2019
Harris
New York
Manufacturers Directory

Exclusive Provider of
Dun & Bradstreet Library Solutions

Published January 2019 next update January 2020

> **WARNING:** Purchasers and users of this directory may not use this directory to compile mailing lists, other marketing aids and other types of data, which are sold or otherwise provided to third parties. Such use is wrongful, illegal and a violation of the federal copyright laws.
>
> **CAUTION:** Because of the many thousands of establishment listings contained in this directory and the possibilities of both human and mechanical error in processing this information, Mergent Inc. cannot assume liability for the correctness of the listings or information on which they are based. Hence, no information contained in this work should be relied upon in any instance where there is a possibility of any loss or damage as a consequence of any error or omission in this volume.

Publisher

Mergent Inc.
444 Madison Ave
New York, NY 10022

©Mergent Inc All Rights Reserved
2019 Mergent Business Press
ISSN 1080-2614
ISBN 978-1-64141-219-3

TABLE OF CONTENTS

Summary of Contents & Explanatory Notes 4
User's Guide to Listings 6

Geographic Section
County/City Cross-Reference Index 9
Firms Listed by Location City 13

Standard Industrial Classification (SIC) Section
SIC Alphabetical Index 641
SIC Numerical Index 643
Firms Listed by SIC 645

Alphabetic Section
Firms Listed by Firm Name 813

Product Section
Product Index 1023
Firms Listed by Product Category 1047

SUMMARY OF CONTENTS

Number of Companies 16,836
Number of Decision Makers 37,073
Minimum Number of Employees 5

EXPLANATORY NOTES

How to Cross-Reference in This Directory

Sequential Entry Numbers. Each establishment in the Geographic Section is numbered sequentially (G-0000). The number assigned to each establishment is referred to as its "entry number." To make cross-referencing easier, each listing in the Geographic, SIC, Alphabetic and Product Sections includes the establishment's entry number. To facilitate locating an entry in the Geographic Section, the entry numbers for the first listing on the left page and the last listing on the right page are printed at the top of the page next to the city name.

Source Suggestions Welcome

Although all known sources were used to compile this directory, it is possible that companies were inadvertently omitted. Your assistance in calling attention to such omissions would be greatly appreciated. A special form on the facing page will help you in the reporting process.

Analysis

Every effort has been made to contact all firms to verify their information. The one exception to this rule is the annual sales figure, which is considered by many companies to be confidential information. Therefore, estimated sales have been calculated by multiplying the nationwide average sales per employee for the firm's major SIC/NAICS code by the firm's number of employees. Nationwide averages for sales per employee by SIC/NAICS codes are provided by the U.S. Department of Commerce and are updated annually. All sales—sales (est)—have been estimated by this method. The exceptions are parent companies (PA), division headquarters (DH) and headquarter locations (HQ) which may include an actual corporate sales figure—sales (corporate-wide) if available.

Types of Companies

Descriptive and statistical data are included for companies in the entire state. These comprise manufacturers, machine shops, fabricators, assemblers and printers. Also identified are corporate offices in the state.

Employment Data

This directory contains companies with 5 or more employees in the manufacturing industry. The employment figure shown in the Geographic Section includes male and female employees and embraces all levels of the company: administrative, clerical, sales and maintenance. This figure is for the facility listed and does not include other plants or offices. It should be recognized that these figures represent an approximate year-round average. These employment figures are broken into codes A through G and used in the Product and SIC Sections to further help you in qualifying a company. Be sure to check the footnotes on the bottom of pages for the code breakdowns.

Standard Industrial Classification (SIC)

The Standard Industrial Classification (SIC) system used in this directory was developed by the federal government for use in classifying establishments by the type of activity they are engaged in. The SIC classifications used in this directory are from the 1987 edition published by the U.S. Government's Office of Management and Budget. The SIC system separates all activities into broad industrial divisions (e.g., manufacturing, mining, retail trade). It further subdivides each division. The range of manufacturing industry classes extends from two-digit codes (major industry group) to four-digit codes (product).

For example:

Industry Breakdown	Code	Industry, Product, etc.
*Major industry group	20	Food and kindred products
Industry group	203	Canned and frozen foods
*Industry	2033	Fruits and vegetables, etc.

*Classifications used in this directory

Only two-digit and four-digit codes are used in this directory.

Arrangement

1. The **Geographic Section** contains complete in-depth corporate data. This section is sorted by cities listed in alphabetical order and companies listed alphabetically within each city. A County/City Index for referencing cities within counties precedes this section.

> IMPORTANT NOTICE: It is a violation of both federal and state law to transmit an unsolicited advertisement to a facsimile machine. Any user of this product that violates such laws may be subject to civil and criminal penalties, which may exceed $500 for each transmission of an unsolicited facsimile. Mergent Inc. provides fax numbers for lawful purposes only and expressly forbids the use of these numbers in any unlawful manner.

2. The **Standard Industrial Classification (SIC) Section** lists companies under approximately 500 four-digit SIC codes. An alphabetical and a numerical index precedes this section. A company can be listed under several codes. The codes are in numerical order with companies listed alphabetically under each code.

3. The **Alphabetic Section** lists all companies with their full physical or mailing addresses and telephone number.

4. The **Product Section** lists companies under unique Harris categories. An index preceding this section lists all product categories in alphabetical order. Companies can be listed under several categories.

USER'S GUIDE TO LISTINGS

GEOGRAPHIC SECTION

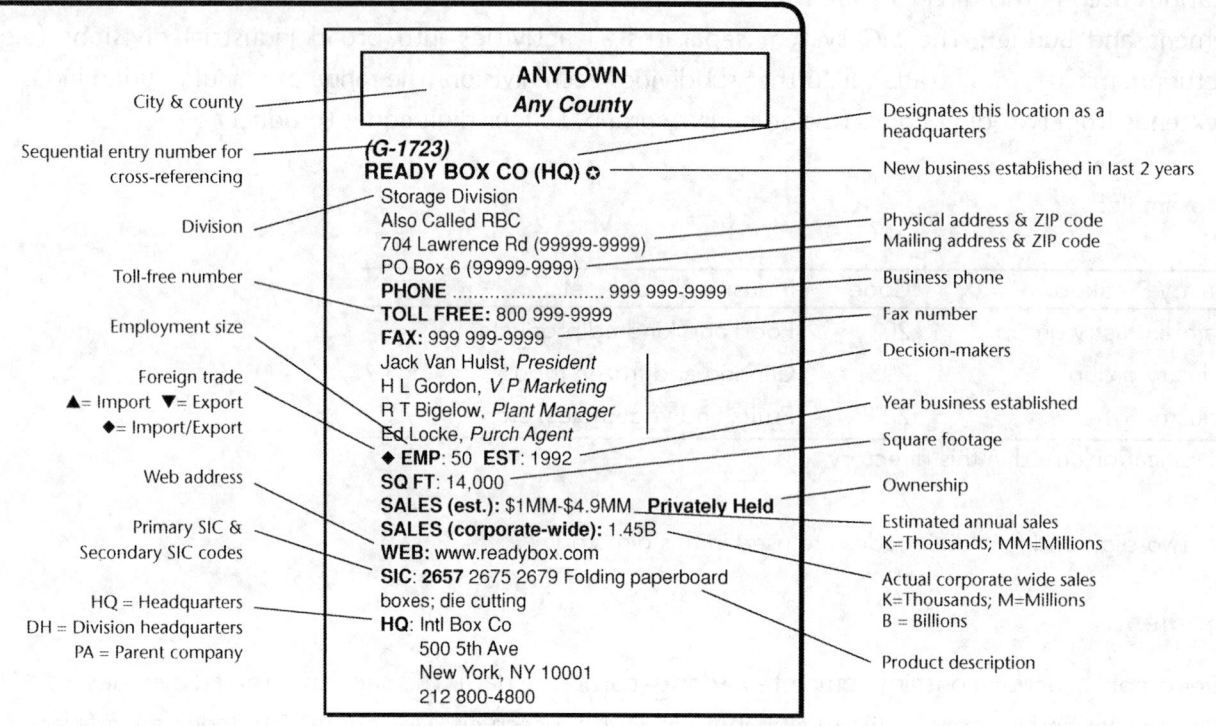

- City & county
- Sequential entry number for cross-referencing
- Division
- Toll-free number
- Employment size
- Foreign trade ▲= Import ▼= Export ◆= Import/Export
- Web address
- Primary SIC & Secondary SIC codes
- HQ = Headquarters
- DH = Division headquarters
- PA = Parent company

- Designates this location as a headquarters
- New business established in last 2 years
- Physical address & ZIP code
- Mailing address & ZIP code
- Business phone
- Fax number
- Decision-makers
- Year business established
- Square footage
- Ownership
- Estimated annual sales K=Thousands; MM=Millions
- Actual corporate wide sales K=Thousands; M=Millions B = Billions
- Product description

SIC SECTION

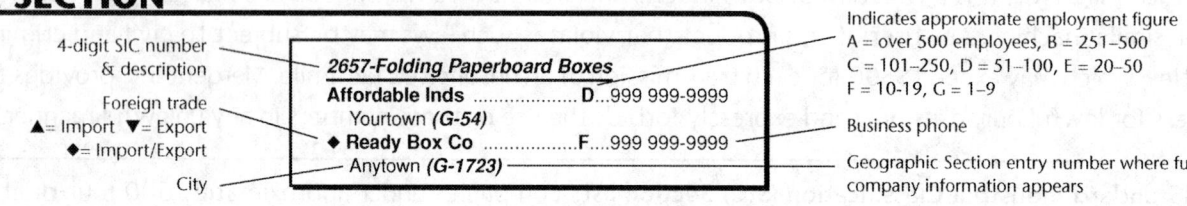

- 4-digit SIC number & description
- Foreign trade ▲= Import ▼= Export ◆= Import/Export
- City

- Indicates approximate employment figure A = over 500 employees, B = 251–500 C = 101–250, D = 51–100, E = 20–50 F = 10-19, G = 1–9
- Business phone
- Geographic Section entry number where full company information appears

ALPHABETIC SECTION

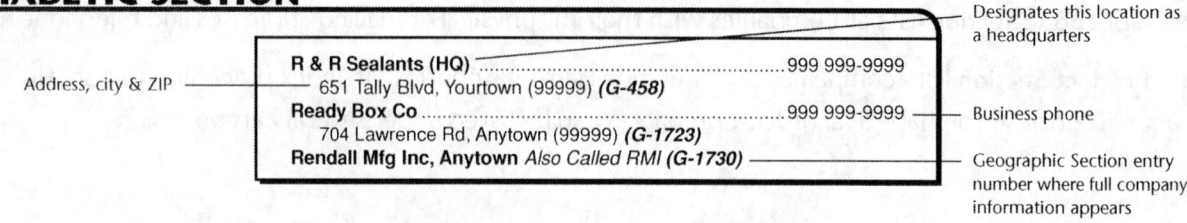

- Address, city & ZIP

- Designates this location as a headquarters
- Business phone
- Geographic Section entry number where full company information appears

PRODUCT SECTION

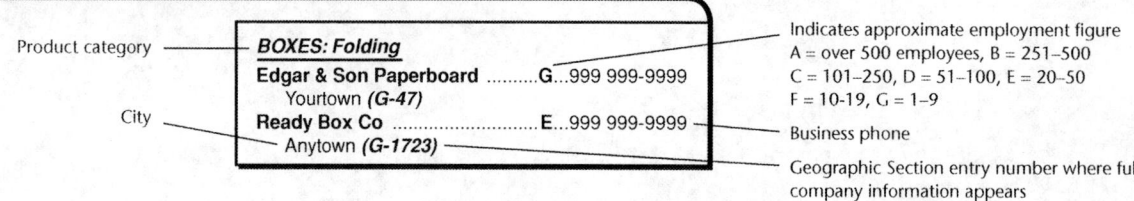

- Product category
- City

- Indicates approximate employment figure A = over 500 employees, B = 251–500 C = 101–250, D = 51–100, E = 20–50 F = 10-19, G = 1–9
- Business phone
- Geographic Section entry number where full company information appears

GEOGRAPHIC SECTION
Companies sorted by city in alphabetical order
In-depth company data listed

STANDARD INDUSTRIAL CLASSIFICATIONS
Alphabetical index of classifcation descriptions
Numerical index of classifcation descriptions
Companies sorted by SIC product groupings

ALPHABETIC SECTION
Company listings in alphabetical order

PRODUCT INDEX
Product categories listed in alphabetical order

PRODUCT SECTION
Companies sorted by product and manufacturing service classifications

New York
County Map

COUNTY/CITY CROSS-REFERENCE INDEX

Albany
City	Entry #
Albany	(G-27)
Alcove	(G-165)
Altamont	(G-194)
Coeymans	(G-3609)
Cohoes	(G-3610)
Colonie	(G-3677)
Delmar	(G-4077)
East Berne	(G-4212)
Feura Bush	(G-4935)
Glenmont	(G-5410)
Green Island	(G-5602)
Guilderland	(G-5654)
Guilderland Center	(G-5656)
Latham	(G-7061)
Medusa	(G-7993)
Menands	(G-8077)
Ravena	(G-13452)
Selkirk	(G-14767)
Slingerlands	(G-14889)
South Bethlehem	(G-14924)
Troy	(G-15594)
Voorheesville	(G-15879)
Watervliet	(G-16040)
Westerlo	(G-16389)

Allegany
City	Entry #
Alfred	(G-184)
Alfred Station	(G-185)
Almond	(G-193)
Angelica	(G-366)
Belmont	(G-817)
Bolivar	(G-1111)
Canaseraga	(G-3238)
Cuba	(G-3917)
Fillmore	(G-4937)
Friendship	(G-5210)
Scio	(G-14735)
Wellsville	(G-16111)

Bronx
City	Entry #
Bronx	(G-1197)

Broome
City	Entry #
Binghamton	(G-858)
Castle Creek	(G-3294)
Chenango Bridge	(G-3465)
Conklin	(G-3724)
Deposit	(G-4106)
Endicott	(G-4580)
Endwell	(G-4616)
Johnson City	(G-6808)
Kirkwood	(G-6937)
Vestal	(G-15808)
Whitney Point	(G-16554)
Windsor	(G-16604)

Cattaraugus
City	Entry #
Allegany	(G-188)
Cattaraugus	(G-3311)
Delevan	(G-4070)
Ellicottville	(G-4444)
Franklinville	(G-5122)
Freedom	(G-5131)
Gowanda	(G-5493)
Hinsdale	(G-6162)
Kill Buck	(G-6878)
Limestone	(G-7157)
Little Valley	(G-7221)
Machias	(G-7706)
Olean	(G-12592)
Portville	(G-13316)
Randolph	(G-13447)
Salamanca	(G-14523)
South Dayton	(G-14927)

Cayuga
City	Entry #
Auburn	(G-462)
Aurora	(G-511)
Cato	(G-3301)
Genoa	(G-5338)
King Ferry	(G-6881)
Locke	(G-7281)
Moravia	(G-8332)
Port Byron	(G-13188)
Scipio Center	(G-14736)
Weedsport	(G-16110)

Chautauqua
City	Entry #
Ashville	(G-415)
Bemus Point	(G-818)
Brocton	(G-1195)
Cassadaga	(G-3291)
Clymer	(G-3599)
Dunkirk	(G-4162)
Ellington	(G-4448)
Falconer	(G-4669)
Findley Lake	(G-4939)
Forestville	(G-5085)
Fredonia	(G-5125)
Frewsburg	(G-5206)
Gerry	(G-5340)
Irving	(G-6501)
Jamestown	(G-6694)
Kennedy	(G-6866)
Lakewood	(G-6988)
Mayville	(G-7920)
Portland	(G-13315)
Ripley	(G-13562)
Sheridan	(G-14814)
Sherman	(G-14815)
Silver Creek	(G-14860)
Sinclairville	(G-14864)
Westfield	(G-16390)

Chemung
City	Entry #
Big Flats	(G-855)
Chemung	(G-3463)
Elmira	(G-4472)
Elmira Heights	(G-4509)
Horseheads	(G-6305)
Millport	(G-8195)
Pine City	(G-12999)
Pine Valley	(G-13006)

Chenango
City	Entry #
Afton	(G-7)
Bainbridge	(G-534)
Earlville	(G-4188)
Greene	(G-5612)
Mount Upton	(G-8371)
New Berlin	(G-8487)
Norwich	(G-12477)
Oxford	(G-12807)
Sherburne	(G-14803)
Smyrna	(G-14912)
South Otselic	(G-14943)

Clinton
City	Entry #
Champlain	(G-3406)
Chazy	(G-3432)
Ellenburg Depot	(G-4436)
Keeseville	(G-6850)
Mooers	(G-8330)
Mooers Forks	(G-8331)
Peru	(G-12972)
Plattsburgh	(G-13105)
Rouses Point	(G-14467)

Columbia
City	Entry #
Ancram	(G-365)
Canaan	(G-3206)
Chatham	(G-3427)
Copake	(G-3746)
Germantown	(G-5339)
Ghent	(G-5357)
Hudson	(G-6335)
Kinderhook	(G-6879)
Livingston	(G-7275)
New Lebanon	(G-8574)
Philmont	(G-12986)
Stottville	(G-15181)
Stuyvesant	(G-15182)
Stuyvesant Falls	(G-15183)
Valatie	(G-15740)

Cortland
City	Entry #
Cortland	(G-3858)
Homer	(G-6252)
Marathon	(G-7788)
Mc Graw	(G-7926)

Delaware
City	Entry #
Arkville	(G-400)
Bloomville	(G-960)
Davenport	(G-3928)
Delhi	(G-4072)
Halcottsville	(G-5657)
Hancock	(G-5709)
Hobart	(G-6163)
Margaretville	(G-7798)
Masonville	(G-7814)
Sidney	(G-14848)
Stamford	(G-15029)
Walton	(G-15910)

Dutchess
City	Entry #
Amenia	(G-205)
Barrytown	(G-606)
Beacon	(G-754)
Clinton Corners	(G-3590)
Dover Plains	(G-4143)
Fishkill	(G-4942)
Hopewell Junction	(G-6282)
Hyde Park	(G-6467)
Lagrangeville	(G-6956)
Millbrook	(G-8187)
Millerton	(G-8192)
Pawling	(G-12892)
Pine Plains	(G-13004)
Pleasant Valley	(G-13172)
Poughkeepsie	(G-13325)
Poughquag	(G-13374)
Red Hook	(G-13457)
Rhinebeck	(G-13485)
Staatsburg	(G-15022)
Stanfordville	(G-15033)
Stormville	(G-15179)
Wappingers Falls	(G-15928)
Wassaic	(G-15965)
Wingdale	(G-16606)

Erie
City	Entry #
Akron	(G-16)
Alden	(G-166)
Amherst	(G-208)
Angola	(G-368)
Blasdell	(G-924)
Bowmansville	(G-1122)
Buffalo	(G-2675)
Chaffee	(G-3402)
Cheektowaga	(G-3434)
Clarence	(G-3524)
Clarence Center	(G-3543)
Colden	(G-3633)
Collins	(G-3672)
Depew	(G-4079)
Derby	(G-4113)
East Amherst	(G-4189)
East Aurora	(G-4193)
East Concord	(G-4214)
Eden	(G-4386)
Elma	(G-4449)
Getzville	(G-5343)
Glenwood	(G-5448)
Grand Island	(G-5494)
Hamburg	(G-5672)
Holland	(G-6218)
Kenmore	(G-6857)
Lackawanna	(G-6947)
Lake View	(G-6982)
Lancaster	(G-7000)
North Collins	(G-12383)
Orchard Park	(G-12694)
Springville	(G-15015)
Tonawanda	(G-15517)
Wales Center	(G-15900)
West Falls	(G-16208)
West Seneca	(G-16292)
Williamsville	(G-16565)

Essex
City	Entry #
Crown Point	(G-3916)
Elizabethtown	(G-4430)
Jay	(G-6773)
Lake Placid	(G-6975)
Lewis	(G-7137)
Mineville	(G-8253)
Ticonderoga	(G-15510)
Upper Jay	(G-15674)
Willsboro	(G-16597)
Wilmington	(G-16600)

Franklin
City	Entry #
Akwesasne	(G-26)
Burke	(G-3142)
Chateaugay	(G-3426)
Hogansburg	(G-6165)
Malone	(G-7717)
Moira	(G-8261)
Saranac Lake	(G-14560)
Tupper Lake	(G-15650)

Fulton
City	Entry #
Broadalbin	(G-1187)
Gloversville	(G-5449)
Johnstown	(G-6823)
Mayfield	(G-7919)
Northville	(G-12476)

Genesee
City	Entry #
Alexander	(G-179)
Batavia	(G-608)
Bergen	(G-819)
Byron	(G-3145)
Corfu	(G-3806)
East Bethany	(G-4213)
Le Roy	(G-7112)
Oakfield	(G-12523)
Pavilion	(G-12889)
Stafford	(G-15026)

Greene
City	Entry #
Athens	(G-451)
Cairo	(G-3146)
Catskill	(G-3302)
Coxsackie	(G-3906)
Durham	(G-4182)
East Durham	(G-4216)
Elka Park	(G-4433)
Greenville	(G-5635)
Hannacroix	(G-5716)
Palenville	(G-12844)
Prattsville	(G-13378)
Round Top	(G-14466)
Surprise	(G-15207)

Hamilton
City	Entry #
Lake Pleasant	(G-6979)
Speculator	(G-14973)

Herkimer
City	Entry #
Dolgeville	(G-4133)
Frankfort	(G-5104)
Herkimer	(G-6039)
Ilion	(G-6473)
Jordanville	(G-6844)
Little Falls	(G-7208)
Middleville	(G-8186)
Mohawk	(G-8255)
Newport	(G-12255)
Old Forge	(G-12589)
Poland	(G-13184)
Van Hornesville	(G-15802)
West Winfield	(G-16305)

Jefferson
City	Entry #
Adams	(G-2)
Adams Center	(G-4)
Alexandria Bay	(G-182)
Brownville	(G-2671)
Cape Vincent	(G-3259)
Carthage	(G-3285)
Clayton	(G-3552)
Dexter	(G-4115)
Felts Mills	(G-4930)
Fort Drum	(G-5091)
Great Bend	(G-5526)
La Fargeville	(G-6942)
Philadelphia	(G-12985)
Three Mile Bay	(G-15509)

COUNTY/CITY CROSS-REFERENCE

	ENTRY #		ENTRY #		ENTRY #		ENTRY #		ENTRY #

Watertown .... (G-15999)
Woodville .... (G-16689)

Kings
Brooklyn .... (G-1433)

Lewis
Beaver Falls .... (G-766)
Castorland .... (G-3298)
Croghan .... (G-3908)
Harrisville .... (G-5740)
Lowville .... (G-7649)
Lyons Falls .... (G-7689)

Livingston
Avon .... (G-517)
Caledonia .... (G-3152)
Conesus .... (G-3708)
Dansville .... (G-3925)
Geneseo .... (G-5313)
Hemlock .... (G-6004)
Lakeville .... (G-6984)
Leicester .... (G-7126)
Lima .... (G-7149)
Livonia .... (G-7277)
Mount Morris .... (G-8366)
Nunda .... (G-12497)
Piffard .... (G-12995)
Retsof .... (G-13480)
York .... (G-16813)

Madison
Canastota .... (G-3240)
Cazenovia .... (G-3316)
Chittenango .... (G-3500)
De Ruyter .... (G-3929)
Erieville .... (G-4621)
Hamilton .... (G-5698)
Morrisville .... (G-8336)
Munnsville .... (G-8457)
Oneida .... (G-12609)
Wampsville .... (G-15917)
West Edmeston .... (G-16207)

Monroe
Brockport .... (G-1190)
Churchville .... (G-3505)
East Rochester .... (G-4280)
Fairport .... (G-4625)
Gates .... (G-5310)
Hamlin .... (G-5700)
Henrietta .... (G-6029)
Hilton .... (G-6156)
Honeoye Falls .... (G-6262)
Mendon .... (G-8093)
North Chili .... (G-12381)
Penfield .... (G-12939)
Pittsford .... (G-13007)
Rochester .... (G-13590)
Rush .... (G-14471)
Scottsville .... (G-14748)
Spencerport .... (G-14975)
Webster .... (G-16074)
West Henrietta .... (G-16227)

Montgomery
Amsterdam .... (G-325)
Canajoharie .... (G-3207)
Esperance .... (G-4622)
Fonda .... (G-5065)
Fort Plain .... (G-5102)
Fultonville .... (G-5234)
Nelliston .... (G-8481)

Palatine Bridge .... (G-12842)
Saint Johnsville .... (G-14517)
Sprakers .... (G-14987)

Nassau
Albertson .... (G-146)
Atlantic Beach .... (G-455)
Baldwin .... (G-538)
Bayville .... (G-753)
Bellmore .... (G-784)
Bethpage .... (G-836)
Carle Place .... (G-3260)
Cedarhurst .... (G-3330)
East Meadow .... (G-4246)
East Norwich .... (G-4271)
East Rockaway .... (G-4292)
East Williston .... (G-4382)
Elmont .... (G-4516)
Farmingdale .... (G-4704)
Floral Park .... (G-4953)
Franklin Square .... (G-5114)
Freeport .... (G-5133)
Garden City .... (G-5249)
Garden City Park ..... (G-5285)
Glen Cove .... (G-5358)
Glen Head .... (G-5379)
Great Neck .... (G-5527)
Greenvale .... (G-5628)
Hempstead .... (G-6005)
Hewlett .... (G-6045)
Hicksville .... (G-6056)
Inwood .... (G-6484)
Island Park .... (G-6510)
Jericho .... (G-6780)
Lawrence .... (G-7102)
Levittown .... (G-7130)
Lido Beach .... (G-7147)
Locust Valley .... (G-7345)
Long Beach .... (G-7356)
Lynbrook .... (G-7658)
Manhasset .... (G-7763)
Massapequa .... (G-7876)
Massapequa Park .... (G-7889)
Merrick .... (G-8095)
Mineola .... (G-8199)
New Hyde Park .... (G-8514)
North Baldwin .... (G-12362)
North Bellmore .... (G-12372)
Oceanside .... (G-12529)
Old Bethpage .... (G-12581)
Old Westbury .... (G-12590)
Oyster Bay .... (G-12809)
Plainview .... (G-13030)
Port Washington ..... (G-13239)
Rockville Centre ..... (G-14230)
Roosevelt .... (G-14434)
Roslyn .... (G-14443)
Roslyn Heights .... (G-14453)
Sea Cliff .... (G-14755)
Seaford .... (G-14757)
South Hempstead .... (G-14941)
Syosset .... (G-15208)
Uniondale .... (G-15662)
Valley Stream .... (G-15771)
Wantagh .... (G-15919)
West Hempstead .... (G-16212)
Westbury .... (G-16308)
Williston Park .... (G-16594)
Woodbury .... (G-16613)
Woodmere .... (G-16639)

New York
New York .... (G-8664)

Niagara
Barker .... (G-599)
Burt .... (G-3143)
Gasport .... (G-5304)
Lewiston .... (G-7138)
Lockport .... (G-7282)
Middleport .... (G-8131)
Newfane .... (G-12252)
Niagara Falls .... (G-12257)
North Tonawanda ..... (G-12409)
Ransomville .... (G-13451)
Sanborn .... (G-14540)
Wilson .... (G-16601)
Youngstown .... (G-16836)

Oneida
Barneveld .... (G-601)
Blossvale .... (G-963)
Boonville .... (G-1113)
Camden .... (G-3185)
Chadwicks .... (G-3400)
Clayville .... (G-3554)
Clinton .... (G-3585)
Forestport .... (G-5083)
Holland Patent .... (G-6224)
Marcy .... (G-7796)
Mc Connellsville ...... (G-7925)
New Hartford .... (G-8501)
New York Mills .... (G-12185)
Oriskany .... (G-12750)
Oriskany Falls .... (G-12767)
Rome .... (G-14245)
Sangerfield .... (G-14559)
Sauquoit .... (G-14621)
Sherrill .... (G-14818)
Stittville .... (G-15160)
Utica .... (G-15675)
Vernon .... (G-15803)
Vernon Center .... (G-15807)
Waterville .... (G-16038)
Westmoreland .... (G-16407)
Whitesboro .... (G-16526)
Yorkville .... (G-16827)

Onondaga
Baldwinsville .... (G-547)
Brewerton .... (G-1149)
Bridgeport .... (G-1182)
Camillus .... (G-3194)
Cicero .... (G-3513)
Clay .... (G-3551)
De Witt .... (G-3930)
East Syracuse .... (G-4316)
Elbridge .... (G-4426)
Fabius .... (G-4624)
Fayetteville .... (G-4927)
Jamesville .... (G-6763)
Jordan .... (G-6842)
Kirkville .... (G-6934)
La Fayette .... (G-6945)
Liverpool .... (G-7222)
Manlius .... (G-7774)
Marcellus .... (G-7792)
Memphis .... (G-8076)
Nedrow .... (G-8478)
North Syracuse .... (G-12398)
Skaneateles .... (G-14866)
Skaneateles Falls .... (G-14879)

Solvay .... (G-14916)
Syracuse .... (G-15235)
Tully .... (G-15647)

Ontario
Bloomfield .... (G-947)
Canandaigua .... (G-3210)
Clifton Springs .... (G-3582)
Farmington .... (G-4909)
Fishers .... (G-4940)
Geneva .... (G-5316)
Hall .... (G-5671)
Honeoye .... (G-6260)
Manchester .... (G-7760)
Naples .... (G-8470)
Oaks Corners .... (G-12527)
Phelps .... (G-12974)
Seneca Castle .... (G-14772)
Shortsville .... (G-14847)
Stanley .... (G-15034)
Victor .... (G-15827)

Orange
Bullville .... (G-3139)
Central Valley .... (G-3394)
Chester .... (G-3467)
Cornwall .... (G-3829)
Cornwall On Hudson (G-3838)
Florida .... (G-4968)
Goshen .... (G-5476)
Greenwood Lake ..... (G-5647)
Harriman .... (G-5719)
Highland Falls .... (G-6149)
Highland Mills .... (G-6150)
Huguenot .... (G-6385)
Middletown .... (G-8135)
Monroe .... (G-8262)
Montgomery .... (G-8308)
Mountainville .... (G-8455)
New Hampton .... (G-8497)
New Windsor .... (G-8632)
Newburgh .... (G-12212)
Pine Bush .... (G-12997)
Pine Island .... (G-13002)
Port Jervis .... (G-13225)
Rock Tavern .... (G-14224)
Salisbury Mills .... (G-14539)
Slate Hill .... (G-14885)
Southfields .... (G-14966)
Sparrow Bush .... (G-14972)
Sugar Loaf .... (G-15200)
Tuxedo Park .... (G-15656)
Unionville .... (G-15673)
Walden .... (G-15890)
Warwick .... (G-15948)
Washingtonville ...... (G-15963)
West Point .... (G-16283)
Westtown .... (G-16413)

Orleans
Albion .... (G-154)
Holley .... (G-6226)
Kendall .... (G-6856)
Lyndonville .... (G-7679)
Medina .... (G-7970)

Oswego
Bernhards Bay .... (G-833)
Central Square .... (G-3389)
Cleveland .... (G-3561)
Constantia .... (G-3739)
Fulton .... (G-5212)

Hannibal .... (G-5717)
Lacona .... (G-6955)
Mexico .... (G-8108)
Oswego .... (G-12775)
Parish .... (G-12860)
Phoenix .... (G-12988)
Pulaski .... (G-13379)
Sandy Creek .... (G-14558)
West Monroe .... (G-16262)
Williamstown .... (G-16564)

Otsego
Cherry Valley .... (G-3466)
Colliersville .... (G-3671)
Cooperstown .... (G-3742)
Edmeston .... (G-4425)
Fly Creek .... (G-5063)
Garrattsville .... (G-5302)
Morris .... (G-8335)
Oneonta .... (G-12624)
Richfield Springs .... (G-13492)
Schenevus .... (G-14729)
Unadilla .... (G-15660)
West Burlington .... (G-16206)

Putnam
Brewster .... (G-1153)
Carmel .... (G-3274)
Cold Spring .... (G-3625)
Garrison .... (G-5303)
Mahopac .... (G-7707)
Patterson .... (G-12880)
Putnam Valley .... (G-13401)

Queens
Arverne .... (G-413)
Astoria .... (G-419)
Bayside .... (G-740)
Bayside Hills .... (G-752)
Bellerose .... (G-780)
Cambria Heights .... (G-3176)
College Point .... (G-3634)
Corona .... (G-3839)
Douglaston .... (G-4139)
East Elmhurst .... (G-4217)
Elmhurst .... (G-4462)
Far Rockaway .... (G-4698)
Floral Park .... (G-4966)
Flushing .... (G-4977)
Forest Hills .... (G-5069)
Fresh Meadows ..... (G-5194)
Glen Oaks .... (G-5386)
Glendale .... (G-5389)
Hollis .... (G-6231)
Howard Beach .... (G-6330)
Jackson Heights .... (G-6618)
Jamaica .... (G-6622)
Kew Gardens .... (G-6869)
Laurelton .... (G-7099)
Little Neck .... (G-7217)
Long Island City .... (G-7362)
Maspeth .... (G-7816)
Middle Village .... (G-8119)
Oakland Gardens .... (G-12526)
Ozone Park .... (G-12821)
Queens Village .... (G-13402)
Rego Park .... (G-13461)
Richmond Hill .... (G-13494)
Ridgewood .... (G-13526)
Rockaway Beach .... (G-14225)
Rockaway Park ..... (G-14227)
Rosedale .... (G-14440)

COUNTY/CITY CROSS-REFERENCE

	ENTRY #
Saint Albans	(G-14506)
South Ozone Park	(G-14944)
South Richmond Hill	(G-14945)
Springfield Gardens	(G-15014)
Sunnyside	(G-15201)
Whitestone	(G-16533)
Woodhaven	(G-16636)
Woodside	(G-16644)

Rensselaer
Averill Park	(G-512)
Berlin	(G-830)
Castleton On Hudson	(G-3295)
Cropseyville	(G-3909)
Eagle Bridge	(G-4184)
East Greenbush	(G-4227)
Hoosick Falls	(G-6275)
Nassau	(G-8476)
Petersburg	(G-12973)
Poestenkill	(G-13179)
Rensselaer	(G-13470)
Stephentown	(G-15154)
Troy	(G-15599)
Valley Falls	(G-15770)
West Sand Lake	(G-16284)

Richmond
Staten Island	(G-15036)

Rockland
Airmont	(G-10)
Blauvelt	(G-933)
Chestnut Ridge	(G-3492)
Congers	(G-3709)
Garnerville	(G-5298)
Haverstraw	(G-5979)
Hillburn	(G-6153)
Monsey	(G-8283)
Nanuet	(G-8459)
New City	(G-8489)
Nyack	(G-12499)
Orangeburg	(G-12667)
Palisades	(G-12846)
Pearl River	(G-12895)
Piermont	(G-12994)
Pomona	(G-13185)
Sloatsburg	(G-14892)
Spring Valley	(G-14988)
Stony Point	(G-15171)
Suffern	(G-15184)
Tallman	(G-15462)
Tappan	(G-15465)
Thiells	(G-15499)
Tomkins Cove	(G-15516)
Valley Cottage	(G-15750)
West Haverstraw	(G-16210)
West Nyack	(G-16263)

Saratoga
Ballston Lake	(G-565)
Ballston Spa	(G-574)
Clifton Park	(G-3562)
Corinth	(G-3808)
Galway	(G-5241)
Gansevoort	(G-5242)
Greenfield Center	(G-5619)
Halfmoon	(G-5660)
Malta	(G-7730)
Mechanicville	(G-7929)
Middle Grove	(G-8115)
Rexford	(G-13481)
Rock City Falls	(G-14222)
Round Lake	(G-14464)
Saratoga Springs	(G-14565)
Schuylerville	(G-14733)
South Glens Falls	(G-14933)
Stillwater	(G-15157)
Waterford	(G-15973)

Schenectady
Delanson	(G-4067)
Duanesburg	(G-4154)
Glenville	(G-5444)
Niskayuna	(G-12352)
Pattersonville	(G-12888)
Rotterdam Junction	(G-14462)
Schenectady	(G-14647)
Scotia	(G-14738)

Schoharie
Central Bridge	(G-3353)
Charlotteville	(G-3425)
Cobleskill	(G-3600)
Howes Cave	(G-6334)
Middleburgh	(G-8129)
Richmondville	(G-13518)
Schoharie	(G-14731)
Sharon Springs	(G-14796)
Sloansville	(G-14891)
Warnerville	(G-15939)

Schuyler
Beaver Dams	(G-765)
Burdett	(G-3140)
Cayuta	(G-3315)
Hector	(G-5999)
Montour Falls	(G-8325)
Odessa	(G-12567)
Rock Stream	(G-14223)
Watkins Glen	(G-16058)
Wayne	(G-16073)

Seneca
Fayette	(G-4926)
Interlaken	(G-6480)
Lodi	(G-7353)
Ovid	(G-12790)
Romulus	(G-14280)
Seneca Falls	(G-14773)
Waterloo	(G-15991)

St. Lawrence
Brasher Falls	(G-1125)
Canton	(G-3254)
Childwold	(G-3490)
Cranberry Lake	(G-3907)
Gouverneur	(G-5486)
Hammond	(G-5701)
Heuvelton	(G-6044)
Massena	(G-7897)
Norfolk	(G-12356)
North Lawrence	(G-12393)
Norwood	(G-12495)
Ogdensburg	(G-12568)
Potsdam	(G-13317)
South Colton	(G-14925)
Star Lake	(G-15035)
Waddington	(G-15882)

Steuben
Addison	(G-5)
Arkport	(G-399)
Avoca	(G-516)
Bath	(G-640)
Campbell	(G-3203)
Corning	(G-3809)
Hammondsport	(G-5702)
Hornell	(G-6294)
Lindley	(G-7207)
Painted Post	(G-12835)
Wayland	(G-16070)
Woodhull	(G-16638)

Suffolk
Amagansett	(G-203)
Amityville	(G-262)
Aquebogue	(G-373)
Babylon	(G-523)
Bay Shore	(G-650)
Bayport	(G-735)
Bellport	(G-796)
Blue Point	(G-964)
Bohemia	(G-966)
Brentwood	(G-1126)
Bridgehampton	(G-1179)
Brightwaters	(G-1185)
Brookhaven	(G-1427)
Calverton	(G-3161)
Center Moriches	(G-3338)
Centereach	(G-3342)
Centerport	(G-3347)
Central Islip	(G-3354)
Cold Spring Harbor	(G-3629)
Commack	(G-3680)
Copiague	(G-3747)
Coram	(G-3796)
Cutchogue	(G-3921)
Deer Park	(G-3931)
Dix Hills	(G-4117)
East Hampton	(G-4232)
East Islip	(G-4244)
East Moriches	(G-4257)
East Northport	(G-4259)
East Patchogue	(G-4273)
East Quogue	(G-4277)
East Setauket	(G-4298)
Eastport	(G-4384)
Edgewood	(G-4391)
Farmingville	(G-4922)
Great River	(G-5601)
Greenlawn	(G-5620)
Greenport	(G-5625)
Halesite	(G-5658)
Hampton Bays	(G-5708)
Hauppauge	(G-5752)
Holbrook	(G-6167)
Holtsville	(G-6236)
Huntington	(G-6389)
Huntington Station	(G-6428)
Islandia	(G-6520)
Islip	(G-6543)
Islip Terrace	(G-6552)
Jamesport	(G-6693)
Kings Park	(G-6882)
Lake Grove	(G-6967)
Lake Ronkonkoma	(G-6980)
Lindenhurst	(G-7159)
Lloyd Harbor	(G-7279)
Manorville	(G-7782)
Mastic	(G-7911)
Mastic Beach	(G-7912)
Mattituck	(G-7913)
Medford	(G-7936)
Melville	(G-7994)
Middle Island	(G-8116)
Miller Place	(G-8191)
Montauk	(G-8304)
Mount Sinai	(G-8368)
Nesconset	(G-8483)
North Babylon	(G-12360)
Northport	(G-12464)
Oakdale	(G-12514)
Patchogue	(G-12861)
Peconic	(G-12914)
Port Jeff STA	(G-13212)
Port Jefferson	(G-13220)
Quogue	(G-13446)
Ridge	(G-13520)
Riverhead	(G-13564)
Ronkonkoma	(G-14284)
Sag Harbor	(G-14497)
Sagaponack	(G-14504)
Saint James	(G-14509)
Sayville	(G-14625)
Selden	(G-14760)
Setauket	(G-14791)
Shelter Island	(G-14800)
Shirley	(G-14826)
Smithtown	(G-14893)
Southampton	(G-14949)
Southold	(G-14967)
Speonk	(G-14984)
Stony Brook	(G-15163)
Wading River	(G-15883)
Wainscott	(G-15889)
Water Mill	(G-15968)
West Babylon	(G-16124)
West Islip	(G-16257)
West Sayville	(G-16287)
Westhampton	(G-16401)
Westhampton Beach	(G-16403)
Wyandanch	(G-16690)
Yaphank	(G-16703)

Sullivan
Barryville	(G-607)
Bethel	(G-834)
Callicoon	(G-3160)
Cochecton	(G-3605)
Ferndale	(G-4931)
Harris	(G-5722)
Hurleyville	(G-6466)
Jeffersonville	(G-6778)
Kauneonga Lake	(G-6849)
Liberty	(G-7143)
Livingston Manor	(G-7276)
Long Eddy	(G-7361)
Monticello	(G-8320)
Narrowsburg	(G-8474)
Roscoe	(G-14439)
South Fallsburg	(G-14930)
Thompsonville	(G-15500)
Westbrookville	(G-16307)
Wht Sphr Spgs	(G-16557)
Woodridge	(G-16643)

Tioga
Apalachin	(G-372)
Berkshire	(G-828)
Candor	(G-3252)
Lockwood	(G-7344)
Nichols	(G-12351)
Owego	(G-12795)
Spencer	(G-14974)
Waverly	(G-16063)

Tompkins
Dryden	(G-4148)
Etna	(G-4623)
Freeville	(G-5191)
Groton	(G-5649)
Ithaca	(G-6554)
Lansing	(G-7055)
Trumansburg	(G-15637)

Ulster
Accord	(G-1)
Bearsville	(G-764)
Bloomington	(G-959)
Boiceville	(G-1110)
Ellenville	(G-4437)
Gardiner	(G-5291)
High Falls	(G-6139)
Highland	(G-6142)
Kerhonkson	(G-6867)
Kingston	(G-6887)
Lake Katrine	(G-6972)
Marlboro	(G-7812)
Milton	(G-8196)
Mount Marion	(G-8363)
New Paltz	(G-8575)
Rifton	(G-13559)
Saugerties	(G-14602)
Shokan	(G-14846)
Stone Ridge	(G-15161)
Tillson	(G-15515)
Ulster Park	(G-15658)
Wallkill	(G-15902)
Wawarsing	(G-16069)
West Hurley	(G-16256)
Woodstock	(G-16684)

Warren
Bakers Mills	(G-537)
Bolton Landing	(G-1112)
Brant Lake	(G-1124)
Chestertown	(G-3490)
Glens Falls	(G-5414)
Lake George	(G-6964)
Lake Luzerne	(G-6974)
North Creek	(G-12391)
Queensbury	(G-13414)
Silver Bay	(G-14859)
Warrensburg	(G-15940)

Washington
Argyle	(G-397)
Cambridge	(G-3177)
Cossayuna	(G-3905)
Fort Ann	(G-5089)
Fort Edward	(G-5093)
Granville	(G-5518)
Greenwich	(G-5636)
Hartford	(G-5741)
Hudson Falls	(G-6376)
Middle Granville	(G-8109)
Salem	(G-14536)
Whitehall	(G-16523)

Wayne
Clyde	(G-3591)
Lyons	(G-7682)
Macedon	(G-7691)
Marion	(G-7800)
Newark	(G-12191)
North Rose	(G-12394)
Ontario	(G-12647)
Palmyra	(G-12850)

COUNTY/CITY CROSS-REFERENCE

	ENTRY #		ENTRY #		ENTRY #		ENTRY #		ENTRY #
Red Creek	(G-13455)	Cortlandt Manor	(G-3898)	Mohegan Lake	(G-8257)	Somers	(G-14919)	North Java	(G-12392)
Savannah	(G-14623)	Cross River	(G-3910)	Montrose	(G-8329)	South Salem	(G-14948)	Perry	(G-12967)
Sodus	(G-14913)	Croton Falls	(G-3911)	Mount Kisco	(G-8337)	Tarrytown	(G-15472)	Portageville	(G-13314)
Walworth	(G-15914)	Croton On Hudson	(G-3912)	Mount Vernon	(G-8372)	Thornwood	(G-15501)	Silver Springs	(G-14863)
Williamson	(G-16558)	Dobbs Ferry	(G-4129)	New Rochelle	(G-8585)	Tuckahoe	(G-15642)	Warsaw	(G-15944)
Wolcott	(G-16608)	Eastchester	(G-4383)	North Salem	(G-12397)	Valhalla	(G-15741)	Wyoming	(G-16698)

Westchester

		Elmsford	(G-4527)	Ossining	(G-12769)	Waccabuc	(G-15881)	**Yates**	
Amawalk	(G-204)	Goldens Bridge	(G-5475)	Peekskill	(G-12917)	White Plains	(G-16415)		
Ardsley	(G-392)	Harrison	(G-5723)	Pelham	(G-12932)	Yonkers	(G-16730)	Branchport	(G-1123)
Armonk	(G-401)	Hartsdale	(G-5742)	Pleasantville	(G-13173)	Yorktown Heights	(G-16814)	Dresden	(G-4146)
Baldwin Place	(G-546)	Hastings On Hudson	(G-5747)	Port Chester	(G-13191)	**Wyoming**		Dundee	(G-4156)
Bedford	(G-768)	Hawthorne	(G-5983)	Pound Ridge	(G-13375)	Arcade	(G-376)	Himrod	(G-6160)
Bedford Hills	(G-772)	Irvington	(G-6502)	Purchase	(G-13386)	Attica	(G-458)	Penn Yan	(G-12948)
Briarcliff Manor	(G-1177)	Jefferson Valley	(G-6776)	Rye	(G-14478)	Bliss	(G-946)	Rushville	(G-14477)
Bronxville	(G-1423)	Katonah	(G-6845)	Rye Brook	(G-14490)	Castile	(G-3292)		
Buchanan	(G-2672)	Larchmont	(G-7057)	Scarsdale	(G-14636)	Gainesville	(G-5240)		
Chappaqua	(G-3419)	Mamaroneck	(G-7734)	Sleepy Hollow	(G-14886)	Java Village	(G-6772)		

GEOGRAPHIC SECTION

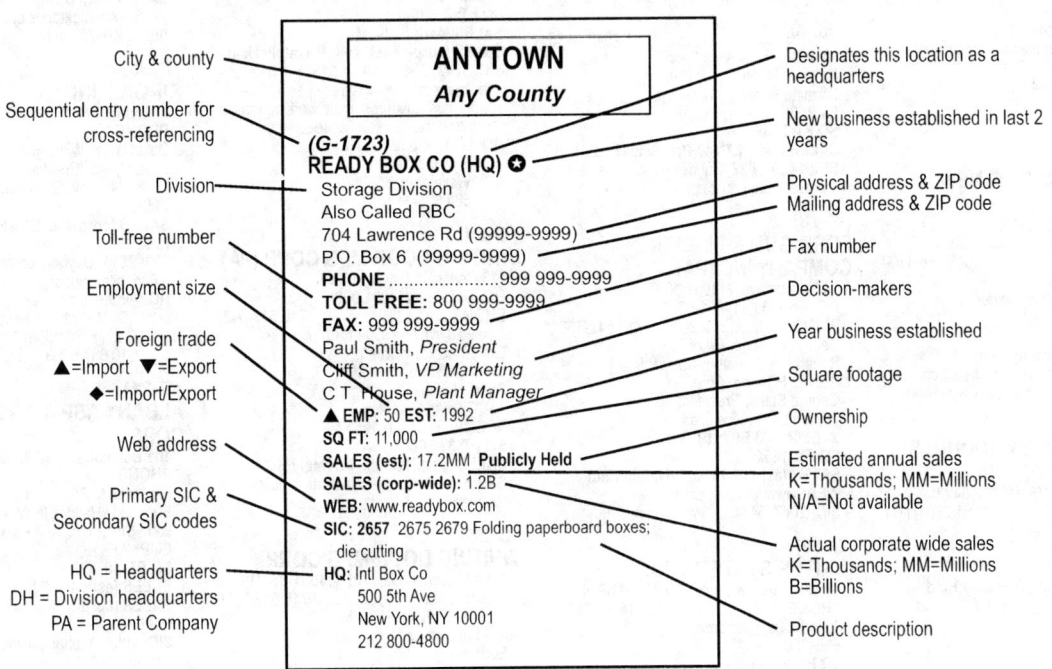

See footnotes for symbols and codes identification.
- This section is in alphabetical order by city.
- Companies are sorted alphabetically under their respective cities.
- To locate cities within a county refer to the County/City Cross Reference Index.

IMPORTANT NOTICE: It is a violation of both federal and state law to transmit an unsolicited advertisement to a facsimile machine. Any user of this product that violates such laws may be subject to civil and criminal penalties which may exceed $500 for each transmission of an unsolicited facsimile. Harris InfoSource provides fax numbers for lawful purposes only and expressly forbids the use of these numbers in any unlawful manner.

Accord
Ulster County

(G-1)
VIC DEMAYOS INC
4967 Us Highway 209 (12404-5723)
P.O. Box 253 (12404-0253)
PHONE.....................................845 626-4343
Vic De Mayo, *President*
Eugene De Mayo, *President*
EMP: 6 **EST:** 1964
SQ FT: 4,000
SALES (est): 225K **Privately Held**
SIC: 3111 5941 Accessory products, leather; sporting goods & bicycle shops

Adams
Jefferson County

(G-2)
BENJAMIN PRINTING INC
Also Called: Minuteman Press
60 E Church St (13605-1103)
PHONE.....................................315 788-7922
Charles Adams, *President*
Michael Biolsi, *General Mgr*
Vitusa Adams, *Vice Pres*
Ed Yancey, *Graphic Designe*
Laura Biolsi,
EMP: 14
SQ FT: 4,000
SALES (est): 1.1MM **Privately Held**
WEB: www.benjaminprinting.com
SIC: 2752 Commercial printing, lithographic

(G-3)
GREAT LAKES CHEESE NY INC
23 Phelps St (13605-1096)
PHONE.....................................315 232-4511
Gary Vanic, *Ch of Bd*
Hans Epprecht, *President*
John Epprecht, *Vice Pres*
Grant Crumb, *Plant Mgr*
John Jennings, *Plant Mgr*
EMP: 79
SQ FT: 88,000
SALES (est): 19.2MM
SALES (corp-wide): 1.6B **Privately Held**
WEB: www.greatlakescheese.com
SIC: 2022 Cheese, natural & processed
PA: Great Lakes Cheese Co., Inc.
17825 Great Lakes Pkwy
Hiram OH 44234
440 834-2500

Adams Center
Jefferson County

(G-4)
R G KING GENERAL CONSTRUCTION
Also Called: Kings Quarry
13018 County Route 155 (13606-3104)
PHONE.....................................315 583-3560
Ronald King, *President*
Bill King, *Vice Pres*
EMP: 5 **EST:** 1959
SALES (est): 508.2K **Privately Held**
SIC: 1442 Construction sand & gravel

Addison
Steuben County

(G-5)
CRAWFORD PRINT SHOP INC
6120 Herrington Rd (14801-9235)
PHONE.....................................607 359-4970
Adam Crawford, *President*
EMP: 5
SALES: 220K **Privately Held**
WEB: www.crawfordsprintshop.com
SIC: 2752 Color lithography

(G-6)
HES INC
6303 Symonds Hill Rd (14801-9564)
PHONE.....................................607 359-2974
John J Crane, *President*
EMP: 8
SQ FT: 10,000
SALES: 450K **Privately Held**
SIC: 3621 3599 Electric motor & generator parts; machine shop, jobbing & repair

Afton
Chenango County

(G-7)
BABYSAFE USA LLC
251 County Road 17 (13730-3111)
PHONE.....................................877 367-4141
Sagi Ben-Dov, *Mng Member*
Jamie Baciuska,
Lynn Baciuska,
▲ **EMP:** 5
SQ FT: 8,000
SALES: 235K **Privately Held**
SIC: 3944 Baby carriages & restraint seats

(G-8)
COBRA OPERATING INDUSTRIES LLC
37 Main St (13730-3164)
PHONE.....................................607 639-1700
Richard W Wagner, *Principal*
Barbara A Wagner,
Barbara Wagner,
EMP: 6
SALES (est): 400K **Privately Held**
SIC: 3441 Fabricated structural metal

(G-9)
WAGNER NINEVEH INC
224 County Rd 26 (13730)
PHONE.....................................607 693-2689
Rebecca Spencer, *Manager*
EMP: 10 **EST:** 2007
SALES (est): 1.3MM **Privately Held**
SIC: 2421 Sawmills & planing mills, general

Airmont
Rockland County

(G-10)
901 D LLC
360 Route 59 Ste 3 (10952-3416)
PHONE.....................................845 369-1111
Kevin Syska, *Engineer*
Fred Sainclivier, *Project Engr*
Aldric Seguin, *Sales Executive*
Andrew Eisenberg, *Program Mgr*
Francois Duverne,

Airmont - Rockland County (G-11)   GEOGRAPHIC SECTION

EMP: 48
SALES (est): 14.9MM
SALES (corp-wide): 17.6MM **Privately Held**
WEB: www.901d.com
SIC: 3553 Cabinet makers' machinery
PA: Graycliff Partners, Lp
500 5th Ave Fl 47
New York NY 10110
212 300-2900

(G-11)
ART ESSENTIALS OF NEW YORK (PA)
25 Church Rd (10952-4108)
P.O. Box 38, Tallman (10982-0038)
PHONE 845 368-1100
Bella Jacobs, *President*
Arnold A Jacobs, *Shareholder*
EMP: 3
SQ FT: 1,400
SALES: 1MM **Privately Held**
WEB: www.artessentialsofnewyork.com
SIC: 2499 Decorative wood & woodwork

(G-12)
HANDY LAUNDRY PRODUCTS CORP (PA)
382 Route 59 Ste 318 (10952-3422)
PHONE 845 701-1111
Shlome Masri, *President*
Aron Braun, *Principal*
▲ **EMP:** 6
SALES (est): 490.4K **Privately Held**
SIC: 2392 Laundry, garment & storage bags

(G-13)
I TRADE TECHNOLOGY LTD
3 Rustic Dr (10952-4722)
PHONE 845 357-4943
Malkie Lebrecht, *Ch of Bd*
EMP: 22
SALES (est): 6.4MM **Privately Held**
SIC: 3678 Electronic connectors

(G-14)
JOMAR INDUSTRIES INC
382 Route 59 Ste 352 (10952-3484)
P.O. Box 379, Monsey (10952-0379)
PHONE 845 357-5773
Alan Marks, *President*
▲ **EMP:** 20
SQ FT: 4,000
SALES (est): 1.6MM **Privately Held**
WEB: www.jomarindustries.com
SIC: 3993 2395 5961 2759 Advertising novelties; art needlework: made from purchased materials; gift items, mail order; commercial printing

(G-15)
MINTED GREEN INC
85 Regina Rd (10952-4527)
PHONE 845 458-1845
Chaim Rosenberg, *Ch of Bd*
EMP: 6 EST: 2015
SQ FT: 1,200
SALES (est): 2.8MM **Privately Held**
SIC: 3942 5092 5945 Dolls & stuffed toys; toys & games; toys & games

Akron
Erie County

(G-16)
AAKRON RULE CORP (PA)
8 Indianola Ave (14001-1199)
P.O. Box 418 (14001-0418)
PHONE 716 542-5483
Danielle Robillard, *Ch of Bd*
Jon Merrick, *Vice Pres*
Devin Piscitelli, *Vice Pres*
Angel Alicea, *Plant Mgr*
George Vancleef, *Opers Mgr*
◆ **EMP:** 150 EST: 1967
SQ FT: 16,000
SALES (est): 45.8MM **Privately Held**
WEB: www.aakronline.com
SIC: 2499 3993 3952 3951 Rulers & rules, wood; paint sticks, wood; signs & advertising specialties; lead pencils & art goods; pens & mechanical pencils

(G-17)
COUNTY LINE STONE CO INC
4515 Crittenden Rd (14001-9517)
P.O. Box 150 (14001-0150)
PHONE 716 542-5435
John Buyers Jr, *Vice Pres*
Bruce M Buyers, *Vice Pres*
Lorraine Pixley, *Finance Mgr*
EMP: 30
SQ FT: 20,000
SALES (est): 4.7MM **Privately Held**
SIC: 1429 5032 Sandstone, crushed & broken-quarrying; asphalt mixture

(G-18)
FORD GUM & MACHINE COMPANY INC (PA)
18 Newton Ave (14001-1099)
P.O. Box 330 (14001-0330)
PHONE 716 542-4561
George H Stege, *Ch of Bd*
Robert A R Clouston, *Ch of Bd*
George H Stege, *Ch of Bd*
George Stege, *President*
Warren Clark, *Vice Pres*
▲ **EMP:** 100 EST: 1913
SQ FT: 125,000
SALES (est): 59.7MM **Privately Held**
WEB: www.fordgum.com
SIC: 2067 5441 Chewing gum; candy

(G-19)
IGNITER SYSTEMS INC
12600 Clarence Center Rd (14001-9749)
PHONE 716 542-5511
John Davis, *President*
EMP: 20
SQ FT: 90,000
SALES (est): 1.9MM **Privately Held**
WEB: www.ignitersystems.com
SIC: 3567 Heating units & devices, industrial: electric

(G-20)
NIAGARA LABEL COMPANY INC
12715 Lewis Rd (14001-9668)
P.O. Box 90 (14001-0090)
PHONE 716 542-3000
Michael C Witmarsh, *CEO*
Marjorie Witmarsh, *Corp Secy*
Connie Ribbeck, *Prdtn Mgr*
Tina Lemley, *Accounts Mgr*
Michele Vanderlinden, *Cust Mgr*
▲ **EMP:** 17
SQ FT: 5,000
SALES (est): 3MM **Privately Held**
WEB: www.niagaralabel.com
SIC: 2754 2759 Labels: gravure printing; labels & seals: printing

(G-21)
PERRYS ICE CREAM COMPANY INC
1 Ice Cream Plz (14001-1031)
PHONE 716 542-5492
Robert Denning, *President*
Chas Staebell, *Regional Mgr*
Brian Perry, *Exec VP*
Joel Bearfield, *Mfg Staff*
Olivia Largis, *QA Dir*
▲ **EMP:** 300
SQ FT: 135,000
SALES (est): 69MM **Privately Held**
SIC: 2024 5145 Ice cream, bulk; snack foods

(G-22)
RE-AL INDUSTRIAL CORP
Also Called: D & E Industrial
5391 Crittenden Rd (14001-9598)
P.O. Box 37, Newfane (14108-0037)
PHONE 716 542-4556
Richard Bottom, *President*
EMP: 8
SQ FT: 8,000
SALES: 700K **Privately Held**
WEB: www.d-eind.com
SIC: 3535 1796 Conveyors & conveying equipment; machinery installation

(G-23)
STRIPPIT INC (DH)
Also Called: L V D
12975 Clarence Center Rd (14001-1371)
PHONE 716 542-4511
John P Lesebbre, *President*
Bruce Turner, *CFO*
◆ **EMP:** 200
SQ FT: 255,000
SALES (est): 64.8MM
SALES (corp-wide): 76K **Privately Held**
SIC: 3542 3544 3549 3545 Machine tools, metal forming type; special dies, tools, jigs & fixtures; metalworking machinery; machine tool accessories
HQ: L.V.D. Company Nv
Nijverheidslaan 2
Wevelgem 8560
564 305-11

(G-24)
WHITING DOOR MFG CORP (PA)
113 Cedar St (14001-1038)
P.O. Box 388 (14001-0388)
PHONE 716 542-5427
Donald J Whiting, *Ch of Bd*
Greg Marek, *President*
Chris Ericksen, *Area Mgr*
Steve Hazard, *Area Mgr*
Joe Olszta, *Area Mgr*
▼ **EMP:** 330 EST: 1953
SQ FT: 371,000
SALES (est): 128MM **Privately Held**
SIC: 3714 Motor vehicle parts & accessories

(G-25)
WHITING DOOR MFG CORP
13550 Bloomingdale Rd (14001-9801)
PHONE 716 542-3070
Michael Whiting, *Manager*
Joe Lukasiewizd, *Info Tech Dir*
EMP: 60
SALES (corp-wide): 128MM **Privately Held**
SIC: 3493 Coiled flat springs
PA: Whiting Door Mfg Corp
113 Cedar St
Akron NY 14001
716 542-5427

Akwesasne
Franklin County

(G-26)
OHSERASE MANUFACTURING LLC
26 Eagle Dr (13655)
P.O. Box 1221 (13655-1221)
PHONE 518 358-9309
Justin Tarbell, *Vice Pres*
▲ **EMP:** 23
SALES (est): 3MM **Privately Held**
SIC: 3999 Barber & beauty shop equipment

Albany
Albany County

(G-27)
ACCESSIBLE BATH TECH LLC
6 Albright Ave (12203-4802)
PHONE 518 937-1518
Craig La Londe, *President*
EMP: 15
SALES: 950K **Privately Held**
SIC: 3999 Manufacturing industries

(G-28)
ACCUPRINT (PA)
2005 Western Ave Ste 1 (12203-5073)
PHONE 518 456-2431
Donald Blais, *Owner*
Denise Denton, *Director*
EMP: 6
SALES (est): 537.1K **Privately Held**
SIC: 2752 Commercial printing, offset

(G-29)
ADIRONDACK SPCLTY ADHSIVES INC
4258 Albany St (12205-4614)
P.O. Box 13283 (12212-3283)
PHONE 518 869-5736
Jerald Casey, *President*
EMP: 15
SQ FT: 7,500
SALES (est): 3.5MM **Privately Held**
WEB: www.adktapes.com
SIC: 2891 Adhesives

(G-30)
AIRGAS INC
84 Karner Rd (12205-4730)
PHONE 518 690-0068
David Boyle, *Manager*
F Gay Dunn, *Co-Mgr*
Lester Mackey, *Executive*
EMP: 14
SALES (corp-wide): 164.2MM **Privately Held**
SIC: 2813 Oxygen, compressed or liquefied; nitrogen; argon
HQ: Airgas, Inc.
259 N Radnor Chester Rd # 100
Radnor PA 19087
610 687-5253

(G-31)
ALBANY ASP & AGGREGATES CORP
101 Dunham Dr (12202-2106)
PHONE 518 436-8916
Frederick M Stutzman, *President*
Eugene D Hallock III, *Vice Pres*
John Stutzman, *Vice Pres*
EMP: 20
SQ FT: 10,000
SALES (est): 4.2MM
SALES (corp-wide): 14MM **Privately Held**
SIC: 2951 Asphalt paving mixtures & blocks
PA: Hudson River Construction Co., Inc.
101 Dunham Dr
Albany NY 12202
518 434-6677

(G-32)
ALBANY CATHOLIC PRESS ASSOC
Also Called: Evangelist, The
40 N Main Ave Ste 2 (12203-1481)
PHONE 518 453-6688
James Breig, *Principal*
Bishop Hubbard, *Principal*
Stephanie Zebrowski, *Manager*
Barbra Oliver, *Manager*
EMP: 9
SQ FT: 10,000
SALES: 1MM **Privately Held**
SIC: 2711 8661 Newspapers: publishing only, not printed on site; religious organizations

(G-33)
ALBANY LETTER SHOP INC
16 Van Zandt St Ste 20 (12207-1448)
P.O. Box 1003 (12201-1003)
PHONE 518 434-1172
Fax: 518 434-6261
EMP: 6
SQ FT: 2,900
SALES (est): 41.6K **Privately Held**
SIC: 2752 Offset Printing

(G-34)
ALBANY MOLECULAR RESEARCH INC
21 Corporate Cir (12203-5154)
PHONE 518 512-2234
Mark Stier, *General Mgr*
Ben Seisler, *Counsel*
Michael Pettersson, *Vice Pres*
Geoff Flavell, *Production*
Tracey Block, *Research*
EMP: 7
SALES (corp-wide): 124.9MM **Privately Held**
SIC: 2836 8731 Biological products, except diagnostic; commercial physical research
HQ: Albany Molecular Research, Inc.
26 Corporate Cir
Albany NY 12203

GEOGRAPHIC SECTION
Albany - Albany County (G-61)

(G-35)
ALBANY MOLECULAR RESEARCH INC (HQ)
Also Called: Amri
26 Corporate Cir (12203-5121)
P.O. Box 15098 (12212-5098)
PHONE..................518 512-2000
Michael Mulhern, *CEO*
Kathy Saybe, *General Mgr*
Julianne Zaremba, *General Mgr*
George Svokos, *COO*
Margalit Fine, *Exec VP*
▲ **EMP:** 277
SQ FT: 159,000
SALES: 570.4MM
SALES (corp-wide): 124.9MM **Privately Held**
SIC: 2836 8731 Biological products, except diagnostic; biotechnical research, commercial

(G-36)
ALBANY MTAL FBRCATION HOLDINGS
67 Henry Johnson Blvd (12210-1413)
PHONE..................518 463-5161
Dave Warzek, *Principal*
EMP: 7 **EST:** 2008
SALES (est): 1.1MM **Privately Held**
SIC: 3444 Sheet metalwork

(G-37)
ALBANY STUDENT PRESS INC
Also Called: A S P
1400 Washington Ave Cc329 (12222-0100)
PHONE..................518 442-5665
Carey Qeen, *Manager*
EMP: 30
SALES: 12.4MM **Privately Held**
SIC: 2711 2741 Newspapers; miscellaneous publishing

(G-38)
ALL-LIFTS INCORPORATED
27-39 Thatcher St (12207-5016)
PHONE..................518 465-3461
Steven R Dewey, *President*
Patrick Dewey, *Vice Pres*
Janis Scott, *Purchasing*
Beth Wilson, *Accountant*
Brian Dewey, *Sales Staff*
EMP: 25 **EST:** 1966
SQ FT: 12,400
SALES (est): 6MM **Privately Held**
WEB: www.all-lifts.com
SIC: 2298 5063 3496 Slings, rope; electrical construction materials; chain, welded

(G-39)
ALO ACQUISITION LLC (DH)
26 Corporate Cir (12203-5121)
PHONE..................518 464-0279
Thomas E D'Ambra, *Ch of Bd*
EMP: 4
SALES (est): 92.5MM
SALES (corp-wide): 124.9MM **Privately Held**
SIC: 2833 5122 8733 Medicinals & botanicals; drugs & drug proprietaries; research institute

(G-40)
AMERICAN BOILER TANK WLDG INC
53 Pleasant St (12207-1385)
PHONE..................518 463-5012
William A Novak, *President*
Bill Engel, *Buyer*
Paul Engel, *Manager*
Brenda Longe, *Manager*
EMP: 20
SQ FT: 30,000
SALES: 5MM **Privately Held**
WEB: www.americanboiler.com
SIC: 3443 Fabricated plate work (boiler shop)

(G-41)
ANDREW J GEORGE
Also Called: Cardinal Data/Lark Graphics
457 Madison Ave (12210-1002)
PHONE..................518 462-4662
Andrew J George, *Owner*
James Smith, *Sales Staff*
EMP: 5
SQ FT: 1,750
SALES (est): 534.7K **Privately Held**
SIC: 2759 Commercial printing

(G-42)
ARCY PLASTIC LAMINATES INC (PA)
555 Patroon Creek Blvd (12206-5007)
PHONE..................518 235-0753
Robert Cecucci, *Asst Sec*
EMP: 48 **EST:** 1952
SQ FT: 31,000
SALES (est): 3.4MM **Privately Held**
SIC: 2541 Counter & sink tops

(G-43)
ARDENT MILLS LLC
Cargill
101 Normanskill St (12202-2155)
PHONE..................518 447-1700
Cody Meyers, *Manager*
EMP: 100
SALES (corp-wide): 631.7MM **Privately Held**
WEB: www.cargill.com
SIC: 2041 0723 Flour & other grain mill products; flour milling custom services
PA: Ardent Mills, Llc
1875 Lawrence St Ste 1400
Denver CO 80202
800 851-9618

(G-44)
BARKER STEEL LLC
126 S Port Rd (12202-1087)
P.O. Box 800, Coeymans (12045-0800)
PHONE..................518 465-6221
Scott Henricks, *Safety Mgr*
David Legenbauer, *Branch Mgr*
EMP: 20
SALES (corp-wide): 20.2B **Publicly Held**
WEB: www.barker.com
SIC: 3449 8742 3441 Bars, concrete reinforcing; fabricated steel; management consulting services; fabricated structural metal
HQ: Barker Steel Llc
55 Sumner St Ste 1
Milford MA 01757
800 363-3953

(G-45)
BEN WEITSMAN OF ALBANY LLC
300 Smith Blvd (12202-1090)
PHONE..................518 462-4444
Adam Weitsman, *Mng Member*
Stephnen Green,
Daniel Innarella,
Joel Root,
EMP: 22 **EST:** 2013
SALES: 21MM
SALES (corp-wide): 156.2MM **Privately Held**
SIC: 3559 3341 Recycling machinery; copper smelting & refining (secondary)
PA: Weitsman Shredding, Llc
1 Recycle Dr
Owego NY 13827
607 687-7777

(G-46)
BENWAY-HAWORTH-LWLR-LACOSTA HE
Also Called: Hearing Aid Office, The
21 Everett Rd (12205-1437)
PHONE..................518 432-4070
Robert Lacosta, *President*
EMP: 12
SQ FT: 2,000
SALES (est): 1.4MM **Privately Held**
SIC: 3842 5999 Hearing aids; hearing aids

(G-47)
BEST PALLET & CRATE LLC
22 Railroad Ave (12205-5727)
PHONE..................518 438-2945
Neil Manasse,
EMP: 6
SALES (est): 901K **Privately Held**
SIC: 2448 Pallets, wood & wood with metal

(G-48)
BIMBO BAKERIES
78 N Manning Blvd (12206-2294)
PHONE..................518 463-2221
Joe Rebholtz, *Principal*
EMP: 16
SALES (est): 2.6MM **Privately Held**
SIC: 2051 Bread, cake & related products

(G-49)
BIMBO BAKERIES USA INC
40 Fuller Rd (12205-5122)
PHONE..................518 489-4053
EMP: 18 **Privately Held**
WEB: www.gwbakeries.com
SIC: 2051 Bakery: wholesale or wholesale/retail combined
HQ: Bimbo Bakeries Usa, Inc
255 Business Center Dr # 200
Horsham PA 19044
215 347-5500

(G-50)
BRIGAR X-PRESS SOLUTIONS INC
Also Called: Digital X-Press
5 Sand Creek Rd Ste 100 (12205-1400)
PHONE..................518 438-7817
John J Mc Grath III, *CEO*
Jodi Hess, *President*
Thomas Newkirk, *Principal*
EMP: 70 **EST:** 1989
SQ FT: 60,000
SALES (est): 24.4MM **Privately Held**
WEB: www.brigarxpress.com
SIC: 2752 Commercial printing, lithographic

(G-51)
BULLEX INC (DH)
Also Called: Bullex Digital Safety
20 Corporate Cir Ste 3 (12203-5153)
PHONE..................518 689-2023
Ryan O Donnell, *CEO*
Tom Rossi,
▲ **EMP:** 10
SALES (est): 12.6MM **Privately Held**
WEB: www.bullexsafety.com
SIC: 3569 8748 Firefighting apparatus; safety training service
HQ: Lion Training Resources Group, Inc.
7200 Poe Ave Ste 400
Dayton OH 45414
937 898-1949

(G-52)
BULLEX INC
Also Called: Bullex Digital Safety
20 Corporate Cir Ste 3 (12203-5153)
PHONE..................518 689-2023
Thomas Roffi, *Branch Mgr*
EMP: 50 **Privately Held**
WEB: www.bullexsafety.com
SIC: 3999 Fire extinguishers, portable
HQ: Bullex, Inc.
20 Corporate Cir Ste 3
Albany NY 12203
518 689-2023

(G-53)
C H EVANS BREWING CO
Also Called: Albany Pump Station
19 Quackenbush Sq (12207-2311)
PHONE..................518 447-9000
Neil Evans, *CEO*
Ryan Demler, *Manager*
Adam Sopris, *Manager*
EMP: 15
SQ FT: 13,587
SALES (est): 1.6MM **Privately Held**
WEB: www.evansale.com
SIC: 2082 Malt beverages

(G-54)
CALLANAN INDUSTRIES INC (DH)
8 Southwoods Blvd Ste 4 (12211-2554)
P.O. Box 15097 (12212-5097)
PHONE..................518 374-2222
Jonas Havens, *President*
Todd Anson, *Plant Mgr*
Tim Hauck, *Plant Mgr*
Dominick Testo, *Plant Mgr*
Bruce Gumlaw, *Manager*
▲ **EMP:** 205
SQ FT: 24,000
SALES (est): 113.6MM
SALES (corp-wide): 29.7B **Privately Held**
WEB: www.callanan.com
SIC: 3272 2951 Concrete products, precast; asphalt paving mixtures & blocks

(G-55)
CAPITAL REGION WKLY NEWSPAPERS
Also Called: Advertiser
645 Albany Shaker Rd (12211-1158)
P.O. Box 1450, Clifton Park (12065-0806)
PHONE..................518 877-7160
Patrick Smith, *President*
EMP: 29
SQ FT: 4,000
SALES (est): 1.6MM **Privately Held**
SIC: 2711 Commercial printing & newspaper publishing combined

(G-56)
CAPITOL CITY SPECIALTIES CO
10 Burdick Dr (12205-1467)
PHONE..................518 486-8935
Michael Campagna, *Principal*
EMP: 8 **EST:** 2013
SALES (est): 759K **Privately Held**
SIC: 2099 Peanut butter

(G-57)
CHAMPLAIN HUDSON POWER EX INC
600 Broadway Fl 3 (12207-2235)
PHONE..................518 465-0710
John Douglas, *CEO*
Donald Jensson, *President*
Scott Hargreaves, *CFO*
Nancy Clarke, *Director*
EMP: 7
SQ FT: 500
SALES (est): 540K **Privately Held**
SIC: 3568 Power transmission equipment

(G-58)
CHARLES FREIHOFER BAKING CO
1 Prospect Rd (12206-2229)
PHONE..................518 463-2221
Peter Rollins, *President*
Eileen Connor, *Accounting Mgr*
EMP: 8
SALES (est): 1MM **Privately Held**
SIC: 2499 Bakers' equipment, wood

(G-59)
CLEAR VIEW BAG COMPANY INC
5 Burdick Dr (12205-1405)
P.O. Box 11160 (12211-0160)
PHONE..................518 458-7153
William J Romer, *Ch of Bd*
Deborah S Romer, *Vice Pres*
Len Smith, *QC Mgr*
Sherri Smith, *Administration*
EMP: 156 **EST:** 1957
SQ FT: 45,000
SALES (est): 27.9MM **Privately Held**
WEB: www.clearviewbag.com
SIC: 3081 2673 Polyethylene film; bags; plastic, laminated & coated

(G-60)
CMC-KUHNKE INC
90 State St Ste 601 (12207-1706)
PHONE..................518 694-3310
Heinz Grossjohann, *President*
Alex Grossjohann, *Vice Pres*
Edward L Shively, *Technical Mgr*
Nathan Zerrahn, *Sales Staff*
Jason Cooper, *Info Tech Mgr*
EMP: 12
SQ FT: 10,000
SALES (est): 2.4MM **Privately Held**
SIC: 3411 Food & beverage containers

(G-61)
CMP EXPORT CO INC
Also Called: Ticoniun
413 N Pearl St (12207-1311)
P.O. Box 350 (12201-0350)
PHONE..................518 434-3147
Devon Howe, *President*
Ed Civiok, *Treasurer*
Edward Civiok Jr, *Treasurer*

Albany - Albany County (G-62)

▲ **EMP:** 42
SALES (est): 3.9MM **Privately Held**
WEB: www.cmpindustries.com
SIC: 3843 Dental equipment & supplies

(G-62)
CMP INDUSTRIES LLC (PA)
Also Called: Ticonium Division
413 N Pearl St (12207-1311)
PHONE 518 434-3147
Alla Slutskaya, *Export Mgr*
Greg Smith, *Engineer*
Scott Mayshaw, *Marketing Staff*
Devon Howe, *Mng Member*
Mathew Lane, *Technical Staff*
◆ **EMP:** 40 **EST:** 1889
SQ FT: 90,000
SALES (est): 8.4MM **Privately Held**
WEB: www.cmpindustry.com
SIC: 3843 Dental equipment & supplies

(G-63)
CMP INDUSTRIES LLC
Also Called: Nobilium
413 N Pearl St (12207-1311)
PHONE 518 434-3147
William Regan, *Branch Mgr*
EMP: 5
SALES (corp-wide): 8.4MM **Privately Held**
WEB: www.cmpindustry.com
SIC: 3843 Dental laboratory equipment
PA: Cmp Industries Llc
413 N Pearl St
Albany NY 12207
518 434-3147

(G-64)
COCA-COLA BTLG CO OF NY INC
38 Warehouse Row (12205-5757)
PHONE 518 459-2010
Dwayne St Claire, *COO*
Dwayne St Clair, *Opers Mgr*
Julie Francis, *Sales/Mktg Mgr*
EMP: 11
SALES (corp-wide): 35.4B **Publicly Held**
SIC: 2086 5149 Soft drinks: packaged in cans, bottles, etc.; groceries & related products
HQ: The Coca-Cola Bottling Company Of New York Inc
2500 Windy Ridge Pkwy Se
Atlanta GA 30339
770 989-3000

(G-65)
COCCADOTTS INC
1179 Central Ave (12205-5436)
PHONE 518 438-4937
Rachel Dott, *Owner*
Luke Dott, *Treasurer*
EMP: 11
SALES (est): 982K **Privately Held**
SIC: 2051 Cakes, bakery: except frozen

(G-66)
COMMERCEHUB INC (HQ)
201 Fuller Rd Fl 6 (12203-3621)
PHONE 518 810-0700
Francis Poore, *President*
Mike Amend, *COO*
John Hinkle, *Exec VP*
Michael Trimarchi, *CFO*
Richard Jones, *CTO*
EMP: 15 **EST:** 1997
SQ FT: 49,500
SALES: 111.1MM **Privately Held**
SIC: 7372 Prepackaged software
PA: Great Dane Parent, Llc
201 Fuller Rd Fl 6
Albany NY 12203
518 810-0700

(G-67)
DAVIES OFFICE REFURBISHING INC (PA)
40 Loudonville Rd (12204-1513)
PHONE 518 426-7188
William E Davies, *President*
Evelyn Davies, *Vice Pres*
David Wyman, *Accounts Exec*
Sean Davies, *Sales Staff*
Michael Nguyen, *CIO*
▲ **EMP:** 123
SQ FT: 96,000
SALES (est): 41.4MM **Privately Held**
WEB: www.daviesoffice.com
SIC: 2522 7641 Office furniture, except wood; office furniture repair & maintenance

(G-68)
DIGITAL PAGE LLC
75 Benjamin St (12202-1137)
PHONE 518 446-9129
Eugene R Spada II,
EMP: 11
SQ FT: 2,000
SALES (est): 174.4K **Privately Held**
SIC: 2791 Typesetting

(G-69)
DYNAMIC SCREENPRINTING
12 Vatrano Rd (12205-3404)
PHONE 518 487-4256
Jeff Serge, *Mng Member*
EMP: 9
SALES (est): 829.3K **Privately Held**
SIC: 2261 Screen printing of cotton broadwoven fabrics

(G-70)
EASY BOOK PUBLISHING INC
260 Osborne Rd Ste 3 (12211-1856)
PHONE 518 459-6281
Nydia Russum, *President*
John Russum, *Vice Pres*
EMP: 6
SQ FT: 1,500
SALES (est): 622.5K **Privately Held**
WEB: www.easy-book.net
SIC: 2741 Directories: publishing only, not printed on site

(G-71)
EDP RENEWABLES NORTH AMER LLC
1971 Western Ave 230 (12203-5066)
PHONE 518 426-1650
Patrick Doyle, *Branch Mgr*
EMP: 8
SALES (corp-wide): 3.1B **Privately Held**
SIC: 3621 Windmills, electric generating
HQ: Edp Renewables North America Llc
808 Travis St Ste 700
Houston TX 77002
713 265-0350

(G-72)
EMPIRE AIR SPECIALTIES INC
40 Kraft Ave (12205-5428)
PHONE 518 689-4440
Robert J Miner, *President*
Rebecca Miner, *Treasurer*
EMP: 25
SQ FT: 5,500
SALES (est): 5.1MM **Privately Held**
SIC: 3444 Sheet metalwork

(G-73)
FASTSIGNS
1593 Central Ave (12205-2457)
PHONE 518 456-7446
James Pritchard, *Principal*
EMP: 10
SALES (est): 1.1MM **Privately Held**
SIC: 3993 Signs & advertising specialties

(G-74)
FINGERPRINT AMERICA INC
1843 Central Ave (12205-4796)
P.O. Box 12542 (12212-2542)
PHONE 518 435-1609
Chris Migliaro, *President*
EMP: 6
SQ FT: 3,000
SALES (est): 733.2K **Privately Held**
WEB: www.fingerprintamerica.com
SIC: 3999 Fingerprint equipment

(G-75)
FORT ORANGE PRESS INC
11 Sand Creek Rd (12205-1442)
PHONE 518 489-3233
Robert F Witko, *Ch of Bd*
Frank P Witko, *Ch of Bd*
Michael P Witko, *President*
William Dorsman, *Vice Pres*
Kenneth L Pleat, *Vice Pres*
EMP: 37 **EST:** 1905
SQ FT: 33,000
SALES (est): 11.4MM **Privately Held**
WEB: www.fortorangepress.com
SIC: 2752 2791 Commercial printing, offset; typesetting

(G-76)
GCOM SOFTWARE INC (PA)
24 Madison Avenue Ext (12203-5396)
PHONE 518 869-1671
Girish Bhatia, *CEO*
Riyaz Ladkhan, *COO*
Sunil Bhatia, *Vice Pres*
Abid Bargeer, *CTO*
EMP: 50
SQ FT: 3,500
SALES: 60.5MM **Privately Held**
WEB: www.gcomsoft.com
SIC: 7372 Prepackaged software

(G-77)
GENERAL ELECTRIC COMPANY
11 Anderson Dr (12205-1401)
PHONE 518 459-4110
James Miner, *Safety Mgr*
Gautam Naik, *Engineer*
Mark Seus, *Design Engr*
Robert Hitchcock, *Manager*
David Testo, *Manager*
EMP: 50
SQ FT: 1,680
SALES (corp-wide): 122B **Publicly Held**
SIC: 3629 7694 Electronic generation equipment; electric motor repair
PA: General Electric Company
41 Farnsworth St
Boston MA 02210
617 443-3000

(G-78)
GREAT DANE PARENT LLC (PA) ○
201 Fuller Rd Fl 6 (12203-3621)
PHONE 518 810-0700
Francis Poore, *President*
EMP: 2 **EST:** 2018
SALES (est): 111.1MM **Privately Held**
SIC: 7372 Prepackaged software

(G-79)
GREENBUSH TAPE & LABEL INC
40 Broadway Unit 31 (12202-1174)
P.O. Box 1488 (12201-1488)
PHONE 518 465-2389
James Chenot, *Vice Pres*
Alfred Chenot, *Treasurer*
EMP: 35 **EST:** 1966
SQ FT: 75,000
SALES (est): 4.6MM **Privately Held**
WEB: www.greenbushlabel.com
SIC: 2759 2672 Labels & seals: printing; coated & laminated paper

(G-80)
HANES SUPPLY INC
156 Railroad Ave Ste 3 (12205-5773)
PHONE 518 438-0139
Bill Kenny, *Manager*
EMP: 13
SALES (est): 2.3MM
SALES (corp-wide): 97.5MM **Privately Held**
SIC: 3496 Miscellaneous fabricated wire products
PA: Hanes Supply, Inc.
55 James E Casey Dr
Buffalo NY 14206
716 826-2636

(G-81)
HANGER INC
1315 Central Ave (12205-5282)
PHONE 518 435-0840
EMP: 26
SALES (corp-wide): 1B **Publicly Held**
SIC: 3842 Surgical appliances & supplies
PA: Hanger, Inc.
10910 Domain Dr Ste 300
Austin TX 78758
512 777-3800

(G-82)
HEARST CORPORATION
Capital Newspaper Div
645 Albany Shaker Rd (12211-1158)
P.O. Box 15000 (12212-5000)
PHONE 518 454-5694
Gary Hahn, *Publisher*
Lisa Stevens, *Editor*
Will Waldron, *Editor*
Joseph Russo, *District Mgr*
David P White, *Vice Pres*
EMP: 550
SALES (corp-wide): 6.6B **Privately Held**
WEB: www.hearstcorp.com
SIC: 2721 2752 2711 Periodicals: publishing only; commercial printing, lithographic; newspapers
PA: The Hearst Corporation
300 W 57th St Fl 42
New York NY 10019
212 649-2000

(G-83)
HOCKEY FACILITY
830 Albany Shaker Rd (12211-1054)
PHONE 518 452-7396
Paul Hebert, *Manager*
EMP: 5
SALES (est): 494.1K **Privately Held**
SIC: 2329 Hockey uniforms: men's, youths' & boys'

(G-84)
HOEHN INC
Also Called: Hoehn.us
159 Chestnut St (12210-1905)
PHONE 518 463-8900
James G Hoehn Jr, *President*
Melissa Nigro, *Vice Pres*
EMP: 15
SALES (est): 1.6MM **Privately Held**
WEB: www.hoehn.com
SIC: 2339 2389 Women's & misses' accessories; men's miscellaneous accessories

(G-85)
HP INC
5 Computer Dr S (12205-1608)
PHONE 650 857-1501
Charlene D Fitzgerald, *Branch Mgr*
EMP: 43
SALES (corp-wide): 52B **Publicly Held**
SIC: 3571 Personal computers (microcomputers)
PA: Hp Inc.
1501 Page Mill Rd
Palo Alto CA 94304
650 857-1501

(G-86)
ION OPTICS INC
Also Called: Cosmo Optics
75 Benjamin St (12202-1137)
PHONE 518 339-6853
Brian Sebastian, *Principal*
EMP: 13
SALES (est): 1.1MM **Privately Held**
SIC: 3229 Lens blanks, optical

(G-87)
ISIMULATE LLC
43 New Scotland Ave (12208-3412)
PHONE 877 947-2831
EMP: 5
SQ FT: 1,000
SALES (est): 500K **Privately Held**
SIC: 3845 Arc lamp units, electrotherapeutic (except IR & UV)

(G-88)
JASON LADANYE GUITAR PIANO & H
605 Park Ave (12208-3217)
PHONE 518 527-3973
Jason Ladanye, *Owner*
EMP: 50
SALES (est): 90.9K **Privately Held**
SIC: 3931 Harmonicas

(G-89)
JOHNSON CONTROLS INC
130 Railroad Ave (12205-5701)
PHONE 518 694-4822
John Desare, *Manager*
EMP: 9 **Privately Held**
SIC: 2531 Seats, automobile
HQ: Johnson Controls, Inc.
5757 N Green Bay Ave
Milwaukee WI 53209
414 524-1200

▲ = Import ▼ = Export
◆ = Import/Export

Albany - Albany County (G-117)

(G-90)
KAL-HARBOUR INC
Also Called: Harbour Roads
11 Villa Rd (12204-2213)
P.O. Box 4087 (12204-0087)
PHONE.................................518 266-0690
Laura Harbour, *President*
EMP: 10 **Privately Held**
WEB: www.harbourroads.com
SIC: 2951 Asphalt paving mixtures & blocks
PA: Kal-Harbour Inc
21 Arch St
Watervliet NY 12189

(G-91)
KING ROAD MATERIALS INC (DH)
Also Called: King Paving
8 Southwoods Blvd (12211-2554)
P.O. Box 15097 (12212-5097)
PHONE.................................518 381-9995
Donald E Fane, *President*
Martin Reff, *Vice Pres*
EMP: 35 **EST:** 1959
SQ FT: 2,552
SALES (est): 21.8MM
SALES (corp-wide): 29.7B **Privately Held**
SIC: 2951 Asphalt & asphaltic paving mixtures (not from refineries)

(G-92)
KING ROAD MATERIALS INC
Cordell Rd (12212)
P.O. Box 12699 (12212-2699)
PHONE.................................518 382-5354
Mellisa Bennett, *Principal*
EMP: 15
SALES (corp-wide): 29.7B **Privately Held**
SIC: 3273 Ready-mixed concrete
HQ: King Road Materials, Inc.
8 Southwoods Blvd
Albany NY 12211
518 381-9995

(G-93)
KOEPPELS KUSTOM KITCHENS INC
16 Van Rensselaer Rd (12205-1413)
PHONE.................................518 489-0092
Carl J Koeppel Jr, *President*
EMP: 5
SQ FT: 4,500
SALES (est): 520K **Privately Held**
SIC: 2541 1751 Counter & sink tops; cabinet building & installation

(G-94)
KRONOS INCORPORATED
16 Sage Est Ste 206 (12204-2241)
PHONE.................................518 459-5545
Frank Shipp, *Manager*
EMP: 36
SALES (corp-wide): 1B **Privately Held**
WEB: www.kronos.com
SIC: 7372 Prepackaged software
HQ: Kronos Incorporated
900 Chelmsford St # 312
Lowell MA 01851
978 250-9800

(G-95)
LIDS CORPORATION
131 Colonie Ctr Spc 429 (12205-2751)
PHONE.................................518 459-7060
Dinelle Jackson, *Manager*
EMP: 5
SALES (corp-wide): 2.9B **Publicly Held**
WEB: www.hatworld.com
SIC: 2253 Hats & headwear, knit
HQ: Lids Corporation
7555 Woodland Dr
Indianapolis IN 46278

(G-96)
M&G DURAVENT INC
10 Jupiter Ln (12205-4947)
PHONE.................................518 463-7284
Mike Winn, *President*
EMP: 22 **Privately Held**
SIC: 3444 Metal ventilating equipment
HQ: M&G Duravent, Inc.
877 Cotting Ct
Vacaville CA 95688
707 446-1786

(G-97)
MCD METALS LLC
20 Corporate Cir Ste 2 (12203-5175)
PHONE.................................518 456-9694
Kevin Gleason, *President*
Jacek Wozniak, *Opers Mgr*
EMP: 11
SALES (est): 734.5K **Privately Held**
SIC: 3499 Shims, metal

(G-98)
MECHANICAL TECHNOLOGY INC (PA)
325 Washington Avenue Ext (12205-5581)
PHONE.................................518 218-2550
David C Michaels, *Ch of Bd*
Frederick W Jones, *President*
Linda Rogers, *Office Mgr*
EMP: 27 **EST:** 1961
SQ FT: 17,400
SALES: 7MM **Publicly Held**
SIC: 3829 Stress, strain & flaw detecting/measuring equipment; vibration meters, analyzers & calibrators

(G-99)
MOHAWK INNOVATIVE TECH INC (PA)
1037 Watervliet Shaker Rd (12205-2032)
PHONE.................................518 862-4290
Hooshang Heshmat, *President*
James F Walton II, *Chairman*
Tiffany Truong, *Business Mgr*
Melissa D Heshmat, *CFO*
Michael Tomaszewski, *Admin Sec*
EMP: 12
SQ FT: 18,000
SALES (est): 3MM **Privately Held**
WEB: www.mohawkinnovative.com
SIC: 3714 8711 Axle housings & shafts, motor vehicle; engineering services

(G-100)
MOTOROLA SOLUTIONS INC
251 New Karner Rd (12205-4627)
PHONE.................................518 869-9517
EMP: 142
SALES (corp-wide): 5.7B **Publicly Held**
SIC: 3663 Mfg Communication Equipment
PA: Motorola Solutions, Inc.
1303 E Algonquin Rd
Schaumburg IL 60661
847 576-5000

(G-101)
MTI INSTRUMENTS INC
325 Washington Ave 3 (12206-3012)
PHONE.................................518 218-2550
Kevin G Lynch, *Principal*
Rick Jones, *Chairman*
Don Welch, *Engineer*
Maribel Lape, *Sales Staff*
George Raylin, *Manager*
EMP: 10
SALES (est): 4.7MM
SALES (corp-wide): 7MM **Publicly Held**
WEB: www.mtiinstruments.com
SIC: 3829 8731 Stress, strain & flaw detecting/measuring equipment; vibration meters, analyzers & calibrators; commercial research laboratory; engineering laboratory, except testing; energy research
PA: Mechanical Technology Incorporated
325 Washington Avenue Ext
Albany NY 12205
518 218-2550

(G-102)
NEW YORK STATE ASSOC
Also Called: NYSASBO
453 New Karner Rd (12205-3821)
PHONE.................................518 434-2281
Michael Borges, *Exec Dir*
EMP: 10
SALES: 2MM **Privately Held**
SIC: 7372 8699 Application computer software; membership organizations

(G-103)
NEWKIRK PRODUCTS INC (DH)
15 Corporate Cir (12203-5177)
PHONE.................................518 862-3200
Raymond Newkirk, *CEO*
Peter Newkirk, *President*
John J Graham, *CFO*
Dennis Donohue, *CIO*
EMP: 240
SQ FT: 135,000
SALES (est): 28.9MM
SALES (corp-wide): 1.6B **Publicly Held**
WEB: www.newkirk.com
SIC: 2731 Pamphlets: publishing & printing
HQ: Dst Systems, Inc.
333 W 11th St
Kansas City MO 64105
816 435-1000

(G-104)
NEWSPAPER TIMES UNION
Also Called: Capitol Newspaper
645 Albany Shaker Rd (12211-1158)
P.O. Box 15000 (12212-5000)
PHONE.................................518 454-5676
David White, *President*
Darrell Foster, *Prdtn Mgr*
Kim Holland, *Finance*
Jennifer Morrell, *Cust Mgr*
Renee Bernard, *Sales Staff*
EMP: 12
SALES (est): 690K **Privately Held**
WEB: www.saratogasignature.com
SIC: 2711 Newspapers, publishing & printing

(G-105)
NINE PIN CIDERWORKS LLC
929 Broadway (12207-1305)
PHONE.................................518 449-9999
Alejandro Del Peral, *Mng Member*
EMP: 10 **EST:** 2013
SALES (est): 911.4K **Privately Held**
SIC: 2099 Cider, nonalcoholic

(G-106)
NORTHEAST COMMERCIAL PRTG INC (PA)
Also Called: Eastern Offset
1237 Central Ave Ste 3 (12205-5328)
PHONE.................................518 459-5047
Anthony Mosca, *President*
EMP: 7
SQ FT: 4,000
SALES (est): 768.6K **Privately Held**
WEB: www.northeastcommercial.com
SIC: 2752 Commercial printing, offset

(G-107)
NORTHEASTERN AIR QUALITY INC
730 3rd St (12206-2007)
PHONE.................................518 857-3641
Robert Kelley, *President*
EMP: 12
SALES: 5MM **Privately Held**
SIC: 1389 Testing, measuring, surveying & analysis services

(G-108)
ORACLE AMERICA INC
Also Called: Sun Microsystems
7 Southwoods Blvd Ste 1 (12211-2526)
PHONE.................................518 427-9353
Leslie Woodin, *Sales/Mktg Mgr*
EMP: 52
SALES (corp-wide): 39.8B **Publicly Held**
SIC: 7372 Prepackaged software
HQ: Oracle America, Inc.
500 Oracle Pkwy
Redwood City CA 94065
650 506-7000

(G-109)
OUR DAILY EATS LLC
10 Burdick Dr Ste 1 (12205-1457)
PHONE.................................518 810-8412
EMP: 12
SALES (est): 1.8MM **Privately Held**
SIC: 2068 Mfg Salted/Roasted Nuts/Seeds

(G-110)
PARK-OHIO INDS TRSRY CO INC (DH)
Also Called: Supply Technologies NY, Inc.
80 State St (12207-2541)
PHONE.................................212 966-3310
John A Chrzanowski, *Ch of Bd*
Samuel Laufer, *President*
▲ **EMP:** 18 **EST:** 1953
SQ FT: 10,000
SALES (est): 15.2MM
SALES (corp-wide): 1.4B **Publicly Held**
SIC: 3452 3599 5072 3451 Bolts, metal; rivets, metal; washers, metal; screws, metal; machine shop, jobbing & repair; bolts; rivets; washers (hardware); screws; screw machine products
HQ: Supply Technologies Llc
6065 Parkland Blvd Ste 2
Cleveland OH 44124
440 947-2100

(G-111)
PATRICK RYANS MODERN PRESS
1 Colonie St (12207-2434)
PHONE.................................518 434-2921
Michael Ryan, *President*
Patrick Ryan, *Vice Pres*
EMP: 10 **EST:** 1946
SQ FT: 6,000
SALES (est): 1MM **Privately Held**
WEB: www.modernpress.com
SIC: 2752 2759 2791 Commercial printing, offset; letterpress printing; typesetting

(G-112)
PBR GRAPHICS INC
20 Railroad Ave Ste 1 (12205-5785)
PHONE.................................518 458-2909
Robert Cullum Jr, *President*
Robert G Cullum Sr, *Vice Pres*
Barbara Cullum, *Treasurer*
EMP: 9
SQ FT: 11,000
SALES: 920K **Privately Held**
SIC: 2752 Commercial printing, offset

(G-113)
PENGUIN RANDOM HOUSE LLC
80 State St (12207-2541)
PHONE.................................212 366-2377
David Shanks, *CEO*
EMP: 200
SALES (corp-wide): 82.3MM **Privately Held**
SIC: 2731 5942 Books: publishing only; book stores
HQ: Penguin Random House Llc
1745 Broadway
New York NY 10019
212 782-9000

(G-114)
PHARMACEUTIC LABS LLC
15 Walker Way (12205-4945)
PHONE.................................518 608-1060
Ernesto Samuel, *CEO*
Raleigh Hamilton, *CFO*
Gilbert L Carey, *General Counsel*
Elmise Jean-Pierre, *Officer*
Trevor Lewis PHD, *Officer*
▲ **EMP:** 14
SALES (est): 2.4MM **Privately Held**
SIC: 2834 Pharmaceutical preparations

(G-115)
PHYLJOHN DISTRIBUTORS INC
Also Called: Gillette Creamery
6 Interstate Ave (12205-5309)
PHONE.................................518 459-2775
Richard H Gillette, *Supervisor*
EMP: 10
SALES (corp-wide): 33.6MM **Privately Held**
WEB: www.gillettecreamery.com
SIC: 2024 Ice cream & frozen desserts
PA: Phyljohn Distributors, Inc.
47 Steves Ln
Gardiner NY 12525
845 419-0900

(G-116)
PINE BUSH PRINTING CO INC
2005 Western Ave (12203-7016)
PHONE.................................518 456-2431
Don Blais, *President*
EMP: 7
SALES (est): 651.8K **Privately Held**
SIC: 2752 Commercial printing, offset

(G-117)
PRAXAIR INC
120 Railroad Ave (12205-5701)
PHONE.................................518 482-4360
EMP: 20

Albany - Albany County (G-118)

SALES (corp-wide): 11.4B **Privately Held**
SIC: 2813 Industrial gases
PA: Praxair, Inc.
  10 Riverview Dr
  Danbury CT 06810
  203 837-2000

(G-118)
PRECISION N AMER FD MCHY LLC
60 Commerce Ave Ste 42 (12206-2043)
PHONE..................518 462-3387
Mark Altarac, *President*
▲ EMP: 12
SQ FT: 57,000
SALES (est): 2.4MM **Privately Held**
SIC: 3556 Food products machinery

(G-119)
PRINTING RESOURCES INC
Also Called: The Printing Company
100 Fuller Rd Ste 1 (12205-5760)
PHONE..................518 482-2470
Darcy Harding, *President*
EMP: 20
SQ FT: 15,000
SALES (est): 2MM **Privately Held**
SIC: 2759 2791 2789 2752 Commercial printing; typesetting; bookbinding & related work; commercial printing, lithographic

(G-120)
R & J SHEET METAL DISTRIBUTORS
Also Called: R and J Sheet Metal
156 Orange St (12210)
PHONE..................518 433-1525
Robert Gardner, *President*
EMP: 6
SALES (est): 969.1K **Privately Held**
SIC: 3444 Sheet metalwork

(G-121)
R R DONNELLEY & SONS COMPANY
Moore Graphics Services
4 Executive Park Dr Ste 2 (12203-3717)
PHONE..................518 438-9722
Joe Benoit, *Manager*
EMP: 100
SALES (corp-wide): 6.9B **Publicly Held**
WEB: www.moore.com
SIC: 2759 Screen printing
PA: R. R. Donnelley & Sons Company
  35 W Wacker Dr Ste 3650
  Chicago IL 60601
  312 326-8000

(G-122)
RAFF ENTERPRISES
12 Petra Ln Ste 6 (12205-4973)
PHONE..................518 218-7883
Sean Raff, *Owner*
EMP: 8
SALES (est): 788.4K **Privately Held**
SIC: 2511 China closets

(G-123)
RATIONAL RETENTION LLC (PA)
Also Called: Rational Enterprises
2 Tower Pl Ste 13 (12203-3726)
PHONE..................518 489-3000
Melissa Faas, *Controller*
William W Duker, *Mng Member*
EMP: 31
SALES (est): 2.5MM **Privately Held**
SIC: 7372 7374 Business oriented computer software; data processing & preparation

(G-124)
RATIONAL RETENTION LLC
2 Tower Pl Ste 13 (12203-3726)
PHONE..................518 489-3000
Michael McCreary, *Branch Mgr*
EMP: 5
SALES (corp-wide): 2.5MM **Privately Held**
SIC: 7372 Prepackaged software
PA: Rational Retention, Llc
  2 Tower Pl Ste 13
  Albany NY 12203
  518 489-3000

(G-125)
REM PRINTING INC
55 Railroad Ave (12205-5947)
PHONE..................518 438-7338
Paul Remmert, *President*
Matthew Remmert, *VP Sales*
EMP: 6
SQ FT: 5,000
SALES: 600K **Privately Held**
WEB: www.remprinting.com
SIC: 2752 Commercial printing, offset

(G-126)
SCARANO BOAT BUILDING INC
194 S Port Rd (12202-1075)
PHONE..................518 463-3401
John S Scarano, *President*
EMP: 45
SALES: 950K **Privately Held**
WEB: www.scaranoboat.com
SIC: 3732 Boat building & repairing

(G-127)
SCARANO BOATBUILDING INC
194 S Port Rd (12202-1075)
PHONE..................518 463-3401
John Scarano, *President*
Rick Scarano, *Vice Pres*
EMP: 27
SQ FT: 90,000
SALES (est): 4.3MM **Privately Held**
SIC: 3732 Boat building & repairing

(G-128)
SOMML HEALTH INC
43 New Scotland Ave Mc25 (12208-3412)
PHONE..................518 880-2170
Kira Novakofski, *Research*
EMP: 5 EST: 2015
SQ FT: 200
SALES (est): 171.6K **Privately Held**
SIC: 7372 Prepackaged software

(G-129)
STANLEY PAPER CO INC
1 Terminal St (12206-2283)
PHONE..................518 489-1131
Matthew Jasinski II, *President*
Pearl Jasinski, *Corp Secy*
EMP: 11 EST: 1942
SQ FT: 6,000
SALES (est): 2.4MM **Privately Held**
SIC: 2679 5113 Conduits, fiber (pressed pulp): from purchased material; industrial & personal service paper

(G-130)
STEIN FIBERS LTD (PA)
4 Computer Dr W Ste 200 (12205-1630)
PHONE..................518 489-5700
Sidney J Stein III, *Ch of Bd*
Peter J Spitalny, *President*
Allen Greenberg, *CFO*
Allen Greenburg, *CFO*
Jeremy Loden, *Sales Staff*
◆ EMP: 18
SQ FT: 4,600
SALES (est): 259.4MM **Privately Held**
WEB: www.steinfibers.com
SIC: 2824 Polyester fibers

(G-131)
STOP N SHOP LLC
911 Central Ave Ste 149 (12206-1350)
PHONE..................518 512-9657
Efasto Bowl, *Mng Member*
EMP: 6
SALES (est): 148.8K **Privately Held**
SIC: 7372 Business oriented computer software

(G-132)
TECHNICAL WLDG FABRICATORS LLC
27 Thatcher St (12207-5052)
PHONE..................518 463-2229
Carol Boyer,
EMP: 10
SALES (est): 1.4MM **Privately Held**
SIC: 3315 Welded steel wire fabric

(G-133)
TEL TECHNOLOGY CENTER AMER LLC (DH)
255 Fuller Rd Ste 244 (12203-3663)
PHONE..................512 424-4200
Hiroshi Takenaka,
▲ EMP: 22
SALES (est): 5.7MM
SALES (corp-wide): 10.6B **Privately Held**
SIC: 3674 Semiconductors & related devices
HQ: Tokyo Electron U.S. Holdings, Inc.
  2400 Grove Blvd
  Austin TX 78741
  512 424-1000

(G-134)
THERMOAURA INC
132b Railroad Ave Ste B (12205-5701)
PHONE..................518 813-4997
Rutvik J Mehta, *President*
Ganpati Ramanath, *Director*
EMP: 11
SQ FT: 4,800
SALES: 500K **Privately Held**
SIC: 3674 Wafers (semiconductor devices)

(G-135)
TOKYO ELECTRON AMERICA INC
255 Fuller Rd Ste 214 (12203-3603)
PHONE..................518 292-4200
Chris Krammer, *Branch Mgr*
EMP: 9
SALES (corp-wide): 10.6B **Privately Held**
WEB: www.telusa.com
SIC: 3674 Semiconductors & related devices
HQ: Tokyo Electron America, Inc.
  2400 Grove Blvd
  Austin TX 78741
  512 424-1000

(G-136)
U ALL INC
9 Interstate Ave (12205-5320)
PHONE..................518 438-2558
James Holodak, *President*
Susan Holodak, *Admin Sec*
EMP: 25
SQ FT: 10,000
SALES (est): 3.7MM **Privately Held**
WEB: www.allu.com
SIC: 2759 2395 5199 2396 Screen printing; embroidery & art needlework; advertising specialties; automotive & apparel trimmings

(G-137)
UCC GUIDE INC (PA)
Also Called: Ernst Publishing Co
99 Washington Ave (12210-2822)
PHONE..................518 434-0909
Gregory E Teal, *CEO*
Jan Clark, *Vice Pres*
Kathryn Teal, *Vice Pres*
EMP: 10
SQ FT: 4,000
SALES (est): 2.3MM **Privately Held**
WEB: www.ernstinfo.com
SIC: 2741 Miscellaneous publishing

(G-138)
ULTREPET LLC
136c Fuller Rd (12205-5604)
PHONE..................781 275-6400
M Scott Mellen, *President*
Carol C Forman, *Principal*
David B Spencer, *Chairman*
Leigh A Peritz, *Vice Pres*
Paul C Zordan, *Vice Pres*
▲ EMP: 65
SALES (est): 13.4MM
SALES (corp-wide): 51.9MM **Privately Held**
SIC: 3559 Plastics working machinery
PA: Wte Corporation
  7 Alfred Cir
  Bedford MA 01730
  781 275-6400

(G-139)
UTC FIRE SEC AMERICAS CORP INC
10 Walker Way Ste 3 (12205-4964)
PHONE..................518 456-0444
EMP: 54
SALES (corp-wide): 59.8B **Publicly Held**
SIC: 3669 Burglar alarm apparatus, electric
HQ: Utc Fire & Security Americas Corporation, Inc.
  8985 Town Center Pkwy
  Lakewood Ranch FL 34202

(G-140)
VERTICAL LAX INC
20 Corporate Cir Ste 4 (12203-5157)
PHONE..................518 669-3699
Curt Styres, *CEO*
Paul Gait, *President*
Lewis Staats, *Treasurer*
▲ EMP: 7 EST: 2010
SALES (est): 632.2K **Privately Held**
SIC: 3949 7389 Sporting & athletic goods;

(G-141)
WEST END IRON WORKS INC
4254 Albany St (12205-4684)
PHONE..................518 456-1105
Eric R Frey, *President*
EMP: 5 EST: 1890
SQ FT: 9,000
SALES (est): 721.6K **Privately Held**
SIC: 3446 Architectural metalwork

(G-142)
WILD WORKS INCORPORATED
30 Railroad Ave (12205-5721)
PHONE..................716 891-4197
William C Smith, *CEO*
EMP: 5
SALES (est): 536.4K **Privately Held**
SIC: 2891 Adhesives & sealants

(G-143)
XEROX CORPORATION
80 State St Ste 3 (12207-2505)
PHONE..................518 434-6543
Gabriela Baron, *President*
Randy Burrows, *President*
Craig Freeman, *Vice Pres*
EMP: 50
SALES (corp-wide): 10.2B **Publicly Held**
WEB: www.xerox.com
SIC: 3861 Photographic equipment & supplies
PA: Xerox Corporation
  201 Merritt 7
  Norwalk CT 06851
  203 968-3000

(G-144)
YOGIBO LLC
120 Washington Avenue Ext # 23 (12203-5367)
PHONE..................518 456-1762
David Ozmon, *Branch Mgr*
EMP: 14 **Privately Held**
SIC: 2519 Household furniture, except wood or metal: upholstered
PA: Yogibo Llc
  16 Celina Ave Unit 13
  Nashua NH 03063

(G-145)
ZELA INTERNATIONAL CO
13 Manor St (12207-3008)
PHONE..................518 436-1833
Ike Sukljian, *President*
Cristina Samuels, *VP Sales*
▲ EMP: 25
SQ FT: 60,000
SALES (est): 2.3MM **Privately Held**
WEB: www.zela.com
SIC: 2844 5122 Cosmetic preparations; cosmetics

GEOGRAPHIC SECTION

Alden - Erie County (G-171)

Albertson
Nassau County

(G-146)
BRAUN INDUSTRIES INC (PA)
Also Called: Braun Brush Company
43 Albertson Ave (11507-2102)
PHONE..................................516 741-6000
Lance W Cheney, *CEO*
Jerilyn Leis, *Cust Mgr*
Adam Czerniawski, *Manager*
▲ **EMP:** 19 **EST:** 1875
SQ FT: 15,000
SALES: 3.2MM **Privately Held**
WEB: www.brush.com
SIC: 3991 Brooms & brushes

(G-147)
BURT MILLWORK CORPORATION
85 Fairview Dr (11507-1007)
PHONE..................................718 257-4601
Eli Gordon, *President*
Seymour Gordon, *Vice Pres*
▲ **EMP:** 22
SQ FT: 42,500
SALES (est): 5.4MM **Privately Held**
SIC: 2431 Doors, wood; door shutters, wood; windows, wood

(G-148)
DAIGE PRODUCTS INC
1 Albertson Ave Ste 3 (11507-1444)
PHONE..................................516 621-2100
I M Harris, *President*
Richard Fchinkel, *Vice Pres*
Ira Harris, *Personnel*
EMP: 15
SQ FT: 3,500
SALES (est): 2.6MM **Privately Held**
WEB: www.daige.com
SIC: 3555 Printing trades machinery

(G-149)
GEMSON GRAPHICS INC
820 Willis Ave Ste 2c (11507-1979)
PHONE..................................516 873-8400
Emanuel Manicone, *Chairman*
EMP: 5
SALES (est): 854.4K **Privately Held**
SIC: 2752 2759 Commercial printing, offset; flexographic printing

(G-150)
PATSY STROCCHIA & SONS IRON WO
Also Called: Strocchia Iron Works
175 I U Willets Rd Ste 4 (11507-1342)
PHONE..................................516 625-8800
Ralph J Strocchia, *Ch of Bd*
Leonard D Strocchia, *Vice Pres*
Ralph Strocchia Jr, *Admin Sec*
EMP: 18 **EST:** 1922
SALES: 3.2MM **Privately Held**
SIC: 3441 Fabricated structural metal

(G-151)
PAYA PRINTING OF NY INC
87 Searingtown Rd (11507-1125)
PHONE..................................516 625-8346
Mohammad Samii, *President*
EMP: 5
SQ FT: 1,000
SALES (est): 472.3K **Privately Held**
SIC: 2754 2752 Commercial printing, gravure; commercial printing, lithographic

(G-152)
PELLA CORPORATION
Also Called: Pella Window Door
77 Albertson Ave Ste 2 (11507-2127)
PHONE..................................516 385-3622
Shanade Alton, *Branch Mgr*
EMP: 316
SALES (corp-wide): 1.9B **Privately Held**
SIC: 2431 Windows, wood
PA: Pella Corporation
102 Main St
Pella IA 50219
641 621-1000

(G-153)
PELLA CORPORATION
Also Called: Pella Window Door
77 Albertson Ave Ste 2 (11507-2127)
PHONE..................................516 385-3622
EMP: 316
SALES (corp-wide): 663.7MM **Privately Held**
SIC: 2431 Mfg Millwork
PA: Pella Corporation
102 Main St
Pella IA 50219
641 621-1000

Albion
Orleans County

(G-154)
ALBION-HOLLEY PENNYSAVER INC
Also Called: Lake Country Media
170 N Main St (14411-1063)
P.O. Box 231 (14411-0231)
PHONE..................................585 589-5641
Karen Sawicz, *President*
Gary Hill, *Editor*
Brad London, *Sales Associate*
Marissa Olles, *Art Dir*
Privitera Jayme, *Graphic Designe*
EMP: 48
SQ FT: 22,000
SALES (est): 6.8MM **Privately Held**
SIC: 2791 2711 2741 Typesetting; job printing & newspaper publishing combined; miscellaneous publishing

(G-155)
AUSTIN INDUSTRIES INC (PA)
3871 Oak Orchard Rd (14411-9536)
PHONE..................................585 589-1353
Alan Austin, *President*
Vernon Carl Austin, *Vice Pres*
Denise Austin, *Treasurer*
Beverly Walthew, *Admin Sec*
EMP: 7
SQ FT: 7,200
SALES (est): 931.1K **Privately Held**
SIC: 3542 5085 Machine tools, metal forming type; welding supplies; industrial tools

(G-156)
CDL MANUFACTURING INC
15661 Telegraph Rd (14411)
PHONE..................................585 589-2533
Kaz Laszewski, *President*
Steve Chiruck, *Vice Pres*
Steve Chirvck, *Plant Mgr*
EMP: 5
SQ FT: 8,000
SALES (est): 662.1K **Privately Held**
WEB: www.cdlmfg.com
SIC: 3599 Machine shop, jobbing & repair

(G-157)
FREEZE-DRY FOODS INC
111 West Ave Ste 2 (14411-1500)
PHONE..................................585 589-6399
Alasdair Grant, *CEO*
Karen Richardson, *President*
Anna Marie Clift, *Controller*
▲ **EMP:** 40
SALES (est): 7.2MM **Privately Held**
WEB: www.freeze-dry.com
SIC: 2038 Frozen specialties
PA: Freeze-Dry Foods Limited
115-710 Dorval Dr
Oakville ON L6K 3
905 844-1471

(G-158)
J PAHURA CONTRACTORS
415 East Ave (14411-1620)
PHONE..................................585 589-5793
James Pahura, *Owner*
EMP: 5
SALES (est): 210K **Privately Held**
SIC: 2951 Asphalt paving mixtures & blocks

(G-159)
L&M SPECIALTY FABRICATION
3816 Oak Orchard Rd (14411-9536)
P.O. Box 426, Elba (14058-0426)
PHONE..................................585 283-4847
Lee Shuknecht, *Managing Prtnr*
Sarah Geissler, *Partner*
Matt Geissler, *Partner*
EMP: 7
SALES (est): 666.4K **Privately Held**
SIC: 3523 Cabs, tractors & agricultural machinery

(G-160)
ORLEANS PALLET COMPANY INC
227 West Ave (14411-1520)
PHONE..................................585 589-0781
Shawn R Malark, *President*
EMP: 11
SQ FT: 65,000
SALES: 954K **Privately Held**
SIC: 2448 Pallets, wood

(G-161)
PENASACK MACHINE COMPANY INC
49 Sanford St (14411-1117)
P.O. Box 396 (14411-0396)
PHONE..................................585 589-7044
Gerard Damore, *Ch of Bd*
Jessica Tobin, *Manager*
EMP: 40 **EST:** 1967
SQ FT: 35,000
SALES (est): 7.9MM **Privately Held**
SIC: 3441 Fabricated structural metal

(G-162)
RS AUTOMATION
Also Called: Richard Stacey Rs Automation
4015 Oak Orchard Rd (14411-9326)
PHONE..................................585 589-0199
Richard Stacey, *Owner*
Christina Farabella, *Purchasing*
EMP: 17
SQ FT: 12,000
SALES (est): 4.6MM **Privately Held**
SIC: 3441 5084 Fabricated structural metal; industrial machinery & equipment

(G-163)
SAINT-GOBAIN ADFORS AMER INC
14770 East Ave (14411-9709)
PHONE..................................585 589-4401
Joel Allen, *Branch Mgr*
EMP: 52
SALES (corp-wide): 213.5MM **Privately Held**
SIC: 2297 Nonwoven fabrics
HQ: Saint-Gobain Adfors America, Inc.
1795 Baseline Rd
Grand Island NY 14072
716 775-3900

(G-164)
WOODSIDE GRANITE INDUSTRIES
Also Called: Brigden Memorials
13890 Ridge Rd W (14411-9160)
PHONE..................................585 589-6500
Leo Lacroix, *President*
▲ **EMP:** 9
SQ FT: 1,500
SALES (est): 1.6MM **Privately Held**
SIC: 3272 5999 Grave markers, concrete; gravestones, finished

Alcove
Albany County

(G-165)
NEW YORK QUARRIES INC
305 Rte 111 (12007)
PHONE..................................518 756-3138
Nancy O'Brien, *President*
▲ **EMP:** 15
SQ FT: 1,200
SALES: 1.5MM **Privately Held**
WEB: www.newyorkquarries.com
SIC: 3281 1411 Granite, cut & shaped; limestone, dimension-quarrying

Alden
Erie County

(G-166)
AGRI SERVICES CO
13899 North Rd (14004-9779)
PHONE..................................716 937-6618
James Guarino, *Owner*
EMP: 5
SALES (est): 125K **Privately Held**
SIC: 3714 5531 Automotive wiring harness sets; truck equipment & parts

(G-167)
ALDEN AURORA GAS COMPANY INC
Also Called: Reserve Gas Company
13441 Railroad St (14004-1389)
P.O. Box 207 (14004-0207)
PHONE..................................716 937-9484
Edward Harris, *Ch of Bd*
James C Gorom, *President*
Paul Tryanowski, *Treasurer*
Jacqueline Harris, *Shareholder*
Bernice Rosenbloom, *Shareholder*
EMP: 8
SQ FT: 1,200
SALES (est): 575.6K **Privately Held**
SIC: 1381 Drilling oil & gas wells

(G-168)
BENNETT MANUFACTURING CO INC
13315 Railroad St (14004-1390)
PHONE..................................716 937-9161
Steven L Yellen, *Ch of Bd*
Richard D Yellen, *Vice Pres*
Bill Stobnicki, *Purchasing*
Toby F Yellen, *Treasurer*
Patricia Miller, *Human Res Mgr*
▲ **EMP:** 150
SQ FT: 100,000
SALES (est): 32.3MM **Privately Held**
WEB: www.bennettmfg.com
SIC: 3441 2842 Fabricated structural metal; specialty cleaning, polishes & sanitation goods

(G-169)
D J CROWELL CO INC
2815 Town Line Rd (14004-9676)
PHONE..................................716 684-3343
David C Bressette, *President*
Jeffroy Minotti, *Vice Pres*
EMP: 6 **EST:** 1900
SQ FT: 6,000
SALES: 500K **Privately Held**
SIC: 3599 Machine shop, jobbing & repair

(G-170)
DUNDAS-JAFINE INC
11099 Broadway St (14004-9517)
PHONE..................................716 681-9690
Debbie Patterson, *General Mgr*
Bill Szajn, *CFO*
Colleen Ference, *Human Resources*
Dave Rockwell, *Sales Staff*
Teresa Hart, *Marketing Staff*
EMP: 50 **Privately Held**
WEB: www.dundasjafine.com
SIC: 3585 3564 3444 Heating equipment, complete; air conditioning equipment, complete; blowers & fans; sheet metalwork
PA: Dundas Jafine Inc
80 West Dr
Brampton ON L6T 3
905 450-7200

(G-171)
GAMMA NORTH CORPORATION
13595 Broadway St (14004-9736)
PHONE..................................716 902-5100
Matthew Baum, *President*
James Mitchell, *President*
Elliot Kracko, *Chairman*
Juan J Alpizar, *Senior VP*
Jose M Rodriguez, *Senior VP*
EMP: 50 **EST:** 2012
SALES (est): 9.3MM **Privately Held**
SIC: 3442 Store fronts, prefabricated, metal

Alden - Erie County (G-172)

(G-172)
HUBCO INC
2885 Commerce Dr (14004-8538)
PHONE..................................716 683-5940
Craig Huber, *President*
Paul Huber, *Vice Pres*
Mark Richardson, *Info Tech Mgr*
▲ **EMP:** 6
SQ FT: 6,000
SALES (est): 1MM **Privately Held**
WEB: www.hubcopads.com
SIC: 3569 3589 Assembly machines, non-metalworking; floor sanding machines, commercial

(G-173)
INTEGER HOLDINGS CORPORATION
Also Called: Greatbatch Medical
11900 Walden Ave (14004-9706)
PHONE..................................716 937-5100
Ed Voboril, *Chairman*
Robert Sprinkle, *COO*
Mike Druding, *Vice Pres*
Sue Pettigrew, *Senior Buyer*
Scott Bowers, *Engineer*
EMP: 21
SALES (corp-wide): 1.4B **Publicly Held**
SIC: 3675 Electronic capacitors
PA: Integer Holdings Corporation
5830 Gran Pkwy Ste 1150
Plano TX 75024
214 618-5243

(G-174)
PHELINGER TOOL & DIE CORP
1254 Town Line Rd (14004-9672)
PHONE..................................716 685-1780
Gordon Phelinger, *President*
Scott Phelinger, *Vice Pres*
EMP: 7
SQ FT: 1,000
SALES (est): 1MM **Privately Held**
WEB: www.phelingertool.com
SIC: 3544 Special dies & tools; jigs & fixtures

(G-175)
RESERVE GAS COMPANY INC
13441 Railroad St (14004-1338)
P.O. Box 207 (14004-0207)
PHONE..................................716 937-9484
Sterlin Harris, *CEO*
James C Gorom, *President*
EMP: 8
SQ FT: 3,200
SALES (est): 1.2MM **Privately Held**
SIC: 1311 Natural gas production

(G-176)
SDR TECHNOLOGY INC
1613 Lindan Dr (14004-1113)
PHONE..................................716 583-1249
Charles Chauncey, *President*
EMP: 5
SALES (est): 381.2K **Privately Held**
SIC: 3663 Radio & TV communications equipment

(G-177)
TURBOPRO INC
1284 Town Line Rd (14004-9672)
PHONE..................................716 681-8651
Joseph Bantle, *President*
Brenda Bantle, *Vice Pres*
EMP: 4
SALES (est): 1MM **Privately Held**
SIC: 3563 Air & gas compressors

(G-178)
WEISBECK PUBLISHING PRINTING
Also Called: Alden Advertiser
13200 Broadway St (14004-1313)
PHONE..................................716 937-9226
Leonard A Weisbeck Jr, *President*
EMP: 5 **EST:** 1948
SQ FT: 1,748
SALES (est): 341.7K **Privately Held**
WEB: www.aldenadvertiser.com
SIC: 2711 Commercial printing & newspaper publishing combined; job printing & newspaper publishing combined

Alexander
Genesee County

(G-179)
LENAPE ENERGY INC (PA)
Also Called: Leape Resources,
9489 Alexander Rd (14005-9795)
PHONE..................................585 344-1200
John Holko, *President*
Amy Holko, *Vice Pres*
Jack Crooks, *Supervisor*
EMP: 5
SQ FT: 3,200
SALES (est): 921.8K **Privately Held**
WEB: www.lenaperesources.com
SIC: 1381 1389 1382 4923 Drilling oil & gas wells; haulage, oil field; gas compressing (natural gas) at the fields; oil & gas exploration services; gas transmission & distribution

(G-180)
LENAPE RESOURCES INC
9489 Alexander Rd (14005-9795)
PHONE..................................585 344-1200
John Holko, *President*
Amy Holko, *Vice Pres*
EMP: 10
SALES: 1MM
SALES (corp-wide): 921.8K **Privately Held**
WEB: www.lenaperesources.com
SIC: 1382 4923 Oil & gas exploration services; gas transmission & distribution
PA: Lenape Energy Inc
9489 Alexander Rd
Alexander NY 14005
585 344-1200

(G-181)
RICHARD BAUER LOGGING
3936 Cookson Rd (14005-9718)
PHONE..................................585 343-4149
Richard Bauer, *Owner*
EMP: 5 **EST:** 1962
SALES (est): 292.4K **Privately Held**
SIC: 2411 Logging camps & contractors

Alexandria Bay
Jefferson County

(G-182)
THOUSAND ISLANDS PRINTING CO
Also Called: Thousand Islands Sun
45501 St Rt 12 (13607)
PHONE..................................315 482-2581
Jeanne Roy Snow, *President*
William F Roy, *Vice Pres*
Helethea Roy, *Treasurer*
EMP: 9 **EST:** 1901
SQ FT: 3,250
SALES (est): 633.6K **Privately Held**
SIC: 2711 Job printing & newspaper publishing combined

(G-183)
THOUSAND ISLANDS WINERY LLC
43298 Seaway Ave Ste 1 (13607-2141)
PHONE..................................315 482-9306
Steven J Conaway,
Erika Conaway,
EMP: 22
SQ FT: 4,771
SALES (est): 3.3MM **Privately Held**
WEB: www.thousandislandswinery.com
SIC: 2084 Wines

Alfred
Allegany County

(G-184)
SAXON GLASS TECHNOLOGIES INC
200 N Main St Ste 114 (14802-1000)
P.O. Box 575 (14802-0575)
PHONE..................................607 587-9630
Arun Varshneya, *President*
Darshana Varshneya, *Vice Pres*
EMP: 10
SQ FT: 4,500
SALES (est): 1.2MM **Privately Held**
WEB: www.saxonglass.com
SIC: 3211 Strengthened or reinforced glass

Alfred Station
Allegany County

(G-185)
ASK CHEMICALS HI-TECH LLC
6329 Rte 21 (14803)
P.O. Box 788, Alfred (14802-0788)
PHONE..................................607 587-9146
Luiz Totti, *Exec VP*
Edward Holzlein, *Plant Mgr*
Paul Bronson, *Plant Engr*
Rick Glenn, *Controller*
Robert Gage, *Marketing Mgr*
▲ **EMP:** 112
SALES: 18MM **Privately Held**
SIC: 2899 Chemical preparations
HQ: Ask Chemicals Gmbh
Reisholzstr. 16-18
Hilden 40721
211 711-030

(G-186)
BUFFALO CRUSHED STONE INC
638 State Route 244 (14803-9766)
P.O. Box 38 (14803-0038)
PHONE..................................607 587-8102
Douglas Drake, *Manager*
EMP: 9
SALES (corp-wide): 651.9MM **Privately Held**
SIC: 1442 Construction sand mining; gravel mining
HQ: Buffalo Crushed Stone, Inc.
500 Como Park Blvd
Buffalo NY 14227
716 826-7310

(G-187)
NORTHERN TIMBER HARVESTING LLC
6042 State Route 21 (14803)
PHONE..................................585 233-7330
Adam Ricci,
EMP: 11
SQ FT: 10,000
SALES: 2.9MM **Privately Held**
SIC: 2411 Logging

Allegany
Cattaraugus County

(G-188)
ALLEGANY LAMINATING AND SUPPLY
158 W Main St (14706-1235)
PHONE..................................716 372-2424
Charles Cousins, *President*
Wanda Cousins, *Corp Secy*
Athena Silluzio, *Admin Sec*
Kimberly Roth, *Clerk*
EMP: 5
SQ FT: 8,300
SALES (est): 460K **Privately Held**
SIC: 2541 3088 Table or counter tops, plastic laminated; partitions for floor attachment, prefabricated: wood; cabinets, except refrigerated: show, display, etc.: wood; tubs (bath, shower & laundry), plastic

(G-189)
E F LIPPERT CO INC
4451 S Nine Mile Rd (14706-9790)
PHONE..................................716 373-1100
Mary Stayer, *President*
Tom Stayer, *Vice Pres*
Cinda Warner, *Admin Sec*
EMP: 13 **EST:** 1945
SQ FT: 500
SALES (est): 725.7K **Privately Held**
SIC: 1442 5261 Common sand mining; gravel mining; sod; top soil

(G-190)
HANSON AGGREGATES EAST LLC
4419 S Nine Mile Rd (14706-9790)
PHONE..................................716 372-1574
EMP: 6
SALES (est): 326.8K **Privately Held**
SIC: 3272 Mfg Concrete Products

(G-191)
I & S OF NY INC
4174 Route 417 (14706-9787)
P.O. Box 380 (14706-0380)
PHONE..................................716 373-7001
Frank Steven, *President*
Mary Stephens, *Manager*
EMP: 10
SQ FT: 6,000
SALES (est): 1.5MM **Privately Held**
SIC: 1389 Servicing oil & gas wells

(G-192)
POTTER LUMBER CO INC
3786 Potter Rd (14706-9410)
P.O. Box 10 (14706-0010)
PHONE..................................716 373-1260
Robert G Potter, *President*
Theodore Potter, *Vice Pres*
Mary Frances Potter, *Treasurer*
Lucy Benson, *Admin Sec*
EMP: 40 **EST:** 1910
SQ FT: 700
SALES (est): 5.8MM **Privately Held**
SIC: 2421 2426 Lumber: rough, sawed or planed; hardwood dimension & flooring mills

Almond
Allegany County

(G-193)
HANSON AGGREGATES NEW YORK LLC
Also Called: Hanson Ready Mix Concrete
546 Clark Rd (14804)
PHONE..................................607 276-5881
Jeff Feenaughty, *Site Mgr*
Jeffrey Feenaughty, *Manager*
EMP: 5
SALES (corp-wide): 20.3B **Privately Held**
SIC: 3271 Concrete block & brick
HQ: Hanson Aggregates New York Llc
8505 Freport Pkwy Ste 500
Irving TX 75063

Altamont
Albany County

(G-194)
ALFRED B PARELLA
Also Called: Latham Seamless Gutters
20 Reservoir Rd (12009-3230)
P.O. Box 448 (12009-0448)
PHONE..................................518 872-1238
Alfred B Parella, *President*
EMP: 5
SALES: 400K **Privately Held**
SIC: 3444 Gutters, sheet metal

GEOGRAPHIC SECTION
Amherst - Erie County (G-219)

(G-195)
ALTAMONT SPRAY WELDING INC
133 Lewis Rd (12009-3220)
PHONE.....................518 861-8870
Mark C Schrowang, *President*
Sandra E Schrowang, *Vice Pres*
EMP: 9
SQ FT: 9,000
SALES (est): 1.2MM **Privately Held**
WEB: www.altamontspraywelding.com
SIC: 3599 Machine shop, jobbing & repair

(G-196)
CARVER SAND & GRAVEL LLC (PA)
494 Western Tpke Ste 1 (12009-2095)
PHONE.....................518 355-6034
Sybil Lindstead, *CFO*
Nancy Laraway, *Mng Member*
Michael Bath,
Carver Laraway,
EMP: 35 **EST:** 1995
SQ FT: 1,000
SALES (est): 17MM **Privately Held**
SIC: 1442 Construction sand & gravel

(G-197)
INDIAN LADDER FARMSTEAD BREWER
287 Altamont Rd (12009-3542)
PHONE.....................518 577-1484
Dietrich Gehring,
EMP: 5
SQ FT: 875
SALES (est): 185.3K **Privately Held**
SIC: 2082 Beer (alcoholic beverage)

(G-198)
INOVA LLC
6032 Depot Rd (12009-4313)
P.O. Box 644 (12009-0644)
PHONE.....................518 861-3400
EMP: 15
SALES (est): 2.5MM **Privately Held**
SIC: 2599 Mfg Furniture/Fixtures

(G-199)
MET WELD INTERNATIONAL LLC
5727 Ostrander Rd (12009-4209)
PHONE.....................518 765-2318
Dan Hill, *Opers Staff*
Jim Carter, *Purch Mgr*
Scott Kniffin, *Purch Mgr*
Jeff Porubcan, *Engineer*
Kevin Shaw, *Engineer*
EMP: 70
SQ FT: 55,000
SALES (est): 17.8MM
SALES (corp-wide): 79.4MM **Privately Held**
WEB: www.metweldintl.com
SIC: 3498 Fabricated pipe & fittings
PA: Gavial Holdings, Inc.
1435 W Mccoy Ln
Santa Maria CA 93455
805 614-0060

(G-200)
REMARKABLE LIQUIDS LLC
6032 Depot Rd (12009-4313)
P.O. Box 122, Guilderland Center (12085-0122)
PHONE.....................518 861-5351
Jason Napoleon, *Opers Staff*
Sarah Carruthers, *Sales Staff*
Ben English, *Sales Staff*
Todd Harmon, *Sales Staff*
Jeremy Irving, *Sales Staff*
EMP: 70
SALES (est): 13.1MM **Privately Held**
SIC: 2082 Beer (alcoholic beverage)

(G-201)
ROBERT PIKCILINGIS
Also Called: Candy Kraft
2575 Western Ave (12009-9288)
PHONE.....................518 355-1860
Robert Pikcilingis, *Owner*
EMP: 10
SQ FT: 4,000
SALES (est): 1MM **Privately Held**
SIC: 2064 2066 Chocolate candy, except solid chocolate; chocolate & cocoa products

(G-202)
RSB ASSOCIATES INC
Also Called: Bruno Associates
488 Picard Rd (12009-3519)
P.O. Box 14825, Albany (12212-4825)
PHONE.....................518 281-5067
Robert S Bruno Sr, *President*
Sean Bruno, *Vice Pres*
EMP: 11
SQ FT: 4,000
SALES: 650K **Privately Held**
SIC: 3554 Die cutting & stamping machinery, paper converting

Amagansett
Suffolk County

(G-203)
COSMETICS PLUS LTD
Also Called: Pixy Dust
23 Deep Wood Ln (11930)
PHONE.....................516 768-7250
Rose Evangelista, *President*
EMP: 8
SQ FT: 10,000
SALES (est): 579.5K **Privately Held**
SIC: 3942 Dolls & stuffed toys

Amawalk
Westchester County

(G-204)
PIC NIC LLC
51 Mahopac Ave (10501-1005)
PHONE.....................914 245-6500
Rick Rezzenico, *Partner*
EMP: 8
SALES (est): 947.6K **Privately Held**
SIC: 3556 Ice cream manufacturing machinery

Amenia
Dutchess County

(G-205)
CASCADE MOUNTAIN WINERY & REST
835 Cascade Rd (12501)
PHONE.....................845 373-9021
William Wetmore, *President*
EMP: 10 **EST:** 1972
SALES (est): 680K **Privately Held**
SIC: 2084 5812 Wines; eating places

(G-206)
GREY HOUSE PUBLISHING INC (PA)
4919 Route 22 (12501-5585)
P.O. Box B, Millerton (12546-0640)
PHONE.....................518 789-8700
Richard H Gottlieb, *Ch of Bd*
Leslie McKenzie, *Vice Pres*
Eric Auld, *Marketing Staff*
EMP: 26
SALES (est): 5.4MM **Privately Held**
WEB: www.greyhouse.com
SIC: 2741 2731 Miscellaneous publishing; book publishing

(G-207)
TIA LATTRELL
13 Powder House Rd (12501-5517)
PHONE.....................845 373-9494
Tia Lattrell, *Owner*
Frederic Latrell, *Owner*
EMP: 5
SALES (est): 261.5K **Privately Held**
SIC: 2024 Ice cream & frozen desserts

Amherst
Erie County

(G-208)
AIRSEP CORPORATION
Airsep Commercial Products Div
260 Creekside Dr Ste 100 (14228-2075)
PHONE.....................716 691-0202
EMP: 100
SALES (corp-wide): 1.1B **Publicly Held**
SIC: 3569 Mfg Oxygen Generators
HQ: Airsep Corporation
401 Creekside Dr
Amherst NY 14228
716 691-0202

(G-209)
ALLIED MOTION CONTROL CORP
495 Commerce Dr Ste 3 (14228-2311)
PHONE.....................716 242-7535
Richard Smith, *Principal*
EMP: 5
SALES (est): 504.7K **Privately Held**
SIC: 3621 Motors & generators

(G-210)
ALLIED MOTION SYSTEMS CORP (DH)
Also Called: Hathaway Prcess Instrmentation
495 Commerce Dr Ste 3 (14228-2311)
PHONE.....................716 242-5868
Ronald Meyer, *President*
EMP: 15
SQ FT: 13,000
SALES (est): 2.2MM
SALES (corp-wide): 6.6B **Publicly Held**
SIC: 3825 Electrical power measuring equipment
HQ: Qualitrol Company Llc
1385 Fairport Rd
Fairport NY 14450
586 643-3717

(G-211)
ALLIED MOTION TECHNOLOGIES INC (PA)
495 Commerce Dr Ste 3 (14228-2311)
PHONE.....................716 242-8634
Richard S Warzala, *Ch of Bd*
Robert P Maida, *Vice Pres*
Kenneth R Wyman, *Vice Pres*
Michael R Leach, *CFO*
▲ **EMP:** 201 **EST:** 1962
SQ FT: 6,000
SALES: 252MM **Publicly Held**
WEB: www.alliedmotion.com
SIC: 3621 3825 Motors, electric; rotary converters (electrical equipment); function generators

(G-212)
ALLSAFE TECHNOLOGIES INC
290 Creekside Dr (14228-2031)
PHONE.....................716 691-0400
James Pokornowski, *President*
Mary Koteras, *Opers Mgr*
Mike Chown, *Production*
Brian Hamp, *Production*
Robert P Pokornowski, *Treasurer*
▲ **EMP:** 65
SQ FT: 35,000
SALES (est): 13.5MM **Privately Held**
WEB: www.allsafe.com
SIC: 3089 2759 Identification cards, plastic; commercial printing

(G-213)
AMERICAN BUSINESS FORMS INC
3840 E Robinson Rd # 249 (14228-2001)
PHONE.....................716 836-5111
Larry Zavadil, *Branch Mgr*
EMP: 30
SALES (corp-wide): 325MM **Privately Held**
SIC: 2752 Commercial printing, lithographic
PA: American Business Forms, Inc.
31 E Minnesota Ave
Glenwood MN 56334
320 634-5471

(G-214)
AMERICAN PRECISION INDS INC (HQ)
45 Hazelwood Dr (14228-2224)
PHONE.....................716 691-9100
Brian Buzzard, *Engineer*
Brian Johnson, *Administration*
◆ **EMP:** 200
SQ FT: 106,800
SALES: 509MM
SALES (corp-wide): 6.6B **Publicly Held**
WEB: www.apischmidtbretten.com
SIC: 3677 3621 3625 3443 Coil windings, electronic; inductors, electronic; motors & generators; electromagnetic clutches or brakes; heat exchangers: coolers (after, inter), condensers, etc.; condensers, steam; separators, industrial process: metal plate
PA: Fortive Corporation
6920 Seaway Blvd
Everett WA 98203
425 446-5000

(G-215)
AMHERST STNLESS FBRICATION LLC
60 John Glenn Dr (14228-2118)
PHONE.....................716 691-7012
Gerald J Bogdan, *President*
Joseph B Huber, *Corp Secy*
Jim Mazur, *Engineer*
Mike Huber, *Manager*
▼ **EMP:** 40 **EST:** 1945
SQ FT: 35,000
SALES (est): 7.5MM
SALES (corp-wide): 9.4MM **Privately Held**
WEB: www.avinsfab.com
SIC: 3443 Tanks, lined: metal plate
PA: General Oil Equipment Co., Inc.
60 John Glenn Dr
Amherst NY 14228
716 691-7012

(G-216)
BEKAERT CORPORATION
Also Called: Advanced Coating Technologies
6000 N Bailey Ave Ste 9 (14226-5102)
PHONE.....................716 830-1321
Chandra Venkatraman, *Branch Mgr*
EMP: 20
SALES (corp-wide): 483.3MM **Privately Held**
WEB: www.bekaert.com
SIC: 3315 Wire & fabricated wire products; fencing made in wiredrawing plants
HQ: Bekaert Corporation
1395 S Marietta Pkwy Se 500-100
Marietta GA 30067
770 421-8520

(G-217)
BFC PRINT NETWORK INC (PA)
455 Commerce Dr Ste 6 (14228-2313)
PHONE.....................716 838-4532
John Crainer, *President*
Nancy Zabka, *Treasurer*
EMP: 1 **EST:** 1974
SQ FT: 5,800
SALES (est): 1.2MM **Privately Held**
WEB: www.bfcprintnetwork.com
SIC: 2759 Business forms: printing

(G-218)
BIRDAIR INC (HQ)
65 Lawrence Bell Dr # 100 (14221-7182)
PHONE.....................716 633-9500
Mitsuo Sugimoto, *President*
Carl Hoffner, *Manager*
◆ **EMP:** 60 **EST:** 1956
SQ FT: 20,000
SALES (est): 12.3MM
SALES (corp-wide): 306.6MM **Privately Held**
SIC: 3448 Prefabricated metal buildings
PA: Taiyo Kogyo Corporation
4-8-4, Kikawahigashi, Yodogawa-Ku
Osaka OSK 532-0
663 063-032

(G-219)
BROOK & WHITTLE LIMITED
215 John Glenn Dr (14228-2227)
PHONE.....................716 691-4348

Amherst - Erie County (G-220)

Paul Johnson, *CFO*
EMP: 21
SALES (corp-wide): 7.1MM **Privately Held**
SIC: 2671 Plastic film, coated or laminated for packaging
HQ: Brook & Whittle Limited
260 Branford Rd
North Branford CT 06471

(G-220)
CCA HOLDING INC
300 Corporate Pkwy (14226-1207)
PHONE...................716 446-8800
Edward Bredniak, *President*
William F Sullivan, *Vice Pres*
◆ **EMP:** 245
SALES (est): 11.6MM **Privately Held**
SIC: 3313 Ferroalloys

(G-221)
CENTER FOR INQUIRY INC (PA)
Also Called: Councel For Sclar Hmnism Cscop
3965 Rensch Rd (14228-2743)
P.O. Box 664, Buffalo (14226-0664)
PHONE...................716 636-4869
Paul Kurtz, *President*
Christopher Fix, *Finance*
Lauren Foster, *Manager*
Nora Hurley, *Producer*
Nicole Scott, *Assoc Editor*
EMP: 15
SALES (est): 3.1MM **Privately Held**
WEB: www.centerforinquiry.net
SIC: 2721 Magazines: publishing only, not printed on site

(G-222)
CHART INDUSTRIES INC
Also Called: Airsep
260 Creekside Dr Ste 100 (14228-2047)
PHONE...................716 691-0202
Ravi Bansal PHD, *CEO*
EMP: 25 **Publicly Held**
SIC: 3443 Fabricated plate work (boiler shop)
PA: Chart Industries, Inc.
3055 Torrington Dr
Ball Ground GA 30107

(G-223)
CRANE EQUIPMENT & SERVICE INC (HQ)
140 John Jmes Adubon Pkwy (14228-1183)
PHONE...................716 689-5400
Jena Buer, *President*
Karen L Howard, *CFO*
Rakesh A Jobanputra, *Treasurer*
Timothy R Harvey, *Admin Sec*
EMP: 3 **EST:** 1997
SQ FT: 3,000
SALES (est): 29.9MM
SALES (corp-wide): 839.4MM **Publicly Held**
WEB: www.broussardla.com
SIC: 3531 Crane carriers
PA: Columbus Mckinnon Corporation
205 Crosspoint Pkwy
Getzville NY 14068
716 689-5400

(G-224)
DELPHI AUTOMOTIVE LLP
Also Called: Delphi Amherst Test Operations
4326 Ridge Lea Rd (14226-1016)
PHONE...................716 438-4886
EMP: 6
SALES (corp-wide): 21.2MM **Privately Held**
SIC: 3714 Motor vehicle parts & accessories
PA: Aptiv International Holdings (Uk) Llp
Courteney Road
Gillingham ME8 0

(G-225)
ENHANCED TOOL INC
90 Pineview Dr (14228-2120)
PHONE...................716 691-5200
Michael Emmert, *CEO*
David M Healey, *Vice Pres*
EMP: 20
SQ FT: 6,000
SALES (est): 3.7MM **Privately Held**
WEB: www.enhancedtool.com
SIC: 3544 Special dies & tools

(G-226)
ESM GROUP INC (DH)
Also Called: E S M
300 Corporate Pkwy 118n (14226-1258)
PHONE...................716 446-8914
Gregory P Marzec, *Ch of Bd*
William F Sullivan, *Exec VP*
Charles A Zak, *Exec VP*
◆ **EMP:** 15 **EST:** 1988
SQ FT: 15,000
SALES (est): 31MM
SALES (corp-wide): 241.5MM **Privately Held**
WEB: www.esmgroup.com
SIC: 2819 Industrial inorganic chemicals
HQ: Skw Stahl-Metallurgie Gmbh
Rathausplatz 11
Unterneukirchen 84579
863 462-7203

(G-227)
ESM II INC (DH)
300 Corporate Pkwy 118n (14226-1258)
PHONE...................716 446-8888
Charles F Wright, *President*
▲ **EMP:** 50
SALES (est): 11.8MM
SALES (corp-wide): 241.5MM **Privately Held**
SIC: 3549 Metalworking machinery
HQ: Esm Group Inc.
300 Corporate Pkwy 118n
Amherst NY 14226
716 446-8914

(G-228)
ESM SPECIAL METALS & TECH INC
300 Corporate Pkwy 118n (14226-1207)
PHONE...................716 446-8914
Hartmut Meyer-Grnow, *CEO*
Sandyee Whipple, *Principal*
EMP: 20
SALES (est): 2.7MM **Privately Held**
SIC: 2819 Industrial inorganic chemicals

(G-229)
GENERAL OIL EQUIPMENT CO INC (PA)
60 John Glenn Dr (14228-2118)
PHONE...................716 691-7012
Gerald Bogdan, *Ch of Bd*
Joseph B Huber, *President*
Bob Gladwell, *Purch Mgr*
Christopher Bogdan, *Project Engr*
Karl B Huber Jr, *Treasurer*
EMP: 50
SQ FT: 34,000
SALES (est): 9.4MM **Privately Held**
WEB: www.goe-avins.com
SIC: 3625 5084 7699 3443 Electric controls & control accessories, industrial; oil refining machinery, equipment & supplies; industrial machinery & equipment repair; tanks, lined: metal plate

(G-230)
GROVER CLEVELAND PRESS INC
2676 Sweet Home Rd (14228-2128)
PHONE...................716 564-2222
Michael Degen, *President*
Tom Degen, *Vice Pres*
EMP: 10
SQ FT: 12,800
SALES (est): 2MM **Privately Held**
WEB: www.grovercllevelandpress.com
SIC: 2752 2759 Commercial printing, offset; photo-offset printing; letterpress printing; embossing on paper

(G-231)
I-EVOLVE TECHONOLOGY SERVICES (PA)
501 John James Audubon Pk (14228-1143)
PHONE...................801 566-5268
Dan Larkin, *President*
Joshua Randle, *Vice Pres*
Dave Blaszak, *Opers Mgr*
Gerald Natiella, *Engineer*
Kevin Stack, *Senior Engr*
EMP: 12
SALES (est): 5.9MM **Privately Held**
SIC: 3433 Solar heaters & collectors

(G-232)
INTERNATIONAL IMAGING MTLS INC (PA)
Also Called: limak
310 Commerce Dr (14228-2396)
PHONE...................716 691-6333
Douglas Wagner, *CEO*
Richard Marshall, *Ch of Bd*
Susan R Stamp, *Senior VP*
Joe Perna, *CFO*
◆ **EMP:** 370
SQ FT: 250,000
SALES (est): 144.9MM **Privately Held**
SIC: 3955 3555 Ribbons, inked: typewriter, adding machine, register, etc.; printing trades machinery

(G-233)
INTRI-CUT INC
90 Pineview Dr (14228-2120)
PHONE...................716 691-5200
Ronald Janson, *President*
EMP: 12
SQ FT: 6,000
SALES (est): 1.6MM **Privately Held**
WEB: www.intri-cut.com
SIC: 3544 Special dies & tools

(G-234)
KISTLER INSTRUMENT CORPORATION
75 John Glenn Dr (14228-2171)
PHONE...................716 691-5100
Michael Murphy, *General Mgr*
Nick Wilks, *Managing Dir*
Mark Burzik, *Opers Mgr*
Nancy Woomer, *Purch Mgr*
Rande Caroll, *Purch Agent*
EMP: 63 **Privately Held**
SIC: 3829 Measuring & controlling devices
HQ: Kistler Instrument Corporation
30280 Hudson Dr
Novi MI 48377
248 668-6900

(G-235)
LIBERTY DISPLAYS INC
4230b Ridge Lea Rd # 110 (14226-1063)
PHONE...................716 743-1757
Dean Rainer, *President*
EMP: 30
SQ FT: 57,000
SALES: 5MM **Privately Held**
SIC: 3999 Forms: display, dress & show

(G-236)
LOOMIS ROOT INC
135 Pineview Dr (14228-2231)
PHONE...................716 564-7668
Steven E Root, *President*
Judith Ryczek, *Controller*
▲ **EMP:** 11 **EST:** 1915
SQ FT: 13,000
SALES (est): 2.5MM **Privately Held**
SIC: 3053 5014 5084 Gaskets, packing & sealing devices; tire & tube repair materials; recapping machinery, for tires

(G-237)
MAHLE INDSTRBETEILIGUNGEN GMBH
Also Called: Delphi-T Compressor Engrg Ctr
4236 Ridge Lea Rd (14226-1016)
PHONE...................716 319-6700
Tim Skinner, *Manager*
EMP: 75 **Privately Held**
SIC: 3563 Air & gas compressors
HQ: Mahle Industriebeteiligungen Gmbh
Pragstr. 26-46
Stuttgart
711 501-0

(G-238)
MAHLE INDUSTRIES INCORPORATED
4236 Ridge Lea Rd (14226-1016)
PHONE...................248 735-3623
EMP: 14 **Privately Held**
SIC: 3714 Motor vehicle parts & accessories

HQ: Mahle Industries, Incorporated
23030 Mahle Dr
Farmington Hills MI 48335
248 305-8200

(G-239)
MOTIVAIR CORPORATION
85 Woodridge Dr (14228-2221)
PHONE...................716 691-9222
Graham Whitmore, *President*
Dan Arnold, *Opers Mgr*
Jayne Baldwin, *Manager*
Olena Olenych, *Technology*
Pete Peresie, *Director*
▲ **EMP:** 20
SQ FT: 25,000
SALES (est): 6.1MM **Privately Held**
SIC: 3585 3443 Air conditioning condensers & condensing units; separators, industrial process: metal plate

(G-240)
NEXSTAR HOLDING CORP
Also Called: PHASE IL MARKETING DBA
275 Northpointe Pkwy (14228-1895)
PHONE...................716 929-9000
Gary Robinson, *President*
Richard S Elliott, *Vice Pres*
Danny Jayes, *Production*
Paula Bednarz, *Admin Asst*
EMP: 5
SALES (est): 1MM **Privately Held**
SIC: 3564 Filters, air: furnaces, air conditioning equipment, etc.

(G-241)
NK MEDICAL PRODUCTS INC (PA)
80 Creekside Dr (14228-2027)
PHONE...................716 759-7200
Norman V Kurlander, *President*
▲ **EMP:** 5
SQ FT: 1,600
SALES (est): 1.2MM **Privately Held**
WEB: www.nkmedicalproducts.com
SIC: 2514 2599 Cribs: metal; hospital beds

(G-242)
NOVUM MEDICAL PRODUCTS INC
80 Creekside Dr (14228-2027)
PHONE...................716 759-7200
Joe Mandella, *President*
Jennifer Cappello, *Manager*
▲ **EMP:** 10 **EST:** 2008
SALES (est): 1MM **Privately Held**
SIC: 2514 2599 Cribs: metal; hospital beds

(G-243)
OERLIKON BLZERS CATING USA INC
6000 N Bailey Ave Ste 9 (14226-5102)
PHONE...................716 270-2228
EMP: 40
SALES (corp-wide): 2.8B **Privately Held**
SIC: 3479 Coating of metals & formed products
HQ: Oerlikon Balzers Coating Usa Inc.
1700 E Golf Rd Ste 200
Schaumburg IL 60173
847 619-5541

(G-244)
OERLIKON BLZERS CATING USA INC
6000 N Bailey Ave Ste 9 (14226-5102)
PHONE...................716 270-2228
EMP: 40
SALES (corp-wide): 2.8B **Privately Held**
SIC: 3479 Coating of metals & formed products
HQ: Oerlikon Balzers Coating Usa Inc.
1700 E Golf Rd Ste 200
Schaumburg IL 60173
847 619-5541

(G-245)
OERLIKON METCO (US) INC
6000 N Bailey Ave (14226-5102)
PHONE...................716 270-2228
Dan Wisniewski, *Branch Mgr*
EMP: 8

GEOGRAPHIC SECTION

Amityville - Suffolk County (G-272)

SALES (corp-wide): 2.8B **Privately Held**
SIC: 3399 Powder, metal
HQ: Oerlikon Metco (Us) Inc.
   1101 Prospect Ave
   Westbury NY 11590
   516 334-1300

(G-246)
ONY BIOTECH INC
1576 Sweet Home Rd (14228-2710)
PHONE..................716 636-9096
Edmund Egan, *President*
Cathleen Conley, *Business Mgr*
Arthur Elm, *Business Mgr*
Jonathan Miller, *Sales Staff*
Walter Klein, *Director*
EMP: 26
SQ FT: 8,000
SALES (est): 5.8MM **Privately Held**
WEB: www.ony.com
SIC: 2834 Pharmaceutical preparations

(G-247)
ORIGINAL CRUNCH ROLL FCTRY LLC
90 Sylvan Pkwy (14228-1109)
PHONE..................716 402-5030
Zachary Bohn, *President*
EMP: 5 EST: 2016
SALES (est): 199.1K **Privately Held**
SIC: 2013 Frozen meats from purchased meat

(G-248)
PROMETHEUS BOOKS INC
59 John Glenn Dr (14228-2197)
PHONE..................716 691-2158
Paul Kurtz, *President*
Jonathan Kurtz, *Vice Pres*
Steven Mitchell, *Manager*
Gretchen Kurtz, *Director*
▲ EMP: 30
SQ FT: 28,000
SALES (est): 3.6MM **Privately Held**
WEB: www.prometheusbooks.com
SIC: 2731 Books: publishing only

(G-249)
SAINT-GBAIN ADVNCED CRMICS LLC
Boron Nitride Div
168 Creekside Dr (14228-2037)
PHONE..................716 691-2000
William Hill, *Manager*
EMP: 50
SALES (corp-wide): 213.5MM **Privately Held**
WEB: www.hexoloy.com
SIC: 3291 Abrasive products
HQ: Saint-Gobain Advanced Ceramics Llc
   23 Acheson Dr
   Niagara Falls NY 14303

(G-250)
SIEMENS INDUSTRY INC
85 Northpointe Pkwy (14228-1886)
PHONE..................716 568-0983
EMP: 87
SALES (corp-wide): 97.7B **Privately Held**
SIC: 3822 Air conditioning & refrigeration controls
HQ: Siemens Industry, Inc.
   100 Technology Dr
   Alpharetta GA 30005
   770 740-3000

(G-251)
STATURE ELECTRIC INC
495 Commerce Dr (14228-2311)
PHONE..................716 242-7535
Richard D Smith, *President*
Richard S Warzala, *Vice Pres*
Kenneth R Wyman, *Treasurer*
Susan M Chiarmonte, *Admin Sec*
EMP: 55
SALES (est): 1.7MM
SALES (corp-wide): 252MM **Publicly Held**
SIC: 3546 3621 Power-driven handtools; electric motor & generator parts; motors, electric
PA: Allied Motion Technologies Inc.
   495 Commerce Dr Ste 3
   Amherst NY 14228
   716 242-8634

(G-252)
SUITE SOLUTIONS INC
100 Corporate Pkwy # 338 (14226-1200)
PHONE..................716 929-3050
Alan Perlmutter, *President*
Edward F O'Gara, *Bd of Directors*
EMP: 25
SALES (est): 1.1MM **Privately Held**
SIC: 7372 7371 Prepackaged software; custom computer programming services

(G-253)
SYNERGY TOOLING SYSTEMS INC (PA)
287 Commerce Dr (14228-2302)
PHONE..................716 834-4457
Richard E Morrison Jr, *President*
EMP: 35
SQ FT: 20,000
SALES (est): 5.8MM **Privately Held**
SIC: 3544 Special dies & tools

(G-254)
TARGETPROCESS INC (PA)
1325 Millersport Hwy (14221-2932)
P.O. Box 1845 (14226-7845)
PHONE..................877 718-2617
Michael Dubakov, *President*
John Manuele, *Accounts Exec*
Peter Strasser, *Sales Staff*
EMP: 10
SALES (est): 827.5K **Privately Held**
SIC: 7372 Prepackaged software

(G-255)
THOMSON INDUSTRIES INC (PA)
45 Hazelwood Dr (14228-2224)
PHONE..................716 691-9100
Dan Daniel, *CEO*
Brian Buzzard, *Engineer*
EMP: 19
SALES (est): 10.9MM **Privately Held**
SIC: 3585 Heating equipment, complete

(G-256)
TRANSCONTINENTAL PRINTING GP
300 International Dr # 200 (14221-5781)
PHONE..................716 626-3078
Louis J Continelli, *Branch Mgr*
EMP: 5 **Privately Held**
SIC: 2752 Commercial printing, lithographic
PA: Imprimeries Transcontinental 2005 S.E.N.C
   1 Place Ville-Marie Bureau 3240
   Montreal QC H3B 0
   514 954-4000

(G-257)
TRI-METAL INDUSTRIES INC
100 Pineview Dr (14228-2120)
PHONE..................716 691-3323
Donald Chatwin Jr, *President*
Douglas B Chatwin, *Treasurer*
EMP: 38 EST: 1960
SQ FT: 33,000
SALES: 2MM **Privately Held**
SIC: 3444 Sheet metal specialties, not stamped

(G-258)
UFC BIOTECHNOLOGY
1576 Sweet Home Rd # 225 (14228-2710)
PHONE..................716 777-3776
Levent Cosan, *Technology*
EMP: 9
SALES (est): 1.8MM **Privately Held**
SIC: 2835 Microbiology & virology diagnostic products

(G-259)
ULTRA-SCAN CORPORATION
4240 Ridge Lea Rd Ste 10 (14226-1083)
PHONE..................716 832-6269
John K Schneider, *President*
Stephen Gojevic, *Design Engr*
David C Horan, *Admin Sec*
EMP: 11
SQ FT: 12,500
SALES (est): 2MM **Privately Held**
WEB: www.ultra-scan.com
SIC: 3575 Mfg Computer Terminals

(G-260)
WATSON BOWMAN ACME CORP
95 Pineview Dr (14228-2121)
PHONE..................716 691-8162
Markus Burri, *President*
◆ EMP: 150
SALES (est): 35MM
SALES (corp-wide): 76B **Privately Held**
WEB: www.wbacorp.com
SIC: 3441 2899 3568 Expansion joints (structural shapes), iron or steel; concrete curing & hardening compounds; power transmission equipment
HQ: Basfin Corporation
   100 Park Ave
   Florham Park NJ 07932
   973 245-6000

(G-261)
WELCOME MAGAZINE INC
4511 Harlem Rd (14226-3803)
PHONE..................716 839-3121
Julie Kianof More, *President*
Margaret Ashley, *Manager*
EMP: 10
SQ FT: 500
SALES (est): 1MM **Privately Held**
WEB: www.welcome-magazine.com
SIC: 2721 Magazines: publishing only, not printed on site

Amityville
Suffolk County

(G-262)
A & G PRECISION CORP
680 Albany Ave (11701-1123)
PHONE..................631 957-5613
Gus Georgopoulos, *President*
Nick Georgopoulos, *Vice Pres*
EMP: 15
SALES: 1.5MM **Privately Held**
SIC: 3599 Machine shop, jobbing & repair

(G-263)
ACTION ENVELOPE & PRTG CO INC
5300 New Horizons Blvd (11701-1145)
PHONE..................631 225-3900
Sharon Newman, *President*
EMP: 10
SQ FT: 8,000
SALES (est): 1.9MM **Privately Held**
WEB: www.actionenvelope.com
SIC: 2759 Commercial printing

(G-264)
ANCON GEAR & INSTRUMENT CORP (PA)
29 Seabro Ave (11701-1201)
PHONE..................631 694-5255
Joseph Markiewicz, *President*
Ed Markiewicz, *Vice Pres*
Donna Scalice, *Admin Sec*
EMP: 18
SQ FT: 6,000
SALES (est): 2.1MM **Privately Held**
WEB: www.ancongear.com
SIC: 3728 Aircraft parts & equipment

(G-265)
BIGNAME COMMERCE LLC
5300 New Horizons Blvd (11701-1145)
PHONE..................631 693-1070
Seth Newman, *President*
EMP: 95 EST: 2017
SALES (est): 3.9MM **Privately Held**
SIC: 2679 Converted paper products

(G-266)
CALICO COTTAGE INC
210 New Hwy (11701-1116)
PHONE..................631 841-2100
Mark Wurzel, *President*
Mark L Wurzel, *President*
David A Sank, *Exec VP*
Larry Wurzel, *Vice Pres*
Lawrence J Wurzel, *Vice Pres*
▼ EMP: 50
SQ FT: 45,000
SALES (est): 15.4MM **Privately Held**
WEB: www.calicocottage.com
SIC: 2064 Candy & other confectionery products

(G-267)
CALPAC INCORPORATED
44 Seabro Ave (11701-1202)
PHONE..................631 789-0502
Pierre Lintault, *President*
EMP: 10
SQ FT: 11,000
SALES (est): 704.6K **Privately Held**
SIC: 3086 2653 Packaging & shipping materials, foamed plastic; display items, corrugated: made from purchased materials

(G-268)
CONTINENTAL INSTRUMENTS LLC
Also Called: Continental Access
355 Bayview Ave (11701-2801)
PHONE..................631 842-9400
Bob Weinstein, *Opers Staff*
Richard Soloway, *Mng Member*
John Banks,
EMP: 34
SQ FT: 90,000
SALES (est): 2.7MM
SALES (corp-wide): 87.3MM **Publicly Held**
SIC: 3625 Control equipment, electric
PA: Napco Security Technologies, Inc.
   333 Bayview Ave
   Amityville NY 11701
   631 842-9400

(G-269)
CONTROL RESEARCH INC
Also Called: Cri Graphic
385 Bayview Ave Unit C (11701-2801)
PHONE..................631 225-1111
Robert Slomkowski, *President*
Sheryl Young, *Office Mgr*
EMP: 5 EST: 1963
SQ FT: 10,000
SALES (est): 606.8K **Privately Held**
WEB: www.stageresearch.com
SIC: 2759 2395 Screen printing; embroidery & art needlework

(G-270)
CRAFTMASTER FLAVOR TECHNOLOGY
23 Albany Ave (11701-2829)
PHONE..................631 789-8607
Thomas Massetti, *President*
Ellen McDonald, *Vice Pres*
Joseph Massetti, *Treasurer*
EMP: 10
SQ FT: 4,000
SALES (est): 1.4MM **Privately Held**
SIC: 2869 2087 Flavors or flavoring materials, synthetic; extracts, flavoring

(G-271)
DANIEL DEMARCO AND ASSOC INC
25 Greene Ave (11701-2943)
PHONE..................631 598-7000
Daniel Demarco, *Ch of Bd*
Dano Demarco, *General Mgr*
Rob Herzog, *Project Mgr*
Tom Whalen, *Project Mgr*
Eileen Hohorst, *Bookkeeper*
EMP: 35
SALES (est): 8.9MM **Privately Held**
WEB: www.danieldemarco.com
SIC: 3429 1751 2499 Cabinet hardware; cabinet building & installation; decorative wood & woodwork

(G-272)
EDO LLC (HQ)
Also Called: Mine Defense Systems
1500 New Horizons Blvd (11701-1130)
PHONE..................631 630-4000
Charles Greene, *CEO*
Lawrence Schwartz, *Principal*
Jon A Anderson, *Senior VP*
Frank W Otto, *Senior VP*
Roy R Byrd, *Vice Pres*
◆ EMP: 9 EST: 1925
SQ FT: 6,000

Amityville - Suffolk County (G-273)

SALES (est): 754.3MM
SALES (corp-wide): 6.1B **Publicly Held**
WEB: www.nycedo.com
SIC: 3728 3663 3679 3812 Military aircraft equipment & armament; countermeasure dispensers, aircraft; research & dev by manuf., aircraft parts & auxiliary equip; antennas, transmitting & communications; satellites, communications; electronic crystals; piezoelectric crystals; sonar systems & equipment
PA: Harris Corporation
  1025 W Nasa Blvd
  Melbourne FL 32919
  321 727-9100

(G-273)
EDO LLC
1500 New Horizons Blvd (11701-1130)
PHONE..................................631 630-4200
James Smith, *President*
EMP: 1000
SALES (corp-wide): 6.1B **Publicly Held**
SIC: 3825 3812 3761 3699 Instruments to measure electricity; search & navigation equipment; guided missiles & space vehicles; electrical equipment & supplies; radio & TV communications equipment
HQ: Edo Llc
  1500 New Horizons Blvd
  Amityville NY 11701
  631 630-4000

(G-274)
EDO LLC
1500 New Horizons Blvd (11701-1130)
PHONE..................................631 630-4000
Frank Otto, *Branch Mgr*
John Gandia, *Manager*
EMP: 123
SALES (corp-wide): 6.1B **Publicly Held**
WEB: www.nycedo.com
SIC: 3625 Control equipment, electric
HQ: Edo Llc
  1500 New Horizons Blvd
  Amityville NY 11701
  631 630-4000

(G-275)
FOLDER FACTORY INC
Also Called: Folders.com
5300 New Horizons Blvd (11701-1145)
PHONE..................................540 477-3852
Mark Gentile, *President*
William David Gentile, *Vice Pres*
Lee Wells, *Sales Dir*
Schericka Fairchild, *Accounts Mgr*
Vincent Roy, *Sales Staff*
EMP: 16
SQ FT: 40,000
SALES: 2.6MM **Privately Held**
WEB: www.folder.com
SIC: 2752 2759 2782 2396 Commercial printing, offset; commercial printing; blankbooks & looseleaf binders; automotive & apparel trimmings

(G-276)
G MARKS HDWR LIQUIDATING CORP
Also Called: Marks USA
333 Bayview Ave (11701-2801)
PHONE..................................631 225-5400
George Marks, *President*
Donna Gallagher, *Purch Mgr*
Bert Weichselbaum, *Finance Mgr*
EMP: 90 EST: 1977
SQ FT: 35,000
SALES: 12.6MM
SALES (corp-wide): 87.3MM **Publicly Held**
WEB: www.marksusa.com
SIC: 3429 Locks or lock sets
PA: Napco Security Technologies, Inc.
  333 Bayview Ave
  Amityville NY 11701
  631 842-9400

(G-277)
GKN AEROSPACE MONITOR INC
1000 New Horizons Blvd (11701-1138)
PHONE..................................562 619-8558
Daniele Cagnatel, *CEO*
Kevin L Cummings, *Ch of Bd*
Fran Novak, *President*
Paul Kowack, *Vice Pres*
Patrick Powers, *Vice Pres*
▲ EMP: 275 EST: 1947
SQ FT: 238,000
SALES (est): 80.7MM
SALES (corp-wide): 12.7B **Privately Held**
WEB: www.monair.com
SIC: 3728 3769 Aircraft assemblies, sub-assemblies & parts; guided missile & space vehicle parts & auxiliary equipment
PA: Gkn Limited
  Po Box 55
  Redditch WORCS B98 0
  152 751-7715

(G-278)
GRAND KNITTING MILLS INC (PA)
7050 New Horizons Blvd # 1 (11701-1179)
PHONE..................................631 226-5000
Fax: 631 226-8336
▲ EMP: 40 EST: 1910
SQ FT: 35,000
SALES (est): 2.9MM **Privately Held**
SIC: 2361 5137 Mfg Girl/Youth Dresses/Blouses Whol Women's/Child's Clothing

(G-279)
HABCO CORP
Also Called: Habco Sales
41 Ranick Dr E (11701-2844)
PHONE..................................631 789-1400
Herb Auleta, *CEO*
Steven Auleta, *President*
Philip Auleta, *Vice Pres*
▲ EMP: 50
SQ FT: 19,175
SALES: 9MM **Privately Held**
SIC: 2022 Processed cheese

(G-280)
HARRIS CORPORATION
Also Called: Exelis
1500 New Horizons Blvd (11701-1130)
PHONE..................................631 630-4000
EMP: 33
SALES (est): 7MM **Privately Held**
SIC: 3812 Search & navigation equipment

(G-281)
HART SPECIALTIES INC
Also Called: New York Eye
5000 New Horizons Blvd (11701-1143)
P.O. Box 9003 (11701-9003)
PHONE..................................631 226-5600
Arthur Jankolovits, *Ch of Bd*
Stella Rossman, *President*
Lucy Korn, *Vice Pres*
Shannon Melendez, *Vice Pres*
Jan Phillips, *Vice Pres*
◆ EMP: 70
SQ FT: 25,000
SALES: 19.4MM **Privately Held**
WEB: www.newyorkeye.net
SIC: 3827 5995 Optical instruments & apparatus; optical goods stores

(G-282)
HEALTH CARE PRODUCTS
369 Bayview Ave (11701-2801)
PHONE..................................631 789-8228
Bruce Kutinsky, *President*
EMP: 6 EST: 2017
SALES (est): 531.1K **Privately Held**
SIC: 2834 Pharmaceutical preparations

(G-283)
HELGEN INDUSTRIES INC
Also Called: De Santis Holster and Lea Gds
431 Bayview Ave (11701-2638)
PHONE..................................631 841-6300
Gene De Santis, *Ch of Bd*
Helen De Santis, *Vice Pres*
▲ EMP: 125
SQ FT: 14,000
SALES (est): 20.5MM **Privately Held**
WEB: www.desantisholster.com
SIC: 3199 3172 Holsters, leather; personal leather goods

(G-284)
HI-TECH PHARMACAL CO INC (HQ)
Also Called: Hi-Tech Pharmacal - An Akorn
369 Bayview Ave (11701-2801)
PHONE..................................631 789-8228
David S Seltzer, *President*
Gary M April, *President*
April Caccavale, *Counsel*
April Polikoff, *Counsel*
Kamel Egbaria, *Exec VP*
▲ EMP: 237
SALES (est): 101.7MM
SALES (corp-wide): 841MM **Publicly Held**
WEB: www.hitechpharm.com
SIC: 2834 Pharmaceutical preparations
PA: Akorn, Inc.
  1925 W Field Ct Ste 300
  Lake Forest IL 60045
  847 279-6100

(G-285)
HI-TECH PHARMACAL CO INC
Also Called: Hi-Tech Pharmacal - An Akorn
26 Edison St (11701-2839)
PHONE..................................631 789-8228
Bernard Seltzer, *President*
Edwin Berrios, *Vice Pres*
Lisa Natalie, *Opers Staff*
Mike Paul, *Accountant*
Serap Ozelkan, *Director*
EMP: 12
SALES (corp-wide): 841MM **Publicly Held**
SIC: 2834 Pharmaceutical preparations
HQ: Hi-Tech Pharmacal Co., Inc.
  369 Bayview Ave
  Amityville NY 11701
  631 789-8228

(G-286)
IMC TEDDY FOOD SERVICE
Also Called: Sefi Fabricator
50 Ranick Dr E (11701-2822)
P.O. Box 338 (11701-0338)
PHONE..................................631 789-8881
Rasik Patel, *Partner*
Madelin Fernandez, *Purch Agent*
Jorge Abril, *Engineer*
EMP: 48
SALES (est): 6.6MM **Privately Held**
WEB: www.imcteddy.com
SIC: 3589 Commercial cooking & food-warming equipment

(G-287)
INNOGENIX INC
8200 New Horizons Blvd (11701-1152)
PHONE..................................631 450-4704
Manish Potti, *President*
EMP: 10
SALES (est): 542.7K **Privately Held**
SIC: 2834 Pharmaceutical preparations

(G-288)
INTERSTATE WOOD PRODUCTS INC
Also Called: Interstate Wood & Vinyl Pdts
1084 Sunrise Hwy (11701-2526)
PHONE..................................631 842-4488
Jennifer Cerullo, *CEO*
John Hokanson, *Manager*
EMP: 25
SQ FT: 8,500
SALES (est): 4MM
SALES (corp-wide): 28.2MM **Privately Held**
SIC: 2499 5031 3496 1799 Fencing, wood; fencing, wood; miscellaneous fabricated wire products; fence construction
PA: Amendola Industries, Inc.
  1084 Sunrise Hwy
  Amityville NY 11701
  631 842-4427

(G-289)
ISLAND LITE LOUVERS INC
35 Albany Ave (11701-2828)
PHONE..................................631 608-4250
Kristin Hill, *Ch of Bd*
EMP: 25
SALES (est): 3.6MM **Privately Held**
WEB: www.islandlitelouver.com
SIC: 3648 Mfg Lighting Equipment

(G-290)
JAXSON ROLLFORMING INC
145 Dixon Ave Ste 1 (11701-2836)
PHONE..................................631 842-7775
Alexander Trink, *President*
▲ EMP: 37
SALES (est): 8MM **Privately Held**
WEB: www.jaxsonrollforming.com
SIC: 3446 5031 Fences, gates, posts & flagpoles; partitions & supports/studs, including accoustical systems; molding, all materials

(G-291)
JEFFREY JOHN
Also Called: Creative Compositions
25 Elm Pl (11701-2815)
PHONE..................................631 842-2850
John Jeffrey, *Owner*
EMP: 6
SALES (est): 349.6K **Privately Held**
SIC: 2499 Decorative wood & woodwork

(G-292)
KABCO PHARMACEUTICALS INC
2000 New Horizons Blvd (11701-1137)
PHONE..................................631 842-3600
Abu Kabir, *Ch of Bd*
Saiful Kibria, *President*
Liton Kabir, *Buyer*
Amir Hossain, *QC Mgr*
Miran Noor, *Cust Mgr*
▲ EMP: 4
SQ FT: 30,000
SALES (est): 1.6MM **Privately Held**
WEB: www.kabco.org
SIC: 2834 Vitamin preparations

(G-293)
KDO INDUSTRIES INC
32 Ranick Dr W (11701-2825)
PHONE..................................631 608-4612
Lucelle Del Rosaio, *CEO*
George Koenig, *Vice Pres*
EMP: 7
SQ FT: 10,000
SALES (est): 1.5MM **Privately Held**
SIC: 3441 Fabricated structural metal

(G-294)
KEY CAST STONE COMPANY INC
113 Albany Ave (11701-2632)
PHONE..................................631 789-2145
Filippo Pedalino, *President*
John Gonzalez, *Treasurer*
Carmelo Cicero, *Admin Sec*
▲ EMP: 20 EST: 1958
SQ FT: 20,000
SALES (est): 3MM **Privately Held**
WEB: www.keycaststone.com
SIC: 3272 Precast terrazo or concrete products; steps, prefabricated concrete; sills, concrete

(G-295)
KLEER-FAX INC
750 New Horizons Blvd (11701-1130)
PHONE..................................631 225-1100
Elias Cruz, *CEO*
Louis Nigro, *President*
◆ EMP: 97
SQ FT: 50,000
SALES (est): 21.8MM **Privately Held**
WEB: www.kleer-fax.com
SIC: 2678 2677 3089 5943 Stationery products; envelopes; extruded finished plastic products; office forms & supplies; die-cut paper & board

(G-296)
LAMBRO INDUSTRIES INC (PA)
115 Albany Ave (11701-2632)
P.O. Box 367 (11701-0367)
PHONE..................................631 842-8088
Shiv Anand CPA, *Ch of Bd*
Scott Condello, *Natl Sales Mgr*
Garry Speight, *Natl Sales Mgr*
Robert Lange, *Mktg Dir*
▲ EMP: 100
SQ FT: 56,000
SALES (est): 17.7MM **Privately Held**
WEB: www.lambro.net
SIC: 3444 Ventilators, sheet metal

GEOGRAPHIC SECTION

Amityville - Suffolk County (G-324)

(G-297)
LEMODE CONCEPTS INC
19 Elm Pl (11701-2815)
PHONE 631 841-0796
Robert Tolda, *President*
Bob Tolda, *President*
Susan Tolda, *Vice Pres*
EMP: 6
SALES (est): 430K **Privately Held**
WEB: www.lemodeconcepts.com
SIC: 2511 Kitchen & dining room furniture

(G-298)
LYNMAR PRINTING CORP
8600 New Horizons Blvd (11701-1154)
PHONE 631 957-8500
Lou Dilorenzo, *President*
Anthony Lisanti, *Vice Pres*
EMP: 8
SQ FT: 8,000
SALES: 1MM **Privately Held**
WEB: www.lynmarprinting.com
SIC: 2752 Commercial printing, offset

(G-299)
M & D MILLWORK LLC
178 New Hwy (11701-1117)
PHONE 631 789-1439
Darren Winter,
Marek Zaleski,
EMP: 10
SQ FT: 14,000
SALES (est): 1.6MM **Privately Held**
SIC: 2431 Millwork

(G-300)
MADJEK INC
185 Dixon Ave (11701-2840)
PHONE 631 842-4475
R Freeman, *Vice Pres*
Eric Anderson, *Project Mgr*
Robert Cummings, *Project Mgr*
Elaine Moore, *Human Resources*
Phil Erickson, *Legal Staff*
▲ **EMP:** 85
SALES (est): 14.4MM **Privately Held**
WEB: www.madjek.com
SIC: 2541 Store fixtures, wood

(G-301)
MAGNIFLOOD INC
7200 New Horizons Blvd (11701-1150)
PHONE 631 226-1000
Kenneth Greene, *President*
Anita Greene, *Admin Sec*
▲ **EMP:** 20 **EST:** 1977
SQ FT: 27,500
SALES (est): 4.7MM **Privately Held**
WEB: www.magniflood.com
SIC: 3646 Commercial indusl & institutional electric lighting fixtures

(G-302)
MASSAPQUA PRCSION MCHINING LTD
30 Seabro Ave (11701-1202)
PHONE 631 789-1485
Richard Beleski, *President*
EMP: 9
SQ FT: 7,000
SALES: 1.9MM **Privately Held**
SIC: 3599 Machine shop, jobbing & repair

(G-303)
METRO IRON CORP
4 Seabro Ave (11701-1202)
PHONE 631 842-5929
John Valente, *President*
Melissa Szatkowski, *Project Mgr*
Daniel Valente, *Project Mgr*
EMP: 7
SALES (est): 2MM **Privately Held**
WEB: www.metroiron.com
SIC: 3441 Fabricated structural metal

(G-304)
NAPCO SECURITY TECH INC (PA)
333 Bayview Ave (11701-2801)
PHONE 631 842-9400
Richard L Soloway, *Ch of Bd*
Michael Carrieri, *Senior VP*
Jorge Hevia, *Senior VP*
Byron Thurmond, *Vice Pres*
Kevin S Buchel, *Treasurer*
EMP: 250 **EST:** 1969
SQ FT: 90,000
SALES: 87.3MM **Publicly Held**
WEB: www.napcosecurity.com
SIC: 3669 3699 3429 1731 Emergency alarms; fire alarm apparatus, electric; security control equipment & systems; door locks, bolts & checks; safety & security specialization; systems software development services

(G-305)
NATURAL ORGANICS LABS INC
Also Called: Universal Proteins
9500 New Horizons Blvd (11701-1155)
PHONE 631 957-5600
Gerald Kessler, *President*
Suzanne Tenn, *Export Mgr*
Patrick Brady, *QC Mgr*
Hashem Khan, *QC Mgr*
Nancy Devera, *Research*
EMP: 500
SALES (est): 57.7MM **Privately Held**
SIC: 2834 2087 Vitamin preparations; flavoring extracts & syrups

(G-306)
NEW BUSINESS SOLUTIONS INC
Also Called: Nbs
31 Sprague Ave (11701-2618)
PHONE 631 789-1500
Michele Ruggeri, *CEO*
George J Ruggeri, *President*
Michael Filangeri, *Project Mgr*
Justina Gartner, *Manager*
▲ **EMP:** 28
SALES (est): 5.7MM **Privately Held**
WEB: www.newbusinesssolutions.com
SIC: 2542 2541 7389 Fixtures: display, office or store: except wood; store & office display cases & fixtures; window trimming service

(G-307)
OFFICIAL OFFSET CORPORATION
8600 New Horizons Blvd (11701-1183)
PHONE 631 957-8500
Benjamin Paulino, *Ch of Bd*
Frank Paulino, *Vice Pres*
Tom Gebhardt, *Plant Mgr*
Philene Abraham, *Production*
Mary Paulino, *Admin Sec*
▼ **EMP:** 20 **EST:** 1957
SQ FT: 20,000
SALES: 4.5MM **Privately Held**
WEB: www.officialoffset.com
SIC: 2752 2791 Commercial printing, offset; typesetting

(G-308)
OIL AND LUBRICANT DEPOT LLC
Also Called: Oil Depot, The
61 Ranick Dr S (11701-2823)
PHONE 718 258-9220
Steven Krausman, *Mng Member*
EMP: 10 **EST:** 2011
SALES (est): 1.8MM **Privately Held**
SIC: 2992 Lubricating oils & greases

(G-309)
OIL SOLUTIONS INTL INC
35 Mill St (11701-2819)
PHONE 631 608-8889
Dennis Traina, *Chairman*
EMP: 8
SALES (est): 160.7K **Privately Held**
SIC: 2911 Oils, lubricating

(G-310)
P & M LLC
Also Called: Sefi Fabricators
50 Ranick Dr E (11701-2822)
P.O. Box 338 (11701-0338)
PHONE 631 842-2200
Tony Cabrera, *Sales Mgr*
Rasik Patel, *Mng Member*
Tom Zebrowski, *Associate*
EMP: 46 **EST:** 1997
SQ FT: 17,000
SALES (est): 10.2MM **Privately Held**
SIC: 3556 Food products machinery

(G-311)
PAULIN INVESTMENT COMPANY
8600 New Horizons Blvd (11701-1154)
PHONE 631 957-8500
Ben M Paulino, *Owner*
EMP: 27
SALES (est): 2.9MM **Privately Held**
SIC: 2759 Commercial printing

(G-312)
PEPSI BOTTLING VENTURES LLC
Also Called: Pepsico
550 New Horizons Blvd (11701-1139)
PHONE 631 226-9000
Carl Cariffunior, *General Mgr*
EMP: 40
SALES (corp-wide): 76.5MM **Privately Held**
SIC: 2086 Carbonated soft drinks, bottled & canned
HQ: Pepsi Bottling Ventures Llc
      4141 Parklake Ave Ste 600
      Raleigh NC 27612
      919 865-2300

(G-313)
PORTFAB LLC
Also Called: Wenig Company, The
45 Ranick Dr E (11701-2821)
PHONE 718 542-3600
William Friedman, *Mng Member*
Rosemarie Friedman,
EMP: 32
SQ FT: 38,000
SALES (est): 5.2MM **Privately Held**
WEB: www.portfab.com
SIC: 3441 Fabricated structural metal

(G-314)
PRECISION SIGNSCOM INC
Also Called: Precision Engraving Company
243 Dixon Ave (11701-2830)
PHONE 631 841-7500
Michael Anzalone, *Ch of Bd*
EMP: 51
SQ FT: 23,500
SALES (est): 8.2MM **Privately Held**
SIC: 3993 Signs, not made in custom sign painting shops

(G-315)
SARAGA INDUSTRIES CORP
Also Called: Lenco
690 Albany Ave Unit D (11701-1199)
PHONE 631 842-4049
Robert Saraga, *President*
EMP: 6
SQ FT: 4,000
SALES (est): 988K **Privately Held**
WEB: www.lencocoolers.com
SIC: 3443 Heat exchangers, condensers & components

(G-316)
STEIN INDUSTRIES INC
22 Sprague Ave (11701-2634)
PHONE 631 789-2222
Stuart Stein, *President*
Andrew Stein, *Vice Pres*
Andrew Jinks, *Manager*
Jane McCaffrey, *Manager*
EMP: 40 **EST:** 1937
SQ FT: 30,000
SALES (est): 5.8MM **Privately Held**
WEB: www.steinindustries.com
SIC: 2541 Wood partitions & fixtures

(G-317)
STRUCTURED 3D INC
188 Dixon Ave (11701-2812)
PHONE 346 704-2614
Mitchell Proux, *President*
EMP: 5
SALES (est): 190.4K **Privately Held**
SIC: 2759 Commercial printing

(G-318)
SUNDIAL BRANDS LLC
11 Ranick Dr S (11701-2823)
PHONE 631 842-8800
Richelieu Dennis, *CEO*
Nyema Tudman, *President*
Brendan Holden, *Senior VP*
Cyrus Dennis, *Vice Pres*
Richard Gallucci, *Vice Pres*
▲ **EMP:** 215
SALES (est): 102.4MM
SALES (corp-wide): 63B **Privately Held**
SIC: 2844 Cosmetic preparations
PA: Unilever Plc
      Unilever House
      London EC4Y
      207 822-5252

(G-319)
SUNDIAL FRAGRANCES & FLAVORS
11 Ranick Dr S (11701-2823)
PHONE 631 842-8800
Richelieu Dennis, *CEO*
Nyema S Tubman, *Ch of Bd*
Mary Dennis, *Treasurer*
EMP: 24
SQ FT: 50,000
SALES (est): 7.8MM **Privately Held**
WEB: www.nhexec.com
SIC: 2869 5122 Perfumes, flavorings & food additives; perfumes

(G-320)
SUNDIAL GROUP LLC
Also Called: Sundial Creations
11 Ranick Dr S (11701-2823)
PHONE 631 842-8800
Marry Dennis, *CEO*
Dennis Richelieu, *CEO*
Richard Gallucci, *Senior VP*
Dennis Layer, *Purch Agent*
Christine Williams, *Research*
EMP: 40
SQ FT: 50,000
SALES (est): 16.9MM **Privately Held**
SIC: 2844 Cosmetic preparations; perfumes & colognes

(G-321)
TOPIDERM INC (PA)
5200 New Horizons Blvd (11701-1189)
PHONE 631 226-7979
Burt Shaffer, *Ch of Bd*
Bob Arnaiz, *Prdtn Mgr*
Carol Donaldson, *Purch Mgr*
Kathleen Sieger, *Purch Mgr*
Steven Pinsky, *CFO*
▲ **EMP:** 200
SALES (est): 58.4MM **Privately Held**
SIC: 2834 2844 Pharmaceutical preparations; cosmetic preparations

(G-322)
TOPIX PHARMACEUTICALS INC (PA)
5200 New Horizons Blvd (11701-1189)
PHONE 631 226-7979
Burt Shaffer, *President*
Jody Manganiello, *Human Resources*
Joe Ragosta, *VP Sales*
Ewelina Aiossa, *Mktg Dir*
Olivia Mullins, *Marketing Staff*
▲ **EMP:** 150
SALES: 45MM **Privately Held**
WEB: www.topixpharm.com
SIC: 2834 Pharmaceutical preparations

(G-323)
TRITON BUILDERS INC
645 Broadway Ste T (11701-2118)
PHONE 631 841-2534
Stacy Guercia-Baldea, *President*
EMP: 20
SQ FT: 2,000
SALES: 6MM **Privately Held**
SIC: 3441 Fabricated structural metal

(G-324)
TRUE TYPE PRINTING CO INC
8600 New Horizons Blvd (11701-1154)
PHONE 718 706-6900
Lee Forlenza, *President*
EMP: 5
SALES (est): 431.8K **Privately Held**
SIC: 2752 Commercial printing, offset

Amsterdam
Montgomery County

(G-325)
AMSTERDAM PRINTING & LITHO INC
Go Promos
166 Wallins Corners Rd (12010-1817)
PHONE..............................518 842-6000
Melissa Santamaria, *Branch Mgr*
EMP: 15
SALES (corp-wide): 3.4B **Privately Held**
WEB: www.amsterdamprinting.com
SIC: 3993 2752 2761 Advertising novelties; commercial printing, lithographic; manifold business forms
HQ: Amsterdam Printing & Litho, Inc.
  166 Wallins Corners Rd
  Amsterdam NY 12010
  518 842-6000

(G-326)
AMSTERDAM PRINTING & LITHO INC
Baldwin Cooke
166 Wallins Corners Rd (12010-1817)
PHONE..............................518 842-6000
EMP: 49
SALES (corp-wide): 3.4B **Privately Held**
WEB: www.amsterdamprinting.com
SIC: 3993 2752 2761 Advertising novelties; commercial printing, lithographic; manifold business forms
HQ: Amsterdam Printing & Litho, Inc.
  166 Wallins Corners Rd
  Amsterdam NY 12010
  518 842-6000

(G-327)
BECKMANN CONVERTING INC (PA)
14 Park Dr (12010-5340)
P.O. Box 390 (12010-0390)
PHONE..............................518 842-0073
Klaus Beckmann, *CEO*
Peter Piusz, *Vice Pres*
Bill Wood, *Engineer*
Tony Tangerone, *Controller*
Scott Ayers, *Marketing Staff*
▲ **EMP:** 40
SQ FT: 100,000
SALES (est): 5.5MM **Privately Held**
WEB: www.beckmannconverting.com
SIC: 2295 2262 Leather, artificial or imitation; fire resistance finishing: manmade & silk broadwoven

(G-328)
BEECH-NUT NUTRITION COMPANY (DH)
1 Nutritious Pl (12010-8105)
PHONE..............................518 839-0300
Jeffrey Boutelle, *President*
Tami Colby, *Editor*
Ray Gosselin, *Vice Pres*
Evan Fish, *Mfg Mgr*
Chris Darling, *Engineer*
◆ **EMP:** 295
SALES (est): 131.1MM
SALES (corp-wide): 1.2B **Privately Held**
SIC: 2032 Baby foods, including meats: packaged in cans, jars, etc.
HQ: Hero Ag
  Karl Roth-Strasse 8
  Lenzburg AG 5600
  628 855-111

(G-329)
BRETON INDUSTRIES INC (PA)
1 Sam Stratton Rd (12010-5243)
PHONE..............................518 842-3030
Alfred Damofal, *CEO*
Peter A Lewis, *Senior VP*
G Eric Lewis, *Vice Pres*
G Richard Lewis, *Treasurer*
EMP: 110
SQ FT: 55,000
SALES (est): 18.9MM **Privately Held**
WEB: www.bretonindustries.com
SIC: 2394 2399 3443 2295 Tarpaulins, fabric: made from purchased materials; canvas awnings & canopies; canvas covers & drop cloths; shades, canvas: made from purchased materials; aprons, breast (harness); fabricated plate work (boiler shop); coated fabrics, not rubberized; narrow fabric mills

(G-330)
CAPITOL CUPS INC
1030 Riverfront Ctr (12010-4616)
PHONE..............................518 627-0051
Robert S Abrams, *President*
John Belfance Jr, *COO*
Robert N Sawyer, *CFO*
Robert L Thompson, *Controller*
EMP: 26
SQ FT: 10,000
SALES (est): 4.4MM **Privately Held**
WEB: www.capitolcups.com
SIC: 3089 Cups, plastic, except foam

(G-331)
CAPITOL PLASTIC PRODUCTS INC
1030 Riverfront Ctr (12010-4616)
P.O. Box 710 (12010-0710)
PHONE..............................518 627-0051
Robert Abrams, *Principal*
▼ **EMP:** 210
SALES (est): 9.2MM
SALES (corp-wide): 114.6MM **Privately Held**
SIC: 3085 Plastics bottles
PA: Cv Holdings, Llc
  1030 Riverfront Ctr
  Amsterdam NY 12010
  518 627-0051

(G-332)
COBLESKILL RED E MIX & SUPPLY
Also Called: Cobleskill Concrete Ready Mix
774 State Highway 5s (12010-7668)
PHONE..............................518 234-2015
John Tesiero, *President*
Carol Whelly, *Admin Sec*
EMP: 10
SQ FT: 15,000
SALES (est): 16.4MM **Privately Held**
SIC: 3273 Ready-mixed concrete

(G-333)
CRANESVILLE BLOCK CO INC (PA)
Also Called: Cranesville Ready-Mix
1250 Riverfront Ctr (12010-4602)
PHONE..............................518 684-6154
John A Tesiero III, *Ch of Bd*
Elizabeth Tesiero, *Corp Secy*
Joe Nolan, *Opers Mgr*
Brian Olpalka, *Store Mgr*
Steve Dillenbeck, *Purch Mgr*
▲ **EMP:** 45 **EST:** 1947
SALES (est): 45.6MM **Privately Held**
SIC: 3271 3273 5211 Blocks, concrete or cinder: standard; ready-mixed concrete; concrete & cinder block; cement; masonry materials & supplies

(G-334)
CSP TECHNOLOGIES INC (HQ)
1031 Riverfront Ctr (12010)
PHONE..............................518 627-0051
Robert Abrams, *CEO*
▲ **EMP:** 45
SALES (est): 14.5MM
SALES (corp-wide): 114.6MM **Privately Held**
SIC: 3089 Plastic processing
PA: Cv Holdings, Llc
  1030 Riverfront Ctr
  Amsterdam NY 12010
  518 627-0051

(G-335)
ELECTRIC CITY CONCRETE CO INC (HQ)
774 State Highway 5s (12010-7668)
PHONE..............................518 887-5560
John A Tesiero Jr, *President*
Carol Whelly, *Vice Pres*
EMP: 25 **EST:** 1977
SALES (est): 1.5MM
SALES (corp-wide): 45.6MM **Privately Held**
SIC: 3273 Ready-mixed concrete
PA: Cranesville Block Co., Inc.
  1250 Riverfront Ctr
  Amsterdam NY 12010
  518 684-6154

(G-336)
EMBASSY MILLWORK INC
3 Sam Stratton Rd (12010-5243)
PHONE..............................518 839-0965
Michael Caruso, *President*
EMP: 12
SALES (est): 1.1MM **Privately Held**
SIC: 2421 Planing mill, independent: except millwork

(G-337)
FIBER GLASS INDUSTRIES INC (PA)
Also Called: Fgi
69 Edson St (12010-5247)
PHONE..............................518 842-4000
John Menzel, *CEO*
Mike Lanham, *President*
◆ **EMP:** 75 **EST:** 1957
SQ FT: 60,000
SALES (est): 22.7MM **Privately Held**
SIC: 2221 Fiberglass fabrics; glass broadwoven fabrics

(G-338)
FULMONT READY-MIX COMPANY INC (PA)
774 State Highway 5s (12010-7668)
PHONE..............................518 887-5560
Elizabeth Tesiero, *President*
John Tesiero III, *Vice Pres*
EMP: 16 **EST:** 1947
SALES (est): 1.1MM **Privately Held**
SIC: 3273 Ready-mixed concrete

(G-339)
GREAT ADIRONDACK YARN COMPANY
950 County Highway 126 (12010-6287)
PHONE..............................518 843-3381
Patti Subik, *Owner*
Paul Subik, *Vice Pres*
EMP: 10
SALES: 400K **Privately Held**
SIC: 2281 2253 5949 5199 Natural & animal fiber yarns, spun; sweaters & sweater coats, knit; sewing & needlework; yarns

(G-340)
HYPERBARIC TECHNOLOGIES INC
1 Sam Stratton Rd (12010-5243)
P.O. Box 69 (12010-0069)
PHONE..............................518 842-3030
Peter Lewis, *President*
Richard Lewis, *CFO*
EMP: 2
SQ FT: 5,000
SALES (est): 3.2MM **Privately Held**
SIC: 3443 Chambers & caissons

(G-341)
J H BUHRMASTER COMPANY INC
Also Called: Amsterdam Oil Heat
164 W Main St (12010-3130)
PHONE..............................518 843-1700
Donald L Hosier, *Sales/Mktg Mgr*
EMP: 8
SALES (corp-wide): 8.6MM **Privately Held**
SIC: 3567 Industrial furnaces & ovens
PA: J. H. Buhrmaster Company, Inc.
  421 Sacandaga Rd
  Scotia NY 12302
  518 382-0260

(G-342)
KAPSTONE CONTAINER CORPORATION
28 Park Dr (12010-5340)
PHONE..............................518 842-2450
Edward H Poulin, *Manager*
Teresa Vasquez, *Manager*
EMP: 60
SALES (corp-wide): 3.3B **Publicly Held**
SIC: 2411 2674 2621 2631 Wooden logs; shipping & shopping bags or sacks; kraft paper; container board; boxes, corrugated: made from purchased materials; boxes, solid fiber: made from purchased materials
HQ: Kapstone Container Corporation
  1601 Blairs Ferry Rd Ne
  Cedar Rapids IA 52402
  319 393-3610

(G-343)
KC TAG CO
108 Edson St (12010-7213)
PHONE..............................518 842-6666
Kevin Collins, *Ch of Bd*
EMP: 8
SALES (est): 1.1MM **Privately Held**
SIC: 3089 Plastics products

(G-344)
KEEP AMERICA BEAUTIFUL INC
Also Called: For A Safer America
1 Prospect St (12010-3637)
P.O. Box 229 (12010-0229)
PHONE..............................518 842-4388
Anna Podolec, *Branch Mgr*
EMP: 6
SALES (est): 434.3K
SALES (corp-wide): 8.8MM **Privately Held**
WEB: www.kab.org
SIC: 3993 Advertising novelties
PA: Keep America Beautiful, Inc.
  1010 Washington Blvd 22-1
  Stamford CT 06901
  203 659-3000

(G-345)
LOSURDO FOODS INC
78 Sam Stratton Rd (12010-5244)
PHONE..............................518 842-1500
Maria Hammill, *Branch Mgr*
EMP: 25
SALES (corp-wide): 73.5MM **Privately Held**
WEB: www.losurdofoods.com
SIC: 2041 Doughs & batters
PA: Losurdo Foods, Inc.
  20 Owens Rd
  Hackensack NJ 07601
  201 343-6680

(G-346)
MCCLARY MEDIA INC
Also Called: Port Jackson Media
1 Venner Rd (12010-5617)
PHONE..............................800 453-6397
Kevin McClary, *Principal*
Geoff Dylong, *Principal*
Rich Kretser, *Principal*
Dave Warner, *Principal*
EMP: 5
SALES (est): 203.3K **Privately Held**
SIC: 2711 7313 Newspapers: publishing only, not printed on site; magazine advertising representative; newspaper advertising representative

(G-347)
MHXCO FOAM COMPANY LLC
120 Edson St (12010-7213)
P.O. Box 579 (12010-0579)
PHONE..............................518 843-8400
Stephen Trembley, *Mng Member*
EMP: 14
SALES: 3MM **Privately Held**
SIC: 3069 Foam rubber

(G-348)
MILLER PRINTING & LITHO INC
97 Guy Park Ave (12010-3225)
PHONE..............................518 842-0001
Scott Miller, *President*
EMP: 6
SQ FT: 9,000
SALES (est): 914.7K **Privately Held**
SIC: 2752 Commercial printing, offset

▲ = Import ▼ = Export
◆ = Import/Export

GEOGRAPHIC SECTION

(G-349)
MILNOT HOLDING CORPORATION
1 Nutritious Pl (12010-8105)
PHONE..............................518 839-0300
Amy McGrath, *Human Res Dir*
EMP: 5
SALES (est): 502.2K
SALES (corp-wide): 1.2B **Privately Held**
SIC: 2099 Food preparations
HQ: Hero Ag
    Karl Roth-Strasse 8
    Lenzburg AG 5600
    628 855-111

(G-350)
MOHAWK FABRIC COMPANY INC
96 Guy Park Ave (12010-3241)
P.O. Box 587 (12010-0587)
PHONE..............................518 842-3090
Gregory Needham, *President*
Dominic Wade, *Principal*
EMP: 15 **EST:** 1922
SQ FT: 35,000
SALES (est): 4.4MM **Privately Held**
WEB: www.mohawkfabric.com
SIC: 2258 Lace & warp knit fabric mills

(G-351)
MOHAWK RESOURCES LTD
65 Vrooman Ave (12010-5321)
P.O. Box 110 (12010-0110)
PHONE..............................518 842-1431
Steven Perlstein, *President*
Andrea Baldomar, *General Mgr*
Nancy Rogers, *Business Mgr*
Ben Blanchette, *Opers Staff*
David Sutter, *Production*
▲ **EMP:** 70
SQ FT: 55,000
SALES (est): 40.9MM **Privately Held**
WEB: www.mohawklifts.com
SIC: 3536 Hoists

(G-352)
MOHAWK SIGN SYSTEMS INC
5 Dandreano Dr (12010-5253)
P.O. Box 966, Schenectady (12301-0966)
PHONE..............................518 842-5303
Bettina Dill, *President*
Neale Dill, *Vice Pres*
EMP: 30
SQ FT: 10,000
SALES (est): 2.5MM **Privately Held**
WEB: www.mohawksign.com
SIC: 3993 Signs, not made in custom sign painting shops

(G-353)
NATIONWIDE TARPS INCORPORATED (PA)
Also Called: NTI Global
50 Willow St (12010-4219)
P.O. Box 189 (12010-0189)
PHONE..............................518 843-1545
Stephen Raeburn, *Ch of Bd*
Anita Raeburn, *Vice Pres*
Edward Davis, *CFO*
April Smida, *Human Res Mgr*
Benal Raeburn, *Agent*
▲ **EMP:** 75
SQ FT: 195,000
SALES (est): 15.9MM **Privately Held**
WEB: www.ntiglobal.com
SIC: 3081 2821 2394 2392 Polyethylene film; plastics materials & resins; canvas & related products; household furnishings; solar cells

(G-354)
NORTH E RGGERS ERECTORS NY INC
178 Clizbe Ave (12010-2935)
PHONE..............................518 842-6377
Scott Egan, *President*
Michael Egan, *Vice Pres*
Charles Egan, *Treasurer*
Thomas Egan, *Admin Sec*
EMP: 40
SQ FT: 6,000
SALES (est): 7.7MM **Privately Held**
SIC: 3441 Fabricated structural metal

(G-355)
NORTHEASTERN WATER JET INC
4 Willow St (12010-4219)
PHONE..............................518 843-4988
Lenny Laporte, *President*
Andre Laporte, *Vice Pres*
EMP: 18
SQ FT: 176,000
SALES (est): 3.5MM **Privately Held**
WEB: www.newj.com
SIC: 3599 Machine shop, jobbing & repair

(G-356)
NOTEWORTHY INDUSTRIES INC
Also Called: Noteworthy Company, The
336 Forest Ave (12010-2723)
P.O. Box 490 (12010-0490)
PHONE..............................518 842-2662
Anthony Constantino, *President*
Elsa Buseck, *President*
Tim Gralewski, *General Mgr*
John P Colangelo, *Vice Pres*
Nicholas Costantino, *Vice Pres*
▲ **EMP:** 148 **EST:** 1971
SQ FT: 400,000
SALES (est): 18MM **Privately Held**
WEB: www.noteworthy.com
SIC: 2673 2679 Plastic bags: made from purchased materials; paper products, converted

(G-357)
POWER AND COMPOSITE TECH LLC
Also Called: P C T
200 Wallins Corners Rd (12010-1819)
PHONE..............................518 843-6825
Robert Mylott, *CEO*
Chun-Bin Yap, *General Mgr*
Phil Day, *Managing Dir*
Charlie Athanasia, *Vice Pres*
Joseph Day, *Vice Pres*
▲ **EMP:** 90
SQ FT: 55,000
SALES (est): 23.8MM **Privately Held*
WEB: www.pactinc.com
SIC: 3621 Electric motor & generator parts
PA: Thayer Capital Partners, L.P.
    1455 Penn Ave Nw Ste 350
    Washington DC 20004

(G-358)
RAYCO OF SCHENECTADY INC
4 Sam Stratton Rd (12010)
PHONE..............................518 212-5113
Ed Legere, *President*
Michael Kilgallen, *Managing Prtnr*
Janis Legere, *Vice Pres*
EMP: 13
SQ FT: 6,000
SALES (est): 1.8MM **Privately Held**
SIC: 3471 Electroplating of metals or formed products; polishing, metals or formed products

(G-359)
SARATOGA HORSEWORKS LTD
57 Edson St (12010-5238)
P.O. Box 549 (12010-0549)
PHONE..............................518 843-6756
Michael Libertucci, *President*
Adrienne Libertucci, *Treasurer*
EMP: 25
SQ FT: 15,000
SALES (est): 1.2MM **Privately Held**
WEB: www.horseworks.com
SIC: 2399 Horse & pet accessories, textile

(G-360)
TONCHE TIMBER LLC
3959 State Highway 30 (12010-6509)
PHONE..............................845 389-3489
Ronald Cohen, *Owner*
EMP: 6 **EST:** 2007
SALES (est): 398.1K **Privately Held**
SIC: 2411 Timber, cut at logging camp

(G-361)
TRI-VILLAGE PUBLISHERS INC
Also Called: Recorder, The
1 Venner Rd (12010-5617)
PHONE..............................518 843-1100
Sidney Lafavour, *Publisher*
Kevin Mc Clary, *Publisher*
Nicole Antonucci, *Editor*
Nicole Bronk, *District Mgr*
Charles Tobey, *Controller*
EMP: 60
SALES (est): 2.7MM **Privately Held**
WEB: www.recordernews.com
SIC: 2711 Newspapers: publishing only, not printed on site

(G-362)
UNIVERSAL CUSTOM MILLWORK INC
3 Sam Stratton Rd (12010-5243)
PHONE..............................518 330-6622
Stephen R Chapman, *Ch of Bd*
Jeffrey W Pahl, *Vice Pres*
EMP: 60
SQ FT: 50,000
SALES (est): 6.2MM **Privately Held**
WEB: www.ucmillwork.com
SIC: 2431 Millwork

(G-363)
VIDA-BLEND LLC
1430 State Highway 5s (12010-8184)
PHONE..............................518 627-4138
Freddy Luna, *Mng Member*
Edward Pragliabento, *Mng Member*
Michael Pragliabento, *Mng Member*
EMP: 20 **EST:** 2013
SALES (est): 3.4MM **Privately Held**
SIC: 2834 Vitamin, nutrient & hematinic preparations for human use

(G-364)
WILLIAM J KLINE & SON INC (PA)
Also Called: Hamilton County News
1 Venner Rd (12010-5617)
PHONE..............................518 843-1100
Sidney Lefavour, *President*
EMP: 90 **EST:** 1878
SQ FT: 30,000
SALES (est): 4.3MM **Privately Held**
SIC: 2711 2752 Newspapers: publishing only, not printed on site; commercial printing, lithographic

Ancram
Columbia County

(G-365)
SCHWEITZER-MAUDUIT INTL INC
2424 Route 82 (12502-5414)
P.O. Box 10 (12502-0010)
PHONE..............................518 329-4222
Gary Kennedy, *Manager*
EMP: 135 **Publicly Held**
SIC: 2141 2111 2621 Tobacco stemming & redrying; cigarettes; cigarette paper
PA: Schweitzer-Mauduit International, Inc.
    100 N Point Ctr E Ste 600
    Alpharetta GA 30022

Angelica
Allegany County

(G-366)
ANGELICA FOREST PRODUCTS INC
54 Closser Ave (14709-8746)
P.O. Box 685 (14709-0685)
PHONE..............................585 466-3205
David Chamberlain, *Principal*
EMP: 9 **EST:** 2011
SALES (est): 1MM **Privately Held**
SIC: 2421 Sawmills & planing mills, general

(G-367)
ANGELICA SPRING COMPANY INC
99 West Ave (14709-8713)
P.O. Box 681 (14709-0681)
PHONE..............................585 466-7892
William Geoppner, *President*
EMP: 17
SQ FT: 4,400
SALES (est): 3.2MM **Privately Held**
WEB: www.angelicaspringcompany.com
SIC: 3493 3496 Coiled flat springs; flat springs, sheet or strip stock; miscellaneous fabricated wire products

Angola
Erie County

(G-368)
ANGOLA PENNY SAVER INC
19 Center St (14006-1305)
PHONE..............................716 549-1164
James Austin, *Publisher*
Kristen Biondi, *Consultant*
EMP: 12 **EST:** 1922
SQ FT: 5,950
SALES (est): 909.2K **Privately Held**
SIC: 2711 Newspapers, publishing & printing

(G-369)
GOYA FOODS INC
Also Called: Goya Foods Great Lakes
200 S Main St (14006-1534)
P.O. Box 152 (14006-0152)
PHONE..............................716 549-0076
Robert J Drago Sr, *Principal*
Greg Drago, *Opers Staff*
Elizabeth Rudyk, *QC Mgr*
EMP: 75
SALES (corp-wide): 1B **Privately Held**
SIC: 2033 2032 2035 2034 Canned fruits & specialties; canned specialties; pickles, sauces & salad dressings; dehydrated fruits, vegetables, soups; poultry slaughtering & processing
PA: Goya Foods, Inc.
    350 County Rd
    Jersey City NJ 07307
    201 348-4900

(G-370)
POLYTEX INC
1305 Eden Evans Center Rd (14006-8839)
PHONE..............................716 549-5100
Jacob H Ilioha, *President*
▲ **EMP:** 100
SQ FT: 8,000
SALES (est): 5.9MM **Privately Held**
SIC: 2221 Fiberglass fabrics

(G-371)
TX RX SYSTEMS INC
8625 Industrial Pkwy (14006-9692)
PHONE..............................716 549-4700
David J Hessler, *Ch of Bd*
Anthony Delgobbo, *Plant Mgr*
Wayne Newman, *Plant Mgr*
James Levesque, *Engineer*
Ken Pokigo, *Engineer*
▲ **EMP:** 115 **EST:** 1976
SQ FT: 31,000
SALES (est): 22.5MM **Privately Held**
WEB: www.txrx.com
SIC: 3669 Intercommunication systems, electric
PA: Bird Technologies Group Inc.
    30303 Aurora Rd
    Solon OH 44139

Apalachin
Tioga County

(G-372)
TAYLOR BROTHERS INC
6 Jacobs Rd (13732-2542)
P.O. Box 248 (13732-0248)
PHONE..............................607 625-2828
Douglas Weist, *President*
EMP: 12
SQ FT: 10,000
SALES: 600K **Privately Held**
SIC: 2448 Pallets, wood; skids, wood

Aquebogue
Suffolk County

(G-373)
ALTAIRE PHARMACEUTICALS INC
311 West Ln (11931)
P.O. Box 849 (11931-0849)
PHONE.................................631 722-5988
Teresa Sawaya, *President*
Al Sawaya, *President*
Joseph Sawaya, *Vice Pres*
▲ **EMP:** 130
SALES (est): 26.8MM **Privately Held**
SIC: 2834 Pharmaceutical preparations

(G-374)
CRESCENT DUCK FARM INC
10 Edgar Ave (11931)
P.O. Box 500 (11931-0500)
PHONE.................................631 722-8700
Douglas H Corwin, *President*
Douglas Corwin, *Vice Pres*
Jeffrey Corwin, *Treasurer*
Blake Corwin, *Manager*
Janet Wedel, *Admin Sec*
▼ **EMP:** 50 EST: 1959
SQ FT: 6,000
SALES (est): 7.9MM **Privately Held**
SIC: 2015 4222 2011 Ducks, processed: fresh; refrigerated warehousing & storage; meat packing plants

(G-375)
PAUMANOK VINEYARDS LTD
1074 Main Rd Rte 25 (11931)
P.O. Box 741 (11931-0741)
PHONE.................................631 722-8800
Charles Massoud, *President*
Ursula Massoud, *Vice Pres*
Nabeel Massoud, *Human Res Mgr*
Salim Massoud, *Manager*
John Perry, *Manager*
▲ **EMP:** 20
SQ FT: 9,000
SALES (est): 2.8MM **Privately Held**
WEB: www.paumanok.com
SIC: 2084 Wines; wine cellars, bonded: engaged in blending wines

Arcade
Wyoming County

(G-376)
AMERICAN PRECISION INDS INC
Surface Mounted Devices Div
95 North St (14009-9196)
P.O. Box 38 (14009-0038)
PHONE.................................585 496-5755
Kevin Heffler, *Branch Mgr*
EMP: 100
SALES (corp-wide): 6.6B **Publicly Held**
WEB: www.apischmidtbretten.com
SIC: 3677 Coil windings, electronic; inductors, electronic
HQ: American Precision Industries Inc.
45 Hazelwood Dr
Amherst NY 14228
716 691-9100

(G-377)
API HEAT TRANSFER INC
A P I Airtech Division
91 North St (14009-9196)
PHONE.................................585 496-5755
Jack Bellomo, *President*
Jason Williams, *Buyer*
Debbie Dixon, *Human Resources*
Karl Anderson, *Branch Mgr*
EMP: 200
SQ FT: 85,000
SALES (corp-wide): 492.5MM **Privately Held**
WEB: www.apiheattransfer.com
SIC: 3443 Heat exchangers: coolers (after, inter), condensers, etc.
HQ: Api Heat Transfer Inc.
2777 Walden Ave Ste 1
Buffalo NY 14225
716 684-6700

(G-378)
BATAVIA ENCLOSURES INC
636 Main St (14009-1037)
PHONE.................................585 344-1797
Toll Free:.................................877 -
Leonard Roberto, *President*
EMP: 6
SQ FT: 10,000
SALES (est): 1MM **Privately Held**
WEB: www.bataviaenclosures.com
SIC: 3444 Mfg Sheet Metalwork

(G-379)
BLISS MACHINE INC
260 North St (14009-1206)
P.O. Box 145 (14009-0145)
PHONE.................................585 492-5128
William Kanner, *President*
Randy Kanner, *Vice Pres*
EMP: 18
SQ FT: 9,500
SALES (est): 3.6MM **Privately Held**
WEB: www.blissmachine.net
SIC: 3599 Machine shop, jobbing & repair

(G-380)
BRAUEN CONSTRUTION
1087 Chaffee Rd (14009-9779)
PHONE.................................585 492-0042
Floyd Brauen, *President*
EMP: 7 EST: 1983
SQ FT: 16,000
SALES (est): 1.1MM **Privately Held**
WEB: www.brauenmillwork.com
SIC: 2431 Woodwork, interior & ornamental

(G-381)
DEVIN MFG INC
40 Edward St (14009-1012)
P.O. Box 97 (14009-0097)
PHONE.................................585 496-5770
William A Devin, *President*
Anne Devin, *Vice Pres*
Erica Bigos, *Admin Sec*
▼ **EMP:** 17 EST: 1959
SQ FT: 17,400
SALES (est): 3.1MM **Privately Held**
WEB: www.devinmfg.com
SIC: 3599 3537 3494 3949 Machine shop, jobbing & repair; engine stands & racks, metal; valves & pipe fittings; target shooting equipment; targets, archery & rifle shooting

(G-382)
EMKAY TRADING CORP
Also Called: Emkay Bordeaux
58 Church St (14009-1117)
P.O. Box 174 (14009-0174)
PHONE.................................585 492-3800
Cathy Golman, *Branch Mgr*
EMP: 30
SQ FT: 51,500
SALES (corp-wide): 1.9MM **Privately Held**
WEB: www.emkaytrading.org
SIC: 2022 2026 Cheese, natural & processed; cream, sweet
PA: Emkay Trading Corp
250 Clearbrook Rd Ste 127
Elmsford NY 10523
914 592-9000

(G-383)
GM PALMER INC
51 Edward St (14009-1012)
P.O. Box 343 (14009-0343)
PHONE.................................585 492-2990
Greg Palmer, *President*
Mary Palmer, *Corp Secy*
◆ **EMP:** 15
SQ FT: 47,500
SALES (est): 10MM **Privately Held**
SIC: 2421 Fuelwood, from mill waste

(G-384)
GOWANDA - BTI LLC
Also Called: Chiptek
7426a Tanner Pkwy (14009-9758)
PHONE.................................716 492-4081
Stephen Sodaro, *Engineer*
Don McElheny,
EMP: 66
SALES: 7.6MM **Privately Held**
SIC: 3677 Electronic coils, transformers & other inductors

(G-385)
J A YANSICK LUMBER CO INC
16 Rule Dr (14009-1019)
PHONE.................................585 492-4312
James Yansick, *President*
EMP: 30 EST: 1966
SQ FT: 1,979
SALES (est): 3.1MM **Privately Held**
SIC: 2421 2426 Lumber: rough, sawed or planed; hardwood dimension & flooring mills

(G-386)
MAPLE GROVE CORP
Also Called: Maple Grove and Enterprises
7075 Route 98 (14009-9756)
P.O. Box 156 (14009-0156)
PHONE.................................585 492-5286
Phillip M Hobin, *Ch of Bd*
Rachel Bookmiller, *COO*
Ted Hobin Jr, *Vice Pres*
Jen Hobin, *CFO*
Michelle Hobin, *Admin Sec*
EMP: 25
SQ FT: 1,200
SALES (est): 4.9MM **Privately Held**
SIC: 7692 7213 Welding repair; coat supply

(G-387)
NEIGHBOR TO NEIGHBOR NEWS INC
Also Called: Arcade Herald
223 Main St (14009-1209)
PHONE.................................585 492-2525
Grant Hamilton, *President*
EMP: 9
SQ FT: 1,200
SALES (est): 360K **Privately Held**
SIC: 2711 Newspapers: publishing only, not printed on site

(G-388)
NEW EAGLE SILO CORP
7648 Hurdville Rd (14009-1021)
PHONE.................................585 492-1300
Leonard Johnson, *President*
EMP: 8 EST: 1967
SQ FT: 6,000
SALES: 400K **Privately Held**
SIC: 3531 Cement silos (batch plant)

(G-389)
STEEL & OBRIEN MFG INC
7869 Route 98 (14009-9601)
PHONE.................................585 492-5800
Bryan Wells, *President*
Pete Beyette, *Vice Pres*
Michael Lovelace, *Vice Pres*
Scott Wells, *Vice Pres*
Tim Bainbridge, *Project Mgr*
▲ **EMP:** 72
SQ FT: 55,000
SALES (est): 15.6MM **Privately Held**
WEB: www.steelobrien.com
SIC: 3494 3492 Valves & pipe fittings; fluid power valves & hose fittings

(G-390)
TPI ARCADE INC
7888 Route 98 (14009-9601)
PHONE.................................585 492-0122
Jack Pohlman, *Ch of Bd*
Gerald Byrne, *Chairman*
EMP: 75
SALES (est): 15.4MM
SALES (corp-wide): 501.5MM **Privately Held**
WEB: www.tpicast.com
SIC: 3363 Aluminum die-castings
PA: Ligon Industries, Llc
1927 1st Ave N Ste 500
Birmingham AL 35203
205 322-3302

(G-391)
WHATS NEXT MANUFACTURING INC
4 Rule Dr (14009-1019)
PHONE.................................585 492-1014
Brad Countryman, *President*
EMP: 20
SQ FT: 20,000
SALES (est): 2MM **Privately Held**
SIC: 3944 Games, toys & children's vehicles

Ardsley
Westchester County

(G-392)
ACORDA THERAPEUTICS INC (PA)
420 Saw Mill River Rd (10502-2605)
PHONE.................................914 347-4300
Ron Cohen, *President*
Heather O'Neil, *General Mgr*
David Lawrence, *Principal*
Danielle Leonis, *Business Mgr*
Juanita Brown, *Project Mgr*
▲ **EMP:** 234
SQ FT: 138,000
SALES: 588.2MM **Publicly Held**
WEB: www.acorda.com
SIC: 2834 8731 2836 Drugs acting on the central nervous system & sense organs; biotechnical research, commercial; biological products, except diagnostic

(G-393)
ADVANCED COMM SOLUTIONS
38 Ridge Rd (10502-2226)
PHONE.................................914 693-5076
EMP: 5
SALES: 900K **Privately Held**
SIC: 3663 Mfg Radio/Tv Communication Equipment

(G-394)
BIOTIE THERAPIES INC
420 Saw Mill River Rd (10502-2605)
PHONE.................................650 244-4850
Timo Veromaa, *CEO*
Ian Massey, *President*
Mehdi Paborji, *COO*
Christopher Kenney, *Vice Pres*
Fred Kerwood, *Vice Pres*
EMP: 12
SQ FT: 5,500
SALES (est): 2.6MM **Publicly Held**
WEB: www.synosia.com
SIC: 2834 Druggists' preparations (pharmaceuticals); tranquilizers or mental drug preparations
PA: Acorda Therapeutics, Inc.
420 Saw Mill River Rd
Ardsley NY 10502

(G-395)
IRTRONICS INSTRUMENTS INC
132 Forest Blvd (10502-1031)
PHONE.................................914 693-6291
John Jenkofsky, *President*
EMP: 10
SQ FT: 1,200
SALES: 870K **Privately Held**
SIC: 3822 3355 3672 Temperature sensors for motor windings; aluminum wire & cable; printed circuit boards

(G-396)
SUPRESTA US LLC (DH)
420 Saw Mill River Rd (10502-2605)
PHONE.................................914 674-9434
Peggy Viehweger, *CEO*
Thomas Emignanelli, *CFO*
▼ **EMP:** 21
SALES (est): 19.9MM **Privately Held**
SIC: 2899 Fire retardant chemicals
HQ: Perimeter Solutions Lp
373 Marshall Ave
Saint Louis MO 63119
314 983-7500

Argyle
Washington County

(G-397)
ADIRONDACK PLAS & RECYCL INC (PA)
453 County Route 45 (12809-3514)
PHONE.................................518 746-9212

GEOGRAPHIC SECTION

Astoria - Queens County (G-420)

John Aspland, *CEO*
Johr S Clair, *Manager*
◆ **EMP:** 21
SQ FT: 125,000
SALES (est): 5.2MM **Privately Held**
SIC: 3089 3559 Plastic processing; recycling machinery

(G-398)
ADIRONDACK SCENIC INC
Also Called: Adirondack Studios
439 County Route 45 Ste 1 (12809-3514)
PHONE.................................518 638-8000
David Thomas Lloyd, *CEO*
Louis Allen, *Vice Pres*
Stephen Detmer, *Project Mgr*
Ryan McLaughlin, *Project Mgr*
Dean Schermerhorn, *Project Mgr*
▲ **EMP:** 100
SQ FT: 128,000
SALES: 180MM **Privately Held**
WEB: www.adirondackscenic.com
SIC: 2599 Factory furniture & fixtures

Arkport
Steuben County

(G-399)
HP HOOD LLC
25 Hurlbut St (14807-9706)
P.O. Box 474 (14807-0474)
PHONE.................................607 295-8134
Freeman Covert, *Manager*
EMP: 100
SQ FT: 5,184
SALES (corp-wide): 2.1B **Privately Held**
WEB: www.hphood.com
SIC: 2026 2099 2022 Cottage cheese; cream, sour; yogurt; food preparations; cheese, natural & processed
PA: Hp Hood Llc
6 Kimball Ln Ste 400
Lynnfield MA 01940
617 887-8441

Arkville
Delaware County

(G-400)
CATSKILL MOUNTAIN PUBLISHING
Also Called: Catskill Mountain News
43414 State Hwy 28 (12406)
PHONE.................................845 586-2601
Richard D Sanford, *President*
Laurie Sanford, *Vice Pres*
Linda Schebesta, *Manager*
EMP: 11 **EST:** 1903
SALES (est): 845.7K **Privately Held**
WEB: www.catskillmountainnews.com
SIC: 2711 Newspapers: publishing only, not printed on site

Armonk
Westchester County

(G-401)
ARUMAI TECHNOLOGIES INC (PA)
175 King St (10504-1606)
PHONE.................................914 217-0038
P Stephen Lamont, *CEO*
David J Colter, *CTO*
Gregory B Thagard, *CTO*
EMP: 12
SALES (est): 652.1K **Privately Held**
SIC: 7372 Prepackaged software

(G-402)
COLUMBIA CABINETS LLC (PA)
20 Maple Ave Ste F (10504-1859)
PHONE.................................212 972-5550
Evan H Levey, *CEO*
EMP: 6
SALES (est): 1.1MM **Privately Held**
SIC: 2434 Wood kitchen cabinets

(G-403)
IBM WORLD TRADE CORPORATION (HQ)
1 New Orchard Rd Ste 1 # 1 (10504-1722)
PHONE.................................914 765-1900
Virginia M Rometty, *CEO*
Asif Samad, *Partner*
John P Gianukakis, *Principal*
James W Boyken, *Vice Pres*
David L Johnson, *Vice Pres*
EMP: 8
SQ FT: 417,000
SALES (est): 24.5B
SALES (corp-wide): 79.1B **Publicly Held**
WEB: www.Inn.com
SIC: 3577 3571 7377 7379 Computer peripheral equipment; electronic computers; computer rental & leasing; computer related maintenance services
PA: International Business Machines Corporation
1 New Orchard Rd Ste 1 # 1
Armonk NY 10504
914 499-1900

(G-404)
INTERNATIONAL BUS MCHS CORP
Also Called: IBM
1 New Orchard Rd Ste 1 # 1 (10504-1722)
PHONE.................................914 345-5219
Sid Singh, *Managing Dir*
Stephen Ward, *Senior VP*
James J Kelly, *Engineer*
Tim Russell, *Engineer*
Raymond Wagner, *Engineer*
EMP: 21
SALES (corp-wide): 79.1B **Publicly Held**
SIC: 7372 Prepackaged software
PA: International Business Machines Corporation
1 New Orchard Rd Ste 1 # 1
Armonk NY 10504
914 499-1900

(G-405)
INTERNATIONAL BUS MCHS CORP
Also Called: IBM
20 Old Post Rd (10504-1314)
PHONE.................................914 499-2000
David Leftwich, *General Mgr*
Jim Gregory, *Vice Pres*
Nancy Lewis, *Manager*
Scott Whelehan, *Director*
EMP: 50
SALES (corp-wide): 79.1B **Publicly Held**
WEB: www.ibm.com
SIC: 7372 Prepackaged software
PA: International Business Machines Corporation
1 New Orchard Rd Ste 1 # 1
Armonk NY 10504
914 499-1900

(G-406)
JINGLEBELL INC
Also Called: JINGLENOG DBA
190 Byram Lake Rd (10504-1509)
PHONE.................................914 219-5395
Melissa Byrne, *President*
▲ **EMP:** 6 **EST:** 2008
SALES: 200K **Privately Held**
SIC: 3229 3231 7389 Christmas tree ornaments, from glass produced on-site; Christmas tree ornaments: made from purchased glass; design services

(G-407)
MAIN STREET CONNECT LLC
Also Called: Daily Voice
200 Business Park Dr # 209 (10504-1719)
PHONE.................................203 803-4110
John Haffey, *Editor*
Jeanne Muchnick, *Editor*
Elizabeth Rivers, *Accounts Mgr*
Kathryn Desilva, *Sales Staff*
Carll Tucker,
EMP: 10
SALES (est): 684.8K **Privately Held**
SIC: 2711 Newspapers, publishing & printing

(G-408)
PRODUCTION RESOURCE GROUP LLC (PA)
Also Called: Prg Integrated Solutions
200 Business Park Dr # 109 (10504-1751)
PHONE.................................877 774-7088
Jeremiah Harris, *CEO*
Matthew Carson, *CEO*
Stephan Paridaen, *President*
John Hovis, *COO*
Robert Manners, *Exec VP*
▲ **EMP:** 100
SQ FT: 140,000
SALES (est): 314.2MM **Privately Held**
WEB: www.prg.com
SIC: 3999 7922 Theatrical scenery; equipment rental, theatrical; lighting, theatrical

(G-409)
SUMMIT COMMUNICATIONS
28 Half Mile Rd (10504-1306)
PHONE.................................914 273-5504
Russell Dekker, *Owner*
EMP: 6
SALES (est): 283.9K **Privately Held**
SIC: 2741 Miscellaneous publishing

(G-410)
SURGICAL DESIGN CORP
Also Called: S D C
3 Macdonald Ave (10504-1935)
PHONE.................................914 273-2445
William Banko MD, *President*
Stanislava Banko, *Corp Secy*
Clara Santos, *Purchasing*
EMP: 15
SQ FT: 10,000
SALES (est): 2.1MM **Privately Held**
WEB: www.surgical.com
SIC: 3841 3851 3827 Surgical instruments & apparatus; instruments, microsurgical: except electromedical; ophthalmic goods; optical instruments & lenses

(G-411)
TRINITY PACKAGING CORPORATION (HQ)
357 Main St (10504-1717)
PHONE.................................914 273-4111
John H Freund, *CEO*
Peter Freund, *President*
Bob Rotolo, *CFO*
▲ **EMP:** 18
SQ FT: 9,000
SALES (est): 161.5MM
SALES (corp-wide): 224MM **Privately Held**
SIC: 2673 2679 Plastic bags: made from purchased materials; paper products, converted
PA: Proampac Pg Borrower Llc
12025 Tricon Rd
Cincinnati OH 45246
513 671-1777

(G-412)
VISANT SECONDARY HOLDINGS CORP (DH)
357 Main St (10504-1808)
PHONE.................................914 595-8200
Paul B Carousso, *Vice Pres*
EMP: 31
SALES (est): 831.7MM
SALES (corp-wide): 14.7B **Publicly Held**
SIC: 2741 Yearbooks: publishing & printing
HQ: Visant Holding Corp.
3601 Minnesota Dr Ste 400
Minneapolis MN 55435
914 595-8200

Arverne
Queens County

(G-413)
ARMOUR BEARER GROUP INC
Also Called: 2fish 5loaves Comminty Pantry
424 Beach 65th St (11692-1440)
PHONE.................................646 812-4487
Clinton Nixon, *President*
EMP: 5 **EST:** 2014
SALES (est): 234.8K **Privately Held**
SIC: 2099 Food preparations

(G-414)
DARRELL MITCHELL
Also Called: D.A.M. Construction, Company
704 Beach 67th St (11692-1314)
PHONE.................................646 659-7075
Darrell Mitchell, *Owner*
EMP: 5
SALES (est): 163.7K **Privately Held**
SIC: 1389 1799 8741 8742 Construction, repair & dismantling services; construction site cleanup; construction management; construction project management consultant

Ashville
Chautauqua County

(G-415)
CASTELLI AMERICA LLC
5151 Fairbanks Rd (14710-9796)
PHONE.................................716 782-2101
Jay Arcata, *Branch Mgr*
EMP: 80
SALES (corp-wide): 534MM **Privately Held**
SIC: 2022 Cheese, natural & processed
HQ: Castelli America, Llc
277 Fairfield Rd Ste 208
Fairfield NJ 07004
973 227-0002

(G-416)
CHAUTAUQUA MACHINE SPC LLC
1880 Open Meadows Rd (14710-9793)
PHONE.................................716 782-3276
Dennis Furlow,
EMP: 10
SQ FT: 8,000
SALES (est): 750K **Privately Held**
SIC: 3441 7692 Fabricated structural metal; automotive welding

(G-417)
CHAUTQUA PRCSION MACHINING INC
1287 Hunt Rd (14710-9612)
PHONE.................................716 763-3752
Jeff Christie, *President*
Eric Hewitt, *Facilities Mgr*
Craig Lassinger, *Engineer*
Mary Ann Attard, *Administration*
EMP: 12
SALES (est): 1.7MM **Privately Held**
SIC: 3599 Machine shop, jobbing & repair

(G-418)
THAYER TOOL & DIE INC
1718 Blckvlle Watts Flts (14710-9538)
PHONE.................................716 782-4841
John Thayer, *President*
EMP: 15
SQ FT: 5,000
SALES: 577.6K **Privately Held**
SIC: 3544 Special dies & tools

Astoria
Queens County

(G-419)
4 OVER 4COM INC
1941 46th St (11105-1101)
PHONE.................................718 932-2700
Taso Panagiotopoulos, *President*
Elizabeth Salazar, *Prdtn Mgr*
Nancy Savescu, *Cust Mgr*
Hary Ayala, *CTO*
Chris Nava, *Executive Asst*
EMP: 6
SALES (est): 801.9K **Privately Held**
SIC: 2759 Post cards, picture: printing

(G-420)
AKI CABINETS INC
2636 2nd St (11102-4130)
PHONE.................................718 721-2541
Mujo Todic, *Ch of Bd*
Gloria Henderson, *Principal*
▲ **EMP:** 22

Astoria - Queens County (G-421)

SALES (est): 2.6MM **Privately Held**
SIC: 2434 Wood kitchen cabinets

(G-421)
ALPS PROVISION CO INC
2270 45th St (11105-1336)
PHONE..............................718 721-4477
Giulio Sottovia, *President*
Leonardo Castorina, *Vice Pres*
Remo Tozzi, *Treasurer*
EMP: 27 **EST:** 1928
SQ FT: 12,500
SALES (est): 4.1MM **Privately Held**
WEB: www.alpsinstyle.com
SIC: 2013 5143 5147 Sausages & other prepared meats; cheese; meats, fresh

(G-422)
D & S SUPPLIES INC
2067 21st St (11105-3507)
PHONE..............................718 721-5256
Paul Melky, *President*
EMP: 17
SALES (est): 1.2MM **Privately Held**
SIC: 3679 Electronic loads & power supplies

(G-423)
D-LITE DONUTS
4519 Broadway (11103-1625)
PHONE..............................718 626-5953
George Kaparakos, *Owner*
EMP: 5
SALES (est): 150K **Privately Held**
SIC: 2051 Doughnuts, except frozen

(G-424)
DF MAVENS INC
2420 49th St (11103-1017)
PHONE..............................347 813-4705
WEI Lo, *President*
Malcolm Stogo, *COO*
EMP: 20 **EST:** 2013
SALES (est): 970K **Privately Held**
SIC: 2024 Ice cream & frozen desserts

(G-425)
ECONOMY PUMP & MOTOR REPR INC
3652 36th St (11106-1304)
PHONE..............................718 433-2600
Elsie Domagala, *President*
EMP: 6
SALES (est): 835.5K **Privately Held**
SIC: 3433 3585 3586 5999 Heating equipment, except electric; heat pumps, electric; compressors for refrigeration & air conditioning equipment; measuring & dispensing pumps; motors, electric

(G-426)
ELECTROTECH SERVICE EQP CORP
2450 46th St (11103-1008)
PHONE..............................718 626-7700
Joseph Amendalara, *CEO*
Robert Strayer, *Sales Mgr*
EMP: 46
SQ FT: 15,000
SALES (est): 19.1MM **Privately Held**
SIC: 3613 5731 Switchgear & switchgear accessories; switchboard apparatus, except instruments; consumer electronic equipment

(G-427)
EMPIRE METAL FINISHING INC
2469 46th St (11103-1007)
PHONE..............................718 545-6700
Michael Vetrone, *President*
Lisa Thorsen, *Vice Pres*
Lisa Vetrone, *Vice Pres*
Gina Aponte, *Technology*
EMP: 30 **EST:** 1922
SQ FT: 5,000
SALES (est): 2.9MM **Privately Held**
SIC: 3471 3499 3449 Gold plating; fire- or burglary-resistive products; miscellaneous metalwork

(G-428)
EXQUISITE GLASS & STONE INC
3117 12th St (11106-4801)
PHONE..............................718 937-9266
Buz Vaultz, *President*
EMP: 5
SQ FT: 900
SALES (est): 500K **Privately Held**
SIC: 3231 Decorated glassware: chipped, engraved, etched, etc.

(G-429)
FAME CONSTRUCTION INC
2388 Brklyn Queens Expy W (11103-1023)
PHONE..............................718 626-1000
Michael Andreou, *President*
EMP: 50
SQ FT: 1,700
SALES (est): 2MM **Privately Held**
SIC: 1389 Construction, repair & dismantling services

(G-430)
HELLAS STONE INC
3344 9th St (11106-4902)
PHONE..............................718 545-4716
Esdavros Cayioulis, *CEO*
▲ **EMP:** 5
SALES (est): 555.7K **Privately Held**
SIC: 2514 Kitchen cabinets: metal

(G-431)
INTER CRAFT CUSTOM FURNITURE
1431 Astoria Blvd (11102-3691)
PHONE..............................718 278-2573
Chipiv Savva, *President*
EMP: 9
SALES (est): 840K **Privately Held**
SIC: 2511 Wood household furniture

(G-432)
KJ ASTORIA GOURMET INC
3720 Broadway (11103-4057)
PHONE..............................718 545-6900
Kwang Hee Lee, *Principal*
EMP: 5
SALES (est): 179.4K **Privately Held**
SIC: 2037 Frozen fruits & vegetables

(G-433)
LEMODE PLUMBING & HEATING
3455 11th St (11106-5011)
PHONE..............................718 545-3336
Angelo Lemodetis, *Owner*
EMP: 30
SALES (est): 4.7MM **Privately Held**
SIC: 3494 Plumbing & heating valves

(G-434)
LENS LAB EXPRESS SOUTHERN BLVD
3097 Steinway St Ste 301 (11103-3820)
PHONE..............................718 626-5184
Jeffery Nesses, *President*
EMP: 7
SALES (est): 925.8K **Privately Held**
SIC: 3851 5048 Ophthalmic goods; ophthalmic goods

(G-435)
MELITA CORP
3330 14th St (11106-4624)
PHONE..............................718 392-7280
Emanuel Darmanin, *Ch of Bd*
Joann Atek, *COO*
Michelle D' Oleivra, *Purchasing*
Michael Cassar, *CFO*
EMP: 201
SQ FT: 44,000
SALES (est): 40.8MM **Privately Held**
SIC: 2051 5411 Bread, cake & related products; grocery stores

(G-436)
MODERN ART FOUNDRY INC
Also Called: Jeffrey Spring Modern Art
1870 41st St (11105-1025)
PHONE..............................718 728-2030
Robert Spring, *President*
Jeffrey Spring, *Vice Pres*
Mary Jo Bursig, *Controller*
▲ **EMP:** 30
SQ FT: 14,000
SALES (est): 5MM **Privately Held**
WEB: www.modernartfoundry.com
SIC: 3366 3446 Castings (except die): bronze; architectural metalwork

(G-437)
NIEBYLSKI BAKERY INC
2364 Steinway St (11105-1913)
PHONE..............................718 721-5152
Anthony Niebylski, *President*
Rose Niebylski, *Vice Pres*
EMP: 7
SALES (est): 500K **Privately Held**
SIC: 2051 5461 Bakery: wholesale or wholesale/retail combined; bakeries

(G-438)
NY PHRMACY COMPOUNDING CTR INC
3715 23rd Ave (11105-1993)
PHONE..............................201 403-5151
Wesam Abdrabouh, *President*
EMP: 5 **EST:** 2014
SALES (est): 549.5K **Privately Held**
SIC: 2834 Pharmaceutical preparations

(G-439)
OMNICARE ANESTHESIA PC (PA)
3636 33rd St Ste 211 (11106-2329)
PHONE..............................718 433-0044
Evans Crevecoeur MD, *Ch of Bd*
Gina Duval, *Principal*
EMP: 23
SALES (est): 4.9MM **Privately Held**
SIC: 3841 Anesthesia apparatus

(G-440)
PILATES DESIGNS LLC
3517 31st St (11106-2320)
PHONE..............................718 721-5929
Silvia Fuster, *Principal*
Sylvia Adamopoulos, *Vice Pres*
EMP: 9
SALES (est): 963.5K **Privately Held**
SIC: 3949 Sporting & athletic goods

(G-441)
RAGO FOUNDATIONS LLC (PA)
1815 27th Ave (11102-3744)
PHONE..............................718 728-8436
Justin Chernoff,
▼ **EMP:** 32 **EST:** 1944
SALES (est): 5.5MM **Privately Held**
WEB: www.ragoshapewear.com
SIC: 2342 Foundation garments, women's

(G-442)
ROSENWACH TANK CO INC (PA)
Also Called: Rosenwach Group, The
4302 Ditmars Blvd (11105-1337)
PHONE..............................212 972-4411
Andrew Rosenwach, *Ch of Bd*
Wallace Rosenwach, *Principal*
George Vassiliades, *Principal*
Artur Freire, *Project Mgr*
Alice Rosenwach, *Treasurer*
EMP: 35 **EST:** 1945
SQ FT: 23,000
SALES (est): 18MM **Privately Held**
SIC: 2449 3443 2531 Tanks, wood: coopered; fabricated plate work (boiler shop); public building & related furniture

(G-443)
SINGLECUT BEERSMITHS LLC
1933 37th St (11105-1118)
PHONE..............................718 606-0788
Daniel Bronson, *General Mgr*
Val Lang, *Finance*
Rich Bueceta, *Mng Member*
EMP: 14 **EST:** 2012
SALES (est): 1.2MM **Privately Held**
SIC: 3556 Brewers' & maltsters' machinery

(G-444)
SITECRAFT INC
Also Called: Rosenwach Tank Co
4302 Ditmars Blvd (11105-1337)
PHONE..............................718 729-4900
Andrew Rosenwach, *President*
EMP: 5
SQ FT: 10,000
SALES (est): 791.4K
SALES (corp-wide): 18MM **Privately Held**
SIC: 2511 Wood lawn & garden furniture

PA: Rosenwach Tank Co. Inc.
4302 Ditmars Blvd
Astoria NY 11105
212 972-4411

(G-445)
SPONGEBATH LLC
2334 28th St Apt 2r (11105-2877)
PHONE..............................917 475-1347
Susette Franklin, *COO*
Matthew Flannery, *Mng Member*
Tod Maitland, *Mng Member*
EMP: 6
SQ FT: 2,200
SALES (est): 2MM **Privately Held**
SIC: 2842 Disinfectants, household or industrial plant

(G-446)
STEINWAY AWNING II LLC (PA)
Also Called: Steinway Awnings
4230 24th St (11101-4608)
PHONE..............................718 729-2965
Cuzana Michalovicoug, *Executive*
EMP: 6
SQ FT: 4,000
SALES (est): 300K **Privately Held**
SIC: 2394 5999 Awnings, fabric: made from purchased materials; canopies, fabric: made from purchased materials; awnings

(G-447)
VSHIP CO
3636 33rd St Ste 207 (11106-2329)
PHONE..............................718 706-8566
Vindu Koil, *President*
Ali Siddiqui, *Manager*
◆ **EMP:** 12 **EST:** 2000
SALES (est): 1.1MM **Privately Held**
SIC: 3443 Containers, shipping (bombs, etc.): metal plate

(G-448)
WAINLAND INC
2460 47th St (11103-1010)
PHONE..............................718 626-2233
Donald Wainland, *President*
Mark Wainland, *Vice Pres*
Neil Wainland, *Vice Pres*
Amel Mustajbasic, *Purch Mgr*
Martha Villacis, *Office Mgr*
▲ **EMP:** 45
SALES (est): 8.9MM **Privately Held**
WEB: www.wainlands.com
SIC: 3645 3444 Residential lighting fixtures; sheet metalwork

(G-449)
WHITE COFFEE CORP
1835 38th St (11105-1076)
PHONE..............................718 204-7900
Carole White, *Ch of Bd*
Al Gaviria, *President*
Jonathan White, *Exec VP*
Greg White, *Vice Pres*
Gregory White, *Vice Pres*
▲ **EMP:** 85 **EST:** 1939
SALES (est): 32.9MM **Privately Held**
SIC: 2095 5149 Coffee roasting (except by wholesale grocers); tea

(G-450)
WLF FOUNDERS CORPORATION
Also Called: Water Lilies
4510 19th Ave (11105-1034)
PHONE..............................718 777-8899
Ginbin Chang, *President*
Chan Chin LI, *Chairman*
Tina Lee, *Purch Mgr*
Gary Cheung, *Natl Sales Mgr*
Peter Lee, *Info Tech Mgr*
▲ **EMP:** 100
SQ FT: 48,000
SALES (est): 18.3MM **Privately Held**
WEB: www.waterliliesfood.com
SIC: 2038 Frozen specialties

Athens
Greene County

(G-451)
NORTHEAST TREATERS INC
796 Schoharie Tpke (12015-4306)
PHONE.................................518 945-2660
Frank Crowe, *Manager*
EMP: 25
SALES (corp-wide): 17MM **Privately Held**
WEB: www.netreaters.com
SIC: 2491 Wood preserving
PA: Northeast Treaters, Inc.
   201 Springfield Rd
   Belchertown MA 01007
   413 323-7811

(G-452)
NORTHEAST TREATERS NY LLC
796 Schoharie Tpke (12015-4306)
PHONE.................................518 945-2660
David A Reed, *Mng Member*
Douglas C Elder,
Charles Geiger,
Henry G Page Jr,
Richard White,
EMP: 20
SQ FT: 884
SALES (est): 2.4MM **Privately Held**
WEB: www.otda.state.ny.us
SIC: 2491 Structural lumber & timber, treated wood

(G-453)
PECKHAM INDUSTRIES INC
Uninn St (12015)
PHONE.................................518 945-1120
John R Peckham, *Branch Mgr*
EMP: 5
SALES (corp-wide): 200.6MM **Privately Held**
SIC: 2951 Asphalt paving mixtures & blocks
PA: Peckham Industries, Inc.
   20 Haarlem Ave Ste 200
   White Plains NY 10603
   914 949-2000

(G-454)
PECKHAM MATERIALS CORP
2 Union St Ext (12015-1298)
PHONE.................................518 945-1120
Chris Zeh, *Opers Mgr*
Mark Libruk, *Terminal Mgr*
Joe Widermuth, *Manager*
Art Coe, *Manager*
EMP: 20
SQ FT: 242
SALES (corp-wide): 200.6MM **Privately Held**
SIC: 2951 Asphalt paving mixtures & blocks
HQ: Peckham Materials Corp
   20 Haarlem Ave Ste 200
   White Plains NY 10603
   914 686-2045

Atlantic Beach
Nassau County

(G-455)
ANCHOR COMMERCE TRADING CORP
53 Dutchess Blvd (11509-1223)
P.O. Box 238 (11509-0238)
PHONE.................................516 881-3485
Meryl P Benin, *President*
EMP: 6 **EST:** 1976
SALES (est): 266.2K **Privately Held**
SIC: 3714 3533 2819 3823 Motor vehicle parts & accessories; oil field machinery & equipment; industrial inorganic chemicals; computer interface equipment for industrial process control

(G-456)
HORIZON APPAREL MFG INC
115 Bayside Dr (11509-1608)
PHONE.................................516 361-4878
Mark Hassin, *President*
Bonnie Hassin, *Vice Pres*
▲ **EMP:** 5
SQ FT: 800
SALES: 25MM **Privately Held**
SIC: 2211 Apparel & outerwear fabrics, cotton

(G-457)
SMALL BUSINESS ADVISORS INC
2005 Park St (11509-1235)
PHONE.................................516 374-1387
Joseph Gelb, *President*
Barbara Goetz Gelb, *Shareholder*
EMP: 10
SALES (est): 465.8K **Privately Held**
SIC: 2721 8721 Periodicals; accounting, auditing & bookkeeping

Attica
Wyoming County

(G-458)
ATTICA MILLWORK INC
71 Market St (14011-1023)
P.O. Box 118 (14011-0118)
PHONE.................................585 591-2333
Kevin Demars, *President*
Justin Papucci, *Vice Pres*
Thomas Wackenheim, *Shareholder*
▲ **EMP:** 19 **EST:** 1945
SQ FT: 65,000
SALES (est): 2.4MM **Privately Held**
WEB: www.atticamillwork.com
SIC: 2431 Millwork

(G-459)
ATTICA PACKAGE COMPANY INC
45 Windsor St (14011-1208)
P.O. Box 295 (14011-0295)
PHONE.................................585 591-0510
Douglas W Domes, *President*
EMP: 10 **EST:** 1917
SQ FT: 16,000
SALES (est): 1.4MM **Privately Held**
SIC: 2411 5199 5211 Logging; sawdust; millwork & lumber

(G-460)
HLW ACRES LLC
Also Called: Hlw Acres Poultry Processing
1727 Exchange Street Rd (14011-9627)
PHONE.................................585 591-0795
Hermann Weber, *Owner*
EMP: 9
SALES (est): 548.4K **Privately Held**
SIC: 2015 Poultry slaughtering & processing

(G-461)
PRECISION FABRICATION LLC
40 S Pearl St (14011-1207)
PHONE.................................585 591-3449
Donald McCulloch, *Owner*
EMP: 5
SALES: 530K **Privately Held**
SIC: 3444 3448 Sheet metalwork; prefabricated metal components

Auburn
Cayuga County

(G-462)
4M PRECISION INDUSTRIES INC
4000 Technology Park Blvd (13021-9030)
PHONE.................................315 252-8415
Margaret Morin, *President*
Megan Byrne, *Sales Staff*
Daniel Morin, *Executive*
Stephen C Morin, *Shareholder*
Edith Carroll Morin, *Admin Sec*
EMP: 44 **EST:** 1968
SQ FT: 55,000
SALES (est): 10.6MM **Privately Held**
WEB: www.4mprecision.com
SIC: 3469 Stamping metal for the trade

(G-463)
AUBURN CUSTOM MILLWORK INC
Also Called: SLC
4022 Technology Park Blvd (13021-9014)
PHONE.................................315 253-3843
Christopher Colella, *President*
EMP: 8
SALES (est): 1.2MM **Privately Held**
SIC: 2431 2541 Millwork; cabinets, lockers & shelving

(G-464)
AUBURN FOUNDRY INC
15 Wadsworth St (13021-2257)
P.O. Box 715 (13021-0715)
PHONE.................................315 253-4441
David Boglione, *President*
Denise Boglione, *Admin Sec*
EMP: 17 **EST:** 1947
SQ FT: 60,000
SALES (est): 2.1MM **Privately Held**
WEB: www.auburnfoundry.com
SIC: 3321 Gray iron castings

(G-465)
AUBURN PUBLISHING CO
Also Called: Citizen , The
25 Dill St (13021-3605)
PHONE.................................315 253-5311
Richard J Emanuel, *President*
David Wilcox, *Editor*
Lee Cunningham, *Creative Dir*
Jordan Farrell, *Graphic Designe*
EMP: 85
SALES (est): 5.1MM
SALES (corp-wide): 566.9MM **Publicly Held**
SIC: 2711 Newspapers: publishing only, not printed on site; newspapers, publishing & printing
HQ: Lee Publications, Inc.
   201 N Harrison St Ste 600
   Davenport IA 52801
   563 383-2100

(G-466)
AUBURN TANK & MANUFACTURING CO
Also Called: Atco EZ Dock
24 Mcmaster St (13021-2442)
P.O. Box 488 (13021-0488)
PHONE.................................315 255-2788
Carl Weber, *President*
EMP: 14
SQ FT: 12,000
SALES (est): 2.2MM **Privately Held**
WEB: www.auburntank.com
SIC: 3444 Sheet metalwork

(G-467)
AUBURN VACUUM FORMING CO INC
40 York St (13021-1251)
P.O. Box 489 (13021-0489)
PHONE.................................315 253-2440
Martin Pelchat, *President*
Rich Berlinski, *Opers Mgr*
Paul Pucek, *CFO*
Jack Hutson, *Sales Staff*
EMP: 19 **EST:** 1969
SQ FT: 71,000
SALES: 2.1MM
SALES (corp-wide): 3.2MM **Privately Held**
SIC: 3089 Injection molding of plastics
PA: Plastique M.P. Inc
   250 Rue Gouin
   Richmond QC J0B 2
   819 826-5921

(G-468)
AVSTAR FUEL SYSTEMS INC
15 Brookfield Pl (13021-2209)
PHONE.................................315 255-1955
EMP: 7
SALES (est): 737.8K **Privately Held**
SIC: 2869 Fuels

(G-469)
BCS ACCESS SYSTEMS US LLC
2150 Crane Brook Dr (13021-9516)
PHONE.................................315 258-3469
Jeffrey Webster, *Officer*
John Andrew Dale,
EMP: 278
SALES: 55MM **Privately Held**
SIC: 3469 Metal stampings
HQ: Bcs Automotive Interface Solutions Limited
   3rd Floor 35 Soho Square
   London
   121 526-4441

(G-470)
BLAIR CNSTR FABRICATION SP
13 Brae Ridge Rd (13021-9672)
PHONE.................................315 253-2321
Blair Longo, *President*
EMP: 6
SQ FT: 6,000
SALES (est): 685.2K **Privately Held**
SIC: 3599 Machine shop, jobbing & repair

(G-471)
BO-MER PLASTICS LLC
13 Pulaski St (13021-1105)
PHONE.................................315 252-7216
Thomas R Herbert, *President*
Scott Morin, *Engineer*
▼ **EMP:** 46 **EST:** 2001
SQ FT: 44,000
SALES (est): 10.5MM **Privately Held**
WEB: www.bo-mer.com
SIC: 3089 Thermoformed finished plastic products; plastic processing

(G-472)
BROOK NORTH FARMS INC
Also Called: Igk Equestrian
89 York St (13021-1135)
P.O. Box 1239, Weedsport (13166-1239)
PHONE.................................315 834-9390
Carolyn Kyle, *CEO*
Peter Kyle, *President*
▲ **EMP:** 12
SALES (est): 2MM **Privately Held**
WEB: www.northbrookfarms.com
SIC: 2515 3496 5083 Mattresses & bedsprings; mats & matting; dairy machinery & equipment

(G-473)
COPPER JOHN CORPORATION
173 State St (13021-1841)
PHONE.................................315 258-9269
Douglas A Springer, *President*
Eric Springer, *Vice Pres*
▲ **EMP:** 19
SQ FT: 11,000
SALES (est): 2.1MM **Privately Held**
WEB: www.copperjohn.com
SIC: 3949 Archery equipment, general

(G-474)
CURRIER PLASTICS INC
101 Columbus St (13021-3101)
PHONE.................................315 255-1779
John Currier, *Ch of Bd*
Massimo A Leone, *President*
Ron Ringleben, *President*
James E Currier, *Vice Pres*
Kyle Jones, *QC Mgr*
▲ **EMP:** 99
SQ FT: 60,000
SALES (est): 25.2MM **Privately Held**
WEB: www.currierplastics.com
SIC: 3089 Injection molding of plastics

(G-475)
DAIKIN APPLIED AMERICAS INC
Also Called: Applied Terminal Systems
4900 Technology Park Blvd (13021-8592)
PHONE.................................315 253-2771
Steve Henry, *Vice Pres*
Rich Savage, *Plant Mgr*
Nancy Russo, *Sales Staff*
Jim Cullin, *Manager*
Alan Youker, *Manager*
EMP: 55
SALES (corp-wide): 21.5B **Privately Held**
SIC: 3585 3822 3564 3561 Heating & air conditioning combination units; auto controls regulating residntl & coml environmt & applncs; blowers & fans; pumps & pumping equipment; fabricated pipe & fittings
HQ: Daikin Applied Americas Inc.
   13600 Industrial Pk Blvd
   Minneapolis MN 55441
   763 553-5330

Auburn - Cayuga County (G-476)

(G-476)
DEWITT PLASTICS INC
28 Aurelius Ave (13021-2231)
PHONE..................315 255-1209
David M Hess, *President*
Keith Kowal, *Prdtn Mgr*
Beatrice Hess, *Accounting Mgr*
Phil Hess, *Accounts Exec*
Traci Kowal, *Marketing Staff*
▲ **EMP:** 11 **EST:** 1972
SALES (est): 2.7MM **Privately Held**
WEB: www.dewittplastics.com
SIC: 2821 Plasticizer/additive based plastic materials

(G-477)
EMCOM INC
Also Called: Electomechanical Componets
62 Columbus St Ste 4 (13021-3161)
PHONE..................315 255-5300
Endy China, *President*
Joseph Reding, *President*
Tony Pongipat, *Vice Pres*
Debra Johnston, *Materials Mgr*
Sue Galbally, *Buyer*
▲ **EMP:** 100
SQ FT: 10,000
SALES (est): 36.8MM **Privately Held**
WEB: www.em-com.com
SIC: 3699 Electrical equipment & supplies

(G-478)
FINGER LAKES LEA CRAFTERS LLC
Also Called: Auburn Leathercrafters
42 Washington St (13021-2479)
PHONE..................315 252-4107
Anita Dungey, *President*
Alan Dungey, *Vice Pres*
Walter Dungey, *VP Sales*
▼ **EMP:** 15
SQ FT: 13,000
SALES: 1.2MM **Privately Held**
WEB: www.auburndirect.com
SIC: 3199 Dog furnishings: collars, leashes, muzzles, etc.: leather

(G-479)
FIRST PRESBYTERIAN CHURCH
112 South St (13021-4891)
PHONE..................315 252-3861
Gerald Rife Jr, *Pastor*
EMP: 6
SALES (est): 500.9K **Privately Held**
SIC: 3281 Cut stone & stone products

(G-480)
FLP GROUP LLC
301 Clark St (13021-2236)
PHONE..................315 252-7583
Greg Kanane, *President*
Joe Mirabito, *Prdtn Mgr*
EMP: 11 **EST:** 1928
SQ FT: 20,000
SALES (est): 1.7MM
SALES (corp-wide): 3.6MM **Privately Held**
WEB: www.fingerlakespress.com
SIC: 2752 2791 2789 2759 Commercial printing, offset; typesetting; bookbinding & related work; commercial printing; automotive & apparel trimmings
PA: Kinaneco., Inc.
   2925 Milton Ave
   Syracuse NY 13209
   315 468-6201

(G-481)
GEN-WEST ASSOCIATES LLC
101 Columbus St (13021-3121)
PHONE..................315 255-1779
Louri Hapkins, *Principal*
Pat Craine, *Accountant*
EMP: 5
SALES (est): 569.3K **Privately Held**
SIC: 3089 Injection molding of plastics

(G-482)
HAMMOND & IRVING INC (PA)
254 North St (13021-1129)
PHONE..................315 253-6265
Edward Gallager, *President*
Edward C Gallagher, *Exec VP*
Barbara Zach, *Treasurer*
Crystal Reyes, *Sales Staff*
Mary Vanacore, *Sales Staff*
▲ **EMP:** 85
SQ FT: 20,000
SALES (est): 23.8MM **Privately Held**
WEB: www.hammond-irving.com
SIC: 3462 Iron & steel forgings

(G-483)
INTERNATIONAL FIRE-SHIELD INC
194 Genesee St (13021-3360)
P.O. Box 7305 (13022-7305)
PHONE..................315 255-1006
Patrick D Bumpus, *CEO*
George Murray, *Ch of Bd*
EMP: 12
SALES (est): 2.2MM **Privately Held**
WEB: www.nyfs.com
SIC: 2899 Fire retardant chemicals

(G-484)
ITT LLC
Also Called: ITT Water Technology
1 Goulds Dr (13021-3134)
PHONE..................315 258-4904
Louis Juliano, *Branch Mgr*
Scott Liscum, *Manager*
EMP: 58
SALES (corp-wide): 2.5B **Publicly Held**
SIC: 3625 Control equipment, electric
HQ: Itt Llc
   1133 Westchester Ave N-100
   White Plains NY 10604
   914 641-2000

(G-485)
JACOBS PRESS INC
87 Columbus St (13021-3121)
P.O. Box 580 (13021-0580)
PHONE..................315 252-4861
Michael K Trapani, *President*
David Verdi, *Opers Mgr*
Pat Nation, *Sales Staff*
Stacy Feocco, *Office Mgr*
Molly Trapani, *Admin Sec*
EMP: 10 **EST:** 1915
SQ FT: 7,228
SALES: 1.1MM **Privately Held**
WEB: www.jacobspress.com
SIC: 2752 Commercial printing, offset

(G-486)
JOHN G RUBINO INC
Also Called: Gleason-Avery
45 Aurelius Ave (13021-2249)
PHONE..................315 253-7396
John G Rubino, *CEO*
John Rubino, *President*
Barbara Zelehowski, *Mktg Dir*
Barbara Zelehowsky, *Manager*
◆ **EMP:** 30
SQ FT: 32,000
SALES (est): 3.7MM **Privately Held**
WEB: www.gleasonavery.com
SIC: 3621 3566 Motors, electric; speed changers, drives & gears

(G-487)
JOHNSTON PRECISION INC
7 Frank Smith St (13021-1145)
PHONE..................315 253-4181
Theodore Johnston, *President*
EMP: 5
SQ FT: 2,400
SALES (est): 602.3K **Privately Held**
SIC: 3599 Machine shop, jobbing & repair

(G-488)
LOLLIPOP TREE INC
181 York St (13021-9009)
PHONE..................845 471-8733
Laurie V Lynch, *Ch of Bd*
Robert Lynch, *President*
EMP: 20
SQ FT: 18,200
SALES (est): 2.6MM **Privately Held**
WEB: www.lolliptree.com
SIC: 2045 2033 2099 2035 Prepared flour mixes & doughs; preserves, including imitation: in cans, jars, etc.; food preparations; pickles, sauces & salad dressings

(G-489)
MACK STUDIOS DISPLAYS INC
5500 Technology Park Blvd (13021-8555)
P.O. Box 917 (13021-0917)
PHONE..................315 252-7542
Peter Maciulewicz, *CEO*
EMP: 45
SQ FT: 125,000
SALES: 10.9MM **Privately Held**
WEB: www.mackstudios.com
SIC: 3999 Advertising display products

(G-490)
MATTEO & ANTONIO BARTOLOTTA
Also Called: Bartolotta Furniture
282 State St (13021-1144)
PHONE..................315 252-2220
Matteo Bartolotta, *President*
EMP: 10 **EST:** 1976
SQ FT: 4,000
SALES (est): 1MM **Privately Held**
SIC: 2512 2521 2434 Upholstered household furniture; wood office furniture; wood kitchen cabinets

(G-491)
NEW HOPE MILLS INC
181 York St (13021-9009)
PHONE..................315 252-2676
Dale E Weed, *President*
David J Weed, *Vice Pres*
EMP: 12
SQ FT: 11,500
SALES (est): 1.1MM **Privately Held**
WEB: www.newhopemills.com
SIC: 2045 0723 Pancake mixes, prepared: from purchased flour; flour milling custom services

(G-492)
NEW HOPE MILLS MFG INC (PA)
181 York St (13021-9009)
PHONE..................315 252-2676
Douglas Weed, *CEO*
Dale Weed, *President*
EMP: 50
SQ FT: 30,000
SALES (est): 9MM **Privately Held**
SIC: 2051 5461 Bakery products, partially cooked (except frozen); bakeries

(G-493)
NUCOR STEEL AUBURN INC
25 Quarry Rd (13021-1146)
P.O. Box 2008 (13021-1077)
PHONE..................315 253-4561
Del Benzenhafer, *General Mgr*
Dan Dimicco, *Chairman*
Lamor Henry, *Safety Mgr*
Luke Scott, *Safety Mgr*
Troy Green, *Buyer*
▲ **EMP:** 290
SQ FT: 300,000
SALES (est): 130.2MM
SALES (corp-wide): 20.2B **Publicly Held**
WEB: www.nucorauburn.com
SIC: 3312 Stainless steel
PA: Nucor Corporation
   1915 Rexford Rd Ste 400
   Charlotte NC 28211
   704 366-7000

(G-494)
OWENS-BROCKWAY GLASS CONT INC
7134 County House Rd (13021-5901)
PHONE..................315 258-3211
Steven Gabel, *Manager*
EMP: 210
SALES (corp-wide): 6.8B **Publicly Held**
SIC: 3221 Glass containers
HQ: Owens-Brockway Glass Container Inc.
   1 Michael Owens Way
   Perrysburg OH 43551
   567 336-8449

(G-495)
PREDATOR MOUNTAINWEAR INC
324 Fire Lane 15 (13021-8680)
PHONE..................315 727-3241
Lee Crossley, *President*
EMP: 5
SQ FT: 1,500
SALES: 1MM **Privately Held**
SIC: 2329 Ski & snow clothing: men's & boys'

(G-496)
PRINTERY
55 Arterial W (13021-2730)
PHONE..................315 253-7403
Pam Flaherty, *Owner*
EMP: 5
SALES (est): 190K **Privately Held**
SIC: 2261 Screen printing of cotton broadwoven fabrics

(G-497)
R P M INDUSTRIES INC
Also Called: RPM Displays
26 Aurelius Ave (13021-2212)
PHONE..................315 255-1105
Roger P Mueller, *President*
David Hess, *Vice Pres*
Martin Lynch, *Asst Treas*
Roy P Mueller, *VP Sales*
▲ **EMP:** 50 **EST:** 1925
SQ FT: 60,000
SALES (est): 49.2K **Privately Held**
WEB: www.rpmdisplays.com
SIC: 3089 5046 2499 Boxes, plastic; plastic hardware & building products; mannequins; shoe trees

(G-498)
ROBINSON CONCRETE INC (PA)
Also Called: Vitale Ready Mix Concrete
3486 Franklin Street Rd (13021-9348)
PHONE..................315 253-6666
Michael Vitale Jr, *President*
Norman Chirco, *Counsel*
Vincent Vitale, *Vice Pres*
Donny Smith, *Manager*
Paul F Vitale, *Admin Sec*
EMP: 50 **EST:** 1865
SQ FT: 2,500
SALES (est): 24MM **Privately Held**
SIC: 3273 3272 1442 Ready-mixed concrete; concrete products, precast; construction sand & gravel

(G-499)
SCHOTT CORPORATION
Also Called: Fiber Optics Schott America
62 Columbus St (13021-3167)
PHONE..................315 255-2791
Hinz Keiser, *Plant Mgr*
EMP: 64 **Privately Held**
SIC: 3229 3827 3674 Pressed & blown glass; optical instruments & lenses; semiconductors & related devices
HQ: Schott Corporation
   555 Taxter Rd Ste 470
   Elmsford NY 10523
   914 831-2200

(G-500)
SIMPLEX MANUFACTURING CO INC
105 Dunning Ave (13021-4403)
P.O. Box 279 (13021-0279)
PHONE..................315 252-7524
Robert C Merritt, *President*
Bob Merritt, *Editor*
Richard C Merritt, *Vice Pres*
Dan Bird, *Marketing Staff*
EMP: 19 **EST:** 1918
SQ FT: 25,000
SALES (est): 3.2MM **Privately Held**
WEB: www.simplexco.com
SIC: 3469 Metal stampings

(G-501)
SUNNYCREST INC (PA)
58 Prospect St (13021-1699)
PHONE..................315 252-7214
Robert Atkinson, *President*
William Atkinson, *Vice Pres*
Ron Shortsleeve, *Finance Mgr*
Eleanor Atkinson, *Admin Sec*
EMP: 30 **EST:** 1969
SQ FT: 53,000
SALES (est): 4.2MM **Privately Held**
WEB: www.sunnycrest.com
SIC: 3272 7261 Concrete products, precast; funeral service & crematories

▲ = Import ▼ = Export
◆ = Import/Export

GEOGRAPHIC SECTION

Babylon - Suffolk County (G-526)

(G-502)
T SHORE PRODUCTS LTD
Also Called: Shore Products Co
5 Eagle Dr (13021-8695)
PHONE...............315 252-9174
Thomas H Tutt II, *President*
Marlene Tutt, *Vice Pres*
EMP: 6
SQ FT: 8,500
SALES: 800K **Privately Held**
SIC: 3536 3448 5461 Hoists; boat lifts; docks; prefabricated metal; bakeries

(G-503)
TARO MANUFACTURING COMPANY INC
114 Clark St (13021-3325)
PHONE...............315 252-9430
Mario Buttaro, *President*
Mark Buttaro, *Vice Pres*
Steve Buttaro, *Vice Pres*
Roxanne Foster, *Manager*
▲ **EMP:** 19
SQ FT: 17,000
SALES (est): 3.3MM **Privately Held**
WEB: www.taromfg.com
SIC: 3621 3694 3678 Rotors, for motors; ignition apparatus & distributors; electronic connectors

(G-504)
TMS INTERNATIONAL LLC
25 Quarry Rd (13021-1146)
PHONE...............315 253-8925
EMP: 5 **Privately Held**
SIC: 3312 Blast furnaces & steel mills
HQ: Tms International, Llc
    12 Monongahela Ave
    Glassport PA 15045
    412 678-6141

(G-505)
TOWPATH MACHINE CORP
31 Allen St (13021-9004)
PHONE...............315 252-0112
Patricia Hanford, *President*
George Hanford, *Treasurer*
EMP: 7
SQ FT: 3,000
SALES: 500K **Privately Held**
WEB: www.towpathmachine.com
SIC: 3599 Machine shop, jobbing & repair

(G-506)
TRW AUTOMOTIVE INC
TRW Manufacturing
2150 Crane Brook Dr (13021-9516)
PHONE...............315 255-3311
Mike Stefanski, *Purch Agent*
Dennis Leitch, *Engineer*
Larry Trent, *Branch Mgr*
EMP: 300 **Privately Held**
SIC: 3469 3714 Metal stampings; motor vehicle parts & accessories
HQ: Trw Automotive Inc.
    12001 Tech Center Dr
    Livonia MI 48150
    734 855-2600

(G-507)
UFP NEW YORK LLC (HQ)
Also Called: Universal Forest Products
11 Allen St (13021-9004)
PHONE...............315 253-2758
Ralph Gschwind, *Principal*
EMP: 20
SALES (est): 7.5MM
SALES (corp-wide): 3.9B **Publicly Held**
WEB: www.ufpinc.com
SIC: 2439 Trusses, wooden roof
PA: Universal Forest Products, Inc.
    2801 E Beltline Ave Ne
    Grand Rapids MI 49525
    616 364-6161

(G-508)
VOLPI MANUFACTURING USA CO INC
5 Commerce Way (13021-8557)
PHONE...............315 255-1737
Max Kunz, *CEO*
Scott Kittelberger, *COO*
James Casasanta, *Engineer*
Thomas Baumann, *CFO*
Carla Vorreuter, *Cust Mgr*

◆ **EMP:** 38
SQ FT: 37,000
SALES (est): 6.4MM **Privately Held**
WEB: www.volpiusa.com
SIC: 3229 Glass fiber products
HQ: Volpi Ag
    Wiesenstrasse 33
    Schlieren ZH
    447 324-343

(G-509)
WEAVER MACHINE & TOOL CO INC
44 York St (13021-1136)
PHONE...............315 253-4422
Victor Ianno, *President*
Scott Bourgeois, *QC Mgr*
Timothy Braun, *Engineer*
Joe Artman, *Officer*
EMP: 15
SQ FT: 26,000
SALES (est): 3.1MM **Privately Held**
WEB: www.weavermachine.com
SIC: 3599 Machine shop, jobbing & repair

(G-510)
XYLEM INC
1 Goulds Dr (13021-3134)
PHONE...............315 258-4949
Marianne Vannostrand, *Purchasing*
Robert Prayne, *Engineer*
Sally Dorado, *Branch Mgr*
Lucas Fisher, *Manager*
Tom Flood, *Administration*
EMP: 150 **Publicly Held**
SIC: 3561 Pumps & pumping equipment
PA: Xylem Inc.
    1 International Dr
    Rye Brook NY 10573

Aurora
Cayuga County

(G-511)
MACKENZIE-CHILDS LLC (PA)
3260 State Route 90 (13026-9769)
PHONE...............315 364-6118
Lee Feldman, *CEO*
Howard Cohen, *CFO*
Carolyn Becker, *Manager*
◆ **EMP:** 150
SQ FT: 70,000
SALES (est): 37.3MM **Privately Held**
WEB: www.mackenzie-childs.com
SIC: 3263 2512 2511 Cookware, fine earthenware; upholstered household furniture; wood household furniture

Averill Park
Rensselaer County

(G-512)
518 PRINTS LLC
1548 Burden Lake Rd Ste 4 (12018-2818)
P.O. Box 632 (12018-0632)
PHONE...............518 674-5346
Jesse Brust, *Owner*
EMP: 6
SALES (est): 656.5K **Privately Held**
SIC: 2752 Commercial printing, lithographic

(G-513)
CAPITAL REG WKLY NEWSPPR GROUP
Also Called: Advertiser, The
29 Sheer Rd (12018-4722)
P.O. Box 70 (12018-0070)
PHONE...............518 674-2841
Charles Hug, *Principal*
Alyson Regan, *Principal*
Karen Demis, *Manager*
EMP: 10
SALES (est): 850K **Privately Held**
SIC: 2721 Periodicals: publishing only

(G-514)
GARMENT CARE SYSTEMS LLC
Also Called: Laura Star Service Center
55 Blue Heron Dr (12018-4600)
PHONE...............518 674-1826
James E Wells, *Mng Member*
▲ **EMP:** 6
SALES (est): 654.5K **Privately Held**
WEB: www.garmentcaresystems.com
SIC: 3499 Ironing boards, metal

(G-515)
L J VALENTE INC
8957 Ny Highway 66 (12018-5822)
PHONE...............518 674-3750
Anthony Valente, *President*
Steve A Valente, *Vice Pres*
EMP: 8
SALES (est): 1.5MM **Privately Held**
SIC: 2421 Building & structural materials, wood

Avoca
Steuben County

(G-516)
HAINES EQUIPMENT INC
20 Carrington St (14809-9766)
PHONE...............607 566-8531
Patricia Haines, *President*
EMP: 50
SQ FT: 50,000
SALES (est): 9.9MM **Privately Held**
WEB: www.hainesequipment.com
SIC: 3523 3565 3556 3535 Farm machinery & equipment; packaging machinery; food products machinery; conveyors & conveying equipment; tire cord & fabrics

Avon
Livingston County

(G-517)
B & B PRECISION MFG INC (PA)
310 W Main St (14414-1150)
P.O. Box 279 (14414-0279)
PHONE...............585 226-6226
Gerald Macintyre, *President*
Steve Megliore, *Plant Supt*
Lawrence Bailey, *Treasurer*
Shelly Guerin, *Accounts Mgr*
EMP: 32 **EST:** 1976
SQ FT: 15,900
SALES (est): 5.5MM **Privately Held**
WEB: www.bbprecision.com
SIC: 3599 Machine shop, jobbing & repair

(G-518)
BARILLA AMERICA NY INC
100 Horseshoe Blvd (14414-1164)
PHONE...............585 226-5600
Kirk Trofholz, *Principal*
▲ **EMP:** 121
SALES (est): 18.5MM **Privately Held**
SIC: 2099 Packaged combination products: pasta, rice & potato
HQ: Barilla America Inc.
    885 Sunset Ridge Rd
    Northbrook IL 60062

(G-519)
KRAFT HEINZ FOODS COMPANY
140 Spring St (14414-1153)
PHONE...............585 226-4400
Greg Manning, *Manager*
EMP: 450
SALES (corp-wide): 26.2B **Publicly Held**
WEB: www.kraftfoods.com
SIC: 2038 2099 Whipped topping, frozen; food preparations
HQ: Kraft Heinz Foods Company
    1 Ppg Pl Ste 3200
    Pittsburgh PA 15222
    412 456-5700

(G-520)
MONROE INDUSTRIES INC
5611 Tec Dr (14414-9562)
PHONE...............585 226-8230
John C Webster, *President*

EMP: 8
SALES (est): 720K **Privately Held**
SIC: 3281 Marble, building: cut & shaped

(G-521)
PENNY LANE PRINTING INC
Also Called: Penny Express
1471 Rte 15 (14414)
P.O. Box 340 (14414-0340)
PHONE...............585 226-8111
Steven Harrison, *President*
Kimberly Dougherty, *Vice Pres*
EMP: 54
SQ FT: 25,000
SALES: 4.5MM **Privately Held**
SIC: 2759 7319 Screen printing; distribution of advertising material or sample services

(G-522)
STAR HEADLIGHT LANTERN CO INC (PA)
455 Rochester St (14414-9503)
PHONE...............585 226-9500
Christopher D Jacobs, *Ch of Bd*
Christopher D Jacob, *President*
David W Jacobs, *President*
Michael Barbato, *Engineer*
Elvis Pacavar, *Engineer*
◆ **EMP:** 146
SQ FT: 85,000
SALES (est): 31.6MM **Privately Held**
WEB: www.star1889.com
SIC: 3648 3669 Strobe lighting systems; railroad signaling devices, electric

Babylon
Suffolk County

(G-523)
A C J COMMUNICATIONS INC
Also Called: Beacon
65 Deer Park Ave Ste 2 (11702-2820)
PHONE...............631 587-5612
Carolyn James, *Principal*
◆ **EMP:** 15
SALES (est): 87.5K **Privately Held**
SIC: 2711 Newspapers: publishing only, not printed on site

(G-524)
ADVANCED COATING TECHNIQUES
313 Wyandanch Ave (11704-1501)
PHONE...............631 643-4555
Anthony Gaitan, *President*
Maria Gaitan, *Corp Secy*
EMP: 20
SQ FT: 50,000
SALES (est): 2.4MM **Privately Held**
WEB: www.advancedcoatingtech.com
SIC: 3479 Galvanizing of iron, steel or end-formed products; coating of metals & formed products

(G-525)
BEDROCK LANDSCAPING MTLS CORP (PA)
Also Called: Bedrock Plus
454 Sunrise Hwy (11704-5906)
PHONE...............631 587-4950
David Cannetti, *President*
EMP: 9
SALES (est): 781.8K **Privately Held**
WEB: www.bedrockmaterial.com
SIC: 3291 Abrasive buffs, bricks, cloth, paper, stones, etc.

(G-526)
EAST PENN MANUFACTURING CO
790 Railroad Ave (11704-7820)
PHONE...............631 321-7161
Timothy Dunn, *Principal*
EMP: 6
SALES (corp-wide): 2.5B **Privately Held**
SIC: 3999 Barber & beauty shop equipment
PA: East Penn Manufacturing Co.
    102 Deka Rd
    Lyon Station PA 19536
    610 682-6361

Babylon - Suffolk County (G-527)

(G-527)
EDM MFG
141 John St Ste 600 (11702-2945)
PHONE..........................631 669-1966
Dariusz Mejer, *Chairman*
EMP: 8
SALES (est): 833.9K **Privately Held**
SIC: 3599 Machine shop, jobbing & repair

(G-528)
JEWELERS MACHINIST CO INC
400 Columbus Ave (11704-5599)
PHONE..........................631 661-5020
Raymond Pawloski, *President*
John Pawloski, *Vice Pres*
Kathleen Pawloski, *Admin Sec*
EMP: 7 **EST:** 1946
SQ FT: 3,000
SALES (est): 1MM **Privately Held**
WEB: www.threadgrind.com
SIC: 3599 Machine shop, jobbing & repair

(G-529)
M C PACKAGING CORPORATION
Also Called: M C Packaging Corp Plant
300 Governor Ave (11704-1900)
PHONE..........................631 643-3763
EMP: 40
SALES (corp-wide): 22.9MM **Privately Held**
SIC: 2679 5113 2759 2657 Mfg Converted Paper Prdt Whol Indstl/Svc Paper Commercial Printing Mfg Folding Paperbrd Box Mfg Corrugated/Fiber Box
PA: M C Packaging Corporation
200 Adams Blvd
Farmingdale NY 11735
631 414-7840

(G-530)
NSJ GROUP LTD
Also Called: Edible Arragement
80 W Main St Ste A (11702-3442)
PHONE..........................631 893-9300
Jason Varach, *Managing Prtnr*
Lindsey Ohland, *Manager*
EMP: 11
SALES (est): 624K **Privately Held**
SIC: 3999 Artificial flower arrangements

(G-531)
PHARMAVANTAGE LLC
15 Lakeland Ave (11702-1409)
PHONE..........................631 321-8171
Susan Capie, *Managing Dir*
▲ **EMP:** 6
SALES (est): 584.9K **Privately Held**
SIC: 2834 Druggists' preparations (pharmaceuticals)

(G-532)
PREMIER SYSTEMS LLC
41 John St Ste 6 (11702-2932)
PHONE..........................631 587-9700
Joseph Pegno,
EMP: 6
SALES (est): 670K **Privately Held**
SIC: 3679 Electronic circuits

(G-533)
PREMIUM PROCESSING CORP
30 Kittiwake Ln (11702-4215)
PHONE..........................631 232-1105
Keith Schmidt, *President*
EMP: 52
SQ FT: 30,000
SALES (est): 654.9K **Privately Held**
SIC: 2834 Vitamin preparations

Bainbridge
Chenango County

(G-534)
SHEHAWKEN ARCHERY CO INC
40 S Main St (13733-1216)
P.O. Box 187 (13733-0187)
PHONE..........................607 967-8333
Fax: 607 967-2828
EMP: 12
SQ FT: 17,000
SALES (est): 720K **Privately Held**
SIC: 3949 Mfg Archery Equipment

(G-535)
TRIMAC MOLDING SERVICES
13 Pruyn St (13733-1155)
P.O. Box 176 (13733-0176)
PHONE..........................607 967-2900
Linda Pickwick, *Partner*
Harold Pickwick, *Partner*
EMP: 9
SQ FT: 60,000
SALES (est): 1.1MM **Privately Held**
WEB: www.trimacmolding.com
SIC: 3089 Injection molding of plastics

(G-536)
UPTURN INDUSTRIES INC
2-4 Whitney Way (13733)
PHONE..........................607 967-2923
Mike Horoszewski, *CEO*
Donna L Enck, *CEO*
Tomas Mahar, *Business Mgr*
Sharon Delello, *Manager*
Nicole Vanpelt, *Administration*
▲ **EMP:** 31
SQ FT: 12,000
SALES (est): 5.1MM **Privately Held**
WEB: www.upturnindustries.com
SIC: 3599 Machine shop, jobbing & repair

Bakers Mills
Warren County

(G-537)
CHAD PIERSON
Also Called: Chad Pierson Logging & Trckg
Chad Pierson (12811)
P.O. Box 29 (12811-0029)
PHONE..........................518 251-0186
Chad Pierson, *President*
EMP: 7
SQ FT: 5,600
SALES (est): 701K **Privately Held**
SIC: 2411 Logging

Baldwin
Nassau County

(G-538)
ELLIQUENCE LLC
2455 Grand Ave (11510-3556)
PHONE..........................516 277-9000
Anthony Carone, *Controller*
Dale Mammina, *Office Mgr*
Alan Ellman, *Mng Member*
Scott Goldsmith, *Manager*
Jackie Weber, *Manager*
▲ **EMP:** 19
SALES (est): 3.2MM **Privately Held**
SIC: 3841 Surgical & medical instruments

(G-539)
JAL SIGNS INC
Also Called: Sign-A-Rama
540 Merrick Rd (11510-3439)
PHONE..........................516 536-7280
Agnes Lidner, *President*
Jim Lindner, *Manager*
James Lidner, *Admin Sec*
Melissa Policaro, *Graphic Designe*
EMP: 10 **EST:** 1999
SALES (est): 1.3MM **Privately Held**
SIC: 3993 Signs & advertising specialties

(G-540)
MAKS PHARMA & DIAGNOSTICS INC
2365 Milburn Ave Bldg 2 (11510-3349)
PHONE..........................631 270-1528
Sadathulla Shareef, *President*
Mohammad Ullah, *Vice Pres*
Sylwia Jabysz, *Admin Sec*
EMP: 3 **EST:** 2012
SQ FT: 2,200
SALES: 1MM **Privately Held**
SIC: 2834 Pharmaceutical preparations

(G-541)
ROSE FENCE INC
345 Sunrise Hwy (11510)
PHONE..........................516 223-0777
Scott Rose, *Branch Mgr*
EMP: 10
SALES (corp-wide): 20.2MM **Privately Held**
WEB: www.rosefence.com
SIC: 2499 5211 3496 3315 Fencing, wood; fencing; miscellaneous fabricated wire products; steel wire & related products
PA: Rose Fence, Inc.
345 W Sunrise Hwy
Freeport NY 11520
516 223-0777

(G-542)
RUSSCO METAL SPINNING CO INC
1020 Archer Pl (11510-3604)
PHONE..........................516 872-6055
William Russ, *President*
Mary Russ, *Corp Secy*
EMP: 10
SQ FT: 5,300
SALES (est): 1.2MM **Privately Held**
SIC: 3469 Metal Spinning

(G-543)
SONIQUENCE LLC
2473 Grand Ave (11510-3531)
PHONE..........................516 267-6400
Alan Ellman,
EMP: 10
SALES (est): 377.1K **Privately Held**
SIC: 3841 Surgical & medical instruments

(G-544)
SPORTSDEPOT INC
891 Hayes St (11510-4646)
PHONE..........................516 543-5018
Sheryl Smalley, *CEO*
Robert Smalley, *CEO*
EMP: 2
SALES: 1MM **Privately Held**
SIC: 3993 Signs & advertising specialties

(G-545)
TECHNICAL PACKAGING INC
2365 Milburn Ave (11510-3349)
P.O. Box 504 (11510-0504)
PHONE..........................516 223-2300
Don Romig, *President*
James Kane, *Vice Pres*
EMP: 15
SALES (est): 3.2MM **Privately Held**
WEB: www.technicalpackaging.com
SIC: 2653 2441 3053 3086 Boxes, corrugated: made from purchased materials; packing cases, wood: nailed or lock corner; packing materials; packaging & shipping materials, foamed plastic; packaging materials; corrugated & solid fiber boxes

Baldwin Place
Westchester County

(G-546)
GOODWILL INDS OF GREATER NY
80 Route 6 Unit 605 (10505-1033)
PHONE..........................914 621-0781
Herbert Wright, *Principal*
EMP: 160
SALES (corp-wide): 117.3MM **Privately Held**
SIC: 3999 Barber & beauty shop equipment
PA: Goodwill Industries Of Greater New York Inc
421 27th Ave
Astoria NY 11102
718 728-5400

Baldwinsville
Onondaga County

(G-547)
ACME SIGNS OF BALDWINSVILLE
3 Marble St (13027-2918)
PHONE..........................315 638-4865
Dennis Sick, *Owner*
EMP: 6
SALES (est): 276.4K **Privately Held**
SIC: 3993 4226 Signs & advertising specialties; special warehousing & storage

(G-548)
ADVANCED RECOVERY & RECYCL LLC
3475 Linda Ln (13027-9217)
PHONE..........................315 450-3301
Byron Tietjen, *President*
Peter Stockmann,
EMP: 10
SALES (est): 669.1K **Privately Held**
SIC: 2611 Pulp mills, mechanical & recycling processing

(G-549)
ANHEUSER-BUSCH LLC
2780 Brundage Rd (13027)
PHONE..........................315 638-0365
EMP: 5
SALES (est): 171.4K **Privately Held**
SIC: 2082 Malt beverages

(G-550)
ANHEUSER-BUSCH LLC
2885 Belgium Rd (13027-2797)
P.O. Box 200 (13027-0200)
PHONE..........................315 638-0365
Howard Triche, *General Mgr*
Chris Lukaczyk, *Area Mgr*
Jesse Randolph, *Opers Mgr*
Josh Zabek, *Opers Mgr*
Adon Allen, *Warehouse Mgr*
EMP: 162
SALES (corp-wide): 1.9B **Privately Held**
WEB: www.hispanicbud.com
SIC: 2082 Beer (alcoholic beverage)
HQ: Anheuser-Busch, Llc
1 Busch Pl
Saint Louis MO 63118
314 632-6777

(G-551)
BACO CONTROLS INC (PA)
8431 Loop Rd (13027-1304)
PHONE..........................315 635-2500
Thomas C Rogers, *President*
EMP: 10
SQ FT: 1,500
SALES (est): 1.8MM **Privately Held**
WEB: www.bacocontrols.com
SIC: 3625 Relays & industrial controls

(G-552)
CAPCO MARKETING
Also Called: Gourmet Connection
8417 Oswego Rd 177 (13027-8813)
P.O. Box 1727, Cicero (13039-1727)
PHONE..........................315 699-1687
Kirk Capece, *Owner*
EMP: 10
SALES (est): 452.4K **Privately Held**
WEB: www.capcomarketing.com
SIC: 2721 5812 Magazines: publishing & printing; eating places

(G-553)
COMPLEX BIOSYSTEMS INC
8417 Oswego Rd 201 (13027-8813)
PHONE..........................315 464-8007
Jacques Beaumont, *Owner*
EMP: 7
SQ FT: 600
SALES (est): 336K **Privately Held**
SIC: 3845 7371 7373 8711 Electrotherapeutic apparatus; computer software systems analysis & design, custom; computer-aided engineering (CAE) systems service; consulting engineer

(G-554)
FINGER LKES STIRS CABINETS LLC
7496 Kingdom Rd (13027-8782)
PHONE..........................315 638-3150
Jack Barton, *Principal*
Jason Barton, *Principal*
Brad Crosby, *Principal*
EMP: 5
SALES (est): 476.7K **Privately Held**
SIC: 2434 Wood kitchen cabinets

GEOGRAPHIC SECTION

(G-555)
GIOVANNI FOOD CO INC (PA)
8800 Sixty Rd (13027-1235)
PHONE....................315 457-2373
Louis J Dement, *Vice Pres*
◆ EMP: 70
SQ FT: 25,000
SALES (est): 13.9MM **Privately Held**
WEB: www.giovannifoods.com
SIC: 2033 Tomato products: packaged in cans, jars, etc.

(G-556)
INDIAN SPRINGS MFG CO INC
2095 W Genesee Rd (13027-8649)
P.O. Box 469 (13027-0469)
PHONE....................315 635-6101
Maurice J Ferguson, *CEO*
Shawn Ferguson, *President*
Robert Wolniak, *Vice Pres*
Patricia Ferguson, *Admin Sec*
EMP: 18
SQ FT: 9,000
SALES (est): 4.9MM **Privately Held**
WEB: www.indiansprings.com
SIC: 2812 3599 Chlorine, compressed or liquefied; machine & other job shop work

(G-557)
KAYLON INDUSTRIES LLC
15 Downer St (13027-2819)
PHONE....................315 303-2119
Christopher Leonard,
EMP: 5
SALES: 100K **Privately Held**
SIC: 3999 Manufacturing industries

(G-558)
METROPOLITAN SIGNS INC
3760 Patchett Rd (13027-9454)
P.O. Box 3062, Liverpool (13089-3062)
PHONE....................315 638-1448
David R Razzante, *President*
EMP: 10 EST: 1970
SQ FT: 4,000
SALES: 600K **Privately Held**
WEB: www.metropolitansigns.com
SIC: 3993 Electric signs

(G-559)
PAPERWORKS INDUSTRIES INC
2900 Mclane Rd (13027-1319)
PHONE....................913 621-0922
Ronald Jenkins, *Principal*
Ryan Bednarek, *Network Analyst*
EMP: 10
SALES (est): 1.2MM
SALES (corp-wide): 13.6B **Privately Held**
SIC: 3999 2671 Barber & beauty shop equipment; packaging paper & plastics film, coated & laminated
HQ: Ros-Mar Litho Inc
19500 Av Clark-Graham
Baie-D'urfe QC H9X 3
514 694-2178

(G-560)
PATIENT PORTAL TECH INC (PA)
8276 Willett Pkwy Ste 200 (13027-1328)
PHONE....................315 638-2030
Brian Kelly, *CEO*
John O'Mara, *President*
Thomas Hagan, *CFO*
Daniel Thompson, *Finance*
Kim Kinney, *Admin Asst*
EMP: 19
SALES (est): 7.1MM **Publicly Held**
WEB: www.gambinoapparel.com
SIC: 7372 Prepackaged software

(G-561)
SPECIALIZED PACKG GROUP INC (DH)
Also Called: Paperworks
2900 Mclane Rd (13027-1319)
PHONE....................315 638-4355
Carlton Highsmith, *Chairman*
▲ EMP: 2
SALES (est): 48.3MM
SALES (corp-wide): 13.6B **Privately Held**
SIC: 2653 2657 Corrugated & solid fiber boxes; folding paperboard boxes

(G-562)
SPECIALIZED PACKG RADISSON LLC
8800 Sixty Rd (13027-1235)
PHONE....................315 638-4355
Thomas Garland,
Carlton Highsmith,
EMP: 150 EST: 1998
SALES (est): 37.3MM
SALES (corp-wide): 13.6B **Privately Held**
SIC: 2653 2657 Boxes, solid fiber: made from purchased materials; folding paperboard boxes
HQ: The Specialized Packaging Group Inc
2900 Mclane Rd
Baldwinsville NY 13027
315 638-4355

(G-563)
SSAC INC
8242 Loop Rd (13027-1391)
PHONE....................800 843-8848
Fax: 315 638-0333
EMP: 21
SALES (est): 3.3MM **Privately Held**
SIC: 3625 Mfg Relays/Industrial Controls

(G-564)
SYRASOFT LLC
6 Canton St (13027-2300)
PHONE....................315 708-0341
Thomas Gardener, *Partner*
EMP: 10
SALES (est): 1.1MM **Privately Held**
WEB: www.syrasoft.com
SIC: 7372 7371 Prepackaged software; custom computer programming services

Ballston Lake
Saratoga County

(G-565)
ASTRO CHEMICAL COMPANY INC
3 Mill Rd (12019-2022)
P.O. Box 1250 (12019-0250)
PHONE....................518 399-5338
Duane A Ball, *Ch of Bd*
▲ EMP: 20
SQ FT: 24,000
SALES (est): 5.6MM **Privately Held**
WEB: www.astrochemical.com
SIC: 2891 Adhesives & sealants

(G-566)
BENNETT STAIR COMPANY INC
1021 State Route 50 (12019-1915)
PHONE....................518 384-1554
Dave Bennett, *President*
Gayle Bennett, *Office Mgr*
EMP: 8
SQ FT: 2,800
SALES: 650K **Privately Held**
SIC: 2431 Staircases & stairs, wood; staircases, stairs & railings

(G-567)
CBM FABRICATIONS INC
15 Westside Dr (12019-2025)
PHONE....................518 399-8023
Charles B McCormack II, *Ch of Bd*
EMP: 30
SQ FT: 8,100
SALES (est): 8.4MM **Privately Held**
WEB: www.cbmfab.com
SIC: 3441 7692 3599 3444 Fabricated structural metal; welding repair; machine shop, jobbing & repair; sheet metalwork

(G-568)
LAKESIDE CIDER MILL FARM INC
336 Schauber Rd (12019-2104)
PHONE....................518 399-8359
Richard Pearce, *President*
Jeffrey Pearce, *Vice Pres*
EMP: 8 EST: 1944
SQ FT: 5,000
SALES (est): 1MM **Privately Held**
SIC: 2099 5812 5431 Cider, nonalcoholic; eating places; vegetable stands or markets

(G-569)
MERCURY PEN COMPANY INC
245 Eastline Rd (12019-1810)
PHONE....................518 899-9653
Jody Gentilesco, *President*
▲ EMP: 7
SQ FT: 5,000
SALES: 216.6K **Privately Held**
WEB: www.mercurypen.com
SIC: 3951 Ball point pens & parts; penholders & parts; pencils & pencil parts, mechanical

(G-570)
NORTHEAST TONER INC
26 Walden Gln Fl 2 (12019-9234)
PHONE....................518 899-5545
Gail Trietiak, *President*
Paul Trietiak, *Vice Pres*
EMP: 7
SALES (est): 1.1MM **Privately Held**
SIC: 3955 Print cartridges for laser & other computer printers

(G-571)
SIXNET LLC
331 Ushers Rd Ste 14 (12019-1546)
P.O. Box 767, Clifton Park (12065-0767)
PHONE....................518 877-5173
Steve Schoenberg, *CEO*
Michael Mokay, *Engineer*
Laura La Prairie, *Sales Dir*
Skip Turiel, *Manager*
Ryan Jacksland, *Technology*
EMP: 80
SQ FT: 20,000
SALES (est): 12.3MM
SALES (corp-wide): 2B **Privately Held**
WEB: www.sixnetio.com
SIC: 3823 Computer interface equipment for industrial process control
HQ: Red Lion Controls, Inc.
20 Willow Springs Cir
York PA 17406
717 767-6961

(G-572)
SIXNET HOLDINGS LLC
331 Ushers Rd Ste 10 (12019-1546)
PHONE....................518 877-5173
Hilton Nicholson,
▲ EMP: 5
SALES (est): 7.9MM
SALES (corp-wide): 2B **Privately Held**
SIC: 3823 Industrial instrmnts msrmnt display/control process variable
PA: Spectris Plc
Heritage House
Egham TW20
178 447-0470

(G-573)
TJB SUNSHINE ENTERPRISES INC
6 Redwood Dr (12019-2631)
PHONE....................518 384-6483
Tom Brundige, *President*
EMP: 14
SALES (est): 1.1MM **Privately Held**
SIC: 2842 Window cleaning preparations

Ballston Spa
Saratoga County

(G-574)
ADVANCED COMFORT SYSTEMS INC
Also Called: ACS
12b Commerce Dr (12020-3631)
PHONE....................518 884-8444
Roger M Kerr, *President*
EMP: 10
SALES (est): 1.7MM **Privately Held**
WEB: www.advancedcomfortsys.com
SIC: 7372 1742 Application computer software; insulation, buildings

(G-575)
ALBATROS NORTH AMERICA INC
Also Called: Sepsa North America
6 Mccrea Hill Rd (12020-5515)
PHONE....................518 381-7100
John Hanrahan, *CEO*
Nicholas Fuster, *President*
William D Kolberg, *Finance*
▲ EMP: 45
SQ FT: 36,000
SALES (est): 11.8MM
SALES (corp-wide): 609MM **Privately Held**
WEB: www.sepsa.es
SIC: 3679 3699 Static power supply converters for electronic applications; security control equipment & systems
HQ: Albatros Sl
Calle De Albatros (Pol Ind La Estacion), 7 - 9
Pinto 28320
914 957-000

(G-576)
ALLYTEX LLC
540 Acland Blvd (12020-3074)
PHONE....................518 376-7539
Alison Arakelian,
EMP: 5
SALES (est): 310.6K **Privately Held**
SIC: 2311 Men's & boys' suits & coats

(G-577)
APPLIED MATERIALS INC
10 Stonebreak Rd Ste 2 (12020-4505)
PHONE....................518 245-1400
EMP: 6
SALES (corp-wide): 14.5B **Publicly Held**
SIC: 3674 Semiconductors & related devices
PA: Applied Materials, Inc.
3050 Bowers Ave
Santa Clara CA 95054
408 727-5555

(G-578)
BURNT HILLS FABRICATORS INC
318 Charlton Rd B (12020-3412)
P.O. Box 2, Burnt Hills (12027-0002)
PHONE....................518 885-1115
James Fantauzzi, *President*
EMP: 15
SQ FT: 7,000
SALES (est): 3.1MM **Privately Held**
SIC: 3441 Fabricated structural metal

(G-579)
DEATH WISH COFFEE COMPANY LLC
100 Saratoga Village Blvd # 3 (12020-3737)
PHONE....................518 400-1050
Michael Brown, *CEO*
Kane Grogan, *Marketing Staff*
EMP: 12 EST: 2015
SALES (est): 1.8MM **Privately Held**
SIC: 2095 5499 Coffee extracts; coffee roasting (except by wholesale grocers); coffee

(G-580)
DIGITAL IMAGING TECH LLC
425 Eastline Rd D (12020-3617)
PHONE....................518 885-4400
Michael Marino, *Mng Member*
Richard Siciliano,
EMP: 6 EST: 1997
SQ FT: 5,000
SALES (est): 1MM **Privately Held**
WEB: www.digimtech.com
SIC: 2752 Commercial printing, lithographic

(G-581)
DIT PRINTS INCORPORATED
Also Called: Digital Imiging Technologies
27 Kent St Ste 53 (12020-1543)
PHONE....................518 885-4400
Deborah Libratore Le Blanc, *President*
Paul Le Blanc, *General Mgr*
EMP: 5
SQ FT: 2,400
SALES (est): 452.7K **Privately Held**
SIC: 2759 Commercial printing

(G-582)
DURA-MILL INC
Also Called: Newco Products Division
16 Stonebreak Rd (12020)
PHONE....................518 899-2255
Richard J Walrath, *President*

Ballston Spa - Saratoga County (G-583)

David Walrath, *Vice Pres*
EMP: 33
SALES (est): 7.5MM **Privately Held**
WEB: www.duramill.com
SIC: 3545 5085 Cutting tools for machine tools; industrial supplies; abrasives; bearings, bushings, wheels & gears; industrial wheels

(G-583)
GLOBALFOUNDRIES US INC
107 Hermes Rd (12020-4534)
PHONE..................408 462-3900
Debra Leach, *Vice Pres*
Buren Jason VA, *Mfg Mgr*
Jason Cargin, *Engineer*
Scott Michalski, *Engineer*
Aaron Sinnott, *Engineer*
EMP: 19
SALES (corp-wide): 8.5B **Privately Held**
SIC: 3369 3674 Nonferrous foundries; integrated circuits, semiconductor networks, etc.
HQ: Globalfoundries U.S. Inc.
 2600 Great America Way
 Santa Clara CA 95054

(G-584)
GREAT AMERICAN AWNING & PATIO
43 Round Lake Rd (12020)
PHONE..................518 899-2300
Frank Rasalik, *President*
EMP: 15
SALES (est): 1.2MM **Privately Held**
SIC: 3271 Blocks, concrete: chimney or fireplace

(G-585)
HARVEST TECHNOLOGIES INC
36 Featherfoil Way (12020-4371)
PHONE..................518 899-7124
Donna Morris, *Partner*
Turk Ellis, *Partner*
EMP: 2
SALES (est): 2MM **Privately Held**
SIC: 2611 Pulp manufactured from waste or recycled paper

(G-586)
JOHNSON CONTROLS INC
339 Brownell Rd (12020-3705)
PHONE..................518 884-8313
David Bardsley, *Branch Mgr*
EMP: 95 **Privately Held**
SIC: 2531 Seats, automobile
HQ: Johnson Controls, Inc.
 5757 N Green Bay Ave
 Milwaukee WI 53209
 414 524-1200

(G-587)
LANE ENTERPRISES INC
825 State Route 67 (12020-3604)
PHONE..................518 885-4385
M J Cathers, *Branch Mgr*
EMP: 20
SALES (corp-wide): 70.5MM **Privately Held**
WEB: www.lanepipe.com
SIC: 3444 3449 Pipe, sheet metal; miscellaneous metalwork
PA: Lane Enterprises, Inc.
 3905 Hartzdale Dr Ste 514
 Camp Hill PA 17011
 717 761-8175

(G-588)
LEMANS CORPORATION
Also Called: Drag Specialties
10 Mccrea Hill Rd (12020-5515)
PHONE..................518 885-7500
Mike Cornell, *Manager*
EMP: 9
SALES (corp-wide): 677.5MM **Privately Held**
SIC: 3714 Acceleration equipment, motor vehicle
PA: Lemans Corporation
 3501 Kennedy Rd
 Janesville WI 53545
 608 758-1111

(G-589)
MAGSOFT CORPORATION
2715 State Route 9 # 102 (12020-5306)
PHONE..................518 877-8390
Sheppard Salon, *President*
Philippe F Wendling, *Exec VP*
EMP: 9
SQ FT: 3,500
SALES: 840K
SALES (corp-wide): 333.3MM **Publicly Held**
WEB: www.magsoft-flux.com
SIC: 7372 7371 Prepackaged software; computer software development & applications
PA: Altair Engineering Inc.
 1820 E Big Beaver Rd
 Troy MI 48083
 248 614-2400

(G-590)
MERIDIAN MANUFACTURING INC
27 Kent St Ste 103a (12020-1543)
PHONE..................518 885-0450
Paul Michael, *President*
Rob Guarino, *Vice Pres*
Robin Guarino, *Vice Pres*
EMP: 7
SQ FT: 8,100
SALES (est): 1.2MM **Privately Held**
SIC: 3599 Machine shop, jobbing & repair

(G-591)
MESSENGER PRESS
1826 Amsterdam Rd (12020-3323)
P.O. Box 376 (12020-0376)
PHONE..................518 885-9231
Ed Bellamy, *Owner*
EMP: 8
SALES (est): 460K **Privately Held**
SIC: 2752 7336 Lithographing on metal; commercial art & graphic design

(G-592)
NORTH AMERICAN SVCS GROUP LLC (HQ)
Also Called: North American Service Group
1240 Saratoga Rd (12020-3500)
PHONE..................518 885-1820
Frank Zilka, *President*
Tim Zilka, *COO*
Alvaro Ramirez, *Manager*
Michael Pickering, *Director*
Gina Sherman, *Executive Asst*
EMP: 15
SQ FT: 40,000
SALES (est): 5.6MM **Privately Held**
SIC: 3443 1799 Cryogenic tanks, for liquids & gases; service station equipment installation, maintenance & repair

(G-593)
NORTHWIND GRAPHICS
2453 State Route 9 (12020-4407)
PHONE..................518 899-9651
Steve Richardson, *Owner*
EMP: 5
SQ FT: 3,500
SALES (est): 420.9K **Privately Held**
SIC: 2759 Screen printing

(G-594)
PREMIUM BLDG COMPONENTS INC
831 Rt 67 Bldg 46 (12020)
PHONE..................518 885-0194
John Buyaskas, *Principal*
EMP: 20
SALES (corp-wide): 7.1MM **Privately Held**
SIC: 3713 Truck & bus bodies
PA: Premium Building Components, Inc.
 527 Queensbury Ave
 Queensbury NY 12804
 518 792-0189

(G-595)
SAND HILL INDUSTRIES INC
Also Called: T-Shirt Graphics
12 Grove St (12020-1814)
PHONE..................518 885-7991
Dennis Albright, *President*
Eileen Albright, *Vice Pres*
EMP: 6

SQ FT: 10,000
SALES (est): 560K **Privately Held**
WEB: www.t-shirtgraphics.com
SIC: 2759 2395 2752 3081 Screen printing; embroidery & art needlework; commercial printing, offset; unsupported plastics film & sheet

(G-596)
SPECIALTY SILICONE PDTS INC
3 Mccrea Hill Rd (12020-5511)
PHONE..................518 885-8826
Susan Premo, *CEO*
Paul Dicaprio, *President*
Patricia S Babbie, *Senior VP*
Ned REO, *Senior VP*
Frederic E Sober, *Senior VP*
▲ **EMP:** 70
SQ FT: 52,000
SALES (est): 13.6MM **Publicly Held**
WEB: www.sspinc.com
SIC: 2869 2822 3714 2992 Silicones; silicone rubbers; motor vehicle parts & accessories; lubricating oils & greases
HQ: Heico Electronic Technologies Corp.
 3000 Taft St
 Hollywood FL 33021
 954 987-6101

(G-597)
STEWARTS PROCESSING CORP (PA)
2907 State Route 9 (12020-4201)
P.O. Box 435, Saratoga Springs (12866-0435)
PHONE..................518 581-1200
Gary C Dake, *Ch of Bd*
Michael Cocca, *Treasurer*
Alison Becktoft, *Human Resources*
Chad Kiesow, *Marketing Staff*
Scott Corey, *Branch Mgr*
EMP: 85
SALES: 61.9MM **Privately Held**
SIC: 2026 2024 2086 Fluid milk; ice cream & ice milk; soft drinks: packaged in cans, bottles, etc.

(G-598)
WINDOW TECH SYSTEMS INC
15 Old Stonebreak Rd (12020-4900)
P.O. Box 2260 (12020-8260)
PHONE..................518 899-9000
David L Bangert, *President*
Dave Bangert, *President*
Tracy Carpenter, *Sales Staff*
Tracy Mason, *Admin Asst*
EMP: 22 **EST:** 1952
SQ FT: 30,000
SALES (est): 4.8MM **Privately Held**
WEB: www.windowtechsystems.net
SIC: 3442 3089 Screens, window, metal; windows, plastic

Barker
Niagara County

(G-599)
ATLANTIC TRANSFORMER INC
1674 Quaker Rd (14012-9616)
P.O. Box 276 (14012-0276)
PHONE..................716 795-3258
John Khorrami, *President*
EMP: 10
SQ FT: 8,500
SALES: 400K **Privately Held**
WEB: www.mgs4u.com
SIC: 3677 Electronic transformers

(G-600)
JT PRECISION INC
8701 Haight Rd (14012-9630)
PHONE..................716 795-3860
Jeff Thuman Sr, *President*
Richard Meyers, *Principal*
Sarah Munn, *Principal*
Cristine O'Keefe, *Officer*
EMP: 34
SALES: 3MM **Privately Held**
SIC: 3599 Machine shop, jobbing & repair

Barneveld
Oneida County

(G-601)
ABDO SHTMTL & FABRICATION INC
11470 N Gage Rd (13304-1930)
PHONE..................315 894-4664
Michael Abdo, *President*
EMP: 7
SQ FT: 8,000
SALES (est): 1.5MM **Privately Held**
WEB: www.abdosheetmetal.com
SIC: 3444 1721 1799 Sheet metal specialties, not stamped; painting & paper hanging; welding on site

(G-602)
JET SEW CORPORATION
8119 State Route 12 (13304)
PHONE..................315 896-2683
Edward Wiehl, *President*
EMP: 15
SQ FT: 65,000
SALES: 550K **Privately Held**
WEB: www.jetsew.com
SIC: 3599 Custom machinery

(G-603)
MOHAWK ELECTRO TECHNIQUES INC
7677 Cameron Hill Rd (13304-1917)
PHONE..................315 896-2661
Lee Broomfield, *President*
Fred Ingo, *Vice Pres*
EMP: 90
SQ FT: 5,000
SALES (est): 9.1MM **Privately Held**
SIC: 3677 Coil windings, electronic; electronic transformers

(G-604)
ROLLING STAR MANUFACTURING INC
125 Liberty Ln (13304-2537)
P.O. Box 471 (13304-0471)
PHONE..................315 896-4767
Jamie R Servello, *President*
Dean Beck, *Vice Pres*
EMP: 20
SQ FT: 2,728
SALES (est): 3.8MM **Privately Held**
WEB: www.customizedtrailers.com
SIC: 3799 Trailers & trailer equipment

(G-605)
SQUARE STAMPING MFG CORP
108 Old Remsen Rd (13304)
PHONE..................315 896-2641
David Allen, *President*
Dan Hart, *General Mgr*
Jeffrey Gouger, *Treasurer*
EMP: 35 **EST:** 1926
SQ FT: 25,000
SALES (est): 7MM **Privately Held**
WEB: www.squarestamping.com
SIC: 3469 Stamping metal for the trade

Barrytown
Dutchess County

(G-606)
STATION HILL OF BARRYTOWN
120 Station Hill Rd (12507-5018)
PHONE..................845 758-5293
George Quasha, *President*
Susan Quasha, *Vice Pres*
EMP: 6
SALES (est): 423.6K **Privately Held**
SIC: 2731 5961 Book publishing; book club, mail order; record &/or tape (music or video) club, mail order

▲ = Import ▼ = Export
◆ = Import/Export

Barryville
Sullivan County

(G-607)
N A R ASSOCIATES INC
128 Rte 55 (12719)
P.O. Box 233 (12719-0233)
PHONE..................845 557-8713
Nick A Roes, *President*
Nancy Bennett, *Vice Pres*
EMP: 6
SALES (est): 537.5K Privately Held
WEB: www.nickroes.com
SIC: 2731 Book publishing

Batavia
Genesee County

(G-608)
ALICIA F HERDLEIN
Also Called: Extreme Streetwear
5450 E Main Street Rd (14020-9625)
PHONE..................585 344-4411
Herdlein F Alicia, *Owner*
Alicia Herdlein, *Owner*
EMP: 5
SALES: 500K Privately Held
SIC: 2759 Screen printing

(G-609)
ALPINA FOODS INC
5011 Agpark Dr W (14020-3446)
PHONE..................855 886-1914
Carlos Mejia, *Principal*
EMP: 13
SALES (est): 1.7MM Privately Held
SIC: 2023 Dry, condensed, evaporated dairy products
PA: Alpina Productos Alimenticios S A
Via Briceno Sopo Kilometro 3
Sopo

(G-610)
AMADA TOOL AMERICA INC
4 Treadeasy Ave Ste A (14020-3010)
PHONE..................585 344-3900
Hitoshi Iizuka, *President*
Michael Guerin, *Corp Secy*
▲ EMP: 55
SQ FT: 50,000
SALES (est): 9.4MM
SALES (corp-wide): 2.8B Privately Held
SIC: 3544 Special dies & tools
HQ: Amada North America, Inc
7025 Firestone Blvd
Buena Park CA 90621

(G-611)
AUTOMOTIVE LLC
4320 Federal Dr (14020-4104)
PHONE..................248 728-8642
EMP: 15
SALES (est): 2.2MM
SALES (corp-wide): 1.3B Privately Held
WEB: www.automotivecorporation.com
SIC: 3465 Body parts, automobile: stamped metal
HQ: Chassix, Inc.
300 Galleria Ofcntr # 501
Southfield MI 48034
248 728-8642

(G-612)
BATAVIA PRESS LLC
3817 W Main Street Rd (14020-9402)
PHONE..................585 343-4429
Becky Almeter, *Partner*
Debbie Clark, *General Mgr*
Robert Hodgins,
EMP: 32
SALES (est): 1.5MM Privately Held
SIC: 2752 7389 2759 Business form & card printing, lithographic; document embossing; engrossing: diplomas, resolutions, etc.; invitation & stationery printing & engraving; security certificates: engraved

(G-613)
BILL SHEA ENTERPRISES INC
Also Called: Deluxe Machine & Tool Co
8825 Alexander Rd (14020-9581)
PHONE..................585 343-2284
William Shea, *President*
Steven Shea, *Vice Pres*
EMP: 2
SQ FT: 20,000
SALES (est): 1.1MM Privately Held
WEB: www.trojanloaders.com
SIC: 3599 Machine shop, jobbing & repair

(G-614)
BONSAL AMERICAN INC
102 Cedar St (14020-3337)
PHONE..................585 343-4741
David Trzybinski, *Branch Mgr*
EMP: 13
SQ FT: 28,069
SALES (corp-wide): 29.7B Privately Held
WEB: www.bonsalamerican.com
SIC: 3272 Concrete products
HQ: Bonsal American, Inc.
625 Griffith Rd Ste 100
Charlotte NC 28217
704 525-1621

(G-615)
BRACH MACHINE INC
4814 Ellicott Street Rd (14020-3420)
PHONE..................585 343-9134
William H Brach, *President*
Nancy E Brach, *Vice Pres*
Nancy Brach, *Vice Pres*
▲ EMP: 12
SQ FT: 15,000
SALES (est): 1.7MM Privately Held
WEB: www.brachmachine.com
SIC: 3469 Machine parts, stamped or pressed metal

(G-616)
CARGILL INCORPORATED
8849 Wortendyke Rd (14020-9558)
PHONE..................585 345-1160
Brent Brinegar, *Opers-Prdtn-Mfg*
Joe Washburn, *Manager*
EMP: 70
SALES (corp-wide): 51.2B Privately Held
WEB: www.cargill.com
SIC: 2048 Prepared feeds
PA: Cargill, Incorporated
15407 Mcginty Rd W
Wayzata MN 55391
952 742-7575

(G-617)
CHAPIN INTERNATIONAL INC
700 Ellicott St (14020-3744)
P.O. Box 549 (14021-0549)
PHONE..................585 343-3140
Andris K Chapin, *Ch of Bd*
James W Campbell, *President*
James Grant, *Vice Pres*
Valerie De Lagenest, *Mktg Dir*
◆ EMP: 225
SQ FT: 710,000
SALES (est): 24.7MM
SALES (corp-wide): 50.1MM Privately Held
SIC: 3499 3524 3085 3563 Aerosol valves, metal; lawn & garden equipment; plastics bottles; air & gas compressors
PA: Chapin Manufacturing, Inc
700 Ellicott St Ste 3
Batavia NY 14020
585 343-3140

(G-618)
CHAPIN MANUFACTURING INC (PA)
700 Ellicott St Ste 3 (14020-3794)
P.O. Box 549 (14021-0549)
PHONE..................585 343-3140
James W Campbell, *Ch of Bd*
Andris K Chapin, *Ch of Bd*
James Grant, *Vice Pres*
William Campbell, *Plant Mgr*
Edward Horeth, *Engineer*
◆ EMP: 220
SQ FT: 710,000
SALES (est): 50.1MM Privately Held
WEB: www.chapinmfg.com
SIC: 3499 3524 3085 3563 Aerosol valves, metal; lawn & garden equipment; plastics bottles; air & gas compressors; spraying outfits: metals, paints & chemicals (compressor); spreaders, fertilizer

(G-619)
CHASSIX AUTOMOTIVE CORP
4320 Federal Dr (14020-4104)
PHONE..................585 815-1700
EMP: 16
SALES (est): 2.2MM Privately Held
SIC: 3599 Machine shop, jobbing & repair

(G-620)
CONSOLIDATED CONTAINER CO LLC
Also Called: Liquitane
14 Hall St (14020-3216)
PHONE..................585 343-9351
Bob Henry, *Facilities Mgr*
Michael Campbell, *Manager*
Robert Henri, *Manager*
Sharon Cummings, *Office Admin*
James Cervi, *Executive*
EMP: 15
SALES (corp-wide): 13.7B Publicly Held
WEB: www.ccllc.com
SIC: 3089 Plastic containers, except foam
HQ: Consolidated Container Company, Llc
2500 Windy Ridge Pkwy Se
Atlanta GA 30339
678 742-4600

(G-621)
COUNTRY FOLKS
123 N Spruce St (14020-2611)
PHONE..................585 343-9721
Patrick Berg, *Principal*
EMP: 5
SALES (est): 196.4K Privately Held
SIC: 2711 Newspapers

(G-622)
DAIRY FARMERS AMERICA INC
Also Called: Muller Quaker Dairy
5140 Agi Business Pk Dr W (14020)
PHONE..................585 409-2200
EMP: 85
SALES (corp-wide): 14.6B Privately Held
SIC: 2026 Fluid milk
PA: Dairy Farmers Of America, Inc.
1405 N 98th St
Kansas City KS 66111
816 801-6455

(G-623)
EXIDE TECHNOLOGIES
Also Called: Exide Batteries
4330 Commerce Dr (14020-4102)
PHONE..................585 344-0656
Deborah Cravatta, *Manager*
George Hoffman, *Manager*
Michael Ellis, *Supervisor*
EMP: 9
SALES (corp-wide): 2.6B Privately Held
WEB: www.exideworld.com
SIC: 3691 Lead acid batteries (storage batteries)
PA: Exide Technologies
13000 Deerfield Pkwy # 200
Milton GA 30004
678 566-9000

(G-624)
FONTRICK DOOR INC
9 Apollo Dr (14020-3001)
PHONE..................585 345-6032
Michael J Fontaine, *CEO*
Jacob Mingle, *Engineer*
EMP: 30
SQ FT: 26,000
SALES (est): 5.2MM Privately Held
WEB: www.fontrickdoor.com
SIC: 2431 1751 Doors & door parts & trim, wood; cabinet building & installation

(G-625)
GEORGIA-PACIFIC CORRUGARED LLC
4 Etreadeasy Ave (14020)
PHONE..................585 343-3800
Andrew Perkins, *Manager*
EMP: 65
SALES (est): 10.3MM
SALES (corp-wide): 42.9B Privately Held
WEB: www.gp.com
SIC: 2611 Pulp manufactured from waste or recycled paper
HQ: Georgia-Pacific Llc
133 Peachtree St Nw
Atlanta GA 30303
404 652-4000

(G-626)
GRAHAM CORPORATION (PA)
20 Florence Ave (14020-3318)
PHONE..................585 343-2216
James J Malvaso, *Ch of Bd*
James R Lines, *President*
Alan E Smith, *Vice Pres*
Keith Sheron, *Purch Mgr*
Wendy Park, *Buyer*
EMP: 277
SQ FT: 45,000
SALES: 77.5MM Publicly Held
WEB: www.graham-mfg.com
SIC: 3563 3585 3443 Vacuum pumps, except laboratory; compressors for refrigeration & air conditioning equipment; condensers, refrigeration; heat exchangers, condensers & components; heat exchangers, plate type; heat exchangers: coolers (after, inter), condensers, etc.

(G-627)
HEATH MANUFACTURING COMPANY
Also Called: Heath Outdoors Products
700 Ellicott St (14020-3744)
PHONE..................800 444-3140
EMP: 6
SALES (corp-wide): 50.1MM Privately Held
SIC: 2048 Bird food, prepared
HQ: Heath Manufacturing Company
140 Mill St Ste A
Coopersville MI 49404
616 997-8181

(G-628)
HODGINS ENGRAVING CO INC
3817 W Main Street Rd (14020-9402)
PHONE..................585 343-4444
Robert Hodgins, *President*
Becky Almeter, *Project Mgr*
Jeremy Almeter, *Prdtn Mgr*
Elaine Skoczylas, *Purch Agent*
Karen Kelley, *Accounting Mgr*
◆ EMP: 70
SQ FT: 36,000
SALES (est): 13MM Privately Held
WEB: www.hodginsengraving.com
SIC: 3555 3953 Printing trades machinery; marking devices

(G-629)
LICKITY SPLITS
238 East Ave (14020-2704)
PHONE..................585 345-6091
Fred Hamilton, *Partner*
Craig Hargrades, *Partner*
EMP: 8
SALES (est): 508K Privately Held
SIC: 2024 Ice cream & frozen desserts

(G-630)
MONDELEZ GLOBAL LLC
Also Called: Nabisco
4303 Federal Dr (14020-4105)
PHONE..................585 345-3300
Phil Barter, *Branch Mgr*
Anthony Del Duca, *Maintence Staff*
EMP: 9 Publicly Held
SIC: 2099 5141 Food preparations; groceries, general line
HQ: Mondelez Global Llc
3 N Pkwy Ste 300
Deerfield IL 60015
847 943-4000

(G-631)
N Y WESTERN CONCRETE CORP
638 E Main St (14020-2812)
PHONE..................585 343-6850
Joseph Penepent, *President*
Eugene Penepent, *Vice Pres*
Vincent Penepent, *Treasurer*
Christopher Coriale, *Accountant*

Batavia - Genesee County (G-632)

EMP: 5 EST: 1950
SQ FT: 2,000
SALES (est): 1.3MM Privately Held
SIC: 3273 Ready-mixed concrete

(G-632)
O-AT-KA MILK PRODUCTS COOP INC (PA)
700 Ellicott St (14020-3744)
P.O. Box 718 (14021-0718)
PHONE.................585 343-0536
Robert Hall, *CEO*
Herbert Nobles, *Ch of Bd*
Dan Wolf, *COO*
Clyde Rutherford, *Vice Pres*
Michael Patterson, *CFO*
◆ EMP: 302 EST: 1956
SQ FT: 205,000
SALES: 319.3MM Privately Held
WEB: www.oatkamilk.com
SIC: 2023 2021 2026 Concentrated skim milk; evaporated milk; dried nonfat milk; creamery butter; fluid milk

(G-633)
PINNACLE MANUFACTURING CO INC
56 Harvester Ave (14020-3357)
P.O. Box 1446 (14021-1446)
PHONE.................585 343-5664
Kim Kisiel, *President*
Kevin Kisiel, *Vice Pres*
Luis Pulvino, *Plant Mgr*
Kathleen Dunlap, *Office Mgr*
▲ EMP: 25
SQ FT: 35,000
SALES (est): 6.1MM Privately Held
WEB: www.pinnaclemanufacturing.com
SIC: 3363 3364 Aluminum die-castings; zinc & zinc-base alloy die-castings

(G-634)
SEVEN SPRINGS GRAVEL PDTS LLC
8479 Seven Springs Rd (14020-9632)
PHONE.................585 343-4336
Mike Doyle,
Carmen Pariso,
EMP: 6
SALES (est): 570K Privately Held
SIC: 1442 Gravel mining

(G-635)
STRONG FORGE & FABRICATION
20 Liberty St (14020-3208)
P.O. Box 803 (14021-0803)
PHONE.................585 343-5251
Mitchell Strong, *President*
Brian Delillo, *Manager*
Deb Buchinger, *Executive*
EMP: 37
SALES (est): 7.2MM Privately Held
WEB: www.strongforge.com
SIC: 3599 Machine shop, jobbing & repair

(G-636)
SUMMIT LUBRICANTS INC
4d Treadeasy Ave (14020-3010)
P.O. Box 966 (14021-0966)
PHONE.................585 815-0798
Ronald Krol, *President*
Allan Ulrich, *Opers Mgr*
Danielle Brinkman, *Administration*
Dan Sharek, *Maintence Staff*
▲ EMP: 47
SQ FT: 50,000
SALES: 14.7MM
SALES (corp-wide): 820MM Publicly Held
WEB: www.summitlubricants.com
SIC: 2992 Lubricating oils & greases
PA: Quaker Chemical Corporation
 901 E Hector St
 Conshohocken PA 19428
 610 832-4000

(G-637)
TOMPKINS METAL FINISHING INC
6 Apollo Dr (14020-3002)
PHONE.................585 344-2600
Allen C Tompkins, *President*
John Tompkins, *Vice Pres*
John Abdoo, *Prdtn Mgr*

Bill Schuler, *Safety Mgr*
Jim McCarrick, *QC Mgr*
EMP: 80
SALES (est): 14.6MM Privately Held
SIC: 3471 Electroplating of metals or formed products

(G-638)
TRACO MANUFACTURING INC
4300 Commerce Dr (14020-4102)
PHONE.................585 343-2434
Tracy Jachimowicz, *President*
Daniel Jachimowicz, *Vice Pres*
Alicia Jachimowicz, *Office Mgr*
EMP: 5
SQ FT: 16,500
SALES (est): 640.2K Privately Held
WEB: www.tracomfg.com
SIC: 2542 Partitions & fixtures, except wood

(G-639)
VISUAL IMPACT GRAPHICS INC
653 Ellicott St Ste 6 (14020-3746)
P.O. Box 236, Byron (14422-0236)
PHONE.................585 548-7118
Tom Chapell, *President*
EMP: 6
SALES (est): 527.9K Privately Held
WEB: www.visualimpactonline.com
SIC: 3993 Signs & advertising specialties

Bath
Steuben County

(G-640)
BABCOCK CO INC
36 Delaware Ave (14810-1607)
PHONE.................607 776-3341
Mark McConnell, *President*
J Ward McConnell, *Chairman*
EMP: 25
SQ FT: 107,000
SALES (est): 4.9MM Privately Held
SIC: 2499 Ladders, wood

(G-641)
BOMBARDIER TRNSP HOLDINGS USA
7940 State Route 415 (14810-7571)
PHONE.................607 776-4791
Carl Drum, *Branch Mgr*
EMP: 60
SALES (corp-wide): 16.2B Privately Held
SIC: 3441 8711 3799 3585 Fabricated structural metal; engineering services; cars, off-highway: electric; refrigeration & heating equipment; electrical apparatus & equipment; electrical equipment & supplies
HQ: Bombardier Transportation (Holdings) Usa Inc
 1501 Lebanon Church Rd
 Pittsburgh PA 15236
 412 655-5700

(G-642)
CLARK SPECIALTY CO INC
7185 State Route 54 (14810-9502)
PHONE.................607 776-3193
James L Presley, *Ch of Bd*
Robert Schuck, *Plant Mgr*
Harry Mulholland, *Manager*
Susan Weaver, *Admin Sec*
EMP: 37 EST: 1946
SQ FT: 90,000
SALES (est): 6.2MM Privately Held
WEB: www.clarkspecialty.com
SIC: 2542 3444 Telephone booths: except wood; sheet metalwork

(G-643)
GATEHOUSE MEDIA LLC
Also Called: Steuben Courier Advocate
10 W Steuben St (14810-1512)
PHONE.................607 776-2121
Karen Causer, *Manager*
EMP: 7
SQ FT: 3,700
SALES (corp-wide): 1.3B Publicly Held
WEB: www.gatehousemedia.com
SIC: 2711 Newspapers, publishing & printing

HQ: Gatehouse Media, Llc
 175 Sullys Trl Ste 300
 Pittsford NY 14534
 585 598-0030

(G-644)
HANGER PRSTHETCS & ORTHO INC
47 W Steuben St (14810-1540)
PHONE.................607 776-8013
Erico Webster, *General Mgr*
EMP: 7
SALES (corp-wide): 1B Publicly Held
SIC: 3842 Orthopedic appliances
HQ: Hanger Prosthetics & Orthotics, Inc.
 10910 Domain Dr Ste 300
 Austin TX 78758
 512 777-3800

(G-645)
KEELER SERVICES
47 W Steuben St Ste 4 (14810-1540)
PHONE.................607 776-5757
Mathew Keeler, *Owner*
EMP: 6
SQ FT: 6,270
SALES (est): 412.1K Privately Held
SIC: 3585 Heating & air conditioning combination units

(G-646)
KNIGHT STTLEMENT SAND GRAV LLC
7291 County Route 15 (14810-8245)
P.O. Box 191 (14810-0191)
PHONE.................607 776-2048
Bryan Dickson,
Brett Dickson,
L Jay Dickson,
EMP: 38
SQ FT: 9,408
SALES (est): 6.3MM Privately Held
SIC: 3273 Ready-mixed concrete

(G-647)
LANE ENTERPRISES INC
Also Called: Lane Metal Products
16 May St (14810-9716)
PHONE.................607 776-3366
Richard A Walter, *Manager*
EMP: 10
SQ FT: 18,416
SALES (corp-wide): 70.5MM Privately Held
WEB: www.lanepipe.com
SIC: 3443 Culverts, metal plate
PA: Lane Enterprises, Inc.
 3905 Hartzdale Dr Ste 514
 Camp Hill PA 17011
 717 761-8175

(G-648)
PHILIPS ELEC N AMER CORP
Philips Lighting
7265 State Route 54 (14810-9586)
PHONE.................607 776-3692
Tom Mason, *Engineer*
Tony Stuart, *Manager*
EMP: 110
SALES (corp-wide): 20.9B Privately Held
WEB: www.usa.philips.com
SIC: 3645 3641 Residential lighting fixtures; electric lamps
HQ: Philips North America Llc
 3000 Minuteman Rd Ms1203
 Andover MA 01810
 978 659-3000

(G-649)
SMART SYSTEMS INC
320 E Washington St (14810-1323)
P.O. Box 158, Bohemia (11716-0158)
PHONE.................607 776-5380
Marven Smith, *President*
EMP: 20
SALES (est): 2.2MM Privately Held
WEB: www.smartsystemsinc.org
SIC: 3711 5012 Mfg Motor Vehicle/Car Bodies Whol Autos/Motor Vehicles

Bay Shore
Suffolk County

(G-650)
3DFLAM INC
Also Called: LPI Envelope
1460 N Clinton Ave Ste I9 (11706-4057)
PHONE.................631 647-2694
Frank Owad, *President*
Victoria Heikkila, *Treasurer*
EMP: 10 EST: 2008
SQ FT: 7,500
SALES (est): 1.9MM Privately Held
SIC: 2677 Envelopes

(G-651)
ABS TALKX INC
34 Cleveland Ave (11706-1223)
PHONE.................631 254-9100
EMP: 8
SQ FT: 7,300
SALES (est): 1.2MM Privately Held
SIC: 3661 5999 4813 Mfg Telephone/Telegraph Apparatus Ret Misc Merchandise Telephone Communications

(G-652)
ADEPTRONICS INCORPORATED
Also Called: Ziptswitch
281 Skip Ln Ste C (11706-1215)
PHONE.................631 667-0659
EMP: 6
SALES: 850K Privately Held
SIC: 3625 Mfg Relays/Industrial Controls

(G-653)
AIR INDUSTRIES MACHINING CORP
1460 5th Ave (11706-4147)
PHONE.................631 328-7000
Michael N Taglich, *Ch of Bd*
Luciano Melluzzo, *President*
▲ EMP: 115
SQ FT: 76,000
SALES (est): 17.9MM Publicly Held
SIC: 3728 Aircraft assemblies, subassemblies & parts
PA: Air Industries Group
 360 Motor Pkwy Ste 100
 Hauppauge NY 11788

(G-654)
ALL STAR CARTS & VEHICLES INC
1565 5th Industrial Ct B (11706-3434)
PHONE.................631 666-5581
Steven Kronrad, *President*
Gregory Kronrad, *Vice Pres*
Robert Kronrad, *Vice Pres*
EMP: 51
SQ FT: 25,000
SALES (est): 8.7MM Privately Held
WEB: www.allstarcarts.com
SIC: 2599 3792 3444 2451 Carts, restaurant equipment; travel trailers & campers; sheet metalwork; mobile homes

(G-655)
ALTEC DATACOM LLC
70 Corbin Ave Ste I (11706-1039)
PHONE.................631 242-2417
Abraham Mendez,
Teresa Mendez,
EMP: 8
SQ FT: 1,500
SALES (est): 857.5K Privately Held
SIC: 3679 Harness assemblies for electronic use: wire or cable

(G-656)
AMERICAN PRIDE FASTENERS LLC
195 S Fehr Way (11706-1207)
PHONE.................631 940-8292
Lynda Zacpal, *President*
George W Hughes III, *Vice Pres*
Nicholas Zacpal, *QC Mgr*
Kathy Sheridan, *Office Mgr*
▲ EMP: 20
SQ FT: 10,000

GEOGRAPHIC SECTION
Bay Shore - Suffolk County (G-684)

SALES: 4.2MM **Privately Held**
SIC: 3965 3452 5085 Fasteners; bolts, nuts, rivets & washers; fasteners & fastening equipment

(G-657)
ANBRIELLA SAND & GRAVEL CORP
145 S 4th St (11706-1230)
PHONE..................631 586-2111
Ricky Starr, *President*
EMP: 42
SALES (est): 2MM **Privately Held**
SIC: 3273 Ready-mixed concrete

(G-658)
ANTENNA & RADOME RES ASSOC (PA)
15 Harold Ct (11706-2220)
P.O. Box 113, Old Bethpage (11804-0113)
PHONE..................631 231-8400
Florence Isaacson, *President*
EMP: 50
SQ FT: 20,000
SALES (est): 19.6MM **Privately Held**
WEB: www.arra.com
SIC: 3679 Microwave components

(G-659)
ARTISTIC IRON WORKS INC
94 Saxon Ave Ste A (11706-7005)
PHONE..................631 665-4285
Rick Portera, *President*
EMP: 8
SQ FT: 5,500
SALES: 1.5MM **Privately Held**
SIC: 3446 3312 2431 Stairs, fire escapes, balconies, railings & ladders; rails, steel or iron; staircases, stairs & railings

(G-660)
ASTRO ELECTROPLATING INC
171 4th Ave (11706-7303)
PHONE..................631 968-0656
Neil Weinstein, *CEO*
John Jodoin, *Opers Mgr*
Jennifer Calderone, *Human Resources*
Nicole Wright, *Manager*
EMP: 36
SALES (est): 5.1MM **Privately Held**
SIC: 3471 Electroplating of metals or formed products

(G-661)
BAIRD MOLD MAKING INC
195 N Fehr Way Ste C (11706-1234)
PHONE..................631 667-0322
John Baird, *President*
Henry Quintin, *Vice Pres*
▲ EMP: 6
SQ FT: 3,000
SALES (est): 803.6K **Privately Held**
SIC: 3089 Molding primary plastic; injection molding of plastics

(G-662)
BFG MARINE INC
200 Candlewood Rd (11706-2217)
PHONE..................631 586-5500
Glenn Burgos, *President*
Ellis W Konkel III, *Vice Pres*
EMP: 10 EST: 1959
SQ FT: 20,000
SALES (est): 2.3MM **Privately Held**
WEB: www.bfgmarine.com
SIC: 3429 5085 Marine hardware; industrial supplies

(G-663)
BIMBO BAKERIES USA INC
Also Called: Transportation Department
14 Spence St (11706-2207)
PHONE..................631 951-5183
Phil Paturzo, *Vice Pres*
Anthony Maiorano, *Branch Mgr*
Henry Valerio, *Admin Asst*
EMP: 32 **Privately Held**
WEB: www.gwbakeries.com
SIC: 2051 Bread, cake & related products
HQ: Bimbo Bakeries Usa, Inc
255 Business Center Dr # 200
Horsham PA 19044
215 347-5500

(G-664)
BIMBO BAKERIES USA INC
30 Inez Dr (11706-2204)
PHONE..................203 531-2311
James Montgomery, *Branch Mgr*
EMP: 50 **Privately Held**
WEB: www.englishmuffin.com
SIC: 2051 Doughnuts, except frozen; cakes, bakery: except frozen; pies, bakery: except frozen
HQ: Bimbo Bakeries Usa, Inc
255 Business Center Dr # 200
Horsham PA 19044
215 347-5500

(G-665)
BIMBO FOODS BAKERIES INC (DH)
Also Called: Bimbo Bakeries USA
40 Harold Ct (11706-2220)
PHONE..................631 273-6000
▲ EMP: 150
SQ FT: 600,000
SALES (est): 2B
SALES (corp-wide): 13B **Privately Held**
WEB: www.gwbakeries.com
SIC: 2051 Mfg Bread/Related Products
HQ: Bimbo Bakeries Usa, Inc
255 Business Center Dr # 200
Horsham PA 19044
215 347-5500

(G-666)
BONDY PRINTING CORP
Also Called: Sir Speedy
267 W Main St (11706-8319)
PHONE..................631 242-1510
William Bondy Jr, *President*
Donna Bondy, *Vice Pres*
EMP: 5
SALES (est): 845.4K **Privately Held**
SIC: 2752 2791 2789 2759 Commercial printing, offset; typesetting; bookbinding & related work; commercial printing; automotive & apparel trimmings

(G-667)
CABLE MANAGEMENT SOLUTIONS INC
Also Called: Jette Group
291 Skip Ln (11706-1206)
PHONE..................631 674-0004
Roger Jette, *President*
▲ EMP: 30
SQ FT: 3,500
SALES (est): 7.1MM **Privately Held**
WEB: www.snaketray.com
SIC: 3496 Miscellaneous fabricated wire products

(G-668)
CCS MACHINERY INC
2175 Union Blvd (11706-8016)
PHONE..................631 968-0900
Mark Wilenkin, *Ch of Bd*
EMP: 14 EST: 2001
SALES (est): 2.5MM **Privately Held**
SIC: 3531 Construction machinery

(G-669)
CENTURY METAL PARTS CORP
230 S Fehr Way (11706-1208)
PHONE..................631 667-0800
Frank Swierzbin, *President*
Thomas Larkin, *IT/INT Sup*
EMP: 25
SQ FT: 17,000
SALES (est): 4MM **Privately Held**
SIC: 3663 3451 Antennas, transmitting & communications; screw machine products

(G-670)
CHEM-TEK SYSTEMS INC
Also Called: Moldedtanks.com
208 S Fehr Way (11706-1208)
P.O. Box 222, Nesconset (11767-0222)
PHONE..................631 253-3010
Shawn Sprague, *President*
EMP: 10
SQ FT: 4,000
SALES (est): 1MM **Privately Held**
SIC: 3089 Plastic & fiberglass tanks

(G-671)
CLAD METAL SPECIALTIES INC
1516 5th Industrial Ct (11706-3402)
PHONE..................631 666-7750
Denise Marcoccia, *Exec VP*
Dominick Bodami, *Vice Pres*
EMP: 19
SQ FT: 13,500
SALES (est): 3.9MM **Privately Held**
WEB: www.cladmetal.com
SIC: 3479 Bonderizing of metal or metal products; aluminum coating of metal products

(G-672)
COLONIAL LABEL SYSTEMS INC
Also Called: Colonial Rapid
50 Corbin Ave Ste L (11706-1047)
P.O. Box 812, Deer Park (11729-0976)
PHONE..................631 254-0111
Ron Afzelius, *President*
EMP: 25
SALES (est): 4MM **Privately Held**
SIC: 2759 Commercial printing

(G-673)
COLONIE PLASTICS CORP
188 Candlewood Rd (11706-2219)
PHONE..................631 434-6969
Paul Gurbatri, *President*
Laura Arzeno, *Opers Mgr*
Louie Passi, *Manager*
▲ EMP: 130
SQ FT: 11,500
SALES (est): 16.6MM **Privately Held**
WEB: www.colonieplastics.com
SIC: 3089 Injection molding of plastics

(G-674)
COLORFULLY YOURS INC
11 Grant Ave (11706-1007)
PHONE..................631 242-8600
Joseph Lindner, *President*
Deborah Lindner, *Vice Pres*
Ginny Ciccone, *Office Mgr*
EMP: 10
SQ FT: 5,000
SALES: 1.2MM **Privately Held**
WEB: www.colorfullyyours.com
SIC: 2752 Commercial printing, offset

(G-675)
COMMAND COMPONENTS CORPORATION
6 Cherry St (11706-7325)
PHONE..................631 666-4411
Jerry Sukman, *President*
EMP: 8
SQ FT: 3,000
SALES (est): 1.2MM **Privately Held**
WEB: www.commandcomponents.com
SIC: 3643 Electric connectors

(G-676)
CYNCAL STEEL FABRICATORS INC
225 Pine Aire Dr (11706-1147)
PHONE..................631 254-5600
Cynthia Callahan, *Owner*
EMP: 12
SALES (est): 1.2MM **Privately Held**
SIC: 3441 Fabricated structural metal

(G-677)
D K P WOOD RAILINGS & STAIRS
1971 Union Blvd (11706-7956)
PHONE..................631 665-8656
Dmitri Onishchuk, *President*
EMP: 11
SALES (est): 1MM **Privately Held**
SIC: 2431 Stair railings, wood

(G-678)
DAVID PEYSER SPORTSWEAR INC (PA)
Also Called: Weatherproof
90 Spence St (11706-2230)
P.O. Box 9171 (11706-9171)
PHONE..................631 231-7788
Paul Peyser, *President*
Joshua Peyser, *Corp Secy*
Irwin Hosea, *Vice Pres*
Hunter McMillan, *Vice Pres*
Alan Peyser, *Vice Pres*
▲ EMP: 245
SQ FT: 110,000
SALES: 54.7MM **Privately Held**
WEB: www.mvsport.com
SIC: 2329 Men's & boys' sportswear & athletic clothing

(G-679)
DECAL TECHNIQUES INC
40 Corbin Ave Ste I (11706-1048)
PHONE..................631 491-1800
Eugene P Snyder, *President*
Terry Lomanto, *Vice Pres*
Helen Rider, *Admin Sec*
EMP: 8
SQ FT: 4,000
SALES (est): 600K **Privately Held**
WEB: www.decaltech.com
SIC: 2752 Decals, lithographed; posters, lithographed

(G-680)
DEER PARK SAND & GRAVEL CORP
145 S 4th St (11706-1200)
PHONE..................631 586-2323
David Ciardullo, *President*
Joe Ciardullo, *Vice Pres*
EMP: 20
SQ FT: 4,000
SALES (est): 3.6MM **Privately Held**
SIC: 3273 5032 Ready-mixed concrete; gravel; sand, construction

(G-681)
DELTA POLYMERS INC
130 S 2nd St (11706-1036)
PHONE..................631 254-6240
Razia Rana, *President*
Riasat Rana, *Vice Pres*
EMP: 8
SQ FT: 10,000
SALES (est): 1.5MM **Privately Held**
WEB: www.deltapolymers.com
SIC: 2851 1752 Epoxy coatings; floor laying & floor work

(G-682)
DURO DYNE CORPORATION (HQ)
81 Spence St (11706-2206)
P.O. Box 9117 (11706-9117)
PHONE..................631 249-9000
Randall Hinden, *President*
▲ EMP: 150 EST: 1952
SQ FT: 130,000
SALES (est): 34.2MM
SALES (corp-wide): 125.5MM **Privately Held**
SIC: 3585 Air conditioning equipment, complete; heating equipment, complete

(G-683)
DURO DYNE MACHINERY CORP
81 Spence St (11706-2206)
P.O. Box 9117 (11706-9117)
PHONE..................631 249-9000
Milton Hinden, *CEO*
Randall Hinden, *President*
Carole D'Agosta, *Vice Pres*
William Watman, *Vice Pres*
◆ EMP: 40 EST: 1952
SQ FT: 25,000
SALES: 9.8MM
SALES (corp-wide): 125.5MM **Privately Held**
SIC: 3585 Air conditioning units, complete: domestic or industrial; heating equipment, complete
PA: Dyne Duro National Corp
81 Spence St
Bay Shore NY 11706

(G-684)
E F IRON WORKS & CONSTRUCTION
241 N Fehr Way Ste 3 (11706-1233)
PHONE..................631 242-4766
Ed Frage, *President*
EMP: 6

Bay Shore - Suffolk County (G-685) — GEOGRAPHIC SECTION

SALES: 390K **Privately Held**
WEB: www.efiron.com
SIC: 3446 1799 Architectural metalwork; ornamental metal work

(G-685)
EMPIRE INDUSTRIAL SYSTEMS CORP (PA)
40 Corbin Ave (11706-1048)
PHONE..................631 242-4619
Shali Roufberg, *President*
EMP: 10
SQ FT: 7,500
SALES (est): 1.1MM **Privately Held**
SIC: 3443 1711 7699 3441 Boilers: industrial, power, or marine; industrial vessels, tanks & containers; boiler & furnace contractors; boiler repair shop; fabricated structural metal

(G-686)
FENIX FURNITURE CO
Also Called: Mica America
35 Drexel Dr (11706-2235)
PHONE..................631 273-3500
Jared Fenigstein, *President*
EMP: 30
SQ FT: 24,000
SALES (est): 3.3MM **Privately Held**
SIC: 2511 Wood household furniture

(G-687)
FOOD BASKET USA COMPANY LTD
30 Inez Dr (11706-2204)
PHONE..................631 231-8999
Charlie Gao, *Principal*
Eddie Leung, *CFO*
EMP: 20 EST: 2015
SALES (est): 891K **Privately Held**
SIC: 2038 Frozen specialties

(G-688)
FRED M LAWRENCE CO INC (PA)
45 Drexel Dr (11706-2201)
PHONE..................718 786-7227
Vincent Lanci, *President*
▲ EMP: 26
SQ FT: 22,000
SALES (est): 4MM **Privately Held**
WEB: www.photoframes.net
SIC: 2499 Picture & mirror frames, wood

(G-689)
INTER MOLDS INC
26 Cleveland Ave (11706-1223)
PHONE..................631 667-8580
Victor Goncalves, *President*
Francisco Silva, *Vice Pres*
Douglas Cooper, *Treasurer*
Mario Santiago, *Admin Sec*
EMP: 6
SQ FT: 5,000
SALES (est): 700K **Privately Held**
WEB: www.intermolds.com
SIC: 3544 Forms (molds), for foundry & plastics working machinery

(G-690)
INTERFACE PRODUCTS CO INC
215 N Fehr Way Ste C (11706-1209)
PHONE..................631 242-4605
George Miller, *President*
Mary Ann Harrell, *Office Mgr*
EMP: 8
SQ FT: 2,125
SALES (est): 770K **Privately Held**
SIC: 3534 Elevators & equipment

(G-691)
ISLIP MINITURE GOLF
500 E Main St (11706-8502)
PHONE..................631 940-8900
Mike Flemming,
EMP: 8
SALES (est): 355.8K **Privately Held**
SIC: 3999 Miniatures

(G-692)
JERRY CARDULLO IRON WORKS INC
Also Called: Cardullo, J Iron Works
101 Spence St (11706-2208)
PHONE..................631 242-8881
Jerry Cardullo, *President*
EMP: 12
SQ FT: 3,000
SALES (est): 880K **Privately Held**
SIC: 3446 Architectural metalwork

(G-693)
LAMINATED WINDOW PRODUCTS INC
211 N Fehr Way (11706-1203)
PHONE..................631 242-6883
Ismael Santiago, *President*
EMP: 10
SQ FT: 4,000
SALES: 800K **Privately Held**
SIC: 2391 2394 Draperies, plastic & textile: from purchased materials; shades, canvas: made from purchased materials

(G-694)
LANWOOD INDUSTRIES INC
Also Called: Fred Lawrence Co
45 Drexel Dr (11706-2201)
PHONE..................718 786-3000
EMP: 30
SQ FT: 25,000
SALES (est): 193.4K **Privately Held**
SIC: 2499 2782 Mfg Wood Products Mfg Blankbooks/Binders

(G-695)
LASTICKS AEROSPACE INC
35 Washington Ave Ste E (11706-1027)
PHONE..................631 242-8484
Guy T Russo, *President*
Keith Johns, *Vice Pres*
Luciano De Biassi, *QC Mgr*
Gregory Nasta, *Software Dev*
EMP: 14
SQ FT: 5,000
SALES (est): 2.9MM **Privately Held**
WEB: www.lasticksaero.com
SIC: 3599 Machine shop, jobbing & repair

(G-696)
LEXAN INDUSTRIES INC
Also Called: Struthers Electronics
15 Harold Ct (11706-2220)
PHONE..................631 434-7586
Florence Isaacson, *President*
EMP: 19
SQ FT: 11,000
SALES (est): 1.3MM **Privately Held**
SIC: 3679 3825 Microwave components; test equipment for electronic & electrical circuits

(G-697)
M F L B INC
Also Called: S D S of Long Island
7 Grant Ave (11706-1007)
PHONE..................631 254-8300
Frank Baubille, *Vice Pres*
Michael Cafiero, *Admin Sec*
EMP: 13
SQ FT: 2,500
SALES: 450K **Privately Held**
WEB: www.mflb.com
SIC: 3677 Electronic coils, transformers & other inductors

(G-698)
MARKS CORPEX BANKNOTE CO (PA)
1440 5th Ave (11706-4149)
PHONE..................631 968-0277
Henri Bertuch, *Principal*
Rhoda Bertuch, *Treasurer*
EMP: 8
SQ FT: 12,000
SALES (est): 828.4K **Privately Held**
WEB: www.corpexnet.com
SIC: 2752 5085 Commercial printing, offset; industrial supplies

(G-699)
MBA ORTHOTICS INC
60 Corbin Ave Unit 60g (11706-1046)
PHONE..................631 392-4755
Andrea Tamayo, *President*
Adriana Salcedo, *General Mgr*
EMP: 5
SALES: 300K **Privately Held**
SIC: 3131 Sole parts for shoes

(G-700)
METAL IMPROVEMENT COMPANY LLC
210 Candlewood Rd (11706-2217)
PHONE..................631 567-2610
Jim Groark, *Manager*
EMP: 14
SALES (corp-wide): 2.2B **Publicly Held**
WEB: www.mic-houston.com
SIC: 3398 Shot peening (treating steel to reduce fatigue)
HQ: Metal Improvement Company, Llc
  80 E Rte 4 Ste 310
  Paramus NJ 07652
  201 843-7800

(G-701)
MILEX PRECISION INC
66 S 2nd St Ste G (11706-1000)
PHONE..................631 595-2393
Aeric Misko, *President*
Dagmar Misko, *Vice Pres*
EMP: 14
SQ FT: 4,000
SALES: 1.5MM **Privately Held**
SIC: 3728 3599 Aircraft parts & equipment; machine shop, jobbing & repair

(G-702)
MINICO INDUSTRIES INC
66a S 2nd St Ste A (11706)
PHONE..................631 595-1455
Nicholas Chonis, *President*
Constantine Chonis, *Vice Pres*
Michael Chonis, *Treasurer*
EMP: 9
SQ FT: 4,500
SALES (est): 1.3MM **Privately Held**
WEB: www.minicoindustries.com
SIC: 3089 Injection molding of plastics

(G-703)
MV CORP INC
Also Called: M V Sport
88 Spence St Ste 90 (11706-2229)
P.O. Box 9171 (11706-9171)
PHONE..................631 273-8020
Joshua Peyser, *Ch of Bd*
Alan Peyser, *Principal*
Paul Peyser, *Principal*
David Chin, *Assistant*
▲ EMP: 150
SQ FT: 40,000
SALES: 15.1MM
SALES (corp-wide): 54.7MM **Privately Held**
WEB: www.mvsport.com
SIC: 2311 2262 2759 2339 Men's & boys' suits & coats; screen printing: man-made fiber & silk broadwoven fabrics; screen printing; women's & misses' outerwear
PA: David Peyser Sportswear, Inc.
  90 Spence St
  Bay Shore NY 11706
  631 231-7788

(G-704)
NASSAU SUFFOLK BRD OF WOMENS
145 New York Ave (11706-3209)
PHONE..................631 666-8835
Cris McNamara, *President*
EMP: 50
SALES (est): 1.7MM **Privately Held**
SIC: 2387 Apparel belts

(G-705)
NASSAU TOOL WORKS INC
1479 N Clinton Ave (11706-4051)
PHONE..................631 328-7031
Michael N Taglich, *Ch of Bd*
Luciano Melluzzo, *President*
EMP: 50 EST: 1956
SQ FT: 60,000
SALES (est): 7.7MM **Publicly Held**
SIC: 3599 3728 Machine shop, jobbing & repair; aircraft landing assemblies & brakes
PA: Air Industries Group
  360 Motor Pkwy Ste 100
  Hauppauge NY 11788

(G-706)
PLATINUM CARTING CORP
1806 Carleton Ave (11706-1632)
PHONE..................631 649-4322
Carol Key, *President*
Zed Key, *Treasurer*
EMP: 15
SALES (est): 1.3MM **Privately Held**
SIC: 3639 Garbage disposal units, household

(G-707)
POLY SCIENTIFIC R&D CORP
70 Cleveland Ave (11706-1282)
PHONE..................631 586-0400
John J Caggiano, *Ch of Bd*
John H Arnold, *Exec VP*
Joseph Caggiano, *Vice Pres*
Delio Dicuffa, *Manager*
EMP: 40 EST: 1969
SQ FT: 22,000
SALES (est): 8.8MM **Privately Held**
WEB: www.polyrnd.com
SIC: 2869 5169 2819 Industrial organic chemicals; chemicals & allied products; industrial inorganic chemicals

(G-708)
POLYCAST INDUSTRIES INC
130 S 2nd St (11706-1036)
PHONE..................631 595-2530
Razia Rana, *President*
Riasat Rana, *Vice Pres*
EMP: 5
SQ FT: 100,000
SALES: 1MM **Privately Held**
SIC: 3679 2992 2891 2821 Electronic circuits; lubricating oils & greases; adhesives & sealants; plastics materials & resins

(G-709)
PRECISION METALS CORP
221 Skip Ln (11706-1206)
PHONE..................631 586-5032
Thomas J Figlozzi, *Ch of Bd*
Anna Maria Figlozzi, *Corp Secy*
Tony Figlozzi, *Vice Pres*
EMP: 45
SQ FT: 16,000
SALES (est): 13MM **Privately Held**
WEB: www.precisionmetalscorp.com
SIC: 3441 3599 3444 Fabricated structural metal; machine & other job shop work; sheet metalwork

(G-710)
PRESTIGELINE INC
5 Inez Dr (11706-2203)
P.O. Box 100 (11706-0703)
PHONE..................631 273-3636
Scott Roth, *President*
Stuart Goldstein, *Senior VP*
Kenneth Golden, *Vice Pres*
▲ EMP: 82
SQ FT: 150,000
SALES (est): 11.1MM **Privately Held**
WEB: www.prestigelineinc.com
SIC: 3645 5063 Residential lighting fixtures; lighting fixtures, residential

(G-711)
PROTO MACHINE INC
60 Corbin Ave Ste D (11706-1046)
PHONE..................631 392-1159
EMP: 11
SQ FT: 3,600
SALES: 1.2MM **Privately Held**
SIC: 3599 Machining Full Service Job Shop

(G-712)
R G FLAIR CO INC
199 S Fehr Way (11706-1207)
PHONE..................631 586-7311
Gerhard Raible, *President*
Dieter Thole, *Corp Secy*
Soraya Rodrigues, *Senior VP*
Martin Sievers, *Vice Pres*
Chris Thole, *Manager*
▲ EMP: 22 EST: 1976
SQ FT: 13,000
SALES (est): 3.7MM **Privately Held**
WEB: www.rgflair.com
SIC: 3469 3915 Stamping metal for the trade; jewelers' materials & lapidary work

GEOGRAPHIC SECTION

Bayport - Suffolk County (G-739)

(G-713)
RAN MAR ENTERPRISES LTD
143 Anchor Ln (11706-8121)
PHONE..................631 666-4754
Melvin Small, *President*
EMP: 12
SQ FT: 13,000
SALES (est): 1.4MM **Privately Held**
SIC: 2891 Manufacturer Converter And Packaging Of Self-Stick Adhesive Products

(G-714)
RFN INC
40 Drexel Dr (11706-2202)
PHONE..................516 764-5100
Alex Treyger, *President*
EMP: 18
SQ FT: 28,000
SALES: 1.5MM **Privately Held**
SIC: 2759 8742 Commercial printing; marketing consulting services

(G-715)
RIT PRINTING CORP
250 N Fairway (11706)
PHONE..................631 586-6220
Anthony Buono, *President*
EMP: 10
SQ FT: 8,000
SALES (est): 1.7MM **Privately Held**
WEB: www.ritprinting.com
SIC: 2752 2759 Commercial printing, offset; commercial printing

(G-716)
ROCKET TECH FUEL CORP
20 Corbin Ave (11706-1004)
PHONE..................516 810-8947
Richard Miller, *President*
Joseph Silhan, *Vice Pres*
EMP: 10 **EST:** 2004
SQ FT: 1,800
SALES: 90MM **Privately Held**
SIC: 1311 Crude petroleum & natural gas

(G-717)
ROMAN STONE CONSTRUCTION CO
85 S 4th St (11706-1210)
PHONE..................631 667-0566
Thomas Montalbine, *President*
Anna Faia, *Vice Pres*
Layne Urbas, *Treasurer*
Lori Messina, *Bookkeeper*
Ryan Camberdella, *Sales Mgr*
EMP: 45 **EST:** 1903
SQ FT: 25,000
SALES (est): 9.3MM **Privately Held**
WEB: www.romanstoneco.com
SIC: 3272 Pipe, concrete or lined with concrete

(G-718)
ROYAL WINDOWS MFG CORP
Also Called: Royal Windows and Doors
1769 5th Ave Unit A (11706-1735)
PHONE..................631 435-8888
Solomos Hajicharalambo's, *Ch of Bd*
George Efthymiou, *Treasurer*
Efthymios Efthymiou, *Controller*
Solon Efthymiou, *Manager*
EMP: 27
SQ FT: 60,000
SALES: 4.4MM **Privately Held**
WEB: www.royalwindow.com
SIC: 2431 5031 1751 Windows, wood; doors, wood; doors & windows; window & door (prefabricated) installation

(G-719)
RUBIES COSTUME COMPANY INC
Also Called: Collegeville Imagineering
158 Candlewood Rd (11706-2219)
PHONE..................631 777-3300
EMP: 100
SALES (corp-wide): 464.8MM **Privately Held**
SIC: 2389 7299 Mfg Costumes
PA: Rubie's Costume Company, Inc.
 12008 Jamaica Ave
 Richmond Hill NY 11418
 718 846-1008

(G-720)
RUBIES COSTUME COMPANY INC
Also Called: Rubie's Distribution Center
1 Holloween Hwy (11706)
PHONE..................631 951-3688
Marc Beige, *Manager*
EMP: 120
SALES (corp-wide): 364.6MM **Privately Held**
SIC: 2389 7299 Costumes; costume rental
PA: Rubie's Costume Company, Inc.
 12008 Jamaica Ave
 Richmond Hill NY 11418
 718 846-1008

(G-721)
RUBIES COSTUME COMPANY INC
158 Candlewood Rd (11706-2219)
PHONE..................631 435-7912
Philip Nastasi, *Manager*
EMP: 10
SALES (corp-wide): 364.6MM **Privately Held**
SIC: 2389 Costumes
PA: Rubie's Costume Company, Inc.
 12008 Jamaica Ave
 Richmond Hill NY 11418
 718 846-1008

(G-722)
RUBIES COSTUME COMPANY INC
158 Candlewood Rd (11706-2219)
PHONE..................516 326-1500
Howard Biege, *Vice Pres*
EMP: 40
SALES (corp-wide): 364.6MM **Privately Held**
SIC: 2389 5199 7299 Costumes; fabrics, yarns & knit goods; costume rental
PA: Rubie's Costume Company, Inc.
 12008 Jamaica Ave
 Richmond Hill NY 11418
 718 846-1008

(G-723)
SIW INC
271 Skip Ln (11706-1206)
PHONE..................631 888-0130
Lisa Gurcan, *President*
Dominic Amorosa, *Vice Pres*
Dominick Amorosa, *Vice Pres*
▲ **EMP:** 12
SQ FT: 11,500
SALES (est): 2.1MM **Privately Held**
SIC: 3449 Bars, concrete reinforcing; fabricated steel

(G-724)
SMART USA INC (PA)
1440 5th Ave (11706-4147)
PHONE..................631 969-1111
Jim Soleiman, *Ch of Bd*
Yosi Soleimany, *Vice Pres*
EMP: 15
SALES (est): 2.3MM **Privately Held**
SIC: 2671 3365 Thermoplastic coated paper for packaging; cooking/kitchen utensils, cast aluminum

(G-725)
SNAKE TRAY INTERNATIONAL LLC
Also Called: Snake Tray
291 Skip Ln (11706-1206)
PHONE..................631 674-0004
Roger Jette, *Mng Member*
▲ **EMP:** 50
SALES (est): 633.3K **Privately Held**
SIC: 3661 Telephone & telegraph apparatus

(G-726)
STANDARD INDUSTRIAL WORKS INC
271 Skip Ln (11706-1206)
PHONE..................631 888-0130
Paul Spotts, *President*
Donna Kaelin, *Office Mgr*
Lisa Gurcan, *Software Dev*
EMP: 10
SQ FT: 11,800
SALES: 700K **Privately Held**
SIC: 3444 Sheet metalwork

(G-727)
SUFFOLK COPY CENTER INC
Also Called: Suffolk Printing
26 W Main St (11706-8383)
PHONE..................631 665-0570
William Beitch, *President*
Florence Beitch, *Corp Secy*
Charles Beitch, *Vice Pres*
EMP: 6 **EST:** 1971
SQ FT: 4,000
SALES (est): 947.6K **Privately Held**
WEB: www.suffolkprinting.com
SIC: 2752 Commercial printing, offset

(G-728)
SUMMIT MANUFACTURING LLC (HQ)
Also Called: Summit Plastics
100 Spence St (11706-2231)
PHONE..................631 952-1570
Louis Marinello, *President*
◆ **EMP:** 7 **EST:** 2015
SALES (est): 6MM **Privately Held**
SIC: 3089 Plastic containers, except foam
PA: Array Canada Inc
 45 Progress Ave
 Scarborough ON M1P 2
 416 299-4865

(G-729)
SUMNER INDUSTRIES INC
Also Called: Ateco Products
309 Orinoco Dr (11706-7111)
PHONE..................631 666-7290
Jonathan Sumner, *President*
Sharon Hendricks, *General Mgr*
▼ **EMP:** 15
SQ FT: 10,000
SALES (est): 3.2MM **Privately Held**
SIC: 3728 Aircraft parts & equipment

(G-730)
TAPE-IT INC
233 N Fehr Way (11706-1203)
PHONE..................631 243-4100
Arnold Rabinowitz, *President*
Lorie Amuro, *Human Res Mgr*
Scott Rabinowitz, *Marketing Staff*
Rabinowitz Arnold, *Data Proc Staff*
◆ **EMP:** 50
SQ FT: 55,000
SALES (est): 14.8MM **Privately Held**
WEB: www.tapeit.com
SIC: 2672 5113 5122 Tape, pressure sensitive: made from purchased materials; pressure sensitive tape; drugs, proprietaries & sundries

(G-731)
TENSATOR INC
Also Called: Tensator Group
260 Spur Dr S (11706-3917)
P.O. Box 400 (11706-0779)
PHONE..................631 666-0300
Alan McPherson, *CEO*
Ben Gale, *CEO*
David Cohen, *Business Mgr*
William Goebel, *Business Mgr*
Christopher Begina, *Prdtn Mgr*
◆ **EMP:** 94
SQ FT: 81,000
SALES (est): 24.5MM
SALES (corp-wide): 35.6MM **Privately Held**
WEB: www.lawrencemetal.com
SIC: 3446 Ornamental metalwork
HQ: Tensator Group Limited
 Unit 7 Danbury Court
 Milton Keynes BUCKS MK14
 190 863-4600

(G-732)
TROJAN METAL FABRICATION INC (PA)
Also Called: Trojan Powder Coating
2215 Union Blvd (11706-8015)
PHONE..................631 968-5040
Carl Troiano, *CEO*
Keith Rein, *Vice Pres*
Claudia Troiano, *Office Mgr*
EMP: 46
SQ FT: 80,000
SALES (est): 6.4MM **Privately Held**
WEB: www.trojanpowder.com
SIC: 3479 Coating of metals & formed products

(G-733)
ULTIMATE STYLES OF AMERICA
27 Garfield Ave Unit A (11706-1052)
PHONE..................631 254-0219
David Goldstein, *President*
EMP: 12
SQ FT: 4,000
SALES (est): 1.3MM **Privately Held**
SIC: 2499 5712 Kitchen, bathroom & household ware: wood; cabinet work, custom

(G-734)
WOOD TALK
Also Called: Woodtalk Stairs & Rails
203 N Fehr Way Ste C (11706-1235)
PHONE..................631 940-3085
Scott Braun, *Principal*
EMP: 5
SALES (est): 487.2K **Privately Held**
SIC: 2431 Staircases, stairs & railings

Bayport
Suffolk County

(G-735)
CARE ENTERPRISES INC
435 Renee Dr (11705-1237)
PHONE..................631 472-8155
Lina Torre, *Vice Pres*
EMP: 6
SALES (est): 650K **Privately Held**
SIC: 3822 Air conditioning & refrigeration controls

(G-736)
CGW CORP (PA)
102 S Gillette Ave (11705-2239)
PHONE..................631 472-6600
George Werner, *President*
EMP: 7
SALES: 800K **Privately Held**
WEB: www.cgwcorp.com
SIC: 3825 Network analyzers

(G-737)
CHIMNEY DOCTORS AMERICAS CORP
738a Montauk Hwy (11705-1621)
PHONE..................631 868-3586
Nicole Newberg, *President*
EMP: 5
SQ FT: 500
SALES (est): 275.3K **Privately Held**
SIC: 3259 3271 3272 1799 Clay chimney products; blocks, concrete: chimney or fireplace; fireplace & chimney material: concrete; prefabricated fireplace installation

(G-738)
PLASTIC SOLUTIONS INC
158 Schenck Ave (11705)
PHONE..................631 234-9013
AVI Ben-Bassat, *Ch of Bd*
EMP: 32
SALES (est): 4.6MM **Privately Held**
SIC: 3089 3544 Plastic containers, except foam; special dies, tools, jigs & fixtures

(G-739)
STICKERSHOPCOM INC
Also Called: Labels, Stickers and More
582 Middle Rd (11705-1900)
PHONE..................631 563-4323
Stacy Ianson, *CEO*
EMP: 5
SALES (est): 741.2K **Privately Held**
SIC: 2679 5999 3993 2759 Tags & labels, paper; banners, flags, decals & posters; letters for signs, metal; poster & decal printing & engraving

Bayside
Queens County

(G-740)
A & G FOOD DISTRIBUTORS LLC
21610 47th Ave Apt 3b (11361-3412)
PHONE..................917 939-3457
Rocco Macri, *President*
▲ **EMP:** 3 **EST:** 2009
SALES: 1.5MM **Privately Held**
SIC: 2032 Italian foods: packaged in cans, jars, etc.

(G-741)
A T A BAGEL SHOPPE INC
Also Called: Bagel Club
20814 Cross Island Pkwy (11360-1187)
PHONE..................718 352-4948
Anthony Lombardo, *President*
EMP: 5
SALES (est): 270K **Privately Held**
SIC: 2051 5812 5461 Bagels, fresh or frozen; eating places; bagels

(G-742)
ABSOLUTE FITNESS US CORP
21337 39th Ave Ste 322 (11361-2071)
PHONE..................732 979-8582
Salvatore Naimo, *CEO*
Dina Destafano, *Director*
EMP: 100
SALES (est): 4.7MM **Privately Held**
SIC: 3949 Sporting & athletic goods

(G-743)
BAGEL CLUB INC
20521 35th Ave (11361-1245)
PHONE..................718 423-6106
Rosa Lombardo, *President*
EMP: 13
SALES (est): 1.5MM **Privately Held**
SIC: 2051 Bagels, fresh or frozen

(G-744)
CANAAN PRINTING INC
20007 46th Ave (11361-3018)
PHONE..................718 729-3100
Sang Miung Kim, *President*
EMP: 10 **EST:** 1980
SQ FT: 5,000
SALES (est): 840K **Privately Held**
WEB: www.canaanprinting.com
SIC: 2752 Commercial printing, offset

(G-745)
FREEMAN TECHNOLOGY INC
2355 Bell Blvd Apt 2h (11360-2051)
PHONE..................732 829-8345
Tim Freeman, *President*
EMP: 20 **EST:** 2012
SQ FT: 1,500
SALES: 2MM
SALES (corp-wide): 2.4MM **Privately Held**
SIC: 3829 Measuring & controlling devices
PA: Freeman Technology Limited
1 Miller Court
Tewkesbury GLOS GL20

(G-746)
G PESSO & SONS INC
20320 35th Ave (11361-1110)
PHONE..................718 224-9130
Gidon Pesso, *Principal*
EMP: 8
SALES (est): 537.2K **Privately Held**
SIC: 2024 Ice cream, bulk

(G-747)
KASTOR CONSULTING INC
3919 218th St (11361-2331)
PHONE..................718 224-9109
Greg Manaris, *President*
EMP: 9
SALES (est): 780K **Privately Held**
WEB: www.kastor.com
SIC: 7372 Prepackaged software

(G-748)
NATIONAL PROSTHETIC ORTHOT
21441 42nd Ave Ste 3a (11361-2963)
PHONE..................718 767-8400
Fernando Perez, *President*
EMP: 9
SQ FT: 1,500
SALES (est): 900K **Privately Held**
SIC: 3842 Limbs, artificial; braces, orthopedic

(G-749)
SCHNEPS PUBLICATIONS INC (PA)
Also Called: Forest Hills Courier
3815 Bell Blvd Ste 38 (11361-2058)
PHONE..................718 224-5863
Victoria A Schneps, *President*
Victoria Schneps, *Publisher*
Katrina Medoff, *Editor*
Celeste Alamin, *Vice Pres*
Bob Brennan, *Sales Executive*
EMP: 50
SALES (est): 3.9MM **Privately Held**
SIC: 2711 Newspapers, publishing & printing

(G-750)
UL CORP
3812 Corporal Stone St # 2 (11361-2141)
PHONE..................201 203-4453
Hyung Ho Kim, *President*
EMP: 8
SALES: 1.2MM **Privately Held**
SIC: 3953 Marking devices

(G-751)
VF IMAGEWEAR INC
333 Pratt Ave (11359-1119)
PHONE..................718 352-2363
Martin Soto, *Manager*
EMP: 21
SALES (corp-wide): 11.8B **Publicly Held**
WEB: www.vfsolutions.com
SIC: 2311 2326 2339 Men's & boys' uniforms; work uniforms; women's & misses' outerwear
HQ: Vf Imagewear, Inc.
545 Marriott Dr Ste 200
Nashville TN 37214
615 565-5000

Bayside Hills
Queens County

(G-752)
CATHAY GLOBAL CO INC
Also Called: Vactronics
5815 215th St (11364-1839)
PHONE..................718 229-0920
Fu Geng, *President*
Janet Jiang, *Vice Pres*
EMP: 6 **EST:** 1991
SQ FT: 2,000
SALES (est): 406.5K **Privately Held**
SIC: 3699 Electrical equipment & supplies

Bayville
Nassau County

(G-753)
PLURIBUS PRODUCTS INC
1 Overlook Ave (11709-2113)
PHONE..................718 852-1614
Peter V Martino, *President*
John V Martino, *Purchasing*
EMP: 32 **EST:** 1966
SQ FT: 50,000
SALES (est): 4.3MM **Privately Held**
SIC: 2531 2449 3341 Public building & related furniture; wood containers; secondary nonferrous metals

Beacon
Dutchess County

(G-754)
ARCHITECTURAL GLASS INC
71 Maple St Apt 2 (12508-2034)
PHONE..................845 831-3116
Michael Benzer, *President*
Jennifer Smith, *Vice Pres*
EMP: 10
SQ FT: 8,000
SALES (est): 605K **Privately Held**
WEB: www.glasstiles.com
SIC: 3229 Glassware, art or decorative

(G-755)
CHEMPRENE INC
483 Fishkill Ave (12508-1251)
P.O. Box 471 (12508-0471)
PHONE..................845 831-2800
John Nicoletti, *President*
▲ **EMP:** 110
SQ FT: 200,000
SALES (est): 41.1MM
SALES (corp-wide): 103.2K **Privately Held**
WEB: www.chemprene.com
SIC: 3496 3069 3535 2295 Conveyor belts; rubberized fabrics; rubber hardware; conveyors & conveying equipment; coated fabrics, not rubberized; investment holding companies, except banks
HQ: Ammeraal Beltech International Beheer B.V.
Comeniusstraat 8
Alkmaar
725 751-212

(G-756)
CHEMPRENE HOLDING INC
483 Fishkill Ave (12508-1251)
PHONE..................845 831-2800
Jami Goud, *Ch of Bd*
Paul Hamilton, *President*
▲ **EMP:** 180
SALES (est): 19.8MM **Privately Held**
SIC: 3496 3069 3535 2295 Conveyor belts; rubberized fabrics; rubber hardware; conveyors & conveying equipment; coated fabrics, not rubberized

(G-757)
DOREL HAT CO (PA)
1 Main St (12508)
PHONE..................845 831-5231
Salvatore Cumella, *CEO*
Ramon Moreno, *Vice Pres*
EMP: 35
SQ FT: 28,000
SALES (est): 1.6MM **Privately Held**
WEB: www.aldohats.com
SIC: 2353 Hats, trimmed: women's, misses' & children's

(G-758)
FCR LLC
Also Called: Recommunity
508 Fishkill Ave (12508-1255)
PHONE..................845 926-1071
EMP: 8 **Privately Held**
SIC: 2611 Pulp manufactured from waste or recycled paper
HQ: Fcr, Llc
809 W Hill St Ste B
Charlotte NC 28208
704 332-1603

(G-759)
HUDSON VALLEY CHOCOLATIER INC (PA)
Also Called: Alps Sweet Shop
269 Main St (12508-2735)
PHONE..................845 831-8240
Sally Craft, *President*
Terry Craft, *Vice Pres*
EMP: 14
SALES (est): 1.8MM **Privately Held**
WEB: www.alpssweetshop.com
SIC: 2064 5441 Candy & other confectionery products; candy

(G-760)
METAL CONCEPTS
9 Hanna Ln 12 (12508-2868)
PHONE..................845 592-1863
Herman Roggeman, *Owner*
Jan Roggeman, *Co-Owner*
EMP: 3
SALES: 1.5MM **Privately Held**
SIC: 3441 Fabricated structural metal

(G-761)
NICHE DESIGN INC
Also Called: Niche Modern
310 Fishkill Ave Unit 11 (12508-2073)
P.O. Box 311 (12508-0311)
PHONE..................212 777-2101
Mary Welch, *President*
Lauren Osterman, *Sales Staff*
Marisa Lomonaco, *Marketing Staff*
Britney Malave, *Marketing Staff*
EMP: 15
SALES (est): 18.2K **Privately Held**
WEB: www.nichenyc.com
SIC: 3229 Glass lighting equipment parts

(G-762)
SIEGFRIEDS CALL INC
20 Kent St 109 (12508-2042)
PHONE..................845 765-2275
Scott H Bacon, *Partner*
Andrea Bacon, *Officer*
EMP: 6
SALES (est): 133.1K **Privately Held**
SIC: 3931 Brass instruments & parts

(G-763)
TIGA HOLDINGS INC
74 Dennings Ave (12508-3624)
PHONE..................845 838-3000
Gary Santagata, *President*
Timothy Hochberj, *Vice Pres*
Michael J Siciliano, *Director*
EMP: 24
SQ FT: 2,300
SALES (est): 2.3MM **Privately Held**
WEB: www.tigallc.com
SIC: 3911 Jewelry, precious metal

Bearsville
Ulster County

(G-764)
LIFELINK MONITORING CORP (PA)
3201 Route 212 (12409-5224)
PHONE..................845 336-2098
Arthur G Avedisian, *President*
John K Holland, *Chairman*
EMP: 15 **EST:** 1994
SQ FT: 25,000
SALES (est): 1.1MM **Privately Held**
WEB: www.llmi.com
SIC: 2835 In vitro & in vivo diagnostic substances

Beaver Dams
Schuyler County

(G-765)
M & H RESEARCH AND DEV CORP
Also Called: M&H Soaring
471 Post Creek Rd (14812-9124)
P.O. Box 368, Big Flats (14814-0368)
PHONE..................607 734-2346
Claude M Sullivan, *President*
Hinz Weissembuehler, *Principal*
Karen Schlosser, *Vice Pres*
EMP: 6
SALES: 450K **Privately Held**
WEB: www.mandhsoaring.com
SIC: 3721 Gliders (aircraft)

GEOGRAPHIC SECTION

Beaver Falls
Lewis County

(G-766)
INTERFACE PERFORMANCE MTLS
9635 Main St (13305)
PHONE...............315 346-3100
John Tabolt, *Principal*
EMP: 15
SALES (est): 448.3K **Privately Held**
SIC: 2679 Paper products, converted

(G-767)
OMNIAFILTRA LLC
9567 Main St (13305)
P.O. Box 410 (13305-0410)
PHONE...............315 346-7300
Gino Fronzoni, *President*
John Wheeler, *Controller*
◆ **EMP:** 37
SQ FT: 70,000
SALES: 12MM **Privately Held**
SIC: 2621 Paper mills

Bedford
Westchester County

(G-768)
BEDFORD WDWRK INSTLLATIONS INC
200 Pound Ridge Rd (10506-1243)
PHONE...............914 764-9434
EMP: 6
SALES (est): 440K **Privately Held**
SIC: 2493 Mfg Reconstituted Wood Products

(G-769)
JSD COMMUNICATIONS INC
Also Called: Remodeling News
10 Colonel Thomas Ln (10506-1521)
P.O. Box 911 (10506-0911)
PHONE...............914 588-1841
James F Duffy, *President*
EMP: 13
SALES: 500K **Privately Held**
WEB: www.remodelingconnection.com
SIC: 2721 Magazines: publishing only, not printed on site

(G-770)
LESANNE LIFE SCIENCES LLC
47 Brook Farm Rd (10506-1309)
PHONE...............914 234-0860
Robert J Beckman,
Robert Beckman,
EMP: 5
SALES: 300K **Privately Held**
SIC: 2835 In vitro & in vivo diagnostic substances

(G-771)
TORY ELECTRIC
641 Old Post Rd (10506-1218)
PHONE...............914 292-5036
EMP: 7
SALES (est): 174.6K **Privately Held**
SIC: 3699 Electrical equipment & supplies

Bedford Hills
Westchester County

(G-772)
BEDFORD PRECISION PARTS CORP
290 Adams St (10507-1910)
P.O. Box 357 (10507-0357)
PHONE...............914 241-2211
Daniel L Kleinman, *President*
Paul Kleinman, *Chairman*
Evalyn S Kleinman, *Corp Secy*
David Kleinman, *Vice Pres*
Robert Kleinman, *Vice Pres*
EMP: 36 **EST:** 1965
SQ FT: 14,000
SALES (est): 5MM **Privately Held**
WEB: www.bedfordprecision.com
SIC: 3993 3563 Signs & advertising specialties; spraying outfits: metals, paints & chemicals (compressor)

(G-773)
CUSTOM SPORTSWEAR CORP
Also Called: Sportswear Unlimited
375 Adams St (10507-2001)
PHONE...............914 666-9200
Adam Giardina, *President*
Len Schlangel, *CFO*
EMP: 5 **EST:** 1988
SQ FT: 6,000
SALES (est): 500K **Privately Held**
WEB: www.sptunl.com
SIC: 2759 5136 Screen printing; uniforms, men's & boys'

(G-774)
DAVID HOWELL PRODUCT DESIGN
Also Called: David Howell & Company
405 Adams St (10507-2066)
PHONE...............914 666-4080
David Howell, *President*
Susan Howell, *Admin Sec*
EMP: 20 **EST:** 1978
SQ FT: 6,000
SALES: 2MM **Privately Held**
WEB: www.davidhowell.com
SIC: 3911 Jewelry, precious metal

(G-775)
DISPERSION TECHNOLOGY INC
364 Adams St (10507-2048)
PHONE...............914 241-4777
Andrei Dukhin, *President*
EMP: 4
SQ FT: 3,000
SALES (est): 1.8MM **Privately Held**
SIC: 3829 Measuring & controlling devices

(G-776)
EYEGLASS SERVICE INDUSTRIES
Also Called: Vision World
777 Bedford Rd (10507-1504)
PHONE...............914 666-3150
Patricia Ausiello, *CEO*
EMP: 5
SALES (corp-wide): 7.3MM **Privately Held**
WEB: www.visionworld.com
SIC: 3841 5995 Surgical & medical instruments; opticians
PA: Eyeglass Service Industries Inc
420 Sunrise Hwy
Lynbrook NY 11563
516 561-3937

(G-777)
MALCON INC
405 Adams St (10507-2066)
P.O. Box 463 (10507-0463)
PHONE...............914 666-7146
Peter Malavenda, *President*
Frances Malavenda, *Corp Secy*
EMP: 18
SQ FT: 15,000
SALES (est): 439.6K **Privately Held**
WEB: www.malcon.com
SIC: 3823 Panelboard indicators, recorders & controllers; receiver

(G-778)
PRODUCTION MILLING COMPANY
364 Adams St Ste 5 (10507-2047)
PHONE...............914 666-0792
Frank G Servidio, *President*
EMP: 5
SQ FT: 1,900
SALES (est): 544.5K **Privately Held**
SIC: 3599 Machine shop, jobbing & repair

(G-779)
RAINBEAU RIDGE FARM
49 Davids Way (10507-2531)
PHONE...............914 234-2197
Lisa Schwartz, *Owner*
Karen Sabath, *Partner*
Mark Schwartz, *Co-Owner*
EMP: 9
SQ FT: 6,000
SALES (est): 443.3K **Privately Held**
SIC: 2022 8299 Cheese, natural & processed; educational services

Bellerose
Queens County

(G-780)
ADVANTEX SOLUTIONS INC
24845 Jericho Tpke (11426-1912)
PHONE...............718 278-2290
Giovanni Natale, *President*
Antonio Sferrazz, *Vice Pres*
Christopher Lowther, *Engineer*
EMP: 6
SALES (est): 1MM **Privately Held**
SIC: 3822 Temperature controls, automatic

(G-781)
LEIGH SCOTT ENTERPRISES INC
Also Called: Minuteman Press
24802 Union Tpke (11426-1837)
PHONE...............718 343-5440
Scott Levine, *President*
Fred Morante, *Sales Staff*
EMP: 6
SALES (est): 986.2K **Privately Held**
WEB: www.minutemanbellrose.com
SIC: 2752 2791 Commercial printing, offset; typesetting

(G-782)
RITNOA INC
24019 Jamaica Ave Fl 2 (11426-1054)
PHONE...............212 660-2148
Shabbir Khan, *President*
EMP: 38 **EST:** 2006
SQ FT: 12,000
SALES (est): 3.1MM **Privately Held**
SIC: 7372 Business oriented computer software

(G-783)
ZINNIAS INC
24520 Grand Central Pkwy 4l (11426-2712)
PHONE...............718 746-8551
▲ **EMP:** 12
SQ FT: 3,800
SALES: 1.4MM **Privately Held**
SIC: 2369 2361 Girls And Childrens Outerwear, Nec, Nsk

Bellmore
Nassau County

(G-784)
ANDERSENS SPRING & WLDG CORP
2374 Merrick Rd (11710-3821)
PHONE...............516 785-7337
Walter A Andersen Jr, *President*
EMP: 6 **EST:** 1951
SQ FT: 11,000
SALES (est): 421.4K **Privately Held**
SIC: 7692 7539 Welding repair; automotive welding; automotive springs, rebuilding & repair

(G-785)
ARNOLD TAYLOR PRINTING INC
2218 Brody Ln (11710-5102)
PHONE...............516 781-0564
Carey Platt, *President*
EMP: 5 **EST:** 1963
SALES (est): 350K **Privately Held**
SIC: 2752 Commercial printing, offset

(G-786)
BELLMORE STEEL PRODUCTS CORP
2282 Bellmore Ave (11710-5627)
P.O. Box 825 (11710-0825)
PHONE...............516 785-9667
Glenn S Suskind, *Ch of Bd*
EMP: 16
SQ FT: 3,000
SALES: 2.7MM **Privately Held**
SIC: 3443 Fabricated plate work (boiler shop)

(G-787)
CLPA EMBROIDERY
2635 Pettit Ave (11710-3630)
PHONE...............516 409-0002
Joseph Clabby, *Owner*
EMP: 5 **EST:** 2001
SALES (est): 250.8K **Privately Held**
SIC: 2395 Art needlework: made from purchased materials

(G-788)
DECAL MAKERS INC
2477 Merrick Rd (11710-5751)
PHONE...............516 221-7200
Audrey J Hastingscooper, *President*
Leslie A Hastings-Bensi, *Corp Secy*
Linda Hennessy, *Vice Pres*
EMP: 25 **EST:** 1923
SALES (est): 2.3MM **Privately Held**
SIC: 2752 3993 2396 Lithographic Commercial Printing Mfg Signs/Advertising Specialties Mfg Auto/Apparel Trimming

(G-789)
METRO CITY GROUP INC
2283 Bellmore Ave (11710-5623)
PHONE...............516 781-2500
Carlos Jaramillo, *President*
EMP: 4
SALES: 4.5MM **Privately Held**
SIC: 3423 1711 Plumbers' hand tools; carpenters' hand tools, except saws: levels, chisels, etc.; plumbing contractors

(G-790)
PAPERWORLD INC
3054 Lee Pl (11710-5034)
PHONE...............516 221-2702
Carol Grubman, *President*
▲ **EMP:** 37
SALES (est): 7.3MM **Privately Held**
SIC: 2679 2675 Adding machine rolls, paper: made from purchased material; die-cut paper & board

(G-791)
PARABIT SYSTEMS INC
2677 Grand Ave (11710-3552)
P.O. Box 481, Roosevelt (11575-0481)
PHONE...............516 378-4800
Robert Leiponis, *President*
Dennis Schmitz, *Opers Staff*
Luckner Badio, *Accountant*
Olesya Maggio, *Accountant*
Bob Hricisak, *VP Sales*
▲ **EMP:** 50
SQ FT: 25,000
SALES (est): 11.5MM **Privately Held**
SIC: 3699 3661 3578 2542 Security devices; telephone & telegraph apparatus; telephone station equipment & parts, wire; automatic teller machines (ATM); telephone booths: except wood

(G-792)
PURE KEMIKA LLC
2156 Legion St (11710-4915)
PHONE...............718 745-2200
Luis F Becker, *Mng Member*
EMP: 6 **EST:** 2013
SQ FT: 1,000
SALES: 1.5MM **Privately Held**
SIC: 2899 Chemical preparations

(G-793)
RUSH GOLD MANUFACTURING LTD
Also Called: G R M
2400 Merrick Rd (11710-3821)
PHONE...............516 781-3155
Harold Lazar, *President*
Shirley Lazar, *Admin Sec*
▲ **EMP:** 74
SQ FT: 10,000
SALES: 5MM **Privately Held**
SIC: 3499 3961 Novelties & giftware, including trophies; costume jewelry

(G-794)
SALISBURY SPORTSWEAR INC
2523 Marine Pl (11710-5107)
PHONE...............516 221-9519

Bellmore - Nassau County (G-795)

Herbert Margolis, *President*
EMP: 50
SALES (est): 3MM **Privately Held**
SIC: 2339 Sportswear, women's

(G-795)
SPEEDY SIGN A RAMA USA INC
Also Called: Sign-A-Rama
2956 Merrick Rd (11710-5760)
PHONE.................516 783-1075
Michael Bolz, *President*
EMP: 5
SALES (est): 389.3K **Privately Held**
SIC: 3993 Signs & advertising specialties

Bellport
Suffolk County

(G-796)
50+ LIFESTYLE
146 S Country Rd Ste 4 (11713-2530)
PHONE.................631 286-0058
Hon Frank C Trotta, *President*
Frank C Trotta, *Owner*
Mary Alice Graham, *Finance*
EMP: 8
SALES: 750K **Privately Held**
SIC: 2711 Newspapers, publishing & printing

(G-797)
ABLE ELECTRONICS INC
18 Sawgrass Dr (11713-1549)
PHONE.................631 924-5386
Loraine Leverock, *CEO*
Elizabeth Padrazo, *Chairman*
Ann Konon, *Vice Pres*
Kenneth Levebrock, *Vice Pres*
Cody Valentin, *Sales Mgr*
EMP: 12
SQ FT: 995
SALES: 3.1MM **Privately Held**
SIC: 3674 Semiconductors & related devices

(G-798)
ALTERNATIVE SERVICE INC
Also Called: Alternative Parts
7 Sawgrass Dr (11713-1547)
PHONE.................631 345-9500
Russell Drake, *President*
Ruseell Drake, *President*
John Cochrane, *Vice Pres*
▲ **EMP:** 15
SQ FT: 15,000
SALES (est): 1.9MM **Privately Held**
SIC: 3444 5084 7699 3541 Sheet metalwork; industrial machine parts; industrial machinery & equipment repair; machine tools, metal cutting type

(G-799)
AVS LAMINATES INC
Also Called: Steigercraft
99 Bellport Ave (11713-2106)
PHONE.................631 286-2136
Alan Steiger, *President*
▲ **EMP:** 25
SQ FT: 20,800
SALES (est): 5.4MM **Privately Held**
WEB: www.steigercraft.com
SIC: 3732 Fishing boats: lobster, crab, oyster, etc.: small

(G-800)
C HOWARD COMPANY INC
1007 Station Rd (11713-1552)
PHONE.................631 286-7940
Fax: 631 286-7947
EMP: 9 **EST:** 1934
SQ FT: 10,000
SALES (est): 520K **Privately Held**
SIC: 2064 Mfg Candy/Confectionery

(G-801)
CRAZ WOODWORKING ASSOC INC
24 Sawgrass Dr (11713-1549)
PHONE.................631 205-1890
Peter Craz, *President*
Steve Lineberger, *Office Mgr*
EMP: 12
SQ FT: 12,000
SALES (est): 1.8MM **Privately Held**
SIC: 2499 Decorative wood & woodwork

(G-802)
EASTERN PRECISION MACHINING
11 Farber Dr Ste I (11713-1500)
PHONE.................631 286-4758
Norbert G Schreiber, *President*
Annmarie Schreiber, *Vice Pres*
EMP: 5
SQ FT: 6,000
SALES (est): 653.8K **Privately Held**
WEB: www.easternprecisionmachining.com
SIC: 3728 3599 Aircraft parts & equipment; machine shop, jobbing & repair

(G-803)
EDGE DISPLAY GROUP ENTP INC
35 Sawgrass Dr Ste 2 (11713-1577)
PHONE.................631 498-1373
Philip J Zellner, *President*
▼ **EMP:** 10
SALES (est): 1MM **Privately Held**
SIC: 3993 Displays & cutouts, window & lobby

(G-804)
FIREWORKS BY GRUCCI INC
20 Pinehurst Dr (11713-1573)
PHONE.................631 286-0088
Phil Grucci, *President*
Felix Grucci Jr, *President*
Donna Butler, *Vice Pres*
◆ **EMP:** 30
SQ FT: 6,000
SALES (est): 6.4MM **Privately Held**
SIC: 2899 Fireworks

(G-805)
HEINECK ASSOCIATES INC
28 Curtis Ave (11713-1120)
PHONE.................631 207-2347
Andrew Heineck, *President*
EMP: 6 **EST:** 2000
SALES: 500K **Privately Held**
SIC: 7372 Prepackaged software

(G-806)
K INDUSTRIES INC (PA)
1107 Station Rd Ste 5a (11713-1562)
P.O. Box 542 (11713-0542)
PHONE.................631 897-2125
Victor Schneider, *President*
EMP: 5
SQ FT: 10,000
SALES: 1MM **Privately Held**
SIC: 3443 Tanks, standard or custom fabricated: metal plate

(G-807)
MAEHR INDUSTRIES INC
14 Sawgrass Dr (11713-1549)
PHONE.................631 924-1661
Michael Maehr, *President*
EMP: 6
SQ FT: 5,000
SALES (est): 760K **Privately Held**
WEB: www.maehr.com
SIC: 3469 3599 Machine parts, stamped or pressed metal; machine shop, jobbing & repair

(G-808)
MCKEON ROLLING STL DOOR CO INC (PA)
44 Sawgrass Dr (11713-1549)
PHONE.................631 803-3000
Joseph J McKeon, *President*
Magid S Shata, *Managing Dir*
David L Dodge, *Vice Pres*
David Dodge, *Vice Pres*
Ashraf Gomaa, *Vice Pres*
▲ **EMP:** 48 **EST:** 1986
SALES (est): 7MM **Privately Held**
SIC: 3442 Metal doors; rolling doors for industrial buildings or warehouses, metal; fire doors, metal

(G-809)
MOTION MESSAGE INC
22 Sawgrass Dr Ste 4 (11713-1571)
PHONE.................631 924-9500
William Sheridan, *President*
Irene Sheridan, *Admin Sec*
EMP: 10
SQ FT: 12,000
SALES (est): 1.1MM **Privately Held**
SIC: 3993 Electric signs

(G-810)
OPTISOURCE INTERNATIONAL INC
Also Called: Nu-Chem Laboratories
40 Sawgrass Dr Ste 1 (11713-1564)
PHONE.................631 924-8360
Daryl Squicciarini, *President*
Anthony Zanghi, *Project Mgr*
John Delligatti, *Purch Agent*
Roseann Ullman, *Accounting Mgr*
John Perez, *Credit Staff*
▲ **EMP:** 30
SQ FT: 30,000
SALES: 13MM **Privately Held**
WEB: www.1-800-optisource.com
SIC: 3851 Lens coating, ophthalmic
HQ: Essilor Laboratories Of America, Inc.
13515 N Stemmons Fwy
Dallas TX 75234
972 241-4141

(G-811)
PALLETS R US INC
555 Woodside Ave (11713-1220)
PHONE.................631 758-2360
Nicholas Sorge, *Ch of Bd*
Thomas Sorge, *Vice Pres*
EMP: 50
SQ FT: 10,000
SALES (est): 11MM **Privately Held**
SIC: 2448 Pallets, wood

(G-812)
PINPOINT SYSTEMS INTL INC (PA)
10 Pinehurst Dr (11713-1573)
PHONE.................631 775-2100
William Silhan, *President*
EMP: 100
SALES (est): 8.5MM **Privately Held**
WEB: www.destdirect.com
SIC: 3699 Electrical equipment & supplies

(G-813)
POLYMAG INC
685 Station Rd Ste 2 (11713-1697)
PHONE.................631 286-4111
Devineni Ratnam, *President*
▲ **EMP:** 20
SQ FT: 15,000
SALES (est): 2.9MM **Privately Held**
WEB: www.polymaginc.com
SIC: 3499 Magnets, permanent: metallic

(G-814)
THEGO CORPORATION
Also Called: Acme Marine Hoist
2 Mooring Dr (11713-2810)
PHONE.................631 776-2472
EMP: 5 **EST:** 1948
SQ FT: 11,500
SALES: 1MM **Privately Held**
SIC: 3536 Mfg Marine Hoists

(G-815)
TORINO INDUS FABRICATION INC
4 Pinehurst Dr (11713-1573)
PHONE.................631 509-1640
Maria Passanante, *President*
Joseph Passanante, *Vice Pres*
EMP: 9
SALES (est): 459.7K **Privately Held**
SIC: 3441 Building components, structural steel

(G-816)
TORINO INDUSTRIAL INC
Also Called: Torino Industrial Fabrication
4 Pinehurst Dr (11713-1573)
PHONE.................631 509-1640
Vincent Sette, *Ch of Bd*
Keith Passanante, *Vice Pres*
Maria Passanante, *Treasurer*
Palmina Sette, *Shareholder*
EMP: 13
SQ FT: 10,000
SALES (est): 2.4MM **Privately Held**
WEB: www.torinoindustrial.com
SIC: 3449 Bars, concrete reinforcing: fabricated steel

Belmont
Allegany County

(G-817)
SUIT-KOTE CORPORATION
5628 Tuckers Corners Rd (14813-9604)
PHONE.................585 268-7127
Paul Suit, *Branch Mgr*
Brian Gates, *Branch Mgr*
EMP: 10
SALES (corp-wide): 234.8MM **Privately Held**
SIC: 2911 Asphalt or asphaltic materials, made in refineries
PA: Suit-Kote Corporation
1911 Lorings Crossing Rd
Cortland NY 13045
607 753-1100

Bemus Point
Chautauqua County

(G-818)
LAKESIDE INDUSTRIES INC
Also Called: Point Industrial
2 Lakeside Dr (14712-9310)
P.O. Box 9130 (14712-0913)
PHONE.................716 386-3031
Roy Benson, *CEO*
Brad Benson, *President*
Timothy Benson, *Vice Pres*
EMP: 10
SQ FT: 2,000
SALES: 950K **Privately Held**
SIC: 3599 Amusement park equipment

Bergen
Genesee County

(G-819)
DIEHL DEVELOPMENT INC
Also Called: Diehl Sand & Gravel
5922 N Lake Rd (14416-9507)
PHONE.................585 494-2920
Keith Diehl, *President*
EMP: 5
SQ FT: 500
SALES (est): 1.6MM **Privately Held**
SIC: 1442 Gravel mining

(G-820)
GT INNOVATIONS LLC
7674 Swamp Rd (14416-9352)
PHONE.................585 739-7659
Daniel Grastorf, *Owner*
EMP: 5
SALES (est): 693K **Privately Held**
SIC: 3444 Concrete forms, sheet metal

(G-821)
GUTHRIE HELI-ARC INC
6276 Clinton Street Rd (14416-9738)
PHONE.................585 548-5053
Will Guthrie, *President*
EMP: 8
SQ FT: 4,500
SALES (est): 715K **Privately Held**
SIC: 7692 Welding repair

(G-822)
K2 PLASTICS INC
8210 Buffalo Rd (14416-9444)
PHONE.................585 494-2727
Klaus Kremmin II, *President*
EMP: 5
SALES (est): 749.3K **Privately Held**
WEB: www.k2plasticsinc.com
SIC: 3089 Molding primary plastic; injection molding of plastics

▲ = Import ▼ = Export
◆ = Import/Export

GEOGRAPHIC SECTION

Bethpage - Nassau County (G-848)

(G-823)
LEWIS & MYERS INC (PA)
Also Called: LMI
7307 S Lake Rd (14416-9357)
PHONE..................585 494-1410
Lawrence Lewis, *President*
EMP: 5
SQ FT: 33,000
SALES (est): 1.5MM **Privately Held**
WEB: www.lmipacking.com
SIC: 3086 Packaging & shipping materials, foamed plastic

(G-824)
LIBERTY PUMPS INC
7000 Appletree Ave (14416-9446)
PHONE..................800 543-2550
Charles E Cook, *Principal*
Allan Davis, *Vice Pres*
Tammy Wells, *Buyer*
Jeff Cook, *Purchasing*
Mike Schuff, *QC Mgr*
◆ EMP: 130 EST: 1965
SQ FT: 120,000
SALES: 109.6MM **Privately Held**
WEB: www.libertypumps.com
SIC: 3561 Pumps, domestic: water or sump

(G-825)
MILLERS MILLWORKS INC
Also Called: Millers Presentation Furniture
29 N Lake Ave (14416-9528)
P.O. Box 175 (14416-0175)
PHONE..................585 494-1420
Greg Lumb, *President*
Jon Finch, *General Mgr*
EMP: 20 EST: 1996
SQ FT: 6,192
SALES: 2.1MM **Privately Held**
WEB: www.millersmillwork.com
SIC: 2521 Wood office furniture

(G-826)
ODYSSEY CONTROLS INC
6256 Clinton Street Rd (14416-9738)
P.O. Box 613 (14416-0613)
PHONE..................585 548-9800
Danie T Harmon Jr, *Ch of Bd*
Andy Meyer, *Engineer*
EMP: 6
SALES (est): 974.7K **Privately Held**
SIC: 3613 Control panels, electric

(G-827)
SCOMAC INC
8629 Buffalo Rd (14416)
P.O. Box 455 (14416-0455)
PHONE..................585 494-2200
Lawrence Scott, *President*
EMP: 12
SQ FT: 12,000
SALES (est): 1.9MM **Privately Held**
WEB: www.scomac.com
SIC: 3545 Diamond dressing & wheel crushing attachments

Berkshire
Tioga County

(G-828)
TIOGA HARDWOODS INC (PA)
12685 State Route 38 (13736-1930)
P.O. Box 195 (13736-0195)
PHONE..................607 657-8686
Kevin Gillette, *President*
Randy Bowers, *Vice Pres*
Scott Snyder, *Vice Pres*
◆ EMP: 1
SQ FT: 20,000
SALES (est): 5.2MM **Privately Held**
WEB: www.tiogahardwoods.com
SIC: 2861 Hardwood distillates

(G-829)
TREIMAN PUBLICATIONS CORP
12724 State Route 38 (13736-1911)
PHONE..................607 657-8473
Dov Trieman, *President*
EMP: 1
SALES (est): 287.1K **Privately Held**
SIC: 2741 Miscellaneous publishing

Berlin
Rensselaer County

(G-830)
COWEE FOREST PRODUCTS INC
28 Taylor Ave (12022)
PHONE..................518 658-2233
William Stallkamp, *President*
Arthur Bogen, *Vice Pres*
▲ EMP: 20 EST: 1898
SQ FT: 100,000
SALES: 2MM **Privately Held**
WEB: www.cowee.com
SIC: 2499 Novelties, wood fiber; carved & turned wood

(G-831)
GREEN RENEWABLE INC
28 Taylor Ave (12022)
PHONE..................518 658-2233
Sean M Gallivan, *President*
EMP: 40
SALES: 4.7MM **Privately Held**
SIC: 2499 Clothespins, wood

(G-832)
MILANESE COMMERCIAL DOOR LLC
28 Taylor Ave (12022-7740)
P.O. Box 560 (12022-0560)
PHONE..................518 658-0398
Brian Milanese, *Principal*
EMP: 10 EST: 2007
SALES (est): 1.4MM **Privately Held**
SIC: 3442 5031 Metal doors; door frames, all materials

Bernhards Bay
Oswego County

(G-833)
MCINTOSH BOX & PALLET CO INC
741 State Route 49 (13028)
P.O. Box 76 (13028-0076)
PHONE..................315 675-8511
Michael Milson, *Branch Mgr*
EMP: 60
SALES (est): 5MM
SALES (corp-wide): 35.3MM **Privately Held**
WEB: www.mcintoshbox.com
SIC: 2448 2441 Pallets, wood; nailed wood boxes & shook
PA: Mcintosh Box & Pallet Co., Inc.
5864 Pyle Dr
East Syracuse NY 13057
315 446-9350

Bethel
Sullivan County

(G-834)
ALEXY ASSOCIATES INC
86 Jim Stephenson Rd (12720)
PHONE..................345 482-3000
Cornelius Alexy, *President*
Sharon Alexy, *Admin Sec*
EMP: 20 EST: 1974
SALES: 200K **Privately Held**
WEB: www.aaultrasoniccleaners.com
SIC: 3699 7629 Cleaning equipment, ultrasonic, except medical & dental; electronic equipment repair

(G-835)
CAMPANELLIS POULTRY FARM INC
4 Perry Rd (12720)
PHONE..................845 482-2222
Anthony Campanelli, *Owner*
EMP: 5
SALES: 1.7MM **Privately Held**
SIC: 2015 Poultry slaughtering & processing

Bethpage
Nassau County

(G-836)
A & M LITHO INC
4 Hunt Pl (11714-6411)
PHONE..................516 342-9727
Anna Laperuta, *President*
EMP: 25
SALES: 2.5MM **Privately Held**
SIC: 2752 Commercial printing, offset

(G-837)
ABBLE AWNING CO INC
313 Broadway Ste 315 (11714-3003)
PHONE..................516 822-1200
Thomas Catalano, *President*
John Catalano, *Vice Pres*
EMP: 9
SQ FT: 2,400
SALES: 500K **Privately Held**
WEB: www.abbleawning.com
SIC: 2394 Awnings, fabric: made from purchased materials; canopies, fabric: made from purchased materials

(G-838)
AC MOORE INCORPORATED
3988 Hempstead Tpke (11714-5603)
PHONE..................516 796-5831
Fax: 516 796-5852
EMP: 5
SALES (corp-wide): 546.1MM **Privately Held**
SIC: 2499 5023 Mfg Wood Products Whol Homefurnishings
HQ: A.C. Moore Incorporated
130 A C Moore Dr
Berlin NJ 08009
856 768-4930

(G-839)
AGUA ENERVIVA LLC
Also Called: Agua Brands
15 Grumman Rd W Ste 1300 (11714-5029)
P.O. Box 1018 (11714-0019)
PHONE..................516 597-5440
Michael Venuti, *President*
Carol Dollard, *COO*
John Borelli, *Marketing Staff*
EMP: 12
SALES (est): 1.5MM **Privately Held**
SIC: 2087 Beverage bases, concentrates, syrups, powders & mixes

(G-840)
BRUNSCHWIG & FILS LLC (HQ)
245 Central Ave (11714-3922)
PHONE..................800 538-1880
Peter Smith,
▲ EMP: 14
SALES (est): 28.7MM
SALES (corp-wide): 300.6MM **Privately Held**
SIC: 2329 2211 Ski & snow clothing: men's & boys'; upholstery, tapestry & wall coverings: cotton
PA: Kravet Inc.
225 Cent Ave S
Bethpage NY 11714
516 293-2000

(G-841)
DRIMARK
999 S Oyster Bay Rd (11714-1038)
PHONE..................516 484-6200
Charles Reichmann, *President*
EMP: 15
SALES (est): 3MM **Privately Held**
SIC: 2678 Stationery products

(G-842)
GRUMMAN FIELD SUPPORT SERVICES
S Oyster Bay Rd (11714)
PHONE..................516 575-0574
Ed Sax, *Principal*
Brian Boyer, *Vice Pres*
Tony Miller, *Finance*
EMP: 70
SALES (est): 11.7MM **Publicly Held**
WEB: www.sperry.ngc.com
SIC: 3721 8731 Aircraft; commercial physical research
HQ: Northrop Grumman Systems Corporation
2980 Fairview Park Dr
Falls Church VA 22042
703 280-2900

(G-843)
HOWE MACHINE & TOOL CORP
236 Park Ave (11714-3709)
PHONE..................516 931-5687
Paul Howe, *President*
Ryan Howe, *Vice Pres*
Sue Howe, *Manager*
EMP: 11
SQ FT: 11,500
SALES: 11.5MM **Privately Held**
WEB: www.howemachine.com
SIC: 3724 Aircraft engines & engine parts

(G-844)
KREON INC
999 S Oyster Bay Rd # 105 (11714-1041)
PHONE..................516 470-9522
Thomas Mindt, *CEO*
Darin Fowler, *President*
Sacha Benadon, *Technical Staff*
▲ EMP: 5
SALES (est): 1MM **Privately Held**
SIC: 3641 Electric lamps
HQ: Kreon Nv
Industrieweg-Noord 1152
Opglabbeek 3660
898 197-80

(G-845)
LOGIC CONTROLS INC
Also Called: Bematech
999 S Oyster Bay Rd (11714-1038)
PHONE..................516 248-0400
Juliet Derby, *President*
Waldirio Alvarez, *Principal*
◆ EMP: 33
SQ FT: 10,000
SALES (est): 7.4MM **Privately Held**
WEB: www.logiccontrols.com
SIC: 3578 Accounting machines & cash registers; cash registers; point-of-sale devices; registers, credit account
HQ: Bematech S/A.
Av. Rui Barbosa 2.529
Sao Jose Dos Pinhais PR 83055

(G-846)
MARK DRI PRODUCTS INC
999 S Oyster Bay Rd # 312 (11714-1038)
PHONE..................516 484-6200
Charles Reichmann, *CEO*
Andre Reichmann, *President*
Lydia Mojica, *Human Res Mgr*
Kathy Bromer, *Marketing Staff*
Benny Varghese, *Manager*
▲ EMP: 200
SQ FT: 54,000
SALES (est): 23.5MM **Privately Held**
WEB: www.drimark.com
SIC: 3951 5112 Markers, soft tip (felt, fabric, plastic, etc.); pens &/or pencils

(G-847)
MELMONT FINE PRINGNG/GRAPHICS
6 Robert Ct Ste 24 (11714-1415)
P.O. Box 395, Old Bethpage (11804-0395)
PHONE..................516 939-2253
Angela Melledy, *President*
EMP: 6
SALES: 150K **Privately Held**
SIC: 2711 7389 Newspapers, publishing & printing; printing broker

(G-848)
MLS SALES
226 10th St (11714-1703)
PHONE..................516 681-2736
Mary Lafauci, *Owner*
EMP: 6
SALES: 120K **Privately Held**
SIC: 3679 Electronic components

Bethpage - Nassau County (G-849)

(G-849)
NORTHROP GRUMMAN CORPORATION
660 Grumman Rd W (11714)
PHONE..................703 280-2900
James Eng, *Engineer*
Sam Ghannadi, *Engineer*
EMP: 702 **Publicly Held**
SIC: 3812 Search & navigation equipment
PA: Northrop Grumman Corporation
2980 Fairview Park Dr
Falls Church VA 22042

(G-850)
NORTHROP GRUMMAN SYSTEMS CORP
925 S Oyster Bay Rd (11714-3582)
PHONE..................516 575-0574
Patsy Wolf, *Managing Dir*
Dominic Anton, *Project Mgr*
Robert Klein, *VP Engrg*
Thomas Chyczewski, *Research*
Rich Turner, *Chief Engr*
EMP: 1659 **Publicly Held**
WEB: www.sperry.ngc.com
SIC: 3721 8731 Aircraft; commercial physical research
HQ: Northrop Grumman Systems Corporation
2980 Fairview Park Dr
Falls Church VA 22042
703 280-2900

(G-851)
PACS SWITCHGEAR LLC (PA)
1211 Stewart Ave (11714-1601)
PHONE..................516 465-7100
Neil Minihane, *CEO*
Larry Bloom, *CFO*
Glen Ring, *Controller*
EMP: 9
SALES (est): 5MM **Privately Held**
SIC: 3613 Switchgear & switchboard apparatus

(G-852)
RAIN CATCHERS SEAMLESS GUTTERS
39 Park Ln (11714-5226)
PHONE..................516 520-1956
Robert Dambrosio, *CEO*
EMP: 5
SALES (est): 413.1K **Privately Held**
SIC: 3272 Floor slabs & tiles, precast concrete

(G-853)
VENGO INC
999 S Oyster Bay Rd # 407 (11714-1044)
PHONE..................866 526-7054
Brian Shimmerlik, *CEO*
Adam Gargenderg, *Vice Pres*
Anthony Gelsi, *Opers Staff*
Brian Bofill, *Engineer*
Sethi Shawn, *Sr Software Eng*
EMP: 6
SALES (est): 1.1MM **Privately Held**
SIC: 3581 Automatic vending machines

(G-854)
WILSONART INTL HOLDINGS LLC
999 S Oyster Bay Rd # 3305 (11714-1038)
PHONE..................516 935-6980
Greg Martino, *Manager*
EMP: 20
SALES (corp-wide): 14.3B **Publicly Held**
WEB: www.wilsonart.com
SIC: 2821 2541 Plastics materials & resins; table or counter tops, plastic laminated
HQ: Wilsonart International Holdings Llc
2501 Wilsonart Dr
Temple TX 76504
254 207-7000

Big Flats
Chemung County

(G-855)
KG MOTORS INC
Also Called: Notubes.com
202 Daniel Zenker Dr (14814-8944)
PHONE..................607 562-2877
Stan Koziatek, *CEO*
James Malta, *Vice Pres*
Erich Farnham, *Purch Agent*
Derek Bissett, *Engineer*
Mike Bush, *Engineer*
▲ **EMP:** 30
SALES: 15MM **Privately Held**
SIC: 3751 Bicycles & related parts

(G-856)
REYNOLDS MANUFACTURING INC
3298 State Rte 352 (14814)
PHONE..................607 562-8936
Kasandra Reynolds, *Ch of Bd*
EMP: 17
SQ FT: 11,000
SALES (est): 3.9MM **Privately Held**
SIC: 3444 3469 Sheet metalwork; machine parts, stamped or pressed metal

(G-857)
X-GEN PHARMACEUTICALS INC (PA)
300 Daniel Zenker Dr (14814)
P.O. Box 445 (14814-0445)
PHONE..................607 562-2700
Susan E Badia, *Ch of Bd*
Robin Liles, *Vice Pres*
Tony Dowd, *Safety Mgr*
Catherine Liles, *Treasurer*
April King, *Manager*
▲ **EMP:** 3
SQ FT: 53,000
SALES (est): 3.6MM **Privately Held**
SIC: 2834 Pharmaceutical preparations

Binghamton
Broome County

(G-858)
A-LINE TECHNOLOGIES INC
197 Corporate Dr (13904-3214)
PHONE..................607 772-2439
Alex Boyce, *President*
Frank J Boyce, *Vice Pres*
Frank Boyce, *Vice Pres*
EMP: 10
SQ FT: 10,000
SALES: 1.1MM **Privately Held**
SIC: 3714 3599 Motor vehicle transmissions, drive assemblies & parts; machine shop, jobbing & repair

(G-859)
ALL AMERICAN BUILDING
109 Crestmont Rd (13905-3951)
PHONE..................607 797-7123
Douglas E Hamm, *Owner*
EMP: 8
SALES (est): 783.7K **Privately Held**
SIC: 3448 Prefabricated metal buildings

(G-860)
ALL SPEC FINISHING INC
219 Clinton St (13905-2236)
PHONE..................607 770-9174
Anthony Milasi, *President*
Dennis Smith, *President*
Shirley Milasi, *Admin Sec*
EMP: 50
SQ FT: 80,000
SALES (est): 5.6MM **Privately Held**
WEB: www.allspecfinishing.com
SIC: 3479 7699 Painting, coating & hot dipping; painting of metal products; plastics products repair

(G-861)
AMERICAN QUALITY TECHNOLOGY
6 Emma St (13905-2508)
PHONE..................607 777-9488
Gary Crounse, *President*
Jerome Luchuk, *CFO*
EMP: 12
SALES: 980K **Privately Held**
SIC: 3672 3679 3825 Printed circuit boards; electronic circuits; instruments to measure electricity

(G-862)
AMETEK INC
33 Lewis Rd Ste 6 (13905-1045)
PHONE..................607 763-4700
Susan Dodge, *Materials Mgr*
Greg Shepherd, *Engineer*
Robert Glydon, *Finance Mgr*
Kevin McLoughlin, *Comptroller*
Robert Hyland, *Branch Mgr*
EMP: 68
SALES (corp-wide): 4.3B **Publicly Held**
SIC: 3621 Motors & generators
PA: Ametek, Inc.
1100 Cassatt Rd
Berwyn PA 19312
610 647-2121

(G-863)
ARNOLD-DAVIS LLC
Also Called: Harris Assembly Group
187 Indl Pk Dr (13904)
PHONE..................607 772-1201
Thomas Davis, *CEO*
Mike Novak, *Engineer*
Kenneth Tinklepaugh, *Engineer*
David Arnold, *Treasurer*
Doug Griffis, *Technology*
▲ **EMP:** 125
SQ FT: 30,000
SALES (est): 28.7MM **Privately Held**
WEB: www.harrisasm.com
SIC: 3679 Harness assemblies for electronic use: wire or cable

(G-864)
BARRETT PAVING MATERIALS INC
14 Brandywine St (13901-2203)
P.O. Box 2368 (13902-2368)
PHONE..................607 723-5367
Bill Lallier, *Facilities Mgr*
Gary Hoyt, *Manager*
EMP: 6
SQ FT: 1,144
SALES (corp-wide): 95.5MM **Privately Held**
WEB: www.barrettpaving.com
SIC: 2951 1442 Asphalt & asphaltic paving mixtures (not from refineries); construction sand & gravel
HQ: Barrett Paving Materials Inc.
3 Becker Farm Rd Ste 307
Roseland NJ 07068
973 533-1001

(G-865)
BINGHAMTON BURIAL VAULT CO INC
1114 Porter Ave (13901-1688)
PHONE..................607 722-4931
Brian Abbey, *President*
Janet Evenson, *Vice Pres*
EMP: 14
SQ FT: 10,000
SALES (est): 2MM **Privately Held**
SIC: 3272 Steps, prefabricated concrete; burial vaults, concrete or precast terrazzo

(G-866)
BINGHAMTON KNITTING CO INC
11 Alice St (13904-1587)
P.O. Box 1646 (13902-1646)
PHONE..................607 722-6941
Douglas W Hardler, *President*
Craig Hardler, *Shareholder*
Julia Sherwood, *Admin Sec*
▲ **EMP:** 20
SQ FT: 23,200
SALES: 1.1MM **Privately Held**
WEB: www.brimwick.com
SIC: 2253 Sweaters & sweater coats, knit

(G-867)
BINGHAMTON PRECAST & SUP CORP
18 Phelps St (13901-1858)
PHONE..................607 722-0334
Jay Abbey, *Ch of Bd*
EMP: 50
SALES (est): 10.5MM **Privately Held**
WEB: www.binghamtonprecast.com
SIC: 3272 Pipe, concrete or lined with concrete; culvert pipe, concrete

(G-868)
BINGHAMTON SIMULATOR CO INC
Also Called: B S C
151 Court St (13901-3502)
PHONE..................607 321-2980
John Matthews, *CEO*
E Terry Lewis, *President*
Robin Laabs, *Principal*
Greg Stanton, *COO*
Ronald Strony, *Engrg Dir*
▲ **EMP:** 40
SQ FT: 14,000
SALES (est): 5.9MM **Privately Held**
WEB: www.bsc.com
SIC: 3571 3577 7699 7373 Electronic computers; graphic displays, except graphic terminals; aircraft & heavy equipment repair services; systems integration services; electrical equipment & supplies

(G-869)
BOCES BUSINESS OFFICE
Also Called: Broom Tioga Boces
435 Glenwood Rd (13905-1699)
PHONE..................607 763-3300
Sandra Ruffo, *President*
EMP: 19
SALES (est): 2.2MM **Privately Held**
SIC: 2761 Continuous forms, office & business

(G-870)
BOKA PRINTING INC
12 Hall St (13903-2114)
PHONE..................607 725-3235
Bob Carr, *Principal*
EMP: 7 **EST:** 2013
SALES (est): 931.9K **Privately Held**
SIC: 2752 Commercial printing, lithographic

(G-871)
BRAND BOX USA LLC
1 Chamberlain St (13904-1314)
PHONE..................607 584-7682
EMP: 6
SALES (est): 569.1K **Privately Held**
SIC: 2653 Corrugated & solid fiber boxes

(G-872)
BSC ASSOCIATES LLC
151 Court St (13901-3502)
PHONE..................607 321-2980
Greg Stanton, *Branch Mgr*
Barbara Blincoe,
EMP: 19
SALES (est): 1.5MM **Privately Held**
SIC: 3699 Flight simulators (training aids), electronic

(G-873)
BW ELLIOTT MFG CO LLC
11 Beckwith Ave (13901-1726)
P.O. Box 773 (13902-0773)
PHONE..................607 772-0404
Richard Allbritton, *CEO*
George Scherer, *President*
Brian Jeker, *Engineer*
Paul Smith, *Engineer*
Sonia Moore, *Finance*
▲ **EMP:** 295
SQ FT: 250,000
SALES (est): 87.5MM
SALES (corp-wide): 1.1B **Publicly Held**
WEB: www.elliottmfg.com
SIC: 3492 3531 3568 Control valves, fluid power: hydraulic & pneumatic; construction machinery; shafts, flexible
PA: Actuant Corporation
N86w12500 Westbrook Xing
Menomonee Falls WI 53051
262 293-1500

▲ = Import ▼ = Export
◆ = Import/Export

GEOGRAPHIC SECTION

Binghamton - Broome County (G-898)

(G-874)
C H THOMPSON COMPANY INC
69-93 Eldredge St (13902)
PHONE.................................607 724-1094
Stacy Cacialli, *President*
Thomas Talerico, *President*
Stacy Schraeder, *Vice Pres*
Joseph Talerico, *CFO*
EMP: 65
SQ FT: 75,000
SALES (est): 8.7MM **Privately Held**
SIC: 3471 2396 3479 Anodizing (plating) of metals or formed products; automotive & apparel trimmings; painting, coating & hot dipping

(G-875)
CMP ADVNCED MECH SLTONS NY LLC
Also Called: Cmp New York
90 Bevier St (13904-1020)
PHONE.................................607 352-1712
Ian Kelly, *Plant Mgr*
Steven Zimmermann, *Mng Member*
Steven Zimmerman, *Mng Member*
Larry Farr, *Manager*
EMP: 130
SALES (est): 1.3MM **Privately Held**
SIC: 3824 Mechanical & electromechanical counters & devices
PA: Cmp Ams (International) Limitee
1241 Rue Des Cascades
Chateauguay QC J6J 4
450 691-5510

(G-876)
CREATIVE ORTHOTICS PROSTHETICS
65 Pennsylvania Ave 207 (13903-1651)
PHONE.................................607 771-4672
Thomas Kirk PHD, *CEO*
EMP: 9
SALES (corp-wide): 1B **Publicly Held**
SIC: 3842 5999 Limbs, artificial; orthopedic & prosthesis applications
HQ: Creative Orthotics & Prosthetics, Inc.
1300 College Ave Ste 1
Elmira NY 14901
607 734-7215

(G-877)
CROWLEY FOODS INC (HQ)
93 Pennsylvania Ave (13903-1645)
PHONE.................................800 637-0019
John Kaned, *President*
▼ **EMP:** 31 **EST:** 1904
SALES (est): 185.8MM
SALES (corp-wide): 2.1B **Privately Held**
WEB: www.crowleyfoods.com
SIC: 2024 2026 Ice cream & frozen desserts; fermented & cultured milk products
PA: Hp Hood Llc
6 Kimball Ln Ste 400
Lynnfield MA 01940
617 887-8441

(G-878)
D D & L INC
Also Called: E D I Window Systems
3 Alice St (13904-1502)
P.O. Box 2949 (13902-2949)
PHONE.................................607 729-9131
David P Smith, *President*
Richard Perry, *Vice Pres*
EMP: 17
SQ FT: 15,120
SALES (est): 1.7MM **Privately Held**
SIC: 3442 5211 Window & door frames; door & window products

(G-879)
DBASE LLC
100 Emerson Pkwy (13905-6625)
P.O. Box 917, Oxford (13830-0917)
PHONE.................................607 729-0234
Robert Thompson, *Principal*
Paul McGee, *Sales Dir*
Martin Kay, *CTO*
Michael Rozlog,
Cheryl Thompson,
EMP: 8 **EST:** 2011
SALES (est): 715.9K **Privately Held**
SIC: 7372 Application computer software

(G-880)
ECK PLASTIC ARTS INC
87 Prospect Ave (13901-2616)
PHONE.................................607 722-3227
Robert L Eck Jr, *President*
Philip Willson, *Project Mgr*
▲ **EMP:** 25
SQ FT: 30,000
SALES (est): 5.5MM **Privately Held**
WEB: www.eckplastics.com
SIC: 3089 Injection molding of plastics; injection molded finished plastic products

(G-881)
ELECTRO FORM CORP
128 Bevier St (13904-1094)
PHONE.................................607 722-6404
Auguste Mathey Jr, *President*
Donna Kadaronak, *Office Mgr*
Donna Jadarondak, *Admin Sec*
EMP: 11
SQ FT: 6,000
SALES (est): 1.3MM **Privately Held**
SIC: 3599 Machine shop, jobbing & repair

(G-882)
EMS TECHNOLOGIES INC
71 Frederick St (13901-2563)
PHONE.................................607 723-3676
Clarence Hotchkiss, *Ch of Bd*
Mark Hotchkiss, *President*
Robert Phillips, *President*
Tom Costello, *Principal*
EMP: 40
SQ FT: 36,000
SALES (est): 9.7MM
SALES (corp-wide): 11.1MM **Privately Held**
WEB: www.emstech.com
SIC: 3672 Printed circuit boards
PA: Nelson Holdings Ltd
71 Frederick St
Binghamton NY 13901
607 772-1794

(G-883)
ENJOY CITY NORTH INC
Also Called: Save Around
100 Emerson Pkwy (13905-6625)
P.O. Box 2399 (13902-2399)
PHONE.................................607 584-5061
Luke Stanton, *President*
Vik Mehta, *Partner*
Janine Drew, *Regional Mgr*
Jennifer Jones, *Regional Mgr*
Erika Nelson, *Regional Mgr*
EMP: 64
SALES (est): 5.9MM **Privately Held**
SIC: 2741 Miscellaneous publishing

(G-884)
FELCHAR MANUFACTURING CORP (HQ)
Also Called: Norwich Manufacturing Division
196 Corporate Dr (13904-3295)
PHONE.................................607 723-3106
Jonathan Miller, *President*
Vince Bungo, *Vice Pres*
Steve Cole, *Vice Pres*
Mike Carr, *Plant Mgr*
◆ **EMP:** 650
SQ FT: 40,000
SALES (est): 146.2MM
SALES (corp-wide): 304.9MM **Privately Held**
WEB: www.felchar.com
SIC: 3678 3089 3621 Electronic connectors; injection molding of plastics; motors & generators
PA: Shop Vac Corporation
2323 Reach Rd
Williamsport PA 17701
570 326-0502

(G-885)
FRATELLIS LLC
Also Called: New Horizons Bakery
20 Campbell Rd (13905-4304)
PHONE.................................607 722-5663
Anthony Roma, *Principal*
Mary Roma, *Mng Member*
EMP: 21
SQ FT: 23,000
SALES (est): 850K **Privately Held**
SIC: 2051 2053 5142 5149 Bread, cake & related products; frozen bakery products, except bread; croissants, frozen; bakery products, frozen; bakery products

(G-886)
FRITO-LAY NORTH AMERICA INC
10 Spud Ln (13904-3299)
PHONE.................................607 775-7000
Brian Stringer, *Opers-Prdtn-Mfg*
Jeff Hadwin, *Manager*
EMP: 85
SQ FT: 4,906
SALES (corp-wide): 63.5B **Publicly Held**
WEB: www.fritolay.com
SIC: 2096 2099 Potato chips & other potato-based snacks; food preparations
HQ: Frito-Lay North America, Inc.
7701 Legacy Dr
Plano TX 75024

(G-887)
GLOWA MANUFACTURING INC
6 Emma St (13905-2508)
PHONE.................................607 770-0811
Jerry Glowa, *President*
Karen Glowa, *Vice Pres*
William Pomeroy, *Shareholder*
EMP: 47
SQ FT: 10,000
SALES (est): 5.3MM **Privately Held**
SIC: 3577 Computer peripheral equipment

(G-888)
GOLUB CORPORATION
Also Called: Price Chopper Pharmacy 234
33 Chenango Bridge Rd (13901-1233)
PHONE.................................607 235-7240
EMP: 28
SALES (corp-wide): 3.3B **Privately Held**
SIC: 3751 Motorcycles & related parts
PA: The Golub Corporation
461 Nott St
Schenectady NY 12308
518 355-5000

(G-889)
HANGER PRSTHETCS & ORTHO INC
65 Pennsylvania Ave (13903-1651)
PHONE.................................607 771-4672
EMP: 7
SALES (corp-wide): 1B **Publicly Held**
SIC: 3842 Limbs, artificial
HQ: Hanger Prosthetics & Orthotics, Inc.
10910 Domain Dr Ste 300
Austin TX 78758
512 777-3800

(G-890)
HP HOOD LLC
Also Called: Crowley Foods
93 Pennsylvania Ave (13903-1645)
PHONE.................................607 772-6580
Joe Cervantes, *Senior VP*
EMP: 1660
SALES (corp-wide): 2.1B **Privately Held**
WEB: www.hphood.com
SIC: 2024 2026 Ice cream & frozen desserts; fermented & cultured milk products
PA: Hp Hood Llc
6 Kimball Ln Ste 400
Lynnfield MA 01940
617 887-8441

(G-891)
I 3 MANUFACTURING SERVICES INC
100 Eldredge St (13901-2631)
PHONE.................................607 238-7077
James T Matthews, *President*
EMP: 5
SALES (est): 384.1K **Privately Held**
SIC: 3672 Printed circuit boards

(G-892)
I3 ASSEMBLY LLC
100 Eldredge St (13901-2631)
PHONE.................................607 238-7077
James Matthews, *Mng Member*
EMP: 70 **EST:** 2015
SQ FT: 185,000
SALES (est): 12.4MM
SALES (corp-wide): 117.3MM **Privately Held**
SIC: 3679 Harness assemblies for electronic use: wire or cable
PA: I3 Electronics, Inc.
100 Eldredge St
Binghamton NY 13901
607 238-7077

(G-893)
I3 ELECTRONICS INC (PA)
100 Eldredge St (13901-2631)
PHONE.................................607 238-7077
Jim Matthews Jr, *President*
Jay Simonis, *Facilities Dir*
James Thornton, *Opers Staff*
Colleen Hawthorne, *Mfg Staff*
Matthew Coppola, *Production*
◆ **EMP:** 133 **EST:** 2013
SALES (est): 117.3MM **Privately Held**
SIC: 3672 Printed circuit boards

(G-894)
IHD MOTORSPORTS LLC
Also Called: Independence Harley-Davidson
1152 Upper Front St (13905-1119)
PHONE.................................979 690-1669
James E Booth, *Mng Member*
EMP: 15 **EST:** 2014
SQ FT: 15,000
SALES (est): 2.6MM **Privately Held**
SIC: 3751 2396 Motorcycles & related parts; motorcycle accessories; automotive & apparel trimmings

(G-895)
ILLINOIS TOOL WORKS INC
33 Lewis Rd (13905-1048)
PHONE.................................607 770-4945
Ron Skeeles, *General Mgr*
EMP: 20
SALES (corp-wide): 14.3B **Publicly Held**
SIC: 3444 Metal housings, enclosures, casings & other containers
PA: Illinois Tool Works Inc.
155 Harlem Ave
Glenview IL 60025
847 724-7500

(G-896)
INSULATING COATINGS CORP
27 Link Dr Ste D (13904-3208)
PHONE.................................607 723-1727
David Ziebarth, *Branch Mgr*
EMP: 14
SALES (corp-wide): 3.9MM **Privately Held**
WEB: www.insulatingcoatings.com
SIC: 2851 Lacquers, varnishes, enamels & other coatings
PA: Insulating Coatings Corp.
956 S Us Highway 41
Inverness FL 34450
352 344-8741

(G-897)
IVI SERVICES INC
Also Called: Indian Valley
5 Pine Camp Dr (13904-3109)
PHONE.................................607 729-5111
Wayne A Rozen, *CEO*
Phil March, *Vice Pres*
◆ **EMP:** 72 **EST:** 1940
SQ FT: 250,000
SALES (est): 13.8MM **Privately Held**
WEB: www.iviindustries.com
SIC: 2299 4225 4953 2673 Bagging, jute; general warehousing; recycling, waste materials; bags: plastic, laminated & coated; textile bags; broadwoven fabric mills, manmade

(G-898)
JANE LEWIS
Also Called: Sun Valley Printing
82 Castle Creek Rd (13901-1004)
PHONE.................................607 722-0584
Jane Lewis, *Owner*
David A Lewis, *Co-Owner*
EMP: 6
SQ FT: 2,400
SALES: 250K **Privately Held**
SIC: 2752 2791 2789 Commercial printing, offset; typesetting; bookbinding & related work

Binghamton - Broome County (G-899)

(G-899)
JOHNSON OUTDOORS INC
Eureka Tents
625 Conklin Rd (13903-2700)
P.O. Box 966 (13902-0966)
PHONE 607 779-2200
Mark Pecora, *Warehouse Mgr*
William Kelly, *Branch Mgr*
EMP: 175
SALES (corp-wide): 490.5MM **Publicly Held**
SIC: 2394 2393 5091 5941 Tents: made from purchased materials; knapsacks, canvas: made from purchased materials; camping equipment & supplies; camping equipment; canoe & kayak dealers; sporting & athletic goods
PA: Johnson Outdoors Inc.
  555 Main St
  Racine WI 53403
  262 631-6600

(G-900)
JONES HUMDINGER
204 Hayes Rd (13905-5918)
PHONE 607 771-6501
Steve Kallfelz, *Owner*
EMP: 15
SALES: 180K **Privately Held**
SIC: 2024 Ice cream & frozen desserts

(G-901)
LABRADOR STONE INC
11 Dutchess Rd (13901-1411)
PHONE 570 465-2120
EMP: 7
SALES (est): 912.6K **Privately Held**
SIC: 1429 7389 Crushed & broken stone;

(G-902)
LEO P CALLAHAN INC
229 Lwer Stlla Ireland Rd (13905)
PHONE 607 797-7314
James Callahan, *President*
EMP: 10 **EST:** 1960
SQ FT: 1,600
SALES (est): 1MM **Privately Held**
SIC: 2796 Color separations for printing

(G-903)
MECHANICAL PWR CONVERSION LLC
Also Called: E&M Power
6 Emma St (13905-2508)
PHONE 607 766-9620
William Peterson, *Vice Pres*
David Eddy, *Mng Member*
EMP: 12
SQ FT: 10,000
SALES: 5MM **Privately Held**
WEB: www.eandmpower.com
SIC: 3679 Electronic loads & power supplies

(G-904)
MELLEM CORPORATION
Also Called: Goldsmith
31 Lewis St Ste 1 (13901-3018)
PHONE 607 723-0001
Gina McHugh, *President*
▲ **EMP:** 15
SQ FT: 750
SALES (est): 1.9MM **Privately Held**
SIC: 3911 5944 Jewelry, precious metal; jewelry, precious stones & precious metals

(G-905)
METAL FAB LLC
13 Spud Ln (13904-3210)
PHONE 607 775-3200
Janet Beal, *Mng Member*
Rick Simon,
Eugene Taren,
EMP: 5
SQ FT: 9,500
SALES: 857K **Privately Held**
SIC: 3441 Fabricated structural metal

(G-906)
MORO CORPORATION
Also Called: Titchener Iron Works Division
23 Griswold St (13904-1511)
PHONE 607 724-4241
Douglas Wilcox, *Branch Mgr*
EMP: 25
SQ FT: 7,368
SALES (corp-wide): 62MM **Publicly Held**
WEB: www.mcgregorindustries.com
SIC: 3446 Architectural metalwork
PA: Moro Corporation
  994 Old Eagle School Rd # 1000
  Wayne PA 19087
  484 367-0300

(G-907)
MS MACHINING INC
Also Called: Mechanical Specialties Co
2 William St (13904-1418)
PHONE 607 723-1105
Eugene Mazza, *President*
Jo Ann Risley, *Office Mgr*
EMP: 9 **EST:** 1956
SQ FT: 10,000
SALES (est): 1.4MM **Privately Held**
SIC: 3544 3599 Special dies & tools; custom machinery; machine shop, jobbing & repair

(G-908)
NELSON HOLDINGS LTD (PA)
71 Frederick St (13901-2529)
PHONE 607 772-1794
Clarence Hotchkiss Jr, *Ch of Bd*
Mark Hotchkiss, *President*
Frederick Hotchkiss, *Vice Pres*
EMP: 1
SQ FT: 180,000
SALES (est): 11.1MM **Privately Held**
SIC: 3679 5261 7699 Electronic circuits; lawn & garden equipment; lawn mower repair shop

(G-909)
PARLOR CITY PAPER BOX CO INC
2 Eldredge St (13901-2600)
P.O. Box 756 (13902-0756)
PHONE 607 772-0600
David L Culver, *Ch of Bd*
Bruce Culver, *Vice Pres*
Brian Culver, *Human Res Mgr*
EMP: 56
SQ FT: 140,000
SALES (est): 13MM **Privately Held**
WEB: www.pghcitypaper.com
SIC: 2653 2652 Corrugated & solid fiber boxes; setup paperboard boxes

(G-910)
PETER PAPASTRAT
Also Called: A A P C O Screen Prntng/Sprtwr
193 Main St (13905-2619)
P.O. Box 285 (13905-0285)
PHONE 607 723-8112
Peter Papastrat, *Owner*
EMP: 5
SQ FT: 6,000
SALES (est): 326.2K **Privately Held**
SIC: 2759 5699 Screen printing; customized clothing & apparel

(G-911)
RB CONVERTING INC
28 Track Dr (13904-2717)
PHONE 607 777-1325
Paul Haslett, *Branch Mgr*
EMP: 5 **Privately Held**
SIC: 2679 Paper products, converted
HQ: Rb Converting, Inc.
  12855 Valley Branch Ln
  Dallas TX 75234
  800 543-7690

(G-912)
REYNOLDS BOOK BINDERY LLC
37 Milford St (13904-1615)
PHONE 607 772-8937
Fax: 607 772-0152
EMP: 11
SQ FT: 15,000
SALES (est): 720K **Privately Held**
SIC: 2789 Book Bindery Company

(G-913)
S L C INDUSTRIES INCORPORATED
63 Barlow Rd (13904-2722)
P.O. Box 116, Kirkwood (13795-0116)
PHONE 607 775-2299
Adam Milligan, *President*
Art Boyle, *President*
Michael Prozeralik, *Treasurer*
Mary Milligan, *Technology*
Thomas O Milligan, *Admin Sec*
EMP: 10
SQ FT: 20,000
SALES (est): 1.5MM **Privately Held**
WEB: www.slcindustries.com
SIC: 2759 2789 Screen printing; bookbinding & related work

(G-914)
SENSOR & DECONTAMINATION INC
Also Called: S D I
892 Powderhouse Rd (13903-7104)
P.O. Box 132 (13903-0132)
PHONE 301 526-8389
Barry R Jones, *President*
David Doetschman, *Corp Secy*
EMP: 10
SALES (est): 710K **Privately Held**
WEB: www.sensoranddecon.com
SIC: 2842 7389 Specialty cleaning preparations;

(G-915)
SOUTHERN TIER PLASTICS INC
Kirkwood Industrial Park (13902)
P.O. Box 2015 (13902-2015)
PHONE 607 723-2601
John Gwyn, *CEO*
Joyce Gray, *President*
Douglas Gray, *Treasurer*
Barbara Gwyn, *Admin Sec*
▲ **EMP:** 72
SQ FT: 30,000
SALES (est): 15.6MM **Privately Held**
WEB: www.southerntierplastics.com
SIC: 3089 Injection molding of plastics

(G-916)
SUNY AT BINGHAMTON
Also Called: School of Management
Vestal Pkwy E (13901)
PHONE 607 777-2316
Gary Roodman, *Dean*
EMP: 73 **Privately Held**
SIC: 2731 8221 9411 Books: publishing only; university; administration of educational programs;
HQ: Suny At Binghamton
  4400 Vestal Pkwy
  Binghamton NY 13902
  607 777-2000

(G-917)
SURESCAN CORPORATION
Also Called: X1000
100 Eldredge St (13901-2631)
PHONE 607 321-0042
John Percival, *President*
EMP: 23
SALES (est): 5.7MM **Privately Held**
WEB: www.surescaneds.com
SIC: 3844 X-ray apparatus & tubes

(G-918)
TCMF INC
Also Called: C.H.thompson Finishing
69-93 Eldredge St (13901)
PHONE 607 724-1094
George Morgan, *President*
Charles Morgan, *Vice Pres*
Trevor Morgan, *Admin Sec*
EMP: 75
SALES (est): 3.7MM **Privately Held**
SIC: 3471 2759 Plating & polishing; commercial printing

(G-919)
THOMAS F EGAN
Also Called: Craftsmen/Access Unlimited
570 Hance Rd (13903-5700)
PHONE 607 669-4822
Thomas Egan, *Owner*
Nancy Garrett, *Manager*
EMP: 26
SALES (est): 3.5MM **Privately Held**
WEB: www.accessunlimited.com
SIC: 3842 3999 Technical aids for the handicapped; wheelchair lifts

(G-920)
TJ POWDER COATERS LLC
24 Broad St (13904-1017)
PHONE 607 724-4779
Jim Foran,
EMP: 7
SQ FT: 7,500
SALES (est): 885.9K **Privately Held**
SIC: 3479 Coating of metals with plastic or resins

(G-921)
TRI CITY HIGHWAY PRODUCTS INC
111 Bevier St (13904-1013)
PHONE 607 722-2967
Martin A Galasso Jr, *CEO*
EMP: 30
SQ FT: 2,500
SALES (est): 5.2MM **Privately Held**
SIC: 2951 1442 Asphalt paving mixtures & blocks; construction sand & gravel

(G-922)
VIRTUSPHERE INC
7 Hillside Ave (13903-2025)
PHONE 607 760-2207
Nourakhmed Latypov, *CEO*
Nurulla Latypov, *President*
EMP: 11
SALES: 150K **Privately Held**
SIC: 7372 Educational computer software

(G-923)
WESTCODE INCORPORATED
2226 Airport Rd (13905-5912)
PHONE 607 766-9881
Edward J Widdowson, *CEO*
EMP: 25
SALES (corp-wide): 11MM **Privately Held**
WEB: www.westcodeus.com
SIC: 3743 Railroad equipment
PA: Westcode Incorporated
  3 Dickinson Dr Ste 100
  Chadds Ford PA 19317
  610 738-1200

Blasdell
Erie County

(G-924)
B F G ELCPLTG AND MFG CO
3949 Jeffrey Blvd (14219-2334)
P.O. Box 825, Hamburg (14075-0825)
PHONE 716 362-0888
Minta Marie, *CEO*
EMP: 32
SALES (est): 255K **Privately Held**
SIC: 3999 Manufacturing industries

(G-925)
CARBON ACTIVATED CORPORATION
3774 Hoover Rd (14219-2302)
PHONE 716 677-6661
Chris Allen, *Branch Mgr*
EMP: 22 **Privately Held**
SIC: 2819 Industrial inorganic chemicals
PA: Carbon Activated Corporation
  2250 S Central Ave
  Compton CA 90220

(G-926)
EVERLASTING MEMORIES
3701 Mckinley Pkwy # 210 (14219-2695)
PHONE 716 833-1111
Dennis Field, *Owner*
EMP: 6
SALES (est): 284.1K **Privately Held**
SIC: 2335 Wedding gowns & dresses

(G-927)
RAPISTAK CORPORATION
2025 Electric Ave (14219-1045)
PHONE 716 822-2804
Nathan Pautorek, *CEO*
EMP: 7
SALES (est): 1.8MM **Privately Held**
WEB: www.rapistak.com
SIC: 3531 Dozers, tractor mounted: material moving

GEOGRAPHIC SECTION

Bloomfield - Ontario County (G-952)

(G-928)
REPUBLIC STEEL INC
Also Called: Lackawanna Hot Rolled Plant
3049 Lake Shore Rd (14219-1447)
PHONE..................716 827-2800
Tom Tyrrell, *Branch Mgr*
William Kilinskas, *Technician*
David Madigan, *Maintence Staff*
EMP: 360 **Privately Held**
SIC: 3312 Blast furnaces & steel mills
HQ: Republic Steel
2633 8th St Ne
Canton OH 44704
330 438-5435

(G-929)
SAMUEL SON & CO INC
250 Lake Ave Ste 3 (14219-1500)
PHONE..................716 656-6500
Don Clark, *Branch Mgr*
EMP: 8 **Privately Held**
SIC: 3312 Blast furnaces & steel mills
HQ: Samuel Son & Co. Inc.
4334 Walden Ave
Lancaster NY 14086

(G-930)
SOTEK INC
3590 Jeffrey Blvd (14219-2390)
PHONE..................716 821-5961
John E Maurer, *President*
Michael Maurer, *Vice Pres*
Jim Carroll, *Opers Mgr*
▲ **EMP:** 52
SQ FT: 45,000
SALES (est): 9.3MM **Privately Held**
WEB: www.sotek.com
SIC: 3599 Machine shop, jobbing & repair

(G-931)
TRANSCO RAILWAY PRODUCTS INC
Milestrip Rd (14219)
P.O. Box 1968, Buffalo (14219-0168)
PHONE..................716 824-1219
Tom Jakubowski, *Manager*
EMP: 23
SALES (corp-wide): 96.7MM **Privately Held**
SIC: 3743 Railroad equipment, except locomotives
HQ: Transco Railway Products Inc.
200 N La Salle St # 1550
Chicago IL 60601
312 427-2818

(G-932)
VALENTI DISTRIBUTING
84 Maple Ave (14219-1624)
PHONE..................716 824-2304
John Valenti, *Principal*
EMP: 7
SALES (est): 23.6K **Privately Held**
SIC: 2064 Candy & other confectionery products

Blauvelt
Rockland County

(G-933)
AERCO INTERNATIONAL INC (HQ)
100 Oritani Dr (10913-1022)
PHONE..................845 580-8000
James F Dagley, *President*
Fred Depuy, *Vice Pres*
Bree McQuillan, *Vice Pres*
Lou Vorsteveld, *Vice Pres*
Debra Day, *Production*
▲ **EMP:** 153
SQ FT: 150,000
SALES (est): 36.5MM
SALES (corp-wide): 1.4B **Publicly Held**
WEB: www.aerco.com
SIC: 3443 3492 Heat exchangers, plate type; heat exchangers: coolers (after, inter), condensers, etc.; boilers: industrial, power, or marine; control valves, fluid power: hydraulic & pneumatic
PA: Watts Water Technologies, Inc.
815 Chestnut St
North Andover MA 01845
978 688-1811

(G-934)
CWS POWDER COATINGS COMPANY LP
2234 Bradley Hill Rd # 12 (10913-1014)
PHONE..................845 398-2911
Cws Powder Coatings, *Partner*
Jonathan Abrams, *Director*
▲ **EMP:** 9
SQ FT: 2,500
SALES (est): 2.4MM
SALES (corp-wide): 71.2MM **Privately Held**
SIC: 3399 Powder, metal
HQ: Cws Powder Coatings Gmbh
Katharinenstr. 61
Duren 52353
242 198-30

(G-935)
ERT SOFTWARE INC
4 Pine Glen Dr (10913-1150)
PHONE..................845 358-5721
Roman Tenenbaum, *President*
EMP: 5
SALES (est): 1.5MM **Privately Held**
WEB: www.alivest.com
SIC: 7372 Prepackaged software

(G-936)
K-BINET INC
624 Route 303 (10913-1170)
PHONE..................845 348-1149
Jay Kim, *President*
Ann Degli, *Admin Sec*
EMP: 8 **EST:** 2001
SALES (est): 680K **Privately Held**
SIC: 2434 Wood kitchen cabinets

(G-937)
LIGHTING N BEYOND LLC
628 Ste 303 (10913)
P.O. Box 539, Spring Valley (10977-0539)
PHONE..................718 669-9142
Mike Oberlander,
EMP: 5
SQ FT: 6,000
SALES: 150K **Privately Held**
SIC: 3648 Lighting equipment

(G-938)
NEXBEV INDUSTRIES LLC
600 Bradley Hill Rd Ste 2 (10913-1171)
PHONE..................646 648-1255
Charles Sessoms,
Antonio Johnson,
EMP: 10
SQ FT: 750
SALES: 50K **Privately Held**
SIC: 2086 Carbonated beverages, nonalcoholic: bottled & canned

(G-939)
RBHAMMERS CORP
Also Called: Heatherdell RB Hammers
500 Bradley Hill Rd (10913-1134)
PHONE..................845 353-5042
Richard Tegtmeier, *President*
◆ **EMP:** 10
SQ FT: 1,500
SALES (est): 6.4MM **Privately Held**
SIC: 3546 Hammers, portable: electric or pneumatic, chipping, etc.

(G-940)
RYAN PRINTING INC
300 Corporate Dr Ste 6 (10913-1162)
PHONE..................845 535-3235
Al Ryan, *President*
EMP: 26
SQ FT: 35,000
SALES (est): 5MM **Privately Held**
SIC: 2752 Commercial printing, offset

(G-941)
SWIVELIER COMPANY INC
Also Called: Point Electric Div
600 Bradley Hill Rd Ste 3 (10913-1171)
PHONE..................845 353-1455
Michael I Schwartz, *President*
Louis M Cafarchio, *Admin Sec*
EMP: 70
SQ FT: 125,000
SALES (est): 10.8MM **Privately Held**
WEB: www.swivelier.com
SIC: 3646 3645 3643 Commercial indusl & institutional electric lighting fixtures; residential lighting fixtures; current-carrying wiring devices

(G-942)
TAPPAN WIRE & CABLE INC (HQ)
100 Bradley Hill Rd (10913-1000)
P.O. Box 4000, Carrollton GA (30112-5050)
PHONE..................845 353-9000
Stuart W Thorn, *Ch of Bd*
Darren Krych, *President*
Mike Luterzo, *Vice Pres*
Jerry Rosen, *CFO*
▲ **EMP:** 189 **EST:** 1978
SQ FT: 180,000
SALES (est): 46.5MM
SALES (corp-wide): 2.4B **Privately Held**
WEB: www.tappanwire.com
SIC: 3315 3643 3357 Wire & fabricated wire products; current-carrying wiring devices; nonferrous wiredrawing & insulating
PA: Southwire Company, Llc
1 Southwire Dr
Carrollton GA 30119
770 832-4242

(G-943)
TRI-SEAL HOLDINGS INC
900 Bradley Hill Rd (10913-1163)
PHONE..................845 353-3300
Paul Young, *Ch of Bd*
Diane Schweitzer, *Owner*
F Patrick Smith, *Chairman*
EMP: 63 **EST:** 1946
SQ FT: 58,000
SALES (est): 9.1MM
SALES (corp-wide): 1.1B **Privately Held**
WEB: www.tri-seal.com
SIC: 3081 2821 Packing materials, plastic sheet; plastics materials & resins
PA: Tekni-Plex, Inc.
460 E Swedesford Rd # 3000
Wayne PA 19087
484 690-1520

(G-944)
TRI-SEAL INTERNATIONAL INC (HQ)
900 Bradley Hill Rd (10913-1163)
PHONE..................845 353-3300
Anatoly Verdel, *President*
▲ **EMP:** 3
SALES (est): 1MM
SALES (corp-wide): 1.1B **Privately Held**
SIC: 2679 Egg cartons, molded pulp: made from purchased material
PA: Tekni-Plex, Inc.
460 E Swedesford Rd # 3000
Wayne PA 19087
484 690-1520

(G-945)
VITS INTERNATIONAL INC
200 Corporate Dr (10913-1119)
PHONE..................845 353-5000
Deirdre Ryder, *President*
John Friedl, *Plant Mgr*
Nina Shapiro, *Office Mgr*
Kim Markovich, *Director*
◆ **EMP:** 40
SQ FT: 22,000
SALES (est): 20MM **Privately Held**
WEB: www.vitsamerica.com
SIC: 3555 Printing trades machinery

Bliss
Wyoming County

(G-946)
FIVE CORNERS REPAIR INC
6653 Hardys Rd (14024-9714)
PHONE..................585 322-7369
Jason Sampson, *President*
Scott Lester, *Vice Pres*
EMP: 12
SALES: 950K **Privately Held**
SIC: 3441 Fabricated structural metal

Bloomfield
Ontario County

(G-947)
BENJAMIN SHERIDAN CORPORATION (DH)
7629 State Route 5 And 20 (14469-9210)
PHONE..................585 657-6161
Ken D'Arcy, *President*
Kathy Chapman, *Executive*
EMP: 5
SQ FT: 224,000
SALES (est): 9.3MM **Publicly Held**
SIC: 3484 3482 Pellets & BB's, pistol & air rifle ammunition; pellet & BB guns
HQ: Crosman Corporation
7629 State Route 5 And 20
Bloomfield NY 14469
585 657-6161

(G-948)
BRISTOL METALS INC
7817 State Route 5 And 20 (14469-9352)
PHONE..................585 657-7665
Edward Gilligan, *President*
Kelly Gilligan, *Corp Secy*
EMP: 14
SQ FT: 15,000
SALES: 1.5MM **Privately Held**
SIC: 3441 Fabricated structural metal

(G-949)
CARVER CREEK ENTERPRISES INC
2524 Cannan Rd (14469-9655)
PHONE..................585 657-7511
Donald Dean, *President*
Thomas Dean, *Vice Pres*
EMP: 5
SQ FT: 1,764
SALES (est): 706.5K **Privately Held**
WEB: www.carvercreekent.com
SIC: 2511 Wood household furniture

(G-950)
COMMODORE MACHINE CO INC
26 Maple Ave (14469-9228)
PHONE..................585 657-6916
George Brandoon, *Ch of Bd*
▲ **EMP:** 21 **EST:** 1970
SALES (est): 3.6MM **Privately Held**
SIC: 3089 Trays, plastic

(G-951)
CROSMAN CORPORATION (DH)
7629 State Route 5 And 20 (14469-9210)
PHONE..................585 657-6161
Robert Beckwith, *CEO*
Bob Hampton, *Vice Pres*
Sonia Nau, *Vice Pres*
David Swanson, *Vice Pres*
Wallace Malheiros, *Engineer*
▲ **EMP:** 29
SQ FT: 224,000
SALES (est): 20.6MM **Publicly Held**
WEB: www.crosman.com
SIC: 3484 3482 3563 Pellet & BB guns; pellets & BB's, pistol & air rifle ammunition; shot, steel (ammunition); air & gas compressors
HQ: Cbcp Acquisition Corp.
60 One Wilton Rd Fl 2 Sixty
Westport CT 06880
203 221-1703

(G-952)
DOLCO LLC
Also Called: Commodore
26 Maple Ave (14469-9228)
PHONE..................585 657-7777
George Braddon, *CEO*
Fritz Seager, *President*
Jeffrey Braddon, *Vice Pres*
Bruce Hayward, *Vice Pres*
Suzanne Wright, *Production*
▲ **EMP:** 50
SQ FT: 35,000
SALES (est): 14.5MM
SALES (corp-wide): 1.1B **Privately Held**
SIC: 3089 2671 7336 Injection molding of plastics; packaging paper & plastics film, coated & laminated; package design

HQ: Dolco Packaging Corp.
101 Railroad Ave
Ridgefield NJ 07657

(G-953)
ELAM SAND & GRAVEL CORP (PA)
8222 State Route 5 And 20 (14469-9567)
P.O. Box 65, West Bloomfield (14585-0065)
PHONE.................585 657-8000
Joseph Spezio, *President*
Ritamarie Dreimiller, *Vice Pres*
EMP: 40 **EST:** 1892
SQ FT: 9,000
SALES (est): 9.3MM **Privately Held**
SIC: 1442 Construction sand mining

(G-954)
FURNITURE DOCTOR INC
7007 State Route 5 And 20 (14469-9322)
P.O. Box 519 (14469-0519)
PHONE.................585 657-6941
Thomas Baker, *President*
Marfa Baker, *Corp Secy*
EMP: 9
SQ FT: 16,000
SALES (est): 847K **Privately Held**
WEB: www.thefurnituredoctoronline.com
SIC: 2511 2514 5712 5021 Wood household furniture; metal household furniture; furniture stores; furniture; reupholstery & furniture repair; interior decorating

(G-955)
GULLO MACHINE & TOOL INC
4 E Main St (14469-9334)
P.O. Box 273 (14469-0273)
PHONE.................585 657-7318
Nancy Gullo, *President*
EMP: 10
SQ FT: 15,000
SALES: 500K **Privately Held**
SIC: 3599 Machine shop, jobbing & repair

(G-956)
TERPHANE HOLDINGS LLC (DH)
2754 W Park Dr (14469-9385)
PHONE.................585 657-5800
Richard Composto, *Plant Mgr*
Linda Wilson, *Purch Mgr*
Renan Bergmann,
▼ **EMP:** 7
SALES (est): 17.1MM
SALES (corp-wide): 1B **Publicly Held**
SIC: 2821 5199 Plastics materials & resins; packaging materials
HQ: Tredegar Film Products Corporation
1100 Boulders Pkwy # 200
North Chesterfield VA 23225
804 330-1000

(G-957)
TERPHANE LLC
Also Called: Terphane Inc.
2754 W Park Dr (14469-9385)
PHONE.................585 657-5800
Renan Bergmann, *CEO*
Dan Roy, *General Mgr*
Glen Vonwald, *Production*
Gabriel Caridade, *Technical Mgr*
Scott Hachten, *Technical Mgr*
◆ **EMP:** 52
SQ FT: 100,000
SALES (est): 17.1MM
SALES (corp-wide): 1B **Publicly Held**
WEB: www.terphane.com
SIC: 2821 Polyesters
HQ: Terphane Holdings Llc
2754 W Park Dr
Bloomfield NY 14469

(G-958)
VELMEX INC
7550 State Route 5 And 20 (14469-9389)
PHONE.................585 657-6151
Mitchel Evans, *President*
Rick Yurick, *Vice Pres*
Tim Luzeckyj, *Production*
Alan Lane, *Engineer*
Alayne Evans, *Treasurer*
EMP: 32
SQ FT: 15,500

SALES: 5.4MM **Privately Held**
WEB: www.velmex.com
SIC: 3545 Machine tool attachments & accessories

Bloomington
Ulster County

(G-959)
COBRA SYSTEMS INC
2669 New York 32 (12411)
PHONE.................845 338-6675
Michael V Pavlov, *President*
▼ **EMP:** 10
SQ FT: 2,400
SALES (est): 1.6MM **Privately Held**
WEB: www.cobracoil.com
SIC: 3496 Barbed wire, made from purchased wire

Bloomville
Delaware County

(G-960)
ED BEACH FOREST MANAGEMENT
2042 Scott Rd (13739-1203)
PHONE.................607 538-1745
Edwin R Beach, *Principal*
EMP: 6
SALES (est): 512.3K **Privately Held**
SIC: 2411 Logging

(G-961)
G HAYNES HOLDINGS INC
Also Called: Catskill Castings Co
51971 State Highway 10 (13739-2242)
PHONE.................607 538-1160
George Haynes, *President*
EMP: 9
SQ FT: 3,500
SALES (est): 385K **Privately Held**
WEB: www.catskillcastings.com
SIC: 3543 Foundry patternmaking

(G-962)
GREENE BRASS & ALUM FNDRY LLC
51971 State Highway 10 (13739-2242)
P.O. Box 752 (13739-0752)
PHONE.................607 656-4204
Thomas Dodd, *Mng Member*
George Heynes,
EMP: 7
SALES (est): 1.1MM **Privately Held**
SIC: 3334 3363 7389 Primary aluminum; aluminum die-castings;

Blossvale
Oneida County

(G-963)
BLUEBAR OIL CO INC
8446 Mill Pond Way (13308)
PHONE.................315 245-4328
David Link, *President*
EMP: 11
SQ FT: 2,000
SALES (est): 1MM **Privately Held**
SIC: 1389 5983 5172 Oil field services; fuel oil dealers; gasoline; fuel oil

Blue Point
Suffolk County

(G-964)
DEER PK STAIR BLDG MLLWK INC
51 Kennedy Ave (11715-1009)
P.O. Box 107 (11715-0107)
PHONE.................631 363-5000
Michael Souto, *President*
Leita Souto, *Admin Sec*
EMP: 45
SQ FT: 30,000

SALES (est): 7.9MM **Privately Held**
WEB: www.deerparkstairs.com
SIC: 2431 5211 5031 Stair railings, wood; staircases & stairs, wood; lumber products; cabinets, kitchen; kitchen cabinets

(G-965)
SPECIALTY INK CO INC (PA)
Also Called: Aero Brand Inks
40 Harbour Dr (11715-1421)
P.O. Box 778, Deer Park (11729-0778)
PHONE.................631 586-3666
Gary Werwa, *President*
▲ **EMP:** 16 **EST:** 1934
SQ FT: 15,000
SALES (est): 1.7MM **Privately Held**
WEB: www.specialtyink.com
SIC: 2899 3953 2893 Ink or writing fluids; pads, inking & stamping; printing ink

Bohemia
Suffolk County

(G-966)
A P MANUFACTURING
21 Floyds Run (11716-2155)
PHONE.................909 228-3049
Jane P Sobota, *Owner*
EMP: 7
SALES (est): 340.7K **Privately Held**
SIC: 3599 Industrial machinery

(G-967)
ABACO STEEL PRODUCTS INC
40 Aero Rd Ste 4 (11716-2194)
PHONE.................631 589-1800
Kenneth Podd, *President*
EMP: 4 **EST:** 1972
SQ FT: 10,000
SALES: 1.2MM **Privately Held**
WEB: www.abacosteel.com
SIC: 2542 2541 Shelving, office & store: except wood; partitions for floor attachment, prefabricated: except wood; cabinets, lockers & shelving

(G-968)
ABLE ENVIRONMENTAL SERVICES
1599 Ocean Ave (11716-1947)
PHONE.................631 567-6585
Faith Barnard, *President*
EMP: 5
SALES (est): 550K **Privately Held**
SIC: 1382 Oil & gas exploration services

(G-969)
ABSOLUTE MANUFACTURING INC
Also Called: Absolute Engineering Company
210 Knickerbocker Ave (11716-3175)
PHONE.................631 563-7466
Val Palzzynski, *President*
Carissa Pelczynski, *Accounts Exec*
EMP: 8
SQ FT: 5,000
SALES (est): 1MM **Privately Held**
SIC: 3599 Machine shop, jobbing & repair

(G-970)
ACCURATE MARINE SPECIALTIES
2200 Artic Ave (11716-2414)
PHONE.................631 589-5502
Gary Lucas, *President*
Chip Watkins, *Corp Secy*
EMP: 6
SQ FT: 5,900
SALES (est): 959.8K **Privately Held**
SIC: 7694 5541 Motor repair services; marine service station

(G-971)
ACE CNTRACTING CONSULTING CORP
Also Called: Island Chimney Service
1650 Sycamore Ave Ste 18 (11716-1731)
PHONE.................631 567-4752
Marc Jagerman, *President*
EMP: 9

SALES (est): 843.6K **Privately Held**
SIC: 3271 Blocks, concrete: chimney or fireplace

(G-972)
ACE MOLDING & TOOL INC
51 Floyds Run (11716-2155)
PHONE.................631 567-2355
Americo Carnaxide, *President*
EMP: 5
SALES (est): 40K **Privately Held**
SIC: 3089 Molding primary plastic

(G-973)
ADVANCED CYBER SECURITY CORP
3880 Veterans Memorial Hw (11716-1038)
PHONE.................866 417-9155
Daniel Delgiorno, *CEO*
EMP: 20
SALES (est): 1.1MM **Privately Held**
SIC: 7372 Operating systems computer software

(G-974)
AEROSPACE LIGHTING CORPORATION (DH)
355 Knickerbocker Ave (11716-3103)
PHONE.................631 563-6400
Werner Lieberherr, *President*
Thomas P McCaffrey, *Senior VP*
Sean Cromie, *Vice Pres*
Wayne R Exton, *Vice Pres*
Steve Scover, *Vice Pres*
EMP: 100 **EST:** 1987
SQ FT: 60,000
SALES (est): 17MM **Publicly Held**
SIC: 3647 5063 Aircraft lighting fixtures; electrical apparatus & equipment
HQ: B/E Aerospace, Inc.
1400 Corporate Center Way
Wellington FL 33414
561 791-5000

(G-975)
ALL AMERICAN AWARDS INC
Also Called: All American Uniform
331 Knickerbocker Ave (11716-3134)
PHONE.................631 567-2025
Frank Coppola, *President*
Jean Coppola, *Vice Pres*
Gina Fecile, *Office Mgr*
Dominic Coppola, *Manager*
EMP: 11
SQ FT: 10,000
SALES (est): 1.4MM **Privately Held**
SIC: 3914 5699 5199 2395 Trophies; uniforms & work clothing; advertising specialties; embroidery & art needlework

(G-976)
ALL ISLAND BLOWER & SHTMTL
1585 Smithtown Ave Unit C (11716-2406)
PHONE.................631 567-7070
Brian Levine, *President*
Brian Higgins, *President*
EMP: 10
SQ FT: 4,000
SALES (est): 1.1MM **Privately Held**
SIC: 3444 Sheet metal specialties, not stamped

(G-977)
AM CAST INC (PA)
34 Aero Rd (11716-2902)
PHONE.................631 750-1644
Tomaso Veneroso, *Ch of Bd*
Stephanie Veneroso, *Vice Pres*
Davide Berretti, *CFO*
▲ **EMP:** 11
SQ FT: 3,500
SALES (est): 2MM **Privately Held**
WEB: www.amcastonline.com
SIC: 3364 Nonferrous die-castings except aluminum

(G-978)
AMPLITECH INC
620 Johnson Ave Ste 2 (11716-2658)
PHONE.................631 521-7738
Fawad Maqbool, *CEO*
Shaf Khan, *Purchasing*
Don Sartorius, *QC Mgr*
Louisa Sanfratello, *CFO*

GEOGRAPHIC SECTION
Bohemia - Suffolk County (G-1005)

EMP: 8
SQ FT: 5,500
SALES: 1.2MM Privately Held
WEB: www.amplitechinc.com
SIC: 3663 Microwave communication equipment

(G-979)
AMPLITECH GROUP INC
620 Johnson Ave Ste 2 (11716-2658)
PHONE..................................631 521-7831
Fawad Maqbool, *Ch of Bd*
Louisa Sanfratello, *CFO*
EMP: 6 EST: 2002
SALES: 1.3MM Privately Held
SIC: 3651 3663 Amplifiers: radio, public address or musical instrument; microwave communication equipment

(G-980)
ANDREA ELECTRONICS CORPORATION (PA)
620 Johnson Ave Ste 1b (11716-2636)
PHONE..................................631 719-1800
Douglas J Andrea, *Ch of Bd*
Corisa L Guiffre, *CFO*
◆ EMP: 9 EST: 1934
SQ FT: 3,000
SALES: 6.9MM Publicly Held
WEB: www.andreaelectronics.com
SIC: 3651 3663 3577 Microphones; mobile communication equipment; computer peripheral equipment

(G-981)
APEX SIGNAL CORPORATION
110 Wilbur Pl (11716-2402)
PHONE..................................631 567-1100
William Forman, *President*
Wayne Grandner, *COO*
Patty Angelos, *Manager*
Ernie Keith, *Officer*
EMP: 90
SALES (est): 9.5MM Privately Held
SIC: 3669 5065 Traffic signals, electric; electronic parts & equipment
PA: North Atlantic Industries, Inc.
110 Wilbur Pl
Bohemia NY 11716

(G-982)
ARCHIMEDES PRODUCTS INC
21 Floyds Run (11716-2155)
PHONE..................................631 589-1215
Jane Sobota, *President*
EMP: 8
SQ FT: 6,000
SALES (est): 760K Privately Held
WEB: www.cncarch.com
SIC: 3599 Machine shop, jobbing & repair

(G-983)
ARLAN DAMPER CORPORATION
1598 Lakeland Ave (11716-2198)
PHONE..................................631 589-7431
Albert A Sapio, *President*
Valerie Cooper, *Office Mgr*
EMP: 25 EST: 1961
SQ FT: 6,400
SALES (est): 4.8MM Privately Held
SIC: 3444 Sheet metal specialties, not stamped

(G-984)
B & H PRECISION FABRICATORS
95 Davinci Dr (11716-2601)
PHONE..................................631 563-9620
Dan Barthelomew, *President*
Deborah Barthelomew, *Vice Pres*
Jared Bartholomew, *VP Opers*
Debbie Bartholomew, *Officer*
EMP: 15
SQ FT: 5,000
SALES: 1MM Privately Held
SIC: 3444 Sheet metal specialties, not stamped

(G-985)
B/E AEROSPACE INC
355 Knickerbocker Ave (11716-3103)
PHONE..................................631 563-6400
Amin J Khoury, *Ch of Bd*
EMP: 29 Publicly Held
SIC: 2531 3728 3647 Seats, aircraft; aircraft parts & equipment; aircraft lighting fixtures
HQ: B/E Aerospace, Inc.
1400 Corporate Center Way
Wellington FL 33414
561 791-5000

(G-986)
B/E AEROSPACE INC
355 Knickerbocker Ave (11716-3103)
PHONE..................................631 589-0877
Steve Scover, *Vice Pres*
Vincent Cipolla, *Electrical Engi*
Peggy Knapp, *MIS Mgr*
Elaine Frank, *Admin Asst*
Gail Reissig, *Admin Asst*
EMP: 230 Publicly Held
SIC: 3812 Search & navigation equipment
HQ: B/E Aerospace, Inc.
1400 Corporate Center Way
Wellington FL 33414
561 791-5000

(G-987)
BETA TRANSFORMER TECH CORP (DH)
40 Orville Dr Ste 2 (11716-2529)
PHONE..................................631 244-7393
Terrance M Paradie, *CEO*
Vincent Buffa, *President*
Sean P Maroney, *Treasurer*
Keith McDonald, *Controller*
Halle F Terrion, *Admin Sec*
EMP: 33
SQ FT: 30,000
SALES (est): 5.9MM
SALES (corp-wide): 3.5B Publicly Held
WEB: www.bttc-beta.com
SIC: 3677 Electronic transformers
HQ: Data Device Corporation
105 Wilbur Pl
Bohemia NY 11716
631 567-5600

(G-988)
BGA TECHNOLOGY LLC
116 Wilbur Pl (11716-2402)
PHONE..................................631 750-4600
Michael Cody, *President*
Ralph Prescott, *Vice Pres*
Bill Kaspar, *Sales Staff*
Jayanth Kygonhalli, *CTO*
EMP: 40
SALES: 3.6MM Privately Held
SIC: 3674 8734 Semiconductors & related devices; testing laboratories

(G-989)
BMG PRINTING AND PROMOTION LLC
170 Wilbur Pl Ste 700 (11716-2416)
PHONE..................................631 231-9200
Paulette Desimone, *Principal*
John L Melillo,
EMP: 8
SALES: 50K Privately Held
SIC: 2761 3993 2732 2752 Manifold business forms; signs & advertising specialties; pamphlets: printing & binding, not published on site; commercial printing, offset; promotional printing, lithographic

(G-990)
BULLITT MOBILE LLC
Also Called: Bullitt Group
80 Orville Dr Ste 100 (11716-2505)
PHONE..................................631 424-1749
Eliana Santos, *President*
Bryan Bourff, *Vice Pres*
Janelle Stoner, *Vice Pres*
Gareth Drewery, *Technical Mgr*
Liam Marriott, *Sls & Mktg Exec*
EMP: 56
SQ FT: 1,200
SALES (est): 5.1MM Privately Held
SIC: 3663 Cellular radio telephone
HQ: Bullitt Mobile Limited
One Valpy Valpy Street
Reading BERKS RG1 1
118 958-0449

(G-991)
C & H MACHINING INC
281 Knickerbocker Ave (11716-3103)
PHONE..................................631 582-6737
Cliff W Havel, *President*
Phillip A Russo, *Vice Pres*
EMP: 13
SQ FT: 6,000
SALES: 1.3MM Privately Held
SIC: 3599 Machine shop, jobbing & repair

(G-992)
C & M CIRCUITS INC
50 Orville Dr (11716-2548)
PHONE..................................631 589-0208
Charles Gwynn, *Ch of Bd*
EMP: 24
SQ FT: 7,500
SALES (est): 1.7MM Privately Held
SIC: 3629 Mfg Electrical Industrial Apparatus

(G-993)
CERTIFIED PRCSION MCHINING INC
70 Knickerbocker Ave # 4 (11716-3166)
PHONE..................................631 244-3671
Michael Staib, *President*
James Turano, *Vice Pres*
EMP: 6
SQ FT: 8,000
SALES (est): 784.2K Privately Held
SIC: 3599 Machine shop, jobbing & repair

(G-994)
CLIMATRONICS CORP (HQ)
606 Johnson Ave Ste 28 (11716-2419)
PHONE..................................541 471-7111
Thomas Pottberg, *President*
Joann Pottberg, *Corp Secy*
David W Gilmore, *Vice Pres*
James Riley Loftin, *CFO*
EMP: 14
SQ FT: 16,500
SALES: 1.3MM
SALES (corp-wide): 25.3MM Privately Held
WEB: www.climatronics.com
SIC: 3829 Meteorological instruments
PA: Met One Instruments, Inc.
1600 Nw Washington Blvd
Grants Pass OR 97526
541 471-7111

(G-995)
CLINTRAK CLINICAL LABELING S (PA)
Also Called: Eagle Business Systems
2800 Veterans Hwy (11716-1002)
PHONE..................................888 479-3900
Bob Scarth, *General Mgr*
Brianne Teemsma, *Project Mgr*
Jamie Pieron, *Opers Mgr*
Pamela Jones-Nill, *QC Mgr*
Darlene Lombardo, *Human Res Dir*
▲ EMP: 55
SQ FT: 45,000
SALES (est): 10.1MM Privately Held
WEB: www.clintrak.com
SIC: 2754 Letter, circular & form: gravure printing

(G-996)
CMB WIRELESS GROUP LLC (PA)
116 Wilbur Pl (11716-2402)
PHONE..................................631 750-4700
Joseph Lucania, *CEO*
Rich Meigh, *Exec VP*
Vincent Vivolo Jr, *Exec VP*
James McGuirk, *Vice Pres*
Tom Doherty, *CFO*
▲ EMP: 280
SALES (est): 43.9MM Privately Held
SIC: 3663 Mobile communication equipment

(G-997)
CMS HEAT TRANSFER DIVISION INC
273 Knickerbocker Ave (11716-3103)
PHONE..................................631 968-0084
Chris Mauro, *President*
Marek Dolat, *Vice Pres*
Steve White, *Vice Pres*
Steven White, *Vice Pres*
Kathy Beers, *Project Mgr*
EMP: 25
SQ FT: 16,000
SALES (est): 5.3MM Privately Held
WEB: www.cmsheattransfer.com
SIC: 3443 Finned tubes, for heat transfer; heat exchangers, plate type

(G-998)
COLOR CRAFT FINISHING CORP
30 Floyds Run Ste A (11716-2212)
PHONE..................................631 563-3230
Angelo Zegarelli, *President*
EMP: 10
SALES: 1.2MM Privately Held
SIC: 3479 3089 Painting of metal products; coloring & finishing of plastic products

(G-999)
COS TEC MANUFACTURING CORP
Also Called: K C Technical Services
390 Knickerbocker Ave # 1 (11716-3123)
PHONE..................................631 589-7170
Guy A Cosmo, *President*
Elizabeth Cosmo, *Vice Pres*
▲ EMP: 7
SQ FT: 11,000
SALES (est): 500K Privately Held
SIC: 2678 Stationery products

(G-1000)
COTTONWOOD METALS INC
1625 Sycamore Ave Ste A (11716-1728)
PHONE..................................646 807-8674
Christopher Smith, *Chairman*
EMP: 20
SQ FT: 15,000
SALES (est): 2.2MM Privately Held
SIC: 3441 Fabricated structural metal

(G-1001)
CRAFT-TECH MFG CORP
1750 Artic Ave (11716-2423)
PHONE..................................631 563-4949
Joseph Desantis, *CEO*
Ralph Desantis Jr, *Vice Pres*
Ralph Desantis Sr, *Treasurer*
EMP: 7 EST: 1978
SQ FT: 19,500
SALES (est): 840K Privately Held
SIC: 3444 Casings, sheet metal

(G-1002)
CREATIVE METAL FABRICATORS
360 Knickerbocker Ave # 13 (11716-3124)
PHONE..................................631 567-2266
Richard W Donovan, *President*
EMP: 7
SQ FT: 8,500
SALES (est): 600K Privately Held
SIC: 3446 Architectural metalwork

(G-1003)
CUSTOM DESIGN METALS INC
1612 Locust Ave Ste C (11716-2100)
PHONE..................................631 563-2444
Robert Lyon, *President*
Richard Mellace, *Vice Pres*
EMP: 5
SQ FT: 7,500
SALES (est): 697.1K Privately Held
SIC: 3399 Metal powders, pastes & flakes

(G-1004)
CUSTOM HOUSE ENGRAVERS INC
Also Called: Village Plaquesmith, Ththe
104 Keyland Ct (11716-2656)
PHONE..................................631 567-3004
Terry McLean, *President*
Terry Mc Lean, *Principal*
Brian McLean, *Vice Pres*
▲ EMP: 6
SQ FT: 3,200
SALES: 1MM Privately Held
SIC: 2796 3089 3479 Engraving platemaking services; engraving of plastic; etching & engraving

(G-1005)
CUSTOM NUTRACEUTICALS LLC (PA)
80 Orville Dr Ste 112 (11716-2505)
PHONE..................................631 755-1388
Steven Coello, *Controller*

Bohemia - Suffolk County (G-1006)

Jason Mancuso,
EMP: 24
SALES (est): 4.2MM **Privately Held**
SIC: 2833 Drugs & herbs: grading, grinding & milling

(G-1006)
CYGNUS AUTOMATION INC
1605 9th Ave (11716-1202)
PHONE....................................631 981-0909
Sharon Dietrich, *President*
John Alessandro, *Vice Pres*
Mark Salerno, *Vice Pres*
Christian Dietrich, *Admin Sec*
EMP: 20
SQ FT: 6,000
SALES (est): 2.8MM **Privately Held**
SIC: 3629 3672 5063 Electronic generation equipment; printed circuit boards; wire & cable

(G-1007)
D & I FINISHING INC
1560 Ocean Ave Ste 7 (11716-1951)
PHONE....................................631 471-3034
Danny Guerrier, *President*
Barbara Guerrier, *General Mgr*
EMP: 6
SQ FT: 4,500
SALES: 400K **Privately Held**
SIC: 3479 1721 3471 Painting of metal products; painting & paper hanging; finishing, metals or formed products

(G-1008)
DATA DEVICE CORPORATION
(DH)
105 Wilbur Pl (11716-2426)
PHONE....................................631 567-5600
Terrance M Paradie, *CEO*
Vincent Buffa, *President*
Charles Frazer, *President*
Frank Bloomfield, *Vice Pres*
John Santini, *Vice Pres*
▲ **EMP:** 320
SQ FT: 104,000
SALES (est): 118.8MM
SALES (corp-wide): 3.5B **Publicly Held**
WEB: www.ddc-web.com
SIC: 3577 3674 3677 Data conversion equipment, media-to-media: computer; modules, solid state; electronic transformers
HQ: Ilc Industries, Llc
105 Wilbur Pl
Bohemia NY 11716
631 567-5600

(G-1009)
DAVIDSON GRINDING CORP
220 Mccormick Dr (11716-2906)
PHONE....................................631 563-3982
Jonathan Davidson, *President*
EMP: 10
SQ FT: 6,500
SALES: 1MM **Privately Held**
SIC: 3599 Machine shop, jobbing & repair

(G-1010)
DAVIS AIRCRAFT PRODUCTS CO INC
1150 Walnut Ave Ste 1 (11716-2168)
P.O. Box 525 (11716-0525)
PHONE....................................631 563-1500
Bruce T Davis, *CEO*
Douglas Davis, *Vice Pres*
Jill Davis, *Vice Pres*
Judy Bender, *Purchasing*
Stephanie Johnson, *Purchasing*
▲ **EMP:** 143 **EST:** 1967
SQ FT: 30,000
SALES (est): 32.5MM **Privately Held**
WEB: www.davisaircraftproducts.com
SIC: 3724 3728 Aircraft engines & engine parts; aircraft parts & equipment

(G-1011)
DAYTON T BROWN INC (PA)
Also Called: D T B
1175 Church St (11716-5014)
PHONE....................................631 589-6300
Dayton T Brown Jr, *Ch of Bd*
Richard Dunne, *President*
Louise Loyst, *Business Mgr*
Virginia Stone, *Business Mgr*
Tom Volpe, *Business Mgr*
EMP: 273 **EST:** 1950
SQ FT: 250,000
SALES (est): 74.4MM **Privately Held**
WEB: www.daytontbrown.com
SIC: 3444 2741 8711 8734 Sheet metal specialties, not stamped; technical manuals: publishing only, not printed on site; technical papers: publishing only, not printed on site; engineering services; testing laboratories; measuring & controlling devices

(G-1012)
DELTA LOCK COMPANY LLC
366 Central Ave (11716-3105)
PHONE....................................631 238-7035
▲ **EMP:** 12
SALES (est): 2.1MM **Privately Held**
SIC: 3429 Locks or lock sets

(G-1013)
DENTON ADVERTISING INC
1650 Sycamore Ave Ste 28 (11716-1731)
PHONE....................................631 586-4333
Dennis Dornan, *President*
Patty Lyons, *Admin Sec*
EMP: 12
SQ FT: 8,000
SALES: 1.4MM **Privately Held**
WEB: www.dentonadvertising.com
SIC: 2752 Lithographing on metal; advertising posters, lithographed

(G-1014)
DEROSA FABRICATIONS INC
250 Knickerbocker Ave (11716-3112)
PHONE....................................631 563-0640
Tony Derosa, *President*
Lorry Derosa, *Vice Pres*
EMP: 20
SQ FT: 12,500
SALES (est): 2.3MM **Privately Held**
SIC: 3599 Machine shop, jobbing & repair

(G-1015)
DESIGN WORKS CRAFT INC
(PA)
70 Orville Dr Ste 1 (11716-2547)
PHONE....................................631 244-5749
Susan Goldsmith, *Ch of Bd*
Daniel Knopp, *President*
▲ **EMP:** 10
SQ FT: 24,500
SALES (est): 4.6MM **Privately Held**
WEB: www.designworkscrafts.com
SIC: 3944 Craft & hobby kits & sets

(G-1016)
DESIGNS FOR VISION INC
4000 Veterans Mem Hwy (11716-1024)
PHONE....................................631 585-3300
Richard Feinbloom, *Chairman*
Kelly McKinnon, *Vice Pres*
Herb Schwartz, *Vice Pres*
Janelle Norton, *Design Engr*
Peter Murphy, *Treasurer*
▲ **EMP:** 130
SQ FT: 30,000
SALES (est): 27.4MM **Privately Held**
WEB: www.designsforvision.com
SIC: 3841 3851 Surgical & medical instruments; ophthalmic goods

(G-1017)
EAGLE TELEPHONICS INC
3880 Veterans Mem Hwy (11716-1038)
PHONE....................................631 471-3600
Richard J Riccoboni, *Ch of Bd*
Don H Coleman, *COO*
Alexander Wenger, *Exec VP*
Frederic H Chapus, *Vice Pres*
EMP: 15
SQ FT: 10,000
SALES (est): 3.3MM **Privately Held**
WEB: www.eagletelephonics.com
SIC: 3661 6794 Telephones & telephone apparatus; patent owners & lessors

(G-1018)
EASTERN COLOR STRIPPING INC
Also Called: Eastern Color Imaging
666 Lanson St (11716-3427)
PHONE....................................631 563-3700
Michael Catera, *President*
Laura Catera, *Admin Sec*
EMP: 10
SQ FT: 3,000
SALES (est): 1.1MM **Privately Held**
WEB: www.easterncolor.com
SIC: 2796 7335 Digital 4 Color Printing And Service Bureau

(G-1019)
EASTERN EXTERIOR WALL
869 Lincoln Ave (11716-4105)
PHONE....................................631 589-3880
Mike Collier, *Project Mgr*
Charlie Bona, *Manager*
EMP: 20
SALES (corp-wide): 172.4MM **Privately Held**
SIC: 2452 Prefabricated wood buildings
HQ: Wall Eastern Exterior Systems Inc
645 Hamilton St Ste 300
Allentown PA 18101
610 868-5522

(G-1020)
EDO LLC
Also Called: Edo Crprtion-Fiber Science Div
5852 Johnson Ave (11716)
PHONE....................................631 218-1413
Weily Tung, *Branch Mgr*
EMP: 17
SALES (corp-wide): 6.1B **Publicly Held**
SIC: 3825 Instruments to measure electricity
HQ: Edo Llc
1500 New Horizons Blvd
Amityville NY 11701
631 630-4000

(G-1021)
EL-GEN LLC
7 Shirley St Unit 1 (11716-1735)
PHONE....................................631 218-3400
Gerard Verbiar, *Treasurer*
Roy J Mc Keen,
EMP: 5
SQ FT: 7,500
SALES (est): 400K **Privately Held**
WEB: www.elgenmfg.com
SIC: 2023 Dietary supplements, dairy & non-dairy based

(G-1022)
ELAN UPHOLSTERY INC
120b Wilbur Pl Ste B (11716-2404)
PHONE....................................631 563-0650
Alan Fogg, *President*
Ann Fogg, *President*
EMP: 10
SQ FT: 7,500
SALES (est): 1MM **Privately Held**
SIC: 2512 7641 Upholstered household furniture; upholstery work

(G-1023)
ELECTRO ALLOY RECOVERY INC
Also Called: Electro Waste Systems
130 Knickerbocker Ave M (11716-3171)
PHONE....................................631 879-7530
John Wellman, *President*
EMP: 8
SQ FT: 15,000
SALES: 2MM **Privately Held**
SIC: 3339 Gold refining (primary); platinum group metal refining (primary)

(G-1024)
FOSTER - GORDON MANUFACTURING
55 Knickerbocker Ave G (11716-3131)
PHONE....................................631 589-6776
Jonathan Gordon, *President*
Louren Gordon, *Vice Pres*
EMP: 8
SQ FT: 9,000
SALES (est): 978.2K **Privately Held**
SIC: 2789 2782 5112 5999 Beveling of cards; blankbooks & looseleaf binders; blank books; alcoholic beverage making equipment & supplies

(G-1025)
FURNITURE BY CRAFTMASTER LTD
1595 Ocean Ave Ste A9 (11716-1962)
PHONE....................................631 750-0658
Michael Ruggiero, *President*
Donna Agate, *Corp Secy*
EMP: 5
SQ FT: 3,600
SALES (est): 622.1K **Privately Held**
SIC: 2521 2512 Wood office furniture; upholstered household furniture

(G-1026)
GE AVIATION SYSTEMS LLC
1000 Macarthur Mem Hwy (11716)
PHONE....................................631 467-5500
Kathleen Moosmueller, *General Mgr*
Predrag Hadzibabic, *Engineer*
Brett Rowles, *Manager*
EMP: 250
SALES (corp-wide): 122B **Publicly Held**
SIC: 3728 Aircraft parts & equipment
HQ: Ge Aviation Systems Llc
1 Neumann Way
Cincinnati OH 45215
937 898-9600

(G-1027)
GE AVIATION SYSTEMS LLC
1000 Macarthur Mem Hwy (11716)
PHONE....................................513 243-9104
Rebecca Everett, *Branch Mgr*
EMP: 99
SALES (corp-wide): 122B **Publicly Held**
SIC: 3812 8731 Search & navigation equipment; electronic research
HQ: Ge Aviation Systems Llc
1 Neumann Way
Cincinnati OH 45215
937 898-9600

(G-1028)
GFH ORTHOTIC & PROSTHETIC LABS
Also Called: Hutnick Rehab
161 Keyland Ct (11716-2621)
PHONE....................................631 467-3725
Glenn F Hutnick, *Ch of Bd*
Todd Schaffhauser, *Director*
EMP: 5 **EST:** 1979
SALES (est): 609.6K **Privately Held**
SIC: 3842 Limbs, artificial; braces, orthopedic

(G-1029)
GLENN WAYNE WHOLESALE BKY INC
Also Called: Glenn Wayne Bakery
1800 Artic Ave (11716-2443)
PHONE....................................631 289-9200
Glenn Alessi, *Ch of Bd*
Wayne Stelz, *President*
EMP: 85
SQ FT: 15,000
SALES (est): 18.5MM **Privately Held**
WEB: www.glennwayne.com
SIC: 2051 Bakery: wholesale or wholesale/retail combined

(G-1030)
GLOBAL PAYMENT TECH INC
(PA)
Also Called: Gpt
170 Wilbur Pl Ste 600 (11716-2433)
PHONE....................................631 563-2500
Andre Soussa, *Ch of Bd*
William McMahon, *President*
Janina Aniolowska, *Opers Staff*
Dennys Noriega, *Opers Staff*
▲ **EMP:** 25
SQ FT: 25,550
SALES (est): 11.8MM **Publicly Held**
WEB: www.gptx.com
SIC: 3581 Mechanisms & parts for automatic vending machines

(G-1031)
GUIDANCE GROUP INC
40 Aero Rd Ste 2 (11716-2900)
PHONE....................................631 619-2600
Jon D Werz, *CEO*
EMP: 8
SALES (est): 577.8K **Privately Held**
SIC: 2711 Newspapers, publishing & printing

GEOGRAPHIC SECTION — Bohemia - Suffolk County

(G-1032)
HIGH FREQUENCY TECH CO INC
1531 Smithtown Ave Ste 1 (11716-2448)
PHONE.....................................631 242-3020
Andrew Amabile, *President*
Mary Ann Amabile, *Shareholder*
▲ EMP: 12
SQ FT: 10,000
SALES (est): 2.3MM **Privately Held**
WEB: www.hftinc.com
SIC: 3559 5065 5084 Plastics working machinery; electronic parts & equipment; materials handling machinery

(G-1033)
HW SPECIALTIES CO INC
210 Knickerbocker Ave B (11716-3175)
PHONE.....................................631 589-0745
Kevin Anderson, *President*
Fred Wichelman, *Vice Pres*
EMP: 18 EST: 1969
SQ FT: 2,500
SALES: 1.4MM **Privately Held**
SIC: 3599 Machine shop, jobbing & repair

(G-1034)
ILC HOLDINGS INC (HQ)
105 Wilbur Pl (11716-2426)
PHONE.....................................631 567-5600
Clifford P Lane, *CEO*
EMP: 9
SALES (est): 118.8MM
SALES (corp-wide): 3.5B **Publicly Held**
SIC: 3674 Semiconductors & related devices
PA: Transdigm Group Incorporated
1301 E 9th St Ste 3000
Cleveland OH 44114
216 706-2960

(G-1035)
ILC INDUSTRIES INC
105 Wilbur Pl (11716-2426)
PHONE.....................................631 567-5600
John Stith, *Engineer*
Frank Haunstein, *Senior Engr*
Derek Pulis, *Senior Engr*
Diane Spooner, *Accounts Exec*
Ivette Cruz, *Mktg Dir*
EMP: 20 EST: 2016
SALES (est): 861.9K **Privately Held**
SIC: 3999 Manufacturing industries

(G-1036)
ILC INDUSTRIES LLC (DH)
Also Called: I L C
105 Wilbur Pl (11716-2426)
PHONE.....................................631 567-5600
Clifford P Lane, *CEO*
Roy Heyder, *Senior Engr*
Ken Sheedy, *CFO*
Nancy Henzel, *Accountant*
Jerry Kessler, *Product Mgr*
▲ EMP: 17 EST: 2010
SQ FT: 150,000
SALES (cst): 118.8MM
SALES (corp-wide): 3.5B **Publicly Held**
WEB: www.ilcindustries.com
SIC: 3674 Semiconductors & related devices
HQ: Ilc Holdings, Inc.
105 Wilbur Pl
Bohemia NY 11716
631 567-5600

(G-1037)
INTELLIGENT TRAFFIC SYSTEMS
140 Keyland Ct Unit 1 (11716-2646)
PHONE.....................................631 567-5994
Joseph Battista, *President*
Karen Battista, *Admin Sec*
EMP: 8
SQ FT: 3,200
SALES: 400K **Privately Held**
SIC: 3669 Signaling apparatus, electric

(G-1038)
J PERCOCO INDUSTRIES INC
Also Called: Mjs Woodworking
1546 Ocean Ave Ste 4 (11716-1938)
PHONE.....................................631 312-4572
Jerolamo Percoco, *President*
George Lisk, *Engineer*
EMP: 8
SQ FT: 15,000
SALES: 1MM **Privately Held**
SIC: 2511 2434 2431 Wood household furniture; wood kitchen cabinets; millwork

(G-1039)
JAMES D RUBINO INC
20 Jules Ct Ste 5 (11716-4106)
PHONE.....................................631 244-8730
James D Rubino, *President*
EMP: 24
SALES (est): 3.3MM **Privately Held**
SIC: 3499 Fabricated metal products

(G-1040)
JANCO PRESS INC
20 Floyds Run (11716-2154)
PHONE.....................................631 563-3003
Maurice Janco, *President*
Florence Janco, *Vice Pres*
Seth Janco, *Vice Pres*
EMP: 15
SQ FT: 10,000
SALES (est): 3.6MM **Privately Held**
SIC: 2754 2759 Labels: gravure printing; labels & seals: printing; embossing on paper

(G-1041)
JEROME STVENS PHRMCUTICALS INC
Also Called: Jsp
60 Davinci Dr (11716-2633)
PHONE.....................................631 567-1113
Ronald Steinlauf, *Chairman*
EMP: 15
SQ FT: 20,000
SALES (est): 4.6MM **Privately Held**
SIC: 2834 Druggists' preparations (pharmaceuticals)

(G-1042)
JOLIN MACHINING CORP
1561 Smithtown Ave (11716-2409)
PHONE.....................................631 589-1305
John Lutjen, *President*
EMP: 12
SQ FT: 7,000
SALES (est): 2.1MM **Privately Held**
SIC: 3599 Machine shop, jobbing & repair

(G-1043)
JONATHAN LORD CORP
87 Carlough Rd Unit A (11716-2921)
PHONE.....................................631 563-4445
Carole Kentrup, *President*
Kathleen Dancik, *Co-President*
EMP: 12
SQ FT: 8,000
SALES (est): 2MM **Privately Held**
WEB: www.jonathanlord.com
SIC: 2052 2051 Cookies & crackers; cakes, bakery: except frozen

(G-1044)
L & J INTERIORS INC
35 Orville Dr Ste 3 (11716-2533)
PHONE.....................................631 218-0838
Jerry Esquibel, *President*
Leon Esquibel, *Vice Pres*
EMP: 8
SALES (est): 870K **Privately Held**
WEB: www.ljinteriors.com
SIC: 2541 1742 Store fixtures, wood; drywall

(G-1045)
LED LUMINA USA LLC
116 Wilbur Pl (11716-2402)
PHONE.....................................631 750-4433
Christina Bonlarron, *CFO*
John Bonlarron, *Mng Member*
▲ EMP: 1
SALES: 1MM **Privately Held**
SIC: 3229 Bulbs for electric lights

(G-1046)
LEETECH MANUFACTURING INC
105 Carlough Rd Unit C (11716-2914)
PHONE.....................................631 563-1442
Fred Vasta, *President*
EMP: 5
SALES (est): 480K **Privately Held**
SIC: 3599 Machine shop, jobbing & repair

(G-1047)
LEIDEL CORPORATION (PA)
Also Called: Pentaplastics
95 Orville Dr (11716-2501)
PHONE.....................................631 244-0900
Warren H Leidel, *Ch of Bd*
Roger D Leidel, *President*
EMP: 26 EST: 1902
SQ FT: 14,000
SALES: 5.9MM **Privately Held**
WEB: www.leidelcorp.com
SIC: 3089 Injection molded finished plastic products; molding primary plastic

(G-1048)
LOGITEK INC
110 Wilbur Pl (11716-2402)
PHONE.....................................631 567-1100
William Forman, *CEO*
EMP: 90 EST: 1969
SALES: 20MM **Privately Held**
WEB: www.naii.com
SIC: 3679 3825 3812 3674 Electronic circuits; instruments to measure electricity; search & navigation equipment; semiconductors & related devices; relays & industrial controls
PA: North Atlantic Industries, Inc.
110 Wilbur Pl
Bohemia NY 11716

(G-1049)
LONG ISLANDS BEST INC
1650 Sycamore Ave Ste 4b (11716-1731)
PHONE.....................................855 542-3785
John Bosco, *President*
EMP: 7
SALES: 119K **Privately Held**
SIC: 2741 Telephone & other directory publishing

(G-1050)
LOUGHLIN MANUFACTURING CORP
1601 9th Ave (11716-1202)
PHONE.....................................631 585-4422
Martin Loughlin, *President*
EMP: 14 EST: 1970
SQ FT: 5,000
SALES (est): 2.5MM **Privately Held**
SIC: 3599 Machine shop, jobbing & repair

(G-1051)
LSC PERIPHERALS INCORPORATED
415 Central Ave Ste F (11716-3118)
PHONE.....................................631 244-0707
Roger Strolin, *Vice Pres*
Frank Villa, *Officer*
EMP: 4
SQ FT: 4,000
SALES (est): 1.5MM **Privately Held**
SIC: 3577 Printers, computer

(G-1052)
LUCAS DENTAL EQUIPMENT CO INC
360 Knickerbocker Ave # 4 (11716-3124)
PHONE.....................................631 244-2807
Richard Lucas, *Ch of Bd*
Joyce Lucas, *President*
EMP: 14 EST: 1930
SQ FT: 20,000
SALES (est): 1.9MM **Privately Held**
SIC: 3843 Dental equipment

(G-1053)
MAGELLAN AEROSPACE NY INC
25 Aero Rd (11716-2901)
PHONE.....................................631 589-2440
Rickie Pennington, *Engineer*
John Thuren, *Accountant*
Jerry Myszka, *Manager*
Russell Gerkitz, *Manager*
Gilead Zfira, *Business Dir*
EMP: 250
SALES (corp-wide): 759.1MM **Privately Held**
SIC: 3599 3728 5088 Machine shop, jobbing & repair; aircraft parts & equipment; aircraft equipment & supplies
HQ: Magellan Aerospace, New York, Inc.
9711 50th Ave
Corona NY 11368
718 699-4000

(G-1054)
MAGNAWORKS TECHNOLOGY INC
36 Carlough Rd Unit H (11716-2905)
PHONE.....................................631 218-3431
Stan Stromski, *Director*
EMP: 7
SALES (est): 638.4K **Privately Held**
WEB: www.magnaworkstechnology.com
SIC: 3499 Magnets, permanent: metallic

(G-1055)
MALHAME PUBLS & IMPORTERS INC
Also Called: Regina Press
180 Orville Dr Unit A (11716-2546)
PHONE.....................................631 694-8600
Robert Malhame, *President*
George E Malhame, *President*
Robert E Malhame, *Treasurer*
▲ EMP: 22 EST: 1889
SALES (est): 3.9MM **Privately Held**
WEB: www.malhame.com
SIC: 2731 5049 Books: publishing only; religious supplies

(G-1056)
MASS MDSG SELF SELECTION EQP
35 Orville Dr Ste 2 (11716-2533)
PHONE.....................................631 234-3300
Stephen D Jaha, *Ch of Bd*
Bob Panagos, *Vice Pres*
▲ EMP: 20 EST: 1961
SQ FT: 4,000
SALES (est): 3.4MM **Privately Held**
WEB: www.masmerch.com
SIC: 2542 1751 Partitions & fixtures, except wood; store fixture installation

(G-1057)
MCGUIGAN INC
Also Called: Concept Components
210 Knickerbocker Ave (11716-3175)
PHONE.....................................631 750-6222
James W McGuigan, *Ch of Bd*
EMP: 25
SQ FT: 9,000
SALES (est): 6.2MM **Privately Held**
WEB: www.mcguigan.com
SIC: 3566 3599 3724 Gears, power transmission, except automotive; custom machinery; aircraft engines & engine parts

(G-1058)
MED SERVICES INC
100 Knickerbocker Ave C (11716-3127)
PHONE.....................................631 218-6450
Steven Cortese, *President*
EMP: 78
SQ FT: 1,800
SALES (est): 155MM **Privately Held**
SIC: 3845 7699 Electromedical equipment; medical equipment repair, non-electric

(G-1059)
MONARCH METAL FABRICATION INC
1625 Sycamore Ave Ste A (11716-1728)
PHONE.....................................631 563-8967
James Carter, *President*
▼ EMP: 8
SQ FT: 17,000
SALES (est): 1.5MM **Privately Held**
WEB: www.monarchmetal.com
SIC: 3444 Sheet metalwork

(G-1060)
MPE GRAPHICS INC
Also Called: Milburn Printing
120 Wilbur Pl Ste A (11716-2440)
PHONE.....................................631 582-8900
Keith Quinn, *President*
Lisa Quinn, *Director*
EMP: 11 EST: 2004
SQ FT: 5,000
SALES (est): 1.5MM **Privately Held**
SIC: 2759 Commercial printing

(G-1061)
MTWLI PRECISION CORP
1605 Sycamore Ave Unit B (11716-1734)
PHONE.....................................631 244-3767
EMP: 5

Bohemia - Suffolk County (G-1062)

SQ FT: 2,100
SALES: 200K **Privately Held**
SIC: 3549 Mfg Metalworking Machinery

(G-1062)
NATURES BOUNTY (NY) INC
90 Orville Dr (11716-2521)
PHONE.....................631 567-9500
EMP: 9 **Publicly Held**
SIC: 2834 Vitamin preparations
HQ: Nature's Bounty (Ny), Inc.
2100 Smithtown Ave
Ronkonkoma NY 11779
631 200-2000

(G-1063)
NEW KIT ON THE BLOCK
100 Knickerbocker Ave K (11716-3127)
PHONE.....................631 757-5655
Lee Holcomb, *President*
EMP: 5
SQ FT: 4,000
SALES (est): 369.2K **Privately Held**
WEB: www.thenewkitontheblock.com
SIC: 3993 5099 Signs & advertising specialties; signs, except electric

(G-1064)
NEWPORT BUSINESS SOLUTIONS INC
61 Keyland Ct (11716-2654)
PHONE.....................631 319-6129
Gina Lanzillotta, *President*
EMP: 18 EST: 2010
SALES (est): 2.2MM **Privately Held**
SIC: 3555 5045 2759 Printing trades machinery; printers, computer; promotional printing

(G-1065)
NORTH ATLANTIC INDUSTRIES INC
50 Orville Dr Ste 3 (11716-2548)
PHONE.....................631 567-1100
EMP: 38 **Privately Held**
SIC: 3825 Instruments to measure electricity
PA: North Atlantic Industries, Inc.
110 Wilbur Pl
Bohemia NY 11716

(G-1066)
NORTH ATLANTIC INDUSTRIES INC (PA)
110 Wilbur Pl (11716-2402)
PHONE.....................631 567-1100
William Forman, *President*
Ernie Keith, *COO*
Lino Massafra, *Vice Pres*
Edward Doepp, *Plant Mgr*
Valerie Auciello, *Research*
EMP: 137
SQ FT: 30,000
SALES: 62MM **Privately Held**
SIC: 3825 Instruments to measure electricity

(G-1067)
NORTH HILLS SIGNAL PROC CORP
40 Orville Dr (11716-2504)
PHONE.....................631 244-7393
Estro Vitantonio, *CEO*
Warren Esanu, *Ch of Bd*
Richard Schwarz, *General Mgr*
Leslie Brand, *CFO*
Ann Martinico, *Info Tech Mgr*
▲ EMP: 23
SQ FT: 12,000
SALES (est): 708.8K
SALES (corp-wide): 6.3MM **Privately Held**
WEB: www.northhills-sp.com
SIC: 3679 Harness assemblies for electronic use: wire or cable
PA: North Hills Holding Company Llc
6851 Jericho Tpke Ste 170
Syosset NY 11791
516 682-7705

(G-1068)
NORTHROCK INDUSTRIES INC
31 Crossway E (11716-1204)
PHONE.....................631 924-6130
Brian F Robertson, *President*
Alan Browning, *Treasurer*
Eric Rueb, *Admin Sec*
▲ EMP: 21
SQ FT: 12,000
SALES (est): 3.8MM **Privately Held**
WEB: www.northrockindustries.com
SIC: 3531 Construction machinery

(G-1069)
NYCON DIAMOND & TOOLS CORP
55 Knickerbocker Ave A (11716-3120)
PHONE.....................855 937-6922
John Pierpaoli, *President*
EMP: 7
SQ FT: 2,000
SALES (est): 344.4K **Privately Held**
SIC: 3559 Concrete products machinery

(G-1070)
OLD WORLD MOULDINGS INC
821 Lincoln Ave (11716-4103)
PHONE.....................631 563-8660
Alan D Havranek, *President*
EMP: 8
SQ FT: 20,000
SALES (est): 2.4MM **Privately Held**
WEB: www.oldworldmouldings.com
SIC: 2431 Moldings, wood: unfinished & prefinished

(G-1071)
PACKAGING DYNAMICS LTD
35 Carlough Rd Ste 2 (11716-2913)
PHONE.....................631 563-4499
Daniel Lehmann, *CEO*
Eric Lehmann, *President*
Darrin Tosh, *Prdtn Mgr*
Pat Lehmann, *Admin Sec*
◆ EMP: 15
SALES (est): 3.5MM **Privately Held**
SIC: 3565 Packaging machinery

(G-1072)
PASSUR AEROSPACE INC
35 Orville Dr Ste 1 (11716-2533)
PHONE.....................631 589-6800
G S Beckwith Gilbert, *Ch of Bd*
James T Barry, *President*
Keith Wichman, *President*
Renee Alter, *Vice Pres*
John Keller, *Vice Pres*
EMP: 6
SQ FT: 3,000
SALES (est): 1.7MM
SALES (corp-wide): 13.8MM **Publicly Held**
WEB: www.passur.com
SIC: 3671 Cathode ray tubes, including rebuilt
PA: Passur Aerospace, Inc.
1 Landmark Sq Ste 1900
Stamford CT 06901
203 622-4086

(G-1073)
PDA PANACHE CORP
Also Called: P D A Panache
70 Knickerbocker Ave # 7 (11716-3151)
P.O. Box 577, Bellport (11713-0577)
PHONE.....................631 776-0523
Paul Schiller, *President*
Lynn Schiller, *Vice Pres*
EMP: 5
SALES (est): 580K **Privately Held**
WEB: www.pdapanache.com
SIC: 3577 5941 5112 Input/output equipment, computer; sporting goods & bicycle shops; pens &/or pencils

(G-1074)
PERVI PRECISION COMPANY INC
220 Knickerbocker Ave # 1 (11716-3181)
PHONE.....................631 589-5557
Carlos Perez, *Owner*
EMP: 6
SQ FT: 4,100
SALES (est): 888K **Privately Held**
SIC: 3469 3599 Machine parts, stamped or pressed metal; machine shop, jobbing & repair

(G-1075)
POWER CONNECTOR INC
140 Wilbur Pl Ste 4 (11716-2400)
PHONE.....................631 563-7878
Andrew S Linder, *President*
Arlene R Linder, *Vice Pres*
▲ EMP: 38
SQ FT: 32,000
SALES: 10MM **Privately Held**
SIC: 3678 Electronic connectors

(G-1076)
PRECISION ASSEMBLY TECH INC
Also Called: P.A.t
160 Wilbur Pl Ste 500 (11716-2437)
PHONE.....................631 699-9400
Lorraine Caruso, *Principal*
Russell Gulotta, *Chairman*
Thomas Gulotta, *Vice Pres*
Rob Gulotta, *Manager*
▲ EMP: 50
SQ FT: 25,000
SALES (est): 16.6MM **Privately Held**
WEB: www.pat-inc.com
SIC: 3679 Electronic circuits; harness assemblies for electronic use: wire or cable

(G-1077)
PRECISION CHARTS INC
Also Called: P C I
130 Wilbur Pl (11716-2404)
P.O. Box 456 (11716-0456)
PHONE.....................631 244-8295
Barry Spencer, *President*
◆ EMP: 25
SQ FT: 30,000
SALES (est): 5.1MM **Privately Held**
WEB: www.pcicharts.com
SIC: 2621 Book, bond & printing papers

(G-1078)
PRIMOPLAST INC
1555 Ocean Ave Ste E (11716-1933)
PHONE.....................631 750-0680
Eugene Ruoff, *President*
William Hayes, *Admin Sec*
EMP: 12
SQ FT: 1,000
SALES: 950K **Privately Held**
SIC: 3089 3531 Injection molded finished plastic products; construction machinery attachments

(G-1079)
PRO TORQUE
Also Called: J Rivera
1440 Church St (11716-5027)
PHONE.....................631 218-8700
Joseph Rivera, *President*
Susan Rivera, *Vice Pres*
Lynn Dimino, *CFO*
EMP: 25
SQ FT: 165,000
SALES: 1.7MM **Privately Held**
WEB: www.jrivera.com
SIC: 3714 Motor vehicle transmissions, drive assemblies & parts

(G-1080)
PROTEX INTERNATIONAL CORP
Also Called: Securax
366 Central Ave (11716-3105)
PHONE.....................631 563-4250
David Wachsman, *CEO*
Rodney Surratt, *CFO*
▲ EMP: 75
SQ FT: 34,000
SALES (est): 13MM **Privately Held**
WEB: www.protex-intl.com
SIC: 3699 Security control equipment & systems

(G-1081)
QUEUE SOLUTIONS LLC
250 Knickerbocker Ave (11716-3112)
PHONE.....................631 750-6440
Richard Prigg, *Mng Member*
EMP: 10
SALES: 5MM **Privately Held**
SIC: 3842 Personal safety equipment

(G-1082)
REPELLEM CONSUMER PDTS CORP
Also Called: Ecosmartplastics
1626 Locust Ave Ste 6 (11716-2159)
PHONE.....................631 273-3992
Terry Feinberg, *President*
EMP: 10
SALES (est): 29.2K **Privately Held**
SIC: 2673 2392 Trash bags (plastic film): made from purchased materials; tablecloths: made from purchased materials

(G-1083)
ROAD CASES USA INC
1625 Sycamore Ave Ste A (11716-1728)
PHONE.....................631 563-0633
Lucille Maielna, *Office Mgr*
EMP: 20
SALES: 106.3K **Privately Held**
SIC: 3523 Farm machinery & equipment

(G-1084)
S G NEW YORK LLC (PA)
Also Called: Pennysaver News
2950 Vtrans Mem Hwy Ste 1 (11716-1030)
PHONE.....................631 665-4000
Richard Megenedy Jr,
Murray Rossby,
EMP: 33
SQ FT: 4,000
SALES (est): 5.3MM **Privately Held**
SIC: 2741 2711 Shopping news: publishing & printing; newspapers, publishing & printing

(G-1085)
SCIENTIFIC INDUSTRIES INC (PA)
80 Orville Dr Ste 102 (11716-2505)
PHONE.....................631 567-4700
Joseph G Cremonese, *Ch of Bd*
Helena R Santos, *President*
Robert P Nichols, *Admin Sec*
EMP: 33 EST: 1954
SQ FT: 19,000
SALES: 8.4MM **Publicly Held**
WEB: www.scind.com
SIC: 3821 Shakers & stirrers

(G-1086)
SECURITY DYNAMICS INC
Also Called: Sdi Cable
217 Knickerbocker Ave # 4 (11716-3132)
PHONE.....................631 392-1701
Huihua Wang, *Ch of Bd*
William Wang, *President*
▲ EMP: 12
SQ FT: 3,000
SALES (est): 3.3MM **Privately Held**
SIC: 3699 Security control equipment & systems

(G-1087)
SELECT CONTROLS INC
45 Knickerbocker Ave # 3 (11716-3119)
PHONE.....................631 567-9010
Robert Ufer, *President*
Tom Morris, *General Mgr*
Diane Morris, *Corp Secy*
Ken Brinkley, *Representative*
EMP: 32
SQ FT: 2,500
SALES (est): 5.7MM **Privately Held**
WEB: www.select-controls.com
SIC: 3823 3625 8711 3613 Industrial flow & liquid measuring instruments; industrial electrical relays & switches; consulting engineer; switchgear & switchboard apparatus

(G-1088)
SHAR-MAR MACHINE COMPANY
1648 Locust Ave Ste F (11716-2156)
PHONE.....................631 567-8040
Myron Rubin, *Owner*
EMP: 5
SQ FT: 3,200
SALES (est): 439.3K **Privately Held**
SIC: 3599 Machine shop, jobbing & repair

(G-1089)
SHORT RUN FORMS INC
171 Keyland Ct (11716-2621)
PHONE.....................631 567-7171

Steven Looney, *President*
Andrew Boccio, *Senior VP*
Robert Stumpo, *Vice Pres*
Jerry Gagliardo, *Foreman/Supr*
EMP: 60
SQ FT: 17,000
SALES (est): 8.3MM **Privately Held**
WEB: www.shortrunforms.com
SIC: 2759 5943 Business forms: printing; office forms & supplies

(G-1090)
SMART HIGH VOLTAGE SOLUTIONS
390 Knickerbocker Ave # 6 (11716-3123)
P.O. Box 5135, Hauppauge (11788-0001)
PHONE 631 563-6724
Kevin R Smith, *President*
Hersh Ochakovski, *Exec VP*
▼ **EMP:** 16
SQ FT: 1,825
SALES: 2.5MM **Privately Held**
SIC: 3542 High energy rate metal forming machines

(G-1091)
SPECTRUM CRAFTS INC
Also Called: Janlynn Corporation, The
70 Orville Dr Ste 1 (11716-2547)
PHONE 631 244-5749
Daniel Knopp, *President*
EMP: 25 **EST:** 2013
SALES (est): 155.7K
SALES (corp-wide): 4.6MM **Privately Held**
SIC: 3944 Craft & hobby kits & sets
PA: Design Works Craft Inc.
70 Orville Dr Ste 1
Bohemia NY 11716
631 244-5749

(G-1092)
STRUCTURAL INDUSTRIES INC
2950 Veterans Memorial Hw (11716-1030)
PHONE 631 471-5200
Stanley Hirsch, *CEO*
Jamie Hirsch, *President*
Cliff Burger, *Exec VP*
Judy Hirsch, *Vice Pres*
Judy Vietheer, *CFO*
▲ **EMP:** 180 **EST:** 1966
SQ FT: 70,000
SALES (est): 22.9MM **Privately Held**
WEB: www.structuralindustries.com
SIC: 2499 3089 3499 Picture frame molding, finished; plastic processing; picture frames, metal

(G-1093)
SYMBOL TECHNOLOGIES LLC
110 Orville Dr (11716-2506)
PHONE 631 738-2400
Ron Goldman, *Branch Mgr*
EMP: 15
SALES (corp-wide): 3.7B **Publicly Held**
WEB: www.symbol.com
SIC: 3577 Computer peripheral equipment
HQ: Symbol Technologies, Llc
1 Zebra Plz
Holtsville NY 11742
631 737-6851

(G-1094)
T R P MACHINE INC
35 Davinci Dr Ste B (11716-2666)
PHONE 631 567-9620
Patrick Price, *President*
Roger Price, *Principal*
Thomas Price, *Vice Pres*
EMP: 25
SQ FT: 8,500
SALES (est): 3.9MM **Privately Held**
WEB: www.trpmachine.com
SIC: 3599 Machine shop, jobbing & repair

(G-1095)
TEMRICK INC
1605 Sycamore Ave Unit B (11716-1734)
PHONE 631 567-8860
Trevor Glausen Jr, *President*
Melissa Glausen, *Vice Pres*
EMP: 5 **EST:** 1978
SQ FT: 5,000
SALES: 550K **Privately Held**
SIC: 3599 7389 Machine shop, jobbing & repair; grinding, precision: commercial or industrial

(G-1096)
TOUCH ADJUST CLIP CO INC
1687 Roosevelt Ave (11716-1428)
PHONE 631 589-3077
Richard Haug Sr, *President*
Richard C Haug, *President*
▲ **EMP:** 9
SQ FT: 10,000
SALES: 1.3MM **Privately Held**
WEB: www.touchadjustclip.com
SIC: 3915 Jewel cutting, drilling, polishing, recutting or setting

(G-1097)
TREO INDUSTRIES INC
Also Called: Genie Fastener Mfg Co
35 Carlough Rd Ste 1 (11716-2913)
PHONE 631 737-4022
Thomas W Blank, *Ch of Bd*
Tim Blank, *President*
Eugenia Blank, *Treasurer*
EMP: 7
SQ FT: 8,000
SALES (est): 957.7K **Privately Held**
SIC: 3452 Bolts, nuts, rivets & washers

(G-1098)
TRIAD COUNTER CORP
1225 Church St (11716-5014)
PHONE 631 750-0615
Frank Simone, *President*
Peter Amari, *Vice Pres*
Kirk Ibsen, *Treasurer*
EMP: 20
SQ FT: 20,000
SALES (est): 2.8MM **Privately Held**
SIC: 2541 5031 1799 Counter & sink tops; kitchen cabinets; kitchen & bathroom remodeling

(G-1099)
TRIANGLE RUBBER CO INC
50 Aero Rd (11716-2909)
PHONE 631 589-9400
Thomas Barresi, *President*
Joseph Barresi Jr, *Vice Pres*
▲ **EMP:** 25
SQ FT: 13,000
SALES (est): 4.3MM **Privately Held**
WEB: www.trianglerubber.com
SIC: 3069 5085 3061 Molded rubber products; rubber goods, mechanical; mechanical rubber goods

(G-1100)
TRIPAR MANUFACTURING CO INC
1620 Ocean Ave Ste 1 (11716-1930)
PHONE 631 563-0855
John M McNamara, *President*
EMP: 7
SQ FT: 8,000
SALES: 1.3MM **Privately Held**
SIC: 3444 3599 Sheet metalwork; machine shop, jobbing & repair

(G-1101)
TRIPLE POINT MANUFACTURING
1371 Church St Ste 6 (11716-5026)
PHONE 631 218-4988
Bernard Lichtenberger, *President*
Erwin Stropagel, *Treasurer*
EMP: 7
SQ FT: 4,000
SALES: 671K **Privately Held**
WEB: www.tpmny.com
SIC: 3451 3599 Screw machine products; machine & other job shop work

(G-1102)
TUSK MANUFACTURING INC
1371 Church St Ste 1 (11716-5026)
PHONE 631 567-3349
Kevin Zorn, *Vice Pres*
Karl Zorn, *Vice Pres*
EMP: 17 **EST:** 1979
SQ FT: 8,000
SALES: 2.2MM **Privately Held**
WEB: www.tuskmfg.com
SIC: 3812 Search & navigation equipment

(G-1103)
UNITED MACHINING INC
1595 Smithtown Ave Ste D (11716-2418)
P.O. Box 480 (11716-0480)
PHONE 631 589-6751
Corey Vercellone, *President*
EMP: 6
SALES: 430K **Privately Held**
SIC: 3599 Machine shop, jobbing & repair

(G-1104)
UPTEK SOLUTIONS CORP
130 Knickerbocker Ave A (11716-3171)
PHONE 631 256-5565
Lin Xu, *President*
Jeffrey Tian, *Vice Pres*
EMP: 13 **EST:** 2012
SALES (est): 1.9MM **Privately Held**
SIC: 3699 Laser scientific & engineering instruments; laser systems & equipment

(G-1105)
VELP SCIENTIFIC INC
155 Keyland Ct (11716-2621)
PHONE 631 573-6002
Stefano Casiraghi, *Sales Staff*
Stefano Casirachi, *Admin Sec*
EMP: 5
SALES (est): 602.7K **Privately Held**
SIC: 3826 Analytical instruments

(G-1106)
VJ TECHNOLOGIES INC (PA)
Also Called: Vjt
89 Carlough Rd (11716-2903)
PHONE 631 589-8800
Vijay Alreia, *Chairman*
Satya Korlipara, *Admin Sec*
◆ **EMP:** 35
SQ FT: 30,000
SALES (est): 0 **Privately Held**
SIC: 3844 3812 3829 X-ray apparatus & tubes; search & detection systems & instruments; nuclear radiation & testing apparatus

(G-1107)
VYTEK INC
271 Knickerbocker Ave (11716-3103)
PHONE 631 750-1770
Joan Crisafulli, *President*
EMP: 10
SALES (est): 1.2MM **Privately Held**
SIC: 3599 7539 Machine shop, jobbing & repair; machine shop, automotive

(G-1108)
WEMCO CASTING LLC
20 Jules Ct Ste 2 (11716-4106)
PHONE 631 563-8050
Sharen Fenchel, *Owner*
EMP: 70
SQ FT: 2,000
SALES (est): 9.5MM **Privately Held**
WEB: www.wemcocastingllc.com
SIC: 3369 Nonferrous foundries

(G-1109)
Z WORKS INC
1395 Lakeland Ave Ste 10 (11716-3318)
PHONE 631 750-0612
Zoltan Mata, *Owner*
Katalin Gergely, *Owner*
EMP: 5 **EST:** 2001
SALES (est): 552.4K **Privately Held**
WEB: www.z-works.com
SIC: 3544 Special dies, tools, jigs & fixtures

Boiceville
Ulster County

(G-1110)
STUCKI EMBROIDERY WORKS INC (PA)
Also Called: Am-Best Emblems
Rr 28 Box W (12412)
PHONE 845 657-2308
Murray Fenwick, *President*
Ilse Fenwick, *Corp Secy*
Arthur Stucki, *Vice Pres*
EMP: 18 **EST:** 1924
SQ FT: 17,000
SALES (est): 2.3MM **Privately Held**
SIC: 2395 Swiss loom embroideries; emblems, embroidered

Bolivar
Allegany County

(G-1111)
KLEIN CUTLERY LLC
Also Called: Scissor Online
7971 Refinery Rd (14715-9605)
PHONE 585 928-2500
Wayne J West,
▲ **EMP:** 60
SQ FT: 18,000
SALES (est): 8.4MM **Privately Held**
WEB: www.scissorsonline.com
SIC: 3421 Scissors, hand; shears, hand

Bolton Landing
Warren County

(G-1112)
NORTHERN LIFTS ELEVATOR CO LLC (PA)
45 Indian Brook Hollow Rd (12814-3813)
P.O. Box 1117 (12814-1117)
PHONE 518 644-2831
Jennifer Jackson, *Accounting Mgr*
Shirley Tennent,
EMP: 8
SALES (est): 1.5MM **Privately Held**
SIC: 3534 Elevators & equipment

Boonville
Oneida County

(G-1113)
3B TIMBER COMPANY INC
8745 Industrial Dr (13309-4845)
P.O. Box 761 (13309-0761)
PHONE 315 942-6580
Mark S Bourgeois, *President*
Gary S Bourgeois, *Vice Pres*
Gary Bourgeois, *Vice Pres*
Janet F Bourgeois, *Treasurer*
EMP: 19
SQ FT: 5,400
SALES (est): 1.5MM **Privately Held**
SIC: 2411 Poles, wood: untreated; posts, wood: hewn, round or split; piling, wood: untreated; wood chips, produced in the field

(G-1114)
BAILEY BOONVILLE MILLS INC
123 Mill St (13309-1115)
P.O. Box 257 (13309-0257)
PHONE 315 942-2131
Delbert C Bailey, *President*
EMP: 7 **EST:** 1968
SALES (est): 721.6K **Privately Held**
SIC: 2048 5999 Prepared feeds; feed & farm supply

(G-1115)
BOONVILLE HERALD INC
Also Called: Boonvlle Hrald Adrndack Turist
105 E Schuyler St (13309-1103)
PHONE 315 942-4449
Joe Kelly, *President*
EMP: 7 **EST:** 1800
SALES (est): 348.3K **Privately Held**
SIC: 2711 Newspapers, publishing & printing

(G-1116)
BOONVILLE MANUFACTURING CORP
13485 State Route 12 (13309-3530)
P.O. Box 301 (13309-0301)
PHONE 315 942-4368
Randy Anderson, *President*
EMP: 7
SQ FT: 8,000
SALES (est): 1MM **Privately Held**
SIC: 3053 Gaskets, all materials

(G-1117)
C J LOGGING EQUIPMENT INC
Also Called: CJ Motor Sports
8730 Industrial Dr (13309-4828)
P.O. Box 661 (13309-0661)
PHONE..................315 942-5431
Mark S Bourgeois, *Ch of Bd*
J Yates Hudson, *President*
Robert Martin Calfee III, *Chairman*
Gary S Bourgeois, *Vice Pres*
Linda Bourgeois, *Treasurer*
▲ EMP: 25
SALES (est): 7.7MM Privately Held
WEB: www.cjlogequip.com
SIC: 2411 Logging

(G-1118)
NORTHERN FOREST PDTS CO INC
9833 Crolius Dr (13309-5001)
PHONE..................315 942-6955
Jeffrey Crolius, *President*
Jay Crolius, *Vice Pres*
EMP: 7
SQ FT: 2,800
SALES (est): 530K Privately Held
SIC: 2431 2499 Millwork; decorative wood & woodwork

(G-1119)
PRESERVING CHRSTN PUBLICATIONS (PA)
12614 State Route 46 (13309)
P.O. Box 221 (13309-0221)
PHONE..................315 942-6617
Gerard Maicher, *President*
John Parrot, *Admin Sec*
EMP: 8
SQ FT: 6,300
SALES: 169.1K Privately Held
WEB: www.pcpbooks.com
SIC: 2731 Book publishing

(G-1120)
QUALITY DAIRY FARMS INC
Also Called: Mercer's Dairy
13584 State Route 12 (13309-3532)
PHONE..................315 942-2611
Dalton Givens, *President*
Ruth Mignerey, *Shareholder*
▼ EMP: 24
SQ FT: 9,600
SALES (est): 4.1MM Privately Held
SIC: 2024 Ice cream, bulk

(G-1121)
S M S C INC
Also Called: Central Adirondack Textiles
101 Water St (13309-1327)
PHONE..................315 942-4394
Fax: 315 942-4394
EMP: 6
SALES (est): 588.4K Privately Held
SIC: 3321 Gray/Ductile Iron Foundry

Bowmansville
Erie County

(G-1122)
PRECISION DENTAL CERAMICS OF B
5204 Genesee St (14026-1038)
PHONE..................716 681-4133
James Mantzanis, *President*
EMP: 11
SQ FT: 2,298
SALES: 700K Privately Held
SIC: 3843 Dental equipment & supplies

Branchport
Yates County

(G-1123)
HUNT COUNTRY VINEYARDS
4021 Italy Hill Rd (14418-9615)
PHONE..................315 595-2812
Art Hunt, *Owner*
Joyce Hunt, *Owner*
Matt Kelly, *Marketing Staff*
EMP: 25
SQ FT: 2,256
SALES (est): 880K Privately Held
WEB: www.huntcountryvineyards.com
SIC: 2084 Wines

Brant Lake
Warren County

(G-1124)
GAR WOOD CUSTOM BOATS
20 Duell Hill Rd (12815-2026)
PHONE..................518 494-2966
Thomas Turcotte, *Mng Member*
EMP: 8
SALES (est): 993.4K Privately Held
WEB: www.garwoodcustomboats.com
SIC: 3732 Boats, fiberglass: building & repairing

Brasher Falls
St. Lawrence County

(G-1125)
TRI-TOWN PACKING CORP
Helena Rd (13613)
P.O. Box 387, Winthrop (13697-0387)
PHONE..................315 389-5101
John Liberty, *President*
Thomas Liberty, *President*
Jeff Liberty, *Vice Pres*
EMP: 15
SQ FT: 5,300
SALES: 1MM Privately Held
WEB: www.adirondacksmokedmeats.com
SIC: 2011 5147 Meat packing plants; meats & meat products

Brentwood
Suffolk County

(G-1126)
ALLIED AERO SERVICES INC
506 Grand Blvd (11717-7902)
PHONE..................631 277-9368
Larry Soech, *President*
Steven Leonard, *Vice Pres*
EMP: 6
SALES (est): 444.4K Privately Held
SIC: 3295 Minerals, ground or treated

(G-1127)
APPLAUSE COATING LLC
8b Grand Blvd (11717-5117)
PHONE..................631 231-5223
Barbara Pinto, *Mng Member*
EMP: 11
SALES: 750K Privately Held
SIC: 3479 Coating of metals & formed products

(G-1128)
BECKS CLASSIC MFG INC
50 Emjay Blvd Ste 7 (11717-3300)
PHONE..................631 435-3800
Warren Beck, *CEO*
Steven Beck, *President*
Kevin Beck, *Vice Pres*
EMP: 100
SQ FT: 60,000
SALES (est): 11.8MM Privately Held
SIC: 2399 2341 2322 2676 Diapers, except disposable: made from purchased materials; panties: women's, misses', children's & infants'; underwear, men's & boys': made from purchased materials; sanitary paper products

(G-1129)
CUBITEK INC
95 Emjay Blvd Ste 2 (11717-3330)
PHONE..................631 665-6900
Daniel Hartman, *President*
Peter Hartman, *Vice Pres*
Judy Hartman, *Treasurer*
▼ EMP: 15
SQ FT: 500
SALES: 3.1MM Privately Held
SIC: 3599 Machine shop, jobbing & repair

(G-1130)
DATAGRAPHIC BUSINESS SYSTEMS
79 Emjay Blvd (11717-3323)
PHONE..................516 485-9069
Glenn M Schuster, *President*
EMP: 6
SQ FT: 3,000
SALES (est): 1.4MM Privately Held
WEB: www.datagraphicdesign.com
SIC: 2621 5943 Business form paper; office forms & supplies

(G-1131)
DELSUR PARTS
112 Pheasant Cir (11717-5047)
PHONE..................631 630-1606
Carlos Fuentes, *Owner*
EMP: 5
SALES: 150K Privately Held
SIC: 3556 Food products machinery

(G-1132)
DORMITORY AUTHORITY - STATE NY
998 Crooked Hill Rd # 26 (11717-1019)
PHONE..................631 434-1487
Terry McGowan, *Director*
EMP: 8
SALES (corp-wide): 2.1B Privately Held
SIC: 3599 Pump governors, for gas machines
PA: Dormitory Authority - State Of New York
515 Broadway Ste 100
Albany NY 12207
518 257-3000

(G-1133)
EXPRESS CONCRETE INC
1250 Suffolk Ave (11717-4507)
PHONE..................631 273-4224
Bruno Palmieri, *President*
EMP: 6
SQ FT: 3,000
SALES (est): 706.5K Privately Held
SIC: 3272 Concrete products

(G-1134)
HY CERT SERVICES INC
122 Cain Dr (11717-1266)
P.O. Box 534, Miller Place (11764-0534)
PHONE..................631 231-7005
Richard Pecchio, *President*
EMP: 5
SALES (est): 517.4K Privately Held
SIC: 3491 Industrial valves

(G-1135)
I MEGLIO CORP
151 Alkier St (11717-5135)
PHONE..................631 617-6900
Barbara Khanat, *President*
David Suarez, *Vice Pres*
EMP: 30
SQ FT: 65,000
SALES: 67MM Privately Held
SIC: 2431 5031 Millwork; millwork

(G-1136)
INTERSTATE LITHO CORP
151 Alkier St (11717-5135)
PHONE..................631 232-6025
Henry Becker, *President*
Richard Becker, *Vice Pres*
EMP: 100 EST: 1975
SQ FT: 100,000
SALES (est): 8.3MM Privately Held
SIC: 2752 2791 2789 Commercial printing, lithographic; typesetting; bookbinding & related work

(G-1137)
INTERSTATE WINDOW CORPORATION
Also Called: Mannix
345 Crooked Hill Rd Ste 1 (11717-1020)
PHONE..................631 231-0800
Robert Salzer, *President*
Paul Greenstein, *Vice Pres*
Sue Hausner, *Vice Pres*
▲ EMP: 100
SQ FT: 51,000
SALES (est): 29MM Privately Held
WEB: www.mannixwindows.com
SIC: 3442 Window & door frames

(G-1138)
J & A USA INC
335 Crooked Hill Rd (11717-1041)
PHONE..................631 243-3336
Yunho Kim, *President*
Sidney Park, *CFO*
◆ EMP: 9
SQ FT: 15,000
SALES (est): 1.6MM Privately Held
WEB: www.jausa.com
SIC: 3999 Barber & beauty shop equipment

(G-1139)
KENNEY MANUFACTURING DISPLAYS
Also Called: Kenny Mfg
12 Grand Blvd (11717-5117)
PHONE..................631 231-5563
Robert Kenney Jr, *President*
Michael Kenney, *Vice Pres*
Brian Ohara, *Purch Mgr*
Robin Douglas, *Buyer*
David LI, *Buyer*
EMP: 11
SQ FT: 7,500
SALES (est): 1.8MM Privately Held
WEB: www.kenneydisplays.com
SIC: 3089 3578 Plastic containers, except foam; point-of-sale devices

(G-1140)
LAURICELLA PRESS INC
Also Called: Imperial Color
81 Emjay Blvd (11717-3329)
PHONE..................516 931-5906
Arthur Lauricella, *President*
Marc Lauricella, *Vice Pres*
EMP: 20
SALES: 500K Privately Held
SIC: 2759 Commercial printing

(G-1141)
LLOYDS FASHIONS INC (PA)
335 Crooked Hill Rd (11717-1041)
P.O. Box 1162, Syosset (11791-0489)
PHONE..................631 435-3353
Lloyd Goldberg, *President*
Rita Goldberg, *Vice Pres*
▲ EMP: 60 EST: 1958
SQ FT: 22,000
SALES: 2.6MM Privately Held
SIC: 2353 2253 5137 Millinery; shawls, knit; women's & children's clothing

(G-1142)
MICHBI DOORS INC
Also Called: Open & Shut Doors
75 Emjay Blvd (11717-3323)
PHONE..................631 231-9050
Michelle Bianculli, *President*
Doug Hommel, *Vice Pres*
Suzanne Mutone, *Vice Pres*
Jeannette Cambridge, *Project Mgr*
Craig Gough, *Project Mgr*
EMP: 56 EST: 1981
SQ FT: 30,000
SALES (est): 8.6MM Privately Held
WEB: www.michbidoors.com
SIC: 2431 3231 3442 Millwork; products of purchased glass; metal doors, sash & trim

(G-1143)
PLASTIRUN CORPORATION
70 Emjay Blvd Bldg A (11717-3394)
PHONE..................631 273-2626
Jack Elyahouzadeh, *President*
Jacob Y Lavi, *Treasurer*
Jerry Faivushevitz, *Accounts Mgr*
◆ EMP: 35 EST: 1982
SQ FT: 51,000
SALES (est): 13.6MM Privately Held
WEB: www.plastirun.com
SIC: 2656 2621 Straws, drinking: made from purchased material; paper mills; towels, tissues & napkins: paper & stock

(G-1144)
T S O GENERAL CORP
81 Emjay Blvd Unit 1 (11717-3329)
P.O. Box 552 (11717-0552)
PHONE..................631 952-5320
Kirk Malandrakis, *President*
EMP: 20
SQ FT: 30,000

SALES: 2MM Privately Held
WEB: www.tsogen.com
SIC: 2759 Commercial printing

(G-1145)
THURO METAL PRODUCTS INC (PA)
21-25 Grand Blvd N (11717)
PHONE..................................631 435-0444
Albert Thuro, *Ch of Bd*
David Thuro, *President*
Louis Krieger, *General Mgr*
Carolyn Thuro, *Corp Secy*
Dan Rivera, *Engineer*
▲ EMP: 40 EST: 1971
SQ FT: 25,000
SALES (est): 12.2MM Privately Held
WEB: www.thurometal.com
SIC: 3451 3545 Screw machine products; machine tool attachments & accessories

(G-1146)
UNIWARE HOUSEWARE CORP (PA)
120 Wilshire Blvd Ste B (11717-8333)
PHONE..................................631 242-7400
Lily Hsu, *President*
Roger Hsu, *Vice Pres*
◆ EMP: 23
SALES (est): 8.5MM Privately Held
SIC: 3634 Electric housewares & fans

(G-1147)
US NONWOVENS CORP (PA)
100 Emjay Blvd (11717-3322)
PHONE..................................631 952-0100
Shervin Mehdizadeh, *CEO*
Samuel Mehdizadeh, *Ch of Bd*
Martin Khagan, *Chairman*
Rody Mehdizadeh, *COO*
◆ EMP: 600
SQ FT: 35,000
SALES (est): 462.2MM Privately Held
WEB: www.usnonwovens.com
SIC: 2842 Specialty cleaning, polishes & sanitation goods

(G-1148)
V E POWER DOOR CO INC
140 Emjay Blvd (11717-3322)
P.O. Box 663, Commack (11725-0663)
PHONE..................................631 231-4500
James Lanzarone, *CEO*
Philip Lanzarone, *President*
Evelyn Semar, *Corp Secy*
Susan Cruz, *Vice Pres*
Edward Lanzarone, *Vice Pres*
▲ EMP: 40
SQ FT: 23,000
SALES (est): 9.4MM Privately Held
SIC: 3699 Door opening & closing devices, electrical

Brewerton
Onondaga County

(G-1149)
AE FUND INC
Also Called: Frigo Design
5860 Mckinley Rd (13029-9691)
PHONE..................................315 698-7650
Eric J Gantley, *President*
Anthony Verdi, *Exec VP*
Allan Issacs, *Vice Pres*
Rob Buell, *VP Sales*
Melissa Govendo, *Executive Asst*
EMP: 30
SQ FT: 15,000
SALES (est): 6.6MM Privately Held
WEB: www.frigodesign.com
SIC: 3632 Refrigerator cabinets, household: metal & wood

(G-1150)
GEORDIE MAGEE UPHL & CANVAS
Also Called: Magee Canvas & Trailer Sales
Weber Rd (13029)
P.O. Box 656 (13029-0656)
PHONE..................................315 676-7679
Geordie H Magee, *President*
EMP: 6
SQ FT: 4,400
SALES: 1.1MM Privately Held
WEB: www.mageetrailers.com
SIC: 2211 5999 Canvas; canvas products

(G-1151)
IRENE CERONE
Also Called: Brewerton Special Tee's
9600 Brewerton Rd (13029-8798)
P.O. Box 670 (13029-0670)
PHONE..................................315 668-2899
Michael Cerone, *Owner*
Irene Cerone, *Co-Owner*
EMP: 7
SALES (est): 594.8K Privately Held
SIC: 2396 Screen printing on fabric articles

(G-1152)
ROBINSON CONCRETE INC
7020 Corporate Park Dr (13029)
PHONE..................................315 676-4662
Michael J Vitale, *Principal*
EMP: 10
SALES (corp-wide): 24MM Privately Held
SIC: 3273 Ready-mixed concrete
PA: Robinson Concrete, Inc.
    3486 Franklin Street Rd
    Auburn NY 13021
    315 253-6666

Brewster
Putnam County

(G-1153)
AAAAAR ORTHOPEDICS INC
141 Main St (10509-1476)
PHONE..................................845 278-4938
Elizabeth Hawkins, *President*
Richard Dipompo, *Vice Pres*
EMP: 5
SALES (est): 360K Privately Held
SIC: 3842 Limbs, artificial

(G-1154)
ADVANCED PRECISION TECHNOLOGY
577 N Main St Ste 7 (10509-1240)
PHONE..................................845 279-3540
Olaf Brauer, *President*
Christine Brauer, *Vice Pres*
EMP: 10
SQ FT: 6,800
SALES (est): 1.1MM Privately Held
SIC: 3444 3341 Sheet metalwork; secondary nonferrous metals

(G-1155)
AKZO NOBEL FUNCTIONAL CHEM LLC
281 Fields Ln (10509-2676)
PHONE..................................845 276-8200
Ton B Chner, *Branch Mgr*
EMP: 88
SALES (corp-wide): 11.3B Privately Held
SIC: 2869 Industrial organic chemicals
HQ: Akzo Nobel Functional Chemical, Llc
    525 W Van Buren St # 1600
    Chicago IL 60607
    312 544-7000

(G-1156)
ALLIANCE CONTROL SYSTEMS INC
577 N Main St Ste 9 (10509-1240)
PHONE..................................845 279-4430
Doug Homberg, *President*
▲ EMP: 8
SALES (est): 943.6K Privately Held
SIC: 3629 Electronic generation equipment

(G-1157)
AMPRO INTERNATIONAL INC
30 Coventry Ln (10509-4808)
PHONE..................................845 278-4910
Floyd Pircio, *President*
Laura Arone, *Admin Secy*
EMP: 2
SQ FT: 1,000
SALES: 1MM Privately Held
SIC: 3679 Antennas, receiving

(G-1158)
BASE SYSTEMS INC
Also Called: Tower Computers
1606 Route 22 (10509-4014)
PHONE..................................845 278-1991
EMP: 2
SQ FT: 3,000
SALES: 2MM Privately Held
SIC: 7372 5045 Ret & Whol Of Prepackaged Software

(G-1159)
BLACK & DECKER (US) INC
Also Called: Powers Fasteners
2 Powers Ln (10509-3633)
PHONE..................................914 235-6300
Matthew Chamberlain, *Vice Pres*
Erica Duttera, *Opers Mgr*
William Taylor, *Branch Mgr*
Matt Henderson, *Branch Mgr*
EMP: 375
SALES (corp-wide): 12.7B Publicly Held
SIC: 3546 Power-driven handtools
HQ: Black & Decker (U.S.) Inc.
    1000 Stanley Dr
    New Britain CT 06053
    860 225-5111

(G-1160)
BREWSTER TRANSIT MIX CORP (PA)
31 Fields Ln (10509-3507)
P.O. Box 410 (10509-0410)
PHONE..................................845 279-3738
Ted Petrillo, *President*
Henry Paparazzo, *Vice Pres*
Curtis Mc Gann, *Admin Sec*
▲ EMP: 80
SQ FT: 1,000
SALES (est): 10.6MM Privately Held
SIC: 3273 5032 Ready-mixed concrete; gravel; sand, construction

(G-1161)
BREWSTER TRANSIT MIX CORP
Fields Ln (10509)
P.O. Box 410 (10509-0410)
PHONE..................................845 279-3738
Jeff Chattin, *General Mgr*
EMP: 35
SALES (corp-wide): 10.6MM Privately Held
SIC: 3273 Ready-mixed concrete
PA: Brewster Transit Mix Corp
    31 Fields Ln
    Brewster NY 10509
    845 279-3738

(G-1162)
DAIRY CONVEYOR CORP (PA)
38 Mount Ebo Rd S (10509-4005)
P.O. Box 411 (10509-0411)
PHONE..................................845 278-7878
Gary Freudenberg, *Chairman*
Roland Debald, *Vice Pres*
Karl Horberg, *CFO*
Peter Debald, *Treasurer*
Jose Gomez, *VP Sales*
◆ EMP: 86 EST: 1954
SQ FT: 68,000
SALES (est): 29.4MM Privately Held
SIC: 3535 7699 Conveyors & conveying equipment; industrial machinery & equipment repair

(G-1163)
DUNMORE CORPORATION
3633 Danbury Rd (10509-4516)
PHONE..................................845 279-5061
Terry Jones, *Manager*
Edward J Mitchell, *Director*
Paul Hill, *Maintence Staff*
EMP: 75
SQ FT: 49,432 Privately Held
WEB: www.dunmore.com
SIC: 2621 3081 2672 Paper mills; plastic film & sheet; coated & laminated paper
HQ: Dunmore Corporation
    145 Wharton Rd
    Bristol PA 19007
    215 781-8895

(G-1164)
ELSAG NORTH AMERICA LLC
7 Sutton Pl Ste A (10509-3537)
PHONE..................................877 773-5724
EMP: 5
SALES (corp-wide): 6.3MM Privately Held
SIC: 3829 Photogrammetrical instruments
PA: Elsag North America Llc
    205 Creek Ridge Rd Ste H
    Greensboro NC 27406
    336 379-7135

(G-1165)
FEYEM USA INC
7 Sutton Pl (10509-3536)
PHONE..................................845 363-6253
Palma Settini, *President*
EMP: 5
SALES (est): 202.9K Privately Held
SIC: 2329 2331 Men's & boys' sportswear & athletic clothing; women's & misses' blouses & shirts

(G-1166)
HEALTHY N FIT INTL INC (PA)
7 Sutton Pl Ste A (10509-3537)
PHONE..................................800 338-5200
Robert Sepe Jr, *Ch of Bd*
Irene Sepe, *Vice Pres*
EMP: 13 EST: 1976
SALES (est): 2.5MM Privately Held
SIC: 2833 5122 Vitamins, natural or synthetic: bulk, uncompounded; vitamins & minerals

(G-1167)
HIPOTRONICS INC (HQ)
1650 Route 22 (10509-4013)
P.O. Box 414 (10509-0414)
PHONE..................................845 279-8091
Timothy H Powers, *CEO*
Richard Davies, *President*
Jeff Brown, *Vice Pres*
Reinold Grob, *Vice Pres*
Charles Consalvo, *Opers Mgr*
▲ EMP: 115 EST: 1962
SQ FT: 90,000
SALES (est): 35.2MM
SALES (corp-wide): 3.6B Publicly Held
WEB: www.hipotronics.com
SIC: 3825 3679 3829 3677 Test equipment for electronic & electrical circuits; test equipment for electronic & electric measurement; power supplies, all types: static; measuring & controlling devices; electronic coils, transformers & other inductors; electronic capacitors; semiconductors & related devices
PA: Hubbell Incorporated
    40 Waterview Dr
    Shelton CT 06484
    475 882-4000

(G-1168)
HUDSON MACHINE WORKS INC
Also Called: H M W
30 Branch Rd (10509-4522)
PHONE..................................845 279-1413
Daniel R Ferguson, *Ch of Bd*
Michael Ferguson, *General Mgr*
Jennifer Ferguson, *Vice Pres*
Glenn Moss, *CFO*
Nancy Dally, *Mktg Dir*
EMP: 110
SQ FT: 25,000
SALES (est): 18.4MM Privately Held
WEB: www.hudsonmachine.com
SIC: 3743 Railroad equipment

(G-1169)
LAMOTHERMIC CORP
391 Route 312 (10509-2328)
PHONE..................................845 278-6118
Amos Noach, *Ch of Bd*
Gideon Noach, *Vice Pres*
Taylor Seymour, *Director*
EMP: 97
SQ FT: 42,000
SALES: 12MM Privately Held
WEB: www.lamothermic.com
SIC: 3369 Castings, except die-castings, precision

(G-1170)
MATERION ADVANCED MATERIALS
42 Mount Ebo Rd S (10509-4005)
PHONE..................................800 327-1355
Raymond Chan, *Branch Mgr*

Brewster - Putnam County (G-1171) GEOGRAPHIC SECTION

EMP: 6
SALES (corp-wide): 1.1B **Publicly Held**
SIC: 3339 Primary nonferrous metals
HQ: Materion Advanced Materials Technologies And Services Inc.
2978 Main St
Buffalo NY 14214
800 327-1355

(G-1171)
MATERION BREWSTER LLC
42 Mount Ebo Rd S (10509-4005)
P.O. Box 1950 (10509-8950)
PHONE.................................845 279-0900
Richard Fager, *Mng Member*
Matthew Willson,
▲ EMP: 75
SQ FT: 36,000
SALES (est): 26.4MM
SALES (corp-wide): 1.1B **Publicly Held**
WEB: www.puretechinc.com
SIC: 3499 3674 Friction material, made from powdered metal; semiconductors & related devices
HQ: Materion Advanced Materials Technologies And Services Inc.
2978 Main St
Buffalo NY 14214
800 327-1355

(G-1172)
MIGGINS SCREW PRODUCTS INC
66 Putnam Ave (10509-1114)
PHONE.................................845 279-2307
Merle Delfay, *President*
John H Miggins, *President*
Merle Delsay, *Post Master*
EMP: 9 EST: 1946
SQ FT: 2,500
SALES (est): 1MM **Privately Held**
SIC: 3451 Screw machine products

(G-1173)
PEDIFIX INC
301 Fields Ln (10509-2621)
PHONE.................................845 277-2850
Dennis Case, *President*
Jon Case, *Vice Pres*
▲ EMP: 25
SQ FT: 15,000
SALES (est): 4.9MM **Privately Held**
WEB: www.pedifix.com
SIC: 3144 3143 Orthopedic shoes, women's; orthopedic shoes, men's

(G-1174)
PRE CYCLED INC
1689 Route 22 (10509-4022)
P.O. Box 341 (10509-0341)
PHONE.................................845 278-7611
Daniel Horkan, *President*
Carol Horkan, *Vice Pres*
EMP: 5
SQ FT: 3,000
SALES (est): 887.9K **Privately Held**
WEB: www.pre-cycled.com
SIC: 2752 Commercial printing, lithographic

(G-1175)
UNILOCK NEW YORK INC (HQ)
51 International Blvd (10509-2343)
PHONE.................................845 278-6700
Edward Bryant, *President*
Brian Kallmeyer, *General Mgr*
Sean O' Lary, *General Mgr*
Glenn Wiley, *General Mgr*
Joseph Kerr, *Vice Pres*
▲ EMP: 8
SALES (est): 10.4MM **Privately Held**
WEB: www.unilock.com
SIC: 3281 5211 3272 3271 Paving blocks, cut stone; paving stones; concrete products; concrete block & brick; asphalt paving mixtures & blocks
PA: Unilock Ltd
401 The West Mall Suite 610
Etobicoke ON M9C 5
416 646-5180

(G-1176)
VISTALAB TECHNOLOGIES INC
2 Geneva Rd (10509-2340)
PHONE.................................914 244-6226
Richard Scordato, *Ch of Bd*
David Marks, *Regional Mgr*
Jeff Calhoun, *Vice Pres*
Jeffrey E Calhoun, *Vice Pres*
Edward Flynn, *CFO*
▲ EMP: 34
SQ FT: 25,000
SALES (est): 8.5MM **Privately Held**
SIC: 3821 Pipettes, hemocytometer

Briarcliff Manor
Westchester County

(G-1177)
THALLE INDUSTRIES INC (PA)
51 Route 100 (10510-1441)
PHONE.................................914 762-3415
Gregg J Pacchiana, *Ch of Bd*
Glenn Pacchiana, *Principal*
George Pacchiana, *Corp Secy*
Jeff Manganello, *Vice Pres*
John Amato, *Sales Mgr*
EMP: 35
SQ FT: 720
SALES (est): 4.5MM **Privately Held**
SIC: 2951 3281 Asphalt paving mixtures & blocks; stone, quarrying & processing of own stone products

(G-1178)
YOGOLICIOUS INC
516 N State Rd (10510-1526)
PHONE.................................914 236-3455
EMP: 5
SALES (est): 273.3K
SALES (corp-wide): 559K **Privately Held**
SIC: 2026 Yogurt
PA: Yogolicious Inc.
59 Marble Ave Ste 1
Pleasantville NY

Bridgehampton
Suffolk County

(G-1179)
BRIDGEHAMPTON STEEL & WLDG INC
Also Called: Aand D Maintenance
27 Foster Ave (11932)
P.O. Box 19 (11932-0019)
PHONE.................................631 537-2486
John Parry, *President*
Suzanne Parry, *Vice Pres*
EMP: 10
SQ FT: 3,000
SALES (est): 1.2MM **Privately Held**
SIC: 3443 1799 Fabricated plate work (boiler shop); welding on site

(G-1180)
COMERFORD HENNESSY AT HOME INC
Also Called: Comerford Collection
2442 Main St (11932)
P.O. Box 44 (11932-0044)
PHONE.................................631 537-6200
Karen Comerford, *President*
Michael Hennessy, *Vice Pres*
EMP: 5
SQ FT: 1,500
SALES (est): 584.1K **Privately Held**
SIC: 2511 Wood household furniture

(G-1181)
IRON HORSE GRAPHICS LTD
112 Maple Ln (11932)
PHONE.................................631 537-3400
Grover Gatewood, *President*
EMP: 9
SQ FT: 2,200
SALES: 782.1K **Privately Held**
SIC: 2752 2759 Offset & photolithographic printing; commercial printing

Bridgeport
Onondaga County

(G-1182)
POWER GNERATION INDUS ENGS INC
8927 Tyler Rd (13030-9727)
PHONE.................................315 633-9389
Mike Verdow, *President*
EMP: 22
SALES (est): 2.9MM **Privately Held**
SIC: 3621 Power generators

(G-1183)
ROBERT M VAULT
1360 Lestina Beach Rd (13030-9722)
PHONE.................................315 243-1447
Robert M Vault, *Principal*
EMP: 5 EST: 2013
SALES (est): 365.6K **Privately Held**
SIC: 3272 Burial vaults, concrete or precast terrazzo

(G-1184)
SYRACUSE LETTER COMPANY INC
Also Called: Lettergraphics
1179 Oak Ln (13030-9779)
PHONE.................................315 476-8328
Nancy Osborn, *President*
David L Osborn, *Chairman*
Bill Davidson, *Vice Pres*
▲ EMP: 15
SQ FT: 24,500
SALES (est): 1.7MM **Privately Held**
SIC: 2759 7331 7389 Promotional printing; direct mail advertising services; coupon redemption service

Brightwaters
Suffolk County

(G-1185)
ALLEN FIELD CO INC
256 Orinoco Dr Ste A (11718-1823)
PHONE.................................631 665-2782
Andrew Franzone, *CEO*
Andrew Franzone Jr, *Ch of Bd*
David Kassel, *Ch of Bd*
Harry Goodman, *Vice Pres*
▲ EMP: 12 EST: 1945
SQ FT: 20,000
SALES: 6MM **Privately Held**
WEB: www.allenfield.com
SIC: 3089 Handles, brush or tool: plastic; injection molded finished plastic products

(G-1186)
INDUSTRIAL MUNICIPAL EQUIPMENT (PA)
146 Concourse E (11718-1502)
PHONE.................................631 665-6712
Peter E Rising, *President*
Mary Rising, *Corp Secy*
EMP: 13
SQ FT: 3,000
SALES (est): 1.6MM **Privately Held**
WEB: www.imetest.com
SIC: 3826 Water testing apparatus

Broadalbin
Fulton County

(G-1187)
BROADALBIN MANUFACTURING CORP
Also Called: BMC
8 Pine St (12025-3128)
P.O. Box 398 (12025-0398)
PHONE.................................518 883-5131
James C Stark, *President*
Michael Deuel, *President*
Mike Deuel, *Vice Pres*
Karen Deuel, *Manager*
EMP: 23 EST: 1970
SQ FT: 8,000
SALES (est): 4.2MM **Privately Held**
SIC: 3599 7692 1761 Machine shop, jobbing & repair; welding repair; sheet metalwork

(G-1188)
EMVI INC
Also Called: Emvi Chocolate
111 Bellen Rd Ste 2 (12025-2101)
PHONE.................................518 883-5111
Irina Gelman, *Principal*
EMP: 5
SALES (est): 459.6K **Privately Held**
SIC: 2066 Chocolate

(G-1189)
GL & RL LOGGING INC
713 Union Mills Rd (12025-1988)
PHONE.................................518 883-3936
George Lee, *President*
EMP: 15
SALES (est): 985.3K **Privately Held**
SIC: 2411 Timber, cut at logging camp

Brockport
Monroe County

(G-1190)
CUSTOM SERVICE SOLUTIONS INC
1900 Transit Way (14420-3006)
PHONE.................................585 637-3760
Paul Guglielmi, *CEO*
Diana Petranek, *CFO*
Tiffany Petranek, *Office Mgr*
Earl Luce, *Technical Staff*
Dallas Wadsworth, *Technical Staff*
EMP: 6
SQ FT: 4,200
SALES: 1.4MM **Privately Held**
WEB: www.customservicesolutions.com
SIC: 3545 Machine tool accessories

(G-1191)
HAMILTON MARKETING CORPORATION
5211 Lake Rd S (14420-9753)
PHONE.................................585 395-0678
Edward Hamilton, *President*
EMP: 5
SQ FT: 5,000
SALES (est): 564.9K **Privately Held**
SIC: 3825 Microwave test equipment

(G-1192)
HAMLIN BOTTLE & CAN RETURN INC
3423 Redman Rd (14420-9478)
PHONE.................................585 259-1301
Andriy Basisty, *President*
EMP: 7
SALES: 240K **Privately Held**
SIC: 2611 Pulp mills, mechanical & recycling processing

(G-1193)
JETS LEFROIS CORP
Also Called: Jets Lefrois Foods
56 High St (14420-2058)
PHONE.................................585 637-5003
Duncan Tsay, *President*
Rosalinc Tsay, *Vice Pres*
EMP: 6
SQ FT: 6,000
SALES (est): 626K **Privately Held**
SIC: 2033 2035 Barbecue sauce: packaged in cans, jars, etc.; relishes, vinegar

(G-1194)
ROCK IROQUOIS PRODUCTS INC
5251 Sweden Walker Rd (14420-9716)
PHONE.................................585 637-6834
Chris Pangrizio, *Manager*
EMP: 20
SALES (corp-wide): 29.7B **Privately Held**
SIC: 1429 Dolomitic marble, crushed & broken-quarrying
HQ: Iroquois Rock Products Inc.
1150 Penfield Rd
Rochester NY 14625
585 381-7010

Brocton
Chautauqua County

(G-1195)
CARBON GRAPHITE MATERIALS INC
Also Called: Cgm
115 Central Ave (14716-9771)
PHONE..................716 792-7979
Ryan Walker, *President*
▲ EMP: 9
SALES (est): 2.2MM **Privately Held**
SIC: 3624 Carbon & graphite products

(G-1196)
JAMESTOWN PLASTICS INC (PA)
8806 Highland Ave (14716-9791)
P.O. Box U (14716-0680)
PHONE..................716 792-4144
Jay J Baker, *Ch of Bd*
Brandy Smith, *QC Mgr*
James Barry, *Engineer*
Kurk Holm, *Maintence Staff*
EMP: 90
SQ FT: 87,000
SALES (est): 18.1MM **Privately Held**
WEB: www.jamestownplastics.com
SIC: 3089 Plastic containers, except foam; plastic processing

Bronx
Bronx County

(G-1197)
527 FRANCO BAKERY CORPORATION
Also Called: Caribe Bakery
527 E 138th St (10454-4971)
PHONE..................718 993-4200
Franco Guillermo, *President*
EMP: 5
SALES (est): 351.7K **Privately Held**
SIC: 2051 Bakery: wholesale or wholesale/retail combined

(G-1198)
872 HUNTS POINT PHARMACY INC
872 Hunts Point Ave (10474-5402)
PHONE..................718 991-3519
EMP: 7
SALES (est): 631.6K **Privately Held**
SIC: 2834 Mfg Pharmaceutical Preparations

(G-1199)
A & L DOORS & HARDWARE LLC
375 E 163rd St Frnt 2 (10451-4391)
PHONE..................718 585-8400
Nathan Lax, *Buyer*
David Katina, *Sales Associate*
Mark Kraus, *Office Mgr*
Leo Lichstein,
EMP: 14
SQ FT: 16,000
SALES (est): 2.3MM **Privately Held**
WEB: www.urban-architectural-interiors.com
SIC: 3442 3429 7699 Metal doors; window & door frames; locks or lock sets; locksmith shop

(G-1200)
A & L SHTMTL FABRICATIONS CORP
1243 Oakpoint Ave (10474-6803)
PHONE..................718 842-1600
Anatoly Lekhter, *President*
Marat Golnick, *Vice Pres*
EMP: 45
SQ FT: 37,500
SALES (est): 10MM **Privately Held**
WEB: www.aandlsheetmetal.com
SIC: 3444 Sheet metalwork

(G-1201)
A L EASTMOND & SONS INC (PA)
Also Called: Easco Boiler
1175 Leggett Ave (10474-6246)
PHONE..................718 378-3000
Arlington Leon Eastmond, *Chairman*
Neil Thomasetti, *Manager*
EMP: 80 EST: 1914
SQ FT: 50,000
SALES (est): 15.4MM **Privately Held**
WEB: www.easco.com
SIC: 3443 7699 7629 Boilers: industrial, power, or marine; boiler repair shop; electrical repair shops

(G-1202)
A&A MARBLE & GRANITE
1190 Commerce Ave (10462-5506)
PHONE..................347 810-9595
Jimmy Avdyli, *Principal*
EMP: 11
SALES (est): 1.4MM **Privately Held**
SIC: 3281 Furniture, cut stone

(G-1203)
A&S REFRIGERATION EQUIPMENT
557 Longfellow Ave (10474-6913)
PHONE..................718 993-6030
Alexander Savinon, *President*
EMP: 5
SALES: 98K **Privately Held**
SIC: 3585 Refrigeration & heating equipment

(G-1204)
A1 INTERNATIONAL HEAT TREATING
905 Brush Ave (10465-1810)
P.O. Box 93, Valhalla (10595-0093)
PHONE..................718 863-5552
Peter Palmero, *President*
John Palmero, *Vice Pres*
Theresa Palmero, *Manager*
EMP: 5
SQ FT: 2,000
SALES (est): 814.7K **Privately Held**
SIC: 3398 Metal heat treating

(G-1205)
ABOVE THE REST BAKING CORP
531-533 Bryant Ave (10474)
PHONE..................718 313-9222
Natalie Darmanin, *President*
EMP: 60 EST: 2016
SALES: 7MM **Privately Held**
SIC: 2051 Bakery: wholesale or wholesale/retail combined

(G-1206)
AC AIR COOLING CO INC
Also Called: Air Conditioning
1637 Stillwell Ave (10461-2216)
PHONE..................718 933-1011
Cac Dong Bui, *President*
Deonarine Sooknarain, *Vice Pres*
Maritza Matos, *Manager*
EMP: 15
SALES (est): 1.9MM **Privately Held**
SIC: 3585 Air conditioning units, complete: domestic or industrial

(G-1207)
ACA QUALITY BUILDING PDTS LLC
1322 Garrison Ave (10474-4710)
PHONE..................718 991-2423
Rubin Goldklang, *Manager*
EMP: 25
SALES (corp-wide): 4.3MM **Privately Held**
SIC: 3446 Partitions & supports/studs, including accoustical systems
PA: Aca Quality Building Products Llc
920 Longfellow Ave
Bronx NY 10474
718 991-2423

(G-1208)
ACE DROP CLOTH CANVAS PDTS INC
Also Called: Ace Drop Cloth Co
4216 Park Ave (10457-4201)
PHONE..................718 731-1550
Jerry Mathios, *President*
Adam Mathios, *Vice Pres*
David Mathios, *Vice Pres*
Marc Mathios, *Vice Pres*
▲ EMP: 31
SQ FT: 35,000
SALES (est): 4.3MM **Privately Held**
WEB: www.acedropcloth.com
SIC: 2299 2326 2394 2393 Fibers, textile: recovery from textile mill waste & rags; work pants; work shirts: men's, youths' & boys'; cloth, drop (fabric): made from purchased materials; textile bags; socks

(G-1209)
ACE FIRE DOOR CORP
4000 Park Ave (10457-7318)
PHONE..................718 901-0001
Aharon Blum, *President*
Joseph Strulovich, *Vice Pres*
Irving Bauer, *Treasurer*
EMP: 20
SQ FT: 20,000
SALES (est): 4MM **Privately Held**
SIC: 3442 2431 Fire doors, metal; doors, wood

(G-1210)
ACME AWNING CO INC
435 Van Nest Ave (10460-2876)
PHONE..................718 409-1881
Lawrence Loiacono, *President*
Jay Loiacono, *Vice Pres*
EMP: 15 EST: 1924
SQ FT: 25,000
SALES: 1MM **Privately Held**
WEB: www.acmeawn.com
SIC: 2394 3089 5039 5999 Awnings, fabric: made from purchased materials; awnings, fiberglass & plastic combination; awnings; awnings

(G-1211)
ACTION PAPER CO INC
429 E 164th St (10456-6602)
P.O. Box 210 (10456-0210)
PHONE..................718 665-1652
Larry Rossman, *President*
EMP: 8
SQ FT: 20,000
SALES (est): 1.3MM **Privately Held**
SIC: 2653 Boxes, corrugated: made from purchased materials

(G-1212)
ADDEO BAKERS INC
2372 Hughes Ave (10458-8148)
PHONE..................718 367-8316
Lawrence Addeo, *President*
EMP: 12
SQ FT: 2,300
SALES (est): 730K **Privately Held**
SIC: 2051 5461 Bread, all types (white, wheat, rye, etc): fresh or frozen; bread

(G-1213)
ADVANCED CMPT SFTWR CONSULTING
2236 Pearsall Ave (10469-5436)
PHONE..................718 300-3577
Mohammed Ziauddin, *President*
EMP: 5
SALES: 241.7K **Privately Held**
SIC: 7372 Prepackaged software

(G-1214)
ALBA FUEL CORP
2135 Wllmsbrdge Rd Fl 2 Flr 2 (10461)
PHONE..................718 931-1700
Esad Kukaj, *President*
EMP: 5
SALES (est): 927.1K **Privately Held**
SIC: 1389 5172 Oil field services; fuel oil

(G-1215)
ALBERT MENIN INTERIORS LTD
2417 3rd Ave Fl 3 (10451-6339)
PHONE..................212 876-3041
Emil Shikh, *President*
Clara Silva, *Manager*
EMP: 12
SQ FT: 1,500
SALES (est): 1.2MM **Privately Held**
WEB: www.albertmenin.com
SIC: 2519 5023 5713 5714 Household furniture, except wood or metal: upholstered; carpets; draperies; carpets; draperies

(G-1216)
ALLIED METAL SPINNING CORP
1290 Viele Ave (10474-7133)
PHONE..................718 893-3300
Arlene Saunders, *Ch of Bd*
▲ EMP: 60
SQ FT: 80,000
SALES (est): 10.7MM **Privately Held**
WEB: www.alliedmetalusa.com
SIC: 3469 Cooking ware, except porcelain enamelled

(G-1217)
ALLWAY TOOLS INC
1255 Seabury Ave (10462-5534)
PHONE..................718 792-3636
Brent Swenson, *President*
EMP: 100
SALES (est): 6.8MM
SALES (corp-wide): 12.9MM **Privately Held**
SIC: 3423 3425 Hand & edge tools; saw blades & handsaws
HQ: Linzer Products Corp.
248 Wyandanch Ave
West Babylon NY 11704
631 253-3333

(G-1218)
ALTYPE FIRE DOOR CORPORATION
886 E 149th St (10455-5012)
PHONE..................718 292-3500
Harold Halman, *President*
Douglas Halamn, *Corp Secy*
Gary Halman, *Vice Pres*
EMP: 5
SQ FT: 12,000
SALES (est): 818.1K **Privately Held**
WEB: www.altypefiredoor.com
SIC: 3442 Fire doors, metal

(G-1219)
AMERICAN REFUSE SUPPLY INC
Also Called: American Hose & Hydralics
521 Longfellow Ave (10474-6913)
PHONE..................718 893-8157
Tim Butler, *Manager*
EMP: 7
SALES (corp-wide): 2.1MM **Privately Held**
SIC: 3714 3562 Motor vehicle parts & accessories; ball & roller bearings
PA: American Refuse Supply Inc
700 21st Ave
Paterson NJ 07513
973 684-3225

(G-1220)
ANASIA INC
1175 Jerome Ave (10452-3331)
PHONE..................718 588-1407
Victor Florencio, *President*
EMP: 5
SALES (est): 406.5K **Privately Held**
SIC: 2671 Packaging paper & plastics film, coated & laminated

(G-1221)
ANHEUSER-BUSCH COMPANIES LLC
510 Food Center Dr (10474-7047)
PHONE..................718 589-2610
Nelson Jamel, *Vice Pres*
Ed Fitzmaurice, *Manager*
EMP: 7
SALES (corp-wide): 1.9B **Privately Held**
SIC: 2082 3411 Beer (alcoholic beverage); aluminum cans
HQ: Anheuser-Busch Companies, Llc
1 Busch Pl
Saint Louis MO 63118
314 632-6777

(G-1222)
ATLAS COATINGS CORP
820 E 140th St (10454-1904)
PHONE................................718 402-2000
Michael Landau, *President*
Stephan Landau, *Vice Pres*
EMP: 64
SQ FT: 25,000
SALES (est): 5.9MM **Privately Held**
SIC: 2893 Printing ink

(G-1223)
AURA DETERGENT LLC (PA)
1746 Crosby Ave (10461-4902)
PHONE................................718 824-2162
John Poppola, *Mng Member*
EMP: 8
SALES (est): 1.2MM **Privately Held**
SIC: 2841 Soap & other detergents

(G-1224)
BACO ENTERPRISES INC (PA)
1190 Longwood Ave (10474-5714)
P.O. Box 740487 (10474-0009)
PHONE................................718 589-6225
Barry L Cohen, *President*
Gregg Walker, *General Mgr*
Brian Cohen, *Vice Pres*
David Cohen, *VP Opers*
▲ **EMP:** 80
SQ FT: 60,000
SALES (est): 27.6MM **Privately Held**
WEB: www.bacoent.com
SIC: 3449 3452 Bars, concrete reinforcing; fabricated steel; bolts, metal

(G-1225)
BANDIT INTERNATIONAL LTD
600 E 132nd St (10454-4639)
PHONE................................718 402-2100
Albert Berkner, *President*
Sophie Berkner, *Vice Pres*
EMP: 15
SQ FT: 50,000
SALES (est): 1.1MM **Privately Held**
SIC: 2329 2339 5136 5137 Men's & boys' sportswear & athletic clothing; sportswear, women's; sportswear, men's & boys'; women's & children's sportswear & swimsuits

(G-1226)
BEEHIVE PRESS INC
3742 Boston Rd (10469-2633)
P.O. Box 409 (10469-0409)
PHONE................................718 654-1200
Roger Denhoff, *President*
Peter Kirkel, *Vice Pres*
EMP: 7 **EST:** 1927
SQ FT: 4,500
SALES: 1.2MM **Privately Held**
WEB: www.beehivepress.com
SIC: 2752 2791 Commercial printing, offset; typesetting

(G-1227)
BELMET PRODUCTS INC (PA)
1350 Garrison Ave (10474-4807)
PHONE................................718 542-8220
Fred Collins, *President*
Angelo Demauro, *Vice Pres*
John Collins, *Opers Mgr*
Sal Monteleone, *Sales Mgr*
Hector Medina, *Info Tech Mgr*
EMP: 48 **EST:** 1919
SQ FT: 39,000
SALES (est): 3MM **Privately Held**
WEB: www.belmetproducts.com
SIC: 3469 3312 Stamping metal for the trade; blast furnaces & steel mills

(G-1228)
BEYOND BETTER FOODS LLC
Also Called: Eaten Lightened
101 Lincoln Ave Frnt 2 (10454-4415)
PHONE................................212 888-1120
Michael Shoretz, *CEO*
Carol Finkelstein, *Marketing Staff*
Caroline Lahey, *Manager*
EMP: 6 **EST:** 2012
SQ FT: 5,000
SALES (est): 1.9MM **Privately Held**
SIC: 2024 Ice cream, packaged: molded, on sticks, etc.

(G-1229)
BIMBO BAKERIES USA INC
5625 Broadway Frnt 2 (10463-5548)
PHONE................................718 601-1561
EMP: 5
SALES (corp-wide): 13.7B **Privately Held**
SIC: 2051 Mfg Bread/Related Products
HQ: Bimbo Bakeries Usa, Inc
255 Business Center Dr # 200
Horsham PA 19044
215 347-5500

(G-1230)
BONK SAM UNFORMS CIVILIAN CAP
Also Called: Sam Bonk Uniform
131 Rose Feiss Blvd Fl 2 (10454-3662)
PHONE................................718 585-0665
Sarah Bonk, *President*
Harry Bonk, *General Mgr*
Rachel B Jones, *Vice Pres*
Judy Bonk, *Manager*
EMP: 50 **EST:** 1963
SQ FT: 18,000
SALES (est): 5.4MM **Privately Held**
SIC: 2353 Uniform hats & caps

(G-1231)
BORGATTIS RAVIOLI EGG NOODLES
632 E 187th St (10458)
PHONE................................718 367-3799
Mario John Borgatti, *President*
Christopher Borgatti, *Vice Pres*
EMP: 5
SQ FT: 500
SALES: 500K **Privately Held**
WEB: www.borgattis.com
SIC: 2098 2032 Noodles (e.g. egg, plain & water); dry; ravioli: packaged in cans, jars, etc.

(G-1232)
BRANDT EQUIPMENT LLC
Also Called: Brandt Industries
4461 Bronx Blvd (10470-1407)
PHONE................................718 994-0800
Abe Reich,
EMP: 9
SQ FT: 10,000
SALES (est): 1.5MM **Privately Held**
WEB: www.brandtind.com
SIC: 2599 3843 Hospital furniture, except beds; dental equipment

(G-1233)
BRONX NEW WAY CORP
113 E Kingsbridge Rd (10468-7510)
PHONE................................347 431-1385
Adel Maflahi, *Principal*
EMP: 6
SALES (est): 459.1K **Privately Held**
SIC: 3643 Outlets, electric: convenience

(G-1234)
BUILDING MANAGEMENT ASSOC INC
998 E 167th St Ofc (10459-2054)
PHONE................................718 542-4779
Jaime Diaz, *Manager*
EMP: 36
SALES (corp-wide): 11.8MM **Privately Held**
SIC: 3822 Building services monitoring controls, automatic
PA: Building Management Associates, Inc.
885 Bruckner Blvd
Bronx NY 10459
718 617-2800

(G-1235)
CASA REDIMIX CONCRETE CORP
886 Edgewater Rd (10474-4906)
PHONE................................718 589-1555
Lucy Figueroa, *President*
EMP: 14
SALES (est): 2.4MM **Privately Held**
SIC: 3273 Ready-mixed concrete

(G-1236)
CEC ELEVATOR CAB CORP
540 Manida St (10474-6818)
PHONE................................718 328-3632
Carlos Vanga Sr, *President*
Nick Gretsuk, *Vice Pres*
Sharlette Leslie, *Production*
Joyce Yan, *Production*
Rakesh Rampersaud, *Purch Agent*
EMP: 65
SQ FT: 30,000
SALES (est): 16.1MM **Privately Held**
WEB: www.cecelevator.com
SIC: 3534 7699 Elevators & equipment; elevators: inspection, service & repair

(G-1237)
CENTER SHEET METAL INC
1371 E Bay Ave (10474-7025)
PHONE................................718 378-4476
Maureen O'Connor, *CEO*
Victor Gany, *President*
Keith Oliveri, *Technology*
EMP: 150
SQ FT: 45,000
SALES (est): 21.7MM **Privately Held**
SIC: 3444 Sheet metalwork

(G-1238)
CFS ENTERPRISES INC
Also Called: CFS Steel Company
650 E 132nd St (10454-4603)
PHONE................................718 585-0500
James R Melvin Jr, *Ch of Bd*
EMP: 20
SQ FT: 40,000
SALES (est): 4.7MM
SALES (corp-wide): 94.6MM **Privately Held**
WEB: www.cfssteel.com
SIC: 3315 Wire & fabricated wire products
PA: Re-Steel Supply Company, Inc.
2000 Eddystone Indus Park
Eddystone PA 19022
610 876-8216

(G-1239)
CHARLES H BECKLEY INC (PA)
749 E 137th St (10454-3402)
PHONE................................718 665-2218
Theodore W Marschke, *President*
Charles L Beckley, *Principal*
Ken Marschke, *Marketing Staff*
▲ **EMP:** 18 **EST:** 1932
SQ FT: 12,000
SALES (est): 2.1MM **Privately Held**
WEB: www.chbeckley.com
SIC: 2515 2511 Box springs, assembled; mattresses & foundations; wood household furniture

(G-1240)
CITY EVOLUTIONARY
336 Barretto St (10474-6718)
PHONE................................718 861-7585
Matt Tan, *General Mgr*
EMP: 8
SALES (est): 546.6K **Privately Held**
SIC: 3449 Bars, concrete reinforcing: fabricated steel

(G-1241)
CITY JEANS INC
845 White Plins Rd Frnt 1 (10473)
PHONE................................718 239-5353
Kyle Christianson, *Owner*
EMP: 5
SALES (corp-wide): 35.8MM **Privately Held**
SIC: 2329 Men's & boys' sportswear & athletic clothing
PA: City Jeans Inc
1515 132nd St Fl 2nd
College Point NY 11356
718 359-2489

(G-1242)
COCA-COLA REFRESHMENTS USA INC
977 E 149th St (10455-5090)
PHONE................................718 401-5200
Tom Druell, *Branch Mgr*
EMP: 20
SALES (corp-wide): 35.4B **Publicly Held**
WEB: www.cokecce.com
SIC: 2086 5149 Soft drinks: packaged in cans, bottles, etc.; groceries & related products
HQ: Coca-Cola Refreshments Usa, Inc.
2500 Windy Ridge Pkwy Se
Atlanta GA 30339
770 989-3000

(G-1243)
COLOR CARTON CORP
341 Canal Pl (10451-6091)
PHONE................................718 665-0840
Nicholas F Loprinzi, *President*
Vincent Loprinzi, *Corp Secy*
Nicholas V Loprinzi, *Vice Pres*
Jimmy Martinelli, *Warehouse Mgr*
Paul Locascio, *Sales Mgr*
▲ **EMP:** 60 **EST:** 1960
SQ FT: 90,000
SALES: 7.3MM **Privately Held**
WEB: www.colorcarton.com
SIC: 2752 2653 2657 Commercial printing, offset; corrugated & solid fiber boxes; folding paperboard boxes

(G-1244)
COLUMBIA POOL ACCESSORIES INC
111 Bruckner Blvd (10454-4514)
PHONE................................718 993-0389
Fax: 718 993-8323
▲ **EMP:** 5
SALES (est): 504K **Privately Held**
SIC: 3585 Mfg Refrigeration/Heating Equipment

(G-1245)
COMPLETE FIBER SOLUTIONS INC
1459 Bassett Ave (10461-2309)
PHONE................................718 828-8900
Victor Desantis, *Principal*
Josh Brite, *Principal*
Chris Richard, *Principal*
EMP: 8
SALES (est): 161K **Privately Held**
SIC: 3357 3229 1731 Fiber optic cable (insulated); fiber optics strands; fiber optic cable installation

(G-1246)
CORAL MANAGEMENT CORP
Also Called: Total Machine and Welding
923 Bryant Ave (10474-4701)
PHONE................................718 893-9286
EMP: 5
SALES: 320K **Privately Held**
SIC: 3449 Mfg Misc Structural Metalwork

(G-1247)
COVINGTON SOUND
2705 Kingsbridge Ter (10463-7456)
PHONE................................646 256-7486
Velma Harris, *Owner*
EMP: 6
SALES: 570K **Privately Held**
SIC: 3651 Speaker systems

(G-1248)
CROSS BRONX OPTICAL
961 E 174th St (10460-5060)
PHONE................................917 667-6611
Marina Pritsker, *Owner*
EMP: 5
SALES (est): 240.8K **Privately Held**
SIC: 3827 Optical instruments & lenses

(G-1249)
CUSTOM 101 PRINTS INC
3601 Bronxwood Ave (10469-1143)
PHONE................................718 708-4425
Anthony Matthews, *CEO*
EMP: 10
SQ FT: 2,000
SALES: 300K **Privately Held**
SIC: 2759 Screen printing

(G-1250)
D B F ASSOCIATES
Also Called: August Graphics
1150 E 156th St (10474-6227)
PHONE................................718 328-0005
Bruce Feldman, *President*
Debra Feldman, *General Mgr*
Debra Bashore, *Assistant VP*
EMP: 8 **EST:** 2001

SALES: 460K *Privately Held*
WEB: www.dbfassociates.com
SIC: 2759 Screen printing

(G-1251)
D W HABER & SON INC
825 E 140th St (10454-1930)
PHONE.................718 993-6405
Robert H Haber, *President*
David Haber, *Vice Pres*
▲ EMP: 25
SQ FT: 40,000
SALES (est): 4MM *Privately Held*
WEB: www.habersilver.com
SIC: 3914 Silversmithing; holloware, plated (all metals)

(G-1252)
DA ELECTRIC
6 E Clarke Pl (10452-7501)
PHONE.................347 270-3422
Damal Dudley, *Owner*
EMP: 45
SALES (est): 4MM *Privately Held*
SIC: 3699 Electrical equipment & supplies

(G-1253)
DALE PRESS INC
Also Called: Riverdale Press, The
5676 Riverdale Ave # 311 (10471-2138)
PHONE.................718 543-6200
Bernard L Stein, *President*
Michael Hinman, *Editor*
Richard L Stein, *Vice Pres*
EMP: 25
SQ FT: 2,500
SALES (est): 1.5MM *Privately Held*
WEB: www.riverdalepress.com
SIC: 2711 Newspapers: publishing only, not printed on site

(G-1254)
DAYTON INDUSTRIES INC
1350 Garrison Ave (10474-4807)
PHONE.................718 542-8144
J Fred Collins, *CEO*
John Collins, *Opers Staff*
Milovan Petrovic, *QC Dir*
Barbara Agovino, *Human Resources*
Catherine Goetz, *Office Mgr*
▲ EMP: 45 EST: 1980
SQ FT: 45,000
SALES (est): 11.9MM *Privately Held*
WEB: www.daytonind.com
SIC: 3469 3442 Stamping metal for the trade; metal doors, sash & trim

(G-1255)
DELBIA DO COMPANY INC (PA)
2550 Park Ave (10451-6014)
PHONE.................718 585-2226
Daryl Do, *Vice Pres*
Jerry Chow, *Vice Pres*
▲ EMP: 20
SQ FT: 8,000
SALES (est): 1.8MM *Privately Held*
SIC: 2087 2844 Flavoring extracts & syrups; perfumes, natural or synthetic

(G-1256)
DELBIA DO COMPANY INC
11 Canal Pl (10451-6009)
PHONE.................718 585-2226
Delbia Do, *Branch Mgr*
EMP: 13
SALES (corp-wide): 1.8MM *Privately Held*
SIC: 2844 2087 Perfumes & colognes; flavoring extracts & syrups
PA: Delbia Do Company Inc.
2550 Park Ave
Bronx NY 10454
718 585-2226

(G-1257)
DELICIOSO COCO HELADO INC
849 Saint Anns Ave (10456-7633)
PHONE.................718 292-1930
Alfred Thiebaud, *President*
Sophia Thiebaud, *Admin Sec*
EMP: 15
SQ FT: 20,000
SALES (est): 2.4MM *Privately Held*
SIC: 2024 5451 Ice cream, bulk; ice cream (packaged)

(G-1258)
DOMINIC DE NIGRIS INC
3255 E Tremont Ave Frnt (10461-5790)
PHONE.................718 597-4460
Dominic De Nigris, *President*
Dan A De Nigris, *Vice Pres*
Dan C De Nigris, *Admin Sec*
EMP: 30
SQ FT: 2,910
SALES (est): 2.7MM *Privately Held*
SIC: 3281 1411 Monuments, cut stone (not finishing or lettering only); dimension stone

(G-1259)
DRYVE LLC
4515 Waldo Ave (10471-3933)
PHONE.................646 279-3648
Erika Boyer,
EMP: 5 EST: 2016
SALES (est): 130.5K *Privately Held*
SIC: 2741 Miscellaneous publishing

(G-1260)
DUFOUR PASTRY KITCHENS INC
251 Locust Ave (10454-2004)
PHONE.................718 402-8800
Fax: 718 402-7002
EMP: 24
SALES (est): 3.7MM *Privately Held*
SIC: 2038 2053 Mfg Frozen Specialties Mfg Frozen Bakery Products

(G-1261)
DUN-RITE SPCLIZED CARRIERS LLC
1561 Southern Blvd (10460-5602)
PHONE.................718 991-1100
Brett Deutsch, *Vice Pres*
Phil Bracco, *Project Mgr*
Carl Panepinto, *Warehouse Mgr*
Dominick Conetta, *Opers Staff*
Anthony Conetta, *VP Finance*
EMP: 12
SALES: 1MM *Privately Held*
SIC: 3536 Hoists, cranes & monorails

(G-1262)
E & J IRON WORKS INC
801 E 136th St (10454-3546)
PHONE.................718 665-6040
Gerhard Teicht, *President*
Edmund Teicht, *General Mgr*
EMP: 20
SQ FT: 22,000
SALES (est): 3.8MM *Privately Held*
SIC: 3446 Gates, ornamental metal

(G-1263)
E H HURWITZ & ASSOCIATES
3000 Kingsbridge Ave (10463-5101)
PHONE.................718 884-3766
EMP: 9 EST: 1978
SALES (est): 720K *Privately Held*
SIC: 7372 Prepackaged Software Services

(G-1264)
EASCO BOILER CORP
1175 Leggett Ave (10474-6294)
PHONE.................718 378-3000
Arlington Leon Eastmond, *Ch of Bd*
Leon Eastmond, *President*
EMP: 30
SQ FT: 15,000
SALES (est): 5.3MM *Privately Held*
SIC: 3443 Fabricated plate work (boiler shop)

(G-1265)
EDWARD C LYONS COMPANY INC
Also Called: E C Lyons
3646 White Plains Rd Frnt (10467-5717)
PHONE.................718 515-5361
Gary Owens, *President*
Cheryl Owens, *Vice Pres*
EMP: 7 EST: 1958
SQ FT: 5,000
SALES: 500K *Privately Held*
WEB: www.eclyons.com
SIC: 3423 Engravers' tools, hand

(G-1266)
EDWARD C MULLER CORP
Also Called: Edward C. Lyons
3646 White Plains Rd Frnt (10467-5717)
PHONE.................718 881-7270
Gary Owens, *President*
Cheryl D Owens, *Vice Pres*
EMP: 15 EST: 1898
SQ FT: 3,600
SALES: 70CK *Privately Held*
SIC: 3423 Engravers' tools, hand

(G-1267)
EDWARDS GRAPHIC CO INC
3801 Hudson Manor Ter 4s (10463-1105)
PHONE.................718 548-6858
Jackie Ginsberg, *President*
Ed Edwards, *Vice Pres*
EMP: 5
SALES (est): 424.8K *Privately Held*
SIC: 2752 Commercial printing, lithographic

(G-1268)
EMILIOR PHRM COMPOUNDING INC
Also Called: Haldey Phrm Compounding
2510 Westchester Ave # 207 (10461-3585)
PHONE.................855 426-6768
Emil J Haldey, *President*
EMP: 40
SALES (est): 6MM *Privately Held*
SIC: 2834 5912 Pharmaceutical preparations; drug stores & proprietary stores

(G-1269)
EVE SALES CORP
945 Close Ave (10473-4906)
PHONE.................718 589-6800
Stuart Gale, *President*
Larry Leffler, *Vice Pres*
◆ EMP: 13
SQ FT: 22,000
SALES (est): 3MM *Privately Held*
WEB: www.evesales.com
SIC: 2032 Mexican foods: packaged in cans, jars, etc.

(G-1270)
FINEST CC CORP
3111 E Tremont Ave (10461-5705)
PHONE.................917 574-4525
Larry Derasmo, *President*
EMP: 6
SQ FT: 1,000
SALES (est): 274.8K *Privately Held*
SIC: 3471 Electroplating of metals or formed products

(G-1271)
FIVE ISLANDS PUBLISHING INC
Also Called: Fire Island News
8 Fort Charles Pl (10463-6705)
PHONE.................631 583-5345
Shawn Beqaj, *President*
Nicole Pressly, *Treasurer*
EMP: 10
SQ FT: 1,000
SALES (est): 398.1K *Privately Held*
SIC: 2711 Newspapers: publishing only, not printed on site

(G-1272)
FLAIR DISPLAY INC
3920 Merritt Ave (10466-2502)
PHONE.................718 324-9330
Eugene Dilorenzo, *President*
Chris Dilorenzo, *Vice Pres*
Raymond Hand, *Vice Pres*
Betty Hood, *Assistant*
▲ EMP: 60 EST: 1953
SQ FT: 50,000
SALES (est): 9MM *Privately Held*
WEB: www.flairdisplay.com
SIC: 3993 Displays & cutouts, window & lobby; displays, paint process

(G-1273)
FOAM PRODUCTS INC
360 Southern Blvd (10454-1711)
PHONE.................718 292-4830
Karen Ippolito, *President*
Frank Ippolito, *Vice Pres*
EMP: 20
SQ FT: 32,000
SALES (est): 4.3MM *Privately Held*
SIC: 3069 3086 Foam rubber; insulation or cushioning material, foamed plastic

(G-1274)
FOUR SASONS MULTI-SERVICES INC
3525 Decatur Ave Apt 2k (10467-1729)
PHONE.................347 843-6262
Gabriel Gomez, *CEO*
EMP: 5
SQ FT: 100
SALES (est): 518.1K *Privately Held*
SIC: 2842 Specialty cleaning preparations

(G-1275)
FRA-RIK FORMICA FABG CO INC
1464 Blondell Ave Fl 2 (10461-2688)
PHONE.................718 597-3335
Philip De Candido, *President*
Frank Maiore, *Vice Pres*
EMP: 9 EST: 1965
SQ FT: 5,000
SALES (est): 866.3K *Privately Held*
SIC: 2434 3299 Wood kitchen cabinets; mica products

(G-1276)
FUEL WATCHMAN SALES & SERVICE
Also Called: Full Timer
364 Jackson Ave (10454-1698)
P.O. Box 202, Garden City (11530-0202)
PHONE.................718 665-6100
Benjamin Strysko, *President*
Tom Strysco, *Vice Pres*
Joan Strysko, *Admin Sec*
EMP: 10 EST: 1944
SALES (est): 1.8MM *Privately Held*
SIC: 3822 3669 Auto controls regulating residntl & coml environmt & applncs; smoke detectors

(G-1277)
G&J GRAPHICS INC
Also Called: Bronx Design Group, The
2914 Westchester Ave (10461-4504)
PHONE.................718 409-9874
Geri Sciortino, *President*
John Sciortino, *Vice Pres*
EMP: 7
SQ FT: 3,100
SALES (est): 894.2K *Privately Held*
WEB: www.bronxdesign.com
SIC: 2759 Commercial printing

(G-1278)
GAL MANUFACTURING CO LLC (HQ)
50 E 153rd St (10451-2104)
PHONE.................718 292-9000
Angelo Messina, *Mng Member*
Mark Boelhouwer, *Mng Member*
EMP: 51 EST: 2017
SALES (corp-wide): 2B *Privately Held*
SIC: 3534 Elevators & moving stairways
PA: Golden Gate Private Equity Incorporated
1 Embarcadero Ctr Fl 39
San Francisco CA 94111
415 983-2706

(G-1279)
GARY PLASTIC PACKAGING CORP (PA)
Also Called: Garyline
1340 Viele Ave (10474-7134)
PHONE.................718 893-2200
Gary Hellinger, *Ch of Bd*
Richard Hellinger, *President*
Gustavo Thet, *Opers Mgr*
Paul Hanney, *Sales Mgr*
Heather Greene, *Accounts Mgr*
◆ EMP: 400 EST: 1962
SQ FT: 300,000
SALES (est): 80.2MM *Privately Held*
WEB: www.plasticboxes.com
SIC: 3089 Plastic containers, except foam

(G-1280)
GENERAL FIRE-PROOF DOOR CORP
913 Edgewater Rd (10474-4930)
PHONE.................718 893-5500

Aaron Szabo, *President*
Rubin Kuszel, *Vice Pres*
EMP: 50 **EST:** 1921
SALES (est): 7.5MM **Privately Held**
SIC: 3442 Fire doors, metal

(G-1281)
GENERAL GALVANIZING SUP CO INC (PA)
652 Whittier St Fl Mezz (10474-6194)
PHONE 718 589-4300
Anthony Visentin, *President*
EMP: 53 **EST:** 1935
SQ FT: 10,000
SALES (est): 5.2MM **Privately Held**
SIC: 3471 5085 Electroplating & plating; fasteners & fastening equipment

(G-1282)
GLOBUS CORK INC
741 E 136th St (10454-3410)
PHONE 347 963-4059
Jen Biscoe, *Vice Pres*
▲ **EMP:** 11
SALES (est): 1.5MM **Privately Held**
WEB: www.globuscork.com
SIC: 2499 Tiles, cork

(G-1283)
GOLDEN GLOW COOKIE CO INC
Also Called: Cookie Factory
1844 Givan Ave (10469-3155)
PHONE 718 379-6223
Rose Florio, *President*
Joan Florio, *Vice Pres*
Salvatore Florio Jr, *Vice Pres*
EMP: 20
SQ FT: 15,000
SALES (est): 3.1MM **Privately Held**
SIC: 2051 2052 Bakery: wholesale or wholesale/retail combined; cookies

(G-1284)
GOOD-O-BEVERAGE INC
Also Called: Coco Rico Southeast
1801 Boone Ave (10460-5101)
PHONE 718 328-6400
Steven Kucerak, *Principal*
Kersia Corporation, *Principal*
▲ **EMP:** 18 **EST:** 1942
SQ FT: 53,000
SALES (est): 5.1MM **Privately Held**
WEB: www.good-o.com
SIC: 2086 Soft drinks: packaged in cans, bottles, etc.

(G-1285)
GRAPHIC PRINTING
2376 Jerome Ave (10468-6401)
PHONE 718 701-4433
Joao Oliveira, *Owner*
EMP: 5
SALES (est): 213.3K **Privately Held**
SIC: 2759 Publication printing

(G-1286)
GRUBER DISPLAY CO INC
3920g Merritt Ave (10466-2502)
PHONE 718 882-8220
Jay Merkel, *President*
EMP: 15
SQ FT: 10,000
SALES (est): 750K **Privately Held**
SIC: 2759 Screen printing

(G-1287)
H W WILSON COMPANY INC
950 University Ave (10452-4297)
P.O. Box 602, Ipswich MA (01938-0602)
PHONE 718 588-8635
F Dixon Brooke Jr, *President*
J David Walker, *President*
Tim Collins, *Vice Pres*
EMP: 450
SQ FT: 150,000
SALES (est): 24.2MM
SALES (corp-wide): 2.8B **Privately Held**
WEB: www.hwwilson.com
SIC: 2721 2731 Periodicals: publishing & printing; books: publishing & printing
HQ: Ebsco Publishing, Inc.
10 Estes St
Ipswich MA 01938
978 356-6500

(G-1288)
HAT ATTACK INC (PA)
Also Called: Hat Attack I Bujibaja
4643 Bullard Ave Ste A (10470-1415)
PHONE 718 994-1000
William Gedney, *President*
Barbara J Gedney, *Vice Pres*
Bill Gedney, *Office Mgr*
◆ **EMP:** 20
SQ FT: 11,000
SALES: 5MM **Privately Held**
WEB: www.hatattack.com
SIC: 3111 2353 Bag leather; hats, caps & millinery

(G-1289)
HEALTHEE ENDEAVORS INC
3565c Boston Rd (10469-2500)
P.O. Box 690159 (10469-0761)
PHONE 718 653-5499
Junior Blake, *President*
Jennifer Blake, *Vice Pres*
Julian Reynolds, *Administration*
EMP: 7 **EST:** 1985
SALES (est): 400K **Privately Held**
SIC: 2833 Vitamins, natural or synthetic: bulk, uncompounded

(G-1290)
HEATING & BURNER SUPPLY INC
479 Walton Ave (10451-5337)
PHONE 718 665-0006
Bob Broker, *President*
Terrance Broker, *Vice Pres*
Eric Nelson, *Sales Staff*
EMP: 7
SQ FT: 10,000
SALES (est): 1.8MM **Privately Held**
WEB: www.heatingandburner.com
SIC: 3822 5063 Auto controls regulating residntl & coml environmt & applncs; motors, electric

(G-1291)
HENDRICKSON CUSTOM CABINETRY
132 Saint Anns Ave Fl 2 (10454-4600)
PHONE 718 401-0137
Felix Hendrickson, *President*
Lisa Hendrickson, *Vice Pres*
Kevin Swinderman, *Corp Comm Staff*
Gerry Remus, *Administration*
EMP: 10
SQ FT: 8,000
SALES (est): 627.3K **Privately Held**
WEB: www.hccco.com
SIC: 2434 Wood kitchen cabinets

(G-1292)
HIGH RIDGE NEWS LLC
5818 Broadway (10463-4105)
PHONE 718 548-7412
Atul Patel, *Owner*
EMP: 5
SALES (est): 268.4K **Privately Held**
SIC: 2711 Newspapers, publishing & printing

(G-1293)
IDEAL SIGNS INC
538 Wales Ave (10455-4510)
PHONE 718 292-9196
Yeudy Diaz, *President*
EMP: 5
SQ FT: 3,000
SALES (est): 396.1K **Privately Held**
SIC: 3993 Mfg Signs/Advertising Specialties

(G-1294)
IMPERIAL DAMPER & LOUVER CO
907 E 141st St (10454-2009)
PHONE 718 731-3800
Brad Mattes, *President*
Tom Tulley, *Vice Pres*
Aida Rivera, *Office Mgr*
EMP: 35
SQ FT: 16,500
SALES (est): 6.6MM **Privately Held**
WEB: www.imperialdamper.com
SIC: 3444 3446 Metal ventilating equipment; louvers, ventilating

(G-1295)
INDEX INCORPORATED
415 Concord Ave (10455-4801)
PHONE 440 632-5400
Elias Wexler, *President*
Tom McCartney, *General Mgr*
EMP: 13
SQ FT: 3,500
SALES (est): 1.4MM **Privately Held**
WEB: www.zerointernational.com
SIC: 3052 Rubber & plastics hose & beltings
HQ: Schlage Lock Company Llc
11819 N Pennsylvania St
Carmel IN 46032
317 810-3700

(G-1296)
INDUSTRIAL PAPER TUBE INC
1335 E Bay Ave (10474-6992)
PHONE 718 893-5000
Howard Kramer, *President*
John Costello, *Vice Pres*
EMP: 19
SQ FT: 50,000
SALES (est): 3.5MM **Privately Held**
WEB: www.mailingtubes-ipt.com
SIC: 3089 2655 Closures, plastic; tubes, for chemical or electrical uses: paper or fiber

(G-1297)
INFORM STUDIO INC
480 Austin Pl Frnt E (10455-5023)
PHONE 718 401-6149
Patrick Eck, *President*
Emad Ebrahim, *Vice Pres*
EMP: 10
SQ FT: 7,000
SALES (est): 1.7MM **Privately Held**
SIC: 2431 Interior & ornamental woodwork & trim

(G-1298)
INNOVA INTERIORS INC
780 E 134th St Fl 2 (10454-3527)
PHONE 718 401-2122
Leon Mace Natenzon, *President*
EMP: 20
SALES (est): 1.2MM **Privately Held**
SIC: 2499 1751 Decorative wood & woodwork; carpentry work

(G-1299)
IWEB DESIGN INC
1491 Metro Ave Ste 3i (10462)
PHONE 805 243-8305
John Horne, *CEO*
Jon Jaskiel, *Vice Pres*
EMP: 10
SALES (est): 460K **Privately Held**
SIC: 3577 Encoders, computer peripheral equipment

(G-1300)
JAB CONCRETE SUPPLY CORP
1465 Bronx River Ave (10472-1001)
P.O. Box 1223 (10472-0965)
PHONE 718 842-5250
Carmine Valente, *President*
EMP: 30 **EST:** 1994
SALES (est): 2.3MM **Privately Held**
SIC: 3272 Concrete products

(G-1301)
JEM THREADING SPECIALTIES INC
1059 Washington Ave (10456-6636)
P.O. Box 491, Lake Peekskill (10537-0491)
PHONE 718 665-3341
Michael Rottenkolber, *President*
John Rottenkolber, *Vice Pres*
EMP: 5
SQ FT: 17,500
SALES (est): 652.8K **Privately Held**
SIC: 3965 3354 3452 Fasteners; rods, extruded, aluminum; bolts, metal

(G-1302)
JENNA CONCRETE CORPORATION
1465 Bronx River Ave (10472-1001)
PHONE 718 842-5250
Carmine Valente, *President*
EMP: 30

SQ FT: 1,000
SALES (est): 6.3MM
SALES (corp-wide): 1.3B **Publicly Held**
SIC: 3272 3273 3271 Concrete products; ready-mixed concrete; concrete block & brick
PA: U.S. Concrete, Inc.
331 N Main St
Euless TX 76039
817 835-4105

(G-1303)
JENNA HARLEM RIVER INC
1465 Bronx River Ave (10472-1001)
PHONE 718 842-5997
Carmine Valente, *President*
EMP: 5
SQ FT: 1,000
SALES (est): 454.9K **Privately Held**
SIC: 3272 3273 3271 Concrete products; ready-mixed concrete; concrete block & brick

(G-1304)
JOHN LANGENBACHER CO INC
888 Longfellow Ave (10474-4804)
PHONE 718 328-0141
Harry Boyd, *President*
William Boyd, *President*
Larry Scherer, *Exec VP*
William Hudspeth, *CFO*
EMP: 50 **EST:** 1907
SQ FT: 100,000
SALES (est): 4.6MM **Privately Held**
SIC: 2431 5712 Millwork; custom made furniture, except cabinets

(G-1305)
KD DIDS INC
Also Called: K D Dance
140 E 144th St (10451-5434)
PHONE 718 402-2012
David E Lee, *President*
David Lee, *President*
EMP: 22
SQ FT: 6,000
SALES (est): 5.3MM **Privately Held**
WEB: www.kddance.com
SIC: 2253 5961 Shirts (outerwear), knit; fitness & sporting goods, mail order

(G-1306)
KEMET PROPERTIES LLC
1179 E 224th St (10466-5834)
PHONE 718 654-8079
Douglas Malcolm, *Principal*
EMP: 5
SALES (est): 529.7K **Privately Held**
SIC: 3675 Mfg Electronic Capacitors

(G-1307)
KENMAR SHIRTS INC (PA)
1415 Blondell Ave (10461-2622)
PHONE 718 824-3880
Mark Greene, *President*
Karen Greene, *Corp Secy*
Irwin Haberman, *Vice Pres*
EMP: 20
SQ FT: 8,000
SALES (est): 1.7MM **Privately Held**
WEB: www.kenmarshirts.com
SIC: 2759 5136 5137 2396 Screen printing; men's & boys' clothing; women's & children's clothing; automotive & apparel trimmings

(G-1308)
KICKS CLOSET SPORTSWEAR INC
1031 Southern Blvd Frnt 2 (10459-3435)
PHONE 347 577-0857
Ismail Abadi, *President*
EMP: 6 **EST:** 2014
SQ FT: 1,800
SALES: 2.7MM **Privately Held**
SIC: 2329 3149 2339 Men's & boys' sportswear & athletic clothing; athletic shoes, except rubber or plastic; women's & misses athletic clothing & sportswear

(G-1309)
KIRSCHNER BRUSH LLC
Also Called: Kbc
605 E 132nd St Frnt 3 (10454-4638)
PHONE 718 292-1809
Israel Kirschner,

▲ = Import ▼ = Export
◆ = Import/Export

▲ **EMP**: 15 **EST**: 1939
SQ FT: 20,000
SALES: 900K **Privately Held**
SIC: 3991 Paint brushes

(G-1310)
KNJ FABRICATORS LLC
4341 Wickham Ave (10466-1809)
PHONE.................................347 234-6985
Krishnadatt N Joe,
EMP: 10
SQ FT: 4,000
SALES: 900K **Privately Held**
SIC: 3441 Fabricated structural metal

(G-1311)
L & D MANUFACTURING CORP
Also Called: D & L Manufacturing
366 Canal Pl Frnt (10451-5911)
PHONE.................................718 665-5226
Larry Weisel, *President*
Leon Weisel, *Vice Pres*
EMP: 6
SALES (est): 624.9K **Privately Held**
SIC: 2599 Restaurant furniture, wood or metal

(G-1312)
L A S REPLACEMENT PARTS INC
1645 Webster Ave (10457-8096)
P.O. Box 873 (10457-0873)
PHONE.................................718 583-4700
Alan Siegel, *President*
Lloyd Siegel, *Corp Secy*
EMP: 10 **EST**: 1946
SQ FT: 10,000
SALES (est): 1.6MM **Privately Held**
WEB: www.lasparts.com
SIC: 3432 1711 Plumbing fixture fittings & trim; plumbing, heating, air-conditioning contractors

(G-1313)
LA PRIMA BAKERY INC (PA)
765 E 182nd St (10460-1140)
PHONE.................................718 584-4442
Sal Attina, *President*
Rocco Attina, *Vice Pres*
EMP: 19
SQ FT: 18,000
SALES (est): 1.2MM **Privately Held**
SIC: 2051 Bread, all types (white, wheat, rye, etc): fresh or frozen

(G-1314)
LEADER SHEET METAL INC
759 E 133rd St 2 (10454-3425)
PHONE.................................347 271-4961
Jenny Dashevsky, *President*
EMP: 17 **EST**: 2009
SALES (est): 3.2MM **Privately Held**
SIC: 3444 Sheet metalwork

(G-1315)
LEGACY USA LLC
Also Called: Legacy Manufacturing
415 Concord Ave (10455-4801)
PHONE.................................718 292-5333
Jacob Wexler, *Mng Member*
EMP: 15 **EST**: 2016
SQ FT: 20,000
SALES: 700K **Privately Held**
SIC: 2891 Adhesives & sealants

(G-1316)
LEMON BROTHERS FOUNDATION INC
Also Called: Not For Profit Chari
23b Debs Pl (10475-2575)
PHONE.................................347 920-2749
Mohammed Rahman, *Principal*
EMP: 15
SALES: 24K **Privately Held**
SIC: 3999 Education aids, devices & supplies

(G-1317)
LENS LAB
2124 Bartow Ave (10475-4615)
PHONE.................................718 379-2020
Janet Bennis, *Manager*
EMP: 6
SALES (est): 266.2K **Privately Held**
SIC: 3851 Ophthalmic goods

(G-1318)
LINDA CAMPBELL
Also Called: Campbell's Print Shop
4420 Richardson Ave (10470-1545)
PHONE.................................718 994-4026
Linda Campbell, *Owner*
EMP: 7 **EST**: 1998
SALES (est): 349.4K **Privately Held**
SIC: 2759 Circulars: printing

(G-1319)
LINO PRESS INC
652 Southern Blvd (10455-3637)
PHONE.................................718 665-2625
Franklin Nunez, *Owner*
EMP: 20
SALES (est): 1.2MM **Privately Held**
SIC: 2741 Miscellaneous publishing

(G-1320)
M J M TOOLING CORP
Also Called: Sutter Machine Tool and Die
1059 Washington Ave (10456-6636)
PHONE.................................718 292-3590
John Rottenkolber, *President*
Michael Rottenkolber, *Treasurer*
EMP: 9
SALES (est): 1.1MM **Privately Held**
SIC: 3544 Special dies & tools

(G-1321)
MARATHON ENTERPRISES INC
Also Called: House O'Weenies
787 E 138th St (10454-1989)
PHONE.................................718 665-2560
Allan Thoreson, *Manager*
EMP: 60
SALES (corp-wide): 24.4MM **Privately Held**
WEB: www.sabrett.com
SIC: 2013 Frankfurters from purchased meat
PA: Marathon Enterprises, Inc.
9 Smith St
Englewood NJ 07631
201 935-3330

(G-1322)
MARINE BOILER & WELDING INC
1428 Sheridan Expy (10459-2106)
PHONE.................................718 378-1900
William Falco, *President*
Thomas Falco, *Vice Pres*
EMP: 12
SQ FT: 5,000
SALES (est): 1MM **Privately Held**
SIC: 3443 1799 Boiler & boiler shop work; welding on site

(G-1323)
MARS FASHIONS INC
780 E 134th St Fl 5 (10454-3527)
PHONE.................................718 402-2200
Rafael Sanchez, *President*
Sam Mann, *Treasurer*
Stuart Mann, *Admin Sec*
EMP: 50
SQ FT: 25,000
SALES: 756.9K **Privately Held**
SIC: 2339 2253 Women's & misses' athletic clothing & sportswear; knit outerwear mills

(G-1324)
MASON TRANSPARENT PACKAGE INC
1180 Commerce Ave (10462-5506)
PHONE.................................718 792-6000
Richard Cole, *President*
Ellen Cole, *Vice Pres*
Kevin O'Connell, *Vice Pres*
Sylvia A Cole, *Admin Sec*
EMP: 30 **EST**: 1947
SQ FT: 25,000
SALES (est): 3.8MM **Privately Held**
WEB: www.masontransparent.com
SIC: 2671 2673 2759 Plastic film, coated or laminated for packaging; plastic bags: made from purchased materials; commercial printing

(G-1325)
MATERIALS DESIGN WORKSHOP
830 Barry St (10474-5707)
PHONE.................................718 893-1954
Eugene Black, *President*
David Black, *Vice Pres*
James Black, *Opers Mgr*
EMP: 14
SQ FT: 11,000
SALES (est): 2.1MM **Privately Held**
SIC: 2521 Cabinets, office: wood

(G-1326)
MENSCH MILL & LUMBER CORP (PA)
Also Called: Mensch Supply
1261 Commerce Ave (10462-5527)
PHONE.................................718 359-7500
Jeff Solomon, *CEO*
Howard Kahn, *Ch of Bd*
Yvette Menendez, *Controller*
Nate Daniels, *Manager*
Ravi Ghandi, *Manager*
EMP: 20 **EST**: 1947
SQ FT: 20,000
SALES: 24.7MM **Privately Held**
WEB: www.menschmill.com
SIC: 2431 5211 Millwork; lumber products

(G-1327)
MERCURY LOCK AND DOOR SERVICE
529 C Wortham St (10474)
PHONE.................................718 542-7048
Howard Levine, *President*
EMP: 29
SALES (est): 2.8MM **Privately Held**
SIC: 3442 Fire doors, metal

(G-1328)
METALLINE FIRE DOOR CO INC (PA)
4110 Park Ave (10457-6017)
PHONE.................................718 583-2320
Lydia Rodriguez, *President*
William Rodriguez, *Vice Pres*
EMP: 20
SQ FT: 12,500
SALES (est): 4.7MM **Privately Held**
SIC: 3442 5072 Fire doors, metal; window & door frames; hardware

(G-1329)
METALWORKS INC
1303 Herschell St (10461-3622)
PHONE.................................718 319-0011
Michael Josephs, *Ch of Bd*
Jeff Dynhas, *Vice Pres*
Denise Joseph, *Admin Sec*
Denise Josephs, *Admin Sec*
EMP: 30
SQ FT: 15,000
SALES (est): 3.6MM **Privately Held**
SIC: 3446 Architectural metalwork

(G-1330)
MIL & MIR STEEL PRODUCTS CO
1210 Randall Ave (10474-6399)
PHONE.................................718 328-7596
William Miraglia, *President*
EMP: 6 **EST**: 1958
SQ FT: 5,000
SALES: 350K **Privately Held**
SIC: 3537 Lift trucks, industrial: fork, platform, straddle, etc.

(G-1331)
MILLENNIUM RMNFCTRED TONER INC
7 Bruckner Blvd (10454-4411)
PHONE.................................718 585-9887
Frank Garcia, *President*
Charles Baker, *Senior VP*
EMP: 11
SALES (est): 920K **Privately Held**
WEB: www.mrtoners.com
SIC: 2893 Printing ink

(G-1332)
MILLER BLAKER INC
620 E 132nd St (10454-4603)
PHONE.................................718 665-0500
Cliff Blaker, *Ch of Bd*
Lee Miller, *Senior VP*
Rabin Ramcharan, *Vice Pres*
Steve Samuels, *Project Mgr*
Rachel Lime, *Purch Agent*
▲ **EMP**: 100
SQ FT: 50,000
SALES (est): 15.4MM **Privately Held**
WEB: www.millerblaker.com
SIC: 2431 2521 Interior & ornamental woodwork & trim; wood office furniture

(G-1333)
MISS GRIMBLE ASSOCIATES INC
Also Called: Grimble Bakery
909 E 135th St (10454-3611)
PHONE.................................718 665-2253
Errol Bier, *President*
EMP: 12
SQ FT: 15,000
SALES (est): 720K **Privately Held**
WEB: www.missgrimble.com
SIC: 2051 Bakery: wholesale or wholesale/retail combined

(G-1334)
MODULAR MEDICAL CORP
1513 Olmstead Ave (10462-4254)
PHONE.................................718 829-2626
Jeffery S Offner, *President*
Peter Wachs, *Vice Pres*
EMP: 30 **EST**: 1978
SQ FT: 30,000
SALES (est): 1.3MM **Privately Held**
SIC: 3841 Surgical & medical instruments

(G-1335)
MONARCH ELECTRIC PRODUCTS INC
Also Called: Vicron Electronic Mfg
4077 Park Ave Fl 5 (10457-7310)
PHONE.................................718 583-7996
Fax: 718 299-9121
▲ **EMP**: 6 **EST**: 1946
SQ FT: 5,000
SALES (est): 500K **Privately Held**
SIC: 3643 Mfg Fluorescent Starting Switches

(G-1336)
MONTE PRESS INC
4808 White Plains Rd (10470-1102)
PHONE.................................718 325-4999
Barbara Deangelo, *President*
EMP: 5
SQ FT: 2,400
SALES (est): 320K **Privately Held**
SIC: 2752 Commercial printing, offset

(G-1337)
N & L FUEL CORP
2014 Blackrock Ave (10472-6104)
PHONE.................................718 863-3538
Nick Leandro, *Principal*
EMP: 9
SALES (est): 1MM **Privately Held**
SIC: 2869 Fuels

(G-1338)
NATIONAL EQUIPMENT CORPORATION
Also Called: Union Standard & Un Conf McHy
801 E 141st St (10454-1917)
PHONE.................................718 585-0200
Eddie Greenberg, *Manager*
EMP: 30
SALES (corp-wide): 10.6MM **Privately Held**
SIC: 3559 3565 5084 3556 Chemical machinery & equipment; pharmaceutical machinery; packaging machinery; processing & packaging equipment; confectionery machinery
PA: National Equipment Corporation
600 Mmaroneck Ave Ste 400
Harrison NY 10528
718 585-0200

(G-1339)
NATIONAL STEEL RULE DIE INC
441 Southern Blvd (10455-4906)
PHONE.................................718 402-1396
Frank G Curatolo, *President*
EMP: 14 **EST**: 1945

Bronx - Bronx County (G-1340)

SQ FT: 5,000
SALES: 900K **Privately Held**
SIC: 3544 Dies, steel rule; special dies & tools

(G-1340)
NEW YORK BOTTLING CO INC
Also Called: Mayim Chaim Beverages
626 Whittier St (10474-6121)
PHONE.................718 963-3232
Zvi Hold, *President*
Joseph Hold, *Vice Pres*
Racheal Hold, *Admin Sec*
Esta Kohn, *Admin Sec*
EMP: 12 EST: 1967
SQ FT: 10,000
SALES (est): 2.6MM **Privately Held**
SIC: 2086 Soft drinks: packaged in cans, bottles, etc.

(G-1341)
NEW YORK INDUSTRIAL WORKS INC
796 E 140th St (10454-1915)
PHONE.................718 292-0615
James Brady, *President*
Gary Mahoni, *Corp Secy*
EMP: 14 EST: 1979
SQ FT: 6,000
SALES (est): 2.6MM **Privately Held**
WEB: www.newdraulictools.com
SIC: 3546 Guns, pneumatic; chip removal

(G-1342)
NEX-GEN READY MIX CORP
530 Faile St (10474-6908)
PHONE.................347 231-0073
Salvatore Bullaro, *Chairman*
EMP: 7
SALES (est): 752K **Privately Held**
SIC: 3273 Ready-mixed concrete

(G-1343)
NICHOLAS DFINE FURN DECORATORS
546 E 170th St 48 (10456-2302)
PHONE.................914 245-8982
Helen Savastano, *President*
Frank Savastano, *Owner*
Vincent Savastano, *Corp Secy*
Nicholas Savastano, *Vice Pres*
EMP: 15
SQ FT: 6,600
SALES (est): 1.7MM **Privately Held**
SIC: 2511 2512 2521 7641 Wood household furniture; upholstered household furniture; wood office furniture; antique furniture repair & restoration

(G-1344)
NOROC ENTERPRISES INC
415 Concord Ave (10455-4801)
PHONE.................718 585-3230
Elias Wexler, *CEO*
Jerry Heid, *Vice Pres*
◆ EMP: 150 EST: 1928
SQ FT: 27,000
SALES (est): 20MM **Privately Held**
WEB: www.zerointernational.com
SIC: 3251 3053 Fireproofing tile, clay; gasket materials

(G-1345)
NORTH BRONX RETINAL & OPHTHLMI
3725 Henry Hudson Pkwy (10463-1527)
PHONE.................347 535-4932
Daniel Chechik MD, *Ch of Bd*
EMP: 8
SALES (est): 849.8K **Privately Held**
SIC: 3851 Ophthalmic goods

(G-1346)
NYC BRONX INC
2490 Grand Concourse (10458-5201)
PHONE.................917 417-0509
Prosper Ozies, *President*
EMP: 5
SQ FT: 2,000
SALES (est): 588K **Privately Held**
SIC: 2369 Girls' & children's outerwear

(G-1347)
OMC INC
4010 Park Ave (10457-7397)
PHONE.................718 731-5001
James O'Halpin, *President*
Mike Checci, *Corp Secy*
Robert Moteti, *Vice Pres*
EMP: 110
SQ FT: 25,000
SALES (est): 19.1MM **Privately Held**
WEB: www.omcdrafting.com
SIC: 3444 Sheet metalwork

(G-1348)
OPERATIVE CAKE CORP
Also Called: Lady Linda Cakes
711 Brush St (10465-1839)
P.O. Box 1017 (10465-0623)
PHONE.................718 278-5600
Matthew Jacobson, *President*
Mark Jacobson, *President*
Sam Jacobson, *Vice Pres*
EMP: 50
SQ FT: 60,000
SALES (est): 6.1MM
SALES (corp-wide): 41.6MM **Privately Held**
WEB: www.groceryhaulers.com
SIC: 2051 5149 Bread, cake & related products; bakery products
PA: Grocery Haulers, Inc.
485 Route 1 S
Iselin NJ 08830
732 499-3745

(G-1349)
P H CUSTOM WOODWORKING CORP
830 Barry St Fl 2nd (10474-5707)
PHONE.................917 801-1444
Kazimierz Sperling, *President*
Daniel Sperling, *Principal*
Anna Sperling, *Vice Pres*
EMP: 23
SQ FT: 8,000
SALES: 3.2MM **Privately Held**
SIC: 2431 Interior & ornamental woodwork & trim; exterior & ornamental woodwork & trim

(G-1350)
PACIFIC DESIGNS INTL INC
2743 Webster Ave (10458-3705)
PHONE.................718 364-2867
Edward Nerenberg, *President*
EMP: 6
SALES (est): 452.4K **Privately Held**
SIC: 3081 Floor or wall covering, unsupported plastic

(G-1351)
PARADIGM GROUP LLC
1357 Lafayette Ave Frnt 1 (10474-4847)
PHONE.................718 860-1538
Vuac Heflaz, *Principal*
EMP: 5
SALES (est): 519.6K **Privately Held**
SIC: 3471 3479 Finishing, metals or formed products; hot dip coating of metals or formed products

(G-1352)
PARKCHESTER DPS LLC
2000 E Tremont Ave (10462-5703)
PHONE.................718 823-4411
Richard Vargas, *Manager*
EMP: 107
SALES (est): 9.1MM **Privately Held**
SIC: 3841 Surgical & medical instruments

(G-1353)
PATIENT-WEAR LLC
3940 Merritt Ave (10466-2502)
PHONE.................914 740-7770
Thomas A Keith, *President*
EMP: 8
SALES (est): 950K **Privately Held**
SIC: 2389 Apparel & accessories

(G-1354)
PELICAN PRODUCTS CO INC (PA)
1049 Lowell St (10459-2608)
PHONE.................718 860-3220
Kenneth Silver, *President*
David Silver, *Vice Pres*
▲ EMP: 23 EST: 1946
SQ FT: 20,000
SALES (est): 2.8MM **Privately Held**
WEB: www.pelicanproducts.com
SIC: 3951 3089 Pens & mechanical pencils; novelties, plastic

(G-1355)
PEPSI-COLA BOTTLING CO NY INC
650 Brush Ave (10465-1804)
PHONE.................718 892-1570
Michael Moral, *Manager*
Robert Vanzandt, *Manager*
EMP: 75
SALES (corp-wide): 500MM **Privately Held**
SIC: 2086 Soft drinks: packaged in cans, bottles, etc.
PA: Pepsi-Cola Bottling Company Of New York, Inc.
11202 15th Ave
College Point NY 11356
718 392-1000

(G-1356)
PERRIGO COMPANY
1625 Bathgate Ave (10457-8101)
PHONE.................718 960-9900
Ange Francois, *Project Mgr*
Alexis Wloch, *Engineer*
Joseph C Papa, *Branch Mgr*
Agron Collaku, *Manager*
Emmy Delgado, *Manager*
EMP: 22 **Privately Held**
SIC: 2834 Analgesics
HQ: Perrigo Company
515 Eastern Ave
Allegan MI 49010
269 673-8451

(G-1357)
PERRIGO NEW YORK INC
455 Claremont Pkwy (10457-8301)
PHONE.................718 901-2800
Oscar Camejo, *Manager*
EMP: 15 **Privately Held**
WEB: www.agis-group.com
SIC: 2834 Ointments
HQ: Perrigo New York, Inc.
1700 Bathgate Ave
Bronx NY 10457
718 960-9900

(G-1358)
PERRIGO NEW YORK INC (DH)
Also Called: Suppositoria Laboratory
1700 Bathgate Ave (10457-7512)
PHONE.................718 960-9900
Joseph C Papa, *Ch of Bd*
Giora Carni, *President*
Juan Guzman, *COO*
Sharon Kochan, *Exec VP*
Ofir Sova, *Vice Pres*
◆ EMP: 500
SQ FT: 300,000
SALES (est): 97MM **Privately Held**
WEB: www.agis-group.com
SIC: 2834 Ointments
HQ: Perrigo Company
515 Eastern Ave
Allegan MI 49010
269 673-8451

(G-1359)
POLYSEAL PACKAGING CORP
1178 E 180th St (10460-2401)
P.O. Box 1171, New York (10035-0807)
PHONE.................718 792-5530
Lewis Matthews, *President*
Carol Smith, *Vice Pres*
EMP: 20
SQ FT: 20,000
SALES (est): 1.9MM **Privately Held**
SIC: 2673 2674 Plastic bags: made from purchased materials; paper bags: made from purchased materials

(G-1360)
PONCIO SIGNS
3007 Albany Cres (10463-5960)
PHONE.................718 543-4851
Poncio Salcedo, *Owner*
EMP: 7 EST: 1962
SQ FT: 700
SALES (est): 290K **Privately Held**
SIC: 3993 Signs, not made in custom sign painting shops

(G-1361)
POORAN PALLET INC
319 Barretto St (10474-6722)
PHONE.................718 938-7970
Zainool Pooran, *President*
EMP: 5
SQ FT: 5,000
SALES: 300K **Privately Held**
SIC: 2448 Pallets, wood & wood with metal

(G-1362)
PORK KING SAUSAGE INC
F22 Hunts Point Co Op Mkt (10474-7568)
PHONE.................718 542-2810
Dominick Puntolillo, *President*
Frank Puntolillo, *Vice Pres*
EMP: 25
SQ FT: 10,000
SALES (est): 5.1MM **Privately Held**
SIC: 2013 Sausages & other prepared meats

(G-1363)
PRECISION ORNA IR WORKS INC
Also Called: Precision Furniture
1838 Adee Ave (10469-3245)
PHONE.................718 379-5200
Joseph Napolitano, *President*
Anthony Napolitano, *Vice Pres*
Philip Napolitano, *Admin Sec*
EMP: 9
SQ FT: 40,000
SALES: 700K **Privately Held**
WEB: www.precisionfurniture.com
SIC: 2514 Household furniture: upholstered on metal frames

(G-1364)
PREMIER BRANDS OF AMERICA INC
555 E 242nd St (10470-1007)
PHONE.................718 325-3000
Glenn Lee, *President*
EMP: 9
SALES (est): 1.1MM
SALES (corp-wide): 34.6MM **Privately Held**
SIC: 3131 2842 3842 Footwear cut stock; shoe polish or cleaner; orthopedic appliances
PA: Premier Brands Of America Inc.
31 South St Ste 2s1
Mount Vernon NY 10550
914 667-6200

(G-1365)
PREMIUM OCEAN LLC
1271 Ryawa Ave (10474-7114)
PHONE.................917 231-1061
Esraim Basson,
Juliana Paparizou,
▲ EMP: 15
SALES (est): 4.1MM **Privately Held**
SIC: 2091 Seafood products: packaged in cans, jars, etc.

(G-1366)
PRONTO GAS HEATING SUPS INC
Also Called: Johnson Contrls Authorized Dlr
431 E 165th St Fl 2 (10456-6644)
PHONE.................718 292-0707
Trifone A Demarinis, *Branch Mgr*
EMP: 9
SALES (est): 1.3MM
SALES (corp-wide): 4MM **Privately Held**
WEB: www.prontosupplies.com
SIC: 3829 5075 5074 Measuring & controlling devices; warm air heating & air conditioning; plumbing & hydronic heating supplies
PA: Pronto Gas Heating Supplies Inc.
181 Chrystie St Frnt
New York NY 10002
212 777-3366

GEOGRAPHIC SECTION
Bronx - Bronx County (G-1396)

(G-1367)
PULSE PLASTICS PRODUCTS INC
1156 E 165th St (10459-2613)
P.O. Box 427, New City (10956-0427)
PHONE.................................718 328-5224
Alan J Backelman, *President*
EMP: 25
SQ FT: 23,000
SALES: 1.5MM **Privately Held**
WEB: www.pulseplastics.com
SIC: 3089 Molding primary plastic; injection molding of plastics

(G-1368)
QUALITY HM BRANDS HOLDINGS LLC (PA)
125 Rose Feiss Blvd (10454-3624)
PHONE.................................718 292-2024
Maurice Feiss, *Mng Member*
Thomas Bilbrough,
William J Haley,
▲ EMP: 3
SALES (est): 160.8MM **Privately Held**
SIC: 3645 5063 Residential lighting fixtures; lighting fixtures; lighting fixtures, residential

(G-1369)
QUALITY MILLWORK CORP
425 Devoe Ave (10460-2309)
P.O. Box 479 (10460-0241)
PHONE.................................718 892-2250
Anthony Guarino, *President*
▲ EMP: 28
SQ FT: 45,000
SALES (est): 3.6MM **Privately Held**
SIC: 2431 Doors, wood

(G-1370)
R GOLDSMITH
1974 Mayflower Ave (10461-4007)
PHONE.................................718 239-1396
Claudine Bryan, *Branch Mgr*
EMP: 10
SALES (est): 486.8K **Privately Held**
SIC: 3914 Silversmithing

(G-1371)
REEFER TEK LLC
885a E 149th St Fl 2 (10455)
PHONE.................................347 590-1067
Michael Liedman, *Managing Dir*
EMP: 12 EST: 2010
SQ FT: 12,000
SALES (est): 1.3MM **Privately Held**
SIC: 3559 Mfg Misc Industry Machinery

(G-1372)
RM BAKERY LLC
Also Called: Rollo Mio Artisan Bakery
220 Coster St (10474-7121)
PHONE.................................718 472-3036
Christian Mattheus, *Mng Member*
EMP: 28
SALES (est): 5.3MM **Privately Held**
SIC: 2051 Bread, cake & related products

(G-1373)
ROANWELL CORPORATION
2564 Park Ave (10451-6014)
PHONE.................................718 401-0288
Barbara Labarre, *CEO*
Jonathan Labarre, *President*
William Rathban, *Principal*
Marcelle Wahba, *Purch Mgr*
Gerardo Sevilla, *Engineer*
▼ EMP: 45
SQ FT: 28,000
SALES: 6MM **Privately Held**
WEB: www.roanwellcorp.com
SIC: 3669 Intercommunication systems, electric

(G-1374)
ROCKING THE BOAT INC
812 Edgewater Rd (10474-4902)
PHONE.................................718 466-5799
Amy Kantroitz, *President*
Adam Green, *Exec Dir*
EMP: 10
SALES: 3MM **Privately Held**
WEB: www.rockingtheboat.org
SIC: 3732 Non-motorized boat, building & repairing

(G-1375)
S & S FASHIONS INC
941 Longfellow Ave (10474-4810)
PHONE.................................718 328-0001
Sageev Mangal, *President*
▲ EMP: 5
SQ FT: 18,000
SALES: 4MM **Privately Held**
SIC: 2329 Men's & boys' sportswear & athletic clothing

(G-1376)
S & S SOAP CO INC
815 E 135th St (10454-3584)
PHONE.................................718 585-2900
Zvi Sebrow, *President*
Joseph Sebrow, *Admin Sec*
EMP: 20 EST: 1930
SQ FT: 40,000
SALES (est): 4.6MM **Privately Held**
WEB: www.blutex.com
SIC: 2841 Detergents, synthetic organic or inorganic alkaline

(G-1377)
S & V RESTAURANT EQP MFRS INC
Also Called: Custom Cool
4320 Park Ave (10457-2442)
PHONE.................................718 220-1140
Sam Zeltzer, *CEO*
Shlomo Zeltzer, *President*
Vyacheslav Ulman, *Corp Secy*
Zelig Zeltzer, *Vice Pres*
Michael Bardin, *Engineer*
EMP: 46
SQ FT: 35,000
SALES (est): 9.7MM **Privately Held**
WEB: www.customcool.com
SIC: 3585 Refrigeration equipment, complete

(G-1378)
SACCOMIZE INC
1554 Stillwell Ave (10461-2212)
PHONE.................................818 287-3000
Anthony Saccommanno, *President*
Thomas Saccommanno, *Vice Pres*
EMP: 9
SQ FT: 5,000
SALES (est): 789K **Privately Held**
WEB: www.saccomize.com
SIC: 3471 7542 Finishing, metals or formed products; washing & polishing, automotive

(G-1379)
SANJAY PALLETS INC
424 Coster St (10474-6811)
PHONE.................................347 590-2485
Mohamed Salem Shaheed, *CEO*
EMP: 8
SALES (est): 1.1MM **Privately Held**
SIC: 2448 Pallets, wood & wood with metal

(G-1380)
SARABETHS KITCHEN LLC
1161 E 156th St (10474-6226)
PHONE.................................718 589-2900
Sarabeth Levine,
EMP: 7
SALES (est): 110.5K **Privately Held**
SIC: 2033 Jams, jellies & preserves: packaged in cans, jars, etc.

(G-1381)
SBK PRESERVES INC
Also Called: Sarabeth's Bakery
1161 E 156th St (10474-6226)
PHONE.................................800 773-7378
William Levine, *Ch of Bd*
Suzanne B Levine, *Vice Pres*
▲ EMP: 40
SQ FT: 15,000
SALES (est): 6.4MM **Privately Held**
SIC: 2033 5149 5961 Jams, including imitation: packaged in cans, jars, etc.; preserves, including imitation: in cans, jars, etc.; pickles, preserves, jellies & jams; food, mail order

(G-1382)
SCACCIANOCE INC
Also Called: Daisy Brand Confectionery
1165 Burnett Pl (10474-5716)
PHONE.................................718 991-4462
Donald Beck, *President*
Anthony Scaccianoce, *Vice Pres*
▲ EMP: 10 EST: 1904
SQ FT: 10,000
SALES (est): 964.8K **Privately Held**
SIC: 2064 2068 Candy & other confectionery products; salted & roasted nuts & seeds

(G-1383)
SIDCO FOOD DISTRIBUTION CORP
2324 Webster Ave (10458-7506)
P.O. Box 379, Fort Lee NJ (07024-0379)
PHONE.................................718 733-3939
Jose Negron, *Ch of Bd*
Lois Rodriguez, *Vice Pres*
EMP: 15
SQ FT: 10,000
SALES (est): 6MM **Privately Held**
SIC: 3556 1541 Food products machinery; food products manufacturing or packing plant construction

(G-1384)
SIGMA MANUFACTURING INDS INC
1361 E Bay Ave (10474-7025)
PHONE.................................718 842-9180
Fax: 718 991-4094
EMP: 13
SQ FT: 12,000
SALES (est): 3MM **Privately Held**
SIC: 3599 Mfg Industrial Machinery

(G-1385)
SIGNATURE METAL MBL MAINT LLC
791 E 132nd St (10454-3512)
PHONE.................................718 292-8280
Gary Swartz,
EMP: 100 EST: 2000
SALES (est): 16MM **Privately Held**
SIC: 3449 Miscellaneous metalwork

(G-1386)
SKECHERS USA INC
Also Called: Skechers Factory Outlet 315
651 River Ave (10451-2113)
PHONE.................................718 585-3024
Daniel Lugo, *Branch Mgr*
EMP: 18 **Publicly Held**
SIC: 3021 Rubber & plastics footwear
PA: Skechers U.S.A., Inc.
228 Manhattan Beach Blvd # 200
Manhattan Beach CA 90266

(G-1387)
SML BROTHERS HOLDING CORP
820 E 140th St (10454-1904)
PHONE.................................718 402-2000
Michael Landau, *CEO*
Stephen Landau, *Admin Sec*
▲ EMP: 85 EST: 1976
SALES (est): 15.9MM **Privately Held**
WEB: www.polytexink.com
SIC: 3952 2851 2865 Ink, drawing: black & colored; paints & paint additives; color pigments, organic

(G-1388)
SPACE AGE PLSTIC FBRCATORS INC
4519 White Plains Rd (10470-1680)
PHONE.................................718 324-4062
Arthur Barsky, *President*
Joel Barsky, *Vice Pres*
EMP: 15
SQ FT: 12,000
SALES: 2.6MM **Privately Held**
WEB: www.plastic64.com
SIC: 3089 Plastic hardware & building products; plastic processing

(G-1389)
SPARROW MINING CO (PA)
3743 White Plains Rd (10467-5754)
PHONE.................................718 519-6600
Randolph Silverstein, *Partner*
David Silverstein, *Partner*
EMP: 7
SALES (est): 1.4MM **Privately Held**
SIC: 1442 Sand mining

(G-1390)
SPECIALTY STEEL FABG CORP
Also Called: Specialty Steel of America.
544 Casanova St (10474-6712)
PHONE.................................718 893-6326
Gregory Burns, *President*
Warren Wilhelm, *Vice Pres*
EMP: 14
SQ FT: 12,000
SALES (est): 2.4MM **Privately Held**
WEB: www.specialtysteelinternational.com
SIC: 3441 5051 5084 Fabricated structural metal; metals service centers & offices; industrial machinery & equipment

(G-1391)
ST RAYMOND MONUMENT CO
2727 Lafayette Ave (10465-2228)
PHONE.................................718 824-3600
Raymond Carotenuto, *President*
Ethel Carotenuto, *Corp Secy*
EMP: 5
SQ FT: 1,200
SALES (est): 403.6K **Privately Held**
SIC: 3272 5999 Monuments, concrete; tombstones, precast terrazzo or concrete; monuments, finished to custom order

(G-1392)
STANDARD PAPER BOX MACHINE CO
347 Coster St Fl 2 (10474-6813)
PHONE.................................718 328-3300
Aaron Adams, *Ch of Bd*
Bruce Adams, *President*
Larry Wilson, *Vice Pres*
Vicki Adams, *Treasurer*
▲ EMP: 25
SQ FT: 35,000
SALES (est): 3.6MM **Privately Held**
SIC: 3554 3542 Box making machines, paper; die cutting & stamping machinery, paper converting; machine tools, metal forming type

(G-1393)
STARLITE PNT & VARNISH CO INC
Also Called: Starlight Paint Factory
724 E 140th St (10454-2405)
PHONE.................................718 292-6420
Peter J Gorynski Jr, *President*
EMP: 5 EST: 1938
SQ FT: 9,000
SALES: 2.5MM **Privately Held**
SIC: 2851 5231 Paints & paint additives; paint

(G-1394)
STEVEN JOHN OPTICIANS
5901 Riverdale Ave (10471-1602)
PHONE.................................718 543-3336
Steven John, *Owner*
EMP: 9
SALES (est): 670K **Privately Held**
SIC: 3827 Optical instruments & lenses

(G-1395)
SUPERMARKET EQUIPMENT DEPO INC
1135 Bronx River Ave (10472-3101)
P.O. Box 368, Mountain Dale (12763-0368)
PHONE.................................718 665-6200
Daniel Resnick, *President*
EMP: 7
SALES: 2.5MM **Privately Held**
SIC: 3585 Mfg Refrigeration/Heating Equipment

(G-1396)
SUPREME FIRE PROOF DOOR CO
391 Rider Ave (10451-5905)
PHONE.................................718 665-4224
Wazier Mahmood, *President*
EMP: 10 EST: 1942
SQ FT: 2,500
SALES (est): 1.2MM **Privately Held**
SIC: 3442 Fire doors, metal

Bronx - Bronx County (G-1397)

(G-1397)
SVYZ TRADING CORP
4320 Park Ave (10457-2442)
PHONE..................................718 220-1140
Sam Zeltser, *Principal*
Zelk Zeltser, *Vice Pres*
Steve Ulman, *Admin Sec*
▲ **EMP:** 6
SQ FT: 5,000
SALES (est): 797.5K **Privately Held**
SIC: 3822 Refrigeration/air-conditioning defrost controls

(G-1398)
T J RONAN PAINT CORP
Also Called: Ronan Paints
749 E 135th St (10454-3408)
PHONE..................................718 292-1100
Dennis Doran, *Ch of Bd*
John A Doran Jr, *Corp Secy*
▼ **EMP:** 25 EST: 1984
SQ FT: 35,000
SALES (est): 5MM **Privately Held**
WEB: www.ronanpaints.com
SIC: 2851 Paints & paint additives

(G-1399)
T M INTERNATIONAL LLC
Also Called: Mazzella Blasting Mat Co
413 Faile St 15 (10474-6907)
P.O. Box 10930, Fairfield NJ (07004-6930)
PHONE..................................718 842-0949
Frank Stagnito, *President*
EMP: 7
SQ FT: 45,000
SALES (est): 1MM **Privately Held**
WEB: www.tmi2001.com
SIC: 2298 Blasting mats, rope

(G-1400)
TANNENS
363 E 149th St (10455-3983)
PHONE..................................718 292-4646
Mary Tannen, *Owner*
EMP: 7 EST: 1938
SQ FT: 1,875
SALES (est): 716.4K **Privately Held**
SIC: 2759 5943 Letterpress printing; office forms & supplies

(G-1401)
TARA RIFIC SCREEN PRINTING INC
4197 Park Ave (10457-6033)
PHONE..................................718 583-6864
Sandy Stein, *President*
Jason Holden, *Manager*
EMP: 7
SALES: 170K **Privately Held**
SIC: 2759 Screen printing

(G-1402)
THEWAVE COMMUNICATIONS LLC
3933 White Plains Rd (10466-3025)
PHONE..................................646 973-8294
Chino Plieto, *CEO*
Christopher Vargas, *CEO*
EMP: 8
SALES: 150K **Privately Held**
SIC: 3663 Radio & TV communications equipment

(G-1403)
TIRADO DISTILLERY INC
1646 Hering Ave (10461-2006)
PHONE..................................718 620-2244
EMP: 6
SALES (est): 377.1K **Privately Held**
SIC: 2085 Distilled & blended liquors

(G-1404)
TREMONT OFFSET INC
1500 Ericson Pl (10461-5414)
PHONE..................................718 892-7333
Robert Del Greco, *President*
Janet Del Greco, *Vice Pres*
Janet Delgrecio, *Vice Pres*
EMP: 9
SQ FT: 2,000
SALES (est): 1.3MM **Privately Held**
SIC: 2752 Commercial printing, offset

(G-1405)
TRENCH & MARINE PUMP CO INC
3466 Park Ave (10456-4307)
P.O. Box 543 (10456-0525)
PHONE..................................212 423-9098
Herman Azia, *President*
Malcolm Azia, *Vice Pres*
Yvette Azia, *Treasurer*
EMP: 40 EST: 1918
SQ FT: 10,000
SALES (est): 1.8MM **Privately Held**
SIC: 3561 3594 Pumps, domestic: water or sump; fluid power pumps & motors

(G-1406)
TRICEUTICAL INC
1652 Hering Ave (10461-2006)
PHONE..................................631 249-0003
Richard Zhang, *President*
EMP: 12 EST: 2009
SALES (est): 1.1MM **Privately Held**
SIC: 2834 Druggists' preparations (pharmaceuticals)

(G-1407)
TROY SIGN & PRINTING
Also Called: Troy Sign Printing Center
4827 White Plains Rd (10470-1125)
PHONE..................................718 994-4482
Leslie Peterson, *Owner*
EMP: 6
SALES (est): 497.8K **Privately Held**
SIC: 2752 Commercial printing, lithographic

(G-1408)
TRUXTON CORP
Also Called: Howard Formed Steel Pdts Div
1357 Lafayette Ave (10474-4846)
P.O. Box 225, Yonkers (10704-0225)
PHONE..................................718 842-6000
Howard Schwartz, *President*
Steve Meier, *Sales Staff*
EMP: 5
SQ FT: 5,000
SALES (est): 809.3K **Privately Held**
WEB: www.mailcart.com
SIC: 3799 Pushcarts & wheelbarrows

(G-1409)
TRYLON WIRE & METAL WORKS INC
526 Tiffany St (10474-6614)
PHONE..................................718 542-4472
Mark Herrmann, *President*
EMP: 25
SQ FT: 20,000
SALES (est): 3.3MM **Privately Held**
SIC: 2542 3496 3444 Stands, merchandise display: except wood; miscellaneous fabricated wire products; sheet metalwork

(G-1410)
TWI-LAQ INDUSTRIES INC
Also Called: Stone Glo Products
1345 Seneca Ave (10474-4611)
PHONE..................................718 638-5860
Lorin Wels, *President*
Steven Wels, *Exec VP*
Robert Wels, *Vice Pres*
EMP: 30
SQ FT: 30,000
SALES (est): 6.3MM **Privately Held**
WEB: www.stoneglo.com
SIC: 2842 Sanitation preparations

(G-1411)
UNITED FARM PROCESSING CORP (PA)
4366 Park Ave (10457-2442)
PHONE..................................718 933-6060
Marvin Weinhaus, *President*
Stephen Leibowitz, *Vice Pres*
EMP: 150
SQ FT: 31,000
SALES: 5.2MM **Privately Held**
SIC: 2035 Pickled fruits & vegetables

(G-1412)
UNITED PICKLE PRODUCTS CORP
4366 Park Ave (10457-2442)
PHONE..................................718 933-6060
Marvin Weinhaus, *President*
Stephen Leibowitz, *Vice Pres*
EMP: 49
SQ FT: 60,000
SALES (est): 25MM **Privately Held**
SIC: 2035 Vegetables, pickled

(G-1413)
VANITY FAIR BATHMART INC
2971 Webster Ave (10458-2424)
PHONE..................................718 584-6700
John P O'Boyle, *President*
EMP: 10
SQ FT: 3,500
SALES (est): 1MM **Privately Held**
WEB: www.vanityfairbathmart.com
SIC: 3431 3469 5023 5031 Bathroom fixtures, including sinks; kitchen fixtures & equipment: metal, except cast aluminum; kitchenware; lumber, plywood & millwork

(G-1414)
VELVET HEALING BY ALMA CORP
645 Melrose Ave Frnt 1 (10455-2552)
PHONE..................................347 271-4220
Alfonsina Pena, *Owner*
EMP: 5
SALES (est): 265.8K **Privately Held**
SIC: 3221 Medicine bottles, glass

(G-1415)
VICTORIA PLATING CO INC
650 Tiffany St (10474-6289)
P.O. Box 740486 (10474-0009)
PHONE..................................718 589-1550
Charles Antmann, *President*
Jeffrey S Higdon, *Vice Pres*
▲ **EMP:** 51
SQ FT: 45,000
SALES (est): 5.3MM **Privately Held**
WEB: www.victoriaplating.com
SIC: 3471 Electroplating of metals or formed products

(G-1416)
VIELE MANUFACTURING CORP
Also Called: Gary Plastic
1340 Viele Ave (10474-7134)
PHONE..................................718 893-2200
Gary Hellinger, *CEO*
Marilyn Hellinger, *Vice Pres*
Jason Barretto, *Prdtn Mgr*
◆ **EMP:** 500
SQ FT: 25,000
SALES (est): 59.5MM **Privately Held**
SIC: 3089 Injection molding of plastics

(G-1417)
WALDORF BAKERS INC
Also Called: Festival Bakers
909 E 135th St (10454-3611)
PHONE..................................718 665-2253
Milton Bier, *Ch of Bd*
Errol M Bier, *President*
Nancy Bier, *Vice Pres*
EMP: 15
SQ FT: 13,328
SALES (est): 1MM **Privately Held**
SIC: 2051 Bread, cake & related products

(G-1418)
WALTERS & WALTERS INC
961 E 224th St (10466-4677)
PHONE..................................347 202-8535
EMP: 7 EST: 2013
SALES (est): 92.3K **Privately Held**
SIC: 7692 Welding repair

(G-1419)
WENIG CORPORATION
230 Manida St Fl 2 (10474-7199)
PHONE..................................718 542-3600
Fax: 718 542-3979
EMP: 30 EST: 1924
SQ FT: 50,000
SALES (est): 5.1MM **Privately Held**
SIC: 3444 Mfg Sheet Metalwork

(G-1420)
YANKEE CORP
Also Called: Yankee Wiping Cloth
1180 Randall Ave (10474-6217)
PHONE..................................718 589-1377
Todd W Hooper, *Chairman*
Richard Kocher, *Vice Pres*
▲ **EMP:** 10
SQ FT: 16,250
SALES (est): 1.2MM **Privately Held**
SIC: 2299 5093 7218 Fabrics: linen, jute, hemp, ramie; waste rags; wiping towel supply

(G-1421)
YULA CORPORATION
330 Bryant Ave (10474-7197)
PHONE..................................718 991-0900
Larry Feldman, *CEO*
Fred Feldman, *President*
Alberto Pea, *Engineer*
Daphne Henry, *Manager*
Matthew Feldman, *Director*
▲ **EMP:** 40 EST: 1926
SQ FT: 20,000
SALES (est): 10.1MM **Privately Held**
WEB: www.yulacorp.com
SIC: 3443 Heat exchangers, plate type

(G-1422)
ZARO BAKE SHOP INC (PA)
Also Called: Zaro's Bread Basket
138 Bruckner Blvd (10454-4620)
PHONE..................................718 993-7327
Stuart D Zaro, *Ch of Bd*
Philip Zaro, *Ch of Bd*
Stewart Zaro, *President*
Joseph Zaro, *Vice Pres*
EMP: 110
SQ FT: 40,000
SALES (est): 72.3MM **Privately Held**
WEB: www.zaro.com
SIC: 2051 2052 Bread, cake & related products; cookies & crackers

Bronxville
Westchester County

(G-1423)
ARTISANAL BRANDS INC
42 Forest Ln (10708-1936)
PHONE..................................914 441-3591
Daniel W Dowe, *President*
EMP: 34
SQ FT: 10,000
SALES (est): 3.9MM **Privately Held**
SIC: 2022 5451 Natural cheese; cheese

(G-1424)
CLARK BOTANICALS INC
9 Paradise Rd (10708-2205)
P.O. Box 988 (10708-0988)
PHONE..................................914 826-4319
Frangesco Clark, *President*
EMP: 10
SALES (est): 1.4MM **Privately Held**
SIC: 2844 Cosmetic preparations

(G-1425)
NOMAD EDITIONS LLC
123 Ellison Ave (10708-2728)
PHONE..................................212 918-0992
Mark Edminston, *CEO*
Marjorie Martay, *Exec VP*
Samuel Spivy, *Vice Pres*
Cristine De Pedro, *CTO*
EMP: 18
SALES (est): 1MM **Privately Held**
SIC: 2759 Advertising literature: printing

(G-1426)
SOVEREIGN SERVICING SYSTEM LLC
1 Stone Pl Ste 200 (10708-3431)
PHONE..................................914 779-1400
Stewart Alpert, *Principal*
EMP: 18
SALES (est): 1MM **Privately Held**
SIC: 1389 Roustabout service

Brookhaven
Suffolk County

(G-1427)
AMNEAL PHARMACEUTICALS LLC
50 Horseblock Rd (11719-9509)
PHONE..................................908 231-1911

GEOGRAPHIC SECTION

Brooklyn - Kings County (G-1458)

EMP: 50
SALES (corp-wide): 430MM Privately Held
SIC: 2834 Mfg Pharmaceutical Preparations
PA: Amneal Pharmaceuticals, Llc
400 Crossing Blvd Fl 3
Bridgewater NJ 08807
631 952-0214

(G-1428)
AMNEAL PHARMACEUTICALS LLC
50 Horseblock Rd (11719-9509)
PHONE..................631 952-0214
EMP: 41
SALES (corp-wide): 1B Publicly Held
SIC: 2834 5122 Pharmaceutical preparations; pharmaceuticals
HQ: Amneal Pharmaceuticals Of New York, Llc
50 Horseblock Rd
Brookhaven NY 11719
908 947-3120

(G-1429)
AMNEAL PHARMACEUTICALS NY LLC (DH)
50 Horseblock Rd (11719-9509)
PHONE..................908 947-3120
Chintu Patel, CEO
Chirag Patel, President
Shankar Hariharan, Exec VP
Jim Luce, Exec VP
Johnny Mikell, Senior VP
▲ EMP: 50
SQ FT: 75,000
SALES (est): 103.2MM
SALES (corp-wide): 1B Publicly Held
WEB: www.amneal.com
SIC: 2834 5122 Pharmaceutical preparations; pharmaceuticals

(G-1430)
GEOTECH ASSOCIATES LTD
20 Stiriz Rd (11719-9717)
PHONE..................631 286-0251
Michael Verruto Jr, President
Linda Billski, Bookkeeper
EMP: 6
SQ FT: 1,500
SALES: 600K Privately Held
SIC: 3272 Concrete stuctural support & building material

(G-1431)
LONG ISLAND PRECAST INC
20 Stiriz Rd (11719-9717)
PHONE..................631 286-0240
Michael Verruto, Ch of Bd
Dan Lambertson, Sales Engr
EMP: 30
SQ FT: 1,500
SALES (est): 6.1MM Privately Held
WEB: www.li-precast.com
SIC: 3272 Concrete products, precast

(G-1432)
SALSBURG DIMENSIONAL STONE
18 Pine St (11719-9409)
PHONE..................631 653-6790
Jay Salsburg, President
EMP: 11
SALES (est): 1MM Privately Held
SIC: 3281 Marble, building: cut & shaped; granite, cut & shaped

Brooklyn
Kings County

(G-1433)
12PT PRINTING LLC
2053 E 1st St (11223-4026)
PHONE..................718 376-2120
Joseph Sutton, Owner
EMP: 5 EST: 2014
SALES (est): 205.1K Privately Held
SIC: 2752 Commercial printing, lithographic

(G-1434)
212KIDDISH INC
168 Spencer St (11205-3929)
PHONE..................718 705-7227
Nachum Weberman, President
EMP: 5 EST: 2010
SALES (est): 344K Privately Held
SIC: 2099 5149 2052 Food preparations; cookies; cookies

(G-1435)
21ST CENTURY SPIRITS CORP
137 12th St (11215)
PHONE..................718 499-0606
Byung J Park, Ch of Bd
EMP: 6
SALES (est): 479.7K Privately Held
SIC: 2085 Gin (alcoholic beverage)

(G-1436)
2P AGENCY USA INC
1674 E 22nd St Apt 3a (11229-1534)
PHONE..................212 203-5586
Robert Azaryev, CEO
EMP: 2
SQ FT: 1,000
SALES (est): 26.5MM
SALES (corp-wide): 221.1MM Privately Held
SIC: 3663 5999 Mobile communication equipment; mobile telephones & equipment
PA: 2p Commercial Agency S.R.O.
U Zvonarky 291/3
Praha - Vinohrady

(G-1437)
388 ASSOCIATES INC
385 Harman St (11237-4701)
PHONE..................267 367-0990
Ci Wang, Manager
EMP: 5
SALES (est): 156.7K Privately Held
SIC: 2392 Household furnishings

(G-1438)
3PHASE INDUSTRIES LLC
Also Called: Token
481 Van Buren St Unit 9a (11221-3046)
PHONE..................347 763-2942
ABI Scholz, Manager
Will Kavesh,
Nicole Cornell,
EMP: 6
SQ FT: 4,000
SALES: 500K Privately Held
SIC: 2522 2519 Office furniture, except wood; household furniture, except wood or metal: upholstered

(G-1439)
3RD AVENUE DOUGHNUT INC
7111 3rd Ave (11209-1308)
PHONE..................718 748-3294
Ahmesh Bratea, President
EMP: 10
SALES (est): 505.5K Privately Held
SIC: 2051 Mfg Bread/Related Products

(G-1440)
3V COMPANY INC
Also Called: Three V
110 Bridge St Ste 3 (11201-1575)
PHONE..................718 858-7333
Clara Crombo, CEO
Sam Gombo, President
Dan Gombo, Vice Pres
EMP: 47
SQ FT: 22,000
SALES (est): 7.7MM Privately Held
WEB: www.threev.com
SIC: 2087 2834 2099 2086 Syrups, flavoring (except drink); pharmaceutical preparations; food preparations; bottled & canned soft drinks

(G-1441)
40 STREET BAKING INC
8617 17th Ave (11214-3601)
PHONE..................212 683-4700
Mohammed Irfan,
EMP: 8
SALES (est): 467.5K Privately Held
SIC: 2051 Bread, cake & related products

(G-1442)
461 NEW LOTS AVENUE LLC
461 New Lots Ave (11207-6411)
P.O. Box 20540 (11202-0540)
PHONE..................347 303-9305
Desmond R John,
EMP: 6
SALES (est): 335.4K Privately Held
SIC: 2759 7991 Commercial printing; spas

(G-1443)
5TH AVENUE PHARMACY INC
4818 5th Ave Ste 1 (11220-1936)
PHONE..................718 439-8585
Avraham Pudel, President
EMP: 9
SALES (est): 1.2MM Privately Held
SIC: 2834 Pharmaceutical preparations

(G-1444)
6727 11TH AVE CORP
Also Called: Prestige Printing Company
6727 11th Ave (11219-5904)
PHONE..................718 837-8787
Vincent Costanza, President
Luke Spano, Vice Pres
EMP: 10 EST: 1973
SQ FT: 3,200
SALES (est): 1.5MM Privately Held
SIC: 2752 2759 Commercial printing, offset; offset & photolithographic printing; letterpress printing

(G-1445)
72 STEEL AND ALUMINIUM WORK
220 42nd St (11232-2814)
PHONE..................917 667-3033
Cheng X Lin, Principal
EMP: 5 EST: 2017
SALES (est): 351K Privately Held
SIC: 3479 Aluminum coating of metal products

(G-1446)
786 IRON WORKS CORP
50 Morgan Ave (11237-1605)
PHONE..................718 418-4808
Baudin Canka, President
EMP: 5
SQ FT: 5,000
SALES (est): 806.8K Privately Held
SIC: 3446 Fences or posts, ornamental iron or steel

(G-1447)
888 PHARMACY INC
4821 8th Ave (11220-2213)
PHONE..................718 871-8833
Larisa Golubets, President
EMP: 10 EST: 2012
SALES (est): 1.5MM Privately Held
SIC: 2834 Pharmaceutical preparations

(G-1448)
999 BAGELS INC
1410 86th St (11228-3408)
PHONE..................718 915-0742
Stefano Mannino, CEO
Salvatore Mannino, Director
EMP: 8
SALES (est): 678.7K Privately Held
SIC: 2051 5461 Bagels, fresh or frozen; bagels

(G-1449)
A & B FINISHING INC
401 Park Ave (11205-1406)
PHONE..................718 522-4702
Fax: 718 624-4916
EMP: 40
SQ FT: 20,000
SALES: 800K Privately Held
SIC: 2253 5199 2339 Knit Outerwear Mill Whol Nondurable Goods Mfg Women's/Misses' Outerwear

(G-1450)
A & L ASSET MANAGEMENT LTD
143 Alabama Ave (11207-2911)
PHONE..................718 566-1500
Meir Akerman, CEO
Eugene Loevinger, Admin Sec
EMP: 150

SQ FT: 120,000
SALES (est): 12MM Privately Held
SIC: 3999 Candles

(G-1451)
A & MT REALTY GROUP LLC
1979 Pacific St Fl 1 (11233-3803)
PHONE..................718 974-5871
Aboubacar Tounkara, Mng Member
EMP: 10
SALES: 1MM Privately Held
SIC: 1389 8741 Construction, repair & dismantling services; management services

(G-1452)
A & S ELECTRIC
952 Flushing Ave (11206-4720)
PHONE..................212 228-2030
EMP: 7 EST: 2011
SALES (est): 1.2MM Privately Held
SIC: 3699 1731 Mfg Electrical Equipment/Supplies Electrical Contractor

(G-1453)
A B C ELASTIC CORP
889 Metropolitan Ave (11211-2513)
PHONE..................718 388-2953
Morris Freund, President
Herman Freund, Admin Sec
EMP: 8 EST: 1966
SQ FT: 10,000
SALES: 2MM Privately Held
SIC: 2221 Elastic fabrics, manmade fiber & silk

(G-1454)
A B S BRASS PRODUCTS INC
185 Moore St (11206-3707)
PHONE..................718 497-2115
Mark Azerrad, President
EMP: 11 EST: 1971
SQ FT: 6,000
SALES (est): 970K Privately Held
SIC: 3432 Plumbers' brass goods: drain cocks, faucets, spigots, etc.

(G-1455)
A G M DECO INC
305 Wallabout St 307 (11206-4325)
PHONE..................718 624-6200
Leib Rosenberg, Manager
EMP: 15 Privately Held
SIC: 3442 Sash, door or window: metal
PA: A. G. M. Deco Inc.
741 Myrtle Ave
Brooklyn NY 11205

(G-1456)
A G M DECO INC (PA)
Also Called: Steiner Doors
741 Myrtle Ave (11205-3924)
PHONE..................718 624-6200
Gabrielle Steiner, President
▲ EMP: 92
SQ FT: 2,000
SALES (est): 120MM Privately Held
SIC: 3442 Sash, door or window: metal

(G-1457)
A HEALTH OBSESSION LLC
2184 Mcdonald Ave (11223-3926)
PHONE..................347 850-4587
Joseph Chehebar,
EMP: 30
SALES (est): 2.2MM
SALES (corp-wide): 9MM Privately Held
SIC: 2086 5149 Fruit drinks (less than 100% juice): packaged in cans, etc.; beverages, except coffee & tea
PA: Jusbyjulie.Com Llc
2184 Mcdonald Ave
Brooklyn NY 11223
917 270-6040

(G-1458)
A TO Z KOSHER MEAT PRODUCTS CO
Also Called: Empire National
123 Borinquen Pl (11211)
PHONE..................718 384-7400
Edward Weinberg, President
Karen Weinberg, Manager
EMP: 20
SQ FT: 20,000
SALES (est): 2.6MM Privately Held
SIC: 2011 Meat packing plants

Brooklyn - Kings County (G-1459)

(G-1459)
A VAN HOEK WOODWORKING LIMITED
71 Montrose Ave (11206-2005)
PHONE..................................718 599-4388
Andre Van Hoek, *President*
EMP: 5
SALES: 300K **Privately Held**
SIC: 2499 5712 Decorative wood & woodwork; cabinet work, custom

(G-1460)
A&B IRON WORKS INC
137 Conover St (11231-1102)
PHONE..................................347 466-3193
Ashley Beygelman, *President*
Boris Beygelman, *Vice Pres*
EMP: 9
SALES: 150K **Privately Held**
SIC: 3315 Fence gates posts & fittings: steel

(G-1461)
A-1 IRON WORKS INC
2413 Atlantic Ave (11233-3416)
PHONE..................................718 927-4766
Mario Palermo, *CEO*
Alberto Palermo, *President*
EMP: 6 EST: 1997
SQ FT: 4,000
SALES (est): 1.1MM **Privately Held**
SIC: 3312 Hot-rolled iron & steel products

(G-1462)
A-1 PRODUCTS INC
165 Classon Ave (11205-2636)
PHONE..................................718 789-1818
Imre David Kaufman, *President*
EMP: 9
SQ FT: 7,000
SALES (est): 1.3MM **Privately Held**
WEB: www.a1prepaid.com
SIC: 3111 2789 3089 Cutting of leather; paper cutting; plastic processing

(G-1463)
A-1 SKULL CAP CORP
Also Called: A1 Skullcaps
1212 36th St (11218-2010)
PHONE..................................718 633-9333
Henny Blau, *President*
▲ EMP: 25
SALES (est): 1.3MM **Privately Held**
WEB: www.skullcap.com
SIC: 2353 5999 Hats & caps; religious goods

(G-1464)
A-ONE LAMINATING CORP
1636 Coney Island Ave 2b (11230-5808)
PHONE..................................718 266-6002
Sol Chaimovits, *CEO*
Reizel Chaimovits, *Admin Sec*
▲ EMP: 6
SALES: 3MM **Privately Held**
SIC: 2295 2621 2672 Laminating of fabrics; asphalt paper, laminated; coated & laminated paper

(G-1465)
A-ONE MOVING & STORAGE INC
1725 Avenue M (11230-5303)
PHONE..................................718 266-6002
EMP: 25
SQ FT: 35,000
SALES (est): 3.5MM **Privately Held**
SIC: 2295 2257 Mfg Coated Fabrics Weft Knit Fabric Mill

(G-1466)
A-PLUS RESTAURANT EQUIPMENT
623 Sackett St (11217-3116)
PHONE..................................718 522-2656
Alex Picav, *Principal*
▼ EMP: 8
SALES (est): 879.2K **Privately Held**
SIC: 2599 Carts, restaurant equipment

(G-1467)
A1 ORNAMENTAL IRON WORKS INC
61 Jefferson St (11206-6108)
PHONE..................................718 265-3055
Matt Barsily, *President*
EMP: 5
SALES (est): 386.2K **Privately Held**
SIC: 3446 Architectural metalwork

(G-1468)
AB FIRE INC
1554 61st St (11219-5431)
P.O. Box 230581 (11223-0581)
PHONE..................................917 416-6444
Ave Kay, *President*
EMP: 8
SALES (est): 618.8K **Privately Held**
SIC: 3711 Fire department vehicles (motor vehicles), assembly of

(G-1469)
ABETTER PROCESSING CORP
984 E 35th St (11210-3423)
PHONE..................................718 252-2223
EMP: 15
SALES (est): 919.1K **Privately Held**
SIC: 3471 Plating/Polishing Service

(G-1470)
ABLE ANODIZING CORP
1767 Bay Ridge Ave (11204-5016)
PHONE..................................718 252-0660
Brenda Clark, *Vice Pres*
Mary Di Nicola, *Treasurer*
EMP: 13
SQ FT: 8,000
SALES: 2.3MM **Privately Held**
SIC: 3471 Anodizing (plating) of metals or formed products

(G-1471)
ABLE NATIONAL CORP
49 Wyckoff Ave (11237-8001)
PHONE..................................718 386-8801
Abraham Katz, *President*
EMP: 20
SQ FT: 150,000
SALES (est): 4MM **Privately Held**
WEB: www.ablenational.com
SIC: 2675 3469 2891 Paper die-cutting; metal stampings; adhesives & sealants

(G-1472)
ACCURATE KNITTING CORP
1478 E 26th St (11210-5233)
PHONE..................................646 552-2216
Chajim Philip Franzos, *President*
EMP: 7
SQ FT: 5,800
SALES (est): 1.2MM **Privately Held**
SIC: 2253 Sweaters & sweater coats, knit

(G-1473)
ACCURATE PRECAST
1957 Pitkin Ave (11207-3305)
PHONE..................................718 345-2910
Fred Lermer, *Principal*
EMP: 18
SALES (est): 2MM **Privately Held**
SIC: 3272 Precast terrazo or concrete products

(G-1474)
ACCURATE SIGNS & AWNINGS INC
247 Prospect Ave Ste 2 (11215-8403)
PHONE..................................718 788-0302
Jim Coppersmith, *President*
EMP: 10
SQ FT: 4,000
SALES: 2MM **Privately Held**
SIC: 3993 Mfg Signs/Advertising Specialties

(G-1475)
ACE & JIG LLC (PA)
323 Dean St Ste 2 (11217-1906)
PHONE..................................347 227-0318
EMP: 8
SALES (est): 871.9K **Privately Held**
SIC: 2335 5137 Ensemble dresses: women's, misses' & juniors'; scarves, women's & children's; women's & children's dresses, suits, skirts & blouses

(G-1476)
ACME ARCHITECTURAL PRODUCTS
513 Porter Ave (11222)
PHONE..................................718 360-0700
Jack Teich, *President*
EMP: 500
SQ FT: 15,000
SALES (est): 25.4MM **Privately Held**
WEB: www.acmesteel.com
SIC: 3469 Spinning metal for the trade; stamping metal for the trade

(G-1477)
ACME ARCHITECTURAL PDTS INC (PA)
Also Called: Acme Architectural Walls
251 Lombardy St (11222-5516)
PHONE..................................718 384-7800
Jack Teich, *President*
Joel Licari, *Vice Pres*
Michael Teich, *Vice Pres*
Mark Teich, *Treasurer*
▲ EMP: 51
SQ FT: 250,000
SALES (est): 50.8MM **Privately Held**
WEB: www.acmearchitecturalwalls.com
SIC: 3442 3444 3446 Metal doors; sheet metalwork; partitions & supports/studs, including accoustical systems

(G-1478)
ACME PARTS INC
901 Elton St (11208-5315)
PHONE..................................718 649-1750
Allan Rodolitz, *President*
EMP: 26
SQ FT: 20,000
SALES (est): 3.3MM **Privately Held**
WEB: www.acmeparts.com
SIC: 3432 Plumbers' brass goods: drain cocks, faucets, spigots, etc.

(G-1479)
ACME SMOKED FISH CORP (PA)
30 Gem St 56 (11222-2804)
PHONE..................................954 942-5598
Eric Caslow, *Ch of Bd*
Mark Brownstein, *Vice Pres*
David Caslow, *Vice Pres*
Robert Caslow, *Vice Pres*
Eduardo Carbajosa, *CFO*
◆ EMP: 100
SQ FT: 70,000
SALES (est): 23.2MM **Privately Held**
WEB: www.acmesmokedfish.com
SIC: 2091 Fish, smoked; fish, cured

(G-1480)
ACTIVE WORLD SOLUTIONS INC
Also Called: M/Wbe
609 Fountain Ave (11208-6006)
PHONE..................................718 922-9404
Alvaro Vazquez, *President*
Maria Vazquez, *Principal*
▲ EMP: 6
SALES (est): 696.9K **Privately Held**
SIC: 2759 2395 7389 Screen printing; embroidery & art needlework; advertising, promotional & trade show services

(G-1481)
ADAR MEDICAL UNIFORM LLC
307 Richardson St (11222-5709)
PHONE..................................718 935-1197
Mayer Teitelbauml, *Owner*
Rachel Jacobs, *VP Sales*
Tzvi Novak, *Comms Mgr*
▲ EMP: 10
SALES (est): 891.5K **Privately Held**
SIC: 2337 2326 Uniforms, except athletic: women's, misses' & juniors'; medical & hospital uniforms, men's

(G-1482)
ADEL ROOTSTEIN (USA) INC
145 18th St (11215-5313)
PHONE..................................718 499-5650
Patty Marino, *Manager*
EMP: 42
SQ FT: 16,572
SALES (corp-wide): 116.3MM **Privately Held**
SIC: 3999 Mannequins

HQ: Adel Rootstein (Usa) Inc
205 W 19th St
New York NY
212 645-2020

(G-1483)
ADIR PUBLISHING CO
1212 36th St (11218-2010)
PHONE..................................718 633-9437
Matt Fef, *Owner*
EMP: 10
SALES: 910K **Privately Held**
WEB: www.a1skullcap.com
SIC: 2731 Books: publishing & printing

(G-1484)
ADRIATIC WOOD PRODUCTS INC
1994 Industrial Park Rd (11207-3335)
PHONE..................................718 922-4621
Anthony Grbic, *President*
John Grbic, *Vice Pres*
John Grisie, *CIO*
Miljenka Grbic, *Admin Sec*
▲ EMP: 38
SQ FT: 80,000
SALES (est): 4.5MM **Privately Held**
WEB: www.adriaticwood.com
SIC: 2431 Moldings, wood: unfinished & prefinished

(G-1485)
ADS-N-COLOR INC
20 Jay St Ste 530 (11201-8324)
PHONE..................................718 797-0900
Anthony Masi, *President*
Nicholas Masi, *Vice Pres*
EMP: 50 EST: 1971
SQ FT: 5,000
SALES (est): 3.5MM **Privately Held**
SIC: 2752 Commercial printing, offset

(G-1486)
ADSMAIN LLC
1072 Bedford Ave Pmb 107 (11216-1116)
PHONE..................................347 560-5060
David Pereplyotchik, *CEO*
Andrew Rush, *Accounts Mgr*
Vlad Troy, *Senior Mgr*
EMP: 8
SALES (est): 900K **Privately Held**
SIC: 2741

(G-1487)
ADVANCE CHEMICALS USA INC
1230 57th St (11219-4523)
PHONE..................................718 633-1030
Heldon Eross, *President*
EMP: 4
SQ FT: 2,000
SALES (est): 1MM **Privately Held**
SIC: 3087 Custom compound purchased resins

(G-1488)
ADVANCED READY MIX CORP
239 Ingraham St (11237-1512)
PHONE..................................718 497-5020
Rocco Mancione, *President*
EMP: 17
SALES (est): 2.8MM **Privately Held**
SIC: 3273 Ready-mixed concrete

(G-1489)
ADVANCED TRANSIT MIX CORP
610 Johnson Ave (11237-1312)
PHONE..................................718 497-5020
Milo Silberstein, *Principal*
EMP: 5
SALES (est): 259.6K **Privately Held**
SIC: 3273 Ready-mixed concrete

(G-1490)
ADVANTAGE WHOLESALE SUPPLY LLC
172 Empire Blvd Brooklyn (11225)
PHONE..................................718 284-5346
Sarah Ahmaz, *Bookkeeper*
Sruli Leader, *Mktg Dir*
David Smetana, *Mgr*
EMP: 55
SALES (est): 10.2MM **Privately Held**
SIC: 3429 Manufactured hardware (general)

▲ = Import ▼ = Export
◆ = Import/Export

(G-1491)
AEON AMERICA INC
66 Jay St Ste 201 (11201-8359)
PHONE..................................914 584-0275
Paul Hains, *President*
Kellen Quinn, *Director*
EMP: 8
SALES (est): 306.3K **Privately Held**
SIC: 2721 Magazines: publishing only, not printed on site

(G-1492)
AESTHONICS INC
Also Called: Remains Lighting
21 Belvidere St Fl 3 (11206-4501)
PHONE..................................646 723-2463
David Callegaros, *President*
Jerod Hugghins, *Manager*
▲ **EMP:** 100
SQ FT: 50,000
SALES (est): 15.9MM **Privately Held**
SIC: 3645 3646 Residential lighting fixtures; commercial indusl & institutional electric lighting fixtures

(G-1493)
AFRO TIMES NEWSPAPER
Also Called: New American
1195 Atlantic Ave (11216-2709)
P.O. Box 160397 (11216-0397)
PHONE..................................718 636-9500
Tom Watkins, *Owner*
▲ **EMP:** 10
SQ FT: 7,500
SALES (est): 341.1K **Privately Held**
WEB: www.newamerican.com
SIC: 2711 Newspapers

(G-1494)
AGE MANUFACTURERS INC
10624 Avenue D (11236-1910)
PHONE..................................718 927-0048
Yosel Avtzon, *President*
▲ **EMP:** 65 **EST:** 1958
SQ FT: 43,000
SALES (est): 5.6MM **Privately Held**
SIC: 3999 3131 2339 2337 Hair & hair-based products; footwear cut stock; trimmings (leather), shoe; scarves, hoods, headbands, etc.: women's; women's & misses' suits & coats

(G-1495)
AIR FLOW PUMP CORP
Also Called: Air Flow Pump Supply
8412 Foster Ave (11236-3205)
PHONE..................................718 241-2800
Joseph Weinstock, *President*
David Weinstock, *Vice Pres*
EMP: 8
SQ FT: 6,000
SALES (est): 1.5MM **Privately Held**
SIC: 3561 5084 Pumps & pumping equipment; water pumps (industrial)

(G-1496)
AIR SKATE & AIR JUMP CORP (PA)
Also Called: Solo
2208 E 5th St (11223-4827)
P.O. Box 7453, New York (10116-7453)
PHONE..................................212 967-1201
Morris Tawil, *CEO*
▲ **EMP:** 12
SALES (est): 6.2MM **Privately Held**
SIC: 3143 5139 Men's footwear, except athletic; footwear, athletic

(G-1497)
AJMADISON CORP
3605 13th Ave (11218-3707)
PHONE..................................718 532-1800
Michael Gross, *Ch of Bd*
Matthew Ortiz, *Editor*
Robert Zuckerman, *CFO*
Jacob Dahan, *Sales Staff*
◆ **EMP:** 55
SALES (est): 17.3MM **Privately Held**
SIC: 3639 7389 Major kitchen appliances, except refrigerators & stoves;

(G-1498)
ALADDIN BAKERS INC (PA)
240 25th St (11232-1338)
PHONE..................................718 499-1818
Joseph Ayoub, *President*
Ed Curran, *Production*
Jennifer McBride, *Purch Mgr*
Wendy Perez, *Sales Associate*
Barbara Adams, *Office Mgr*
EMP: 125
SALES (est): 26.8MM **Privately Held**
WEB: www.aladdinbakers.com
SIC: 2051 Bread, all types (white, wheat, rye, etc): fresh or frozen

(G-1499)
ALBERT KEMPERLE INC
890 E 51st St (11203-6736)
PHONE..................................718 629-1084
Albert Kemperle, *Owner*
EMP: 21
SALES (corp-wide): 182MM **Privately Held**
SIC: 3465 Body parts, automobile: stamped metal
PA: Albert Kemperle, Inc.
8400 New Horizons Blvd
Amityville NY 11701
631 841-1241

(G-1500)
ALBEST METAL STAMPING CORP
1 Kent Ave (11249-1000)
PHONE..................................718 388-6000
Alexander Fischer, *President*
Nathan Hirsch, *Corp Secy*
Yakov Fischer, *Vice Pres*
Cheryl Francis, *Buyer*
▲ **EMP:** 65
SQ FT: 120,000
SALES (est): 14.9MM **Privately Held**
WEB: www.albest.com
SIC: 3469 3364 3089 3496 Stamping metal for the trade; nonferrous die-castings except aluminum; casting of plastic; miscellaneous fabricated wire products; aluminum die-castings

(G-1501)
ALBRIZIO INC
Also Called: Albrizio Couture
257 Varet St Ste Mgmt (11206-3859)
PHONE..................................212 719-5290
David Cicalese, *Chairman*
Ann Albrizio, *Executive*
EMP: 6 **EST:** 2010
SALES (est): 657.5K **Privately Held**
SIC: 2353 Millinery

(G-1502)
ALDO FRUSTACCI IRON WORKS INC
165 27th St (11232-1624)
PHONE..................................718 768-0707
Aldo Frustaci, *President*
EMP: 10
SQ FT: 8,000
SALES (est): 1.3MM **Privately Held**
SIC: 3444 3441 3446 Sheet metalwork; fabricated structural metal; stairs, staircases, stair treads: prefabricated metal

(G-1503)
ALDOS IRON WORKS INC
75 Van Brunt St (11231-1428)
PHONE..................................718 834-0408
Enzo Frustaci, *President*
EMP: 7 **EST:** 1974
SQ FT: 2,700
SALES: 950K **Privately Held**
SIC: 3446 Architectural metalwork

(G-1504)
ALETA INDUSTRIES INC
40 Ash St (11222)
PHONE..................................718 349-0040
Zinovy Malinov, *President*
Michael Guitonowitz, *Vice Pres*
Alex Sandler, *Treasurer*
EMP: 18
SQ FT: 15,000
SALES (est): 2.9MM **Privately Held**
WEB: www.aletastjames.com
SIC: 3444 Sheet metalwork

(G-1505)
ALGEMEINER JOURNAL INC
508 Montgomery St (11225-3023)
P.O. Box 250746 (11225-0746)
PHONE..................................718 771-0400
Gershon Jacobson, *President*
Sagy Braun, *Manager*
EMP: 5
SALES (est): 374.5K **Privately Held**
WEB: www.algemeiner.com
SIC: 2711 Newspapers: publishing only, not printed on site

(G-1506)
ALL AMERICAN CONCRETE CORP
239 Ingraham St (11237-1512)
PHONE..................................718 497-3301
Walter Charles, *President*
Anne Kresse, *Vice Pres*
EMP: 4
SALES (est): 1.6MM **Privately Held**
SIC: 3271 Concrete block & brick

(G-1507)
ALL AMERICAN TRANSIT MIX CORP
46 Knickerbocker Ave (11237-1410)
PHONE..................................718 417-3654
Catherine Manzione, *President*
EMP: 9
SALES (est): 800K **Privately Held**
SIC: 3273 Ready-mixed concrete

(G-1508)
ALL OUT DIE CUTTING INC
49 Wyckoff Ave Ste 1 (11237-2650)
PHONE..................................718 346-6666
Abraham Katc, *President*
EMP: 25 **EST:** 1980
SQ FT: 20,000
SALES (est): 1.9MM **Privately Held**
SIC: 3544 3469 2891 2675 Special dies & tools; metal stampings; adhesives & sealants; die-cut paper & board

(G-1509)
ALL UNITED WINDOW CORP
97 Classon Ave (11205-1401)
PHONE..................................718 624-0490
Cooper Eng, *President*
EMP: 21
SQ FT: 10,000
SALES (est): 3.1MM **Privately Held**
WEB: www.allunitedwindow.com
SIC: 3442 5211 Storm doors or windows, metal; windows, storm: wood or metal

(G-1510)
ALLIED FOOD PRODUCTS INC
251 Saint Marks Ave (11238-3503)
P.O. Box 380305 (11238-0305)
PHONE..................................718 230-4227
Ernest Stern, *President*
David Weill, *Marketing Mgr*
Isaac Stern, *Director*
▲ **EMP:** 10
SQ FT: 10,000
SALES (est): 1.3MM **Privately Held**
WEB: www.alliedfoodproducts.com
SIC: 2034 2024 Dried & dehydrated soup mixes; pudding pops, frozen; gelatin pops, frozen

(G-1511)
ALLIED SAMPLE CARD CO INC
140 58th St Ste 7a (11220-2524)
PHONE..................................718 238-0523
Marc Trager, *President*
Thomas Firavanti, *Vice Pres*
EMP: 30 **EST:** 1938
SQ FT: 22,000
SALES (est): 1MM **Privately Held**
SIC: 2675 Cards, folders & mats: die-cut

(G-1512)
ALPHA INCORPORATED
265 80th St (11209-3611)
PHONE..................................718 765-1614
Michael Gerovich, *Owner*
EMP: 6 **EST:** 2010
SALES (est): 414.7K **Privately Held**
SIC: 3089 Identification cards, plastic

(G-1513)
ALPHA KNITTING MILLS INC
41 Varick Ave Ste Mgmt (11237-1521)
PHONE..................................718 628-6300
Rose Fuchs, *President*
Bernard Fried, *Corp Secy*
Alex Fried, *Vice Pres*
William Fried, *Vice Pres*
EMP: 15
SQ FT: 15,000
SALES (est): 1.2MM **Privately Held**
SIC: 2253 Knit outerwear mills

(G-1514)
ALPINE PAPER BOX CO INC
2246 Fulton St (11233-3306)
PHONE..................................718 345-4040
Anthony Caggiano, *President*
EMP: 30 **EST:** 1953
SQ FT: 15,000
SALES (est): 4.5MM **Privately Held**
SIC: 3499 2631 Boxes for packing & shipping, metal; paperboard mills

(G-1515)
ALTRONIX CORP
140 58th St Bldg A3w (11220-2521)
PHONE..................................718 567-8181
Jonathan Sohnis, *Ch of Bd*
Alan Forman, *President*
Thomas Chiantia, *Electrical Engi*
Gary Zatz, *Natl Sales Mgr*
Jessy Castro, *Sales Staff*
◆ **EMP:** 100
SQ FT: 52,000
SALES (est): 32.1MM **Privately Held**
SIC: 3699 3625 5063 Security control equipment & systems; control equipment, electric; burglar alarm systems

(G-1516)
AMBER BEVER INC
8604 Avenue M 1 (11236-4918)
PHONE..................................212 391-4911
Beverly Brown, *CEO*
Mark Brown, *President*
▲ **EMP:** 4
SQ FT: 1,500
SALES (est): 2MM **Privately Held**
SIC: 2339 Women's & misses' athletic clothing & sportswear

(G-1517)
AMBY INTERNATIONAL INC
1460 E 12th St (11230-6606)
PHONE..................................718 645-0964
Ben Wallerstein, *President*
▲ **EMP:** 5
SALES (est): 786.8K **Privately Held**
SIC: 2673 Plastic bags: made from purchased materials

(G-1518)
AMCO INTL MFG & DESIGN INC
10 Conselyea St (11211-2202)
PHONE..................................718 388-8668
Adam Milewski, *President*
EMP: 26
SALES: 950K **Privately Held**
SIC: 3691 Storage batteries

(G-1519)
AMERICAN ALMOND PDTS CO INC (PA)
103 Walworth St (11205-2807)
P.O. Box 5247, Parsippany NJ (07054-6247)
PHONE..................................718 875-8310
Victor Frumolt, *President*
Patrick Holsgrove, *Plant Engr*
▲ **EMP:** 77 **EST:** 1924
SQ FT: 23,000
SALES (est): 9MM **Privately Held**
SIC: 2087 2099 2068 Pastes, flavoring; almond pastes; salted & roasted nuts & seeds

(G-1520)
AMERICAN CRAFT JEWELERS INC (PA)
3611 14th Ave Ste 522 (11218-3750)
PHONE..................................718 972-0945
Stanley Grimstein, *President*
EMP: 9
SQ FT: 2,000

Brooklyn - Kings County (G-1521) GEOGRAPHIC SECTION

SALES: 8MM **Privately Held**
SIC: 3911 Jewelry, precious metal

(G-1521)
AMERICAN DIES INC
37 Provost St (11222-1813)
PHONE..................718 387-1900
Joel Lefkowitz, *President*
EMP: 14
SALES (est): 1.5MM **Privately Held**
SIC: 3544 Dies & die holders for metal cutting, forming, die casting

(G-1522)
AMERICAN INTL TRIMMING
80 39th St (11232-2604)
PHONE..................718 369-9643
Tony Wu, *President*
▲ EMP: 6
SQ FT: 32,000
SALES (est): 565.5K **Privately Held**
WEB: www.aiglifeus.com
SIC: 3089 3496 Clothes hangers, plastic; garment hangers, made from purchased wire

(G-1523)
AMERICAN LEATHER SPECIALTIES
87 34th St Unit 1 (11232-2009)
PHONE..................800 556-6488
Paul Weinberg, *President*
George Schuman, *Vice Pres*
Alan Weinberg, *Vice Pres*
Joel Weinberg, *Vice Pres*
Robert Weinberg, *Treasurer*
▲ EMP: 100 EST: 1931
SQ FT: 70,000
SALES (est): 7.9MM **Privately Held**
WEB: www.americanleatherspecialties.com
SIC: 2399 5199 Pet collars, leashes, etc.; non-leather; pet supplies

(G-1524)
AMERICAN MTAL STMPING SPINNING
72 N 15th St (11222-2802)
PHONE..................718 384-1500
Stephanie Eisenberg, *President*
EMP: 15
SALES (est): 1.7MM **Privately Held**
SIC: 3469 Stamping metal for the trade; spinning metal for the trade

(G-1525)
AMERICAN PACKAGE COMPANY INC
Also Called: Ampaco
226 Franklin St (11222-1382)
PHONE..................718 389-4444
Martin C Kofman, *President*
EMP: 40 EST: 1921
SQ FT: 120,000
SALES (est): 7.1MM **Privately Held**
SIC: 2652 3089 Setup paperboard boxes; boxes, plastic

(G-1526)
AMERICAN PRINT SOLUTIONS INC
561 President St (11215-1018)
PHONE..................718 246-7800
Steven Klein, *Branch Mgr*
EMP: 5
SALES (est): 343K
SALES (corp-wide): 3.9MM **Privately Held**
SIC: 2752 Commercial printing, offset
PA: American Print Solutions Inc.
    2233 Nostrand Ave Ste 7
    Brooklyn NY 11210
    718 208-2309

(G-1527)
AMERICAN PRINT SOLUTIONS INC (PA)
2233 Nostrand Ave Ste 7 (11210-3029)
PHONE..................718 208-2309
Erica Braun, *President*
Isaac Braun, *Vice Pres*
Malki Lipshitz, *Treasurer*
Israel Izzy Braun, *Finance Dir*
Israel I Braun, *Finance*
EMP: 5
SQ FT: 20,000

SALES (est): 3.9MM **Privately Held**
SIC: 2754 5112 Business forms: gravure printing; business forms

(G-1528)
AMERICAN WOOD COLUMN CORP
913 Grand St (11211-2785)
PHONE..................718 782-3163
Thomas Lupo, *President*
EMP: 8 EST: 1916
SQ FT: 12,000
SALES (est): 944.9K **Privately Held**
SIC: 2431 3299 Woodwork, interior & ornamental; ornamental & architectural plaster work

(G-1529)
AMIRAM DROR INC (PA)
Also Called: Black Hound
226 India St (11222-1804)
P.O. Box 170, Short Hills NJ (07078-0170)
PHONE..................212 979-9505
Amiram Dror, *President*
EMP: 16
SQ FT: 7,500
SALES: 1.8MM **Privately Held**
WEB: www.blackhoundny.com
SIC: 2051 2064 2066 2033 Bakery: wholesale or wholesale/retail combined; chocolate candy, except solid chocolate; chocolate bars, solid; chocolate candy, solid; fruits & fruit products in cans, jars, etc.; chocolate; canned goods: fruit, vegetables, seafood, meats, etc.; candy

(G-1530)
AMJ DOT LLC
Also Called: City Fashion, The
1726 E 7th St (11223-2216)
PHONE..................718 775-3288
Assaf Joseth, *CEO*
Assaf Joseph, *CEO*
Ruth Elmann, *COO*
David Yakobov, *CFO*
▲ EMP: 7
SQ FT: 1,200
SALES (est): 2.7MM **Privately Held**
SIC: 2335 5621 Women's, juniors' & misses' dresses; women's clothing stores

(G-1531)
AMPLE HILLS CREAMERY INC (PA)
305 Nevins St (11215-1015)
PHONE..................347 725-4061
Brian Smith, *CEO*
EMP: 28
SALES (est): 8.7MM **Privately Held**
SIC: 2024 Ice cream & frozen desserts

(G-1532)
AMPLE HILLS CREAMERY INC
623 Vanderbilt Ave (11238-3502)
PHONE..................718 809-1678
EMP: 47
SALES (corp-wide): 8.7MM **Privately Held**
SIC: 2024 Ice cream & frozen desserts
PA: Ample Hills Creamery, Inc.
    305 Nevins St
    Brooklyn NY 11215
    347 725-4061

(G-1533)
AMPLE HILLS HOLDINGS INC
305 Nevins St (11215-1015)
PHONE..................347 725-4061
Brian Smith, *CEO*
EMP: 9
SALES (est): 957.6K **Privately Held**
SIC: 2024 6719 Ice cream & frozen desserts; investment holding companies, except banks

(G-1534)
ANGEL-MADE IN HEAVEN INC
Also Called: 116 26 Street
116 26th St (11232-1405)
PHONE..................718 832-4778
Morris Dahan, *President*
EMP: 9
SQ FT: 29,800

SALES (corp-wide): 1.3MM **Privately Held**
WEB: www.angelmih.com
SIC: 2339 Women's & misses' outerwear
PA: Angel-Made In Heaven, Inc.
    525 Fashion Ave Rm 1710
    New York NY 10018
    212 869-5678

(G-1535)
ANIIWE INC
774 Rockaway Ave Apt 3k (11212-5830)
PHONE..................347 683-1891
Tamaris King, *President*
Tiffany King, *Principal*
EMP: 5
SALES (est): 318.9K **Privately Held**
SIC: 3961 5139 2679 Bracelets, except precious metal; shoe accessories; wallboard, decorated: made from purchased material

(G-1536)
ANNE TAINTOR INC
Also Called: ATI
137 Montague St (11201-3548)
PHONE..................718 483-9312
Anne Taintor, *President*
Nathan Janoff, *Vice Pres*
▲ EMP: 6
SALES (est): 643K **Privately Held**
WEB: www.annetaintor.com
SIC: 2771 2752 2678 7389 Greeting cards; post cards, picture: lithographed; poster & decal printing, lithographic; notebooks: made from purchased paper;

(G-1537)
ANNOINTED BUTY MINISTRIES LLC
1697 E 54th St (11234-3921)
P.O. Box 340437 (11234-0437)
PHONE..................646 867-3796
Rachel Ineus, *CEO*
EMP: 5
SALES (est): 235.7K **Privately Held**
SIC: 2721 Periodicals

(G-1538)
ANYAS LICORICE INC
1027 Grand St (11211-1748)
PHONE..................917 935-1916
Anya Skwarek, *Principal*
EMP: 7
SALES (est): 434.4K **Privately Held**
SIC: 2064 Candy & other confectionery products

(G-1539)
APEX AIRTRONICS INC (PA)
2465 Atlantic Ave (11207-2346)
P.O. Box 353, Woodmere (11598-0353)
PHONE..................718 485-8560
William Rosenblum, *President*
▲ EMP: 28 EST: 1948
SQ FT: 14,000
SALES (est): 4.9MM **Privately Held**
SIC: 3663 Radio broadcasting & communications equipment

(G-1540)
APEX REAL HOLDINGS INC
Also Called: Pak 21
1640 40th St Ste A (11218-5541)
PHONE..................877 725-2150
Mark Loewy, *President*
EMP: 8
SQ FT: 2,000
SALES (est): 105.2K **Privately Held**
WEB: www.pak21.com
SIC: 2392 Bags, garment storage: except paper or plastic film

(G-1541)
APOLLO WINDOWS & DOORS INC
1003 Metropolitan Ave (11211-2605)
PHONE..................718 386-3326
Hang Hsin Cheng, *President*
Wen Tsui Ping, *Admin Sec*
EMP: 9
SQ FT: 20,000

SALES (est): 1MM **Privately Held**
WEB: www.apollowindows.com
SIC: 2431 Doors & door parts & trim, wood; windows & window parts & trim, wood

(G-1542)
APPLE CORE ELECTRONICS INC
991 Flushing Ave (11206-4721)
PHONE..................718 628-4068
Michael Arnold, *President*
Gregory Arnold, *Vice Pres*
EMP: 11
SQ FT: 4,000
SALES (est): 1.8MM **Privately Held**
SIC: 3669 5065 Intercommunication systems, electric; intercommunication equipment, electronic

(G-1543)
APPLIED MINERALS INC (PA)
55 Washington St Ste 301 (11201-1077)
PHONE..................212 226-4265
Mario Concha, *Ch of Bd*
John F Levy, *Vice Ch Bd*
Andre Zeitoun, *President*
Christopher T Carney, *CFO*
William Gleeson, *General Counsel*
EMP: 11
SALES: 2.4MM **Publicly Held**
WEB: www.atlasmining.com
SIC: 1459 2816 Clays, except kaolin & ball; iron oxide pigments (ochers, siennas, umbers)

(G-1544)
APPSBIDDER INC
55 Clark St 772 (11201-2415)
PHONE..................917 880-4269
Oladapo Ajayi, *CEO*
EMP: 5
SALES (est): 166.2K **Privately Held**
SIC: 7372 Prepackaged Software Services

(G-1545)
APSCO SPORTS ENTERPRISES INC
Also Called: Abercrombie & Fitch
50th St & 1st Av Bg 57 F5 (11232)
PHONE..................718 965-9500
Philip Livoti, *President*
Phillip Livoti, *President*
Philip Di Pietro, *Vice Pres*
Vincent Dipietro, *Opers Mgr*
Christine De Chirico, *Controller*
▲ EMP: 60 EST: 1968
SQ FT: 30,000
SALES (est): 7.4MM **Privately Held**
SIC: 2396 Screen printing on fabric articles

(G-1546)
ARCHITCTRAL DSIGN ELEMENTS LLC
52 Box St (11222-1150)
PHONE..................718 218-7800
Alan Paulenoff, *Mng Member*
Tess Cross, *Manager*
EMP: 7
SALES: 850K **Privately Held**
SIC: 3083 Laminated plastics plate & sheet

(G-1547)
ARCHITECTURAL COATINGS INC
538 Johnson Ave (11237-1226)
PHONE..................718 418-9584
Nick Comaianni, *President*
Daniel France, *Vice Pres*
Margaret Karnick, *Admin Sec*
EMP: 18
SALES: 1.2MM **Privately Held**
SIC: 3599 Machine & other job shop work

(G-1548)
ARCTIC GLACIER NEWBURGH INC
335 Moffat St (11237-6408)
PHONE..................718 456-2013
Vincent Losquadro, *Branch Mgr*
EMP: 7
SALES (corp-wide): 3.6B **Publicly Held**
SIC: 2097 Manufactured ice

GEOGRAPHIC SECTION

Brooklyn - Kings County (G-1578)

HQ: Arctic Glacier Newburgh Inc.
225 Lake St
Newburgh NY 12550
845 561-0549

(G-1549)
ARES BOX LLC
63 Flushing Ave Unit 224 (11205-1073)
PHONE..................................718 858-8760
Mary Filippidis,
EMP: 85
SALES (est): 4.9MM **Privately Held**
SIC: 2671 Packaging paper & plastics film, coated & laminated

(G-1550)
ARES PRINTING AND PACKG CORP
Brooklyn Navy Yard Bldg (11205)
PHONE..................................718 858-8760
Mary Filippidis, *President*
Bob Filippidis, *Vice Pres*
George Filippidis, *Vice Pres*
Jerry Filippidis, *Vice Pres*
EMP: 125
SQ FT: 150,000
SALES (est): 16.6MM **Privately Held**
WEB: www.aresny.com
SIC: 2752 2653 Commercial printing, offset; corrugated & solid fiber boxes; boxes, corrugated: made from purchased materials; display items, corrugated: made from purchased materials

(G-1551)
ARIMED ORTHOTICS PROSTHETICS (PA)
302 Livingston St (11217-1002)
PHONE..................................718 875-8754
Steven Mirones, *President*
EMP: 14
SQ FT: 10,000
SALES (est): 3.4MM **Privately Held**
WEB: www.arimed.com
SIC: 3842 5661 5999 7251 Orthopedic appliances; shoes, orthopedic; orthopedic & prosthesis applications; shoe repair shop

(G-1552)
ARISTA STEEL DESIGNS CORP
788 3rd Ave (11232-1418)
PHONE..................................718 965-7077
Steve Viglis, *President*
EMP: 5
SALES: 1,000K **Privately Held**
SIC: 3449 Bars, concrete reinforcing: fabricated steel

(G-1553)
ARISTOCRAT LIGHTING INC
104 Halleck St (11231-2100)
PHONE..................................718 522-0003
Leon Gross, *President*
Michael Gross, *Vice Pres*
EMP: 12 **EST:** 1983
SQ FT: 18,000
SALES (est): 1.5MM **Privately Held**
SIC: 3646 Commercial indusl & institutional electric lighting fixtures

(G-1554)
ARNOLDS MEAT FOOD PRODUCTS
274 Heyward St (11206-2994)
PHONE..................................718 384-8071
Sheldon Dosik, *President*
Jason Judd, *Vice Pres*
EMP: 25
SALES (est): 3.8MM **Privately Held**
SIC: 2013 Sausages from purchased meat

(G-1555)
AROMASONG USA INC
35 Frost St (11211-1202)
PHONE..................................718 838-9669
Sam Neustein, *President*
EMP: 10
SALES (est): 599.5K **Privately Held**
SIC: 2844 2099 Bath salts; seasonings & spices

(G-1556)
ART BEDI-MAKKY FOUNDRY CORP
227 India St Ste 31 (11222-1803)
PHONE..................................718 383-4191
Istvan Makky, *President*
EMP: 8
SQ FT: 7,500
SALES: 400K **Privately Held**
SIC: 3366 Castings (except die): bronze

(G-1557)
ART DIGITAL TECHNOLOGIES LLC
85 Debevoise Ave (11222-5608)
PHONE..................................646 649-4820
Dan Bright,
EMP: 11
SALES (est): 1.2MM **Privately Held**
WEB: www.artdigitaltech.com
SIC: 2752 7336 Commercial printing, lithographic; commercial art & graphic design

(G-1558)
ARTEMIS STUDIOS INC
Also Called: Diane Artemis Studios
34 35th St Ste 2b (11232-2212)
PHONE..................................718 788-6022
Martin Kurant, *President*
EMP: 70 **EST:** 1964
SQ FT: 30,000
SALES (est): 5MM **Privately Held**
WEB: www.artemisstudios.com
SIC: 3999 3645 Shades, lamp or candle; residential lighting fixtures

(G-1559)
ARTHUR GLUCK SHIRTMAKERS INC
871 E 24th St (11210-2821)
PHONE..................................212 755-8165
Michael Spitzer, *President*
EMP: 10
SALES: 1.5MM **Privately Held**
WEB: www.shirtcreations.com
SIC: 2321 Men's & boys' dress shirts

(G-1560)
ASA MANUFACTURING INC
3611 14th Ave (11218-3773)
PHONE..................................718 853-3033
Alex Klein, *President*
Sam Hershkovich, *Vice Pres*
EMP: 20
SQ FT: 4,000
SALES (est): 3.8MM **Privately Held**
WEB: www.par4shelters.com
SIC: 3915 Jewelry parts, unassembled

(G-1561)
ASAP RACK RENTAL INC
33 35th St St5 (11232-2022)
PHONE..................................718 499-4495
David Fox, *President*
EMP: 7
SQ FT: 6,000
SALES: 969.3K **Privately Held**
SIC: 2542 3537 5051 5021 Garment racks; except wood; industrial trucks & tractors; pipe & tubing, steel; racks

(G-1562)
ASHCO MANAGEMENT INC
1937 Mcdonald Ave (11223-1805)
PHONE..................................212 960-8428
Isaac Ashkenazie, *CEO*
EMP: 10 **EST:** 2011
SQ FT: 5,000
SALES (est): 396.5K **Privately Held**
SIC: 3732 5023 5731 Kayaks, building & repairing; kitchen tools & utensils; radio, television & electronic stores

(G-1563)
ASHLEY RESIN CORP
1171 59th St (11219-4909)
P.O. Box 190733 (11219-0733)
PHONE..................................718 851-8111
Nathan Freedman, *President*
Misem Moskobics, *Admin Sec*
▼ **EMP:** 5
SALES (est): 1.3MM **Privately Held**
WEB: www.ashleypoly.com
SIC: 2821 Plastics materials & resins

(G-1564)
ASPECT PRINTING INC
904 E 51st St (11203-6736)
PHONE..................................347 789-4284
Olga Belenkaya, *Ch of Bd*
Anatoly Fusman, *Manager*
EMP: 20
SALES (est): 3MM **Privately Held**
SIC: 2711 2759 Commercial printing & newspaper publishing combined; magazines: printing

(G-1565)
ASTRO LABEL & TAG LTD
5820 Fort Hamilton Pkwy (11219)
PHONE..................................718 435-4474
Sheldon Kustin, *President*
Lew Kustin, *Vice Pres*
Ellis Amies, *Admin Sec*
EMP: 5
SQ FT: 5,000
SALES: 600K **Privately Held**
SIC: 2759 Flexographic printing; tags: printing; labels & seals: printing

(G-1566)
AT COPY INC
Also Called: Save Mor Copy Center
25 Flatbush Ave (11217-1101)
PHONE..................................718 624-6136
Bartholemew Tesoriero, *President*
Roberta Tesoriero, *Vice Pres*
EMP: 9
SQ FT: 3,300
SALES (est): 1.6MM **Privately Held**
SIC: 2752 Commercial printing, offset

(G-1567)
ATALLA HANDBAGS INC
559 79th St (11209-3709)
PHONE..................................718 965-5500
Sami Atalla, *President*
EMP: 4
SQ FT: 1,300
SALES (est): 1.1MM **Privately Held**
SIC: 3171 Handbags, women's

(G-1568)
ATELIER VIOLLET CORP
505 Driggs Ave (11211-2020)
PHONE..................................718 782-1727
Jean Paul Viollet, *President*
EMP: 6
SQ FT: 7,500
SALES (est): 778.7K **Privately Held**
WEB: www.atelierviollet.com
SIC: 2511 5712 2499 Wood household furniture; custom made furniture, except cabinets; decorative wood & woodwork

(G-1569)
ATERES PUBLISHING & BK BINDERY
Also Called: Ateres Book Binding
845 Bedford Ave (11205-2801)
PHONE..................................718 935-9355
Sam Greenfield, *President*
Simon Pollak, *Sales Executive*
Joseph Greenfield, *Admin Sec*
▲ **EMP:** 14 **EST:** 1975
SQ FT: 20,000
SALES (est): 1.6MM **Privately Held**
SIC: 2789 2731 Bookbinding & repairing: trade, edition, library, etc.; book publishing

(G-1570)
ATLANTIC ELECTRONIC TECH LLC
Also Called: Atlantic Electronic Technology
285 5th Ave Apt 2b (11215-2421)
PHONE..................................800 296-2177
Absalam Ottafa,
▲ **EMP:** 5
SQ FT: 1,500
SALES: 500K **Privately Held**
SIC: 3699 Security control equipment & systems

(G-1571)
ATLANTIC STAIRS CORP
Also Called: Design Interiors
284a Meserole St (11206-2242)
PHONE..................................718 417-8818
Stanley Majkut, *President*

Elizabeth Wozniak, *Admin Sec*
EMP: 6
SQ FT: 3,000
SALES (est): 797.4K **Privately Held**
WEB: www.atlanticstairs.com
SIC: 2431 Doors & door parts & trim, wood; staircases, stairs & railings

(G-1572)
ATLAS COATINGS GROUP CORP (PA)
4808 Farragut Rd (11203-6612)
PHONE..................................718 469-8787
Ben Berman, *CEO*
Jeff Berman, *President*
Lance Berman, *Vice Pres*
EMP: 75 **EST:** 2001
SALES (est): 4.7MM **Privately Held**
SIC: 2851 5231 Paints & paint additives; paint

(G-1573)
ATTIAS OVEN CORP
Also Called: Cannon Co
926 3rd Ave (11232-2002)
PHONE..................................718 499-0145
Simon Attias, *President*
Carrie Gorelick, *Manager*
▲ **EMP:** 6
SQ FT: 5,000
SALES (est): 1MM **Privately Held**
WEB: www.attiasco.com
SIC: 3589 Commercial cooking & food-warming equipment

(G-1574)
AUDIBLE DIFFERENCE INC
Also Called: ADI
110 8th St (11215-3116)
PHONE..................................212 662-4848
Erich R Bechtel, *President*
EMP: 25
SALES (est): 3.4MM **Privately Held**
SIC: 3699 Electric sound equipment
PA: Audible Difference, Inc.
110 8th St
Brooklyn NY 11215

(G-1575)
AUDIBLE DIFFERENCE INC (PA)
Also Called: Audible Difference Lnc
110 8th St (11215-3116)
PHONE..................................212 662-4848
Erich R Bechtel, *President*
EMP: 2
SALES (est): 2.8MM **Privately Held**
WEB: www.adigroup.net
SIC: 3699 Electric sound equipment

(G-1576)
AUDIO TECHNOLOGY NEW YORK INC
Also Called: Audiology
129 31st St (11232-1824)
PHONE..................................718 369-7528
Alan Safdiah, *Senior VP*
Charles Safdiah, *CFO*
Jamie Safdiah, *Director*
▲ **EMP:** 10
SQ FT: 30,000
SALES (est): 1.7MM **Privately Held**
SIC: 3651 Mfg Home Audio/Video Equipment

(G-1577)
AZURRX BIOPHARMA INC
760 Parkside Ave Ste 304 (11226-1784)
PHONE..................................646 699-7855
Edward J Borkowski, *Ch of Bd*
Johan M Spoor, *President*
Maged Shenouda, *CFO*
James E Pennington, *Chief Mktg Ofcr*
Alastair Riddell, *Bd of Directors*
EMP: 13
SQ FT: 687
SALES (est): 2.1MM **Privately Held**
SIC: 2834 Pharmaceutical preparations

(G-1578)
B & B SWEATER MILLS INC (PA)
1160 Flushing Ave (11237-1747)
PHONE..................................718 456-8693
Berl Biderman, *President*
Sol Biderman, *Corp Secy*
▲ **EMP:** 10 **EST:** 1954
SQ FT: 42,000

Brooklyn - Kings County (G-1579)   **GEOGRAPHIC SECTION**

SALES (est): 975.4K Privately Held
SIC: 2253 5137 Sweaters & sweater coats, knit; sweaters, women's & children's

(G-1579)
B & K DYE CUTTING INC
245 Varet St (11206-3823)
PHONE..............................718 497-5216
EMP: 6
SQ FT: 5,000
SALES: 300K Privately Held
SIC: 2261 Dyeing & Cutting Materials

(G-1580)
B D B TYPEWRITER SUPPLY WORKS
6215 14th Ave (11219-5338)
PHONE..............................718 232-4800
Albert Brauner, Owner
EMP: 25 EST: 1948
SQ FT: 3,160
SALES (est): 1.3MM Privately Held
SIC: 2521 2752 Wood office furniture; commercial printing, lithographic

(G-1581)
BABY CENTRAL LLC
2436 Mcdonald Ave (11223-5231)
PHONE..............................718 372-2229
Mike Seda, Principal
EMP: 6 EST: 2007
SALES (est): 620K Privately Held
SIC: 2023 Baby formulas

(G-1582)
BACKSTAGE LLC (PA)
45 Main St Ste 416 (11201-1093)
PHONE..............................212 493-4243
James Reynolds, President
Lisa Hamil, Editor
Briana Rodriguez, Editor
Michael Rieck, Senior VP
Luke Crowe, Vice Pres
EMP: 26
SALES (est): 11.5MM Privately Held
SIC: 2721 Magazines: publishing only, not printed on site

(G-1583)
BADER ENTERPRISE INC
Also Called: Better Candy Company
115 27th St (11232-1504)
PHONE..............................718 965-9434
Younis Bader, President
Fuad Bader, Vice Pres
EMP: 8
SQ FT: 9,000
SALES (est): 993.6K Privately Held
SIC: 2064 Candy & other confectionery products

(G-1584)
BANNER SMOKED FISH INC
2715 W 15th St (11224-2705)
PHONE..............................718 449-1992
Abraham A Attias, Ch of Bd
Eddie Flores, Asst Controller
Alan Levitz, Admin Sec
▲ EMP: 54
SQ FT: 20,000
SALES (est): 6.3MM Privately Held
SIC: 2091 Fish, smoked

(G-1585)
BANNERBOY CORPORATION
20 Jay St Ste 432 (11201-8311)
PHONE..............................646 691-6524
Katie Holliday McVeay, Manager
EMP: 6
SALES (est): 209.6K Privately Held
SIC: 3993 Neon signs

(G-1586)
BARCLAY BROWN CORP
47 Lancaster Ave (11223-5533)
PHONE..............................718 376-7166
Gladys Hedaya, President
Maurice Hedaya, Vice Pres
EMP: 10
SALES (est): 792.5K Privately Held
WEB: www.barclaybrowncorp.com
SIC: 3161 3086 Satchels; packaging & shipping plastic, foamed plastic

(G-1587)
BASS OIL & CHEMICAL LLC
136 Morgan Ave (11237-1220)
PHONE..............................718 628-4444
Leonard Roz, CEO
EMP: 17
SALES (est): 1.5MM Privately Held
SIC: 1389 Oil field services

(G-1588)
BASS OIL COMPANY INC
136 Morgan Ave (11237-1220)
PHONE..............................718 628-4444
Gregory Bass, Ch of Bd
EMP: 30
SQ FT: 28,000
SALES (est): 6.3MM Privately Held
SIC: 2899 5172 Antifreeze compounds; engine fuels & oils

(G-1589)
BATAMPTE PICKLE PRODUCTS INC (PA)
77 Brooklyn Terminal Mkt (11236-1511)
PHONE..............................718 251-2100
Barry Silberstein, President
Howard Silberstein, Corp Secy
Scott Silberstein, Vice Pres
EMP: 60 EST: 1955
SQ FT: 12,000
SALES (est): 8.7MM Privately Held
SIC: 2035 5149 Pickles, vinegar; pickles, preserves, jellies & jams

(G-1590)
BATOR BINTOR INC
42 Delevan St (11231-1808)
PHONE..............................347 546-6503
Max Connolly, President
EMP: 10
SALES (est): 528.9K Privately Held
WEB: www.batorbintor.com
SIC: 2431 2541 1521 Windows & window parts & trim, wood; cabinets, lockers & shelving; general remodeling, single-family houses

(G-1591)
BAYIT HOME AUTOMATION CORP
2299 Mcdonald Ave (11223-4737)
PHONE..............................973 988-2638
Eliav Scaba, CEO
Marco Scaba, Principal
EMP: 30
SQ FT: 180,000
SALES (est): 4.3MM Privately Held
SIC: 3651 Video camera-audio recorders, household use

(G-1592)
BEDESSEE IMPORTS LTD
140 Varick Ave (11237-1219)
PHONE..............................718 272-1300
Verman Bedessee, Branch Mgr
EMP: 20 Privately Held
SIC: 2098 Noodles (e.g. egg, plain & water), dry
PA: Bedessee Imports Ltd
2 Golden Gate Crt
Scarborough ON M1P 3
416 292-2400

(G-1593)
BEDFORD DOWNING GLASS
220 Ingraham St Ste 2 (11237-1514)
PHONE..............................718 418-6409
Ingo Williams, Owner
▼ EMP: 9
SQ FT: 25,000
SALES (est): 605K Privately Held
SIC: 3229 5999 Glassware, art or decorative; art, picture frames & decorations

(G-1594)
BEIS MOSHIACH INC
744 Eastern Pkwy (11213-3409)
PHONE..............................718 778-8000
Menachem Hendel, President
Naftoli Greenfield, Admin Sec
EMP: 35
SALES (est): 3.3MM Privately Held
SIC: 2759 Publication printing

(G-1595)
BELTRAN ASSOCIATES INC
1133 E 35th St Ste 1 (11210-4243)
PHONE..............................718 252-2996
Michael Beltran, Ch of Bd
Ichael Beltran, Ch of Bd
Michael R Beltran, Ch of Bd
Atanu Bose, Technology
EMP: 40
SQ FT: 10,000
SALES (est): 9.1MM Privately Held
WEB: www.beltranassociates.com
SIC: 3564 Air purification equipment

(G-1596)
BELTRAN TECHNOLOGIES INC
1133 E 35th St (11210-4243)
PHONE..............................718 338-3311
Michael R Beltran, Ch of Bd
▲ EMP: 25
SALES (est): 4.9MM Privately Held
SIC: 3564 8711 Precipitators, electrostatic; engineering services

(G-1597)
BENCHMARK FURNITURE MFG
300 Dewitt Ave (11236-1912)
PHONE..............................718 257-4707
Sandy Marks, President
▲ EMP: 70
SQ FT: 50,000
SALES (est): 8.1MM Privately Held
WEB: www.benchmarkfurnituremfg.com
SIC: 2511 Wood household furniture

(G-1598)
BENNETT MULTIMEDIA INC
1087 Utica Ave (11203-5318)
PHONE..............................718 629-1454
David Newman, President
EMP: 10
SQ FT: 4,000
SALES (est): 870K Privately Held
SIC: 2752 Commercial printing, lithographic

(G-1599)
BENNETT PRINTING CORPORATION
1087 Utica Ave (11203-5390)
PHONE..............................718 629-1454
Lawrence Newman, President
David Newman, Vice Pres
Ellen Newman, Treasurer
EMP: 10
SQ FT: 5,800
SALES: 950K Privately Held
SIC: 2752 Commercial printing, offset

(G-1600)
BENSON MILLS INC (PA)
140 58th St Ste 7j (11220-2538)
PHONE..............................718 236-6743
Keith Levy, Ch of Bd
Gabriel Levy, President
Ralph Levy, Vice Pres
◆ EMP: 22
SQ FT: 5,000
SALES (est): 2.4MM Privately Held
SIC: 2299 Fabrics: linen, jute, hemp, ramie

(G-1601)
BERKMAN BROS INC
538 Johnson Ave (11237-1226)
PHONE..............................718 782-1827
Gerald R Berkman, President
▲ EMP: 21
SQ FT: 20,000
SALES (est): 1.6MM Privately Held
WEB: www.berkmanbrothers.com
SIC: 3471 3479 Electroplating of metals or formed products; lacquering of metal products

(G-1602)
BEST BOILERS INC
2402 Neptune Ave (11224-2316)
P.O. Box 240607 (11224-0607)
PHONE..............................718 372-4210
Aaron Ganguli, President
Raymond Miele, Treasurer
EMP: 10

SALES (est): 815K Privately Held
WEB: www.bestboilers.com
SIC: 3433 Boilers, low-pressure heating: steam or hot water

(G-1603)
BEST MEDICAL WEAR LTD
34 Franklin Ave Ste 301 (11205-1222)
P.O. Box 50221 (11205-0221)
PHONE..............................718 858-5544
Herman Schwartz, CEO
Gitty Schwartz, President
Gittel Schwartz, President
▲ EMP: 8 EST: 1997
SALES (est): 2.5MM Privately Held
WEB: www.bestmedicalwear.com
SIC: 2326 Work uniforms; medical & hospital uniforms, men's

(G-1604)
BESTEC CONCEPT INC
Also Called: Maxivision
140 58th St Ste 8d (11220-2560)
PHONE..............................718 937-5848
Helen M Han, President
EMP: 6
SALES (est): 841.4K Privately Held
SIC: 2326 2311 2337 2339 Work uniforms; men's & boys' uniforms; military uniforms, men's & youths': purchased materials; policemen's uniforms: made from purchased materials; uniforms, except athletic: women's, misses' & juniors'; service apparel, washable: women's

(G-1605)
BESTMADE PRINTING LLC
Also Called: B M Printing
205 Keap St Apt 2 (11211-7970)
PHONE..............................718 384-0719
Shia Ostreicher, Owner
EMP: 10
SALES (est): 1MM Privately Held
SIC: 2759 Commercial printing

(G-1606)
BETTER FRESH CORP
41 Varick Ave (11237-1521)
PHONE..............................718 628-3682
Hamish McCall, Finance Dir
EMP: 5
SQ FT: 600
SALES (est): 169.2K Privately Held
SIC: 2087 Beverage bases

(G-1607)
BEVERAGE WORKS INCORPORATED
70 Hamilton Ave 8 (11231-1305)
PHONE..............................718 834-0500
Steve Dimario, Opers Mgr
Pat Mezzatesta, Office Mgr
EMP: 6
SALES (est): 426.9K Privately Held
SIC: 2086 Carbonated beverages, nonalcoholic: bottled & canned

(G-1608)
BEVERAGE WORKS NY INC
70 Hamilton Ave 8 (11231-1305)
PHONE..............................718 812-2034
Gerald Ponfiglsione, Principal
EMP: 20 Privately Held
WEB: www.beverageworks.com
SIC: 2086 Bottled & canned soft drinks
PA: The Beverage Works Nj Inc
1800 State Route 34 # 203
Wall Township NJ 07719

(G-1609)
BIEN CUIT LLC
120 Smith St (11201-6217)
PHONE..............................718 852-0200
Alex Copeland, Office Mgr
David Golper, Mng Member
Elyse Hinojosa, Manager
EMP: 41 EST: 2011
SALES: 3MM Privately Held
SIC: 2051 Bakery: wholesale or wholesale/retail combined

(G-1610)
BIG APPLE WELDING SUPPLY
236 47th St (11220-1010)
PHONE..............................718 439-3959
Vincent Pampillonia, President

GEOGRAPHIC SECTION

Brooklyn - Kings County (G-1642)

EMP: 5
SALES (est): 691.7K **Privately Held**
SIC: 7692 Automotive welding

(G-1611)
BIGROW PAPER MFG CORP
Also Called: Bigrow Paper Product
930 Bedford Ave (11205-4502)
PHONE..................718 624-4439
David Greenwald, *President*
▲ EMP: 10
SQ FT: 13,000
SALES (est): 1.4MM **Privately Held**
SIC: 2621 Business form paper; envelope paper

(G-1612)
BILLIE-ANN PLASTICS PKG CORP
360 Troutman St (11237-2614)
PHONE..................718 497-3409
Toll Free:..................888 -
William Rubinstein, *President*
Joan Rubinstein, *Vice Pres*
▲ EMP: 30
SQ FT: 15,000
SALES (est): 5.6MM **Privately Held**
WEB: www.billieannplastics.com
SIC: 3089 Plastic containers, except foam

(G-1613)
BILLING CODING AND PRTG INC
455 Grant Ave (11208-3056)
PHONE..................718 827-9409
Omirta Rickheeram, *President*
EMP: 7
SALES (est): 673.1K **Privately Held**
SIC: 2752 Commercial printing, lithographic

(G-1614)
BINAH MAGAZINES CORP
207 Foster Ave (11230-2195)
PHONE..................718 305-5200
Ruth Lichtenstein, *Principal*
Mendy Loevy, *Asst Controller*
Chanie Berger, *Marketing Staff*
EMP: 50
SALES (est): 698K **Privately Held**
SIC: 2721 Magazines: publishing & printing

(G-1615)
BINDLE AND KEEP
47 Hall St Ste 109 (11205-1315)
PHONE..................917 740-5002
Daniel Friedman, *Owner*
EMP: 8 EST: 2013
SALES (est): 680K **Privately Held**
SIC: 2311 2337 Suits, men's & boys': made from purchased materials; women's & misses' suits & skirts

(G-1616)
BIOBAT INC (PA)
450 Clarkson Ave Msc129 (11203-2012)
PHONE..................718 270-1011
Eva Cramer, *President*
EMP: 1 EST: 2011
SQ FT: 500
SALES (est): 1.7MM **Privately Held**
SIC: 2833 Medicinal chemicals

(G-1617)
BKLYNFAVORS PARTY PRINT
49 Sheridan Ave (11208-3022)
PHONE..................718 277-0233
Dashawn Gables, *Sales Staff*
EMP: 5 EST: 2014
SALES (est): 366.3K **Privately Held**
SIC: 2752 Commercial printing, lithographic

(G-1618)
BLACKBIRDS BROOKLYN LLC
Also Called: Four &TWenty Blackbirds
597 Sackett St (11217-3116)
PHONE..................917 362-4080
Kathryn Morrissette, *Administration*
Emily Elsen,
Melissa Elsen,
EMP: 25
SALES (est): 979.1K **Privately Held**
SIC: 2051 Bakery: wholesale or wholesale/retail combined

(G-1619)
BLUE MARBLE ICE CREAM LLC
220 36th St Unit 33 (11232-2405)
PHONE..................718 858-5551
Alexis Miesen, *Co-Owner*
Jennie Dundas, *Mng Member*
Sarah Green, *Manager*
Vincent Biscaye, *Director*
EMP: 8
SALES (est): 1.2MM **Privately Held**
SIC: 2024 5451 Ice cream, bulk; ice cream (packaged)

(G-1620)
BLUE OCEAN FOOD TRADING LLC
154 42nd St (11232-3317)
PHONE..................718 689-4291
Guo Wen Lin, *Mng Member*
EMP: 6
SALES (est): 445.5K **Privately Held**
SIC: 2091 Canned & cured fish & seafoods

(G-1621)
BLUE SKY PLASTIC PRODUCTION
305 Johnson Ave (11206-2804)
PHONE..................718 366-3966
Bao Gui Zhuo, *CEO*
▲ EMP: 10
SALES (est): 1.5MM **Privately Held**
SIC: 3083 Plastic finished products, laminated

(G-1622)
BLUE STAR BEVERAGES CORP
1099 Flushing Ave (11237-1830)
PHONE..................718 381-3535
Albert Shtainer, *Principal*
▲ EMP: 9
SALES (est): 921.2K **Privately Held**
SIC: 2086 Carbonated beverages, nonalcoholic: bottled & canned

(G-1623)
BLUEBERRY KNITTING INC (PA)
138 Ross St (11211-7705)
PHONE..................718 599-6520
Phillip Werzberger, *President*
EMP: 2
SQ FT: 1,000
SALES (est): 2.2MM **Privately Held**
SIC: 2253 Sweaters & sweater coats, knit

(G-1624)
BNC INNOVATIVE WOODWORKING
555 Liberty Ave (11207-3109)
PHONE..................718 277-2800
Hyman Cassuto, *Owner*
EMP: 11
SQ FT: 11,202
SALES (est): 1.1MM **Privately Held**
SIC: 2431 Millwork

(G-1625)
BNEI ARAM SOBA INC
Also Called: Community Magazine
1616 Ocean Pkwy (11223-2144)
PHONE..................718 645-4460
Jack Cohen, *President*
Alan Epstein, *Opers Staff*
David Sitt, *Treasurer*
Max Sharp, *Controller*
EMP: 11
SQ FT: 8,000
SALES (est): 1.1MM **Privately Held**
WEB: www.communitym.com
SIC: 2721 Magazines: publishing only, not printed on site

(G-1626)
BNH LEAD EXAMINER CORP
199 Lee Ave Ste 481 (11211-8919)
PHONE..................718 807-1365
Naftali Burger, *Ch of Bd*
EMP: 6
SALES (est): 280K **Privately Held**
SIC: 2711 Newspapers, publishing & printing

(G-1627)
BODY BUILDERS INC
Also Called: Red Line Networx Screen Prtg
5518 3rd Ave (11220-2609)
PHONE..................718 492-7997
Richard Baez, *Ch of Bd*
EMP: 6
SALES (est): 565.7K **Privately Held**
SIC: 2759 Commercial printing

(G-1628)
BOOKLINKS PUBLISHING SVCS LLC
55 Washington St Ste 253c (11201-1073)
PHONE..................718 852-2116
Maria Villela, *President*
Jada Gorrell, *Project Mgr*
Nina Fielder, *Manager*
Jose Schettino, *Bd of Directors*
EMP: 6
SQ FT: 5,000
SALES (est): 2MM **Privately Held**
SIC: 2731 Textbooks: publishing only, not printed on site

(G-1629)
BOOKLYN ARTISTS ALLIANCE INC
140 58th St Bldg B-7g (11220-2521)
PHONE..................718 383-9621
Bridget Elmer, *President*
Chris Wilde, *President*
M Ober, *Business Mgr*
Mark Wagner, *Treasurer*
ARI Misfeldt, *Manager*
EMP: 5
SALES (est): 700K **Privately Held**
WEB: www.booklyn.org
SIC: 2731 Books: publishing & printing

(G-1630)
BRACCI IRONWORKS INC
1440 Utica Ave (11203-6617)
PHONE..................718 629-2374
Cory Bracci, *President*
Charlie Smith, *General Mgr*
Jonathan Bracci, *Vice Pres*
Michael Bracci, *Admin Sec*
EMP: 10
SQ FT: 9,000
SALES (est): 1.6MM **Privately Held**
SIC: 3446 7692 Stairs, staircases, stair treads: prefabricated metal; welding repair

(G-1631)
BRAGLEY MFG CO INC
Also Called: Bragley Shipg Carrying Cases
924 Bergen St (11238-3301)
PHONE..................718 622-7469
Neil Lurie, *President*
Vincent Lorello, *Vice Pres*
Leila Lurie, *Admin Sec*
EMP: 50 EST: 1946
SQ FT: 20,000
SALES (est): 4.3MM **Privately Held**
WEB: www.bragleycases.com
SIC: 2441 3089 3161 Cases, wood; cases, plastic; luggage

(G-1632)
BRAZEN STREET LLC
734 Pennsylvania Ave (11207-6903)
PHONE..................516 305-7951
Dr Ade Bushansky, *CEO*
Dr Tyrone Johnson, *CFO*
EMP: 50
SALES (est): 4.1MM **Privately Held**
SIC: 2082 Beer (alcoholic beverage)

(G-1633)
BRIDGE ENTERPRISES INC
544 Park Ave (11205-1600)
PHONE..................718 625-6622
Sara Lev, *President*
EMP: 5
SALES (est): 415.9K **Privately Held**
SIC: 2732 Book music: printing & binding, not published on site

(G-1634)
BRIDGE FULFILLMENT INC
445 Park Ave 204 (11205-2735)
PHONE..................718 625-6622
Chaim Eigner, *Ch of Bd*

EMP: 3
SQ FT: 500
SALES (est): 2MM **Privately Held**
SIC: 2759 Commercial printing

(G-1635)
BRIGHT WAY SUPPLY INC
6302 Fort Hamilton Pkwy (11219-5122)
PHONE..................718 833-2882
Phillip Lee, *Ch of Bd*
▲ EMP: 15
SQ FT: 10,000
SALES (est): 1.8MM **Privately Held**
SIC: 3677 Transformers power supply, electronic type

(G-1636)
BRODER MFG INC
566 Johnson Ave (11237-1305)
P.O. Box 370182 (11237-0182)
PHONE..................718 366-1667
Martin Broder, *President*
▲ EMP: 6
SQ FT: 6,000
SALES (est): 513.5K **Privately Held**
SIC: 2392 5162 Tablecloths & table settings; plastics products

(G-1637)
BROOKLYN BANGERS LLC
111 Atlantic Ave Ste 1r (11201-6726)
PHONE..................718 875-3535
Joseph Del Prete, *Mng Member*
Saul Bolton,
Ben Daitz,
EMP: 17
SQ FT: 1,800
SALES (est): 186.3K **Privately Held**
SIC: 2013 5147 Sausages & other prepared meats; meats & meat products

(G-1638)
BROOKLYN BREW SHOP LLC
81 Prospect St (11201-1473)
PHONE..................718 874-0119
Stephen Valand,
▲ EMP: 12
SQ FT: 2,000
SALES (est): 3.5MM **Privately Held**
SIC: 3556 5084 Beverage machinery; industrial machinery & equipment

(G-1639)
BROOKLYN CASING CO INC
412 3rd St (11215-2882)
PHONE..................718 522-0866
Morris Klasbole, *President*
EMP: 6
SALES (est): 410K **Privately Held**
SIC: 2013 Sausage casings, natural

(G-1640)
BROOKLYN CIRCUS (PA)
150 Nevins St (11217-2986)
PHONE..................718 858-0919
Ouigi Theordore, *Owner*
Nicole Moutis, *Manager*
Delon George, *Director*
EMP: 10
SALES (est): 760.7K **Privately Held**
SIC: 2752 Letters, circular or form: lithographed

(G-1641)
BROOKLYN CSTM MET FBRCTION INC
48 Prospect Park Sw (11215-5915)
PHONE..................718 499-1573
David Stanavich, *President*
EMP: 5
SALES (est): 498.4K **Privately Held**
SIC: 3499 Fabricated metal products

(G-1642)
BROOKLYN DENIM CO
85 N 3rd St (11249-3944)
PHONE..................718 782-2600
Frank Pizzurro, *Principal*
EMP: 10
SALES (est): 980K **Privately Held**
SIC: 2211 2389 5651 Denims; apparel for handicapped; jeans stores

Brooklyn - Kings County (G-1643)   GEOGRAPHIC SECTION

(G-1643)
BROOKLYN INDUSTRIES LLC
328 7th Ave (11215-4105)
PHONE..................................718 788-5250
Lindsey Stamps, *Manager*
EMP: 7
SALES (corp-wide): 20.6MM **Privately Held**
SIC: 3999 Barber & beauty shop equipment
PA: Brooklyn Industries Llc
45 Main St Ste 413
Brooklyn NY 11201
718 801-8900

(G-1644)
BROOKLYN JOURNAL PUBLICATIONS
Also Called: Brooklyn Heights Press
16 Court St 30 (11241-0102)
PHONE..................................718 422-7400
John Dozier Hasty, *President*
EMP: 20
SALES (est): 1MM **Privately Held**
WEB: www.brooklyneagle.net
SIC: 2711 Newspapers, publishing & printing

(G-1645)
BROOKLYN RAIL INC
99 Commercial St Apt 15 (11222-1081)
PHONE..................................718 349-8427
Theodore Hann, *President*
Phong Bui, *Publisher*
Sara Christoph, *Managing Dir*
Taylor Dafoe, *Assistant*
Kara Rooney, *Associate*
EMP: 12
SALES: 751K **Privately Held**
WEB: www.brooklynrail.org
SIC: 2711 Newspapers

(G-1646)
BROOKLYN REMEMBERS INC
9201 4th Ave (11209-7006)
PHONE..................................718 491-1705
Patrick Condon, *Admin Sec*
Lisa Deljanin, *Administration*
EMP: 17
SALES (est): 721.7K **Privately Held**
SIC: 3299 Architectural sculptures: gypsum, clay, papier mache, etc.

(G-1647)
BROOKLYN ROASTING WORKS LLC
45 Washington St (11201-1029)
PHONE..................................718 855-1000
EMP: 6 **Privately Held**
SIC: 2095 Coffee extracts
PA: Brooklyn Roasting Works Llc
50 John St
Brooklyn NY 11201

(G-1648)
BROOKLYN SIGNS LLC
Also Called: Signs New York
6404 14th Ave (11219-5314)
PHONE..................................718 252-7575
Tahir Salemi, *President*
EMP: 6
SQ FT: 1,200
SALES (est): 351.1K **Privately Held**
SIC: 3993 Letters for signs, metal; neon signs; displays & cutouts, window & lobby; name plates: except engraved, etched, etc.: metal

(G-1649)
BROOKLYN SWEET SPOT INC
366 Myrtle Ave Ste A (11205-2694)
PHONE..................................718 522-2577
Kiyomi Rodgers, *President*
EMP: 5 **EST:** 2013
SALES (est): 316.5K **Privately Held**
SIC: 2051 Cakes, pies & pastries

(G-1650)
BROOKLYN WINERY LLC (PA)
213 N 8th St (11211-2007)
PHONE..................................347 763-1506
Pam Wroblewski, *Finance Mgr*
Dorann Gutierrez, *Sales Mgr*
Marisa Malgieri, *Sales Mgr*
Lillyann Singer, *Sales Mgr*
Kara Taylor, *Sales Mgr*
EMP: 11
SALES (est): 2MM **Privately Held**
SIC: 2084 Wines

(G-1651)
BROOKLYNS BEST PASTA CO INC ◆
7520 Avenue V (11234-6217)
PHONE..................................917 881-3007
Elena Trotta, *Principal*
EMP: 5 **EST:** 2018
SALES (est): 139.9K **Privately Held**
SIC: 2099 2033 5149 Pasta, uncooked: packaged with other ingredients; spaghetti & other pasta sauce: packaged in cans, jars, etc.; pasta & rice

(G-1652)
BROOKLYNWRAP INC
Also Called: Brooklynwrap Fresh Wraps
4714 Avenue N (11234-3710)
PHONE..................................718 258-8088
Yuewei Chen, *CEO*
Asone Waterman, *Manager*
EMP: 5
SALES (est): 451.2K **Privately Held**
SIC: 2099 5812 Dessert mixes & fillings; eating places

(G-1653)
BSD ALUMINUM FOIL LLC
260 Hewest St (11211)
PHONE..................................347 689-3875
Esther Klein, *President*
EMP: 25 **EST:** 2009
SQ FT: 100,000
SALES (est): 1.8MM **Privately Held**
SIC: 2621 3421 3353 Towels, tissues & napkins: paper & stock; table & food cutlery, including butchers'; aluminum sheet, plate & foil

(G-1654)
BUDD WOODWORK INC
54 Franklin St (11222-2089)
PHONE..................................718 389-1110
Serafin Caamano, *President*
Belen Caamano, *Shareholder*
EMP: 15 **EST:** 1952
SQ FT: 14,000
SALES (est): 2.3MM **Privately Held**
SIC: 2499 Decorative wood & woodwork

(G-1655)
BUNA BESTA TORTILLAS
219 Johnson Ave (11206-2713)
PHONE..................................347 987-3995
Francis Forgione, *Principal*
EMP: 6
SALES (est): 444.3K **Privately Held**
SIC: 2099 Tortillas, fresh or refrigerated

(G-1656)
BUPERIOD PBC
5414 6th Ave 2 (11220-3119)
PHONE..................................917 406-9804
Vanessa Siverls, *CEO*
EMP: 5
SALES (est): 177.6K **Privately Held**
SIC: 2299 7389 Pads, fiber: henequen, sisal, istle;

(G-1657)
BUSHWICK BAKERY CORP
127 Central Ave Ste A (11221-2760)
PHONE..................................917 460-5994
Jean Pierre Marquet, *Principal*
EMP: 5 **EST:** 2010
SALES (est): 233.2K **Privately Held**
SIC: 2051 Bread, cake & related products

(G-1658)
BUSHWICK BOTTLING LLC
465 Johnson Ave (11237-1201)
PHONE..................................929 666-3618
Randy Bresil,
EMP: 10 **EST:** 2017
SALES (est): 283.1K **Privately Held**
SIC: 3999 Manufacturing industries

(G-1659)
BUSHWICK KITCHEN LLC
630 Flushing Ave Fl 5 (11206-5026)
PHONE..................................917 297-1045
Casey Elsas, *Mng Member*
Ped Barbeau,
EMP: 5
SQ FT: 1,400
SALES: 500K **Privately Held**
SIC: 2035 Seasonings & sauces, except tomato & dry

(G-1660)
BUSINESS DIRECTORY INC
Also Called: Community Directory
137 Division Ave Ste A (11211-8270)
PHONE..................................718 486-8099
Shie Krausz, *President*
EMP: 10
SALES (est): 850K **Privately Held**
SIC: 2741 Telephone & other directory publishing

(G-1661)
BUSINESS MANAGEMENT SYSTEMS
Also Called: Fisau
1675 W 9th St Apt 4d (11223-1220)
PHONE..................................914 245-8558
Zak Kogan, *CEO*
Leonid Kogan, *President*
Mark Milyavsky, *Exec VP*
Yakov Rudman, *Project Leader*
Scott Oldham, *Director*
EMP: 11
SALES (est): 782.6K **Privately Held**
WEB: www.fisau.com
SIC: 7372 Business oriented computer software

(G-1662)
BUST INC
Also Called: Bust Magazine
253 36th St Unit 3 (11232-2415)
P.O. Box 1016, New York (10276-1016)
PHONE..................................212 675-1707
Laura Henzel, *President*
Debbie Stoller, *Vice Pres*
EMP: 5
SALES (est): 644.5K **Privately Held**
WEB: www.bust.com
SIC: 2721 Magazines: publishing & printing

(G-1663)
C B S FOOD PRODUCTS CORP
770 Chauncey St (11207-1120)
PHONE..................................718 452-2500
Bernard Steinberg, *Ch of Bd*
Chaim Stein, *President*
Phillip Shapiro, *Vice Pres*
EMP: 15 **EST:** 1939
SQ FT: 34,000
SALES (est): 5.6MM **Privately Held**
SIC: 2079 Cooking oils, except corn: vegetable refined; shortening & other solid edible fats

(G-1664)
C K PRINTING
267 41st St (11232-2811)
PHONE..................................718 965-0388
Bo Chen, *Owner*
EMP: 7
SALES (est): 777.2K **Privately Held**
SIC: 2752 Commercial printing, lithographic

(G-1665)
C T A DIGITAL INC
36 Taaffe Pl (11205-1409)
PHONE..................................718 963-9845
Sol Markowitz, *Vice Pres*
EMP: 12
SALES (corp-wide): 12.7K **Privately Held**
SIC: 3944 Video game machines, except coin-operated
PA: C T A Digital Inc.
326 State Route 208
Monroe NY 10950
845 513-0433

(G-1666)
CAB SIGNS INC
Also Called: Cab Plastics
38 Livonia Ave (11212-4011)
PHONE..................................718 479-2424
Christopher Bayer, *President*
Charles Bayer, *Vice Pres*
Joseph Bayer, *Sales Staff*
EMP: 26
SQ FT: 14,000
SALES (est): 3.6MM **Privately Held**
WEB: www.cabplastics.com
SIC: 3993 Signs, not made in custom sign painting shops

(G-1667)
CABEZON DESIGN GROUP INC
197 Waverly Ave (11205-3605)
PHONE..................................718 488-9868
Kurt Lebeck, *President*
EMP: 7
SALES (est): 220K **Privately Held**
WEB: www.cabezondesign.com
SIC: 3446 7389 Architectural metalwork; business services

(G-1668)
CABINETS BY STANLEY INC
46 Hall St (11205)
PHONE..................................718 222-5861
Stanley Stryszowski, *CEO*
Lukasz Stryszowski, *Exec VP*
Tom Stryszowski, *Project Mgr*
EMP: 7
SALES (est): 517.2K **Privately Held**
SIC: 2434 Wood kitchen cabinets

(G-1669)
CALIPER STUDIO INC
75 Scott Ave (11237-1320)
PHONE..................................718 302-2427
Jonathan Taylor, *President*
Steve Lynch, *Vice Pres*
Kevin Matre, *Manager*
Michael Conlon, *Admin Sec*
EMP: 37
SALES (est): 1.4MM **Privately Held**
SIC: 3446 Architectural metalwork

(G-1670)
CAMEO METAL PRODUCTS INC
127 12th St (11215-3891)
PHONE..................................718 788-1106
Vito Di Maio, *Ch of Bd*
Antonio D Maio, *President*
Frank Spodnick, *General Mgr*
Anthony Di Maio, *Vice Pres*
Adolspoll Cruz, *Finance*
▲ **EMP:** 40
SQ FT: 48,988
SALES (est): 8.2MM **Privately Held**
WEB: www.cameometal.com
SIC: 3559 3469 Metal finishing equipment for plating, etc.; metal stampings

(G-1671)
CANARSIE COURIER INC
1142 E 92nd St 44 (11236-3698)
PHONE..................................718 257-0600
Donna Marra, *Publisher*
Sandra Greco, *Principal*
Catherine Rosa, *Business Mgr*
EMP: 10
SALES (est): 706.1K **Privately Held**
WEB: www.canarsiecourier.com
SIC: 2711 Newspapers, publishing & printing

(G-1672)
CANDLE IN THE WINDOW INC
Also Called: Aura Essence
43 Hall St Ste C10 (11205-1393)
P.O. Box 230123, New York (10023-0003)
PHONE..................................718 852-5743
Marni Bouchardy, *Ch of Bd*
▲ **EMP:** 16
SQ FT: 8,000
SALES (est): 1.1MM **Privately Held**
SIC: 3999 5199 Candles; candles

(G-1673)
CANNIZZARO SEAL & ENGRAVING CO
435 Avenue U (11223-4007)
P.O. Box 230304 (11223-0304)
PHONE..................................718 513-6125
Janet Cannizzaro, *President*
▲ **EMP:** 5
SQ FT: 1,200
SALES (est): 672K **Privately Held**
WEB: www.cannizzaroseal.com
SIC: 3953 5199 Embossing seals & hand stamps; gifts & novelties

GEOGRAPHIC SECTION
Brooklyn - Kings County (G-1702)

(G-1674)
CAPITOL POLY CORP
101 Spencer St (11205-2805)
P.O. Box 270, Haverstraw (10927-0270)
PHONE..................................718 855-6000
Benny Green, *President*
EMP: 20 **EST:** 1995
SALES (est): 2.6MM **Privately Held**
WEB: www.capitolpoly.com
SIC: 2673 Plastic bags: made from purchased materials

(G-1675)
CAPUTO BAKERY INC
Also Called: Caputo's Bake Shop
329 Court St Ste 1 (11231-4390)
PHONE..................................718 875-6871
John Caputo, *President*
Francis Tunzi, *Vice Pres*
EMP: 5
SQ FT: 2,000
SALES (est): 300K **Privately Held**
SIC: 2051 5461 Bakery: wholesale or wholesale/retail combined; bakeries

(G-1676)
CARDINAL TANK CORP
Also Called: Cardinal Boiler and Tank
700 Hicks St (11231-1823)
PHONE..................................718 625-4350
William J Weidmann, *President*
EMP: 50
SQ FT: 31,000
SALES (est): 9.5MM **Privately Held**
WEB: www.cardinal-detecto.centralcarolinascale.co
SIC: 3443 Fuel tanks (oil, gas, etc.): metal plate

(G-1677)
CARECONNECTOR
177 Concord St Apt 2a (11201-2091)
PHONE..................................919 360-2987
Sima Pendharkar, *Principal*
EMP: 5 **EST:** 2015
SALES (est): 199.7K **Privately Held**
SIC: 7372 Business oriented computer software

(G-1678)
CARRY-ALL CANVAS BAG CO INC
1983 Coney Island Ave (11223-2328)
PHONE..................................718 375-4230
Michel Kraut, *President*
▲ **EMP:** 7
SQ FT: 3,800
SALES (est): 500K **Privately Held**
WEB: www.carryallbag.com
SIC: 3161 Traveling bags

(G-1679)
CARTER ENTERPRISES LLC (PA)
Also Called: Mil-Spec. Enterprises
4610 12th Ave (11219-2556)
PHONE..................................718 853-5052
Chaim Wolf, *Mng Member*
▲ **EMP:** 32
SALES (est): 61.2MM **Privately Held**
WEB: www.carterny.com
SIC: 2389 Men's miscellaneous accessories

(G-1680)
CARTS MOBILE FOOD EQP CORP
Also Called: Cfe
113 8th St (11215-3115)
PHONE..................................718 788-5540
Jeno Rosenberg, *President*
Florence Rosenberg, *Corp Secy*
Dave Nader, *Exec VP*
Joe Revitte, *Design Engr*
EMP: 22
SQ FT: 15,000
SALES (est): 4.1MM **Privately Held**
WEB: www.cartsfoodeqp.com
SIC: 2599 3589 3556 Food wagons, restaurant; carts, restaurant equipment; commercial cooking & foodwarming equipment; food products machinery

(G-1681)
CASA COLLECTION INC
106 Ferris St (11231-1066)
PHONE..................................718 694-0272
Roberto Gil, *President*
Fili Perez, *Mfg Staff*
EMP: 5
SALES (est): 480K **Privately Held**
WEB: www.casacollection.com
SIC: 2434 5712 Wood kitchen cabinets; juvenile furniture

(G-1682)
CASA INNOVATIONS INC
Also Called: Shredder Essentials
155 Bay Ridge Ave (11220-5108)
PHONE..................................718 965-6600
Aron Abramson, *CEO*
Charles Sued, *President*
▲ **EMP:** 6
SQ FT: 5,300
SALES (est): 1.1MM **Privately Held**
SIC: 3678 Electronic connectors

(G-1683)
CATALINA PRODUCTS CORP (PA)
2455 Mcdonald Ave (11223-5232)
PHONE..................................718 336-8288
Victor Salama, *President*
Marie Mireille Salama, *Corp Secy*
Linda Reyzis, *Vice Pres*
Paul Yedin, *Vice Pres*
▲ **EMP:** 35 **EST:** 1968
SQ FT: 75,000
SALES (est): 2.1MM **Privately Held**
WEB: www.catalinabath.com
SIC: 2392 Shower curtains: made from purchased materials

(G-1684)
CCC PUBLICATIONS INC
12020 Flatlands Ave (11207-8203)
PHONE..................................718 306-1008
AR Bernard, *CEO*
Robin Hogan, *General Mgr*
Karen Bernard, *Vice Pres*
EMP: 11
SQ FT: 2,500
SALES (est): 600K **Privately Held**
SIC: 2731 Book publishing
PA: Christian Cultural Center, Inc.
12020 Flatlands Ave
Brooklyn NY 11207

(G-1685)
CELONIS INC
1820 Avenue M Unit 544 (11230-5347)
PHONE..................................941 615-9670
Alexander Rinke, *CEO*
Panayiotis Vitakis, *Senior VP*
Anthony Deighton, *Chief Mktg Ofcr*
EMP: 5
SALES (est): 261.9K **Privately Held**
SIC: 7372 Prepackaged software

(G-1686)
CERTIFIED HEALTH PRODUCTS INC
67 35th St Unit 12 (11232-2200)
PHONE..................................718 339-7498
Gene Kisselman, *President*
Steve Zeltser, *Vice Pres*
Denis Korablev, *QC Mgr*
EMP: 35
SQ FT: 12,000
SALES (est): 3.9MM **Privately Held**
SIC: 3069 Orthopedic sundries, molded rubber

(G-1687)
CHAMBORD LLC
4302 Farragut Rd (11203-6520)
PHONE..................................718 859-1110
Daniel Faks, *President*
EMP: 20
SQ FT: 12,000
SALES (est): 1.3MM **Privately Held**
SIC: 2051 Bread, cake & related products

(G-1688)
CHAN & CHAN (USA) CORP
2 Rewe St (11211-1708)
PHONE..................................718 388-9633
EMP: 8
SALES (est): 569.6K **Privately Held**
SIC: 2099 3999 Food preparations; atomizers, toiletry

(G-1689)
CHAN KEE DRIED BEAN CURD INC
71 Steuben St (11205-2608)
PHONE..................................718 622-0820
Alex Luk, *President*
Tan Muneng Sing, *Principal*
Tran Van Track, *Principal*
EMP: 6
SQ FT: 1,000
SALES (est): 500K **Privately Held**
SIC: 2099 Tofu, except frozen desserts

(G-1690)
CHARLOTTE NEUVILLE DESIGN LLC
Also Called: Fashion Chef, The
882 3rd Ave (11232-1904)
PHONE..................................646 530-4570
Charlotte Neuville, *President*
EMP: 6
SQ FT: 2,000
SALES (est): 539.2K **Privately Held**
SIC: 2051 Cakes, bakery: except frozen

(G-1691)
CHEFS DELIGHT PACKING CO
94 N 8th St (11249-2802)
PHONE..................................718 388-8581
Bradford Karroll, *President*
Doug Karroll, *Vice Pres*
EMP: 13 **EST:** 1956
SQ FT: 3,000
SALES (est): 1.6MM **Privately Held**
SIC: 2011 Meat packing plants

(G-1692)
CIC INTERNATIONAL LTD
1118 42nd St (11219-1213)
P.O. Box 533, New York (10011)
PHONE..................................212 213-0089
S G Fassoulis, *President*
David Ceva, *Exec VP*
James Chladek, *Vice Pres*
Robert Perry, *Vice Pres*
Larry Thompson, *Vice Pres*
EMP: 98
SQ FT: 14,656
SALES (est): 6.3MM **Privately Held**
SIC: 3812 3711 3482 3483 Aircraft/aerospace flight instruments & guidance systems; military motor vehicle assembly; small arms ammunition; ammunition components; rocket launchers; helicopters

(G-1693)
CIOCCOLATO 7 LLC
Also Called: Butterfly 7
336 Malcolm X Blvd G (11233-1842)
PHONE..................................347 240-7115
Rick Shorter, *Owner*
EMP: 5
SALES (est): 153.2K **Privately Held**
SIC: 3944 5023 Games, toys & children's vehicles; decorative home furnishings & supplies

(G-1694)
CITY COOLING ENTERPRISES INC
1624 61st St (11204-2109)
PHONE..................................718 331-7400
Derick Pearlin, *President*
EMP: 8
SQ FT: 5,000
SALES (est): 1.1MM **Privately Held**
SIC: 3444 1711 Sheet metalwork; heating & air conditioning contractors

(G-1695)
CITY OF NEW YORK
Also Called: HRA Poster Project
4014 1st Ave Fl 3 (11232-2700)
PHONE..................................718 965-8787
David Hall, *Branch Mgr*
EMP: 30 **Privately Held**
WEB: www.nyc.gov
SIC: 2741 9199 Shopping news: publishing & printing; general government administration;
PA: City Of New York
City HI
New York NY 10007
212 788-3000

(G-1696)
CITY OF NEW YORK
Also Called: Department of Sanitation
5602 19th Ave (11204-2049)
PHONE..................................718 236-2693
Jay Ryan, *Superintendent*
EMP: 117 **Privately Held**
WEB: www.nyc.gov
SIC: 2842 9511 Sanitation preparations; waste management program administration, government;
PA: City Of New York
City HI
New York NY 10007
212 788-3000

(G-1697)
CITY SIGNS INC
1940 Mcdonald Ave (11223-1829)
PHONE..................................718 375-5933
Yehuda Mizrahi, *President*
Eyal Mizrahi, *Vice Pres*
Smadar Mizrahi, *Treasurer*
EMP: 5
SQ FT: 12,000
SALES (est): 636.1K **Privately Held**
WEB: www.citysignsinc.com
SIC: 3993 2399 5999 Signs, not made in custom sign painting shops; neon signs; flags, fabric; awnings

(G-1698)
CITY SITES SPORTSWEAR INC (PA)
2421 Mcdonald Ave (11223-5230)
P.O. Box 230187 (11223-0187)
PHONE..................................718 375-2990
Sui Tong MA, *President*
David Schwitzer, *Corp Secy*
▲ **EMP:** 24
SQ FT: 8,000
SALES (est): 2.6MM **Privately Held**
SIC: 2339 Sportswear, women's

(G-1699)
CLASSIC ALBUM
343 Lorimer St (11206-1998)
PHONE..................................718 388-2818
Barry Himmel, *President*
EMP: 30
SQ FT: 12,500
SALES (est): 2.7MM **Privately Held**
SIC: 2782 7221 2789 2759 Blankbooks & looseleaf binders; photographic studios, portrait; bookbinding & related work; commercial printing

(G-1700)
CLASSIC ALBUM LLC
343 Lorimer St (11206-1998)
PHONE..................................718 388-2818
Barry Himmel,
▲ **EMP:** 75 **EST:** 1952
SQ FT: 10,000
SALES (est): 9.3MM **Privately Held**
SIC: 2782 7221 Albums; photographic studios, portrait

(G-1701)
CLEANSE TEC
1000 Linwood St (11208-5320)
PHONE..................................718 346-9111
Steven Feig, *President*
Jonathan Spaude, *District Mgr*
Bob Clark, *Senior VP*
Bruce Hittner, *Vice Pres*
Rui Cruz, *Manager*
EMP: 29
SQ FT: 14,000
SALES (est): 7.2MM **Privately Held**
WEB: www.soapman.com
SIC: 2841 2842 Detergents, synthetic organic or inorganic alkaline; specialty cleaning, polishes & sanitation goods

(G-1702)
CNV ARCHITECTURAL COATINGS INC
538 Johnson Ave (11237-1226)
PHONE..................................718 418-9584
Nicola Comaianni, *President*

Brooklyn - Kings County (G-1703)

EMP: 6 EST: 2015
SQ FT: 10,000
SALES (est): 297.5K **Privately Held**
SIC: 3479 Metal coating & allied service

(G-1703)
CODA RESOURCES LTD (PA)
Also Called: Cambridge Resources
960 Alabama Ave (11207-8327)
PHONE..................718 649-1666
Hillel Tropper, *CEO*
Kurtis Feil, *Vice Pres*
Larry Lasher, *Vice Pres*
Moshe Tropper, *Vice Pres*
Dov Feder, *Project Mgr*
▲ EMP: 95
SQ FT: 100,000
SALES (est): 33.9MM **Privately Held**
WEB: www.codaresources.com
SIC: 3469 2821 Metal stampings; molding compounds, plastics

(G-1704)
COFFEE HOLDING COMPANY INC
4425 1st Ave (11232-4201)
PHONE..................718 832-0800
R Gordon, *Principal*
David Gordon, *Exec VP*
Sam Elway, *Human Res Mgr*
Antero Baez, *Sales Staff*
James Bensley, *Manager*
▼ EMP: 8
SALES (est): 737.5K **Privately Held**
SIC: 2095 Roasted coffee

(G-1705)
COLONIAL REDI RECORD CORP
1225 36th St (11218-2023)
PHONE..................718 972-7433
Joe Berkobits, *President*
EMP: 25
SQ FT: 12,000
SALES: 2.5MM **Privately Held**
SIC: 3993 Signs & advertising specialties

(G-1706)
COLUMBIA BUTTON NAILHEAD CORP
306 Stagg St 316 (11206-1702)
PHONE..................718 386-3414
Robert Matz, *President*
Charles J Matz Jr, *Corp Secy*
EMP: 17 EST: 1946
SQ FT: 20,000
SALES (est): 2.2MM **Privately Held**
SIC: 3965 Studs, shirt, except precious/semiprecious metal or stone; buttons & parts; buckles & buckle parts

(G-1707)
COMBOLAND PACKING CORP
2 Cumberland St (11205-1040)
PHONE..................718 858-4200
Marvin Eisenstadt, *President*
Ira Eisenstadt, *Vice Pres*
Matthew Causco, *Planning*
EMP: 99
SALES (est): 8.8MM **Privately Held**
SIC: 2869 Perfumes, flavorings & food additives

(G-1708)
COMET INTL TRDG CO INC
993 Flatbush Ave Ste 4-A (11226-5006)
PHONE..................731 599-2430
Emilie Kraft, *President*
EMP: 12
SQ FT: 3,500
SALES: 13MM **Privately Held**
SIC: 3089 2211 5719 Plastic kitchenware, tableware & houseware; apparel & outerwear fabrics, cotton; cookware, except aluminum

(G-1709)
COMMODORE MANUFACUTRING CORP
Also Called: Commodore Tool
3913 2nd Ave (11232-2707)
PHONE..................718 788-2600
Abraham Damast, *Branch Mgr*
EMP: 50
SALES (corp-wide): 26.8MM **Privately Held**
SIC: 3542 Machine tools, metal forming type
PA: Commodore Manufacutring Corporation
4312 2nd Ave
Brooklyn NY 11232
718 788-2600

(G-1710)
COMMUNITY NEWS GROUP LLC (PA)
Also Called: Bronx Times Reporter
1 Metrotech Ctr Fl 10 (11201-3949)
PHONE..................718 260-2500
Les Goodstein, *CEO*
Jennifer Goodstein, *President*
Bill Egbert, *Editor*
Ralph D'Onofrio, *Vice Pres*
Cynthia Soto, *Office Mgr*
EMP: 105
SQ FT: 14,000
SALES (est): 20.1MM **Privately Held**
SIC: 2711 Commercial printing & newspaper publishing combined; newspapers, publishing & printing

(G-1711)
CONFRTRNITY OF PRESCIOUS BLOOD
5300 Fort Hamilton Pkwy (11219)
PHONE..................718 436-1120
Susan Pergolizzi, *Principal*
Austin Bennett, *Director*
EMP: 8
SALES (est): 690K **Privately Held**
WEB: www.confraternitypb.org
SIC: 2731 Books: publishing only

(G-1712)
CONSUMER FLAVORING EXTRACT CO
921 Mcdonald Ave (11218-5611)
PHONE..................718 435-0201
Louis Fontana, *President*
EMP: 14 EST: 1962
SQ FT: 5,000
SALES (est): 1.8MM **Privately Held**
WEB: www.consumersflavoring.com
SIC: 2079 2087 Edible oil products, except corn oil; concentrates, flavoring (except drink)

(G-1713)
CONTINENTAL LATEX CORP
1489 Shore Pkwy Apt 1g (11214-6321)
PHONE..................718 783-7883
George Miller, *President*
EMP: 10 EST: 1953
SALES (est): 800K **Privately Held**
SIC: 3069 3089 Air-supported rubber structures; plastic processing

(G-1714)
CONTROL ELECTROPOLISHING CORP
109 Walworth St (11205-2897)
P.O. Box 790385, Middle Village (11379-0385)
PHONE..................718 858-6634
Nancy Zapata, *President*
EMP: 15 EST: 1959
SQ FT: 7,000
SALES: 1.2MM **Privately Held**
SIC: 3471 Polishing, metals or formed products

(G-1715)
CONVERGENT MED MGT SVCS LLC
7513 3rd Ave (11209-3103)
PHONE..................718 921-6159
Anthony Pennacchio, *President*
EMP: 5
SALES (est): 553.2K **Privately Held**
SIC: 3674 Semiconductors & related devices

(G-1716)
COPY CAT
3177 Coney Island Ave A (11235-6443)
PHONE..................718 934-2192
Horace Bryan, *President*
Araceli Bryan, *Vice Pres*
EMP: 5 EST: 1977
SQ FT: 3,000
SALES (est): 415.2K **Privately Held**
SIC: 3647 Vehicular lighting equipment

(G-1717)
COPY CORNER INC
200 Division Ave (11211-7108)
PHONE..................718 388-4545
Zalman Eizikovits, *President*
EMP: 5
SQ FT: 1,500
SALES (est): 410K **Privately Held**
SIC: 2754 2789 Commercial printing, gravure; bookbinding & related work

(G-1718)
CORNELL BEVERAGES INC
105 Harrison Pl (11237-1403)
PHONE..................718 381-3000
Helene Hoffman, *President*
Allan Hoffman, *Vice Pres*
Donna Hoffman, *Treasurer*
EMP: 10
SALES (est): 1MM **Privately Held**
WEB: www.cornellbev.com
SIC: 2086 Soft drinks: packaged in cans, bottles, etc.

(G-1719)
CORONADO
349 Covert St (11237-6319)
PHONE..................718 386-7425
Coronado, *Principal*
EMP: 5
SALES (est): 282.4K **Privately Held**
SIC: 3272 Concrete products

(G-1720)
CORONET PARTS MFG CO INC (PA)
883 Elton St (11208-5315)
PHONE..................718 649-1750
Allan Rodolitz, *President*
Jeffrey Rodolitz, *President*
Mark Silfen, *General Mgr*
Joseph Thomas, *Purch Mgr*
Armand Salvati, *Sales Staff*
EMP: 20 EST: 1945
SQ FT: 15,000
SALES (est): 7.3MM **Privately Held**
WEB: www.coronetparts.com
SIC: 3432 5074 Plumbers' brass goods: drain cocks, faucets, spigots, etc.; plumbers' brass goods & fittings

(G-1721)
CORONET PARTS MFG CO INC
901 Elton St Fl 1 (11208-5315)
PHONE..................718 649-1750
Joel Poretz, *Branch Mgr*
EMP: 20
SALES (corp-wide): 7.3MM **Privately Held**
WEB: www.coronetparts.com
SIC: 3432 Plumbers' brass goods: drain cocks, faucets, spigots, etc.
PA: Coronet Parts Mfg. Co. Inc.
883 Elton St
Brooklyn NY 11208
718 649-1750

(G-1722)
COSMIC ENTERPRISE
147 Rockaway Ave Ste A (11233-3289)
PHONE..................718 342-6257
Marjorie Thorne, *Owner*
EMP: 6
SALES (est): 320K **Privately Held**
SIC: 2833 5499 Drugs & herbs: grading, grinding & milling; health & dietetic food stores

(G-1723)
COUNTY ENERGY CORP
65 S 11th St Apt 1e (11249-7003)
PHONE..................718 626-7000
David Rosner, *President*
EMP: 4
SALES: 20MM **Privately Held**
SIC: 1311 4911 Natural gas production; electric services

(G-1724)
COURIER-LIFE INC
Also Called: Courier Life Publications
1 Metrotech Ctr (11201-3948)
PHONE..................718 260-2500
Les Goodstein, *CEO*
Jennifer Goodstein, *President*
Vince Dimiceli, *Senior Editor*
EMP: 218
SQ FT: 11,300
SALES (est): 10.9MM
SALES (corp-wide): 20.1MM **Privately Held**
WEB: www.courierlife.net
SIC: 2711 Newspapers: publishing only, not printed on site; newspapers, publishing & printing
PA: Community News Group Llc
1 Metrotech Ctr Fl 10
Brooklyn NY 11201
718 260-2500

(G-1725)
CRAFT PACKAGING INC
1274 49th St Ste 350 (11219-3011)
PHONE..................718 633-4045
Fhia Rothstein, *President*
Rothstein Shia, *Owner*
EMP: 5
SALES (est): 445K **Privately Held**
SIC: 2671 Packaging paper & plastics film, coated & laminated

(G-1726)
CREAM BEBE
694 Myrtle Ave Ste 220 (11205-3916)
PHONE..................917 578-2088
Yossi Greenburg, *Owner*
EMP: 10
SALES (est): 380K **Privately Held**
SIC: 2361 Shirts: girls', children's & infants'

(G-1727)
CREATIONS IN LUCITE INC
165 Franklin Ave Apt 5 (11205-2760)
PHONE..................718 871-2000
Davin Rand, *President*
David Rand, *President*
Shaye Gross, *Vice Pres*
EMP: 9
SALES: 150K **Privately Held**
WEB: www.creationsinlucite.com
SIC: 2821 Acrylic resins

(G-1728)
CREATIVE GOLD LLC
1425 37th St Ste 5 (11218-3771)
PHONE..................718 686-2225
▲ EMP: 23 EST: 2003
SALES: 500K **Privately Held**
SIC: 3911 Manufacture Precious Metals

(G-1729)
CREATIVE SCENTS USA INC
183 Wilson St Ste 106 (11211-7578)
PHONE..................718 522-5901
Adolf Kraus, *CEO*
EMP: 3
SALES: 2MM **Privately Held**
SIC: 2392 Household furnishings

(G-1730)
CREPINI LLC
Also Called: Crepe Team, The
5600 1st Ave (11220-2550)
PHONE..................347 422-0829
Paula Rimer, *CEO*
Charles Rabinovich, *President*
Sam Shkolnik, *Sales Staff*
Eugene Tulman, *Officer*
Eric Shkolnik,
▲ EMP: 30
SQ FT: 12,000
SALES (est): 12MM **Privately Held**
WEB: www.crepini.com
SIC: 2024 5084 Food product manufacturing machinery; dairy based frozen desserts

(G-1731)
CREST LOCK CO INC
342 Herzl St (11212-4442)
PHONE..................718 345-9898
Samuel Sheiman, *President*
▲ EMP: 15 EST: 1938
SQ FT: 20,000

SALES (est): 1.4MM **Privately Held**
WEB: www.crestlock.net
SIC: 3429 Luggage hardware

(G-1732)
CRITERION BELL & SPECIALTY
4312 2nd Ave (11232-3306)
PHONE 718 788-2600
Abraham Damast, *President*
Donald Damast, *Corp Secy*
Gary Damast, *Vice Pres*
EMP: 40
SQ FT: 30,000
SALES (est): 3.6MM **Privately Held**
SIC: 3499 3999 Novelties & specialties, metal; Christmas tree ornaments, except electrical & glass

(G-1733)
CROWN WOODWORKING CORP
583 Montgomery St (11225-3009)
PHONE 718 974-6415
Mendel Barber, *President*
EMP: 9
SALES: 350K **Privately Held**
SIC: 2431 Millwork

(G-1734)
CROWNBROOK ACC LLC (PA)
Also Called: American Conveyor
478 Albany Ave 113 (11203-1002)
PHONE 718 626-0760
Ron Schinik, *Mng Member*
Richard Dauphin,
◆ **EMP:** 40
SQ FT: 30,000
SALES (est): 9.7MM **Privately Held**
SIC: 3535 1799 Conveyors & conveying equipment; welding on site

(G-1735)
CRUSADER CANDLE CO INC
325 Nevins St Ste 327329 (11215-1084)
PHONE 718 625-0005
Paul J Morra, *President*
◆ **EMP:** 28 **EST:** 1946
SQ FT: 14,500
SALES: 5MM **Privately Held**
SIC: 3999 Candles

(G-1736)
CRYE PRECISION LLC
63 Flushing Ave (11205-1005)
PHONE 718 246-3838
Eric Correll, *Engineer*
Steven Filipelli, *Controller*
Beth Rodriguez, *Cust Mgr*
Jeremy Morton, *Sales Staff*
Brad Thomas, *Manager*
▲ **EMP:** 185
SQ FT: 90,000
SALES (est): 53MM **Privately Held**
SIC: 3842 2311 5632 5699 Clothing, fire resistant & protective; military uniforms, men's & youths': purchased materials; policemen's uniforms: made from purchased materials; apparel accessories; customized clothing & apparel; textile & apparel services

(G-1737)
CT INDUSTRIAL SUPPLY CO INC
305 Ten Eyck St (11206-1724)
P.O. Box 60338 (11206-0338)
PHONE 718 417-3226
Charles Tolkin, *President*
EMP: 10
SALES (est): 1MM **Privately Held**
SIC: 3089 Garbage containers, plastic

(G-1738)
CTAC HOLDINGS LLC
68 35th Street Brooklyn (11232)
PHONE 212 924-2280
Anthony Cirone, *President*
EMP: 20
SALES (est): 2.4MM **Privately Held**
SIC: 2066 Chocolate

(G-1739)
CUMBERLAND PACKING CORP (PA)
2 Cumberland St (11205-1000)
PHONE 718 858-4200
Steven Eisenstadt, *CEO*
Jeffrey Eisenstadt, *Principal*
Rob Bowen, *Exec VP*
Ira Eisenstadt, *Senior VP*
Jeff Eisenstadt, *Vice Pres*
◆ **EMP:** 390
SQ FT: 13,000
SALES: 150MM **Privately Held**
WEB: www.cpack.com
SIC: 2869 Sweeteners, synthetic; flavors or flavoring materials, synthetic

(G-1740)
CURRICULUM ASSOCIATES LLC
55 Prospect St (11201-1497)
PHONE 978 313-1355
Stephanie Lawkins, *Manager*
EMP: 12
SALES (corp-wide): 14MM **Privately Held**
SIC: 2731 Book publishing
PA: Curriculum Associates, Llc
153 Rangeway Rd
North Billerica MA 01862
978 667-8000

(G-1741)
CUSTOM FIXTURES INC
129 13th St (11215-4603)
PHONE 718 965-1141
Michael Lerich, *President*
EMP: 9
SQ FT: 8,000
SALES (est): 960K **Privately Held**
WEB: www.customfixturesonline.com
SIC: 2542 Fixtures: display, office or store: except wood

(G-1742)
CUSTOM LAMPSHADES INC
Also Called: Creative Custom Shades
544 Park Ave Ste 503 (11205-1788)
P.O. Box 50186 (11205-0186)
PHONE 718 254-0500
Nachman Heller, *President*
EMP: 16 **EST:** 1979
SALES (est): 1.8MM **Privately Held**
SIC: 3645 5719 Lamp & light shades; lamps & lamp shades

(G-1743)
CUSTOM LUCITE CREATIONS INC
165 Franklin Ave Apt 5 (11205-2760)
PHONE 718 871-2000
David L Rand, *CEO*
EMP: 10
SALES (est): 943K **Privately Held**
SIC: 3089 Injection molding of plastics; plastic processing

(G-1744)
CUSTOM WOOD INC
770 E 94th St (11236-1817)
PHONE 718 927-4700
James Campo, *President*
EMP: 8 **EST:** 1980
SQ FT: 3,200
SALES: 750K **Privately Held**
SIC: 2541 2431 Store fixtures, wood; woodwork, interior & ornamental

(G-1745)
D & H AMAZING DEALS INC (PA)
Also Called: D&H
1233 39th St (11218-1932)
PHONE 347 318-3805
Daniel Fuchs, *President*
▲ **EMP:** 5
SALES: 5MM **Privately Held**
SIC: 2844 5731 Cosmetic preparations; radio, television & electronic stores

(G-1746)
D BEST SERVICE CO INC
Also Called: D Best Glass & Mirror
729 Church Ave (11218-3305)
PHONE 718 972-6133
William Omalley Jr, *President*
Grace Fradella O'Malley, *Admin Sec*
EMP: 7
SQ FT: 400
SALES (est): 947K **Privately Held**
SIC: 3429 1751 7699 Metal fasteners; window & door installation & erection; mirror repair shop

(G-1747)
D MALDARI & SONS INC
557 3rd Ave (11215-4600)
PHONE 718 499-3555
Chris Maldari, *President*
Daniel Maldari, *Vice Pres*
▲ **EMP:** 30 **EST:** 1902
SQ FT: 16,000
SALES (est): 4.6MM **Privately Held**
WEB: www.maldari.com
SIC: 3544 Extrusion dies

(G-1748)
D V S IRON & ALUMINUM WORKS
117 14th St (11215-4607)
PHONE 718 768-7961
Louis Di Janic, *President*
EMP: 9 **EST:** 1969
SQ FT: 1,000
SALES (est): 1.4MM **Privately Held**
SIC: 3446 Railings, prefabricated metal

(G-1749)
DADDARIO & COMPANY INC
Also Called: D'Addario & Company Inc
1000 Dean St Ste 410 (11238-3385)
PHONE 718 599-6660
EMP: 22
SALES (corp-wide): 193.1MM **Privately Held**
SIC: 3931 Musical instruments
PA: D'addario & Company, Inc.
595 Smith St
Farmingdale NY 11735
631 439-3300

(G-1750)
DAHILL DISTRIBUTORS INC
975 Dahill Rd (11204-1738)
PHONE 347 371-9453
Hirsch Stengel, *President*
EMP: 8
SQ FT: 500
SALES: 800K **Privately Held**
WEB: www.filmart.com
SIC: 3699 5199 Electrical equipment & supplies; general merchandise, non-durable

(G-1751)
DAILY WEAR SPORTSWEAR CORP (PA)
2308 Mcdonald Ave (11223-4739)
PHONE 718 972-0533
Isaac Abed, *President*
Joey Abed, *Vice Pres*
Michael Abed, *Vice Pres*
▲ **EMP:** 8
SQ FT: 20,000
SALES (est): 1MM **Privately Held**
SIC: 2339 Sportswear, women's

(G-1752)
DALY MEGHAN
78 5th Ave (11217-4647)
PHONE 347 699-3259
Meghan Daly, *Owner*
EMP: 10
SALES (est): 283.4K **Privately Held**
SIC: 2051 Bakery: wholesale or wholesale/retail combined

(G-1753)
DAMASCUS BAKERY INC (PA)
56 Gold St (11201-1297)
PHONE 718 855-1456
Edward Mafoud, *President*
David Mafoud, *Exec VP*
Wanda Hightower, *Human Res Mgr*
EMP: 91 **EST:** 1930
SQ FT: 20,000
SALES (est): 23.4MM **Privately Held**
WEB: www.damascusbakery.com
SIC: 2051 5149 Bakery: wholesale or wholesale/retail combined; bread, all types (white, wheat, rye, etc): fresh or frozen; bakery products

(G-1754)
DANDELION ENERGY INC
15 Metrotech Ctr Fl 19 (11201-3818)
PHONE 603 781-2663
Kathleen Hannun, *CEO*
Rajeev Quazi, *President*
EMP: 12
SALES (est): 486.9K **Privately Held**
SIC: 3433 Heating equipment, except electric

(G-1755)
DANET INC
Also Called: Russian Bazaar
8518 17th Ave Fl 2 (11214-2810)
PHONE 718 266-4444
Nathasha Shapiro, *President*
Anatoli Shapiro, *Vice Pres*
Margarita Shapiro, *Director*
EMP: 12
SALES (est): 490K **Privately Held**
WEB: www.danet.com
SIC: 2711 7319 Newspapers: publishing only, not printed on site; transit advertising services

(G-1756)
DANIEL O REICH INCORPORATED
Also Called: Reich Paper
7518 3rd Ave (11209-3104)
PHONE 718 748-6000
Dan Reich, *CEO*
Daniel K Reich, *President*
Duke Reich, *President*
▲ **EMP:** 10
SQ FT: 4,800
SALES (est): 2MM **Privately Held**
WEB: www.oliveart.com
SIC: 2621 Paper mills

(G-1757)
DAPPER DADS INC
45 Rochester Ave (11233-3011)
PHONE 917 903-8045
Mario Daniels, *President*
Geayse Williams, *Vice Pres*
EMP: 5
SALES (est): 204.3K **Privately Held**
SIC: 2741 7389 Miscellaneous publishing;

(G-1758)
DAS YIDISHE LICHT INC
66 Middleton St Apt 1 (11206-5088)
PHONE 718 387-3166
Mike Kraus, *President*
EMP: 5
SQ FT: 1,500
SALES (est): 290K **Privately Held**
SIC: 2711 Newspapers: publishing only, not printed on site

(G-1759)
DAVEL SYSTEMS INC
1314 Avenue M (11230-5206)
PHONE 718 382-6024
David Liberman, *President*
EMP: 6
SALES (est): 477.1K **Privately Held**
SIC: 7372 Prepackaged software

(G-1760)
DAWNEX INDUSTRIES INC
861 Park Ave (11206-7300)
PHONE 718 384-0199
Fax: 718 709-1331
EMP: 10
SALES (est): 600K **Privately Held**
SIC: 3089 Mfg Plastic Products

(G-1761)
DBG MEDIA
358 Classon Ave (11238-1306)
PHONE 718 599-6828
David Greaves, *Owner*
EMP: 8
SQ FT: 900
SALES (est): 230K **Privately Held**
WEB: www.ourtimepress.com
SIC: 2711 Newspapers: publishing only, not printed on site

(G-1762)
DE ANS PORK PRODUCTS INC (PA)
899 4th Ave (11232-2150)
PHONE 718 788-2464
Frank De Angelis, *President*
Anthony Gaglia, *Vice Pres*
Guy De Angelis, *Treasurer*
EMP: 25

Brooklyn - Kings County (G-1763)   **GEOGRAPHIC SECTION**

SQ FT: 13,000
SALES (est): 2.8MM **Privately Held**
SIC: 2013 Sausages from purchased meat

(G-1763)
DEAN TRADING CORP
200 Junius St (11212-8103)
PHONE.................................718 485-0600
Robert Clemente, *Ch of Bd*
EMP: 18 **EST:** 1966
SQ FT: 20,000
SALES (est): 6.7MM **Privately Held**
SIC: 2299 Textile mill waste & remnant processing

(G-1764)
DELLET INDUSTRIES INC
1 43rd St Ste L8 (11232-2621)
PHONE.................................718 965-0101
Mike Brown, *Manager*
EMP: 16
SALES (est): 1.5MM **Privately Held**
SIC: 2599 Furniture & fixtures

(G-1765)
DELLS CHERRIES LLC
Also Called: Dell's Maraschino Cherries Co
175 Dikeman St Ste 177 (11231-1199)
PHONE.................................718 624-4380
Dana Bentz, *President*
Steve Leffler, *General Mgr*
Dominique Mondella, *Vice Pres*
Urb Brinker, *Natl Sales Mgr*
EMP: 30 **EST:** 2016
SQ FT: 30,000
SALES (est): 942.1K **Privately Held**
SIC: 2033 Maraschino cherries: packaged in cans, jars, etc.

(G-1766)
DELLS CHERRIES LLC
81 Ferris St (11231-1105)
PHONE.................................718 624-4380
Dana Bentz, *President*
EMP: 30
SQ FT: 17,540 **Privately Held**
WEB: www.dellscherry.com
SIC: 2033 Maraschino cherries: packaged in cans, jars, etc.

(G-1767)
DELUXE TRAVEL STORE INC
Also Called: Deluxe Passport Express
5014 12th Ave (11219-3407)
PHONE.................................718 435-8111
Yitzchok Isaac Stern, *CEO*
EMP: 5
SALES (est): 282.8K **Privately Held**
SIC: 3161 3199 5099 Luggage; corners, luggage: leather; luggage

(G-1768)
DENVIN INC
6520 New Utrecht Ave (11219-5725)
PHONE.................................718 232-3389
Joseph Otranto, *President*
Vinny Mongelli, *Vice Pres*
Dennis Otranto, *Treasurer*
EMP: 50 **EST:** 1941
SQ FT: 16,000
SALES (est): 5MM **Privately Held**
WEB: www.empiresilver.com
SIC: 3914 Silversmithing

(G-1769)
DER YID INC
Also Called: Der Yid Publication
84 Bay St (11231)
P.O. Box 110556 (11211-0556)
PHONE.................................718 797-3900
Moses Freidman, *Owner*
Aron Friedman, *Editor*
EMP: 35
SQ FT: 2,900
SALES: 1.7MM **Privately Held**
SIC: 2731 Book publishing

(G-1770)
DESIGNS BY ROBERT SCOTT INC
Also Called: Closet Systems Group, The
810 Humboldt St Ste 3 (11222-1913)
PHONE.................................718 609-2535
Robert S Feingold, *President*
Jason Kesselman, *Vice Pres*
EMP: 20

SQ FT: 16,000
SALES: 1.8MM **Privately Held**
WEB: www.robertscottinc.com
SIC: 2511 2521 2499 Wood household furniture; wood office furniture; kitchen, bathroom & household ware: wood

(G-1771)
DESKU GROUP INC
7206 7th Ave (11209-2617)
PHONE.................................646 436-1464
Kriste Desku, *President*
EMP: 8
SQ FT: 5,000
SALES: 30MM **Privately Held**
SIC: 1241 Coal mining services

(G-1772)
DIANA KANE INCORPORATED
229 5th Ave Ste B (11215-7708)
PHONE.................................718 638-6520
Diana Kane, *President*
EMP: 5
SQ FT: 600
SALES: 500K **Privately Held**
WEB: www.dianakane.com
SIC: 3911 5094 Jewelry, precious metal; jewelry

(G-1773)
DIANE STUDIOS INC (PA)
34 35th St Ste 2b (11232-2212)
PHONE.................................718 788-6007
Martin Kurant, *President*
EMP: 55
SQ FT: 30,000
SALES (est): 4.9MM **Privately Held**
WEB: www.dianestudios.com
SIC: 3999 Shades, lamp or candle

(G-1774)
DIB MANAGMNT INC
Also Called: Airtech Lab
251 53rd St (11220-1716)
PHONE.................................718 439-8190
Rollads Dib, *President*
Ramona Luckert, *CFO*
EMP: 10
SALES (est): 1.1MM **Privately Held**
SIC: 2869 Fuels

(G-1775)
DICK BAILEY SERVICE INC
Also Called: Dick Bailey Printers
25 Chapel St Ste 602 (11201-1916)
PHONE.................................718 522-4363
Richard Bailey, *President*
William Bailey, *Vice Pres*
EMP: 14
SALES (est): 1.9MM **Privately Held**
SIC: 2752 8111 Commercial printing, offset; legal services

(G-1776)
DIGIORANGE INC
Also Called: Shhhmouse
5620 1st Ave Ste 4 (11220-2519)
PHONE.................................718 787-1500
▲ **EMP:** 7
SALES (est): 222.9K **Privately Held**
SIC: 3577 Computer peripheral equipment

(G-1777)
DIGITAC INC (PA)
2076 Ocean Pkwy (11223-4045)
PHONE.................................732 215-4020
Jacob Berman, *Ch of Bd*
▲ **EMP:** 15
SQ FT: 80,000
SALES (est): 2.5MM **Privately Held**
SIC: 3651 3089 3827 Video camera-audio recorders, household use; plastic kitchenware, tableware & houseware; spyglasses

(G-1778)
DIJIFI LLC
1166 Manhattan Ave # 100 (11222-1035)
PHONE.................................646 519-2447
Jesse Crowder,
EMP: 11
SALES (est): 1.1MM **Privately Held**
SIC: 2754 Photogravure printing

(G-1779)
DIME TRADING INC
787 Kent Ave (11205-1517)
PHONE.................................718 797-0303
Isamar Margareten, *President*
▲ **EMP:** 8
SALES (est): 1.5MM **Privately Held**
WEB: www.dimetrading.com
SIC: 2789 Trade binding services

(G-1780)
DINETTE DEPOT LTD
Also Called: Dining Furniture
350 Dewitt Ave (11207-6618)
P.O. Box 696, Bay Shore (11706-0845)
PHONE.................................516 515-9623
Walter Lustig, *Partner*
Barry Lustig, *Partner*
▲ **EMP:** 75 **EST:** 1919
SQ FT: 60,000
SALES (est): 8.9MM **Privately Held**
SIC: 2511 Kitchen & dining room furniture

(G-1781)
DISPLAY PRESENTATIONS LTD
16 Court St Fl 14 (11241-1014)
PHONE.................................631 951-4050
Stanley Zaneski, *Ch of Bd*
Fabian Zaneski, *President*
Stan Zaneski, *Vice Pres*
EMP: 52
SQ FT: 56,000
SALES (est): 6.1MM **Privately Held**
WEB: www.displaypresentations.net
SIC: 3993 Displays & cutouts, window & lobby

(G-1782)
DIVINE ART FURNITURE INC
43 Hall St Ste C9 (11205-1393)
PHONE.................................718 834-0111
David Masarsky, *President*
EMP: 8
SQ FT: 6,000
SALES: 100K **Privately Held**
WEB: www.davineartwood.com
SIC: 2521 Wood office furniture

(G-1783)
DLC COMPREHENSIVE MEDICAL PC
979 Fulton St (11238-2346)
P.O. Box 216, Old Westbury (11568-0216)
PHONE.................................718 857-1200
Katie Cheng, *Manager*
EMP: 10 **EST:** 1997
SALES (est): 692K **Privately Held**
SIC: 2741 5961 Miscellaneous publishing; magazines, mail order

(G-1784)
DLX INDUSTRIES INC
Also Called: Columbia Seal N Sew
225 25th St (11232-1337)
PHONE.................................718 272-9420
Martin Prince, *President*
Marc Stewart, *Vice Pres*
Luis Soto, *Director*
◆ **EMP:** 100 **EST:** 1950
SQ FT: 70,000
SALES (est): 12MM **Privately Held**
SIC: 3161 Attache cases; briefcases; cases, carrying

(G-1785)
DOLCE VITE INTERNATIONAL LLC
386 12th St (11215-5002)
PHONE.................................713 962-5767
Christina Summers, *Mng Member*
EMP: 5 **EST:** 2015
SALES (est): 227.9K **Privately Held**
SIC: 2066 Chocolate

(G-1786)
DOMANI FASHIONS CORP
86 S 1st St (11249-4171)
PHONE.................................718 797-0505
Moses Rosenberg, *President*
Benjamin Schlesinger, *Vice Pres*
▲ **EMP:** 9
SQ FT: 3,000
SALES (est): 840K **Privately Held**
SIC: 2369 2253 Girls' & children's outerwear; sweaters & sweater coats, knit

(G-1787)
DOMESTIC CASING CO
410 3rd Ave (11215-3179)
PHONE.................................718 522-1902
Morris Klagsbald, *Partner*
Harold Klagsbald, *Partner*
▲ **EMP:** 6 **EST:** 1956
SQ FT: 12,000
SALES (est): 1.9MM **Privately Held**
SIC: 2013 2011 Sausage casings, natural; meat packing plants

(G-1788)
DONNE DIEU PAPER MILL INC
Also Called: DIEU DONNE
63 Flushing Ave Unit 112 (11205-1069)
PHONE.................................212 226-0573
Susan Gosin, *President*
Paul Wong, *Treasurer*
Kathleen Flynn, *Exec Dir*
Dona Warner, *Director*
Eric Costello, *Admin Sec*
EMP: 7
SQ FT: 8,000
SALES: 666.2K **Privately Held**
WEB: www.dieudonne.org
SIC: 2621 8999 7999 Art paper; artist's studio; arts & crafts instruction

(G-1789)
DOORTEC ARCHTCTURAL MET GL LLC
234 46th St (11220-1008)
PHONE.................................718 567-2730
Boris Barskiy,
Natalya Yanovska, *Contractor*
EMP: 27
SALES (corp-wide): 4.8MM **Privately Held**
SIC: 3444 Sheet metalwork
PA: Doortec Architectural Metal & Glass, L.L.C.
303 Martin St
River Vale NJ 07675
201 497-5056

(G-1790)
DOVELIN PRINTING COMPANY INC
43 Hall St Ste C2 (11205-1393)
PHONE.................................718 302-3951
Stanley Darmachman, *President*
EMP: 12
SQ FT: 12,000
SALES (est): 970K **Privately Held**
SIC: 2752 Commercial printing, lithographic

(G-1791)
DR JACOBS NATURALS LLC
2615 Coney Island Ave 2nd (11223-5501)
PHONE.................................718 265-1522
Joe Aini, *Mng Member*
EMP: 24
SALES (est): 263.5K **Privately Held**
SIC: 2841 Soap & other detergents

(G-1792)
DREAM STATUARY INC
Also Called: Original Dream Statuary
251 Cleveland St (11208-1004)
PHONE.................................718 647-2024
Kumar Budhu, *President*
EMP: 6
SALES: 100K **Privately Held**
SIC: 3299 Statuary: gypsum, clay, papier mache, metal, etc.; art goods: plaster of paris, papier mache & scagliola

(G-1793)
DREAMS TO PRINT
Also Called: Hard Ten
10101 Foster Ave (11236-2107)
PHONE.................................718 483-8020
Michael Azafrani, *Owner*
EMP: 1
SALES (est): 3MM **Privately Held**
SIC: 2731 Book clubs: publishing & printing

(G-1794)
DRESSER-ARGUS INC
36 Bridge St (11201-1170)
PHONE.................................718 643-1540
Warren Frank, *Ch of Bd*

▲ = Import ▼=Export
◆ =Import/Export

Bonita Wetmore, *Admin Sec*
▲ **EMP**: 5
SQ FT: 6,000
SALES (est): 938.9K **Privately Held**
SIC: 3728 3423 Military aircraft equipment & armament; hand & edge tools

(G-1795)
DRNS CORP
Also Called: Carousel ADS
140 58th St Ste 3f (11220-2561)
PHONE.................................718 369-4530
Mark Nacson, *President*
Joan Kalmanowitz, *Admin Sec*
▲ **EMP**: 11
SQ FT: 19,500
SALES (est): 1.3MM **Privately Held**
WEB: www.directpromos.com
SIC: 2759 8743 Letterpress & screen printing; screen printing; promotion service

(G-1796)
DURALL DOLLY LLC
48 Spencer St (11205-1737)
PHONE.................................802 728-7122
EMP: 15 EST: 1981
SQ FT: 14,000
SALES (est): 990K **Privately Held**
SIC: 2599 Mfg Harwood Dollies

(G-1797)
DWECK INDUSTRIES INC (PA)
Also Called: Stephen Dweck Industries
2455 Mcdonald Ave Fl 2 (11223-5232)
PHONE.................................718 615-1695
Edmond Dweck, *President*
Gregory Dweck, *Corp Secy*
Stephen Dweck, *Vice Pres*
EMP: 2
SQ FT: 8,000
SALES (est): 3.3MM **Privately Held**
WEB: www.stephendweck.com
SIC: 3911 Pearl jewelry, natural or cultured

(G-1798)
DWECK INDUSTRIES INC
2247 E 16th St Fl 2 (11229-4424)
PHONE.................................718 615-1695
Edmond Dweck, *Branch Mgr*
EMP: 36
SALES (corp-wide): 3.3MM **Privately Held**
WEB: www.stephendweck.com
SIC: 3915 Lapidary work, contract or other
PA: Dweck Industries, Inc.
2455 Mcdonald Ave Fl 2
Brooklyn NY 11223
718 615-1695

(G-1799)
DYNAMIC HEALTH LABS INC
Also Called: Pet Authority
110 Bridge St Ste 2 (11201-1575)
PHONE.................................718 858-0100
Bruce Burwick, *President*
Vlad Goykow, *Purch Mgr*
▲ **EMP**: 33
SQ FT: 24,000
SALES (est): 10.5MM **Privately Held**
SIC: 2037 Fruit juices

(G-1800)
DYNAMIC PACKAGING INC
1567 39th St (11218-4424)
PHONE.................................718 388-0800
Stanley Freund, *Ch of Bd*
EMP: 10
SQ FT: 10,000
SALES (est): 1.1MM **Privately Held**
WEB: www.dynamicpackaging.net
SIC: 2759 5113 Bags, plastic: printing; bags, paper & disposable plastic

(G-1801)
DYNATABS LLC
Also Called: Www.dynatabs.com
1600 Ocean Pkwy Apt 1f (11230-7037)
PHONE.................................718 376-6084
Harold Baum, *Managing Dir*
Setty Baum, *CFO*
EMP: 11
SQ FT: 3,900
SALES (est): 1.3MM **Privately Held**
WEB: www.dynatabs.com
SIC: 2023 Dietary supplements, dairy & non-dairy based

(G-1802)
E & F HOME FASHIONS INC (PA)
2154 E 71st St (11234-6225)
PHONE.................................718 968-9719
Elaine Roth, *President*
Fred Roth, *Corp Secy*
▲ **EMP**: 6
SALES (est): 456.5K **Privately Held**
SIC: 2392 5023 Tablecloths & table settings; shower curtains: made from purchased materials; linens & towels

(G-1803)
E G M RESTAURANT EQUIPMENT MFG
688 Flushing Ave (11206-5025)
PHONE.................................718 782-9800
Scott Michaels, *President*
EMP: 7 EST: 1971
SQ FT: 2,500
SALES (est): 640K **Privately Held**
SIC: 3444 Restaurant sheet metalwork

(G-1804)
E GRAPHICS CORPORATION
160 Havemeyer St (11211-8772)
PHONE.................................718 486-9767
Esmeralda Lora, *President*
Edwin Lora, *General Mgr*
EMP: 5
SALES (est): 405.6K **Privately Held**
SIC: 2732 Book printing

(G-1805)
E S P METAL CRAFTS INC
379 Harman St (11237-4701)
PHONE.................................718 381-2443
Edward Grancagnolo, *President*
▲ **EMP**: 9
SALES (est): 1MM **Privately Held**
SIC: 3446 Railings, bannisters, guards, etc.: made from metal pipe

(G-1806)
E-Z GLOBAL WHOLESALE INC
925 E 14th St (11230-3648)
PHONE.................................888 769-7888
Shakhim Mamedov, *President*
EMP: 5
SALES (est): 174.3K **Privately Held**
SIC: 3999 Manufacturing industries

(G-1807)
EAGLE FINISHING
Also Called: Eagle Fashions U S A
49 Wyckoff Ave (11237-8001)
PHONE.................................718 497-7875
Ariam Kurti, *Principal*
EMP: 20
SALES (est): 605.5K **Privately Held**
SIC: 2396 Apparel findings & trimmings

(G-1808)
EAST WEST GLOBAL SOURCING INC
425 Neptune Ave Apt 22a (11224-4587)
PHONE.................................917 887-2286
Michael Zeidner, *CEO*
EMP: 8
SQ FT: 2,000
SALES (est): 371K **Privately Held**
SIC: 3199 Leather garments

(G-1809)
EASTERN FEATHER & DOWN CORP
Also Called: Yugo Landau
1027 Metropolitan Ave (11211-2710)
PHONE.................................718 387-4100
Joseph Landau, *President*
Yehoshua Weiner, *Vice Pres*
▲ **EMP**: 8
SQ FT: 45,000
SALES (est): 4MM **Privately Held**
SIC: 3999 Down (feathers)

(G-1810)
EASTERN SILVER OF BORO PARK
4901 16th Ave (11204-1115)
PHONE.................................718 854-5600
Bernard Gelbstein, *President*
EMP: 5
SQ FT: 4,500
SALES (est): 1MM **Privately Held**
SIC: 3479 Engraving jewelry silverware, or metal

(G-1811)
ECOPLAST & PACKAGING LLC
4619 Surf Ave (11224-1047)
PHONE.................................718 996-0800
Shifra Lefkowitz, *CEO*
Larry Lefkowitz,
EMP: 6 EST: 2009
SALES (est): 2.2MM **Privately Held**
SIC: 2671 2673 3081 2754 Plastic film, coated or laminated for packaging; bags: plastic, laminated & coated; unsupported plastics film & sheet; commercial printing, gravure

(G-1812)
ED NEGRON FINE WOODWORKING
43 Hall St Fl 5 (11205-1315)
PHONE.................................718 246-1016
Ed Negron, *President*
EMP: 8
SALES (est): 722.4K **Privately Held**
SIC: 2431 2499 Millwork; decorative wood & woodwork

(G-1813)
EDCO SUPPLY CORPORATION
323 36th St (11232-2599)
PHONE.................................718 788-8108
Carl Freyer, *CEO*
Joaquin Celis, *Safety Mgr*
Arlene Amuso, *Human Res Mgr*
Louisa Susman, *Sales Staff*
Justin Daniels, *Marketing Staff*
EMP: 53 EST: 1955
SQ FT: 25,000
SALES (est): 9.5MM **Privately Held**
WEB: www.edcosupply.com
SIC: 3081 5113 2673 Packing materials, plastic sheet; pressure sensitive tape; bags: plastic, laminated & coated

(G-1814)
EDISON POWER & LIGHT CO INC
204 Van Dyke St 207 (11231-1038)
PHONE.................................718 522-0002
Leon Gross, *President*
EMP: 14
SQ FT: 36,000
SALES (est): 1.8MM **Privately Held**
SIC: 3648 5719 Lighting equipment; lighting fixtures

(G-1815)
EDSAL MACHINE PRODUCTS INC (PA)
126 56th St (11220-2575)
PHONE.................................718 439-9163
Evangelos S Tsevdos, *Ch of Bd*
Steven Tsevdos, *President*
Dessie Tsevdos, *Admin Sec*
▲ **EMP**: 12
SQ FT: 20,000
SALES (est): 1.8MM **Privately Held**
SIC: 3599 Machine shop, jobbing & repair

(G-1816)
EFS DESIGNS LLC
610 Smith St Ste 3 (11231-2113)
PHONE.................................718 852-9511
Udoro Suarez, *Mng Member*
EMP: 6
SQ FT: 20,000
SALES: 591K **Privately Held**
SIC: 2262 2759 Screen printing: man-made fiber & silk broadwoven fabrics; screen printing

(G-1817)
EKS MANUFACTURING INC
577 Wortman Ave (11208-5415)
P.O. Box 21325 (11202-1325)
PHONE.................................917 217-0784
William Socolov, *Owner*
EMP: 10
SALES (est): 1.1MM **Privately Held**
SIC: 3652 Phonograph records, prerecorded

(G-1818)
EL DIARIO LLC
1 Metrotech Ctr Fl 1801 (11201-3949)
PHONE.................................212 807-4600
Rossana Rosado, *CEO*
Pedro Frisneda, *Editor*
Ramon Vera, *Opers Staff*
Gladys Ruiz, *Accounts Exec*
Denny Pena, *Director*
EMP: 122
SQ FT: 28,000
SALES (est): 7.5MM **Privately Held**
WEB: www.eldiariony.com
SIC: 2711 Newspapers, publishing & printing

(G-1819)
EL ERMAN INTERNATIONAL LTD
1205 E 29th St (11210-4630)
PHONE.................................212 444-9440
Shelley Cohen, *President*
Moshe Cohen, *Vice Pres*
David Elan, *Vice Pres*
◆ **EMP**: 3
SALES: 2MM **Privately Held**
SIC: 2844 5122 Face creams or lotions; hair preparations
PA: E.L. Erman Cosmetic Production Ltd
3 Haplada
Ashdod
885 325-37

(G-1820)
ELECTRIC MOTORS AND PUMPS INC
466 Carroll St (11215-1012)
PHONE.................................718 935-9118
Jorge Fraticelli, *President*
Maria Fraticelli, *Vice Pres*
EMP: 7
SQ FT: 4,500
SALES (est): 790K **Privately Held**
SIC: 3469 5999 5084 Machine parts, stamped or pressed metal; engine & motor equipment & supplies; motors, electric; plumbing & heating supplies; pumps & pumping equipment

(G-1821)
ELECTRONIC DIE CORP
19th St Fl 2 Flr 2 (11232)
PHONE.................................718 455-3200
Joseph Assenza, *President*
Michael Reiss, *Principal*
Alfred Torez, *Treasurer*
EMP: 10
SQ FT: 10,000
SALES (est): 1.1MM **Privately Held**
WEB: www.electronicdiecorp.com
SIC: 3544 Special dies & tools

(G-1822)
ELEGANT DESSERTS BY METRO INC
868 Kent Ave (11205-2702)
PHONE.................................718 388-1323
Martin Weisz, *President*
Benjamin Weisz, *Principal*
EMP: 12
SQ FT: 7,500
SALES (est): 830K **Privately Held**
SIC: 2024 Ices, flavored (frozen dessert)

(G-1823)
ELEGANT LINEN INC
200 60th St (11220-3712)
PHONE.................................718 492-0297
Benjamin Barber, *President*
Richard Citron, *Vice Pres*
▲ **EMP**: 30
SQ FT: 4,000

Brooklyn - Kings County (G-1824)

SALES (est): 3.3MM **Privately Held**
WEB: www.elegantlinen.com
SIC: 2392 Sheets, fabric: made from purchased materials

(G-1824)
ELEMENT ST JOHNS CORP
764 Saint Johns Pl (11216-4694)
PHONE.................................917 349-2139
Michelle Abreu, *Principal*
EMP: 9
SALES (est): 1.1MM **Privately Held**
SIC: 2819 Industrial inorganic chemicals

(G-1825)
ELEPATH INC
110 Kent Ave 9 (11249-2812)
PHONE.................................347 417-4975
Bryan Goldberg, *CFO*
EMP: 5
SALES (est): 333.2K **Privately Held**
SIC: 7372 Application computer software

(G-1826)
ELEPHANTS CUSTOM FURNITURE INC
67 Van Dam St (11222-3806)
PHONE.................................917 509-3581
Gokhan Doguer, *President*
EMP: 51
SQ FT: 10,000
SALES (est): 8.3MM **Privately Held**
SIC: 2499 Decorative wood & woodwork

(G-1827)
ELRAMIDA HOLDINGS INC
2555 E 29th St (11235-2020)
PHONE.................................646 280-0503
Mark Harris, *CEO*
Eldar Rakhamineov, *Ch of Bd*
EMP: 22
SALES (est): 4.5MM **Privately Held**
SIC: 3537 Trucks, tractors, loaders, carriers & similar equipment

(G-1828)
EMCO CHEMICAL (USA) CORP
334 Douglass St (11217-3114)
PHONE.................................718 797-3652
Andy Uchitel, *President*
Mary Ellen Limer, *Vice Pres*
EMP: 25
SQ FT: 6,000
SALES (est): 3.1MM **Privately Held**
SIC: 2819 Industrial inorganic chemicals

(G-1829)
EMERALD HOLDINGS INC
Also Called: Emerald Knitting
63 Flushing Ave Unit 201 (11205-1072)
PHONE.................................718 797-4404
Michael Engle, *President*
Arnold Shulman, *Vice Pres*
▲ **EMP:** 5
SALES (est): 611.6K **Privately Held**
SIC: 2339 2253 Women's & misses' outerwear; knit outerwear mills

(G-1830)
EMES MOTOR INC
876 Metropolitan Ave (11211-2515)
PHONE.................................718 387-2445
Abraham Mertz, *President*
EMP: 5
SALES (est): 600K **Privately Held**
SIC: 3621 5999 Motors & generators; motors, electric

(G-1831)
EMILIA INTERIORS INC (PA)
867 E 52nd St (11203-6701)
PHONE.................................718 629-4202
Nicholas Vignapiano, *President*
Jennie Vignapiano, *Corp Secy*
EMP: 19
SQ FT: 20,000
SALES (est): 1.5MM **Privately Held**
WEB: www.girardemilia.com
SIC: 2511 Wood household furniture

(G-1832)
EMPIRE AIR SYSTEMS LLC
Also Called: Empire Air Hvac
2535 65th St (11204-3528)
PHONE.................................718 377-1549

Lior Binyamin,
Shmuel Cohen Zada,
EMP: 15
SALES (est): 1.5MM **Privately Held**
SIC: 3585 Air conditioning equipment, complete

(G-1833)
EMPIRE PRESS CO (PA)
550 Empire Blvd (11225-3131)
PHONE.................................718 756-9500
Mordechai Chein, *Owner*
Joe Katz, *Office Mgr*
EMP: 5
SQ FT: 6,000
SALES (est): 513.4K **Privately Held**
WEB: www.empirepress.com
SIC: 2791 2752 Typesetting; commercial printing, offset

(G-1834)
EMPIRE TRANSIT MIX INC
430 Maspeth Ave (11211-1704)
PHONE.................................718 384-3000
Rocco Tomassetti, *Ch of Bd*
Dina Tammaro, *Office Mgr*
Michael Serrano, *Office Admin*
Rocco Pomassetti, *Info Tech Dir*
EMP: 40
SALES (est): 7.9MM **Privately Held**
SIC: 3273 Ready-mixed concrete

(G-1835)
EMUNAS SALES INC
947 E 27th St (11210-3727)
PHONE.................................718 621-3138
Usher Orzel, *President*
EMP: 16
SQ FT: 3,000
SALES (est): 422.2K **Privately Held**
SIC: 2323 Men's & boys' neckwear

(G-1836)
ENERGY CONSERVATION & SUP INC
Also Called: Ecs Global
55 Washington St Ste 324 (11201-1070)
PHONE.................................718 855-5888
Luther Garcia, *CEO*
Anthony Huggett, *COO*
Ricky Dweck, *Vice Pres*
James Crespo, *Treasurer*
Gretchen Sanchez, *Finance Dir*
EMP: 35
SQ FT: 2,200
SALES (est): 13.5MM **Privately Held**
WEB: www.enerconsupply.com
SIC: 3646 Commercial indusl & institutional electric lighting fixtures

(G-1837)
ENTERPRISE WOOD PRODUCTS INC
4712 18th Ave (11204-1260)
PHONE.................................718 853-9243
Jan Koegel, *President*
Leonard Rosenberg, *Treasurer*
EMP: 11
SQ FT: 7,500
SALES (est): 1.3MM **Privately Held**
SIC: 2434 Wood kitchen cabinets

(G-1838)
ENTICING LINGERIE INC
166 Gravesend Neck Rd (11223-4707)
PHONE.................................718 998-8625
David Gindi, *President*
Arlette Gindi, *Corp Secy*
EMP: 20
SQ FT: 5,000
SALES (est): 5MM **Privately Held**
WEB: www.enticinglingerie.com
SIC: 2341 2342 Women's & children's underwear; bras, girdles & allied garments

(G-1839)
ENZO MANZONI LLC
2896 W 12th St (11224-2907)
PHONE.................................212 464-7000
Gene Isaac, *Director*
EMP: 7
SQ FT: 5,000
SALES (est): 400K **Privately Held**
SIC: 2326 5136 Work apparel, except uniforms; men's & boys' clothing; men's & boys' sportswear & work clothing

(G-1840)
EPNER TECHNOLOGY INC
25 Division Pl (11222-5204)
PHONE.................................718 782-8722
David Epner, *Owner*
EMP: 5
SALES (est): 480.1K **Privately Held**
SIC: 3471 Plating & polishing

(G-1841)
EPNER TECHNOLOGY INCORPORATED (PA)
279 Frost St (11222-5601)
PHONE.................................718 782-5948
David Epner, *President*
Paul J Brancato, *General Mgr*
Stephen V Candiloro, *Corp Secy*
Steven A Candiloro Sr, *Vice Pres*
Heather Michella, *Manager*
▼ **EMP:** 40
SQ FT: 40,000
SALES (est): 6.1MM **Privately Held**
WEB: www.epner.com
SIC: 3471 Electroplating of metals or formed products

(G-1842)
EPNER TECHNOLOGY INCORPORATED
78 Kingsland Ave (11222-5603)
PHONE.................................718 782-8722
David Epner, *Marketing Staff*
Stephen V Candiloro, *Systems Mgr*
EMP: 35
SALES (est): 2.2MM
SALES (corp-wide): 6.1MM **Privately Held**
WEB: www.epner.com
SIC: 3471 Plating & polishing
PA: Epner Technology Incorporated
  279 Frost St
  Brooklyn NY 11222
  718 782-5948

(G-1843)
EPONYM INC
85 N 3rd St 112 (11249-3944)
PHONE.................................646 918-4586
EMP: 5
SALES (est): 576.6K **Privately Held**
SIC: 3851 Eyeglasses, lenses & frames

(G-1844)
EPUFFER INC
2348 80th St Fl 1 (11214-2025)
PHONE.................................718 374-6030
Shawn Shalmiev, *President*
EMP: 5
SQ FT: 2,000
SALES (est): 45MM **Privately Held**
SIC: 2111 Cigarettes

(G-1845)
EQUITYARCADE LLC
33 Nassau Ave (11222-3132)
PHONE.................................678 232-1301
Aaron Kaplan, *CEO*
Ponsius Odaga, *Manager*
EMP: 5
SALES (est): 143.6K **Privately Held**
SIC: 2741

(G-1846)
ERCOLE NYC INC (PA)
142 26th St (11232)
PHONE.................................212 675-2218
Ornella Pisano, *President*
▲ **EMP:** 18
SQ FT: 15,000
SALES (est): 1.8MM **Privately Held**
WEB: www.ercolehome.com
SIC: 3253 2511 Ceramic wall & floor tile; tables, household: wood

(G-1847)
ESER REALTY CORP (PA)
62 Greenpoint Ave 64 (11222-2057)
PHONE.................................718 383-0565
Robert Frenkel, *Ch of Bd*
Morton Frenkel, *President*
◆ **EMP:** 50
SQ FT: 30,000
SALES (est): 5.4MM **Privately Held**
SIC: 3999 Feathers, renovating

(G-1848)
ESKAYEL INC
75 S 6th St (11249-6027)
PHONE.................................347 703-8084
Shannan Campanaro, *Principal*
EMP: 5
SALES (est): 411.9K **Privately Held**
SIC: 2299 2273 2679 8999 Broadwoven fabrics: linen, jute, hemp & ramie; dyeing & finishing of tufted rugs & carpets; wallpaper; artist's studio

(G-1849)
ESQUIRE MECHANICAL CORP
79 Sandford St (11205)
PHONE.................................718 625-4006
Geoffrey Thaw, *President*
EMP: 7
SQ FT: 5,000
SALES (est): 1.2MM **Privately Held**
WEB: www.dunhill-esquire.com
SIC: 3556 Mfg Rotisseries

(G-1850)
ESS BEE INDUSTRIES INC
95 Evergreen Ave (11206-6124)
PHONE.................................718 894-5202
Alex Stein, *President*
Iza Stein, *Vice Pres*
EMP: 30
SQ FT: 40,000
SALES (est): 2.3MM **Privately Held**
SIC: 2221 2392 5023 Manmade Broadwoven Fabric Mill Mfg Household Furnishings Whol Homefurnishings

(G-1851)
ESSENCE COMMUNICATIONS INC (PA)
Also Called: Essence Magazine
241 37th St Fl 1 (11232-2410)
PHONE.................................212 522-1212
Michelle Ebanks, *CEO*
Christian Juhl, *CEO*
Barbara Britton, *President*
Clarence O Smith, *President*
Joy C Profet, *General Mgr*
▲ **EMP:** 119
SQ FT: 30,000
SALES (est): 20.9MM **Privately Held**
SIC: 2721 Magazines: publishing only, not printed on site

(G-1852)
ESSEX WORKS LTD
446 Riverdale Ave (11207-6121)
PHONE.................................718 495-4575
Douglas Schickler, *President*
EMP: 19 **EST:** 1995
SQ FT: 3,000
SALES (est): 1.8MM **Privately Held**
WEB: www.essexworks.com
SIC: 3299 Architectural sculptures: gypsum, clay, papier mache, etc.

(G-1853)
EURO WOODWORKING INC
303 Park Ave Fl 8 (11205-1307)
PHONE.................................718 246-9172
Wolfgang Michelitsch, *President*
EMP: 6
SALES (est): 644.5K **Privately Held**
SIC: 3089 Prefabricated plastic buildings

(G-1854)
EVER-NU-METAL PRODUCTS INC
471 20th St (11215-6294)
PHONE.................................646 423-5833
Frank Gagliardi Jr, *President*
John Gagliardi, *General Mgr*
Rocco Gagliardi, *Corp Secy*
▲ **EMP:** 12
SQ FT: 14,000
SALES (est): 1.4MM **Privately Held**
WEB: www.evernumetal.com
SIC: 3471 Finishing, metals or formed products

(G-1855)
EVERLAST SEALS AND SUPPLY LLC
41 Montrose Ave (11206-2381)
PHONE.................................718 388-7373
Joshua Benjamin, *Managing Prtnr*

John Martini, *Sls & Mktg Exec*
Barry Himmel,
▲ **EMP:** 10
SQ FT: 15,000
SALES: 1MM **Privately Held**
SIC: 3053 Gaskets, all materials

(G-1856)
EXCELLENT POLY INC
820 4th Ave (11232-1612)
PHONE 718 768-6555
Joshua Silber, *CEO*
Isaac Stern, *President*
Harry Weingarten, *Exec VP*
EMP: 15 **EST:** 1959
SQ FT: 55,000
SALES (est): 3.7MM **Privately Held**
WEB: www.excellentpoly.com
SIC: 2673 3081 Plastic bags: made from purchased materials; unsupported plastics film & sheet

(G-1857)
EXCELLENT PRINTING INC
Also Called: Excellent Photoccpies
165 Hooper St (11211-7911)
PHONE 718 384-7272
Gubor Rubin, *President*
Joseph Weinburger, *Vice Pres*
EMP: 6
SALES (est): 540.4K **Privately Held**
WEB: www.yeshivanet.com
SIC: 2759 Commercial printing

(G-1858)
EXECUTIVE MACHINES INC
Also Called: Jeam Imports
882 3rd Ave Unit 8 (11232-1902)
P.O. Box 320150 (11232-0150)
PHONE 718 965-6600
Aron Abramson, *CEO*
Charles Sued, *President*
▲ **EMP:** 30
SQ FT: 20,000
SALES: 20K **Privately Held**
WEB: www.executivemachines.com
SIC: 3678 Electronic connectors

(G-1859)
EXPERT INDUSTRIES INC
848 E 43rd St (11210-3502)
PHONE 718 434-6060
Cynthia Rubinberg, *President*
Michael Rubinberg, *Vice Pres*
EMP: 25
SQ FT: 25,000
SALES (est): 4MM **Privately Held**
SIC: 3443 3556 3444 Tanks, standard or custom fabricated: metal plate; vessels, process or storage (from boiler shops): metal plate; mixers, commercial, food; sheet metalwork

(G-1860)
EY INDUSTRIES INC
Also Called: Ruckel Manufacturing Co
63 Flushing Ave Unit 331 (11205-1083)
PHONE 718 624-9122
Joseph Friedman, *President*
Aaron Parnes, *COO*
EMP: 15 **EST:** 1937
SQ FT: 15,000
SALES (est): 980K **Privately Held**
WEB: www.yarmulka.com
SIC: 2392 Comforters & quilts: made from purchased materials; pillowcases: made from purchased materials; mattress protectors, except rubber; sheets, fabric: made from purchased materials

(G-1861)
EZ NEWSLETTER LLC
1449 Bay Ridge Ave 2 (11219-6232)
PHONE 412 943-7777
Eric V Hileman, *Mng Member*
EMP: 10
SALES (est): 890K **Privately Held**
SIC: 7372 Prepackaged software

(G-1862)
EZ SYSTEMS US INC
215 Water St Gf (11201-1131)
PHONE 929 295-0699
Bertrand Maugain, *CEO*
Morten Ingebrigtsen, *Ch of Bd*
Eivind Hesjadalen, *CFO*

Monika Zimmermann, *Manager*
EMP: 105
SALES (est): 5MM
SALES (corp-wide): 9.5MM **Privately Held**
SIC: 7372 Business oriented computer software
PA: Ez Systems As
Porselesvegen 18
Porsgrunn 3920
355 870-20

(G-1863)
F R A M TECHNOLOGIES INC
3048 Bedford Ave (11210-3714)
PHONE 718 338-6230
Mordechai Plotsker, *President*
EMP: 6
SALES (est): 50.2K **Privately Held**
WEB: www.framtech.com
SIC: 7372 Prepackaged software

(G-1864)
FACTORY EAST
Also Called: Factory Nyc
723 Kent Ave (11249-7807)
PHONE 718 280-1558
Paul Outlaw, *Owner*
Jonathan Epstein, *Project Mgr*
Jim Wines, *Project Mgr*
Shane Jezowski, *Engineer*
EMP: 20
SALES (est): 2.4MM **Privately Held**
SIC: 3499 Fabricated metal products

(G-1865)
FAIRVIEW BELL AND INTERCOM
502 Gravesend Neck Rd B (11223-4800)
PHONE 718 627-8621
Grzegorz Butny, *President*
Florence Kachman, *Manager*
EMP: 5
SQ FT: 600
SALES (est): 200K **Privately Held**
SIC: 3699 Security devices

(G-1866)
FALCONES COOKIE LAND LTD (PA)
Also Called: Falcone Food Distribution
1648 61st St (11204)
PHONE 718 236-4200
Carmine Falcone Jr, *Ch of Bd*
Angelo Falcone, *President*
Francis Falcone, *Vice Pres*
EMP: 40
SQ FT: 24,000
SALES (est): 5.4MM **Privately Held**
SIC: 2052 Cookies

(G-1867)
FAMILY FUEL CO INC
1571 W 10th St (11204-6302)
PHONE 718 232-2009
Carol Maiden, *Chairman*
EMP: 5
SALES (est): 359.8K **Privately Held**
SIC: 2869 Fuels

(G-1868)
FANCY WINDOWS & DOORS MFG CORP
Also Called: Fancy Window & Door
312 Ten Eyck St (11206-1723)
PHONE 718 366-7800
Jin Hu Ye, *Ch of Bd*
Jackson Ye, *President*
Jian Xu Chong, *Shareholder*
▲ **EMP:** 7
SQ FT: 4,000
SALES (est): 935.5K **Privately Held**
SIC: 2431 Doors & door parts & trim, wood; windows & window parts & trim, wood

(G-1869)
FAUCETS AND MORE INCORPORATED
5318a 16th Ave Ste 106 (11204-1425)
PHONE 734 328-2387
Jack Branson, *President*
EMP: 6
SALES: 7MM **Privately Held**
SIC: 3432 Faucets & spigots, metal & plastic

(G-1870)
FAVORITE PLASTIC CORP
1465 Utica Ave (11234-1108)
PHONE 718 253-7000
Hershey Friedman, *President*
Mitch Kirschner, *Vice Pres*
▲ **EMP:** 110 **EST:** 1956
SQ FT: 75,000
SALES (est): 16.8MM **Privately Held**
WEB: www.favoriteplastics.com
SIC: 3081 3083 Plastic film & sheet; laminated plastics plate & sheet

(G-1871)
FAYE BERNARD LOUNGEWEAR
2604 Avenue M (11210-4611)
PHONE 718 951-7245
Faye Zola, *Partner*
Bernard Zola, *Partner*
EMP: 8
SQ FT: 2,000
SALES (est): 600K **Privately Held**
SIC: 2341 Nightgowns & negligees: women's & children's

(G-1872)
FELDMAN JEWELRY CREATIONS INC
4821 16th Ave (11204-1109)
PHONE 718 438-8895
Susan Feldman, *President*
Mordecai Feldman, *Vice Pres*
EMP: 5
SQ FT: 650
SALES (est): 490K **Privately Held**
SIC: 3911 Necklaces, precious metal; rings, finger: precious metal

(G-1873)
FELDWARE INC
250 Avenue W (11223-5288)
PHONE 718 372-0486
Sidney Feldman, *President*
Charles Feldman, *Vice Pres*
▲ **EMP:** 25 **EST:** 1959
SQ FT: 15,000
SALES (est): 4MM **Privately Held**
SIC: 3469 Stamping metal for the trade

(G-1874)
FENCE PLAZA CORP
1601 Nostrand Ave (11226-5101)
PHONE 718 469-2200
George Prince, *President*
EMP: 6
SQ FT: 300
SALES (est): 1.1MM **Privately Held**
WEB: www.fenceplaza.com
SIC: 3446 1799 5211 3441 Fences or posts, ornamental iron or steel; fence construction; fencing; fabricated structural metal

(G-1875)
FERRO FABRICATORS INC
1117 38th St (11218-1926)
PHONE 718 703-0007
Gregory Dec, *President*
EMP: 13 **EST:** 2003
SQ FT: 10,000
SALES (est): 2.4MM **Privately Held**
SIC: 3449 Bars, concrete reinforcing: fabricated steel

(G-1876)
FEVERTREE USA INC
77 Front St Fl 2 (11201-1006)
PHONE 718 852-5577
Charles Gibb, *CEO*
EMP: 10
SQ FT: 200
SALES: 45MM **Privately Held**
SIC: 2086 Carbonated beverages, nonalcoholic: bottled & canned

(G-1877)
FIBERWAVE CORPORATION
140 58th St Ste 37 (11220-2524)
PHONE 718 802-9011
John Romeo, *President*
Ed Kirchgessner, *CFO*
▲ **EMP:** 200

SALES (est): 31.8MM **Privately Held**
WEB: www.fiberwave.com
SIC: 3661 Fiber optics communications equipment

(G-1878)
FIELD WARES LLC
Also Called: Field Company
53 Bridge St Apt 410 (11201-7901)
PHONE 508 380-6545
Stephen Muscarella, *Mng Member*
Chris Muscarella,
EMP: 6
SQ FT: 1,000
SALES (est): 2MM **Privately Held**
SIC: 3321 Cooking utensils, cast iron

(G-1879)
FIL DOUX INC
227 5th Ave (11215-1202)
PHONE 212 202-1459
Leonardo Novik, *Ch of Bd*
Jeremy Chang, *COO*
Hannah Rice, *Project Mgr*
Juliette Ozkalfayan, *Mktg Coord*
Audrey Pincus, *Creative Dir*
EMP: 10
SALES (est): 3MM **Privately Held**
SIC: 2299 Broadwoven fabrics: linen, jute, hemp & ramie

(G-1880)
FILTA CLEAN CO INC
Also Called: Belton Industries
107 Georgia Ave (11207-2489)
PHONE 718 495-3800
Tommy Weber, *President*
Ron Weber, *Vice Pres*
EMP: 35
SQ FT: 10,000
SALES (est): 9.1MM **Privately Held**
WEB: www.multidisplayandpanel.com
SIC: 3564 7349 Filters, air: furnaces, air conditioning equipment, etc.; air duct cleaning

(G-1881)
FINE AND RAW CHOCOLATE
288 Seigel St (11206-3813)
PHONE 718 366-3633
Daniel Sklaar, *Owner*
EMP: 5
SALES (est): 150K **Privately Held**
SIC: 2064 Candy bars, including chocolate covered bars

(G-1882)
FINELINE THERMOGRAPHERS INC
544 Park Ave Ste 308 (11205-1647)
PHONE 718 643-1100
Samuel Fried, *President*
Themmy Sixler, *Admin Sec*
EMP: 7
SQ FT: 7,000
SALES (est): 817.5K **Privately Held**
SIC: 2759 Thermography

(G-1883)
FINESSE CREATIONS INC
3004 Avenue J (11210-3838)
PHONE 718 692-2100
Esther Machlis, *President*
▲ **EMP:** 10
SQ FT: 2,500
SALES (est): 2.6MM **Privately Held**
WEB: www.finessecreations.com
SIC: 3599 5044 3569 Custom machinery; office equipment; baling machines, for scrap metal, paper or similar material

(G-1884)
FIRE FOX SECURITY CORP
2070 72nd St Apt B1 (11204-5823)
PHONE 917 981-9280
John Mansi, *President*
EMP: 5
SQ FT: 800
SALES: 250K **Privately Held**
SIC: 3699 5045 Security control equipment & systems; computers, peripherals & software

Brooklyn - Kings County (G-1885)

(G-1885)
FIVE BORO HOLDING LLC
1425 37th St Ste 3 (11218-3771)
PHONE..................................718 431-9500
Joey Cohen, *Mng Member*
EMP: 10
SQ FT: 18,000
SALES (est): 138.2K **Privately Held**
WEB: www.fiveboroughprinting.com
SIC: 2761 Computer forms, manifold or continuous

(G-1886)
FIVE BURROUGHS BREWING CO
215 47th St (11220-1009)
PHONE..................................718 355-8575
Blake W Tomnitz, *CEO*
EMP: 6
SALES (est): 91.3K **Privately Held**
SIC: 2082 Beer (alcoholic beverage)

(G-1887)
FLARE MULTICOPY CORP
Also Called: Flare Multi Copy
1840 Flatbush Ave (11210-4831)
PHONE..................................718 258-8860
Steven Zeller, *President*
Sam Stempler, *Treasurer*
EMP: 22
SALES (est): 3.2MM **Privately Held**
SIC: 2752 2791 2789 2732 Commercial printing, offset; typesetting; bookbinding & related work; book printing

(G-1888)
FLATCUT LLC
68 Jay St Ste 901 (11201-8364)
PHONE..................................212 542-5732
Tomer Ben-Gal, *Principal*
Jay Schainholz, *Principal*
Deven Pravin Shah, *Marketing Staff*
EMP: 5 **EST:** 2010
SALES (est): 523.8K **Privately Held**
SIC: 3498 3532 3496 Fabricated pipe & fittings; mining machinery; miscellaneous fabricated wire products

(G-1889)
FLAVOR PAPER LTD
Also Called: Flavor League
216 Pacific St (11201-5888)
PHONE..................................718 422-0230
Emily Cangie, *COO*
Walt Vayo, *VP Prdtn*
Clare Colton, *Marketing Staff*
Julia Heydemann, *Director*
Jon Sherman, *Administration*
EMP: 13
SQ FT: 3,500
SALES (est): 1.4MM **Privately Held**
WEB: www.flavorleague.com
SIC: 2679 Wallpaper

(G-1890)
FLEAHEART INC
61 Greenpoint Ave Ste 403 (11222-1526)
PHONE..................................718 521-4958
Andrew Woodrum, *Ch of Bd*
EMP: 11
SALES (est): 1.3MM **Privately Held**
SIC: 2759 Commercial printing

(G-1891)
FLEETWOOD CABINET CO INC (PA)
673 Livonia Ave (11207-5407)
PHONE..................................516 379-2139
Eric Belgraier, *President*
EMP: 8 **EST:** 1948
SQ FT: 12,000
SALES (est): 1MM **Privately Held**
SIC: 2541 Cabinets, except refrigerated: show, display, etc.: wood; counters or counter display cases, wood; table or counter tops, plastic laminated; sink tops, plastic laminated

(G-1892)
FLICKINGER GLASSWORKS INC
175 Van Dyke St Ste 321ap (11231-1079)
PHONE..................................718 875-1531
Charles Flickinger, *President*
EMP: 8
SQ FT: 7,000
SALES (est): 1.1MM **Privately Held**
WEB: www.flickingerglassworks.com
SIC: 3231 5231 Glass sheet, bent: made from purchased glass; glass, leaded or stained

(G-1893)
FLUSHING BOILER & WELDING CO
8720 Ditmas Ave (11236-1606)
PHONE..................................718 463-1266
EMP: 7
SALES (est): 470K **Privately Held**
SIC: 7692 7699 5074 1799 Welding Repair Services Whol Plumbing Equip/Supp Special Trade Contractor

(G-1894)
FLUSHING PHARMACY INC
414 Flushing Ave Ste 1 (11205-1548)
PHONE..................................718 260-8999
Michell Wifemen, *President*
EMP: 250
SALES (est): 326.2K **Privately Held**
SIC: 2834 5813 Druggists' preparations (pharmaceuticals); night clubs

(G-1895)
FOLENE PACKAGING LLC
2509 Avenue M (11210-4544)
P.O. Box 300965 (11230-0965)
PHONE..................................917 626-6740
Edward Weiss,
▲ **EMP:** 5
SALES (est): 586.6K **Privately Held**
SIC: 2671 Plastic film, coated or laminated for packaging

(G-1896)
FOLIO GRAPHICS CO INC
2759 E 66th St (11234-6806)
PHONE..................................718 763-2076
Stanley Drate, *President*
Rochelle Drate, *Vice Pres*
EMP: 6
SQ FT: 780
SALES (est): 420K **Privately Held**
SIC: 2731 7335 Books: publishing only; commercial photography

(G-1897)
FORD REGULATOR VALVE CORP
199 Varet St (11206-3704)
PHONE..................................718 497-3255
Joseph Tuzzolo, *President*
Paula Tuzollo, *Treasurer*
EMP: 5 **EST:** 1889
SQ FT: 5,000
SALES (est): 520K **Privately Held**
WEB: www.fordregulatorvalve.com
SIC: 3494 5085 Valves & pipe fittings; industrial supplies

(G-1898)
FORO MARBLE CO INC
166 2nd Ave (11215-4619)
PHONE..................................718 852-2322
Joseph P Guido, *President*
Joseph A Guido Jr, *Exec VP*
Joan Foro, *Vice Pres*
Joan Guido, *Sales Executive*
EMP: 25 **EST:** 1965
SQ FT: 25,000
SALES (est): 4.4MM **Privately Held**
WEB: www.foromarble.net
SIC: 3272 5032 Tile, precast terrazzo or concrete; slabs, crossing: concrete; tile, clay or other ceramic, excluding refractory

(G-1899)
FORTUNE SIGN
1334 39th St (11218-3616)
PHONE..................................646 383-8682
Anatoliy Kreychmar, *Principal*
EMP: 5 **EST:** 2011
SALES (est): 479.2K **Privately Held**
SIC: 3993 Signs & advertising specialties

(G-1900)
FOSTER REEVE & ASSOCIATES INC (PA)
1155 Manhattan Ave # 1011 (11222-6161)
PHONE..................................718 609-0090
Foster Reeve, *President*
Cathy Reilly, *CFO*
▲ **EMP:** 6
SQ FT: 4,000
SALES (est): 3.7MM **Privately Held**
WEB: www.fraplaster.com
SIC: 3299 1742 Moldings, architectural: plaster of paris; plastering, plain or ornamental

(G-1901)
FOUNTAIN TILE OUTLET INC
609 Fountain Ave Ste A (11208-6007)
PHONE..................................718 927-4555
Frank Lapetina, *Principal*
EMP: 6
SALES (est): 297.3K **Privately Held**
SIC: 2426 Flooring, hardwood

(G-1902)
FOUR S SHOWCASE MANUFACTURING
1044 Linwood St (11208-5422)
PHONE..................................718 649-4900
Tony Razi, *President*
Isabel Razi, *Vice Pres*
EMP: 8
SQ FT: 12,000
SALES (est): 931.7K **Privately Held**
WEB: www.4sshowcase.com
SIC: 2542 Office & store showcases & display fixtures

(G-1903)
FOX 416 CORP
Also Called: Fox's U-Bet Syrups
416 Thatford Ave (11212-5810)
PHONE..................................718 385-4600
David Fox, *Ch of Bd*
Karen Fox, *Corp Secy*
EMP: 30 **EST:** 1900
SQ FT: 36,000
SALES (est): 6.7MM **Privately Held**
WEB: www.foxs-u-bet.com
SIC: 2087 2066 Syrups, flavoring (except drink); chocolate coatings & syrup

(G-1904)
FRANKLIN POLY FILM INC
1149 56th St (11219-4504)
PHONE..................................718 492-3523
Isidore Handler, *President*
Rose Frankel, *Principal*
Angela Rice, *Plant Mgr*
Israel Kahan, *Admin Sec*
▼ **EMP:** 39 **EST:** 1970
SQ FT: 26,000
SALES (est): 5.4MM **Privately Held**
SIC: 2673 3082 3081 Plastic bags: made from purchased materials; unsupported plastics profile shapes; unsupported plastics film & sheet

(G-1905)
FRANZ FISCHER INC
1267 Flushing Ave (11237-2302)
P.O. Box 370715 (11237-0715)
PHONE..................................718 821-1300
Franz Fischer, *President*
EMP: 10
SQ FT: 14,000
SALES (est): 1.5MM **Privately Held**
WEB: www.franzfischer.com
SIC: 2511 Wood household furniture

(G-1906)
FRENCH & ITLN FURN CRAFTSMEN
Also Called: French Itln Furn Craftsmen Cor
999 Grand St (11211-2704)
PHONE..................................718 599-5000
Patrick F Molloy, *President*
EMP: 7
SQ FT: 6,000
SALES (est): 490K **Privately Held**
WEB: www.frenchanditalian.com
SIC: 2511 5712 Wood household furniture; furniture stores

(G-1907)
FRESH FANATIC INC
88 Washington Ave (11205-1202)
PHONE..................................516 521-6574
Andrew Goldin, *CEO*
David Goldin, *President*
EMP: 8
SALES (est): 1MM **Privately Held**
SIC: 2033 5146 5149 Fruit juices: fresh; fish, fresh; sandwiches

(G-1908)
FRESH ICE CREAM COMPANY LLC
630 Flushing Ave 4 (11206-5026)
PHONE..................................347 603-6021
Gerard Tucci, *Manager*
EMP: 10 **Privately Held**
SIC: 2024 5143 Ice cream & frozen desserts; ice cream & ices
PA: The Fresh Ice Cream Company Llc
278 6th St Apt 3b
Brooklyn NY 11215

(G-1909)
FRIENDLY STAR FUEL INC
889 3rd Ave (11232-1907)
PHONE..................................718 369-8801
Gurpal Cheema, *Principal*
EMP: 7
SALES (est): 674.4K **Privately Held**
SIC: 2869 Fuels

(G-1910)
FUTURE DIAGNOSTICS LLC
266 47th St (11220-1010)
PHONE..................................347 434-6700
Hindy Sobel, *Mng Member*
Charles Sobel, *Mng Member*
◆ **EMP:** 42
SQ FT: 20,000
SALES: 15MM **Privately Held**
SIC: 3841 Medical instruments & equipment, blood & bone work

(G-1911)
FUTURE STAR DIGATECH
713 Monroe St (11221-2813)
PHONE..................................718 666-0350
Kertena Seabrook, *Owner*
EMP: 10
SALES (est): 760.6K **Privately Held**
SIC: 3577 Printers, computer

(G-1912)
FUZION CREATIONS INTL LLC
Also Called: Dj Expression
140 58th St Ste A (11220-2539)
PHONE..................................718 369-8800
Maney Douek, *President*
EMP: 50
SQ FT: 1,500
SALES (est): 4.8MM **Privately Held**
SIC: 3911 5094 Jewelry apparel; jewelry

(G-1913)
G S COMMUNICATIONS USA INC
Also Called: Gs Communications USA
179 Greenpoint Ave (11222-7088)
PHONE..................................718 389-7371
Helen Juszczak, *President*
David Pasirstein, *Vice Pres*
Louis Makowski, *Network Mgr*
EMP: 22
SQ FT: 11,250
SALES (est): 2MM **Privately Held**
WEB: www.gscomm.com
SIC: 3571 5734 Personal computers (microcomputers); computer & software stores

(G-1914)
G Z G REST & KIT MET WORKS
120 13th St (11215-4604)
PHONE..................................718 788-8621
Gregory Uchatel, *President*
Alex Blyustein, *Vice Pres*
EMP: 15
SQ FT: 5,500
SALES (est): 920K **Privately Held**
SIC: 2599 Bar, restaurant & cafeteria furniture; carts, restaurant equipment

(G-1915)
GAC EXPRESS INC
1310 52nd St (11219-3860)
PHONE..................................718 438-2227
EMP: 5
SALES (est): 343K **Privately Held**
SIC: 3661 Message concentrators

▲ = Import ▼ = Export ◆ = Import/Export

GEOGRAPHIC SECTION

Brooklyn - Kings County (G-1946)

(G-1916)
GALIVA INC
236 Broadway Ste 214 (11211-8415)
PHONE..................903 600-5755
Simon Gelb, *Ch of Bd*
Joel Gelb, *COO*
EMP: 4
SQ FT: 10,000
SALES (est): 1.4MM **Privately Held**
SIC: 2252 Socks

(G-1917)
GARCO MANUFACTURING CORP INC
4802 Farragut Rd (11203-6612)
PHONE..................718 287-3330
EMP: 7 EST: 1960
SQ FT: 4,000
SALES (est): 64.5K **Privately Held**
SIC: 2851 Mfg Paints/Allied Products

(G-1918)
GARY GELBFISH MD
2502 Avenue I (11210-2830)
PHONE..................718 258-3004
Gary Gelbfish, *Owner*
EMP: 8
SALES (est): 690K **Privately Held**
SIC: 3845 Surgical support systems: heart-lung machine, exc. iron lung

(G-1919)
GCM METAL INDUSTRIES INC
454 Troutman St (11237-2604)
PHONE..................718 386-4059
Baldo Ciaravino, *President*
EMP: 15
SALES (est): 1.4MM **Privately Held**
SIC: 3449 1791 5051 1799 Bars, concrete reinforcing; fabricated steel; structural steel erection; structural shapes, iron or steel; ornamental metal work

(G-1920)
GCNS TECHNOLOGY GROUP INC (PA)
597 Rutland Rd (11203-1703)
PHONE..................347 713-8160
Onyike Adjaero, *President*
EMP: 6
SALES (est): 1.3MM **Privately Held**
SIC: 3825 Network analyzers

(G-1921)
GENERAL VY-COAT LLC
1636 Coney Island Ave 2b (11230-5808)
PHONE..................718 266-6002
Sol Chaimovits,
▲ EMP: 40
SQ FT: 80,000
SALES (est): 5.2MM **Privately Held**
SIC: 2851 3086 2821 Vinyl coatings, strippable; plastics foam products; plastics materials & resins

(G-1922)
GENIUS MEDIA GROUP INC
Also Called: Rap Genius
92 3rd St (11231-4808)
PHONE..................509 670-7502
Thomas Lehman, *President*
EMP: 15
SALES (est): 1.4MM **Privately Held**
SIC: 2741 Miscellaneous publishing

(G-1923)
GERI-GENTLE CORPORATION (PA)
3841 Ocean View Ave (11224-1343)
PHONE..................917 804-7807
Joseph Grun, *CEO*
Harold Rubin, *President*
▲ EMP: 2
SQ FT: 5,000
SALES: 2MM **Privately Held**
SIC: 3069 Medical & laboratory rubber sundries & related products

(G-1924)
GFL USA INC
Also Called: Gfl Amenities
81 Prospect St (11201-1473)
PHONE..................917 297-8701
Guido Bonadonna, *CEO*
Katie Childs, *Sales Staff*
EMP: 2
SQ FT: 100
SALES (est): 1MM **Privately Held**
SIC: 2841 2844 Soap & other detergents; shampoos, rinses, conditioners: hair; towelettes, premoistened
PA: Gfl Sa
Via Per Sorengo 1
Lugano TI
919 607-500

(G-1925)
GHANI TEXTILES INC
2459 Coyle St Fl 2 (11235-1207)
PHONE..................718 859-4561
Muhammad Aslam, *CEO*
▲ EMP: 1
SALES: 1MM **Privately Held**
SIC: 2299 Acoustic felts

(G-1926)
GHOSTEK LLC
140 58th St Ste 2g (11220-2486)
PHONE..................855 310-3439
Vadim Mikhailov,
David Khanatayev,
EMP: 17 EST: 2015
SALES (est): 106.6K **Privately Held**
SIC: 3663 5731 Cellular radio telephone; sound equipment, automotive

(G-1927)
GILLIES COFFEE COMPANY
150 19th St (11232-1005)
PHONE..................718 499-7766
Donald N Schoenholt, *President*
Hy Chabbott, *Treasurer*
EMP: 25
SQ FT: 14,000
SALES (est): 3.3MM **Privately Held**
WEB: www.gilliescoffee.com
SIC: 2095 2099 Coffee roasting (except by wholesale grocers); tea blending

(G-1928)
GIULIETTA LLC
649 Morgan Ave Ste 3h (11222-3765)
PHONE..................212 334-1859
Sofia Sizzi, *Principal*
EMP: 5 EST: 2011
SALES (est): 489.4K **Privately Held**
SIC: 2339 Women's & misses' accessories

(G-1929)
GIUMENTA CORP (PA)
Also Called: Utility Brass & Bronze Div
42 2nd Ave (11215-3102)
PHONE..................718 832-1200
Anthony J Giumenta, *President*
Anthony F Giumenta, *Vice Pres*
Stephen Giumenta, *Treasurer*
▼ EMP: 46
SQ FT: 55,000
SALES (est): 12.8MM **Privately Held**
SIC: 3446 Ornamental metalwork

(G-1930)
GIUMENTA CORP
Architectural Grille Division
42 2nd Ave (11215-3102)
PHONE..................718 832-1200
Anthony Giumenta, *President*
EMP: 46
SALES (corp-wide): 12.8MM **Privately Held**
SIC: 3446 Architectural metalwork
PA: Giumenta Corp.
42 2nd Ave
Brooklyn NY 11215
718 832-1200

(G-1931)
GLENWOOD CAST STONE INC
Also Called: Glenwood Mason Supply
4106 Glenwood Rd (11210-2025)
PHONE..................718 859-6500
Constance M Cincotta, *President*
EMP: 5
SALES (est): 445.2K **Privately Held**
SIC: 3272 Concrete products, precast

(G-1932)
GLISSEN CHEMICAL CO INC (PA)
1321 58th St (11219-4594)
P.O. Box 190034 (11219-0034)
PHONE..................718 436-4200
Joseph W Lehr, *President*
Barbara Lehr, *Exec VP*
Rosita Barca, *Administration*
EMP: 27 EST: 1930
SQ FT: 25,000
SALES (est): 8.1MM **Privately Held**
SIC: 2841 Detergents, synthetic organic or inorganic alkaline

(G-1933)
GLOBMARBLE LLC
2201 Neptune Ave Ste 5 (11224-2362)
PHONE..................347 717-4088
Iryna Semenenko, *Mng Member*
▲ EMP: 6 EST: 2010
SALES (est): 316.8K **Privately Held**
SIC: 3544 5031 Industrial molds; molding, all materials

(G-1934)
GMS HICKS STREET CORPORATION
214 Hicks St (11201-4110)
PHONE..................718 858-1010
Greg Markman, *Principal*
EMP: 40
SALES (est): 2.3MM **Privately Held**
SIC: 3088 Plastics plumbing fixtures

(G-1935)
GNI COMMERCE INC
Also Called: Yourhealth911.com
458 Neptune Ave Apt 11f (11224-4319)
PHONE..................347 275-1155
Vladimir Gouliaev, *President*
Bella Bomze, *Vice Pres*
▼ EMP: 7
SQ FT: 3,500
SALES: 3.1MM **Privately Held**
WEB: www.gnicommerce.com
SIC: 2023 Dietary supplements, dairy & non-dairy based

(G-1936)
GODDARL DESIGN CO
51 Nassau Ave Ste 1b (11222-3171)
PHONE..................718 599-0170
Robert Goddard, *President*
Rosemary Heath, *Office Mgr*
EMP: 7
SQ FT: 2,000
SALES: 500K **Privately Held**
WEB: www.goddarddesign.com
SIC: 3648 3625 3669 Lighting equipment; control equipment, electric; intercommunication systems, electric

(G-1937)
GOLD & DIAMONDS WHOLESALE OUTL
4417 5th Ave (11220-6834)
PHONE..................718 438-7888
Alex Gattif, *President*
EMP: 4
SALES: 2MM **Privately Held**
SIC: 3911 5094 Jewel settings & mountings, precious metal; diamonds (gems)

(G-1938)
GOLDEN LEAVES KNITWEAR INC
43 Hall St Ste B3 (11205-1395)
PHONE..................718 875-8235
Cheskel Gluck, *President*
▲ EMP: 40
SQ FT: 25,000
SALES: 2.3MM **Privately Held**
SIC: 2253 2339 Sweaters & sweater coats, knit; women's & misses' outerwear

(G-1939)
GOLDMARK INC
Also Called: Gold Mark Mfg Co
3611 14th Ave Ste B01 (11218-3750)
PHONE..................718 438-0295
Shimson Jalas, *President*
EMP: 20
SQ FT: 20,000
SALES (est): 3.3MM **Privately Held**
WEB: www.goldmark.com
SIC: 3915 Jewelers' findings & materials

(G-1940)
GOODMAN MAIN STOPPER MFG CO
523 Atlantic Ave (11217-1913)
PHONE..................718 875-5140
Joseph Petrone, *President*
EMP: 12 EST: 1897
SQ FT: 10,000
SALES (est): 159.6K **Privately Held**
SIC: 3494 5999 Valves & pipe fittings; medical apparatus & supplies

(G-1941)
GOTENNA INC
81 Willoughby St Ste 302 (11201-5291)
PHONE..................415 894-2616
Daniela Perdomo, *President*
John Levy, *Principal*
Russ Dauer, *COO*
Mike Nolfi, *Mfg Staff*
Raphael Abrams, *Engineer*
EMP: 13
SALES (est): 1.4MM **Privately Held**
SIC: 3679 Headphones, radio

(G-1942)
GOURMET CRAFTS INC
152 Highlawn Ave (11223-2636)
P.O. Box 200006 (11220-0006)
PHONE..................718 372-0505
Borris Tulman, *President*
Eugene Tulman, *Vice Pres*
Eric Shkolnik, *CFO*
EMP: 16
SQ FT: 4,000
SALES: 925K **Privately Held**
WEB: www.thecrepeteam.com
SIC: 2099 Food preparations

(G-1943)
GOURMET NUT INC
3611 14th Ave Ste 654 (11218-3787)
PHONE..................877 830-9030
Morris Elbaz, *President*
▲ EMP: 32
SALES: 11.2MM **Privately Held**
SIC: 2064 Candy & other confectionery products

(G-1944)
GOURMET TOAST CORP
345 Park Ave (11205-1389)
PHONE..................718 852-4536
Jack Feld, *President*
EMP: 8 EST: 1958
SQ FT: 8,000
SALES: 600K **Privately Held**
SIC: 2099 2051 Bread crumbs, not made in bakeries; bread, cake & related products

(G-1945)
GOVERNMENT DATA PUBLICATION
1661 Mcdonald Ave (11230-6312)
PHONE..................347 789-8719
Siegfried Lobel, *President*
EMP: 35
SQ FT: 10,000
SALES (est): 3MM **Privately Held**
WEB: www.govdata.com
SIC: 2731 2741 2721 2752 Books: publishing only; miscellaneous publishing; directories: publishing only, not printed on site; periodicals: publishing only; commercial printing, lithographic

(G-1946)
GRADO LABORATORIES INC
4614 7th Ave Ste 1 (11220-1499)
PHONE..................718 435-5340
John A Grado, *President*
John Chen, *Vice Pres*
Jonathan Grado, *Vice Pres*
▲ EMP: 10 EST: 1953
SQ FT: 10,000
SALES (est): 1.8MM **Privately Held**
SIC: 3679 Phonograph needles; headphones, radio

Brooklyn - Kings County (G-1947)

(G-1947)
GRANADA ELECTRONICS INC
485 Kent Ave (11249-5927)
PHONE 718 387-1157
Nachman Brach, *President*
EMP: 6
SQ FT: 55,000
SALES (est): 540K **Privately Held**
SIC: 3651 Audio electronic systems; television receiving sets

(G-1948)
GRAND PROCESSING INC
1050 Grand St (11211-1701)
PHONE 718 388-0600
Iggy Panadora, *President*
EMP: 30
SQ FT: 30,000
SALES (est): 1.3MM **Privately Held**
SIC: 2253 Dyeing & finishing knit outerwear, excl. hosiery & glove

(G-1949)
GREEN BEAM LED INC
Also Called: Greenbeam Led
4601b 1st Ave (11232-4200)
PHONE 718 439-6262
Elliot Gellar, *CEO*
EMP: 3
SALES: 5MM **Privately Held**
SIC: 3646 Ceiling systems, luminous

(G-1950)
GREEN WAVE INTERNATIONAL INC
5423 1st Ave (11220-2503)
P.O. Box 90288 (11209-0288)
PHONE 718 499-3371
Kay Dan Wong, *President*
Ivan Hui, *Manager*
Abel Leung, *Technical Staff*
John Calarese Sr, *Exec Dir*
◆ **EMP:** 7
SQ FT: 12,000
SALES (est): 1MM **Privately Held**
SIC: 3263 Commercial tableware or kitchen articles, fine earthenware

(G-1951)
GREENEBUILD LLC
390a Lafayette Ave (11238)
PHONE 917 562-0556
Winston Greene,
EMP: 12
SALES (est): 755.8K **Privately Held**
SIC: 1442 Construction sand & gravel

(G-1952)
GREENTREE PHARMACY INC
291 7th Ave (11215-7263)
PHONE 718 768-2700
Julia Nudelman, *Owner*
EMP: 10 **EST:** 2013
SALES (est): 1.6MM **Privately Held**
SIC: 2834 5961 Pharmaceutical preparations; pharmaceuticals, mail order

(G-1953)
GROW COMPUTER INC
448 15th St Apt 1r (11215-5778)
PHONE 646 535-2037
Daniel Nelson, *CEO*
EMP: 7
SALES: 95K **Privately Held**
SIC: 3429 Manufactured hardware (general)

(G-1954)
GUERNICA
Also Called: Guernica Magazine
63 3rd Pl Apt 4r (11231-4047)
PHONE 914 414-7318
Joel Whitney, *Principal*
Elizabeth Onusko, *Principal*
EMP: 15
SALES: 20K **Privately Held**
SIC: 2721 Periodicals

(G-1955)
H & H LABORATORIES INC (PA)
61 4th St (11231-4809)
PHONE 718 624-8041
George Hoffmann, *President*
▲ **EMP:** 14
SQ FT: 5,000
SALES (est): 1.6MM **Privately Held**
WEB: www.hhlabs.com
SIC: 2844 2841 Toilet preparations; soap & other detergents

(G-1956)
H & H LABORATORIES INC
409 Hoyt St (11231-4858)
PHONE 718 624-8041
George Hoffman, *Branch Mgr*
EMP: 5
SALES (corp-wide): 1.6MM **Privately Held**
SIC: 2844 2841 Toilet preparations; soap & other detergents
PA: H & H Laboratories Inc.
61 4th St
Brooklyn NY 11231
718 624-8041

(G-1957)
H T L & S LTD
Also Called: Peerless Envelopes & Prtg Co
5820 Fort Hamilton Pkwy (11219)
PHONE 718 435-4474
Sheldon Kustin, *Partner*
Lewis Kustin, *Partner*
EMP: 11 **EST:** 1933
SQ FT: 20,000
SALES: 700K **Privately Held**
SIC: 2752 2759 Commercial printing, offset; letterpress printing; flexographic printing

(G-1958)
H2GEAR FASHIONS LLC
1065 Shepherd Ave (11208-5713)
PHONE 347 787-7508
Henry Guindi,
Henry Naftali,
▲ **EMP:** 5
SQ FT: 350
SALES (est): 2.2MM **Privately Held**
SIC: 2339 Women's & misses' athletic clothing & sportswear

(G-1959)
HADDAD BROS INC
1200 Mcdonald Ave (11230-3321)
PHONE 718 377-5505
Michael Hollander, *VP Sales*
John Isseco, *Branch Mgr*
EMP: 50
SALES (corp-wide): 7.2MM **Privately Held**
WEB: www.haddadbros.com
SIC: 2361 2369 2335 Girls' & children's dresses, blouses & shirts; girls' & children's outerwear; women's, juniors' & misses' dresses
PA: Haddad Bros. Inc.
28 W 36th St Rm 1026
New York NY 10018
212 563-2117

(G-1960)
HAGADAH PASSOVER BAKERY
814 Bergen St (11238-3702)
PHONE 718 638-1589
P Woodsberger, *Owner*
EMP: 8
SALES (est): 453.6K **Privately Held**
SIC: 2051 Bread, cake & related products

(G-1961)
HALMARK ARCHITECTURAL FINSHG
353 Stanley Ave (11207-7601)
PHONE 718 272-1831
Hal Spergel, *President*
EMP: 24
SQ FT: 10,000
SALES (est): 2.9MM **Privately Held**
SIC: 3471 2843 3449 Finishing, metals or formed products; surface active agents; miscellaneous metalwork

(G-1962)
HAMODIA CORP
324 Avenue I (11230-2618)
PHONE 718 338-5637
Ruth Lichtenstein, *Ch of Bd*
EMP: 5
SALES (est): 246.5K **Privately Held**
SIC: 2711 Newspapers, publishing & printing

(G-1963)
HAMODIA CORP
Also Called: Daily Newsppr For Torah Jewry
207 Foster Ave (11230-2195)
PHONE 718 853-9094
Ruth Lichtenstein, *CEO*
EMP: 17 **EST:** 1998
SALES (est): 1MM **Privately Held**
SIC: 2711 Newspapers, publishing & printing

(G-1964)
HANA PASTRIES INC
34 35th St Unit 9 (11232-2212)
P.O. Box 320154 (11232-0154)
PHONE 718 369-7593
EMP: 6
SALES (est): 757.2K **Privately Held**
SIC: 2051 5411 Mfg Bread/Related Products Ret Groceries

(G-1965)
HANCO METAL PRODUCTS INC
25 Jay St (11201-1139)
PHONE 212 787-5992
Mark Meyer Hantman, *President*
Myles Hantman, *General Mgr*
Debra Hantman, *Corp Secy*
EMP: 10 **EST:** 1934
SQ FT: 2,000
SALES (est): 800K **Privately Held**
SIC: 3451 3432 Screw machine products; faucets & spigots, metal & plastic

(G-1966)
HANDMADE FRAMES INC
1013 Grand St Ste 2 (11211-1720)
PHONE 718 782-8364
Paul Baumann, *President*
Angel Lopez, *General Mgr*
Marilyn Gold, *Vice Pres*
EMP: 14
SQ FT: 9,000
SALES (est): 983.6K **Privately Held**
SIC: 3999 3952 Framed artwork; frames for artists' canvases

(G-1967)
HANDY TOOL & MFG CO INC
1205 Rockaway Ave (11236-2132)
P.O. Box 360524 (11236-0524)
PHONE 718 478-9203
Gennady Nekritin, *Project Engr*
Rochelle Sherman, *Treasurer*
Raquel Genao, *Admin Asst*
EMP: 22 **EST:** 1948
SQ FT: 13,600
SALES (est): 5.8MM **Privately Held**
SIC: 3728 3544 Aircraft assemblies, sub-assemblies & parts; special dies, tools, jigs & fixtures

(G-1968)
HAVE YOUR CAKE KITCHEN LLC
Also Called: Rule Breaker Snacks
291 Union St Phb (11231)
PHONE 646 820-8074
Nancy Kalish, *Mng Member*
EMP: 7
SALES (est): 515K **Privately Held**
SIC: 2051 7389 Bakery: wholesale or wholesale/retail combined;

(G-1969)
HEALTHONE PHARMACY INC
119 Pennsylvania Ave (11207-2428)
PHONE 718 495-9015
Mel Springer, *President*
EMP: 15
SALES (est): 3.5MM **Privately Held**
SIC: 2834 Pharmaceutical preparations

(G-1970)
HEALTHY WAY OF LIFE MAGAZINE
1529 Voorhies Ave (11235-3912)
PHONE 718 616-1681
Boris Zat, *President*
EMP: 5
SALES (est): 287.8K **Privately Held**
SIC: 2721 Periodicals

(G-1971)
HECHT & SOHN GLASS CO INC
406 Willoughby Ave (11205-4509)
PHONE 718 782-8295
Abe Sabel, *President*
▲ **EMP:** 6
SQ FT: 11,000
SALES (est): 754K **Privately Held**
WEB: www.entrances.com
SIC: 3211 3231 Flat glass; doors, glass: made from purchased glass

(G-1972)
HENRYS DEALS INC
Also Called: Allstateelectronics
1002 Quentin Rd Ste 2009 (11223-2248)
PHONE 347 821-4685
David Matts, *CEO*
Simon Sarweh, *CEO*
EMP: 20
SALES: 1MM **Privately Held**
SIC: 3861 Photographic equipment & supplies

(G-1973)
HERCULES HEAT TREATING CORP
101 Classon Ave 113 (11205-1401)
PHONE 718 625-1266
Anthony Rizzo Jr, *President*
Joseph Rizzo, *COO*
EMP: 27
SQ FT: 25,000
SALES (est): 5.9MM **Privately Held**
WEB: www.herculesht.com
SIC: 3398 Metal heat treating

(G-1974)
HERMAN H STICHT COMPANY INC
Also Called: Megohmer Vbrating Reed Standco
45 Main St Ste 401 (11201-1084)
PHONE 718 852-7602
Paul H Plotkin, *President*
Glenn A Butterfield, *Vice Pres*
Edna E Brown, *Treasurer*
EMP: 6
SQ FT: 6,000
SALES (est): 1.1MM **Privately Held**
WEB: www.stichtco.com
SIC: 3825 3823 3829 Measuring instruments & meters, electric; industrial instrmnts msrmnt display/control process variable; measuring & controlling devices

(G-1975)
HERMAN HALL COMMUNICATIONS
Also Called: Everybodys Carribbean Magazine
1630 Nostrand Ave (11226-5516)
PHONE 718 941-1879
Herman Hall, *President*
Helen Lucas, *Treasurer*
EMP: 12
SQ FT: 5,000
SALES: 500K **Privately Held**
SIC: 2721 Magazines: publishing only, not printed on site

(G-1976)
HERRIS GOURMET INC
536 Grand St (11211-3503)
PHONE 917 578-2308
Herman Franczoz, *Vice Pres*
EMP: 5
SQ FT: 2,500
SALES (est): 297.2K **Privately Held**
SIC: 2051 5812 5499 Bread, cake & related products; contract food services; gourmet food stores

(G-1977)
HERTLING TROUSERS INC
236 Greenpoint Ave (11222-2493)
PHONE 718 784-6100
Julius Hertling, *President*
▲ **EMP:** 40
SQ FT: 8,000
SALES (est): 4.4MM **Privately Held**
SIC: 2325 2253 Men's & boys' trousers & slacks; pants, slacks or trousers, knit

GEOGRAPHIC SECTION
Brooklyn - Kings County (G-2007)

(G-1978)
HMO BEVERAGE CORPORATION
68 33rd St Unit 4 (11232-1912)
PHONE..................................917 371-6100
Georgios Papanastasatos, *Principal*
EMP: 8
SALES (est): 617.9K **Privately Held**
SIC: 2086 Carbonated beverages, nonalcoholic: bottled & canned

(G-1979)
HNC ENTERPRISES LLC
10624 Avenue D (11236-1910)
PHONE..................................904 448-9387
Isaac Autzon,
EMP: 5 **EST:** 2017
SQ FT: 4,000
SALES (est): 1.5MM **Privately Held**
SIC: 2844 5122 Toilet preparations; cosmetics

(G-1980)
HOLLYWOOD SIGNS INC
388 3rd Ave (11215-2705)
PHONE..................................917 577-7333
Steve Kokonovich, *President*
EMP: 9
SALES (est): 690K **Privately Held**
SIC: 3993 Signs & advertising specialties

(G-1981)
HOLYOKE FITTINGS INC
850 Stanley Ave (11208-5226)
PHONE..................................718 649-0710
Allan Rodolitz, *President*
Jamie Hamm, *Natl Sales Mgr*
EMP: 15
SQ FT: 18,000
SALES (est): 2.3MM **Privately Held**
WEB: www.holyokefittings.com
SIC: 3494 Valves & pipe fittings

(G-1982)
HOME REPORTER INC
Also Called: Home Reporter & Sunset News
8723 3rd Ave (11209-5103)
PHONE..................................718 238-6600
James F Griffin Jr, *President*
Josh Schneps, *Publisher*
Alex Kalas, *Corp Secy*
Marvile Griffin, *Vice Pres*
EMP: 50 **EST:** 1956
SQ FT: 2,000
SALES (est): 2.3MM **Privately Held**
WEB: www.homereporter.net
SIC: 2711 Commercial printing & newspaper publishing combined

(G-1983)
HOME4U INC
152 Skillman St Apt 8 (11205-3906)
PHONE..................................347 262-7214
Abraham Goldstein, *CEO*
Joel Teitelbaum, *CFO*
▲ **EMP:** 7
SQ FT: 2,000
SALES (est): 413.3K **Privately Held**
SIC: 2541 Cabinets, lockers & shelving

(G-1984)
HONEYBEE ROBOTICS LTD (HQ)
Also Called: Honeybee Rbtics Cft Mechanisms
Suit Bldg 128 (11205)
PHONE..................................212 966-0661
Kiel Davis, *President*
Stephen Gorvan, *Chairman*
Jason Herman, *Vice Pres*
Erik Mumm, *Vice Pres*
Kris Zacny, *Vice Pres*
EMP: 44
SQ FT: 110,000
SALES (est): 9.1MM
SALES (corp-wide): 185.7MM **Privately Held**
WEB: www.honeybeerobotics.com
SIC: 3569 Robots, assembly line: industrial & commercial
PA: Ensign-Bickford Industries, Inc.
125 Powder Forest Drive 3 Flr 3
Simsbury CT 06070
860 843-2000

(G-1985)
HOSKIE CO INC
132 Harrison Pl (11237-1522)
PHONE..................................718 628-8672
Glenn Ho, *CEO*
◆ **EMP:** 80 **EST:** 2000
SQ FT: 38,000
SALES (est): 17.4MM **Privately Held**
WEB: www.hoskiecompanyinc.com
SIC: 2015 3999 Poultry slaughtering & processing; atomizers, toiletry

(G-1986)
HPI CO INC (PA)
1656 41st St (11218-5512)
PHONE..................................718 851-2753
Moshe Kenner, *President*
Peggy Oberland, *Vice Pres*
▲ **EMP:** 5
SQ FT: 3,000
SALES (est): 100K **Privately Held**
WEB: www.hpico.net
SIC: 3567 Industrial furnaces & ovens

(G-1987)
HUDSON POWER TRANSMISSION CO
241 Halsey St (11216-2403)
PHONE..................................718 622-3869
Lawrence Saft, *President*
EMP: 5
SQ FT: 880
SALES (est): 440K **Privately Held**
SIC: 3568 Power transmission equipment

(G-1988)
HUNTINGTON ICE & CUBE CORP (PA)
335 Moffat St (11237-6408)
PHONE..................................718 456-2013
Gaspar Piccolo, *Vice Pres*
EMP: 10
SALES (est): 1.1MM **Privately Held**
SIC: 2097 Block ice

(G-1989)
HYGRADE
30 Warsoff Pl (11205-1638)
PHONE..................................718 488-9000
Follman Lazar, *President*
EMP: 7
SALES (est): 139.5K **Privately Held**
SIC: 3842 7218 4959 Personal safety equipment; wiping towel supply; environmental cleanup services

(G-1990)
HYMAN PODRUSNICK CO INC
212 Foster Ave (11230-2197)
P.O. Box 300158 (11230-0158)
PHONE..................................718 853-4502
David Binder, *President*
Mae Binder, *Vice Pres*
▲ **EMP:** 5
SQ FT: 5,000
SALES (est): 410K **Privately Held**
SIC: 3469 3821 Household cooking & kitchen utensils, porcelain enameled; laboratory apparatus & furniture

(G-1991)
HYPERLINE SYSTEMS INC
9322 3rd Ave Ste 406 (11209-6802)
PHONE..................................613 736-8500
Gregory Shields, *Branch Mgr*
EMP: 8
SALES (est): 1MM **Privately Held**
SIC: 3357 5063 Coaxial cable, nonferrous; wire & cable
PA: Hyperline Systems Inc.
700 Pinnacle Ct Ste 170
Norcross GA 30071

(G-1992)
IAMMALIAMILLS LLC
Also Called: Malia Mills
32 33rd St Unit 13 (11232-1924)
PHONE..................................805 845-2137
Malian Mills,
Malia Mills,
EMP: 6
SALES (est): 646.2K **Privately Held**
SIC: 2253 Bathing suits & swimwear, knit

(G-1993)
ICESTONE LLC
63 Flushing Ave Unit 283b (11205-1079)
PHONE..................................718 624-4900
Dal Lamagna, *CEO*
Jana Milcikova, *Managing Prtnr*
Arti Bhatt, *Vice Pres*
Alison Tester, *Purch Dir*
Raymond Chen, *Research*
▲ **EMP:** 37
SQ FT: 55,000
SALES (est): 6.7MM **Privately Held**
SIC: 3281 2541 1752 3499 Building stone products; counter & sink tops; ceramic floor tile installation; furniture parts, metal

(G-1994)
IEH CORPORATION
140 58th St Ste 8e (11220-2525)
PHONE..................................718 492-4440
David Offerman, *Ch of Bd*
Mark Iskin, *Purchasing*
Robert Romeo, *VP Engrg*
Robert Knoth, *CFO*
EMP: 168 **EST:** 1937
SQ FT: 20,400
SALES (est): 23.4MM **Privately Held**
WEB: www.iehcorp.com
SIC: 3678 Electronic connectors

(G-1995)
IMPERIAL FRAMES & ALBUMS LLC
8200 21st Ave (11214-2506)
PHONE..................................718 832-9793
Moshe Wigdder, *Mng Member*
▲ **EMP:** 5
SALES (est): 2.5MM **Privately Held**
WEB: www.imperialframes.com
SIC: 2499 Woodenware, kitchen & household

(G-1996)
IMPERIAL POLYMERS INC
534 Grand St (11211-3503)
PHONE..................................718 387-4741
Joseph Freund, *President*
EMP: 6
SALES (est): 550K **Privately Held**
SIC: 2821 3089 Molding compounds, plastics; plastic processing

(G-1997)
IMPREMEDIA LLC (PA)
Also Called: La Raza
1 Metrotech Ctr Fl 18 (11201-3948)
PHONE..................................212 807-4600
Patricia Prieto, *Editor*
Ramon Vera, *Opers Staff*
Marcelo Caro, *Sales Dir*
John Paton, *Mng Member*
Monica Lozano,
▲ **EMP:** 99
SALES (est): 66.1MM **Privately Held**
WEB: www.impremedia.com
SIC: 2711 Newspapers: publishing only, not printed on site

(G-1998)
INDIAN LARRY LEGACY
400 Union Ave (11211-3429)
PHONE..................................718 609-9184
EMP: 5
SALES (est): 500K **Privately Held**
SIC: 3751 Mfg Motorcycles/Bicycles

(G-1999)
INDUSTRIAL ELECTRONIC HARDWARE
140 58th St Ste 8e (11220-2525)
PHONE..................................718 492-4440
Bob Offman, *President*
EMP: 70
SALES (est): 6MM **Privately Held**
SIC: 3429 Manufactured hardware (general)

(G-2000)
INDUSTRIAL FINISHING PRODUCTS
820 Remsen Ave (11236-1611)
PHONE..................................718 342-4871
Andrew Galgano, *Manager*
EMP: 12
SALES (corp-wide): 12.4MM **Privately Held**
WEB: www.industrialfinishings.com
SIC: 2851 Plastics base paints & varnishes
PA: Industrial Finishing Products Inc
465 Logan St
Brooklyn NY 11208
718 277-3333

(G-2001)
INFANT FORMULA LABORATORY SVC
711 Livonia Ave (11207-5497)
PHONE..................................718 257-3000
Richard C Miller, *President*
EMP: 10 **EST:** 1947
SQ FT: 20,000
SALES (est): 1MM **Privately Held**
SIC: 2023 5149 Bottled baby formula; groceries & related products

(G-2002)
INFOMIR LLC
2626 E 14th St Ste 101f (11235-3976)
PHONE..................................631 482-6636
Gregory Goldsedib, *CEO*
EMP: 10
SALES (est): 669.6K **Privately Held**
SIC: 7372 Application computer software

(G-2003)
INK PUBLISHING CORPORATION
68 Jay St Ste 315 (11201-8360)
PHONE..................................347 294-1220
Kristian Knapp, *Sales Dir*
Phyll Castle, *Branch Mgr*
Robert Albacete, *Executive*
EMP: 6 **Privately Held**
SIC: 2721 Magazines: publishing only, not printed on site
HQ: Ink Publishing Corporation
800 Suth Dglas Rd Ste 250
Coral Gables FL 33134

(G-2004)
INK WELL
1440 Coney Island Ave (11230-4120)
PHONE..................................718 253-9736
Yosef Oratz, *Owner*
EMP: 5
SQ FT: 4,000
SALES (est): 340K **Privately Held**
SIC: 2752 Commercial printing, lithographic

(G-2005)
INLAND PAPER PRODUCTS CORP
Also Called: Wew Container
444 Liberty Ave (11207)
P.O. Box 70137 (11207-0137)
PHONE..................................718 827-8150
Daniel Weicher, *President*
Joel Einbinoer, *Corp Secy*
▲ **EMP:** 20
SQ FT: 30,000
SALES (est): 3.6MM **Privately Held**
SIC: 3083 Laminated plastics plate & sheet

(G-2006)
INTEGRA MICROSYSTEM 1988 INC
Also Called: All-Tech
61 Greenpoint Ave Ste 412 (11222-1526)
PHONE..................................718 609-6099
Israel Haber, *Ch of Bd*
EMP: 5
SQ FT: 1,000
SALES (est): 826.8K **Privately Held**
SIC: 3575 Computer terminals, monitors & components

(G-2007)
INTER METAL FABRICATORS INC
161 Dikeman St (11231-1105)
P.O. Box 290718 (11229-0718)
PHONE..................................718 852-4000
Beatrice Degliuomini, *Ch of Bd*
Pat De Gliuomni Sr, *President*
Pat Degliuomini, *Opers Staff*
EMP: 13
SQ FT: 10,000

Brooklyn - Kings County (G-2008) **GEOGRAPHIC SECTION**

SALES (est): 1.9MM **Privately Held**
SIC: 3441 Structural Metal Fabrication

(G-2008)
INTERIOR METALS
Also Called: M&A Metals
255 48th St (11220-1011)
PHONE..................718 439-7324
Michael Tommasi, *President*
Antonella Tommasi, *Treasurer*
EMP: 27
SQ FT: 13,000
SALES (est): 4.7MM **Privately Held**
WEB: www.interiormetals.com
SIC: 3444 Radiator shields or enclosures, sheet metal

(G-2009)
INTERNATIONAL AIDS VACCINE INI
140 58th St (11220-2521)
PHONE..................646 381-8066
EMP: 97
SALES (corp-wide): 72.3MM **Privately Held**
SIC: 2836 8731 Vaccines; commercial physical research
PA: International Aids Vaccine Initative Inc.
125 Broad St Fl 9th
New York NY 10004
212 847-1111

(G-2010)
INTERNATIONAL FIREPROOF DOOR
1005 Greene Ave (11221-2910)
PHONE..................718 783-1310
Eric Arrow, *President*
EMP: 10
SQ FT: 7,500
SALES (est): 1.4MM **Privately Held**
WEB: www.firedoor.com
SIC: 3442 5251 Fire doors, metal; window & door frames; hardware

(G-2011)
INTERNATIONAL IDENTITY LLC
824 Park Ave Apt 1c (11206-5324)
PHONE..................787 864-0379
Pedroalberto Sanchez, *President*
EMP: 5
SALES (est): 215.8K **Privately Held**
SIC: 7372 Prepackaged software

(G-2012)
INTERNATIONAL STONE ACCESSRS
703 Myrtle Ave (11205-3903)
PHONE..................718 522-5399
Abraham Levy, *President*
Sanny Levy, *Vice Pres*
▲ EMP: 6
SQ FT: 7,500
SALES (est): 931.6K **Privately Held**
WEB: www.stonecityexpo.com
SIC: 3281 Marble, building: cut & shaped

(G-2013)
INTERNTNAL AUTO VOLUNTARY UNTD
1956 Bay Ridge Ave Fl 2 (11204-4544)
PHONE..................718 743-8732
Yuri Artemenko, *President*
EMP: 6
SALES (est): 292.2K **Privately Held**
SIC: 3714 Motor vehicle parts & accessories

(G-2014)
IQUIT CIG LLC
4014 13th Ave (11218-3502)
PHONE..................718 475-1422
Zelman Pollak,
EMP: 6
SQ FT: 250
SALES (est): 335.6K **Privately Held**
SIC: 3999 Cigarette & cigar products & accessories

(G-2015)
IRX THERAPUETICS INC
140 58th St (11220-2521)
PHONE..................347 442-0640
EMP: 6

SALES (est): 439.7K **Privately Held**
SIC: 2834 Pharmaceutical preparations

(G-2016)
ISSACS YISROEL
Also Called: Benchers Unlimited
4424 18th Ave (11204-1201)
PHONE..................718 851-7430
Yisroel Issacs, *Owner*
Grant Gray, *Bd of Directors*
EMP: 5
SALES: 600K **Privately Held**
WEB: www.benchers.com
SIC: 2759 5947 Imprinting; gifts & novelties

(G-2017)
IT COMMODITY SOURCING INC
Also Called: Federal Contract MGT Svcs
1640 E 22nd St (11210-5125)
PHONE..................718 677-1577
EMP: 5
SALES (est): 370K **Privately Held**
SIC: 3663 Mfg Radio/Tv Communication Equipment

(G-2018)
ITAC LABEL & TAG CORP
179 Lexington Ave (11216-1114)
PHONE..................718 625-2148
ARI Adler, *President*
EMP: 7
SQ FT: 17,500
SALES: 700K **Privately Held**
SIC: 2672 Labels (unprinted), gummed: made from purchased materials

(G-2019)
ITIN SCALE CO INC
4802 Glenwood Rd (11234-1106)
PHONE..................718 336-5900
Samuel Racer, *President*
Lance Gregor, *Sales Mgr*
Philip Levinson, *Manager*
◆ EMP: 20 EST: 1970
SQ FT: 4,500
SALES (est): 5.1MM **Privately Held**
WEB: www.itinscales.com
SIC: 3829 3699 3596 3821 Measuring & controlling devices; electrical equipment & supplies; scales & balances, except laboratory; laboratory apparatus & furniture; scales, except laboratory; commercial cooking & food service equipment

(G-2020)
IVALUA INC
195 Montague St (11201-3628)
PHONE..................650 930-9710
Daniel Olivier Amzallag, *CEO*
EMP: 10
SALES (corp-wide): 19.6MM **Privately Held**
SIC: 7372 Business oriented computer software
HQ: Ivalua, Inc.
805 Veterans Blvd Ste 203
Redwood City CA 94063

(G-2021)
J & J BRONZE & ALUMINUM CAST
Also Called: All Cast Foundry
249 Huron St (11222-1801)
PHONE..................718 383-2111
Vincent Grosso, *Vice Pres*
EMP: 34
SQ FT: 23,000
SALES (est): 4.2MM **Privately Held**
SIC: 3366 3365 3369 Castings (except die): bronze; aluminum & aluminum-based alloy castings; nonferrous foundries

(G-2022)
J H C FABRICATIONS INC (PA)
Also Called: Jhc Labresin
595 Berriman St (11208-5203)
P.O. Box 80377 (11208-0377)
PHONE..................718 649-0065
Henry L Calamari, *President*
John Calamari, *Corp Secy*
▲ EMP: 28 EST: 1986
SQ FT: 16,000

SALES (est): 3.9MM **Privately Held**
WEB: www.jhclabresin.com
SIC: 3821 3644 Laboratory furniture; insulators & insulation materials, electrical

(G-2023)
J H M ENGINEERING
4014 8th Ave (11232-3706)
PHONE..................718 871-1810
J H Maliga, *Owner*
EMP: 25 EST: 1966
SQ FT: 15,000
SALES (est): 2MM **Privately Held**
SIC: 3841 3843 3845 3699 Surgical & medical instruments; dental equipment; electromedical equipment; electrical equipment & supplies

(G-2024)
J LOWY CO
Also Called: J Lowy Lea Skullcaps Mfg Co
940 E 19th St (11230-3805)
PHONE..................718 338-7324
Jerry Lowy, *Owner*
▲ EMP: 8
SALES: 1MM **Privately Held**
WEB: www.kippott.com
SIC: 2386 5999 Hats & caps, leather; religious goods

(G-2025)
J M L PRODUCTIONS INC
162 Spencer St (11205-3929)
PHONE..................718 643-1674
Jay Cohen, *President*
Michael Dymburt, *Admin Sec*
EMP: 60
SQ FT: 30,000
SALES (est): 2.3MM **Privately Held**
SIC: 2396 2759 Screen printing on fabric articles; screen printing

(G-2026)
J M P DISPLAY FIXTURE CO INC
760 E 96th St (11236-1821)
PHONE..................718 649-0333
Joseph Cangelosi, *President*
Rosalie Angelosi, *Vice Pres*
EMP: 7
SQ FT: 7,200
SALES (est): 1.2MM **Privately Held**
SIC: 2541 Display fixtures, wood

(G-2027)
J R COOPERAGE CO INC
125 Division Pl (11222-5325)
PHONE..................718 387-1664
Gustav Rosenberg, *President*
EMP: 8
SQ FT: 40,000
SALES: 170K **Privately Held**
SIC: 3412 Metal barrels, drums & pails

(G-2028)
JACKS GOURMET LLC
1000 Dean St Ste 214 (11238-3382)
PHONE..................718 954-4681
Jack Silberstein, *CEO*
EMP: 12
SALES: 1.5MM **Privately Held**
SIC: 2013 Sausages & other prepared meats

(G-2029)
JACMAX INDUSTRIES LLC
Also Called: Expressive Scent
473 Wortman Ave (11208-5425)
PHONE..................718 439-3743
Max Antar, *CEO*
Jack Eida, *President*
EMP: 7
SQ FT: 150,000
SALES (est): 455.6K **Privately Held**
SIC: 2677 Envelopes

(G-2030)
JACOB INC
287 Keap St (11211-7477)
PHONE..................646 450-3067
Solomon Breuer, *CEO*
EMP: 40
SQ FT: 8,000
SALES: 20MM **Privately Held**
SIC: 3554 Paper industries machinery

(G-2031)
JACOBS JUICE CORP
388 Avenue X Apt 2h (11223-6025)
PHONE..................646 255-2860
Jacob Prig, *President*
EMP: 5
SALES (est): 183.4K **Privately Held**
SIC: 3999 Novelties, bric-a-brac & hobby kits

(G-2032)
JACOBY ENTERPRISES LLC
1615 54th St (11204-1438)
PHONE..................718 435-0289
Abraham Jacobowitz,
▲ EMP: 7
SQ FT: 1,500
SALES (est): 1.2MM **Privately Held**
WEB: www.jacobygems.com
SIC: 3911 5094 Bracelets, precious metal; cigarette lighters, precious metal; precious stones & metals; jewelry

(G-2033)
JAKES SNEAKERS INC
845 Classon Ave (11238-6103)
PHONE..................718 233-1132
Jake Zebak, *President*
EMP: 1
SALES: 1.2MM **Privately Held**
SIC: 2393 5661 Cushions, except spring & carpet: purchased materials; children's shoes

(G-2034)
JAXIS INC (PA)
Also Called: Jaxi's Sportswear
1365 38th St (11218-3634)
PHONE..................212 302-7611
Ezra Abed, *President*
Nathan Mann, *Vice Pres*
Eddy Mann, *Admin Sec*
EMP: 6
SQ FT: 1,100
SALES (est): 560K **Privately Held**
SIC: 2339 5137 Sportswear, women's; sportswear, women's & children's

(G-2035)
JAY TUROFF
Also Called: Jay-Art Nvelties/Tower Grafics
681 Coney Island Ave (11218-4306)
PHONE..................718 856-7300
Jay Turoff, *Owner*
EMP: 11 EST: 1965
SQ FT: 3,500
SALES: 1.2MM **Privately Held**
SIC: 3993 7336 3961 Signs & advertising specialties; commercial art & graphic design; costume novelties

(G-2036)
JERRY TOMASELLI
Also Called: Express Tag & Label
141 32nd St (11232-1809)
PHONE..................718 965-1400
Jerry Tomaselli, *Owner*
EMP: 10
SQ FT: 10,000
SALES: 500K **Privately Held**
SIC: 2679 Tags, paper (unprinted): made from purchased paper

(G-2037)
JEWELERS SOLDER SUPPLY INC
Also Called: Jewler's Solder Sheet & Wire
1362 54th St (11219-4219)
P.O. Box 190141 (11219-0141)
PHONE..................718 637-1256
Michael Goldenberg, *Owner*
Connie Klinger, *Principal*
Rachel Goldenberg, *Vice Pres*
EMP: 11
SQ FT: 10,000
SALES: 145.2K **Privately Held**
SIC: 3356 Solder: wire, bar, acid core, & rosin core

(G-2038)
JEWISH HERITAGE FOR BLIND
1655 E 24th St (11229-2401)
PHONE..................718 338-4999
Rabbi David Toiv, *President*
EMP: 8

GEOGRAPHIC SECTION Brooklyn - Kings County (G-2069)

SQ FT: 2,000
SALES (est): 607.1K **Privately Held**
WEB: www.jhftb.org
SIC: 2741 Miscellaneous publishing

(G-2039)
JEWISH JOURNAL
7014 13th Ave (11228-1604)
PHONE..................718 630-9350
EMP: 5
SALES (est): 160K **Privately Held**
SIC: 2711 Newspapers-Publishing/Printing

(G-2040)
JEWISH PRESS INC
4915 16th Ave (11204-1115)
PHONE..................718 330-1100
Sidney Klass, *President*
Jerry Greenwald, *Vice Pres*
Harry Rosenthal, *Vice Pres*
Irene Klass, *Admin Sec*
Jodie Maoz, *Associate*
EMP: 149 EST: 1949
SQ FT: 40,000
SALES (est): 9.6MM **Privately Held**
WEB: www.jewishpress.com
SIC: 2711 Newspapers: publishing only, not printed on site

(G-2041)
JO-MART CANDIES CORP
Also Called: Jo Mart Chocolates
2917 Avenue R (11229-2525)
PHONE..................718 375-1277
Michael Rogak, *President*
EMP: 11 EST: 1946
SQ FT: 3,000
SALES (est): 1.4MM **Privately Held**
WEB: www.jomartchocolates.com
SIC: 2064 5441 2066 Candy & other confectionery products; candy; chocolate & cocoa products

(G-2042)
JOEL ZELCER
102 S 8th St (11249-8632)
PHONE..................917 525-6790
Joel Zelcer, *Owner*
EMP: 10
SALES (est): 520.7K **Privately Held**
SIC: 3944 7389 Games, toys & children's vehicles;

(G-2043)
JOHN AUGULIARO PRINTING CO
Also Called: John V Aguliaro Printing
2533 Mcdonald Ave (11223-5232)
PHONE..................718 382-5283
Justin Aguliaro, *President*
EMP: 8
SALES (est): 760K **Privately Held**
SIC: 2759 Commercial printing

(G-2044)
JOMAT NEW YORK INC
4100 1st Ave Ste 3 (11232-3303)
PHONE..................718 369-7641
Marc Landman, *President*
EMP: 35
SQ FT: 12,000
SALES (est): 1MM **Privately Held**
SIC: 2339 2369 Women's & misses' outerwear; girls' & children's outerwear

(G-2045)
JORDACHE WOODWORKING CORP
276 Greenpoint Ave # 1303 (11222-2451)
PHONE..................718 349-3373
Nicholas Jordache, *President*
EMP: 14
SALES (est): 500K **Privately Held**
SIC: 2434 2499 Wood kitchen cabinets; decorative wood & woodwork

(G-2046)
JOS H LOWENSTEIN AND SONS INC (PA)
420 Morgan Ave (11222-5705)
PHONE..................718 388-5410
Stephen J Lowenstein, *Ch of Bd*
David Lowenstein, *President*
Sue Papish, *Exec VP*
Richard Cahayla-Wynne, *Vice Pres*

Thomas Sowpel, *Vice Pres*
◆ EMP: 85
SQ FT: 100,000
SALES (est): 14.5MM **Privately Held**
WEB: www.jhlowenstein.com
SIC: 2869 2865 Industrial organic chemicals; dyes, synthetic organic

(G-2047)
JOSEPH PAUL
Also Called: Perfect Publications
1064 Rogers Ave Apt 5 (11226-6234)
P.O. Box 1087, New York (10163-1087)
PHONE..................718 693-4269
Joseph Paul, *Owner*
A Bourne, *Manager*
◆ EMP: 6
SALES (est): 340K **Privately Held**
SIC: 2752 Commercial printing, lithographic

(G-2048)
JOSEPH SHALHOUB & SON INC
1258 Prospect Ave (11218-1304)
PHONE..................718 871-6300
Joseph Shalhoub Jr, *President*
Ray Shalhoub, *Vice Pres*
EMP: 14
SQ FT: 15,000
SALES (est): 710K **Privately Held**
SIC: 2064 Fruits: candied, crystallized, or glazed

(G-2049)
JOSEPH ZAKON WINERY LTD
Also Called: Kesser Wine
586 Montgomery St (11225-3130)
PHONE..................718 604-1430
Joseph Zakon, *President*
EMP: 3
SQ FT: 5,000
SALES (est): 1.5MM **Privately Held**
SIC: 2084 Wines

(G-2050)
JOY OF LEARNING
992 Gates Ave (11221-3602)
PHONE..................718 443-6463
C Clay Berry, *Owner*
EMP: 7
SALES (est): 200K **Privately Held**
SIC: 2211 Broadwoven fabric mills, cotton

(G-2051)
JOYA LLC
Also Called: Joya Studio
19 Vanderbilt Ave (11205-1113)
PHONE..................718 852-6979
Bernard Bouchardy, *CEO*
Mayra Miranda, *Manager*
EMP: 15
SALES (est): 1.2MM **Privately Held**
SIC: 3999 Candles

(G-2052)
JOYVA CORP (PA)
53 Varick Ave (11237-1523)
PHONE..................718 497-0170
Sanford Wiener, *CEO*
Sandra Quinones, *Office Mgr*
Richard Radutzky, *Manager*
◆ EMP: 75 EST: 1906
SQ FT: 26,370
SALES (est): 12.2MM **Privately Held**
WEB: www.joyva.com
SIC: 2099 2066 2064 Food preparations; chocolate & cocoa products; halvah (candy)

(G-2053)
JTA USA INC
63 Flushing Ave Unit 339 (11205-1084)
PHONE..................718 722-0902
Alex Rub, *President*
EMP: 7
SQ FT: 2,000
SALES (est): 731.9K **Privately Held**
SIC: 3291 Wheels, abrasive

(G-2054)
JUDAICA PRESS INC
123 Ditmas Ave (11218-4930)
PHONE..................718 972-6202
Gloria Goldman, *President*
Chaim Schneider, *Sales Mgr*
Aryeh Mezzi, *Manager*

▲ EMP: 8 EST: 1963
SQ FT: 2,325
SALES (est): 1.1MM **Privately Held**
WEB: www.judaicapress.com
SIC: 2731 Books: publishing only

(G-2055)
JUDIS LAMPSHADES INC
1495 E 22nd St (11210-5122)
PHONE..................917 561-3921
Judith Sadan, *President*
Judi Sadan, *President*
EMP: 5 EST: 1998
SQ FT: 1,000
SALES (est): 310K **Privately Held**
WEB: www.judislampshades.com
SIC: 3645 Lamp shades, metal

(G-2056)
JUICES ENTERPRISES INC
1142 Nostrand Ave (11225-5414)
PHONE..................718 953-1860
Patrick Brown, *President*
Juliet McNaughton, *President*
EMP: 6
SALES (est): 437.1K **Privately Held**
SIC: 2086 Carbonated beverages, nonalcoholic: bottled & canned

(G-2057)
JULIANS RECIPE LLC
128 Norman Ave (11222-3382)
PHONE..................888 640-8880
Alexander Dzieduszycki, *Mng Member*
▲ EMP: 8
SQ FT: 1,100
SALES (est): 9.2MM **Privately Held**
SIC: 2038 Frozen specialties

(G-2058)
JULIUS COHEN JEWELERS INC
169 Richardson St (11222-5016)
PHONE..................212 371-3050
Leslie Steinweiss, *President*
Anderson King, *Manager*
Parsley Steinweiss, *Director*
EMP: 7 EST: 1956
SALES (est): 909.8K **Privately Held**
WEB: www.juliuscohen.com
SIC: 3911 5944 Bracelets, precious metal; rings, finger: precious metal; pins (jewelry), precious metal; jewelry stores

(G-2059)
JUNIORS CHEESECAKE INC (PA)
386 Flatbush Avenue Ext (11201-5331)
PHONE..................718 852-5257
Alan Rosen, *President*
Walter Rosen, *Chairman*
Kevin Rosen, *Vice Pres*
Anna Poselenova, *Opers Staff*
Nancy Weinberger, *Marketing Staff*
EMP: 7
SQ FT: 30,000
SALES (est): 1.6MM **Privately Held**
WEB: www.juniorscheesecake.com
SIC: 2051 Cakes, pies & pastries

(G-2060)
JUS BY JULIE LLC (PA)
2184 Mcdonald Ave (11223-3926)
PHONE..................718 266-3906
Sesar Maleh,
Elliot Maleh,
EMP: 2
SALES (est): 1.1MM **Privately Held**
SIC: 2033 Vegetable juices: fresh; fruit juices: fresh

(G-2061)
K & R ALLIED INC
Also Called: Allied K & R Broom & Brush Co
39 Pearl St Fl 2 (11201-8302)
PHONE..................718 625-6610
Karl Chang, *President*
Kam Lau, *Vice Pres*
Cathy Chang, *Prgrmr*
EMP: 10
SQ FT: 18,000
SALES (est): 1.1MM **Privately Held**
WEB: www.alliedkr.com
SIC: 3991 Brooms

(G-2062)
K & S CHILDRENS WEAR INC
Also Called: Elegant Sportswear
204 Wallabout St (11206-5418)
PHONE..................718 624-0006
Thomas Klein, *President*
Jacob Klein, *Vice Pres*
EMP: 47
SQ FT: 20,000
SALES (est): 7.5MM **Privately Held**
SIC: 2253 2369 Sweaters & sweater coats, knit; jackets: girls', children's & infants'

(G-2063)
K DISPLAYS
1363 47th St (11219-2612)
PHONE..................718 854-6045
Malvin Boehm, *President*
EMP: 10
SALES (est): 486.4K **Privately Held**
SIC: 3172 Cases, jewelry

(G-2064)
K M DRIVE LINE INC
966 Grand St (11211-2707)
PHONE..................718 599-0628
Salvatore Bucchio Jr, *President*
John Smith, *Accounts Mgr*
EMP: 8
SQ FT: 5,000
SALES (est): 1.2MM **Privately Held**
WEB: www.kmdriveline.com
SIC: 3714 5013 5531 Drive shafts, motor vehicle; motor vehicle supplies & new parts; automobile & truck equipment & parts

(G-2065)
K T A V PUBLISHING HOUSE INC
527 Empire Blvd (11225-3121)
PHONE..................201 963-9524
Sol Scharfstein, *President*
Bernard Scharfstein, *Corp Secy*
▲ EMP: 13
SQ FT: 25,000
SALES (est): 1.3MM **Privately Held**
WEB: www.ktav.com
SIC: 2731 Books: publishing only

(G-2066)
KALE FACTORY INC
790 Washington Ave (11238-7706)
PHONE..................917 363-6361
EMP: 6
SALES (est): 474.4K **Privately Held**
SIC: 2099 Food preparations

(G-2067)
KARO SHEET METAL INC
Also Called: Karosheet Metal
229 Russell St (11222-3004)
PHONE..................718 542-8420
Kathleen Portman, *President*
EMP: 40
SQ FT: 10,000
SALES (est): 5.9MM **Privately Held**
SIC: 3444 Ducts, sheet metal; ventilators, sheet metal

(G-2068)
KENDI IRON WORKS INC (PA)
236 Johnson Ave (11206-2819)
PHONE..................718 821-2722
Zadok Zvi, *President*
Anna Zvi, *Vice Pres*
EMP: 8
SQ FT: 16,500
SALES (est): 680.6K **Privately Held**
SIC: 3446 Ornamental metalwork

(G-2069)
KEURIG DR PEPPER INC
212 Wolcott St (11231-1130)
PHONE..................718 246-6200
Joseph Poli, *CEO*
M McCrodden, *Financial Exec*
EMP: 8 **Publicly Held**
SIC: 2086 Soft drinks: packaged in cans, bottles, etc.
PA: Keurig Dr Pepper Inc.
53 South Ave
Burlington MA 01803

Brooklyn - Kings County (G-2070)   **GEOGRAPHIC SECTION**

(G-2070)
KINFOLK STUDIOS INC
Also Called: Kinfolk Store, The
94 Wythe Ave (11249-1923)
PHONE 770 617-5592
Maceo McNeff, *President*
EMP: 14 **Privately Held**
SIC: 2599 Bar, restaurant & cafeteria furniture
PA: Kinfolk Studios Inc.
    90 Wythe Ave
    Brooklyn NY 11249

(G-2071)
KINFOLK STUDIOS INC (PA)
Also Called: Kinfolk Store
90 Wythe Ave (11249-1923)
PHONE 347 799-2946
Ryan Carney, *President*
Olivia Hayes, *Director*
Jeremiah Mandel, *Director*
EMP: 16
SQ FT: 900
SALES: 950K **Privately Held**
SIC: 2599 Bar, restaurant & cafeteria furniture

(G-2072)
KING RESEARCH INC
114 12th St Ste 1 (11215-3892)
PHONE 718 788-0122
Bernard R King, *President*
Carol Ordyk, *Asst Sec*
◆ **EMP:** 23 **EST:** 1947
SQ FT: 23,500
SALES (est): 3.2MM **Privately Held**
SIC: 2842 2841 2844 3229 Mfg Polish/Sanitation Gd Mfg Soap/Other Detergent Mfg Toilet Preparations Mfg Pressed/Blown Glass

(G-2073)
KING SALES INC
284 Wallabout St (11206-4927)
PHONE 718 301-9862
David Schwimmer, *Owner*
▲ **EMP:** 10
SALES (est): 480.7K **Privately Held**
SIC: 2329 Athletic (warmup, sweat & jogging) suits: men's & boys'

(G-2074)
KING STEEL IRON WORK CORP
2 Seneca Ave (11237)
PHONE 718 384-7500
Eliran Galapo, *Vice Pres*
EMP: 15
SALES (est): 2.9MM **Privately Held**
SIC: 3441 Fabricated structural metal

(G-2075)
KINGS CNTY BRWERS CLLCTIVE LLC
381 Troutman St (11237-2613)
PHONE 917 207-2739
Anthony Bellis,
EMP: 10
SALES (est): 1.8MM **Privately Held**
SIC: 3556 2082 Brewers' & maltsters' machinery; brewers' grain

(G-2076)
KINGS FILM & SHEET INC
Also Called: Kings Specialty Co
482 Baltic St (11217-2508)
P.O. Box 170144 (11217-0144)
PHONE 718 624-7510
Forrest T Weisburst, *President*
Joel Leonard, *General Mgr*
EMP: 24
SQ FT: 15,000
SALES (est): 3.8MM **Privately Held**
WEB: www.kingsspecialty.com
SIC: 3081 Plastic film & sheet

(G-2077)
KMS CONTRACTING INC
Also Called: Sure Iron Works
86 Georgia Ave (11207-2402)
PHONE 718 495-6500
Steven Horn, *President*
EMP: 14
SQ FT: 11,500
SALES (est): 2.6MM **Privately Held**
WEB: www.sureiron.com
SIC: 3446 Architectural metalwork

(G-2078)
KNIGHT LIFE ENTERTAINMENT
674 Lincoln Pl Apt 9 (11216-4434)
P.O. Box 160525 (11216-0525)
PHONE 646 733-8911
Keisha Knight, *Owner*
EMP: 6 **EST:** 2010
SALES: 3.8K **Privately Held**
SIC: 7372 Application computer software

(G-2079)
KO FRO FOODS INC
4418 18th Ave 4420 (11204-1201)
PHONE 718 972-6480
Kalman Mendelsohn, *President*
Abraham Mendelsohn, *Chairman*
Heshy Mendelsohn, *Treasurer*
EMP: 20
SQ FT: 4,300
SALES (est): 2MM **Privately Held**
WEB: www.mendelsohns.com
SIC: 2053 Frozen bakery products, except bread

(G-2080)
KODIAK STUDIOS INC
3030 Emmons Ave Apt 3t (11235-2226)
PHONE 718 769-5399
Alex Tish, *President*
EMP: 5
SALES (est): 384.4K **Privately Held**
WEB: www.kodiakstudios.com
SIC: 3299 Architectural sculptures: gypsum, clay, papier mache, etc.

(G-2081)
KON TAT GROUP CORPORATION
Also Called: Ametal International
1491 E 34th St (11234-2601)
PHONE 718 207-5022
Kong Tat Yee, *CEO*
David Kong, *Exec VP*
▼ **EMP:** 8
SQ FT: 4,000
SALES (est): 179.7K **Privately Held**
SIC: 7692 Welding repair

(G-2082)
KURRIER INC
145 Java St (11222-1602)
PHONE 718 389-3018
Wladyslaw Wawrzonek, *President*
EMP: 5
SALES (est): 310K **Privately Held**
WEB: www.kurrier.com
SIC: 2759 5813 Newspapers: printing; drinking places

(G-2083)
KWADAIR LLC
137 Kent St (11222-2127)
PHONE 646 824-2511
▲ **EMP:** 5
SALES (est): 457.1K **Privately Held**
SIC: 3812 Aircraft/aerospace flight instruments & guidance systems

(G-2084)
KWESI LEGESSE LLC
Also Called: K.E.Y.S. Publishers
203 Remsen Ave (11212-1342)
PHONE 347 581-9872
Kayode Smith, *Co-Owner*
EMP: 5
SALES (est): 180.3K **Privately Held**
SIC: 2731 Book publishing

(G-2085)
KWIK TICKET INC (PA)
Also Called: Jon Barry Company Division
4101 Glenwood Rd (11210-2024)
PHONE 718 421-3800
Larry Spiewak, *Principal*
Vivian Martinez, *Opers Mgr*
Brian Katz, *Sales Staff*
Malky Jacobovits, *Office Mgr*
Ike Betesh, *Executive*
◆ **EMP:** 15
SQ FT: 30,000
SALES (est): 2MM **Privately Held**
WEB: www.kwikticket.com
SIC: 2752 Tags, lithographed; tickets, lithographed

(G-2086)
KWONG CHI METAL FABRICATION
166 41st St (11232-3320)
PHONE 718 369-6429
Larry Lang, *President*
EMP: 8
SALES (est): 400K **Privately Held**
SIC: 3479 3499 Metal coating & allied service; fabricated metal products

(G-2087)
L & M UNISERV CORP
4416 18th Ave Pmb 133 (11204-1201)
PHONE 718 854-3700
Morris Wizel, *President*
EMP: 6
SALES (est): 585.9K **Privately Held**
SIC: 2759 Magazines: printing; catalogs: printing

(G-2088)
L Y Z CREATIONS LTD INC
78 18th St (11232-1010)
PHONE 718 768-2977
Amram Weinstock, *President*
EMP: 20
SQ FT: 10,000
SALES (est): 350K **Privately Held**
SIC: 3172 3993 Wallets; watch straps, except metal; leather money holders; signs & advertising specialties

(G-2089)
LADYBIRD BAKERY INC
1112 8th Ave (11215-4314)
PHONE 718 499-8108
Mary L Clemens, *Ch of Bd*
EMP: 6
SQ FT: 750
SALES (est): 634.9K **Privately Held**
WEB: www.twolittleredhens.com
SIC: 2051 2052 Bakery: wholesale or wholesale/retail combined; cookies & crackers

(G-2090)
LAGE INDUSTRIES CORPORATION
9814 Ditmas Ave (11236-1914)
PHONE 718 342-3400
Daniel Lage, *Owner*
EMP: 12
SALES: 2MM **Privately Held**
SIC: 3273 Ready-mixed concrete

(G-2091)
LAGUNATIC MUSIC & FILMWORKS
Also Called: Blackheart Records
456 Johnson Ave 202 (11237-1202)
PHONE 212 353-9600
Kenny Laguna, *President*
Meryl Laguna, *Corp Secy*
Joan Jett, *Vice Pres*
Alena Amante, *CFO*
Ed Sargent, *Manager*
EMP: 10
SALES (est): 878.9K **Privately Held**
WEB: www.blackheart.com
SIC: 2741 Music book & sheet music publishing

(G-2092)
LAMM INDUSTRIES INC
2513 E 21st St (11235-2903)
PHONE 718 368-0181
Vladimir Lamm, *President*
EMP: 6
SALES (est): 922.9K **Privately Held**
WEB: www.lammindustries.com
SIC: 3651 5731 Audio electronic systems; radio, television & electronic stores

(G-2093)
LANCASTER QUALITY PORK INC
5600 1st Ave Ste 6 (11220-2558)
PHONE 718 439-8822
David Kaplan, *President*
EMP: 16
SALES (est): 2.3MM **Privately Held**
SIC: 2013 5147 5421 Prepared pork products from purchased pork; meat brokers; meat markets, including freezer provisioners

(G-2094)
LANOVES INC
72 Anthony St (11222-5329)
PHONE 718 384-1880
Sebastian Antoniuk, *President*
EMP: 8
SALES (est): 710K **Privately Held**
SIC: 2511 Wood household furniture

(G-2095)
LAYTON MANUFACTURING CORP (PA)
864 E 52nd St (11203-6702)
PHONE 718 498-6000
Steve Layton, *President*
Antonia Layton, *Vice Pres*
EMP: 24
SQ FT: 9,000
SALES (est): 5.3MM **Privately Held**
WEB: www.laytonmfg.com
SIC: 3585 1711 5075 Air conditioning equipment, complete; heating & air conditioning contractors; air conditioning & ventilation equipment & supplies

(G-2096)
LAZER MARBLE & GRANITE CORP
1053 Dahill Rd (11204-1741)
PHONE 718 859-9644
Lazer Mechlovitz, *CEO*
Nachman Mechlovitz, *President*
Leo Leifer, *General Mgr*
Rafi Kramer, *Opers Mgr*
Rene Shleifer, *Sales Staff*
▲ **EMP:** 7
SQ FT: 4,200
SALES (est): 1.2MM **Privately Held**
SIC: 3211 3253 Building glass, flat; ceramic wall & floor tile

(G-2097)
LDI LIGHTING INC (PA)
240 Broadway Ste C (11211-8409)
PHONE 718 384-4490
Allen Mundle, *President*
EMP: 9
SQ FT: 5,000
SALES (est): 2.5MM **Privately Held**
SIC: 3646 Ornamental lighting fixtures, commercial

(G-2098)
LDI LIGHTING INC
193 Williamsburg St W A (11211-7984)
PHONE 718 384-4490
Alex Menzlowitz, *Branch Mgr*
EMP: 5
SALES (corp-wide): 2.5MM **Privately Held**
SIC: 3646 Commercial indusl & institutional electric lighting fixtures
PA: Ldi Lighting, Inc
    240 Broadway Ste C
    Brooklyn NY 11211
    718 384-4490

(G-2099)
LE HOOK ROUGE LLC
275 Conover St Ste 3q-3p (11231-1035)
PHONE 212 947-6272
Esther Chen, *President*
▲ **EMP:** 1 **EST:** 2014
SQ FT: 10,000
SALES: 8MM **Privately Held**
SIC: 3911 Jewelry apparel

(G-2100)
LE LABO HOLDING LLC (HQ)
Also Called: Le Labo Fragrances
122 N 6th St Fl 2 (11249-3002)
PHONE 646 490-6200
Fabrice Penot,
▲ **EMP:** 30
SALES (est): 9.3MM **Publicly Held**
SIC: 2844 Perfumes & colognes

▲ = Import   ▼ = Export
◆ = Import/Export

GEOGRAPHIC SECTION
Brooklyn - Kings County (G-2130)

(G-2101)
LE LABO HOLDING LLC
80 39th St Fl Ground (11232-2614)
PHONE..................................646 719-1740
Jean B Mondesir Jr, *Principal*
EMP: 25 **Publicly Held**
SIC: 2844 Perfumes & colognes
HQ: Le Labo Holding Llc
122 N 6th St Fl 2
Brooklyn NY 11249
646 490-6200

(G-2102)
LEARNINGATEWAY LLC
106 Saint James Pl (11238-1831)
PHONE..................................212 920-7969
Catherine Gichenje, *President*
EMP: 5
SALES (est): 347.2K **Privately Held**
SIC: 7372 Educational computer software

(G-2103)
LED WAVES INC
4100 1st Ave Ste 3n (11232-3303)
PHONE..................................347 416-6182
Joel Slavis, *CEO*
Nancy Ahn, *Marketing Staff*
▲ **EMP:** 12
SALES (est): 2.6MM **Privately Held**
SIC: 3641 5063 Electric lamps; light bulbs & related supplies

(G-2104)
LEE PRINTING INC
188 Lee Ave (11211-8028)
PHONE..................................718 237-1651
Leo Wollner, *President*
EMP: 5
SQ FT: 1,800
SALES: 800K **Privately Held**
SIC: 2752 Commercial printing, offset

(G-2105)
LEE SPRING COMPANY LLC (HQ)
140 58th St Ste 3c (11220-2522)
PHONE..................................718 362-5183
Al Mangels Jr, *President*
Ralph Mascolo, *Vice Pres*
Jamie Collazo, *Plant Mgr*
Laura Hoffman, *Prdtn Mgr*
Elvis Jarvis, *QC Mgr*
▲ **EMP:** 150
SQ FT: 33,000
SALES (est): 43.6MM
SALES (corp-wide): 45.3MM **Privately Held**
WEB: www.leespring.com
SIC: 3495 3493 3315 5085 Mechanical springs, precision; steel springs, except wire; wire & fabricated wire products; springs
PA: Unimex Corporation
54 E 64th St
New York NY 10065
212 755-8800

(G-2106)
LEE SPRING LLC (PA)
140 58th St Ste 3c (11220-2522)
PHONE..................................718 236-2222
Al Amangels, *President*
Chris Emick, *Plant Mgr*
Christian Chavez, *Engineer*
Calvin Lin, *Engineer*
Kedar Muzumdar, *Engineer*
EMP: 37 **EST:** 1918
SALES (est): 7.6MM **Privately Held**
SIC: 3495 Wire springs

(G-2107)
LEGION LIGHTING CO INC
221 Glenmore Ave (11207-3307)
PHONE..................................718 498-1770
Sheldon Bellovin, *President*
Evan Bellovin, *Vice Pres*
Michael Bellovin, *Vice Pres*
Wayne Cowell, *Engineer*
▲ **EMP:** 30 **EST:** 1946
SQ FT: 75,000
SALES: 7.3MM **Privately Held**
WEB: www.legionlighting.com
SIC: 3646 Fluorescent lighting fixtures, commercial

(G-2108)
LEITER SUKKAHS INC
1346 39th St (11218-3616)
PHONE..................................718 436-0303
Gitel Goldman, *President*
▲ **EMP:** 7
SQ FT: 8,000
SALES (est): 989.2K **Privately Held**
WEB: www.leiterssukkah.com
SIC: 2394 5049 5999 Tents: made from purchased materials; religious supplies; tents; religious goods

(G-2109)
LEMRAL KNITWEAR INC
70 Franklin Ave (11205-1504)
PHONE..................................718 210-0175
Eva Freund, *President*
Andrew Freund, *Treasurer*
A Schon, *Admin Sec*
EMP: 60 **EST:** 1968
SQ FT: 30,000
SALES (est): 3.6MM **Privately Held**
SIC: 2257 2339 Weft knit fabric mills; women's & misses' outerwear

(G-2110)
LENS LAB EXPRESS
Also Called: Vision Quest
482 86th St (11209-4708)
PHONE..................................718 921-5488
Sherri Smith, *Owner*
EMP: 6
SALES (est): 496.5K **Privately Held**
SIC: 3851 5995 5049 Ophthalmic goods; opticians; optical goods

(G-2111)
LENS LAB EXPRESS OF GRAHAM AVE
28 Graham Ave (11206-4008)
PHONE..................................718 486-0117
Candido Diaz, *Principal*
EMP: 5
SQ FT: 7,600
SALES (est): 643.6K **Privately Held**
SIC: 3851 Ophthalmic goods

(G-2112)
LEO INTERNATIONAL INC
471 Sutter Ave (11207-3905)
PHONE..................................718 290-8005
Gary Stern, *President*
Kate Armbrust, *Art Dir*
Richard Ward, *Officer*
▲ **EMP:** 25
SQ FT: 65,000
SALES (est): 6.4MM **Privately Held**
WEB: www.leointernational.com
SIC: 3498 Fabricated pipe & fittings

(G-2113)
LEWIS AVENUE LLC
172 5th Ave 111 (11217-3597)
PHONE..................................718 669-0579
Joseph Abdallah, *President*
EMP: 15
SALES (est): 586.5K **Privately Held**
SIC: 3429 Keys, locks & related hardware

(G-2114)
LEWIS MACHINE CO INC
Also Called: Lewis, S J Machine Co
209 Congress St (11201-6415)
PHONE..................................718 625-0799
Gene Wayda, *President*
EMP: 8 **EST:** 1933
SQ FT: 2,000
SALES: 750K **Privately Held**
SIC: 3599 Machine shop, jobbing & repair

(G-2115)
LIBERTY FABRICATION INC
226 Glenmore Ave (11207-3323)
PHONE..................................718 495-5735
Jimmy Hsu, *President*
EMP: 5
SALES (est): 757.8K **Privately Held**
SIC: 3315 Wire & fabricated wire products

(G-2116)
LIBERTY PANEL CENTER INC (PA)
Also Called: Liberty Panel & Home Center
1009 Liberty Ave (11208-2812)
PHONE..................................718 647-2763
Irwin Kandel, *President*
Cory Kandel, *Vice Pres*
Craig Kandel, *Vice Pres*
EMP: 19
SQ FT: 25,000
SALES (est): 2.4MM **Privately Held**
SIC: 2851 Paints & paint additives

(G-2117)
LIDDABIT SWEETS
330 Wythe Ave Apt 2g (11249-4153)
PHONE..................................917 912-1370
Liz Gutman, *Principal*
EMP: 6
SALES (est): 501.1K **Privately Held**
SIC: 2053 Buns, sweet: frozen

(G-2118)
LIFESTYLE-TRIMCO (PA)
Also Called: Lifestyle-Trimco Viaggo
323 Malta St (11207-8210)
PHONE..................................718 257-9101
Charles Rosenthal, *President*
Chuck Rosenthal, *Principal*
Lloyd Kielson, *Vice Pres*
Ricardo Olton, *Project Mgr*
▲ **EMP:** 39
SQ FT: 12,000
SALES: 18MM **Privately Held**
SIC: 3999 2542 2541 5046 Mannequins; garment racks: except wood; garment racks, wood; mannequins; display equipment, except refrigerated; signs & advertising specialties

(G-2119)
LIGHT BLUE USA LLC
1421 Locust Ave (11230-5220)
PHONE..................................718 475-2515
Isaac Markowitz, *Director*
EMP: 8 **EST:** 2012
SALES (est): 390.5K **Privately Held**
SIC: 3674 3648 1731 Light emitting diodes; lighting equipment; lighting contractor

(G-2120)
LIGHT PHONE INC (PA)
49 Bogart St Apt 44 (11206-3837)
PHONE..................................415 595-0044
Joe Hollier, *Founder*
Kaiwei Tang, *Founder*
EMP: 5
SALES: 500K **Privately Held**
SIC: 3669 Communications equipment

(G-2121)
LIGHT WAVES CONCEPT INC
Also Called: Led Waves
4100 1st Ave (11232-2609)
PHONE..................................212 677-6400
Joel Slavis, *President*
▲ **EMP:** 13
SALES: 2MM **Privately Held**
WEB: www.lightwavesconcept.com
SIC: 3646 3544 Commercial indusl & institutional electric lighting fixtures: special dies, tools, jigs & fixtures

(G-2122)
LIGHTING COLLABORATIVE INC
275 Park Ave Apt 6k (11205-2562)
PHONE..................................212 253-7220
Lewis Herman, *Ch of Bd*
Amelia Froom, *Vice Pres*
EMP: 6
SQ FT: 1,600
SALES (est): 974.2K **Privately Held**
WEB: www.lightingcollaborative.com
SIC: 3648 Lighting fixtures, except electric: residential

(G-2123)
LILLYS HOMESTYLE BAKESHOP INC
6210 9th Ave (11220-4726)
PHONE..................................718 491-2904
Ethan Lieberman, *Ch of Bd*
Mendel Brach, *President*
EMP: 60 **EST:** 2003
SALES (est): 9.8MM **Privately Held**
SIC: 2051 Bakery: wholesale or wholesale/retail combined

(G-2124)
LIN JIN FENG
7718 18th Ave (11214-1110)
PHONE..................................718 232-3039
Lin Jinfeng, *Owner*
EMP: 7 **EST:** 2010
SALES (est): 579.2K **Privately Held**
SIC: 2674 Grocers' bags: made from purchased materials

(G-2125)
LINDA TOOL & DIE CORPORATION
163 Dwight St (11231-1539)
PHONE..................................718 522-2066
Michael Di Marino, *President*
Linda Cataffo, *Vice Pres*
Arlene Di Marino, *Vice Pres*
David Holmes, *Prdtn Mgr*
Sandy Wise, *Office Mgr*
▲ **EMP:** 23
SQ FT: 17,500
SALES (est): 4.5MM **Privately Held**
WEB: www.lindatool.com
SIC: 3599 Machine shop, jobbing & repair

(G-2126)
LINDEN FORMS & SYSTEMS INC
40 S 6th St (11249-5938)
PHONE..................................212 219-1100
Leo Green, *President*
EMP: 25 **EST:** 1975
SQ FT: 8,000
SALES (est): 2MM **Privately Held**
SIC: 2761 2759 Computer forms, manifold or continuous; commercial printing

(G-2127)
LION DIE-CUTTING CO INC
95 Dobbin St Ste 1 (11222-2851)
PHONE..................................718 383-8841
Leo Friedman, *President*
Moshe Lieberman, *Vice Pres*
EMP: 27 **EST:** 1958
SQ FT: 40,000
SALES: 3MM **Privately Held**
SIC: 2675 2621 Cutouts, cardboard, die-cut: from purchased materials; card paper

(G-2128)
LION IN THE SUN PARK SLOPE LTD
232 7th Ave (11215-3041)
PHONE..................................718 369-4006
Melinda Morris, *CEO*
David Morris, *Vice Pres*
EMP: 9
SQ FT: 2,000
SALES (est): 1.2MM **Privately Held**
WEB: www.lioninthesuninvitations.com
SIC: 2759 Invitation & stationery printing & engraving; invitations: printing

(G-2129)
LITE BRITE MANUFACTURING INC
575 President St (11215)
PHONE..................................718 855-9797
David Kabasso, *President*
Shaul Kabasso, *Vice Pres*
EMP: 15
SQ FT: 20,000
SALES (est): 1.2MM **Privately Held**
SIC: 3646 3643 Fluorescent lighting fixtures, commercial; current-carrying wiring devices

(G-2130)
LIVID MAGAZINE
1055 Bedford Ave Apt 4c (11216-4730)
PHONE..................................929 340-7123
Daniel Watson, *Owner*
EMP: 11
SALES (est): 473.1K **Privately Held**
SIC: 2721 Magazines: publishing & printing

Brooklyn - Kings County (G-2131)

(G-2131)
LLCS PUBLISHING CORP
2071 Flatbush Ave Ste 189 (11234-4340)
PHONE...................................718 569-2703
Matt Cunningham, *Owner*
EMP: 10
SALES (est): 547.3K **Privately Held**
WEB: www.llcpublishing.com
SIC: 2741 Miscellaneous publishing

(G-2132)
LO & SONS INC
55 Prospect St (11201-1497)
PHONE...................................917 775-4025
Helen Lo, *CEO*
Jan Lo, *President*
▲ **EMP:** 10
SALES (est): 211.4K **Privately Held**
SIC: 3161 Traveling bags

(G-2133)
LONDON PARIS LTD
4211 13th Ave (11219-1334)
PHONE...................................718 564-4793
Elias Brach, *President*
▲ **EMP:** 7
SALES: 1.4MM **Privately Held**
SIC: 2329 Men's & boys' sportswear & athletic clothing

(G-2134)
LOPEZ RESTORATIONS INC (PA)
394 Mcguinness Blvd Ste 4 (11222-1201)
PHONE...................................718 383-1555
Angel Lopez, *President*
EMP: 11
SQ FT: 3,500
SALES (est): 1.5MM **Privately Held**
SIC: 3952 Frames for artists' canvases

(G-2135)
LOPOPOLO IRON WORKS INC
2495 Mcdonald Ave (11223-5232)
PHONE...................................718 339-0572
Joseph Lopopolo, *President*
Mike Lopopolo, *Shareholder*
EMP: 7 **EST:** 1965
SQ FT: 4,000
SALES (est): 1.2MM **Privately Held**
SIC: 3446 Gates, ornamental metal

(G-2136)
LOTUS AWNINGS ENTERPRISES INC
157 11th St (11215-3815)
PHONE...................................718 965-4824
Susana Merchan, *President*
EMP: 7
SQ FT: 5,000
SALES (est): 867K **Privately Held**
SIC: 3444 5999 Awnings & canopies; awnings

(G-2137)
LOWEL-LIGHT MANUFACTURING INC
140 58th St Ste 8c (11220-2524)
PHONE...................................718 921-0600
Marvin Seligman, *President*
▲ **EMP:** 40
SQ FT: 34,000
SALES (est): 5.2MM **Privately Held**
WEB: www.lowel.com
SIC: 3861 3641 Photographic equipment & supplies; electric lamps

(G-2138)
LYN JO KITCHENS INC
1679 Mcdonald Ave (11230-6312)
PHONE...................................718 336-6060
Hal Grosshandler, *President*
EMP: 5
SQ FT: 2,400
SALES: 260K **Privately Held**
SIC: 2434 Wood kitchen cabinets

(G-2139)
LYNCH KNITTING MILLS INC
538 Johnson Ave (11237-1226)
PHONE...................................718 821-3436
Joseph Rotstein, *President*
EMP: 35 **EST:** 1965
SQ FT: 15,000
SALES (est): 3.3MM **Privately Held**
SIC: 2253 Knit Outerwear Mill

(G-2140)
M & C FURNITURE
Also Called: M C Kitchen & Bath
375 Park Ave (11205-2635)
PHONE...................................718 422-2136
Moshe Chayun, *President*
Erez Chayun, *Vice Pres*
▲ **EMP:** 6
SQ FT: 9,000
SALES (est): 846.2K **Privately Held**
WEB: www.fintec-usa.com
SIC: 2511 5031 1751 Wood household furniture; kitchen cabinets; cabinet & finish carpentry

(G-2141)
M & D INSTALLERS INC (PA)
Also Called: M & D Fire Door
70 Flushing Ave Ste 1 (11205-1067)
PHONE...................................718 782-6978
Moshe Deutsch, *Ch of Bd*
David Posner, *President*
Jay Posner, *CFO*
Mendel Mandel, *Sales Staff*
▼ **EMP:** 52
SQ FT: 50,000
SALES (est): 30MM **Privately Held**
WEB: www.mdfiredoor.com
SIC: 3442 5211 5031 Fire doors, metal; door & window products; metal doors, sash & trim

(G-2142)
M & M FOOD PRODUCTS INC
Also Called: Flaum Appetizing
286 Scholes St (11206-1728)
PHONE...................................718 821-1970
Morris Grunhut, *Ch of Bd*
EMP: 14
SQ FT: 23,000
SALES (est): 940K **Privately Held**
WEB: www.flaumappetizing.com
SIC: 2099 Salads, fresh or refrigerated

(G-2143)
M & R WOODWORKING & FINISHING
49 Withers St (11211-6891)
PHONE...................................718 486-5480
Robert Wieczorkowski, *President*
Milgorzata Wieczorkowski, *Vice Pres*
EMP: 7
SQ FT: 5,625
SALES: 500K **Privately Held**
SIC: 2499 Decorative wood & woodwork

(G-2144)
M A M KNITTING MILLS CORP
Also Called: Mam Knitg
43 Hall St (11205-1315)
PHONE...................................800 570-0093
Michael Engel, *President*
Pinchas Brach, *Treasurer*
▲ **EMP:** 40
SQ FT: 32,000
SALES (est): 1.6MM **Privately Held**
SIC: 2253 2329 2339 Sweaters & sweater coats, knit; sweaters & sweater jackets: men's & boys'; women's & misses' outerwear

(G-2145)
M B C METAL INC
Also Called: Milgo Industrial
68 Lombardy St (11222-5207)
PHONE...................................718 384-6713
Bruce Gitlin, *President*
EMP: 10
SQ FT: 5,000
SALES: 750K **Privately Held**
SIC: 3446 Architectural metalwork

(G-2146)
M B M MANUFACTURING INC
331 Rutledge St Ste 203 (11211-7546)
PHONE...................................718 769-4148
David Goldstein, *President*
Susan Goldstein, *Vice Pres*
▲ **EMP:** 15 **EST:** 1978
SQ FT: 25,000
SALES (est): 1.2MM **Privately Held**
SIC: 2253 Sweaters & sweater coats, knit

(G-2147)
M FACTORY USA INC (HQ)
32 33rd St Unit 5 (11232-1911)
PHONE...................................917 410-7878
Alessandro Lanaro, *President*
Tara Montoneri, *Director*
Rebecca Gieser, *Admin Sec*
EMP: 4 **EST:** 2016
SQ FT: 6,000
SALES: 4MM
SALES (corp-wide): 18.8MM **Privately Held**
SIC: 3851 Eyeglasses, lenses & frames
PA: Tworoger Associates, Ltd.
594 Broadway Rm 801
New York NY 10012
212 965-4900

(G-2148)
MAC ARTSPRAY FINISHING CORP
Also Called: Mac-Artspray Finshg
799 Sheffield Ave (11207-7797)
PHONE...................................718 649-3800
Howard Moskowitz, *President*
EMP: 12
SQ FT: 10,000
SALES: 800K **Privately Held**
SIC: 3479 Painting of metal products

(G-2149)
MACEDONIA LTD
Also Called: Carlton Ice Cream Co
34 E 29th St (11226-5027)
PHONE...................................718 462-3596
Aristides Saketos, *President*
Zeno Gianopoulos, *Vice Pres*
▲ **EMP:** 12
SQ FT: 8,500
SALES (est): 2.1MM **Privately Held**
WEB: www.macedonia.com
SIC: 2024 5143 Ice cream, bulk; ice cream & ices

(G-2150)
MAD SCNTSTS BRWING PRTNERS LLC
Also Called: Sixpoint Brewery
40 Van Dyke St (11231-1529)
PHONE...................................347 766-2739
Shane Welch, *President*
David Ranly, *Supervisor*
Sheetal Aiyer, *Officer*
▲ **EMP:** 25
SALES (est): 7.5MM **Privately Held**
SIC: 2082 Beer (alcoholic beverage)

(G-2151)
MADE CLOSE LLC
141 Meserole Ave (11222-2744)
PHONE...................................917 837-1357
David Mehlman, *CEO*
EMP: 6
SALES (est): 185.1K **Privately Held**
SIC: 2051 Bakery: wholesale or wholesale/retail combined

(G-2152)
MAJESTIC HOME IMPRVS DISTR
5620 Fort Hamilton Pkwy (11219-4834)
PHONE...................................718 853-5079
Man L Wong, *President*
▲ **EMP:** 5
SALES (est): 399.3K **Privately Held**
WEB: www.majesticimprovements.com
SIC: 2514 1521 Kitchen cabinets: metal; single-family home remodeling, additions & repairs

(G-2153)
MAKERBOT INDUSTRIES LLC (DH)
1 Metrotech Ctr Fl 21 (11201-3949)
PHONE...................................347 334-6800
Jenny Lawton, *CEO*
Valentin Storz, *General Mgr*
Lucas Levin, *Vice Pres*
Gil Maman, *Vice Pres*
Adam Lederfarb, *Opers Staff*
▲ **EMP:** 150
SQ FT: 15,000
SALES (est): 94.9MM
SALES (corp-wide): 2.9B **Privately Held**
SIC: 3621 3625 5084 Motors & generators; actuators, industrial; industrial machinery & equipment
HQ: Stratasys, Inc.
7665 Commerce Way
Eden Prairie MN 55344
952 937-3000

(G-2154)
MALIA MILLS INC
32 33rd St Unit 13 (11232-1924)
PHONE...................................212 354-4200
EMP: 11
SALES (est): 654.2K **Privately Held**
SIC: 2339 5699 Mfg Women's/Misses' Outerwear Ret Misc Apparel/Accessories

(G-2155)
MANDALAY FOOD PRODUCTS INC
640 Dean St (11238-3021)
PHONE...................................718 230-3370
U Han Kyu, *President*
EMP: 5
SQ FT: 300
SALES (est): 356.5K **Privately Held**
WEB: www.mandalay.org
SIC: 2099 5411 Food preparations; grocery stores, independent

(G-2156)
MANGO USA INC
5620 1st Ave Ste 1 (11220-2519)
PHONE...................................718 998-6050
Kheder Fatiha, *CEO*
▲ **EMP:** 20 **EST:** 2006
SALES (est): 3.8MM **Privately Held**
SIC: 3144 3021 3149 2339 Dress shoes, women's; canvas shoes, rubber soled; athletic shoes, except rubber or plastic; women's & misses' athletic clothing & sportswear; women's & children's clothing

(G-2157)
MANHATTAN COMFORT INC (PA)
1482 Carroll St (11213-4514)
PHONE...................................908 888-0818
Schneur Lang, *President*
▲ **EMP:** 8
SALES: 10MM **Privately Held**
SIC: 2521 5712 Wood office furniture; furniture stores

(G-2158)
MANHATTAN POLY BAG CORPORATION
1228 47th St (11219-2501)
PHONE...................................917 689-7549
William Kaufman, *President*
Sylvia Kaufman, *Vice Pres*
Gary Kaufman, *Controller*
EMP: 32
SQ FT: 88,500
SALES (est): 4.1MM **Privately Held**
SIC: 2673 Plastic bags: made from purchased materials

(G-2159)
MANHATTAN SPECIAL BOTTLING
342 Manhattan Ave (11211-2404)
PHONE...................................718 388-4144
Aurora Passaro, *President*
Louis Passaro, *Exec VP*
EMP: 10 **EST:** 1895
SQ FT: 7,500
SALES (est): 930K **Privately Held**
WEB: www.manhattanspecial.com
SIC: 2086 Soft drinks: packaged in cans, bottles, etc.

(G-2160)
MANNING LEWIS DIV RUBICON INDS
848 E 43rd St (11210-3502)
PHONE...................................908 687-2400
Michael Rubinberg, *President*
EMP: 25
SALES (est): 1.2MM **Privately Held**
SIC: 3585 Refrigeration & heating equipment

GEOGRAPHIC SECTION

Brooklyn - Kings County (G-2191)

(G-2161)
MANCR ELECTRIC SUPPLY CORP
2737 Ocean Ave (11229-4700)
PHONE.................................718 648-8003
Kenneth Rabinowitz, *Ch of Bd*
Lawrence Rafalovich, *President*
EMP: 10
SQ FT: 10,000
SALES (est): 2.4MM **Privately Held**
SIC: 3699 Electrical equipment & supplies

(G-2162)
MANZIONE READY MIX CORP
Also Called: Manzione Enterprises
46 Knickerbocker Ave (11237-1410)
PHONE.................................718 628-3837
Rocco Manzione, *President*
Gary Snolpava, *President*
EMP: 4 **EST:** 1999
SQ FT: 45,000
SALES (est): 3MM **Privately Held**
SIC: 3273 Ready-mixed concrete

(G-2163)
MARAMONT CORPORATION (PA)
5600 1st Ave (11220-2550)
PHONE.................................718 439-8900
George Chivari, *President*
Linda Jannzzkowski, *CFO*
▲ **EMP:** 420
SQ FT: 65,000
SALES (est): 101MM **Privately Held**
SIC: 2099 8322 Ready-to-eat meals, salads & sandwiches; salads, fresh or refrigerated; sandwiches, assembled & packaged: for wholesale market; individual & family services

(G-2164)
MARBLE KNITS INC
Also Called: Marble Knitting Mills
544 Park Ave Ste 3 (11205-1608)
PHONE.................................718 237-7990
Kalman Sinay, *President*
David Bark, *Vice Pres*
EMP: 20
SQ FT: 55,000
SALES (est): 2.6MM **Privately Held**
SIC: 2253 Sweaters & sweater coats, knit

(G-2165)
MARCY BUSINESS FORMS INC
1468 40th St (11218-3510)
PHONE.................................718 935-9100
Samuel Roth, *Ch of Bd*
EMP: 5
SALES (est): 550K **Privately Held**
WEB: www.marcybusinessforms.com
SIC: 2761 Manifold business forms

(G-2166)
MARCY PRINTING INC
777 Kent Ave Ste A (11205-1543)
P.O. Box 110199 (11211-0199)
PHONE.................................718 935-9100
Charles H Laufer, *President*
Jano Roth, *Manager*
EMP: 5
SQ FT: 12,000
SALES (est): 808.9K **Privately Held**
SIC: 2752 Commercial printing, offset; letters, circular or form: lithographed

(G-2167)
MARINA HOLDING CORP
Also Called: Venice Marina
3939 Emmons Ave (11235-1001)
PHONE.................................718 646-9283
Chuck Rondot, *Manager*
EMP: 15
SQ FT: 6,000
SALES (est): 1.3MM
SALES (corp-wide): 1.4B **Privately Held**
WEB: www.venicemarina.com
SIC: 2339 5551 5541 Women's & misses' outerwear; boat dealers; gasoline service stations
PA: Jordache Enterprises Inc.
1400 Broadway Rm 1400 # 1400
New York NY 10018
212 643-8400

(G-2168)
MARINA ICE CREAM
888 Jamaica Ave (11208-1525)
PHONE.................................718 235-3000
Frank Birone, *Owner*
EMP: 6 **EST:** 2007
SALES (est): 407.5K **Privately Held**
SIC: 2024 5143 Ice cream, bulk; ice cream & ices

(G-2169)
MARK POSNER
1950 52nd St (11204-1731)
PHONE.................................718 258-6241
Mark Posner, *Owner*
EMP: 5
SALES (est): 218.2K **Privately Held**
SIC: 3432 Plastic plumbing fixture fittings, assembly

(G-2170)
MARLBOROUGH JEWELS INC
67 35th St Unit 2 (11232-2200)
P.O. Box 320673 (11232-0673)
PHONE.................................718 768-2000
Donald Calaman, *President*
EMP: 8
SALES (est): 1MM **Privately Held**
SIC: 3961 5094 3911 Costume jewelry, ex. precious metal & semiprecious stones; jewelry; jewelry, precious metal

(G-2171)
MARLOW PRINTING CO INC
Also Called: Nap Industries
667 Kent Ave (11249-7530)
PHONE.................................718 625-4948
Jack Freund, *President*
Morris Lowy, *Vice Pres*
EMP: 30 **EST:** 1977
SQ FT: 35,000
SALES (est): 3.9MM **Privately Held**
WEB: www.napind.com
SIC: 2759 2752 Flexographic printing; commercial printing, lithographic

(G-2172)
MARLY HOME INDUSTRIES USA INC
181 Lombardy St (11222-5417)
PHONE.................................718 388-3030
EMP: 9
SALES (est): 172.9K **Privately Held**
SIC: 2824 2221 Polyester fibers; polyester broadwoven fabrics

(G-2173)
MAROVATO INDUSTRIES INC
108 Dobbin St (11222-2806)
PHONE.................................718 389-0800
Margaret Rotondi, *Ch of Bd*
Marty Pietanza, *Opers Mgr*
Gabriel Xu, *Engineer*
Rosemarie Rotondi, *Treasurer*
Nannette Buchelli, *Sales Associate*
▲ **EMP:** 15
SALES (est): 4MM **Privately Held**
WEB: www.marovato.com
SIC: 3441 8711 Building components, structural steel; structural engineering; mechanical engineering

(G-2174)
MARTIN GREENFIELD CLOTHIERS
Also Called: Greenfield Martin Clothiers
239 Varet St (11206-3823)
PHONE.................................718 497-5480
Martin Greenfield, *President*
Jay Greenfield, *Exec VP*
Todd Greenfield, *Vice Pres*
▲ **EMP:** 140
SQ FT: 40,000
SALES (est): 15MM **Privately Held**
SIC: 2311 2325 Suits, men's & boys': made from purchased materials; jackets, tailored suit-type: men's & boys'; topcoats, men's & boys': made from purchased materials; slacks, dress: men's, youths' & boys'

(G-2175)
MARVEL EQUIPMENT CORP INC
215 Eagle St (11222-1210)
PHONE.................................718 383-6597
Carl Ungenheuer, *President*
Barbara Maxwell, *Vice Pres*
Emma Ungenheuer, *Admin Sec*
EMP: 7
SALES (est): 200K **Privately Held**
SIC: 3612 Generator voltage regulators

(G-2176)
MASON WOODWORKS LLC
127 Chester Ave (11218-3021)
PHONE.................................917 363-7052
Robert Mason, *Principal*
EMP: 5
SALES (est): 380.9K **Privately Held**
SIC: 2431 Millwork

(G-2177)
MASS APPEAL MAGAZINE
261 Vandervoort Ave (11211-1718)
PHONE.................................718 858-0979
Adrian Moeller, *Partner*
Patrick Elasik, *Partner*
EMP: 7 **EST:** 1998
SQ FT: 1,100
SALES (est): 830.6K **Privately Held**
SIC: 2721 Magazines: publishing only, not printed on site

(G-2178)
MATCHABLES INC
Also Called: Bara Fashions
106 Green St Ste G1 (11222-1352)
PHONE.................................718 389-9318
Raphael Blumenstock, *President*
Ruth Malach, *Vice Pres*
EMP: 10
SQ FT: 8,000
SALES (est): 750K **Privately Held**
SIC: 2253 Sweaters & sweater coats, knit

(G-2179)
MATERIAL PROCESS SYSTEMS INC
87 Richardson St Ste 2 (11211-1319)
PHONE.................................718 302-3081
Steven Urbatsch, *President*
Matthew Josephs, *Vice Pres*
▲ **EMP:** 14
SALES (est): 1.6MM **Privately Held**
WEB: www.materialprocess.com
SIC: 2434 3446 Wood kitchen cabinets; architectural metalwork

(G-2180)
MATRIX STEEL COMPANY INC
50 Bogart St (11206-3818)
PHONE.................................718 381-6800
EMP: 6
SALES (est): 1.5MM **Privately Held**
SIC: 3312 3321 Fabrication Structural Steel/Miscellaneous Ironworks

(G-2181)
MATTHEWS HATS
99 Kenilworth Pl Fl 1 (11210-2423)
PHONE.................................718 859-4683
Larry S Matthews, *Partner*
Merrill Matthews, *Partner*
EMP: 7
SALES (est): 410K **Privately Held**
SIC: 2353 Hats, trimmed: women's, misses' & children's

(G-2182)
MAXWELL BAKERY INC
2700 Atlantic Ave (11207-2893)
PHONE.................................718 498-2200
George Jograj, *Owner*
Earl Wheelin, *General Mgr*
EMP: 25
SQ FT: 10,000
SALES (est): 1.2MM **Privately Held**
WEB: www.maxwellbakery.com
SIC: 2051 Bakery: wholesale or wholesale/retail combined

(G-2183)
MDCARE911 LLC
Also Called: Gocare247
30 Main St Apt 5c (11201-8213)
PHONE.................................917 640-4869
Anthony Schweinzer,
EMP: 5
SALES (est): 128.9K **Privately Held**
SIC: 7372 Home entertainment computer software

(G-2184)
MDS HOT BAGELS DELI INC
127 Church Ave (11218-3917)
PHONE.................................718 438-5650
Alex Esalias, *President*
EMP: 7
SQ FT: 1,000
SALES (est): 435K **Privately Held**
SIC: 2051 5461 5411 Bagels, fresh or frozen; bagels; delicatessens

(G-2185)
MECHANICAL DISPLAYS INC
4420 Farragut Rd (11203-6522)
PHONE.................................718 258-5588
Hugo Paulucci, *President*
Lou Nasti, *Vice Pres*
▲ **EMP:** 7
SQ FT: 7,500
SALES (est): 1MM **Privately Held**
WEB: www.mechanicaldisplays.com
SIC: 3944 7389 Trains & equipment, toy: electric & mechanical; convention & show services

(G-2186)
MECHON BEISS UVAS
1130 40th St (11218-2745)
PHONE.................................718 436-1489
Shie Weisblum, *President*
EMP: 5
SALES (est): 291.6K **Privately Held**
SIC: 2791 Typesetting

(G-2187)
MEDI-TECH INTERNATIONAL CORP (PA)
Also Called: Spandage
26 Court St Ste 1301 (11242-1113)
PHONE.................................800 333-0109
Jacqueline Fortunato, *CEO*
Marilyn Geiger, *Principal*
Derrick Brown, *Regional Mgr*
Carol Callahan, *Regional Mgr*
Steve Dejoe, *Regional Mgr*
▲ **EMP:** 4
SQ FT: 1,000
SALES (est): 2.6MM **Privately Held**
WEB: www.medi-techintl.com
SIC: 3842 2339 Bandages: plastic, muslin, plaster of paris, etc.; dressings, surgical; maternity clothing

(G-2188)
MEEKER SALES CORP
551 Sutter Ave (11207-4001)
PHONE.................................718 384-5400
Harvey Worth, *President*
EMP: 1
SQ FT: 150
SALES: 1.2MM **Privately Held**
SIC: 2514 Metal household furniture

(G-2189)
MEISEL-PESKIN CO INC (PA)
349 Scholes St 353 (11206-1787)
PHONE.................................718 497-1840
Garry Meisel, *President*
▲ **EMP:** 78 **EST:** 1934
SQ FT: 18,000
SALES (est): 4.9MM **Privately Held**
SIC: 3999 Furs, dressed: bleached, curried, scraped, tanned or dyed

(G-2190)
MENPIN SUPPLY CORP
1229 60th St (11219-4930)
PHONE.................................718 415-4168
David Hiehs, *President*
EMP: 18 **EST:** 2016
SALES (est): 2.8MM **Privately Held**
SIC: 3589 Water filters & softeners, household type

(G-2191)
MENROSE USA LLC
Also Called: Milkboy
605 Montgomery St (11225-3129)
PHONE.................................718 221-5540
EMP: 5 **EST:** 2014
SALES (est): 289.7K **Privately Held**
SIC: 2066 Chocolate

Brooklyn - Kings County (G-2192) — GEOGRAPHIC SECTION

(G-2192)
MENUCHA PUBLISHERS INC
1221 38th St (11218-1928)
PHONE.................718 232-0856
Hirsch Traube, *President*
▲ **EMP:** 16
SALES: 1.6MM **Privately Held**
SIC: 2741 Miscellaneous publishing

(G-2193)
MERCADO GLOBAL INC
254 36th St Unit 41 (11232-2499)
PHONE.................718 838-9908
Garrard Beeney, *Partner*
Meg Koglin, *Principal*
Leah Vinton, *Principal*
Ruth Degolia, *Exec Dir*
Delia Mendoza, *Director*
EMP: 4
SALES: 1.1MM **Privately Held**
WEB: www.mercadoglobal.org
SIC: 3961 Jewelry apparel, non-precious metals

(G-2194)
MERCURY PAINT CORPORATION (PA)
4808 Farragut Rd (11203-6612)
PHONE.................718 469-8787
Jeff Berman, *President*
Wyatt Tichner, *Opers Mgr*
▲ **EMP:** 75 **EST:** 1961
SQ FT: 100,000
SALES (est): 23.2MM **Privately Held**
WEB: www.mercurypaintcorp.com
SIC: 2851 5231 Paints & paint additives; paint

(G-2195)
MERCURY PLASTICS CORP
989 Utica Ave 995 (11203-4399)
PHONE.................718 498-5400
William Wright, *President*
George Wright Jr, *Corp Secy*
▲ **EMP:** 20
SQ FT: 8,000
SALES (est): 3MM **Privately Held**
SIC: 3089 Molding primary plastic

(G-2196)
MERKOS LINYONEI CHINUCH INC
Also Called: Merkos Bookstore
291 Kingston Ave (11213-3402)
PHONE.................718 778-0226
Malka Ahern, *Manager*
EMP: 20
SALES (corp-wide): 950K **Privately Held**
WEB: www.chabad.org
SIC: 2731 Books: publishing only
PA: Merkos L'inyonei Chinuch, Inc.
770 Eastern Pkwy
Brooklyn NY 11213
718 774-4000

(G-2197)
MERZON LEATHER CO INC
810 Humboldt St Ste 2 (11222-1913)
PHONE.................718 782-6260
Richard Merzon, *President*
▲ **EMP:** 150 **EST:** 1943
SQ FT: 50,000
SALES (est): 16.3MM **Privately Held**
SIC: 3161 3172 Cases, carrying; suitcases; camera carrying bags; personal leather goods

(G-2198)
MESORAH PUBLICATIONS LTD
4401 2nd Ave (11232-4212)
PHONE.................718 921-9000
Martin Zlotowitz, *President*
Jacob Brander, *Vice Pres*
Efraim Perlowitz, *Marketing Staff*
Bernard Kempler, *MIS Dir*
Nosson Scherman, *Admin Sec*
▲ **EMP:** 43
SQ FT: 20,000
SALES (est): 8MM **Privately Held**
WEB: www.artscroll.com
SIC: 2731 Books: publishing only; pamphlets: publishing only, not printed on site

(G-2199)
METAL CRAFTS INC
Also Called: Metalcraft By N Barzel
650 Berriman St (11208-5304)
PHONE.................718 443-3333
Norman Barzel, *President*
Norman Barsi, *President*
EMP: 6
SALES (est): 590K **Privately Held**
SIC: 3441 Fabricated structural metal

(G-2200)
METRO KITCHENS CORP
1040 E 45th St (11203-6542)
PHONE.................718 434-1166
John Ciavattoni, *President*
Kevin Taflin, *Vice Pres*
▲ **EMP:** 11
SQ FT: 10,000
SALES (est): 880K **Privately Held**
WEB: www.metro-kitchens.com
SIC: 2434 5031 1751 Wood kitchen cabinets; kitchen cabinets; cabinet & finish carpentry

(G-2201)
METRO PRODUCTS & SERVICES LLC (PA)
Also Called: Gumbusters of New York
1424 74th St (11228-2208)
PHONE.................866 846-8486
Anthony Mule, *Owner*
Andrea Mule, *Co-Owner*
▲ **EMP:** 14
SQ FT: 5,000
SALES (est): 1.2MM **Privately Held**
SIC: 2861 Gum & wood chemicals

(G-2202)
METROPOLITAN PACKG MFG CORP
68 Java St (11222-1519)
PHONE.................718 383-2700
Malka Katz, *President*
Herman Katz, *Vice Pres*
Abraham Katz, *VP Sales*
▲ **EMP:** 35 **EST:** 1964
SQ FT: 20,000
SALES (est): 6.8MM **Privately Held**
WEB: www.metropack.com
SIC: 2673 Plastic bags: made from purchased materials

(G-2203)
MICHAEL BERNSTEIN DESIGN ASSOC
361 Stagg St Fl 4 (11206-1734)
PHONE.................718 456-9277
Michael Bernstein, *President*
EMP: 20
SQ FT: 10,000
SALES (est): 1.6MM **Privately Held**
WEB: www.mbda.org
SIC: 2431 2434 Mfg Millwork Mfg Wood Kitchen Cabinets

(G-2204)
MICHAEL STUART INC
199 Cook St (11206-3701)
P.O. Box 60267 (11206-0267)
PHONE.................718 821-0704
Michael Stuart Fuchs, *President*
EMP: 20 **EST:** 1975
SQ FT: 20,000
SALES (est): 1.4MM **Privately Held**
SIC: 2369 2392 2211 2361 Girls' & children's outerwear; tablecloths: made from purchased materials; bathmats, cotton; girls' & children's dresses, blouses & shirts

(G-2205)
MICRO ESSENTIAL LABORATORY
4224 Avenue H (11210-3518)
P.O. Box 100824 (11210-0824)
PHONE.................718 338-3618
Joel Florin, *President*
Mark Florin, *Vice Pres*
Evelyn La Nier, *Office Mgr*
EMP: 30
SQ FT: 7,500
SALES (est): 7.3MM **Privately Held**
WEB: www.microessentiallab.com
SIC: 2672 Chemically treated papers: made from purchased materials

(G-2206)
MILGO INDUSTRIAL INC (PA)
Also Called: Milgo/Bufkin
68 Lombardy St (11222-5234)
PHONE.................718 388-6476
Bruce J Gitlin, *President*
Rose Gitlin, *Vice Pres*
Gina Jordan, *Vice Pres*
Barbara Kanter, *CFO*
Don Mancuso, *Director*
EMP: 70 **EST:** 1918
SQ FT: 30,000
SALES (est): 11.6MM **Privately Held**
WEB: www.milgo-bufkin.com
SIC: 3446 3442 3398 Architectural metalwork; metal doors, sash & trim; store fronts, prefabricated, metal; brazing (hardening) of metal

(G-2207)
MILGO INDUSTRIAL INC
514 Varick Ave (11222-5400)
PHONE.................718 387-0406
Alex Kveton, *Branch Mgr*
EMP: 5
SALES (corp-wide): 11.6MM **Privately Held**
WEB: www.milgo-bufkin.com
SIC: 3446 3442 3398 Architectural metalwork; metal doors, sash & trim; brazing (hardening) of metal
PA: Milgo Industrial Inc.
68 Lombardy St
Brooklyn NY 11222
718 388-6476

(G-2208)
MILLENNIUM STL RACK RNTALS INC (PA)
253 Bond St (11217-2919)
PHONE.................718 965-4736
Toll Free:.................877 -
David Fox, *President*
▲ **EMP:** 9 **EST:** 1999
SALES (est): 1.1MM **Privately Held**
WEB: www.millenniumsteelservice.com
SIC: 2542 7359 Garment racks: except wood; equipment rental & leasing

(G-2209)
MINDBODYGREEN LLC
45 Main St Ste 422 (11201-1093)
PHONE.................347 529-6952
Jason Wacob,
Stephen Anderson,
EMP: 29
SQ FT: 2,500
SALES (est): 2.3MM **Privately Held**
SIC: 2741

(G-2210)
MINI-CIRCUITS FORT WAYNE LLC
13 Neptune Ave (11235-4404)
P.O. Box 350166 (11235-0166)
PHONE.................718 934-4500
Gerard Crepeau, *Purch Mgr*
Wing Shum, *Engineer*
Marc Sweet, *Controller*
Lynn Fogel, *CTO*
Harvey Kaylie,
EMP: 500
SALES (est): 66.2MM **Privately Held**
WEB: www.matchingpad.com
SIC: 3679 3678 3677 3674 Attenuators; electronic connectors; electronic coils, transformers & other inductors; semiconductors & related devices; radio & TV communications equipment; current-carrying wiring devices

(G-2211)
MISHPACHA MAGAZINE INC
5809 16th Ave (11204-2112)
PHONE.................718 686-9339
Eli Peli, *President*
Rachel Bachrach, *Editor*
Barbara Bensoussan, *Editor*
Nomee Shaingarten, *COO*
Nina Feiner, *Adv Mgr*
EMP: 5

SALES (est): 512.5K **Privately Held**
SIC: 2721 Magazines: publishing & printing

(G-2212)
MISS SPORTSWEAR INC
117 9th St (11215-3108)
PHONE.................212 391-2535
Moses Fallas, *Ch of Bd*
EMP: 9 **Privately Held**
SIC: 2339 Women's & misses' athletic clothing & sportswear
PA: M.I.S.S. Sportswear, Inc.
117 9th St
Brooklyn NY 11215

(G-2213)
MISS SPORTSWEAR INC (PA)
Also Called: Miss Group, The
117 9th St (11215-3108)
PHONE.................212 391-2535
Moses Fallas, *Ch of Bd*
Alan Fallas, *Vice Pres*
▲ **EMP:** 3
SQ FT: 8,000
SALES (est): 22MM **Privately Held**
SIC: 2339 Women's & misses' athletic clothing & sportswear

(G-2214)
MISS SPORTSWEAR INC
Also Called: Miss Group, The
117 9th St (11215-3108)
PHONE.................718 369-6012
Sammy Fallas, *Branch Mgr*
EMP: 13 **Privately Held**
SIC: 2339 Women's & misses' athletic clothing & sportswear
PA: M.I.S.S. Sportswear, Inc.
117 9th St
Brooklyn NY 11215

(G-2215)
MISSIONTEX INC
236 Greenpoint Ave Ste 12 (11222-2495)
PHONE.................718 532-9053
Jay McLaughlin, *Principal*
▲ **EMP:** 5
SALES (est): 320K **Privately Held**
SIC: 2281 5949 5632 5651 Yarn spinning mills; fabric stores piece goods; fur apparel; family clothing stores

(G-2216)
MJK CUTTING INC
Also Called: M J K
117 9th St (11215-3108)
PHONE.................718 384-7613
Wing Lau, *President*
EMP: 10
SALES (est): 750K **Privately Held**
SIC: 3552 Jacquard card cutting machines

(G-2217)
MJK ENTERPRISES LLC
Also Called: M & J Custom Lampshade Company
34 35th St (11232-2021)
PHONE.................917 653-9042
Martin Kuranc, *Managing Prtnr*
EMP: 8 **EST:** 2011
SALES: 50MM **Privately Held**
SIC: 3648 Lanterns: electric, gas, carbide, kerosene or gasoline

(G-2218)
MJM JEWELRY CORP
Also Called: Berry Jewelry Company
400 3rd Ave (11215-2738)
PHONE.................718 596-1600
Percival S Mijares, *Branch Mgr*
EMP: 70
SALES (corp-wide): 14.6MM **Privately Held**
WEB: www.berryjewelry.com
SIC: 3911 Jewelry, precious metal
PA: Mjm Jewelry Corp.
29 W 38th St Rm 1601
New York NY 10018
212 354-5014

(G-2219)
MKJ COMMUNICATIONS CORP
850 3rd Ave Ste 402 (11232-1523)
PHONE.................212 206-0072
Jennifer Herman, *President*
EMP: 11

GEOGRAPHIC SECTION

Brooklyn - Kings County (G-2250)

SQ FT: 3,500
SALES: 7.2MM **Privately Held**
SIC: 3699 Security control equipment & systems

(G-2220)
MNN HOLDING COMPANY LLC
Also Called: Mother Nature & Partners
155 Water St Ste 616 (11201-1016)
PHONE..............................404 558-5251
Michael Jacobson, *CFO*
EMP: 18 **Privately Held**
SIC: 7372 8748 Publishers' computer software; publishing consultant
PA: Mnn Holding Company, Llc
191 Peachtree St Ne Ste 4
Atlanta GA 30303

(G-2221)
MODERN PLASTIC BAGS MFG INC
63 Flushing Ave Unit 303 (11205-1080)
PHONE..............................718 237-2985
Abrahm Stossel, *President*
EMP: 5
SQ FT: 3,000
SALES: 450K **Privately Held**
SIC: 2673 Plastic & plioflim bags

(G-2222)
MOES WEAR APPAREL INC
1020 E 48th St Ste 8 (11203-6605)
PHONE..............................718 940-1597
Selly Nessry, *President*
Jeff Saad, *Vice Pres*
Morris Saad, *Vice Pres*
▲ EMP: 13
SQ FT: 50,000
SALES (est): 2.1MM **Privately Held**
SIC: 2339 Women's & misses' outerwear

(G-2223)
MOLDOVA PICKLES & SALADS INC
1060 E 46th St (11203-6516)
PHONE..............................718 284-2220
Naum Zozulya, *President*
Vitaliy Pinchev, *Vice Pres*
▲ EMP: 5
SALES (est): 420K **Privately Held**
SIC: 2035 Pickles, vinegar

(G-2224)
MONFEFO LLC
630 Flushing Ave 5q (11206-5026)
PHONE..............................347 779-2600
Justin Monsul, *Mng Member*
EMP: 5 EST: 2016
SQ FT: 600
SALES: 300K **Privately Held**
SIC: 2086 Soft drinks: packaged in cans, bottles, etc.

(G-2225)
MONTROSE EQUIPMENT SALES INC
Also Called: Ace
202 N 10th St (11211-1109)
PHONE..............................718 388-7446
Emil Romotzki, *President*
Jack Pivovarov, *Corp Secy*
▲ EMP: 12
SQ FT: 8,000
SALES (est): 1.2MM **Privately Held**
SIC: 3541 Machine tools, metal cutting type

(G-2226)
MORCO PRODUCTS CORP
556 39th St (11232-3002)
PHONE..............................718 853-4005
Michael Morgan, *President*
Neil Falcone, *Vice Pres*
EMP: 15
SQ FT: 6,200
SALES (est): 1.1MM **Privately Held**
SIC: 3599 Machine shop, jobbing & repair

(G-2227)
MORRIS KITCHEN INC
30 Chester Ct (11225-5605)
PHONE..............................646 413-5186
Kari Morris, *Owner*
EMP: 15

SALES (est): 2.2MM **Privately Held**
SIC: 2099 2032 2033 Food preparations; chicken soup: packaged in cans, jars, etc.; tomato products: packaged in cans, jars, etc.

(G-2228)
MOTI INC
4118 13th Ave (11219-1333)
PHONE..............................718 436-4280
Mordechai Fleicher, *President*
▲ EMP: 16
SQ FT: 8,000
SALES (est): 1.2MM **Privately Held**
SIC: 3999 Wigs, including doll wigs, toupees or wiglets

(G-2229)
MOZNAIM PUBLISHING CO INC
Also Called: Moznaim Co
4304 12th Ave (11219-1301)
PHONE..............................718 853-0525
Menachem Wagshol, *President*
Monshe Sternlicht, *Vice Pres*
▲ EMP: 6
SALES (est): 360K **Privately Held**
WEB: www.moznaim.com
SIC: 2731 5192 5999 Books: publishing only; books; religious goods

(G-2230)
MPL METAL INC
1560 Troy Ave (11203-6536)
PHONE..............................718 338-4952
Moises Robles, *Vice Pres*
EMP: 5
SALES (est): 512K **Privately Held**
SIC: 3499 Aerosol valves, metal

(G-2231)
MR DISPOSABLE INC
101 Richardson St Ste 2 (11211-1344)
PHONE..............................718 388-8574
Raymond Cora, *CEO*
Victor Morales, *Vice Pres*
Debbie Cora, *Admin Sec*
▲ EMP: 10
SALES: 400K **Privately Held**
WEB: www.mrdisposable.com
SIC: 2676 Diapers, paper (disposable): made from purchased paper

(G-2232)
MR GLASS TEMPERING LLC
38 15th St (11215-4610)
PHONE..............................718 576-3826
Raymond Gao,
Robert Liao,
EMP: 12
SQ FT: 10,000
SALES (est): 1.6MM **Privately Held**
SIC: 3211 Tempered glass

(G-2233)
MR PIEROGI LLC
126 12th St (11215-3817)
PHONE..............................718 499-7821
Leonard Sherman,
EMP: 11
SALES (est): 1.2MM **Privately Held**
SIC: 2013 Sausages & other prepared meats

(G-2234)
MR SIGN USA INC
1920 Atlantic Ave (11233-3004)
PHONE..............................718 218-3321
Michael Leivowitz, *President*
EMP: 15
SALES (est): 1.2MM **Privately Held**
SIC: 3993 Signs & advertising specialties

(G-2235)
MRCHOCOLATECOM LLC
Also Called: Jacques Torres Chocolate
66 Water St Ste 2 (11201-1048)
PHONE..............................718 875-9772
Jacques Torres, *Partner*
Keitaro Goto, *Partner*
Kris Kruid, *Partner*
Linda Lee, *Sales Dir*
Brittany Hall, *Asst Mgr*
▲ EMP: 18

SALES (est): 910K **Privately Held**
WEB: www.jacquestorres.com
SIC: 2064 5145 5441 Candy & other confectionery products; confectionery; candy, nut & confectionery stores

(G-2236)
MS PAPER PRODUCTS CO INC
930 Bedford Ave (11205-4502)
PHONE..............................718 624-0248
Solomon Schwimmer, *President*
EMP: 6 EST: 1970
SQ FT: 12,000
SALES: 500K **Privately Held**
SIC: 2631 Paperboard mills

(G-2237)
MTZ ENTERPRISES INC
870 39th St (11232)
PHONE..............................347 834-2716
Sam Brody, *President*
EMP: 10
SQ FT: 1,200
SALES: 2MM **Privately Held**
SIC: 3646 Commercial indusl & institutional electric lighting fixtures

(G-2238)
MY HANKY INC
680 81st St Apt 4d (11228-2833)
PHONE..............................646 321-0869
Frank Marino, *President*
EMP: 10
SQ FT: 500
SALES: 500K **Privately Held**
SIC: 2389 Handkerchiefs, except paper

(G-2239)
MYSTIC DISPLAY CO INC
909 Remsen Ave (11236-1624)
PHONE..............................718 485-2651
David Censi, *President*
Barry Censi, *Corp Secy*
Hank Lombardi, *Vice Pres*
▼ EMP: 2
SQ FT: 47,000
SALES: 8MM **Privately Held**
WEB: www.mysticdisplay.com
SIC: 3993 7319 Displays & cutouts, window & lobby; display advertising service

(G-2240)
N C IRON WORKS INC
1117 60th St (11219-4925)
PHONE..............................718 633-4660
Nicholas Sorrentino, *President*
EMP: 5
SQ FT: 3,900
SALES (est): 976.6K **Privately Held**
SIC: 3312 Hot-rolled iron & steel products

(G-2241)
NAGAD CABINETS INC
1039 Mcdonald Ave (11230-1020)
PHONE..............................718 382-7200
Naftali Grueberger, *President*
EMP: 5
SQ FT: 2,000
SALES (est): 745.6K **Privately Held**
SIC: 2434 Vanities, bathroom: wood

(G-2242)
NANOTRONICS IMAGING INC
63 Flushing Ave Unit 128 (11205-1059)
PHONE..............................212 401-6209
Matthew Putman, *CEO*
Jonathan Yancey, *Technology*
EMP: 20
SALES (corp-wide): 2.4MM **Privately Held**
SIC: 3826 Analytical instruments
PA: Nanotronics Imaging, Inc.
2251 Front St Ste 109-111
Cuyahoga Falls OH 44221
330 926-9809

(G-2243)
NAP INDUSTRIES INC
Also Called: N A P
667 Kent Ave (11249-7500)
PHONE..............................718 625-4948
Leopold Lowy, *President*
Morris Lowy, *Chairman*
Jack Freund, *Vice Pres*
Leiby Freund, *Manager*
▲ EMP: 90

SQ FT: 55,000
SALES (est): 18.4MM **Privately Held**
SIC: 2673 Plastic bags: made from purchased materials

(G-2244)
NARRATIVELY INC
30 John St (11201-1122)
PHONE..............................203 536-0332
Noah Rosenberg, *President*
EMP: 25 EST: 2012
SQ FT: 20,000
SALES (est): 1.3MM **Privately Held**
SIC: 2741

(G-2245)
NATIONAL DIE & BUTTON MOULD CO
Also Called: Eisen Bros
1 Kent Ave (11249-1014)
PHONE..............................201 939-7800
Louis Eisenpresser, *Chairman*
George Eisenpresser, *Chairman*
EMP: 50 EST: 1911
SQ FT: 65,000
SALES (est): 5.1MM **Privately Held**
WEB: www.nailheads.com
SIC: 3965 3469 Buttons & parts; buckles & buckle parts; eyelets, metal: clothing, fabrics, boots or shoes; metal stampings

(G-2246)
NATIONAL PRFMCE SOLUTIONS INC
Also Called: Squeaky Clean
1043 78th St (11228-2611)
PHONE..............................718 833-4767
Lola Bizas, *Ch of Bd*
Jacob Kahle, *Principal*
Greg Bowman, *Co-Owner*
Michell Bowman, *Co-Owner*
EMP: 100
SQ FT: 400
SALES (est): 20.1MM **Privately Held**
SIC: 3993 Advertising artwork

(G-2247)
NATIONWIDE DAIRY INC
792 E 93rd St (11236-1831)
PHONE..............................347 689-8148
Eduard Magidov, *CEO*
◆ EMP: 5
SQ FT: 9,000
SALES (est): 423.4K **Privately Held**
SIC: 2023 Dry, condensed, evaporated dairy products

(G-2248)
NATURAL STONE & CABINET INC
1365 Halsey (11237-6102)
PHONE..............................718 388-2988
Sally Lee, *Owner*
▲ EMP: 5
SALES (est): 423.1K **Privately Held**
SIC: 2522 Cabinets, office: except wood

(G-2249)
NAUTICAL MARINE PAINT CORP
Also Called: Nautical Paint
4802 Farragut Rd (11203-6690)
PHONE..............................718 462-7000
Michael Schnurr, *President*
EMP: 25
SQ FT: 4,000
SALES (corp-wide): 15.8MM **Privately Held**
SIC: 2851 5231 Mfg Paints/Allied Products Ret Paint/Glass/Wallpaper
PA: Nautical Marine Paint Corp
1999 Elizabeth St
North Brunswick NJ 08902
732 821-3200

(G-2250)
NB ELCTRCAL ENCLSURES MFRS INC
902 903 Shepherd Ave (11208)
PHONE..............................718 272-8792
Neville Bearam, *President*
Travis Maynard, *Business Mgr*
EMP: 7
SALES: 2MM **Privately Held**
SIC: 3441 Fabricated structural metal

Brooklyn - Kings County (G-2251)

(G-2251)
NCC NY LLC
1840 Mcdonald Ave (11223-1827)
PHONE..................................718 943-7000
Joey Haber,
Joe Nakash,
Ralph Nakash,
▲ EMP: 20 EST: 1999
SQ FT: 9,000
SALES (est): 4.8MM Privately Held
WEB: www.ehalacha.com
SIC: 3699 Extension cords
PA: Nakash Five Points Llc
1400 Broadway Fl 15
New York NY 10018

(G-2252)
NEO CABINETRY LLC
400 Liberty Ave (11207-3061)
PHONE..................................718 403-0456
Louis Doucet, Owner
EMP: 10
SALES (est): 1MM Privately Held
SIC: 2434 Wood kitchen cabinets

(G-2253)
NEO PLASTICS LLC
1007 Sheffield Ave (11207-8341)
PHONE..................................646 542-1499
Isak Bengiyat,
EMP: 12
SALES (est): 607.7K Privately Held
SIC: 3089 Plastic containers, except foam

(G-2254)
NEPTUNE MACHINE INC
521 Carroll St (11215-1011)
PHONE..................................718 852-4100
Nicholas G Karkas, President
John Karkas, Vice Pres
Jerry Lachance, Sales Engr
Aris Fotopoulos, Manager
Farrah Ficco-Vasquez, Admin Asst
EMP: 20
SQ FT: 12,500
SALES (est): 3.8MM Privately Held
WEB: www.neptunemachine.com
SIC: 3599 Machine shop, jobbing & repair

(G-2255)
NEW AGE IRONWORKS INC
183 Van Siclen Ave (11207-2605)
PHONE..................................718 277-1895
Yair Tapia, President
EMP: 13
SALES (est): 1.5MM Privately Held
SIC: 7692 Welding repair

(G-2256)
NEW ART PUBLICATIONS INC
Also Called: BOMB MAGAZINE
80 Hanson Pl Ste 703 (11217-2998)
PHONE..................................718 636-9100
Betsy Sussler, President
Ryan Chapman, Managing Dir
Alexis Boehmler, Principal
Raluca Albu, Editor
Ted Dodson, Director
EMP: 10
SALES: 1.8MM Privately Held
WEB: www.bombsite.com
SIC: 2721 Magazines: publishing only, not printed on site

(G-2257)
NEW CONCEPTS OF NEW YORK LLC
89 19th St 91 (11232-1055)
PHONE..................................212 695-4999
Robert Schwartz,
▲ EMP: 20
SALES (est): 2.4MM Privately Held
WEB: www.newconceptsllc.com
SIC: 2339 Women's & misses' accessories

(G-2258)
NEW DIMENSION AWARDS INC (PA)
Also Called: New Dimension Trophies
6505 11th Ave (11219-5602)
PHONE..................................718 236-8200
Joseph S Cardinale, President
EMP: 9
SQ FT: 16,000
SALES (est): 1MM Privately Held
WEB: www.newdimensioninc.com
SIC: 3499 Trophies, metal, except silver; novelties & specialties, metal

(G-2259)
NEW DIMENSIONS OFFICE GROUP
Also Called: Acme Office Group
540 Morgan Ave (11222-5227)
PHONE..................................718 387-0995
Ernest Eager, President
Bertran Teich, Vice Pres
Buddy Martin, Treasurer
Jack Teich, Admin Sec
EMP: 52
SQ FT: 20,000
SALES (est): 3.6MM Privately Held
SIC: 3446 2541 2522 2521 Architectural metalwork; wood partitions & fixtures; office furniture, except wood; panel systems & partitions (free-standing), office: wood

(G-2260)
NEW YORK CHRISTAN TIMES INC
1061 Atlantic Ave (11238-2902)
P.O. Box 381066 (11238-8066)
PHONE..................................718 638-6397
Dennis Dillon, President
Karen Granger, Vice Pres
EMP: 6
SALES (est): 492.3K Privately Held
SIC: 2759 Publication printing

(G-2261)
NEW YORK DAILY CHALLENGE INC (PA)
1195 Atlantic Ave Fl 2 (11216-2709)
P.O. Box 160252 (11216-0252)
PHONE..................................718 636-9500
Thomas H Watkins Jr, President
Duwad Philip, Manager
EMP: 20
SQ FT: 1,000
SALES (est): 1MM Privately Held
SIC: 2711 Newspapers: publishing only, not printed on site

(G-2262)
NEW YORK HOSPITAL DISPOSABLE
101 Richardson St Ste 1 (11211-1344)
PHONE..................................718 384-1620
Rosa Ramos, President
Victor Cora, President
Zitzor Cora, Admin Sec
EMP: 20
SQ FT: 12,000
SALES (est): 1.7MM Privately Held
SIC: 2389 2326 Hospital gowns; men's & boys' work clothing

(G-2263)
NEW YORK PASTA AUTHORITY INC
640 Parkside Ave (11226-1506)
PHONE..................................347 787-2130
Chavi Katzman, Exec Dir
EMP: 10
SALES (est): 629.3K Privately Held
SIC: 2033 Spaghetti & other pasta sauce: packaged in cans, jars, etc.

(G-2264)
NEW YORK POPLIN LLC
4611 1st Ave (11232-4200)
PHONE..................................718 768-3296
Wayne Yip, Mng Member
▲ EMP: 8
SQ FT: 8,000
SALES (est): 4.5MM Privately Held
SIC: 2221 Apparel & outerwear fabric, manmade fiber or silk

(G-2265)
NEW YORK QRTRLY FOUNDATION INC
322 76th St (11209-3106)
P.O. Box 2015, New York (10113-2015)
PHONE..................................917 843-8825
Raymond Hammond, President
Neil Smith, Vice Pres
Linda Tieber, Treasurer
Andrea Lockett, Admin Sec
EMP: 12
SALES: 52K Privately Held
SIC: 2731 7389 Book publishing;

(G-2266)
NEWCASTLE FABRICS CORP
Also Called: Newtown Finishing
86 Beadel St (11222-5232)
PHONE..................................718 388-6600
Daniel Aldalezo, Manager
EMP: 5
SALES (corp-wide): 3.3MM Privately Held
WEB: www.newcastlefabrics.com
SIC: 2269 7389 Finishing plants; textile & apparel services
PA: Newcastle Fabrics Corp.
140 58th St Ste 112
Brooklyn NY 11220
718 782-5560

(G-2267)
NEWS REPORT INC
Also Called: Diyzeitung
1281 49th St Ste 3 (11219-3055)
PHONE..................................718 851-6607
Albert Friedman, Ch of Bd
Rose Friedman, Vice Pres
EMP: 25
SALES (est): 1MM Privately Held
SIC: 2711 Newspapers: publishing only, not printed on site; newspapers, publishing & printing

(G-2268)
NEWYORK PEDORTHIC ASSOCIATES
Also Called: Rosenbaum Foot
2102 63rd St (11204-3058)
PHONE..................................718 236-7700
Mark Rosenbaum, President
EMP: 6
SALES (est): 854.9K Privately Held
SIC: 3069 Orthopedic sundries, molded rubber

(G-2269)
NIFT GROUP INC
14 Woodbine St (11221-4302)
PHONE..................................504 505-1144
Timothee Dumain, Principal
EMP: 1 EST: 2016
SALES: 3MM Privately Held
SIC: 7372 Business oriented computer software

(G-2270)
NLHE LLC
Also Called: Nanette Lepore
141 Flushing Ave 906 (11205-1338)
PHONE..................................212 594-0012
Robert Savage, CEO
Erica Wolf, President
EMP: 50 EST: 2014
SALES (est): 265K Privately Held
SIC: 2339 5137 Sportswear, women's; women's & children's clothing

(G-2271)
NOBLE CHECKS INC
1682 43rd St Apt 2 (11204-1059)
PHONE..................................212 537-6241
Isaac Dresdner, Ch of Bd
EMP: 5
SALES (est): 678.1K Privately Held
WEB: www.noblechecks.com
SIC: 2759 Commercial printing

(G-2272)
NORDIC INTERIOR INC
26 Court St Ste 2211 (11242-1122)
PHONE..................................718 456-7000
Helge Halvorsen, President
Lloyd Jacobsen, Corp Secy
Harald Haegeland, Vice Pres
▲ EMP: 150
SQ FT: 55,000
SALES (est): 20.7MM Privately Held
WEB: www.nordicinterior.com
SIC: 2431 1742 Woodwork, interior & ornamental; drywall

(G-2273)
NORTHSIDE MEDIA GROUP LLC (HQ)
55 Washington St Ste 652 (11201-1063)
PHONE..................................917 318-6513
Jesse Smith, Vice Pres
Dangelo Laura, Marketing Mgr
Scott Stedman, Mng Member
Daniel Stedman,
EMP: 14
SALES (est): 2.3MM
SALES (corp-wide): 8.5MM Privately Held
SIC: 2721 Magazines: publishing & printing
PA: Zealot Networks, Inc.
2114 Narcissus Ct
Venice CA 90291
310 821-3737

(G-2274)
NORTHSIDE MEDIA GROUP LLC
55 Washington St Ste 652 (11201-1063)
PHONE..................................917 318-6513
Scott Stedman, Branch Mgr
EMP: 25
SALES (corp-wide): 8.5MM Privately Held
SIC: 2721 Magazines: publishing & printing
HQ: Northside Media Group Llc
55 Washington St Ste 652
Brooklyn NY 11201
917 318-6513

(G-2275)
NOVEL BOX COMPANY LTD
659 Berriman St (11208-5303)
PHONE..................................718 965-2222
Moishe Sternhill, President
Abe Kwadrat, Vice Pres
▲ EMP: 25
SQ FT: 41,000
SALES (est): 4.7MM Privately Held
WEB: www.novelbox.com
SIC: 2657 3469 3089 Folding paperboard boxes; boxes, stamped metal; boxes, plastic

(G-2276)
NOVOYE RSSKOYE SLOVO PUBG CORP
Also Called: Russian Daily
2614 Voorhies Ave (11235-2414)
PHONE..................................646 460-4566
Yuri Ivnitsky, Ch of Bd
Lawrence Weinberg, President
Sophia Theodossiou, Sales Staff
EMP: 52
SQ FT: 16,000
SALES (est): 2MM Privately Held
WEB: www.nrs.com
SIC: 2711 Newspapers: publishing only, not printed on site

(G-2277)
NUVITE CHEMICAL COMPOUNDS CORP
213 Freeman St 215 (11222-1400)
PHONE..................................718 383-8351
Clifford Lester, President
EMP: 11 EST: 1949
SQ FT: 7,000
SALES (est): 1MM Privately Held
WEB: www.nuvitechemical.com
SIC: 2842 Cleaning or polishing preparations

(G-2278)
NY CABINET FACTORY INC
6901 14th Ave (11228-1701)
PHONE..................................718 256-6541
Vin Burratto, President
Frank Burratto, Vice Pres
EMP: 11 EST: 2015
SQ FT: 2,500
SALES: 2MM Privately Held
SIC: 2434 5211 Wood kitchen cabinets; counter tops

(G-2279)
NY ORTHOPEDIC USA INC
63 Flushing Ave Unit 333 (11205-1083)
PHONE..................................718 852-5330
Michael Rozenberg, President
Michael Blatt, Vice Pres
▲ EMP: 80

SQ FT: 24,000
SALES (est): 10MM Privately Held
WEB: www.nyorthousa.com
SIC: 3842 2389 5999 Personal safety equipment; uniforms & vestments; medical apparatus & supplies

(G-2280)
NY TILEMAKERS
331 Grand St (11211-4464)
PHONE..................989 278-8453
Andru Eron, Owner
EMP: 5 EST: 2012
SALES: 80K Privately Held
SIC: 3253 Ceramic wall & floor tile

(G-2281)
NYC COMMUNITY MEDIA LLC
Also Called: Villager, The
1 Metrotech Ctr N Fl 10 (11201-3875)
PHONE..................212 229-1890
Alexis Avedisian, Comms Mgr
Amy Chen, Manager
Michael Shirey, Art Dir
Jennifer Goodstein,
EMP: 18 EST: 2012
SQ FT: 1,200
SALES (est): 1.2MM Privately Held
SIC: 2711 Newspapers, publishing & printing

(G-2282)
NYP HOLDINGS INC
Also Called: New York Post
1 Metrotech Ctr N Fl 10 (11201-3875)
PHONE..................718 260-2500
Cliff Luster, Principal
EMP: 60
SALES (corp-wide): 9B Publicly Held
SIC: 2711 Newspapers, publishing & printing
HQ: Nyp Holdings, Inc.
1211 Ave Of The Americas
New York NY 10036

(G-2283)
OBOUT SOFTWARE INC
728 Ocean View Ave Apt A1 (11235-6325)
PHONE..................212 380-3500
Oleg Boutorine, President
EMP: 10
SALES (est): 488.8K Privately Held
SIC: 7372 Prepackaged software

(G-2284)
OFFICE GRABS LLC
Also Called: Officegrabscom
1245 50th St Apt 4d (11219-3561)
PHONE..................347 678-3993
Moshe Rosenberg, CFO
EMP: 7
SALES (est): 94K Privately Held
SIC: 3577 Computer peripheral equipment

(G-2285)
OFFICE GRABS NY INC
1303 53rd St 105 (11219-3823)
PHONE..................212 444-1331
Meir Barminka, CEO
Moshe Rosenberg, President
EMP: 6
SALES (est): 695K Privately Held
SIC: 2752 Commercial printing, lithographic

(G-2286)
OGOSPORT LLC
63 Flushing Ave Unit 137 (11205-1070)
PHONE..................718 554-0777
Matthew Romano, Project Mgr
Jenie Fu,
Kevin Williams,
▲ EMP: 5
SQ FT: 5,000
SALES (est): 580K Privately Held
WEB: www.ogosport.com
SIC: 3944 Games, toys & children's vehicles

(G-2287)
OLOLLO INC
43 Hall St Ste B8 (11205-1395)
PHONE..................877 701-0110
Regan Chen, President
▲ EMP: 7 EST: 2009
SQ FT: 10,000

SALES (est): 1MM Privately Held
SIC: 2519 Household furniture, except wood or metal: upholstered

(G-2288)
OMG CLEANERS INC
565 Coney Island Ave (11218-4303)
PHONE..................718 282-2011
EMP: 5
SALES (est): 431.2K Privately Held
SIC: 2842 Drycleaning preparations

(G-2289)
ONE STORY INC
232 3rd St Ste A108 (11215-2708)
PHONE..................917 816-3659
Maribeth Batcha, President
Hannah Tinti, Vice Pres
EMP: 2
SALES (est): 355.4K Privately Held
SIC: 2741 Miscellaneous publishing

(G-2290)
ORCHARD SAUSAGES INC
340 Johnson Ave (11206-2802)
PHONE..................718 381-9388
Tom Sat, President
Zhao Ming SA, Vice Pres
EMP: 10
SQ FT: 10,000
SALES: 3MM Privately Held
SIC: 2013 Sausages & other prepared meats

(G-2291)
ORTEX HOME TEXTILE INC
Also Called: Ortex Home Textiles
523 E 82nd St (11236-3118)
PHONE..................718 241-7298
Merry Lati, President
David Ausi, Vice Pres
▲ EMP: 6
SQ FT: 15,000
SALES (est): 6.4MM Privately Held
SIC: 2211 Sheets, bedding & table cloths: cotton

(G-2292)
ORTHOCRAFT INC
1477 E 27th St (11210-5308)
PHONE..................718 951-1700
Herschel Sauber, President
Avrumi Friedman, COO
Nina Sauber, Manager
EMP: 6
SQ FT: 800
SALES (est): 973.5K Privately Held
SIC: 3842 5999 Limbs, artificial; orthopedic appliances; orthopedic & prosthesis applications

(G-2293)
ORTHOPEDIC ARTS LABORATORY INC
141 Atlantic Ave Apt 1 (11201-5516)
PHONE..................718 858-2400
Stephan Manucharian, CEO
EMP: 5
SQ FT: 850
SALES (est): 898.3K Privately Held
SIC: 3842 Limbs, artificial; prosthetic appliances

(G-2294)
OSO INDUSTRIES INC
1205 Manhattan Ave (11222-6154)
PHONE..................917 709-2050
Eric Weil, Principal
Klara Bernabe, Manager
EMP: 8
SALES (est): 318.5K Privately Held
SIC: 3999 Manufacturing industries

(G-2295)
OTHER HALF BREWING CO
195 Centre St (11231-3907)
PHONE..................347 987-3527
EMP: 5
SALES (est): 218.8K Privately Held
SIC: 2082 Mfg Malt Beverages

(G-2296)
OUTREACH PUBLISHING CORP
546 Montgomery St (11225-3023)
PHONE..................718 773-0525

Shlomo Lakein, President
Reuven Lakein, General Mgr
Reuben Lakein, Vice Pres
EMP: 7
SALES (est): 660K Privately Held
WEB: www.outreach770.com
SIC: 2741 Miscellaneous publishing

(G-2297)
P M BELTS USA INC
131 32nd St (11232-1809)
PHONE..................800 762-3580
Gregory O'Neil, President
EMP: 45 EST: 1986
SQ FT: 12,500
SALES (est): 1.9MM Privately Held
WEB: www.pmbelt.com
SIC: 2387 Apparel belts

(G-2298)
P8H INC
Also Called: Paddle8
81 Prospect St 7 (11201-1473)
PHONE..................212 343-1142
EMP: 40 EST: 2017
SALES (est): 20MM Privately Held
SIC: 7372 7389 Prepackaged Software Services Business Services

(G-2299)
PALAGONIA BAKERY CO INC
Also Called: Palagonia Italian Bread
508 Junius St (11212-7199)
PHONE..................718 272-5400
Christopher Palagonia, President
▲ EMP: 100
SQ FT: 25,000
SALES (est): 13MM Privately Held
SIC: 2051 Bread, cake & related products

(G-2300)
PANOPLY MEDIA LLC (HQ)
15 Metrotech Ctr Fl 8 (11201-3826)
PHONE..................646 382-5423
Brendan Monaghan, CEO
Ava Lubell, General Mgr
Christopher Landry, Director
EMP: 20 EST: 2016
SQ FT: 21,000
SALES (est): 2.8MM
SALES (corp-wide): 2.5B Publicly Held
SIC: 2741
PA: Graham Holdings Company
1300 17th St N Ste 1700
Arlington VA 22209
703 345-6300

(G-2301)
PAP CHAT INC
3105 Quentin Rd (11234-4234)
PHONE..................516 350-1888
Justin Schwartz, CEO
EMP: 5
SALES (est): 207.7K Privately Held
SIC: 7372 7389 Prepackaged software;

(G-2302)
PARADISE PLASTICS LLC
116 39th St (11232-2712)
PHONE..................718 788-3733
Max Berg,
Judith Berg,
Ernest Grossberger,
Gabriella Grossberger,
EMP: 25 EST: 1952
SQ FT: 40,000
SALES (est): 5MM Privately Held
WEB: www.paradiseplastics.com
SIC: 2673 Plastic bags: made from purchased materials

(G-2303)
PARAGON PUBLISHING INC
97 Harrison Ave (11206-2918)
PHONE..................718 302-2093
Mendel Sicherman, President
EMP: 5
SALES (est): 440K Privately Held
SIC: 2741 Miscellaneous publishing

(G-2304)
PARK AVE BLDG & ROOFG SUPS LLC
2120 Atlantic Ave (11233-3162)
PHONE..................718 403-0100
Bob Groeninger, CEO

Raymond Rivera, President
Eddy Philippe, Vice Pres
Joseph Colwell, Store Mgr
Tom Hussey, CFO
EMP: 40
SQ FT: 15,000
SALES (est): 40.2MM Privately Held
SIC: 3531 5033 Aerial work platforms: hydraulic/elec. truck/carrier mounted; roofing & siding materials

(G-2305)
PARK AVENUE SPORTSWEAR LTD (PA)
820 4th Ave (11232-1612)
PHONE..................718 369-0520
Joseph Steg, President
Martin Perlstein, Vice Pres
EMP: 12 EST: 1962
SQ FT: 15,000
SALES (est): 2.1MM Privately Held
SIC: 2339 Sportswear, women's

(G-2306)
PARK SLOPE COPY CENTER
123 7th Ave (11215-1301)
PHONE..................718 783-0268
Bob Kalb, Owner
Jon Kalb, General Mgr
EMP: 11
SALES: 123.6K Privately Held
SIC: 2752 Commercial printing, offset

(G-2307)
PATRICK MACKIN CUSTOM FURN
Also Called: Art Boards
612 Degraw St (11217-3112)
PHONE..................718 237-2592
Patrick Mackin, President
▲ EMP: 7
SALES (est): 600K Privately Held
WEB: www.art-boards.com
SIC: 2511 Wood household furniture

(G-2308)
PECORARO DAIRY PRODUCTS INC (PA)
287 Leonard St (11211-3618)
PHONE..................718 388-2379
Cesare Pecoraro, President
Ralph Parlato, Vice Pres
EMP: 6
SQ FT: 4,000
SALES (est): 959.9K Privately Held
SIC: 2022 Natural cheese

(G-2309)
PEKING FOOD LLC
47 Stewart Ave (11237-1517)
PHONE..................718 628-8080
Lawrence Wu, Mng Member
Teresa Wu,
▼ EMP: 30
SQ FT: 28,000
SALES (est): 4MM Privately Held
SIC: 2051 Bread, cake & related products

(G-2310)
PENN SIGNS INC
Also Called: Mr Sign
1920 Atlantic Ave (11233-3004)
PHONE..................718 797-1112
Shulm Miller, President
Leo Lew, Manager
EMP: 20
SALES (est): 2.1MM Privately Held
SIC: 3993 Signs, not made in custom sign painting shops

(G-2311)
PENN STATE METAL FABRI
810 Humboldt St Ste 9 (11222-1913)
PHONE..................718 786-8814
Herbert Engler, President
EMP: 4
SQ FT: 7,500
SALES: 1MM Privately Held
SIC: 3531 3463 Construction machinery; pump & compressor forgings, nonferrous

(G-2312)
PERALTA METAL WORKS INC
602 Atkins Ave (11208-5202)
PHONE..................718 649-8661

Brooklyn - Kings County (G-2313)

Omar Peralta, *President*
Yvette Peralta, *Vice Pres*
EMP: 8
SQ FT: 3,500
SALES (est): 1.5MM **Privately Held**
SIC: 3441 Fabricated structural metal

(G-2313)
PERFECT PRINT INC
220 36th St Unit 2a (11232-2413)
PHONE..................718 832-5280
Orly Masry, *President*
EMP: 20
SALES: 250K **Privately Held**
SIC: 2211 Print cloths, cotton

(G-2314)
PHILLIP TISSICHER
Also Called: Fao Printing
1688 Utica Ave (11234-1525)
PHONE..................718 282-3310
Phillip Tissicher, *Owner*
EMP: 12
SALES (est): 113.7K **Privately Held**
SIC: 2752 Commercial printing, lithographic

(G-2315)
PHOENIX METAL DESIGNS INC
100 Hinsdale St (11207-2902)
PHONE..................516 597-4100
Voula Nikitopoulos, *Chairman*
EMP: 5 **EST:** 2016
SALES (est): 747.7K **Privately Held**
SIC: 3446 Architectural metalwork

(G-2316)
PICTURE PERFECT FRAMING
1758 50th St (11204-1220)
PHONE..................718 851-1884
Harry Gruber, *Owner*
Chaya Gruber, *Owner*
EMP: 5 **EST:** 1990
SALES: 30K **Privately Held**
SIC: 2499 3499 Picture & mirror frames, wood; picture frames, metal

(G-2317)
PILGRIM SURF & SUPPLY
68 N 3rd St (11249-3925)
PHONE..................718 218-7456
Chris Gentile, *Owner*
Chelsea Burcz, *Editor*
EMP: 7
SALES (est): 580.2K **Privately Held**
SIC: 3949 Surfboards

(G-2318)
PILLOW PERFECTIONS LTD INC
252 Norman Ave Ste 101 (11222-6412)
PHONE..................718 383-2259
Kenny Fried, *President*
▼ **EMP:** 8
SQ FT: 7,000
SALES: 700K **Privately Held**
SIC: 2511 5712 Wood household furniture; furniture stores

(G-2319)
PINK BOX ACCESSORIES LLC
Also Called: Blue Box
940 40th St (11219-1025)
PHONE..................718 435-2821
Mariano Uy,
Michael Uy,
▲ **EMP:** 5
SALES: 500K **Privately Held**
SIC: 3911 7389 Jewelry, precious metal;

(G-2320)
PINTRILL LLC
231 Grand St (11211-4302)
PHONE..................718 782-1000
Jordan Roswell, *Mng Member*
EMP: 11 **EST:** 2014
SQ FT: 600
SALES (est): 1MM **Privately Held**
SIC: 3951 Pens & mechanical pencils

(G-2321)
PIROKE TRADE INC
1430 35th St Fl 2 (11218-3706)
PHONE..................646 515-1537
Keitaro Maruyama, *President*
EMP: 5

SALES (est): 280K **Privately Held**
SIC: 2789 Trade binding services

(G-2322)
PIVOT RECORDS LLC
600 Johnson Ave (11237-1318)
P.O. Box 70276 (11207-0276)
PHONE..................718 417-1213
EMP: 11
SALES (est): 490K **Privately Held**
SIC: 3652 Mfg Prerecorded Records/Tapes

(G-2323)
PLASTPAC INC
32 Walton St (11206-5056)
PHONE..................908 272-7200
Mark Porges, *President*
EMP: 38
SALES (corp-wide): 9.3MM **Privately Held**
SIC: 3086 Plastics foam products
PA: Plastpac Inc
30 Boright Ave
Kenilworth NJ 07033
908 272-7200

(G-2324)
PLATFORM EXPERTS INC
2938 Quentin Rd (11229-1825)
PHONE..................646 843-7100
Joshua Newman, *President*
EMP: 8
SQ FT: 4,000
SALES (est): 775.2K **Privately Held**
WEB: www.platformexperts.com
SIC: 7372 Prepackaged software

(G-2325)
PLAYGROUND NY INC
55 Hope St Apt 212 (11211-4865)
PHONE..................505 920-7236
Linda Yang, *CEO*
EMP: 11
SALES (est): 239.1K **Privately Held**
SIC: 7372 7389 Application computer software;

(G-2326)
POLYTECH POOL MFG INC
Also Called: Wet & Wild Pools & Spas
262 48th St 262 (11220-1012)
P.O. Box 544, Cedarhurst (11516-0544)
PHONE..................718 492-8991
Fax: 718 439-1254
EMP: 10 **EST:** 1975
SQ FT: 60,000
SALES (est): 870K **Privately Held**
SIC: 3949 Mfg Sporting/Athletic Goods

(G-2327)
PONTI ROSSI INC
186 Franklin St Apt C16 (11222-1690)
PHONE..................347 506-9616
Alessandro Capuano, *President*
EMP: 6
SALES (est): 227.7K **Privately Held**
SIC: 2099 Food preparations

(G-2328)
POP PRINTING INCORPORATED
288 Hamilton Ave (11231-3208)
PHONE..................212 808-7800
Stephen Stein, *Ch of Bd*
EMP: 14
SALES (est): 1.8MM **Privately Held**
SIC: 2752 Commercial printing, offset

(G-2329)
POTENTIAL POLY BAG INC
1253 Coney Island Ave (11230-3520)
PHONE..................718 258-0800
Mark Katz, *President*
Jerry Millman, *Vice Pres*
▲ **EMP:** 9
SQ FT: 10,000
SALES (est): 1.6MM **Privately Held**
WEB: www.potentialpolybag.com
SIC: 3081 Polyethylene film

(G-2330)
POWERHOUSE CULTURAL ENTRMT INC
Also Called: Powerhouse Books
126a Front St (11201-1116)
PHONE..................212 604-9074

Daniel Power, *CEO*
Craig Cohen, *President*
▲ **EMP:** 17
SQ FT: 10,200
SALES (est): 2.8MM **Privately Held**
WEB: www.powerhousebooks.com
SIC: 2731 Book publishing

(G-2331)
POWERMATE CELLULAR
140 58th St Ste 1d (11220-2525)
PHONE..................718 833-9400
Fax: 718 567-7020
▲ **EMP:** 7
SALES (est): 730.8K **Privately Held**
SIC: 3661 Mfg Telephone/Telegraph Apparatus

(G-2332)
PPR DIRECT MARKETING LLC (PA)
74 20th St (11232-1101)
PHONE..................718 965-8600
Robert Notine,
Richard Carvalho,
Margaret Hickey,
▲ **EMP:** 8 **EST:** 2010
SALES (est): 3.9MM **Privately Held**
SIC: 2389 Men's miscellaneous accessories

(G-2333)
PR & STONE & TILE INC
Also Called: Stone Crafters International
17 Beadel St (11222-5110)
PHONE..................718 383-1115
Edward Rynkosky, *President*
Arakdiusz Rakowski, *Vice Pres*
EMP: 5
SALES: 900K **Privately Held**
SIC: 3281 Granite, cut & shaped

(G-2334)
PRECISION DIAMOND CUTTERS INC
1410 E 22nd St (11210-5111)
PHONE..................212 719-4438
David Lew, *President*
Kathy Paykany, *Vice Pres*
EMP: 6
SALES (est): 522.3K **Privately Held**
WEB: www.bellnor.com
SIC: 3915 Diamond cutting & polishing

(G-2335)
PRECISION MTAL FABRICATORS INC
Also Called: PMF
236 39th St (11232-2820)
PHONE..................718 832-9805
Dimitrios Theodoru, *President*
EMP: 12
SQ FT: 8,000
SALES (est): 2.1MM **Privately Held**
SIC: 3444 Sheet metalwork

(G-2336)
PRECISION PRODUCT INC
18 Steuben St (11205-1306)
PHONE..................718 852-7127
Sonny K Chan, *President*
▲ **EMP:** 5 **EST:** 1997
SQ FT: 6,000
SALES (est): 650.5K **Privately Held**
SIC: 3531 Construction machinery

(G-2337)
PREEBRO PRINTING
5319 Fort Hamilton Pkwy (11219-4036)
PHONE..................718 633-7300
Zur Getter, *Owner*
EMP: 5
SALES (est): 537.4K **Privately Held**
WEB: www.preebroprinting.com
SIC: 2752 Commercial printing, lithographic

(G-2338)
PREMIUM ASSURE INC
1726 Mcdonald Ave Ste 201 (11230-6942)
PHONE..................605 252-9999
Shulem Iskowitz, *Ch of Bd*
Nick Hager, *Principal*
EMP: 5 **EST:** 2017

SALES (est): 182.3K **Privately Held**
SIC: 3999 Hair & hair-based products

(G-2339)
PRESSED JUICE LLC (PA)
Also Called: East Coast Copacking
205 Clinton Ave Apt 12a (11205-3555)
PHONE..................646 573-9157
Paul Baudier,
Donaldo Aragon,
EMP: 2
SALES: 1MM **Privately Held**
SIC: 2033 Fruit juices: packaged in cans, jars, etc.

(G-2340)
PRESSER KOSHER BAKING CORP
1720 Avenue M (11230-5304)
PHONE..................718 375-5088
Sam Klein, *President*
EMP: 20
SQ FT: 2,500
SALES: 750K **Privately Held**
SIC: 2051 5461 Bakery: wholesale or wholesale/retail combined; bakeries

(G-2341)
PRESTIGE HANGERS STR FIXS CORP
1026 55th St (11219-4024)
PHONE..................718 522-6777
Abe Minkosf, *President*
Mozes Parnes, *Principal*
EMP: 5
SQ FT: 5,000
SALES: 370K **Privately Held**
WEB: www.prestigestorefixtures.com
SIC: 3089 Clothes hangers, plastic

(G-2342)
PRIME FOOD PROCESSING CORP
300 Vandervoort Ave (11211-1715)
PHONE..................718 963-2323
Albert Chan, *Ch of Bd*
Yee Hung Chan, *President*
▲ **EMP:** 80
SQ FT: 35,000
SALES (est): 12.5MM **Privately Held**
SIC: 2013 2037 Frozen meats from purchased meat; vegetables, quick frozen & cold pack, excl. potato products

(G-2343)
PRIMO FROZEN DESSERTS INC
Also Called: Ices Queen
1633 Utica Ave (11234-1524)
PHONE..................718 252-2312
Dan Lazzaro, *CEO*
Dominick Lazzaro, *Vice Pres*
EMP: 8
SQ FT: 4,500
SALES: 400K **Privately Held**
SIC: 2024 Ices, flavored (frozen dessert)

(G-2344)
PRIMO PLASTICS INC
162 Russell St (11222-3619)
P.O. Box 220187 (11222-0187)
PHONE..................718 349-1000
John Primo, *President*
Pete Krutros, *Vice Pres*
▲ **EMP:** 20
SQ FT: 7,800
SALES (est): 2.6MM **Privately Held**
SIC: 2673 5113 Plastic bags: made from purchased materials; bags, paper & disposable plastic

(G-2345)
PRINCE SEATING CORP
1355 Atlantic Ave (11216-2810)
PHONE..................718 363-2300
Abe Belsky, *President*
Henry Bodner, *Vice Pres*
Paul Olendzki, *Opers Staff*
▲ **EMP:** 25
SQ FT: 80,000
SALES: 4.4MM **Privately Held**
WEB: www.chairfactory.net
SIC: 2521 Wood office chairs, benches & stools; chairs, office: padded, upholstered or plain; wood; stools, office: wood

GEOGRAPHIC SECTION
Brooklyn - Kings County (G-2376)

(G-2346)
PRINT HOUSE INC
Also Called: Printhouse, The
538 Johnson Ave (11237-1226)
PHONE.....................718 443-7500
Sholom Laine, *Ch of Bd*
Yaakov Laine, *Executive*
▲ **EMP:** 60
SQ FT: 71,000
SALES (est): 13.5MM **Privately Held**
SIC: 2752 Commercial printing, lithographic

(G-2347)
PRINT MALL
4122 16th Ave (11204-1052)
PHONE.....................718 437-7700
Sara Olewski, *Owner*
EMP: 5
SALES (est): 450.4K **Privately Held**
WEB: www.invitations123.com
SIC: 2759 Invitation & stationery printing & engraving

(G-2348)
PRINT SEFORIM BZUL INC
8 Lynch St Apt 6r (11206-5528)
PHONE.....................718 679-1011
EMP: 6
SALES (est): 135.1K **Privately Held**
SIC: 2752 Commercial printing, lithographic

(G-2349)
PRINTING FACTORY LLC
1940 Utica Ave (11234-3214)
PHONE.....................718 451-0500
Lisa Blitman,
EMP: 12
SALES (est): 891K **Privately Held**
SIC: 2732 Book printing

(G-2350)
PRINTING MAX NEW YORK INC
2282 Flatbush Ave (11234-4518)
PHONE.....................718 692-1400
George Blair, *Principal*
EMP: 6
SALES (est): 546.7K **Privately Held**
SIC: 2759 Screen printing

(G-2351)
PRINTING SALES GROUP LIMITED
Also Called: Flair Printers
1856 Flatbush Ave (11210-4831)
PHONE.....................718 258-8860
Steven Zuller, *President*
EMP: 20
SALES (est): 1.7MM **Privately Held**
SIC: 2752 Commercial printing, offset

(G-2352)
PRINTUTOPIA
393 Prospect Ave (11215-5608)
P.O. Box 150528 (11215-0528)
PHONE.....................718 788-1545
Hamlet Villa, *General Mgr*
EMP: 10
SALES (est): 810.9K **Privately Held**
SIC: 2752 Commercial printing, offset

(G-2353)
PRODUCTAND DESIGN INC
63 Flushing Ave Unit 322 (11205-1082)
PHONE.....................718 858-2440
John Milich, *President*
▲ **EMP:** 10
SALES: 2MM **Privately Held**
SIC: 3441 8712 Fabricated structural metal; architectural services

(G-2354)
PROFOOT INC
74 20th St Fl 2 (11232-1101)
PHONE.....................718 965-8600
Leonard Feldman, *President*
Robert Notine, *Corp Secy*
Larry Brown, *Vice Pres*
Richard Jefairjian, *Vice Pres*
Donoghue Jessica, *Vice Pres*
▲ **EMP:** 45
SQ FT: 35,000
SALES (est): 9.6MM **Privately Held**
WEB: www.profootcare.com
SIC: 3842 Orthopedic appliances; foot appliances, orthopedic

(G-2355)
PROFORMANCE FOODS INC
44 Dobbin St Fl 1 (11222-3110)
PHONE.....................703 869-3413
Ryan Wiltse, *President*
EMP: 7
SALES: 2MM **Privately Held**
SIC: 2096 Potato chips & similar snacks

(G-2356)
PROJECT ENERGY SAVERS LLC
Also Called: PES Group
68 Jay St Ste 516 (11201-8362)
PHONE.....................718 596-4231
Joshua Wolfe, *Mng Member*
Mark Wolfe,
EMP: 14
SALES (est): 1.2MM **Privately Held**
SIC: 2731 8748 Textbooks: publishing only, not printed on site; energy conservation consultant

(G-2357)
PROMOTIONAL DEVELOPMENT INC
Also Called: P D I
909 Remsen Ave (11236-1624)
PHONE.....................718 485-8550
Henry Lombardi, *President*
Anthony Valentine, *Vice Pres*
David Censi, *CFO*
Barry Censi, *Treasurer*
Dorothy Sylvester, *Manager*
▲ **EMP:** 80
SQ FT: 60,000
SALES (est): 12.9MM **Privately Held**
WEB: www.promotionaldevelopment.com
SIC: 3999 3993 Advertising display products; signs & advertising specialties

(G-2358)
PROTECTIVE LINING CORP
601 39th St (11232-3101)
PHONE.....................718 854-3838
Steven Howard, *President*
Morton Howard, *Vice Pres*
▲ **EMP:** 65 **EST:** 1950
SQ FT: 28,000
SALES (est): 18.5MM **Privately Held**
WEB: www.prolining.com
SIC: 3089 Plastic containers, except foam

(G-2359)
PROVISION SUPPLY LLC (PA)
Also Called: Ezcontacts.com
1153 55th St (11219-4117)
PHONE.....................347 623-0237
Joel Lefkowitz, *President*
EMP: 13
SALES (est): 13.1MM **Privately Held**
SIC: 3851 Protective eyeware

(G-2360)
PROVISIONAIRE & CO LLC
Also Called: Field Trip Jerky
630 Flushing Ave Fl 4 (11206-5026)
PHONE.....................646 681-8600
Todd Tolis, *Sales Dir*
Thomas Donigan, *Manager*
Maxwell Fiedel, *Manager*
Ross Shepard, *Manager*
M Scott Fiesinger,
EMP: 20
SALES (est): 1.9MM **Privately Held**
SIC: 2013 Snack sticks, including jerky: from purchased meat

(G-2361)
PURE ACOUSTICS INC
18 Fuller Pl (11215-6007)
PHONE.....................718 788-4411
Rami Ezratty, *CEO*
EMP: 7 **EST:** 2003
SALES: 2MM **Privately Held**
SIC: 3651 Speaker systems

(G-2362)
PURE PLANET WATERS LLC
4809 Avenue N Ste 185 (11234-3711)
PHONE.....................718 676-7900
Denise Piccolo,
Gary Cucuza,
EMP: 10
SQ FT: 2,000
SALES: 1MM **Privately Held**
SIC: 3589 5999 5078 5074 Water filters & softeners, household type; water purification equipment, household type; water treatment equipment, industrial; water purification equipment; drinking water coolers, mechanical; water purification equipment

(G-2363)
PUTNAM ROLLING LADDER CO INC
444 Jefferson St (11237-2326)
PHONE.....................718 381-8219
Henry Skiba, *Manager*
EMP: 17
SALES (corp-wide): 3.4MM **Privately Held**
WEB: www.putnamrollingladder.com
SIC: 2499 Ladders, wood
PA: Putnam Rolling Ladder Co Inc
32 Howard St
New York NY 10013
212 226-5147

(G-2364)
PYX INC
Also Called: Pyx Enterprise
143 E 29th St (11226-5505)
PHONE.....................718 469-4253
Omega Ashanti, *President*
EMP: 9
SALES: 250K **Privately Held**
SIC: 3993 Advertising artwork

(G-2365)
QUALITY CARPET ONE FLOOR & HM
214 Ditmas Ave (11218-4900)
PHONE.....................718 941-4200
Herbert Frank, *Principal*
EMP: 9
SALES (est): 193K **Privately Held**
SIC: 2273 1743 5023 Carpets & rugs; tile installation, ceramic; floor coverings

(G-2366)
QUALITY FOAM INC
137 Gardner Ave (11237-1107)
PHONE.....................718 381-3644
Paul Minarsky, *President*
Kyle Minarsky, *Vice Pres*
◆ **EMP:** 12
SALES (est): 1.5MM **Privately Held**
WEB: www.qualityfoamproducts.com
SIC: 2515 Mattresses, containing felt, foam rubber, urethane, etc.

(G-2367)
QUALITY NATURE INC
8225 5th Ave Ste 215 (11209-4508)
PHONE.....................718 484-4666
Sagie Gernshteyn, *President*
EMP: 5
SQ FT: 300
SALES: 733.6K **Privately Held**
SIC: 2834 Vitamin, nutrient & hematinic preparations for human use

(G-2368)
QUALITY STAINLESS STEEL NY INC (PA)
865 63rd St (11220-4727)
PHONE.....................718 748-1785
Hong Guang Huang, *Ch of Bd*
EMP: 10
SALES (est): 1.1MM **Privately Held**
SIC: 3312 Stainless steel

(G-2369)
QUALITY STRAPPING INC
55 Meadow St (11206-1700)
PHONE.....................718 418-1111
Imre Oberlander, *President*
Aharon L Grossman, *Vice Pres*
Abraham Stern, *CFO*
▲ **EMP:** 58
SQ FT: 60,000
SALES: 6.7MM **Privately Held**
WEB: www.qualitystrapping.com
SIC: 3559 Plastics working machinery

(G-2370)
QUALITY WOODWORKING CORP
260 Butler St (11217-3006)
PHONE.....................718 875-3437
Joseph Borruso Sr, *President*
Denise Jacob, *Office Mgr*
Anthony Borruso, *Admin Sec*
EMP: 19 **EST:** 1943
SQ FT: 16,000
SALES (est): 2.5MM **Privately Held**
SIC: 2441 Boxes, wood

(G-2371)
QUEEN ANN MACARONI MFG CO INC
Also Called: Queen Ann Ravioli
7205 18th Ave (11204-5634)
PHONE.....................718 256-1061
Alfred Ferrara, *President*
Anna Ferrara, *Vice Pres*
EMP: 7
SQ FT: 4,000
SALES (est): 628.1K **Privately Held**
WEB: www.queenannravioliandmacaroni.com
SIC: 2098 5499 Macaroni products (e.g. alphabets, rings & shells), dry; gourmet food stores

(G-2372)
QUIP NYC INC
45 Main St Ste 616 (11201-1099)
PHONE.....................917 331-3993
Simon Enever, *President*
Shane Pittson, *Marketing Mgr*
EMP: 9
SALES (est): 463.5K **Privately Held**
SIC: 2844 3634 Toothpastes or powders, dentifrices; toothbrushes, electric

(G-2373)
QUIST INDUSTRIES LTD
204 Van Dyke St Ste 320a (11231-1005)
P.O. Box 150083 (11215-0083)
PHONE.....................718 243-2800
Rebecca Steinman, *President*
EMP: 10
SQ FT: 3,500
SALES (est): 837.3K **Privately Held**
WEB: www.quistindustries.com
SIC: 2759 2395 Letterpress & screen printing; emblems, embroidered

(G-2374)
R & F BOARDS & DIVIDERS INC
1678 57th St (11204-1800)
PHONE.....................718 331-1529
Regina Frankl, *Ch of Bd*
EMP: 5
SALES (est): 350.7K **Privately Held**
SIC: 3081 Mfg Unsupported Plastic Film/Sheet

(G-2375)
R & H BAKING CO INC
19 5th St (11231-4514)
PHONE.....................718 852-1768
Humayun Kabir, *Owner*
EMP: 25 **EST:** 2003
SQ FT: 15,000
SALES: 1.5MM **Privately Held**
WEB: www.kabirbakery.com
SIC: 2051 Bakery: wholesale or wholesale/retail combined

(G-2376)
R H GUEST INCORPORATED
Also Called: Guesthouse Division
1300 Church Ave (11226-2602)
PHONE.....................718 675-7600
Robert Guest, *President*
Gloria Caprio, *Treasurer*
EMP: 8
SQ FT: 1,000
SALES: 1.7MM **Privately Held**
WEB: www.rhgexhibits.com
SIC: 2542 2541 Showcases (not refrigerated): except wood; showcases, except refrigerated: wood

Brooklyn - Kings County (G-2377)

(G-2377)
R HOCHMAN PAPERS INCORPORATED
1000 Dean St Ste 315 (11238-3384)
PHONE..................516 466-6414
Ronald Hochman, *President*
Erik Rimalovski, *COO*
▲ **EMP:** 11
SQ FT: 2,100
SALES (est): 10.9MM **Privately Held**
WEB: www.hochmanpapers.com
SIC: 2752 Commercial printing, offset

(G-2378)
RAGS KNITWEAR LTD
850 Metropolitan Ave (11211-2515)
P.O. Box 420, Lynbrook (11563-0420)
PHONE..................718 782-8417
Paul Gross, *President*
EMP: 40
SQ FT: 40,000
SALES (est): 980K **Privately Held**
SIC: 2253 Sweaters & sweater coats, knit

(G-2379)
RAHARNEY CAPITAL LLC
325 Gold St Fl 502 (11201-3040)
PHONE..................212 220-9084
Sean Murray, *Mng Member*
EMP: 5
SALES (est): 171.1K **Privately Held**
SIC: 2721 Magazines: publishing only, not printed on site

(G-2380)
RAILINGS BY NEW STAR BRASS
Also Called: J Ironwork
26 Cobeck Ct (11223-6147)
PHONE..................516 358-1153
Carlo Lopopolo, *President*
Al Grancagnolo, *President*
Mary Ann Harmon, *Purchasing*
EMP: 20
SQ FT: 25,000
SALES (est): 3.8MM **Privately Held**
SIC: 3446 Architectural metalwork

(G-2381)
RAINBOW PLASTICS INC
371 Vandervoort Ave (11211-1712)
PHONE..................718 218-7288
Maggie Zheng, *Vice Pres*
▲ **EMP:** 13
SALES (est): 2MM **Privately Held**
SIC: 3089 Garbage containers, plastic

(G-2382)
RAINBOW POLY BAG CO INC
179 Morgan Ave (11237-1015)
PHONE..................718 386-3500
Gladys Harmanoglu, *President*
Hikmet Harmanoglu, *Vice Pres*
EMP: 40
SQ FT: 50,000
SALES (est): 7.5MM **Privately Held**
WEB: www.rainbowpolybag.com
SIC: 2673 3081 Plastic bags: made from purchased materials; unsupported plastics film & sheet

(G-2383)
RALPH PAYNE
Also Called: A-R Payne Cabinet Comp
475 Van Buren St Ste 11c (11221-3009)
PHONE..................718 222-4200
Ralph Payne, *Owner*
EMP: 7
SQ FT: 5,000
SALES: 300K **Privately Held**
WEB: www.ralphpayne.com
SIC: 2434 5087 1751 Wood kitchen cabinets; beauty parlor equipment & supplies; cabinet & finish carpentry

(G-2384)
RAPID-LITE FIXTURE CORPORATION
249 Huron St (11222-1801)
PHONE..................347 599-2600
Joel Eskin, *Ch of Bd*
EMP: 10 **EST:** 1946
SQ FT: 4,500
SALES (est): 1.5MM **Privately Held**
WEB: www.rapidlite.com
SIC: 3645 3646 5063 5719 Residential lighting fixtures; commercial indusl & institutional electric lighting fixtures; lighting fixtures, residential; lighting fixtures, commercial & industrial; lighting fixtures

(G-2385)
RAWPOTHECARY INC
630 Flushing Ave (11206-5026)
PHONE..................917 783-7770
Stephanie Walzack, *President*
EMP: 8
SALES (est): 722.5K **Privately Held**
SIC: 2099 5812 Ready-to-eat meals, salads & sandwiches; eating places

(G-2386)
RAY GOLD SHADE INC
16 Wellington Ct (11230-2424)
PHONE..................718 377-8892
Martin Rosenbaum, *President*
Sonia Rosenbaum, *Vice Pres*
EMP: 10
SQ FT: 18,000
SALES (est): 560K **Privately Held**
WEB: www.goldrayshades.com
SIC: 3999 Shades, lamp or candle

(G-2387)
RB WYATT MFG CO INC
2518 Ralph Ave (11234-5519)
P.O. Box 340296 (11234-0296)
PHONE..................718 209-9682
Joseph Dalcamo Jr, *President*
Joseph Accetulli, *Vice Pres*
Brian Grant, *Vice Pres*
EMP: 10
SQ FT: 4,000
SALES (est): 2MM **Privately Held**
SIC: 3231 Doors, glass: made from purchased glass

(G-2388)
RBW STUDIO LLC
Also Called: Rich Brilliant Willing
67 34th St Unit 5 (11232-2010)
PHONE..................212 388-1621
Theodore Richardson, *President*
Charles Brill, *Vice Pres*
Alex Williams, *Vice Pres*
Wesley Damgo, *Bookkeeper*
Elizabeth Tisdahl, *Natl Sales Mgr*
EMP: 25 **EST:** 2009
SQ FT: 2,000
SALES: 4.2MM **Privately Held**
SIC: 3699 Christmas tree lighting sets, electric

(G-2389)
REAR VIEW SAFETY INC
1797 Atlantic Ave (11233-3040)
PHONE..................855 815-3842
Gila Newman, *CEO*
Joseph Schechter, *Exec VP*
▲ **EMP:** 25
SQ FT: 6,000
SALES (est): 554.2K
SALES (corp-wide): 24.3MM **Privately Held**
SIC: 3861 Cameras & related equipment
PA: Safe Fleet Investments Llc
6800 E 163rd St
Belton MO 64012
844 258-8178

(G-2390)
RECORDED ANTHLOGY OF AMRCN MUS
Also Called: New World Records
20 Jay St Ste 1001 (11201-8346)
PHONE..................212 290-1695
Herman E Krawitz, *President*
Auther Moorhaed, *Treasurer*
Russell Platt, *Controller*
Robert McNeill, *Manager*
Paul Tai, *Director*
▲ **EMP:** 12
SALES: 1.2MM **Privately Held**
WEB: www.newworldrecords.org
SIC: 3652 Pre-recorded records & tapes

(G-2391)
RECYCLED BROOKLYN GROUP LLC
236 Van Brunt St (11231-1211)
PHONE..................917 902-0662
Matthew Lostice,
Alberto Baudo,
Nilesh Dawda,
Andrea De Sanctis,
Marco Gentilucci,
EMP: 14
SQ FT: 8,000
SALES (est): 1MM **Privately Held**
SIC: 2511 5712 Wood household furniture; furniture stores

(G-2392)
REDI RECORDS PAYROLL
1225 36th St (11218-2023)
PHONE..................718 854-6990
Joe Burke, *President*
EMP: 10
SALES (est): 594.9K **Privately Held**
SIC: 2752 Calendars, lithographed

(G-2393)
REGIONAL MGT & CONSULTING INC
79 Bridgewater St (11222-3818)
PHONE..................718 599-3718
Henryk Jarosz, *President*
Bogdan Szczurek, *Exec VP*
EMP: 10
SQ FT: 4,200
SALES (est): 1.3MM **Privately Held**
SIC: 3292 5033 Asbestos products; insulation materials

(G-2394)
REISMAN BROS BAKERY INC
Also Called: Reismans Bros. Bakery
110 Avenue O (11204-6501)
P.O. Box 40112 (11204-0112)
PHONE..................718 331-1975
Bernat Reisman, *Ch of Bd*
Larry Fisler, *Vice Pres*
Esther Friedman, *Admin Sec*
EMP: 15
SQ FT: 4,000
SALES (est): 4MM **Privately Held**
WEB: www.reismansbakery.com
SIC: 2051 5411 Bakery: wholesale or wholesale/retail combined; cakes, bakery: except frozen; supermarkets

(G-2395)
REMARKETY INC (PA)
81 Prospect St (11201-1473)
PHONE..................800 570-7564
Yoel Presman, *President*
EMP: 2
SQ FT: 600
SALES: 1.2MM **Privately Held**
SIC: 7372 Home entertainment computer software

(G-2396)
REMEDIES SURGICAL SUPPLIES
331 Rutledge St Ste 204 (11211-7546)
PHONE..................718 599-5301
Mordchai Hirsch, *President*
EMP: 7
SQ FT: 2,000
SALES (est): 4.5MM **Privately Held**
SIC: 3634 3069 Humidifiers, electric: household; medical & laboratory rubber sundries & related products

(G-2397)
REMSEN GRAPHICS CORP
52 Court St 2 (11201-4901)
PHONE..................718 643-7500
Greg Vellanti, *President*
Frank Vellanti, *Vice Pres*
Piero Galluzzo, *Admin Sec*
EMP: 5
SQ FT: 1,200
SALES (est): 1MM **Privately Held**
SIC: 2752 7389 Offset & photolithographic printing

(G-2398)
RENE PORTIER INC
3611 14th Ave Ste 6 (11218-3750)
PHONE..................718 853-7896
Charlotte Fixler, *President*
Aaron Fixler, *Vice Pres*
EMP: 9
SQ FT: 6,000
SALES (est): 1MM **Privately Held**
SIC: 2339 Mfg Women's/Misses' Outerwear

(G-2399)
REVIVN PUBLIC BENEFIT CORP
63 Flushing Ave Unit 231 (11205-1074)
PHONE..................347 762-8193
John Fazzolari, *President*
EMP: 15
SALES (est): 1.9MM **Privately Held**
SIC: 7372 3571 Application computer software; electronic computers

(G-2400)
RHOSEY LLC
Also Called: Rose Gourmet
1677 Mcdonald Ave (11230-6312)
PHONE..................718 382-1226
Kevin Ronan,
EMP: 5
SALES (est): 469.1K **Privately Held**
SIC: 2045 2038 5142 Doughs, frozen or refrigerated: from purchased flour; ethnic foods, frozen; packaged frozen goods

(G-2401)
RICHARD MANUFACTURING CO INC
63 Flushing Ave Unit 327 (11205-1083)
PHONE..................718 254-0958
Solomon Mayer, *President*
Janet Mayer, *Admin Sec*
EMP: 8 **EST:** 1943
SALES: 200K **Privately Held**
SIC: 2326 2339 Aprons, work, except rubberized & plastic: men's; aprons, except rubber or plastic: women's, misses, juniors'

(G-2402)
RINI TANK & TRUCK SERVICE
327 Nassau Ave (11222-3811)
PHONE..................718 384-6606
Richard V Rini, *President*
EMP: 16
SQ FT: 10,000
SALES (est): 978.7K **Privately Held**
SIC: 7692 Welding repair

(G-2403)
RIOT NEW MEDIA GROUP INC
147 Prince St Ste 1 (11201-3022)
PHONE..................604 700-4896
Jeffrey O'Neal, *CEO*
Josh Corman, *Editor*
Amanda Nelson, *Editor*
Alex Baker, *Director*
Clinton Kabler, *Officer*
EMP: 6
SALES (est): 516.3K **Privately Held**
SIC: 2741

(G-2404)
RIP VAN WAFELS INC
67 West St Ste 705 (11222-5393)
PHONE..................415 529-5403
Abhishek Pruisken, *CEO*
Marco De Leon, *Co-CEO*
EMP: 22
SQ FT: 1,600
SALES (est): 3.1MM **Privately Held**
SIC: 2066 5947 Chocolate; gifts & novelties

(G-2405)
RIVA JEWELRY MANUFACTURING INC
140 58th St Ste 8b (11220-2524)
PHONE..................718 361-3100
Ted Doudak, *President*
Lauren Bartlow, *COO*
Edgar Andrade, *Materials Mgr*
John Badee, *Engineer*
Remon Soliman, *Security Mgr*
▲ **EMP:** 125
SQ FT: 20,000

GEOGRAPHIC SECTION

Brooklyn - Kings County (G-2434)

SALES (est): 21.3MM **Privately Held**
WEB: www.rivajewelry.com
SIC: 3911 Jewelry apparel

(G-2406)
RIVERSIDE MACHINERY COMPANY (PA)
Also Called: Sns Machinery
140 53rd St (11232-4319)
PHONE 718 492-7400
Simon Srybnik, *President*
Louis Srybnik, *Vice Pres*
Saul Waller, *Treasurer*
Jay B Srybnik, *Admin Sec*
EMP: 5
SQ FT: 30,000
SALES (est): 4.3MM **Privately Held**
SIC: 3599 Machine shop, jobbing & repair

(G-2407)
RIVERSIDE MACHINERY COMPANY
132 54th St (11220-2506)
PHONE 718 492-7400
Simon Srybnik, *Manager*
EMP: 20
SQ FT: 35,060
SALES (corp-wide): 4.3MM **Privately Held**
SIC: 3549 5084 Metalworking machinery; industrial machinery & equipment
PA: Riverside Machinery Company Inc
140 53rd St
Brooklyn NY 11232
718 492-7400

(G-2408)
ROB HERSCHENFELD DESIGN INC
304 Boerum St (11206-3590)
PHONE 718 456-6801
Rob Herschenfeld, *President*
EMP: 10
SQ FT: 10,000
SALES (est): 1.2MM **Privately Held**
SIC: 2512 1522 Upholstered household furniture; remodeling, multi-family dwellings

(G-2409)
ROBERT STRAHAN CUSTOM WDWKG
Also Called: Robert Strahan Woodworks
810 Humboldt St Ste 9 (11222-1913)
PHONE 718 349-3570
Robert Strahan, *Owner*
EMP: 5
SQ FT: 4,000
SALES: 500K **Privately Held**
WEB: www.robertstrahan.com
SIC: 2431 Millwork

(G-2410)
ROBIN INDUSTRIES LTD
56 N 3rd St (11249-3925)
PHONE 718 218-9616
Monica Vega, *President*
EMP: 11
SQ FT: 10,000
SALES (est): 1.2MM **Privately Held**
WEB: www.robinindustries.com
SIC: 3632 1711 Household refrigerators & freezers; heating & air conditioning contractors

(G-2411)
ROGER MICHAEL PRESS INC (PA)
499 Van Brunt St Ste 6b (11231-1053)
P.O. Box 27176 (11202-7176)
PHONE 732 752-0800
Michael Held, *President*
Deborah Held, *Vice Pres*
Amy Neufeld, *Marketing Staff*
▲ **EMP:** 61
SQ FT: 20,000
SALES (est): 200K **Privately Held**
WEB: www.mrogerpress.com
SIC: 2782 2789 Bookbinding & related work; looseleaf binders & devices

(G-2412)
ROMANTIC TIMES INC
Also Called: Romantic Times Magazine
9 Ridgewood Pl (11237-5912)
PHONE 718 237-1097
Kathryn Falk, *President*
EMP: 17
SQ FT: 6,000
SALES (est): 2.1MM **Privately Held**
WEB: www.romantictimes.com
SIC: 2721 5942 Magazines: publishing & printing; book stores

(G-2413)
ROODE HOEK & CO INC
55 Ferris St (11231-1194)
PHONE 718 522-5921
EMP: 13 **EST:** 2000
SALES: 750K **Privately Held**
SIC: 2431 Mfg Wooden Architectural Components
PA: E.R. Butler & Co., Inc.
55 Prince St Frnt A
New York NY 10012

(G-2414)
ROOM AT THE TOP INC
Also Called: Hat Depot
632 Hegeman Ave (11207-7111)
PHONE 718 257-0766
Shellie McDowell, *President*
EMP: 5
SALES (est): 630.3K **Privately Held**
SIC: 2353 Hats, caps & millinery

(G-2415)
ROSE SOLOMON CO
63 Flushing Ave Unit 330 (11205-1083)
PHONE 718 855-1788
Mendel Reichman, *President*
▲ **EMP:** 21 **EST:** 1908
SQ FT: 7,000
SALES (est): 1.1MM **Privately Held**
SIC: 2389 5049 2869 Burial garments; religious supplies; industrial organic chemicals

(G-2416)
ROTH CLOTHING CO INC (PA)
300 Penn St (11211-7405)
PHONE 718 384-4927
Mates Roth, *President*
▲ **EMP:** 3
SQ FT: 30,000
SALES: 1.2MM **Privately Held**
SIC: 2389 2311 Clergymen's vestments; suits, men's & boys' made from purchased materials

(G-2417)
ROTH DESIGN & CONSULTING INC
Also Called: Roth's Metal Works
132 Bogart St (11206)
PHONE 718 209-0193
Arnold Roth, *President*
Jake Roth, *Vice Pres*
EMP: 40
SQ FT: 40,000
SALES (est): 7MM **Privately Held**
SIC: 3441 8711 1791 Fabricated structural metal; building construction consultant; structural engineering; structural steel erection

(G-2418)
ROYAL CLOTHING CORP
1316 48th St Apt 1 (11219-3167)
PHONE 718 436-5841
Abraham Sports, *President*
Joseph Schwartz, *Buyer*
EMP: 6
SQ FT: 2,000
SALES: 2MM **Privately Held**
SIC: 2311 5611 Suits, men's & boys': made from purchased materials; suits, men's

(G-2419)
ROYAL CROWN FINANCIAL
1028 Dahill Rd (11204-1742)
PHONE 718 234-7237
Milton Schwartz, *Vice Pres*
EMP: 6
SALES (est): 201.4K **Privately Held**
SIC: 2086 Soft drinks: packaged in cans, bottles, etc.

(G-2420)
ROYAL INDUSTRIES INC (PA)
Also Called: Royal Line The
225 25th St (11232-1337)
PHONE 718 369-3046
Michael Rudensky, *President*
ARI Rudensky, *Vice Pres*
Jonathan Rudensky, *Vice Pres*
◆ **EMP:** 39 **EST:** 1985
SQ FT: 75,000
SALES (est): 13.3MM **Privately Held**
WEB: www.royalindustries.com
SIC: 3089 3161 Novelties, plastic; luggage

(G-2421)
ROYAL KOSHER FOODS LLC
1464 45th St Ste 1a (11219-2243)
PHONE 347 221-1867
Yitzchok Podrigal,
EMP: 6
SALES (est): 110.5K **Privately Held**
SIC: 2099 Food preparations

(G-2422)
ROYAL MOLDS INC
1634 Marine Pkwy (11234-4217)
PHONE 718 382-7686
EMP: 15 **EST:** 1946
SQ FT: 10,000
SALES (est): 1.1MM **Privately Held**
SIC: 3544 3423 Mfg Dies/Tools/Jigs/Fixtures Mfg Hand/Edge Tools

(G-2423)
ROYAL PLASTICS CORP
2840 Atlantic Ave Ste 1 (11207-2692)
PHONE 718 647-7500
Donald Marchese, *President*
▲ **EMP:** 19 **EST:** 1958
SQ FT: 40,000
SALES (est): 2.7MM **Privately Held**
WEB: www.royalplastics.com
SIC: 3089 Plastic processing

(G-2424)
ROYAL SWEET BAKERY INC
119 49th St (11232-4229)
PHONE 718 567-7770
Mikhail Yusim, *President*
◆ **EMP:** 10
SALES (est): 1.1MM **Privately Held**
SIC: 2051 Bakery: wholesale or wholesale/retail combined

(G-2425)
RUBICON INDUSTRIES CORP (PA)
848 E 43rd St (11210-3500)
PHONE 718 434-4700
Michael Rubinberg, *President*
Matthew Rubinberg, *General Mgr*
▲ **EMP:** 24
SQ FT: 20,000
SALES (est): 4.7MM **Privately Held**
WEB: www.rubiconhx.com
SIC: 3585 Evaporative condensers, heat transfer equipment

(G-2426)
RUBY ENGINEERING LLC
354 Sackett St (11231-4702)
PHONE 646 391-4600
Phillip Roach, *Vice Pres*
Dennis Roach,
EMP: 5
SQ FT: 1,000
SALES (est): 310K **Privately Held**
WEB: www.rubyengineering.com
SIC: 1442 Construction sand mining

(G-2427)
RUS AUTO PARTS INC
Also Called: Bdtrims
508 Coney Island Ave (11218-3409)
PHONE 800 410-2669
Alex Kobzar, *President*
EMP: 5
SALES (est): 388.7K **Privately Held**
SIC: 3089 Automotive parts, plastic

(G-2428)
RUSSIAN MIX INC
2225 Benson Ave Apt 74 (11214-5245)
PHONE 347 385-7198
EMP: 5
SALES (est): 345.8K **Privately Held**
SIC: 3273 Ready-mixed concrete

(G-2429)
RUSSKAYA REKLAMA INC
2699 Coney Island Ave (11235-5004)
PHONE 718 769-3000
Paul Reklama, *President*
EMP: 20
SALES (est): 1.1MM **Privately Held**
SIC: 2711 Newspapers, publishing & printing

(G-2430)
RYBA GENERAL MERCHANDISE INC
63 Flushing Ave Unit 332 (11205-1083)
PHONE 718 522-2028
Sam Ryba, *President*
Marvin Ryba, *Vice Pres*
Chaya Knopfler, *Admin Sec*
◆ **EMP:** 7
SQ FT: 25,000
SALES (est): 710K **Privately Held**
WEB: www.rybagen.com
SIC: 2325 5136 Slacks, dress: men's, youths' & boys'; men's & boys' clothing; shirts, men's & boys'

(G-2431)
S & J SHEET METAL SUPPLY
70 Grand Ave (11205-2505)
PHONE 718 384-0800
David Gottlieb, *Branch Mgr*
EMP: 5
SALES (corp-wide): 111.2MM **Privately Held**
SIC: 3444 5033 Sheet metalwork; roofing & siding materials
PA: S. & J. Sheet Metal Supply Inc
608 E 133rd St
Bronx NY 10454
718 993-0460

(G-2432)
S & S MACHINERY CORP (PA)
Also Called: CAM Machinery Co
140 53rd St (11232-4319)
PHONE 718 492-7400
Simon Srybnik, *President*
Louis Srybnik, *Vice Pres*
▲ **EMP:** 30
SQ FT: 100,000
SALES (est): 6.4MM **Privately Held**
WEB: www.sandsmachinery.com
SIC: 3541 3549 5084 3545 Machine tools, metal cutting type; metalworking machinery; metalworking machinery; machine tools & accessories; machine tool accessories

(G-2433)
S & S MACHINERY CORP
132 54th St (11220-2506)
PHONE 718 492-7400
Al Testa, *Branch Mgr*
EMP: 40
SALES (corp-wide): 6.4MM **Privately Held**
WEB: www.sandsmachinery.com
SIC: 3541 3549 5084 Machine tools, metal cutting type; metalworking machinery; machine tools & accessories; metalworking machinery
PA: S. & S. Machinery Corp.
140 53rd St
Brooklyn NY 11232
718 492-7400

(G-2434)
S & S PRTG DIE-CUTTING CO INC
488 Morgan Ave Ste A (11222-5703)
PHONE 718 388-8990
Felix Sikar, *President*
▲ **EMP:** 14
SQ FT: 21,000

Brooklyn - Kings County (G-2435)

SALES: (est) 1.4MM **Privately Held**
WEB: www.printdiecut.com
SIC: 3469 7389 2759 2675 Stamping metal for the trade; metal cutting services; letterpress printing; die-cut paper & board; coated & laminated paper

(G-2435)
S & T MACHINE INC
970 E 92nd St Fl 1 (11236-1720)
PHONE.................................718 272-2484
Saverio Accardi, *President*
Tinal Accardi, *Vice Pres*
EMP: 15
SQ FT: 5,000
SALES: (est) 1.5MM **Privately Held**
SIC: 3444 Sheet metal specialties, not stamped

(G-2436)
S & W KNITTING MILLS INC
703 Bedford Ave Fl 3 (11206)
PHONE.................................718 237-2416
Henry Weiss, *President*
Manachem Samuel, *Treasurer*
EMP: 50 EST: 1977
SQ FT: 35,000
SALES: (est) 2.9MM **Privately Held**
SIC: 2253 2329 2339 2257 Sweaters & sweater coats, knit; sweaters & sweater jackets: men's & boys'; women's & misses' outerwear; weft knit fabric mills

(G-2437)
S & W LADIES WEAR
3611 14th Ave Ste 601 (11218-3750)
PHONE.................................718 431-2800
Elias Bochner, *Owner*
EMP: 7 EST: 2015
SALES: (est) 124.7K **Privately Held**
SIC: 3144 Boots, canvas or leather: women's

(G-2438)
S & W METAL TRADING CORP
1601 E 7th St (11230-7002)
PHONE.................................212 719-5070
Abraham Slomovics, *President*
Abraham Weisz, *Vice Pres*
EMP: 8
SQ FT: 1,000
SALES: (est) 960.6K **Privately Held**
SIC: 3339 3341 Primary nonferrous metals; secondary nonferrous metals

(G-2439)
S D Z METAL SPINNING STAMPING
1807 Pacific St (11233-3505)
PHONE.................................718 778-3600
Kenny Mersand, *President*
EMP: 15
SQ FT: 10,000
SALES: 971.2K **Privately Held**
SIC: 3469 Spinning metal for the trade; stamping metal for the trade

(G-2440)
S HELLERMAN INC (PA)
242 Green St (11222-1208)
PHONE.................................718 622-2995
Robert Hellerman, *President*
Joseph Hellerman, *Vice Pres*
EMP: 11
SQ FT: 20,000
SALES: 750K **Privately Held**
SIC: 2299 Textile mill waste & remnant processing

(G-2441)
S2 SPORTSWEAR INC
4100 1st Ave Ste 5n (11232-3303)
PHONE.................................347 335-0713
Saul Chakkall, *CEO*
Albert Zayat, *Vice Pres*
Ronnie Chakkall, *CFO*
▲ EMP: 10 EST: 2014
SQ FT: 6,000
SALES: 1.3MM **Privately Held**
SIC: 2339 5137 Sportswear, women's; sportswear, women's & children's

(G-2442)
SABBSONS INTERNATIONAL INC
Also Called: Simple Elegance New York
474 50th St (11220-1913)
PHONE.................................718 360-1947
Isaac Sabbagh, *CEO*
Abraham I Sabbagh, *Vice Pres*
Victor Sabbagh, *CFO*
◆ EMP: 10
SALES: (est) 492.2K **Privately Held**
SIC: 2299 Linen fabrics

(G-2443)
SAFCORE LLC
23 Van Dam St (11222-4509)
PHONE.................................917 627-5263
Safwat Riad,
EMP: 10
SALES: (est) 322.9K **Privately Held**
SIC: 2519 Household furniture

(G-2444)
SAGA INTERNATIONAL RECYCL LLC
6623 13th Ave (11219-6122)
PHONE.................................718 621-5900
Akiva Klein, *Principal*
▲ EMP: 6
SQ FT: 3,000
SALES: (est) 1MM **Privately Held**
SIC: 2821 Plastics materials & resins

(G-2445)
SAHADI FINE FOODS INC
4215 1st Ave (11232-3300)
PHONE.................................718 369-0100
Pat Whelan, *Managing Dir*
Audrey Sahadi, *Director*
Charles Sahadi, *Director*
Robert Sahadi, *Director*
Ron Sahadi, *Director*
◆ EMP: 22
SQ FT: 116,000
SALES: (est) 4.8MM **Privately Held**
WEB: www.sahadifinefoods.com
SIC: 2068 2032 5149 5145 Nuts: dried, dehydrated, salted or roasted; seeds: dried, dehydrated, salted or roasted; beans & bean sprouts, canned, jarred, etc.; fruits, dried; nuts, salted or roasted

(G-2446)
SALTY ROAD INC
190 Bedford Ave 404 (11249-2904)
PHONE.................................347 673-3925
Marisa Wu, *CEO*
EMP: 8
SALES: (est) 696.3K **Privately Held**
SIC: 2064 Candy & other confectionery products

(G-2447)
SANGSTER FOODS INC
225 Parkside Ave Apt 3p (11226-1352)
PHONE.................................212 993-9129
Lily Golberg, *Director*
Peter Sangster, *Director*
Tania Sangster, *Director*
EMP: 10
SALES: (est) 324.6K **Privately Held**
SIC: 2032 2043 2091 5149 Ethnic foods: canned, jarred, etc.; infants' foods, cereal type; canned & cured fish & seafoods; health foods; instant coffee

(G-2448)
SARUG INC
2055 Mcdonald Ave (11223-2821)
PHONE.................................718 339-2791
Henrik Zylberstein, *President*
EMP: 55
SQ FT: 3,000
SALES: (est) 3.3MM **Privately Held**
SIC: 2253 Sweaters & sweater coats, knit

(G-2449)
SAS MAINTENANCE SERVICES INC
8435 Bay 16th St Ste A (11214-2844)
PHONE.................................718 837-2124
Maria Locascio, *President*
EMP: 17

SALES: (est) 2.8MM **Privately Held**
WEB: www.sasmaint.com
SIC: 3471 Cleaning, polishing & finishing

(G-2450)
SCHLESS BOTTLES INC (PA)
4616 16th Ave (11204-1104)
PHONE.................................718 236-2790
Mark Schlesinger, *Ch of Bd*
Judy Schlesinger, *President*
▲ EMP: 16
SQ FT: 40,000
SALES: (est) 3.8MM **Privately Held**
SIC: 3085 Plastics bottles

(G-2451)
SCHWARTZ TEXTILE LLC
Also Called: Tag Manufacturing
160 7th St (11215-3107)
PHONE.................................718 499-8243
Mitchell Schwartz, *President*
Kewal Sukhoo, *Business Mgr*
Marc Schwartz, *Vice Pres*
Irving Schwartz,
▲ EMP: 25
SQ FT: 60,000
SALES: (est) 2MM **Privately Held**
SIC: 2329 2321 Sweaters & sweater jackets: men's & boys'; men's & boys' furnishings

(G-2452)
SCIENTIFIC COMPONENTS CORP (PA)
Also Called: Mini-Circuits
13 Neptune Ave (11235-4404)
P.O. Box 350199 (11235-0199)
PHONE.................................718 934-4500
Harvey Kaylie, *President*
Marina Gokhtel, *Partner*
Elkhan Meirov, *Partner*
Pauline Morris, *Partner*
Carlos Perez, *Partner*
▲ EMP: 475
SQ FT: 50,000
SALES: (est) 141.6MM **Privately Held**
WEB: www.minicircuits.com
SIC: 3679 Electronic switches; electronic circuits

(G-2453)
SCIENTIFIC COMPONENTS CORP
Also Called: Mini Circuits
2450 Knapp St (11235-1006)
PHONE.................................718 368-2060
EMP: 264
SALES: (corp-wide): 141.6MM **Privately Held**
SIC: 3679 Electronic circuits
PA: Scientific Components Corp
13 Neptune Ave
Brooklyn NY 11235
718 934-4500

(G-2454)
SEASONS SOYFOOD INC
605 Degraw St (11217-3120)
PHONE.................................718 797-9896
Johnny Hong, *President*
▲ EMP: 8
SALES: (est) 500K **Privately Held**
SIC: 2099 Tofu, except frozen desserts

(G-2455)
SEETIN DESIGN GROUP INC
57 Grand Street Ext (11211)
PHONE.................................718 486-5610
Robert Seetin, *Ch of Bd*
◆ EMP: 10
SQ FT: 2,000
SALES: (est) 202.7K **Privately Held**
SIC: 3499 Furniture parts, metal

(G-2456)
SEPHARDIC YELLOW PAGES
2150 E 4th St (11223-4037)
PHONE.................................718 998-0299
David Benhorren, *Owner*
EMP: 20 EST: 1998
SALES: (est) 1.6MM **Privately Held**
SIC: 2759 2741 Publication printing; miscellaneous publishing

(G-2457)
SERGE DUCT DESIGNS INC
535 Dean St Apt 124 (11217-5207)
PHONE.................................718 783-7799
Serge Rozenbaum, *President*
Micha Rozenbaug, *Vice Pres*
EMP: 20
SALES: (est) 3.3MM **Privately Held**
SIC: 3549 Metalworking machinery

(G-2458)
SETTEPANI INC (PA)
Also Called: Settepani Bakery
602 Lorimer St (11211-2220)
PHONE.................................718 349-6524
Nino Settepani, *President*
Biagio Settepani, *Vice Pres*
Antonio Settepani, *Admin Sec*
EMP: 28
SQ FT: 5,000
SALES: 700K **Privately Held**
WEB: www.settepani.com
SIC: 2051 5461 Bakery: wholesale or wholesale/retail combined; bakeries

(G-2459)
SFOGLINI LLC
630 Flushing Ave Fl 2 (11206-5026)
PHONE.................................646 872-1035
Steven Gonzalez, *Mng Member*
Scott Ketchum, *Mng Member*
Steve Gonzalez, *Food Svc Dir*
EMP: 10
SQ FT: 4,000
SALES: (est) 1.2MM **Privately Held**
SIC: 2099 Pasta, uncooked: packaged with other ingredients

(G-2460)
SG BLOCKS INC (PA)
195 Montague St Fl 14 (11201-3631)
PHONE.................................615 585-2639
Paul M Galvin, *CEO*
Mahesh Shetty, *President*
Scott Hill, *Vice Pres*
Brian Wasserman, *CFO*
Kevin King, *Controller*
▼ EMP: 7
SALES: 5MM **Publicly Held**
WEB: www.newvalley.com
SIC: 2448 5032 8711 8741 Cargo containers, wood & metal combination; building blocks; engineering services; construction management

(G-2461)
SH LEATHER NOVELTY COMPANY
123 Clymer St Bsmt (11249-6708)
PHONE.................................718 387-7742
Shiee Handler, *President*
Solmen Delowitz, *Vice Pres*
Feiga Handler, *Treasurer*
EMP: 3 EST: 1954
SQ FT: 4,000
SALES: 1MM **Privately Held**
SIC: 2387 Apparel belts

(G-2462)
SHAKUFF LLC
34 35th St Unit 29 (11232-2209)
PHONE.................................212 675-0383
Joseph Sidof,
EMP: 6
SALES: (est) 142.3K **Privately Held**
SIC: 3648 Lighting equipment

(G-2463)
SHALAM IMPORTS INC (PA)
Also Called: Shalamex
1552 Dahill Rd Ste B (11204-3572)
PHONE.................................718 686-6271
Sasson Shalam, *President*
Abraham Shalam, *Vice Pres*
◆ EMP: 12 EST: 1955
SQ FT: 1,800
SALES: (est) 1.2MM **Privately Held**
SIC: 2674 Shipping bags or sacks, including multiwall & heavy duty

(G-2464)
SHANGHAI STOVE INC
78 Gerry St 82 (11206-4326)
PHONE.................................718 599-4583
James Wong, *President*

EMP: 15
SALES (est): 1.6MM **Privately Held**
SIC: 3444 Restaurant sheet metalwork

(G-2465)
SHIELD SECURITY DOORS LTD
169 Columbia Hts Apt 6b (11201-2240)
PHONE..................202 468-3308
EMP: 6
SALES (est): 576.7K **Privately Held**
SIC: 3699 5072 Security control equipment & systems; security devices; security devices, locks

(G-2466)
SHOWERAY CO (PA)
1857 E 8th St (11223-3234)
PHONE..................718 965-3633
Abraham Grazi, *President*
Jack Grazi, *Vice Pres*
Maurice Grazi, *Admin Sec*
EMP: 100 EST: 1938
SQ FT: 60,000
SALES (est): 3.9MM **Privately Held**
SIC: 2392 2391 Shower curtains: made from purchased materials; tablecloths: made from purchased materials; mattress protectors, except rubber; curtains & draperies

(G-2467)
SIGN & SIGNS
785 Coney Island Ave (11218-5309)
PHONE..................718 941-6200
Ali Chashir, *Principal*
EMP: 6
SALES (est): 388.6K **Privately Held**
SIC: 3993 Electric signs

(G-2468)
SIGN GROUP INC
Also Called: Boro Park Signs
5215 New Utrecht Ave (11219-3829)
PHONE..................718 438-7103
Ushe Steinmetz, *President*
Solomon Gutter, *Admin Sec*
EMP: 25
SQ FT: 9,000
SALES (est): 3MM **Privately Held**
WEB: www.signgroup.com
SIC: 3993 Electric signs

(G-2469)
SIGN WORLD INC
1194 Utica Ave (11203-5997)
PHONE..................212 619-9000
Herman Weiss, *President*
Carl Weiss, *Treasurer*
EMP: 25 EST: 1964
SQ FT: 10,000
SALES (est): 1.9MM **Privately Held**
SIC: 3993 2752 Signs & advertising specialties; commercial printing, lithographic

(G-2470)
SIGNS & DECAL CORP
410 Morgan Ave (11211-1640)
PHONE..................718 486-6400
Abdulrasul M Khalfan, *President*
Abdulrasul Khalfan, *President*
Tazzim Khalfan, *Vice Pres*
Andres Carrera, *Project Mgr*
Babu M Khalfan, *Info Tech Dir*
▲ EMP: 30
SQ FT: 25,000
SALES (est): 5.7MM **Privately Held**
WEB: www.signsanddecal.com
SIC: 3993 Displays & cutouts, window & lobby; signs, not made in custom sign painting shops

(G-2471)
SILLY PHILLIE CREATIONS INC
Also Called: Swisse Cheeks
140 58th St Ste 6f (11220-2526)
PHONE..................718 492-6300
Richard S'Dao, *President*
Phyllis G S'Dao, *Vice Pres*
Phyllis S'Dao, *Vice Pres*
▲ EMP: 30
SQ FT: 30,000
SALES (est): 2.9MM **Privately Held**
WEB: www.sillyphillie.com
SIC: 2392 2361 2369 Household furnishings; girls' & children's dresses, blouses & shirts; sun suits: girls', children's & infants'

(G-2472)
SILVER OAK PHARMACY INC
5105 Church Ave (11203-3511)
PHONE..................718 922-3400
Axay B Joshi, *Principal*
Milind Suvarnakar, *Pharmacist*
EMP: 6
SALES (est): 536.7K **Privately Held**
SIC: 2834 Pharmaceutical preparations

(G-2473)
SILVERMAN & GORF INC
60 Franklin Ave (11205-1594)
PHONE..................718 625-1309
Edward Gorf, *President*
Harry Moorer, *Vice Pres*
EMP: 6
SQ FT: 30,000
SALES (est): 490K **Privately Held**
SIC: 3471 Plating of metals or formed products

(G-2474)
SILVERSTONE SHTMTL FBRICATIONS
66 Huntington St (11231)
PHONE..................718 422-0380
Rustem Duka, *President*
EMP: 5
SQ FT: 10,000
SALES (est): 1MM **Privately Held**
SIC: 3441 Fabricated structural metal

(G-2475)
SIMON LIU INC
280 24th St (11232-1310)
PHONE..................718 567-2011
Simon Liu, *President*
▲ EMP: 12
SQ FT: 7,500
SALES (est): 907.5K **Privately Held**
WEB: www.simonliuinc.com
SIC: 3952 5999 Artists' equipment; artists' supplies & materials

(G-2476)
SIMON S DECORATING INC
1670 E 19th St (11229-1312)
PHONE..................718 339-2931
Simon Poldanl, *President*
EMP: 5
SALES (est): 402.7K **Privately Held**
SIC: 2512 Upholstered household furniture

(G-2477)
SIMPLE ELEGANCE NEW YORK INC
474 50th St (11220-1913)
PHONE..................718 360-1947
Isaac Sabbagh, *President*
Victor Sabbagh, *Vice Pres*
Abraham Sabbagh, *CFO*
▲ EMP: 15
SQ FT: 6,000
SALES (est): 1MM **Privately Held**
SIC: 2299 5131 Linen fabrics; linen piece goods, woven

(G-2478)
SINCERUS LLC
2478 Mcdonald Ave (11223-5233)
PHONE..................800 419-2804
Marc Poirier,
EMP: 5
SQ FT: 5,000
SALES (est): 229.7K **Privately Held**
SIC: 2834 Pharmaceutical preparations

(G-2479)
SING AH POULTRY
114 Sackett St (11231-1414)
PHONE..................718 625-7253
Perry Chen, *Owner*
EMP: 5
SQ FT: 2,400
SALES (est): 311.4K **Privately Held**
SIC: 2015 Poultry, slaughtered & dressed

(G-2480)
SING TAO NEWSPAPERS NY LTD
5317 8th Ave (11220-3259)
PHONE..................212 431-9030
Rick Ho, *Manager*
EMP: 10 **Privately Held**
WEB: www.nysingtao.com
SIC: 2711 Newspapers
PA: Sing Tao Newspapers New York Ltd.
188 Lafayette St
New York NY 10013

(G-2481)
SING TAO NEWSPAPERS NY LTD
905 Flushing Ave Fl 2 (11206-4602)
PHONE..................718 821-0123
Patrick Seto, *Facilities Mgr*
EMP: 30
SQ FT: 20,900 **Privately Held**
WEB: www.nysingtao.com
SIC: 2711 Newspapers, publishing & printing
PA: Sing Tao Newspapers New York Ltd.
188 Lafayette St
New York NY 10013

(G-2482)
SITA FINISHING INC
Also Called: Sita Knitting
207 Starr St Ste 1 (11237-2639)
PHONE..................718 417-5295
Loan Sita, *President*
Ioan Sita, *President*
George Sita, *Vice Pres*
▲ EMP: 10
SQ FT: 8,000
SALES (est): 1MM **Privately Held**
WEB: www.sitafashion.com
SIC: 2211 Canvas

(G-2483)
SLAVA INDUSTRIES INCORPORATED (PA)
Also Called: Nfk International
555 16th St (11215-5914)
PHONE..................718 499-4850
Nevio Kovacevic, *Principal*
Ilaria Sialino, *CFO*
▲ EMP: 2
SQ FT: 1,200
SALES: 38MM **Privately Held**
SIC: 2512 2514 Upholstered household furniture; metal household furniture

(G-2484)
SLEEPING PARTNERS INTL INC
Also Called: Sleeping Partners Home Fashion
140 58th St Ste 3e (11220-2522)
PHONE..................212 254-1515
Salvatore Stoch, *Ch of Bd*
Terry Pierson, *Bookkeeper*
▲ EMP: 15
SQ FT: 25,000
SALES (est): 5MM **Privately Held**
SIC: 2392 Household furnishings

(G-2485)
SLEEPY HEAD INC
230 3rd St (11215-2714)
PHONE..................718 237-9655
Victor Daniels, *President*
Haim Zeitoune, *Vice Pres*
EMP: 10
SQ FT: 17,000
SALES (est): 720K **Privately Held**
WEB: www.sleepyheadinc.com
SIC: 2369 Mfg Girl/Youth Outerwear

(G-2486)
SLN GROUP INC
2172 E 26th St (11229-4955)
PHONE..................718 677-5969
Luiza Shamilova, *Principal*
EMP: 5
SALES (est): 421.2K **Privately Held**
SIC: 3679 Electronic components

(G-2487)
SLOANE DESIGN INC
226 52nd St (11220-1715)
PHONE..................212 539-0184
Sloane Madureira, *President*
Tim Chapman, *Vice Pres*

EMP: 5 EST: 2005
SALES (est): 275.4K **Privately Held**
SIC: 2752 Commercial printing, lithographic

(G-2488)
SMARTONERS INC (PA)
289 Keap St Ste A (11211-7459)
PHONE..................718 975-0197
Aidel Appel, *President*
EMP: 4
SQ FT: 3,000
SALES (est): 8MM **Privately Held**
SIC: 3955 Print cartridges for laser & other computer printers

(G-2489)
SMITH STREET BREAD CO LLC
17 5th St (11231-4514)
PHONE..................718 797-9712
Mark Rubin, *Mng Member*
EMP: 12
SQ FT: 500
SALES (est): 1MM **Privately Held**
SIC: 2051 Bread, cake & related products

(G-2490)
SOCIAL BICYCLES INC (PA)
Also Called: Sobi
55 Prospect St Ste 304 (11201-1497)
PHONE..................917 746-7624
Stephen Ryan Rzepecki, *CEO*
Edward Rayner, *CFO*
Colin Hughes, *Director*
Mark Miretsky, *Director*
Jay Lee, *General Counsel*
▲ EMP: 25
SQ FT: 700
SALES (est): 5.3MM **Privately Held**
SIC: 3751 7372 Bicycles & related parts; prepackaged software

(G-2491)
SOCKBIN
718 Avenue U (11223-4134)
PHONE..................917 519-1119
Andrew Muller, *Owner*
EMP: 6
SALES (est): 247.4K **Privately Held**
SIC: 2252 Socks

(G-2492)
SOCKS AND MORE OF NY INC
1605 Avenue Z Fl 1 (11235-3809)
PHONE..................718 769-1785
Irene Dubrovsky, *Chairman*
EMP: 9
SALES (est): 997.4K **Privately Held**
SIC: 2252 Socks

(G-2493)
SOHO LETTERPRESS INC
68 35th St Unit 6 (11232-2211)
PHONE..................718 788-2518
Anne Noonan, *President*
EMP: 12
SALES (est): 1MM **Privately Held**
WEB: www.soholetterpress.com
SIC: 2759 Letterpress printing

(G-2494)
SOLA HOME EXPO INC
172 Neptune Ave (11235-5317)
PHONE..................718 646-3383
Sergiy Orlov, *President*
▲ EMP: 6
SALES: 80K **Privately Held**
SIC: 3431 Bathroom fixtures, including sinks

(G-2495)
SOLAR ENERGY SYSTEMS LLC (PA)
1205 Manhattan Ave # 1210 (11222-6156)
PHONE..................718 389-1545
David Buckner, *President*
Christopher Moustakis, *Vice Pres*
Nadja Bruder, *Admin Asst*
EMP: 12
SQ FT: 1,300
SALES (est): 4MM **Privately Held**
WEB: www.solarsystems.com
SIC: 3433 1711 Solar heaters & collectors; solar energy contractor

Brooklyn - Kings County (G-2496)

(G-2496)
SOLARWATERWAY INC
Also Called: Solarelectricway
254 36th St Ste C453 (11232-2544)
PHONE..................888 998-5337
Jacqueline Sarway, *President*
Murray Sarway, *Vice Pres*
▲ **EMP:** 33
SQ FT: 9,000
SALES (est): 4MM **Privately Held**
SIC: 3645 3646 5063 Residential lighting fixtures; commercial indusl & institutional electric lighting fixtures; lighting fixtures

(G-2497)
SOLARZ BROS PRINTING CORP
231 Norman Ave Ste 105 (11222-1559)
PHONE..................718 383-1330
Sbigniew Solarz, *Principal*
EMP: 5
SALES (est): 363.4K **Privately Held**
SIC: 2759 Commercial printing

(G-2498)
SOLENIS LLC
Also Called: Ashland Water Technologies
761 Humboldt St (11222-3001)
PHONE..................718 383-1717
Peter Coster, *Branch Mgr*
EMP: 9
SALES (corp-wide): 667.2MM **Privately Held**
SIC: 2899 Water treating compounds
HQ: Solenis Llc
3 Beaver Valley Rd # 500
Wilmington DE 19803
866 337-1533

(G-2499)
SONAAL INDUSTRIES INC
210 Kingsland Ave (11222-4303)
PHONE..................718 383-3860
Rana P Mukhopadhyay, *Principal*
EMP: 7
SALES (est): 205.5K **Privately Held**
SIC: 3999 Manufacturing industries

(G-2500)
SOURCE TECHNOLOGIES
9728 3rd Ave (11209-7742)
PHONE..................718 708-0305
Nick Anthony, *Owner*
EMP: 12
SQ FT: 2,000
SALES: 1MM **Privately Held**
SIC: 3599 Machine & other job shop work

(G-2501)
SOUTH CENTRAL BOYZ
2568 Bedford Ave Apt 1a (11226-7071)
PHONE..................718 496-7270
Keith Bessor, *President*
EMP: 5
SALES (est): 280K **Privately Held**
SIC: 2389 7389 Costumes;

(G-2502)
SPACE 150
20 Jay St Ste 928 (11201-8354)
PHONE..................612 332-6458
EMP: 120 **EST:** 2003
SALES (est): 11.6MM **Privately Held**
SIC: 2741 Misc Publishing

(G-2503)
SPFM CORP (PA)
Also Called: Spray Market, The
162 2nd Ave (11215-4619)
PHONE..................718 788-6800
Jacob Kloc, *President*
Ann Marie Wolf, *Administration*
EMP: 5
SALES: 500K **Privately Held**
SIC: 3563 Spraying & dusting equipment

(G-2504)
SPREAD-MMMS LLC
545 Prospect Pl Apt 10d (11238-4271)
P.O. Box 4, New York (10029-0004)
PHONE..................917 727-8116
EMP: 6
SALES (est): 414.9K **Privately Held**
SIC: 2099 Mfg Food Preparations

(G-2505)
SPRING PUBLISHING CORPORATION
Also Called: Polska Gazeta
419 Manhattan Ave (11222-4914)
PHONE..................718 782-0881
Janus Czuj, *President*
EMP: 6
SALES (est): 451.1K **Privately Held**
WEB: www.polskagazeta.com
SIC: 2711 Newspapers, publishing & printing

(G-2506)
ST JOHN
1700 Saint Johns Pl (11233-4906)
PHONE..................718 771-4541
EMP: 5 **EST:** 2010
SALES (est): 363.4K **Privately Held**
SIC: 2339 Mfg Women's/Misses' Outerwear

(G-2507)
STAG BROTHERS CAST STONE CO
909 E 51st St (11203-6735)
PHONE..................718 629-0975
Sal Stagliano, *President*
EMP: 8
SALES (est): 310K **Privately Held**
SIC: 3272 Concrete products

(G-2508)
STAPLEX COMPANY INC
777 5th Ave (11232-1695)
PHONE..................718 768-3333
James J Cussani Jr, *President*
Gregory Cussani, *Vice Pres*
David Hill, *Vice Pres*
R Powers, *Vice Pres*
Joe Crosby, *Engineer*
▲ **EMP:** 20 **EST:** 1949
SQ FT: 20,000
SALES (est): 4.3MM **Privately Held**
SIC: 3579 3821 Stapling machines (hand or power); laboratory apparatus & furniture

(G-2509)
STAR COMPOSITION SERVICES INC
170 Hewes St (11211-8001)
PHONE..................212 684-4001
Jacob Weiss, *President*
▲ **EMP:** 5 **EST:** 1970
SQ FT: 800
SALES: 500K **Privately Held**
SIC: 2791 7374 Typesetting, computer controlled; computer graphics service

(G-2510)
STAR POLY BAG INC (PA)
200 Liberty Ave (11207-2904)
PHONE..................718 384-3130
Rachel Posen, *CEO*
Joel Posen, *Principal*
EMP: 17 **EST:** 1961
SQ FT: 22,000
SALES (est): 5.1MM **Privately Held**
WEB: www.starpoly.com
SIC: 2673 Plastic bags: made from purchased materials

(G-2511)
STAR POLY BAG INC
96 Snediker Ave (11207-2908)
PHONE..................718 384-5342
Rachel Posen, *CEO*
EMP: 5
SALES (est): 240.1K **Privately Held**
SIC: 2673 Plastic bags: made from purchased materials

(G-2512)
STARBROOK INCORPORATED
141 Neptune Ave A (11235-5315)
PHONE..................212 514-5212
Elvira Pasternak, *President*
EMP: 6
SALES (corp-wide): 662.9K **Privately Held**
SIC: 2759 Commercial printing
PA: Starbrook Incorporated
3208 W Lake St
Minneapolis MN 55416
212 514-5212

(G-2513)
STARLINER SHIPPING & TRAVEL
5305 Church Ave Ste 1 (11203-3638)
PHONE..................718 385-1515
Rhea Murray, *President*
Leighton Murray, *Vice Pres*
Blueth Murray-Ogunnoiki, *Vice Pres*
Anthia Murray, *Treasurer*
▼ **EMP:** 7
SALES (est): 540K **Privately Held**
SIC: 2599 Ship furniture

(G-2514)
STEALTH ARCHTCTRAL WINDOWS INC
Also Called: Stealth Window
232 Varet St (11206-3862)
PHONE..................718 821-6666
Barry Borgen, *President*
EMP: 19
SQ FT: 52,000
SALES (est): 2.1MM **Privately Held**
WEB: www.avantguards.com
SIC: 2431 Windows, wood

(G-2515)
STEALTH INC
1129 E 27th St (11210-4620)
PHONE..................718 252-7900
Jack Edelstein, *President*
EMP: 16
SQ FT: 3,000
SALES: 1.7MM **Privately Held**
SIC: 2326 Industrial garments, men's & boys'

(G-2516)
STEELCRAFT MANUFACTURING CO
Also Called: Steel Craft
352 Pine St (11208-2807)
PHONE..................718 277-2404
Louis Massa, *President*
EMP: 11 **EST:** 1945
SQ FT: 9,000
SALES (est): 990.1K **Privately Held**
SIC: 3444 2541 2514 Radiator shields or enclosures, sheet metal; wood partitions & fixtures; kitchen cabinets: metal

(G-2517)
STEELDECK NY INC
141 Banker St (11222-3147)
PHONE..................718 599-3700
Philip Parsons, *President*
Gail Moorcroft, *Vice Pres*
Alexandra Berch, *Production*
Allan Dias, *Production*
Jeremiah Brown, *Manager*
▲ **EMP:** 15 **EST:** 2001
SQ FT: 20,000
SALES: 3.2MM **Privately Held**
SIC: 3999 5049 2541 2531 Stage hardware & equipment, except lighting; theatrical equipment & supplies; partitions for floor attachment, prefabricated: wood; theater furniture

(G-2518)
STEELMASTERS INC
135 Liberty Ave (11212-8008)
PHONE..................718 498-2854
Matthew Rosio, *President*
Anthony Masi, *Vice Pres*
EMP: 23 **EST:** 1994
SQ FT: 14,000
SALES (est): 3MM **Privately Held**
SIC: 3442 Rolling doors for industrial buildings or warehouses, metal

(G-2519)
STEELSTONE GROUP LLC
Also Called: Gourmia
1425 37th St (11218-3767)
PHONE..................888 552-0033
EMP: 5
SALES (est): 90.3K **Privately Held**
SIC: 3631 Household cooking equipment

(G-2520)
STEINBOCK-BRAFF INC
Also Called: Kat Nap Products
3611 14th Ave (11218-3773)
PHONE..................718 972-6500
Corey Steinbock, *President*
▲ **EMP:** 30 **EST:** 1933
SQ FT: 80,000
SALES (est): 3.8MM **Privately Held**
WEB: www.sleepmattress.com
SIC: 2515 5021 Mattresses & foundations; household furniture

(G-2521)
STEVE & ANDYS ORGANICS INC
630 Flushing Ave (11206-5026)
PHONE..................718 499-7933
Michelle Schwartz, *President*
Arjan Khiani, *Vice Pres*
Steve Marino, *Treasurer*
Quinn Rhone, *Director*
EMP: 5
SALES (est): 339.9K **Privately Held**
SIC: 2064 Candy & other confectionery products

(G-2522)
STIEGELBAUER ASSOCIATES INC (PA)
Bldg 280 (11205)
PHONE..................718 624-0835
Michael Stiegelbauer, *President*
Dawn Stiegelbauer, *Corp Secy*
Steven Paone, *Vice Pres*
Butch Huerta, *Project Mgr*
Kimberly Amato, *Mktg Dir*
EMP: 22
SQ FT: 180,000
SALES (est): 3MM **Privately Held**
SIC: 3999 Theatrical scenery

(G-2523)
STONE AND BATH GALLERY
868 39th St (11232-3230)
PHONE..................718 438-4500
Samuel Stru, *Owner*
▲ **EMP:** 8
SALES (est): 298.7K **Privately Held**
SIC: 3261 3251 Bathroom accessories/fittings, vitreous china or earthenware; brick & structural clay tile

(G-2524)
STREET BEAT SPORTSWEAR INC (PA)
Also Called: Visual F-X
462 Kent Ave Fl 2 (11249-5922)
PHONE..................718 302-1500
Albert Papouchado, *President*
Allen Smith, *CFO*
Micheal Amar, *Treasurer*
▲ **EMP:** 10
SQ FT: 66,000
SALES (est): 3.6MM **Privately Held**
SIC: 2339 Sportswear, women's

(G-2525)
STUDIO 21 LA INC
13 42nd St Fl 5 (11232-2616)
PHONE..................718 965-6579
▲ **EMP:** 20
SQ FT: 5,000
SALES (est): 1.4MM **Privately Held**
SIC: 2531 5399 5712 Mfg Public Building Furniture Ret Misc General Merchandise Ret Furniture

(G-2526)
STUDIO 40 INC
810 Humboldt St Ste 4 (11222-1913)
PHONE..................212 420-8631
Richard Temerian, *President*
EMP: 6
SALES (est): 842.1K **Privately Held**
SIC: 3446 Architectural metalwork
PA: Studio 40 Inc
40 Great Jones St Apt 1
New York NY 10012

(G-2527)
STUHRLING ORIGINAL LLC
449 20th St (11215-6247)
PHONE..................718 840-5760
Israel Jacobson, *Controller*
Shifra Birnhack, *Accounts Mgr*

GEOGRAPHIC SECTION

Brooklyn - Kings County (G-2558)

Tali Brach, *Accounts Mgr*
Yiddy Lemmer, *Info Tech Dir*
Chaim Fischer, *Executive*
◆ **EMP:** 25
SQ FT: 20,000
SALES (est): 10MM **Privately Held**
SIC: 3873 5094 Watches, clocks, watchcases & parts; clocks, watches & parts; watches & parts

(G-2528)
STURDY STORE DISPLAYS INC
110 Beard St (11231-1502)
PHONE...............................718 389-9919
Michael Fried, *President*
Jacob Brauner, *Vice Pres*
Moshe Nathan Neuman, *Controller*
▲ **EMP:** 23
SQ FT: 35,000
SALES (est): 3.2MM **Privately Held**
WEB: www.sturdystoredisplays.com
SIC: 2542 Partitions & fixtures, except wood

(G-2529)
STYLIST PLEATING CORP
107 Vanderveer St Apt 3b (11207-2155)
PHONE...............................718 384-8181
Kenneth Stier, *President*
EMP: 18 **EST:** 1938
SQ FT: 11,000
SALES (est): 879.8K **Privately Held**
SIC: 2395 Permanent pleating & pressing, for the trade

(G-2530)
SUE & SAM CO INC (PA)
Also Called: W & G Manufacturing
720 39th St 720 # 720 (11232-3200)
PHONE...............................718 436-1672
Howard Wollman, *President*
▲ **EMP:** 25
SQ FT: 37,000
SALES (est): 5.1MM **Privately Held**
SIC: 2321 2361 Polo shirts, men's & boys': made from purchased materials; shirts: girls', children's & infants'

(G-2531)
SUN MING JAN INC
145 Noll St (11206-4714)
PHONE...............................718 418-8221
Ben Chen, *CEO*
▲ **EMP:** 10 **EST:** 1999
SALES (est): 949.6K **Privately Held**
SIC: 2013 Sausages & other prepared meats

(G-2532)
SUNBURST STUDIOS INC
584 3rd Ave (11215-4612)
PHONE...............................718 768-6360
Ihor Nykolak, *President*
Peter Friedman, *Treasurer*
EMP: 5 **EST:** 1976
SQ FT: 3,600
SALES: 400K **Privately Held**
WEB: www.sunburststudio.com
SIC: 3231 8999 Stained glass: made from purchased glass; cut & engraved glassware: made from purchased glass; art restoration

(G-2533)
SUNWIRE ELECTRIC CORP
70 Wyckoff Ave Apt 4h (11237-3385)
PHONE...............................718 456-7500
Chen Birbaul, *Vice Pres*
EMP: 5
SALES: 700K **Privately Held**
SIC: 3699 Electrical equipment & supplies

(G-2534)
SUPER NEON LIGHT CO INC
7813 16th Ave (11214-1003)
PHONE...............................718 236-5667
James Coccaro Jr, *President*
EMP: 8 **EST:** 1939
SQ FT: 1,600
SALES (est): 550K **Privately Held**
SIC: 3993 Neon signs

(G-2535)
SUPERFLEX LTD
152 44th St (11232-3310)
PHONE...............................718 768-1400

Shimon Elbaz, *Ch of Bd*
Yigal Elbaz, *President*
▲ **EMP:** 50
SQ FT: 60,000
SALES (est): 19.6MM **Privately Held**
WEB: www.superflex.com
SIC: 3644 3052 Electric conduits & fittings; plastic hose

(G-2536)
SUPERIOR BLOCK CORP
Also Called: Glenwood Masonry Products
761 E 42nd St (11210-2012)
PHONE...............................718 421-0900
Constance Cincotta, *President*
EMP: 10 **EST:** 1997
SQ FT: 75,000
SALES (est): 1.8MM **Privately Held**
SIC: 3271 Concrete block & brick

(G-2537)
SUPERIOR ELEC ENCLOSURE INC
16 Spencer St (11205-1605)
PHONE...............................718 797-9090
Harris Grant, *President*
EMP: 7
SALES (est): 1MM **Privately Held**
SIC: 3444 Metal housings, enclosures, casings & other containers

(G-2538)
SUPERIOR FIBER MILLS INC
181 Lombardy St (11222-5417)
P.O. Box 306, East Norwich (11732-0306)
PHONE...............................718 782-7500
Helen Burney, *President*
Henry Burney, *Vice Pres*
EMP: 40
SQ FT: 125,000
SALES (est): 5.1MM **Privately Held**
WEB: www.superiorfibers.com
SIC: 2299 2221 Batts & batting: cotton mill waste & related material; broadwoven fabric mills, manmade

(G-2539)
SUPERLEAF LLC
Also Called: Detox Water
212 7th St 1 (11215-3208)
PHONE...............................888 887-4318
Kenneth Park, *CEO*
EMP: 5
SQ FT: 1,300
SALES (est): 169.2K **Privately Held**
SIC: 2086 Water, pasteurized: packaged in cans, bottles, etc.

(G-2540)
SUPREME BOILERS INC
9221 Ditmas Ave (11236-1711)
PHONE...............................718 342-2220
Aaron Ganguli, *President*
David Rakst, *Vice Pres*
EMP: 5 **EST:** 2007
SALES (est): 540K **Privately Held**
SIC: 3443 Boiler & boiler shop work

(G-2541)
SUPREME POLY PLASTICS INC
299 Meserole St (11206-1732)
PHONE...............................718 456-9300
Abe Eilander, *President*
EMP: 25
SQ FT: 45,000
SALES (est): 3.9MM **Privately Held**
WEB: www.supremepoly.com
SIC: 2673 Plastic bags: made from purchased materials

(G-2542)
SURE-KOL REFRIGERATOR CO INC
490 Flushing Ave (11205-1615)
PHONE...............................718 625-0601
Steven Waslin, *President*
David J Waslin, *Corp Secy*
Jack Waslin, *Vice Pres*
EMP: 10 **EST:** 1947
SQ FT: 13,000
SALES (est): 1.5MM **Privately Held**
SIC: 3632 Household refrigerators & freezers

(G-2543)
SURPRISE PLASTICS INC
124 57th St (11220-2576)
PHONE...............................718 492-6355
Fax: 718 492-0258
▲ **EMP:** 115
SQ FT: 48,000
SALES (est): 16.8MM **Privately Held**
SIC: 3089 Mfg Plastic Products

(G-2544)
SURTIC MINING COMPANY LLC
1825 Foster Ave (11230-1834)
PHONE...............................718 434-0477
Herman Graham, *CEO*
Bruce Benn, *COO*
Venicia Fletchman, *Exec VP*
EMP: 14
SALES (est): 31.2MM **Privately Held**
SIC: 1041 7389 Open pit gold mining;

(G-2545)
SWEATER BRAND INC
Also Called: Domain
86 S 1st St (11249-4171)
PHONE...............................718 797-0505
Moshe Rosenberg, *Manager*
EMP: 6
SALES (corp-wide): 3.2MM **Privately Held**
SIC: 2253 Sweaters & sweater coats, knit
PA: Sweater Brand Inc.
22 Wallenberg Cir
Monsey NY
718 797-0505

(G-2546)
SYNERGY DIGITAL
43 Hall St (11205-1315)
PHONE...............................718 643-2742
Fax: 718 643-9212
EMP: 15
SALES (est): 720K **Privately Held**
SIC: 3691 Mfg Storage Batteries

(G-2547)
T & L TRADING CO
17 Meserole St (11206-1901)
PHONE...............................718 782-5550
David Tang, *Owner*
▲ **EMP:** 5
SQ FT: 5,000
SALES (est): 675.8K **Privately Held**
SIC: 2621 Stationery, envelope & tablet papers; bond paper

(G-2548)
T M I PLASTICS INDUSTRIES INC
28 Wythe Ave (11249-1036)
PHONE...............................718 383-0363
Sam Yuen, *President*
▲ **EMP:** 15
SALES (est): 2.2MM **Privately Held**
SIC: 2673 Plastic bags: made from purchased materials

(G-2549)
T MIX INC
6217 5th Ave (11220-4611)
PHONE...............................646 379-6814
Lin Jian, *CEO*
EMP: 6
SALES (est): 688.6K **Privately Held**
SIC: 3273 Ready-mixed concrete

(G-2550)
T&K PRINTING INC
Also Called: T & K Printing
262 44th St (11232-2816)
PHONE...............................718 439-9454
Hien Khuu, *President*
EMP: 10
SALES (est): 1.8MM **Privately Held**
SIC: 3577 2759 Optical scanning devices; commercial printing

(G-2551)
TAAM TOV FOODS INC
Also Called: Ko-Sure Food Distributors
188 28th St (11232-1604)
PHONE...............................718 788-8880
Meyer Thurm, *President*
Max Thurm, *Vice Pres*
Sam Sherer, *Treasurer*
▲ **EMP:** 7

SALES (est): 723.9K **Privately Held**
SIC: 2022 Cheese spreads, dips, pastes & other cheese products

(G-2552)
TABLE TOPS PAPER CORP
47 Hall St Ste C-2 (11205-1315)
P.O. Box 220443 (11222-0443)
PHONE...............................718 831-6440
Ben Ruiz, *President*
EMP: 8
SALES (est): 660K **Privately Held**
SIC: 2759 5111 5999 Financial note & certificate printing & engraving; printing & writing paper; alarm signal systems

(G-2553)
TABLET PUBLISHING COMPANY INC
Also Called: Tablet Newspaper, The
1712 10th Ave (11215-6215)
PHONE...............................718 965-7333
Monsignor Anthony Danna, *Publisher*
Ed Wilkinson, *Principal*
Leonard W Kaiser, *Business Mgr*
Carrie White, *Manager*
EMP: 25
SQ FT: 18,000
SALES (est): 1.4MM **Privately Held**
SIC: 2711 2741 Newspapers: publishing only, not printed on site; miscellaneous publishing

(G-2554)
TAI SENG
106 Lexington Ave (11238-1412)
PHONE...............................718 399-6311
▲ **EMP:** 6
SALES (est): 330K **Privately Held**
SIC: 2673 Mfg Bags-Plastic/Coated Paper

(G-2555)
TALMU NY LLC
266 47th St (11220-1010)
PHONE...............................347 434-6700
Reuven Sobel,
Warren Vogel,
EMP: 6
SALES (est): 330.7K **Privately Held**
SIC: 3639 5149 Major kitchen appliances, except refrigerators & stoves; coffee & tea

(G-2556)
TARGUM PRESS USA INC
Also Called: Horizons Magazine
1946 59th St (11204-2340)
PHONE...............................248 355-2266
Sydney Choncow, *President*
David Dombey, *Admin Sec*
EMP: 8
SALES (est): 584.8K **Privately Held**
SIC: 2731 Book publishing

(G-2557)
TAYLOR TANK COMPANY INC
848 E 43rd St (11210-3502)
PHONE...............................718 434-1300
Michael Rubinberg, *President*
Cynthia Rubinberg, *Admin Sec*
EMP: 30 **EST:** 1947
SQ FT: 20,000
SALES (est): 4.7MM
SALES (corp-wide): 4.7MM **Privately Held**
WEB: www.rubiconhx.com
SIC: 3443 Tanks, standard or custom fabricated: metal plate
PA: Rubicon Industries Corp.
848 E 43rd St
Brooklyn NY 11210
718 434-4700

(G-2558)
TECHNICAL LIBRARY SERVICE INC
Also Called: Talas
330 Morgan Ave (11211-2716)
PHONE...............................212 219-0770
Jacob Salik, *Ch of Bd*
Marjorie Salik, *President*
EMP: 11 **EST:** 1962
SQ FT: 25,000

Brooklyn - Kings County (G-2559) GEOGRAPHIC SECTION

SALES (est): 1.3MM **Privately Held**
WEB: www.talas-nyc.com
SIC: 2653 8231 5199 Corrugated boxes, partitions, display items, sheets & pad; boxes, corrugated: made from purchased materials; libraries; law library; packaging materials

(G-2559)
TECHNIPOLY MANUFACTURING INC
Also Called: T M I of New York
20 Wythe Ave (11249-1036)
PHONE 718 383-0363
Kam S Yuen, *Owner*
Lip Foo Yee, *Vice Pres*
Allen Yuen, *Admin Sec*
EMP: 28
SQ FT: 16,000
SALES (est): 4.4MM **Privately Held**
SIC: 2673 2752 Plastic bags: made from purchased materials; commercial printing, lithographic

(G-2560)
TECNOLUX INCORPORATED
103 14th St (11215-4607)
PHONE 718 369-3900
David Ablon, *President*
▲ EMP: 7
SQ FT: 10,000
SALES (est): 710K **Privately Held**
WEB: www.tecnolux.com
SIC: 3648 Lighting equipment

(G-2561)
TEKA FINE LINE BRUSHES INC
3691 Bedford Ave (11229-1703)
PHONE 718 692-2928
Terry Ettkins, *President*
EMP: 7
SALES (est): 860.6K **Privately Held**
WEB: www.tekabrush.com
SIC: 3991 Hair pencils (artists' brushes)

(G-2562)
TELLER PRINTING CORP
317 Division Ave (11211-7307)
PHONE 718 486-3662
James Teller, *President*
EMP: 6
SALES (est): 595.1K **Privately Held**
SIC: 2752 Commercial printing, lithographic

(G-2563)
THATS MY GIRL INC (PA)
80 39th St Ste 501 (11232-2604)
P.O. Box 230317 (11223-0317)
PHONE 212 695-0020
Salomon Salem, *President*
Raymond Kassin, *Vice Pres*
Connie LI, *Bookkeeper*
Chelsea Reizner, *Accounts Exec*
EMP: 2
SQ FT: 800
SALES (est): 1.7MM **Privately Held**
SIC: 2361 Girls' & children's dresses, blouses & shirts

(G-2564)
THE EARTH TIMES FOUNDATION
195 Adams St Apt 6j (11201-1808)
PHONE 718 297-0488
Pranay Gupte, *President*
Ranjit Sahni, *Treasurer*
Jon Quint, *Director*
EMP: 5
SALES: 984.9K **Privately Held**
SIC: 2711 Newspapers, publishing & printing

(G-2565)
THEMIS CHIMNEY INC
190 Morgan Ave (11237-1014)
PHONE 718 937-4716
Mark Papadimitriou, *President*
EMP: 12
SQ FT: 12,000
SALES (est): 2.4MM **Privately Held**
SIC: 3443 3444 Liners/lining; sheet metalwork

(G-2566)
THOMPSON OVERHEAD DOOR CO INC
47 16th St (11215-4613)
PHONE 718 788-2470
Olav M Thompson, *President*
Edward Thompson, *Corp Secy*
Lynn Murray, *Treasurer*
Robert Kligman, *Sales Mgr*
EMP: 15
SQ FT: 16,000
SALES (est): 2.3MM **Privately Held**
SIC: 3442 5211 Rolling doors for industrial buildings or warehouses, metal; door & window products

(G-2567)
TIE KING INC (PA)
Also Called: Jimmy Sales
243 44th St (11232-2815)
PHONE 718 768-8484
Jimmy Azizo, *President*
David Azizo, *General Mgr*
Solomon Azizo, *Treasurer*
Steven Azizo, *Manager*
Jack Azizo, *Admin Sec*
▲ EMP: 50
SQ FT: 20,000
SALES (est): 5.6MM **Privately Held**
WEB: www.thetieking.com
SIC: 2323 Men's & boys' neckties & bow ties

(G-2568)
TLI IMPORT INC
151 2nd Ave (11215-4615)
PHONE 917 578-4568
Nouri Arabi, *President*
EMP: 6 EST: 2010
SALES (est): 315.9K **Privately Held**
SIC: 2221 Textile warping, on a contract basis

(G-2569)
TONER-N-MORE INC
2220 65th St Ste 103 (11204-4035)
PHONE 718 232-6200
Yoni Glatzer, *President*
EMP: 5
SQ FT: 10,000
SALES (est): 650.3K **Privately Held**
WEB: www.tonernmore.com
SIC: 3861 Toners, prepared photographic (not made in chemical plants)

(G-2570)
TOOLS & STAMPING CORP
Also Called: Balint Tool
48 Eagle St (11222-1013)
P.O. Box 220375 (11222-0375)
PHONE 718 392-4040
Ernest Feldman, *President*
Judah Feldman, *Vice Pres*
EMP: 5 EST: 1960
SALES (est): 390K **Privately Held**
WEB: www.jnet.com
SIC: 3469 3544 3429 Stamping metal for the trade; special dies & tools; luggage hardware

(G-2571)
TOOTTER INC
1470 Royce St (11234-5924)
PHONE 212 204-7937
Sade Metellus, *Vice Pres*
EMP: 25
SQ FT: 1,200
SALES (est): 654.8K **Privately Held**
SIC: 7372 Application computer software

(G-2572)
TOPOO INDUSTRIES INCORPORATED
7815 16th Ave (11214-1003)
PHONE 718 331-3755
▲ EMP: 8
SALES (est): 826.4K **Privately Held**
SIC: 3999 Manufacturing industries

(G-2573)
TOPRINT LTD
6110 7th Ave (11220-4107)
PHONE 718 439-0469
Thomas Corey, *Principal*
EMP: 5
SALES (est): 340K **Privately Held**
SIC: 2759 Commercial printing

(G-2574)
TORTILLERIA CHINANTLA INC
975 Grand St (11211-2704)
PHONE 718 302-0101
Erasmo Ponce, *Manager*
EMP: 7
SALES (corp-wide): 2.2MM **Privately Held**
SIC: 2096 Potato chips & similar snacks
PA: Tortilleria Chinantla Inc.
  86 Central Ave
  Brooklyn NY 11206
  718 456-2828

(G-2575)
TOTAL METAL RESOURCE
Also Called: Pmrnyc
175 Bogart St (11206-1720)
PHONE 718 384-7818
Scott Behr, *President*
EMP: 10
SALES (est): 1.5MM **Privately Held**
SIC: 3499 Fabricated metal products

(G-2576)
TOURA LLC
392 2nd St 2 (11215-2404)
PHONE 646 652-8668
Kathleen Schnoor, *Principal*
Aaron Radin, *Principal*
EMP: 10
SALES (est): 730.4K **Privately Held**
SIC: 3663 Mobile communication equipment

(G-2577)
TOWER ISLES FROZEN FOODS LTD
Also Called: Tower Isles Patties
2025 Atlantic Ave (11233-3131)
P.O. Box 330625 (11233-0625)
PHONE 718 495-2626
Patrick Jolly, *President*
James Jobson, *Vice Pres*
EMP: 73 EST: 1969
SQ FT: 32,600
SALES (est): 20MM **Privately Held**
WEB: www.towerislespatties.com
SIC: 2013 Boneless meat, from purchased meat

(G-2578)
TRADE MARK GRAPHICS INC
4502 Avenue N (11234-3613)
PHONE 718 306-0001
Avery Marder, *President*
EMP: 7
SQ FT: 24,000
SALES (est): 924.2K **Privately Held**
SIC: 2752 Commercial printing, offset

(G-2579)
TRANSCNTINENTAL ULTRA FLEX INC
975 Essex St (11208-5419)
PHONE 718 272-9100
Eli Blatt, *CEO*
Todd Addison, *Treasurer*
Radek Danialawicz, *Info Tech Dir*
Radek Danielawicz, *Info Tech Mgr*
◆ EMP: 270
SQ FT: 115,000
SALES: 53.2MM
SALES (corp-wide): 1.6B **Privately Held**
WEB: www.ultraflex.com
SIC: 2759 2671 2752 Flexographic printing; packaging paper & plastics film, coated & laminated; commercial printing, lithographic
PA: Transcontinental Inc
  1 Place Ville-Marie Bureau 3240
  Montreal QC H3B 0
  514 954-4000

(G-2580)
TRANSLAND SOURCING LLC
5 Lynch St (11249-9223)
PHONE 718 596-5704
Jacob Frankl, *CEO*
EMP: 4
SALES: 5MM **Privately Held**
SIC: 3571 Mfg Electronic Computers

(G-2581)
TRI STATE SHEARING BENDING INC
366 Herzl St (11212-4442)
P.O. Box 120002 (11212-0002)
PHONE 718 485-2200
Alan Blaier, *President*
Michele Blaier, *Vice Pres*
EMP: 15
SQ FT: 12,000
SALES (est): 3.7MM **Privately Held**
SIC: 3446 Stairs, staircases, stair treads: prefabricated metal

(G-2582)
TRI-STATE FOOD JOBBERS INC
5600 1st Ave Unit A5 (11220-2550)
PHONE 718 921-1211
Maor Ohana, *President*
EMP: 6 EST: 2009
SALES (est): 2.6MM **Privately Held**
SIC: 3497 Foil containers for bakery goods & frozen foods

(G-2583)
TRIANGLE LABEL TAG INC
525 Dekalb Ave (11205-4818)
PHONE 718 875-3030
Joseph Kahan, *President*
Herman Frankel, *Vice Pres*
EMP: 8
SQ FT: 5,000
SALES (est): 1.3MM **Privately Held**
SIC: 2672 2759 5131 2241 Adhesive papers, labels or tapes: from purchased material; labels & seals: printing; piece goods & notions; labels; labels, woven

(G-2584)
TRICO MANUFACTURING CORP
196 Dupont St (11222-1241)
PHONE 718 349-6565
Elizabeth Fling, *President*
EMP: 6 EST: 2000
SQ FT: 7,000
SALES (est): 484.1K **Privately Held**
SIC: 3429 Door locks, bolts & checks; door opening & closing devices, except electrical

(G-2585)
TRIMET COAL LLC
1615 Avenue I Apt 420 (11230-3041)
PHONE 718 951-3654
EMP: 21
SALES (est): 1.3MM **Privately Held**
SIC: 1241 Coal Mining Services

(G-2586)
TRIPI ENGRAVING CO INC
Also Called: Royal Engraving
60 Meserole Ave (11222-2638)
PHONE 718 383-6500
Phil Tripi, *President*
EMP: 25
SQ FT: 10,000
SALES (est): 2.2MM **Privately Held**
SIC: 2759 5112 5943 2796 Engraving; stationery; stationery stores; platemaking services; typesetting; commercial printing, lithographic

(G-2587)
TRIPLE J BEDDING LLC
63 Flushing Ave Unit 331 (11205-1083)
PHONE 718 643-8005
Joseph Friedman, *CEO*
▲ EMP: 7
SALES (est): 26K **Privately Held**
SIC: 2511 Wood household furniture

(G-2588)
TRM LINEN INC
1546 59th St (11219-5028)
PHONE 718 686-6075
Chaim Cohen, *Ch of Bd*
▼ EMP: 5
SALES (est): 547.5K **Privately Held**
SIC: 2299 5961 Linen fabrics; mail order house

(G-2589)
TROVE INC
20 Jay St Ste 846 (11201-8306)
PHONE 212 268-2046

GEOGRAPHIC SECTION

Brooklyn - Kings County (G-2617)

Randall Buck, *Buyer*
EMP: 14
SALES (est): 1.4MM **Privately Held**
SIC: 3999 5199 Fire extinguishers, portable; gifts & novelties

(G-2590)
TRU-TONE METAL PRODUCTS INC
1261 Willoughby Ave (11237-2904)
P.O. Box 370711 (11237-0711)
PHONE 718 386-5960
James P Murtha, *President*
Catherine Murtha, *Vice Pres*
Nick Murtha, *Director*
EMP: 20
SQ FT: 5,000
SALES (est): 2.5MM **Privately Held**
SIC: 3471 Anodizing (plating) of metals or formed products; coloring & finishing of aluminum or formed products

(G-2591)
TUNECORE INC (PA)
45 Main St Ste 705 (11201-1075)
P.O. Box 20256 (11202-0256)
PHONE 646 651-1060
Scott Ackerman, *CEO*
Troy Denkinger, *Vice Pres*
Elise Holzheimer, *Vice Pres*
Gillian Morris, *Vice Pres*
Matt Barrington, *Controller*
EMP: 32
SALES (est): 1.6MM **Privately Held**
SIC: 3651 Music distribution apparatus

(G-2592)
TUNECORE INC
63 Pearl St (11201-1147)
PHONE 646 651-1060
Scott Ackermann, *CEO*
Jeremy Crowther, *Director*
EMP: 16
SALES (corp-wide): 1.6MM **Privately Held**
SIC: 2741 Miscellaneous publishing
PA: Tunecore, Inc.
45 Main St Ste 705
Brooklyn NY 11201
646 651-1060

(G-2593)
TUROFF TOWER GRAPHICS INC
Also Called: Tower Sales Co
681 Coney Island Ave (11218-4306)
PHONE 718 856-7300
Jay Turoff, *President*
Rose Turoff, *Corp Secy*
Georgina Snyder, *Vice Pres*
EMP: 14 **EST:** 1969
SQ FT: 1,000
SALES (est): 1.3MM **Privately Held**
SIC: 3993 Neon signs

(G-2594)
TUV TAAM CORP
502 Flushing Ave (11205-1616)
PHONE 718 855-2207
Aaron Nutovich, *President*
Rivka Nutovich, *Treasurer*
Lea Gold, *Admin Sec*
▲ **EMP:** 50
SQ FT: 10,000
SALES (est): 7.1MM **Privately Held**
SIC: 2099 2038 Tortillas, fresh or refrigerated; salads, fresh or refrigerated; frozen specialties

(G-2595)
TWI WATCHES LLC
Also Called: Akribos Watches
4014 1st Ave (11232-2606)
PHONE 718 663-3969
Ben Rosenbaum, *Sales Dir*
Chaim Sischer, *Mng Member*
▲ **EMP:** 35
SALES (est): 2MM **Privately Held**
SIC: 3873 Watches, clocks, watchcases & parts

(G-2596)
TWIN MARQUIS INC (HQ)
7 Bushwick Pl (11206-2815)
PHONE 718 386-6868
Hyung Kyun Kim, *Ch of Bd*
Susie Moy, *Marketing Staff*
Chung Pun Tang, *Admin Sec*
▲ **EMP:** 65
SQ FT: 33,000
SALES: 40.3MM
SALES (corp-wide): 4.8B **Privately Held**
WEB: www.twinmarquis.com
SIC: 2098 2099 2035 Noodles (e.g. egg, plain & water), dry; noodles, fried (Chinese); pickles, sauces & salad dressings
PA: Cj Cheiljedang Corporation
330 Dongho-Ro, Jung-Gu
Seoul 04560
822 674-0111

(G-2597)
TWO WORLDS ARTS LTD
307 Kingsland Ave (11222-3708)
PHONE 212 929-2210
Jean Chau, *Manager*
EMP: 6
SALES (corp-wide): 931.1K **Privately Held**
SIC: 2512 Upholstered household furniture
PA: Two Worlds Arts Ltd
122 W 18th St
New York NY 10011
212 929-2210

(G-2598)
ULTRAPEDICS LTD (PA)
355 Ovington Ave Ste 104 (11209-1457)
P.O. Box 90384 (11209-0384)
PHONE 718 748-4806
Eric Schwelke, *President*
EMP: 7
SQ FT: 3,400
SALES (est): 1.1MM **Privately Held**
SIC: 3842 5999 Prosthetic appliances; artificial limbs

(G-2599)
UNIFIED SOLUTIONS FOR CLG INC
1829 Pacific St (11233-3505)
PHONE 718 782-8800
Mendel Jacobowitz, *President*
Lipa Jacobowitz, *Vice Pres*
EMP: 15
SALES (est): 3MM **Privately Held**
SIC: 2869 Butadiene (industrial organic chemical)

(G-2600)
UNIFORMS BY PARK COATS INC
790 3rd Ave (11232-1510)
PHONE 718 499-1182
Nick Haymandos, *President*
Despina Haymandos, *Vice Pres*
EMP: 28 **EST:** 1973
SQ FT: 8,000
SALES (est): 2.7MM **Privately Held**
WEB: www.uniformsbypark.com
SIC: 2311 2337 Men's & boys' uniforms; uniforms, except athletic; women's, misses' & juniors'

(G-2601)
UNIMEX CORPORATION
Lee Spring Company Division
1462 62nd St (11219-5413)
PHONE 718 236-2222
Albert Mangels, *President*
EMP: 160
SALES (corp-wide): 45.3MM **Privately Held**
SIC: 3495 Mechanical springs, precision
PA: Unimex Corporation
54 E 64th St
New York NY 10065
212 755-8500

(G-2602)
UNITED GEMDIAM INC
Also Called: UGI
1537 52nd St (11219-3910)
PHONE 718 851-5083
Morris Friedman, *President*
Isaac Friedman, *Office Mgr*
EMP: 43
SQ FT: 5,000
SALES (est): 2.8MM **Privately Held**
WEB: www.ugi.com
SIC: 3915 5094 Diamond cutting & polishing; diamonds (gems)

(G-2603)
UNITED PLASTICS INC
640 Humboldt St Ste 1 (11222-4121)
P.O. Box 220363 (11222-0363)
PHONE 718 389-2255
Mike Reno, *Vice Pres*
Gary Mayo, *Manager*
EMP: 7
SALES (corp-wide): 1.6MM **Privately Held**
SIC: 2673 3089 Plastic bags: made from purchased materials; plastic processing
PA: United Plastics, Inc
219 Nassau Ave
Brooklyn NY
718 389-2255

(G-2604)
UNITED TRANSIT MIX INC
318 Boerum St (11206-3505)
P.O. Box 370647 (11237-0647)
PHONE 718 416-3400
Tony Mastronardi, *President*
EMP: 14
SALES (est): 4MM **Privately Held**
SIC: 3273 Ready-mixed concrete

(G-2605)
UNITED WIND INC
195 Plymouth St (11201-1123)
PHONE 888 313-3353
Russell Tencer, *CEO*
Aaron Lubowitz, *COO*
Ryan Storke, *Vice Pres*
Jodhi Tarr, *Vice Pres*
Guy Brooks, *Sales Staff*
EMP: 16 **EST:** 2013
SALES (est): 3.4MM **Privately Held**
SIC: 3443 Wind tunnels

(G-2606)
UNIVERSAL COOLERS INC
120 13th St (11215-4604)
PHONE 718 788-8621
Gregory Uchitel, *Ch of Bd*
▲ **EMP:** 6 **EST:** 1995
SALES (est): 1.2MM **Privately Held**
SIC: 3585 Parts for heating, cooling & refrigerating equipment

(G-2607)
UNIVERSAL FIRE PROOF DOOR
1171 Myrtle Ave (11206-6007)
PHONE 718 455-8442
Abelardo Galicia, *President*
EMP: 25 **EST:** 1924
SQ FT: 24,000
SALES (est): 5.4MM **Privately Held**
SIC: 3442 Fire doors, metal

(G-2608)
UNIVERSAL PARENT AND YOUTH
Also Called: Upayori
1530 Pa Ave Apt 17e (11239-2620)
PHONE 917 754-2426
Vincent Riggins, *Exec Dir*
EMP: 10
SALES (est): 537.8K **Privately Held**
SIC: 3585 Refrigeration & heating equipment

(G-2609)
UNIVERSAL SCREENING ASSOCIATES
Also Called: USA Tees.com
6509 11th Ave (11219-5602)
PHONE 718 232-2744
David Cardinale, *President*
Jodi Cardinale, *Sales Executive*
Adam Kokoni, *Graphic Designe*
▲ **EMP:** 12
SQ FT: 500
SALES: 500K **Privately Held**
SIC: 2759 Screen printing

(G-2610)
UNIVERSAL STEEL FABRICATORS
90 Junius St (11212-8029)
PHONE 718 342-0782
Harvinder Paul, *President*
Emilio Franza, *Treasurer*
EMP: 15
SQ FT: 3,500
SALES: 1MM **Privately Held**
SIC: 3446 5051 1799 Architectural metalwork; structural shapes, iron or steel; fence construction

(G-2611)
URBAN WOODWORKS LTD
18 Crescent St (11208-1516)
PHONE 718 827-1570
Gewan Bharatlall, *President*
Gabriela Bharatlall, *Vice Pres*
EMP: 5
SALES: 1.8MM **Privately Held**
SIC: 2431 Millwork

(G-2612)
US CONCRETE INC
Also Called: Kings Material
692 Mcdonald Ave (11218-4914)
PHONE 718 438-6800
Robert Bruzzese, *Branch Mgr*
EMP: 20
SALES (corp-wide): 1.3B **Publicly Held**
SIC: 3273 Ready-mixed concrete
PA: U.S. Concrete, Inc.
331 N Main St
Euless TX 76039
817 835-4105

(G-2613)
US SWEETENERS CORP
133-48 St (11232)
PHONE 718 854-8714
Raizy Geller, *President*
Moses Geller, *CFO*
Joel Geller, *Officer*
EMP: 35
SALES: 35MM **Privately Held**
SIC: 2061 Granulated cane sugar

(G-2614)
VAAD LHAFOTZAS SICHOES
788 Eastern Pkwy (11213-3409)
PHONE 718 778-5436
Zalmen Chanin, *President*
Nachman Shapiro, *Treasurer*
Sholom Jacobson, *Admin Sec*
▲ **EMP:** 13
SQ FT: 10,000
SALES: 1MM **Privately Held**
SIC: 2731 Books: publishing only

(G-2615)
VAN BLARCOM CLOSURES INC (PA)
156 Sanford St (11205)
PHONE 718 855-3810
Vincent Scuderi Jr, *Ch of Bd*
Ron Camuto, *Vice Pres*
Anthony Scuderi, *QC Mgr*
John Scuderi, *Treasurer*
Nella Rockford, *Accountant*
▲ **EMP:** 195 **EST:** 1947
SQ FT: 160,000
SALES: 49.3MM **Privately Held**
WEB: www.vbcpkg.com
SIC: 3089 3466 3549 Closures, plastic; caps, plastic; closures, stamped metal; bottle caps & tops, stamped metal; jar tops & crowns, stamped metal; assembly machines, including robotic

(G-2616)
VAN LEEUWEN ARTISAN ICE CREAM
56 Dobbin St (11222-3110)
PHONE 718 701-1630
Ben Van Leeuwen, *Principal*
▲ **EMP:** 7
SALES (est): 446K **Privately Held**
SIC: 2024 Ice cream & frozen desserts

(G-2617)
VANS INC
25 Franklin St (11222-2007)
PHONE 718 349-2311
EMP: 10
SALES (corp-wide): 11.8B **Publicly Held**
SIC: 3021 Canvas shoes, rubber soled
HQ: Vans, Inc.
1588 S Coast Dr
Costa Mesa CA 92626
855 909-8267

Brooklyn - Kings County (G-2618)

(G-2618)
VENTURE RESPIRATORY INC
1413 38th St (11218-3613)
PHONE.................................718 437-3633
Moshe Richard, *President*
Judah Schiller, *Exec VP*
ARI Pearl, *Office Mgr*
EMP: 13
SQ FT: 5,000
SALES (est): 2.8MM **Privately Held**
WEB: www.venturerespiratory.com
SIC: 3842 Respiratory protection equipment, personal

(G-2619)
VERSO INC
20 Jay St Ste 1010 (11201-8346)
PHONE.................................718 246-8160
Jacob Stevens, *Director*
EMP: 8
SQ FT: 2,500
SALES: 959.9K
SALES (corp-wide): 2.2MM **Privately Held**
SIC: 2731 Book publishing
PA: New Left Books Limited
6 Meard Street
London W1F 0
207 437-3546

(G-2620)
VIAMEDIA CORPORATION
2610 Atlantic Ave (11207-2415)
PHONE.................................718 485-7792
James Underwood, *President*
Michael Underwood, *Vice Pres*
EMP: 5
SQ FT: 3,200
SALES (est): 254.1K **Privately Held**
WEB: www.via-indy.com
SIC: 2741 Miscellaneous publishing

(G-2621)
VICTORIA FINE FOODS LLC (DH)
443 E 100th St (11236-2103)
PHONE.................................718 649-1635
Tim Shanley, *CEO*
Brian Dean, *President*
Robin Puskas, *Research*
Marcia Todd, *Accounting Mgr*
Scott Davis, *Sales Staff*
◆ **EMP:** 100 **EST:** 2011
SQ FT: 90,000
SALES (est): 39.3MM
SALES (corp-wide): 1.6B **Publicly Held**
SIC: 2035 2099 2033 5149 Pickles, sauces & salad dressings; spices, including grinding; canned fruits & specialties; pasta & rice
HQ: Victoria Fine Foods Holding Company
443 E 100th St
Brooklyn NY 11236
718 649-1635

(G-2622)
VICTORIA FINE FOODS HOLDING CO (HQ)
443 E 100th St (11236-2103)
PHONE.................................718 649-1635
Tim Shanley, *CEO*
Brian Dean, *President*
EMP: 4
SQ FT: 90,000
SALES: 39.3MM
SALES (corp-wide): 1.6B **Publicly Held**
SIC: 2035 2099 2033 5149 Pickles, sauces & salad dressings; spices, including grinding; canned fruits & specialties; pasta & rice
PA: B&G Foods, Inc.
4 Gatehall Dr Ste 110
Parsippany NJ 07054
973 401-6500

(G-2623)
VIKING MAR WLDG SHIP REPR LLC
14 Raleigh Pl (11226-4218)
PHONE.................................718 758-4116
Floyd Ricketts,
EMP: 10
SALES (est): 520.5K **Privately Held**
SIC: 3731 Shipbuilding & repairing

(G-2624)
VINEGAR HILL ASSET LLC
436 E 34th St (11203-5034)
PHONE.................................718 469-0342
EMP: 5 **EST:** 2015
SALES (est): 83K **Privately Held**
SIC: 2099 Vinegar

(G-2625)
VINELAND KOSHER POULTRY INC
Also Called: Poultry Dist
5600 1st Ave A7 (11220-2550)
PHONE.................................718 921-1347
David Lefkowitz, *Systems Mgr*
EMP: 10
SALES (corp-wide): 8.4MM **Privately Held**
WEB: www.vinelandkosherpoultry.com
SIC: 2015 5144 Poultry Processing Whol Poultry/Products
PA: Vineland Kosher Poultry Inc
1050 S Mill Rd
Vineland NJ 08360
856 692-1871

(G-2626)
VIRGINIA DARE EXTRACT CO INC (PA)
Also Called: V & E Kohnstamm & Co Div
882 3rd Ave Unit 2 (11232-1902)
PHONE.................................718 788-6320
Howard Smith Jr, *President*
Stephen Balter, *Vice Pres*
Laura McCord, *Purchasing*
Scott Taylor, *Accounts Exec*
Chrisandra Harvey,
◆ **EMP:** 152
SQ FT: 165,000
SALES (est): 42.9MM **Privately Held**
SIC: 2087 Extracts, flavoring

(G-2627)
VIRTUALAPT CORP
45 Main St Ste 613 (11201-1099)
PHONE.................................917 293-3173
Bryan Colin, *CEO*
Filippo Alimonda, *Officer*
EMP: 14
SALES (est): 440.2K **Privately Held**
SIC: 3812 Search & detection systems & instruments; distance measuring equipment

(G-2628)
VIRTUVENT INC
81 Prospect St Fl 7 (11201-1473)
PHONE.................................855 672-8677
Devin Drake, *Chairman*
EMP: 7 **EST:** 2012
SQ FT: 2,000
SALES (est): 409.6K **Privately Held**
SIC: 7372 7389 Business oriented computer software;

(G-2629)
VISITAINER CORP
Also Called: Plastifold Industries Division
148 Classon Ave (11205-2637)
PHONE.................................718 636-0300
William Lefkovitz, *President*
EMP: 25 **EST:** 1962
SQ FT: 30,000
SALES (est): 2.5MM **Privately Held**
SIC: 2657 3089 Folding paperboard boxes; plastic containers, except foam

(G-2630)
VITAROSE CORP OF AMERICA
2615 Nostrand Ave Ste 1 (11210-4643)
PHONE.................................718 951-9700
Joe Derose, *President*
EMP: 6 **EST:** 1959
SQ FT: 2,625
SALES: 1MM **Privately Held**
SIC: 2541 3231 3089 3444 Window backs, store or lunchroom, prefabricated: wood; products of purchased glass; awnings, fiberglass & plastic combination; awnings & canopies

(G-2631)
VITO & SONS BAKERY
Also Called: Mima S Bakery
1423 72nd St (11228-1711)
PHONE.................................201 617-8501
Fax: 201 864-3088
EMP: 10
SALES (est): 612.1K **Privately Held**
SIC: 2051 Mfg Bread/Related Products

(G-2632)
VLINE INC
81 Prospect St (11201-1473)
PHONE.................................512 222-5464
Jack Strong, *CEO*
EMP: 5
SALES (est): 295.8K **Privately Held**
SIC: 7372 Utility computer software

(G-2633)
VOLCKENING INC (PA)
6700 3rd Ave (11220-5296)
PHONE.................................718 748-0294
William J Schneider, *Ch of Bd*
Frederick C Schneider, *President*
Henry Schneider, *Vice Pres*
Robert McDonough, *VP Mktg*
EMP: 45
SQ FT: 30,000
SALES (est): 6.6MM **Privately Held**
WEB: www.volckening.com
SIC: 3565 3991 Packaging machinery; brushes, household or industrial

(G-2634)
VOODOO MANUFACTURING INC
361 Stagg St Ste 408 (11206-1743)
PHONE.................................646 893-8366
Max Friefeld, *CEO*
Travis Lopes, *Sales Staff*
Mike Baumgarten, *Marketing Staff*
Nicole Hartmann, *Executive*
EMP: 30
SALES (est): 100K **Privately Held**
SIC: 3555 Printing trades machinery

(G-2635)
VPULSE INC
191 Nassau Ave (11222-3509)
PHONE.................................646 729-5675
William Ruhnke, *CEO*
EMP: 5
SALES (est): 369.7K **Privately Held**
SIC: 3089 Ducting, plastic

(G-2636)
VSG INTERNATIONAL LLC
Also Called: Kustom Collabo
196 Clinton Ave Apt A2 (11205-3411)
PHONE.................................718 300-8171
Yusef Sirius-El, *Mng Member*
Nicholas Vasilopoulos,
▲ **EMP:** 5 **EST:** 2012
SQ FT: 5,000
SALES (est): 298.1K **Privately Held**
SIC: 3149 Athletic shoes, except rubber or plastic

(G-2637)
W E W CONTAINER CORPORATION
189 Wyona St (11207-3009)
PHONE.................................718 827-8150
Daniel Weicher, *Branch Mgr*
EMP: 20
SALES (corp-wide): 3.5MM **Privately Held**
SIC: 2673 2671 Bags: plastic, laminated & coated; plastic film, coated or laminated for packaging
PA: W E W Container Corporation
200 Bradford St
Brooklyn NY
718 827-8150

(G-2638)
WALTER P SAUER LLC
Also Called: Morris Fine Furniture Workshop
276 Grndpint Ave Ste 8400 (11222)
PHONE.................................718 937-0600
Anthony Morris,
EMP: 43
SQ FT: 2,100
SALES (est): 2.4MM **Privately Held**
WEB: www.walterpsauer.com
SIC: 2511 Wood household furniture

(G-2639)
WARNACO INC
70 Washington St Fl 10 (11201-1442)
PHONE.................................718 722-3000
Smitty Seelall, *Branch Mgr*
EMP: 10
SALES (corp-wide): 8.9B **Publicly Held**
WEB: www.warnaco.com
SIC: 2341 2321 2253 2329 Panties: women's, misses, children's & infants'; women's & children's nightwear; men's & boys' dress shirts; shirts (outerwear), knit; sweaters & sweater coats, knit; athletic (warmup, sweat & jogging) suits: men's & boys'; underwear, men's & boys': made from purchased materials; brassieres
HQ: Warnaco Inc.
501 Fashion Ave Fl 14
New York NY 10018
212 287-8000

(G-2640)
WATERMARK DESIGNS HOLDINGS LTD
350 Dewitt Ave (11207-6618)
PHONE.................................718 257-2800
AVI Abel, *President*
Jack Abel, *Vice Pres*
▲ **EMP:** 55
SQ FT: 20,000
SALES (est): 10.5MM **Privately Held**
SIC: 3431 3432 Bathroom fixtures, including sinks; plumbing fixture fittings & trim

(G-2641)
WEINFELD SKULL CAP MFG CO INC
Also Called: A Weinfeld Skull Cap Mfg
6022 14th Ave (11219-5006)
PHONE.................................718 854-3864
Mendel Weinfeld, *President*
▲ **EMP:** 8
SQ FT: 180
SALES (est): 804.2K **Privately Held**
SIC: 2353 Hats & caps

(G-2642)
WETLOOK DETAILING INC
1125 Banner Ave Apt 11a (11235-5267)
PHONE.................................212 390-8877
Dylan Valentine, *COO*
EMP: 8 **EST:** 2016
SALES (est): 400.6K **Privately Held**
SIC: 3589 Car washing machinery

(G-2643)
WG SHEET METAL CORP
341 Amber St (11208-5104)
PHONE.................................718 235-3093
Andy Tolta, *Admin Sec*
EMP: 5
SALES: 700K **Privately Held**
SIC: 3444 Sheet metalwork

(G-2644)
WHITLEY EAST LLC
Brooklyn Navy Yd Bg 2 Fl (11205)
PHONE.................................718 403-0050
William McShane, *General Mgr*
EMP: 79 **Privately Held**
WEB: www.capsyscorp.com
SIC: 2452 Modular homes, prefabricated, wood
HQ: Whitley East, Llc
64 Hess Rd
Leola PA 17540
717 656-2081

(G-2645)
WIDE FLANGE INC
176 27th St (11232-1625)
PHONE.................................718 492-8705
Joyce Cavagnaro, *President*
Blaze Bono, *Vice Pres*
EMP: 11
SQ FT: 5,500
SALES: 1.8MM **Privately Held**
SIC: 3449 Bars, concrete reinforcing: fabricated steel

GEOGRAPHIC SECTION

Buchanan - Westchester County (G-2674)

(G-2646)
WIGGBY PRECISION MACHINE CORP
140 58th St Ste 56 (11220-2526)
PHONE..................................718 439-6900
Ronald Wiggberg, *CEO*
Robert G Wiggberg, *Corp Secy*
EMP: 30 **EST:** 1949
SALES (est): 4.4MM **Privately Held**
SIC: 3599 Machine shop, jobbing & repair

(G-2647)
WILLIAM BROOKS WOODWORKING
856 Saratoga Ave (11212-4350)
PHONE..................................718 495-9767
William Brooks, *Owner*
EMP: 10
SALES: 275K **Privately Held**
SIC: 2434 Wood kitchen cabinets

(G-2648)
WILLIAM HARVEY STUDIO INC
214 N 8th St (11211-2008)
PHONE..................................718 599-4343
William Harvey, *President*
Reed Harvey, *Admin Sec*
EMP: 5
SQ FT: 2,500
SALES (est): 290K **Privately Held**
WEB:␣w.w.williamharveydesign.com
SIC: 2392 Household furnishings

(G-2649)
WILLIAM KANES MFG CORP
23 Alabama Ave (11207-2303)
PHONE..................................718 346-1515
William Kanes, *President*
EMP: 7
SQ FT: 5,000
SALES: 500K **Privately Held**
SIC: 3444 3599 Sheet metalwork; machine shop, jobbing & repair

(G-2650)
WILLIAMSBURG BULLETIN
136 Ross St (11211-7705)
PHONE..................................718 387-0123
EMP: 6
SALES (est): 376.3K **Privately Held**
SIC: 2711 Commercial printing & newspaper publishing combined

(G-2651)
WINDOW-FIX INC
331 37th St Fl 1 (11232-2505)
PHONE..................................718 854-3475
Ernesto Cappello, *President*
John Cappello, *Vice Pres*
EMP: 20
SALES (est): 3.3MM **Privately Held**
SIC: 3211 1751 7699 Window glass, clear & colored; window & door installation & erection; window blind repair services

(G-2652)
WINDOWMAN INC (USA)
460 Kingsland Ave (11222-1906)
PHONE..................................718 246-2626
Bruce Schmutter, *President*
EMP: 6
SALES: 2MM **Privately Held**
WEB: www.windowmanusa.com
SIC: 3442 3699 1796 1751 Metal doors, sash & trim; door opening & closing devices, electrical; installing building equipment; window & door installation & erection; safety & security specialization

(G-2653)
WINDOWS MEDIA PUBLISHING LLC
369 Remsen Ave (11212-1245)
PHONE..................................917 732-7892
Mark McLean,
EMP: 25
SALES (est): 834.9K **Privately Held**
SIC: 2731 Books: publishing & printing

(G-2654)
WINTER WATER FACTORY
191 33rd St (11232-2109)
PHONE..................................646 387-3247
Stefanie Lynen, *Owner*
Todd Warnock, *Opers Staff*

EMP: 6
SALES (est): 250K **Privately Held**
SIC: 2253 Dresses, knit

(G-2655)
WONTON FOOD INC (PA)
220 Moore St 222 (11206-3708)
PHONE..................................718 628-6868
Norman Wong, *CEO*
Ching Sun Wong, *Ch of Bd*
Alice Mok, *Assistant VP*
Foo Kam Wong, *Vice Pres*
Jian Chen, *VP Opers*
▲ **EMP:** 160
SQ FT: 55,000
SALES (est): 76.5MM **Privately Held**
WEB: www.wontonfood.com
SIC: 2099 2052 5149 Noodles, fried (Chinese); cookies; canned goods: fruit, vegetables, seafood, meats, etc.

(G-2656)
WOODWARD/WHITE INC
45 Main St Ste 820 (11201-1076)
PHONE..................................718 509-6082
Bradley Silberberg, *Branch Mgr*
EMP: 10
SALES (corp-wide): 11.3MM **Privately Held**
SIC: 2731 Book publishing
PA: Woodward/White, Inc.
  237 Park Ave Sw Ste 101
  Aiken SC 29801
  803 648-0300

(G-2657)
WORLD CHEESE CO INC
178 28th St (11232-1604)
PHONE..................................718 965-1700
Leo S Thurm, *President*
Meyer Thurm, *President*
Sruly Sherer, *VP Sales*
Jay Sherer, *Marketing Staff*
Florence Greenberg, *Exec Sec*
◆ **EMP:** 16
SQ FT: 25,000
SALES (est): 4.9MM **Privately Held**
SIC: 2022 Natural cheese; cheese spreads, dips, pastes & other cheese products

(G-2658)
WORLD JOURNAL LLC
6007 8th Ave (11220-4337)
PHONE..................................718 871-5000
Boby Chou, *CEO*
EMP: 12
SALES (corp-wide): 53.3MM **Privately Held**
WEB: www.wjnews.net
SIC: 2711 Newspapers, publishing & printing
HQ: World Journal Llc
  14107 20th Ave Fl 2
  Whitestone NY 11357
  718 746-8889

(G-2659)
WORLDWIDE RESOURCES INC
1908 Avenue O (11230-6721)
PHONE..................................718 760-5000
David Pick, *President*
EMP: 16 **EST:** 2012
SQ FT: 1,200
SALES (est): 1MM **Privately Held**
SIC: 3324 Aerospace investment castings, ferrous

(G-2660)
XSTATIC PRO INC
Proxcases
901 Essex St (11208-5317)
PHONE..................................718 237-2299
Gabriel Menashe, *Branch Mgr*
EMP: 13
SALES (corp-wide): 1.3MM **Privately Held**
SIC: 3161 Musical instrument cases
PA: Xstatic Pro, Inc.
  901 Essex St
  Brooklyn NY 11208
  718 237-2299

(G-2661)
Y & A TRADING INC
Also Called: Sukkah Center
1365 38th St (11218-3634)
PHONE..................................718 436-6333
Joe Biston, *President*
▲ **EMP:** 10
SALES (est): 771.9K **Privately Held**
WEB: www.sukkah.com
SIC: 2394 5999 Canvas & related products; religious goods

(G-2662)
YALOZ MOULD & DIE CO INC
Also Called: Yaloz Mold & Die
239 Java St Fl 2 (11222-1893)
PHONE..................................718 389-1131
Yehuda Leon Yaloz, *President*
EMP: 30
SQ FT: 45,000
SALES (est): 2.6MM **Privately Held**
SIC: 2542 3429 Fixtures, store: except wood; manufactured hardware (general)

(G-2663)
YEPES FINE FURNITURE
72 Van Dam St (11222-3807)
PHONE..................................718 383-0221
Tiberio Yepes, *Owner*
EMP: 20
SALES (est): 1.4MM **Privately Held**
SIC: 2512 5712 Upholstered household furniture; furniture stores

(G-2664)
YOFAH RELIGIOUS ARTICLES INC
2001 57th St Ste 1 (11204-2035)
PHONE..................................718 435-3288
Jacob Leser, *President*
▲ **EMP:** 13
SQ FT: 2,000
SALES: 1.4MM **Privately Held**
SIC: 3911 Rosaries or other small religious articles, precious metal

(G-2665)
YOLAND CORPORATION
253 36th St Unit 2 (11232-2415)
PHONE..................................718 499-4803
Ayal Adler, *President*
Roni Ginat, *General Mgr*
Tal Ganet, *Vice Pres*
ADI Ginat, *Manager*
EMP: 40
SQ FT: 8,000
SALES (est): 4.8MM **Privately Held**
WEB: www.yolandcorp.com
SIC: 2399 Parachutes
PA: D. Yoland Ltd.
  17 Hamasger
  Netanya
  986 161-03

(G-2666)
YORK FUEL INCORPORATED
1760 Flatbush Ave (11210-4203)
PHONE..................................718 951-0202
Gurmeet Singh Buttar, *President*
EMP: 6
SALES (est): 598.7K **Privately Held**
SIC: 2869 Fuels

(G-2667)
YS MARKETING INC
Also Called: Numed Pharmaceuticals
2004 Mcdonald Ave (11223-2819)
PHONE..................................718 778-6080
Joel Silberstein, *President*
EMP: 20
SALES: 20MM **Privately Held**
SIC: 2834 Pharmaceutical preparations

(G-2668)
Z-STUDIOS DSIGN FBRICATION LLC
30 Haven Pl (11233-3408)
PHONE..................................347 512-4210
Zachary Zaus,
EMP: 5
SQ FT: 2,500
SALES: 200K **Privately Held**
SIC: 3446 Architectural metalwork

(G-2669)
ZIPARI INC
45 Main St Ste 406 (11201-1084)
PHONE..................................855 558-7884
Mark Nathan, *CEO*
Rob Graney, *Vice Pres*
Jyoti Mokal, *Engineer*
Dylan Carroll, *Sales Staff*
Janelle Taylor, *Marketing Staff*
EMP: 50
SALES (est): 814K **Privately Held**
SIC: 7372 Application computer software

(G-2670)
ZOOMERS INC (PA)
Also Called: Liz Lange
32 33rd St (11232-1901)
PHONE..................................718 369-2656
Gary Jay Schulman, *CEO*
Deborah Schulman, *President*
Wayne Sternberg, *Vice Pres*
▲ **EMP:** 28
SQ FT: 20,000
SALES (est): 5.2MM **Privately Held**
SIC: 2339 Maternity clothing; sportswear, women's

Brownville
Jefferson County

(G-2671)
FLORELLE TISSUE CORPORATION
1 Bridge St (13615-7765)
PHONE..................................647 997-7405
Harry Minas, *President*
▲ **EMP:** 50
SALES (est): 1.2MM **Privately Held**
SIC: 2676 Towels, napkins & tissue paper products

Buchanan
Westchester County

(G-2672)
CONTINENTAL BUCHANAN LLC
350 Broadway (10511-1000)
PHONE..................................703 480-3800
Ike Preston, *President*
Georganne Elkins, *Purch Agent*
Dennis Romps, *CFO*
Robbe Pearson, *Director*
▲ **EMP:** 100
SALES (est): 9.3MM **Privately Held**
SIC: 2493 3275 2891 Building board & wallboard, except gypsum; building board, gypsum; sealing compounds for pipe threads or joints

(G-2673)
LAFARGE NORTH AMERICA INC
350 Broadway (10511-1000)
PHONE..................................914 930-3027
Criss Fraley, *Opers-Prdtn-Mfg*
EMF: 100
SALES (corp-wide): 26.4B **Privately Held**
SIC: 3241 3275 Cement, hydraulic; gypsum products
HQ: Lafarge North America Inc.
  8700 W Bryn Mawr Ave
  Chicago IL 60631
  773 372-1000

(G-2674)
SILVA CABINETRY INC
12 White St Ste C (10511-1665)
PHONE..................................914 737-7697
Antonio Dasilva, *President*
EMP: 25
SALES (est): 2.9MM **Privately Held**
SIC: 2434 Wood kitchen cabinets

Buffalo
Erie County

(G-2675)
240 MICHIGAN STREET INC
Also Called: Garb-El Products Co
96 Darwin Dr (14226-4509)
PHONE.................................716 434-6010
James Carbone, *President*
EMP: 10
SQ FT: 19,000
SALES (est): 2MM **Privately Held**
WEB: www.garb-el.com
SIC: 3589 Garbage disposers & compactors, commercial

(G-2676)
260 OAK STREET INC
260 Oak St (14203-1626)
PHONE.................................877 852-4676
Glenn Snyder, *Ch of Bd*
EMP: 5
SQ FT: 6,233
SALES (est): 376.8K **Privately Held**
SIC: 2542 Cabinets: show, display or storage: except wood

(G-2677)
5TH & OCEAN CLOTHING INC
160 Delaware Ave (14202-2404)
PHONE.................................716 604-9000
Luis Leiter Jr, *Mng Member*
Alex A Leiter, *Director*
◆ **EMP:** 115
SQ FT: 40,000
SALES (est): 10.4MM
SALES (corp-wide): 563.7MM **Privately Held**
WEB: www.5thocean.com
SIC: 2339 Women's & misses' accessories
PA: New Era Cap Co., Inc.
160 Delaware Ave
Buffalo NY 14202
716 604-9000

(G-2678)
760 NL HOLDINGS
760 Northland Ave (14211-1041)
PHONE.................................716 821-1391
Tim George, *Principal*
EMP: 30 **EST:** 1996
SQ FT: 20,000
SALES (est): 8.4MM **Privately Held**
WEB: www.nfcf.net
SIC: 3441 Fabricated structural metal

(G-2679)
A J M ENTERPRISES
348 Cayuga Rd (14225-1927)
PHONE.................................716 626-7294
Jarek Chelpinski, *Partner*
EMP: 10
SALES (est): 546.9K **Privately Held**
SIC: 3915 Jewelers' castings

(G-2680)
A-FAB INITIATIVES INC
99 Bud Mil Dr (14206-1801)
PHONE.................................716 877-5257
Edward Raimonde, *President*
◆ **EMP:** 12
SALES (est): 975.1K **Privately Held**
SIC: 3441 3354 Fabricated structural metal; aluminum extruded products

(G-2681)
ACCENTA INCORPORATED
150 Lawrence Bell Dr # 108 (14221-8403)
P.O. Box 99 (14223-0099)
PHONE.................................716 565-6262
Ulf Ernetoft, *President*
EMP: 5 **EST:** 2012
SALES (est): 399.8K **Privately Held**
SIC: 3999 Advertising display products

(G-2682)
ACCESS PRODUCTS INC
241 Main St Ste 100 (14203-2703)
PHONE.................................800 679-4022
Kenneth E J Szekely, *President*
Sean Morrison, *Principal*
David Murray, *Vice Pres*
Lance Mitchell, *Sales Mgr*
EMP: 6
SALES: 5.3MM **Privately Held**
SIC: 3272 Building materials, except block or brick: concrete

(G-2683)
ACME NIPPLE MFG CO INC
1930 Elmwood Ave (14207-1902)
PHONE.................................716 873-7491
John Hurley, *President*
EMP: 8
SQ FT: 10,000
SALES (est): 1MM **Privately Held**
SIC: 3321 Pressure pipe & fittings, cast iron

(G-2684)
ACME SCREENPRINTING LLC
247 Cayuga Rd Ste 25e (14225-1949)
PHONE.................................716 565-1052
Joe Strepason,
EMP: 7
SALES (est): 275.7K **Privately Held**
SIC: 2759 Screen printing

(G-2685)
ADCO CIRCUITS INC
Also Called: E J E Research Div
160 Lawrence Bell Dr # 122 (14221-7897)
PHONE.................................716 668-6600
John Nemcek, *Vice Pres*
Edward Vrana, *Vice Pres*
EMP: 6
SALES (corp-wide): 28.9MM **Privately Held**
WEB: www.adcocircuits.com
SIC: 3674 3679 3672 Microprocessors; electronic circuits; printed circuit boards
PA: Adco Circuits, Inc.
2868 Bond St
Rochester Hills MI 48309
248 853-6620

(G-2686)
ADM MILLING CO
250 Ganson St (14203-3048)
P.O. Box 487 (14240-0487)
PHONE.................................716 849-7333
Charles Bayless, *Vice Pres*
Andreas Martin, *Vice Pres*
Brad Heald, *Plant Mgr*
Yvette Ceser, *Manager*
George Siradis, *Manager*
EMP: 75
SALES (corp-wide): 60.8B **Publicly Held**
WEB: www.admmilling.com
SIC: 2041 Grain mills (except rice)
HQ: Adm Milling Co.
8000 W 110th St Ste 300
Overland Park KS 66210
913 491-9400

(G-2687)
ADPRO SPORTS LLC
55 Amherst Villa Rd (14225-1432)
PHONE.................................716 854-5116
Ron Raccuia, *President*
Thomas Naples, *Exec VP*
Jeffrey Diebel, *Senior VP*
Paul Schintzius, *Senior VP*
EMP: 76 **EST:** 2010
SALES (est): 1MM **Privately Held**
SIC: 2329 2339 3949 Men's & boys' sportswear & athletic clothing; women's & misses' athletic clothing & sportswear; team sports equipment

(G-2688)
ADSCO MANUFACTURING CORP
4979 Lake Ave (14219-1398)
PHONE.................................716 827-5450
Gustav Linda, *President*
James Treantis, *Controller*
EMP: 60
SQ FT: 32,000
SALES (est): 12.1MM **Privately Held**
WEB: www.adscomfg.com
SIC: 3441 Expansion joints (structural shapes), iron or steel

(G-2689)
ADVANCED MACHINE DESIGN CO INC
45 Roberts Ave (14206-3130)
PHONE.................................716 826-2000
Heinrich Moelbert, *Ch of Bd*
Reiner Moelbert, *President*
Ursula Moelbert, *Corp Secy*
EMP: 30
SQ FT: 102,000
SALES (est): 5.9MM **Privately Held**
WEB: www.amd-co.com
SIC: 3541 3542 8711 3549 Machine tool replacement & repair parts, metal cutting types; machine tools, metal forming type; presses; hydraulic & pneumatic, mechanical & manual; shearing machines, power; industrial engineers; metalworking machinery; cutlery

(G-2690)
AEP ENVIRONMENTAL LLC
2495 Main St Ste 230 (14214-2156)
PHONE.................................716 446-0739
Lynn Zier, *Mng Member*
Anthony Zier, *Admin Sec*
Scott Meacham,
Kenneth Pronti,
EMP: 10
SALES (est): 500K **Privately Held**
SIC: 3646 2844 5122 5047 Commercial indusl & institutional electric lighting fixtures; toilet preparations; drugs, proprietaries & sundries; medical & hospital equipment; household furnishings

(G-2691)
ALLEN BOAT CO INC
370 Babcock St Rear (14206-2802)
PHONE.................................716 842-0800
Thomas Allen Jr, *President*
Michael Huffman, *Vice Pres*
Sharon Hicok, *Controller*
EMP: 6 **EST:** 1961
SQ FT: 10,000
SALES (est): 997.3K **Privately Held**
WEB: www.allenboatco.com
SIC: 3732 2394 Sailboats, building & repairing; sails: made from purchased materials

(G-2692)
ALLIED CIRCUITS LLC
22 James E Casey Dr (14206-2367)
PHONE.................................716 551-0285
Chris Aquiline,
Chris Scinta,
Tom Wagner,
EMP: 50
SQ FT: 10,400
SALES: 9.6MM **Privately Held**
WEB: www.alliedcircuits.com
SIC: 3613 Panelboards & distribution boards, electric

(G-2693)
AMBIND CORP
Cheektowaga (14225)
P.O. Box 886 (14231-0886)
PHONE.................................716 836-4365
David Spiezer, *President*
EMP: 5
SALES (est): 660.1K **Privately Held**
SIC: 2241 Bindings, textile

(G-2694)
AMERICAN CITY BUS JOURNALS INC
465 Main St Ste 100 (14203-1717)
PHONE.................................716 541-1654
Jack Connors, *Principal*
Bo Sunshine, *Marketing Staff*
EMP: 32
SALES (corp-wide): 1.4B **Privately Held**
SIC: 2711 Newspapers: publishing only, not printed on site
HQ: American City Business Journals, Inc.
120 W Morehead St Ste 400
Charlotte NC 28202
704 973-1000

(G-2695)
AMERICAN DOUGLAS METALS INC
Also Called: Afab Initiative
99 Bud Mil Dr (14206-1801)
PHONE.................................716 856-3170
Edward Raimonde, *CEO*
Kevin Blake, *Branch Mgr*
EMP: 12
SQ FT: 29,700
SALES (corp-wide): 27.4MM **Privately Held**
WEB: www.americandouglasmetals.com
SIC: 1099 3353 3291 Aluminum ore mining; aluminum sheet, plate & foil; abrasive products
PA: American Douglas Metals, Inc.
783 Thorpe Rd
Orlando FL 32824
407 855-6590

(G-2696)
AMERICAN IMAGES INC
25 Imson St (14210-1615)
PHONE.................................716 825-8888
Steve Wojtkowiak, *President*
EMP: 10
SALES (est): 1.4MM **Privately Held**
SIC: 2397 Schiffli machine embroideries

(G-2697)
AMETA INTERNATIONAL CO LTD
2221 Kenmore Ave Ste 108 (14207-1360)
PHONE.................................416 992-8036
EMP: 6 **EST:** 2013
SALES (est): 571.4K **Privately Held**
SIC: 3699 Security control equipment & systems
PA: Ameta International Co. Ltd
80 Shields Crt
Markham ON L3R 9
905 415-1234

(G-2698)
AMHERST MEDIA INC
175 Rano St Ste 200 (14207-2176)
P.O. Box 538 (14213-0538)
PHONE.................................716 874-4450
Craig Alesse, *President*
Barbara Lynch-Johnt, *Assoc Editor*
EMP: 5
SALES (est): 705K **Privately Held**
WEB: www.amherstmedia.com
SIC: 2731 7812 Books: publishing only; video production

(G-2699)
AMSCO INC
925 Bailey Ave (14206-2338)
PHONE.................................716 823-4213
Norm Brodfuhrersin, *President*
Jack Kraus, *Vice Pres*
Linda Nowak, *Treasurer*
EMP: 16
SQ FT: 18,000
SALES (est): 1.3MM **Privately Held**
SIC: 3544 3444 Jigs & fixtures; sheet metalwork

(G-2700)
ANDUJAR ASBESTOS AND LEAD
473 4th St (14201-1603)
PHONE.................................716 228-6757
Alfredo Andjujar, *President*
EMP: 9 **EST:** 2015
SQ FT: 24,000
SALES: 200K **Privately Held**
SIC: 3292 Asbestos products

(G-2701)
ANNESE & ASSOCIATES INC
500 Corporate Pkwy # 106 (14226-1263)
PHONE.................................716 972-0076
Raymond Apy, *Branch Mgr*
EMP: 7
SALES (corp-wide): 887.7MM **Publicly Held**
SIC: 3577 Data conversion equipment, media-to-media: computer
HQ: Annese & Associates, Inc.
747 Pierce Rd Ste 2
Clifton Park NY 12065
518 877-7058

(G-2702)
ANTIQUES & COLLECTIBLE AUTOS
35 Dole St (14210-1603)
PHONE.................................716 825-3990
Joseph Trombley, *President*
EMP: 3
SALES: 1.6MM **Privately Held**
WEB: www.acrods.com
SIC: 3711 Automobile bodies, passenger car, not including engine, etc.

GEOGRAPHIC SECTION

Buffalo - Erie County (G-2729)

(G-2703)
ANTONICELLI VITO RACE CAR
3883 Broadway St (14227-1105)
PHONE..................................716 684-2205
Vito Antonicelli, *Owner*
EMP: 5
SQ FT: 6,000
SALES (est): 75K **Privately Held**
SIC: 3711 Motor vehicles & car bodies

(G-2704)
API HEAT TRANSF THERMASYS CORP (HQ)
2777 Walden Ave (14225-4788)
PHONE..................................716 684-6700
Joseph Cordosi, *President*
◆ EMP: 664
SALES (est): 37.4K
SALES (corp-wide): 492.5MM **Privately Held**
SIC: 3443 3714 Heat exchangers: coolers (after, inter), condensers, etc.; radiators & radiator shells & cores, motor vehicle
PA: Api Heat Transfer Company
2777 Walden Ave Ste 1
Buffalo NY 14225
716 684-6700

(G-2705)
API HEAT TRANSFER COMPANY (PA)
2777 Walden Ave Ste 1 (14225-4788)
PHONE..................................716 684-6700
Mike Laisure, *President*
EMP: 9 EST: 2005
SALES (est): 492.5MM **Privately Held**
SIC: 3443 Heat exchangers: coolers (after, inter), condensers, etc.

(G-2706)
APPLE IMPRINTS APPAREL INC
2336 Bailey Ave (14211-1738)
PHONE..................................716 893-1130
Jack Lipomi, *President*
Kevin Lipomi, *Vice Pres*
▲ EMP: 22 EST: 1981
SQ FT: 15,000
SALES (est): 2.8MM **Privately Held**
WEB: www.appleimprints.com
SIC: 2396 7319 Screen printing on fabric articles; display advertising service

(G-2707)
APPLINCE INSTALLATION SVC CORP (PA)
3190 Genesee St (14225 2607)
PHONE..................................716 884-7425
Paul Glowlacki, *CEO*
Wayne Stoutner, *President*
Kim Carney, *Warehouse Mgr*
Gene Tomczyk, *Manager*
EMP: 24
SALES (est): 14MM **Privately Held**
SIC: 3631 5085 7699 Household cooking equipment; industrial supplies; restaurant equipment repair

(G-2708)
ARCHER-DANIELS-MIDLAND COMPANY
Also Called: ADM
250 Ganson St (14203-3048)
P.O. Box 487 (14240-0487)
PHONE..................................716 849-7333
Brad Heald, *Branch Mgr*
Andrew Van Thyne, *Manager*
EMP: 100
SALES (corp-wide): 60.8B **Publicly Held**
WEB: www.admworld.com
SIC: 2041 Flour & other grain mill products
PA: Archer-Daniels-Midland Company
77 W Wacker Dr Ste 4600
Chicago IL 60601
312 634-8100

(G-2709)
ARMOR MACHINING SERVICES, INC.
343 Elk St (14210-2105)
P.O. Box 1135 (14220-8185)
PHONE..................................716 825-0190
EMP: 22
SQ FT: 25,000

SALES (est): 3.6MM **Privately Held**
SIC: 7694 5063 5084 Electric motor repair; motors, electric; cranes, industrial

(G-2710)
ASSOCIATED PUBLISHING COMPANY (HQ)
61 John Muir Dr (14228-1147)
PHONE..................................325 676-4032
Robert N Allen III, *President*
EMP: 40
SALES (est): 6.8MM
SALES (corp-wide): 6.6B **Privately Held**
WEB: www.associatedpublishingcompany.com
SIC: 2741 Directories, telephone: publishing only, not printed on site; telephone & other directory publishing
PA: The Hearst Corporation
300 W 57th St Fl 42
New York NY 10019
212 649-2000

(G-2711)
ATECH-SEH METAL FABRICATOR
330 Greene St (14206-1025)
PHONE..................................716 895-8888
EMP: 20
SALES (est): 2MM **Privately Held**
SIC: 3444 Sheet metalwork

(G-2712)
ATHENEX INC (PA)
1001 Main St Ste 600 (14203-1009)
PHONE..................................716 427-2950
Johnson Y N Lau, *Ch of Bd*
William Zuo, *President*
Jeffrey Yordon, *COO*
Timothy Cook, *Senior VP*
Joe Mase, *Vice Pres*
EMP: 86
SQ FT: 51,000
SALES: 38MM **Publicly Held**
WEB: www.kinexpharma.com
SIC: 2834 8731 Pharmaceutical preparations; medical research, commercial

(G-2713)
ATHENEX PHARMACEUTICAL DIV LLC (PA)
1001 Main St Ste 600 (14203-1009)
PHONE..................................877 463-7823
Tom Moutvic, *Principal*
James Bennett, *Consultant*
EMP: 14
SALES (est): 2.9MM **Privately Held**
SIC: 2834 Powders, pharmaceutical; solutions, pharmaceutical

(G-2714)
AURUBIS BUFFALO INC
600 Military Rd (14207)
PHONE..................................716 879-6700
Raymond Mercer, *President*
EMP: 11
SALES (corp-wide): 12.9B **Privately Held**
SIC: 3351 Copper rolling & drawing
HQ: Aurubis Buffalo, Inc.
70 Sayre St
Buffalo NY 14207
716 879-6700

(G-2715)
AURUBIS BUFFALO INC (HQ)
70 Sayre St (14207-2225)
P.O. Box 981 (14240-0981)
PHONE..................................716 879-6700
Raymond Mercer, *President*
Richard Lyons, *Vice Pres*
Bonnie Rizzo, *Vice Pres*
Karl Sholtz, *Production*
Christian Wojciechowski, *Purchasing*
▲ EMP: 264
SQ FT: 1,214,500
SALES (est): 203.7MM
SALES (corp-wide): 12.9B **Privately Held**
WEB: www.luvata.com
SIC: 3351 Copper rolling & drawing
PA: Aurubis Ag
Hovestr. 50
Hamburg 20539
407 883-0

(G-2716)
AUSTIN AIR SYSTEMS LIMITED
500 Elk St (14210-2208)
PHONE..................................716 856-3700
Richard Taylor, *President*
Joyce Taylor, *Vice Pres*
Brian Popovich, *Prdtn Mgr*
Jason Armstrong, *Mfg Staff*
Lauren Bert, *Sales Mgr*
◆ EMP: 60
SQ FT: 173,000
SALES (est): 19.5MM **Privately Held**
SIC: 3564 Air purification equipment

(G-2717)
AVALON COPY CENTERS AMER INC
Also Called: Avalon Document Services
741 Main St (14203-1321)
PHONE..................................716 995-7777
Hilary Kleppe, *Branch Mgr*
EMP: 25
SALES (corp-wide): 19.6MM **Privately Held**
SIC: 2741 7375 7336 7334 Art copy: publishing & printing; information retrieval services; commercial art & graphic design; photocopying & duplicating services
PA: Avalon Copy Centers Of America, Inc.
901 N State St
Syracuse NY 13208
315 471-3333

(G-2718)
AVANTI ADVANCED MFG CORP
673 Ontario St (14207-1614)
PHONE..................................716 791-9001
Jim WEI, *Ch of Bd*
▲ EMP: 10 EST: 2013
SALES (est): 810.6K **Privately Held**
SIC: 3089 Injection molding of plastics

(G-2719)
AZ-LIGHT INC
3349 Sheridan Dr (14226-1440)
PHONE..................................716 837-5533
William Watson, *General Mgr*
EMP: 6 EST: 2016
SALES (est): 500K **Privately Held**
SIC: 3645 1731 Fluorescent lighting fixtures, residential; lighting contractor

(G-2720)
B & K COMPONENTS LTD
2100 Old Union Rd (14227-2725)
PHONE..................................323 776-4277
John L Beyer III, *President*
Dr Charles A Marchetta, *Admin Sec*
▲ EMP: 70 EST: 1981
SQ FT: 18,500
SALES (est): 9.5MM **Privately Held**
WEB: www.bkcomp.com
SIC: 3651 Audio electronic systems

(G-2721)
B & P JAYS INC
Also Called: Mecca Printing
19 N Hill Dr (14224-2582)
PHONE..................................716 668-8408
EMP: 5
SQ FT: 1,400
SALES: 200K **Privately Held**
SIC: 2752 Offset Printing

(G-2722)
BAK USA TECHNOLOGIES CORP
425 Michigan Ave (14203-2240)
PHONE..................................716 248-2704
J P Folsgaard Bak, *CEO*
Ulla Bak, *President*
Andrew Murphy, *Vice Pres*
Jennifer Mazurkiewicz, *Accounts Exec*
Sara Vanhoose, *Sales Staff*
EMP: 32
SQ FT: 15,000
SALES (est): 4MM **Privately Held**
SIC: 3571 Electronic computers

(G-2723)
BARRON GAMES INTL CO LLC
84 Aero Dr Ste 5 (14225-1435)
PHONE..................................716 630-0054
Gregory Bacorn, *President*
Ann Zykina, *Vice Pres*

Anna Zykina, *Vice Pres*
Alyssa Chawgo, *Office Mgr*
◆ EMP: 11
SQ FT: 4,500
SALES: 2MM **Privately Held**
WEB: www.barrongames.com/
SIC: 3944 5092 Electronic games & toys; video games

(G-2724)
BATAVIA PRECISION GLASS LLC
231 Currier Ave (14212-2262)
PHONE..................................585 343-6050
Steve Barber,
EMP: 6
SQ FT: 9,000
SALES: 63K **Privately Held**
SIC: 3231 8748 Leaded glass; business consulting

(G-2725)
BATES JACKSON ENGRAVING CO INC
17 Elm St 21 (14203-2605)
PHONE..................................716 854-3000
Rozanne Flammer, *CEO*
Edward Flammer, *President*
Carolyn Owen, *VP Finance*
EMP: 35 EST: 1903
SQ FT: 19,000
SALES (est): 3.7MM **Privately Held**
SIC: 2759 2752 2791 Engraving; commercial printing, offset; typesetting

(G-2726)
BATTENFELD-AMERICAN INC
1575 Clinton St (14206-3064)
P.O. Box 728, North Tonawanda (14120-0728)
PHONE..................................716 822-8410
John A Bellanti Sr, *CEO*
Barbara A Bellanti, *Ch of Bd*
Barbara Bellanti, *President*
Debbi Carpenter, *Vice Pres*
Florence Bellanti, *Admin Sec*
▼ EMP: 38
SQ FT: 110,000
SALES (est): 9.2MM
SALES (corp-wide): 44.4MM **Privately Held**
WEB: www.battenfeld-grease.com
SIC: 2992 Oils & greases, blending & compounding
PA: Battenfeld Management, Inc.
1174 Erie Ave
North Tonawanda NY 14120
716 695-2100

(G-2727)
BEAR METAL WORKS INC
39 Scoville Ave (14206-2932)
P.O. Box 2528 (14240-2528)
PHONE..................................716 824-4350
Barrett E Price, *Ch of Bd*
Gloria Gau, *Project Mgr*
January Delaney, *Office Mgr*
Catherine Jasinski, *Admin Sec*
EMP: 10 EST: 1999
SALES (est): 2.4MM **Privately Held**
SIC: 3441 Fabricated structural metal

(G-2728)
BEKA WORLD LP
258 Sonwil Dr (14225-5516)
PHONE..................................905 821-1050
EMP: 7
SALES (corp-wide): 1.5MM **Privately Held**
SIC: 2992 Lubricating oils & greases
PA: Beka World Lp
2775 N Hills Dr Ne
Atlanta GA 30305
404 841-1133

(G-2729)
BELRIX INDUSTRIES INC
3590 Jeffrey Blvd (14219-2390)
PHONE..................................716 821-5964
Gail Maurer, *President*
EMP: 6
SQ FT: 15,000
SALES (est): 1.1MM **Privately Held**
WEB: www.belrix.com
SIC: 3469 Machine parts, stamped or pressed metal

Buffalo - Erie County (G-2730)

(G-2730)
BEMCO OF WESTERN NY INC
122 Roberts Ave (14206-3120)
PHONE..................................716 823-8400
Barry E Medwin, *President*
Paul Kunkes, *Vice Pres*
EMP: 6
SQ FT: 60,000
SALES (est): 1.1MM **Privately Held**
SIC: 3625 Motor control accessories, including overload relays

(G-2731)
BETTER WIRE PRODUCTS INC
680 New Babcock St (14206-2201)
PHONE..................................716 883-3377
William Breeser, *President*
Lynn Youngman, *Sales Staff*
Steven Bennett, *Director*
▲ **EMP:** 35 **EST:** 1952
SQ FT: 30,000
SALES (est): 8.2MM **Privately Held**
SIC: 3496 Miscellaneous fabricated wire products

(G-2732)
BFG MANUFACTURING SERVICES INC
3949 Jeffrey Blvd (14219-2334)
P.O. Box 825, Hamburg (14075-0825)
PHONE..................................716 362-0888
Minta Marie, *Branch Mgr*
EMP: 27
SALES (est): 3.5MM
SALES (corp-wide): 12.6MM **Privately Held**
WEB: www.bfgelectroplating.com
SIC: 3471 Electroplating of metals or formed products
PA: Bfg Manufacturing Services, Inc.
701 Martha St
Punxsutawney PA 15767
814 938-9164

(G-2733)
BIG HEART PET BRANDS
Del Monte Foods
243 Urban St (14211-1532)
PHONE..................................716 891-6566
Greg Pastore, *General Mgr*
Todd Verost, *Opers Mgr*
Sean McGloin, *Purch Mgr*
Barbara Schumacher, *Purch Agent*
Richard Aumiller, *Engineer*
EMP: 31
SALES (corp-wide): 7.3B **Publicly Held**
WEB: www.kraftfoods.com
SIC: 2066 Chocolate & cocoa products
HQ: Big Heart Pet Brands
1 Maritime Plz Fl 2
San Francisco CA 94111
415 247-3000

(G-2734)
BLACK & DECKER (US) INC
881 W Delavan Ave (14209-1297)
PHONE..................................716 884-6220
Mike Eaton, *Manager*
EMP: 6
SQ FT: 4,112
SALES (corp-wide): 12.7B **Publicly Held**
WEB: www.dewalt.com
SIC: 3546 Power-driven handtools
HQ: Black & Decker (U.S.) Inc.
1000 Stanley Dr
New Britain CT 06053
860 225-5111

(G-2735)
BMC LLC
3155 Broadway St (14227-1034)
PHONE..................................716 681-7755
Richard Neal, *President*
▲ **EMP:** 24
SQ FT: 4,500
SALES (est): 2.5MM **Privately Held**
SIC: 3084 Plastics pipe

(G-2736)
BROOK & WHITTLE LIMITED
215 John Glenn Dr (14228-2227)
PHONE..................................716 853-1688
Andrew Sharp, *Sales Mgr*
EMP: 120
SALES (corp-wide): 7.1MM **Privately Held**
SIC: 2671 4789 Plastic film, coated or laminated for packaging; cargo loading & unloading services
HQ: Brook & Whittle Limited
260 Branford Rd
North Branford CT 06471

(G-2737)
BRYANT MACHINE & DEVELOPMENT
63 Stanley St (14206-1017)
PHONE..................................716 894-8282
Michael Denz, *President*
Matthew Bryant Jr, *Corp Secy*
Cindy White, *Office Mgr*
EMP: 10
SQ FT: 8,000
SALES: 200K **Privately Held**
SIC: 3599 Machine shop, jobbing & repair

(G-2738)
BRYANT MACHINE CO INC
63 Stanley St (14206-1017)
PHONE..................................716 894-8282
Kip Laviolette, *President*
Erica Laviolette, *Office Mgr*
EMP: 10 **EST:** 1946
SQ FT: 5,000
SALES (est): 1MM **Privately Held**
WEB: www.bryantmachine.com
SIC: 3599 Machine shop, jobbing & repair

(G-2739)
BRYANT MANUFACTURING WNY INC
63 Stanley St (14206-1017)
PHONE..................................716 894-8282
Kip A Laviolette, *CEO*
EMP: 6
SALES: 950K **Privately Held**
SIC: 3599 Machine shop, jobbing & repair

(G-2740)
BUFFALO ARMORY LLC
1050 Military Rd (14217-2528)
PHONE..................................716 935-6346
John Bastiste, *President*
EMP: 5
SALES (est): 832.4K **Privately Held**
SIC: 3398 Metal heat treating

(G-2741)
BUFFALO BLENDS INC (PA)
1400 William St (14206-1813)
PHONE..................................716 825-4422
Timothy Sheehy, *President*
Kevin Prise, *Treasurer*
▲ **EMP:** 22 **EST:** 1999
SQ FT: 35,000
SALES (est): 3.2MM **Privately Held**
WEB: www.buffaloblends.com
SIC: 2087 Beverage bases, concentrates, syrups, powders & mixes

(G-2742)
BUFFALO CRUSHED STONE INC (HQ)
500 Como Park Blvd (14227-1606)
PHONE..................................716 826-7310
Steven B Detwiler, *Ch of Bd*
David Firmstone, *Vice Pres*
Jamie Hypnarowski, *Vice Pres*
Melissa Garman, *Shareholder*
EMP: 40
SQ FT: 25,000
SALES (est): 33.1MM
SALES (corp-wide): 651.9MM **Privately Held**
SIC: 3272 Concrete products
PA: New Enterprise Stone & Lime Co., Inc.
3912 Brumbaugh Rd
New Enterprise PA 16664
814 224-6883

(G-2743)
BUFFALO FINISHING WORKS INC
1255 Niagara St (14213-1501)
PHONE..................................716 893-5266
John Warchocki, *President*
Ulrike Warchocki, *Vice Pres*
EMP: 5
SQ FT: 7,000
SALES: 250K **Privately Held**
SIC: 3479 Painting of metal products; enameling, including porcelain, of metal products

(G-2744)
BUFFALO GAMES LLC
220 James E Casey Dr (14206-2362)
PHONE..................................716 827-8393
Nagendra Raina, *Mng Member*
EMP: 75
SQ FT: 88,000
SALES (est): 1.9MM **Privately Held**
SIC: 3944 Games, toys & children's vehicles
HQ: Buffalo Holding Corp.
220 James E Casey Dr
Buffalo NY 14206
716 464-5263

(G-2745)
BUFFALO LAW JOURNAL
465 Main St Ste 100 (14203-1717)
PHONE..................................716 541-1600
Kim Schaus, *General Mgr*
EMP: 6
SALES (est): 310K **Privately Held**
WEB: www.buffalolawjournal.com
SIC: 2711 Newspapers: publishing only, not printed on site

(G-2746)
BUFFALO LINING & FABRICATING
73 Gillette Ave (14214-2702)
PHONE..................................716 883-6500
Bruce F Meyers, *President*
James Meyers, *Vice Pres*
EMP: 6 **EST:** 1956
SQ FT: 12,000
SALES (est): 695.3K **Privately Held**
SIC: 3069 Molded rubber products

(G-2747)
BUFFALO METAL CASTING CO INC
1875 Elmwood Ave (14207-1997)
PHONE..................................716 874-6211
John Klodzinski, *President*
Justin Klodzinski, *General Mgr*
Jennifer Patterson, *Manager*
Chris Chadbourne, *Supervisor*
EMP: 40
SQ FT: 80,000
SALES (est): 7.6MM **Privately Held**
WEB: www.buffalometalcasting.com
SIC: 3369 Castings, except die-castings, precision

(G-2748)
BUFFALO METAL FABRICATING CORP
50 Wecker St (14215-3897)
PHONE..................................716 892-7800
Nicholas Moroczko, *President*
Alfreda Moroczko, *Corp Secy*
Morgan Moroczko, *Vice Pres*
EMP: 15
SQ FT: 50,000
SALES (est): 2.4MM **Privately Held**
WEB: www.buffalometalfab.com
SIC: 3441 Fabricated structural metal

(G-2749)
BUFFALO METAL FINISHING CO (PA)
135 Dart St (14213-1087)
P.O. Box 1012 (14213-7012)
PHONE..................................716 883-2751
Frank Bonare, *President*
EMP: 8 **EST:** 1941
SQ FT: 11,000
SALES: 500K **Privately Held**
SIC: 3471 3479 Plating of metals or formed products; polishing, metals or formed products; anodizing (plating) of metals or formed products; painting of metal products

(G-2750)
BUFFALO NEWS INC
1 News Plz (14203-2994)
P.O. Box 100 (14240-0100)
PHONE..................................716 849-4401
Stanford Lipsey, *CEO*
Karen Colville, *President*
Warren Colville, *President*
Joan Adamski, *General Mgr*
Jane Mayer, *General Mgr*
▲ **EMP:** 900 **EST:** 2009
SQ FT: 1,000
SALES: 186.5K
SALES (corp-wide): 242.1B **Publicly Held**
WEB: www.berkshirehathaway.com
SIC: 2711 Newspapers, publishing & printing
PA: Berkshire Hathaway Inc.
3555 Farnam St Ste 1140
Omaha NE 68131
402 346-1400

(G-2751)
BUFFALO NEWSPRESS INC
200 Broadway St (14204-1439)
P.O. Box 648 (14240-0648)
PHONE..................................716 852-1600
Warren T Colville, *President*
Mark Korzelius, *President*
Michael A Kibler, *Chairman*
Joan Holzman, *Vice Pres*
Marcus Regoord, *Vice Pres*
EMP: 120
SQ FT: 80,000
SALES (est): 22.8MM **Privately Held**
WEB: www.buffalonewspress.com
SIC: 2759 Newspapers: printing; advertising literature: printing

(G-2752)
BUFFALO SPREE PUBLISHING INC (PA)
1738 Elmwood Ave Ste 103 (14207-2465)
PHONE..................................716 783-9119
Laurence Levite, *CEO*
Chastity Oshei, *Vice Pres*
Theresa Clair, *CFO*
Louis Aguglia, *Accounts Exec*
Wendy Burns, *Accounts Exec*
EMP: 25
SQ FT: 10,000
SALES (est): 2.3MM **Privately Held**
WEB: www.buffalospree.com
SIC: 2721 Magazines: publishing only, not printed on site

(G-2753)
BUFFALO STANDARD PRINTING CORP
Also Called: Am-Pol Eagle
3620 Harlem Rd Ste 5 (14215-2042)
PHONE..................................716 835-9454
Irene Harzewski, *President*
EMP: 10 **EST:** 1958
SALES (est): 709.7K **Privately Held**
SIC: 2711 Commercial printing & newspaper publishing combined; job printing & newspaper publishing combined

(G-2754)
BUFFALO STRUCTURAL STEEL INC
60 Bryant Woods S (14228-3605)
PHONE..................................814 827-1350
Tim Powell, *Branch Mgr*
EMP: 25 **Privately Held**
WEB: www.buffalostructural.com
SIC: 3441 Fabricated structural metal
PA: Buffalo Structural Steel, Inc.
60 Bryant Woods S
Amherst NY 14228

(G-2755)
BUFLOVAK LLC (PA)
750 E Ferry St (14211-1106)
PHONE..................................716 895-2100
Mike Durusky, *Plant Mgr*
Tami McNamara, *Purch Mgr*
Maliek Likely, *Engineer*
Kevin Sonner, *Design Engr*
Dave Bielecki, *Controller*
◆ **EMP:** 28
SQ FT: 225,000
SALES (est): 11.7MM **Privately Held**
WEB: www.buflovatechnologies.com
SIC: 3556 5084 3567 3443 Food products machinery; industrial machinery & equipment; industrial furnaces & ovens; fabricated plate work (boiler shop)

GEOGRAPHIC SECTION
Buffalo - Erie County (G-2779)

(G-2756)
BUSINESS FIRST OF NEW YORK (DH)
465 Main St Ste 100 (14203-1793)
PHONE..................716 854-5822
Jack Connors, *President*
Jeff Wright, *Editor*
Shelley Rohauer, *Advt Staff*
EMP: 44
SQ FT: 10,000
SALES (est): 4.5MM
SALES (corp-wide): 1.4B **Privately Held**
SIC: 2711 Newspapers: publishing only, not printed on site
HQ: American City Business Journals, Inc.
  120 W Morehead St Ste 400
  Charlotte NC 28202
  704 973-1000

(G-2757)
BUXTON MACHINE AND TOOL CO INC
2181 Elmwood Ave (14216-1002)
PHONE..................716 876-2312
James P Hettrick, *President*
Mildred Di Luca, *Admin Sec*
EMP: 12 **EST:** 1984
SQ FT: 12,000
SALES (est): 1.8MM **Privately Held**
SIC: 3599 Machine shop, jobbing & repair

(G-2758)
CALSPAN CORPORATION (HQ)
4455 Genesee St (14225-1955)
P.O. Box 400 (14225)
PHONE..................716 631-6955
Robert Jacobson, *President*
Louis H Knotts, *President*
John Yurtchuk, *Chairman*
Peter Sauer, *COO*
Ruthanne Armstrong, *Senior VP*
◆ **EMP:** 129
SQ FT: 170,200
SALES (est): 44.1MM
SALES (corp-wide): 79.2MM **Privately Held**
WEB: www.windtunnel.com
SIC: 3721 Research & development on aircraft by the manufacturer
PA: Calspan Holdings, Llc
  4455 Genesee St
  Buffalo NY 14225
  716 631-6955

(G-2759)
CALSPAN HOLDINGS LLC (PA)
4455 Genesee St (14225-1955)
P.O. Box 400 (14225)
PHONE..................716 631-6955
Louis Knotts, *CEO*
Peter Sauer, *CFO*
EMP: 12
SQ FT: 170,200
SALES (est): 79.2MM **Privately Held**
SIC: 3721 Research & development on aircraft by the manufacturer

(G-2760)
CAMELLIA GENERAL PROVISION CO
Also Called: Camellia Foods
1333 Genesee St (14211-2227)
PHONE..................716 893-5352
Peter J Cichocki, *Ch of Bd*
Edmund J Cichocki Jr, *President*
Eric Cichocki, *Vice Pres*
Patrick Cichocki, *Vice Pres*
Adam Cichocki, *Opers Staff*
EMP: 46 **EST:** 1937
SQ FT: 40,000
SALES: 10MM **Privately Held**
WEB: www.camelliafoods.com
SIC: 2013 5147 Sausage casings, natural; bologna from purchased meat; smoked meats from purchased meat; meats, fresh; meats, cured or smoked

(G-2761)
CARAUSTAR INDUSTRIES INC
25 Dewberry Ln (14227-2709)
PHONE..................716 874-0393
Lynn Ramsey, *Branch Mgr*
EMP: 8
SALES (corp-wide): 1.7B **Privately Held**
SIC: 2655 Tubes, fiber or paper: made from purchased material
PA: Caraustar Industries, Inc.
  5000 Astell Pwdr Sprng Rd
  Austell GA 30106
  770 948-3101

(G-2762)
CCL LABEL INC
685 Howard St (14206-2210)
P.O. Box 550 (14240-0550)
PHONE..................716 852-2155
Roy Graham, *Plant Mgr*
Joe Langan, *Plant Mgr*
Matt Piejda, *Buyer*
Gale Podsiadlo, *Buyer*
Peter Lowry, *Engineer*
EMP: 150
SQ FT: 25,883
SALES (corp-wide): 3.7B **Privately Held**
WEB: www.avery.com
SIC: 2672 2671 Adhesive papers, labels or tapes: from purchased material; packaging paper & plastics film, coated & laminated
HQ: Ccl Label, Inc.
  161 Worcester Rd Ste 504
  Framingham MA 01701
  508 872-4511

(G-2763)
CENO TECHNOLOGIES INC
1234 Delaware Ave (14209-1430)
PHONE..................716 885-5050
Scott Patrick, *President*
Alan Rowdon, *Vice Pres*
EMP: 5
SALES (est): 661.9K **Privately Held**
SIC: 3531 Construction machinery

(G-2764)
CERTAINTEED CORPORATION
Pipe and Plastic Div
231 Ship Canal Pkwy (14218-1026)
PHONE..................716 827-7560
Bob Kearful, *Branch Mgr*
EMP: 400
SALES (corp-wide): 213.5MM **Privately Held**
WEB: www.certainteed.net
SIC: 3089 Extruded finished plastic products
HQ: Certainteed Corporation
  20 Moores Rd
  Malvern PA 19355
  610 893-5000

(G-2765)
CHOCOLATE DELIVERY SYSTEMS INC (PA)
1800 Elmwood Ave (14207-2410)
PHONE..................716 877-3146
Timothy Thill, *President*
Anne Rosa, *Vice Pres*
▲ **EMP:** 29
SALES (est): 18.4MM **Privately Held**
SIC: 2064 Candy bars, including chocolate covered bars

(G-2766)
CILYOX INC
Also Called: New Rosen Printing
345 Broadway St (14204-1541)
PHONE..................716 853-3809
Michael Cimato, *President*
Bryan Knox, *Vice Pres*
EMP: 10 **EST:** 1963
SQ FT: 43,000
SALES (est): 1.3MM **Privately Held**
SIC: 2752 Commercial printing, offset

(G-2767)
CLEARVIEW SOCIAL INC
77 Goodell St Ste 430 (14203-1257)
PHONE..................801 414-7675
Adrian Dayton, *CEO*
Chris Lafleur, *COO*
Alex Fenner, *Regl Sales Mgr*
Seth Weinert, *Sales Staff*
Desiree Hernandez, *Consultant*
EMP: 5 **EST:** 2013
SALES (est): 188.8K **Privately Held**
SIC: 7372 Business oriented computer software

(G-2768)
CLEVELAND BIOLABS INC (PA)
73 High St (14203-1149)
PHONE..................716 849-6810
Yakov Kogan, *CEO*
Lea Verny, *Ch of Bd*
Olga Krasnova, *Purch Mgr*
Inna Shyshynova, *Research*
Langdon Miller, *Chief Mktg Ofcr*
EMP: 25
SQ FT: 32,000
SALES: 1.9MM **Publicly Held**
WEB: www.cbiolabs.com
SIC: 2834 8731 Pharmaceutical preparations; biological research

(G-2769)
COBEY INC (PA)
1 Ship Canal Pkwy (14218-1024)
PHONE..................716 362-9550
John J Obey, *Ch of Bd*
Robert J Castle, *Vice Pres*
Neil Ackerman, *Project Mgr*
Matt Klinczar, *Project Mgr*
Dean Rozler, *Purch Mgr*
▲ **EMP:** 110
SQ FT: 117,000
SALES (est): 48.1MM **Privately Held**
WEB: www.cobey.com
SIC: 3498 Fabricated pipe & fittings

(G-2770)
COGNIGEN CORPORATION
Also Called: Cognigen Acquisition
1780 Wehrle Dr Ste 110 (14221-7000)
PHONE..................716 633-3463
Ted Grasela, *President*
Jill Fiedler-Kelly, *Vice Pres*
Cindy Walawander, *Vice Pres*
Rebecca Humphrey, *Manager*
Andrew Rokitka, *Manager*
EMP: 65
SALES (est): 8.8MM **Publicly Held**
SIC: 2834 8999 Druggists' preparations (pharmaceuticals); scientific consulting
PA: Simulations Plus, Inc.
  42505 10th St W Ste 103
  Lancaster CA 93534

(G-2771)
COHENS BAKERY INC
Also Called: Al Cohens Famous Rye Bread Bky
1132 Broadway St (14212-1502)
PHONE..................716 892-8149
Mark Didomenico, *President*
John J Blando, *Vice Pres*
Gary East Abrook, *Accountant*
EMP: 45
SQ FT: 25,000
SALES (est): 5.7MM **Privately Held**
SIC: 2045 5149 2051 Doughs & batters: from purchased flour; groceries & related products; bread, cake & related products

(G-2772)
COLAD GROUP LLC
693 Seneca St Fl 5 (14210-1324)
PHONE..................716 961-1776
F Martin Anson, *Mng Member*
J Todd Anson,
EMP: 81
SALES (est): 7.6MM
SALES (corp-wide): 17.8MM **Privately Held**
WEB: www.colad.com
SIC: 2782 2671 2752 2759 Blankbooks & looseleaf binders; packaging paper & plastics, coated & laminated; commercial printing, lithographic; commercial printing; signs & advertising specialties
PA: Bindagraphics, Inc.
  2701 Wilmarco Ave
  Baltimore MD 21223
  410 362-7200

(G-2773)
COMET FLASHER INC (PA)
1 Babcock St (14210-2253)
PHONE..................716 821-9595
James Casey, *President*
Devon Saltsman, *Project Mgr*
Jamie Rybij, *Admin Sec*
EMP: 9
SALES (est): 1.5MM **Privately Held**
SIC: 3669 Traffic signals, electric

(G-2774)
COMMERCIAL PRINT & IMAGING
4778 Main St (14226-4020)
PHONE..................716 597-0100
Kevin Preston, *President*
John A Polvino, *Vice Pres*
EMP: 25
SQ FT: 6,500
SALES (est): 3.4MM **Privately Held**
SIC: 2752 Commercial printing, offset

(G-2775)
COMMITMENT 2000 INC
Also Called: Father Sam's Bakery
105 Msgr Valente Dr (14206-1815)
PHONE..................716 439-1206
William A Sam, *Ch of Bd*
Samuel Sam, *Vice Pres*
Nick Sam, *Plant Mgr*
Samuel A Sam II, *Treasurer*
Glenn Povitz, *VP Sales*
EMP: 40 **EST:** 1977
SQ FT: 40,000
SALES (est): 8.9MM **Privately Held**
WEB: www.fathersams.com
SIC: 2051 Bread, all types (white, wheat, rye, etc): fresh or frozen

(G-2776)
COMPLEMAR PRINT LLC
Also Called: Merrill Press
3034 Genesee St (14225-2641)
PHONE..................716 875-7238
Michael Gotthelf, *President*
Christine Gotthelf, *Vice Pres*
Joan Gotthelf, *Admin Sec*
EMP: 12
SQ FT: 7,000
SALES (est): 1.8MM
SALES (corp-wide): 29.9MM **Privately Held**
WEB: www.quickbizcards.com
SIC: 2752 Commercial printing, offset
PA: Complemar Partners, Inc.
  500 Lee Rd Ste 200
  Rochester NY 14606
  585 647-5800

(G-2777)
CONAX TECHNOLOGIES LLC (PA)
2300 Walden Ave (14225-4765)
PHONE..................716 684-4500
Ed Wilson, *Mfg Mgr*
Gary Barnhard, *Engineer*
Sue Blaszynski, *Human Res Dir*
Michael J Valachos, *Sales Mgr*
Ron Miller, *Sales Engr*
EMP: 126
SQ FT: 83,000
SALES (est): 18.5MM **Privately Held**
WEB: www.conaxbuffalo.com
SIC: 3823 Industrial process control instruments

(G-2778)
CONNIES LAUNDRY
1494 S Park Ave (14220-1075)
PHONE..................716 822-2800
Froncell Clifton, *Owner*
EMP: 5
SQ FT: 1,000
SALES: 500K **Privately Held**
SIC: 2842 Laundry cleaning preparations

(G-2779)
CONTRACT PHRMCTCALS LTD NAGARA
100 Forest Ave (14213-1064)
PHONE..................716 887-3400
David Tyler, *Business Mgr*
John Ross, *Branch Mgr*
EMP: 200 **Privately Held**
WEB: www.cplltd.com
SIC: 2834 Mfg Pharmaceutical Preparations
PA: Contract Pharmaceuticals Limited Canada
  7600 East Danbro Cres
  Mississauga ON L5N 6
  905 821-7600

(G-2780)
COOKIEBAKER LLC
1 Robert Rich Way (14213-1701)
PHONE..................................716 878-8000
Sam Stolbun, *President*
EMP: 6
SALES (est): 498.8K **Privately Held**
SIC: 2099 Food preparations

(G-2781)
COOPER TURBOCOMPRESSOR INC (DH)
3101 Broadway St (14227-1034)
P.O. Box 209 (14225-0209)
PHONE..................................716 896-6600
Jeff Altamari, *Vice Pres*
Frank Athearn, *Vice Pres*
Ron Flecknoe, *Vice Pres*
Ray Plachta, *Vice Pres*
Ed Roper, *Vice Pres*
▲ **EMP:** 485
SQ FT: 273,000
SALES (est): 61MM **Publicly Held**
SIC: 3511 3563 Turbines & turbine generator sets; air & gas compressors

(G-2782)
COSTANZOS BAKERY INC
30 Innsbruck Dr (14227-2736)
PHONE..................................716 656-9093
Jeffrey A Costanzo, *Ch of Bd*
Michael Costanzo, *Vice Pres*
George Martone, *Vice Pres*
Chris Clark, *Opers Mgr*
Mike Costanzo, *Opers Mgr*
EMP: 130 **EST:** 1933
SQ FT: 20,000
SALES (est): 25.4MM **Privately Held**
WEB: www.costanzosbakery.com
SIC: 2051 5461 5149 Bakery: wholesale or wholesale/retail combined; bakeries; bakery products

(G-2783)
CRANDALL FILLING MACHINERY INC
80 Gruner Rd (14227-1007)
PHONE..................................716 897-3486
David Reed, *President*
Heather Wood, *Corp Secy*
Charles Wood, *Sales Staff*
Dian Reed, *Shareholder*
EMP: 6 **EST:** 1906
SQ FT: 7,000
SALES (est): 804.5K **Privately Held**
SIC: 3565 Packaging machinery

(G-2784)
CROSBY COMPANY
183 Pratt St (14204-1519)
PHONE..................................716 852-3522
Peter W Crosby, *CEO*
Jack Spencer, *Buyer*
Art Machuca, *Engineer*
Richard Daeing, *Admin Sec*
EMP: 50
SQ FT: 300,000
SALES (est): 10.5MM **Privately Held**
WEB: www.crosbycompany.com
SIC: 3469 Stamping metal for the trade

(G-2785)
CRYSTAL ROCK LLC
100 Stradtman St Ste 1 (14206-2665)
PHONE..................................716 626-7460
Tom Gawel, *Division Mgr*
EMP: 25
SALES (corp-wide): 2.2B **Privately Held**
SIC: 2086 Water, pasteurized: packaged in cans, bottles, etc.
HQ: Crystal Rock Llc
1050 Buckingham St
Watertown CT 06795

(G-2786)
CS BUSINESS SYSTEMS INC (PA)
1236 Main St (14209-2197)
PHONE..................................716 886-6521
Michael I Choo, *Ch of Bd*
Elaine Sigismondi, *Human Resources*
Mike Mooney, *Accounts Mgr*
Kim Cooper, *Sales Staff*
Will Blakeslee, *Sales Executive*
▲ **EMP:** 25
SQ FT: 35,000
SALES (est): 8.8MM **Privately Held**
WEB: www.csbusiness.com
SIC: 3678 3357 5045 Electronic connectors; nonferrous wiredrawing & insulating; computer peripheral equipment

(G-2787)
CURTIS L MACLEAN L C (HQ)
Also Called: Maclean Curtis
50 Thielman Dr (14206-2364)
PHONE..................................716 898-7800
Duncan Mac Lean, *CEO*
Paul Hojnacki, *President*
Joseph Manzella, *General Mgr*
Robert Craft, *Maint Spvr*
Zachary Dailey, *Engineer*
EMP: 300
SALES (est): 48.9MM
SALES (corp-wide): 1.3B **Privately Held**
SIC: 3714 Motor vehicle engines & parts
PA: Mac Lean-Fogg Company
1000 Allanson Rd
Mundelein IL 60060
847 566-0010

(G-2788)
CURTIS SCREW CO INC
50 Thielman Dr (14206-2364)
PHONE..................................716 898-7800
John Hoskins, *Chairman*
EMP: 36
SALES (est): 7.9MM **Privately Held**
SIC: 3451 Screw machine products

(G-2789)
CUSTOM CANVAS MANUFACTURING CO
775 Seneca St (14210-1487)
PHONE..................................716 852-6372
Anthony L Guido Jr, *President*
Phyllis Guido, *Vice Pres*
William Sal Guido, *Prdtn Mgr*
▲ **EMP:** 28 **EST:** 1961
SQ FT: 32,000
SALES (est): 3.2MM **Privately Held**
SIC: 2394 7699 Canvas covers & drop cloths; liners & covers, fabric: made from purchased materials; tarpaulins, fabric: made from purchased materials; tents: made from purchased materials; tent repair shop

(G-2790)
D & G WELDING INC
249 Hertel Ave (14207-2153)
PHONE..................................716 873-3088
Toll Free:...........................888 -
David M Black, *President*
EMP: 5
SQ FT: 2,300
SALES (est): 566.6K **Privately Held**
SIC: 7692 3498 Welding repair; pipe fittings, fabricated from purchased pipe

(G-2791)
D-C THEATRICKS
747 Main St (14203-1321)
PHONE..................................716 847-0180
David Dejac, *Partner*
Douglas Caskey, *Partner*
EMP: 5
SQ FT: 4,500
SALES (est): 430K **Privately Held**
WEB: www.costume.com
SIC: 2389 5699 5136 5137 Theatrical costumes; costumes, masquerade or theatrical; men's & boys' clothing; women's & children's clothing

(G-2792)
DAN TRENT COMPANY INC
Also Called: D & D Printing
1728 Clinton St (14206-3151)
PHONE..................................716 822-1422
Daniel Trent, *President*
EMP: 5 **EST:** 1970
SQ FT: 5,610
SALES (est): 1MM **Privately Held**
SIC: 2752 Commercial printing, offset

(G-2793)
DARLING INGREDIENTS INC
2000 William St (14206-2415)
PHONE..................................716 895-0655
Robert Fader, *Manager*
EMP: 19
SALES (est): 8.8MM **Privately Held**
SALES (corp-wide): 3.6B **Publicly Held**
SIC: 2077 Animal & marine fats & oils
PA: Darling Ingredients Inc.
251 Oconnor Ridge Blvd
Irving TX 75038
972 717-0300

(G-2794)
DAVIS
283 Minnesota Ave (14215-1013)
PHONE..................................716 833-4678
Arthur L Davis, *Principal*
EMP: 9
SALES (est): 668.9K **Privately Held**
SIC: 2389 Clergymen's vestments

(G-2795)
DECK BROS INC
222 Chicago St (14204-2249)
PHONE..................................716 852-0262
Ronald P Kellner, *President*
Karl J Kellner, *Vice Pres*
Doug Deschamps, *Sales Staff*
EMP: 25 **EST:** 1952
SQ FT: 45,000
SALES (est): 3MM **Privately Held**
SIC: 3599 7692 Machine shop, jobbing & repair; welding repair

(G-2796)
DELAWARE VALLEY FORGE CO INC
247 Rano St (14207-2149)
PHONE..................................716 447-9140
Margaret Duggan, *President*
Michael Duggan, *Vice Pres*
William Simon Jr, *Vice Pres*
EMP: 5
SALES (est): 497.6K **Privately Held**
SIC: 3462 Iron & steel forgings

(G-2797)
DELAWARE VALLEY FORGE INC
241 Rano St (14207-2149)
P.O. Box 220, Kenmore (14217-0220)
PHONE..................................716 447-9140
Margaret Duggan, *President*
EMP: 20
SALES (est): 1.7MM **Privately Held**
SIC: 3462 Iron & steel forgings

(G-2798)
DENNY MACHINE CO INC
20 Norris St (14207-2207)
PHONE..................................716 873-6865
Leonard Deni, *President*
Frank Deni, *Vice Pres*
Joseph Deni, *Vice Pres*
Jennie Deni, *Admin Sec*
EMP: 45 **EST:** 1957
SQ FT: 10,000
SALES (est): 7.6MM **Privately Held**
WEB: www.deni.com
SIC: 3599 Machine shop, jobbing & repair

(G-2799)
DERRICK CORPORATION (PA)
Also Called: Derrick Equipment
590 Duke Rd (14225-5102)
PHONE..................................716 683-9010
James W Derrick, *Ch of Bd*
William W Derrick, *President*
Alan Bishop, *Division Mgr*
John J Bakula, *Exec VP*
John Bakula, *Exec VP*
◆ **EMP:** 200 **EST:** 1951
SQ FT: 210,000
SALES (est): 185.2MM **Privately Held**
WEB: www.derrickcorp.com
SIC: 3533 Oil & gas field machinery

(G-2800)
DESIGNERS FOLDING BOX CORP
84 Tennessee St (14204-2797)
PHONE..................................716 853-5141
Jeffrey P Winney, *President*
Brian Webb, *Opers Mgr*
Jeff Winney, *Pub Rel Mgr*
James Winney, *Treasurer*
Teri McAndrews, *Admin Sec*
EMP: 25 **EST:** 1950
SQ FT: 38,000
SALES (est): 2.5MM **Privately Held**
WEB: www.designersfoldingbox.com
SIC: 2657 Folding paperboard boxes

(G-2801)
DILESE INTERNATIONAL INC
Also Called: Choco-Logo
141 Broadway St (14203-1629)
PHONE..................................716 855-3500
Daniel Johnson, *President*
EMP: 10
SQ FT: 10,000
SALES (est): 942.2K **Privately Held**
WEB: www.chocologo.com
SIC: 2066 2064 Chocolate; candy & other confectionery products

(G-2802)
DKM SALES LLC
Also Called: Dkm Ad Art
1352 Genesee St (14211-2296)
PHONE..................................716 893-7777
Ken Krzeminski, *Partner*
Scott Tanyi, *Plant Mgr*
Jason Ackerman, *Opers Staff*
Jan Gannon, *Sales Staff*
Karen McKnight, *Sales Staff*
EMP: 40
SQ FT: 65,000
SALES (est): 5.2MM **Privately Held**
WEB: www.dkm-sales.com
SIC: 2759 3993 2399 Screen printing; advertising novelties; banners, made from fabric

(G-2803)
DORIC VAULT OF WNY INC
73 Gilbert St (14206-2948)
PHONE..................................716 828-1776
Dennis Schultz, *President*
Carol Schultz, *Vice Pres*
EMP: 12
SQ FT: 27,000
SALES (est): 1MM **Privately Held**
SIC: 3272 Burial vaults, concrete or precast terrazzo

(G-2804)
DUALL FINISHING INC
53 Hopkins St (14220-2130)
PHONE..................................716 827-1707
Richard Duman, *President*
EMP: 8
SALES (est): 325K **Privately Held**
SIC: 3549 Metalworking machinery

(G-2805)
DURO-SHED INC (PA)
721 Center Rd (14224-2181)
PHONE..................................585 344-0800
Dave Delagrange, *President*
EMP: 33
SQ FT: 6,000
SALES (est): 2.6MM **Privately Held**
WEB: www.duro-shed.com
SIC: 2452 Prefabricated wood buildings

(G-2806)
E B ATLAS STEEL CORP
120 Tonawanda St (14207-3117)
PHONE..................................716 876-0900
Brian Hogle, *President*
EMP: 16
SQ FT: 7,000
SALES (est): 3.5MM **Privately Held**
SIC: 3441 Fabricated structural metal

(G-2807)
E I DU PONT DE NEMOURS & CO
Also Called: Dupont
3115 River Rd (14207-1059)
P.O. Box 88 (14207-0088)
PHONE..................................716 876-4420
Betty Czyz, *Area Mgr*
Theresa Yates, *Purch Mgr*
Candie Strom, *Buyer*
Charles Desjardins, *Engineer*
Russell Thomas, *Engineer*
EMP: 50
SALES (corp-wide): 62.4B **Publicly Held**
WEB: www.dupont.com
SIC: 2823 2253 2821 Cellulosic man-made fibers; knit outerwear mills; plastics materials & resins

GEOGRAPHIC SECTION

Buffalo - Erie County (G-2836)

HQ: E. I. Du Pont De Nemours And Company
974 Centre Rd
Wilmington DE 19805
302 774-1000

(G-2808)
EAC HOLDINGS OF NY CORP
701 Willet Rd (14218-3756)
PHONE..................................716 822-2500
Kristine Ramming, *President*
Betty Ramming, *Chairman*
James Kintzel, *Corp Secy*
▼ **EMP:** 73
SQ FT: 70,000
SALES (est): 3MM **Privately Held**
WEB: www.electroabrasives.com
SIC: 3291 Abrasive grains

(G-2809)
EAST CAST ORTHTICS PROSTHETICS
505 Delaware Ave (14202-1309)
PHONE..................................716 856-5192
Vincent Benenati, *President*
Larry Benenati, *Vice Pres*
EMP: 12
SALES (est): 1.1MM **Privately Held**
SIC: 3842 Orthopedic appliances

(G-2810)
EAST COAST TOOL & MFG
1 Alliance Dr (14218-2529)
PHONE..................................716 826-5183
Richard R Stjohn, *President*
Robert Dewey, *Treasurer*
Bernie Pruchniewski, *Admin Sec*
Michael Bauer, *Administration*
Jeanine St John, *Administration*
EMP: 6
SQ FT: 5,000
SALES (est): 984K **Privately Held**
SIC: 3541 Grinding machines, metalworking

(G-2811)
EASTERN NIAGRA RADIOLOGY
899 Main St (14203-1109)
PHONE..................................716 882-6544
Joseph Serghany MD, *Partner*
Cynithia Selmensburger, *Admin Sec*
EMP: 22
SALES: 300K **Privately Held**
SIC: 3829 Medical diagnostic systems, nuclear

(G-2812)
EASTMAN MACHINE COMPANY
779 Washington St (14203-1396)
PHONE..................................716 856-2200
Robert L Stevenson, *CEO*
Marla Coniglio, *Exec VP*
Wade Stevenson, *Vice Pres*
Michael Herman, *Opers Mgr*
Kristina Ettinger, *Export Mgr*
◆ **EMP:** 110 **EST:** 1888
SQ FT: 130,000
SALES (est): 36.3MM **Privately Held**
WEB: www.eastmancuts.com
SIC: 3552 Textile machinery

(G-2813)
EDWIN J MCKENICA & SONS INC
Also Called: E.J. McKenica & Sons
1200 Clinton St (14206-2824)
PHONE..................................716 823-4646
Trent McKenica, *CEO*
Richard E McKenica, *Ch of Bd*
Glenn Milbrand, *President*
Bob Brigham, *General Mgr*
Robert Brigham, *General Mgr*
▲ **EMP:** 15 **EST:** 1974
SQ FT: 28,000
SALES (est): 3.6MM **Privately Held**
SIC: 3599 Machine shop, jobbing & repair

(G-2814)
ELECTRO ABRASIVES LLC
701 Willet Rd (14218-3798)
PHONE..................................716 822-2500
Kristine L Ramming, *President*
Brian Hauer, *Manager*
Jim Pierowicz, *Manager*
Kathy Robinson, *Manager*
◆ **EMP:** 20

SALES (est): 3.3MM **Privately Held**
SIC: 3291 Abrasive products

(G-2815)
ELWOOD SPECIALTY PRODUCTS INC
2180 Elmwood Ave (14216-1003)
PHONE..................................716 877-6622
Peter McGennis Jr, *President*
Bill Easton, *Mfg Staff*
EMP: 13
SQ FT: 20,000
SALES (est): 1.5MM **Privately Held**
WEB: www.coolsac.com
SIC: 3842 Clothing, fire resistant & protective

(G-2816)
EM-KAY MOLDS INC
398 Ludington St (14206-1446)
PHONE..................................716 895-6180
Richard Boehler, *President*
C F Boehler, *Vice Pres*
EMP: 6
SQ FT: 24,000
SALES: 400K **Privately Held**
SIC: 3089 Injection molding of plastics; molding primary plastic

(G-2817)
EMCOM INDUSTRIES INC
235 Genesee St (14204-1456)
PHONE..................................716 852-3711
Daniel A Higgins, *President*
EMP: 5
SQ FT: 40,000
SALES: 290K **Privately Held**
SIC: 3322 3599 Malleable iron foundries; machine shop, jobbing & repair

(G-2818)
EMPIRE INNOVATION GROUP LLC
410 Main St Ste 5 (14202-3735)
PHONE..................................716 852-5000
Nicolas Knab,
EMP: 10
SALES (est): 1MM **Privately Held**
SIC: 7372 Application computer software

(G-2819)
ENGINEERED COMPOSITES INC
Also Called: Armor Tile
55 Roberts Ave (14206-3119)
PHONE..................................716 362-0295
Daniel Bolubash, *President*
Roman Bolubash, *Vice Pres*
Jeff Hansen, *Prdtn Mgr*
David Holmes, *Manager*
▲ **EMP:** 30
SQ FT: 40,000
SALES (est): 11.8MM **Privately Held**
WEB: www.armortile.com
SIC: 3089 Floor coverings, plastic; injection molding of plastics

(G-2820)
ENRG INC
155 Chandler St 5 (14207-2405)
PHONE..................................716 873-2939
John Olenick, *President*
Kevin Keefe, *Engineer*
Tim Curry, *Manager*
Viswanathan Venkateswaran, *Manager*
EMP: 15
SQ FT: 13,000
SALES: 1.5MM **Privately Held**
WEB: www.enrg-inc.com
SIC: 3299 3674 Ceramic fiber; solid state electronic devices

(G-2821)
ENTERPRISE FOLDING BOX CO INC
75 Isabelle St (14207-1739)
PHONE..................................716 876-6421
Andrew Baranyi, *CEO*
Lynette Ovitt, *President*
Aj Baranyi, *Office Mgr*
Lynette Lodestro, *Branch Mgr*
EMP: 24
SQ FT: 100,000
SALES (est): 8.9MM **Privately Held**
WEB: www.enterprisebox.com
SIC: 2631 Folding boxboard

(G-2822)
ESM GROUP INC
300 Corporate Pkwy 118n (14226-1258)
P.O. Box 128, Valencia PA (14059-0128)
PHONE..................................724 265-1766
Charles Wright, *President*
EMP: 6
SALES (corp-wide): 241.5MM **Privately Held**
WEB: www.esmgroup.com
SIC: 2819 Industrial inorganic chemicals
HQ: Esm Group Inc.
300 Corporate Pkwy 118n
Amherst NY 14226
716 446-8914

(G-2823)
F X GRAPHIX INC
3043 Delaware Ave (14217-2059)
PHONE..................................716 871-1511
Thomas Giambra, *Partner*
Pamela Gittins, *Partner*
EMP: 6
SQ FT: 1,600
SALES (est): 686.4K **Privately Held**
WEB: www.fxgraphix.com
SIC: 2395 7336 Embroidery products, except schiffli machine; commercial art & graphic design

(G-2824)
FAMOUS DOUGHNUTS INC
3043 Main St (14214-1333)
PHONE..................................716 834-6356
Richard Roehm Sr, *President*
EMP: 8
SQ FT: 6,000
SALES (est): 791.7K **Privately Held**
SIC: 2051 Doughnuts, except frozen

(G-2825)
FARTHING PRESS INC
260 Oak St (14203-1676)
PHONE..................................716 852-4674
David W Snyder, *President*
Carolyn Snyder, *Vice Pres*
EMP: 9 **EST:** 1908
SQ FT: 6,800
SALES (est): 1.1MM **Privately Held**
SIC: 2752 2759 Commercial printing, offset; letterpress & screen printing; letterpress printing; screen printing

(G-2826)
FIBRON PRODUCTS INC
Also Called: Real Wood Tiles
170 Florida St (14208-1250)
PHONE..................................716 886-2378
Robert C Oshei Jr, *President*
EMP: 50 **EST:** 1949
SQ FT: 65,000
SALES (est): 3.5MM **Privately Held**
SIC: 2499 2426 Handles, wood; hardwood dimension & flooring mills

(G-2827)
FLASHFLO MANUFACTURING INC
88 Hopkins St (14220-2131)
PHONE..................................716 826-9500
Lawrence Speiser, *President*
EMP: 10
SALES (est): 1.7MM **Privately Held**
SIC: 3545 Machine tool accessories

(G-2828)
FLETCHER ENTERPRISES INC
Also Called: Fastsigns
4913 Genesee St (14225-2411)
PHONE..................................716 837-7446
Mary Ellen Fletcher, *President*
EMP: 5
SALES (est): 508.9K **Privately Held**
SIC: 3993 Signs & advertising specialties

(G-2829)
FLEXIBLE LIFELINE SYSTEMS INC
100 Stradtman St (14206-2666)
PHONE..................................716 896-4949
Murry Mike Mumau, *President*
Austin Townsend, *General Mgr*
Megan Quinn, *Vice Pres*
EMP: 44 **EST:** 2017

SALES (est): 1.7MM **Privately Held**
SIC: 3842 Surgical appliances & supplies

(G-2830)
FLEXLUME SIGN CORPORATION
1464 Main St (14209-1780)
P.O. Box 804 (14209-0804)
PHONE..................................716 884-2020
Alfred P Rowell Sr, *CEO*
Alfred P Rowell Jr, *President*
Shirley J Rowell, *Corp Secy*
Michelle Holland, *Administration*
EMP: 9
SQ FT: 22,000
SALES (est): 1.2MM **Privately Held**
WEB: www.flexlume.com
SIC: 3993 1799 Electric signs; sign installation & maintenance

(G-2831)
FORSYTH INDUSTRIES INC
1195 Colvin Blvd (14223-1909)
PHONE..................................716 652-1070
Joseph Takats III, *President*
EMP: 29 **EST:** 1890
SQ FT: 50,000
SALES (est): 4.2MM **Privately Held**
SIC: 3469 3315 Mfg Metal Stampings Mfg Steel Wire/Related Products

(G-2832)
FPPF CHEMICAL CO INC (PA)
117 W Tupper St Ste 1 (14201-2171)
PHONE..................................716 856-9607
Christopher Lory, *President*
Jim Thurston, *Buyer*
Mark Jacobs, *Sales Staff*
EMP: 8
SQ FT: 4,000
SALES (est): 1.4MM **Privately Held**
WEB: www.fppf.com
SIC: 2911 2899 Fuel additives; antifreeze compounds

(G-2833)
FRANK WARDYNSKI & SONS INC
336 Peckham St (14206-1717)
PHONE..................................716 854-6083
Raymond F Wardynski, *Ch of Bd*
Michael Wardynski, *Manager*
EMP: 40
SQ FT: 24,000
SALES (est): 6.8MM **Privately Held**
WEB: www.wardynski.com
SIC: 2013 5149 2011 Sausage casings, natural; canned goods: fruit, vegetables, seafood, meats, etc.; meat packing plants

(G-2834)
FREDERICK MACHINE REPAIR INC
405 Ludington St (14206-1445)
PHONE..................................716 332-0104
Alan Frederick, *President*
EMP: 8 **EST:** 1945
SQ FT: 11,000
SALES (est): 1.3MM **Privately Held**
SIC: 3599 Machine shop, jobbing & repair

(G-2835)
FRONTIER HT-DIP GLVANIZING INC
1740 Elmwood Ave (14207-2410)
P.O. Box 199 (14207-0199)
PHONE..................................716 875-2091
Lewis G Pierce, *President*
Lewis Pierce, *Sales Executive*
▲ **EMP:** 18
SQ FT: 65,000
SALES (est): 3.2MM **Privately Held**
WEB: www.frontierhdgalvanizing.com
SIC: 3479 Galvanizing of iron, steel or endformed products

(G-2836)
FRONTIER HYDRAULICS CORP
1738 Elmwood Ave Ste 2 (14207-2465)
PHONE..................................716 694-2070
Steve M Jackson, *President*
EMP: 12
SQ FT: 10,000
SALES: 750K **Privately Held**
WEB: www.frontierhydraulics.com
SIC: 3511 Hydraulic turbines

Buffalo - Erie County (G-2837)

(G-2837)
FULL CIRCLE STUDIOS LLC
710 Main St (14202-1915)
PHONE..................716 875-7740
Kevin Crosby, *General Mgr*
Cole Bielecki, *Editor*
Jim Phillips, *Founder*
Terry Fisher,
EMP: 7
SALES (est): 864.1K **Privately Held**
WEB: www.fullcirclestudios.com
SIC: 3699 Electronic training devices

(G-2838)
GALLAGHER PRINTING INC
Also Called: Rocket Communications
2518 Delaware Ave (14216-1702)
PHONE..................716 873-2434
David Gallagher, *President*
Dean Gallagher, *Corp Secy*
Daryl Gallagher, *Vice Pres*
Dennis Gallagher, *Treasurer*
EMP: 30 EST: 1969
SQ FT: 30,000
SALES (est): 3.6MM **Privately Held**
WEB: www.gallagherprinting.com
SIC: 2752 2711 6513 Commercial printing, offset; newspapers; apartment building operators

(G-2839)
GALLE & ZINTER INC
Also Called: Galle Mamorial
3405 Harlem Rd (14225-2019)
PHONE..................716 833-4212
Paul Zinter, *President*
Rick Zinter, *Principal*
Tina Zinter, *Admin Sec*
EMP: 7
SQ FT: 2,198
SALES (est): 534.7K **Privately Held**
SIC: 3272 Monuments & grave markers, except terrazo

(G-2840)
GARLAND TECHNOLOGY LLC (PA)
199 Delaware Ave (14202-2102)
P.O. Box 711 (14205-0711)
PHONE..................716 242-8500
Christopher Bihary, *CEO*
Erica Tank, *President*
George Bouchard, *Engineer*
Renee Straney, *Engineer*
Pam Makofski, *Finance*
EMP: 20
SALES (est): 4.5MM **Privately Held**
SIC: 3572 Computer storage devices

(G-2841)
GAS TCHNLOGY ENRGY CNCEPTS LLC
Also Called: G Tech Natureul Gasses Systems
201 Dutton Ave (14211-1011)
PHONE..................716 831-9695
David Reichard, *Mng Member*
Sam Ho, *Business Dir*
William Hess,
EMP: 8
SQ FT: 5,000
SALES (est): 1.3MM **Privately Held**
SIC: 3563 Air & gas compressors

(G-2842)
GAY SHEET METAL DIES INC
301 Hinman Ave (14216-1093)
PHONE..................716 877-0208
Dolores Dewey, *President*
EMP: 8 EST: 1936
SQ FT: 6,500
SALES (est): 1.3MM **Privately Held**
SIC: 3469 3544 Stamping metal for the trade; die sets for metal stamping (presses)

(G-2843)
GEAR MOTIONS INCORPORATED
Also Called: Oliver Gear
1120 Niagara St (14213-1714)
PHONE..................716 885-1080
Mike Barron, *Branch Mgr*
EMP: 22
SALES (corp-wide): 18MM **Privately Held**
WEB: www.gearmotions.com
SIC: 3462 Gears, forged steel
PA: Gear Motions Incorporated
1750 Milton Ave
Syracuse NY 13209
315 488-0100

(G-2844)
GEMTROL INC
1800 Broadway St Bldg 1c (14212-2001)
PHONE..................716 894-0716
Jeffrey Dombek, *President*
EMP: 8
SQ FT: 4,400
SALES (est): 1.4MM **Privately Held**
WEB: www.gemtrol.com
SIC: 3625 Electric controls & control accessories, industrial

(G-2845)
GENERAL MILLS INC
54 S Michigan Ave (14203-3086)
PHONE..................716 856-6060
Allen Brown, *Director*
EMP: 50
SALES (corp-wide): 15.7B **Publicly Held**
WEB: www.generalmills.com
SIC: 2041 Flour: blended, prepared or self-rising; flour mixes
PA: General Mills, Inc.
1 General Mills Blvd
Minneapolis MN 55426
763 764-7600

(G-2846)
GENERAL MILLS INC
315 Ship Canal Pkwy (14218-1018)
PHONE..................716 856-6060
EMP: 58
SALES (corp-wide): 15.7B **Publicly Held**
SIC: 2043 Wheat flakes: prepared as cereal breakfast food
PA: General Mills, Inc.
1 General Mills Blvd
Minneapolis MN 55426
763 764-7600

(G-2847)
GENERAL MOTORS LLC
2995 River Rd 2 (14207-1059)
PHONE..................716 879-5000
Joseph Felong, *Superintendent*
Kevin Hamilton, *VP Opers*
Mark Gramza, *Opers Mgr*
Lewis Campbell, *Prdtn Mgr*
Darla Flatt, *Mfg Mgr*
EMP: 900 **Publicly Held**
SIC: 3714 Motor vehicle parts & accessories
HQ: General Motors Llc
300 Renaissance Ctr L1
Detroit MI 48243

(G-2848)
GENESEE RESERVE BUFFALO LLC
300 Bailey Ave (14210-2211)
P.O. Box 20619, Rochester (14602-0619)
PHONE..................716 824-3116
Bob Victor,
EMP: 30
SALES (est): 2.5MM **Privately Held**
SIC: 2491 Structural lumber & timber, treated wood

(G-2849)
GIBRALTAR INDUSTRIES INC (PA)
3556 Lake Shore Rd # 100 (14219-1400)
P.O. Box 2028 (14219-0228)
PHONE..................716 826-6500
William P Montague, *Ch of Bd*
Frank G Heard, *President*
Paul Soucier, *President*
Bill Wark, *General Mgr*
Timothy Heasley, *Principal*
◆ EMP: 82
SALES: 986.9MM **Publicly Held**
WEB: www.gibraltar1.com
SIC: 3499 3316 3441 3398 Strapping, metal; cold finishing of steel shapes; strip steel, cold-rolled: from purchased hot-rolled; sheet, steel, cold-rolled: from purchased hot-rolled; bars, steel, cold finished, from purchased hot-rolled; fabricated structural metal; metal heat treating

(G-2850)
GLAXOSMITHKLINE LLC
17 Mahogany Dr (14221-2420)
PHONE..................716 913-5679
EMP: 26
SALES (corp-wide): 39.8B **Privately Held**
SIC: 2834 Pharmaceutical preparations
HQ: Glaxosmithkline Llc
5 Crescent Dr
Philadelphia PA 19112
215 751-4000

(G-2851)
GLOBALQUEST SOLUTIONS INC
2813 Wehrle Dr Ste 3 (14221-7384)
PHONE..................716 601-3524
Aaron Fox, *President*
Chris Lorenz, *Sales Executive*
Michael Morlock, *CTO*
EMP: 12
SQ FT: 2,000
SALES (est): 3.4MM **Privately Held**
WEB: www.globalquestinc.com
SIC: 7372 Business oriented computer software

(G-2852)
GOERGEN-MACKWIRTH CO INC
765 Hertel Ave (14207-1992)
P.O. Box 750 (14207-0750)
PHONE..................716 874-4800
Jeffrey Mertz, *President*
Patricia Mertz, *Admin Sec*
Nicole Watson, *Administration*
EMP: 45
SQ FT: 24,000
SALES (est): 11.1MM **Privately Held**
WEB: www.goergenmackwirth.com
SIC: 3444 1761 Sheet metalwork; sheet metalwork

(G-2853)
GRAPHIC CNTRLS ACQISITION CORP (DH)
400 Exchange St (14204-2064)
P.O. Box 1271 (14240-1271)
PHONE..................716 853-7500
Sam Heleba, *CEO*
Gina Lapiante, *Vice Pres*
John Belotti, *VP Mfg*
Dan Fallin, *VP Mfg*
Wayne Harper, *Opers Dir*
▲ EMP: 275
SQ FT: 235,000
SALES (est): 136.6MM
SALES (corp-wide): 1.4B **Privately Held**
WEB: www.graphiccontrols.com
SIC: 2752 2679 Tag, ticket & schedule printing: lithographic; paper products, converted
HQ: Graphic Controls Holdings, Inc.
400 Exchange St
Buffalo NY 14204
716 853-7500

(G-2854)
GRAPHIC CONTROLS HOLDINGS INC (HQ)
400 Exchange St (14204-2064)
P.O. Box 1271 (14240-1271)
PHONE..................716 853-7500
Samuel Heleba, *CEO*
Ryokei Tsuryta, *Ch of Bd*
Thomas Reardon, *Treasurer*
Karl Shoop, *Info Tech Mgr*
EMP: 12
SQ FT: 235,000
SALES: 138MM
SALES (corp-wide): 1.4B **Privately Held**
SIC: 2752 6719 2679 Tag, ticket & schedule printing: lithographic; investment holding companies, except banks; paper products, converted

PA: Nissha Co.,Ltd.
3, Hanaicho, Mibu, Nakagyo-Ku
Kyoto KYO 604-8
758 118-111

(G-2855)
GREAT LAKES ORTHPD LABS INC
1031 Main St (14203-1014)
PHONE..................716 878-7307
Blanche Daley, *Manager*
EMP: 5 **Privately Held**
SIC: 3842 Limbs, artificial; orthopedic appliances; braces, orthopedic
PA: Great Lakes Orthopedic Labs Inc.
1031 Main St
Buffalo NY 14203

(G-2856)
GREAT LAKES PLASTICS CO INC
2371 Broadway St (14212-2313)
PHONE..................716 896-3100
Thomas Barzycki, *CEO*
Curtis Rice, *President*
Catherine Barzycki, *Vice Pres*
Amy Nelson, *Treasurer*
Donna Michalski, *Manager*
EMP: 28 EST: 1946
SQ FT: 28,000
SALES (est): 4.9MM **Privately Held**
WEB: www.greatlakesplastic.com
SIC: 3082 3081 Rods, unsupported plastic; unsupported plastics film & sheet

(G-2857)
GREAT LAKES PRESSED STEEL CORP
1400 Niagara St (14213-1302)
PHONE..................716 885-4037
Timothy O Nichols, *President*
Maryjane Nichols, *Vice Pres*
Mary Jane Nichols, *Admin Sec*
EMP: 20
SQ FT: 25,000
SALES (est): 3.6MM **Privately Held**
WEB: www.glpscorp.com
SIC: 3469 3544 Stamping metal for the trade; dies, steel rule

(G-2858)
GREEN APPLE COURAGE INC
Also Called: BP Magazine
374 Delaware Ave Ste 240 (14202-1623)
P.O. Box 59 (14205-0059)
PHONE..................716 614-4673
Joanne Doan, *Ch of Bd*
EMP: 3 EST: 2004
SALES: 1.3MM **Privately Held**
SIC: 2721 Magazines: publishing & printing

(G-2859)
GTI AMERICA INC
1207 Del Ave Unit 214 (14209)
PHONE..................716 332-6151
Brian Grundy, *President*
EMP: 9
SQ FT: 300
SALES (est): 421K **Privately Held**
SIC: 3663 1799 Antennas, transmitting & communications; television antennas (transmitting) & ground equipment; antenna installation

(G-2860)
HABASIT AMERICA INC
1400 Clinton St (14206-2919)
PHONE..................716 824-8484
Tim Eldridge, *Branch Mgr*
Mike Berdysiak, *Info Tech Mgr*
John Berdysiak, *MIS Staff*
EMP: 75
SQ FT: 50,000
SALES (corp-wide): 708MM **Privately Held**
WEB: www.habasit.com
SIC: 3496 3052 Conveyor belts; rubber & plastics hose & beltings
HQ: Habasit America, Inc.
805 Satellite Blvd Nw
Suwanee GA 30024
678 288-3600

GEOGRAPHIC SECTION

Buffalo - Erie County (G-2888)

(G-2861)
HADLEY EXHIBITS INC (PA)
1700 Elmwood Ave (14207-2408)
PHONE.................................716 874-3666
Theodore K Johnson, *President*
Ralph Allen, *Vice Pres*
Robert Riehle, *Project Mgr*
Greg Kerl, *Prdtn Mgr*
Lynn Olson, *CFO*
EMP: 87
SQ FT: 180,000
SALES (est): 13.1MM **Privately Held**
WEB: www.hadleyexhibits.com
SIC: 3993 Displays & cutouts, window & lobby

(G-2862)
HAGNER INDUSTRIES INC
95 Botsford Pl (14216-2601)
PHONE.................................716 873-5720
Peter Hagner, *President*
EMP: 8
SQ FT: 3,800
SALES (est): 400K **Privately Held**
SIC: 3599 1799 Machine shop, jobbing & repair; welding on site

(G-2863)
HAKSON SAFETY WEARS INC
111 Colgate Ave (14220)
PHONE.................................613 667-3015
Muhamad Aslam, *President*
EMP: 10
SQ FT: 3,000
SALES: 500K **Privately Held**
SIC: 3842 Clothing, fire resistant & protective

(G-2864)
HANKIN BROTHERS CAP CO
Also Called: Han-Kraft Uniform Headwear
1910 Genesee St (14211-1818)
PHONE.................................716 892-8840
Benjamin Hankin, *Partner*
Richard Hankin, *Partner*
EMP: 10
SQ FT: 2,800
SALES (est): 1MM **Privately Held**
SIC: 2353 Uniform hats & caps

(G-2865)
HARD MANUFACTURING CO INC
230 Grider St (14215-3797)
PHONE.................................716 893-1800
Marjorie Bryem, *CEO*
◆ **EMP:** 45
SQ FT: 180,000
SALES: 7MM **Privately Held**
WEB: www.hardmfg.com
SIC: 2514 2599 2515 2511 Cribs: metal; hospital beds; mattresses & bedsprings; wood household furniture

(G-2866)
HARMAC MEDICAL PRODUCTS INC (PA)
2201 Bailey Ave (14211-1797)
PHONE.................................716 897-4500
John F Somers, *President*
David Rozanski, *Buyer*
Lou Ann Digiacomo, *Manager*
▲ **EMP:** 400
SQ FT: 80,000
SALES (est): 104.9MM **Privately Held**
WEB: www.harmac.com
SIC: 3841 Surgical & medical instruments

(G-2867)
HAROLD WOOD CO INC
329 Hinman Ave (14216-1096)
PHONE.................................716 873-1535
Richard L Wood, *President*
Jane Wood, *Admin Sec*
EMP: 5 **EST:** 1927
SQ FT: 3,200
SALES (est): 607.9K **Privately Held**
WEB: www.haroldwood.com
SIC: 3479 Name plates: engraved, etched, etc.

(G-2868)
HARPER INTERNATIONAL CORP
4455 Genesee St Ste 123 (14225-1965)
PHONE.................................716 276-9900
Tom Kittell, *CEO*
Charles Miller, *President*
Elizabeth Wruck, *Purchasing*
James Fry, *Engineer*
Amrik Malhi, *Engineer*
◆ **EMP:** 100 **EST:** 1988
SALES: 50MM **Privately Held**
WEB: www.harperintl.com
SIC: 3567 Industrial furnaces & ovens

(G-2869)
HEALTH MATTERS AMERICA INC
2501 Broadway St Ste 2 (14227-1054)
P.O. Box 1482 (14225-8482)
PHONE.................................716 235-8772
Jerry Zeifman, *President*
▲ **EMP:** 14
SALES (est): 1.6MM **Privately Held**
SIC: 2393 Tea bags, fabric: made from purchased materials

(G-2870)
HEINTZ & WEBER CO INC
150 Reading St (14220-2156)
PHONE.................................716 852-7171
Steven D Desmond, *CEO*
Suzanne M Desmond, *Exec VP*
EMP: 7 **EST:** 1922
SQ FT: 12,500
SALES (est): 860.7K **Privately Held**
WEB: www.webersmustard.com
SIC: 2035 Pickles, vinegar; mustard, prepared (wet); relishes, fruit & vegetable

(G-2871)
HERITAGE CONTRACT FLOORING LLC
29 Depot St (14206-2203)
PHONE.................................716 853-1555
William H Russell, *CEO*
Don Faltisio, *CEO*
Bill Russell, *CEO*
Jeff Friedman, *Vice Pres*
Joe Pantano, *Vice Pres*
EMP: 45
SALES (est): 8.5MM **Privately Held**
SIC: 3996 Hard surface floor coverings

(G-2872)
HI-TEMP FABRICATION INC
15 Lawrence Bell Dr (14221-7075)
PHONE.................................716 852-5655
Shelly Kent, *President*
Dave Schedlbauer, *Vice Pres*
John Lent, *Sales Mgr*
EMP: 13
SQ FT: 40,000
SALES (est): 2.1MM **Privately Held**
WEB: www.hi-tempfab.com
SIC: 2493 Hardboard & fiberboard products

(G-2873)
HOHL MACHINE & CONVEYOR CO INC
Also Called: Hohlveyor
1580 Niagara St (14213-1102)
PHONE.................................716 882-7210
Richard Milazzo, *President*
Carl Milazzo, *Principal*
EMP: 50 **EST:** 1945
SQ FT: 30,000
SALES (est): 14.8MM **Privately Held**
SIC: 3599 3535 Machine & other job shop work; belt conveyor systems, general industrial use

(G-2874)
HOOD INDUSTRIES INC
580 Tifft St (14220-1813)
PHONE.................................716 836-0301
Steven R Doraski, *President*
EMP: 10
SQ FT: 60,000
SALES (est): 1.4MM **Privately Held**
SIC: 2449 Shipping cases & drums, wood: wirebound & plywood

(G-2875)
HOSPIRA INC
2501 Walden Ave (14225)
PHONE.................................716 684-9400
Carlos E Simon, *Opers Mgr*
Wayne Dreibelbis, *Mfg Spvr*
Paul Lesniak, *Opers Staff*
Steve Wisniewski, *Engineer*
Jane Jontz, *Human Res Dir*
EMP: 193
SALES (corp-wide): 52.5B **Publicly Held**
SIC: 2834 Druggists' preparations (pharmaceuticals)
HQ: Hospira, Inc.
  275 N Field Dr
  Lake Forest IL 60045
  224 212-2000

(G-2876)
HUTCHINSON INDUSTRIES INC
Rodgard
92 Msgr Valente Dr (14206-1822)
PHONE.................................716 852-1435
Bill Barrett, *Branch Mgr*
EMP: 30
SALES (corp-wide): 8.3B **Publicly Held**
SIC: 3069 Medical & laboratory rubber sundries & related products
HQ: Hutchinson Industries, Inc.
  460 Southard St
  Trenton NJ 08638
  609 394-1010

(G-2877)
HYDRO-AIR COMPONENTS INC
Also Called: Zehnder Rittling
100 Rittling Blvd (14220-1885)
PHONE.................................716 827-6510
Scott Pallotta, *CEO*
Robert Daigler, *Vice Pres*
Jim Blount, *Engineer*
Jeffrey Prynn, *Engineer*
Dave Polisoto, *Senior Engr*
▲ **EMP:** 130
SQ FT: 80,000
SALES (est): 37.2MM
SALES (corp-wide): 686.7MM **Privately Held**
SIC: 3585 1711 Refrigeration & heating equipment; plumbing, heating, air-conditioning contractors
PA: Zehnder Group Ag
  Moortalstrasse 1
  GrAnichen AG
  628 551-500

(G-2878)
I ON YOUTH
115 Godfrey St (14215-2361)
PHONE.................................716 832-6509
Marilyn Nixon, *President*
EMP: 5
SALES (est): 304.6K **Privately Held**
SIC: 2721 Periodicals

(G-2879)
ICYNENE US ACQUISITION CORP (HQ)
438 Main St Ste 100 (14202-3207)
PHONE.................................800 758-7325
Bill Sommers, *CFO*
EMP: 3
SALES (est): 2.3MM
SALES (corp-wide): 11.9MM **Publicly Held**
SIC: 2899 Foam charge mixtures
PA: Ffl Partners, Llc
  1 Maritime Plz Fl 22
  San Francisco CA 94111
  415 402-2100

(G-2880)
IMAGE TECH
96 Donna Lea Blvd (14221-3104)
PHONE.................................716 635-0167
Joan Hudack, *Owner*
EMP: 15
SALES (est): 520K **Privately Held**
SIC: 3999 Pet supplies

(G-2881)
IMMCO DIAGNOSTICS INC
640 Ellicott St Fl 3 (14203-1245)
PHONE.................................716 691-0091
EMP: 9 **Privately Held**
SIC: 3231 2835 8071 Mfg Products-Purchased Glass Mfg Diagnostic Substances Medical Laboratory
HQ: Immco Diagnostics, Inc.
  60 Pineview Dr
  Buffalo NY 14228
  716 691-0091

(G-2882)
IN ROOM PLUS INC
2495 Main St Ste 217 (14214-2154)
PHONE.................................716 838-9433
Mike Amrose, *CEO*
Wanda Jones, *President*
Kim Hamilton, *Director*
Elizabeth Jones, *Director*
Lori Kempski, *Director*
▼ **EMP:** 32
SQ FT: 21,000
SALES (est): 5.3MM **Privately Held**
WEB: www.inroomplus.com
SIC: 2064 Candy & other confectionery products

(G-2883)
INDUSTRIAL SUPPORT INC
36 Depot St (14206-2204)
PHONE.................................716 662-2954
David P Sullivan, *President*
▲ **EMP:** 75
SQ FT: 55,000
SALES (est): 16.9MM **Privately Held**
WEB: www.industrialsupportinc.com
SIC: 3441 5999 2541 Fabricated structural metal; electronic parts & equipment; wood partitions & fixtures

(G-2884)
INGERSOLL-RAND COMPANY
3101 Broadway St (14227-1034)
P.O. Box 209 (14217-0209)
PHONE.................................716 896-6600
Joseph Manzella, *VP Opers*
Pasquale Cariello, *Project Mgr*
Brian Fleming, *Project Mgr*
Duane Schmitz, *Project Mgr*
Peter Quartararo, *Opers Mgr*
EMP: 40 **Privately Held**
SIC: 3563 Air & gas compressors
HQ: Ingersoll-Rand Company
  800 Beaty St Ste B
  Davidson NC 28036
  704 655-4000

(G-2885)
INSTANTWHIP OF BUFFALO INC
2117 Genesee St (14211-1907)
PHONE.................................716 892-7031
John Beck, *General Mgr*
EMP: 20
SALES (corp-wide): 47.5MM **Privately Held**
SIC: 2099 2035 2026 2022 Food preparations; pickles, sauces & salad dressings; fluid milk; cheese, natural & processed; sample distribution
HQ: Instantwhip Of Buffalo, Inc
  2200 Cardigan Ave
  Columbus OH 43215
  614 488-2536

(G-2886)
INSTY-PRINTS OF BUFFALO INC (PA)
265 Franklin St (14202-1901)
PHONE.................................716 853-6483
David Metz, *President*
Jim Metz, *Vice Pres*
Tom Metz, *Treasurer*
EMP: 7
SQ FT: 3,500
SALES (est): 1.2MM **Privately Held**
SIC: 2752 Commercial printing, lithographic

(G-2887)
INTERIOR SOLUTIONS OF WNY LLC
472 Franklin St (14202-1302)
PHONE.................................716 332-0372
Jan Malof,
EMP: 9
SALES (est): 1MM **Privately Held**
SIC: 2521 Chairs, office: padded, upholstered or plain: wood

(G-2888)
INTERNATIONAL PAPER COMPANY
100 Bud Mil Dr (14206-1802)
PHONE.................................716 852-2144
Pam Regans, *Branch Mgr*
EMP: 15

Buffalo - Erie County (G-2889)   GEOGRAPHIC SECTION

SALES (corp-wide): 21.7B **Publicly Held**
WEB: www.tin.com
SIC: 2653 Corrugated & solid fiber boxes
PA: International Paper Company
6400 Poplar Ave
Memphis TN 38197
901 419-9000

(G-2889)
J D COUSINS INC
667 Tifft St (14220-1890)
PHONE 716 824-1098
Gregory N Pauly, *CEO*
Mike Heim, *Foreman/Supr*
Gary Bailey, *Opers Staff*
Jonathan Whitehead, *Project Engr*
Jim Howard, *Bookkeeper*
EMP: 24 **EST:** 1904
SQ FT: 30,000
SALES (est): 5.1MM **Privately Held**
WEB: www.jdcousins.com
SIC: 3599 Machine shop, jobbing & repair

(G-2890)
JAYS FURNITURE PRODUCTS INC
321 Ramsdell Ave (14216-1030)
PHONE 716 876-8854
James Gianni, *President*
Dean Gianni, *Plant Mgr*
Janie Gianni, *Admin Sec*
EMP: 30
SQ FT: 25,000
SALES (est): 5.2MM **Privately Held**
WEB: www.jaysfurnitureproducts.com
SIC: 2531 2512 2431 Benches for public buildings; upholstered household furniture; millwork

(G-2891)
JBREN CORP
Also Called: Lancaster Tanks and Steel Pdts
107 Dorothy St (14206-2939)
PHONE 716 332-5928
John Brennan, *CEO*
EMP: 16
SALES (est): 2.6MM **Privately Held**
SIC: 3443 Water tanks, metal plate

(G-2892)
JENTSCH & CO INC
107 Dorothy St (14206-2939)
PHONE 716 852-4111
Christopher Jentsch, *President*
Walter Peters, *Corp Secy*
EMP: 6 **EST:** 1931
SQ FT: 28,500
SALES (est): 944.3K **Privately Held**
WEB: www.jentschandcompany.com
SIC: 3441 Fabricated structural metal

(G-2893)
JERRY MILLER MOLDED SHOES INC (PA)
Also Called: Jerry Miller I.D. Shoes
36 Mason St (14213-1505)
PHONE 716 881-3920
Hussain Syed, *President*
Sarah Syed, *Vice Pres*
◆ **EMP:** 11
SQ FT: 26,000
SALES (est): 1.2MM **Privately Held**
WEB: www.jerrymillershoes.com
SIC: 3143 3144 Orthopedic shoes, men's; orthopedic shoes, women's

(G-2894)
JERSEY EXPRESS INC
3080 Main St (14214-1304)
PHONE 716 834-6151
Nancy Miranda, *President*
Scott Simard, *Principal*
Michael Miranda, *Vice Pres*
EMP: 15
SALES (est): 1.4MM **Privately Held**
WEB: www.jerseyexpress.com
SIC: 2389 Mfg Apparel/Accessories

(G-2895)
JET-BLACK SEALERS INC
Also Called: Sealmaster
555 Ludwig Ave (14227-1026)
P.O. Box 7257 (14240-7257)
PHONE 716 891-4197
William C Smith, *Ch of Bd*
Eric Moggaffin, *Sales Mgr*
Rosemary Smith, *Admin Sec*
EMP: 6
SQ FT: 6,400
SALES (est): 1.4MM **Privately Held**
WEB: www.sealmasterbuffalo.com
SIC: 2951 Asphalt paving mixtures & blocks

(G-2896)
JOHNSON CONTROLS INC
130 John Muir Dr Ste 100 (14228-1139)
PHONE 716 688-7340
Harold Witschi, *Branch Mgr*
EMP: 50 **Privately Held**
SIC: 3822 Auto controls regulating residntl & coml environmt & applncs
HQ: Johnson Controls, Inc.
5757 N Green Bay Ave
Milwaukee WI 53209
414 524-1200

(G-2897)
JOHNSON MANUFACTURING COMPANY
Also Called: SA Day Buffalo Flux Facility
1489 Niagara St (14213-1103)
P.O. Box 1084, Tonawanda (14151-1084)
PHONE 716 881-3030
Jackson Bowling, *General Mgr*
Gary Lampka, *Engineer*
EMP: 10 **Privately Held**
WEB: www.johnsonmfg.com
SIC: 2899 Fluxes: brazing, soldering, galvanizing & welding
PA: Johnson Manufacturing Company, Inc
114 Lost Grove Rd
Princeton IA 52768

(G-2898)
JUST LAMPS OF NEW YORK INC
334 Harris Hill Rd Apt 1 (14221-7473)
PHONE 716 626-2240
Dave Bethell, *CEO*
Eric Lanham, *President*
Eric Laham, *General Mgr*
Mark Murray, *CFO*
Jonathan Pittman, *Sales Staff*
EMP: 12
SALES (est): 2.2MM **Privately Held**
WEB: www.justlamps.us.com
SIC: 3861 Projectors, still or motion picture, silent or sound

(G-2899)
K & E FABRICATING COMPANY INC
40 Stanley St (14206-1018)
PHONE 716 829-1829
Peter Fasolino, *President*
EMP: 12 **EST:** 1922
SQ FT: 10,000
SALES (est): 2.7MM **Privately Held**
SIC: 3441 Fabricated structural metal

(G-2900)
K D M DIE COMPANY INC
620 Elk St (14210-2237)
PHONE 716 828-9000
Gary Posluszny, *CEO*
Carl Posluszny, *Treasurer*
EMP: 17
SQ FT: 32,000
SALES (est): 2.5MM **Privately Held**
SIC: 3544 3599 Special dies & tools; machine shop, jobbing & repair

(G-2901)
K-TECHNOLOGIES INC
4090 Jeffrey Blvd (14219-2338)
PHONE 716 828-4444
Jeffrey Kryszak, *President*
Edward Tierney, *Vice Pres*
Guy Allan, *Manager*
Terry Metzger, *Manager*
Andrew Sauciunac, *Manager*
EMP: 40
SQ FT: 5,400
SALES: 4MM **Privately Held**
WEB: www.k-technologies.net
SIC: 3824 Electromechanical counters

(G-2902)
KEHR-BUFFALO WIRE FRAME CO INC
Also Called: Rogers Industrial Spring
127 Kehr St (14211-1522)
P.O. Box 806, Grand Island (14072-0806)
PHONE 716 897-2288
George Rogers, *President*
James Rogers III, *Vice Pres*
EMP: 30
SQ FT: 27,000
SALES (est): 4.7MM **Privately Held**
WEB: www.kbwf.net
SIC: 3496 Miscellaneous fabricated wire products

(G-2903)
KELLER BROS & MILLER INC
401 Franklin St (14202-1586)
PHONE 716 854-2374
Ralph Salerno, *President*
EMP: 9
SQ FT: 8,600
SALES (est): 1.6MM **Privately Held**
WEB: www.kbmprinting.com
SIC: 2752 Commercial printing, offset

(G-2904)
KEY TECH FINISHING
2929 Main St Ste 2 (14214-1760)
PHONE 716 832-1232
Jack Karet, *President*
Jennifer Masse, *General Mgr*
Joan Karet, *Corp Secy*
Melanie Sandquist, *Plant Mgr*
EMP: 30
SQ FT: 80,000
SALES (est): 2.2MM
SALES (corp-wide): 8.9MM **Privately Held**
WEB: www.keyfinishing.com
SIC: 3471 Electroplating of metals or formed products; electroplating & plating
PA: Keystone Corporation
144 Milton St
Buffalo NY 14210
716 832-1232

(G-2905)
KEYNOTE SYSTEMS CORPORATION
2810 Sweet Home Rd (14228-1347)
PHONE 716 564-1332
Leonard Gostowski, *President*
EMP: 5
SALES (est): 560.8K **Privately Held**
SIC: 7372 Prepackaged software

(G-2906)
KEYSTONE CORPORATION (PA)
144 Milton St (14210-1644)
PHONE 716 832-1232
Jack A Karet, *President*
Joan Karet, *Corp Secy*
Michael Karet, *Vice Pres*
Sam Goorevich, *Sales Mgr*
Karen Mongiello,
EMP: 40 **EST:** 1923
SQ FT: 45,000
SALES (est): 8.9MM **Privately Held**
WEB: www.keyfinishing.com
SIC: 3471 Electroplating of metals or formed products; electroplating & plating; anodizing (plating) of metals or formed products

(G-2907)
KITTINGER COMPANY INC
4675 Transit Rd (14221-6022)
PHONE 716 876-1000
Raymond C Bialkowski, *CEO*
EMP: 50
SQ FT: 60,000
SALES (est): 7.8MM **Privately Held**
WEB: www.kittingerfurniture.com
SIC: 2521 2512 2511 Wood office furniture; upholstered household furniture; wood household furniture

(G-2908)
KNOLL INC
Also Called: Datesweiser
1700 Broadway St (14212-2031)
PHONE 716 891-1700
EMP: 60 **Publicly Held**
SIC: 2521 Wood office furniture
PA: Knoll, Inc.
1235 Water St
East Greenville PA 18041

(G-2909)
KOCH METAL SPINNING CO INC
74 Jewett Ave (14214-2421)
PHONE 716 835-3631
Eric Koch, *President*
McManigle Robert, *Purch Mgr*
▼ **EMP:** 52 **EST:** 1939
SQ FT: 50,000
SALES: 4.2MM **Privately Held**
WEB: www.kochmetalspinning.com
SIC: 3469 Spinning metal for the trade

(G-2910)
KOEHLR-GIBSON MKG GRAPHICS INC
Also Called: Koehler-Gibson Mkg & Graphics
875 Englewood Ave (14223-2334)
PHONE 716 838-5960
David Koehler, *President*
EMP: 20
SQ FT: 13,000
SALES (est): 2.7MM **Privately Held**
SIC: 3953 2796 Date stamps, hand: rubber or metal; postmark stamps, hand: rubber or metal; printing dies, rubber or plastic, for marking machines; photoengraving plates, linecuts or halftones

(G-2911)
KOHLER AWNING INC
2600 Walden Ave (14225-4736)
PHONE 716 685-3333
John M Kohler III, *President*
Craig Kohler, *Corp Secy*
Jesse W Kohler, *Vice Pres*
EMP: 30 **EST:** 1924
SQ FT: 2,182
SALES (est): 4.4MM **Privately Held**
WEB: www.kohlerawning.com
SIC: 2394 7699 Awnings, fabric: made from purchased materials; awning repair shop

(G-2912)
KREPE KRAFT INC
Also Called: Krepe-Kraft
1801 Elmwood Ave (14207-2463)
P.O. Box 1907 (14219-0107)
PHONE 716 826-7086
Daniel Keane, *President*
Leo Eckman, *President*
Kevin T Keane, *Principal*
Donna Eckman, *Vice Pres*
John M Yessa, *Treasurer*
EMP: 370
SQ FT: 47,300
SALES: 23.5MM
SALES (corp-wide): 59.2MM **Privately Held**
WEB: www.krepekraft.com
SIC: 2754 5947 Gift, novelty & souvenir shop; invitations: gravure printing
PA: Mod-Pac Corp.
1801 Elmwood Ave Ste 1
Buffalo NY 14207
716 898-8480

(G-2913)
KYNTEC CORPORATION
2100 Old Union Rd (14227-2725)
PHONE 716 810-6956
Patrick Lee, *Ch of Bd*
Scott Taylor, *President*
Gerald Spyche, *Vice Pres*
Rich Ryan, *Treasurer*
EMP: 6 **EST:** 2012
SALES (est): 1.3MM **Privately Held**
SIC: 3569 3484 3429 3531 Industrial shock absorbers; rifles or rifle parts, 30 mm. & below; aircraft hardware; marine related equipment

(G-2914)
L LLC
106 Soldiers Pl (14222-1261)
PHONE 716 885-3918
Mohsen Lachaal, *Mng Member*
EMP: 20 **EST:** 2001
SALES (est): 2.1MM **Privately Held**
SIC: 2079 Olive oil

▲ = Import   ▼ = Export
◆ = Import/Export

GEOGRAPHIC SECTION
Buffalo - Erie County (G-2941)

(G-2915)
LABATT USA LLC
79 Perry St Ste 1 (14203-3079)
PHONE..............................716 604-1050
Glen Walter, *President*
Thomas Cardella, *Vice Pres*
James Pendegrat,
▲ **EMP:** 60
SALES (est): 8.8MM **Privately Held**
SIC: 2082 Beer (alcoholic beverage)
HQ: North American Breweries, Inc.
    445 Saint Paul St
    Rochester NY 14605

(G-2916)
LACTALIS AMERICAN GROUP INC
2375 S Park Ave (14220-2653)
PHONE..............................716 827-2622
Sean Paul Quiblier, *Principal*
Sharon Pusateri, *Assistant*
Laurie Siwy, *Clerk*
EMP: 100
SALES (corp-wide): 98.8K **Privately Held**
SIC: 2022 Natural cheese
HQ: Lactalis American Group, Inc.
    2376 S Park Ave
    Buffalo NY 14220
    716 823-6262

(G-2917)
LACTALIS AMERICAN GROUP INC (DH)
Also Called: Sorrento Lactalis
2376 S Park Ave (14220-2670)
PHONE..............................716 823-6262
Frederick Bouisset, *CEO*
Aliza Manzella, *Business Mgr*
Alain Gerard, *Vice Pres*
Paul Peterson, *Vice Pres*
Elena Umanskaya, *Vice Pres*
◆ **EMP:** 500
SALES (est): 564.9MM
SALES (corp-wide): 98.8K **Privately Held**
WEB: www.lactalisamericangroup.com
SIC: 2022 Natural cheese
HQ: Parmalat Spa
    Via Delle Nazioni Unite 4
    Collecchio PR 43044
    052 180-81

(G-2918)
LAFARGE NORTH AMERICA INC
575 Ohio St (14203-3119)
PHONE..............................716 854-5791
Robert Hafner, *Manager*
EMP: 5
SALES (corp-wide): 26.4B **Privately Held**
WEB: www.lafargenorthamerica.com
SIC: 3241 Cement, hydraulic
HQ: Lafarge North America Inc.
    8700 W Bryn Mawr Ave
    Chicago IL 60631
    773 372-1000

(G-2919)
LAKESHORE CARBIDE INC
1959 Maple Rd (14221-2754)
PHONE..............................716 462-4349
Carl Ciesla, *Chairman*
EMP: 6 **EST:** 2009
SALES (est): 694.6K **Privately Held**
SIC: 2819 Carbides

(G-2920)
LANDIES CANDIES CO INC
2495 Main St Ste 350 (14214-2154)
PHONE..............................716 834-8212
Larry Szrama, *President*
Andrew Gaiek, *Vice Pres*
Matthew Halizak, *Facilities Mgr*
Dennis Hussak, *Marketing Staff*
Mark Miller, *Manager*
▲ **EMP:** 10
SALES (est): 1.8MM **Privately Held**
WEB: www.landiescandies.com
SIC: 2064 Candy & other confectionery products

(G-2921)
LASEOPTICS CORP
300 International Dr # 100 (14221-5783)
PHONE..............................716 462-5078
Samuel John, *President*
Samuel Kassey, *Vice Pres*
EMP: 14
SALES (est): 1.1MM **Privately Held**
SIC: 2298 Cable, fiber

(G-2922)
LAURUS DEVELOPMENT INC
3556 Lake Shore Rd # 121 (14219-1460)
PHONE..............................716 823-1202
Vincent Coppola, *President*
John Feuerstein, *Vice Pres*
EMP: 14
SALES (est): 1MM **Privately Held**
WEB: www.laurusdevelopment.com
SIC: 7372 7371 8748 7379 Business oriented computer software; computer software systems analysis & design, custom; computer software development & applications; systems engineering consultant, ex. computer or professional; computer related maintenance services

(G-2923)
LIME ENERGY CO
1a Elk Terminal (14204-4200)
PHONE..............................704 892-4442
Adam Procell, *Branch Mgr*
EMP: 7
SALES (corp-wide): 112.6MM **Privately Held**
SIC: 3274 Lime
PA: Lime Energy Co.
    4 Gateway Ctr Fl 4 # 4
    Newark NJ 07102
    201 416-2575

(G-2924)
LINDE LLC
101 Katherine St (14210-2005)
PHONE..............................716 847-0748
Jack Pederson, *Opers-Prdtn-Mfg*
EMP: 40
SALES (corp-wide): 20.1B **Privately Held**
SIC: 2813 Nitrogen; oxygen, compressed or liquefied
HQ: Linde Llc
    200 Somerset Corporate Bl
    Bridgewater NJ 08807
    908 464-8100

(G-2925)
LINE WARD CORPORATION
157 Seneca Creek Rd (14224-2347)
PHONE..............................716 675-7373
Cheryl Gustavel, *President*
Roger Gustavel, *Vice Pres*
EMP: 5
SQ FT: 3,000
SALES (est): 1.4MM **Privately Held**
WEB: www.lineward.com
SIC: 3531 Construction machinery

(G-2926)
LITELAB CORP (PA)
251 Elm St (14203-1603)
PHONE..............................716 856-4300
Frederick A Spaulding, *CEO*
Dawn M Casati, *Corp Secy*
Lawrence Christ, *COO*
Dawn Csati, *Controller*
Audrey Mingle, *Human Res Mgr*
▲ **EMP:** 135
SQ FT: 80,000
SALES (est): 25.7MM **Privately Held**
WEB: www.litelab.com
SIC: 3646 3645 Commercial indusl & institutional electric lighting fixtures; residential lighting fixtures

(G-2927)
LOCKHOUSE DISTILLERY
41 Columbia St Ste 200 (14204-2133)
PHONE..............................716 768-4898
Chad Vosseller, *President*
Thomas Jablonski, *Partner*
Jon Mirro, *Vice Pres*
EMP: 6
SALES (est): 292.6K **Privately Held**
SIC: 2085 Distilled & blended liquors

(G-2928)
LOY L PRESS INC
Also Called: Allegra Printing
3959 Union Rd (14225-4253)
PHONE..............................716 634-5966
Richard Delong, *President*
Joyce S Delong, *Vice Pres*
EMP: 5
SQ FT: 1,894
SALES (est): 887.2K **Privately Held**
SIC: 2752 2791 2789 2759 Commercial printing, offset; typesetting; bookbinding & related work; commercial printing

(G-2929)
M A MOSLOW & BROS INC
375 Norfolk Ave (14215-3108)
PHONE..............................716 896-2950
David Moslow, *President*
Joe Moslow, *Vice Pres*
▲ **EMP:** 40
SQ FT: 21,000
SALES (est): 4.3MM **Privately Held**
WEB: www.moslowbros.com
SIC: 2499 Trophy bases, wood

(G-2930)
M K ULRICH CONSTRUCTION INC
1601 Harlem Rd (14206-1923)
PHONE..............................716 893-5777
Don Ulrich, *President*
Marie Ulrich, *Vice Pres*
EMP: 12
SQ FT: 4,800
SALES: 900K **Privately Held**
SIC: 3272 1799 Ornamental metal work; steps, prefabricated concrete

(G-2931)
MAC INNES ENTERPRISES INC
Also Called: Associated Publishing Co
61 John Muir Dr (14228-1147)
PHONE..............................325 676-4032
Robert Allen III, *President*
Richard Rayburn, *Vice Pres*
EMP: 20 **EST:** 1986
SALES (est): 733.1K **Privately Held**
SIC: 2741 Directories, telephone: publishing only, not printed on site; telephone & other directory publishing

(G-2932)
MACNEIL POLYMERS INC (PA)
3155 Broadway St (14227-1034)
PHONE..............................716 681-7755
Richard Neil, *President*
EMP: 15 **EST:** 2000
SQ FT: 35,097
SALES (est): 1MM **Privately Held**
WEB: www.macneilpolymers.com
SIC: 2821 Plastics materials & resins

(G-2933)
MAGAZINES & BROCHURES INC
Also Called: Labels X Press
2205 Kenmore Ave Ste 107 (14214-1329)
PHONE..............................716 875-9699
Craig Boggs, *President*
Scott Boggs, *Treasurer*
EMP: 5
SALES (est): 538.7K **Privately Held**
WEB: www.labelsxpress.com
SIC: 2759 2752 Labels & seals: printing; commercial printing, lithographic

(G-2934)
MAGNESIUM TECHNOLOGIES CORP
266 Elmwood Ave (14222-2202)
P.O. Box 818 (14222)
PHONE..............................905 689-7361
Bernie Rumbold, *CEO*
EMP: 13
SALES (corp-wide): 1.2B **Privately Held**
SIC: 3295 Magnesite, crude: ground, calcined or dead-burned
HQ: Opta Minerals (Usa) Inc.
    4807 Rockside Rd Ste 400
    Independence OH 44131
    330 659-3003

(G-2935)
MAGTROL INC
70 Gardenville Pkwy W (14224-1394)
PHONE..............................716 668-5555
William A Mulroy III, *President*
◆ **EMP:** 50 **EST:** 1953
SQ FT: 35,000
SALES (est): 12.1MM **Privately Held**
WEB: www.magtrol.com
SIC: 3625 3568 3825 3823 Brakes, electromagnetic; clutches, except vehicular; instruments to measure electricity; industrial instrmnts msrmnt display/control process variable; motor vehicle parts & accessories; aircraft & motor vehicle measurement equipment

(G-2936)
MAKE-WAVES INSTRUMENT CORP (PA)
4172 Vinewood Dr (14221-7518)
PHONE..............................716 681-7524
John R Patterson, *President*
Brian Cory, *Vice Pres*
Richard Rang, *Controller*
▲ **EMP:** 25
SQ FT: 36,000
SALES (est): 2.4MM **Privately Held**
WEB: www.makewavesinstrumentcorp.com
SIC: 3825 3829 3641 3545 Tachometer generators; gauges, motor vehicle: oil pressure, water temperature; electric lamps; machine tool accessories; valves & pipe fittings; gaskets, packing & sealing devices

(G-2937)
MARKIN TUBING LP
Also Called: Markin Tubing Division
400 Ingham Ave (14218-2536)
PHONE..............................585 495-6211
Ivan Zahariev, *Production*
Joel Sack, *Engineer*
Tom Stamper, *Manager*
EMP: 17 **Privately Held**
SIC: 3312 3317 Tubes, steel & iron; steel pipe & tubes
PA: Markin Tubing, Lp
    1 Markin Ln
    Wyoming NY 14591

(G-2938)
MASSIMO FRIEDMAN INC
Also Called: Great Arrow Graphics
2495 Main St Ste 457 (14214-2154)
PHONE..............................718 836-0408
Alan Friedman, *President*
Donna M Massimo, *Corp Secy*
Lisa Samar, *Vice Pres*
EMP: 20
SALES (est): 2.2MM **Privately Held**
WEB: www.greatarrow.com
SIC: 2771 Greeting cards

(G-2939)
MATERION ADVANCED MATERIALS (DH)
2978 Main St (14214-1004)
PHONE..............................800 327-1355
Donald Klinkowicz, *President*
Amy Maundrell, *General Mgr*
Scott Haluska, *Vice Pres*
Charisse Brown, *Opers Mgr*
William Kirchmyer, *Materials Mgr*
▲ **EMP:** 198 **EST:** 1912
SQ FT: 150,000
SALES (est): 109.5MM
SALES (corp-wide): 1.1B **Publicly Held**
WEB: www.williams-adv.com
SIC: 3674 Semiconductors & related devices
HQ: Materion Brush Inc.
    6070 Parkland Blvd Ste 1
    Mayfield Heights OH 44124
    216 486-4200

(G-2940)
MAXSECURE SYSTEMS INC
300 International Dr # 100 (14221-5781)
PHONE..............................800 657-4336
Ken Szekely, *President*
Ken Lawrence, *Admin Sec*
EMP: 3
SALES: 1.3MM **Privately Held**
WEB: www.max-secure.com
SIC: 2531 Public building & related furniture

(G-2941)
MC IVOR MANUFACTURING INC
400 Ingham Ave (14218-2536)
P.O. Box 13 (14220-0013)
PHONE..............................716 825-1808

Buffalo - Erie County (G-2942)   GEOGRAPHIC SECTION

Bruce Mc Ivor, *President*
EMP: 6
SQ FT: 13,000
SALES (est): 632.2K **Privately Held**
SIC: 3599 Machine shop, jobbing & repair

(G-2942)
MCINTOSH BOX & PALLET CO INC
11 Hubbard St (14206-2922)
PHONE..................716 825-4122
Tim Mack, *Sales Staff*
Mark Jerreld, *Branch Mgr*
EMP: 6
SALES (est): 440.8K
SALES (corp-wide): 35.3MM **Privately Held**
SIC: 2448 Pallets, wood
PA: Mcintosh Box & Pallet Co., Inc.
5864 Pyle Dr
East Syracuse NY 13057
315 446-9350

(G-2943)
MEDICAL ACOUSTICS LLC
640 Ellicott St Ste 407 (14203-1253)
P.O. Box 327, Bowmansville (14026-0327)
PHONE..................716 218-7353
Stephen Ostrow, *Vice Pres*
Nicolaas Smith, *Vice Pres*
Frank Codella, *Mng Member*
Joel Castlevetere,
EMP: 12
SALES: 1MM **Privately Held**
SIC: 3842 Respirators

(G-2944)
MERZ METAL & MACHINE CORP
237 Chelsea Pl (14211-1003)
PHONE..................716 893-7786
Dave Nieman, *President*
Joe Huefner, *Vice Pres*
Joesph Huefner, *Vice Pres*
Kathy Charczuk, *Human Resources*
Steve Korsh, *Technology*
EMP: 22 **EST:** 1948
SQ FT: 13,000
SALES (est): 5MM **Privately Held**
WEB: www.merzmetal.com
SIC: 3444 1711 Ventilation & duct work contractor; ventilators, sheet metal

(G-2945)
MIBRO GROUP
Also Called: Allied
4039 Genesee St (14225-1904)
PHONE..................716 631-5713
Leon Lapidus, *President*
Barry J Smith, *CFO*
Deb Pacione, *Sales Staff*
Michael Smits, *Mktg Dir*
Cristina Chang, *Graphic Designe*
◆ **EMP:** 75 **EST:** 1954
SQ FT: 100,000
SALES (est): 11.8MM **Privately Held**
WEB: www.mibro.com
SIC: 3545 Drill bits, metalworking
PA: Mibro Partners
111 Sinnott Rd
Scarborough ON M1L 4
416 285-9000

(G-2946)
MIKEN COMPANIES INC
75 Boxwood Ln (14227-2707)
P.O. Box 178 (14231-0178)
PHONE..................716 668-6311
Walter J Jaworski, *CEO*
Michael Bolas, *President*
Pauline Jaworski, *Vice Pres*
Douglas Kirkpatrick, *Admin Sec*
EMP: 100 **EST:** 1929
SQ FT: 65,000
SALES (est): 13.5MM **Privately Held**
WEB: www.mikencompanies.com
SIC: 2752 2759 2675 2672 Commercial printing, lithographic; commercial printing; die-cut paper & board; coated & laminated paper

(G-2947)
MINEO & SAPIO MEATS INC
Also Called: Minero & Sapio Sausage
410 Connecticut St (14213-2641)
PHONE..................716 884-2398
Michael Pierro, *President*
Nadine Pierro, *Treasurer*
EMP: 6
SALES (est): 1.4MM **Privately Held**
WEB: www.mineosapio.com
SIC: 2013 5421 Sausages & other prepared meats; meat markets, including freezer provisioners

(G-2948)
MIRION TECH CONAX NUCLEAR INC
Also Called: Ist Conax Nuclear
402 Sonwil Dr (14225-5530)
PHONE..................716 681-1973
Iain Wilson, *CEO*
Steven Karnyski, *General Mgr*
Jack Pacheco, *CFO*
Seth B Rosen, *Admin Sec*
EMP: 23
SQ FT: 26,200
SALES (est): 4.8MM **Privately Held**
WEB: www.mirion.com
SIC: 3829 Nuclear radiation & testing apparatus
HQ: Mirion Technologies (Ist) Corporation
315 Daniel Zenker Dr # 204
Horseheads NY 14845
607 562-4300

(G-2949)
MM OF EAST AURORA LLC
Also Called: Buffalo Hardwood Floor Center
3801 Harlem Rd (14215-1907)
PHONE..................716 651-9663
Marlena Maloney, *Mng Member*
James Maloney,
EMP: 10
SALES (est): 1.5MM **Privately Held**
SIC: 2426 Hardwood dimension & flooring mills

(G-2950)
MOBILEAPP SYSTEMS LLC
4 Grand View Trl (14217)
PHONE..................716 667-2780
EMP: 5 **EST:** 2012
SALES (est): 310.6K **Privately Held**
SIC: 7372 Prepackaged software

(G-2951)
MOD-PAC CORP (PA)
1801 Elmwood Ave Ste 1 (14207-2496)
PHONE..................716 898-8480
Kevin T Keane, *Ch of Bd*
Daniel G Keane, *President*
Robert J McKenna, *Principal*
Howard Zemsky, *Principal*
David B Lupp, *COO*
◆ **EMP:** 160
SQ FT: 333,000
SALES: 59.2MM **Privately Held**
WEB: www.modpac.com
SIC: 2657 5999 Food containers, folding: made from purchased material; alarm & safety equipment stores

(G-2952)
MOD-PAC CORP
1801 Elmwood Ave Ste 1 (14207-2496)
P.O. Box 1907, Blasdell (14219-0107)
PHONE..................716 447-9013
Leo Eckman, *Manager*
EMP: 100
SALES (corp-wide): 59.2MM **Privately Held**
WEB: www.modpac.com
SIC: 2754 2752 Commercial printing, gravure; commercial printing, lithographic
PA: Mod-Pac Corp.
1801 Elmwood Ave Ste 1
Buffalo NY 14207
716 898-8480

(G-2953)
MONO-SYSTEMS INC
180 Hopkins St (14220-1854)
PHONE..................716 821-1344
Jim Sutton, *Manager*
EMP: 30
SALES (est): 4.6MM
SALES (corp-wide): 27.1MM **Privately Held**
WEB: www.monosystems.com
SIC: 3443 3643 3549 Cable trays, metal plate; current-carrying wiring devices; metalworking machinery
PA: Mono-Systems, Inc.
4 International Dr # 280
Rye Brook NY 10573
914 934-2075

(G-2954)
MOZZARELLA FRESCA INCORPORATED
2376 S Park Ave (14220-2670)
PHONE..................559 752-4823
Brandy Benderson, *President*
EMP: 5 **EST:** 2008
SALES (est): 306.8K
SALES (corp-wide): 98.8K **Privately Held**
SIC: 2022 Cheese, natural & processed
HQ: Lactalis American Group, Inc.
2376 S Park Ave
Buffalo NY 14220
716 823-6262

(G-2955)
MRI NORTHTOWNS GROUP PC
Also Called: Northtown Imaging
199 Park Club Ln Ste 300 (14221-5269)
PHONE..................716 836-4646
James Rinaldi, *Manager*
Victor Regenbogen, *Diag Radio*
EMP: 11
SALES (corp-wide): 2.2MM **Privately Held**
WEB: www.lockportmri.com
SIC: 3231 Medical & laboratory glassware: made from purchased glass
PA: Mri Northtown's Group Pc
1020 Youngs Rd Ste 120w
Williamsville NY 14221
716 689-4406

(G-2956)
MULLER TOOL INC
74 Anderson Rd (14225-4979)
PHONE..................716 895-3658
Gary D Reisweber, *President*
Bruce Reisweber, *Vice Pres*
Paul Banko, *QC Mgr*
EMP: 20 **EST:** 1941
SQ FT: 12,000
SALES (est): 3.3MM **Privately Held**
WEB: www.mullertool.com
SIC: 3599 3451 Machine shop, jobbing & repair; screw machine products

(G-2957)
MULTISORB TECH INTL LLC (PA)
325 Harlem Rd (14224-1825)
PHONE..................716 824-8900
James Renda, *President*
Rich Burke, *Opers Staff*
Sarah Cook, *Opers Staff*
Deb Hasley, *Buyer*
Shawn Masterson, *Engineer*
EMP: 1
SALES (est): 30.6MM **Privately Held**
SIC: 2819 Industrial inorganic chemicals

(G-2958)
MULTISORB TECHNOLOGIES INC
Also Called: Ecto Tech Automation
10 French Rd (14227)
PHONE..................716 656-1402
John S Cullen, *CEO*
EMP: 30
SALES (corp-wide): 320.9MM **Privately Held**
SIC: 2819 Industrial inorganic chemicals
HQ: Multisorb Technologies, Inc.
325 Harlem Rd
Buffalo NY 14224
716 824-8900

(G-2959)
MUNSCHAUER INC
330 Greene St (14206-1025)
P.O. Box 686 (14240-0686)
PHONE..................716 895-8888
Grace W Munschauer, *Ch of Bd*
Grace Munschauer, *President*
EMP: 16 **EST:** 2008
SALES (est): 3MM **Privately Held**
SIC: 3442 Window & door frames

(G-2960)
N MAKE MOLD INC
Also Called: Chocolate Delivery Systems
85 River Rock Dr Ste 202 (14207-2170)
PHONE..................716 877-3146
Timothy Thill, *President*
▲ **EMP:** 50
SALES (est): 17.8MM
SALES (corp-wide): 18.4MM **Privately Held**
SIC: 2064 Candy bars, including chocolate covered bars
PA: Chocolate Delivery Systems, Inc.
1800 Elmwood Ave
Buffalo NY 14207
716 877-3146

(G-2961)
NAS QUICK SIGN INC
Also Called: North American Signs Buffalo
1628 Elmwood Ave (14207-3014)
PHONE..................716 876-7599
Frank Strada, *President*
Agnes Strada, *Shareholder*
EMP: 9
SQ FT: 7,000
SALES (est): 1.3MM **Privately Held**
SIC: 3993 Signs, not made in custom sign painting shops; electric signs

(G-2962)
NEW AVON LLC
433 Thorncliff Rd (14223-1128)
PHONE..................716 572-4842
Kathy Gleason, *Principal*
EMP: 12
SALES (corp-wide): 31.2B **Privately Held**
SIC: 2844 Toilet preparations
HQ: New Avon Llc
1 Liberty Plz Fl 25
New York NY 10006
212 282-6000

(G-2963)
NEW BUFFALO SHIRT FACTORY INC
1979 Harlem Rd (14212-2410)
PHONE..................716 436-5839
John Weiss, *President*
David Swart, *Director*
Pamela Thayer, *Director*
EMP: 8
SQ FT: 14,000
SALES: 1MM **Privately Held**
SIC: 2759 Screen printing

(G-2964)
NEW ERA CAP CO INC
160 Delaware Ave (14202-2404)
PHONE..................716 604-9000
Michael Thorton, *Manager*
EMP: 300
SALES (corp-wide): 563.7MM **Privately Held**
WEB: www.neweracap.com
SIC: 2353 Uniform hats & caps; baseball caps
PA: New Era Cap Co., Inc.
160 Delaware Ave
Buffalo NY 14202
716 604-9000

(G-2965)
NEW ERA CAP CO INC (PA)
160 Delaware Ave (14202-2404)
P.O. Box 208, Derby (14047-0208)
PHONE..................716 604-9000
Christopher Koch, *Ch of Bd*
Peter M Augustine, *President*
Valerie Koch, *Corp Secy*
Kenneth Berg, *Director*
◆ **EMP:** 326 **EST:** 1920
SQ FT: 120,000
SALES (est): 563.7MM **Privately Held**
WEB: www.neweracap.com
SIC: 2353 Uniform hats & caps; baseball caps

(G-2966)
NIAGARA FIBERGLASS INC
88 Okell St (14220-2133)
PHONE..................716 822-3921
Stephen Gale, *President*
Philip O'Donnell, *Vice Pres*
EMP: 45
SQ FT: 23,000

▲ = Import ▼=Export
◆ =Import/Export

SALES: 2.3MM **Privately Held**
SIC: 3089 3544 Molding primary plastic; special dies, tools, jigs & fixtures

(G-2967)
NIAGARA GEAR CORPORATION
941 Military Rd (14217-2590)
PHONE...................................716 874-3131
Matthew Babisz, *President*
Robert C Barden, *Vice Pres*
Marcia Iore, *Finance Mgr*
EMP: 25 EST: 1952
SQ FT: 30,000
SALES (est): 4.2MM **Privately Held**
WEB: www.niagaragear.com
SIC: 3566 Gears, power transmission, except automotive

(G-2968)
NIAGARA LASALLE CORPORATION
110 Hopkins St (14220-2195)
P.O. Box 399 (14240-0399)
PHONE...................................716 827-7010
Dave Belin, *Vice Pres*
Mike Slood, *Manager*
Mike Flood, *Executive*
EMP: 75
SALES (corp-wide): 482.4MM **Privately Held**
SIC: 3316 Bars, steel, cold finished, from purchased hot-rolled
HQ: Niagara Lasalle Corporation
 1412 150th St
 Hammond IN 46327
 219 853-6000

(G-2969)
NIAGARA PUNCH & DIE CORP
176 Gruner Rd (14227-1090)
PHONE...................................716 896-7619
Jay Czerniak, *President*
Jean Czerniak, *Admin Sec*
EMP: 8 EST: 1956
SQ FT: 5,000
SALES (est): 1.7MM **Privately Held**
WEB: www.npd123.com
SIC: 3544 Special dies & tools

(G-2970)
NIAGARA TRANSFORMER CORP
1747 Dale Rd (14225-4964)
P.O. Box 233 (14225-0233)
PHONE...................................716 896-6500
John F Darby, *President*
Sheldon Kennedy, *Vice Pres*
Stan Hatch, *Opers Mgr*
Rose Joralemon, *Opers Staff*
Robert Blake, *Engineer*
▲ EMP: 85 EST: 1928
SQ FT: 100,000
SALES (est): 28MM **Privately Held**
WEB: www.niagaratransformer.com
SIC: 3612 Power transformers, electric

(G-2971)
NIAGARA TYING SERVICE INC
176 Dingens St (14206-2308)
PHONE...................................716 825-0066
Albert J Barrato, *President*
Antoinette Barrato, *Admin Sec*
▲ EMP: 38
SALES (est): 5.8MM **Privately Held**
WEB: www.niagaratyingservice.com
SIC: 2013 Sausage casings, natural

(G-2972)
NICKEL CITY STUDIOS PHOTO JOUR
45 Linwood Ave (14209-2203)
PHONE...................................716 200-0956
Rich Mattingly, *Principal*
EMP: 5
SALES (est): 430.3K **Privately Held**
SIC: 3356 Nickel

(G-2973)
NORAZZA INC (PA)
3938 Broadway St (14227-1104)
PHONE...................................716 706-1160
Thomas J Sperazza, *CEO*
Gregory Tramont, *Controller*
Cindy Judd, *Accounting Mgr*
Beth Bloomquist, *Manager*
▲ EMP: 4

SALES (est): 1.6MM **Privately Held**
WEB: www.norazza.com
SIC: 3577 3861 Computer peripheral equipment; photographic equipment & supplies

(G-2974)
NORSE ENERGY CORP USA
3556 Lake Shore Rd # 700 (14219-1445)
PHONE...................................716 568-2048
EMP: 5 EST: 1993
SALES (est): 690K **Privately Held**
SIC: 1382 Oil/Gas Exploration Services

(G-2975)
NORTHROP GRUMMAN INTL TRDG INC
Also Called: Land Self Prtction Systems Div
1740 Wehrle Dr (14221-7032)
PHONE...................................716 626-7233
Patrick Duffey, *General Mgr*
Michael Clark, *Senior Engr*
Brian Schmidt, *Sales Staff*
Joseph Downie, *Director*
EMP: 6
SALES (est): 569.5K **Publicly Held**
SIC: 3699 Flight simulators (training aids), electronic
HQ: Northrop Grumman Overseas Holding, Inc.
 2980 Fairview Park Dr
 Falls Church VA 22042
 703 280-4069

(G-2976)
NORTHROP GRUMMAN SYSTEMS CORP
1740 Wehrle Dr (14221-7032)
PHONE...................................716 626-4600
Tim Green, *Principal*
David J Ellis, *Business Mgr*
Gabriel Abdella, *Opers Mgr*
Lisa Lane, *Opers Mgr*
Susan Murphy, *Research*
EMP: 99 **Publicly Held**
SIC: 3721 Aircraft
HQ: Northrop Grumman Systems Corporation
 2980 Fairview Park Dr
 Falls Church VA 22042
 703 280-2900

(G-2977)
OEHLERS WLDG & FABRICATION INC
242 Elk St (14210-2102)
PHONE...................................716 821-1800
Mark Appelbaum, *President*
EMP: 15
SQ FT: 45,000
SALES: 1.4MM **Privately Held**
SIC: 3441 Fabricated structural metal

(G-2978)
OERLIKON BLZERS CATING USA INC
6000 N Bailey Ave Ste 3 (14226-5102)
PHONE...................................716 564-8557
John Jesnowski, *Branch Mgr*
EMP: 30
SALES (corp-wide): 2.8B **Privately Held**
WEB: www.balzers.com
SIC: 3479 3471 Coating of metals & formed products; finishing, metals or formed products
HQ: Oerlikon Balzers Coating Usa Inc.
 1700 E Golf Rd Ste 200
 Schaumburg IL 60173
 847 619-5541

(G-2979)
OLIVER GEAR INC
1120 Niagara St (14213-1790)
PHONE...................................716 885-1080
Sam Haines, *President*
Mike Barron, *Vice Pres*
Barbara Stone, *CFO*
EMP: 25
SQ FT: 21,000

SALES (est): 6MM
SALES (corp-wide): 18MM **Privately Held**
WEB: www.gearmotions.com
SIC: 3566 7699 Gears, power transmission, except automotive; industrial equipment services
PA: Gear Motions Incorporated
 1750 Milton Ave
 Syracuse NY 13209
 315 488-0100

(G-2980)
ONEIDA SALES & SERVICE INC
Also Called: Oneida Concrete Products
155 Commerce Dr (14218-1041)
PHONE...................................716 822-8205
Frederick Saia, *President*
EMP: 40
SALES (est): 9.4MM **Privately Held**
WEB: www.oneidagroup.com
SIC: 3531 1799 3496 Concrete plants; fence construction; miscellaneous fabricated wire products

(G-2981)
ONY INC BAIRD RESEARCHPARK
1576 Sweet Home Rd (14228-2710)
PHONE...................................716 636-9096
Edmond Egan, *President*
EMP: 30 EST: 2010
SALES (est): 1.7MM **Privately Held**
SIC: 2834 Druggists' preparations (pharmaceuticals)

(G-2982)
ORBITAL HOLDINGS INC
2775 Broadway St Ste 200 (14227-1043)
PHONE...................................951 360-7100
Jerry Jacobs, *Vice Pres*
▲ EMP: 20
SQ FT: 35,160
SALES (est): 3MM
SALES (corp-wide): 20.6MM **Privately Held**
WEB: www.avf.com
SIC: 3449 3429 Miscellaneous metalwork; manufactured hardware (general)
HQ: Avf Group Inc.
 2775 Broadway St Ste 200
 Cheektowaga NY 14227

(G-2983)
OTIS BEDDING MFG CO INC (PA)
80 James E Casey Dr (14206-2367)
PHONE...................................716 825-2599
John Roma Sr, *President*
John Roma Jr, *Vice Pres*
Carol Roma, *Treasurer*
▲ EMP: 20 EST: 1882
SQ FT: 40,000
SALES (est): 2.5MM **Privately Held**
WEB: www.otisbed.com
SIC: 2515 5712 Mattresses, innerspring or box spring; mattresses

(G-2984)
P J R INDUSTRIES INC
Also Called: Southside Precast Products
1951 Hamburg Tpke Ste 17 (14218-1047)
PHONE...................................716 825-9300
Richard Workman, *President*
EMP: 32
SQ FT: 18,500
SALES: 3.5MM **Privately Held**
WEB: www.southsideprecast.com
SIC: 3272 Concrete products, precast

(G-2985)
P P I BUSINESS FORMS INC
94 Spaulding St (14220-1238)
PHONE...................................716 825-1241
Fax: 716 685-4740
EMP: 9
SQ FT: 9,500
SALES (est): 900K **Privately Held**
SIC: 2761 Manifold Business Forms

(G-2986)
P&G METAL COMPONENTS CORP
54 Gruner Rd (14227-1007)
PHONE...................................716 896-7900
Scott Bauer, *General Mgr*
David E Ponkow, *Chairman*

Andrew Ponkow, *Exec VP*
Thomas Brush, *CFO*
▲ EMP: 100 EST: 1955
SQ FT: 75,000
SALES (est): 35.6MM **Privately Held**
WEB: www.pgsteel.com
SIC: 3469 3544 4961 Stamping metal for the trade; special dies, tools, jigs & fixtures; steam & air-conditioning supply

(G-2987)
P&G STEEL INC
54 Gruner Rd (14227-1092)
PHONE...................................716 896-7900
EMP: 11
SALES (est): 2MM **Privately Held**
SIC: 3469 Metal stampings

(G-2988)
PACKAGE PRINT TECHNOLOGIES
1831 Niagara St (14207-3112)
PHONE...................................716 871-9905
Kim Koehler, *President*
Tony Collini, *General Mgr*
▲ EMP: 10
SQ FT: 5,000
SALES (est): 3.7MM **Privately Held**
WEB: www.packageprinttech.com
SIC: 3555 3069 Printing trades machinery; printers' rolls & blankets: rubber or rubberized fabric

(G-2989)
PACLINE CONVEYORS INC
15 Charlotte Rd (14225-1205)
PHONE...................................716 932-7858
Carol Scholz, *President*
Paul Geddes, *President*
Robert Stern, *Engineer*
Robert Campana, *CFO*
EMP: 40
SQ FT: 500
SALES (est): 343.6K **Privately Held**
WEB: www.pacline.com
SIC: 3535 Conveyors & conveying equipment

(G-2990)
PAR-FOAM PRODUCTS INC
239 Van Rensselaer St (14210-1345)
PHONE...................................716 855-2066
Kaushik A Shah, *President*
Rolandd J Nauffer, *Vice Pres*
EMP: 130
SQ FT: 64,000
SALES (est): 14.7MM **Privately Held**
SIC: 3069 3714 3086 Foam rubber; motor vehicle parts & accessories; plastics foam products

(G-2991)
PARK AVENUE IMPRINTS LLC (PA)
2955 S Park Ave (14218-2613)
PHONE...................................716 822-5737
James Roorda, *Mng Member*
EMP: 6
SQ FT: 1,200
SALES (est): 592.2K **Privately Held**
SIC: 2759 Screen printing

(G-2992)
PARKSIDE CANDY CO INC (PA)
3208 Main St Ste 1 (14214-1379)
PHONE...................................716 833-7540
Phillip J Buffamonte, *President*
EMP: 17 EST: 1978
SALES (est): 1.8MM **Privately Held**
WEB: www.parksidecandy.com
SIC: 2066 5441 Chocolate bars, solid; chocolate candy, solid; candy

(G-2993)
PARRINELLO PRINTING INC
84 Aero Dr (14225-1435)
PHONE...................................716 633-7780
Colleen Parrinello, *President*
EMP: 14
SALES (est): 2.1MM **Privately Held**
SIC: 2752 Commercial printing, offset

Buffalo - Erie County (G-2994)   GEOGRAPHIC SECTION

(G-2994)
PDI CONE CO INC
Also Called: Dutchtreat
69 Leddy St (14210-2134)
PHONE..................................716 825-8750
Geoge Page, *Principal*
EMP: 67
SALES (est): 8.2MM Privately Held
SIC: 2052 Cones, ice cream

(G-2995)
PELLICANO SPECIALTY FOODS INC
195 Reading St (14220-2157)
P.O. Box 34, Lake View (14085-0034)
PHONE..................................716 822-2366
Mario Pellicano, *President*
Jim Kalec, *Vice Pres*
EMP: 18 **EST:** 1996
SALES: 4MM Privately Held
SIC: 2099 Food preparations

(G-2996)
PENINSULA PLASTICS LTD
161 Marine Dr Apt 6e (14202-4214)
P.O. Box 1179 (14202)
PHONE..................................716 854-3050
Craig Bolton, *Owner*
EMP: 54
SALES (est): 2.1MM Privately Held
WEB: www.penplast.com
SIC: 3089 Injection molding of plastics

(G-2997)
PEOPLES CHOICE M R I
125 Galileo Dr (14221-2776)
PHONE..................................716 681-7377
Vafeem Iqbal, *President*
EMP: 10
SALES (est): 827.1K Privately Held
WEB: www.peoplesmri.com
SIC: 3577 Magnetic ink & optical scanning devices

(G-2998)
PERAFLEX HOSE INC
155 Great Arrow Ave Ste 4 (14207-3010)
PHONE..................................716 876-8806
Newell Kraik, *President*
Mark Montgomery, *Director*
◆ **EMP:** 15
SQ FT: 13,000
SALES (est): 3MM Privately Held
WEB: www.peraflex.com
SIC: 3052 5085 Rubber & plastics hose & beltings; industrial supplies

(G-2999)
PERKINS INTERNATIONAL INC (HQ)
672 Delaware Ave (14209-2202)
PHONE..................................309 675-1000
Michael J Baunton, *CEO*
Dan Hagan, *Analyst*
EMP: 5
SALES (est): 3.1MM
SALES (corp-wide): 45.4B Publicly Held
WEB: www.tuckaway.com
SIC: 3519 Internal combustion engines
PA: Caterpillar Inc.
510 Lake Cook Rd Ste 100
Deerfield IL 60015
224 551-4000

(G-3000)
PERMA TECH INC
363 Hamburg St (14204-2086)
PHONE..................................716 854-0707
Richard E Lund Jr, *President*
EMP: 22
SQ FT: 45,000
SALES (est): 3MM Privately Held
WEB: www.permatechinc.com
SIC: 2394 3441 3089 Awnings, fabric: made from purchased materials; fabricated structural metal; doors, folding: plastic or plastic coated fabric

(G-3001)
PHILCOM LTD
1144 Military Rd (14217-2232)
PHONE..................................716 875-8005
Bruce G Phillips, *Ch of Bd*
Karen Phillips, *Vice Pres*
EMP: 1
SALES (est): 3.8MM Privately Held
SIC: 3089 Boxes, plastic

(G-3002)
PHILPAC CORPORATION (PA)
1144 Military Rd (14217-2232)
PHONE..................................716 875-8005
Bruce G Phillips, *President*
Karen Phillips, *Corp Secy*
Courtney Gorman, *Materials Mgr*
Rich Taber, *Purchasing*
Jason Sleggs, *Sales Staff*
EMP: 50
SALES (est): 14.1MM Privately Held
SIC: 2653 5085 3086 2655 Boxes, corrugated: made from purchased materials; packing, industrial; padding, foamed plastic; fiber cans, drums & similar products; nailed wood boxes & shook

(G-3003)
PIERCE ARROW DRAPERY MFG
Also Called: Pierce Arrow Draperies
1685 Elmwood Ave Ste 312 (14207-2435)
PHONE..................................716 876-3023
Robert Merkel, *President*
EMP: 5
SQ FT: 2,000
SALES (est): 526.5K Privately Held
SIC: 2221 Draperies & drapery fabrics, manmade fiber & silk

(G-3004)
PII HOLDINGS INC (DH)
2150 Elmwood Ave (14207-1910)
PHONE..................................716 876-9951
Mike McLelland, *CEO*
Ray Baran, *Treasurer*
EMP: 2
SALES (est): 208MM
SALES (corp-wide): 2.9B Privately Held
SIC: 3089 3822 6719 Molding primary plastic; temperature controls, automatic; investment holding companies, except banks
HQ: Berwind Consolidated Holdings, Inc.
3000 Ctr Sq W 1500 Mkt St 1500 W
Philadelphia PA 19102
215 563-2800

(G-3005)
PINE HILL FABRICATORS
2731 Seneca St (14224-1895)
PHONE..................................716 823-2474
Joseph L Neuner, *Owner*
Liz Eichelberger, *Office Mgr*
EMP: 6
SQ FT: 4,000
SALES (est): 840.3K Privately Held
SIC: 2541 Counter & sink tops

(G-3006)
PLASLOK CORP
3155 Broadway St (14227-1034)
PHONE..................................716 681-7755
Richard A Neil, *President*
EMP: 43
SQ FT: 75,000
SALES: 7MM Privately Held
SIC: 2821 Molding compounds, plastics

(G-3007)
PLASTIC SYS/GR BFLO INC
465 Cornwall Ave (14215-3125)
PHONE..................................716 835-7555
Daniel McNamara, *President*
Sean Lobue, *General Mgr*
EMP: 5 **EST:** 1980
SQ FT: 9,200
SALES (est): 697.1K Privately Held
WEB: www.plasticsystems.com
SIC: 3089 Plastic containers, except foam; trays, plastic; thermoformed finished plastic products; cases, plastic

(G-3008)
POINTMAN LLC (PA)
Also Called: Swremote
403 Main St Ste 200 (14203-2107)
PHONE..................................716 842-1439
Stephen Kiernan, *President*
Steven Raines, *Vice Pres*
Steve Kiernan, *Director*
EMP: 5
SQ FT: 18,000
SALES: 1.6MM Privately Held
SIC: 7372 5734 5045 Business oriented computer software; software, business & non-game; computer software

(G-3009)
POL-TEK INDUSTRIES LTD
2300 Clinton St (14227-1735)
PHONE..................................716 823-1502
Martin Ostrowski, *CEO*
Wanda Ostrowski, *Corp Secy*
Natalie Handzlik, *Office Mgr*
EMP: 15
SQ FT: 11,000
SALES (est): 2MM Privately Held
WEB: www.pol-tek.com
SIC: 3599 Machine shop, jobbing & repair

(G-3010)
POWERFLOW INC
1714 Broadway St (14212-2090)
P.O. Box 905 (14240-0905)
PHONE..................................716 892-1014
Douglas K Ward, *Ch of Bd*
▲ **EMP:** 66 **EST:** 1978
SQ FT: 55,000
SALES: 33MM Privately Held
WEB: www.powerflowinc.com
SIC: 3714 Motor vehicle parts & accessories

(G-3011)
PRECISION PHOTO-FAB INC
Also Called: Switzer
4020 Jeffrey Blvd (14219-2393)
PHONE..................................716 821-9393
Bernie Switzer, *President*
Joseph Dunlop, *Vice Pres*
Adam Switzer, *Vice Pres*
EMP: 55
SQ FT: 20,000
SALES (est): 12.4MM Privately Held
WEB: www.precisionphotofab.com
SIC: 3469 Metal stampings

(G-3012)
PRECISION SPCLTY FBRCTIONS LLC
51 N Gates Ave (14218-1029)
PHONE..................................716 824-2108
Dennis Switzer,
John Maher,
EMP: 20
SALES (est): 2.6MM Privately Held
SIC: 3499 Strapping, metal

(G-3013)
PREMIER MACHINING TECH INC
2100 Old Union Rd (14227-2725)
PHONE..................................716 608-1311
William G Belcher, *President*
Kimberly Belcher, *Admin Sec*
EMP: 8
SQ FT: 18,500
SALES: 1.2MM Privately Held
SIC: 3599 Machine shop, jobbing & repair

(G-3014)
PRINCE RUBBER & PLAS CO INC (PA)
137 Arthur St (14207-2098)
PHONE..................................225 272-1653
S Warren Prince Jr, *Ch of Bd*
John G Putnam, *Admin Sec*
▲ **EMP:** 45
SQ FT: 35,000
SALES (est): 10.7MM Privately Held
WEB: www.princerp.com
SIC: 3069 3089 3084 3053 Hard rubber & molded rubber products; plastic processing; plastics pipe; gaskets, packing & sealing devices

(G-3015)
PRINTED IMAGE
1906 Clinton St (14206-3206)
PHONE..................................716 821-1880
Richard Zavarella, *Owner*
EMP: 5
SQ FT: 3,000
SALES (est): 451.1K Privately Held
SIC: 2759 Screen printing

(G-3016)
PRO-GEAR CO INC
1120 Niagara St (14213-1714)
PHONE..................................716 684-3811
Gary Rackley, *President*
EMP: 5
SQ FT: 6,500
SALES (est): 377.2K
SALES (corp-wide): 18MM Privately Held
SIC: 3462 Gears, forged steel
PA: Gear Motions Incorporated
1750 Milton Ave
Syracuse NY 13209
315 488-0100

(G-3017)
PROTECTIVE INDUSTRIES INC (DH)
Also Called: Caplugs
2150 Elmwood Ave (14207-1910)
PHONE..................................716 876-9951
David Williams, *President*
Susan McElliggott, *Vice Pres*
Kennery Rob, *Vice Pres*
Thomas Valentine, *Vice Pres*
James Ray, *VP Opers*
◆ **EMP:** 250
SQ FT: 80,000
SALES: 208MM
SALES (corp-wide): 2.9B Privately Held
WEB: www.mokon.com
SIC: 3089 3822 Molding primary plastic; temperature controls, automatic
HQ: Pii Holdings, Inc.
2150 Elmwood Ave
Buffalo NY 14207
716 876-9951

(G-3018)
PROTECTIVE INDUSTRIES INC
Also Called: Caplugs
2150 Elmwood Ave (14207-1910)
PHONE..................................716 876-9855
Jeff Smith, *Branch Mgr*
EMP: 238
SALES (corp-wide): 2.9B Privately Held
WEB: www.mokon.com
SIC: 3089 Molding primary plastic
HQ: Protective Industries, Inc.
2150 Elmwood Ave
Buffalo NY 14207
716 876-9951

(G-3019)
PROTECTIVE INDUSTRIES INC
Mokon
2510 Elmwood Ave (14217-2223)
PHONE..................................716 876-9951
Robert Kennery, *General Mgr*
EMP: 55
SALES (corp-wide): 2.9B Privately Held
WEB: www.mokon.com
SIC: 3822 Temperature controls, automatic
HQ: Protective Industries, Inc.
2150 Elmwood Ave
Buffalo NY 14207
716 876-9951

(G-3020)
PVS CHEMICAL SOLUTIONS INC
55 Lee St (14210-2109)
PHONE..................................716 825-5762
Patrick Murphy, *Opers Mgr*
Jane Lamanna, *Engineer*
Chris Cancilla, *Manager*
EMP: 51
SALES (corp-wide): 500.1MM Privately Held
SIC: 2819 2899 Sulfur chloride; chemical preparations
HQ: Pvs Chemical Solutions, Inc.
10900 Harper Ave
Detroit MI 48213

(G-3021)
PVS TECHNOLOGIES INC
Also Called: PVS Chemical Solutions
55 Lee St (14210-2109)
PHONE..................................716 825-5762
William Decker, *Manager*
EMP: 48
SQ FT: 65,268

GEOGRAPHIC SECTION

Buffalo - Erie County (G-3048)

SALES (corp-wide): 500.1MM **Privately Held**
SIC: 2819 Metal salts & compounds, except sodium, potassium, aluminum
HQ: Pvs Technologies, Inc.
10900 Harper Ave
Detroit MI 48213
313 571-1100

(G-3022)
QLS SOLUTIONS GROUP INC
701 Seneca St Ste 600 (14210-1361)
PHONE 716 852-2203
Gary Skalyo, *President*
EMP: 24
SQ FT: 30,000
SALES (est): 4.3MM **Privately Held**
WEB: www.qualitylaser.com
SIC: 3955 3861 Print cartridges for laser & other computer printers; reproduction machines & equipment

(G-3023)
QTA MACHINING INC
Also Called: Quick Turn Around Machining
876 Bailey Ave (14206-2300)
PHONE 716 862-8108
Suzanne M Pelczynski, *President*
Roxanne Pelczynski, *Vice Pres*
EMP: 12
SQ FT: 10,000
SALES (est): 2.1MM **Privately Held**
WEB: www.qtanow.com
SIC: 3599 Machine shop, jobbing & repair

(G-3024)
QUAKER BONNET INC
54 Irving Pl (14201-1521)
PHONE 716 885-7208
Elizabeth Kolken, *President*
Ben Kolken, *Vice Pres*
EMP: 5 EST: 1930
SQ FT: 4,400
SALES (est): 494.2K **Privately Held**
WEB: www.quakerbonnet.com
SIC: 2051 2052 2024 Bakery: wholesale or wholesale/retail combined; cookies; ice cream & frozen desserts

(G-3025)
QUALITY BINDERY SERVICE INC
501 Amherst St (14207-2913)
PHONE 716 883-5185
Kathleen Hartmans, *President*
EMP: 34
SQ FT: 4,000
SALES (est): 4.1MM **Privately Held**
SIC: 2789 Trade binding services

(G-3026)
QUANTUM ASSET RECOVERY
482 Niagara Falls Blvd (14223-2634)
PHONE 716 393-2712
EMP: 7
SALES (est): 359.6K **Privately Held**
SIC: 3572 Computer storage devices

(G-3027)
QUEEN CITY MALTING LLC
644 N Forest Rd (14221-4965)
PHONE 716 481-1313
Joseph S Kirby Jr, *CEO*
EMP: 7
SALES (est): 262.8K **Privately Held**
SIC: 2083 Malt

(G-3028)
QUEEN CITY MANUFACTURING INC
333 Henderson Ave (14217-1538)
PHONE 716 877-1102
Robert Maranto, *President*
Joseph Mallare, *Vice Pres*
Steve Nappo, *Vice Pres*
▲ EMP: 5
SALES (est): 1.4MM **Privately Held**
WEB: www.queencitymanufacturing.com
SIC: 2821 Melamine resins, melamine-formaldehyde

(G-3029)
R & A INDUSTRIAL PRODUCTS
Also Called: R&A Prods
30 Cornelia St (14210-1202)
PHONE 716 823-4300
Tony Onello, *President*
EMP: 5
SQ FT: 2,600
SALES: 376.6K **Privately Held**
SIC: 3061 Mechanical rubber goods

(G-3030)
R & B MACHINERY CORP
400 Kennedy Rd Ste 3 (14227-1073)
PHONE 716 894-3332
Fax: 716 894-3335
EMP: 4
SQ FT: 28,000
SALES (est): 2.2MM **Privately Held**
SIC: 3559 Mfg Misc Industry Machinery

(G-3031)
RAPID RAYS PRINTING & COPYING
300 Broadway St (14204-1433)
P.O. Box 442 (14205-0442)
PHONE 716 852-0550
Raymond Wellence, *President*
Kathleen Wellence, *Vice Pres*
EMP: 9 EST: 1973
SQ FT: 4,100
SALES (est): 1.1MM **Privately Held**
WEB: www.rapidrays.com
SIC: 2752 Photo-offset printing

(G-3032)
RAPID SERVICE ENGRAVING CO
1593 Genesee St (14211-1634)
PHONE 716 896-4555
James F Egloff, *President*
John F Egloff, *Admin Sec*
EMP: 6
SQ FT: 6,000
SALES (est): 578.8K **Privately Held**
SIC: 2796 2752 Photoengraving plates, linecuts or halftones; commercial printing, lithographic

(G-3033)
REALTIMETRADERSCOM
1325 N Forest Rd Ste 240 (14221-2143)
P.O. Box 387, Getzville (14068-0387)
PHONE 716 632-6600
Andrew Marthiasan, *President*
EMP: 33 EST: 1995
SQ FT: 2,000
SALES (est): 1.4MM **Privately Held**
SIC: 2711 7375 Newspapers; information retrieval services

(G-3034)
REIMANN & GEORGER CORPORATION
1849 Harlem Rd (14212-2401)
P.O. Box 681 (14240-0681)
PHONE 716 895-1156
E Eric Von Dungen, *Principal*
Joseph Quadrone, *Opers Mgr*
Mark Mickiewicz, *Buyer*
Donna Cooke, *Supervisor*
▲ EMP: 42
SQ FT: 38,000
SALES (est): 18.9MM **Privately Held**
WEB: www.rgcproducts.com
SIC: 3536 3546 Hoists; boat lifts; power-driven handtools

(G-3035)
REUSE ACTION INCORPORATED
279 Northampton St (14208-2304)
PHONE 716 949-0900
Michael Gainer, *Principal*
EMP: 5 EST: 2011
SALES (est): 579.6K **Privately Held**
SIC: 3822 Building services monitoring controls, automatic

(G-3036)
RICH HOLDINGS INC
1 Robert Rich Way (14213-1701)
PHONE 716 878-8000
Christopher T Dunstan, *Principal*
◆ EMP: 75
SALES (est): 7.5MM **Privately Held**
SIC: 2053 Frozen bakery products, except bread

(G-3037)
RICH PRODUCTS CORPORATION (PA)
1 Robert Rich Way (14213-1701)
P.O. Box 245 (14240-0245)
PHONE 716 878-8000
Bill Gisel, *CEO*
Richard Ferranti, *President*
Kim Burke, *President*
Ray Burke, *President*
Jeff Kim, *President*
◆ EMP: 1375 EST: 1993
SQ FT: 60,000
SALES (est): 4B **Privately Held**
WEB: www.richs.com
SIC: 2053 2092 2023 2099 Frozen bakery products, except bread; fresh or frozen packaged fish; shrimp, frozen: prepared; shellfish, frozen: prepared; dry, condensed, evaporated dairy products; whipped topping, dry mix; cream substitutes; dessert mixes & fillings

(G-3038)
RIGIDIZED METALS CORPORATION
Also Called: Rigidized-Metal
658 Ohio St (14203-3185)
PHONE 716 849-4703
Richard S Smith Jr, *Ch of Bd*
Richard S Smith III, *President*
Fred Deuschle, *Engineer*
Douglas F Lum, *Treasurer*
▲ EMP: 48 EST: 1940
SQ FT: 58,060
SALES (est): 22.2MM **Privately Held**
WEB: www.rigidized.com
SIC: 3469 3444 2796 Rigidizing metal; sheet metalwork; platemaking services

(G-3039)
RLP HOLDINGS INC
Also Called: Belt Maintenance Systems
1049 Military Rd (14217-2228)
PHONE 716 852-0832
Joe Hooley, *President*
Brian RE, *VP Sales*
▲ EMP: 8
SQ FT: 18,000
SALES (est): 2.4MM **Privately Held**
SIC: 3535 Conveyors & conveying equipment

(G-3040)
ROBERTS-GORDON LLC (DH)
Also Called: RG
1250 William St (14206-1819)
P.O. Box 44 (14240-0044)
PHONE 716 852-4400
Mark J Dines, *President*
Richard G Jasiura, *CFO*
▲ EMP: 100 EST: 1998
SQ FT: 107,000
SALES (est): 90MM
SALES (corp-wide): 297MM **Privately Held**
WEB: www.rg-inc.com
SIC: 3675 3433 Condensers, electronic; unit heaters, domestic
HQ: Specified Air Solutions Llc
1250 William St
Buffalo NY 14206
716 852-4400

(G-3041)
ROBINSON KNIFE
2615 Walden Ave (14225-4735)
PHONE 716 685-6300
Robert Skerker, *CEO*
Larry Skerker, *Vice Pres*
EMP: 11
SALES (est): 1.5MM **Privately Held**
SIC: 3089 Plastic kitchenware, tableware & houseware

(G-3042)
ROCKET COMMUNICATIONS INC
Also Called: Buffalo Rocket
2507 Delaware Ave (14216)
PHONE 716 873-2594
David Gallagher, *CEO*
Dennis Gallagher, *Vice Pres*
Dean Gallagher, *Treasurer*
Daryl Gallagher, *Admin Sec*
EMP: 12 EST: 1996
SQ FT: 30,000
SALES (est): 727.5K **Privately Held**
WEB: www.buffalorocket.com
SIC: 2711 Newspapers, publishing & printing

(G-3043)
RODGARD CORPORATION
92 Msgr Valente Dr (14206-1822)
PHONE 716 852-1435
Richard E Hauck, *Ch of Bd*
EMP: 30
SALES (est): 32.4K
SALES (corp-wide): 624.4MM **Publicly Held**
WEB: www.rodgard.com
SIC: 2821 Elastomers, nonvulcanizable (plastics)
PA: Astronics Corporation
130 Commerce Way
East Aurora NY 14052
716 805-1599

(G-3044)
ROLLERS INC
2495 Main St Ste 359 (14214-2154)
PHONE 716 837-0700
Frank Reppenhagen, *Owner*
EMP: 9
SALES (est): 640K **Privately Held**
WEB: www.rollers.com
SIC: 2515 3555 5085 Mattresses, containing felt, foam rubber, urethane, etc.; printing trade parts & attachments; industrial supplies

(G-3045)
ROSINA FOOD PRODUCTS INC
Also Called: Ceoentano
170 French Rd (14227-2777)
PHONE 716 668-0123
Russell A Corigliano, *Ch of Bd*
James Corigliano, *Ch of Bd*
John Zimmerman, *President*
Frank Corigliano, *Exec VP*
Jose Cabanin, *Vice Pres*
EMP: 178
SQ FT: 60,000
SALES (est): 40.1MM **Privately Held**
SIC: 2013 5812 Sausages & other prepared meats; eating places
PA: Rosina Holding, Inc.
170 French Rd
Buffalo NY 14227

(G-3046)
ROSINA HOLDING INC (PA)
170 French Rd (14227-2717)
PHONE 716 668-0123
Russell A Corigliano, *Ch of Bd*
Todd Palczewski, *Research*
Frank Corigliano, *Treasurer*
Randy Bernick, *Manager*
Dennis Delaney, *Programmer Anys*
EMP: 3
SQ FT: 40,000
SALES (est): 50.8MM **Privately Held**
SIC: 2013 Sausages & other prepared meats

(G-3047)
ROSS L SPORTS SCREENING INC
2756 Seneca St (14224-1866)
PHONE 716 824-5350
Dave Cellino, *Owner*
EMP: 15 EST: 1973
SALES (est): 443.6K **Privately Held**
SIC: 2395 Embroidery & art needlework

(G-3048)
ROUGH BROTHERS HOLDING CO (HQ)
Also Called: Sunlight US Co., Inc.
3556 Lake Shore Rd # 100 (14219-1445)
PHONE 716 826-6500
Frank Heard, *President*
Paul M Murray, *Senior VP*
Kenneth W Smith, *CFO*
Timothy F Murphy, *Treasurer*
EMP: 8

Buffalo - Erie County (G-3049)

SALES (est): 113.4MM
SALES (corp-wide): 986.9MM **Publicly Held**
SIC: **3499** 3316 3441 3398 Strapping, metal; cold finishing of steel shapes; fabricated structural metal; metal heat treating
PA: Gibraltar Industries, Inc.
3556 Lake Shore Rd # 100
Buffalo NY 14219
716 826-6500

(G-3049)
ROYAL BEDDING CO BUFFALO INC
Also Called: Restonic
201 James E Casey Dr (14206-2363)
PHONE.....................716 895-1414
Thomas Comer Jr, *President*
Jennifer Beaman, *Executive*
▲ EMP: 25
SQ FT: 110,000
SALES (est): 5MM **Privately Held**
SIC: **2515** Mattresses, innerspring or box spring; box springs, assembled

(G-3050)
RWB CONTROLS INC
471 Connecticut St (14213-2645)
PHONE.....................716 897-4341
Fax: 716 882-1575
EMP: 6
SQ FT: 4,000
SALES (est): 600K **Privately Held**
SIC: **3823** 5063 Mfg Industrial Process Control Instruments & Displays

(G-3051)
S & H MACHINE COMPANY INC
83 Clyde Ave (14215-2237)
PHONE.....................716 834-1194
EMP: 5
SQ FT: 5,500
SALES (est): 400K **Privately Held**
SIC: **3599** Machine Shop

(G-3052)
S J B FABRICATION
430 Kennedy Rd (14227-1032)
PHONE.....................716 895-0281
Sean Brubckman, *Owner*
EMP: 10
SALES (est): 310.1K **Privately Held**
SIC: **7692** Welding repair

(G-3053)
S J MCCULLAGH INC (PA)
Also Called: McCullagh Coffee
245 Swan St (14204-2051)
PHONE.....................716 856-3473
Warren E Emblidge Jr, *President*
Daniel Phillips, *Executive*
Carol Emblidge, *Admin Sec*
▲ EMP: 50
SQ FT: 16,000
SALES (est): 11.7MM **Privately Held**
SIC: **2095** 5113 5149 Coffee roasting (except by wholesale grocers); cups, disposable plastic & paper; groceries & related products; dried or canned foods; sugar, refined; chocolate

(G-3054)
SAFETEC OF AMERICA INC
887 Kensington Ave (14215-2720)
PHONE.....................716 895-1822
Scott A Weinstein, *CEO*
Peter Weinstein, *Vice Pres*
Nadine Martz, *Research*
Allyson Devonshire, *Human Res Mgr*
Marc Colonna, *Accounts Mgr*
▲ EMP: 60
SQ FT: 80,000
SALES: 10.3MM **Privately Held**
WEB: www.safetec.com
SIC: **2842** 2834 Specialty cleaning, polishes & sanitation goods; drugs affecting parasitic & infective diseases

(G-3055)
SAFETY-KLEEN SYSTEMS INC
60 Katherine St (14210-2006)
PHONE.....................716 855-2212
James Drozdowski, *Branch Mgr*
EMP: 16
SQ FT: 24,259
SALES (corp-wide): 2.9B **Publicly Held**
SIC: **2992** Re-refining lubricating oils & greases
HQ: Safety-Kleen Systems, Inc.
2600 N Central Expy # 400
Richardson TX 75080
972 265-2000

(G-3056)
SAHLEN PACKING COMPANY INC
318 Howard St (14206-2760)
P.O. Box 280 (14240-0280)
PHONE.....................716 852-8677
Joseph E Sahlen, *Ch of Bd*
Christopher Cauley, *Vice Pres*
Deborah Howell, *VP Opers*
David Miller, *Controller*
James Bowen, *CPA*
▲ EMP: 85 EST: 1869
SQ FT: 53,789
SALES (est): 16.3MM **Privately Held**
WEB: www.sahlen.com
SIC: **2011** Sausages from meat slaughtered on site; hams & picnics from meat slaughtered on site; bacon, slab & sliced from meat slaughtered on site

(G-3057)
SALIT SPECIALTY REBAR INC
1050 Military Rd (14217-2528)
PHONE.....................716 299-1990
Steven Cohen, *CEO*
James Terhune, *General Mgr*
Kevin Cornell, *VP Sales*
Sheri Otis, *Manager*
▼ EMP: 25
SALES (est): 15MM **Privately Held**
SIC: **3441** Fabricated structural metal

(G-3058)
SCHULER-SUBRA INC
Also Called: Eskay Metal Fabricating
83 Doat St (14211-2048)
PHONE.....................716 893-3100
Jeff Subra, *President*
EMP: 6 EST: 1944
SQ FT: 16,500
SALES (est): 648.9K **Privately Held**
WEB: www.specialtystainless.com
SIC: **3441** Fabricated structural metal

(G-3059)
SCHUTTE-BUFFALO HAMMERMILL LLC
Also Called: Schutte-Buffalo Hammer Mill
61 Depot St (14206-2203)
PHONE.....................716 855-1202
Thomas E Warne, *President*
James Klopser,
▲ EMP: 25 EST: 1933
SQ FT: 22,500
SALES (est): 8.9MM **Privately Held**
WEB: www.hammermills.com
SIC: **3531** Hammer mills (rock & ore crushing machines), portable

(G-3060)
SCREW COMPRESSOR TECH INC
158 Ridge Rd (14218-1035)
PHONE.....................716 827-6600
John Zahner, *President*
EMP: 13
SALES (est): 2.3MM **Privately Held**
SIC: **3563** Air & gas compressors

(G-3061)
SECOND AMENDMENT FOUNDATION
Also Called: Gun Week
267 Linwood Ave Ste A (14209-1816)
PHONE.....................716 885-6408
Joseph Tartaro, *President*
Peggy Tartaro, *Editor*
EMP: 5
SALES (corp-wide): 873.3K **Privately Held**
WEB: www.saf.org
SIC: **2711** Newspapers, publishing & printing
PA: Second Amendment Foundation Inc
12500 Ne 10th Pl
Bellevue WA 98005
425 454-7012

(G-3062)
SERVICE CANVAS CO INC
149 Swan St Unit 155 (14203-2624)
PHONE.....................716 853-0558
Jerald H Eron, *President*
EMP: 12 EST: 1946
SQ FT: 80,000
SALES (est): 1.2MM **Privately Held**
WEB: www.servicecanvas.com
SIC: **2394** Canopies, fabric: made from purchased materials
PA: Synthetic Textiles Inc
398 Broadway St
Buffalo NY 14204

(G-3063)
SERVICE MFG GROUP INC (PA)
400 Scajaquada St (14211-1722)
PHONE.....................716 893-1482
Linda Casoni, *CEO*
Vito Casoni, *President*
Sal Alagna, *Sales Mgr*
Bridget Kashmer, *Info Tech Mgr*
EMP: 12
SQ FT: 150,000
SALES (est): 8.4MM **Privately Held**
WEB: www.t-smg.com
SIC: **3625** 3444 Relays & industrial controls; sheet metal specialties, not stamped

(G-3064)
SERVICE MFG GROUP INC
Also Called: Smg Control Systems
400 Scajaquada St (14211-1722)
PHONE.....................716 893-1482
George Smith, *Opers-Prdtn-Mfg*
EMP: 35
SALES (est): 4.4MM
SALES (corp-wide): 8.4MM **Privately Held**
WEB: www.t-smg.com
SIC: **3444** Sheet metalwork
PA: The Service Manufacturing Group Inc
400 Scajaquada St
Buffalo NY 14211
716 893-1482

(G-3065)
SIEMENS INDUSTRY INC
85 Northpointe Pkwy Ste 8 (14228-1886)
PHONE.....................716 568-0983
Tom Strollo, *General Mgr*
Patrick Parlane, *Branch Mgr*
EMP: 50
SALES (corp-wide): 97.7B **Privately Held**
WEB: www.sibt.com
SIC: **3585** 7373 1541 Heating equipment, complete; computer integrated systems design; industrial buildings & warehouses
HQ: Siemens Industry, Inc.
100 Technology Dr
Alpharetta GA 30005
770 740-3000

(G-3066)
SIMREX CORPORATION
1223 William St (14206-1805)
PHONE.....................716 206-0174
Donna Neuperger, *President*
Michael Aquilino, *Exec VP*
Frank Neuperger, *Vice Pres*
Dan Smyntek, *Design Engr*
▼ EMP: 8
SQ FT: 3,200
SALES (est): 1.3MM **Privately Held**
SIC: **3669** 3661 Intercommunication systems, electric; modems

(G-3067)
SMARTPILL CORPORATION
847 Main St (14203-1109)
PHONE.....................716 882-0701
David Barthel, *President*
EMP: 31
SQ FT: 7,500
SALES (est): 3.7MM **Privately Held**
WEB: www.smartpill.com
SIC: **3826** Analytical instruments

(G-3068)
SOMERSET PRODUCTION CO LLC
338 Harris Hill Rd # 102 (14221-7470)
PHONE.....................716 932-6480
Thomas H O'Neil Jr, *Principal*
Suzan Willhauck, *Webmaster*
William A Ziegler,
EMP: 7
SQ FT: 6,000
SALES (est): 620K **Privately Held**
SIC: **1382** Oil & gas exploration services

(G-3069)
SOMMER AND SONS PRINTING INC
2222 S Park Ave (14220-2296)
P.O. Box 3, Bowmansville (14026-0003)
PHONE.....................716 822-4311
Dennis Sommer, *President*
EMP: 11
SQ FT: 10,000
SALES (est): 1.6MM **Privately Held**
SIC: **2754** Commercial Printing

(G-3070)
SOPARK CORP (PA)
3300 S Park Ave (14218-3530)
PHONE.....................716 822-0434
Gerald Murak, *Ch of Bd*
Kiruba Hanmugam, *President*
Andrea Heinold, *Controller*
▲ EMP: 85
SQ FT: 28,000
SALES: 11MM **Privately Held**
WEB: www.sopark.com
SIC: **3672** 3679 3621 3694 Printed circuit boards; electronic circuits; motors, electric; engine electrical equipment

(G-3071)
SOROC TECHNOLOGY CORP
1051 Clinton St (14206-2823)
PHONE.....................716 849-5913
Rudy Cheddie, *President*
EMP: 2
SALES (est): 1MM **Privately Held**
WEB: www.soroc.com
SIC: **7372** Prepackaged software
PA: Soroc Technology Inc
607 Chrislea Rd
Woodbridge ON L4L 8
905 265-8000

(G-3072)
SORRENTO LACTALIS INC
2375 S Park Ave (14220-2653)
PHONE.....................716 823-6262
Leslie Pankow, *Business Mgr*
James Foriest, *Administration*
EMP: 8
SALES (est): 576.7K
SALES (corp-wide): 98.8MM **Privately Held**
SIC: **2022** Natural cheese
HQ: Lactalis American Group, Inc.
2376 S Park Ave
Buffalo NY 14220
716 823-6262

(G-3073)
SOUND VIDEO SYSTEMS WNY LLC
1720 Military Rd (14217-1148)
PHONE.....................716 684-8200
Bob Courtney, *Accounts Exec*
Joseph Caprino,
▲ EMP: 10
SALES (est): 1.4MM **Privately Held**
SIC: **3651** Household audio & video equipment

(G-3074)
SPECIFIED AIR SOLUTIONS LLC (HQ)
1250 William St (14206-1819)
P.O. Box 44 (14240-0044)
PHONE.....................716 852-4400
Charley Brown, *CEO*
EMP: 26
SALES (est): 90.1MM
SALES (corp-wide): 297MM **Privately Held**
SIC: **3585** 3567 Heating equipment, complete; paint baking & drying ovens
PA: Madison Industries Holdings Llc
500 W Madison St Ste 3890
Chicago IL 60661
312 277-0156

GEOGRAPHIC SECTION
Buffalo - Erie County (G-3102)

(G-3075)
SPEEDWAYS CONVEYORS INC
1210 E Ferry St (14211-1615)
PHONE..................716 893-2222
John T Thorn, *President*
John Jacobowitz, *Exec VP*
EMP: 47 **EST:** 1945
SQ FT: 100,000
SALES: 4.3MM **Privately Held**
SIC: 3535 5084 3537 Conveyors & conveying equipment; industrial machinery & equipment; industrial trucks & tractors

(G-3076)
STEPHEN M KIERNAN
Also Called: Big Bear
701 Seneca St Ste 300 (14210-1351)
PHONE..................716 836-6300
Stephen M Kiernan, *CEO*
David M Thiemecke, *COO*
EMP: 40
SALES (est): 1.6MM **Privately Held**
SIC: 2395 Embroidery & art needlework

(G-3077)
STETRON INTERNATIONAL INC (PA)
90 Broadway St Ste 1 (14203-1687)
PHONE..................716 854-3443
Edward R Steger, *Ch of Bd*
Monique Steger, *President*
Caroline A Steger, *Exec VP*
Roy T Chao, *Senior VP*
▲ **EMP:** 14
SQ FT: 13,000
SALES (est): 3MM **Privately Held**
WEB: www.stetron.com
SIC: 3679 8734 3676 3674 Electronic circuits; electronic loads & power supplies; electronic switches; testing laboratories; electronic resistors; semiconductors & related devices; printed circuit boards; relays & industrial controls

(G-3078)
STORYBOOKS FOREVER
4 Magnolia Ave (14220-2005)
P.O. Box 1234 (14220-8234)
PHONE..................716 822-7845
Dan Devlin, *Owner*
EMP: 14 **EST:** 2001
SALES (est): 530.2K **Privately Held**
SIC: 2731 Book publishing

(G-3079)
SUIT-KOTE CORPORATION
505 Como Park Blvd (14227-1605)
PHONE..................716 683-8850
Scott Harris, *Opers Staff*
Gary Thompson, *Branch Mgr*
EMP: 15
SALES (corp-wide): 234.8MM **Privately Held**
WEB: www.suit-kote.com
SIC: 2843 Surface active agents
PA: Suit-Kote Corporation
1911 Lorings Crossing Rd
Cortland NY 13045
607 753-1100

(G-3080)
SUPER PRICE CHOPPER INC
1580 Genesee St (14211-1635)
PHONE..................716 893-3323
AK Kaid, *President*
EMP: 11
SALES (est): 485.7K **Privately Held**
SIC: 3751 Motorcycles & related parts

(G-3081)
SURMET CERAMICS CORPORATION
699 Hertel Ave Ste 290 (14207-2341)
PHONE..................716 875-4091
Timothy Davis, *CEO*
Tom Mroz, *Manager*
EMP: 17
SALES (est): 2.1MM
SALES (corp-wide): 14MM **Privately Held**
SIC: 3297 Graphite refractories: carbon bond or ceramic bond
PA: Surmet, Corp.
31 B St
Burlington MA 01803
781 345-5721

(G-3082)
SWEETWORKS INC (PA)
Also Called: Niagara Chocolates
3500 Genesee St (14225-5015)
PHONE..................716 634-4545
Philip Terranova, *CEO*
Leanne Khoury, *Business Mgr*
Pascal Bieri, *Opers Mgr*
Andrew Ingham, *Opers Mgr*
Jeffrey Geiger, *Prdtn Mgr*
◆ **EMP:** 153
SQ FT: 115,000
SALES (est): 131.4MM **Privately Held**
WEB: www.sweetworks.net
SIC: 2066 2067 2064 Chocolate; chewing gum; candy & other confectionery products; chocolate candy, except solid chocolate; lollipops & other hard candy

(G-3083)
SYNTHETIC TEXTILES INC (PA)
398 Broadway St (14204-1546)
P.O. Box 1465 (14240-1465)
PHONE..................716 842-2598
Jerald H Eron, *President*
EMP: 2
SQ FT: 88,000
SALES (est): 1.2MM **Privately Held**
WEB: www.synthetictextile.com
SIC: 3083 Plastic finished products, laminated

(G-3084)
SYSTEMS DRS C3 INC (DH)
485 Cayuga Rd (14225-1368)
PHONE..................716 631-6200
Alan Dietrich, *President*
Jason Rinsky, *Vice Pres*
Richard A Schneider, *Treasurer*
Mark S Newman, *Director*
EMP: 300
SQ FT: 300,000
SALES: 137.6MM
SALES (corp-wide): 9.2B **Privately Held**
WEB: www.drs-ewns.com
SIC: 3812 8713 Radar systems & equipment;
HQ: Leonardo Drs, Inc.
2345 Crystal Dr Ste 1000
Arlington VA 22202
703 416-8000

(G-3085)
T M MACHINE INC
176 Reading St (14220-2198)
PHONE..................716 822-0817
Theodore S Michalski, *President*
Dennis Michalski, *Vice Pres*
EMP: 9
SQ FT: 7,000
SALES: 1.5MM **Privately Held**
SIC: 3599 Machine shop, jobbing & repair

(G-3086)
TAILORED COATINGS INC
1800 Brdwy St Bldg 2a (14212)
PHONE..................716 893-4869
David R Mohamed, *Ch of Bd*
Fred Tafelski, *Principal*
EMP: 24
SALES (est): 4MM **Privately Held**
SIC: 3479 Painting of metal products

(G-3087)
TCHNOLOGIES N MRC AMEERICA LLC
Also Called: M R C
25 Roberts Ave (14206-3130)
PHONE..................716 822-4300
Lynn Leimkuehler, *Vice Pres*
Bruce McLean, *Office Mgr*
James Leimkuehler,
EMP: 9 **EST:** 1980
SQ FT: 150,000
SALES (est): 1.3MM **Privately Held**
SIC: 3599 7699 Machine shop, jobbing & repair; industrial machinery & equipment repair

(G-3088)
TECTRAN MFG INC (HQ)
2345 Walden Ave Ste 1 (14225-4770)
PHONE..................800 776-5549
Bruce McKie, *Ch of Bd*
▲ **EMP:** 86
SALES: 19.4MM **Privately Held**
WEB: www.tectran.com
SIC: 3713 Truck bodies & parts

(G-3089)
TEGNA INC
Also Called: W G R Z - T V Channel 2
259 Delaware Ave (14202-2008)
PHONE..................716 849-2222
Jim Toellner, *General Mgr*
Chris Hoffman, *Technology*
Pam Bork, *Regional*
EMP: 130
SALES (corp-wide): 1.9B **Publicly Held**
WEB: www.gannett.com
SIC: 2711 4833 Newspapers; television broadcasting stations
PA: Tegna Inc.
7950 Jones Branch Dr
Mc Lean VA 22102
703 873-6600

(G-3090)
TENT AND TABLE COM LLC
2845 Bailey Ave (14215-3242)
PHONE..................716 570-0258
▲ **EMP:** 15
SALES: 7MM **Privately Held**
SIC: 3999 Mfg Misc Products

(G-3091)
TERRAPIN STATION LTD
1172 Hertel Ave (14216-2704)
PHONE..................716 874-6677
Barry Cohen, *President*
Robert Colsanti, *Vice Pres*
EMP: 13
SALES (est): 1.2MM **Privately Held**
WEB: www.terrapinstationbuffalo.com
SIC: 2337 Women's & misses' suits & coats

(G-3092)
THE CHOCOLATE SHOP
871 Niagara St (14213-2114)
PHONE..................716 882-5055
Vincent Caruana, *Owner*
James Vincent, *Manager*
EMP: 6
SQ FT: 3,500
SALES (est): 381.6K **Privately Held**
WEB: www.chocolateshopandmore.com
SIC: 2066 5441 Chocolate & cocoa products; candy

(G-3093)
THERMAL FOAMS/SYRACUSE INC (PA)
2101 Kenmore Ave (14207-1695)
PHONE..................716 874-6474
William F Wopperer, *Ch of Bd*
John P Jeffery, *President*
David Wopperer, *Vice Pres*
Larry Brady, *Treasurer*
▲ **EMP:** 2
SQ FT: 150,000
SALES (est): 5.8MM **Privately Held**
SIC: 3086 Insulation or cushioning material, foamed plastic

(G-3094)
THERMOTECH CORP
3 Bradford St (14210-1601)
PHONE..................716 823-3311
Fred Muhitch, *President*
Bruce Smith, *Vice Pres*
EMP: 9
SQ FT: 18,000
SALES (est): 1.2MM **Privately Held**
WEB: www.thermalprecision.com
SIC: 3443 Air coolers, metal plate

(G-3095)
TIEDEMANN WALDEMAR INC
Also Called: Roofing Consultant
1720 Military Rd Ste 2 (14217-1148)
PHONE..................716 875-5665
Waldemar Tiedemann, *President*
EMP: 11 **EST:** 1964

SALES (est): 1.1MM **Privately Held**
SIC: 2431 1761 Millwork; roofing contractor

(G-3096)
TIME RELEASE SCIENCES INC
Also Called: Trs Packaging
205 Dingens St (14206-2309)
PHONE..................716 823-4580
Jeffrey Dorn, *Ch of Bd*
Dennis McGee, *Supervisor*
▲ **EMP:** 22
SALES (est): 4.6MM **Privately Held**
SIC: 2671 Packaging paper & plastics film, coated & laminated

(G-3097)
TMP TECHNOLOGIES INC (PA)
Also Called: Advanced Foam Products Div
1200 Northland Ave (14215-3835)
PHONE..................716 895-6100
Jeffrey T Doran, *Ch of Bd*
Gary R Ashe, *Vice Pres*
Kirk Dorn, *Vice Pres*
Don Phister, *Vice Pres*
Matthew Mantelli, *Engineer*
▼ **EMP:** 65
SQ FT: 47,000
SALES (est): 19.7MM **Privately Held**
WEB: www.tmptech.com
SIC: 3069 3086 2834 2821 Sponge rubber & sponge rubber products; molded rubber products; foam rubber; plastics foam products; pharmaceutical preparations; plastics materials & resins

(G-3098)
TOMRIC SYSTEMS INC
85 River Rock Dr (14207-2178)
PHONE..................716 854-6050
Timothy Thill, *Ch of Bd*
◆ **EMP:** 14
SALES: 443.1K
SALES (corp-wide): 18.4MM **Privately Held**
SIC: 2064 Candy & other confectionery products
PA: Chocolate Delivery Systems, Inc.
1800 Elmwood Ave
Buffalo NY 14207
716 877-3146

(G-3099)
TOOLING ENTERPRISES INC
680 New Babcock St Ste 1 (14206-2285)
PHONE..................716 842-0445
Eugene Joseph, *President*
EMP: 10
SQ FT: 21,000
SALES (est): 1.3MM **Privately Held**
SIC: 3469 3544 Stamping metal for the trade; special dies, tools, jigs & fixtures

(G-3100)
TOVIE ASARESE ROYAL PRTG CO
351 Grant St (14213-1423)
PHONE..................716 885-7692
Ottoviano Asarese, *President*
EMP: 7 **EST:** 1952
SQ FT: 1,500
SALES (est): 964.4K **Privately Held**
SIC: 2752 2759 Commercial printing, offset; letterpress printing

(G-3101)
TRANE US INC
45 Earhart Dr Ste 103 (14221-7809)
PHONE..................716 626-1260
Joseph Goungo, *Sales Engr*
Ronald Gerster, *Branch Mgr*
EMP: 50 **Privately Held**
SIC: 3585 Refrigeration & heating equipment
HQ: Trane U.S. Inc.
3600 Pammel Creek Rd
La Crosse WI 54601
608 787-2000

(G-3102)
TRANSCO RAILWAY PRODUCTS INC
Milestrip Rd Rr 179 (14219)
P.O. Box 1968, Blasdell (14219-0168)
PHONE..................716 825-1663
Rfick Heldt, *Manager*

Buffalo - Erie County (G-3103) — GEOGRAPHIC SECTION

EMP: 20
SALES (corp-wide): 96.7MM **Privately Held**
SIC: 3743 Railroad equipment
HQ: Transco Railway Products Inc.
200 N La Salle St # 1550
Chicago IL 60601
312 427-2818

(G-3103) TRINITY PACKAGING CORPORATION
Cello-Pack Spclty Flms Lmntion
55 Innsbruck Dr (14227-2703)
PHONE 716 668-3111
Craig Miller, *Vice Pres*
EMP: 26
SALES (corp-wide): 224MM **Privately Held**
SIC: 3081 2673 Unsupported plastics film & sheet; bags: plastic, laminated & coated
HQ: Trinity Packaging Corporation
357 Main St
Armonk NY 10504
914 273-4111

(G-3104) TRIPP PLATING WORKS INC
1491 William St (14206-1807)
PHONE 716 894-2424
Steven E Jagielo, *President*
Cherie Jagielo, *Vice Pres*
EMP: 7 **EST:** 1922
SQ FT: 6,000
SALES (est): 776.4K **Privately Held**
SIC: 3471 Electroplating of metals or formed products; polishing, metals or formed products; buffing for the trade

(G-3105) TRU MOLD SHOES INC
42 Breckenridge St (14213-1555)
PHONE 716 881-4484
Ahmed Syed, *President*
Wayne Weisedel, *General Mgr*
Andrea Syed, *Vice Pres*
Sarah Syed, *Vice Pres*
EMP: 15
SQ FT: 11,000
SALES (est): 4.3MM **Privately Held**
WEB: www.trumold.com
SIC: 3143 3144 Orthopedic shoes, men's; orthopedic shoes, women's

(G-3106) TWENTY-FIRST CENTURY PRESS INC
501 Cornwall Ave (14215-3125)
PHONE 716 837-0800
Tracy B Lach, *President*
Mary Crimmen, *Vice Pres*
▲ **EMP:** 18 **EST:** 1979
SQ FT: 40,000
SALES (est): 3.4MM **Privately Held**
SIC: 2752 2789 Commercial printing, offset; photo-offset printing; binding only: books, pamphlets, magazines, etc.

(G-3107) U S SUGAR CO INC
692 Bailey Ave (14206-3003)
PHONE 716 828-1170
Tom Ferlito, *CEO*
Meaghan Johnson, *President*
Ed Jackson, *Senior VP*
Vernessa Roberts, *Vice Pres*
Steve Ward, *Vice Pres*
◆ **EMP:** 50
SQ FT: 300,000
SALES (est): 18.6MM **Privately Held**
SIC: 2099 Sugar

(G-3108) UC COATINGS LLC (PA)
2250 Fillmore Ave (14214-2119)
P.O. Box 1066 (14215-6066)
PHONE 716 833-9366
Thomas D Johel, *CEO*
Thuy N Murray, *Corp Secy*
Dave Sondel, *Sales Staff*
Christine Babin, *Marketing Staff*
▼ **EMP:** 27 **EST:** 1951
SQ FT: 30,000
SALES (est): 4.3MM **Privately Held**
WEB: www.uccoatings.com
SIC: 2851 Wood fillers or sealers; lacquers, varnishes, enamels & other coatings

(G-3109) UNICELL BODY COMPANY INC (PA)
571 Howard St (14206-2195)
PHONE 716 853-8628
Roger J Martin, *Ch of Bd*
Scott Vader, *President*
Ernie Deufemi, *General Mgr*
Anthony Lista, *General Mgr*
Alan Thach, *Project Mgr*
EMP: 45 **EST:** 1963
SQ FT: 67,000
SALES: 20MM **Privately Held**
WEB: www.unicell.com
SIC: 3713 5013 Truck bodies (motor vehicles); truck parts & accessories

(G-3110) UNIFORM NAMEMAKERS INC
55 Amherst Villa Rd (14225-1432)
PHONE 716 626-5474
Warren Clark, *President*
EMP: 10
SQ FT: 7,000
SALES (est): 550K **Privately Held**
WEB: www.uniformnamemakers.com
SIC: 2395 Embroidery & art needlework

(G-3111) UNILOCK LTD
510 Smith St (14210-1288)
PHONE 716 822-6074
David Mc Intyre, *Branch Mgr*
EMP: 20 **Privately Held**
SIC: 3271 Paving blocks, concrete
PA: Unilock Ltd
401 The West Mall Suite 610
Etobicoke ON M9C 5
416 646-5180

(G-3112) UNITED RICHTER ELECTRICAL MTRS
106 Michigan Ave (14204-2111)
PHONE 716 855-1945
Thomas Weiner, *President*
John Cook, *Vice Pres*
Judith Weiner, *Admin Sec*
EMP: 10
SQ FT: 10,000
SALES (est): 1.7MM **Privately Held**
SIC: 7694 5063 Electric motor repair; power transmission equipment, electric

(G-3113) UPSTATE NIAGARA COOP INC (PA)
Also Called: Bison Products
25 Anderson Rd (14225-4905)
P.O. Box 650 (14225-0650)
PHONE 716 892-3156
Larry Webster, *CEO*
Daniel Wolf, *President*
Kim Pickard, *General Mgr*
Kim Pickard-Dudley, *General Mgr*
Doug Ricketts, *General Mgr*
EMP: 55 **EST:** 1930
SALES: 893.9MM **Privately Held**
SIC: 2026 Fermented & cultured milk products

(G-3114) UPSTATE NIAGARA COOP INC
Also Called: Upstate Milk Co-Operatives
1730 Dale Rd (14225-4921)
P.O. Box 650 (14225-0650)
PHONE 716 892-2121
Larry Darch, *Principal*
EMP: 200
SQ FT: 53,690
SALES (corp-wide): 893.9MM **Privately Held**
SIC: 2023 2026 Ice cream mix, unfrozen: liquid or dry; fluid milk
PA: Upstate Niagara Cooperative, Inc.
25 Anderson Rd
Buffalo NY 14225
716 892-3156

(G-3115) V LAKE INDUSTRIES INC
1555 Niagara St (14213-1101)
PHONE 716 885-9141
Keith McCoy, *President*
David Russell, *Project Mgr*
EMP: 8
SQ FT: 24,000
SALES (est): 1.2MM **Privately Held**
SIC: 3599 Machine & other job shop work

(G-3116) VENT-A-KILN CORPORATION
Also Called: Vent-A-Fume
51 Botsford Pl (14216-2601)
PHONE 716 876-2023
Susan Lee, *President*
Jay Tolbert, *Vice Pres*
EMP: 5
SQ FT: 1,200
SALES (est): 882.5K **Privately Held**
WEB: www.ventakiln.com
SIC: 3564 Blowers & fans

(G-3117) VERMED INC
400 Exchange St (14204-2064)
PHONE 800 669-6905
Sam Heleba, *President*
▲ **EMP:** 85
SQ FT: 45,000
SALES (est): 9.6MM
SALES (corp-wide): 1.4B **Privately Held**
WEB: www.vermed.com
SIC: 3845 3825 Electromedical equipment; instruments for measuring electrical quantities
HQ: Graphic Controls Acquisition Corp.
400 Exchange St
Buffalo NY 14204
716 853-7500

(G-3118) VERMONT MEDICAL INC
Also Called: Vermed
400 Exchange St (14204-2064)
PHONE 802 463-9976
Hurley Blakeney, *CEO*
Rich Kalich, *President*
Thomas Salmon, *Vice Pres*
Patrick Boylan, *Treasurer*
George Nostrand, *Admin Sec*
▲ **EMP:** 160
SQ FT: 44,800
SALES (est): 30.4MM **Privately Held**
SIC: 3823 3845 Electrodes used in industrial process measurement; electromedical equipment

(G-3119) VINCENT MARTINO DENTAL LAB
74 Ransier Dr (14224-2244)
PHONE 716 674-7800
Vincent Martino, *President*
Deborah Martino, *Admin Sec*
EMP: 10 **EST:** 1976
SQ FT: 800
SALES: 300K **Privately Held**
SIC: 3843 8072 Orthodontic appliances; orthodontic appliance production

(G-3120) VISIMETRICS CORPORATION
2290 Kenmore Ave (14207-1312)
PHONE 716 871-7070
Kenneth Luczkiewicz, *President*
William Umiker, *Vice Pres*
EMP: 8
SQ FT: 22,000
SALES (est): 1MM **Privately Held**
WEB: www.visicnc.com
SIC: 3599 Machine shop, jobbing & repair

(G-3121) VOYAGER EMBLEMS INC
Also Called: Voyager Custom Products
701 Seneca St Ste D (14210-1351)
PHONE 416 255-3421
Donald B Grant, *Ch of Bd*
Sally Grant, *President*
Thomas Maloney, *Admin Sec*
EMP: 108
SQ FT: 38,000
SALES (est): 5.3MM **Privately Held**
WEB: www.voyager-emblems.com
SIC: 2395 Emblems, embroidered
HQ: Grant Emblems Limited
55 Fieldway Rd Suite A
Etobicoke ON M8Z 3
416 255-3421

(G-3122) VULCAN STEAM FORGING CO
247 Rano St (14207-2189)
P.O. Box 87 (14207-0087)
PHONE 716 875-3680
Michael Duggan, *President*
Jered Fitch, *Opers Mgr*
▲ **EMP:** 27
SQ FT: 30,000
SALES (est): 5.6MM **Privately Held**
WEB: www.vulcansf.com
SIC: 3462 Flange, valve & pipe fitting forgings, ferrous

(G-3123) WARD INDUSTRIAL EQUIPMENT INC (PA)
Also Called: Ward Iron Works Limited
1051 Clinton St (14206-2823)
PHONE 716 856-6966
Guy Nelson, *President*
▲ **EMP:** 1
SQ FT: 500
SALES (est): 4.3MM **Privately Held**
WEB: www.devansco.com
SIC: 3535 5084 Bulk handling conveyor systems; industrial machinery & equipment

(G-3124) WARNER
514 Hopkins Rd (14221-2415)
PHONE 716 446-0663
Alan Warner, *Principal*
EMP: 9
SALES (est): 573.7K **Privately Held**
SIC: 2389 Clergymen's vestments

(G-3125) WEB ASSOCIATES INC
1255 Niagara St (14213-1501)
PHONE 716 883-3377
William E Breeser, *President*
EMP: 6
SALES (est): 480.3K **Privately Held**
WEB: www.betterwire.com
SIC: 3315 3469 Wire & fabricated wire products; metal stampings

(G-3126) WEBB-MASON INC
300 Airborne Pkwy Ste 210 (14225-1491)
PHONE 716 276-8792
Jon Webber, *Manager*
EMP: 23
SALES (corp-wide): 113.5MM **Privately Held**
SIC: 2752 Business form & card printing, lithographic
PA: Webb-Mason, Inc.
10830 Gilroy Rd
Hunt Valley MD 21031
410 785-1111

(G-3127) WENDT CORPORATION
2555 Walden Ave (14225-4737)
PHONE 716 391-1200
Thomas A Wendt Sr, *CEO*
Mike Fialkowski, *President*
Pmp Koksal, *Project Mgr*
Jody Cramer, *Purch Agent*
Srdjan Sikirica, *Research*
◆ **EMP:** 100
SQ FT: 66,000
SALES (est): 37.4MM **Privately Held**
SIC: 3599 Custom machinery

(G-3128) WEST METAL WORKS INC
Also Called: W M W
68 Hayes Pl (14210-1614)
PHONE 716 895-4900
James Stermer, *President*
Jennifer Stermer, *Vice Pres*
David Wojtkowiak, *Marketing Staff*
EMP: 20 **EST:** 1946

GEOGRAPHIC SECTION

Caledonia - Livingston County (G-3153)

SALES (est): 3.5MM Privately Held
WEB: www.westmetalworks.com
SIC: 7692 3559 3443 3449 Welding repair; chemical machinery & equipment; plate work for the metalworking trade; miscellaneous metalwork

(G-3129)
WESTERN NEW YORK FAMILY MAG
3147 Delaware Ave Ste B (14217-2002)
PHONE..................................716 836-3486
Michelle J Miller, Owner
Susan Lojacono, Graphic Designe
EMP: 5
SALES (est): 517.2K Privately Held
WEB: www.wnyfamilymagazine.com
SIC: 2721 Magazines: publishing only, not printed on site

(G-3130)
WILCRO INC
90 Earhart Dr Ste 19 (14221-7802)
PHONE..................................716 632-4204
Richard Crooks Sr, President
Richard Crooks Jr, Vice Pres
Robert Crooks, Admin Sec
EMP: 9
SALES (est): 514.8K Privately Held
WEB: www.wilcro.com
SIC: 3571 2796 Personal computers (microcomputers); engraving on copper, steel, wood or rubber; printing plates

(G-3131)
WILLARD MACHINE
73 Forest Ave (14213-1093)
PHONE..................................716 885-1630
Jeffrey Rathmann, President
EMP: 13
SQ FT: 10,000
SALES (est): 1.2MM Privately Held
WEB: www.willardmachine.com
SIC: 3599 Machine shop, jobbing & repair

(G-3132)
WILLIAM S HEIN & CO INC
Also Called: Metro Center Western New York
1575 Main St (14209-1513)
PHONE..................................716 882-2600
Kevin Marmion, President
EMP: 100
SALES (corp-wide): 40.4K Privately Held
WEB: www.foreign-law.com
SIC: 2731 Books: publishing only
PA: William S. Hein & Co., Inc.
   2350 N Forest Rd Ste 14a
   Getzville NY 14068
   716 882-2600

(G-3133)
WINTERS INSTRUMENTS INC (HQ)
Also Called: Winters Instruments
455 Cayuga Rd Ste 650 (14225-1317)
PHONE..................................281 880-8607
Jeffrey Smith, President
Dharmesh Bhardwaj, Regional Mgr
Brian McClure, Exec VP
John Bernotas, Regl Sales Mgr
Ray McKeown, Regl Sales Mgr
▲ EMP: 45
SQ FT: 10,000
SALES (est): 5.1MM Privately Held
SIC: 3823 5084 Industrial instrmnts msrmnt display/control process variable; instruments & control equipment
PA: Winters Instruments Ltd
   121 Railside Rd
   North York ON M3A 1
   416 444-2345

(G-3134)
X-L ENVELOPE AND PRINTING INC
701 Seneca St Ste 100 (14210-1376)
P.O. Box 344 (14224-0344)
PHONE..................................716 852-2135
Terry Allen, CEO
Bob Woollacott, Treasurer
EMP: 11
SQ FT: 20,000
SALES (est): 2.3MM Privately Held
SIC: 2677 2752 Mfg Envelopes Lithographic Commercial Printing

(G-3135)
YOU FIRST SERVICES INC
485 Cayuga Rd (14225-1368)
PHONE..................................716 204-7215
Arti Goswami, Principal
EMP: 17
SALES (est): 2.9MM Privately Held
SIC: 3549 5122 2834 Assembly machines, including robotic; pharmaceuticals; solutions, pharmaceutical

(G-3136)
YOUNG & SWARTZ INC
39 Cherry St (14204-1298)
PHONE..................................716 852-2171
Raphael Winzig, President
EMP: 10 EST: 1886
SQ FT: 15,000
SALES (est): 1.2MM Privately Held
SIC: 3991 5198 Brushes, household or industrial; paint brushes, rollers, sprayers

(G-3137)
YR BLANC & CO LLC
Also Called: Renovatio Med & Surgical Sups
25 Eltham Dr (14226-4108)
PHONE..................................716 800-3999
Yves-Richard Blanc, CEO
EMP: 5
SALES (est): 764.4K Privately Held
SIC: 2899 3589 1781 5078 ; sewage & water treatment equipment; water well servicing; drinking water coolers, mechanical

(G-3138)
ZEPTOMETRIX CORPORATION (PA)
847 Main St (14203-1109)
PHONE..................................716 882-0920
Shawn R Smith, President
Gregory Chiklis, COO
Chris Collins, Vice Pres
John Paul, Vice Pres
Ronald Urmson, CFO
▼ EMP: 80
SQ FT: 20,000
SALES (est): 20.3MM Privately Held
WEB: www.zeptometrix.com
SIC: 2836 Biological products, except diagnostic

Bullville
Orange County

(G-3139)
WOODARDS CONCRETE PRODUCTS INC
629 Lybolt Rd (10915)
P.O. Box 8 (10915-0008)
PHONE..................................845 361-3471
Robert Zwart, President
Gayle Cortright, Corp Secy
Allen Zwart, Vice Pres
Steve Zwart, Vice Pres
EMP: 25 EST: 1955
SQ FT: 14,000
SALES (est): 4.3MM Privately Held
WEB: www.woodardsconcrete.com
SIC: 3272 Concrete products, precast; septic tanks, concrete; steps, prefabricated concrete

Burdett
Schuyler County

(G-3140)
ATWATER ESTATE VINEYARDS LLC
5055 State Route 414 (14818-9816)
PHONE..................................607 546-8463
Ted Marks, Partner
Stacy Yeater, Accountant
Denise Clappier, Manager
Chaz Coney, Manager
George Nosisi, Assistant
EMP: 20 EST: 2000
SQ FT: 672

SALES (est): 2.3MM Privately Held
WEB: www.atwatervineyards.com
SIC: 2084 Wines

(G-3141)
FINGER LAKES DISTILLING
4676 State Route 414 (14818-9730)
PHONE..................................607 546-5510
Brian McKenzie, President
EMP: 15
SALES (est): 2.1MM Privately Held
SIC: 2085 Distilled & blended liquors

Burke
Franklin County

(G-3142)
CREST HAVEN PRECAST INC
4925 State Route 11 (12917-2410)
PHONE..................................518 483-4750
Gary Boileau, President
Eva Boileau, Vice Pres
EMP: 7
SALES: 800K Privately Held
SIC: 3271 Blocks, concrete or cinder: standard

Burt
Niagara County

(G-3143)
AKZO NOBEL CHEMICALS LLC
2153 Lockport Olcott Rd (14028-9788)
PHONE..................................716 778-8554
Gordon Martens, Manager
EMP: 8
SALES (corp-wide): 11.3B Privately Held
WEB: www.akzo-nobel.com
SIC: 2869 2899 Industrial organic chemicals; chemical preparations
HQ: Akzo Nobel Chemicals Llc
   525 W Van Buren St # 1600
   Chicago IL 60607
   312 544-7000

(G-3144)
SCHULZE VINEYARDS & WINERY LLC
2090 Coomer Rd (14028-9733)
PHONE..................................716 778-8090
Anne Schulze,
EMP: 13
SALES: 578K Privately Held
SIC: 2084 Wines

Byron
Genesee County

(G-3145)
OXBO INTERNATIONAL CORPORATION (DH)
7275 Batavia Byron Rd (14422-9599)
PHONE..................................585 548-2665
Gary C Stich, CEO
Richard Glazier, Ch of Bd
Paul Dow, Vice Pres
Andrew Talbott, Vice Pres
James Nowicki, CFO
▲ EMP: 100
SQ FT: 43,500
SALES (est): 51MM
SALES (corp-wide): 98.9K Privately Held
WEB: www.oxbocorp.com
SIC: 3523 5083 Farm machinery & equipment; farm & garden machinery
HQ: Ploeger Oxbo Group B.V.
   Electronweg 5
   Roosendaal
   165 319-333

Cairo
Greene County

(G-3146)
B & B FOREST PRODUCTS LTD
251 Route 145 (12413-2659)
P.O. Box 907 (12413-0907)
PHONE..................................518 622-0811
William Fabian, President
▼ EMP: 13 EST: 1993
SALES (est): 1.3MM Privately Held
SIC: 2411 Logging

(G-3147)
BILBEE CONTROLS INC
628 Main St (12413)
PHONE..................................518 622-3033
Robert Levinn, President
Barbara Powell, Owner
EMP: 12
SQ FT: 12,000
SALES: 1.5MM Privately Held
WEB: www.bilbeecontrols.com
SIC: 3822 Mfg Environmental Controls

(G-3148)
HIGHLAND MUSEUM & LIGHTHOUSE
111 M Simons Rd (12413-3135)
PHONE..................................508 487-1121
Dan Sanders, President
Gordon S Russell, President
Francine Webster, Treasurer
EMP: 15 EST: 1997
SALES: 180.5K Privately Held
SIC: 3731 Lighthouse tenders, building & repairing

(G-3149)
JRS FUELS INC
8037 Route 32 (12413-2526)
PHONE..................................518 622-9939
John Vandenburgh, Principal
EMP: 5 EST: 2009
SALES (est): 652.4K Privately Held
SIC: 2869 Fuels

(G-3150)
K & B WOODWORKING INC
133 Rolling Meadow Rd (12413-2201)
PHONE..................................518 634-7253
Peter Vogel, President
Richard Vogel, Corp Secy
Rick Vogel, Treasurer
EMP: 9
SQ FT: 10,000
SALES (est): 726K Privately Held
WEB: www.kbwoodworking.com
SIC: 2511 2499 Wood household furniture; decorative wood & woodwork

(G-3151)
OAK VALLEY LOGGING INC
558 Frank Hitchcock Rd (12413-2626)
P.O. Box 1260 (12413-1260)
PHONE..................................518 622-8249
Glenn Defrancesco, Chairman
EMP: 5
SALES (est): 346.9K Privately Held
SIC: 2411 Logging

Caledonia
Livingston County

(G-3152)
ADVIS INC
2218 River Rd (14423-9518)
PHONE..................................585 568-0100
Mark F Bocko, CEO
Donna REA, Business Mgr
EMP: 9
SALES: 950K Privately Held
SIC: 3674 Semiconductors & related devices

(G-3153)
APPLIED ENERGY SOLUTIONS LLC
1 Technology Pl (14423-1246)
PHONE..................................585 538-3270

Jennifer Morgan, *Opers Staff*
Mark Corcoran, *QC Mgr*
Rhonda Skrzypek, *Agent*
Vern Fleming,
EMP: 44
SQ FT: 60,000
SALES (est): 12.5MM **Privately Held**
WEB: www.appliedenergysol.com
SIC: 3629 Battery chargers, rectifying or nonrotating

(G-3154)
COMMODITY RESOURCE CORPORATION
2773 Caledonia Leroy Rd (14423-9538)
P.O. Box 576, Lakeville (14480-0576)
PHONE................................585 538-9500
Leslie Cole, *President*
EMP: 12
SALES (est): 1.7MM **Privately Held**
WEB: www.crcconnect.com
SIC: 2875 2048 Fertilizers, mixing only; feed premixes

(G-3155)
GULDENSCHUH LOGGING & LBR LLC
143 Wheatland Center Rd (14423-9750)
P.O. Box 191 (14423-0191)
PHONE................................585 538-4750
Don Guldenschuh, *Mng Member*
Garrett Guldenschuh,
EMP: 9
SQ FT: 50,000
SALES (est): 1.4MM **Privately Held**
SIC: 2426 2411 5099 5211 Furniture stock & parts, hardwood; logging; timber products, rough; lumber products

(G-3156)
HORNS & HALOS CFT BREWING LLC
3154 State St (14423-1222)
PHONE................................585 507-7248
Justin Caccamise,
John Kabrovski,
EMP: 20
SQ FT: 8,200
SALES (est): 671.8K **Privately Held**
SIC: 2082 Near beer

(G-3157)
RHETT M CLARK INC
Also Called: Gregson-Clark
3213 Lehigh St (14423-1073)
PHONE................................585 538-9570
Rhett M Clark, *President*
EMP: 6
SQ FT: 5,000
SALES (est): 1MM **Privately Held**
SIC: 3524 5083 Lawn & garden equipment; lawn & garden machinery & equipment

(G-3158)
SPECIALIZED PRINTED FORMS INC
Also Called: Spforms
352 Center St (14423-1202)
P.O. Box 118 (14423-0118)
PHONE................................585 538-2381
Kevin Johnston, *General Mgr*
Russell Shepard, *Plant Mgr*
Mike Randall, *Sales Staff*
▲ **EMP:** 20 **EST:** 1951
SQ FT: 135,000
SALES (est): 3.3MM
SALES (corp-wide): 370.1MM **Publicly Held**
WEB: www.spforms.com
SIC: 2761 Continuous forms, office & business
PA: Ennis, Inc.
2441 Presidential Pkwy
Midlothian TX 76065
972 775-9801

(G-3159)
TSS FOAM INDUSTRIES CORP
2770 W Main St (14423-9560)
P.O. Box 119 (14423-0119)
PHONE................................585 538-2321
Samuel L Dilberto Jr, *Ch of Bd*
Terri Laurie, *Human Res Mgr*
EMP: 15

SQ FT: 60,000
SALES (est): 2.7MM **Privately Held**
SIC: 3086 5047 7389 Packaging & shipping materials, foamed plastic; medical & hospital equipment; sewing contractor

Callicoon
Sullivan County

(G-3160)
CATSKILL DELAWARE PUBLICATIONS (PA)
Also Called: Sullivan County Democrat
5 Lower Main St (12723-5000)
P.O. Box 308 (12723-0308)
PHONE................................845 887-5200
Frederick W Stabbert III, *President*
EMP: 19 **EST:** 1900
SQ FT: 5,704
SALES: 1MM **Privately Held**
WEB: www.sc-democrat.com
SIC: 2711 2752 Commercial printing & newspaper publishing combined; commercial printing, lithographic

Calverton
Suffolk County

(G-3161)
ACME MARINE HOIST INC
Also Called: Thego
800 Burman Blvd (11933-3024)
PHONE................................631 472-3030
Norman Marcioch, *President*
▼ **EMP:** 8 **EST:** 1958
SQ FT: 11,500
SALES (est): 719.2K **Privately Held**
WEB: www.acmemarinehoist.com
SIC: 3536 Hoists, cranes & monorails

(G-3162)
BONSAL AMERICAN INC
931 Burman Blvd (11933-3027)
PHONE................................631 208-8073
John Cardona, *Principal*
EMP: 20
SALES (corp-wide): 29.7B **Privately Held**
WEB: www.bonsalamerican.com
SIC: 3272 Concrete products
HQ: Bonsal American, Inc.
625 Griffith Rd Ste 100
Charlotte NC 28217
704 525-1621

(G-3163)
COASTAL PIPELINE PRODUCTS CORP
55 Twomey Ave (11933-1374)
P.O. Box 575 (11933-0575)
PHONE................................631 369-4000
Alexander Koke, *President*
Chris Young, *QC Mgr*
▲ **EMP:** 50
SQ FT: 32,000
SALES (est): 10.6MM **Privately Held**
WEB: www.coastalpipeline.com
SIC: 3272 Concrete products, precast

(G-3164)
COOKING WITH CHEF MICHELLE LLC
Also Called: Ms. Michelles
4603 Middle Country Rd (11933-4104)
PHONE................................516 662-2324
Michelle Gilette-Kelly, *President*
Michelle Marie Gilette-Kelly, *President*
Christopher Kelly, *CFO*
EMP: 6
SQ FT: 8,400
SALES: 229.6K **Privately Held**
SIC: 2052 5149 Cookies; crackers, cookies & bakery products

(G-3165)
EAST END COUNTRY KITCHENS INC
Also Called: Pezera Associates
121 Edwards Ave (11933-1602)
PHONE................................631 727-2258
Henry Pazera, *President*

EMP: 10
SALES (est): 1.2MM **Privately Held**
SIC: 2434 Wood kitchen cabinets

(G-3166)
GLOBAL MARINE POWER INC
Also Called: Hustler Powerboats
221 Scott Ave (11933-3039)
PHONE................................631 208-2933
Joe Logiudice, *Owner*
Richard Logiudice, *Vice Pres*
EMP: 40
SQ FT: 32,000
SALES (est): 8.3MM **Privately Held**
WEB: www.hustlerpowerboats.com
SIC: 3089 3732 5551 Plastic boats & other marine equipment; boat building & repairing; boat dealers

(G-3167)
LUMINATI AEROSPACE LLC
400 David Ct (11933-3007)
PHONE................................631 574-2616
Daniel Preston, *CEO*
April Chapple, *Vice Pres*
EMP: 16
SALES (est): 998.5K **Privately Held**
SIC: 3721 Research & development on aircraft by the manufacturer

(G-3168)
PELLA CORPORATION
Also Called: Reilly Windows & Doors
901 Burman Blvd (11933-3027)
PHONE................................631 208-0710
Brian Goodale, *General Mgr*
Michael P Reilly, *Chairman*
EMP: 126
SALES (corp-wide): 1.9B **Privately Held**
SIC: 2431 5211 5031 2499 Millwork; millwork & lumber; doors & windows; decorative wood & woodwork; window & door (prefabricated) installation
PA: Pella Corporation
102 Main St
Pella IA 50219
641 621-1000

(G-3169)
RACING INDUSTRIES INC
901 Scott Ave (11933-3033)
PHONE................................631 905-0100
Ameet Bambami, *President*
▲ **EMP:** 20
SQ FT: 20,000
SALES (est): 4.5MM **Privately Held**
WEB: www.racingindustries.com
SIC: 3465 Body parts, automobile: stamped metal

(G-3170)
ROAR BIOMEDICAL INC
4603 Middle Country Rd (11933-4104)
PHONE................................631 591-2749
Robert Brocia, *Branch Mgr*
EMP: 5
SALES (est): 335.5K
SALES (corp-wide): 2.4MM **Privately Held**
SIC: 2836 5122 Biological products, except diagnostic; biologicals & allied products
PA: Roar Biomedical Inc
3960 Broadway
New York NY 10032
212 280-2983

(G-3171)
STONY BROOK MFG CO INC (PA)
652 Scott Ave (11933-3046)
PHONE................................631 369-9530
Ella Scaife, *President*
Marek Hyrycz, *Vice Pres*
Graham Scaife, *Vice Pres*
Peter Day, *Project Mgr*
Diane Reycroft, *Sales Mgr*
EMP: 30
SQ FT: 11,000
SALES (est): 5.1MM **Privately Held**
WEB: www.stonybrookmfg.com
SIC: 3317 Steel pipe & tubes

(G-3172)
SUFFOLK CEMENT PRECAST INC (PA)
1813 Middle Rd (11933)
P.O. Box 261 (11933-0261)
PHONE................................631 727-4432
Kenneth Lohr, *President*
EMP: 9
SQ FT: 500
SALES (est): 1MM **Privately Held**
SIC: 3273 Ready-mixed concrete

(G-3173)
SUFFOLK CEMENT PRODUCTS INC
1843 Middle Rd (11933-1450)
PHONE................................631 727-2317
Mark A Lohr, *Ch of Bd*
Linda Hagen, *Vice Pres*
EMP: 29
SQ FT: 4,500
SALES (est): 14.6MM **Privately Held**
WEB: www.suffolkcement.com
SIC: 3273 3271 Ready-mixed concrete; blocks, concrete or cinder: standard

(G-3174)
TEBBENS STEEL LLC
800 Burman Blvd (11933-3024)
PHONE................................631 208-8330
Thomas A Tebbens II, *Mng Member*
Elsie Tebbens,
EMP: 18 **EST:** 1959
SQ FT: 9,000
SALES (est): 4.8MM **Privately Held**
SIC: 3449 8711 Miscellaneous metalwork; structural engineering

(G-3175)
US HOISTS CORP
Also Called: Acme Marine
800 Burman Blvd (11933-3024)
PHONE................................631 472-3030
Thomas A Tebbens II, *President*
Kelly Tebbens, *Vice Pres*
◆ **EMP:** 7
SALES (est): 1.1MM **Privately Held**
SIC: 3536 Hoists, cranes & monorails

Cambria Heights
Queens County

(G-3176)
MADISON ELECTRIC
21916 Linden Blvd (11411-1619)
PHONE................................718 358-4121
Pete Danielsson, *Owner*
EMP: 18
SQ FT: 2,000
SALES: 300K **Privately Held**
SIC: 3699 Electrical equipment & supplies

Cambridge
Washington County

(G-3177)
B & J LUMBER CO INC
1075 State Route 22 (12816-2501)
P.O. Box 40 (12816-0040)
PHONE................................518 677-3845
John Merriman, *President*
Barbara Merriman, *Vice Pres*
EMP: 5 **EST:** 1955
SALES: 100K **Privately Held**
SIC: 2421 5989 0115 Sawmills & planing mills, general; wood (fuel); corn

(G-3178)
CAMBRIDGE-PACIFIC INC
Also Called: CTX Printing
891 State Rd 22 (12816)
P.O. Box 159 (12816-0159)
PHONE................................518 677-5988
Chris Belnap, *President*
▲ **EMP:** 33 **EST:** 1986
SQ FT: 12,000
SALES (est): 6.7MM **Privately Held**
WEB: www.cpacific.com
SIC: 2677 Envelopes

GEOGRAPHIC SECTION

Campbell - Steuben County (G-3205)

(G-3179)
COMMON SENSE NATURAL SOAP
7 Pearl St (12816-1127)
PHONE..................................518 677-0224
Robert Racine, *Owner*
EMP: 30 EST: 2014
SALES: 5.5MM **Privately Held**
SIC: 2844 Toilet preparations

(G-3180)
EASTERN CASTINGS CO
2 Pearl St (12816-1107)
P.O. Box 129 (12816-0129)
PHONE..................................518 677-5610
Anthony McDonald, *President*
Andrew Nolan, *Treasurer*
EMP: 15
SQ FT: 25,000
SALES (est): 1.5MM **Privately Held**
SIC: 3365 Aluminum & aluminum-based alloy castings

(G-3181)
ED LEVIN INC
Also Called: Ed Levin Jewelry
52 W Main St (12816-1158)
PHONE..................................518 677-8595
Peter Tonjes, *President*
EMP: 25
SQ FT: 10,000
SALES: 2MM **Privately Held**
WEB: www.edlevinjewelry.com
SIC: 3911 Jewelry, precious metal

(G-3182)
MORCON INC (PA)
879 State Rd 22 (12816)
PHONE..................................518 677-8511
Joseph Raccuia, *President*
Brian Stidd, *Controller*
EMP: 90
SALES: 40MM **Privately Held**
SIC: 2621 Tissue paper

(G-3183)
ROBERT RACINE (PA)
Also Called: Common Sense Natural Soap
41 N Union St (12816-1025)
PHONE..................................518 677-0224
Robert Racine, *Owner*
▲ **EMP:** 37
SALES (est): 7MM **Privately Held**
WEB: www.commonsensefarm.com
SIC: 2841 2844 Soap & other detergents; toilet preparations

(G-3184)
WAYMOR1 INC
Hc 22 (12816)
PHONE..................................518 677-8511
Susan H Morris, *Owner*
Wayne R Morris, *Owner*
EMP: 50
SALES (corp-wide): 46.7MM **Privately Held**
SIC: 2679 2676 Paper products, converted; sanitary paper products
PA: Waymor1, Inc.
879 State Rte 22
Cambridge NY 12816

Camden
Oneida County

(G-3185)
CAMDEN NEWS INC
Also Called: Queens Central News
39 Main St (13316-1301)
P.O. Box 117 (13316-0117)
PHONE..................................315 245-1849
James Van Winkle, *President*
EMP: 5 EST: 1974
SQ FT: 7,000
SALES (est): 400.5K **Privately Held**
SIC: 2711 Newspapers: publishing only, not printed on site

(G-3186)
CAMDEN WIRE CO INC
Also Called: International Wire Group
12 Masonic Ave (13316-1294)
PHONE..................................315 245-3800
Rodney Kent, *President*
Donald De Kay, *VP Finance*
EMP: 700 EST: 1929
SQ FT: 400,000
SALES (est): 120.2MM
SALES (corp-wide): 455.4MM **Privately Held**
SIC: 3351 3357 Wire, copper & copper alloy; nonferrous wiredrawing & insulating
HQ: International Wire Group, Inc.
12 Masonic Ave
Camden NY 13316

(G-3187)
DAVIS LOGGING & LUMBER
1450 Curtiss Rd (13316-5006)
PHONE..................................315 245-1040
Leonard Davis, *Principal*
EMP: 5 EST: 1985
SALES (est): 354.8K **Privately Held**
SIC: 2411 Logging

(G-3188)
INTERNATIONAL WIRE GROUP (PA)
12 Masonic Ave (13316-1202)
PHONE..................................315 245-3800
Rodney Kent, *CEO*
Donald Dekay, *CFO*
EMP: 12 EST: 2011
SALES (est): 455.4MM **Privately Held**
SIC: 3351 Wire, copper & copper alloy

(G-3189)
INTERNATIONAL WIRE GROUP INC (HQ)
Also Called: Bare Wire Division
12 Masonic Ave (13316-1202)
PHONE..................................315 245-2000
Rodney D Kent, *Ch of Bd*
Geoff Kent, *Vice Pres*
Glenn J Holler, *CFO*
Donald F Dekay, *VP Finance*
▲ **EMP:** 300
SALES (est): 455.4MM **Privately Held**
SIC: 3357 Nonferrous wiredrawing & insulating
PA: International Wire Group
12 Masonic Ave
Camden NY 13316
315 245-3800

(G-3190)
KEVIN REGAN LOGGING LTD
1011 Hillsboro Rd (13316-4518)
P.O. Box 439 (13316-0439)
PHONE..................................315 245-3890
Kevin Regan, *President*
EMP: 5
SALES (est): 585.6K **Privately Held**
SIC: 2411 1629 Logging; land clearing contractor

(G-3191)
OMEGA WIRE INC (DH)
Also Called: Bare Wire Div
12 Masonic Ave (13316-1202)
P.O. Box 131 (13316-0131)
PHONE..................................315 245-3800
Rodney D Kent, *President*
Peter Ernenwein, *Vice Pres*
Donald De Kay, *VP Finance*
▲ **EMP:** 325
SQ FT: 200,000
SALES (est): 95.9MM
SALES (corp-wide): 455.4MM **Privately Held**
WEB: www.omegawire.com
SIC: 3351 Wire, copper & copper alloy

(G-3192)
OWI CORPORATION
Also Called: Bare Wire Division
12 Masonic Ave (13316-1202)
P.O. Box 131 (13316-0131)
PHONE..................................315 245-4305
Rodney Kent, *President*
Donald De Kay, *VP Finance*
▲ **EMP:** 6
SALES (est): 907.4K
SALES (corp-wide): 455.4MM **Privately Held**
SIC: 3351 Wire, copper & copper alloy
HQ: International Wire Group, Inc.
12 Masonic Ave
Camden NY 13316

(G-3193)
PERFORMANCE WIRE & CABLE INC
9482 State Route 13 (13316-4947)
P.O. Box 126 (13316-0126)
PHONE..................................315 245-2594
Steven Benjamin, *President*
EMP: 13
SQ FT: 37,500
SALES (est): 2.3MM **Privately Held**
WEB: www.performancewire.com
SIC: 3357 Nonferrous wiredrawing & insulating

Camillus
Onondaga County

(G-3194)
AQUARII INC
17 Genesee St (13031-1126)
PHONE..................................315 672-8807
Ray Carrock, *President*
Hannah Carrock, *Marketing Mgr*
Charles Shatzkin, *Director*
EMP: 8
SALES (est): 1.6MM **Privately Held**
SIC: 3646 Commercial indusl & institutional electric lighting fixtures

(G-3195)
CLEARSTEP TECHNOLOGIES LLC
213 Emann Dr (13031-2009)
PHONE..................................315 952-3628
Scott Buehler,
EMP: 7 EST: 2007
SQ FT: 2,000
SALES: 1.8MM **Privately Held**
WEB: www.clearsteptech.com
SIC: 2741 Technical manual & paper publishing

(G-3196)
KSA MANUFACTURING LLC
5050 Smoral Rd (13031-9726)
PHONE..................................315 488-0809
Adam Kudlick,
Jane Kudlick,
▲ **EMP:** 12
SQ FT: 8,500
SALES (est): 1.4MM **Privately Held**
WEB: www.ksamanufacturing.com
SIC: 3492 Hose & tube fittings & assemblies, hydraulic/pneumatic

(G-3197)
STEVE POLI SALES
Also Called: Imprinted Sportswear
102 Farmington Dr (13031-2113)
PHONE..................................315 487-0394
Steve Poli, *Owner*
EMP: 5
SALES (est): 283.6K **Privately Held**
SIC: 2261 Screen printing of cotton broadwoven fabrics

(G-3198)
TOSCH PRODUCTS LTD
25 Main St (13031-1126)
PHONE..................................315 672-3040
Todd Oudemool, *President*
Dirk J Oudemool,
EMP: 6
SQ FT: 12,000
SALES: 500K **Privately Held**
WEB: www.toschltd.com
SIC: 3949 Lacrosse equipment & supplies, general

(G-3199)
UPSTATE TUBE INC
5050 Smoral Rd (13031-9726)
PHONE..................................315 488-5636
Michael Kudlick, *President*
Kristy Kudlick, *Principal*
Tyler Kudlick, *Vice Pres*
EMP: 5
SALES (est): 424.5K **Privately Held**
SIC: 3492 Fluid power valves & hose fittings

(G-3200)
WESTROCK - SOUTHERN CONT LLC
100 Southern Dr (13031-1578)
PHONE..................................315 487-6111
Dave Atkwell, *Manager*
EMP: 120
SALES (corp-wide): 14.8B **Publicly Held**
WEB: www.southerncontainer.com
SIC: 2653 3412 Boxes, corrugated: made from purchased materials; metal barrels, drums & pails
HQ: Westrock - Southern Container, Llc
133 River Rd
Cos Cob CT 06807
631 232-5704

(G-3201)
WESTROCK RKT LLC
100 Southern Dr (13031-1578)
PHONE..................................315 487-6111
David Ray, *Manager*
EMP: 12
SALES (corp-wide): 14.8B **Publicly Held**
SIC: 2653 Corrugated & solid fiber boxes
HQ: Westrock Rkt, Llc
1000 Abernathy Rd Ste 125
Atlanta GA 30328
770 448-2193

(G-3202)
WESTROCK RKT COMPANY
4914 W Genesee St (13031-2374)
PHONE..................................770 448-2193
David Atwell, *Plant Mgr*
EMP: 161
SALES (corp-wide): 14.8B **Publicly Held**
WEB: www.rocktenn.com
SIC: 2653 Partitions, solid fiber: made from purchased materials
HQ: Westrock Rkt, Llc
1000 Abernathy Rd Ste 125
Atlanta GA 30328
770 448-2193

Campbell
Steuben County

(G-3203)
FT SEISMIC SUPPORT INC
5596 Mills Rd (14821-9534)
PHONE..................................607 527-8595
Melinda A Comstock, *President*
EMP: 130
SALES (est): 19.3MM **Privately Held**
SIC: 1382 Oil & gas exploration services

(G-3204)
KRAFT HEINZ FOODS COMPANY
8596 Main St (14821-9636)
PHONE..................................607 527-4584
Kenneth Blake, *Principal*
Henry Mapes, *Branch Mgr*
EMP: 350
SALES (corp-wide): 26.2B **Publicly Held**
WEB: www.kraftfoods.com
SIC: 2022 2026 Cheese, natural & processed; fluid milk
HQ: Kraft Heinz Foods Company
1 Ppg Pl Ste 3200
Pittsburgh PA 15222
412 456-5700

(G-3205)
UPSTATE FARMS CHEESE LLC
8600 Main St (14821)
PHONE..................................607 527-4584
Tim Reagan, *Plant Mgr*
EMP: 180
SALES (est): 4.2MM
SALES (corp-wide): 893.9MM **Privately Held**
SIC: 2022 Processed cheese
PA: Upstate Niagara Cooperative, Inc.
25 Anderson Rd
Buffalo NY 14225
716 892-3156

Canaan
Columbia County

(G-3206)
HILLTOWN PORK INC (PA)
12948 State Route 22 (12029-2118)
PHONE.................................518 781-4050
Richard A Beckwith, *President*
Edwin S Beckwith, *Vice Pres*
Robert A Beckwith, *Admin Sec*
EMP: 22
SALES (est): 3.3MM **Privately Held**
SIC: 2011 2013 Pork products from pork slaughtered on site; sausages & other prepared meats

Canajoharie
Montgomery County

(G-3207)
GRAVYMASTER INC
Also Called: Dryden & Palmer Co
101 Erie Blvd (13317-1148)
PHONE.................................203 453-1893
Stephen A Besse, *President*
EMP: 44
SQ FT: 31,000
SALES (est): 4.6MM **Privately Held**
WEB: www.gravy.com
SIC: 2064 2035 2099 Candy & other confectionery products; seasonings & sauces, except tomato & dry; food preparations

(G-3208)
RICHARDSON BRANDS COMPANY (HQ)
Also Called: Richardson Foods
101 Erie Blvd (13317-1148)
PHONE.................................800 839-8938
Arnold J D'Angelo, *CEO*
Cheri Hines, *Vice Pres*
Tracey Burton, *VP Opers*
John Almaviva, *Opers Mgr*
Harold Rabe, *Warehouse Mgr*
▲ **EMP:** 150
SQ FT: 180,000
SALES (est): 30.1MM
SALES (corp-wide): 477MM **Privately Held**
WEB: www.richardsonbrands.com
SIC: 2064 Candy & other confectionery products
PA: Founders Equity, Inc.
545 5th Ave Rm 401
New York NY 10017
212 829-0900

(G-3209)
W W CUSTOM CLAD INC
75 Creek St (13317-1446)
PHONE.................................518 673-3322
EMP: 62
SQ FT: 23,804
SALES (corp-wide): 5.2MM **Privately Held**
WEB: www.wwcustomclad.com
SIC: 3479 Coating of metals & formed products
PA: W. W. Custom Clad, Inc.
337 E Main St
Canajoharie NY

Canandaigua
Ontario County

(G-3210)
AKOUSTIS INC
5450 Campus Dr Ste 100 (14424-8260)
PHONE.................................585 919-3073
Mary Winters, *Opers Staff*
EMP: 30
SALES (corp-wide): 1.2MM **Publicly Held**
SIC: 3674 4813 Integrated circuits, semiconductor networks, etc.; data telephone communications
HQ: Akoustis, Inc.
9805 Northcross Center Ct
Huntersville NC 28078
704 997-5735

(G-3211)
BADGE MACHINE PRODUCTS INC
2491 Brickyard Rd (14424-7969)
PHONE.................................585 394-0330
Gail Flugel, *President*
Christian Flugel, *Vice Pres*
Dan Pospula, *QA Dir*
Francis Flugel, *Treasurer*
Allison Leet, *Controller*
EMP: 30
SQ FT: 24,000
SALES (est): 5.2MM **Privately Held**
WEB: www.badgemachine.com
SIC: 3599 Machine shop, jobbing & repair

(G-3212)
BRISTOL CORE INC
5310 North St (14424-6900)
P.O. Box 507 (14424-0507)
PHONE.................................585 919-0302
Morgan Curtice, *President*
EMP: 18
SALES (est): 3.5MM **Privately Held**
SIC: 2621 Bristols

(G-3213)
CANANDAIGUA MSGNR INCORPORATED (PA)
Also Called: Daily Messenger
73 Buffalo St (14424-1001)
PHONE.................................585 394-0770
George Ewing Jr, *President*
George Ewing Sr, *Chairman*
Andrew Kavulich, *Vice Pres*
Lynn Brown, *Sls & Mktg Exec*
Lesley Stevens, *Accounts Exec*
EMP: 200 **EST:** 1910
SALES (est): 12.2MM **Privately Held**
SIC: 2711 2752 Newspapers: publishing only, not printed on site; commercial printing, lithographic

(G-3214)
CARGES ENTPS OF CANANDAIGUA
Also Called: Canandaigua Quick Print
330 S Main St (14424-2117)
PHONE.................................585 394-2600
Elizabeth Carges, *President*
Kevin Carges, *Vice Pres*
Robert Carges, *Vice Pres*
EMP: 6
SQ FT: 2,000
SALES (est): 1.1MM **Privately Held**
WEB: www.quickprintny.com
SIC: 2752 7334 Commercial printing, offset; photocopying & duplicating services

(G-3215)
CONSTELLATION BRANDS INC
3325 Marvin Sands Dr (14424-8405)
PHONE.................................585 393-4880
EMP: 31
SALES (corp-wide): 7.5B **Publicly Held**
WEB: www.cbrands.com
SIC: 2084 Wines, brandy & brandy spirits
PA: Constellation Brands, Inc.
207 High Point Dr # 100
Victor NY 14564
585 678-7100

(G-3216)
CONSTELLATION BRANDS US OPRS
116 Buffalo St (14424-1012)
PHONE.................................585 396-7600
Sue Bachorski, *Vice Pres*
Phil Piwko, *Finance*
Christopher Benziger, *Branch Mgr*
Brian Meath, *CTO*
Ron Fondiller, *Info Tech Dir*
EMP: 773
SALES (corp-wide): 7.5B **Publicly Held**
SIC: 2084 Wines
HQ: Constellation Brands U.S. Operations, Inc.
235 N Bloomfield Rd
Canandaigua NY 14424
585 396-7600

(G-3217)
CONSTELLATION BRANDS US OPRS (HQ)
Also Called: Centerra Wine Company
235 N Bloomfield Rd (14424-1059)
PHONE.................................585 396-7600
John Wright, *CEO*
Lou Applebaum, *President*
William F Hackett, *President*
Scott McCain, *District Mgr*
Michael Bell, *Opers Staff*
▲ **EMP:** 277
SALES (est): 740.3MM
SALES (corp-wide): 7.5B **Publicly Held**
SIC: 2084 Wines
PA: Constellation Brands, Inc.
207 High Point Dr # 100
Victor NY 14564
585 678-7100

(G-3218)
DENNIES MANUFACTURING INC
2543 State Route 21 (14424-8718)
PHONE.................................585 393-4646
Richard Warkentin, *President*
EMP: 27
SQ FT: 10,000
SALES (est): 5.2MM **Privately Held**
SIC: 3599 3441 7692 Machine shop, jobbing & repair; fabricated structural metal; welding repair

(G-3219)
DOUGS MACHINE SHOP INC
2304 Brickyard Rd (14424-7975)
PHONE.................................585 905-0004
Douglas Leonard, *Ch of Bd*
EMP: 8 **EST:** 2008
SALES (est): 1.1MM **Privately Held**
SIC: 3599 Machine shop, jobbing & repair

(G-3220)
EXFO BURLEIGH PDTS GROUP INC
181 S Main St Ste 10 (14424-1911)
PHONE.................................585 301-1530
Germain Lamonde, *Ch of Bd*
Sue Yoffee, *Principal*
Pierre Plamondon, *Vice Pres*
Yevgeniy Gelfand, *Software Dev*
EMP: 87
SQ FT: 20,000
SALES (est): 12.8MM **Privately Held**
WEB: www.burleigh.com
SIC: 3625 3827 3699 3826 Relays & industrial controls; optical instruments & lenses; laser systems & equipment; analytical optical instruments

(G-3221)
FINGER LAKES EXTRUSION CORP
Also Called: Flex Tubing
2437 State Route 21 (14424-8716)
PHONE.................................585 905-0632
William Scott, *President*
Erika Ray, *Vice Pres*
Erica Wright, *Vice Pres*
▲ **EMP:** 21 **EST:** 1998
SQ FT: 56,000
SALES: 5.6MM **Privately Held**
WEB: www.flextubing.com
SIC: 3089 3082 Extruded finished plastic products; tubes, unsupported plastic

(G-3222)
GATEHOUSE MEDIA LLC
Mpnnow
73 Buffalo St (14424-1001)
PHONE.................................585 394-0770
Carl Helbig, *Branch Mgr*
EMP: 100
SALES (corp-wide): 1.3B **Publicly Held**
WEB: www.gatehousemedia.com
SIC: 2711 2752 Newspapers, publishing & printing; commercial printing, lithographic
HQ: Gatehouse Media, Llc
175 Sullys Trl Ste 300
Pittsford NY 14534
585 598-0030

(G-3223)
GROSSGLOCKNER INC
Also Called: Artisan Meats
2640 Brickyard Rd (14424-7966)
PHONE.................................585 266-4960
Josef Brunner, *CEO*
Craig Funk, *General Mgr*
EMP: 6
SALES (est): 476.3K **Privately Held**
SIC: 2013 Sausages from purchased meat

(G-3224)
JUST RIGHT CARBINES LLC
231 Saltonstall St (14424-8301)
PHONE.................................585 261-5331
Richard J Cutri,
EMP: 6
SALES: 900K **Privately Held**
SIC: 3999 Manufacturing industries

(G-3225)
MOORE PRINTING COMPANY INC
9 Coy St (14424-1595)
PHONE.................................585 394-1533
Donna Miller, *President*
Burton Moore, *President*
EMP: 8
SQ FT: 3,500
SALES (est): 1MM **Privately Held**
SIC: 2752 2759 Commercial printing, offset; letterpress printing

(G-3226)
MURCADOM CORPORATION
Also Called: Fire Curtain Technologies
5711 Thomas Rd (14424-7988)
PHONE.................................585 412-2176
Jason Murphy, *CEO*
Timothy Wigton, *Opers Staff*
Paul Yarnall, *Director*
EMP: 10
SALES (est): 1MM **Privately Held**
SIC: 3272 7389 Building materials, except block or brick; concrete;

(G-3227)
NUPRO TECHNOLOGIES LLC
23 Coach St Ste 2a (14424-1529)
P.O. Box 182 (14424-0182)
PHONE.................................412 422-5922
Sam Altman, *Mng Member*
Marro Vidal,
▲ **EMP:** 15
SQ FT: 2,500
SALES (est): 2.7MM **Privately Held**
SIC: 3315 Wire & fabricated wire products

(G-3228)
PACTIV LLC
2651 Brickyard Rd (14424-7990)
PHONE.................................585 394-5125
Sam Aversa, *Engineer*
Margaret Finucane, *Branch Mgr*
Steve Hutchinson, *Info Tech Mgr*
EMP: 238 **Privately Held**
SIC: 2673 3089 5113 Food storage & frozen food bags, plastic; food storage & trash bags (plastic); food casings, plastic; containers, paper & disposable plastic; cups, disposable plastic & paper; dishes, disposable plastic & paper
HQ: Pactiv Llc
1900 W Field Ct
Lake Forest IL 60045
847 482-2000

(G-3229)
PACTIV LLC
5310 North St (14424-6900)
PHONE.................................847 482-2000
Phil Korenscra, *Manager*
EMP: 8 **Privately Held**
WEB: www.pactiv.com
SIC: 3089 Plastic containers, except foam
HQ: Pactiv Llc
1900 W Field Ct
Lake Forest IL 60045
847 482-2000

(G-3230)
PACTIV LLC
Also Called: Canandaigua Technology Center
5250 North St (14424-1026)
PHONE.................................585 393-3149

David Class, *Branch Mgr*
EMP: 800 Privately Held
WEB: www.pactiv.com
SIC: 3089 Tableware, plastic; composition stone, plastic; doors, folding: plastic or plastic coated fabric
HQ: Pactiv Llc
1900 W Field Ct
Lake Forest IL 60045
847 482-2000

(G-3231)
PLURES TECHNOLOGIES INC (PA)
4070 County Road 16 (14424-8314)
PHONE 585 905-0554
Aaron Dobrinsky, *President*
EMP: 1
SALES: 5.5MM Privately Held
SIC: 3674 Integrated circuits, semiconductor networks, etc.

(G-3232)
QUICKPRINT
330 S Main St (14424-2117)
PHONE 585 394-2600
Kevin Carges, *CEO*
Jim Paro, *Sales Mgr*
EMP: 5
SALES (est): 362.8K Privately Held
SIC: 2752 Commercial printing, offset

(G-3233)
SELECT FABRICATORS INC
5310 North St Ste 5 (14424-6900)
P.O. Box 119 (14424-0119)
PHONE 585 393-0650
David A Yearsley, *President*
Eleanor Yearsley, *Vice Pres*
Kristin Lupien, *Production*
Gary W Winch, *CFO*
Sandra Winch, *Admin Sec*
▼ **EMP: 15 EST: 2000**
SQ FT: 19,728
SALES (est): 2.3MM Privately Held
WEB: www.selectfabricatorsinc.com
SIC: 2393 3812 2673 2394 Duffle bags, canvas: made from purchased materials; aircraft/aerospace flight instruments & guidance systems; bags: plastic, laminated & coated; tents: made from purchased materials

(G-3234)
SKYOP LLC
5297 Parkside Dr Ste 440c (14424-7501)
PHONE 585 598-4737
Brian Pitre,
Daniel Albert,
EMP: 10 EST: 2013
SALES (est): 157.1K Privately Held
SIC: 7372 Educational computer software

(G-3235)
TIMBER FRAMES INC
5557 State Route 64 (14424-9382)
PHONE 585 374-6405
Alan R Milanette, *President*
EMP: 7 EST: 1976
SQ FT: 800
SALES (est): 1.4MM Privately Held
WEB: www.timberframesinc.com
SIC: 2439 1751 Structural wood members; framing contractor

(G-3236)
WOLFE PUBLICATIONS INC (PA)
Also Called: Messenger Post Media
73 Buffalo St (14424-1001)
PHONE 585 394-0770
Kathy Hammond, *President*
Beth Kesel, *General Mgr*
Rick Jensen, *Editor*
Marie Ewing, *Vice Pres*
John Bowman, *Prdtn Mgr*
EMP: 104 EST: 1956
SQ FT: 17,500
SALES (est): 7.7MM Privately Held
WEB: www.mpnewspapers.com
SIC: 2711 Commercial printing & newspaper publishing combined

(G-3237)
YOUNG EXPLOSIVES CORP
Also Called: Display Fireworks
2165 North Michigan Rd (14424-7918)
P.O. Box 18653, Rochester (14618-0653)
PHONE 585 394-1783
James R Young, *President*
▲ **EMP: 70 EST: 1949**
SQ FT: 400
SALES (est): 12.2MM Privately Held
WEB: www.youngexplosives.com
SIC: 2899 7999 Fireworks; fireworks display service

Canaseraga
Allegany County

(G-3238)
BEAVER CREEK INDUSTRIES INC
11530 White Rd (14822-9607)
PHONE 607 545-6382
Gary Bajus, *President*
Gary Bajus II, *Vice Pres*
Mary Bajus, *Treasurer*
Ethan Flint, *Associate*
EMP: 9
SQ FT: 8,000
SALES: 1MM Privately Held
SIC: 2431 Interior & ornamental woodwork & trim

(G-3239)
WILSON BEEF FARMS LLC
10751 Hess Rd (14822-9701)
PHONE 607 545-8308
Christopher Wilson, *Owner*
Chris Wilson, *Mng Member*
EMP: 10
SQ FT: 6,000
SALES (est): 886.2K Privately Held
WEB: www.wilsonbeeffarms.com
SIC: 2013 5421 Sausages & other prepared meats; meat markets, including freezer provisioners

---

Canastota
Madison County

(G-3240)
BLADING SERVICES UNLIMITED LLC
40 Madison Blvd (13032-3500)
PHONE 315 875-5313
Stephen Stevens,
EMP: 12
SALES (est): 2.2MM Privately Held
SIC: 3599 Machine shop, jobbing & repair

(G-3241)
CALLANAN INDUSTRIES INC
6375 Tuttle Rd (13032-4168)
PHONE 315 697-9569
Tim Hauck, *Principal*
EMP: 25
SALES (corp-wide): 29.7B Privately Held
SIC: 3272 Concrete products, precast
HQ: Callanan Industries, Inc.
8 Southwoods Blvd Ste 4
Albany NY 12211
518 374-2222

(G-3242)
CANASTOTA PUBLISHING CO INC
130 E Center St (13032-1307)
PHONE 315 697-9010
Patrick Milmoe, *President*
EMP: 5
SQ FT: 3,200
SALES (est): 695.4K Privately Held
SIC: 2752 Commercial printing, offset

(G-3243)
DEBRUCQUE CLEVELAND TRAMRAIL S
3 Technology Blvd (13032-3517)
PHONE 315 697-5160
Ron Debrucque, *Mng Member*
EMP: 6
SQ FT: 4,500
SALES (est): 1MM Privately Held
SIC: 3536 Cranes & monorail systems

(G-3244)
OWL WIRE & CABLE LLC
3127 Seneca Tpke (13032-3514)
PHONE 315 697-2011
Philip J Kemper, *President*
Robert J Ratti, *Chairman*
Frank Russo, *CFO*
▲ **EMP: 180 EST: 1951**
SQ FT: 400,000
SALES (est): 71MM
SALES (corp-wide): 242.1B Publicly Held
WEB: www.owlwire.com
SIC: 3496 Miscellaneous fabricated wire products
HQ: The Marmon Group Llc
181 W Madison St Ste 2600
Chicago IL 60602

(G-3245)
PRIME MATERIALS RECOVERY INC
51 Madison Blvd (13032-3501)
PHONE 315 697-5251
Francis Pratt, *Branch Mgr*
EMP: 8
SALES (corp-wide): 184.7MM Privately Held
SIC: 3441 Fabricated structural metal
PA: Prime Materials Recovery Inc.
99 E River Dr
East Hartford CT 06108
860 622-7626

(G-3246)
S K CIRCUITS INC (PA)
340 Rosewood Cir (13032-1556)
PHONE 703 376-8718
Vijay K Kodali, *President*
EMP: 11
SALES (est): 1.6MM Privately Held
SIC: 3672 Printed circuit boards

(G-3247)
SALARINOS ITALIAN FOODS INC
Also Called: Basilio's
110 James St (13032-1410)
PHONE 315 697-9766
Vincent Salamone Jr, *President*
Debra Salamone, *Vice Pres*
EMP: 10
SQ FT: 4,050
SALES (est): 1.1MM Privately Held
SIC: 2013 2038 Sausages from purchased meat; pizza, frozen

(G-3248)
SIDE HILL FARMERS COOP INC
8275 State Route 13 (13032-4470)
PHONE 315 447-4693
Paul O'Mara, *President*
Kirsten Tolman, *Treasurer*
EMP: 6
SALES: 1MM Privately Held
SIC: 2011 Meat packing plants

(G-3249)
THERMOLD CORPORATION
7059 Harp Rd (13032-4583)
PHONE 315 697-3924
Jeremy Schwimmer, *Ch of Bd*
Dan Emmons, *President*
▲ **EMP: 106 EST: 1945**
SQ FT: 35,000
SALES (est): 29.5MM Privately Held
WEB: www.thermold.com
SIC: 3089 Molding primary plastic; injection molding of plastics

(G-3250)
TRICON PIPING SYSTEMS INC
2 Technology Blvd (13032-3520)
P.O. Box 361 (13032-0361)
PHONE 315 697-8787
Hugh Roszel, *President*
Sara Jeffris, *Manager*
▼ **EMP: 12 EST: 1999**
SALES (est): 3.2MM Privately Held
WEB: www.triconpiping.com
SIC: 3317 Steel pipe & tubes

(G-3251)
VICTORY SIGNS INC
8915 Old State Route 13 (13032-5417)
PHONE 315 762-0220
Anthony Deperno, *President*
Jennifer Deperno, *Vice Pres*
EMP: 8
SQ FT: 2,000
SALES (est): 1.1MM Privately Held
SIC: 3993 Signs, not made in custom sign painting shops

Candor
Tioga County

(G-3252)
H L ROBINSON SAND & GRAVEL (PA)
535 Ithaca Rd (13743)
P.O. Box 121 (13743-0121)
PHONE 607 659-5153
Hannah L Robinson, *President*
EMP: 18
SQ FT: 5,000
SALES (est): 2.6MM Privately Held
SIC: 1442 Sand mining; gravel mining

(G-3253)
MARCELLUS ENERGY SERVICES LLC
3 Mill St Ste 6 (13743)
PHONE 607 236-0038
Gloria Tubbs, *Mng Member*
EMP: 20
SALES (est): 1.3MM Privately Held
SIC: 1389 Oil field services

Canton
St. Lawrence County

(G-3254)
BIMBO BAKERIES USA INC
19 Miner St Ste D (13617-1231)
PHONE 315 379-9069
Jeff Ward, *Manager*
EMP: 18 Privately Held
SIC: 2051 Bakery: wholesale or wholesale/retail combined
HQ: Bimbo Bakeries Usa, Inc
255 Business Center Dr # 200
Horsham PA 19044
215 347-5500

(G-3255)
COMMERCIAL PRESS INC
6589 Us Highway 11 (13617-3980)
PHONE 315 274-0028
David Charleson, *President*
Tracy Charleson, *Vice Pres*
EMP: 6
SQ FT: 1,200
SALES (est): 620K Privately Held
SIC: 2752 2759 Commercial printing, offset; commercial printing

(G-3256)
CORNING INCORPORATED
334 County Route 16 (13617-3135)
PHONE 315 379-3200
Joseph Neubert, *Plant Mgr*
Daniel Cassavaw, *Engineer*
Jared Thibodeau, *Engineer*
Donna Marshall, *Manager*
Dale Johnson, *Technology*
EMP: 86
SALES (corp-wide): 10.1B Publicly Held
WEB: www.corning.com
SIC: 3229 3211 Pressed & blown glass; flat glass
PA: Corning Incorporated
1 Riverfront Plz
Corning NY 14831
607 974-9000

(G-3257)
FRAZER COMPUTING INC
6196 Us Highway 11 (13617-3967)
P.O. Box 569 (13617-0569)
PHONE 315 379-3500
Michael Frazer, *Owner*

Canton - St. Lawrence County (G-3258) — GEOGRAPHIC SECTION

Chris Havens, *Project Mgr*
Josh Clark, *Marketing Staff*
David Aeschbacher, *Prgrmr*
Corey Griffin, *Software Dev*
EMP: 26
SALES (est): 4MM **Privately Held**
WEB: www.frazercomputing.com
SIC: 7372 Business oriented computer software

(G-3258)
ST LAWRENCE COUNTY NEWSPAPERS (HQ)
Also Called: Courier Observer
1 Main St Ste 103 (13617-1279)
PHONE 315 393-1003
Chuck Kelley, *General Mgr*
Eileen Kast, *Purch Agent*
Brenda La Brake, *VP Finance*
Debra Peters, *Accounts Exec*
▲ **EMP:** 60
SQ FT: 15,000
SALES (est): 6.3MM
SALES (corp-wide): 32MM **Privately Held**
WEB: www.courierobserver.com
SIC: 2711 2752 Commercial printing & newspaper publishing combined; commercial printing, lithographic
PA: Johnson Newspaper Corporation
260 Washington St
Watertown NY
315 782-1000

Cape Vincent
Jefferson County

(G-3259)
METALCRAFT MARINE US INC
583 E Broadway St (13618)
PHONE 315 501-4015
Tom Wroe, *President*
Michael Allen, *General Mgr*
Paul Cooledge, *Project Mgr*
Rob Phippen, *Controller*
Bob Clark, *Admin Sec*
▼ **EMP:** 17
SQ FT: 4,000
SALES: 547K **Privately Held**
SIC: 3732 3731 Boat building & repairing; shipbuilding & repairing; barges, building & repairing; combat vessels, building & repairing; fireboats, building & repairing
PA: Metal Craft Marine Incorporated
347 Wellington St
Kingston ON K7K 6
613 549-7747

Carle Place
Nassau County

(G-3260)
ALPHA WOLF LLC
241 Rushmore Ave (11514-1428)
PHONE 516 778-5812
Michael Chalavoutis, *President*
Lorraine Chalavoutis, *Vice Pres*
EMP: 5 **EST:** 2015
SALES: 100K **Privately Held**
SIC: 2086 Mineral water, carbonated: packaged in cans, bottles, etc.

(G-3261)
APOLLO ORTHOTICS CORP
320 Westbury Ave (11514-1607)
PHONE 516 333-3223
Caleb Lee, *CEO*
EMP: 5
SALES: 500K **Privately Held**
SIC: 3842 Orthopedic appliances

(G-3262)
BEE GREEN INDUSTRIES INC
322 Westbury Ave (11514-1607)
PHONE 516 334-3525
Harold Livine, *President*
EMP: 6
SALES (est): 312.1K **Privately Held**
SIC: 3999 Manufacturing industries

(G-3263)
BIOTEMPER
Also Called: Biotemper Plus
516 Mineola Ave (11514-1716)
PHONE 516 302-7985
Nadeem Khan, *Administration*
EMP: 5 **EST:** 2015
SALES (est): 229.7K **Privately Held**
SIC: 2833 Medicinal chemicals

(G-3264)
FORMED PLASTICS INC
207 Stonehinge Ln (11514-1743)
P.O. Box 347 (11514-0347)
PHONE 516 334-2300
Patrick K Long, *President*
Stephen Zamprelli, *President*
Beth Long, *Exec VP*
David Long, *Exec VP*
Matthew Desmond, *Vice Pres*
EMP: 80 **EST:** 1946
SQ FT: 74,000
SALES (est): 20.3MM **Privately Held**
WEB: www.formedplastics.com
SIC: 3089 Plastic processing

(G-3265)
GENNARIS ITLN FRENCH BKY INC
Also Called: Cardinali Bakery
465 Westbury Ave (11514-1401)
PHONE 516 997-8968
Giuseppe A Mauro, *President*
Mary Lou Makelski, *Admin Sec*
EMP: 6 **EST:** 1935
SALES (est): 759.1K **Privately Held**
SIC: 2051 5461 Bread, cake & related products; bakeries

(G-3266)
JEFF COOPER INC
288 Westbury Ave (11514-1605)
P.O. Box 361 (11514-0361)
PHONE 516 333-8200
Jeff Cooper, *President*
Laurie Cooper, *Vice Pres*
David Cooper, *Manager*
EMP: 12
SALES (est): 1.8MM **Privately Held**
WEB: www.jcplatinum.com
SIC: 3911 Rings, finger: precious metal

(G-3267)
JOHNSON & HOFFMAN LLC
40 Voice Rd (11514-1511)
P.O. Box 343 (11514-0343)
PHONE 516 742-3333
Brad Ansary, *President*
Joan Hill, *Senior VP*
Jerry Bentivegna, *Vice Pres*
Larry Zettwoch, *Vice Pres*
Albert Costabile, *Purch Mgr*
EMP: 70
SQ FT: 65,000
SALES (est): 14.3MM **Privately Held**
WEB: www.aecjh.com
SIC: 3469 Metal stampings

(G-3268)
LOW-COST MFG CO INC
318 Westbury Ave (11514-1607)
P.O. Box 147 (11514-0147)
PHONE 516 627-3282
Harold Rothlin, *President*
Freddy Malamud, *General Mgr*
▲ **EMP:** 6
SQ FT: 4,000
SALES (est): 1MM **Privately Held**
WEB: www.lowcostmfg.com
SIC: 3564 5087 Purification & dust collection equipment; laundry equipment & supplies

(G-3269)
M&M PRINTING INC
Also Called: MARsid-M&m Group, The
245 Westbury Ave (11514-1604)
PHONE 516 796-3020
Barry Caputo, *President*
Sidney Halpern, *Vice Pres*
Dan Magorrian, *Marketing Mgr*
James Fritz, *IT/INT Sup*
Adham Zaid, *Art Dir*
EMP: 15
SALES (est): 1.6MM **Privately Held**
SIC: 2752 Commercial printing, offset

(G-3270)
MARKET PLACE PUBLICATIONS
Also Called: J & F Advertising
234 Silverlake Blvd Ste 2 (11514-1644)
PHONE 516 997-7909
Gonzalez Jose, *Principal*
EMP: 40 **EST:** 1987
SALES (est): 1.5MM **Privately Held**
SIC: 2711 7313 Newspapers; newspaper advertising representative

(G-3271)
MARSID GROUP LTD
Also Called: Marsid Press
245 Westbury Ave (11514-1604)
PHONE 516 334-1603
Sidney Halpern, *President*
▼ **EMP:** 9
SALES (est): 1.3MM **Privately Held**
WEB: www.mmprint.com
SIC: 2752 Commercial printing, offset

(G-3272)
SCIENTIFIC SOLUTIONS GLOBL LLC
326 Westbury Ave (11514-1607)
PHONE 516 543-3376
Felicia Accius, *Manager*
Aurangzeb Pirzada,
EMP: 10 **EST:** 2017
SQ FT: 3,600
SALES (est): 500K **Privately Held**
SIC: 2844 Cosmetic preparations

(G-3273)
VINCENTS FOOD CORP
179 Old Country Rd (11514-1907)
PHONE 516 481-3544
Anthony Marisi, *President*
Robert Marisi, *Treasurer*
EMP: 12
SALES (est): 720K **Privately Held**
SIC: 2033 Tomato sauce: packaged in cans, jars, etc.

Carmel
Putnam County

(G-3274)
BIODESIGN INC OF NEW YORK (PA)
1 Sunset Rdg (10512-1118)
P.O. Box 1050 (10512-8050)
PHONE 845 454-6610
Susanne Ruddnick PHD, *President*
Michael Payne PHD, *Vice Pres*
EMP: 15
SQ FT: 26,000
SALES (est): 1.2MM **Privately Held**
WEB: www.biodesignofny.com
SIC: 3821 3829 Laboratory apparatus & furniture; measuring & controlling devices

(G-3275)
EASTERN JUNGLE GYM INC (PA)
30 Commerce Dr (10512-3026)
PHONE 845 878-9800
Scott Honigsberg, *President*
Rolf Zimmerman, *President*
Mark Honigsberg, *Vice Pres*
Naim Brahimi, *Store Mgr*
Barbara Hobbs,
◆ **EMP:** 35
SQ FT: 30,000
SALES (est): 6MM **Privately Held**
WEB: www.playsystem.com
SIC: 3949 5941 Playground equipment; playground equipment

(G-3276)
J & J TL DIE MFG & STAMPG CORP
594 Horsepound Rd (10512-4703)
PHONE 845 228-0242
Ronald C Johnson, *President*
EMP: 5 **EST:** 1981
SQ FT: 4,800
SALES (est): 554.9K **Privately Held**
SIC: 3599 Machine shop, jobbing & repair

(G-3277)
JAMES A STALEY CO INC
5 Bowen Ct (10512-4535)
PHONE 845 878-3344
James A Staley, *President*
J David Mori, *Vice Pres*
Kevin Loffredo, *Engineer*
Chris Prax, *Project Engr*
Jeff Salisbury, *Project Engr*
EMP: 18
SQ FT: 15,800
SALES (est): 5.2MM **Privately Held**
WEB: www.staleyco.com
SIC: 3829 7699 Aircraft & motor vehicle measurement equipment; testers for checking hydraulic controls on aircraft; fuel system instruments, aircraft; aircraft & heavy equipment repair services; hydraulic equipment repair

(G-3278)
NORTHEAST MESA LLC (PA)
10 Commerce Dr (10512-3026)
PHONE 845 878-9344
Denise Persek, *Sales Staff*
Giulio Burra,
Phil Waylonis,
EMP: 6 **EST:** 1995
SQ FT: 8,400
SALES (est): 1.2MM **Privately Held**
WEB: www.northeastmesa.com
SIC: 3271 Blocks, concrete: landscape or retaining wall

(G-3279)
PATTERSON BLACKTOP CORP
Also Called: Peckham Materials
1181 Route 6 (10512-1645)
PHONE 845 628-3425
Kurt Gabrielson, *Branch Mgr*
EMP: 6
SALES (corp-wide): 200.6MM **Privately Held**
SIC: 3531 Asphalt plant, including gravel-mix type
HQ: Patterson Blacktop Corp
20 Haarlem Ave
White Plains NY 10603

(G-3280)
PRECISION ARMS INC
Also Called: Time Precision
421 Route 52 (10512-6063)
PHONE 845 225-1130
Art Cocchia, *President*
Steven Cocchia, *Vice Pres*
EMP: 6
SQ FT: 3,500
SALES (est): 524.2K **Privately Held**
WEB: www.precisionarms.com
SIC: 3599 7699 Machine shop, jobbing & repair; gunsmith shop

(G-3281)
SILARX PHARMACEUTICALS INC (HQ)
Also Called: Lannett Company
1033 Stoneleigh Ave (10512-2414)
P.O. Box 449, Spring Valley (10977-0449)
PHONE 845 352-4020
Rohit Desai, *President*
Vipin Patel, *Vice Pres*
Nayan Raval, *Vice Pres*
Joseph Ortiz, *Mfg Spvr*
John Matthew, *Human Res Dir*
▲ **EMP:** 98
SQ FT: 30,000
SALES: 17.6MM
SALES (corp-wide): 684.5MM **Publicly Held**
SIC: 2834 Pharmaceutical preparations
PA: Lannett Company, Inc.
9000 State Rd
Philadelphia PA 19136
215 333-9000

(G-3282)
TPA COMPUTER CORP
531 Route 52 Apt 4 (10512-6073)
PHONE 877 866-6044
Steven Barnes, *President*
EMP: 10
SQ FT: 1,000

GEOGRAPHIC SECTION

Catskill - Greene County (G-3306)

SALES: 1.2MM **Privately Held**
WEB: www.tpacomputer.com
SIC: 7372 5734 Application computer software; computer & software stores

(G-3283)
TRAFFIC LANE CLOSURES LLC
1214 Route 52 Ste 1 (10512-4569)
P.O. Box 726, Brewster (10509-0326)
PHONE.................845 228-6100
Ralph M Rosenfeld, *General Mgr*
Teresa Rosenfeld, *Mng Member*
EMP: 13
SQ FT: 3,800
SALES (est): 1.7MM **Privately Held**
WEB: www.trafficlaneclosures.com
SIC: 3669 1611 7359 3679 Highway signals, electric; highway signs & guardrails; work zone traffic equipment (flags, cones, barrels, etc.); attenuators; soil erosion control fabrics

(G-3284)
WATSON LABORATORIES INC
1033 Stoneleigh Ave (10512-2414)
PHONE.................951 493-5300
Lillian Denunzio, *Buyer*
Robert Greco, *Branch Mgr*
EMP: 11 **Privately Held**
SIC: 2834 Pharmaceutical preparations
HQ: Watson Laboratories, Inc.
400 Interpace Pkwy
Parsippany NJ 07054

Carthage
Jefferson County

(G-3285)
A B C MC CLEARY SIGN CO INC
40230 State Route 3 (13619-9727)
PHONE.................315 493-3550
Ronald Moore, *President*
Jo Anne Moore, *Corp Secy*
EMP: 11
SQ FT: 15,000
SALES (est): 792.9K **Privately Held**
SIC: 3993 Electric signs

(G-3286)
CARTHAGE FIBRE DRUM INC (PA)
14 Hewitt Dr (13619-1101)
P.O. Box 109 (13619-0109)
PHONE.................315 493-2730
Timothy Wright, *President*
Ford Wright Sr, *Vice Pres*
Cathy Wright, *Treasurer*
EMP: 20 **EST:** 1915
SQ FT: 1,509
SALES (est): 5.5MM **Privately Held**
SIC: 2655 Fiber cans, drums & similar products

(G-3287)
CARTHAGE SPECIALTY PPRBD INC
Also Called: Climax Paperboard
30 Champion St (13619-1156)
PHONE.................315 493-2120
Patrick Purdy, *CEO*
Jeneen Labeau, *Purch Mgr*
Tina Pomerville, *Sales Mgr*
Michael Lambert, *Sales Staff*
EMP: 5
SALES (est): 22MM **Privately Held**
SIC: 2631 Paperboard mills
PA: Ox Industries, Inc.
600 W Elm Ave
Hanover PA 17331
717 698-3329

(G-3288)
CEM MACHINE INC (PA)
571 W End Ave (13619-1038)
PHONE.................315 493-4258
Mark Robinson, *President*
Roxanne Robinson, *Corp Secy*
Jason Flint, *Engineer*
Timothy Nettles, *Treasurer*
◆ **EMP:** 48
SQ FT: 80,000

SALES (est): 7.7MM **Privately Held**
WEB: www.cem-machine.com
SIC: 3599 Machine & other job shop work

(G-3289)
CHAMPION MATERIALS INC (PA)
502 S Washington St (13619-1533)
P.O. Box 127 (13619-0127)
PHONE.................315 493-2654
James D Uhlinger Jr, *Ch of Bd*
Jason Uhlinger, *Vice Pres*
Kellie O'Connor, *Controller*
Heather Walker, *Admin Asst*
EMP: 6
SALES (est): 6.8MM **Privately Held**
WEB: www.championmaterials.com
SIC: 3273 5211 Ready-mixed concrete; sand & gravel

(G-3290)
DAVID JOHNSON
Also Called: Poly Can
Deer River Rd (13619)
PHONE.................315 493-4735
David Johnson, *Owner*
EMP: 12
SQ FT: 12,000
SALES: 2MM **Privately Held**
SIC: 3085 Plastics bottles

Cassadaga
Chautauqua County

(G-3291)
WRIGHTS HARDWOODS INC
Also Called: Livermoore Logging
6868 Route 60 (14718-9706)
P.O. Box 1021, Sinclairville (14782-1021)
PHONE.................716 595-2345
Michael A Livermore, *President*
L Phillip Wright, *Vice Pres*
EMP: 22
SQ FT: 2,832
SALES (est): 1.6MM **Privately Held**
SIC: 2426 Dimension, hardwood

Castile
Wyoming County

(G-3292)
DON BECK INC
5249 State Route 39 (14427-9518)
PHONE.................585 493-3040
Richard T Beck, *President*
EMP: 6
SALES (est): 994.1K **Privately Held**
SIC: 3523 Farm machinery & equipment

(G-3293)
ELITSAC INC
Also Called: Elitsac Lumber
103 S Main St (14427-9722)
PHONE.................585 493-2628
Sara Bliss, *President*
William R Bliss, *Vice Pres*
EMP: 18
SQ FT: 25,000
SALES (est): 3.9MM **Privately Held**
WEB: www.elitsac.com
SIC: 3444 5211 7359 5251 Metal roofing & roof drainage equipment; lumber & other building materials; stores & yards equipment rental; snowblowers

Castle Creek
Broome County

(G-3294)
A D BOWMAN & SON LUMBER CO
1737 Us Highway 11 (13744-1107)
PHONE.................607 692-2595
Melvin Bowman, *Ch of Bd*
Joanne Bowman, *President*
Joel Bowman, *Vice Pres*
EMP: 28

SALES (est): 4.3MM **Privately Held**
SIC: 2426 2448 2421 Lumber, hardwood dimension; pallets, wood & wood with metal; sawmills & planing mills, general

Castleton On Hudson
Rensselaer County

(G-3295)
CELL-NIQUE CORPORATION
22 Hamilton Way (12033-1015)
PHONE.................203 856-8550
Dan Ratner, *CEO*
Donna Ratner, *COO*
Kol Ratner, *Associate*
▲ **EMP:** 1
SQ FT: 1,000,000
SALES (est): 3.5MM **Privately Held**
WEB: www.cell-nique.com
SIC: 2086 Iced tea & fruit drinks, bottled & canned

(G-3296)
MOORADIAN HYDRAULICS & EQP CO (PA)
1190 Route 9 (12033-9686)
PHONE.................518 766-3866
Richard Mooradian, *President*
Thomas Mooradian, *Vice Pres*
EMP: 12
SQ FT: 17,200
SALES (est): 2.5MM **Privately Held**
SIC: 7692 7699 5085 Welding repair; hydraulic equipment repair; hose, belting & packing

(G-3297)
SAXTON CORPORATION
1320 Route 9 (12033-9686)
PHONE.................518 732-7705
Mike Kellog, *President*
EMP: 30
SALES (est): 2.7MM **Privately Held**
SIC: 3993 Signs & advertising specialties

Castorland
Lewis County

(G-3298)
BLACK RIVER WOODWORKING LLC
4773 State Route 410 (13620-2301)
PHONE.................315 376-8405
Melvin Hess,
Brian Ball,
Ronald Hess,
EMP: 5 **EST:** 1993
SQ FT: 6,000
SALES (est): 550K **Privately Held**
SIC: 2511 Wood household furniture

(G-3299)
DANIEL & LOIS LYNDAKER LOGGING
10460 Monnat School Rd (13620-1270)
PHONE.................315 346-6527
Lois Lyndaker, *Principal*
EMP: 8 **EST:** 2010
SALES (est): 806K **Privately Held**
SIC: 2411 Logging

(G-3300)
LYNDAKER TIMBER HARVESTING LLC
10204 State Route 812 (13620-1268)
PHONE.................315 346-1328
David R Lyndaker,
Anita Lyndaker,
EMP: 11
SALES (est): 1.2MM **Privately Held**
SIC: 2411 Timber, cut at logging camp

Cato
Cayuga County

(G-3301)
ZAPPALA FARMS AG SYSTEMS INC
11404 Schuler Rd (13033-4276)
PHONE.................315 626-6293
James R Zappala, *President*
Samuel Zappala, *Vice Pres*
John R Zappala, *Admin Sec*
EMP: 30
SALES (est): 2.4MM **Privately Held**
SIC: 3523 5531 Farm machinery & equipment; automotive accessories

Catskill
Greene County

(G-3302)
CIMENT ST-LAURENT INC
Also Called: St Lawrence Cement Co
6446 Route 9w (12414-5322)
P.O. Box 31 (12414-0031)
PHONE.................518 943-4040
Georges Hubin, *Branch Mgr*
EMP: 140
SALES (corp-wide): 29.7B **Privately Held**
SIC: 3241 Masonry cement
HQ: Crh Canada Group Inc
2300 Steeles Ave W Suite 300
Concord ON L4K 5
905 532-3000

(G-3303)
GOLUB CORPORATION
Also Called: Price Chopper Pharmacy
320 W Bridge St (12414-1730)
PHONE.................518 943-3903
Kathleen Bryant, *Branch Mgr*
EMP: 21
SALES (corp-wide): 3.3B **Privately Held**
SIC: 3751 Motorcycles & related parts
PA: The Golub Corporation
461 Nott St
Schenectady NY 12308
518 355-5000

(G-3304)
HILL CREST PRESS
Also Called: E & G Press
138 Grandview Ave (12414-1934)
PHONE.................518 943-0671
Christine French, *Principal*
EMP: 8 **EST:** 1965
SQ FT: 1,500
SALES (est): 1.1MM **Privately Held**
SIC: 2752 2759 Commercial printing, offset; letterpress printing

(G-3305)
LEHIGH CEMENT COMPANY
120 Alpha Rd (12414-6902)
PHONE.................518 943-5940
Cheryl McElroy, *Manager*
EMP: 20
SALES (corp-wide): 287.7MM **Privately Held**
WEB: www.gfcement.com
SIC: 3273 5032 Ready-mixed concrete; cement
HQ: Lehigh Cement Company
313 Warren St
Glens Falls NY 12801
518 792-1137

(G-3306)
MARK T WESTINGHOUSE
Also Called: Pro Printers of Greene County
138 Grandview Ave (12414-1934)
PHONE.................518 678-3262
Mark T Westinghouse, *Owner*
EMP: 6 **EST:** 1970
SQ FT: 2,000
SALES: 600K **Privately Held**
SIC: 2752 2759 Commercial printing, offset; letterpress printing

Catskill - Greene County (G-3307)

(G-3307)
MOUNTAIN T-SHIRTS INC
Also Called: Mountain T-Shirts & Sign Works
8 W Bridge St (12414-1620)
PHONE..................518 943-4533
Craig Remaley, *President*
Daniel Webster, *Corp Secy*
Michael Marciante, *Treasurer*
EMP: 6 **EST:** 1984
SALES (est): 380K **Privately Held**
WEB: www.mountaintshirts.com
SIC: 2396 2261 5136 5199 Printing & embossing on plastics fabric articles; printing of cotton broadwoven fabrics; men's & boys' clothing; gifts & novelties

(G-3308)
PECKHAM INDUSTRIES INC
7065 Us Highway 9w (12414-5311)
P.O. Box 146, Ashland (12407-0146)
PHONE..................518 943-0155
Gary Metcalf, *Principal*
EMP: 18
SALES (corp-wide): 200.6MM **Privately Held**
SIC: 2951 Concrete, asphaltic (not from refineries)
PA: Peckham Industries, Inc.
20 Haarlem Ave Ste 200
White Plains NY 10603
914 949-2000

(G-3309)
WILLIAM MOON IRON WORKS INC
Also Called: Moon, Wm
80 Main St (12414-1805)
PHONE..................518 943-3861
Paul Moon, *President*
EMP: 10
SQ FT: 6,000
SALES: 450K **Privately Held**
SIC: 3599 Machine shop, jobbing & repair

(G-3310)
WOLFGANG B GOURMET FOODS INC
117 Cauterskill Ave (12414-1748)
PHONE..................518 719-1727
Wolfgang Brandl, *President*
Penelope Queen, *Vice Pres*
Dr Fereidoon Behin, *Shareholder*
EMP: 14
SQ FT: 10,000
SALES (est): 2.4MM **Privately Held**
SIC: 2033 Spaghetti & other pasta sauce: packaged in cans, jars, etc.

Cattaraugus
Cattaraugus County

(G-3311)
ADAMS LUMBER CO INC
6052 Adams Rd (14719-9567)
PHONE..................716 358-2815
John Adams, *President*
Dennis Adams, *Treasurer*
EMP: 16 **EST:** 1961
SQ FT: 10,000
SALES (est): 2.1MM **Privately Held**
SIC: 2421 Lumber: rough, sawed or planed

(G-3312)
CHESTER-JENSEN COMPANY
124 S Main St (14719-1240)
PHONE..................610 876-6276
Albert Gimbrone, *Opers-Prdtn-Mfg*
EMP: 40
SQ FT: 52,232
SALES (corp-wide): 5.2MM **Privately Held**
WEB: www.chester-jensen.com
SIC: 3556 Food products machinery
PA: Chester-Jensen Company
345 Tilghman St
Chester PA 19013
610 876-6276

(G-3313)
P & C GAS MEASUREMENTS SERVICE
Also Called: P & C Service
9505 Tannery Rd (14719-9761)
PHONE..................716 257-3412
James Perkins, *CEO*
Marie Robbons, *Manager*
EMP: 11
SQ FT: 5,000
SALES (est): 826.6K **Privately Held**
SIC: 1389 Oil sampling service for oil companies

(G-3314)
SETTERSTIX INC
261 S Main St (14719-1312)
PHONE..................716 257-3451
Eric Pritchard, *President*
Ron Wasmund, *Controller*
EMP: 43
SALES: 12.2MM **Privately Held**
SIC: 2679 Paperboard products, converted

Cayuta
Schuyler County

(G-3315)
WAGNER HARDWOODS LLC
6307 St Route 224 (14824)
P.O. Box 68 (14824-0068)
PHONE..................607 594-3321
Les Wagner, *Branch Mgr*
EMP: 200 **Privately Held**
WEB: www.wagner-hardwoods.com
SIC: 2421 Sawmills & planing mills, general
PA: Wagner Hardwoods Llc
6052 County Road 20
Friendship NY 14739

Cazenovia
Madison County

(G-3316)
BYS PUBLISHING LLC
118 Albany St (13035-1257)
PHONE..................315 655-9431
Brent Selleck,
◆ **EMP:** 5
SALES (est): 316.5K **Privately Held**
SIC: 2741 Miscellaneous publishing

(G-3317)
CONTINENTAL CORDAGE CORP (DH)
75 Burton St (13035-1156)
P.O. Box 623 (13035-0623)
PHONE..................315 655-9800
Rodney D Kent, *President*
▲ **EMP:** 100
SQ FT: 60,000
SALES (est): 5.8MM
SALES (corp-wide): 455.4MM **Privately Held**
WEB: www.iwgbwd.com
SIC: 2298 3357 3496 3356 Cordage: abaca, sisal, henequen, hemp, jute or other fiber; nonferrous wiredrawing & insulating; miscellaneous fabricated wire products; nonferrous rolling & drawing; copper rolling & drawing; steel wire & related products

(G-3318)
D R CORNUE WOODWORKS
3206 Us Route 20 (13035-8408)
PHONE..................315 655-9463
Dale R Cornue, *Owner*
EMP: 6
SQ FT: 6,000
SALES: 600K **Privately Held**
SIC: 2431 Doors, wood; woodwork, interior & ornamental; windows, wood

(G-3319)
FITZSIMMONS SYSTEMS INC
53 Nelson St (13035-1306)
PHONE..................315 214-7010
Lowell Todd Fitzsimmons, *President*

▼ **EMP:** 13
SQ FT: 1,500
SALES (est): 2.2MM **Privately Held**
WEB: www.fuelstoragetank.com
SIC: 2899 Chemical preparations

(G-3320)
KNOWLES CAZENOVIA INC (HQ)
Also Called: Dli
2777 Us Route 20 (13035-8444)
PHONE..................315 655-8710
Michael P Busse, *Ch of Bd*
David Wightman, *President*
Jon Keenan, *Production*
Brian Nagle, *QC Mgr*
Vicky Thurston, *QC Mgr*
▲ **EMP:** 179
SQ FT: 120,000
SALES (est): 34MM
SALES (corp-wide): 744.2MM **Publicly Held**
WEB: www.dilabs.com
SIC: 3675 Electronic capacitors
PA: Knowles Corporation
1151 Maplewood Dr
Itasca IL 60143
630 250-5100

(G-3321)
MADISON COUNTY DISTILLERY LLC
2420 Rte 20 (13035-8438)
PHONE..................315 391-6070
Patrick Ruddy,
EMP: 5
SALES (est): 205K **Privately Held**
SIC: 2085 Gin (alcoholic beverage); vodka (alcoholic beverage)

(G-3322)
MALL INC
4876 Bethel Rd (13035-9621)
PHONE..................315 751-9490
Peter Burr, *CEO*
Steven Petrocelli, *President*
EMP: 2
SALES: 5.5MM **Privately Held**
SIC: 7372 Application computer software

(G-3323)
MARQUARDT SWITCHES INC (DH)
2711 Us Route 20 (13035-9405)
PHONE..................315 655-8050
Harold Marquardt, *Ch of Bd*
Kirk Wardell, *President*
John Jelfo, *CFO*
Peter Mitchell, *Admin Sec*
▲ **EMP:** 200 **EST:** 1975
SQ FT: 98,000
SALES: 219.7MM **Privately Held**
WEB: www.switches.com
SIC: 3625 3613 Switches, electric power; switchgear & switchboard apparatus
HQ: Marquardt Gmbh
SchloBstr. 16
Rietheim-Weilheim 78604
742 499-0

(G-3324)
PDJ INC
Also Called: Johnson Bros Lumber
2550 E Ballina Rd (13035-8475)
PHONE..................315 655-8824
Paul Johnson, *President*
Judith Johnson, *Vice Pres*
Kara Connellan, *Office Spvr*
Heather Johnson, *Admin Sec*
EMP: 30
SQ FT: 39,400
SALES (est): 5.3MM **Privately Held**
SIC: 2421 Lumber: rough, sawed or planed

(G-3325)
PEAKS COFFEE COMPANY
3264 Rte 20 (13035-8408)
PHONE..................315 565-1900
Kelsey Ball, *Co-Owner*
Samuel Bender, *Co-Owner*
EMP: 5
SQ FT: 1,100
SALES (est): 153.8K **Privately Held**
SIC: 2095 Coffee roasting (except by wholesale grocers)

(G-3326)
PRICET PRINTING
3852 Charles Rd (13035-4505)
PHONE..................315 655-0369
Nathan Hoak, *President*
EMP: 6
SALES (est): 726.3K **Privately Held**
SIC: 2752 Commercial printing, lithographic

(G-3327)
STK ELECTRONICS INC
Also Called: Air-O-Tronics
2747 Rte 20 (13035-8444)
PHONE..................315 655-8476
Bill Merlini, *Ch of Bd*
Peter M Kip, *Principal*
Peter Mitchell, *Principal*
William Merlini, *CFO*
▲ **EMP:** 40
SQ FT: 20,000
SALES (est): 9.4MM **Privately Held**
WEB: www.stkelectronics.com
SIC: 3675 5063 Electronic capacitors; electrical apparatus & equipment; circuit breakers

(G-3328)
TRONSER INC
3066 John Trush Jr Blvd (13035-9541)
PHONE..................315 655-9528
Michael Tronser, *President*
Mike Beckett, *General Mgr*
James Dowd, *Vice Pres*
Peter Mitchell, *Admin Sec*
▲ **EMP:** 6
SQ FT: 7,000
SALES (est): 1.4MM
SALES (corp-wide): 11.6MM **Privately Held**
WEB: www.tronser.com
SIC: 3675 Electronic capacitors
PA: Alfred Tronser Gmbh
Quellenweg 14
Engelsbrand 75331
708 279-80

(G-3329)
VOLTRONICS LLC
Also Called: Trimmer Capacitor Company, The
2777 Us Route 20 (13035-8444)
PHONE..................410 749-2424
Aaron Goldberg, *General Mgr*
EMP: 48 **EST:** 1963
SQ FT: 200,000
SALES (est): 8.2MM
SALES (corp-wide): 7.8B **Publicly Held**
WEB: www.variablecap.com
SIC: 3675 Electronic capacitors
PA: Dover Corporation
3005 Highland Pkwy # 200
Downers Grove IL 60515
630 541-1540

Cedarhurst
Nassau County

(G-3330)
ABLE KITCHEN
Also Called: Able Kitchen Supplies
540 Willow Ave Unit B (11516-2211)
PHONE..................877 268-1264
Schulman Joseph, *Owner*
Raquel Walt, *Marketing Mgr*
EMP: 15
SALES (est): 994.2K **Privately Held**
SIC: 2434 Wood kitchen cabinets

(G-3331)
ELMAT QUALITY PRINTING LTD
79 Columbia Ave (11516-2011)
PHONE..................516 569-5722
Matt Friedman, *President*
Ellen Friedman, *Treasurer*
EMP: 16 **EST:** 1979
SQ FT: 4,000
SALES: 1.5MM **Privately Held**
SIC: 2752 Commercial printing, offset

GEOGRAPHIC SECTION

Central Islip - Suffolk County (G-3360)

(G-3332)
GLOBAL SECURITY TECH LLC
123 Grove Ave Ste 222 (11516-2302)
PHONE..................917 838-4507
Yoram Curiel, *CEO*
Victor Franco, *President*
Samuel Franco, *VP Sales*
Victor S Franco, *Manager*
Victor Dabah,
EMP: 10
SALES (est): 73.2K **Privately Held**
SIC: 3089 Identification cards, plastic

(G-3333)
M & M BAGEL CORP
Also Called: Bagelry
507 Central Ave (11516-2010)
PHONE..................516 295-1222
Vincent Matuozzi, *President*
Robert Madorsky, *Vice Pres*
EMP: 12
SALES (est): 1MM **Privately Held**
SIC: 2051 5461 Bagels, fresh or frozen; bagels

(G-3334)
MARK F ROSENHAFT N A O
538 Central Ave (11516-2127)
PHONE..................516 374-1010
Mark F Rosenhaft, *Owner*
EMP: 8
SALES (est): 429.8K **Privately Held**
SIC: 3851 5999 Eyes, glass & plastic; miscellaneous retail stores

(G-3335)
NANO VIBRONIX INC
601 Chestnut St (11516-2228)
PHONE..................516 374-8330
Harold Jacobs, *President*
EMP: 5
SALES (est): 16K **Privately Held**
SIC: 3841 Surgical & medical instruments

(G-3336)
NJR MEDICAL DEVICES
390 Oak Ave (11516-1824)
P.O. Box 582, New York (10021-0034)
PHONE..................440 258-8204
Nicholas Pastron, *CEO*
EMP: 20
SALES (est): 1.9MM **Privately Held**
SIC: 3841 Suction therapy apparatus

(G-3337)
SOLAR THIN FILMS INC (PA)
Also Called: Stf
445 Central Ave Unit 366 (11516-2077)
PHONE..................212 629-8260
Robert M Bubin, *CEO*
▲ **EMP:** 28
SALES (est): 3.9MM **Publicly Held**
SIC: 3674 Photovoltaic devices, solid state

Center Moriches
Suffolk County

(G-3338)
DIAMOND PRECAST PRODUCTS INC
170 Railroad Ave (11934-1906)
PHONE..................631 874-3777
Rick Cerrone, *President*
Dominic Iannuci, *Treasurer*
Ronald Notaranonio, *Admin Sec*
EMP: 15 **EST:** 1999
SALES (est): 1.8MM **Privately Held**
SIC: 3272 Precast terrazo or concrete products

(G-3339)
ISLAND READY MIX INC
170 Railroad Ave (11934-1906)
PHONE..................631 874-3777
Rice Cerrone, *President*
Dominic Iannuci, *Treasurer*
Ronald Notarantonio, *Admin Sec*
EMP: 25 **EST:** 1961
SALES (est): 4.5MM **Privately Held**
WEB: www.islandreadymix.com
SIC: 3273 3272 Ready-mixed concrete; concrete products, precast

(G-3340)
RED TAIL MOULDING & MLLWK LLC
23 Frowein Rd Ste 1 (11934-1606)
PHONE..................516 852-4613
Tom Smith,
EMP: 3
SALES: 1.2MM **Privately Held**
SIC: 2431 Doors & door parts & trim, wood

(G-3341)
SPECIALTY PRODUCTS INC
15 Frowein Rd Bldg E2 (11934-1609)
P.O. Box 1164, Westhampton Beach (11978-7164)
PHONE..................866 869-4335
Vincent Immordino, *CEO*
Linda Bonhof, *President*
EMP: 20
SQ FT: 10,000
SALES: 10MM **Privately Held**
SIC: 3089 5199 Plastic processing; general merchandise, non-durable

Centereach
Suffolk County

(G-3342)
A M S SIGN DESIGNS
2360 Middle Country Rd (11720-3523)
PHONE..................631 467-7722
Mark Saccone, *Owner*
Suzanna Saccone, *Co-Owner*
EMP: 5
SALES (est): 415.3K **Privately Held**
SIC: 3993 Signs & advertising specialties

(G-3343)
CALIBRATION TECHNOLOGIES INC
30 Woodland Blvd (11720-3636)
PHONE..................631 676-6133
Thomas J Accardi, *President*
EMP: 5
SALES (est): 526K **Privately Held**
SIC: 3629 Electrical industrial apparatus

(G-3344)
I FIX SCREEN
203 Centereach Mall (11720-2751)
PHONE..................631 421-1938
Alberto Cruz, *Principal*
EMP: 6
SALES (est): 421.2K **Privately Held**
SIC: 3442 Screen & storm doors & windows

(G-3345)
QUANTA ELECTRONICS INC
48 Fran Ln (11720-4441)
PHONE..................631 961-9953
Martin Czerniewski, *President*
Marcin Czerniewski, *Chief Engr*
EMP: 12
SALES (est): 1.4MM **Privately Held**
SIC: 3663 Radio & TV communications equipment

(G-3346)
WIN SET TECHNOLOGIES LLC
2364 Middle Country Rd (11720-3502)
P.O. Box 2007, Miller Place (11764-8786)
PHONE..................631 234-7077
Philip Settepani,
Frederick Winter III,
▼ **EMP:** 10
SQ FT: 3,000
SALES: 750K **Privately Held**
WEB: www.winset.net
SIC: 3542 Presses: forming, stamping, punching, sizing (machine tools)

Centerport
Suffolk County

(G-3347)
BLONDIE S BAKESHOP INC
90 Washington Dr (11721-1831)
PHONE..................631 424-4545
Jeff Kennaugh, *President*
EMP: 8
SALES (est): 592.2K **Privately Held**
SIC: 2051 Bakery: wholesale or wholesale/retail combined

(G-3348)
FORUM PUBLISHING CO
Also Called: Marketer's Forum Magazine
383 E Main St (11721-1538)
PHONE..................631 754-5000
Martin B Stevens, *Owner*
EMP: 9 **EST:** 1976
SQ FT: 3,000
SALES: 1.4MM **Privately Held**
WEB: www.forum123.com
SIC: 2721 Trade journals: publishing & printing

(G-3349)
LEESA DESIGNS LTD
31 Glenn Cres (11721-1715)
P.O. Box 488 (11721-0488)
PHONE..................631 261-3991
Helen L Dello-Iacona, *President*
Helen L Dello-Iacora, *President*
Sara Mazzola, *Treasurer*
EMP: 5
SALES: 200K **Privately Held**
SIC: 2339 Neckwear & ties; women's, misses' & juniors'

(G-3350)
LIBERTY INSTALL INC
100 Centershore Rd (11721-1527)
PHONE..................631 651-5655
Sheri Stevens, *President*
EMP: 11
SALES (est): 423.3K **Privately Held**
SIC: 3841 Surgical & medical instruments

(G-3351)
MSP TECHNOLOGYCOM LLC
77 Bankside Dr (11721-1738)
PHONE..................631 424-7542
Walter Stark, *CEO*
Jeanne Connor-Stark,
EMP: 3
SQ FT: 1,200
SALES (est): 1.2MM **Privately Held**
WEB: www.msptechnology.com
SIC: 3585 5075 Humidifiers & dehumidifiers; dehumidifiers, except portable

(G-3352)
SURVIVAL INC
90 Washington Dr Ste C (11721-1831)
PHONE..................631 385-5060
Sanjay Lakhani, *President*
Rebecca Lakhani, *Vice Pres*
▲ **EMP:** 8
SALES (est): 1.1MM **Privately Held**
WEB: www.survivalrules.com
SIC: 2339 Women's & misses' outerwear

Central Bridge
Schoharie County

(G-3353)
AMERICAN STANDARD MFG INC
Also Called: Asm
106 Industrial Park Ln (12035)
P.O. Box 164 (12035-0164)
PHONE..................518 868-2512
Coleman Vickary, *Chairman*
Aaron Haig, *Prdtn Mgr*
William Cleveland, *Director*
Connie Vickary, *Admin Sec*
Dominic Vickary, *Associate*
EMP: 25
SQ FT: 28,000
SALES: 6MM **Privately Held**
WEB: www.amrstd.com
SIC: 3499 2542 Machine bases, metal; partitions & fixtures, except wood

Central Islip
Suffolk County

(G-3354)
AH ELCTRONIC TEST EQP REPR CTR
7 Olive St (11722-4017)
PHONE..................631 234-8979
Audley Haynes, *Principal*
EMP: 12 **Privately Held**
WEB: www.ahelectronics.com
SIC: 1389 3825 7629 Testing, measuring, surveying & analysis services; standards & calibration equipment for electrical measuring; electronic equipment repair
PA: Ah Electronic Test Equipment Repair Center Inc
374 Islip Ave Ste 201
Islip NY 11751

(G-3355)
ALPHAMED BOTTLES INC
300 S Technology Dr (11722-4400)
PHONE..................631 524-5577
Subhakar Viyala, *President*
Pavan Vemula, *Opers Mgr*
▲ **EMP:** 21
SQ FT: 26,000
SALES: 8MM **Privately Held**
SIC: 3085 Plastics bottles

(G-3356)
ASCENT PHARMACEUTICALS INC (HQ)
400 S Technology Dr (11722-4402)
PHONE..................631 851-0550
Sudhakar Viviyala, *CEO*
▲ **EMP:** 72
SALES (est): 25.3MM **Privately Held**
SIC: 2834 Pharmaceutical preparations

(G-3357)
AUTRONIC PLASTICS INC
Also Called: API
1150 Motor Pkwy (11722-1217)
PHONE..................516 333-7577
Michael Lax, *President*
Tim Keuning, *President*
Agjah I Libohova, *Research*
Fred Van Koot, *Engineer*
Rosemarie Romano, *Controller*
▲ **EMP:** 70
SQ FT: 55,000
SALES (est): 27.4MM **Privately Held**
WEB: www.apisolution.com
SIC: 3089 5162 Injection molding of plastics; plastics products

(G-3358)
AVCO INDUSTRIES INC
120 Windsor Pl (11722-3331)
P.O. Box 416, Huntington Station (11746-0338)
PHONE..................631 851-1555
Gil Korine, *Ch of Bd*
▼ **EMP:** 15
SQ FT: 40,000
SALES (est): 9.8MM **Privately Held**
SIC: 2679 Pressed fiber & molded pulp products except food products

(G-3359)
BERKSHIRE TRANSFORMER (PA)
Also Called: Custom Power Systems
77 Windsor Pl Ste 18 (11722-3334)
PHONE..................631 467-5328
Paul Alessandrini, *Owner*
EMP: 5
SALES (est): 916.7K **Privately Held**
SIC: 3679 3612 Electronic loads & power supplies; transformers, except electric

(G-3360)
BI NUTRACEUTICALS INC
120 Hoffman Ln (11749-5008)
PHONE..................631 232-1105
Robin Corcella, *Purchasing*
Christoph Kirchner, *CFO*
Matthew Overholser, *Sales Staff*
Bob Harvey, *Manager*
EMP: 52 **Privately Held**

WEB: www.botanicals.com
SIC: 2834 Vitamin preparations
HQ: Bi Nutraceuticals, Inc.
2384 E Pacifica Pl
Rancho Dominguez CA 90220
310 669-2100

(G-3361)
CELLU TISSUE - LONG ISLAND LLC
555 N Research Pl (11722-4417)
PHONE..............................631 232-2626
Russell C Taylor,
▲ EMP: 210
SALES (est): 22.5MM Publicly Held
SIC: 2676 Sanitary paper products
HQ: Cellu Tissue Holdings, Inc.
12725 Morris Road Ext
Alpharetta GA 30004

(G-3362)
CENTRAL ISLIP PHARMACY INC
1629 Islip Ave (11722-2701)
PHONE..............................631 234-6039
Ronald Goodstadt, Principal
EMP: 7
SALES (est): 847.4K Privately Held
SIC: 2834 Adrenal pharmaceutical preparations

(G-3363)
COLOR CARD LLC
Also Called: Limo-Print.com
1065 Islip Ave (11722-4203)
PHONE..............................631 232-1300
Robert Haller Sr, President
Marilyn Haller, Vice Pres
EMP: 18
SQ FT: 110,000
SALES (est): 1.5MM Privately Held
SIC: 2752 5961 2759 Business form & card printing, lithographic; cards, mail order; invitations: printing

(G-3364)
CREATIVE HOME FURNISHINGS (PA)
Also Called: Dakotah
250 Creative Dr (11722-4404)
PHONE..............................631 582-8000
Gunther Bartsch, President
▲ EMP: 3
SALES (est): 9MM Privately Held
WEB: www.dakotah.com
SIC: 2392 Cushions & pillows

(G-3365)
CVD EQUIPMENT CORPORATION (PA)
Also Called: C V D
355 S Technology Dr (11722-4416)
PHONE..............................631 981-7081
Leonard A Rosenbaum, Ch of Bd
Steven Aragon, COO
Max Shatalov, Vice Pres
Karlheinz Strobl, Vice Pres
Glen R Charles, CFO
▲ EMP: 173
SQ FT: 130,000
SALES: 41.1MM Publicly Held
WEB: www.cvdequipment.com
SIC: 3674 Semiconductors & related devices

(G-3366)
CVD EQUIPMENT CORPORATION
Also Called: Conceptronic
355 S Technology Dr (11722-4416)
PHONE..............................631 582-4365
Leonard Rosenbaum, President
EMP: 15
SALES (corp-wide): 41.1MM Publicly Held
WEB: www.cvdequipment.com
SIC: 3559 3567 Semiconductor manufacturing machinery; heating units & devices, industrial: electric
PA: Cvd Equipment Corporation
355 S Technology Dr
Central Islip NY 11722
631 981-7081

(G-3367)
D & R SILK SCREENING LTD
201 Creative Dr (11722-4405)
PHONE..............................631 234-7464
Dominick De Ricco, President
Rose De Ricco, Admin Sec
EMP: 15
SQ FT: 4,000
SALES (est): 1.2MM Privately Held
SIC: 2261 2396 Screen printing of cotton broadwoven fabrics; automotive & apparel trimmings

(G-3368)
EUGENE G DANNER MFG INC
Also Called: Danner, Eg Mfg
160 Oval Dr (11749-1403)
PHONE..............................631 234-5261
Eugene G Danner, President
Josephine Danner, Corp Secy
Michael Danner, Vice Pres
▲ EMP: 38 EST: 1948
SQ FT: 31,000
SALES (est): 7.9MM Privately Held
WEB: www.dannermfg.com
SIC: 3089 Aquarium accessories, plastic

(G-3369)
FAR EASTERN COCONUT COMPANY
200 Corporate Plz 201a (11749-1552)
PHONE..............................631 851-8800
Richard Martino, President
Rich Martino, Vice Pres
Mitchell Bauman, Treasurer
▲ EMP: 10
SQ FT: 2,000
SALES (est): 640K Privately Held
SIC: 2099 Coconut, desiccated & shredded

(G-3370)
FREEPORT PAPER INDUSTRIES INC
120 Windsor Pl (11722-3331)
PHONE..............................631 851-1555
Gil Korine, Ch of Bd
Jon Giambruno, Software Dev
◆ EMP: 60
SQ FT: 40,000
SALES (est): 14.1MM Privately Held
SIC: 2621 Paper mills

(G-3371)
GMR MANUFACTURING INC
Also Called: George Raum Manufacturing
101 Windsor Pl Unit D (11722-3329)
PHONE..............................631 582-2600
George Raum, President
EMP: 6 EST: 1976
SQ FT: 2,300
SALES (est): 520.4K Privately Held
SIC: 3599 Machine shop, jobbing & repair

(G-3372)
INVAGEN PHARMACEUTICALS INC
550 S Research Pl (11722-4415)
PHONE..............................631 949-6367
Fakiha Rana, Branch Mgr
EMP: 150 Privately Held
SIC: 2834 Tablets, pharmaceutical
HQ: Invagen Pharmaceuticals Inc.
7 Oser Ave Ste 4
Hauppauge NY 11788
631 231-3233

(G-3373)
ISLAND RECYCLING CORP
228 Blydenburg Rd (11749-5006)
PHONE..............................631 234-6688
Mary Dimatteo, President
EMP: 5
SQ FT: 10,000
SALES (est): 572.3K Privately Held
SIC: 3341 Recovery & refining of nonferrous metals

(G-3374)
ISLANDIA MRI ASSOCIATES PC
200 Corporate Plz Ste 203 (11749-1507)
PHONE..............................631 234-2828
Joel Reiter, President
Maggie Hernandez, Office Mgr
EMP: 15

SALES (est): 1.5MM Privately Held
SIC: 3826 Magnetic resonance imaging apparatus

(G-3375)
J&R FUEL OF LI INC
97 W Suffolk Ave (11722-2143)
PHONE..............................631 234-1959
James R Reed, Owner
EMP: 5
SALES (est): 385.2K Privately Held
SIC: 2869 Fuels

(G-3376)
LENARO PAPER CO INC
31 Windsor Pl (11722-3301)
P.O. Box 9024 (11722-9024)
PHONE..............................631 439-8800
Leonard Aronica, Ch of Bd
Anthony J Aronica, Vice Pres
◆ EMP: 18
SQ FT: 143,000
SALES (est): 10.3MM Privately Held
WEB: www.lenaropaper.com
SIC: 2621 5111 Paper mills; fine paper

(G-3377)
M & M MOLDING CORP
250 Creative Dr (11722-4404)
PHONE..............................631 582-1900
Mathias Meinzinger, President
John McLaughlin, CFO
Gunther Bartsch, Treasurer
▲ EMP: 200 EST: 1977
SQ FT: 50,000
SALES (est): 27.2MM Privately Held
SIC: 3089 Injection molded finished plastic products

(G-3378)
MONARCH GRAPHICS INC
1065 Islip Ave (11722-4203)
PHONE..............................631 232-1300
Marilyn Haller, President
Robert Haller, Vice Pres
EMP: 18
SQ FT: 11,000
SALES (est): 2.6MM Privately Held
WEB: www.monarchgraphics.com
SIC: 2752 Commercial printing, offset

(G-3379)
NATIONWIDE EXHIBITOR SVCS INC
Also Called: Nationwide Displays
110 Windsor Pl (11722-3331)
PHONE..............................631 467-2034
Steven Griffith, President
William Griffith, Vice Pres
Frank Vesce, Project Mgr
Matthew Houck, Accounts Exec
John Griffith, Manager
EMP: 10
SQ FT: 20,000
SALES (est): 2MM Privately Held
SIC: 3993 3999 2542 Displays & cutouts, window & lobby; advertising display products; fixtures: display, office or store: except wood

(G-3380)
NETEGRITY INC (DH)
1 Ca Plz (11749-5305)
PHONE..............................631 342-6000
Barry N Bycoff, President
William C Bartow, Vice Pres
Gregory L Zelo, Vice Pres
Nicholas Rosati, QA Dir
Regina O Sommer, CFO
EMP: 160
SALES (est): 22.8MM
SALES (corp-wide): 17.6B Publicly Held
WEB: www.netegrity.com
SIC: 7372 Prepackaged software
HQ: Ca, Inc.
520 Madison Ave Fl 22
New York NY 10022
800 225-5224

(G-3381)
NORTH AMERICAN ENCLOSURES INC (PA)
Also Called: Nae
85 Jetson Ln Ste B (11722-1202)
P.O. Box 913, Westbury (11590-0126)
PHONE..............................631 234-9500

Richard Schwartz, Ch of Bd
Norman S Grafstein, President
Marie Neubert, Corp Secy
▲ EMP: 40 EST: 1962
SQ FT: 55,000
SALES (est): 66.3MM Privately Held
WEB: www.naeframes.com
SIC: 2499 3827 Picture & mirror frames, wood; mirrors, optical

(G-3382)
QUALITY ENCLOSURES INC (PA)
101 Windsor Pl Unit H (11722-3339)
PHONE..............................631 234-0115
Manny Schwartz, Ch of Bd
Michael Schwartz, President
Steve Schwartz, General Mgr
◆ EMP: 23
SQ FT: 27,000
SALES (est): 6.2MM Privately Held
WEB: www.qualityenclosures.com
SIC: 3088 3231 Plastics plumbing fixtures; products of purchased glass

(G-3383)
RICHARD RUFFNER
Also Called: Dynamic Printing
69 Carleton Ave (11722-3018)
PHONE..............................631 234-4600
Richard Ruffner, Owner
Rosie Dejesus, Exec Dir
EMP: 15
SQ FT: 6,000
SALES (est): 1.1MM Privately Held
SIC: 2759 7349 5943 2789 Commercial printing; building maintenance services; office forms & supplies; bookbinding & related work; manifold business forms; commercial printing, lithographic

(G-3384)
SPECTRUM CATALYSTS INC
69 Windsor Pl (11722-3300)
P.O. Box 472, Smithtown (11787-0472)
PHONE..............................631 560-3683
John Plunkett, President
Michael Plunkett, Senior VP
EMP: 5 EST: 2001
SQ FT: 100,000
SALES: 1MM Privately Held
SIC: 3559 Chemical machinery & equipment

(G-3385)
SYNERGY RESOURCES INC
320 Carleton Ave Ste 6200 (11722-4538)
PHONE..............................631 665-2050
Gene Caiola, Ch of Bd
Mark Lilly, Principal
EMP: 65
SQ FT: 3,500
SALES: 12MM Privately Held
WEB: www.synergyresources.net
SIC: 7372 Business oriented computer software

(G-3386)
SYSTEM OF AME BINDING
95 Hoffman Ln (11749-5020)
PHONE..............................631 390-8560
William Stross, Vice Pres
EMP: 9
SALES (est): 1.5MM Privately Held
SIC: 3111 Bookbinders' leather

(G-3387)
UNITED BAKING CO INC
16 Bronx Ave (11722-2406)
PHONE..............................631 413-5116
EMP: 17 Privately Held
SIC: 2052 Cookies & crackers
PA: United Baking Co., Inc.
41 Natcon Dr
Shirley NY 11967

(G-3388)
VANGUARD METALS INC
135 Brightside Ave (11722-2709)
P.O. Box 666 (11722-0666)
PHONE..............................631 234-6500
Joel Frank, President
Helene Frank, Vice Pres
EMP: 15
SQ FT: 6,000

▲ = Import ▼ = Export
◆ = Import/Export

GEOGRAPHIC SECTION

Champlain - Clinton County (G-3415)

SALES: 1.6MM Privately Held
WEB: www.vanguardmetals.com
SIC: 3451 3599 Screw machine products; machine shop, jobbing & repair

Central Square
Oswego County

(G-3389)
ALLOY METAL PRODUCTS LLC
193 Us Route 11 (13036-9760)
P.O. Box 2 (13036-0002)
PHONE..............................315 676-2405
James Thayer, *Mng Member*
▲ EMP: 10
SQ FT: 14,000
SALES: 1MM Privately Held
WEB: www.alloymetalproducts.com
SIC: 3714 Motor vehicle parts & accessories

(G-3390)
AMERITOOL MFG INC
64 Corporate Park Dr (13036-9595)
P.O. Box 213 (13036-0213)
PHONE..............................315 668-2172
Jerome E Beck, *President*
Cheryl Joyce, *Vice Pres*
▲ EMP: 20
SALES (est): 3.9MM Privately Held
SIC: 3593 Fluid power cylinders & actuators

(G-3391)
NASIFF ASSOCIATES INC
841 County Route 37 (13036-2133)
P.O. Box 88, Brewerton (13029-0088)
PHONE..............................315 676-2346
Roger Nasiff, *President*
Anita Bourdeau, *Marketing Mgr*
Anita M Bourdeau, *Corp Comm Staff*
EMP: 6
SALES (est): 1.1MM Privately Held
WEB: www.nasiff.com
SIC: 3841 8711 Diagnostic apparatus, medical; professional engineer

(G-3392)
TORRINGTON INDUSTRIES INC
Also Called: Mid-State Ready Mix
90 Corporate Park Dr (13036-9595)
PHONE..............................315 676-4662
Theodore Zoli, *President*
EMP: 6
SALES (corp-wide): 1.9MM Privately Held
SIC: 3273 Ready-mixed concrete
PA: Torrington Industries Inc
 112 Wall St
 Torrington CT 06790
 860 489-9261

(G-3393)
UPSTATE INSULATED GLASS INC
47 Weber Rd (13036-2109)
PHONE..............................315 475-4960
James R Markert, *President*
EMP: 6
SQ FT: 3,100
SALES: 800K Privately Held
SIC: 3231 1793 5231 Insulating units, multiple-glazed: made from purchased glass; glass & glazing work; glass

Central Valley
Orange County

(G-3394)
CROCS INC
498 Red Apple Ct (10917-6620)
PHONE..............................845 928-3002
Debbie Heffern, *Manager*
EMP: 14
SALES (corp-wide): 1B Publicly Held
SIC: 3021 Shoes, rubber or rubber soled fabric uppers
PA: Crocs, Inc.
 7477 Dry Creek Pkwy
 Niwot CO 80503
 303 848-7000

(G-3395)
DAVID YURMAN ENTERPRISES LLC
484 Evergreen Ct (10917-6716)
PHONE..............................845 928-8660
EMP: 9
SALES (corp-wide): 46.9MM Privately Held
SIC: 3911 Mfg Precious Metal Jewelry
PA: David Yurman Enterprises Llc
 24 Vestry St
 New York NY 10013
 212 896-1550

(G-3396)
ELIZABETH ARDEN INC
214 Red Apple Ct (10917-6605)
PHONE..............................845 810-2175
April Lee, *Principal*
EMP: 199 Publicly Held
SIC: 2844 Toilet preparations
HQ: Elizabeth Arden, Inc.
 880 Sw 145th Ave Ste 200
 Pembroke Pines FL 33027

(G-3397)
SCHILLER STORES INC
Also Called: Lecreuset of America
869 Adirondack Way (10917-6205)
PHONE..............................845 928-4316
Marcia York, *Branch Mgr*
EMP: 5 Privately Held
WEB: www.lecreusetofamerica.com
SIC: 3269 Cookware: stoneware, coarse earthenware & pottery
PA: Schiller Stores Inc
 509 Tanger Mall Dr
 Riverhead NY 11901

(G-3398)
VF OUTDOOR LLC
Also Called: North Face
461 Dune Rd (10917-6201)
PHONE..............................845 928-4900
Justin Dobson, *Manager*
Justin Dodson, *Manager*
EMP: 25
SALES (corp-wide): 11.8B Publicly Held
WEB: www.thenorthface.com
SIC: 2329 2339 Men's & boys' leather, wool & down-filled outerwear; women's & misses' outerwear
HQ: Vf Outdoor, Llc
 2701 Harbor Bay Pkwy
 Alameda CA 94502
 510 618-3500

(G-3399)
WOODBURY PRINTING PLUS + INC
96 Turner Rd (10917-4001)
PHONE..............................845 928-6610
Frank Collins, *President*
EMP: 7
SQ FT: 3,800
SALES (est): 832.4K Privately Held
WEB: www.wprintingplus.com
SIC: 2752 7334 2791 3993 Commercial printing, offset; photocopying & duplicating services; typesetting; signs & advertising specialties

Chadwicks
Oneida County

(G-3400)
NEW YORK STATE TOOL CO INC
3343 Oneida St (13319)
PHONE..............................315 737-8985
David Wilsey, *President*
Matthew Wilsey, *President*
EMP: 11
SQ FT: 6,000
SALES (est): 1.7MM Privately Held
WEB: www.nystool.com
SIC: 3599 Machine shop, jobbing & repair

(G-3401)
WILLIAMS TOOL INC
9372 Elm St (13319-3515)
P.O. Box 430 (13319-0430)
PHONE..............................315 737-7226
Ray Williams, *President*

Bob Prichard, *Prdtn Mgr*
Michele Dingle, *Manager*
Dan Petrie, *Manager*
EMP: 38 EST: 1957
SQ FT: 17,000
SALES: 3.3MM Privately Held
WEB: www.wmstool.com
SIC: 3599 Machine shop, jobbing & repair

Chaffee
Erie County

(G-3402)
DIAMOND SAW WORKS INC (PA)
12290 Olean Rd (14030-9767)
PHONE..............................716 496-7417
James Ziemer, *President*
James M Ziemer, *President*
Ed Duschen, *Engineer*
Roy Culleton, *Regl Sales Mgr*
Al Epperson, *Regl Sales Mgr*
▲ EMP: 50
SQ FT: 55,000
SALES (est): 4.8MM Privately Held
WEB: www.diamondsaw.com
SIC: 3425 Saw blades & handsaws

(G-3403)
DONALD STEFAN
Also Called: Stefan & Sons Welding
3428 W Yorkshire Rd (14030-9619)
PHONE..............................716 492-1110
Donald Stefan, *Owner*
EMP: 5
SALES (est): 140.3K Privately Held
SIC: 7692 3441 Welding repair; fabricated structural metal

(G-3404)
HART TO HART INDUSTRIES INC
Also Called: Arcade Glass Works
13520 Chaffee Curriers Rd (14030-9701)
PHONE..............................716 492-2709
Bill Harter, *President*
EMP: 5
SQ FT: 3,500
SALES: 516.1K Privately Held
SIC: 3444 3089 Awnings & canopies; window frames & sash, plastic

(G-3405)
UFP NEW YORK LLC
Also Called: Universal Forest Products
13989 E Schutt Rd (14030-9763)
PHONE..............................716 496-5484
Steve Slowik, *Branch Mgr*
EMP: 40
SQ FT: 18,720
SALES (corp-wide): 3.9B Publicly Held
WEB: www.ufpinc.com
SIC: 2439 Trusses, wooden roof
HQ: Ufp New York, Llc
 11 Allen St
 Auburn NY 13021
 315 253-2758

Champlain
Clinton County

(G-3406)
BOW INDUSTRIAL CORPORATION
178 W Service Rd (12919-4440)
PHONE..............................518 561-0190
Samuel Bern, *President*
▼ EMP: 96
SQ FT: 60,000
SALES (est): 1.4MM Privately Held
SIC: 3088 Plastics plumbing fixtures

(G-3407)
BURTON CORPORATION
Also Called: Burton Snowboards
21 Lawrence Paquette Dr (12919-4857)
PHONE..............................802 862-4500
EMP: 100

SALES (corp-wide): 149.4MM Privately Held
WEB: www.burton.com
SIC: 3949 Sporting & athletic goods
PA: The Burton Corporation
 80 Industrial Pkwy
 Burlington VT 05401
 802 862-4500

(G-3408)
ELEGANCE COATING LTD
33 W Service Rd 100 (12919-4438)
PHONE..............................386 668-8379
Mario Morin, *CEO*
EMP: 25 EST: 2007
SALES (est): 2.4MM Privately Held
SIC: 3479 Coating of metals & formed products

(G-3409)
GREAT WESTERN MALTING CO
16 Beeman Way (12919-4965)
PHONE..............................800 496-7732
Will Jackson, *President*
▲ EMP: 9
SALES (est): 412.1K Privately Held
SIC: 2083 Malt

(G-3410)
HUMANWARE USA INC (PA)
1 Ups Way (12919-4569)
P.O. Box 800 (12919-0800)
PHONE..............................800 722-3393
Phillip Rance, *President*
Greg Brown, *CFO*
EMP: 21
SQ FT: 3,800
SALES (est): 5.5MM Privately Held
SIC: 3851 Eyeglasses, lenses & frames

(G-3411)
KOREGON ENTERPRISES INC
Also Called: Nite Train R
102 W Service Rd (12919-4440)
PHONE..............................450 218-6836
H J Park, *President*
▲ EMP: 5
SQ FT: 3,300
SALES (est): 655.4K Privately Held
WEB: www.nitetrain-r.com
SIC: 3699 5047 Electrical equipment & supplies; incontinent care products & supplies

(G-3412)
MODERN MECHANICAL FAB INC
100 Walnut St Ste 7 (12919-5337)
PHONE..............................518 298-5177
Heather Trombly, *President*
John Trombly, *Corp Secy*
▲ EMP: 9
SALES (est): 1.5MM Privately Held
WEB: www.modmechfab.com
SIC: 7692 Welding repair

(G-3413)
STARCYL USA CORP
348 State Route 11 (12919-4816)
PHONE..............................877 782-7295
Terry Allardin, *President*
EMP: 15
SQ FT: 10,000
SALES (est): 3.6MM Privately Held
SIC: 3593 Fluid power cylinders, hydraulic or pneumatic

(G-3414)
TESTORI INTERIORS INC
107 Lwrnce Paqtte Indstrl (12919)
PHONE..............................518 298-4400
Lindo Lapegna, *CEO*
Peter George, *Principal*
Ajay Thakker, *CFO*
◆ EMP: 43 EST: 2000
SQ FT: 100,000
SALES (est): 8.9MM Privately Held
SIC: 2531 Public building & related furniture

(G-3415)
UNI SOURCE TECHNOLOGY
1320 Rt 9 (12919)
PHONE..............................514 748-8888
Lawrence Rutenberg, *Branch Mgr*
EMP: 10 Privately Held
SIC: 3812 Defense systems & equipment

Champlain - Clinton County (G-3416) — GEOGRAPHIC SECTION

PA: Unisource Technology Inc
9010 Av Ryan
Dorval QC H9P 2
514 748-8888

(G-3416)
UNIQUE PACKAGING CORPORATION
11320 State Route 9 # 3807 (12919-5062)
P.O. Box 219, Plattsburgh (12901-0219)
PHONE 514 341-5872
Fred Povitz, *President*
Earl Povitz, *Opers Staff*
EMP: 5
SALES (est): 496.8K **Privately Held**
SIC: 3053 3172 Packing materials; cases, jewelry

(G-3417)
UNIVERSAL INTERIORS LLC
107 Lawrence Paquette Dr (12919-4862)
PHONE 518 298-4400
Ajay Thakkar, *President*
EMP: 11
SALES (est): 349.6K **Privately Held**
SIC: 2519 2531 Fiberglass & plastic furniture; public building & related furniture

(G-3418)
WATER SPLASH INC
25 Locust St Ste 421 (12919-5001)
PHONE 800 936-3430
Gokhan Celik, *CEO*
Tara Menon, *Manager*
▲ **EMP:** 5
SALES (est): 364.4K **Privately Held**
SIC: 3999 Manufacturing industries

Chappaqua
Westchester County

(G-3419)
AIR ENGINEERING FILTERS INC
17 Memorial Dr (10514-3528)
P.O. Box 174 (10514-0174)
PHONE 914 238-5945
Pam Rubin, *President*
EMP: 9
SQ FT: 2,000
SALES (est): 1.3MM **Privately Held**
SIC: 3564 Filters, air: furnaces, air conditioning equipment, etc.

(G-3420)
CONSTRUCTION TECHNOLOGY INC (PA)
17 Green Ln (10514-2739)
PHONE 914 747-8900
Richard Levine, *President*
EMP: 22
SQ FT: 1,000
SALES (est): 1.9MM **Privately Held**
SIC: 7372 Prepackaged software

(G-3421)
DECORATIVE HARDWARE
180 Hunts Ln (10514-2602)
P.O. Box 627 (10514-0627)
PHONE 914 238-5251
Ronald Lawrence Prezener, *President*
Marie Anne Prezener, *Vice Pres*
▲ **EMP:** 10
SQ FT: 2,000
SALES (est): 1.3MM **Privately Held**
WEB: www.decorative-hardware.com
SIC: 3429 Furniture builders' & other household hardware; furniture hardware

(G-3422)
INSIGHT UNLIMITED INC
660 Quaker Rd (10514-1505)
PHONE 914 861-2090
Shmuel Kliger, *President*
EMP: 6
SALES (est): 282K **Privately Held**
SIC: 7372 Prepackaged software

(G-3423)
NANORX INC
6 Devoe Pl (10514-3601)
PHONE 914 671-0224
Palayakopai Raghavan, *President*
EMP: 2

SALES: 1MM **Privately Held**
SIC: 2834 Medicines, capsuled or ampuled

(G-3424)
WIDGETWORKS UNLIMITED LLC
395 Millwood Rd (10514-1100)
PHONE 914 666-6395
Russell Todd,
EMP: 5
SALES: 100K **Privately Held**
SIC: 3651 Speaker systems

Charlotteville
Schoharie County

(G-3425)
FLY-TYERS CARRY-ALL LLC
Also Called: Folstaf Company, The
112 Meade Rd (12036-1612)
PHONE 607 821-1460
Lee Stoliar,
EMP: 5
SQ FT: 850
SALES (est): 611.9K **Privately Held**
WEB: www.folstaf.com
SIC: 3949 5091 Fishing equipment; fishing tackle, general; fishing equipment & supplies; fishing tackle

Chateaugay
Franklin County

(G-3426)
AGRI-MARK INC
39 Mccadam Ln (12920-4306)
P.O. Box 900 (12920-0900)
PHONE 518 497-6644
Matt Helm, *Safety Mgr*
Ron Davis, *Manager*
Tom Sorrell, *Director*
Tony Green, *Maintence Staff*
EMP: 100
SALES (corp-wide): 319MM **Privately Held**
WEB: www.agrimark.net
SIC: 2022 Natural cheese
PA: Agri-Mark, Inc.
40 Shattuck Rd Ste 301
Andover MA 01810
978 552-5500

Chatham
Columbia County

(G-3427)
CRAFTECH
5 Dock St (12037)
PHONE 518 828-5011
Linda Geblanski, *CEO*
Erwin Gerard, *Owner*
EMP: 55
SALES (est): 2.6MM **Privately Held**
SIC: 2821 3089 Molding compounds, plastics; molding primary plastic

(G-3428)
KLING MAGNETICS INC
343 State Route 295 (12037-3713)
P.O. Box 348 (12037-0348)
PHONE 518 392-4000
Jody Rael, *President*
▲ **EMP:** 20
SQ FT: 20,000
SALES (est): 2.2MM **Privately Held**
SIC: 3993 3089 2752 3944 Advertising novelties; novelties, plastic; commercial printing, lithographic; games, toys & children's vehicles

(G-3429)
RAPID INTELLECT GROUP INC
77b Church St (12037-1319)
P.O. Box 131, Stuyvesant Falls (12174-0131)
PHONE 518 929-3210
Steve Grzeskow, *President*
Peter Grzeskow, *Vice Pres*
EMP: 12 **EST:** 1997

SALES (est): 766.1K **Privately Held**
SIC: 2731 Books: publishing only

(G-3430)
SONOCO PRODUCTS COMPANY
87 Center St (12037-1032)
PHONE 518 392-2000
Scott Lundy, *Manager*
EMP: 100
SALES (corp-wide): 5B **Publicly Held**
SIC: 2631 Paperboard mills
PA: Sonoco Products Company
1 N 2nd St
Hartsville SC 29550
843 383-7000

(G-3431)
SONOCO-CRELLIN INTL INC (HQ)
87 Center St (12037-1032)
PHONE 518 392-2000
Bob Puechl, *Vice Pres*
David Marche, *Vice Pres*
Michael Tucker, *Vice Pres*
▲ **EMP:** 500
SQ FT: 70,000
SALES (est): 175.1MM
SALES (corp-wide): 5B **Publicly Held**
SIC: 3089 Molding primary plastic
PA: Sonoco Products Company
1 N 2nd St
Hartsville SC 29550
843 383-7000

Chazy
Clinton County

(G-3432)
JP SIGNS
9592 State Route 9 (12921-3102)
PHONE 518 569-3907
Jessica Macnerland, *Owner*
EMP: 5
SALES: 150K **Privately Held**
SIC: 3993 7389 5699 Signs & advertising specialties; printers' services: folding, collating; T-shirts, custom printed

(G-3433)
PLASTITEL USA INC
641 Ridge Rd (12921-2420)
PHONE 450 687-0600
Denis Deshaies, *CEO*
Mathieu Perreault, *Managing Dir*
EMP: 9 **EST:** 2014
SALES (est): 1.2MM **Privately Held**
SIC: 3089 Thermoformed finished plastic products

Cheektowaga
Erie County

(G-3434)
ACCOLADE USA INC
Also Called: Level Wear
60 Industrial Pkwy # 397 (14227-2774)
PHONE 866 423-5071
Hilton Ngo, *President*
EMP: 200
SQ FT: 100,000
SALES: 1MM **Privately Held**
SIC: 2211 Apparel & outerwear fabrics, cotton

(G-3435)
AVF GROUP INC (DH)
2775 Broadway St Ste 200 (14227-1043)
PHONE 951 360-7111
Jerry Jacobs, *President*
▲ **EMP:** 14
SALES (est): 3MM
SALES (corp-wide): 20.6MM **Privately Held**
WEB: www.avf.com
SIC: 2542 Partitions & fixtures, except wood

(G-3436)
BUFFALO COMPRESSED AIR INC
2727 Broadway St Ste 3a (14227-1070)
P.O. Box 1215, Lockport (14095-1215)
PHONE 716 783-8673
Greg Fuer, *Principal*
EMP: 7
SALES (est): 1.1MM **Privately Held**
SIC: 3563 Air & gas compressors

(G-3437)
COMAIRCO EQUIPMENT INC (DH)
3250 Union Rd (14227-1044)
PHONE 716 656-0211
Roland Nadeau, *President*
Edward Murphy, *Vice Pres*
EMP: 7
SQ FT: 6,000
SALES (est): 6.5MM **Privately Held**
WEB: www.comairco.com
SIC: 3563 Air & gas compressors
HQ: Equipement Comairco Ltee
5535 Rue Ernest-Cormier
Montreal QC H7C 2
450 665-8780

(G-3438)
CRS NUCLEAR SERVICES LLC
840 Aero Dr Ste 150 (14225-1451)
PHONE 716 810-0688
Kevin Connor, *Mng Member*
▲ **EMP:** 12
SALES (est): 5.4MM **Privately Held**
SIC: 2834 Pharmaceutical preparations

(G-3439)
CULINARY ARTS SPECIALTIES INC
Also Called: Cas
2268 Union Rd (14227-2726)
PHONE 716 656-8943
Arthur L Keller, *President*
Andrew P Keller, *Vice Pres*
Jonathan Polly, *Purch Mgr*
Thomas Dagonese, *Controller*
Gus Walters, *Manager*
EMP: 85
SQ FT: 50,000
SALES (est): 20.5MM **Privately Held**
SIC: 2053 Cakes, bakery: frozen

(G-3440)
DERRICK CORPORATION
2540 Walden Ave (14225-4744)
PHONE 716 685-4892
EMP: 297
SALES (corp-wide): 185.2MM **Privately Held**
SIC: 3533 Derricks, oil or gas field
PA: Derrick Corporation
590 Duke Rd
Buffalo NY 14225
716 683-9010

(G-3441)
DORM COMPANY CORPORATION
Also Called: Dorm Co.
575 Kennedy Rd Ste 2 (14227-1040)
P.O. Box 485, Clarence Center (14032-0485)
PHONE 502 551-6195
Jeff Gawronski, *President*
▲ **EMP:** 5
SQ FT: 6,000
SALES (est): 1MM **Privately Held**
SIC: 2431 Dormers, wood

(G-3442)
DUAL PRINT & MAIL LLC
340 Nagel Dr (14225-4731)
PHONE 716 684-3825
Thomas Salisbury, *Ch of Bd*
Tom Salisbury, *CFO*
Deron Bauer, *Accounts Exec*
EMP: 73
SALES (corp-wide): 29MM **Privately Held**
SIC: 2752 Commercial printing, lithographic

GEOGRAPHIC SECTION

Chester - Orange County (G-3467)

HQ: Dual Print & Mail, Llc
3235 Grand Island Blvd
Grand Island NY 14072
716 775-8001

(G-3443)
ECOLAB INC
3719 Union Rd Ste 121 (14225-4250)
PHONE 716 683-6298
Dave Beckwith, *Branch Mgr*
EMP: 17
SALES (corp-wide): 13.8B **Publicly Held**
WEB: www.ecolab.com
SIC: 2841 Soap & other detergents
PA: Ecolab Inc.
1 Ecolab Pl
Saint Paul MN 55102
800 232-6522

(G-3444)
FLUID HANDLING LLC
Standard Xchange
175 Standard Pkwy (14227-1233)
PHONE 716 897-2800
Joseph McMara, *Branch Mgr*
EMP: 240 **Publicly Held**
WEB: www.ittind.com
SIC: 3443 Industrial vessels, tanks & containers
HQ: Fluid Handling, Llc
175 Standard Pkwy
Cheektowaga NY 14227
716 897-2800

(G-3445)
FLUID HANDLING LLC (HQ)
Also Called: Xylem
175 Standard Pkwy (14227-1233)
PHONE 716 897-2800
Ken Napolitano, *President*
Shobha Nair, *General Mgr*
Jim Peterson, *General Mgr*
David W Webber, *Managing Dir*
Domkowski Bob, *Business Mgr*
▲ EMP: 1
SALES (est): 266.3MM **Publicly Held**
SIC: 3561 Pumps & pumping equipment

(G-3446)
GEMINI MANUFACTURES
160 Holtz Dr (14225)
PHONE 716 633-0306
Todd Lehmann, *Partner*
Irene Turski, *Partner*
EMP: 14
SQ FT: 4,200
SALES: 860K **Privately Held**
SIC: 3915 Jewelers' materials & lapidary work

(G-3447)
GF PACKAGING LLC (PA)
2727 Broadway St Ste 3 (14227-1070)
PHONE 716 692-2705
Val Sracine, *Mng Member*
▲ EMP: 30 EST: 1946
SQ FT: 50,000
SALES (est): 3MM **Privately Held**
SIC: 2542 Counters or counter display cases: except wood

(G-3448)
HAMMOND MANUFACTURING CO INC
475 Cayuga Rd (14225-1309)
PHONE 716 630-7030
Robert F Hammond, *CEO*
Marc A Dube, *Principal*
Kevin Bond, *COO*
Doug Hutt, *Engineer*
Judy Kowal, *Finance*
▲ EMP: 14
SQ FT: 17,000
SALES (est): 3.5MM
SALES (corp-wide): 85.5MM **Privately Held**
WEB: www.hammfg.com
SIC: 3677 5063 Transformers power supply, electronic type; electrical apparatus & equipment; transformers, electric
PA: Hammond Manufacturing Company Limited
394 Edinburgh Rd N
Guelph ON N1H 1
519 822-2960

(G-3449)
HONEYWELL INTERNATIONAL INC
307 Cayuga Rd Ste 160 (14225-1985)
PHONE 716 631-2197
Susan Jackson, *Manager*
EMP: 5
SALES (corp-wide): 40.5B **Publicly Held**
WEB: www.honeywell.com
SIC: 3724 Aircraft engines & engine parts
PA: Honeywell International Inc.
115 Tabor Rd
Morris Plains NJ 07950
973 455-2000

(G-3450)
HUGH F MCPHERSON INC
Also Called: Franklin's Printing
70 Innsbruck Dr (14227-2735)
PHONE 716 668-6107
Hugh F McPherson, *President*
Barbara L McPherson, *Vice Pres*
EMP: 7
SALES (est): 825K **Privately Held**
SIC: 2752 2791 7331 Commercial printing, offset; typesetting; mailing service

(G-3451)
LEO SCHULTZ
Also Called: Cuore Technology
1144 Maryvale Dr (14225-2312)
PHONE 716 969-0945
Kevin Ryan, *Branch Mgr*
EMP: 5
SALES (corp-wide): 1.5MM **Privately Held**
SIC: 3822 Auto controls regulating residntl & coml environmt & applncs
PA: Leo Rue Schultz
821 Panelli Pl
Santa Clara CA 95050
716 969-0945

(G-3452)
MP CAROLL INC
4822 Genesee St (14225-2494)
PHONE 716 683-8520
Michael Carrol, *President*
◆ EMP: 12
SALES (est): 2.2MM **Privately Held**
SIC: 2426 Flooring, hardwood

(G-3453)
MULTI-HEALTH SYSTEMS INC
Indus Pkwy Ste 70660 60 (14227)
PHONE 800 456-3003
James Henebry, *Sales Staff*
Steven J Stein, *Branch Mgr*
Heba Ahmed, *Research Analys*
EMP: 90 **Privately Held**
WEB: www.mhs.com
SIC: 3695 2741 Computer software tape & disks: blank, rigid & floppy; miscellaneous publishing
PA: Multi-Health Systems Inc
3770 Victoria Park Ave
North York ON M2H 3
416 492-2627

(G-3454)
NEVILLE MFG SVC & DIST INC (PA)
2320 Clinton St (14227-1735)
PHONE 716 834-3038
Patrick Crowe, *President*
Kevin Ohora, *Sls & Mktg Exec*
Russ Villa, *Director*
EMP: 24 EST: 1951
SQ FT: 4,000
SALES (est): 4MM **Privately Held**
SIC: 2448 Pallets, wood; skids, wood

(G-3455)
NOVATECH INC
190 Gruner Rd (14227-1022)
PHONE 716 892-6682
John Popovich Sr, *President*
John Popovich Jr, *Vice Pres*
EMP: 20
SQ FT: 8,000
SALES (est): 3.4MM **Privately Held**
WEB: www.novatechmachining.com
SIC: 3545 Precision tools, machinists'

(G-3456)
PROSTHETICS BY NELSON INC (PA)
Also Called: Nelson Prsthtics Orthotics Lab
2959 Genesee St (14225-2653)
PHONE 716 894-6666
Christopher Vandusen, *President*
EMP: 16
SQ FT: 8,500
SALES (est): 2.2MM **Privately Held**
SIC: 3842 5999 Limbs, artificial; orthopedic appliances; orthopedic & prosthesis applications

(G-3457)
REDLAND FOODS CORP
40 Sonwil Dr (14225-2425)
PHONE 716 288-9061
Eva Mounsteven, *Director*
▲ EMP: 12
SALES (est): 982K **Privately Held**
SIC: 2099 Emulsifiers, food

(G-3458)
SMG METAL PRODUCTS LLC
390 Cayuga Rd (14225-1940)
PHONE 716 633-6439
Dave Schmelz, *Purchasing*
Jay Bozer, *Manager*
EMP: 8
SALES (est): 1.6MM **Privately Held**
SIC: 3444 Sheet metalwork

(G-3459)
STEREO ADVANTAGE INC
Also Called: Advantage Wood Shop
45 Boxwood Ln (14227-2707)
PHONE 716 656-7161
Anthony Ragusa Jr, *Partner*
EMP: 10
SALES (corp-wide): 42.3MM **Privately Held**
SIC: 2541 Store & office display cases & fixtures
PA: Stereo Advantage, Inc.
1955 Wehrle Dr Ste B
Williamsville NY 14221
716 204-2346

(G-3460)
SUPERIOR GLOVE WORKS USA LTD
2345 Walden Ave Ste 600 (14225-4752)
PHONE 716 626-9500
Lynne Jordan, *Principal*
EMP: 30
SALES (est): 2.8MM **Privately Held**
SIC: 3842 Gloves, safety

(G-3461)
TECTRAN INC
2345 Walden Ave Ste 100 (14225-4770)
PHONE 800 776-5549
Bruce McKie, *President*
EMP: 9
SALES (est): 1.1MM **Privately Held**
SIC: 3699 3799 Cleaning equipment, ultrasonic, except medical & dental; carriages, horse drawn

(G-3462)
USA SEALING INC
356 Sonwil Dr (14225-5520)
PHONE 716 288-9952
David Cassert, *President*
Matthew Healy, *Director*
EMP: 50
SALES (est): 2MM **Privately Held**
SIC: 3053 2891 Gaskets & sealing devices; sealing compounds, synthetic rubber or plastic

Chemung
Chemung County

(G-3463)
DALRYMPLE GRAV & CONTG CO INC
Chemung Flats Rd (14825)
P.O. Box 278 (14825-0278)
PHONE 607 529-3235
Hank Dalrymple, *President*
EMP: 30
SALES (corp-wide): 105.9MM **Privately Held**
SIC: 1442 5032 Gravel mining; stone, crushed or broken
HQ: Dalrymple Gravel And Contracting Company, Inc.
2105 S Broadway
Pine City NY 14871
607 739-0391

(G-3464)
VULCRAFT OF NEW YORK INC (HQ)
621 M St (14825)
P.O. Box 280 (14825-0280)
PHONE 607 529-9000
Peggy Peters, *Regional Mgr*
Alex Herbitter, *Regional Mgr*
Ray Napolitan, *Exec VP*
Paige Freeman, *Project Mgr*
John Giovenco, *Traffic Mgr*
EMP: 119
SQ FT: 300,000
SALES: 60.9MM
SALES (corp-wide): 20.2B **Publicly Held**
WEB: www.nucor.com
SIC: 3441 Expansion joints (structural shapes), iron or steel
PA: Nucor Corporation
1915 Rexford Rd Ste 400
Charlotte NC 28211
704 366-7000

Chenango Bridge
Broome County

(G-3465)
ATWOOD TOOL & MACHINE INC
39 Kattelville Rd (13745)
PHONE 607 648-6543
H Blair Atwood, *President*
Brent Atwood, *Vice Pres*
David Atwood, *Treasurer*
Laurie Atwood, *Treasurer*
Cindy Hood, *Admin Sec*
EMP: 22 EST: 1963
SQ FT: 23,000
SALES (est): 3.7MM **Privately Held**
WEB: www.atwoodknives.com
SIC: 3599 Machine shop, jobbing & repair

Cherry Valley
Otsego County

(G-3466)
THISTLE HILL WEAVERS
143 Baxter Rd (13320-2431)
PHONE 518 284-2729
Rabbit Goody, *Owner*
Jill Maney, *Manager*
EMP: 5
SALES (est): 465.2K **Privately Held**
WEB: www.thistlehillweavers.com
SIC: 2299 Hand woven fabrics

Chester
Orange County

(G-3467)
ADVERTISER PUBLICATIONS INC
Also Called: Marketplace, The
148 State Route 17m (10918)
PHONE 845 783-1111
Howard Kaplan, *President*
Seth Kaplan, *Vice Pres*
Steve Herman, *Manager*
EMP: 13
SQ FT: 2,200
SALES: 1.9MM **Privately Held**
SIC: 2711 7331 7313 Newspapers; direct mail advertising services; newspaper advertising representative

Chester - Orange County

(G-3468)
AMSCAN INC
Also Called: Amscan Everyday Warehouse
47 Elizabeth Dr (10918-1367)
PHONE..........................845 469-9116
EMP: 11
SALES (corp-wide): 2.3B **Publicly Held**
SIC: 2656 Plates, paper: made from purchased material
HQ: Amscan Inc.
80 Grasslands Rd Ste 3
Elmsford NY 10523
914 345-2020

(G-3469)
BRAKEWELL STL FABRICATORS INC
55 Leone Ln (10918-1363)
PHONE..........................845 469-9131
Dan Doyle, *President*
Dave Bendlin, *Project Mgr*
Robert McGrath, *Project Mgr*
William Valentin, *Project Mgr*
Frank Versace, *Project Mgr*
EMP: 45
SQ FT: 26,000
SALES: 7MM **Privately Held**
WEB: www.brakewell.com
SIC: 3411 3499 Metal cans; metal ladders

(G-3470)
BYK USA INC
48 Leone Ln (10918-1362)
PHONE..........................845 469-5800
Stephan Glander, *Branch Mgr*
EMP: 29 **Privately Held**
SIC: 2819 Industrial inorganic chemicals
HQ: Byk Usa Inc.
524 S Cherry St
Wallingford CT 06492
203 265-2086

(G-3471)
COMMUNITY PRODUCTS LLC
Also Called: Community Playthings
359 Gibson Hill Rd (10918-2321)
PHONE..........................845 658-7720
Gary Frase, *Purchasing*
William Wiser, *Purchasing*
John Rhodes, *Branch Mgr*
EMP: 24
SALES (corp-wide): 93.4MM **Privately Held**
SIC: 3842 Surgical appliances & supplies
PA: Community Products, Llc
101 Woodcrest Dr
Rifton NY 12471
845 658-8799

(G-3472)
COMMUNITY PRODUCTS LLC
24 Elizabeth Dr (10918-1366)
PHONE..........................845 572-3433
Ben Maendel, *Branch Mgr*
EMP: 20
SALES (corp-wide): 93.4MM **Privately Held**
SIC: 3842 Orthopedic appliances
PA: Community Products, Llc
101 Woodcrest Dr
Rifton NY 12471
845 658-8799

(G-3473)
DURASOL SYSTEMS INC (HQ)
445 Bellvale Rd (10918-3115)
PHONE..........................845 610-1100
Vince Best, *President*
Paolo Galliani, *President*
Frank Dorr, *Vice Pres*
Trace Feinstein, *Vice Pres*
Tim Robinson, *Vice Pres*
◆ EMP: 51
SQ FT: 65,000
SALES (est): 19.8MM
SALES (corp-wide): 33.2MM **Privately Held**
WEB: www.durasol.com
SIC: 2394 Awnings, fabric: made from purchased materials
PA: Bat Spa
Via H. Ford 2
Noventa Di Piave VE 30020
042 165-672

(G-3474)
F A ALPINE WINDOWS MFG
1683 State Route 17m (10918-1020)
PHONE..........................845 469-5700
Larry Maddaloni, *President*
▲ EMP: 10
SALES (est): 1.6MM **Privately Held**
WEB: www.faalpinewindowmfg.com
SIC: 3442 Metal doors

(G-3475)
G SCHIRMER INC
Also Called: Music Sales
2 Old Rt 17 (10918)
P.O. Box 572 (10918-0572)
PHONE..........................845 469-4699
Ella Winfield, *Manager*
EMP: 50
SALES (corp-wide): 13.6MM **Privately Held**
WEB: www.schirmer.com
SIC: 2741 Music books: publishing only, not printed on site
HQ: G Schirmer Inc
180 Madison Ave Ste 2400
New York NY 10016
212 254-2100

(G-3476)
GREEN ENERGY CONCEPTS INC
37 Elkay Dr Ste 51 (10918-3025)
P.O. Box 1023, Harriman (10926-1023)
PHONE..........................845 238-2574
Richard Mueller, *President*
▲ EMP: 6
SALES: 950K **Privately Held**
SIC: 3646 Commercial indusl & institutional electric lighting fixtures

(G-3477)
KE DURASOL AWNINGS INC
445 Bellvale Rd (10918-3115)
PHONE..........................845 610-1100
Paolo Galliani, *President*
Vince Best, *Principal*
EMP: 11
SALES (est): 1MM **Privately Held**
SIC: 2394 Canvas & related products

(G-3478)
NEXANS ENERGY USA INC
Also Called: Industrial Cables
25 Oakland Ave (10918-1011)
PHONE..........................845 469-2141
Gordon Thursfield, *President*
Steve Hall, *Principal*
Sande Aivaliotis, *Vice Pres*
Julie Land, *CFO*
Marianne Calicchio, *Human Resources*
▲ EMP: 160
SQ FT: 350,000
SALES (est): 56.3MM
SALES (corp-wide): 32.3MM **Privately Held**
SIC: 3496 Cable, uninsulated wire: made from purchased wire
HQ: Nexans Canada Inc
140 Allstate Pky Suite 300
Markham ON L3R 0
905 944-4300

(G-3479)
PDJ COMPONENTS INC
35 Brookside Ave (10918-1409)
PHONE..........................845 469-9191
George W Ketchum, *CEO*
Pamela Ketchum, *Vice Pres*
Christin Keating, *Accountant*
Dave Crandall, *Manager*
EMP: 40
SQ FT: 30,000
SALES (est): 7.2MM **Privately Held**
WEB: www.pdjtruss.com
SIC: 2439 2499 Trusses, wooden roof; trusses, except roof: laminated lumber; decorative wood & woodwork

(G-3480)
REPRO MED SYSTEMS INC
Also Called: RMS Medical Products
24 Carpenter Rd Ste 1 (10918-1065)
PHONE..........................845 469-2042
Daniel S Goldberger, *Ch of Bd*
Donald B Pettigrew, *President*
Karen Fisher, *CFO*
Fred MA, *Chief Mktg Ofcr*
EMP: 73
SALES: 13.3MM **Privately Held**
SIC: 3841 Suction therapy apparatus

(G-3481)
RIC-LO PRODUCTIONS LTD
Also Called: Lycian Stage Lighting
1144 Kings Hwy (10918-3100)
P.O. Box 214, Sugar Loaf (10981-0214)
PHONE..........................845 469-2285
Richard F Logothetis, *Chairman*
▲ EMP: 43
SQ FT: 17,400
SALES (est): 8.3MM **Privately Held**
SIC: 3648 3641 Stage lighting equipment; electric lamps

(G-3482)
S A BAXTER LLC (PA)
37 Elkay Dr Ste 33 (10918-3025)
PHONE..........................845 469-7995
Colin Gentle, *Manager*
Scott Baxter,
▲ EMP: 3
SALES: 2MM **Privately Held**
SIC: 3446 5072 Architectural metalwork; builders' hardware

(G-3483)
SATIN FINE FOODS INC
32 Leone Ln (10918-1362)
PHONE..........................845 469-1034
Kevin O' Reilly, *Ch of Bd*
◆ EMP: 75
SQ FT: 96,000
SALES (est): 5.5MM **Privately Held**
SIC: 2064 Candy & other confectionery products

(G-3484)
STERIS CORPORATION
23 Elizabeth Dr (10918-1367)
PHONE..........................845 469-4087
EMP: 7
SALES (corp-wide): 2.6B **Privately Held**
SIC: 3842 Surgical appliances & supplies
HQ: Steris Corporation
5960 Heisley Rd
Mentor OH 44060
440 354-2600

(G-3485)
STRAUS COMMUNICATIONS
Also Called: Straus Newspaper
20 West Ave Ste 201 (10918-1053)
PHONE..........................845 782-4000
Stan Martin, *Manager*
EMP: 15
SALES (est): 806.9K
SALES (corp-wide): 2.5MM **Privately Held**
WEB: www.strausnews.com
SIC: 2711 Newspapers, publishing & printing
PA: Straus Communications
57 W 57th St Ste 1204
New York NY
212 751-0400

(G-3486)
STRAUS NEWSPAPERS INC
20 West Ave (10918-1032)
PHONE..........................845 782-4000
Jeanne Straus, *President*
Juan Ayala, *Principal*
Vincent Gardino, *Vice Pres*
Rick Sophia, *Director*
EMP: 24 EST: 1991
SALES (est): 1.7MM **Privately Held**
SIC: 2711 Newspapers

(G-3487)
TELE-VUE OPTICS INC
32 Elkay Dr (10918-3001)
PHONE..........................845 469-4551
Albert Nagler, *CEO*
David Nagler, *President*
Sandy Nagler, *Vice Pres*
▲ EMP: 20
SQ FT: 14,000
SALES (est): 4.3MM **Privately Held**
WEB: www.televue.com
SIC: 3827 Optical instruments & apparatus

(G-3488)
THEODORE A RAPP ASSOCIATES
728 Craigville Rd (10918-4014)
PHONE..........................845 469-2100
Theodore A Rapp, *President*
EMP: 7
SALES (est): 718.8K **Privately Held**
SIC: 3651 Microphones

(G-3489)
TRISTATE CONTRACT SALES LLC
164 Dug Rd (10918-2652)
PHONE..........................845 782-2614
Ross Elliot, *Principal*
EMP: 5
SALES (est): 442.6K **Privately Held**
SIC: 2434 Vanities, bathroom: wood

Chestertown
Warren County

(G-3490)
CETTEL STUDIO OF NEW YORK INC
636 Atateka Dr (12817-2010)
PHONE..........................518 494-3622
Peter Heonis, *President*
EMP: 6
SALES: 350K **Privately Held**
SIC: 3843 Orthodontic appliances

(G-3491)
PECKHAM MATERIALS CORP
5983 State Route 9 (12817-2513)
PHONE..........................518 494-2313
John McClure, *Opers-Prdtn-Mfg*
EMP: 10
SQ FT: 208
SALES (corp-wide): 200.6MM **Privately Held**
SIC: 2951 5032 Asphalt paving mixtures & blocks; brick, stone & related material
HQ: Peckham Materials Corp
20 Haarlem Ave Ste 200
White Plains NY 10603
914 686-2045

Chestnut Ridge
Rockland County

(G-3492)
GENERICS BIDCO I LLC
Also Called: Par Pharmaceutical
1 Ram Ridge Rd (10977-6714)
P.O. Box 456, Devault PA (19432-0456)
PHONE..........................256 859-4011
Marvin Samson, *CEO*
Phil Cupero,
Robert Mills,
William S Propst Sr,
▲ EMP: 4
SQ FT: 5,800
SALES (est): 31.9MM **Privately Held**
WEB: www.qualitestrx.com
SIC: 2834 5122 5961 Pharmaceutical preparations; pharmaceuticals; pharmaceuticals, mail order
HQ: Generics International (Us), Inc.
1400 Atwater Dr
Malvern PA 19355

(G-3493)
MEHRON INC
Also Called: Lechler Labs
100 Red Schoolhouse Rd C2 (10977-7056)
PHONE..........................845 426-1700
Martin Melik, *President*
Jimmy Varghese, *Research*
Gene Flaharty, *Sales Mgr*
▲ EMP: 35 EST: 1932
SQ FT: 15,000
SALES (est): 12MM **Privately Held**
WEB: www.mehron.com
SIC: 2844 Cosmetic preparations

GEOGRAPHIC SECTION

Cicero - Onondaga County (G-3517)

(G-3494)
PAR PHARMACEUTICAL INC (DH)
1 Ram Ridge Rd (10977-6714)
PHONE 845 573-5500
Paul V Campanelli, *CEO*
Thomas J Haughey, *President*
Kenneth I Sawyer, *Principal*
Terry Coughlin, *COO*
Michael A Tropiano, *Exec VP*
▲ **EMP:** 277 **EST:** 1978
SQ FT: 92,000
SALES (est): 185.7MM **Privately Held**
SIC: 2834 Druggists' preparations (pharmaceuticals)
HQ: Par Pharmaceutical Companies, Inc.
1 Ram Ridge Rd
Chestnut Ridge NY 10977
845 573-5500

(G-3495)
PAR PHRMCEUTICAL COMPANIES INC (DH)
1 Ram Ridge Rd (10977-6714)
PHONE 845 573-5500
Paul V Campanelli, *CEO*
Tony Pera, *President*
Terrance J Coughlin, *COO*
Sarah Dobson, *Research*
Michael Tropiano, *CFO*
EMP: 50 **EST:** 2012
SALES (est): 339.7MM **Privately Held**
SIC: 2834 Pharmaceutical preparations
HQ: Endo Health Solutions Inc.
1400 Atwater Dr
Malvern PA 19355
484 216-0000

(G-3496)
PAR STERILE PRODUCTS LLC (DH)
6 Ram Ridge Rd (10977-6713)
PHONE 845 573-5500
Paul V Campanelli, *CEO*
Eric Bruce, *Opers Staff*
Michael Tropiano, *CFO*
Melissa Williams, *Controller*
Thomas J Haughey,
EMP: 32
SALES (est): 71.2MM **Privately Held**
WEB: www.jhppharma.com
SIC: 2834 Pharmaceutical preparations
HQ: Par Pharmaceutical, Inc.
1 Ram Ridge Rd
Chestnut Ridge NY 10977
845 573-5500

(G-3497)
TELEDYNE LECROY INC (HQ)
700 Chestnut Ridge Rd (10977-6435)
PHONE 845 425-2000
Thomas H Reslewic, *President*
Tyler Cox, *Vice Pres*
David G Graef, *Vice Pres*
Douglas Lee, *Vice Pres*
James Mueller, *Vice Pres*
▲ **EMP:** 204
SQ FT: 95,000
SALES: 204.6MM
SALES (corp-wide): 2.6B **Publicly Held**
WEB: www.lecroy.com
SIC: 3825 3829 Oscillographs & oscilloscopes; measuring & controlling devices
PA: Teledyne Technologies Inc
1049 Camino Dos Rios
Thousand Oaks CA 91360
805 373-4545

(G-3498)
U S PLYCHMICAL OVERSEAS CORP
584 Chestnut Ridge Rd # 586 (10977-5646)
PHONE 845 356-5530
David Cherry, *President*
Bruce W Gebhardt, *General Mgr*
Richard E Knipe Jr, *VP Sales*
EMP: 20
SQ FT: 20,000
SALES (est): 3.2MM **Privately Held**
WEB: www.uspoly.com
SIC: 2842 Cleaning or polishing preparations; sanitation preparations

Childwold
St. Lawrence County

(G-3499)
LEATHER ARTISAN
Also Called: Artisan Bags
9740 State Highway 3 (12922-2028)
PHONE 518 359-3102
Thomas Amoroso, *Partner*
EMP: 5
SQ FT: 7,000
SALES (est): 610.7K **Privately Held**
WEB: www.leatherartisan.com
SIC: 3172 5699 5199 Personal leather goods; leather garments; leather, leather goods & furs

Chittenango
Madison County

(G-3500)
A L SEALING
2280 Osborne Rd (13037-8791)
PHONE 315 699-6900
John C Thomas, *Ch of Bd*
EMP: 5
SALES (est): 312.3K **Privately Held**
SIC: 3053 Gaskets & sealing devices

(G-3501)
ARISE AT MARSHALL FARMS INC
1972 New Boston Rd (13037-9600)
PHONE 315 687-6727
Jennifer Schulz, *Branch Mgr*
Ron Champion, *Info Tech Mgr*
EMP: 5
SALES (est): 378K
SALES (corp-wide): 298.6K **Privately Held**
SIC: 3699 Grids, electric
PA: Arise At Marshall Farms, Inc.
635 James St Ste 1
Syracuse NY 13203
315 472-3171

(G-3502)
CONSOLDTED PRECISION PDTS CORP
901 E Genesee St (13037-1325)
PHONE 315 687-0014
Renae Wallace, *Mfg Mgr*
Paula Busa, *Materials Mgr*
James Scholefield, *QC Mgr*
Mark Gaspari, *Manager*
EMP: 350
SALES (corp-wide): 6.3B **Privately Held**
SIC: 3365 3324 Aluminum foundries; steel investment foundries
HQ: Consolidated Precision Products Corp.
1621 Euclid Ave Ste 1850
Cleveland OH 44115
216 453-4800

(G-3503)
CPP - GUAYMAS
901 E Genesee St (13037-1325)
PHONE 315 687-0014
Ramses Valdes, *Manager*
EMP: 200
SQ FT: 1,000
SALES (est): 25.1MM
SALES (corp-wide): 6.3B **Privately Held**
WEB: www.escocorp.com
SIC: 3321 Foundry, smelting, refining & similar machinery
HQ: Cpp-Syracuse, Inc.
901 E Genesee St
Chittenango NY 13037
315 687-0014

(G-3504)
CPP-SYRACUSE INC (DH)
901 E Genesee St (13037-1325)
PHONE 315 687-0014
James Stewart, *CEO*
David A Bishop, *Manager*
Michelle Bingham, *Technology*
▲ **EMP:** 30 **EST:** 1947
SQ FT: 95,000
SALES (est): 78.4MM
SALES (corp-wide): 6.3B **Privately Held**
SIC: 3324 3369 3356 Aerospace investment castings, ferrous; nonferrous foundries; nonferrous rolling & drawing
HQ: Consolidated Precision Products Corp.
1621 Euclid Ave Ste 1850
Cleveland OH 44115
216 453-4800

Churchville
Monroe County

(G-3505)
AMA PRECISION SCREENING INC
456 Sanford Rd N (14428-9503)
PHONE 585 293-0820
George Pietropaolo, *President*
EMP: 18
SALES (est): 2.3MM **Privately Held**
WEB: www.amatech.com
SIC: 2759 Screen printing

(G-3506)
AMERICAN PACKAGING CORPORATION
100 Apc Dr (14428)
PHONE 585 537-4650
Brendan O'Hara, *Manager*
EMP: 113
SALES (corp-wide): 231.8MM **Privately Held**
SIC: 2671 Paper coated or laminated for packaging
PA: American Packaging Corporation
100 Apc Way
Columbus WI 53925
920 623-2291

(G-3507)
BURNT MILL SMITHING
127 Burnt Mill Rd (14428-9405)
PHONE 585 293-2380
Dennis Schrieber, *Owner*
Dennis Schriber, *Owner*
EMP: 5
SALES (est): 295K **Privately Held**
WEB: www.burnt-mill.com
SIC: 3949 5941 Sporting & athletic goods; sporting goods & bicycle shops

(G-3508)
CUSTOM MOLDING SOLUTIONS INC
456 Sanford Rd N (14428-9503)
PHONE 585 293-1702
Dwight Campbell, *President*
EMP: 22
SALES (est): 4.7MM **Privately Held**
SIC: 3089 Injection molding of plastics

(G-3509)
DYNAK INC
530 Savage Rd (14428-9614)
PHONE 585 271-2255
Bob Vorndran, *President*
Barbara Klink, *Vice Pres*
EMP: 13
SQ FT: 25,000
SALES (est): 2MM **Privately Held**
WEB: www.dynak.com
SIC: 3599 Mfg Industrial Machinery

(G-3510)
INLAND VACUUM INDUSTRIES INC (PA)
35 Howard Ave (14428-8008)
P.O. Box 373 (14428-0373)
PHONE 585 293-3330
Peter C Yu, *Ch of Bd*
Lusanne Lam, *Vice Pres*
Peter Yu, *Vice Pres*
▲ **EMP:** 12
SQ FT: 1,000
SALES (est): 1.7MM **Privately Held**
WEB: www.inlandvacuum.com
SIC: 2992 Lubricating oils & greases

(G-3511)
INTEK PRECISION
539 Attridge Rd (14428-9712)
PHONE 585 293-0853
Susan Kurucz, *Partner*
Paul Kurucz, *Partner*
EMP: 8
SQ FT: 3,000
SALES: 200K **Privately Held**
WEB: www.intekprecision.com
SIC: 3544 Special dies, tools, jigs & fixtures

(G-3512)
QUALICOAT INC
14 Sanford Rd N (14428-9503)
PHONE 585 293-2650
Michael Pontarelli, *Ch of Bd*
Joe Pontarelli, *Engineer*
Sharon Cubitt, *Manager*
Ross Mazzola, *Director*
▲ **EMP:** 80
SQ FT: 48,000
SALES (est): 10.2MM **Privately Held**
WEB: www.qualicoat.com
SIC: 3479 Coating of metals & formed products; painting of metal products

Cicero
Onondaga County

(G-3513)
ADD ASSOCIATES INC
Also Called: Image Press, The
6333 Daedalus Rd (13039-8889)
PHONE 315 449-3474
Toll Free: .... 888 -
Chris Arnone, *President*
Lonnie Dahl, *Vice Pres*
EMP: 8
SQ FT: 10,000
SALES (est): 1.3MM **Privately Held**
SIC: 2741 Miscellaneous publishing

(G-3514)
AWNING MART INC
5665 State Route 31 (13039-8513)
PHONE 315 699-5928
Doug Loguidice, *President*
EMP: 7
SQ FT: 4,400
SALES (est): 749.3K **Privately Held**
SIC: 2394 1799 5199 5999 Awnings, fabric: made from purchased materials; awning installation; canvas products; awnings; canvas products

(G-3515)
CLINTONS DITCH COOP CO INC
8478 Pardee Rd (13039-8531)
PHONE 315 699-2695
Ronald Anania, *President*
Michael Moehringer, *General Mgr*
Bill Fitzgerald, *Vice Pres*
Tim Tenney, *Vice Pres*
Melissa Moshier, *Plant Mgr*
EMP: 155
SQ FT: 250,000
SALES: 62.6MM **Privately Held**
WEB: www.clintonsditch.com
SIC: 2086 Soft drinks: packaged in cans, bottles, etc.

(G-3516)
DAF OFFICE NETWORKS INC
6121 Jemola Runne (13039-8238)
PHONE 315 699-7070
David A Farabee, *President*
EMP: 9
SALES (est): 1MM **Privately Held**
SIC: 2521 5112 5044 Wood office furniture; office supplies; office equipment

(G-3517)
EJ GROUP INC
6177 S Bay Rd (13039-9303)
PHONE 315 699-2601
EMP: 9 **Privately Held**
SIC: 3446 Architectural metalwork
PA: Ej Group, Inc.
301 Spring St
East Jordan MI 49727

Cicero - Onondaga County (G-3518)

(G-3518)
GIBAR INC
7838 Brewerton Rd (13039-9536)
PHONE...................315 452-5656
EMP: 244
SALES (corp-wide): 9MM Privately Held
SIC: 3421 Table & food cutlery, including butchers'
PA: Gibar, Inc
1 Technology Pl
East Syracuse NY 13057
315 432-4546

(G-3519)
LIBERTY MACHINE & TOOL
7908 Ontario Ave (13039-9759)
PHONE...................315 699-3242
Thomas Burgmeier, Owner
EMP: 1
SQ FT: 2,500
SALES: 1MM Privately Held
SIC: 3599 Machine shop, jobbing & repair

(G-3520)
PAUL DE LIMA COMPANY INC
8550 Pardee Rd (13039-8519)
PHONE...................315 457-3725
Jim Sarner, Vice Pres
Steve Zaremba, CFO
Peter Sansone, Human Res Dir
Karen Huntley, Mktg Dir
W Drescher, Branch Mgr
EMP: 23
SALES (corp-wide): 14.9MM Privately Held
SIC: 2095 Roasted coffee
PA: Paul De Lima Company, Inc.
7546 Morgan Rd Ste 1
Liverpool NY 13090
315 457-3725

(G-3521)
PAUL DELIMA COFFEE COMPANY
8550 Pardee Rd (13039-8519)
PHONE...................315 457-3725
Paul De Lima, Principal
Jim Von Holtz, Maintence Staff
▲ EMP: 9
SALES (est): 1.1MM Privately Held
SIC: 2095 Roasted coffee

(G-3522)
R & B FABRICATION INC
7282 State Route 31 (13039-9708)
PHONE...................315 640-9901
Robert Bellinger, President
Robert Schneider, Vice Pres
Carly Barrett, Manager
EMP: 10 EST: 2017
SALES: 50K Privately Held
SIC: 7692 7699 7353 1541 Welding repair; automotive welding; industrial equipment services; cranes & aerial lift equipment, rental or leasing; prefabricated building erection, industrial

(G-3523)
THERMAL FOAMS/SYRACUSE INC
6173 S Bay Rd (13039-9303)
P.O. Box 1981 (13039-1981)
PHONE...................315 699-8734
John Jeffery, Branch Mgr
EMP: 25 Privately Held
SIC: 3086 Plastics foam products
PA: Thermal Foams/Syracuse, Inc.
2101 Kenmore Ave
Buffalo NY 14207

Clarence
Erie County

(G-3524)
ANABEC INC
9393 Main St (14031-1912)
P.O. Box 433 (14031-0433)
PHONE...................716 759-1674
Stephen Meyers, President
Nancy Ewing, Vice Pres
EMP: 5 EST: 1995
SQ FT: 3,200
SALES (est): 792.5K Privately Held
WEB: www.anabec.com
SIC: 2899 Chemical preparations

(G-3525)
ATHENEX PHARMA SOLUTIONS LLC
11342 Main St (14031-1718)
PHONE...................877 463-7823
Stephen A Panaro, CEO
Ryan Downey, Director
Leanne Kisicki, Director
EMP: 8 EST: 2012
SQ FT: 18,000
SALES (est): 2.5MM
SALES (corp-wide): 38MM Publicly Held
SIC: 2834 Pharmaceutical preparations
PA: Athenex, Inc.
1001 Main St Ste 600
Buffalo NY 14203
716 427-2950

(G-3526)
BUFFALO CRUSHED STONE INC
91 Barton Rd (14031-1837)
P.O. Box 827, Buffalo (14231-0827)
PHONE...................716 632-6963
Greg Kramer, President
EMP: 32
SQ FT: 3,895
SALES (corp-wide): 651.9MM Privately Held
SIC: 1422 Crushed & broken limestone
HQ: Buffalo Crushed Stone, Inc.
500 Como Park Blvd
Buffalo NY 14227
716 826-7310

(G-3527)
DIMAR MANUFACTURING CORP
10123 Main St (14031-2164)
P.O. Box 597 (14031-0597)
PHONE...................716 759-0351
Gregory A Fry, President
Thomas J Kowalski, CFO
EMP: 140
SQ FT: 93,000
SALES: 16.2MM Privately Held
WEB: www.dimarmfg.com
SIC: 3499 3444 Furniture parts, metal; sheet metalwork

(G-3528)
DRESCHER PAPER BOX INC
10425 Keller Rd (14031-1057)
PHONE...................716 854-0288
J Baird Langworthy, President
John Langworthy, Exec VP
EMP: 14 EST: 1867
SALES (est): 2.5MM Privately Held
WEB: www.drescherpuzzle.com
SIC: 2652 3944 Setup paperboard boxes; games, toys & children's vehicles; puzzles

(G-3529)
DYNABRADE INC (PA)
8989 Sheridan Dr (14031-1490)
PHONE...................716 631-0100
Walter N Welsch, Ch of Bd
Ned T Librock, President
Steven D Briggs, Vice Pres
Hardy Hamann, Vice Pres
Clyde Tulowitzki, Purch Mgr
▲ EMP: 175
SQ FT: 95,000
SALES (est): 39.4MM Privately Held
WEB: www.dynabrade.com
SIC: 3546 Power-driven handtools

(G-3530)
EASTERN HILLS PRINTING (PA)
9195 Main St (14031-1931)
PHONE...................716 741-3300
Geoffrey Mohring, CEO
EMP: 9
SQ FT: 400
SALES (est): 954.2K Privately Held
SIC: 2752 Commercial printing, offset

(G-3531)
EASTERN MANUFACTURING INC
9530 Cobblestone Dr (14031-2413)
PHONE...................716 741-4572
Barbara Gomlar, President
EMP: 10
SQ FT: 8,000
SALES (est): 1.3MM Privately Held
SIC: 3441 Fabricated structural metal

(G-3532)
ELECTROCHEM SOLUTIONS INC (DH)
10000 Wehrle Dr (14031-2086)
PHONE...................716 759-5800
Joseph Flanagan, Exec VP
Capodanno Mathieu, Engineer
Thomas J Mazza, Treasurer
Timothy G McEvoy, Admin Sec
◆ EMP: 53
SALES (est): 45.9MM
SALES (corp-wide): 1.4B Publicly Held
SIC: 3692 Primary batteries, dry & wet
HQ: Greatbatch Ltd.
10000 Wehrle Dr
Clarence NY 14031
612 331-6750

(G-3533)
EXCEL INDUSTRIES INC
11737 Main St (14031)
P.O. Box 409 (14031-0409)
PHONE...................716 542-5468
Francis Nicholas, President
Mark Steck, General Mgr
Donald Nicholas, Vice Pres
Diana Fiske, Treasurer
Craig Nicholas, Office Mgr
EMP: 40
SQ FT: 35,000
SALES (est): 6.2MM Privately Held
WEB: www.excelindustriesinc.com
SIC: 3599 3441 Machine shop, jobbing & repair; fabricated structural metal

(G-3534)
INTEGER HOLDINGS CORPORATION
Engineered Components Division
4098 Barton Rd (14031-1814)
PHONE...................716 759-5200
Charles Wemhoff, Manager
EMP: 100
SALES (corp-wide): 1.4B Publicly Held
WEB: www.greatbatch.com
SIC: 3841 3842 Surgical instruments & apparatus; surgical appliances & supplies
PA: Integer Holdings Corporation
5830 Gran Pkwy Ste 1150
Plano TX 75024
214 618-5243

(G-3535)
MEDIMA LLC
Also Called: Medima Metals
5727 Strickler Rd (14031-1372)
PHONE...................716 741-0400
Barry Lazar, Mng Member
◆ EMP: 250
SALES: 425MM Privately Held
SIC: 3339 3313 Silicon & chromium; ferroalloys

(G-3536)
OEM SOLUTIONS INC
4995 Rockhaven Dr (14031-2438)
PHONE...................716 864-9324
▲ EMP: 4
SQ FT: 3,000
SALES: 1MM Privately Held
SIC: 3469 3699 Metal Stampings And Electrical Equipment And Supplies

(G-3537)
PALLET SERVICES INC (PA)
4055 Casillio Pkwy (14031-2047)
P.O. Box 911, Tonawanda (14151-0911)
PHONE...................716 873-7700
Donald Matre, CEO
Ronald A Matre, Vice Pres
Dan O'Leary, Sales Executive
EMP: 120 EST: 1997
SALES (est): 23MM Privately Held
WEB: www.palletservices.com
SIC: 2448 Wood pallets & skids

(G-3538)
PEAK MOTION INC
11190 Main St (14031-1702)
PHONE...................716 534-4925
Douglas Webster, President
EMP: 7
SALES (est): 1.7MM Privately Held
WEB: www.peakmotion.com
SIC: 3499 3544 Aerosol valves, metal; special dies, tools, jigs & fixtures

(G-3539)
PRECIMED INC
Also Called: Greatbatch Medical
10000 Wehrle Dr (14031-2086)
PHONE...................716 759-5600
Patrick White, CEO
Patrick Berdoz, President
EMP: 46
SQ FT: 2,000
SALES (est): 4.5MM
SALES (corp-wide): 1.4B Publicly Held
WEB: www.precimed.com
SIC: 3841 5047 Surgical & medical instruments; medical & hospital equipment
HQ: Greatbatch Ltd.
10000 Wehrle Dr
Clarence NY 14031
612 331-6750

(G-3540)
RLS HOLDINGS INC
11342 Main St (14031-1718)
PHONE...................716 418-7274
Stephen A Panaro PHD, President
EMP: 5
SALES (est): 799K Privately Held
SIC: 2834 Pharmaceutical preparations

(G-3541)
RODAC USA CORP
5605 Kraus Rd (14031-1342)
PHONE...................716 741-3931
Daniel Primeau, CEO
EMP: 25
SALES (est): 2.2MM Privately Held
SIC: 3648 Mfg Lighting Equipment

(G-3542)
WAVE FLOAT ROOMS LLC
4817 Kraus Rd (14031-1507)
PHONE...................844 356-2876
Craig Silver,
EMP: 8
SALES: 1.4MM Privately Held
SIC: 3999 Hot tub & spa covers

Clarence Center
Erie County

(G-3543)
CLARENCE RESINS AND CHEMICALS
9585 Keller Rd (14032-9230)
PHONE...................716 406-9804
James G Lawrence, President
EMP: 8
SQ FT: 800
SALES (est): 1.2MM Privately Held
SIC: 2821 5169 Plastics materials & resins; synthetic resins, rubber & plastic materials

(G-3544)
EXACTA LLC
8955 Williams Ct (14032-9414)
PHONE...................716 406-2303
Peter Buchbinder, Owner
James B Schleer, Mng Member
EMP: 9
SQ FT: 1,200
SALES (est): 640K Privately Held
WEB: www.exacta.com
SIC: 3555 Copy holders, printers'

▲ = Import ▼= Export
◆ = Import/Export

GEOGRAPHIC SECTION

(G-3545)
ITALIAN MARBLE & GRANITE INC
8526 Roll Rd (14032-9761)
PHONE.................................716 741-1800
Mark K Zografos, *President*
▲ EMP: 16
SQ FT: 21,000
SALES (est): 2.4MM Privately Held
SIC: 3281 Marble, building; cut & shaped

(G-3546)
J R PRODUCTS INC
9680 County Rd (14032-9240)
PHONE.................................716 633-7565
Doug Rouba, *President*
Vedant Sandhya, *Opers Staff*
Brian Roba, *VP Sales*
▲ EMP: 9
SALES (est): 730K Privately Held
WEB: www.jrprvinc.com
SIC: 3949 Camping equipment & supplies

(G-3547)
JW BURG MACHINE & TOOL INC
7430 Rapids Rd (14032-9501)
P.O. Box 372 (14032-0372)
PHONE.................................716 434-0015
Joe Burg, *President*
EMP: 8
SALES (est): 265.7K Privately Held
SIC: 3599 Machine shop, jobbing & repair

(G-3548)
MALYN INDUSTRIAL CERAMICS INC
8640 Roll Rd (14032-9139)
P.O. Box 469 (14032-0469)
PHONE.................................716 741-1510
Michael Malyn, *President*
Pat Malyn, *Vice Pres*
EMP: 7
SQ FT: 7,000
SALES (est): 930K Privately Held
WEB: www.malyn.com
SIC: 3291 3432 Grinding balls, ceramic; plumbing fixture fittings & trim

(G-3549)
TECHNIFLO CORPORATION
9730 County Rd (14032-9651)
P.O. Box 307, Clarence (14031-0307)
PHONE.................................716 741-3500
Richard F Whitesell, *CEO*
EMP: 9 EST: 1975
SQ FT: 8,000
SALES (est): 1.8MM Privately Held
SIC: 3625 Noise control equipment

(G-3550)
UNICENTER MILLWORK INC
9605 Clarence Center Rd (14032-9748)
PHONE.................................716 741-8201
Terrance Reilly, *President*
EMP: 9
SALES (est): 680K Privately Held
SIC: 2431 Millwork

Clay
Onondaga County

(G-3551)
MS SPARES LLC
8055 Evesborough Dr (13041-9140)
PHONE.................................607 223-3024
Michael Slater, *President*
EMP: 5
SALES (est): 559.5K Privately Held
SIC: 3061 3599 3444 7692 Mechanical rubber goods; machine & other job shop work; sheet metalwork; welding repair

Clayton
Jefferson County

(G-3552)
AMERICAN METALCRAFT MARINE
690 Riverside Dr (13624-1043)
P.O. Box 961, Cape Vincent (13618-0961)
PHONE.................................315 686-9891
Kenneth I Johnson, *President*
Leon Rusho Jr, *Vice Pres*
▼ EMP: 7 EST: 1997
SALES (est): 567.9K Privately Held
WEB: www.americanmetalcraftmarine.com
SIC: 3732 Boat building & repairing

(G-3553)
COYOTE MOON LLC (PA)
Also Called: Coyote Moon Vineyards
17371 County Route 3 (13624-2193)
P.O. Box 497 (13624-0497)
PHONE.................................315 686-5600
David Countryman, *Manager*
Phillip Randazzo,
EMP: 12
SALES (est): 2.2MM Privately Held
SIC: 2084 5182 5921 Wines; wine; wine

Clayville
Oneida County

(G-3554)
BARRETT PAVING MATERIALS INC
363 Rasbach Rd (13322-2538)
PHONE.................................315 737-9471
Doug Henry, *Facilities Mgr*
Robert Bard, *Branch Mgr*
Bob Bard, *Manager*
EMP: 13
SALES (corp-wide): 95.5MM Privately Held
WEB: www.barrettpaving.com
SIC: 2951 1429 3272 1422 Asphalt & asphaltic paving mixtures (not from refineries); igneous rock, crushed & broken-quarrying; concrete products; crushed & broken limestone
HQ: Barrett Paving Materials Inc.
3 Becker Farm Rd Ste 307
Roseland NJ 07068
973 533-1001

(G-3555)
BARRETT PAVING MATERIALS INC
1223 Albany Rd (13322-2523)
PHONE.................................315 737-8310
Robert Bard, *Manager*
EMP: 14
SALES (corp-wide): 95.5MM Privately Held
WEB: www.barrettpaving.com
SIC: 2951 Asphalt paving mixtures & blocks
HQ: Barrett Paving Materials Inc.
3 Becker Farm Rd Ste 307
Roseland NJ 07068
973 533-1001

(G-3556)
CLAYVILLE ICE CO INC
2514 Foundry Pl (13322-1600)
P.O. Box 12 (13322-0012)
PHONE.................................315 839-5405
Gareth A Evans, *President*
EMP: 8
SQ FT: 17,000
SALES: 340.1K Privately Held
SIC: 2097 Block ice; ice cubes

(G-3557)
HMI METAL POWDERS
Also Called: Pratt With ME Hmi Met Powders
2395 Main St (13322-1102)
P.O. Box 294 (13322-0294)
PHONE.................................315 839-5421
John Letisky, *Treasurer*
EMP: 120
SQ FT: 140,000
SALES (est): 14.7MM Privately Held
SIC: 3312 Blast furnaces & steel mills

(G-3558)
HOMOGENEOUS METALS INC
Also Called: Hmi Metal Powders
2395 Main St (13322-1102)
P.O. Box 294 (13322-0294)
PHONE.................................315 839-5421
Mark Hewko, *Ch of Bd*
Greg Treacy, *Ch of Bd*
Mark Huwko, *General Mgr*
▲ EMP: 56 EST: 1965
SQ FT: 129,000
SALES (est): 14.3MM
SALES (corp-wide): 59.8B Publicly Held
WEB: www.hmipowder.com
SIC: 3312 Billets, steel
PA: United Technologies Corporation
10 Farm Springs Rd
Farmington CT 06032
860 728-7000

(G-3559)
VALLEY CREEK SIDE INC
Also Called: Valley Signs
1960 State Route 8 (13322-1312)
P.O. Box 287 (13322-0287)
PHONE.................................315 839-5526
EMP: 7
SALES: 240K Privately Held
SIC: 3993 Mfg Signs/Advertising Specialties

(G-3560)
WOLAK INC
2360 King Rd (13322-1214)
PHONE.................................315 839-5366
J Wolak, *President*
EMP: 7 EST: 1941
SQ FT: 20,000
SALES (est): 560K Privately Held
SIC: 2541 Counter & sink tops

Cleveland
Oswego County

(G-3561)
GOT WOOD LLC
28 North St (13042-3278)
P.O. Box 337, Central Square (13036-0337)
PHONE.................................315 440-8857
Michael Fullmer, *Owner*
EMP: 6
SALES (est): 410.3K Privately Held
SIC: 2411 3531 Timber, cut at logging camp; rakes, land clearing: mechanical

Clifton Park
Saratoga County

(G-3562)
ADVANCED MFG TECHNIQUES
453 Kinns Rd (12065-2408)
P.O. Box 617 (12065-0617)
PHONE.................................518 877-8560
Steve Petronis, *President*
Richard Carusone, *Vice Pres*
EMP: 7
SQ FT: 10,000
SALES (est): 1.1MM Privately Held
WEB: www.advmfgtech.com
SIC: 3599 3699 Machine shop, jobbing & repair; electrical equipment & supplies

(G-3563)
ANTHROPOSOPHIC PRESS INC (PA)
15 Greenridge Dr (12065-6628)
PHONE.................................518 851-2054
Gordon Edwards, *Ch of Bd*
Michael Dobson, *President*
Christopher Bamford, *Admin Sec*
▲ EMP: 2
SQ FT: 6,500
SALES: 1.1MM Privately Held
SIC: 2731 5192 5961 Books: publishing only; books; books, mail order (except book clubs)

(G-3564)
ATLANTIC PROJECTS COMPANY INC
5 Southside Dr Ste 11s (12065-3870)
P.O. Box 782 (12065-0782)
PHONE.................................518 878-2065
Judith Brodeur, *CFO*
EMP: 10 EST: 1999
SALES (est): 1.6MM
SALES (corp-wide): 892.8MM Publicly Held
SIC: 3511 Hydraulic turbines
HQ: Atlantic Projects Company Limited
3 Marine Road
Dun Laoghaire

(G-3565)
BOBRICK WASHROOM EQUIPMENT INC
200 Commerce Dr (12065-1399)
PHONE.................................518 877-7444
Rich Ross, *Manager*
EMP: 100
SALES (corp-wide): 97.9MM Privately Held
SIC: 2542 5074 3446 Partitions & fixtures, except wood; plumbing & hydronic heating supplies; architectural metalwork
HQ: Bobrick Washroom Equipment, Inc.
6901 Tujunga Ave
North Hollywood CA 91605
818 764-1000

(G-3566)
G&G LED LLC
10 Corprate Dr Clifton Pa Clifton Park (12065)
PHONE.................................800 285-6780
Matthew Sloan, *Principal*
EMP: 24 EST: 2010
SQ FT: 12,000
SALES (est): 5.8MM Privately Held
SIC: 3646 Commercial indusl & institutional electric lighting fixtures

(G-3567)
HECTOR PT SR REHAB SVC PLLC
1 Wall St (12065-3851)
PHONE.................................518 371-5554
Hector Jasen, *Branch Mgr*
EMP: 5
SALES (est): 283K Privately Held
SIC: 3949 Sporting & athletic goods
PA: Hector Pt Sr Rehab Service Pllc
1 Wall St
Clifton Park NY 12065

(G-3568)
JOHNSON CONTROLS
1399 Vischer Ferry Rd (12065)
PHONE.................................518 952-6040
Dan Bullis, *Manager*
EMP: 30 Privately Held
WEB: www.simplexgrinnell.com
SIC: 3669 Emergency alarms
HQ: Johnson Controls Fire Protection Lp
4700 Exchange Ct Ste 300
Boca Raton FL 33431
561 988-7200

(G-3569)
LASERTECH CRTRIDGE RE-BUILDERS
7 Longwood Dr (12065-7614)
PHONE.................................518 373-1246
Enn Epner, *Owner*
William Hougeich, *Vice Pres*
EMP: 9
SALES: 400K Privately Held
SIC: 3861 5734 Toners, prepared photographic (not made in chemical plants); computer & software stores

(G-3570)
M MANASTRIP-M CORPORATION
821 Main St (12065-1002)
PHONE.................................518 664-2089
David Scagnelli, *President*
EMP: 5
SQ FT: 3,000

Clifton Park - Saratoga County (G-3571)

SALES (est): 503.7K **Privately Held**
WEB: www.manastrip.com
SIC: 3498 3451 3494 Manifolds, pipe: fabricated from purchased pipe; screw machine products; valves & pipe fittings

(G-3571)
MICROB PHASE SERVICES
Also Called: Brittish American Envmtl
14 Nottingham Way S (12065-1727)
PHONE..................................518 877-8948
Ron Shongar, *Owner*
EMP: 15
SALES (est): 830K **Privately Held**
SIC: 3822 Mfg Environmental Controls

(G-3572)
NYI BUILDING PRODUCTS INC (PA)
5 Southside Dr Ste 204 (12065-3870)
PHONE..................................518 458-7500
Jay Torani, *Principal*
Susanne Brook, *Vice Pres*
▲ EMP: 16
SQ FT: 1,500
SALES (est): 4.1MM **Privately Held**
WEB: www.nyionline.com
SIC: 3315 5169 Nails, spikes, brads & similar items; adhesives & sealants

(G-3573)
PRINT & GRAPHICS GROUP
12 Fire Rd (12065-3110)
PHONE..................................518 371-4649
Frank Papasso, *Owner*
EMP: 6
SALES (est): 468.9K **Privately Held**
SIC: 2752 Commercial printing, offset

(G-3574)
PVC INDUSTRIES INC
107 Pierce Rd (12065-1310)
PHONE..................................518 877-8670
Louis F Simonini, *President*
EMP: 30
SQ FT: 65,000
SALES (est): 864.9K **Privately Held**
WEB: www.pvcindustries.com
SIC: 3089 Windows, plastic; window frames & sash, plastic
PA: Sturbridge Associates Iii Llc
185 Union Ave
Providence RI 02909

(G-3575)
ROBAT INC
1 Fairchild Sq Ste 114 (12065-1266)
PHONE..................................518 812-6244
Gregory Miczek, *Vice Pres*
EMP: 5
SALES: 400K **Privately Held**
SIC: 3823 Industrial process measurement equipment

(G-3576)
SENSIO AMERICA
800 Route 146 Ste 175 (12065-3945)
PHONE..................................877 501-5337
Paul Bardwell, *General Mgr*
Terry V Delong, *Principal*
Terry Delong, *Branch Mgr*
EMP: 15
SALES (est): 2.3MM **Privately Held**
SIC: 3648 Lighting equipment

(G-3577)
SENSIO AMERICA LLC (PA)
800 Route 146 Ste 175 (12065-3945)
PHONE..................................877 501-5337
Terry Delong, *Vice Pres*
Adam Giordano, *Opers Mgr*
Gary Rutherford, *CTO*
▲ EMP: 14
SQ FT: 7,000
SALES: 5.2MM **Privately Held**
SIC: 3648 Lighting equipment

(G-3578)
ST SILICONES CORPORATION
821 Main St (12065-1002)
PHONE..................................518 406-3208
David A Scagnelli, *President*
EMP: 15
SALES (est): 1MM **Privately Held**
SIC: 3841 Surgical & medical instruments

(G-3579)
THE GRAMECY GROUP
4 Gramecy Ct (12065-2329)
PHONE..................................518 348-1325
Bill Sommers, *Owner*
EMP: 8
SALES (est): 721.5K **Privately Held**
WEB: www.gramecy.com
SIC: 2759 3479 Commercial printing; name plates: engraved, etched, etc.

(G-3580)
WESTCHESTER VALVE & FITTING CO
741 Pierce Rd (12065-1302)
PHONE..................................914 762-6600
Tom Selfridge, *Owner*
EMP: 5
SALES (est): 280.2K **Privately Held**
SIC: 3494 Valves & pipe fittings

(G-3581)
WORLDWIDE GAS TURBINE PDTS INC
Also Called: Gt Parts & Services
300 Commerce Dr (12065-1317)
PHONE..................................518 877-7200
Anthony Campana, *CEO*
Stephen P Campana, *Ch of Bd*
Antoinette Campana, *Admin Sec*
EMP: 8
SQ FT: 1,200
SALES (est): 1.9MM **Privately Held**
SIC: 3511 Turbines & turbine generator sets

Clifton Springs
Ontario County

(G-3582)
MERCHANDISER INC
70 Stephens St (14432-1051)
P.O. Box 642 (14432-0642)
PHONE..................................315 462-6411
Cheryl Tears, *President*
James Tears, *Vice Pres*
EMP: 5
SQ FT: 1,792
SALES: 450K **Privately Held**
WEB: www.themerchandiser.net
SIC: 2759 2711 Publication printing; newspapers

(G-3583)
RJ WELDING & FABRICATING INC
2300 Wheat Rd (14432-9312)
PHONE..................................315 523-1288
Robert Crosby, *Principal*
EMP: 5
SALES (est): 556.2K **Privately Held**
SIC: 7692 Welding repair

(G-3584)
TOWNLINE MACHINE CO INC
3151 Manchester (14432)
PHONE..................................315 462-3413
Scott Converse, *President*
Patrick Converse, *Treasurer*
EMP: 22
SQ FT: 25,000
SALES: 3MM **Privately Held**
SIC: 3545 Precision tools, machinists'

Clinton
Oneida County

(G-3585)
GERMANIUM CORP AMERICA INC
34 Robinson Rd (13323-1419)
PHONE..................................315 853-4900
Gregory P Evans, *Ch of Bd*
▲ EMP: 11
SALES (est): 1.5MM
SALES (corp-wide): 245.7MM **Privately Held**
WEB: www.indium.com
SIC: 3341 2819 Secondary nonferrous metals; chemicals, high purity: refined from technical grade
PA: Indium Corporation Of America
34 Robinson Rd
Clinton NY 13323
800 446-3486

(G-3586)
INDIUM CORPORATION OF AMERICA (PA)
34 Robinson Rd (13323-1419)
P.O. Box 269, Utica (13503-0269)
PHONE..................................800 446-3486
Gregory P Evans, *CEO*
William N Macartney III, *Ch of Bd*
Ross Bemtson, *President*
Ning-Cheng Lee, *Vice Pres*
Mike McKenna, *Vice Pres*
▲ EMP: 45 EST: 1934
SQ FT: 12,000
SALES (est): 245.7MM **Privately Held**
WEB: www.indium.com
SIC: 3356 Solder: wire, bar, acid core, & rosin core

(G-3587)
POWER LINE CONSTRUCTORS INC
24 Robinson Rd (13323-1419)
P.O. Box 385 (13323-0385)
PHONE..................................315 853-6183
David L Critelli, *President*
En M Critelli, *Exec VP*
Steven M Critelli, *Exec VP*
Steve Bonsted, *Vice Pres*
Allen Kobbe, *Vice Pres*
EMP: 30
SQ FT: 7,500
SALES (est): 7.4MM **Privately Held**
WEB: www.powerlineconstructors.com
SIC: 3669 Traffic signals, electric

(G-3588)
SANTUCCI CUSTOM LIGHTING ◯
2943 Lumbard Rd (13323-4527)
PHONE..................................866 853-1929
Marilyn Santucci, *CEO*
EMP: 10 EST: 2018
SALES: 1MM **Privately Held**
SIC: 3646 Chandeliers, commercial

(G-3589)
TENNEY MEDIA GROUP (PA)
Also Called: Omp Printing & Graphics
28 Robinson Rd (13323-1419)
P.O. Box 325 (13323-0325)
PHONE..................................315 853-5569
Claudia Cleary, *Ch of Bd*
Robert Tenney, *Admin Sec*
EMP: 67
SQ FT: 25,000
SALES (est): 27.8MM **Privately Held**
WEB: www.psaver.com
SIC: 2741 2711 Shopping news: publishing & printing; newspapers

Clinton Corners
Dutchess County

(G-3590)
CLINTON VINEYARDS INC
450 Schultzville Rd (12514-2402)
PHONE..................................845 266-5372
Phyllis Feder, *President*
EMP: 5
SALES (est): 425.6K **Privately Held**
WEB: www.clintonvineyards.com
SIC: 2084 Wines

Clyde
Wayne County

(G-3591)
ADVANCED ATOMIZATION TECH LLC
Also Called: Aatech
124 Columbia St (14433-1049)
PHONE..................................315 923-2341
Leanne Collazzo, *General Mgr*
Christopher Harrison, *CFO*
James Mazzarell, *CTO*
EMP: 300 EST: 2012
SQ FT: 60,000
SALES (est): 136MM
SALES (corp-wide): 14.3B **Publicly Held**
SIC: 3724 Aircraft engines & engine parts
PA: Parker-Hannifin Corporation
6035 Parkland Blvd
Cleveland OH 44124
216 896-3000

(G-3592)
ENERGY PANEL STRUCTURES INC
Also Called: Fingerlakes Construction
10269 Old Route 31 (14433-9777)
PHONE..................................315 923-7777
Kirt Burghdorf, *Vice Pres*
EMP: 7
SALES (corp-wide): 206.5MM **Privately Held**
SIC: 3448 2452 Prefabricated metal buildings; prefabricated wood buildings
HQ: Energy Panel Structures, Inc.
603 N Van Gordon Ave
Graettinger IA 51342
712 859-3219

(G-3593)
ENERGY PANEL STRUCTURES INC
Also Called: Fingerlakes Construction
10269 Old Route 31 (14433-9777)
PHONE..................................585 343-1777
Kirt Burghdorf, *Vice Pres*
EMP: 7
SALES (corp-wide): 206.5MM **Privately Held**
SIC: 3448 2452 Prefabricated metal buildings; prefabricated wood buildings
HQ: Energy Panel Structures, Inc.
603 N Van Gordon Ave
Graettinger IA 51342
712 859-3219

(G-3594)
FUEL EFFICIENCY LLC
101 Davis Pkwy (14433)
PHONE..................................315 923-2511
Joseph Connelly,
Karen Connelly,
EMP: 8
SQ FT: 12,700
SALES (est): 1.4MM **Privately Held**
WEB: www.fuelefficiency.com
SIC: 3443 Boilers: industrial, power, or marine; boiler shop products: boilers, smokestacks, steel tanks

(G-3595)
MEADE MACHINE CO INC
31 Ford St (14433-1306)
PHONE..................................315 923-1703
Mark Clinton Meade, *President*
Elizabeth Meade, *Vice Pres*
EMP: 6 EST: 1943
SQ FT: 8,000
SALES: 800K **Privately Held**
SIC: 3599 7539 Machine shop, jobbing & repair; machine shop, automotive

(G-3596)
MODERN BLOCK LLC
2440 Wyne Zandra Rose Vly (14433)
PHONE..................................315 923-7443
Andy Martin,
Glen S Martin,
EMP: 8
SALES: 600K **Privately Held**
SIC: 3271 Concrete block & brick

GEOGRAPHIC SECTION

(G-3597)
PARKER-HANNIFIN CORPORATION
Also Called: Parker-Hannifin Aerospace
124 Columbia St (14433-1049)
PHONE.....................631 231-3737
Dave Wright, *Plant Mgr*
Horace Bassaragh, *Engineer*
Mark Bushart, *Engineer*
Brian Cario, *Engineer*
AVI Korenshtein, *Engineer*
EMP: 248
SALES (corp-wide): 14.3B **Publicly Held**
SIC: 3728 Aircraft parts & equipment
PA: Parker-Hannifin Corporation
6035 Parkland Blvd
Cleveland OH 44124
216 896-3000

(G-3598)
THOMAS ELECTRONICS INC (PA)
208 Davis Pkwy (14433-9550)
PHONE.....................315 923-2051
David A Ketchum, *President*
Dennis Young, *President*
Jeff Culmo, *General Mgr*
Douglas Ketchum, *Exec VP*
Doug Ketchum, *Vice Pres*
▲ **EMP:** 160
SQ FT: 71,180
SALES (est): 22.5MM **Privately Held**
SIC: 3671 Cathode ray tubes, including rebuilt

Clymer
Chautauqua County

(G-3599)
CUSTOM SHIPPING PRODUCTS INC
8661 Knowlton Rd (14724-9706)
P.O. Box 245 (14724-0245)
PHONE.....................716 355-4437
John Holthouse, *President*
Shelly Schenck, *Corp Secy*
Mike Schenck, *Vice Pres*
EMP: 10
SQ FT: 3,000
SALES: 890K **Privately Held**
SIC: 2448 Pallets, wood

Cobleskill
Schoharie County

(G-3600)
CLAPPER HOLLOW DESIGNS INC
369 N Grand St (12043-4140)
PHONE.....................518 234-9561
Michael Lambert, *President*
Brigette Belka, *Vice Pres*
EMP: 20
SQ FT: 10,000
SALES (est): 1.6MM **Privately Held**
SIC: 3952 Frames for artists' canvases

(G-3601)
COBLESKILL STONE PRODUCTS INC (PA)
112 Rock Rd (12043-5738)
P.O. Box 220 (12043-0220)
PHONE.....................518 234-0221
Emil Galasso, *Chairman*
Michael Galasso, *Vice Pres*
Daniel Kleeschulte, *Vice Pres*
Michael Moore, *Vice Pres*
Craig Watson, *Admin Sec*
EMP: 15 **EST:** 1954
SQ FT: 5,000
SALES (est): 115.2MM **Privately Held**
WEB: www.cobleskillstone.com
SIC: 1422 Crushed & broken limestone

(G-3602)
EFJ INC
Also Called: Mill Services
128 Macarthur Ave (12043-3603)
P.O. Box 577 (12043-0577)
PHONE.....................518 234-4799
Daniel W Holt, *President*
James Place, *Vice Pres*
EMP: 60 **EST:** 1993
SQ FT: 80,000
SALES: 10.6MM **Privately Held**
WEB: www.millservices.com
SIC: 2431 Millwork

(G-3603)
KELLEY FARM & GARDEN INC
Also Called: Agway
239 W Main St (12043-1713)
P.O. Box 37 (12043-0037)
PHONE.....................518 234-2332
Scott F Kelley, *President*
Kathy Kelley, *Corp Secy*
EMP: 20
SQ FT: 3,700
SALES (est): 6.6MM **Privately Held**
SIC: 3546 5191 5261 Saws & sawing equipment; animal feeds; lawnmowers & tractors

(G-3604)
T A S SALES SERVICE LLC
105 Kenyon Rd (12043-5713)
PHONE.....................518 234-4919
Thomas Sachs, *Principal*
EMP: 9
SALES (est): 1.1MM **Privately Held**
SIC: 1389 Gas field services

Cochecton
Sullivan County

(G-3605)
COCHECTON MILLS INC (PA)
30 Depot Rd (12726-5221)
PHONE.....................845 932-8282
Dennis E Nearing, *President*
Sean Nearing, *Manager*
EMP: 20
SQ FT: 8,500
SALES (est): 2.1MM **Privately Held**
SIC: 2048 2041 Poultry feeds; livestock feeds; flour & other grain mill products

(G-3606)
JML QUARRIES INC
420 Bernas Rd (12726-5423)
PHONE.....................845 932-8206
Rodney Cornelius, *President*
EMP: 25
SQ FT: 2,000
SALES (est): 3.2MM **Privately Held**
SIC: 1422 Crushed & broken limestone

(G-3607)
MASTEN ENTERPRISES LLC (PA)
420 Bernas Rd (12726-5423)
PHONE.....................845 932-8206
John Bernas, *Principal*
Mauren Cowger, *Manager*
EMP: 150 **EST:** 2000
SQ FT: 2,000
SALES (est): 12.2MM **Privately Held**
SIC: 1429 Grits mining (crushed stone)

(G-3608)
SULLIVAN CONCRETE INC
Also Called: Sullivan Structures
420 Bernas Rd (12726-5423)
PHONE.....................845 888-2235
John Bernas, *President*
EMP: 12
SQ FT: 2,000
SALES (est): 2.7MM **Privately Held**
WEB: www.sullivanstructures.com
SIC: 3273 Ready-mixed concrete

Coeymans
Albany County

(G-3609)
TRACEY WELDING CO INC
29 Riverview Dr (12045-7719)
P.O. Box 799 (12045-0799)
PHONE.....................518 756-6309
Richard Tracey, *President*
Richard J Tracey, *Vice Pres*
EMP: 8
SQ FT: 15,200
SALES (est): 1.3MM **Privately Held**
WEB: www.traceywelding.com
SIC: 7692 Welding repair

Cohoes
Albany County

(G-3610)
ELECTRONIC COATING TECH INC (PA)
1 Mustang Dr Ste 4 (12047-4867)
PHONE.....................518 688-2048
Tom Charlton, *President*
Mark Fonda, *Manager*
▲ **EMP:** 10
SALES (est): 1.6MM **Privately Held**
SIC: 3479 3672 Coating of metals & formed products; coating of metals with silicon; printed circuit boards

(G-3611)
JAY MOULDING CORPORATION
7 Bridge Ave Ste 1 (12047-4799)
PHONE.....................518 237-4200
Christy Smagala, *President*
Richard Smagala, *Shareholder*
EMP: 10
SQ FT: 9,000
SALES: 1MM **Privately Held**
WEB: www.jaymoulding.com
SIC: 3083 Thermosetting laminates: rods, tubes, plates & sheet; thermoplastic laminates: rods, tubes, plates & sheet

(G-3612)
LINDE GAS NORTH AMERICA LLC
Also Called: Lifegas
10 Arrowhead Ln (12047-4812)
PHONE.....................518 713-2015
Casey Hilligas, *Branch Mgr*
EMP: 40
SALES (corp-wide): 20.1B **Privately Held**
SIC: 2813 Nitrogen; oxygen, compressed or liquefied
HQ: Linde Gas North America Llc
200 Somerset Corp Blvd # 7000
Bridgewater NJ 08807

(G-3613)
MATHESON TRI-GAS INC
15 Green Mountain Dr (12047-4807)
PHONE.....................518 203-5003
Scott Kallman, *Branch Mgr*
EMP: 6
SALES (corp-wide): 34.9B **Privately Held**
SIC: 2813 Nitrogen
HQ: Matheson Tri-Gas, Inc.
150 Allen Rd Ste 302
Basking Ridge NJ 07920
908 991-9200

(G-3614)
MOHAWK FINE PAPERS INC (PA)
465 Saratoga St (12047-4626)
P.O. Box 497 (12047-0497)
PHONE.....................518 237-1740
Thomas D O'Connor, *Ch of Bd*
John F Haren, *President*
Walter Duignan, *Vice Chairman*
Kevin P Richard, *COO*
George Milner, *Senior VP*
▲ **EMP:** 300 **EST:** 1876
SQ FT: 207,000
SALES (est): 253.1MM **Privately Held**
WEB: www.mohawkpaper.com
SIC: 2672 2621 Coated & laminated paper; paper mills; uncoated paper

(G-3615)
MOHAWK FINE PAPERS INC
465 Saratoga St (12047-4626)
PHONE.....................518 237-1741
Dave Raley, *Manager*
EMP: 30
SALES (est): 253.1MM **Privately Held**
WEB: www.mohawkpaper.com
SIC: 2621 Paper mills
PA: Mohawk Fine Papers Inc.
465 Saratoga St
Cohoes NY 12047
518 237-1740

(G-3616)
NORLITE LLC
Also Called: Norlite Corporation
628 Saratoga St (12047-4644)
P.O. Box 694 (12047-0694)
PHONE.....................518 235-0030
Michael Ferraro, *Corp Secy*
Robert O'Brien, *Mng Member*
EMP: 325 **EST:** 1973
SQ FT: 5,000
SALES (est): 84MM
SALES (corp-wide): 137.1K **Privately Held**
WEB: www.norliteagg.com
SIC: 3295 Shale, expanded
HQ: Tradebe Environmental Services, Llc
1433 E 83rd Ave Ste 200
Merrillville IN 46410

(G-3617)
PRECISION VALVE & AUTOMTN INC (PA)
Also Called: PVA
1 Mustang Dr Ste 3 (12047-4867)
PHONE.....................518 371-2684
Anthony J Hynes, *Ch of Bd*
Ryan Livingston, *Regional Mgr*
Craig Tuttle, *Mfg Dir*
Rich Degonza, *Mfg Mgr*
Peter Howe, *Facilities Mgr*
◆ **EMP:** 190
SQ FT: 115,000
SALES (est): 34.1MM **Privately Held**
WEB: www.pva.net
SIC: 3491 Industrial valves

(G-3618)
REO WELDING INC
5 New Cortland St (12047-2628)
PHONE.....................518 238-1022
Robert J REO Jr, *President*
Michael REO, *Vice Pres*
EMP: 17
SQ FT: 6,000
SALES (est): 4.7MM **Privately Held**
WEB: www.reowelding.com
SIC: 3441 7692 Fabricated structural metal; welding repair

(G-3619)
ROBERTS NICHOLS FIRE APPARATUS
84 Island View Rd (12047-4995)
PHONE.....................518 431-1945
Harry Roberts, *CEO*
EMP: 9
SALES (est): 1.3MM **Privately Held**
SIC: 3711 Motor vehicles & car bodies

(G-3620)
SCHONWETTER ENTERPRISES INC
Also Called: Bilinski Sausage Mfg Co
41 Lark St (12047-4618)
PHONE.....................518 237-0171
Steven M Schonwetter, *Ch of Bd*
Carrie Coddington, *Transptn Dir*
Sagar Agarwal, *QC Mgr*
Cathie Schonwetter, *Sales Executive*
Steven Schonwetter, *Executive*
EMP: 25
SQ FT: 20,000
SALES (est): 5MM **Privately Held**
WEB: www.bilinski.com
SIC: 2013 Sausages from purchased meat

Cohoes - Albany County (G-3621) GEOGRAPHIC SECTION

(G-3621)
SHELTER ENTERPRISES INC
8 Saratoga St (12047-3109)
P.O. Box 618 (12047-0618)
PHONE.................................518 237-4100
Jeffory J Myers, *Principal*
▲ EMP: 60
SQ FT: 110,000
SALES (est): 14.7MM **Privately Held**
WEB: www.shelter-ent.com
SIC: 3086 2452 Insulation or cushioning material, foamed plastic; prefabricated buildings, wood

(G-3622)
TROYS LANDSCAPE SUPPLY CO INC
1266 Loudon Rd (12047)
PHONE.................................518 785-1526
Troy Miller, *President*
Monica Mickman, *Vice Pres*
EMP: 11
SQ FT: 2,520
SALES (est): 1MM **Privately Held**
SIC: 3271 Blocks, concrete: landscape or retaining wall

(G-3623)
VITAL SIGNS & GRAPHICS CO INC
251 Saratoga St (12047-3120)
PHONE.................................518 237-8372
Alexander Coloruotolo, *President*
EMP: 5
SQ FT: 1,200
SALES (est): 546K **Privately Held**
SIC: 3993 7336 Signs, not made in custom sign painting shops; graphic arts & related design

(G-3624)
W N VANALSTINE & SONS INC (PA)
Also Called: Macaran Printed Products
18 New Cortland St (12047-2628)
P.O. Box 380 (12047-0380)
PHONE.................................518 237-1436
Nicholas V Alstine, *President*
William N Van Astine III, *Chairman*
Edward Wixted, *CFO*
Patrick Degnan, *Accounts Exec*
Carol Wilcox, *Manager*
EMP: 65 EST: 1952
SQ FT: 52,000
SALES (est): 14.5MM **Privately Held**
WEB: www.printandapply.com
SIC: 2759 5199 Flexographic printing; packaging materials

Cold Spring
Putnam County

(G-3625)
MID-HUDSON CONCRETE PDTS INC
3504 Route 9 (10516-3862)
PHONE.................................845 265-3141
Joe Giachinta, *President*
Katie Demarco, *Marketing Staff*
EMP: 10
SQ FT: 3,000
SALES (est): 1.5MM **Privately Held**
WEB: www.midhudsonconcreteproducts.com
SIC: 3272 Concrete products, precast; septic tanks, concrete

(G-3626)
PUTNAM CNTY NEWS RECORDER LLC
3 Stone St (10516-3020)
P.O. Box 185 (10516-0185)
PHONE.................................845 265-2468
Kimberly Hyatt, *Assoc Editor*
Elizabeth Ailes, *
EMP: 12 EST: 1939
SALES (est): 639.1K **Privately Held**
WEB: www.pcnr.com
SIC: 2711 Newspapers: publishing only, not printed on site

(G-3627)
RIVERVIEW INDUSTRIES INC
3012 Route 9 Ste 1 (10516-3675)
PHONE.................................845 265-5284
Kevin Reichard, *President*
Paul Reichard, *Vice Pres*
EMP: 7
SALES (est): 949.4K **Privately Held**
SIC: 3548 7538 7549 Welding apparatus; general truck repair; high performance auto repair & service

(G-3628)
SCANGA WOODWORKING CORP
22 Corporate Park W (10516)
PHONE.................................845 265-9115
Laura Hammond, *Ch of Bd*
Hugo Scanga, *President*
John Scanga, *Vice Pres*
Mark Scanga, *Vice Pres*
Ian Malings, *Purchasing*
▲ EMP: 38
SQ FT: 9,000
SALES (est): 6.2MM **Privately Held**
SIC: 2431 Moldings, wood: unfinished & prefinished; interior & ornamental woodwork & trim; panel work, wood

Cold Spring Harbor
Suffolk County

(G-3629)
CIRRUS HEALTHCARE PRODUCTS LLC (PA)
60 Main St (11724-1433)
P.O. Box 220 (11724-0220)
PHONE.................................631 692-7600
Malcolm Boothman, *Director*
Drew O'Connell,
▲ EMP: 28
SALES (est): 6MM **Privately Held**
WEB: www.cirrushealthcare.com
SIC: 3842 Ear plugs

(G-3630)
DANI ACCESSORIES INC
204 Lawrence Hill Rd (11724-1910)
PHONE.................................631 692-4505
Daniel Montefusco, *President*
EMP: 30
SQ FT: 4,000
SALES (est): 2MM **Privately Held**
SIC: 3171 Handbags, women's

(G-3631)
INFOSERVICES INTERNATIONAL
Also Called: Itelinso
1 Saint Marks Pl (11724-1825)
PHONE.................................631 549-1805
Michael Dohan, *President*
EMP: 15
SALES (est): 840K **Privately Held**
WEB: www.infoservices.com
SIC: 2741 Telephone & other directory publishing

(G-3632)
PRINT CENTER INC
3 Harbor Rd Ste 21 (11724-1514)
PHONE.................................718 643-9559
Robert Hershon, *President*
EMP: 6
SALES (est): 479K **Privately Held**
WEB: www.rhinography.com
SIC: 2752 Commercial printing, lithographic

Colden
Erie County

(G-3633)
O & S MACHINE & TOOL CO INC
8143 State Rd (14033-9713)
P.O. Box 303 (14033-0303)
PHONE.................................716 941-5542
Philip J Schueler, *President*
EMP: 9 EST: 1977
SQ FT: 5,000
SALES (est): 1MM **Privately Held**
SIC: 3599 Machine shop, jobbing & repair

College Point
Queens County

(G-3634)
A ANGONOA INC (PA)
11505 15th Ave (11356-1597)
P.O. Box 560089 (11356-0089)
PHONE.................................718 762-4466
Peter Zampieri, *President*
John Armao, *Plant Mgr*
Gregg Desantis, *Natl Sales Mgr*
Christopher Desantis, *Sales Staff*
Michael Kroczynski, *Manager*
EMP: 110
SQ FT: 60,000
SALES (est): 14.5MM **Privately Held**
WEB: www.angonoa.com
SIC: 2051 Bread, cake & related products

(G-3635)
AABACS GROUP INC
1509 132nd St (11356-2441)
PHONE.................................718 961-3577
Michael Shin, *Principal*
EMP: 10
SALES (est): 990.8K **Privately Held**
SIC: 3699 Security control equipment & systems

(G-3636)
ABC WINDOWS AND SIGNS CORP
12606 18th Ave (11356-2326)
PHONE.................................718 353-6210
Lin Yang, *Ch of Bd*
EMP: 12 EST: 2010
SALES (est): 1.3MM **Privately Held**
SIC: 3993 Signs, not made in custom sign painting shops

(G-3637)
AEROSPACE WIRE & CABLE INC
12909 18th Ave (11356-2407)
PHONE.................................718 358-2345
Richard Chen, *President*
Leo Tong, *Sales Mgr*
CHI Chung Chen, *Shareholder*
CHI Chen, *Shareholder*
▲ EMP: 30
SQ FT: 3,500
SALES (est): 7.2MM **Privately Held**
WEB: www.aerospacewire.com
SIC: 3315 Wire, steel: insulated or armored; cable, steel: insulated or armored

(G-3638)
AFC INDUSTRIES INC
1316 133rd Pl Ste 1 (11356-2024)
PHONE.................................718 747-0237
Anat Barnes, *Chairman*
Len Pushkantser, *Exec VP*
Dileep Jacob, *Opers Staff*
Gary Jacobs, *Controller*
Michael Shepard, *Accounts Mgr*
▲ EMP: 100
SQ FT: 20,000
SALES (est): 11MM **Privately Held**
WEB: www.afcindustries.com
SIC: 2599 Hospital furniture, except beds

(G-3639)
AMERICAN ORTHOTIC LAB CO INC
924 118th St (11356-1557)
PHONE.................................718 961-6487
Kevin John Renart, *President*
EMP: 7
SQ FT: 1,080
SALES (est): 917.5K **Privately Held**
SIC: 3544 Industrial molds

(G-3640)
BEL AIRE OFFSET CORP
Also Called: Bel Aire Printing
1853 College Point Blvd (11356-2220)
PHONE.................................718 539-8333
Carmine Nicoletti, *President*
EMP: 5 EST: 1973
SQ FT: 5,000
SALES (est): 693.5K **Privately Held**
WEB: www.belaireprintingcorp.com
SIC: 2752 Commercial printing, offset

(G-3641)
CAPITAL KIT CAB & DOOR MFRS
Also Called: Capital Ktchens Cab Doors Mfrs
1425 128th St (11356-2335)
PHONE.................................718 886-0303
Tom Catalanotto Sr, *President*
Steven Catalanotto, *Corp Secy*
Tom Catalanotto Jr, *Vice Pres*
EMP: 7
SQ FT: 10,000
SALES: 700K **Privately Held**
WEB: www.capitalkitchens.com
SIC: 2434 2431 5031 1751 Wood kitchen cabinets; doors, wood; kitchen cabinets; cabinet & finish carpentry

(G-3642)
CITY STORE GATES MFG CORP
Also Called: None
1520 129th St (11356-2400)
PHONE.................................718 939-9700
Vincent Greco Jr, *Ch of Bd*
▲ EMP: 25
SQ FT: 35,000
SALES (est): 6MM **Privately Held**
SIC: 3446 5211 1799 3429 Gates, ornamental metal; door & window products; fence construction; manufactured hardware (general); millwork

(G-3643)
EAST COAST THERMOGRAPHERS INC
1558 127th St Ste 1 (11356-2347)
PHONE.................................718 321-3211
Barry Schwartz, *President*
EMP: 30
SQ FT: 6,000
SALES (est): 2MM **Privately Held**
SIC: 2759 3953 2752 Thermography; marking devices; commercial printing, lithographic

(G-3644)
FILLING EQUIPMENT CO INC
1539 130th St (11356-2481)
PHONE.................................718 445-2111
Robert A Hampton, *President*
EMP: 11 EST: 1959
SQ FT: 6,800
SALES (est): 2.7MM **Privately Held**
WEB: www.fillingequipment.com
SIC: 3565 5084 Bottling machinery: filling, capping, labeling; industrial machinery & equipment

(G-3645)
GMD INDUSTRIES INC
Also Called: Designer Glass
12920 18th Ave (11356-2408)
PHONE.................................718 445-8779
Jorge Rodriguez, *President*
Maria Rodriguez, *Vice Pres*
Raquel Rodriguez, *Sales Staff*
Diego Rodriguez, *Data Proc Staff*
▲ EMP: 8
SQ FT: 1,500
SALES (est): 1.1MM **Privately Held**
WEB: www.gmdindustries.com
SIC: 3231 Decorated glassware: chipped, engraved, etched, etc.; mirrored glass

(G-3646)
IN-HOUSE INC
1535 126th St Ste 3 (11356-2346)
PHONE.................................718 445-9007
Joseph Passarella, *President*
Alexandra Gross, *Consultant*
EMP: 10
SQ FT: 5,000
SALES: 1.5MM **Privately Held**
SIC: 2752 2791 2789 2732 Commercial printing, offset; typesetting; bookbinding & related work; book printing

(G-3647)
INK-IT PRINTING INC
Also Called: Ink-It Prtg Inc/Angle Offset
1535 126th St Ste 1 (11356-2346)
PHONE.................................718 229-5590
Michael Igoe, *President*

▲ = Import ▼ = Export
◆ = Import/Export

GEOGRAPHIC SECTION

Collins - Erie County (G-3675)

EMP: 8
SQ FT: 750
SALES (est): 701.8K Privately Held
SIC: 2752 Commercial printing, offset

(G-3648)
INTER-FENCE CO INC
1520 129th St (11356-2400)
PHONE.................718 939-9700
Vincent Greco Sr, *President*
Vincent Greco Jr, *Vice Pres*
Thomas A Greco, *Treasurer*
Thomas Greco, *Treasurer*
Angela Greco, *Admin Sec*
EMP: 40
SQ FT: 35,000
SALES (est): 5.4MM Privately Held
SIC: 3442 3446 Metal doors; gates, ornamental metal

(G-3649)
ISLAND CIRCUITS INTERNATIONAL
1318 130th St Fl 2 (11356-1917)
PHONE.................516 625-5555
Maurizio Lanza, *Branch Mgr*
EMP: 7
SALES (corp-wide): 1.8MM Privately Held
SIC: 3679 Electronic circuits
PA: Island Circuits International
100 E 2nd St Ste 201
Mineola NY 11501
516 625-5555

(G-3650)
JAD CORP OF AMERICA
2048 119th St (11356-2123)
PHONE.................718 762-8900
Joseph A Dussich Jr, *President*
James Jozkowski, *Purchasing*
Henry Schaeffer, *CFO*
Trina Yapching, *Controller*
Chris Panzarella, *Sales Mgr*
EMP: 50
SQ FT: 45,000
SALES (est): 24.4MM Privately Held
WEB: www.jad.com
SIC: 2673 5087 5169 Trash bags (plastic film); made from purchased materials; cleaning & maintenance equipment & supplies; chemicals & allied products

(G-3651)
JPMORGAN CHASE BANK NAT ASSN
13207 14th Ave (11356-2001)
PHONE.................718 767-3592
EMP: 6
SALES (corp-wide): 99.6B Publicly Held
SIC: 3578 Automatic teller machines (ATM)
HQ: Jpmorgan Chase Bank, National Association
1111 Polaris Pkwy
Columbus OH 43240
614 436-3055

(G-3652)
LAHOYA ENTERPRISE INC
Also Called: Kourosh
1842 College Point Blvd (11356-2221)
PHONE.................718 886-8799
Kourosh Tehrani, *Ch of Bd*
▲ EMP: 30
SALES (est): 2MM Privately Held
SIC: 2339 Women's & misses' outerwear

(G-3653)
LIBERTY CONTROLS INC
1505 132nd St Fl 2 (11356-2441)
PHONE.................718 461-0600
Charles Papalcure, *President*
Chris Kellner, *Vice Pres*
David Derose, *Project Mgr*
EMP: 7 EST: 1998
SALES (est): 660K Privately Held
WEB: www.liberty-controls.com
SIC: 3829 Measuring & controlling devices

(G-3654)
M T M PRINTING CO INC
2321 College Point Blvd (11356-2596)
PHONE.................718 353-3297
Steven Kolman, *President*
Tracy Kolman, *Vice Pres*
EMP: 14 EST: 1940
SQ FT: 5,500
SALES (est): 2.7MM Privately Held
WEB: www.mtmprinting.com
SIC: 2752 2759 Commercial printing, offset; letterpress printing

(G-3655)
MATIC INDUSTRIES INC
1540 127th St (11356-2332)
PHONE.................718 886-5470
Roland Tatzel, *President*
EMP: 7
SALES (est): 580K Privately Held
SIC: 3599 Machine shop, jobbing & repair

(G-3656)
MINT-X PRODUCTS CORPORATION
2048 119th St (11356-2123)
PHONE.................877 646-8224
Joseph Dussich, *President*
Gary Price, *General Mgr*
James Dussich, *Vice Pres*
Frank Fernandez, *Opers Mgr*
Rich Wilson, *Director*
EMP: 10
SALES: 10MM Privately Held
SIC: 2673 Food storage & trash bags (plastic)

(G-3657)
NAS CP CORP (DH)
Also Called: Interplex Nas Electronics
1434 110th St Apt 4a (11356-1445)
PHONE.................718 961-6757
Jack Seidler, *President*
John Pease, *Exec VP*
Irving Klein, *Treasurer*
▲ EMP: 50
SQ FT: 41,000
SALES (est): 24.6MM
SALES (corp-wide): 223.2MM Privately Held
SIC: 3544 3471 3825 Dies & die holders for metal cutting, forming, die casting; plating of metals or formed products; test equipment for electronic & electric measurement
HQ: Interplex Industries, Inc.
231 Ferris Ave
Rumford RI 02916
718 961-6212

(G-3658)
OLIVE LED LIGHTING INC
1310 111th St (11356-1453)
PHONE.................718 746-0830
Junho Lee, *President*
◆ EMP: 7
SQ FT: 8,800
SALES (est): 977.1K Privately Held
SIC: 3648 5063 Lighting equipment; light bulbs & related supplies

(G-3659)
PARKMATIC CAR PRKG SYSTEMS LLC
2025 130th St (11356-2700)
PHONE.................800 422-5438
EMP: 5
SALES (corp-wide): 3.5MM Privately Held
SIC: 3559 Parking facility equipment & supplies
PA: Parkmatic Car Parking Systems, Llc
47-10 A 32nd Pl
Long Island City NY 11101
516 224-7700

(G-3660)
PEPSI-COLA BOTTLING CO NY INC (PA)
11202 15th Ave (11356-1496)
PHONE.................718 392-1000
William Wilson, *Ch of Bd*
Shan Lin, *Opers Staff*
Thomas Obrien, *Opers Staff*
Ronald Belanger, *Research*
Pratibha Nagarajan, *Financial Analy*
EMP: 550 EST: 1987
SQ FT: 400,000
SALES (est): 500MM Privately Held
SIC: 2086 Soft drinks: packaged in cans, bottles, etc.

(G-3661)
PRECISION GEAR INCORPORATED
11207 14th Ave (11356-1407)
PHONE.................718 321-7200
M Briggs Forelli, *President*
▲ EMP: 147
SQ FT: 56,000
SALES (est): 46.6MM Privately Held
WEB: www.precisiongearinc.com
SIC: 3728 Aircraft power transmission equipment; beaching gear, aircraft

(G-3662)
QUALITY LIFE INC
2047 129th St (11356-2725)
PHONE.................718 939-5787
Ping Ping Huang, *Ch of Bd*
▲ EMP: 15
SALES (est): 1.1MM Privately Held
SIC: 3634 Massage machines, electric, except for beauty/barber shops

(G-3663)
RAINBOW LEATHER INC
1415 112th St (11356-1435)
PHONE.................718 939-8762
Richard Lipson, *President*
Maria Ll, *Production*
Danny Pilpe, *Sales Staff*
Doron Richman, *Web Dvlpr*
▲ EMP: 10 EST: 1981
SQ FT: 8,000
SALES (est): 1.8MM Privately Held
WEB: www.rainbowleather.com
SIC: 3111 Embossing of leather

(G-3664)
SCHUSTER & RICHARD LABORTORIES
Also Called: Schuster & Richard Lab
1420 130th St (11356-2416)
PHONE.................718 358-8607
Charles Boudiette, *President*
EMP: 6 EST: 1946
SQ FT: 1,500
SALES (est): 540K Privately Held
SIC: 3842 Foot appliances, orthopedic

(G-3665)
SESCO INDUSTRIES INC
11019 15th Ave (11356-1425)
P.O. Box 560242 (11356-0242)
PHONE.................718 939-5137
Steven Shulman, *President*
Allen Franceschi, *QC Mgr*
▲ EMP: 11 EST: 1976
SQ FT: 4,000
SALES (est): 1.8MM Privately Held
WEB: www.sescoindustries.com
SIC: 3452 Bolts, nuts, rivets & washers

(G-3666)
SIGN CITY OF NEW YORK INC
13212 11th Ave (11356-1958)
P.O. Box 527015, Flushing (11352-7015)
PHONE.................718 661-1118
EMP: 5
SALES (est): 74.2K Privately Held
SIC: 3993 Signs & advertising specialties

(G-3667)
SPACE SIGN
1525 132nd St (11356-2441)
PHONE.................718 961-1112
Chang Kon Hahn, *President*
Joyce Hahn, *Vice Pres*
EMP: 11
SQ FT: 5,000
SALES (est): 1.3MM Privately Held
WEB: www.spacesign.com
SIC: 3993 3089 3444 1799 Electric signs; awnings, fiberglass & plastic combination; awnings, sheet metal; awning installation; awnings

(G-3668)
SRTECH INDUSTRY CORP
12019 Ketch Ct (11356-1151)
PHONE.................718 496-7001
S Chung, *President*
EMP: 25
SQ FT: 5,000
SALES: 3MM Privately Held
SIC: 3663 Amplifiers, RF power & IF

(G-3669)
TAG ENVELOPE CO INC
1419 128th St (11356-2335)
P.O. Box 220372, Brooklyn (11222-0372)
PHONE.................718 389-6844
Geraldine Wald, *President*
Eric Wald, *Vice Pres*
Ian Wald, *Vice Pres*
EMP: 22 EST: 1919
SQ FT: 10,000
SALES: 3MM Privately Held
SIC: 2621 2679 Envelope paper; tags, paper (unprinted); made from purchased paper

(G-3670)
ZERED INC (PA)
12717 20th Ave (11356-2317)
PHONE.................718 353-7464
Hakjin Han, *President*
James Han, *Director*
▲ EMP: 10
SALES (est): 1.3MM Privately Held
SIC: 3211 Plate glass, polished & rough

Colliersville
Otsego County

(G-3671)
C & F FABRICATORS & ERECTORS
Rr 7 (13747)
PHONE.................607 432-3520
Matthew Centofante, *President*
EMP: 6
SQ FT: 2,000
SALES (est): 580K Privately Held
SIC: 3443 Fabricated plate work (boiler shop)

Collins
Erie County

(G-3672)
COUNTRY SIDE SAND & GRAVEL (HQ)
Taylor Hollow Rd (14034)
PHONE.................716 988-3271
Daniel Gernatt Jr, *President*
EMP: 1
SQ FT: 10,000
SALES (est): 1.2MM
SALES (corp-wide): 37.6MM Privately Held
SIC: 1442 Sand mining; gravel mining
PA: Gernatt Asphalt Products, Inc.
13870 Taylor Hollow Rd
Collins NY 14034
716 532-3371

(G-3673)
EAST END
1995 Lenox Rd (14034-9785)
PHONE.................716 532-2622
Cheryl Whiteparker, *Owner*
EMP: 10
SALES (est): 1.1MM Privately Held
WEB: www.eastend.com
SIC: 2111 Cigarettes

(G-3674)
GERNATT ASPHALT PRODUCTS INC (PA)
Also Called: Gernatt Companies
13870 Taylor Hollow Rd (14034-9713)
P.O. Box 400 (14034-0400)
PHONE.................716 532-3371
Daniel R Gernatt Jr, *Ch of Bd*
Randall Best, *Vice Pres*
Susan Degolier, *Office Mgr*
EMP: 20
SQ FT: 10,000
SALES (est): 37.6MM Privately Held
WEB: www.gernatt.com
SIC: 1442 Construction sand & gravel

(G-3675)
STEEL CITY SALT LLC
13870 Taylor Hollow Rd (14034-9713)
PHONE.................716 532-0000

Bill Schmitz, *Principal*
EMP: 6
SALES: 500K **Privately Held**
SIC: 1479 Rock salt mining

(G-3676)
ZEBROWSKI INDUSTRIES INC
4345 Route 39 (14034-9765)
PHONE.................716 532-3911
Peter Zebrowski, *Chairman*
EMP: 9
SALES (est): 755.2K **Privately Held**
SIC: 3999 Chairs, hydraulic, barber & beauty shop

Colonie
Albany County

(G-3677)
COLONIE BLOCK AND SUPPLY CO
124 Lincoln Ave (12205-4917)
PHONE.................518 869-8411
Thomas Gentile, *President*
Donald Countermine, *Vice Pres*
Marlene Countermine, *Treasurer*
EMP: 5 **EST:** 1935
SQ FT: 5,000
SALES (est): 693.3K **Privately Held**
SIC: 3271 5032 Blocks, concrete or cinder: standard; masons' materials

(G-3678)
GERALD MCGLONE
17 Zoar Ave (12205-3531)
PHONE.................518 482-2613
Gerald McGlone, *Owner*
EMP: 5
SALES (est): 423.6K **Privately Held**
SIC: 2679 Wallpaper

(G-3679)
SNYDERS NEON DISPLAYS INC
Also Called: Snyder Neon & Plastic Signs
5 Highland Ave (12205-5458)
PHONE.................518 857-4100
Mary Elizabeth Orminski, *President*
Mark Orminski, *Vice Pres*
EMP: 6 **EST:** 1931
SQ FT: 5,800
SALES: 230K **Privately Held**
SIC: 3993 7389 Signs & advertising specialties; crane & aerial lift service

Commack
Suffolk County

(G-3680)
AVENTURA TECHNOLOGIES INC (PA)
48 Mall Dr (11725-5704)
PHONE.................631 300-4000
Frances Cabasso, *CEO*
Lavonne Lazarus, *Vice Pres*
Kevin A Lichtman, *Vice Pres*
Kevin Lichtman, *Vice Pres*
Matt Rice, *Project Mgr*
▲ **EMP:** 40
SQ FT: 40,000
SALES (est): 15.5MM **Privately Held**
WEB: www.ati247.com
SIC: 3577 3812 1731 Computer peripheral equipment; search & navigation equipment; voice, data & video wiring contractor; closed circuit television installation

(G-3681)
AVERY BIOMEDICAL DEVICES INC
61 Mall Dr Ste 1 (11725-5725)
PHONE.................631 864-1600
Martin Dobelle, *CEO*
Antonio Martins, *CEO*
Claire Dobelle, *President*
George Lapinski, *Prdtn Mgr*
Rommel Caguicla, *Technical Mgr*
EMP: 16
SQ FT: 4,000
SALES (est): 1.7MM **Privately Held**
WEB: www.dobelle.com
SIC: 3841 Surgical instruments & apparatus

(G-3682)
BEYER GRAPHICS INC
30 Austin Blvd Ste A (11725-5747)
PHONE.................631 543-3900
Jose Beyer, *CEO*
William Beyer Sr, *Ch of Bd*
Daniel Byer, *CFO*
Greg Hansen, *Sales Staff*
Doreen Ullger, *Sales Staff*
▲ **EMP:** 99
SQ FT: 40,000
SALES (est): 35.9MM **Privately Held**
SIC: 2752 2791 2789 7374 Commercial printing, offset; typesetting; bookbinding & related work; computer graphics service

(G-3683)
BREN-TRNICS BATTERIES INTL INC
10 Brayton Ct (11725-3104)
PHONE.................631 499-5155
Leo A Brenna, *President*
EMP: 6
SALES (est): 805K **Privately Held**
SIC: 3691 Batteries, rechargeable

(G-3684)
BREN-TRNICS BATTERIES INTL LLC
10 Brayton Ct (11725-3104)
PHONE.................631 499-5155
Leo Brenna,
EMP: 20
SQ FT: 94,000
SALES (est): 2.4MM **Privately Held**
SIC: 3691 Alkaline cell storage batteries

(G-3685)
BREN-TRONICS INC
10 Brayton Ct (11725-3104)
PHONE.................631 499-5155
SAI W Fung, *President*
Gregor Ritchie, *President*
Trish Sturiale, *General Mgr*
Sylvain Lhuissier, *Vice Pres*
Leigh Straub, *Opers Staff*
◆ **EMP:** 200
SQ FT: 80,000
SALES (est): 56.2MM **Privately Held**
WEB: www.bren-tronics.com
SIC: 3691 3692 3699 Storage batteries; primary batteries, dry & wet; electrical equipment & supplies

(G-3686)
CLEAN GAS SYSTEMS INC
368 Veterans Memorial Hwy 3a (11725-4338)
PHONE.................631 467-1600
Anil M Shah, *President*
EMP: 20
SQ FT: 4,000
SALES (est): 4.3MM **Privately Held**
WEB: www.cgscgs.com
SIC: 3564 8711 7389 Air purification equipment; pollution control engineering; air pollution measuring service

(G-3687)
COMFORT CARE TEXTILES INC (HQ)
368 Veterans Memorial Hwy # 5 (11725-4322)
PHONE.................631 543-0531
Scott Janicola, *Chairman*
▲ **EMP:** 40
SQ FT: 26,000
SALES (est): 6.5MM
SALES (corp-wide): 11.9MM **Privately Held**
SIC: 2295 Coated fabrics, not rubberized
PA: Jan Lew Textile Corp
368 Veterans Memorial Hwy # 5
Commack NY 11725
631 543-0531

(G-3688)
CORAL COLOR PROCESS LTD
50 Mall Dr (11725-5704)
PHONE.................631 543-5200

Edward Aiello, *President*
Ediedie D Npolis, *Vice Pres*
EMP: 37
SQ FT: 20,000
SALES (est): 13MM **Privately Held**
SIC: 2752 Commercial printing, offset

(G-3689)
DOCTOR PAVERS
34 Redleaf Ln (11725-5516)
PHONE.................516 342-6016
Roberto A Mendonca, *Owner*
EMP: 5
SALES (est): 346.2K **Privately Held**
SIC: 2951 Asphalt paving mixtures & blocks

(G-3690)
FOREST LABORATORIES LLC
500 Commack Rd (11725-5020)
P.O. Box 9025 (11725)
PHONE.................631 858-6010
Richard Overt, *Vice Pres*
Lori J Nuckols, *Project Mgr*
James Hamilton, *Opers Staff*
Bob Gilmartin, *QC Mgr*
John Dibella, *Controller*
EMP: 130 **Privately Held**
WEB: www.frx.com
SIC: 2834 Antibiotics, packaged
HQ: Forest Laboratories, Llc
909 3rd Ave Fl 23
New York NY 10022
212 421-7850

(G-3691)
FOREST RESEARCH INSTITUTE INC
49 Mall Dr (11725-5722)
PHONE.................631 858-5200
Forest Labs, *Principal*
Richard Del Bosco, *Manager*
EMP: 11 **EST:** 2008
SALES (est): 1.4MM **Privately Held**
SIC: 2834 Pharmaceutical preparations

(G-3692)
GASSER & SONS INC (PA)
440 Moreland Rd (11725-5778)
PHONE.................631 543-6600
Richard F Gasser, *Chairman*
Jack Gasser, *Vice Pres*
Robert Perez, *Mfg Staff*
▲ **EMP:** 125 **EST:** 1916
SQ FT: 30,000
SALES (est): 22.2MM **Privately Held**
WEB: www.gasser.com
SIC: 3469 Stamping metal for the trade

(G-3693)
GEMINI PHARMACEUTICALS INC
87 Modular Ave Ste 1 (11725-5718)
PHONE.................631 543-3334
Andrew Finamore, *President*
Michael Finamore, *Vice Pres*
Brian Finamore, *Treasurer*
Anthony Finamore, *Admin Sec*
▲ **EMP:** 260
SALES: 36.4MM **Privately Held**
WEB: www.geminipharm.com
SIC: 2834 2833 Pharmaceutical preparations; vitamins, natural or synthetic: bulk, uncompounded

(G-3694)
HAROME DESIGNS LLC
75 Modular Ave (11725-5705)
PHONE.................631 864-1900
Alan J Cohen, *Mng Member*
EMP: 22
SALES (est): 1.2MM **Privately Held**
SIC: 2519 Household furniture, except wood or metal: upholstered

(G-3695)
HOBART CORPORATION
71 Mall Dr Ste 1 (11725-5728)
PHONE.................631 864-3440
Paul Todoro, *Manager*
EMP: 24

SALES (corp-wide): 14.3B **Publicly Held**
WEB: www.hobartcorp.com
SIC: 3639 5084 7629 7699 Major kitchen appliances, except refrigerators & stoves; food product manufacturing machinery; electrical repair shops; restaurant equipment repair
HQ: Hobart Llc
701 S Ridge Ave
Troy OH 45374
937 332-3000

(G-3696)
ISLAND AUDIO ENGINEERING
7 Glenmere Ct (11725-5607)
PHONE.................631 543-2372
George Alexandrovich, *Owner*
EMP: 5 **EST:** 1972
SALES (est): 397.3K **Privately Held**
SIC: 3677 Inductors, electronic

(G-3697)
MALOYA LASER INC
65a Mall Dr Ste 1 (11725-5726)
PHONE.................631 543-2327
Reto Hug, *President*
Marc Anderes, *Vice Pres*
Roger Hug, *VP Sales*
EMP: 27
SQ FT: 22,500
SALES (est): 6.1MM **Privately Held**
WEB: www.maloyalaser.com
SIC: 3444 Mail (post office) collection or storage boxes, sheet metal

(G-3698)
MOBILE MINI INC
1158 Jericho Tpke (11725-3020)
PHONE.................631 543-4900
Ryan Catarelli, *Branch Mgr*
EMP: 20
SALES (corp-wide): 533.5MM **Publicly Held**
WEB: www.mobilemini.com
SIC: 3448 Buildings, portable: prefabricated metal
PA: Mobile Mini, Inc.
4646 E Van Buren St # 400
Phoenix AZ 85008
480 894-6311

(G-3699)
RCE MANUFACTURING LLC
10 Brayton Ct (11725-3104)
PHONE.................631 856-9005
SAI Fung, *Mng Member*
EMP: 5
SQ FT: 5,000
SALES (est): 384.1K **Privately Held**
SIC: 3672 Printed circuit boards

(G-3700)
ROPACK USA INC
49 Mall Dr (11725-5722)
PHONE.................631 482-7777
Yves Massicotta, *CEO*
EMP: 10 **EST:** 2015
SALES (est): 1.8MM **Privately Held**
SIC: 2834 Pharmaceutical preparations

(G-3701)
RPF ASSOCIATES INC
Also Called: Signs By Tomorrow
2155 Jericho Tpke Ste A (11725-2919)
PHONE.................631 462-7446
Ron Facchiano, *President*
EMP: 5
SQ FT: 1,250
SALES (est): 665.5K **Privately Held**
SIC: 3993 Signs & advertising specialties

(G-3702)
SETTONS INTL FOODS INC (PA)
Also Called: Setton Farms
85 Austin Blvd (11725-5701)
PHONE.................631 543-8090
Joshua Setton, *CEO*
Morris Setton, *Exec VP*
Assees Joshua, *Vice Pres*
Jeff Gibbons, *Plant Mgr*
Banu Sinar, *Export Mgr*
◆ **EMP:** 70 **EST:** 1971
SQ FT: 55,000

GEOGRAPHIC SECTION

SALES (est): 23.6MM **Privately Held**
WEB: www.settonfarms.com
SIC: 2034 2068 2099 2066 Dried & dehydrated fruits; nuts: dried, dehydrated, salted or roasted; food preparations; chocolate & cocoa products; candy & other confectionery products

(G-3703)
SIMPLY NATURAL FOODS LLC
Also Called: Simply Lite Foods
74 Mall Dr (11725-5711)
PHONE 631 543-9600
Solomon Gluck, *Controller*
Abe Rach,
Russ Asaro,
▲ EMP: 200
SQ FT: 55,000
SALES (est): 20.9MM **Privately Held**
WEB: www.simplylite.com
SIC: 3556 2064 2066 Food products machinery; candy & other confectionery products; chocolate & cocoa products

(G-3704)
VEHICLE TRACKING SOLUTIONS LLC
152 Veterans Memorial Hwy (11725-3634)
PHONE 631 586-7400
John Cunningham, *President*
Glenn Reed, *COO*
Marty Cruz, *Opers Mgr*
Karen Cunningham, *CFO*
Pete Desiderio, *Consultant*
EMP: 50
SQ FT: 17,000
SALES (est): 13.9MM **Privately Held**
WEB: www.vehicletrackingsolutions.com
SIC: 7372 Prepackaged software

(G-3705)
VITA-GEN LABORATORIES LLC
71s Mall Dr (11725-5703)
PHONE 631 450-4357
EMP: 5
SALES (est): 460.1K **Privately Held**
SIC: 2834 Vitamin, nutrient & hematinic preparations for human use; medicines, capsuled or ampuled

(G-3706)
WELLMILL LLC
Also Called: VITAMIX LABORATORIES
69 Mall Dr (11725-5727)
PHONE 631 465-9245
Michael Kochitz, *Mng Member*
David Grudzinski, *Administration*
Angelica Rodriguez, *Administration*
Steven Browne,
EMP: 25
SQ FT: 25,000
SALES: 3MM **Privately Held**
SIC: 2834 Vitamin preparations

(G-3707)
WICKERS SPORTSWEAR INC (PA)
Also Called: Wickers Performance Wear
88 Wyandanch Blvd (11725-4310)
PHONE 631 543-1700
Anthony Mazzenga, *CEO*
Diane Basso, *President*
Carol Mazzenga, *Principal*
Maryann D'Erario, *Treasurer*
▲ EMP: 7
SQ FT: 2,000
SALES (est): 1.1MM **Privately Held**
WEB: www.wickers.com
SIC: 2322 2341 Underwear, men's & boys': made from purchased materials; women's & children's underwear

Conesus
Livingston County

(G-3708)
EAGLE CREST VINEYARD LLC
Also Called: O-Neh-Da Vineyard
7107 Vineyard Rd (14435-9521)
PHONE 585 346-5760
Sally Brown, *Manager*
Elizabeth Goldstone,
▲ EMP: 5

SQ FT: 20,000
SALES (est): 605.7K **Privately Held**
SIC: 2084 0172 Wines; grapes

Congers
Rockland County

(G-3709)
ANKA TOOL & DIE INC
150 Wells Ave (10920-2096)
PHONE 845 268-4116
Agnes Karl, *Corp Secy*
Anton Karl Jr, *Vice Pres*
Anthony Pisello, *Engineer*
Ingrid Capasso, *Office Mgr*
▲ EMP: 35 EST: 1970
SQ FT: 6,400
SALES (est): 5.8MM **Privately Held**
WEB: www.ankatool.com
SIC: 3544 3089 Special dies & tools; injection molding of plastics

(G-3710)
APTARGROUP INC
Also Called: Aptar Congers
250 N Route 303 (10920-1450)
PHONE 845 639-3700
Raymond Scheire, *Project Mgr*
Alex Theodorakis, *Branch Mgr*
Danielle Petrow, *Manager*
Paula Brunner, *Director*
Eric Arico, *Recruiter*
EMP: 150 **Publicly Held**
SIC: 3586 Measuring & dispensing pumps
PA: Aptargroup, Inc.
 475 W Terra Cotta Ave E
 Crystal Lake IL 60014

(G-3711)
BEAN KING INTERNATIONAL LLC
36 N Route 9w (10920-2459)
PHONE 845 268-3135
Faustino Larios, *Principal*
Jose Moreno, *Mng Member*
▲ EMP: 10
SALES: 4MM **Privately Held**
SIC: 3523 Driers (farm): grain, hay & seed

(G-3712)
BOURGHOL BROTHERS INC
73 Lake Rd (10920-2323)
P.O. Box 80 (10920-0080)
PHONE 845 268-9752
Charles Bourghol, *President*
Alexander Bourghol, *Treasurer*
EMP: 7
SQ FT: 1,200
SALES (est): 1.1MM **Privately Held**
WEB: www.bourgholbrosjewelers.com
SIC: 3911 5944 Jewelry, precious metal; jewelry, precious stones & precious metals

(G-3713)
CHARTWELL PHARMA NDA B2 HOLDIN
77 Brenner Dr (10920-1307)
PHONE 845 268-5000
Kimberly Ezdebski, *Vice Pres*
EMP: 5
SALES (est): 229.7K **Privately Held**
SIC: 2834 Tablets, pharmaceutical

(G-3714)
CHARTWELL PHARMACEUTICALS LLC
77 Brenner Dr (10920-1307)
PHONE 845 268-5000
David I Chipkin, *COO*
Francis Ezdebski, *Vice Pres*
EMP: 75
SALES (est): 18.2MM **Privately Held**
SIC: 2834 Pharmaceutical preparations

(G-3715)
CHARTWELL RX LLC
77 Brenner Dr (10920-1307)
PHONE 845 268-5000
Kimberly Ezdebski,
EMP: 40
SQ FT: 40,000

SALES (est): 3.3MM **Privately Held**
SIC: 2834 Pharmaceutical preparations

(G-3716)
F M GROUP INC
100 Wells Ave (10920-2042)
PHONE 845 589-0102
Josef Feldman, *President*
Solomon Feldman, *Marketing Staff*
EMP: 10
SALES (est): 1.7MM **Privately Held**
WEB: www.functionalmaterials.com
SIC: 2899 2865 Ink or writing fluids; dyes & pigments

(G-3717)
HUDSON VALLEY COATINGS LLC
175 N Route 9w Ste 12 (10920-1780)
PHONE 845 398-1778
Joseph Montana,
EMP: 5 EST: 2008
SALES (est): 396.2K **Privately Held**
SIC: 3479 Coating of metals with plastic or resins

(G-3718)
INDUS PRECISION MANUFACTURING
50 N Harrison Ave Ste 9 (10920-1952)
PHONE 845 268-0782
Shylamma Mathew, *Chairman*
Abraham Mathew, *Vice Pres*
Manju Mathew, *Sales Staff*
EMP: 14
SALES: 450K **Privately Held**
SIC: 3599 Machine shop, jobbing & repair

(G-3719)
LINDEN COOKIES INC
25 Brenner Dr (10920-1307)
PHONE 845 268-5050
Paul L Sturz, *President*
C Ronald Sturz, *Vice Pres*
EMP: 50 EST: 1960
SQ FT: 33,000
SALES (est): 10.1MM **Privately Held**
WEB: www.lindencookies.com
SIC: 2052 Cookies

(G-3720)
STAR KAY WHITE INC (PA)
151 Wells Ave (10920-1398)
PHONE 845 268-2600
Walter Katzenstein, *Principal*
Benjamin Katzenstein, *Vice Pres*
James Katzenstein, *Treasurer*
Paul Casino, *Director*
◆ EMP: 65 EST: 1890
SQ FT: 45,000
SALES (est): 14.3MM **Privately Held**
WEB: www.starkaywhite.com
SIC: 2087 Flavoring extracts & syrups

(G-3721)
VALOIS OF AMERICA INC
250 N Route 303 (10920-1450)
PHONE 845 639-3700
Alex Thoedorakis, *President*
Carl Lund, *Opers Staff*
Pamela Moran, *Sales Staff*
▲ EMP: 150
SQ FT: 3,500
SALES (est): 19.4MM **Publicly Held**
WEB: www.aptargroup.com
SIC: 3586 Measuring & dispensing pumps
PA: Aptargroup, Inc.
 475 W Terra Cotta Ave E
 Crystal Lake IL 60014

(G-3722)
VITANE PHARMACEUTICALS INC
125 Wells Ave (10920-2036)
PHONE 845 267-6700
Mohammed Hassan, *CEO*
Ezz Hamza, *President*
◆ EMP: 24
SQ FT: 15,000
SALES: 7.4MM **Privately Held**
SIC: 2834 Pharmaceutical preparations

(G-3723)
WYNN STARR FLAVORS INC (PA)
225 N Route 303 Ste 109 (10920-3001)
PHONE 845 584-3080
Steven B Zavagli, *Chairman*
Harold Alberts, *Director*
Earl J Gilmartin Jr, *Director*
Wesley Delaney, *Admin Sec*
Dorothy Zavagli, *Admin Sec*
EMP: 80
SQ FT: 12,000
SALES (est): 10.2MM **Privately Held**
WEB: www.wynnstarr.com
SIC: 2087 Beverage bases

Conklin
Broome County

(G-3724)
ARDAGH METAL PACKAGING USA INC
379 Broome Corporate Pkwy (13748-1513)
PHONE 607 584-3300
Steven Walker, *Manager*
EMP: 126 **Privately Held**
SIC: 3411 Metal cans
HQ: Ardagh Metal Packaging Usa Inc.
 600 N Bell Ave
 Carnegie PA 15106

(G-3725)
CBA GROUP LLC
33 Broome Corporate Pkwy (13748-1510)
P.O. Box 825, Binghamton (13902-0825)
PHONE 607 779-7522
Jeroen Schmits, *President*
Patrick J Gillard, *President*
Koen A Gieskes, *Vice Pres*
EMP: 1000
SALES (est): 4.7MM
SALES (corp-wide): 1.7B **Privately Held**
SIC: 3559 Electronic component making machinery
HQ: Francisco Partners, L.P.
 1 Letterman Dr Bldg C
 San Francisco CA 94129
 415 418-2900

(G-3726)
DOLMEN
216 Broome Corporate Pkwy (13748-1506)
PHONE 912 596-1537
Steve Hanratty, *Principal*
EMP: 10
SALES (est): 400K **Privately Held**
SIC: 3999 Manufacturing industries

(G-3727)
E-SYSTEMS GROUP LLC (HQ)
Also Called: SMC
100 Progress Pkwy (13748-1320)
PHONE 607 775-1100
Michael David, *General Mgr*
Karen Greene, *Sales Staff*
Harry Dradley, *Mng Member*
Frans De Coster, *Manager*
Christopher Larocca, *Senior Mgr*
▲ EMP: 26 EST: 1952
SQ FT: 30,000
SALES (est): 6.1MM
SALES (corp-wide): 48.4MM **Privately Held**
WEB: www.smcplus.com
SIC: 2521 2522 5045 3571 Wood office furniture; office furniture, except wood; computers, peripherals & software; computer peripheral equipment; electronic computers; partitions & fixtures, except wood
PA: Engineered Data Products Holdings, Llc
 6800 W 117th Ave
 Broomfield CO 80020
 303 465-2800

(G-3728)
INTERNATIONAL PAPER COMPANY
1240 Conklin Rd (13748-1407)
PHONE 607 775-1550
Don Bonualas, *Engineer*
David Davenport, *Sls & Mktg Exec*

Edward Badyna, *Manager*
EMP: 150
SALES (corp-wide): 21.7B **Publicly Held**
SIC: 2653 2656 2631 2611 Boxes, corrugated: made from purchased materials; food containers (liquid tight), including milk cartons; cartons, milk: made from purchased material; container, packaging & boxboard; container board; packaging board; pulp mills; printing paper
PA: International Paper Company
6400 Poplar Ave
Memphis TN 38197
901 419-9000

(G-3729)
IRVING WOODLANDS LLC
53 Shaw Rd (13748)
PHONE...................607 723-4862
Michael Senneway, *General Mgr*
EMP: 28
SQ FT: 63,350
SALES (corp-wide): 1.3B **Privately Held**
WEB: www.jdirving.com
SIC: 3441 Fabricated structural metal
HQ: Irving Woodlands Llc
1798 St John Rd
St John Plt ME 04743
207 834-5767

(G-3730)
NEWSPAPER PUBLISHER LLC
Also Called: Independent Baptist Voice
1035 Conklin Rd (13748-1102)
P.O. Box 208 (13748-0208)
PHONE...................607 775-0472
Don Einstein, *President*
EMP: 10
SQ FT: 15,000
SALES (est): 540.1K **Privately Held**
WEB: www.automarketpaper.com
SIC: 2711 2791 7011 Newspapers: publishing only, not printed on site; typesetting; bed & breakfast inn

(G-3731)
PERFORATED SCREEN SURFACES
216 Broome Corporate Pkwy (13748-1506)
PHONE...................866 866-8690
Davis Fleming, *President*
EMP: 20
SALES (est): 3.2MM **Privately Held**
◆ **SIC: 3443** Perforating on heavy metal

(G-3732)
S & T KNITTING CO INC (PA)
Also Called: Derby Fashion Center
1010 Conklin Rd (13748-1004)
P.O. Box 1512, Binghamton (13902-1512)
PHONE...................607 722-7558
Richard Horner, *President*
Bridgette Harvey, *Admin Sec*
EMP: 27 **EST:** 1958
SQ FT: 65,000
SALES (est): 1.9MM **Privately Held**
SIC: 2253 5651 Sweaters & sweater coats, knit; family clothing stores

(G-3733)
SAMSCREEN INC
216 Broome Corporate Pkwy (13748-1506)
PHONE...................607 722-3979
Fintan D Fleming, *CEO*
Bill McMahon, *Plant Mgr*
Roland Ryan, *Mfg Staff*
William McMahon, *Research*
Eileen Fleming, *Admin Sec*
▼ **EMP:** 28
SQ FT: 30,000
SALES (est): 7.3MM **Privately Held**
WEB: www.samscreen.com
SIC: 3429 Piano hardware

(G-3734)
TIN INC
1240 Conklin Rd (13748-1407)
PHONE...................607 775-1550
Edward Badyna, *Manager*
EMP: 88
SALES (corp-wide): 21.7B **Publicly Held**
WEB: www.tin.com
SIC: 2653 Boxes, corrugated: made from purchased materials

HQ: Tin Inc.
6400 Poplar Ave
Memphis TN 38197

(G-3735)
TOOLROOM EXPRESS INC
Also Called: Four Square Tool
1010 Conklin Rd (13748-1004)
PHONE...................607 723-5373
Richard Haddock, *President*
Michelle Gordon, *Office Mgr*
Shelly Haddock, *Manager*
▲ **EMP:** 55
SQ FT: 20,000
SALES (est): 11.2MM **Privately Held**
WEB: www.toolroomexpress.com
SIC: 3089 3599 Injection molding of plastics; machine shop, jobbing & repair

(G-3736)
UI ACQUISITION HOLDING CO (PA)
33 Broome Corporate Pkwy (13748-1510)
PHONE...................607 779-7522
Jean-Luc Pelissier, *President*
Keith O'Leary, *Vice Pres*
EMP: 2
SALES (est): 143.3MM **Privately Held**
SIC: 3559 Electronic component making machinery

(G-3737)
UI HOLDING COMPANY (HQ)
33 Broome Corporate Pkwy (13748-1510)
PHONE...................607 779-7522
Jeroen Schmits, *President*
Koen A Gieskes, *Vice Pres*
Patrick J Gillard, *CFO*
EMP: 3
SALES (est): 143.3MM **Privately Held**
SIC: 3559 Electronic component making machinery

(G-3738)
UNIVERSAL INSTRUMENTS CORP (DH)
33 Broome Corporate Pkwy (13748-1510)
PHONE...................800 842-9732
Jean-Luc Pelissier, *CEO*
Lynn Tilton, *CEO*
Keith O'Leary, *CFO*
Lisa D'Angelo, *Treasurer*
◆ **EMP:** 200
SALES (est): 127.2MM **Privately Held**
WEB: www3.uic.com
SIC: 3559 Electronic component making machinery

Constantia
Oswego County

(G-3739)
BRIDGEPORT METALCRAFT INC
567 County Route 23 (13044-2737)
P.O. Box 470 (13044-0470)
PHONE...................315 623-9597
Donald Deitz Jr, *President*
Cristy Deitz, *Vice Pres*
EMP: 5 **EST:** 1965
SQ FT: 5,000
SALES (est): 550K **Privately Held**
WEB: www.bridgeportmetalcraft.com
SIC: 3469 Spinning metal for the trade

(G-3740)
MICHAEL P MMARR
Also Called: Mike's Custom Cabinets
1358 State Route 49 (13044-2769)
P.O. Box 91 (13044-0091)
PHONE...................315 623-9380
Michael Marr, *Owner*
Michael P Marr, *Owner*
EMP: 9
SALES: 325K **Privately Held**
SIC: 2434 5211 2541 Wood kitchen cabinets; cabinets, kitchen; wood partitions & fixtures

(G-3741)
UNITED WIRE TECHNOLOGIES INC
1804 State Route 49 (13044-2604)
P.O. Box 502, Cleveland (13042-0502)
PHONE...................315 623-7203
James E Ransom, *Ch of Bd*
Paul Coates, *President*
Donald Ransom, *Vice Pres*
Michael Ransom, *CFO*
▲ **EMP:** 15
SQ FT: 17,000
SALES (est): 2.6MM **Privately Held**
SIC: 3357 Nonferrous wiredrawing & insulating

Cooperstown
Otsego County

(G-3742)
BREWERY OMMEGANG LTD
656 County Highway 33 (13326-4737)
PHONE...................607 286-4144
Simon Thorpe, *President*
Tara Aitchison, *COO*
Sean Bolger, *Store Mgr*
Bobbie Boehler, *QC Mgr*
Rick Debar, *Technical Mgr*
▲ **EMP:** 30
SQ FT: 35,000
SALES (est): 6.6MM **Privately Held**
WEB: www.ommegang.com
SIC: 2082 Beer (alcoholic beverage)

(G-3743)
COOPERSTOWN BAT COMPANY INC
118 Main St (13326-1225)
P.O. Box 415 (13326-0415)
PHONE...................607 547-2415
Timothy Haney, *President*
Sharon Oberriter, *President*
Don Oberriter, *Vice Pres*
EMP: 15
SQ FT: 4,000
SALES: 1.6MM **Privately Held**
WEB: www.cooperstownbat.com
SIC: 3949 Baseball equipment & supplies, general

(G-3744)
DUVEL MORTGAGE USA INC
656 County Highway 33 (13326-4737)
PHONE...................607 267-6121
Tom Gardner, *Executive*
EMP: 5
SALES (est): 238.4K **Privately Held**
SIC: 2082 Malt beverages

(G-3745)
VANBERG & DEWULF CO INC
52 Pioneer St Ste 4 (13326-1231)
PHONE...................607 547-8184
Don Feinberg, *Principal*
▲ **EMP:** 6
SALES (est): 399.9K **Privately Held**
SIC: 2082 Beer (alcoholic beverage)

Copake
Columbia County

(G-3746)
HIGH VOLTAGE INC
31 County Route 7a (12516-1214)
PHONE...................518 329-3275
Stephen S Peschel, *Ch of Bd*
Michael Peschel, *Chairman*
James Grayson, *Vice Pres*
EMP: 37
SQ FT: 23,760
SALES: 10MM **Privately Held**
WEB: www.hvinc.com
SIC: 3826 Analytical instruments

Copiague
Suffolk County

(G-3747)
ACTAVIS LABORATORIES NY INC
33 Ralph Ave (11726-1532)
PHONE...................631 693-8000
Brenton Saunders, *CEO*
EMP: 80
SALES (est): 8.5MM **Privately Held**
SIC: 2834 Druggists' preparations (pharmaceuticals)
HQ: Allergan Finance, Llc
400 Interpace Pkwy
Parsippany NJ 07054
862 261-7000

(G-3748)
ACTION MACHINED PRODUCTS INC
1355 Bangor St (11726-2911)
PHONE...................631 842-2333
Edward G Korndoerfer, *President*
EMP: 13
SQ FT: 8,750
SALES (est): 2.3MM **Privately Held**
SIC: 3451 Screw machine products

(G-3749)
AJES PHARMACEUTICALS LLC
11a Lincoln St (11726-1530)
PHONE...................631 608-1728
Asha Patel,
Jatendra Patel,
▼ **EMP:** 20
SQ FT: 25,000
SALES (est): 4.1MM **Privately Held**
SIC: 2833 5499 Vitamins, natural or synthetic: bulk, uncompounded; health & dietetic food stores

(G-3750)
ARCHITECTURAL FIBERGLASS CORP
1395 Marconi Blvd (11726-2814)
P.O. Box 116 (11726-0116)
PHONE...................631 842-4772
Charles Wittman, *President*
EMP: 22
SALES (est): 2.1MM **Privately Held**
WEB: www.afcornice.com
SIC: 2295 5999 Varnished glass & coated fiberglass fabrics; fiberglass materials, except insulation

(G-3751)
ARGENCORD MACHINE CORP INC
10 Reith St (11726-1414)
PHONE...................631 842-8990
Emilio Benenati, *Ch of Bd*
Gustavo Sanchez, *COO*
Steven Peltier, *CFO*
EMP: 7 **EST:** 1967
SQ FT: 10,000
SALES: 300K **Privately Held**
SIC: 3599 Machine shop, jobbing & repair

(G-3752)
ART PRECISION METAL PRODUCTS
1465 S Strong Ave (11726-3253)
PHONE...................631 842-8889
Steven Triola, *President*
EMP: 10
SQ FT: 13,500
SALES (est): 1.8MM **Privately Held**
SIC: 3599 3469 3444 3544 Machine shop, jobbing & repair; spinning metal for the trade; sheet metalwork; special dies & tools

(G-3753)
ASTRA PRODUCTS INC
6 Bethpage Rd (11726-1413)
P.O. Box 479, Baldwin (11510-0479)
PHONE...................631 464-4747
Mark Bogin, *President*
Jeffrey Bogin, *Vice Pres*
▲ **EMP:** 6
SQ FT: 4,000

GEOGRAPHIC SECTION

Copiague - Suffolk County (G-3785)

SALES: 3MM **Privately Held**
SIC: 3081 5162 Plastic film & sheet; plastics sheets & rods

(G-3754)
BALDWIN MACHINE WORKS INC
20 Grant Ave 2040 (11726-3817)
PHONE.................................631 842-9110
Kenneth Roblin, *President*
▲ EMP: 6
SQ FT: 6,000
SALES (est): 758.2K **Privately Held**
SIC: 3541 3545 Drill presses; machine tool accessories; drills (machine tool accessories); drilling machine attachments & accessories

(G-3755)
CHIVVIS ENTERPRISES INC
10 Grant St (11726-1504)
PHONE.................................631 842-9055
Floyd G Chivvis, *President*
Douglas J Chivvis, *Treasurer*
EMP: 10
SQ FT: 10,000
SALES (est): 2MM **Privately Held**
WEB: www.chivvisent.com
SIC: 3469 Metal stampings

(G-3756)
D & C CLEANING INC
1095 Campagnoli Ave (11726-2309)
PHONE.................................631 789-5659
Joan Estrella, *President*
EMP: 12
SALES (est): 763.6K **Privately Held**
SIC: 3635 Mfg Home Vacuum Cleaners

(G-3757)
ELWOOD INTERNATIONAL INC
Also Called: Elwood, William J
89 Hudson St (11726-1505)
P.O. Box 180 (11726-0180)
PHONE.................................631 842-6600
Stuart Roll, *Ch of Bd*
Richard Roll, *President*
EMP: 18
SQ FT: 37,000
SALES (est): 4.4MM **Privately Held**
WEB: www.elwoodintl.com
SIC: 2035 Seasonings & sauces, except tomato & dry

(G-3758)
ENGINEERED METAL PRODUCTS INC
10 Reith St (11726-1414)
PHONE.................................631 842-3780
Gustavo Sanchez, *President*
EMP: 9
SALES (est): 549.3K **Privately Held**
SIC: 3728 Aircraft assemblies, subassemblies & parts

(G-3759)
GABILA & SONS MFG INC
Also Called: Gabila's Knishes
100 Wartburg Ave (11726-2919)
PHONE.................................631 789-2220
Elliott Gabay, *President*
Sophie Levy, *Chairman*
EMP: 50 EST: 1921
SQ FT: 20,000
SALES (est): 7.4MM **Privately Held**
SIC: 2051 Bakery: wholesale or wholesale/retail combined; knishes, except frozen

(G-3760)
GABILA FOOD PRODUCTS INC
100 Wartburg Ave (11726-2919)
PHONE.................................631 789-2220
Elliot Gabay, *President*
EMP: 50
SALES: 7MM **Privately Held**
SIC: 2043 Cereal breakfast foods

(G-3761)
H & M LEASING CORP
1245 Marconi Blvd (11726-2815)
PHONE.................................631 225-5246
Mark Field, *President*
Marc B Field, *President*
EMP: 6
SALES (est): 670K **Privately Held**
SIC: 3444 Bins, prefabricated sheet metal

(G-3762)
HARBOR WLDG & FABRICATION CORP
30 Railroad Ave (11726-2708)
PHONE.................................631 667-1880
Joseph Awing, *President*
EMP: 11
SALES: 1.8MM **Privately Held**
SIC: 3449 Bars, concrete reinforcing: fabricated steel

(G-3763)
HERMANN GERDENS INC
1725 N Strongs Rd (11726-2926)
PHONE.................................631 841-3132
Joseph Gerdens, *President*
EMP: 6 EST: 1987
SALES (est): 735.1K **Privately Held**
SIC: 3444 Sheet metalwork

(G-3764)
HOLLYWOOD ADVERTISING BANNERS
Also Called: Hollywood Banners
539 Oak St (11726-3215)
PHONE.................................631 842-3000
Timothy Cox, *President*
EMP: 24
SALES (est): 1.3MM **Privately Held**
SIC: 2396 Fabric printing & stamping

(G-3765)
HOLLYWOOD BANNERS INC
539 Oak St (11726-3261)
PHONE.................................631 842-3000
Daniel F Mahoney, *Ch of Bd*
Mike Hartman, *Sales Staff*
Christopher O'Shea, *Sales Staff*
Tony Connelli, *Graphic Designe*
EMP: 30
SQ FT: 22,000
SALES (est): 3.6MM **Privately Held**
WEB: www.hollywoodbanners.com
SIC: 2399 Banners, made from fabric

(G-3766)
JAF CONVERTERS INC
60 Marconi Blvd (11726-2098)
PHONE.................................631 842-3131
John Flandina, *CEO*
Emily Flandina, *Admin Sec*
▲ EMP: 45
SQ FT: 10,000
SALES (est): 5.9MM **Privately Held**
WEB: www.jafstamp.com
SIC: 3993 Signs & advertising specialties

(G-3767)
LONG ISLAND TOOL & DIE INC
1445 S Strong Ave (11726-3227)
PHONE.................................631 225-0600
Richard Cohen, *Principal*
EMP: 5
SALES (est): 396.8K **Privately Held**
SIC: 3544 Special dies & tools

(G-3768)
MALISA BRANKO INC
95 Garfield Ave (11726-3222)
PHONE.................................631 225-9741
Branko Malisa, *President*
Regina Malisa, *Treasurer*
EMP: 12
SQ FT: 5,600
SALES (est): 1.3MM **Privately Held**
SIC: 3599 Machine shop, jobbing & repair

(G-3769)
MARK - 10 CORPORATION
11 Dixon Ave (11726-1902)
PHONE.................................631 842-9200
William Fridman, *President*
EMP: 20
SQ FT: 12,000
SALES (est): 5.2MM **Privately Held**
WEB: www.mark-10.com
SIC: 3823 5084 8731 Electrolytic conductivity instruments, industrial process; industrial process control instruments; industrial machinery & equipment; electronic research

(G-3770)
NELL-JOY INDUSTRIES INC (PA)
8 Reith St Ste 10 (11726-1414)
PHONE.................................631 842-8989
Emilio L Benenati, *CEO*
Steven Peltier, *President*
Regina Booker, *General Mgr*
Stephen Manz, *QC Mgr*
Melissa Gavin, *Controller*
EMP: 32
SQ FT: 35,000
SALES (est): 3.4MM **Privately Held**
SIC: 3724 5088 Aircraft engines & engine parts; aircraft & space vehicle supplies & parts; aeronautical equipment & supplies

(G-3771)
NORTH EAST FINISHING CO INC
Also Called: Nefco
245 Ralph Ave (11726-1514)
PHONE.................................631 789-8000
Bill Dechirico, *President*
Donna Ward, *Corp Secy*
Joseph Ricchetti, *Vice Pres*
EMP: 11
SQ FT: 7,500
SALES (est): 1.2MM **Privately Held**
SIC: 3471 Finishing, metals or formed products

(G-3772)
PIPER PLASTICS CORP
102 Ralph Ave (11726-1510)
PHONE.................................631 842-6889
Andrew Weiss, *President*
Charles Weiss, *Vice Pres*
EMP: 29 EST: 1963
SQ FT: 16,000
SALES (est): 5.4MM **Privately Held**
WEB: www.piper-plastics.com
SIC: 3089 3479 Molding primary plastic; coating of metals with plastic or resins

(G-3773)
PIPER PLASTICS CORP
105 Ralph Ave (11726-1511)
PHONE.................................631 842-6889
Andrew Weiss, *President*
EMP: 6
SALES (est): 375.4K **Privately Held**
SIC: 3089 Molding primary plastic

(G-3774)
PRECISION ELECTRONICS INC
1 Di Tomas Ct (11726-1943)
PHONE.................................631 842-4900
Dominick Scaringella, *President*
Joseph Corrigan, *Vice Pres*
Joseph A Whalen Jr, *Treasurer*
Rita Scaringella, *Admin Sec*
EMP: 15 EST: 1955
SQ FT: 13,000
SALES: 3.5MM **Privately Held**
WEB: www.precisionelect.com
SIC: 3677 3625 3612 Coil windings, electronic; electronic transformers; relays, for electronic use; voltage regulators, transmission & distribution

(G-3775)
PROTOFAST HOLDING CORP
182 N Oak St (11726-1223)
PHONE.................................631 753-2549
Marco Gil, *President*
EMP: 6
SQ FT: 5,600
SALES (est): 700K **Privately Held**
SIC: 3444 Sheet metalwork

(G-3776)
QUALITY CANDLE MFG CO INC
121 Cedar St (11726-1201)
PHONE.................................631 842-8475
Joseph Arnone, *President*
EMP: 10 EST: 1955
SQ FT: 6,000
SALES (est): 870K **Privately Held**
WEB: www.qualitycandlecompany.com
SIC: 3999 Candles

(G-3777)
REESE MANUFACTURING INC
16 Reith St (11726-1414)
PHONE.................................631 842-3780
Emilio Benenati, *President*
Terri Martin, *Vice Pres*
EMP: 8
SALES (est): 367.8K **Privately Held**
SIC: 3728 Aircraft body assemblies & parts

(G-3778)
RMW FILTRATION PRODUCTS CO LLC
230 Lambert Ave (11726-3207)
P.O. Box 573, Lindenhurst (11757-0573)
PHONE.................................631 226-9412
EMP: 3
SQ FT: 4,000
SALES: 2MM **Privately Held**
SIC: 3599 Custom Machine Shop

(G-3779)
SCAN-A-CHROME COLOR INC
555 Oak St (11726-3215)
PHONE.................................631 532-6146
Brian Geiger, *President*
EMP: 5
SALES (est): 697.5K **Privately Held**
SIC: 2759 7336 7389 Commercial printing; commercial art & graphic design;

(G-3780)
SEAL REINFORCED FIBERGLASS INC (PA)
19 Bethpage Rd (11726-1421)
PHONE.................................631 842-2230
Patrick Kaler, *President*
Kevin Kaler, *Vice Pres*
Timothy Kaler, *Shareholder*
Helen Kaler, *Admin Sec*
Laura Kaler, *Admin Asst*
EMP: 28 EST: 1961
SQ FT: 20,000
SALES: 3MM **Privately Held**
WEB: www.sealfiberglass.com
SIC: 3089 Molding primary plastic; plastic processing

(G-3781)
SEAL REINFORCED FIBERGLASS INC
23 Bethpage Rd (11726-1421)
PHONE.................................631 842-2230
Thomas Kaler, *Branch Mgr*
EMP: 9
SQ FT: 11,000
SALES (corp-wide): 3MM **Privately Held**
WEB: www.sealfiberglass.com
SIC: 3089 Molding primary plastic
PA: Seal Reinforced Fiberglass, Inc.
  19 Bethpage Rd
  Copiague NY 11726
  631 842-2230

(G-3782)
SIGN SHOP INC
1272 Montauk Hwy Ste A (11726-4908)
PHONE.................................631 226-4145
John Prete, *President*
Bill Prete, *Vice Pres*
EMP: 6
SQ FT: 6,500
SALES: 500K **Privately Held**
WEB: www.thesignshopinc.com
SIC: 2759 7389 2752 Screen printing; lettering & sign painting services; commercial printing, lithographic

(G-3783)
STEEL CRAFT ROLLING DOOR
5 Di Tomas Ct (11726-1943)
PHONE.................................631 608-8662
Joan Palmieri, *General Mgr*
EMP: 10
SALES (est): 1.3MM **Privately Held**
SIC: 3325 Steel foundries

(G-3784)
SUNRISE DOOR SOLUTIONS
Also Called: Sunrise Installation
1215 Sunrise Hwy (11726-1405)
PHONE.................................631 464-4139
EMP: 5
SALES (est): 466.7K **Privately Held**
SIC: 3442 Mfg Metal Doors/Sash/Trim

(G-3785)
SWISS TOOL CORPORATION
100 Court St (11726-1287)
PHONE.................................631 842-7766
Anton Croenlein, *President*

Copiague - Suffolk County (G-3786)

Anna Croenlein, *Corp Secy*
EMP: 40
SQ FT: 20,000
SALES (est): 7.5MM **Privately Held**
WEB: www.swisstoolcorp.com
SIC: 3354 Aluminum extruded products

(G-3786)
TATRA MFG CORPORATION
30 Railroad Ave (11726-2717)
PHONE 631 691-1184
Joseph Tyminski, *President*
Lana Tyminski, *Corp Secy*
EMP: 15
SQ FT: 10,000
SALES (est): 2.5MM **Privately Held**
SIC: 3444 Sheet metalwork

(G-3787)
TII INDUSTRIES INC
1385 Akron St (11726-2932)
PHONE 631 789-5000
T Roach, *Principal*
Walter R Fay, *Vice Pres*
Gerald Smith, *QC Dir*
Jaclyn Porter, *Accounting Mgr*
Maribel Rivera, *Sales Associate*
EMP: 11 **EST:** 2013
SALES (est): 803.9K **Privately Held**
SIC: 3999 Manufacturing industries

(G-3788)
TOBAY PRINTING CO INC
1361 Marconi Blvd (11726-2898)
PHONE 631 842-3300
Robert Rogers, *President*
Jean Rogers, *Vice Pres*
Chuck Williams, *Sales Executive*
EMP: 40
SALES (est): 6.1MM **Privately Held**
WEB: www.tobayprinting.com
SIC: 2732 2752 2796 2791 Book printing; commercial printing, lithographic; platemaking services; typesetting; bookbinding & related work

(G-3789)
TRIL INC
320 Pioxi St (11726-2132)
PHONE 631 645-7989
Sushe Zhang, *Principal*
Xiaoling Wang, *Vice Pres*
EMP: 9
SALES (est): 651.2K **Privately Held**
SIC: 3841 Surgical & medical instruments

(G-3790)
VALLE SIGNS AND AWNINGS
55 Decker St (11726-1401)
PHONE 516 408-3440
Oscar Valle, *Owner*
Neal McLendon, *Officer*
EMP: 10
SALES (est): 1.1MM **Privately Held**
SIC: 3993 Electric signs

(G-3791)
VIBRATION ELIMINATOR CO INC (PA)
15 Dixon Ave (11726-1902)
PHONE 631 841-4000
Stuart Levy, *President*
Don Warick Jr, *Vice Pres*
▲ **EMP:** 41 **EST:** 1933
SQ FT: 13,000
SALES (est): 6.3MM **Privately Held**
WEB: www.veco-ny.com
SIC: 3625 Noise control equipment

(G-3792)
VIN MAR PRECISION METALS INC
1465 S Strong Ave (11726-3210)
PHONE 631 563-6608
Catherine Leo, *President*
Anthony Leo, *Vice Pres*
EMP: 15
SQ FT: 6,000
SALES (est): 2.5MM **Privately Held**
WEB: www.vin-mar.com
SIC: 3444 Sheet metal specialties, not stamped

(G-3793)
W A BAUM CO INC
620 Oak St (11726-3217)
P.O. Box 209 (11726-0209)
PHONE 631 226-3940
William A Baum Jr, *Ch of Bd*
John C Baum Sr, *President*
James M Baum, *Vice Pres*
Michael Hayes, *Vice Pres*
Margaret Faber, *Export Mgr*
▲ **EMP:** 80 **EST:** 1916
SQ FT: 31,000
SALES (est): 11.7MM **Privately Held**
WEB: www.wabaum.com
SIC: 3841 Blood pressure apparatus

(G-3794)
WORLDWIDE ARNTCAL CMPNENTS INC (PA)
10 Reith St (11726-1414)
PHONE 631 842-3780
Steven Peltier, *President*
Carol Peltier, *Treasurer*
▼ **EMP:** 25 **EST:** 1965
SQ FT: 10,000
SALES: 4MM **Privately Held**
WEB: www.aeronauticalcomponents.com
SIC: 3812 5088 Search & navigation equipment; aircraft equipment & supplies

(G-3795)
WORLDWIDE ARNTCAL CMPNENTS INC
Also Called: Beryllium Manufacturing
10 Reith St (11726-1414)
P.O. Box 407, Lindenhurst (11757-0407)
PHONE 631 842-3780
Steve Paltier, *CFO*
EMP: 6
SALES (corp-wide): 4MM **Privately Held**
WEB: www.aeronauticalcomponents.com
SIC: 3812 5088 Search & navigation equipment; transportation equipment & supplies
PA: Worldwide Aeronautical Components Inc.
10 Reith St
Copiague NY 11726
631 842-3780

Coram
Suffolk County

(G-3796)
BAYSHORE WIRE PRODUCTS CORP
480 Mill Rd (11727-4108)
PHONE 631 451-8825
Socratis Stavropoulos, *President*
EMP: 11
SQ FT: 11,000
SALES (est): 1.3MM **Privately Held**
SIC: 3496 Miscellaneous fabricated wire products

(G-3797)
G L 7 SALES PLUS LTD
Also Called: Land and Sea Trailer Shop
125 Middle Country Rd F (11727-4474)
PHONE 631 696-8290
George Applescott, *Owner*
EMP: 6
SALES (est): 532.2K **Privately Held**
SIC: 3715 Truck trailers

(G-3798)
HAMPTON TRANSPORT INC
3655 Route 112 (11727-4123)
PHONE 631 716-4445
Keith Lewin, *President*
EMP: 12 **EST:** 1993
SALES: 100K **Privately Held**
SIC: 2399 4119 Horse harnesses & riding crops, etc.: non-leather; local passenger transportation

(G-3799)
ISLAND INDUSTRIES CORP
480 Mill Rd (11727-4108)
PHONE 631 451-8825
Socratis Stavropoulos, *President*
▲ **EMP:** 7
SQ FT: 20,000
SALES (est): 1.3MM **Privately Held**
SIC: 3315 Wire & fabricated wire products

(G-3800)
NATURES VALUE INC (PA)
468 Mill Rd (11727-4108)
PHONE 631 846-2500
Oscar Ramjeet, *CEO*
Joe Kramer, *CFO*
▲ **EMP:** 300
SQ FT: 224,000
SALES (est): 82.3MM **Privately Held**
WEB: www.naturesvalue.com
SIC: 2834 Vitamin preparations

(G-3801)
NEW YORK FAN COIL LLC
7 Chesapeake Bay Rd (11727-2004)
PHONE 646 580-1344
Seth Rubin,
EMP: 8
SALES (est): 862.9K **Privately Held**
SIC: 3677 Electronic coils, transformers & other inductors

(G-3802)
NOTO INDUSTRIAL CORP
11 Thomas St (11727-3153)
PHONE 631 736-7600
John Noto, *President*
EMP: 8
SALES (est): 1MM **Privately Held**
SIC: 3535 Conveyors & conveying equipment

(G-3803)
PREMIUM MULCH & MATERIALS INC
482 Mill Rd (11727-4108)
PHONE 631 320-3666
Nicholas Sorge, *President*
EMP: 10
SALES (est): 91K **Privately Held**
SIC: 2499 Mulch or sawdust products, wood

(G-3804)
SHARONANA ENTERPRISES INC
52 Sharon Dr (11727-1923)
PHONE 631 875-5619
Orlando Vizcaino, *Principal*
EMP: 20
SALES: 1MM **Privately Held**
SIC: 2541 Store & office display cases & fixtures

(G-3805)
SUFFOLK INDUS RECOVERY CORP
Also Called: Pk Metals
3542 Route 112 (11727-4101)
PHONE 631 732-6403
Philip L Fava, *CEO*
Richard Smith, *Vice Pres*
Cathy Finn, *Payroll Mgr*
Mike Eberl, *Manager*
EMP: 65 **EST:** 1934
SALES (est): 14.7MM **Privately Held**
WEB: www.pkmetals.com
SIC: 2611 4212 Pulp mills, mechanical & recycling processing; garbage collection & transport, no disposal

Corfu
Genesee County

(G-3806)
DELAVAL INC
Also Called: Beck, Don
850 Main Rd (14036-9753)
PHONE 585 599-4696
Donald M Beck, *Branch Mgr*
John Donnelly, *Branch Mgr*
EMP: 18
SQ FT: 8,100
SALES (corp-wide): 7.5B **Privately Held**
WEB: www.donbeckinc.com
SIC: 3556 Milk processing machinery

HQ: Delaval Inc.
11100 N Congress Ave
Kansas City MO 64153
816 891-7700

(G-3807)
IDEAL BURIAL VAULT COMPANY
1166 Vision Pkwy (14036-9794)
PHONE 585 599-2242
George Tilley, *President*
Greg Tilley, *Vice Pres*
EMP: 8 **EST:** 1953
SQ FT: 4,500
SALES (est): 1.2MM **Privately Held**
SIC: 3272 Burial vaults, concrete or pre-cast terrazzo

Corinth
Saratoga County

(G-3808)
CURTIS/PALMER HYDROELECTRIC LP
15 Pine St (12822-1319)
PHONE 518 654-6297
David Liebetreu, *Plant Mgr*
EMP: 11
SALES (est): 1.6MM **Publicly Held**
SIC: 3629 Power conversion units, a.c. to d.c.: static-electric
PA: Atlantic Power Corporation
3 Allied Dr Ste 220
Dedham MA 02026

Corning
Steuben County

(G-3809)
CORNING INCORPORATED (PA)
1 Riverfront Plz (14831-0002)
PHONE 607 974-9000
Wendell P Weeks, *Ch of Bd*
James P Clappin, *Exec VP*
Clark S Kinlin, *Exec VP*
David L Morse, *Exec VP*
Eric S Musser, *Exec VP*
◆ **EMP:** 3014 **EST:** 1851
SALES: 10.1B **Publicly Held**
WEB: www.corning.com
SIC: 3229 3357 3661 3674 Glass fiber products; glass tubes & tubing; TV tube blanks, glass; fiber optic cable (insulated); telephone & telegraph apparatus; semiconductors & related devices

(G-3810)
CORNING INCORPORATED
Decker Bldg (14831-0001)
PHONE 607 974-9000
Jamie Houghton, *Branch Mgr*
EMP: 51
SALES (corp-wide): 10.1B **Publicly Held**
WEB: www.corning.com
SIC: 3229 Pressed & blown glass
PA: Corning Incorporated
1 Riverfront Plz
Corning NY 14831
607 974-9000

(G-3811)
CORNING INCORPORATED
1 Riverfront Plz (14831-0002)
PHONE 607 974-9000
Dick Jack, *General Mgr*
EMP: 45
SALES (corp-wide): 10.1B **Publicly Held**
WEB: www.corning.com
SIC: 3229 Pressed & blown glass
PA: Corning Incorporated
1 Riverfront Plz
Corning NY 14831
607 974-9000

(G-3812)
CORNING INCORPORATED
Hp-Ab-01-A9b (14831-0001)
PHONE 607 248-1200
Kirk Gregg, *Officer*
EMP: 48

GEOGRAPHIC SECTION

Cornwall - Orange County (G-3837)

SALES (corp-wide): 10.1B **Publicly Held**
SIC: 3229 3661 3674 3357 Glass fiber products; glass tubes & tubing; TV tube blanks, glass; telephone & telegraph apparatus; semiconductors & related devices; fiber optic cable (insulated)
PA: Corning Incorporated
    1 Riverfront Plz
    Corning NY 14831
    607 974-9000

(G-3813)
CORNING INCORPORATED
1 W Market St Ste 601 (14830-2673)
PHONE 607 974-4488
Olajuwon Ogunsanwo, *Electrical Engi*
John Holliday, *Branch Mgr*
EMP: 6
SALES (corp-wide): 10.1B **Publicly Held**
WEB: www.corning.com
SIC: 3229 Pressed & blown glass
PA: Corning Incorporated
    1 Riverfront Plz
    Corning NY 14831
    607 974-9000

(G-3814)
CORNING INCORPORATED
1 Museum Way (14830-2253)
PHONE 607 974-8496
Sean Keenan, *Engineer*
Rashid Rahman, *Engineer*
Pete Knott, *Manager*
Ryan Ehrhart, *Project Leader*
Eric Corrigan, *Supervisor*
EMP: 20
SQ FT: 7,500
SALES (corp-wide): 10.1B **Publicly Held**
WEB: www.corning.com
SIC: 3229 Pressed & blown glass
PA: Corning Incorporated
    1 Riverfront Plz
    Corning NY 14831
    607 974-9000

(G-3815)
CORNING INTERNATIONAL CORP (HQ)
1 Riverfront Plz (14831-0002)
PHONE 607 974-9000
Wendell P Weeks, *CEO*
John W Loose, *Ch of Bd*
James W Wheat, *President*
Kirk P Gregg, *Vice Pres*
Kenneth C KAO, *Vice Pres*
▼ EMP: 7
SQ FT: 15,000
SALES (est): 626.5MM
SALES (corp-wide): 10.1B **Publicly Held**
WEB: www.corningware.com
SIC: 3229 5945 Pressed & blown glass; ceramics supplies
PA: Corning Incorporated
    1 Riverfront Plz
    Corning NY 14831
    607 974-9000

(G-3816)
CORNING OPTCAL CMMNCATIONS LLC
22 W 3rd St (14830-3114)
P.O. Box 2306, Hickory NC (28603-2306)
PHONE 607 974-7543
Lin He, *Research*
Tony Tripeny, *Manager*
Kim Hamilton, *Manager*
EMP: 12
SALES (corp-wide): 10.1B **Publicly Held**
WEB: www.corningcablesystems.com
SIC: 3357 Communication wire
HQ: Corning Optical Communications Llc
    800 17th St Nw
    Hickory NC 28601
    828 901-5000

(G-3817)
CORNING SPECIALTY MTLS INC
1 Riverfront Plz (14831-0002)
PHONE 607 974-9000
Wendell P Weeks, *Ch of Bd*
EMP: 6

SALES (est): 2.1MM
SALES (corp-wide): 10.1B **Publicly Held**
SIC: 3357 3229 3674 Fiber optic cable (insulated); glass fiber products; glass tubes & tubing; TV tube blanks, glass; semiconductors & related devices
PA: Corning Incorporated
    1 Riverfront Plz
    Corning NY 14831
    607 974-9000

(G-3818)
CORNING VITRO CORPORATION
Also Called: Corning Consumer Products Co
1 Riverfront Plz (14830-2556)
PHONE 607 974-8605
Peter Campanella, *President*
John W Loose, *President*
Hayward R Gipson, *Senior VP*
Thomas E Blumer, *Vice Pres*
Dawn M Cross, *Vice Pres*
◆ EMP: 4593
SALES (est): 228.8MM
SALES (corp-wide): 10.1B **Publicly Held**
WEB: www.corning.com
SIC: 3229 3469 Pressed & blown glass; household cooking & kitchen utensils, metal
PA: Corning Incorporated
    1 Riverfront Plz
    Corning NY 14831
    607 974-9000

(G-3819)
GATEHOUSE MEDIA LLC
Also Called: Leader, The
34 W Pulteney St (14830-2211)
P.O. Box 1017 (14830-0817)
PHONE 607 936-4651
Denny Bruen, *Principal*
Becky Jenkins, *Bookkeeper*
Heather Falkey, *Manager*
Breenna Hilton, *Manager*
EMP: 85
SALES (corp-wide): 1.3B **Publicly Held**
WEB: www.the-leader.com
SIC: 2711 Newspapers, publishing & printing
HQ: Gatehouse Media, Llc
    175 Sullys Trl Ste 300
    Pittsford NY 14534
    585 598-0030

(G-3820)
HERFF JONES LLC
262 W 2nd St (14830-2438)
PHONE 607 936-2366
Virginia Caumlake, *Manager*
EMP: 25
SALES (corp-wide): 1.1B **Privately Held**
WEB: www.herffjones.com
SIC: 2741 Yearbooks: publishing & printing
HQ: Herff Jones, Llc
    4501 W 62nd St
    Indianapolis IN 46268
    800 419-5462

(G-3821)
KABRICS
2737 Forest Hill Dr (14830-3690)
PHONE 607 962-6344
Kathy Wilson, *Owner*
EMP: 8
SALES (est): 300K **Privately Held**
SIC: 2395 Embroidery & art needlework

(G-3822)
MULTIMEDIA SERVICES INC
11136 River Rd 40 (14830-9324)
PHONE 607 936-3186
Richard Bartholomew, *President*
Daniel Flatt, *Vice Pres*
Rose Flatt, *Vice Pres*
Belinda Wilcox, *VP Finance*
Rick Bartholomew, *Human Res Mgr*
EMP: 21
SQ FT: 13,000
SALES (est): 4.8MM **Privately Held**
SIC: 2752 Commercial printing, offset

(G-3823)
PANELOGIC INC
366 Baker Street Ext (14830-1639)
PHONE 607 962-6319
George Welch, *CEO*
Douglas Brown, *President*

EMP: 32
SQ FT: 14,500
SALES (est): 8.1MM **Privately Held**
WEB: www.panelogic.com
SIC: 3625 Electric controls & control accessories, industrial

(G-3824)
RISING SONS 6 BREWING COINC
196 Baker St (14830-2074)
P.O. Box 1064 (14830-0864)
PHONE 607 368-4836
Nadia Mauer, *Principal*
Mark Mauer, *Principal*
EMP: 5
SQ FT: 5,400
SALES (est): 271.7K **Privately Held**
SIC: 2082 Ale (alcoholic beverage)

(G-3825)
RYERS CREEK CORP
Also Called: Mill, The
1330 Mill Dr (14830-9020)
PHONE 607 523-6617
Graham Howard, *Manager*
EMP: 20
SQ FT: 7,500
SALES (est): 2.2MM **Privately Held**
WEB: www.gotothemill.com
SIC: 2499 3999 Novelties, wood fiber; tobacco pipes, pipestems & bits

(G-3826)
STORFLEX HOLDINGS INC
Also Called: Storflex Fixture
392 Pulteney St (14830-2134)
PHONE 607 962-2137
Timothy Purdie, *Ch of Bd*
Connie Santell, *Treasurer*
EMP: 152
SQ FT: 160,000
SALES (est): 41.3MM **Privately Held**
WEB: www.storflex.com
SIC: 2542 Partitions & fixtures, except wood

(G-3827)
TOBEYCO MANUFACTURING CO INC
165 Cedar St (14830-2603)
PHONE 607 962-2446
Stephen Tobey, *President*
EMP: 12
SQ FT: 16,000
SALES (est): 880K **Privately Held**
SIC: 3599 3479 Machine & other job shop work; machine shop, jobbing & repair; painting, coating & hot dipping

(G-3828)
VITRIX INC
Also Called: Vitrix Hot Glass and Crafts
77 W Market St (14830-2526)
PHONE 607 936-8707
Thomas Kelly, *President*
EMP: 6
SALES (est): 683.4K **Privately Held**
WEB: www.vitrixhotglass.com
SIC: 3231 5719 Products of purchased glass; glassware

Cornwall
Orange County

(G-3829)
ADVANCE D TECH INC
2 Mill St Stop 19 (12518-1265)
P.O. Box 38 (12518-0038)
PHONE 845 534-8248
Samuel Brach, *President*
EMP: 10
SQ FT: 6,000
SALES: 1.5MM **Privately Held**
SIC: 3545 Diamond cutting tools for turning, boring, burnishing, etc.

(G-3830)
ASPIRE ONE COMMUNICATIONS LLC
245 Main St Ste 8 (12518-1564)
PHONE 201 281-2998

Steven Mandel,
EMP: 12
SQ FT: 20,000
SALES (est): 4MM **Privately Held**
SIC: 2721 8999 Magazines: publishing & printing; communication services

(G-3831)
ASPIRE ONE COMMUNICATIONS INC
246 Main St (12518-1568)
PHONE 845 534-6110
Steven Mandel, *President*
Sophia Koutsiaftis, *Publisher*
Laura Soles, *Creative Dir*
EMP: 9
SALES (est): 2MM **Privately Held**
SIC: 2721 7389 Magazines: publishing & printing;

(G-3832)
COSTUME ARMOUR INC
Also Called: Christo Vac
2 Mill St Stop 1 (12518-1265)
P.O. Box 85 (12518-0085)
PHONE 845 534-9120
Nino Novellino, *President*
Susan Truncale, *Admin Asst*
EMP: 16 EST: 1962
SQ FT: 20,000
SALES (est): 1.7MM **Privately Held**
WEB: www.costumearmour.com
SIC: 2389 3999 Theatrical costumes; theatrical scenery

(G-3833)
KLX INC
Also Called: Klx Aerospace Solutions
45 Quaker Ave Ste 203 (12518-2146)
PHONE 845 534-0401
Joan Nissen, *Branch Mgr*
EMP: 15
SALES (corp-wide): 93.3B **Publicly Held**
SIC: 3812 Search & navigation equipment
HQ: Klx Inc.
    1300 Corp Ctr Way Ste 200
    Wellington FL 33414
    561 383-5100

(G-3834)
MOMN POPS INC
13 Orr Hatch (12518-1727)
PHONE 845 567-0640
EMP: 25
SALES (est): 3.6MM **Privately Held**
SIC: 2064 2066 Mfg Candy/Confectionery & Chocolate/Cocoa Products

(G-3835)
NEW YORK STATE FOAM ENRGY LLC
2 Commercial Dr (12518-1484)
P.O. Box 175 (12518-0175)
PHONE 845 534-4656
Dennis Bender, *General Mgr*
Bryan Bender, *Financial Exec*
Jeanine Nicholson, *Office Mgr*
EMP: 8
SALES (est): 1.2MM **Privately Held**
SIC: 3086 1742 Insulation or cushioning material, foamed plastic; acoustical & insulation work

(G-3836)
NEWS OF THE HIGHLANDS INC (PA)
Also Called: Cornwall Local
35 Hasbrouck Ave (12518-1603)
P.O. Box 518 (12518-0518)
PHONE 845 534-7771
Constantine Eristoff, *President*
Anne Phipps Sidamon-Eristoff, *Vice Pres*
Henry J Sylvestri, *Treasurer*
EMP: 14
SALES (est): 767.4K **Privately Held**
WEB: www.newsofthehighlands.com
SIC: 2711 Commercial printing & newspaper publishing combined; newspapers, publishing & printing

(G-3837)
RANDOB LABS LTD
45 Quaker Ave Ste 207 (12518-2146)
P.O. Box 440 (12518-0440)
PHONE 845 534-2197

Cornwall On Hudson - Orange County (G-3838)

GEOGRAPHIC SECTION

Jim Creagan, *President*
EMP: 3
SALES (est): 1.6MM **Privately Held**
SIC: 2834 Vitamin, nutrient & hematinic preparations for human use

Cornwall On Hudson
Orange County

(G-3838)
EXECUTIVE SIGN CORP
43 Boulevard (12520-1809)
PHONE 212 397-4050
Isaac Goldman, *Owner*
EMP: 6
SALES (est): 385.1K **Privately Held**
WEB: www.executivesigncorp.com
SIC: 3993 Signs, not made in custom sign painting shops

Corona
Queens County

(G-3839)
BONO SAWDUST SUPPLY CO INC
Also Called: Bono Sawdust Co
3330 127th Pl (11368-1508)
PHONE 718 446-1374
Fax: 718 446-6715
EMP: 6 **EST:** 1931
SQ FT: 12,000
SALES (est): 750K **Privately Held**
SIC: 2421 2842 Mfg Sawdust & Shavings

(G-3840)
CAZAR PRINTING & ADVERTISING
4215 102nd St (11368-2460)
PHONE 718 446-4606
Herman Cazar, *Owner*
▲ **EMP:** 5
SALES (est): 320K **Privately Held**
SIC: 2752 Commercial printing, lithographic

(G-3841)
CORONA PLUMBING & HTG SUP INC
10466 Roosevelt Ave (11368-2328)
PHONE 718 424-4133
Apolinar A Ferreira, *Ch of Bd*
EMP: 5
SALES (est): 118.3K **Privately Held**
SIC: 3432 1711 Plumbing fixture fittings & trim; hydronics heating contractor

(G-3842)
CORONA READY MIX INC
5025 97th Pl (11368-3028)
PHONE 718 271-5940
Paul Melis, *President*
John Vasilantonakis, *Vice Pres*
EMP: 10
SQ FT: 6,500
SALES (est): 1.5MM **Privately Held**
SIC: 3273 Ready-mixed concrete

(G-3843)
DELICIOUS FOODS INC
11202 Roosevelt Ave (11368-2624)
PHONE 718 446-9352
Berminder Chahal, *President*
EMP: 11
SALES (est): 910.2K **Privately Held**
WEB: www.deliciousasianfood.com
SIC: 2038 2032 5812 Ethnic foods, frozen; ethnic foods: canned, jarred, etc.; caterers

(G-3844)
GREEN ZONE FOOD SERVICE INC
9906 Christie Ave 3a (11368-3149)
PHONE 917 709-1728
Jian Lin, *CEO*
Ryan Su, *Vice Pres*
EMP: 6 **EST:** 2015
SQ FT: 2,000
SALES (est): 243.4K **Privately Held**
SIC: 2086 Carbonated beverages, nonalcoholic: bottled & canned; soft drinks: packaged in cans, bottles, etc.

(G-3845)
IMAGE IRON WORKS INC
5050 98th St (11368-3023)
PHONE 718 592-8276
Sigi Fredo Gomez, *President*
EMP: 8
SALES (est): 720K **Privately Held**
SIC: 3312 Hot-rolled iron & steel products

(G-3846)
JASON & JEAN PRODUCTS INC
104 Corona Ave (11368)
PHONE 718 271-8300
Chin Ho Kim, *President*
EMP: 10
SQ FT: 6,000
SALES (est): 710K **Privately Held**
SIC: 3999 Hair & hair-based products

(G-3847)
KENAN INTERNATIONAL TRADING
Also Called: Moo Goong Hwa
10713 Northern Blvd (11368-1235)
PHONE 718 672-4922
Young Kim, *Owner*
▲ **EMP:** 5
SQ FT: 6,720
SALES (est): 648.1K **Privately Held**
WEB: www.kenandigital.com
SIC: 3444 3993 2759 5999 Awnings, sheet metal; signs & advertising specialties; commercial printing; awnings

(G-3848)
MAGELLAN AEROSPACE BETHEL INC
9711 50th Ave (11368-2740)
PHONE 203 798-9373
James Butyniec, *CEO*
Paul Heide, *General Mgr*
Jose Lima, *Opers Staff*
Phuong Lam, *Engineer*
Dean Boeckholt, *Controller*
▲ **EMP:** 125
SQ FT: 37,250
SALES (est): 19.4MM
SALES (corp-wide): 759.1MM **Privately Held**
WEB: www.ambel.net
SIC: 3728 3599 3724 Aircraft assemblies, subassemblies & parts; machine & other job shop work; aircraft engines & engine parts
PA: Magellan Aerospace Corporation
3160 Derry Rd E
Mississauga ON L4T 1
905 677-1889

(G-3849)
MAGELLAN AEROSPACE NY INC (HQ)
9711 50th Ave (11368-2740)
P.O. Box 847256, Boston MA (02284-7256)
PHONE 718 699-4000
N Murray Edwards, *Ch of Bd*
John Marcello, *Ch of Bd*
James S Butyniec, *President*
Jo-Ann Ball, *Vice Pres*
Jim Stauffer, *Vice Pres*
▲ **EMP:** 200 **EST:** 1939
SQ FT: 205,000
SALES: 45.1MM
SALES (corp-wide): 759.1MM **Privately Held**
WEB: www.magellan.aero
SIC: 3812 3769 3489 3728 Search & navigation equipment; guided missile & space vehicle parts & auxiliary equipment; ordnance & accessories; aircraft assemblies, subassemblies & parts
PA: Magellan Aerospace Corporation
3160 Derry Rd E
Mississauga ON L4T 1
905 677-1889

(G-3850)
MILAN PROVISION CO INC
10815 Roosevelt Ave (11368-2538)
PHONE 718 899-7678
Sal Laurita, *President*
EMP: 20
SQ FT: 3,000
SALES (est): 2.3MM **Privately Held**
SIC: 2013 Sausages & other prepared meats

(G-3851)
MOGA TRADING COMPANY INC
57 Granger St (11368)
PHONE 718 760-2966
Paul Cheng, *President*
EMP: 7
SALES (est): 571.2K **Privately Held**
SIC: 2392 Household furnishings

(G-3852)
NATURAL DREAMS LLC
5312 104th St (11368-3222)
PHONE 718 760-4202
Kaston Etal, *President*
EMP: 5
SALES (est): 334.8K **Privately Held**
SIC: 2515 Mattresses & bedsprings

(G-3853)
RUTCARELE INC
3449 110th St (11368-1333)
PHONE 347 830-5353
Alex Rovira, *CEO*
EMP: 8
SALES (est): 950K **Privately Held**
SIC: 3999 Manufacturing industries

(G-3854)
S S PRECISION GEAR & INSTR
4512 104th St (11368-2890)
PHONE 718 457-7474
Salvatore Silvestri, *President*
Michael Silvestri, *General Mgr*
EMP: 7
SQ FT: 2,500
SALES (est): 500K **Privately Held**
SIC: 3545 Machine tool accessories

(G-3855)
SOLAR SCREEN CO INC
5311 105th St (11368-3297)
PHONE 718 592-8222
Miles Joseph, *President*
EMP: 9 **EST:** 1955
SQ FT: 10,000
SALES: 2MM **Privately Held**
WEB: www.solar-screen.com
SIC: 2591 Window shades

(G-3856)
UNITED STEEL PRODUCTS INC
3340 127th Pl (11368-1508)
PHONE 718 478-5330
Fred Budetti, *President*
Alfred Franza, *Vice Pres*
Alfredo Franza, *Vice Pres*
Todd Rigolli, *CFO*
Nicholas Henry, *Marketing Staff*
▲ **EMP:** 80
SQ FT: 22,000
SALES: 9.1MM **Privately Held**
WEB: www.unitedsteelproducts.com
SIC: 3442 1542 7699 Metal doors; commercial & office building contractors; door & window repair

(G-3857)
YONG JI PRODUCTIONS INC
10219 44th Ave (11368-2430)
PHONE 917 559-4616
Wanchang Yin, *President*
EMP: 20
SALES (est): 1.2MM **Privately Held**
SIC: 2311 Men's & boys' suits & coats

Cortland
Cortland County

(G-3858)
ACTUANT CORPORATION
Also Called: Cortland
44 River St (13045-2311)
PHONE 607 753-8276
John Stidd, *CEO*
EMP: 47
SALES (corp-wide): 1.1B **Publicly Held**
SIC: 3593 Fluid power cylinders, hydraulic or pneumatic
PA: Actuant Corporation
N86w12500 Westbrook Xing
Menomonee Falls WI 53051
262 293-1500

(G-3859)
ALPLA INC
106 Central Ave (13045)
PHONE 607 250-8101
EMP: 5
SALES (est): 416.3K **Privately Held**
SIC: 3085 Plastics bottles

(G-3860)
BESTWAY ENTERPRISES INC (PA)
3877 Luker Rd (13045-9339)
PHONE 607 753-8261
Karl D Ochs, *CEO*
Steve Everle, *Sales Staff*
Bob Leet, *Sales Staff*
Jim Fish, *Sales Associate*
Cindy Johnson, *Office Mgr*
EMP: 50
SQ FT: 200,000
SALES (est): 52.9MM **Privately Held**
SIC: 2491 5031 Structural lumber & timber, treated wood; building materials, exterior

(G-3861)
BESTWAY OF NEW YORK INC
3877 Luker Rd (13045-9385)
PHONE 607 753-8261
Karl D Ochs, *President*
David Ondich, *Sales Mgr*
EMP: 1
SALES (est): 6.1MM
SALES (corp-wide): 52.9MM **Privately Held**
SIC: 2491 Structural lumber & timber, treated wood
PA: Bestway Enterprises Inc.
3877 Luker Rd
Cortland NY 13045
607 753-8261

(G-3862)
BFMA HOLDING CORPORATION
37 Huntington St (13045-3096)
PHONE 607 753-6746
Barry W Florescue, *Ch of Bd*
Donna Southworth, *Opers Staff*
EMP: 9
SQ FT: 3,000
SALES (est): 1.1MM **Privately Held**
SIC: 2841 5122 5131 5139 Soap: granulated, liquid, cake, flaked or chip; toiletries; sewing accessories; shoe accessories; display equipment, except refrigerated; packaging & labeling services

(G-3863)
BORGWARNER MORSE TEC LLC
3690 Luker Rd (13045-9397)
PHONE 607 257-6700
Roger Wood, *Branch Mgr*
EMP: 90
SALES (corp-wide): 9.8B **Publicly Held**
WEB: www.borgwarnermorsetec.com
SIC: 3714 Motor vehicle parts & accessories
HQ: Borgwarner Morse Tec Llc
800 Warren Rd
Ithaca NY 14850
607 257-6700

(G-3864)
BP DIGITAL IMAGING LLC
Also Called: Carbon Copies
87 Main St (13045-2610)
P.O. Box 5396 (13045-5396)
PHONE 607 753-0022
Ted Morrison, *Purchasing*
Betsy Allen, *Mng Member*
Jeff Czimmer, *Technology*
Paul Allen, *
▼ **EMP:** 8
SQ FT: 1,800
SALES: 500K **Privately Held**
SIC: 2752 Photolithographic printing

(G-3865)
CORTLAND CABLE COMPANY INC
44 River St (13045-2335)
P.O. Box 330 (13045-0330)
PHONE..................607 753-8276
John Stidd, *CEO*
Richard Nye, *Vice Pres*
◆ **EMP:** 50
SALES (est): 49.7K
SALES (corp-wide): 1.1B **Publicly Held**
WEB: www.cortlandcable.com
SIC: 3496 3357 2823 Cable, uninsulated wire: made from purchased wire; nonferrous wiredrawing & insulating; cellulosic manmade fibers
HQ: Cortland Company, Inc.
44 River St
Cortland NY 13045

(G-3866)
CORTLAND COMPANY INC (HQ)
44 River St (13045-2311)
P.O. Box 330 (13045-0330)
PHONE..................607 753-8276
John A Stidd, *CEO*
John Thomas, *President*
Sam Bull, *Vice Pres*
John G Greco, *Vice Pres*
Stephen A Breen, *CFO*
EMP: 79
SALES (est): 37MM
SALES (corp-wide): 1.1B **Publicly Held**
WEB: www.actuant.com
SIC: 2298 5063 Ropes & fiber cables; wire & cable; electronic wire & cable
PA: Actuant Corporation
N86w12500 Westbrook Xing
Menomonee Falls WI 53051
262 293-1500

(G-3867)
CORTLAND LINE MFG LLC
3736 Kellogg Rd (13045-8818)
PHONE..................607 756-2851
Randy Brown, *President*
Ralph Canfield, *CFO*
EMP: 30
SALES (est): 2.3MM **Privately Held**
SIC: 3949 Fishing equipment

(G-3868)
CORTLAND MACHINE AND TOOL CO
60 Grant St (13045-2173)
P.O. Box 27 (13045-0027)
PHONE..................607 756-5852
Stan Pierce, *President*
Debbie Hoyt, *Human Res Mgr*
Scott Rogers, *Technology*
EMP: 11 **EST:** 1913
SQ FT: 10,000
SALES: 900K **Privately Held**
SIC: 3599 Machine shop, jobbing & repair

(G-3869)
CORTLAND PLASTICS INTL LLC
211 S Main St (13045)
PHONE..................607 662-0120
Fritz Kern, *Engineer*
Kay Breed, *Controller*
Patrick Dessein, *Mng Member*
David Erwin,
Rick Esposito,
EMP: 26
SALES (est): 5.6MM **Privately Held**
SIC: 3085 Plastics bottles

(G-3870)
CORTLAND READY MIX INC
6 Locust Ave Ofc Rte 13 (13045-1412)
PHONE..................607 753-3063
Michael Saunders, *President*
EMP: 12 **EST:** 1944
SQ FT: 4,000
SALES: 200K
SALES (corp-wide): 7.8MM **Privately Held**
WEB: www.saundersconcrete.com
SIC: 3273 Ready-mixed concrete
PA: Saunders Concrete Co. Inc.
5126 S Onondaga Rd
Nedrow NY 13120
315 469-3217

(G-3871)
CORTLAND STANDARD PRINTING CO
110 Main St (13045-6607)
P.O. Box 5548 (13045-5548)
PHONE..................607 756-5665
Kevin R Howe, *President*
Kevin Conlon, *Editor*
F M Catalano, *Chief*
Ann G Howe, *Vice Pres*
Rachel Costanpino, *Human Res Mgr*
EMP: 65 **EST:** 1867
SQ FT: 15,000
SALES (est): 4.4MM **Privately Held**
WEB: www.cortlandstandard.com
SIC: 2711 2791 Newspapers: publishing only, not printed on site; typesetting

(G-3872)
FORKEY CONSTRUCTION & FABG INC
3690 Luker Rd (13045-9397)
PHONE..................607 849-4879
Charles Forkey, *President*
EMP: 30
SQ FT: 27,000
SALES (est): 7.9MM **Privately Held**
SIC: 3469 Machine parts, stamped or pressed metal

(G-3873)
GRAPH-TEX INC
46 Elm St (13045-2225)
P.O. Box 109 (13045-0109)
PHONE..................607 756-7791
Brent Riley, *President*
EMP: 10
SALES (corp-wide): 3.1MM **Privately Held**
WEB: www.graph-tex.com
SIC: 2759 Screen printing
PA: Graph-Tex, Inc.
24 Court St
Cortland NY 13045
607 756-1875

(G-3874)
GRAPH-TEX INC (PA)
24 Court St (13045-2685)
P.O. Box 109 (13045-0109)
PHONE..................607 756-1875
Brent Riley, *President*
EMP: 8
SQ FT: 3,600
SALES (est): 3.1MM **Privately Held**
WEB: www.graph-tex.com
SIC: 2759 5941 5091 Screen printing; sporting goods & bicycle shops; sporting & recreation goods

(G-3875)
GRAPHICS PLUS PRINTING INC
215 S Main St (13045-3266)
PHONE..................607 299-0500
Robert Eckard, *President*
EMP: 24
SQ FT: 47,000
SALES (est): 5.6MM **Privately Held**
SIC: 2752 2759 7336 Commercial printing, offset; screen printing; art design services

(G-3876)
GUTCHESS LUMBER CO INC (PA)
890 Mclean Rd (13045-9393)
PHONE..................607 753-3393
Gary H Gutchess, *Ch of Bd*
Matthew F Gutchess, *President*
Jeffrey D Breed, *Treasurer*
John Tracy, *Human Res Dir*
Bryan Conklin, *Sales Mgr*
◆ **EMP:** 250 **EST:** 1904
SQ FT: 3,500
SALES: 150MM **Privately Held**
WEB: www.gutchess.com
SIC: 2421 2426 Building & structural materials, wood; lumber, hardwood dimension

(G-3877)
ITHACA PREGANCY CENTER
4 Church St (13045-2710)
PHONE..................607 753-3909
EMP: 5
SALES (est): 477K
SALES (corp-wide): 183.1K **Privately Held**
SIC: 2835 Pregnancy test kits
PA: Ithaca Pregancy Center
210 W Green St
Ithaca NY 14850
607 273-4673

(G-3878)
JACKSONS WELDING LLC
Also Called: Jacksons Welding Service & Sls
215 N Homer Ave (13045)
PHONE..................607 756-2725
EMP: 7
SQ FT: 8,000
SALES (est): 252.2K **Privately Held**
SIC: 7692 5084 1799 Welding Repair Whol Industrial Equipment Trade Contractor

(G-3879)
JM MURRAY CENTER INC (PA)
823 State Route 13 Ste 1 (13045-8731)
PHONE..................607 756-9913
Floyd Moon, *President*
Judy O Brien, *Vice Pres*
Dale Davis, *Vice Pres*
Gerald Gebhard, *Vice Pres*
Patricia Willyard, *Vice Pres*
▲ **EMP:** 110
SQ FT: 110,000
SALES (est): 17.8MM **Privately Held**
WEB: www.jmmurray.com
SIC: 2673 3843 7349 Bags: plastic, laminated & coated; dental equipment & supplies; building maintenance services

(G-3880)
JM MURRAY CENTER INC
4057 West Rd (13045-1637)
PHONE..................607 756-0246
Judy O'Brien, *Branch Mgr*
EMP: 110
SALES (est): 4.1MM
SALES (corp-wide): 17.8MM **Privately Held**
WEB: www.jmmurray.com
SIC: 2673 3843 7349 Bags: plastic, laminated & coated; dental equipment & supplies; building maintenance services
PA: J.M. Murray Center, Inc.
823 State Route 13 Ste 1
Cortland NY 13045
607 756-9913

(G-3881)
MARIETTA CORPORATION (HQ)
37 Huntington St (13045-3098)
P.O. Box 5250 (13045-5250)
PHONE..................607 753-6746
Donald W Sturdivant, *CEO*
Chris Calhoun, *Senior VP*
Beth Corl, *Senior VP*
Ray Ferretti, *Senior VP*
David Hempson, *Senior VP*
◆ **EMP:** 500
SQ FT: 550,000
SALES (est): 397.5MM
SALES (corp-wide): 256.4MM **Privately Held**
SIC: 2844 2834 2541 Cosmetic preparations; toilet preparations; druggists' preparations (pharmaceuticals); store & office display cases & fixtures
PA: Marietta Holding Corporation, Inc.
37 Huntington St
Cortland NY 13045
607 753-6746

(G-3882)
MARIETTA CORPORATION
106 Central Ave (13045)
PHONE..................607 753-0982
Greg Rudy, *Branch Mgr*
EMP: 350
SALES (corp-wide): 284.9MM **Privately Held**
SIC: 2841 7389 Soap: granulated, liquid, cake, flaked or chip; packaging & labeling services
HQ: Marietta Corporation
37 Huntington St
Cortland NY 13045
607 753-6746

(G-3883)
MARIETTA CORPORATION
Also Called: Packaging Avantage/Marietta La
37 Huntington St (13045-3098)
P.O. Box 5006 (13045-5006)
PHONE..................323 589-8181
Greg Mullen, *Branch Mgr*
Eden Sebhatu, *Lab Dir*
EMP: 600
SALES (corp-wide): 284.9MM **Privately Held**
SIC: 2841 5122 5131 5139 Soap: granulated, liquid, cake, flaked or chip; toiletries; toilet articles; toilet preparations; perfumes; sewing accessories; hair accessories; shoe accessories; display equipment, except refrigerated; packaging & labeling services
HQ: Marietta Corporation
37 Huntington St
Cortland NY 13045
607 753-6746

(G-3884)
MCCONNAUGHAY TECHNOLOGIES
Also Called: Cortland Asphalt Products
1911 Lorings Crossing Rd (13045-9747)
PHONE..................607 753-1100
Frank Suits Jr, *President*
Larry Ostermeyer, *Vice Pres*
▲ **EMP:** 8
SQ FT: 15,000
SALES (est): 1.4MM
SALES (corp-wide): 234.8MM **Privately Held**
WEB: www.mcconnaughay.com
SIC: 2951 Asphalt paving mixtures & blocks
PA: Suit-Kote Corporation
1911 Lorings Crossing Rd
Cortland NY 13045
607 753-1100

(G-3885)
PALL CORPORATION
Also Called: Pall Trinity Micro
3643 State Route 281 (13045-3591)
P.O. Box 2030 (13045-0930)
PHONE..................607 753-6041
David Berger, *President*
Steven Chisolm, *Vice Pres*
Carl Boise, *Opers Staff*
Chris Montreuil, *Mfg Staff*
Randy Button, *Engineer*
EMP: 750
SALES (corp-wide): 18.3B **Publicly Held**
WEB: www.pall.com
SIC: 3842 3841 3569 3599 Surgical appliances & supplies; surgical & medical instruments; IV transfusion apparatus; filters; filters, general line: industrial; filter elements, fluid, hydraulic line; air intake filters, internal combustion engine, except auto; gasoline filters, internal combustion engine, except auto; oil filters, internal combustion engine, except automotive; filters: oil, fuel & air, motor vehicle; perforated metal, stamped
HQ: Pall Corporation
25 Harbor Park Dr
Port Washington NY 11050
516 484-5400

(G-3886)
PALL CORPORATION
3669 State Route 281 (13045-8957)
PHONE..................607 753-6041
Angela Griffin, *Engineer*
Brian Palermo, *Engineer*
Jacques Joseph, *Branch Mgr*
Tim Pierce, *Manager*
Pam Stack, *Technology*
EMP: 750
SALES (corp-wide): 18.3B **Publicly Held**
WEB: www.pall.com
SIC: 3842 Surgical appliances & supplies
HQ: Pall Corporation
25 Harbor Park Dr
Port Washington NY 11050
516 484-5400

Cortland - Cortland County (G-3887)

(G-3887)
PALL CORPORATION
Also Called: Pall's Advnced Sprtons Systems
839 State Route 13 Ste 12 (13045-8998)
P.O. Box 2030 (13045-0930)
PHONE..................607 753-6041
Carl Boise, *Principal*
Charles Casterline, *Mfg Staff*
Lance Benjamin, *Engineer*
Michael Fox, *Engineer*
Stephen Smith, *Engineer*
EMP: 750
SALES (corp-wide): 18.3B **Publicly Held**
SIC: 3842 Surgical appliances & supplies
HQ: Pall Corporation
25 Harbor Park Dr
Port Washington NY 11050
516 484-5400

(G-3888)
PAUL BUNYAN PRODUCTS INC
890 Mclean Rd (13045-9393)
PHONE..................315 696-6164
Judith Greene, *President*
William Oustad, *Vice Pres*
Margaret Hudson, *Treasurer*
EMP: 20
SQ FT: 36,000
SALES (est): 3.8MM **Privately Held**
SIC: 2448 Pallets, wood

(G-3889)
PRECISION EFORMING LLC
839 State Route 13 Ste 1 (13045-8999)
PHONE..................607 753-7730
Scott Selbach,
Doug Ondrack,
EMP: 13
SQ FT: 7,000
SALES (est): 2MM **Privately Held**
WEB: www.precisioneforming.com
SIC: 3542 Electroforming machines

(G-3890)
PYROTEK INCORPORATED
641 State Route 13 (13045-8836)
PHONE..................607 756-3050
Thomas Howard, *Manager*
EMP: 97
SALES (corp-wide): 588.8MM **Privately Held**
SIC: 3365 Aluminum foundries
PA: Pyrotek Incorporated
705 W 1st Ave
Spokane WA 99201
509 926-6212

(G-3891)
QUADRA FLEX CORP
Also Called: Quadra Flex Quality Labels
1955 State Route 13 (13045-9619)
P.O. Box 286 (13045-0286)
PHONE..................607 758-7066
David Masri, *President*
Christopher Meddaugh, *Vice Pres*
Theresa Meddaugh, *Vice Pres*
Thresa Meddaugh, *Treasurer*
Ben Masri, *Director*
EMP: 5
SQ FT: 2,500
SALES: 700K **Privately Held**
WEB: www.quadraflex.com
SIC: 2759 2679 Labels & seals: printing; labels, paper: made from purchased material

(G-3892)
REDDING-HUNTER INC
Also Called: Redding Reloading Equipment
1089 Starr Rd (13045-8806)
PHONE..................607 753-3331
Richard W Beebe, *President*
Robin Sharpless, *Exec VP*
▼ **EMP:** 25
SQ FT: 15,000
SALES (est): 4.7MM **Privately Held**
WEB: www.redding-reloading.com
SIC: 3484 3599 Small arms; machine shop, jobbing & repair

(G-3893)
SAUNDERS CONCRETE CO INC
Also Called: Cortland Ready Mix
6 Locust Ave (13045-1412)
PHONE..................607 756-7905
Wilbur Hayes, *Manager*
EMP: 15
SALES (corp-wide): 7.8MM **Privately Held**
SIC: 3273 Ready-mixed concrete
PA: Saunders Concrete Co. Inc.
5126 S Onondaga Rd
Nedrow NY 13120
315 469-3217

(G-3894)
SELLCO INDUSTRIES INC
58 Grant St (13045-2174)
P.O. Box 70 (13045-0070)
PHONE..................607 756-7594
George Delorenzo Jr, *President*
Marilyn De Lorenzo, *Vice Pres*
EMP: 20
SQ FT: 19,000
SALES (est): 2.5MM **Privately Held**
WEB: www.sellcoinc.com
SIC: 3993 2782 2399 2396 Signs & advertising specialties; looseleaf binders & devices; banners, made from fabric; automotive & apparel trimmings

(G-3895)
SUIT-KOTE CORPORATION (PA)
1911 Lorings Crossing Rd (13045-9775)
PHONE..................607 753-1100
Frank H Suits Jr, *President*
Brian Hinkley, *General Mgr*
Scott Harris, *Vice Pres*
Dan Quinlan, *Vice Pres*
Steve Rebman, *Vice Pres*
◆ **EMP:** 200
SQ FT: 10,000
SALES (est): 234.8MM **Privately Held**
WEB: www.suit-kote.com
SIC: 2951 1611 Asphalt & asphaltic paving mixtures (not from refineries); highway & street paving contractor

(G-3896)
TECHNOLOGIES APPLICATION LLC
Also Called: Glyph Production Technologies
3736 Kellogg Rd (13045-8818)
PHONE..................607 275-0345
Rebecca Ebhardt, *Marketing Mgr*
Liran Shathi,
Eyal Shathi,
▲ **EMP:** 14
SQ FT: 15,000
SALES: 7MM **Privately Held**
WEB: www.glyphtech.com
SIC: 3572 Computer storage devices

(G-3897)
WILBEDONE INC
1133 State Route 222 (13045-9352)
PHONE..................607 756-8813
Thomas L Beames, *President*
Diana Simpson, *Human Resources*
Rusty Perkins, *Office Mgr*
David Motyl, *Manager*
Sally Young, *Consultant*
EMP: 33
SQ FT: 18,000
SALES (est): 5.2MM **Privately Held*
WEB: www.wilbedone.com
SIC: 2541 Counter & sink tops

Cortlandt Manor
Westchester County

(G-3898)
ABLE INDUSTRIES INC
Also Called: Able Wire Co
18 Brook Ln (10567-6502)
PHONE..................914 739-5685
Warren Button, *President*
Patricia Button, *Admin Sec*
▲ **EMP:** 12 **EST:** 1980
SQ FT: 18,000
SALES (est): 1.1MM **Privately Held**
WEB: www.ablewire.com
SIC: 3315 Wire, steel: insulated or armored

(G-3899)
DURANM INC
101 Dale Ave (10567-1617)
PHONE..................914 774-3367
Martin F Duran, *CEO*
EMP: 5
SALES (est): 626.1K **Privately Held**
SIC: 3272 Floor slabs & tiles, precast concrete

(G-3900)
ELMSFORD SHEET METAL WORKS INC
23 Arlo Ln (10567-2631)
PHONE..................914 739-6300
Donald J Trier, *President*
Joseph Jasiel, *Manager*
Mark Dipasquale, *Director*
EMP: 75
SQ FT: 24,000
SALES (est): 12.6MM
SALES (corp-wide): 24.2B **Privately Held**
WEB: www.elmsfordsheetmetal.com
SIC: 3444 7389 7699 Sheet metal specialties, not stamped; metal cutting services; metal reshaping & replating services
HQ: Engie North America Inc.
1990 Post Oak Blvd # 1900
Houston TX 77056
713 636-0000

(G-3901)
GC MOBILE SERVICES INC
Also Called: G C Mobile Svcs
32 William Puckey Dr (10567-6216)
PHONE..................914 736-9730
Garth Cooperman, *President*
EMP: 6
SALES: 250K **Privately Held**
SIC: 7692 Welding repair

(G-3902)
HIGHRANGE FUELS INC
96 Oregon Rd (10567-1246)
PHONE..................914 930-8300
Sajan Augustine, *Principal*
EMP: 7
SALES (est): 457.8K **Privately Held**
SIC: 2869 Fuels

(G-3903)
MINES PRESS INC
231 Croton Ave (10567-5284)
PHONE..................914 788-1800
Steven Mines, *Ch of Bd*
Daniel Mines, *Ch of Bd*
Cynthia Mines, *Corp Secy*
Suzanne Shwab, *Purch Agent*
Carl Hutt, *CFO*
▲ **EMP:** 115 **EST:** 1933
SQ FT: 100,000
SALES (est): 30.7MM **Privately Held**
WEB: www.minespress.com
SIC: 2752 2759 2789 2791 Commercial printing, offset; letterpress printing; gold stamping on books; typesetting

(G-3904)
PRONTO PRINTER
2085 E Main St Ste 3 (10567-2616)
PHONE..................914 737-0800
John P Marvin, *Owner*
EMP: 6 **EST:** 1974
SQ FT: 7,000
SALES: 650K **Privately Held**
SIC: 2752 Photo-offset printing

Cossayuna
Washington County

(G-3905)
FRONHOFER TOOL COMPANY INC
4197 County Rd 48 (12823)
P.O. Box 84 (12823-0084)
PHONE..................518 692-2496
Paul Fronhofer II, *Ch of Bd*
Kyle Fronhofer, *Vice Pres*
Heidi Griffin, *Manager*
EMP: 30
SQ FT: 10,000
SALES: 5MM **Privately Held**
WEB: www.fronhofertool.com
SIC: 3599 Machine shop, jobbing & repair

Coxsackie
Greene County

(G-3906)
DUCOMMUN AEROSTRUCTURES NY INC
171 Stacey Rd (12051-2613)
PHONE..................518 731-2791
Michael D Grosso, *CEO*
Anthony J Reardon, *Ch of Bd*
Hugh J Quigley, *President*
Paul Burton, *Vice Pres*
EMP: 270
SQ FT: 65,000
SALES (est): 52.8MM
SALES (corp-wide): 558.1MM **Publicly Held**
WEB: www.dynabil.com
SIC: 3728 Aircraft parts & equipment
HQ: Ducommun Aerostructures, Inc.
268 E Gardena Blvd
Gardena CA 90248
310 380-5390

Cranberry Lake
St. Lawrence County

(G-3907)
FORM A ROCKLAND PLASTICS INC
7152 Main St (12927)
P.O. Box 670 (12927-0670)
PHONE..................315 848-3300
Donald Lashomb II, *President*
Cynthia Whitmore Lashomb, *Treasurer*
EMP: 5 **EST:** 1963
SQ FT: 6,000
SALES (est): 623.7K **Privately Held**
SIC: 3089 3172 Plastic containers, except foam; key cases

Croghan
Lewis County

(G-3908)
GRAND SLAM SAFETY LLC
9793 S Bridge St (13327-2329)
P.O. Box 35 (13327-0035)
PHONE..................315 766-7008
Robert K Lyndaker, *President*
Brian Graves, *Plant Engr*
Robert Chamberlain,
Mick Lehman,
David Moore,
EMP: 6
SALES: 300K **Privately Held**
SIC: 3949 Sporting & athletic goods

Cropseyville
Rensselaer County

(G-3909)
R J VALENTE GRAVEL INC
3349 Rte 2 (12052)
PHONE..................518 279-1001
Tim Banks, *Branch Mgr*
EMP: 29
SALES (corp-wide): 17.7MM **Privately Held**
SIC: 1442 Construction sand & gravel
PA: R. J. Valente Gravel, Inc.
1 Madison St
Troy NY 12180
518 432-4470

Cross River
Westchester County

(G-3910)
VEPO SOLUTIONS LLC
3 Fairview Ct (10518-1127)
PHONE..................914 384-2121

Alan Seiler, *President*
EMP: 5 **EST:** 2017
SALES: 2MM **Privately Held**
SIC: 3824 7371 Water meters; computer software development & applications

Croton Falls
Westchester County

(G-3911)
GARY STOCK CORPORATION
597 Rte 22 (10519)
P.O. Box 609 (10519-0609)
PHONE 914 276-2700
Gary Stock, *President*
Michele Ryan, *Mktg Dir*
EMP: 7
SALES (est): 1MM **Privately Held**
WEB: www.gstockco.com
SIC: 2759 Promotional printing

Croton On Hudson
Westchester County

(G-3912)
BLUE PIG ICE CREAM FACTORY
121 Maple St (10520-2538)
PHONE 914 271-3850
Julia Horowitz, *Owner*
EMP: 5
SALES: 250K **Privately Held**
SIC: 2024 5812 Ice cream & frozen desserts; ice cream stands or dairy bars

(G-3913)
DALEE BOOKBINDING CO INC
Also Called: Creations In Canvas
10 Croton Lake Rd (10520-3615)
PHONE 914 965-1660
David Hutter, *President*
EMP: 16 **EST:** 1965
SQ FT: 12,000
SALES (est): 2MM **Privately Held**
WEB: www.daleebook.com
SIC: 2789 2782 Binding only: books, pamphlets, magazines, etc.; blankbooks

(G-3914)
GENERAL SPLICE CORPORATION
Hwy 129 (10520)
PHONE 914 271-5131
Ralph Milano, *President*
Nicole Milano, *Treasurer*
EMP: 6
SQ FT: 7,000
SALES (est): 917.7K **Privately Held**
SIC: 3535 Conveyors & conveying equipment

(G-3915)
NK ELECTRIC LLC
22 Scenic Dr (10520-1848)
P.O. Box 171 (10520-0171)
PHONE 914 271-0222
James Brophy, *Principal*
EMP: 7
SALES (est): 1.1MM **Privately Held**
SIC: 3699 Electrical equipment & supplies

Crown Point
Essex County

(G-3916)
MOUNTAIN FOREST PRODUCTS INC
3281 Nys Route 9n (12928-2405)
PHONE 518 597-3674
Kevin Mero, *President*
Vicki Mero, *Corp Secy*
EMP: 6
SQ FT: 1,152
SALES (est): 733.8K **Privately Held**
SIC: 2411 Logging

Cuba
Allegany County

(G-3917)
D F STAUFFER BISCUIT CO INC
8670 Farnsworth Rd (14727-9720)
P.O. Box 12002, York PA (17402-0672)
PHONE 585 968-2700
Maria Defaria, *Human Res Mgr*
Jeff Howard, *Office Mgr*
Larry Chandler, *Maintence Staff*
Petra Bartel, *Master*
EMP: 50
SALES (corp-wide): 11.6B **Privately Held**
WEB: www.stauffers.net
SIC: 2052 Mfg Cookies/Crackers
HQ: D F Stauffer Biscuit Co Inc
360 S Belmont St
York PA 17403
717 815-4600

(G-3918)
DEMING ELECTRO-PLATING CORP
5 Woodruff St (14727-1020)
PHONE 585 968-2355
Barbara Deming, *President*
Bruce L Deming, *Vice Pres*
Michael L Demming, *Vice Pres*
EMP: 6 **EST:** 1947
SQ FT: 22,000
SALES: 500K **Privately Held**
SIC: 3471 Electroplating of metals or formed products

(G-3919)
EMPIRE CHEESE INC
4520 County Road 6 (14727-9598)
PHONE 585 968-1552
Gary Vanic, *CEO*
John Epprecht, *Corp Secy*
Russell Mullins, *Vice Pres*
Shelley Williamson, *Purch Agent*
Tom Eastham, *Plant Engr*
EMP: 175
SQ FT: 100,000
SALES (est): 83.2MM
SALES (corp-wide): 1.6B **Privately Held**
WEB: www.empirecheese.com
SIC: 2022 Cheese, natural & processed
PA: Great Lakes Cheese Co., Inc.
17825 Great Lakes Pkwy
Hiram OH 44234
440 834-2500

(G-3920)
SPS MEDICAL SUPPLY CORP
Also Called: Sterilator Company
31 Water St Ste 1 (14727-1030)
PHONE 585 968-2377
Shawn Doyle, *Branch Mgr*
EMP: 10
SALES (corp-wide): 871.9MM **Publicly Held**
SIC: 3842 3821 Sterilizers, hospital & surgical; autoclaves, laboratory
HQ: Sps Medical Supply Corp.
6789 W Henrietta Rd
Rush NY 14543
585 359-0130

Cutchogue
Suffolk County

(G-3921)
DI BORGHESE CASTELLO LLC
17150 County Road 48 (11935-1041)
P.O. Box 957 (11935-0957)
PHONE 631 734-5111
Marco Borghese, *Mng Member*
EMP: 10
SALES (est): 811.1K **Privately Held**
WEB: www.castellodiborghese.com
SIC: 2084 Wines

(G-3922)
PELLEGRINI VINEYARDS LLC
23005 Main Rd (11935-1331)
PHONE 631 734-4111
Rita Pellegrini, *Partner*
Robert Pellegrini, *Partner*
John Larsen, *Manager*
EMP: 5
SALES (est): 533.4K **Privately Held**
WEB: www.pellegrinivineyards.com
SIC: 2084 Wines

(G-3923)
PUGLIESE VINEYARDS INC
34515 Main Rd Rte 25 (11935)
P.O. Box 467 (11935-0467)
PHONE 631 734-4057
Patricia Pugliese, *President*
EMP: 5
SALES (est): 473.3K **Privately Held**
WEB: www.pugliesevineyards.com
SIC: 2084 Wines

(G-3924)
VEDELL NORTH FORK LLC
Also Called: Corey Creek Vineyards
36225 Main Rd (11935-1346)
PHONE 631 323-3526
Peggy Lauber,
Jean Partridge,
EMP: 7
SALES (est): 590K **Privately Held**
SIC: 2084 Wines

Dansville
Livingston County

(G-3925)
DANSVILLE LOGGING & LUMBER
10903 State Route 36 (14437-9444)
PHONE 585 335-5879
Timothy Rauber, *President*
EMP: 23
SQ FT: 900
SALES: 1.4MM **Privately Held**
SIC: 2421 Lumber: rough, sawed or planed

(G-3926)
GPM ASSOCIATES LLC
Also Called: Forbes Products
10 Forbes St (14437-9268)
PHONE 585 335-3940
Linda Demartinis, *Purch Agent*
Ron Van Duyne, *Engineer*
Kathy Boldt, *Supervisor*
Mark McDermott,
Kevin Young, *Maintence Staff*
EMP: 20
SALES (est): 3.7MM
SALES (corp-wide): 15.8MM **Privately Held**
SIC: 2782 3089 2752 2393 Blankbooks & looseleaf binders; novelties, plastic; commercial printing, lithographic; textile bags
PA: Gpm Associates Llc
45 High Tech Dr
Rush NY 14543
585 334-4800

(G-3927)
JUST IN TIME CNC MACHINING
88 Ossian St (14437-9101)
PHONE 585 335-2010
Kelly Alexander, *President*
EMP: 14
SQ FT: 10,000
SALES (est): 1.6MM **Privately Held**
SIC: 3599 Machine shop, jobbing & repair

Davenport
Delaware County

(G-3928)
GREENE LUMBER CO LP
16991 State Highway 23 (13750-8304)
PHONE 607 278-6101
Jeffrey Meyer,
EMP: 35 **EST:** 1984
SQ FT: 13,888
SALES: 5.8MM
SALES (corp-wide): 344.3MM **Privately Held**
SIC: 2421 Lumber: rough, sawed or planed
PA: Baillie Lumber Co., L.P.
4002 Legion Dr
Hamburg NY 14075
800 950-2850

De Ruyter
Madison County

(G-3929)
USA BODY INC
994 Middle Lake Rd (13052-1244)
PHONE 315 852-6123
Bruce Macrae, *President*
Kristine Macrae, *Admin Sec*
EMP: 8
SALES (est): 1.5MM **Privately Held**
SIC: 3713 Truck bodies (motor vehicles)

De Witt
Onondaga County

(G-3930)
MAXI COMPANIES INC
4317 E Genesee St (13214-2114)
PHONE 315 446-1002
Charles C Giancola, *President*
▼ **EMP:** 6
SALES (est): 536.3K **Privately Held**
SIC: 3582 Dryers, laundry: commercial, including coin-operated

Deer Park
Suffolk County

(G-3931)
ABLE WELDBUILT INDUSTRIES INC
1050 Grand Blvd (11729-5710)
PHONE 631 643-9700
Steve Laganas, *President*
EMP: 15
SALES (est): 3.4MM **Privately Held**
SIC: 3713 Truck & bus bodies

(G-3932)
ABRA-KA-DATA SYSTEMS LTD
39 W Jefryn Blvd Ste 1 (11729-5792)
PHONE 631 667-5550
Robert A Berding, *Ch of Bd*
Kenneth Berding, *President*
Dorothy Berding, *Admin Sec*
▲ **EMP:** 22
SQ FT: 15,000
SALES (est): 2.2MM **Privately Held**
SIC: 2761 Manifold business forms

(G-3933)
AD MAKERS LONG ISLAND INC
60 E Jefryn Blvd Ste 3 (11729-5798)
PHONE 631 595-9100
Arthur Lituchy, *President*
Henry Houston, *Vice Pres*
EMP: 10
SQ FT: 1,500
SALES (est): 930K **Privately Held**
WEB: www.admadvertising.com
SIC: 3993 7311 Signs & advertising specialties; advertising agencies

(G-3934)
ADVANCED STRUCTURES CORP (PA)
235 W Industry Ct (11729-4688)
PHONE 631 667-5000
Linda Frank, *President*
Tina Lang, *Controller*
EMP: 15
SQ FT: 22,000
SALES (est): 3.8MM **Privately Held**
WEB: www.advancedstructurescorp.com
SIC: 3469 3083 Metal stampings; laminated plastic sheets

Deer Park - Suffolk County (G-3935)   GEOGRAPHIC SECTION

(G-3935)
AERO SPECIALTIES MANUFACTURING
20 Burt Dr (11729-5770)
PHONE..................631 242-7200
Donald Carter, *President*
Elizabeth A Smith, *Vice Pres*
EMP: 12 EST: 1999
SQ FT: 1,400
SALES: 3.4MM **Privately Held**
SIC: 3599 Machine shop, jobbing & repair

(G-3936)
ALL COLOR BUSINESS SPC LTD
305 Suburban Ave (11729-6806)
PHONE..................516 420-0649
William Bogue, *Ch of Bd*
EMP: 6
SALES (est): 760K **Privately Held**
SIC: 2752 Commercial printing, lithographic

(G-3937)
ALLSTATE GASKET & PACKING INC
31 Prospect Pl (11729-3713)
PHONE..................631 254-4050
Angelo Romano, *President*
▲ **EMP:** 17
SQ FT: 2,000
SALES (est): 2.4MM **Privately Held**
WEB: www.allstategasket.com
SIC: 3053 5085 3443 Gaskets, all materials; industrial supplies; fabricated plate work (boiler shop)

(G-3938)
ALLSTATE SIGN & PLAQUE CORP
70 Burt Dr (11729-5702)
P.O. Box 725 (11729-0725)
PHONE..................631 242-2828
David Fick, *President*
Mark Fick, *Vice Pres*
Peter Fick, *Treasurer*
EMP: 15 EST: 1956
SQ FT: 15,000
SALES: 2.6MM **Privately Held**
WEB: www.allstatesign.com
SIC: 3993 2796 Signs, not made in custom sign painting shops; engraving platemaking services

(G-3939)
AMERICAN CASINO EQUIPMENT MFG
Also Called: Acem
45 W Jefryn Blvd Ste 107 (11729-5722)
PHONE..................631 242-2440
John Makowski, *CEO*
EMP: 10
SALES: 2.5MM **Privately Held**
WEB: www.acemcasino.com
SIC: 2499 Laundry products, wood

(G-3940)
AMERICAN RACING HEADERS INC
Also Called: Arh
880 Grand Blvd (11729-5708)
PHONE..................631 608-1427
Nick Filippides, *CEO*
Jose Cruz, *Principal*
EMP: 30 EST: 2011
SALES (est): 6.8MM **Privately Held**
SIC: 3542 Headers

(G-3941)
AMERICAN SEALING TECHNOLOGY
31 Prospect Pl (11729-3713)
P.O. Box 545, Levittown (11756-0545)
PHONE..................631 254-0019
EMP: 12
SQ FT: 10,000
SALES (est): 960K **Privately Held**
SIC: 3053 Mfg Gaskets/Packing/Sealing Devices

(G-3942)
ANAND PRINTING MACHINERY INC
188 W 16th St (11729-4909)
PHONE..................631 667-3079
Amand Kumar, *President*
EMP: 1
SALES: 8MM **Privately Held**
SIC: 3555 Printing trades machinery

(G-3943)
ANTHONY MANNO & CO INC
307 Skidmore Rd Ste 2 (11729-7117)
P.O. Box 32, Freeport (11520-0032)
PHONE..................631 445-1834
Anthony Manno, *President*
Russell Fragala, *Senior VP*
EMP: 7
SQ FT: 5,000
SALES (est): 644.2K **Privately Held**
SIC: 3452 Screws, metal

(G-3944)
APOGEE TRANSLITE INC
593 Acorn St Ste B (11729-3613)
PHONE..................631 254-6975
Lynn Nicoali, *President*
Michael Boyd, *COO*
Marty Gaon, *Exec VP*
Dominick Persichilli, *Production*
Tina Giordano, *Purch Agent*
EMP: 25
SQ FT: 30,000
SALES (est): 8.4MM **Privately Held**
WEB: www.apogeetranslite.com
SIC: 3548 3646 Welding apparatus; commercial indusl & institutional electric lighting fixtures

(G-3945)
ARMA CONTAINER CORP
65 N Industry Ct (11729-4601)
PHONE..................631 254-1200
Bruce Margolis, *CEO*
Howard Gottfried, *Vice Pres*
Jack Hausman, *Treasurer*
Howard Glass, *Admin Sec*
▼ **EMP:** 50 EST: 1946
SQ FT: 70,000
SALES (est): 12.7MM **Privately Held**
WEB: www.armacontainer.com
SIC: 2653 Boxes, corrugated: made from purchased materials

(G-3946)
ARTHUR BROWN W MFG CO
49 E Industry Ct Ste I (11729-4711)
PHONE..................631 243-5594
Philip Sabatino, *President*
Anthony Sabatino, *Vice Pres*
EMP: 15
SQ FT: 8,000
SALES (est): 2MM **Privately Held**
WEB: www.arthurwbrown.com
SIC: 2511 Wood household furniture

(G-3947)
ARTSAICS STUDIOS INC
1006 Grand Blvd (11729-5710)
PHONE..................631 254-2558
Nelson Londono, *President*
EMP: 6
SALES (est): 649.3K **Privately Held**
WEB: www.artsaics.com
SIC: 3253 Mosaic tile, glazed & unglazed: ceramic

(G-3948)
AUTO DATA SYSTEMS INC (PA)
Also Called: Auto Data Labels
44 W Jefryn Blvd Ste K (11729-4721)
PHONE..................631 667-2382
Scott Saal, *President*
▼ **EMP:** 21
SQ FT: 3,000
SALES: 2.2MM **Privately Held**
SIC: 2679 5131 Tags & labels, paper; labels

(G-3949)
AUTO MARKET PUBLICATIONS INC
1641 Deer Park Ave Ste 5 (11729-5209)
PHONE..................631 667-0500
Corey Franklin, *President*
EMP: 8
SALES (est): 640.2K **Privately Held**
SIC: 2741 Telephone & other directory publishing

(G-3950)
BEST WAY TOOLS BY ANDERSON INC
171 Brook Ave (11729-7204)
PHONE..................631 586-4702
Arleen Anderson CPA, *CEO*
Wayne Anderson, *President*
Warren Anderson, *Vice Pres*
Paul Cassutti, *Vice Pres*
Austen Anderson, *VP Sales*
EMP: 4
SQ FT: 15,000
SALES: 8MM **Privately Held**
WEB: www.bestwaytools.com
SIC: 3423 5072 Hand & edge tools; hardware

(G-3951)
BIMBO BAKERIES
955 Grand Blvd (11729-5707)
PHONE..................631 274-4906
EMP: 8
SALES (est): 545.2K **Privately Held**
SIC: 2051 Bread, cake & related products

(G-3952)
BLI INTERNATIONAL INC
Also Called: Allegiant Health
75 N Industry Ct (11729-4601)
PHONE..................631 940-9000
Brian LI, *President*
Robert Naughton, *General Mgr*
Lee Rudibaugh, *Senior VP*
Jerry Maleh, *Vice Pres*
John Zhong, *Vice Pres*
EMP: 130
SALES (est): 42.5MM **Privately Held**
SIC: 2834 Tablets, pharmaceutical

(G-3953)
BLUE SKIES
859 Long Island Ave (11729-3426)
PHONE..................631 392-1140
Lisa Delvecchio, *Owner*
EMP: 5
SALES (est): 419.7K **Privately Held**
SIC: 3577 Printers & plotters

(G-3954)
BRENSEKE GEORGE WLDG IR WORKS
Also Called: Brenseke's
915 Long Island Ave Ste A (11729-3731)
PHONE..................631 271-4870
Carol Brenseke, *President*
George Brenseke, *Vice Pres*
EMP: 6
SALES: 800K **Privately Held**
SIC: 7692 Welding repair

(G-3955)
BROOKS LITHO DIGITAL GROUP INC
35 W Jefryn Blvd Ste A (11729-5784)
PHONE..................631 789-4500
David Brooks, *President*
Linda Brooks, *Vice Pres*
EMP: 5
SQ FT: 500
SALES (est): 929.2K **Privately Held**
WEB: www.brookslitho.com
SIC: 2752 2791 2789 2759 Commercial printing, offset; typesetting; bookbinding & related work; commercial printing

(G-3956)
CHALLENGE GRAPHICS SVCS INC (PA)
22 Connor Ln (11729-7234)
PHONE..................631 586-0171
Anthony Brancato, *Ch of Bd*
Jim McLoone, *General Mgr*
Joseph Brancato, *Vice Pres*
Kurt Hochreiter, *Prdtn Mgr*
Roseann Brancato, *Treasurer*
EMP: 42
SQ FT: 32,000
SALES (est): 6.6MM **Privately Held**
SIC: 2752 2791 2789 Lithographing on metal; typesetting; bookbinding & related work

(G-3957)
CHAPMAN SKATEBOARD CO INC
Also Called: New York Skateboards
87 N Industry Ct Ste A (11729-4607)
PHONE..................631 321-4773
Greg Chapman, *President*
Christine Chapman, *Vice Pres*
Chappy Chapman, *Sales Mgr*
Glenn Chapman, *Administration*
▲ **EMP:** 25
SQ FT: 2,000
SALES (est): 582.4K **Privately Held**
WEB: www.chapmanskateboards.com
SIC: 3949 5941 Skates & parts, roller; skateboarding equipment

(G-3958)
CONTINENTAL KNITTING MILLS
Also Called: La-Mar Fashions
156 Brook Ave (11729-7251)
PHONE..................631 242-5330
Pat Marini, *President*
Jennifer Marini, *Vice Pres*
EMP: 5
SQ FT: 4,000
SALES: 300K **Privately Held**
SIC: 2329 2339 5131 Men's & boys' sportswear & athletic clothing; women's & misses' athletic clothing & sportswear; sportswear, women's; knit fabrics

(G-3959)
COUSINS FURNITURE & HM IMPRVS
Also Called: Cousin's Furniture
515 Acorn St (11729-3601)
PHONE..................631 254-3752
Joaquim L Rodrigues, *President*
Ilidio Rodrigues, *Vice Pres*
Barton Bienenstock, *Executive*
EMP: 42
SQ FT: 10,200
SALES (est): 5.6MM **Privately Held**
SIC: 2511 2431 Wood household furniture; millwork

(G-3960)
CTI SOFTWARE INC
44 W Jefryn Blvd Ste P (11729-4721)
PHONE..................631 253-3550
Eric Meyn, *Ch of Bd*
EMP: 13
SALES (est): 1MM **Privately Held**
WEB: www.ctisoftware.com
SIC: 7372 Prepackaged software

(G-3961)
D W S ASSOCIATES INC
Also Called: D W S Printing
89 N Industry Ct (11729-4601)
PHONE..................631 667-6666
Thomas Staib, *President*
Andrew Staib, *Vice Pres*
Dave Tascarella, *VP Opers*
Courtney Casey, *Asst Controller*
Craig Pace, *Sales Dir*
EMP: 36
SQ FT: 20,000
SALES (est): 10.7MM **Privately Held**
WEB: www.dwsprinting.com
SIC: 2752 Commercial printing, offset

(G-3962)
DAVINCI DESIGNS INC
Also Called: Davinci Dsgns Distinctive Furn
20 Lucon Dr Unit A (11729-5789)
PHONE..................631 595-1095
Ralph Vinci, *CEO*
Chris Vinci, *Vice Pres*
Patricia Kennedy, *Manager*
EMP: 15
SQ FT: 3,000
SALES (est): 1.5MM **Privately Held**
WEB: www.davincidesigns.com
SIC: 2522 2521 Office furniture, except wood; wood office furniture

(G-3963)
DEER PARK DRIVESHAFT & HOSE
Also Called: Deer Park Drv Shaft & Hose Co
85 Brook Ave Ste C (11729-7202)
PHONE..................631 667-4091
Nick Monastero, *President*

Richard Desena, *Vice Pres*
EMP: 4
SALES: 1MM **Privately Held**
SIC: 3714 3052 5013 Drive shafts, motor vehicle; axles, motor vehicle; automobile hose, plastic; automotive supplies & parts

(G-3964)
DEER PARK MACARONI CO INC (PA)
Also Called: Dpr Food Service
1882 Deer Park Ave (11729-4318)
PHONE.................................631 667-4600
Ernest Oliviero, *President*
Tom McDonald, *Vice Pres*
Christopher Litrel, *Admin Sec*
EMP: 12 **EST:** 1949
SQ FT: 5,000
SALES (est): 2MM **Privately Held**
WEB: www.deerparkravioli.com
SIC: 2098 Macaroni & spaghetti

(G-3965)
DEER PARK MACARONI CO INC
Also Called: Deer Park Ravioli & Macaroni
1882 Deer Park Ave (11729-4318)
PHONE.................................631 667-4600
Earnest Olivero, *Manager*
EMP: 10
SALES (est): 833.4K
SALES (corp-wide): 2MM **Privately Held**
WEB: www.deerparkravioli.com
SIC: 2098 5149 Noodles (e.g. egg, plain & water), dry; pasta & rice
PA: Deer Park Macaroni Co Inc
1882 Deer Park Ave
Deer Park NY 11729
631 667-4600

(G-3966)
DESIGN DISTRIBUTORS INC
300 Marcus Blvd (11729-4500)
PHONE.................................631 242-2000
Stuart J Avrick, *Ch of Bd*
Adam G Avrick, *President*
Mark F Rice, *Vice Pres*
Michael Glanzman, *VP Opers*
Mark Rice, *Marketing Mgr*
▲ **EMP:** 85 **EST:** 1962
SQ FT: 80,000
SALES (est): 19.1MM **Privately Held**
SIC: 2759 2752 7331 Envelopes: printing; commercial printing, lithographic; direct mail advertising services

(G-3967)
DOVER MARINE MFG & SUP CO INC
98 N Industry Ct (11729-4602)
PHONE.................................631 667-4300
Theodore Cerrito, *President*
Lisa Cerrito, *Treasurer*
EMP: 5
SQ FT: 5,000
SALES (est): 480K **Privately Held**
WEB: www.dovermfg.com
SIC: 3429 Marine hardware

(G-3968)
DP MURPHY CO INC
945 Grand Blvd (11729-5707)
PHONE.................................631 673-9400
Timothy M Schratwieser, *President*
John Van Wyk, *Opers Mgr*
Hiram Quezada, *Prgrmr*
Adriane Gray, *Director*
EMP: 66 **EST:** 1873
SQ FT: 20,000
SALES (est): 8.8MM **Privately Held**
WEB: www.dpmurphy.com
SIC: 2752 7374 7331 2791 Commercial printing, offset; data processing service; mailing service; typesetting; bookbinding & related work

(G-3969)
EAST COAST EMBROIDERY LTD
74 Brook Ave Ste 1 (11729-7227)
PHONE.................................631 254-3878
Susan Simione, *President*
EMP: 7
SALES: 750K **Privately Held**
SIC: 2395 Embroidery products, except schiffli machine

(G-3970)
EAST COAST ORTHOIC & PROS COR (PA)
75 Burt Dr (11729-5701)
PHONE.................................516 248-5566
Vincent A Benenati, *CEO*
Lawrence J Benenati, *President*
John Fernandez, *Opers Mgr*
Robert Lea, *Facilities Mgr*
Joanne Giordano, *Purchasing*
▲ **EMP:** 70 **EST:** 1997
SALES (est): 12.7MM **Privately Held**
WEB: www.ec-op.com
SIC: 3842 Orthopedic appliances

(G-3971)
EC WOOD & COMPANY INC
110 E Industry Ct (11729-4706)
PHONE.................................718 388-2287
Joseph Fontana, *President*
EMP: 15
SQ FT: 13,000
SALES (est): 1.4MM **Privately Held**
SIC: 2434 Wood kitchen cabinets

(G-3972)
ELITE CELLULAR ACCESSORIES INC
61 E Industry Ct (11729-4725)
PHONE.................................877 390-2502
John Nordstrom, *President*
Stephen Conlon, *Exec VP*
EMP: 30
SQ FT: 10,000
SALES (est): 2.7MM **Privately Held**
SIC: 3663 5065 5731 Mobile communication equipment; intercommunication equipment, electronic; video cameras, recorders & accessories

(G-3973)
EMBASSY DINETTES INC
78 E Industry Ct (11729-4704)
PHONE.................................631 253-2292
Michael Walman, *Vice Pres*
◆ **EMP:** 5
SQ FT: 15,000
SALES (est): 456.8K **Privately Held**
SIC: 2514 Dinette sets: metal

(G-3974)
EMPIRE INDUSTRIAL BURNER SVC
550 Brook Ave (11729-6802)
PHONE.................................631 242-4619
Edward Roufberg, *President*
Rose Marie Price, *Administration*
EMP: 10
SQ FT: 37,000
SALES (est): 1MM
SALES (corp-wide): 1.1MM **Privately Held**
SIC: 3433 1711 Burners, furnaces, boilers & stokers; boiler maintenance contractor; heating systems repair & maintenance
PA: Empire Industrial Systems Corp.
40 Corbin Ave
Bay Shore NY 11706
631 242-4619

(G-3975)
EURO MARMOL GRAN
2 Saxwood St Ste G (11729-4710)
PHONE.................................631 940-9165
Guillermo Mazariegos, *President*
EMP: 6
SALES (est): 483.1K **Privately Held**
SIC: 1411 Granite dimension stone

(G-3976)
FLOW X RAY CORPORATION
Also Called: Flow Dental
100 W Industry Ct (11729-4604)
PHONE.................................631 242-9729
Howard Wolf, *President*
Martin B Wolf, *Chairman*
Arlene Wolf, *Vice Pres*
Carolyn Price, *CFO*
Carol Price Camiola, *Info Tech Mgr*
▲ **EMP:** 96 **EST:** 1974
SQ FT: 70,000
SALES (est): 13.4MM **Privately Held**
SIC: 3844 X-ray apparatus & tubes

(G-3977)
FORCE DIGITAL MEDIA INC
39 W Jefryn Blvd Ste 2 (11729-5792)
PHONE.................................631 243-0243
John Mazzio, *President*
EMP: 5
SALES (est): 189.8K **Privately Held**
SIC: 2759 7336 Commercial printing; package design

(G-3978)
FORMATS UNLIMITED INC
Also Called: Mf Digital
19 W Jefryn Blvd Ste 2 (11729-5749)
PHONE.................................631 249-9200
Anthony Cosentino, *Ch of Bd*
Joyce Cosentino, *Vice Pres*
Rob Derita, *Sales Mgr*
John McGrath, *Sales Staff*
Jayne Hessel, *Officer*
EMP: 10
SQ FT: 2,500
SALES (est): 1.9MM **Privately Held**
WEB: www.formats-unlimited.com
SIC: 7372 5045 3572 5065 Prepackaged software; disk drives; disk drives, computer; diskettes, computer

(G-3979)
FOSSIL INDUSTRIES INC
44 W Jefryn Blvd Ste A (11729-4721)
PHONE.................................631 254-9200
Howard Decesare, *President*
Mark Decesare, *Vice Pres*
Steven Melisi, *VP Opers*
Linda Peters, *Accounts Exec*
Alyssa Alaia, *Graphic Designe*
▼ **EMP:** 25
SQ FT: 25,000
SALES (est): 3MM **Privately Held**
WEB: www.fossilinc.com
SIC: 3993 Signs, not made in custom sign painting shops

(G-3980)
FUTURE SPRAY FINISHING CO
78 Brook Ave Ste A (11729-7226)
PHONE.................................631 242-6252
Josephine Galea, *Owner*
EMP: 5
SQ FT: 4,500
SALES (est): 364K **Privately Held**
SIC: 3479 Coating of metals & formed products

(G-3981)
GLOBAL STEEL PRODUCTS CORP (HQ)
95 Marcus Blvd (11729-4501)
PHONE.................................631 586-3455
Peter Rolla, *President*
Adrienne Rolla, *Treasurer*
◆ **EMP:** 150
SQ FT: 85,000
SALES (est): 19.1MM
SALES (corp-wide): 201.6MM **Privately Held**
WEB: www.globalpartitions.com
SIC: 2542 3446 3443 3442 Partitions for floor attachment, prefabricated: except wood; architectural metalwork; fabricated plate work (boiler shop); metal doors, sash & trim
PA: Itr Industries, Inc
441 Saw Mill River Rd
Yonkers NY 10701
914 964-7063

(G-3982)
GLOBAL TECHNOLOGIES INC (PA)
81 E Jefryn Blvd Ste D (11729-5733)
PHONE.................................631 243-7924
Stan Lichenstein, *President*
Ann Marie Longo, *Vice Pres*
Joseph Rotbard, *Admin Sec*
EMP: 80
SQ FT: 12,000
SALES (est): 13.4MM **Privately Held**
WEB: www.globaltec.com
SIC: 3357 5063 3669 5065 Communication wire; electronic wire & cable; intercommunication systems, electric; communication equipment; printed circuit boards

(G-3983)
HI-TEMP BRAZING INC
539 Acorn St (11729-3601)
PHONE.................................631 491-4917
Raymond M Gentner, *President*
Raymond M Gentner III, *Opers Mgr*
EMP: 30
SQ FT: 7,500
SALES (est): 6.3MM **Privately Held**
WEB: www.hitempbrazing.com
SIC: 3398 Brazing (hardening) of metal

(G-3984)
HIGHLAND ORGANIZATION CORP
435 Unit 23 Brook Ave (11729)
PHONE.................................631 991-3240
Marc Piacenti, *President*
Jennifer McGee, *Comptroller*
EMP: 35 **EST:** 1999
SQ FT: 3,200
SALES: 5MM **Privately Held**
SIC: 2431 Millwork

(G-3985)
HRD METAL PRODUCTS INC
120 E Jefryn Blvd Ste A (11729-5723)
PHONE.................................631 243-6700
Hector Lasalle, *President*
Martin Michie, *Vice Pres*
EMP: 8
SQ FT: 4,000
SALES (est): 800K **Privately Held**
SIC: 3444 Sheet metalwork

(G-3986)
ICE CUBE INC (PA)
171 E Industry Ct Ste B (11729-4732)
PHONE.................................613 254-0071
Conn Simino, *President*
EMP: 7
SALES (est): 848.3K **Privately Held**
SIC: 2097 Ice cubes

(G-3987)
ISLAND INSTRUMENT CORP
65 Burt Dr (11729-5701)
PHONE.................................631 243-0550
Patrick McKeever, *President*
Dawn Bannwarth, *Office Mgr*
EMP: 9
SQ FT: 12,500
SALES (est): 1.3MM **Privately Held**
WEB: www.sonnart.com
SIC: 3599 Machine shop, jobbing & repair

(G-3988)
J & J SWISS PRECISION INC
160 W Industry Ct Ste F (11729-4677)
P.O. Box 408 (11729-0408)
PHONE.................................631 243-5584
John Dojlidko, *President*
Tom Mak, *QC Mgr*
John Mroz, *Treasurer*
EMP: 30
SQ FT: 10,000
SALES (est): 4.7MM **Privately Held**
SIC: 3599 3451 Machine shop, jobbing & repair; screw machine products

(G-3989)
JAMAR PRECISION PRODUCTS CO
5 Lucon Dr (11729-5711)
PHONE.................................631 254-0234
James Lewandoski, *President*
Joy Lewandoski, *Vice Pres*
EMP: 12
SQ FT: 10,500
SALES (est): 726K **Privately Held**
SIC: 3599 Machine shop, jobbing & repair

(G-3990)
JAMCO AEROSPACE INC
121a E Industry Ct (11729-4705)
PHONE.................................631 586-7900
Jack Lee, *CEO*
Linette Lee, *President*
Ronald Lee, *Project Engr*
Hanna LI, *Admin Sec*
EMP: 50
SQ FT: 30,000
SALES (est): 11MM **Privately Held**
WEB: www.jamco-aerospace.com
SIC: 3728 Aircraft parts & equipment

Deer Park - Suffolk County (G-3991)

(G-3991)
JAVCON MACHINE INC
255 Skidmore Rd (11729-7102)
PHONE 631 586-1890
Eric Clauss, *President*
EMP: 9 **EST:** 1977
SALES: 1.5MM **Privately Held**
SIC: 3599 Machine shop, jobbing & repair

(G-3992)
JED LIGHTS INC (HQ)
10 Connor Ln (11729-7210)
PHONE 516 812-5001
Doug Flank, *Manager*
EMP: 10
SQ FT: 10,000
SALES (est): 4.9MM
SALES (corp-wide): 10.1MM **Privately Held**
SIC: 3648 5063 3053 3052 Lighting equipment; lighting fittings & accessories; gasket materials; rubber & plastics hose & beltings
PA: Green Logic Led Electrical Supply Inc.
75 Marine St
Farmingdale NY 11735
516 280-2854

(G-3993)
JOHN J MAZUR INC
94 E Jefryn Blvd Ste K (11729-5728)
PHONE 631 242-4554
John J Mazur Jr, *President*
Peter Strouse, *QC Mgr*
Alice Mazur, *Admin Sec*
EMP: 15 **EST:** 1957
SQ FT: 15,000
SALES (est): 2.3MM **Privately Held**
SIC: 3599 Machine shop, jobbing & repair

(G-3994)
JUSTIN GREGORY INC
94 E Jefryn Blvd Ste E (11729-5728)
PHONE 631 249-5187
Justin Gregory, *CEO*
Renee Levin, *President*
EMP: 6
SALES (est): 639.9K **Privately Held**
SIC: 3111 Accessory products, leather

(G-3995)
KENWIN SALES CORP
Also Called: Levitt Industrial Textile
86 W Industry Ct (11729-4610)
PHONE 516 933-7553
Beth Foley, *CEO*
Andrew Kanter, *President*
EMP: 8
SQ FT: 6,000
SALES (est): 1MM **Privately Held**
WEB: www.levittextiles.com
SIC: 3965 Fasteners

(G-3996)
KONAR PRECISION MFG INC
62 S 2nd St Ste F (11729-4716)
PHONE 631 242-4466
Daruisz Konarski, *President*
Slawomir Konarski, *Vice Pres*
Monika Konarska, *Accounting Mgr*
Karol Konarski, *Office Mgr*
EMP: 5
SQ FT: 2,000
SALES (est): 500K **Privately Held**
SIC: 3599 Machine shop, jobbing & repair

(G-3997)
L & K GRAPHICS INC
Also Called: Minuteman Press
1917 Deer Park Ave (11729-3302)
PHONE 631 667-2269
Richard Crockett, *Ch of Bd*
Robert Mason, *President*
EMP: 6 **EST:** 1975
SQ FT: 2,000
SALES (est): 1MM **Privately Held**
SIC: 2752 Commercial printing, lithographic

(G-3998)
L MILLER DESIGN INC
Also Called: Bank Displays.com
100 E Jefryn Blvd Ste F (11729-5729)
PHONE 631 242-1163
Robert L Miller, *President*
Leena Miller, *Corp Secy*
Mike Malone, *Vice Pres*
John Giachetti, *Director*
EMP: 7
SALES: 650K **Privately Held**
WEB: www.lmillerdesign.com
SIC: 3993 7319 Signs & advertising specialties; display advertising service

(G-3999)
LA STRADA DANCE FOOTWEAR INC
770 Grand Blvd Ste 1 (11729-5725)
PHONE 631 242-1401
Daniel Cerasuolo, *President*
Linda O'Shea, *Corp Secy*
EMP: 6
SQ FT: 3,300
SALES: 350K **Privately Held**
SIC: 3149 2252 Ballet slippers; socks

(G-4000)
LESLY ENTERPRISE & ASSOCIATES
29 Columbo Dr (11729-1808)
P.O. Box 190 (11729-0190)
PHONE 631 988-1301
Lesly Senat, *Principal*
EMP: 5
SALES: 50K **Privately Held**
SIC: 3721 Aircraft

(G-4001)
LEVON GRAPHICS CORP
500 Brook Ave (11729-6835)
P.O. Box 9073, Farmingdale (11735-9073)
PHONE 631 753-2022
Donna A Dickran, *Ch of Bd*
Harry L Dickran, *President*
Larry Dupkin, *Opers Staff*
Debbie Kubler, *Admin Asst*
Elizabeth Meisser, *Admin Asst*
EMP: 80
SQ FT: 42,000
SALES (est): 15.1MM **Privately Held**
WEB: www.levongraphics.com
SIC: 2752 2759 Commercial printing, offset; commercial printing

(G-4002)
LIGHTING SCULPTURES INC
Also Called: Versaponents
66 N Industry Ct (11729-4602)
PHONE 631 242-3387
Chet Yaswen, *President*
Laura Yaswen, *Vice Pres*
EMP: 10
SALES (est): 2.3MM **Privately Held**
SIC: 3648 Lighting equipment

(G-4003)
LONG ISLAND METALFORM INC
12 Lucon Dr (11729-5712)
PHONE 631 242-9088
George Seitz Jr, *President*
EMP: 14
SQ FT: 14,000
SALES (est): 2.8MM **Privately Held**
WEB: www.longislandmetalform.com
SIC: 3469 Spinning metal for the trade

(G-4004)
LUCIA GROUP INC
45 W Jefryn Blvd Ste 108 (11729-5722)
PHONE 631 392-4900
Craig Lucia, *President*
Guly Rothwell, *Project Mgr*
▲ **EMP:** 5 **EST:** 1994
SQ FT: 1,000
SALES (est): 610K **Privately Held**
WEB: www.theluciagroup.com
SIC: 2522 2542 Office furniture, except wood; shelving, office & store: except wood

(G-4005)
M H STRYKE CO INC
181 E Industry Ct Ste A (11729-4718)
PHONE 631 242-2660
Kenneth Winter, *President*
EMP: 10 **EST:** 1931
SQ FT: 3,000
SALES (est): 760.5K **Privately Held**
SIC: 3965 Fasteners, snap

(G-4006)
MARKSMEN MANUFACTURING CORP
355 Marcus Blvd (11729-4509)
PHONE 800 305-6942
Peter Guttieri, *President*
◆ **EMP:** 48
SQ FT: 14,800
SALES (est): 11.1MM **Privately Held**
WEB: www.marksmenmfg.com
SIC: 3452 3599 Bolts, metal; machine shop, jobbing & repair

(G-4007)
MASTER CRAFT FINISHERS INC
30 W Jefryn Blvd Ste 1 (11729-4730)
PHONE 631 586-0540
Roger J Fox, *President*
Jay Adriaenssens, *VP Opers*
EMP: 40 **EST:** 1969
SQ FT: 15,000
SALES (est): 4.5MM **Privately Held**
SIC: 3479 3471 2396 Coating of metals & formed products; finishing, metals or formed products; automotive & apparel trimmings

(G-4008)
MCG ELECTRONICS INC
Also Called: McG Surge Protection
12 Burt Dr (11729-5778)
PHONE 631 586-5125
Michael Coyle, *President*
Suzanne Baron, *General Mgr*
Cecilia Coyle, *Vice Pres*
Kim Connors, *Purch Mgr*
Dion Neri, *Engng Exec*
▼ **EMP:** 50
SQ FT: 10,000
SALES (est): 7.9MM **Privately Held**
WEB: www.mcgsurge.com
SIC: 3674 Semiconductors & related devices

(G-4009)
MD INTERNATIONAL INDUSTRIES
Also Called: M D I Industries
120 E Jefryn Blvd Ste Aa (11729-5739)
PHONE 631 254-3100
Martin Michie, *Owner*
Blanche Michie, *Shareholder*
EMP: 24
SQ FT: 10,000
SALES (est): 4.5MM **Privately Held**
WEB: www.mdiindustries.com
SIC: 3728 3444 Aircraft parts & equipment; sheet metalwork

(G-4010)
MINI-MAX DNTL REPR EQPMNTS INC
25 W Jefryn Blvd Ste B (11729-5740)
PHONE 631 242-0322
Brad Vollmer, *Principal*
Michael Gavris, *Principal*
EMP: 7
SALES: 1.2MM **Privately Held**
SIC: 3843 Dental equipment & supplies

(G-4011)
MODERN PACKAGING INC
505 Acorn St (11729-3601)
PHONE 631 595-2437
Syed Zaki Hossai, *Ch of Bd*
Syed Zaki Hossain, *Ch of Bd*
Towhidul Islam, *General Mgr*
Jaroslaw Dabek, *Vice Pres*
Jerry Dabek, *Vice Pres*
▲ **EMP:** 62
SQ FT: 20,000
SALES (est): 14.1MM **Privately Held**
WEB: www.modernpackaginginc.com
SIC: 3599 3565 5084 Custom machinery; packaging machinery; packaging machinery & equipment

(G-4012)
NANZ CUSTOM HARDWARE INC
105 E Jefryn Blvd (11729-5713)
PHONE 212 367-7000
EMP: 125
SALES (corp-wide): 28.3MM **Privately Held**
WEB: www.nanz.com
SIC: 3429 5031 Door opening & closing devices, except electrical; building materials, interior
PA: Nanz Custom Hardware, Inc.
20 Vandam St Fl 5l
New York NY 10013
212 367-7000

(G-4013)
NATIONAL COMPUTER & ELECTRONIC
Also Called: Nceec
367 Bay Shore Rd Ste D (11729-7244)
PHONE 631 242-7222
Neal Morofsky, *Chairman*
Lynn Nicolai, *Vice Pres*
EMP: 8
SQ FT: 5,000
SALES (est): 859K **Privately Held**
WEB: www.ncee.com
SIC: 3469 Electronic enclosures, stamped or pressed metal

(G-4014)
NELCO LABORATORIES INC
154 Brook Ave (11729-7251)
P.O. Box 58 (11729-0058)
PHONE 631 242-0082
April Catanzaro, *President*
Noelle Park, *Vice Pres*
EMP: 22 **EST:** 1971
SQ FT: 6,800
SALES (est): 3.2MM **Privately Held**
WEB: www.nelcolabs.com
SIC: 2836 Allergens, allergenic extracts

(G-4015)
NEW WOP RECORDS
Also Called: Artists, Doo Wop
317 W 14th St (11729-6301)
PHONE 631 617-9732
Giro Manuele, *Owner*
EMP: 5
SALES (est): 210K **Privately Held**
SIC: 3651 Household audio & video equipment

(G-4016)
NIJON TOOL CO INC
12 Evergreen Pl 12 # 12 (11729-3708)
PHONE 631 242-3434
Franklin Trama, *President*
John Burns, *Vice Pres*
EMP: 10
SQ FT: 12,500
SALES (est): 870K **Privately Held**
SIC: 3544 Special dies & tools

(G-4017)
NIKE INC
102 The Arches Cir (11729-7057)
PHONE 631 242-3014
EMP: 38
SALES (corp-wide): 36.4B **Publicly Held**
SIC: 3021 Rubber & plastics footwear
PA: Nike, Inc.
1 Sw Bowerman Dr
Beaverton OR 97005
503 671-6453

(G-4018)
NUTEC COMPONENTS INC
81 E Jefryn Blvd Ste A (11729-5733)
PHONE 631 242-1224
Rene H Schnetzler, *President*
Glenn Stanley, *Vice Pres*
EMP: 15
SQ FT: 10,500
SALES (est): 3.6MM **Privately Held**
WEB: www.nutec1.com
SIC: 3823 Industrial instrmnts msrmnt display/control process variable

(G-4019)
NUTRA SOLUTIONS USA INC
Also Called: Nsusa
1019 Grand Blvd (11729-5709)
PHONE 631 392-1900
Latiful Hakue, *CEO*
Kalsar Sultana, *Principal*
EMP: 25

SALES (est): 9.5MM **Privately Held**
SIC: 2833 7389 Vitamins, natural or synthetic: bulk, uncompounded; packaging & labeling services

(G-4020)
NY FROYO LLC
324 W 19th St (11729-6342)
PHONE 516 312-4588
EMP: 5
SALES (est): 254.2K **Privately Held**
SIC: 2024 Yogurt desserts, frozen

(G-4021)
OCEAN CARDIAC MONITORING
38 W 17th St (11729-3902)
PHONE 631 777-3700
Roberto Garcia, *Owner*
EMP: 5
SALES (est): 561.6K **Privately Held**
SIC: 3845 Patient monitoring apparatus

(G-4022)
OVERNIGHT LABELS INC
151 W Industry Ct Ste 15 (11729-4600)
PHONE 631 242-4240
Donald Earl, *President*
Tony De Moraes, *Art Dir*
▲ **EMP:** 20
SQ FT: 3,400
SALES (est): 5.3MM **Privately Held**
WEB: www.overnightlabels.com
SIC: 2672 Labels (unprinted), gummed: made from purchased materials

(G-4023)
PAULS RODS & RESTOS INC
131 Brook Ave Ste 13 (11729-7221)
PHONE 631 665-7637
Paul R Dimauro, *Principal*
EMP: 6
SALES (est): 830.5K **Privately Held**
SIC: 3531 Automobile wrecker hoists

(G-4024)
PDF SEAL INCORPORATED
503 Acorn St (11729-3601)
PHONE 631 595-7035
Jaroslaw Dabek, *Ch of Bd*
Syed Zaki Hossain, *Vice Pres*
Jeremy Bank, *Opers Mgr*
Adeeb Hakim, *Prdtn Mgr*
EMP: 25
SQ FT: 16,000
SALES: 10MM **Privately Held**
SIC: 2631 Container, packaging & boxboard

(G-4025)
PHOTO MEDIC EQUIPMENT INC
Also Called: Precise Optics
3 Saxwood St Ste E (11729-4700)
PHONE 631 242-6600
Len Corso, *Ch of Bd*
R Hannington, *Purchasing*
Ann Alonzo, *Controller*
R Corso, *Marketing Staff*
Gordon Kellogg, *Systems Mgr*
EMP: 90
SQ FT: 50,000
SALES (est): 7.7MM **Privately Held**
WEB: www.preciseoptics.com
SIC: 3844 X-ray apparatus & tubes

(G-4026)
PLX INC (PA)
Also Called: P L X
25 W Jefryn Blvd Ste A (11729-5740)
PHONE 631 586-4190
Jack Lipkins, *President*
Zvi Bleier, *Vice Pres*
Doinel Blaj, *Engineer*
Zechariah Gajadhar, *Engineer*
Mary Youssef, *Bookkeeper*
EMP: 40 **EST:** 1953
SQ FT: 15,000
SALES (est): 7.1MM **Privately Held**
WEB: www.plxinc.com
SIC: 3827 Optical instruments & apparatus

(G-4027)
PNC SPORTS
1880 Deer Park Ave (11729-4318)
PHONE 516 665-2244
Richard Knowles, *Principal*
EMP: 7

SALES (est): 688.1K **Privately Held**
SIC: 3949 Sporting & athletic goods

(G-4028)
PRECISION CNC
71 E Jefryn Blvd (11729-5713)
PHONE 631 847-3999
Sal Napolitano, *Owner*
EMP: 6
SALES (est): 782.4K **Privately Held**
SIC: 3728 Aircraft parts & equipment

(G-4029)
PRINT MARKET INC
66 E Jefryn Blvd Ste 1 (11729-5760)
PHONE 631 940-8181
EMP: 8
SALES (est): 62.8K **Privately Held**
SIC: 2752 Lithographic Commercial Printing

(G-4030)
PROFESSIONAL MANUFACTURERS
475 Brook Ave (11729-7208)
P.O. Box 282 (11729-0282)
PHONE 631 586-2440
Richard Lizio, *President*
EMP: 10
SALES (est): 960K **Privately Held**
SIC: 3843 Dental equipment & supplies

(G-4031)
PVH CORP
Also Called: Van Heusen
1358 The Arches Cir (11729-7069)
PHONE 631 254-8200
Shannon Wright, *Branch Mgr*
EMP: 9
SALES (corp-wide): 8.9B **Publicly Held**
SIC: 2321 Men's & boys' dress shirts
PA: Pvh Corp.
200 Madison Ave Bsmt 1
New York NY 10016
212 381-3500

(G-4032)
R E F PRECISION PRODUCTS
517 Acorn St Ste A (11729-3610)
PHONE 631 242-4471
Robert Fleece, *Partner*
Raymond Crisafulli, *Partner*
EMP: 17
SQ FT: 3,600
SALES (est): 2.2MM **Privately Held**
WEB: www.refprecisionproducts.com
SIC: 3599 Custom machinery; machine shop, jobbing & repair

(G-4033)
R J S DIRECT MARKETING INC
561 Acorn St Ste E (11729-3600)
PHONE 631 667-5768
Micheal Manfre, *President*
EMP: 15
SALES (est): 1.5MM **Privately Held**
WEB: www.rjsmarketingonline.com
SIC: 2834 Solutions, pharmaceutical

(G-4034)
RAINBOW POWDER COATING CORP
86 E Industry Ct (11729-4704)
PHONE 631 586-4019
Ron Vincent, *President*
EMP: 5
SQ FT: 5,800
SALES (est): 496.4K **Privately Held**
SIC: 3471 Finishing, metals or formed products

(G-4035)
REFLEX OFFSET INC
305 Suburban Ave (11729-6806)
PHONE 516 746-4142
John Banks, *President*
Richard Banks, *Vice Pres*
EMP: 8
SQ FT: 5,400
SALES (est): 1MM **Privately Held**
WEB: www.reflexoffset.com
SIC: 2752 Commercial printing, offset

(G-4036)
RINALDI PRECISION MACHINE
Also Called: R P M
43 Crossway Dr (11729-6225)
PHONE 631 242-4141
Angelo Rinaldi, *President*
EMP: 10
SQ FT: 1,700
SALES (est): 1.6MM **Privately Held**
SIC: 3599 Machine shop, jobbing & repair

(G-4037)
ROSEMONT PRESS INCORPORATED
35 W Jefryn Blvd Ste A (11729-5784)
PHONE 212 239-4770
Czarina Anif, *Branch Mgr*
EMP: 9
SALES (corp-wide): 8.2MM **Privately Held**
WEB: www.rosemontpress.com
SIC: 2741 Miscellaneous publishing
PA: Rosemont Press Incorporated
253 Church St Apt 2
New York NY 10013
212 239-4770

(G-4038)
ROSS METAL FABRICATORS INC
225 Marcus Blvd (11729-4503)
P.O. Box 12308, Hauppauge (11788-0615)
PHONE 631 586-7000
Richard Ross, *President*
Ron Reid, *Vice Pres*
Lawrence Perez, *Treasurer*
EMP: 40 **EST:** 1969
SQ FT: 30,000
SALES (est): 6.6MM
SALES (corp-wide): 39.2MM **Privately Held**
SIC: 3443 Metal parts
PA: Charles Ross & Son Company
710 Old Willets Path
Hauppauge NY 11788
631 234-0500

(G-4039)
RSM ELECTRON POWER INC (PA)
Also Called: Sensitron Semiconductor
221 W Industry Ct (11729-4605)
PHONE 631 586-7600
Steve Saunders, *President*
Mary Saunders, *Admin Sec*
▲ **EMP:** 90 **EST:** 1969
SQ FT: 20,000
SALES (est): 23.8MM **Privately Held**
WEB: www.sensitron.com
SIC: 3674 Integrated circuits, semiconductor networks, etc.

(G-4040)
SCHENCK CORPORATION (DH)
535 Acorn St (11729-3698)
PHONE 631 242-4010
Lars Kuenne, *President*
Uwe Grimm, *CFO*
Patrise Heins, *Manager*
◆ **EMP:** 70
SQ FT: 40,000
SALES (est): 33.4MM
SALES (corp-wide): 4.3B **Privately Held**
SIC: 3545 3829 Balancing machines (machine tool accessories); measuring & controlling devices
HQ: Schenck Industrie-Beteiligungen Ag
C/O Dr. Thomas Hefti
Glarus GL
556 402-544

(G-4041)
SCHENCK TREBEL CORP (DH)
535 Acorn St (11729-3616)
PHONE 631 242-4010
Lars Kuenne, *President*
Uwe Grimm, *CFO*
Patrise Heins, *Manager*
◆ **EMP:** 60
SQ FT: 44,000

SALES (est): 20MM
SALES (corp-wide): 4.3B **Privately Held**
WEB: www.schenck-usa.com
SIC: 3545 3829 Balancing machines (machine tool accessories); measuring & controlling devices
HQ: Schenck Corporation
535 Acorn St
Deer Park NY 11729
631 242-4010

(G-4042)
SCIENTIFIC COMPONENTS CORP
Also Called: Mini Circuits Lab
161 E Industry Ct (11729-4705)
PHONE 631 243-4901
Al Chasinov, *Branch Mgr*
Robert Jasinkonis, *Manager*
EMP: 40
SALES (corp-wide): 141.6MM **Privately Held**
SIC: 3825 Instruments to measure electricity
PA: Scientific Components Corp
13 Neptune Ave
Brooklyn NY 11235
718 934-4500

(G-4043)
SECTOR MICROWAVE INDS INC
999 Grand Blvd (11729-5799)
PHONE 631 242-2245
Victor H Nelson, *President*
Thomas J Nelson, *Vice Pres*
Tom Nelson, *Vice Pres*
Jim Tracy, *Info Tech Mgr*
Patricia Nelson, *Admin Sec*
▼ **EMP:** 55
SQ FT: 28,000
SALES: 8.7MM **Privately Held**
SIC: 3643 Electric switches

(G-4044)
SHANKER INDUSTRIES REALTY INC (PA)
301 Suburban Ave (11729-6806)
PHONE 631 940-9889
John Shanker, *President*
Francine Shanker, *Exec VP*
Frances Shanker, *Vice Pres*
▲ **EMP:** 5
SQ FT: 5,700
SALES (est): 1.3MM **Privately Held**
WEB: www.shanko.com
SIC: 3446 Ornamental metalwork

(G-4045)
SHARON MANUFACTURING CO INC
540 Brook Ave (11729-6802)
PHONE 631 242-8870
Robert Stamm, *President*
William Stamm, *Vice Pres*
John Zaikowski, *Purch Agent*
EMP: 8
SQ FT: 7,500
SALES (est): 1.7MM **Privately Held**
SIC: 3469 3565 Machine parts, stamped or pressed metal; bag opening, filling & closing machines

(G-4046)
SOMERS STAIN GLASS INC
108 Brook Ave Ste A (11729-7238)
PHONE 631 586-7772
Ronald Somers, *President*
Tricia Somers, *Office Mgr*
EMP: 10
SQ FT: 10,000
SALES: 700K **Privately Held**
SIC: 3231 3229 Stained glass: made from purchased glass; lamp parts & shades, glass

(G-4047)
SOUNDCOAT COMPANY INC (DH)
1 Burt Dr (11729-5756)
PHONE 631 242-2200
Louis Nenninger, *CEO*
◆ **EMP:** 65 **EST:** 1963
SQ FT: 70,000

Deer Park - Suffolk County (G-4048)

SALES (est): 14.9MM
SALES (corp-wide): 385.7MM **Privately Held**
WEB: www.soundcoat.com
SIC: **3086** 2299 3625 3296 Insulation or cushioning material, foamed plastic; acoustic felts; noise control equipment; mineral wool

(G-4048)
SPEAQUA CORP
46 W Jefryn Blvd (11729-4736)
PHONE..................................858 334-9042
Steven Patsis, *President*
Steve Patsis, *Vice Pres*
EMP: 40
SQ FT: 20,000
SALES (est): 1.7MM **Privately Held**
SIC: **3651** Loudspeakers, electrodynamic or magnetic

(G-4049)
SUFFOLK COMMUNITY COUNCIL INC (PA)
819 Grand Blvd Ste 1 (11729-5780)
PHONE..................................631 434-9277
Judith Pannullo, *Director*
EMP: 9
SQ FT: 2,000
SALES (est): 194.3K **Privately Held**
WEB: www.suffolkcommunitycouncil.org
SIC: **2721** 8322 Periodicals: publishing only; individual & family services

(G-4050)
SUPER STEELWORKS CORPORATION
12 Lucon Dr (11729-5712)
PHONE..................................718 386-4770
Carlos Mery, *Principal*
▲ EMP: 5
SALES (est): 391.2K **Privately Held**
SIC: **3317** Steel pipe & tubes

(G-4051)
TEK PRECISION CO LTD
205 W Industry Ct (11729-4613)
PHONE..................................631 242-0330
John Krause, *CEO*
Steve Longobardi, *President*
Randall Strauss, *Vice Pres*
Pat Sweeney, *Production*
Sharon Valles, *Purch Mgr*
EMP: 24
SQ FT: 21,000
SALES: 10.4MM **Privately Held**
WEB: www.tekprecision.com
SIC: **3728** Aircraft assemblies, subassemblies & parts

(G-4052)
TRI-STATE WINDOW FACTORY CORP
360 Marcus Blvd (11729-4504)
PHONE..................................631 667-8600
John Kypreos, *President*
EMP: 75
SQ FT: 31,000
SALES (est): 13.8MM **Privately Held**
SIC: **3089** 1761 1751 Windows, plastic; siding contractor; window & door (prefabricated) installation

(G-4053)
ULTRA THIN READY TO BAKE PIZZA
Also Called: Ultra Thin Pzza Shlls Fltbrads
151 E Industry Ct (11729-4705)
PHONE..................................516 679-6655
Douglas Bronsky, *Mng Member*
Cherise Kramer,
EMP: 30
SQ FT: 15,000
SALES (est): 5.6MM **Privately Held**
SIC: **2099** Pizza, refrigerated: except frozen

(G-4054)
UNICEL CORPORATION
235 W Industry Ct (11729-4605)
PHONE..................................760 741-3912
Michael Henderson, *President*
▲ EMP: 30 EST: 1978
SQ FT: 13,000
SALES (est): 4.8MM **Privately Held**
WEB: www.unicelcorp.com
SIC: **3469** Honeycombed metal

(G-4055)
UNIVERSAL SHIELDING CORP
20 W Jefryn Blvd (11729-5769)
PHONE..................................631 667-7900
Irwin Newman, *Ch of Bd*
Lois Newman, *Vice Pres*
Michael Newman, *Vice Pres*
EMP: 50
SQ FT: 20,000
SALES (est): 12.7MM **Privately Held**
WEB: www.universalshielding.com
SIC: **3448** 3469 3444 Buildings, portable: prefabricated metal; metal stampings; sheet metalwork

(G-4056)
UNIVERSAL SIGNS AND SVC INC
435 Brook Ave Unit 2 (11729-6826)
PHONE..................................631 446-1121
Marcos Marmol, *President*
EMP: 27
SQ FT: 20,000
SALES (est): 3MM **Privately Held**
SIC: **3993** Signs, not made in custom sign painting shops

(G-4057)
USA SIGNS OF AMERICA INC
172 E Industry Ct (11729-4706)
PHONE..................................631 254-6900
John Prahalis, *President*
Lynn Loder, *Vice Pres*
EMP: 75
SALES (est): 7.3MM **Privately Held**
WEB: www.usasignsofamerica.com
SIC: **3993** Signs & advertising specialties

(G-4058)
VEJA ELECTRONICS INC (PA)
Also Called: Stack Electronics
46 W Jefryn Blvd Ste A (11729-4736)
PHONE..................................631 321-6086
Steven Patsis, *CEO*
Steve Patsis, *President*
▲ EMP: 100
SQ FT: 40,000
SALES (est): 32.6MM **Privately Held**
WEB: www.stackny.com
SIC: **3644** 5063 5065 Terminal boards; electrical fittings & construction materials; electronic parts

(G-4059)
VERSAPONENTS INC
Also Called: Writing Sculptures
66 N Industry Ct (11729-4602)
PHONE..................................631 242-3387
Chet Yaswen, *President*
Laura Yaswen, *Vice Pres*
EMP: 16
SQ FT: 4,500
SALES (est): 2.5MM **Privately Held**
SIC: **3646** Commercial indusl & institutional electric lighting fixtures

(G-4060)
VINYL MATERIALS INC
365 Bay Shore Rd (11729-7201)
PHONE..................................631 586-9444
Alex Folkman, *President*
Joseph Folkman, *Vice Pres*
Roop Narine Dhanrag, *Controller*
EMP: 50
SQ FT: 65,000
SALES (est): 8.2MM **Privately Held**
SIC: **3081** 5162 3089 Vinyl film & sheet; plastics products; plastic processing

(G-4061)
VISUAL MILLWORK & FIX MFG INC
95 Marcus Blvd (11729-4501)
PHONE..................................718 267-7800
Mario Fichera Sr, *CEO*
Mario Fichera Jr, *Vice Pres*
Lydia Fichara, *CFO*
Roy White, *CFO*
EMP: 60
SQ FT: 50,000
SALES (est): 6MM **Privately Held**
WEB: www.visualdisplayinc.com
SIC: **2542** Office & store showcases & display fixtures

(G-4062)
WESTROCK RKT LLC
140 W Industry Ct (11729-4604)
PHONE..................................631 586-6000
Ron Byers, *General Mgr*
EMP: 130
SQ FT: 120,000
SALES (corp-wide): 14.8B **Publicly Held**
WEB: www.rocktenn.com
SIC: **2653** 5113 Boxes, corrugated: made from purchased materials; bags, paper & disposable plastic
HQ: Westrock Rkt, Llc
1000 Abernathy Rd Ste 125
Atlanta GA 30328
770 448-2193

(G-4063)
WOLF X-RAY CORPORATION
100 W Industry Ct (11729-4604)
PHONE..................................631 242-9729
Martin Wolf, *President*
Carol Price, *Credit Mgr*
Melissa Ferguson, *Executive Asst*
Andrea Rowen, *Executive Asst*
◆ EMP: 60 EST: 1931
SQ FT: 80,000
SALES (est): 10.2MM **Privately Held**
WEB: www.wolfxray.com
SIC: **3844** X-ray apparatus & tubes

(G-4064)
WOLO MFG CORP
1 Saxwood St Ste 1 # 1 (11729-4779)
PHONE..................................631 242-0333
Stanley Solow, *President*
◆ EMP: 21
SQ FT: 10,000
SALES (est): 4.1MM **Privately Held**
SIC: **3429** 3714 3647 Motor vehicle hardware; motor vehicle parts & accessories; vehicular lighting equipment

(G-4065)
WORLD LLC
Also Called: Wmw Machinery Company
513 Acorn St Ste B (11729-3611)
PHONE..................................631 940-9121
Cornel Circiumaru, *Mng Member*
▼ EMP: 15
SQ FT: 8,000
SALES: 1.5MM **Privately Held**
SIC: **3541** Machine tools, metal cutting type

(G-4066)
ZACMEL GRAPHICS LLC
500 Brook Ave Ste B (11729-6835)
PHONE..................................631 944-6031
Alex Nartowicz, *Prdtn Mgr*
Chuck Schleifer, *Cust Mgr*
David Warheit,
EMP: 7 EST: 2003
SALES (est): 1MM **Privately Held**
SIC: **2752** 7336 Commercial printing, lithographic; commercial art & graphic design

Delanson
Schenectady County

(G-4067)
BENZSAY & HARRISON INC
Railroad Ave (12053)
PHONE..................................518 895-2311
Rudolph Benzsay, *President*
Sema Benzsay, *Admin Sec*
EMP: 6
SQ FT: 25,000
SALES: 900.1K **Privately Held**
WEB: www.bh-inc.com
SIC: **2819** Aluminum compounds

(G-4068)
ELECTRCAL INSTRUMENTATION CTRL
1253 Youngs Rd (12053-1711)
P.O. Box 24, Duanesburg (12056-0024)
PHONE..................................518 861-5789
Michael Weiss, *President*
EMP: 11
SALES: 2MM **Privately Held**
SIC: **3823** Industrial process control instruments

(G-4069)
HARVEST HOMES INC
1331 Cole Rd (12053-3109)
PHONE..................................518 895-2341
Timothy O Brien, *Ch of Bd*
Henry Walthery, *General Mgr*
Robert A Guay, *Vice Pres*
Christian Guay, *Sales Mgr*
EMP: 35
SQ FT: 27,000
SALES: 4.5MM **Privately Held**
SIC: **2452** 2439 Panels & sections, prefabricated, wood; structural wood members

Delevan
Cattaraugus County

(G-4070)
HALEY CONCRETE INC (PA)
10413 Delevan Elton Rd (14042-9613)
PHONE..................................716 492-0849
Lawrence Haley II, *President*
Lawrence Haley III, *Admin Sec*
EMP: 15
SQ FT: 1,250
SALES (est): 2MM **Privately Held**
SIC: **3273** 4212 Ready-mixed concrete; local trucking, without storage

(G-4071)
KENDOR MUSIC INC
21 Grove St (14042-9682)
P.O. Box 278 (14042-0278)
PHONE..................................716 492-1254
Craig Cornwall, *President*
EMP: 12
SQ FT: 10,000
SALES (est): 1MM **Privately Held**
WEB: www.kendormusic.com
SIC: **2741** Music, sheet: publishing & printing

Delhi
Delaware County

(G-4072)
DELAWARE COUNTY TIMES INC
56 Main St (13753-1121)
PHONE..................................607 746-2176
Donald F Bishop II, *President*
Jackyln Losie, *Director*
EMP: 6
SALES (est): 468.8K **Privately Held**
SIC: **2711** 2721 Newspapers: publishing only, not printed on site; periodicals

(G-4073)
EXCELSIOR PUBLICATIONS
133 Main St (13753-1219)
PHONE..................................607 746-7600
Francis P Ruggiero, *President*
EMP: 5 EST: 1999
SALES (est): 479.5K **Privately Held**
SIC: **2721** Magazines: publishing & printing

(G-4074)
FRIESLNDCMPINA INGRDNTS N AMER
40196 State Hwy 10 Delhi (13753)
PHONE..................................607 746-0196
Don Combs, *Principal*
EMP: 35
SALES (corp-wide): 14.2B **Privately Held**
SIC: **2023** Dry, condensed, evaporated dairy products
HQ: Frieslandcampina Ingredients North America, Inc
61 S Paramus Rd Ste 535
Paramus NJ 07652
201 655-7780

GEOGRAPHIC SECTION

(G-4075)
SAPUTO DAIRY FOODS USA LLC
Also Called: Morningstar Foods
40236 State Highway 10 (13753-3207)
P.O. Box 1 (13753-0001)
PHONE 607 746-2141
Elizabeth Banburen, *Manager*
EMP: 100 Privately Held
WEB: www.morningstarfoods.com
SIC: 2026 Milk processing (pasteurizing, homogenizing, bottling)
HQ: Saputo Dairy Foods Usa, Llc
2711 N Haske Ave Ste 3700
Dallas TX 75204
214 863-2300

(G-4076)
SPORTSFIELD SPECIALTIES INC (PA)
Also Called: Promats Athletics
41155 State Highway 10 (13753-3213)
P.O. Box 231 (13753-0231)
PHONE 607 746-8911
Wayne Oliver, *President*
Ed Rosa, *Vice Pres*
Michelle Macintyre, *Purch Mgr*
Paige Hanselman, *Purch Agent*
Jennifer Schwerin, *Purch Agent*
EMP: 45
SQ FT: 46,000
SALES (est): 10.8MM **Privately Held**
WEB: www.sportsfieldspecialties.com
SIC: 3949 Sporting & athletic goods

Delmar
Albany County

(G-4077)
COMMUNITY MEDIA GROUP LLC (PA)
Also Called: Spotlight Newspaper
125 Adams St (12054-3211)
PHONE 518 439-4949
Bo Berezansky, *Vice Pres*
Bill Decker, *Consultant*
John A McIntyre Jr,
Daniel E Alexander,
David B Tyler Jr,
EMP: 26
SALES (est): 1.3MM **Privately Held**
SIC: 2711 Newspapers, publishing & printing

(G-4078)
SANZDRANZ LLC (PA)
Also Called: Gatherer's Gourmet Granola
83 Dumbarton Dr (12054-4418)
PHONE 518 894-8625
Sandro Gerbini, *President*
EMP: 5 EST: 2010
SQ FT: 3,700
SALES (est): 231K **Privately Held**
SIC: 2043 Cereal breakfast foods

Depew
Erie County

(G-4079)
AUBURN-WATSON CORP (PA)
3295 Walden Ave (14043-2313)
PHONE 716 876-8000
Wayne Watson, *President*
Natalie Watson, *Vice Pres*
EMP: 10 EST: 1946
SQ FT: 8,000
SALES (est): 754.5K **Privately Held**
SIC: 2434 1751 Wood kitchen cabinets; cabinet building & installation

(G-4080)
BISON STEEL INCORPORATED
2 Main St Ste 103 (14043-0323)
P.O. Box 454 (14043-0454)
PHONE 716 683-0900
Edwin C Bailey, *President*
Gus Schiralli, *Admin Sec*
▲ **EMP: 5**
SQ FT: 27,000
SALES (est): 786.2K **Privately Held**
SIC: 3496 Miscellaneous fabricated wire products

(G-4081)
BMG SYSTEMS
4779 Transit Rd 169 (14043-4915)
P.O. Box 1307, Orchard Park (14127-8307)
PHONE 716 432-5160
EMP: 13
SALES (est): 2.5MM **Privately Held**
SIC: 3444 Sheet metalwork

(G-4082)
BUFFALO ENVELOPE INC
Also Called: Buffalo Envelope Company
2914 Walden Ave Ste 300 (14043-2694)
PHONE 716 686-0100
Lorne Hill, *Managing Dir*
Dany Paradis, *Principal*
EMP: 12
SQ FT: 12,800
SALES (est): 2.8MM
SALES (corp-wide): 118.7MM **Privately Held**
SIC: 2677 5112 Envelopes; envelopes
PA: Supremex Inc
7213 Rue Cordner
Lasalle QC H8N 2
514 595-0555

(G-4083)
BUFFALO POWER ELECTRONICS CTR
166 Taylor Dr Ste 1 (14043-2021)
PHONE 716 651-1600
William Gates, *Ch of Bd*
Dennis M Cascio, *President*
Frank Stasio, *Vice Pres*
EMP: 15
SQ FT: 38,000
SALES (est): 4.9MM **Privately Held**
WEB: www.buffalopower.com
SIC: 3612 5065 Transformers, except electric; transformers, electronic

(G-4084)
BUFFALO TUNGSTEN INC
Also Called: Bti
2 Main St (14043-3323)
P.O. Box 397 (14043-0397)
PHONE 716 683-9170
Ralph V Showalter, *Ch of Bd*
Jeffrey Showalter, *Engineer*
Diane Shopwalter, *Admin Sec*
◆ **EMP: 60**
SQ FT: 500,000
SALES (est): 17.6MM **Privately Held**
WEB: www.buffalotungsten.com
SIC: 3399 2819 Powder, metal; tungsten carbide powder, except abrasive or metallurgical

(G-4085)
CUSTOM COUNTERTOPS INC (PA)
3192 Walden Ave (14043-2846)
PHONE 716 685-2871
Gloria Marino, *President*
EMP: 8
SALES: 750K **Privately Held**
WEB: www.customcountertops.com
SIC: 3131 2541 Counters; wood partitions & fixtures

(G-4086)
D R M MANAGEMENT INC (PA)
Also Called: Fresh Bake Pizza Co
3430 Transit Rd (14043-4853)
PHONE 716 668-0333
Ronald Digiore, *President*
Daniel J Digiore, *Vice Pres*
Mark Digiore, *Admin Sec*
EMP: 48
SQ FT: 1,200
SALES (est): 5.4MM **Privately Held**
WEB: www.drminc.us
SIC: 2038 8741 2099 Pizza, frozen; restaurant management; pizza, refrigerated; except frozen

(G-4087)
DESU MACHINERY CORPORATION
200 Gould Ave (14043-3134)
P.O. Box 245 (14043-0245)
PHONE 716 681-5798
Martin W Golden II, *CEO*
Mark L Dalquist, *President*
Thomas Depczynski, *Sls & Mktg Exec*
Jim Dahlquist, *Marketing Mgr*
EMP: 85
SALES (est): 8MM **Privately Held**
SIC: 3556 3565 Packing house machinery; bottling machinery: filling, capping, labeling

(G-4088)
ELMAR INDUSTRIES INC
200 Gould Ave (14043-3138)
P.O. Box 245 (14043-0245)
PHONE 716 681-5650
Martin W Golden II, *Ch of Bd*
Mark L Dahlquist, *Ch of Bd*
David Zolnowski, *Purch Mgr*
Mark Vaughan, *Engineer*
James Krypel, *Design Engr*
▲ **EMP: 62**
SQ FT: 21,000
SALES (est): 19.2MM **Privately Held**
WEB: www.elmarworldwide.com
SIC: 3565 Packaging machinery

(G-4089)
FIBRIX LLC
Buffalo Batt A Div of Polyeste
3307 Walden Ave (14043-2347)
PHONE 716 683-4100
Bob Heilman, *Manager*
EMP: 50
SQ FT: 43,000
SALES (corp-wide): 74MM **Privately Held**
WEB: www.leggett.com
SIC: 2299 2824 2221 Batting, wadding, padding & fillings; pillow fillings: curled hair, cotton waste, moss, hemp tow; organic fibers, noncellulosic; broadwoven fabric mills, manmade
HQ: Fibrix, Llc
1820 Evans St Ne
Conover NC 28613

(G-4090)
FLADO ENTERPRISES INC
Also Called: Quality Quick Signs
1380 French Rd Ste 6 (14043-4800)
PHONE 716 668-6400
Christopher R Flejtuch, *President*
EMP: 7
SQ FT: 7,000
SALES (est): 794.3K **Privately Held**
WEB: www.qualityquicksigns.com
SIC: 3993 Signs, not made in custom sign painting shops

(G-4091)
HARPER INTERNATIONAL CORP
99 Sheldon Ave (14043-3532)
PHONE 716 276-9900
Charles Miller, *President*
EMP: 6
SALES (est): 779.4K **Privately Held**
SIC: 3567 Industrial furnaces & ovens

(G-4092)
HOWDEN NORTH AMERICA INC (DH)
Also Called: Howdens
2475 George Urban Blvd # 120 (14043-2022)
PHONE 803 741-2700
Matthew Ingle, *CEO*
Karl Kimmerling, *President*
Will Samuel, *Chairman*
Kyle Greenzweig, *Engineer*
Manuel Rubio, *Sales Mgr*
◆ **EMP: 85 EST: 1980**
SALES (est): 277.2MM
SALES (corp-wide): 3.3B **Publicly Held**
WEB: www.howdenbuffalo.com
SIC: 3564 3568 Exhaust fans: industrial or commercial; couplings, shaft: rigid, flexible, universal joint, etc.

(G-4093)
HOWDEN NORTH AMERICA INC
Also Called: Howden Fan Company
2475 George Urban Blvd # 120 (14043-2022)
PHONE 716 817-6900
Darryl Halter, *Principal*
Tina Cramer, *Project Mgr*
Jim Raczkowski, *Buyer*
Phil Nowicki, *Technical Mgr*
Leona Backus, *Human Resources*
EMP: 100
SALES (corp-wide): 3.3B **Publicly Held**
WEB: www.howdenbuffalo.com
SIC: 3564 8711 Ventilating fans: industrial or commercial; engineering services
HQ: Howden North America Inc.
2475 George Urban Blvd # 120
Depew NY 14043
803 741-2700

(G-4094)
LEGNO VENETO USA
3283 Walden Ave (14043-2311)
PHONE 716 651-9169
James Carol II, *Owner*
James Caroll, *Owner*
▲ **EMP: 9**
SQ FT: 26,000
SALES (est): 1MM **Privately Held**
WEB: www.lvwoodfloors.com
SIC: 2426 Flooring, hardwood

(G-4095)
LEICA MICROSYSTEMS INC
Also Called: Opd
3362 Walden Ave (14043-2475)
P.O. Box 123, Cragsmoor (12420-0123)
PHONE 716 686-3000
Tom Tonner, *QC Mgr*
John Burgess, *Branch Mgr*
EMP: 8
SALES (corp-wide): 18.3B **Publicly Held**
SIC: 3827 Optical instruments & apparatus; microscopes, except electron, proton & corneal
HQ: Leica Microsystems Inc.
1700 Leider Ln
Buffalo Grove IL 60089
847 405-0123

(G-4096)
MOLDCRAFT INC
240 Gould Ave (14043-3130)
PHONE 716 684-1126
John Chase, *President*
Henry Lewandowski, *Treasurer*
Sharon Winkler, *Manager*
Jimmy Gray, *Admin Sec*
EMP: 20
SQ FT: 8,000
SALES: 3.8MM **Privately Held**
WEB: www.moldcraftinc.com
SIC: 3544 Forms (molds), for foundry & plastics working machinery

(G-4097)
NIAGARA REFINING LLC
5661 Transit Rd (14043-3227)
P.O. Box 398 (14043-0398)
PHONE 716 706-1400
▲ **EMP: 27**
SALES (est): 7.9MM **Privately Held**
SIC: 2819 Tungsten carbide powder, except abrasive or metallurgical

(G-4098)
NORTHEAST METROLOGY CORP
4490 Broadway (14043-2904)
PHONE 716 827-3770
Basil Korbut, *President*
Ursula Korbut, *Office Mgr*
EMP: 10
SQ FT: 6,120
SALES (est): 2MM **Privately Held**
WEB: www.vantek-nem.com
SIC: 3825 8734 Test equipment for electronic & electric measurement; testing laboratories

(G-4099)
OSMOSE HOLDINGS INC
2475 George Urban Blvd # 160 (14043-2022)
PHONE 716 882-5905

Depew - Erie County (G-4100)

James R Spengler Jr, *President*
David L Bradley, *Vice Pres*
Julie Pettus, *Safety Dir*
Joel Rowe, *Opers Mgr*
Mark Lehner, *Transportation*
◆ **EMP:** 1335
SALES (est): 228.8MM **Publicly Held**
WEB: www.fireretardanttreatedwood.com
SIC: 2491 Preserving (creosoting) of wood
HQ: Oaktree Capital Management, L.P.
  333 S Grand Ave Ste 2800
  Los Angeles CA 90071

(G-4100)
PCB GROUP INC
Also Called: ICP
3425 Walden Ave (14043-2417)
PHONE 716 684-0001
Mike Lally, *CEO*
James F Lally, *Ch of Bd*
John Betzig, *Opers Mgr*
Larry Dick, *Opers Mgr*
Nikki Kapilevich, *Purch Agent*
EMP: 50
SQ FT: 64,000
SALES (est): 138.2MM
SALES (corp-wide): 787.9MM **Publicly Held**
SIC: 3679 3823 Transducers, electrical; industrial instrmnts msrmnt display/control process variable
PA: Mts Systems Corporation
  14000 Technology Dr
  Eden Prairie MN 55344
  952 937-4000

(G-4101)
PCB PIEZOTRONICS INC
Larson Davis
3425 Walden Ave (14043-2495)
PHONE 716 684-0001
Chris Rasmussen, *Buyer*
EMP: 10
SALES (corp-wide): 787.9MM **Publicly Held**
SIC: 3829 Measuring & controlling devices
HQ: Pcb Piezotronics, Inc.
  3425 Walden Ave
  Depew NY 14043
  716 684-0001

(G-4102)
PCB PIEZOTRONICS INC
Industrl Mntrng Instrmntatn Dv
3425 Walden Ave (14043-2495)
PHONE 716 684-0003
Erick Yax, *Manager*
EMP: 400
SALES (corp-wide): 787.9MM **Publicly Held**
WEB: www.pcb.com
SIC: 3679 5063 Electronic circuits; electrical apparatus & equipment
HQ: Pcb Piezotronics, Inc.
  3425 Walden Ave
  Depew NY 14043
  716 684-0001

(G-4103)
QMC TECHNOLOGIES INC
4388 Broadway (14043-2998)
PHONE 716 681-0810
James A Serafin, *President*
Rachael S Serafin, *General Mgr*
Bob Serafin, *Vice Pres*
James S Serafin, *Purch Mgr*
Cathy Wawrzyniak, *Bookkeeper*
▲ **EMP:** 16
SQ FT: 5,500
SALES (est): 4.8MM **Privately Held**
WEB: www.qmctechnologies.com
SIC: 3599 Machine shop, jobbing & repair

(G-4104)
REICHERT INC
Also Called: Reichert Technologies
3362 Walden Ave (14043-2437)
PHONE 716 686-4500
Bruce Wilson, *Ch of Bd*
Timothy Levindofske, *President*
Scott Parks, *President*
Karen Garbacz, *General Mgr*
Jerry C Cirino, *Vice Pres*
▲ **EMP:** 147
SQ FT: 48,000

SALES (est): 42.2MM
SALES (corp-wide): 4.3B **Publicly Held**
WEB: www.leicams.com
SIC: 3841 Surgical & medical instruments
PA: Ametek, Inc.
  1100 Cassatt Rd
  Berwyn PA 19312
  610 647-2121

(G-4105)
RMF PRINT MANAGEMENT GROUP
786 Terrace Blvd Ste 3 (14043-3729)
P.O. Box 329, Lancaster (14086-0329)
PHONE 716 683-4351
Sharon Doherty, *Manager*
EMP: 13
SALES (est): 1.7MM **Privately Held**
SIC: 2752 Commercial printing, offset

Deposit
Broome County

(G-4106)
CANNONSVILLE LUMBER INC
199 Old Route 10 (13754-2100)
PHONE 607 467-3380
Adolf Schaffer Jr, *President*
EMP: 5 **EST:** 1998
SALES (est): 695.9K **Privately Held**
SIC: 2421 Sawmills & planing mills, general
PA: Schaefer Enterprises Of Deposit, Inc.
  315 Old Route 10
  Deposit NY 13754

(G-4107)
COURIER PRINTING CORP
24 Laurel Bank Ave Ste 2 (13754-1244)
PHONE 607 467-2191
Hilton Evans, *President*
Sarah Evans, *Admin Sec*
EMP: 30 **EST:** 1848
SQ FT: 55,000
SALES (est): 1.8MM **Privately Held**
WEB: www.courierprintingcorp.com
SIC: 2752 Commercial printing, offset

(G-4108)
INTEGRATED WOOD COMPONENTS INC
Also Called: Iwci
791 Airport Rd (13754-1277)
P.O. Box 145 (13754-0145)
PHONE 607 467-1739
John Kamp, *President*
Tom Stobert, *Corp Secy*
Gerard Kamp, *Vice Pres*
Cork Faulkner, *Accounts Exec*
Charlie Hopkins, *Accounts Exec*
EMP: 49
SQ FT: 2,800
SALES (est): 5.3MM **Privately Held**
SIC: 2541 Wood partitions & fixtures

(G-4109)
SANFORD STONE LLC
185 Latham Rd (13754-1271)
P.O. Box 313 (13754-0313)
PHONE 607 467-1313
George W Sanford,
EMP: 21
SALES (est): 2.5MM **Privately Held**
SIC: 3281 Cut stone & stone products

(G-4110)
SCHAEFER ENTPS DEPOSIT INC (PA)
315 Old Route 10 (13754-2106)
PHONE 607 467-4990
Larry Schaefer, *President*
EMP: 30
SALES (est): 7.6MM **Privately Held**
SIC: 1422 Cement rock, crushed & broken-quarrying

(G-4111)
SCHAEFER LOGGING INC
315 Old Route 10 (13754-2106)
PHONE 607 467-4990
Larry Schaefer, *President*
EMP: 10

SALES (est): 1MM **Privately Held**
SIC: 2411 5411 Logging; convenience stores
PA: Schaefer Enterprises Of Deposit, Inc.
  315 Old Route 10
  Deposit NY 13754

(G-4112)
WALTER R TUCKER ENTPS LTD
Also Called: E-Z Red Co
8 Leonard Way (13754-1240)
P.O. Box 80 (13754-0080)
PHONE 607 467-2866
Mark Tucker, *President*
Bob Cacciabeve, *Exec VP*
▲ **EMP:** 25 **EST:** 1966
SQ FT: 13,000
SALES (est): 6.1MM **Privately Held**
WEB: www.ezred.com
SIC: 3825 3824 3991 3629 Battery testers, electrical; test equipment for electronic & electric measurement; liquid meters; brushes, except paint & varnish; battery chargers, rectifying or nonrotating; motor vehicle supplies & new parts; testing equipment, electrical: automotive

Derby
Erie County

(G-4113)
GREYLINE SIGNS INC
6681 Schuyler Dr (14047-9644)
PHONE 716 947-4526
Linda Scritchfield, *President*
Everett Scritchfield, *Vice Pres*
EMP: 5
SALES (est): 430K **Privately Held**
SIC: 3993 Signs & advertising specialties

(G-4114)
NEW ERA CAP CO INC
8061 Erie Rd (14047-9503)
PHONE 716 549-0445
Eileen Beiter, *COO*
EMP: 10
SALES (corp-wide): 563.7MM **Privately Held**
SIC: 2353 Uniform hats & caps; baseball caps
PA: New Era Cap Co., Inc.
  160 Delaware Ave
  Buffalo NY 14202
  716 604-9000

Dexter
Jefferson County

(G-4115)
HANA SPORTSWEAR INC
321 Lakeview Dr (13634)
PHONE 315 639-6332
Robert Hartz, *President*
Beth Laster, *Treasurer*
▲ **EMP:** 20
SQ FT: 13,000
SALES (est): 2MM **Privately Held**
SIC: 3949 2339 2311 Sporting & athletic goods; women's & misses' outerwear; men's & boys' suits & coats

(G-4116)
VENUS MANUFACTURING CO INC (PA)
349 Lakeview Dr (13634)
P.O. Box 551 (13634-0551)
PHONE 315 639-3100
Roger Reifensnyder, *CEO*
Michael J Hennegan, *President*
▲ **EMP:** 90
SQ FT: 14,000
SALES (est): 6.2MM **Privately Held**
WEB: www.venusswimwear.com
SIC: 2339 Bathing suits: women's, misses' & juniors'

Dix Hills
Suffolk County

(G-4117)
A & D TOOL INC
30 Pashen Pl (11746-6600)
PHONE 631 243-4339
Dimitrios Margiellos, *President*
Tatiana Labate, *Corp Secy*
EMP: 7
SALES: 360K **Privately Held**
WEB: www.adtool.com
SIC: 3544 Forms (molds), for foundry & plastics working machinery

(G-4118)
AKA SPORT INC
16 Princeton Dr (11746-4826)
P.O. Box 1088, Commack (11725-0942)
PHONE 631 858-9888
Jon Bihn, *President*
Xiping Bihn, *Corp Secy*
▲ **EMP:** 11
SALES: 2MM **Privately Held**
SIC: 2393 3161 7389 Canvas bags; traveling bags;

(G-4119)
ALTERNATIVES FOR CHILDREN
600 S Service Rd (11746-6015)
PHONE 631 271-0777
Vivienne Viera, *Director*
EMP: 31
SALES (corp-wide): 15.9MM **Privately Held**
SIC: 3949 Windsurfing boards (sailboards) & equipment
PA: Alternatives For Children
  14 Research Way
  East Setauket NY 11733
  631 331-6400

(G-4120)
AUTHORITY TRANSPORTATION INC
Also Called: Authority On Transportation
167 Oakfield Ave (11746-6327)
PHONE 888 933-1268
Jinya Kato, *Principal*
David Lipsky, *Principal*
EMP: 12
SQ FT: 40,000
SALES (est): 1MM **Privately Held**
SIC: 3716 Motor homes

(G-4121)
MAYFLOWER SPLINT CO
16 Arbor Ln (11746-5127)
P.O. Box 381, Huntington Station (11746-0309)
PHONE 631 549-5131
Inge Krueger, *Owner*
EMP: 25
SALES (est): 1.6MM **Privately Held**
SIC: 3842 Surgical appliances & supplies

(G-4122)
MCG GRAPHICS INC
101 Village Hill Dr (11746-8335)
PHONE 631 499-0730
Michael Goldsmith, *President*
EMP: 6
SQ FT: 800
SALES (est): 747.1K **Privately Held**
SIC: 2752 2754 Commercial printing, lithographic; commercial printing, gravure

(G-4123)
PREMIERE LIVING PRODUCTS LLC
22 Branwood Dr (11746-5710)
PHONE 631 873-4337
Sandy Cohen, *Mng Member*
◆ **EMP:** 10
SALES (est): 477.2K **Privately Held**
SIC: 2511 Storage chests, household: wood

(G-4124)
PRINTING X PRESS IONS
5 Dix Cir (11746-6033)
PHONE 631 242-1992

GEOGRAPHIC SECTION

Dryden - Tompkins County (G-4149)

Christine Sigel, *Owner*
EMP: 7
SALES: 1.5MM **Privately Held**
WEB: www.printingxpresns.com
SIC: 2752 Lithographic Commercial Printing

(G-4125)
SAFE CIRCUITS INC
15 Shoreham Dr W (11746-6580)
PHONE...............................631 586-3682
James Ptucha, *Principal*
EMP: 6
SALES (est): 784.1K **Privately Held**
SIC: 3679 Electronic circuits

(G-4126)
SENTRY DEVICES CORP
33 Rustic Gate Ln (11746-6136)
PHONE...............................631 491-3191
Alex Feibush, *President*
EMP: 5
SALES (est): 400K **Privately Held**
SIC: 3669 1731 Burglar alarm apparatus, electric; marine horns, electric; fire detection & burglar alarm systems specialization

(G-4127)
TREBOR INSTRUMENT CORP
39 Balsam Dr (11746-7724)
PHONE...............................631 423-7026
Zygmunt Grzesiak, *President*
EMP: 8
SQ FT: 2,200
SALES (est): 855.5K **Privately Held**
WEB: www.treborinst.com
SIC: 3599 Machine shop, jobbing & repair

(G-4128)
YING KE YOUTH AGE GROUP INC
1 Campbell Dr (11746-7901)
PHONE...............................929 402-8458
Mark Bestercy, *Vice Pres*
EMP: 12
SALES (est): 241.2K **Privately Held**
SIC: 3751 5137 5065 Motor scooters & parts; women's & children's clothing; electronic parts & equipment

Dobbs Ferry
Westchester County

(G-4129)
AKZO NOBEL CHEMICALS LLC
Also Called: Akzo Nobel Central Research
7 Livingstone Ave (10522-3401)
PHONE...............................914 674-5008
G Thompson, *Branch Mgr*
EMP: 250
SALES (corp-wide): 11.3B **Privately Held**
WEB: www.akzo-nobel.com
SIC: 2819 8731 2899 Industrial inorganic chemicals; commercial physical research; chemical preparations
HQ: Akzo Nobel Chemicals Llc
525 W Van Buren St # 1600
Chicago IL 60607
312 544-7000

(G-4130)
REMBAR COMPANY LLC
67 Main St (10522-2152)
PHONE...............................914 693-2620
Frank H Firor, *CEO*
Walter Pastor, *President*
Audra Haase, *Vice Pres*
▼ EMP: 23 EST: 1950
SQ FT: 8,000
SALES (est): 2.8MM **Privately Held**
WEB: www.rembar.com
SIC: 3297 3399 Nonclay refractories; metal powders, pastes & flakes

(G-4131)
SUN SCIENTIFIC INC
145 Palisade St (10522-1617)
PHONE...............................914 479-5108
Sundram Ravikumar, *President*
Shridhar Shanmugam, *COO*
David Hildenbrand, *Vice Pres*
Arti Ravikumar, *Vice Pres*

Vikram Ravikumar, *Planning*
EMP: 7
SQ FT: 1,500
SALES (est): 660.8K **Privately Held**
SIC: 3845 Electromedical equipment

(G-4132)
W H WHITE PUBLICATIONS INC
Also Called: Rivertowns Enterprise
95 Main St (10522-1673)
PHONE...............................914 725-2500
Deborah White, *President*
Kris DiLorenzo, *Relations*
EMP: 8 EST: 1981
SALES (est): 368.9K **Privately Held**
SIC: 2711 Newspapers, publishing & printing

Dolgeville
Herkimer County

(G-4133)
GEHRING TRICOT CORPORATION (PA)
Also Called: Gehring Textiles
68 Ransom St (13329-1461)
P.O. Box 272 (13329-0272)
PHONE...............................315 429-8551
George G Gehring Jr, *President*
William Christimann, *General Mgr*
Gary Farquhar Jr, *General Mgr*
Brenda Gehring, *Principal*
Marie Bevilaqua, *Vice Pres*
▲ EMP: 71 EST: 1952
SQ FT: 50,000
SALES (est): 64MM **Privately Held**
SIC: 2258 2262 Dyeing & finishing lace goods & warp knit fabric; tricot fabrics; finishing plants, manmade fiber & silk fabrics

(G-4134)
GEHRING TRICOT CORPORATION
68 Ransom St Ste 272 (13329-1461)
PHONE...............................315 429-8551
Robert Lumley, *Vice Pres*
Ray Moissonnier, *QC Dir*
Paul Gutowski, *Controller*
Richard Patrick, *Data Proc Dir*
EMP: 125
SALES (corp-wide): 64MM **Privately Held**
SIC: 2257 2258 Dyeing & finishing circular knit fabrics; warp & flat knit products
PA: Gehring Tricot Corporation
68 Ransom St
Dolgeville NY 13329
315 429-8551

(G-4135)
NORTH HUDSON WOODCRAFT CORP
152 N Helmer Ave (13329-2826)
P.O. Box 192 (13329-0192)
PHONE...............................315 429-3105
Jeffrey C Slifka, *Ch of Bd*
William Slifka, *Treasurer*
Michael Jorrey, *Controller*
EMP: 50 EST: 1871
SQ FT: 100,000
SALES (est): 7.4MM **Privately Held**
WEB: www.northhudsonwoodcraft.com
SIC: 2426 3995 Furniture dimension stock, hardwood; burial caskets

(G-4136)
RAWLINGS SPORTING GOODS CO INC
52 Mckinley Ave (13329-1139)
PHONE...............................315 429-8511
Ronald Van Dergroef, *Principal*
Robert Johnson, *Production*
Kevin Griffin, *Purch Agent*
Kayla Morrill, *Human Resources*
EMP: 52
SQ FT: 62,884
SALES (corp-wide): 49.2MM **Privately Held**
SIC: 3949 Sporting & athletic goods

HQ: Rawlings Sporting Goods Company, Inc.
510 Maryville University
Saint Louis MO 63141

(G-4137)
REAL DESIGN INC
187 S Main St (13329-1455)
PHONE...............................315 429-3071
Sam Camardello, *President*
EMP: 10
SALES: 400K **Privately Held**
WEB: www.realdesigninc.com
SIC: 3429 Furniture hardware

(G-4138)
TUMBLE FORMS INC (PA)
1013 Barker Rd (13329-2401)
PHONE...............................315 429-3101
Dave Faulchner, *General Mgr*
EMP: 20
SQ FT: 25,200
SALES (est): 10.6MM **Privately Held**
SIC: 3842 Surgical appliances & supplies

Douglaston
Queens County

(G-4139)
SALVADOR COLLETTI BLANK
25141 Van Zandt Ave (11362-1735)
PHONE...............................718 217-6725
Salvador Colletti, *Principal*
EMP: 5
SALES (est): 240.9K **Privately Held**
SIC: 2099 Food preparations

(G-4140)
SOLID-LOOK CORPORATION
4628 243rd St (11362-1129)
PHONE...............................917 683-1780
Raffaello Galli, *CEO*
EMP: 2
SQ FT: 2,000
SALES (est): 1MM **Privately Held**
SIC: 3841 Surgical & medical instruments

(G-4141)
SPRINGFIELD CONTROL SYSTEMS
4056 Douglaston Pkwy (11363-1507)
PHONE...............................718 631-0870
William Boettjer, *President*
EMP: 8
SALES (est): 680K **Privately Held**
SIC: 3823 Temperature measurement instruments, industrial

(G-4142)
TAMKA SPORT LLC
225 Beverly Rd (11363-1122)
PHONE...............................718 224-7820
Kathleen Derienzo, *Mng Member*
EMP: 8
SALES: 90K **Privately Held**
SIC: 2329 2339 Men's & boys' athletic uniforms; uniforms, athletic: women's, misses' & juniors'

Dover Plains
Dutchess County

(G-4143)
CENTRAL DOVER DEVELOPMENT
247 Dover Furnace Rd (12522-5773)
PHONE...............................917 709-3266
Wayne Tanner, *President*
Elaine Tanner, *Vice Pres*
EMP: 4
SALES: 1MM **Privately Held**
SIC: 1442 0191 Gravel mining; general farms, primarily crop

(G-4144)
J & J LOG & LUMBER CORP
528 Old State Route 22 (12522-5821)
P.O. Box 1139 (12522-1139)
PHONE...............................845 832-6535
Randolph L Williams, *CEO*

◆ EMP: 80
SQ FT: 10,200
SALES (est): 15.6MM **Privately Held**
SIC: 2421 2426 Sawmills & planing mills, general; hardwood dimension & flooring mills

(G-4145)
PALUMBO BLOCK CO INC
365 Dover Furnace Rd (12522-5775)
P.O. Box 810 (12522-0810)
PHONE...............................845 832-6100
Fortunato Palumbo, *President*
Anthony Palumbo, *Vice Pres*
Mary Palumbo, *Vice Pres*
Tony Palumbo, *Vice Pres*
Mary Palumbo Sprong, *Vice Pres*
EMP: 25
SQ FT: 28,000
SALES (est): 4.6MM **Privately Held**
SIC: 3271 5082 5211 Blocks, concrete or cinder: standard; masonry equipment & supplies; masonry materials & supplies

Dresden
Yates County

(G-4146)
ABTEX CORPORATION
89 Main St (14441-9708)
P.O. Box 188 (14441-0188)
PHONE...............................315 536-7403
D Mark Fultz, *President*
Jason Saner, *Vice Pres*
Christian Donovan, *Opers Mgr*
John Roman, *Engineer*
David Burlew, *Project Engr*
EMP: 21
SQ FT: 20,000
SALES (est): 4.4MM **Privately Held**
WEB: www.abtex.com
SIC: 3991 3541 Brushes, household or industrial; machine tools, metal cutting type

(G-4147)
FAULKNER TRUSS COMPANY INC
1830 King Hill Rd (14441)
P.O. Box 407, Hammondsport (14840-0407)
PHONE...............................315 536-8894
Richard C Faulkner, *Ch of Bd*
EMP: 5
SALES (est): 573.2K **Privately Held**
SIC: 2439 Trusses, wooden roof

Dryden
Tompkins County

(G-4148)
AMISH STRUCTURE
32 North St (13053-8514)
P.O. Box 2 (13053-0002)
PHONE...............................607 257-1070
Virginia Jordan, *Partner*
Christopher Jordan, *Partner*
EMP: 10
SALES (est): 1.1MM **Privately Held**
SIC: 2421 Outdoor wood structural products

(G-4149)
BAGELOVERS INC
42 Elm St (13053-9623)
P.O. Box 62 (13053-0062)
PHONE...............................607 844-3683
Charles Tallman, *President*
Gary Westphal, *Vice Pres*
EMP: 18
SQ FT: 12,500
SALES (est): 2.4MM **Privately Held**
SIC: 2051 5142 Bagels, fresh or frozen; packaged frozen goods

Dryden - Tompkins County (G-4150)

(G-4150)
INTEGRATED WATER MANAGEMENT
Also Called: I W M
289 Cortland Rd (13053-9517)
P.O. Box 523 (13053-0523)
PHONE..................607 844-4276
David Duffett, *President*
▲ EMP: 5
SQ FT: 3,700
SALES (est): 1MM **Privately Held**
SIC: 3589 Water treatment equipment, industrial

(G-4151)
ROSCOE BROTHERS INC
15 Freeville Rd (13053-9537)
PHONE..................607 844-3750
Chris Roscoe, *President*
Nick Roscoe, *Vice Pres*
EMP: 13 EST: 2014
SALES: 1MM **Privately Held**
SIC: 2452 7389 Prefabricated buildings, wood;

(G-4152)
STURGES ELEC PDTS CO INC
Also Called: Sepco-Sturges Electronics
23 North St (13053)
P.O. Box 532 (13053-0532)
PHONE..................607 844-8604
James Koch, *President*
EMP: 45
SQ FT: 15,000
SALES (est): 6.2MM **Privately Held**
WEB: www.sturgeselectronics.com
SIC: 3679 Harness assemblies for electronic use: wire or cable

(G-4153)
STURGES ELECTRONICS LLC
23 North St (13053)
P.O. Box 532 (13053-0532)
PHONE..................607 844-8604
Gary Nelson, *President*
EMP: 16
SALES (est): 232.3K **Privately Held**
SIC: 3679 Harness assemblies for electronic use: wire or cable

Duanesburg
Schenectady County

(G-4154)
AMERICAN CAR SIGNS INC
1483 W Duane Lake Rd (12056-2713)
PHONE..................518 227-1173
Eulaila Kulikoff, *CEO*
EMP: 6
SALES: 50K **Privately Held**
SIC: 3993 Electric signs

(G-4155)
CUSTOM DESIGN KITCHENS INC
1700 Duanesburg Rd (12056-4310)
PHONE..................518 355-4446
Terry Zarrillo, *President*
Dawn Zarrillo, *Corp Secy*
EMP: 10
SQ FT: 10,000
SALES: 920K **Privately Held**
SIC: 2541 5031 5211 3131 Cabinets, except refrigerated: show, display, etc.: wood; kitchen cabinets; cabinets, kitchen; counter tops; counters

Dundee
Yates County

(G-4156)
EAST BRANCH WINERY INC (PA)
Also Called: Mc Gregor Vineyard Winery
5503 Dutch St (14837-9746)
PHONE..................607 292-3999
Robert Mc Gregor, *President*
David Payne, *Shareholder*
Marge Mc Gregor, *Admin Sec*
EMP: 8
SQ FT: 2,000
SALES (est): 402K **Privately Held**
SIC: 2084 0172 Wines; grapes

(G-4157)
FINGER LAKES MEDIA INC
Also Called: The Observer
45 Water St (14837-1029)
P.O. Box 127 (14837-0127)
PHONE..................607 243-7600
George Lawson, *President*
EMP: 12
SALES (est): 529.2K **Privately Held**
WEB: www.fingerlakesmedia.com
SIC: 2711 Newspapers, publishing & printing

(G-4158)
GLENORA FARM INC
Also Called: Glenora Farms
340 Dundee Glenora Rd (14837-8838)
PHONE..................607 243-8383
Jeffrey Morris, *Owner*
EMP: 5 EST: 1996
SALES (est): 325.5K **Privately Held**
WEB: www.glenorafarm.com
SIC: 2084 Wines

(G-4159)
GLENORA WINE CELLARS INC
5435 State Route 14 (14837-8804)
PHONE..................607 243-9500
Eugene Pierce, *President*
Tracey Miller, *Prdtn Mgr*
Scott Welliver, *Treasurer*
Tracey Dwyer, *Controller*
Barbara Stone, *Human Res Mgr*
EMP: 34
SQ FT: 18,000
SALES (est): 5.3MM **Privately Held**
WEB: www.glenora.com
SIC: 2084 Wines

(G-4160)
HERMANN J WIEMER VINEYARD
3962 Rte 14 (14837)
P.O. Box 38 (14837-0038)
PHONE..................607 243-7971
Hermann J Wiemer, *President*
Osker Bynke, *Mktg Dir*
▲ EMP: 5
SALES (est): 514.4K **Privately Held**
WEB: www.wiemer.com
SIC: 2084 0172 Wines; grapes

(G-4161)
HICKORY ROAD LAND CO LLC
Also Called: Hickory Hollow Wind Cellars
5289 Route 14 (14837-8800)
P.O. Box 37 (14837-0037)
PHONE..................607 243-9114
Edward Woodland, *Mng Member*
Suzanne Kendall, *Manager*
EMP: 5
SALES (est): 397.6K **Privately Held**
SIC: 2084 Wine cellars, bonded: engaged in blending wines

Dunkirk
Chautauqua County

(G-4162)
AMCOR RIGID PLASTICS USA LLC
1 Cliffstar Ave (14048-2800)
PHONE..................716 366-2440
Bryan Cotton, *Branch Mgr*
EMP: 50 **Privately Held**
WEB: www.slpcamericas.com
SIC: 3089 Plastic containers, except foam
HQ: Amcor Rigid Plastics Usa, Llc
   935 Technology Dr Ste 100
   Ann Arbor MI 48108

(G-4163)
CHAUTAUQUA CIRCUITS INC
855 Main St (14048-3505)
PHONE..................716 366-5771
William E Wragge, *President*
EMP: 6
SALES: 250K **Privately Held**
SIC: 3672 Printed circuit boards

(G-4164)
CHAUTAUQUA WOODS CORPORATION
134 Franklin Ave (14048-2806)
P.O. Box 130 (14048-0130)
PHONE..................716 366-3808
Bia Khan, *President*
Kerrie Pelittier, *Manager*
EMP: 40
SQ FT: 50,000
SALES (est): 1.2MM **Privately Held**
WEB: www.chautauquawoods.com
SIC: 2431 Doors, wood

(G-4165)
CLIFFSTAR LLC (DH)
Also Called: Cott Beverages
1 Cliffstar Dr (14048-2800)
PHONE..................716 366-6100
Monica Consonery, *Exec VP*
Kevin Sanvidge, *Exec VP*
Richard Star, *Exec VP*
Kevin M Sanvidge, *VP Admin*
Chris Cronje, *CFO*
◆ EMP: 700 EST: 1997
SALES (est): 460MM
SALES (corp-wide): 58.5K **Privately Held**
SIC: 2033 2086 Fruit juices: fresh; bottled & canned soft drinks; pasteurized & mineral waters, bottled & canned
HQ: Refresco Beverages Us Inc.
   8112 Woodland Center Blvd
   Tampa FL 33614
   813 313-1800

(G-4166)
DUNKIRK CONSTRUCTION PRODUCTS
852 Main St (14048-3506)
P.O. Box 149 (14048-0149)
PHONE..................716 366-5220
Patrick Pacos, *President*
James Pacos, *Vice Pres*
Dorothy Pacos, *Treasurer*
EMP: 5
SQ FT: 3,800
SALES (est): 643.3K **Privately Held**
SIC: 3273 Mfg Ready-Mixed Concrete

(G-4167)
DUNKIRK METAL PRODUCTS WNY LLC (PA)
3575 Chadwick Dr (14048-9652)
PHONE..................716 366-2555
Joe Shull, *President*
Jeaai Gaulhv, *Partner*
▼ EMP: 22 EST: 1946
SQ FT: 50,000
SALES (est): 5.2MM **Privately Held**
SIC: 3469 Metal stampings

(G-4168)
DUNKIRK SPECIALTY STEEL LLC
830 Brigham Rd (14048-3473)
P.O. Box 319 (14048-0319)
PHONE..................716 366-1000
Dennis Oates, *President*
Wendel Crosby, *General Mgr*
William W Beible Jr, *Senior VP*
Paul A McGrath, *VP Admin*
Brandon Leach, *Opers Mgr*
◆ EMP: 166
SALES (est): 36.5MM **Publicly Held**
WEB: www.dunkirkspecialtysteel.com
SIC: 3312 Stainless steel
PA: Universal Stainless & Alloy Products, Inc.
   600 Mayer St
   Bridgeville PA 15017

(G-4169)
ECR INTERNATIONAL INC
Dunkirk Division
85 Middle Rd (14048-1311)
P.O. Box 32 (14048-0032)
PHONE..................716 366-5500
Dennis Keppel, *Engineer*
Thomas Poweski, *Manager*
Tom Stall, *Info Tech Dir*
EMP: 130
SQ FT: 17,087
SALES (corp-wide): 107.2MM **Privately Held**
WEB: www.ecrinternational.com
SIC: 3433 3443 Boilers, low-pressure heating: steam or hot water; fabricated plate work (boiler shop)
PA: Ecr International, Inc.
   2201 Dwyer Ave
   Utica NY 13501
   315 797-1310

(G-4170)
FFC HOLDING CORP SUBSIDIARIES (PA)
1 Ice Cream Dr (14048-3300)
PHONE..................716 366-5400
Kenneth A Johnson, *President*
Bob Griewisch, *Vice Pres*
Bob Bogdanowicz, *Purch Mgr*
EMP: 12
SQ FT: 280,000
SALES (est): 110.9MM **Privately Held**
SIC: 2024 Ice cream & frozen desserts

(G-4171)
FIELDBROOK FOODS CORPORATION (HQ)
1 Ice Cream Dr (14048-3300)
P.O. Box 1318 (14048-6318)
PHONE..................716 366-5400
Kenneth A Johnson, *CEO*
Robert Griewisch, *President*
Ronald Odebralski, *Vice Pres*
Jack Fuhrman, *Transptn Dir*
Brenda Tabone, *Purch Mgr*
◆ EMP: 350
SQ FT: 280,000
SALES (est): 146.8MM **Privately Held**
SIC: 2024 Ice cream, bulk

(G-4172)
INX INTERNATIONAL INK CO
3257 Middle Rd (14048-9745)
PHONE..................716 366-6010
Sue Colston, *Branch Mgr*
EMP: 21
SALES (corp-wide): 1.4B **Privately Held**
SIC: 2893 Printing ink
HQ: Inx International Ink Co.
   150 N Martingale Rd # 700
   Schaumburg IL 60173
   630 382-1800

(G-4173)
LAKESIDE PRECISION INC
208 Dove St (14048-1598)
PHONE..................716 366-5030
Christopher Anson, *CEO*
Hugh Graves, *Opers Dir*
EMP: 22 EST: 1963
SQ FT: 11,300
SALES: 1.7MM **Privately Held**
WEB: www.lakesideprecision.com
SIC: 3599 Machine shop, jobbing & repair; custom machinery

(G-4174)
NESTLE PURINA PETCARE COMPANY
Also Called: Nestle Purina Factory
3800 Middle Rd (14048-9750)
PHONE..................716 366-8080
Ron Bowers, *Branch Mgr*
EMP: 300
SALES (corp-wide): 90.8B **Privately Held**
WEB: www.purina.com
SIC: 2047 Dog food
HQ: Nestle Purina Petcare Company
   901 Chouteau Ave
   Saint Louis MO 63102
   314 982-1000

(G-4175)
OBSERVER DAILY SUNDAY NEWSPPR
Also Called: The Observer
10 E 2nd St (14048-1602)
P.O. Box 391 (14048-0391)
PHONE..................716 366-3000
Karl T Davis, *General Mgr*
James Austin, *Plant,Mgr*
Janice Gee, *Director*
EMP: 100

GEOGRAPHIC SECTION

East Aurora - Erie County (G-4200)

SALES (est): 13.8MM **Privately Held**
WEB: www.observertoday.com
SIC: 2752 2711 Commercial printing, lithographic; newspapers

(G-4176)
PERSCH SERVICE PRINT INC (PA)
11 W 3rd St (14048)
PHONE.................................716 366-2677
Robert H Persch, *President*
Margaret T Persch, *Treasurer*
Margaret P Triaga, *Admin Sec*
EMP: 9 EST: 1911
SALES (est): 1.4MM **Privately Held**
SIC: 2752 7334 Commercial printing, offset; photocopying & duplicating services

(G-4177)
REM-TRONICS INC
659 Brigham Rd (14048-2361)
PHONE.................................716 934-2697
Abe M Kadis, *President*
Mathew Karalunas, *General Mgr*
Kathy Rock, *Admin Asst*
EMP: 58
SQ FT: 20,000
SALES (est): 9.7MM **Privately Held**
WEB: www.rem-tronics.com
SIC: 3679 Electronic circuits

(G-4178)
REXFORD SERVICES INC
4849 W Lake Rd (14048-9613)
PHONE.................................716 366-6671
William Rexford, *President*
Trisha Rexford, *Vice Pres*
EMP: 5
SALES (est): 680.7K **Privately Held**
SIC: 3713 Specialty motor vehicle bodies

(G-4179)
SHAANT INDUSTRIES INC
134 Franklin Ave (14048-2806)
P.O. Box 130 (14048-0130)
PHONE.................................716 366-3654
Khalid Khan, *President*
▲ EMP: 40
SQ FT: 50,000
SALES (est): 7.6MM **Privately Held**
WEB: www.ultrapak.net
SIC: 3081 2671 Polyvinyl film & sheet; packaging paper & plastics film, coated & laminated

(G-4180)
SPECIAL METALS CORPORATION
100 Willowbrook Ave (14048-3479)
P.O. Box 304 (14048-0304)
PHONE.................................716 366-5663
Fred A Schweizer, *Opers Staff*
Don Borowski, *Manager*
EMP: 60
SALES (corp-wide): 242.1B **Publicly Held**
SIC: 3542 3463 3462 3341 Forging machinery & hammers; extruding machines (machine tools); metal; die casting machines; nonferrous forgings; iron & steel forgings; secondary nonferrous metals
HQ: Special Metals Corporation
4832 Richmond Rd Ste 100
Warrensville Heights OH 44128
216 755-3030

(G-4181)
X PRESS SCREEN PRINTING
4867 W Lake Rd (14048-9613)
PHONE.................................716 679-7788
Chad Rizzo, *President*
EMP: 7
SALES (est): 584.7K **Privately Held**
SIC: 2759 Commercial printing

Durham
Greene County

(G-4182)
ADVANCED YARN TECHNOLOGIES INC
Also Called: Cidega American Trim
4750 State Hwy 145 (12422-5306)
PHONE.................................518 239-6600
Richard Gangi, *President*
Daniel Gangi, *Vice Pres*
Sebastian Gangi, *Vice Pres*
EMP: 50
SALES (est): 5.8MM **Privately Held**
SIC: 2281 5199 Yarn spinning mills; fabrics, yarns & knit goods

(G-4183)
AMERICAN TRIM MFG INC
4750 State Hwy 145 (12422-5306)
PHONE.................................518 239-8151
Richard Gangi, *President*
Daniel Gangi, *Vice Pres*
Sabastian Gangi, *Vice Pres*
▲ EMP: 50
SQ FT: 30,000
SALES (est): 12.5MM **Privately Held**
SIC: 2241 Trimmings, textile

Eagle Bridge
Rensselaer County

(G-4184)
EAGLE BRIDGE MACHINE & TL INC
135 State Route 67 (12057)
PHONE.................................518 686-4541
Robert Farrara, *President*
Raymond Farrara, *Corp Secy*
▲ EMP: 35 EST: 1965
SQ FT: 12,000
SALES (est): 4.3MM **Privately Held**
WEB: www.eaglebridgemachine.com
SIC: 3599 3743 Machine shop, jobbing & repair; railroad equipment

(G-4185)
PROFESSIONAL PACKG SVCS INC
Also Called: Pro Pack
62 Owlkill Rd (12057-2609)
PHONE.................................518 677-5100
Ronald Dooley, *President*
Lorraine Dooley, *Corp Secy*
EMP: 30
SQ FT: 25,000
SALES (est): 5.6MM **Privately Held**
SIC: 2653 2631 3086 Boxes, corrugated: made from purchased materials; paperboard mills; plastics foam products

(G-4186)
PROPAK INC
70 Owlkill Rd (12057)
PHONE.................................518 677-5100
Jack Baratta, *Principal*
Frank Bowles, *Controller*
EMP: 6
SALES (est): 588.4K **Privately Held**
SIC: 2652 Setup paperboard boxes

(G-4187)
STRATO TRANSIT COMPONENTS LLC
155 State Route 67 (12057)
PHONE.................................518 686-4541
Michael Foxx,
Michael Corridon,
Steven Foxx,
▲ EMP: 9
SALES (est): 1.1MM **Privately Held**
SIC: 3743 Railroad equipment

Earlville
Chenango County

(G-4188)
EARLVILLE PAPER BOX CO INC
19 Clyde St (13332)
PHONE.................................315 691-2131
Richard T Upton, *President*
Marilyn J Upton, *Treasurer*
EMP: 20
SQ FT: 7,200
SALES (est): 4MM **Privately Held**
WEB: www.earlvillepaperbox.com
SIC: 2652 Setup paperboard boxes

East Amherst
Erie County

(G-4189)
ELITE ROASTERS INC (PA)
Also Called: Elite Coffee Roasters
8600 Transit Rd Ste 1b (14051-2615)
PHONE.................................716 626-0307
Gerald Dewes, *CFO*
William Klein, *Director*
EMP: 12 EST: 2015
SALES (est): 1.7MM **Privately Held**
SIC: 2095 5149 7389 Roasted coffee; coffee, green or roasted; packaging & labeling services

(G-4190)
INTEGRTED WORK ENVRONMENTS LLC
Also Called: Iwe
6346 Everwood Ct N (14051-2032)
P.O. Box 1514, Williamsville (14231-1514)
PHONE.................................716 725-5088
Evan M Casey, *Mng Member*
EMP: 7
SALES (est): 974.7K **Privately Held**
SIC: 3821 5047 5049 Laboratory apparatus & furniture; medical laboratory equipment; laboratory equipment, except medical or dental

(G-4191)
SUPERIOR EXTERIORS OF BUFFALO
57 Insbrook Ct (14051-1496)
PHONE.................................716 873-1000
Salvatore Dinatale, *President*
EMP: 10
SQ FT: 15,000
SALES (est): 1MM **Privately Held**
SIC: 3444 Awnings & canopies

(G-4192)
SWEET MELODYS LLC
8485 Transit Rd (14051-1059)
PHONE.................................716 580-3227
Chuck Incorvia,
▲ EMP: 20
SALES (est): 2MM **Privately Held**
SIC: 2024 Dairy based frozen desserts

East Aurora
Erie County

(G-4193)
AMERICAN PRECISION INDS INC
Also Called: API Delevan
270 Quaker Rd (14052-2192)
P.O. Box 449 (14052-0449)
PHONE.................................716 652-3600
Daniel A Raskas, *President*
Joseph Calkins, *QC Mgr*
Jim Bingel, *Branch Mgr*
EMP: 95
SALES (corp-wide): 6.6B **Publicly Held**
WEB: www.apischmidtbretten.com
SIC: 3677 Coil windings, electronic; inductors, electronic
HQ: American Precision Industries Inc.
45 Hazelwood Dr
Amherst NY 14228
716 691-9100

(G-4194)
ASTRONICS CORPORATION (PA)
130 Commerce Way (14052-2164)
PHONE.................................716 805-1599
Kevin T Keane, *Ch of Bd*
Peter J Gundermann, *President*
James F Mulato, *President*
James S Kramer, *Exec VP*
Mark A Peabody, *Exec VP*
▲ EMP: 204
SQ FT: 125,000
SALES: 624.4MM **Publicly Held**
SIC: 3728 3647 Aircraft parts & equipment; aircraft lighting fixtures

(G-4195)
AURORA TECHNICAL SERVICES LTD
11970 Parker Rd (14052-9533)
P.O. Box 103 (14052-0103)
PHONE.................................716 652-1463
Karen Wright, *President*
Steven Wright, *Vice Pres*
EMP: 5
SQ FT: 1,100
SALES (est): 651.1K **Privately Held**
WEB: www.auroratechserv.com
SIC: 3829 3825 Ultrasonic testing equipment; meters: electric, pocket, portable, panelboard, etc.

(G-4196)
COLDEN CLOSET LLC
1375 Boies Rd (14052-9726)
PHONE.................................716 713-6125
Kevin Lindberg, *Owner*
EMP: 9
SALES (est): 1MM **Privately Held**
SIC: 2673 Wardrobe bags (closet accessories): from purchased materials

(G-4197)
DIREKT FORCE LLC
455 Olean Rd Ste 3 (14052-9791)
PHONE.................................716 652-3022
Kurt Knolle, *Mng Member*
EMP: 25 EST: 2001
SQ FT: 7,000
SALES (est): 4.9MM **Privately Held**
WEB: www.direktforce.com
SIC: 3492 3593 3443 Control valves, fluid power: hydraulic & pneumatic; fluid power cylinders, hydraulic or pneumatic; fabricated plate work (boiler shop)

(G-4198)
EVERFAB INC
12928 Big Tree Rd (14052-9524)
PHONE.................................716 655-1550
Alan L Everett, *Ch of Bd*
Lee Everett, *Vice Pres*
Scott Everett, *Vice Pres*
Scott Johnson, *Mfg Mgr*
Jim Leonard, *Production*
EMP: 55
SQ FT: 45,000
SALES (est): 12.7MM **Privately Held**
WEB: www.everfab.com
SIC: 2821 3441 3545 3544 Elastomers, nonvulcanizable (plastics); molding compounds, plastics; fabricated structural metal; machine tool accessories; special dies, tools, jigs & fixtures; machine & other job shop work

(G-4199)
EXTEN II LLC
127 Elm St (14052-2535)
P.O. Box 875, Orchard Park (14127-0875)
PHONE.................................716 895-2214
Richard Swanson, *President*
EMP: 18
SALES (est): 2.1MM **Privately Held**
SIC: 3714 Motor vehicle parts & accessories

(G-4200)
F M EDM INC
210 Pennsylvania Ave (14052-2919)
P.O. Box 773 (14052-0773)
PHONE.................................716 655-1784
Mark Mann, *President*
▲ EMP: 3
SQ FT: 4,000

East Aurora - Erie County (G-4201)

SALES: 1MM **Privately Held**
WEB: www.fmedm.com
SIC: **3544** Special dies & tools

(G-4201)
GRANT HAMILTON (PA)
Also Called: East Aurora Advertiser
710 Main St (14052-2406)
P.O. Box 5 (14052-0005)
PHONE 716 652-0320
Grant Hamilton, *Owner*
EMP: 15
SQ FT: 2,850
SALES (est): 1MM **Privately Held**
WEB: www.eastaurorany.com
SIC: **2741** 5943 Newsletter publishing; office forms & supplies

(G-4202)
GUARDIAN SYSTEMS TECH INC
659 Oakwood Ave (14052-2511)
PHONE 716 481-5597
Edward Seebald, *CEO*
Meighan Lloyd, *Principal*
EMP: 10
SALES (est): 649.6K **Privately Held**
SIC: **3699** Electrical equipment & supplies

(G-4203)
LINE BY LINE DESIGN INC (PA)
425 Olean Rd (14052-9744)
PHONE 716 655-4680
Jim Klein, *President*
▲ EMP: 7
SQ FT: 2,500
SALES (est): 1.1MM **Privately Held**
WEB: www.lbld.com
SIC: **3089** Injection molding of plastics

(G-4204)
LUMINESCENT SYSTEMS INC (HQ)
Also Called: L S I
130 Commerce Way (14052-2191)
PHONE 716 655-0800
Peter Gundermann, *President*
Frank Johns, *Vice Pres*
James Kramer, *Vice Pres*
Richard Miller, *Vice Pres*
Todd Marshall, *Project Engr*
EMP: 300
SALES (est): 63.3MM
SALES (corp-wide): 624.4MM **Publicly Held**
SIC: **3647** 3646 3648 3577 Aircraft lighting fixtures; commercial indusl & institutional electric lighting fixtures; lighting equipment; computer peripheral equipment
PA: Astronics Corporation
130 Commerce Way
East Aurora NY 14052
716 805-1599

(G-4205)
MATTEL INC
609 Girard Ave (14052)
PHONE 716 714-8514
Teresa G Ruiz, *VP Mktg*
Kathleen Hammons, *Branch Mgr*
Lauren Watson, *Recruiter*
EMP: 15
SALES (corp-wide): 4.8B **Publicly Held**
WEB: www.mattel.com
SIC: **3944** 3942 3949 Games, toys & children's vehicles; dolls, except stuffed toy animals; stuffed toys, including animals; sporting & athletic goods
PA: Mattel, Inc.
333 Continental Blvd
El Segundo CA 90245
310 252-2000

(G-4206)
MATTEL INC
Also Called: Fisher-Price
636 Girard Ave (14052-1824)
P.O. Box 1169 (14052-7169)
PHONE 310 252-2000
Jerry Drinkard, *Principal*
Jeanette Volk, *Personnel*
Erik Jobson, *Mktg Dir*
Sarah Kancar, *Marketing Staff*
Tony Sauls, *Manager*
EMP: 34
SALES (corp-wide): 4.8B **Publicly Held**
SIC: **3944** Games, toys & children's vehicles
PA: Mattel, Inc.
333 Continental Blvd
El Segundo CA 90245
310 252-2000

(G-4207)
MOOG INC
Moog Industrial Group
300 Jamison Rd (14052)
PHONE 716 687-4954
Phil Prosser, *Business Mgr*
Rick Crance, *Opers Staff*
Keith Mazierski, *Purch Mgr*
Mark Smith, *Buyer*
Mike Trottier, *Buyer*
EMP: 300
SALES (corp-wide): 2.7B **Publicly Held**
WEB: www.moog.com
SIC: **3492** 3721 Fluid power valves & hose fittings; aircraft
PA: Moog Inc.
400 Jamison Rd
Elma NY 14059
716 652-2000

(G-4208)
MOOG INC
Moog Systems Group
7021 Seneca St (14052)
PHONE 716 805-8100
James Riedel, *Vice Pres*
Gil Hoffman, *Engineer*
Kristi Sydor, *Engineer*
Doug Gallen, *Manager*
Elizabeth V Victor, *Manager*
EMP: 225
SALES (corp-wide): 2.7B **Publicly Held**
WEB: www.moog.com
SIC: **3812** Search & navigation equipment
PA: Moog Inc.
400 Jamison Rd
Elma NY 14059
716 652-2000

(G-4209)
NORTHERN DESIGN INC
12990 Old Big Tree Rd (14052-9525)
PHONE 716 652-7071
Robert Lippert, *President*
Gabor Bertalan, *Vice Pres*
EMP: 6
SQ FT: 550
SALES: 500K **Privately Held**
WEB: www.northerndesign.com
SIC: **3544** Forms (molds), for foundry & plastics working machinery; dies & die holders for metal cutting, forming, die casting

(G-4210)
SLOSSON EDUCTL PUBLICATIONS
538 Buffalo Rd (14052-9404)
P.O. Box 280 (14052-0280)
PHONE 716 652-0930
Steven Slosson, *President*
Janet Slosson, *Chairman*
EMP: 12
SQ FT: 2,400
SALES (est): 1.2MM **Privately Held**
WEB: www.slosson.com
SIC: **2741** 8748 8299 Miscellaneous publishing; publishing consultant; arts & crafts schools

(G-4211)
WEST FALLS MACHINE CO INC
Also Called: West Falls Machine Co 1
11692 E Main Rd (14052-9597)
PHONE 716 655-0440
Matthew Creps, *CEO*
Mary Ann George, *Vice Pres*
EMP: 15
SQ FT: 15,000
SALES (est): 2.7MM **Privately Held**
SIC: **3599** 3471 Machine shop, jobbing & repair; chromium plating of metals or formed products

East Berne
Albany County

(G-4212)
RUDY STEMPEL & FAMILY SAWMILL
73 Stemple Rd (12059-2843)
PHONE 518 872-0431
Rudolph Stempel, *President*
EMP: 6
SALES (est): 440.2K **Privately Held**
SIC: **2421** Sawmills & planing mills, general

East Bethany
Genesee County

(G-4213)
SANDVOSS FARMS LLC
Also Called: First Light Farm & Creamery
10198 East Rd (14054-9754)
PHONE 585 297-7044
Peter R Sandvoss, *Owner*
Peter Sandvoss,
Stephen Sandvoss,
EMP: 8
SALES (est): 378.9K **Privately Held**
SIC: **2022** Natural cheese

East Concord
Erie County

(G-4214)
MCEWAN TRUCKING & GRAV PRODUC
11696 Route 240 (14055-9717)
PHONE 716 609-1828
Mary McEwan, *Principal*
EMP: 6
SALES (est): 545.1K **Privately Held**
SIC: **1442** Construction sand & gravel

(G-4215)
WENDELS POULTRY FARM
12466 Vaughn St (14055-9747)
PHONE 716 592-2299
Martin Wendel, *Partner*
Denise Wandel, *Partner*
David Wendel, *Partner*
EMP: 8
SQ FT: 12,000
SALES (est): 928.6K **Privately Held**
SIC: **2015** 0254 Poultry, processed; poultry hatcheries

East Durham
Greene County

(G-4216)
GLAXOSMITHKLINE LLC
Also Called: Glaxosmthkline Cnsmr Heathcare
3169 Route 145 (12423-1416)
PHONE 518 239-6901
Max Van Veem, *Vice Pres*
Max Van Vessem, *Branch Mgr*
EMP: 75
SALES (corp-wide): 39.8B **Privately Held**
SIC: **3843** 2834 Dental equipment & supplies; procaine pharmaceutical preparations
HQ: Glaxosmithkline Llc
5 Crescent Dr
Philadelphia PA 19112
215 751-4000

East Elmhurst
Queens County

(G-4217)
ARM CONSTRUCTION COMPANY INC
10001 27th Ave (11369-1647)
PHONE 646 235-6520
Abdul Motaleb, *President*
EMP: 5
SALES: 383K **Privately Held**
SIC: **1389** 7389 Construction, repair & dismantling services;

(G-4218)
BROTHERS ROOFING SUPPLIES CO
10514 Astoria Blvd (11369-2097)
PHONE 718 779-0280
Robert Kersch, *Ch of Bd*
Michael Kersch, *Vice Pres*
EMP: 20 EST: 1969
SQ FT: 16,000
SALES (est): 4.3MM **Privately Held**
WEB: www.brothersroofingsupply.com
SIC: **3444** Metal roofing & roof drainage equipment

(G-4219)
CITROS BUILDING MATERIALS CO
10514 Astoria Blvd (11369-2027)
PHONE 718 779-0727
Bobby Kersh, *President*
EMP: 40
SQ FT: 1,600
SALES (est): 5.2MM **Privately Held**
SIC: **3444** Skylights, sheet metal

(G-4220)
DOROSE NOVELTY CO INC
Also Called: Dorose Albums
3107 103rd St (11369-2013)
PHONE 718 451-3088
Sam Krauthamer, *President*
Alex Brodsky, *Vice Pres*
Regina Krauthamer, *Treasurer*
EMP: 14 EST: 1958
SALES (est): 1.1MM **Privately Held**
SIC: **2782** Albums

(G-4221)
I RAUCHS SONS INC
3220 112th St (11369-2590)
PHONE 718 507-8844
Milton Levine, *President*
Joel Levine, *Corp Secy*
EMP: 21 EST: 1903
SQ FT: 12,000
SALES (est): 3.5MM **Privately Held**
SIC: **3444** Sheet metalwork

(G-4222)
KESSO FOODS INC
Also Called: Mediterranean Thick Yogurt
7720 21st Ave (11370-1219)
PHONE 718 777-5303
Fotini Kessissoglou, *President*
EMP: 5
SALES: 100K **Privately Held**
SIC: **2026** 5143 Fluid milk; yogurt

(G-4223)
LIBERTY AWNINGS & SIGNS INC
Also Called: Empire Signs
7705 21st Ave (11370-1250)
PHONE 347 203-1470
Panayiotis Panayi, *CEO*
EMP: 2
SQ FT: 5,000
SALES: 2.3MM **Privately Held**
SIC: **3993** Advertising artwork

(G-4224)
MOON GATES COMPANY
3243 104th St (11369-2515)
PHONE 718 426-0023
Stephen Vieira, *Principal*
EMP: 6
SQ FT: 2,000

GEOGRAPHIC SECTION

East Meadow - Nassau County (G-4252)

SALES (est): 400K **Privately Held**
SIC: 3446 1791 Mfg Architectural Metalwork Structural Steel Erection

(G-4225)
T RJ SHIRTS INC
3050 90th St (11369-1706)
PHONE..................347 642-3071
Femd Rocky, *Principal*
EMP: 6
SALES (est): 487.3K **Privately Held**
SIC: 2331 T-shirts & tops, women's: made from purchased materials

(G-4226)
WESTCHSTR CRNKSHFT GRNDNG
Also Called: Westchester Crankshaft Grinding
3263 110th St (11369-2525)
PHONE..................718 651-3900
Marco Albanese, *Vice Pres*
▲ EMP: 9
SALES (est): 1.1MM **Privately Held**
SIC: 3599 Crankshafts & camshafts, machining

East Greenbush
Rensselaer County

(G-4227)
AUTOMATED & MGT SOLUTIONS LLC
743 Columbia Tpke (12061-2266)
PHONE..................518 833-0315
Francis Clifford, *Mng Member*
Sharon Hemmes, *Information Mgr*
EMP: 7 EST: 2011
SALES: 900K **Privately Held**
SIC: 7372 Application computer software; operating systems computer software

(G-4228)
CURTIS PRTG CO THE DEL PRESS
711 Columbia Tpke (12061-2212)
PHONE..................518 477-4820
Richard Lieberman, *President*
EMP: 5
SQ FT: 4,000
SALES (est): 645.3K **Privately Held**
WEB: www.curtisprinting.com
SIC: 2759 Letterpress printing

(G-4229)
GARELICK FARMS LLC
504 Third Avenue Ext (12061)
PHONE..................518 283-0820
Paul Nero, *Sales Executive*
Bill Hogan, *Branch Mgr*
EMP: 210 **Publicly Held**
SIC: 2026 Cottage cheese
HQ: Garelick Farms, Llc
1199 W Central St Ste 1
Franklin MA 02038
508 528-9000

(G-4230)
LEONARD CARLSON
Also Called: Carlson, L A Co
90 Waters Rd (12061-3422)
PHONE..................518 477-4710
Leonard Carlson, *Owner*
▲ EMP: 6 EST: 1956
SQ FT: 6,000
SALES: 425K **Privately Held**
SIC: 3931 Organs, all types: pipe, reed, hand, electronic, etc.

(G-4231)
SABIC INNOVATIVE PLASTICS
1 Gail Ct (12061-1750)
PHONE..................713 448-7474
Scott Dansey, *General Mgr*
Narendra Mansharamani, *Principal*
Amish Agarwal, *Vice Pres*
Shelia Naab, *Vice Pres*
Ahmet Kizilirmakli, *Plant Mgr*
EMP: 36 EST: 2012
SALES (est): 5.9MM **Privately Held**
SIC: 2821 Plastics materials & resins

East Hampton
Suffolk County

(G-4232)
BISTRIAN CEMENT CORPORATION
225 Springs Fireplace Rd (11937-4823)
P.O. Box 5048 (11937-6079)
PHONE..................631 324-1123
Barry Bistrian, *President*
Betsy Avallone, *Shareholder*
Bruce Bistrian, *Shareholder*
Pat Bistrian, *Shareholder*
Barbara Borg, *Shareholder*
EMP: 12
SQ FT: 20,000
SALES: 1.7MM **Privately Held**
SIC: 3272 3259 Septic tanks, concrete; drain tile, clay

(G-4233)
C E KING & SONS INC
10 Saint Francis Pl (11937-4330)
PHONE..................631 324-4944
Clarence E King III, *President*
David King, *Treasurer*
Deanna Tikkanen, *Admin Sec*
EMP: 7
SQ FT: 1,650
SALES: 600K **Privately Held**
WEB: www.kingsawnings.com
SIC: 2394 5999 Awnings, fabric: made from purchased materials; fire extinguishers

(G-4234)
CHESU INC
81 Newtown Ln (11937-2323)
PHONE..................239 564-2803
Chet Borgida, *President*
Susan Borgida, *Vice Pres*
EMP: 10 EST: 2012
SALES (est): 1MM **Privately Held**
SIC: 3086 5111 7389 Packaging & shipping materials, foamed plastic; printing paper; notary publics

(G-4235)
EAST HAMPTON IND NEWS INC
Also Called: East Hampton Independent The
74 Monlauk Hwy Unit 19 (11937-3268)
PHONE..................631 324-2500
James Mackim, *President*
Kitty Merrill, *Editor*
Jodi Della Femina, *Vice Pres*
Lee Minitree, *Treasurer*
Annemarie Davin, *Sales Staff*
EMP: 28
SQ FT: 1,400
SALES (est): 1.6MM **Privately Held**
WEB: www.indyeastend.com
SIC: 2711 Newspapers, publishing & printing

(G-4236)
EAST HAMPTON STAR INC
153 Main St (11937-2716)
P.O. Box 5002 (11937-6005)
PHONE..................631 324-0002
Helen Rattray, *President*
EMP: 40 EST: 1886
SQ FT: 6,400
SALES (est): 2.9MM **Privately Held**
WEB: www.easthamptonstar.com
SIC: 2711 Commercial printing & newspaper publishing combined; newspapers, publishing & printing

(G-4237)
ELIE TAHARI LTD
1 Main St (11937-2701)
PHONE..................631 329-8883
Brenda Bolin, *Branch Mgr*
EMP: 75
SALES (corp-wide): 178.6MM **Privately Held**
SIC: 2337 Suits: women's, misses' & juniors'
PA: Elie Tahari Ltd.
16 Bleeker St
Millburn NJ 07041
973 671-6300

(G-4238)
IRONY LIMITED INC (PA)
Also Called: Hedges and Gardens
53 Sag Harbor Tpke (11937-4905)
PHONE..................631 329-4065
Robert Linker, *President*
Elizabeth Linker, *Vice Pres*
EMP: 2
SQ FT: 2,200
SALES (est): 1.2MM **Privately Held**
SIC: 3441 7641 3446 1799 Fabricated structural metal; antique furniture repair & restoration; stairs, staircases, stair treads: prefabricated metal; ornamental metal work

(G-4239)
KEENERS EAST END LITHO INC
10 Prospect Blvd (11937-5800)
PHONE..................631 324-8565
Charles Keener, *President*
Lynn Keener, *Corp Secy*
Greg Keener, *Vice Pres*
EMP: 8
SALES (est): 834.6K **Privately Held**
SIC: 2752 Commercial printing, lithographic

(G-4240)
LURIA COMMUNICATIONS INC
Also Called: Card Pak Start Up
31 Shorewood Dr Fl 1 (11937-3402)
PHONE..................631 329-4922
Jay Blatt, *President*
Vicki Luria, *Vice Pres*
EMP: 8
SALES: 500K **Privately Held**
SIC: 2721 7311 7331 Trade journals: publishing only, not printed on site; advertising agencies; mailing list brokers

(G-4241)
NATURPATHICA HOLISTIC HLTH INC
74 Montauk Hwy Unit 23 (11937-3268)
PHONE..................631 329-8792
Barbara Close, *CEO*
Jonathan Keattch, *COO*
Johnny Haas, *Manager*
EMP: 100
SQ FT: 750
SALES (est): 4.4MM **Privately Held**
SIC: 2844 Cosmetic preparations

(G-4242)
SABIN METAL CORPORATION (PA)
300 Pantigo Pl Ste 102 (11937-2630)
PHONE..................631 329-1695
Andrew Sabin, *President*
Jonathan Sabin, *Exec VP*
Kevin Beirne, *Vice Pres*
John Jonat, *Vice Pres*
Yanan Sui, *Research*
▲ EMP: 14 EST: 1945
SQ FT: 4,000
SALES (est): 43.2MM **Privately Held**
WEB: www.sabinmetal.com
SIC: 3341 Secondary precious metals

(G-4243)
STAR READY MIX EAST INC
225 Springs Fireplace Rd (11937-4823)
P.O. Box 371, Medford (11763-0371)
PHONE..................631 289-8787
Thomas Hess, *President*
EMP: 15
SALES (est): 1.1MM **Privately Held**
SIC: 3273 Ready-mixed concrete

East Islip
Suffolk County

(G-4244)
KEY CONTAINER CORP
135 Hollins Ln (11730-3006)
PHONE..................631 582-3847
Frank Giaquinko, *President*
EMP: 6
SALES: 800K **Privately Held**
SIC: 2653 Corrugated & solid fiber boxes

(G-4245)
QUALIFIED MANUFACTURING CORP
15 Amber Ct (11730-3801)
PHONE..................631 249-4440
Donald Wojnar, *President*
EMP: 11 EST: 1970
SQ FT: 7,000
SALES (est): 1.4MM **Privately Held**
SIC: 3599 Mfg Industrial Machinery

East Meadow
Nassau County

(G-4246)
ARTYS SPRNKLR SVC INSTLLATION
234 E Meadow Ave Unit B (11554-2455)
PHONE..................516 538-4371
Arthur R Wolf, *President*
Helen Wolf, *Treasurer*
EMP: 13
SALES: 700K **Privately Held**
SIC: 3432 Lawn hose nozzles & sprinklers

(G-4247)
CHV PRINTED COMPANY
1905 Hempstead Tpke B (11554-1047)
PHONE..................516 997-1101
Andrew Mazzone, *Principal*
Timothy Chant, *Administration*
EMP: 19
SALES (est): 1.8MM **Privately Held**
SIC: 2759 Screen printing

(G-4248)
COMPLETE ORTHOPEDIC SVCS INC
2094 Front St (11554-1709)
PHONE..................516 357-9113
Noreen Diaz, *Ch of Bd*
Alexandra Divito, *Marketing Staff*
Anne Feret, *Practice Mgr*
EMP: 20
SALES (est): 3MM **Privately Held**
SIC: 3842 Braces, orthopedic

(G-4249)
DATASONIC INC
1413 Cleveland Ave (11554-4405)
PHONE..................516 248-7330
Richard Mintz, *President*
EMP: 5
SALES (est): 320K **Privately Held**
SIC: 3669 Burglar alarm apparatus, electric

(G-4250)
E M T MANUFACTURING INC
Also Called: Engineering Mfg & Tech
273 Cherry Pl (11554-2936)
PHONE..................516 333-1917
Ernest Hippner, *President*
Marion Hippner, *Corp Secy*
EMP: 12
SQ FT: 10,000
SALES (est): 1.7MM **Privately Held**
SIC: 3599 3365 Machine shop, jobbing & repair; aerospace castings, aluminum

(G-4251)
EATON CORPORATION
280 Bellmore Rd (11554-3538)
PHONE..................516 353-3017
John Pierro, *Principal*
EMP: 222 **Privately Held**
SIC: 3625 Motor controls & accessories
HQ: Eaton Corporation
1000 Eaton Blvd
Cleveland OH 44122
440 523-5000

(G-4252)
HI TECH SIGNS OF NY INC
415 E Meadow Ave (11554-3952)
PHONE..................516 794-7880
Scott Abrecht, *President*
EMP: 5
SQ FT: 2,000

East Meadow - Nassau County (G-4253)

SALES (est): 615.5K **Privately Held**
SIC: 3993 5999 Signs, not made in custom sign painting shops; banners, flags, decals & posters

(G-4253)
HIBU INC (DH)
90 Merrick Ave Ste 530 (11554-1575)
PHONE..................516 730-1900
Mike Pocock, *CEO*
John Condron, *Ch of Bd*
Joseph Walsh, *President*
Bob Wigley, *Chairman*
Mark Payne, *COO*
◆ **EMP:** 200
SQ FT: 30,000
SALES (est): 1.8B
SALES (corp-wide): 431.4MM **Privately Held**
SIC: 2741 Directories: publishing & printing
HQ: Yell Limited
One Reading Central
Reading BERKS RG1 3
800 555-444

(G-4254)
JOHN PRIOR
2545 Hempstead Tpke # 402 (11554-2144)
PHONE..................516 520-9801
John Prior, *Principal*
Barbara Gordon, *Human Resources*
EMP: 8 **EST:** 2007
SALES (est): 716.9K **Privately Held**
SIC: 3999 Manufacturing industries

(G-4255)
PJ DECORATORS INC
257 Pontiac Pl (11554-1231)
PHONE..................516 735-9693
David Brill, *President*
EMP: 25
SALES (est): 2MM **Privately Held**
SIC: 2591 5023 5719 Drapery hardware & blinds & shades; vertical blinds; vertical blinds

(G-4256)
TRIPLE H CONSTRUCTION INC
832 Bethlynn Ct (11554-4911)
PHONE..................516 280-8252
Hesham Hassane, *President*
Venaal Hassane, *Vice Pres*
EMP: 22
SQ FT: 1,600
SALES: 700K **Privately Held**
SIC: 3446 1751 Fences or posts, ornamental iron or steel; window & door installation & erection

East Moriches
Suffolk County

(G-4257)
KEY SIGNALS
47 Tuthill Point Rd (11940-1216)
PHONE..................631 433-2962
Mark Gartung, *Principal*
EMP: 7
SALES (est): 605K **Privately Held**
SIC: 3629 Electrical industrial apparatus

(G-4258)
TATES WHOLESALE LLC
Also Called: Tate's Bake Shop
62 Pine St (11940-1117)
PHONE..................631 780-6511
Kathleen King, *President*
Robert Panarella, *Warehouse Mgr*
EMP: 130
SALES (est): 21.9MM **Privately Held**
SIC: 2051 Bakery: wholesale or wholesale/retail combined

East Northport
Suffolk County

(G-4259)
ADVANTAGE ORTHOTICS INC
337 Larkfield Rd (11731-2904)
PHONE..................631 368-1754
Claire Ann Ketcham, *Principal*
EMP: 9
SALES (est): 1.1MM **Privately Held**
SIC: 3842 Orthopedic appliances

(G-4260)
ARCHITCTRAL MLLWK INSTALLATION
590 Elwood Rd (11731-5629)
PHONE..................631 499-0755
Shaun Hanley, *President*
EMP: 23
SALES: 2MM **Privately Held**
SIC: 2431 2439 Mfg Millwork Mfg Structural Wood Members

(G-4261)
COMPUTER CONVERSIONS CORP
6 Dunton Ct (11731-1704)
PHONE..................631 261-3300
Stephen Renard, *President*
Dave Varrone, *General Mgr*
Paul Waldman, *Vice Pres*
Les Levy, *Project Engr*
Margaret Librizzi, *Human Res Mgr*
EMP: 32
SQ FT: 5,000
SALES (est): 6.9MM **Privately Held**
WEB: www.computer-conversions.com
SIC: 3571 Electronic computers

(G-4262)
EAST TO WEST ARCHITECTRAL PDTS
103 Tinton Pl Ste 1a (11731-5330)
PHONE..................631 433-9690
Dean Nichol, *President*
EMP: 1
SALES: 3MM **Privately Held**
WEB: www.easttowestsales.com
SIC: 3996 Hard surface floor coverings

(G-4263)
FASTNET SOFTWARE INTL INC
459 Elwood Rd (11731-4006)
PHONE..................888 740-7790
Uzma Abbas, *President*
EMP: 10
SALES (est): 813.4K **Privately Held**
SIC: 7372 Business oriented computer software

(G-4264)
FORTE NETWORK
Also Called: Forte Security Group
75 Lockfield Rd (11731)
PHONE..................631 390-9050
Richard Allen, *President*
EMP: 40
SALES (est): 4.2MM **Privately Held**
SIC: 3699 Security control equipment & systems

(G-4265)
ISLAND SILKSCREEN INC
Also Called: Connie's T Shirt Shop
328 Larkfield Rd (11731-2945)
PHONE..................631 757-4567
Mike Sambur, *President*
EMP: 5
SALES (est): 458.4K **Privately Held**
SIC: 2759 Screen printing

(G-4266)
JORDAN PANEL SYSTEMS CORP (PA)
196 Laurel Rd Unit 2 (11731-1441)
PHONE..................631 754-4900
John A Finamore Sr, *President*
▼ **EMP:** 25
SQ FT: 5,000
SALES (est): 10MM **Privately Held**
WEB: www.jordanpanel.com
SIC: 3499 1761 1793 5033 Aerosol valves, metal; roofing, siding & sheet metal work; glass & glazing work; roofing, asphalt & sheet metal

(G-4267)
LOUDON LTD
Also Called: Minuteman Press
281 Larkfield Rd (11731-2417)
PHONE..................631 757-4447
Kathy Loudon, *President*
David Loudon, *General Mgr*
EMP: 5
SQ FT: 1,800
SALES (est): 740K **Privately Held**
SIC: 2752 2791 Commercial printing, offset; typesetting

(G-4268)
MONASANI SIGNS INC
Also Called: Mr Sign
22 Compton St (11731-5510)
PHONE..................631 266-2635
William Monahan, *President*
EMP: 5
SQ FT: 1,500
SALES: 400K **Privately Held**
SIC: 3993 7532 Signs & advertising specialties; truck painting & lettering

(G-4269)
PROGRESSIVE HARDWARE CO INC
63 Brightside Ave (11731-1903)
PHONE..................631 445-1826
William Zilz, *President*
▲ **EMP:** 9
SQ FT: 11,000
SALES: 960K **Privately Held**
WEB: www.progressive-hardware.com
SIC: 3429 Builders' hardware

(G-4270)
READY CHECK GLO INC
23 Bruce Ln Ste E (11731-2701)
PHONE..................516 547-1849
Celestina Pugliese, *CEO*
EMP: 5 **EST:** 2010
SALES (est): 175K **Privately Held**
SIC: 2752 7389 Menus, lithographed;

East Norwich
Nassau County

(G-4271)
CATHAY RESOURCES INC
38 Cord Pl (11732-1155)
P.O. Box 314 (11732-0314)
PHONE..................516 922-2839
Walter Belous, *President*
▲ **EMP:** 3
SQ FT: 3,000
SALES: 10MM **Privately Held**
SIC: 3356 Tin & tin alloy bars, pipe, sheets, etc.

(G-4272)
GOLDEN EGRET LLC
38 Cord Pl (11732-1155)
P.O. Box 314 (11732-0314)
PHONE..................516 922-2839
Walter Belous, *Mng Member*
▲ **EMP:** 6
SALES (est): 766.7K **Privately Held**
SIC: 3313 Tungsten carbide powder

East Patchogue
Suffolk County

(G-4273)
G & M DEGE INC
250 Orchard Rd Bldg 1 (11772-5535)
PHONE..................631 475-1450
Nick Gallipoli, *President*
Angela Gallipoli, *Vice Pres*
EMP: 14
SQ FT: 3,000
SALES (est): 3.4MM **Privately Held**
SIC: 2851 Removers & cleaners

(G-4274)
GLOBAL HANGER & DISPLAY INC
14 Hewlett Ave (11772-5407)
PHONE..................631 475-5900
Sandy Stoll, *Principal*
▲ **EMP:** 6
SALES (est): 575.9K **Privately Held**
SIC: 3089 Plastics products

(G-4275)
HUNTER METAL INDUSTRIES INC
Also Called: Hunter Displays
14 Hewlett Ave (11772-5499)
PHONE..................631 475-5900
Sandy Stoll, *CEO*
Kevin Kasper, *General Mgr*
Ken Kasper, *Vice Pres*
Linda Roesch, *Purch Mgr*
Susan Anastasia, *Accounting Mgr*
EMP: 100 **EST:** 1951
SQ FT: 75,000
SALES (est): 15.7MM **Privately Held**
WEB: www.hunterdisplays.com
SIC: 2542 2541 Fixtures: display, office or store: except wood; display fixtures, wood

(G-4276)
PROGRESSIVE ORTHOTICS LTD
285 Sills Rd Bldg 8c (11772-8800)
PHONE..................631 447-3860
Bruce Goodman, *Branch Mgr*
EMP: 12
SALES (corp-wide): 905.9K **Privately Held**
WEB: www.progressiveorthotics.com
SIC: 3842 5999 Orthopedic appliances; orthopedic & prosthesis applications
PA: Progressive Orthotics Ltd
280 Middle Country Rd G
Selden NY 11784
631 732-5556

East Quogue
Suffolk County

(G-4277)
EAST COAST MINES LTD
Also Called: East Coast Mines & Material
2 Lewis Rd (11942)
PHONE..................631 653-5445
William Tintle, *President*
EMP: 20
SQ FT: 5,000
SALES (est): 2.9MM **Privately Held**
SIC: 1442 5261 5032 Construction sand & gravel; top soil; brick, stone & related material

(G-4278)
HAMPTON SHIPYARDS INC
7 Carter Ln (11942-4334)
P.O. Box 3007 (11942-2008)
PHONE..................631 653-6777
Fred Scopinich, *President*
Doris Scopinich, *Vice Pres*
EMP: 10 **EST:** 1956
SQ FT: 21,000
SALES (est): 1.1MM **Privately Held**
SIC: 3732 Boat building & repairing

(G-4279)
SITEWATCH TECHNOLOGY LLC
22 Sunset Ave (11942-4200)
PHONE..................207 778-3246
Fred York, *Principal*
David B Horn,
EMP: 6
SALES (est): 590.8K **Privately Held**
SIC: 3678 Electronic connectors

East Rochester
Monroe County

(G-4280)
ART PARTS SIGNS INC
100 Lincoln Pkwy (14445-1450)
PHONE..................585 381-2134
Patricia Ransco, *President*
EMP: 7
SQ FT: 8,000
SALES: 500K **Privately Held**
SIC: 3993 Signs, not made in custom sign painting shops

GEOGRAPHIC SECTION

East Setauket - Suffolk County (G-4306)

(G-4281)
CARPENTIER INDUSTRIES LLC
Also Called: Rochester Magnet
119 Despatch Dr (14445-1447)
PHONE..............................585 385-5550
Andrew Carpentier, *President*
Jennifer Fisher, *Accounts Mgr*
▲ **EMP:** 15 **EST:** 2010
SQ FT: 10,000
SALES (est): 2.2MM **Privately Held**
WEB: www.rochestermagnet.com
SIC: 3499 Magnets, permanent: metallic

(G-4282)
CONNOVER PACKAGING INC
119 Despatch Dr (14445-1447)
PHONE..............................585 377-2510
Andrew Carpentier, *President*
Vic Rauscher, *Sales Dir*
Judy Stephens, *Office Mgr*
Kim Koronas, *Info Tech Mgr*
EMP: 6
SQ FT: 15,000
SALES (est): 1.2MM **Privately Held**
WEB: www.connoverpackaging.com
SIC: 2673 Plastic bags: made from purchased materials

(G-4283)
EKOSTINGER INC
140 Despatch Dr (14445-1448)
PHONE..............................585 739-0450
Parr Wiegel, *CEO*
Aaron Flajsing, *Director*
Steven Chatwin, *Officer*
EMP: 11 **EST:** 2012
SQ FT: 13,500
SALES (est): 1MM **Privately Held**
SIC: 3713 Truck bodies & parts

(G-4284)
FERRO CORPORATION
603 W Commercial St (14445-2253)
P.O. Box 389 (14445-0389)
PHONE..............................585 586-8770
Richard Veeder, *Branch Mgr*
EMP: 35
SQ FT: 30,000
SALES (corp-wide): 1.4B **Publicly Held**
WEB: www.ferro.com
SIC: 2819 Industrial inorganic chemicals
PA: Ferro Corporation
6060 Parkland Blvd # 250
Mayfield Heights OH 44124
216 875-5600

(G-4285)
FILTROS LTD
Also Called: Filtros Plant
603 W Commercial St (14445-2253)
P.O. Box 389 (14445-0389)
PHONE..............................585 586-8770
Byron Anderson, *CEO*
Allan Schilling, *Vice Pres*
Scott Stranford, *QC Mgr*
George Goeller, *Sales Mgr*
Peter Saunders, *Sales Engr*
EMP: 35 **EST:** 1999
SQ FT: 45,000
SALES (est): 5.6MM **Privately Held**
WEB: www.filtrosltd.com
SIC: 3255 3564 3297 3264 Clay refractories; blowers & fans; nonclay refractories; porcelain electrical supplies

(G-4286)
HOERCHER INDUSTRIES INC
A1 Country Club Rd Ste 1 (14445-2230)
PHONE..............................585 398-2982
Lawrence Hoercher, *President*
EMP: 5
SQ FT: 3,500
SALES (est): 360K **Privately Held**
SIC: 3599 Electrical discharge machining (EDM)

(G-4287)
IDEAL MANUFACTURING INC
80 Bluff Dr (14445-1300)
PHONE..............................585 872-7190
Ben Stroyer, *President*
Arthur Stroyer, *Vice Pres*
Jay Stroyer, *Sales Dir*
Bruce Stroyer, *Marketing Staff*
Nancy Balentine, *Office Admin*
▼ **EMP:** 32
SQ FT: 7,000
SALES (est): 9.1MM **Privately Held**
SIC: 2515 Foundations & platforms

(G-4288)
KEMCO SALES LLC
119 Despatch Dr (14445-1447)
PHONE..............................203 762-1902
Andrew Carpentier, *President*
EMP: 15
SQ FT: 15,000
SALES (est): 2.5MM **Privately Held**
WEB: www.securpak.com
SIC: 2673 Bags: plastic, laminated & coated

(G-4289)
KRONENBERGER MFG CORP
115 Despatch Dr (14445-1447)
P.O. Box 650 (14445-0650)
PHONE..............................585 385-2340
Gunter Kronenberger, *President*
Eric Kronenberger, *Vice Pres*
Kevin Kronenberger, *Vice Pres*
EMP: 45
SQ FT: 40,000
SALES (est): 7.5MM **Privately Held**
SIC: 3599 Machine shop, jobbing & repair

(G-4290)
LINCDOC LLC
Also Called: Lincware
401 Main St (14445-1707)
PHONE..............................585 563-1669
Darren Mathis, *CEO*
Rob Tiernan, *Partner*
Donna Moss, *Sales Staff*
Cristin Donaher, *Business Anlyst*
Eileen Gaisser, *Business Anlyst*
EMP: 7
SALES (est): 468.7K **Privately Held**
SIC: 7372 Prepackaged software

(G-4291)
RICHARDS & WEST INC
Also Called: Rw Manufacturing Company
501 W Commercial St Ste 1 (14445-2258)
PHONE..............................585 461-4088
John R Keim, *Ch of Bd*
Gary Keim, *Vice Pres*
John E Miner, *Vice Pres*
John Minr, *Vice Pres*
Patricia Holzgartner, *Human Res Mgr*
EMP: 54 **EST:** 1982
SQ FT: 10,000
SALES (est): 8.5MM **Privately Held**
WEB: www.rwmfg.com
SIC: 3911 7631 5944 Jewelry, precious metal; jewelry repair services; jewelry, precious stones & precious metals

East Rockaway
Nassau County

(G-4292)
ADULTS AND CHILDREN WITH LEARN
22 Alice Ct (11518-1902)
PHONE..............................516 593-8230
EMP: 28
SALES (corp-wide): 78.7MM **Privately Held**
SIC: 3999 Barber & beauty shop equipment
PA: Adults And Children With Learning And Developmental Disabilities, Inc.
807 S Oyster Bay Rd
Bethpage NY 11714
516 822-0028

(G-4293)
CIRCUITS & SYSTEMS INC
Also Called: Arlyn Scales
59 2nd St (11518-1236)
PHONE..............................516 593-4301
Arnold Gordon, *President*
Lynne Gordon, *Treasurer*
▲ **EMP:** 22 **EST:** 1977
SQ FT: 6,000
SALES (est): 5.4MM **Privately Held**
WEB: www.chaverware.com
SIC: 7373 Scales & balances, except laboratory; computer-aided design (CAD) systems service

(G-4294)
DAWN PAPER CO INC (PA)
Also Called: Dawn Printing Company
4 Leonard Dr (11518-1609)
PHONE..............................516 596-9110
Stephen Kucker, *President*
Jonathan Greenberg, *Vice Pres*
Marla Perrino, *Vice Pres*
EMP: 12
SQ FT: 5,000
SALES (est): 2.4MM **Privately Held**
SIC: 2752 5113 5085 Commercial printing, lithographic; bags, paper & disposable plastic; boxes, crates, etc., other than paper

(G-4295)
SEXTET FABRICS INC
21 Ryder Pl Ste 4 (11518-1200)
P.O. Box 10 (11518-0010)
PHONE..............................516 593-0608
Gordon Stern, *CEO*
Barbara Ross, *President*
▲ **EMP:** 12 **EST:** 1971
SQ FT: 8,500
SALES (est): 5MM **Privately Held**
SIC: 2259 Convertors, knit goods

(G-4296)
STERLING PIERCE COMPANY INC
395 Atlantic Ave (11518-1423)
PHONE..............................516 593-1170
William Burke, *President*
Isabel Burke, *Vice Pres*
▼ **EMP:** 29
SQ FT: 5,000
SALES (est): 3.3MM **Privately Held**
WEB: www.sterlingpierce.com
SIC: 2789 2732 2752 Binding only: books, pamphlets, magazines, etc.; book printing; commercial printing, lithographic

(G-4297)
STYLEBUILT ACCESSORIES INC (PA)
Also Called: Stylebuilt Acesries
45 Rose Ln (11518-2126)
PHONE..............................917 439-0578
Jonathan Greenfield, *President*
Jerome Greenfield, *Vice Pres*
Jackie Greenfield, *Treasurer*
▲ **EMP:** 12 **EST:** 1946
SQ FT: 65,000
SALES: 950K **Privately Held**
WEB: www.stylebuilt.com
SIC: 3499 Novelties & specialties, metal

East Setauket
Suffolk County

(G-4298)
B & Z TECHNOLOGIES LLC
Also Called: Bnz Tech
7 Technology Dr (11733-4000)
PHONE..............................631 675-9666
Javed Siddiqui, *President*
David Hlinka, *General Mgr*
Asma Siddiqui, *Officer*
EMP: 7
SQ FT: 2,000
SALES: 2MM **Privately Held**
WEB: www.bnztech.com
SIC: 3812 Antennas, radar or communications; radar systems & equipment

(G-4299)
BASF CORPORATION
Also Called: BASF The Chemical Company
361 Sheep Pasture Rd (11733-3614)
PHONE..............................631 689-0200
Meredith Culver, *Branch Mgr*
Anthony Asselta, *Manager*
EMP: 157
SALES (corp-wide): 76B **Privately Held**
SIC: 2869 Industrial organic chemicals
HQ: Basf Corporation
100 Park Ave
Florham Park NJ 07932
973 245-6000

(G-4300)
EATING EVOLVED INC
10 Technology Dr Unit 4 (11733-4063)
PHONE..............................516 510-2601
EMP: 9 **EST:** 2015
SALES (est): 693.9K **Privately Held**
SIC: 2066 Chocolate & cocoa products

(G-4301)
FLAGPOLES INCORPORATED
95 Gnarled Hollow Rd (11733-1934)
P.O. Box 833 (11733-0643)
PHONE..............................631 751-5500
Jack Seferian, *CEO*
Haig Seferian, *Principal*
Gregory Seferian, *Vice Pres*
Greg Seferian, *Manager*
▼ **EMP:** 90
SQ FT: 96,000
SALES (est): 19.1MM **Privately Held**
WEB: www.flagpole.net
SIC: 3446 3441 3354 Flagpoles, metal; lamp posts, metal; fabricated structural metal; aluminum extruded products

(G-4302)
GOLDBERG PROSTHETIC & ORTHOTIC
9 Technology Dr (11733-4000)
PHONE..............................631 689-6606
Mark E Goldberg, *President*
EMP: 14
SALES (est): 2.1MM **Privately Held**
SIC: 3842 8021 5999 Limbs, artificial; prosthodontist; artificial limbs

(G-4303)
MEDICINE RULES INC
2 Constance Ct (11733-3730)
PHONE..............................631 334-5395
Joseph Agartner, *President*
EMP: 5
SALES (est): 309.6K **Privately Held**
SIC: 3695 Computer software tape & disks: blank, rigid & floppy

(G-4304)
MILLER MOHR DISPLAY INC
12 Technology Dr Unit 6 (11733-4049)
PHONE..............................631 941-2769
Marilyn Mohr, *President*
Miller Mohr, *Principal*
EMP: 5
SALES: 950K **Privately Held**
SIC: 3993 Displays & cutouts, window & lobby

(G-4305)
MML SOFTWARE LTD
Also Called: Finance Manager
45 Research Way Ste 207 (11733-6401)
PHONE..............................631 941-1313
Ron Bovich, *President*
Andrew Miller, *President*
Mercedes Burgos, *Vice Pres*
Wendy Gottlieb, *Mktg Coord*
Gail Andersen, *Admin Asst*
EMP: 20
SQ FT: 5,000
SALES (est): 2.2MM **Privately Held**
WEB: www.financemgr.com
SIC: 7372 6163 Application computer software; loan brokers

(G-4306)
PENETRON INTERNATIONAL LTD
45 Research Way Ste 203 (11733-6401)
PHONE..............................631 941-9700
Robert G Reuera, *CEO*
Grant Urban, *Sales Mgr*
Dale Williams, *Regl Sales Mgr*
Vanessa Georgiades, *Sales Staff*
Michelle Staria, *Sales Staff*
▲ **EMP:** 14
SQ FT: 60,000
SALES (est): 5.5MM **Privately Held**
WEB: www.penetron.com
SIC: 2899 Waterproofing compounds

East Setauket - Suffolk County (G-4307)

(G-4307)
POLE-TECH CO INC
Also Called: Poletech Flagpole Manufacturer
97 Gnarled Hollow Rd (11733-1980)
P.O. Box 715 (11733-0770)
PHONE..................................631 689-5525
Karnik M Seferian, *Ch of Bd*
Ralph Barbarite, *Vice Pres*
Melanie Veen, *Manager*
◆ **EMP:** 17
SQ FT: 20,000
SALES (est): 4.7MM **Privately Held**
WEB: www.poletech.com
SIC: 3446 Flagpoles, metal

(G-4308)
PRINTING SPECTRUM INC
12 Research Way Ste 1 (11733-3531)
PHONE..................................631 689-1010
James Altebrando, *Ch of Bd*
EMP: 12
SQ FT: 10,000
SALES (est): 2MM **Privately Held**
WEB: www.printingspectrum.com
SIC: 2752 Commercial printing, offset

(G-4309)
SARTEK INDUSTRIES INC (PA)
Also Called: Snr Cctv Systems Division
17 N Belle Mead Ave Ste 1 (11733-3466)
PHONE..................................631 473-3555
Carl Saieva, *President*
EMP: 6
SQ FT: 5,200
SALES: 950.3K **Privately Held**
WEB: www.sarind.com
SIC: 3663 1731 Television closed circuit equipment; closed circuit television installation

(G-4310)
SKYLINE LLC
16 Hulse Rd Ste 1 (11733-3645)
PHONE..................................631 403-4131
Louis Bove, *Mng Member*
Lawrence Schreiber,
EMP: 20
SALES: 3.5MM **Privately Held**
SIC: 3295 Perlite, aggregate or expanded

(G-4311)
TECHNOMAG INC
12 Technology Dr Unit 5 (11733-4049)
PHONE..................................631 246-6142
Vujay Katukota, *President*
▲ **EMP:** 5
SALES (est): 665.5K **Privately Held**
SIC: 3499 3577 7319 Magnets, permanent: metallic; computer peripheral equipment; distribution of advertising material or sample services

(G-4312)
TIMES BEACON RECORD NEWSPAPERS (PA)
Also Called: Village Times, The
185 Route 25a Ste 4 (11733-2870)
P.O. Box 707 (11733-0769)
PHONE..................................631 331-1154
Leah E Dunaief, *President*
Leah Dunaief, *Owner*
Marie Murtagh, *Advt Staff*
Ellen Segal, *Manager*
EMP: 16
SALES (est): 2MM **Privately Held**
SIC: 2711 Newspapers: publishing only, not printed on site

(G-4313)
TUCKER JONES HOUSE INC
1 Enterprise Dr (11733-4086)
P.O. Box 231 (11733-0231)
PHONE..................................631 642-9092
Donna Sucilsky, *President*
EMP: 20
SQ FT: 8,000
SALES (est): 2.3MM **Privately Held**
WEB: www.tavernpuzzle.com
SIC: 3944 Puzzles

(G-4314)
VISION QUEST LIGHTING INC
Also Called: E-Quest Lighting
12 Satterly Rd (11733-3722)
PHONE..................................631 737-4800
Larry Lieberman, *Ch of Bd*
Torrey Bievenour, *Vice Pres*
Janelle Norton, *Vice Pres*
▲ **EMP:** 33
SQ FT: 2,500
SALES (est): 8.7MM **Privately Held**
WEB: www.vql.com
SIC: 3645 3646 Residential lighting fixtures; fluorescent lighting fixtures, residential; garden, patio, walkway & yard lighting fixtures: electric; fluorescent lighting fixtures, commercial

(G-4315)
ZEPPELIN ELECTRIC COMPANY INC
26 Deer Ln (11733-3407)
PHONE..................................631 928-9467
William Zeppelin, *President*
EMP: 7
SQ FT: 1,250
SALES: 525.4K **Privately Held**
SIC: 3625 1731 Relays & industrial controls; electronic controls installation

East Syracuse
Onondaga County

(G-4316)
ALBERT F STAGER INC
6805 Crossbow Dr (13057-1006)
PHONE..................................315 434-7240
EMP: 5
SALES (corp-wide): 526.3MM **Privately Held**
SIC: 3081 Plastic film & sheet
HQ: Albert F Stager Inc
3815 California Rd
Orchard Park NY 14127
716 667-6000

(G-4317)
ALLEN TOOL PHOENIX INC
6821 Ellicott Dr (13057-1148)
P.O. Box 3024, Liverpool (13089-3024)
PHONE..................................315 463-7533
Cheryl Maines, *President*
Heath Severn, *Engineer*
Joan Cooney, *Accountant*
Nick Grevelding, *Administration*
EMP: 20
SQ FT: 18,000
SALES (est): 3.5MM **Privately Held**
WEB: www.allentoolphoenix.com
SIC: 3599 7692 Machine shop, jobbing & repair; welding repair

(G-4318)
ANAREN INC (HQ)
6635 Kirkville Rd (13057-9672)
PHONE..................................315 432-8909
Lawrence A Sala, *President*
Mark P Burdick, *President*
David E Kopf, *President*
Jeff Liebl, *President*
Timothy Ross, *President*
▲ **EMP:** 300
SQ FT: 159,000
SALES (est): 108.2MM
SALES (corp-wide): 2.6B **Publicly Held**
WEB: www.anaren.com
SIC: 3679 Electronic circuits; microwave components
PA: Ttm Technologies, Inc.
1665 Scenic Ave Ste 250
Costa Mesa CA 92626
714 327-3000

(G-4319)
ANAREN MICROWAVE INC
6635 Kirkville Rd (13057-9600)
PHONE..................................315 432-8909
Lawrence A Sala, *CEO*
Brian Buyea, *Project Mgr*
Deborah Burgmeier, *Engineer*
Rodrigo Cortes, *Engineer*
Ian Frank, *Engineer*
EMP: 1
SALES (est): 54.7MM
SALES (corp-wide): 2.6B **Publicly Held**
SIC: 3821 Micromanipulator

HQ: Anaren, Inc.
6635 Kirkville Rd
East Syracuse NY 13057
315 432-8909

(G-4320)
ARMSTRONG MOLD CORPORATION (PA)
6910 Manlius Center Rd (13057-8507)
PHONE..................................315 437-1517
John Alfred Armstrong, *CEO*
Peter Armstrong, *President*
Mark Garofano, *President*
Christopher Tiffault, *General Mgr*
Jeffrey Forrest, *COO*
▼ **EMP:** 50
SQ FT: 90,000
SALES (est): 19.6MM **Privately Held**
WEB: www.armstrongmold.com
SIC: 3365 3089 3543 Aluminum & aluminum-based alloy castings; injection molding of plastics; industrial patterns

(G-4321)
ARMSTRONG MOLD CORPORATION
5860 Fisher Rd (13057-2962)
PHONE..................................315 437-1517
John Alfred Armstrong, *Principal*
Greg Mork, *Engineer*
EMP: 75
SQ FT: 31,060
SALES (corp-wide): 19.6MM **Privately Held**
WEB: www.armstrongmold.com
SIC: 3599 3365 3089 3543 Custom machinery; machine shop, jobbing & repair; aluminum & aluminum-based alloy castings; injection molding of plastics; industrial patterns
PA: Armstrong Mold Corporation
6910 Manlius Center Rd
East Syracuse NY 13057
315 437-1517

(G-4322)
ARTISTRY IN WOOD OF SYRACUSE
6804 Manlius Center Rd # 2 (13057-1394)
PHONE..................................315 431-4022
Gregory W McCartney, *President*
EMP: 17
SALES (est): 3.6MM **Privately Held**
SIC: 2599 2531 5046 Factory furniture & fixtures; public building & related furniture; library furniture; store fixtures

(G-4323)
ASSA ABLOY ENTRANCE SYSTEMS US
Also Called: Besam Entrance Solutions
28 Corporate Cir Ste 1 (13057-1283)
PHONE..................................315 492-6600
Shane Stone, *Branch Mgr*
Jim Griswold, *Manager*
EMP: 22
SALES (corp-wide): 9B **Privately Held**
SIC: 3699 1796 3442 Door opening & closing devices, electrical; installing building equipment; metal doors
HQ: Assa Abloy Entrance Systems Us Inc.
1900 Airport Rd
Monroe NC 28110
704 290-5520

(G-4324)
AURORA STONE GROUP LLC
114 Marcy St (13057-2143)
PHONE..................................315 471-6869
Sandra Murphy,
EMP: 10 **EST:** 2011
SALES (est): 900K **Privately Held**
SIC: 3281 1743 Granite, cut & shaped; marble installation, interior

(G-4325)
B P NASH CO INC
5841 Butternut Dr (13057-9514)
PHONE..................................315 445-1310
Barry Nash, *President*
EMP: 15
SQ FT: 12,000
SALES: 1.5MM **Privately Held**
SIC: 3441 Fabricated structural metal

(G-4326)
BK PRINTING INC
Also Called: Speedpro Imaging
6507 Basile Rowe (13057-2928)
PHONE..................................315 565-5396
Robert Kellher, *President*
Lori Parker, *CFO*
EMP: 7 **EST:** 2010
SQ FT: 5,000
SALES: 700K **Privately Held**
SIC: 2752 Commercial printing, lithographic

(G-4327)
BRISTOL-MYERS SQUIBB COMPANY
6000 Thompson Rd (13057-5050)
P.O. Box 4755, Syracuse (13221-4755)
PHONE..................................315 432-2000
Meredith Downescurtis, *Research*
Kirk Wolfgang, *Engineer*
Steven Lee, *Branch Mgr*
Julie Sachar, *Manager*
Jeffrey Titus, *Associate Dir*
EMP: 40
SALES (corp-wide): 20.7B **Publicly Held**
WEB: www.bms.com
SIC: 2834 Druggists' preparations (pharmaceuticals)
PA: Bristol-Myers Squibb Company
430 E 29th St Fl 14
New York NY 10016
212 546-4000

(G-4328)
CARRIER CORPORATION
6390 Fly Rd (13057-9349)
PHONE..................................315 463-5744
Ralph Bott, *Branch Mgr*
Leslie Franklin, *Manager*
EMP: 293
SALES (corp-wide): 59.8B **Publicly Held**
WEB: www.carrier.com
SIC: 3585 Air conditioning equipment, complete
HQ: Carrier Corporation
13995 Pasteur Blvd
Palm Beach Gardens FL 33418
800 379-6484

(G-4329)
CARRIER CORPORATION
Carrier Transicold
Kinne St (13057)
P.O. Box 4805, Syracuse (13221-4805)
PHONE..................................315 432-6000
Nick Pinchuk, *Manager*
Alan Knight, *Manager*
EMP: 293
SALES (corp-wide): 59.8B **Publicly Held**
WEB: www.carrier.com
SIC: 3585 Air conditioning equipment, complete
HQ: Carrier Corporation
13995 Pasteur Blvd
Palm Beach Gardens FL 33418
800 379-6484

(G-4330)
CARRIER CORPORATION
Transicold
Carrier Pkwy Bldg Tr 20 (13057)
P.O. Box 4805, Syracuse (13221-4805)
PHONE..................................315 432-3844
Nick Pinchuk, *President*
Scott Lindsay, *Design Engr*
EMP: 293
SALES (corp-wide): 59.8B **Publicly Held**
WEB: www.carrier.com
SIC: 3585 Lockers, refrigerated
HQ: Carrier Corporation
13995 Pasteur Blvd
Palm Beach Gardens FL 33418
800 379-6484

(G-4331)
CLEARWOOD CUSTOM CARPENTRY AND
617 W Manlius St Ste 1 (13057-2276)
PHONE..................................315 432-8422
Kyle Latray, *Mng Member*
Andrew McDonald,
EMP: 30
SQ FT: 33,856

GEOGRAPHIC SECTION

East Syracuse - Onondaga County (G-4357)

SALES (est): 5.1MM **Privately Held**
WEB: www.clearwoodccm.com
SIC: 2431 2434 Millwork; wood kitchen cabinets

(G-4332)
CONSTRUCTION PARTS WHSE INC
5841 Butternut Dr (13057-9514)
PHONE..................315 445-1310
Bruce P Nash Jr, *President*
Dale Spuches, *Vice Pres*
EMP: 6
SALES: 1MM **Privately Held**
SIC: 3444 Sheet metal specialties, not stamped

(G-4333)
DAIRY FARMERS AMERICA INC
5001 Brittonfield Pkwy (13057-9201)
P.O. Box 4844, Syracuse (13221-4844)
PHONE..................816 801-6440
Jennifer Lastowicka, *Accountant*
David Geisler, *Manager*
EMP: 41
SALES (corp-wide): 14.6B **Privately Held**
WEB: www.dfamilk.com
SIC: 2026 Milk processing (pasteurizing, homogenizing, bottling)
PA: Dairy Farmers Of America, Inc.
  1405 N 98th St
  Kansas City KS 66111
  816 801-6455

(G-4334)
DATACOM SYSTEMS INC
9 Adler Dr (13057-1201)
PHONE..................315 463-9541
Kevin Formby, *President*
Timothy Crofton, *President*
Sam Lanzafane, *Chairman*
Joe Sullivan, *Vice Pres*
Morris De Lorenzo, *Buyer*
EMP: 33
SQ FT: 16,000
SALES (est): 7.1MM **Privately Held**
WEB: www.datacomsystems.com
SIC: 3571 Electronic computers

(G-4335)
DEAN FOODS COMPANY
6867 Schuyler Rd (13057-9752)
PHONE..................315 452-5001
Leah Curcio, *Principal*
EMP: 87 **Publicly Held**
SIC: 2026 Milk processing (pasteurizing, nomogenizing, bottling)
PA: Dean Foods Company
  2711 N Haskell Ave
  Dallas TX 75204

(G-4336)
E F THRESH INC
6000 Galster Rd (13057-2917)
PHONE..................315 437-7301
Eric F Thresh, *President*
Janet Thresh, *Corp Secy*
William Thresh, *Vice Pres*
EMP: 6
SQ FT: 35,000
SALES: 728K **Privately Held**
SIC: 2541 6512 Cabinets, except refrigerated: show, display, etc.: wood; commercial & industrial building operation

(G-4337)
FALK PRECISION INC
5917 Fisher Rd (13057-2912)
PHONE..................315 437-4545
Tracy Foltz, *Ch of Bd*
EMP: 30
SQ FT: 15,000
SALES (est): 3.5MM **Privately Held**
WEB: www.falkprecision.com
SIC: 3599 Chemical milling job shop

(G-4338)
FBM GALAXY INC
6741 Old Collamer Rd (13057-1119)
PHONE..................315 463-5144
Glen Markam, *Manager*
EMP: 18
SALES (corp-wide): 2B **Publicly Held**
WEB: www.spi-co.com
SIC: 3089 3296 3554 Plastic processing; fiberglass insulation; die cutting & stamping machinery, paper converting
HQ: Fbm Galaxy, Inc.
  1650 Manheim Pike Ste 202
  Lancaster PA 17601
  717 569-3900

(G-4339)
FIBERONE LLC
5 Technology Pl Ste 4 (13057-9738)
PHONE..................315 434-8877
Liz Castaneda, *General Mgr*
Craig Mead,
EMP: 15 EST: 2000
SALES (est): 2MM **Privately Held**
SIC: 2298 Cable, fiber

(G-4340)
FLEX-HOSE COMPANY INC
6801 Crossbow Dr (13057-1026)
PHONE..................315 437-1903
Philip Argersinger, *President*
Joanna Carter, *Vice Pres*
Chuck Philips, *Vice Pres*
Jon Golley, *Sales Mgr*
James Hyland, *Sales Associate*
▲ EMP: 28 EST: 1968
SQ FT: 15,000
SALES (est): 7.6MM **Privately Held**
SIC: 3599 Hose, flexible metallic

(G-4341)
FOREST MEDICAL LLC
6700 Old Collamer Rd # 114 (13057-1167)
PHONE..................315 434-9000
Robert Hyland, *Manager*
Raymond Lichorobiec,
EMP: 9
SQ FT: 4,000
SALES (est): 1.1MM **Privately Held**
WEB: www.forestmedical.com
SIC: 3845 Electromedical equipment

(G-4342)
GEI INTERNATIONAL INC (PA)
Also Called: Gaebel Enterprises
100 Ball St (13057-2359)
P.O. Box 6849, Syracuse (13217-6849)
PHONE..................315 463-9261
Peter Anderson, *President*
Maureen Anderson, *Vice Pres*
EMP: 20 EST: 1960
SALES (est): 2.3MM **Privately Held**
WEB: www.geionline.com
SIC: 3423 3531 5199 3829 Rules or rulers, metal; scrapers (construction machinery); art goods & supplies; measuring & controlling devices

(G-4343)
GREENWOOD WINERY LLC
6475 Collamer Rd (13057-1031)
P.O. Box 2949, Syracuse (13220-2949)
PHONE..................315 432-8132
Tom Greenwood, *Owner*
Thomas Greenwood, *Mng Member*
EMP: 30
SALES: 800K **Privately Held**
SIC: 2084 2066 Wines; chocolate

(G-4344)
H F W COMMUNICATIONS INC (HQ)
Also Called: Holstein World
6437 Collamer Rd Ste 1 (13057-1559)
PHONE..................315 703-7979
Scott Smith, *CEO*
Joel Hastings, *President*
John Montandon, *President*
Art Sweum, *Vice Pres*
Suzanne Miller, *CFO*
EMP: 15
SALES (est): 6.4MM
SALES (corp-wide): 6.5MM **Privately Held**
SIC: 2721 Trade journals: publishing & printing
PA: Multi-Ag Media L.L.C.
  6437 Collamer Rd
  East Syracuse NY
  315 703-7979

(G-4345)
HANGER INC
6620 Fly Rd Ste 203 (13057-4282)
PHONE..................518 438-4546
Ramona Fields, *Practice Mgr*
EMP: 26
SALES (corp-wide): 1B **Publicly Held**
SIC: 3842 Surgical appliances & supplies
PA: Hanger, Inc.
  10910 Domain Dr Ste 300
  Austin TX 78758
  512 777-3800

(G-4346)
HERCULES CANDY CO
Also Called: Hercules Gift & Gourmet
720 W Manlius St (13057-2158)
PHONE..................315 463-4339
Terry L Andrianos, *Partner*
EMP: 8
SALES: 232K **Privately Held**
WEB: www.herculescandy.com
SIC: 2064 5441 5149 Candy & other confectionery products; candy; chocolate

(G-4347)
HONEYWELL INTERNATIONAL INC
7000 Airways Park Dr # 4 (13057-9413)
PHONE..................315 463-7208
Michael Lyons, *Manager*
EMP: 10
SALES (corp-wide): 40.5B **Publicly Held**
WEB: www.ondemandcorp.com
SIC: 3724 Aircraft engines & engine parts
PA: Honeywell International Inc.
  115 Tabor Rd
  Morris Plains NJ 07950
  973 455-2000

(G-4348)
INDUSTRIAL FABRICATING CORP (PA)
6201 E Molloy Rd (13057-1021)
PHONE..................315 437-3353
Myron R Kocan, *President*
EMP: 33
SQ FT: 60,000
SALES (est): 14MM **Privately Held**
WEB: www.industrialfabricating.com
SIC: 3441 3444 Fabricated structural metal; sheet metalwork

(G-4349)
INDUSTRIAL FABRICATING CORP
4 Collamer Cir (13057-1102)
PHONE..................315 437-8234
Gary Cristal, *Manager*
EMP: 29
SQ FT: 32,886
SALES (corp-wide): 14MM **Privately Held**
WEB: www.industrialfabricating.com
SIC: 3443 Weldments
PA: Industrial Fabricating Corp
  6201 E Molloy Rd
  East Syracuse NY 13057
  315 437-3353

(G-4350)
INFICON INC (HQ)
2 Technology Pl (13057-9714)
PHONE..................315 434-1100
Darren Lee, *General Mgr*
Jeffrey Newbery, *General Mgr*
Hoang Cao, *Vice Pres*
Terry Perkins, *Vice Pres*
Janice Smeall, *Vice Pres*
▲ EMP: 250 EST: 1970
SQ FT: 135,000
SALES: 149.6K
SALES (corp-wide): 373.5MM **Privately Held**
WEB: www.inficon.com
SIC: 3823 3812 Industrial process control instruments; search & navigation equipment
PA: Inficon Holding Ag
  Hintergasse 15b
  Bad Ragaz SG 7310
  813 004-980

(G-4351)
INFICON HOLDING AG
2 Technology Pl (13057-9714)
PHONE..................315 434-1100
William Busher, *QC Mgr*
Paul Mahunik, *Engineer*
Peter G Maier, *CFO*
Peter Maeir, *CFO*
Janice Smeall, *VP Finance*
EMP: 7
SALES (est): 448K **Privately Held**
SIC: 3823 Industrial process control instruments

(G-4352)
INFITEC INC
6500 Badgley Rd (13057-9667)
P.O. Box 2956, Syracuse (13220-2956)
PHONE..................315 433-1150
George W Ehegartner, *Ch of Bd*
David Lawrie, *Vice Pres*
▲ EMP: 60
SQ FT: 22,000
SALES (est): 3.9MM **Privately Held**
WEB: www.infitec.com
SIC: 3625 3822 Timing devices, electronic; auto controls regulating residntl & coml environmt & applncs

(G-4353)
INTERSURGICAL INCORPORATED (PA)
6757 Kinne St (13057-1215)
PHONE..................315 451-2900
Howard Bellm, *Managing Dir*
Mary Sweeney, *Vice Pres*
Susan Jaeger, *Accountant*
Courtnie Walker, *HR Admin*
Dan White, *Natl Sales Mgr*
EMP: 30
SQ FT: 7,000
SALES (est): 5.5MM **Privately Held**
SIC: 3841 Anesthesia apparatus

(G-4354)
J W STEVENS CO INC
6059 Corporate Dr (13057-1040)
PHONE..................315 472-6311
Jeff Salanger, *Vice Pres*
EMP: 6
SALES (est): 711.8K **Privately Held**
SIC: 3443 Boiler shop products: boilers, smokestacks, steel tanks

(G-4355)
JE MILLER INC
747 W Manlius St (13057-2177)
PHONE..................315 437-6811
Dennis J Hile, *President*
Robert Leroy, *General Mgr*
Barbara Hile, *Vice Pres*
Audrey More, *Train & Dev Mgr*
Lana Woods, *Sales Staff*
EMP: 16 EST: 1951
SQ FT: 15,000
SALES (est): 3.5MM **Privately Held**
WEB: www.jemiller.com
SIC: 3625 3585 Relays & industrial controls; air conditioning units, complete: domestic or industrial

(G-4356)
JOHNSON CONTROLS
6731 Collamer Rd Ste 4 (13057-9715)
PHONE..................607 338-5100
Mike Delsanto, *Manager*
EMP: 10 **Privately Held**
WEB: www.simplexgrinnell.com
SIC: 3669 Emergency alarms
HQ: Johnson Controls Fire Protection Lp
  4700 Exchange Ct Ste 300
  Boca Raton FL 33431
  561 988-7200

(G-4357)
KERNER AND MERCHANT
104 Johnson St (13057-2840)
PHONE..................315 463-8023
Benjamin R Merchant, *President*
Albert H Arnold, *Admin Sec*
EMP: 7
SQ FT: 3,600
SALES: 300K **Privately Held**
SIC: 3931 7699 Pipes, organ; organ tuning & repair

East Syracuse - Onondaga County (G-4358)

(G-4358)
MICROWAVE FILTER COMPANY INC (PA)
6743 Kinne St (13057-1269)
PHONE..................315 438-4700
Paul W Mears, *CEO*
Robert R Andrews, *Ch of Bd*
Sherry Bell, *General Mgr*
Carl F Fahrenkrug Jr, *Exec VP*
David Barnello, *Opers Mgr*
EMP: 36
SQ FT: 40,000
SALES: 3MM **Publicly Held**
WEB: www.microwavefilter.com
SIC: 3677 3679 Filtration devices, electronic; microwave components

(G-4359)
MUTUAL LIBRARY BINDERY INC
6295 E Molloy Rd Ste 3 (13057-1104)
P.O. Box 6026, Syracuse (13217-6026)
PHONE..................315 455-6638
Otto E Rausch, *President*
Robert Rausch, *Vice Pres*
Stephen Rausch, *Vice Pres*
EMP: 25 **EST:** 1915
SALES (est): 2.6MM **Privately Held**
SIC: 2789 Bookbinding & repairing: trade, edition, library, etc.

(G-4360)
NIAGARA SCIENTIFIC INC
Also Called: Schroeder Machine Div
6743 Kinne St (13057-1215)
P.O. Box 146 (13057-0146)
PHONE..................315 437-0821
Carl Fahrenkrug, *President*
Milo Peterson, *Exec VP*
Richard Jones, *CFO*
EMP: 54
SQ FT: 16,000
SALES (est): 4.3MM
SALES (corp-wide): 3MM **Publicly Held**
WEB: www.microwavefilter.com
SIC: 3565 3826 Carton packing machines; environmental testing equipment
PA: Microwave Filter Company, Inc.
6743 Kinne St
East Syracuse NY 13057
315 438-4700

(G-4361)
NIDEC MOTOR CORPORATION
Advanced Motors & Drives
6268 E Molloy Rd (13057-1047)
PHONE..................315 434-9303
EMP: 15
SALES (corp-wide): 13.9B **Privately Held**
SIC: 3621 Motors, electric
HQ: Nidec Motor Corporation
8050 West Florissant Ave
Saint Louis MO 63136

(G-4362)
POWER-FLO TECHNOLOGIES INC
Also Called: Auburn Armature
6500 New Venture Gear Dr (13057-1076)
PHONE..................315 399-5801
Mike Capfllo, *Manager*
EMP: 93
SALES (corp-wide): 51.8MM **Privately Held**
WEB: www.auburnarmature.com
SIC: 7694 Armature rewinding shops
PA: Power-Flo Technologies, Inc.
270 Park Ave
New Hyde Park NY 11040
516 812-6800

(G-4363)
PPC BROADBAND INC (HQ)
6176 E Molloy Rd (13057-4010)
P.O. Box 278 (13057-0278)
PHONE..................315 431-7200
Dave Jackson, *CEO*
Milos Dvorak, *Area Mgr*
Floyd Backes, *Vice Pres*
Ryan Hagan, *Vice Pres*
Brian Kelly, *Vice Pres*
◆ **EMP:** 500 **EST:** 1992
SALES: 350MM
SALES (corp-wide): 2.3B **Publicly Held**
WEB: www.ppc-online.com
SIC: 3678 Electronic connectors

PA: Belden Inc.
1 N Brentwood Blvd Fl 15
Saint Louis MO 63105
314 854-8000

(G-4364)
RAYMOND CORPORATION
6533 Chrysler Ln (13057-1375)
PHONE..................315 643-5000
Jim Schaefer, *Branch Mgr*
EMP: 30
SALES (corp-wide): 18.8B **Privately Held**
SIC: 3535 3537 7359 Conveyors & conveying equipment; industrial trucks & tractors; equipment rental & leasing
HQ: The Raymond Corporation
22 S Canal St
Greene NY 13778
607 656-2311

(G-4365)
REYNOLDS TECH FABRICATORS INC
6895 Kinne St (13057-1217)
PHONE..................315 437-0532
Joan J Reynolds, *CEO*
EMP: 37
SQ FT: 35,000
SALES (est): 6.8MM **Privately Held**
SIC: 3559 3471 Refinery, chemical processing & similar machinery; plating of metals or formed products

(G-4366)
RICHLAR INDUSTRIES INC
Also Called: Richlar Custom Foam Div
6741 Old Collamer Rd (13057-1119)
PHONE..................315 463-5144
Richard Bruntarger, *President*
EMP: 18
SQ FT: 32,000
SALES (est): 3.1MM **Privately Held**
SIC: 3089 3296 3554 Plastic processing; fiberglass insulation; die cutting & stamping machinery, paper converting

(G-4367)
SAAB DEFENSE AND SEC USA LLC
5717 Enterprise Pkwy (13057-2905)
PHONE..................315 445-5009
Laurence Harris, *Principal*
Luke Nicolette, *Opers Staff*
Christopher Mann, *Engineer*
Nicholas Sadowski, *Engineer*
Todd Shapiro, *Program Mgr*
EMP: 12
SALES (corp-wide): 3.7B **Privately Held**
SIC: 3812 Search & detection systems & instruments
HQ: Saab Defense And Security Usa Llc
20700 Loudoun County Pkwy # 100
Ashburn VA 20147
703 406-7200

(G-4368)
SBB INC
1 Gm Dr Ste 5 (13057)
PHONE..................315 422-2376
Robert McKenty, *Principal*
Tony Meehl, *Project Mgr*
Brian Kearney, *Associate*
EMP: 5
SALES (est): 1.2MM **Privately Held**
SIC: 3564 Air purification equipment

(G-4369)
SEABOARD GRAPHIC SERVICES LLC
Also Called: Minuteman Press
6881 Schuyler Rd (13057-9752)
PHONE..................315 652-4200
Lawrence Kuhn, *Mng Member*
EMP: 25
SALES (est): 4.2MM **Privately Held**
WEB: www.seaboardgraphics.com
SIC: 2752 Commercial printing, lithographic

(G-4370)
SHAKO INC
6191 E Molloy Rd (13057-1038)
PHONE..................315 437-1294
Brian Mayfield, *Principal*
EMP: 8

SALES (est): 892.9K **Privately Held**
SIC: 3535 Pneumatic tube conveyor systems

(G-4371)
STF SERVICES INC
26 Corporate Cir Ste 2 (13057-1105)
PHONE..................315 463-8506
Michael Smith, *President*
John Siedlicki, *COO*
EMP: 50
SQ FT: 20,000
SALES (est): 4.1MM
SALES (corp-wide): 1.9B **Privately Held**
WEB: www.superforms.com
SIC: 2731 2741 Books: publishing only; miscellaneous publishing
HQ: The Bureau Of National Affairs Inc
1801 S Bell St Ste Cn110
Arlington VA 22202
703 341-3000

(G-4372)
SYRACUSE CORRUGATED BOX CORP
302 Stoutenger St (13057-2841)
P.O. Box 126 (13057-0126)
PHONE..................315 437-9901
David R Wilde, *President*
Charles Wilde, *Vice Pres*
John Wilde, *Admin Sec*
EMP: 14 **EST:** 1969
SQ FT: 24,000
SALES (est): 2.5MM **Privately Held**
SIC: 2653 Boxes, corrugated: made from purchased materials

(G-4373)
THE PRS GROUP INC (PA)
Also Called: Political Risk Services, The
5800 Hrtge Lndng Dr Ste E (13057)
PHONE..................315 431-0511
Christopher McKee, *CEO*
Christa Mosher, *Production*
Dianna Spinner, *Treasurer*
Patricia Davis, *Admin Sec*
EMP: 10 **EST:** 2000
SQ FT: 2,100
SALES (est): 737.4K **Privately Held**
WEB: www.prsgroup.com
SIC: 2721 Periodicals: publishing & printing; statistical reports (periodicals): publishing & printing

(G-4374)
TPC INC
6780 Nthrn Blvd Ste 401 (13057)
P.O. Box 2581, Syracuse (13220-2581)
PHONE..................315 438-8605
Max Bablok, *President*
EMP: 6
SALES (est): 24.3MM **Privately Held**
SIC: 3728 Aircraft parts & equipment

(G-4375)
TRANE US INC
15 Technology Pl (13057-9713)
PHONE..................315 234-1500
Tyler Malm, *Sales Engr*
Mike Carey, *Branch Mgr*
EMP: 36
SQ FT: 4,500 **Privately Held**
SIC: 3585 Refrigeration & heating equipment
HQ: Trane U.S. Inc.
3600 Pammel Creek Rd
La Crosse WI 54601
608 787-2000

(G-4376)
TYCO SIMPLEXGRINNELL
6731 Collamer Rd Ste 4 (13057-9715)
PHONE..................315 437-9664
Kevin Hache, *Branch Mgr*
EMP: 40
SALES (corp-wide): 1.3B **Privately Held**
SIC: 3569 3491 Sprinkler systems, fire: automatic; automatic regulating & control valves
PA: Tyco Simplexgrinnell
1501 Nw 51st St
Boca Raton FL 33431
561 988-3658

(G-4377)
U S TECH CORPORATION
6511 Basile Rowe (13057-2928)
P.O. Box 816, Skaneateles (13152-0816)
PHONE..................315 437-7207
Alexander E Gelston II, *President*
Janis J Soule, *Vice Pres*
EMP: 12
SALES: 6MM **Privately Held**
SIC: 3812 Search & detection systems & instruments

(G-4378)
UNITED TECHNOLOGIES CORP
6304 Carrier Pkwy (13057-6300)
PHONE..................315 432-7849
EMP: 9
SALES (corp-wide): 59.8B **Publicly Held**
SIC: 3724 Aircraft engines & engine parts
PA: United Technologies Corporation
10 Farm Springs Rd
Farmington CT 06032
860 728-7000

(G-4379)
UNIVERSAL STEP INC
5970 Butternut Dr (13057-8526)
PHONE..................315 437-7611
David Smith, *President*
EMP: 5 **EST:** 2009
SALES (est): 595.1K **Privately Held**
SIC: 3272 Steps, prefabricated concrete

(G-4380)
VILLAGE DECORATION LTD
20 Corporate Cir (13057-1015)
PHONE..................315 437-2522
Michael Robinson, *President*
Shawn Robinson, *Plant Mgr*
EMP: 30
SQ FT: 13,500
SALES: 1.5MM **Privately Held**
SIC: 3599 Machine & other job shop work

(G-4381)
WERMA (USA) INC
6731 Collamer Rd Ste 1 (13057-9793)
PHONE..................315 414-0200
Michael Oneill, *President*
Peter Gasparini, *Sales Mgr*
Robert Salone, *Sales Mgr*
▲ **EMP:** 4 **EST:** 2011
SQ FT: 4,500
SALES (est): 2.7MM
SALES (corp-wide): 43.3MM **Privately Held**
SIC: 3669 Signaling apparatus, electric
PA: Werma Signaltechnik Gmbh + Co. Kg
Durbheimer Str. 15
Rietheim-Weilheim 78604
742 495-570

East Williston
Nassau County

(G-4382)
NORTH AMERICAN PIPE CORP
Also Called: Jekerda Sales
156 High St (11596-1418)
PHONE..................516 338-2863
Jamie Hebert, *Manager*
EMP: 10 **Publicly Held**
SIC: 3354 3084 Pipe, extruded, aluminum; plastics pipe
HQ: North American Pipe Corporation
2801 Post Oak Blvd # 600
Houston TX 77056

Eastchester
Westchester County

(G-4383)
W D TECHNOLOGY INC
42 Water St Ste B (10709-5502)
PHONE..................914 779-8738
Vincent Rende, *President*
EMP: 6
SQ FT: 1,000

SALES: 1.5MM **Privately Held**
SIC: 3679 3825 Liquid crystal displays (LCD); radio frequency measuring equipment

Eastport
Suffolk County

(G-4384)
EASTPORT FEEDS INC
140 E Moriches Blvd (11941-1122)
P.O. Box 127 (11941-0127)
PHONE 631 325-0077
Donald Dixon, *Sales/Mktg Mgr*
Jed Brambley, *Manager*
EMP: 9
SQ FT: 84,942
SALES (est): 983K
SALES (corp-wide): 711.5K **Privately Held**
SIC: 2048 Prepared feeds
PA: Eastport Feeds, Inc.
  10 Edgar Ave
  Aquebogue NY 11931
  631 722-8700

(G-4385)
MEDIA TECHNOLOGIES LTD
220 Sonata Ct (11941-1617)
PHONE 631 467-7900
Rainer Zopfy, *President*
EMP: 12
SQ FT: 6,800
SALES (est): 2.7MM **Privately Held**
WEB: www.mediatechmail.com
SIC: 3652 5044 Compact laser discs, pre-recorded; duplicating machines

Eden
Erie County

(G-4386)
AARFID LLC (PA)
3780 Yochum Rd (14057-9519)
PHONE 716 992-3999
Chad Carpenter, *President*
EMP: 5
SALES (est): 1MM **Privately Held**
SIC: 7372 3695 Business oriented computer software; magnetic & optical recording media

(G-4387)
E B TROTTNOW MACHINE SPC
8955 Woodside Dr (14057-1460)
PHONE 716 694-0600
Mary Pietsch, *President*
EMP: 18 **EST:** 1948
SQ FT: 55,000
SALES (est): 3MM **Privately Held**
SIC: 3599 Mfg Industrial Machinery

(G-4388)
EDEN TOOL & DIE INC
2721 Hemlock Rd (14057-1390)
P.O. Box 296 (14057-0296)
PHONE 716 992-4240
James Rettig, *President*
Gary Rettig, *Vice Pres*
Raymond Rettig, *Admin Sec*
▼ **EMP:** 8
SALES (est): 1MM **Privately Held**
SIC: 3544 Special dies & tools

(G-4389)
JOHN F RAFTER INC
Also Called: Jf Rafter The Lexington Co
2746 W Church St (14057-1011)
P.O. Box 300 (14057-0300)
PHONE 716 992-3425
John Rafter Jr, *President*
EMP: 5
SQ FT: 2,500
SALES (est): 567.8K **Privately Held**
SIC: 3452 Screws, metal

(G-4390)
MUSTANG-MAJOR TOOL & DIE CO
3243 N Boston Rd (14057-9500)
PHONE 716 992-9200
David Kolodczak, *President*
EMP: 6 **EST:** 1965
SQ FT: 8,200
SALES (est): 800K **Privately Held**
WEB: www.mmtooldie.com
SIC: 3544 Special dies & tools

Edgewood
Suffolk County

(G-4391)
ABH NATURES PRODUCTS INC
131 Heartland Blvd (11717-8315)
PHONE 631 249-5783
Jahirul Islam, *President*
Harsh Vyas, *CFO*
Sahina Islam, *Director*
EMP: 28
SQ FT: 40,000
SALES (est): 9.2MM **Privately Held**
WEB: www.abhnature.com
SIC: 2833 Vitamins, natural or synthetic: bulk, uncompounded

(G-4392)
ABH PHARMA INC
131 Heartland Blvd (11717-8315)
PHONE 866 922-4669
Frank Cantone, *CEO*
Robert Zorn, *Executive*
EMP: 70 **EST:** 2016
SALES (est): 9MM **Privately Held**
SIC: 2834 Pharmaceutical preparations

(G-4393)
ADVANCE FOOD SERVICE CO INC
200 Heartland Blvd (11717-8380)
PHONE 631 242-4800
Milton Schwartz, *Corp Secy*
Daniel Schwartz, *Vice Pres*
EMP: 200 **EST:** 1955
SQ FT: 60,000
SALES (est): 30MM **Privately Held**
SIC: 3589 Cooking equipment, commercial

(G-4394)
ADVANCE TABCO INC (HQ)
200 Heartland Blvd (11717-8379)
PHONE 631 242-8270
Penny Schwartz-Hutner, *President*
Alice Schwartz, *Chairman*
Daniel Schwartz, *Vice Pres*
Chris Pacicca, *Warehouse Mgr*
Ryan Fee, *Purch Mgr*
◆ **EMP:** 85
SQ FT: 70,000
SALES (est): 23.6MM
SALES (corp-wide): 86.3MM **Privately Held**
SIC: 3589 3431 Commercial cooking & foodwarming equipment; metal sanitary ware
PA: Kinplex Corp.
  200 Heartland Blvd
  Edgewood NY 11717
  631 242-4800

(G-4395)
ALL ISLAND MEDIA INC (PA)
Also Called: Pennysaver/Town Crier
1 Rodeo Dr (11717-8318)
PHONE 631 698-8400
Paul E Gregory, *Principal*
Angelo Donofrio, *Vice Pres*
Robert Sussi, *Vice Pres*
Arleen Butler, *Sales Mgr*
Gregg Robinson, *Sales Mgr*
EMP: 110
SQ FT: 20,000
SALES (est): 12.9MM **Privately Held**
WEB: www.allislandmedia.com
SIC: 2711 Newspapers, publishing & printing

(G-4396)
AZTEC TOOL CO INC
180 Rodeo Dr (11717-8340)
PHONE 631 243-1144
Stewart Swiss, *President*
James Evarts, *Vice Pres*
EMP: 20
SQ FT: 24,000
SALES (est): 4.3MM **Privately Held**
WEB: www.aztectool.com
SIC: 3089 Injection molded finished plastic products; injection molding of plastics

(G-4397)
BIOCHEMICAL DIAGNOSTICS INC
180 Heartland Blvd (11717-8314)
PHONE 631 595-9200
Allen Panetz, *President*
Amir Forooqi, *Corp Secy*
EMP: 25
SQ FT: 30,000
SALES (est): 4.1MM **Privately Held**
WEB: www.biochemicaldiagnostics.com
SIC: 3841 2835 Diagnostic apparatus, medical; in vitro & in vivo diagnostic substances

(G-4398)
CASTELLA IMPORTS INC (PA)
120 Wilshire Blvd Ste A (11717-8333)
PHONE 631 231-5500
Vasilios Valsamos, *Ch of Bd*
Chris Valsamos, *Vice Pres*
Gina Berezny, *Purch Agent*
John Roumbos, *CFO*
Thalia Pecaro, *Sales Staff*
◆ **EMP:** 153
SQ FT: 110,000
SALES (est): 71.5MM **Privately Held**
WEB: www.castellaimports.com
SIC: 2099 5149 Food preparations; specialty food items

(G-4399)
CPI AEROSTRUCTURES INC
91 Heartland Blvd (11717-8330)
PHONE 631 586-5200
Terry Stinson, *Ch of Bd*
Douglas McCrosson, *President*
Barry Fratello, *Vice Pres*
Bob Muller, *Vice Pres*
Charles Munna, *VP Opers*
EMP: 259 **EST:** 1980
SQ FT: 171,000
SALES (est): 81.2MM **Privately Held**
WEB: www.cpiaero.com
SIC: 3728 Aircraft assemblies, subassemblies & parts

(G-4400)
FLEXIM AMERICAS CORPORATION (HQ)
250 Executive Dr Ste V (11717-8354)
PHONE 631 492-2300
Jens Hilpert, *President*
John Obrien, *Vice Pres*
EMP: 12
SQ FT: 7,250
SALES (est): 2.4MM
SALES (corp-wide): 23.4MM **Privately Held**
SIC: 3824 Impeller & counter driven flow meters
PA: Flexim Flexible IndustriemeBtechnik Gmbh
  Boxberger Str. 4
  Berlin 12681
  309 366-7660

(G-4401)
FORERUNNER TECHNOLOGIES INC (PA)
150 Executive Dr Ste M (11717-8323)
PHONE 631 337-2100
Jim Wallace, *President*
Michael Viola, *Vice Pres*
Matthew Ali, *Sales Staff*
▲ **EMP:** 45
SQ FT: 8,000
SALES (est): 20.6MM **Privately Held**
SIC: 3661 7371 4813 4899 Telephone & telegraph apparatus; computer software development & applications; telephone communication, except radio; data communication services; electronic parts & equipment; communication services

(G-4402)
GLOBAL MARKET DEVELOPMENT INC
Also Called: Accusonic Voice Systems
200 Executive Dr Ste G (11717-8322)
PHONE 631 667-1000
Anthony Mazzeo, *President*
Philip Glickman, *Exec VP*
Phillip Glickman, *Vice Pres*
Chris Scocco, *Opers Mgr*
Johanna Morales, *Controller*
▲ **EMP:** 30
SQ FT: 4,200
SALES (est): 6.1MM **Privately Held**
WEB: www.accusonicproducts.com
SIC: 3651 Loudspeakers, electrodynamic or magnetic

(G-4403)
IBA INDUSTRIAL INC
Also Called: Rdi
151 Heartland Blvd (11717-8315)
PHONE 631 254-6800
Richard A Galloway, *Ch of Bd*
Frederic Genin, *President*
Rick Galloway, *Vice Pres*
Scott Weglar, *Site Mgr*
Chris McKittrick, *Mfg Staff*
▲ **EMP:** 41 **EST:** 1958
SQ FT: 42,000
SALES (est): 13.2MM
SALES (corp-wide): 244.2MM **Privately Held**
WEB: www.e-beam-rdi.com
SIC: 3699 5065 Electron linear accelerators; electronic parts & equipment
PA: Ion Beam Application Sa
  Chemin Du Cyclotron 3
  Ottignies-Louvain-La-Neuve 1348
  104 758-11

(G-4404)
IMPRESSART
100 Executive Dr Ste D (11717-8328)
PHONE 631 940-9530
EMP: 15
SALES (est): 699.9K **Privately Held**
SIC: 3999 Mfg Misc Products

(G-4405)
INTERNATIONAL LEISURE PDTS INC
191 Rodeo Dr (11717-8319)
PHONE 631 254-2155
Larry Schwimmer, *President*
▲ **EMP:** 20
SALES (est): 1.8MM
SALES (corp-wide): 19.3MM **Privately Held**
SIC: 3949 Billiard & pool equipment & supplies, general
PA: Swimline Corp.
  191 Rodeo Dr
  Edgewood NY 11717
  631 254-2155

(G-4406)
KELTA INC (PA)
141 Rodeo Dr (11717-8378)
PHONE 631 789-5000
Parag Mehta, *President*
Dwight Tabor, *Sales Mgr*
Dana Diffily, *Sales Staff*
Jyotindra Mehta, *Admin Sec*
▲ **EMP:** 22
SQ FT: 25,000
SALES (est): 103.5MM **Privately Held**
SIC: 3089 3643 3661 Plastic hardware & building products; current-carrying wiring devices; telephone & telegraph apparatus

(G-4407)
KINPLEX CORP (PA)
200 Heartland Blvd (11717-8380)
PHONE 631 242-4800
Penny Hunter, *President*
Penny S Hunter, *President*
Daniel Schwartz, *Vice Pres*

Edgewood - Suffolk County (G-4408)

▲ EMP: 50
SQ FT: 70,000
SALES (est): 86.3MM **Privately Held**
SIC: 3589 Commercial cooking & food-warming equipment

(G-4408)
KINPLEX CORP
Also Called: Tables Manufacturing
200 Heartland Blvd (11717-8380)
PHONE..................631 242-4800
Maragret Ramsey, *Manager*
EMP: 50
SALES (corp-wide): 86.3MM **Privately Held**
SIC: 3589 2599 3556 Mfg Service Industry Machinery Mfg Furniture/Fixtures Mfg Food Products Machinery
PA: Kinplex Corp.
 200 Heartland Blvd
 Edgewood NY 11717
 631 242-4800

(G-4409)
MERIT ELECTRONIC DESIGN CO INC
Also Called: Medco
190 Rodeo Dr (11717-8317)
PHONE..................631 667-9699
Guy Intoci, *President*
Cheryl Sickles, *CFO*
▲ EMP: 115
SQ FT: 20,000
SALES (est): 43.7MM **Privately Held**
WEB: www.medcomfg.com
SIC: 3679 Electronic circuits

(G-4410)
POLY-FLEX CORP (PA)
250 Executive Dr Ste S (11717-8354)
PHONE..................631 586-9500
Barry Neustein, *President*
Talbert Paola, *Principal*
▲ EMP: 10 EST: 1977
SQ FT: 8,000
SALES (est): 1.9MM **Privately Held**
WEB: www.poly-flexcorp.com
SIC: 2759 Envelopes: printing

(G-4411)
POLYGEN PHARMACEUTICALS INC
41 Mercedes Way Unit 17 (11717-8334)
PHONE..................631 392-4044
Zhoumin LI, *President*
Bipin Sharma, *Director*
EMP: 25
SQ FT: 32,000
SALES (est): 4.5MM **Privately Held**
SIC: 2834 5122 Pharmaceutical preparations

(G-4412)
PRO-TECH CATINGS SOLUTIONS INC
250 Executive Dr Ste H (11717-8354)
PHONE..................631 707-9400
Alvelio Farington, *President*
EMP: 5
SALES (est): 123.9K **Privately Held**
SIC: 3479 Etching & engraving

(G-4413)
RSQUARED NY INC
100 Heartland Blvd (11717-8313)
P.O. Box 807, Deer Park (11729-0971)
PHONE..................631 521-8700
Altaf Hirji, *President*
◆ EMP: 98
SQ FT: 30,000
SALES (est): 13.7MM **Privately Held**
WEB: www.redvisuals.com
SIC: 3993 Advertising artwork

(G-4414)
S G NEW YORK LLC
Also Called: Penny Saver News
1 Rodeo Dr (11717-8318)
PHONE..................631 698-8400
Bob Sussy, *Manager*
EMP: 17
SALES (corp-wide): 5.3MM **Privately Held**
SIC: 2711 Newspapers, publishing & printing

PA: S G New York Llc
 2950 Vtrans Mem Hwy Ste 1
 Bohemia NY 11716
 631 665-4000

(G-4415)
SATCO PRODUCTS INC (PA)
Also Called: Satco Lighting
110 Heartland Blvd (11717-8303)
PHONE..................631 243-2022
Herbert Gildin, *CEO*
William Gildin, *Ch of Bd*
Phil Alexander, *General Mgr*
Alan Ginsberg, *General Mgr*
Luis Melendez, *General Mgr*
◆ EMP: 63
SQ FT: 80,000
SALES (est): 34.6MM **Privately Held**
WEB: www.satco.com
SIC: 3641 3645 5063 Electric lamps; residential lighting fixtures; lighting fixtures; light bulbs & related supplies

(G-4416)
SWIMLINE CORP (PA)
191 Rodeo Dr (11717-8319)
PHONE..................631 254-2155
Herman Schwimmer, *Ch of Bd*
Larry Schwimmer, *President*
Dennis Smith, *General Mgr*
David Schwartz, *Opers Mgr*
Jordan Mindich, *Director*
◆ EMP: 125
SALES (est): 19.3MM **Privately Held**
SIC: 3949 3081 Swimming pools, plastic; unsupported plastics film & sheet

(G-4417)
SWIMLINE INTERNATIONAL CORP
191 Rodeo Dr (11717-8319)
PHONE..................631 254-2155
Larry Schwimmer, *President*
Cynthia Schwimmer, *Vice Pres*
◆ EMP: 125
SALES (est): 9.7MM
SALES (corp-wide): 19.3MM **Privately Held**
SIC: 3423 Leaf skimmers or swimming pool rakes
PA: Swimline Corp.
 191 Rodeo Dr
 Edgewood NY 11717
 631 254-2155

(G-4418)
SYLHAN LLC (PA)
210 Rodeo Dr (11717-8317)
PHONE..................631 243-6600
Bob Luisi, *Vice Pres*
Ronald Manganiello,
Edward N Epstein,
Steven Paskoff,
▲ EMP: 20
SQ FT: 20,000
SALES (est): 2MM **Privately Held**
WEB: www.sylhan.com
SIC: 3599 Machine shop, jobbing & repair

(G-4419)
TII TECHNOLOGIES INC (HQ)
141 Rodeo Dr (11717-8378)
PHONE..................516 364-9300
Parag Mehta, *President*
Thomas Smith, *President*
Luca Evans, *Vice Pres*
Seamus Gallagher, *Vice Pres*
Kurt Weber, *Opers Staff*
▲ EMP: 29
SQ FT: 25,000
SALES (est): 10.4MM
SALES (corp-wide): 103.5MM **Privately Held**
WEB: www.tiinettech.com
SIC: 3089 3643 3661 Plastic hardware & building products; lightning protection equipment; telephone & telegraph apparatus
PA: Kelta, Inc.
 141 Rodeo Dr
 Edgewood NY 11717
 631 789-5000

(G-4420)
TIME BASE CORPORATION (PA)
Also Called: Time Base Consoles
170 Rodeo Dr (11717-8317)
PHONE..................631 293-4068
Jansen Hahn, *President*
Frank Lapallo, *Vice Pres*
Diana Lukasik, *VP Opers*
Rene Maradiaga, *Foreman/Supr*
Cheryl Johnson, *Accounts Mgr*
EMP: 49
SQ FT: 20,000
SALES (est): 7.9MM **Privately Held**
SIC: 2517 5712 Wood television & radio cabinets; cabinet work, custom

(G-4421)
TOGA MANUFACTURING INC (HQ)
200 Heartland Blvd (11717-8379)
PHONE..................631 242-4800
Alice Schwartz, *President*
Penny Schwartz Hutner, *Vice Pres*
Daniel Schwartz, *Vice Pres*
▲ EMP: 4
SQ FT: 40,000
SALES (est): 11.2MM
SALES (corp-wide): 86.3MM **Privately Held**
SIC: 3589 Commercial cooking & food-warming equipment
PA: Kinplex Corp.
 200 Heartland Blvd
 Edgewood NY 11717
 631 242-4800

(G-4422)
US ALLIANCE PAPER INC
101 Heartland Blvd (11717-8315)
PHONE..................631 254-3030
John Sarraf, *President*
Jeanette Provan, *General Mgr*
Steve Sarrafzadeh, *Vice Pres*
Bogdan Sujka, *Site Mgr*
Steve Saraf, *VP Sales*
▲ EMP: 220
SQ FT: 250,000
SALES (est): 67.4MM **Privately Held**
WEB: www.usalliancepaper.com
SIC: 2621 Paper mills

(G-4423)
WAYNE INTEGRATED TECH CORP
160 Rodeo Dr (11717-8317)
PHONE..................631 242-0213
Helen Moks, *CEO*
Joseph V Moks Jr, *Vice Pres*
Joseph Moks, *VP Opers*
Karen Moks, *Office Mgr*
EMP: 38
SQ FT: 15,000
SALES (est): 8.1MM **Privately Held**
WEB: www.gowayne.com
SIC: 3443 3444 3599 Containers, shipping (bombs, etc.): metal plate; metal housings, enclosures, casings & other containers; machine shop, jobbing & repair

(G-4424)
WEICO WIRE & CABLE INC
Also Called: Magnet Wire Division
161 Rodeo Dr (11717-8359)
PHONE..................631 254-2970
Theodore Weill, *President*
Philip Abshire, *Sales Staff*
Susan Smith, *Administration*
▲ EMP: 28
SQ FT: 35,000
SALES: 12.5K **Privately Held**
SIC: 3496 Cable, uninsulated wire: made from purchased wire

Edmeston
Otsego County

(G-4425)
BISHOP PRINT SHOP INC
Also Called: Ecclesiastical Press
9 East St (13335)
PHONE..................607 965-8155
Michael Lampron, *President*

EMP: 9 EST: 1949
SALES (est): 1.4MM **Privately Held**
WEB: www.bishopprintshop.com
SIC: 2752 2893 Commercial printing, offset; letterpress or offset ink

Elbridge
Onondaga County

(G-4426)
ACCURATE MCHNING INCORPORATION
Also Called: Acrolite
251 State Route 5 (13060-9640)
P.O. Box 1010 (13060-1010)
PHONE..................315 689-1428
Ronald E Drake Sr, *President*
Matt Drake, *Vice Pres*
Heather Moore, *Engineer*
Natalie Duffy, *Office Mgr*
Matthew R Drake, *Admin Sec*
EMP: 19
SQ FT: 13,600
SALES (est): 4.8MM **Privately Held**
WEB: www.acrolite.com
SIC: 3559 Fiber optics strand coating machinery

(G-4427)
ALLRED & ASSOCIATES INC
321 Rte 5 W (13060)
PHONE..................315 252-2559
Jimmie B Allred III, *President*
EMP: 40
SALES (est): 8.1MM **Privately Held**
WEB: www.evi-inc.com
SIC: 3083 Laminated plastic sheets

(G-4428)
DUCK FLATS PHARMA
245 E Main St (13060-8706)
P.O. Box 101 (13060-0101)
PHONE..................315 689-3407
Luana Pescokoplowitz, *Owner*
EMP: 9
SALES (est): 570K **Privately Held**
SIC: 2678 Tablets & pads, book & writing: from purchased materials

(G-4429)
TESSY PLASTICS CORP
488 State Route 5 (13060-9501)
PHONE..................315 689-3924
Roland Beck, *President*
EMP: 750
SALES (corp-wide): 301.6MM **Privately Held**
SIC: 3089 Injection molding of plastics
PA: Tessy Plastics Corp.
 700 Visions Dr
 Skaneateles NY 13152
 315 689-3924

Elizabethtown
Essex County

(G-4430)
DENTON PUBLICATIONS INC (PA)
Also Called: Free Trader
14 Hand Ave (12932)
P.O. Box 338 (12932-0338)
PHONE..................518 873-6368
Daniel Alexander, *President*
Gayle Alexander, *Vice Pres*
Maureen Lindsay, *Accounting Mgr*
Jennifer Valenze, *Manager*
Lin Jones, *Admin Sec*
EMP: 80 EST: 1948
SQ FT: 11,000
SALES (est): 6MM **Privately Held**
WEB: www.denpubs.com
SIC: 2711 2752 Commercial printing & newspaper publishing combined; commercial printing, lithographic

GEOGRAPHIC SECTION

(G-4431)
E C C CORP
7 Church St (12932)
P.O. Box 567 (12932-0567)
PHONE..................518 873-6494
Peter Belzer, *President*
▲ **EMP:** 6
SQ FT: 5,304
SALES: 1MM **Privately Held**
SIC: 3944 Banks, toy

(G-4432)
HALFWAY HOUSE LLC
7158 Us Route 9 (12932)
PHONE..................518 873-2198
Tina Croff, *Partner*
Gifford Croff, *Partner*
EMP: 7
SALES (est): 680.1K **Privately Held**
SIC: 2599 Bar, restaurant & cafeteria furniture

Elka Park
Greene County

(G-4433)
CHURCH COMMUNITIES NY INC
Also Called: Community Playthings
2255 Platte Clove Rd (12427-1014)
PHONE..................518 589-5103
Martin Mathis, *Branch Mgr*
EMP: 40
SALES (corp-wide): 10.8MM **Privately Held**
WEB: www.churchcommunitiesfoundation.org
SIC: 3944 3842 Games, toys & children's vehicles; orthopedic appliances
PA: Church Communities Ny Inc.
  101 Woodcrest Dr
  Rifton NY 12471
  845 658-7700

(G-4434)
CHURCH COMMUNITIES NY INC
Also Called: Community Playthings
Platte Clove Rd (12427)
PHONE..................518 589-5103
Martin Mathis, *Branch Mgr*
EMP: 40
SALES (corp-wide): 10.8MM **Privately Held**
WEB: www.churchcommunitiesfoundation.org
SIC: 3944 3842 Games, toys & children's vehicles; orthopedic appliances
PA: Church Communities Ny Inc.
  101 Woodcrest Dr
  Rifton NY 12471
  845 658-7700

(G-4435)
COMMUNITY PRODUCTS LLC
2255 Platte Clove Rd (12427-1014)
PHONE..................518 589-5103
EMP: 9
SALES (est): 1.1MM
SALES (corp-wide): 93.4MM **Privately Held**
WEB: www.communityplaythings.com
SIC: 3842 3942 Surgical appliances & supplies; dolls & stuffed toys
PA: Community Products, Llc
  101 Woodcrest Dr
  Rifton NY 12471
  845 658-8799

Ellenburg Depot
Clinton County

(G-4436)
ELLENBURG RECYCLERS
Also Called: Baker Commodities
5005 State Route 11 (12935-2229)
PHONE..................518 594-3900
Aaron Rowe, *Manager*
EMP: 10 **EST:** 2000
SQ FT: 2,337
SALES (est): 665.5K **Privately Held**
SIC: 2077 Animal & marine fats & oils

Ellenville
Ulster County

(G-4437)
BROSS QUALITY PAVING
4 Kossar Pl (12428-2414)
PHONE..................845 532-7116
Julio Moya, *Partner*
EMP: 6
SALES (est): 479.2K **Privately Held**
SIC: 2951 Asphalt paving mixtures & blocks

(G-4438)
DEVIL DOG MANUFACTURING CO INC (PA)
23 Market St (12428-2107)
P.O. Box 588 (12428-0588)
PHONE..................845 647-4411
Carl J Rosenstock, *President*
Richard Rosenstock, *Vice Pres*
Herbert Rosenstock, *Treasurer*
Nelson Rosenstock, *Shareholder*
Stanley Rosenstock, *Admin Sec*
▲ **EMP:** 6 **EST:** 1952
SQ FT: 30,000
SALES (est): 18.5MM **Privately Held**
WEB: www.sportwear.com
SIC: 2369 Jeans: girls', children's & infants'

(G-4439)
JM ORIGINALS INC
Also Called: Sbi Enterprises
70 Berme Rd (12428-5605)
P.O. Box 563 (12428-0563)
PHONE..................845 647-3003
Martha Arginsky, *President*
Myrna Jargonsky, *Vice Pres*
◆ **EMP:** 140 **EST:** 1976
SQ FT: 35,000
SALES (est): 13.4MM **Privately Held**
WEB: www.jmoriginals.com
SIC: 2361 5137 5641 2369 Girls' & children's dresses, blouses & shirts; women's & children's clothing; children's wear; girls' & children's outerwear

(G-4440)
MASTER JUVENILE PRODUCTS INC
Also Called: Sbi Enterprises
70 Berme Rd (12428-5605)
P.O. Box 563 (12428-0563)
PHONE..................845 647-8400
Irwin Arginsky, *President*
EMP: 10
SQ FT: 40,000
SALES (est): 966.6K **Privately Held**
WEB: www.pogosticks.com
SIC: 3944 Games, toys & children's vehicles

(G-4441)
OPTIMUM WINDOW MFG CORP
28 Canal St (12428-1226)
PHONE..................845 647-1900
Candido Perez, *Ch of Bd*
Maria E Perez, *Corp Secy*
Paula F Fabbro, *Executive*
◆ **EMP:** 37
SALES (est): 10MM **Privately Held**
WEB: www.optimumwindow.com
SIC: 3442 Screen & storm doors & windows

(G-4442)
REED SYSTEMS LTD
17 Edwards Pl (12428-1601)
P.O. Box 209 (12428-0209)
PHONE..................845 647-3660
James Reed, *President*
Joan E Reed, *Vice Pres*
EMP: 15
SQ FT: 1,600
SALES: 4.9MM **Privately Held**
WEB: www.reedsystemsltd.com
SIC: 3399 Powder, metal

(G-4443)
ROCK MOUNTAIN FARMS INC
11 Spring St (12428-1329)
PHONE..................845 647-9084
Karen Osterhoudt, *President*
Howard Osterhoudt, *Vice Pres*
EMP: 5
SALES (est): 540K **Privately Held**
SIC: 1442 6519 Gravel mining; landholding office

Ellicottville
Cattaraugus County

(G-4444)
AMERICAN LCKR SEC SYSTEMS INC
12 Martha St (14731-9714)
PHONE..................716 699-2773
Fax: 716 699-2775
EMP: 25
SQ FT: 4,800
SALES (corp-wide): 30.1MM **Privately Held**
SIC: 3581 Mfg Vending Machines
PA: American Locker Security Systems, Inc.
  700 Freeport Pkwy Ste 300
  Coppell TX 75019
  817 329-1600

(G-4445)
ELLICOTTVILLE DISTILLERY LLC
5462 Robbins Rd (14731-9764)
P.O. Box 1471 (14731-1471)
PHONE..................716 597-6121
Bryan Scharf, *President*
EMP: 5
SALES (est): 356.8K **Privately Held**
SIC: 2085 Distilled & blended liquors

(G-4446)
FITZPATRICK AND WELLER INC
12 Mill St (14731-9614)
P.O. Box 490 (14731-0490)
PHONE..................716 699-2393
Gregory J Fitzpatrick, *Ch of Bd*
Dana G Fitzpatrick, *Chairman*
Daniel Fitzpatrick, *Vice Pres*
Greg Fitzpatrick, *Vice Pres*
Dave Hellwig, *Prdtn Mgr*
▼ **EMP:** 85 **EST:** 1892
SQ FT: 220,000
SALES (est): 14.9MM **Privately Held**
WEB: www.fitzweller.com
SIC: 2426 Furniture dimension stock, hardwood

(G-4447)
NORTH PK INNOVATIONS GROUP INC (PA)
6442 Route 242 E (14731)
P.O. Box 900 (14731-0900)
PHONE..................716 699-2031
William Northrup, *CEO*
Lori Northrup, *Chairman*
▲ **EMP:** 20
SQ FT: 13,000
SALES (est): 5.4MM **Privately Held**
SIC: 3433 Heating equipment, except electric

Ellington
Chautauqua County

(G-4448)
ELLIOT INDUSTRIES INC
Leach Rd (14732)
PHONE..................716 287-3100
Thomas A Elliot, *President*
Ann Elliot, *Treasurer*
EMP: 8
SQ FT: 5,000
SALES (est): 500K **Privately Held**
SIC: 3296 Fiberglass insulation

Elma
Erie County

(G-4449)
COMGRAPH SALES SERVICE
7491 Clinton St (14059-8807)
PHONE..................716 601-7243
Brian Schiemant, *Owner*
EMP: 5
SALES (est): 542.7K **Privately Held**
SIC: 2759 Commercial printing

(G-4450)
FREDERICK COON INC
Also Called: Elma Press
5751 Clinton St (14059-9424)
PHONE..................716 683-6812
Frederick H Coon Jr, *President*
Douglas Coon, *Vice Pres*
Joel Coon, *Vice Pres*
Betty Coon, *Treasurer*
EMP: 23
SQ FT: 2,708
SALES: 900K **Privately Held**
SIC: 2752 2759 Commercial printing, offset; letterpress printing

(G-4451)
GENERAL WELDING & FABG INC (PA)
991 Maple Rd (14059-9530)
PHONE..................716 652-0033
Mark S Andol, *President*
Steve Mayer, *General Mgr*
Edwin Pierrot, *General Mgr*
Richard Andol, *Info Tech Mgr*
EMP: 3
SQ FT: 14,000
SALES (est): 5.7MM **Privately Held**
SIC: 7692 3715 5531 Welding repair; truck trailers; truck equipment & parts

(G-4452)
KENS SERVICE & SALES INC
11500 Clinton St (14059-8830)
PHONE..................716 683-1155
Kenneth Kelchlin Jr, *President*
Matt Kelchlin, *Vice Pres*
EMP: 14 **EST:** 1955
SQ FT: 25,000
SALES (est): 2.8MM **Privately Held**
SIC: 3799 All terrain vehicles (ATV)

(G-4453)
MOOG INC (PA)
400 Jamison Rd (14059-9596)
P.O. Box 18, East Aurora (14052-0018)
PHONE..................716 652-2000
John R Scannell, *Ch of Bd*
Richard A Aubrecht, *Vice Ch Bd*
Mark Trabert, *President*
Martin Bobak, *General Mgr*
Sean Gartland, *General Mgr*
◆ **EMP:** 2100 **EST:** 1951
SQ FT: 22,000
SALES: 2.7B **Publicly Held**
WEB: www.moog.com
SIC: 3812 3492 3625 3769 Aircraft control systems, electronic; fluid power valves for aircraft; relays & industrial controls; actuators, industrial; guided missile & space vehicle parts & auxiliary equipment; aircraft parts & equipment; surgical & medical instruments

(G-4454)
MOOG INC
160 Jamison Rd (14059)
PHONE..................716 687-4778
Dave Golda, *Manager*
EMP: 25
SALES (corp-wide): 2.7B **Publicly Held**
SIC: 3625 Relays & industrial controls
PA: Moog Inc.
  400 Jamison Rd
  Elma NY 14059
  716 652-2000

(G-4455)
MOOG INC
Also Called: Moog Space and Defense Group
500 Jamison Rd Plt20 (14059-9497)
PHONE..................716 687-5486

David Schabel, *Design Engr*
Bill Watt, *Electrical Engi*
Eileen Tighe, *Human Resources*
Kathy Hall-Zientek, *Manager*
EMP: 453
SALES (corp-wide): 2.7B **Publicly Held**
SIC: 3812 Aircraft control systems, electronic
PA: Moog Inc.
  400 Jamison Rd
  Elma NY 14059
  716 652-2000

(G-4456)
R W PUBLICATIONS DIV OF WTRHS (PA)
Also Called: Akron-Corfu Pennysaver
6091 Seneca St Bldg C (14059-9807)
PHONE................................716 714-5620
Robert Rozeski Sr, *President*
Thomas Rybczynski, *Vice Pres*
Cheryl Kowalski, *Treasurer*
EMP: 30 **EST:** 1961
SQ FT: 5,800
SALES (est): 12.9MM **Privately Held**
WEB: www.rwpennysaver.com
SIC: 2711 2741 Newspapers, publishing & printing; miscellaneous publishing

(G-4457)
R W PUBLICATIONS DIV OF WTRHS
Also Called: Pennysavers Rw Publications
6091 Seneca St Bldg C (14059-9807)
PHONE................................716 714-5620
Meg Bourdette, *General Mgr*
EMP: 20
SALES (corp-wide): 12.9MM **Privately Held**
WEB: www.rwpennysaver.com
SIC: 2711 Commercial printing & newspaper publishing combined; newspapers, publishing & printing
PA: R W Publications Div Of Waterhouse Publication Inc
  6091 Seneca St Bldg C
  Elma NY 14059
  716 714-5620

(G-4458)
SERVOTRONICS INC (PA)
1110 Maple Rd (14059-9573)
PHONE................................716 655-5990
Kenneth D Trbovich, *Ch of Bd*
Salvatore Sanfilippo, *Senior VP*
James C Takacs, *Senior VP*
Lisa F Bencel, *CFO*
EMP: 160 **EST:** 1959
SQ FT: 83,000
SALES: 41.4MM **Publicly Held**
WEB: www.servotronics.com
SIC: 3728 3769 3421 3492 Aircraft parts & equipment; guided missile & space vehicle parts & auxiliary equipment; cutlery; electrohydraulic servo valves, metal

(G-4459)
STEUBEN FOODS INCORPORATED (PA)
1150 Maple Rd (14059-9597)
PHONE................................718 291-3333
Kenneth Schlossberg, *President*
Jeffrey Sokal, *Principal*
Cook Alciati, *Counsel*
Tyson Prince, *Counsel*
Frank Balon, *Exec VP*
EMP: 17
SQ FT: 10,000
SALES (est): 115.3MM **Privately Held**
SIC: 2032 2026 Puddings, except meat: packaged in cans, jars, etc.; yogurt; milk drinks, flavored

(G-4460)
STEUBEN FOODS INCORPORATED
1150 Maple Rd (14059-9597)
PHONE................................716 655-4000
Norman Bower, *Branch Mgr*
EMP: 200
SALES (corp-wide): 115.3MM **Privately Held**
SIC: 2026 Milk processing (pasteurizing, homogenizing, bottling)

PA: Steuben Foods, Incorporated
  1150 Maple Rd
  Elma NY 14059
  718 291-3333

(G-4461)
STONY MANUFACTURING INC
591 Pound Rd (14059-9602)
PHONE................................716 652-6730
James A Wyzykiewicz, *President*
Michael C Wyzykiewicz, *Vice Pres*
Ronald P Wyzykiewicz, *Vice Pres*
EMP: 9
SQ FT: 12,500
SALES (est): 1.5MM **Privately Held**
SIC: 3599 Machine shop, jobbing & repair

Elmhurst
Queens County

(G-4462)
BUFFALO PROVISIONS CO INC
4009 76th St (11373-1033)
PHONE................................718 292-4300
Rene Armendariz, *President*
Staci Armendariz, *Vice Pres*
Andres Mendez, *Manager*
EMP: 15
SQ FT: 10,000
SALES (est): 1.6MM **Privately Held**
SIC: 2013 Sausages from purchased meat

(G-4463)
COACH INC
90 Queens Blvd (11373)
PHONE................................718 760-0624
EMP: 14
SALES (corp-wide): 4.1B **Publicly Held**
SIC: 3171 Mfg Women's Handbags/Purses
PA: Coach, Inc.
  516 W 34th St Bsmt 5
  New York NY 10001
  212 594-1850

(G-4464)
FEDERAL SAMPLE CARD CORP
4520 83rd St (11373-3599)
PHONE................................718 458-1344
Michael Cronin, *President*
EMP: 100
SQ FT: 40,000
SALES (est): 7.4MM **Privately Held**
SIC: 2782 3999 Sample books; advertising display products

(G-4465)
GO GO APPLE INC
4126 Benham St (11373-1750)
PHONE................................646 264-8909
Xiu Qin Lin, *Administration*
EMP: 5
SALES (est): 176.7K **Privately Held**
SIC: 3571 Mfg Electronic Computers

(G-4466)
GODIVA CHOCOLATIER INC
9015 Queens Blvd Ste 2045 (11373-4923)
PHONE................................718 271-3603
Nicole Keaton, *Manager*
EMP: 24 **Privately Held**
SIC: 2066 Chocolate
HQ: Godiva Chocolatier, Inc.
  333 W 34th St Fl 6
  New York NY 10001
  212 984-5900

(G-4467)
GOLDEN BRIDGE GROUP INC
7416 Grand Ave (11373-4127)
PHONE................................718 335-8882
Roger Yang, *President*
▲ **EMP:** 6
SALES (est): 143.4K **Privately Held**
SIC: 3161 Luggage

(G-4468)
LA CALENITA BAKERY & CAFETERIA
4008 83rd St (11373-1307)
PHONE................................718 205-8273
Dilia Lindo, *Owner*
EMP: 8

SALES (est): 377.1K **Privately Held**
SIC: 2051 Bread, cake & related products

(G-4469)
MAJESTIC CURTAINS LLC
4410 Ketcham St Apt 2g (11373-3686)
PHONE................................718 898-0774
Robert Connor,
Barbara Tisdale,
EMP: 7
SALES (est): 660K **Privately Held**
SIC: 2391 1799 Curtains & draperies; window treatment installation

(G-4470)
PENNER ELBOW COMPANY INC
4700 76th St (11373-2946)
PHONE................................718 526-9000
Sheldon Flatow, *President*
EMP: 12
SQ FT: 10,000
SALES (est): 1.4MM **Privately Held**
SIC: 3444 3321 Elbows, for air ducts, stovepipes, etc.: sheet metal; pressure pipe & fittings, cast iron

(G-4471)
ROKON TECH LLC
5223 74th St (11373-4108)
PHONE................................718 429-0729
Manfred Konrad, *Mng Member*
EMP: 5
SALES (est): 611.6K **Privately Held**
SIC: 3534 Elevators & moving stairways

Elmira
Chemung County

(G-4472)
AFI CYBERNETICS CORPORATION
713 Batavia St (14904-2011)
PHONE................................607 732-3244
Kenneth Doyle, *President*
Tracy Haines, *Purch Agent*
Tim Blampied, *Sales Dir*
Jerry Windows, *Info Tech Mgr*
EMP: 28
SQ FT: 25,000
SALES (est): 6MM **Privately Held**
WEB: www.aficybernetics.com
SIC: 3625 Electric controls & control accessories, industrial

(G-4473)
AIR-FLO MFG CO INC
365 Upper Oakwood Ave (14903-1127)
PHONE................................607 733-8284
Charles Musso Jr, *President*
Tom Musso, *Vice Pres*
Kevin Foster, *Opers Mgr*
Velma Andrews, *Accountant*
EMP: 75
SQ FT: 60,000
SALES (est): 33MM **Privately Held**
WEB: www.air-flo.com
SIC: 3531 Construction machinery

(G-4474)
CAMERON BRIDGE WORKS LLC
1051 S Main St (14904-2713)
PHONE................................607 734-9456
Christopher Goll, *President*
EMP: 20
SQ FT: 85,000
SALES (est): 4.4MM
SALES (corp-wide): 28.2MM **Privately Held**
SIC: 3441 Fabricated structural metal for bridges
PA: Cameron Manufacturing & Design, Inc.
  727 Blostein Blvd
  Horseheads NY 14845
  607 739-3606

(G-4475)
CARBAUGH TOOL COMPANY INC
126 Philo Rd W (14903-9755)
PHONE................................607 739-3293
Harold Dota, *President*
EMP: 30 **EST:** 1966

SQ FT: 10,600
SALES (est): 4.6MM **Privately Held**
SIC: 3599 3544 Machine & other job shop work; special dies & tools

(G-4476)
CARBIDE-USA LLC
100 Home St (14904-1859)
P.O. Box 4005 (14904-0005)
PHONE................................607 331-9353
EMP: 8
SALES (est): 1.2MM **Privately Held**
SIC: 2819 Carbides

(G-4477)
CHEMUNG CNTY CHPTER NYSARC INC (HQ)
Also Called: ARC OF CHEMUNG, THE
711 Sullivan St (14901-2322)
PHONE................................607 734-6151
Nikki May, *President*
Joanne Conley-Pease, *Human Res Dir*
Missy Goetschius, *Pub Rel Dir*
Tammy Jackson, *Manager*
Mike Raniewicz, *MIS Dir*
EMP: 150
SQ FT: 33,000
SALES: 21.4MM
SALES (corp-wide): 70.6MM **Privately Held**
WEB: www.chemungarc.org
SIC: 3861 8331 8361 3577 Home for the mentally retarded; computer peripheral equipment; job training & vocational rehabilitation services; wood pallets & skids; photographic equipment & supplies; computer software development & applications
PA: Nysarc, Inc.
  29 British American Blvd # 2
  Latham NY 12110
  518 439-8311

(G-4478)
COMMUNITY GLASS INC
139 W 17th St (14903-1215)
PHONE................................607 737-8860
Patrick M Crouse, *President*
EMP: 7
SALES (est): 624.9K **Privately Held**
SIC: 3231 Products of purchased glass

(G-4479)
CONCRETE DESIGNS INC
2770 County Route 60 (14901-9464)
PHONE................................607 738-0309
Kenneth Elston, *President*
EMP: 8
SALES: 500K **Privately Held**
SIC: 2899 1771 Foam charge mixtures; patio construction, concrete

(G-4480)
COURSER INC
802 County Road 64 # 100 (14903-7984)
PHONE................................607 739-3861
Daniel Herman, *Ch of Bd*
Bob Cleveland, *Mfg Staff*
Christophe Seeley, *Engineer*
Steve Seeley, *Finance Mgr*
Dan Herman, *Human Res Mgr*
EMP: 25
SQ FT: 50,000
SALES (est): 4.6MM **Privately Held**
WEB: www.courser.com
SIC: 3599 Machine shop, jobbing & repair

(G-4481)
CREATIVE ORTHOTICS & PROSTHET (DH)
1300 College Ave Ste 1 (14901-1154)
PHONE................................607 734-7215
Vinit Asar, *Ch of Bd*
John Renz, *President*
EMP: 14
SALES (est): 37.9MM
SALES (corp-wide): 1B **Publicly Held**
WEB: www.creativeoandp.com
SIC: 3842 5999 5047 Limbs, artificial; artificial limbs; hospital equipment & furniture
HQ: Hanger Prosthetics & Orthotics, Inc.
  10910 Domain Dr Ste 300
  Austin TX 78758
  512 777-3800

GEOGRAPHIC SECTION

Elmira - Chemung County (G-4507)

(G-4482)
EASTERN METAL OF ELMIRA INC (PA)
1430 Sullivan St (14901-1698)
PHONE...............................607 734-2295
Kevin Harrison, *Ch of Bd*
Christina Buckley, *Sales Staff*
Rodney Kerrick, *Data Proc Dir*
Rebecca Walker, *Admin Asst*
▼ **EMP:** 80 **EST:** 1947
SALES (est): 20MM **Privately Held**
WEB: www.usa-sign.com
SIC: 3993 7336 Signs & advertising specialties; graphic arts & related design

(G-4483)
EASTSIDE OXIDE CO
211 Judson St (14901-3308)
PHONE...............................607 734-1253
Greg Wheeler, *Principal*
John Short, *Principal*
EMP: 40
SALES (est): 1.7MM **Privately Held**
WEB: www.eastsiderailnow.org
SIC: 3471 Plating of metals or formed products

(G-4484)
ELMIRA HEAT TREATING INC
407 S Kinyon St (14904-2398)
PHONE...............................607 734-1577
Terry Youngs, *CEO*
Richard Youngs, *President*
EMP: 40 **EST:** 1962
SQ FT: 20,000
SALES (est): 9.9MM **Privately Held**
WEB: www.elmiraht.com
SIC: 3398 Tempering of metal

(G-4485)
EXTREME SHALE PERFORMANCE LLC
2285 County Route 60 (14901-9459)
PHONE...............................814 688-7956
Josh Harris,
EMP: 7
SALES (est): 270.4K **Privately Held**
SIC: 3462 5072 Chains, forged steel; chains

(G-4486)
F M HOWELL & COMPANY (PA)
Also Called: Howell Packaging
79 Pennsylvania Ave (14904-1455)
P.O. Box 286 (14902-0286)
PHONE...............................607 734-6291
Katherine H Roehlke, *CEO*
James Haley, *Division Mgr*
Trevor Ball, *Vice Pres*
Keith Baumann, *Vice Pres*
Douglas M McGinnis, *Vice Pres*
▲ **EMP:** 74 **EST:** 1883
SQ FT: 168,000
SALES: 36.3MM **Privately Held**
WEB: www.howellpkg.com
SIC: 2657 2671 7389 2652 Folding paperboard boxes; thermoplastic coated paper for packaging; packaging & labeling services; setup paperboard boxes

(G-4487)
FENNELL INDUSTRIES LLC (PA)
Also Called: United Dividers
108 Stephens Pl (14901-1539)
PHONE...............................607 733-6693
Tom Fennell, *Owner*
Martin Fennell, *Mng Member*
Thomas Fennell,
EMP: 30
SQ FT: 13,500
SALES (est): 9.1MM **Privately Held**
SIC: 2653 Boxes, corrugated: made from purchased materials; partitions, corrugated: made from purchased materials

(G-4488)
GEORGE CHILSON LOGGING
54 Franklin St (14904-1738)
PHONE...............................607 732-1558
George Chilson, *Owner*
EMP: 1
SALES: 1.6MM **Privately Held**
SIC: 2411 Logging camps & contractors

(G-4489)
HANGER PRSTHETCS & ORTHO INC
Also Called: Hanger Clinic
1300 College Ave (14901-1154)
PHONE...............................607 795-1220
Sheryl Price, *Manager*
EMP: 99
SALES (corp-wide): 1B **Publicly Held**
SIC: 3842 Limbs, artificial
HQ: Hanger Prosthetics & Orthotics, Inc.
10910 Domain Dr Ste 300
Austin TX 78758
512 777-3800

(G-4490)
HARDINGE INC (HQ)
1 Hardinge Dr (14903-1946)
PHONE...............................607 734-2281
Christopher Disantis, *Ch of Bd*
Charles P Dougherty, *President*
James P Langa, *Senior VP*
URS Baumgartner, *Vice Pres*
William Sepanik, *Vice Pres*
▲ **EMP:** 277
SALES: 317.9MM **Privately Held**
WEB: www.hardinge.com
SIC: 3541 3545 3553 3549 Machine tools, metal cutting type; lathes; grinding, polishing, buffing, lapping & honing machines; collets (machine tool accessories); lathes, wood turning: including accessories; metalworking machinery
PA: Hardinge Holdings, Llc
79 W Paces Ferry Rd Nw
Atlanta GA 30305
404 419-2670

(G-4491)
HAUN WELDING SUPPLY INC
1100 Sullivan St (14901-1640)
PHONE...............................607 846-2289
Mike Cesaro, *Manager*
EMP: 8
SALES (corp-wide): 65.7MM **Privately Held**
SIC: 7692 5999 5169 Welding repair; welding supplies; industrial gases
PA: Haun Welding Supply, Inc.
5921 Court Street Rd
Syracuse NY 13206
315 463-5241

(G-4492)
HILLIARD CORPORATION (PA)
100 W 4th St (14901-2190)
P.O. Box 866 (14902-0866)
PHONE...............................607 733-7121
Arie J Van Den Blink, *Ch of Bd*
Gene A Ebbrecht, *President*
Laura Blew, *General Mgr*
Steve Chesebro, *Exec VP*
Steven J Chesebro, *Exec VP*
◆ **EMP:** 277 **EST:** 1905
SQ FT: 326,000
SALES (est): 106.5MM **Privately Held**
SIC: 3564 3569 3823 Purification & dust collection equipment; filters; industrial instrmnts msrmnt display/control process variable

(G-4493)
HILLIARD CORPORATION
1420 College Ave (14901-1153)
PHONE...............................607 733-7121
Phil Lazeski, *Engineer*
Greg Tenbus, *Engineer*
Arie J Van Den Blink, *Branch Mgr*
Doug Canfield, *Manager*
Jeffrey Wolowitz, *Manager*
EMP: 9
SALES (corp-wide): 106.5MM **Privately Held**
SIC: 3564 3569 3823 Purification & dust collection equipment; filters; industrial instrmnts msrmnt display/control process variable
PA: The Hilliard Corporation
100 W 4th St
Elmira NY 14901
607 733-7121

(G-4494)
I D MACHINE INC
Also Called: I Do Machining
1580 Lake St (14901-1248)
PHONE...............................607 796-2549
John Meier, *Ch of Bd*
EMP: 7
SALES (est): 1.1MM **Privately Held**
WEB: www.idomachining.com
SIC: 3599 Machine shop, jobbing & repair

(G-4495)
JRSMM LLC
Also Called: Jetwrx Rotable Services
1316 College Ave (14901-1169)
P.O. Box 282 (14902-0282)
PHONE...............................607 331-1549
Robert Salluzzo, *CFO*
EMP: 6 **EST:** 2016
SQ FT: 12,000
SALES (est): 313.4K **Privately Held**
SIC: 3728 Aircraft parts & equipment

(G-4496)
KITCHEN SPECIALTY CRAFTSMEN
2366 Corning Rd (14903-1045)
PHONE...............................607 739-0833
Douglas Wells, *President*
Kenneth Wells, *Vice Pres*
Phillis Wells, *Treasurer*
EMP: 9 **EST:** 1968
SALES (est): 1.1MM **Privately Held**
SIC: 2541 Table or counter tops, plastic laminated

(G-4497)
MCWANE INC
Also Called: Kennedy Valve Division
1021 E Water St (14901-3332)
P.O. Box 931 (14902-0931)
PHONE...............................607 734-2211
Arne Feyling, *General Mgr*
David Adams, *Safety Mgr*
Matt Hicks, *Safety Mgr*
Roberta Hoover, *Safety Mgr*
Thomas Shaw, *Safety Mgr*
EMP: 376
SALES (corp-wide): 1.3B **Privately Held**
WEB: www.mcwane.com
SIC: 3491 3561 3321 5085 Industrial valves; pumps & pumping equipment; gray & ductile iron foundries; valves & fittings
PA: Mcwane, Inc.
2900 Highway 280 S # 300
Birmingham AL 35223
205 414-3100

(G-4498)
MEGA TOOL & MFG CORP
1023 Caton Ave (14904-2620)
PHONE...............................607 734-8398
Craig Spencer, *President*
Mary Lou Spencer, *Admin Sec*
Mary Spencer, *Admin Sec*
EMP: 25 **EST:** 1965
SQ FT: 18,000
SALES (est): 3.4MM **Privately Held**
WEB: www.megatool-mfg.com
SIC: 3599 3469 7692 3544 Machine shop, jobbing & repair; machine parts, stamped or pressed metal; welding repair; special dies, tools, jigs & fixtures

(G-4499)
PC SOLUTIONS & CONSULTING
407 S Walnut St (14904-1637)
PHONE...............................607 735-0466
Roy Brotherhood, *President*
Katherine Brotherhood, *Vice Pres*
EMP: 5
SQ FT: 1,800
SALES (est): 787.8K **Privately Held**
WEB: www.powerpcs.com
SIC: 3575 7371 Computer terminals, monitors & components; custom computer programming services

(G-4500)
QUICKER PRINTER INC
210 W Gray St (14901-2907)
P.O. Box 1257 (14902-1257)
PHONE...............................607 734-8622
Robert Lavarnway Jr, *President*
Tracie Dahl, *Sales Staff*
EMP: 7
SQ FT: 5,000
SALES (est): 1.2MM **Privately Held**
WEB: www.quickerprinter.com
SIC: 2752 2791 Commercial printing, offset; typesetting

(G-4501)
RAINBOW LETTERING
1329 College Ave (14901-1133)
PHONE...............................607 732-5751
George Malone, *Owner*
Tom Wolfe, *Owner*
EMP: 5
SALES: 150K **Privately Held**
SIC: 2396 2759 Screen printing on fabric articles; screen printing

(G-4502)
SEPAC INC
Also Called: Placid Industries
1580 Lake St Ste 1 (14901-1255)
PHONE...............................607 732-2030
John H Meier, *President*
Martha Zoerb, *Accounting Mgr*
Kenneth Seager, *Manager*
▲ **EMP:** 35
SQ FT: 17,352
SALES (est): 9.3MM **Privately Held**
SIC: 3568 Power transmission equipment

(G-4503)
STAR-GAZETTE FUND INC
Also Called: Elmira Star-Gazette
310 E Church St (14901-2704)
PHONE...............................607 734-5151
Monte I Trammer, *President*
EMP: 150
SALES: 20MM
SALES (corp-wide): 3.1B **Publicly Held**
SIC: 2711 Newspapers, publishing & printing
HQ: Gannett Satellite Information Network, Llc
7950 Jones Branch Dr
Mc Lean VA 22102
703 854-6000

(G-4504)
SURFACE FINISH TECHNOLOGY
215 Judson St (14901-3308)
PHONE...............................607 732-2909
John Short, *President*
Linda Short, *Corp Secy*
Jack Slocum, *Engineer*
Carrie Roadarmel, *CFO*
Laura Walters, *Human Res Mgr*
EMP: 35
SQ FT: 18,000
SALES (est): 4.3MM **Privately Held**
WEB: www.surfacefinishtech.com
SIC: 3471 Finishing, metals or formed products

(G-4505)
TDS FITNESS EQUIPMENT CORP
Also Called: New York Barbell
160 Home St (14904-1811)
PHONE...............................607 733-6789
T D Seethapathy,
Thugginni D Seethapathy, *President*
▲ **EMP:** 10
SQ FT: 100,000
SALES (est): 4.2MM **Privately Held**
WEB: www.tdsfitnessequipment.com
SIC: 3949 5091 5941 Dumbbells & other weightlifting equipment; exercise equipment; exercise equipment

(G-4506)
TDS FOUNDRY CORPORATION
160 Home St (14904-1811)
PHONE...............................607 733-6789
EMP: 9
SALES (est): 267.3K **Privately Held**
SIC: 3949 Exercise equipment

(G-4507)
WINCHESTER OPTICAL COMPANY (DH)
1935 Lake St (14901-1239)
P.O. Box 1515 (14902-1515)
PHONE...............................607 734-4251
Ben E Lynch, *President*

Elmira - Chemung County (G-4508)

Karla Lynch, *General Mgr*
Michael P Lynch, *Vice Pres*
Mike Lynch, *Vice Pres*
Deborah Lynch, *Treasurer*
EMP: 41
SQ FT: 32,500
SALES (est): 12.8MM **Privately Held**
WEB: www.winoptical.com
SIC: 3851 5048 Frames, lenses & parts, eyeglass & spectacle; ophthalmic goods
HQ: Essilor Laboratories Of America Holding Co., Inc.
13555 N Stemmons Fwy
Dallas TX 75234
214 496-4141

(G-4508)
WRIGHTCUT EDM & MACHINE INC
951 Carl St (14904-2662)
PHONE.................................607 733-5018
Byron Wright, *President*
Michelle Wright, *Vice Pres*
EMP: 9
SQ FT: 3,500
SALES (est): 1.3MM **Privately Held**
WEB: www.wrightcutedm.com
SIC: 3599 Machine shop, jobbing & repair

Elmira Heights
Chemung County

(G-4509)
ANCHOR GLASS CONTAINER CORP
151 E Mccanns Blvd (14903-1955)
PHONE.................................607 737-1933
Jason Achterberg, *General Mgr*
Rose Wilson, *Controller*
Michael Sopp, *Manager*
EMP: 370
SALES (corp-wide): 264.1K **Privately Held**
WEB: www.anchorglass.com
SIC: 3221 Glass containers
HQ: Anchor Glass Container Corporation
401 E Jackson St Ste 1100
Tampa FL 33602

(G-4510)
CAF USA INC
300 E 18th St (14903-1333)
PHONE.................................607 737-3004
Jesus Isturiz, *General Mgr*
Hoyos V Manuel, *General Mgr*
Stuart Landry, *Area Mgr*
Lou Tartaglia, *Vice Pres*
Kathleen Nunez, *Opers Mgr*
EMP: 100
SALES (corp-wide): 1.1B **Privately Held**
SIC: 3743 Railroad equipment
HQ: Caf Usa, Inc.
1401 K St Nw Ste 1003
Washington DC 20005
202 898-4848

(G-4511)
GOLOS PRINTING INC
110 E 9th St (14903-1733)
PHONE.................................607 732-1896
Thomas L Golos Sr, *President*
Thomas L Corp Sr, *President*
Hank Corp, *Vice Pres*
EMP: 6 **EST:** 1921
SQ FT: 10,000
SALES: 300K **Privately Held**
SIC: 2752 2759 Commercial printing, offset; letterpress printing

(G-4512)
MOTOR COMPONENTS LLC
2243 Corning Rd (14903-1031)
PHONE.................................607 737-8011
Reeve Howland, *Facilities Mgr*
Dave Demarco, *Controller*
Tony Bonfardeci, *Manager*
Kris Miller, *Manager*
Cindy Adams, *MIS Dir*
▲ **EMP:** 68
SQ FT: 300,000

SALES (est): 18.8MM
SALES (corp-wide): 43.3MM **Privately Held**
WEB: www.motorcomponents.com
SIC: 3714 Motor vehicle wheels & parts
PA: Bam Enterprises, Inc.
2937 Alt Blvd
Grand Island NY 14072
716 773-7634

(G-4513)
SERVICE MACHINE & TOOL COMPANY
206 E Mccanns Blvd (14903-1958)
P.O. Box 2118 (14903-0118)
PHONE.................................607 732-0413
Keith Knowlden, *President*
Axieann Knowlden, *Corp Secy*
Hal Fitzsimmons, *Tech/Comp Coord*
▲ **EMP:** 25
SALES (est): 4.8MM **Privately Held**
WEB: www.servicemachinetool.com
SIC: 3599 Machine shop, jobbing & repair

(G-4514)
STAMPED FITTINGS INC
217 Lenox Ave (14903-1118)
PHONE.................................607 733-9988
Shana Graham, *President*
Mike Graham, *Vice Pres*
▲ **EMP:** 25 **EST:** 1997
SQ FT: 25,000
SALES (est): 4.8MM **Privately Held**
WEB: www.stampedfittings.com
SIC: 3469 Stamping metal for the trade

(G-4515)
SWIFT GLASS CO INC
131 22nd St (14903-1329)
P.O. Box 879, Elmira (14902-0879)
PHONE.................................607 733-7166
Daniel J Burke, *President*
Gary Palmowski, *Opers Mgr*
Kevin Wheeler, *Opers Mgr*
Christine Fey, *Asst Controller*
Jim Darling, *Sales Mgr*
▲ **EMP:** 85 **EST:** 1882
SQ FT: 80,000
SALES (est): 18.9MM **Privately Held**
WEB: www.swiftglass.com
SIC: 3231 Scientific & technical glassware: from purchased glass

Elmont
Nassau County

(G-4516)
ARCHITECTURAL SIGN GROUP INC
145 Meacham Ave (11003-2633)
PHONE.................................516 326-1800
Abbas Jaffer, *President*
Rehana Jaffer, *Vice Pres*
EMP: 5
SQ FT: 4,000
SALES (est): 762.3K **Privately Held**
WEB: www.archsigngroup.com
SIC: 3993 Electric signs

(G-4517)
AWT SUPPLY CORP
Also Called: American Printing Eqp & Sup
153 Meacham Ave (11003-2633)
P.O. Box 356, Franklin Square (11010-0356)
PHONE.................................516 437-9105
Greg Mandel, *President*
Josh Solomon, *Vice Pres*
Max Mandel, *Exec Dir*
▲ **EMP:** 8
SQ FT: 45,000
SALES (est): 1.5MM **Privately Held**
WEB: www.americanprintingequipment.com
SIC: 3555 5051 3546 Printing trades machinery; wire; power-driven handtools

(G-4518)
ELMONT NORTH LITTLE LEAGUE
1532 Clay St (11003-1046)
PHONE.................................516 775-8210
Ronald Levin, *Owner*

Tom Laietta, *Vice Pres*
EMP: 7
SALES (est): 462.1K **Privately Held**
SIC: 2721 Trade journals: publishing only, not printed on site

(G-4519)
GM INSULATION CORP
1345 Rosser Ave (11003-3244)
P.O. Box 2188, New Hyde Park (11040-8188)
PHONE.................................516 354-6000
Izabel Skugor, *President*
EMP: 13
SALES (est): 2.4MM **Privately Held**
SIC: 2295 Sealing or insulating tape for pipe: coated fiberglass

(G-4520)
MARTIN ORNA IR WORKS II INC
266 Elmont Rd (11003-1600)
PHONE.................................516 354-3923
Martin Boventre, *President*
Charles Cascio, *Principal*
EMP: 5 **EST:** 1962
SQ FT: 5,000
SALES (est): 630.2K **Privately Held**
SIC: 3446 Architectural metalwork

(G-4521)
MERIDIAN TECHNOLOGIES INC
700 Elmont Rd (11003-4027)
PHONE.................................516 285-1000
Denise Shay, *Ch of Bd*
Michael Barry, *Managing Dir*
Irina Kovaleva, *Engineer*
Rachel Shifrin, *Systems Staff*
▲ **EMP:** 22
SQ FT: 10,000
SALES: 2.2MM **Privately Held**
WEB: www.meridian-tech.com
SIC: 3679 Electronic circuits

(G-4522)
PROFESSNL SPT PBLICATIONS INC
570 Elmont Rd (11003-3535)
PHONE.................................516 327-9500
Michael Shabsels, *Ch of Bd*
EMP: 20
SALES (est): 1.7MM **Privately Held**
SIC: 2741 Miscellaneous publishing

(G-4523)
PROFESSNL SPT PBLICATIONS INC
Also Called: Pspi
570 Elmont Rd Ste 202 (11003-3535)
PHONE.................................516 327-9500
EMP: 100
SALES (corp-wide): 22.6MM **Privately Held**
WEB: www.pspsports.com
SIC: 2721 Periodicals
PA: Professional Sports Publications Inc.
519 8th Ave
New York NY 10018
212 697-1460

(G-4524)
RPC INC
Also Called: RPC Car Service
165 Emporia Ave (11003-1837)
PHONE.................................347 873-3935
Michelle Franklin, *Branch Mgr*
EMP: 39
SALES (corp-wide): 1.6B **Publicly Held**
SIC: 1389 Oil field services
PA: Rpc, Inc.
2801 Buford Hwy Ne # 520
Brookhaven GA 30329
404 321-2140

(G-4525)
SAPIENZA PASTRY INC
Also Called: Sapienza Bake Shop
1376 Hempstead Tpke (11003-2539)
PHONE.................................516 352-5232
Paul Sapienza, *President*
EMP: 25
SQ FT: 3,600
SALES (est): 3.3MM **Privately Held**
SIC: 2051 5461 2099 2052 Bakery: wholesale or wholesale/retail combined; bakeries; food preparations; cookies & crackers

(G-4526)
TIMELY SIGNS INC
2135 Linden Blvd (11003-3901)
PHONE.................................516 285-5339
Eugene Goldsmith, *President*
EMP: 6
SQ FT: 2,000
SALES: 600K **Privately Held**
SIC: 3993 Displays & cutouts, window & lobby

Elmsford
Westchester County

(G-4527)
A GATTY PRODUCTS INC
Also Called: A Gatty Svce
1 Warehouse Ln (10523-1538)
P.O. Box 725 (10523-0725)
PHONE.................................914 592-3903
Andy Gattyan, *President*
Eva Gattyn, *Vice Pres*
EMP: 6
SQ FT: 5,000
SALES (est): 396K **Privately Held**
SIC: 3639 1799 Trash compactors, household; hydraulic equipment, installation & service

(G-4528)
ADL DATA SYSTEMS INC
565 Taxter Rd Ste 100 (10523-2300)
PHONE.................................914 591-1800
David Pollack, *President*
Aaron Weg, *Vice Pres*
EMP: 40
SQ FT: 13,000
SALES (est): 5.1MM **Privately Held**
WEB: www.adldata.com
SIC: 7372 Business oriented computer software

(G-4529)
ANCHOR TECH PRODUCTS CORP
4 Vernon Ln Ste 2 (10523-1947)
PHONE.................................914 592-0240
Dan Esposito, *President*
Steve Ebanks, *Manager*
▲ **EMP:** 20
SQ FT: 3,000
SALES (est): 2MM **Privately Held**
SIC: 3052 Vacuum cleaner hose, rubber; vacuum cleaner hose, plastic; v-belts, rubber

(G-4530)
ARTINA GROUP INC
250 Clearbrook Rd Ste 245 (10523-1332)
P.O. Box 681, Tarrytown (10591-0681)
PHONE.................................914 592-1850
INA Shapiro, *President*
Richard Horn, *Vice Pres*
Mark Spinozza, *Controller*
Ron Mazzarella, *Software Dev*
Stephanie Boyle, *Executive Asst*
EMP: 34 **EST:** 1971
SQ FT: 25,000
SALES (est): 6.4MM **Privately Held**
SIC: 2752 Business forms, lithographed

(G-4531)
BEST PRICED PRODUCTS INC
250 Clearbrook Rd Ste 240 (10523-1332)
P.O. Box 1174, White Plains (10602-1174)
PHONE.................................914 345-3800
Linda Goldberg, *President*
Andrew Goldberg, *Marketing Staff*
EMP: 5
SQ FT: 30,000
SALES (est): 290K **Privately Held**
WEB: www.bpp2.com
SIC: 3999 Novelties, bric-a-brac & hobby kits

(G-4532)
BH COFFEE COMPANY LLC (PA)
Also Called: Barrie House Coffee & Tea
4 Warehouse Ln Ste 121 (10523-1541)
PHONE.................................914 377-2500
David Goldstein, *CEO*
Paul Goldstein, *President*
Miles Lewis, *Business Mgr*

GEOGRAPHIC SECTION

Elmsford - Westchester County (G-4559)

Ronald Goldstein, *Vice Pres*
Karan Magee, *Vice Pres*
▲ **EMP:** 100 **EST:** 1934
SQ FT: 35,000
SALES (est): 24.9MM **Privately Held**
WEB: www.barriehouse.com
SIC: 2095 Coffee roasting (except by wholesale grocers)

(G-4533)
BLINDTEK DESIGNER SYSTEMS INC
1 Hayes St (10523-2531)
PHONE 914 347-7100
Lee Miller, *President*
Anthony Ash, *Vice Pres*
Steve Beamand, *Vice Pres*
▲ **EMP:** 18 **EST:** 1998
SALES (est): 2.7MM **Privately Held**
SIC: 2591 Blinds vertical

(G-4534)
C & F IRON WORKS INC
14 N Payne St Ste 1 (10523-1839)
PHONE 914 592-2450
Fernando Pastilha, *President*
EMP: 15
SQ FT: 1,600
SALES (est): 800K **Privately Held**
SIC: 3446 Railings, bannisters, guards, etc.: made from metal pipe

(G-4535)
C & F STEEL CORP
14 N Payne St Ste 2 (10523-1841)
PHONE 914 592-3928
Arthur Boino, *CEO*
EMP: 18 **EST:** 2000
SALES (est): 2.8MM **Privately Held**
SIC: 3446 Fences, gates, posts & flagpoles

(G-4536)
COCA-COLA BTLG CO OF NY INC
115 Fairview Pk Dr Ste 1 (10523-1535)
PHONE 914 789-1580
Margerite Lopiccollo, *Principal*
EMP: 10
SALES (corp-wide): 35.4B **Publicly Held**
SIC: 2086 Bottled & canned soft drinks
HQ: The Coca-Cola Bottling Company Of New York Inc
2500 Windy Ridge Pkwy Se
Atlanta GA 30339
770 989-3000

(G-4537)
CONWAY IMPORT CO INC
Also Called: Conway Dressing For Success
4 Warehouse Ln Ste 142 (10523-1568)
PHONE 914 592-1312
Leo Maccaro, *Branch Mgr*
EMP: 5
SALES (corp-wide): 14MM **Privately Held**
WEB: www.conwaydressings.com
SIC: 2035 Mayonnaise
PA: Conway Import Co., Inc.
11051 W Addison St
Franklin Park IL 60131
847 455-5600

(G-4538)
CORAL BLOOD SERVICE
525 Executive Blvd # 285 (10523-1240)
PHONE 800 483-4888
Rose Shaw, *Vice Pres*
EMP: 15
SALES (est): 1.7MM **Privately Held**
SIC: 2836 Plasmas

(G-4539)
CRAFTERS WORKSHOP INC
116 S Central Ave Ste 1 (10523-3503)
PHONE 914 345-2838
Jaime Echt, *President*
▼ **EMP:** 9
SQ FT: 3,000
SALES (est): 512.4K **Privately Held**
WEB: www.thecraftersworkshop.com
SIC: 3953 Stencils, painting & marking

(G-4540)
CRONIN ENTERPRISES INC
Also Called: Minuteman Press
70 E Main St Ste 2 (10523-3146)
PHONE 914 345-9600
Gary Cronin, *President*
Jacquiline Cronin, *Vice Pres*
EMP: 9
SQ FT: 4,000
SALES (est): 1.2MM **Privately Held**
SIC: 2752 Commercial printing, lithographic

(G-4541)
EMKAY TRADING CORP (PA)
250 Clearbrook Rd Ste 127 (10523-1332)
P.O. Box 504 (10523-0504)
PHONE 914 592-9000
Howard Kravitz, *President*
Ruth Kravitz, *Vice Pres*
EMP: 2
SQ FT: 2,500
SALES (est): 1.9MM **Privately Held**
WEB: www.emkaytrading.org
SIC: 2022 Cheese, natural & processed

(G-4542)
ENGAGEMENT TECHNOLOGY LLC
33 W Main St Ste 303 (10523-2413)
PHONE 914 591-7600
Gloria Golle, *Controller*
Bruce Bolger,
EMP: 10
SALES (est): 1.5MM **Privately Held**
SIC: 3679 Electronic loads & power supplies

(G-4543)
FABRICATION ENTERPRISES INC
250 Clearbrook Rd Ste 240 (10523-1332)
P.O. Box 1500, White Plains (10602-1500)
PHONE 914 591-9300
Elliott Goldberg, *President*
Linda Green, *VP Prdtn*
Kathleen Renna, *Opers Staff*
Brendan Fahey, *Accounts Mgr*
Greg Guerci, *Accounts Mgr*
◆ **EMP:** 45
SQ FT: 30,000
SALES: 50MM **Privately Held**
WEB: www.fabricationenterprises.com
SIC: 3841 2297 Physiotherapy equipment, electrical; nonwoven fabrics

(G-4544)
HUDSON SOFTWARE CORPORATION
3 W Main St Ste 106 (10523-2414)
PHONE 914 773-0400
Glenn Polin, *President*
Mike Gulley, *COO*
James Mott, *Opers Mgr*
Ralph Santoni, *Manager*
EMP: 35
SQ FT: 6,000
SALES (est): 2.8MM **Privately Held**
WEB: www.hudsonsoft.com
SIC: 7372 7371 7374 Prepackaged software; custom computer programming services; service bureau, computer

(G-4545)
HYPRES INC (PA)
175 Clearbrook Rd (10523-1109)
PHONE 914 592-1190
Richard E Hitt Jr, *Ch of Bd*
Richard Hitt, *President*
Deepnarayan Gupta, *President*
Oleg Mukhanov, *President*
Amir Jafari-Salim, *Research*
EMP: 37
SQ FT: 17,250
SALES (est): 11MM **Privately Held**
WEB: www.hypres.com
SIC: 3679 Electronic circuits

(G-4546)
IRON ART INC
14 N Payne St (10523-1835)
PHONE 914 592-7977
Fernando Pastilha, *President*
EMP: 5
SALES: 200K **Privately Held**
SIC: 3446 Ornamental metalwork

(G-4547)
JAM PRINTING PUBLISHING INC
11 Clearbrook Rd Ste 133 (10523-1126)
PHONE 914 345-8400
Judith Millman, *President*
EMP: 7
SALES (est): 949.8K **Privately Held**
WEB: www.jamprinting.com
SIC: 2752 Commercial printing, lithographic

(G-4548)
KEURIG DR PEPPER INC
55 Hunter Ln (10523-1334)
PHONE 914 846-2300
Sam Suleiman, *Warehouse Mgr*
EMP: 100 **Publicly Held**
SIC: 2086 Soft drinks: packaged in cans, bottles, etc.
PA: Keurig Dr Pepper Inc.
5301 Legacy Dr
Plano TX 01803

(G-4549)
MAGNETIC ANALYSIS CORPORATION (PA)
Also Called: M A C
103 Fairview Pk Dr Ste 2 (10523-1544)
PHONE 914 530-2000
Jl Vitulli, *Ch of Bd*
William S Gould III, *Chairman*
Keith Brandt, *District Mgr*
Alain Dura, *District Mgr*
Fred Fundy, *District Mgr*
▲ **EMP:** 90 **EST:** 1928
SQ FT: 26,000
SALES: 25MM **Privately Held**
WEB: www.mac-ndt.com
SIC: 3829 3825 Testing equipment: abrasion, shearing strength, etc.; instruments to measure electricity

(G-4550)
MASTER IMAGE PRINTING INC
75 N Central Ave Ste 202 (10523-2548)
PHONE 914 347-4400
John Sabatino, *President*
Mary Jane Yollen, *Vice Pres*
EMP: 5
SQ FT: 5,000
SALES: 1MM **Privately Held**
WEB: www.masterimage.com
SIC: 2759 2752 2396 2679 Labels & seals: printing; commercial printing, lithographic; automotive & apparel trimmings; labels, paper: made from purchased material

(G-4551)
MASTERDISK CORPORATION
134 S Central Ave Ste C (10523-3539)
PHONE 212 541-5022
Douglas Levine, *CEO*
Laksham Fernando, *Treasurer*
EMP: 15
SQ FT: 10,000
SALES: 981K **Privately Held**
WEB: www.masterdisk.com
SIC: 3652 3651 2851 Master records or tapes, preparation of; household audio & video equipment; vinyl coatings, strippable

(G-4552)
MOTTS LLP (HQ)
Also Called: Motts
55 Hunter Ln (10523-1334)
P.O. Box 869077, Plano TX (75086-9077)
PHONE 972 673-8088
Jim Baldwin, *General Counsel*
Larry D Young,
◆ **EMP:** 250
SQ FT: 160,000
SALES (est): 318.5MM **Publicly Held**
WEB: www.maunalai.com
SIC: 2033 5149 2087 Fruit juices: packaged in cans, jars, etc.; apple sauce: packaged in cans, jars, etc.; beverage concentrates; cocktail mixes, nonalcoholic

(G-4553)
MYPUBLISHER INC (HQ)
8 Westchester Plz Ste 145 (10523-1604)
PHONE 914 773-4312
Jeffrey T Housenbold, *Ch of Bd*
▲ **EMP:** 19
SALES (est): 4.3MM
SALES (corp-wide): 1.1B **Publicly Held**
WEB: www.mypublisher.com
SIC: 2782 Albums
PA: Shutterfly, Inc.
2800 Bridge Pkwy Ste 100
Redwood City CA 94065
650 610-5200

(G-4554)
NANOVIBRONIX INC
525 Executive Blvd (10523-1240)
PHONE 914 233-3004
William Stern, *CEO*
Jona Zumeris, *Vice Pres*
Stephen Brown, *CFO*
Brian Murphy, *Director*
EMP: 12
SALES (est): 707.1K **Privately Held**
SIC: 3845 Ultrasonic medical equipment, except cleaning

(G-4555)
NANTUCKET ALLSERVE INC
Also Called: Nantucket Nectars
55 Hunter Ln (10523-1334)
PHONE 914 612-4000
Mark Hellendrung, *President*
Thomas First, *Co-COB*
Thomas Scott, *Co-COB*
Tim Chan, *Treasurer*
EMP: 400
SALES (est): 17.9MM **Privately Held**
SIC: 2086 5499 Fruit drinks (less than 100% juice): packaged in cans, etc.; juices, fruit or vegetable

(G-4556)
NOVAMED-USA INC
4 Westchester Plz Ste 137 (10523-1612)
PHONE 914 789-2100
Carol Schuler, *Exec VP*
Maggie Wang, *Purch Mgr*
Deniz Ozgulbas, *QC Mgr*
▲ **EMP:** 40
SQ FT: 30,000
SALES (est): 5.9MM **Privately Held**
SIC: 3841 3845 Catheters; patient monitoring apparatus

(G-4557)
OLYMPIA SPORTS COMPANY INC
Also Called: Olympia Company
500 Executive Blvd # 170 (10523-1239)
PHONE 914 347-4737
Roger Heumann, *President*
Ed Brodsky, *Vice Pres*
Peter Kiernan, *Vice Pres*
▲ **EMP:** 10
SQ FT: 7,200
SALES (est): 1.3MM **Privately Held**
WEB: www.olympiagloves.com
SIC: 3949 Gloves, sport & athletic: boxing, handball, etc.

(G-4558)
PRESS EXPRESS
400 Executive Blvd # 146 (10523-1243)
PHONE 914 592-3790
Al Tiso, *President*
EMP: 5
SALES (est): 408.6K **Privately Held**
SIC: 2741 7313 Miscellaneous publishing; printed media advertising representatives

(G-4559)
RADON TESTING CORP OF AMERICA (PA)
Also Called: R T C A
2 Hayes St (10523-2502)
PHONE 914 345-3380
Michael Osterer, *CEO*
Nancy Bredhoff, *President*
David Bredhoff, *Managing Dir*
Alan S Bandes, *Vice Pres*
Mark A Goodman, *Vice Pres*
EMP: 18
SQ FT: 4,500

Elmsford - Westchester County (G-4560)

SALES (est): 2.6MM **Privately Held**
WEB: www.rtca.com
SIC: 3821 Laboratory apparatus & furniture

(G-4560)
RALPH MARTINELLI
Also Called: Suburban Marketing Assoc
100 Clearbrook Rd Ste 170 (10523-1135)
PHONE..................914 345-3055
Ralph Martinelli, *Owner*
EMP: 30
SALES (est): 1.3MM **Privately Held**
WEB: www.sub-pub.com
SIC: 2721 Magazines: publishing only, not printed on site

(G-4561)
RAW INDULGENCE LTD
Also Called: Raw Revolution
44 Executive Blvd Ste 205 (10523-1336)
P.O. Box 359, Hawthorne (10532-0359)
PHONE..................866 498-4671
David Friedman, *CEO*
Alice Benedetto, *President*
Dorathea Gornie, *Sales Staff*
▲ EMP: 14
SQ FT: 3,000
SALES (est): 2.9MM **Privately Held**
SIC: 2099 Food preparations

(G-4562)
RELIABLE AUTMTC SPRNKLR CO INC (PA)
103 Fairview Pk Dr Ste 1 (10523-1523)
PHONE..................800 431-1588
Frank J Fee III, *President*
Candida M Fee, *Vice Pres*
Kevin T Fee, *Vice Pres*
Michael R Fee, *Vice Pres*
Robert C Hultgren, *Vice Pres*
◆ EMP: 350 EST: 1920
SQ FT: 64,000
SALES (est): 381.2MM **Privately Held**
SIC: 3569 Sprinkler systems, fire: automatic

(G-4563)
SAVE O SEAL CORPORATION INC
90 E Main St (10523-3218)
P.O. Box 553 (10523-0553)
PHONE..................914 592-3031
Tullio Muscariello, *President*
Rose Muscariello, *Vice Pres*
EMP: 7
SQ FT: 3,000
SALES (est): 1.2MM **Privately Held**
SIC: 3565 5085 Packaging machinery; knives, industrial

(G-4564)
SCHOTT CORPORATION (DH)
555 Taxter Rd Ste 470 (10523-2363)
PHONE..................914 831-2200
Linda S Mayer, *Ch of Bd*
Greg Wolters, *Ch of Bd*
Dr Andreas F Liebenberg, *President*
Tony Cappabianca, *Business Mgr*
Nikhil Krishna, *Business Mgr*
◆ EMP: 70
SQ FT: 70,000
SALES (est): 781.5MM **Privately Held**
SIC: 3211 3829 3221 3229 Flat glass; measuring & controlling devices; glass containers; vials, glass; glass fiber products
HQ: Schott Ag
Hattenbergstr. 10
Mainz 55122
613 166-0

(G-4565)
SCHOTT GEMTRON CORPORATION
555 Taxter Rd Ste 470 (10523-2352)
PHONE..................423 337-3522
Linda S Mayer, *President*
Tony Springate, *Accounts Mgr*
EMP: 194 **Privately Held**
SIC: 3211 Flat glass
HQ: Schott Gemtron Corporation
615 Highway 68
Sweetwater TN 37874
423 337-3522

(G-4566)
SCHOTT LITHOTEC USA CORP
555 Taxter Rd Ste 470 (10523-2352)
PHONE..................845 463-5300
Patrick Markschlaeger, *President*
EMP: 80
SQ FT: 36,115
SALES (est): 5.7MM **Privately Held**
SIC: 3674 Semiconductors & related devices

(G-4567)
SCHOTT NORTH AMERICA INC (DH)
555 Taxter Rd Ste 470 (10523-2352)
PHONE..................914 831-2200
Greg Wolters, *CEO*
Patrick Gallagher, *Business Mgr*
Joseph Frankel, *VP Human Res*
Dan Bergman, *Info Tech Mgr*
Manfred Jaeckel, *Admin Sec*
▲ EMP: 60 EST: 1998
SQ FT: 23,000
SALES (est): 506MM **Privately Held**
WEB: www.us.schott.com
SIC: 3229 Pressed & blown glass
HQ: Schott Corporation
555 Taxter Rd Ste 470
Elmsford NY 10523
914 831-2200

(G-4568)
SCHOTT SOLAR PV INC
555 Taxter Rd Ste 470 (10523-2352)
PHONE..................888 457-6527
Mark Finocchario, *President*
Hans-Juergen Gebel, *Vice Pres*
Manfred Jaeckel, *Admin Sec*
▲ EMP: 8
SALES (est): 748.2K **Privately Held**
SIC: 3674 3211 Solar cells; flat glass
HQ: Schott Solar Ag
Hattenbergstr. 10
Mainz
613 166-0

(G-4569)
SIGN WORKS INCORPORATED
150 Clearbrook Rd Ste 118 (10523-1142)
PHONE..................914 592-0700
Lynn Feiner, *President*
Anthony Martinelli, *Marketing Staff*
EMP: 25
SQ FT: 11,000
SALES (est): 2.7MM **Privately Held**
SIC: 3993 1799 Signs, not made in custom sign painting shops; sign installation & maintenance

(G-4570)
SML ACQUISITION LLC
33 W Main St Ste 505 (10523-2453)
PHONE..................914 592-3130
Robert B Wetzel, *President*
EMP: 179 EST: 2011
SQ FT: 35,000
SALES (est): 12.5MM **Privately Held**
SIC: 2844 Toilet preparations

(G-4571)
SPOTLIGHT PUBLICATIONS LLC
100 Clearbrook Rd Ste 170 (10523-1135)
PHONE..................914 345-9473
John Jordan, *Principal*
EMP: 5
SALES (est): 470K **Privately Held**
SIC: 2721 Magazines: publishing only, not printed on site

(G-4572)
SUBURBAN PUBLISHING INC
Also Called: Westchester Magazine
100 Clearbrook Rd Ste 170 (10523-1135)
PHONE..................914 345-0601
Ralph Martinelli, *Branch Mgr*
EMP: 6
SALES (est): 450.7K
SALES (corp-wide): 1MM **Privately Held**
WEB: www.hudsonvalleymagazine.com
SIC: 2721 Magazines: publishing & printing
PA: Suburban Publishing Inc
1 Summit Ct Ste 200a
Fishkill NY 12524
845 463-0542

(G-4573)
TRANE US INC
3 Westchester Plz 198 (10523-1623)
PHONE..................914 593-0303
Terry Connor, *Manager*
EMP: 5 **Privately Held**
SIC: 3585 Refrigeration & heating equipment
HQ: Trane U.S. Inc.
3600 Pammel Creek Rd
La Crosse WI 54601
608 787-2000

(G-4574)
TRI-STATE METALS LLC
Also Called: Tsm
41 N Lawn Ave (10523-2632)
PHONE..................914 347-8157
Patti Carone, *Manager*
Ray Ayerbe, *Webmaster*
EMP: 10
SQ FT: 10,000
SALES (est): 2.2MM **Privately Held**
SIC: 3444 Culverts, flumes & pipes

(G-4575)
U E SYSTEMS INCORPORATED (PA)
14 Hayes St (10523-2536)
PHONE..................914 592-1220
Michael Osterler, *Ch of Bd*
Blake Canham, *Regional Mgr*
Joe Edelen, *Regional Mgr*
Jacob Law, *Regional Mgr*
Mike Naro, *Regional Mgr*
EMP: 30
SALES (est): 5.2MM **Privately Held**
WEB: www.uesystems.com
SIC: 3829 3812 3699 Ultrasonic testing equipment; search & navigation equipment; electrical equipment & supplies

(G-4576)
VITERION CORPORATION
565 Taxter Rd Ste 175 (10523-2371)
PHONE..................914 333-6033
Toru Ide, *President*
EMP: 16 EST: 2012
SALES (est): 2.5MM **Privately Held**
SIC: 3841 Surgical & medical instruments

(G-4577)
WESTINGHOUSE A BRAKE TECH CORP
Also Called: Metro Service Center
4 Warehouse Ln Ste 144 (10523-1556)
PHONE..................914 347-8650
Doug Cavallo, *Manager*
EMP: 13
SALES (corp-wide): 3.8B **Publicly Held**
WEB: www.wabco-rail.com
SIC: 3743 Rapid transit cars & equipment
PA: Westinghouse Air Brake Technologies Corporation
1001 Airbrake Ave
Wilmerding PA 15148
412 825-1000

(G-4578)
WHITE PLAINS MARBLE INC
186 E Main St (10523-3302)
PHONE..................914 347-6000
John Bargellini, *President*
EMP: 7
SQ FT: 5,000
SALES (est): 700K **Privately Held**
SIC: 3281 1743 Marble, building: cut & shaped; statuary, marble; terrazzo, tile, marble, mosaic work

(G-4579)
WILLEMIN-MACODEL INC
5 Westchester Plz (10523-1613)
PHONE..................914 345-3504
Alain Guerdat, *President*
▲ EMP: 6
SQ FT: 1,300
SALES: 500K **Privately Held**
SIC: 3599 Custom machinery

Endicott
Broome County

(G-4580)
311 INDUSTRIES CORP
434 Airport Rd (13760-4406)
PHONE..................607 846-4520
John Galli, *President*
▲ EMP: 6
SALES (est): 193.9K **Privately Held**
SIC: 3089 Boot or shoe products, plastic

(G-4581)
AMPHENOL CABLES ON DEMAND CORP
20 Valley St (13760-3600)
PHONE..................607 321-2115
R Adam Norwitt, *CEO*
▲ EMP: 10
SQ FT: 10,000
SALES: 4MM
SALES (corp-wide): 7B **Publicly Held**
SIC: 3678 Electronic connectors
PA: Amphenol Corporation
358 Hall Ave
Wallingford CT 06492
203 265-8900

(G-4582)
AMPHENOL INTRCONNECT PDTS CORP (HQ)
20 Valley St (13760-3600)
PHONE..................607 754-4444
Richard Adam Norwitt, *CEO*
Martin H Loeffler, *President*
Marybeth Perrino, *COO*
Sue Thompson, *Buyer*
Edward G Jepsen, *CFO*
▲ EMP: 5
SQ FT: 140,000
SALES (est): 79.6MM
SALES (corp-wide): 7B **Publicly Held**
WEB: www.amphenol-aipc.com
SIC: 3679 Harness assemblies for electronic use: wire or cable
PA: Amphenol Corporation
358 Hall Ave
Wallingford CT 06492
203 265-8900

(G-4583)
BAE SYSTEMS CONTROLS INC (DH)
1098 Clark St (13760-2815)
PHONE..................607 770-2000
Terry Crimmins, *President*
James Crouch, *General Mgr*
Katelyn Warren, *General Mgr*
Robert Murphy, *Principal*
William Samuels, *Principal*
▲ EMP: 1400 EST: 2000
SALES (est): 506.7MM
SALES (corp-wide): 24.2B **Privately Held**
WEB: www.baesystemscontrols.com
SIC: 3812 Aircraft/aerospace flight instruments & guidance systems

(G-4584)
CHAKRA COMMUNICATIONS INC
32 Washington Ave (13760-5305)
PHONE..................607 748-7491
Jim Arnold, *Branch Mgr*
EMP: 20 **Privately Held**
WEB: www.chakracentral.com
SIC: 2752 7334 2791 2789 Commercial printing, offset; photocopying & duplicating services; typesetting; bookbinding & related work; commercial printing
HQ: Chakra Communications, Inc.
80 W Drullard Ave
Lancaster NY 14086

(G-4585)
CROWLEY FABG MACHINING CO INC (PA)
403 N Nanticoke Ave (13760-4138)
PHONE..................607 484-0299
Thomas Crowley, *President*
Mike Crowley, *General Mgr*
Tom Crowley, *General Mgr*
Michael Newfrock, *Business Mgr*

▲ = Import ▼ = Export
◆ = Import/Export

Todd Vargason, *Engineer*
EMP: 33
SQ FT: 30,000
SALES (est): 5.6MM **Privately Held**
WEB: www.crowleyfab.com
SIC: 3599 Machine & other job shop work; machine shop, jobbing & repair

(G-4586)
DATUM ALLOYS INC
407 Airport Rd (13760-4405)
PHONE.................607 239-6274
Ben Scott, *President*
Duncan Watey, *Vice Pres*
◆ **EMP:** 6
SQ FT: 800
SALES (est): 746.9K **Privately Held**
SIC: 3291 Abrasive metal & steel products

(G-4587)
EL'TEE TOOL & DIE CO
404 E Franklin St (13760-4124)
PHONE.................607 748-4301
William Andrew Keeler, *Owner*
EMP: 10
SQ FT: 10,000
SALES (est): 1.4MM **Privately Held**
SIC: 3559 Automotive related machinery

(G-4588)
ENDICOTT INTERCONNECT TECH INC
Also Called: Ei
1701 North St (13760-5587)
P.O. Box 5250, Binghamton (13902-5250)
PHONE.................866 820-4820
James J Mc Namara Jr, *Ch of Bd*
Michael Cummings, *President*
William Lynn, *CFO*
Brad Van Brunt, *Sales Staff*
James W Orband, *Admin Sec*
▲ **EMP:** 600
SQ FT: 1,400,000
SALES (est): 90.2K **Privately Held**
WEB: www.endicottinterconnect.com
SIC: 3674 Semiconductors & related devices

(G-4589)
ENDICOTT PRECISION INC
1328-30 Campville Rd (13760-4414)
PHONE.................607 754-7076
Ronald Oliveira, *General Mgr*
Tammie Romich, *General Mgr*
Douglas Walters, *General Mgr*
Manuel Oliveira, *Chairman*
Dolores Oliveira, *Vice Pres*
EMP: 125 **EST:** 1959
SQ FT: 85,000
SALES (est): 16.6MM **Privately Held**
WEB: www.endicottprecision.com
SIC: 3444 3443 3599 3469 Sheet metalwork; fabricated plate work (boiler shop); weldments; custom machinery; metal stampings

(G-4590)
ENDICOTT RESEARCH GROUP INC
2601 Wayne St (13760-3207)
PHONE.................607 754-9187
Nathan Burd, *President*
Michael Kretzmer, *General Mgr*
Scott Barney, *Vice Pres*
Anna Quick, *Mfg Staff*
Scott Dittrich, *Buyer*
EMP: 64
SQ FT: 30,000
SALES (est): 13.9MM **Privately Held**
WEB: www.ergpower.com
SIC: 3629 Power conversion units, a.c. to d.c.: static-electric; inverters, nonrotating: electrical

(G-4591)
ENGINEERING MFG TECH LLC
101 Delaware Ave (13760-6106)
PHONE.................607 754-7111
Patricia Marconi, *President*
Wyoma Chambala, *Vice Pres*
Michael Nowalk, *Vice Pres*
EMP: 90 **EST:** 1946
SQ FT: 80,000
SALES (est): 21MM **Privately Held**
WEB: www.endicottmachine.com
SIC: 3444 3599 3496 3469 Sheet metalwork; machine & other job shop work; miscellaneous fabricated wire products; metal stampings

(G-4592)
FAMBUS INC
Also Called: Village Printing
2800 Watson Blvd (13760-3512)
PHONE.................607 785-3700
David Labelle, *President*
Maureen Labelle, *Office Mgr*
Frank Labelle, *Consultant*
EMP: 6
SQ FT: 2,100
SALES (est): 590K **Privately Held**
WEB: www.fambus.com
SIC: 2752 7334 Commercial printing, offset; photocopying & duplicating services

(G-4593)
FELIX ROMA & SONS INC
2 S Page Ave (13760-4693)
P.O. Box 5547 (13763-5547)
PHONE.................607 748-3336
Eugene F Roma, *President*
Eugene Romask, *Vice Pres*
EMP: 60
SQ FT: 43,000
SALES (est): 8.1MM **Privately Held**
WEB: www.felixroma.com
SIC: 2051 Bakery: wholesale or wholesale/retail combined; bread, all types (white, wheat, rye, etc): fresh or frozen; rolls, bread type: fresh or frozen

(G-4594)
G B INTERNATIONAL TRDG CO LTD
408 Airport Rd (13760-4494)
PHONE.................607 785-0938
August Garufy, *President*
◆ **EMP:** 250
SQ FT: 30,000
SALES (est): 40.9MM **Privately Held**
WEB: www.gbint.com
SIC: 3629 5065 5999 Power conversion units, a.c. to d.c.: static-electric; electronic parts & equipment; electronic parts & equipment

(G-4595)
GEORGE INDUSTRIES LLC (PA)
1 S Page Ave (13760-4695)
PHONE.................607 748-3371
Jon Cohen, *President*
Todd Bushnell, *General Mgr*
John Ferro, *Purch Mgr*
Kellen Kafka, *Engineer*
Don Leonard, *Manager*
EMP: 67 **EST:** 1951
SQ FT: 100,000
SALES (est): 16.8MM **Privately Held**
WEB: www.georgeindustries.com
SIC: 3441 Fabricated structural metal

(G-4596)
I3 ELECTRONICS INC
Huron Campus 1500 1700 (13760)
PHONE.................607 238-7077
Jim Matthews Jr, *Branch Mgr*
EMP: 53
SALES (corp-wide): 117.3MM **Privately Held**
SIC: 3672 Printed circuit boards
PA: I3 Electronics, Inc.
100 Eldredge St
Binghamton NY 13901
607 238-7077

(G-4597)
JARETS STUFFED CUPCAKES
116 Oak Hill Ave (13760-2810)
PHONE.................607 658-9096
EMP: 8 **EST:** 2015
SALES (est): 406.6K **Privately Held**
SIC: 2051 Bread, cake & related products

(G-4598)
JAX SIGNS AND NEON INC
108 Odell Ave (13760)
PHONE.................607 727-3420
James E Taber, *Ch of Bd*
EMP: 7
SALES (est): 831.4K **Privately Held**
SIC: 3993 Electric signs

(G-4599)
JD TOOL INC
205 Harrison Ave (13760-5119)
PHONE.................607 786-3129
Jeffrey Dibble, *President*
Mandy Esposito, *Office Mgr*
EMP: 3
SALES: 1.8MM **Privately Held**
WEB: www.jdtool.net
SIC: 3545 Tools & accessories for machine tools

(G-4600)
JIM ROMAS BAKERY INC
202 N Nanticoke Ave (13760-4135)
PHONE.................607 748-7425
James Roma, *President*
Carl Roma, *Vice Pres*
EMP: 30
SQ FT: 5,200
SALES: 800K **Privately Held**
SIC: 2051 5411 Bakery: wholesale or wholesale/retail combined; delicatessens

(G-4601)
MEDSIM-EAGLE SIMULATION INC
811 North St (13760-5127)
PHONE.................607 658-9354
Nimrod Goor, *President*
Christopher Paulsen, *Vice Pres*
EMP: 12
SALES (est): 692.5K **Privately Held**
WEB: www.medsim.com
SIC: 3571 3577 7373 Electronic computers; graphic displays, except graphic terminals; systems integration services
HQ: Medsim Inc
741 Curlew Rd
Delray Beach FL 33444

(G-4602)
MICROCHIP TECHNOLOGY INC
3301 Country Club Rd (13760-3401)
PHONE.................607 785-5992
EMP: 166
SALES (corp-wide): 3.9B **Publicly Held**
SIC: 3674 Semiconductors & related devices
PA: Microchip Technology Inc
2355 W Chandler Blvd
Chandler AZ 85224
480 792-7200

(G-4603)
NANOMAS TECHNOLOGIES INC
1093 Clark St (13760-2815)
PHONE.................607 821-4208
John J Hannafin, *President*
Tom Xu, *Vice Pres*
Zhihao Yang, *Vice Pres*
EMP: 10
SQ FT: 300
SALES (est): 115.5K **Privately Held**
SIC: 3674 Semiconductor circuit networks

(G-4604)
NEW VISION INDUSTRIES INC
1239 Campville Rd (13760-4424)
P.O. Box 570, Apalachin (13732-0570)
PHONE.................607 687-7700
Michael R Copt, *President*
Betsy Copt, *Vice Pres*
EMP: 18
SQ FT: 4,100
SALES (est): 5.5MM **Privately Held**
WEB: www.newvisionindustries.com
SIC: 3569 3441 Assembly machines, nonmetalworking; fabricated structural metal

(G-4605)
NORTH POINT TECHNOLOGY LLC
816 Buffalo St (13760-1780)
PHONE.................866 885-3377
Robert P Lee,
EMP: 10
SALES (est): 726K **Privately Held**
WEB: www.northpointusa.com
SIC: 3625 Relays & industrial controls

(G-4606)
PALMER INDUSTRIES INC
2320 Lewis St (13760-6157)
PHONE.................607 754-8741
Jeck Palmer Jr, *Manager*
EMP: 7
SALES (corp-wide): 2.2MM **Privately Held**
WEB: www.palmerind.com
SIC: 3842 3534 Wheelchairs; elevators & moving stairways
PA: Palmer Industries Inc
509 Paden St
Endicott NY 13760
607 754-2957

(G-4607)
PALMER INDUSTRIES INC (PA)
509 Paden St (13760-4631)
P.O. Box 5707 (13763-5707)
PHONE.................607 754-2957
Jack Palmer Sr, *President*
Jack Palmer Jr, *General Mgr*
▲ **EMP:** 20
SALES (est): 2.2MM **Privately Held**
WEB: www.palmerind.com
SIC: 3842 Wheelchairs

(G-4608)
PHOTONIX TECHNOLOGIES INC
48 Washington Ave (13760-5305)
PHONE.................607 786-4600
John Urban, *President*
Sam Cucci, *Vice Pres*
EMP: 12
SQ FT: 2,500
SALES: 1,000K **Privately Held**
WEB: www.photonixtechnologies.com
SIC: 3825 Test equipment for electronic & electric measurement

(G-4609)
SAM A LUPO & SONS INC (PA)
1219 Campville Rd (13760-4411)
P.O. Box 5721 (13763-5721)
PHONE.................800 388-5352
Sam A Lupo Jr, *President*
Stephen J Lupo, *Vice Pres*
EMP: 3
SALES (est): 9.7MM **Privately Held**
WEB: www.spiedies.com
SIC: 2011 5411 Meat by-products from meat slaughtered on site; delicatessens

(G-4610)
SMARTYS CORNER
501 W Main St (13760-4621)
PHONE.................607 239-5276
Laura Cla, *Principal*
EMP: 6 **EST:** 2008
SALES (est): 435.9K **Privately Held**
SIC: 2024 Ice cream, bulk

(G-4611)
TIOGA TOOL INC (PA)
160 Glendale Dr (13760-3704)
PHONE.................607 785-6005
Jeff Rudler, *President*
Tracy Smith, *Office Mgr*
EMP: 12 **EST:** 1965
SQ FT: 5,500
SALES (est): 1.7MM **Privately Held**
WEB: www.tiogatool.com
SIC: 3599 1799 Machine & other job shop work; welding on site

(G-4612)
TNTPAVING
1077 Taft Ave (13760-7201)
PHONE.................607 372-4911
Dale Thomas, *Owner*
EMP: 5
SALES (est): 204.9K **Privately Held**
SIC: 2952 Asphalt felts & coatings

(G-4613)
TRUEBITE INC
129 Squires Ave (13760-2936)
PHONE.................607 786-3184
Ed Calafut, *President*
▲ **EMP:** 12
SALES (est): 825K **Privately Held**
WEB: www.fotofiles.com
SIC: 3545 Drills (machine tool accessories)

Endicott - Broome County (G-4614)

(G-4614)
VESTAL ELECTRONIC DEVICES LLC
635 Dickson St (13760-4527)
PHONE..............................607 773-8461
Walter H Kintner Jr, Mng Member
▲ EMP: 17
SQ FT: 110,000
SALES: 3.4MM Privately Held
WEB: www.vestalelectronics.com
SIC: 3679 3356 Electronic circuits; tin & tin alloy bars, pipe, sheets, etc.

(G-4615)
WEDDING GOWN PRESERVATION CO
707 North St (13760-5011)
PHONE..............................607 748-7999
Michael Schapiro, Owner
Susan Schapiro, Vice Pres
Kelly Crapser, Representative
EMP: 60
SALES (est): 7.3MM Privately Held
WEB: www.gownpreservation.com
SIC: 2842 Drycleaning preparations

Endwell
Broome County

(G-4616)
EMPIRE PLASTICS INC
2011 E Main St (13760-5622)
PHONE..............................607 754-9132
John Witinski Sr, President
John Witinski Jr, Vice Pres
EMP: 33 EST: 1958
SQ FT: 11,000
SALES (est): 5.4MM Privately Held
SIC: 3599 3699 2821 Machine shop, jobbing & repair; laser welding, drilling & cutting equipment; thermosetting materials; acrylic resins; nylon resins; polytetrafluoroethylene resins (teflon)

(G-4617)
J T SYSTEMATIC
Also Called: Just In Time Company
39 Valley St (13760-3659)
PHONE..............................607 754-0929
Roger Carr, Owner
EMP: 5
SQ FT: 6,000
SALES: 350K Privately Held
SIC: 3089 3999 3544 3599 Injection molded finished plastic products; models, general, except toy; industrial molds; machine shop, jobbing & repair

(G-4618)
LIGHTSPIN TECHNOLOGIES INC
616 Lowell Dr (13760-2525)
PHONE..............................301 656-7600
Jared Bowling, President
Richard Clayton, Chairman
EMP: 6
SALES: 1MM Privately Held
WEB: www.polychip.com
SIC: 3674 Semiconductors & related devices

(G-4619)
PROGRESSIVE TOOL COMPANY INC
3221 Lawndale St (13760-3593)
PHONE..............................607 748-8294
Gordon E Markoff, CEO
Ronald G Markoff, President
Sandra J Roloson, Corp Secy
Lorraine Markoff, Vice Pres
EMP: 35 EST: 1956
SQ FT: 15,900
SALES (est): 5MM Privately Held
SIC: 3599 Machine shop, jobbing & repair

(G-4620)
PTC PRECISION LLC
3221 Lawndale St (13760-3523)
PHONE..............................607 748-8294
Wayne Keller, CFO
EMP: 21 EST: 2017
SQ FT: 30,000
SALES: 5MM
SALES (corp-wide): 43.3MM Privately Held
SIC: 3545 Precision tools, machinists'
PA: Bam Enterprises, Inc.
2937 Alt Blvd
Grand Island NY 14072
716 773-7634

Erieville
Madison County

(G-4621)
MADISON MFG & MCH INC
3882 Sanderson Rd (13061-4166)
PHONE..............................315 922-4476
Mark Russitano, Principal
EMP: 8 EST: 2017
SALES (est): 235K Privately Held
SIC: 3999 Manufacturing industries

Esperance
Montgomery County

(G-4622)
US SANDER LLC
4131 Rte 20 (12066)
PHONE..............................518 875-9157
Gary Rudolph, Mng Member
David Rudolph,
Peggy Rudolph,
EMP: 9
SQ FT: 10,000
SALES (est): 1.9MM Privately Held
WEB: www.ussander.com
SIC: 3553 Sanding machines, except portable floor sanders: woodworking

Etna
Tompkins County

(G-4623)
W F SAUNDERS & SONS INC
Also Called: Saunders Concrete
30 Pinckney Rd (13062)
PHONE..............................607 257-6930
Bob Saunders, Owner
EMP: 9
SALES (est): 879.6K
SALES (corp-wide): 7.7MM Privately Held
SIC: 3273 Ready-mixed concrete
PA: W F Saunders & Sons Inc
5126 S Onondaga Rd
Nedrow NY 13120
315 469-3217

Fabius
Onondaga County

(G-4624)
VILLAGE WROUGHT IRON INC
7756 Main St (13063-9749)
PHONE..............................315 683-5589
Gary Host, President
Adam Host, Vice Pres
EMP: 12
SQ FT: 15,000
SALES (est): 1.9MM Privately Held
SIC: 3446 Architectural metalwork

Fairport
Monroe County

(G-4625)
BERNARD HALL
Also Called: Minuteman Press
10 Perinton Hills Mall (14450-3621)
PHONE..............................585 425-3340
Bernard Hall, Owner
EMP: 5
SALES (est): 498.5K Privately Held
SIC: 2752 2791 2789 Commercial printing, offset; typesetting; bookbinding & related work

(G-4626)
BREED ENTERPRISES INC
34 Water St (14450-1549)
PHONE..............................585 388-0126
Ronald Reding, President
Bruce Caruana, Vice Pres
EMP: 5
SALES (est): 1.1MM Privately Held
WEB: www.bullittmansparts.com
SIC: 3599 Machine shop, jobbing & repair

(G-4627)
CASA LARGA VINEYARDS (PA)
27 Emerald Hill Cir (14450-9504)
P.O. Box 400 (14450-0400)
PHONE..............................585 223-4210
Ann Colaruotolo, President
Andrew Colaruotolo, President
John Colaruotolo, Vice Pres
EMP: 30
SALES (est): 3.2MM Privately Held
WEB: www.casalarga.com
SIC: 2084 5921 7299 Wines; wine; banquet hall facilities

(G-4628)
CASA LARGA VINEYARDS
2287 Turk Hill Rd (14450-9579)
P.O. Box 400 (14450-0400)
PHONE..............................585 223-4210
Ann Colaruottolo, Manager
EMP: 7
SALES (corp-wide): 3.2MM Privately Held
WEB: www.casalarga.com
SIC: 2084 Wines
PA: Casa Larga Vineyards
27 Emerald Hill Cir
Fairport NY 14450
585 223-4210

(G-4629)
CORNING TROPEL CORPORATION
60 Oconnor Rd (14450-1328)
PHONE..............................585 377-3200
Curt Weinstein, Ch of Bd
John Burning, President
Paul Dewa, General Mgr
Sean Buono, Project Mgr
Mark Stauffer, Opers Spvr
EMP: 195
SQ FT: 100,000
SALES (est): 28.6MM
SALES (corp-wide): 10.1B Publicly Held
WEB: www.tropel.com
SIC: 3841 3827 3229 Ophthalmic instruments & apparatus; optical instruments & lenses; pressed & blown glass
PA: Corning Incorporated
1 Riverfront Plz
Corning NY 14831
607 974-9000

(G-4630)
D BAG LADY INC
183 Perinton Pkwy (14450-9104)
PHONE..............................585 425-8095
Debra Perry, President
EMP: 8
SQ FT: 8,500
SALES (est): 1.1MM Privately Held
WEB: www.dbaglady.com
SIC: 2673 Bags: plastic, laminated & coated

(G-4631)
DAVIS INTERNATIONAL INC
388 Mason Rd (14450-9561)
PHONE..............................585 421-8175
Timothy M McGraw, President
James R Davis, Principal
Timothy McGraw, Marketing Staff
EMP: 7
SQ FT: 5,000
SALES (est): 770K Privately Held
WEB: www.davisinternational.net
SIC: 3555 5084 Printing trades machinery; printing trades machinery, equipment & supplies

(G-4632)
DUNDEE FOODS LLC (PA)
Also Called: Dundeespirits
815 Whitney Rd W (14450-1030)
PHONE..............................585 377-7700
Giovanni Lidestri, CEO
Chris Knapp, Manager
Ed Brillante, Planning
James Manning, Maintence Staff
▲ EMP: 19
SALES (est): 2.9MM Privately Held
SIC: 2099 Food preparations

(G-4633)
FITSMO LLC
108 Packetts Gln (14450-2150)
PHONE..............................585 519-1956
Anthony Messana, Mng Member
EMP: 6
SALES (est): 327.6K Privately Held
SIC: 3949 7389 Sporting & athletic goods;

(G-4634)
HANDONE STUDIOS INC
388 Mason Rd (14450-9561)
PHONE..............................585 421-8175
Jim Davis, President
Anatol Topolewski, Purch Mgr
EMP: 9
SQ FT: 6,000
SALES: 300K Privately Held
SIC: 2759 Screen printing

(G-4635)
IRON SMOKE WHISKEY LLC
111 Parce Ave Ste 5 (14450-1467)
PHONE..............................585 388-7584
Thomas J Brunett, President
EMP: 6 EST: 2015
SALES (est): 566.5K Privately Held
SIC: 2085 Bourbon whiskey

(G-4636)
J & N COMPUTER SERVICES INC
1387 Fairport Rd Ste 900j (14450-2087)
PHONE..............................585 388-8780
Nancy E Jacobsen, Ch of Bd
Jerry Jacobsen, General Mgr
Jonathon Hull, Opers Mgr
Michelle Sexstone, Director
EMP: 11
SQ FT: 3,000
SALES (est): 4.1MM Privately Held
SIC: 3571 5734 Electronic computers; computer & software stores

(G-4637)
JASCO HEAT TREATING INC
75 Macedon Center Rd (14450-9763)
P.O. Box 60620, Rochester (14606-0620)
PHONE..............................585 388-0071
Eugine W Baldino, CEO
Kenneth Marvald, Admin Sec
EMP: 23
SQ FT: 50,000
SALES (est): 5.8MM Privately Held
WEB: www.jascotools.com
SIC: 3398 Metal heat treating

(G-4638)
LAHR RECYCLING & RESINS INC
Also Called: Lahr Plastics
164 Daley Rd (14450-9524)
PHONE..............................585 425-8608
Craig A Lahr, President
EMP: 15
SQ FT: 20,000
SALES (est): 1.8MM Privately Held
SIC: 3087 Custom compound purchased resins

(G-4639)
LIDESTRI FOODS INC (PA)
Also Called: Lidestri Food and Drink
815 Whitney Rd W (14450-1030)
PHONE..............................585 377-7700
John Lidestri, CEO
Phil Viruso, General Mgr
Joe Ferrigno, Principal
Robert Schiefer, Principal
Tony Bash, Vice Pres
◆ EMP: 400 EST: 1974
SQ FT: 260,000

▲ = Import ▼ = Export
◆ = Import/Export

SALES (est): 247.9MM Privately Held
WEB: www.francescorinaldi.com
SIC: 3221 2033 Bottles for packing, bottling & canning: glass; canned fruits & specialties; spaghetti & other pasta sauce: packaged in cans, jars, etc.

(G-4640)
LMG NATIONAL PUBLISHING INC (HQ)
350 Willowbrook Office Pa (14450-4222)
P.O. Box 580, Middletown (10940-0580)
PHONE..................585 598-6874
Leslie Hinton, *Ch of Bd*
EMP: 26
SALES (est): 14MM
SALES (corp-wide): 1.3B Publicly Held
SIC: 2711 2752 Newspapers; commercial printing, lithographic
PA: New Media Investment Group Inc.
   1345 Avenue Of The Americ
   New York NY 10105
   212 479-3160

(G-4641)
MASTERCRAFT DECORATORS INC
Also Called: Caldwell Cor
320 Macedon Center Rd (14450-9759)
PHONE..................585 223-5150
James Yonosko, *President*
◆ EMP: 40
SQ FT: 6,000
SALES (est): 5.5MM Privately Held
WEB: www.guildlines.com
SIC: 2759 Screen printing
PA: Zenan Custom Cresting Inc
   430 Flint Rd
   North York ON M3J 2
   416 736-6652

(G-4642)
MICROGEN SYSTEMS INC
3 Railroad St Ste D (14450-1563)
PHONE..................585 214-2426
Robert Andosca, *CEO*
Michael Perrotta, *Officer*
EMP: 8
SQ FT: 3,000
SALES (est): 758.7K Privately Held
SIC: 3676 Electronic resistors

(G-4643)
MOSER BAER TECHNOLOGIES INC
6 Camborne Cir (14450-8963)
PHONE..................585 749-0480
Gopalan Rajeswaran, *CEO*
EMP: 12
SQ FT: 12,000
SALES (est): 177.4K Privately Held
SIC: 3674 Semiconductors & related devices
PA: Moser Baer India Limited
   No-43/A B, Phase-3
   New Delhi DL 11002

(G-4644)
MURPHY MANUFACTURING CO INC
38 West Ave (14450-2159)
P.O. Box 119 (14450-0119)
PHONE..................585 223-0100
Gordon D Murphy Sr, *President*
Donna Faust, *Database Admin*
▲ EMP: 5 EST: 1946
SQ FT: 6,500
SALES (est): 360K Privately Held
WEB: www.murphymanufacturing.com
SIC: 3451 3491 Screw machine products; industrial valves

(G-4645)
OMEGA TOOL MEASURING MCHS INC (PA)
101 Perinton Pkwy (14450-9104)
PHONE..................585 598-7800
Michael R Nuccitelli, *CEO*
Chris Nuccitelli, *President*
Mark Higgins, *Exec VP*
Ronald S Ricotta, *Vice Pres*
Tom Jenkins, *Purch Agent*
▲ EMP: 35
SQ FT: 100,000

SALES (est): 30MM Privately Held
WEB: www.parlec.com
SIC: 3541 3545 Numerically controlled metal cutting machine tools; machine tool accessories

(G-4646)
ORACLE AMERICA INC
Sun Microsystems
345 Woodcliff Dr Ste 1 (14450-4210)
PHONE..................585 317-4648
Kevin Regan, *Manager*
Jeff Barteld, *Director*
EMP: 55
SALES (corp-wide): 39.8B Publicly Held
SIC: 7372 Prepackaged software
HQ: Oracle America, Inc.
   500 Oracle Pkwy
   Redwood City CA 94065
   650 506-7000

(G-4647)
PARKER-HANNIFIN CORPORATION
Also Called: Chomerics Div
83 Estates Dr W (14450-8425)
PHONE..................585 425-7000
Patrick Malone, *CEO*
Brian Smith, *QC Mgr*
Duane Potter, *Manager*
EMP: 126
SALES (corp-wide): 12B Publicly Held
SIC: 3594 Fluid power pumps & motors
PA: Parker-Hannifin Corporation
   6035 Parkland Blvd
   Cleveland OH 44124
   216 896-3000

(G-4648)
PARLEC LLC
101 Perinton Pkwy Fl 1 (14450-9182)
PHONE..................585 425-4400
Joe Odea, *Mng Member*
EMP: 80 EST: 2017
SQ FT: 100,000
SALES (est): 2.3MM
SALES (corp-wide): 1.8B Privately Held
SIC: 3545 Machine tool accessories
HQ: Techniks, Llc
   9930 E 56th St
   Indianapolis IN 46236

(G-4649)
PENNSAUKEN PACKING COMPANY LLC
815 Whitney Rd W (14450-1030)
PHONE..................585 377-7700
Giovanni Lidestri, *CEO*
EMP: 7
SALES (est): 332.7K
SALES (corp-wide): 247.9MM Privately Held
SIC: 3221 Food containers, glass
PA: Lidestri Foods, Inc.
   815 Whitney Rd W
   Fairport NY 14450
   585 377-7700

(G-4650)
PERFORMANCE DESIGNED BY PETERS
Also Called: Poerformance Design
7 Duxbury Hts (14450-3331)
PHONE..................585 223-9062
Peter R Geib, *President*
Todd Geib, *Vice Pres*
EMP: 19
SALES (est): 5MM Privately Held
SIC: 3714 Motor vehicle parts & accessories

(G-4651)
PRINTER COMPONENTS INC (HQ)
100 Photikon Dr Ste 2 (14450-8430)
PHONE..................585 924-5190
Richard Dipasquale, *Vice Pres*
Rick Dipasquale, *Vice Pres*
◆ EMP: 9
SQ FT: 16,000

SALES (est): 1.6MM
SALES (corp-wide): 61MM Privately Held
WEB: www.pcivictor.com
SIC: 3861 5112 3955 5999 Printing equipment, photographic; laserjet supplies; print cartridges for laser & other computer printers; photocopy machines; printers, computer
PA: Floturn, Inc.
   4236 Thunderbird Ln
   West Chester OH 45014
   513 860-8040

(G-4652)
QIOPTIQ, INC.
78 Schuyler Baldwin Dr (14450-9100)
PHONE..................585 223-2370
▲ EMP: 45
SQ FT: 41,000
SALES (est): 4.1MM Privately Held
SIC: 3826 3827 Analytical optical instruments; optical instruments & lenses

(G-4653)
QUALITROL COMPANY LLC (HQ)
Also Called: Otiwti
1385 Fairport Rd (14450-1399)
PHONE..................586 643-3717
Ronald Meyer, *President*
John Piper, *President*
Jay Cunningham, *Vice Pres*
Brian English, *Vice Pres*
Gene Grace, *Vice Pres*
▲ EMP: 111
SQ FT: 50,000
SALES (est): 118.6MM
SALES (corp-wide): 6.6B Publicly Held
WEB: www.qualitrolcorp.com
SIC: 3829 Measuring & controlling devices
PA: Fortive Corporation
   6920 Seaway Blvd
   Everett WA 98203
   425 446-5000

(G-4654)
QUALTECH TOOL & MACHINE INC
1000 Turk Hill Rd Ste 292 (14450-8755)
P.O. Box 356 (14450-0356)
PHONE..................585 223-9227
Anita Palmer, *President*
Richard T Palmer III, *Vice Pres*
EMP: 10 EST: 1979
SQ FT: 10,500
SALES (est): 1.4MM Privately Held
SIC: 3599 Machine shop, jobbing & repair

(G-4655)
R STEINER TECHNOLOGIES INC
180 Perinton Pkwy (14450-9107)
PHONE..................585 425-5912
Rudolph Steiner, *CEO*
Andy Nolan, *President*
EMP: 20
SQ FT: 12,000
SALES (est): 1.5MM Privately Held
WEB: www.steinertechnologies.com
SIC: 3541 Machine tools, metal cutting type

(G-4656)
SCAIFE ENTERPRISES INC
Also Called: Petrillo's Bakery
4 Chillon Ct (14450-4642)
PHONE..................585 454-5231
Richard W Scaife, *President*
Richard Scaife, *President*
EMP: 18
SALES (est): 2MM Privately Held
SIC: 2051 Mfg Bread/Related Products

(G-4657)
SENDEC CORP
Sendec Corp Product Division
151 Perinton Pkwy (14450-9104)
PHONE..................585 425-5965
David Sestito, *General Mgr*
EMP: 22
SALES (corp-wide): 333.6MM Privately Held
WEB: www.sendec.com
SIC: 3679 Microwave components

HQ: Sendec Corp.
   345 Pomroys Dr
   Windber PA 15963
   585 425-3390

(G-4658)
SENECA TEC INC
73 Country Corner Ln (14450-3034)
PHONE..................585 381-2645
John Kidd, *President*
James Kidd, *Vice Pres*
Art Trimble, *Vice Pres*
EMP: 9 EST: 1967
SQ FT: 1,500
SALES (est): 765.7K Privately Held
WEB: www.senecatec.com
SIC: 3861 3841 Photographic processing equipment & chemicals; surgical & medical instruments

(G-4659)
SIEMENS PRODUCT LIFE MGMT SFTW
345 Woodcliff Dr (14450-4210)
PHONE..................585 389-8699
EMP: 34
SALES (corp-wide): 97.7B Privately Held
SIC: 7372 Business oriented computer software
HQ: Siemens Product Lifecycle Management Software Inc.
   5800 Granite Pkwy Ste 600
   Plano TX 75024
   972 987-3000

(G-4660)
STEINER TECHNOLOGIES INC
180 Perinton Pkwy (14450-9107)
PHONE..................585 425-5910
Andrew Nolan, *President*
Mike Fagan, *Engineer*
EMP: 19 EST: 2008
SALES (est): 3.9MM Privately Held
SIC: 3545 Cutting tools for machine tools

(G-4661)
STREAMLINE PRECISION INC
205 Turk Hill Park (14450-8728)
PHONE..................585 421-9050
Kelly Palladino, *President*
Robert Levitsky, *Vice Pres*
Tom Gore, *Engineer*
EMP: 8
SQ FT: 1,000
SALES (est): 926.4K Privately Held
SIC: 3545 Precision tools, machinists'

(G-4662)
STREAMLINE PRECISION INC
Also Called: Steamline Machine
1000 Turk Hill Rd Ste 205 (14450-8755)
PHONE..................585 421-9050
Robert Levitsky, *President*
EMP: 6
SALES (est): 650K Privately Held
SIC: 3545 Precision tools, machinists'

(G-4663)
SUHOR INDUSTRIES INC (PA)
Also Called: Si Funeral Services
72 Oconnor Rd (14450-1328)
PHONE..................585 377-5100
Joe Suhor, *President*
Ken Moore, *Vice Pres*
▲ EMP: 14
SQ FT: 4,250
SALES (est): 2.2MM Privately Held
WEB: www.wilbertservices.com
SIC: 3272 Burial vaults, concrete or precast terrazzo

(G-4664)
THALES LASER SA
78 Schuyler Baldwin Dr (14450-9100)
PHONE..................585 223-2370
Ariane Andreani, *General Mgr*
EMP: 65
SALES (est): 3.4MM Privately Held
SIC: 3674 Semiconductors & related devices

(G-4665)
VIDEK INC
1387 Fairport Rd 1000c (14450-2004)
PHONE..................585 377-0377
Thomas Slechta, *President*

Moreen Jorjensen, *Controller*
EMP: 25
SQ FT: 14,861
SALES (est): 5.5MM **Privately Held**
WEB: www.videk.com/
SIC: 3827 3829 Optical test & inspection equipment; measuring & controlling devices

(G-4666)
VOLT TEK INC
111 Parce Ave (14450-1467)
PHONE..........................585 377-2050
Fax: 585 377-2654
▲ **EMP:** 15
SALES (est): 1.4MM **Privately Held**
SIC: 3644 Mfg Nonconductive Wiring Devices

(G-4667)
WORKPLACE INTERIORS LLC
400 Packetts Lndg (14450-1576)
PHONE..........................585 425-7420
Chad Mucha, *Project Mgr*
Scott Maccaull, *Mng Member*
Chuck Gannon, *Master*
EMP: 20 **EST:** 2015
SQ FT: 16,000
SALES: 12.2MM **Privately Held**
SIC: 2522 5021 Office furniture, except wood; office furniture

(G-4668)
XACTIV INC
Also Called: Torrey Pines Research
71 Perinton Pkwy (14450-9104)
PHONE..........................585 288-7220
Peter Mason, *President*
Chuck Synborski, *Exec VP*
Ernest Thompson, *Opers Staff*
Jim Mason, *Chief Engr*
David Jackson, *Technician*
EMP: 19
SQ FT: 21,000
SALES (est): 4.4MM **Privately Held**
SIC: 3624 3721 8731 8711 Carbon & graphite products; research & development on aircraft by the manufacturer; commercial physical research; engineering services; scientific consulting

Falconer
Chautauqua County

(G-4669)
AJ GENCO MCH SP MCHY RDOUT SVC
Also Called: A J Gnco Mch Shp/Mchnery Rdout
235 Carter St (14733-1409)
PHONE..........................716 664-4925
Anthony J Genco, *President*
EMP: 10
SQ FT: 23,940
SALES: 610K **Privately Held**
SIC: 3599 7692 3444 Machine shop, jobbing & repair; welding repair; sheet metalwork

(G-4670)
ALLIED INSPECTION SERVICES LLC
4 Carter St (14733-1406)
PHONE..........................716 489-3199
Scott M Lynn, *Director*
EMP: 13
SALES (est): 2MM **Privately Held**
SIC: 3569 Sprinkler systems, fire: automatic

(G-4671)
ARCONIC INC
Also Called: Alcoa
2632 S Work St Ste 24 (14733-1705)
PHONE..........................716 358-6451
EMP: 8
SALES (corp-wide): 12.9B **Publicly Held**
SIC: 3542 Mfg Machine Tools-Forming
PA: Arconic Inc.
390 Park Ave Fl 12
New York NY 10022
212 836-2758

(G-4672)
BARTON TOOL INC
1864 Lyndon Blvd (14733-1735)
P.O. Box 17 (14733-0017)
PHONE..........................716 665-2801
Jo Anne Barton, *President*
John Barton, *Vice Pres*
EMP: 7
SQ FT: 20,000
SALES (est): 1.1MM **Privately Held**
WEB: www.bartontool.com
SIC: 3089 3599 Injection molding of plastics; machine shop, jobbing & repair

(G-4673)
CHAUTAUQUA SIGN CO INC
2164 Allen Street Ext (14733-1703)
PHONE..........................716 665-2222
Gregory J Winter, *President*
EMP: 8
SALES (est): 805.1K **Privately Held**
WEB: www.chautauquasportshalloffame.org
SIC: 3993 Signs & advertising specialties

(G-4674)
CPI OF FALCONER INC
1890 Lyndon Blvd (14733-1731)
PHONE..........................716 664-4444
EMP: 22
SQ FT: 20,000
SALES (est): 266.7K **Privately Held**
SIC: 3089 3965 Mfg Plastic Products Mfg Fasteners/Buttons/Pins

(G-4675)
ELLISON BRONZE INC
125 W Main St (14733-1698)
PHONE..........................716 665-6522
Peter Stark, *Ch of Bd*
Mark Graves, *President*
Billy Emerson, *Vice Pres*
Roger Overend, *Vice Pres*
James Chau, *Purch Mgr*
◆ **EMP:** 59 **EST:** 1913
SQ FT: 65,000
SALES (est): 12.1MM **Privately Held**
WEB: www.ellisonbronze.com
SIC: 3442 Metal doors

(G-4676)
EMC TECH INC
1984 Allen Street Ext (14733-1717)
PHONE..........................716 488-9071
Eric Corey, *Vice Pres*
EMP: 13
SALES (est): 1.4MM **Privately Held**
SIC: 3552 3585 Dyeing, drying & finishing machinery & equipment; air conditioning equipment, complete

(G-4677)
FALCON CHAIR AND TABLE INC
121 S Work St (14733-1433)
P.O. Box 8 (14733-0008)
PHONE..........................716 664-7136
Peter Scheira, *President*
Gary Henry, *Vice Pres*
Joan Erickson, *Admin Sec*
EMP: 49
SQ FT: 23,000
SALES (est): 4.7MM **Privately Held**
SIC: 2511 Mfg Wood Household Furniture

(G-4678)
FALCONER ELECTRONICS INC (PA)
421 W Everett St (14733-1647)
PHONE..........................716 665-4176
Roger E Hall, *President*
Janine Hall, *Vice Pres*
EMP: 61
SQ FT: 20,000
SALES (est): 10.8MM **Privately Held**
WEB: www.falconer-electronics.com
SIC: 3672 5065 Printed circuit boards; electronic parts

(G-4679)
HANSON AGGREGATES EAST LLC
4419 S 9 Mile Rd (14733)
PHONE..........................716 372-1574
Mike Shumack, *Manager*
EMP: 17

SALES (corp-wide): 20.3B **Privately Held**
SIC: 3273 Ready-mixed concrete
HQ: Hanson Aggregates East Llc
3131 Rdu Center Dr
Morrisville NC 27560
919 380-2500

(G-4680)
HANSON SIGN SCREEN PRCESS CORP
Also Called: Hanson Sign Companies
82 Carter St (14733-1406)
PHONE..........................716 661-3900
Edward Sullivan, *CEO*
EMP: 34 **EST:** 1949
SQ FT: 25,000
SALES (est): 4.6MM **Privately Held**
WEB: www.hansonsign.com
SIC: 3993 Signs, not made in custom sign painting shops

(G-4681)
INSCAPE (NEW YORK) INC (HQ)
Also Called: Inscape Archtectural Interiors
221 Lister Ave 1 (14733-1459)
PHONE..........................716 665-6210
Rod Turgeon, *CEO*
Craig Dunlop, *Ch of Bd*
Nic Balderi, *Vice Pres*
Stephen Holland, *Purch Mgr*
Kent Smallwood, *CFO*
◆ **EMP:** 82
SALES (est): 20.7MM
SALES (corp-wide): 71.5MM **Privately Held**
SIC: 2542 3442 3441 3449 Partitions for floor attachment, prefabricated: except wood; metal doors; fabricated structural metal; custom roll formed products;
PA: Inscape Corporation
67 Toll Rd
Holland Landing ON L9N 1
905 836-7676

(G-4682)
INSCAPE INC
221 Lister Ave (14733-1459)
PHONE..........................716 665-6210
Aziz Hirji, *CFO*
EMP: 40
SQ FT: 130,000
SALES (est): 2MM **Privately Held**
SIC: 2522 2542 Office furniture, except wood; partitions & fixtures, except wood

(G-4683)
JAMES TOWN MACADAM INC
1946 New York Ave (14733-1739)
PHONE..........................716 665-4504
Jim Ells, *Principal*
EMP: 56
SQ FT: 2,000
SALES (est): 5.2MM **Privately Held**
SIC: 3273 Ready-mixed concrete

(G-4684)
JAMESTOWN CONTAINER CORP (PA)
14 Deming Dr (14733-1697)
P.O. Box 8, Jamestown (14702-0008)
PHONE..........................716 665-4623
Bruce Janowsky, *Ch of Bd*
Dick Weimer, *Corp Secy*
Joseph R Palmeri, *Vice Pres*
Jill Divincenzo, *Human Resources*
Bill Benedict, *Sales Mgr*
▼ **EMP:** 110
SQ FT: 100,000
SALES (est): 148.3MM **Privately Held**
WEB: www.jamestowncontainer.com
SIC: 2653 3086 Boxes, corrugated: made from purchased materials; packaging & shipping materials, foamed plastic

(G-4685)
JAMESTOWN IRON WORKS INC
2022 Allen Street Ext (14733-1793)
PHONE..........................716 665-2818
David W Maher, *President*
EMP: 16 **EST:** 1881
SQ FT: 3,600
SALES (est): 4.3MM **Privately Held**
SIC: 3321 3599 Ductile iron castings; machine shop, jobbing & repair

(G-4686)
LANDPRO EQUIPMENT LLC (PA)
1756 Lindquist Dr (14733-9710)
PHONE..........................716 665-3110
Tracy Buck, *President*
Ryan Payment, *Vice Pres*
Jonathon Lindstrom, *Sales Mgr*
EMP: 37
SALES: 13.6MM **Privately Held**
SIC: 3523 Farm machinery & equipment

(G-4687)
MONOFRAX LLC
1870 New York Ave (14733-1797)
PHONE..........................716 483-7200
Bill Andrews, *President*
Adam Gorczyca, *Purch Mgr*
Daryl Clendenen, *Marketing Mgr*
Amul Gupta, *Info Tech Mgr*
◆ **EMP:** 250
SQ FT: 300,000
SALES (est): 50.4MM
SALES (corp-wide): 940.5K **Privately Held**
WEB: www.monofrax.com
SIC: 3297 Nonclay refractories
PA: Callista Holdings Gmbh & Co. Kg
Steinstr. 48
Munchen 81667
892 314-1600

(G-4688)
RAND MACHINE PRODUCTS, INC.
2072 Allen Street Ext (14733-1709)
P.O. Box 72 (14733-0072)
PHONE..........................716 665-5217
EMP: 133 **EST:** 1964
SQ FT: 15,000
SALES (est): 27MM **Privately Held**
WEB: www.randmachine.com
SIC: 3544 3494 3743 3599 Special dies, tools, jigs & fixtures; special dies & tools; valves & pipe fittings; industrial locomotives & parts; custom machinery

(G-4689)
RAPID REMOVAL LLC
1599 Route 394 (14733-9716)
P.O. Box 498 (14733-0498)
PHONE..........................716 665-4663
Brian Hasson,
EMP: 10 **EST:** 2010
SALES (est): 563.7K **Privately Held**
SIC: 2851 Removers & cleaners

(G-4690)
REYNOLDS PACKAGING MCHY INC
Also Called: Csi
2632 S Work St Ste 24 (14733-1705)
PHONE..........................716 358-6451
Fax: 716 358-6459
EMP: 55 **Privately Held**
SIC: 3565 3643 3466 Mfg Packaging Machinery Mfg Conductive Wiring Devices Mfg Crowns/Closures
HQ: Reynolds Packaging Machinery Inc.
2632 S Work St Ste 24
Falconer NY 14733

(G-4691)
SKF USA INC
Also Called: SKF Aeroengine North America
1 Maroco St (14733-9705)
P.O. Box 263 (14733-0263)
PHONE..........................716 661-2869
Brandon Green, *Engineer*
Joseph Sienicki, *Engineer*
Wayne Wilson, *Engineer*
Steve Koehler, *Branch Mgr*
Arthur Daligny, *Manager*
EMP: 61
SALES (corp-wide): 9.2B **Privately Held**
WEB: www.skfusa.com
SIC: 3562 3769 Ball bearings & parts; guided missile & space vehicle parts & auxiliary equipment
HQ: Skf Usa Inc.
890 Forty Foot Rd
Lansdale PA 19446
267 436-6000

GEOGRAPHIC SECTION

Farmingdale - Nassau County (G-4718)

(G-4692)
SKF USA INC
Also Called: SKF Aeroengine North America
1 Maroco St (14733-9705)
PHONE.................................716 661-2600
Mark Ragen, *Senior Engr*
Cheryl Fox, *Sales Staff*
Steve Koehler, *Branch Mgr*
Pascal Wanderoild, *Manager*
EMP: 61
SALES (corp-wide): 9.2B **Privately Held**
WEB: www.skfusa.com
SIC: 3562 3769 Ball bearings & parts; guided missile & space vehicle parts & auxiliary equipment
HQ: Skf Usa Inc.
890 Forty Foot Rd
Lansdale PA 19446
267 436-6000

(G-4693)
STUART MOLD & MANUFACTURING
560 N Work St (14733-1115)
PHONE.................................716 488-9765
Randall Stuart, *President*
Charles Stuart, *Vice Pres*
EMP: 12
SQ FT: 10,000
SALES (est): 1.3MM **Privately Held**
WEB: www.stumold.com
SIC: 3089 Injection molding of plastics

(G-4694)
STUART TOOL & DIE INC
600 N Work St (14733-1117)
PHONE.................................716 488-1975
Ronald Rothleder, *President*
Patrick J Degnan, *Vice Pres*
George Watkins, *Engineer*
Corinne Beckstrom, *Bookkeeper*
Dawn Johnson, *Office Mgr*
EMP: 40
SQ FT: 10,000
SALES: 9MM **Privately Held**
WEB: www.stu-t-d.com
SIC: 3544 Industrial molds; special dies & tools; jigs & fixtures

(G-4695)
TRUCK-LITE CO LLC
310 E Elmwood Ave (14733-1421)
PHONE.................................716 665-2614
EMP: 20
SALES (corp-wide): 42.9B **Privately Held**
WEB: www.truck-lite.com
SIC: 3647 3648 Vehicular lighting equipment; lighting equipment
HQ: Truck-Lite Co., Llc
310 E Elmwood Ave
Falconer NY 14733

(G-4696)
TRUCK-LITE CO LLC (HQ)
Also Called: (FORMER NAME: TRUCK-LITE CO., INC.)
310 E Elmwood Ave (14733-1421)
P.O. Box 387, Jamestown (14702-0387)
PHONE.................................716 665-6214
Douglas Wolma, *President*
Brian Kupchella, *COO*
Robert Richard, *Vice Pres*
Robert Willing, *CFO*
David Crawford, *Sales Staff*
◆ **EMP:** 473
SALES (est): 313.7MM
SALES (corp-wide): 42.9B **Privately Held**
SIC: 3647 Vehicular lighting equipment
PA: Koch Industries, Inc.
4111 E 37th St N
Wichita KS 67220
316 828-5500

(G-4697)
TRUCK-LITE SUB INC
310 E Elmwood Ave (14733-1421)
PHONE.................................800 888-7095
George Baldwin, *Principal*
Jeff Caulfield, *Regional Mgr*
Charlie Gang, *Regional Mgr*
John Cecco, *Vice Pres*
Matt Rhinehart, *Engineer*
EMP: 7 EST: 2015
SALES (est): 152.4K **Privately Held**
SIC: 3799 Transportation equipment

Far Rockaway
Queens County

(G-4698)
BUSINESS ADVISORY SERVICES
Also Called: Universal Water Technology
1104 Bay 25th St (11691-1749)
PHONE.................................718 337-3740
Michael Walfish, *President*
David Weis, *Vice Pres*
EMP: 5
SALES: 750K **Privately Held**
SIC: 3589 Water treatment equipment, industrial

(G-4699)
EAZY LOCKS LLC
1914 Mott Ave (11691-4102)
PHONE.................................718 327-7770
Carl Roberts, *CEO*
EMP: 6
SQ FT: 1,700
SALES: 1.1MM **Privately Held**
SIC: 3429 Locks or lock sets

(G-4700)
EMPIRE PUBLISHING INC
Also Called: West End Journal
1525 Central Ave Ste 1 (11691-4020)
PHONE.................................516 829-4000
Jerome Lippman, *President*
EMP: 15
SQ FT: 2,000
SALES (est): 870.4K **Privately Held**
SIC: 2711 Newspapers: publishing only, not printed on site

(G-4701)
FAR ROCKAWAY DRUGS INC
Also Called: Ocean Park Drugs & Surgical
1727 Seagirt Blvd (11691-4513)
PHONE.................................718 471-2500
Russell Shvartsshteyn, *President*
Steven Blick, *Vice Pres*
EMP: 16
SQ FT: 4,000
SALES (est): 2.8MM **Privately Held**
WEB: www.mynucare.com
SIC: 3842 5912 Surgical appliances & supplies; drug stores & proprietary stores

(G-4702)
J P R PHARMACY INC
Also Called: Vista Pharmacy & Surgical
529 Beach 20th St (11691-3645)
PHONE.................................718 327-0600
Jeffrey Rosenberg, *President*
Russell Shvartsshteyn, *Vice Pres*
EMP: 11
SQ FT: 800
SALES: 4.6MM **Privately Held**
SIC: 3842 5912 Surgical appliances & supplies; drug stores & proprietary stores

(G-4703)
ROCKAWAY STAIRS LTD
1011 Bay 24th St (11691-1801)
PHONE.................................718 945-0047
Nollah Pastor, *President*
EMP: 5
SALES (est): 334.7K **Privately Held**
SIC: 2431 Stair railings, wood

Farmingdale
Nassau County

(G-4704)
A & J MACHINE & WELDING INC
6040 New Hwy (11735)
PHONE.................................631 845-7586
Ahalya Narine, *Manager*
EMP: 15 **Privately Held**
SIC: 7692 Welding repair
PA: A & J Machine & Welding Inc.
8776 130th St
Jamaica NY

(G-4705)
A R V PRECISION MFG INC
60 Baiting Place Rd Ste B (11735-6228)
PHONE.................................631 293-9643
Fred Freyre, *President*
EMP: 5
SQ FT: 2,000
SALES (est): 899.8K **Privately Held**
SIC: 3679 3599 3089 Electronic circuits; machine shop, jobbing & repair; injection molded finished plastic products

(G-4706)
AAA CATALYTIC RECYCLING INC
345 Eastern Pkwy (11735-2713)
PHONE.................................631 920-7944
Drew Vecchionem, *CEO*
▲ **EMP:** 10 EST: 2011
SALES: 10MM **Privately Held**
SIC: 3339 Platinum group metal refining (primary)

(G-4707)
ABBE LABORATORIES INC
1095 Broadhollow Rd Ste E (11735-4815)
PHONE.................................631 756-2223
Eleanor Posner, *President*
Robert Posner, *Corp Secy*
EMP: 10
SALES (est): 1.9MM **Privately Held**
WEB: www.abbelabs.com
SIC: 2844 5122 Face creams or lotions; cosmetics

(G-4708)
AFCO SYSTEMS INC
Also Called: Afco Modular Enclosure Systems
200 Finn Ct Ste 1 (11735-1119)
PHONE.................................631 249-9441
Michael Mallia, *CEO*
Gerard Becker, *President*
Lawrence Mallia, *Exec VP*
John Consoli, *CTO*
EMP: 102
SQ FT: 65,000
SALES: 25MM
SALES (corp-wide): 20.7MM **Privately Held**
WEB: www.afcosystems.com
SIC: 2522 3469 3444 Panel systems & partitions, office: except wood; metal stampings; sheet metalwork
HQ: Legrand North America, Llc
60 Woodlawn St
West Hartford CT 06110
860 233-6251

(G-4709)
AIRFLEX CORP
965 Conklin St (11735-2412)
PHONE.................................631 752-1219
Jonathan Fogelman, *President*
EMP: 89
SQ FT: 10,000
SALES (est): 17.7MM **Privately Held**
SIC: 3446 Architectural metalwork

(G-4710)
AIRFLEX INDUSTRIAL INC (PA)
965 Conklin St (11735-2412)
PHONE.................................631 752-1234
Jonathan Fogelman, *Ch of Bd*
EMP: 41
SQ FT: 10,000
SALES (est): 16.4MM **Privately Held**
WEB: www.airflexind.com
SIC: 3446 3822 3365 Louvers, ventilating; damper operators: pneumatic, thermostatic, electric; aluminum & aluminum-based alloy castings

(G-4711)
AIRFLEX INDUSTRIAL INC
937 Conklin St (11735-2412)
PHONE.................................631 752-1234
Jonathan Fogelman, *Branch Mgr*
EMP: 59
SALES (corp-wide): 16.4MM **Privately Held**
SIC: 3446 Louvers, ventilating
PA: Airflex Industrial, Inc.
965 Conklin St
Farmingdale NY 11735
631 752-1234

(G-4712)
ALA SCIENTIFIC INSTRUMENTS INC
60 Marine St Ste 1 (11735-5660)
PHONE.................................631 393-6401
Alan Kriegstein, *President*
Andrew Pomerantz, *Vice Pres*
Kim Forrest, *Administration*
EMP: 13
SQ FT: 6,000
SALES: 2.5MM **Privately Held**
WEB: www.alascience.com
SIC: 3841 5047 Surgical & medical instruments; medical equipment & supplies

(G-4713)
ALL AMERICAN FUNDING & REF LLC
345 Eastern Pkwy (11735-2713)
PHONE.................................516 978-7531
Andrew Vecchione, *Mng Member*
Frank Ponte,
Joe Ponte,
Frank Tuzzo,
EMP: 6
SQ FT: 17,000
SALES: 18MM **Privately Held**
SIC: 3339 5093 Precious metals; metal scrap & waste materials

(G-4714)
ALL COLOR OFFSET PRINTERS INC
Also Called: All Color Business Specialties
51 Henry St Ste A (11735)
PHONE.................................516 420-0649
William Bogue, *President*
Tim Dorman, *Vice Pres*
EMP: 5
SQ FT: 2,500
SALES (est): 912.2K **Privately Held**
SIC: 2752 Commercial printing, offset

(G-4715)
ALL STAR SHEET METAL INC
25 Rome St (11735-6601)
PHONE.................................718 456-1567
Christine Benazic, *CEO*
Enrik Benazic, *President*
EMP: 15
SQ FT: 5,200
SALES (est): 2.5MM **Privately Held**
SIC: 3444 Sheet metalwork

(G-4716)
ALLOY METAL WORKS INC
146 Verdi St (11735-6324)
PHONE.................................631 694-8163
Phillip Rajotte Jr, *President*
EMP: 5
SQ FT: 2,500
SALES: 250K **Privately Held**
SIC: 7692 Welding repair

(G-4717)
ALPHA MANUFACTURING CORP
152 Verdi St (11735-6324)
PHONE.................................631 249-3700
George Sparacio, *President*
EMP: 10
SQ FT: 6,000
SALES: 1MM **Privately Held**
SIC: 3599 Machine shop, jobbing & repair

(G-4718)
AMANA TOOL CORP
Also Called: Age Timberline Mamba
120 Carolyn Blvd (11735-1525)
PHONE.................................631 752-1300
Eitan Spiegel, *CEO*
Aaron Einstein, *Chairman*
John P McInerney, *Vice Pres*
Zygmunt L Milewski, *Vice Pres*
Natalie Einstein, *Treasurer*
◆ **EMP:** 52
SQ FT: 80,000
SALES (est): 10.5MM **Privately Held**
WEB: www.amanatool.com
SIC: 3425 Saw blades & handsaws

Farmingdale - Nassau County (G-4719)

(G-4719)
AMERICAN AEROSPACE CONTRLS INC
Also Called: A A C
570 Smith St (11735-1115)
PHONE..................631 694-5100
Ruth Gitlin, *CEO*
Susan Brosnan, *General Mgr*
Philip Koch, *Opers Staff*
Celeste Morrissey, *QC Mgr*
Piotr Pacholski, *Project Engr*
EMP: 47
SQ FT: 16,000
SALES: 10MM **Privately Held**
WEB: www.a-a-c.com
SIC: 3679 Transducers, electrical

(G-4720)
AMERICAN VISUALS INC
Also Called: American Visual Display
90 Gazza Blvd (11735-1402)
PHONE..................631 694-6104
Morris Charnow, *President*
EMP: 7
SQ FT: 8,200
SALES (est): 825.6K **Privately Held**
WEB: www.americanvisuals.com
SIC: 3993 3089 Displays & cutouts, window & lobby; plastic processing

(G-4721)
ANDREA SYSTEMS LLC
140 Finn Ct (11735-1107)
PHONE..................631 390-3140
Luis Rivera, *Electrical Engi*
Robert J Carton, *Sales Mgr*
Frank Randazzo, *Mng Member*
Robert Carton, *Manager*
Heather Hinkley, *Manager*
EMP: 23
SQ FT: 15,000
SALES: 5MM **Privately Held**
WEB: www.andreasystems.com
SIC: 3669 Intercommunication systems, electric

(G-4722)
ARBE MACHINERY INC
54 Allen Blvd (11735-5623)
PHONE..................631 756-2477
Artin Karakaya, *President*
Burc Karakaya, *Vice Pres*
◆ **EMP:** 10
SQ FT: 30,000
SALES (est): 2.3MM **Privately Held**
SIC: 3559 5084 3599 Jewelers' machines; industrial machinery & equipment; machine shop, jobbing & repair

(G-4723)
AUSCO INC
425 Smith St Ste 1 (11735-1124)
PHONE..................516 944-9882
Kenneth Bram, *Ch of Bd*
Jackie Gregus, *General Mgr*
Thai Tong, *Vice Pres*
Glenn Davis, *Mfg Mgr*
Cliff Lestrange, *QA Dir*
EMP: 100
SQ FT: 11,000
SALES (est): 25.1MM **Privately Held**
WEB: www.auscoinc.com
SIC: 3728 Aircraft assemblies, subassemblies & parts

(G-4724)
AUTEL US INC (HQ)
Also Called: Autel North America
175 Central Ave Ste 200 (11735-6917)
PHONE..................631 923-2620
Arthur Jacobsen, *CEO*
▲ **EMP:** 5 **EST:** 2011
SQ FT: 20,000
SALES (est): 1.8MM
SALES (corp-wide): 60.8MM **Privately Held**
SIC: 3694 Automotive electrical equipment
PA: Autel Intelligent Technology Corp., Ltd.
8th Floor, Building B1, Zhiyuan Xueyuan Road, Xili, Nanshan Shenzhen 51805
755 861-4777

(G-4725)
AVANTI FURNITURE CORP
497 Main St (11735-3579)
PHONE..................516 293-8220
Joan Bagnasco, *President*
Kevin Bagnasco, *Treasurer*
▲ **EMP:** 12
SQ FT: 10,000
SALES (est): 1.6MM **Privately Held**
SIC: 2512 Chairs: upholstered on wood frames

(G-4726)
BDR CREATIVE CONCEPTS INC
141 Central Ave Ste B (11735-6903)
PHONE..................516 942-7768
Ronald Cohen, *President*
Pearl Cohen, *Vice Pres*
Tiffany Unruh, *Manager*
Bruce Beckerman, *Shareholder*
Debra Beckerman, *Shareholder*
EMP: 14
SQ FT: 7,000
SALES (est): 1.4MM **Privately Held**
WEB: www.bdrcc.com
SIC: 2759 Poster & decal printing & engraving; posters, including billboards: printing

(G-4727)
BESCOR VIDEO ACCESSORIES LTD
244 Route 109 (11735-1503)
PHONE..................631 420-1717
Douglas Brandwin, *President*
▲ **EMP:** 16
SQ FT: 8,000
SALES (est): 3.1MM **Privately Held**
SIC: 3861 5065 5043 Cameras & related equipment; video equipment, electronic; photographic cameras, projectors, equipment & supplies

(G-4728)
BEVERAGE WORKS NJ INC
16 Dubon Ct (11735-1008)
PHONE..................631 293-3501
Michael Graciano, *District Mgr*
Ron Sievers, *District Mgr*
Christian Boehm, *Accounts Mgr*
Gary Sklar, *Accounts Mgr*
Christopher Malone, *Sales Staff*
EMP: 20 **Privately Held**
WEB: www.beverageworks.com
SIC: 2086 Bottled & canned soft drinks
PA: The Beverage Works Nj Inc
1800 State Route 34 # 203
Wall Township NJ 07719

(G-4729)
BST UNITED CORP
59 Central Ave Ste 19 (11735-6902)
PHONE..................631 777-2110
Khaled Shahriar, *President*
Sabina Khaleq, *Vice Pres*
Tony Pahm, *Vice Pres*
EMP: 12
SQ FT: 4,000
SALES: 250K **Privately Held**
SIC: 3089 Blow molded finished plastic products

(G-4730)
C & C BINDERY CO INC
Also Called: C&C Diecuts
25 Central Ave Unit B (11735-6920)
PHONE..................631 752-7078
Joe Spalone, *President*
EMP: 30
SQ FT: 11,000
SALES (est): 4.7MM **Privately Held**
SIC: 2789 Binding only: books, pamphlets, magazines, etc.

(G-4731)
C A M GRAPHICS CO INC
24 Central Dr (11735-1202)
PHONE..................631 842-3400
Emanuel Cardinale, *President*
Jorge Reyes, *Vice Pres*
Mike Demartino, *Manager*
Juneth Webson, *Manager*
Elizabeth Heiser, *Admin Sec*
EMP: 27
SQ FT: 20,000
SALES (est): 4.5MM **Privately Held**
WEB: www.camgraphics.com
SIC: 3672 3679 3643 3613 Printed circuit boards; electronic switches; current-carrying wiring devices; switchgear & switchboard apparatus

(G-4732)
CANDID LITHO PRINTING LTD (PA)
210 Route 109 (11735-1503)
PHONE..................212 431-3800
Howard Weinstein, *President*
Scott Weinstein, *Corp Secy*
Lewis Rosenberg, *Vice Pres*
Jhamar Brown, *Controller*
Mary Milazzo, *Human Resources*
EMP: 60 **EST:** 1964
SQ FT: 109,285
SALES (est): 17.5MM **Privately Held**
WEB: www.candidlitho.com
SIC: 2752 Commercial printing, offset

(G-4733)
CANDID WORLDWIDE LLC (HQ)
210 Route 109 (11735-1503)
PHONE..................212 799-5300
David Stadler, *CEO*
Howard Weinstein, *President*
EMP: 6
SALES (est): 6.7MM
SALES (corp-wide): 17.5MM **Privately Held**
SIC: 2759 Posters, including billboards: printing
PA: Candid Litho Printing Ltd.
210 Route 109
Farmingdale NY 11735
212 431-3800

(G-4734)
CHIM-CAP CORP
120 Schmitt Blvd (11735-1424)
PHONE..................800 262-9622
Fred Giumenta Jr, *President*
▲ **EMP:** 20
SQ FT: 40,000
SALES (est): 3.8MM **Privately Held**
WEB: www.chimcapcorp.com
SIC: 3272 Fireplace & chimney material: concrete; chimney caps, concrete

(G-4735)
CIGAR OASIS LLC
79 Heisser Ct (11735-3310)
PHONE..................516 520-5258
Albert P Foundos, *President*
Christine Beno, *Vice Pres*
Donna Oswald, *Vice Pres*
Philip Foundos, *Treasurer*
▲ **EMP:** 5
SQ FT: 2,000
SALES (est): 569.2K **Privately Held**
SIC: 3911 Cigar & cigarette accessories

(G-4736)
COCO ARCHITECTUREAL GRILLES
173 Allen Blvd (11735-5616)
PHONE..................631 482-9449
Jim Coco, *President*
EMP: 5
SALES (est): 675K **Privately Held**
SIC: 3441 Fabricated structural metal

(G-4737)
COLONIAL PRECISION MACHINERY
Also Called: Colonial Electric
134 Rome St (11735-6607)
PHONE..................631 249-0738
James Tormey, *President*
Scott Tormey, *Vice Pres*
EMP: 7
SQ FT: 15,000
SALES (est): 650K **Privately Held**
SIC: 3469 Machine parts, stamped or pressed metal

(G-4738)
COMMERCE SPRING CORP
143 Allen Blvd (11735-5616)
PHONE..................631 293-4844
Bruno Rotellini, *President*
EMP: 12
SQ FT: 10,000
SALES (est): 1.2MM **Privately Held**
WEB: www.commercespring.com
SIC: 3495 Wire springs

(G-4739)
COSMO ELECTRONIC MACHINE CORP
Also Called: D & L Electronic Die
113 Gazza Blvd (11735-1421)
PHONE..................631 249-2535
Kenneth Arutt, *President*
Bruce Mc Kee, *Vice Pres*
EMP: 50
SQ FT: 3,000
SALES (est): 5.2MM **Privately Held**
SIC: 3544 Special dies & tools

(G-4740)
COSMOS ELECTRONIC MACHINE CORP (PA)
140 Schmitt Blvd (11735-1461)
PHONE..................631 249-2535
Kenneth Arutt, *President*
Bruce McKee, *Vice Pres*
EMP: 43
SQ FT: 20,000
SALES (est): 8.6MM **Privately Held**
SIC: 3567 Industrial furnaces & ovens

(G-4741)
CRISRAY PRINTING CORP
50 Executive Blvd Ste A (11735-4712)
PHONE..................631 293-3770
Raymond J Marro, *President*
Angelo Berardi, *General Mgr*
Anthony Conti, *Vice Pres*
Chris Marro, *Vice Pres*
Patricia Marro, *Vice Pres*
EMP: 30 **EST:** 1971
SQ FT: 10,000
SALES (est): 5MM **Privately Held**
WEB: www.crisray.com
SIC: 2759 Labels & seals: printing

(G-4742)
CURTISS-WRIGHT CONTROLS
Also Called: Curtiss-Wrght Intgrted Sensing
175 Central Ave Ste 100 (11735-6917)
P.O. Box 7751, Philadelphia PA (19101-7751)
PHONE..................631 756-4740
Thomas P Quinly, *COO*
EMP: 14
SALES (corp-wide): 2.2B **Publicly Held**
SIC: 3674 Semiconductors & related devices
HQ: Curtiss-Wright Controls Integrated Sensing, Inc.
28965 Avenue Penn
Valencia CA 91355
626 851-3100

(G-4743)
CURTISS-WRIGHT FLOW CTRL CORP (HQ)
Also Called: Target Rock
1966 Broadhollow Rd Ste E (11735-1726)
PHONE..................631 293-3800
Martin Benante, *Ch of Bd*
David Linton, *President*
Frederic Borah, *General Mgr*
David C Adams, *COO*
Joseph Callaghan, *Vice Pres*
◆ **EMP:** 236 **EST:** 1950
SQ FT: 100,000
SALES: 439.4MM
SALES (corp-wide): 2.2B **Publicly Held**
SIC: 3491 3494 Industrial valves; valves & pipe fittings
PA: Curtiss-Wright Corporation
130 Harbour Place Dr # 300
Davidson NC 28036
704 869-4600

(G-4744)
CURTISS-WRIGHT FLOW CTRL CORP
1966 Broadhollow Rd Ste E (11735-1726)
P.O. Box 379 (11735-0379)
PHONE..................631 293-3800
Steve Jung, *Branch Mgr*
EMP: 160
SALES (corp-wide): 2.2B **Publicly Held**
SIC: 3491 Industrial valves

▲ = Import ▼=Export
◆ =Import/Export

GEOGRAPHIC SECTION

HQ: Curtiss-Wright Flow Control Corporation
1966 Broadhollow Rd Ste E
Farmingdale NY 11735
631 293-3800

(G-4745)
CUSTOM DOOR & MIRROR INC
Also Called: Flex Supply
148 Milbar Blvd (11735-1425)
PHONE...................................631 414-7725
Angelo Sciubba, *Ch of Bd*
Philip Sciubba, *Vice Pres*
▲ **EMP:** 20 **EST:** 1996
SQ FT: 17,000
SALES: 3MM **Privately Held**
WEB: www.paniflex.com
SIC: 3089 2431 Doors, folding: plastic or plastic coated fabric; millwork

(G-4746)
CUSTOM SITECOM LLC
Also Called: Buckle Down
470 Smith St (11735-1105)
PHONE...................................631 420-4238
Eric Swope, *COO*
Jason Dorf,
▲ **EMP:** 11
SALES (est): 2MM **Privately Held**
SIC: 3714 Motor vehicle parts & accessories

(G-4747)
DADDARIO & COMPANY INC (PA)
595 Smith St (11735-1120)
P.O. Box 290 (11735-0290)
PHONE...................................631 439-3300
James D'Addario, *Ch of Bd*
Rick Drumm, *President*
John D'Addario III, *Exec VP*
John D'Addario Jr, *Vice Pres*
David Via, *Vice Pres*
◆ **EMP:** 700
SQ FT: 110,000
SALES: 193.1MM **Privately Held**
WEB: www.daddario.com
SIC: 3931 Guitars & parts, electric & non-electric; strings, musical instrument

(G-4748)
DAKOTA SYSTEMS MFG CORP
Also Called: Dakota Wall
1885 New Hwy Ste 2 (11735-1518)
PHONE...................................631 249-5811
Edward Owsinski, *President*
Jimmy Eowinski, *Bookkeeper*
EMP: 6
SQ FT: 3,000
SALES (est): 1.1MM **Privately Held**
SIC: 2542 3312 Partitions & fixtures, except wood; stainless steel

(G-4749)
DANBURY PHARMA LLC
220 Smith St (11735-1024)
PHONE...................................631 393-6333
BJ Harid,
▲ **EMP:** 33
SQ FT: 19,000
SALES (est): 8.2MM **Privately Held**
SIC: 2834 Vitamin preparations

(G-4750)
DESKTOP PUBLISHING CONCEPTS
Also Called: Toledo Graphics Group
855 Conklin St Ste T (11735-2409)
P.O. Box 34 (11735-0034)
PHONE...................................631 752-1934
Nicholas Sachs, *President*
EMP: 12
SQ FT: 2,500
SALES (est): 1.4MM **Privately Held**
WEB: www.toledogroup.com
SIC: 2791 7336 Typesetting; graphic arts & related design

(G-4751)
DIGICOM INTERNATIONAL INC
145 Rome St (11735-6610)
PHONE...................................631 249-8999
Chia I Chen, *CEO*
Jammy Chen, *Executive*
▲ **EMP:** 15
SQ FT: 20,000
SALES (est): 3MM **Privately Held**
SIC: 3571 5045 Electronic computers; computer peripheral equipment

(G-4752)
DIGITAL MATRIX CORP
34 Sarah Dr Ste B (11735-1218)
PHONE...................................516 481-7990
Alex Greenspan, *President*
Jan Berman, *Vice Pres*
Alexsandr Davelman, *Engineer*
Joel Berman, *Treasurer*
Lorraine Berman, *Shareholder*
EMP: 21
SQ FT: 20,000
SALES (est): 3.7MM **Privately Held**
WEB: www.galvanics.com
SIC: 3559 Electroplating machinery & equipment

(G-4753)
DUCON TECHNOLOGIES INC
19 Engineers Ln (11735-1207)
PHONE...................................631 420-4900
Aron Govil, *Branch Mgr*
EMP: 45
SALES (corp-wide): 479.4MM **Privately Held**
SIC: 3564 3537 Blowers & fans; industrial trucks & tractors
PA: Ducon Technologies Inc.
5 Penn Plz Ste 2403
New York NY 10001
631 694-1700

(G-4754)
E B INDUSTRIES LLC (PA)
90 Carolyn Blvd (11735-1525)
PHONE...................................631 293-8565
James Fox, *Engineer*
Dominic Rocco, *Engineer*
John Delalio, *Business Dir*
Steven M Delalio,
Devorah Lisnoff, *Admin Asst*
EMP: 25 **EST:** 1965
SQ FT: 16,000
SALES (est): 3.1MM **Privately Held**
WEB: www.ebindustries.com
SIC: 7692 Welding repair

(G-4755)
E B INDUSTRIES LLC
90 Carolyn Blvd (11735-1525)
PHONE...................................631 293-8565
Steven Delalio, *Mng Member*
EMP: 25
SALES (est): 411.8K
SALES (corp-wide): 3.1MM **Privately Held**
WEB: www.ebindustries.com
SIC: 7692 Welding repair
PA: E B Industries, Llc
90 Carolyn Blvd
Farmingdale NY 11735
631 293-8565

(G-4756)
EAST COAST CYCLE LLC
80 Smith St Ste 1 (11735-1011)
PHONE...................................631 780-5360
Jeffrey Bruno,
▲ **EMP:** 9
SQ FT: 2,500
SALES (est): 900K **Privately Held**
SIC: 3751 5091 Bicycles & related parts; bicycles

(G-4757)
EAST COAST ENVMTL GROUP INC
136 Allen Blvd (11735-5659)
PHONE...................................516 352-1946
Edwin Rincon, *President*
EMP: 5
SQ FT: 15,000
SALES: 1MM **Privately Held**
SIC: 3826 Differential thermal analysis instruments

(G-4758)
EDLAW PHARMACEUTICALS INC
195 Central Ave Ste B (11735-6904)
PHONE...................................631 454-6888
Scott Giroux, *General Mgr*
Bonnie Hilton Green, *Principal*
▼ **EMP:** 20
SQ FT: 6,500
SALES: 3.4MM **Privately Held**
SIC: 2834 Pharmaceutical preparations

(G-4759)
EEG ENTERPRISES INC
586 Main St (11735-3546)
PHONE...................................516 293-7472
Philip McLaughlin, *President*
Bill McLaughlin, *President*
William Jorden, *Vice Pres*
Frank Zovko, *Engineer*
Eric McErlain, *Sales Dir*
EMP: 12
SQ FT: 5,000
SALES (est): 2.1MM **Privately Held**
WEB: www.eegent.com
SIC: 3663 Cable television equipment; television antennas (transmitting) & ground equipment

(G-4760)
ENZO LIFE SCIENCES INC (HQ)
Also Called: Enzo Diagnostics
10 Executive Blvd (11735-4710)
PHONE...................................631 694-7070
Elazar Rabbani, *Ch of Bd*
Michael Garofalo, *General Mgr*
Barry W Weiner, *Exec VP*
Herbert Bass, *Vice Pres*
Michael Mullenix, *Vice Pres*
EMP: 30
SQ FT: 40,000
SALES (est): 12.1MM
SALES (corp-wide): 104.7MM **Publicly Held**
SIC: 2835 2834 5049 In vitro & in vivo diagnostic substances; pharmaceutical preparations; laboratory equipment, except medical or dental
PA: Enzo Biochem, Inc.
527 Madison Ave Rm 901
New York NY 10022
212 583-0100

(G-4761)
ENZO LIFE SCIENCES INTL INC
10 Executive Blvd (11735-4710)
PHONE...................................610 941-0430
Robert Zipkin, *President*
Ira Taffer, *Vice Pres*
◆ **EMP:** 28
SQ FT: 20,000
SALES (est): 2.9MM
SALES (corp-wide): 104.7MM **Publicly Held**
WEB: www.biomol.com
SIC: 2834 Pharmaceutical preparations
HQ: Enzo Life Sciences, Inc.
10 Executive Blvd
Farmingdale NY 11735

(G-4762)
EVANS MANUFACTURING LLC
595 Smith St (11735-1116)
P.O. Box 290 (11735-0290)
PHONE...................................631 439-3300
James D'Addario,
John D'Addario Jr,
Robert Dodaro,
Michael Russo,
Domenick Scarfogliero,
▲ **EMP:** 75 **EST:** 1995
SQ FT: 110,000
SALES (est): 6MM **Privately Held**
WEB: www.dadario.com
SIC: 3931 Heads, drum

(G-4763)
FARMINGDALE IRON WORKS INC
105 Florida St (11735-6305)
PHONE...................................631 249-5995
John Cardullo, *President*
Vita Cardullo, *Corp Secy*
EMP: 6 **EST:** 1959
SQ FT: 4,500
SALES: 642.4K **Privately Held**
SIC: 3441 Fabricated structural metal

(G-4764)
FERRARO MANUFACTURING COMPANY
150 Central Ave (11735-6900)
PHONE...................................631 752-1509
Joseph Ferraro, *President*
EMP: 6
SALES (est): 800.9K **Privately Held**
WEB: www.ferrarofirm.com
SIC: 3599 Machine shop, jobbing & repair

(G-4765)
FIBER FOOT APPLIANCES INC
34 Sarah Dr Ste A (11735-1218)
PHONE...................................631 465-9199
Jeffrey Fiber, *President*
Allan Fiber, *Treasurer*
Helene Fiber, *Admin Sec*
EMP: 13
SQ FT: 6,500
SALES (est): 1.4MM **Privately Held**
SIC: 3842 Foot appliances, orthopedic

(G-4766)
FOREST LABS
210 Sea Ln (11735-3900)
PHONE...................................631 755-1185
Shankar Hariharan, *Exec VP*
EMP: 8
SALES (est): 711.9K **Privately Held**
SIC: 2834 Pharmaceutical preparations

(G-4767)
FRUITCROWN PRODUCTS CORP (PA)
250 Adams Blvd (11735-6615)
PHONE...................................631 694-5800
Robert E Jagenburg, *President*
Bruce Jagenburg, *Vice Pres*
Nick Mendola, *Warehouse Mgr*
Greg Newman, *QC Mgr*
Gary Forbord, *Technical Mgr*
▼ **EMP:** 45
SQ FT: 40,000
SALES (est): 19.5MM **Privately Held**
WEB: www.fruitcrown.com
SIC: 2033 Fruits: packaged in cans, jars, etc.

(G-4768)
FUN INDUSTRIES OF NY
111 Milbar Blvd (11735-1426)
PHONE...................................631 845-3805
Bryan Spodek, *Principal*
EMP: 13
SALES (est): 1.4MM **Privately Held**
SIC: 3999 Manufacturing industries

(G-4769)
GAMMA INSTRUMENT CO INC
34 Sarah Dr Ste B (11735-1218)
PHONE...................................516 486-5526
John Schurr, *President*
William Hansen, *Vice Pres*
EMP: 7 **EST:** 1976
SALES: 500K **Privately Held**
SIC: 3599 Machine shop, jobbing & repair

(G-4770)
GAVIN MFG CORP
25 Central Ave Unit A (11735-6920)
PHONE...................................631 467-0040
Christopher Gavin, *President*
Brian Gavin, *Vice Pres*
Michael Gavin, *Vice Pres*
Ryan Gavin, *Vice Pres*
EMP: 45 **EST:** 1953
SQ FT: 15,000
SALES (est): 7.7MM **Privately Held**
WEB: www.gavinmfgcorp.com
SIC: 2679 2653 2657 Paper products, converted; paperboard products, converted; corrugated & solid fiber boxes; folding paperboard boxes

(G-4771)
GILD-RITE INC
51 Carolyn Blvd (11735-1527)
PHONE...................................631 752-9000
Howard Schneider, *President*
Morris D Schneider, *Chairman*
Roert Schneider, *Vice Pres*
Sylvia K Zang, *Treasurer*
EMP: 5
SQ FT: 7,000
SALES: 250K
SALES (corp-wide): 12.6MM **Privately Held**
SIC: 2789 Gilding books, cards or paper

Farmingdale - Nassau County (G-4772) — GEOGRAPHIC SECTION

PA: Leather Craftsmen, Inc.
6 Dubon Ct
Farmingdale NY 11735
631 752-9000

(G-4772)
GLISSADE NEW YORK LLC
399 Smith St (11735-1106)
PHONE.................................631 756-4800
Jed Leadman,
▲ EMP: 25
SQ FT: 30,000
SALES (est): 3.3MM **Privately Held**
WEB: www.glissade.com
SIC: 2514 2434 Medicine cabinets & vanities: metal; vanities, bathroom: wood

(G-4773)
GOLDMARK PRODUCTS INC
855 Conklin St Ste D (11735-2409)
PHONE.................................631 777-3343
Stanley Dabrowski, *President*
Matthew Paliwoda, *Treasurer*
EMP: 30
SQ FT: 5,000
SALES (est): 3.2MM **Privately Held**
SIC: 3911 3339 Mfg Precious Metal Jewelry Primary Nonferrous Metal Producer

(G-4774)
GREAT ROCK AUTOMATION INC
99 Rome St (11735-6606)
PHONE.................................631 270-1508
Dona Kiessel, *Opers Mgr*
EMP: 13
SALES (est): 2.1MM **Privately Held**
SIC: 3433 5074 Boilers, low-pressure heating: steam or hot water; boilers, steam

(G-4775)
GREEN LOGIC LED ELEC SUP INC (PA)
Also Called: Gllusa
75 Marine St (11735-5604)
PHONE.................................516 280-2854
George Geffen, *CEO*
Daniel Yu, *Vice Pres*
Donald Geffen, *Marketing Staff*
Marvin Yu,
EMP: 38
SALES (est): 10.1MM **Privately Held**
SIC: 3674 Light emitting diodes

(G-4776)
GREENMAKER INDUSTRIES LLC
885 Conklin St (11735-2400)
PHONE.................................866 684-7800
Bruce Respler, *Principal*
Aj Rego, *Buyer*
EMP: 11 EST: 2005
SALES (est): 2MM **Privately Held**
SIC: 2841 2842 Soap & other detergents; rug, upholstery, or dry cleaning detergents or spotters; sanitation preparations, disinfectants & deodorants; degreasing solvent; window cleaning preparations

(G-4777)
GUSTBUSTER LTD
Also Called: Sunbuster
855 Conklin St Ste O (11735-2409)
PHONE.................................631 391-9000
Steven Asman, *President*
▲ EMP: 8
SQ FT: 17,000
SALES: 2MM **Privately Held**
WEB: www.gustbuster.com
SIC: 3999 Umbrellas, canes & parts

(G-4778)
HADES MANUFACTURING CORP
140 Finn Ct (11735-1107)
PHONE.................................631 249-4244
Gary Speiser, *President*
Ken Norris, *Vice Pres*
EMP: 10 EST: 1966
SQ FT: 5,000
SALES (est): 1.8MM **Privately Held**
WEB: www.hadesmfgcorp.com
SIC: 3823 5084 Industrial machinery & equipment; temperature instruments: industrial process type

(G-4779)
HAHNS OLD FASHIONED CAKE CO
75 Allen Blvd (11735-5614)
PHONE.................................631 249-3456
Regina C Hahn, *President*
Andrew M Hahn, *Corp Secy*
Lee Rosenbaum, *Vice Pres*
EMP: 12
SQ FT: 4,550
SALES: 1MM **Privately Held**
WEB: www.crumbcake.net
SIC: 2051 5149 Cakes, bakery: except frozen; bakery products

(G-4780)
HIRSCH OPTICAL CORP
91 Carolyn Blvd (11735-1409)
PHONE.................................516 752-2211
Harold M Rothstein, *President*
Ken Mittel, *Exec VP*
Kenneth Mitel, *Vice Pres*
Michael Weinstein, *Vice Pres*
EMP: 60 EST: 1978
SQ FT: 12,000
SALES (est): 6.8MM **Privately Held**
WEB: www.hirschoptical.com
SIC: 3851 Eyeglasses, lenses & frames

(G-4781)
HORNE PRODUCTS INC
144 Verdi St (11735-6324)
PHONE.................................631 293-0773
John Hind, *President*
Joanne Incalcatera, *Corp Secy*
Patricia A O'Neill, *Vice Pres*
EMP: 6
SQ FT: 2,200
SALES (est): 991.9K **Privately Held**
WEB: www.horneproducts.com
SIC: 3743 5088 Railroad equipment; railroad equipment & supplies

(G-4782)
HURON TL CUTTER GRINDING INC
2045 Wellwood Ave (11735-1212)
PHONE.................................631 420-7000
James Cosenza, *President*
Richard Cosenza, *Vice Pres*
Francisco Adrian, *QC Mgr*
Blanche Silbert, *Admin Sec*
Danielle Avena, *Administration*
EMP: 30 EST: 1955
SQ FT: 25,000
SALES: 4MM **Privately Held**
WEB: www.hurontool.com
SIC: 3545 3841 3568 3423 Tools & accessories for machine tools; knives, surgical; power transmission equipment; hand & edge tools

(G-4783)
I J WHITE CORPORATION
20 Executive Blvd (11735-4710)
PHONE.................................631 293-3788
Peter J White, *Ch of Bd*
Niv Eldor, *COO*
Andy Cohn, *Vice Pres*
Roy Berntsen, *Plant Mgr*
Frank Vecchio, *Purch Mgr*
▼ EMP: 70 EST: 1919
SQ FT: 42,500
SALES (est): 20.7MM **Privately Held**
WEB: www.ijwhite.com
SIC: 3556 3535 Food products machinery; conveyors & conveying equipment

(G-4784)
IMPRESSIVE IMPRINTS INC
195 Central Ave Ste N (11735-6904)
PHONE.................................631 293-6161
Howard Lang, *President*
EMP: 5 EST: 1961
SQ FT: 3,000
SALES (est): 551K **Privately Held**
SIC: 3993 Signs & advertising specialties

(G-4785)
INNOVATIVE AUTOMATION INC
595 Smith St (11735-1116)
P.O. Box 290 (11735-0290)
PHONE.................................631 439-3300
James D'Addario, *President*
John D'Addario Jr, *Vice Pres*
EMP: 12
SQ FT: 25,000
SALES (est): 1.4MM **Privately Held**
WEB: www.innovativeautomation.net
SIC: 3545 Machine tool attachments & accessories

(G-4786)
INSTANT VERTICALS INC
330 Broadhollow Rd (11735-4807)
PHONE.................................631 501-0001
Michael Moran, *President*
John Joy, *Vice Pres*
EMP: 10
SALES (est): 1.2MM **Privately Held**
WEB: www.instantverticals.com
SIC: 2591 1799 Window blinds; window treatment installation

(G-4787)
INTELLIGENT CTRL SYSTEMS LLC
208 Route 109 Ste 211 (11735-1536)
PHONE.................................516 340-1011
Jack Hammer, *Chief Engr*
Michael Ruff,
Celso Monge,
EMP: 5
SALES (est): 382.7K **Privately Held**
SIC: 3699 Electrical equipment & supplies

(G-4788)
INTERNATIONAL KEY SUPPLY LLC
Also Called: Ik Supply
32 Gazza Blvd (11735-1402)
PHONE.................................631 983-6096
Sean McAuliffe, *Partner*
Anna Blinova, *Manager*
EMP: 10
SALES: 1.2MM **Privately Held**
SIC: 3429 3694 3643 Keys & key blanks; automotive electrical equipment; connectors & terminals for electrical devices

(G-4789)
J M HALEY CORP
151 Toledo St Ste 1 (11735-6640)
PHONE.................................631 845-5200
John Ackerson, *President*
Steven Cardona, *Project Mgr*
Pavel Kaliadka, *Project Mgr*
Julia Giangrasso, *HR Admin*
Cynthia Bissoon, *Administration*
EMP: 140 EST: 1972
SQ FT: 10,000
SALES: 16MM **Privately Held**
WEB: www.jmhaleycorp.com
SIC: 3441 Fabricated structural metal

(G-4790)
J P PRINTING INC (PA)
Also Called: Minuteman Press
331 Main St (11735-3508)
PHONE.................................516 293-6110
Jeff Miller, *President*
Susan Miller, *Vice Pres*
EMP: 5
SQ FT: 1,200
SALES: 385K **Privately Held**
SIC: 2752 5943 Commercial printing, offset; office forms & supplies

(G-4791)
JAMES WOERNER INC
130 Allen Blvd (11735-5617)
PHONE.................................631 454-9330
James Woerner, *President*
Barbara Woerner, *Vice Pres*
EMP: 6
SQ FT: 7,000
SALES (est): 1MM **Privately Held**
SIC: 3498 3441 7538 Fabricated pipe & fittings; fabricated structural metal; general automotive repair shops

(G-4792)
JANED ENTERPRISES
48 Allen Blvd Unit B (11735-5642)
PHONE.................................631 694-4494
Joseph Pileri, *CEO*
Claudia Montuori, *President*
EMP: 15
SQ FT: 14,000
SALES (est): 2.5MM **Privately Held**
WEB: www.janed.net
SIC: 3449 Miscellaneous metalwork

(G-4793)
JGM WHOLESALE BAKERY INC
296 Route 109 (11735-1503)
PHONE.................................631 396-0131
Noris Moreira, *President*
Samuel Moreira, *Vice Pres*
EMP: 5
SALES (est): 139.9K **Privately Held**
SIC: 2051 Bakery: wholesale or wholesale/retail combined

(G-4794)
JOE P INDUSTRIES INC
Also Called: Carrmet Industries
6 Commerce Dr (11735-1206)
PHONE.................................631 293-7889
Joseph Parente, *President*
EMP: 17
SQ FT: 3,500
SALES: 1MM **Privately Held**
SIC: 3444 Metal housings, enclosures, casings & other containers

(G-4795)
JUNK IN MY TRUNK INC
266 Route 109 (11735-1503)
PHONE.................................631 420-5865
Tomasz Myszke, *Principal*
EMP: 5
SALES (est): 583.7K **Privately Held**
SIC: 3161 Trunks

(G-4796)
K SIDRANE INC
24 Baiting Place Rd (11735-6227)
PHONE.................................631 393-6974
William Turley, *President*
Michael Liff, *General Mgr*
Neil Sidrane, *Chairman*
Andrew Hersh, *Accounts Mgr*
▲ EMP: 45 EST: 1948
SQ FT: 10,000
SALES (est): 12MM **Privately Held**
SIC: 2679 2671 2672 Tags & labels, paper; packaging paper & plastics film, coated & laminated; coated & laminated paper; adhesive papers, labels or tapes: from purchased material

(G-4797)
KABAR MANUFACTURING CORP (HQ)
140 Schmitt Blvd (11735-1461)
PHONE.................................631 694-6857
Bruce Mc Kee, *President*
Ken Arutt, *Treasurer*
▲ EMP: 45 EST: 1945
SQ FT: 12,000
SALES: 11.2MM
SALES (corp-wide): 8.6MM **Privately Held**
WEB: www.cosmos-kabar.com
SIC: 3565 3559 Packaging machinery; plastics working machinery
PA: Cosmos Electronic Machine Corp.
140 Schmitt Blvd
Farmingdale NY 11735
631 249-2535

(G-4798)
KABAR MANUFACTURING CORP
113 Gazza Blvd (11735-1421)
PHONE.................................631 694-1036
Bruce Mc Kee, *President*
EMP: 30
SALES (corp-wide): 8.6MM **Privately Held**
WEB: www.cosmos-kabar.com
SIC: 3559 Plastics working machinery
HQ: Kabar Manufacturing Corp.
140 Schmitt Blvd
Farmingdale NY 11735
631 694-6857

(G-4799)
KAZAC INC
Also Called: Corzane Cabinets
55 Allen Blvd Ste C (11735-5643)
PHONE.................................631 249-7299
Fax: 631 249-1454
EMP: 5

▲ = Import ▼ = Export
◆ = Import/Export

GEOGRAPHIC SECTION

Farmingdale - Nassau County (G-4825)

SQ FT: 4,200
SALES: 450K Privately Held
SIC: 2511 2521 Mfg Wood Household Furniture Mfg Wood Office Furniture

(G-4800)
KEDCO INC
Also Called: Kedco Wine Storage Systems
564 Smith St (11735-1115)
PHONE..................................516 454-7800
Helene Windt, *President*
David Windt, *Corp Secy*
Ken Windt, *Vice Pres*
EMP: 12 EST: 1970
SQ FT: 20,000
SALES (est): 2MM Privately Held
SIC: 3585 2599 3556 Refrigeration & heating equipment; bar, restaurant & cafeteria furniture; beverage machinery

(G-4801)
KELLY WINDOW SYSTEMS INC
460 Smith St (11735-1105)
PHONE..................................631 420-8500
Carl J Giugliano, *President*
Frank Giugliano, *Vice Pres*
Pat Giugliano, *Vice Pres*
EMP: 32
SQ FT: 20,000
SALES (est): 4.6MM Privately Held
WEB: www.kellywindows.com
SIC: 2431 3442 Windows, wood; metal doors, sash & trim

(G-4802)
KEM MEDICAL PRODUCTS CORP (PA)
400 Broadhollow Rd Ste 2 (11735-4824)
PHONE..................................631 454-6565
Douglas A Kruger, *President*
Joseph Ebenstein, *Vice Pres*
EMP: 3
SQ FT: 2,500
SALES (est): 1.4MM Privately Held
WEB: www.kemmed.com
SIC: 3842 3829 Personal safety equipment; measuring & controlling devices

(G-4803)
KINEMOTIVE CORPORATION
222 Central Ave Ste 1 (11735-6958)
PHONE..................................631 249-6440
Arthur Szeglin, *Ch of Bd*
William Niedzwiecki, *President*
Charles Szeglin, *Principal*
Engin Oge, *Vice Pres*
Robert Skidmore, *Sales Mgr*
EMP: 48 EST: 1959
SQ FT: 20,000
SALES (est): 9.7MM Privately Held
WEB: www.kinemotive.com
SIC: 3492 3452 3599 3568 Fluid power valves & hose fittings; screws, metal; bellows, industrial: metal; couplings, shaft: rigid, flexible, universal joint, etc.; pivots, power transmission; precision springs; pressure transducers

(G-4804)
L AND S PACKING CO
Also Called: Paesana
101 Central Ave (11735-6915)
P.O. Box 709 (11735-0709)
PHONE..................................631 845-1717
Louis J Scaramelli III, *Ch of Bd*
Louis Scarmelli IV, *President*
Stan Staszewski, *General Mgr*
Jacqueline Massaro, *Exec VP*
Lorraine Scaramelli, *Exec VP*
▲ EMP: 72
SQ FT: 73,000
SALES (est): 18.2MM Privately Held
WEB: www.paesana.com
SIC: 2033 2035 Olives: packaged in cans, jars, etc.; vegetables: packaged in cans, jars, etc.; maraschino cherries: packaged in cans, jars, etc.; spaghetti & other pasta sauce: packaged in cans, jars, etc.; pickles, sauces & salad dressings

(G-4805)
L P R PRECISION PARTS & TLS CO
108 Rome St Ste 1 (11735-6637)
PHONE..................................631 293-7334
Tarquin Rattotti Jr, *President*
Tarquin Rattotti Sr, *Principal*
Lucy Rattotti, *Corp Secy*
EMP: 10
SQ FT: 5,000
SALES (est): 1.7MM Privately Held
WEB: www.lprprecision.com
SIC: 3599 Machine shop, jobbing & repair

(G-4806)
LA MAR LIGHTING CO INC
485 Smith St (11735-1106)
P.O. Box 9013 (11735-9013)
PHONE..................................631 777-7700
Jeffrey Goldstein, *CEO*
Barry Kugel, *Ch of Bd*
Liz Ladeveze, *Prdtn Mgr*
Keith Briggs, *Purch Mgr*
Gregory Calise, *Technical Mgr*
▲ EMP: 46 EST: 1957
SQ FT: 40,000
SALES: 13.9MM Privately Held
WEB: www.lamarlighting.com
SIC: 3646 3641 3648 Fluorescent lighting fixtures, commercial; electric lamps; lighting equipment

(G-4807)
LADY BURD EXCLUSIVE COSMT INC (PA)
Also Called: Lady Burd Private Label Cosmt
44 Executive Blvd Ste 1 (11735-4706)
PHONE..................................631 454-0444
Roberta Burd, *Chairman*
Allan Burd, *Vice Pres*
Christina Burd, *Vice Pres*
Lawrence Burd, *Vice Pres*
Tina Burd, *Vice Pres*
▲ EMP: 109
SQ FT: 40,000
SALES (est): 20.8MM Privately Held
WEB: www.ladyburd.com
SIC: 2844 Cosmetic preparations

(G-4808)
LEATHER CRAFTSMEN INC (PA)
6 Dubon Ct (11735-1008)
PHONE..................................631 752-9000
Howard Schneider, *President*
Joseph Fiore, *Vice Pres*
David Willis, *Sales Associate*
Robert Schneider, *Admin Sec*
EMP: 70
SQ FT: 18,000
SALES (est): 12.6MM Privately Held
WEB: www.leathercraftsmen.com
SIC: 2782 Albums

(G-4809)
LOGOMAX INC
242 Route 109 Ste B (11735-1500)
PHONE..................................631 420-0484
Victor Rouse, *President*
Annette Regan, *Sales Staff*
EMP: 4 EST: 1998
SALES (est): 1.1MM Privately Held
WEB: www.logomaxusa.com
SIC: 2759 Screen printing

(G-4810)
LONG BLOCKCHAIN CORP (PA)
12 Dubon Ct Ste 1 (11735-1025)
PHONE..................................855 542-2832
Shamyl Malik, *Ch of Bd*
Peter Dydensborg, *COO*
Tom Cardella, *Bd of Directors*
Richard Roberts, *Bd of Directors*
Paul Vassilakos, *Bd of Directors*
EMP: 18
SQ FT: 5,000
SALES (est): 4.4MM Privately Held
SIC: 2086 Iced tea & fruit drinks, bottled & canned

(G-4811)
LOS OLIVOS LTD
105 Bi County Blvd (11735-3919)
PHONE..................................631 773-6439
Ester Alvarado, *Ch of Bd*
EMP: 135
SALES (est): 3.2MM Privately Held
SIC: 3556 Smokers, food processing equipment

(G-4812)
M C PACKAGING CORPORATION (PA)
120-200 Adams Blvd (11735)
P.O. Box 1031, Melville (11747-0031)
PHONE..................................631 694-3012
Robert M Silverberg, *Ch of Bd*
Marc Silverberg, *President*
▲ EMP: 135 EST: 1966
SQ FT: 9,000
SALES (est): 52.2MM Privately Held
WEB: www.mcpkg.com
SIC: 2679 Cardboard products, except die-cut

(G-4813)
MACHINIT INC
400 Smith St (11735-1105)
PHONE..................................631 454-9297
Tony Kusturic, *President*
Edward Grcic, *General Mgr*
EMP: 4
SALES: 2MM Privately Held
SIC: 2253 Knit outerwear mills

(G-4814)
MAN PRODUCTS INC
99 Milbar Blvd Unit 1 (11735-1407)
PHONE..................................631 789-6500
Attilio Mancusi, *President*
EMP: 30
SALES (est): 4.4MM Privately Held
WEB: www.manproducts.com
SIC: 3448 Prefabricated metal buildings

(G-4815)
MARKEN LLP
123 Smith St (11735-1004)
PHONE..................................631 396-7454
Steve Roese, *Partner*
James Schaitel, *Manager*
EMP: 8
SQ FT: 10,000
SALES (corp-wide): 65.8B Publicly Held
SIC: 2834 4731 Tablets, pharmaceutical; freight forwarding
HQ: Marken Llp
     1009 Slater Rd Ste 120
     Durham NC 27703
     919 474-6892

(G-4816)
MAROTTA DENTAL STUDIO INC
130 Finn Ct (11735-1107)
PHONE..................................631 249-7520
Leonard Marotta, *President*
Steve Pigliacelli, *Vice Pres*
Steven Pigliacelli, *Vice Pres*
Justin Hayes, *Opers Mgr*
Chris Marotta, *Treasurer*
EMP: 40
SQ FT: 15,000
SALES (est): 7MM Privately Held
WEB: www.marottadental.com
SIC: 3843 8021 8072 Dental materials; offices & clinics of dentists; dental laboratories

(G-4817)
MART-TEX ATHLETICS INC
180 Allen Blvd (11735-5617)
PHONE..................................631 454-9583
Richard Marte, *President*
Raymond Marte Jr, *Corp Secy*
Peter Rasp Sr, *Sales Mgr*
EMP: 35
SQ FT: 15,000
SALES (est): 3.5MM Privately Held
WEB: www.mart-tex.com
SIC: 2759 Screen printing

(G-4818)
MAZZA CLASSICS INCORPORATED
117 Gazza Blvd (11735-1415)
PHONE..................................631 390-9060
Jim Rivera, *President*
EMP: 7
SQ FT: 5,000
SALES: 500K Privately Held
SIC: 2512 Upholstered household furniture

(G-4819)
MEMORY PROTECTION DEVICES INC
200 Broadhollow Rd Ste 4 (11735-4814)
PHONE..................................631 249-0001
Thomas Blaha, *President*
Charles Engelstein, *Chairman*
Daniel Lynch, *Vice Pres*
EMP: 10
SQ FT: 3,000
SALES: 7MM Privately Held
WEB: www.memoryprotectiondevices.com
SIC: 3089 Battery cases, plastic or plastic combination

(G-4820)
MERB LLC
Also Called: Belgian Boys USA
140 Carolyn Blvd (11735-1525)
PHONE..................................631 393-3621
Michael Berro, *President*
Ricardo Dellajiovanna, *Vice Pres*
Anouck Gotlib, *Creative Dir*
EMP: 10 EST: 2013
SQ FT: 2,000
SALES: 10MM Privately Held
SIC: 2099 Food preparations

(G-4821)
METADURE PARTS & SALES INC
Also Called: Sbcontract.com
165 Gazza Blvd (11735-1415)
PHONE..................................631 249-2141
Gary Templeton, *President*
Nicholas Picon, *QC Mgr*
EMP: 12
SQ FT: 10,000
SALES (est): 2.2MM Privately Held
SIC: 3728 Military aircraft equipment & armament

(G-4822)
METROPLTAN DATA SLTONS MGT INC
279 Conklin St (11735-2608)
P.O. Box 11394, Newark NJ (07101-4394)
PHONE..................................516 586-5520
John Dankowitz, *President*
Jonathan Friedfertig, *Accounts Mgr*
Patricia Dankowitz, *Administration*
EMP: 11
SQ FT: 1,500
SALES (est): 2MM Privately Held
SIC: 3089 Identification cards, plastic

(G-4823)
MID ISLAND DIE CUTTING CORP
77 Schmitt Blvd (11735-1403)
PHONE..................................631 293-0180
Robert Geier, *President*
Jenny Rivelli, *Controller*
Gerri Rizelli, *Controller*
Ruth Geier, *Admin Sec*
EMP: 200
SQ FT: 12,000
SALES (est): 33.2MM Privately Held
SIC: 2675 Die-cut paper & board

(G-4824)
MID ISLAND GROUP
Also Called: Geier Bindery Co
77 Schmitt Blvd (11735-1403)
PHONE..................................631 293-0180
Robert Geier, *President*
Bob Russo, *Vice Pres*
EMP: 25
SQ FT: 40,000
SALES (est): 4MM Privately Held
WEB: www.midislandgroup.com
SIC: 2789 Binding only: books, pamphlets, magazines, etc.

(G-4825)
MID-ISLAND BINDERY INC
77 Schmitt Blvd (11735-1403)
PHONE..................................631 293-0180
Robert Geier, *CEO*
EMP: 48
SQ FT: 30,000
SALES (est): 6.2MM Privately Held
SIC: 2789 Pamphlets, binding

Farmingdale - Nassau County (G-4826)

GEOGRAPHIC SECTION

(G-4826)
MILLER TECHNOLOGY INC
61 Gazza Blvd (11735-1401)
PHONE..................................631 694-2224
Walter Miller Jr, *President*
Joane Miller, *Treasurer*
EMP: 5 **EST:** 1954
SQ FT: 3,000
SALES: 250K **Privately Held**
SIC: 3089 3369 3599 Casting of plastic; castings, except die-castings, precision; machine shop, jobbing & repair

(G-4827)
MIRAGE MOULDING MFG INC
Also Called: Mirage Moulding & Supply
160 Milbar Blvd (11735-1425)
PHONE..................................631 843-6168
Hashim Ismailzadah, *Ch of Bd*
▲ **EMP:** 11
SALES (est): 1.2MM **Privately Held**
SIC: 3089 Molding primary plastic

(G-4828)
MISONIX INC (PA)
1938 New Hwy (11735-1214)
PHONE..................................631 694-9555
Stavros G Vizirgianakis, *CEO*
Robert S Ludecker, *Senior VP*
Joseph J Brennan, *Vice Pres*
Joseph Brennan, *Vice Pres*
Scott Ludecker, *Vice Pres*
▲ **EMP:** 85
SQ FT: 34,400
SALES: 36.6MM **Publicly Held**
WEB: www.misonix.com
SIC: 3841 3845 3677 Surgical & medical instruments; electromedical equipment; electronic coils, transformers & other inductors

(G-4829)
MKT329 INC
Also Called: Superior Packaging
565 Broadhollow Rd Ste 5 (11735-4826)
P.O. Box 667, North Bellmore (11710-0667)
PHONE..................................631 249-5500
Marlene Tallon, *President*
▲ **EMP:** 21 **EST:** 2014
SQ FT: 121
SALES (est): 3.6MM **Privately Held**
SIC: 2653 Boxes, corrugated: made from purchased materials

(G-4830)
MOREY PUBLISHING
Also Called: Long Island Press
20 Hempstead Tpke Unit B (11735-2043)
PHONE..................................516 284-3300
Jed Morey, *Ch of Bd*
Beverly Fortune, *Publisher*
Jon Sasala, *Editor*
EMP: 30
SALES (est): 4.4MM **Privately Held**
SIC: 2741 Miscellaneous publishing

(G-4831)
NAMEPLATE MFRS OF AMER
65 Toledo St (11735-6620)
PHONE..................................631 752-0055
Bill Williams, *CEO*
Darren Cash, *COO*
EMP: 40
SQ FT: 8,000
SALES (est): 4.9MM **Privately Held**
WEB: www.nameplateamerica.com
SIC: 3479 3993 2752 2671 Name plates: engraved, etched, etc.; signs & advertising specialties; commercial printing, lithographic; packaging paper & plastics film, coated & laminated

(G-4832)
NATIONWIDE SALES AND SERVICE
303 Smith St Ste 4 (11735-1110)
PHONE..................................631 491-6625
Mark Genoa, *Ch of Bd*
Scott Genoa, *Vice Pres*
▲ **EMP:** 10
SQ FT: 10,000
SALES (est): 1.6MM **Privately Held**
WEB: www.shopnss.com
SIC: 3635 5087 5722 Household vacuum cleaners; janitors' supplies; vacuum cleaning systems; vacuum cleaners

(G-4833)
NEIGHBOR NEWSPAPERS
565 Broadhollow Rd Ste 3 (11735-4826)
PHONE..................................631 226-2636
Richard A Freedman, *Principal*
EMP: 7
SALES (est): 402.3K **Privately Held**
SIC: 2711 Commercial printing & newspaper publishing combined

(G-4834)
NEILSON INTERNATIONAL INC
144 Allen Blvd Ste B (11735-5644)
P.O. Box 784, Hicksville (11802-0784)
PHONE..................................631 454-0400
Kamlesh Mehta, *President*
▲ **EMP:** 3
SQ FT: 8,000
SALES: 1MM **Privately Held**
WEB: www.neilsoninc.com
SIC: 2211 Print cloths, cotton

(G-4835)
NESTLE HEALTHCARE NTRTN INC
Also Called: Haagen-Dazs
565 Broadhollow Rd (11735-4831)
PHONE..................................516 249-5085
Bill Boraczek, *Principal*
EMP: 7
SALES (corp-wide): 90.8B **Privately Held**
SIC: 2099 5812 Food preparations; ice cream, soft drink & soda fountain stands
HQ: Nestle Healthcare Nutrition, Inc.
1007 Us Hwy 202206
Bridgewater NJ 08807
952 848-6000

(G-4836)
NETECH CORPORATION
Also Called: Biomedical & Industrial
110 Toledo St (11735-6623)
PHONE..................................631 531-0100
Mohan Das, *President*
EMP: 11
SQ FT: 4,500
SALES (est): 2.1MM **Privately Held**
WEB: www.gonetech.com
SIC: 3845 Electromedical equipment

(G-4837)
NOGA DAIRIES INC
Also Called: Dairy Delite
175 Price Pkwy (11735-1318)
PHONE..................................516 293-5448
Eli Paz, *CEO*
Zami Leinson, *President*
Noa Kahana, *Vice Pres*
▲ **EMP:** 10
SQ FT: 22,000
SALES (est): 1.3MM **Privately Held**
SIC: 2026 2022 Yogurt; spreads, cheese

(G-4838)
NUTRASCIENCE LABS INC
70 Carolyn Blvd (11735-1525)
PHONE..................................631 247-0660
Steve Rolfes, *CEO*
EMP: 27 **EST:** 2014
SALES (est): 1.2MM
SALES (corp-wide): 85.5MM **Privately Held**
SIC: 2833 2834 Botanical products, medicinal: ground, graded or milled; druggists' preparations (pharmaceuticals)
PA: Twinlab Consolidated Holdings Inc.
4800 T Rex Ave Ste 305
Boca Raton FL 33431
561 443-4301

(G-4839)
ORICS INDUSTRIES INC
240 Smith St (11735-1113)
PHONE..................................718 461-8613
Ori Cohen, *Ch of Bd*
▲ **EMP:** 50
SQ FT: 15,000
SALES (est): 24.2MM **Privately Held**
WEB: www.orics.com
SIC: 3565 3841 Packaging machinery; surgical & medical instruments

(G-4840)
ORLANDI INC (PA)
Also Called: Orlandi Scented Products
131 Executive Blvd (11735-4719)
PHONE..................................631 756-0110
Sven Dobler, *Ch of Bd*
Douglas M Whitaker, *Senior VP*
Per Dobler, *Vice Pres*
Russell Ostroff, *Vice Pres*
Lee Johnson, *Prdtn Mgr*
▲ **EMP:** 100
SQ FT: 80,000
SALES (est): 34.5MM **Privately Held**
WEB: www.orlandi-usa.com
SIC: 3993 3999 7389 2752 Signs & advertising specialties; novelties, bric-a-brac & hobby kits; packaging & labeling services; commercial printing, lithographic

(G-4841)
ORLANDI INC
121 Executive Blvd (11735-4719)
PHONE..................................631 756-0110
Sven Dobler, *President*
EMP: 50
SQ FT: 45,500
SALES (corp-wide): 34.5MM **Privately Held**
SIC: 3993 3999 7389 2752 Signs & advertising specialties; novelties, bric-a-brac & hobby kits; packaging & labeling services; commercial printing, lithographic
PA: Orlandi, Inc.
131 Executive Blvd
Farmingdale NY 11735
631 756-0110

(G-4842)
OSI PHARMACEUTICALS LLC
500 Bi County Blvd # 118 (11735-3959)
PHONE..................................631 847-0175
EMP: 84
SALES (corp-wide): 10.4B **Privately Held**
SIC: 2834 Mfg Pharmaceutical Preparations
HQ: Osi Pharmaceuticals, Llc
1 Bioscience Way Dr
Farmingdale NY 11735
631 962-2000

(G-4843)
OSI PHARMACEUTICALS LLC (DH)
1 Bioscience Way Dr (11735)
PHONE..................................631 962-2000
Colin Goddard PHD, *CEO*
Gabriel Leung, *President*
Anker Lundemose MD PHD, *President*
Nancy Irwin, *Editor*
Robert L Simon, *Exec VP*
▼ **EMP:** 5
SALES (est): 83.3MM
SALES (corp-wide): 12.2B **Privately Held**
WEB: www.osip.com
SIC: 2834 8731 Drugs affecting neoplasms & endrocrine systems; drugs acting on the central nervous system & sense organs; commercial physical research
HQ: Astellas Us Holding, Inc.
1 Astellas Way
Northbrook IL 60062
224 205-8800

(G-4844)
PCX AEROSTRUCTURES LLC
60 Milbar Blvd (11735-1406)
PHONE..................................631 467-2632
EMP: 25
SALES (corp-wide): 100MM **Privately Held**
SIC: 3441 Structural Metal Fabrication
PA: Pcx Aerostructures, Llc
300 Fenn Rd
Newington CT 06111
860 666-2471

(G-4845)
PEERLESS INSTRUMENT CO INC
1966 Broadhollow Rd Ste D (11735-1726)
PHONE..................................631 396-6500
Martin R Benante, *CEO*
David Linton, *President*
Frederic Borah, *General Mgr*
Fran Vargas, *Buyer*
George Fkiaras, *Engineer*
▲ **EMP:** 109 **EST:** 1938
SQ FT: 55,000
SALES (est): 24.6MM
SALES (corp-wide): 2.2B **Publicly Held**
WEB: www.peerlessny.com
SIC: 3829 7389 3825 3625 Measuring & controlling devices; design services; instruments to measure electricity; relays & industrial controls
PA: Curtiss-Wright Corporation
130 Harbour Place Dr # 300
Davidson NC 28036
704 869-4600

(G-4846)
PHARBEST PHARMACEUTICALS INC
14 Engineers Ln Ste 1 (11735-1219)
PHONE..................................631 249-5130
Munir Islam, *President*
Intekhab Ahmed, *Manager*
Nishant Parikh, *Manager*
▼ **EMP:** 41
SQ FT: 22,000
SALES (est): 8MM **Privately Held**
WEB: www.pharbestusa.com
SIC: 2834 Druggists' preparations (pharmaceuticals)

(G-4847)
PHARMALIFE INC
130 Gazza Blvd (11735-1420)
PHONE..................................631 249-4040
Larry Sayage, *President*
EMP: 5 **EST:** 1999
SQ FT: 4,300
SALES (est): 692.9K **Privately Held**
SIC: 2834 Vitamin, nutrient & hematinic preparations for human use

(G-4848)
PHOENIX LABORATORIES INC
200 Adams Blvd (11735-6615)
PHONE..................................516 822-1230
Melvin Rich, *President*
Stephen R Stern, *Exec VP*
Charlotte Rich, *Admin Sec*
EMP: 180 **EST:** 1966
SQ FT: 40,000
SALES (est): 25MM **Privately Held**
WEB: www.phoenixlaboratories.com
SIC: 2834 Vitamin, nutrient & hematinic preparations for human use; vitamin preparations

(G-4849)
PINTAIL COFFEE INC
1776 New Hwy (11735-1513)
PHONE..................................631 396-0808
EMP: 5 **EST:** 2013
SALES (est): 169.7K **Privately Held**
SIC: 2095 5149 Coffee roasting (except by wholesale grocers); coffee, green or roasted

(G-4850)
PIRNAT PRECISE METALS INC
Also Called: F & M Precise Metals Co
127 Marine St (11735-5609)
PHONE..................................631 293-9169
Frank Pirnat, *President*
Mark Pirnat, *Vice Pres*
EMP: 7 **EST:** 1967
SQ FT: 10,000
SALES (est): 1.2MM **Privately Held**
SIC: 3444 Sheet metalwork

(G-4851)
PLASCAL CORP
361 Eastern Pkwy (11735-2713)
P.O. Box 590 (11735-0590)
PHONE..................................516 249-2200
Mark Hurd, *CEO*
Fred Hurd, *President*
Sheldon Eskowitz, *Corp Secy*

GEOGRAPHIC SECTION

Farmingdale - Nassau County (G-4881)

Thomas Blackler, *Vice Pres*
Raymond Brown, *Vice Pres*
▲ **EMP:** 4 **EST:** 1975
SQ FT: 75,000
SALES: 6MM **Privately Held**
WEB: www.plascal.com
SIC: 3081 Vinyl film & sheet

(G-4852)
PLATINUM PRINTING & GRAPHICS
70 Carolyn Blvd Ste C (11735-1525)
PHONE 631 249-3325
Paul Currao, *President*
EMP: 5 **EST:** 1996
SALES (est): 474.8K **Privately Held**
SIC: 2752 Commercial printing, lithographic

(G-4853)
POLYPLASTIC FORMS INC
49 Gazza Blvd (11735-1401)
PHONE 631 249-5011
Thomas Garrett, *President*
Diane Garrett, *Corp Secy*
Richa.d Garrett, *Vice Pres*
Nancy Behrens, *Administration*
EMP: 35
SQ FT: 10,000
SALES (est): 5.2MM **Privately Held**
WEB: www.polyplasticforms.com
SIC: 3993 Displays & cutouts, window & lobby; signs, not made in custom sign painting shops

(G-4854)
POSILLICO MATERIALS LLC
1750 New Hwy (11735-1562)
PHONE 631 249-1872
Joseph K Posillico, *CEO*
Michael J Posillico, *President*
Mario A Posillico, *Chairman*
Joseph D Posillico, *Senior VP*
Paul F Posillico, *Senior VP*
EMP: 11 **EST:** 1971
SQ FT: 2,500
SALES: 13.6MM
SALES (corp-wide): 158.9MM **Privately Held**
SIC: 2951 Asphalt & asphaltic paving mixtures (not from refineries)
PA: Posillico Civil, Inc.
   1750 New Hwy
   Farmingdale NY 11735
   631 249-1872

(G-4855)
PRECIPART CORPORATION
120 Finn Ct Ste 2 (11735-1121)
PHONE 631 694-3100
John P Walter, *President*
Lloyd W Miller, *Chairman*
Georges Assimilalo, *COO*
Anna Ferrizz, *Project Mgr*
Andreas Wenger, *Opers Staff*
EMP: 216
SQ FT: 16,200
SALES: 43.5MM **Privately Held**
WEB: www.precipart.com
SIC: 3566 Gears, power transmission, except automotive
PA: Precipart Group, Inc.
   100 Finn Ct
   Farmingdale NY 11735

(G-4856)
PRECISION ENVELOPE CO INC
Also Called: H & R Precision
110 Schmitt Blvd 7a (11735-6961)
PHONE 631 694-3990
Gilbert M Colombo Jr, *President*
Jane Colombo, *Corp Secy*
Diana Hall, *Bookkeeper*
EMP: 9
SQ FT: 7,000
SALES (est): 1.2MM **Privately Held**
SIC: 2759 2752 Envelopes: printing; stationery: printing; business forms, lithographed

(G-4857)
PRECISION LABEL CORPORATION
175 Marine St (11735-5609)
PHONE 631 270-4490
Bradley A Cohn, *CEO*
EMP: 12
SQ FT: 4,000
SALES (est): 1.7MM **Privately Held**
SIC: 2759 2679 Labels & seals: printing; labels, paper: made from purchased material

(G-4858)
PROMPT PRINTING INC
160 Rome St (11735-6609)
PHONE 631 454-6524
Fax: 631 454-6370
EMP: 6 **EST:** 1980
SQ FT: 2,000
SALES: 370K **Privately Held**
SIC: 2752 Lithographic Commercial Printing

(G-4859)
PROOF INDUSTRIES INC
125 Rome St (11735-6606)
PHONE 631 694-7663
Vincent Caciopppo, *President*
EMP: 9
SQ FT: 3,000
SALES (est): 1.3MM **Privately Held**
WEB: www.proofroof.com
SIC: 2439 5999 1751 Trusses, wooden roof; awnings; window & door (prefabricated) installation

(G-4860)
PROPER CHEMICAL LTD
280 Smith St (11735-1113)
PHONE 631 420-8000
Emil Backstrom, *President*
EMP: 5
SQ FT: 20,000
SALES (est): 400K **Privately Held**
SIC: 2833 Medicinal chemicals

(G-4861)
QUALITY STAIR BUILDERS INC
95 Schmitt Blvd (11735-1403)
PHONE 631 694-0711
Esta Topal, *President*
Sherri Sugar, *Corp Secy*
EMP: 16 **EST:** 1955
SQ FT: 10,000
SALES (est): 2.2MM **Privately Held**
SIC: 2431 Staircases & stairs, wood

(G-4862)
QUICK SIGN F X
6 Powell St (11735-4019)
PHONE 516 249-6531
Steve Levine, *President*
EMP: 13
SALES (est): 853.7K **Privately Held**
SIC: 3993 Signs & advertising specialties

(G-4863)
R & J GRAPHICS INC
45 Central Ave (11735-6901)
PHONE 631 293-6611
John Merendino, *President*
Ann Merendino, *Admin Sec*
EMP: 16
SQ FT: 15,000
SALES (est): 2.8MM **Privately Held**
SIC: 2752 Commercial printing, lithographic

(G-4864)
R D PRINTING ASSOCIATES INC
1865 New Hwy Ste 1 (11735-1501)
PHONE 631 390-5964
Ralph Demartino Jr, *President*
EMP: 14
SQ FT: 10,000
SALES (est): 1.4MM **Privately Held**
SIC: 2752 Commercial printing, offset

(G-4865)
RAILWORKS CORPORATION
Signals & Communications
83 Central Ave (11735-6901)
PHONE 904 296-5055
Tim Orlandi, *Branch Mgr*
Marcia Calvitto, *Admin Asst*
Richard Muniz, *Clerk*
EMP: 6
SALES (corp-wide): 1.5B **Privately Held**
SIC: 3612 Signaling transformers, electric
HQ: Railworks Corporation
   5 Penn Plz
   New York NY 10001
   212 502-7900

(G-4866)
RIPI PRECISION CO INC (PA)
92 Toledo St (11735-6623)
PHONE 631 694-2453
Michael Perciballi, *President*
EMP: 12
SQ FT: 12,000
SALES (est): 2.5MM **Privately Held**
SIC: 3728 Aircraft parts & equipment

(G-4867)
ROBOCOM US LLC (HQ)
Also Called: Robocom Systems International
1111 Broadhollow Rd # 100 (11735-4819)
PHONE 631 861-2045
Fred Radcliffe, *President*
Richard Adamo, *Vice Pres*
Raymond Oconnor, *Vice Pres*
Patti Guasta, *Sr Project Mgr*
Michael Ciani, *Prgrmr*
EMP: 13
SQ FT: 4,000
SALES: 7MM
SALES (corp-wide): 219K **Privately Held**
WEB: www.avantce.com
SIC: 7372 Prepackaged software
PA: Avantc, Llc
   3838 Tamiami Trl N # 416
   Naples FL 34103
   407 312-8445

(G-4868)
ROLI RETREADS INC
Also Called: Roli Tire and Auto Repair
212 E Carmans Rd Unit A (11735-4722)
PHONE 631 694-7670
Richard Bucci, *Owner*
Laura Lavender, *Controller*
EMP: 20
SQ FT: 6,500
SALES (est): 4.2MM **Privately Held**
WEB: www.rolitire.com
SIC: 3011 7549 Tire & inner tube materials & related products; automotive maintenance services

(G-4869)
ROTA PACK INC
34 Sarah Dr Ste B (11735-1218)
PHONE 631 274-1037
Adrian Spirea, *Ch of Bd*
EMP: 11
SALES: 525K **Privately Held**
WEB: www.rotaindustries.com
SIC: 3565 3535 Packaging machinery; conveyors & conveying equipment

(G-4870)
ROZAL INDUSTRIES INC
151 Marine St (11735-5609)
PHONE 631 420-4277
Brian Casio, *President*
Gary Grieber, *Vice Pres*
EMP: 47
SALES (est): 4MM **Privately Held**
SIC: 3599 Machine shop, jobbing & repair

(G-4871)
RS PRECISION INDUSTRIES INC
295 Adams Blvd (11735-6632)
PHONE 631 420-0424
Robert Savitzky, *President*
Lily Savitzky, *Admin Sec*
EMP: 24
SQ FT: 6,700
SALES (est): 5.9MM **Privately Held**
WEB: www.rsprecision.com
SIC: 3599 Machine shop, jobbing & repair

(G-4872)
S & V KNITS INC
117 Marine St (11735-5607)
PHONE 631 752-1595
EMP: 30
SQ FT: 14,000
SALES (est): 2.8MM **Privately Held**
SIC: 2253 2339 Knit Outerwear Mill Mfg Women's/Misses' Outerwear

(G-4873)
SEANAIR MACHINE CO INC
95 Verdi St (11735-6320)
PHONE 631 694-2820
Laura Abel Nawrocki, *Ch of Bd*
Dorothy Abel, *President*
Thomas J Nawrochi, *Vice Pres*
Laura Abel, *Info Tech Mgr*
EMP: 18 **EST:** 1955
SQ FT: 16,000
SALES (est): 3.3MM **Privately Held**
SIC: 3599 Machine shop, jobbing & repair

(G-4874)
SIMTEC INDUSTRIES CORPORATION
65 Marine St Ste A (11735-5638)
PHONE 631 293-0080
Jean J Simon, *President*
EMP: 6
SALES: 1MM **Privately Held**
SIC: 3552 Textile machinery

(G-4875)
SKYLINE CUSTOM CABINETRY INC
200 Verdi St Unit A (11735-6337)
PHONE 631 393-2983
Lisa Mumalo, *Principal*
EMP: 5
SALES (est): 506.1K **Privately Held**
SIC: 2434 Wood kitchen cabinets

(G-4876)
SMITH GRAPHICS INC
40 Florida St (11735-6301)
PHONE 631 420-4180
Rick Smith, *President*
Sarah Silva, *Office Mgr*
EMP: 8
SQ FT: 2,500
SALES (est): 1.2MM **Privately Held**
WEB: www.smithgraphicsinc.com
SIC: 3993 Signs & advertising specialties

(G-4877)
SOURCE ENVELOPE INC
104 Allen Blvd Ste I (11735-5627)
PHONE 866 284-0707
EMP: 9
SQ FT: 2,000
SALES (est): 963.4K **Privately Held**
SIC: 2752 2759 Lithographic And Letterpress Printing

(G-4878)
SPACE COAST SEMICONDUCTOR INC
1111 Broadhollow Rd Fl 3 (11735-4881)
PHONE 631 414-7131
Anthony Tamborrino, *Director*
EMP: 10
SALES (est): 682.4K **Privately Held**
WEB: www.spacecoastsemi.com
SIC: 3679 Electronic components

(G-4879)
STANDWILL PACKAGING INC
220 Sherwood Ave (11735-1718)
PHONE 631 752-1236
William Standwill Jr, *President*
Janet Kelso, *Receptionist*
▲ **EMP:** 25 **EST:** 1976
SQ FT: 15,000
SALES (est): 4MM **Privately Held**
WEB: www.standwill.com
SIC: 2752 2759 Commercial printing, offset; commercial printing

(G-4880)
STAR MOLD CO INC
125 Florida St (11735-6307)
PHONE 631 694-2283
Guenther Merz, *President*
EMP: 6
SQ FT: 2,400
SALES: 320K **Privately Held**
SIC: 3544 Industrial molds

(G-4881)
STEPHEN J LIPKINS INC
855 Conklin St Ste A (11735-2409)
PHONE 631 249-8866
Jonathan Lipkins, *President*
EMP: 5 **EST:** 1968

Farmingdale - Nassau County (G-4882)　　　　　　　　　　　　　　　　　　　　　　　　　　　**GEOGRAPHIC SECTION**

SQ FT: 2,800
SALES (est): 420K **Privately Held**
SIC: 3915 Jewel cutting, drilling, polishing, recutting or setting; jewelry polishing for the trade

(G-4882)
STERLING INDUSTRIES INC
410 Eastern Pkwy (11735-2431)
PHONE..................................631 753-3070
Brian Lewis, *President*
EMP: 25
SALES (est): 4.4MM **Privately Held**
SIC: 3444 Sheet metalwork

(G-4883)
SUNDIAL BRANDS
1 Adams Blvd (11735-6611)
PHONE..................................631 842-8800
EMP: 7 **EST:** 2015
SALES (est): 1.4MM **Privately Held**
SIC: 2844 Toilet preparations

(G-4884)
SUPERIOR METAL & WOODWORK INC
70 Central Ave (11735-6906)
PHONE..................................631 465-9004
John Cipri, *President*
Joseph Cipri, *Vice Pres*
James Santora, *Project Mgr*
EMP: 25
SQ FT: 12,500
SALES: 6.5MM **Privately Held**
SIC: 3446 Architectural metalwork

(G-4885)
SUPERIOR MOTION CONTROLS INC
40 Smith St (11735-1005)
PHONE..................................516 420-2921
Frank Grieco, *CEO*
Tony Reda, *Engineer*
Rich Neuman, *Sales Staff*
EMP: 40
SQ FT: 20,000
SALES: 9.6MM **Privately Held**
WEB: www.superior-ny.com
SIC: 3728 3679 3462 Aircraft assemblies, subassemblies & parts; electronic loads & power supplies; iron & steel forgings

(G-4886)
SWIMWEAR ANYWHERE INC (PA)
Also Called: Carmen Mark Valvo Swimwear
85 Sherwood Ave (11735-1717)
PHONE..................................631 420-1400
Rosemarie Dilorenzo, *Chairman*
Joseph Dilorenzo, *COO*
Bob Colasante, *Prdtn Mgr*
Arthur Conway, *Opers Staff*
Joseph Roehrig, *CFO*
◆ **EMP:** 75 **EST:** 1998
SALES: 52MM **Privately Held**
SIC: 2339 Bathing suits: women's, misses' & juniors'

(G-4887)
SYNTHO PHARMACEUTICALS INC
230 Sherwood Ave (11735-1718)
PHONE..................................631 755-9898
Hosneara Malik, *President*
Tithi Malik, *Principal*
EMP: 7
SALES: 2.1MM **Privately Held**
WEB: www.synthopharmaceutical.com
SIC: 2834 Pharmaceutical preparations

(G-4888)
T A TOOL & MOLDING INC
Also Called: Konrad Design
185 Marine St (11735-5609)
PHONE..................................631 293-0172
Ludwig Konrad, *President*
Maryann Konrad, *Vice Pres*
EMP: 18
SALES (est): 2.7MM **Privately Held**
SIC: 3089 3544 Injection molding of plastics; industrial molds

(G-4889)
TANGENT MACHINE & TOOL CORP
108 Gazza Blvd (11735-1489)
PHONE..................................631 249-3088
Joseph Scafidi, *President*
Joseph A Scafidi, *President*
Charles C Piola, *CFO*
EMP: 17 **EST:** 1953
SQ FT: 30,000
SALES (est): 3.5MM **Privately Held**
SIC: 3599 3728 Machine shop, jobbing & repair; aircraft parts & equipment

(G-4890)
TAPE PRINTERS INC
155 Allen Blvd Ste A (11735-5640)
PHONE..................................631 249-5585
Alexander J Kruk, *President*
▲ **EMP:** 15
SQ FT: 10,000
SALES (est): 2.8MM **Privately Held**
WEB: www.tapeprinters.com
SIC: 2759 Bag, wrapper & seal printing & engraving; labels & seals: printing

(G-4891)
TELEPHONICS CORPORATION
Also Called: Communications Systems Div
815 Broadhollow Rd (11735-3937)
PHONE..................................631 755-7659
John Piechowiak, *Engineer*
EMP: 99
SALES (corp-wide): 1.5B **Publicly Held**
SIC: 3661 Telephone & telegraph apparatus
HQ: Telephonics Corporation
　815 Broadhollow Rd
　Farmingdale NY 11735
　631 755-7000

(G-4892)
TELEPHONICS CORPORATION (HQ)
815 Broadhollow Rd (11735-3937)
PHONE..................................631 755-7000
Kevin McSweeney, *President*
Mel French, *President*
Jack Sullivan, *General Mgr*
Alan Bryan, *Principal*
James Colotti, *Vice Chairman*
▲ **EMP:** 667
SQ FT: 160,000
SALES: 260.3MM
SALES (corp-wide): 1.5B **Publicly Held**
SIC: 3669 3661 3679 3812 Intercommunication systems, electric; telephone & telegraph apparatus; electronic circuits; radar systems & equipment; air traffic control systems & equipment, electronic; radio & TV communications equipment
PA: Griffon Corporation
　712 5th Ave Fl 18
　New York NY 10019
　212 957-5000

(G-4893)
TELEPHONICS CORPORATION
Also Called: Command Systems Division
815 Broadhollow Rd (11735-3937)
PHONE..................................631 755-7000
Joseph Battaglia, *CEO*
EMP: 99
SALES (corp-wide): 1.5B **Publicly Held**
SIC: 3699 Electronic training devices
HQ: Telephonics Corporation
　815 Broadhollow Rd
　Farmingdale NY 11735
　631 755-7000

(G-4894)
THERMAL PROCESS CNSTR CO
19 Engineers Ln (11735-1207)
PHONE..................................631 293-6400
Al Gupta, *President*
EMP: 22
SQ FT: 10,000
SALES (est): 1.5MM **Privately Held**
SIC: 3567 3497 Incinerators, metal: domestic or commercial; metal foil & leaf

(G-4895)
TIGER SUPPLY INC
99 Sherwood Ave (11735-1717)
PHONE..................................631 293-2700
Anthony Davanzo, *President*
EMP: 6
SALES (est): 955.2K **Privately Held**
WEB: www.tigersupplyinc.com
SIC: 3843 Dental equipment & supplies

(G-4896)
TIME-CAP LABORATORIES INC
Also Called: Custom Coatings
7 Michael Ave (11735-3921)
PHONE..................................631 753-9090
Mark Saldanha, *Ch of Bd*
Irene McGregor, *President*
Robert Azzara, *COO*
Alex Martinez, *Production*
Sam Chacko, *Manager*
▲ **EMP:** 160
SQ FT: 45,000
SALES (est): 50.9MM **Privately Held**
SIC: 2834 Proprietary drug products
PA: Marksans Pharma Limited
　11th Floor, Opp Gundecha Symphony,
　Oshiwara,
　Mumbai MH 40005

(G-4897)
TIN BOX COMPANY OF AMERICA INC (PA)
216 Sherwood Ave (11735-1718)
PHONE..................................631 845-1600
Lloyd Roth, *President*
Andy Siegel, *Vice Pres*
Michael Siegel, *Vice Pres*
Stephen Siegel, *CFO*
Cathy Callahan-Pallone, *Manager*
▲ **EMP:** 25
SQ FT: 20,000
SALES (est): 6.1MM **Privately Held**
SIC: 2631 5051 Container, packaging & boxboard; tin & tin base metals, shapes, forms, etc.

(G-4898)
TRI-FLEX LABEL CORP
48 Allen Blvd Unit A (11735-5642)
PHONE..................................631 293-0411
Kevin Duckman, *President*
Kevin Duckham, *President*
Rich Arens, *Marketing Staff*
Gene Saraniero, *Manager*
Ed Webster, *Director*
▲ **EMP:** 20
SQ FT: 6,000
SALES (est): 4.4MM **Privately Held**
WEB: www.triflexlabel.com
SIC: 2672 2679 Labels (unprinted), gummed: made from purchased materials; labels, paper: made from purchased material

(G-4899)
TRI-SUPREME OPTICAL LLC
Also Called: Tri Supreme Optical
91 Carolyn Blvd (11735-1527)
PHONE..................................631 249-2020
Jay Graber,
Phil Feldman,
▲ **EMP:** 95
SQ FT: 18,000
SALES (est): 12.5MM **Privately Held**
WEB: www.essilor.us
SIC: 3851 5049 Lenses, ophthalmic; optical goods
HQ: Essilor Of America, Inc.
　13555 N Stemmons Fwy
　Dallas TX 75234
　214 496-4000

(G-4900)
TRONIC PLATING CO INC
37 Potter St (11735-4200)
PHONE..................................516 293-7883
Herbert Buckstone, *President*
Stanley J Buckstone, *Vice Pres*
EMP: 11 **EST:** 1955
SQ FT: 6,000
SALES: 629.2K **Privately Held**
SIC: 3471 Electroplating of metals or formed products; finishing, metals or formed products

(G-4901)
ULTIMATE PRCISION MET PDTS INC
200 Finn Ct (11735-1119)
PHONE..................................631 249-9441
Michael Mallia, *CEO*
Vincent Mallia, *President*
Paul Mallia, *Principal*
Larry Mallia, *Vice Pres*
Joseph Reid, *Vice Pres*
▼ **EMP:** 125
SQ FT: 70,000
SALES (est): 25.3MM **Privately Held**
WEB: www.ultimateprecision.com
SIC: 3469 3544 3444 Stamping metal for the trade; special dies & tools; sheet metalwork

(G-4902)
VELOCITY PHARMA LLC
210-220 Sea Ln (11735)
PHONE..................................631 393-2905
Ankur Shah, *President*
Arthur Valeeva, *Opers Mgr*
Nicholas Monte, *Director*
▲ **EMP:** 8
SQ FT: 20,000
SALES: 5MM **Privately Held**
SIC: 2834 Vitamin, nutrient & hematinic preparations for human use

(G-4903)
VITA-NAT INC
298 Adams Blvd (11735-6615)
PHONE..................................631 293-6000
Mohd M Alam, *President*
Khurshid Anwar, *Vice Pres*
▲ **EMP:** 6
SQ FT: 7,000
SALES: 861.1K **Privately Held**
SIC: 2834 Vitamin, nutrient & hematinic preparations for human use

(G-4904)
W R P WELDING LTD
Also Called: Ramick Welding
126 Toledo St (11735-6625)
PHONE..................................631 249-8859
William R Pontecorvo, *President*
EMP: 6
SQ FT: 3,500
SALES (est): 542.1K **Privately Held**
SIC: 7692 Brazing

(G-4905)
WALNUT PACKAGING INC
450 Smith St (11735-1105)
PHONE..................................631 293-3836
Jose Alvarado, *President*
EMP: 21
SQ FT: 14,000
SALES (est): 3.3MM **Privately Held**
WEB: www.wpiplasticbags.com
SIC: 3086 Packaging & shipping materials, foamed plastic

(G-4906)
WEL MADE ENTERPRISES INC
1630 New Hwy (11735-1510)
PHONE..................................631 752-1238
EMP: 14 **EST:** 1950
SQ FT: 1,800
SALES: 1.1MM **Privately Held**
SIC: 3272 Mfg Concrete Products

(G-4907)
XYLON INDUSTRIES INC
79 Florida St (11735-6305)
PHONE..................................631 293-4717
Joseph Jones, *President*
EMP: 5
SQ FT: 4,200
SALES: 850K **Privately Held**
SIC: 3842 2431 Radiation shielding aprons, gloves, sheeting, etc.; millwork

(G-4908)
ZINGS COMPANY LLC
250 Adams Blvd (11735-6615)
PHONE..................................631 454-0339
Robert Jagenburg,
EMP: 5
SALES (est): 385.1K **Privately Held**
WEB: www.zingsco.com
SIC: 2024 Juice pops, frozen

▲ = Import ▼ = Export
◆ = Import/Export

Farmington
Ontario County

(G-4909)
BADGER TECHNOLOGIES INC
5829 County Road 41 (14425-9103)
PHONE...................585 869-7101
Gary Gray, *Manager*
EMP: 45
SALES (est): 4.3MM **Privately Held**
WEB: www.badgertech.com
SIC: 3679 Harness assemblies for electronic use; wire or cable
PA: Badger Technologies, Inc.
 5829 County Road 41
 Farmington NY 14425

(G-4910)
BADGER TECHNOLOGIES INC (PA)
5829 County Road 41 (14425-9103)
PHONE...................585 869-7101
Manoj Shekar, *President*
Jim Harris, *General Mgr*
▲ **EMP:** 63
SQ FT: 15,000
SALES (est): 9.9MM **Privately Held**
WEB: www.badgertech.com
SIC: 3672 Printed circuit boards

(G-4911)
CROSMAN CORPORATION
1360 Rural Rte 8 (14425)
PHONE...................585 398-3920
Steve Burley, *Branch Mgr*
EMP: 30 **Publicly Held**
SIC: 3484 3482 3563 Pellet & BB guns; pellets & BB's, pistol & air rifle ammunition; shot, steel (ammunition); air & gas compressors
HQ: Crosman Corporation
 7629 State Route 5 And 20
 Bloomfield NY 14469
 585 657-6161

(G-4912)
EBSCO INDUSTRIES INC
Global Point Products
5815 County Road 41 (14425-9103)
PHONE...................585 398-2000
David Testa, *Vice Pres*
EMP: 5
SALES (corp-wide): 2.8B **Privately Held**
WEB: www.ebscoind.com
SIC: 3861 Photographic equipment & supplies
PA: Ebsco Industries, Inc.
 5724 Highway 280 E
 Birmingham AL 35242
 205 991-6600

(G-4913)
EMORY MACHINE & TOOL CO INC
6176 Hunters Dr (14425-1122)
PHONE...................585 436-9610
James Fowler Jr, *President*
EMP: 45
SQ FT: 30,000
SALES (est): 4.4MM **Privately Held**
WEB: www.emory-rockwood.com
SIC: 3599 3451 Mfg Industrial Machinery Mfg Screw Machine Products

(G-4914)
GANNETT CO INC
Also Called: Democrat & Chronicle
6300 Collett Rd (14425-1075)
PHONE...................585 924-3406
Karen Beach, *Manager*
EMP: 8
SALES (corp-wide): 3.1B **Publicly Held**
WEB: www.gannett.com
SIC: 2711 Newspapers: publishing only, not printed on site
PA: Gannett Co., Inc.
 7950 Jones Branch Dr
 Mc Lean VA 22102
 703 854-6000

(G-4915)
HANSEN STEEL
Also Called: Hansen Metal Fabrications
6021 County Road 41 (14425-8938)
PHONE...................585 398-2020
Thomas Hansen, *Owner*
EMP: 25
SQ FT: 13,500
SALES (est): 3.4MM **Privately Held**
SIC: 3441 7692 3444 Fabricated structural metal; welding repair; sheet metalwork

(G-4916)
INGLESIDE MACHINE CO INC
1120 Hook Rd (14425-8956)
PHONE...................585 924-3046
Jan Marie Veomett, *Ch of Bd*
EMP: 80
SQ FT: 40,000
SALES (est): 11.6MM **Privately Held**
WEB: www.inglesidemachine.com
SIC: 7692 3599 Welding repair; machine shop, jobbing & repair

(G-4917)
MINITEC FRAMING SYSTEMS LLC
5602 County Road 41 (14425-9101)
PHONE...................585 924-4690
Susan Paeth, *General Mgr*
Jason Cooley, *Foreman/Supr*
Matt Hoad, *Sales Engr*
Mike Taylor, *Sales Engr*
Andrew Moles,
▲ **EMP:** 26 **EST:** 1998
SQ FT: 53,000
SALES: 3.5MM **Privately Held**
SIC: 3354 Aluminum extruded products

(G-4918)
ROCHESTER ASPHALT MATERIALS
5929 Loomis Rd (14425-9526)
PHONE...................585 924-7360
Daniel Coe, *Branch Mgr*
EMP: 60
SALES (corp-wide): 29.7B **Privately Held**
SIC: 3273 Ready-mixed concrete
HQ: Rochester Asphalt Materials Inc
 1150 Penfield Rd
 Rochester NY 14625
 585 381-7010

(G-4919)
ROCHESTER LUMBER COMPANY
Also Called: Trusses & Trim Division
6080 Collett Rd (14425-9531)
PHONE...................585 924-7171
Paul Rickner, *Branch Mgr*
EMP: 30
SALES (corp-wide): 10.2MM **Privately Held**
SIC: 2439 2431 3442 Trusses, wooden roof; doors, wood; staircases & stairs, wood; metal doors, sash & trim
PA: Rochester Lumber Company
 2040 East Ave
 Rochester NY 14610
 585 473-8080

(G-4920)
TCS ELECTRONICS INC
1124 Corporate Dr (14425-9570)
PHONE...................585 337-4301
Jim Harris, *General Mgr*
Renee Strong, *Manager*
EMP: 27
SALES (est): 6MM **Privately Held**
SIC: 3672 3679 Circuit boards, television & radio printed; harness assemblies for electronic use: wire or cable

(G-4921)
VR FOOD EQUIPMENT INC
5801 County Road 41 (14425-9103)
P.O. Box 25428 (14425-0428)
PHONE...................315 531-8133
Steven A Von Rhedey, *Ch of Bd*
Isaac Von Rhedey, *Vice Pres*
Steven P Von Rhedey, *Vice Pres*
Peter Von Rhedey, *CFO*
▲ **EMP:** 10
SQ FT: 15,000
SALES (est): 2.5MM **Privately Held**
WEB: www.vrfoodequipment.com
SIC: 3556 5084 Food products machinery; food industry machinery

Farmingville
Suffolk County

(G-4922)
A NATIONAL PRINTING CO INC
51 Leeds Blvd (11738-1147)
PHONE...................631 243-3395
Michael Orrach, *President*
EMP: 5
SALES (est): 337.8K **Privately Held**
SIC: 2752 Commercial printing, lithographic

(G-4923)
BUD BARGER ASSOC INC
Also Called: Carduner Sales Company
3 Mount Mckinley Ave (11738-2107)
PHONE...................631 696-6703
Bud Barger, *President*
EMP: 5
SALES (est): 602K **Privately Held**
SIC: 3679 Electronic components

(G-4924)
MIND DESIGNS INC (PA)
5 Gregory Ct (11738-4202)
PHONE...................631 563-3644
Anibal Rodriguez, *President*
Joshua Rodriguez, *COO*
Dorothea Rodriguez, *CFO*
EMP: 8
SQ FT: 8,800
SALES (est): 1.5MM **Privately Held**
WEB: www.mindglow.com
SIC: 2431 5211 Planing mill, millwork; cabinets, kitchen

(G-4925)
PEI/GENESIS INC
Also Called: Pei Genesis International
2410 N Ocean Ave Ste 401 (11738-2917)
PHONE...................631 256-1747
Donald Wood, *Branch Mgr*
EMP: 8
SALES (corp-wide): 307MM **Privately Held**
SIC: 3678 Electronic connectors
PA: Pei/Genesis, Inc.
 2180 Hornig Rd Ste 2
 Philadelphia PA 19116
 215 464-1410

Fayette
Seneca County

(G-4926)
SENECA STONE CORPORATION
Cty Rd 121 Hoster Cors Rd (13065)
P.O. Box 76 (13065-0076)
PHONE...................315 549-8253
Tom Cleare, *Manager*
EMP: 15
SALES (corp-wide): 105.9MM **Privately Held**
SIC: 3281 5032 Cut stone & stone products; stone, crushed or broken
HQ: Seneca Stone Corporation
 2105 S Broadway
 Pine City NY 14871
 607 737-6200

Fayetteville
Onondaga County

(G-4927)
DATA KEY COMMUNICATION LLC
7573 Hunt Ln (13066-2560)
PHONE...................315 445-2347
Judy Flannagan, *Mng Member*
Carole Jesiolowski, *Manager*
Diane Stirling, *Senior Editor*
EMP: 15
SALES (est): 1.5MM **Privately Held**
WEB: www.datakeyllc.com
SIC: 2721 7375 7371 Magazines: publishing only, not printed on site; information retrieval services; custom computer programming services

(G-4928)
JENLOR LTD
523 E Genesee St (13066-1536)
PHONE...................315 637-9080
Joseph Ophir, *President*
▲ **EMP:** 10
SQ FT: 5,000
SALES (est): 1.3MM **Privately Held**
WEB: www.jenlor-samatic.com
SIC: 3679 Electronic circuits

(G-4929)
P B & H MOULDING CORPORATION
7121 Woodchuck Hill Rd (13066-9714)
PHONE...................315 455-1756
Timothy Orcutt, *President*
Douglas Hatch, *Vice Pres*
Jo Dean Hall Orcutt, *Vice Pres*
Patine Ryu, *Executive*
EMP: 22
SQ FT: 33,000
SALES (est): 2.5MM **Privately Held**
WEB: www.pbhmoulding.com
SIC: 2499 Picture frame molding, finished

Felts Mills
Jefferson County

(G-4930)
CRANESVILLE BLOCK CO INC
Also Called: Drum Ready-Mix
23903 Cemetery Rd (13638-3113)
P.O. Box 210 (13638-0210)
PHONE...................315 773-2296
Edward Bailey, *Regional Mgr*
Robert Vancoughnett, *Opers Mgr*
James Buckley, *Sales Executive*
EMP: 35
SALES (corp-wide): 45.6MM **Privately Held**
SIC: 3271 3273 Blocks, concrete or cinder: standard; ready-mixed concrete
PA: Cranesville Block Co., Inc.
 1250 Riverfront Ctr
 Amsterdam NY 12010
 518 684-6154

Ferndale
Sullivan County

(G-4931)
CHIPITA AMERICA INC
Also Called: Mamma Says
1243 Old Route 17 (12734-5422)
PHONE...................845 292-2540
Ed McDermott, *Manager*
EMP: 50 **Privately Held**
SIC: 2052 Cookies
HQ: Chipita America, Inc.
 1 Westbrook Corporate Ctr
 Westchester IL 60154
 708 731-2434

(G-4932)
DC FABRICATION & WELDING INC
17 Radcliff Rd (12734-5300)
PHONE...................845 295-0215
Dan Coutermash, *President*
Bill Fredrick, *Treasurer*
EMP: 6
SQ FT: 8,000
SALES: 600K **Privately Held**
SIC: 7692 Welding repair

(G-4933)
GETEC INC
624 Harris Rd (12734-5135)
P.O. Box 583 (12734-0583)
PHONE...................845 292-0800
Jean Bader, *President*
Hans Bader Jr, *Vice Pres*

Christa Bader, *Project Engr*
▲ EMP: 15
SQ FT: 10,000
SALES: 3.1MM **Privately Held**
WEB: www.getec.com
SIC: 3621 Generators & sets, electric

(G-4934)
HUDSON VALLEY FOIE GRAS LLC
80 Brooks Rd (12734-5101)
PHONE.................845 292-2500
Michael Ginor,
EMP: 12 EST: 2008
SALES (est): 2.2MM **Privately Held**
SIC: 2015 Ducks, processed; ducks, processed: canned; ducks, processed: fresh; ducks, processed: frozen

Feura Bush
Albany County

(G-4935)
LINDE LLC
76 W Yard Rd (12067-9739)
PHONE.................518 439-8187
Paul L Giudice, *Project Mgr*
John Cox, *Branch Mgr*
Debbi Lacey, *Administration*
EMP: 55
SALES (corp-wide): 20.1B **Privately Held**
SIC: 2813 Nitrogen; oxygen, compressed or liquefied
HQ: Linde Llc
    200 Somerset Corporate Bl
    Bridgewater NJ 08807
    908 464-8100

(G-4936)
OWENS CORNING SALES LLC
1277 Feura Bush Rd (12067-1719)
P.O. Box 98, Delmar (12054-0098)
PHONE.................518 475-3600
Craig Burroughs, *Branch Mgr*
EMP: 465
SQ FT: 1,860 **Publicly Held**
WEB: www.owenscorning.com
SIC: 3229 3296 Pressed & blown glass; mineral wool
HQ: Owens Corning Sales, Llc
    1 Owens Corning Pkwy
    Toledo OH 43659
    419 248-8000

Fillmore
Allegany County

(G-4937)
CUBA SPECIALTY MFG CO INC
Also Called: Tackle Factory
81 S Genesee St (14735-8700)
P.O. Box 195 (14735-0195)
PHONE.................585 567-4176
Dana R Pickup, *President*
Stephen Fentz, *President*
Edward Fox, *President*
Michelle Popovice, *Controller*
▲ EMP: 10 EST: 1931
SQ FT: 23,000
SALES (est): 1.6MM **Privately Held**
SIC: 3496 Traps, animal & fish

(G-4938)
PRIMESOUTH INC
11537 Route 19 (14735)
PHONE.................585 567-4191
John Kingston, *Manager*
EMP: 10 EST: 1991
SALES (est): 740K **Privately Held**
SIC: 3825 Electrical power measuring equipment

Findley Lake
Chautauqua County

(G-4939)
OUR OWN CANDLE COMPANY INC (PA)
10349 Main St (14736-9722)
P.O. Box 99 (14736-0099)
PHONE.................716 769-5000
Lawrence S Gross, *President*
Kurt M Duska, *Vice Pres*
◆ EMP: 12
SALES (est): 2MM **Privately Held**
SIC: 3999 Shades, lamp or candle; candles

Fishers
Ontario County

(G-4940)
GORBEL INC (PA)
600 Fishers Run (14453)
P.O. Box 593 (14453-0593)
PHONE.................585 924-6262
David Reh, *CEO*
Brian D Reh, *Ch of Bd*
David Butwid, *Vice Pres*
Brian Peets, *Research*
Chris Adams, *Engineer*
◆ EMP: 130 EST: 1977
SQ FT: 64,000
SALES (est): 75.2MM **Privately Held**
WEB: www.gorbel.com
SIC: 3536 Cranes, industrial plant

(G-4941)
OLDCASTLE APG NORTHEAST INC
735 Wangum Rd (14453)
PHONE.................585 924-2103
Thomas Hill, *Principal*
Lori Wyman, *Executive*
EMP: 29
SALES (corp-wide): 29.7B **Privately Held**
SIC: 3271 Blocks, concrete or cinder: standard
HQ: Oldcastle Apg Northeast, Inc.
    13555 Wellington Cntr Cir
    Gainesville VA 20155
    703 365-7070

Fishkill
Dutchess County

(G-4942)
ACADIA STAIRS
73 Route 9 Ste 3 (12524-2944)
PHONE.................845 765-8600
Michelle Cioffredi, *President*
▲ EMP: 8
SALES (est): 1.3MM **Privately Held**
SIC: 3441 Fabricated structural metal

(G-4943)
BIONIC EYE TECHNOLOGIES INC
4 Willow Lake Dr (12524-2952)
PHONE.................845 505-5254
Richard Birney, *CEO*
EMP: 7
SALES (est): 447.5K **Privately Held**
SIC: 3842 Implants, surgical

(G-4944)
CRANESVILLE BLOCK CO INC
70 Route 9 (12524-2962)
PHONE.................845 896-5687
John Tesrro, *CEO*
EMP: 20
SQ FT: 3,960
SALES (corp-wide): 45.6MM **Privately Held**
SIC: 3273 Ready-mixed concrete
PA: Cranesville Block Co., Inc.
    1250 Riverfront Ctr
    Amsterdam NY 12010
    518 684-6154

(G-4945)
ENTERPRISE BAGELS INC
Also Called: Bagel Shoppe, The
986 Main St Ste 3 (12524-3508)
PHONE.................845 896-3823
Joe Raffele, *CEO*
EMP: 12
SALES (est): 1.4MM **Privately Held**
SIC: 2051 Bagels, fresh or frozen

(G-4946)
FAMILY HEARING CENTER
18 Westage Dr Ste 16 (12524-2289)
PHONE.................845 897-3059
Lori Biasotti, *Owner*
EMP: 5
SALES (est): 440.6K **Privately Held**
SIC: 3842 8049 Hearing aids; audiologist

(G-4947)
LAM RESEARCH CORPORATION
300 Westage Bus Ctr Dr # 190 (12524-4201)
PHONE.................845 896-0606
Craig Bitzell, *Manager*
EMP: 50
SALES (corp-wide): 11B **Publicly Held**
WEB: www.lamrc.com
SIC: 3559 Semiconductor manufacturing machinery
PA: Lam Research Corporation
    4650 Cushing Pkwy
    Fremont CA 94538
    510 572-0200

(G-4948)
LOVINGLY LLC
1399 Route 52 Ste 100 (12524-3250)
PHONE.................845 977-0775
Ken Garland, *Managing Prtnr*
Russ Taylor, *Regional Mgr*
Mahima Kurian, *Engineer*
Edward Castillo, *Sales Staff*
Lindsay Santoro, *Sales Staff*
EMP: 36
SQ FT: 10,000
SALES (est): 379.6K **Privately Held**
WEB: www.unitedfloristnetwork.com
SIC: 7372 Application computer software

(G-4949)
MONTFORT BROTHERS INC
44 Elm St (12524-1804)
PHONE.................845 896-6694
Jacqueline Montfort, *President*
Bob Armstrong, *Prdtn Mgr*
Anita Assenza, *Purchasing*
Melissa Oberle, *Office Mgr*
Karen Piga, *Executive Asst*
EMP: 30
SQ FT: 15,000
SALES (est): 6.4MM **Privately Held**
WEB: www.montfortgroup.com
SIC: 3271 Blocks, concrete or cinder: standard

(G-4950)
N SKETCH BUILD INC
982 Main St Ste 4-130 (12524-3506)
PHONE.................800 975-0597
Jacqueline Ellison, *Ch of Bd*
◆ EMP: 9
SALES (est): 934.3K **Privately Held**
SIC: 2499 Decorative wood & woodwork

(G-4951)
NERAK SYSTEMS INC
4 Stage Door Rd (12524-2423)
PHONE.................914 763-8259
Volker Brandt, *President*
Peter Pralle, *Vice Pres*
Simone Wakefield, *CFO*
▲ EMP: 15
SQ FT: 100,000
SALES (est): 4.5MM **Privately Held**
WEB: www.nerak-systems.com
SIC: 3535 5084 Conveyors & conveying equipment; materials handling machinery
HQ: Nerak Gmbh Fordertechnik
    Brigitta 5
    Hambuhren 29313
    508 494-40

(G-4952)
SUBURBAN PUBLISHING INC (PA)
Also Called: Hudson Valley Magazine
1 Summit Ct Ste 200a (12524-3508)
PHONE.................845 463-0542
Angelo Martinello, *Chairman*
Robert Martinella, *President*
Robert Martinelli, *Vice Pres*
EMP: 12
SQ FT: 3,000
SALES (est): 1MM **Privately Held**
WEB: www.hudsonvalleymagazine.com
SIC: 2721 Magazines: publishing only, not printed on site

Floral Park
Nassau County

(G-4953)
ALLIANCE SERVICES CORP
23 Van Siclen Ave (11001-2012)
PHONE.................516 775-7600
Frank De Oliveira, *President*
Peter Smith, *General Mgr*
Victor De Oliveira, *Vice Pres*
EMP: 14
SQ FT: 18,000
SALES: 1.6MM **Privately Held**
WEB: www.alliancewelding.com
SIC: 7692 Welding repair

(G-4954)
ALLIANCE WELDING & STEEL FABG
15 Van Siclen Ave (11001-2012)
PHONE.................516 775-7600
Victor De Oliveira, *President*
Frank De Oliveira, *Corp Secy*
EMP: 18
SQ FT: 18,000
SALES (est): 2.4MM **Privately Held**
SIC: 3444 7692 Sheet metalwork; welding repair

(G-4955)
ALLOMATIC PRODUCTS COMPANY
Also Called: Sales Department
102 Jericho Tpke Ste 104 (11001-2004)
PHONE.................516 775-0330
Bob Clark, *Vice Pres*
Bob Tichy, *Marketing Mgr*
Israel Tabaksblat, *Marketing Staff*
John Butz, *Manager*
EMP: 5 **Privately Held**
WEB: www.allomatic.com
SIC: 3714 Motor vehicle parts & accessories
HQ: Allomatic Products Company Inc
    609 E Chaney St
    Sullivan IN 47882
    800 686-4729

(G-4956)
AUTOMATED BLDG MGT SYSTEMS INC (PA)
Also Called: Honeywell Authorized Dealer
54 Cherry Ln (11001-1611)
PHONE.................516 216-5603
Alkesh Amin, *President*
EMP: 40
SQ FT: 2,000
SALES: 27.5MM **Privately Held**
WEB: www.abmsys.com
SIC: 3822 Temperature controls, automatic

(G-4957)
BARCLAY TAGG RACING
86 Geranium Ave (11001-3035)
PHONE.................631 404-8269
Barclay Tagg, *Owner*
EMP: 30
SALES (est): 1.1MM **Privately Held**
SIC: 3721 Aircraft

(G-4958)
C & A SERVICE INC (PA)
Also Called: Citrus and Allied Essences
65 S Tyson Ave (11001-1821)
PHONE.................516 354-1200
Richard Pisano Jr, *President*

◆ **EMP**: 5
SALES (est): 1.1MM **Privately Held**
SIC: 2899 2911 Chemical preparations; aromatic chemical products

(G-4959)
CB PUBLISHING LLC
Also Called: CB Products
50 Carnation Ave Bldg 2-1 (11001-1741)
P.O. Box 280, New Hyde Park (11040-0280)
PHONE..................516 354-4888
Clifford Brechner, *President*
EMP: 7
SQ FT: 1,400
SALES (est): 577.4K **Privately Held**
WEB: www.cbproducts.com
SIC: 2731 Books: publishing only

(G-4960)
CITRUS AND ALLIED ESSENCES LTD (PA)
Also Called: C&A Aromatics
65 S Tyson Ave (11001-1898)
PHONE..................516 354-1200
Stephen Pisano, *CEO*
Richard C Pisano Jr, *CEO*
Grace Alloca, *Principal*
Arthur Curran, *Principal*
Ann E Heller, *Principal*
◆ **EMP**: 120
SQ FT: 11,000
SALES (est): 31.1MM **Privately Held**
WEB: www.citrusandallied.com
SIC: 2087 2899 2911 Flavoring extracts & syrups; chemical preparations; aromatic chemical products

(G-4961)
CREATRON SERVICES INC
Also Called: Lanel
504 Cherry Ln (11001-1646)
PHONE..................516 437-5119
Isidore Epstein, *President*
Alan Rosen, *Vice Pres*
EMP: 20
SQ FT: 10,000
SALES (est): 1.4MM **Privately Held**
SIC: 3861 Photographic equipment & supplies

(G-4962)
DECREE SIGNS & GRAPHICS INC
Also Called: Manhattan Signs
91 Tulip Ave Apt Kd1 (11001-1983)
PHONE..................973 278-3603
Anthony Decrescenzo, *President*
EMP: 15
SALES (est): 1.6MM **Privately Held**
SIC: 3993 Signs, not made in custom sign painting shops

(G-4963)
EASTERN UNIT EXCH RMNFACTURING
186 Beech St (11001-3318)
P.O. Box 180346, Richmond Hill (11418-0346)
PHONE..................718 739-7113
Chester Brown, *President*
Mehendra Sarwan, *Manager*
EMP: 15 **EST**: 1976
SQ FT: 5,000
SALES (est): 1.8MM **Privately Held**
SIC: 3694 Alternators, automotive; generators, automotive & aircraft; motors, starting: automotive & aircraft

(G-4964)
P T E INC
36 Ontario Rd (11001-4113)
PHONE..................516 775-3839
Gustave Loos, *President*
EMP: 19 **EST**: 1957
SQ FT: 10,125
SALES (est): 1.3MM **Privately Held**
SIC: 3599 Machine shop, jobbing & repair

(G-4965)
TWO BILLS MACHINE & TOOL CO
17 Concord St (11001-2819)
PHONE..................516 437-2585
Wilhelm Sangen, *President*
Frederick Sangen, *Vice Pres*
EMP: 11
SQ FT: 7,000
SALES (est): 1.3MM **Privately Held**
SIC: 3599 Machine shop, jobbing & repair

Floral Park
Queens County

(G-4966)
INDIRA FOODS INC
25503 Hillside Ave # 255 (11004)
PHONE..................718 343-1500
Indira Mathur, *President*
EMP: 10
SALES (est): 820K **Privately Held**
SIC: 2032 Italian foods: packaged in cans, jars, etc.

(G-4967)
S & J TRADING INC
8030 263rd St (11004-1517)
P.O. Box 40337, Glen Oaks (11004-0337)
PHONE..................718 347-1323
Surinder Chawla, *President*
▲ **EMP**: 8
SALES (est): 800K **Privately Held**
SIC: 3299 5063 5033 Mica products; electrical apparatus & equipment; roofing, siding & insulation

Florida
Orange County

(G-4968)
BRACH KNITTING MILLS INC
12 Roosevelt Ave (10921-1808)
P.O. Box 13 (10921-0013)
PHONE..................845 651-4450
Shea Brach, *President*
EMP: 15 **EST**: 1965
SQ FT: 32,000
SALES: 500K **Privately Held**
SIC: 2251 2331 Panty hose; tights, women's; snirts, women's & juniors': made from purchased materials

(G-4969)
CONVERGENT CNNCTIVITY TECH INC
1751 State Route 17a (10921-1061)
P.O. Box 454 (10921-0454)
PHONE..................845 651-5250
Joseph T Moore, *Ch of Bd*
▲ **EMP**: 5
SALES (est): 789.9K **Privately Held**
SIC: 3357 Nonferrous wiredrawing & insulating

(G-4970)
EMPIRE VENTILATION EQP CO INC (PA)
9 Industrial Dr (10921-1000)
PHONE..................718 728-2143
George R Taylor, *President*
Linda L Taylor, *Vice Pres*
Robert E Warnken, *Treasurer*
Brian G Taylor, *Admin Sec*
EMP: 12 **EST**: 1936
SQ FT: 15,000
SALES: 1.5MM **Privately Held**
WEB: www.empirevent.com
SIC: 3444 Ventilators, sheet metal

(G-4971)
ISLAND NAMEPLATE INC
124 S Main St (10921-1818)
P.O. Box 548 (10921-0548)
PHONE..................845 651-4005
Joseph C Sicina III, *President*
EMP: 5
SQ FT: 1,860
SALES: 260K **Privately Held**
SIC: 3993 Name plates: except engraved, etched, etc.: metal

(G-4972)
REMEE PRODUCTS CORP (PA)
Also Called: Remfo
1751 State Route 17a (10921-1061)
PHONE..................845 651-4431
Elias Muhlrad, *President*
Steve N Luciana, *President*
Eric Muhlrad, *COO*
Bill Cullen, *Vice Pres*
Glenn La Perle, *VP Opers*
◆ **EMP**: 95
SQ FT: 125,000
SALES (est): 31.4MM **Privately Held**
SIC: 3357 Nonferrous wiredrawing & insulating

(G-4973)
ZIRCAR CERAMICS INC (PA)
100 N Main St Ste 2 (10921-1329)
P.O. Box 519 (10921-0519)
PHONE..................845 651-6600
Phil Hamling, *President*
David Hamling, *Vice Pres*
Jay Magnelli, *Prdtn Mgr*
Marilyn Sweeney, *Manager*
▲ **EMP**: 34
SQ FT: 30,000
SALES (est): 8MM **Privately Held**
WEB: www.zircarceramics.com
SIC: 3297 Nonclay refractories

(G-4974)
ZIRCAR REFR COMPOSITES INC
14 Golden Hill Ter (10921-1116)
PHONE..................845 651-2200
Julie Sterns, *Branch Mgr*
EMP: 12 **Privately Held**
WEB: www.zrci.com
SIC: 2493 Reconstituted wood products
PA: Zircar Refractory Composites, Inc.
   46 Jayne St
   Florida NY 10921

(G-4975)
ZIRCAR REFR COMPOSITES INC (PA)
46 Jayne St (10921-1109)
P.O. Box 489 (10921-0489)
PHONE..................845 651-4481
Tom Hamling, *Ch of Bd*
Peter Hamling, *President*
Mike Cauda, *Engineer*
▲ **EMP**: 8
SQ FT: 4,000
SALES (est): 3.3MM **Privately Held**
WEB: www.zrci.com
SIC: 3297 Nonclay refractories

(G-4976)
ZIRCAR ZIRCONIA INC
87 Meadow Rd (10921-1112)
P.O. Box 287 (10921-0287)
PHONE..................845 651-3040
Craig Hamling, *President*
Clare Hamling, *Vice Pres*
Jeff Babcock, *Prdtn Mgr*
Kyra Hamling, *Buyer*
John Koar, *Engineer*
▲ **EMP**: 24
SQ FT: 20,800
SALES (est): 3.8MM **Privately Held**
WEB: www.zircarzirconia.com
SIC: 3297 Nonclay refractories

Flushing
Queens County

(G-4977)
5 STARS PRINTING CORP
13330 32nd Ave (11354-1921)
PHONE..................718 461-4612
S K Han, *President*
EMP: 10
SALES (est): 894.5K **Privately Held**
WEB: www.bocasoccer.com
SIC: 2759 Commercial printing

(G-4978)
AB SEAFOOD TRADING INC
3129 Higgins St (11354-2503)
PHONE..................718 353-8848
Dian Y Lin, *CEO*
EMP: 5
SALES (est): 274.7K **Privately Held**
SIC: 2092 Fresh or frozen packaged fish

(G-4979)
ACCREDO HEALTH INCORPORATED
14330 38th Ave Apt 1f (11354-5720)
PHONE..................718 353-3012
Nakia Jefferson, *Branch Mgr*
EMP: 5
SALES (corp-wide): 100B **Publicly Held**
SIC: 2833 Medicinals & botanicals
HQ: Accredo Health, Incorporated
   1640 Century Center Pkwy # 110
   Memphis TN 38134

(G-4980)
ACE PRINTING & PUBLISHING INC
Also Called: Ace Printing Co
14951 Roosevelt Ave (11354-4939)
PHONE..................718 939-0040
Sung N Kang, *CEO*
EMP: 10
SQ FT: 3,000
SALES (est): 800K **Privately Held**
SIC: 2752 Offset & photolithographic printing

(G-4981)
AIR EXPORT MECHANICAL
4108 Parsons Blvd Apt 4r (11355-1940)
PHONE..................917 709-5310
Gricelio Nosquera, *President*
EMP: 5
SALES (est): 480K **Privately Held**
SIC: 3564 Filters, air: furnaces, air conditioning equipment, etc.

(G-4982)
ALBERT SIY
Also Called: Avant Garde Screen Printing Co
13508 Booth Memorial Ave (11355-5009)
PHONE..................718 359-0389
Albert Siy, *Owner*
EMP: 8
SALES (est): 1MM **Privately Held**
SIC: 2752 2759 2396 Commercial printing, lithographic; screen printing; automotive & apparel trimmings

(G-4983)
ALL ABOUT ART INC
4128 Murray St (11355-1055)
PHONE..................718 321-0755
Gee Book Jeung, *President*
EMP: 11
SALES (est): 900K **Privately Held**
WEB: www.myallaboutart.com
SIC: 2395 2261 Embroidery products, except schiffli machine; finishing plants, cotton

(G-4984)
AMERICAN AUTO ACC INCRPORATION (PA)
3506 Leavitt St Apt Cfc (11354-2967)
PHONE..................718 886-6600
Henry Hsu, *President*
Betty L Hsu, *Vice Pres*
EMP: 20
SQ FT: 50,000
SALES (est): 1.5MM **Privately Held**
WEB: www.3aracing.com
SIC: 3714 5013 Motor vehicle parts & accessories; motor vehicle supplies & new parts

(G-4985)
AMERICAN STD SHTMTL SUP CORP
13324 36th Rd (11354-4413)
PHONE..................718 888-9350
Dezhao Zhao, *Principal*
EMP: 10
SALES (est): 955K **Privately Held**
SIC: 3444 3334 1711 Sheet metalwork; primary aluminum; ventilation & duct work contractor

(G-4986)
ARRINGEMENT INTERNATIONAL INC
16015 45th Ave (11358-3135)
PHONE..................347 323-7974

Flushing - Queens County (G-4987) GEOGRAPHIC SECTION

WEI Huang, *President*
EMP: 6 **EST:** 2013
SQ FT: 1,500
SALES: 200K **Privately Held**
SIC: 3911 Jewelry, precious metal

(G-4987)
ATI TRADING INC
13631 41st Ave Ste 5a (11355-2446)
PHONE..................................718 888-7918
EMP: 18
SALES (est): 3.5MM **Privately Held**
SIC: 3823 Computer interface equipment for industrial process control

(G-4988)
BEST CONCRETE MIX CORP
3510 College Point Blvd (11354-2719)
PHONE..................................718 463-5500
Michael Emanuele, *President*
EMP: 35
SQ FT: 20,000
SALES (est): 6.2MM **Privately Held**
SIC: 3273 Ready-mixed concrete

(G-4989)
CFP PURCHASING INC
4760 197th St (11358-3937)
PHONE..................................705 806-0383
Robert Mantrop, *President*
▼ **EMP:** 2
SALES: 3MM **Privately Held**
SIC: 2499 7389 Yard sticks, wood;

(G-4990)
CHINESE MEDICAL REPORT INC
3907 Prince St Ste 5b (11354-5308)
PHONE..................................718 359-5676
Ava Lee, *President*
▲ **EMP:** 5
SALES (est): 250.9K **Privately Held**
WEB: www.chinesemedical.com
SIC: 2711 Newspapers

(G-4991)
CHRISTIAN PRESS INC
14317 Franklin Ave (11355-2116)
PHONE..................................718 886-4400
Young-Choon Chang, *President*
EMP: 5
SQ FT: 1,200
SALES: 250K **Privately Held**
SIC: 2711 8661 Newspapers, publishing & printing; miscellaneous denomination church

(G-4992)
CITIC INTL (USA) TRAVEL INC
13633 37th Ave Ste 2a (11354-4562)
PHONE..................................718 888-9577
Fuxing Chong, *President*
EMP: 6
SALES: 400K **Privately Held**
SIC: 7372 4724 Application computer software; travel agencies

(G-4993)
COFIRE PAVING CORPORATION
12030 28th Ave (11354-1049)
PHONE..................................718 463-1403
Ross J Holland, *President*
John D Ficarelli, *Treasurer*
Robert Ficarelli, *Admin Sec*
EMP: 30 **EST:** 1946
SQ FT: 29,000
SALES (est): 4.6MM **Privately Held**
SIC: 2951 1611 Asphalt paving mixtures & blocks; surfacing & paving

(G-4994)
COURTLANDT BOOT JACK CO INC
3334 Prince St (11354-2731)
PHONE..................................718 445-6200
John K Parlante Jr, *President*
▲ **EMP:** 35 **EST:** 1940
SQ FT: 30,000
SALES (est): 4.3MM **Privately Held**
SIC: 3199 2387 Holsters, leather; apparel belts

(G-4995)
DELICIAS ANDINAS FOOD CORP
5750 Maspeth Ave (11378-2212)
PHONE..................................718 416-2922

Manuel Midonda, *President*
Juanita Midonda, *Vice Pres*
EMP: 32
SALES (est): 5.5MM **Privately Held**
SIC: 2051 Bakery: wholesale or wholesale/retail combined

(G-4996)
DIGITAL ONE USA INC
Also Called: Akhon Samoy Weekly
7230 Roosevelt Ave (11372-6335)
PHONE..................................718 396-4890
Kazi S Hoque, *President*
EMP: 15
SALES (est): 735.5K **Privately Held**
SIC: 2711 Newspapers

(G-4997)
EASY ANALYTIC SOFTWARE INC (PA)
Also Called: Easi
7359 196th St (11366-1810)
PHONE..................................718 740-7930
Robert Katz, *President*
Edward Sussman, *Vice Pres*
EMP: 9
SALES (est): 849.7K **Privately Held**
WEB: www.easidemographics.com
SIC: 7372 Prepackaged software

(G-4998)
EXCELSIOR MLT-CLTURAL INST INC
13340 Roosevelt Ave 7g (11354-5263)
P.O. Box 14332, Augusta GA (30919-0332)
PHONE..................................706 627-4285
Rhonda Jackson, *CEO*
Ronald Nurse, *Director*
EMP: 14
SALES (est): 741.8K **Privately Held**
SIC: 3812 Cabin environment indicators

(G-4999)
FERRARA BROS LLC (HQ)
12005 31st Ave (11354-2516)
PHONE..................................718 939-3030
William J Sandbrook, *President*
EMP: 20
SQ FT: 16,000
SALES: 14.4MM
SALES (corp-wide): 1.3B **Publicly Held**
WEB: www.ferraraconcrete.com
SIC: 3273 5211 5033 Ready-mixed concrete; masonry materials & supplies; roofing, siding & insulation
PA: U.S. Concrete, Inc.
331 N Main St
Euless TX 76039
817 835-4105

(G-5000)
FIBER USA CORP
13620 38th Ave Ste 11f (11354-4232)
PHONE..................................718 888-1512
Pengyu Zhu, *President*
Leo Zhu, *Manager*
EMP: 8
SQ FT: 3,000
SALES (est): 1.8MM
SALES (corp-wide): 22.6MM **Privately Held**
SIC: 2653 5093 Corrugated & solid fiber boxes; plastics scrap
PA: Jiangyin Mighty Chemical Fiber Co., Ltd.
Mazhen Industrial Park
Wuxi 21440
510 869-2183

(G-5001)
FLUSHING IRON WELD INC
13125 Maple Ave (11355-4224)
PHONE..................................718 359-2208
Dario Toro, *President*
Hector Munoz, *Vice Pres*
Nelson Santander, *Project Mgr*
Paula Munoz, *Manager*
EMP: 20
SQ FT: 5,000
SALES: 2.5MM **Privately Held**
SIC: 3446 Architectural metalwork

(G-5002)
GLOBAL GRAPHICS INC
Also Called: Wen Hwa Printing
3711 Prince St Ste D (11354-4428)
PHONE..................................718 939-4967
Rong Fang, *President*
Chen Wang, *Manager*
EMP: 10
SALES: 500K **Privately Held**
SIC: 2752 Commercial printing, lithographic

(G-5003)
GROUP INTERNATIONAL LLC
14711 34th Ave (11354-3755)
PHONE..................................718 475-8805
John Liriano, *CEO*
EMP: 5
SALES (est): 169.2K **Privately Held**
SIC: 2043 Infants' foods, cereal type

(G-5004)
H H B BAKERY OF LITTLE NECK
Also Called: Richer's Bakery
24914 Horace Harding Expy (11362-2050)
PHONE..................................718 631-7004
Eugene Stanko, *President*
EMP: 5
SALES (est): 230K **Privately Held**
SIC: 2051 Bakery: wholesale or wholesale/retail combined

(G-5005)
H&L COMPUTERS INC
13523 Northern Blvd (11354-4006)
PHONE..................................516 873-8088
Bothen Lin, *President*
EMP: 20
SQ FT: 5,000
SALES (est): 1.6MM **Privately Held**
SIC: 3571 Electronic computers

(G-5006)
HAIR COLOR RESEARCH GROUP INC
13320 Whitestone Expy (11354-2509)
PHONE..................................718 445-6026
Armando Petruccelli, *President*
EMP: 26
SALES: 2.5MM **Privately Held**
SIC: 3999 Hair & hair-based products

(G-5007)
HARVY SURGICAL SUPPLY CORP
Also Called: Harvy Canes
3435 Collins Pl (11354-2720)
PHONE..................................718 939-1122
Harvey Murtha, *President*
Scott Murtha, *General Mgr*
Paul Murtha, *Vice Pres*
◆ **EMP:** 30 **EST:** 1897
SALES (est): 5MM **Privately Held**
SIC: 3842 Canes, orthopedic

(G-5008)
HISUN OPTOELECTRONICS CO LTD
Also Called: Hisun Led
4109 College Point Blvd (11355-4226)
PHONE..................................718 886-6966
Eugene L Yu, *President*
▲ **EMP:** 15
SALES (est): 1.8MM **Privately Held**
SIC: 3674 Light emitting diodes

(G-5009)
HOME IDEAL INC
4528 159th St (11358-3148)
PHONE..................................718 762-8998
Henry Chin, *President*
Cheryl Lyn, *Corp Secy*
Winston Lyn, *Vice Pres*
EMP: 7
SALES: 300K **Privately Held**
SIC: 2434 5712 1751 2541 Wood kitchen cabinets; cabinets, except custom made: kitchen; cabinet building & installation; wood partitions & fixtures

(G-5010)
INTER PACIFIC CONSULTING CORP
Also Called: Ipcc
14055 34th Ave Apt 3n (11354-3038)
PHONE..................................718 460-2787
John Tsao, *President*
▲ **EMP:** 5
SALES: 1MM **Privately Held**
SIC: 3499 5023 Picture frames, metal; frames & framing, picture & mirror

(G-5011)
INTERCULTURAL ALLIANCE ARTISTS
Also Called: Iaas, The
4510 165th St (11358-3229)
P.O. Box 4378, New York (10163-4378)
PHONE..................................917 406-1202
Gabrielle David, *President*
Stephanie Agosto, *Vice Pres*
Michelle Aragon, *Vice Pres*
Joan Edmonds Ashman, *Vice Pres*
Naydene Brickus, *Vice Pres*
EMP: 5
SALES: 11.8K **Privately Held**
SIC: 2721 Magazines: publishing & printing

(G-5012)
INTREPID CONTROL SERVICE INC
2904 Francis Lewis Blvd (11358-1536)
PHONE..................................718 886-8771
William Varrone, *President*
James Colleran, *Corp Secy*
Andrew Manesis, *Vice Pres*
Dean Pecoraro, *Vice Pres*
EMP: 5
SQ FT: 750
SALES (est): 961.1K **Privately Held**
SIC: 3822 Temperature controls, automatic

(G-5013)
J D STEWARD INC
4537 162nd St (11358-3157)
PHONE..................................718 358-0169
Dominick Savino, *President*
Jean Stephens, *Vice Pres*
Joseph Savino, *Treasurer*
EMP: 5
SALES: 900K **Privately Held**
WEB: www.jdsteward.com
SIC: 3498 Fabricated pipe & fittings

(G-5014)
JOHN A VASSILAROS & SON INC
Also Called: Vassilaros Coffee
2905 120th St (11354-2505)
PHONE..................................718 886-4140
John Vassilaros, *President*
Irene Vassilaros, *Vice Pres*
EMP: 42
SQ FT: 25,000
SALES (est): 11MM **Privately Held**
WEB: www.vassilaroscoffee.com
SIC: 2095 Coffee roasting (except by wholesale grocers)

(G-5015)
KALEL PARTNERS LLC
7012 170th St Ste 101 (11365-3332)
PHONE..................................347 561-7804
Todd Friedman, *CEO*
EMP: 15
SALES (est): 474K **Privately Held**
SIC: 2741 Miscellaneous publishing

(G-5016)
KEPCO INC (PA)
13138 Sanford Ave (11354-4245)
PHONE..................................718 461-7000
Martin Kupferberg, *President*
Max Kupferberg, *Chairman*
Saul Kupferberg, *Vice Pres*
Seth Kupferberg, *Vice Pres*
Mark Kupferberg, *VP Mfg*
EMP: 150 **EST:** 1946
SQ FT: 145,000
SALES (est): 34.1MM **Privately Held**
SIC: 3612 Power & distribution transformers

GEOGRAPHIC SECTION

Flushing - Queens County (G-5046)

(G-5017)
KEPCO INC
13140 Maple Ave (11355-4225)
PHONE 718 461-7000
Martin Kupferberg, *President*
EMP: 90
SALES (corp-wide): 34.1MM Privately Held
SIC: 3612 Power & distribution transformers
PA: Kepco, Inc.
    13138 Sanford Ave
    Flushing NY 11355
    718 461-7000

(G-5018)
KEPCO INC
13138 Sanford Ave (11355-4245)
PHONE 718 461-7000
EMP: 50
SALES (corp-wide): 34.1MM Privately Held
SIC: 3612 Power & distribution transformers
PA: Kepco, Inc.
    13138 Sanford Ave
    Flushing NY 11355
    718 461-7000

(G-5019)
KOREA TIMES NEW YORK INC
15408 Nthrn Blvd Ste 2b (11354)
PHONE 718 961-7979
Jae Chang, *President*
EMP: 7
SALES (corp-wide): 83.9MM Privately Held
SIC: 2711 Newspapers: publishing only, not printed on site
HQ: The Korea Times New York Inc
    3710 Skillman Ave
    Long Island City NY 11101
    718 784-4526

(G-5020)
KOREAN YELLOW PAGES
14809 Northern Blvd (11354-4346)
PHONE 718 461-0073
Gwanseo Pak, *Owner*
▲ EMP: 10
SALES: 300K Privately Held
SIC: 2741 Telephone & other directory publishing

(G-5021)
LB LAUNDRY INC
4431 Kissena Blvd (11355-3055)
PHONE 347 399-8030
LI Xinli, *Owner*
EMP: 3
SQ FT: 700
SALES: 2MM Privately Held
SIC: 2842 3582 Laundry cleaning preparations; commercial laundry equipment

(G-5022)
LEVI STRAUSS & CO
13432 Blossom Ave (11355-4639)
PHONE 917 213-6263
Chip Bergh, *Branch Mgr*
EMP: 19
SALES (corp-wide): 4.9B Privately Held
SIC: 2325 Jeans: men's, youths' & boys'
PA: Levi Strauss & Co.
    1155 Battery St
    San Francisco CA 94111
    415 501-6000

(G-5023)
LIFE WATCH TECHNOLOGY INC
Also Called: My Life My Health
42-10 Polen St Ste 412 (11355)
PHONE 917 669-2428
Jiping Zhu, *CEO*
EMP: 56
SQ FT: 1,200
SALES (est): 2MM Privately Held
SIC: 3873 Watches & parts, except crystals & jewels

(G-5024)
LONG ISLAND PIPE SUPPLY INC
5858 56th St (11378-3106)
PHONE 718 456-7877
David Pargon, *Manager*
EMP: 6
SALES (corp-wide): 59.6MM Privately Held
WEB: www.lipipe.com
SIC: 3498 Fabricated pipe & fittings
PA: Long Island Pipe Supply Inc
    586 Commercial Ave
    Garden City NY 11530
    516 222-8008

(G-5025)
LOOSELEAF LAW PUBLICATIONS INC
4308 162nd St (11358-3131)
P.O. Box 650042, Fresh Meadows (11365-0042)
PHONE 718 359-5559
Warren Taylor, *President*
Hilary McKeon, *General Mgr*
Michael Loughrey, *Vice Pres*
Tina Macgowan, *Production*
Hilliary McKeon, *Manager*
EMP: 10
SQ FT: 5,000
SALES: 1MM Privately Held
WEB: www.looseleaflaw.com
SIC: 2731 5961 Books: publishing only; books, mail order (except book clubs)

(G-5026)
NATURAL LAB INC
13538 39th Ave Ste 4 (11354-4423)
PHONE 718 321-8848
Michael Chang, *Manager*
▲ EMP: 6
SALES (est): 543.2K Privately Held
SIC: 2099 5149 Food preparations; organic & diet foods

(G-5027)
NEW STAR BAKERY
4121a Kissena Blvd (11355-3138)
PHONE 718 961-8868
Huantang Liang, *Owner*
EMP: 20
SALES (est): 1.2MM Privately Held
SIC: 2051 Bread, cake & related products

(G-5028)
NEW YORK IL BO INC
Also Called: Korean New York Daily, The
4522 162nd St Fl 2 (11358-3280)
PHONE 718 961-1538
Grace Chung, *CEO*
▲ EMP: 15
SALES: 120K Privately Held
SIC: 2711 Newspapers: publishing only, not printed on site

(G-5029)
NEW YORK TIMES COMPANY
1 New York Times Plz (11354-1200)
PHONE 718 281-7000
Thomas P Lombardo, *Plant Mgr*
Mike Joyce, *Foreman/Supr*
Frank Polgano, *Foreman/Supr*
EMP: 12
SALES (corp-wide): 1.6B Publicly Held
WEB: www.nytco.com
SIC: 2711 Commercial printing & newspaper publishing combined
PA: The New York Times Company
    620 8th Ave
    New York NY 10018
    212 556-1234

(G-5030)
NORTH AMERICA PASTEL ARTISTS
13303 41st Ave Apt 1a (11355-5840)
PHONE 718 463-4701
Jason Chang, *President*
EMP: 8
SALES: 3K Privately Held
SIC: 3952 Pastels, artists'

(G-5031)
NORTH SHORE NEON SIGN CO INC
4649 54th Ave (11378-1011)
PHONE 718 937-4848
Nancy Byrnes, *Accountant*
Tom Brown, *Manager*
EMP: 30
SALES (corp-wide): 13.5MM Privately Held
WEB: www.northshoreneon.com
SIC: 3993 1799 Electric signs; sign installation & maintenance
PA: North Shore Neon Sign Co. Inc.
    295 Skidmore Rd
    Deer Park NY 11729
    631 667-2500

(G-5032)
P S PIBBS INC
Also Called: Pibbs Industries
13315 32nd Ave (11354-1909)
PHONE 718 445-8046
Damiano Petruccelli, *CEO*
Biagio Petruccelli, *President*
Sunny Thomas, *President*
Giulio Pertruccelli, *Vice Pres*
Antonio Petruccelli, *Vice Pres*
◆ EMP: 100
SQ FT: 30,000
SALES (est): 11.8MM Privately Held
WEB: www.pibbs.com
SIC: 3999 2844 Barber & beauty shop equipment; shampoos, rinses, conditioners: hair; hair preparations, including shampoos; face creams or lotions

(G-5033)
PALADINO PRTG & GRAPHICS INC
20009 32nd Ave (11361-1037)
PHONE 718 279-6000
Vincent Paladino, *President*
EMP: 9
SQ FT: 1,000
SALES (est): 1.2MM Privately Held
SIC: 2752 Commercial printing, lithographic

(G-5034)
PALMBAY LTD
4459 Kissena Blvd Apt 6h (11355-3065)
PHONE 718 424-3388
Wenchao Tao, *President*
◆ EMP: 6
SQ FT: 20,000
SALES (est): 817.3K Privately Held
WEB: www.disposablewear.com
SIC: 2384 2252 Robes & dressing gowns; slipper socks

(G-5035)
PARIS WEDDING CENTER CORP (PA)
42-53 42 55 Main St (11355)
PHONE 347 368-4085
Yuki Lin, *President*
▲ EMP: 12
SALES (est): 888.6K Privately Held
SIC: 2335 Wedding gowns & dresses

(G-5036)
PEACE TIMES WEEKLY INC
14527 33rd Ave (11354-3145)
PHONE 718 762-6500
Yongil Park, *President*
Joseph Aahn, *President*
▲ EMP: 5
SALES: 346.3K Privately Held
SIC: 2711 Newspapers: publishing only, not printed on site

(G-5037)
PERRY PLASTICS INC
3050 Whitestone Expy # 300 (11354-1964)
PHONE 718 747-5600
Irwing Laub, *President*
Aaron Laub, *Vice Pres*
▼ EMP: 10
SALES (est): 902.3K Privately Held
SIC: 2295 Chemically coated & treated fabrics

(G-5038)
PORCELAIN REFINISHING CORP
19905 32nd Ave (11358-1205)
P.O. Box 446, Fairless Hills PA (19030-0446)
PHONE 516 352-4841
Paula Weinstock, *President*
EMP: 15
SQ FT: 700
SALES (est): 2.5MM Privately Held
SIC: 3431 5074 Bathtubs: enameled iron, cast iron or pressed metal; sanitary ware, china or enameled iron

(G-5039)
PRIME COOK (WTTC) INC (PA)
15038 Jewel Ave (11367-1434)
PHONE 646 881-0068
Jun Chen, *President*
EMP: 3
SALES (est): 17.8MM Privately Held
SIC: 3262 China cookware

(G-5040)
PRIME RESEARCH SOLUTIONS LLC
Also Called: Turkprime
7328 136th St (11367-2827)
PHONE 917 836-7941
Leonid Litman, *Principal*
Jonathan Robinson, *Principal*
EMP: 11
SALES (est): 155K Privately Held
SIC: 7372 8999 Educational computer software; scientific consulting

(G-5041)
PURE GHEE INC (PA)
5701 225th St (11364-2042)
PHONE 718 224-7399
Mahesh K Maheshwari, *President*
Sucheta Maheshwari, *Senior VP*
EMP: 6 EST: 1988
SQ FT: 9,700
SALES: 1.5MM Privately Held
SIC: 2021 Butter oil; butter

(G-5042)
RAJBHOG FOODS INC
4123 Murray St (11355-1048)
PHONE 718 358-5105
Ajit M Mody, *CEO*
Suzy Mody, *Vice Pres*
Sachin Mody, *Treasurer*
Lata Mody, *Sales Mgr*
▲ EMP: 30
SQ FT: 12,000
SALES (est): 3.6MM Privately Held
WEB: www.rajbhog.com
SIC: 2064 Candy & other confectionery products

(G-5043)
S & L AEROSPACE METALS LLC
12012 28th Ave (11354-1049)
PHONE 718 326-1821
Jerry Wang, *President*
Carlos Quintana, *Vice Pres*
Ted Varvatsas, *Vice Pres*
Alan Wang, *Vice Pres*
EMP: 100 EST: 1946
SQ FT: 50,000
SALES (est): 29.2MM Privately Held
WEB: www.slaerospace.com
SIC: 3728 Aircraft assemblies, subassemblies & parts

(G-5044)
SANFORD PRINTING INC
13335 41st Rd (11355-3667)
PHONE 718 461-1202
Paul Peng, *President*
▲ EMP: 5
SALES (est): 696K Privately Held
SIC: 2752 Commercial printing, offset

(G-5045)
SHENZHEN XNHDINGSHENG TECH LTD
4112a Main St 2fd09 (11355)
PHONE 510 506-5753
Suye Guo,
EMP: 20
SALES (est): 504.6K Privately Held
SIC: 3999 Manufacturing industries

(G-5046)
SNAPP TOO ENTERPRISE
3312 211th St (11361-1523)
PHONE 718 224-5252
Edward Porzelt, *Owner*
EMP: 6
SALES (est): 330K Privately Held
SIC: 2086 Bottled & canned soft drinks

Flushing - Queens County (G-5047)

(G-5047)
SPEEDY ENTERPRISE OF USA CORP
4120 162nd St (11358-4123)
PHONE.................................718 463-3000
Harolyn Paik, *Principal*
EMP: 6
SALES (est): 713K Privately Held
SIC: 2752 Commercial printing, lithographic

(G-5048)
STARK AQUARIUM PRODUCTS CO INC
Also Called: Stark Fish
2914 122nd St (11354-2530)
PHONE.................................718 445-5357
Edith Starkman, *President*
Omiros Gioroukos, *Vice Pres*
Helen Vasili, *Admin Asst*
▲ EMP: 21 EST: 1977
SQ FT: 20,000
SALES (est): 2.7MM Privately Held
WEB: www.starkproducts.com
SIC: 3231 Aquariums & reflectors, glass

(G-5049)
SUEZ ENERGY ASTORIA LLC
17-10 Steinway St (11375)
PHONE.................................718 274-7700
Charles McCall, *CEO*
Louis St-Maurice, *CFO*
EMP: 145 EST: 2007
SALES (est): 167.3K
SALES (corp-wide): 24.2B Privately Held
SIC: 3621 Power generators
HQ: Engie North America Inc.
 1990 Post Oak Blvd # 1900
 Houston TX 77056
 713 636-0000

(G-5050)
SUNRISE TILE INC
13309 35th Ave (11354-2712)
PHONE.................................718 939-0538
Kathy Chen, *Manager*
▲ EMP: 8
SALES (est): 797.4K Privately Held
SIC: 2273 1752 Carpets & rugs; wood floor installation & refinishing

(G-5051)
TABI INC
488 Onderdonk Ave Apt 1l (11385-1547)
PHONE.................................347 701-1051
Diego Tenesaca, *President*
EMP: 6
SALES (est): 199.3K Privately Held
SIC: 7372 Application computer software

(G-5052)
TEMPCO GLASS FABRICATION LLC
13110 Maple Ave (11355-4223)
PHONE.................................718 461-6888
Steven Powell, *General Mgr*
Johnson Chen, *General Mgr*
John Nguyen, *Sales Staff*
Shirley Shaw, *Sales Staff*
▲ EMP: 56 EST: 2012
SALES: 7MM Privately Held
SIC: 3211 Building glass, flat

(G-5053)
TILCON NEW YORK INC
Also Called: Flushing Terminal
3466 College Point Blvd (11354-2717)
PHONE.................................845 480-3249
EMP: 63
SALES (corp-wide): 29.7B Privately Held
SIC: 1429 Dolomitic marble, crushed & broken-quarrying
HQ: Tilcon New York Inc.
 9 Entin Rd
 Parsippany NJ 07054
 800 789-7625

(G-5054)
TONGLI PHARMACEUTICALS USA INC (PA)
4260 Main St Apt 6f (11355-3707)
PHONE.................................212 842-8337
Mingli Yao, *Ch of Bd*
Ailing Zhao, *Admin Sec*
EMP: 11
SALES: 11.1MM Publicly Held
SIC: 2834 Pharmaceutical preparations

(G-5055)
TRIBORO BAGEL CO INC
Also Called: Bagel Oasis
18312 Horace Harding Expy (11365-2123)
PHONE.................................718 359-9245
Abe Moskowitz, *President*
Mike Edelstein, *Corp Secy*
EMP: 20 EST: 1961
SQ FT: 1,200
SALES (est): 1MM Privately Held
WEB: www.bageloasis.com
SIC: 2051 Bakery: wholesale or wholesale/retail combined; bagels, fresh or frozen

(G-5056)
TWINKLE LIGHTING INC
13114 40th Rd (11354-5137)
PHONE.................................718 225-0939
Fuchun Lin, *President*
Cheng Zhi Lai, *Sales Mgr*
EMP: 5
SALES (est): 471.6K Privately Held
SIC: 3646 Commercial indusl & institutional electric lighting fixtures

(G-5057)
UNITED SATCOM INC
4555 Robinson St (11355-3444)
PHONE.................................718 359-4100
Ted Park, *President*
EMP: 7
SQ FT: 3,500
SALES: 1.5MM Privately Held
SIC: 3663 Microwave communication equipment

(G-5058)
UNITED STEEL PRODUCTS INC
Also Called: Ronmar
3340 127th Pl (11368-1508)
PHONE.................................914 968-7782
EMP: 60
SALES (est): 24.8K Privately Held
SIC: 3442 3446 Mfg Metal Doors/Sash/Trim Mfg Architectural Metalwork

(G-5059)
WARODEAN CORPORATION
Also Called: Loosesleeve Law Publications
4308 162nd St (11358-3131)
P.O. Box 650042, Fresh Meadows (11365-0042)
PHONE.................................718 359-5559
Michael Loughrey, *President*
EMP: 8
SQ FT: 1,750
SALES (est): 690K Privately Held
SIC: 2731 Textbooks: publishing & printing

(G-5060)
WOLSKI WOOD WORKS INC
14134 78th Rd Apt 3c (11367-3331)
PHONE.................................718 577-9816
Tadeusz Wolski, *President*
EMP: 7
SALES (est): 177.1K Privately Held
SIC: 2421 Outdoor wood structural products

(G-5061)
YELLOW E HOUSE INC
Also Called: Gatecomusa
18812 Northern Blvd (11358-2811)
PHONE.................................718 888-2000
Stephan Cho, *CEO*
EMP: 7
SQ FT: 3,000
SALES (est): 499.7K Privately Held
SIC: 3571 5045 7629 5945 Electronic computers; computers, peripherals & software; business machine repair, electric; hobby, toy & game shops

(G-5062)
ZENITH SOLUTIONS
6922 Manse St (11375-5850)
PHONE.................................718 575-8570
P Bilello, *Principal*
EMP: 7
SALES (est): 631.8K Privately Held
SIC: 2834 Intravenous solutions

Fly Creek
Otsego County

(G-5063)
ADIRONDACK LEATHER PDTS INC
196 Cemetery Rd (13337)
P.O. Box 180 (13337-0180)
PHONE.................................607 547-5798
Gregory M O Neil, *CEO*
Darlene O Neil, *Vice Pres*
EMP: 10
SALES (est): 1.4MM Privately Held
WEB: www.adirondackleatherproducts.com
SIC: 3199 7389 Holsters, leather; leggings or chaps, canvas or leather; leather belting & strapping;

(G-5064)
FLY CREEK CDER MILL ORCHRD INC
288 Goose St (13337-2314)
PHONE.................................607 547-9692
Brenda Michaels, *President*
Howard Michaels, *Vice Pres*
EMP: 5
SALES (est): 485.8K Privately Held
SIC: 2022 2033 2037 2084 Cheese, natural & processed; canned fruits & specialties; frozen fruits & vegetables; wines; gift shop

Fonda
Montgomery County

(G-5065)
KASSON & KELLER INC
Also Called: Kas-Kel
60 School St (12068-4809)
P.O. Box 777 (12068-0777)
PHONE.................................518 853-3421
William Keller III, *Ch of Bd*
Dan Novak, *COO*
James P Keller, *Exec VP*
Drue Wallach, *Vice Pres*
Linda Kilmartin, *Credit Mgr*
▲ EMP: 900 EST: 1946
SQ FT: 60,000
SALES (est): 169.2MM Privately Held
WEB: www.kas-kel.com
SIC: 3442 3089 1521 3231 Window & door frames; windows, plastic; single-family housing construction; products of purchased glass

(G-5066)
KEYMARK CORPORATION
1188 Cayadutta St (12068)
P.O. Box 626 (12068-0626)
PHONE.................................518 853-3421
William L Keller III, *Ch of Bd*
Kelly Fernet, *General Mgr*
Tony Maiolo, *COO*
James P Keller, *Exec VP*
Sterling Gartung, *Maint Spvr*
▲ EMP: 600 EST: 1964
SQ FT: 250,000
SALES (est): 228.8MM Privately Held
WEB: www.keymarkcorp.com
SIC: 3354 3479 3471 Aluminum extruded products; painting of metal products; anodizing (plating) of metals or formed products

(G-5067)
TEMPER CORPORATION (PA)
544 Persse Rd (12068-7700)
P.O. Box 1127 (12068-1127)
PHONE.................................518 853-3467
John Rode, *President*
Bob Francisco, *Production*
Matt Townes, *Manager*
EMP: 25
SQ FT: 30,000
SALES (est): 4.2MM Privately Held
WEB: www.tempercorp.com
SIC: 3493 3053 Steel springs, except wire; gaskets & sealing devices

(G-5068)
TEMPER CORPORATION
Temper Axle Products
544 Persse Rd (12068-7700)
PHONE.................................518 853-3467
John Rhode, *President*
EMP: 5
SALES (corp-wide): 4.2MM Privately Held
WEB: www.tempercorp.com
SIC: 3714 Axles, motor vehicle
PA: Temper Corporation
 544 Persse Rd
 Fonda NY 12068
 518 853-3467

Forest Hills
Queens County

(G-5069)
2H INTERNATIONAL CORP
6766 108th St Apt D1 (11375-2904)
PHONE.................................347 623-9380
June LI, *Manager*
EMP: 5
SALES: 300K Privately Held
SIC: 2337 Women's & misses' suits & coats

(G-5070)
AIGNER CHOCOLATES (PA)
10302 Metropolitan Ave (11375-6734)
PHONE.................................718 544-1850
Peter Aigner, *Ch of Bd*
EMP: 10
SQ FT: 2,000
SALES (est): 1.1MM Privately Held
WEB: www.aignerchocolates.com
SIC: 2064 2066 Chocolate candy, except solid chocolate; chocolate candy, solid

(G-5071)
ALLROUND LOGISTICS INC (PA)
Also Called: Allround Maritime Services
7240 Ingram St (11375-5927)
PHONE.................................718 544-8945
Roland Meier, *President*
Ellen Meier, *Vice Pres*
Charlie Boon, *Treasurer*
Jody Barton, *Asst Sec*
◆ EMP: 5
SQ FT: 3,600
SALES: 1.7MM Privately Held
WEB: www.allroundlogistics.com
SIC: 3534 Escalators, passenger & freight

(G-5072)
ARIEL TIAN LLC
253 W 35th St Fl 8 Flr 8 (11375)
P.O. Box 296, New York (10018-0005)
PHONE.................................212 457-1266
LI Tian, *Mng Member*
EMP: 5
SALES: 100K Privately Held
SIC: 3111 7389 Accessory products, leather; styling of fashions, apparel, furniture, textiles, etc.

(G-5073)
COMBINE GRAPHICS CORP
10714 Queens Blvd (11375-4249)
PHONE.................................212 695-4044
Charles Caminiti, *President*
Louis Zafonte, *Vice Pres*
EMP: 5
SQ FT: 2,300
SALES: 590.6K Privately Held
SIC: 2752 Commercial printing, offset

(G-5074)
HANGER INC
Also Called: Hanger Prosthectics Orthotics
11835 Queens Blvd Ste Ll3 (11375-7205)
PHONE.................................718 575-5504
Joe Nieto, *Manager*
Michael Sacco, *Manager*
EMP: 8
SALES (corp-wide): 1B Publicly Held
SIC: 3842 5999 Surgical appliances & supplies; artificial limbs

GEOGRAPHIC SECTION

Fort Edward - Washington County (G-5101)

PA: Hanger, Inc.
10910 Domain Dr Ste 300
Austin TX 78758
512 777-3800

(G-5075)
HI-TECH ADVANCED SOLUTIONS INC
10525 65th Ave Apt 4h (11375-1802)
PHONE..................718 926-3488
Nison B Isaak, *President*
EMP: 10
SALES: 100K **Privately Held**
SIC: 3571 Electronic computers

(G-5076)
LOYALTYPLANT INC (PA)
70 23 Juno St (11375)
PHONE..................551 221-2701
Vasilii Diachenko, *President*
EMP: 10
SALES (est): 399.2K **Privately Held**
SIC: 7372 Business oriented computer software

(G-5077)
NATIVE AMERCN ENRGY GROUP INC (PA)
7211 Austin St Ste 288 (11375-5354)
PHONE..................718 408-2323
Raj Nanvaan, *Principal*
Linda Chontos, *Officer*
EMP: 6
SALES (est): 495.9K **Privately Held**
SIC: 1382 Oil & gas exploration services

(G-5078)
NATURE ONLY INC
10420 Queens Blvd Apt 3b (11375-3602)
PHONE..................917 922-6539
EMP: 9
SALES (est): 780K **Privately Held**
SIC: 2844 Mfg Natural Rash Creams For Kids & Facial Creams

(G-5079)
NEW YORK TYPING & PRINTING CO
10816 72nd Ave (11375-5653)
PHONE..................718 268-7900
Jay Goldstin, *President*
EMP: 5 **EST:** 1981
SALES (est): 380K **Privately Held**
SIC: 2752 7338 Commercial printing, offset; secretarial & typing service

(G-5080)
PRESTON GLASS INDUSTRIES INC
Also Called: P G I
10420 Queens Blvd Apt 17a (11375-3610)
PHONE..................718 997-8888
Ashish Karnavat, *President*
EMP: 20 **EST:** 1995
SALES (est): 1.3MM **Privately Held**
SIC: 3641 Electrodes, cold cathode fluorescent lamp

(G-5081)
TWIST IT TOP IT
10309 Metropolitan Ave (11375-6733)
PHONE..................718 793-8947
EMP: 15 **EST:** 2012
SALES (est): 367.6K **Privately Held**
SIC: 2026 Yogurt

(G-5082)
WILSON & WILSON GROUP
Also Called: Wilson N Wilson Group & RES
6514 110th St (11375-1424)
PHONE..................212 729-4736
Pius Wilson, *Principal*
EMP: 5
SALES: 25K **Privately Held**
SIC: 3577 Computer peripheral equipment

Forestport
Oneida County

(G-5083)
NIRVANA INC
1 Nirvana Plz (13338)
PHONE..................315 942-4900
Mozafar Rafizadeh, *President*
Mansur Rafizadeh, *Vice Pres*
MO Rafizadeh, *Vice Pres*
Edward Wiehl, *Vice Pres*
▲ **EMP:** 160
SQ FT: 250,000
SALES (est): 68MM **Privately Held**
WEB: www.nirvanaspring.com
SIC: 2086 Mineral water, carbonated: packaged in cans, bottles, etc.; water, pasteurized: packaged in cans, bottles, etc.

(G-5084)
TOWN OF OHIO
Also Called: Town of Ohio Highway Garage
N Lake Rd (13338)
PHONE..................315 392-2055
Fred Reuter, *Manager*
EMP: 24
SQ FT: 2,066 **Privately Held**
SIC: 3531 Snow plow attachments
PA: Town Of Ohio
234 Nellis Rd
Cold Brook NY 13324
315 826-7912

Forestville
Chautauqua County

(G-5085)
BAILEY MANUFACTURING CO LLC
10987 Bennett State Rd (14062-9714)
P.O. Box 356 (14062-0356)
PHONE..................716 965-2731
John Hines, *President*
Dona Hines,
EMP: 50 **EST:** 2002
SQ FT: 40,000
SALES (est): 11MM **Privately Held**
SIC: 3469 Metal stampings

(G-5086)
MERRITT ESTATE WINERY INC
2264 King Rd (14062-9703)
PHONE..................716 965-4800
William T Merritt, *President*
Jason Merritt, *Corp Secy*
EMP: 15
SQ FT: 20,000
SALES (est): 2.4MM **Privately Held**
WEB: www.merrittestatewinery.com
SIC: 2084 Wines

(G-5087)
P S M GROUP INC
Also Called: Pit Stop Motorsports
17 Main St (14062-9998)
P.O. Box 500 (14062-0500)
PHONE..................716 532-6686
Jeffrey A Furash, *President*
EMP: 20 **EST:** 1978
SALES (est): 1.7MM **Privately Held**
WEB: www.burningasphalt.com
SIC: 2842 7948 Specialty cleaning, polishes & sanitation goods; race track operation

(G-5088)
SHYKAT PROMOTIONS
10561 Creek Rd (14062-9607)
PHONE..................866 574-2757
Krista Miller, *Owner*
EMP: 7
SALES (est): 372.9K **Privately Held**
SIC: 2759 2395 8743 Screen printing; embroidery & art needlework; promotion service

Fort Ann
Washington County

(G-5089)
JEWELRY BY SARAH BELLE
10394 State Route 149 (12827-1900)
PHONE..................518 793-1626
Sarah Maynard, *Principal*
EMP: 5 **EST:** 2010
SALES (est): 362.7K **Privately Held**
SIC: 3911 Jewelry apparel

(G-5090)
PETTEYS LUMBER
Also Called: A Petteys Lumber
10247 State Route 149 (12827-1804)
PHONE..................518 792-5943
Alvin Petteys, *Owner*
EMP: 7
SALES: 370K **Privately Held**
SIC: 2421 2426 Lumber: rough, sawed or planed; hardwood dimension & flooring mills

Fort Drum
Jefferson County

(G-5091)
BLACK RIVER GENERATIONS LLC
Also Called: Reenergy Black River
4515 2nd St (13602)
P.O. Box 849 (13602-0849)
PHONE..................315 773-2314
EMP: 23 **EST:** 2010
SALES (est): 9.8MM **Privately Held**
SIC: 3822 Mfg Environmental Controls

(G-5092)
REENERGY BLACK RIVER LLC
4515 Ephrtes River Vly Rd (13602)
PHONE..................315 773-2314
Larry Richardson, *CEO*
Peter Lister, *Facilities Mgr*
Tom Beck, *Officer*
William Ralson, *Officer*
EMP: 33
SALES (est): 1.1MM **Privately Held**
SIC: 3612 Transformers, except electric
PA: Reenergy Holdings Llc
30 Century Hill Dr # 102
Latham NY 12110

Fort Edward
Washington County

(G-5093)
A HYATT BALL CO LTD
School St (12828)
PHONE..................518 747-0272
Robert Simpson, *President*
EMP: 7
SQ FT: 12,000
SALES (est): 1.2MM **Privately Held**
SIC: 3562 3949 Ball bearings & parts; billiard & pool equipment & supplies, general

(G-5094)
BURNHAM POLYMERIC INC
Also Called: Burnhams, The
1408 Route 9 (12828-2459)
P.O. Box 317, Glens Falls (12801-0317)
PHONE..................518 792-3040
Warren Burnham Jr, *President*
William Wulfken, *President*
Matt Perkins, *Opers Mgr*
EMP: 7
SQ FT: 8,400
SALES (est): 670K **Privately Held**
WEB: www.burnhams.com
SIC: 3089 Extruded finished plastic products

(G-5095)
D K MACHINE INC
48 Sullivan Pkwy (12828-1027)
PHONE..................518 747-0626
Daniel Komarony, *President*
Jim Glacy, *Purchasing*
Scott Lufkin, *Engineer*
Karen Ely, *Office Mgr*
Theresa Komarony, *Admin Sec*
EMP: 10
SQ FT: 8,500
SALES (est): 1.7MM **Privately Held**
WEB: www.dkmachine.com
SIC: 3599 5085 Machine shop, jobbing & repair; industrial supplies

(G-5096)
IRVING CONSUMER PRODUCTS INC (DH)
Also Called: Irving Tissue Div
1 Eddy St (12828-1711)
PHONE..................518 747-4151
J K Irving, *Principal*
Arthur L Irving, *Vice Pres*
John Irving, *Director*
▲ **EMP:** 300
SQ FT: 700,000
SALES (est): 106.9MM **Privately Held**
SIC: 2621 Towels, tissues & napkins: paper & stock
HQ: Irving Consumer Products Limited
100 Prom Midland
Dieppe NB E1A 6
506 858-7777

(G-5097)
PALLETS INC
99 1/2 East St (12828-1813)
P.O. Box 326 (12828-0326)
PHONE..................518 747-4177
Clinton Binley, *President*
Arthur Binley III, *Chairman*
Marvin Horowitz, *Admin Sec*
EMP: 45 **EST:** 1942
SQ FT: 100,000
SALES (est): 6.6MM **Privately Held**
WEB: www.palletsincorporated.com
SIC: 2448 2421 Pallets, wood; sawmills & planing mills, general; lumber: rough, sawed or planed

(G-5098)
PARKER MACHINE COMPANY INC
28 Sullivan Pkwy (12828-1027)
PHONE..................518 747-0675
Tammy Aust, *President*
Patrick A Whaley, *Vice Pres*
Patrick Whaley, *Vice Pres*
EMP: 17
SQ FT: 17,400
SALES (est): 3.4MM **Privately Held**
WEB: www.parkermachine.com
SIC: 3599 5251 Machine shop, jobbing & repair; tools

(G-5099)
REAL BARK MULCH LLC
1380 Towpath Ln (12828-1757)
PHONE..................518 747-3650
Patrick Gulsha,
Patrick Bulsha,
EMP: 9
SALES (est): 1.8MM **Privately Held**
SIC: 3524 Lawn & garden equipment

(G-5100)
RFB ASSOCIATES INC
Also Called: Bruno Associates
35 Sullivan Pkwy (12828-1028)
P.O. Box 14825, Albany (12212-4825)
PHONE..................518 271-0551
Robert Bruno Sr, *President*
Sean P Bruno Sr, *Vice Pres*
EMP: 12
SQ FT: 60,000
SALES: 3MM **Privately Held**
SIC: 3559 3569 3565 3552 Automotive related machinery; assembly machines, non-metalworking; packaging machinery; textile machinery

(G-5101)
STONEGATE STABLESS
106 Reynolds Rd (12828-9244)
PHONE..................518 746-7133
William Johnson, *Owner*
EMP: 8

Fort Plain - Montgomery County (G-5102)
GEOGRAPHIC SECTION

SALES (est): 540.6K **Privately Held**
SIC: 2399 Horse harnesses & riding crops, etc.: non-leather

Fort Plain
Montgomery County

(G-5102)
ELITE PRECISE MANUFACTURER LLC
55 Willett St (13339-1178)
PHONE..................518 993-3040
Ross Stevenson, *Principal*
EMP: 8
SQ FT: 10,000
SALES (est): 430.9K **Privately Held**
SIC: 3599 Machine & other job shop work

(G-5103)
PERFORMANCE PRECISION MFG LLC
55 Willett St (13339-1178)
PHONE..................518 993-3033
Joeseph Stevenson, *Owner*
EMP: 8
SALES (est): 952.2K **Privately Held**
SIC: 3999 Manufacturing industries

Frankfort
Herkimer County

(G-5104)
C-FLEX BEARING CO INC
104 Industrial Dr (13340-1139)
PHONE..................315 895-7454
D Joanne Willcox, *President*
Wayne Smith, *Vice Pres*
EMP: 10 **EST:** 1994
SQ FT: 6,200
SALES: 1.4MM **Privately Held**
WEB: www.c-flex.com
SIC: 3568 3812 3556 3825 Bearings, bushings & blocks; search & navigation equipment; food products machinery; instruments to measure electricity

(G-5105)
DI SANOS CREATIVE CANVAS INC
113 W Main St (13340-1007)
PHONE..................315 894-3137
John Di Sano, *President*
EMP: 5
SQ FT: 2,400
SALES (est): 425.3K **Privately Held**
WEB: www.disanoscreativecanvas.com
SIC: 2394 5999 5091 Awnings, fabric: made from purchased materials; canvas covers & drop cloths; awnings; canvas products; boat accessories & parts

(G-5106)
F E HALE MFG CO
120 Benson Pl (13340-3752)
P.O. Box 186 (13340-0186)
PHONE..................315 894-5490
Jim Benson, *President*
Brooke Benson, *Admin Sec*
EMP: 65 **EST:** 1907
SQ FT: 80,000
SALES (est): 11.6MM **Privately Held**
WEB: www.halebookcases.com
SIC: 2521 Bookcases, office: wood

(G-5107)
FIBERDYNE LABS INC
127 Business Park Dr (13340-3700)
PHONE..................315 895-8470
A Peter Polus III, *CEO*
Carl Fredlund, *President*
Ken Misterka, *President*
Chad A Polus, *President*
Jeffrey Sperl, *General Mgr*
▲ **EMP:** 96
SQ FT: 20,000
SALES (est): 10.5MM **Privately Held**
WEB: www.fiberdyne.com
SIC: 3357 4899 4822 Fiber optic cable (insulated); communication signal enhancement network system; telegraph & other communications

(G-5108)
JBF STAINLESS LLC
148 Industrial Park Dr (13340-4745)
P.O. Box 632, Cazenovia (13035-0632)
PHONE..................315 569-2800
John Feldmeier, *President*
Margaret Feldmeier, *Principal*
EMP: 26
SQ FT: 4,500
SALES (est): 6.5MM **Privately Held**
SIC: 3324 Steel investment foundries

(G-5109)
MAPLEHURST BAKERIES LLC
Also Called: Granny's Kitchens
178 Industrial Park Dr (13340-4745)
PHONE..................315 735-5000
EMP: 280
SALES (corp-wide): 37.8B **Privately Held**
SIC: 2051 2053 Bread, cake & related products; doughnuts, frozen
HQ: Maplehurst Bakeries, Llc
50 Maplehurst Dr
Brownsburg IN 46112
317 858-9000

(G-5110)
MOHAWK VALLEY MANUFACTURING
2237 Broad St (13340-5101)
PHONE..................315 797-0851
EMP: 7
SALES (est): 630K **Privately Held**
SIC: 3556 Mfg Food Products Machinery

(G-5111)
PRECISION POLISH LLC
144 Adams St (13340-3751)
PHONE..................315 894-3792
Jack Dunderdale, *Vice Pres*
Nial Williams, *Mng Member*
Michelle Williams, *Manager*
EMP: 25
SALES: 1.4MM **Privately Held**
SIC: 3441 Fabricated structural metal

(G-5112)
SOFT-NOZE USA INC
2216 Broad St (13340-5100)
PHONE..................315 732-2726
Brett Truett, *President*
Krista Petrowski, *Finance Mgr*
Haris Dervisevic, *Technology*
▲ **EMP:** 5
SQ FT: 4,500
SALES (est): 744.9K **Privately Held**
WEB: www.softnoze.com
SIC: 3625 Electric controls & control accessories, industrial

(G-5113)
TURBO MACHINED PRODUCTS LLC
102 Industrial Dr (13340-1139)
PHONE..................315 895-3010
John A Kabot Jr, *President*
Robert Cartmell, *Vice Pres*
Gordy Black, *Engineer*
Jeff Huey, *Engineer*
Erin Dygert, *Sales Executive*
EMP: 35
SQ FT: 20,000
SALES (est): 8.1MM **Privately Held**
WEB: www.turbomp.com
SIC: 3824 3511 Impeller & counter driven flow meters; turbines & turbine generator sets & parts

Franklin Square
Nassau County

(G-5114)
514 ADAMS CORPORATION
Also Called: Adams Press
781 Hempstead Tpke (11010-4328)
PHONE..................516 352-6948
Daniel Rummo, *President*
Chris Rummo, *Vice Pres*
Theresa Rummo, *Admin Sec*
EMP: 7
SQ FT: 3,000
SALES (est): 1.1MM **Privately Held**
SIC: 2752 2791 2789 Commercial printing, offset; typesetting; bookbinding & related work

(G-5115)
BONURA AND SONS IRON WORKS
957 Lorraine Dr (11010-1812)
PHONE..................718 381-4100
Frank Bonura, *Principal*
Enzo Bonuro, *Principal*
EMP: 15
SALES (est): 1.2MM **Privately Held**
SIC: 3312 1799 Blast Furnace-Steel Works Trade Contractor

(G-5116)
D C I TECHNICAL INC
475 Franklin Ave Fl 2 (11010-1228)
PHONE..................516 355-0464
Andrea Mannheim, *President*
Harold Adler, *Vice Pres*
Merideth Hilton, *Vice Pres*
Sidney Platt, *Vice Pres*
EMP: 12
SQ FT: 2,700
SALES (est): 882.8K **Privately Held**
SIC: 2731 2741 Books: publishing & printing; miscellaneous publishing

(G-5117)
FEMTECH WOMEN POWERED SOFTWARE
1230 Hempstead Tpke (11010-1534)
PHONE..................516 328-2631
Colleen Simeone, *President*
EMP: 99
SALES (est): 2.6MM **Privately Held**
WEB: www.femtech.at
SIC: 7372 Prepackaged software

(G-5118)
LESSOILCOM
672 Dogwood Ave (11010-3247)
P.O. Box 20988, Floral Park (11002-0988)
PHONE..................516 319-5052
Mike Gregoretti, *Principal*
EMP: 6
SALES (est): 343K **Privately Held**
SIC: 1241 Bituminous coal mining services, contract basis

(G-5119)
MOVIN ON SOUNDS AND SEC INC
Also Called: M O S S Communications
636 Hempstead Tpke (11010-3628)
PHONE..................516 489-2350
Bruce Cirillo, *President*
Mark Rock, *Manager*
Jean Ulsheimer, *Manager*
Paul Cirillo, *Officer*
EMP: 35
SALES (est): 6.6MM **Privately Held**
WEB: www.movinon.com
SIC: 3663 Radio & TV communications equipment

(G-5120)
NYCOM BUSINESS SOLUTIONS INC
804 Hempstead Tpke (11010-4321)
PHONE..................516 345-6000
Jerry Sperduto, *President*
EMP: 3
SQ FT: 800
SALES: 1.2MM **Privately Held**
SIC: 3663 Cellular radio telephone

(G-5121)
STUDENT LIFELINE INC
Also Called: Student Safety Books
922 Hempstead Tpke (11010-3628)
P.O. Box 570200, Whitestone (11357-0200)
PHONE..................516 327-0800
Richard Signarino, *President*
EMP: 42
SQ FT: 2,200
SALES (est): 4.1MM **Privately Held**
WEB: www.studentlifeline.com
SIC: 2741 Miscellaneous publishing

Franklinville
Cattaraugus County

(G-5122)
BUFFALO CRUSHED STONE INC
Rr 16 (14737)
P.O. Box 106 (14737-0106)
PHONE..................716 566-9636
John Lentz, *Manager*
EMP: 11
SALES (corp-wide): 651.9MM **Privately Held**
SIC: 1442 5032 Gravel mining; stone, crushed or broken
HQ: Buffalo Crushed Stone, Inc.
500 Como Park Blvd
Buffalo NY 14227
716 826-7310

(G-5123)
CATTARAUGUS CONTAINERS INC
21 Elm St 23 (14737-1052)
P.O. Box 174 (14737-0174)
PHONE..................716 676-2000
Jane Lemke, *President*
Paul Wagner, *Vice Pres*
Tammy Mooney, *Controller*
EMP: 33
SQ FT: 33,000
SALES: 3.8MM **Privately Held**
SIC: 2653 2657 5113 Boxes, corrugated: made from purchased materials; folding paperboard boxes; corrugated & solid fiber boxes

(G-5124)
ONTARIO KNIFE COMPANY
26 Empire St (14737-1099)
PHONE..................716 676-5527
Nicholas D Trbovich Jr, *CEO*
Kenneth Trbovich, *Ch of Bd*
Nicholas D Trbovich, *Chairman*
Cari Jaroslawsky, *Treasurer*
◆ **EMP:** 63
SQ FT: 10,000
SALES: 6.5MM
SALES (corp-wide): 41.4MM **Publicly Held**
WEB: www.ontarioknife.com
SIC: 3421 Knife blades & blanks
PA: Servotronics, Inc.
1110 Maple Rd
Elma NY 14059
716 655-5990

Fredonia
Chautauqua County

(G-5125)
CDF INDSTRIAL PCKG SLTIONS INC
134 Clinton Ave (14063-1406)
PHONE..................716 672-2984
Jeremy Poehler, *Ch of Bd*
Thomas J Ivory, *President*
Richard Ivory, *Vice Pres*
Vickie Ivory, *Treasurer*
Mary Ivory, *Admin Sec*
EMP: 18
SQ FT: 26,000
SALES (est): 3MM **Privately Held**
SIC: 2448 Pallets, wood

(G-5126)
FREDONIA PENNYSAVER INC (PA)
Also Called: Lakeshore Pennysaver
276 W Main St Ste 1 (14063-2099)
P.O. Box 493 (14063-0493)
PHONE..................716 679-1509
Thomas K Webb Jr, *President*
Maureen Webb, *Vice Pres*
EMP: 5
SQ FT: 1,000

▲ = Import ▼=Export
◆ =Import/Export

GEOGRAPHIC SECTION

Freeport - Nassau County (G-5154)

SALES (est): 805.8K **Privately Held**
WEB: www.fredoniapennysaver.com
SIC: 2741 2711 Guides: publishing only, not printed on site; newspapers, publishing & printing

(G-5127)
GREAT LAKES SPECIALITES
9491 Route 60 (14063-9729)
P.O. Box 351 (14063-0351)
PHONE.................................716 672-4622
Michael J Gloss, *Owner*
EMP: 20
SQ FT: 10,000
SALES (est): 1.8MM **Privately Held**
SIC: 2448 2449 2441 Pallets, wood; wood containers; nailed wood boxes & shook

(G-5128)
TUBE FABRICATION COMPANY INC
183 E Main St Ste 10 (14063-1435)
PHONE.................................716 673-1871
Daniel Sturniolo, *President*
EMP: 12
SALES (est): 2.2MM **Privately Held**
SIC: 3498 5051 Tube fabricating (contract bending & shaping); tubing, metal

(G-5129)
URBAN TECHNOLOGIES INC
3451 Stone Quarry Rd (14063-9722)
PHONE.................................716 672-2709
John Urbanik, *President*
EMP: 5
SALES (est): 676.5K **Privately Held**
SIC: 3677 Electronic transformers; inductors, electronic

(G-5130)
WOODBURY VINEYARDS INC
Also Called: Noble Vintages
3215 S Roberts Rd (14063-9417)
PHONE.................................716 679-9463
Joseph Carney, *Branch Mgr*
Maria Pizzino,
EMP: 5
SALES (corp-wide): 2.2MM **Privately Held**
WEB: www.woodburyvineyards.com
SIC: 2084 Wines
PA: Woodbury Vineyards, Inc.
2001 Crocker Rd Ste 440
Westlake OH 44145
440 835-2828

Freedom
Cattaraugus County

(G-5131)
GUTCHESS FREEDOM INC
10699 Maple Grove Rd (14065-9774)
PHONE.................................716 492-2824
Larry Lines, *Manager*
EMP: 70 EST: 2007
SALES (est): 8.3MM
SALES (corp-wide): 150MM **Privately Held**
SIC: 2421 Custom sawmill
PA: Gutchess Lumber Co., Inc.
890 Mclean Rd
Cortland NY 13045
607 753-3393

(G-5132)
GUTCHESS LUMBER CO INC
10699 Maple Grove Rd (14065-9774)
PHONE.................................716 492-2824
EMP: 43
SQ FT: 2,940
SALES (corp-wide): 150MM **Privately Held**
SIC: 2421 Sawmills & planing mills, general
PA: Gutchess Lumber Co., Inc.
890 Mclean Rd
Cortland NY 13045
607 753-3393

Freeport
Nassau County

(G-5133)
5TH AVENUE CHOCOLATIERE LLC
114 Church St (11520-3833)
PHONE.................................516 868-8070
Joseph Whaley,
EMP: 20 EST: 2015
SALES: 3MM **Privately Held**
SIC: 2066 Chocolate

(G-5134)
5TH AVENUE CHOCOLATIERE LTD (PA)
114 Church St (11520-3833)
PHONE.................................212 935-5454
Joseph E Whaley, *President*
John Whaley, *Vice Pres*
▲ EMP: 4
SQ FT: 4,500
SALES: 1.6MM **Privately Held**
SIC: 2064 2066 5441 Candy & other confectionery products; chocolate & cocoa products; candy

(G-5135)
A PROMOS USA INC
Also Called: Aarrow Promotions
143 E Merrick Rd (11520-4017)
PHONE.................................516 377-0186
Mindy Younger, *Principal*
Debbie Mandel, *Vice Pres*
EMP: 12
SQ FT: 1,000
SALES: 1.5MM **Privately Held**
SIC: 2759 Screen printing

(G-5136)
ACCESS DISPLAY GROUP INC
Also Called: Swing Frame
151 S Main St (11520-3845)
PHONE.................................516 678-7772
Charles Abrams, *President*
Barbara Abrams, *Vice Pres*
Jessica Malarkey, *Sales Staff*
Brain McAuley, *Info Tech Dir*
Craig R Abrams, *Exec Dir*
▲ EMP: 14
SQ FT: 6,000
SALES (est): 3MM **Privately Held**
WEB: www.swingframe.com
SIC: 3499 Picture frames, metal

(G-5137)
AIRMARINE ELECTROPLATING CORP
388 Woodcleft Ave (11520-6379)
PHONE.................................516 623-4406
Ernest Rieger III, *President*
EMP: 6
SALES (est): 724.4K **Privately Held**
WEB: www.airmarine.com
SIC: 3471 Electroplating of metals or formed products

(G-5138)
ALABASTER GROUP INC
188 N Main St (11520-2232)
PHONE.................................516 867-8223
Orna Alabaster, *President*
Zeev Alabaster, *Vice Pres*
EMP: 5
SQ FT: 7,300
SALES (est): 356.4K **Privately Held**
SIC: 2791 7336 7389 Typesetting; graphic arts & related design; printing broker

(G-5139)
ALL AMERICAN METAL CORPORATION (PA)
200 Buffalo Ave (11520-4732)
P.O. Box 108 (11520-0108)
PHONE.................................516 223-1760
Bernard Pechter, *President*
▲ EMP: 8
SQ FT: 50,000

SALES (est): 5MM **Privately Held**
WEB: www.allamericanmetal.com
SIC: 2542 Partitions for floor attachment, prefabricated: except wood

(G-5140)
ALL AMERICAN METAL CORPORATION
200 Buffalo Ave (11520-4732)
P.O. Box 108 (11520-0108)
PHONE.................................516 623-0222
Bernard Pechter, *Manager*
EMP: 32
SALES (corp-wide): 5MM **Privately Held**
WEB: www.allamericanmetal.com
SIC: 2542 3446 Mfg Partitions/Fixtures-Nonwood Mfg Architectural Metalwork
PA: All American Metal Corporation
200 Buffalo Ave
Freeport NY 11520
516 223-1760

(G-5141)
ALPHA FASTENERS CORP
154 E Merrick Rd (11520-4020)
PHONE.................................516 867-6188
Koula Perdios, *President*
Archie Perdios, *Vice Pres*
Michael Perdios, *Vice Pres*
▲ EMP: 5
SQ FT: 3,000
SALES (est): 795.3K **Privately Held**
SIC: 3451 Screw machine products

(G-5142)
AMADEO SERRANO
36 Frankel Ave (11520-4846)
PHONE.................................516 608-8359
Amaeeo Serrano, *Owner*
EMP: 6
SALES (est): 733K **Privately Held**
SIC: 3089 Fences, gates & accessories: plastic

(G-5143)
AMERICAN PUFF CORP
225 Buffalo Ave (11520-4794)
PHONE.................................516 379-1300
William Ostrower, *President*
EMP: 100
SQ FT: 70,000
SALES (est): 6.7MM **Privately Held**
SIC: 3172 2399 Personal leather goods; powder puffs & mitts

(G-5144)
ANNA YOUNG ASSOC LTD
Also Called: Lombardi Design & Mfg
100 Doxsee Dr (11520-4716)
PHONE.................................516 546-4400
Carl M Lombardi, *President*
▲ EMP: 150
SQ FT: 50,000
SALES (est): 57.6MM **Privately Held**
WEB: www.lombardi.cc
SIC: 3089 Injection molded finished plastic products

(G-5145)
BELLO LLC
178 Hanse Ave (11520-4609)
PHONE.................................516 623-8800
John Alair Garcia, *Mng Member*
EMP: 144 EST: 2016
SQ FT: 65,000
SALES (est): 17.8MM **Privately Held**
SIC: 2053 Frozen bakery products, except bread

(G-5146)
BRAMSON HOUSE INC
151 Albany Ave (11520-4710)
PHONE.................................516 764-5006
Jules Abramson, *CEO*
Ellis Abramson, *President*
Betty Abramson, *Vice Pres*
Patty Abramson, *Accounting Mgr*
Barry Silverman, *VP Sales*
◆ EMP: 120
SQ FT: 80,000
SALES (est): 17MM **Privately Held**
WEB: www.bramsonhouse.com
SIC: 2392 2391 Bedspreads & bed sets: made from purchased materials; curtains & draperies

(G-5147)
BRUETON INDUSTRIES INC (PA)
146 Hanse Ave Ste 1 (11520-4636)
PHONE.................................516 379-3400
Ralph Somma, *President*
EMP: 60 EST: 1920
SQ FT: 55,000
SALES (est): 6.8MM **Privately Held**
WEB: www.brueton.com
SIC: 2522 2514 2511 2521 Office furniture, except wood; metal household furniture; wood household furniture; wood office furniture

(G-5148)
CASTLEREAGH PRINTCRAFT INC
Also Called: Castle Reagh Print Craft
320 Buffalo Ave (11520-4711)
PHONE.................................516 623-1728
James Vollaro, *President*
Robert Quadrino, *Vice Pres*
Steven Quadrino, *Vice Pres*
Donna Vollaro, *CFO*
EMP: 70
SQ FT: 35,000
SALES (est): 10.5MM **Privately Held**
WEB: www.printcraftonline.com
SIC: 3555 2791 2789 2752 Printing trades machinery; typesetting; bookbinding & related work; commercial printing, lithographic

(G-5149)
CELLGEN INC
55 Commercial St (11520-2831)
PHONE.................................516 889-9300
Nicholas Capriotti, *CEO*
EMP: 9
SALES (est): 332K **Privately Held**
SIC: 3621 Generators & sets, electric

(G-5150)
DART AWNING INC
365 S Main St (11520-5114)
PHONE.................................516 544-2082
Thomas Hart, *President*
Richard Hart, *Admin Sec*
EMP: 7
SQ FT: 5,000
SALES (est): 1.5MM **Privately Held**
WEB: www.dartawnings.com
SIC: 3444 5999 Awnings, sheet metal; awnings

(G-5151)
DORAL REFINING CORP
533 Atlantic Ave (11520-5211)
PHONE.................................516 223-3684
Stephen Faliks, *President*
Alan Zaret, *Vice Pres*
EMP: 20
SQ FT: 10,000
SALES (est): 6MM **Privately Held**
WEB: www.doralcorp.com
SIC: 3339 Precious metals

(G-5152)
EDR INDUSTRIES INC
Also Called: Wil-Nic
100 Commercial St (11520-2832)
PHONE.................................516 868-1928
Don Capriglione, *President*
Christopher Cullinan, *Vice Pres*
EMP: 19
SQ FT: 10,000
SALES (est): 3.4MM **Privately Held**
SIC: 3599 Machine shop, jobbing & repair

(G-5153)
FARBER PLASTICS INC
162 Hanse Ave (11520-4644)
PHONE.................................516 378-4860
Lewis Farber, *President*
David Garfinkel, *Sales Mgr*
Kc Calderone, *Office Mgr*
EMP: 23
SALES (est): 4.5MM **Privately Held**
SIC: 3081 Plastic film & sheet

(G-5154)
FARBER TRUCKING CORP
162 Hanse Ave (11520-4644)
PHONE.................................516 378-4860
Lewis Farber, *President*

(PA)=Parent Co (HQ)=Headquarters (DH)=Div Headquarters
✪ = New Business established in last 2 years

2019 Harris
New York Manufacturers Directory

Freeport - Nassau County (G-5155) GEOGRAPHIC SECTION

EMP: 23
SQ FT: 35,000
SALES (est): 3MM Privately Held
SIC: 3081 Plastic film & sheet

(G-5155)
FORM-TEC INC
216 N Main St Ste E (11520-2200)
PHONE.................................516 867-0200
Howard Lebow, *President*
EMP: 20
SQ FT: 10,000
SALES (est): 3.6MM Privately Held
WEB: www.form-tec.com
SIC: 3089 Molding primary plastic

(G-5156)
FORSYTHE COSMETIC GROUP LTD
Also Called: Forsythe Licensing
10 Niagara Ave (11520-4704)
P.O. Box 431, Lawrence (11559-0431)
PHONE.................................516 239-4200
Harriet Rose, *Ch of Bd*
Michael Rose, *President*
Beth Friedman, *Vice Pres*
Whitney Matza, *Vice Pres*
Cathy Cheong, *Sales Staff*
◆ EMP: 50
SQ FT: 20,000
SALES (est): 16.5MM Privately Held
WEB: www.cosmeticgroup.com
SIC: 2844 Cosmetic preparations

(G-5157)
FREEPORT SCREEN & STAMPING
31 Hanse Ave (11520-4601)
PHONE.................................516 379-0330
Stan Papot, *President*
▲ EMP: 20
SQ FT: 13,500
SALES (est): 2.4MM Privately Held
SIC: 3469 2759 2396 Metal stampings; screen printing; automotive & apparel trimmings

(G-5158)
GLENN FOODS INC (PA)
Also Called: Glenny's
371 S Main St Ste 119-405 (11520-5114)
PHONE.................................516 377-1400
Glenn Schacher, *President*
Philip Fruchter, *Vice Pres*
Steven Fruchter, *Treasurer*
▼ EMP: 10
SALES (est): 880K Privately Held
WEB: www.glennys.com
SIC: 2099 Food preparations

(G-5159)
GREENFIELD DIE CASTING CORP
99 Doxsee Dr (11520-4717)
PHONE.................................516 623-9230
Peter Greenfield, *President*
Michael Greenfield, *Vice Pres*
Douglas Greenfield, *Admin Sec*
EMP: 50
SQ FT: 56,000
SALES (est): 7.3MM Privately Held
SIC: 3364 3369 Zinc & zinc-base alloy die-castings; nonferrous foundries

(G-5160)
GREENFIELD INDUSTRIES INC
99 Doxsee Dr (11520-4717)
PHONE.................................516 623-9230
Peter Greenfield, *President*
Douglas Greenfield, *Vice Pres*
Michael Greenfield, *Vice Pres*
▲ EMP: 75
SQ FT: 70,000
SALES (est): 12.2MM Privately Held
WEB: www.greenfieldny.com
SIC: 3363 Aluminum die-castings

(G-5161)
HARWITT INDUSTRIES INC
61 S Main St Unit A (11520-3864)
PHONE.................................516 623-9787
Louis Harwitt, *President*
EMP: 13 EST: 2002
SALES (est): 920K Privately Held
SIC: 3599 Machine & other job shop work

(G-5162)
INTEX COMPANY INC (PA)
Also Called: Semtex Industrial
80 Commercial St (11520-2832)
PHONE.................................516 223-0200
Henrietta Rivman, *President*
EMP: 61
SQ FT: 20,000
SALES (est): 6.6MM Privately Held
SIC: 3674 5065 Semiconductors & related devices; electronic parts

(G-5163)
LAMAR PLASTICS PACKAGING LTD
216 N Main St Ste F (11520-2200)
PHONE.................................516 378-2500
Lawrence Aronson, *Ch of Bd*
Marc Aronson, *President*
Josh Aronson, *Vice Pres*
Linda Tino, *Traffic Mgr*
Barry Reimel, *VP Sales*
▲ EMP: 60 EST: 1966
SQ FT: 60,000
SALES (est): 10.3MM Privately Held
SIC: 3086 3993 Packaging & shipping materials, foamed plastic; displays & cutouts, window & lobby

(G-5164)
MARCON ELECTRONIC SYSTEMS LLC
152 Westend Ave (11520-5245)
PHONE.................................516 633-6396
Grace Connelly,
EMP: 6
SALES: 750K Privately Held
SIC: 3679 Electronic components

(G-5165)
MARCON SERVICES
152 Westend Ave (11520-5245)
PHONE.................................516 223-8019
Grace Connelly, *Owner*
EMP: 6
SALES (est): 66.5K Privately Held
WEB: www.graceconnelly.com
SIC: 3674 Semiconductors & related devices

(G-5166)
MELTO METAL PRODUCTS CO INC
37 Hanse Ave (11520-4696)
PHONE.................................516 546-8866
Bernard Liebman, *Ch of Bd*
Peter Sheridan, *Vice Pres*
Juan Costa, *Project Mgr*
▲ EMP: 35
SQ FT: 15,000
SALES (est): 8.6MM Privately Held
WEB: www.meltometalproducts.com
SIC: 3444 Sheet metalwork

(G-5167)
MICA INTERNATIONAL LTD
126 Albany Ave (11520-4702)
PHONE.................................516 378-3400
Fax: 516 379-0560
EMP: 12
SQ FT: 5,500
SALES (est): 820K Privately Held
SIC: 2511 Mfg Wood Household Furniture

(G-5168)
MIDBURY INDUSTRIES INC
86 E Merrick Rd (11520-4034)
PHONE.................................516 868-0600
Diane Jones, *President*
Michael Natilli Jr, *Vice Pres*
EMP: 15
SQ FT: 10,000
SALES (est): 900K Privately Held
WEB: www.midbury.com
SIC: 3089 Injection molding of plastics

(G-5169)
NEW YORK VANITY AND MFG CO
10 Henry St (11520-3910)
PHONE.................................718 417-1010
Teddy Foukalas, *President*
Tony Fotou, *Shareholder*
▲ EMP: 25
SQ FT: 30,000
SALES (est): 3.6MM Privately Held
WEB: www.nyvanity.com
SIC: 2434 Vanities, bathroom: wood

(G-5170)
ON TIME PLASTICS INC
121 Henry St (11520-3821)
PHONE.................................516 442-4280
Franklin Toribio, *President*
EMP: 7
SALES: 600K Privately Held
SIC: 3083 Thermoplastic laminates: rods, tubes, plates & sheet

(G-5171)
ONDRIVESUS CORP
Also Called: Rino
216 N Main St Bldg B2 (11520-2200)
PHONE.................................516 771-6777
Dennis G Berg, *CEO*
D Lee Berg, *President*
Jayne Berg, *Vice Pres*
Don Grandone, *Engineer*
◆ EMP: 35
SQ FT: 11,000
SALES (est): 10.4MM Privately Held
WEB: www.ondrives.us
SIC: 3566 Speed changers, drives & gears

(G-5172)
ORAMAAX DENTAL PRODUCTS INC
216 N Main St Ste A (11520-2200)
PHONE.................................516 771-8514
Robert Endelson, *President*
EMP: 15
SQ FT: 12,500
SALES (est): 1.4MM Privately Held
WEB: www.flosscard.com
SIC: 3843 5047 Dental equipment & supplies; dental equipment & supplies

(G-5173)
PENTHOUSE MANUFACTURING CO INC
Also Called: Penthouse Group, The
225 Buffalo Ave (11520-4709)
PHONE.................................516 379-1300
William Ostrower, *President*
▲ EMP: 350 EST: 1974
SALES (est): 36.4MM Privately Held
SIC: 3172 2399 Cosmetic bags; powder puffs & mitts

(G-5174)
PHOENIX METAL PRODUCTS INC
100 Bennington Ave (11520-3927)
PHONE.................................516 546-4200
Robert Wolf, *President*
◆ EMP: 10
SQ FT: 10,000
SALES (est): 1.8MM Privately Held
WEB: www.phoenixmetalproducts.com
SIC: 3469 Metal stampings

(G-5175)
PRESTI READY MIX CONCRETE INC
Also Called: Presti Stone and Mason
210 E Merrick Rd (11520-4029)
PHONE.................................516 378-6006
Joseph Prestigiacomo, *President*
EMP: 7
SQ FT: 2,500
SALES (est): 1.2MM Privately Held
SIC: 3273 3531 Ready-mixed concrete; bituminous, cement & concrete related products & equipment

(G-5176)
PRIMELITE MANUFACTURING CORP
407 S Main St (11520-5194)
PHONE.................................516 868-4411
Benjamin Heit, *President*
EMP: 9 EST: 1962
SQ FT: 12,000
SALES (est): 1.9MM Privately Held
WEB: www.primelite-mfg.com
SIC: 3646 Commercial indusl & institutional electric lighting fixtures

(G-5177)
QUALITY LINEALS USA INC
105 Bennington Ave Ste 1 (11520-3946)
PHONE.................................516 378-6577
Jill Kaiserman, *President*
EMP: 43
SQ FT: 40,000 Privately Held
SIC: 3544 Dies, plastics forming
PA: Quality Lineals Usa, Inc.
1 Kees Pl
Merrick NY 11566

(G-5178)
RAND & PASEKA MFG CO INC
10 Hanse Ave (11520-4602)
PHONE.................................516 867-1500
Marc Schwab, *President*
Andrea Schwab, *Senior VP*
Bogdan Chojnacki, *Manager*
EMP: 22
SQ FT: 19,000
SALES (est): 3.3MM Privately Held
SIC: 3911 Rosaries or other small religious articles, precious metal

(G-5179)
ROSE FENCE INC (PA)
345 W Sunrise Hwy (11520-3120)
PHONE.................................516 223-0777
Janice Rosenzeig, *Ch of Bd*
▲ EMP: 42
SQ FT: 2,000
SALES (est): 20.2MM Privately Held
WEB: www.rosefence.com
SIC: 3496 Fencing, made from purchased wire

(G-5180)
SAJ OF FREEPORT CORP
Also Called: Love & Quiches Desserts
178 Hanse Ave (11520-4609)
PHONE.................................516 623-8800
Irwin Axelrod, *CEO*
Andrew Axelrod, *President*
Susan Axelrod, *Chairman*
Andy Axelrod, *Vice Pres*
Michael Goldstein, *Vice Pres*
▼ EMP: 250 EST: 1974
SALES (est): 69.7MM Privately Held
WEB: www.loveandquiches.com
SIC: 2051 Bread, cake & related products

(G-5181)
SEA ISLE CUSTOM ROD BUILDERS
495 Guy Lombardo Ave (11520-6293)
PHONE.................................516 868-8855
Robert Feuring, *President*
EMP: 7
SQ FT: 1,710
SALES: 900K Privately Held
SIC: 3949 5941 Fishing tackle, general; fishing equipment

(G-5182)
SEMITRONICS CORP (HQ)
80 Commercial St (11520-2832)
PHONE.................................516 223-0200
Henrietta Rivman, *President*
Phil Balducci, *Opers Staff*
Paul Kurland, *QC Mgr*
Brian Jipp, *Manager*
Ken Ehalt, *Technology*
EMP: 45
SQ FT: 10,000
SALES (est): 6.1MM
SALES (corp-wide): 6.6MM Privately Held
WEB: www.semitronics.com
SIC: 3674 5065 Semiconductors & related devices; electronic parts & equipment
PA: Intex Company Inc
80 Commercial St
Freeport NY 11520
516 223-0200

(G-5183)
SEVILLE CENTRAL MIX CORP (PA)
157 Albany Ave (11520-4710)
PHONE.................................516 868-3000
Peter Scalamandre, *Ch of Bd*
Joseph L Scalamandre, *Vice Pres*
EMP: 67 EST: 1979
SQ FT: 8,000

SALES (est): 12.3MM Privately Held
WEB: www.sevillecentralmix.com
SIC: 3273 Ready-mixed concrete

(G-5184)
SIGNATURE INDUSTRIES INC
32 Saint Johns Pl (11520-4618)
PHONE.................................516 679-5177
Emil Petschauer, *President*
Ante Vulin, *Vice Pres*
James Calderon, *Treasurer*
EMP: 15
SALES (est): 1.7MM Privately Held
WEB: www.signatureindustries.com
SIC: 3993 Signs & advertising specialties

(G-5185)
TEENA CREATIONS INC
10 Hanse Ave (11520-4628)
PHONE.................................516 867-1500
Jules Rand, *President*
Michael Rand, *Treasurer*
Mark Schwab, *Admin Sec*
EMP: 5
SQ FT: 19,000
SALES (est): 520K Privately Held
SIC: 3911 Jewelry, precious metal

(G-5186)
TEMREX CORPORATION (PA)
300 Buffalo Ave (11520-4720)
P.O. Box 182 (11520-0182)
PHONE.................................516 868-6221
Alda Levander, *CEO*
Ethan Levander, *President*
Ruth Fusci, *Admin Sec*
EMP: 37
SQ FT: 5,000
SALES (est): 4.5MM Privately Held
WEB: www.temrex.com
SIC: 3843 Dental equipment & supplies

(G-5187)
THREE STAR OFFSET PRINTING
188 N Main St (11520-2232)
PHONE.................................516 867-8223
Zeev Alauaster, *President*
Orna Alabaster, *Corp Secy*
EMP: 10 EST: 1958
SQ FT: 7,300
SALES (est): 1.9MM Privately Held
SIC: 2752 Photo-offset printing; commercial printing, offset

(G-5188)
TRIUMPH ACTUATION SYSTEMS LLC
417 S Main St (11520-5144)
PHONE.................................516 378-0162
EMP: 55
SALES (corp-wide): 3.8B Publicly Held
SIC: 3593 3728 3724 3594 Mfg Fluid Power Cylinder Mfg Aircraft Parts/Equip Mfg Aircraft Engine/Part Mfg Fluid Power Pump/Mtr Whol Industrial Equip
HQ: Triumph Actuation Systems, Llc
4520 Hampton Rd
Clemmons NC 27012
336 766-9036

(G-5189)
UNIQUE DISPLAY MFG CORP (PA)
216 N Main St Ste D (11520-2200)
PHONE.................................516 546-3800
Philip Boxer, *President*
Eleanor Boxer, *Corp Secy*
EMP: 8 EST: 1976
SQ FT: 50,000
SALES (est): 925.1K Privately Held
SIC: 3993 Displays & cutouts, window & lobby

(G-5190)
WL CONCEPTS & PRODUCTION INC
1 Bennington Ave (11520-3953)
PHONE.................................516 538-5300
William Levine, *President*
Walter Nikles, *VP Opers*
Marian Keilson, *Director*
▲ EMP: 7
SQ FT: 4,500

SALES (est): 1MM Privately Held
WEB: www.wlconcepts.com
SIC: 3993 Signs & advertising specialties

Freeville
Tompkins County

(G-5191)
FREEVILLE PUBLISHING CO INC
Also Called: Cortland-Ithaca Subn Shopper
9 Main St (13068-9599)
P.O. Box 210 (13068-0210)
PHONE.................................607 844-9119
Michael Down, *President*
EMP: 10 EST: 1949
SQ FT: 1,998
SALES (est): 809.7K Privately Held
SIC: 2741 2752 2759 Shopping news: publishing only, not printed on site; commercial printing, offset; commercial printing

(G-5192)
GENOA SAND & GRAVEL LNSG
390 Peruville Rd (13068-9732)
PHONE.................................607 533-4551
EMP: 5
SALES (est): 210K Privately Held
SIC: 1442 Construction Sand/Gravel

(G-5193)
WEAVER WIND ENERGY LLC
7 Union St (13068-3201)
PHONE.................................607 379-9463
Art Weaver, *President*
EMP: 5
SQ FT: 5,000
SALES (est): 526.4K Privately Held
SIC: 3511 Turbines & turbine generator sets

Fresh Meadows
Queens County

(G-5194)
AMERICAN CIGAR
6940 Fresh Meadow Ln (11365-3422)
PHONE.................................718 969-0008
Allen Schuster, *President*
EMP: 6
SALES (est): 450K Privately Held
WEB: www.smokeyscigars.com
SIC: 2121 Cigars

(G-5195)
CDML COMPUTER SERVICES LTD
5343 198th St (11365-1719)
PHONE.................................718 428-9063
Leonard Kaplan, *President*
EMP: 6
SALES (est): 281.3K Privately Held
WEB: www.cdml.com
SIC: 7372 7371 Prepackaged software; custom computer programming services

(G-5196)
DYNAMIC DECISIONS INC (PA)
18519 64th Ave (11365-2707)
PHONE.................................908 755-5000
Alan Fan, *President*
▲ EMP: 10
SQ FT: 6,500
SALES (est): 2.7MM Privately Held
WEB: www.ddidynex.com
SIC: 3571 3577 Electronic computers; computer peripheral equipment

(G-5197)
EXCELTECH INC
5317 Hollis Court Blvd (11365-1727)
PHONE.................................718 423-7262
Allan Chan, *CEO*
EMP: 12
SALES (est): 1.3MM Privately Held
SIC: 3674 Semiconductors & related devices

(G-5198)
FRENCH ASSOCIATES INC
Also Called: French Pdts Frnch Pickle Works
7339 172nd St (11366-1420)
PHONE.................................718 387-9880
Seymour Rosen, *President*
Jerry Rosen, *Vice Pres*
EMP: 10 EST: 1919
SQ FT: 20,000
SALES (est): 650K Privately Held
WEB: www.frenchassociates.com
SIC: 2035 5199 5149 Pickles, vinegar; general merchandise, non-durable; groceries & related products

(G-5199)
HACULLA NYC INC
6805 Fresh Meadow Ln (11365-3438)
PHONE.................................718 886-3163
Jonathan Koon, *Principal*
EMP: 10 EST: 2014
SALES (est): 530K Privately Held
SIC: 2329 Men's & boys' sportswear & athletic clothing

(G-5200)
KOON ENTERPRISES LLC
6805 Fresh Madow Ln Ste B (11365)
PHONE.................................718 886-3163
Jonathan M Koon, *Mng Member*
Katherine Koon,
EMP: 5
SALES (est): 1.2MM Privately Held
SIC: 2389 Costumes

(G-5201)
KOONICHI INC
6805 Fresh Meadow Ln Ste B (11365)
PHONE.................................718 886-8338
Jonathan Koon, *President*
Katherine Koon, *Vice Pres*
Raymond Koon, *CFO*
▲ EMP: 7
SQ FT: 2,500
SALES (est): 590K Privately Held
WEB: www.koonichi.com
SIC: 3089 Automotive parts, plastic

(G-5202)
MANIFESTATION-GLOW PRESS INC
7740 164th St (11366-1227)
PHONE.................................718 380-5259
IA Konopiaty, *Ch of Bd*
Abakash Konopiaty, *President*
EMP: 5
SQ FT: 1,800
SALES (est): 540K Privately Held
WEB: www.heart-light.com
SIC: 2752 Commercial printing, offset

(G-5203)
RYBA SOFTWARE INC
7359 186th St (11366-1719)
PHONE.................................718 264-9352
Alexander J Ryba, *Principal*
EMP: 5
SALES (est): 198.4K Privately Held
SIC: 7372 Prepackaged software

(G-5204)
TOROTRON CORPORATION
18508 Union Tpke Ste 101 (11366-1700)
PHONE.................................718 428-6992
Oscar Zanger, *President*
Steve Bortnicker, *Controller*
Miriam Zanger, *Admin Sec*
EMP: 8 EST: 1950
SQ FT: 3,000
SALES: 350K Privately Held
SIC: 3679 Electronic circuits

(G-5205)
VR CONTAINMENT LLC
17625 Union Tpke Ste 175 (11366-1515)
PHONE.................................917 972-3441
EMP: 6
SALES (est): 644K Privately Held
SIC: 3442 3446 Metal doors; gates, ornamental metal

Frewsburg
Chautauqua County

(G-5206)
ARTISAN MANAGEMENT GROUP INC
39 Venman St (14738-9565)
PHONE.................................716 569-4094
Kevin Delong, *President*
EMP: 7
SALES: 950K Privately Held
SIC: 3544 3599 Special dies, tools, jigs & fixtures; machine shop, jobbing & repair

(G-5207)
COLBURNS AC RFRGN
17 White Dr (14738-9553)
P.O. Box 9430 (14738-1443)
PHONE.................................716 569-3695
George M Colburn, *President*
EMP: 10
SQ FT: 3,600
SALES (est): 1.9MM Privately Held
SIC: 3585 7623 Heating & air conditioning combination units; refrigeration repair service

(G-5208)
FREW RUN GRAVEL PRODUCTS INC
984 Frew Run Rd (14738-9746)
PHONE.................................716 569-4712
Michael Nelson, *President*
EMP: 6
SALES (est): 441.4K Privately Held
SIC: 1442 Construction sand & gravel

(G-5209)
MONARCH PLASTICS INC
225 Falconer St (14738-9506)
P.O. Box 648 (14738-0648)
PHONE.................................716 569-2175
Donald Olander, *President*
Charles Moffett, *Engineer*
Bambi L Muro, *Executive*
▲ EMP: 30 EST: 1960
SQ FT: 16,000
SALES (est): 5.7MM Privately Held
WEB: www.monarchplastic.com
SIC: 3089 Molding primary plastic

Friendship
Allegany County

(G-5210)
FRIENDSHIP DAIRIES LLC
6701 County Road 20 (14739-8660)
PHONE.................................585 973-3031
Ron Klein, *President*
Sherry Crawford, *Buyer*
Tim Bentley, *CTO*
EMP: 250
SQ FT: 15,000
SALES (est): 39.8MM Privately Held
WEB: www.deanfoods.com
SIC: 2023 2022 Dry, condensed, evaporated dairy products; cheese, natural & processed
HQ: Saputo Dairy Foods Usa, Llc
2711 N Haske Ave Ste 3700
Dallas TX 75204
214 863-2300

(G-5211)
WAGNER HARDWOODS LLC (PA)
6052 County Road 20 (14739-8664)
PHONE.................................607 229-8198
Les Wagner, *Principal*
EMP: 8
SALES (est): 22.5MM Privately Held
SIC: 2421 Sawmills & planing mills, general

Fulton
Oswego County

(G-5212)
C & C METAL FABRICATIONS INC
159 Hubbard St (13069-1247)
PHONE.....................315 598-7607
Judy Davis, *Manager*
John F Sharkey IV,
EMP: 19
SQ FT: 32,000
SALES (est): 3.2MM **Privately Held**
WEB: www.candcfabrication.com
SIC: 3441 Fabricated structural metal

(G-5213)
CANFIELD MACHINE & TOOL LLC
121 Howard Rd (13069-4278)
PHONE.....................315 593-8062
Chris Canfield, *CIO*
Debra Canfield, *Director*
EMP: 41
SQ FT: 24,000
SALES (est): 5.7MM **Privately Held**
SIC: 3599 Machine shop, jobbing & repair

(G-5214)
D-K MANUFACTURING CORP
Also Called: DK
551 W 3rd St S (13069-2824)
P.O. Box 600 (13069-0600)
PHONE.....................315 592-4327
Norman W Kesterke, *President*
Donald L Kesterke, *General Mgr*
Lorry Bailey, *Manager*
Sue Kesterke, *CIO*
EMP: 20
SQ FT: 30,000
SALES (est): 2MM **Privately Held**
WEB: www.d-kmfg.com
SIC: 3469 3599 Stamping metal for the trade; machine shop, jobbing & repair

(G-5215)
DOT PUBLISHING
Also Called: Fulton Daily News
117 Cayuga St (13069-1709)
PHONE.....................315 593-2510
Monica Mackenzie, *President*
EMP: 10
SQ FT: 2,048
SALES (est): 581.9K **Privately Held**
SIC: 2711 Newspapers, publishing & printing

(G-5216)
FULTON NEWSPAPERS INC
Also Called: Fulton Patriot
67 S 2nd St (13069-1725)
PHONE.....................315 598-6397
Vincent R Caravan, *President*
Ronald Caravan, *Vice Pres*
EMP: 20
SQ FT: 8,000
SALES (est): 928.2K **Privately Held**
SIC: 2711 2752 2791 2789 Newspapers: publishing only, not printed on site; commercial printing, offset; typesetting; bookbinding & related work

(G-5217)
FULTON TOOL CO INC
802 W Broadway Ste 1 (13069-1522)
PHONE.....................315 598-2900
Bruce Phelps, *President*
Barbara Phelps, *Corp Secy*
Peter Russell, *Vice Pres*
EMP: 21 EST: 1959
SQ FT: 32,000
SALES (est): 4.3MM **Privately Held**
WEB: www.fultontool.com
SIC: 3599 Machine shop, jobbing & repair

(G-5218)
GONE SOUTH CONCRETE BLOCK INC
Also Called: John Deere Authorized Dealer
2809 State Route 3 (13069-5805)
P.O. Box 787 (13069-0787)
PHONE.....................315 598-2141
Thomas S Venezia, *President*
Mike Relf, *Vice Pres*
Cory Murray, *Controller*
Mark Lalomia, *Sales Mgr*
EMP: 30
SQ FT: 2,000
SALES (est): 6.7MM **Privately Held**
SIC: 3271 5211 5082 Blocks, concrete or cinder: standard; lumber & other building materials; construction & mining machinery

(G-5219)
HAUN WELDING SUPPLY INC
214 N 4th St (13069-1216)
PHONE.....................315 592-5012
Patty Sasso, *Manager*
EMP: 7
SQ FT: 1,938
SALES (corp-wide): 65.7MM **Privately Held**
SIC: 7692 5084 Welding repair; welding machinery & equipment
PA: Haun Welding Supply, Inc.
5921 Court Street Rd
Syracuse NY 13206
315 463-5241

(G-5220)
HUHTAMAKI INC
Huhtamaki Consumer Packaging
100 State St (13069-2518)
PHONE.....................315 593-5311
Dietmar Johann, *Opers Mgr*
Carl Graf, *Opers Spvr*
Tom Meucci, *Opers Staff*
Patrick Logan, *Engineer*
David Rhodes, *Controller*
EMP: 585
SALES (corp-wide): 35.2B **Privately Held**
SIC: 2621 Pressed pulp products
HQ: Huhtamaki, Inc.
9201 Packaging Dr
De Soto KS 66018
913 583-3025

(G-5221)
INTERFACE PERFORMANCE MTLS INC
2885 State Route 481 (13069-4221)
PHONE.....................315 592-8100
Richard Isbell, *QC Dir*
Debra Morris, *Technology*
EMP: 219
SALES (corp-wide): 698.4MM **Publicly Held**
WEB: www.sealinfo.com
SIC: 3053 Gaskets, packing & sealing devices
HQ: Interface Performance Materials, Inc.
216 Wohlsen Way
Lancaster PA 17603

(G-5222)
IVES FARM MARKET
Also Called: Ives Slaughterhouse
2652 Rr 176 (13069)
PHONE.....................315 592-4880
Ronald Ives, *Owner*
Jean Ives, *Partner*
EMP: 5
SALES (est): 360K **Privately Held**
SIC: 2011 5411 5421 Meat packing plants; grocery stores; meat markets, including freezer provisioners

(G-5223)
JOHN CRANE INC
2314 County Route 4 (13069-3659)
PHONE.....................315 593-6237
John Crane, *Branch Mgr*
EMP: 64
SALES (corp-wide): 4.1B **Privately Held**
SIC: 3053 Gaskets & sealing devices
HQ: John Crane Inc.
227 W Monroe St Ste 1800
Chicago IL 60606
312 605-7800

(G-5224)
K&NS FOODS USA LLC
607 Phillips St (13069-1520)
PHONE.....................315 598-8080
Jimmy Koid, *Mng Member*
▲ EMP: 30 EST: 2012
SALES (est): 7.6MM **Privately Held**
SIC: 2015 Chicken, processed: frozen
PA: K&N's Foods (Private) Limited
Business Centre, Shadman Second Floor
Lahore
423 742-1710

(G-5225)
KENWELL CORPORATION
871 Hannibal St (13069-4186)
P.O. Box 207 (13069-0207)
PHONE.....................315 592-4263
Roger Horning, *President*
Bruce Horning, *Vice Pres*
Bob Flack, *Manager*
Doug Horning, *Info Tech Mgr*
EMP: 52 EST: 1970
SQ FT: 13,000
SALES (est): 10.8MM **Privately Held**
WEB: www.kenwellcorp.com
SIC: 3599 Machine shop, jobbing & repair

(G-5226)
KRENGEL MANUFACTURING CO INC
Also Called: American Marking Systems
121 Fulton Ave Fl 2 (13069)
PHONE.....................212 227-1901
EMP: 18
SALES (est): 980K **Privately Held**
SIC: 3953 Mfg Marking Devices

(G-5227)
LINDE MERCHANT PRODUCTION INC
370 Owens Rd (13069-4619)
PHONE.....................315 593-1360
Richard Olinger, *Principal*
EMP: 8
SALES (corp-wide): 20.1B **Privately Held**
SIC: 2813 Carbon dioxide
HQ: Linde Merchant Production, Inc.
575 Mountain Ave
New Providence NJ 07974

(G-5228)
NET & DIE INC
24 Foster St (13069)
P.O. Box 240 (13069-0240)
PHONE.....................315 592-4311
Richard N Shatrau, *President*
Helena Rockwood, *Corp Secy*
EMP: 38 EST: 1963
SQ FT: 30,000
SALES (est): 6.7MM **Privately Held**
SIC: 3599 Machine shop, jobbing & repair

(G-5229)
NORTH END PAPER CO INC
702 Hannibal St (13069-1020)
PHONE.....................315 593-8100
William F Shafer III, *President*
EMP: 7
SQ FT: 40,000
SALES (est): 1.1MM
SALES (corp-wide): 8.7MM **Privately Held**
WEB: www.flowercitytissue.com
SIC: 2621 Tissue paper
PA: Flower City Tissue Mills Company, Inc.
700 Driving Park Ave
Rochester NY 14613
585 458-9200

(G-5230)
NORTHERN BITUMINOUS MIX INC
32 Silk Rd (13069-4862)
P.O. Box 787 (13069-0787)
PHONE.....................315 598-2141
Thomas Venezia Sr, *President*
EMP: 6
SQ FT: 2,000
SALES (est): 784K **Privately Held**
SIC: 2951 Asphalt & asphaltic paving mixtures (not from refineries)

(G-5231)
PATHFINDER INDUSTRIES INC
117 N 3rd St (13069-1256)
PHONE.....................315 593-2483
Marsha Ives, *President*
Maribeth Myers, *Vice Pres*
Mike Cook, *Foreman/Supr*
Wally Corzett, *Prgrmr*
EMP: 21
SQ FT: 22,000
SALES (est): 4.6MM **Privately Held**
WEB: www.pathfinderind.com
SIC: 3444 Sheet metalwork

(G-5232)
SUNOCO INC
376 Owens Rd (13069)
PHONE.....................315 593-0500
Erin Tones, *Principal*
EMP: 6 EST: 2016
SALES (est): 230K **Privately Held**
SIC: 2869 2046 Ethyl alcohol, ethanol; corn oil products

(G-5233)
UNIVERSAL METAL WORKS LLC
159 Hubbard St (13069-1247)
PHONE.....................315 598-7607
John F Sharkey IV,
EMP: 19
SALES: 4.5MM **Privately Held**
SIC: 3441 Fabricated structural metal

Fultonville
Montgomery County

(G-5234)
ANDERSON INSTRUMENT CO INC (HQ)
156 Auriesville Rd (12072-2031)
PHONE.....................518 922-5315
Andrew Hider, *CEO*
Brigitt Fauve, *Vice Pres*
William Wilson, *Vice Pres*
Deanne Brassard, *Purch Agent*
Peter Cannellos, *Buyer*
▲ EMP: 70
SQ FT: 40,000
SALES (est): 24.8MM
SALES (corp-wide): 6.6B **Publicly Held**
WEB: www.andinst.com
SIC: 3823 5084 3822 3625 Controllers for process variables, all types; industrial machinery & equipment; auto controls regulating residntl & coml environmt & applncs; relays & industrial controls
PA: Fortive Corporation
6920 Seaway Blvd
Everett WA 98203
425 446-5000

(G-5235)
CONSOLIDATED BARRICADES INC
179 Dillenbeck Rd (12072-3311)
PHONE.....................518 922-7944
Joseph Melideo, *President*
EMP: 8
SQ FT: 7,000
SALES (est): 1.2MM **Privately Held**
WEB: www.consolidatedbarricades.com
SIC: 3499 Barricades, metal

(G-5236)
FULTONVILLE MACHINE & TOOL CO
73 Union St (12072-1836)
P.O. Box 426 (12072-0426)
PHONE.....................518 853-4441
Randolf C Snyder, *President*
Patricia Snyder, *Corp Secy*
EMP: 11 EST: 1945
SQ FT: 18,000
SALES: 1.2MM **Privately Held**
SIC: 3599 Machine shop, jobbing & repair

(G-5237)
MOHAWK RIVER LEATHER WORKS
32 Broad St (12072)
PHONE.....................518 853-3900
Joseph H Sicilia, *President*
Robert Hojohn, *Vice Pres*
EMP: 17
SQ FT: 3,534
SALES (est): 2.6MM **Privately Held**
SIC: 3111 Coloring of leather

(G-5238)
PARTLOW CORPORATION
Also Called: Partlow West
156 Auriesville Rd (12072-2031)
PHONE..................................518 922-5315
Craig Purse, *President*
Donald D'Amico, *Vice Pres*
EMP: 175
SQ FT: 60,000
SALES: 34.8MM **Privately Held**
SIC: 3823 Industrial process control instruments

(G-5239)
PERRONE LEATHER LLC (PA)
Also Called: Perrone Aerospace
182a Riverside Dr (12072-1750)
PHONE..................................518 853-4300
Bartle Avery, *CEO*
William T Perrone Jr, *President*
Rick McGinn,
▲ **EMP:** 90
SQ FT: 69,221
SALES (est): 17.1MM **Privately Held**
WEB: www.perroneleather.com
SIC: 3199 5611 Leather garments; men's & boys' clothing stores

Gainesville
Wyoming County

(G-5240)
DRASGOW INC
4150 Poplar Tree Rd (14066-9723)
PHONE..................................585 786-3603
Karl Drasgow, *President*
Bryan Schabloski, *Production*
Crystal Hilton, *Info Tech Mgr*
EMP: 25
SQ FT: 17,946
SALES: 1.7MM **Privately Held**
SIC: 3569 Filters

Galway
Saratoga County

(G-5241)
WHALENS HORSERADISH PRODUCTS
1710 Route 29 (12074-2213)
PHONE..................................518 587-6404
Kim Bibens, *President*
EMP: 5
SALES (est): 450.7K **Privately Held**
SIC: 2035 Horseradish, prepared

Gansevoort
Saratoga County

(G-5242)
AUREONIC
13 Whispering Pines Rd (12831-1443)
PHONE..................................518 791-9331
Shawn Lescault, *CEO*
Nicholas Karker, *Co-Owner*
Patrick Roden, *Co-Owner*
Robert Schramm, *Co-Owner*
Ian Tucker, *CFO*
EMP: 5
SALES (est): 350K **Privately Held**
SIC: 3823 7389 Combustion control instruments;

(G-5243)
GRANITE & MARBLE WORKS INC
8 Commerce Park Dr (12831-2240)
PHONE..................................518 584-2800
Margaret P Roohan, *President*
▲ **EMP:** 20
SALES (est): 2.8MM **Privately Held**
SIC: 3281 Granite, cut & shaped

(G-5244)
PALLETTE STONE CORPORATION
269 Ballard Rd (12831-1597)
PHONE..................................518 584-2421
Thomas Longe, *President*
D Alan Collins, *Corp Secy*
Christopher Weed, *Manager*
EMP: 40
SQ FT: 3,000
SALES (est): 8.3MM
SALES (corp-wide): 37.3MM **Privately Held**
SIC: 3281 2951 3241 5032 Cut stone & stone products; concrete, bituminous; portland cement; stone, crushed or broken; asphalt mixture; concrete & cinder block; paving stones; concrete & cinder block
PA: D. A. Collins Construction Co., Inc.
269 Ballard Rd
Gansevoort NY 12831
518 664-9855

(G-5245)
RASP INCORPORATED
8 Dukes Way (12831-1668)
PHONE..................................518 747-8020
Ronald Richards, *Vice Pres*
Jeff Bruno, *Engineer*
Michael Close, *Treasurer*
EMP: 27 **EST:** 1995
SQ FT: 8,000
SALES (est): 6.4MM **Privately Held**
WEB: www.rasp-controls.com
SIC: 3625 Industrial controls: push button, selector switches, pilot

(G-5246)
ROCK HILL BAKEHOUSE LTD
21 Saratoga Rd (12831)
PHONE..................................518 743-1627
Matthew Funiciello, *President*
Michael London, *Vice Pres*
Adam Witt, *Treasurer*
Wendy London, *Admin Sec*
EMP: 30
SALES (est): 2.7MM **Privately Held**
WEB: www.rockhillbakehouse.com
SIC: 2051 5461 Bread, all types (white, wheat, rye, etc): fresh or frozen; bread

(G-5247)
STONE BRIDGE IRON AND STL INC
426 Purinton Rd (12831-2193)
PHONE..................................518 695-3752
Brian Carmer, *Principal*
Britt Carmer, *Exec VP*
Mark Hutchinson, *Vice Pres*
Daniel Hogan, *Safety Dir*
James Mulholland, *Plant Mgr*
▲ **EMP:** 60
SQ FT: 45,000
SALES (est): 17.3MM **Privately Held**
WEB: www.stonebridgeiron.com
SIC: 3441 Building components, structural steel

(G-5248)
TRUARC FABRICATION
1 Commerce Park Dr (12831-2239)
PHONE..................................518 691-0430
Cris Edgrely, *President*
Bill Lorrain, *Manager*
EMP: 9
SALES (est): 956.8K **Privately Held**
SIC: 3599 Flexible metal hose, tubing & bellows

Garden City
Nassau County

(G-5249)
A G MASTER CRAFTS LTD
5 South St Ste A (11530-4926)
P.O. Box 373, Glen Head (11545-0373)
PHONE..................................516 745-6262
Tom Gardianos, *President*
Diana Gardianos, *Vice Pres*
▲ **EMP:** 15
SALES (est): 2.4MM **Privately Held**
WEB: www.agmastercrafts.com
SIC: 2521 Cabinets, office: wood

(G-5250)
AAR ALLEN SERVICES INC
AAR Aircraft Component
747 Zeckendorf Blvd (11530-2188)
PHONE..................................516 222-9000
Rob Bruinsna, *General Mgr*
Salim Khamze, *Engineer*
James Maczarella, *VP Finance*
EMP: 39
SALES (corp-wide): 1.7B **Publicly Held**
SIC: 3728 Aircraft parts & equipment
HQ: Aar Allen Services, Inc.
1100 N Wood Dale Rd
Wood Dale IL 60191

(G-5251)
ATLAS SWITCH CO INC
969 Stewart Ave (11530-4816)
PHONE..................................516 222-6280
Gina Paradise, *President*
John Paradise, *Engineer*
Art Metz, *Bookkeeper*
Harris Berloe, *Accounts Exec*
Matt Perlow, *Sales Engr*
EMP: 33
SQ FT: 30,000
SALES (est): 11.2MM **Privately Held**
WEB: www.atlasswitch.com
SIC: 3613 3699 Switches, electric power except snap, push button, etc.; electrical equipment & supplies

(G-5252)
BHARAT ELECTRONICS LIMITED
53 Hilton Ave (11530-2806)
PHONE..................................516 248-4021
Siva Muthuswamy, *Manager*
EMP: 7
SALES (corp-wide): 1.5B **Privately Held**
WEB: www.bel-india.com
SIC: 3674 Solid state electronic devices
PA: Bharat Electronics Limited
Outer Ring Road, Nagavara
Bengaluru KA 56004
802 503-9266

(G-5253)
BRISTOL-MYERS SQUIBB COMPANY
1000 Stewart Ave (11530-4814)
PHONE..................................516 832-2191
Richard Serafin, *Branch Mgr*
EMP: 225
SALES (corp-wide): 20.7B **Publicly Held**
WEB: www.bms.com
SIC: 2834 Pharmaceutical preparations
PA: Bristol-Myers Squibb Company
430 E 29th St Fl 14
New York NY 10016
212 546-4000

(G-5254)
CAMPUS COURSE PAKS INC
1 South Ave Fl 1 (11530-4213)
PHONE..................................516 877-3967
Wayne Piskin, *President*
EMP: 5
SQ FT: 1,500
SALES (est): 237.4MM **Privately Held**
WEB: www.ccpaks.com
SIC: 2731 Books: publishing only

(G-5255)
DILLMEIER ENTERPRISES INC
106 7th St Ste 201 (11530-5718)
PHONE..................................800 325-0596
EMP: 18
SALES (corp-wide): 23MM **Privately Held**
SIC: 3231 Products of purchased glass
PA: Dillmeier Enterprises, Inc.
2903 Industrial Park Rd
Van Buren AR 72956
800 325-0596

(G-5256)
DYNA-EMPIRE INC
1075 Stewart Ave (11530-4871)
PHONE..................................516 222-2700
G Patrick Mc Carthy, *President*
Richard Shaper, *Vice Pres*
Syd Crossley, *Opers Staff*
Colin Crossley, *Engineer*
Regina Weller, *Human Res Mgr*
▲ **EMP:** 145 **EST:** 1941
SQ FT: 52,000
SALES (est): 29.4MM **Privately Held**
WEB: www.dyna-empire.com
SIC: 3724 3728 3829 3823 Aircraft engines & engine parts; aircraft landing assemblies & brakes; measuring & controlling devices; industrial instrmnts msrmnt display/control process variable; search & navigation equipment

(G-5257)
EDGEWOOD INDUSTRIES INC
635 Commercial Ave (11530-6409)
PHONE..................................516 227-2447
Frank Suppa, *President*
EMP: 6
SALES (est): 551.9K **Privately Held**
SIC: 3271 Concrete block & brick

(G-5258)
EURO FINE PAPER INC
220 Nassau Blvd (11530-5500)
PHONE..................................516 238-5253
Tom McShea Sr, *President*
EMP: 8
SALES (est): 640K **Privately Held**
SIC: 2621 Paper mills

(G-5259)
EUROPEAN MARBLE WORKS CO INC
Also Called: Puccio Marble and Onyx
54 Nassau Blvd (11530-4139)
PHONE..................................718 387-9778
Paul Puccio, *President*
John Puccio, *Vice Pres*
▲ **EMP:** 12 **EST:** 1956
SQ FT: 70,000
SALES (est): 1.3MM **Privately Held**
SIC: 3281 Cut stone & stone products

(G-5260)
EXERGY LLC
320 Endo Blvd Unit 1 (11530-6747)
PHONE..................................516 832-9300
Jordan Finkelstein, *President*
Bob Scott, *President*
Robert Scott, *Vice Pres*
EMP: 37
SQ FT: 20,000
SALES (est): 7.2MM **Privately Held**
WEB: www.exergyllc.com
SIC: 3443 8711 Heat exchangers, condensers & components; consulting engineer

(G-5261)
H&E SERVICE CORP
Also Called: Gimbel & Associates
400 Garden Cy Plz Ste 405 (11530)
PHONE..................................646 472-1936
Roger Gimbel, *President*
Gail Steiger, *Executive Asst*
Lois Ritarossi, *Sr Consultant*
EMP: 98 **EST:** 1960
SQ FT: 30,000
SALES (est): 5.4MM **Privately Held**
SIC: 2752 Commercial printing, offset

(G-5262)
IMACOR INC
821 Franklin Ave Ste 301 (11530-4519)
PHONE..................................516 393-0970
Scott Roth, *President*
Jenn Kujawski, *Exec VP*
EMP: 20
SALES (est): 3.3MM **Privately Held**
SIC: 3845 Ultrasonic scanning devices, medical

(G-5263)
ISSCO CORPORATION (PA)
Also Called: Industrial SEC Systems Contrls
111 Cherry Valley Ave # 410 (11530-1570)
PHONE..................................212 732-8748
Arthur R Katon, *President*
Marsha Katon, *Corp Secy*
EMP: 18
SQ FT: 14,000
SALES (est): 1.4MM **Privately Held**
SIC: 3699 Security control equipment & systems

Garden City - Nassau County (G-5264)

(G-5264) L & M PUBLICATIONS INC
Also Called: Freeport Baldwin Leader
2 Endo Blvd (11530-6707)
PHONE..................516 378-3133
Linda Laursen Toscano, *President*
Paul Laursen, *Vice Pres*
John Laursen, *Shareholder*
EMP: 33
SALES (est): 1.6MM **Privately Held**
WEB: www.merricklife.com
SIC: 2711 7313 Newspapers: publishing only, not printed on site; newspaper advertising representative

(G-5265) LIFETIME BRANDS INC (PA)
1000 Stewart Ave (11530-4814)
PHONE..................516 683-6000
Robert B Kay, *CEO*
Jeffrey Siegel, *Ch of Bd*
Daniel Siegel, *President*
Ronald Shiftan, *COO*
Laurence Winoker, *CFO*
◆ EMP: 277
SQ FT: 159,000
SALES: 579.4MM **Publicly Held**
WEB: www.lifetimebrands.com
SIC: 3421 5023 5719 Cutlery; home furnishings; kitchen tools & utensils; stainless steel flatware; kitchenware; cutlery; glassware

(G-5266) LITMOR PUBLISHING CORP (PA)
Also Called: Litmor Publications
821 Franklin Ave Ste 208 (11530-4519)
PHONE..................516 931-0012
Margaret Norris, *Publisher*
Edward Norris, *General Mgr*
EMP: 15
SQ FT: 3,000
SALES (est): 1.3MM **Privately Held**
SIC: 2711 2791 2752 Newspapers, publishing & printing; typesetting; commercial printing, lithographic

(G-5267) LONG ISLAND PIPE SUPPLY INC (PA)
Also Called: LI Pipe Supply
586 Commercial Ave (11530-6418)
PHONE..................516 222-8008
Robert Moss, *CEO*
Larry Greenberg, *General Mgr*
Brian Coyle, *Sales Mgr*
Frank Anselmo, *Sales Staff*
Keith Cowan, *Sales Staff*
EMP: 40
SQ FT: 35,000
SALES (est): 22.9MM **Privately Held**
SIC: 3498 Fabricated pipe & fittings

(G-5268) LONG ISLAND PIPE SUPPLY INC (PA)
586 Commercial Ave (11530-6418)
PHONE..................516 222-8008
Robert Moss, *President*
John Freer, *Asst Mgr*
EMP: 28
SQ FT: 35,000
SALES (est): 59.6MM **Privately Held**
WEB: www.lipipe.com
SIC: 3498 5074 Fabricated pipe & fittings; plumbing fittings & supplies

(G-5269) M AND J HAIR CENTER INC
Also Called: Natural Image Hair Concepts
1103 Stewart Ave Ste 100 (11530-4886)
PHONE..................516 872-1010
Jean Dreyfuss, *President*
EMP: 15
SQ FT: 1,600
SALES (est): 1.4MM **Privately Held**
WEB: www.mjhair.com
SIC: 3999 Wigs, including doll wigs, toupees or wiglets

(G-5270) MCQUILLING PARTNERS INC (PA)
1035 Stewart Ave Ste 100 (11530-4825)
PHONE..................516 227-5718
John F Desantes, *Ch of Bd*
Roger Marco, *Managing Dir*
Dick Barnard, *Vice Pres*
Alison Omelio, *Marketing Staff*
David Saginaw, *Director*
EMP: 26 EST: 1964
SALES (est): 3.5MM **Privately Held**
WEB: www.mcquilling.com
SIC: 3731 Tankers, building & repairing

(G-5271) META PHARMACY SYSTEMS INC
401 Franklin Ave Ste 106 (11530-5942)
PHONE..................516 488-6189
Salvatore M Barcia, *President*
EMP: 25
SALES (est): 1.8MM **Privately Held**
WEB: www.metapharmacy.com
SIC: 7372 Prepackaged software

(G-5272) MITCO MANUFACTURING
605 Locust St (11530-6552)
PHONE..................800 338-8908
▲ EMP: 6
SALES (est): 400.9K **Privately Held**
SIC: 3999 Manufacturing industries

(G-5273) OPTIONLINE LLC
100 Hilton Ave Apt 23 (11530-1564)
PHONE..................516 218-3225
Luiz Grossmann, *President*
EMP: 25
SALES (est): 694.2K **Privately Held**
SIC: 2721 7375 Periodicals: publishing only; statistical reports (periodicals): publishing only; on-line data base information retrieval

(G-5274) PINCHARMING INC
215 Brixton Rd (11530-1339)
PHONE..................516 663-5115
Susan Smith, *President*
Barry Smith, *Vice Pres*
EMP: 12
SALES (est): 1MM **Privately Held**
SIC: 3961 Costume jewelry

(G-5275) PRACTICEPRO SOFTWARE SYSTEMS
666 Old Country Rd Bsmt (11530-2079)
PHONE..................516 222-0010
Gary J Balsamo, *President*
EMP: 5
SALES: 313.6K **Privately Held**
WEB: www.practicepro.com
SIC: 7372 Prepackaged software

(G-5276) PROGINET CORPORATION
200 Garden Cy Plz Ste 220 (11530)
PHONE..................516 535-3600
Sandison E Weil, *President*
Stephen M Flynn, *COO*
John W Gazzola, *Senior VP*
Joe Christel, *CFO*
Kevin Bohan, *CIO*
EMP: 37
SALES: 9.3MM **Privately Held**
WEB: www.proginet.com
SIC: 7372 Application computer software; business oriented computer software; operating systems computer software

(G-5277) PUCCIO DESIGN INTERNATIONAL
Also Called: Puccio European Marble & Onyx
54 Nassau Blvd (11530-4139)
PHONE..................516 248-6426
Paul Puccio, *President*
EMP: 15 EST: 1968
SQ FT: 4,000
SALES (est): 170.8K **Privately Held**
WEB: www.puccio.info
SIC: 3281 Furniture, cut stone

(G-5278) RICHNER COMMUNICATIONS INC (PA)
Also Called: Prime Time
2 Endo Blvd (11530-6707)
PHONE..................516 569-4000
Stuart Richner, *CEO*
Robert Kern, *General Mgr*
Tony Bellissimo, *Editor*
Jeff Bessen, *Editor*
Scott Brinton, *Editor*
EMP: 130
SQ FT: 90,000
SALES (est): 14.2MM **Privately Held**
SIC: 2711 Commercial printing & newspaper publishing combined; newspapers, publishing & printing

(G-5279) ROBECO/ASCOT PRODUCTS INC
100 Ring Rd W (11530-3219)
PHONE..................516 248-1521
EMP: 0
SALES (est): 1.2MM **Privately Held**
SIC: 3081 Unsupported Plastics Film And Sheet, Nsk

(G-5280) SAVENERGY INC
645 South St Unit A (11530-4928)
PHONE..................516 239-1958
John Hyung Choi, *President*
▲ EMP: 9 EST: 2010
SALES (est): 1.1MM **Privately Held**
SIC: 3646 Commercial indusl & institutional electric lighting fixtures

(G-5281) SEVIROLI FOODS INC (PA)
601 Brook St (11530-6431)
PHONE..................516 222-6220
Joseph Seviroli Jr, *Ch of Bd*
Paul Vertullo, *COO*
Francesca Kaszuba, *VP Opers*
Ovidio Campos, *Plant Mgr*
Ray Ramnarine, *Purch Mgr*
▲ EMP: 200
SQ FT: 80,000
SALES (est): 76.9MM **Privately Held**
WEB: www.seviroli.com
SIC: 2038 Frozen specialties

(G-5282) STANDARD WEDDING BAND CO
951 Franklin Ave (11530-2909)
PHONE..................516 294-0954
Walter E Soderlund, *President*
Mabel T Soderlund, *Treasurer*
EMP: 6
SALES (est): 500K **Privately Held**
SIC: 3911 Rings, finger: precious metal

(G-5283) THERMAL TECH DOORS INC (PA)
576 Brook St (11530-6416)
PHONE..................516 745-0100
Emanuel Karavas, *President*
Stephanos Kourtis, *Vice Pres*
EMP: 40
SQ FT: 25,000
SALES (est): 5MM **Privately Held**
SIC: 3442 Sash, door or window: metal

(G-5284) WON & LEE INC
Also Called: Unicorn Graphics
971 Stewart Ave (11530-4816)
PHONE..................516 222-0712
Jong Suk Lee, *President*
Jong Hoon Lee, *Vice Pres*
▲ EMP: 35
SQ FT: 30,000
SALES (est): 6.8MM **Privately Held**
WEB: www.unicorngraphics.com
SIC: 2759 2789 2752 2741 Calendars: printing; bookbinding & related work; commercial printing, lithographic; miscellaneous publishing; ink, printers'

Garden City Park
Nassau County

(G-5285) DENTON STONEWORKS INC
94 Denton Ave (11040-4036)
P.O. Box 3807, New Hyde Park (11040-8807)
PHONE..................516 746-1500
Boguslaw Kaczor, *CEO*
EMP: 14
SQ FT: 15,000
SALES (est): 1.8MM **Privately Held**
SIC: 3281 Cut stone & stone products

(G-5286) NEW YORK PACKAGING II LLC
Also Called: Redi Bag USA
135 Fulton Ave (11040-5305)
P.O. Box 1039, New Hyde Park (11040-7039)
PHONE..................516 746-0600
Jeffrey Rabiea, *President*
Michael Zapf, *CFO*
▲ EMP: 25
SALES: 36.8MM **Privately Held**
SIC: 2673 Plastic bags: made from purchased materials

(G-5287) PERFECT GEAR & INSTRUMENT
125 Railroad Ave (11040-5016)
PHONE..................516 873-6122
Karen Hearne, *Principal*
EMP: 24
SALES (corp-wide): 111.3MM **Privately Held**
SIC: 3462 Gears, forged steel
HQ: Perfect Gear & Instrument Corp
250 Duffy Ave
Hicksville NY 11801
516 328-3330

(G-5288) SQUARE ONE PUBLISHERS INC
115 Herricks Rd (11040-5341)
PHONE..................516 535-2010
Rudy Shur, *President*
▲ EMP: 12
SQ FT: 8,000
SALES (est): 2.3MM **Privately Held**
SIC: 2731 Books: publishing only

(G-5289) WINDOWCRAFT INC
77 2nd Ave (11040-5030)
PHONE..................516 294-3580
Joseph Daniels, *President*
▲ EMP: 18
SQ FT: 6,000
SALES (est): 3.1MM **Privately Held**
SIC: 2591 Window shades

(G-5290) YORK INDUSTRIES INC
303 Nassau Blvd (11040-5213)
PHONE..................516 746-3736
Lee E Smith, *Ch of Bd*
Paul Byers, *Vice Pres*
Roseanne Squillace, *Buyer*
Janne Allen, *Purchasing*
Frank Filadelfo, *Engineer*
EMP: 50 EST: 1942
SQ FT: 9,000
SALES (est): 11MM **Privately Held**
WEB: www.york-ind.com
SIC: 3829 3568 3462 3429 Measuring & controlling devices; ball joints, except aircraft & automotive; iron & steel forgings; manufactured hardware (general); hand & edge tools; tire cord & fabrics

Gardiner
Ulster County

(G-5291) ARTHUR LAUER INC
47 Steves Ln (12525-5322)
P.O. Box 745, Dublin OH (43017-0845)
PHONE..................845 255-7871
Jeremy Smith, *President*

Joyce Salimeno, *Partner*
▲ **EMP:** 29
SALES (est): 2.7MM **Privately Held**
WEB: http://www.arthurlauer.com
SIC: 2511 2512 Wood household furniture; upholstered household furniture

(G-5292)
BYCMAC CORP
Also Called: Kiss My Face
144 Main St (12525-5245)
P.O. Box 224 (12525-0224)
PHONE.................................845 255-0884
Robert Macleod, *President*
Steve Byckiewicz, *Exec VP*
Betty Jordan, *Vice Pres*
Amanda Weber, *Prdtn Mgr*
Heather Halpern, *Research*
▲ **EMP:** 45
SQ FT: 20,000
SALES (est): 10.1MM **Privately Held**
WEB: http://www.kissmyface.com
SIC: 2844 Cosmetic preparations

(G-5293)
DAVID KUCERA INC
42 Steves Ln (12525-5319)
PHONE.................................845 255-1044
David Kucera, *President*
Ann Marie Cramer, *Manager*
EMP: 35
SQ FT: 15,000
SALES (est): 6.6MM **Privately Held**
WEB: http://www.davidkucerainc.com
SIC: 3272 Concrete products, precast

(G-5294)
GLASSON SCULPTURE WORKS
23 Shaft Rd (12525-5115)
PHONE.................................845 255-2969
Gregory Glasson, *Branch Mgr*
EMP: 5
SALES (est): 311.9K **Privately Held**
SIC: 3299 Mfg Nonmetallic Mineral Products
PA: Glasson Sculpture Works
  612 S 11th St
  Laramie WY 82070

(G-5295)
S P INDUSTRIES INC
Also Called: Sp Scientific
815 Rte 208 (12525)
P.O. Box 48330, Newark NJ (07101-8530)
PHONE.................................845 255-5000
Dan De Beau, *Branch Mgr*
Paul W Coiteux, *Technical Staff*
EMP: 82
SQ FT: 7,200
SALES (corp-wide): 1.4B **Privately Held**
WEB: http://www.virtis.com
SIC: 3821 Laboratory apparatus & furniture
HQ: S P Industries, Inc.
  935 Mearns Rd
  Warminster PA 18974
  215 672-7800

(G-5296)
TUTHILLTOWN SPIRITS LLC
14 Gristmill Ln (12525-5528)
P.O. Box 320 (12525-0320)
PHONE.................................845 255-1527
Brian Lee,
Ralph Erenzo,
▲ **EMP:** 15
SALES (est): 2.9MM
SALES (corp-wide): 1.5B **Privately Held**
SIC: 2085 Distilled & blended liquors
HQ: William Grant & Sons Limited
  Phoenix Crescent
  Bellshill ML4 3

(G-5297)
UTILITY CANVAS INC (PA)
2686 Route 44 55 (12525)
PHONE.................................845 255-9290
Hal Grano, *President*
Jillian Kaufman, *Vice Pres*
EMP: 6
SQ FT: 4,000
SALES (est): 1MM **Privately Held**
SIC: 2394 Canvas & related products

Garnerville
Rockland County

(G-5298)
A & W METAL WORKS INC
55 W Railroad Ave 5 (10923-1261)
P.O. Box 276 (10923-0276)
PHONE.................................845 352-2346
Martin Weinstock, *Admin Sec*
EMP: 10 EST: 2016
SALES (est): 400K **Privately Held**
SIC: 3999 Manufacturing industries

(G-5299)
AM ARCHITECTURAL METAL & GLASS
5 Bridge St (10923-1201)
PHONE.................................845 942-8848
Paula Maunsell, *CEO*
Greg Raho, *Project Mgr*
Alejandro Ramos, *Project Mgr*
Aura Leon, *Opers Mgr*
Aisling Carney, *Controller*
▲ **EMP:** 35
SALES (est): 1.5MM **Privately Held**
SIC: 3449 Curtain walls for buildings, steel

(G-5300)
FIRST DUE FIRE EQUIPMENT INC
130 W Ramapo Rd (10923-2134)
PHONE.................................845 222-1329
David Leiser, *CEO*
Mike Humphrey, *General Mgr*
Evan Humphrey, *Sales Staff*
EMP: 10
SALES (est): 1.9MM **Privately Held**
WEB: http://www.jeffola.com
SIC: 3569 Firefighting apparatus & related equipment; firefighting apparatus

(G-5301)
SPECTACLE BREWING LLC
55 W Rr Ave Ste 25 (10923)
P.O. Box 395 (10923-0395)
PHONE.................................845 942-8776
Jeff O'Neil,
EMP: 16
SALES (est): 1.8MM **Privately Held**
SIC: 2082 Beer (alcoholic beverage)

Garrattsville
Otsego County

(G-5302)
BUTTERNUTS BEER AND ALE LLC
4021 State Highway 51 (13342-1705)
PHONE.................................607 263-5070
Cahrles Williamson, *Principal*
EMP: 9
SALES (est): 1MM **Privately Held**
SIC: 2082 Malt beverages

Garrison
Putnam County

(G-5303)
ELEANORS BEST
15 Peacock Way (10524-3107)
P.O. Box 9 (10524-0009)
PHONE.................................845 809-5621
Jennifer Mercurio, *Mng Member*
EMP: 10
SALES (est): 639K **Privately Held**
SIC: 2033 Jams, jellies & preserves: packaged in cans, jars, etc.

Gasport
Niagara County

(G-5304)
AG-PAK INC
8416 Telegraph Rd (14067-9246)
P.O. Box 304 (14067-0304)
PHONE.................................716 772-2651
James W Currie, *CEO*
Andy Currie, *President*
◆ **EMP:** 15
SQ FT: 14,000
SALES (est): 3.2MM **Privately Held**
WEB: http://www.agpak.com
SIC: 3556 Food products machinery

(G-5305)
COSMICOAT OF WNY INC
Also Called: Star Seal of New York
8419 East Ave (14067-9102)
P.O. Box 376 (14067-0376)
PHONE.................................716 772-2644
John Rouch, *President*
EMP: 4
SQ FT: 10,000
SALES (est): 1.6MM **Privately Held**
WEB: http://www.starsealny.com
SIC: 2951 Asphalt & asphaltic paving mixtures (not from refineries)

(G-5306)
GASPORT WELDING & FABG INC
8430 Telegraph Rd (14067-9246)
P.O. Box 410 (14067-0410)
PHONE.................................716 772-7205
Edward J Wojtkowski Jr, *President*
Beverly Wojtkowski, *Corp Secy*
EMP: 10
SQ FT: 14,000
SALES (est): 1.6MM **Privately Held**
SIC: 3443 7692 3441 Tanks, standard or custom fabricated: metal plate; hoppers, metal plate; containers, shipping (bombs, etc.): metal plate; welding repair; fabricated structural metal

(G-5307)
MAKIPLASTIC
4904 Gasport Rd (14067-9506)
P.O. Box 2 (14067-0002)
PHONE.................................716 772-2222
Scott Brauer, *Owner*
EMP: 5
SALES (est): 420.7K **Privately Held**
SIC: 3949 Bait, artificial: fishing

(G-5308)
MILNE MFG INC
8411 State St (14067-9246)
P.O. Box 159 (14067-0159)
PHONE.................................716 772-2536
Ann Cain, *Branch Mgr*
Lyle Demmin, *Manager*
EMP: 11 **Privately Held**
WEB: http://www.mmplastics.com
SIC: 3089 7389 Injection molding of plastics; telephone answering service
PA: M M Plastic (Mfg) Company, Inc
  1301 Blundell Rd
  Mississauga ON L4Y 1
  905 277-5514

(G-5309)
WOLFE LUMBER MILL INC
8416 Ridge Rd (14067-9415)
PHONE.................................716 772-7750
David C Caldwell, *President*
Sandy Lawrence, *Admin Sec*
EMP: 7
SQ FT: 11,000
SALES: 800K **Privately Held**
SIC: 2449 2448 2431 Fruit crates, wood: wirebound; pallets, wood; millwork

Gates
Monroe County

(G-5310)
KEYES MACHINE WORKS INC
147 Park Ave (14606-3818)
PHONE.................................585 426-5059
John Ritchie, *President*
Fraser Ritchie, *Vice Pres*
EMP: 5
SQ FT: 2,500
SALES: 490K **Privately Held**
SIC: 3544 3599 7699 Special dies & tools; custom machinery; industrial equipment services

(G-5311)
QSF INC
Also Called: Quality Stainless Fabrication
140 Cherry Rd (14624-2510)
PHONE.................................585 247-6200
Clyde Wingate, *President*
EMP: 7
SQ FT: 10,000
SALES (est): 1MM **Privately Held**
WEB: http://www.qsfportal.com
SIC: 3312 1731 7692 Stainless steel; electronic controls installation; welding repair

(G-5312)
R D A CONTAINER CORPORATION
70 Cherry Rd (14624-2592)
PHONE.................................585 247-2323
Alan P Brant, *Ch of Bd*
Steve Douglass, *Dept Chairman*
Kevin Deyager, *Prdtn Mgr*
Theodre Brant, *Treasurer*
Jay Stewart, *VP Sales*
EMP: 42
SQ FT: 103,000
SALES (est): 9.3MM **Privately Held**
WEB: http://www.rdacontainer.com
SIC: 2653 3086 2449 Boxes, corrugated: made from purchased materials; packaging & shipping materials, foamed plastic; rectangular boxes & crates, wood

Geneseo
Livingston County

(G-5313)
CLARION PUBLICATIONS INC
38 Main St (14454-1216)
P.O. Box 236 (14454-0236)
PHONE.................................585 243-3530
M Corrin Strong, *President*
Howard Appell, *Editor*
Phil Livingston, *Editor*
EMP: 12
SQ FT: 1,600
SALES (est): 603.3K **Privately Held**
WEB: http://www.clarioncall.com
SIC: 2711 2721 2754 7334 Newspapers: publishing only, not printed on site; magazines: publishing & printing; color printing, gravure; photocopying & duplicating services

(G-5314)
DEER RUN ENTERPRISES INC
Also Called: Deer Run Winery
3772 W Lake Rd (14454-9743)
PHONE.................................585 346-0850
George Kuyon, *President*
Joan Kuyon, *Vice Pres*
Scott Kuyon, *Manager*
EMP: 6
SQ FT: 4,000
SALES (est): 684K **Privately Held**
WEB: http://www.deerrunwinery.com
SIC: 2084 Wines

(G-5315)
LIVINGSTON COUNTY NEWS
122 Main St (14454-1230)
PHONE.................................585 243-1234
Tom Turanvull, *President*
EMP: 7

Geneva - Ontario County (G-5316)   **GEOGRAPHIC SECTION**

SALES (est): 442.3K
SALES (corp-wide): 32MM **Privately Held**
WEB: www.ogd.com
SIC: 2711 Newspapers, publishing & printing
PA: Johnson Newspaper Corporation
260 Washington St
Watertown NY
315 782-1000

Geneva
Ontario County

(G-5316)
ALLESON OF ROCHESTER INC
Also Called: Don Alleson Athletic
833 Canandaigua Rd Ste 40 (14456-2015)
PHONE.................................315 548-3635
Lyla Bousfiou, *Opers-Prdtn-Mfg*
EMP: 40
SQ FT: 53,685
SALES (corp-wide): 552.1MM **Privately Held**
SIC: 2329 2339 Athletic (warmup, sweat & jogging) suits: men's & boys'; athletic clothing: women's, misses' & juniors'
HQ: Alleson Of Rochester, Inc.
2921 Brighton Henrietta
Rochester NY 14623
585 272-0606

(G-5317)
BILLSBORO WINERY
4760 State Route 14 (14456-9746)
PHONE.................................315 789-9538
Kim Aliberti, *President*
EMP: 6 EST: 1999
SALES (est): 529.4K **Privately Held**
SIC: 2084 Wines

(G-5318)
CCMI INC
88 Middle St (14456-1836)
PHONE.................................315 781-3270
Wells C Lewis, *President*
Anthony Lewis, *President*
James Hartman, *Treasurer*
Faye Bentley, *Sales Dir*
Rose Hammond Hoose, *Manager*
EMP: 8
SQ FT: 7,500
SALES (est): 931.7K **Privately Held**
WEB: www.ccmi-reedco.com
SIC: 2821 7389 Plastics materials & resins; packaging & labeling services

(G-5319)
CCN INTERNATIONAL INC
200 Lehigh St (14456-1096)
PHONE.................................315 789-4400
Charles Richard Conoyer, *President*
Dick Conoyer, *General Mgr*
Anne Nenneau, *Exec VP*
Tim Bowman, *VP Mfg*
Mike Kelsey, *VP Mfg*
▼ EMP: 74 EST: 1970
SQ FT: 85,000
SALES (est): 10.6MM **Privately Held**
WEB: www.ccnintl.com
SIC: 2521 Desks, office: wood

(G-5320)
CHERIBUNDI INC (PA)
500 Technology Farm Dr # 11 (14456-1333)
PHONE.................................800 699-0460
Steve Pear, *Principal*
Ed Maguire, *Vice Pres*
Mary Sterling, *QC Mgr*
Michelle Grech, *Chief Mktg Ofcr*
Sarah Theis, *Mktg Dir*
EMP: 21
SQ FT: 8,300
SALES (est): 5MM **Privately Held**
SIC: 2037 2033 2086 Fruit juices; fruit juice concentrates, frozen; fruit juices: fresh; fruit drinks (less than 100% juice): packaged in cans, etc.

(G-5321)
COMMUNITY MEDIA GROUP INC
Also Called: Finger Lakes Times
218 Genesee St (14456-2323)
PHONE.................................315 789-3333
EMP: 90 **Privately Held**
SIC: 2711 Newspapers, publishing & printing
PA: Community Media Group Inc.
805 S Logan St
West Frankfort IL 62896

(G-5322)
ENVIROFORM RECYCLED PDTS INC
287 Gambee Rd (14456-1025)
P.O. Box 553 (14456-0553)
PHONE.................................315 789-1810
Robert L Bates, *President*
Joe Bates, *Project Mgr*
EMP: 9
SQ FT: 5,000
SALES (est): 2.5MM **Privately Held**
WEB: www.enviroform.com
SIC: 3069 Molded rubber products; rubber automotive products

(G-5323)
FAHY-WILLIAMS PUBLISHING INC
171 Reed St (14456-2137)
P.O. Box 1080 (14456-8080)
PHONE.................................315 781-6820
Kevin Fahy, *President*
Tim Braden, *Vice Pres*
Trisha McKenna, *Office Mgr*
EMP: 13
SQ FT: 3,200
SALES (est): 2MM **Privately Held**
WEB: www.fwpi.com
SIC: 2721 Magazines: publishing only, not printed on site

(G-5324)
FINGER LAKES RADIOLOGY LLC
196 North St (14456-1651)
PHONE.................................315 787-5399
Andre Forcier,
EMP: 6
SALES (est): 1.3MM **Privately Held**
SIC: 3826 Magnetic resonance imaging apparatus

(G-5325)
GENEVA GRANITE CO INC (PA)
272 Border City Rd (14456-1988)
P.O. Box 834 (14456-0834)
PHONE.................................315 789-8142
Ralph Fratto Jr, *President*
Jean Fratto, *Vice Pres*
Joseph Fratto, *Treasurer*
EMP: 15
SQ FT: 1,200
SALES (est): 2.7MM **Privately Held**
SIC: 3281 1771 Curbing, paving & walkway stone; concrete work; curb construction

(G-5326)
GENEVA PRINTING COMPANY INC
40 Castle St (14456-2679)
PHONE.................................315 789-8191
Ronald Alcock, *President*
Jo Ellen Alcock, *Vice Pres*
Joellen Alcock, *Vice Pres*
EMP: 8
SQ FT: 7,500
SALES (est): 1.2MM **Privately Held**
WEB: www.genevaprinting.com
SIC: 2752 Commercial printing, offset

(G-5327)
GUARDIAN INDUSTRIES LLC
50 Forge Ave (14456-1281)
PHONE.................................315 787-7000
Christopher Housman, *General Mgr*
Dean Cambell, *Principal*
Mark Bennett, *Manager*
Tom Olstead, *Director*
EMP: 332
SALES (corp-wide): 42.9B **Privately Held**
WEB: www.guardian.com
SIC: 3211 Flat glass

HQ: Guardian Industries, Llc
2300 Harmon Rd
Auburn Hills MI 48326
248 340-1800

(G-5328)
HANGER PRSTHETCS & ORTHO INC
787 State Route 5 And 20 (14456-2001)
PHONE.................................315 789-4810
Thomas Kirk PHD, *CEO*
EMP: 5
SALES (corp-wide): 1B **Publicly Held**
SIC: 3842 Limbs, artificial; braces, orthopedic
HQ: Hanger Prosthetics & Orthotics, Inc.
10910 Domain Dr Ste 300
Austin TX 78758
512 777-3800

(G-5329)
MCINTOSH BOX & PALLET CO INC
40 Doran Ave (14456-1224)
PHONE.................................315 789-8750
Vayeli Rivera, *Manager*
EMP: 18
SQ FT: 14,400
SALES (est): 1.5MM
SALES (corp-wide): 35.3MM **Privately Held**
WEB: www.mcintoshbox.com
SIC: 2441 2448 Shipping cases, wood: nailed or lock corner; wood pallets & skids
PA: Mcintosh Box & Pallet Co., Inc.
5864 Pyle Dr
East Syracuse NY 13057
315 446-9350

(G-5330)
NEGYS NEW LAND VINYRD WINERY
Also Called: Three Brothers Winery
623 Lerch Rd Ste 1 (14456-9295)
PHONE.................................315 585-4432
Dave Mansfield, *President*
Nancy Burdick, *President*
Erica Ridley, *General Mgr*
Dale Nagy, *Vice Pres*
Jon Mansfield, *Assistant*
EMP: 7
SALES: 100K **Privately Held**
SIC: 2084 5921 Wines; wine

(G-5331)
R M REYNOLDS
Also Called: Point of Sale Outfitters
504 Exchange St (14456-3407)
PHONE.................................315 789-7365
R M Reynolds, *Owner*
EMP: 5
SQ FT: 5,500
SALES (est): 342.1K **Privately Held**
SIC: 3911 5094 Jewelry, precious metal; jewelry

(G-5332)
SENECA FOODS CORPORATION
Also Called: Vegetable Operations
100 Gambee Rd (14456-1099)
PHONE.................................315 781-8733
Warren Fredericksen, *Plant Mgr*
Gary Hadyk, *Plant Mgr*
Mark Forsting, *Opers-Prdtn-Mfg*
Katie Gushlaw, *Human Res Mgr*
Jocelyn Cinamella, *Sales Staff*
EMP: 150
SALES (corp-wide): 1.3B **Publicly Held**
SIC: 2033 Sauerkraut: packaged in cans, jars, etc.; vegetables: packaged in cans, jars, etc.
PA: Seneca Foods Corporation
3736 S Main St
Marion NY 14505
315 926-8100

(G-5333)
SENECA TRUCK & TRAILER INC
2200 State Route 14 (14456-9511)
PHONE.................................315 781-1100
Patrick O'Connor, *President*
Patrick O Connor, *President*
EMP: 6

SALES (est): 350K **Privately Held**
WEB: www.senecatruck.com
SIC: 3715 Truck trailers

(G-5334)
TRAMWELL INC
Also Called: Graphic Connections
70 State St (14456-1760)
PHONE.................................315 789-2762
William D Whitwell, *President*
Nancy F Whitwell, *Vice Pres*
EMP: 5
SQ FT: 4,000
SALES (est): 300K **Privately Held**
SIC: 2261 Screen printing of cotton broadwoven fabrics

(G-5335)
VANCE METAL FABRICATORS INC
251 Gambee Rd (14456-1025)
PHONE.................................315 789-5626
Joseph A Hennessy, *Ch of Bd*
William Dobbin Jr, *Chairman*
Len Visco, *Opers Mgr*
Brian Mott, *Safety Mgr*
John Sabin, *Foreman/Supr*
▲ EMP: 85 EST: 1880
SQ FT: 36,000
SALES (est): 39MM **Privately Held**
WEB: www.vancemetal.com
SIC: 3441 3444 Fabricated structural metal; sheet metalwork

(G-5336)
VENTOSA VINEYARDS LLC
3440 State Route 96a (14456-9209)
PHONE.................................315 719-0000
Lenny Cecere, *Owner*
Jennifer Fish, *CFO*
Karen Rice, *Manager*
EMP: 6
SALES (est): 1MM **Privately Held**
SIC: 2084 Wines

(G-5337)
ZOTOS INTERNATIONAL INC
Joico Laboritoriies
300 Forge Ave (14456-1294)
PHONE.................................315 781-3207
Herb Nieporent, *Principal*
EMP: 289
SALES (corp-wide): 23.6B **Privately Held**
WEB: www.zotos.com
SIC: 2844 Hair preparations, including shampoos; cosmetic preparations
HQ: Zotos International, Inc.
100 Tokeneke Rd
Darien CT 06820
203 655-8911

Genoa
Cayuga County

(G-5338)
STONE WELL BODIES & MCH INC
625 Sill Rd (13071-4182)
PHONE.................................315 497-3512
Luigi Sposito, *CEO*
Todd Mix, *COO*
Robert Todd Mix, *Vice Pres*
Robert Eckert, *Chief Engr*
▼ EMP: 37
SQ FT: 30,000
SALES (est): 4.7MM **Privately Held**
WEB: www.stonewellbodies.com
SIC: 3715 3441 8711 Truck trailers; fabricated structural metal; engineering services

Germantown
Columbia County

(G-5339)
ON THE DOUBLE INC
Also Called: John Patrick
178 Viewmont Rd (12526-5808)
PHONE.................................518 431-3571
Walter Fleming, *Ch of Bd*

GEOGRAPHIC SECTION

Glen Cove - Nassau County (G-5362)

EMP: 5
SALES (est): 446.8K Privately Held
SIC: 2339 2329 Women's & misses' athletic clothing & sportswear; men's & boys' sportswear & athletic clothing

Gerry
Chautauqua County

(G-5340)
COBBE INDUSTRIES INC
Also Called: Valley Industries
1397 Harris Hollow Rd (14740-9515)
PHONE.................................716 287-2661
Daniel W Cobbe, *President*
EMP: 30 EST: 1976
SQ FT: 22,000
SALES (est): 4.3MM Privately Held
WEB: www.valleyindustries.com
SIC: 3469 3441 Metal stampings; fabricated structural metal

(G-5341)
SWANSON LUMBER
5273 N Hill Rd (14740-9521)
PHONE.................................716 499-1726
Charles Swanson, *Owner*
EMP: 5
SQ FT: 2,688
SALES (est): 352K Privately Held
SIC: 2421 Sawmills & planing mills, general

(G-5342)
UNIVERSAL TOOLING CORPORATION
4533 Route 60 (14740-9540)
P.O. Box 364 (14740-0364)
PHONE.................................716 985-4691
Nichole Segrue, *CEO*
Warren Piazza, *President*
Mike Swanson, *Vice Pres*
Scott Sando, *Manager*
Ray Ord, *Supervisor*
EMP: 13 EST: 1981
SQ FT: 10,630
SALES (est): 1.5MM Privately Held
WEB: www.u-t-c.com
SIC: 3544 3545 Forms (molds), for foundry & plastics working machinery; dies, plastics forming; machine tool accessories

Getzville
Erie County

(G-5343)
C M INSURANCE COMPANY INC
Also Called: Columbus McKinnon
205 Crosspoint Pkwy (14068-1605)
PHONE.................................716 689-5409
Timothy T Tevens, *President*
Robert Friedl, *CFO*
Timothy Harvey, *Admin Sec*
EMP: 4
SQ FT: 2,900
SALES (est): 1MM
SALES (corp-wide): 839.4MM Publicly Held
WEB: www.columbusmckinnon.com
SIC: 3536 Hoists, cranes & monorails
PA: Columbus Mckinnon Corporation
    205 Crosspoint Pkwy
    Getzville NY 14068
    716 689-5400

(G-5344)
COLUMBUS MCKINNON CORPORATION (PA)
205 Crosspoint Pkwy (14068-1605)
PHONE.................................716 689-5400
Ernest R Verebelyi, *Ch of Bd*
Mark D Morelli, *President*
Benjamin Auyeung, *Vice Pres*
Bert A Brant, *Vice Pres*
Ivo Celi, *Vice Pres*
EMP: 145 EST: 1875
SALES: 839.4MM Publicly Held
WEB: www.cmworks.com
SIC: 3536 3496 3535 3537 Hoists; cranes, industrial plant; cranes, overhead traveling; chain, welded; conveyor belts; conveyors & conveying equipment; tables, lift: hydraulic

(G-5345)
COLUMBUS MCKINNON CORPORATION
Also Called: Coffing
205 Crosspoint Pkwy (14068-1605)
PHONE.................................716 689-5400
EMP: 134
SALES (corp-wide): 839.4MM Publicly Held
WEB: www.cmworks.com
SIC: 3536 3496 3535 3537 Hoists; cranes, industrial plant; cranes, overhead traveling; chain, welded; conveyor belts; conveyors & conveying equipment; tables, lift: hydraulic
PA: Columbus Mckinnon Corporation
    205 Crosspoint Pkwy
    Getzville NY 14068
    716 689-5400

(G-5346)
COLUMBUS MCKINNON CORPORATION
Also Called: Yale
205 Crosspoint Pkwy (14068-1605)
PHONE.................................716 689-5400
EMP: 134
SALES (corp-wide): 839.4MM Publicly Held
WEB: www.cmworks.com
SIC: 3536 3496 3535 3537 Hoists; cranes, industrial plant; cranes, overhead traveling; chain, welded; conveyor belts; conveyors & conveying equipment; tables, lift: hydraulic
PA: Columbus Mckinnon Corporation
    205 Crosspoint Pkwy
    Getzville NY 14068
    716 689-5400

(G-5347)
COLUMBUS MCKINNON CORPORATION
Also Called: Columbus McKinnon- Lift TEC Div
205 Crosspoint Pkwy (14068-1605)
PHONE.................................716 689-5400
Linda Riggi, *Manager*
EMP: 100
SALES (corp-wide): 839.4MM Publicly Held
WEB: www.cmworks.com
SIC: 3536 Hoists, cranes & monorails
PA: Columbus Mckinnon Corporation
    205 Crosspoint Pkwy
    Getzville NY 14068
    716 689-5400

(G-5348)
INTEL CORPORATION
55 Dodge Rd (14068-1205)
PHONE.................................408 765-8080
Mike Brunner, *Branch Mgr*
EMP: 60
SALES (corp-wide): 62.7B Publicly Held
WEB: www.intel.com
SIC: 3674 7372 Microprocessors; application computer software
PA: Intel Corporation
    2200 Mission College Blvd
    Santa Clara CA 95054
    408 765-8080

(G-5349)
MISSION CRITICAL ENERGY INC
1801 N French Rd (14068-1032)
PHONE.................................716 276-8465
Mark Dettmer, *President*
EMP: 5 EST: 2012
SALES (est): 478.8K Privately Held
SIC: 3511 Turbines & turbine generator sets

(G-5350)
NINAS CUSTARD
2577 Millersport Hwy (14068-1445)
PHONE.................................716 636-0345
Merry Scioli, *Partner*
EMP: 30
SALES (est): 3.6MM Privately Held
SIC: 2024 Ice cream & frozen desserts

(G-5351)
OLD DUTCHMANS WROUGH IRON INC
2800 Millersport Hwy (14068-1449)
P.O. Box 632 (14068-0632)
PHONE.................................716 688-2034
Keith Deck, *Principal*
▲ EMP: 6
SQ FT: 2,416
SALES: 100K Privately Held
WEB: www.oldutchman.com
SIC: 3446 Architectural metalwork

(G-5352)
PETIT PRINTING CORP
42 Hunters Gln (14068-1264)
PHONE.................................716 871-9490
Richard Petit, *President*
EMP: 8
SQ FT: 14,000
SALES: 540K Privately Held
WEB: www.petitprinting.com
SIC: 2752 Commercial printing, offset

(G-5353)
SPX FLOW US LLC
105 Crosspoint Pkwy (14068-1603)
PHONE.................................716 692-3000
EMP: 900
SALES (corp-wide): 1.9B Publicly Held
SIC: 3556 8742 Food products machinery; food & beverage consultant
HQ: Spx Flow Us, Llc
    135 Mount Read Blvd
    Rochester NY 14611
    585 436-5550

(G-5354)
U S ENERGY DEVELOPMENT CORP (PA)
2350 N Forest Rd (14068-1296)
PHONE.................................716 636-0401
Joseph M Jayson, *Ch of Bd*
Douglas Walch, *President*
Jerry Jones, *Opers Mgr*
Judy Jayson, *Marketing Staff*
Stephanie Christiano, *Manager*
EMP: 53
SQ FT: 5,000
SALES (est): 45.7MM Privately Held
WEB: www.usenergydevcorp.com
SIC: 1382 1381 1389 Oil & gas exploration services; drilling oil & gas wells; oil field services

(G-5355)
VADER SYSTEMS LLC
385 Crsspint Pkwy Ste 104 (14068)
PHONE.................................716 688-1600
Scott Vader, *CEO*
Zachary Vader, *Co-Owner*
Spencer Heyden, *Engineer*
Viktor Sukhotskiy, *Electrical Engi*
EMP: 11
SALES (est): 6.4MM Privately Held
SIC: 3599 3542 3577 3549 Machine & other job shop work; metal deposit forming machines; computer peripheral equipment; metalworking machinery

(G-5356)
WILLIAM S HEIN & CO INC (PA)
Also Called: METRO STORAGE CENTER
2350 N Forest Rd Ste 14a (14068-1296)
PHONE.................................716 882-2600
William S Hein Sr, *Ch of Bd*
Kevin Marmion, *President*
Len Grieco, *Vice Pres*
Susan H Mc Clinton, *Vice Pres*
Bonnie Morton, *Treasurer*
EMP: 115
SQ FT: 140,000
SALES: 40.4K Privately Held
WEB: www.foreign-law.com
SIC: 2731 5942 3572 Books: publishing only; book stores; computer storage devices

Ghent
Columbia County

(G-5357)
J D HANDLING SYSTEMS INC
1346 State Route 9h (12075-3415)
PHONE.................................518 828-9676
Joseph Cardinale Jr, *President*
Joseph Cardinale Sr, *Shareholder*
Diane Cardinale, *Admin Sec*
▲ EMP: 12
SQ FT: 53,000
SALES: 1.5MM Privately Held
WEB: www.jdhand.com
SIC: 3535 5599 Conveyors & conveying equipment; utility trailers

Glen Cove
Nassau County

(G-5358)
A LOSEE & SONS
68 Landing Rd (11542-1844)
PHONE.................................516 676-3060
Allan Losee, *President*
Mark Losee, *Treasurer*
EMP: 7
SQ FT: 3,000
SALES: 500K Privately Held
SIC: 2431 Woodwork, interior & ornamental

(G-5359)
ALLEN PICKLE WORKS INC
36 Garvies Point Rd (11542-2821)
PHONE.................................516 676-0640
Ronald Horman, *President*
Nick Horman, *Vice Pres*
EMP: 19
SQ FT: 20,000
SALES (est): 9MM Privately Held
SIC: 2035 Pickles, vinegar

(G-5360)
ALLIED MAKER
108 Glen Cove Ave (11542-2832)
PHONE.................................516 200-9145
Ryden Rizzo, *Principal*
Kayte Jolly, *Prdtn Mgr*
Aaron Meyers, *Design Engr*
EMP: 14
SALES (est): 1.8MM Privately Held
SIC: 3993 Signs & advertising specialties

(G-5361)
AUGUST THOMSEN CORP
36 Sea Cliff Ave (11542-3635)
PHONE.................................516 676-7100
Jeffrey G Schneider, *President*
Douglas J Schneider, *Vice Pres*
Douglass Schnieder, *Sales Dir*
Ingrid Schneider, *Shareholder*
◆ EMP: 40 EST: 1905
SQ FT: 25,000
SALES (est): 8.3MM Privately Held
WEB: www.atecousa.com
SIC: 3365 Cooking/kitchen utensils, cast aluminum

(G-5362)
AVALONBAY COMMUNITIES INC
1100 Avalon Sq (11542-2877)
PHONE.................................516 484-7766
Karen Griesmann, *Vice Pres*
EMP: 24
SALES (corp-wide): 2.1B Publicly Held
SIC: 3843 Dental equipment & supplies
PA: Avalonbay Communities, Inc.
    671 N Glebe Rd Ste 800
    Arlington VA 22203
    703 329-6300

(G-5363)
COMMUNITY CPONS FRNCHISING INC
100 Carney St Ste 2 (11542-3687)
PHONE 516 277-1968
Matthew Rosencrans, *President*
Dennis Bernstein, *Sales Mgr*
Stu Golden, *Regl Sales Mgr*
EMP: 25
SQ FT: 3,200
SALES: 3.5MM **Privately Held**
SIC: 2741 7313 Miscellaneous publishing; newspaper advertising representative

(G-5364)
COMPS INC
3 School St Ste 101b (11542-2548)
P.O. Box 255, Sea Cliff (11579-0255)
PHONE 516 676-0400
Keith Larson, *President*
EMP: 12
SALES (est): 887.8K **Privately Held**
WEB: www.compsny.com
SIC: 2741 Miscellaneous publishing

(G-5365)
EXPO FURNITURE DESIGNS INC
Also Called: Expo Lighting Design
1 Garvies Point Rd (11542-2821)
PHONE 516 674-1420
Brian Landau, *President*
Maria Landau, *Admin Sec*
▲ EMP: 10
SQ FT: 5,000
SALES: 900K **Privately Held**
WEB: www.expodesigninc.com
SIC: 3648 5063 5072 Lighting fixtures, except electric: residential; lighting fixtures; hardware

(G-5366)
G SICURANZA LTD
4 East Ave (11542-3917)
PHONE 516 759-0259
Gaetano Sicuranza, *Ch of Bd*
EMP: 5
SALES (est): 555.1K **Privately Held**
SIC: 3432 Plumbing fixture fittings & trim

(G-5367)
GADDIS INDUSTRIAL EQUIPMENT
Also Called: Gaddis Engineering
140 Pratt Oval (11542-1482)
P.O. Box 915, Locust Valley (11560-0915)
PHONE 516 759-3100
M Francis Gaddis, *President*
Marie B Gaddis, *Treasurer*
Paul Gaddis, *Asst Treas*
L C Hills, *Admin Sec*
EMP: 12
SALES (est): 1.2MM **Privately Held**
SIC: 3053 Packing materials

(G-5368)
GLEN PLAZA MARBLE & GRAN INC
75 Glen Cove Ave Ste A (11542-3261)
PHONE 516 671-1100
Frank Caruso, *President*
Joe Caruso, *Corp Secy*
Angelo Caruso, *Vice Pres*
▲ EMP: 7
SQ FT: 7,500
SALES (est): 702.1K **Privately Held**
SIC: 3281 5032 5999 5211 Granite, cut & shaped; marble, building: cut & shaped; granite building stone; marble building stone; monuments & tombstones; tile, ceramic

(G-5369)
KCH PUBLICATIONS INC
Also Called: Gold Coast Gazette
57 Glen St Ste 1 (11542-2785)
PHONE 516 671-2360
Kevin Horton, *President*
EMP: 20
SALES (est): 914.5K **Privately Held**
WEB: www.goldcoastgazette.net
SIC: 2711 Commercial printing & newspaper publishing combined; newspapers, publishing & printing

(G-5370)
KORE INFRASTRUCTURE LLC (PA)
4 High Pine (11542-1422)
PHONE 646 532-9060
Cornelius Shields, *Mng Member*
EMP: 3
SQ FT: 3,000
SALES (est): 2.8MM **Privately Held**
SIC: 2869 4953 Fuels; recycling, waste materials

(G-5371)
NORESCO INDUSTRIAL GROUP INC
3 School St Ste 103 (11542-2548)
PHONE 516 759-3355
Daan Hu, *President*
Julie Lee, *Exec VP*
▲ EMP: 40
SALES (est): 9.1MM **Privately Held**
WEB: www.norescoindustrial.com
SIC: 3321 5013 5084 3322 Ductile iron castings; automotive supplies & parts; industrial machinery & equipment; malleable iron foundries

(G-5372)
PLEATCO LLC
28 Garvies Point Rd (11542-2821)
PHONE 516 609-0200
Howard Smith, *President*
John Antretter, *Vice Pres*
Richard Medina, *Vice Pres*
Jeffrey Smith, *Vice Pres*
Mary Villegas, *VP Opers*
▲ EMP: 80
SQ FT: 21,000
SALES (est): 31.2MM **Privately Held**
SIC: 3589 Swimming pool filter & water conditioning systems

(G-5373)
PROFESSIONAL TAPE CORPORATION
100 Pratt Oval (11542-1482)
P.O. Box 234271, Great Neck (11023-4271)
PHONE 516 656-5519
Morris Kamkar, *President*
▲ EMP: 4
SQ FT: 10,000
SALES: 7MM **Privately Held**
WEB: www.proftapeco.com
SIC: 3695 7819 5099 Magnetic tape; video tape or disk reproduction; video & audio equipment

(G-5374)
SHERCO SERVICES LLC
2 Park Pl Ste A (11542-2566)
PHONE 516 676-3028
Shawn Sheridan,
EMP: 10
SALES (est): 1.2MM **Privately Held**
SIC: 3537 Trucks, tractors, loaders, carriers & similar equipment

(G-5375)
SLANTO MANUFACTURING INC
40 Garvies Point Rd (11542-2887)
PHONE 516 759-5721
Mel Dubin, *President*
EMP: 25
SALES (est): 1.6MM **Privately Held**
SIC: 3442 Baseboards, metal

(G-5376)
STEVENSON PRINTING CO INC
1 Brewster St Ste 2 (11542-2556)
PHONE 516 676-1233
Anthony Messineo, *President*
Cindy Messineo Hawxhurst, *Vice Pres*
Glenn Messineo, *Vice Pres*
EMP: 6 EST: 1909
SQ FT: 12,800
SALES (est): 800.8K **Privately Held**
WEB: www.printingedgemarketing.com
SIC: 2752 Commercial printing, offset

(G-5377)
SUNNYSIDE DECORATIVE PRINTS CO
Also Called: Etcetera Wallpapers
67 Robinson Ave (11542-2944)
PHONE 516 671-1935
Douglas Fletcher Jr, *President*
Melissa Wolf, *Manager*
EMP: 9
SQ FT: 12,000
SALES: 1.2MM **Privately Held**
SIC: 2679 Wallpaper

(G-5378)
WELLS RUGS INC
Also Called: Wells, George Ruggery
44 Sea Cliff Ave (11542-3627)
PHONE 516 676-2056
Joseph Misiak, *President*
EMP: 6
SALES (est): 404.7K **Privately Held**
SIC: 2273 Carpets & rugs

Glen Head
Nassau County

(G-5379)
DEANGELIS LTD
262 Glen Head Rd (11545-1974)
PHONE 212 348-8225
Kenneth Deangelis, *President*
Kayel Deangelis, *Vice Pres*
EMP: 50 EST: 1957
SQ FT: 1,500
SALES (est): 4.8MM **Privately Held**
SIC: 2512 2391 Upholstered household furniture; draperies, plastic & textile: from purchased materials

(G-5380)
HALM INSTRUMENT CO INC
180 Glen Head Rd (11545-1924)
PHONE 516 676-6700
Floyd A Lyon, *President*
Steven Lyon, *Vice Pres*
Donald Schanck, *Vice Pres*
EMP: 76 EST: 1945
SQ FT: 32,000
SALES (est): 5MM **Privately Held**
SIC: 3555 Printing presses

(G-5381)
INTERNATIONAL NEWSPPR PRTG CO
Also Called: International Newspaper Prntng
18 Carlisle Dr (11545-2120)
PHONE 516 626-6095
Richard Schwartz, *Vice Pres*
Gilda Schwartz, *Admin Sec*
EMP: 25 EST: 1932
SQ FT: 12,500
SALES (est): 3.1MM **Privately Held**
SIC: 2752 Offset Printing

(G-5382)
LOMIN CONSTRUCTION COMPANY
Also Called: O'Neil Construction
328 Glen Cove Rd (11545-2273)
PHONE 516 759-5734
Steven O'Neil, *Partner*
EMP: 6
SALES (est): 490K **Privately Held**
SIC: 3531 1629 1611 Pavers; tennis court construction; surfacing & paving

(G-5383)
NEW ART SIGNS CO INC
78 Plymouth Dr N (11545-1127)
PHONE 718 443-0900
Steven Weiss, *President*
EMP: 5
SALES (est): 350K **Privately Held**
SIC: 3993 2759 Signs & advertising specialties; screen printing

(G-5384)
NIRX MEDICAL TECHNOLOGIES LLC
15 Cherry Ln (11545-2215)
PHONE 516 676-6479
Doug Maxwell, *Branch Mgr*
EMP: 15
SALES (corp-wide): 1.6MM **Privately Held**
WEB: www.nirx.net
SIC: 3845 Position emission tomography (PET scanner)
PA: Nirx Medical Technologies, Llc
7083 Hollywood Blvd Fl 4
Los Angeles CA 90028
424 264-0556

(G-5385)
NORTH SHORE MONUMENTS INC
667 Cedar Swamp Rd Ste 5 (11545-2267)
PHONE 516 759-2156
Maggie L Tanchuck, *President*
Hugh A Tanchuck, *Vice Pres*
EMP: 6
SQ FT: 3,100
SALES: 734.4K **Privately Held**
WEB: www.northshoremonuments.com
SIC: 3281 5999 1799 Granite, cut & shaped; monuments & tombstones; sandblasting of building exteriors

Glen Oaks
Queens County

(G-5386)
BAYSIDE BEEPERS & CELLULAR
25607 Hillside Ave (11004-1617)
PHONE 718 343-3888
Albert Castro, *Owner*
EMP: 5 EST: 2013
SALES (est): 335.2K **Privately Held**
SIC: 3663 4812 Pagers (one-way); cellular telephone services

(G-5387)
SHINE FOODS USA INC
7824 266th St (11004-1325)
PHONE 516 784-9674
Joby Joseph, *CEO*
▲ EMP: 5
SALES (est): 258.5K **Privately Held**
SIC: 2092 5149 Fresh or frozen fish or seafood chowders, soups & stews; groceries & related products

(G-5388)
WYNCO PRESS ONE INC
Also Called: Minuteman Press
7839 268th St (11004-1330)
PHONE 516 354-6145
Jeff Wheeler, *President*
EMP: 6
SQ FT: 1,000
SALES: 750K **Privately Held**
SIC: 2752 2791 2789 Commercial printing, offset; typesetting; bookbinding & related work

Glendale
Queens County

(G-5389)
A & S WINDOW ASSOCIATES INC
8819 76th Ave (11385-7992)
PHONE 718 275-7900
Alan Herman, *President*
▲ EMP: 20 EST: 1952
SQ FT: 14,000
SALES (est): 3.2MM **Privately Held**
WEB: www.aswindowassociates.com
SIC: 3442 Storm doors or windows, metal

(G-5390)
ALFA CARD INC
7915 Cooper Ave (11385-7528)
PHONE 718 326-7107
George Chase, *President*
Judy Chase, *Vice Pres*
EMP: 8
SQ FT: 1,400

GEOGRAPHIC SECTION

SALES (est): 385K **Privately Held**
WEB: www.alfacard.com
SIC: **2754** Business form & card printing, gravure

(G-5391)
ALLEN WILLIAM & COMPANY INC
Also Called: Alvin J Bart
7119 80th St Ste 8315 (11385-7733)
PHONE.................................212 675-6461
Fax: 718 821-2486
EMP: 200 EST: 1884
SALES (est): 24MM **Privately Held**
SIC: **2678** 2752 Mfg Stationery Products Lithographic Commercial Printing

(G-5392)
BOWE INDUSTRIES INC (PA)
Also Called: Changes
8836 77th Ave (11385-7826)
PHONE.................................718 441-6464
Daniel Barasch, *CEO*
Marek Kiyashka, *President*
Michael Ohlstein, *Senior VP*
Michael Olsten, *Human Res Dir*
Maryanne Messina, *Human Res Mgr*
◆ EMP: 100
SQ FT: 62,000
SALES (est): 56.8MM **Privately Held**
SIC: **2321** 2331 2361 Men's & boys' furnishings; T-shirts & tops, women's: made from purchased materials; shirts, women's & juniors': made from purchased materials; t-shirts & tops: girls', children's & infants'; shirts: girls', children's & infants'

(G-5393)
BOWE INDUSTRIES INC
8836 77th Ave (11385-7826)
PHONE.................................718 441-6464
Michael Ohlstein, *Branch Mgr*
EMP: 75
SALES (corp-wide): 56.8MM **Privately Held**
SIC: **2321** Men's & boys' furnishings
PA: Bowe Industries Inc.
8836 77th Ave
Glendale NY 11385
718 441-6464

(G-5394)
C F PETERS CORP
7030 80th St Ste 2 (11385-7735)
PHONE.................................718 416-7800
Gene Caprioglio, *Vice Pres*
Dr Don Gillespie, *Vice Pres*
Richie Anichiarico, *Warehouse Mgr*
Shili Uddin, *Finance*
Frank Billack, *Sales Dir*
▲ EMP: 27 EST: 1948
SQ FT: 7,200
SALES (est): 3.3MM **Privately Held**
WEB: www.petersedition.com
SIC: **2741** Music book & sheet music publishing

(G-5395)
CIDC CORP
Also Called: Ocs Industries
5605 Cooper Ave (11385)
PHONE.................................718 342-5820
Henry Gutman, *President*
▲ EMP: 15
SALES (est): 2MM **Privately Held**
SIC: **2514** 3433 Cabinets, radio & television: metal; heating equipment, except electric

(G-5396)
COSTUME CULTURE BY FRANCO LLC
7017 83rd St (11385-7716)
PHONE.................................718 821-7100
Michelle Umano, *CEO*
▲ EMP: 1
SALES (est): 1MM **Privately Held**
SIC: **2389** Costumes

(G-5397)
COTTON EMPORIUM INC (PA)
8000 Cooper Ave Ste 8 (11385-7734)
PHONE.................................718 894-3365
Josef Moshevili, *President*
Nana Moshevili, *Vice Pres*

▲ EMP: 8
SQ FT: 8,500
SALES (est): 2MM **Privately Held**
SIC: **2329** Sweaters & sweater jackets: men's & boys'

(G-5398)
DISPLAYS & BEYOND INC
8816 77th Ave (11385-7826)
PHONE.................................718 805-7786
Dilawar Syed, *President*
Mohammed Kazi, *Vice Pres*
EMP: 12
SALES (est): 2MM **Privately Held**
SIC: **2653** 3993 5999 Display items, corrugated: made from purchased materials; signs & advertising specialties; trophies & plaques; banners, flags, decals & posters

(G-5399)
FM BRUSH CO INC
7002 72nd Pl (11385-7307)
PHONE.................................718 821-5939
Fred J Mink Jr, *Ch of Bd*
Beatrice Mink, *Corp Secy*
Jeffrey A Mink, *Vice Pres*
Carolyn Koster, *Traffic Mgr*
Linda Mayer, *Human Res Mgr*
▲ EMP: 120 EST: 1929
SQ FT: 20,000
SALES (est): 16.2MM **Privately Held**
WEB: www.fmbrush.com
SIC: **3991** Brushes, household or industrial

(G-5400)
FRED M VELEPEC CO INC
7172 70th St (11385-7246)
PHONE.................................718 821-6636
Fredric A Velepec, *President*
Gerda Velepec, *Vice Pres*
EMP: 21 EST: 1942
SQ FT: 6,000
SALES (est): 1.8MM **Privately Held**
SIC: **3545** Tools & accessories for machine tools

(G-5401)
GLENDALE ARCHITECTURAL WD PDTS
Also Called: Glendale Products
7102 80th St (11385-7715)
PHONE.................................718 326-2700
Vincenzo Alcamo, *President*
EMP: 30
SALES (est): 4.2MM **Privately Held**
WEB: www.glendalecustomfurniture.com
SIC: **2521** 2511 Wood office furniture; wood household furniture

(G-5402)
GLENRIDGE FABRICATORS INC
7945 77th Ave (11385-7522)
PHONE.................................718 456-2297
Albert Putre, *Ch of Bd*
Kampta Persaud, *Vice Pres*
EMP: 10 EST: 1977
SQ FT: 36,000
SALES (est): 2.1MM **Privately Held**
SIC: **3441** 3443 1799 Fabricated structural metal; weldments; welding on site

(G-5403)
MARK I PUBLICATIONS INC
Also Called: Queens Chronicle
7119 80th St Ste 8201 (11385-7733)
P.O. Box 747769, Rego Park (11374-7769)
PHONE.................................718 205-8000
Mark Wilder, *President*
Rebecca Cooney, *Counsel*
Stanley Merzon, *Vice Pres*
EMP: 50
SQ FT: 1,800
SALES (est): 3.5MM **Privately Held**
WEB: www.qchron.com
SIC: **2711** Newspapers, publishing & printing

(G-5404)
NEW DAY WOODWORK INC
Also Called: John Bossone
8861 76th Ave (11385-7910)
PHONE.................................718 275-1721
Jay Levtow, *President*
EMP: 30
SQ FT: 14,000

SALES (est): 2.5MM **Privately Held**
WEB: www.newdaywoodwork.com
SIC: **2511** Wood household furniture

(G-5405)
NORTH STAR KNITTING MILLS INC
7030 80th St (11385-7737)
PHONE.................................718 894-4848
Todor Stefan, *President*
Marian Stefan, *Admin Sec*
EMP: 7
SQ FT: 12,500
SALES: 900K **Privately Held**
SIC: **2253** 5199 Knit Outerwear Mill Whol Nondurable Goods

(G-5406)
PHOENIX ENVMTL SVCS CORP
7314 88th St (11385-7950)
PHONE.................................718 381-8100
Frank Garibaldi, *President*
Michael Alexander, *Vice Pres*
Michael McLaughlin, *Vice Pres*
EMP: 18
SALES (est): 144.7K **Privately Held**
SIC: **3444** Sheet metalwork

(G-5407)
ROLLING GATE SUPPLY CORP
7919 Cypress Ave (11385-6038)
PHONE.................................718 366-5258
Miguel Molinare, *President*
▲ EMP: 9
SALES (est): 970K **Privately Held**
SIC: **3315** Steel wire & related products

(G-5408)
SUPERIOR DECORATORS INC
Also Called: Superior Plastic Slipcovers
7416 Cypress Hills St (11385-6946)
PHONE.................................718 381-4793
Peter Cassar, *Owner*
Charlie Heavens, *Manager*
EMP: 16
SQ FT: 3,500
SALES (est): 710K **Privately Held**
SIC: **2392** Slipcovers: made of fabric, plastic etc.

(G-5409)
T & R KNITTING MILLS INC (PA)
8000 Cooper Ave Ste 6 (11385-7734)
PHONE.................................718 497-4017
Rocco Marini, *President*
▲ EMP: 40
SQ FT: 100,000
SALES (est): 20MM **Privately Held**
SIC: **2253** Sweaters & sweater coats, knit

Glenmont
Albany County

(G-5410)
AIR PRODUCTS AND CHEMICALS INC
461 River Rd (12077-4307)
PHONE.................................518 463-4273
Micheal Joczak, *Branch Mgr*
EMP: 53
SQ FT: 8,624
SALES (corp-wide): 8.1B **Publicly Held**
WEB: www.airproducts.com
SIC: **2813** Oxygen, compressed or liquefied
PA: Air Products And Chemicals, Inc.
7201 Hamilton Blvd
Allentown PA 18195
610 481-4911

(G-5411)
DEMARTINI OIL EQUIPMENT SVC
214 River Rd (12077-4604)
P.O. Box 9 (12077-0009)
PHONE.................................518 463-5752
James Demartini, *President*
James De Martini, *President*
Marianne Carner, *Vice Pres*
Mathew Carner, *Treasurer*
EMP: 6 EST: 1945
SQ FT: 4,000

SALES (est): 1.1MM **Privately Held**
SIC: **3713** 7699 Truck bodies (motor vehicles); industrial machinery & equipment repair

(G-5412)
INNOVATIVE MUNICIPAL PDTS US
Also Called: Innovative Surface Solutions
454 River Rd (12077-4306)
PHONE.................................800 387-5777
Greg Baun, *President*
▲ EMP: 30
SALES (est): 20MM **Privately Held**
SIC: **2819** Industrial inorganic chemicals
HQ: Innovative Building Products Inc
78 Orchard Rd
Ajax ON L1S 6
905 427-0318

(G-5413)
J & D WALTER DISTRIBUTORS INC
Also Called: J & D Walter Wholesale Distrg
6 Old River Rd (12077-4312)
P.O. Box 340 (12077-0340)
PHONE.................................518 449-1606
James F Walter, *President*
Chris Walter, *Senior VP*
Patricia Walter, *Treasurer*
▲ EMP: 10
SQ FT: 20,000
SALES (est): 1.4MM **Privately Held**
SIC: **2253** 3151 5013 Jackets, knit; leather gloves & mittens; motorcycle parts

Glens Falls
Warren County

(G-5414)
AMES GOLDSMITH CORP
21 Rogers St (12801-3803)
PHONE.................................518 792-7435
Bill Hamelin, *President*
Ben Morrow, *Engineer*
Lisa Davis, *Controller*
Michael Herman, *Controller*
Frank Barber, *Sales Staff*
EMP: 16
SALES (corp-wide): 32.8MM **Privately Held**
SIC: **3399** 2819 3339 2869 Silver powder; flakes, metal; catalysts, chemical; primary nonferrous metals; industrial organic chemicals
PA: Ames Goldsmith Corp.
50 Harrison Ave
South Glens Falls NY 12803
518 792-5808

(G-5415)
ANDRITZ INC
Also Called: Ahlstrom Kamyr
13 Pruyns Island Dr (12801-4706)
PHONE.................................518 745-2988
Michael Kingsley, *Manager*
EMP: 20
SALES (corp-wide): 6.9B **Privately Held**
SIC: **2611** Pulp manufactured from waste or recycled paper
HQ: Andritz Inc.
500 Technology Dr
Canonsburg PA 15317
724 597-7801

(G-5416)
ANGIODYNAMICS INC
10 Glens Fls Technical Pa (12801)
PHONE.................................518 792-4112
Mark Frost, *President*
EMP: 275
SALES (corp-wide): 344.2MM **Publicly Held**
SIC: **3841** Surgical & medical instruments
PA: Angiodynamics, Inc.
14 Plaza Dr
Latham NY 12110
518 795-1400

Glens Falls - Warren County (G-5417) — GEOGRAPHIC SECTION

(G-5417)
ANGIODYNAMICS INC
Also Called: Rita Medical Systems
10 Glens Falls Tech Park (12801-3864)
P.O. Box 627, Manchester GA (31816-0627)
PHONE 706 846-3126
Mario Martinez, Branch Mgr
EMP: 150
SALES (corp-wide): 344.2MM Publicly Held
WEB: www.angiodynamics.com
SIC: 3841 5047 Catheters; medical & hospital equipment
PA: Angiodynamics, Inc.
  14 Plaza Dr
  Latham NY 12110
  518 795-1400

(G-5418)
BARTON MINES COMPANY LLC (PA)
Also Called: Barton International
6 Warren St (12801-4531)
PHONE 518 798-5462
Charles Bracken Jr, Ch of Bd
William Flint, President
Joseph R Ahrberg, Vice Pres
Scott Beavers, Purchasing
Bill Flint, VP Bus Dvlpt
◆ EMP: 150 EST: 1996
SQ FT: 5,000
SALES (est): 145.9MM Privately Held
WEB: www.barton.com
SIC: 1499 3291 5085 Garnet mining; coated abrasive products; abrasives

(G-5419)
BRENNANS QUICK PRINT INC
Also Called: Bqp
6 Collins Dr (12804-1493)
P.O. Box 4221, Queensbury (12804-0221)
PHONE 518 793-4999
Sue Brennan, President
EMP: 6
SALES (est): 685.1K Privately Held
WEB: www.bqprinting.com
SIC: 2752 Commercial printing, offset

(G-5420)
C R BARD INC
Glens Falls Manufacturing
289 Bay Rd (12804-2015)
PHONE 518 793-2531
Jason Gaeve, Branch Mgr
EMP: 960
SALES (corp-wide): 12B Publicly Held
WEB: www.crbard.com
SIC: 3841 3845 Surgical & medical instruments; electromedical equipment
HQ: C. R. Bard, Inc.
  730 Central Ave
  New Providence NJ 07974
  908 277-8000

(G-5421)
CONVERTER DESIGN INC (PA)
25 Murdock Ave (12801-2456)
PHONE 518 745-7138
Jim Wood, President
EMP: 1
SALES: 1.2MM Privately Held
SIC: 3599 Custom machinery

(G-5422)
COOPERS CAVE ALE CO S-CORP
2 Sagamore St (12801-3179)
PHONE 518 792-0007
Edward Bethel, Partner
Patricia Bethel, Partner
EMP: 15 EST: 1999
SALES (est): 2.1MM Privately Held
WEB: www.cooperscaveale.com
SIC: 2082 Beer (alcoholic beverage)

(G-5423)
DOHENY NICE AND EASY
Also Called: Doheny's Mobil
150 Broad St (12801-4253)
PHONE 518 793-1733
EMP: 8
SALES (est): 380K Privately Held
SIC: 2086 Mfg Bottled/Canned Soft Drinks

(G-5424)
ERBESSD RELIABILITY LLC
Also Called: Erbessd Reliability Instrs
2c Glens Falls Tech Park (12801-3864)
PHONE 518 874-2700
Michael Howard, President
EMP: 27
SALES (est): 1.5MM Privately Held
SIC: 3829 Measuring & controlling devices

(G-5425)
FLOMATIC CORPORATION
Also Called: Flomatic Valves
15 Pruyns Island Dr (12801-4706)
PHONE 518 761-9797
Bo Andersson, President
Nick Farrrara, Vice Pres
Nick Farrara, VP Sales
Mike Jones, Sales Staff
Dina Dieckert, Marketing Staff
◆ EMP: 50
SQ FT: 50,000
SALES (est): 12.7MM Privately Held
WEB: www.flomatic.com
SIC: 3494 3491 Valves & pipe fittings; water works valves
HQ: Boshart Industries Inc
  25 Whaley Ave
  Milverton ON N0K 1
  519 595-4444

(G-5426)
GLENS FALLS NEWSPAPERS INC
76 Lawrence St (12801-3741)
P.O. Box 2157 (12801-2157)
PHONE 518 792-3131
James Marshall, Principal
EMP: 6
SALES (est): 358K Privately Held
SIC: 2711 Newspapers, publishing & printing

(G-5427)
GLENS FALLS PRINTING LLC
51 Hudson Ave (12801-4347)
PHONE 518 793-0555
George Beyerbach,
Barbara Beyerbach,
Robert Beyerbach,
EMP: 12 EST: 1966
SQ FT: 4,800
SALES (est): 2.6MM Privately Held
SIC: 2752 Commercial printing, offset

(G-5428)
JUST BEVERAGES LLC
31 Broad St (12801-4301)
P.O. Box 4392, Queensbury (12804-0392)
PHONE 480 388-1133
Jim Jacobs, CFO
EMP: 11
SALES (est): 1.3MM Privately Held
SIC: 2086 Mineral water, carbonated: packaged in cans, bottles, etc.

(G-5429)
KADANT INC
436 Quaker Rd (12804-1535)
PHONE 518 793-8801
Steve Fielding, Opers Staff
Jeff Bachand, Branch Mgr
Thomas Kozloski, Associate
EMP: 12
SALES (corp-wide): 515MM Publicly Held
SIC: 3554 Paper industries machinery
PA: Kadant Inc.
  1 Technology Park Dr # 210
  Westford MA 01886
  978 776-2000

(G-5430)
KMA CORPORATION
153 Maple St Ste 5 (12801-3796)
PHONE 518 743-1330
Eric Ukauf, President
▲ EMP: 9
SALES (est): 1.1MM Privately Held
SIC: 3599 Machine & other job shop work

(G-5431)
LEE ENTERPRISES INCORPORATED
Also Called: Post Star
76 Lawrence St (12801-3741)
P.O. Box 2157 (12801-2157)
PHONE 518 792-3131
Terry Doomes, President
Greg Brownell, Editor
Adam Colver, Editor
Bob Condon, Editor
Nancy Gautier, Editor
EMP: 160
SQ FT: 5,000
SALES (est): 10.3MM
SALES (corp-wide): 566.9MM Publicly Held
SIC: 2711 Newspapers: publishing only, not printed on site
HQ: Lee Publications, Inc.
  201 N Harrison St Ste 600
  Davenport IA 52801
  563 383-2100

(G-5432)
LEHIGH CEMENT COMPANY (DH)
Also Called: Lehigh Northeast Cement
313 Warren St (12801-3820)
P.O. Box 440 (12801-0440)
PHONE 518 792-1137
Helmut S Erhard, Ch of Bd
Dan Harrington, President
Nancy Stevens, Research
Osvaldo Diaz, Manager
David Dreyer, Manager
▲ EMP: 122
SQ FT: 20,000
SALES (est): 21.6MM
SALES (corp-wide): 287.7MM Privately Held
WEB: www.gfcement.com
SIC: 3241 Portland cement; masonry cement
HQ: Dyckerhoff Gmbh
  Biebricher Str. 68
  Wiesbaden 65203
  611 676-0

(G-5433)
MEDTEK SKIN CARE INC (PA)
Also Called: Phototherapeutix
206 Glen St Ste 5 (12801-3585)
PHONE 518 745-7264
Fax: 518 745-1402
EMP: 40
SQ FT: 9,000
SALES (est): 4.4MM Privately Held
SIC: 3648 Mfg U V A Tanning Systems And Ultraviolet Medical Systems

(G-5434)
MILLER MECHANICAL SERVICES INC
55-57 Walnut St (12801)
P.O. Box 504 (12801-0504)
PHONE 518 792-0430
Elizabeth Miller, President
Ken Lofton, Superintendent
Ken Pagels, Opers Staff
Frank Burkhardt, Engineer
Elaine Lambert, Administration
EMP: 20
SQ FT: 2,240
SALES (est): 5.6MM Privately Held
WEB: www.millermech.com
SIC: 3542 Machine tools, metal forming type

(G-5435)
NATIONAL VAC ENVMTL SVCS CORP
80 Park Rd (12804-7614)
PHONE 518 743-0563
Roger Letendre, Branch Mgr
EMP: 20
SALES (corp-wide): 9.6MM Privately Held
SIC: 3589 Vacuum cleaners & sweepers, electric: industrial
PA: National Vacuum Environmental Services Corp.
  408 47th St
  Niagara Falls NY 14304
  716 773-1167

(G-5436)
NAVILYST MEDICAL INC
10 Glens Fls Technical Pa (12801)
PHONE 800 833-9973
▲ EMP: 670
SALES (est): 150.8MM
SALES (corp-wide): 344.2MM Publicly Held
SIC: 3841 Surgical & medical instruments
PA: Angiodynamics, Inc.
  14 Plaza Dr
  Latham NY 12110
  518 795-1400

(G-5437)
OAK LONE PUBLISHING CO INC
Also Called: Chronicle, The
15 Ridge St (12801-3608)
P.O. Box 153 (12801-0153)
PHONE 518 792-1126
Mark Frost, President
Patricia Maddock, Vice Pres
EMP: 27
SQ FT: 5,280
SALES (est): 1.7MM Privately Held
WEB: www.loneoak.com
SIC: 2711 Newspapers: publishing only, not printed on site

(G-5438)
PACTIV CORPORATION
6 Haskell Ave (12801-3854)
P.O. Box 148 (12801-0148)
PHONE 518 743-3100
Christopher G Angus, Vice Pres
EMP: 207 Privately Held
WEB: www.pactiv.com
SIC: 3089 Thermoformed finished plastic products
HQ: Pactiv Llc
  1900 W Field Ct
  Lake Forest IL 60045
  847 482-2000

(G-5439)
PACTIV LLC
18 Peck Ave (12801-3833)
PHONE 518 793-2524
Gene Tomzzac, Plant Mgr
Mitch Brehm, Manager
Paul Ostwald, Manager
Brian Williams, MIS Dir
EMP: 110 Privately Held
WEB: www.pactiv.com
SIC: 2673 3497 3089 Food storage & trash bags (plastic); trash bags (plastic film): made from purchased materials; food storage & frozen food bags, plastic; metal foil & leaf; plastic containers, except foam; plastic kitchenware, tableware & houseware
HQ: Pactiv Llc
  1900 W Field Ct
  Lake Forest IL 60045
  847 482-2000

(G-5440)
PRECISION EXTRUSION INC
12 Glens Fls Technical Pa (12801)
PHONE 518 792-1199
Michael J Badera, Ch of Bd
Barbara Samiley, Human Resources
EMP: 35
SQ FT: 15,000
SALES (est): 6.8MM
SALES (corp-wide): 5.6B Privately Held
WEB: www.precisionextrusion.com
SIC: 3089 Injection molding of plastics
HQ: Pexco Llc
  2500 Northwinds Pkwy # 472
  Alpharetta GA 30009
  404 564-8560

(G-5441)
UMICORE TECHNICAL MATERIALS
9 Pruyns Island Dr (12801-4706)
PHONE 518 792-7700
Marc Grynberg, CEO
Martin Boarder, Chairman
Stephan Csoma, Exec VP
Filip Platteeuw, CFO
▲ EMP: 110
SALES (est): 22.9MM
SALES (corp-wide): 3.3B Privately Held
SIC: 3339 Silver refining (primary)

▲ = Import ▼ = Export
◆ = Import/Export

HQ: Umicore Usa Inc.
3600 Glenwood Ave Ste 250
Raleigh NC 27612

(G-5442)
UMICORE USA INC
9 Pruyns Island Dr (12801-4706)
PHONE..................................919 874-7171
Allen Molvar, *Branch Mgr*
EMP: 25
SALES (corp-wide): 3.3B **Privately Held**
SIC: 3339 5051 5052 5169 Cobalt refining (primary); nonferrous metal sheets, bars, rods, etc.; metallic ores; industrial chemicals; metal scrap & waste materials
HQ: Umicore Usa Inc.
3600 Glenwood Ave Ste 250
Raleigh NC 27612

(G-5443)
VIBRO-LASER INSTRS CORP LLC
2c Glens Falls Tech Park (12801-3864)
PHONE..................................518 874-2700
Megh McCane Howard,
EMP: 5
SALES (est): 284.4K **Privately Held**
SIC: 3823 Analyzers, industrial process type

Glenville
Schenectady County

(G-5444)
BIOSOIL FARM INC
204 Glenville Industrial (12302-1072)
PHONE..................................518 344-4920
Chad Currin, *President*
Andrew McCarty, *CFO*
EMP: 6 EST: 2017
SQ FT: 12,000
SALES: 100K **Privately Held**
SIC: 2875 Fertilizers, mixing only

(G-5445)
DSM NUTRITIONAL PRODUCTS LLC
Fortitech
300 Tech Park (12302-7107)
PHONE..................................518 372-5155
Chris Nulmerrick, *Manager*
EMP: 152
SALES (corp-wide): 10.1B **Privately Held**
SIC: 2834 3295 2087 Vitamin, nutrient & hematinic preparations for human use; vitamin preparations; minerals, ground or treated; flavoring extracts & syrups
HQ: Dsm Nutritional Products, Llc
45 Waterview Blvd
Parsippany NJ 07054
800 526-0189

(G-5446)
INTERNATIONAL PAPER COMPANY
803 Corporation Park (12302-1057)
PHONE..................................518 372-6461
EMP: 92
SALES (corp-wide): 21.7B **Publicly Held**
WEB: www.tin.com
SIC: 2653 Boxes, corrugated: made from purchased materials
PA: International Paper Company
6400 Poplar Ave
Memphis TN 38197
901 419-9000

(G-5447)
STARFIRE SYSTEMS INC
8 Sarnowski Dr (12302-3504)
PHONE..................................518 899-9336
Andrew Skinner, *CEO*
Richard M Saburro, *Ch of Bd*
▲ EMP: 12
SALES (est): 2.3MM **Privately Held**
WEB: www.starfiresystems.com
SIC: 3299 8731 Ceramic fiber; commercial physical research

Glenwood
Erie County

(G-5448)
LK INDUSTRIES INC
9731 Center St (14069-9611)
PHONE..................................716 941-9202
Larry Krzeminski, *President*
Lawrence Krzeminski, *General Mgr*
EMP: 5
SQ FT: 3,000
SALES: 600K **Privately Held**
SIC: 3541 Machine tools, metal cutting type

Gloversville
Fulton County

(G-5449)
ADIRONDACK STAINED GLASS WORKS
29 W Fulton St Ste 6 (12078-2937)
PHONE..................................518 725-0387
Donald Dwyer, *President*
Brenda Dwyer, *Treasurer*
Patrick Duell, *Admin Sec*
EMP: 6
SQ FT: 9,600
SALES: 275K **Privately Held**
SIC: 3231 Stained glass: made from purchased glass

(G-5450)
AMERICAN TARGET MARKETING INC
11 Cayadutta St (12078-3816)
PHONE..................................518 725-4369
Richard Denero, *President*
Al Parillo, *Treasurer*
EMP: 31
SQ FT: 18,000
SALES: 700K **Privately Held**
SIC: 3151 Leather gloves & mittens

(G-5451)
ANDROME LEATHER INC
21 Foster St (12078-1600)
P.O. Box 826 (12078-0826)
PHONE..................................518 773-7945
Frank A Garguilo, *President*
Christopher Garguilo, *Vice Pres*
Lisa Garguilo, *Admin Sec*
▲ EMP: 15
SQ FT: 10,000
SALES (est): 1.9MM **Privately Held**
SIC: 3111 2843 Finishing of leather; leather finishing agents

(G-5452)
AVANTI CONTROL SYSTEMS INC
1 Hamilton St Fl 2 (12078-2321)
P.O. Box 113 (12078-0113)
PHONE..................................518 921-4368
Timothy M Tesiero, *President*
EMP: 6
SALES (est): 1.3MM **Privately Held**
SIC: 3613 8711 Control panels, electric; engineering services

(G-5453)
BEEBIE PRINTING & ART AGCY INC
40 E Pine St (12078-4339)
P.O. Box 1277 (12078-0011)
PHONE..................................518 725-4528
Craig J Beebie, *President*
EMP: 7
SQ FT: 10,000
SALES (est): 846.5K **Privately Held**
SIC: 2759 7336 Commercial printing; graphic arts & related design

(G-5454)
COLONIAL TANNING CORPORATION (PA)
8 Wilson St 810 (12078-1500)
P.O. Box 1068 (12078-0009)
PHONE..................................518 725-7171
William Studenic, *President*
George Bradt, *Opers Mgr*
▲ EMP: 7 EST: 1971
SQ FT: 50,000
SALES (est): 1.1MM **Privately Held**
SIC: 3111 Tanneries, leather

(G-5455)
CURTIN-HEBERT CO INC
Also Called: Curtin-Hebert Machines
11 Forest St (12078-3999)
P.O. Box 511 (12078-0005)
PHONE..................................518 725-7157
James Curtin, *Ch of Bd*
EMP: 11 EST: 1908
SQ FT: 11,000
SALES (est): 1.3MM **Privately Held**
WEB: www.curtinhebert.com
SIC: 3559 Rubber working machinery, including tires; leather working machinery; metal pickling equipment

(G-5456)
FOWNES BROTHERS & CO INC
204 County Highway 157 (12078-6043)
PHONE..................................518 752-4411
Rennie Sanges, *Branch Mgr*
EMP: 30
SALES (corp-wide): 76.1MM **Privately Held**
SIC: 3151 2381 5136 5137 Gloves, leather: dress or semidress; gloves, woven or knit: made from purchased materials; gloves, men's & boys'; gloves, women's & children's; gloves, sport & athletic: boxing, handball, etc.
PA: Fownes Brothers & Co Inc
16 E 34th St Fl 5
New York NY 10016
212 683-0150

(G-5457)
HALO OPTICAL PRODUCTS INC
9 Phair St Ste 1 (12078-4328)
P.O. Box 1369 (12078-0011)
PHONE..................................518 773-4256
Peter Leonardi, *President*
EMP: 65 EST: 1964
SQ FT: 32,000
SALES (est): 8.5MM **Privately Held**
SIC: 3827 Optical instruments & apparatus

(G-5458)
HOHENFORST SPLITTING CO INC
152 W Fulton St (12078-2799)
PHONE..................................518 725-0012
Robert Hohenforst, *President*
Loretta Hohenforst, *Vice Pres*
EMP: 6
SQ FT: 6,000
SALES (est): 780.2K **Privately Held**
SIC: 3111 Cutting of leather

(G-5459)
HUDSON DYING & FINISHING LLC
68 Harrison St (12078-4732)
PHONE..................................518 752-4389
Mark Shore,
EMP: 30
SALES (est): 2MM **Privately Held**
SIC: 2389 Men's miscellaneous accessories

(G-5460)
KENNYETTO GRAPHICS INC
137 E State St Ext (12078-6038)
PHONE..................................518 883-6360
Lawrence Monks, *President*
Shirley Kraft, *Manager*
EMP: 30
SALES (est): 3.5MM **Privately Held**
WEB: www.kennyettographics.com
SIC: 3993 Signs & advertising specialties

(G-5461)
LITCHFIELD FABRICS OF NC (PA)
111 Woodside Ave (12078-2741)
PHONE..................................518 773-9500
William Conroy, *President*
Dale Steenburgh, *CFO*
Morris Evans, *Treasurer*
EMP: 3
SQ FT: 2,000
SALES (est): 3.2MM **Privately Held**
SIC: 2258 Tricot fabrics

(G-5462)
MOHAWK CABINET COMPANY INC
137 E State St (12078-1200)
PHONE..................................518 725-0645
James Law, *President*
EMP: 12
SALES (est): 2.1MM **Privately Held**
SIC: 3585 Cabinets, show & display, refrigerated

(G-5463)
PROTECH (LLC)
Also Called: Pro-TEC V I P
11 Cayadutta St (12078-3816)
PHONE..................................518 725-7785
Al Parillo, *Mng Member*
Richard Denero,
EMP: 26
SALES (est): 2.3MM **Privately Held**
SIC: 3151 5699 Gloves, leather: work; work clothing

(G-5464)
SAMCO LLC
122 S Main St (12078-3821)
PHONE..................................518 725-4705
Richard Warner,
EMP: 50
SQ FT: 30,000
SALES (est): 4.8MM **Privately Held**
SIC: 3151 Gloves, leather: dress or semidress

(G-5465)
SOMERSET DYEING & FINISHING
68 Harrison St (12078-4732)
P.O. Box 1189 (12078-0010)
PHONE..................................518 773-7383
Edward Falk, *Treasurer*
EMP: 42
SQ FT: 24,000
SALES: 5.5MM **Privately Held**
SIC: 2258 Dyeing & finishing lace goods & warp knit fabric

(G-5466)
SOMERSET INDUSTRIES INC (PA)
Also Called: CJ Indstries A Div Smrset Inds
68 Harrison St (12078-4732)
P.O. Box 1189 (12078-0010)
PHONE..................................518 773-7383
Ed Falk, *CEO*
Edward Falk, *Treasurer*
Bruce Dingman, *Controller*
▲ EMP: 32
SQ FT: 35,000
SALES (est): 12.8MM **Privately Held**
WEB: www.somersetindustries.com
SIC: 2258 Lace & warp knit fabric mills

(G-5467)
STEPHEN MILLER GEN CONTRS INC
Also Called: Miller's Ready Mix
301 Riceville Rd (12078-6958)
P.O. Box 291, Mayfield (12117-0291)
PHONE..................................518 661-5601
Stephen Miller, *CEO*
EMP: 25 EST: 1971
SQ FT: 640
SALES (est): 5.8MM **Privately Held**
SIC: 3273 1541 1761 1542 Ready-mixed concrete; industrial buildings, new construction; roofing, siding & sheet metal work; nonresidential construction

(G-5468)
TAYLOR MADE GROUP LLC (DH)
93 South Blvd (12078-4730)
PHONE..................................518 725-0681
Dennis Flint, *CEO*
Jason Pajonk-Taylor, *President*
Robert Khalife, *CFO*
John Taylor, *Admin Sec*
▲ EMP: 46
SQ FT: 5,000

Gloversville - Fulton County (G-5469)

SALES: 15MM
SALES (corp-wide): 2.1B **Publicly Held**
SIC: 3231 3429 Windshields, glass: made from purchased glass; manufactured hardware (general); marine hardware
HQ: Lippert Components, Inc.
3501 County Road 6 E
Elkhart IN 46514
574 312-7480

(G-5469)
TAYLOR PRODUCTS INC (PA)
66 Kingsboro Ave (12078-3415)
P.O. Box 1190 (12078-0190)
PHONE.................................518 773-9312
James W Taylor, *Ch of Bd*
Dennis F Flint, *President*
▲ **EMP:** 2
SQ FT: 20,000
SALES (est): 5.4MM **Privately Held**
SIC: 3231 Tempered glass: made from purchased glass; safety glass: made from purchased glass

(G-5470)
TIC TAC TOES MFG CORP
1 Hamilton St (12078-2321)
P.O. Box 953 (12078-0953)
PHONE.................................518 773-8187
Robert Winig, *President*
▲ **EMP:** 75
SQ FT: 75,000
SALES (est): 9.5MM **Privately Held**
WEB: www.tictactoes.com
SIC: 3143 3144 Men's footwear, except athletic; women's footwear, except athletic

(G-5471)
WADSWORTH LOGGING INC
3095 State Highway 30 (12078-7601)
P.O. Box 177, Northville (12134-0177)
PHONE.................................518 863-6870
Stephen S Wadsworth, *President*
EMP: 10 **EST:** 1996
SALES (est): 910K **Privately Held**
SIC: 2411 Logging camps & contractors

(G-5472)
WASHBURNS DAIRY INC
145 N Main St (12078-3078)
P.O. Box 551 (12078-0005)
PHONE.................................518 725-0629
Richard J Washburn, *President*
Alfred J Washburn, *Corp Secy*
Bill Washburn, *Vice Pres*
William Washburn, *Vice Pres*
EMP: 45
SQ FT: 6,000
SALES (est): 5.3MM **Privately Held**
SIC: 2024 5143 Ice cream & ice milk; ice cream & ices

(G-5473)
WILLIAM B COLLINS COMPANY
Also Called: Leader Herald, The
8 E Fulton St (12078-3227)
PHONE.................................518 773-8272
George Ogden Nutting, *President*
Patricia Older, *Editor*
Robert M Nutting, *Vice Pres*
William C Nutting, *Vice Pres*
Duane D Wittman, *Treasurer*
EMP: 70 **EST:** 1961
SQ FT: 15,000
SALES (est): 7.7MM **Privately Held**
WEB: www.lhprint.com
SIC: 2711 Commercial printing & newspaper publishing combined
HQ: The Ogden Newspapers Inc
1500 Main St
Wheeling WV 26003
304 233-0100

(G-5474)
WOOD & HYDE LEATHER CO INC
68 Wood St (12078-1695)
P.O. Box 786 (12078-0007)
PHONE.................................518 725-7105
Randall Doerter, *CEO*
James Keiffer, *President*
Thomas Porter, *CFO*
◆ **EMP:** 30
SQ FT: 266,000

SALES (est): 3.5MM **Privately Held**
WEB: www.woodandhyde.com
SIC: 3111 Tanneries, leather

Goldens Bridge
Westchester County

(G-5475)
GUITAR SPECIALIST INC
307 Rte 22 (10526-1009)
PHONE.................................914 401-9052
Doug J Proper, *President*
Sharon E Proper, *Admin Sec*
EMP: 5
SQ FT: 1,500
SALES (est): 341.2K **Privately Held**
WEB: www.guitarspecialist.com
SIC: 3931 7699 Guitars & parts, electric & nonelectric; musical instrument repair services

Goshen
Orange County

(G-5476)
BIMBO BAKERIES USA INC
Also Called: Stroehmann Bakeries 72
9 Police Dr (10924-6730)
PHONE.................................845 294-5282
Phil Tobin, *Manager*
EMP: 19 **Privately Held**
SIC: 2051 5149 Breads, rolls & buns; groceries & related products
HQ: Bimbo Bakeries Usa, Inc
255 Business Center Dr # 200
Horsham PA 19044
215 347-5500

(G-5477)
BLASER PRODUCTION INC
31 Hatfield Ln (10924-6712)
PHONE.................................845 294-3200
Peter Blaser, *Ch of Bd*
Nick Blaser, *Vice Pres*
▲ **EMP:** 11
SALES (est): 15.1MM **Privately Held**
WEB: www.blaser.com
SIC: 2992 Lubricating oils
HQ: Blaser Swisslube Holding Corp
31 Hatfield Ln
Goshen NY 10924

(G-5478)
BLASER SWISSLUBE HOLDING CORP (HQ)
31 Hatfield Ln (10924-6712)
PHONE.................................845 294-3200
Peter Blaser, *CEO*
Ulrich Krahenbuhl, *President*
Richard Surico, *Vice Pres*
Linda Aldorasi, *Controller*
◆ **EMP:** 16
SQ FT: 40,000
SALES (est): 73.6MM **Privately Held**
SIC: 2992 Lubricating oils
PA: Koras Ag
Winterseistrasse 22
RUegsauschachen BE
344 600-101

(G-5479)
FG GALASSI MOULDING CO INC
699 Pulaski Hwy (10924)
PHONE.................................845 258-2100
John Petromilli, *President*
Linda Petromilli, *Marketing Staff*
▲ **EMP:** 9
SQ FT: 11,000
SALES (est): 1MM **Privately Held**
WEB: www.fggalassi.com
SIC: 2499 Picture & mirror frames, wood

(G-5480)
JUNO CHEFS
Also Called: Milmar Food Group
1 6 1/2 Station Rd (10924-6723)
PHONE.................................845 294-5400
Julius Spessot, *President*
Luisa Spessot, *President*
Barry Werk, *Purchasing*
Mary Ellermakinen, *Human Res Mgr*

EMP: 65
SQ FT: 25,000
SALES (est): 12.7MM **Privately Held**
WEB: www.junofoundation.org
SIC: 2038 Breakfasts, frozen & packaged

(G-5481)
KONICA MNOLTA SUPS MFG USA INC
51 Hatfield Ln (10924-6712)
PHONE.................................845 294-8400
Miyako Asai, *President*
Aj Sandone, *Sales Mgr*
Eric Berne, *Accounts Exec*
Sara Bruckner, *Accounts Exec*
Eileen Burns, *Accounts Exec*
▲ **EMP:** 75
SQ FT: 88,039
SALES: 100MM
SALES (corp-wide): 9.6B **Privately Held**
WEB: www.konicabt.com
SIC: 3861 Toners, prepared photographic (not made in chemical plants)
HQ: Konica Minolta Holdings U.S.A. Inc.
100 Williams Dr
Ramsey NJ 07446
201 825-4000

(G-5482)
MILMAR FOOD GROUP II LLC
1 6 1/2 Station Rd (10924-6777)
PHONE.................................845 294-5400
Martin Hoffman,
▲ **EMP:** 250
SQ FT: 66,000
SALES (est): 58.3MM **Privately Held**
WEB: www.milmarfoodgroup.com
SIC: 2038 8748 Frozen specialties; business consulting

(G-5483)
SKIN ATELIER INC
Also Called: Skinprint
1997 Route 17m (10924-5229)
PHONE.................................845 294-1202
Robert P Manzo, *President*
James Hannan, *Vice Pres*
Devon Houghtalin, *Cust Mgr*
▼ **EMP:** 10
SQ FT: 4,000
SALES (est): 1.9MM **Privately Held**
WEB: www.skinprint.com
SIC: 2844 Toilet preparations

(G-5484)
TILCON NEW YORK INC
Also Called: Goshen Quarry
2 Quarry Rd (10924-6045)
PHONE.................................845 615-0216
Bob Portice, *Manager*
EMP: 63
SALES (corp-wide): 29.7B **Privately Held**
SIC: 1429 Dolomitic marble, crushed & broken-quarrying
HQ: Tilcon New York Inc.
9 Entin Rd
Parsippany NJ 07054
800 789-7625

(G-5485)
VALUE FRAGRANCES & FLAVORS INC
7 Musket Ct (10924)
PHONE.................................845 294-5726
Alexander Vernon, *President*
Gerald Vernon, *CFO*
EMP: 18 **EST:** 2014
SQ FT: 30,000
SALES (est): 15MM **Privately Held**
SIC: 2869 Perfumes, flavorings & food additives

Gouverneur
St. Lawrence County

(G-5486)
BAKERY & COFFEE SHOP
274 W Main St (13642-1333)
PHONE.................................315 287-1829
John Yerdon, *Owner*
EMP: 5

SALES: 230K **Privately Held**
SIC: 2051 Bakery: wholesale or wholesale/retail combined

(G-5487)
CARGILL INCORPORATED
19 Starbuck St (13642-1626)
P.O. Box 209 (13642-0209)
PHONE.................................315 287-0241
Edward Hoffman, *Sales/Mktg Mgr*
EMP: 20
SQ FT: 3,978
SALES (corp-wide): 51.2B **Privately Held**
WEB: www.cargill.com
SIC: 2048 Prepared feeds
PA: Cargill, Incorporated
15407 Mcginty Rd W
Wayzata MN 55391
952 742-7575

(G-5488)
CIVES CORPORATION
Also Called: Cives Steel Company Nthrn Div
8 Church St (13642-1416)
PHONE.................................315 287-2200
Bill Mayers, *Plant Supt*
Norm Newvine, *Purchasing*
Kim Pistolesi, *Accounting Dir*
Ted Totten, *Manager*
EMP: 150
SALES (corp-wide): 651.3MM **Privately Held**
WEB: www.cives.com
SIC: 3441 1791 Fabricated structural metal; structural steel erection
PA: Cives Corporation
3700 Mansell Rd Ste 500
Alpharetta GA 30022
770 993-4424

(G-5489)
CLEARWATER PAPER CORPORATION
4921 State Highway 58 (13642-3207)
PHONE.................................315 287-1200
Jeremery Bartholomew, *Branch Mgr*
EMP: 85 **Publicly Held**
SIC: 2621 Paper mills
PA: Clearwater Paper Corporation
601 W Riverside Ave # 1100
Spokane WA 99201

(G-5490)
DUNN PAPER - NATURAL DAM INC
4921 St Rt 58 (13642-3207)
PHONE.................................315 287-1200
Brent Earnshaw, *President*
Al Magnan, *CFO*
EMP: 88
SALES: 48MM
SALES (corp-wide): 139.6MM **Privately Held**
SIC: 2621 Specialty papers
HQ: Dunn Paper, Inc.
218 Riverview St
Port Huron MI 48060
810 984-5521

(G-5491)
IMERYS USA INC
16a Main St Hailesboro Rd (13642-3360)
P.O. Box 479 (13642-0479)
PHONE.................................315 287-0780
Bob Snyder, *Branch Mgr*
EMP: 17
SQ FT: 30,000
SALES (corp-wide): 2.6MM **Privately Held**
SIC: 1411 Granite, dimension-quarrying; marble, dimension-quarrying
HQ: Imerys Usa, Inc.
100 Mansell Ct E Ste 300
Roswell GA 30076
770 645-3300

(G-5492)
RIVERSIDE IRON LLC
26 Water St (13642)
PHONE.................................315 535-4864
Eric Tessmer, *President*
EMP: 12
SALES (est): 777.7K **Privately Held**
SIC: 3441 3449 Dam gates, metal plate; architectural metalwork; miscellaneous metalwork

GEOGRAPHIC SECTION

Gowanda
Cattaraugus County

(G-5493)
TTE FILTERS LLC (HQ)
1 Magnetic Pkwy (14070-1526)
P.O. Box 111 (14070-0111)
PHONE..................716 532-2234
Claude Badawy, *President*
Thomas Norsen, *CFO*
Susan Szucs, *Director*
EMP: 16
SALES: 1.5MM
SALES (corp-wide): 18.7MM **Privately Held**
SIC: 3677 Filtration devices, electronic
PA: Gowanda Holdings, Llc
 1 Magnetic Pkwy
 Gowanda NY 14070
 716 532-2234

Grand Island
Erie County

(G-5494)
ABRAXIS BIOSCIENCE LLC
3159 Staley Rd (14072-2028)
PHONE..................716 773-0800
Mark Forell, *Manager*
EMP: 7
SALES (corp-wide): 13B **Publicly Held**
SIC: 2834 Pharmaceutical preparations
HQ: Abraxis Bioscience, Llc
 11755 Wilshire Blvd Fl 20
 Los Angeles CA 90025

(G-5495)
ASI SIGN SYSTEMS INC
2957 Alt Blvd (14072-1220)
PHONE..................716 775-0104
Keith Joslyn, *Plant Mgr*
Robin Wright, *Controller*
Andy Bernatovicz, *Branch Mgr*
EMP: 7
SALES (corp-wide): 20.7MM **Privately Held**
SIC: 3993 Signs & advertising specialties
PA: Asi Sign Systems, Inc.
 8181 Jetstar Dr Ste 110
 Irving TX 75063
 214 352-9140

(G-5496)
BAM ENTERPRISES INC (PA)
2937 Alt Blvd (14072-1285)
PHONE..................716 773-7634
Gary Moose, *CEO*
Victor Alfiero, *CFO*
EMP: 2
SQ FT: 310,000
SALES (est): 43.3MM **Privately Held**
SIC: 3714 Motor vehicle wheels & parts

(G-5497)
DUAL PRINT & MAIL LLC (HQ)
3235 Grand Island Blvd (14072-1284)
PHONE..................716 775-8001
Michael Vitch, *CEO*
Thomas Salisbury, *Ch of Bd*
Rick Bruno, *Vice Pres*
Joanne Sabio, *Vice Pres*
EMP: 76
SALES (est): 12MM
SALES (corp-wide): 29MM **Privately Held**
SIC: 2752 Commercial printing, lithographic
PA: Compu-Mail, Llc
 3235 Grand Island Blvd
 Grand Island NY 14072
 716 775-8001

(G-5498)
DYLIX CORPORATION
347 Lang Blvd (14072-3123)
PHONE..................719 773-2985
Nathaniel G Bargar, *President*
Bryan Barrett, *General Mgr*
Tom Glynn, *Sales Staff*
Kenneth Lenz, *Manager*
EMP: 25
SALES (est): 4.9MM **Privately Held**
WEB: www.dylixcorp.com
SIC: 3829 Pressure transducers

(G-5499)
FAST BY GAST INC
120 Industrial Dr (14072-1270)
PHONE..................716 773-1536
Paul Gast, *President*
Dana Gast, *Vice Pres*
▲ EMP: 9
SQ FT: 4,240
SALES (est): 1.2MM **Privately Held**
WEB: www.fastbygast.com
SIC: 3714 Motor vehicle parts & accessories

(G-5500)
FRESENIUS KABI USA LLC
3159 Staley Rd (14072-2028)
PHONE..................716 773-0053
Peter Martinez, *Vice Pres*
Bob Brockman, *Project Mgr*
Nicholas Bateman, *Production*
Arthur Senf, *Manager*
David Derner, *Supervisor*
EMP: 450
SALES (corp-wide): 39.9B **Privately Held**
WEB: www.appdrugs.com
SIC: 2834 Pharmaceutical preparations
HQ: Fresenius Kabi Usa, Inc.
 3 Corporate Dr
 Lake Zurich IL 60047
 847 969-2700

(G-5501)
FRESENIUS KABI USA LLC
3159 Staley Rd (14072-2028)
PHONE..................716 773-0800
Jonathan Brotka, *Production*
Corey Carpenter, *Production*
Michael Dudek, *Production*
Nicholas Tim, *Production*
Scott Gorenflo, *Engineer*
EMP: 35
SALES (corp-wide): 39.9B **Privately Held**
SIC: 2834 Pharmaceutical preparations
HQ: Fresenius Kabi Usa, Llc
 3 Corporate Dr Fl 3 # 3
 Lake Zurich IL 60047
 847 550-2300

(G-5502)
GRAND ISLAND ANIMAL HOSPITAL
Also Called: Grand Island Research & Dev
2323 Whitehaven Rd (14072-1505)
PHONE..................716 773-7645
Robert Harper, *President*
Lysa P Posner Dvm, *Principal*
EMP: 20
SALES (est): 1.5MM **Privately Held**
SIC: 3999 0742 Pet supplies: veterinary services, specialties

(G-5503)
ISLECHEM LLC
2801 Long Rd (14072-1244)
PHONE..................716 773-8401
Daniel Canavan, *Vice Pres*
Dave Ernst, *Manager*
Patrick Canavan,
▲ EMP: 37
SALES: 8.2MM **Privately Held**
WEB: www.islechem.com
SIC: 2869 8731 Industrial organic chemicals; commercial physical research

(G-5504)
JR ENGINEERING ENTERPRISE LLC
2141 Bedell Rd (14072-1614)
PHONE..................716 909-2693
Tila Roger M, *Vice Pres*
Jessey Rajah Roger, *Mng Member*
EMP: 2
SALES: 1MM **Privately Held**
SIC: 3564 7349 7389 Exhaust fans: industrial or commercial; exhaust hood or fan cleaning;

(G-5505)
LIFE TECHNOLOGIES CORPORATION
3175 Staley Rd (14072-2028)
PHONE..................716 774-6700
Lyle Turner, *Vice Pres*
Jim Godsey, *Vice Pres*
Christoph Hergersberg, *Vice Pres*
Chris Crannell, *Facilities Mgr*
Thomas Rehberg, *Production*
EMP: 100
SALES (corp-wide): 20.9B **Publicly Held**
SIC: 3826 Analytical instruments
HQ: Life Technologies Corporation
 5781 Van Allen Way
 Carlsbad CA 92008
 760 603-7200

(G-5506)
LINDE LLC
3279 Grand Island Blvd (14072-1216)
PHONE..................716 773-7552
Jeff Schutrum, *Manager*
EMP: 60
SALES (corp-wide): 20.1B **Privately Held**
SIC: 3825 3625 3567 3561 Instruments to measure electricity; relays & industrial controls; industrial furnaces & ovens; pumps & pumping equipment; machine tool accessories
HQ: Linde Llc
 200 Somerset Corporate Bl
 Bridgewater NJ 08807
 908 464-8100

(G-5507)
NIDEC INDUS AUTOMTN USA LLC
Also Called: Emerson Control Techniques
359 Lang Blvd Bldg B (14072-3123)
PHONE..................716 774-1193
Jim Hovey, *Technical Mgr*
Diane Thompson, *Branch Mgr*
John Johnson, *Manager*
Ken Siddall, *Manager*
Don Hubbard, *IT/INT Sup*
EMP: 30
SALES (corp-wide): 13.9B **Privately Held**
SIC: 3566 3823 Mfg Indstrl Machinery & Equip Process Control Instrmnts
HQ: Nidec Industrial Automation Usa, Llc
 7078 Shady Oak Rd
 Eden Prairie MN 55344
 952 995-8000

(G-5508)
NRD LLC
2937 Alt Blvd (14072-1292)
P.O. Box 310 (14072-0310)
PHONE..................716 773-7634
Douglas J Fiegel, *President*
Joseph Atwell, *Engineer*
Hironori Awano, *Engineer*
William Demas, *Engineer*
Gary Figi, *Engineer*
▲ EMP: 50
SQ FT: 32,000
SALES (est): 10.4MM
SALES (corp-wide): 43.3MM **Privately Held**
WEB: www.nrdstaticcontrol.com
SIC: 3629 3669 3499 Static elimination equipment, industrial; smoke detectors; fire- or burglary-resistive products
PA: Bam Enterprises, Inc.
 2937 Alt Blvd
 Grand Island NY 14072
 716 773-7634

(G-5509)
OCCIDENTAL CHEMICAL CORP
2801 Long Rd (14072-1244)
PHONE..................716 773-8100
Charles G Radar, *Branch Mgr*
EMP: 30
SALES (corp-wide): 13.2B **Publicly Held**
WEB: www.oxychem.com
SIC: 2812 Alkalies & chlorine
HQ: Occidental Chemical Corporation
 5005 Lyndon B Johnson Fwy
 Dallas TX 75244
 972 404-3800

(G-5510)
R R DONNELLEY & SONS COMPANY
Also Called: Moore Business Forms
300 Lang Blvd (14072-3122)
PHONE..................716 773-0647
Tom Daly, *Sales Staff*
Jeffrey Gebhart, *Branch Mgr*
EMP: 56
SALES (corp-wide): 6.9B **Publicly Held**
WEB: www.moore.com
SIC: 2759 Commercial printing
PA: R. R. Donnelley & Sons Company
 35 W Wacker Dr Ste 3650
 Chicago IL 60601
 312 326-8000

(G-5511)
RR DONNELLEY & SONS COMPANY
Also Called: Moore Research Center
300 Lang Blvd (14072-3122)
PHONE..................716 773-0300
Anthony D Joseph, *Vice Pres*
EMP: 65
SALES (corp-wide): 6.9B **Publicly Held**
WEB: www.moore.com
SIC: 2761 Manifold business forms
PA: R. R. Donnelley & Sons Company
 35 W Wacker Dr Ste 3650
 Chicago IL 60601
 312 326-8000

(G-5512)
SAINT-GOBAIN ADFORS AMER INC (DH)
Also Called: Saint-Gobain-Paris France
1795 Baseline Rd (14072-2010)
PHONE..................716 775-3900
John Bedell, *CEO*
Marilyn Woomer, *Credit Mgr*
◆ EMP: 55
SALES (est): 153.3MM
SALES (corp-wide): 213.5MM **Privately Held**
WEB: www.sgtf.com
SIC: 2297 Nonwoven fabrics

(G-5513)
SIHI PUMPS INC (DH)
303 Industrial Dr (14072-1293)
P.O. Box 460 (14072-0460)
PHONE..................716 773-6450
David P Moran, *Ch of Bd*
Frank Papp, *Vice Pres*
Mike Pastore, *Vice Pres*
Rob Schurr, *Senior Buyer*
Scott Carter, *Sales Staff*
▲ EMP: 47
SQ FT: 37,500
SALES (est): 7.5MM
SALES (corp-wide): 75.8K **Privately Held**
WEB: www.sihi.com
SIC: 3561 Industrial pumps & parts
HQ: S.F. Americas Inc
 303 Industrial Dr
 Grand Island NY
 716 773-6450

(G-5514)
STARLINE USA INC
3036 Alt Blvd (14072-1274)
PHONE..................716 773-0100
Joshua Lapsker, *CEO*
Daniel Norris, *President*
Ron Lapsker, *Chairman*
EMP: 120
SQ FT: 80,000
SALES (est): 15.9MM **Privately Held**
SIC: 2396 Printing & embossing on plastics fabric articles

(G-5515)
THERMO FISHER SCIENTIFIC INC
3175 Staley Rd (14072-2028)
PHONE..................716 774-6700
Michael Barbieri, *Sales Staff*
Pat Cockrill, *Sales Staff*
Deanne Finn, *Sales Staff*
Rich Grabbe, *Sales Staff*
Shelly Guerrero, *Sales Staff*
EMP: 6
SALES (corp-wide): 20.9B **Publicly Held**
SIC: 3826 Analytical instruments

Grand Island - Erie County (G-5516)   **GEOGRAPHIC SECTION**

PA: Thermo Fisher Scientific Inc.
168 3rd Ave
Waltham MA 02451
781 622-1000

(G-5516)
TULLY PRODUCTS INC
2065 Baseline Rd (14072-2060)
PHONE....................716 773-3166
Richard Ray, *President*
EMP: 5
SQ FT: 8,000
SALES: 500K **Privately Held**
SIC: 3089 Trays, plastic

(G-5517)
US PEROXIDE
1815 Love Rd Ste 1 (14072-2248)
PHONE....................716 775-5585
Eric Poomi, *Project Mgr*
Paul Faulise, *Manager*
EMP: 8
SALES (est): 1.3MM **Privately Held**
SIC: 2819 Peroxides, hydrogen peroxide

Granville
Washington County

(G-5518)
CENTRAL TIMBER CO INC
Also Called: Central Timber Research/Devt
9088 State Route 22 (12832-4805)
PHONE....................518 638-6338
Ralph Jameson II, *President*
EMP: 5
SQ FT: 52,704
SALES (est): 326.6K **Privately Held**
SIC: 2411 Logging

(G-5519)
LOCKER MASTERS INC
10329 State Route 22 (12832-5024)
PHONE....................518 288-3203
Martha Lyng, *President*
William Lyng, *Treasurer*
Allan Lyng, *Admin Sec*
EMP: 12
SQ FT: 12,000
SALES: 600K **Privately Held**
SIC: 2542 7699 Lockers (not refrigerated): except wood; industrial machinery & equipment repair

(G-5520)
MANCHESTER NEWSPAPER INC (PA)
Also Called: Whitehall Times
14 E Main St (12832-1334)
P.O. Box 330 (12832-0330)
PHONE....................518 642-1234
John Manchester, *President*
Dee Carroll, *Manager*
Lisa Manchester, *Executive*
EMP: 33 **EST:** 1875
SQ FT: 10,000
SALES (est): 3.8MM **Privately Held**
WEB: www.manchesternewspapers.com
SIC: 2711 Newspapers: publishing only, not printed on site

(G-5521)
MANCHESTER WOOD INC
1159 County Route 24 (12832)
P.O. Box 180 (12832-0180)
PHONE....................518 642-9518
Edward Eriksen, *President*
Luke Eriksen, *Vice Pres*
Priscilla Eriksen, *Treasurer*
Laurie Grottoli, *Accountant*
EMP: 148 **EST:** 1976
SQ FT: 54,000
SALES (est): 21.6MM **Privately Held**
WEB: www.manchesterwood.com
SIC: 2511 Chairs, household, except upholstered: wood

(G-5522)
METTOWEE LUMBER & PLASTICS CO
82 Church St (12832-1662)
PHONE....................518 642-1100
Henry V Derminden IV, *President*
Robert Vandermindem Jr, *Vice Pres*

Rick Doyle, *Manager*
EMP: 250 **EST:** 1936
SQ FT: 20,000
SALES (est): 21.7MM
SALES (corp-wide): 62.8MM **Privately Held**
SIC: 2421 0811 3089 Sawmills & planing mills, general; timber tracts; plastic processing
PA: Telescope Casual Furniture, Inc.
82 Church St
Granville NY 12832
518 642-1100

(G-5523)
NORTH AMERICAN SLATE INC
50 Columbus St (12832-1024)
PHONE....................518 642-1702
Robert Tatko, *President*
EMP: 7 **EST:** 1998
SQ FT: 3,500
SALES (est): 495.1K **Privately Held**
SIC: 3281 Slate products

(G-5524)
SAINT-GOBAIN PRFMCE PLAS CORP
1 Sealants Park (12832-1652)
PHONE....................518 642-2200
Bob Shear, *Branch Mgr*
EMP: 150
SALES (corp-wide): 213.5MM **Privately Held**
SIC: 2891 3086 2821 2671 Sealants; plastics foam products; plastics materials & resins; packaging paper & plastics film, coated & laminated
HQ: Saint-Gobain Performance Plastics Corporation
31500 Solon Rd
Solon OH 44139
440 836-6900

(G-5525)
WINN MANUFACTURING INC
12 Burtis Ave (12832)
P.O. Box 308 (12832-0308)
PHONE....................518 642-3515
Steve Winn, *President*
Sandra Winn, *Vice Pres*
EMP: 6
SQ FT: 4,500
SALES: 500K **Privately Held**
SIC: 3599 Machine shop, jobbing & repair

Great Bend
Jefferson County

(G-5526)
HANSON AGGREGATES EAST LLC
County Rt 47 (13643)
PHONE....................315 493-3721
Dan Oconnor, *Superintendent*
EMP: 15
SQ FT: 910
SALES (corp-wide): 20.3B **Privately Held**
SIC: 3281 Limestone, cut & shaped
HQ: Hanson Aggregates East Llc
3131 Rdu Center Dr
Morrisville NC 27560
919 380-2500

Great Neck
Nassau County

(G-5527)
ADVANCED BARCODE TECH INC
Also Called: ABT
175 E Shore Rd Ste 228 (11023-2434)
PHONE....................516 570-8100
Charles Bibas, *President*
Stephen A Bauman, *President*
Dafna Bibas, *Vice Pres*
EMP: 16
SQ FT: 7,500

SALES (est): 3.8MM **Privately Held**
WEB: www.abtworld.com
SIC: 3577 7371 Bar code (magnetic ink) printers; computer software development

(G-5528)
AFP MANUFACTURING CORP
9 Park Pl (11021-5034)
PHONE....................516 466-6464
Attilio F Petrocelli, *Principal*
EMP: 18 **EST:** 2009
SALES (est): 3.6MM **Privately Held**
SIC: 3999 Manufacturing industries

(G-5529)
ALFRED BUTLER INC
107 Grace Ave (11021-1608)
PHONE....................516 829-7460
Jerome Butler, *President*
▲ **EMP:** 16
SQ FT: 8,000
SALES (est): 1.8MM **Privately Held**
WEB: www.alfredbutler.com
SIC: 3911 Rings, finger: precious metal

(G-5530)
ALFRED KHALILY INC
Also Called: Alfa Chem
2 Harbor Way (11024-2117)
PHONE....................516 504-0059
Alfred Khalily, *President*
Farry Khalily, *Vice Pres*
Freshteh Khalily, *Treasurer*
▲ **EMP:** 14
SQ FT: 5,000
SALES (est): 2.7MM **Privately Held**
WEB: www.alfachem1.com
SIC: 2834 Pharmaceutical preparations

(G-5531)
ALL NET LTD
15 Cuttermill Rd Ste 145 (11021-3252)
PHONE....................516 504-4559
Kishore Hemrajani, *President*
Priya Najrani, *Corp Secy*
EMP: 12
SQ FT: 1,500
SALES (est): 952.9K **Privately Held**
SIC: 2329 5136 Basketball uniforms: men's, youths' & boys'; men's & boys' clothing

(G-5532)
ALLURE FASHIONS INC
8 Barstow Rd Apt 2e (11021-3543)
PHONE....................516 829-2470
Jay Confino, *President*
Abdool S Ali, *Vice Pres*
EMP: 2
SQ FT: 800
SALES: 1.5MM **Privately Held**
SIC: 2341 Women's & children's nightwear

(G-5533)
AMERICAN APPAREL LTD
15 Cuttermill Rd Ste 145 (11021-3252)
PHONE....................516 504-4559
Kishore Hemrajani, *President*
EMP: 8
SQ FT: 1,000
SALES (est): 550.5K **Privately Held**
SIC: 2326 Men's & boys' work clothing

(G-5534)
APPLICATION RESOURCES INC
Also Called: Stratusoft
15 Cuttermill Rd Ste 529 (11021)
PHONE....................516 636-6200
Eran Mertans, *President*
Eran D Mertens, *Manager*
EMP: 5
SALES (est): 438.6K **Privately Held**
WEB: www.stratusoft.com
SIC: 7372 Prepackaged software

(G-5535)
ARCADIA CHEM PRESERVATIVE LLC
100 Great Neck Rd Apt 5b (11021-3349)
PHONE....................516 466-5258
Richard Rofe, *Mng Member*
EMP: 5
SQ FT: 3,000

SALES (est): 5.8MM **Privately Held**
SIC: 2869 5169 Industrial organic chemicals; alkalines & chlorine; drilling mud; industrial chemicals; silicon lubricants

(G-5536)
ARGON CORP (PA)
160 Great Neck Rd (11021-3304)
PHONE....................516 487-5314
Moshe Albaum, *CEO*
Mike Forde, *COO*
Michele Kilcommons, *Purch Mgr*
Cynthia Panter, *QC Mgr*
Leonid Fabisevich, *Engineer*
▲ **EMP:** 18
SQ FT: 10,000
SALES (est): 7MM **Privately Held**
WEB: www.argoncorp.com
SIC: 3571 8731 Electronic computers; computer (hardware) development

(G-5537)
AUTOMOTIVE LEATHER GROUP LLC
17 Barstow Rd Ste 206 (11021-2213)
PHONE....................516 627-4000
Bob Kamali, *Mng Member*
EMP: 10
SQ FT: 5,000
SALES (est): 398.3K **Privately Held**
SIC: 3111 Accessory products, leather

(G-5538)
AVANTE
35 Hicks Ln (11024-2026)
PHONE....................516 782-4888
Arash Ouriel, *Partner*
Albert Alishahi, *Partner*
▲ **EMP:** 6
SALES (est): 567.4K **Privately Held**
WEB: www.avante.net
SIC: 2371 Fur goods

(G-5539)
BEAUTY AMERICA LLC
10 Bond St Ste 296 (11021-2454)
PHONE....................917 744-1430
AVI Sivan,
EMP: 30
SALES: 1.9MM **Privately Held**
SIC: 3823 4813 Viscosimeters, industrial process type;

(G-5540)
BRILLIANT STARS COLLECTION INC
150 Great Neck Rd Ste 400 (11021-3309)
PHONE....................516 365-9000
Rodney Rahmani, *President*
Ellen Moses, *Manager*
EMP: 5
SQ FT: 13,000
SALES (est): 444.9K **Privately Held**
WEB: www.brilliantstars.com
SIC: 3911 Jewelry, precious metal

(G-5541)
CADDY CONCEPTS INC
15 Cuttermill Rd (11021-3252)
PHONE....................516 570-6279
Kishore Hemrajani, *President*
▲ **EMP:** 10
SALES (est): 1MM **Privately Held**
SIC: 2392 Mfg Household Furnishings

(G-5542)
CARDONA INDUSTRIES USA LTD (PA)
505 Northern Blvd Ste 213 (11021-5112)
P.O. Box 7778, Delray Beach FL (33482-7778)
PHONE....................516 466-5200
Ben Feinsod, *President*
Edward Streim, *Chairman*
Douglas Knapp, *Vice Pres*
▲ **EMP:** 8
SQ FT: 2,500
SALES (est): 1.3MM **Privately Held**
SIC: 3369 5094 White metal castings (lead, tin, antimony), except die; jewelers' findings

GEOGRAPHIC SECTION
Great Neck - Nassau County (G-5571)

(G-5543)
CARNELS PRINTING INC
Also Called: Carnel Printing and Copying
21 Schenck Ave Apt 3ba (11021-3644)
PHONE..................516 883-3355
Kay W Ray, *President*
EMP: 6
SQ FT: 2,500
SALES (est): 903.4K **Privately Held**
SIC: 2752 2791 2789 Commercial printing, offset; typesetting; bookbinding & related work

(G-5544)
CHAMELEON GEMS INC
98 Cuttermill Rd Ste 398n (11021-3009)
PHONE..................516 829-3333
Aaron Hakimian, *CEO*
Abraham Hakimian, *President*
EMP: 12
SALES (est): 1.6MM **Privately Held**
SIC: 3911 Jewelry, precious metal

(G-5545)
CLASSIC CREATIONS INC
Also Called: Viducci
1 Linden Pl Ste 409 (11021-2640)
PHONE..................516 498-1991
Tony Nemati, *Owner*
EMP: 5
SALES (est): 412.2K **Privately Held**
SIC: 3915 Jewel cutting, drilling, polishing, recutting or setting

(G-5546)
COLONIAL TAG & LABEL CO INC
425 Northern Blvd Ste 36 (11021-4803)
PHONE..................516 482-0508
Eric Kono, *President*
John Kono, *Executive*
▲ **EMP:** 13 **EST:** 1966
SQ FT: 10,000
SALES (est): 8.7MM **Privately Held**
WEB: www.cdscds.com
SIC: 2241 2759 Labels, woven; tags; printing

(G-5547)
CONFORMER PRODUCTS INC
60 Cuttermill Rd Ste 411 (11021-3104)
PHONE..................516 504-6300
Marvin Makofsky, *CEO*
Bob Makofsky, *General Mgr*
EMP: 13
SALES (est): 2.2MM **Privately Held**
SIC: 2677 Envelopes

(G-5548)
CONNIE FRENCH CLEANERS INC
Also Called: Connie Cleaners
801 Middle Neck Rd (11024-1932)
PHONE..................516 487-1343
Michael Estivo, *President*
EMP: 9 **EST:** 1938
SQ FT: 2,000
SALES (est): 1.1MM **Privately Held**
SIC: 2842 7219 Drycleaning preparations; garment alteration & repair shop

(G-5549)
DALCOM USA LTD
Also Called: Dalfon
11 Middle Neck Rd Ste 301 (11021-2301)
PHONE..................516 466-7733
Fred Hakim, *President*
EMP: 11
SQ FT: 4,000
SALES (est): 2.5MM **Privately Held**
WEB: www.dalfon.com
SIC: 2326 Men's & boys' work clothing

(G-5550)
DSR INTERNATIONAL CORP
107 Northern Blvd Ste 401 (11021-4312)
PHONE..................631 427-2600
Thil NA, *Principal*
Harvey Drill, *Sales Staff*
▲ **EMP:** 6
SALES (est): 628.4K
SALES (corp-wide): 164.5MM **Privately Held**
SIC: 3315 5063 Cable, steel: insulated or armored; electronic wire & cable
PA: Dsr Corp.
  7 Noksansaneopjung-Ro 192beon-Gil, Gangseo-Gu
  Busan 46753
  825 197-9050

(G-5551)
EXPEDI-PRINTING INC
41 Red Brook Rd (11024-1437)
PHONE..................516 513-0919
Shiann Jong Chen, *Chairman*
▲ **EMP:** 145
SQ FT: 130,000
SALES (est): 15.2MM **Privately Held**
WEB: www.expedi.com
SIC: 2759 Newspapers: printing; periodicals: printing

(G-5552)
F L DEMETER INC
12 N Gate Rd (11023-1313)
PHONE..................516 487-5187
Debra Janke, *President*
Mark Crames, *Vice Pres*
▲ **EMP:** 25
SQ FT: 3,000
SALES (est): 5.3MM **Privately Held**
SIC: 2844 5122 Perfumes & colognes; cosmetics, perfumes & hair products

(G-5553)
FAB INDUSTRIES CORP (HQ)
98 Cuttermill Rd Ste 412 (11021-3006)
PHONE..................516 498-3200
Steven Myers, *President*
Sam Hiatt, *Vice Pres*
Beth Myers, *Vice Pres*
Jim Sitterly, *Vice Pres*
Jerry Deese, *CFO*
EMP: 307
SQ FT: 2,409
SALES (est): 27.9MM **Privately Held**
WEB: www.fab-industries.com
SIC: 2258 2211 Warp & flat knit products; lace & lace products; bedspreads, lace: made on lace machines; bed sets, lace; sheets, bedding & table cloths: cotton

(G-5554)
FABRIC RESOURCES INTL LTD (PA)
9 Park Pl (11021-5034)
PHONE..................516 829-4550
Steven Richman, *President*
◆ **EMP:** 16 **EST:** 1939
SQ FT: 5,500
SALES (est): 2.8MM **Privately Held**
SIC: 2221 2262 2231 2295 Broadwoven fabric mills, manmade; finishing plants, manmade fiber & silk fabrics; broadwoven fabric mills, wool; coated fabrics, not rubberized

(G-5555)
FIRST QLTY PACKG SOLUTIONS LLC (PA)
80 Cuttermill Rd Ste 500 (11021-3108)
PHONE..................516 829-3030
EMP: 15
SALES (est): 6.2MM **Privately Held**
SIC: 3086 Packaging & shipping materials, foamed plastic

(G-5556)
FIRST QUALITY HYGIENIC INC
80 Cuttermill Rd Ste 500 (11021-3108)
PHONE..................516 829-3030
Kambiz Damaghi, *President*
EMP: 5
SALES (est): 253.5K **Privately Held**
SIC: 2676 5137 Towels, napkins & tissue paper products; feminine hygiene paper products; diapers

(G-5557)
FIRST QUALITY PRODUCTS INC (HQ)
80 Cuttermill Rd Ste 500 (11021-3108)
P.O. Box 270, Mc Elhattan PA (17748-0270)
PHONE..................516 829-4949
Nasser Damaghi, *Ch of Bd*
Kambiz Damaghi, *Ch of Bd*
Noam Yarimi, *Business Mgr*
Bob Damaghi, *Vice Pres*
Mark Jaros, *Project Dir*
◆ **EMP:** 11
SQ FT: 6,000
SALES (est): 335.1MM **Privately Held**
SIC: 2676 Sanitary paper products

(G-5558)
FLEXTRADE SYSTEMS INC (PA)
111 Great Neck Rd Ste 314 (11021-5403)
PHONE..................516 627-8993
Vijay Kedia, *President*
Vikas Kedia, *Managing Dir*
Vishal Pandya, *COO*
Shailendra Balani, *Senior VP*
Jamie Benincasa, *Senior VP*
EMP: 140
SALES (est): 92.9MM **Privately Held**
WEB: www.flextrade.com
SIC: 7372 Business oriented computer software

(G-5559)
FULLER SPORTSWEAR CO INC
10 Grenfell Dr (11020-1429)
PHONE..................516 773-3353
Robert Feinerman, *President*
Aaron Feinerman, *Corp Secy*
Robin Feinerman, *Vice Pres*
EMP: 6 **EST:** 1960
SQ FT: 50,000
SALES (est): 550K **Privately Held**
SIC: 2331 Blouses, women's & juniors': made from purchased material

(G-5560)
GELBER & MUNDY JEWELRY CO INC
Also Called: Gelber Mundy of Great Neck
5 Bond St Frnt 2 (11021-2420)
PHONE..................516 482-1585
Howard Zuckerman, *Vice Pres*
Herman Zuckerman, *Branch Mgr*
EMP: 7
SALES (est): 783.4K
SALES (corp-wide): 2.2MM **Privately Held**
SIC: 3873 Watches, clocks, watchcases & parts
PA: Gelber & Mundy Jewelry Co Inc
  76 Bowery Unit 11
  New York NY 10013
  212 925-0462

(G-5561)
ILICO JEWELRY INC
98 Cuttermill Rd Ste 396 (11021-3008)
PHONE..................516 482-0201
Michael Ilian, *President*
Rodney Ilian, *Vice Pres*
Rebecca Ilian, *Admin Sec*
EMP: 5
SQ FT: 1,200
SALES (est): 505.2K **Privately Held**
SIC: 3911 Jewelry, precious metal

(G-5562)
INTERNATIONAL CASEIN CORP CAL
111 Great Neck Rd Ste 218 (11021-5408)
PHONE..................516 466-4363
Marvin Match, *President*
Vance Perry, *Vice Pres*
EMP: 5
SQ FT: 1,500
SALES (est): 480.5K **Privately Held**
SIC: 2821 Plastics materials & resins

(G-5563)
IRIDIUM INDUSTRIES INC
Also Called: Artube
17 Barstow Rd Ste 302 (11021-2213)
PHONE..................516 504-9700
Jacques Sassouni, *Principal*
EMP: 50
SALES (corp-wide): 37.5MM **Privately Held**
SIC: 3089 3083 Plastic containers, except foam; laminated plastics plate & sheet
PA: Iridium Industries, Inc.
  147 Forge Rd
  East Stroudsburg PA 18301
  570 476-8800

(G-5564)
JAY-AIMEE DESIGNS INC
1 Great Neck Rd Ste 1 # 1 (11021-3323)
PHONE..................718 609-0333
Isaac Matalon, *CEO*
Shlomi Matalon, *President*
Diana Maldimado, *Bookkeeper*
Roberto Lebron, *Legal Staff*
EMP: 175
SQ FT: 4,000
SALES (est): 25.5MM **Privately Held**
WEB: www.jayaimee.com
SIC: 3911 Earrings, precious metal

(G-5565)
KALATI COMPANY INC
10 Bond St Ste 1 (11021-2455)
PHONE..................516 423-9132
Rami Kalati, *Principal*
EMP: 6
SALES (est): 17.5K **Privately Held**
SIC: 2273 Carpets & rugs

(G-5566)
KAMALI AUTOMOTIVE GROUP INC
17 Barstow Rd Ste 206 (11021-2213)
PHONE..................516 627-4000
Joseph Kamali, *Vice Pres*
EMP: 10
SALES (est): 398.3K **Privately Held**
SIC: 3111 Upholstery leather

(G-5567)
KAMALI GROUP INC
17 Barstow Rd Ste 206 (11021-2213)
PHONE..................516 627-4000
Bahman Kamali, *Ch of Bd*
Bob Kamali, *Principal*
Joseph Kamali, *Vice Pres*
Ruth Kamali, *Vice Pres*
Selena Lau, *Vice Pres*
▲ **EMP:** 5
SQ FT: 3,000
SALES (est): 29.3K **Privately Held**
WEB: www.kamaligroup.com
SIC: 2399 3111 Automotive covers, except seat & tire covers; accessory products, leather

(G-5568)
LE VIAN CORP (PA)
Also Called: Arusha Tanzanite
235 Great Neck Rd (11021-3301)
PHONE..................516 466-7200
Moosa Levian, *President*
Emily Portannese, *Asst Mgr*
▲ **EMP:** 84 **EST:** 1998
SQ FT: 7,000
SALES (est): 32.1MM **Privately Held**
WEB: www.levian.com
SIC: 3911 Jewelry, precious metal

(G-5569)
LINO INTERNATIONAL INC
Also Called: Lino Metal
111 Great Neck Rd 300a (11021-5403)
PHONE..................516 482-7100
Ling Hong LI, *President*
EMP: 7
SALES (est): 5MM **Privately Held**
SIC: 3312 Pipes, iron & steel

(G-5570)
MANHATTAN SHADE & GLASS CO INC (PA)
37 Pond Park Rd (11023-2011)
PHONE..................212 288-5616
Steven Schulman, *President*
Morine Shulman, *Principal*
Douglas Schulman, *Vice Pres*
Mitchell Schulman, *Vice Pres*
Saoirse Finnegan, *Project Mgr*
▼ **EMP:** 30 **EST:** 1964
SQ FT: 3,500
SALES (est): 6.2MM **Privately Held**
WEB: www.manhattanshade.com
SIC: 2591 3211 Shade, curtain & drapery hardware; window glass, clear & colored

(G-5571)
MARCO MOORE INC
825 Northern Blvd Ste 201 (11021-5323)
PHONE..................212 575-2090
David Zar, *President*

EMP: 60
SQ FT: 11,000
SALES: 4MM
SALES (corp-wide): 9.6MM **Privately Held**
SIC: 3911 3873 Jewelry, precious metal; watches, clocks, watchcases & parts
PA: Royal Jewelry Manufacturing Inc.
825 Northern Blvd Fl 2
Great Neck NY 11021
212 302-2500

(G-5572)
MEDISONIC INC
57 Watermill Ln Ste 296 (11021-4234)
PHONE.............................516 653-2345
AVI Sivan, *CEO*
Faiza Masroor, *Admin Sec*
EMP: 10
SQ FT: 850
SALES: 175K **Privately Held**
SIC: 2844 Toilet preparations

(G-5573)
NIBMOR PROJECT LLC
11 Middle Neck Rd (11021-2312)
PHONE.............................718 374-5091
Jennifer Love, *CEO*
EMP: 14
SALES (est): 2.3MM **Privately Held**
SIC: 2066 Chocolate

(G-5574)
NUTEK DISPOSABLES INC
80 Cuttermill Rd Ste 500 (11021-3108)
PHONE.............................516 829-3030
Terry Ahner, *Maint Spvr*
Tiffany Diaz, *Human Res Mgr*
EMP: 6 **Privately Held**
SIC: 2676 Sanitary paper products
HQ: Nutek Disposables, Inc.
121 North Rd
Mc Elhattan PA 17748
570 769-6900

(G-5575)
OAKWOOD PUBLISHING CO
10 Bond St Ste 1 (11021-2455)
PHONE.............................516 482-7720
Richard Weiss, *President*
EMP: 7
SQ FT: 3,000
SALES: 100K **Privately Held**
SIC: 2741 Misc Publishing

(G-5576)
OLD DUTCH MUSTARD CO INC (PA)
Also Called: Pilgrim Foods Co
98 Cuttermill Rd Ste 260s (11021-3033)
PHONE.............................516 466-0522
Charles R Santich, *Ch of Bd*
Paul Santich, *President*
Renate Santich, *Vice Pres*
▼ EMP: 6 EST: 1915
SQ FT: 3,000
SALES (est): 15.2MM **Privately Held**
SIC: 2099 2033 2035 Vinegar; fruit juices: concentrated, hot pack; fruit juices: fresh; fruit juices: packaged in cans, jars, etc.; mustard, prepared (wet)

(G-5577)
ORO AVANTI INC (PA)
250 Kings Point Rd (11024-1022)
PHONE.............................516 487-5185
Hersel Sarraf, *President*
Gidion Sarraf, *Vice Pres*
EMP: 7
SALES (est): 1.7MM **Privately Held**
SIC: 3295 Minerals, ground or treated

(G-5578)
OZ BAKING COMPANY LTD
114 Middle Neck Rd (11021-1245)
PHONE.............................516 466-5114
Ofer Zur, *Ch of Bd*
EMP: 8
SALES (est): 568.7K **Privately Held**
SIC: 2051 Bread, cake & related products

(G-5579)
PAMA ENTERPRISES INC
60 Cuttermill Rd Ste 411 (11021-3104)
PHONE.............................516 504-6300
Marvin A Makofsky, *President*
Sari McConnell, *VP Bus Dvlpt*
EMP: 5
SALES (est): 619.1K **Privately Held**
SIC: 3993 2752 Advertising novelties; commercial printing, lithographic

(G-5580)
PEARL LEATHER GROUP LLC
17 Barstow Rd Ste 206 (11021-2213)
PHONE.............................516 627-4047
Bob Kamali,
John Ruggeiro,
▲ EMP: 50
SQ FT: 4,000
SALES: 10MM **Privately Held**
SIC: 3111 Leather processing

(G-5581)
PENFLI INDUSTRIES INC
11 Woodland Pl (11021-1035)
PHONE.............................212 947-6080
Anton Fischman, *President*
Joe Fischman, *Vice Pres*
▲ EMP: 15 EST: 1978
SALES (est): 1.6MM **Privately Held**
WEB: www.penfliusa.com
SIC: 2326 5136 2339 5137 Men's & boys' work clothing; men's & boys' clothing; women's & misses' athletic clothing & sportswear; women's & children's clothing

(G-5582)
PREMIER INGRIDIENTS INC
3 Johnstone Rd (11021-1507)
PHONE.............................516 641-6763
Dennis Provda, *CEO*
▲ EMP: 4 EST: 2010
SALES: 1.3MM **Privately Held**
SIC: 2999 Waxes, petroleum: not produced in petroleum refineries

(G-5583)
PRESTIGE BOX CORPORATION (PA)
115 Cuttermill Rd (11021-3101)
P.O. Box 220428 (11022-0428)
PHONE.............................516 773-3115
Sherry Warren, *Principal*
Ray Turin, *Vice Pres*
EMP: 38 EST: 1963
SQ FT: 12,000
SALES (est): 49.7MM **Privately Held**
SIC: 2657 2653 2631 2652 Folding paperboard boxes; boxes, corrugated: made from purchased materials; boxboard; setup paperboard boxes

(G-5584)
PROGRESSIVE COLOR GRAPHICS
122 Station Rd (11023-1723)
PHONE.............................212 292-8787
Hugo Saltini, *President*
Stuart Linzer, *Vice Pres*
EMP: 41
SQ FT: 28,000
SALES (est): 4.2MM **Privately Held**
SIC: 2752 Offset & photolithographic printing

(G-5585)
ROSECORE DIVISION
Also Called: Corey Rugs
11 Grace Ave Ste 100 (11021-2417)
P.O. Box 855, Plainview (11803-0855)
PHONE.............................516 504-4530
Fax: 516 504-4542
EMP: 10
SALES (est): 820K **Privately Held**
SIC: 2273 Mfg Carpets/Rugs

(G-5586)
ROYAL JEWELRY MFG INC (PA)
825 Northern Blvd Fl 2 (11021-5321)
PHONE.............................212 302-2500
Parviz Hakimian, *President*
Ben Hakimian, *Vice Pres*
Ronnie Kalatizadeh, *Vice Pres*
David Zar, *Vice Pres*
Ken Hakimian, *Sales Staff*
▲ EMP: 60
SQ FT: 9,000
SALES (est): 9.6MM **Privately Held**
WEB: www.royaljewelrymfg.com
SIC: 3911 5094 5944 Jewelry, precious metal; jewelry; jewelry stores

(G-5587)
S KASHI & SONS INC
175 Great Neck Rd Ste 204 (11021-3313)
PHONE.............................212 869-9393
Sarah Kashi, *President*
Elie Kashi, *Vice Pres*
Ronen Kashi, *Admin Sec*
▲ EMP: 15
SQ FT: 1,300
SALES (est): 2.1MM **Privately Held**
WEB: www.skashi.com
SIC: 3911 5094 Jewelry, precious metal; precious stones & metals

(G-5588)
SAMUEL B COLLECTION INC
98 Cuttermill Rd (11021-3036)
PHONE.............................516 466-1826
Neda Behnam, *President*
▲ EMP: 3
SALES: 3MM **Privately Held**
SIC: 3911 Jewelry, precious metal

(G-5589)
SCARGUARD LABS LLC
15 Barstow Rd (11021-2211)
PHONE.............................516 482-8050
Joel Studin, *CEO*
Jim Dun, *President*
Steve Levinson, *VP Opers*
Richard E Pino, *CFO*
Jaclyn Politi, *Office Admin*
EMP: 12
SQ FT: 5,000
SALES (est): 3.1MM **Privately Held**
SIC: 2834 Pharmaceutical preparations

(G-5590)
SSJJJ MANUFACTURING LLC (PA)
98 Cuttermill Rd Ste 412 (11021-3006)
PHONE.............................516 498-3200
Steven Myers,
Beth Myers,
EMP: 352
SALES (est): 15MM **Privately Held**
SIC: 2258 2211 Warp & flat knit products; lace & lace products; bedspreads, lace: made on lace machines; bed sets, lace; sheets, bedding & table cloths: cotton

(G-5591)
STANDARD GROUP (PA)
Also Called: Southern Standard Cartons
1010 Nthrn Blvd Ste 236 (11021)
PHONE.............................718 335-5500
Louis Cortes, *President*
Richard Armend, *Superintendent*
Zahid Aziz, *Superintendent*
Richard Ezell, *Superintendent*
Matthew Fiocchi, *Superintendent*
▲ EMP: 42
SQ FT: 115,000
SALES (est): 69.6MM **Privately Held**
SIC: 2657 Folding paperboard boxes

(G-5592)
STANDARD GROUP LLC (HQ)
Also Called: Southern Standard Cartoons
1010 Nthrn Blvd Ste 236 (11021)
PHONE.............................718 507-6430
Louis Cortes, *Vice Pres*
Cynthia Sapp, *Human Res Mgr*
Denise Barr, *Manager*
Joseph Rebecca,
Steven Levkoff,
▲ EMP: 235 EST: 2009
SQ FT: 115,000
SALES (est): 54.8MM **Privately Held**
WEB: www.thestandardgroup.com
SIC: 2657 Folding paperboard boxes

(G-5593)
STAR SPORTS CORP
Also Called: American Turf Monthly
747 Middle Neck Rd # 103 (11024-1950)
PHONE.............................516 773-4075
Allen Hakim, *President*
Joe Girardi, *Editor*
EMP: 20
SQ FT: 2,500
SALES: 900K **Privately Held**
WEB: www.carteriley.com
SIC: 2711 Newspapers

(G-5594)
STYLECRAFT INTERIORS INC
22 Watermill Ln (11021-4235)
PHONE.............................516 487-2133
Fred Reindl, *President*
Matthew Reindl, *Treasurer*
EMP: 10 EST: 1944
SQ FT: 5,000
SALES: 600K **Privately Held**
WEB: www.stylecraftinteriors.com
SIC: 3843 2521 Cabinets, dental; cabinets, office: wood

(G-5595)
TODD ENTERPRISES INC
747 Middle Neck Rd # 103 (11024-1955)
PHONE.............................516 773-8087
Alan Sarfaty, *President*
EMP: 100
SQ FT: 16,000
SALES (est): 10.6MM **Privately Held**
WEB: www.scinetcorp.com
SIC: 3571 5045 3577 3572 Electronic computers; computers; computer peripheral equipment; computer storage devices

(G-5596)
TONI INDUSTRIES INC
Also Called: Hbs
111 Great Neck Rd Ste 305 (11021-5403)
PHONE.............................212 921-0700
Ophelia Chung, *President*
Neil Blumstein, *Vice Pres*
EMP: 14 EST: 2002
SALES: 18MM **Privately Held**
SIC: 2339 Athletic clothing: women's, misses' & juniors'

(G-5597)
UNIQUE OVERSEAS INC
425 Northern Blvd Ste 22 (11021-4803)
PHONE.............................516 466-9792
Raju Shewakramani, *President*
Ragu Ramani, *Principal*
◆ EMP: 8
SALES (est): 894K **Privately Held**
WEB: www.uniqueoverseas.com
SIC: 3199 Equestrian related leather articles

(G-5598)
UNIVERSAL METALS INC
98 Cuttermill Rd Ste 428 (11021-3006)
PHONE.............................516 829-0896
Pushpa Kochar, *CEO*
Hira Kochar, *Vice Pres*
◆ EMP: 5
SALES (est): 1.9MM **Privately Held**
SIC: 3399 Metal fasteners

(G-5599)
VARIETY GEM CO INC (PA)
295 Northern Blvd Ste 208 (11021-4701)
PHONE.............................212 921-1820
Effie Bezalel, *President*
Soraya Zabih, *Bookkeeper*
▲ EMP: 10
SQ FT: 2,000
SALES (est): 1.6MM **Privately Held**
WEB: www.varietygem.com
SIC: 3911 Jewelry, precious metal

(G-5600)
WEGO INTERNATIONAL FLOORS LLC
239 Great Neck Rd (11021-3301)
PHONE.............................516 487-3510
Bert Eshaghpour, *CEO*
Barry Okun, *CFO*
EMP: 11 EST: 2015
SALES (est): 604.7K
SALES (corp-wide): 328.3MM **Privately Held**
SIC: 2491 5023 Flooring, treated wood block; wood flooring
PA: Wego Chemical Group Inc.
239 Great Neck Rd
Great Neck NY 11021
516 487-3510

GEOGRAPHIC SECTION

Great River
Suffolk County

(G-5601)
HEARST BUSINESS MEDIA CORP
3500 Sunrise Hwy Ste 100 (11739-1001)
PHONE.................................631 650-6151
Peter Olsen, *Principal*
EMP: 9
SALES (corp-wide): 6.6B **Privately Held**
SIC: 2721 Magazines: publishing only, not printed on site
HQ: Hearst Business Media Corp
    2620 Barrett Rd
    Gainesville GA 30507
    770 532-4111

Green Island
Albany County

(G-5602)
ARCADIA MFG GROUP INC (PA)
80 Cohoes Ave (12183-1505)
PHONE.................................518 434-6213
William T Sumner, *Ch of Bd*
Michael Werner, *President*
Kimberly Maher, *Opers Staff*
Jerry Gibson, *Buyer*
Lou Ann Norelli, *Controller*
▲ **EMP:** 44
SQ FT: 20,000
SALES (est): 10.8MM **Privately Held**
WEB: www.arcadiasupply.com
SIC: 3498 3446 3444 3999 Fabricated pipe & fittings; ornamental metalwork; sheet metalwork; cigar lighters, except precious metal

(G-5603)
CASE GROUP LLC
Also Called: Case Window and Door
195 Cohoes Ave (12183-1501)
PHONE.................................518 720-3100
Russell Brooks, *Mng Member*
Gerhard Loeffel,
◆ **EMP:** 36
SQ FT: 50,000
SALES (est): 5MM **Privately Held**
WEB: www.casewindow.com
SIC: 2431 Doors & door parts & trim, wood; windows & window parts & trim wood

(G-5604)
CRYSTAL IS INC (HQ)
70 Cohoes Ave Ste 1b (12183-1531)
PHONE.................................518 271-7375
Larry Felton, *CEO*
Steven Berger, *President*
Eoin Connolly, *Vice Pres*
Keith Evans, *Vice Pres*
Ben Jamison, *Vice Pres*
EMP: 45
SQ FT: 10,500
SALES (est): 9.8MM
SALES (corp-wide): 19.1B **Privately Held**
WEB: www.crystal-is.com
SIC: 3679 Electronic crystals
PA: Asahi Kasei Corporation
    1-1-2, Yurakucho
    Chiyoda-Ku TKY 100-0
    366 993-000

(G-5605)
GENERAL CONTROL SYSTEMS INC
60 Cohoes Ave Ste 101 (12183-1553)
PHONE.................................518 270-8045
Clay Robinson, *President*
Gregory Pacifico, *General Mgr*
Peter Pritchard, *Business Mgr*
Jason Baniak, *Engineer*
Christen Egan, *Engineer*
EMP: 50
SQ FT: 24,000
SALES (est): 11.5MM
SALES (corp-wide): 4.4B **Privately Held**
WEB: www.gcontrol.net
SIC: 3625 Industrial controls: push button, selector switches, pilot
PA: Talen Energy Corporation
    600 Hamilton St Ste 600 # 600
    Allentown PA 18101
    888 211-6011

(G-5606)
GREEN ISLAND POWER AUTHORITY
20 Clinton St (12183-1117)
PHONE.................................518 273-0661
John J Brown, *Chairman*
Robert Bourgeois, *Fire Chief*
Micheal Cocca, *Vice Chairman*
EMP: 11
SQ FT: 8,400
SALES: 5.8MM **Privately Held**
WEB: www.villageofgreenisland.com
SIC: 3699 Electrical equipment & supplies

(G-5607)
HUERSCH MARKETING GROUP LLC
70 Cohoes Ave Ste 4 (12183-1533)
PHONE.................................518 874-1045
Thomas R Huerter, *CEO*
EMP: 12
SALES (est): 775.2K **Privately Held**
SIC: 2711 Commercial printing & newspaper publishing combined

(G-5608)
LAI INTERNATIONAL INC
1 Tibbits Ave (12183-1430)
PHONE.................................763 780-0060
Michael Dagle, *Plant Mgr*
Michael Bagel, *Manager*
Jim Corrigan, *Manager*
Jim Burnor, *Maintence Staff*
EMP: 27 **Privately Held**
SIC: 3728 Aircraft assemblies, subassemblies & parts
PA: Lai International, Inc.
    4255 Pheasant Ridge Dr Ne # 405
    Minneapolis MN 55449

(G-5609)
LYDALL PERFORMANCE MTL INC
68 George St (12183-1113)
PHONE.................................518 273-6320
Paul Hyde, *Engineer*
John Minnick, *Engineer*
Tim Reilly, *Controller*
Susan Pratt, *Human Res Dir*
Joanne Roscoe, *Accounts Mgr*
◆ **EMP:** 115
SQ FT: 300,000
SALES (est): 28.2MM
SALES (corp-wide): 698.4MM **Publicly Held**
WEB: www.lydall.com
SIC: 2211 Cotton broad woven goods
PA: Lydall, Inc.
    1 Colonial Rd
    Manchester CT 06042
    860 646-1233

(G-5610)
LYDALL PERFORMANCE MTLS INC
68 George St (12183-1113)
PHONE.................................518 273-6320
EMP: 11
SALES (corp-wide): 698.4MM **Publicly Held**
SIC: 3569 Filters
HQ: Lydall Performance Materials, Inc.
    134 Chestnut Hill Rd
    Rochester NH 03867
    603 332-4600

(G-5611)
RELIABLE BROTHERS INC
185 Cohoes Ave (12183-1501)
PHONE.................................518 273-6732
Kyle Buchakjian, *Ch of Bd*
Vahan Buchakjian, *President*
EMP: 30
SALES (est): 5.3MM **Privately Held**
SIC: 2013 5147 Meat extracts from purchased meat; meats, fresh

Greene
Chenango County

(G-5612)
AMERICAN BLADE MFG LLC
Also Called: Greene Brass & Aluminum Fndry
47 Birdsall St (13778-1053)
PHONE.................................607 656-4204
Tom Todd, *Manager*
EMP: 8
SALES (corp-wide): 1.3MM **Privately Held**
WEB: www.charleslay.com
SIC: 3366 3365 Bronze foundry; aluminum foundries
PA: American Blade Manufacturing Llc
    138 Roundhouse Rd
    Oneonta NY 13820
    607 432-4518

(G-5613)
CROSS COUNTRY MFG INC
2355 Rte 206 (13778)
P.O. Box 565 (13778-0565)
PHONE.................................607 656-4103
Frank M Hanrahan, *Branch Mgr*
EMP: 15
SALES (corp-wide): 6.9MM **Privately Held**
WEB: www.crosscountrymfg.com
SIC: 3715 Truck trailers
PA: Cross Country Manufacturing, Inc.
    2355 State Highway 206
    Greene NY 13778
    607 656-4103

(G-5614)
G C CONTROLS INC
1408 County Road 2 (13778-2257)
PHONE.................................607 656-4117
Mert Gilbert, *Ch of Bd*
Steven Gilbert, *Principal*
Dan Snowberger, *Vice Pres*
EMP: 40
SQ FT: 12,000
SALES (est): 8MM **Privately Held**
WEB: www.gccontrols.com
SIC: 3625 Electric controls & control accessories, industrial; control equipment, electric; timing devices, electronic

(G-5615)
GREENE TECHNOLOGIES INC
Grand & Clinton St (13778)
PHONE.................................607 656-4166
Carol M Rosenkrantz, *Chairman*
EMP: 100
SQ FT: 49,000
SALES (est): 18.6MM **Privately Held**
WEB: www.greenetech.biz
SIC: 3444 3479 3471 3469 Sheet metalwork; coating of metals & formed products; electroplating of metals or formed products; polishing, metals or formed products; metal stampings

(G-5616)
RAPP SIGNS INC
3979 State Route 206 (13778-2134)
PHONE.................................607 656-8167
Ronald J Rapp, *President*
David Rapp, *Principal*
EMP: 13
SALES (est): 1.3MM **Privately Held**
SIC: 3993 1799 Signs, not made in custom sign painting shops; sign installation & maintenance

(G-5617)
RAYMOND CORPORATION (DH)
22 S Canal St (13778)
P.O. Box 130 (13778-0130)
PHONE.................................607 656-2311
Michael G Field, *President*
Louis J Callea, *Counsel*
Timothy Combs, *Exec VP*
Rick Harrington, *Senior VP*
Michael Field, *Vice Pres*
◆ **EMP:** 800
SQ FT: 325,000
SALES (est): 740.7MM
SALES (corp-wide): 18.8B **Privately Held**
WEB: www.raymondcorp.com
SIC: 3535 7359 3537 Conveyors & conveying equipment; belt conveyor systems, general industrial use; pneumatic tube conveyor systems; equipment rental & leasing; aircraft & industrial truck rental services; lift trucks, industrial: fork, platform, straddle, etc.
HQ: Raymond Consolidated Corporation
    22 S Canal St
    Greene NY 13778
    800 235-7200

(G-5618)
RAYMOND SALES CORPORATION (DH)
22 S Canal St (13778-1244)
P.O. Box 130 (13778-0130)
PHONE.................................607 656-2311
James Malvaso, *Principal*
EMP: 6
SQ FT: 325,000
SALES (est): 50MM
SALES (corp-wide): 18.8B **Privately Held**
SIC: 3537 5084 Forklift trucks; materials handling machinery
HQ: The Raymond Corporation
    22 S Canal St
    Greene NY 13778
    607 656-2311

Greenfield Center
Saratoga County

(G-5619)
PECKHAM INDUSTRIES INC
430 Coy Rd (12833-1042)
PHONE.................................518 893-2176
William H Peckham, *Branch Mgr*
EMP: 18
SALES (corp-wide): 200.6MM **Privately Held**
SIC: 2951 Concrete, asphaltic (not from refineries)
PA: Peckham Industries, Inc.
    20 Haarlem Ave Ste 200
    White Plains NY 10603
    914 949-2000

Greenlawn
Suffolk County

(G-5620)
ALL CULTURES INC
Also Called: American Culture
12 Gates St (11740-1427)
PHONE.................................631 293-3143
Louis Guaneri, *CEO*
Louis Guarneri, *Manager*
◆ **EMP:** 35
SQ FT: 30,000
SALES (est): 6.7MM **Privately Held**
WEB: www.americanculturehair.com
SIC: 2844 Hair preparations, including shampoos; shampoos, rinses, conditioners: hair

(G-5621)
BAE SYSTEMS INFO & ELEC SYS
450 Pulaski Rd (11740-1606)
PHONE.................................631 912-1525
Patrick T Jennings, *Manager*
Joanne Tranchina, *Manager*
EMP: 8
SALES (corp-wide): 24.2B **Privately Held**
WEB: www.iesi.na.baesystems.com
SIC: 3812 Search & navigation equipment
HQ: Bae Systems Information And Electronic Systems Integration Inc.
    65 Spit Brook Rd
    Nashua NH 03060
    603 885-4321

(G-5622)
BAE SYSTEMS PLC
1 Hazeltine Way (11740)
PHONE.................................631 261-7000
Jon Schweikert, *Engineer*

Greenlawn - Suffolk County (G-5623)

Robert Dabkowski, *Senior Engr*
Ray Daugherty, *Branch Mgr*
Scott Baumstein, *Software Engr*
EMP: 25
SALES (corp-wide): 24.2B **Privately Held**
SIC: 3812 Search & navigation equipment
PA: Bae Systems Plc
6 Carlton Gardens
London
125 237-3232

(G-5623)
MB PLASTICS INC (PA)
130 Stony Hollow Rd (11740-1511)
PHONE.................................718 523-1180
Milton Bassin, *President*
▲ EMP: 14 EST: 1964
SQ FT: 15,000
SALES (est): 1.5MM **Privately Held**
SIC: 2821 3911 Plastics materials & resins; jewelry apparel

(G-5624)
MEDICAL TECHNOLOGY PRODUCTS
33a Smith St (11740-1219)
PHONE.................................631 285-6640
Thomas J Hartnett Jr, *Ch of Bd*
Thomas Hartnett, *COO*
David Hawkins, *Admin Sec*
EMP: 8
SQ FT: 5,000
SALES (est): 1MM **Privately Held**
SIC: 3841 Surgical & medical instruments

Greenport
Suffolk County

(G-5625)
125-127 MAIN STREET CORP
Also Called: Mills, William J & Company
125 Main St 127 (11944-1421)
P.O. Box 2126 (11944-0978)
PHONE.................................631 477-1500
William J Mills III, *President*
Robert Hills, *Vice Pres*
Jamie Mills, *Sales Executive*
Maureen Hills, *Executive*
EMP: 18 EST: 1880
SQ FT: 25,000
SALES (est): 2MM **Privately Held**
WEB: www.millscanvas.com
SIC: 2394 Awnings, fabric: made from purchased materials; sails: made from purchased materials

(G-5626)
STIDD SYSTEMS INC
220 Carpenter St (11944-1406)
P.O. Box 87 (11944-0087)
PHONE.................................631 477-2400
Walter A Gezari, *President*
Robert J Digregorio, *Vice Pres*
David J Wilberding, *Vice Pres*
Deborah Pontino, *Purch Mgr*
Ian Strachan, *Engineer*
▼ EMP: 36
SQ FT: 62,000
SALES: 10MM **Privately Held**
WEB: www.stidd.com
SIC: 2531 Vehicle furniture

(G-5627)
WOODEN BOATWORKS
190 Sterling St Unit 2 (11944-1454)
PHONE.................................631 477-6507
Robert Wahl, *Principal*
EMP: 6
SALES (est): 737.8K **Privately Held**
SIC: 3732 Boat building & repairing

Greenvale
Nassau County

(G-5628)
CALL FORWARDING TECHNOLOGIES
55 Northern Blvd Ste 3b (11548-1301)
PHONE.................................516 621-3600
Charles Hart, *President*
EMP: 7
SQ FT: 600
SALES (est): 810K **Privately Held**
SIC: 3661 Telephones & telephone apparatus

(G-5629)
DALMA DRESS MFG CO INC
3 Carman Rd (11548-1123)
PHONE.................................212 391-8296
Madalin Dipalma, *President*
Madalina Dipalma, *Owner*
Giovanna Darmiani, *Vice Pres*
EMP: 25
SQ FT: 5,500
SALES (est): 1.7MM **Privately Held**
SIC: 2335 2339 Mfg Women's/Misses' Dresses Mfg Women's/Misses' Outerwear

(G-5630)
INCREDIBLE SCENTS INC
1 Plaza Rd Ste 202 (11548-1059)
PHONE.................................516 656-3300
Howard Rabinowitz, *President*
Richard Davi, *Exec VP*
EMP: 5 EST: 1999
SQ FT: 1,500
SALES (est): 10MM **Privately Held**
WEB: www.incrediblescents.com
SIC: 3841 Surgical & medical instruments

(G-5631)
ROMAN IRON WORKS INC
15 Plaza Rd (11548-1085)
PHONE.................................516 621-1103
Maria McKinley, *President*
James Mancuso, *President*
EMP: 12 EST: 1953
SQ FT: 10,000
SALES (est): 2MM **Privately Held**
SIC: 3441 3446 1791 Fabricated structural metal; joists, open web steel: long-span series; architectural metalwork; stairs, fire escapes, balconies, railings & ladders; iron work, structural

(G-5632)
SLANT/FIN CORPORATION (PA)
100 Forest Dr (11548-1295)
P.O. Box 416 (11548-0416)
PHONE.................................516 484-2600
Melvin Dubin, *Ch of Bd*
Adam Dubin, *Chairman*
Neil Segal, *Plant Mgr*
Robert Viets, *Buyer*
Steve Pulaski, *Design Engr*
▲ EMP: 374 EST: 1949
SQ FT: 200,000
SALES (est): 75.9MM **Privately Held**
WEB: www.slantfin.com
SIC: 3433 3443 Heating equipment, except electric; fabricated plate work (boiler shop)

(G-5633)
SLANTCO MANUFACTURING INC (HQ)
100 Forest Dr (11548-1205)
PHONE.................................516 484-2600
Melvin Dubin, *President*
Selwyn Steinberg, *Senior VP*
Donald Brown, *Treasurer*
Maria Matuszewski, *Supervisor*
Delcy Brooks, *Admin Sec*
EMP: 7 EST: 1976
SQ FT: 150,000
SALES (est): 1.3MM
SALES (corp-wide): 75.9MM **Privately Held**
SIC: 3443 Heat exchangers: coolers (after, inter), condensers, etc.
PA: Slant/Fin Corporation
100 Forest Dr
Greenvale NY 11548
516 484-2600

(G-5634)
WIN WOOD CABINETRY INC
200 Forest Dr Ste 7 (11548-1216)
PHONE.................................516 304-2216
Frank Lin, *President*
▲ EMP: 8
SALES (est): 413K **Privately Held**
SIC: 2434 Wood kitchen cabinets

Greenville
Greene County

(G-5635)
CLASSIC AUTO CRAFTS INC
Also Called: Town Line Auto
6501 State Route 32 (12083-2212)
P.O. Box 10 (12083-0010)
PHONE.................................518 966-8003
John Dolce, *President*
EMP: 8
SALES (est): 1.3MM **Privately Held**
WEB: www.townlineauto.com
SIC: 3599 Machine shop, jobbing & repair

Greenwich
Washington County

(G-5636)
BDP INDUSTRIES INC (PA)
Also Called: Belt Dewatering Press
354 State Route 29 (12834-4518)
P.O. Box 118 (12834-0118)
PHONE.................................518 695-6851
Albert J Schmidt, *President*
Socrates Fronhofer, *Vice Pres*
A J Schmidt, *Vice Pres*
Kelly Falk, *Purchasing*
Steven Dobert, *Engineer*
EMP: 49 EST: 1978
SALES: 16.8MM **Privately Held**
WEB: www.bdpindustries.com
SIC: 3523 3545 3542 Turf & grounds equipment; turf equipment, commercial; machine tool accessories; machine tools, metal forming type

(G-5637)
BETTERBEE INC
Also Called: Southern Adirondack Honey Co.
8 Meader Rd (12834-2734)
PHONE.................................518 314-0575
Erica Stevens, *CEO*
Margaret A Stevens, *President*
Justin Stevens, *Exec VP*
John Rath, *Engineer*
Leah Sargood, *Sales Mgr*
◆ EMP: 15
SQ FT: 3,500
SALES (est): 2.4MM **Privately Held**
WEB: www.betterbee.com
SIC: 2499 3999 Beekeeping supplies, wood; candles

(G-5638)
ESSITY PROF HYGIENE N AMER LLC
72 County Route 53 (12834-2214)
PHONE.................................518 692-8434
Michael Bell, *Safety Mgr*
Glenn Jones, *Branch Mgr*
EMP: 50
SALES (corp-wide): 7.6B **Privately Held**
WEB: www.scatissue.com
SIC: 2621 Napkin stock, paper
HQ: Essity Professional Hygiene North America Llc
984 Winchester Rd
Neenah WI 54956
920 727-3770

(G-5639)
FORT MILLER GROUP INC
688 Wilbur Ave (12834-4413)
P.O. Box 98, Schuylerville (12871-0098)
PHONE.................................518 695-5000
John T Hedbring, *Ch of Bd*
John Marcelle, *Exec VP*
Brian Myers, *Safety Mgr*
Keith Carleton, *Site Mgr*
Dave House, *Opers Staff*
▲ EMP: 420
SQ FT: 160,000
SALES (est): 134MM **Privately Held**
WEB: www.fortmiller.com
SIC: 3272 3441 Concrete products, precast; fabricated structural metal
PA: The Fort Miller Service Corp
688 Wilbur Ave
Greenwich NY 12834

(G-5640)
FORT MILLER SERVICE CORP (PA)
688 Wilbur Ave (12834-4413)
P.O. Box 98, Schuylerville (12871-0098)
PHONE.................................518 695-5000
John T Hedbring, *Ch of Bd*
Mary Ann Spiezio, *Vice Pres*
Richard Schumaker, *CFO*
▼ EMP: 12
SQ FT: 10,000
SALES (est): 156.5MM **Privately Held**
SIC: 3272 3271 5211 1799 Concrete products, precast; burial vaults, concrete or precast terrazzo; concrete block & brick; concrete & cinder block; fence construction

(G-5641)
HOLLINGSWORTH & VOSE COMPANY
3235 County Rte 113 (12834)
PHONE.................................518 695-8000
Donald Wagner, *Opers-Prdtn-Mfg*
EMP: 160
SQ FT: 3,594
SALES (corp-wide): 781.1MM **Privately Held**
WEB: www.hovo.com
SIC: 2621 3053 Filter paper; gasket materials
PA: Hollingsworth & Vose Company
112 Washington St
East Walpole MA 02032
508 850-2000

(G-5642)
ICE CREAM MAN INC
417 State Route 29 (12834-4233)
PHONE.................................518 692-8382
Julia Reynolds, *President*
EMP: 20
SALES (est): 200K **Privately Held**
WEB: www.the-ice-cream-man.com
SIC: 2024 Ice cream, bulk

(G-5643)
NORTHAST CTR FOR BEKEEPING LLC
Also Called: Betterbee
8 Meader Rd (12834-2734)
PHONE.................................800 632-3379
Christopher Cripps,
Joseph Cali,
John Rath,
◆ EMP: 19
SALES (est): 1.6MM **Privately Held**
SIC: 2499 5191 3999 Beekeeping supplies, wood; beekeeping supplies (non-durable); beekeepers' supplies

(G-5644)
PHANTOM LABORATORY INC
Also Called: Phantom Laboratory, The
2727 State Route 29 (12834-3212)
P.O. Box 511, Salem (12865-0511)
PHONE.................................518 692-1190
Joshua Levy, *President*
Julie Simms, *Vice Pres*
Bonnie Hanlon, *VP Opers*
Megan Stalter, *Cust Mgr*
EMP: 15
SQ FT: 65,000
SALES (est): 750K **Privately Held**
WEB: www.phantomlab.com
SIC: 3844 X-ray apparatus & tubes

(G-5645)
SOUTHERN ADRNDCK FBR PRDCRS CP
2532 State Route 40 (12834-2300)
PHONE.................................518 692-2700
Mary Jeanne Packer, *President*
EMP: 5
SALES: 50K **Privately Held**
SIC: 2299 Textile goods

(G-5646)
TYMETAL CORP (HQ)
678 Wilbur Ave (12834-4413)
P.O. Box 139, Schuylerville (12871-0139)
PHONE.................................518 692-9930
John T Hedbring, *President*
Rob Douglas, *President*
Douglas Blanchard, *Opers Mgr*

GEOGRAPHIC SECTION

Peg Harrington, *Opers Staff*
Bruce Gill, *Engineer*
EMP: 30
SQ FT: 25,000
SALES: 15MM **Privately Held**
WEB: www.tymetal.com
SIC: 3446 3441 Fences, gates, posts & flagpoles; fabricated structural metal

Greenwood Lake
Orange County

(G-5647)
AUTOMATED ELEVATOR SYSTEMS
659 Jersey Ave (10925-2014)
PHONE 845 595-1063
Jacqueline Doyle, *Principal*
EMP: 20
SALES (est): 527.2K **Privately Held**
SIC: 3534 Elevators & moving stairways

(G-5648)
BARNABY PRINTS INC (PA)
673 Jersey Ave (10925-2014)
P.O. Box 98 (10925-0098)
PHONE 845 477-2501
Robert Brodhurst, *President*
William Neuhaus, *Treasurer*
EMP: 15
SQ FT: 12,000
SALES (est): 1.1MM **Privately Held**
SIC: 2759 2396 Screen printing; automotive & apparel trimmings

Groton
Tompkins County

(G-5649)
BAY HORSE INNOVATIONS NYINC
130 Cayuga St (13073-1002)
PHONE 607 898-3337
Gene Velten, *President*
EMP: 7
SALES (est): 513.2K **Privately Held**
SIC: 3713 Truck & bus bodies

(G-5650)
C & D ASSEMBLY INC
107 Corona Ave (13073-1206)
PHONE 607 898-4275
Jeffrey Cronk, *President*
Michael Hammond, *Vice Pres*
Candice Dann, *Treasurer*
▲ **EMP:** 42
SQ FT: 10,600
SALES (est): 9.5MM **Privately Held**
WEB: www.cdassembly.com
SIC: 3672 8731 Printed circuit boards; electronic research

(G-5651)
CAYUGA TOOL AND DIE INC
182 Newman Rd (13073-8712)
PHONE 607 533-7400
Judson Bailey, *President*
Becky Bailey, *Treasurer*
EMP: 9
SQ FT: 3,680
SALES (est): 664.9K **Privately Held**
SIC: 3599 Machine shop, jobbing & repair

(G-5652)
MARTINEZ SPECIALTIES INC
205 Bossard Rd (13073-9779)
PHONE 607 898-3053
Philip Martinez, *President*
Dorothy Martinez, *Vice Pres*
Jamie Young, *Vice Pres*
EMP: 8
SALES (est): 1.1MM **Privately Held**
SIC: 3694 Ignition apparatus & distributors

(G-5653)
PYLANTIS NEW YORK LLC
102 E Cortland St (13073-1108)
PHONE 310 429-5911
Jeff Toolan, *CEO*
Eli Gill, *COO*

Matt Ruttenberg,
EMP: 5 **EST:** 2012
SALES (est): 348.9K **Privately Held**
SIC: 3089 Injection molding of plastics

Guilderland
Albany County

(G-5654)
CUSTOM PRTRS GUILDERLAND INC
Also Called: Guilderland Printing
2210 Western. Ave (12084-9701)
PHONE 518 456-2811
Joyce Ragone, *President*
Thomas Ragone, *Vice Pres*
Kathleen Szesnat, *Manager*
EMP: 15
SQ FT: 4,000
SALES (est): 2.9MM **Privately Held**
SIC: 2759 Screen printing

(G-5655)
PRICE CHOPPER OPERATING CO
2080 Western Ave Ste 160 (12084-9564)
PHONE 518 456-5115
Cathy Gorman, *Branch Mgr*
EMP: 5
SALES (corp-wide): 3.3B **Privately Held**
SIC: 3751 Motorcycles & related parts
HQ: Price Chopper Operating Co., Inc
501 Duanesburg Rd
Schenectady NY 12306
518 379-1600

Guilderland Center
Albany County

(G-5656)
INOVA LLC
2 Van Buren Blvd Bldg 19 (12085-7703)
P.O. Box 20 (12085-0020)
PHONE 866 528-2804
Loren Sherman,
▲ **EMP:** 35
SQ FT: 39,000
SALES (est): 5.3MM **Privately Held**
SIC: 2511 2599 2531 Bed frames, except water bed frames: wood; hotel furniture; school furniture

Halcottsville
Delaware County

(G-5657)
ALTA INDUSTRIES LTD
Also Called: Alta Log Homes
46966 State Hwy 30 (12438)
PHONE 845 586-3336
Frank Mann, *President*
David S Mann, *Vice Pres*
Heather Davie, *Production*
Kenneth Castle, *Purchasing*
Marleen Gagnon, *Bookkeeper*
EMP: 16
SQ FT: 7,000
SALES (est): 2.2MM **Privately Held**
WEB: www.altaloghomes.com
SIC: 2452 Log cabins, prefabricated, wood

Halesite
Suffolk County

(G-5658)
MANUFACTURERS INDEXING PDTS
Also Called: Mip
53 Gristmill Ln (11743-2134)
PHONE 631 271-0956
Charles Busk Jr, *President*
EMP: 9 **EST:** 1964
SQ FT: 12,000

SALES (est): 787.7K **Privately Held**
SIC: 2821 2675 Vinyl resins; die-cut paper & board

(G-5659)
ROSE FENCE INC
356 Bay Ave (11743-1141)
PHONE 516 790-2308
EMP: 88
SALES (corp-wide): 20.2MM **Privately Held**
SIC: 3496 Fencing, made from purchased wire
PA: Rose Fence, Inc.
345 W Sunrise Hwy
Freeport NY 11520
516 223-0777

Halfmoon
Saratoga County

(G-5660)
ADVANCE ENERGY TECH INC
1 Solar Dr (12065-3402)
PHONE 518 371-2140
Timothy K Carlo, *Ch of Bd*
EMP: 27 **EST:** 1965
SQ FT: 30,000
SALES (est): 6.3MM **Privately Held**
WEB: www.advanceet.com
SIC: 3585 Parts for heating, cooling & refrigerating equipment

(G-5661)
CAPITAL DISTRICT STAIRS INC
45 Dunsbach Rd (12065-7906)
PHONE 518 383-2449
Alex Nikiforov, *President*
EMP: 7
SALES (est): 1MM **Privately Held**
WEB: www.capitaldistrictstairs.com
SIC: 2431 Staircases & stairs, wood; stair railings, wood

(G-5662)
EBELING ASSOCIATES INC (PA)
Also Called: Control Global Solutions
9 Corporate Dr Ste 1 (12065-8636)
PHONE 518 688-8700
Allan Robison, *President*
James Colunio, *CIO*
Scott Ebeling, *Systems Analyst*
EMP: 18
SQ FT: 5,500
SALES (est): 1.9MM **Privately Held**
WEB: www.execontrol.com
SIC: 7372 Prepackaged software

(G-5663)
INFO LABEL INC
12 Enterprise Ave (12065-3424)
PHONE 518 664-0791
Mark Dufort, *President*
EMP: 15
SQ FT: 7,000
SALES (est): 2MM **Privately Held**
WEB: www.infolabel.net
SIC: 2759 5084 Labels & seals: printing; printing trades machinery, equipment & supplies

(G-5664)
INTERSOURCE MANAGEMENT GROUP (PA)
7 Corporate Dr Ste 3 (12065-8612)
PHONE 518 372-6798
Randy Wright, *Sales Staff*
Robert Dybas, *Manager*
EMP: 6
SALES (est): 1.9MM **Privately Held**
SIC: 3511 Turbines & turbine generator sets & parts

(G-5665)
MOTOROLA SOLUTIONS INC
7 Deer Run Holw (12065-5664)
PHONE 518 348-0833
Carolely Urgenson, *Principal*
EMP: 148
SALES (corp-wide): 6.3B **Publicly Held**
WEB: www.motorola.com
SIC: 3663 Radio broadcasting & communications equipment

PA: Motorola Solutions, Inc.
500 W Monroe St Ste 4400
Chicago IL 60661
847 576-5000

(G-5666)
MOVINADS & SIGNS LLC
1771 Route 9 (12065-2413)
PHONE 518 378-3000
Rob Potter, *President*
EMP: 5 **EST:** 2007
SQ FT: 4,000
SALES: 300K **Privately Held**
SIC: 3993 Signs & advertising specialties

(G-5667)
REQUEST INC
Also Called: Request Multimedia
14 Corporate Dr Ste 6 (12065-8607)
PHONE 518 899-1254
Peter M Cholnoky, *President*
Lavoy Gary, *Technology*
EMP: 30
SQ FT: 8,100
SALES (est): 5MM **Privately Held**
WEB: www.request.com
SIC: 3651 Home entertainment equipment, electronic

(G-5668)
REQUEST SERIOUS PLAY LLC
14 Corporate Dr (12065-8607)
PHONE 518 899-1254
Barry Evans, *Principal*
EMP: 7
SALES (est): 680K **Privately Held**
SIC: 3651 Home entertainment equipment, electronic

(G-5669)
SAVE MORE BEVERAGE CORP
Also Called: Uptown
1512 Route 9 Ste 1 (12065-8664)
PHONE 518 371-2520
Harold Rockowitz, *President*
Robert Popp, *Treasurer*
EMP: 8
SALES: 2.5MM **Privately Held**
SIC: 2086 5921 5181 Carbonated beverages, nonalcoholic: bottled & canned; beer (packaged); soft drinks; beer & other fermented malt liquors

(G-5670)
ZAPPONE CHRYSLER JEEP DDGE INC
1780 Route 9 (12065-2402)
PHONE 518 982-0610
James M Zappone, *Ch of Bd*
Ken Pelcher, *Owner*
EMP: 19
SALES (est): 3.5MM **Privately Held**
SIC: 3699 5511 Heat emission operating apparatus; new & used car dealers

Hall
Ontario County

(G-5671)
MILLCO WOODWORKING LLC
1710 Railroad Pl (14463-9005)
P.O. Box 38 (14463-0038)
PHONE 585 526-6844
Charles L Millerd,
Mark M Millerd,
EMP: 11
SQ FT: 6,290
SALES (est): 1.6MM **Privately Held**
WEB: www.millcowoodworking.com
SIC: 2434 2431 Wood kitchen cabinets; millwork

Hamburg
Erie County

(G-5672)
ABASCO INC
5225 Southwestern Blvd (14075-3524)
P.O. Box 247 (14075-0247)
PHONE 716 649-4790

Frank A Saeli Jr, *President*
Michael Saeli, *Vice Pres*
Bill Seipel, *Vice Pres*
Bev Nappo, *Purch Mgr*
William G Seipel, *Marketing Mgr*
▲ **EMP:** 30 **EST:** 1962
SALES (est): 8.4MM **Privately Held**
WEB: www.abasco.net
SIC: 3613 3449 Control panels, electric; miscellaneous metalwork

(G-5673)
CAPITAL CONCRETE INC
5690 Camp Rd (14075-3706)
PHONE..................................716 648-8001
Rosanne Lettieri, *President*
EMP: 6
SALES (est): 912.9K **Privately Held**
SIC: 3273 Ready-mixed concrete

(G-5674)
CLASSIC AWNINGS INC
Also Called: Classic Awnings and Tent Co
1 Elmview Ave (14075-3761)
PHONE..................................716 649-0390
David Vesneske, *President*
EMP: 15
SQ FT: 5,000
SALES: 750K **Privately Held**
WEB: www.classicawnings.com
SIC: 2394 7359 Awnings, fabric: made from purchased materials; tent & tarpaulin rental

(G-5675)
E-ONE INC
4760 Camp Rd (14075-2604)
PHONE..................................716 646-6790
Kevin Nunn, *Regl Sales Mgr*
Jeffrey Hermann, *Branch Mgr*
EMP: 70 **Publicly Held**
SIC: 3537 Industrial trucks & tractors
HQ: E-One, Inc.
    1601 Sw 37th Ave
    Ocala FL 34474
    352 237-1122

(G-5676)
EATON BROTHERS CORP
3530 Lakeview Rd (14075-6160)
P.O. Box 60 (14075-0060)
PHONE..................................716 649-8250
Ralph D Allen, *President*
Gary Allen, *Exec VP*
Christopher Allen, *Shareholder*
▲ **EMP:** 9
SQ FT: 21,000
SALES (est): 2.1MM **Privately Held**
WEB: www.eatonbrothers.com
SIC: 3524 3272 Lawn & garden tractors & equipment; tombstones, precast terrazzo or concrete

(G-5677)
EL-DON BATTERY POST INC
4109 Saint Francis Dr (14075-1722)
PHONE..................................716 627-3697
Gary K Logsdon, *Principal*
EMP: 5
SALES (est): 833.7K **Privately Held**
SIC: 3691 5063 Storage batteries; batteries

(G-5678)
EMCS LLC
4414 Manor Ln (14075-1117)
PHONE..................................716 523-2002
Ed Monacelli, *President*
Rob Haefner, *Vice Pres*
EMP: 7
SALES (est): 839.5K **Privately Held**
SIC: 3572 Computer storage devices

(G-5679)
EVENHOUSE PRINTING
4783 Southwestern Blvd (14075-1926)
PHONE..................................716 649-2666
Robin L Evenhouse, *Partner*
EMP: 7
SALES (est): 783K **Privately Held**
WEB: www.evenhouseprinting.com
SIC: 2752 Commercial printing, lithographic

(G-5680)
GATEWAY PRTG & GRAPHICS INC
3970 Big Tree Rd (14075-1320)
PHONE..................................716 823-3873
Jeffery Donner, *President*
Eugene Donner, *Corp Secy*
Brian Lattimore, *Production*
Brenda Blazevic, *Office Mgr*
Brenda Blazek, *Admin Sec*
EMP: 28
SQ FT: 20,000
SALES (est): 4.8MM **Privately Held**
WEB: www.gatewayprints.com
SIC: 2752 2791 2789 2761 Commercial printing, offset; typesetting; bookbinding & related work; manifold business forms

(G-5681)
GREAT AMERICAN TOOL CO INC
7223 Boston State Rd (14075-6932)
PHONE..................................716 646-5700
John Anthon, *President*
▲ **EMP:** 6
SALES (est): 1.1MM **Privately Held**
WEB: www.timberlineknives.com
SIC: 3546 3421 Power-driven handtools; table & food cutlery, including butchers'

(G-5682)
JOBS WEEKLY INC
Also Called: Wny Jobs.com
31 Buffalo St Ste 2 (14075-5000)
PHONE..................................716 648-5627
Thomas Kluckhohn, *President*
Carl Kluckhohn, *Vice Pres*
Steve Kluckhohn, *Treasurer*
Susan O'Connor, *Manager*
Laura O'Loughlin, *Manager*
EMP: 11
SALES: 1MM **Privately Held**
WEB: www.wnyjobs.com
SIC: 2711 Newspapers, publishing & printing

(G-5683)
K & H INDUSTRIES INC (PA)
160 Elmview Ave (14075-3763)
PHONE..................................716 312-0088
Joseph Pinker Jr, *Ch of Bd*
Karl A Baake, *President*
John Herc, *Vice Pres*
Tim Cooke, *Purchasing*
Joe Powers, *Technical Mgr*
▲ **EMP:** 17 **EST:** 1960
SQ FT: 100,000
SALES (est): 4.7MM **Privately Held**
WEB: www.khindustries.com
SIC: 3641 3643 3599 3089 Lamps, fluorescent, electric; plugs, electric; connectors & terminals for electrical devices; electrical discharge machining (EDM); injection molding of plastics

(G-5684)
K & H INDUSTRIES INC
160 Elmview Ave (14075-3763)
PHONE..................................716 312-0088
Klaus Baake, *Branch Mgr*
EMP: 20
SALES (corp-wide): 4.7MM **Privately Held**
WEB: www.khindustries.com
SIC: 3089 3641 Injection molding of plastics; lamps, fluorescent, electric
PA: K & H Industries, Inc.
    160 Elmview Ave
    Hamburg NY 14075
    716 312-0088

(G-5685)
KRAGEL CO INC
Also Called: Custom Bags Unlimited
23 Lake St (14075-4940)
P.O. Box 71 (14075-0071)
PHONE..................................716 648-1344
Jim Bednasz, *President*
EMP: 7
SQ FT: 4,980
SALES (est): 181.5K **Privately Held**
SIC: 2221 2393 2394 Nylon broadwoven fabrics; textile bags; liners & covers, fabric: made from purchased materials

(G-5686)
KUSTOM KORNER
Also Called: West Herr Automotive Group
5140 Camp Rd (14075-2704)
PHONE..................................716 646-0173
Scott Beiler, *President*
Eric Zimmerman, *General Mgr*
EMP: 13
SALES (est): 1.3MM **Privately Held**
SIC: 3465 Body parts, automobile: stamped metal

(G-5687)
NITRO MANUFACTURING LLC
106 Evans St Ste E (14075-6169)
PHONE..................................716 646-9900
Bill Frascella, *Manager*
EMP: 10
SALES (est): 246.8K **Privately Held**
SIC: 3999 Barber & beauty shop equipment

(G-5688)
NORTHEASTERN TRANSPARTS INC
5727 S Park Ave (14075-3022)
PHONE..................................716 833-0792
Ronald Gutowski, *Owner*
Wendy Gutowski, *Manager*
EMP: 13
SQ FT: 13,500
SALES (est): 1.2MM **Privately Held**
WEB: www.northeasterntransparts.com
SIC: 3714 Transmission housings or parts, motor vehicle

(G-5689)
ON THE MARK DIGITAL PRINTING &
5758 S Park Ave (14075-3739)
PHONE..................................716 823-3373
Mark Poydock, *President*
EMP: 5
SALES (est): 626.7K **Privately Held**
SIC: 3993 Signs & advertising specialties

(G-5690)
PRAXAIR INC
5322 Scranton Rd (14075-2935)
PHONE..................................716 649-1600
Jim Hodgson, *Manager*
EMP: 20
SALES (corp-wide): 11.4B **Privately Held**
SIC: 2813 Industrial gases
PA: Praxair, Inc.
    10 Riverview Dr
    Danbury CT 06810
    203 837-2000

(G-5691)
QUEST MANUFACTURING INC
5600 Camp Rd (14075-3706)
PHONE..................................716 312-8000
Michael J O'Brien, *President*
Matt Sharpless, *Sales Staff*
Gloria Obrien, *Manager*
John Kennedy, *Technology*
EMP: 30 **EST:** 1998
SQ FT: 17,700
SALES (est): 702.2K **Privately Held**
WEB: www.questmanufacturing.com
SIC: 3312 Stainless steel

(G-5692)
QUEST MANUFACTURING INC
5600 Camp Rd (14075-3706)
PHONE..................................716 312-8000
Kimberly M Leach, *Principal*
EMP: 20
SALES (est): 2.8MM **Privately Held**
SIC: 3999 Manufacturing industries

(G-5693)
RIEFLER CONCRETE PRODUCTS LLC
5690 Camp Rd (14075-3706)
PHONE..................................716 649-3260
Michael Sheehan, *President*
Echarles Cotten, *Vice Pres*
David J Lichner, *VP Opers*
Thomas Noonan, *Treasurer*
William C Haas, *VP Sales*
EMP: 170
SQ FT: 6,700
SALES (est): 20.4MM **Privately Held**
SIC: 3273 5999 3271 3272 Ready-mixed concrete; concrete products, pre-cast; blocks, concrete or cinder: standard; concrete products

(G-5694)
ROLY DOOR SALES INC
5659 Herman Hill Rd (14075-6909)
PHONE..................................716 877-1515
EMP: 5 **EST:** 1952
SALES (est): 328.6K **Privately Held**
SIC: 3442 Mfg Metal Doors/Sash/Trim

(G-5695)
SINCLAIR TECHNOLOGIES INC (DH)
5811 S Park Ave 3 (14075-3738)
PHONE..................................716 874-3682
Valerie Sinclair, *Ch of Bd*
David Ralston, *President*
David Savel, *CFO*
Andrea Sinclair, *Treasurer*
Dorothy F Sinclair, *Admin Sec*
EMP: 21 **EST:** 1960
SQ FT: 36,000
SALES (est): 1.7MM
SALES (corp-wide): 807.6MM **Privately Held**
WEB: www.sinctech.com
SIC: 3663 5065 3674 3643 Antennas, transmitting & communications; communication equipment; amateur radio communications equipment; semiconductors & related devices; current-carrying wiring devices; switchgear & switchboard apparatus; nonferrous wiredrawing & insulating
HQ: Sinclair Technologies Inc
    85 Mary St
    Aurora ON L4G 6
    905 727-0165

(G-5696)
STAUB MACHINE COMPANY INC
Also Called: Staub Square
206 Lake St (14075-4471)
PHONE..................................716 649-4211
Anthony J Staub, *Ch of Bd*
Tony Staub, *President*
Jim Staub, *Opers Mgr*
Rhonda Bachert, *Controller*
Erik Bauerlein, *Marketing Mgr*
EMP: 20
SQ FT: 1,500
SALES (est): 4.1MM **Privately Held**
WEB: www.staubmachine.com
SIC: 3599 Machine shop, jobbing & repair

(G-5697)
WILLIAM R SHOEMAKER INC
399 Pleasant Ave (14075-4719)
PHONE..................................716 649-0511
William R Shoemaker, *President*
EMP: 5
SQ FT: 1,800
SALES (est): 708.8K **Privately Held**
SIC: 3569 Firefighting apparatus

Hamilton
Madison County

(G-5698)
COSSITT CONCRETE PRODUCTS INC
6543 Middleport Rd (13346-2275)
P.O. Box 379 (13346-0379)
PHONE..................................315 824-2700
Lance Kenyon, *President*
EMP: 10 **EST:** 1947
SQ FT: 1,500
SALES (est): 1.9MM **Privately Held**
SIC: 3272 3273 5211 3271 Concrete stuctural support & building material; ready-mixed concrete; lumber & other building materials; architectural concrete: block, split, fluted, screen, etc.

(G-5699)
JAMES MORRIS
Also Called: Madison Manufacturing
6697 Airport Rd (13346-2118)
PHONE..................................315 824-8519

James Morris, *Owner*
Bob Britton, *General Mgr*
EMP: 30
SQ FT: 6,000
SALES (est): 2.8MM **Privately Held**
WEB: www.jamesmorris.net
SIC: 3559 Electronic component making machinery

Hamlin
Monroe County

(G-5700)
HF TECHNOLOGIES LLC
810 Martin Rd (14464-9743)
PHONE..................585 254-5030
David Fletcher,
Angela Fletcher,
EMP: 20 **EST:** 2001
SQ FT: 25,000
SALES (est): 2.3MM **Privately Held**
WEB: www.hftechnologies.com
SIC: 3577 3955 Printers, computer; print cartridges for laser & other computer printers

Hammond
St. Lawrence County

(G-5701)
YESTERYEARS VINTAGE DOORS LLC
66 S Main St (13646-3201)
PHONE..................315 324-5250
Howard Demick, *Owner*
Erica Demick, *Natl Sales Mgr*
EMP: 9
SQ FT: 5,760
SALES (est): 1.2MM **Privately Held**
WEB: www.vintagedoors.com
SIC: 2431 Doors, wood

Hammondsport
Steuben County

(G-5702)
ATLAS METAL INDUSTRIES INC
17 Wheeler Ave (14840-9566)
PHONE..................607 776-2048
EMP: 1 **EST:** 2012
SALES (est): 3.1MM
SALES (corp-wide): 105MM **Privately Held**
SIC: 3999 Manufacturing industries
PA: Mercury Aircraft Inc.
   8126 County Route 88
   Hammondsport NY 14840
   607 569-4200

(G-5703)
CUSTOM MANUFACTURING INC
Also Called: CMI Microclimates
93 Lake St (14840-9563)
PHONE..................607 569-2738
Carmen J Waters, *President*
Michael Waters, *Vice Pres*
▲ **EMP:** 5
SALES: 700K **Privately Held**
WEB: www.archivalboxes.com
SIC: 2655 Containers, liquid tight fiber: from purchased material

(G-5704)
HEARTWOOD SPECIALTIES INC
10249 Gibson Rd (14840-9431)
PHONE..................607 654-0102
Bruce G Bozman, *President*
EMP: 7 **EST:** 1983
SQ FT: 5,000
SALES (est): 680K **Privately Held**
SIC: 2521 2541 Wood office furniture; wood partitions & fixtures

(G-5705)
HERON HILL VINEYARDS INC (PA)
Also Called: Heron Hill Winery
9301 County Route 76 (14840-9685)
PHONE..................607 868-4241
John Engle Jr, *CEO*
Eric Frarey, *Managing Prtnr*
Christy Dann, *CFO*
Don Riesenberger, *Manager*
Tambi Schweizer, *Manager*
EMP: 33
SQ FT: 8,640
SALES (est): 2.5MM **Privately Held**
WEB: www.heronhill.com
SIC: 2084 5812 0172 Wines; eating places; grapes

(G-5706)
KEUKA BREWING CO LLC
8572 Briglin Rd (14840-9633)
PHONE..................607 868-4648
Richard Musso, *President*
EMP: 8
SALES (est): 678K **Privately Held**
SIC: 2082 Beer (alcoholic beverage)

(G-5707)
KONSTANTIN D FRANK& SONS VINI
Also Called: Vinifera Wine Cellard
9749 Middle Rd (14840-9462)
PHONE..................607 868-4884
Fred Frank, *President*
Meaghan Frank, *General Mgr*
Hilda Volz, *Admin Sec*
▲ **EMP:** 30
SALES (est): 3.9MM **Privately Held**
WEB: www.drfrankwines.com
SIC: 2084 0172 Wines; grapes

Hampton Bays
Suffolk County

(G-5708)
BROCK AWNINGS LTD
211 E Montauk Hwy Ste 1 (11946-2035)
PHONE..................631 765-5200
Earl Brock, *President*
EMP: 10 **EST:** 1975
SQ FT: 8,000
SALES: 693.1K **Privately Held**
WEB: www.brockawnings.com
SIC: 2394 5999 5199 5091 Awnings, fabric: made from purchased materials; canvas products; canvas products; boat accessories & parts

Hancock
Delaware County

(G-5709)
BEAVER MOUNTAIN LOG HOMES INC
200 Beaver Mountain Dr (13783-1748)
PHONE..................607 467-2700
Kenneth Clark, *Branch Mgr*
EMP: 5
SALES (corp-wide): 5.2MM **Privately Held**
SIC: 2452 Log cabins, prefabricated, wood
PA: Beaver Mountain Log Homes Inc
   1740 County Highway 48
   Deposit NY
   607 467-2758

(G-5710)
COBLESKILL STONE PRODUCTS INC
Also Called: Hancock Quarry/Asphalt
1565 Green Flats Rd (13783)
PHONE..................607 637-4271
Ray Althiser, *Branch Mgr*
EMP: 10
SALES (corp-wide): 115.2MM **Privately Held**
WEB: www.cobleskillstone.com
SIC: 1422 2951 Crushed & broken limestone; asphalt & asphaltic paving mixtures (not from refineries)
PA: Cobleskill Stone Products, Inc.
   112 Rock Rd
   Cobleskill NY 12043
   518 234-0221

(G-5711)
COMPREHENSIVE DENTAL TECH
Rr 1 Box 69 (13783)
PHONE..................607 467-4456
Marie Benjamin, *President*
Mike Archer, *Vice Pres*
EMP: 4
SQ FT: 2,700
SALES: 1.3MM **Privately Held**
SIC: 7372 8021 Prepackaged software; offices & clinics of dentists

(G-5712)
MALLERY LUMBER LLC
158 Labarre St (13783)
PHONE..................607 637-2236
Les Wagner, *President*
EMP: 7
SQ FT: 2,000
SALES (est): 69.2K **Privately Held**
SIC: 2421 Kiln drying of lumber

(G-5713)
PETERS LLC
5259 Peas Eddy Rd (13783-4237)
PHONE..................607 637-5470
Van Peters,
Beverly Peters,
EMP: 5
SALES (est): 360K **Privately Held**
SIC: 2411 Logging

(G-5714)
RUSSELL BASS
Also Called: Russell Bass & Son Lumber
59 Saw Mill Rd (13783)
P.O. Box 718 (13783-0718)
PHONE..................607 637-5253
Russell Bass, *Partner*
EMP: 15
SALES (est): 1.3MM **Privately Held**
SIC: 2421 2411 Sawmills & planing mills, general; logging

(G-5715)
VAN CPETERS LOGGING INC
4480 Peas Eddy Rd (13783-4232)
PHONE..................607 637-3574
Van Peters, *Principal*
EMP: 6
SALES (est): 515.7K **Privately Held**
SIC: 2411 Logging

Hannacroix
Greene County

(G-5716)
MODERN METAL FABRICATORS INC
799 Cr 111 (12087)
PHONE..................518 966-4142
Brian Kinn, *President*
EMP: 7
SALES (est): 228.5K **Privately Held**
SIC: 2522 Office furniture, except wood

Hannibal
Oswego County

(G-5717)
ACRO-FAB LTD
55 Rochester St (13074-3139)
P.O. Box 184 (13074-0184)
PHONE..................315 564-6688
Mike Combes, *Ch of Bd*
Martin Victory, *Corp Secy*
Darrell Baker, *Vice Pres*
EMP: 23
SQ FT: 12,000
SALES (est): 3.1MM **Privately Held**
WEB: www.acro-fab.com
SIC: 7692 3444 3599 Welding repair; sheet metalwork; machine shop, jobbing & repair

(G-5718)
WOOD-MIZER HOLDINGS INC
8604 State Route 104 (13074-2125)
PHONE..................315 564-5722
Parker Rittgers, *Branch Mgr*
EMP: 7
SQ FT: 7,200
SALES (corp-wide): 127.3MM **Privately Held**
WEB: www.lastec.com
SIC: 3553 Woodworking machinery
PA: Wood-Mizer Holdings, Inc.
   8180 W 10th St
   Indianapolis IN 46214
   317 271-1542

Harriman
Orange County

(G-5719)
HOME MAIDE INC
1 Short St (10926-3311)
PHONE..................845 837-1700
Edward Fennessy, *President*
EMP: 14
SALES (est): 2.8MM **Privately Held**
SIC: 3556 Ovens, bakery

(G-5720)
JOHNSON CONTROLS
4 Commerce Dr S Ste 3 (10926-3101)
PHONE..................845 774-4120
Steve Walsh, *Manager*
EMP: 5 **Privately Held**
WEB: www.simplexgrinnell.com
SIC: 3669 5087 1731 1711 Emergency alarms; firefighting equipment; fire detection & burglar alarm systems specialization; fire sprinkler system installation
HQ: Johnson Controls Fire Protection Lp
   4700 Exchange Ct Ste 300
   Boca Raton FL 33431
   561 988-7200

(G-5721)
PREMIER INK SYSTEMS INC
2 Commerce Dr S (10926-3101)
PHONE..................845 782-5802
Tyring Marcus, *Owner*
EMP: 48
SALES (corp-wide): 16.5MM **Privately Held**
SIC: 2759 Screen printing
PA: Premier Ink Systems, Inc.
   10420 N State St
   Harrison OH 45030
   513 367-2300

Harris
Sullivan County

(G-5722)
JUS-SAR FUEL INC
Also Called: Black Bear Fuels Oil
884 Old Route 17 (12742-5016)
P.O. Box 289 (12742-0289)
PHONE..................845 791-8900
Darren Mapes, *President*
EMP: 5
SALES (est): 793.8K **Privately Held**
SIC: 3433 Heaters, swimming pool: oil or gas

Harrison
Westchester County

(G-5723)
CASTLE FUELS CORPORATION
440 Mamaroneck Ave (10528-2418)
PHONE..................914 381-6600
Michael Romita, *CEO*
EMP: 39
SALES (est): 4.6MM **Privately Held**
SIC: 2869 Fuels

Harrison - Westchester County (G-5724)

(G-5724)
CEMAC FOODS CORP
8 Cayuga Trl (10528-1820)
PHONE..............................914 835-0526
Thomas May, *President*
Helen Nash May, *Corp Secy*
Mel Persily, *Vice Pres*
Mildred Nash, *CFO*
EMP: 16
SQ FT: 3,000
SALES (est): 1.6MM Privately Held
WEB: www.cemacfoods.com
SIC: 2022 Natural cheese; imitation cheese

(G-5725)
CHEMLUBE INTERNATIONAL LLC (PA)
500 Mmaroneck Ave Ste 306 (10528)
PHONE..............................914 381-5800
Robert Nobel, *CEO*
Robert Cowen, *Vice Pres*
Rob Kress, *Vice Pres*
Connie Grossman, *Finance Dir*
Scott Ruliffson, *Manager*
◆ EMP: 13 EST: 2012
SQ FT: 5,300
SALES (est): 4.7MM Privately Held
SIC: 2992 5172 5169 Lubricating oils & greases; lubricating oils & greases; chemicals & allied products

(G-5726)
CHEMLUBE MARKETING INC
500 Mamaroneck Ave (10528-1633)
PHONE..............................914 381-5800
Robert Nobel, *Ch of Bd*
◆ EMP: 13
SQ FT: 5,300
SALES (est): 5.4MM Privately Held
WEB: www.sopetra.com
SIC: 2992 5172 5169 Lubricating oils & greases; lubricating oils & greases; chemicals & allied products

(G-5727)
DAL-TILE CORPORATION
31 Oakland Ave (10528-3709)
PHONE..............................914 835-1801
Brian Scocio, *Manager*
EMP: 7
SALES (corp-wide): 9.4B Publicly Held
WEB: www.mohawk.com
SIC: 3253 5032 Ceramic wall & floor tile; ceramic wall & floor tile
HQ: Dal-Tile Corporation
7834 C F Hawn Fwy
Dallas TX 75217
214 398-1411

(G-5728)
GGP PUBLISHING INC
105 Calvert St Ste 201 (10528-3138)
P.O. Box 635, Larchmont (10538-0635)
PHONE..............................914 834-8896
Generosa Gina Protano, *Partner*
EMP: 10
SALES: 1MM Privately Held
WEB: www.ggppublishing.com
SIC: 2731 Books: publishing only

(G-5729)
GRACE ASSOCIATES INC
470 West St (10528-2510)
PHONE..............................718 767-9000
Anthony Grace, *President*
Richard Grace, *Vice Pres*
EMP: 5
SQ FT: 1,500
SALES (est): 639.3K Privately Held
SIC: 3271 3272 2951 Concrete block & brick; concrete products; asphalt paving mixtures & blocks

(G-5730)
MARTINELLI HOLDINGS LLC
Also Called: Today Media
4 Ellsworth Ave Apt 2 (10528-3142)
PHONE..............................302 504-1361
Dianne Green, *Branch Mgr*
EMP: 50
SALES (corp-wide): 15K Privately Held
SIC: 2721 Magazines: publishing only, not printed on site
PA: Martinelli Holdings Llc
3301 Lancaster Pike 5c
Wilmington DE 19805
302 656-1809

(G-5731)
NATIONAL EQUIPMENT CORPORATION (PA)
Also Called: Union Standard Eqp Co Div
600 Mmaroneck Ave Ste 400 (10528)
PHONE..............................718 585-0200
Arthur A Greenberg, *Ch of Bd*
Andrew Greenberg, *President*
John Greenberg, *President*
Charles Greenberg, *Exec VP*
David Feinne, *Sales Engr*
◆ EMP: 18
SQ FT: 260,000
SALES (est): 10.6MM Privately Held
SIC: 3559 5084 3556 Chemical machinery & equipment; processing & packaging equipment; confectionery machinery

(G-5732)
PACE POLYETHYLENE MFG CO INC (PA)
46 Calvert St (10528-3238)
P.O. Box 385 (10528-0385)
PHONE..............................914 381-3000
Stan Nathanson, *President*
Marc Lawrence, *Vice Pres*
EMP: 20
SQ FT: 1,500
SALES (est): 5.2MM Privately Held
SIC: 3081 Polyethylene film

(G-5733)
PROFESSIONAL MEDICAL DEVICES
10 Century Trl (10528-1702)
PHONE..............................914 835-0614
EMP: 10
SALES: 500K Privately Held
SIC: 3841 Mfg Surgical/Medical Instruments

(G-5734)
SPRINGFIELD OIL SERVICES INC (PA)
550 Mmaroneck Ave Ste 503 (10528)
PHONE..............................914 315-6812
Bentley Blum, *President*
Mary Irwin, *Vice Pres*
▲ EMP: 18
SQ FT: 1,000
SALES (est): 1.2MM Privately Held
SIC: 1382 Oil & gas exploration services

(G-5735)
SS&C FINANCIAL SERVICES LLC (DH)
1 South Rd (10528-3309)
PHONE..............................914 670-3600
William Stone, *CEO*
David Jonassen, *Managing Dir*
Hans Hufschmid, *Principal*
Vernon Barback, *COO*
Anderson Jon, *Vice Pres*
EMP: 105
SQ FT: 24,000
SALES (est): 66MM
SALES (corp-wide): 1.6B Publicly Held
WEB: www.globeop.com
SIC: 7372 Prepackaged software
HQ: Ss&C Technologies, Inc.
80 Lamberton Rd
Windsor CT 06095
860 298-4500

(G-5736)
STILLTHEONE DISTILLERY LLC
500 Mmaroneck Ave Ste 205 (10528)
PHONE..............................914 217-0347
EMP: 6
SALES (est): 448.9K Privately Held
SIC: 2085 Distilled & blended liquors

(G-5737)
TREO BRANDS LLC
106 Calvert St (10528-3131)
PHONE..............................914 341-1850
Robert Golten, *CEO*
Brian O'Byrne, *President*
EMP: 8
SQ FT: 3,800
SALES (est): 284.7K Privately Held
SIC: 2086 Carbonated beverages, nonalcoholic: bottled & canned

(G-5738)
UNIVERSAL REMOTE CONTROL INC (PA)
500 Mmaroneck Ave Ste 502 (10528)
PHONE..............................914 630-4343
Chang Park, *Chairman*
Tim Brendlin, *Engineer*
Lars Granoe, *VP Sales*
Scott Srolis, *Sales Mgr*
Steve Gobern, *Accounts Mgr*
▲ EMP: 57
SQ FT: 11,000
SALES (est): 12.8MM Privately Held
WEB: www.universalremote.com
SIC: 3678 Electronic connectors

(G-5739)
VALUE SPRING TECHNOLOGY INC
521 Harrison Ave (10528-1431)
PHONE..............................917 705-4658
EMP: 15
SALES (est): 305.2K Privately Held
SIC: 7372 Prepackaged Software Services

Harrisville
Lewis County

(G-5740)
CIVES CORPORATION
Also Called: Viking-Cives
14331 Mill St (13648-3331)
PHONE..............................315 543-2321
Larry Jeroscko, *General Mgr*
Steve Rider, *General Mgr*
Terri Luther, *Purchasing*
Mike Jackson, *Engineer*
Tim Ireland, *Regl Sales Mgr*
EMP: 75
SQ FT: 46,000
SALES (corp-wide): 651.3MM Privately Held
WEB: www.cives.com
SIC: 3531 Snow plow attachments
PA: Cives Corporation
3700 Mansell Rd Ste 500
Alpharetta GA 30022
770 993-4424

Hartford
Washington County

(G-5741)
RICHARD STEWART
4495 State Rte 149 (12838)
P.O. Box 18 (12838-0018)
PHONE..............................518 632-5363
Richard Stewart, *Owner*
Mary Stewart, *Owner*
EMP: 5
SALES (est): 445.1K Privately Held
SIC: 3523 Dairy equipment (farm)

Hartsdale
Westchester County

(G-5742)
APOGEE POWER USA INC
7 Verne Pl (10530-1026)
PHONE..............................202 746-2890
Michael Harper, *CEO*
John Hollins, *President*
Dr Kc Tsai, *Mfg Mgr*
EMP: 10
SALES (est): 14.6K Privately Held
SIC: 3825 3621 Electrical energy measuring equipment; storage battery chargers, motor & engine generator type

(G-5743)
FRISCH PLASTICS CORP
7 Joyce Rd (10530-2929)
PHONE..............................973 685-5936
Ruth Lefkowitz, *President*
Irwin Lefkowitz, *Vice Pres*
EMP: 20
SALES: 500K Privately Held
WEB: www.frischplastics.com
SIC: 3089 Novelties, plastic

(G-5744)
SIGN HERE ENTERPRISES LLC
Also Called: Sign-A-Rama
28 N Central Ave Rear (10530-2430)
PHONE..............................914 328-3111
David Reichenberg,
EMP: 5
SALES (est): 350K Privately Held
SIC: 3993 Signs & advertising specialties

(G-5745)
TAPEMAKER SUPPLY COMPANY LLC
22 Sherbrooke Rd (10530-2938)
PHONE..............................914 693-3407
Ronald Huppert, *Mng Member*
EMP: 7
SALES (est): 407.8K Privately Held
WEB: www.tapemakersupply.com
SIC: 2759 Commercial printing

(G-5746)
TLC VISION (USA) CORPORATION
Also Called: Blinds To Go
150 Central Park Ave (10530)
PHONE..............................914 395-3949
Steven Shiller, *Owner*
EMP: 5 Privately Held
SIC: 2591 Window blinds
HQ: Tlc Vision (Usa) Corporation
16305 Swingley Ridge Rd # 300
Chesterfield MO 63017
636 534-2300

Hastings On Hudson
Westchester County

(G-5747)
ALTERNATIVE TECHNOLOGY CORP
Also Called: Marketfax Information Services
1 North St Ste 1 # 1 (10706-1542)
P.O. Box 357 (10706-0357)
PHONE..............................914 478-5900
Tom Kadala, *CEO*
EMP: 5
SQ FT: 3,000
SALES: 1.2MM Privately Held
WEB: www.marketfax.com
SIC: 3661 5065 4822 7375 Facsimile equipment; facsimile equipment; facsimile transmission services; information retrieval services

(G-5748)
FLOGIC INC
Also Called: F Logic
25 Chestnut Dr (10706-1901)
PHONE..............................914 478-1352
Julius Funaro, *President*
Michael Piscatelli, *Vice Pres*
EMP: 13
SALES (est): 1.2MM Privately Held
WEB: www.flinc.com
SIC: 7372 Prepackaged software

(G-5749)
IN2GREEN LLC
14 Bellair Dr (10706-1102)
PHONE..............................914 693-5054
Jill Dietz, *Sales Dir*
Lori Slater, *Mng Member*
EMP: 5 EST: 2009
SALES (est): 533.4K Privately Held
SIC: 2211 Blankets & blanketings, cotton

(G-5750)
JAMES RICHARD SPECIALTY CHEM
24 Ridge St (10706-2702)
PHONE..............................914 478-7500
Katrine Barth, *President*
EMP: 6
SQ FT: 1,300

SALES: 3MM **Privately Held**
WEB: www.rjsconline.com
SIC: 2842 Specialty cleaning, polishes & sanitation goods

(G-5751)
LORENA CANALS USA INC
104 Burnside Dr (10706-3013)
PHONE..............................844 567-3622
Delia Elbaum, *General Mgr*
▲ EMP: 3
SQ FT: 3,000
SALES: 1MM
SALES (corp-wide): 3.2MM **Privately Held**
SIC: 2273 5023 Carpets & rugs; rugs
PA: Lorena Canals Sl.
Calle Alexandre Goicoechea, 6 - Loc 8
Sant Just Desvern

Hauppauge
Suffolk County

(G-5752)
A & Z PHARMACEUTICAL INC
180 Oser Ave (11788-3736)
PHONE..............................631 952-3802
Frank Berstler, *Vice Pres*
EMP: 90
SALES (est): 5.6MM **Privately Held**
SIC: 2834 8734 Pills, pharmaceutical; testing laboratories
PA: A & Z Pharmaceutical Inc.
350 Wireless Blvd Ste 200
Hauppauge NY 11788

(G-5753)
A & Z PHARMACEUTICAL INC (PA)
350 Wireless Blvd Ste 200 (11788-3947)
PHONE..............................631 952-3800
Emma LI, *CEO*
Xu Xiaoxian, *Ch of Bd*
Frank Berstler, *Senior VP*
Xian Chen, *Vice Pres*
Denis Decarie, *Vice Pres*
◆ EMP: 450
SQ FT: 73,000
SALES (est): 148.3MM **Privately Held**
SIC: 2834 Vitamin, nutrient & hematinic preparations for human use

(G-5754)
ADVANCED BACK TECHNOLOGIES
89 Ste F Cabot Ct (11788)
PHONE..............................631 231-0076
David F Cuccia, *President*
EMP: 5 EST: 1997
SALES (est): 867.8K **Privately Held**
SIC: 3069 Orthopedic sundries, molded rubber

(G-5755)
ADVANCED TESTING TECH INC (PA)
Also Called: A T T I
110 Ricefield Ln (11788-2008)
PHONE..............................631 231-8777
Hector M Gavilla, *Chairman*
Eli Levi, *Exec VP*
Tom Lingenfelter, *Vice Pres*
Angelo Stano, *Prdtn Mgr*
EMP: 180
SQ FT: 6,000
SALES (est): 32.7MM **Privately Held**
WEB: www.attinet.com
SIC: 3825 8711 Test equipment for electronic & electric measurement; electrical or electronic engineering

(G-5756)
AEROFLEX PLAINVIEW INC
Integrted Electronic Solutions
350 Kennedy Dr (11788-4014)
PHONE..............................631 231-9100
Harsad Shah, *Engineer*
Nandakumar Thirunarayan, *Senior Engr*
William Billbrown, *Branch Mgr*
EMP: 120

SALES (corp-wide): 2.7B **Privately Held**
SIC: 3679 3621 3674 3577 Electronic circuits; motors & generators; semiconductors & related devices; computer peripheral equipment
HQ: Aeroflex Plainview, Inc.
35 S Service Rd
Plainview NY 11803
516 694-6700

(G-5757)
AIPING PHARMACEUTICAL INC
350w Wireless Blvd (11788-3959)
PHONE..............................631 952-3802
Jing Zou, *Principal*
Frank Berstler, *Vice Pres*
EMP: 5
SALES (est): 408.6K **Privately Held**
SIC: 2834 2899 Tablets, pharmaceutical; gelatin: edible, technical, photographic or pharmaceutical

(G-5758)
AIR INDUSTRIES GROUP (PA)
360 Motor Pkwy Ste 100 (11788-5193)
PHONE..............................631 881-4920
Luciano Melluzzo, *CEO*
Michael N Taglich, *Chairman*
Michael E Recca, *CFO*
Michael Brand, *Bd of Directors*
David Buonanno, *Bd of Directors*
EMP: 58
SALES: 49.8MM **Publicly Held**
SIC: 3728 Aircraft body assemblies & parts; aircraft landing assemblies & brakes; aircraft assemblies, subassemblies & parts

(G-5759)
ALADDIN PACKAGING LLC
115 Engineers Rd Ste 100 (11788-4005)
PHONE..............................631 273-4747
Bill Dowd, *Plant Mgr*
Moshe Wortzberger, *Sales Associate*
Jerry Levovitz, *Marketing Staff*
Abraham Mandell, *Mng Member*
Joel Endzweig,
▲ EMP: 60
SQ FT: 40,000
SALES (est): 16.2MM **Privately Held**
SIC: 2673 Cellophane bags, unprinted: made from purchased materials

(G-5760)
ALLCRAFT FABRICATORS INC
150 Wireless Blvd (11788-3955)
PHONE..............................631 951-4100
Douglas Donaldson, *President*
Darren J Winter, *Exec VP*
Tyler Kerby, *Purch Agent*
Matthew Schumacher, *Controller*
Margaret Manzo, *Administration*
EMP: 75 EST: 1964
SALES (est): 12.1MM **Privately Held**
SIC: 2522 Office furniture, except wood

(G-5761)
ALLEN MACHINE PRODUCTS INC
120 Ricefield Ln Ste 100 (11788-2033)
PHONE..............................631 630-8800
Peter Allen, *Ch of Bd*
Richard Pettenato, *Vice Pres*
Chris Bonadonna, *Mfg Dir*
Michael Kellwick, *Purch Mgr*
Ray Haase, *QC Mgr*
▲ EMP: 50
SQ FT: 30,000
SALES: 5.9MM **Privately Held**
WEB: www.allenmachine.com
SIC: 3469 3444 Machine parts, stamped or pressed metal; sheet metalwork

(G-5762)
ALUFOIL PRODUCTS CO INC
135 Oser Ave Ste 3 (11788-3722)
PHONE..............................631 231-4141
Howard Lent, *Ch of Bd*
Elliot Lent, *Vice Pres*
Estelle Lent, *Shareholder*
Barbara Sherman, *Shareholder*
◆ EMP: 18 EST: 1945
SQ FT: 45,000

SALES: 3.7MM **Privately Held**
WEB: www.alufoil.com
SIC: 3497 3353 Foil, laminated to paper or other materials; foil, aluminum

(G-5763)
AMERICAN ACCESS CARE LLC
32 Central Ave (11788-4734)
PHONE..............................631 582-9729
Thea Hemback, *Manager*
EMP: 11
SALES (corp-wide): 20.9B **Privately Held**
WEB: www.americanaccesscare.com
SIC: 3844 X-ray apparatus & tubes
HQ: American Access Care, Llc
40 Valley Stream Pkwy
Malvern PA 19355
717 235-0181

(G-5764)
AMERICAN CHIMNEY SUPPLIES INC
129 Oser Ave Ste B (11788-3813)
PHONE..............................631 434-2020
Chris Arbucci, *President*
▲ EMP: 6 EST: 1993
SQ FT: 21,000
SALES (est): 1.1MM **Privately Held**
SIC: 3312 3272 3259 Stainless steel; chimney caps, concrete; clay chimney products

(G-5765)
AMERICAN DIAGNOSTIC CORP
Also Called: A D C
55 Commerce Dr (11788-3931)
PHONE..............................631 273-6155
Marc Blitstein, *President*
Neal Weingart, *Vice Pres*
◆ EMP: 77
SALES (est): 15.8MM **Privately Held**
WEB: www.adctoday.com
SIC: 3841 Blood pressure apparatus; stethoscopes & stethographs

(G-5766)
AMERICAN HLTH FORMULATIONS INC (HQ)
Also Called: Summit Vitamins
45 Adams Ave (11788-3605)
PHONE..............................631 392-1756
Jimmy Wang, *President*
Lisa Wang, *CFO*
John Mullins, *Sales Dir*
Giancarlo Denegri, *Sales Mgr*
Hank Cheatham, *Sales Staff*
EMP: 6
SQ FT: 20,000
SALES (est): 1.2MM **Privately Held**
SIC: 2834 2869 Vitamin preparations; sweeteners, synthetic

(G-5767)
AMERICAN INTRMDAL CONT MFG LLC
Also Called: Aicm
150 Motor Pkwy Ste 401 (11788-5108)
PHONE..............................631 774-6790
Pat Marron, *President*
EMP: 8
SQ FT: 200
SALES (est): 888.5K **Privately Held**
SIC: 2655 Fiber shipping & mailing containers

(G-5768)
ARC SYSTEMS INC
2090 Joshuas Path (11788-4764)
PHONE..............................631 582-8020
Robert Miller, *President*
Clifford Miller, *Treasurer*
▲ EMP: 33 EST: 1967
SQ FT: 12,000
SALES (est): 6.3MM **Privately Held**
WEB: www.arcsystemsinc.com
SIC: 3621 3694 3724 Motors, electric; electric motor & generator parts; battery charging alternators & generators; aircraft engines & engine parts

(G-5769)
ARKAY PACKAGING CORPORATION (PA)
100 Marcus Blvd Ste 2 (11788-3749)
PHONE..............................631 273-2000

Mitchell Kaneff, *Chairman*
Walter Shiels, *COO*
Brian Hopkins, *Plant Mgr*
Mel Bohince, *Project Mgr*
Brian Jermyn, *Sales Staff*
▲ EMP: 40
SQ FT: 5,000
SALES (est): 42.9MM **Privately Held**
WEB: www.arkay.com
SIC: 2657 Folding paperboard boxes

(G-5770)
ARTEMIS INC
36 Central Ave (11788-4734)
PHONE..............................631 232-2424
Yuly Margulis, *CEO*
Alex Margulis, *Vice Pres*
Alexander Margulis, *Vice Pres*
Mike Schorr, *Engineer*
William Roe, *Design Engr*
▲ EMP: 7 EST: 1999
SQ FT: 9,000
SALES (est): 1.4MM **Privately Held**
WEB: www.artemis.com
SIC: 3674 3812 Integrated circuits, semiconductor networks, etc.; radar systems & equipment

(G-5771)
ARTISTIC PRODUCTS LLC
345 Oser Ave (11788-3607)
PHONE..............................631 435-0200
Richard Leifer,
Bradley Brighton,
▲ EMP: 45
SQ FT: 50,000
SALES (est): 7MM **Privately Held**
WEB: www.artistic-products.com
SIC: 2522 Desks, office: except wood

(G-5772)
ATLANTIC ESSENTIAL PDTS INC
7 Oser Ave Ste 1 (11788-3811)
PHONE..............................631 434-8333
Maxim G Uvarov, *Ch of Bd*
Pailla Rebby, *Vice Pres*
Selven Sam, *Vice Pres*
EMP: 57 EST: 1999
SQ FT: 22,000
SALES (est): 11.2MM **Privately Held**
WEB: www.atlanticep.com
SIC: 2834 7389 Vitamin preparations; packaging & labeling services

(G-5773)
ATLANTIC ULTRAVIOLET CORP
375 Marcus Blvd (11788-2026)
PHONE..............................631 234-3275
Hilary Boehme, *President*
Thomas Dituro, *Vice Pres*
Celeste Kopp, *Treasurer*
Ronald Henderson, *Director*
Anne Wysocki, *Admin Sec*
◆ EMP: 30 EST: 1963
SALES (est): 7.1MM **Privately Held**
WEB: www.ultraviolet.com
SIC: 3589 3641 Water purification equipment, household type; ultraviolet lamps

(G-5774)
AUTOMATIC CONNECTOR INC
375 Oser Ave (11788-3607)
PHONE..............................631 543-5000
David Lax, *President*
EMP: 19
SALES (est): 3.1MM **Privately Held**
WEB: www.automaticconnector.com
SIC: 3678 3643 Electronic connectors; electric connectors

(G-5775)
AVM PRINTING INC
Also Called: Printers 3
43 Corporate Dr (11788-2048)
PHONE..............................631 351-1331
Anthony Viscuso, *President*
EMP: 13
SQ FT: 6,000
SALES: 2MM **Privately Held**
SIC: 2752 Commercial printing, lithographic

Hauppauge - Suffolk County (G-5776)

(G-5776)
AVON REPRODUCTIONS INC
Also Called: Avon Press
175 Engineers Rd (11788-4020)
PHONE.................................631 273-2400
Brad Peters, *President*
James Gibb, *Vice Pres*
▲ **EMP:** 35 **EST:** 1958
SQ FT: 10,000
SALES (est): 3.6MM **Privately Held**
WEB: www.avonpress.com
SIC: 2752 Lithographing on metal

(G-5777)
BACTOLAC PHARMACEUTICAL INC
7 Oser Ave Ste 1 (11788-3811)
PHONE.................................631 951-4908
Pailla M Reddy, *President*
Renee Reynolds, *Vice Pres*
Pylla Reddy, *Prdtn Mgr*
Chandana Angitipalli, *Purchasing*
Chiru Reddy, *Purchasing*
▲ **EMP:** 400
SALES (est): 636.3K **Privately Held**
WEB: www.bactolac.com
SIC: 2834 Vitamin preparations

(G-5778)
BARRONS EDUCATIONAL SERIES INC (PA)
250 Wireless Blvd (11788-3924)
PHONE.................................631 434-3311
Manuel H Barron, *Chairman*
Jackie Raab, *Sales Staff*
◆ **EMP:** 125
SQ FT: 75,000
SALES (est): 26.4MM **Privately Held**
WEB: www.barronseduc.com
SIC: 2731 5942 Books: publishing only; book stores

(G-5779)
BETAPAST HOLDINGS LLC
110 Nicon Ct (11788-4212)
PHONE.................................631 582-6740
Wayne R Demmons, *CEO*
Joseph Yanosik, *President*
Linda Okvist, *Production*
Mark Adelman, *Purch Mgr*
Brian Rosengrant, *QC Dir*
EMP: 70 **EST:** 1966
SQ FT: 10,000
SALES (est): 11.7MM **Privately Held**
WEB: www.betatronix.com
SIC: 3823 3676 Potentiometric self-balancing inst., except X-Y plotters; electronic resistors

(G-5780)
BIO-BOTANICA INC (PA)
75 Commerce Dr (11788-3943)
PHONE.................................631 231-0987
Frank D'Amelio Sr, *CEO*
Josephine Perricone, *President*
Frank D'Amelio Jr, *Vice Pres*
Jonathan Selzer, *Vice Pres*
Kasra Hoshmand, *Project Mgr*
◆ **EMP:** 100
SQ FT: 100,000
SALES (est): 19.6MM **Privately Held**
SIC: 2833 2834 2844 Alkaloids & other botanical based products; drugs & herbs: grading, grinding & milling; botanical products, medicinal: ground, graded or milled; extracts of botanicals: powdered, pilular, solid or fluid; toilet preparations

(G-5781)
BLACK & DECKER (US) INC
180 Oser Ave Ste 100 (11788-3709)
PHONE.................................631 952-2008
Joe Rufino, *Branch Mgr*
EMP: 7
SALES (corp-wide): 12.7B **Publicly Held**
WEB: www.dewalt.com
SIC: 3546 Power-driven handtools
HQ: Black & Decker (U.S.) Inc.
1000 Stanley Dr
New Britain CT 06053
860 225-5111

(G-5782)
BLUE STAR PRODUCTS INC
355 Marcus Blvd Ste 2 (11788-2027)
PHONE.................................631 952-3204
Gerald Jacino Sr, *President*
Tom Jacino, *Chief Mktg Ofcr*
EMP: 12
SQ FT: 15,000
SALES (est): 1.3MM **Privately Held**
WEB: www.bluestar-products.com
SIC: 3559 Automotive maintenance equipment

(G-5783)
BRICK-IT INC
17 Central Ave (11788-4733)
PHONE.................................631 244-3993
Ronald F Trezza, *President*
James Kulp, *Sales Staff*
▼ **EMP:** 5
SQ FT: 10,000
SALES (est): 1MM **Privately Held**
WEB: www.brickit.com
SIC: 3291 5211 Coated abrasive products; brick

(G-5784)
BRICKIT
17 Central Ave (11788-4733)
PHONE.................................631 727-8977
Oscar Hernandez, *Sales Staff*
Robert Dolinsk,
Robert Dolinsky,
EMP: 20
SALES (est): 3.3MM **Privately Held**
SIC: 3271 Brick, concrete

(G-5785)
C & C CUSTOM METAL FABRICATORS
2 N Hoffman Ln (11788-2735)
PHONE.................................631 235-9646
Chris Drago, *President*
EMP: 6
SQ FT: 1,500
SALES (est): 483.7K **Privately Held**
SIC: 3441 Fabricated structural metal

(G-5786)
CENTRAL SEMICONDUCTOR CORP
145 Adams Ave (11788-3603)
PHONE.................................631 435-1110
W S Radgowski, *CEO*
Susan M Ryan, *President*
Steven Radgowski, *Vice Pres*
Thomas Radgowski, *Vice Pres*
Al Simon, *Vice Pres*
▲ **EMP:** 80
SQ FT: 30,000
SALES (est): 23.9MM **Privately Held**
WEB: www.centralsemi.com
SIC: 3674 Integrated circuits, semiconductor networks, etc.

(G-5787)
CHARL INDUSTRIES INC
225 Engineers Rd (11788-4020)
PHONE.................................631 234-0100
Richard Coronato Sr, *President*
Kitt Tyson, *Manager*
Charlotte Coronato, *Admin Sec*
EMP: 40
SQ FT: 44,000
SALES (est): 8.1MM **Privately Held**
WEB: www.charlco.com
SIC: 3599 Machine shop, jobbing & repair

(G-5788)
CHARLES ROSS & SON COMPANY (PA)
Also Called: Ross Metal Fabricators Div
710 Old Willets Path (11788-4193)
P.O. Box 12308 (11788-0615)
PHONE.................................631 234-0500
Richard Ross, *President*
Bogard Lagman, *Exec VP*
Joseph Martorana, *Vice Pres*
Ronald Reid, *Vice Pres*
Ed Stock, *Project Mgr*
▲ **EMP:** 60 **EST:** 1840
SQ FT: 50,000
SALES (est): 39.2MM **Privately Held**
WEB: www.cosmeticmixers.com
SIC: 3443 3586 3559 5084 Fabricated plate work (boiler shop); measuring & dispensing pumps; chemical machinery & equipment; pharmaceutical machinery; industrial machinery & equipment

(G-5789)
CIRCOR AEROSPACE INC
Aerodyne Controls
425 Rabro Dr Ste 1 (11788-4245)
PHONE.................................631 737-1900
Daniel R Godin, *Division Mgr*
Frank Filangeri, *Mfg Staff*
Charlie Geiser, *Production*
Patrick Martone, *Buyer*
Joe Sparacio, *Buyer*
EMP: 70
SALES (corp-wide): 661.7MM **Publicly Held**
SIC: 3483 3829 3728 Ammunition, except for small arms; measuring & controlling devices; aircraft parts & equipment
HQ: Circor Aerospace, Inc.
2301 Wardlow Cir
Corona CA 92880

(G-5790)
CITATION HEALTHCARE LABELS LLC (HQ)
55 Engineers Rd (11788-4007)
PHONE.................................631 293-4646
Richard Bolnick, *President*
Frederick Youngs, *COO*
EMP: 2
SALES (est): 4.7MM
SALES (corp-wide): 29.1MM **Privately Held**
SIC: 2759 Labels & seals: printing
PA: Advanced Web Technologies, Llc
600 Hoover St Ne Ste 500
Minneapolis MN 55413
612 706-3700

(G-5791)
CLICK IT INC
85 Corporate Dr (11788-2021)
PHONE.................................631 686-2900
James J Carey, *CEO*
Venkat Sarvasya, *Technology*
EMP: 60
SALES (est): 10.8MM **Privately Held**
WEB: www.clickitinc.com
SIC: 3663 Television closed circuit equipment

(G-5792)
COCA-COLA BTLG CO OF NY INC
375 Wireless Blvd (11788-3940)
PHONE.................................631 434-3535
Mike Chidester, *Manager*
EMP: 50
SALES (corp-wide): 35.4B **Publicly Held**
SIC: 2086 Bottled & canned soft drinks
HQ: The Coca-Cola Bottling Company Of New York Inc
2500 Windy Ridge Pkwy Se
Atlanta GA 30339
770 989-3000

(G-5793)
COLONIAL WIRE & CABLE CO INC (PA)
40 Engineers Rd (11788-4079)
PHONE.................................631 234-8500
Thomas J Walsh III, *President*
Thomas J Walsh Jr, *Chairman*
George Stubbs, *Corp Secy*
Peter Spaeth, *Manager*
EMP: 55 **EST:** 1944
SQ FT: 100,000
SALES (est): 11.3MM **Privately Held**
WEB: www.colonialwire.com
SIC: 3357 Nonferrous wiredrawing & insulating

(G-5794)
COLONIAL WIRE CABLE CO NJ INC (PA)
40 Engineers Rd (11788-4079)
PHONE.................................631 234-8500
Thomas Walsh II, *Ch of Bd*
EMP: 5
SALES (est): 853.4K **Privately Held**
SIC: 3357 Nonferrous wiredrawing & insulating

(G-5795)
COMME-CI COMME-CA AP GROUP
Also Called: Male Power Apparel
380 Rabo Dr (11788)
PHONE.................................631 300-1035
Sam Baker, *President*
Marybeth Healy, *Vice Pres*
▲ **EMP:** 21
SQ FT: 12,000
SALES (est): 3.5MM **Privately Held**
WEB: www.malepower.com
SIC: 2322 2329 2339 2341 Underwear, men's & boys': made from purchased materials; bathing suits & swimwear: men's & boys'; bathing suits: women's, misses' & juniors'; panties: women's, misses', children's & infants'

(G-5796)
COMMUNICATION POWER CORP
80 Davids Dr Ste 3 (11788-2002)
PHONE.................................631 434-7306
Daniel P Myer, *President*
Richard Myer, *General Mgr*
John Foglio, *Engineer*
Fred Winter, *Engineer*
Tuna Djemil, *Manager*
▲ **EMP:** 36
SQ FT: 11,000
SALES (est): 8.6MM **Privately Held**
WEB: www.cpcamps.com
SIC: 3663 3651 5065 Amplifiers, RF power & IF; household audio & video equipment; communication equipment

(G-5797)
COMPAC DEVELOPMENT CORPORATION
Also Called: Miller Stuart
110 Plant Ave Ste 1 (11788-3830)
PHONE.................................631 881-4903
Scott Cullen, *General Mgr*
John Canova, *General Mgr*
EMP: 85 **EST:** 1976
SQ FT: 84,000
SALES (est): 13.2MM **Publicly Held**
WEB: www.compac-rf.com
SIC: 3469 Electronic enclosures, stamped or pressed metal
PA: Air Industries Group
360 Motor Pkwy Ste 100
Hauppauge NY 11788

(G-5798)
CONTRACT PHARMACAL CORP
110 Plant Ave (11788-3830)
PHONE.................................631 231-4610
Donna Murray, *QC Mgr*
Mark Wolf, *Manager*
EMP: 20
SQ FT: 48,000
SALES (corp-wide): 310.4MM **Privately Held**
SIC: 2834 Pharmaceutical preparations
PA: Contract Pharmacal Corp.
135 Adams Ave
Hauppauge NY 11788
631 231-4610

(G-5799)
CONTRACT PHARMACAL CORP
1324 Motor Pkwy (11749-5262)
PHONE.................................631 231-4610
Jeff Reingold, *Mktg Dir*
Mark Wolf, *Manager*
EMP: 125
SALES (corp-wide): 310.4MM **Privately Held**
SIC: 2834 Pharmaceutical preparations
PA: Contract Pharmacal Corp.
135 Adams Ave
Hauppauge NY 11788
631 231-4610

(G-5800)
CONTRACT PHARMACAL CORP
250 Kennedy Dr (11788-4002)
PHONE.................................631 231-4610
Matt Wolf, *CEO*

GEOGRAPHIC SECTION

Hauppauge - Suffolk County (G-5825)

EMP: 50
SALES (corp-wide): 310.4MM **Privately Held**
SIC: 2834 Pharmaceutical preparations
PA: Contract Pharmacal Corp.
135 Adams Ave
Hauppauge NY 11788
631 231-4610

(G-5801)
CONTRACT PHARMACAL CORP
145 Oser Ave (11788-3725)
PHONE..................631 231-4610
Mark Wolf, *President*
EMP: 79
SALES (corp-wide): 309.4MM **Privately Held**
SIC: 2834 Pharmaceutical preparations
PA: Contract Pharmacal Corp.
135 Adams Ave
Hauppauge NY 11788
631 231-4610

(G-5802)
CONTRACT PHARMACAL CORP
160 Commerce Dr (11788-3944)
PHONE..................631 231-4610
Glenn Simonin, *Maintenance Dir*
Mark Wolf, *Manager*
EMP: 181
SALES (corp-wide): 309.4MM **Privately Held**
SIC: 2834 Vitamin preparations
PA: Contract Pharmacal Corp.
135 Adams Ave
Hauppauge NY 11788
631 231-4610

(G-5803)
CONTRACT PHARMACAL CORP
150 Commerce Dr (11788-3930)
PHONE..................631 231-4610
Mark Wolf, *Manager*
EMP: 19
SALES (corp-wide): 310.4MM **Privately Held**
SIC: 2834 Pharmaceutical preparations
PA: Contract Pharmacal Corp.
135 Adams Ave
Hauppauge NY 11788
631 231-4610

(G-5804)
COUNTRY LIFE LLC
101 Corporate Dr (11788-2021)
PHONE..................631 231-1031
Wendy Lucas, *President*
EMP: 102
SALES (corp-wide): 4B **Privately Held**
SIC: 2833 Vitamins, natural or synthetic: bulk, uncompounded
HQ: Country Life, Llc
180 Vanderbilt Motor Pkwy
Hauppauge NY 11788
631 232-5400

(G-5805)
CROSSTEX INTERNATIONAL INC (HQ)
10 Ranick Rd (11788-4209)
PHONE..................631 582-6777
Gary Steinberg, *CEO*
Bill French, *General Mgr*
Sheldon Fisher, *Vice Pres*
Dan Pitkowsky, *Vice Pres*
Ken Plunkett, *Vice Pres*
◆ EMP: 75
SQ FT: 63,000
SALES (est): 60.9MM
SALES (corp-wide): 871.9MM **Publicly Held**
WEB: www.crosstex.com
SIC: 3843 2621 5047 2842 Dental equipment & supplies; toweling tissue, paper; dentists' professional supplies; specialty cleaning, polishes & sanitation goods; soap & other detergents; sanitary paper products
PA: Cantel Medical Corp.
150 Clove Rd Ste 36
Little Falls NJ 07424
973 890-7220

(G-5806)
CROSSTEX INTERNATIONAL INC
2095 Express Dr N (11788-5308)
PHONE..................631 582-6777
Jessica Lauper, *Manager*
EMP: 10
SALES (corp-wide): 871.9MM **Publicly Held**
SIC: 3843 Dental equipment & supplies
HQ: Crosstex International, Inc.
10 Ranick Rd
Hauppauge NY 11788
631 582-6777

(G-5807)
CURRAN MANUFACTURING CORP (PA)
Also Called: Royal Products
200 Oser Ave (11788-3724)
PHONE..................631 273-1010
F Allan Curran, *Ch of Bd*
Christopher Jakubowsky, *VP Opers*
Linda Michaels, *Purch Mgr*
Lynn Telis, *Director*
Ana Andrade,
▲ EMP: 49 EST: 1946
SALES (est): 10.2MM **Privately Held**
WEB: www.airchucks.com
SIC: 3545 5084 Machine tool attachments & accessories; machine tools & accessories

(G-5808)
CURRAN MANUFACTURING CORP
Also Called: Royal Products
210 Oser Ave (11788-3724)
PHONE..................631 273-1010
Allan Curran, *President*
EMP: 50
SALES (est): 5.8MM
SALES (corp-wide): 10.2MM **Privately Held**
WEB: www.airchucks.com
SIC: 3545 Machine tool attachments & accessories
PA: Curran Manufacturing Corp
200 Oser Ave
Hauppauge NY 11788
631 273-1010

(G-5809)
DEPCO INC
20 Newton Pl (11788-4752)
PHONE..................631 582-1995
Greg Minuto, *CEO*
David W Bean, *President*
▲ EMP: 10
SQ FT: 20,000
SALES (est): 1.9MM **Privately Held**
SIC: 2822 Silicone rubbers

(G-5810)
DEUTSCH RELAYS
55 Engineers Rd (11788-4007)
PHONE..................631 342-1700
Thomas M Sadusky, *President*
Serge Belot, *Vice Pres*
EMP: 14
SALES (est): 1.8MM **Privately Held**
SIC: 3625 Relays & industrial controls

(G-5811)
DISC GRAPHICS INC
30 Gilpin Ave (11788-4724)
PHONE..................631 300-1129
Margaret Krumholz, *President*
EMP: 150
SALES (corp-wide): 64.8MM **Privately Held**
SIC: 2657 Folding paperboard boxes
PA: Disc Graphics, Inc.
10 Gilpin Ave
Hauppauge NY 11788
631 234-1400

(G-5812)
DISC GRAPHICS INC (PA)
10 Gilpin Ave (11788-4770)
PHONE..................631 234-1400
Donald Sinkin, *Ch of Bd*
Margaret Krumholz, *President*
Stephen Frey, *Senior VP*
John A Rebecchi, *Senior VP*
John Rebecchi, *Vice Pres*
▲ EMP: 215
SALES (est): 64.8MM **Privately Held**
WEB: www.discgraphics.com
SIC: 2657 Folding paperboard boxes

(G-5813)
DISPLAY LOGIC USA INC
40 Oser Ave Ste 4 (11788-3807)
PHONE..................631 406-1922
Keith Morton, *CEO*
Andrew Blum, *Partner*
EMP: 9 EST: 2012
SALES (est): 1.4MM **Privately Held**
SIC: 3823 Digital displays of process variables

(G-5814)
DOCTOR PRINT INC (PA)
Also Called: Dr Print
18 Commerce Dr Ste 1 (11788-3975)
PHONE..................631 873-4560
Mitch Cohen, *CEO*
Anthony Bulla, *Vice Pres*
Brendan Sweeney, *Executive*
Marilyn Kovol, *Administration*
EMP: 20
SQ FT: 4,000
SALES (est): 2.7MM **Privately Held**
SIC: 2759 Laser printing

(G-5815)
DRI RELAYS INC (HQ)
60 Commerce Dr (11788-3929)
PHONE..................631 342-1700
Michel Nespoulous, *President*
Steve Byun, *Project Mgr*
Tracy Gu, *Production*
Gary Smith, *Purch Mgr*
Phyllis Beatman, *Buyer*
▲ EMP: 100
SALES (est): 23.7MM **Privately Held**
SIC: 3625 Relays, for electronic use
PA: Financiere De Societes Techniques
17 Rue Vicq D Azir
Paris
142 039-420

(G-5816)
DRIVE SHAFT SHOP INC
210 Blydenburg Rd Unit A (11749-5022)
PHONE..................631 348-1818
Frank J Rehak III, *President*
EMP: 10
SQ FT: 1,600
SALES (est): 840K **Privately Held**
WEB: www.driveshaftshop.com
SIC: 3714 Drive shafts, motor vehicle; axle housings & shafts, motor vehicle; axles, motor vehicle; hydraulic fluid power pumps for auto steering mechanism

(G-5817)
EBC TECHNOLOGIES LLC
Also Called: Theautopartsshop.com
200 Motor Pkwy Ste D26 (11788-5116)
PHONE..................631 729-8182
Jay Talluri, *CEO*
EMP: 55
SALES: 5MM **Privately Held**
SIC: 3571 Electronic computers

(G-5818)
ELECTRONIC MACHINE PARTS LLC
Also Called: Emp
400 Oser Ave Ste 2000 (11788-3658)
PHONE..................631 434-3700
Tim McAdam, *Vice Pres*
Maureen McAdam, *Mng Member*
Maureen Ramert,
EMP: 13
SQ FT: 2,100
SALES (est): 3.1MM **Privately Held**
WEB: www.empregister.com
SIC: 3625 3823 3714 Control equipment, electric; industrial instrmnts msrmnt display/control process variable; motor vehicle parts & accessories

(G-5819)
ELECTRONIC PRINTING INC
1200 Prime Pl (11788-4761)
P.O. Box 1439, New York (10276-1439)
PHONE..................631 218-2200
John Kwiecinski, *President*
Eileen Abrams, *Office Mgr*
Paul Kwiecinski, *Shareholder*
EMP: 7
SQ FT: 9,000
SALES (est): 1.2MM **Privately Held**
WEB: www.epi-printing.com
SIC: 2752 Commercial printing, lithographic

(G-5820)
EMBASSY INDUSTRIES INC
Also Called: Franklin Manufacturing Div
315 Oser Ave Ste 1 (11788-3680)
PHONE..................631 435-0209
Robert Ramistella, *President*
Richard Horowitz, *Chairman*
Richard Cisek, *COO*
Jamie Nella, *Natl Sales Mgr*
▲ EMP: 170 EST: 1950
SQ FT: 75,000
SALES (est): 58.6MM
SALES (corp-wide): 58.9MM **Publicly Held**
WEB: www.embassyind.com
SIC: 3433 1711 3567 Heating equipment, except electric; plumbing, heating, air-conditioning contractors; industrial furnaces & ovens
PA: P & F Industries, Inc.
445 Broadhollow Rd # 100
Melville NY 11747
631 694-9800

(G-5821)
ET OAKES CORPORATION
686 Old Willets Path (11788-4102)
PHONE..................631 232-0002
W Peter Oakes, *Ch of Bd*
Noel Oakes, *Corp Secy*
Robert Peck, *Vice Pres*
EMP: 20
SQ FT: 25,000
SALES (est): 5.2MM **Privately Held**
WEB: www.oakes.com
SIC: 3556 3531 5084 3599 Cutting, chopping, grinding, mixing & similar machinery; construction machinery; food product manufacturing machinery; machine shop, jobbing & repair

(G-5822)
F & T GRAPHICS INC
690 Old Willets Path (11788-4102)
PHONE..................631 643-1000
John M Leone, *President*
EMP: 17
SQ FT: 15,000
SALES (est): 4.3MM **Privately Held**
SIC: 2752 Commercial printing, offset

(G-5823)
FB LABORATORIES INC
Also Called: Futurebiotics
70 Commerce Dr (11788-3962)
PHONE..................631 750-0000
Saiful Kibria, *President*
▲ EMP: 50 EST: 2010
SALES (est): 9.9MM **Privately Held**
SIC: 2834 Vitamin preparations

(G-5824)
FINISH LINE TECHNOLOGIES INC (PA)
50 Wireless Blvd (11788-3954)
PHONE..................631 666-7300
Henry J Krause, *President*
◆ EMP: 28
SQ FT: 60,000
SALES: 11.3MM **Privately Held**
SIC: 2992 Lubricating oils & greases

(G-5825)
FIXTURES 2000 INC
Also Called: Premier Store Fixtures
400 Oser Ave Ste 350 (11788-3632)
P.O. Box 14177 (11788-0401)
PHONE..................631 236-4100
Jose Tellez, *President*
Oswaldo Zurita, *Senior VP*
Nelson Goodman, *Vice Pres*
◆ EMP: 280
SQ FT: 230,978
SALES (est): 67.2MM **Privately Held**
WEB: www.premierfixtures.com
SIC: 2542 Fixtures, store: except wood

Hauppauge - Suffolk County (G-5826)

(G-5826)
FLUID MECHANISMS HAUPPAUGE INC
225 Engineers Rd (11788-4020)
PHONE..................................631 234-0100
Richard Coronato, *President*
Charlotte Coronato, *Corp Secy*
EMP: 35 **EST:** 1962
SQ FT: 44,000
SALES (est): 9.8MM **Privately Held**
SIC: 3728 Aircraft parts & equipment

(G-5827)
FORECAST CONSOLES INC
681 Old Willets Path (11788-4109)
PHONE..................................631 253-9000
William Haberman, *President*
V Decesare, *Prdtn Mgr*
Janet Haberman, *CFO*
Ryan Haberman, *Sales Staff*
▲ **EMP:** 24
SQ FT: 21,000
SALES (est): 3.7MM **Privately Held**
WEB: www.forecast-consoles.com
SIC: 2511 2531 2521 2541 Console tables: wood; public building & related furniture; wood office furniture; shelving, office & store, wood; office furniture, except wood

(G-5828)
FOREST LABORATORIES LLC
45 Adams Ave (11788-3605)
PHONE..................................212 421-7850
Elaine Hochberg, *Branch Mgr*
EMP: 54 **Privately Held**
WEB: www.frx.com
SIC: 2834 Mfg Pharmaceutical Preparations
HQ: Forest Laboratories, Llc
909 3rd Ave Fl 23
New York NY 10022
212 421-7850

(G-5829)
FUNGILAB INC
89 Cabot Ct Ste K (11788-3719)
PHONE..................................631 750-6361
Ernest Buira, *CEO*
Joan Buira, *President*
◆ **EMP:** 5
SQ FT: 10,000
SALES: 1MM
SALES (corp-wide): 3MM **Privately Held**
SIC: 3821 Laboratory apparatus & furniture
PA: Fungi Lab Sa
Calle Constitucio (Pg Ind Les Grases),
64 - Nave 15
Sant Feliu De Llobregat 08980
936 853-500

(G-5830)
FUTUREBIOTICS LLC
70 Commerce Dr (11788-3936)
PHONE..................................631 273-6300
Steve Welling, *COO*
Steve Tuohey, *Research*
Michelle Coscia, *Controller*
Bob Weinstein, *VP Sales*
Saiful Kaibria, *Mng Member*
▲ **EMP:** 25
SALES (est): 5.8MM **Privately Held**
WEB: www.futurebiotics.com
SIC: 2834 Medicines, capsuled or ampuled

(G-5831)
GENERAL SEMICONDUCTOR INC
150 Motor Pkwy Ste 101 (11788-5167)
PHONE..................................631 300-3818
Linda Perry, *Executive*
EMP: 6 **EST:** 2015
SALES (est): 313.3K **Privately Held**
SIC: 3674 Semiconductors & related devices

(G-5832)
GENERIC PHARMACEUTICAL SVCS
Also Called: Gpsi
1324 Motor Pkwy Ste 114 (11749-5226)
PHONE..................................631 348-6900
Harold Grossman, *President*
James Hassenfeld, *Corp Secy*
▲ **EMP:** 38
SQ FT: 20,000
SALES (est): 6.7MM **Privately Held**
WEB: www.poucher.com
SIC: 2834 Pharmaceutical preparations

(G-5833)
GEOSYNC MICROWAVE INC
320 Oser Ave (11788-3608)
PHONE..................................631 760-5567
Arthur Faverio, *President*
Stephen Philips, *Vice Pres*
Tim Jahn, *Engineer*
Israel Moskovitch, *Engineer*
M Zahidi, *Engineer*
EMP: 5
SQ FT: 4,000
SALES (est): 950K **Privately Held**
WEB: www.geosyncmicrowave.com
SIC: 3663 Satellites, communications

(G-5834)
GES GES
89 Cabot Ct Ste A (11788-3719)
PHONE..................................631 291-9624
EMP: 5
SALES (est): 604.7K **Privately Held**
SIC: 2834 Liniments

(G-5835)
GLARO INC
735 Calebs Path Ste 1 (11788-4201)
PHONE..................................631 234-1717
Neal Glass, *President*
Robert Betensky, *Exec VP*
Kerry Betensky, *Treasurer*
Lin Hou, *Admin Asst*
Andrea Perry, *Representative*
▲ **EMP:** 60 **EST:** 1945
SQ FT: 50,000
SALES (est): 9.6MM **Privately Held**
WEB: www.glaro.com
SIC: 2542 Office & store showcases & display fixtures

(G-5836)
GOURMET FACTORY INC
55 Corporate Dr (11788-2021)
PHONE..................................631 231-4548
Andromahi Kangadis, *Owner*
Andrew Marsano, *Director*
EMP: 5
SALES (est): 110.5K **Privately Held**
SIC: 2079 Cooking oils, except corn: vegetable refined

(G-5837)
GSE COMPOSITES INC
110 Oser Ave (11788-3820)
P.O. Box 13248 (11788-0593)
PHONE..................................631 389-1300
EMP: 14
SALES (est): 1.9MM **Privately Held**
SIC: 3089 Mfg Plastic Products

(G-5838)
HAIG PRESS INC
Also Called: Haig Graphic Communications
690 Old Willets Path (11788-4102)
PHONE..................................631 582-5800
James Kalousdian, *Ch of Bd*
Steve Kalousdian, *Vice Pres*
EMP: 44
SQ FT: 30,000
SALES (est): 7.3MM **Privately Held**
WEB: www.haiggraphic.com
SIC: 2752 2789 2759 Commercial printing, offset; bookbinding & related work; commercial printing

(G-5839)
HALLMARK HLTH CARE SLTIONS LLC
200 Motor Pkwy Ste D26 (11788-5116)
PHONE..................................516 513-0959
Isaac Ullatil, *CEO*
William Reau, *Officer*
Shiv Prakash Bidlur,
Jayasekhar Talluri,
EMP: 10
SQ FT: 2,400
SALES (est): 3MM **Privately Held**
SIC: 7372 Prepackaged software

(G-5840)
HARMONIC DRIVE LLC
89 Cabot Ct Ste A (11788-3719)
PHONE..................................631 231-6630
Douglas Olson, *President*
EMP: 6
SALES (corp-wide): 510MM **Privately Held**
WEB: www.harmonic-drive.com
SIC: 3566 Speed changers, drives & gears
HQ: Harmonic Drive L.L.C.
247 Lynnfield St
Peabody MA 01960

(G-5841)
HAUPPAUGE COMPUTER WORKS INC (HQ)
Also Called: Hauppuge Cmpt Dgtal Erope Sarl
909 Motor Pkwy (11788-5250)
PHONE..................................631 434-1600
Kenneth Plotkin, *Ch of Bd*
Gerald Tucciarone, *CFO*
Charlie Hynes, *Supervisor*
Kim Wild, *CTO*
▲ **EMP:** 25
SQ FT: 85,000
SALES (est): 9MM **Publicly Held**
WEB: www.happage.com
SIC: 3577 7371 Computer peripheral equipment; custom computer programming services

(G-5842)
HAUPPAUGE DIGITAL INC (PA)
909 Motor Pkwy (11788-5250)
PHONE..................................631 434-1600
Kenneth Plotkin, *Ch of Bd*
John Casey, *President*
Yehia Oweiss, *VP Sls/Mktg*
Gerald Tucciarone, *CFO*
Cheryl Willins, *Controller*
▲ **EMP:** 28
SALES (est): 34MM **Publicly Held**
WEB: www.hauppauge.com
SIC: 3577 Computer peripheral equipment

(G-5843)
HAWK-I SECURITY INC
355 Oser Ave (11788-3607)
P.O. Box 672, Smithtown (11787-0672)
PHONE..................................631 656-1056
Joseph Smith, *CEO*
Eric Foreman, *Vice Pres*
Doug Miller, *CFO*
◆ **EMP:** 5
SQ FT: 1,000
SALES (est): 448.9K **Privately Held**
WEB: www.hawkisecurity.com
SIC: 3699 Security devices

(G-5844)
HI-TRON SEMICONDUCTOR CORP
85 Engineers Rd (11788-4003)
PHONE..................................631 231-1500
Mel Lax, *President*
Mindy Lax, *Admin Sec*
EMP: 20 **EST:** 1964
SQ FT: 42,000
SALES (est): 1.4MM **Privately Held**
SIC: 3674 Semiconductors & related devices

(G-5845)
HILORD CHEMICAL CORPORATION
70 Engineers Rd (11788-4076)
PHONE..................................631 234-7373
Donald Balbinder, *President*
Cody Sickle, *Vice Pres*
Shawnee Sicke, *Treasurer*
Rommel Gloria, *Manager*
Michael Lani, *Information Mgr*
▲ **EMP:** 26 **EST:** 1970
SQ FT: 37,000
SALES (est): 6.3MM **Privately Held**
WEB: www.hilord.com
SIC: 3861 2822 3479 Toners, prepared photographic (not made in chemical plants); ethylene-propylene rubbers, EPDM polymers; coating electrodes

(G-5846)
HOHMANN & BARNARD INC (DH)
30 Rasons Ct (11788-4206)
P.O. Box 5270 (11788-0270)
PHONE..................................631 234-0600
Ronald P Hohmann, *Principal*
Christopher Hohmann, *Treasurer*
Joseph C Carr, *Director*
Gene Toombs, *Director*
◆ **EMP:** 25
SQ FT: 55,000
SALES (est): 43.4MM
SALES (corp-wide): 242.1B **Publicly Held**
WEB: www.foamfiller.com
SIC: 3496 3462 3315 Clips & fasteners, made from purchased wire; iron & steel forgings; steel wire & related products
HQ: Mitek Industries, Inc.
16023 Swinly Rdg
Chesterfield MO 63017
314 434-1200

(G-5847)
HUCKLEBERRY INC
Also Called: Minuteman Press
655 Old Willets Path (11788-4105)
PHONE..................................631 630-5450
Robin Eschenberg, *President*
Hayley Eschenberg, *Managing Prtnr*
EMP: 6
SALES (est): 1.1MM **Privately Held**
SIC: 2752 Commercial printing, lithographic

(G-5848)
ICONIX INC
40 Oser Ave Ste 4 (11788-3807)
PHONE..................................516 513-1420
Jacob Kohn, *Ch of Bd*
Steve Molstad, *QC Mgr*
James Scanlan, *Sales Executive*
Yaffa Kahan, *Info Tech Mgr*
EMP: 18
SQ FT: 6,200
SALES (est): 9.1MM **Privately Held**
SIC: 3699 5065 Electrical equipment & supplies; electronic parts & equipment

(G-5849)
INNOVATIVE LABS LLC
85 Commerce Dr (11788-3902)
PHONE..................................631 231-5522
Frank Amelio Sr, *CEO*
Frank D Amelio Jr, *President*
Ahsanul Aziz, *Purch Mgr*
EMP: 60
SQ FT: 25,000
SALES: 10MM **Privately Held**
WEB: www.innovativelabsny.com
SIC: 2834 Tablets, pharmaceutical; medicines, capsuled or ampuled

(G-5850)
INNOVATIVE VIDEO TECH INC
Also Called: Invid Tech
355 Oser Ave (11788-3607)
PHONE..................................631 388-5700
Joe Troiano, *President*
Lou Giannizzero, *Accounts Mgr*
EMP: 13
SQ FT: 10,000
SALES (est): 1.3MM **Privately Held**
SIC: 3699 Security control equipment & systems

(G-5851)
INVAGEN PHARMACEUTICALS INC (DH)
7 Oser Ave Ste 4 (11788-3811)
PHONE..................................631 231-3233
Sudhakar Vidiyala, *President*
Madhava U Reddy, *COO*
Amina Ali, *Human Res Mgr*
Bala Vattikuti, *Manager*
▲ **EMP:** 330
SQ FT: 150,000
SALES (est): 129MM **Privately Held**
SIC: 2834 5122 Pharmaceutical preparations; pharmaceuticals

GEOGRAPHIC SECTION

Hauppauge - Suffolk County (G-5877)

(G-5852)
J & M PACKAGING INC
Also Called: Baron Packaging
21 Newton Rd (11788-1646)
P.O. Box 5783 (11788-0164)
PHONE..................631 608-3069
Melissa Vincente, CEO
John Vincente, Vice Pres
EMP: 10
SQ FT: 7,500
SALES (est): 162.8K Privately Held
SIC: 2653 2449 3086 Boxes, corrugated: made from purchased materials; rectangular boxes & crates, wood; plastics foam products

(G-5853)
JACK MERKEL INC
1720 Express Dr S (11788-5302)
PHONE..................631 234-2600
Jack Merkel, President
Scott Merkel, General Mgr
EMP: 5
SQ FT: 6,000
SALES: 800K Privately Held
SIC: 3599 7538 Machine shop, jobbing & repair; engine repair; engine rebuilding: automotive

(G-5854)
JOSH PACKAGING INC
245 Marcus Blvd Ste 1 (11788-2000)
PHONE..................631 822-1660
Abraham Golshirazian, Ch of Bd
Abe Gulsh, President
Nejat Rahmani, Vice Pres
▲ EMP: 20
SQ FT: 30,000
SALES (est): 5MM Privately Held
SIC: 2673 5113 5162 Plastic bags: made from purchased materials; industrial & personal service paper; plastics materials

(G-5855)
KILTRONX ENVIRO SYSTEMS LLC
330 Motor Pkwy Ste 201 (11788-5118)
PHONE..................917 971-7177
Gabriel Kaszovitz,
Arlen Cabale,
EMP: 30
SQ FT: 1,500
SALES (est): 9MM Privately Held
SIC: 2295 Chemically coated & treated fabrics

(G-5856)
KINGS PARK ASPHALT CORPORATION
201 Moreland Rd Ste 2 (11788-3922)
PHONE..................631 269-9774
Michael Farino, President
James Farino, Corp Secy
Paul Farino, Vice Pres
EMP: 5
SQ FT: 1,000
SALES (est): 649.2K Privately Held
SIC: 2951 Asphalt paving blocks (not from refineries)

(G-5857)
KLD LABS INC
55 Cabot Ct (11788-3717)
PHONE..................631 549-4222
Steven Magnus, President
Bob Bencivenga, Project Mgr
Marc Wegel, Project Mgr
Bettye Stephens, Purch Mgr
Kevin Koestner, Engineer
EMP: 40
SQ FT: 20,000
SALES (est): 9.4MM Privately Held
WEB: www.kldlabs.com
SIC: 3829 7373 Measuring & controlling devices; computer integrated systems design

(G-5858)
L3 TECHNOLOGIES INC
Narda-Miteq Division
435 Moreland Rd (11788-3926)
PHONE..................631 231-1700
Joe Merenda, President
John Mega, Division Pres
Tim Fowler, Vice Pres

John H Reilly, Purchasing
Todd Zubris, Engineer
EMP: 300
SALES (corp-wide): 9.5B Publicly Held
SIC: 3663 Telemetering equipment, electronic
PA: L3 Technologies, Inc.
600 3rd Ave Fl 34
New York NY 10016
212 697-1111

(G-5859)
L3 TECHNOLOGIES INC
Also Called: L-3 Narda-Miteq
100 Davids Dr (11788-2043)
PHONE..................631 436-7400
Steven Skpock, President
EMP: 700
SALES (corp-wide): 9.5B Publicly Held
SIC: 3663 3769 3661 3651 Radio & TV communications equipment; guided missile & space vehicle parts & auxiliary equipment; telephone & telegraph apparatus; household audio & video equipment; current-carrying wiring devices
PA: L3 Technologies, Inc.
600 3rd Ave Fl 34
New York NY 10016
212 697-1111

(G-5860)
L3 TECHNOLOGIES INC
435 Moreland Rd (11788-3926)
PHONE..................631 231-3994
EMP: 9
SALES (corp-wide): 9.5B Publicly Held
SIC: 3812 Search & navigation equipment
PA: L3 Technologies, Inc.
600 3rd Ave Fl 34
New York NY 10016
212 697-1111

(G-5861)
L3 TECHNOLOGIES INC
Also Called: Narda Satellite Networks
435 Moreland Rd (11788-3926)
PHONE..................631 231-1700
Margaret Pawelko, Administration
EMP: 100
SQ FT: 60,000
SALES (corp-wide): 9.5B Publicly Held
SIC: 3663 8748 5731 Telemetering equipment, electronic; communications consulting; antennas, satellite dish
PA: L3 Technologies, Inc.
600 3rd Ave Fl 34
New York NY 10016
212 697-1111

(G-5862)
L3 TECHNOLOGIES INC
Also Called: L-3 Narda-Miteq
330 Oser Ave (11788-3630)
PHONE..................631 436-7400
Aksel Kiiss, Manager
EMP: 100
SALES (corp-wide): 9.5B Publicly Held
SIC: 3663 Radio broadcasting & communications equipment
PA: L3 Technologies, Inc.
600 3rd Ave Fl 34
New York NY 10016
212 697-1111

(G-5863)
LA FLOR PRODUCTS COMPANY INC (PA)
Also Called: La Flor Spices
25 Hoffman Ave (11788-4717)
PHONE..................631 851-9601
Ruben La Torre Sr, President
Dan La Torre, Exec VP
Ruben La Torre Jr, Vice Pres
Chris Pappas, Vice Pres
▲ EMP: 44
SQ FT: 90,000
SALES: 9MM Privately Held
WEB: www.laflor.com
SIC: 2099 Seasonings & spices; seasonings: dry mixes

(G-5864)
LEHNEIS ORTHOTICS PROSTHETIC
517 Route 111 Ste 300 (11788-4338)
PHONE..................516 790-1897

Alfred Lehneis, President
EMP: 9
SALES (corp-wide): 5MM Privately Held
WEB: www.lehneis.com
SIC: 3842 5047 5999 Limbs, artificial; medical equipment & supplies; artificial limbs
PA: Lehneis Orthotics & Prosthetic Associates Ltd
13 Bedells Landing Rd
Roslyn NY
516 621-7277

(G-5865)
LISTEC VIDEO CORP (PA)
90 Oser Ave (11788-3800)
PHONE..................631 273-3029
William J Littler, Ch of Bd
Joanne Camarda, President
Raymond Blumenthal, Vice Pres
EMP: 5
SQ FT: 3,000
SALES (est): 450.1K Privately Held
WEB: www.listecny.com
SIC: 3663 5099 Radio & TV communications equipment; video & audio equipment

(G-5866)
LIVING WELL INNOVATIONS INC
115 Engineers Rd (11788-4005)
PHONE..................646 517-3200
Arthur Danziger, President
EMP: 6
SQ FT: 4,000
SALES (est): 4MM Privately Held
SIC: 2731 5192 Book publishing; books

(G-5867)
LNK INTERNATIONAL INC
22 Arkay Dr (11788-3708)
PHONE..................631 435-3500
EMP: 100
SALES (corp-wide): 105.4MM Privately Held
SIC: 2834 Pharmaceutical preparations
PA: L.N.K. International Inc.
60 Arkay Dr
Hauppauge NY 11788
631 435-3500

(G-5868)
LNK INTERNATIONAL INC
100 Ricefield Ln (11788-2008)
PHONE..................631 435-3500
Chudgar Pk, Manager
EMP: 100
SALES (corp-wide): 105.4MM Privately Held
SIC: 2834 Pharmaceutical preparations
PA: L.N.K. International Inc.
60 Arkay Dr
Hauppauge NY 11788
631 435-3500

(G-5869)
LNK INTERNATIONAL INC
325 Kennedy Dr (11788-4006)
PHONE..................631 435-3500
Joseph J Mollica, President
EMP: 100
SALES (corp-wide): 105.4MM Privately Held
SIC: 2834 Pharmaceutical preparations
PA: L.N.K. International Inc.
60 Arkay Dr
Hauppauge NY 11788
631 435-3500

(G-5870)
LNK INTERNATIONAL INC
145 Ricefield Ln (11788-2007)
PHONE..................631 543-3787
Pk Chudgar, Manager
EMP: 100
SALES (corp-wide): 105.4MM Privately Held
SIC: 2834 Pharmaceutical preparations
PA: L.N.K. International Inc.
60 Arkay Dr
Hauppauge NY 11788
631 435-3500

(G-5871)
LNK INTERNATIONAL INC
40 Arkay Dr (11788-3708)
PHONE..................631 435-3500

Shaji Kumar Varghese, Branch Mgr
EMP: 100
SALES (corp-wide): 105.4MM Privately Held
SIC: 2834 Pharmaceutical preparations
PA: L.N.K. International Inc.
60 Arkay Dr
Hauppauge NY 11788
631 435-3500

(G-5872)
LNK INTERNATIONAL INC
55 Arkay Dr (11788-3707)
PHONE..................631 231-4020
Joseph J Mollica Sr, Branch Mgr
EMP: 100
SALES (corp-wide): 105.4MM Privately Held
SIC: 2834 Pharmaceutical preparations
PA: L.N.K. International Inc.
60 Arkay Dr
Hauppauge NY 11788
631 435-3500

(G-5873)
LOURDES INDUSTRIES INC (PA)
65 Hoffman Ave (11788-4798)
PHONE..................631 234-6600
William J Jakobsen, Ch of Bd
Bruce Jacobson, President
Peter McKenna, Vice Pres
Paul Vaughan, Opers Mgr
Douglas Benzenuto, Purch Agent
EMP: 90 EST: 1954
SQ FT: 26,000
SALES (est): 21.4MM Privately Held
SIC: 3795 3492 3643 3724 Tanks & tank components; fluid power valves & hose fittings; current-carrying wiring devices; aircraft engines & engine parts; engineering services

(G-5874)
LOURDES SYSTEMS INC
21 Newton Pl (11788-4815)
PHONE..................631 234-7077
George Powell, Ch of Bd
Peter Maguire, President
George Meyerle, Vice Pres
Peter McKenna, Treasurer
EMP: 12
SQ FT: 5,000
SALES (est): 1.3MM Privately Held
SIC: 3542 Machine tools, metal forming type

(G-5875)
M&C ASSOCIATES LLC
700 Vets Memrl Hwy 335 (11788)
PHONE..................631 467-8760
Lou Marianacci, President
Leanora Gordon, Principal
Karen Ferraro, Vice Pres
Joseph Cutillo, Engineer
Kelly Palacios, Sales Dir
EMP: 40
SALES (est): 6.9MM Privately Held
SIC: 3571 Electronic computers

(G-5876)
MACHINERY MOUNTINGS INC
41 Sarah Dr (11788)
PHONE..................631 851-0480
Bernard H Kass, President
Steven Kass, Vice Pres
Wayne Kass, Vice Pres
EMP: 14
SALES (est): 1.6MM Privately Held
SIC: 3499 Machine bases, metal

(G-5877)
MAGGIO DATA FORMS
1735 Express Dr S (11788)
PHONE..................631 348-0343
Robert Maggio, President
James Maggio, Vice Pres
EMP: 110
SQ FT: 30,000
SALES (est): 16MM Privately Held
WEB: www.maggio.com
SIC: 2761 Manifold business forms

Hauppauge - Suffolk County (G-5878)

(G-5878)
MAKAMAH ENTERPRISES INC
Also Called: S.W.H. Precision Industries
89 Cabot Ct Ste C (11788-3719)
PHONE................................631 231-0200
Christopher J Thomas, *President*
▲ EMP: 10
SALES (est): 1.2MM **Privately Held**
SIC: 3599 Machine shop, jobbing & repair

(G-5879)
MAKERS NUTRITION LLC (PA)
315 Oser Ave Ste 3 (11788-3680)
PHONE................................631 456-5397
Jason Provenzano, *President*
Stephen Finnegan, *Senior VP*
EMP: 25 EST: 2014
SALES: 25MM **Privately Held**
SIC: 2834 Pharmaceutical preparations

(G-5880)
MANHATTAN SHADE & GLASS CO INC
135 Ricefield Ln (11788-2046)
PHONE................................212 288-5616
EMP: 35
SALES (corp-wide): 6.2MM **Privately Held**
WEB: www.manhattanshade.com
SIC: 3231 3211 2591 Products of purchased glass; window glass, clear & colored; shade, curtain & drapery hardware
PA: Manhattan Shade & Glass Co. Inc.
  37 Pond Park Rd
  Great Neck NY 11023
  212 288-5616

(G-5881)
MASON INDUSTRIES INC (PA)
Also Called: M I
350 Rabro Dr (11788-4237)
P.O. Box 410, Smithtown (11787-0410)
PHONE................................631 348-0282
Norm Mason, *Ch of Bd*
Patrick Lama, *Vice Pres*
Doug Valerio, *Vice Pres*
Armando Gamble, *Safety Mgr*
Jenny King, *Purchasing*
◆ EMP: 350 EST: 1958
SQ FT: 60,000
SALES (est): 64.7MM **Privately Held**
WEB: www.mercer-rubber.com
SIC: 3625 3829 3052 3069 Noise control equipment; measuring & controlling devices; rubber hose; hard rubber & molded rubber products; fabricated structural metal; electronic connectors

(G-5882)
MASON INDUSTRIES INC
33 Ranick Rd Ste 1 (11788-4250)
PHONE................................631 348-0282
Patricia Gowicki, *Manager*
EMP: 7
SALES (corp-wide): 64.7MM **Privately Held**
SIC: 3625 Noise control equipment
PA: Mason Industries, Inc.
  350 Rabro Dr
  Hauppauge NY 11788
  631 348-0282

(G-5883)
MCKEE FOODS CORPORATION
111 Serene Pl (11788-3534)
PHONE................................631 979-9364
John Meyer, *Branch Mgr*
EMP: 609
SALES (corp-wide): 1.7B **Privately Held**
WEB: www.mckeefoods.com
SIC: 2051 Cakes, bakery: except frozen
PA: Mckee Foods Corporation
  10260 Mckee Rd
  Collegedale TN 37315
  423 238-7111

(G-5884)
MEDICAL ACTION INDUSTRIES INC
150 Motor Pkwy Ste 205 (11788-5180)
PHONE................................631 231-4600
Paul Meringola, *Manager*
EMP: 215 **Publicly Held**
WEB: www.medical-action.com
SIC: 3842 4226 5999 5047 Sponges, surgical; sterilizers, hospital & surgical; surgical appliances & supplies; special warehousing & storage; medical apparatus & supplies; hospital equipment & furniture
HQ: Medical Action Industries Inc.
  25 Heywood Rd
  Arden NC 28704
  631 231-4600

(G-5885)
MELLAND GEAR INSTR OF HUPPAUGE
225 Engineers Rd (11788-4020)
PHONE................................631 234-0100
Richard Coronato Sr, *CEO*
Richard C Coronato, *CEO*
Charlotte Coronato, *Admin Sec*
EMP: 35 EST: 1959
SQ FT: 44,000
SALES (est): 5.7MM **Privately Held**
SIC: 3824 3545 Mechanical counters; precision tools, machinists'

(G-5886)
MERCER RUBBER CO
350 Rabro Dr (11788-4257)
PHONE................................631 348-0282
Norman J Mason, *President*
Mary P Ryan, *Corp Secy*
Pat Lama, *Vice Pres*
▲ EMP: 150 EST: 1866
SQ FT: 60,000
SALES (est): 20.6MM
SALES (corp-wide): 64.7MM **Privately Held**
WEB: www.mercer-rubber.com
SIC: 3069 3052 Expansion joints, rubber; rubber hose
PA: Mason Industries, Inc.
  350 Rabro Dr
  Hauppauge NY 11788
  631 348-0282

(G-5887)
MERGENCE STUDIOS LTD
135 Ricefield Ln (11788-2046)
PHONE................................212 288-5616
▲ EMP: 12
SALES (est): 1.5MM **Privately Held**
SIC: 2241 Narrow Fabric Mill Misc Personal Services

(G-5888)
METAL DYNAMICS INTL CORP
Also Called: Mdi
25 Corporate Dr (11788-2021)
P.O. Box 13248 (11788-0593)
PHONE................................631 231-1153
Daniel Shybunko, *President*
Anne D Shybunko-Moore, *President*
Tim Austin, *Vice Pres*
Tom Scully, *Sales Mgr*
◆ EMP: 5
SQ FT: 28,600
SALES (est): 892.7K **Privately Held**
WEB: www.metaldynamicsintl.com
SIC: 3728 Aircraft parts & equipment

(G-5889)
MICROCAD TRNING CONSULTING INC
77 Arkay Dr Ste C2 (11788-3742)
PHONE................................631 291-9484
Michael F Frey, *Branch Mgr*
EMP: 7 **Privately Held**
SIC: 7372 Prepackaged software
PA: Microcad Training & Consulting, Inc.
  440 Arsenal St Ste 3
  Watertown MA

(G-5890)
MICROCHIP TECHNOLOGY INC
80 Arkay Dr Ste 100 (11788-3705)
PHONE................................631 233-3280
Daniel Thornton, *Engineer*
Dan Levesser, *Manager*
Marco Forcone, *Senior Mgr*
EMP: 6
SALES (corp-wide): 3.9B **Publicly Held**
WEB: www.microchip.com
SIC: 3674 Microcircuits, integrated (semiconductor)
PA: Microchip Technology Inc
  2355 W Chandler Blvd
  Chandler AZ 85224
  480 792-7200

(G-5891)
MICROSOFT CORPORATION
2929 Expressway Dr N # 300 (11749-5302)
PHONE................................516 380-1531
Brett Tanzer, *Manager*
EMP: 100
SALES (corp-wide): 110.3B **Publicly Held**
WEB: www.microsoft.com
SIC: 7372 Application computer software
PA: Microsoft Corporation
  1 Microsoft Way
  Redmond WA 98052
  425 882-8080

(G-5892)
MILSO INDUSTRIES INC
25 Engineers Rd (11788-4019)
PHONE................................631 234-1133
Al Orsi, *Branch Mgr*
EMP: 12
SQ FT: 10,000
SALES (corp-wide): 1.5B **Publicly Held**
SIC: 3995 5087 Burial caskets; caskets
HQ: Milso Industries Inc.
  534 Union St
  Brooklyn NY 11215
  718 624-4593

(G-5893)
MINI GRAPHICS INC
Also Called: Mgi
140 Commerce Dr (11788-3948)
PHONE................................516 223-6464
James Delise, *CEO*
Charles J Delise, *Principal*
Steven Delise, *Principal*
Mark Dlhopolsky, *Project Mgr*
Jerry Clark, *QA Dir*
EMP: 100
SALES (est): 23.3MM **Privately Held**
WEB: www.minigraphics.net
SIC: 2759 Commercial printing

(G-5894)
MMC ENTERPRISES CORP
175 Commerce Dr Ste E (11788-3920)
PHONE................................800 435-1088
Jin Sun, *President*
▲ EMP: 8
SALES (est): 972.6K **Privately Held**
SIC: 3826 Instruments measuring magnetic & electrical properties

(G-5895)
MMC MAGNETICS CORP
175 Commerce Dr Ste E (11788-3920)
PHONE................................631 435-9888
Huai Sheu Zhou, *Ch of Bd*
EMP: 17
SALES (est): 1.4MM **Privately Held**
SIC: 3674 3499 Photoelectric magnetic devices; magnets, permanent: metallic

(G-5896)
MOBILE FLEET INC (PA)
10 Commerce Dr (11788-3968)
P.O. Box 1240, Farmingdale (11735-0855)
PHONE................................631 206-2920
Robert E Squicciarini Sr, *CEO*
Jennifer Clark, *Principal*
Kevin Walker, *Vice Pres*
Matt Tannenbaum, *CFO*
Daniel Bittner, *Cust Mgr*
▼ EMP: 8
SQ FT: 16,500
SALES: 15MM **Privately Held**
SIC: 3647 Automotive lighting fixtures

(G-5897)
MONITOR ELEVATOR PRODUCTS LLC
Also Called: Monitor Controls
125 Ricefield Ln (11788-2007)
PHONE................................631 543-4334
Paul Horney, *President*
Steve Goldberg, *General Mgr*
Kathryn Byszewski, *Vice Pres*
Louise Russo, *Purchasing*
Osmond Koksal, *Engineer*
▲ EMP: 65 EST: 2011
SQ FT: 30,000
SALES (est): 16.6MM
SALES (corp-wide): 22.6MM **Privately Held**
WEB: www.mcontrols.com
SIC: 3534 Elevators & equipment
PA: Innovation Industries, Inc.
  3500 E Main St
  Russellville AR 72802
  800 843-1004

(G-5898)
MULTIFOLD DIE CTNG FINSHG CORP
120 Ricefield Ln Ste B (11788-2033)
PHONE................................631 232-1235
William Collins, *Ch of Bd*
Christine Collins, *President*
EMP: 5
SALES (est): 561.8K **Privately Held**
SIC: 3544 Special dies & tools

(G-5899)
NATUS MEDICAL INCORPORATED
Also Called: Neometrics
150 Motor Pkwy Ste 106 (11788-5167)
PHONE................................631 457-4430
Joe Amato, *Principal*
Doni Antonelli, *Project Mgr*
Christina Rossi, *Consultant*
EMP: 8
SALES (corp-wide): 500.9MM **Publicly Held**
SIC: 3845 Electromedical equipment
PA: Natus Medical Incorporated
  6701 Koll Center Pkwy # 120
  Pleasanton CA 94566
  925 223-6700

(G-5900)
NEOPOST USA INC
415 Oser Ave Ste K (11788-3637)
PHONE................................631 435-9100
Joanne Lafrance, *Principal*
Chris Jensen, *Executive*
EMP: 50
SALES (corp-wide): 53.4MM **Privately Held**
SIC: 3579 7359 7629 Postage meters; business machine & electronic equipment rental services; business machine repair, electric
HQ: Neopost Usa Inc.
  478 Wheelers Farms Rd
  Milford CT 06461
  203 301-3400

(G-5901)
NEW HORIZON GRAPHICS INC
1200 Prime Pl (11788-4761)
PHONE................................631 231-8055
Anthony Guida, *Chairman*
Paul Santos, *Mfg Mgr*
Annette Guida, *Treasurer*
EMP: 45
SQ FT: 25,000
SALES (est): 10.4MM **Privately Held**
WEB: www.newhorizongraphic.com
SIC: 2752 2675 Commercial printing, offset; cards, folders & mats: die-cut

(G-5902)
NOVA SCIENCE PUBLISHERS INC
400 Oser Ave Ste 1600 (11788-3667)
PHONE................................631 231-7269
Frank Columbus, *President*
Nadya Columbus, *General Mgr*
Nadezhda Columbus, *Vice Pres*
Nese Kaya, *Marketing Staff*
Gaff Pierre, *Marketing Staff*
EMP: 12
SQ FT: 1,500
SALES (est): 1.7MM **Privately Held**
SIC: 2721 2731 Magazines: publishing only, not printed on site; book publishing

(G-5903)
NUBIAN HERITAGE
367 Old Willets Path (11788-1217)
PHONE................................631 265-3551
Edwin McCray, *Owner*
EMP: 5

SALES (est): 274.2K Privately Held
SIC: 3999 5199 Fire extinguishers, portable; gifts & novelties

(G-5904)
OLAN LABORATORIES INC
Also Called: Prolocksusa
20 Newton Pl (11788-4752)
PHONE.................................631 582-2082
Maurice Gregory Minuto, President
Lisa Minuto, Vice Pres
EMP: 9
SQ FT: 20,000
SALES: 1.7MM Privately Held
SIC: 2844 Cosmetic preparations; hair preparations, including shampoos

(G-5905)
OLDCASTLE BUILDINGENVELOPE INC
895 Motor Pkwy (11788-5232)
P.O. Box 18039 (11788-8839)
PHONE.................................631 234-2200
Daniel Dahill, Branch Mgr
EMP: 125
SALES (corp-wide): 29.7B Privately Held
WEB: www.crh.ie
SIC: 3231 5231 Tempered glass: made from purchased glass; insulating glass: made from purchased glass; glass
HQ: Oldcastle Buildingenvelope, Inc.
5005 Lndn B Jnsn Fwy 10
Dallas TX 75244
214 273-3400

(G-5906)
OLYMPIC MANUFACTURING INC
195 Marcus Blvd (11788-3702)
PHONE.................................631 231-8900
Donald Molloy Jr. President
EMP: 20
SQ FT: 6,000
SALES (est): 2.1MM Privately Held
SIC: 3444 Sheet metalwork

(G-5907)
ORBIT INTERNATIONAL CORP (PA)
80 Cabot Ct (11788-3771)
PHONE.................................631 435-8300
Mitchell Binder, President
David Goldman, CFO
John Goodfellow, Manager
Mark Tublisky, Admin Sec
Phyllis Smith, Assistant
EMP: 90 EST: 1957
SQ FT: 60,000
SALES (est): 26.4MM Publicly Held
WEB: www.orbitintl.com
SIC: 3679 3674 3643 3577 Power supplies, all types: static; solid state electronic devices; current-carrying wiring devices; computer peripheral equipment; computer terminals

(G-5908)
ORBIT INTERNATIONAL CORP
Tulip Development Laboratory
80 Cabot Ct (11788-3771)
PHONE.................................631 435-8300
Mitchell Binder, Branch Mgr
EMP: 53
SALES (corp-wide): 26.4MM Publicly Held
SIC: 3679 Static power supply converters for electronic applications
PA: Orbit International Corp.
80 Cabot Ct
Hauppauge NY 11788
631 435-8300

(G-5909)
PARKER-HANNIFIN CORPORATION
Also Called: Electronics Systems Division
300 Marcus Blvd (11788-2044)
PHONE.................................631 231-3737
Donald Washkewicz, President
Andrew Antone, Mfg Staff
Steve Rooney, Purchasing
Pete Ho, Engineer
Elliott Kurbec, Engineer
EMP: 335
SQ FT: 150,000
SALES (corp-wide): 14.3B Publicly Held
WEB: www.parker.com
SIC: 3594 Fluid power pumps & motors
PA: Parker-Hannifin Corporation
6035 Parkland Blvd
Cleveland OH 44124
216 896-3000

(G-5910)
PDK LABS INC
145 Ricefield Ln (11788-2007)
PHONE.................................631 273-2630
Reginald Spinello, President
EMP: 80
SQ FT: 44,000
SALES (est): 1.5MM Privately Held
SIC: 2844 2834 Toilet preparations; oral preparations; cosmetic preparations; vitamin, nutrient & hematinic preparations for human use

(G-5911)
PEELLE COMPANY (PA)
373 Smithtown Byp 311 (11788-2516)
PHONE.................................631 231-6000
R B Peelle Jr, Ch of Bd
Henry E Peelle III, President
Michael J Ryan, Vice Pres
▲ EMP: 7
SQ FT: 6,000
SALES (est): 10.9MM Privately Held
SIC: 3499 Aerosol valves, metal

(G-5912)
PEER SOFTWARE INCORPORATED (PA)
1363 Veterans Hwy Ste 44 (11788-3046)
PHONE.................................631 979-1770
Paul J Marsala, Principal
EMP: 8
SALES (est): 2.7MM Privately Held
SIC: 7372 Prepackaged software

(G-5913)
PETER KWASNY INC
400 Oser Ave Ste 1650 (11788-3669)
PHONE.................................727 641-1462
Hans Peter Kwasny, President
▲ EMP: 6
SALES (est): 657K
SALES (corp-wide): 75.8MM Privately Held
SIC: 2851 Paints & allied products
PA: Peter Kwasny Gmbh
Heilbronner Str. 96
Gundelsheim 74831
626 995-0

(G-5914)
PHOENIX MCH PDTS OF HAUPPAUGE
225 Engineers Rd (11788-4020)
PHONE.................................631 234-0100
Richard F Coronato Sr, President
EMP: 5
SQ FT: 15,000
SALES (est): 342.7K Privately Held
SIC: 3599 Machine shop, jobbing & repair

(G-5915)
PINDER INTERNATIONAL INC (PA)
1140 Motor Pkwy Ste A (11788-5255)
PHONE.................................631 273-0324
Jatinder Dhall, Ch of Bd
▲ EMP: 5
SQ FT: 15,000
SALES (est): 769.4K Privately Held
SIC: 2231 Apparel & outerwear broadwoven fabrics

(G-5916)
PIROD INC
Also Called: Valmont Site Pro 1
15 Oser Ave (11788-3808)
PHONE.................................631 231-7660
Joe Catapano, General Mgr
Joseph Cadapano, Branch Mgr
EMP: 33
SALES (corp-wide): 2.7B Publicly Held
SIC: 3441 Fabricated structural metal
HQ: Pirod Inc.
1545 Pidco Dr
Plymouth IN 46563
574 936-7221

(G-5917)
PNEUMERCATOR COMPANY INC
1785 Express Dr N (11788-5303)
PHONE.................................631 293-8450
Jonathan Levy, President
▲ EMP: 35 EST: 1914
SQ FT: 11,500
SALES (est): 7.1MM Privately Held
WEB: www.pneumercator.com
SIC: 3823 Gas flow computers, industrial process type; pressure gauges, dial & digital

(G-5918)
POLY CRAFT INDUSTRIES CORP
40 Ranick Rd (11788-4209)
PHONE.................................631 630-6731
Samuel Brach, President
Sylvia Brach, Admin Sec
▲ EMP: 25
SQ FT: 13,000
SALES (est): 5.9MM Privately Held
SIC: 2673 5113 Plastic bags: made from purchased materials; bags, paper & disposable plastic

(G-5919)
PRECARE CORP
Also Called: Premier Care Industries
150 Marcus Blvd (11788-3723)
PHONE.................................631 524-5171
Abraham Micheal, Branch Mgr
EMP: 5 Privately Held
SIC: 2676 Sanitary paper products
PA: Precare Corp.
150 Marcus Blvd
Hauppauge NY 11788

(G-5920)
PRECARE CORP (PA)
Also Called: Premier Care Industries
150 Marcus Blvd (11788-3723)
PHONE.................................631 667-1055
Ouri Neman, CEO
Matthew Neman, Vice Pres
Gregg Walker, Vice Pres
Bill Lutz, VP Sales
Ariana Bonetti, Manager
▲ EMP: 5
SQ FT: 35,000
SALES: 20.5MM Privately Held
SIC: 2621 2676 Tissue paper; napkins, sanitary: made from purchased paper; diapers, paper (disposable): made from purchased paper; tampons, sanitary: made from purchased paper

(G-5921)
PRELOAD CONCRETE STRUCTURES
60 Commerce Dr (11788-3929)
PHONE.................................631 231-8100
Andrew E Tripp Jr, President
Nancy Coll, Corp Secy
Jack Hornstein, Vice Pres
EMP: 42
SQ FT: 29,000
SALES (est): 6.9MM Privately Held
WEB: www.preload.com
SIC: 3272 Tanks, concrete

(G-5922)
PREMIER WOODWORKING INC
400 Oser Ave (11788-3619)
P.O. Box 14177 (11788-0401)
PHONE.................................631 236-4100
Jose Tellez, President
Carlos Zurita, Vice Pres
▲ EMP: 35
SQ FT: 230,000
SALES: 2.5MM Privately Held
SIC: 2541 Wood partitions & fixtures

(G-5923)
PRINTERS 3 INC
43 Corporate Dr Ste 2 (11788-2048)
PHONE.................................631 351-1331
Sal Viscuso, Ch of Bd
Anthony Viscuso, President
Christal Viscuso, Corp Secy
EMP: 10
SQ FT: 4,200
SALES (est): 1.7MM Privately Held
SIC: 2752 Commercial printing, offset

(G-5924)
PROFESSIONAL BUTY HOLDINGS INC
150 Motor Pkwy Ste 401 (11788-5108)
PHONE.................................631 787-8576
Bruce Kowalsky, Managing Prtnr
Gari Dawn Tingler, Treasurer
EMP: 10
SQ FT: 100,000
SALES: 10MM Privately Held
SIC: 2844 Toilet preparations

(G-5925)
PROFESSIONAL SOLUTIONS PRINT
300 Wheeler Rd Ste 303 (11788-4300)
PHONE.................................631 231-9300
Karl Snyder, President
EMP: 6
SALES: 750K Privately Held
SIC: 2752 Commercial printing, lithographic

(G-5926)
PROFILE PRINTING & GRAPHICS (PA)
275 Marcus Blvd (11788-2022)
PHONE.................................631 273-2727
Michael Munda, President
EMP: 7
SQ FT: 3,000
SALES (est): 558.9K Privately Held
WEB: www.profileprinting.com
SIC: 2752 Commercial printing, offset

(G-5927)
QUOIZEL INC
590 Old Willets Path # 1 (11788-4119)
PHONE.................................631 436-4402
Carolyn Fredrickson, Cust Mgr
Toni Phillips, Branch Mgr
EMP: 27
SALES (corp-wide): 165.2MM Privately Held
WEB: www.quoizel.com
SIC: 3645 5063 8741 Mfg Residential Lighting Fixtures Whol Electrical Equipment Management Services
PA: Quoizel, Inc.
6 Corporate Pkwy
Goose Creek SC 29445
843 553-6700

(G-5928)
RENTSCHLER BIOTECHNOLOGIE GMBH
400 Oser Ave Ste 1650 (11788-3669)
PHONE.................................631 656-7137
Nikolaus F Rentschler, CEO
EMP: 5
SALES (est): 426.6K Privately Held
SIC: 2836 Biological products, except diagnostic

(G-5929)
RODALE WIRELESS INC
Also Called: Rodale Electronics
20 Oser Ave Ste 2 (11788-3815)
PHONE.................................631 231-0044
John B Clement, President
Vince Maida, Vice Pres
Mary Licciardi, Purch Dir
Robert Ponzio, Buyer
EMP: 25
SQ FT: 10,000
SALES: 4.7MM Privately Held
SIC: 3825 3812 3663 3643 Instruments to measure electricity; search & navigation equipment; radio & TV communications equipment; current-carrying wiring devices; computer peripheral equipment; countermeasure simulators, electric

(G-5930)
ROTRONIC INSTRUMENT CORP (DH)
135 Engineers Rd Ste 150 (11788-4018)
P.O. Box 11241 (11788-0703)
PHONE.................................631 348-6844
David Love, Managing Dir
Patrick J Lafarie, Senior VP
David P Love, Vice Pres
Anthony Cordero, Sales Mgr
Steve Chenal, Regl Sales Mgr

Hauppauge - Suffolk County (G-5931) — GEOGRAPHIC SECTION

▲ **EMP:** 18
SALES (est): 2.2MM **Privately Held**
WEB: www.rotronic-usa.com
SIC: 3823 Temperature measurement instruments, industrial; temperature instruments: industrial process type; humidity instruments, industrial process type
HQ: Rotronic Ag
Grindelstrasse 6
Bassersdorf ZH 8303
448 381-111

(G-5931)
RSM ELECTRON POWER INC
Also Called: Sensitron Semiconductor
100 Engineers Rd Ste 100 # 100 (11788-4023)
PHONE 631 586-7600
Steve Saunders, *Branch Mgr*
EMP: 90
SALES (corp-wide): 23.8MM **Privately Held**
SIC: 3674 Semiconductors & related devices
PA: Rsm Electron Power, Inc.
221 W Industry Ct
Deer Park NY 11729
631 586-7600

(G-5932)
SANTA FE MANUFACTURING CORP
225 Engineers Rd (11788-4020)
PHONE 631 234-0100
Richard Coronato Sr, *President*
Charlotte Coronato, *Vice Pres*
EMP: 5
SQ FT: 44,000
SALES (est): 605.2K **Privately Held**
SIC: 3728 3827 Aircraft parts & equipment; optical instruments & lenses

(G-5933)
SAPTALIS PHARMACEUTICALS LLC (PA)
45 Davids Dr (11788-2038)
PHONE 631 231-2751
Polireddy Dondeti, *President*
Tatiana Akimova, *Exec VP*
EMP: 22
SQ FT: 10,000
SALES (est): 3.6MM **Privately Held**
SIC: 2834 Pharmaceutical preparations

(G-5934)
SCALAMANDRE WALLPAPER INC
Also Called: Scalamandre Silks
350 Wireless Blvd (11788-3947)
PHONE 631 467-8800
▲ **EMP:** 401
SQ FT: 30,000
SALES (est): 40.2MM **Privately Held**
SIC: 2621 5198 2231 2221 Paper Mill Whol Paints/Varnishes Wool Brdwv Fabric Mill Manmad Brdwv Fabric Mill Cotton Brdwv Fabric Mill

(G-5935)
SCHNEIDER OPTICS INC (HQ)
285 Oser Ave (11788-3616)
PHONE 631 761-5000
Dwight Lindsey, *CEO*
Stuart Singer, *Vice Pres*
Ira Tiffen, *Vice Pres*
Ron Engvaldsen, *Mfg Dir*
Joe Lee, *Purchasing*
▲ **EMP:** 26
SQ FT: 11,000
SALES: 16MM
SALES (corp-wide): 66.9MM **Privately Held**
WEB: www.schneideroptics.com
SIC: 3827 Optical instruments & lenses
PA: Jos. Schneider Optische Werke Gmbh
Ringstr. 132
Bad Kreuznach 55543
671 601-0

(G-5936)
SCIEGEN PHARMACEUTICALS INC (PA)
330 Oser Ave (11788-3630)
PHONE 631 434-2723
Pailla Malla Reddy, *CEO*
Siva Reddy, *Vice Pres*
Venkata Reddy, *Vice Pres*
Krishna Chilakamarphy, *Opers Mgr*
Amit Rathi, *Warehouse Mgr*
▲ **EMP:** 70
SQ FT: 89,000
SALES: 15MM **Privately Held**
SIC: 2834 Vitamin preparations

(G-5937)
SCOTTS COMPANY LLC
65 Engineers Rd (11788-4003)
PHONE 631 478-6843
Peter Pirro, *Principal*
EMP: 8
SALES (corp-wide): 2.6B **Publicly Held**
SIC: 2873 Fertilizers: natural (organic), except compost
HQ: The Scotts Company Llc
14111 Scottslawn Rd
Marysville OH 43040
937 644-3729

(G-5938)
SIEMENS INDUSTRY INC
Process Instrmntation Bus Unit
155 Plant Ave (11788-3801)
PHONE 631 231-3600
Allan Cottrell, *Manager*
Jens Grebner, *Manager*
EMP: 120
SALES (corp-wide): 97.7B **Privately Held**
WEB: www.sea.siemens.com
SIC: 3824 Totalizing meters, consumption registering
HQ: Siemens Industry, Inc.
100 Technology Dr
Alpharetta GA 30005
770 740-3000

(G-5939)
SIGN A RAMA INC
Also Called: Sign-A-Rama
663 Old Willets Path C (11788-4117)
PHONE 631 952-3324
Jim Reardon, *Manager*
EMP: 6
SALES (corp-wide): 91.3MM **Privately Held**
WEB: www.franchisemart.com
SIC: 3993 Signs & advertising specialties
HQ: Sign A Rama Inc.
2121 Vista Pkwy
West Palm Beach FL 33411
561 640-5570

(G-5940)
SIMA TECHNOLOGIES LLC
345 Oser Ave (11788-3607)
PHONE 412 828-9130
Richard Leifer,
Robert S Leifer,
▲ **EMP:** 7
SQ FT: 27,000
SALES (est): 976K **Privately Held**
WEB: www.simacorp.com
SIC: 3651 3861 5999 3577 Household audio & video equipment; photographic processing equipment & chemicals; mobile telephones & equipment; computer peripheral equipment; electrical equipment & supplies; motors & generators

(G-5941)
SIR INDUSTRIES INC
208 Blydenburg Rd Unit C (11749-5023)
PHONE 631 234-2444
Stanley Rabinowitz, *President*
▲ **EMP:** 6
SQ FT: 7,000
SALES: 30.4K **Privately Held**
SIC: 3648 5063 5719 Stage lighting equipment; light bulbs & related supplies; lighting fixtures

(G-5942)
SPACE-CRAFT WORLDWIDE INC
47 Wireless Blvd (11788)
PHONE 631 603-3000
Mazher Khalfan, *President*
Shawn Gomes, *Design Engr*
Eddy Vasquez, *Design Engr*
Megan Howard, *Director*
Kevin Ewanyk, *Officer*
▲ **EMP:** 40

SALES (est): 10.5MM **Privately Held**
SIC: 2541 Store & office display cases & fixtures

(G-5943)
SPECTRON GLASS & ELECTRONICS
595 Old Willets Path A (11788-4112)
PHONE 631 582-5600
Robert S Marshall, *Ch of Bd*
Pascal Lemarie, *Vice Pres*
Randy Bublitz, *QC Mgr*
Jennifer Marshall, *Human Res Mgr*
Kevin Berghauser, *Sales Staff*
▲ **EMP:** 17
SQ FT: 16,000
SALES (est): 3.1MM **Privately Held**
WEB: www.spectronsensors.com
SIC: 3679 3674 Electronic switches; semiconductors & related devices
PA: Spectron Systems Technology Inc
595 Old Willets Path A
Hauppauge NY 11788
631 582-5600

(G-5944)
SPECTRON SYSTEMS TECHNOLOGY (PA)
595 Old Willets Path A (11788-4113)
PHONE 631 582-5600
Robert Marshall, *President*
Nancy Chereb, *Treasurer*
EMP: 13
SQ FT: 14,000
SALES (est): 3.1MM **Privately Held**
WEB: www.tiltsensors.com
SIC: 3674 Semiconductors & related devices

(G-5945)
SPECTRUM BRANDS INC
Also Called: United Pet Group
2100 Pacific St (11788-4737)
PHONE 631 232-1200
Mark Stern, *Branch Mgr*
EMP: 275
SALES (corp-wide): 5B **Publicly Held**
SIC: 3999 Pet supplies
HQ: Spectrum Brands, Inc.
3001 Deming Way
Middleton WI 53562
608 275-3340

(G-5946)
SPECTRUM THIN FILMS INC
135 Marcus Blvd (11788-3702)
PHONE 631 901-1010
Anthony Pirera, *President*
Carlos Penalbert, *Opers Staff*
Derek Schomburg, *Sales Engr*
Kenneth Riccardi, *Technical Staff*
EMP: 35
SQ FT: 3,400
SALES (est): 12.6MM **Privately Held**
WEB: www.spectrumthinfilms.com
SIC: 3827 5049 Lenses, optical: all types except ophthalmic; optical goods

(G-5947)
SPELLMAN HGH-VOLTAGE ELEC CORP (PA)
475 Wireless Blvd (11788-3951)
PHONE 631 630-3000
Yolanda Gonzalez, *Purchasing*
Shalom Cohen, *Engineer*
EMP: 500
SQ FT: 100,000
SALES (est): 290.9MM **Privately Held**
SIC: 3679 Electronic loads & power supplies

(G-5948)
STANDARD MICROSYSTEMS CORP (HQ)
Also Called: Smsc
80 Arkay Dr Ste 100 (11788-3774)
PHONE 631 435-6000
Christine King, *President*
Ian Harris, *President*
Jennifer Innella, *Principal*
David Coller, *Senior VP*
Aaron L Fisher, *Senior VP*
▲ **EMP:** 68 **EST:** 1971
SQ FT: 200,000

SALES (est): 126.9MM
SALES (corp-wide): 3.9B **Publicly Held**
SIC: 3674 Microcircuits, integrated (semiconductor)
PA: Microchip Technology Inc
2355 W Chandler Blvd
Chandler AZ 85224
480 792-7200

(G-5949)
STAR QUALITY PRINTING INC
Also Called: Star Communications
270 Oser Ave (11788-3610)
PHONE 631 273-1900
Alka Parikh, *Ch of Bd*
Kalpesh Parikh, *President*
Adhish Parikh, *Vice Pres*
Fernando Basurto, *Production*
▲ **EMP:** 12
SQ FT: 7,500
SALES (est): 2.8MM **Privately Held**
WEB: www.sqprinting.com
SIC: 2752 Commercial printing, offset

(G-5950)
STERLING NORTH AMERICA INC
270 Oser Ave (11788-3610)
PHONE 631 243-6933
Ed McAllister, *Ch of Bd*
EMP: 28
SQ FT: 40,000
SALES (est): 7.2MM **Privately Held**
SIC: 2752 Commercial printing, offset

(G-5951)
SUMMIT APPAREL INC (PA)
Also Called: Royal Apparel
91 Cabot Ct (11788-3717)
PHONE 631 213-8299
Morad Mayeri, *Ch of Bd*
Abraham Mayeri, *Vice Pres*
▲ **EMP:** 48
SQ FT: 25,000
SALES (est): 10MM **Privately Held**
WEB: www.summitapparel.com
SIC: 2253 Dresses, knit

(G-5952)
SUPERIOR WASHER & GASKET CORP (PA)
170 Adams Ave (11788-3612)
P.O. Box 5407 (11788-0407)
PHONE 631 273-8282
Allan Lippolis, *Principal*
Robert Lippolis, *Purchasing*
Peter Anderson, *Sales Staff*
Michelle Card, *Sales Associate*
Courtney Gautier, *Sales Associate*
EMP: 65 **EST:** 1972
SQ FT: 42,000
SALES (est): 16.5MM **Privately Held**
WEB: www.superiorwasher.com
SIC: 3452 Washers, metal; washers

(G-5953)
SUPERITE GEAR INSTR OF HPPAUGE (PA)
225 Engineers Rd (11788-4020)
PHONE 631 234-0100
Richard Coronato Sr, *President*
Charlotte Coronato, *Admin Sec*
EMP: 8
SQ FT: 44,000
SALES (est): 2.4MM **Privately Held**
SIC: 3462 Gears, forged steel

(G-5954)
SYMWAVE INC (DH)
80 Arkay Dr (11788-3705)
PHONE 949 542-4400
Yossi Cohen, *President*
Jun Ye, *Vice Pres*
Adam Spice, *CFO*
Christopher Thomas, *CTO*
EMP: 6
SALES (est): 733K
SALES (corp-wide): 3.9B **Publicly Held**
WEB: www.symwave.com
SIC: 3674 Semiconductors & related devices
HQ: Standard Microsystems Corporation
80 Arkay Dr Ste 100
Hauppauge NY 11788
631 435-6000

GEOGRAPHIC SECTION

(G-5955)
TARSIA TECHNICAL INDUSTRIES
Also Called: TTI
93 Marcus Blvd (11788-3712)
PHONE.................................631 231-8322
Joe Tarsia, *President*
EMP: 7
SALES (est): 664.2K Privately Held
WEB: www.ttiind.com
SIC: 3599 Machine shop, jobbing & repair

(G-5956)
TECHNIMETAL PRECISION INDS
195 Marcus Blvd (11788-3796)
PHONE.................................631 231-8900
Donald T Molloy, *President*
Stephen J Miller, *Exec VP*
EMP: 50 EST: 1967
SQ FT: 27,000
SALES (est): 8.9MM Privately Held
WEB: www.tpimetals.com
SIC: 3444 Sheet metal specialties, not stamped

(G-5957)
TELEBYTE INC (PA)
355 Marcus Blvd Ste 2 (11788-2027)
PHONE.................................631 423-3232
Dr Kenneth S Schneider, *CEO*
Michael Breneisen, *President*
EMP: 25
SQ FT: 3,500
SALES (est): 4.8MM Privately Held
WEB: www.telebyteusa.com
SIC: 3663 Radio & TV communications equipment

(G-5958)
THREAD CHECK INC
390 Oser Ave Ste 2 (11788-3682)
PHONE.................................631 231-1515
Hyman Jack Kipnes, *President*
Irving Kipnes, *Vice Pres*
EMP: 99
SQ FT: 74,000
SALES (est): 11.5MM Privately Held
WEB: www.threadcheck.com
SIC: 3552 5084 3823 Thread making machines, spinning machinery; industrial machinery & equipment; industrial instrmnts msrmnt display/control process variable

(G-5959)
TIFFEN COMPANY LLC
Also Called: Tiffen Co, The
80 Oser Ave (11788-3809)
PHONE.................................631 273-2500
EMP: 9
SALES (corp-wide): 24.1MM Privately Held
SIC: 3861 Photographic equipment & supplies
PA: The Tiffen Company Llc
   90 Oser Ave
   Hauppauge NY 11788
   631 273-2500

(G-5960)
TIFFEN COMPANY LLC (PA)
90 Oser Ave (11788-3809)
PHONE.................................631 273-2500
Bill Funicello, *Opers Dir*
Andrew Tiffen, *Prdtn Mgr*
Steve Tiffen, *Mng Member*
Leigh Boden, *Manager*
Karen Romanelli,
▲ EMP: 60
SALES (est): 24.1MM Privately Held
WEB: www.tiffen.com
SIC: 3861 Photographic equipment & supplies

(G-5961)
TOTAL DEFENSE INC
1393 Veterans Memorial Hw (11788-3068)
PHONE.................................631 257-3258
Robert Walters, *CEO*
Lawrence Guerin, *Vice Pres*
EMP: 65
SQ FT: 3,947
SALES (est): 2.4MM
SALES (corp-wide): 60MM Privately Held
SIC: 7372 Prepackaged software

PA: Appriver, Llc
   1101 Glf Brz Pkwy Ste 200
   Gulf Breeze FL 32561
   850 932-5338

(G-5962)
TUNAVERSE MEDIA INC
750 Veterans Hwy Ste 200 (11788-2943)
PHONE.................................631 778-8350
Ross Pirtle, *President*
Hal Denton, *Vice Pres*
Tom Diemidil, *Vice Pres*
EMP: 8
SALES: 500K Privately Held
SIC: 7372 Prepackaged software

(G-5963)
TWINCO MFG CO INC
30 Commerce Dr (11788-3904)
PHONE.................................631 231-0022
John A Schatz, *President*
Ellen Wilcken, *Vice Pres*
▲ EMP: 44 EST: 1965
SQ FT: 50,000
SALES: 9.3MM Privately Held
WEB: www.twincomfg.com
SIC: 3669 3469 3599 3743 Railroad signaling devices, electric; machine parts, stamped or pressed metal; machine & other job shop work; railroad equipment

(G-5964)
UNIFLEX HOLDINGS LLC (PA)
1600 Caleds Ext Ste 135 (11788)
PHONE.................................516 932-2000
Rob Cunningham,
▲ EMP: 10
SALES (est): 13.5MM Privately Held
WEB: www.uflineart.com
SIC: 2673 2674 2672 Plastic & pliofilm bags; bags: uncoated paper & multiwall; coated & laminated paper

(G-5965)
UNITED-GUARDIAN INC (PA)
230 Marcus Blvd (11788-3731)
P.O. Box 18050 (11788-8850)
PHONE.................................631 273-0900
Kenneth H Globus, *Ch of Bd*
Peter A Hiltunen, *Vice Pres*
Robert S Rubinger, *CFO*
Andrea Young, *Controller*
EMP: 31
SQ FT: 50,000
SALES: 12.9MM Publicly Held
WEB: www.u-g.com
SIC: 2844 2834 Pharmaceutical preparations; cosmetic preparations

(G-5966)
UNIVERSAL PACKG SYSTEMS INC (PA)
Also Called: Paklab
380 Townline Rd Ste 130 (11788-2800)
PHONE.................................631 543-2277
Andrew Young III, *Ch of Bd*
Alan Kristel, *COO*
Jeffery Morlando, *CFO*
Megan Johnson, *Executive Asst*
William Wachtel, *Admin Sec*
▲ EMP: 750
SQ FT: 115,000
SALES (est): 423.8MM Privately Held
SIC: 2844 7389 3565 2671 Cosmetic preparations; packaging & labeling services; bottling machinery: filling, capping, labeling, plastic film, coated or laminated for packaging

(G-5967)
UNLIMITED INK INC
595 Old Willets Path B (11788-4114)
PHONE.................................631 582-0696
Josh Disamone, *President*
EMP: 20
SALES (est): 934.8K Privately Held
SIC: 2759 5699 Screen printing; sports apparel

(G-5968)
VEHICLE MANUFACTURERS INC
Also Called: Skyguard
400 Oser Ave Ste 100 (11788-3600)
PHONE.................................631 851-1700
George J Wafer, *CEO*

Scott Wafer, *President*
Judith Kaye, *Business Mgr*
Angelo Addesso, *COO*
Jill Murray, *Manager*
EMP: 22
SQ FT: 3,000
SALES: 10MM Privately Held
SIC: 3069 Rubber automotive products

(G-5969)
VETRA SYSTEMS CORPORATION
275 Marcus Blvd Unit J (11788-2022)
PHONE.................................631 434-3185
Jonas Ulenas, *President*
Paul Sabatino, *Vice Pres*
Valdas Douba, *Shareholder*
Nigole Ulenas, *Shareholder*
EMP: 8
SALES (est): 1.3MM Privately Held
WEB: www.vetra.com
SIC: 3823 5084 Computer interface equipment for industrial process control; controllers for process variables, all types; conveyor systems

(G-5970)
VICON INDUSTRIES INC (PA)
135 Fell Ct (11788-4351)
PHONE.................................631 952-2288
Saagar Govil, *Ch of Bd*
John M Badke, *COO*
Bret M McGowan, *Senior VP*
Peter A Horn, *Vice Pres*
EMP: 117
SQ FT: 30,000
SALES (est): 26.6MM Privately Held
WEB: www.viconindustries.com
SIC: 3663 3669 Security systems services

(G-5971)
VISIONTRON CORP
720 Old Willets Path (11788-4102)
PHONE.................................631 582-8600
Lisa Torsiello, *President*
Donna Goroshko, *General Mgr*
Joseph Torsiello, *Vice Pres*
Laurence Torsiello, *Vice Pres*
Charles Hansen, *Mfg Dir*
◆ EMP: 25
SQ FT: 20,000
SALES (est): 6.1MM Privately Held
WEB: www.visiontron.com
SIC: 3669 Intercommunication systems, electric

(G-5972)
W & H STAMPINGS INC
45 Engineers Rd (11788-4019)
PHONE.................................631 234-6161
Ernest E Hoffmann, *President*
Ron Marcisak, *General Mgr*
EMP: 28 EST: 1956
SQ FT: 33,000
SALES: 1MM Privately Held
WEB: www.whstamp.com
SIC: 3469 Stamping metal for the trade

(G-5973)
WATSON PRODUCTIONS LLC
Also Called: Skyline New York
740 Old Willets Path # 400 (11788-4121)
PHONE.................................516 334-9766
Robert Watson,
▼ EMP: 12
SALES (est): 2.4MM Privately Held
WEB: www.watsonproductions.com
SIC: 3577 Graphic displays, except graphic terminals

(G-5974)
WELDING METALLURGY INC (HQ)
360 Motor Pkwy Ste 100 (11788-5193)
PHONE.................................631 253-0500
Gary Settoducato, *Ch of Bd*
Scott Glassman, *CFO*
Scott A Glassman, *CFO*
Chuck Layne, *Manager*
EMP: 47
SQ FT: 35,000
SALES (est): 11.6MM Publicly Held
WEB: www.weldingmet.com
SIC: 3441 Fabricated structural metal

(G-5975)
WIDEX USA INC (DH)
Also Called: Widex International
185 Commerce Dr (11788-3916)
P.O. Box 6077, Long Island City (11106-0077)
PHONE.................................718 360-1000
Jake Haycock, *President*
▲ EMP: 87
SALES (est): 22.9MM
SALES (corp-wide): 739.4MM Privately Held
SIC: 3842 Hearing aids
HQ: Widex A/S
   Nymollevej 6
   Lynge 3540
   443 556-00

(G-5976)
WILBAR INTERNATIONAL INC
50 Cabot Ct (11788-3716)
PHONE.................................631 951-9800
Steven Cohen, *President*
Richard Sobel, *Vice Pres*
Peter Rizzo, *Plant Mgr*
Brian Kelley, *CIO*
▲ EMP: 100
SQ FT: 20,000
SALES (est): 27.1MM Privately Held
SIC: 3949 Swimming pools, plastic; swimming pools, except plastic

(G-5977)
WOODBINE PRODUCTS INC
110 Plant Ave (11788-3830)
PHONE.................................631 586-3770
Vincent J Conforti, *President*
Johanna Conforti, *Admin Sec*
EMP: 20
SQ FT: 20,000
SALES (est): 2.4MM Publicly Held
WEB: www.woodbineproducts.com
SIC: 3812 Operates As A Manufacturer Of Navigation Equipment Specializing In Aerospace Acceleration Indicators Or Systems Components
HQ: Welding Metallurgy, Inc.
   360 Motor Pkwy Ste 100
   Hauppauge NY 11788
   631 253-0500

(G-5978)
WORLD TRADING CENTER INC
115 Engineers Rd Fl 2 (11788-4005)
PHONE.................................631 273-3330
Arthur W Danziger Jr, *President*
◆ EMP: 8
SQ FT: 4,000
SALES (est): 1.6MM Privately Held
WEB: www.wtcco.com
SIC: 2511 3699 3634 Wood household furniture; household electrical equipment; housewares, excluding cooking appliances & utensils

Haverstraw
Rockland County

(G-5979)
JAGUAR INDUSTRIES INC
89 Broadway (10927-1144)
P.O. Box 385 (10927-0385)
PHONE.................................845 947-1800
Marvin Kigler, *President*
EMP: 15
SQ FT: 15,000
SALES: 8MM Privately Held
SIC: 3351 5065 3643 3357 Wire, copper & copper alloy; electronic parts & equipment; current-carrying wiring devices; nonferrous wiredrawing & insulating; laminated plastics plate & sheet

(G-5980)
ROCKLAND INSULATED WIRE CABLE
87 Broadway (10927-1144)
P.O. Box 111 (10927-0111)
PHONE.................................845 429-3103
Lawrence Kigler, *President*
EMP: 7 EST: 1956
SQ FT: 10,000

SALES (est): 1.2MM **Privately Held**
SIC: 3357 Nonferrous wiredrawing & insulating

(G-5981)
ROSS ELECTRONICS LTD
12 Maple Ave (10927-1824)
PHONE..................................718 569-6643
Reuven Lakein, *President*
▲ EMP: 20 EST: 2010
SALES: 12MM **Privately Held**
SIC: 3699 5999 Electrical equipment & supplies; electronic parts & equipment

(G-5982)
TILCON NEW YORK INC
Also Called: Haverstraw Quarry
66 Scratchup Rd (10927)
PHONE..................................845 638-3594
EMP: 63
SALES (corp-wide): 29.7B **Privately Held**
SIC: 2951 Asphalt paving mixtures & blocks
HQ: Tilcon New York Inc.
   9 Entin Rd
   Parsippany NJ 07054
   800 789-7625

Hawthorne
Westchester County

(G-5983)
ASTRA TOOL & INSTRUMENT MFG
369 Bradhurst Ave (10532-1141)
PHONE..................................914 747-3863
Greg Unmann, *President*
Greg Unman, *President*
EMP: 22 EST: 1950
SQ FT: 10,000
SALES: 2.9MM **Privately Held**
WEB: www.astratool.net
SIC: 3841 3599 Surgical & medical instruments; machine shop, jobbing & repair

(G-5984)
BIOMED PHARMACEUTICALS INC
Also Called: Soleo Health
4 Skyline Dr Ste 5 (10532-2192)
PHONE..................................914 592-0525
Drew Walk, *CEO*
John Ginzler, *CFO*
EMP: 8
SALES (est): 1.1MM
SALES (corp-wide): 42.3MM **Privately Held**
SIC: 2834 5912 Druggists' preparations (pharmaceuticals); drug stores & proprietary stores
PA: Soleo Health Holdings, Inc.
   950 Calcon Hook Rd Ste 19
   Sharon Hill PA 19079
   888 244-2340

(G-5985)
COCA-COLA REFRESHMENTS USA INC
3 Skyline Dr (10532-2174)
PHONE..................................914 592-0806
John Krause, *Project Mgr*
Brian Winn, *Branch Mgr*
EMP: 8
SALES (corp-wide): 35.4B **Publicly Held**
SIC: 2086 Bottled & canned soft drinks
HQ: Coca-Cola Refreshments Usa, Inc.
   2500 Windy Ridge Pkwy Se
   Atlanta GA 30339
   770 989-3000

(G-5986)
FOUR BROTHERS ITALIAN BAKERY
Also Called: Sinapi's Italian Ice
332 Elwood Ave (10532-1217)
PHONE..................................914 741-5434
Pat Sinapi, *President*
Angelo Sinapi, *Vice Pres*
Anthony Sinapi, *Treasurer*
Luigi Sinapi, *Admin Sec*
EMP: 5

SALES (est): 469.6K **Privately Held**
SIC: 2024 5143 Ices, flavored (frozen dessert); ice cream & ices

(G-5987)
GAS TURBINE CONTROLS CORP
6 Skyline Dr Ste 150 (10532-8102)
P.O. Box 104, Ardsley (10502-0104)
PHONE..................................914 693-0830
Peter Zinman, *Ch of Bd*
▲ EMP: 25
SALES (est): 2.5MM **Privately Held**
SIC: 3511 Turbines & turbine generator sets

(G-5988)
J JAMNER SURGICAL INSTRS INC
Also Called: Jarit Surgical Instruments
40 Saw Mill River Rd # 12 (10532-1535)
PHONE..................................914 592-9051
Robert Rogowski, *President*
Lori Sebeth, *Manager*
EMP: 23
SQ FT: 15,000
SALES (est): 3.1MM **Publicly Held**
WEB: www.jarit.com
SIC: 3841 Mfg Surgical/Medical Instruments
PA: Integra Lifesciences Holdings Corporation
   311 Enterprise Dr
   Plainsboro NJ 08536

(G-5989)
JOHNSON CONTROLS INC
8 Skyline Dr Ste 115 (10532-2151)
PHONE..................................914 593-5200
Rick Salon, *Manager*
EMP: 20 **Privately Held**
SIC: 3822 Energy cutoff controls, residential or commercial types
HQ: Johnson Controls, Inc.
   5757 N Green Bay Ave
   Milwaukee WI 53209
   414 524-1200

(G-5990)
KRYTEN IRON WORKS INC
3 Browns Ln Ste 201 (10532-1546)
PHONE..................................914 345-0990
EMP: 8
SALES (est): 1.4MM **Privately Held**
SIC: 3441 3446 Structural Metal Fabrication Mfg Architectural Metalwork

(G-5991)
LITHO DYNAMICS INC
17 Saw Mill River Rd (10532-1503)
PHONE..................................914 769-1759
Kenneth Giustino, *President*
Ed Martin, *Vice Pres*
Joseph Giustino, *Shareholder*
EMP: 6
SQ FT: 10,000
SALES: 400K **Privately Held**
SIC: 2752 Commercial printing, offset

(G-5992)
LUDL ELECTRONIC PRODUCTS LTD
Also Called: Lep
171 Brady Ave (10532-2216)
PHONE..................................914 769-6111
Helmut Ludl, *Ch of Bd*
Dirk Ludl, *President*
Mark Ludl, *President*
Petra H Ludl, *Corp Secy*
Nicholas Kucharik, *Mfg Staff*
▼ EMP: 25
SQ FT: 23,000
SALES: 2K **Privately Held**
WEB: www.ludl.com
SIC: 3825 Instruments to measure electricity

(G-5993)
MWSI INC (PA)
12 Skyline Dr Ste 230 (10532-2138)
PHONE..................................914 347-4200
Mark Wasserman, *President*
EMP: 70
SQ FT: 12,160

SALES (est): 3.9MM **Privately Held**
SIC: 3961 5094 3911 Costume jewelry, ex. precious metal & semiprecious stones; jewelry; jewelry, precious metal

(G-5994)
NYSCO PRODUCTS LLC
211 Saw Mill River Rd (10532-1509)
P.O. Box 725, Bronx (10473-0725)
PHONE..................................718 792-9000
Barry Kramer, *Principal*
Charles Levin, *Vice Pres*
Glenn Smith, *Vice Pres*
Patricia Albright, *Human Res Dir*
Albert Lian, *VP Sales*
▲ EMP: 60
SQ FT: 80,000
SALES (est): 13.1MM **Privately Held**
WEB: www.nysco.com
SIC: 3993 Signs & advertising specialties

(G-5995)
PEPSICO
3 Skyline Dr (10532-2174)
PHONE..................................419 252-0247
EMP: 17
SALES (est): 2.8MM **Privately Held**
SIC: 2086 Carbonated soft drinks, bottled & canned

(G-5996)
PRINCETEL INC
Also Called: Wendon Engineering
200 Saw Mill River Rd (10532-1523)
PHONE..................................914 579-2410
Boying Zhang, *Branch Mgr*
EMP: 14
SALES (corp-wide): 8.5MM **Privately Held**
SIC: 3678 3621 Electronic connectors; sliprings, for motors or generators
PA: Princetel Inc.
   2560 E State Street Ext
   Hamilton NJ 08619
   609 588-8801

(G-5997)
SCHMERSAL INC
15 Skyline Dr Ste 230 (10532-2152)
PHONE..................................914 347-4775
Philip Schmersal, *General Mgr*
Gary Ferguson, *Managing Dir*
Sagar Bhosale, *Managing Dir*
Joe Bussie, *Regional Mgr*
David Upton, *Business Mgr*
◆ EMP: 26
SQ FT: 10,000
SALES (est): 5.2MM
SALES (corp-wide): 225.7MM **Privately Held**
WEB: www.schmersal.com
SIC: 3625 Motor control accessories, including overload relays
HQ: K. A. Schmersal Gmbh & Co. Kg
   Moddinghofe 30
   Wuppertal 42279
   202 647-40

(G-5998)
U X WORLD INC
245 Saw Mill River Rd # 106 (10532-1547)
PHONE..................................914 375-6167
Vinod Pulkayath, *President*
EMP: 5
SQ FT: 300
SALES: 140K **Privately Held**
SIC: 7372 Prepackaged software

Hector
Schuyler County

(G-5999)
HAZLITTS 1852 VINEYARDS INC
Also Called: Hazlitt 1852 Vineyards
5712 State Route 414 (14841-9714)
P.O. Box 53 (14841-0053)
PHONE..................................607 546-9463
Doug Hazlitt, *CEO*
Elaine Hazlitt, *President*
Jerome Hazlitt, *President*
Fred Wickham, *Vice Pres*
Leigh Triner, *Treasurer*
EMP: 48
SQ FT: 4,500

SALES (est): 7.1MM **Privately Held**
WEB: www.hazlitt1852.com
SIC: 2084 0172 Wines; grapes

(G-6000)
LAFAYETTE CHATEAU
Also Called: Chateau La Fayette Reneau
Rr 414 (14841)
PHONE..................................607 546-2062
Richard Reno, *Owner*
EMP: 25
SQ FT: 5,000
SALES (est): 2MM **Privately Held**
WEB: www.clrwine.com
SIC: 2084 Wines

(G-6001)
RED NEWT CELLARS INC
3675 Tichenor Rd (14841-9675)
PHONE..................................607 546-4100
David Whiting, *President*
Terri Myers, *Business Mgr*
Katie Thompson, *Manager*
EMP: 10
SQ FT: 13,000
SALES (est): 2.8MM **Privately Held**
WEB: www.rednewt.com
SIC: 2084 Wines

(G-6002)
STANDING STONE VINEYARDS
9934 State Route 414 (14841-9727)
PHONE..................................607 582-6051
Martha Macinski, *Owner*
Tom Macinski, *Co-Owner*
EMP: 6
SALES (est): 438.6K **Privately Held**
WEB: www.standingstonewines.com
SIC: 2084 5921 Wines; wine

(G-6003)
TICKLE HILL WINERY
3831 Ball Diamond Rd (14841-9629)
PHONE..................................607 546-7740
Valerie Rosbaugh, *Owner*
EMP: 5
SALES (est): 283.8K **Privately Held**
SIC: 2084 Wine cellars, bonded: engaged in blending wines

Hemlock
Livingston County

(G-6004)
ITT CORPORATION
4847 Main St (14466-9714)
PHONE..................................585 269-7109
Rosario Pitta, *Branch Mgr*
EMP: 46
SALES (corp-wide): 2.5B **Publicly Held**
WEB: www.ittind.com
SIC: 3625 Control equipment, electric
HQ: Itt Llc
   1133 Westchester Ave N-100
   White Plains NY 10604
   914 641-2000

Hempstead
Nassau County

(G-6005)
ANHUI SKYWORTH LLC
44 Kensington Ct (11550-2126)
PHONE..................................917 940-6903
Fuzhen Ang, *Mng Member*
Fuzhen Wang, *Mng Member*
▲ EMP: 65
SALES (est): 1.8MM **Privately Held**
SIC: 2392 5023 Cushions & pillows; pillowcases

(G-6006)
ARIC SIGNS & AWNINGS INC
153 Baldwin Rd (11550-6818)
PHONE..................................516 350-0409
Ivan Arizaga-Rodrig, *Owner*
EMP: 5
SALES (est): 347.6K **Privately Held**
SIC: 3993 Signs & advertising specialties

GEOGRAPHIC SECTION
Henrietta - Monroe County (G-6034)

(G-6007)
ARNELL INC
73 High St (11550-3817)
PHONE 516 486-7098
Doug Riebl, *President*
Ron Riebl, *Vice Pres*
EMP: 6 **EST:** 1956
SQ FT: 4,300
SALES (est): 910.3K **Privately Held**
SIC: 3469 3544 Metal stampings; special dies, tools, jigs & fixtures

(G-6008)
BP BEYOND PRINTING INC
117 Fulton Ave (11550-3706)
PHONE 516 328-2700
Christine Persaud, *Ch of Bd*
EMP: 6
SALES (est): 859K **Privately Held**
SIC: 2752 2759 Commercial printing, offset; commercial printing

(G-6009)
CENTURY-TECH INC
32 Intersection St (11550-1306)
PHONE 718 326-9400
EMP: 13 **Privately Held**
SIC: 3561 Mfg Pumps/Pumping Equipment
PA: Century-Tech Inc.
  5825 63rd St
  Hempstead NY 11550

(G-6010)
CENTURY-TECH INC
32 Intersection St (11550-1306)
PHONE 516 493-9800
Peter Terranova, *President*
Jack Terranova, *Corp Secy*
Ronald Wiggberg, *Corp Secy*
Louis Mastrangelo, *Vice Pres*
◆ **EMP:** 25
SQ FT: 30,000
SALES (est): 5MM **Privately Held**
WEB: www.century-techinc.com
SIC: 3559 Plastics working machinery

(G-6011)
GENERAL REFINING & SMELTING
Also Called: Grc
106 Taft Ave (11550-4887)
PHONE 516 538-4747
Richard Spera, *President*
EMP: 7
SQ FT: 10,000
SALES (est): 1MM **Privately Held**
SIC: 3339 3341 Gold refining (primary); silver refining (primary); platinum group metal refining (primary); secondary non-ferrous metals

(G-6012)
GENERAL REFINING CORPORATION
59 Madison Ave (11550-4813)
PHONE 516 538-4747
Peter Spera, *Principal*
EMP: 8
SALES (est): 850K **Privately Held**
SIC: 3339 Gold refining (primary)

(G-6013)
HEMPSTEAD SENTINEL INC
Also Called: Sentinel Printing
55 Chasner St (11550-4807)
P.O. Box 305 (11551-0305)
PHONE 516 486-5000
Glenn Boehmer, *President*
Joan Boehmer, *Admin Sec*
EMP: 13
SQ FT: 7,000
SALES (est): 3.1MM **Privately Held**
SIC: 2752 Commercial printing, offset

(G-6014)
ICELL INC
133 Fulton Ave (11550-3710)
PHONE 516 590-0007
Arpreet Sanhi, *President*
EMP: 127
SQ FT: 4,000
SALES: 10MM **Privately Held**
SIC: 3663 Mobile communication equipment

(G-6015)
JEM SIGN CORP (PA)
Also Called: Tee Pee Signs
470 S Franklin St (11550-7419)
PHONE 516 867-4466
Jeraldine Eid, *President*
Teddy Eid, *Vice Pres*
EMP: 5
SQ FT: 3,700
SALES (est): 725.6K **Privately Held**
WEB: www.teepeesigns.com
SIC: 3993 7532 5999 1799 Electric signs; truck painting & lettering; trophies & plaques; sign installation & maintenance

(G-6016)
JONICE INDUSTIRES
95 Angevine Ave (11550-5618)
PHONE 516 640-4283
EMP: 5
SALES (est): 232.3K **Privately Held**
SIC: 2299 Broadwoven fabrics: linen, jute, hemp & ramie

(G-6017)
KING CRACKER CORP
Also Called: Cristina
307 Peninsula Blvd (11550-4912)
PHONE 516 539-9251
Leonard Morales, *President*
EMP: 15
SALES (est): 450K **Privately Held**
SIC: 2051 5149 Bread, cake & related products; bakery products

(G-6018)
LONG ISLAND READY MIX
75 Chasner St (11550-4807)
PHONE 516 485-5260
Steve Welti, *Owner*
EMP: 5
SALES (est): 223.5K **Privately Held**
SIC: 3273 Ready-mixed concrete

(G-6019)
MAGER & GOUGELMAN INC
230 Hilton Ave Ste 112 (11550-8116)
PHONE 212 661-3939
Henry P Gougleman, *President*
EMP: 8
SALES (corp-wide): 855.4K **Privately Held**
WEB: www.artificial-eyes.com
SIC: 3851 Eyes, glass & plastic
PA: Mager & Gougelman Inc
  345 E 37th St Rm 316
  New York NY 10016
  212 661-3939

(G-6020)
MAGER & GOUGELMAN INC
230 Hilton Ave Ste 112 (11550-8116)
PHONE 516 489-0202
Denise Gougelmann, *Manager*
EMP: 9
SALES (corp-wide): 855.4K **Privately Held**
WEB: www.artificial-eyes.com
SIC: 3851 Eyes, glass & plastic
PA: Mager & Gougelman Inc
  345 E 37th St Rm 316
  New York NY 10016
  212 661-3939

(G-6021)
MILLENNIUM SIGNS & DISPLAY INC
90 W Graham Ave (11550-6102)
PHONE 516 292-8000
Sajjad Khalfan, *President*
Reyaz Khalfan, *Vice Pres*
▲ **EMP:** 25
SQ FT: 35,000
SALES (est): 4MM **Privately Held**
WEB: www.msdny.com
SIC: 3993 Signs & advertising specialties

(G-6022)
NASSAU COUNTY PUBLICATIONS
Also Called: Beacon Newspapers
5 Centre St (11550-2422)
PHONE 516 481-5400
Peter Hoegl, *President*
EMP: 5
SALES (est): 352.4K **Privately Held**
SIC: 2711 Newspapers: publishing only, not printed on site

(G-6023)
PLANT-TECH2O INC
30 Chasner St (11550-4808)
P.O. Box 520 (11551-0520)
PHONE 516 483-7845
William Lyon, *President*
EMP: 5
SQ FT: 5,000
SALES: 500K **Privately Held**
SIC: 3523 7359 7389 1791 Farm machinery & equipment; live plant rental; plant care service; exterior wall system installation

(G-6024)
PURE GOLDS FAMILY CORP
1 Brooklyn Rd (11550-6619)
PHONE 516 483-5600
Steven Gold, *Ch of Bd*
Howard Gold, *Vice Pres*
Marc Gold, *Vice Pres*
Neil Gold, *CFO*
Paul Altamore, *Natl Sales Mgr*
▲ **EMP:** 75 **EST:** 1932
SQ FT: 75,000
SALES (est): 16.8MM **Privately Held**
WEB: www.goldshorseradish.com
SIC: 2035 2099 Seasonings & sauces, except tomato & dry; horseradish, prepared; Worcestershire sauce; mustard, prepared (wet); food preparations

(G-6025)
RELIABLE PRESS II INC
Also Called: Printing
73 Sealey Ave (11550-1240)
PHONE 718 840-5812
Ira Cohen, *President*
▲ **EMP:** 16
SALES (est): 1.1MM **Privately Held**
SIC: 2741 Miscellaneous publishing

(G-6026)
T-REX SUPPLY CORPORATION
1 Fulton Ave Ste 120 (11550-3646)
PHONE 516 308-0505
EMP: 6
SALES (est): 967.7K **Privately Held**
SIC: 3559 Special Industry Machinery, Nec, Nsk

(G-6027)
ULTIMATE SIGNS & DESIGNS INC
86 Sewell St (11550-5432)
PHONE 516 481-0800
Michael Peras, *President*
Chris Hays, *General Mgr*
Shanna Peras, *Vice Pres*
Nicholas Georgetti, *Opers Staff*
Marguerite Martinek, *Accounting Mgr*
EMP: 26
SQ FT: 10,000
SALES (est): 3.8MM **Privately Held**
WEB: www.ultimatesigns.com
SIC: 3993 Electric signs

(G-6028)
WOODMOTIF INC
Also Called: Woodmotif Cabinetry
42 Chasner St (11550-4820)
PHONE 516 564-8325
George Dimitriadis, *President*
EMP: 10
SALES (est): 1.3MM **Privately Held**
SIC: 2521 2511 2499 Wood office furniture; wood household furniture; decorative wood & woodwork

Henrietta
Monroe County

(G-6029)
AGRINETIX CMPT SYSTEMS LLC
Also Called: Agrinetix, LLC
370 Summit Point Dr 1a (14467-9629)
PHONE 877 978-5477
Richard Wildman, *CEO*
EMP: 12
SALES (est): 1.5MM **Privately Held**
SIC: 7372 Business oriented computer software

(G-6030)
ANGIOTECH BIOCOATINGS CORP
336 Summit Point Dr (14467-9607)
PHONE 585 321-1130
Richard Whitbourne, *Ch of Bd*
Richard Richmond, *President*
John F Lanzafame, *President*
Carolyn Eastman, *Vice Pres*
Gerard Whitbourne, *Vice Pres*
▲ **EMP:** 45
SQ FT: 13,000
SALES (est): 4MM **Privately Held**
WEB: www.angiotech.com
SIC: 3479 2891 2851 Painting, coating & hot dipping; adhesives & sealants; paints & allied products
PA: Angiotech Pharmaceuticals, Inc
  355 Burrard St Suite 1100
  Vancouver BC V6C 2
  604 221-7676

(G-6031)
ARGON MEDICAL DEVICES INC
336 Summit Point Dr (14467-9607)
PHONE 585 321-1130
EMP: 8
SALES (corp-wide): 268.3MM **Privately Held**
SIC: 3845 3842 3841 Electromedical equipment; surgical appliances & supplies; surgical & medical instruments
HQ: Argon Medical Devices, Inc.
  2600 Dallas Pkwy Ste 440
  Frisco TX 75034
  903 675-9321

(G-6032)
HYDROACOUSTICS INC
999 Lehigh Station Rd # 100 (14467-9389)
PHONE 585 359-1000
Michael J Czora, *Vice Pres*
Jim Rall, *Mfg Staff*
Ken Wittlief, *Engineer*
EMP: 16
SQ FT: 45,000
SALES (est): 4.3MM
SALES (corp-wide): 3.7MM **Privately Held**
WEB: www.hydroacoustics.com
SIC: 3594 Fluid power pumps & motors
PA: Hai Technologies Inc.
  999 Lehigh Station Rd # 100
  Henrietta NY 14467
  281 598-3940

(G-6033)
KONECRANES INC
1020 Lehigh Station Rd # 4 (14467-9369)
PHONE 585 359-4450
Christina Moss, *Manager*
EMP: 12
SALES (corp-wide): 3.7B **Privately Held**
WEB: www.kciusa.com
SIC: 3536 7699 Cranes, industrial plant; industrial machinery & equipment repair
HQ: Konecranes, Inc.
  4401 Gateway Blvd
  Springfield OH 45502

(G-6034)
LAKE IMAGE SYSTEMS INC
205 Summit Point Dr Ste 2 (14467-9631)
PHONE 585 321-3630
Scott Stevens, *President*
Martin Keats, *President*
Paul Stinson, *Exec VP*
Paul Smith, *Senior VP*
Alain Almeras, *Opers Mgr*
EMP: 17
SQ FT: 7,500
SALES: 5.5MM **Privately Held**
WEB: www.lakeimage.com
SIC: 3861 3554 7371 Cameras & related equipment; paper industries machinery; computer software development
PA: Lake Image Systems Limited
  1 The Forum Icknield Way Industrial Estate
  Tring HERTS HP23

Henrietta - Monroe County (G-6035)

(G-6035)
MAGPUMP LLC
235 Middle Rd Ste 600 (14467-9302)
PHONE.................................585 444-9812
David Reitano,
EMP: 6
SALES (est): 261.5K **Privately Held**
SIC: 3484 Guns (firearms) or gun parts, 30 mm. & below

(G-6036)
ORAFOL AMERICAS INC
Also Called: Reflexite Precision Tech Ctr
200 Park Centre Dr (14467)
PHONE.................................585 272-0309
Stephen Meissner, *Engineer*
Steven Scott, *Branch Mgr*
EMP: 25
SALES (corp-wide): 561.4MM **Privately Held**
WEB: www.reflexite.com
SIC: 3081 Vinyl film & sheet
HQ: Orafol Americas Inc.
1100 Oracal Pkwy
Black Creek GA 31308
912 851-5000

(G-6037)
TUCKER PRINTERS INC
270 Middle Rd (14467-9312)
PHONE.................................585 359-3030
Joe R Davis, *CEO*
Daniel A Tucker, *President*
Glenn Marino, *Vice Pres*
Jennifer Collier, *Project Mgr*
Kathy Howell, *Purch Agent*
EMP: 82 **EST:** 1997
SQ FT: 60,000
SALES (est): 18.7MM
SALES (corp-wide): 6.9B **Publicly Held**
WEB: www.tuckerprinters.com
SIC: 2752 Commercial printing, offset
HQ: Consolidated Graphics, Inc.
5858 Westheimer Rd # 400
Houston TX 77057
713 787-0977

(G-6038)
TURNER UNDGRD INSTLLATIONS INC
1233 Lehigh Station Rd (14467-9228)
PHONE.................................585 739-0238
Robert Turner, *President*
Rhett Turner, *Vice Pres*
Abraham Brouk, *Project Mgr*
Jane Peers, *Admin Sec*
EMP: 12
SQ FT: 11,000
SALES: 3.4MM **Privately Held**
SIC: 1381 Directional drilling oil & gas wells

Herkimer
Herkimer County

(G-6039)
GATEHOUSE MEDIA LLC
Also Called: Evening Telegram
111 Green St (13350-1914)
P.O. Box 551 (13350-0551)
PHONE.................................315 866-2220
Beth Brewer, *Adv Dir*
EMP: 10
SALES (corp-wide): 1.3B **Publicly Held**
WEB: www.gatehousemedia.com
SIC: 2711 Newspapers, publishing & printing
HQ: Gatehouse Media, Llc
175 Sullys Trl Ste 300
Pittsford NY 14534
585 598-0030

(G-6040)
HEIDELBERG GROUP INC
3056 State Hwy Rte 28 N (13350)
PHONE.................................315 866-0999
Boyd Bissell, *President*
▲ **EMP:** 40
SQ FT: 8,000
SALES (est): 6.6MM **Privately Held**
WEB: www.heidelbergbakingco.com
SIC: 2051 Bakery: wholesale or wholesale/retail combined

(G-6041)
HERKIMER DIAMOND MINES INC
800 Mohawk St (13350-2261)
PHONE.................................315 891-7355
Renee Scialdo Schevat, *Ch of Bd*
EMP: 25
SALES (est): 3.2MM **Privately Held**
WEB: www.herkimerdiamond.com
SIC: 1499 5094 Gemstone & industrial diamond mining; diamonds (gems)

(G-6042)
HERKIMER TOOL & MACHINING CORP
Also Called: Herkimer Tool & Equipment Co
125 Marginal Rd (13350-2305)
PHONE.................................315 866-2110
F Ellis Green Jr, *President*
Francis E Green III, *Vice Pres*
Nancy J Green, *Admin Sec*
EMP: 10
SQ FT: 14,000
SALES (est): 1.3MM **Privately Held**
SIC: 3599 Machine shop, jobbing & repair

(G-6043)
LENNONS LITHO INC
Also Called: Mohawk Valley Printing Co
234 Kast Hill Rd (13350-4402)
PHONE.................................315 866-3156
Robert J Lennon, *Ch of Bd*
Elfrieda Lennon, *Treasurer*
EMP: 10
SQ FT: 6,400
SALES (est): 730K **Privately Held**
WEB: www.mohawkvalleyprinting.com
SIC: 2752 2759 Commercial printing, offset; commercial printing; letterpress printing

Heuvelton
St. Lawrence County

(G-6044)
LOSURDO FOODS INC
Also Called: Losurdo Creamery
34 Union St (13654-2200)
PHONE.................................315 344-2444
Michael Losurdo Sr, *President*
Antonio Fazzino, *Vice Pres*
Marc Losurdo, *Vice Pres*
Michael Losurdo Jr, *Vice Pres*
Maria Losurdo, *Treasurer*
EMP: 150
SQ FT: 75,000
SALES (est): 19.1MM
SALES (corp-wide): 73.5MM **Privately Held**
WEB: www.losurdofoods.com
SIC: 2022 Natural cheese
PA: Losurdo Foods, Inc.
20 Owens Rd
Hackensack NJ 07601
201 343-6680

Hewlett
Nassau County

(G-6045)
ABS METAL CORP
58 Holly Rd (11557-1411)
PHONE.................................646 302-9018
Alan Minchenberg, *Principal*
EMP: 5 **EST:** 2012
SALES (est): 491.2K **Privately Held**
SIC: 3471 Finishing, metals or formed products

(G-6046)
ALGAFUEL AMERICA
289 Meadowview Ave (11557-2106)
PHONE.................................516 295-2257
Allan Roffe, *Principal*
EMP: 7
SALES (est): 464.7K **Privately Held**
SIC: 2911 Diesel fuels

(G-6047)
LADY BRASS CO INC
1717 Broadway Unit 2 (11557-1682)
PHONE.................................516 887-8040
Lauren Brasco, *President*
EMP: 6
SALES (est): 1MM **Privately Held**
SIC: 2337 2326 Uniforms, except athletic: women's, misses' & juniors'; work uniforms

(G-6048)
LIFEWATCH INC
Also Called: Lifewatch Personal Mergency
1344 Broadway Ste 106 (11557-1356)
PHONE.................................800 716-1433
Evan Sirlin, *President*
Art Sirlin, *Vice Pres*
Art Mitchell, *Treasurer*
EMP: 10
SALES (est): 700K **Privately Held**
WEB: www.lifewatch.net
SIC: 3669 5063 5999 Emergency alarms; alarm systems; alarm signal systems

(G-6049)
NEW PRIMECARE
1184 Broadway (11557-2322)
PHONE.................................516 822-4031
Fred Tylutki, *CFO*
EMP: 6 **EST:** 2007
SALES (est): 403.2K **Privately Held**
SIC: 3845 Laser systems & equipment, medical

(G-6050)
S & M RING CORP
1080 Channel Dr (11557-2638)
PHONE.................................212 382-0900
Wally Schafran, *President*
▲ **EMP:** 12
SALES (est): 684.2K **Privately Held**
SIC: 3911 Rings, finger: precious metal

(G-6051)
TORSAF PRINTERS INC
Also Called: Minuteman Press
1313 Broadway (11557-2115)
PHONE.................................516 569-5577
David Toron, *President*
Michael Toron, *Corp Secy*
EMP: 6
SQ FT: 4,800
SALES (est): 981.6K **Privately Held**
SIC: 2752 2791 Commercial printing, offset; typesetting

(G-6052)
UNITED PIPE NIPPLE CO INC
1602 Lakeview Dr (11557-1818)
PHONE.................................516 295-2468
Roger Desimone, *CEO*
Selma Dolgov, *President*
▲ **EMP:** 15
SQ FT: 25,000
SALES: 5MM **Privately Held**
WEB: www.unitedpipenipple.com
SIC: 3494 Pipe fittings

(G-6053)
VENUS PRINTING COMPANY
1420 Kew Ave (11557-1413)
PHONE.................................212 967-8900
Erwin Goodman, *President*
Carol Goodman, *Treasurer*
Tom Shields, *Manager*
EMP: 15
SALES (est): 1MM **Privately Held**
SIC: 2759 Commercial printing

(G-6054)
WASHINGTON FOUNDRIES INC
1434 Vian Ave (11557-1423)
PHONE.................................516 374-8447
Jyotsna Kejriwal, *CEO*
Ramesh Kejriwal, *President*
EMP: 4
SQ FT: 2,100
SALES (est): 1.1MM **Privately Held**
SIC: 3674 Semiconductors & related devices

(G-6055)
YES WERE NUTS LTD
Also Called: I'M Nuts
1215 Broadway (11557-2001)
PHONE.................................516 374-1940
Catherine Davi, *President*
EMP: 6
SQ FT: 2,500
SALES (est): 423.3K **Privately Held**
SIC: 2066 Chocolate

Hicksville
Nassau County

(G-6056)
AJAX WIRE SPECIALTY CO INC
119 Bloomingdale Rd (11801-6508)
PHONE.................................516 935-2333
Patricia Ellner, *CEO*
David Ellner, *President*
EMP: 15
SQ FT: 5,000
SALES: 1MM **Privately Held**
SIC: 3495 Wire springs

(G-6057)
ALL ISLAND MEDIA INC
Also Called: Carrier News
325 Duffy Ave Unit 2 (11801-3644)
PHONE.................................516 942-8400
Daniel Mikos, *Marketing Staff*
Robert Sussi, *Branch Mgr*
EMP: 26
SALES (corp-wide): 12.9MM **Privately Held**
WEB: www.allislandmedia.com
SIC: 2711 Newspapers, publishing & printing
PA: All Island Media, Inc.
1 Rodeo Dr
Edgewood NY 11717
631 698-8400

(G-6058)
ALL THE RAGE INC
147 W Cherry St Unit 1 (11801-3885)
P.O. Box 20249, Huntington Station (11746-0854)
PHONE.................................516 605-2001
Michael J Demarco, *President*
EMP: 7
SQ FT: 3,000
SALES (est): 4MM **Privately Held**
SIC: 3911 Jewelry apparel

(G-6059)
APPLIED POWER SYSTEMS INC
Also Called: A P S
124 Charlotte Ave (11801-2620)
PHONE.................................516 935-2230
James Murphy, *CEO*
Les Doti, *Vice Pres*
Andres Romay, *Vice Pres*
Randall Kramer, *Med Doctor*
Richard Radocha, *Med Doctor*
▲ **EMP:** 25
SALES (est): 4.8MM **Privately Held**
WEB: www.appliedps.com
SIC: 3679 3677 3629 3823 Power supplies, all types: static; transformers power supply, electronic type; inverters, nonrotating: electrical; controllers for process variables, all types; frequency converters (electric generators)

(G-6060)
APX TECHNOLOGIES INC
264 Duffy Ave (11801-3605)
PHONE.................................516 433-1313
Yuval Ofek, *President*
Talia Ofek, *Director*
▲ **EMP:** 20
SQ FT: 3,500
SALES (est): 3MM **Privately Held**
SIC: 3679 Harness assemblies for electronic use: wire or cable; electronic loads & power supplies

Hicksville - Nassau County (G-6087)

(G-6061)
ARSTAN PRODUCTS INTERNATIONAL
Also Called: Apx Arstan Products
264 Duffy Ave (11801-3605)
PHONE.....................516 433-1313
Yuval Ofek, *President*
EMP: 15
SQ FT: 3,500
SALES (est): 969.3K **Privately Held**
WEB: www.apxonline.com
SIC: 3679 3612 Power supplies, all types: static; transformers, except electric

(G-6062)
AUTO-MAT COMPANY INC
69 Hazel St (11801-5340)
PHONE.....................516 938-7373
Timothy S Browner, *President*
Marilyn Browner, *Corp Secy*
Roger Browner, *Vice Pres*
EMP: 21 EST: 1956
SQ FT: 12,000
SALES (est): 1.5MM **Privately Held**
SIC: 2273 5013 7532 Automobile floor coverings, except rubber or plastic; automotive supplies & parts; interior repair services

(G-6063)
BALANCE ENTERPRISES INC
12 W Cherry St (11801-3802)
PHONE.....................516 822-3183
Robert Philips, *President*
Robert Phillips, *Store Dir*
EMP: 8
SALES (est): 455.5K **Privately Held**
SIC: 3999 Education aids, devices & supplies

(G-6064)
BATTSCO LLC
190 Lauman Ln Unit A (11801-6570)
PHONE.....................516 586-6544
Fred Hentschel, *Managing Prtnr*
John R Garnett, *Mng Member*
▲ **EMP:** 5
SQ FT: 2,500
SALES: 2MM **Privately Held**
SIC: 3691 Storage batteries

(G-6065)
BEBITZ USA INC
2 Reiter Ave (11801-5234)
PHONE.....................516 280-8378
Dhruv Kochhar, *President*
Daulat R Tannan, *Vice Pres*
Ashish Tannan, *Manager*
▲ **EMP:** 7
SALES (est): 646.1K
SALES (corp-wide): 22.1MM **Privately Held**
SIC: 3312 Hot-rolled iron & steel products
HQ: Flanschenwerk Bebitz Gmbh
Lebendorfer StraBe 1
Konnern 06420
346 914-00

(G-6066)
C Q COMMUNICATIONS INC
Also Called: Cq Magazine
17 W John St Unit 1 (11801-1004)
PHONE.....................516 681-2922
Richard Ross, *President*
S Del Grosso, *Accounting Dir*
Catherine M Ross, *Admin Secy*
EMP: 22
SQ FT: 10,000
SALES (est): 3.1MM **Privately Held**
WEB: www.cq-vhf.com
SIC: 2721 Magazines: publishing only, not printed on site

(G-6067)
CAMBRIDGE KITCHENS MFG INC
280 Duffy Ave Unit 1 (11801-3656)
PHONE.....................516 935-5100
Neoklis Vasiliades, *President*
Barbara Narene, *Admin Secy*
EMP: 15
SQ FT: 32,000
SALES: 2.6MM **Privately Held**
WEB: www.cambridgekitchens.com
SIC: 2434 Wood kitchen cabinets

(G-6068)
CLASSIC COLOR GRAPHICS INC (PA)
268 N Broadway Unit 8 (11801-2923)
P.O. Box 599, Jericho (11753-0599)
PHONE.....................516 822-9090
Daniel Fischer, *President*
Meryl Fischer, *Treasurer*
EMP: 7
SALES (est): 508.8K **Privately Held**
SIC: 2752 Commercial printing, offset

(G-6069)
CLASSIC COLOR GRAPHICS INC
87 Broadway (11801-4272)
PHONE.....................516 822-9090
Dan Fisher, *President*
Barry Moscowitz, *Accountant*
EMP: 5
SALES (corp-wide): 508.8K **Privately Held**
SIC: 2752 Commercial printing, lithographic
PA: Classic Color Graphics, Inc
268 N Broadway Unit 8
Hicksville NY 11801
516 822-9090

(G-6070)
CLEARY CUSTOM CABINETS INC
794 S Broadway (11801-5017)
PHONE.....................516 939-2475
Tom Cleary, *President*
Lora Cleary, *Vice Pres*
EMP: 15
SALES (est): 2.1MM **Privately Held**
WEB: www.clearycustomcabinets.com
SIC: 2434 Wood kitchen cabinets

(G-6071)
COOPER LIGHTING LLC
Also Called: Neo Ray Lighting Products
100 Andrews Rd Ste 1 (11801-1725)
PHONE.....................516 470-1000
Harry Mangru, *Buyer*
Aida Rivera, *Design Engr*
Dennis Detore, *Controller*
Lisa Goodman,
▲ **EMP:** 110 EST: 2007
SALES (est): 16.7MM **Privately Held**
WEB: www.neoray-lighting.com
SIC: 3646 3645 Commercial indusl & institutional electric lighting fixtures; residential lighting fixtures
HQ: Cooper Industries Unlimited Company
41 A B Drury Street
Dublin

(G-6072)
CORAL GRAPHIC SERVICES INC (DH)
Also Called: Coral Graphic Svce
840 S Broadway (11801-5066)
PHONE.....................516 576-2100
David Liess, *Ch of Bd*
Frank Cappo, *President*
Mike Borden, *Vice Pres*
Michelle Desjardin, *Accounts Mgr*
Erin Sommerfeld, *Sales Associate*
▲ **EMP:** 182
SQ FT: 56,000
SALES: 73.9MM
SALES (corp-wide): 82.3MM **Privately Held**
SIC: 2752 Commercial printing, offset
HQ: Dynamic Graphic Finishing, Inc.
945 Horsham Rd
Horsham PA 19044
215 441-8880

(G-6073)
CORAL GRAPHIC SERVICES INC
840 S Broadway (11801-5066)
PHONE.....................516 576-2100
Dave Lieff, *President*
EMP: 102
SALES (corp-wide): 82.3MM **Privately Held**
SIC: 2752 Commercial printing, offset
HQ: Coral Graphic Services, Inc.
840 S Broadway
Hicksville NY 11801
516 576-2100

(G-6074)
CRAIG ENVELOPE CORP
220 Miller Pl (11801-1826)
PHONE.....................718 786-4277
Lawrence Aaronson, *President*
Susan Aaronson, *Corp Secy*
Robert Aaronson, *VP Opers*
John Lundgren, *Human Res Mgr*
EMP: 39
SQ FT: 20,000
SALES (est): 6MM **Privately Held**
SIC: 2752 2759 Commercial printing, offset; letterpress printing

(G-6075)
CREATIVE MODELS & PROTOTYPES
160 Lauman Ln Unit A (11801-6557)
PHONE.....................516 433-6828
Deborah Dinoia, *President*
William Dinoia, *Manager*
EMP: 8
SALES: 40K **Privately Held**
SIC: 3999 Models, general, except toy

(G-6076)
CROWN EQUIPMENT CORPORATION
Also Called: Crown Lift Trucks
5 Charlotte Ave Ste 1 (11801-3607)
PHONE.....................516 822-5100
Jim Casey, *Manager*
EMP: 68
SALES (corp-wide): 3.1B **Privately Held**
SIC: 3537 Lift trucks, industrial: fork, platform, straddle, etc.
PA: Crown Equipment Corporation
44 S Washington St
New Bremen OH 45869
419 629-2311

(G-6077)
CULICOVER & SHAPIRO INC
270 Duffy Ave Ste K (11801-3600)
PHONE.....................516 597-4888
Richard Shapiro, *President*
David Shapiro, *Treasurer*
▲ **EMP:** 4
SALES: 1.2MM **Privately Held**
SIC: 3991 Brushes, household or industrial

(G-6078)
CYNOSURE INC
Also Called: Ellman International
400 Karin Ln (11801-5352)
PHONE.....................516 594-3333
Tom Oliveri, *VP Opers*
EMP: 7
SALES (corp-wide): 3B **Publicly Held**
SIC: 3841 3843 Surgical & medical instruments; dental equipment & supplies
HQ: Cynosure, Inc.
5 Carlisle Rd
Westford MA 01886

(G-6079)
DESIGNATRONICS INCORPORATED (PA)
Also Called: Sdp/Si
250 Duffy Ave Unit A (11801-3654)
P.O. Box 5416, New Hyde Park (11042-5416)
PHONE.....................516 328-3300
Michael Walsh, *Ch of Bd*
Richard Kufner, *President*
Sue Anderson, *Exec VP*
Robert Lindemann, *Vice Pres*
Daniel Raleigh, *Vice Pres*
▲ **EMP:** 2
SQ FT: 40,000
SALES (est): 111.3MM **Privately Held**
WEB: www.designatronics.com
SIC: 3824 3559 3545 3625 Mechanical & electromechanical counters & devices; electronic component making machinery; cams (machine tool accessories); relays & industrial controls; iron & steel forgings

(G-6080)
DESIGNATRONICS INCORPORATED
Also Called: Stock Drive Products Div
250 Duffy Ave Unit A (11801-3654)
PHONE.....................516 328-3300
Anthony Pagliughi, *Principal*
Janice Iburg, *Buyer*
EMP: 296
SALES (corp-wide): 111.3MM **Privately Held**
WEB: www.designatronics.com
SIC: 3625 3621 3568 3566 Motor controls & accessories; motors & generators; power transmission equipment; speed changers, drives & gears; manufactured hardware (general); tire cord & fabrics
PA: Designatronics Incorporated
250 Duffy Ave Unit A
Hicksville NY 11801
516 328-3300

(G-6081)
E-BEAM SERVICES INC (PA)
270 Duffy Ave Ste H (11801-3600)
PHONE.....................516 622-1422
Paul R Minbiole, *President*
Mary C Daly, *Vice Pres*
Mary Daly, *Admin Sec*
▲ **EMP:** 4
SQ FT: 2,000
SALES: 5MM **Privately Held**
WEB: www.e-beamservices.com
SIC: 3671 Electron beam (beta ray) generator tubes

(G-6082)
EDGIAN PRESS INC
10 Bethpage Rd (11801-1512)
PHONE.....................516 931-2114
Edward E Giannelli, *President*
Ian R Fuller, *Principal*
Edward G Giannelli, *Principal*
EMP: 8
SQ FT: 6,000
SALES (est): 1.1MM **Privately Held**
SIC: 2752 2759 Commercial printing, offset; letterpress printing

(G-6083)
EISEMAN-LUDMAR CO INC
56 Bethpage Dr (11801-1502)
PHONE.....................516 932-6990
Andrew Ludmar, *President*
Carol Ludmar, *Vice Pres*
David Ludmar, *Vice Pres*
EMP: 10
SQ FT: 4,200
SALES (est): 891.8K **Privately Held**
WEB: www.elcaccessories.com
SIC: 2395 2241 Embroidery & art needlework; lace & decorative trim, narrow fabric

(G-6084)
EMPIRE STEEL WORKS INC
110a New South Rd (11801-5223)
P.O. Box 111, Lynbrook (11563-0111)
PHONE.....................516 561-3500
Shaneeza Lila, *President*
EMP: 10
SALES (est): 1.7MM **Privately Held**
SIC: 3312 3446 Structural shapes & pilings, steel; fences or posts, ornamental iron or steel

(G-6085)
ESCHEN PRSTHETIC ORTHOTIC LABS
299 Duffy Ave (11801-3653)
PHONE.....................516 871-0029
Andrew Meyers, *President*
EMP: 10
SALES (est): 1.6MM **Privately Held**
SIC: 3842 Surgical appliances & supplies

(G-6086)
FLEXFIT LLC
350 Karin Ln Unit A (11801-5360)
PHONE.....................516 932-8800
Alan Schneidman, *General Mgr*
Leslie Umphrey, *General Mgr*
Mike Son, *Design Engr*
John Michael, *Credit Mgr*
Daniel Kim, *Accounts Exec*
▲ **EMP:** 60
SALES (est): 78.5MM **Privately Held**
SIC: 2353 Hats & caps

(G-6087)
FOOT LOCKER RETAIL INC
Also Called: Champs Sports
358 Broadway Mall (11801-2709)
PHONE.....................516 827-5306

Hicksville - Nassau County (G-6088)   GEOGRAPHIC SECTION

Jamie Blas, *Manager*
EMP: 10
SALES (corp-wide): 7.7B **Publicly Held**
WEB: www.venatorgroup.com
SIC: 2389 5611 Men's miscellaneous accessories; clothing, sportswear, men's & boys'
HQ: Foot Locker Retail, Inc.
 330 W 34th St
 New York NY 10001

(G-6088)
FOUGERA PHARMACEUTICALS INC
55 Cantiague Rock Rd (11801-1126)
P.O. Box 2006, Melville (11747-0103)
PHONE 631 454-7677
Robert Faivre, *Managing Dir*
EMP: 158
SALES (corp-wide): 49.1B **Privately Held**
SIC: 2834 Druggists' preparations (pharmaceuticals)
HQ: Fougera Pharmaceuticals Inc.
 60 Baylis Rd
 Melville NY 11747
 631 454-7677

(G-6089)
GE POLYMERSHAPES
120 Andrews Rd (11801-1704)
PHONE 516 433-4092
Mike Grimm, *Manager*
◆ **EMP:** 10
SALES (est): 878.8K **Privately Held**
SIC: 2295 Resin or plastic coated fabrics

(G-6090)
GIM ELECTRONICS CORP
270 Duffy Ave Ste H (11801-3600)
PHONE 516 942-3382
Mark Douenias, *President*
William Cardenas, *Vice Pres*
Mike Moran, *CTO*
EMP: 15
SQ FT: 7,800
SALES (est): 10MM **Privately Held**
WEB: www.gimelectronics.com
SIC: 3572 5961 Computer storage devices; computer equipment & electronics, mail order

(G-6091)
GLOBAL GLASS CORP
134 Woodbury Rd (11801-3025)
PHONE 516 681-2309
Jack Flax, *President*
▲ **EMP:** 6
SQ FT: 2,000
SALES (est): 662.4K **Privately Held**
SIC: 3211 3231 5231 5719 Flat glass; products of purchased glass; glass; mirrors; glass & glazing work

(G-6092)
GLOPAK USA CORP (PA)
35 Engel St Ste B (11801-2648)
PHONE 844 445-6725
Kenneth Wang, *CEO*
▲ **EMP:** 34
SALES (est): 35MM **Privately Held**
SIC: 3221 Bottles for packing, bottling & canning; glass

(G-6093)
GOLFING MAGAZINE
Also Called: Long Island Golfer Magazine
22 W Nicholai St Ste 200 (11801-3881)
PHONE 516 822-5446
John Glozek Jr, *President*
▲ **EMP:** 8
SALES (est): 411K **Privately Held**
WEB: www.ligolfer.com
SIC: 2721 5736 Magazines: publishing only, not printed on site; sheet music

(G-6094)
HANAN PRODUCTS COMPANY INC
196 Miller Pl (11801-1826)
PHONE 516 938-1000
Stuart M Hanan, *President*
Francis Hanan, *Vice Pres*
Doris Hanan, *Admin Sec*
▼ **EMP:** 20 **EST:** 1950
SQ FT: 23,000
SALES (est): 3.9MM **Privately Held**
WEB: www.hananproducts.com
SIC: 2026 Whipped topping, except frozen or dry mix

(G-6095)
HESPERUS NAUTICALS INC (HQ)
115 N Broadway Ste 206 (11801-2926)
PHONE 516 974-3016
Munira Khumri, *CEO*
EMP: 5
SALES (est): 316.8K **Privately Held**
SIC: 3429 Marine hardware

(G-6096)
HICKSVILLE MACHINE WORKS CORP
761 S Broadway (11801-5098)
PHONE 516 931-1524
Gioachino Jack Spiezio, *Ch of Bd*
Betty Spiezio, *Admin Sec*
EMP: 18
SQ FT: 35,000
SALES (est): 3.8MM **Privately Held**
WEB: www.hicksvillemachine.com
SIC: 3728 Aircraft assemblies, subassemblies & parts

(G-6097)
JOHN E POTENTE & SONS INC
114 Woodbury Rd Unit 1 (11801-3047)
PHONE 516 935-8585
Eugene Potente, *CEO*
Ralph J Potente, *President*
Saverio Potente, *Vice Pres*
EMP: 6 **EST:** 1925
SQ FT: 5,000
SALES (est): 929.9K **Privately Held**
SIC: 3272 Concrete products

(G-6098)
KINGFORM CAP COMPANY INC
121 New South Rd (11801-5230)
PHONE 516 822-2501
Leonard Ochs, *President*
▲ **EMP:** 60 **EST:** 1955
SQ FT: 33,000
SALES (est): 6.7MM **Privately Held**
WEB: www.kingformcap.com
SIC: 2353 Uniform hats & caps

(G-6099)
KOZY SHACK ENTERPRISES LLC (HQ)
83 Ludy St (11801-5114)
PHONE 516 870-3000
Robert Striano, *Principal*
Joanne Caridi, *Admin Sec*
◆ **EMP:** 250 **EST:** 1967
SQ FT: 70,000
SALES: 90.2MM
SALES (corp-wide): 12.8B **Privately Held**
WEB: www.kozyshack.com
SIC: 2099 5149 Desserts, ready-to-mix; gelatin dessert preparations; groceries & related products
PA: Land O'lakes, Inc.
 4001 Lexington Ave N
 Arden Hills MN 55126
 651 375-2222

(G-6100)
KOZY SHACK ENTERPRISES LLC
Also Called: Freshway Distributors
50 Ludy St (11801-5115)
PHONE 516 870-3000
John Ievolo, *Manager*
EMP: 200
SALES (corp-wide): 12.8B **Privately Held**
WEB: www.kozyshack.com
SIC: 2099 5149 2024 Desserts, ready-to-mix; gelatin dessert preparations; groceries & related products; ice cream & frozen desserts
HQ: Kozy Shack Enterprises, Llc
 83 Ludy St
 Hicksville NY 11801
 516 870-3000

(G-6101)
KUNO STEEL PRODUCTS CORP
132 Duffy Ave (11801-3640)
PHONE 516 938-8500
Kuno Weckenmann, *President*
Irmgard Weckenmann, *Corp Secy*
EMP: 10
SQ FT: 1,500
SALES: 1.2MM **Privately Held**
WEB: www.kunosteel.com
SIC: 3441 Building components, structural steel

(G-6102)
LAND OLAKES INC
50 Ludy St (11801-5115)
PHONE 516 681-2980
EMP: 9
SALES (corp-wide): 12.8B **Privately Held**
SIC: 2099 Food preparations
PA: Land O'lakes, Inc.
 4001 Lexington Ave N
 Arden Hills MN 55126
 651 375-2222

(G-6103)
LEATHER INDEXES CORP
174a Miller Pl (11801-1826)
P.O. Box 1350, Port Washington (11050-7350)
PHONE 516 827-1900
Paul Ellenberg, *President*
Kay Ellenberg, *Vice Pres*
EMP: 60
SQ FT: 15,000
SALES: 1.5MM **Privately Held**
SIC: 2678 2782 2675 Stationery products; blankbooks & looseleaf binders; die-cut paper & board

(G-6104)
M F MANUFACTURING ENTERPRISES
2 Ballad Ln (11801-4529)
PHONE 516 822-5135
Michael Funk, *CEO*
Fern Funk, *Vice Pres*
EMP: 5
SALES (est): 325K **Privately Held**
SIC: 3469 Machine parts, stamped or pressed metal

(G-6105)
MARCAL PRINTING INC
Also Called: PIP Printing
85 N Broadway (11801-2948)
PHONE 516 942-9500
Marc Saltzman, *President*
Alan Smith, *Vice Pres*
EMP: 6
SQ FT: 3,000
SALES (est): 940.3K **Privately Held**
SIC: 2752 Offset Printing

(G-6106)
MARIAH METAL PRODUCTS INC
89 Tec St (11801-3618)
PHONE 516 938-9783
Raymond O Leary, *President*
EMP: 5
SQ FT: 2,000
SALES (est): 676.2K **Privately Held**
SIC: 3444 Sheet metalwork

(G-6107)
MARIGOLD SIGNS INC
Also Called: Sign-A-Rama
485 S Broadway Ste 34 (11801-5071)
PHONE 516 433-7446
Vincent Marino, *President*
Robert Goldaber, *Vice Pres*
EMP: 10
SALES (est): 1.3MM **Privately Held**
SIC: 3993 Signs & advertising specialties

(G-6108)
MARKWIK CORP
309 W John St (11801-1024)
PHONE 516 470-1990
Jane A Groene, *President*
Taylor Groene, *General Mgr*
EMP: 18 **EST:** 1949
SQ FT: 9,000
SALES (est): 2.3MM **Privately Held**
WEB: www.markwik.com
SIC: 3089 Plastic hardware & building products

(G-6109)
MICRO CONTACTS INC (PA)
1 Enterprise Pl Unit E (11801-2694)
PHONE 516 433-4830
Gerald F Tucci, *Ch of Bd*
Michael F Tucci, *President*
Robert Stinson, *General Mgr*
Steven Klekman, *Vice Pres*
Philip Uruburu, *Vice Pres*
▲ **EMP:** 50 **EST:** 1963
SQ FT: 40,000
SALES (est): 10MM **Privately Held**
WEB: www.microcontacts.com
SIC: 3643 Contacts, electrical

(G-6110)
MISON CONCEPTS INC
485 S Broadway Ste 33 (11801-5071)
PHONE 516 933-8000
Joseph Jaroff, *President*
Bhavani Morganstern, *Vice Pres*
▲ **EMP:** 8
SQ FT: 2,000
SALES (est): 690K **Privately Held**
WEB: www.mison.com
SIC: 3446 Architectural metalwork

(G-6111)
MOD-A-CAN INC (PA)
178 Miller Pl (11801-1890)
PHONE 516 931-8545
Stan Buoninfante, *President*
Stan L Buoninfante, *President*
Bill Sammon, *General Mgr*
Roberta Wolfe, *General Mgr*
Michael Iannotta, *Vice Pres*
EMP: 55 **EST:** 1966
SQ FT: 19,400
SALES (est): 11.5MM **Privately Held**
WEB: www.modacan.com
SIC: 3812 Aircraft flight instruments

(G-6112)
MULTI PACKAGING SOLUTIONS INC
325 Duffy Ave Unit 1 (11801-3644)
PHONE 516 488-2000
Michael Greenberg, *Branch Mgr*
EMP: 113
SALES (corp-wide): 14.8B **Publicly Held**
SIC: 2671 Packaging paper & plastics film, coated & laminated
HQ: Multi Packaging Solutions, Inc.
 150 E 52nd St Fl 28
 New York NY 10022

(G-6113)
NASSAU CANDY DISTRIBUTORS INC (HQ)
Also Called: Nassau Candy Specialty
530 W John St (11801-1039)
PHONE 516 433-7100
Lesley Stier, *President*
Barry Rosenbaum, *President*
Bonnie Cohen, *Managing Dir*
Les Stier, *COO*
Pashka Bellia, *Vice Pres*
▲ **EMP:** 180
SQ FT: 300,000
SALES (est): 213.9MM **Privately Held**
WEB: www.nassaucandy.com
SIC: 2064 Candy & other confectionery products
PA: Nassau-Sosnick Distribution Company Llc
 258 Littlefield Ave
 South San Francisco CA 94080
 650 952-2226

(G-6114)
NOASPENCE INC
Also Called: Edible Arrangement Store 1373
1040 S Broadway Unit 6 (11801-5027)
PHONE 516 433-7848
Hillary B Friedland, *President*
EMP: 6
SALES (est): 499K **Privately Held**
SIC: 2099 5441 Dessert mixes & fillings; confectionery

(G-6115)
NU - COMMUNITEK LLC
108 New South Rd Ste A (11801-5262)
PHONE 516 433-3553
Gary Calmenson,

GEOGRAPHIC SECTION

Highland - Ulster County (G-6143)

Jarret Calmenson,
EMP: 10
SQ FT: 1,500
SALES (est): 2.4MM **Privately Held**
WEB: www.loyaltykiosk.com
SIC: 3575 Computer terminals

(G-6116)
NY EMBROIDERY INC
Also Called: New York Embroidery & Monogram
25 Midland Ave (11801-1509)
PHONE..................516 822-6456
John La Rocca, *President*
▲ **EMP**: 20
SALES (est): 1.5MM **Privately Held**
WEB: www.nyembroidery.com
SIC: 2395 Embroidery & art needlework

(G-6117)
OLMSTEAD PRODUCTS CORP
1 Jefry Ln (11801-5394)
PHONE..................516 681-3700
Jack Tepper, *President*
Nicholas Lucarello, *Vice Pres*
▲ **EMP**: 12 EST: 1954
SQ FT: 7,000
SALES (est): 2.1MM **Privately Held**
SIC: 3556 Food products machinery

(G-6118)
OXYGEN INC (PA)
Also Called: Rodan
6 Midland Ave (11801-1510)
PHONE..................516 433-1144
Daniel Joory, *President*
Ronnie Zubli, *CFO*
Ann Dee, *Sales Staff*
Alex Calleia, *Graphic Designe*
◆ **EMP**: 9
SQ FT: 2,000
SALES (est): 1.1MM **Privately Held**
SIC: 2369 Bathing suits & swimwear: girls', children's & infants'; leggings: girls', children's & infants'

(G-6119)
OYSTER BAY PUMP WORKS INC
78 Midland Ave Unit 1 (11801-1537)
P.O. Box 725 (11802-0725)
PHONE..................516 933-4500
Patrick Gaillard, *CEO*
Andrew Mancura, *Purch Mgr*
Debbie D'Ambrosio, *Buyer*
▲ **EMP**: 18
SALES (est): 5.2MM **Privately Held**
WEB: www.obpw.com
SIC: 3561 3829 3589 Pumps & pumping equipment; medical diagnostic systems, nuclear; liquor dispensing equipment & systems

(G-6120)
P & F BAKERS INC
640 S Broadway (11801-5016)
PHONE..................516 931-6821
P Zamparelli, *CEO*
EMP: 9
SALES (est): 494.4K **Privately Held**
SIC: 2026 Bakers' cheese

(G-6121)
PAL ALUMINUM INC (PA)
Also Called: Pal Industries
230 Duffy Ave Unit A (11801-3641)
PHONE..................516 937-1990
Pana Giotis Mar Neris, *President*
Laurel Marneris, *Vice Pres*
EMP: 3
SQ FT: 70,000
SALES (est): 4.7MM **Privately Held**
SIC: 3444 5033 5031 Metal roofing & roof drainage equipment; gutters, sheet metal; roof deck, sheet metal; siding, except wood; doors

(G-6122)
PAL MANUFACTURING CORP
230 Duffy Ave Unit B (11801-3641)
PHONE..................516 937-1990
Laurel Marneris, *President*
Panagiotis Marneris, *Vice Pres*
EMP: 28
SQ FT: 70,000

SALES (est): 4.5MM **Privately Held**
WEB: www.palwindows.com
SIC: 3442 3231 Storm doors or windows, metal; products of purchased glass

(G-6123)
PB08 INC
40 Bloomingdale Rd (11801-6507)
PHONE..................347 866-7353
Jajtar Kular, *Owner*
Neeraj Sherma, *Principal*
EMP: 2
SALES (est): 3MM **Privately Held**
SIC: 3537 Trucks: freight, baggage, etc.: industrial, except mining

(G-6124)
PEDRE CORP (PA)
Also Called: Pedre Watch
270 Duffy Ave Ste G (11801-3600)
PHONE..................212 868-2935
R Peter Gunshor, *President*
Anthony Scott, *Prdtn Mgr*
◆ **EMP**: 31
SQ FT: 10,000
SALES (est): 5.5MM **Privately Held**
WEB: www.pedrewatch.com
SIC: 3873 Watches, clocks, watchcases & parts

(G-6125)
PERFECT GEAR & INSTRUMENT (HQ)
250 Duffy Ave (11801-3654)
PHONE..................516 328-3330
Morton Hoffman, *President*
Joseph Rubenfeld, *Vice Pres*
EMP: 10
SALES (est): 1.9MM
SALES (corp-wide): 111.3MM **Privately Held**
SIC: 3462 Gears, forged steel
PA: Designatronics Incorporated
250 Duffy Ave Unit A
Hicksville NY 11801
516 328-3300

(G-6126)
PETRO INC
477 W John St (11801-1029)
PHONE..................516 686-1900
Rodney Roberts, *Branch Mgr*
EMP: 9 **Publicly Held**
SIC: 1389 Oil field services
HQ: Petro, Inc.
9 W Broad St Ste 430
Stamford CT 06902
203 325-5400

(G-6127)
PIONEER WINDOW HOLDINGS INC (PA)
Also Called: Pioneer Windows Manufacturing
15 Frederick Pl (11801-4205)
PHONE..................516 822-7000
Vincent Amato, *Ch of Bd*
Anthony J Ross, *President*
Tony Fabbricatore, *Vice Pres*
Dennis Dolan, *Project Mgr*
Brian Holodar, *Project Mgr*
EMP: 12
SALES (est): 14.8MM **Privately Held**
WEB: www.pwindows.com
SIC: 3442 Storm doors or windows, metal

(G-6128)
REPAPERS CORPORATION (PA)
268 N Broadway Unit 9 (11801-2923)
PHONE..................305 691-1635
Andres Patino, *Principal*
Deisy Bonilla, *Purchasing*
◆ **EMP**: 14
SALES (est): 5MM **Privately Held**
SIC: 2611 Pulp manufactured from waste or recycled paper

(G-6129)
RUI XING INTERNATIONAL TRDG CO
89 Jerusalem Ave (11801-4950)
PHONE..................516 298-2667
Ke Yi Sun, *Ch of Bd*
Katie Huang, *Manager*
▲ **EMP**: 5

SALES (est): 500K **Privately Held**
SIC: 3089 Boxes, plastic

(G-6130)
SAMSON TECHNOLOGIES CORP (HQ)
278 Duffy Ave Unit B (11801-3642)
PHONE..................631 784-2200
Richard Ash, *Ch of Bd*
Scott Goodman, *President*
David Hakim, *General Mgr*
Derek Ash, *Business Mgr*
David Ash, *COO*
◆ **EMP**: 70
SALES (est): 15.8MM
SALES (corp-wide): 273.1MM **Privately Held**
WEB: www.samsontech.com
SIC: 3651 3931 5099 5065 Sound reproducing equipment; musical instruments; musical instruments; sound equipment, electronic
PA: Sam Ash Music Corporation
278 Duffy Ave Unit A
Hicksville NY 11801
516 932-6400

(G-6131)
SCIARRA LABORATORIES INC
48509 S Broadway (11801)
PHONE..................516 933-7853
John J Sciarra, *President*
Christopher J Sciarra, *Vice Pres*
Christopher Sciarra, *Vice Pres*
Neil Brown, *Plant Mgr*
Sara Beaulieu, *Office Mgr*
EMP: 6
SALES (est): 1.3MM **Privately Held**
WEB: www.sciarralabs.com
SIC: 2834 Pharmaceutical preparations

(G-6132)
SI PARTNERS INC
15 E Carl St Unit 1 (11801-4290)
PHONE..................516 433-1415
Amit Singhvi, *President*
▲ **EMP**: 7
SALES (est): 837.8K **Privately Held**
SIC: 3355 Aluminum wire & cable

(G-6133)
STS REFILL AMERICA LLC
399 W John St Unit A (11801-1043)
PHONE..................516 934-8008
Shahar Turgeman,
Mark Freedman,
Uri Hason,
Scott Robert,
▲ **EMP**: 6
SQ FT: 2,500
SALES (est): 451K **Privately Held**
WEB: www.stsrefill.com
SIC: 3951 Cartridges, refill: ball point pens

(G-6134)
SUMMIT INSTRUMENT CORP
99 Engineers Dr (11801-6594)
PHONE..................516 433-0140
Arthur Petschauer, *CEO*
Tom Petschauer, *President*
Stefanie Petschauer, *Corp Secy*
EMP: 8
SQ FT: 7,500
SALES (est): 750K **Privately Held**
SIC: 3599 Machine shop, jobbing & repair

(G-6135)
SUNQUEST PHARMACEUTICALS INC
385 W John St Ste 1 (11801-1033)
PHONE..................855 478-6779
Atul Sharma, *President*
EMP: 17
SALES (est): 4.2MM **Privately Held**
SIC: 2834 Pharmaceutical preparations

(G-6136)
TAMPERPROOF SCREW COMPANY INC
30 Laurel St (11801-2641)
PHONE..................516 931-1616
Lewis Friedman, *President*
George Friedman, *Corp Secy*
Alaina Picitelli, *Vice Pres*
▲ **EMP**: 12

SQ FT: 5,000
SALES (est): 2.3MM **Privately Held**
WEB: www.tamperproof.com
SIC: 3452 Screws, metal

(G-6137)
TJ SIGNS UNLIMITED LLC
Also Called: American Signcrafters
327 New South Rd (11801-5226)
PHONE..................631 273-4800
Jeffrey Petersen, *CEO*
Jonathan Bell, *President*
Lisa Johnson, *President*
EMP: 130
SALES (est): 276.5K **Privately Held**
SIC: 3993 Signs & advertising specialties

(G-6138)
VIRAJ - USA INC (DH)
2 Reiter Ave (11801-5234)
PHONE..................516 280-8380
Dhruv Kochhar, *President*
Daulat Tannan, *Vice Pres*
Imran Hassan, *Admin Asst*
◆ **EMP**: 6
SALES (est): 879.7K **Privately Held**
SIC: 3312 Stainless steel

High Falls
Ulster County

(G-6139)
ALE-TECHNIQUES INC
2452 Lucas Tpke Ste B (12440-5926)
PHONE..................845 687-7200
Daniel Ale, *CEO*
EMP: 15
SQ FT: 35,000
SALES (est): 1.3MM **Privately Held**
SIC: 3545 Machine tool accessories

(G-6140)
DELTA PRESS INC
2426 Lucas Tpke (12440-5920)
PHONE..................212 989-3445
Joel Sachs, *President*
EMP: 30
SALES (est): 2.5MM **Privately Held**
WEB: www.deltapress.com
SIC: 2752 Commercial printing, offset

(G-6141)
ULSTER COUNTY PRESS OFFICE
Also Called: Blue Stone Press
1209 State Route 213 (12440-5714)
P.O. Box 149, Stone Ridge (12484-0149)
PHONE..................845 687-4480
Lori Childerss, *President*
Gregory Childress, *Principal*
Rochelle Riservato, *Associate*
EMP: 5
SALES (est): 463.5K **Privately Held**
WEB: www.ulstercountypress.com
SIC: 2711 Commercial printing & newspaper publishing combined; newspapers, publishing & printing

Highland
Ulster County

(G-6142)
BORABORA FRUIT JUICES INC
255 Milton Xrds (12528-2256)
P.O. Box 383, Pound Ridge (10576-0383)
PHONE..................914 438-8744
Michael Heath, *President*
EMP: 8
SQ FT: 10,000
SALES (est): 1MM **Privately Held**
SIC: 2086 Bottled & canned soft drinks

(G-6143)
GORDON FIRE EQUIPMENT LLC
3199 Us Highway 9w (12528-2633)
PHONE..................845 691-5700
Mary Anne Hein, *Mng Member*
EMP: 5
SALES (est): 807K **Privately Held**
SIC: 2899 Fire retardant chemicals

Highland - Ulster County (G-6144)

(G-6144)
HUDSON VALLEY TECH DEV CTR INC
Also Called: Manufacturing & Tech Entp Ctr
180 South St (12528-2439)
PHONE.................845 391-8214
Tom Phillips, *Exec Dir*
Lindsay Thompson, *Administration*
EMP: 15
SQ FT: 5,000
SALES: 1.3MM **Privately Held**
WEB: www.hvtdc.org
SIC: 3679 8711 Electronic circuits; consulting engineer

(G-6145)
M M TOOL AND MANUFACTURING
175 Chapel Hill Rd (12528-2105)
PHONE.................845 691-4140
Matt Mc Cluskey, *President*
Kenneth P Castelo, *Director*
EMP: 8
SQ FT: 10,000
SALES: 1.2MM **Privately Held**
SIC: 3585 Air conditioning equipment, complete; air conditioning units, complete; domestic or industrial

(G-6146)
PRISM SOLAR TECHNOLOGIES INC (HQ)
180 South St (12528-2439)
PHONE.................845 883-4200
Kevin R Stewart, *CEO*
David Waserstein, *Ch of Bd*
Carolyn Lewandowski, *Corp Secy*
Jeff Rosenberg, *Opers Mgr*
John Neidhardt, *Facilities Mgr*
▲ **EMP:** 38
SQ FT: 93,000
SALES (est): 4.9MM **Publicly Held**
SIC: 3433 Solar heaters & collectors

(G-6147)
SELUX CORPORATION
5 Lumen Ln (12528-1903)
P.O. Box 1060 (12528-8060)
PHONE.................845 691-7723
Juergen Hess, *Ch of Bd*
Peter Stanway, *President*
Norman Emery, *Managing Dir*
Michael Seckler, *Vice Pres*
Donna Rose, *Purchasing*
▲ **EMP:** 164
SQ FT: 85,000
SALES: 42.5MM
SALES (corp-wide): 190.4K **Privately Held**
WEB: www.selux.com
SIC: 3646 Commercial indusl & institutional electric lighting fixtures
HQ: Selux Benelux Nv
  Grotesteenweg 50
  Kontich 2550

(G-6148)
ZUMTOBEL LIGHTING INC (DH)
3300 Route 9w (12528-2630)
PHONE.................845 691-6262
Kevin Maddy, *CEO*
Mark Hegeman, *Purch Mgr*
Rick Meyer, *Purchasing*
Deborah Lampitok, *Controller*
James Coles, *Sales Mgr*
▲ **EMP:** 130
SQ FT: 80,000
SALES: 44MM
SALES (corp-wide): 54.5MM **Privately Held**
WEB: www.zumtobel.com
SIC: 3646 Commercial indusl & institutional electric lighting fixtures
HQ: Zumtobel Lighting Gmbh
  SchweizerstraBe 30
  Dornbirn 6850
  557 239-00

Highland Falls
Orange County

(G-6149)
SKD TACTICAL INC
291 Main St (10928-1803)
PHONE.................845 897-2889
Dani Seuk, *CEO*
Joe Seuk, *Vice Pres*
Sean Seuk, *Cust Mgr*
Jo Seuk, *Administration*
▲ **EMP:** 6 **EST:** 1999
SALES: 1.5MM **Privately Held**
SIC: 2399 Military insignia, textile

Highland Mills
Orange County

(G-6150)
ALL MERCHANDISE DISPLAY CORP
Also Called: AM Display
4 Pheasant Run (10930-2140)
PHONE.................718 257-2221
Eddie Minkoff, *President*
Abraham J Minkoff, *Vice Pres*
EMP: 7
SALES (est): 627.8K **Privately Held**
SIC: 2541 Display fixtures, wood

(G-6151)
M &L INDUSTRY OF NY INC
583 State Route 32 Ste 1u (10930-5229)
PHONE.................845 827-6255
EMP: 9
SALES (est): 770K **Privately Held**
SIC: 2441 Mfg Wood Boxes/Shook

(G-6152)
SPEYSIDE HOLDINGS LLC
911 State Route 32 (10930-2309)
P.O. Box 1007 (10930-1007)
PHONE.................845 928-2221
Anthony Williams, *Chairman*
EMP: 25
SALES (est): 855.3K **Privately Held**
SIC: 1442 Construction sand & gravel

Hillburn
Rockland County

(G-6153)
HILLBURN GRANITE COMPANY INC
166 Sixth St (10931)
P.O. Box 832, Tuxedo Park (10987-0832)
PHONE.................845 357-8900
Leeann Matthews, *Info Tech Mgr*
EMP: 5
SQ FT: 1,000
SALES (est): 285.4K **Privately Held**
SIC: 1411 Granite dimension stone

(G-6154)
MERCO HACKENSACK INC
Also Called: Merco Tape
201 Route 59 Ste D2 (10931-1189)
P.O. Box 875 (10931-0875)
PHONE.................845 357-3699
David Rose, *President*
Adam Riskin, *Vice Pres*
Eleanor Rose, *Sales Staff*
Joshua Rose, *Sales Staff*
Celeste Tenore, *Admin Asst*
◆ **EMP:** 6 **EST:** 1972
SQ FT: 18,000
SALES: 4.7MM **Privately Held**
WEB: www.maskingtape.com
SIC: 2672 Tape, pressure sensitive: made from purchased materials

(G-6155)
SYMMETRY MEDICAL INC
201 Route 59 Bldg E (10931-1190)
P.O. Box 1187 (10931-1187)
PHONE.................845 368-4573
EMP: 8
SALES (corp-wide): 871.2MM **Privately Held**
SIC: 3841 Surgical & medical instruments
HQ: Symmetry Medical Inc.
  3724 N State Road 15
  Warsaw IN 46582

Hilton
Monroe County

(G-6156)
CUDDEBACK MACHINING INC
18 Draffin Rd (14468-9708)
PHONE.................585 392-5889
Lawrence Cuddeback, *President*
Michael Ahl, *Managing Dir*
Sandra Cuddeback, *Admin Sec*
EMP: 7
SQ FT: 4,200
SALES (est): 1.1MM **Privately Held**
WEB: www.cuddebackmachining.com
SIC: 3496 3544 Miscellaneous fabricated wire products; special dies & tools

(G-6157)
MONROE FLUID TECHNOLOGY INC
36 Draffin Rd (14468-9717)
PHONE.................585 392-3434
Alan Christodaro, *President*
Jeff Cliff, *VP Mfg*
Paul Silloway, *Prdtn Mgr*
Fred Kane, *Accounts Mgr*
Manny Bright, *Director*
▲ **EMP:** 25
SALES: 10MM **Privately Held**
SIC: 2992 2899 2841 Lubricating oils; cutting oils, blending: made from purchased materials; chemical preparations; soap & other detergents

(G-6158)
OMEGA CONSOLIDATED CORPORATION
101 Heinz St (14468-1226)
PHONE.................585 392-9262
Martin Hunte, *President*
Robert Hunte, *Vice Pres*
Thomas Hunte, *Vice Pres*
▼ **EMP:** 20 **EST:** 1981
SQ FT: 30,000
SALES (est): 3.1MM **Privately Held**
WEB: www.omegacon.com
SIC: 3541 Machine tools, metal cutting type

(G-6159)
WILLIAM J RYAN
Also Called: Ryan Printing
1365 Hamlin Parma Townlne (14468-9749)
PHONE.................585 392-6200
William Ryan, *Owner*
EMP: 5
SQ FT: 3,000
SALES: 200K **Privately Held**
WEB: www.ryanprinting.com
SIC: 2752 7334 2759 Commercial printing, lithographic; photocopying & duplicating services; commercial printing

Himrod
Yates County

(G-6160)
LAPP MANAGEMENT CORP
Also Called: Wood-Tex Products
3700 Route 14 (14842-9802)
PHONE.................607 243-5141
Barbara Lapp, *President*
EMP: 7
SQ FT: 12,000
SALES (est): 1.2MM **Privately Held**
WEB: www.woodtexproducts.com
SIC: 2452 Prefabricated buildings, wood

(G-6161)
WOOD TEX PRODUCTS LLC
3700 Route 14 (14842-9802)
PHONE.................607 243-5141
Ben Lapp, *Exec VP*

Meredith Marsh, *Manager*
Matt Camacho, *Senior Mgr*
Brian Fisher, *Info Tech Mgr*
Kent Lapp,
EMP: 54
SALES: 7.2MM **Privately Held**
SIC: 2452 Prefabricated buildings, wood

Hinsdale
Cattaraugus County

(G-6162)
SIMPLICITY BANDSAW INC
3674 Main St (14743-9817)
PHONE.................716 557-8805
Norbert J Witzigman, *Principal*
EMP: 7
SALES (est): 717.2K **Privately Held**
SIC: 2421 Sawmills & planing mills, general

Hobart
Delaware County

(G-6163)
HATHERLEIGH COMPANY LTD
62545 State Highway 10 (13788-3019)
PHONE.................607 538-1092
Frederic Flach, *Ch of Bd*
Anna Krusinski, *Manager*
EMP: 9
SALES: 8.7K **Privately Held**
WEB: www.bodysculptingbible.com
SIC: 2721 7812 Trade journals: publishing only, not printed on site; audio-visual program production

(G-6164)
SPECGX LLC
Also Called: Mallinckrodt Pharmaceuticals
172 Railroad Ave (13788)
PHONE.................607 538-9124
Jacqueline Murphy, *Project Mgr*
Seth Merwin, *Opers Mgr*
Tammi Tully, *Purch Agent*
Paul Dibble, *Engineer*
Carolyn Ehrhart, *Engineer*
EMP: 630
WEB: www.mallinckrodt.com
SIC: 2834 Pharmaceutical preparations
HQ: Specgx Llc
  385 Marshall Ave
  Saint Louis MO 63119
  314 654-2000

Hogansburg
Franklin County

(G-6165)
JACOBS TOBACCO COMPANY
Also Called: Jacobs Manufacturing
344 Frogtown Rd (13655-3137)
PHONE.................518 358-4948
Roseley Jacobs, *Owner*
Tisha Thompson, *Marketing Mgr*
EMP: 24
SALES (est): 4.3MM **Privately Held**
SIC: 2111 Cigarettes

(G-6166)
OHSERASE MANUFACTURING LLC
393 Frogtown Rd (13655-3138)
PHONE.................518 358-9309
Justin Tarbell, *Vice Pres*
▲ **EMP:** 7
SALES (est): 85K **Privately Held**
SIC: 3999 Barber & beauty shop equipment

Holbrook
Suffolk County

(G-6167)
ACCENT SPEAKER TECHNOLOGY LTD
Also Called: Nola Speaker
1511 Lincoln Ave (11741-2216)
PHONE 631 738-2540
Carl Marchisotto, *CEO*
▲ EMP: 7
SALES (est): 1MM Privately Held
SIC: 3651 Speaker systems

(G-6168)
ACCURATE INDUSTRIAL MACHINING
1711 Church St (11741-5921)
PHONE 631 242-0566
Jerome Bricker, *President*
Marguerite Bricker, *Corp Secy*
▲ EMP: 20
SQ FT: 30,000
SALES (est): 2.7MM Privately Held
SIC: 3599 5084 Machine shop, jobbing & repair; industrial machinery & equipment

(G-6169)
ADVANCED DOOR SOLUTIONS INC
Also Called: Advanced Doors
1363 Lincoln Ave Ste 7 (11741-2274)
PHONE 631 773-6100
James McGonigle, *President*
EMP: 7
SQ FT: 2,300
SALES: 1MM Privately Held
SIC: 3442 7699 1796 1793 Metal doors, sash & trim; lock & key services; lock parts made to individual order; installing building equipment; glass & glazing work; window & door installation & erection

(G-6170)
ADVANCED PLACEMENT L LC
60 Lorraine Ct (11741-1540)
PHONE 949 281-9086
Dr Mark Resasco,
EMP: 49 EST: 2016
SQ FT: 2,850
SALES: 6.2MM Privately Held
SIC: 3841 Surgical & medical instruments

(G-6171)
ALWAYS BAKED FRESH
331 Dante Ct Ste F (11741-3800)
PHONE 631 648-0811
Victoria Kim, *Principal*
EMP: 8 EST: 2009
SALES (est): 432.7K Privately Held
SIC: 2051 Cakes, bakery: except frozen

(G-6172)
BNM PRODUCT SERVICE
1561 Lincoln Ave (11741-2217)
PHONE 631 750-1586
Sergio Lorenzo, *President*
EMP: 5
SALES (est): 673.5K Privately Held
SIC: 3545 Machine tool accessories

(G-6173)
BRZOZKA INDUSTRIES INC
Also Called: Felber Metal Fabricators
790 Broadway Ave (11741-4906)
PHONE 631 588-8164
Waldmar Brazozka, *CEO*
Hans Felber, *President*
EMP: 10
SQ FT: 3,600
SALES (est): 1.8MM Privately Held
SIC: 3444 Sheet metalwork

(G-6174)
CALMETRICS INC
1340 Lincoln Ave Ste 6 (11741-2255)
PHONE 631 580-2522
Frank Ferrandino, *President*
David Cernese, *Vice Pres*
Tina Korpus, *Manager*
Justina Kortus, *Manager*
Justina Corpus, *Admin Sec*
EMP: 6
SQ FT: 1,650
SALES (est): 585.6K Privately Held
SIC: 3825 Standards & calibrating equipment, laboratory

(G-6175)
CAREFREE KITCHENS INC
925 Lincoln Ave Ste 1 (11741-2200)
PHONE 631 567-2120
Leonard Daino, *President*
Carolina Daino, *Vice Pres*
EMP: 5
SALES (est): 440K Privately Held
SIC: 2434 5031 5211 Wood kitchen cabinets; kitchen cabinets; cabinets, kitchen

(G-6176)
CJN MACHINERY CORP
917 Lincoln Ave Ste 13 (11741-2250)
PHONE 631 244-8030
Josephine Chillemi, *President*
Josephine Chllemi, *President*
EMP: 7
SQ FT: 4,000
SALES (est): 1.6MM Privately Held
SIC: 3599 Machine shop, jobbing & repair

(G-6177)
CLEAN ROOM DEPOT INC
1730 Church St (11741-5918)
PHONE 631 589-3033
Ken Lorello, *President*
Alexis Lorello, *Vice Pres*
EMP: 10
SQ FT: 3,600
SALES (est): 1.9MM Privately Held
WEB: www.cleanroomdepot.com
SIC: 3822 Auto controls regulating residntl & coml environmt & applncs

(G-6178)
COIL STAMPING INC
1340 Lincoln Ave Ste 1 (11741-2255)
PHONE 631 588-3040
Edward Kiss, *President*
EMP: 15
SALES (est): 1.6MM Privately Held
WEB: www.coilstamping.com
SIC: 3469 Metal stampings

(G-6179)
COLORSPEC COATINGS INTL INC
1716 Church St (11741-5918)
P.O. Box 493, Bohemia (11716-0493)
PHONE 631 472-8251
Lisa Bancalari, *President*
Robert Pein, *Vice Pres*
▲ EMP: 10
SQ FT: 5,200
SALES (est): 1.2MM Privately Held
WEB: www.colorspeccoatings.com
SIC: 2491 Preserving (creosoting) of wood

(G-6180)
CRYSTALIZATIONS SYSTEMS INC
1401 Lincoln Ave (11741-2215)
PHONE 631 467-0090
Patricia Ellenwood, *President*
Alexis Young, *Production*
Nelson Young, *Admin Sec*
EMP: 15
SQ FT: 12,000
SALES (est): 2.3MM Privately Held
SIC: 3499 Fire- or burglary-resistive products

(G-6181)
CTB ENTERPRISE LLC
1170 Lincoln Ave Unit 7 (11741-2286)
PHONE 631 563-0088
Tom Passaro, *Mng Member*
EMP: 10
SALES (est): 814.3K Privately Held
WEB: www.ctbenterprise.com
SIC: 3826 Instruments measuring magnetic & electrical properties

(G-6182)
DATA DISPLAY USA INC
1330 Lincoln Ave Ste 2 (11741-2268)
P.O. Box 5135, Brookings SD (57006-5135)
PHONE 631 218-2130
Marie Neville, *CEO*
Kevin Neville, *President*
▲ EMP: 120
SQ FT: 5,000
SALES (est): 14.8MM
SALES (corp-wide): 610.5MM Publicly Held
WEB: www.data-display.com
SIC: 3674 Light emitting diodes
HQ: Daktronics Ireland Co. Limited Deerpark Industrial Estate Ennis V95 X

(G-6183)
DYNOCOAT INC
1738 Church St (11741-5918)
PHONE 631 244-9344
Patrick Dimaio, *President*
Donald Cowdell, *Vice Pres*
EMP: 10
SQ FT: 6,500
SALES (est): 850K Privately Held
WEB: www.dynocoat.com
SIC: 3479 Coating of metals & formed products

(G-6184)
ELECTRONIC SYSTEMS INC
Also Called: Esi
1742 Church St (11741-5918)
PHONE 631 589-4389
Gregory Quirk, *President*
EMP: 4 EST: 1997
SALES (est): 1.2MM Privately Held
SIC: 3571 Electronic computers

(G-6185)
ENCORE REFINING AND RECYCLEING
1120 Lincoln Ave (11741-2260)
PHONE 631 319-1910
Joseph Crisera, *Partner*
Robert Gaslindo, *Partner*
EMP: 9
SALES (est): 432.3K Privately Held
SIC: 3341 Secondary precious metals

(G-6186)
GEOMETRIC CIRCUITS INC
920 Lincoln Ave Unit 1 (11741-2257)
PHONE 631 249-0230
John Pollina, *President*
Kurt J Meyer, *Treasurer*
EMP: 60
SQ FT: 36,000
SALES (est): 7.5MM Privately Held
WEB: www.geometriccircuits.com
SIC: 3672 Printed circuit boards

(G-6187)
GRAND PRIX LITHO INC
101 Colin Dr Unit 5 (11741-4332)
PHONE 631 242-4182
Craig Lennon, *President*
Starr Maynard, *Prdtn Mgr*
EMP: 25 EST: 1968
SQ FT: 6,000
SALES (est): 4MM Privately Held
WEB: www.grandprixlitho.com
SIC: 2752 Commercial printing, offset

(G-6188)
IMAGE TYPOGRAPHY INC
Also Called: Starfire Printing
751 Coates Ave Ste 31 (11741-6039)
P.O. Box 5250, Miller Place (11764-7901)
PHONE 631 218-6932
James Bryant, *President*
EMP: 5 EST: 2001
SALES (est): 484K Privately Held
WEB: www.starfireprinting.com
SIC: 2759 Commercial printing

(G-6189)
INGHAM INDUSTRIES INC
Also Called: Authentic Parts
1363 Lincoln Ave Ste 1 (11741-2274)
PHONE 631 242-2493
Donna Miller, *President*
EMP: 3
SQ FT: 2,500
SALES: 1MM Privately Held
WEB: www.authelectric.com
SIC: 3699 5065 5251 3429 Chimes, electric; intercommunication equipment, electronic; builders' hardware; manufactured hardware (general)

(G-6190)
INNOVATIVE POWER PRODUCTS INC
1170 Lincoln Ave Unit 7 (11741-2286)
PHONE 631 563-0088
Thomas Passaro Jr, *President*
Thomas Dowling, *Vice Pres*
EMP: 30
SQ FT: 5,200
SALES (est): 3.4MM Privately Held
SIC: 3679 Passive repeaters; electronic circuits

(G-6191)
ISLAND COMPONENTS GROUP INC
101 Colin Dr Unit 4 (11741-4332)
PHONE 631 563-4224
Demetris Agrotis, *CEO*
Roy Koch, *General Mgr*
Bob Jorglewich, *Purch Agent*
EMP: 17
SQ FT: 5,000
SALES: 2MM Privately Held
WEB: www.islandcomponents.com
SIC: 3621 Motors, electric; electric motor & generator parts; electric motor & generator auxillary parts

(G-6192)
JAGS MANUFACTURING NETWORK INC
13403 Lincoln Ave (11741)
PHONE 631 750-6367
Ubalco Filippetti, *CEO*
Pat Filippetti, *General Mgr*
EMP: 6 EST: 2010
SQ FT: 3,200
SALES (est): 680K Privately Held
SIC: 3999 Barber & beauty shop equipment

(G-6193)
LATIUM USA TRADING LLC (PA)
Also Called: Four Seasons Buildings Pdts
5005 Veterans Mem Hwy (11741-4506)
PHONE 631 563-4000
Shaun Kennedy, *President*
Mike Bonasoro, *Sales Staff*
Lauren Lafranca, *Marketing Staff*
Larry Berryhill, *Regional*
EMP: 70
SALES (est): 50.6MM Privately Held
SIC: 3448 Sunrooms, prefabricated metal

(G-6194)
LAWN ELEMENTS INC
1150 Lincoln Ave Ste 4 (11741-2251)
PHONE 631 656-9711
Veronica Concilio, *Principal*
EMP: 11
SALES (est): 1.5MM Privately Held
SIC: 2819 Industrial inorganic chemicals

(G-6195)
LIBERTY LABEL MFG INC
21 Peachtree Ct (11741-4615)
PHONE 631 737-2365
Mike Fernandez, *President*
Lawrence Fernandez, *Vice Pres*
Sandra Iannuzzi, *Office Mgr*
EMP: 15
SALES (est): 1.9MM Privately Held
WEB: www.libertylabel.com
SIC: 2754 2672 Labels: gravure printing; commercial printing, lithographic; coated & laminated paper

(G-6196)
LONG ISLAND ANALYTICAL LABS
110 Colin Dr (11741-4306)
PHONE 631 472-3400
Mike Veraldi, *President*
Domenik Veraldi Jr, *Vice Pres*
Jim Aufiero, *Manager*

Holbrook - Suffolk County (G-6197)

Michael Veraldi, *Director*
Nancy Fava, *Analyst*
EMP: 18 **EST:** 1998
SQ FT: 6,000
SALES (est): 3.7MM **Privately Held**
WEB: www.lialinc.com
SIC: 3822 Auto controls regulating residntl & coml environmt & applncs

(G-6197)
M C PRODUCTS
Also Called: Division of Emergency Services
1330 Lincoln Ave Ste 2 (11741-2268)
P.O. Box 821 (11741-0821)
PHONE 631 471-4070
William Barnes, *President*
Jennifer Riccobono, *Mktg Dir*
EMP: 25
SALES (est): 4.2MM **Privately Held**
WEB: www.mcproducts.com
SIC: 3674 Semiconductors & related devices

(G-6198)
MARKETPLACE SLUTIONS GROUP LLC
48 Nimbus Rd Ste 303 (11741-4417)
PHONE 631 868-0111
Paul Pensabene, *Mng Member*
EMP: 25
SQ FT: 30,000
SALES: 4MM **Privately Held**
SIC: 2032 8742 8748 Italian foods: packaged in cans, jars, etc.; management consulting services; business consulting

(G-6199)
METALS BUILDING PRODUCTS
5005 Veterans Mem Hwy (11741-4506)
PHONE 844 638-2527
Shaun Kennedy, *President*
Bill Kaufmann, *Manager*
EMP: 37
SALES (est): 8MM
SALES (corp-wide): 50.6MM **Privately Held**
SIC: 3448 Prefabricated metal buildings
PA: Latium Usa Trading Llc
   5005 Veterans Mem Hwy
   Holbrook NY 11741
   631 563-4000

(G-6200)
METALSMITH INC
1340 Lincoln Ave Ste 13 (11741-2255)
PHONE 631 467-1500
Jeff Smith, *President*
EMP: 5
SQ FT: 3,500
SALES (est): 420K **Privately Held**
SIC: 3444 Sheet metalwork

(G-6201)
MICROMATTER TECH INC USA
Also Called: Calmetrics
1340 Lincoln Ave Ste 6 (11741-2255)
PHONE 631 580-2522
Frank Ferrandino, *Branch Mgr*
EMP: 9
SALES (corp-wide): 783.8K **Privately Held**
SIC: 3479 Aluminum coating of metal products
PA: Micrommatter Technologies Inc. Usa
   603 Davis St Apt 2008
   Austin TX 78701
   631 580-2522

(G-6202)
NATURES BOUNTY CO
4320 Veterans Mem Hwy (11741-4501)
PHONE 631 588-3492
Duran Magdy, *Plant Mgr*
Albert Anastafi, *Manager*
EMP: 19 **Publicly Held**
SIC: 2833 Vitamins, natural or synthetic: bulk, uncompounded
HQ: The Nature's Bounty Co
   2100 Smithtown Ave
   Ronkonkoma NY 11779
   631 200-2000

(G-6203)
NBTY INC
4320 Veterans Mem Hwy (11741-4504)
PHONE 631 200-2062
Denise Roman, *Marketing Staff*
Joseph Barreca, *Manager*
Kelly Brett, *Manager*
Kristi Latuso, *Manager*
Dragos Lynn, *Manager*
EMP: 9
SALES (est): 563.4K **Privately Held**
SIC: 2833 Medicinals & botanicals

(G-6204)
OMICRON TECHNOLOGIES INC
1736 Church St (11741-5918)
PHONE 631 434-7697
Bob Levine, *President*
John Kennedy, *Vice Pres*
EMP: 20
SALES (est): 901.2K **Privately Held**
SIC: 3999 Manufacturing industries

(G-6205)
READ MANUFACTURING COMPANY INC
330 Dante Ct (11741-3845)
PHONE 631 567-4487
Ronald H Read Sr, *CEO*
Heather Read-Connor, *President*
EMP: 21
SQ FT: 10,000
SALES: 2.6MM **Privately Held**
WEB: www.readmfg.com
SIC: 3444 3479 Sheet metal specialties, not stamped; painting, coating & hot dipping

(G-6206)
ROADIE PRODUCTS INC
Also Called: Hybrid Cases
1121 Lincoln Ave Unit 20 (11741-2264)
P.O. Box 98, Oakdale (11769-0098)
PHONE 631 567-8588
Frank Maiella, *President*
▲ **EMP:** 25
SQ FT: 15,000
SALES (est): 4.7MM **Privately Held**
WEB: www.islandcases.com
SIC: 3161 3171 Musical instrument cases; handbags, women's

(G-6207)
RV PRINTING
39 Portside Dr (11741-5814)
PHONE 631 567-8658
Robert Viola, *Owner*
EMP: 7
SALES (est): 1.4MM **Privately Held**
SIC: 2752 Commercial printing, lithographic

(G-6208)
SELECT-A-FORM INC
4717 Veterans Mem Hwy (11741-4515)
PHONE 631 981-3076
Dave Walters, *President*
John Candia, *Vice Pres*
Gwen Little, *Office Mgr*
EMP: 52
SQ FT: 17,000
SALES (est): 4.2MM **Privately Held**
SIC: 2759 2761 2752 Business forms: printing; manifold business forms; color lithography

(G-6209)
SOLAR METROLOGY LLC
1340 Lincoln Ave Ste 6 (11741-2255)
PHONE 845 247-4701
Francis Reilly,
EMP: 9
SALES (est): 640.8K **Privately Held**
SIC: 3823 Industrial instrmnts msrmnt display/control process variable

(G-6210)
SPEEDCARD INC
Also Called: B C T
133 Glenmere Way (11741-5013)
PHONE 631 472-1904
Jeffery Lewis, *President*
Sharon Lewis, *Manager*
EMP: 8
SQ FT: 3,000
SALES: 320K **Privately Held**
WEB: www.speedcard.com
SIC: 2752 Commercial printing, lithographic

(G-6211)
STERLING SHELF LINERS INC
836 Grundy Ave (11741-2606)
PHONE 631 676-5175
Jason Sterling, *President*
EMP: 5
SALES (est): 187.6K **Privately Held**
SIC: 2542 2392 Shelving, office & store: except wood; placemats, plastic or textile

(G-6212)
SUMMIT TECHNOLOGIES LLC
Also Called: Summit Laser Products
723 Broadway Ave (11741-4955)
PHONE 631 590-1040
Steven Hecht, *Mng Member*
Mike Kosiah,
▲ **EMP:** 38
SQ FT: 25,300
SALES (est): 3.7MM **Privately Held**
WEB: www.uninetimaging.com
SIC: 3955 Print cartridges for laser & other computer printers
PA: Uninet Imaging, Inc.
   3232 W El Segundo Blvd
   Hawthorne CA 90250

(G-6213)
SUPERIOR WELDING
331 Dante Ct Ste G (11741-3800)
PHONE 631 676-2751
Steve Takats, *Executive*
EMP: 7
SALES (est): 802.6K **Privately Held**
SIC: 3599 Machine shop, jobbing & repair

(G-6214)
SYMBOL TECHNOLOGIES LLC
25 Andrea Rd (11741-4310)
PHONE 631 218-3907
James Rawson, *Manager*
EMP: 16
SALES (corp-wide): 3.7B **Publicly Held**
WEB: www.symbol.com
SIC: 3577 Magnetic ink & optical scanning devices
HQ: Symbol Technologies, Llc
   1 Zebra Plz
   Holtsville NY 11742
   631 737-6851

(G-6215)
TENS MACHINE COMPANY INC
800 Grundy Ave (11741-2606)
PHONE 631 981-3321
Toni Coffaro, *President*
Fabio Berlingieri, *Vice Pres*
Mike Berlingieri, *Vice Pres*
Salvatore Berlingieri, *Vice Pres*
Alexandrea Martin, *Prdtn Mgr*
EMP: 28
SQ FT: 9,620
SALES: 5.5MM **Privately Held**
WEB: www.tensmachine.com
SIC: 3728 Aircraft parts & equipment

(G-6216)
TRUSTFORT LLC
4250 Veterans Memorial Hw (11741-4020)
PHONE 781 787-0906
Atindra Barua, *Mng Member*
Marguerite Larkin, *Manager*
EMP: 3
SALES: 1MM **Privately Held**
SIC: 7372 Business oriented computer software

(G-6217)
UNISOURCE FOOD EQP SYSTEMS INC
1505 Lincoln Ave (11741-2216)
PHONE 516 681-0537
Ronald Mondello, *President*
▲ **EMP:** 9
SALES (est): 896.7K **Privately Held**
SIC: 3556 2499 Bakery machinery; bakers' equipment, wood

Holland
Erie County

(G-6218)
BUFFALO POLYMER PROCESSORS INC
42 Edgewood Dr (14080-9784)
PHONE 716 537-3153
Miro O Staroba, *Ch of Bd*
EMP: 40
SQ FT: 180,000
SALES (est): 7MM **Privately Held**
SIC: 3089 Injection molding of plastics; plastic processing

(G-6219)
INEX INC
9229 Olean Rd (14080-9773)
PHONE 716 537-2270
Michael Kasprzyk, *CEO*
Curt Colopy, *Vice Pres*
Corry McCluer, *Info Tech Mgr*
EMP: 9
SALES (est): 1.6MM **Privately Held**
WEB: www.schunk-inex.com
SIC: 3443 Fabricated plate work (boiler shop)

(G-6220)
MULLICAN FLOORING LP
209 Vermont St (14080-9735)
P.O. Box 342 (14080-0342)
PHONE 716 537-2642
Rick Tyburski, *Manager*
EMP: 45
SALES (corp-wide): 344.3MM **Privately Held**
WEB: www.mullicanlumberco.com
SIC: 2426 Flooring, hardwood
HQ: Mullican Flooring, L.P.
   655 Woodlyn Rd
   Johnson City TN 37601
   423 262-8440

(G-6221)
PRO-TECK COATING INC
7785 Olean Rd (14080-9709)
P.O. Box 372 (14080-0372)
PHONE 716 537-2619
Wayne Rutkowski Sr, *President*
Jeff Weber, *Vice Pres*
EMP: 13
SQ FT: 22,000
SALES (est): 1.1MM **Privately Held**
WEB: www.proteckcoating.com
SIC: 3479 Coating of metals with plastic or resins; coating of metals & formed products

(G-6222)
STAROBA PLASTICS INC
42 Edgewood Dr (14080-9784)
PHONE 716 537-3153
Miro Staroba, *CEO*
Barbara Staroba, *Vice Pres*
Ed Staroba, *Manager*
EMP: 125
SALES (est): 17.9MM **Privately Held**
SIC: 3089 Injection molding of plastics

(G-6223)
UHMAC INC
136 N Main St (14080-9704)
PHONE 716 537-2343
James McBride, *President*
Rhonda B Juhasz, *Corp Secy*
EMP: 10
SQ FT: 9,973
SALES (est): 1.6MM **Privately Held**
WEB: www.uhmac.com
SIC: 3542 Rebuilt machine tools, metal forming types

GEOGRAPHIC SECTION

Holtsville - Suffolk County (G-6250)

Holland Patent
Oneida County

(G-6224)
CUSTOM KLEAN CORP
Also Called: Pressure Washer Sales
8890 Boak Rd E (13354-3608)
PHONE.................................315 865-8101
Paul Sears, *President*
EMP: 15
SQ FT: 30,000
SALES (est): 1.8MM **Privately Held**
WEB: www.pressurewashersales.com
SIC: 3589 7363 High pressure cleaning equipment; domestic help service

(G-6225)
STEFFEN PUBLISHING INC
Also Called: Adirondack Home News
9584 Main St (13354-3819)
P.O. Box 403 (13354-0403)
PHONE.................................315 865-4100
Fax: 315 865-4000
EMP: 100
SQ FT: 20,000
SALES (est): 4.4MM **Privately Held**
SIC: 2711 2752 2732 2731 Newspapers-Publish/Print Lithographic Coml Print Book Printing Book-Publishing/Printing Periodical-Publish/Print

Holley
Orleans County

(G-6226)
AMY PAK PUBLISHING INC
3997 Roosevelt Hwy (14470-9201)
PHONE.................................585 964-8188
Amy Pak, *Principal*
EMP: 8
SALES (est): 742.3K **Privately Held**
SIC: 2741 Miscellaneous publishing

(G-6227)
ORLEANS CUSTOM PACKING INC
101 Cadbury Way (14470-1079)
PHONE.................................585 314-8227
Donald Ward, *Ch of Bd*
EMP: 6
SALES (est): 622.4K **Privately Held**
SIC: 2011 Meat packing plants

(G-6228)
PRECISION PACKAGING PDTS INC
88 Nesbitt Dr (14470-1078)
PHONE.................................585 638-8200
Michael Evans, *CEO*
▲ EMP: 110
SQ FT: 68,000
SALES (est): 13.6MM
SALES (corp-wide): 14.7B **Publicly Held**
WEB: www.prepackpro.com
SIC: 3089 Plastic containers, except foam
PA: Newell Brands Inc.
221 River St Ste 13
Hoboken NJ 07030
201 610-6600

(G-6229)
SEAWARD CANDIES
3588 N Main Street Rd (14470-9305)
PHONE.................................585 638-6761
Donna Seaward,
EMP: 6
SALES: 75K **Privately Held**
SIC: 2064 5441 Candy & other confectionery products; candy

(G-6230)
WADDINGTON NORTH AMERICA INC
Also Called: Wna Holley
88 Nesbitt Dr (14470-1078)
PHONE.................................585 638-8200
EMP: 13
SALES (corp-wide): 2.9B **Privately Held**
SIC: 3089 Plastic kitchenware, tableware & houseware; plastic processing

HQ: Waddington North America, Inc.
50 E Rivercenter Blvd # 650
Covington KY 41011

Hollis
Queens County

(G-6231)
BORDEN & RILEY PAPER CO INC
18410 Jamaica Ave Ste W3 (11423-2434)
PHONE.................................718 454-9494
Zoila P Woodward, *President*
Juan Guerra, *Vice Pres*
▲ EMP: 25
SQ FT: 31,500
SALES (est): 5.3MM **Privately Held**
WEB: www.bordenandriley.com
SIC: 2675 Die-cut paper & board

(G-6232)
CHINA RUITAI INTL HOLDINGS LTD
8710 Clover Pl (11423-1252)
PHONE.................................718 740-2278
James Herbst, *Principal*
EMP: 3
SALES: 43.1MM **Privately Held**
SIC: 2869 Industrial organic chemicals

(G-6233)
CRUMBRUBBER TECHNOLOGY INC
18740 Hollis Ave (11423-2808)
PHONE.................................718 468-3988
Angelo Reali, *President*
Michael Reali, *Vice Pres*
EMP: 10
SQ FT: 60,000
SALES: 5MM **Privately Held**
SIC: 3559 4953 Recycling machinery; recycling, waste materials

(G-6234)
G & J RDYMX & MASNRY SUP INC
18330 Jamaica Ave (11423-2302)
PHONE.................................718 454-0800
John Cervoni, *President*
John Cerzoni, *President*
EMP: 12
SQ FT: 80,000
SALES (est): 1.2MM **Privately Held**
SIC: 3273 Ready-mixed concrete

(G-6235)
NEW ATLANTIC READY MIX CORP
18330 Jamaica Ave (11423-2302)
PHONE.................................718 812-0739
John Cervoni, *President*
EMP: 7
SALES (est): 1MM **Privately Held**
SIC: 3273 Ready-mixed concrete

Holtsville
Suffolk County

(G-6236)
ADVANCE PHARMACEUTICAL INC (PA)
895 Waverly Ave (11742-1109)
PHONE.................................631 981-4600
Tasrin Hossain, *President*
Liaquat Hossain, *Vice Pres*
EMP: 85
SQ FT: 80,000
SALES: 9MM **Privately Held**
SIC: 2834 Druggists' preparations (pharmaceuticals)

(G-6237)
BROOKHAVEN INSTRUMENTS CORP
750 Blue Point Rd (11742-1896)
PHONE.................................631 758-3200
Walther Tscharnuter, *CEO*
Joe Pozzolano, *Ch of Bd*
Bruce Weiner, *President*

Eric Farrell, *General Mgr*
Joseph Pozzolano, *General Mgr*
EMP: 24
SQ FT: 15,000
SALES (est): 5MM **Privately Held**
WEB: www.bic.com
SIC: 3826 Analytical instruments

(G-6238)
C & H PRECISION TOOLS INC
194 Morris Ave Ste 20 (11742-1451)
PHONE.................................631 758-3806
Donald Schwabe, *President*
EMP: 20
SALES (est): 1.9MM **Privately Held**
SIC: 3469 Metal stampings

(G-6239)
CUTTING EDGE METAL WORKS
12 Long Island Ave (11742-1803)
PHONE.................................631 981-8333
Tom Richards, *Owner*
Lou Tancredi, *Vice Pres*
EMP: 24
SALES: 3.1MM **Privately Held**
SIC: 3444 Sheet metalwork

(G-6240)
KOEHLER INSTRUMENT COMPANY INC (PA)
85 Corporate Dr (11742-2007)
PHONE.................................631 589-3800
Roy Westerhaus, *Ch of Bd*
Chris Koenig, *Engineer*
Peter Brey, *Treasurer*
Virginia Chambers, *Sales Staff*
Christina Corbitt, *Sales Staff*
▲ EMP: 55
SQ FT: 28,500
SALES (est): 10.8MM **Privately Held**
WEB: www.koehlerinstrument.com
SIC: 3823 Industrial instrmnts msrmnt display/control process variable

(G-6241)
OASIS COSMETIC LABS INC
182 Long Island Ave (11742-1815)
PHONE.................................631 758-0038
Thomas Murray, *President*
EMP: 10
SALES: 2MM **Privately Held**
SIC: 2844 Cosmetic preparations

(G-6242)
PAVCO ASPHALT INC
615 Furrows Rd (11742-2001)
PHONE.................................631 289-3223
Ronald Marone, *President*
Ronald Fehr, *Treasurer*
Sally Marone, *Admin Sec*
EMP: 20
SQ FT: 2,000
SALES (est): 2.3MM **Privately Held**
SIC: 2951 1611 Asphalt paving mixtures & blocks; highway & street paving contractor

(G-6243)
PRIMA ASPHALT AND CONCRETE
615 Furrows Rd (11742-2099)
PHONE.................................631 289-3223
William Fehr, *Vice Pres*
Ronald Fehr, *Treasurer*
Sally Marone, *Admin Sec*
EMP: 11
SQ FT: 2,000
SALES (est): 3.3MM **Privately Held**
SIC: 2951 Asphalt paving mixtures & blocks

(G-6244)
SCREEN THE WORLD INC
Also Called: Crazy Hatter
658 Blue Point Rd (11742-1848)
PHONE.................................631 475-0023
Jeff Liebowitz, *President*
EMP: 12
SQ FT: 5,000
SALES (est): 1.5MM **Privately Held**
WEB: www.crazyhatter.com
SIC: 2759 2395 Screen printing; art needlework; made from purchased materials

(G-6245)
STARFIRE PRINTING INC
28 Washington Ave (11742-1027)
PHONE.................................631 736-1495
EMP: 5
SALES (est): 230K **Privately Held**
SIC: 2759 Commercial Printing

(G-6246)
SYMBOL TECHNOLOGIES LLC (HQ)
Also Called: Symbol Technologies Delaware
1 Zebra Plz (11742-1300)
PHONE.................................631 737-6851
Edward Fitzpatrick, *CEO*
Paul Kiernen, *Principal*
Timothy T Yates, *CFO*
Cary Schmiedel, *Treasurer*
▲ EMP: 1800 EST: 1987
SQ FT: 299,000
SALES (est): 1.4B
SALES (corp-wide): 3.7B **Publicly Held**
WEB: www.symbol.com
SIC: 3577 Optical scanning devices
PA: Zebra Technologies Corporation
3 Overlook Pt
Lincolnshire IL 60069
847 634-6700

(G-6247)
TANGRAM COMPANY LLC
125 Corporate Dr (11742-2007)
PHONE.................................631 758-0460
Amber Cuttone, *Office Mgr*
Philip Gillette,
John Takakjian,
▼ EMP: 25
SQ FT: 32,000
SALES: 6.4MM **Privately Held**
WEB: www.tangramco.com
SIC: 2819 2899 Industrial inorganic chemicals; chemical preparations

(G-6248)
TELXON CORPORATION (DH)
1 Zebra Plz (11742-1300)
PHONE.................................631 738-2400
John W Paxton, *Ch of Bd*
Kenneth A Cassady, *President*
David H Briggs, *Vice Pres*
Woody M McGee, *CFO*
▲ EMP: 35
SALES (est): 83.8MM
SALES (corp-wide): 3.7B **Publicly Held**
WEB: www.telxon.com
SIC: 3571 7373 3663 Personal computers (microcomputers); systems integration services; radio & TV communications equipment
HQ: Symbol Technologies, Llc
1 Zebra Plz
Holtsville NY 11742
631 737-6851

(G-6249)
TOPAZ INDUSTRIES INC
130 Corporate Dr (11742-2005)
PHONE.................................631 207-0700
Craig Stowell, *President*
▲ EMP: 10
SQ FT: 3,000
SALES (est): 2MM **Privately Held**
SIC: 2899 Salt

(G-6250)
WEISS INSTRUMENTS INC
905 Waverly Ave (11742-1109)
PHONE.................................631 207-1200
William Weiss, *CEO*
John Weiss, *President*
Kenneth Goodwin, *General Mgr*
Andrea Rocco, *Editor*
Phillip J Weiss, *Chairman*
▲ EMP: 100 EST: 1882
SQ FT: 50,000
SALES (est): 25.6MM **Privately Held**
WEB: www.weissinstruments.com
SIC: 3823 3829 Temperature instruments: industrial process type; pressure gauges, dial & digital; measuring & controlling devices

Holtsville - Suffolk County (G-6251)

(G-6251)
ZEBRA TECHNOLOGIES ENTP CORP
1 Zebra Plz (11742-1325)
PHONE...................................800 722-6234
Anders Gustafsson, *CEO*
Darrin Bouck, *Engineer*
Kenneth Rivalsi, *Engineer*
Ming Sun, *Senior Engr*
Michael Smiley, *CFO*
EMP: 39
SALES (est): 23MM
SALES (corp-wide): 3.7B **Publicly Held**
SIC: 3577 1541 5088 Computer peripheral equipment; prefabricated building erection, industrial; transportation equipment & supplies
PA: Zebra Technologies Corporation
3 Overlook Pt
Lincolnshire IL 60069
847 634-6700

Homer
Cortland County

(G-6252)
ALBANY INTERNATIONAL CORP
156 S Main St (13077-1600)
PHONE...................................607 749-7226
Tim Stevens, *Safety Mgr*
Glen Gutierrez, *Buyer*
Gary R Seales, *Manager*
EMP: 115
SALES (corp-wide): 863.7MM **Publicly Held**
WEB: www.albint.com
SIC: 2298 3089 2284 Cordage & twine; extruded finished plastic products; thread mills
PA: Albany International Corp.
216 Airport Dr
Rochester NH 03867
603 330-5850

(G-6253)
DEWEY MACHINE & TOOL INC
49 James St (13077-1221)
PHONE...................................607 749-3930
Chris Dewey, *President*
EMP: 6
SQ FT: 2,000
SALES (est): 864.4K **Privately Held**
SIC: 3599 Machine shop, jobbing & repair

(G-6254)
F M L INDUSTRIES INC
10 Hudson St (13077-1043)
P.O. Box 398 (13077-0398)
PHONE...................................607 749-7273
Paul Dries, *President*
EMP: 9
SQ FT: 12,000
SALES (est): 1.4MM **Privately Held**
SIC: 7692 3444 3599 Welding repair; sheet metalwork; machine shop, jobbing & repair

(G-6255)
HASKELL MACHINE & TOOL INC
5 S Fulton St (13077-1232)
PHONE...................................607 749-2421
James E Harris, *President*
Roberta J Harris, *Vice Pres*
EMP: 10 **EST:** 1947
SQ FT: 7,000
SALES (est): 1.4MM **Privately Held**
WEB: www.haskellmachine.com
SIC: 3599 7692 Machine shop, jobbing & repair; welding repair

(G-6256)
HOMER IRON WORKS LLC
5130 Us Route 11 (13077-9528)
PHONE...................................607 749-3963
Mike Park,
EMP: 7
SQ FT: 2,100
SALES: 700K **Privately Held**
SIC: 3441 7692 7538 Fabricated structural metal; welding repair; general automotive repair shops

(G-6257)
HOMER LOGGING CONTRACTOR
6176 Sunnyside Dr (13077-9321)
PHONE...................................607 753-8553
Steve Hubbard, *Principal*
EMP: 5
SALES (est): 339.5K **Privately Held**
SIC: 2411 Logging camps & contractors

(G-6258)
PHOTON VISION SYSTEMS INC (PA)
1 Technology Pl (13077-1526)
PHONE...................................607 749-2689
Thomas L Vogelsong, *President*
Jeffrey J Zarnowski, *COO*
EMP: 15 **EST:** 1997
SALES (est): 1.6MM **Privately Held**
SIC: 3571 Electronic computers

(G-6259)
SOLIDUS INDUSTRIES INC
Also Called: Pb Industries
6849 N Glen Haven Rd (13077-9522)
PHONE...................................607 749-4540
Frank Girardi, *President*
EMP: 96
SQ FT: 28,000
SALES (est): 13MM **Privately Held**
WEB: www.pb-industries.com
SIC: 3444 3469 3479 2396 Sheet metalwork; machine parts, stamped or pressed metal; coating of metals & formed products; automotive & apparel trimmings

Honeoye
Ontario County

(G-6260)
CY PLASTICS WORKS INC
8601 Main St (14471-9603)
P.O. Box 560 (14471-0560)
PHONE...................................585 229-2555
Andy Molodetz, *President*
John Cavagnaro, *Engineer*
Julie Molodetz, *Controller*
▲ **EMP:** 40
SQ FT: 35,000
SALES (est): 10.6MM **Privately Held**
SIC: 3089 3544 3842 3949 Injection molding of plastics; special dies, tools, jigs & fixtures; industrial molds; surgical appliances & supplies; sporting & athletic goods

(G-6261)
ROOME TECHNOLOGIES INC
4796 Honeoye Business Par (14471-8808)
P.O. Box 742 (14471-0742)
PHONE...................................585 229-4437
David Roome, *President*
EMP: 7
SQ FT: 8,500
SALES: 2MM **Privately Held**
WEB: www.roometechnologies.com
SIC: 3564 Filters, air: furnaces, air conditioning equipment, etc.

Honeoye Falls
Monroe County

(G-6262)
BRANSON ULTRASONICS CORP
475 Quaker Meeting Hse Rd (14472-9754)
PHONE...................................585 624-8000
John Bielaski, *Project Engr*
Craig Birrittella, *Manager*
EMP: 20
SQ FT: 78,580
SALES (corp-wide): 15.2B **Publicly Held**
WEB: www.bransonic.com
SIC: 3699 Cleaning equipment, ultrasonic, except medical & dental
HQ: Branson Ultrasonics Corporation
41 Eagle Rd Ste 1
Danbury CT 06810
203 796-0400

(G-6263)
CUSTOM BREWCRAFTERS INC
300 Village Square Blvd (14472-1180)
PHONE...................................585 624-4386
Walter Alcorn, *President*
Jim Perdue, *Finance Dir*
Kurt Kipfer, *Administration*
Logan Abplanalp, *Relations*
EMP: 12
SQ FT: 4,800
SALES (est): 1.7MM **Privately Held**
WEB: www.custombrewcrafters.com
SIC: 2082 Beer (alcoholic beverage)

(G-6264)
EQUICENTER INC
3247 Rush Mendon Rd (14472-9333)
PHONE...................................585 742-2522
Jonathan Friedlander, *President*
EMP: 30
SALES: 622.2K **Privately Held**
SIC: 3199 Equestrian related leather articles

(G-6265)
GRAVER TECHNOLOGIES LLC
300 W Main St (14472-1197)
PHONE...................................585 624-1330
Herbert J Ego, *General Mgr*
EMP: 40
SQ FT: 34,000
SALES (est): 9.4MM
SALES (corp-wide): 242.1B **Publicly Held**
SIC: 3569 Filters, general line: industrial
HQ: Graver Technologies Llc
200 Lake Dr
Newark DE 19702

(G-6266)
HANSON AGGREGATES PA LLC
2049 County Rd 6 (14472)
PHONE...................................585 624-3800
Douglas Fuess, *Manager*
EMP: 35
SALES (corp-wide): 20.3B **Privately Held**
SIC: 2951 1442 5032 Asphalt & asphaltic paving mixtures (not from refineries); gravel mining; brick, stone & related material
HQ: Hanson Aggregates Pennsylvania, Llc
7660 Imperial Way
Allentown PA 18195
610 366-4626

(G-6267)
HANSON AGGREGATES PA LLC
2049 Honeoye Falls 6 Rd (14472-8913)
P.O. Box 151 (14472-0151)
PHONE...................................585 624-1220
Mike Clark, *Branch Mgr*
EMP: 30
SALES (corp-wide): 20.3B **Privately Held**
SIC: 1442 5999 1422 5032 Gravel mining; stones, crystalline: rough; crushed & broken limestone; asphalt mixture
HQ: Hanson Aggregates Pennsylvania, Llc
7660 Imperial Way
Allentown PA 18195
610 366-4626

(G-6268)
HONEOYE FALLS DISTILLERY LLC (PA)
168 W Main St (14472-1135)
PHONE...................................201 780-4618
Scott M Stanton, *Mng Member*
John D Marshall,
Robert Teal Schlegel,
EMP: 11 **EST:** 2014
SQ FT: 7,000
SALES: 200K **Privately Held**
SIC: 2085 Applejack (alcoholic beverage)

(G-6269)
K & H PRECISION PRODUCTS INC
45 Norton St (14472-1032)
PHONE...................................585 624-4894
Steven Hogarth, *President*
Alex Ferguson, *Vice Pres*
George Reeners, *CFO*
Colin Hogarth, *Manager*
EMP: 40
SQ FT: 20,000
SALES (est): 8.1MM **Privately Held**
WEB: www.kandhprecision.com
SIC: 3543 3089 3599 3544 Industrial patterns; injection molded finished plastic products; machine shop, jobbing & repair; special dies, tools, jigs & fixtures; nonferrous foundries

(G-6270)
KADDIS MANUFACTURING CORP
Enerco Plant
1175 Bragg St (14472-8602)
P.O. Box 92985, Rochester (14692-9085)
PHONE...................................585 624-3070
Bruce Whitmore, *Manager*
Robert Dardenne, *Supervisor*
EMP: 8
SALES (corp-wide): 11.2MM **Privately Held**
WEB: www.kaddis.com
SIC: 3451 3621 3568 Screw machine products; motors & generators; power transmission equipment
PA: Kaddis Manufacturing Corp.
293 Patriot Way
Rochester NY 14624
585 464-9000

(G-6271)
MICROPEN TECHNOLOGIES CORP
Also Called: MICROPEN DIVISION
93 Papermill St (14472-1252)
PHONE...................................585 624-2610
Edwin P Petrazzolo, *CEO*
William Grande, *Vice Pres*
Eric Van Wormer, *Vice Pres*
Randy Greig, *Engineer*
Nathan Mercuri, *Engineer*
▼ **EMP:** 75
SQ FT: 38,000
SALES: 13.6MM **Privately Held**
WEB: www.ohmcraft.com
SIC: 3676 3625 Electronic resistors; resistors & resistor units

(G-6272)
RUSH GRAVEL CORP
130 Kavanaugh Rd (14472-9599)
PHONE...................................585 533-1740
Marie Schillinger, *Treasurer*
David Schillinger Jr, *Shareholder*
Timothy Schillinger, *Shareholder*
EMP: 8
SALES (est): 770K **Privately Held**
WEB: www.rushgravel.com
SIC: 1442 Sand mining; gravel mining

(G-6273)
SOUTHCO INC
Honeoye Falls Div
250 East St (14472-1298)
PHONE...................................585 624-2545
Terry Graham, *Engineer*
Joseph Werner, *Engineer*
John Kilpatrick, *Senior Engr*
Karen Lewis, *Treasurer*
Scott Hammond, *Human Res Mgr*
EMP: 400
SQ FT: 40,000
SALES (corp-wide): 681.3MM **Privately Held**
WEB: www.southco.com
SIC: 3429 3452 Metal fasteners; bolts, nuts, rivets & washers
HQ: Southco, Inc.
210 N Brinton Lake Rd
Concordville PA 19331
610 459-4000

(G-6274)
STEVER-LOCKE INDUSTRIES INC
Also Called: Metal Stampings
179 N Main St (14472-1056)
PHONE...................................585 624-3450
Elaine R Davin, *President*
▲ **EMP:** 9
SQ FT: 33,000
SALES (est): 6.2MM **Privately Held**
WEB: www.steverlocke.com
SIC: 3469 3672 3643 Metal stampings; wiring boards; current-carrying wiring devices

GEOGRAPHIC SECTION

Hoosick Falls
Rensselaer County

(G-6275)
GRAPHITEK INC
4883 State Route 67 (12090-4829)
P.O. Box 131, Glenmont (12077-0131)
PHONE..................518 686-5966
Al Randle, *President*
Thierry Guerlain, *Vice Pres*
Peggy Cottrell, *Office Mgr*
EMP: 18
SQ FT: 8,500
SALES: 3.5MM **Privately Held**
WEB: www.graphitek.com
SIC: 3993 Signs & advertising specialties

(G-6276)
INTERFACE PERFORMANCE MTLS INC
12 Davis St (12090-1006)
PHONE..................518 686-3400
James Lynch, *Branch Mgr*
EMP: 60
SALES (corp-wide): 698.4MM **Publicly Held**
WEB: www.sealinfo.com
SIC: 2631 3053 Paperboard mills; gaskets, packing & sealing devices
HQ: Interface Performance Materials, Inc.
216 Wohlsen Way
Lancaster PA 17603

(G-6277)
LOVEJOY CHAPLET CORPORATION
12 River St (12090-1815)
P.O. Box 66 (12090-0066)
PHONE..................518 686-5232
Peter McGuire, *President*
Lisa McGuire, *Vice Pres*
Mallory McGuire, *Sales Mgr*
Margaret Sargood, *Admin Asst*
EMP: 28 EST: 1911
SQ FT: 20,000
SALES (est): 4.5MM **Privately Held**
WEB: www.lovejoychaplet.com
SIC: 3599 Machine shop, jobbing & repair

(G-6278)
OAK-MITSUI INC
1 Mechanic St Bldg 2 (12090-1011)
PHONE..................518 686-8060
EMP: 54
SALES (corp-wide): 4.8B **Privately Held**
SIC: 3497 Copper foil
HQ: Oak Mitsui, Inc.
29 Battleship Road Ext
Camden SC 29020
518 686-4961

(G-6279)
OAK-MITSUI TECHNOLOGIES LLC
80 1st St (12090-1631)
P.O. Box 501 (12090-0501)
PHONE..................518 686-4961
Fujio Kuwako,
▲ EMP: 30
SALES (est): 4.6MM
SALES (corp-wide): 4.8B **Privately Held**
WEB: www.oakmitsui.com
SIC: 3497 Copper foil
HQ: Oak Mitsui, Inc.
29 Battleship Road Ext
Camden SC 29020
518 686-4961

(G-6280)
SAINT-GOBAIN PRFMCE PLAS CORP
14 Mccaffrey St (12090-1819)
PHONE..................518 686-7301
Chris Lower, *Manager*
EMP: 177
SALES (corp-wide): 213.5MM **Privately Held**
SIC: 2821 Plastics materials & resins

HQ: Saint-Gobain Performance Plastics Corporation
31500 Solon Rd
Solon OH 44139
440 836-6900

(G-6281)
SAINT-GOBAIN PRFMCE PLAS CORP
1 Liberty St (12090-1019)
P.O. Box 320 (12090)
PHONE..................518 686-7301
Pat Traynor, *Branch Mgr*
EMP: 190
SALES (corp-wide): 213.5MM **Privately Held**
SIC: 2821 Polytetrafluoroethylene resins (teflon)
HQ: Saint-Gobain Performance Plastics Corporation
31500 Solon Rd
Solon OH 44139
440 836-6900

Hopewell Junction
Dutchess County

(G-6282)
APPLIED MATERIALS INC
2531 Route 52 (12533-3227)
PHONE..................845 227-5000
Ofer Nakash, *Opers Mgr*
Mark Gilliam, *Manager*
James Hartman, *Manager*
EMP: 50
SALES (corp-wide): 14.5B **Publicly Held**
WEB: www.appliedmaterials.com
SIC: 3559 Semiconductor manufacturing machinery
PA: Applied Materials, Inc.
3050 Bowers Ave
Santa Clara CA 95054
408 727-5555

(G-6283)
BEECH GROVE TECHNOLOGY INC
11 Sandy Pines Blvd (12533-8211)
P.O. Box 406, Stormville (12582-0406)
PHONE..................845 223-6844
Carol Petvai, *President*
Steve Petvai, *Vice Pres*
EMP: 5
SQ FT: 1,500
SALES (est): 480K **Privately Held**
SIC: 3674 Semiconductors & related devices

(G-6284)
EMAGIN CORPORATION (PA)
2070 Route 52 Bldg 334 (12533-3507)
PHONE..................845 838-7900
Jill J Wittels, *Ch of Bd*
Andrew G Sculley, *President*
Jeffrey P Lucas, *President*
Christopher Brody, *Principal*
Paul Cronson, *Principal*
EMP: 90
SQ FT: 37,000
SALES: 22MM **Publicly Held**
WEB: www.emagin.com
SIC: 3674 Light emitting diodes

(G-6285)
FRITTERS & BUNS INC
236 Blue Hill Rd (12533-6659)
PHONE..................845 227-6609
EMP: 8 EST: 1985
SALES (est): 400K **Privately Held**
SIC: 2051 Mfg Bread/Related Products

(G-6286)
GLOBALFOUNDRIES US 2 LLC (DH)
2070 Route 52 (12533-3507)
PHONE..................512 457-3900
Sanjay Jha, *CEO*
EMP: 118
SALES (est): 972.9K
SALES (corp-wide): 8.5B **Privately Held**
SIC: 3674 Semiconductors & related devices

(G-6287)
GLOBALFOUNDRIES US INC
2070 Route 52 (12533-3507)
PHONE..................512 457-3900
David Brown, *Manager*
James Doyle, *Manager*
Kohji Ono, *Manager*
Thomas Schulze, *Technical Staff*
EMP: 21
SALES (corp-wide): 8.5B **Privately Held**
SIC: 3559 3674 Semiconductor manufacturing machinery; semiconductors & related devices
HQ: Globalfoundries U.S. Inc.
2600 Great America Way
Santa Clara CA 95054

(G-6288)
HOPEWELL PRECISION INC
19 Ryan Rd (12533-8322)
P.O. Box 551 (12533-0551)
PHONE..................845 221-2737
Richard Skeen, *President*
Donna Cznarty, *Admin Sec*
EMP: 22
SQ FT: 25,000
SALES (est): 4.1MM **Privately Held**
WEB: www.hopewell-precision.com
SIC: 3663 Studio equipment, radio & television broadcasting

(G-6289)
INTERNATIONAL BUS MCHS CORP
Also Called: IBM
10 North Dr (12533)
PHONE..................800 426-4968
Michael Baldwin, *Engineer*
Rich Burda, *Engineer*
Ethan Gallagher, *Engineer*
Jeffrey Yang, *Engineer*
Louis Fasano, *Senior Engr*
EMP: 170
SALES (corp-wide): 79.1B **Publicly Held**
WEB: www.ibm.com
SIC: 3674 Semiconductors & related devices
PA: International Business Machines Corporation
1 New Orchard Rd Ste 1 # 1
Armonk NY 10504
914 499-1900

(G-6290)
KLA-TENCOR CORPORATION
20 Corporate Park Rd C (12533-6557)
PHONE..................845 897-1723
Matt Brown, *Manager*
Megha Saraf, *Associate*
EMP: 12
SALES (corp-wide): 4B **Publicly Held**
WEB: www.tencor.com
SIC: 3674 Semiconductors & related devices
PA: Kla-Tencor Corporation
1 Technology Dr
Milpitas CA 95035
408 875-3000

(G-6291)
LIFE MEDICAL TECHNOLOGIES LLC
2070 Rte 52 21a Bldg 320a (12533)
PHONE..................845 894-2121
EMP: 10
SALES (est): 660K **Privately Held**
SIC: 3069 Mfg Fabricated Rubber Products

(G-6292)
PHILLIP J ORTIZ MANUFACTURING
44 Railroad Ave (12533-7318)
P.O. Box 116 (12533-0116)
PHONE..................845 226-7030
Barry Ortiz, *President*
EMP: 6
SQ FT: 10,000
SALES (est): 506.7K **Privately Held**
SIC: 7692 3714 Welding repair; motor vehicle parts & accessories

(G-6293)
SPECTRAL SYSTEMS LLC (PA)
35 Corporate Park Rd (12533-6558)
PHONE..................845 896-2200
Scott Little, *President*
Carlos Guajardo, *Sales Mgr*
Bruce Capuano,
Frank Wesley,
EMP: 47
SALES: 11MM **Privately Held**
SIC: 3827 Optical instruments & apparatus

Hornell
Steuben County

(G-6294)
BOMBARDIER TRANSPORTATION
1 William K Jackson Ln (14843-1457)
PHONE..................607 324-0216
Dave Sharma, *Branch Mgr*
EMP: 60
SALES (corp-wide): 16.2B **Privately Held**
SIC: 3441 3743 Fabricated structural metal; railroad equipment, except locomotives
HQ: Bombardier Transportation (Holdings) Usa Inc
1501 Lebanon Church Rd
Pittsburgh PA 15236
412 655-5700

(G-6295)
DOLOMITE PRODUCTS COMPANY INC
Also Called: A.L. Blades
7610 County Road 65 (14843-9626)
PHONE..................607 324-3636
Robert Blades, *Branch Mgr*
EMP: 16
SALES (corp-wide): 29.7B **Privately Held**
SIC: 2951 Paving mixtures
HQ: Dolomite Products Company Inc.
1150 Penfield Rd
Rochester NY 14625
315 524-1998

(G-6296)
DYCO ELECTRONICS INC
7775 Industrial Park Rd (14843-9673)
PHONE..................607 324-2030
Gregory D Georgek, *President*
Randy Drake, *General Mgr*
Roque Santiago, *General Mgr*
Jeff Wilkins, *Opers Mgr*
Allan Klus, *Engineer*
EMP: 80
SQ FT: 30,000
SALES (est): 14.7MM **Privately Held**
WEB: www.dycoelectronics.com
SIC: 3612 Specialty transformers

(G-6297)
DYCO MANUFACTURING LLC
Also Called: Dyco Electronics
7775 Industrial Park Rd (14843-9673)
PHONE..................607 324-2030
Thomas Norsen,
Gregory Georgek,
Donald McElheny,
EMP: 63
SALES (est): 1.7MM **Privately Held**
SIC: 3999 Manufacturing industries

(G-6298)
FORTITUDE INDUSTRIES INC
Also Called: A T M
7200 County Route 70a (14843-9303)
PHONE..................607 324-1500
Margaret E Walsh, *President*
Randy Harkenrider, *President*
Tom Connors, *Vice Pres*
Barry Walsh, *Vice Pres*
Rob Crowley, *Prdtn Mgr*
EMP: 65
SQ FT: 13,500
SALES (est): 11MM **Privately Held**
SIC: 3625 Electromagnetic clutches or brakes

Hornell - Steuben County (G-6299)

(G-6299)
GATEHOUSE MEDIA LLC
Also Called: Evening Tribune
32 Broadway Mall (14843-1920)
PHONE 607 324-1425
Lynn Brennan, *Editor*
Kelly Luvinson, *Manager*
Sandy Eveland, *Director*
EMP: 101
SALES (corp-wide): 1.3B **Publicly Held**
WEB: www.gatehousemedia.com
SIC: 2711 Newspapers, publishing & printing
HQ: Gatehouse Media, Llc
 175 Sullys Trl Ste 300
 Pittsford NY 14534
 585 598-0030

(G-6300)
GRAY MANUFACTURING INDS LLC
Also Called: G M I
6258 Ice House Rd (14843-9739)
P.O. Box 126 (14843-0126)
PHONE 607 281-1325
David Gray, *CEO*
Denny Mullikin, *Vice Pres*
Tim Wilcox, *Project Engr*
Marie Stewart, *Administration*
Richard Head,
▲ **EMP:** 17
SQ FT: 15,000
SALES (est): 6.3MM **Privately Held**
SIC: 3743 Railroad equipment

(G-6301)
LOGO PRINT COMPANY
135 Seneca St (14843-1329)
PHONE 607 324-5403
Chris O'Dell, *President*
EMP: 7
SALES (est): 23.6K **Privately Held**
SIC: 2752 Commercial printing, lithographic

(G-6302)
SENECA MEDIA INC (PA)
Also Called: Genesee County Express
32 Broadway Mall (14843-1920)
PHONE 607 324-1425
George Sample, *President*
Micheal Wnek, *President*
EMP: 152
SALES (est): 8.5MM **Privately Held**
WEB: www.eveningtribune.com
SIC: 2711 8661 Newspapers, publishing & printing; religious organizations

(G-6303)
STERN & STERN INDUSTRIES INC
188 Thacher St (14843-1293)
P.O. Box 556 (14843-0556)
PHONE 607 324-4485
Peter B Thornton, *Ch of Bd*
Stanley Cone, *Vice Pres*
Lee Kessler, *Vice Pres*
Joanne Prouty, *Vice Pres*
Terry Bartel, *Manager*
EMP: 100
SALES (est): 28.3MM **Privately Held**
WEB: www.sternandstern.com
SIC: 2221 Manmade & synthetic broadwoven fabrics

(G-6304)
TRANSIT AIR INC
Also Called: Transitair Systems
1 William K Jackson Ln (14843-1693)
PHONE 607 324-0216
Dave Sharma, *President*
Thomas J Martin, *Vice Pres*
Dhruv Sharma, *Vice Pres*
Allen Wright, *Vice Pres*
Doug Schuster, *Sales Executive*
▲ **EMP:** 25 **EST:** 1991
SQ FT: 50,000
SALES (est): 8.2MM **Privately Held**
SIC: 3585 3822 3613 Air conditioning equipment, complete; auto controls regulating residntl & coml environmt & applncs; control panels, electric

Horseheads
Chemung County

(G-6305)
BEECHER EMSSN SLTN TCHNLGS LLC (PA)
Also Called: Ward Diesel Filter Systems
1250 Schweizer Rd (14845-9017)
PHONE 607 796-0149
Scott Beecher, *President*
EMP: 17
SQ FT: 12,000
SALES (est): 2.4MM **Privately Held**
WEB: www.warddiesel.com
SIC: 3564 Air purification equipment

(G-6306)
BELDEN INC
Also Called: Lrc Electronics
224 N Main St Ste 4 (14845-1766)
PHONE 607 796-5600
Larry Zuber, *Branch Mgr*
Sue Berg, *Technology*
EMP: 400
SALES (corp-wide): 2.3B **Publicly Held**
WEB: www.tnb.com
SIC: 3663 3678 3643 Cable television equipment; electronic connectors; current-carrying wiring devices
PA: Belden Inc.
 1 N Brentwood Blvd Fl 15
 Saint Louis MO 63105
 314 854-8000

(G-6307)
BENNETT DIE & TOOL INC
130 Wygant Rd (14845-1564)
PHONE 607 739-5629
Jim Mc Millen, *President*
Brian Bennett, *Vice Pres*
Jim Pittman, *Plant Mgr*
Jim McMillen, *Mktg Dir*
Jane Mc Millen, *Manager*
EMP: 40
SQ FT: 25,000
SALES (est): 6.6MM **Privately Held**
WEB: www.bdandt.com
SIC: 3544 Special dies & tools; jigs & fixtures

(G-6308)
CAMERON MFG & DESIGN INC (PA)
727 Blostein Blvd (14845-2739)
P.O. Box 478 (14845-0478)
PHONE 607 739-3606
Christopher Goll, *President*
Ronald Johnson, *President*
Guy Loomis, *Plant Mgr*
Joshua Roloson, *Plant Mgr*
Ken Antes, *Project Mgr*
▲ **EMP:** 205
SQ FT: 106,000
SALES (est): 28.2MM **Privately Held**
WEB: www.camfab.com
SIC: 3444 Sheet metalwork

(G-6309)
CEMECON INC
315 Daniel Zenker Dr (14845-1008)
PHONE 607 562-2363
Gary Lake, *President*
Jason Habecker, *Purchasing*
John Makovitch, *QC Mgr*
Mary E Hosey, *Controller*
Andrew Brayer, *Sales Staff*
▲ **EMP:** 40
SALES (est): 4.7MM **Privately Held**
SIC: 3999 Manufacturing industries

(G-6310)
CROWN TANK COMPANY LLC
60 Electric Pkwy (14845-1424)
PHONE 855 276-9682
EMP: 10
SALES (est): 1.1MM **Privately Held**
SIC: 3443 Fuel tanks (oil, gas, etc.): metal plate

(G-6311)
DAVID HELSING
Also Called: Horseheads Printing
2077 Grand Central Ave (14845-2893)
PHONE 607 796-2681
David Helsing, *Owner*
EMP: 5
SQ FT: 3,200
SALES (est): 320K **Privately Held**
SIC: 2752 7336 2789 Lithographing on metal; commercial art & graphic design; bookbinding & related work

(G-6312)
DEPUY SYNTHES INC
Also Called: Synthes USA
35 Airport Rd (14845-1067)
PHONE 607 271-2500
Eric May, *Engineer*
Ron Lerner, *Manager*
EMP: 150
SALES (corp-wide): 76.4B **Publicly Held**
SIC: 3842 Surgical appliances & supplies
HQ: Depuy Synthes, Inc.
 700 Orthopaedic Dr
 Warsaw IN 46582

(G-6313)
EM PFAFF & SON INC
204 E Franklin St (14845-2425)
PHONE 607 739-3691
Susan Alexander, *President*
John Alexander, *Vice Pres*
EMP: 19 **EST:** 1944
SQ FT: 21,000
SALES (est): 2.7MM **Privately Held**
SIC: 2431 2434 Millwork; wood kitchen cabinets

(G-6314)
EMHART GLASS MANUFACTURING INC
74 Kahler Rd (14845-1022)
PHONE 607 734-3671
Jonathan Chan, *Project Mgr*
Jeff Chapman, *Facilities Mgr*
Alice Nichols, *Mfg Staff*
Celeste Quint, *Purch Mgr*
Melissa Hill, *Buyer*
EMP: 150
SALES (corp-wide): 2.6B **Privately Held**
WEB: www.emhartglass.com
SIC: 3559 Glass making machinery: blowing, molding, forming, etc.
HQ: Emhart Glass Manufacturing Inc.
 123 Great Pond Dr
 Windsor CT 06095
 860 298-7340

(G-6315)
FENNELL SPRING COMPANY LLC
295 Hemlock St (14845-2721)
PHONE 607 739-3541
Thomas Fennell, *Mng Member*
Martin Fennell,
EMP: 60
SQ FT: 75,000
SALES (est): 10MM **Privately Held**
SIC: 3495 Precision springs

(G-6316)
FUEL ENERGY SERVICES USA LTD
250 Ltta Brook Indus Pkwy (14845)
PHONE 607 846-2650
Mitchell Liivam, *CEO*
EMP: 22
SALES (est): 5.3MM **Privately Held**
SIC: 2869 1389 2911 7699 Fuels; oil field services; oils, fuel; pumps & pumping equipment repair; industrial equipment cleaning

(G-6317)
GAS FIELD SPECIALISTS INC
224 N Main St (14845-1766)
PHONE 716 378-6422
Brad West, *Branch Mgr*
Lisa Springstead, *Manager*
EMP: 51
SALES (corp-wide): 44.6MM **Privately Held**
SIC: 1389 Oil field services; gas field services
PA: Gas Field Specialists, Inc.
 2107 State Route 44 S
 Shinglehouse PA 16748
 814 698-2122

(G-6318)
HEADS & TAILS LURE CO
283 Hibbard Rd (14845-7930)
PHONE 607 739-7900
Clint Kellar, *Owner*
EMP: 5 **EST:** 2007
SQ FT: 4,000
SALES (est): 238.3K **Privately Held**
SIC: 3949 Lures, fishing: artificial

(G-6319)
MICATU INC
315 Daniel Zenker Dr # 202 (14845-1008)
PHONE 888 705-8836
Michael Oshetski, *CEO*
EMP: 5
SALES (est): 1.3MM **Privately Held**
SIC: 3827 Optical instruments & lenses

(G-6320)
MIRION TECH IMAGING LLC
Also Called: Mirion Tech Imging Systems Div
315 Daniel Zenker Dr (14845-1008)
PHONE 607 562-4300
David Stewart, *President*
Seth Rosen, *Admin Sec*
Emmanuelle Lee, *Asst Sec*
EMP: 23 **EST:** 2015
SQ FT: 15,000
SALES (est): 3.6MM **Privately Held**
SIC: 3663 Radio & TV communications equipment
PA: Mirion Technologies, Inc.
 3000 Executive Pkwy # 518
 San Ramon CA 94583

(G-6321)
MIRION TECHNOLOGIES IST CORP (HQ)
Also Called: Imaging and Sensing Technology
315 Daniel Zenker Dr # 204 (14845-1008)
PHONE 607 562-4300
Thomas Logan, *CEO*
David Stewart, *President*
Tim Pelot, *Vice Pres*
Jack Pacheco, *CFO*
Bryant Hozempa, *Manager*
EMP: 70
SQ FT: 105,000
SALES (est): 26.8MM **Privately Held**
WEB: www.mirion.com
SIC: 3679 3861 3829 3812 Electronic circuits; photographic equipment & supplies; nuclear radiation & testing apparatus; search & navigation equipment; computer peripheral equipment

(G-6322)
MRC GLOBAL (US) INC
224 N Main St Bldg 13-1 (14845-1766)
PHONE 607 739-8575
James Griffith, *Branch Mgr*
EMP: 11 **Publicly Held**
SIC: 1311 Crude petroleum & natural gas
HQ: Mrc Global (Us) Inc.
 1301 Mckinney St Ste 2300
 Houston TX 77010
 877 294-7574

(G-6323)
ORTHSTAR ENTERPRISES INC
119 Sing Sing Rd (14845-1073)
P.O. Box 459, Big Flats (14814-0459)
PHONE 607 562-2100
James E Orsillo, *Ch of Bd*
Joseph E Strykowski, *President*
EMP: 65
SALES (est): 3.5MM **Privately Held**
WEB: www.orthstar.com
SIC: 7372 7379 3812 3823 Prepackaged Software Svc Computer Related Svcs Mfg Search/Navgatn Equip Mfg Process Cntrl Instr

(G-6324)
PHOTONIC CONTROLS LLC
500 1st Ctr Ste 2 (14845)
PHONE 607 562-4585
Ronald S Karfelt, *President*
EMP: 14
SQ FT: 6,250

GEOGRAPHIC SECTION

Hudson - Columbia County (G-6347)

SALES: 1.8MM **Privately Held**
WEB: www.photoniccontrols.com
SIC: **3229** Electronic & Optical Product Design Services

(G-6325)
REPSOL OIL & GAS USA LLC
337 Daniel Zenker Dr (14845-1008)
PHONE.....................607 562-4000
Pat Minor, *Plant Mgr*
Dominik Wells, *Engineer*
Corinne Bugamelli, *Accountant*
Robert A Broen, *Branch Mgr*
Ron Holm, *Consultant*
EMP: 5
SALES (corp-wide): 1B **Privately Held**
SIC: **1311** Natural gas production
HQ: Repsol Oil & Gas Usa, Llc
2455 Tech Forest Blvd
Spring TX 77381
832 442-1000

(G-6326)
RIMCO PLASTICS CORP
316 Colonial Dr (14845-9034)
PHONE.....................607 739-3864
Robert Reimsnyder, *President*
Lester Reimsnyder III, *Vice Pres*
Nancy Kosalek, *Treasurer*
EMP: 25 EST: 1966
SQ FT: 48,000
SALES (est): 4.6MM **Privately Held**
WEB: www.rimcoplastics.com
SIC: **3089** **3086** Plastic processing; plastics foam products

(G-6327)
ROCHESTER COCA COLA BOTTLING
Also Called: Coca-Cola
210 Industrial Park Rd (14845-9024)
PHONE.....................607 739-5678
John Kelley, *Branch Mgr*
George Keim, *Manager*
EMP: 35
SQ FT: 23,000
SALES (corp-wide): 35.4B **Publicly Held**
SIC: **2086** Soft drinks: packaged in cans, bottles, etc.
HQ: Rochester Coca Cola Bottling Corp
300 Oak St
Pittston PA 18640
570 655-2874

(G-6328)
SCHLUMBERGER TECHNOLOGY CORP
224 N Main St Bldg S (14845-1766)
PHONE.....................607 378-0105
EMP: 200 **Publicly Held**
SIC: **1382** **1389** **3825** **3824** Geophysical exploration, oil & gas field; geological exploration, oil & gas field; well logging; cementing oil & gas well casings; pumping of oil & gas wells; oil field services; measuring instruments & meters, electric; meters: electric, pocket, portable, panelboard, etc.; controls, revolution & timing instruments; counters, revolution; oil & gas field machinery; measuring & dispensing pumps
HQ: Schlumberger Technology Corp
100 Gillingham Ln
Sugar Land TX 77478
281 285-8500

(G-6329)
SILICON CARBIDE PRODUCTS INC
361 Daniel Zenker Dr (14845-1008)
PHONE.....................607 562-8599
Martin Metzger, *President*
Joshua Dahlman, *General Mgr*
Mark Whitmer, *Vice Pres*
▲ EMP: 30
SALES (est): 4.8MM **Privately Held**
WEB: www.siliconcarbideproducts.com
SIC: **3297** Cement: high temperature, refractory (nonclay)

Howard Beach
Queens County

(G-6330)
GRILLMASTER INC
15314 83rd St (11414-1826)
PHONE.....................718 272-9191
Anne Cohen, *CEO*
Sherman Moss, *President*
Evelyn Kelly, *Manager*
EMP: 50
SQ FT: 20,000
SALES (est): 7.8MM **Privately Held**
SIC: **3585** **3822** **3446** Parts for heating, cooling & refrigerating equipment; auto controls regulating residntl & coml environmt & applncs; architectural metalwork

(G-6331)
RAK FINISHING CORP
15934 83rd St (11414-2933)
PHONE.....................718 416-4242
John Muncan, *CEO*
Jon Muncan, *CEO*
Julianna Muncan, *President*
EMP: 48
SQ FT: 7,000
SALES (est): 3MM **Privately Held**
SIC: **2339** **7389** Service apparel, washable: women's; textile & apparel services

(G-6332)
VIP PRINTING
16040 95th St (11414-3801)
PHONE.....................718 641-9361
Victor Ingrassia, *Owner*
EMP: 5
SALES: 150K **Privately Held**
SIC: **2752** Commercial printing, lithographic

(G-6333)
VPJ PUBLICATION INC
Also Called: Forum South, The
15519 Lahn St (11414-2858)
PHONE.....................718 845-3221
Patricia Adams, *President*
EMP: 25
SQ FT: 1,000
SALES (est): 948.3K **Privately Held**
SIC: **2711** Newspapers, publishing & printing

Howes Cave
Schoharie County

(G-6334)
W KINTZ PLASTICS INC (HQ)
Also Called: K P I Plastics
165 Caverns Rd (12092-1907)
PHONE.....................518 296-8513
Edwin Kintz, *Ch of Bd*
Roger Cusano, *Engineer*
Lawrence Kath, *CFO*
William Oliver, *Manager*
Stanley Scharling, *Info Tech Dir*
◆ EMP: 10 EST: 1976
SQ FT: 60,000
SALES (est): 2.4MM
SALES (corp-wide): 21.3MM **Privately Held**
WEB: www.kintz.com
SIC: **3089** Injection molding of plastics; plastic processing
PA: Universal Plastics Corporation
75 Whiting Farms Rd
Holyoke MA 01040
413 592-4791

Hudson
Columbia County

(G-6335)
A & S WOODWORKING INC
9 Partition St (12534-3111)
PHONE.....................518 821-0832
Arthur Cincotti, *CEO*
EMP: 7

SQ FT: 900
SALES: 5MM **Privately Held**
SIC: **2511** Wood household furniture

(G-6336)
A COLARUSSO AND SON INC (PA)
Also Called: Colarusso Blacktop Co
91 Newman Rd (12534-4040)
P.O. Box 302 (12534-0302)
PHONE.....................518 828-3218
Peter G Colarusso Jr, *President*
Robert Colarusso, *Corp Secy*
Gary Graziano, *Vice Pres*
Dave Laspada, *Vice Pres*
Robert Butler, *Project Mgr*
EMP: 20 EST: 1912
SQ FT: 10,000
SALES (est): 11.7MM **Privately Held**
WEB: www.acolarusso.com
SIC: **2951** **5032** **1611** **1771** Asphalt & asphaltic paving mixtures (not from refineries); asphalt mixture; stone, crushed or broken; highway & street construction; concrete work; construction sand & gravel

(G-6337)
ACME KITCHENETTES CORP
4269 Us Route 9 (12534-4031)
PHONE.....................518 828-4191
Nick Peros, *President*
EMP: 20
SALES (est): 3.4MM **Privately Held**
WEB: www.acme3in1.com
SIC: **3469** **3632** **2434** **5064** Kitchen fixtures & equipment: metal, except cast aluminum; household refrigerators & freezers; wood kitchen cabinets; refrigerators & freezers

(G-6338)
AMERICAN SPACER TECHNOLOGIES
6 Joslen Heights Rd (12534-1027)
PHONE.....................518 828-1339
Paul Donofrio, *President*
EMP: 8 EST: 2008
SALES (est): 1MM **Privately Held**
SIC: **3089** Injection molding of plastics

(G-6339)
ARCHER-DANIELS-MIDLAND COMPANY
Also Called: ADM
201 State Route 23b (12534-4009)
P.O. Box 398 (12534-0398)
PHONE.....................518 828-4691
Andy Spirek, *Branch Mgr*
EMP: 50
SALES (corp-wide): 60.8B **Publicly Held**
SIC: **2041** Flour & other grain mill products
PA: Archer-Daniels-Midland Company
77 W Wacker Dr Ste 4600
Chicago IL 60601
312 634-8100

(G-6340)
ARCHER-DANIELS-MIDLAND COMPANY
Also Called: ADM
Ste B Rr 23 (12534)
P.O. Box 398 (12534-0398)
PHONE.....................518 828-4691
Mark Eisler, *Manager*
EMP: 52
SALES (corp-wide): 60.8B **Publicly Held**
WEB: www.admworld.com
SIC: **2041** **5149** Flour & other grain mill products; flour
PA: Archer-Daniels-Midland Company
77 W Wacker Dr Ste 4600
Chicago IL 60601
312 634-8100

(G-6341)
ATLANTIC ENGINEER PRODUCTS LLC
239 State Route 23b (12534-4009)
P.O. Box 639, Kinderhook (12106-0639)
PHONE.....................518 822-1800
Robert Peloke,
Thomas Smith Sr,
Tucker Smith,
EMP: 25

SALES (est): 2.7MM **Privately Held**
SIC: **3537** Loading docks: portable, adjustable & hydraulic

(G-6342)
ATMOST REFRIGERATION CO INC (PA)
Also Called: R T F Manufacturing
793 Route 66 (12534-3410)
PHONE.....................518 828-2180
Thomas Finck, *Principal*
Bob Walsh, *Sls & Mktg Exec*
Ashley Finck, *Marketing Staff*
▲ EMP: 5
SQ FT: 25,000
SALES (est): 3.3MM **Privately Held**
WEB: www.rtfmanufacturing.com
SIC: **3585** Refrigeration equipment, complete

(G-6343)
BERKSHIRE BUSINESS FORMS INC
829 Route 66 (12534-3406)
P.O. Box 118, Troy (12181-0118)
PHONE.....................518 828-2600
Nancy Linton, *President*
Jeffrey C Linton, *Vice Pres*
John S Linton, *VP Mfg*
EMP: 12 EST: 1960
SQ FT: 15,000
SALES: 1.2MM **Privately Held**
SIC: **2759** Commercial printing

(G-6344)
CRAFTECH INDUSTRIES INC
8 Dock St (12534-2003)
P.O. Box 636 (12534-0636)
PHONE.....................518 828-5001
Barbara Gerard, *President*
Ronald Prior, *General Mgr*
Irving Gerard, *Vice Pres*
Linda Jabanski, *Human Res Mgr*
Linda Jablanski, *Human Resources*
EMP: 55 EST: 1966
SQ FT: 18,500
SALES (est): 13.1MM **Privately Held**
WEB: www.craftechind.com
SIC: **3451** **3089** **3452** Screw machine products; injection molding of plastics; bolts, nuts, rivets & washers

(G-6345)
DAILY MAIL & GREENE CNTY NEWS (HQ)
1 Hudson City Ctr Ste 202 (12534-2355)
PHONE.....................518 943-2100
Roger Coleman, *President*
Raymond Pignone, *Principal*
EMP: 15 EST: 1951
SQ FT: 5,000
SALES (est): 3.1MM
SALES (corp-wide): 32MM **Privately Held**
WEB: www.thedailymail.org
SIC: **2711** Newspapers, publishing & printing
PA: Johnson Newspaper Corpcration
260 Washington St
Watertown NY
315 782-1000

(G-6346)
DIGITAL FABRICATION WKSHP INC
99 S 3rd St Ste 2 (12534-2171)
PHONE.....................518 249-6500
EMP: 6
SALES (est): 424.1K **Privately Held**
SIC: **2499** Decorative wood & woodwork

(G-6347)
DINOSAW INC (PA)
340 Power Ave (12534-2442)
PHONE.....................518 828-9942
Henry J Warchol Jr, *CEO*
Gregg S Warchol, *President*
Scott Myers, *Sales Mgr*
Henry Warchol, *Manager*
Allison Coon, *Admin Sec*
EMP: 25
SQ FT: 14,000

Hudson - Columbia County (G-6348)

SALES (est): 3.9MM **Privately Held**
WEB: www.dinosaw.com
SIC: **3425** 3545 5085 3541 Saw blades & handsaws; machine tool accessories; industrial tools; machine tools, metal cutting type

(G-6348)
EMSIG MANUFACTURING CORP
160 Fairview Ave Ste 916 (12534-8404)
PHONE.................................518 828-7301
James Feane, *Manager*
EMP: 11
SALES (corp-wide): 25.5MM **Privately Held**
SIC: **3965** 5131 Buttons & parts; buttons
PA: Emsig Manufacturing Corp.
    263 W 38th St Fl 5
    New York NY 10018
    718 784-7717

(G-6349)
FLANDERS PRECISIONAIRE NY
1 Vapor Trl (12534-4077)
PHONE.................................518 751-5640
Philip L Whitaker, *Chairman*
EMP: 5
SALES (est): 905K **Privately Held**
SIC: **3564** Air cleaning systems

(G-6350)
FOSTER REFRIGERATORS ENTP
300 Fairview Ave (12534-1214)
PHONE.................................518 671-6036
James Dinardi, *President*
EMP: 10
SALES (est): 1.8MM **Privately Held**
SIC: **3585** 7623 Refrigeration equipment, complete; refrigeration service & repair

(G-6351)
GOLUB CORPORATION
Also Called: Price Chopper Pharmacy
351 Fairview Ave Ste 3 (12534-1259)
PHONE.................................518 822-0076
Stacey McGovern, *Branch Mgr*
EMP: 35
SALES (corp-wide): 3.3B **Privately Held**
SIC: **3751** Motorcycles & related parts
PA: The Golub Corporation
    461 Nott St
    Schenectady NY 12308
    518 355-5000

(G-6352)
H & H HULLS INC
35 Industrial Tract Anx (12534-1505)
PHONE.................................518 828-1339
Thomas Halpin, *President*
EMP: 5
SQ FT: 2,604
SALES (est): 290K **Privately Held**
SIC: **3089** Injection molded finished plastic products

(G-6353)
HOLCIM (US) INC
4303 Us Route 9 (12534-4032)
PHONE.................................518 828-8478
Melanie Pulcher, *Principal*
EMP: 6
SALES (corp-wide): 26.4B **Privately Held**
SIC: **3241** Portland cement
HQ: Holcim (Us) Inc.
    8700 W Bryn Mawr Ave
    Chicago IL 60631
    773 372-1000

(G-6354)
HRI METALS LLC
1233 Us Route 9 (12534-3226)
PHONE.................................518 822-1013
Paul Harpis, *President*
EMP: 5
SALES (est): 223.9K **Privately Held**
SIC: **3444** 5211 Metal roofing & roof drainage equipment; roofing material

(G-6355)
HUDSON FABRICS LLC
128 2nd Street Ext (12534-1626)
PHONE.................................518 671-6100
Mark Schur,
EMP: 15
SALES (est): 1.6MM **Privately Held**
SIC: **2258** Tricot fabrics

(G-6356)
HUDSON VALLEY CREAMERY LLC
2986 Us Route 9 (12534-4407)
PHONE.................................518 851-2570
Bonnie Kelleher, *Purch Agent*
Veronica Madey,
▲ **EMP:** 10 **EST:** 2010
SALES (est): 1.2MM **Privately Held**
SIC: **2022** Cheese, natural & processed

(G-6357)
J V PRECISION INC
3031 Us Route 9 (12534-4320)
PHONE.................................518 851-3200
Dorothy Jahns, *President*
Scott Valentine, *Vice Pres*
Lisa Valentine, *Treasurer*
EMP: 6
SQ FT: 5,400
SALES (est): 999.2K **Privately Held**
WEB: www.jvprecision.com
SIC: **3624** Electrodes, thermal & electrolytic uses: carbon, graphite

(G-6358)
JEM WDWKG & CABINETS INC
250 Falls Rd (12534-3323)
PHONE.................................518 828-5361
Neil Schnelwar, *Chairman*
EMP: 17 **EST:** 2007
SALES (est): 2.2MM **Privately Held**
SIC: **2434** Wood kitchen cabinets

(G-6359)
JOHNNYS IDEAL PRINTING CO
Also Called: Johnny's Ideal Prntng Co
352 Warren St (12534-2419)
PHONE.................................518 828-6666
John Brodowski, *President*
Virginia Brodowski, *Treasurer*
EMP: 5
SQ FT: 5,000
SALES (est): 460K **Privately Held**
SIC: **2752** 2759 2791 2789 Commercial printing, offset; letterpress printing; typesetting; bookbinding & related work

(G-6360)
JOHNSON ACQUISITION CORP (HQ)
Also Called: Chatham Courier, The
364 Warren St (12534-2419)
PHONE.................................518 828-1616
Roger Coleman, *President*
Karrie Allen, *Editor*
EMP: 13
SQ FT: 35,000
SALES: 401.9K
SALES (corp-wide): 32MM **Privately Held**
WEB: www.registerstar.com
SIC: **2711** Commercial printing & newspaper publishing combined
PA: Johnson Newspaper Corporation
    260 Washington St
    Watertown NY
    315 782-1000

(G-6361)
JONAS LOUIS PAUL STUDIOS INC
304 Miller Rd (12534-4522)
PHONE.................................518 851-2211
David Merritt, *President*
Pam Merritt, *Admin Sec*
EMP: 6 **EST:** 1942
SQ FT: 10,000
SALES (est): 429.3K **Privately Held**
WEB: www.jonasstudios.com
SIC: **3299** Statuary: gypsum, clay, papier mache, metal, etc.

(G-6362)
LB FURNITURE INDUSTRIES LLC
99 S 3rd St (12534-2172)
PHONE.................................518 828-1501
Wayne Amburgh, *Purch Agent*
Jenny Decker, *Cust Svc Dir*
Simon F Segal,
Baruch Singer,
▲ **EMP:** 150
SQ FT: 300,000

SALES (est): 13.2MM **Privately Held**
WEB: www.lbempire.com
SIC: **2599** 3469 Restaurant furniture, wood or metal; household cooking & kitchen utensils, metal

(G-6363)
MELTZ LUMBER CO OF MELLENVILLE
483 Route 217 (12534-3640)
PHONE.................................518 672-7021
Emil Meltz Jr, *President*
Jeffory Meltz, *Vice Pres*
Betty Lou Meltz, *Admin Sec*
EMP: 20
SALES (est): 2.7MM **Privately Held**
SIC: **2421** 5211 Sawmills & planing mills, general; millwork & lumber

(G-6364)
MICOSTA ENTERPRISES INC
Also Called: Easy H2b
3007 County Route 20 (12534-3384)
PHONE.................................518 822-9708
Steven A McKay, *President*
EMP: 8
SQ FT: 350
SALES (est): 811.4K **Privately Held**
WEB: www.micostaent.com
SIC: **2053** 2066 Pies, bakery: frozen; chocolate bars, solid

(G-6365)
MODERN FARMER MEDIA INC
403 Warren St (12534-2414)
PHONE.................................518 828-7447
Ann M Gardner, *CEO*
Jo Liguori, *Editor*
Lavender Halsey, *Director*
Renee Lewin, *Director*
Glen Fuenmayor, *Creative Dir*
EMP: 10 **EST:** 2012
SALES (est): 1.3MM **Privately Held**
SIC: **2721** 7371 Periodicals-Publishing/Printing Custom Computer Programing

(G-6366)
OVERHEAD DOOR CORPORATION
W McGuire Co
1 Hudson Ave (12534-2807)
PHONE.................................518 828-7652
Rich Moore, *Manager*
EMP: 100
SALES (corp-wide): 3.6B **Privately Held**
WEB: www.overheaddoor.com
SIC: **3442** 2431 5084 3842 Garage doors, overhead: metal; doors, wood; materials handling machinery; surgical appliances & supplies; packaging machinery; prefabricated metal buildings
HQ: Overhead Door Corporation
    2501 S State Hwy 121 Ste
    Lewisville TX 75067
    469 549-7100

(G-6367)
PERIODICAL SERVICES CO INC
351 Fairview Ave Ste 300 (12534-1259)
PHONE.................................518 822-9300
Marcia Scneider, *President*
Rob Koskey, *Vice Pres*
EMP: 15 **EST:** 2013
SALES: 3MM **Privately Held**
SIC: **2721** Magazines: publishing only, not printed on site

(G-6368)
PGS MILLWORK INC (PA)
32 Hickory Ln (12534-1297)
PHONE.................................518 828-2608
Thomas Spurge, *CEO*
Mara Lopez, *Counsel*
Scott Manchester, *Vice Pres*
Larry Hess, *Project Mgr*
▲ **EMP:** 65
SQ FT: 44,000
SALES (est): 6.6MM **Privately Held**
WEB: www.pgsmillwork.com
SIC: **2431** 2434 2499 5211 Woodwork, interior & ornamental; wood kitchen cabinets; decorative wood & woodwork; millwork & lumber

(G-6369)
PRINCTON ARCHTCTURAL PRESS LLC (HQ)
202 Warren St (12534-2118)
PHONE.................................518 671-6100
Kevin Lippert,
▲ **EMP:** 16
SALES: 5.2MM
SALES (corp-wide): 30.2MM **Privately Held**
SIC: **2731** 2678 Books: publishing only; stationery products
PA: The Mcevoy Group Llc
    680 2nd St
    San Francisco CA 94107
    415 537-4200

(G-6370)
SATURN INDUSTRIES INC (PA)
157 Union Tpke (12534-1524)
P.O. Box 367 (12534-0367)
PHONE.................................518 828-9956
Maryanne Lee, *President*
John Lee, *Vice Pres*
EMP: 40 **EST:** 1959
SQ FT: 25,000
SALES (est): 3.5MM **Privately Held**
SIC: **3624** 3599 3544 3769 Electrodes, thermal & electrolytic uses: carbon, graphite; machine & other job shop work; special dies, tools, jigs & fixtures; guided missile & space vehicle parts & auxiliary equipment; current-carrying wiring devices

(G-6371)
SAUSBIERS AWNING SHOP INC
43 8th St (12534-2901)
PHONE.................................518 828-3748
William M Harp, *President*
EMP: 8 **EST:** 1902
SQ FT: 4,000
SALES: 700K **Privately Held**
SIC: **2394** 5999 7532 Awnings, fabric: made from purchased materials; fire extinguishers; upholstery & trim shop, automotive; tops (canvas or plastic), installation or repair: automotive

(G-6372)
SERVOTEC USA LLC
1 Industrial Tract Anx # 3 (12534-1514)
PHONE.................................518 671-6120
Thomas Tanguay,
Will N Page,
EMP: 6
SALES (est): 900.9K **Privately Held**
WEB: www.servotecusa.com
SIC: **3542** Presses: hydraulic & pneumatic, mechanical & manual

(G-6373)
SMITH CONTROL SYSTEMS INC
1839 Route 9h (12534-3374)
PHONE.................................518 828-7646
Thomas H Smith Sr, *President*
Kirt Coonradt, *Vice Pres*
Michael Keating, *Vice Pres*
Renee Gordon, *Purchasing*
Thomas H Smith Jr, *Treasurer*
EMP: 17
SQ FT: 10,000
SALES (est): 4.5MM **Privately Held**
WEB: www.smithcontrol.com
SIC: **3613** Control panels, electric

(G-6374)
TWIN COUNTIES PRO PRINTERS INC
59 Fairview Ave (12534-2334)
PHONE.................................518 828-3278
David Scott, *President*
Linda D Scott, *CFO*
EMP: 10
SQ FT: 3,500
SALES (est): 1.1MM **Privately Held**
WEB: www.pro-printers.com
SIC: **2752** 7334 Commercial printing, offset; photocopying & duplicating services

(G-6375)
UFP NEW YORK LLC
Also Called: Universal Forest Products
11 Falls Industrial Pk Rd (12534-3377)
PHONE.................................518 828-2888

Rich Flinn, *General Mgr*
EMP: 35
SALES (corp-wide): 3.9B **Publicly Held**
WEB: www.ufpinc.com
SIC: 2439 Trusses, wooden roof
HQ: Ufp New York, Llc
 11 Allen St
 Auburn NY 13021
 315 253-2758

Hudson Falls
Washington County

(G-6376)
COLOR-AID CORPORATION
38 La Fayette St Ste 2 (12839-1247)
PHONE.................................212 673-5500
Richard O'Brien, *President*
Raymond O'Brien, *Vice Pres*
EMP: 8
SQ FT: 8,500
SALES (est): 1.2MM **Privately Held**
WEB: www.coloraid.com
SIC: 2752 Commercial printing, lithographic

(G-6377)
DIMENSIONAL MILLS INC
337 Main St (12839-1513)
PHONE.................................518 746-1047
David Lafountain, *President*
EMP: 5 **EST:** 1992
SALES (est): 600K **Privately Held**
SIC: 2448 Wood pallets & skids

(G-6378)
DWA PALLET INC
Also Called: Dimensional Mills
337 Main St (12839-1513)
PHONE.................................518 746-1047
Daniel Ellsworth, *President*
EMP: 9
SALES (est): 951K **Privately Held**
SIC: 2448 Pallets, wood

(G-6379)
GENERAL ELECTRIC COMPANY
446 Lock 8 Way 8th (12839)
PHONE.................................518 746-5750
John Cozzens, *Engineer*
Stephen Smith, *Branch Mgr*
Todd Campbell, *Senior Mgr*
EMP: 425
SALES (corp-wide): 122B **Publicly Held**
SIC: 3629 Capacitors, fixed or variable
PA: General Electric Company
 41 Farnsworth St
 Boston MA 02210
 617 443-3000

(G-6380)
GL&V USA INC
27 Allen St (12839-1901)
PHONE.................................518 747-2444
Eve Lacroix, *General Mgr*
EMP: 103
SALES (corp-wide): 110MM **Privately Held**
WEB: www.glv.com
SIC: 3554 Paper industries machinery
HQ: Gl&V Usa Inc.
 1 Cellu Dr Ste 200
 Nashua NH 03063
 603 882-2711

(G-6381)
GRANVILLE GLASS & GRANITE
131 Revere Rd (12839)
PHONE.................................518 812-0492
Kyle Suchan, *President*
Scott Suchan, *Vice Pres*
EMP: 5
SALES (est): 514.4K **Privately Held**
SIC: 3231 Products of purchased glass

(G-6382)
HAANEN PACKARD MACHINERY INC (PA)
16 Allen St (12839-1941)
PHONE.................................518 747-2330
Michael Haanen, *President*
Tony Rouleau, *Prgrmr*
EMP: 8

SQ FT: 3,500
SALES (est): 1.8MM **Privately Held**
SIC: 3554 3559 Paper industries machinery; plastics working machinery

(G-6383)
NORTH-EAST MACHINE INC
4160 State Route 4 (12839-3716)
PHONE.................................518 746-1837
Tracy Stevenson, *President*
EMP: 7
SQ FT: 4,000
SALES: 450K **Privately Held**
SIC: 3599 Machine shop, jobbing & repair

(G-6384)
PECKHAM MATERIALS CORP
438 Vaughn Rd (12839-9644)
PHONE.................................518 747-3353
John R Peckham, *President*
EMP: 30
SALES (corp-wide): 200.6MM **Privately Held**
SIC: 1429 3531 2952 2951 Igneous rock, crushed & broken-quarrying; asphalt plant, including gravel-mix type; asphalt felts & coatings; asphalt paving mixtures & blocks; highway & street construction
HQ: Peckham Materials Corp
 20 Haarlem Ave Ste 200
 White Plains NY 10603
 914 686-2045

Huguenot
Orange County

(G-6385)
ELEMENTIS SRL INC (DH)
Also Called: Summitreheis
15 Big Pond Rd (12746-5003)
P.O. Box 626 (12746-0626)
PHONE.................................845 692-3914
Piyush J Patel, *Ch of Bd*
Suresh Patel, *President*
EMP: 110
SQ FT: 106,000
SALES (est): 19.6MM
SALES (corp-wide): 782.7MM **Privately Held**
SIC: 2819 Industrial inorganic chemicals
HQ: Srlh Holdings, Inc.
 15 Big Pond Rd
 Huguenot NY 12746
 929 529-7951

(G-6386)
SOMERVILLE ACQUISITIONS CO INC
Also Called: Summit Research Laboratories
15 Big Pond Rd (12746-5003)
P.O. Box F (12746-0626)
PHONE.................................845 856-5261
EMP: 10
SALES (corp-wide): 27.3MM **Privately Held**
SIC: 2819 Manufactures Aluminum Compounds
PA: Somerville Acquisitions Co., Inc.
 45 River Rd Ste 300
 Flemington NJ 08822
 908 782-9500

(G-6387)
SOMERVILLE TECH GROUP INC
15 Big Pond Rd (12746-5003)
P.O. Box F (12746-0626)
PHONE.................................908 782-9500
Piyush J Patel, *CEO*
EMP: 100
SALES (est): 5.9MM **Privately Held**
SIC: 2819 Aluminum compounds

(G-6388)
SRLH HOLDINGS INC (HQ)
15 Big Pond Rd (12746-5003)
PHONE.................................929 529-7951
Piyush J Patel, *CEO*
Suresh Patel, *President*
Michael Dodds, *CFO*
EMP: 111

SALES (est): 22MM
SALES (corp-wide): 782.7MM **Privately Held**
SIC: 2819 Industrial inorganic chemicals
PA: Elementis Plc
 Caroline House
 London WC1V
 207 067-2999

Huntington
Suffolk County

(G-6389)
ACWORTH FOUNDATION
775 Park Ave Ste 255 (11743-7538)
PHONE.................................631 784-7802
Brian Acworth, *Owner*
EMP: 3
SALES: 1.2MM **Privately Held**
SIC: 2515 Foundations & platforms

(G-6390)
ADL DESIGN INC
4 W Mall Dr (11743-6440)
PHONE.................................516 949-6658
David Pollack, *CEO*
▲ **EMP:** 2
SALES: 2MM **Privately Held**
SIC: 3144 Dress shoes, women's

(G-6391)
ANIMAL PANTRY
741 W Jericho Tpke (11743-6150)
PHONE.................................631 673-3666
Andrew Mistler, *Owner*
EMP: 5 **EST:** 2013
SALES (est): 250.8K **Privately Held**
SIC: 3999 Pet supplies

(G-6392)
APS ENTERPRISE SOFTWARE INC
775 Park Ave (11743-3976)
PHONE.................................631 784-7720
Peter Thiermann, *President*
Michael Sullivan, *Principal*
Steffen Heinke, *Treasurer*
EMP: 22
SALES (est): 1.2MM **Privately Held**
SIC: 7372 Prepackaged software

(G-6393)
AXLE TEKNOLOGY LLC (PA)
226 New York Ave Ste 301 (11743-2748)
PHONE.................................631 423-3044
Nicolas Sanders, *COO*
◆ **EMP:** 9
SALES (est): 1.3MM **Privately Held**
SIC: 3714 5013 Axles, motor vehicle; automotive supplies & parts

(G-6394)
BERJEN METAL INDUSTRIES LTD
645 New York Ave Unit 1 (11743-4266)
PHONE.................................631 673-7979
Robert Sentura, *President*
Barbara Santoro, *Vice Pres*
Robert J Santoro, *Admin Sec*
EMP: 6
SALES (est): 935.8K **Privately Held**
WEB: www.berjen.com
SIC: 3444 1761 Sheet metalwork; sheet metalwork

(G-6395)
BOA SECURITY TECHNOLOGIES CORP
Also Called: Boa Handcuff Company
586 New York Ave Unit 3 (11743-4269)
PHONE.................................516 576-0295
Alan Lurie, *President*
Alvin MA, *Vice Pres*
EMP: 6
SQ FT: 4,000
SALES: 535.4K **Privately Held**
WEB: www.cuffmaxx.com
SIC: 3429 Handcuffs & leg irons

(G-6396)
COOCOO SMS INC
356 New York Ave Ste 1 (11743-3304)
PHONE.................................646 459-4260
John J Tunney III, *Mng Member*
Larry Prager,
Ryan Thompson,
EMP: 11
SALES (est): 500K **Privately Held**
SIC: 7372 Prepackaged software

(G-6397)
DEJANA TRCK UTILITY EQP CO LLC
Also Called: Dejana Truck & Utility Eqp Co
743 Park Ave (11743-3912)
PHONE.................................631 549-0944
Fax: 631 549-0945
EMP: 25 **Publicly Held**
SIC: 3711 Mfg Motor Vehicle/Car Bodies
HQ: Dejana Truck & Utility Equipment Company, Llc
 490 Pulaski Rd
 Kings Park NY 11754
 631 544-9000

(G-6398)
FAD INC
Also Called: Fad Treasures
630 New York Ave Ste B (11743-4289)
PHONE.................................631 385-2460
Allan Axelowitz, *President*
Donna Axelowitz, *Admin Sec*
▲ **EMP:** 27
SQ FT: 6,000
SALES (est): 3.3MM **Privately Held**
WEB: www.fad-treasures.com
SIC: 2339 5137 5632 Women's & misses' accessories; women's & children's accessories; women's accessory & specialty stores

(G-6399)
HARBORSIDE PRESS
94 N Woodhull Rd (11743-2829)
PHONE.................................631 470-4967
Anthony Cutrone, *President*
Claudine Kiffer, *Editor*
Leslie Dubin, *Vice Pres*
Elizabeth Janetschek, *Assoc Editor*
Frank Buchner, *CTO*
EMP: 7
SALES (est): 92.3K **Privately Held**
SIC: 2741 Miscellaneous publishing

(G-6400)
INTEGRATED CONTROL CORP
748 Park Ave (11743-3900)
PHONE.................................631 673-5100
Roberta Vaccaro Salerno, *President*
Roberta Salerno, *President*
John Patti, *Manager*
Phil Salerno, *Manager*
Mark Salerno, *CTO*
▲ **EMP:** 34
SQ FT: 5,000
SALES (est): 8.4MM **Privately Held**
WEB: www.integratedcontrol.com
SIC: 3823 Industrial instrmnts msrmnt display/control process variable

(G-6401)
J A T PRINTING INC
Also Called: Minuteman Press
46 Gerard St Unit 2 (11743-6944)
PHONE.................................631 427-1155
John Titus, *President*
Gina Titus, *Vice Pres*
EMP: 6
SALES (est): 777.9K **Privately Held**
SIC: 2752 Commercial printing, lithographic

(G-6402)
JURIS PUBLISHING INC
52 Elm St Ste 7 (11743-3488)
PHONE.................................631 351-5430
Charles Kitzen, *President*
Michael Kitzen, *Vice Pres*
▲ **EMP:** 12 **EST:** 1994
SALES (est): 1.4MM **Privately Held**
WEB: www.jurispub.com
SIC: 2731 Books: publishing only

Huntington - Suffolk County (G-6403) — GEOGRAPHIC SECTION

(G-6403)
LADY-N-TH-WNDOW CHOCOLATES INC
Also Called: Bon Bons Chocolatier
319 Main St (11743-6914)
PHONE..................631 549-1059
Mary Alice Meinersman, *President*
Susanna Fasolino, *Vice Pres*
EMP: 10
SQ FT: 4,200
SALES (est): 1.3MM **Privately Held**
WEB: www.bonbonschocolatier.com
SIC: 2066 2064 5441 5947 Chocolate; candy & other confectionery products; candy; gift, novelty & souvenir shop

(G-6404)
LONG ISLAND CMNTY NWSPPERS INC
Also Called: Long Islndr Nrth/Sth Pblctns
322 Main St (11743-6923)
PHONE..................631 427-7000
Peter Sloggatt, *Manager*
EMP: 12
SALES (corp-wide): 7.4MM **Privately Held**
WEB: www.antonnews.com
SIC: 2711 Newspapers, publishing & printing
PA: Long Island Community Newspapers Inc.
  132 E 2nd St
  Mineola NY 11501
  516 482-4490

(G-6405)
LONG ISLANDER NEWSPAPERS LLC
14 Wall St Ste A (11743-7622)
PHONE..................631 427-7000
Michael Schenkler,
EMP: 7
SALES (est): 366.1K **Privately Held**
SIC: 2711 Newspapers

(G-6406)
NORTHROP GRUMMAN SYSTEMS CORP
70 Dewey St (11743-7126)
PHONE..................631 423-1014
Ray Schubnel, *Manager*
Mary Westerling, *Administration*
EMP: 7 **Publicly Held**
WEB: www.sperry.ngc.com
SIC: 3721 Aircraft
HQ: Northrop Grumman Systems Corporation
  2980 Fairview Park Dr
  Falls Church VA 22042
  703 280-2900

(G-6407)
PASSIVE-PLUS INC
48 Elm St (11743-3402)
PHONE..................631 425-0938
Lisa Beyel, *President*
Steve Beyel, *Vice Pres*
▲ EMP: 18
SALES (est): 1.7MM **Privately Held**
SIC: 3679 3675 3676 3674 Microwave components; electronic capacitors; electronic resistors; magnetohydrodynamic (MHD) devices

(G-6408)
QUANTUM MECHANICS NY LLC
40 Hennessey Dr (11743-3828)
PHONE..................917 519-7077
EMP: 7
SALES (est): 347.4K **Privately Held**
SIC: 3572 Computer storage devices

(G-6409)
RED ONYX INDUSTRIAL PDTS LLC
23 Green St Ste 310 (11743-3363)
PHONE..................516 459-6035
▲ EMP: 5 EST: 2009
SALES (est): 326.8K **Privately Held**
SIC: 3493 Leaf springs: automobile, locomotive, etc.

(G-6410)
ROAR BEVERAGES LLC
125 W Shore Rd (11743-2042)
PHONE..................631 683-5565
Roland Neffey, *CEO*
John Behling, *General Mgr*
Vincent Nesi, *COO*
Andrew Zambratto, *Vice Pres*
▼ EMP: 21
SALES: 7MM **Privately Held**
SIC: 2087 Concentrates, drink

(G-6411)
ROBOT FRUIT INC
40 Radcliff Dr (11743-2649)
PHONE..................631 423-7250
Thomas Vieweg, *CEO*
EMP: 12 EST: 2012
SALES (est): 603.1K **Privately Held**
SIC: 7372 Application computer software

(G-6412)
ROLLSON INC
10 Smugglers Cv (11743-1616)
PHONE..................631 423-9578
Rudolph Creteur, *President*
Tom Perry, *Vice Pres*
EMP: 25 EST: 1938
SQ FT: 15,000
SALES (est): 2.7MM **Privately Held**
WEB: www.rollson.com
SIC: 3429 3444 3446 Marine hardware; sheet metalwork; architectural metalwork

(G-6413)
ROTRONIC INSTRUMENT CORP
160 E Main St Ste 1 (11743-7401)
PHONE..................631 427-3898
Jay Crum, *Regl Sales Mgr*
Karl Szymanski, *Regl Sales Mgr*
Bob Hayes, *Sales Associate*
J Lafarie, *Branch Mgr*
EMP: 8 **Privately Held**
SIC: 3823 Industrial instrmnts msrmnt display/control process variable
HQ: Rotronic Instrument Corp.
  135 Engineers Rd Ste 150
  Hauppauge NY 11788
  631 348-6844

(G-6414)
SC TEXTILES INC
Also Called: Affiliated Services Group
434 New York Ave (11743-3438)
PHONE..................631 944-6262
Stephen S Cohen, *President*
EMP: 2
SQ FT: 3,500
SALES: 4MM **Privately Held**
SIC: 3679 Electronic loads & power supplies

(G-6415)
SECURITY OFFSET SERVICES INC
11 Grandview St (11743-3534)
PHONE..................631 944-6031
George Hirsch, *President*
EMP: 9
SQ FT: 10,000
SALES (est): 939.4K **Privately Held**
SIC: 2752 Commercial printing, offset

(G-6416)
SELECT PRODUCTS HOLDINGS LLC (PA)
1 Arnold Dr Unit 3 (11743-3981)
P.O. Box 707 (11743-0707)
PHONE..................631 421-6000
Simon Roozrokh, *CEO*
David Darouvar, *CFO*
▲ EMP: 49
SQ FT: 80,000
SALES (est): 12.6MM **Privately Held**
SIC: 2676 Towels, napkins & tissue paper products

(G-6417)
STEVEN KRAUS ASSOCIATES INC
9 Private Rd (11743-2243)
PHONE..................631 923-2033
Steven Kraus, *President*
EMP: 5
SQ FT: 2,500
SALES: 475K **Privately Held**
SIC: 2542 Office & store showcases & display fixtures

(G-6418)
TELEPHONICS CORPORATION
Tlsi Division
770 Park Ave (11743-3974)
PHONE..................631 549-6000
Mark Supko, *President*
Peter A Wolfe, *Senior VP*
Joseph Obiedzenski, *Opers Staff*
Jerry Golden, *Purch Agent*
Rob Walker, *Purch Agent*
EMP: 30
SALES (corp-wide): 1.5B **Publicly Held**
SIC: 3679 3674 Electronic circuits; semiconductors & related devices
HQ: Telephonics Corporation
  815 Broadhollow Rd
  Farmingdale NY 11735
  631 755-7000

(G-6419)
TELEPHONICS CORPORATION
770 Park Ave (11743-3974)
PHONE..................631 755-7000
Doug Miller, *Engineer*
Dominic Nocera, *Controller*
Christina Radzewsky, *Admin Asst*
EMP: 12
SALES (corp-wide): 1.5B **Publicly Held**
SIC: 3669 Emergency alarms
HQ: Telephonics Corporation
  815 Broadhollow Rd
  Farmingdale NY 11735
  631 755-7000

(G-6420)
TELEPHONICS CORPORATION
780 Park Ave (11743-4516)
PHONE..................631 470-8800
Stephen Maroney, *Director*
EMP: 99
SALES (corp-wide): 1.5B **Publicly Held**
SIC: 3699 Electronic training devices
HQ: Telephonics Corporation
  815 Broadhollow Rd
  Farmingdale NY 11735
  631 755-7000

(G-6421)
TELEPHONICS TLSI CORP
780 Park Ave (11743-4516)
PHONE..................631 470-8854
Zhigang MA, *President*
Marshall Lacoff, *Senior VP*
Dan McGovern, *Engineer*
Rudy Rupe, *Engineer*
Gustavo Taboada, *Engineer*
EMP: 200
SQ FT: 20,000
SALES (est): 5.6MM
SALES (corp-wide): 1.5B **Publicly Held**
SIC: 3674 Microcircuits, integrated (semiconductor)
HQ: Telephonics Corporation
  815 Broadhollow Rd
  Farmingdale NY 11735
  631 755-7000

(G-6422)
TLSI INCORPORATED
780 Park Ave (11743-4516)
PHONE..................631 470-8880
Zhigang MA, *President*
Kevin McSweeney, *COO*
Keith Keating, *Senior Mgr*
EMP: 65
SALES (est): 8.2MM
SALES (corp-wide): 1.5B **Publicly Held**
SIC: 3674 3679 Semiconductors & related devices; electronic circuits
HQ: Telephonics Corporation
  815 Broadhollow Rd
  Farmingdale NY 11735
  631 755-7000

(G-6423)
UNITED DATA SYSTEMS INC
Also Called: American Lpg Systems
202 E Main St Ste 302 (11743-2966)
PHONE..................631 549-6900
Erling Kristiansen, *Ch of Bd*
▲ EMP: 8
SQ FT: 11,500
SALES (est): 565.8K **Privately Held**
WEB: www.udsystems.com
SIC: 7372 5045 Prepackaged software; computer software

(G-6424)
VALLEY INDUSTRIAL PRODUCTS INC
152 New York Ave (11743-2185)
PHONE..................631 385-9300
Laurel B Phelan, *CEO*
Laurel Phelan, *Ch of Bd*
Alberta Barth Dwyer, *Treasurer*
EMP: 35 EST: 1965
SQ FT: 14,000
SALES (est): 12.5MM **Privately Held**
WEB: www.valleyindustrialtape.com
SIC: 2672 2671 2241 Tape, pressure sensitive: made from purchased materials; packaging paper & plastics film, coated & laminated; narrow fabric mills

(G-6425)
VDC ELECTRONICS INC
155 W Carver St Ste 2 (11743-3376)
PHONE..................631 683-5850
Sheryl Ross, *Ch of Bd*
▲ EMP: 13
SALES (est): 1.9MM **Privately Held**
SIC: 3621 Storage battery chargers, motor & engine generator type

(G-6426)
VENCO SALES INC
755 Park Ave Ste 300 (11743-3979)
PHONE..................631 754-0782
John Venini, *President*
Gary Bosma, *Sales Staff*
Frank Brecher, *Sales Staff*
Jim Finan, *Sales Staff*
Rob Morrision, *Sales Staff*
EMP: 20
SALES (est): 2.5MM **Privately Held**
SIC: 3494 Plumbing & heating valves

(G-6427)
WEBINFINITY AMERICAS INC (PA)
315 Main St Unit 4 (11743-6941)
PHONE..................516 331-5180
James F Hodgkinson, *Ch of Bd*
Chris Becwar, *Partner*
EMP: 12 EST: 2012
SALES (est): 7.3MM **Privately Held**
SIC: 3823 Digital displays of process variables

Huntington Station
Suffolk County

(G-6428)
AEROBIC WEAR INC
16 Depot Rd (11746-1737)
PHONE..................631 673-1830
Bradley Rosen, *President*
EMP: 5
SQ FT: 6,200
SALES: 527.8K **Privately Held**
WEB: www.aerobicwear.com
SIC: 2339 2369 Athletic clothing: women's, misses' & juniors'; girls' & children's outerwear

(G-6429)
AMERICAN CULTURE HAIR INC
159 E 2nd St (11746-1430)
PHONE..................631 242-3142
Louis Guarneri, *President*
Arlene Benza, *Comms Dir*
Alicyn McDermott, *Education*
▲ EMP: 22
SALES (est): 2.1MM **Privately Held**
SIC: 3999 Hair & hair-based products

(G-6430)
AMERICAN TCHNCAL CERAMICS CORP (DH)
Also Called: Atc
1 Norden Ln (11746-2140)
PHONE..................631 622-4700
John Lawing, *CEO*
John S Gilbertson, *Principal*
Richard Monsorno, *Senior VP*

▲ = Import ▼=Export ◆ =Import/Export

GEOGRAPHIC SECTION

Huntington Station - Suffolk County (G-6460)

David B Ott, *Senior VP*
Kathleen M Kelly, *Vice Pres*
◆ **EMP:** 440
SQ FT: 18,000
SALES (est): 184.5MM
SALES (corp-wide): 14.8B **Publicly Held**
WEB: www.atceramics.com
SIC: 3672 3675 Printed circuit boards; electronic capacitors
HQ: Avx Corporation
  1 Avx Blvd
  Fountain Inn SC 29644
  864 967-2150

(G-6431)
AMERICAN TECHICAL CERAMICS
11 Stepar Pl (11746-2103)
PHONE 631 622-4758
Eduardo Sayers, *Manager*
▲ **EMP:** 5
SALES (est): 431K **Privately Held**
SIC: 3675 Electronic capacitors

(G-6432)
AMERICAN TECHNICAL CERAMICS
17 Stepar Pl (11746-2141)
PHONE 631 622-4700
Skip Wiese, *Facilities Mgr*
James Navas, *Foreman/Supr*
Ned Patel, *Production*
Yardley Cornet, *Purch Agent*
Robert Clark, *QC Mgr*
EMP: 400
SALES (corp-wide): 14.8B **Publicly Held**
WEB: www.atceramics.com
SIC: 3675 Electronic capacitors
HQ: American Technical Ceramics Corp.
  1 Norden Ln
  Huntington Station NY 11746
  631 622-4700

(G-6433)
AUTO SPORT DESIGNS INC
203 W Hills Rd (11746-3147)
PHONE 631 425-1555
Tom Papadopoulos, *President*
Tomas Papadopoulos, *President*
▲ **EMP:** 11
SQ FT: 30,000
SALES (est): 2.1MM **Privately Held**
WEB: www.autosportdesigns.com
SIC: 3713 5511 5531 Automobile assembly, including specialty automobiles; new & used car dealers; speed shops, including race car supplies

(G-6434)
BC COMMUNICATIONS INC
Also Called: Sign Depot Distribution
211 Depot Rd (11746-2488)
PHONE 631 549-8833
Suzanne Cranz, *President*
William F Cranz, *President*
Suzanne Vautier, *Vice Pres*
EMP: 1
SQ FT: 10,500
SALES (est): 1MM **Privately Held**
WEB: www.signdepotsales.com
SIC: 3993 Signs & advertising specialties

(G-6435)
CALIFORNIA FRAGRANCE COMPANY
Also Called: Aromafloria
171 E 2nd St (11746-1430)
PHONE 631 424-4023
Sharon Christie, *President*
Tracy Gunther, *Purchasing*
Elizebeth Flaherty, *Controller*
Susan Marchese, *Accounting Mgr*
Rosemary Gaynor, *Cust Mgr*
▲ **EMP:** 30
SQ FT: 30,000
SALES (est): 7.2MM **Privately Held**
SIC: 2844 Cosmetic preparations

(G-6436)
COMCO PLASTICS INC
11 Stepar Pl (11746-2103)
PHONE 718 849-9000
Michael French, *President*
John C French, *President*
Rovena Prifti, *Controller*
▲ **EMP:** 36 **EST:** 1956
SQ FT: 20,000
SALES (est): 4.3MM **Privately Held**
WEB: www.comcoplastics.com
SIC: 3081 3082 Unsupported plastics film & sheet; rods, unsupported plastic

(G-6437)
COMPLETE SEC & CONTRLS INC
100 Hillwood Dr (11746-1345)
PHONE 631 421-7200
Steve Krishnayah, *President*
EMP: 18
SQ FT: 7,000
SALES (est): 175.3K **Privately Held**
WEB: www.completesecuritycorp.com
SIC: 3644 Noncurrent-carrying wiring services

(G-6438)
DC CONTRACTING & BUILDING CORP
136 Railroad St (11746-1540)
PHONE 631 385-1117
Dean Confessore, *President*
EMP: 13
SQ FT: 5,000
SALES (est): 1.7MM **Privately Held**
SIC: 2431 Woodwork, interior & ornamental

(G-6439)
DILLNER PRECAST INC
200 W 9th St (11746-1667)
PHONE 631 421-9130
John Dillner, *President*
EMP: 5
SQ FT: 4,000
SALES (corp-wide): 1MM **Privately Held**
SIC: 3272 Concrete products, precast
PA: Dillner Precast Inc
  14 Meadow Ln
  Lloyd Harbor NY 11743
  631 421-9130

(G-6440)
FERACO INDUSTRIES
3 Plumb Ct (11746-1128)
PHONE 631 547-8120
Ray Albini, *Owner*
EMP: 8
SALES (est): 734.4K **Privately Held**
SIC: 3999 Manufacturing industries

(G-6441)
FORMAC WELDING INC
42 W Hills Rd (11746-2304)
PHONE 631 421-5525
Joel Mc Elearney, *President*
Maureen Mc Elearney, *Admin Sec*
EMP: 7
SQ FT: 3,800
SALES (est): 866.2K **Privately Held**
SIC: 7692 Welding repair

(G-6442)
FOUR-WAY PALLET CORP
191 E 2nd St (11746-1430)
PHONE 631 351-3401
Leonard Koppelman, *President*
EMP: 28
SALES (est): 3.5MM **Privately Held**
SIC: 2448 7699 5084 Pallets, wood & wood with metal; pallet repair; materials handling machinery

(G-6443)
HART SPORTS INC
4 Roxanne Ct (11746-1122)
PHONE 631 385-1805
James Hart, *President*
EMP: 6
SALES (est): 411.7K **Privately Held**
SIC: 3949 Hockey equipment & supplies, general

(G-6444)
HERCULES INTERNATIONAL INC
95 W Hills Rd (11746-3119)
PHONE 631 423-6900
Michael Flaxman, *President*
EMP: 20
SALES (est): 2.2MM **Privately Held**
WEB: www.herculesintlcorp.com
SIC: 3589 Car washing machinery

(G-6445)
HUNTINGTON WELDING & IRON
139 W Pulaski Rd (11746-1693)
PHONE 631 423-3331
Andrew Blondrage, *Owner*
EMP: 5
SALES (est): 301.5K **Privately Held**
SIC: 7692 Welding repair

(G-6446)
HUNTINGTON WOODWORKING INC
Also Called: Mica World
691 E Jericho Tpke (11746-7501)
PHONE 631 271-7897
Anthony Perico Jr, *President*
Marie Perico, *Vice Pres*
EMP: 5
SALES (est): 725.7K **Privately Held**
WEB: www.mica-world.com
SIC: 2434 Wood kitchen cabinets

(G-6447)
I A S NATIONAL INC
Also Called: Hercules
95 W Hills Rd (11746-3197)
PHONE 631 423-6900
Michael Flaxman, *President*
Lynn Kramer, *Manager*
▼ **EMP:** 20
SALES (est): 2.8MM **Privately Held**
WEB: www.hercules.com
SIC: 3589 2899 Car washing machinery; chemical preparations

(G-6448)
ISLAND AUTOMATED GATE CO LLC
125 W Hills Rd (11746-3144)
PHONE 631 425-0196
Stan Osowski,
EMP: 3
SALES: 1MM **Privately Held**
SIC: 3569 Bridge or gate machinery, hydraulic

(G-6449)
JOHN LAROCCA & SON INC
Also Called: E C Sumereau & Sons
290 Broadway (11746-1403)
PHONE 631 423-5256
John Larocca, *President*
EMP: 6 **EST:** 1856
SQ FT: 10,000
SALES (est): 741.9K **Privately Held**
WEB: www.ecsumereau.com
SIC: 3471 Electroplating of metals or formed products

(G-6450)
KELMAR SYSTEMS INC
284 Broadway (11746-1497)
PHONE 631 421-1230
Andrew Marglin, *President*
Laurie Franz, *Vice Pres*
Joan Marglin, *Admin Sec*
EMP: 16
SQ FT: 4,500
SALES: 1.4MM **Privately Held**
WEB: www.kelmarsystems.com
SIC: 3861 Sound recording & reproducing equipment, motion picture

(G-6451)
MELBOURNE C FISHER YACHT SAILS
Also Called: Doyle Sails
1345 New York Ave Ste 2 (11746-1751)
PHONE 631 673-5055
Mark Washeim, *President*
Diana Malkin'washeim, *Vice Pres*
▼ **EMP:** 6
SALES (est): 722.7K **Privately Held**
SIC: 2394 Sails: made from purchased materials

(G-6452)
MICROSOFT CORPORATION
160 Walt Whitman Rd 1006b (11746-4160)
PHONE 631 760-2340
EMP: 5
SALES (corp-wide): 110.3B **Publicly Held**
SIC: 7372 Prepackaged software
PA: Microsoft Corporation
  1 Microsoft Way
  Redmond WA 98052
  425 882-8080

(G-6453)
NEW YORK DIGITAL CORPORATION
33 Walt Whitman Rd # 117 (11746-3678)
PHONE 631 630-9798
Salil Bandy, *President*
EMP: 11
SQ FT: 30,000
SALES (est): 830K **Privately Held**
SIC: 3679 Electronic loads & power supplies

(G-6454)
NORTH SHORE PALLET INC
191 E 2nd St (11746-1430)
PHONE 631 673-4700
EMP: 8
SALES (est): 1.1MM **Privately Held**
SIC: 2448 Pallets, wood & wood with metal

(G-6455)
ROTTKAMP TENNIS INC
100 Broadway (11746-1448)
PHONE 631 421-0040
Richard Rottkamp, *President*
EMP: 25
SALES (est): 1.7MM **Privately Held**
SIC: 3949 Tennis equipment & supplies

(G-6456)
RUBBER STAMP X PRESS
7 Bradford Pl (11747-1043)
PHONE 631 423-1322
Ilene Schleichkorn, *Chairman*
EMP: 5
SALES (est): 380.4K **Privately Held**
SIC: 3953 Embossing seals & hand stamps

(G-6457)
SCENT-A-VISION INC
171 E 2nd St (11746-1430)
PHONE 631 424-4905
Sharon Christie, *President*
EMP: 23
SQ FT: 5,000
SALES (est): 3.3MM **Privately Held**
WEB: www.aromafloria.com
SIC: 2844 5122 Toilet preparations; perfumes

(G-6458)
SELECTRODE INDUSTRIES INC (PA)
230 Broadway (11746-1403)
PHONE 631 547-5470
Joe Paternoster, *Ch of Bd*
Paul Paternoster, *President*
Matthew Garuccio, *Director*
▲ **EMP:** 95
SQ FT: 26,000
SALES (est): 20.9MM **Privately Held**
WEB: www.selectrode.com
SIC: 3356 3496 Nonferrous rolling & drawing; miscellaneous fabricated wire products

(G-6459)
SUPER SWEEP INC (PA)
Also Called: SMS
20 Railroad St Unit 1 (11746-1296)
PHONE 631 223-8205
Michael Marglin, *Ch of Bd*
EMP: 12
SALES (est): 2.6MM **Privately Held**
SIC: 3354 Aluminum extruded products

(G-6460)
SWISSWAY INC
123 W Hills Rd (11746-3155)
PHONE 631 351-5350
Gerard Cavalier Jr, *President*
Rosemary Schwinn, *Asst Office Mgr*
EMP: 25 **EST:** 1963
SQ FT: 10,000

Huntington Station - Suffolk County (G-6461)

SALES (est): 3.7MM **Privately Held**
WEB: www.swisswayinc.com
SIC: 3599 Machine shop, jobbing & repair

(G-6461)
TECHNOPAVING NEW YORK INC
270 Broadway (11746-1561)
PHONE.................................631 351-6472
Christine Brown, *President*
EMP: 7
SALES (est): 716.1K **Privately Held**
SIC: 3531 Pavers

(G-6462)
TEQUIPMENT INC
Also Called: T E Q
7 Norden Ln (11746-2102)
PHONE.................................516 922-3508
Robert Sugarman, *President*
Richard Acheampong, *Area Mgr*
Christine Sugarman, *Corp Secy*
Robert-Wayne Harris, *Vice Pres*
Russell Keach, *Production*
EMP: 100
SQ FT: 40,000
SALES (est): 22.6MM **Privately Held**
WEB: www.tequipment.com
SIC: 7372 Educational computer software

(G-6463)
VAIRE LLC
200 E 2nd St Ste 34 (11746-1464)
PHONE.................................631 271-4933
Robert Pearl,
EMP: 6
SQ FT: 23,000
SALES (est): 1.1MM **Privately Held**
SIC: 3652 5211 Compact laser discs, prerecorded; bathroom fixtures, equipment & supplies

(G-6464)
WALSH & HUGHES INC (PA)
Also Called: Velvetop Products
1455 New York Ave (11746-1706)
PHONE.................................631 427-5904
John B Walsh, *President*
Linda J Walsh, *Treasurer*
EMP: 8 **EST:** 1968
SQ FT: 3,800
SALES (est): 1.7MM **Privately Held**
WEB: www.velvetop.com
SIC: 2891 5941 5032 5091 Sealants; tennis goods & equipment; clay construction materials, except refractory; sporting & recreation goods

(G-6465)
Z-CAR-D CORP
Also Called: Sign-A-Rama
403 Oakwood Rd (11746-7207)
PHONE.................................631 424-2077
Dawn M Tiritter-Bent, *Ch of Bd*
Michael Ziccardi, *Vice Pres*
EMP: 28
SQ FT: 15,000
SALES (est): 3.1MM **Privately Held**
WEB: www.ssar.com
SIC: 3993 Signs & advertising specialties

Hurleyville
Sullivan County

(G-6466)
MONGIELLO SALES INC
250 Hilldale Rd (12747-5301)
P.O. Box 320 (12747-0320)
PHONE.................................845 436-4200
Anthony Mongiello, *President*
Felicia Ramos-Peters, *Pub Rel Mgr*
Gary Kudrowitz, *Manager*
▼ **EMP:** 40
SALES (est): 4.1MM **Privately Held**
SIC: 2022 Natural cheese

Hyde Park
Dutchess County

(G-6467)
ABE POOL SERVICE
793 Violet Ave (12538-1952)
PHONE.................................845 473-7730
Abraham Stewart, *President*
EMP: 5
SALES (est): 618.4K **Privately Held**
SIC: 3589 Swimming pool filter & water conditioning systems

(G-6468)
CASTINO CORPORATION
1300 Route 9g (12538-2076)
PHONE.................................845 229-0341
Eric Castaldo, *Principal*
EMP: 6 **EST:** 2011
SALES (est): 590.9K **Privately Held**
SIC: 3089 Plastics products

(G-6469)
HYDE PARK BREWING CO INC
4076 Albany Post Rd (12538-1934)
PHONE.................................845 229-8277
Carmelo Decicco, *President*
EMP: 20
SQ FT: 4,000
SALES (est): 2MM **Privately Held**
WEB: www.hydeparkbrewing.com
SIC: 2082 5812 Beer (alcoholic beverage); eating places

(G-6470)
NEW CITY PRESS INC
202 Comforter Blvd (12538-2977)
PHONE.................................845 229-0335
Patrick Markey, *General Mgr*
Gary Brandal, *Manager*
EMP: 5
SALES (est): 441.2K **Privately Held**
WEB: www.newcitypress.com
SIC: 2731 Books: publishing only

(G-6471)
RIVERWOOD SIGNS BY DANDEV DESI
7 Maple Ln (12538-1223)
PHONE.................................845 229-0282
Kathleen Hinz-Shaffer, *President*
EMP: 5
SALES: 100K **Privately Held**
SIC: 3993 7336 7389 Signs & advertising specialties; commercial art & graphic design; design, commercial & industrial

(G-6472)
VICTORIA PRECISION INC
78 Travis Rd (12538-2753)
PHONE.................................845 473-9309
Vincent Slaninka, *President*
Ray Forman, *Sales Staff*
EMP: 5
SQ FT: 3,000
SALES (est): 270K **Privately Held**
WEB: www.victoriaprecisioninc.com
SIC: 3599 Machine shop, jobbing & repair

Ilion
Herkimer County

(G-6473)
ACORN PRODUCTS CORP
27 Pleasant Ave (13357-1115)
PHONE.................................315 894-4868
John Thayer, *President*
EMP: 15 **EST:** 2008
SALES (est): 1.5MM **Privately Held**
SIC: 2396 Printing & embossing on plastics fabric articles

(G-6474)
FERMER PRECISION INC
114 Johnson Rd (13357-3899)
PHONE.................................315 822-6371
Stewart Bunce, *President*
Rick Bunce, *General Mgr*
John Tofani, *Vice Pres*
Chris Hoover, *Engineer*
Steve Scheibel, *Sales Staff*
EMP: 72
SQ FT: 60,000
SALES: 8MM **Privately Held**
WEB: www.fermerprecision.com
SIC: 3599 Electrical discharge machining (EDM); machine shop, jobbing & repair

(G-6475)
ILION PLASTICS INC
27 Pleasant Ave (13357-1115)
PHONE.................................315 894-4868
Steve Quinn, *President*
Kathy Quinn, *President*
EMP: 16
SQ FT: 10,000
SALES: 800K **Privately Held**
SIC: 3089 Injection molding of plastics

(G-6476)
JAMES WIRE DIE CO
138 West St (13357-2250)
PHONE.................................315 894-3233
R B Roux, *President*
Alex Roux, *Vice Pres*
EMP: 5
SALES: 100K **Privately Held**
SIC: 3544 Special dies & tools

(G-6477)
ORIGINAL HRKMER CNTY CHESE INC
Also Called: Herkimer Cheese
2745 State Route 51 (13357-4299)
P.O. Box 310, Herkimer (13350-0310)
PHONE.................................315 895-7428
Sheldon Basloe, *President*
Norma Basloe, *Corp Secy*
Robert Basloe, *Vice Pres*
Nora Ray, *Safety Mgr*
Jacob Basloe, *Purch Mgr*
EMP: 60 **EST:** 1949
SQ FT: 22,913
SALES (est): 7.7MM **Privately Held**
WEB: www.herkimerfoods.com
SIC: 2022 2099 Natural cheese; gelatin dessert preparations; dessert mixes & fillings

(G-6478)
REMINGTON ARMS COMPANY LLC
14 Hoefler Ave (13357-1888)
PHONE.................................315 895-3482
Laird G Williams, *Principal*
Steven Taylor, *Safety Dir*
Kyle Luke, *Opers Mgr*
Joseph Nolan, *Opers Staff*
Rosann Barone, *Buyer*
EMP: 850
SALES (corp-wide): 31.2B **Privately Held**
WEB: www.remington.com
SIC: 3484 8711 Guns (firearms) or gun parts, 30 mm. & below; engineering services
HQ: Remington Arms Company, Llc
870 Remington Dr
Madison NC 27025
336 548-8700

(G-6479)
REVIVAL INDUSTRIES INC
126 Old Forge Rd (13357-4200)
PHONE.................................315 868-1085
Richard Jackson, *President*
Edward R Jackson, *Vice Pres*
EMP: 17
SQ FT: 16,000
SALES (est): 1MM **Privately Held**
WEB: www.revivalindustries.com
SIC: 2426 2499 Gun stocks, wood; handles, poles, dowels & stakes: wood; novelties, wood fiber

Interlaken
Seneca County

(G-6480)
AMERICANA VINEYARDS & WINERY
4367 E Covert Rd (14847-9720)
PHONE.................................607 387-6801
Joseph Gober, *President*
EMP: 15
SALES: 750K **Privately Held**
SIC: 2084 Wines

(G-6481)
HIPSHOT PRODUCTS INC
Also Called: Melissa
8248 State Route 96 (14847-9655)
PHONE.................................607 532-9404
David Borisoff, *President*
Zack Singer, *Engineer*
▲ **EMP:** 15
SALES (est): 2MM **Privately Held**
WEB: www.hipshotproducts.com
SIC: 3931 5736 Guitars & parts, electric & nonelectric; musical instrument stores

(G-6482)
LUCAS VINEYARDS INC
3862 County Road 150 (14847-9805)
PHONE.................................607 532-4825
Ruth Lucas, *President*
Jeffrey Houck, *Vice Pres*
EMP: 12
SALES (est): 1.8MM **Privately Held**
WEB: www.lucasvineyards.com
SIC: 2084 0172 5921 Wines; grapes; liquor stores

(G-6483)
PINE TREE FARMS INC
3714 Cayuga St (14847-9607)
P.O. Box 254 (14847-0254)
PHONE.................................607 532-4312
Mark Stillions, *President*
Joelle Stillions, *Corp Secy*
Neal Stillions, *Vice Pres*
Michelle Griego-Stillions, *Sales Mgr*
EMP: 30
SQ FT: 14,000
SALES (est): 4.7MM **Privately Held**
WEB: www.pinetreefarmsinc.com
SIC: 2048 Bird food, prepared

Inwood
Nassau County

(G-6484)
APEX ARIDYNE CORP
168 Doughty Blvd (11096-2010)
P.O. Box 960670 (11096-0670)
PHONE.................................516 239-4400
Edward Schlussel, *President*
EMP: 5
SALES (corp-wide): 8.6MM **Privately Held**
SIC: 2258 2257 Lace & warp knit fabric mills; weft knit fabric mills
PA: Apex Aridyne Corp.
2350 Long Dairy Rd
Graham NC
516 239-4400

(G-6485)
ARLEE LIGHTING CORP
125 Doughty Blvd (11096-2003)
PHONE.................................516 595-8558
Pinchaf Gralla, *President*
▲ **EMP:** 4
SALES (est): 2.7MM **Privately Held**
SIC: 3646 Commercial indusl & institutional electric lighting fixtures

(G-6486)
AUDIOSAVINGS INC
Also Called: Rockville Pro
600 Bayview Ave Ste 200 (11096-1625)
PHONE.................................888 445-1555
▼ **EMP:** 14
SALES (est): 2.5MM **Privately Held**
SIC: 3651 Mfg Home Audio/Video Equipment

(G-6487)
BEL TRANSFORMER INC (HQ)
Also Called: Signal Transformer
500 Bayview Ave (11096-1702)
P.O. Box 36129, Newark NJ (07188-6106)
PHONE.................................516 239-5777
Daniel Bernstein, *President*
Colin Dunn, *Vice Pres*
▲ **EMP:** 60
SQ FT: 40,000

GEOGRAPHIC SECTION

Island Park - Nassau County (G-6514)

SALES: 17MM
SALES (corp-wide): 491.6MM **Publicly Held**
WEB: www.signaltransformer.com
SIC: 3677 Electronic coils, transformers & other inductors
PA: Bel Fuse Inc.
206 Van Vorst St
Jersey City NJ 07302
201 432-0463

(G-6488)
EXCEL PAINT APPLICATORS INC
555 Doughty Blvd (11096-1031)
PHONE..................347 221-1968
P C Sekar, *President*
▲ EMP: 45
SQ FT: 48,000
SALES (est): 5.4MM **Privately Held**
SIC: 3991 Brooms & brushes

(G-6489)
EXCELLENT ART MFG CORP
Also Called: Neva Slip
531 Bayview Ave (11096-1703)
PHONE..................718 388-7075
Marshall Korn, *President*
David Korn, *Vice Pres*
▲ EMP: 16 EST: 1929
SQ FT: 25,000
SALES (est): 1.8MM **Privately Held**
SIC: 3949 2273 2392 Sporting & athletic goods; carpets & rugs; mattress pads

(G-6490)
FIBERALL CORP
449 Sheridan Blvd (11096-1203)
PHONE..................516 371-5200
Isaac Zilber, *President*
Sophie Zilber, *Vice Pres*
Tony Recchia, *VP Sales*
▲ EMP: 25
SQ FT: 8,000
SALES (est): 5MM **Privately Held**
WEB: www.fiberall.com
SIC: 3357 Nonferrous wiredrawing & insulating

(G-6491)
GENERAL DIARIES CORPORATION
56 John St (11096-1353)
PHONE..................516 371-2244
Mark Lebo, *President*
▲ EMP: 15 EST: 1953
SALES (est): 2MM **Privately Held**
WEB: www.dallasnews.com
SIC: 2782 2678 Memorandum books, printed; diaries; desk pads, paper: made from purchased materials

(G-6492)
HASTINGS HIDE INC
Also Called: A J Hollander Enterprises
372 Doughty Blvd (11096-1337)
PHONE..................516 295-2400
Howard Ganz, *President*
EMP: 6
SALES (est): 891.1K
SALES (corp-wide): 1.7MM **Privately Held**
SIC: 3111 5159 4731 Leather tanning & finishing; hides; agents, shipping
PA: Hastings Hide, Inc.
231 Road 3168
Hastings NE 68901
402 463-5308

(G-6493)
INWOOD MATERIAL
1 Sheridan Blvd (11096-1807)
PHONE..................516 371-1842
Frank Sciarrino, *President*
EMP: 11
SALES (est): 1.7MM **Privately Held**
SIC: 3273 5082 Ready-mixed concrete; masonry equipment & supplies

(G-6494)
LES CHATEAUX DE FRANCE INC
1 Craft Ave (11096-1609)
PHONE..................516 239-6795
Gerald Shapiro, *President*
Marie Cuscianna, *Vice Pres*
EMP: 28
SQ FT: 7,000
SALES (est): 3.1MM **Privately Held**
SIC: 2038 Snacks, including onion rings, cheese sticks, etc.

(G-6495)
MGR EQUIPMENT CORP
22 Gates Ave (11096-1612)
PHONE..................516 239-3030
Gerald Ross, *President*
Robert Ross, *Corp Secy*
George Mauder, *Vice Pres*
▼ EMP: 25
SQ FT: 40,000
SALES (est): 4.3MM **Privately Held**
WEB: www.mgrequip.com
SIC: 3585 Ice making machinery

(G-6496)
N3A CORPORATION
345 Doughty Blvd (11096-1348)
PHONE..................516 284-6799
Niall Alli, *CEO*
Adrienne Alli, *CFO*
▲ EMP: 100 EST: 2007
SQ FT: 100,000
SALES (est): 9.3MM **Privately Held**
SIC: 2676 2599 Towels, napkins & tissue paper products; hotel furniture

(G-6497)
NEA MANUFACTURING CORP
315 Doughty Blvd (11096-1348)
PHONE..................516 371-4200
Sheik Alli, *President*
▲ EMP: 37
SQ FT: 4,000
SALES (est): 4.6MM **Privately Held**
SIC: 3672 3679 3677 3678 Printed circuit boards; electronic switches; electronic transformers; electronic connectors; household audio & video equipment; current-carrying wiring devices

(G-6498)
NOEL ASSOC
114 Henry St Ste A (11096-2350)
PHONE..................516 371-5420
EMP: 5
SALES (est): 300K **Privately Held**
SIC: 3993 Mfg Signs/Advertising Specialties

(G-6499)
PLUSLUX LLC
Also Called: Wascomat of America
461 Doughty Blvd (11096-1344)
PHONE..................516 371-4400
Neal Milch,
EMP: 7
SALES (est): 337.5K **Privately Held**
SIC: 3633 Household laundry machines, including coin-operated

(G-6500)
SCY MANUFACTURING INC
600 Bayview Ave Ste 200 (11096-1625)
PHONE..................516 986-3083
Shmuel Freund, *President*
Chagai Freund, *Vice Pres*
Isaac Freund, *Vice Pres*
◆ EMP: 3 EST: 2013
SQ FT: 900
SALES: 8MM **Privately Held**
SIC: 3651 Mfg Home Audio/Video Equipment

Irving
Chautauqua County

(G-6501)
SENECA NATION ENTERPRISE
11482 Route 20 (14081-9539)
PHONE..................716 934-7430
EMP: 12
SALES (est): 1.3MM **Privately Held**
SIC: 2111 5172 Cigarettes; gasoline

Irvington
Westchester County

(G-6502)
ABYRX INC
1 Bridge St Ste 121 (10533-1553)
PHONE..................914 357-2600
John Pacifico, *President*
Aniq Darr, *Vice Pres*
Jenny Enrico, *Opers Mgr*
Richard Kronenthal, *Officer*
EMP: 11 EST: 2013
SALES (est): 1.5MM **Privately Held**
SIC: 3841 Surgical instruments & apparatus

(G-6503)
CITY GEAR INC
213 Taxter Rd (10533-1111)
PHONE..................914 450-4746
John Clark, *President*
Ingred Roberg, *Vice Pres*
▼ EMP: 6
SQ FT: 3,000
SALES (est): 510K **Privately Held**
SIC: 3599 Machine shop, jobbing & repair

(G-6504)
FEINKIND INC
Also Called: REFINEDKIND PET PRODUCTS
17 Algonquin Dr (10533-1007)
PHONE..................800 289-6136
Josh Feinkind, *CEO*
▲ EMP: 1
SQ FT: 65,000
SALES: 1MM **Privately Held**
SIC: 2511 Novelty furniture: wood

(G-6505)
GUTTZ CORPORATION OF AMERICA
Also Called: Gutts Corporation of America
50 S Buckhout St Ste 104 (10533-2217)
PHONE..................914 591-9600
Robert H Cohen, *President*
Ronald Roemer, *Vice Pres*
Jane Berger, *Manager*
EMP: 13
SQ FT: 7,000
SALES (est): 1.5MM **Privately Held**
WEB: www.marketvis.com
SIC: 3955 Print cartridges for laser & other computer printers

(G-6506)
HAIR VENTURES LLC (PA)
Also Called: Hairstory
94 Fargo Ln (10533-1202)
PHONE..................718 664-7689
Eli Halliwell, *CEO*
Erica Halliwell, *CFO*
EMP: 11
SALES (est): 1.1MM **Privately Held**
SIC: 2844 Hair preparations, including shampoos

(G-6507)
ISP OPTICS CORPORATION (HQ)
50 S Buckhout St (10533-2203)
PHONE..................914 591-3070
Mark Lifshotz, *CEO*
Joseph Menaker, *President*
▲ EMP: 61
SQ FT: 22,000
SALES: 14.2MM
SALES (corp-wide): 32.5MM **Publicly Held**
WEB: www.ispoptics.com
SIC: 3827 Optical instruments & apparatus
PA: Lightpath Technologies, Inc.
2603 Challenger Tech Ct # 100
Orlando FL 32826
407 382-4003

(G-6508)
ORTHOCON INC
1 Bridge St Ste 121 (10533-1553)
PHONE..................914 357-2600
John J Pacifico, *President*
David J Hart, *Vice Pres*
Stephen Hall, *CFO*
EMP: 23 EST: 2006
SALES (est): 2.9MM **Privately Held**
SIC: 3841 Surgical & medical instruments

(G-6509)
PECO PALLET INC (HQ)
2 Bridge St Ste 210 (10533-1594)
PHONE..................914 376-5444
Joseph Dagnese, *CEO*
David Lee, *President*
Jeff Euritt, *Vice Pres*
Adrian Potgieter, *Vice Pres*
Eric Sobanski, *Vice Pres*
EMP: 24
SQ FT: 5,000
SALES (est): 31.2MM **Privately Held**
WEB: www.pecopallet.com
SIC: 2448 7359 Pallets, wood; pallet rental services

Island Park
Nassau County

(G-6510)
A-1 MANHATTAN CUSTOM FURN INC
Also Called: Manhattan Cabinets
4315 Austin Blvd (11558-1627)
PHONE..................212 750-9800
Eric Heim, *Manager*
EMP: 5
SALES (corp-wide): 3.7MM **Privately Held**
WEB: www.manhattancabinetry.com
SIC: 2434 Wood kitchen cabinets
PA: A-1 Manhattan Custom Furniture Inc.
4315 Austin Blvd
Island Park NY 11558
718 937-4780

(G-6511)
A-1 MANHATTAN CUSTOM FURN INC (PA)
Also Called: Manhattan Cabinetry
4315 Austin Blvd (11558-1627)
PHONE..................718 937-4780
Michael Koullias, *President*
John Koullias, *Vice Pres*
Taki Koullias, *Human Res Mgr*
EMP: 45
SQ FT: 44,000
SALES (est): 3.7MM **Privately Held**
WEB: www.manhattancabinetry.com
SIC: 2511 Wood household furniture

(G-6512)
BHI ELEVATOR CABS INC
74 Alabama Ave (11558-1116)
PHONE..................516 431-5665
Rick Hart, *President*
Brian Holodar, *Principal*
EMP: 15
SALES (est): 3.2MM **Privately Held**
SIC: 3534 Elevators & equipment

(G-6513)
ECOLOGICAL LABORATORIES INC (PA)
4 Waterford Rd (11558-1022)
P.O. Box 184, Malverne (11565-0184)
PHONE..................516 823-3441
Barry Richter, *President*
Doug Dent, *Vice Pres*
Mark Krupka, *Vice Pres*
Matthew Richter, *Vice Pres*
Domenic Simone, *Vice Pres*
▲ EMP: 55
SQ FT: 5,500
SALES (est): 14.3MM **Privately Held**
WEB: www.propump.com
SIC: 2899 2836 5169 Water treating compounds; biological products, except diagnostic; chemicals & allied products

(G-6514)
F & B PHOTO OFFSET CO INC (PA)
4 California Pl N (11558-2215)
P.O. Box 366 (11558-0366)
PHONE..................516 431-5433
Frank Naudus, *President*
EMP: 5
SQ FT: 6,000

Island Park - Nassau County (G-6515)

SALES: 1MM **Privately Held**
SIC: 2752 2759 Commercial printing, offset; letterpress printing

(G-6515)
H D M LABS INC
153 Kingston Blvd (11558-1926)
PHONE..................................516 431-8357
Hardat Singh, *President*
Natashia Singh, *COO*
EMP: 5 EST: 1993
SQ FT: 1,600
SALES (est): 879.9K **Privately Held**
WEB: www.hdmlabsinc.com
SIC: 3829 Medical diagnostic systems, nuclear

(G-6516)
NATHAN BERRIE & SONS INC
Also Called: Naomi Manufacturing
3956 Long Beach Rd (11558-1146)
P.O. Box 240 (11558-0240)
PHONE..................................516 432-8500
Stanley Berrie, *President*
Suzanne Berrie, *Admin Sec*
EMP: 9 EST: 1944
SQ FT: 4,000
SALES (est): 1.1MM **Privately Held**
SIC: 3915 Jewelers' findings & materials

(G-6517)
NORTHFELD PRECISION INSTR CORP
Also Called: NORTH FIELD
4400 Austin Blvd (11558-1621)
P.O. Box 550 (11558-0550)
PHONE..................................516 431-1112
Donald Freedman, *Ch of Bd*
Paul Defeo, *COO*
Ken Sprenger, *VP Sales*
Charles Florio, *Sales Staff*
Gilbert Decosimo, *Manager*
EMP: 32
SQ FT: 15,000
SALES: 7.2MM **Privately Held**
WEB: www.northfield.com
SIC: 3545 Chucks: drill, lathe or magnetic (machine tool accessories)

(G-6518)
SOUTH SHORE TRIBUNE INC
4 California Pl N (11558-2215)
P.O. Box 366 (11558-0366)
PHONE..................................516 431-5628
Frank Naudus, *President*
EMP: 6
SQ FT: 6,000
SALES (est): 253.5K
SALES (corp-wide): 1MM **Privately Held**
SIC: 2711 Commercial printing & newspaper publishing combined; newspapers, publishing & printing
PA: F & B Photo Offset Co Inc
4 California Pl N
Island Park NY 11558
516 431-5433

(G-6519)
WOOD DESIGNS DELUXE CORP
4090 Austin Blvd (11558-1241)
PHONE..................................917 414-4640
Patricia Parra, *President*
EMP: 7
SALES (est): 589.5K **Privately Held**
SIC: 2782 Checkbooks

Islandia
Suffolk County

(G-6520)
A & L MACHINE COMPANY INC
200 Blydenburg Rd Ste 9 (11749-5011)
PHONE..................................631 463-3111
Horst Ehinger, *President*
George Ramos, *Principal*
EMP: 7 EST: 1963
SQ FT: 4,000
SALES (est): 1MM **Privately Held**
WEB: www.anlmachine.com
SIC: 3599 Machine shop, jobbing & repair

(G-6521)
ARK SCIENCES INC
1601 Veterans Hwy Ste 315 (11749-1543)
PHONE..................................646 943-1520
Joseph Tosini, *President*
EMP: 5
SALES (est): 621.3K **Privately Held**
SIC: 2834 Veterinary pharmaceutical preparations

(G-6522)
BIG APPLE SIGN CORP
Also Called: Big Apple Visual Group
3 Oval Dr (11749-1402)
PHONE..................................631 342-0303
Amir Khalfan, *Branch Mgr*
EMP: 35
SALES (corp-wide): 18.2MM **Privately Held**
WEB: www.bigapplegroup.com
SIC: 3993 2399 3552 Signs, not made in custom sign painting shops; displays & cutouts, window & lobby; banners, made from fabric; silk screens for textile industry
PA: Big Apple Sign Corp.
247 W 35th St Rm 400
New York NY 10001
212 629-3650

(G-6523)
CA INC
1 Ca Plz Ste 100 (11749-5303)
PHONE..................................800 225-5224
Michael P Gregoire, *CEO*
Richard Philyaw, *Assistant VP*
Brian Burba, *Vice Pres*
George Cox, *Vice Pres*
Edward Dziadzio, *Vice Pres*
EMP: 5
SALES (corp-wide): 17.6B **Publicly Held**
SIC: 7372 Business oriented computer software; application computer software
HQ: Ca, Inc.
520 Madison Ave Fl 22
New York NY 10022
800 225-5224

(G-6524)
CENTURY DIRECT LLC
15 Enter Ln (11749-4811)
PHONE..................................212 763-0600
Michael Kellogg, *Principal*
Eric Seid, *COO*
Martin Rego, *Vice Pres*
Michael Vignola, *Vice Pres*
Thomas McNeill, *CFO*
▲ EMP: 200
SQ FT: 80,000
SALES (est): 41.6MM **Privately Held**
WEB: www.centltr.com
SIC: 2759 7331 7379 Commercial printing; direct mail advertising services; computer related maintenance services

(G-6525)
CES INDUSTRIES INC
95 Hoffman Ln Ste S (11749-5020)
PHONE..................................631 782-7088
Mitchell B Nesenoff, *CEO*
Edward J Ermler, *Vice Pres*
EMP: 40
SQ FT: 20,000
SALES (est): 6.7MM **Privately Held**
WEB: www.cesindustries.com
SIC: 3699 Electronic training devices

(G-6526)
DISPLAY MARKETING GROUP INC
170 Oval Dr Ste B (11749-1419)
PHONE..................................631 348-4450
Steven Larit, *President*
EMP: 35
SQ FT: 24,000
SALES (est): 5.2MM **Privately Held**
SIC: 3993 Displays & cutouts, window & lobby

(G-6527)
DUETTO INTEGRATED SYSTEMS INC
Also Called: Dis
85 Hoffman Ln Ste Q (11749-5019)
PHONE..................................631 851-0102
Carmela Faraci, *Office Mgr*
Gary Sortino, *Manager*
Michael Faraci, *Technician*
EMP: 10
SQ FT: 2,000
SALES (est): 1.5MM **Privately Held**
SIC: 3599 Custom machinery

(G-6528)
FLEXBAR MACHINE CORPORATION
Also Called: Mediflex
250 Gibbs Rd (11749-2697)
PHONE..................................631 582-8440
Jon Adler, *President*
Juanita Adler, *Corp Secy*
Robert Adler, *Vice Pres*
Julia Mullen, *Opers Mgr*
Keith Donaldson, *Purchasing*
▲ EMP: 27
SQ FT: 10,500
SALES (est): 6.3MM **Privately Held**
WEB: www.flexbar.com
SIC: 3545 3841 Machine tool attachments & accessories; surgical & medical instruments

(G-6529)
I E D CORP
88 Bridge Rd (11749)
PHONE..................................631 348-0424
Martin Ramage, *President*
Robert Jaffe, *Engineer*
EMP: 10
SQ FT: 5,000
SALES (est): 1.5MM **Privately Held**
SIC: 3674 3625 Microprocessors; relays & industrial controls

(G-6530)
ICD PUBLICATIONS INC (PA)
Also Called: Hotel Business
1377 Motor Pkwy Ste 410 (11749-5258)
PHONE..................................631 246-9300
Ian Gittlitz, *President*
James Schultz, *Publisher*
Nicole Carlino, *Editor*
Corris Little, *Editor*
Christina Trauthwein, *Editor*
EMP: 25
SQ FT: 10,000
SALES (est): 3.5MM **Privately Held**
WEB: www.icdnet.com
SIC: 2721 7313 Magazines: publishing only, not printed on site; magazine advertising representative

(G-6531)
INNOVANT INC (PA)
Also Called: Innovant Group
135 Oval Dr (11749-1402)
PHONE..................................631 348-1900
Charles Braham, *President*
Garrett Pluck, *Vice Pres*
Mary Hudson, *Controller*
Carl Clark, *Branch Mgr*
Joan Gullans, *Admin Sec*
▲ EMP: 6
SALES (est): 48MM **Privately Held**
WEB: www.innovant.com
SIC: 2521 Wood office furniture

(G-6532)
JOMART ASSOCIATES INC
170 Oval Dr Ste A (11749-1419)
PHONE..................................212 627-2153
Walter Waltman, *President*
Peter Batterson, *Vice Pres*
Evelyn Giman, *Admin Sec*
EMP: 30
SQ FT: 1,200
SALES (est): 2.8MM **Privately Held**
WEB: www.jomartassociates.com
SIC: 2759 Commercial printing

(G-6533)
LIF DISTRIBUTING INC
155 Oval Dr (11749-1402)
PHONE..................................631 630-6900
Steven Frielander, *President*
Gerard Mach, *Vice Pres*
EMP: 13
SQ FT: 8,000
SALES (est): 1.9MM **Privately Held**
SIC: 2541 Table or counter tops, plastic laminated

(G-6534)
M & M CANVAS & AWNINGS INC
Also Called: M & M Signs & Awnings
180 Oval Dr (11749-1403)
PHONE..................................631 424-5370
Mike Mere, *President*
EMP: 7
SALES (est): 888.7K **Privately Held**
WEB: www.mmawning.com
SIC: 2394 Awnings, fabric: made from purchased materials

(G-6535)
METRO DOOR INC (DH)
Also Called: Metro Service Solutions
2929 Express Dr N 300b (11749-5306)
PHONE..................................800 669-3667
Scott McCermott, *President*
Scott McDermott, *President*
Jim Karcher, *Co-Founder*
Christine M Vetrano, *CFO*
▼ EMP: 80
SQ FT: 17,200
SALES (est): 22.4MM
SALES (corp-wide): 6.4B **Publicly Held**
WEB: www.metrodoor.com
SIC: 3446 1799 Fences, gates, posts & flagpoles; fence construction

(G-6536)
OLIVE BRANCH FOODS LLC
3124 Express Dr S (11749-5013)
PHONE..................................631 343-7070
Jeffrey Siegel, *CEO*
Ron Loeb, *President*
Harry Shufrin, *CFO*
Patty Amato, *Director*
Ron Logiudice, *Director*
EMP: 8
SALES (est): 83K **Privately Held**
SIC: 2033 Olives: packaged in cans, jars, etc.

(G-6537)
PRINTEX PACKAGING CORPORATION
555 Raymond Dr (11749-4844)
PHONE..................................631 234-4300
David Heller, *President*
Joel Heller, *President*
Carol Heller, *Vice Pres*
Tom Vollmuth, *Vice Pres*
Alex Diaz, *Manager*
▲ EMP: 70
SQ FT: 40,000
SALES (est): 22MM **Privately Held**
WEB: www.printexpackaging.com
SIC: 3089 3086 2671 Boxes, plastic; packaging & shipping materials, foamed plastic; packaging paper & plastics film, coated & laminated

(G-6538)
SOCKET PRODUCTS MFG CORP
175 Bridge Rd (11749-5202)
PHONE..................................631 232-9870
Sol Kellner, *President*
EMP: 5
SQ FT: 5,000
SALES (est): 759.1K **Privately Held**
SIC: 3452 3545 Screws, metal; nuts, metal; bolts, metal; sockets (machine tool accessories)

(G-6539)
SONOTEC US INC
190 Blydenburg Rd (11749-5015)
PHONE..................................631 415-4758
Christopher Portelli, *President*
Cristy Baldwin, *Executive Asst*
EMP: 120 EST: 2013
SALES: 1MM
SALES (corp-wide): 20MM **Privately Held**
SIC: 3674 Solid state electronic devices
PA: Sonotec Ultraschallsensorik Halle Gmbh
Nauendorfer Str. 2
Halle (Saale) 06112
345 133-170

GEOGRAPHIC SECTION

Ithaca - Tompkins County (G-6565)

(G-6540)
WHITSONS FOOD SVC BRONX CORP
1800 Motor Pkwy (11749-5216)
PHONE..................................631 424-2700
Robert Whitcomb, *President*
Beth Bunster, *Corp Secy*
Douglas Whitcomb, *Vice Pres*
John Whitcomb, *Vice Pres*
Andrew Whitcomb, *Shareholder*
EMP: 350
SQ FT: 65,000
SALES (est): 47.7MM **Privately Held**
SIC: 2068 2099 Salted & roasted nuts & seeds; food preparations; peanut butter

(G-6541)
ZAHK SALES INC
Also Called: Project Visual
75 Hoffman Ln Ste A (11749-5027)
PHONE..................................631 851-0851
Husein Kermalli, *President*
▲ **EMP:** 7
SALES (est): 623K **Privately Held**
WEB: www.zahk.com
SIC: 3444 1752 Sheet metalwork; wood floor installation & refinishing

(G-6542)
ZYDOC MED TRANSCRIPTION LLC
1455 Veterans Memorial Hw (11749-4836)
PHONE..................................631 273-1963
Lisa Robbins, *Opers Mgr*
Sue Schmitt, *Opers Staff*
Norbert Stumm, *Human Res Mgr*
Kevin Ross, *VP Sales*
James Maisel, *Mng Member*
EMP: 11
SQ FT: 2,500
SALES (est): 636.1K **Privately Held**
WEB: www.transcriber.org
SIC: 7372 Prepackaged software

Islip
Suffolk County

(G-6543)
ADVANCED PAVEMENT GROUP CORP (PA)
2 W Beech St (11751-1513)
PHONE..................................631 277-8400
Ken Roy Jr, *President*
EMP: 9
SALES (est): 7.2MM **Privately Held**
SIC: 2951 Asphalt paving mixtures & blocks

(G-6544)
AINES MANUFACTURING CORP
96 E Bayberry Rd (11751-4903)
PHONE..................................631 471-3900
▼ **EMP:** 30
SQ FT: 10,000
SALES (est): 4.3MM **Privately Held**
SIC: 3661 Mfg Telephone/Telegraph Apparatus

(G-6545)
COOKIES UNITED LLC
141 Freeman Ave (11751-1428)
PHONE..................................631 581-4000
Louis Avignone, *Mng Member*
▲ **EMP:** 120
SQ FT: 80,000
SALES (est): 6.4MM **Privately Held**
SIC: 2052 Cookies & crackers
PA: United Baking Co., Inc.
41 Natcon Dr
Shirley NY 11967

(G-6546)
EUGENIA SELECTIVE LIVING INC
122 Freeman Ave (11751-1417)
PHONE..................................631 277-1461
Edward Smith, *President*
Eugenia Smith, *Admin Sec*
EMP: 10
SQ FT: 5,000
SALES (est): 1.2MM **Privately Held**
WEB: www.selectiveliving.com
SIC: 2511 2519 2521 2522 Wood household furniture; furniture, household: glass, fiberglass & plastic; wood office furniture; office furniture, except wood; laboratory equipment, except medical or dental; cabinet & finish carpentry

(G-6547)
JIMCO LAMP & MANUFACTURING CO
Also Called: Jimco Lamp Company
181 Freeman Ave (11751-1400)
PHONE..................................631 218-2152
Marlo Lorenz, *Branch Mgr*
EMP: 8 **Privately Held**
SIC: 3999 3645 Shades, lamp or candle; table lamps
HQ: Jimco Lamp & Manufacturing Co
11759 Highway 63 N Ste B
Bono AR 72416
870 935-6820

(G-6548)
MEADES WELDING AND FABRICATING
331 Islip Ave (11751)
PHONE..................................631 581-1555
Michelle Mede, *President*
EMP: 5
SALES (est): 195.3K **Privately Held**
SIC: 7692 5046 Welding repair; commercial cooking & food service equipment

(G-6549)
MJB PRINTING CORP
Also Called: Mod Printing
280 Islip Ave (11751-2818)
PHONE..................................631 581-0177
Jeanine Bazata, *President*
Michael Bazata, *Treasurer*
EMP: 5 **EST:** 1960
SQ FT: 2,800
SALES (est): 717.9K **Privately Held**
SIC: 2752 Commercial printing, offset

(G-6550)
RIKE ENTERPRISES INC
Also Called: Corpkit Legal Supplies
46 Taft Ave (11751-2112)
PHONE..................................631 277-8338
Richard Jansen, *President*
▲ **EMP:** 15
SALES (est): 1.7MM **Privately Held**
WEB: www.corpkit.com
SIC: 2759 5112 Commercial printing; office supplies

(G-6551)
T J SIGNS UNLIMITED LLC (PA)
Also Called: American Signcrafters
171 Freeman Ave (11751-1430)
PHONE..................................631 273-4800
Jeff Petersen, *President*
Thomas Garatina, *Business Mgr*
Jonathan Bell, *Vice Pres*
Anthony Lipari, *Vice Pres*
Valerie Mayer, *Vice Pres*
EMP: 50
SQ FT: 20,000
SALES: 25MM **Privately Held**
WEB: www.americansigncrafters.com
SIC: 3993 1799 7389 Electric signs; neon signs; sign installation & maintenance; personal service agents, brokers & bureaus

Islip Terrace
Suffolk County

(G-6552)
BARRASSO & SONS TRUCKING INC
160 Floral Park St (11752-1399)
PHONE..................................631 581-0360
Michael Barrasso, *President*
Joseph Longo, *Corp Secy*
Anthony Barrasso, *Director*
EMP: 30 **EST:** 1996
SQ FT: 2,500
SALES (est): 7.2MM **Privately Held**
SIC: 3271 5211 5032 Blocks, concrete or cinder: standard; brick; brick, stone & related material

(G-6553)
NIKE INC
2675 Sunrise Hwy (11752-2119)
PHONE..................................631 960-0184
John Grasselino, *Branch Mgr*
EMP: 38
SALES (corp-wide): 36.4B **Publicly Held**
SIC: 3021 Rubber & plastics footwear
PA: Nike, Inc.
1 Sw Bowerman Dr
Beaverton OR 97005
503 671-6453

Ithaca
Tompkins County

(G-6554)
ADVANCED DIGITAL INFO CORP
10 Brown Rd (14850-1287)
PHONE..................................607 266-4000
James H Watson Jr, *Principal*
EMP: 50
SALES (corp-wide): 505.3MM **Publicly Held**
SIC: 3672 Printed circuit boards
HQ: Advanced Digital Information Corporation
11431 Willows Rd Ne
Redmond WA 98052
425 881-8004

(G-6555)
ADVION INC (PA)
61 Brown Rd (14850-1247)
PHONE..................................607 266-9162
David Patterson, *President*
Thomas R Kurz, *President*
Rosemary French, *General Mgr*
Mark Allen PH, *Vice Pres*
Gary Williams, *Vice Pres*
EMP: 20
SQ FT: 16,500
SALES (est): 12.4MM **Privately Held**
SIC: 3826 Mass spectrometers

(G-6556)
ALPINE MACHINE INC
1616 Trumansburg Rd (14850)
PHONE..................................607 272-1344
Richard Hoffman, *President*
David Osburn, *Corp Secy*
William Osburn, *Vice Pres*
Russell Timblin, *Vice Pres*
EMP: 15 **EST:** 1981
SQ FT: 6,000
SALES (est): 2MM **Privately Held**
WEB: www.alpinemachine.com
SIC: 3599 7692 3541 3444 Machine shop, jobbing & repair; welding repair; machine tools, metal cutting type; sheet metalwork

(G-6557)
ARNOLD PRINTING CORP
604 W Green St (14850-5250)
PHONE..................................607 272-7800
Robert Becker Jr, *President*
Chris Becker, *Vice Pres*
Christian J Becker, *Vice Pres*
EMP: 18 **EST:** 1963
SQ FT: 8,000
SALES (est): 2.6MM **Privately Held**
SIC: 2752 Commercial printing, offset

(G-6558)
BEETNPATH LLC
Also Called: Grainful
950 Danby Rd Ste 180 (14850-5663)
PHONE..................................607 319-5585
Andrew Scirri, *President*
Emily Eisenhut, *Sales Staff*
Katie Long, *Marketing Mgr*
Anthony Eisenhut, *Mng Member*
Jeannine Sacco, *Officer*
EMP: 6
SQ FT: 1,200
SALES (est): 150K **Privately Held**
SIC: 2038 Breakfasts, frozen & packaged; lunches, frozen & packaged; dinners, frozen & packaged

(G-6559)
BENNETT DIE & TOOL INC
113 Brewery Ln (14850-8814)
PHONE..................................607 273-2836
James McMillen, *President*
Brian Bennett, *Vice Pres*
EMP: 16
SALES (est): 1.2MM **Privately Held**
SIC: 3544 Dies & die holders for metal cutting, forming, die casting; special dies & tools

(G-6560)
BIGWOOD SYSTEMS INC
35 Thornwood Dr Ste 400 (14850-1284)
PHONE..................................607 257-0915
Hsiao-Dong Chiang, *President*
Pat Causgrove, *General Mgr*
Gilburt Chiang, *Director*
EMP: 7
SALES (est): 651.6K **Privately Held**
WEB: www.bigwood-systems.com
SIC: 7372 Application computer software

(G-6561)
BIN OPTICS
20 Thornwood Dr Ste 100 (14850-1265)
PHONE..................................604 257-3200
Chet Warzynski, *Director*
EMP: 5
SALES (est): 332.6K **Privately Held**
SIC: 3089 Lenses, except optical: plastic

(G-6562)
BINOPTICS LLC (DH)
9 Brown Rd (14850-1247)
PHONE..................................607 257-3200
Alex Behfar, *CEO*
William Fritz, *COO*
Norman Kwong, *Exec VP*
Christopher Smith, *CFO*
▼ **EMP:** 35
SQ FT: 28,600
SALES (est): 16.9MM **Publicly Held**
WEB: www.binoptics.com
SIC: 3827 Optical instruments & lenses

(G-6563)
BOLTON POINT WTR TRTMNT PLANT
1402 E Shore Dr (14850-8506)
PHONE..................................607 277-0660
Paul Tunison, *Manager*
Steve Ridole, *Manager*
Pamela Van Gelder, *Bd of Directors*
EMP: 5 **EST:** 2008
SALES (est): 509.3K **Privately Held**
SIC: 3589 Water treatment equipment, industrial

(G-6564)
BORGWARNER INC
800 Warren Rd (14850-1266)
PHONE..................................607 257-6700
Larry Wilcox, *Principal*
Angela Hawken, *Manager*
Robert West, *Supervisor*
EMP: 19
SALES (corp-wide): 9.8B **Publicly Held**
SIC: 3714 Motor vehicle parts & accessories
PA: Borgwarner Inc.
3850 Hamlin Rd
Auburn Hills MI 48326
248 754-9200

(G-6565)
BORGWARNER INC
780 Warren Rd (14850-1242)
PHONE..................................607 257-1800
Roger Wood, *President*
Patrick McNamara, *Maint Spvr*
Ken Degraff, *Engineer*
Magaly Wooten, *Engineer*
Jay Stearns, *Manager*
EMP: 30
SALES (corp-wide): 9.8B **Publicly Held**
SIC: 3714 Motor vehicle parts & accessories

Ithaca - Tompkins County (G-6566)   GEOGRAPHIC SECTION

PA: Borgwarner Inc.
3850 Hamlin Rd
Auburn Hills MI 48326
248 754-9200

(G-6566)
BORGWARNER ITHACA LLC
Also Called: Morse Systems
800 Warren Rd (14850-1266)
PHONE..................607 257-6700
James R Verrier, *President*
Steven G Carlson, *Vice Pres*
John J Gasparovic, *Vice Pres*
Brian Petak, *Production*
Cathy Barron, *Buyer*
EMP: 300
SQ FT: 100,000
SALES (est): 42.4MM
SALES (corp-wide): 9.8B **Publicly Held**
SIC: 3714 Motor vehicle parts & accessories
PA: Borgwarner Inc.
3850 Hamlin Rd
Auburn Hills MI 48326
248 754-9200

(G-6567)
BORGWARNER MORSE TEC INC
780 Warren Rd (14850-1242)
PHONE..................607 266-5111
Timothy M Manganello, *CEO*
Jason Moss, *Engineer*
EMP: 90
SALES (corp-wide): 9.8B **Publicly Held**
WEB: www.borgwarnermorsetec.com
SIC: 3714 Motor vehicle parts & accessories
HQ: Borgwarner Morse Tec Llc
800 Warren Rd
Ithaca NY 14850
607 257-6700

(G-6568)
BORGWARNER MORSE TEC LLC (HQ)
800 Warren Rd (14850-1266)
PHONE..................607 257-6700
James R Verrier, *President*
Ronald M Ruzic, *President*
Timothy M Manganello, *Chairman*
Thomas Malone, *Area Mgr*
Steve G Carlson, *Vice Pres*
▲ EMP: 184
SALES (est): 133.6MM
SALES (corp-wide): 9.8B **Publicly Held**
WEB: www.borgwarnermorsetec.com
SIC: 3714 3462 3568 Motor vehicle parts & accessories; iron & steel forgings; power transmission equipment
PA: Borgwarner Inc.
3850 Hamlin Rd
Auburn Hills MI 48326
248 754-9200

(G-6569)
BSU INC
445 E State St (14850-4409)
PHONE..................607 272-8100
Catalina Chamseddine, *CEO*
Ahmad Chamseddine, *COO*
Dorothy Slocum, *Controller*
Dottie Highfield, *Accounts Mgr*
EMP: 42
SQ FT: 17,000
SALES (est): 7.5MM **Privately Held**
WEB: www.bsuinc.com
SIC: 3672 8711 Printed circuit boards; electronic parts & equipment; engineering services

(G-6570)
CAYUGA WOODEN BOATWORKS INC
381 Enfield Main Rd (14850-9346)
P.O. Box 301, Cayuga (13034-0301)
PHONE..................315 253-7447
Phil Walker, *General Mgr*
Ken Anderson, *Principal*
Kenneth Anderson, *Manager*
EMP: 21
SQ FT: 10,000
SALES (est): 3.4MM **Privately Held**
WEB: www.cwbw.com
SIC: 3732 7699 Boat building & repairing; boat repair

(G-6571)
CBORD GROUP INC (HQ)
950 Danby Rd Ste 100c (14850-5795)
PHONE..................607 257-2410
Max Steinhardt, *President*
Tim Tighe, *President*
Bruce Lane, *Exec VP*
Karen Sammon, *Senior VP*
Larry Delaney, *Vice Pres*
EMP: 250
SQ FT: 40,000
SALES (est): 147.9MM
SALES (corp-wide): 4.6B **Publicly Held**
WEB: www.cbord.com
SIC: 7372 5045 Application computer software; computer peripheral equipment; computers
PA: Roper Technologies, Inc.
6901 Prof Pkwy E Ste 200
Sarasota FL 34240
941 556-2601

(G-6572)
CORNELL UNIVERSITY
Also Called: Cornell University Press
512 E State St (14850-4412)
PHONE..................607 277-2338
John G Ackerman, *Director*
EMP: 51
SALES (corp-wide): 4B **Privately Held**
SIC: 2731 8221 Textbooks: publishing only, not printed on site; university
PA: Cornell University
308 Duffield Hall
Ithaca NY 14853
607 254-4636

(G-6573)
CORNELL UNIVERSITY
Also Called: Cornell Laboratory Ornithology
159 Sapsucker Woods Rd (14850-1923)
PHONE..................607 254-2473
John Fitzpatrick, *Director*
Patrick V Gallagher, *Associate Dir*
Harry De Gorter, *Professor*
EMP: 20
SALES (corp-wide): 4B **Privately Held**
SIC: 2721 8221 Periodicals; university
PA: Cornell University
308 Duffield Hall
Ithaca NY 14853
607 254-4636

(G-6574)
DAILY CORNELL SUN
Also Called: Dail Cornell Sun, The
139 W State St (14850-5427)
PHONE..................607 273-0746
John Marcham, *President*
Cameron Pollack, *Editor*
Amanda Soule, *Business Mgr*
John Schroeder, *Prdtn Mgr*
Walter Rose, *Marketing Staff*
EMP: 25
SQ FT: 7,020
SALES (est): 1.4MM **Privately Held**
WEB: www.cornellsun.com
SIC: 2711 Newspapers: publishing only, not printed on site; newspapers, publishing & printing

(G-6575)
DUKE COMPANY
7 Hall Rd (14850-8732)
PHONE..................607 347-4455
Steven Dudley, *Principal*
EMP: 8
SALES (est): 178K **Privately Held**
SIC: 3272 7353 Building materials, except block or brick: concrete; earth moving equipment, rental or leasing

(G-6576)
F M ABDULKY INC (PA)
527 W Seneca St (14850-4033)
PHONE..................607 272-7373
Fareed M Abdulky, *President*
Fareed Abdulky, *President*
Lamia Abdulky, *Vice Pres*
Don Covert, *Manager*
EMP: 13 EST: 1974
SQ FT: 4,000
SALES (est): 1.2MM **Privately Held**
WEB: www.abdulky.com
SIC: 3911 Jewelry, precious metal

(G-6577)
F M ABDULKY INC
Also Called: Buffalo Finishing Company
527 W Seneca St (14850-4033)
PHONE..................607 272-7373
Don Covert, *Manager*
EMP: 6
SQ FT: 2,616
SALES (corp-wide): 1.2MM **Privately Held**
WEB: www.abdulky.com
SIC: 3911 Jewelry, precious metal
PA: F M Abdulky Inc
527 W Seneca St
Ithaca NY 14850
607 272-7373

(G-6578)
GLYCOBIA INC
33 Thornwood Dr Ste 104 (14850-1275)
PHONE..................607 339-0051
Matthew Delisa, *President*
EMP: 5
SALES (est): 299K **Privately Held**
SIC: 2834 Pharmaceutical preparations

(G-6579)
GRATITUDE & COMPANY INC
215 N Cayuga St Ste 71 (14850-4323)
PHONE..................607 277-3188
Julie Umbach, *President*
EMP: 6
SALES (est): 895K **Privately Held**
WEB: www.giftsofgratitude.com
SIC: 2621 Specialty papers

(G-6580)
HANGER PRSTHETCS & ORTHO INC
Also Called: Creative Orthotics Prosthetics
310 Taughannock Blvd 1a (14850-3251)
PHONE..................607 277-6620
Thomas Kirk PHD, *CEO*
EMP: 10
SALES (corp-wide): 1B **Publicly Held**
SIC: 3842 Surgical appliances & supplies
HQ: Hanger Prosthetics & Orthotics, Inc.
10910 Domain Dr Ste 300
Austin TX 78758
512 777-3800

(G-6581)
HENRY NEWMAN LLC
Also Called: Ithaca Ice Company, The
312 4th St (14850-3481)
P.O. Box 333 (14851-0333)
PHONE..................607 273-8512
Henry Newman, *Owner*
Charles Everhart, *Principal*
EMP: 10
SQ FT: 8,000
SALES (est): 284.7K **Privately Held**
SIC: 2097 5999 Ice cubes; ice

(G-6582)
INCODEMA INC
407 Cliff St (14850-2009)
PHONE..................607 277-7070
Sean Whittaker, *CEO*
Mike Wargo, *COO*
Will Elmer, *Buyer*
Jeremy Woodman, *QC Mgr*
Chris Hern, *Engineer*
▼ EMP: 47
SQ FT: 30,000
SALES (est): 11.3MM **Privately Held**
SIC: 3444 Sheet metal specialties, not stamped

(G-6583)
INCODEMA3D LLC
407 Cliff St (14850-2009)
P.O. Box 429, Freeville (13068-0429)
PHONE..................607 269-4390
Terry Posecznick, *Controller*
Scott Volk, *Director*
EMP: 38
SALES (est): 5MM **Privately Held**
SIC: 2759 Commercial printing

(G-6584)
INDUSTRIAL MACHINE REPAIR
1144 Taughannock Blvd (14850-9573)
PHONE..................607 272-0717
Martin J Sullivan, *Owner*
EMP: 6
SALES (est): 219.6K **Privately Held**
SIC: 3823 Computer interface equipment for industrial process control

(G-6585)
INTERNATIONAL CENTER FOR POSTG
Also Called: Icpme-Ithaca Center
179 Graham Rd Ste E (14850-1141)
PHONE..................607 257-5860
Kenneth Zeserson,
EMP: 9
SALES (est): 772.7K
SALES (corp-wide): 87.5MM **Privately Held**
WEB: www.radinfonet.com
SIC: 2721 8741 Periodicals: publishing only; management services
PA: Jobson Medical Information Llc
440 9th Ave Fl 14
New York NY 10001
212 274-7000

(G-6586)
INTERNATIONAL CLIMBING MCHS
630 Elmira Rd (14850-8745)
PHONE..................607 288-4001
Samuel J Maggio, *President*
Carolina Osorio Gil, *Manager*
EMP: 5
SALES (est): 644.5K **Privately Held**
SIC: 3599 Custom machinery

(G-6587)
ITHACA BEER COMPANY INC
122 Ithaca Beer Dr (14850-8813)
PHONE..................607 272-1305
Dan Mitchell, *President*
Pete Browning, *Vice Pres*
Paul Wagner, *Admin Sec*
EMP: 30
SQ FT: 6,100
SALES (est): 5.8MM **Privately Held**
WEB: www.ithacabeer.com
SIC: 2082 Beer (alcoholic beverage)

(G-6588)
ITHACA JOURNAL NEWS CO INC
123 W State St Ste 1 (14850-5479)
PHONE..................607 272-2321
Sherman Bodner, *President*
EMP: 50 EST: 1815
SQ FT: 6,000
SALES (est): 2.9MM
SALES (corp-wide): 3.1B **Publicly Held**
WEB: www.ithaca.gannett.com
SIC: 2711 Commercial printing & newspaper publishing combined; newspapers, publishing & printing
PA: Gannett Co., Inc.
7950 Jones Branch Dr
Mc Lean VA 22102
703 854-6000

(G-6589)
JOE MORO
Also Called: Moro Design
214 Fayette St (14850-5263)
PHONE..................607 272-0591
Joe Moro, *Owner*
EMP: 5
SALES (est): 170K **Privately Held**
SIC: 3949 Bowling equipment & supplies

(G-6590)
KIONIX INC
36 Thornwood Dr (14850-1263)
PHONE..................607 257-1080
Nader Sadrzadeh, *President*
Paul Bryan, *Exec VP*
Timothy J Davis, *Exec VP*
Kenneth N Salky, *Exec VP*
Kenneth Hager, *Vice Pres*
▲ EMP: 185
SQ FT: 60,000
SALES (est): 52.4MM
SALES (corp-wide): 3.7B **Privately Held**
WEB: www.kionix.com
SIC: 3674 Semiconductors & related devices

GEOGRAPHIC SECTION
Ithaca - Tompkins County (G-6617)

PA: Rohm Company Limited
21, Mizosakicho, Saiin, Ukyo-Ku
Kyoto KYO 615-0
753 112-121

(G-6591) M2 RACE SYSTEMS INC
53 Enfield Main Rd (14850-9367)
PHONE..................607 882-9078
Ron Mielbrecht, *President*
Beth Mielbrecht, *Vice Pres*
EMP: 6
SQ FT: 7,500
SALES (est): 706.3K Privately Held
WEB: www.m2race.com
SIC: 3714 Cylinder heads, motor vehicle

(G-6592) MADISON PRINTING CORP
Also Called: Instant Printing Service
704 W Buffalo St (14850-3300)
PHONE..................607 273-3535
Angelo Digiacomo, *President*
Mclly Digiacomo, *Vice Pres*
EMP: 5 **EST**: 1972
SQ FT: 1,600
SALES (est): 592.3K Privately Held
SIC: 2752 Commercial printing, offset

(G-6593) MAG INC
Also Called: Momentummedia Sports Pubg
20 Eastlake Rd (14850-9786)
PHONE..................607 257-6970
Mark Goldberg, *President*
Maria Bise, *Prdtn Dir*
Penny Small, *Financial Exec*
Diedra Harkenrider, *Sales Staff*
Mike Townsend, *Advt Staff*
EMP: 25
SQ FT: 3,600
SALES (est): 3.3MM Privately Held
WEB: www.momentummedia.com
SIC: 2721 Magazines: publishing only, not printed on site

(G-6594) MCBOOKS PRESS INC
520 N Meadow St 2 (14850-3229)
PHONE..................607 272-2114
Alexander G Skutt, *President*
▲ **EMP**: 5
SQ FT: 750
SALES: 1.2MM Privately Held
WEB: www.mcbooks.com
SIC: 2731 Books: publishing only

(G-6595) MEZMERIZ INC
33 Thornwood Dr Ste 100 (14850-1275)
PHONE..................607 216-8140
Bradley N Treat, *President*
Scott Adams, *Vice Pres*
Shahyaan Desai, *CTO*
EMP: 5
SALES (est): 935K Privately Held
SIC: 3679 Electronic components

(G-6596) MITEGEN LLC
95 Brown Rd Ste 1034 (14850-1277)
P.O. Box 3867 (14852-3867)
PHONE..................607 266-8877
Ben Apker, *Director*
Robert E Thorne,
EMP: 5
SALES: 200K Privately Held
WEB: www.mitegen.com
SIC: 3844 X-ray apparatus & tubes

(G-6597) MPL INC
41 Dutch Mill Rd (14850-9785)
PHONE..................607 266-0480
Shane French, *CEO*
Michelle French, *Ch of Bd*
EMP: 39
SQ FT: 15,000
SALES (est): 11.1MM Privately Held
WEB: www.mplinc.com
SIC: 3672 Printed circuit boards

(G-6598) MULTIWIRE LABORATORIES LTD
95 Brown Rd 1018266a (14850-1294)
PHONE..................607 257-3378
Donald Bilderback, *President*
Becky Bilderback, *Vice Pres*
▼ **EMP**: 6
SQ FT: 2,668
SALES (est): 855.4K Privately Held
WEB: www.multiwire.com
SIC: 3844 3826 X-ray apparatus & tubes; analytical instruments

(G-6599) NCR CORPORATION
950 Danby Rd (14850-5778)
PHONE..................607 273-5310
Malcom Unsworth, *Branch Mgr*
EMP: 247
SALES (corp-wide): 6.5B Publicly Held
WEB: www.ncr.com
SIC: 2752 3577 Commercial printing, lithographic; computer peripheral equipment
PA: Ncr Corporation
864 Spring St Nw
Atlanta GA 30308
937 445-5000

(G-6600) NEW SKI INC
Also Called: Ithaca Times
109 N Cayuga St Ste A (14850-4340)
P.O. Box 27 (14851-0027)
PHONE..................607 277-7000
James Belinski, *President*
EMP: 30
SQ FT: 2,000
SALES (est): 1.3MM Privately Held
WEB: www.ithacatimes.com
SIC: 2711 Newspapers: publishing only, not printed on site

(G-6601) NEWCHEM INC
Also Called: Newcut
407 Cliff St (14850-2009)
PHONE..................315 331-7680
Sean Whittaker, *President*
Dick Boerman, *Export Mgr*
Pete Engel, *Engineer*
Illa Burbank, *CFO*
Kirk Cranston, *Manager*
EMP: 22
SALES: 4MM Privately Held
SIC: 3479 Etching, photochemical

(G-6602) ONGWEOWEH CORP (PA)
5 Earr Rd (14850-9117)
P.O. Box 3300 (14852-3300)
PHONE..................607 266-7070
Frank C Bonamie, *Ch of Bd*
Justin M Bennett, *President*
Alison Meyer, *Manager*
Doreen Gebhard, *Representative*
Susan Luss, *Representative*
EMP: 56
SQ FT: 1,000
SALES (est): 225MM Privately Held
WEB: www.ongweoweh.com
SIC: 2448 Wood pallets & skids

(G-6603) PERFORMANCE SYSTEMS CONTG INC
124 Brindley St (14850-5002)
PHONE..................607 277-6240
Greg Thomas, *President*
EMP: 50
SQ FT: 20,000
SALES (est): 4.5MM Privately Held
WEB: www.pscontracting.com
SIC: 3825 Energy measuring equipment, electrical

(G-6604) PETRUNIA LLC
Also Called: Petrune
126 E State St (14850-5542)
PHONE..................607 277-1930
Dominica Brookman, *Mng Member*
EMP: 5
SALES (est): 628.5K Privately Held
SIC: 2339 Women's & misses' accessories

(G-6605) POROUS MATERIALS INC
Also Called: Advance Pressure Products
20 Dutch Mill Rd (14850-9199)
PHONE..................607 257-5544
Krishna M Gupta, *President*
Sam Wright, *Info Tech Mgr*
Sudha Gupta, *Admin Sec*
Terri Murray, *Technician*
EMP: 17
SQ FT: 10,000
SALES (est): 2MM Privately Held
WEB: www.pmiapp.com
SIC: 3826 Laser scientific & engineering instruments

(G-6606) PRECISION FILTERS INC (PA)
240 Cherry St (14850-5099)
PHONE..................607 277-3550
Douglas Firth, *Ch of Bd*
Donald Chandler, *President*
John Morris, *General Mgr*
Paul Costantini, *Vice Pres*
Alan Szary, *Vice Pres*
EMP: 35
SQ FT: 15,500
SALES (est): 6.6MM Privately Held
WEB: www.pfinc.com
SIC: 3825 Test equipment for electronic & electric measurement

(G-6607) PURITY ICE CREAM CO INC
700 Cascadilla St Ste A (14850-3255)
PHONE..................607 272-1545
Bruce Lane, *President*
Heather Lane, *Vice Pres*
EMP: 18 **EST**: 1936
SQ FT: 10,000
SALES (est): 2MM Privately Held
WEB: www.purityicecream.com
SIC: 2024 5143 5812 2026 Ice cream, bulk; ice cream & ices; ice cream stands or dairy bars; fluid milk

(G-6608) RHEONIX INC (PA)
10 Brown Rd Ste 103 (14850-1287)
PHONE..................607 257-1242
Gregory J Galvin PHD, *Ch of Bd*
Richard A Montagna PHD, *Senior VP*
Peng Zhou PHD, *Senior VP*
John Brenner Ms, *Vice Pres*
Jeff Button, *Project Mgr*
EMP: 60
SALES (est): 13.3MM Privately Held
WEB: www.rheonix.com
SIC: 3826 Analytical instruments

(G-6609) RPS HOLDINGS INC
99 Eastlake Rd (14850-9786)
PHONE..................607 257-7778
David Johnson, *President*
EMP: 22
SALES (est): 1.6MM Privately Held
WEB: www.rpsolutions.com
SIC: 7372 Business oriented computer software

(G-6610) STORK H & E TURBO BLADING INC
334 Comfort Rd (14850-8626)
P.O. Box 177 (14851-0177)
PHONE..................607 277-4968
John Slocum, *Ch of Bd*
Ben Tepeek, *CFO*
▲ **EMP**: 170 **EST**: 1976
SQ FT: 49,046
SALES (est): 42.4MM
SALES (corp-wide): 19.5B Publicly Held
WEB: www.he-machinery.com
SIC: 3511 Turbines & turbine generator sets
HQ: Stork Turbo Blading B.V.
Kamerlingh Onnesstraat 21
Sneek
880 891-290

(G-6611) THERM INCORPORATED
1000 Hudson Street Ext (14850-5999)
PHONE..................607 272-8500
Robert R Sprole III, *Ch of Bd*
Valerie Daugherty, *General Mgr*
Rodney Ross, *Purch Agent*
Dexter Cross, *Design Engr*
Bruce Honeywell, *Accountant*
▲ **EMP**: 200
SQ FT: 130,000
SALES (est): 52.3MM Privately Held
WEB: www.therm.com
SIC: 3724 Aircraft engines & engine parts

(G-6612) TOMPKINS WEEKLY INC
36 Besemer Rd (14850-9638)
P.O. Box 6404 (14851-6404)
PHONE..................607 539-7100
James Graney, *Principal*
EMP: 6
SALES (est): 296.5K Privately Held
SIC: 2711 Newspapers

(G-6613) TRANSACT TECHNOLOGIES INC
Also Called: Ithaca Peripherals
20 Bomax Dr (14850-1200)
PHONE..................607 257-8901
Dick Cole, *Vice Pres*
Dave Ritchie, *Vice Pres*
Andy Hoffman, *Purch Agent*
Sarah Jones, *Accountant*
Ann Dell, *Manager*
EMP: 94
SQ FT: 70,000 Publicly Held
WEB: www.transact-tech.com
SIC: 3577 Printers, computer
PA: Transact Technologies Incorporated
2319 Whitney Ave Ste 3b
Hamden CT 06518

(G-6614) TRANSACTION PRINTER GROUP
108 Woodcrest Ter (14850-6224)
PHONE..................607 274-2500
Dana Wardlaw, *Principal*
EMP: 5 **EST**: 2009
SALES (est): 522.2K Privately Held
SIC: 2752 Commercial printing, lithographic

(G-6615) VANGUARD GRAPHICS LLC
Also Called: Vanguard Printing
17 Hallwoods Rd (14850-8787)
PHONE..................607 272-1212
Steve Rossi, *President*
Bob Polledri, *President*
William Post, *Vice Pres*
Lynn Hickey, *Purch Agent*
Al Chaffee, *Purchasing*
EMP: 140
SALES (est): 4.5MM
SALES (corp-wide): 7.1MM Privately Held
SIC: 2752 Commercial printing, offset
PA: Kappa Media, Llc
40 Skippack Pike
Fort Washington PA 19034
215 643-5800

(G-6616) VECTOR MAGNETICS LLC
236 Cherry St (14850-5023)
PHONE..................607 273-8351
Arthur Kuckes, *CEO*
Rahn Pitzer, *President*
David Mohler, *VP Opers*
David Mohlet, *VP Opers*
Justin Armstrong, *Engineer*
EMP: 25
SQ FT: 12,000
SALES (est): 4.4MM Privately Held
SIC: 3829 Magnetometers

(G-6617) ZYMTRNIX CATALYTIC SYSTEMS INC
526 N Campus (14853-6007)
PHONE..................607 351-2639
Stephane Corgie, *CEO*
EMP: 6 **EST**: 2013
SALES (est): 729.3K Privately Held
SIC: 2869 Enzymes
PA: Zymtronix, Llc
526 N Campus 414a 1 Weill
Ithaca NY 14853
607 351-2639

Jackson Heights
Queens County

(G-6618)
BORNOMALA USA INC
Also Called: Weekly Bornomal
3766 72nd St Fl 3 (11372-6143)
PHONE..................347 753-2355
Mahfuzur Rahman, *President*
EMP: 5 **EST:** 2015
SALES (est): 92.2K **Privately Held**
SIC: 2711 Newspapers, publishing & printing; newspapers: publishing only, not printed on site

(G-6619)
CITYPHARMA INC
7316 Roosevelt Ave (11372-6336)
PHONE..................917 832-6035
Lynn Youn, *President*
EMP: 5
SALES (est): 392.1K **Privately Held**
SIC: 2834 Pharmaceutical preparations

(G-6620)
KARISHMA FASHIONS INC
Also Called: Lavanya
3708 74th St (11372-6338)
PHONE..................718 565-5404
Shiv Dass, *President*
EMP: 5
SQ FT: 1,500
SALES: 300K **Privately Held**
SIC: 2395 Embroidery & art needlework

(G-6621)
WEEKLY AJKAL
3707 74th St Ste 8 (11372-6308)
PHONE..................718 565-2100
Jakaria Masud, *Owner*
EMP: 10
SALES (est): 375.8K **Privately Held**
SIC: 2711 Newspapers

Jamaica
Queens County

(G-6622)
ABBOTT INDUSTRIES INC (PA)
Also Called: Woodmaster Industries
9525 149th St (11435-4511)
PHONE..................718 291-0800
Leonard Grossman, *Ch of Bd*
Jeffrey Grossman, *Vice Pres*
Robert Candea, *Engineer*
Cindy Ackerman, *Controller*
Pat Iaonne, *Manager*
▲ **EMP:** 350 **EST:** 1958
SQ FT: 225,000
SALES (est): 36.8MM **Privately Held**
SIC: 2499 2541 3089 2542 Woodenware, kitchen & household; store fixtures, wood; plastic hardware & building products; office & store showcases & display fixtures; fryers, electric: household; heating units, for electric appliances; can openers, electric; food mixers, electric: household; miscellaneous fabricated wire products

(G-6623)
ACCORD PIPE FABRICATORS INC
9226 180th St (11433-1427)
PHONE..................718 657-3900
Harry Schwarz, *President*
Thomas S Bloom, *Vice Pres*
EMP: 35
SQ FT: 40,000
SALES (est): 5.5MM **Privately Held**
SIC: 3498 5051 Fabricated pipe & fittings; pipe & tubing, steel

(G-6624)
AMERICAN STEEL GATE CORP
10510 150th St (11435-5018)
PHONE..................718 291-4050
Tony Lohay, *President*
Anthony Lohay, *President*
EMP: 6
SQ FT: 3,000
SALES (est): 638.3K **Privately Held**
WEB: www.americansteelgate.com
SIC: 3442 Rolling doors for industrial buildings or warehouses, metal

(G-6625)
AMERICAN TORQUE INC
10522 150th St (11435-5018)
PHONE..................718 526-2433
Marsha McCarthy, *President*
EMP: 10
SQ FT: 4,000
SALES (est): 1MM **Privately Held**
SIC: 3566 Torque converters, except automotive

(G-6626)
ATLANTIC PORK & PROVISIONS INC
14707 94th Ave (11435-4513)
PHONE..................718 272-9550
Jack Antinori, *President*
Ronald Romeo, *Vice Pres*
Susan Antinori, *Treasurer*
EMP: 40 **EST:** 1948
SQ FT: 30,000
SALES (est): 3.9MM **Privately Held**
SIC: 2013 Bologna from purchased meat; ham, boiled: from purchased meat; ham, roasted: from purchased meat; ham, smoked: from purchased meat

(G-6627)
ATLAS CONCRETE BATCHING CORP
9511 147th Pl (11435-4507)
PHONE..................718 523-3000
Thomas Polsinelli, *Principal*
EMP: 100
SQ FT: 12,000
SALES (est): 9MM **Privately Held**
SIC: 3273 Ready-mixed concrete

(G-6628)
ATLAS TRANSIT MIX CORP
9511 147th Pl (11435-4507)
PHONE..................718 523-3000
Mary Polsinelli, *President*
Vincent Polsinelli, *Corp Secy*
Tom Polsinelli, *Vice Pres*
EMP: 150
SQ FT: 12,000
SALES (est): 900K **Privately Held**
SIC: 3273 Ready-mixed concrete

(G-6629)
B & R SHEET
10652 157th St (11433-2050)
PHONE..................718 558-5544
Rohan Rampersaud, *Principal*
EMP: 5 **EST:** 2014
SALES (est): 502.1K **Privately Held**
SIC: 3444 1761 Sheet metalwork; sheet metalwork

(G-6630)
BAUERSCHMIDT & SONS INC
11920 Merrick Blvd (11434-2296)
PHONE..................718 528-3500
Fred Bauerschmidt, *Ch of Bd*
Robert Bauerschmidt, *Treasurer*
Christina Vicario, *Bookkeeper*
Patricia Bauerschmidt, *Manager*
Douglas Wefer, *Admin Asst*
▲ **EMP:** 70 **EST:** 1948
SQ FT: 28,000
SALES (est): 11.4MM **Privately Held**
WEB: www.bauerschmidtandsons.com
SIC: 2541 2431 2521 2434 Office fixtures, wood; cabinets, except refrigerated: show, display, etc.: wood; woodwork, interior & ornamental; wood office furniture; wood kitchen cabinets

(G-6631)
CAPITOL AWNING CO INC
Also Called: Capitol Awning & Shade Co
10515 180th St (11434-1818)
PHONE..................212 505-1717
Michael Catalano, *President*
Fred Catalano Jr, *President*
Phil Catalano, *Vice Pres*
Ryan Catalano, *Treasurer*
Michael Grosso, *Accounts Exec*
EMP: 18
SQ FT: 8,000
SALES (est): 2MM **Privately Held**
WEB: www.capitolawning.com
SIC: 2394 Awnings, fabric: made from purchased materials

(G-6632)
CENTURY TOM INC
10416 150th St (11435-4924)
PHONE..................347 654-3179
Yanru Lin, *CEO*
EMP: 4 **EST:** 2012
SALES (est): 1.7MM **Privately Held**
SIC: 2023 Dietary supplements, dairy & non-dairy based

(G-6633)
CHEMCLEAN CORPORATION
13045 180th St (11434-4107)
PHONE..................718 525-4500
Bernard Esquenet, *President*
Brian Alexander, *Sales Executive*
Miriam Ramos, *Office Mgr*
▲ **EMP:** 28 **EST:** 1943
SQ FT: 30,000
SALES (est): 5.8MM **Privately Held**
WEB: www.chemclean.com
SIC: 2842 Cleaning or polishing preparations

(G-6634)
CIRCLE 5 DELI CORP
13440 Guy R Brewer Blvd (11434-3728)
PHONE..................718 525-5687
Yahya Alsaidi, *Principal*
EMP: 8
SALES (est): 455.7K **Privately Held**
SIC: 2051 Bakery, for home service delivery

(G-6635)
CITY MASON CORP
Also Called: Three Star Supply
10417 148th St (11435-4921)
PHONE..................718 658-3796
Anthony Scaccia, *Ch of Bd*
Frank Landen Jr, *President*
EMP: 15
SQ FT: 20,000
SALES (est): 1.1MM **Privately Held**
SIC: 3272 Concrete products

(G-6636)
CITY POST EXPRESS INC
17518 147th Ave (11434-5402)
P.O. Box 405, Fairfield CT (06824-0405)
PHONE..................718 995-8690
Robert Swords, *Principal*
▲ **EMP:** 9
SALES (est): 866.5K **Privately Held**
SIC: 2741 Miscellaneous publishing

(G-6637)
CLASSIQUE PERFUMES INC
139 01 Archer Ave (11435)
PHONE..................718 657-8200
EMP: 3
SQ FT: 9,500
SALES: 1.2MM **Privately Held**
SIC: 2844 Mfrs Colognes Perfumes & Cosmetics

(G-6638)
CONCORD EXPRESS CARGO INC
17214 119th Ave (11434-2260)
PHONE..................718 276-7200
Chris Okafor, *CEO*
Margaret Jones, *Admin Sec*
▼ **EMP:** 5
SALES (est): 642.5K **Privately Held**
SIC: 2448 Cargo containers, wood & wood with metal

(G-6639)
CORKHILL MANUFACTURING CO INC
Also Called: Corkhill Grp
13121 Merrick Blvd (11434-4133)
PHONE..................718 528-7413
Dennis Wugalter, *President*
EMP: 8 **EST:** 1947
SQ FT: 7,000
SALES (est): 1.5MM **Privately Held**
SIC: 3442 Storm doors or windows, metal

(G-6640)
CRS REMANUFACTURING CO INC
9440 158th St (11433-1017)
PHONE..................718 739-1720
Pratab Angira, *President*
Balkrishna Angira, *Vice Pres*
▲ **EMP:** 10
SALES (est): 920K **Privately Held**
SIC: 3714 Power steering equipment, motor vehicle

(G-6641)
D AND D SHEET METAL CORP
9510 218th St Ste 4 (11429-1216)
PHONE..................718 465-7585
EMP: 12
SALES (est): 960K **Privately Held**
SIC: 3444 Mfg Sheet Metalwork

(G-6642)
EXPRESSIONS PUNCHING & DIGITIZ
Also Called: Expression Embroidery
9315 179th Pl (11433-1425)
PHONE..................718 291-1177
George Hanakis, *President*
Evelyn Hanakis, *Vice Pres*
EMP: 9
SQ FT: 7,000
SALES: 980K **Privately Held**
SIC: 2395 Embroidery products, except schiffli machine; embroidery & art needlework

(G-6643)
FORTUNE POLY PRODUCTS INC
17910 93rd Ave (11433-1406)
PHONE..................718 361-0767
Roger Truong, *President*
▲ **EMP:** 14
SQ FT: 25,000
SALES (est): 2.8MM **Privately Held**
SIC: 2673 Plastic bags: made from purchased materials

(G-6644)
FRANCHET METAL CRAFT INC
17832 93rd Ave (11433-1489)
PHONE..................718 658-6400
Frank Grodio, *President*
EMP: 6
SQ FT: 4,000
SALES: 700K **Privately Held**
SIC: 3444 Sheet metal specialties, not stamped

(G-6645)
FRANKLIN ELECTRIC CO INC
17501 Rockaway Blvd # 309 (11434-5502)
PHONE..................718 244-7744
EMP: 563
SALES (corp-wide): 1.1B **Publicly Held**
SIC: 3621 Motors, electric
PA: Franklin Electric Co., Inc.
9255 Coverdale Rd
Fort Wayne IN 46809
260 824-2900

(G-6646)
GLEANER COMPANY LTD
Also Called: Jamaican Weekly Gleaner
9205 172nd St Fl 2 (11433-1218)
PHONE..................718 657-0788
Sheila Alexander, *Director*
EMP: 5
SALES (est): 510.2K **Privately Held**
WEB: www.gleaner-classifieds.com
SIC: 2711 Newspapers, publishing & printing
HQ: Gleaner Company (Canada) Inc, The
1390 Eglinton Ave W Suite 2
Toronto ON M6C 2
416 784-3002

(G-6647)
GOURMET BOUTIQUE LLC (PA)
14402 158th St (11434-4214)
PHONE..................718 977-1200
Robert Liberto, *CEO*
Jan Sussman, *President*
Hugh Anderson, *Maint Spvr*

Sergio Tenaglia, *Opers Staff*
Jere Dudley, *VP Sales*
▲ **EMP:** 217
SQ FT: 60,000
SALES: 64MM **Privately Held**
WEB: www.gourmetboutique.com
SIC: 2099 Food preparations

(G-6648)
H & H FURNITURE CO
11420 101st Ave (11419-1139)
PHONE.................................718 850-5252
John Hassan, *Manager*
EMP: 5
SALES (est): 330K **Privately Held**
SIC: 2512 Upholstered household furniture

(G-6649)
H G MAYBECK CO INC
17930 93rd Ave Ste 2 (11433-1405)
PHONE.................................718 297-4410
John Arapis, *President*
Chris Arapis, *Vice Pres*
Len Golombek, *Sales Mgr*
▲ **EMP:** 30
SQ FT: 26,000
SALES (est): 4.2MM **Privately Held**
SIC: 2393 2673 Canvas bags; bags: plastic, laminated & coated

(G-6650)
HILLSIDE PRINTING INC
Also Called: Printing Express
16013 Hillside Ave (11432-3982)
PHONE.................................718 658-6719
Joseph Randazzo, *President*
EMP: 10
SQ FT: 2,000
SALES: 1MM **Privately Held**
WEB: www.hillsideprinting.com
SIC: 2752 Commercial printing, offset

(G-6651)
IMPLADENT LTD (PA)
19845 Foothill Ave (11423-1611)
PHONE.................................718 465-1810
Maurice Valen, *President*
Virginia Valen, *Vice Pres*
Gisele Sasson, *Admin Sec*
EMP: 22
SALES (est): 2MM **Privately Held**
WEB: www.impladentltd.com
SIC: 3843 3069 5047 Dental equipment & supplies; medical & laboratory rubber sundries & related products; dental equipment & supplies

(G-6652)
J SUSSMAN INC
10910 180th St (11433-2622)
PHONE.................................718 297-0228
David Sussman, *President*
Steve Sussman, *Vice Pres*
Bibi Ortiz, *Executive*
▼ **EMP:** 45 **EST:** 1906
SQ FT: 55,000
SALES (est): 11.4MM **Privately Held**
WEB: www.jsussmaninc.com
SIC: 3442 3354 Window & door frames; aluminum extruded products

(G-6653)
JAMAICA IRON WORKS INC
10847 Merrick Blvd (11433-2992)
PHONE.................................718 657-4849
Robert Pape, *President*
EMP: 10 **EST:** 1927
SQ FT: 2,000
SALES (est): 830K **Privately Held**
SIC: 3446 Fences or posts, ornamental iron or steel

(G-6654)
JONATHAN METAL & GLASS LTD
17818 107th Ave (11433-1802)
PHONE.................................718 846-8000
Wilfred Smith, *President*
Nerone Qela, *Project Mgr*
Antonio Gonzalez, *Purchasing*
Shakero Porter, *Office Mgr*
Leila Zhu, *Asst Office Mgr*
▲ **EMP:** 151
SQ FT: 32,000

SALES: 44.3MM **Privately Held**
SIC: 3446 Bank fixtures, ornamental metal; brasswork, ornamental: structural; grillwork, ornamental metal

(G-6655)
LIBERTY READY MIX INC
9533 150th St (11435-4501)
PHONE.................................718 526-1700
Giabomo Gisonda, *President*
EMP: 12
SALES (est): 1.6MM **Privately Held**
SIC: 3273 Ready-mixed concrete

(G-6656)
LITE-MAKERS INC
10715 180th St (11433-2617)
PHONE.................................718 739-9300
John Iorio, *President*
Gary Iorio, *Treasurer*
▲ **EMP:** 30
SQ FT: 12,000
SALES (est): 4.7MM **Privately Held**
WEB: www.litemakers.com
SIC: 3646 Chandeliers, commercial

(G-6657)
MACHINA DEUS LEX INC
15921 Grand Central Pkwy (11432-1128)
PHONE.................................917 577-0972
Glen Kieser, *President*
EMP: 6
SALES: 150K **Privately Held**
SIC: 2421 Silo stock, wood: sawed

(G-6658)
MAIA SYSTEMS LLC
8344 Parsons Blvd Ste 101 (11432-1642)
PHONE.................................718 206-0100
Jack Najyb, *President*
EMP: 6
SALES (est): 846.4K **Privately Held**
SIC: 3661 3577 5734 Telephone sets, all types except cellular radio; computer peripheral equipment; computer & software stores

(G-6659)
MAUCERI SIGN INC
Also Called: Mauceri Sign & Awning Co
16725 Rockaway Blvd (11434-5222)
PHONE.................................718 656-7700
James V Mauceri, *President*
Carol Caruso, *General Mgr*
EMP: 18
SQ FT: 14,000
SALES (est): 2.6MM **Privately Held**
SIC: 3993 2394 5999 Signs, not made in custom sign painting shops; awnings, fabric: made from purchased materials; awnings

(G-6660)
METAL WORKS OF NY INC
11603 Merrick Blvd (11434-1825)
PHONE.................................718 525-9440
Vincent Sabatino, *President*
Danny Sabatino, *Treasurer*
EMP: 5
SALES (est): 520K **Privately Held**
SIC: 3441 Fabricated structural metal

(G-6661)
METEOR EXPRESS INC
16801 Rockaway Blvd # 202 (11434-5287)
PHONE.................................718 551-9177
Ning Fang, *CEO*
EMP: 15
SALES (est): 1.2MM **Privately Held**
SIC: 3537 Trucks: freight, baggage, etc.: industrial, except mining

(G-6662)
MINUTEMAN PRESS INTL INC
24814 Union Tpke (11426)
PHONE.................................718 343-5440
Rob Schiffman, *Manager*
EMP: 5
SALES (corp-wide): 23.4MM **Privately Held**
SIC: 2752 Commercial printing, lithographic
PA: Minuteman Press International, Inc.
   61 Executive Blvd
   Farmingdale NY 11735
   631 249-1370

(G-6663)
MMS H& F INC
8745 144th St (11435-3122)
PHONE.................................718 785-6663
Hamida Begun, *Principal*
Mohhammed Rahaman, *Vice Pres*
EMP: 6 **EST:** 2012
SQ FT: 1,200
SALES: 350K **Privately Held**
SIC: 2392 Household furnishings

(G-6664)
MOUNTAIN SIDE FARMS INC
15504 Liberty Ave (11433-1038)
PHONE.................................718 526-3442
Henry Schwartz, *President*
EMP: 30 **EST:** 1981
SQ FT: 500
SALES (est): 29.8K **Privately Held**
SIC: 2026 Milk processing (pasteurizing, homogenizing, bottling)

(G-6665)
NEW YORK STEEL SERVICES CO
18009 Liberty Ave (11433-1434)
PHONE.................................718 291-7770
George Cromwell, *Owner*
EMP: 5
SALES (est): 390K **Privately Held**
SIC: 3449 Bars, concrete reinforcing: fabricated steel

(G-6666)
PAL ALUMINUM INC
Also Called: Pal Industries
10620 180th St (11433-1828)
PHONE.................................718 262-0091
Pana Giotis Mar Neris, *Branch Mgr*
EMP: 22
SALES (corp-wide): 4.7MM **Privately Held**
SIC: 3444 Metal roofing & roof drainage equipment
PA: Pal Aluminum, Inc.
   230 Duffy Ave Unit B
   Hicksville NY 11801
   516 937-1990

(G-6667)
PATI INC
Also Called: Airport Press, The
Jfk Intl Airprt Hngar 16 (11430)
PHONE.................................718 244-6788
Fax: 718 995-3432
EMP: 10
SQ FT: 1,000
SALES (est): 790K **Privately Held**
SIC: 2721 Periodicals-Publishing/Printing

(G-6668)
PRECISION READY MIX INC
14707 Liberty Ave (11435-4727)
PHONE.................................718 658-5600
Frank Scaccia, *President*
EMP: 6
SQ FT: 700
SALES (est): 500K **Privately Held**
SIC: 3273 Ready-mixed concrete

(G-6669)
PREMIUM SWEETS USA INC
16803 Hillside Ave (11432-4340)
PHONE.................................718 739-6000
Babu Khan, *CEO*
EMP: 8
SALES (est): 602.4K **Privately Held**
SIC: 2064 5145 Candy & other confectionery products; candy

(G-6670)
QUEENS READY MIX INC
14901 95th Ave (11435-4521)
PHONE.................................718 526-4919
Tony Mastronardi, *President*
Jerry Mastronardi, *Vice Pres*
EMP: 7
SALES (est): 1MM **Privately Held**
SIC: 3273 Ready-mixed concrete

(G-6671)
R & M THERMOFOIL DOORS INC
14830 94th Ave (11435-4516)
PHONE.................................718 206-4991
Robby Moyal, *Ch of Bd*

EMP: 5
SALES (est): 643.2K **Privately Held**
SIC: 2434 Wood kitchen cabinets

(G-6672)
RAYCO MANUFACTURING CO INC
Also Called: Rayco Manufacturing Div
10715 180th St (11433-2617)
PHONE.................................516 431-2006
Sidney L Friedman, *President*
John Iannuzzo, *Treasurer*
EMP: 12
SQ FT: 15,000
SALES (est): 1.6MM **Privately Held**
SIC: 3444 3469 Sheet metalwork; machine parts, stamped or pressed metal

(G-6673)
RAYS RESTAURANT & BAKERY INC
12325 Jamaica Ave (11418-2640)
PHONE.................................718 441-7707
Ray Manharalall, *CEO*
▲ **EMP:** 6
SQ FT: 3,100
SALES (est): 320K **Privately Held**
SIC: 2051 Bakery: wholesale or wholesale/retail combined

(G-6674)
REHABILITATION INTERNATIONAL
15350 89th Ave Apt 1101 (11432-3977)
PHONE.................................212 420-1500
Tomas Lagerwall, *President*
EMP: 5
SQ FT: 4,000
SALES: 182.2K **Privately Held**
SIC: 3663

(G-6675)
ROSCO INC (PA)
9021 144th Pl (11435-4227)
PHONE.................................718 526-2601
Sol Englander, *Chairman*
Gertrude Englander, *Corp Secy*
Ben Englander, *Vice Pres*
Danny Englander, *Vice Pres*
Joe Ippolito, *Plant Mgr*
◆ **EMP:** 170
SQ FT: 85,000
SALES (est): 37.5MM **Privately Held**
WEB: www.roscomirrors.com
SIC: 3231 3714 3429 Mirrors, truck & automobile: made from purchased glass; motor vehicle parts & accessories; manufactured hardware (general)

(G-6676)
ROSCO COLLISION AVOIDANCE INC
9021 144th Pl (11435-4227)
PHONE.................................718 526-2601
Daniel Englander, *VP Finance*
EMP: 8
SALES: 2MM **Privately Held**
SIC: 3861 Cameras & related equipment

(G-6677)
SKY LAUNDROMAT INC
8615 Ava Pl Apt 4e (11432-2954)
PHONE.................................718 639-7070
David Mendoza, *President*
EMP: 33
SQ FT: 5,000
SALES: 660K **Privately Held**
SIC: 2211 7215 Laundry nets; laundry, coin-operated

(G-6678)
SSRJA LLC
Also Called: Five Star Printing
10729 180th St (11433-2617)
PHONE.................................718 725-7020
Savithri Somwaru,
Anand Jagessar,
Seelochini S Liriano,
Javier Rojas,
EMP: 11
SQ FT: 10,000
SALES: 3MM **Privately Held**
SIC: 2711 Newspapers, publishing & printing

Jamaica - Queens County (G-6679)

(G-6679)
STAR MOUNTAIN JFK INC
Also Called: Star Mountain Coffee
Federal Cir Bldg 141 (11430)
PHONE..................................718 553-6787
Carmen Ham, *President*
EMP: 5
SALES: 350K **Privately Held**
SIC: 2095 Roasted coffee

(G-6680)
SUGARBEAR CUPCAKES
14552 159th St (11434-4220)
PHONE..................................917 698-9005
Louise Torbert, *Principal*
Tiffany Thompson, *Recruiter*
Richelle Ryan, *Media Spec*
EMP: 8
SALES (est): 315K **Privately Held**
SIC: 2051 Bread, cake & related products

(G-6681)
SUNBILT SOLAR PDTS BY SUSSMAN
10910 180th St (11433-2622)
PHONE..................................718 297-0228
Steven Sussman, *President*
David Sussman, *Vice Pres*
EMP: 55
SQ FT: 80,000
SALES (est): 5.7MM **Privately Held**
SIC: 3448 Sunrooms, prefabricated metal

(G-6682)
TECHNICAL SERVICE INDUSTRIES
Also Called: ABC Casting
17506 Devonshire Rd 5n (11432-2949)
PHONE..................................212 719-9800
Mitch Altman, *President*
Michael Hooks, *Vice Pres*
EMP: 27
SQ FT: 3,500
SALES (est): 3MM **Privately Held**
SIC: 3911 Jewelry, precious metal

(G-6683)
TEE PEE FENCE AND RAILING
Also Called: Tee Pee Fence & Rail
9312 179th Pl (11433-1426)
PHONE..................................718 658-8323
Tom Pendergast, *President*
Jim Pendergast, *Manager*
EMP: 15
SQ FT: 15,000
SALES: 1.3MM **Privately Held**
SIC: 3446 Fences or posts, ornamental iron or steel; railings, prefabricated metal

(G-6684)
THE SANDHAR CORP
16427 Highland Ave (11432-3555)
PHONE..................................718 523-0819
Hardev Sandhu, *President*
Shawinder Sandhu, *Vice Pres*
EMP: 7 **EST:** 1990
SALES (est): 413.8K **Privately Held**
SIC: 2711 Newspapers

(G-6685)
TRU-ART SIGN CO INC
Also Called: Signs By Sunrise
10515 180th St (11433-1818)
PHONE..................................718 658-5068
Lawrence Amatulli, *President*
EMP: 12
SALES (corp-wide): 1.3MM **Privately Held**
SIC: 3993 Signs & advertising specialties
PA: Tru-Art Sign Co. Inc.
187 N Main St
Freeport NY
516 378-0066

(G-6686)
TURBO EXPRESS INC
16019 Rockaway Blvd Ste D (11434-5100)
PHONE..................................718 723-3686
Gilberto Rosario, *Principal*
EMP: 5
SALES (est): 239.2K **Privately Held**
SIC: 2741 Miscellaneous publishing

(G-6687)
UNIKE PRODUCTS INC
18230 Wexford Ter Apt 2m (11432-3119)
PHONE..................................347 686-4616
Nancy Roger, *CEO*
▼ **EMP:** 5
SALES: 100K **Privately Held**
SIC: 2844 Hair preparations, including shampoos; shampoos, rinses, conditioners; hair; oral preparations; toothpastes or powders, dentifrices

(G-6688)
URDU TIMES
16920 Hillside Ave (11432-4435)
PHONE..................................718 297-8700
Khalil Ur Rehman, *President*
EMP: 6
SALES (est): 198.5K **Privately Held**
SIC: 2711 Newspapers

(G-6689)
VISUAL EFFECTS INC
15929 Jamaica Ave 2 (11432-6002)
PHONE..................................718 324-0011
Thomas Murphy, *President*
Henry Kwitel, *Vice Pres*
▲ **EMP:** 10 **EST:** 1968
SALES (est): 1.5MM **Privately Held**
SIC: 3648 5063 3993 Lighting equipment; lighting fixtures; electric signs; displays & cutouts, window & lobby

(G-6690)
WAYNE DECORATORS INC
14409 Rockaway Blvd Apt 1 (11436-1602)
PHONE..................................718 529-4200
Louis Sapodin, *President*
Alex Greenberg, *Vice Pres*
EMP: 8
SQ FT: 2,000
SALES (est): 617.1K **Privately Held**
SIC: 2391 2392 2393 Draperies, plastic & textile: from purchased materials; bedspreads & bed sets: made from purchased materials; pillows, bed: made from purchased materials; cushions, except spring & carpet: purchased materials

(G-6691)
WHITNEY FOODS INC
Also Called: Kissle
15504 Liberty Ave (11433-1038)
PHONE..................................718 291-3333
Henry Schwartz, *Ch of Bd*
Kenneth Schlossberg, *Vice Ch Bd*
D Bruce Budinoff, *Vice Pres*
Robert E Braks, *Treasurer*
EMP: 16
SALES (est): 1.5MM
SALES (corp-wide): 115.3MM **Privately Held**
SIC: 2026 Yogurt
PA: Steuben Foods, Incorporated
1150 Maple Rd
Elma NY 14059
718 291-3333

(G-6692)
X-TREME READY MIX INC
17801 Liberty Ave (11433-1432)
PHONE..................................718 739-3384
Michael Falco, *Ch of Bd*
EMP: 9
SALES (est): 1.2MM **Privately Held**
SIC: 3531 Mixers, concrete

Jamesport
Suffolk County

(G-6693)
NORTH HOUSE VINEYARDS INC
Also Called: Jamesport Vineyards
1216 Main Rd Rte 25a (11947)
P.O. Box 842 (11947-0842)
PHONE..................................631 779-2817
Ronald B Goerler, *President*
Ann Marie Goerler, *Treasurer*
▲ **EMP:** 5
SALES (est): 427.4K **Privately Held**
WEB: www.jamesportvineyards.com
SIC: 2084 Wines

Jamestown
Chautauqua County

(G-6694)
ACCESS ELEVATOR & LIFT INC (PA)
1209 E 2nd St (14701-1952)
PHONE..................................716 483-3696
Sean Fenton, *President*
EMP: 1
SALES: 1.8MM **Privately Held**
SIC: 3534 Elevators & equipment

(G-6695)
ACU-RITE COMPANIES INC
1 Precision Way (14701-9630)
PHONE..................................716 661-1700
Thomas Wright, *CEO*
Chris Bartkowiak, *Engineer*
Jerry Reynolds, *Controller*
Kenneth Cramer, *Software Engr*
◆ **EMP:** 5
SALES (est): 525.7K **Privately Held**
SIC: 3545 Machine tool accessories
HQ: Heidenhain Corporation
333 E State Pkwy
Schaumburg IL 60173
847 490-1191

(G-6696)
ALL METAL SPECIALTIES INC
300 Livingston Ave (14701-2665)
PHONE..................................716 664-6009
Raymond Anderson, *President*
EMP: 21 **EST:** 1953
SQ FT: 18,500
SALES (est): 3.2MM **Privately Held**
WEB: www.allmetalspecialties.com
SIC: 3444 Sheet metalwork

(G-6697)
ALLIED INDUSTRIAL PRODUCTS CO
Also Called: Allied Industries
880 E 2nd St (14701-3824)
PHONE..................................716 664-3893
Greg Bender, *Manager*
EMP: 6
SALES: 292.7K
SALES (corp-wide): 90K **Privately Held**
SIC: 3599 Machine & other job shop work
PA: Allied Industrial Products Co
180 W Olive St
Long Beach NY

(G-6698)
ANDERSON PRECISION INC
20 Livingston Ave (14701-2844)
PHONE..................................716 484-1148
Steven Godfrey, *President*
Jason Carlson, *Prdtn Mgr*
Mike Potter, *Engineer*
Steve Godfrey, *CFO*
David Archer, *VP Sales*
▲ **EMP:** 83
SQ FT: 80,000
SALES (est): 22MM **Privately Held**
WEB: www.andersonprecision.com
SIC: 3451 3494 Screw machine products; valves & pipe fittings

(G-6699)
ARTONE LLC
Also Called: Artone Furniture By Design
1089 Allen St (14701-2327)
PHONE..................................716 664-2232
Michael Calimeri, *President*
Sebastian Calimeri, *Exec VP*
Sebastion Calimeri, *Vice Pres*
James Tharp, *Plant Engr*
Sally Donisi, *Controller*
▲ **EMP:** 85
SQ FT: 240,000
SALES: 12.3MM **Privately Held**
WEB: www.artonemfg.com
SIC: 2521 2522 2531 2541 Wood office furniture; office furniture, except wood; public building & related furniture; wood partitions & fixtures; wood kitchen cabinets; upholstered household furniture

(G-6700)
BELLA INTERNATIONAL INC
111 W 2nd St Ste 4000 (14701-5207)
PHONE..................................716 484-0102
Stephen Pownell, *Principal*
EMP: 5
SALES (est): 508.3K **Privately Held**
WEB: www.bellayre.com
SIC: 2835 In vitro & in vivo diagnostic substances

(G-6701)
BIOPOOL US INC
Also Called: Trinity Biotech Distribution
2823 Girts Rd (14701-9666)
P.O. Box 1059 (14702-1059)
PHONE..................................716 483-3851
Ian Woodwards, *CEO*
Peter Coyne, *Bd of Directors*
William Reese, *Admin Sec*
▲ **EMP:** 48
SALES (est): 7MM **Privately Held**
SIC: 2835 In vitro & in vivo diagnostic substances
HQ: Trinity Biotech, Inc.
2823 Girts Rd
Jamestown NY 14701
800 325-3424

(G-6702)
BLACKSTONE ADVANCED TECH LLC
86 Blackstone Ave (14701-2202)
PHONE..................................716 665-5410
Richard Turner, *CEO*
EMP: 101
SALES: 26.8MM **Privately Held**
SIC: 3444 3441 3443 Sheet metalwork; fabricated structural metal; fabricated plate work (boiler shop)

(G-6703)
BNO INTL TRDG CO INC
505 Chautauqua Ave (14701-7615)
P.O. Box 97 (14702-0097)
PHONE..................................716 487-1900
Benjamin N Okwumabua, *President*
Benjamin Okwumabua, *President*
Constance Okwumabua, *Vice Pres*
EMP: 4
SQ FT: 100,000
SALES: 2.5MM **Privately Held**
WEB: www.bnointl.com
SIC: 3669 5063 Highway signals, electric; signaling equipment, electrical

(G-6704)
BUSH INDUSTRIES INC (PA)
1 Mason Dr (14701-9200)
P.O. Box 460 (14702-0460)
PHONE..................................716 665-2000
Jim Garde, *CEO*
Stephen Pettia, *President*
Jill Curley-Holshous, *Vice Pres*
Wendy Gricius, *Vice Pres*
Wende Parrish, *Vice Pres*
◆ **EMP:** 234 **EST:** 1959
SQ FT: 440,000
SALES (est): 99.8MM **Privately Held**
WEB: www.bushindustries.com
SIC: 2511 2521 Wood household furniture; desks, office: wood; cabinets, office: wood; bookcases, office: wood; panel systems & partitions (free-standing), office: wood

(G-6705)
CITY OF JAMESTOWN
Also Called: Jamestown Public Works
200 E 3rd St Ste 4 (14701-5433)
PHONE..................................716 483-7545
Jeffrey Lehman, *Director*
EMP: 55 **Privately Held**
SIC: 3531 Road construction & maintenance machinery
PA: City Of Jamestown
200 E 3rd St
Jamestown NY 14701
716 483-7538

GEOGRAPHIC SECTION
Jamestown - Chautauqua County (G-6731)

(G-6706)
CLARK LABORATORIES INC (DH)
Also Called: Trinity Biotech USA
2823 Girts Rd (14701-9666)
P.O. Box 1059 (14702-1059)
PHONE..................................716 483-3851
Ian M Woodwards, *CEO*
▲ **EMP:** 11
SQ FT: 25,000
SALES (est): 13MM **Privately Held**
SIC: 2835 In vitro & in vivo diagnostic substances
HQ: Trinity Biotech, Inc.
  2823 Girts Rd
  Jamestown NY 14701
  800 325-3424

(G-6707)
CLEANING TECH GROUP LLC
Blackstone-Ney Ultrasonics
9 N Main St (14701-5213)
P.O. Box 220 (14702-0220)
PHONE..................................716 665-2340
Timothy Piazza, *President*
EMP: 50 **Privately Held**
SIC: 3569 3559 Blast cleaning equipment, dustless; degreasing machines, automotive & industrial
HQ: Cleaning Technologies Group, Llc
  4933 Provident Dr
  West Chester OH 45246

(G-6708)
CNTRY CROSS COMMUNICATIONS LLC
Also Called: W K Z A 106.9 K I S S-F M
106 W 3rd St Ste 106 # 106 (14701-5105)
PHONE..................................386 758-9696
John Newman, *Mng Member*
EMP: 10
SALES (est): 1.1MM **Privately Held**
WEB: www.1069kissfm.com
SIC: 3663 Radio receiver networks

(G-6709)
CONTAINER TSTG SOLUTIONS LLC
17 Tiffany Ave (14701-1953)
PHONE..................................716 487-3300
Brian Johnson, *Branch Mgr*
EMP: 12 **Privately Held**
SIC: 2834 Solutions, pharmaceutical
PA: Container Testing Solutions Llc
  17 Lester St
  Sinclairville NY 14782

(G-6710)
COPPER RIDGE OIL INC
111 W 2nd St Ste 404 (14701-5229)
P.O. Box 626, Olean (14760-0626)
PHONE..................................716 372-4021
Greg Thropp, *President*
EMP: 8
SALES (est): 950K **Privately Held**
SIC: 1381 Drilling oil & gas wells

(G-6711)
DAWSON METAL COMPANY INC
Also Called: Dawson Doors
825 Allen St (14701-3998)
P.O. Box 278 (14702-0278)
PHONE..................................716 664-3811
David G Dawson, *Principal*
Roxie Barnes, *COO*
Rick Carlson, *Vice Pres*
Mike Restivo, *Vice Pres*
Jill Barber, *Purch Mgr*
EMP: 110 **EST:** 1945
SQ FT: 100,000
SALES: 13.1MM **Privately Held**
WEB: www.dawsondoors.com
SIC: 3444 3442 Sheet metalwork; metal doors, sash & trim; sash, door or window: metal; moldings & trim, except automobile: metal

(G-6712)
ECKO FIN & TOOLING INC
221 Hopkins Ave Ste 2 (14701-2252)
PHONE..................................716 487-0200
Steve Rauschenberger, *CEO*
Lance Rauschenberger, *Vice Pres*
▼ **EMP:** 11
SALES: 1.3MM **Privately Held**
SIC: 3542 Machine tools, metal forming type

(G-6713)
EL GRECO WOODWORKING INC (PA)
106 E 1st St Ste 1 (14701-5499)
PHONE..................................716 483-0315
George Theofilactidis, *President*
Constantina Kathleen Theofilac, *Corp Secy*
Dimitri Theofilactidis, *Vice Pres*
EMP: 20 **EST:** 1975
SQ FT: 100,000
SALES (est): 2.7MM **Privately Held**
WEB: www.elgrecofurniture.com
SIC: 2511 Chairs, household, except upholstered: wood

(G-6714)
ELECTRIC MOTOR SPECIALTY INC
Also Called: Electric Motor Specialties
490 Crescent St (14701-3828)
P.O. Box 111, Dewittville (14728-0111)
PHONE..................................716 487-1458
William L Allen, *President*
EMP: 6
SALES (est): 551.3K **Privately Held**
SIC: 7694 5063 Electric motor repair; motors, electric

(G-6715)
EMCO FINISHING PRODUCTS INC
470 Crescent St (14701-3897)
PHONE..................................716 483-1176
Daniel S Alexander, *President*
Barbara L Sheldon, *Admin Sec*
▲ **EMP:** 9 **EST:** 1999
SQ FT: 14,000
SALES (est): 2.3MM **Privately Held**
SIC: 2851 Lacquer: bases, dopes, thinner

(G-6716)
FRED SANTUCCI INC
Also Called: Industrial Welding & Fabg Co
121 Jackson Ave E (14701-2441)
PHONE..................................716 483-1411
Frederick A Santucci, *President*
Marybeth Santucci, *Corp Secy*
Susan Wilston, *Manager*
EMP: 14
SQ FT: 12,000
SALES (est): 2.6MM **Privately Held**
SIC: 3441 7692 Fabricated structural metal; welding repair

(G-6717)
GENCO JOHN
Also Called: S & S Enterprises
71 River St (14701-3806)
PHONE..................................716 483-5446
John Genco, *Owner*
EMP: 6
SQ FT: 21,000
SALES (est): 588.9K **Privately Held**
SIC: 3599 1541 7692 3541 Machine shop, jobbing & repair; dry cleaning plant construction; welding repair; machine tools, metal cutting type

(G-6718)
GRACE WHEELER
Also Called: Superior Bat Company
118 E 1st St (14701-5430)
P.O. Box 3331 (14702-3331)
PHONE..................................716 483-1254
Grace Wheeler, *Owner*
EMP: 6
SQ FT: 26,000
SALES (est): 522.3K **Privately Held**
SIC: 3949 Baseball equipment & supplies, general; softball equipment & supplies

(G-6719)
GREEN PROSTHETICS & ORTHOTICS
1290 E 2nd St (14701-1915)
PHONE..................................716 484-1088
Michelle Lohrke, *Opers-Prdtn-Mfg*
EMP: 7
SALES (corp-wide): 1.9MM **Privately Held**
SIC: 3842 5999 Limbs, artificial; artificial limbs
PA: Green Prosthetics & Orthotics, Inc
  2241 Peninsula Dr
  Erie PA 16506
  814 833-2311

(G-6720)
H & H METAL SPECIALTY INC
153 Hopkins Ave (14701-2289)
PHONE..................................716 665-2110
Paul W Harris Jr, *President*
Bruce W Harris, *Vice Pres*
EMP: 21 **EST:** 1953
SQ FT: 15,000
SALES (est): 2.4MM **Privately Held**
WEB: www.hhmetalspecialty.com
SIC: 3498 Fabricated pipe & fittings

(G-6721)
HANSON AGGREGATES NEW YORK LLC
2237 Allen Street Ext (14701-9632)
PHONE..................................716 665-4620
Scott Wheaton, *Manager*
Linda Olson, *Administration*
EMP: 15
SALES (corp-wide): 20.3B **Privately Held**
SIC: 3273 Ready-mixed concrete
HQ: Hanson Aggregates New York Llc
  8505 Freport Pkwy Ste 500
  Irving TX 75063

(G-6722)
HOPES WINDOWS INC
84 Hopkins Ave (14701-2223)
P.O. Box 580 (14702-0580)
PHONE..................................716 665-5124
Randy Manita, *President*
John Brown, *Vice Pres*
Mary Lausterer, *Vice Pres*
Randall Manitta, *Vice Pres*
Brian Whalen, *Vice Pres*
▲ **EMP:** 250
SQ FT: 228,000
SALES (est): 54.5MM **Privately Held**
SIC: 3442 Sash, door or window: metal

(G-6723)
HYTECH TOOL & DIE INC
2202 Washington St (14701-2028)
PHONE..................................716 488-2796
William Swanson, *President*
David Reiser, *General Mgr*
▲ **EMP:** 8
SQ FT: 6,625
SALES (est): 1.3MM
SALES (corp-wide): 4.2MM **Privately Held**
WEB: www.hytechmold.com
SIC: 3544 Dies & die holders for metal cutting, forming, die casting; industrial molds
PA: Hytech Tool & Design Co
  12076 Edinboro Rd
  Edinboro PA 16412
  814 734-6000

(G-6724)
INTERNATIONAL ORD TECH INC
101 Harrison St (14701-6614)
PHONE..................................716 664-1100
Tammy H Snyder, *President*
Fred Callahan, *Vice Pres*
John Hedman, *Vice Pres*
Sandy Alexander, *Cust Mgr*
◆ **EMP:** 90
SALES (est): 13.3MM **Privately Held**
WEB: www.iotusa.net
SIC: 3469 3398 2874 Metal stampings; metal heat treating; phosphates

(G-6725)
JAMESTOWN ADVANCED PDTS CORP
2855 Girts Rd (14701-9666)
PHONE..................................716 483-3406
Wendi Lodestro, *Ch of Bd*
Wendi A Lodestro, *Ch of Bd*
Lee Lodestro, *Vice Pres*
EMP: 46
SALES (est): 16.2MM **Privately Held**
WEB: www.jamestownadvanced.com
SIC: 3444 Sheet metalwork

(G-6726)
JAMESTOWN AWNING INC
313 Steele St (14701-6287)
PHONE..................................716 483-1435
Mark Saxton, *President*
EMP: 9 **EST:** 1964
SQ FT: 5,000
SALES (est): 896.4K **Privately Held**
SIC: 2394 Awnings, fabric: made from purchased materials

(G-6727)
JAMESTOWN BRONZE WORKS INC
174 Hopkins Ave (14701-2290)
PHONE..................................716 665-2302
Robert R Knobloch, *President*
Wolfgang Michael Dunker, *Vice Pres*
Rexford Knapp, *Foreman/Supr*
▼ **EMP:** 5
SQ FT: 10,000
SALES: 500K **Privately Held**
WEB: www.jamestownbronze.com
SIC: 3369 3479 Nonferrous foundries; etching on metals

(G-6728)
JAMESTOWN FAB STL & SUP INC
1034 Allen St (14701-2302)
PHONE..................................716 665-2227
Mel Duggan, *President*
Malachai Ives, *Vice Pres*
Lee Luce, *Vice Pres*
Sue Livermore, *HR Admin*
EMP: 6
SQ FT: 20,000
SALES (est): 1.2MM **Privately Held**
SIC: 3446 Fire escapes, metal; railings, bannisters, guards, etc.: made from metal pipe; stairs, staircases, stair treads: prefabricated metal; fences or posts, ornamental iron or steel

(G-6729)
JAMESTOWN KITCHEN & BATH INC
1085 E 2nd St (14701-2243)
PHONE..................................716 665-2299
Donald Proctor, *President*
Andy Proctor, *Vice Pres*
Lora Proctor, *Admin Sec*
EMP: 7
SQ FT: 15,000
SALES (est): 1.2MM **Privately Held**
SIC: 3281 5712 Bathroom fixtures, cut stone; cabinet work, custom

(G-6730)
JAMESTOWN MACADAM INC (PA)
Also Called: Corbett Hill Gravel Products
74 Walden Ave (14701-2751)
P.O. Box 518, Celoron (14720-0518)
PHONE..................................716 664-5108
Michael Wellman, *Ch of Bd*
Roger R Olson, *President*
Tim Sickles, *Managing Dir*
Thomas Olson, *Vice Pres*
Chip Nelsen, *VP Opers*
EMP: 15
SQ FT: 3,000
SALES (est): 9MM **Privately Held**
WEB: www.jamestownmacadam.com
SIC: 2951 5032 Asphalt paving mixtures & blocks; gravel

(G-6731)
JAMESTOWN METAL PRODUCTS LLC
178 Blackstone Ave (14701-2297)
PHONE..................................716 665-5313
Richard McLeod, *President*
Christian Davis, *Project Mgr*
Mike Cook, *Opers Mgr*
Richard Brader, *Purchasing*
David Gniwecki, *Engineer*
▲ **EMP:** 105
SQ FT: 165,000
SALES (est): 26.6MM
SALES (corp-wide): 78.4MM **Privately Held**
SIC: 3821 Laboratory equipment: fume hoods, distillation racks, etc.

PA: Institutional Casework, Incorporated
1865 Hwy 641 North Paris
Paris TN 38242
731 642-4251

(G-6732)
JAMESTOWN SCIENTIFIC INDS LLC
1300 E 2nd St (14701-1915)
PHONE.................................716 665-3224
Bob Trusler, *Safety Mgr*
Kelly Haight, *Facilities Mgr*
Duane Smith, *Prgrmr*
John Pflaumer,
EMP: 13
SALES (est): 2.1MM **Privately Held**
WEB: www.jamestownscientific.com
SIC: 3069 Medical & laboratory rubber sundries & related products

(G-6733)
JEFFREY D MENOFF
785 Fairmount Ave (14701-2608)
PHONE.................................716 665-1468
Jeffrey D Menoff, *Owner*
EMP: 7
SALES (est): 619.4K **Privately Held**
SIC: 3843 Enamels, dentists'

(G-6734)
JOHNSON MCH & FIBR PDTS CO INC
142 Hopkins Ave (14701-2208)
PHONE.................................716 665-2003
Michael Marshall, *President*
Dale L Marshall, *Principal*
Richard D Thorpe, *Vice Pres*
Brian Maloy, *Manager*
EMP: 15
SQ FT: 11,000
SALES (est): 2.8MM **Privately Held**
SIC: 3599 3541 Machine shop, jobbing & repair; screw machines, automatic

(G-6735)
LAKESIDE CAPITAL CORPORATION
Also Called: Dahlstrom Roll Form
402 Chandler St Ste 2 (14701-3890)
P.O. Box 446 (14702-0446)
PHONE.................................716 664-2555
Robert G White, *Ch of Bd*
▲ EMP: 21
SQ FT: 73,800
SALES (est): 6.5MM **Privately Held**
WEB: www.dahlstromrollform.com
SIC: 3449 Custom roll formed products

(G-6736)
LARSON METAL MANUFACTURING CO
Also Called: Design Craft Division
1831 Mason Dr (14701-9290)
P.O. Box 1182 (14702-1182)
PHONE.................................716 665-6807
Melda W Larson, *President*
William E Larson, *Vice Pres*
EMP: 6
SQ FT: 31,000
SALES: 1MM **Privately Held**
SIC: 2522 Office furniture, except wood

(G-6737)
MASON CARVINGS INC
2871 Ivystone Dr (14701-9783)
PHONE.................................716 484-7884
Sam Mason, *President*
Thomas Mason, *Vice Pres*
Robert Parasiliti, *Manager*
Mary Jo Mason, *Admin Sec*
EMP: 8 EST: 1927
SQ FT: 18,000
SALES: 350K **Privately Held**
SIC: 2426 Carvings, furniture; wood

(G-6738)
MASTER MACHINE INCORPORATED
155 Blackstone Ave (14701-2203)
PHONE.................................716 487-2555
Steven Carolus, *President*
▲ EMP: 14
SQ FT: 15,000
SALES (est): 1.4MM **Privately Held**
SIC: 3599 Machine shop, jobbing & repair

(G-6739)
MILES MACHINE INC
85 Jones And Gifford Ave (14701-2826)
PHONE.................................716 484-6026
Richard Page, *President*
Michael Page, *Vice Pres*
Diane Start, *Office Mgr*
EMP: 11
SQ FT: 5,000
SALES: 1MM **Privately Held**
SIC: 3599 Machine shop, jobbing & repair

(G-6740)
NATIONAL WIRE & METAL TECH INC
22 Carolina St (14701-2311)
PHONE.................................716 661-9180
Bump Hedman, *President*
John Hedman, *Vice Pres*
Tammy Snyder, *Vice Pres*
Lucy Hedman, *Treasurer*
Sara Hays, *Info Tech Mgr*
▲ EMP: 25
SQ FT: 80,000
SALES (est): 4.4MM **Privately Held**
SIC: 3469 2392 Perforated metal, stamped; mops, floor & dust

(G-6741)
OGDEN NEWSPAPERS INC
Also Called: Post-Journal, The
15 W 2nd St (14701-5215)
P.O. Box 190 (14702-0190)
PHONE.................................716 487-1111
Michael Bird, *President*
Debbie Brunner, *Marketing Staff*
James Austin, *Manager*
EMP: 200 **Privately Held**
SIC: 2711 Commercial printing & newspaper publishing combined
HQ: The Ogden Newspapers Inc
1500 Main St
Wheeling WV 26003
304 233-0100

(G-6742)
POST JOURNAL
412 Murray Ave (14701-4742)
PHONE.................................716 487-1111
Debra Brunner, *Principal*
EMP: 14
SALES (est): 1.1MM **Privately Held**
SIC: 2711 Commercial printing & newspaper publishing combined; newspapers, publishing & printing

(G-6743)
PREMIER FINISHING INC
85 Jones And Gifford Ave (14701-2826)
PHONE.................................716 484-6271
Jack Sase, *President*
Gary Samson, *General Mgr*
EMP: 11 EST: 2013
SALES (est): 548.3K **Privately Held**
SIC: 3471 Plating of metals or formed products

(G-6744)
PRODUCTO CORPORATION
Also Called: Ring Division Producto Machine
2980 Turner Rd (14701-9024)
P.O. Box 490 (14702)
PHONE.................................716 484-7131
Newman Marsilius, *President*
Alan Smith, *Engineer*
Maynard L Cotter, *Branch Mgr*
EMP: 113
SQ FT: 40,800
SALES (corp-wide): 65.8MM **Privately Held**
WEB: www.ringprecision.com
SIC: 3541 3542 3544 Machine tools, metal cutting type; machine tools, metal forming type; special dies, tools, jigs & fixtures
HQ: The Producto Corporation
800 Union Ave
Bridgeport CT 06607
203 366-3224

(G-6745)
ROLLFORM OF JAMESTOWN INC
Also Called: Precision Locker
181 Blackstone Ave (14701-2203)
PHONE.................................716 665-5310
Edward F Ruttenberg, *President*
Mike Mattern, *General Mgr*
▲ EMP: 17
SQ FT: 43,000
SALES (est): 4.9MM **Privately Held**
WEB: www.rollform.com
SIC: 3449 Custom roll formed products

(G-6746)
SHRED CENTER
20 Carroll St (14701-4755)
PHONE.................................716 664-3052
Ronald Mazonie, *Owner*
Monica Mazany, *Vice Pres*
EMP: 6 EST: 2008
SALES (est): 557K **Privately Held**
SIC: 3559 Tire shredding machinery

(G-6747)
SKF USA INC
Also Called: MRC Bearings
402 Chandler St (14701-3890)
P.O. Box 263, Falconer (14733-0263)
PHONE.................................716 661-2600
Tom Lunz, *Engineer*
Rolf Jacobson, *Branch Mgr*
Ned Baudo, *Training Spec*
EMP: 61
SALES (corp-wide): 9.2B **Privately Held**
WEB: www.skfusa.com
SIC: 3053 3829 3562 Gaskets & sealing devices; oil seals, rubber; vibration meters, analyzers & calibrators; ball bearings & parts
HQ: Skf Usa Inc.
890 Forty Foot Rd
Lansdale PA 19446
267 436-6000

(G-6748)
SPARTAN PUBLISHING INC
Also Called: Southern Tier Pennysaver
2 Harding Ave (14701-4778)
PHONE.................................716 664-7373
Robert V Stanley, *President*
Sandra Stanley, *Treasurer*
EMP: 12
SQ FT: 4,000
SALES (est): 530K **Privately Held**
SIC: 2711 Newspapers, publishing & printing

(G-6749)
SPRAY-TECH FINISHING INC
443 Buffalo St (14701-2262)
P.O. Box 278 (14702-0278)
PHONE.................................716 664-6317
David Dawson, *President*
Guy Lombardo, *Treasurer*
Harold Andersen, *Admin Sec*
EMP: 8
SQ FT: 80,000
SALES: 1.1MM **Privately Held**
WEB: www.spraytechfinishing.com
SIC: 2952 Coating compounds, tar

(G-6750)
STAR TUBING CORP
53 River St (14701-3806)
P.O. Box 904 (14702-0904)
PHONE.................................716 483-1703
Gary F Johnson, *President*
Gary Johnson, *President*
Sandra Johnson, *Vice Pres*
Charles A Lawson, *Shareholder*
EMP: 6
SQ FT: 46,000
SALES (est): 1.3MM **Privately Held**
WEB: www.startubing.com
SIC: 3498 Tube fabricating (contract bending & shaping)

(G-6751)
SUHOR INDUSTRIES INC
Also Called: GM Pre Cast Products
584 Buffalo St (14701-2307)
PHONE.................................716 483-6818
Joel Suhor, *President*
EMP: 5

SALES (corp-wide): 2.2MM **Privately Held**
WEB: www.wilberservices.com
SIC: 3272 Burial vaults, concrete or precast terrazzo
PA: Suhor Industries, Inc.
72 Oconnor Rd
Fairport NY 14450
585 377-5100

(G-6752)
SUIT-KOTE CORPORATION
57 Lister St (14701-2701)
PHONE.................................716 664-3750
George Ginter, *Branch Mgr*
EMP: 35
SALES (corp-wide): 234.8MM **Privately Held**
WEB: www.suit-kote.com
SIC: 2951 1611 Asphalt & asphaltic paving mixtures (not from refineries); highway & street paving contractor
PA: Suit-Kote Corporation
1911 Lorings Crossing Rd
Cortland NY 13045
607 753-1100

(G-6753)
SUNSET RIDGE HOLDINGS INC
Also Called: Electric Motor Specialty
490-496 Crescent St (14701)
PHONE.................................716 487-1458
Rebecca Ames, *President*
EMP: 5
SALES: 230K **Privately Held**
SIC: 7694 7699 Armature rewinding shops; pumps & pumping equipment repair

(G-6754)
SUPERIOR ENERGY SERVICES INC
1720 Foote Avenue Ext (14701-9385)
PHONE.................................716 483-0100
EMP: 7 **Publicly Held**
SIC: 1389 Servicing oil & gas wells
PA: Superior Energy Services, Inc.
1001 La St Ste 2900
Houston TX 77002

(G-6755)
SUPERIOR STL DOOR TRIM CO INC
154 Fairmount Ave (14701-2866)
PHONE.................................716 665-3256
Ellen Connell, *President*
Bevan Connell, *Vice Pres*
EMP: 15
SALES: 5MM **Privately Held**
SIC: 3442 Metal doors, sash & trim

(G-6756)
SUPERIOR WOOD TURNINGS
118 E 1st St (14701-5430)
P.O. Box 3341 (14702-3341)
PHONE.................................716 483-1254
Shane Goodwill, *Partner*
Doug Wheeler, *Partner*
EMP: 16
SQ FT: 30,000
SALES (est): 1.9MM **Privately Held**
WEB: www.superiorwoodturnings.com
SIC: 2499 Carved & turned wood

(G-6757)
TILAROS BAKERY INC
32 Willard St Ste 34 (14701-6937)
PHONE.................................716 488-3209
Robert Tilaro, *President*
Donald Sholl, *Treasurer*
EMP: 7
SQ FT: 1,250
SALES (est): 709K **Privately Held**
SIC: 2051 Bakery: wholesale or wholesale/retail combined

(G-6758)
TITANX ENGINE COOLING INC
2258 Allen Street Ext (14701-2330)
PHONE.................................716 665-7129
Stefan Nordstrm, *CEO*
Matthew Moore, *President*
Arnaud Contet, *Vice Pres*
Ulf Hellgesson, *Vice Pres*
Mats Hman, *Vice Pres*
▲ EMP: 320

SALES (est): 148.5MM
SALES (corp-wide): 237.5MM **Privately Held**
SIC: 3714 Air conditioner parts, motor vehicle
HQ: Titanx Engine Cooling Ab
Klockskogsvagen 9
Solvesborg 294 7
456 550-00

(G-6759)
UPSTATE NIAGARA COOP INC
223 Fluvanna Ave (14701-2050)
PHONE.................................716 484-7178
Michael Conklin, *Manager*
EMP: 20
SALES (corp-wide): 893.9MM **Privately Held**
SIC: 2026 0241 5143 Milk processing (pasteurizing, homogenizing, bottling); milk production; dairy products, except dried or canned
PA: Upstate Niagara Cooperative, Inc.
25 Anderson Rd
Buffalo NY 14225
716 892-3156

(G-6760)
VAC AIR SERVICE INC
Also Called: Ameri Serv South
1295 E 2nd St (14701-1914)
P.O. Box 940 (14702-0940)
PHONE.................................716 665-2206
EMP: 11
SQ FT: 4,000
SALES (est): 1.4MM **Privately Held**
SIC: 3563 Mfg Air/Gas Compressors

(G-6761)
WEBER-KNAPP COMPANY (PA)
441 Chandler St (14701-3895)
PHONE.................................716 484-9135
Rex Mc Cray, *Ch of Bd*
Donald Pangborn, *Senior VP*
Larry Troxell, *Foreman/Supr*
Alex Pickett, *Engineer*
Kory Slye, *Engineer*
▲ **EMP:** 110 **EST:** 1920
SQ FT: 146,000
SALES (est): 23MM **Privately Held**
WEB: www.weberknapp.com
SIC: 3429 Furniture hardware

(G-6762)
WILSTON ENTERPRISES INC
Also Called: Industrial Welding & Fabg Co
121 Jackson Ave (14701-2441)
PHONE.................................716 483-1411
Susan L Wilston, *President*
Eugene Wilston, *Vice Pres*
EMP: 18 **EST:** 2007
SALES (est): 1.6MM **Privately Held**
SIC: 3441 Building components, structural steel

Jamesville
Onondaga County

(G-6763)
B & B LUMBER COMPANY INC (PA)
4800 Solvay Rd (13078-9530)
P.O. Box 420 (13078-0420)
PHONE.................................866 282-0582
Jeffrey H Booher, *Ch of Bd*
Brent Booher, *Principal*
Brigham Booher, *Principal*
Pat Buff, *Principal*
Gary R Booher, *Vice Pres*
EMP: 130
SQ FT: 300,000
SALES (est): 21.4MM **Privately Held**
SIC: 2448 2421 2426 Pallets, wood; lumber: rough, sawed or planed; hardwood dimension & flooring mills

(G-6764)
B&B ALBANY PALLET COMPANY LLC
4800 Solvay Rd (13078-9530)
P.O. Box 420 (13078-0420)
PHONE.................................315 492-1786
Ruth Manasse, *Vice Pres*

Michael Parvis, *Mfg Staff*
Jane Diehl, *Accountant*
Eric Smith,
EMP: 30 **EST:** 1966
SQ FT: 9,500
SALES: 3.7MM
SALES (corp-wide): 21.4MM **Privately Held**
SIC: 2448 Pallets, wood
PA: B & B Lumber Company Inc.
4800 Solvay Rd
Jamesville NY 13078
866 282-0582

(G-6765)
CHRISTIANA MILLWORK INC (PA)
4755 Jamesville Rd (13078)
PHONE.................................315 492-9099
Lawrence J Christiana, *President*
Ross Tuzzo Lino, *President*
EMP: 26
SQ FT: 26,000
SALES (est): 4.1MM **Privately Held**
SIC: 2431 Millwork

(G-6766)
HANSON AGGREGATES NEW YORK LLC
2237 Allen St (13078)
PHONE.................................716 665-4620
Scott Wheaton, *Manager*
EMP: 10
SALES (corp-wide): 20.3B **Privately Held**
SIC: 3241 Natural cement
HQ: Hanson Aggregates New York Llc
8505 Freport Pkwy Ste 500
Irving TX 75063

(G-6767)
HANSON AGGREGATES NEW YORK LLC
4800 Jamesville Rd (13078)
PHONE.................................315 469-5501
Dan Meehan, *Vice Pres*
Daniel Meehan, *Vice Pres*
Liz Simmons, *Office Mgr*
EMP: 120
SALES (corp-wide): 20.3B **Privately Held**
SIC: 3273 Ready-mixed concrete
HQ: Hanson Aggregates New York Llc
8505 Freport Pkwy Ste 500
Irving TX 75063

(G-6768)
HANSON AGGREGATES PA LLC
4800 Jamesville Rd (13078)
PHONE.................................315 469-5501
Dan Meehan, *Vice Pres*
Gary Eno, *Branch Mgr*
EMP: 20
SALES (corp-wide): 20.3B **Privately Held**
SIC: 1442 1422 Common sand mining; crushed & broken limestone
HQ: Hanson Aggregates Pennsylvania, Llc
7660 Imperial Way
Allentown PA 18195
610 366-4626

(G-6769)
PREMIER HARDWOOD PRODUCTS INC
4800 Solvay Rd (13078-9530)
P.O. Box 420 (13078-0420)
PHONE.................................315 492-1786
Brigham Booher, *Ch of Bd*
Lawrence G English, *President*
Jeffrey Booher, *Vice Pres*
Russ Shamblen, *Purch Agent*
Gary Booher, *Treasurer*
EMP: 50
SQ FT: 80,000
SALES (est): 9.5MM **Privately Held**
WEB: www.premierhardwood.com
SIC: 2426 Hardwood dimension & flooring mills

(G-6770)
ROBINSON CONCRETE INC
3537 Apulia Rd (13078-9663)
PHONE.................................315 492-6200
Micheal Vitale, *President*
EMP: 12

SALES (corp-wide): 24MM **Privately Held**
SIC: 3273 Ready-mixed concrete
PA: Robinson Concrete, Inc.
3486 Franklin Street Rd
Auburn NY 13021
315 253-6666

(G-6771)
U-CUT ENTERPRISES INC
4800 Solvay Rd (13078-9530)
P.O. Box 420 (13078-0420)
PHONE.................................315 492-9316
John R Storrier Jr, *President*
Gay Vadala, *Office Mgr*
EMP: 22
SQ FT: 8,000
SALES: 2.5MM **Privately Held**
WEB: www.u-cut.com
SIC: 3599 Machine shop, jobbing & repair

Java Village
Wyoming County

(G-6772)
FARRANT SCREW MACHINE PRODUCTS
Gulf Rd (14083)
PHONE.................................585 457-3213
Thomas Farrant, *President*
EMP: 7
SQ FT: 13,000
SALES: 1MM **Privately Held**
SIC: 3599 Machine shop, jobbing & repair

Jay
Essex County

(G-6773)
ADIRONDACK LIFE INC (PA)
Also Called: Adirondack Life Magazine
Rr 9 Box North (12941)
P.O. Box 410 (12941-0410)
PHONE.................................518 946-2191
Barry Silverstein, *President*
Janine Sorrell, *Business Mgr*
Marty Kilburn, *Director*
Kelly Hofschneider, *Art Dir*
Betsy Folwell, *Creative Dir*
EMP: 18
SALES (est): 1.8MM **Privately Held**
WEB: www.adirondacklife.com
SIC: 2721 Magazines: publishing only, not printed on site

(G-6774)
ADIRONDACK LIFE INC
Also Called: Adirondack Life Magazine
12961 Nys Route 9n (12941-5715)
PHONE.................................518 946-2191
Linda Bedard, *Advt Staff*
Barry Silverstein, *Branch Mgr*
EMP: 8
SALES (est): 790.9K
SALES (corp-wide): 1.8MM **Privately Held**
SIC: 2721 Magazines: publishing only, not printed on site
PA: Adirondack Life Inc
Rr 9 Box North
Jay NY 12941
518 946-2191

(G-6775)
WILLIAM WARD LOGGING
Valley Rd (12941)
P.O. Box 300 (12941-0300)
PHONE.................................518 946-7826
William L Ward Sr, *Owner*
EMP: 17
SALES (est): 1.1MM **Privately Held**
SIC: 2411 Logging

Jefferson Valley
Westchester County

(G-6776)
GEORGE PONTE INC
Also Called: Gpi Equipment Company
500 E Main St (10535-1100)
PHONE.................................914 243-4202
George Ponte, *President*
EMP: 5
SQ FT: 4,000
SALES (est): 792.4K **Privately Held**
WEB: www.gpiusa.com
SIC: 3559 5084 Pharmaceutical machinery; materials handling machinery

(G-6777)
LONGSTEM ORGANIZERS INC
380 E Main St (10535-1200)
P.O. Box 22 (10535-0022)
PHONE.................................914 777-2174
Alison Albanese, *President*
Gregery Alabnese, *Vice Pres*
▲ **EMP:** 6
SQ FT: 4,500
SALES (est): 600K **Privately Held**
SIC: 3449 Miscellaneous metalwork

Jeffersonville
Sullivan County

(G-6778)
A S A PRECISION CO INC
295 Jffersonville N Br Rd (12748-5825)
PHONE.................................845 482-4870
Steve Schmidt, *President*
Rich Schmidt, *Vice Pres*
EMP: 6 **EST:** 1961
SQ FT: 6,400
SALES (est): 780K **Privately Held**
SIC: 3826 Analytical instruments

(G-6779)
JEFFERSONVILLE VOLUNTEER
49 Callicoon Center Rd (12748)
P.O. Box 396 (12748-0396)
PHONE.................................845 482-3110
Dawnrenee Hauschild, *Chairman*
EMP: 50
SALES: 534.6K **Privately Held**
SIC: 3713 Ambulance bodies

Jericho
Nassau County

(G-6780)
BAMBERGER POLYMERS INTL CORP
2 Jericho Plz Ste 109 (11753-1681)
PHONE.................................516 622-3600
Steven Goldberg, *President*
Dennis Don, *Exec VP*
Alfonso Garcia, *Vice Pres*
Christine Levy, *Vice Pres*
Paul Coco, *CFO*
◆ **EMP:** 10
SQ FT: 11,000
SALES (est): 1.1MM **Privately Held**
WEB: www.bambergerpolymers.com
SIC: 2821 Plasticizer/additive based plastic materials
PA: Bamberger Polymers Corp.
2 Jericho Plz Ste 109
Jericho NY 11753

(G-6781)
CFFCO USA INC
55 Jericho Tpke Ste 302 (11753-1013)
PHONE.................................718 747-1118
James Yan, *CEO*
Juan Lopez, *Vice Pres*
▲ **EMP:** 7
SQ FT: 1,800
SALES: 11MM **Privately Held**
WEB: www.cffco.com
SIC: 2499 Fencing, docks & other outdoor wood structural products

Jericho - Nassau County (G-6782)

(G-6782)
CLOUDSCALE365 INC (PA)
30 Jericho Executive Plz (11753-1057)
PHONE..................888 608-6245
Pat Hannon, *COO*
Eric Church, *CTO*
EMP: 3 **EST:** 2015
SALES (est): 1.7MM **Privately Held**
SIC: 7372 Business oriented computer software

(G-6783)
CONTINENTAL KRAFT CORP
100 Jericho Quadrangle # 219 (11753-2708)
PHONE..................516 681-9090
Peter J Bogan, *Ch of Bd*
David Landau, *President*
Steve Roth, *Treasurer*
▼ **EMP:** 6
SQ FT: 2,264
SALES (est): 998.3K **Privately Held**
WEB: www.continentalkraft.com
SIC: 2631 Kraft linerboard

(G-6784)
D SQUARED TECHNOLOGIES INC
71 Birchwood Park Dr (11753-2238)
PHONE..................516 932-7319
David Delman, *President*
EMP: 5
SALES (est): 246.2K **Privately Held**
WEB: www.d2tech.net
SIC: 3949 Exercise equipment

(G-6785)
DARBY DENTAL SUPPLY
105 Executive Ct (11753)
PHONE..................516 688-6421
Gary Rosenberg, *Principal*
Anthony Ricigilano, *Vice Pres*
Rich Parent, *Analyst*
EMP: 9
SALES (est): 1.7MM **Privately Held**
SIC: 3843 Dental equipment & supplies

(G-6786)
ELARA FDSRVICE DISPOSABLES LLC
Also Called: Elara Brands
420 Jericho Tpke Ste 320 (11753-1319)
PHONE..................877 893-3244
Daniel Grinberg, *President*
Ernesto Grinberg, *Chairman*
Donna Cherulnik, *Vice Pres*
Darci Rodriguez, *Vice Pres*
Maria Buono, *Controller*
▲ **EMP:** 7
SALES: 12MM **Privately Held**
SIC: 3089 5113 Work gloves, plastic; bags, paper & disposable plastic

(G-6787)
EVENT JOURNAL INC
366 N Broadway Ste 209 (11753-2000)
PHONE..................516 470-1811
Dawn Strain, *President*
Marisa Kerby, *Opers Staff*
Laura Miller, *Manager*
EMP: 10
SALES (est): 570.5K **Privately Held**
SIC: 2711 Newspapers, publishing & printing

(G-6788)
EXCHANGE MY MAIL INC
30 Jericho Executive Plz 100c (11753-1025)
PHONE..................516 605-1835
Sal Dipiazza, *CEO*
Steven Daneshgar, *Exec VP*
EMP: 15
SQ FT: 2,500
SALES (est): 1.7MM **Privately Held**
WEB: www.exchangemymail.com
SIC: 7372 Application computer software

(G-6789)
FIRETRONICS INC (PA)
50 Jericho Tpke (11753-1014)
PHONE..................516 997-5151
Gail Miller, *President*
John Moreno, *Accountant*
EMP: 7

SALES (est): 610.7K **Privately Held**
SIC: 3669 Fire detection systems, electric

(G-6790)
HEALTH CARE COMPLIANCE (HQ)
30 Jericho Executive Plz 400c (11753-1098)
PHONE..................516 478-4100
Mitchell Diamond, *CEO*
Benjamin Diamond, *President*
Lise Rauzi Chc, *Vice Pres*
EMP: 17
SQ FT: 5,350
SALES (est): 3.3MM
SALES (corp-wide): 247.6MM **Publicly Held**
WEB: www.hccsonline.com
SIC: 7372 Educational computer software
PA: Healthstream, Inc.
209 10th Ave S Ste 450
Nashville TN 37203
615 301-3100

(G-6791)
INTERNATIONAL TIME PRODUCTS
410 Jericho Tpke Ste 110 (11753-1318)
PHONE..................516 931-0005
Raymond T D'Alessio, *Owner*
EMP: 6
SALES (est): 240K **Privately Held**
SIC: 3172 Watch straps, except metal

(G-6792)
JPM FINE WOODWORKING LLC
103 Estate Dr (11753-2829)
PHONE..................516 236-7605
Mitchell Kahn,
EMP: 6
SALES (est): 265.3K **Privately Held**
SIC: 3999 Novelties, bric-a-brac & hobby kits

(G-6793)
KPP LTD
Also Called: Admor Blinds & Window Fashion
200 Robbins Ln Unit C2 (11753-2341)
PHONE..................516 338-5201
Michael Parker, *President*
Dan Kossman, *Vice Pres*
Rita Parker, *Treasurer*
EMP: 7
SQ FT: 1,700
SALES (est): 1MM **Privately Held**
WEB: www.admorblinds.com
SIC: 2591 7641 Blinds vertical; reupholstery & furniture repair

(G-6794)
NAK INTERNATIONAL CORP (PA)
131 Jericho Tpke Ste 204 (11753-1017)
PHONE..................516 334-6245
Allan Seligson, *President*
Dean Musi, *Vice Pres*
▲ **EMP:** 58 **EST:** 1986
SALES (est): 14.8MM **Privately Held**
SIC: 3463 Nonferrous forgings

(G-6795)
NCR CORPORATION
30 Jericho Executive Plz (11753-1057)
PHONE..................516 876-7200
Paul Buscemi, *Manager*
EMP: 200
SALES (corp-wide): 6.5B **Publicly Held**
WEB: www.ncr.com
SIC: 3571 7622 Electronic computers; radio & television repair
PA: Ncr Corporation
864 Spring St Nw
Atlanta GA 30308
937 445-5000

(G-6796)
PARKSIDE PRINTING CO INC
4 Tompkins Ave (11753-1920)
PHONE..................516 933-5423
William Goldstein, *President*
Ellen Goldstein, *Corp Secy*
EMP: 10
SQ FT: 10,000

SALES (est): 1MM **Privately Held**
SIC: 2752 Commercial printing, lithographic

(G-6797)
PITNEY BOWES INC
200 Robbins Ln Unit B2 (11753-2341)
PHONE..................516 822-0900
Dan Hindman, *Branch Mgr*
EMP: 35
SALES (corp-wide): 3.5B **Publicly Held**
SIC: 3579 7359 Postage meters; business machine & electronic equipment rental services
PA: Pitney Bowes Inc.
3001 Summer St Ste 3
Stamford CT 06905
203 356-5000

(G-6798)
PRODUCT STATION INC
366 N Broadway Ste 410 (11753-2000)
PHONE..................516 942-4220
Scott Roberts, *President*
Peter Oliveto, *Vice Pres*
EMP: 11
SALES (est): 1.1MM **Privately Held**
SIC: 3613 Distribution cutouts

(G-6799)
RESOURCE CAPITAL FUNDS LP
2 Jericho Plz Ste 103 (11753-1661)
PHONE..................631 692-9111
Sherri Croasdale, *Branch Mgr*
EMP: 5
SALES (corp-wide): 110.1K **Privately Held**
SIC: 1481 Mine development, nonmetallic minerals
PA: Resource Capital Funds Lp
1400 16th St Ste 200
Denver CO 80202
720 946-1444

(G-6800)
ROYCE ASSOCIATES A LTD PARTNR
366 N Broadway Ste 400 (11753-2000)
PHONE..................516 367-6298
Joanna Moskowitz, *Manager*
EMP: 5
SALES (corp-wide): 18.3MM **Privately Held**
SIC: 2869 3089 2842 2851 Industrial organic chemicals; plastic processing; polishing preparations & related products; varnishes; chemical preparations
PA: Royce Associates, A Limited Partnership
35 Carlton Ave
East Rutherford NJ 07073
201 438-5200

(G-6801)
SATNAM DISTRIBUTORS LLC
Also Called: Lion & Bear Distributors
200 Robbins Ln Unit B (11753-2341)
PHONE..................516 802-0600
Rachna Sachdev,
EMP: 3
SQ FT: 6,000
SALES: 4.5MM **Privately Held**
SIC: 2834 Tablets, pharmaceutical

(G-6802)
SC MEDICAL OVERSEAS INC
Also Called: Orfit Industries America
350 Jericho Tpke Ste 302 (11753-1317)
PHONE..................516 935-8500
Steven A Cuypres, *President*
Martin Ratner, *Vice Pres*
▲ **EMP:** 9
SQ FT: 3,000
SALES: 780K **Privately Held**
WEB: www.orfit.com
SIC: 2821 Plastics materials & resins

(G-6803)
SD EAGLE GLOBAL INC
2 Kay St (11753-2648)
PHONE..................516 822-1778
Shaojun Liu, *President*
EMP: 7
SALES (est): 409.9K **Privately Held**
SIC: 2211 Denims

(G-6804)
SJ ASSOCIATES INC (PA)
500 N Broadway Ste 159 (11753-2111)
PHONE..................516 942-3232
Bruce Joseph, *President*
EMP: 25
SQ FT: 3,000
SALES (est): 5.7MM **Privately Held**
SIC: 3559 5065 Electronic component making machinery; electronic parts

(G-6805)
SKD DISTRIBUTION CORP
28 Westchester Ave (11753-1442)
PHONE..................718 525-6000
Richard Marks, *President*
Harold Marks, *Vice Pres*
Rachel Marks, *Art Dir*
▲ **EMP:** 30
SQ FT: 45,000
SALES (est): 4.9MM **Privately Held**
SIC: 3089 3086 Novelties, plastic; plastics foam products

(G-6806)
VERTARIB INC
Also Called: Thermacon Tank Insulation
471 N Broadway Ste 196 (11753-2106)
PHONE..................561 683-0888
Alan Dinow, *CEO*
EMP: 5 **Privately Held**
SIC: 3443 Tank towers, metal plate
PA: Vertarib Inc.
9005 Southern Blvd
West Palm Beach FL 33411

(G-6807)
WAGNERS LLC (PA)
366 N Broadway Ste 402 (11753-2027)
P.O. Box 54 (11753-0054)
PHONE..................516 933-6580
Harry Tyre, *President*
Donald P Corr, *Senior VP*
Danielle Traietta, *Engineer*
Maggie Keller, *Controller*
Brenda Lontine, *Manager*
EMP: 6
SQ FT: 1,500
SALES: 50MM **Privately Held**
WEB: www.wagnerproducts.com
SIC: 2048 Bird food, prepared

Johnson City
Broome County

(G-6808)
GAGNE ASSOCIATES INC
41 Commercial Dr (13790-4111)
P.O. Box 487 (13790-0487)
PHONE..................800 800-5954
Mary Ann Holland, *Ch of Bd*
Jeff Sampson, *President*
William Coak, *Vice Pres*
Kim Prentice, *Vice Pres*
Bill Clark, *Marketing Mgr*
▲ **EMP:** 25 **EST:** 1961
SQ FT: 37,250
SALES (est): 5.3MM **Privately Held**
WEB: www.gagneinc.com
SIC: 3089 5063 Plastic hardware & building products; lighting fittings & accessories

(G-6809)
GANNETT CO INC
Also Called: Gannett NY Production Facility
10 Gannett Dr (13790-2260)
PHONE..................607 352-2702
Kevin Crane, *Manager*
EMP: 100
SALES (corp-wide): 3.1B **Publicly Held**
WEB: www.gannett.com
SIC: 2741 Miscellaneous publishing
PA: Gannett Co., Inc.
7950 Jones Branch Dr
Mc Lean VA 22102
703 854-6000

(G-6810)
HI-TECH INDUSTRIES NY INC
23 Ozalid Rd (13790-2306)
PHONE..................607 217-7361
Douglas Gardner, *Ch of Bd*

GEOGRAPHIC SECTION

Johnstown - Fulton County (G-6834)

Douglas P Sterns, *President*
EMP: 28
SQ FT: 8,900
SALES (est): 3.7MM **Privately Held**
SIC: 3444 3599 Sheet metalwork; machine shop, jobbing & repair

(G-6811)
INNOVATION ASSOCIATES INC
530 Columbia Dr Ste 101 (13790-1096)
PHONE..................................607 798-9376
Mary Reno, *CEO*
Joseph Harry Boyer, *Chairman*
Thomas Boyer, *COO*
Doyle Jensen, *Exec VP*
Phil L Samples, *Vice Pres*
▲ EMP: 150
SQ FT: 18,700
SALES (est): 62.7MM **Privately Held**
WEB: www.innovat.com
SIC: 3559 8711 Pharmaceutical machinery; consulting engineer

(G-6812)
J H ROBOTICS INC
109 Main St (13790-2482)
PHONE..................................607 729-3758
John F Hartman, *Ch of Bd*
Jason Colsten, *Engineer*
Gerald Sensenig, *Engineer*
Cindy Warner, *VP Finance*
EMP: 35
SQ FT: 41,000
SALES (est): 9.7MM **Privately Held**
WEB: www.jhrobotics.com
SIC: 3494 3569 3545 Valves & pipe fittings; robots, assembly line: industrial & commercial; machine tool accessories

(G-6813)
KLEMMT ORTHOTICS & PROSTHETICS
Also Called: Klemmt Orthopaedic Services
130 Oakdale Rd (13790-1758)
PHONE..................................607 770-4400
Marcus Klemmt, *President*
Julie Klemmt, *Principal*
EMP: 8
SQ FT: 3,000
SALES (est): 680K **Privately Held**
SIC: 3842 5999 Orthopedic appliances; prosthetic appliances; orthopedic & prosthesis applications

(G-6814)
KNUCKLEHEAD EMBROIDERY INC
800 Valley Plz Ste 4 (13790-1046)
PHONE..................................607 797-2725
Dave Cobb, *President*
Diane Cobb, *Vice Pres*
Matt Heier, *Treasurer*
Bridget Heier, *Admin Sec*
EMP: 5
SQ FT: 1,500
SALES (est): 500K **Privately Held**
WEB: www.knuckleheadinc.com
SIC: 2262 5699 2759 2395 Embossing: manmade fiber & silk broadwoven fabrics; customized clothing & apparel; screen printing; art needlework: made from purchased materials

(G-6815)
NORTH POINT TECHNOLOGIES
520 Columbia Dr Ste 105 (13790-3305)
PHONE..................................607 238-1114
Robert Lee, *Owner*
Lisa Lee, *Co-Owner*
Richard J Wrobleski, *Administration*
EMP: 26
SALES (est): 3.9MM **Privately Held**
SIC: 3625 Industrial controls: push button, selector switches, pilot

(G-6816)
PELLA CORPORATION
Also Called: Pella Window Door
800 Valley Plz Ste 5 (13790-1046)
PHONE..................................607 223-2023
Chris Ward, *Branch Mgr*
EMP: 316
SALES (corp-wide): 1.9B **Privately Held**
SIC: 2431 Windows, wood
PA: Pella Corporation
 102 Main St
 Pella IA 50219
 641 621-1000

(G-6817)
PELLA CORPORATION
Also Called: Pella Window Door
800 Valley Plz Ste 5 (13790-1046)
PHONE..................................607 231-8550
Chris Ward, *Branch Mgr*
EMP: 316
SALES (corp-wide): 1.9B **Privately Held**
SIC: 2431 Windows, wood
PA: Pella Corporation
 102 Main St
 Pella IA 50219
 641 621-1000

(G-6818)
PELLA CORPORATION
Also Called: Pella Window Door
800 Valley Plz Ste 5 (13790-1046)
PHONE..................................607 238-2812
Chris Ward, *Branch Mgr*
EMP: 316
SALES (corp-wide): 1.9B **Privately Held**
SIC: 2431 Windows, wood
PA: Pella Corporation
 102 Main St
 Pella IA 50219
 641 621-1000

(G-6819)
PELLA CORPORATION
Also Called: Pella Window Door
800 Valley Plz Ste 5 (13790-1046)
PHONE..................................607 238-2812
Chris Ward, *Branch Mgr*
EMP: 316
SALES (corp-wide): 1.9B **Privately Held**
SIC: 2431 Windows, wood
PA: Pella Corporation
 102 Main St
 Pella IA 50219
 641 621-1000

(G-6820)
PELLA CORPORATION
Also Called: Pella Window Door
800 Valley Plz Ste 5 (13790-1046)
PHONE..................................607 231-8550
Chris Ward, *Branch Mgr*
EMP: 316
SALES (corp-wide): 1.9B **Privately Held**
SIC: 2431 Windows, wood
PA: Pella Corporation
 102 Main St
 Pella IA 50219
 641 621-1000

(G-6821)
ROB SALAMIDA COMPANY INC
71 Pratt Ave Ste 1 (13790-2255)
PHONE..................................607 729-4868
Robert A Salamida, *President*
▲ EMP: 19 EST: 1975
SQ FT: 9,136
SALES (est): 4.3MM **Privately Held**
WEB: www.spiedie.com
SIC: 2035 2099 Seasonings & sauces, except tomato & dry; food preparations

(G-6822)
UPSTATE OFFICE LIQUIDATORS INC
Also Called: Upstate Office Furniture
718 Azon Rd (13790-1725)
PHONE..................................607 722-9234
Sylvia J Kerber, *President*
Wayne Kerber Jr, *Vice Pres*
▲ EMP: 11
SQ FT: 45,000
SALES (est): 1.9MM **Privately Held**
WEB: www.upstateofficefurniture.com
SIC: 2521 Wood office furniture

Johnstown
Fulton County

(G-6823)
ARROW LEATHER FINISHING INC
228 Pleasant Ave (12095-1107)
PHONE..................................518 762-3121
Joseph De Cristofaro, *President*
▲ EMP: 50
SQ FT: 18,000
SALES (est): 6.7MM **Privately Held**
SIC: 3111 Finishing of leather

(G-6824)
BENJAMIN MOORE & CO
Union Ave Ext (12095)
P.O. Box 220 (12095-0220)
PHONE..................................518 736-1723
Robert Nowicki, *Manager*
EMP: 40
SQ FT: 2,403
SALES (corp-wide): 242.1B **Publicly Held**
WEB: www.benjaminmoore.com
SIC: 2851 5198 Paints & allied products; paints
HQ: Benjamin Moore & Co.
 101 Paragon Dr
 Montvale NJ 07645
 201 573-9600

(G-6825)
ELECTRO-METRICS CORPORATION
231 Enterprise Rd (12095-3340)
PHONE..................................518 762-2600
Leslie Apple, *CEO*
▼ EMP: 34
SQ FT: 42,500
SALES (est): 7.8MM **Privately Held**
WEB: www.emihq.com
SIC: 3663 Radio & TV communications equipment

(G-6826)
EMPIRE ARCHTCTURAL SYSTEMS INC
125 Belzano Rd (12095-9755)
PHONE..................................518 773-5109
Paul Lusenhop, *President*
EMP: 35
SQ FT: 40,000
SALES (est): 4.1MM **Privately Held**
SIC: 2541 3442 Store fronts, prefabricated: wood; store fronts, prefabricated, metal

(G-6827)
EUPHRATES INC
230 Enterprise Rd (12095-3338)
P.O. Box 977 (12095-0977)
PHONE..................................518 762-3488
Hamdi Ulukaya, *President*
▲ EMP: 87
SALES: 34MM **Privately Held**
WEB: www.euphrates.com
SIC: 2022 Natural cheese

(G-6828)
FAGE USA DAIRY INDUSTRY INC
Also Called: Fage USA Yogurt Mfg Plant
1 Opportunity Dr (12095-3349)
PHONE..................................518 762-5912
Athanasios Filippou, *CEO*
Ryan Joy, *Business Mgr*
Jeff Scipione, *Business Mgr*
Robert Shea, *Corp Secy*
Spyridon Giantatas, *Vice Pres*
▲ EMP: 265
SALES (est): 94.6MM
SALES (corp-wide): 169.1MM **Privately Held**
WEB: www.fageusa.com
SIC: 2026 Yogurt
HQ: Fage Usa Holdings
 1 Opportunity Dr
 Johnstown NY 12095
 518 762-5912

(G-6829)
FAGE USA HOLDINGS (HQ)
1 Opportunity Dr (12095-3349)
PHONE..................................518 762-5912
Anthanasios Filippou, *CEO*
Ioannis Ravanis, *Exec VP*
Bernard McConaghy, *Safety Mgr*
Tim McClarren, *Purch Mgr*
Christos Koloventzos, *Treasurer*
◆ EMP: 5 EST: 2000
SALES (est): 94.6MM
SALES (corp-wide): 169.1MM **Privately Held**
SIC: 2026 5143 Yogurt; yogurt
PA: Fage Dairy Industry S.A.
 35 Ermou
 Metamorfosi 14452
 210 289-2555

(G-6830)
HAWKINS FABRICS INC (PA)
328 N Perry St (12095-1210)
P.O. Box 351, Gloversville (12078-0351)
PHONE..................................518 773-9550
Alex Willart, *President*
James Batty, *President*
▲ EMP: 38
SQ FT: 50,000
SALES (est): 13.4MM **Privately Held**
WEB: www.safeind.com
SIC: 2259 2231 Gloves, knit, except dress & semidress gloves; mittens, knit; work gloves, knit; broadwoven fabric mills, wool

(G-6831)
HUDSON INDUSTRIES CORPORATION
Also Called: Milligan & Higgins Div
100 Maple Ave (12095-1041)
P.O. Box 506 (12095-0506)
PHONE..................................518 762-4638
Ron Kormanek, *Branch Mgr*
EMP: 40
SQ FT: 36,025 **Privately Held**
WEB: www.milligan1868.com
SIC: 2891 Glue
HQ: Hudson Industries Corporation
 271 Us Highway 46 F207
 Fairfield NJ 07004
 973 402-0100

(G-6832)
JAG MANUFACTURING INC
26 Grecco Dr (12095-1067)
P.O. Box 957 (12095-0957)
PHONE..................................518 762-9558
Joseph A Galea, *President*
Kelly L Galea, *Vice Pres*
▲ EMP: 45
SQ FT: 10,000
SALES (est): 5.2MM **Privately Held**
SIC: 3949 3732 2394 2393 Golf equipment; boat building & repairing; canvas & related products; textile bags; broadwoven fabric mills, manmade

(G-6833)
KAMALI LEATHER LLC
204 Harrison St (12095-4072)
PHONE..................................518 762-2522
Mark Towne, *Manager*
EMP: 9
SALES (est): 1.1MM
SALES (corp-wide): 4.6MM **Privately Held**
SIC: 3199 Boxes, leather
PA: Kamali Leather Llc
 44 Hillside Ave
 Manhasset NY 11030
 516 627-6505

(G-6834)
LEE DYEING COMPANY NC INC
Also Called: Merrimac Leasing
328 N Perry St (12095-1210)
P.O. Box 100 (12095-0100)
PHONE..................................518 736-5232
Morris Evans, *President*
John Henley, *Manager*
EMP: 10
SQ FT: 76,063
SALES (est): 1.3MM **Privately Held**
WEB: www.leedyeing.com
SIC: 2261 Embossing cotton broadwoven fabrics

Johnstown - Fulton County (G-6835)

(G-6835)
PEACEFUL VALLEY MAPLE FARM (PA)
116 Lagrange Rd (12095-4031)
PHONE..................518 762-0491
Stephen M Savage, *Owner*
EMP: 5
SALES: 100K **Privately Held**
SIC: 2099 Maple syrup

(G-6836)
PEARL LEATHER FINISHERS INC (PA)
11 Industrial Pkwy 21 (12095-1046)
PHONE..................518 762-4543
Carmen F Ruggiero, *CEO*
Chuck Frascatore, *Plant Mgr*
Kimberly Holt, *QC Mgr*
Harry Downing, *Associate*
▲ EMP: 17
SQ FT: 20,000
SALES (est): 7.1MM **Privately Held**
WEB: www.pearlleather.com
SIC: 3111 Leather tanning & finishing

(G-6837)
PIONEER WINDOW HOLDINGS INC
200 Union Ave (12095-3336)
P.O. Box 70 (12095-0070)
PHONE..................518 762-5526
Vincent Amato, *President*
EMP: 50 **Privately Held**
WEB: www.pwindows.com
SIC: 3442 3354 Storm doors or windows, metal; aluminum extruded products
PA: Pioneer Window Holdings, Inc.
15 Frederick Pl
Hicksville NY 11801

(G-6838)
R H CROWN CO INC
100 N Market St (12095-2126)
PHONE..................518 762-4589
Michael Gray, *President*
Richard Reynolds, *Exec VP*
EMP: 30 EST: 1965
SQ FT: 58,000
SALES (est): 9.6MM **Privately Held**
SIC: 2911 7349 Oils, lubricating; janitorial service, contract basis

(G-6839)
SILK SCREEN ART INC
1 School St (12095-2198)
PHONE..................518 762-8423
David P Sponenberg, *President*
Guy B Sponenberg, *Vice Pres*
EMP: 12
SQ FT: 20,000
SALES (est): 870K **Privately Held**
SIC: 2759 Screen printing

(G-6840)
SIMCO LEATHER CORPORATION
99 Pleasant Ave (12095-1720)
P.O. Box 509 (12095-0509)
PHONE..................518 762-7100
Gerald Simek, *President*
▲ EMP: 20
SQ FT: 45,000
SALES (est): 3MM **Privately Held**
SIC: 3111 Tanneries, leather

(G-6841)
SPRAY NINE CORPORATION
309 W Montgomery St (12095-2435)
PHONE..................800 477-7299
Greg Mostooler, *General Mgr*
EMP: 80
SQ FT: 82,000
SALES (est): 12MM **Privately Held**
WEB: www.spraynine.com
SIC: 2842 Cleaning or polishing preparations

Jordan
Onondaga County

(G-6842)
OMEGA WIRE INC
Also Called: Bare Wire Div
24 N Beaver St (13080-9531)
PHONE..................315 689-7115
C Knapp, *Manager*
EMP: 90
SALES (corp-wide): 455.4MM **Privately Held**
WEB: www.omegawire.com
SIC: 3351 3366 3315 Wire, copper & copper alloy; copper foundries; steel wire & related products
HQ: Omega Wire, Inc.
12 Masonic Ave
Camden NY 13316
315 245-3800

(G-6843)
WECARE ORGANICS LLC (PA)
9293 Bonta Bridge Rd (13080-9430)
PHONE..................315 689-1937
Jeffrey Leblanc, *President*
EMP: 24
SALES (est): 9.5MM **Privately Held**
SIC: 2869 Plasticizers, organic: cyclic & acyclic

Jordanville
Herkimer County

(G-6844)
HANSON AGGREGATES PA INC
237 Kingdom Rd (13361-2603)
PHONE..................315 858-1100
Kevin Smith, *Superintendent*
EMP: 30
SQ FT: 2,944
SALES (corp-wide): 20.3B **Privately Held**
SIC: 1442 1422 Common sand mining; crushed & broken limestone
HQ: Hanson Aggregates Pennsylvania, Llc
7660 Imperial Way
Allentown PA 18195
610 366-4626

Katonah
Westchester County

(G-6845)
NOVA PACKAGING LTD INC
7 Sunrise Ave (10536-2301)
P.O. Box 785, Goldens Bridge (10526-0785)
PHONE..................914 232-8406
Greg Scott, *President*
EMP: 37
SALES (est): 5.3MM **Privately Held**
SIC: 2671 3081 2673 Packaging paper & plastics film, coated & laminated; unsupported plastics film & sheet; bags: plastic, laminated & coated

(G-6846)
RECORD REVIEW LLC
Also Called: Bedford Pund Rdge Rcord Review
16 The Pkwy Fl 3 (10536-1550)
P.O. Box 455, Bedford Hills (10507-0455)
PHONE..................914 244-0533
Deborah White, *Mng Member*
Rob Astorino, *Executive*
EMP: 10
SALES (est): 448.1K **Privately Held**
SIC: 2711 Newspapers, publishing & printing

(G-6847)
US AUTHENTIC LLC
11 Mt Holly Rd E (10536-2400)
PHONE..................914 767-0295
Shaul Dover, *Mng Member*
▲ EMP: 6 EST: 2000
SQ FT: 4,000
SALES (est): 600.5K **Privately Held**
WEB: www.flightjacket.com
SIC: 2386 Garments, sheep-lined

(G-6848)
WORDWISE INC
1 Brady Ln (10536-2503)
PHONE..................914 232-5366
Karen Gotimer, *CEO*
EMP: 3
SALES (est): 1.8MM **Privately Held**
WEB: www.wordwiseinc.com
SIC: 2731 Textbooks: publishing only, not printed on site

Kauneonga Lake
Sullivan County

(G-6849)
B H M METAL PRODUCTS CO
Horseshoe Lake Rd (12749)
PHONE..................845 292-5297
Robert Gordon, *Owner*
EMP: 6 EST: 1947
SQ FT: 15,000
SALES: 100K **Privately Held**
SIC: 3469 3441 3312 3679 Metal stampings; fabricated structural metal; tool & die steel & alloys; electronic circuits

Keeseville
Clinton County

(G-6850)
ESSEX BOX & PALLET CO INC
49 Industrial Park Rd (12944-2936)
PHONE..................518 834-7279
Michael Lemza, *President*
EMP: 22 EST: 1966
SQ FT: 19,000
SALES (est): 2.8MM **Privately Held**
WEB: www.essexboxandpallet.com
SIC: 2449 2448 2499 Wood containers; pallets, wood; handles, poles, dowels & stakes: wood

(G-6851)
INTERNATIONAL MTLS & SUPS INC
56 Industrial Park Rd (12944-2937)
PHONE..................518 834-9899
David Kruse, *President*
John Burns, *Vice Pres*
Martin Caouette, *Vice Pres*
Jeffrey Kinblom, *Vice Pres*
David Rumble, *Vice Pres*
▼ EMP: 5 EST: 2001
SALES (est): 454.7K
SALES (corp-wide): 1.2B **Privately Held**
SIC: 2869 Industrial organic chemicals
HQ: Virginia Materials Inc.
3306 Peterson St
Norfolk VA 23509
800 321-2282

(G-6852)
LOREMANSS EMBROIDERY ENGRAV
Also Called: Loreman's
1599 Front St (12944-3510)
P.O. Box 546 (12944-0546)
PHONE..................518 834-9205
Jim Reisdorf, *Sales Staff*
Thomas H Loreman, *Mng Member*
Donald Loreman Sr,
EMP: 12
SQ FT: 7,000
SALES: 1.7MM **Privately Held**
WEB: www.loremans.com
SIC: 2261 2759 7389 2395 Screen printing of cotton broadwoven fabrics; screen printing; engraving service; embroidery & art needlework; automotive & apparel trimmings

(G-6853)
MURRAY LOGGING LLC
1535 Route 9 (12944-2848)
PHONE..................518 834-7372
Robert Murray,
James Murray,
EMP: 5
SALES (est): 379.4K **Privately Held**
SIC: 2411 Logging camps & contractors

(G-6854)
PEPSI-COLA METRO BTLG CO INC
Also Called: Pepsico
1524 Route 9 (12944-2890)
PHONE..................518 834-7811
Michael Armstrong, *Warehouse Mgr*
Michael Bear,
Jim Banker, *Manager*
EMP: 400
SALES (corp-wide): 63.5B **Publicly Held**
WEB: www.pbg.com
SIC: 2086 Carbonated soft drinks, bottled & canned
HQ: Pepsi-Cola Metropolitan Bottling Company, Inc.
1111 Westchester Ave
White Plains NY 10604
914 767-6000

(G-6855)
UPSTATE RECORDS MANAGEMENT LLC
1729 Front St (12944-3620)
PHONE..................518 834-1144
Barbara Davidson,
EMP: 5
SALES: 125K **Privately Held**
SIC: 7372 Prepackaged software

Kendall
Orleans County

(G-6856)
DMD MACHINING TECHNOLOGY INC
17231 Roosevelt Hwy (14476-9762)
PHONE..................585 659-8180
David Hofer, *President*
EMP: 5
SALES: 250K **Privately Held**
SIC: 3599 Machine & other job shop work

Kenmore
Erie County

(G-6857)
ARMENTO INCORPORATED
Also Called: Armento Architectural Arts
1011 Military Rd (14217-2225)
P.O. Box 39, Buffalo (14217-0039)
PHONE..................716 875-2423
Robert W Pierce, *President*
EMP: 6 EST: 1946
SQ FT: 5,000
SALES (est): 1MM **Privately Held**
SIC: 3446 Ornamental metalwork

(G-6858)
DENNYS DRIVE SHAFT SERVICE
1189 Military Rd (14217-1845)
PHONE..................716 875-6640
Dennis Bringhurst, *President*
Mary Bringhurst, *Vice Pres*
EMP: 8
SALES (est): 1MM **Privately Held**
WEB: www.dennysdriveshaft.com
SIC: 3714 7538 Drive shafts, motor vehicle; general automotive repair shops

(G-6859)
HARGRAVE DEVELOPMENT
Also Called: Hargraves Bus MGT Consulting
84 Shepard Ave (14217-1914)
PHONE..................716 877-7880
Lawrence Tanner, *Owner*
Lloyd Tanner, *Principal*
EMP: 15
SALES (est): 597.2K **Privately Held**
SIC: 1499 8742 Miscellaneous nonmetallic minerals; business consultant

(G-6860)
HERRMANN GROUP LLC
Also Called: Identity Ink & Custom Tee
2320 Elmwood Ave (14217-2645)
PHONE..................716 876-9798
William Herrmann,
EMP: 5
SALES (est): 473.6K **Privately Held**
SIC: 2759 3552 3949 5136 Screen printing; embroidery machines; sporting & athletic goods; men's & boys' clothing; clothing, sportswear, men's & boys'

(G-6861)
HORACE J METZ
Also Called: Insty Trints
2385 Elmwood Ave (14217-2648)
PHONE..................716 873-9103
Horace J Metz, Owner
Jim Metz, Manager
EMP: 7 **EST:** 1976
SALES (est): 280.2K **Privately Held**
SIC: 2759 Commercial printing

(G-6862)
HULLEY HOLDING COMPANY INC (PA)
Also Called: Hulley Woodworking Company
2500 Elmwood Ave (14217-2223)
PHONE..................716 332-3982
John Hulley, President
EMP: 13
SQ FT: 6,400
SALES: 1MM **Privately Held**
WEB: www.hulleywoodworking.com
SIC: 2431 Millwork

(G-6863)
KEN-TON OPEN MRI PC
2882 Elmwood Ave (14217-1325)
PHONE..................716 876-7000
Joseph Serghany, Ch of Bd
Dr H Chen Park, Principal
EMP: 7
SALES (est): 670K **Privately Held**
SIC: 3841 8071 2835 Diagnostic apparatus, medical; testing laboratories; in vivo diagnostics

(G-6864)
W H JONES & SON INC
1208 Military Rd (14217-1833)
PHONE..................716 875-8233
Elizabeth Jones, Ch of Bd
W Todd Jones, President
Kevin B Jones, Vice Pres
Peter W Jones, Vice Pres
EMP: 10 **EST:** 1941
SQ FT: 6,800
SALES: 737.7K **Privately Held**
SIC: 3599 Custom machinery

(G-6865)
ZENGER PARTNERS LLC
1881 Kenmore Ave (14217-2523)
PHONE..................716 876-2284
Joseph Zenger,
EMP: 37 **EST:** 1947
SQ FT: 12,000
SALES: 3.1MM **Privately Held**
SIC: 2752 2791 2789 Commercial printing, offset; typesetting; bookbinding & related work

Kennedy
Chautauqua County

(G-6866)
CARGILL INCORPORATED
1029 Poland Center Rd (14747-9708)
PHONE..................716 665-6570
Tim Decker, Branch Mgr
EMP: 7
SALES (corp-wide): 51.2B **Privately Held**
WEB: www.growmarkfs.com
SIC: 2048 Prepared feeds
PA: Cargill, Incorporated
15407 Mcginty Rd W
Wayzata MN 55391
952 742-7575

Kerhonkson
Ulster County

(G-6867)
BARRA & TRUMBORE INC
40 Old Mine Rd (12446-2641)
PHONE..................845 626-5442
David Barra, President
Martin Trumbore, Vice Pres
▲ **EMP:** 8
SALES (est): 725.2K **Privately Held**
WEB: www.barratrumbore.com
SIC: 3281 Cut stone & stone products

(G-6868)
DAVES PRECISION MACHINE SHOP
56 Webster Ave (12446-2672)
PHONE..................845 626-7263
David Seymour, Owner
EMP: 12
SQ FT: 1,500
SALES (est): 540K **Privately Held**
SIC: 3599 Machine shop, jobbing & repair

Kew Gardens
Queens County

(G-6869)
A & B COLOR CORP (DEL) (PA)
Also Called: Soho Guilds
8204 Lefferts Blvd # 356 (11415-1731)
PHONE..................718 441-5482
William Rabinowitz, President
EMP: 6
SQ FT: 2,500
SALES (est): 198K **Privately Held**
SIC: 2851 5198 Paints & allied products; paints

(G-6870)
AD-VANTAGE PRINTING INC
12034 Queens Blvd Vd (11415-1230)
PHONE..................718 820-0688
Francene Biderman, President
Angelica Rozon, Prdtn Mgr
Ruth Sommer, Production
EMP: 11
SALES (est): 2.1MM **Privately Held**
WEB: www.advantages.net
SIC: 2752 5199 7336 Commercial printing, offset; advertising specialties; graphic arts & related design

(G-6871)
CUMMINS - ALLISON CORP
8002 Kew Gardens Rd # 402 (11415-3613)
PHONE..................718 263-2482
EMP: 64
SALES (corp-wide): 383.8MM **Privately Held**
SIC: 3579 3519 Perforators (office machines); internal combustion engines
PA: Cummins - Allison Corp.
852 Feehanville Dr
Mount Prospect IL 60056
847 759-6403

(G-6872)
CUZINS DUZIN CORP
8420 Austin St Apt 3a (11415-2213)
P.O. Box 313073, Jamaica (11431-3073)
PHONE..................347 724-6200
Todd Jones, Manager
EMP: 8
SALES (est): 76K **Privately Held**
SIC: 2051 Doughnuts, except frozen

(G-6873)
I D E PROCESSES CORPORATION (PA)
106 81st Ave (11415-1108)
PHONE..................718 544-1177
Fax: 718 575-8050
▲ **EMP:** 17
SQ FT: 500
SALES: 2.1MM **Privately Held**
SIC: 3625 Mfg Silencers & Industrial Noise Control Equipment

(G-6874)
ISRAELI YELLOW PAGES
12510 Queens Blvd Ste 14 (11415-1522)
PHONE..................718 520-1000
Assaf Ran, CEO
EMP: 20
SALES (est): 756.9K **Privately Held**
SIC: 2741 Telephone & other directory publishing

(G-6875)
JACK L POPKIN & CO INC
12510 84th Rd (11415-2202)
PHONE..................718 361-6700
Leonard F Popkin, President
Debra Z Popkin, Admin Sec
EMP: 8 **EST:** 1947
SQ FT: 6,000
SALES: 1.6MM **Privately Held**
SIC: 3861 7699 Printing equipment, photographic; printing trades machinery & equipment repair

(G-6876)
JG INNOVATIVE INDUSTRIES INC
8002 Kew Gardens Rd # 5002 (11415-3600)
PHONE..................718 784-7300
Joseph Gottlieb, Ch of Bd
Anat Geula, COO
EMP: 8
SALES (est): 964.5K **Privately Held**
SIC: 3999 Advertising display products

(G-6877)
MANHOLE BRRIER SEC SYSTEMS INC
Also Called: Mbss
8002 Kew Gardens Rd # 901 (11415-3600)
PHONE..................516 741-1032
Michael Manoussos, CEO
John Messer, President
EMP: 22 **EST:** 2001
SQ FT: 5,000
SALES (est): 3.6MM **Privately Held**
SIC: 3699 Security devices

Kill Buck
Cattaraugus County

(G-6878)
DONVER INCORPORATED
4185 Killbuck Rd (14748)
P.O. Box 181 (14748-0181)
PHONE..................716 945-1910
Donald A Vershay, President
Patricia B Vershay, Vice Pres
EMP: 18
SQ FT: 900
SALES: 4.3MM **Privately Held**
SIC: 2421 3713 2491 2426 Sawmills & planing mills, general; truck & bus bodies; wood preserving; hardwood dimension & flooring mills

Kinderhook
Columbia County

(G-6879)
AMERICAN BIO MEDICA CORP (PA)
122 Smith Rd (12106-2819)
PHONE..................518 758-8158
Melissa A Waterhouse, CEO
Richard P Koskey, Ch of Bd
Edmund M Jaskiewicz, President
Douglas Casterlin, Vice Pres
Heidi Dillenbeck, QA Dir
EMP: 65
SQ FT: 30,000
SALES: 4.9MM **Publicly Held**
WEB: www.americanbiomedica.com
SIC: 2834 3841 Pharmaceutical preparations; diagnostic apparatus, medical

(G-6880)
MAPLE HILL CREAMERY LLC
5 Hudson St (12106-7709)
PHONE..................518 758-7777
Peter T Joseph, Mng Member
EMP: 6
SALES (est): 628.5K
SALES (corp-wide): 8MM **Privately Held**
SIC: 2026 Yogurt
PA: Maple Hill Creamery Llc
285 Allendale Rd W
Stuyvesant NY 12173
518 758-7777

King Ferry
Cayuga County

(G-6881)
LAKE VIEW MANUFACTURING LLC
Also Called: Aurora Shoe Company
1690 State Route 90 N (13081-9713)
P.O. Box 430, Aurora (13026-0430)
PHONE..................315 364-7892
David Binns, President
EMP: 10
SQ FT: 5,000
SALES (est): 1.3MM **Privately Held**
SIC: 3143 3144 Men's footwear, except athletic; women's footwear, except athletic

Kings Park
Suffolk County

(G-6882)
DEJANA TRCK UTILITY EQP CO LLC (HQ)
490 Pulaski Rd (11754-1317)
PHONE..................631 544-9000
Peter Dejana, President
Greg Markert, Business Mgr
Mike Sitkin, Prdtn Mgr
Liz Jannell, Purch Mgr
Nicholas Allen, Parts Mgr
EMP: 150
SQ FT: 25,000
SALES (est): 36.1MM **Publicly Held**
SIC: 3711 5531 Truck & tractor truck assembly; truck equipment & parts

(G-6883)
HANSA PLASTICS INC
8 Meadow Glen Rd (11754-1312)
PHONE..................631 269-9050
Harold Schmidt, President
Nellie Schmidt, Corp Secy
Peter Schmidt Jr, Vice Pres
▲ **EMP:** 10 **EST:** 1961
SQ FT: 5,000
SALES (est): 1.8MM **Privately Held**
WEB: www.hansasystemsusa.com
SIC: 3089 Injection molding of plastics

(G-6884)
KINGS PARK READY MIX CORP
140 Old Northport Rd E (11754-4211)
PHONE..................631 269-4330
Claudio Valente, President
EMP: 15
SALES: 2MM **Privately Held**
SIC: 3273 Ready-mixed concrete

(G-6885)
PELKOWSKI PRECAST CORP
294a Old Northport Rd (11754-4200)
PHONE..................631 269-5727
Tom Pelkowski, President
Bob Pelkowski, Vice Pres
Bryan Pelkowski, Treasurer
Bill Pelkowski, Admin Sec
EMP: 17
SQ FT: 400
SALES (est): 2.7MM **Privately Held**
SIC: 3272 Concrete products, precast; septic tanks, concrete; manhole covers or frames, concrete: covers, catch basin: concrete

(G-6886)
R SCHLEIDER CONTRACTING CORP
135 Old Northport Rd (11754-4200)
PHONE..................631 269-4249

Kingston - Ulster County (G-6887)

GEOGRAPHIC SECTION

Ray Schleider, *President*
Loretta Schleider, *Vice Pres*
EMP: 5 **EST:** 1969
SQ FT: 2,500
SALES (est): 853.6K **Privately Held**
SIC: 2951 5169 Road materials, bituminous (not from refineries); industrial salts & polishes

Kingston
Ulster County

(G-6887)
ALCOA FASTENING SYSTEMS
1 Corporate Dr (12401-5536)
PHONE..................845 334-7203
Klaus Kleinfeld, *Principal*
▲ **EMP:** 130
SQ FT: 40,000
SALES (est): 21.5MM **Privately Held**
SIC: 3452 Bolts, nuts, rivets & washers

(G-6888)
ARMOR DYNAMICS INC
138 Maple Hill Rd (12401-8616)
PHONE..................845 658-9200
Bernard C Schaeffer, *President*
EMP: 15
SALES: 1.5MM **Privately Held**
SIC: 3711 Cars, armored, assembly of

(G-6889)
BESICORP LTD (PA)
1151 Flatbush Rd (12401-7011)
PHONE..................845 336-7700
William Seils, *President*
Frederic M Zinn Sr, *President*
Michael F Zinn, *Chairman*
Jim Waleur, *Plant Mgr*
EMP: 13 **EST:** 1998
SQ FT: 8,000
SALES (est): 6.2MM **Privately Held**
SIC: 3674 4911 3585 Photovoltaic devices, solid state; electric services; refrigeration & heating equipment

(G-6890)
C & G OF KINGSTON INC
25 Cornell St (12401-3625)
P.O. Box 1458 (12402-1458)
PHONE..................845 331-0148
Clyde E Wonderly, *CEO*
Gloria M Wonderly, *Admin Sec*
EMP: 60
SQ FT: 20,000
SALES (est): 5.7MM **Privately Held**
WEB: www.wonderlys.com
SIC: 2391 2392 Curtains & draperies; bedspreads & bed sets: made from purchased materials

(G-6891)
C S I G INC
721 Broadway Ste 270 (12401-3449)
PHONE..................845 383-3800
Andrew Peck, *CEO*
Jonathan Peck, *CEO*
Tim Peck, *Vice Pres*
Timothy Peck, *Vice Pres*
Andy Peck, *Human Res Mgr*
EMP: 9
SQ FT: 1,450
SALES (est): 650K **Privately Held**
WEB: www.csiginc.com
SIC: 7372 Application computer software

(G-6892)
CALLANAN INDUSTRIES INC
737 Flatbush Rd (12401-7313)
PHONE..................845 331-6868
Lew A Anthony, *Marketing Staff*
Randy Anson, *Manager*
EMP: 25
SALES (corp-wide): 29.7B **Privately Held**
WEB: www.callanan.com
SIC: 3272 3281 2951 1442 Concrete products, precast; stone, quarrying & processing of own stone products; asphalt paving mixtures & blocks; construction sand & gravel
HQ: Callanan Industries, Inc.
8 Southwoods Blvd Ste 4
Albany NY 12211
518 374-2222

(G-6893)
CENTER FOR PROSTHETIC
144 Pine St Ste 110 (12401-4946)
PHONE..................845 336-7762
Jones Zinter, *Branch Mgr*
EMP: 5
SALES (est): 396.4K **Privately Held**
SIC: 3842 Prosthetic appliances
PA: Center For Prosthetic & Orthotic Design, Inc.
149 S Lake Ave
Albany NY 12208

(G-6894)
CHARLTON PRECISION PRODUCTS
461 Sawkill Rd (12401-1229)
P.O. Box 500, Mount Marion (12456-0500)
PHONE..................845 338-2351
Robert Charlton, *President*
Bonnie Charlton, *Vice Pres*
Nancy Charlton, *Shareholder*
Katherine Charlton, *Admin Sec*
EMP: 8 **EST:** 1962
SQ FT: 4,000
SALES (est): 1.2MM **Privately Held**
WEB: www.charltonprecision.com
SIC: 3643 Current-carrying wiring devices

(G-6895)
CITY OF KINGSTON
Also Called: Kingston Wste Wtr Trment Plant
91 E Strand St (12401-6001)
PHONE..................845 331-2490
Allen Winchell, *Director*
EMP: 11 **Privately Held**
WEB: www.kingstonez.com
SIC: 3589 9511 Sewage & water treatment equipment;
PA: City Of Kingston
420 Broadway
Kingston NY 12401
845 334-3935

(G-6896)
CRANESVILLE BLOCK CO INC
637 E Chester St (12401-1738)
PHONE..................845 331-1775
Will Longto, *Principal*
EMP: 25
SQ FT: 4,262
SALES (corp-wide): 45.6MM **Privately Held**
SIC: 3273 Ready-mixed concrete
PA: Cranesville Block Co., Inc.
1250 Riverfront Ctr
Amsterdam NY 12010
518 684-6154

(G-6897)
DAILY FREEMAN
79 Hurley Ave (12401-2898)
PHONE..................845 331-5000
Jan Dewey, *Principal*
Sam Daleo, *Principal*
EMP: 11
SALES (est): 486K **Privately Held**
SIC: 2711 Newspapers, publishing & printing

(G-6898)
DIRT T SHIRTS INC
444 Old Neighborhood Rd (12401-1508)
PHONE..................845 336-4230
John Stote, *President*
Scott Winter, *Vice Pres*
William Stote, *Treasurer*
John Stote III, *Admin Sec*
EMP: 40
SQ FT: 25,000
SALES (est): 3.5MM **Privately Held**
SIC: 2396 2395 Screen printing on fabric articles; art goods for embroidering, stamped: purchased materials

(G-6899)
EAST COAST CULTURES LLC
906 State Route 28 (12401-7264)
P.O. Box 220147, Brooklyn (11222-0147)
PHONE..................917 261-3010
EMP: 10
SALES (est): 932K **Privately Held**
SIC: 2086 Mfg Bottled/Canned Soft Drinks

(G-6900)
EXCELSIOR WOOD PRODUCTS LLC
401b Sawkill Rd (12401-1229)
PHONE..................845 339-6630
Ron Sauer, *President*
EMP: 10
SQ FT: 1,750
SALES (est): 1.5MM **Privately Held**
WEB: www.excelsiorwood.com
SIC: 2431 Millwork

(G-6901)
HEALTHALLIANCE HOSPITAL
Also Called: Benedictine Hospital
105 Marys Ave (12401-5848)
PHONE..................845 338-2500
Joseph Christiana, *Med Doctor*
Jeffrey Murphy, *Manager*
Fan Yang, *Pathologist*
Richard Parrish, *Director*
Arlene Cohen, *Oncology*
EMP: 7 **Privately Held**
SIC: 3821 Laboratory apparatus & furniture
HQ: Healthalliance Hospital Mary's Avenue Campus
105 Marys Ave
Kingston NY 12401
845 338-2500

(G-6902)
HUCK INTERNATIONAL INC
Also Called: Arconic Fstening Systems Rings
1 Corporate Dr (12401-5536)
PHONE..................845 331-7300
Garvin Wells, *Opers Mgr*
Steven Boderck, *Branch Mgr*
EMP: 203
SALES (corp-wide): 12.9B **Publicly Held**
WEB: www.huck.com
SIC: 3452 3594 3546 Bolts, nuts, rivets & washers; fluid power pumps & motors; power-driven handtools
HQ: Huck International, Inc.
3724 E Columbia St
Tucson AZ 85714
520 519-7400

(G-6903)
KEEGAN ALES LLC
20 Saint James St (12401-4534)
PHONE..................845 331-2739
Tommy Keegan, *Mng Member*
Lisa Hantes, *Manager*
EMP: 13
SALES (est): 1.1MM **Privately Held**
WEB: www.keeganales.com
SIC: 2082 Beer (alcoholic beverage)

(G-6904)
KINGSTON HOOPS SUMMER
68 Glen St (12401-6406)
P.O. Box 2606 (12402-2606)
PHONE..................845 401-6830
Charlene Laday Hill, *Owner*
EMP: 8
SALES (est): 24K **Privately Held**
SIC: 3494 Valves & pipe fittings

(G-6905)
KNIGHTLY ENDEAVORS
319 Wall St Ste 2 (12401-3884)
PHONE..................845 340-0949
John Reeder, *Owner*
EMP: 11 **EST:** 1996
SALES (est): 789.1K **Privately Held**
WEB: www.knightly.com
SIC: 2211 Apparel & outerwear fabrics, cotton

(G-6906)
LABELLA PASTA INC
906 State Route 28 (12401-7264)
PHONE..................845 331-9130
Nancy Covello, *President*
Dennis Covello, *President*
EMP: 7
SQ FT: 4,800
SALES (est): 709.5K **Privately Held**
WEB: www.labellapasta.com
SIC: 2099 Pasta, uncooked: packaged with other ingredients

(G-6907)
LHV PRECAST INC
540 Ulster Landing Rd (12401-6963)
PHONE..................845 336-8880
Henry Killian, *CEO*
Robert Willis, *President*
James Willis, *Vice Pres*
Mike Venett, *Plant Engr*
Karen Bennett, *Admin Asst*
EMP: 50
SQ FT: 30,000
SALES (est): 8.9MM **Privately Held**
WEB: www.lhvprecast.com
SIC: 3272 Concrete products, precast

(G-6908)
LOCAL MEDIA GROUP INC
Also Called: Times Herald-Record
34 John St (12401-3822)
PHONE..................845 340-4910
EMP: 12
SALES (corp-wide): 1.2B **Publicly Held**
SIC: 2711 Newspapers-Publishing/Printing
HQ: Local Media Group, Inc.
40 Mulberry St
Middletown NY 10940
845 341-1100

(G-6909)
LUMINARY PUBLISHING INC
314 Wall St (12401-3820)
PHONE..................845 334-8600
Jason Stern, *President*
Amara Projansky, *Vice Pres*
Robert Pina, *Accounts Exec*
Brian Mahoney, *Director*
David Perry, *Art Dir*
EMP: 15
SQ FT: 1,000
SALES (est): 1.8MM **Privately Held**
WEB: www.chronogram.com
SIC: 2721 2741 Magazines: publishing & printing; art copy & poster publishing

(G-6910)
M & E MFG CO INC
19 Progress St (12401-3611)
P.O. Box 1548 (12402-1548)
PHONE..................845 331-7890
Jeffrey Weinberger, *CEO*
Don Hall, *President*
EMP: 55
SQ FT: 54,000
SALES (est): 6.1MM **Privately Held**
WEB: www.zframerack.com
SIC: 3441 Fabricated structural metal

(G-6911)
MILLROCK TECHNOLOGY INC
39 Kieffer Ln Ste 2 (12401-2210)
PHONE..................845 339-5700
Taylor Thompson, *Chairman*
Mary Anne Whitnas, *Accounts Mgr*
◆ **EMP:** 20
SQ FT: 12,000
SALES (est): 4.4MM **Privately Held**
WEB: www.millrocktech.com
SIC: 3585 Refrigeration equipment, complete

(G-6912)
NORTHAST COML WIN TRTMENTS INC
Also Called: Wonderly Company, The
25 Cornell St (12401-3625)
PHONE..................845 331-0148
Al Parsons, *CEO*
Cheryl Jansen, *Prdtn Mgr*
Pat Schweikart, *CFO*
EMP: 65
SALES (est): 6.6MM **Privately Held**
SIC: 2391 Cottage sets (curtains): made from purchased materials

(G-6913)
NORTHEAST DATA
619 State Route 28 (12401-7466)
P.O. Box 316, West Hurley (12491-0316)
PHONE..................845 331-5554
Mark Wachtel, *Principal*
EMP: 7
SALES (est): 1MM **Privately Held**
SIC: 3559 Tire shredding machinery

PA: National Waste Management Holdings, Inc.
5920 N Florida Ave
Hernando FL 34442
352 489-6912

(G-6914)
PEARSON EDUCATION INC
317 Wall St (12401-3819)
PHONE.....................................845 340-8700
Dan Cooper, *Manager*
EMP: 27
SALES (corp-wide): 5.9B **Privately Held**
WEB: www.phgenit.com
SIC: 2731 Book publishing
HQ: Pearson Education, Inc.
221 River St
Hoboken NJ 07030
201 236-7000

(G-6915)
R & F HANDMADE PAINTS INC
84 Ten Broeck Ave (12401-3921)
PHONE.....................................845 331-3112
Richard Frumess, *President*
Kevin Lavin, *Vice Pres*
Darin Seim, *Opers Staff*
Jim Haskin, *Treasurer*
▲ **EMP:** 12
SQ FT: 5,000
SALES (est): 1MM **Privately Held**
SIC: 3952 5199 Lead pencils & art goods; artists' materials

(G-6916)
ROBERT TABATZNIK ASSOC INC (PA)
Also Called: American Printing and Off Sups
867 Flatbush Rd (12401-7315)
PHONE.....................................845 336-4555
Patricia Tabatznik, *Ch of Bd*
EMP: 10
SQ FT: 7,300
SALES (est): 3.7MM **Privately Held**
WEB: www.rtachicago.com
SIC: 2752 5112 Commercial printing, offset; office supplies

(G-6917)
SOLVENTS COMPANY INC
9 Cornell St (12401-3623)
P.O. Box 2376 (12402-2376)
PHONE.....................................631 595-9300
Batia Shellef, *President*
EMP: 10 **EST:** 2013
SALES (est): 1.8MM **Privately Held**
SIC: 2911 2869 2899 2842 Solvents; non-aromatic chemical products; industrial organic chemicals; chlorinated solvents; orange oil; degreasing solvent

(G-6918)
SPIEGEL WOODWORKS INC
Also Called: S A W
418 Old Neighborhood Rd (12401-1508)
PHONE.....................................845 336-8090
Gary Spiegel, *President*
EMP: 10
SQ FT: 12,000
SALES: 1.6MM **Privately Held**
WEB: www.sawmoulding.com
SIC: 2431 2421 Moldings, wood: unfinished & prefinished; doors, wood; sawmills & planing mills, general

(G-6919)
STATEBOOK LLC
185 Fair St Ste 2 (12401-0503)
P.O. Box 3659 (12402-3659)
PHONE.....................................845 383-1991
Calandra Cruickshank, *Principal*
Teresa Cecd, *Vice Pres*
EMP: 5
SALES (est): 315.8K **Privately Held**
SIC: 2741

(G-6920)
STAVO INDUSTRIES INC (PA)
Also Called: Ertel Alsop
132 Flatbush Ave (12401-2202)
PHONE.....................................845 331-4552
George T Quigley, *Vice Pres*
Jason Neese, *Purch Mgr*
Bill Kearney, *VP Sales*
Scott Benson, *Sales Staff*
Dave Bower, *Chief Mktg Ofcr*
▲ **EMP:** 17 **EST:** 1966
SQ FT: 15,000
SALES (est): 9.8MM **Privately Held**
WEB: www.ertelalsop.com
SIC: 3569 3561 3443 Filters, general line: industrial; industrial pumps & parts; tanks, standard or custom fabricated: metal plate

(G-6921)
STAVO INDUSTRIES INC
Also Called: Ertel Engineering Co
132 Flatbush Ave (12401-2202)
PHONE.....................................845 331-5389
George Quigley, *Vice Pres*
EMP: 45
SALES (est): 6.3MM
SALES (corp-wide): 9.8MM **Privately Held**
WEB: www.ertelalsop.com
SIC: 3569 Filters
PA: Stavo Industries, Inc.
132 Flatbush Ave
Kingston NY 12401
845 331-4552

(G-6922)
TIMELY SIGNS OF KINGSTON INC
154 Clinton Ave Fl 1 (12401-4922)
PHONE.....................................845 331-8710
Gerard Beichert, *President*
Jeff Zduniak, *Principal*
Joe Beichert, *Vice Pres*
EMP: 12
SQ FT: 15,000
SALES (est): 1.6MM **Privately Held**
WEB: www.timelysigns.com
SIC: 3993 Signs & advertising specialties

(G-6923)
TONNER DOLL COMPANY INC (PA)
1094 Morton Blvd (12401-8110)
P.O. Box 4410 (12402-4410)
PHONE.....................................845 339-9537
Robert Tonner, *CEO*
Jack Kralik, *Vice Pres*
▲ **EMP:** 24
SQ FT: 8,500
SALES (est): 2.5MM **Privately Held**
WEB: www.tonnerdoll.com
SIC: 3942 Miniature dolls, collectors'

(G-6924)
TORTILLA HEAVEN INC
Also Called: Armadillo Bar & Grill
97 Abeel St (12401-6009)
PHONE.....................................845 339-1550
Merle Borenstein, *President*
EMP: 20
SQ FT: 3,200
SALES (est): 2.2MM **Privately Held**
SIC: 2099 5812 Tortillas, fresh or refrigerated; Mexican restaurant

(G-6925)
ULSTER PRECISION INC
100 Lipton St (12401-2600)
PHONE.....................................845 338-0995
Selma Boris, *President*
Harold Hill, *Exec VP*
Dan Smith, *Sales Staff*
Jill Boris, *Admin Sec*
Lou Distasi,
EMP: 20
SQ FT: 16,000
SALES (est): 3.8MM **Privately Held**
SIC: 3444 3441 3645 Sheet metal specialties, not stamped; fabricated structural metal; residential lighting fixtures

(G-6926)
ULSTER PUBLISHING CO INC (PA)
Also Called: Woodstock Times
322 Wall St Fl 1 (12401-3820)
P.O. Box 3329 (12402-3329)
PHONE.....................................845 334-8205
Geddy Sveikauskas, *President*
EMP: 20 **EST:** 1972
SQ FT: 2,500
SALES (est): 3.5MM **Privately Held**
WEB: www.ulsterpublishing.com
SIC: 2711 2721 Newspapers: publishing only, not printed on site; magazines: publishing only, not printed on site

(G-6927)
UNIVERSAL METAL FABRICATORS
Also Called: Reliance Gayco
27 Emerick St (12401-3009)
PHONE.....................................845 331-8248
James Hassett, *President*
EMP: 10
SQ FT: 50,000
SALES (est): 2MM **Privately Held**
WEB: www.urminc.com
SIC: 3555 3599 3569 3532 Printing trades machinery; machine shop, jobbing & repair; separators for steam, gas, vapor or air (machinery); mining machinery

(G-6928)
URBAN PRECAST LLC
6 Kieffer Ln (12401-2206)
PHONE.....................................845 331-6299
Tom Auringer,
EMP: 50 **EST:** 2012
SALES (est): 177.7K **Privately Held**
SIC: 3272 Concrete products, precast

(G-6929)
US HEALTH EQUIPMENT COMPANY
138 Maple Hill Rd (12401-8616)
PHONE.....................................845 658-7576
Bernard Schaeffer, *President*
Wayne Schaeffer, *President*
EMP: 20 **EST:** 1961
SALES (est): 2.3MM **Privately Held**
WEB: www.saunex.com
SIC: 3634 Sauna heaters, electric

(G-6930)
USHECO INC
138 Maple Hill Rd (12401-8616)
PHONE.....................................845 658-9200
Bernarr C Schaeffer, *CEO*
Wayne M Schaeffer, *President*
Lorene Schaeffer, *Vice Pres*
EMP: 16
SQ FT: 40,000
SALES (est): 1.3MM **Privately Held**
WEB: www.usheco.com
SIC: 3089 Injection molding of plastics; plastic processing

(G-6931)
VINCENT CONIGLIARO
Also Called: Salvin Company
308 State Route 28 (12401-7445)
PHONE.....................................845 340-0489
Vincent Conigliaro, *Owner*
EMP: 15
SQ FT: 12,000
SALES (est): 860K **Privately Held**
SIC: 3648 5719 1731 5731 Lighting equipment: lighting, lamps & accessories; lighting contractor; radio, television & electronic stores; audio electronic systems

(G-6932)
WORKSHOP ART FABRICATION
117 Tremper Ave (12401-3619)
P.O. Box 1009 (12402-1009)
PHONE.....................................845 331-0385
Vincent Didonato, *President*
Andrew Tharmer, *President*
EMP: 12
SALES: 1MM **Privately Held**
SIC: 3562 Casters

(G-6933)
YUM YUM NOODLE BAR
275 Fair St Ste 17 (12401-3882)
PHONE.....................................845 679-7992
Dorothy Lee, *Owner*
EMP: 8
SALES (est): 672.9K **Privately Held**
SIC: 2098 Noodles (e.g. egg, plain & water), dry

Kirkville
Onondaga County

(G-6934)
MANTH-BROWNELL INC
1120 Fyler Rd (13082-9445)
PHONE.....................................315 687-7263
Wesley R Skinner Jr, *Ch of Bd*
Rob Pike, *Vice Pres*
Glenn Spaarling, *CFO*
Glenn Sparling, *CFO*
John Skinner, *Admin Sec*
EMP: 180 **EST:** 1951
SQ FT: 140,000
SALES (est): 45.2MM **Privately Held**
WEB: www.manth.com
SIC: 3451 Screw machine products

(G-6935)
STANLEY INDUSTRIAL EQP LLC
8094 Saintsville Rd (13082-9325)
PHONE.....................................315 656-8733
Thomas Stanley, *Mng Member*
EMP: 6
SQ FT: 5,200
SALES (est): 1.2MM **Privately Held**
SIC: 3537 Forklift trucks

(G-6936)
TITAN STEEL CORP
6333 N Kirkville Rd (13082-3300)
P.O. Box 10 (13082-0010)
PHONE.....................................315 656-7046
Gretchen K Conway, *President*
Jeff Kealin, *Vice Pres*
EMP: 12
SALES (est): 2.7MM **Privately Held**
SIC: 3441 Building components, structural steel

Kirkwood
Broome County

(G-6937)
ACTIVE MANUFACTURING INC
32 Laughlin Rd (13795)
P.O. Box 332 (13795-0332)
PHONE.....................................607 775-3162
Frank Sweetay, *President*
EMP: 12
SQ FT: 2,000
SALES (est): 1.4MM **Privately Held**
SIC: 3599 3999 Machine shop, jobbing & repair; models, general, except toy

(G-6938)
AKRATURN MFG INC
1743 Us Route 11 (13795-1637)
PHONE.....................................607 775-2802
Douglas Gardner, *President*
Douglas Sterns, *Corp Secy*
David Gardner, *Vice Pres*
EMP: 51
SQ FT: 60,000
SALES (est): 5.2MM **Privately Held**
WEB: www.akraturn.com
SIC: 3599 Machine shop, jobbing & repair

(G-6939)
BELDEN MANUFACTURING INC
Also Called: Dan Ann Associates
1813 Us Route 11 (13795-1608)
PHONE.....................................607 238-0998
Jerry Wilson, *President*
Kate Molesky, *Office Mgr*
EMP: 20
SQ FT: 6,000
SALES (est): 3MM **Privately Held**
SIC: 3599 Machine shop, jobbing & repair

(G-6940)
FUSE ELECTRONICS INC
1223 Us Route 11 (13795-1641)
PHONE.....................................607 352-3222
Susane Lewis, *CEO*
Patricia Mancinelli, *Ch of Bd*
Susanne Lewis, *Manager*
EMP: 7
SALES (est): 1MM **Privately Held**
SIC: 3677 Electronic coils, transformers & other inductors

(G-6941)
TRINIC LLC
40 Grossett Dr (13795-1006)
PHONE..................607 655-1517
EMP: 15
SALES (est): 2.7MM **Privately Held**
SIC: 3272 Concrete products

La Fargeville
Jefferson County

(G-6942)
HP HOOD LLC
20700 State Route 411 (13656-3228)
PHONE..................315 658-2132
Bob Shrader, *IT/INT Sup*
EMP: 300
SALES (corp-wide): 2.1B **Privately Held**
SIC: 2026 Fluid milk
PA: Hp Hood Llc
  6 Kimball Ln Ste 400
  Lynnfield MA 01940
  617 887-8441

(G-6943)
JOHNSON S SAND GRAVEL INC
23284 County Route 3 (13656-3111)
PHONE..................315 771-1450
Rusty Johnson, *Principal*
EMP: 6
SALES (est): 542.4K **Privately Held**
SIC: 1442 Construction sand & gravel

(G-6944)
THOUSAND ISLAND READY MIX CON
38760 State Route 180 (13656-3108)
PHONE..................315 686-3203
Thomas Dillenbeck, *President*
Steven Dillenbeck, *Vice Pres*
EMP: 8 **EST:** 1964
SQ FT: 2,988
SALES (est): 1.3MM **Privately Held**
WEB: www.thousandislandsconcrete.com
SIC: 3273 Ready-mixed concrete

La Fayette
Onondaga County

(G-6945)
BOULAY FABRICATION INC
Rr 20 Box West (13084)
P.O. Box 508 (13084-0508)
PHONE..................315 677-5247
Timothy Foody, *President*
Daniel Foody, *Vice Pres*
Connie Foody, *Admin Sec*
EMP: 12
SQ FT: 14,000
SALES (est): 2.1MM **Privately Held**
WEB: www.boulayfab.com
SIC: 3613 Control panels, electric

(G-6946)
BYRNE DAIRY INC (PA)
2394 Us Route 11 (13084-9583)
P.O. Box 176 (13084-0176)
PHONE..................315 475-2121
Carl Byrne, *Ch of Bd*
Scott Smith, *General Mgr*
William M Byrne Jr, *Principal*
Scott Matukas, *COO*
Mark Byrne, *Vice Pres*
EMP: 300 **EST:** 1932
SQ FT: 32,000
SALES (est): 269.4MM **Privately Held**
WEB: www.byrnedairy.com
SIC: 2026 2024 Milk processing (pasteurizing, homogenizing, bottling); ice cream, packaged: molded, on sticks, etc.; ice cream, bulk

Lackawanna
Erie County

(G-6947)
ALLIANCE INNOVATIVE MFG INC
1 Alliance Dr (14218-2529)
PHONE..................716 822-1626
Richard St John, *President*
Jeanine Zaleski, *Controller*
EMP: 34 **EST:** 2007
SQ FT: 35,000
SALES: 7MM **Privately Held**
SIC: 3599 Machine shop, jobbing & repair

(G-6948)
CERTAINTEED CORPORATION
231 Ship Canal Pkwy (14218-1026)
PHONE..................716 823-3684
EMP: 226
SALES (corp-wide): 213.5MM **Privately Held**
SIC: 3221 Glass containers
HQ: Certainteed Corporation
  20 Moores Rd
  Malvern PA 19355
  610 893-5000

(G-6949)
LINITA DESIGN & MFG CORP
1951 Hamburg Tpke Ste 24 (14218-1047)
P.O. Box 1101, Buffalo (14201-6101)
PHONE..................716 566-7753
Carlos Vera, *President*
Sean Greenhouse, *Sales Staff*
Andrea Vera, *Info Tech Mgr*
Eva Vera, *Shareholder*
EMP: 50
SQ FT: 80,000
SALES: 10.6MM **Privately Held**
SIC: 3441 7389 7692 8711 Dam gates, metal plate; design services; welding repair; engineering services

(G-6950)
PAGE FRONT GROUP INC
2703 S Park Ave (14218-1511)
P.O. Box 756, Buffalo (14205-0756)
PHONE..................716 823-8222
William Delmont, *President*
Beverly Mazur, *Corp Secy*
EMP: 6
SQ FT: 1,500
SALES (est): 400.8K **Privately Held**
SIC: 2711 Newspapers: publishing only, not printed on site

(G-6951)
QUIKRETE COMPANIES LLC
Also Called: Quikrete-Buffalo
11 N Steelawanna Ave (14218-1114)
PHONE..................716 213-2027
Tom Kostelny, *Sales Mgr*
Chuck Olgin, *Manager*
EMP: 30
SQ FT: 26,293 **Privately Held**
WEB: www.quikrete.com
SIC: 3272 Concrete products
HQ: The Quikrete Companies Llc
  5 Concourse Pkwy Ste 1900
  Atlanta GA 30328
  404 634-9100

(G-6952)
RJS MACHINE WORKS INC
1611 Electric Ave (14218-3021)
PHONE..................716 826-1778
Ronald J Szewczyk, *President*
EMP: 6
SQ FT: 9,000
SALES: 470K **Privately Held**
SIC: 3599 Machine shop, jobbing & repair

(G-6953)
SAMPLA BELTING NORTH AMER LLC
61 N Gates Ave (14218-1029)
PHONE..................716 667-7450
Andrew Carducci, *Opers Mgr*
Lucio Depaoli, *Mng Member*
Stefan Cristian Balint,
David Gordon,
Enrico Minelli,
▲ **EMP:** 20
SQ FT: 40,000
SALES (est): 4.3MM **Privately Held**
SIC: 3199 3052 Transmission belting, leather; transmission belting, rubber

(G-6954)
WELDED TUBE USA INC
2537 Hamburg Tpke (14218-2557)
PHONE..................716 828-1111
Robert Mandel, *CEO*
▲ **EMP:** 60 **EST:** 2013
SALES (est): 19MM **Privately Held**
SIC: 3317 Steel pipe & tubes
PA: Welded Tube Of Canada Corp
  111 Rayette Rd
  Concord ON L4K 2
  905 669-1111

Lacona
Oswego County

(G-6955)
VANHOUTEN MOTORSPORTS
27 Center Rd (13083-4127)
PHONE..................315 387-6312
Henry E Van Houten, *Principal*
EMP: 6
SALES (est): 656.9K **Privately Held**
SIC: 3531 Automobile wrecker hoists

Lagrangeville
Dutchess County

(G-6956)
GRAPHICS SLUTION PROVIDERS INC (PA)
Also Called: Brewster Coachworks
115 Barmore Rd (12540-6601)
P.O. Box 55 (12540-0055)
PHONE..................845 677-5088
Theresa Brewster, *President*
Alexander S Brewster, *Vice Pres*
Jack Brewster, *Vice Pres*
EMP: 10 **EST:** 1977
SQ FT: 2,500
SALES: 2.5MM **Privately Held**
WEB: www.graphics-solutions.com
SIC: 2499 7373 Novelties, wood fiber; value-added resellers, computer systems

(G-6957)
INTENTIONS JEWELRY LLC
83 Miller Hill Dr (12540-5641)
PHONE..................845 226-4650
Bob Baff,
Shareane Baff,
EMP: 5
SALES (est): 406.6K **Privately Held**
SIC: 3911 Jewelry, precious metal

(G-6958)
MACRO TOOL & MACHINE COMPANY
1397 Route 55 (12540-5118)
PHONE..................845 223-3824
Daniel Siegel, *President*
Roland Siegel, *Vice Pres*
Gisela Siegel, *Treasurer*
EMP: 8
SQ FT: 30,000
SALES: 500K **Privately Held**
WEB: www.macrotool.com
SIC: 3599 Amusement park equipment; machine shop, jobbing & repair

(G-6959)
MICROCAD TRNING CONSULTING INC
1110 Route 55 Ste 209 (12540-5048)
PHONE..................617 923-0500
Agustin Fernandez, *Principal*
EMP: 7 **Privately Held**
SIC: 7372 8243 Prepackaged software; software training, computer
PA: Microcad Training & Consulting, Inc.
  440 Arsenal St Ste 3
  Watertown MA

(G-6960)
PARAGON AQUATICS
Also Called: KDI Paragon
1351 Route 55 Unit 1 (12540-5128)
PHONE..................845 452-5500
Thomas A Saldarelli, *Principal*
Devin Hare, *Safety Mgr*
▲ **EMP:** 50 **EST:** 1969
SQ FT: 38,000
SALES: 8.1MM
SALES (corp-wide): 1.2B **Privately Held**
WEB: www.paragonaquatics.com
SIC: 3449 3446 Miscellaneous metalwork; railings, prefabricated metal
HQ: Pentair Water Pool And Spa, Inc.
  1620 Hawkins Ave
  Sanford NC 27330
  919 566-8000

(G-6961)
PENTAIR WATER POOL AND SPA INC
Paragon Aquatics
341 Route 55 (12540)
PHONE..................845 452-5500
Thomas Saldarelli, *President*
EMP: 45
SALES (corp-wide): 1.2B **Privately Held**
WEB: www.pentairpool.com
SIC: 3589 3561 Swimming pool filter & water conditioning systems; pumps, domestic: water or sump
HQ: Pentair Water Pool And Spa, Inc.
  1620 Hawkins Ave
  Sanford NC 27330
  919 566-8000

(G-6962)
STYLES AVIATION INC (PA)
Also Called: Sky Geek
30 Airway Dr Ste 2 (12540-5254)
PHONE..................845 677-8185
Steven T Styles, *CEO*
Virginia R Styles, *Vice Pres*
Sherri Palm, *Treasurer*
Jeffery Cross, *Manager*
▲ **EMP:** 5
SQ FT: 5,000
SALES (est): 5.9MM **Privately Held**
SIC: 3728 5088 Aircraft parts & equipment; aircraft equipment & supplies

(G-6963)
TYMOR PARK
249 Duncan Rd (12540-5845)
PHONE..................845 724-5691
Robert Mattes, *Director*
EMP: 5
SALES: 7.9K **Privately Held**
WEB: www.unionvaleny.us
SIC: 2531 Picnic tables or benches, park

Lake George
Warren County

(G-6964)
LEATHER OUTLET
1656 State Route 9 (12845-3440)
PHONE..................518 668-0328
Kevin Clint, *Owner*
EMP: 8
SALES (est): 653.7K **Privately Held**
SIC: 3199 Leather goods

(G-6965)
PERFORMANCE CUSTOM TRAILER
230 Lockhart Mountain Rd (12845-4904)
P.O. Box 106, Hadley (12835-0106)
PHONE..................518 504-4021
William Bunting, *President*
Diane Bunting, *Treasurer*
EMP: 7
SQ FT: 3,000
SALES (est): 1.2MM **Privately Held**
SIC: 3799 Boat trailers

(G-6966)
UNDER ARMOUR INC
1444 State Route 9 (12845-3480)
PHONE..................518 761-6787
EMP: 29

SALES (corp-wide): 4.9B **Publicly Held**
SIC: 2329 Men's & boys' sportswear & athletic clothing
PA: Under Armour, Inc.
1020 Hull St Ste 300
Baltimore MD 21230
410 454-6428

Lake Grove
Suffolk County

(G-6967)
LUCKY LOUS INC
24 State St (11755-1714)
PHONE 631 672-1932
Lou T Camassa, *President*
Maria Camassa, *Treasurer*
EMP: 7
SALES: 80K **Privately Held**
SIC: 2099 Dessert mixes & fillings

(G-6968)
S&B ALTERNATIVE FUELS INC
1232 Stony Brook Rd (11755-1624)
PHONE 631 585-6637
Scott Kunz, *Principal*
EMP: 5 **EST:** 2009
SALES (est): 464.7K **Privately Held**
SIC: 2869 Fuels

(G-6969)
SPEEDWAY LLC
2825 Middle Country Rd (11755-2105)
PHONE 631 738-2536
Jaswante Kor, *Branch Mgr*
EMP: 15 **Publicly Held**
SIC: 1311 Crude petroleum production
HQ: Speedway Llc
500 Speedway Dr
Enon OH 45323
937 864-3000

(G-6970)
SUNDOWN SKI & SPORT SHOP INC (PA)
3060 Middle Country Rd (11755-2106)
PHONE 631 737-8600
Winfred Breuer, *President*
Michael Rahatigan, *Vice Pres*
Michael Rhatigan, *Vice Pres*
▲ **EMP:** 20
SQ FT: 13,000
SALES (est): 10.9MM **Privately Held**
SIC: 2511 5091 Wood lawn & garden furniture; skiing equipment

(G-6971)
VANS INC
313 Smith Haven Mall (11755-1201)
PHONE 631 724-1011
Sean Dunne, *Branch Mgr*
EMP: 10
SALES (corp-wide): 11.8B **Publicly Held**
SIC: 3021 5699 Canvas shoes, rubber soled; uniforms & work clothing
HQ: Vans, Inc.
1588 S Coast Dr
Costa Mesa CA 92626
855 909-8267

Lake Katrine
Ulster County

(G-6972)
COBRA MANUFACTURING CORP
68 Leggs Mills Rd (12449-5145)
P.O. Box 209, Bloomington (12411-0209)
PHONE 845 514-2505
Michael V Pavlov, *President*
Hillarie Pavlov, *Treasurer*
▲ **EMP:** 9 **EST:** 2000
SALES (est): 1.2MM **Privately Held**
SIC: 3315 Barbed & twisted wire

(G-6973)
WCD WINDOW COVERINGS INC
1711 Ulster Ave (12449-5426)
P.O. Box 723 (12449-0723)
PHONE 845 336-4511
Drew Wonderly, *President*
EMP: 50
SQ FT: 14,000
SALES: 1.3MM **Privately Held**
WEB: www.wcd-drapery.com
SIC: 2391 5021 2591 Draperies, plastic & textile: from purchased materials; beds & bedding; drapery hardware & blinds & shades

Lake Luzerne
Warren County

(G-6974)
KETCHUM MANUFACTURING CO INC
11 Town Shed Rd (12846)
P.O. Box 10 (12846-0010)
PHONE 518 696-3331
Gary Powers, *President*
Lisa Podwirny, *Vice Pres*
Helen A Powers, *Admin Sec*
EMP: 13 **EST:** 1964
SQ FT: 8,000
SALES: 1.2MM **Privately Held**
WEB: www.ketchummfg.com
SIC: 3999 Identification tags, except paper

Lake Placid
Essex County

(G-6975)
COMSEC VENTURES INTERNATIONAL
17 Tamarack Ave (12946-1607)
PHONE 518 523-1600
William H Borland, *President*
Tina Preston, *Manager*
EMP: 6
SQ FT: 1,700
SALES (est): 458.2K **Privately Held**
SIC: 3699 4822 4215 7929 Security control equipment & systems; telegraph & other communications; courier services, except by air; entertainers & entertainment groups

(G-6976)
LAKE PLACID ADVERTISERS WKSHP
Also Called: Sir Speedy
Cold Brook Plz (12946)
PHONE 518 523-3359
Tom Connors, *President*
Adele Pierce, *Vice Pres*
EMP: 20
SQ FT: 2,000
SALES: 4.5MM **Privately Held**
SIC: 2752 2759 2791 Commercial printing, lithographic; commercial printing; typesetting

(G-6977)
PEAK PERFORMANCE DESIGN LLC
Also Called: Create Prosthetics
7 Old Military Rd (12946-1614)
PHONE 518 302-9198
Daniel Kelleher, *CFO*
EMP: 7 **EST:** 2016
SALES (est): 248.5K **Privately Held**
SIC: 3842 3577 Prosthetic appliances; printers & plotters

(G-6978)
SUGAR SHACK DESERT COMPANY INC
2567 Main St (12946-3305)
PHONE 518 523-7540
Gina D Cimaglia, *CEO*
EMP: 6
SALES (est): 290K **Privately Held**
SIC: 2099 Sugar

Lake Pleasant
Hamilton County

(G-6979)
WILT INDUSTRIES INC
2452 State Route 8 (12108)
PHONE 518 548-4961
Daniel Wilt, *President*
Richard Wilt, *Vice Pres*
EMP: 6 **EST:** 1949
SQ FT: 10,000
SALES: 1MM **Privately Held**
WEB: www.wiltindustries.com
SIC: 3559 Glass making machinery: blowing, molding, forming, etc.

Lake Ronkonkoma
Suffolk County

(G-6980)
HONEYWELL INTERNATIONAL INC
1859 Lakeland Ave (11779-7420)
PHONE 631 471-2202
Gail Cino, *Manager*
EMP: 5
SALES (corp-wide): 40.5B **Publicly Held**
WEB: www.adilink.com
SIC: 3724 Aircraft engines & engine parts
PA: Honeywell International Inc.
115 Tabor Rd
Morris Plains NJ 07950
973 455-2000

(G-6981)
J F B & SONS LITHOGRAPHERS
1700 Ocean Ave (11779-6570)
PHONE 631 467-1444
Joseph Brown, *President*
Randall Brown, *Corp Secy*
Gary Brown, *Vice Pres*
Dennis Ganzak, *CFO*
EMP: 75
SQ FT: 43,000
SALES (est): 3.9MM
SALES (corp-wide): 189.9MM **Privately Held**
SIC: 2752 Commercial printing, lithographic
HQ: Earth Color New York, Inc.
249 Pomeroy Rd
Parsippany NJ 07054
973 884-1300

Lake View
Erie County

(G-6982)
DEEDEE DESSERTS LLC
6969 Southwestern Blvd (14085-9644)
P.O. Box 353 (14085-0353)
PHONE 716 627-2330
Dawn Davis,
EMP: 7
SALES (est): 330K **Privately Held**
SIC: 2099 Dessert mixes & fillings

(G-6983)
EFFECTIVE SLLING SOLUTIONS LLC
1898 Hanley Dr (14085-9704)
PHONE 716 771-8503
Ben Kaukus, *Mng Member*
EMP: 5
SALES: 94K **Privately Held**
SIC: 2759 Screen printing

Lakeville
Livingston County

(G-6984)
ARCHER-DANIELS-MIDLAND COMPANY
Also Called: ADM
3401 Rochester Rd (14480-9762)
PHONE 585 346-2311
Lee Robinson, *Branch Mgr*
EMP: 7
SALES (corp-wide): 60.8B **Publicly Held**
WEB: www.admworld.com
SIC: 2041 Flour & other grain mill products
PA: Archer-Daniels-Midland Company
77 W Wacker Dr Ste 4600
Chicago IL 60601
312 634-8100

(G-6985)
CONESUS LAKE ASSOCIATION INC
5828 Big Tree Rd (14480-9737)
P.O. Box 637 (14480-0637)
PHONE 585 346-6864
Greg Foust, *Ch of Bd*
George Coolbaugh, *President*
Burt Lyon, *Treasurer*
EMP: 30
SALES: 47.4K **Privately Held**
SIC: 3599 2511 Machine & other job shop work; wood household furniture

(G-6986)
S & R TOOL INC
6066 Stone Hill Rd (14480-9712)
PHONE 585 346-2029
Samuel Dandrea, *President*
Richard Panipinto, *Vice Pres*
EMP: 6
SQ FT: 10,428
SALES (est): 1MM **Privately Held**
SIC: 3599 Machine shop, jobbing & repair

(G-6987)
SWEETENERS PLUS INC
5768 Sweeteners Blvd (14480-9741)
P.O. Box 520 (14480-0520)
PHONE 585 728-3770
Carlton Myers, *President*
Mark Rudolph, *QC Mgr*
Kyle Whitford, *Sales Staff*
Michael Burke, *Marketing Staff*
Ann Coffey, *Admin Sec*
▲ **EMP:** 70
SQ FT: 30,000
SALES (est): 41.4MM **Privately Held**
WEB: www.sweetenersplus.com
SIC: 2062 Cane sugar refining

Lakewood
Chautauqua County

(G-6988)
ARCHROCK INC
305 E Fairmount Ave Ste 4 (14750-2000)
PHONE 716 763-1553
Mike Czernika, *Manager*
EMP: 15 **Publicly Held**
WEB: www.exterran.com
SIC: 1389 5084 Gas compressing (natural gas) at the fields; compressors, except air conditioning
PA: Archrock Inc.
9807 Katy Fwy Ste 100
Houston TX 77024

(G-6989)
ARRO MANUFACTURING LLC
4687 Gleason Rd (14750)
P.O. Box 19 (14750-0019)
PHONE 716 763-6203
Scott Bauer, *President*
Deborah Bauer,
EMP: 18
SALES (est): 695.5K **Privately Held**
SIC: 3544 3469 Punches, forming & stamping; metal stampings

Lakewood - Chautauqua County (G-6990) — GEOGRAPHIC SECTION

(G-6990)
ARRO TOOL & DIE INC
4687 Gleason Rd (14750)
P.O. Box 7 (14750-0007)
PHONE..................716 763-6203
James R Lindell, *President*
Eric Corey, *Vice Pres*
Jeff A Lindell, *Vice Pres*
Richard Morris, *Vice Pres*
Timothy Raynor, *Engineer*
EMP: 19 **EST:** 1952
SQ FT: 23,000
SALES (est): 2.6MM **Privately Held**
WEB: www.arrotool.com
SIC: 3544 3469 Special dies & tools; metal stampings

(G-6991)
CLASSIC BRASS INC
2051 Stoneman Cir (14750-9779)
P.O. Box 3563, Jamestown (14702-3563)
PHONE..................716 763-1400
J Christopher Creighton, *President*
▲ **EMP:** 56
SQ FT: 30,050
SALES (est): 9.2MM **Privately Held**
SIC: 3429 Furniture builders' & other household hardware

(G-6992)
CUMMINS INC
Also Called: Jamestown Engine Plant
4720 Baker St (14750-9772)
PHONE..................716 456-2676
Karine Ramsey, *Principal*
Jordan Elliss, *Opers Mgr*
Adam Moss, *Mfg Mgr*
Mike Abbate, *Materials Mgr*
Eric Fransen, *Warehouse Mgr*
◆ **EMP:** 62
SALES (est): 14.1MM **Privately Held**
SIC: 3519 Internal combustion engines

(G-6993)
CUMMINS INC
4720 Baker St (14750-9772)
PHONE..................716 456-2111
Maria Jones, *Opers Mgr*
Dan Nelson, *Purchasing*
Cecil Rhoades, *Engineer*
Dana Bogt, *Branch Mgr*
Pratik Sing, *Info Tech Mgr*
EMP: 800
SQ FT: 1,733
SALES (corp-wide): 20.4B **Publicly Held**
WEB: www.cummins.com
SIC: 3519 3714 Internal combustion engines; motor vehicle parts & accessories
PA: Cummins Inc,
 500 Jackson St
 Columbus IN 47201
 812 377-5000

(G-6994)
DLH ENERGY SERVICE LLC
4422 W Fairmount Ave (14750-9705)
P.O. Box 40, Ashville (14710-0040)
PHONE..................716 410-0028
Kim Helffrich, *Manager*
Scott Motter, *Manager*
Charles Dubose,
EMP: 3
SQ FT: 1,000
SALES: 5MM **Privately Held**
SIC: 1311 Crude petroleum & natural gas

(G-6995)
QUALITY MANUFACTURING SYS LLC
1995 Stoneman Cir (14750-9776)
PHONE..................716 763-0988
Patsy Jo Kosinski, *Partner*
EMP: 6
SQ FT: 12,000
SALES (est): 1.1MM **Privately Held**
SIC: 3569 Assembly machines, non-metal-working

(G-6996)
R R DONNELLEY & SONS COMPANY
Also Called: Moore Business Forms
112 Winchester Rd (14750-1739)
P.O. Box 137 (14750-0137)
PHONE..................716 763-2613
Kevin Diluca, *Manager*
Dan Caruso, *Manager*
EMP: 12
SALES (corp-wide): 6.9B **Publicly Held**
WEB: www.moore.com
SIC: 2759 Commercial Printing
PA: R. R. Donnelley & Sons Company
 35 W Wacker Dr Ste 3650
 Chicago IL 60601
 312 326-8000

(G-6997)
R-CO PRODUCTS CORPORATION
1855 Big Tree Rd (14750-9759)
PHONE..................800 854-7657
Edward Roemer Jr, *President*
Erika Roemer, *Treasurer*
Katy Lord, *Admin Sec*
EMP: 13 **EST:** 1975
SQ FT: 30,000
SALES (est): 2.5MM **Privately Held**
SIC: 2891 Sealants

(G-6998)
ULRICH PLANFILING EQP CORP
2120 4th Ave (14750-9727)
P.O. Box 135 (14750-0135)
PHONE..................716 763-1815
Daniel Berry, *President*
Jamie Carlson, *Vice Pres*
Reid Van Every, *Plant Mgr*
Barbara Sauer, *Purch Mgr*
Joni Drocy, *Engineer*
▼ **EMP:** 40
SQ FT: 42,400
SALES (est): 7.7MM **Privately Held**
WEB: www.ulrichcorp.com
SIC: 2522 Office cabinets & filing drawers: except wood

(G-6999)
WATER STREET BRASS CORPORATION
4515 Gleason Rd (14750-9748)
P.O. Box 463 (14750-0463)
PHONE..................716 763-0059
Mathew Churchill, *President*
▲ **EMP:** 22
SALES (est): 2.7MM **Privately Held**
SIC: 3429 Furniture hardware

Lancaster
Erie County

(G-7000)
A & T TOOLING LLC
91 Beach Ave (14086-1658)
PHONE..................716 601-7299
Maureen Hassenbohler,
EMP: 5
SALES: 250K **Privately Held**
SIC: 3543 Industrial patterns

(G-7001)
ADVANCED ASSEMBLY SERVICES INC
44 Knollwood Dr (14086-4459)
PHONE..................716 217-8144
Tim Kosmowski, *President*
Ra Kosmowski, *Vice Pres*
EMP: 6 **EST:** 2000
SQ FT: 5,000
SALES (est): 890.9K **Privately Held**
WEB: www.advancedassemblyservices.com
SIC: 3999 Barber & beauty shop equipment

(G-7002)
ADVANCED THERMAL SYSTEMS INC
15 Enterprise Dr (14086-9773)
PHONE..................716 681-1800
Edward W Patnode, *Ch of Bd*
Eugene Miliczky, *President*
EMP: 40
SQ FT: 31,000
SALES (est): 8.5MM **Privately Held**
WEB: www.advancedthermal.net
SIC: 3494 3568 3498 3441 Expansion joints pipe; ball joints, except aircraft & automotive; fabricated pipe & fittings; fabricated structural metal

(G-7003)
AFTER 50 INC
5 W Main St Rear (14086-2109)
PHONE..................716 832-9300
Bonnie Degweck, *President*
Phyllis Goasiti, *Vice Pres*
EMP: 5
SALES: 500K **Privately Held**
SIC: 2711 Newspapers, publishing & printing

(G-7004)
AIR SYSTEM PRODUCTS INC
Also Called: AFP Industries
51 Beach Ave (14086-1658)
PHONE..................716 683-0435
Patrick Scanlon, *President*
Henry Bourg, *Vice Pres*
Mike Zacharko, *Accounts Mgr*
▲ **EMP:** 12
SQ FT: 17,000
SALES (est): 1.7MM **Privately Held**
WEB: www.airsyspro.com
SIC: 3491 Industrial valves

(G-7005)
ALCO PLASTICS INC
35 Ward Rd (14086-9779)
PHONE..................716 683-3020
Raymond Mazurczyk, *President*
EMP: 20 **EST:** 1971
SQ FT: 25,000
SALES (est): 3.1MM **Privately Held**
SIC: 2673 Plastic bags: made from purchased materials

(G-7006)
ALDEN OPTICAL LABORATORY INC
6 Lancaster Pkwy (14086-9713)
PHONE..................716 937-9181
Charles H Creighton, *President*
Helen Creighton, *Treasurer*
EMP: 16
SQ FT: 8,000
SALES (est): 2.4MM **Privately Held**
WEB: www.aldenoptical.com
SIC: 3851 Contact lenses

(G-7007)
APPLE RUBBER PRODUCTS INC (PA)
Also Called: Express Seal Div
310 Erie St (14086-9504)
PHONE..................716 684-6560
Steven L Apple, *President*
Carol Malaney, *Vice Pres*
Chris Chiodo, *Engineer*
Brian Webb, *Engineer*
Joe Divissich, *Project Engr*
▲ **EMP:** 130
SQ FT: 11,000
SALES (est): 32.8MM **Privately Held**
WEB: www.applerubber.com
SIC: 3069 Molded rubber products

(G-7008)
APPLE RUBBER PRODUCTS INC
Also Called: Expresseal
204 Cemetery Rd (14086-9798)
PHONE..................716 684-7649
Steven Apple, *President*
Mark Trzepacz, *Manager*
Ray Eldernayer, *CIO*
EMP: 110
SQ FT: 49,668
SALES (est): 12.2MM
SALES (corp-wide): 32.8MM **Privately Held**
WEB: www.applerubber.com
SIC: 3069 3061 3053 Hard rubber & molded rubber products; molded rubber products; mechanical rubber goods; gaskets, packing & sealing devices
PA: Apple Rubber Products, Inc.
 310 Erie St
 Lancaster NY 14086
 716 684-6560

(G-7009)
BABULA CONSTRUCTION INC
5136 William St (14086-9447)
PHONE..................716 681-0886
Stanley Babula, *President*
Janet Babula, *Vice Pres*
EMP: 7
SALES: 300K **Privately Held**
SIC: 1389 Construction, repair & dismantling services

(G-7010)
BIMBO BAKERIES USA INC
2900 Commerce Pkwy (14086-1741)
PHONE..................716 706-0450
George Weston, *Owner*
EMP: 18 **Privately Held**
WEB: www.gwbakeries.com
SIC: 2051 Bakery: wholesale or wholesale/retail combined
HQ: Bimbo Bakeries Usa, Inc
 255 Business Center Dr # 200
 Horsham PA 19044
 215 347-5500

(G-7011)
BUFFALO FILTER LLC
5900 Genesee St (14086-9024)
PHONE..................716 835-7000
Samantha Bonano, *CEO*
Samantha Palmerton, *Vice Pres*
Greg Pepe, *Vice Pres*
David McKay, *Opers Staff*
Michael Fuszara, *Mfg Staff*
▲ **EMP:** 85
SQ FT: 15,000
SALES (est): 17.8MM **Privately Held**
WEB: www.buffalofilter.com
SIC: 3841 3845 3699 3564 Surgical & medical instruments; laser systems & equipment, medical; electrical equipment & supplies; blowers & fans

(G-7012)
CASEY MACHINE CO INC
74 Ward Rd (14086-9779)
PHONE..................716 651-0150
Thomas Radziwon, *Ch of Bd*
Ronald C Radziwon, *President*
Tom Radziwon, *Vice Pres*
Peter Szulc, *Vice Pres*
Bill Gillan, *Purch Agent*
EMP: 95 **EST:** 1976
SQ FT: 15,000
SALES (est): 18.4MM **Privately Held**
WEB: www.caseymachine.com
SIC: 3599 Machine shop, jobbing & repair

(G-7013)
CHAKRA COMMUNICATIONS INC
80 W Drullard Ave (14086-1649)
PHONE..................716 505-7300
Sharique Ansari, *Branch Mgr*
EMP: 50 **Privately Held**
WEB: www.chakracentral.com
SIC: 2796 2791 7812 7375 Lithographic plates, positives or negatives; typesetting; motion picture & video production; information retrieval services; color lithography
HQ: Chakra Communications, Inc.
 80 W Drullard Ave
 Lancaster NY 14086

(G-7014)
CLASSIC & PERFORMANCE SPC
Also Called: Classic Tube
80 Rotech Dr (14086-9755)
PHONE..................716 759-1800
Paul Fix, *President*
Lauren J Fix, *Vice Pres*
EMP: 24
SQ FT: 20,000
SALES (est): 4MM **Privately Held**
WEB: www.classictube.com
SIC: 3714 Exhaust systems & parts, motor vehicle

GEOGRAPHIC SECTION

Lancaster - Erie County (G-7040)

(G-7015)
DELFT PRINTING INC
1000 Commerce Pkwy (14086-1707)
PHONE..................................716 683-1100
Kamal C Jowdy, *President*
EMP: 7
SQ FT: 2,200
SALES: 800K **Privately Held**
WEB: www.delftprinting.com
SIC: 2759 Commercial printing

(G-7016)
DIVERSIFIED MANUFACTURING INC
4401 Walden Ave (14086-9013)
PHONE..................................716 681-7670
Walt Kempa, *Branch Mgr*
EMP: 15
SALES (corp-wide): 20.5MM **Privately Held**
WEB: www.dmimfg.com
SIC: 3441 Fabricated structural metal
PA: Diversified Manufacturing Inc.
  410 Ohio St
  Lockport NY 14094
  716 434-5585

(G-7017)
EASTERN AIR PRODUCTS LLC
Also Called: Engineered Air Products
41 Ward Rd (14086-9779)
PHONE..................................716 391-1866
Jeffrey Browne, *President*
Peter Baran, *Vice Pres*
Michael Arno, *CFO*
▲ **EMP:** 18
SQ FT: 12,500
SALES: 3.2MM **Privately Held**
SIC: 3563 Air & gas compressors including vacuum pumps

(G-7018)
ERIE ENGINEERED PRODUCTS INC
3949 Walden Ave (14086-1472)
PHONE..................................716 206-0204
Barry Newman, *Ch of Bd*
Thomas Kilpatrick, *General Mgr*
Mark Folmsbee, *Vice Pres*
Lorne Weil, *Shareholder*
Sandra Whiteford,
EMP: 47
SQ FT: 88,000
SALES: 3.9MM **Privately Held**
WEB: www.containers-cases.com
SIC: 3443 3441 3412 3411 Containers, shipping (bombs, etc.): metal plate; fabricated structural metal; metal barrels, drums & pails; metal cans; plastic containers, except foam; battery cases, plastic or plastic combination; boxes, plastic; buckets, plastic

(G-7019)
FBC CHEMICAL CORPORATION
4111 Walden Ave (14086-1599)
PHONE..................................716 681-1581
Joe Villafranca, *Manager*
EMP: 5
SQ FT: 4,000
SALES (corp-wide): 60MM **Privately Held**
WEB: www.fbcchem.com
SIC: 2842 5169 Cleaning or polishing preparations; chemicals & allied products
PA: Fbc Chemical Corporation
  634 Route 228
  Mars PA 16046
  724 625-3116

(G-7020)
FLOWNET LLC
580 Lake Ave (14086-9627)
PHONE..................................716 685-4036
EMP: 6
SALES (est): 288K **Privately Held**
SIC: 1311 Natural gas production

(G-7021)
GOOD EARTH INC
5960 Broadway St (14086-9531)
PHONE..................................716 684-8111
Gunter Burkhardt, *President*
Cornelia Orffeo, *Vice Pres*
EMP: 6
SALES (est): 824.5K **Privately Held**
WEB: www.goodearth.net
SIC: 2833 Organic medicinal chemicals: bulk, uncompounded

(G-7022)
GOOD EARTH ORGANICS CORP (PA)
5960 Broadway St (14086-9531)
PHONE..................................716 684-8111
Guenter H Burkhardt, *Ch of Bd*
Andreas G Burkhardt, *Vice Pres*
Bernhard G Burkhardt, *Vice Pres*
Eva Burkhardt, *Vice Pres*
Cornelia Orffeo, *Purchasing*
EMP: 20
SQ FT: 180,000
SALES: 17MM **Privately Held**
WEB: www.goodearth.org
SIC: 3523 Planting machines, agricultural

(G-7023)
HC BRILL CO INC
3765 Walden Ave (14086-1405)
PHONE..................................716 685-4000
Bob Craiglow, *Vice Pres*
EMP: 8
SALES (est): 1.2MM **Privately Held**
SIC: 2033 Canned fruits & specialties

(G-7024)
ILLINOIS TOOL WORKS INC
United Silicone Div
4471 Walden Ave (14086-9754)
PHONE..................................716 681-8222
Joseph Wukovits, *Branch Mgr*
EMP: 155
SALES (corp-wide): 14.3B **Publicly Held**
SIC: 3559 Plastics working machinery
PA: Illinois Tool Works Inc.
  155 Harlem Ave
  Glenview IL 60025
  847 724-7500

(G-7025)
JRB MACHINE-TOOL INC
11 Embry Pl (14086-1703)
P.O. Box 285 (14086-0285)
PHONE..................................716 206-0355
Richard Betschen, *President*
Jane Betschen, *Vice Pres*
▲ **EMP:** 7
SQ FT: 2,000
SALES (est): 800.4K **Privately Held**
SIC: 3599 Machine shop, jobbing & repair

(G-7026)
KZ PRECISION INC
Also Called: K Z Precision
1 Mason Pl (14086-1615)
PHONE..................................716 683-3202
Kenneth Zwara, *President*
EMP: 15
SQ FT: 7,500
SALES (est): 931.7K **Privately Held**
WEB: www.kzprecision.com
SIC: 3599 Machine shop, jobbing & repair

(G-7027)
LAFARGE NORTH AMERICA INC
6125 Genesee St (14086-9722)
PHONE..................................716 651-9235
Ken King, *Regl Sales Mgr*
Ron Morgan, *Manager*
EMP: 25
SALES (corp-wide): 26.4B **Privately Held**
WEB: www.lafargenorthamerica.com
SIC: 3241 1442 Cement, hydraulic: construction sand & gravel
HQ: Lafarge North America Inc.
  8700 W Bryn Mawr Ave
  Chicago IL 60631
  773 372-1000

(G-7028)
LAKESIDE CONCRETE SERVICES INC
89 Brandel Ave (14086-1932)
PHONE..................................716 681-7510
James Bates, *President*
EMP: 7
SALES (est): 1MM **Privately Held**
SIC: 3273 Ready-mixed concrete

(G-7029)
LANCASTER KNIVES INC (PA)
165 Court St (14086-2399)
PHONE..................................716 683-5050
Scott C Cant, *President*
Allen A Turton, *Engineer*
Rick Sinnott, *Supervisor*
▲ **EMP:** 45 **EST:** 1896
SQ FT: 46,000
SALES (est): 5.5MM **Privately Held**
WEB: www.lancasterknives.com
SIC: 3423 3545 3469 3541 Knives, agricultural or industrial; shear knives; machine parts, stamped or pressed metal; machine tools, metal cutting type

(G-7030)
LANCE VALVES
15 Enterprise Dr (14086-9749)
PHONE..................................716 681-5825
Eugene Miliczky, *Vice Pres*
Geoffrey Schrott, *Manager*
EMP: 8 **EST:** 1974
SQ FT: 6,000
SALES (est): 966.3K **Privately Held**
WEB: www.lancevalves.com
SIC: 3494 Valves & pipe fittings

(G-7031)
MANHASSET TOOL & DIE CO INC
4270 Walden Ave (14086-9770)
PHONE..................................716 684-6066
Mark Fenimore, *President*
EMP: 10 **EST:** 1955
SALES (est): 1MM **Privately Held**
WEB: www.manhassettool.com
SIC: 3544 3542 Jigs & fixtures; jigs: inspection, gauging & checking; die sets for metal stamping (presses); dies & die holders for metal cutting, forming, die casting; punching & shearing machines; bending machines

(G-7032)
MARKAR ARCHITECTURAL PRODUCTS
Also Called: Adams Ridge
68 Ward Rd (14086-9779)
PHONE..................................716 685-4104
Fax: 716 685-3919
EMP: 8 **Privately Held**
SIC: 3442 Mfg Metal Doors/Sash/Trim

(G-7033)
MOLDTECH INC
1900 Commerce Pkwy (14086-1735)
PHONE..................................716 685-3344
H Wayne Gerhart, *Ch of Bd*
Rob Paladichuk, *Vice Pres*
James H Wittman, *CFO*
James Wittman, *CFO*
▲ **EMP:** 45
SQ FT: 35,000
SALES (est): 15.7MM **Privately Held**
SIC: 3069 3061 Molded rubber products; mechanical rubber goods

(G-7034)
ORFFEO PRINTING & IMAGING INC
99 Cambria St (14086-1952)
P.O. Box 426 (14086-0426)
PHONE..................................716 681-5757
Gregory Orffeo, *Ch of Bd*
Darci Abel, *Graphic Designe*
EMP: 5
SQ FT: 27,000
SALES (est): 2.7MM **Privately Held**
SIC: 2752 7331 Commercial printing, offset; direct mail advertising services

(G-7035)
PALMA TOOL & DIE COMPANY INC
40 Ward Rd (14086-9779)
PHONE..................................716 681-4464
William D Tate Sr, *President*
Jeff Parks, *General Mgr*
Thomas Owczarak, *Vice Pres*
Stanley Blaszak, *Admin Sec*
Ed Schmidt,
EMP: 42
SQ FT: 23,000
SALES (est): 7.5MM **Privately Held**
WEB: www.palmatool.com
SIC: 3544 Special dies & tools

(G-7036)
PARKER-HANNIFIN CORPORATION
4087 Walden Ave (14086-1512)
PHONE..................................716 686-6400
Justin Scricco, *Marketing Staff*
Craig Dillworth, *Manager*
William Allhusen, *Sr Software Eng*
EMP: 126
SALES (corp-wide): 12B **Publicly Held**
SIC: 3594 Fluid power pumps
PA: Parker-Hannifin Corporation
  6035 Parkland Blvd
  Cleveland OH 44124
  216 896-3000

(G-7037)
PARKER-HANNIFIN CORPORATION
Finite Airtek Filtration
4087 Walden Ave (14086-1512)
PHONE..................................716 685-4040
Dale Zimmerman, *Regional Mgr*
Rick Woodring, *Branch Mgr*
EMP: 82
SALES (corp-wide): 12B **Publicly Held**
WEB: www.parker.com
SIC: 3569 3714 3564 Filters; motor vehicle parts & accessories; blowers & fans
PA: Parker-Hannifin Corporation
  6035 Parkland Blvd
  Cleveland OH 44124
  216 896-3000

(G-7038)
PARKER-HANNIFIN CORPORATION
Purification, Dehydration
4087 Walden Ave (14086-1512)
PHONE..................................716 685-4040
Jon Hilberg, *Branch Mgr*
EMP: 85
SALES (corp-wide): 12B **Publicly Held**
WEB: www.parker.com
SIC: 3585 3567 Refrigeration & heating equipment; industrial furnaces & ovens
PA: Parker-Hannifin Corporation
  6035 Parkland Blvd
  Cleveland OH 44124
  216 896-3000

(G-7039)
PERFORMANCE ADVANTAGE CO INC
6 W Main St Lowr Rear (14086-2110)
PHONE..................................716 683-7413
Richard Young, *President*
James Everett, *General Mgr*
Barb Kozurkiewicz, *Accounting Mgr*
Jared Enser, *Sales Staff*
Michael McGuire, *Sales Staff*
EMP: 15
SQ FT: 13,000
SALES (est): 2.2MM **Privately Held**
WEB: www.pactoolmounts.com
SIC: 3089 Plastic hardware & building products

(G-7040)
PFANNENBERG INC
68 Ward Rd (14086-9779)
PHONE..................................716 685-6866
Andreas Pfannenberg, *President*
Earl Rogalski, *Vice Pres*
Ken Surdej, *Prdtn Mgr*
Brian Glynn, *Buyer*
Joe Wagner, *Buyer*
◆ **EMP:** 52
SQ FT: 65,000
SALES: 15.5MM
SALES (corp-wide): 1.6MM **Privately Held**
WEB: www.pfannenbergusa.com
SIC: 3585 Air conditioning units, complete: domestic or industrial
PA: Pfannenberg Group Holding Gmbh
  Werner-Witt-Str. 1
  Hamburg 21035
  407 341-20

Lancaster - Erie County (G-7041)

(G-7041)
PFANNENBERG MANUFACTURING LLC
68 Ward Rd (14086-9779)
PHONE..................716 685-6866
William Baron, *President*
Laura Chasalow, *Vice Pres*
Jennifer Bialasik, *Vice Pres*
Earl Rogalski, *Vice Pres*
EMP: 60
SQ FT: 57,000
SALES (est): 1.9MM **Privately Held**
SIC: 3585 Refrigeration & heating equipment

(G-7042)
PRZ TECHNOLOGIES INC
5490 Broadway St (14086-2220)
P.O. Box 369 (14086-0369)
PHONE..................716 683-1300
Walt Przybyl, *President*
Danielle McGraw, *Opers Mgr*
Karan Andrea, *Accountant*
EMP: 15
SALES (est): 2.8MM **Privately Held**
SIC: 3545 Machine tool attachments & accessories

(G-7043)
RAM PRECISION TOOL INC
139 Gunnville Rd (14086-9017)
PHONE..................716 759-8722
Joseph Walter, *President*
Barbara M Walter, *Vice Pres*
EMP: 6
SQ FT: 6,000
SALES (est): 836K **Privately Held**
WEB: www.ramprecisiontool.com
SIC: 3599 Machine shop, jobbing & repair

(G-7044)
RICHARDS MACHINE TOOL CO INC
36 Nichter Rd (14086-9708)
PHONE..................716 683-3380
Dennis Richards, *President*
Betsy Richards, *Vice Pres*
EMP: 23
SQ FT: 18,000
SALES (est): 2.5MM **Privately Held**
SIC: 3599 Machine shop, jobbing & repair

(G-7045)
RMF PRINTING TECHNOLOGIES INC
Also Called: Ogilvie Press
50 Pearl St (14086-1922)
PHONE..................716 683-7500
Monica Castano, *Ch of Bd*
Juan Carlos Yanez, *CFO*
▲ **EMP:** 50
SQ FT: 140,000
SALES (est): 19.3MM **Privately Held**
WEB: www.rmfprinttechnology.com
SIC: 2752 Commercial printing, lithographic

(G-7046)
ROLITE MFG INC
10 Wendling Ct (14086-9766)
PHONE..................716 683-0259
Ron Roberts, *President*
Ronald Roberts, *President*
Thomas Debbins, *Vice Pres*
Nick Debbins, *Project Mgr*
Mike Bailey, *Sales Staff*
▲ **EMP:** 25
SQ FT: 65,000
SALES (est): 7MM **Privately Held**
WEB: www.rolitemfg.com
SIC: 3469 3449 Stamping metal for the trade; custom roll formed products

(G-7047)
S3J ELECTRONICS LLC
2000 Commerce Pkwy (14086-1733)
PHONE..................716 206-1309
EMP: 20
SALES (est): 4.2MM **Privately Held**
SIC: 3674 Mfg Semiconductors/Related Devices

(G-7048)
SECURE INTERNATIONAL
100 W Drullard Ave Ste 3 (14086-1670)
PHONE..................716 206-2500
Robert Eising, *President*
◆ **EMP:** 8
SALES (est): 688.7K **Privately Held**
SIC: 2051 Bakery: wholesale or wholesale/retail combined

(G-7049)
SEIBEL MODERN MFG & WLDG CORP
38 Palmer Pl (14086-2144)
PHONE..................716 683-1536
Leon A Seibel, *Ch of Bd*
Mark Seibel, *Vice Pres*
Jeff Heath, *Engineer*
Lynne M Sobkowiak, *Manager*
▲ **EMP:** 85 **EST:** 1945
SQ FT: 70,000
SALES (est): 20.9MM **Privately Held**
WEB: www.seibelmodern.com
SIC: 3441 3443 Fabricated structural metal; fabricated plate work (boiler shop)

(G-7050)
SILICONE PRODUCTS & TECHNOLOGY
4471 Walden Ave (14086-9754)
PHONE..................716 684-1155
Kim Jackson, *President*
EMP: 150
SALES (est): 11.1MM **Privately Held**
SIC: 2822 3544 Silicone rubbers; special dies, tools, jigs & fixtures

(G-7051)
STUTZMAN MANAGEMENT CORP
11 Saint Joseph St (14086-1800)
PHONE..................800 735-2013
Gerard Sheldon, *President*
EMP: 15
SQ FT: 32,000
SALES (est): 2.3MM **Privately Held**
SIC: 3443 Fuel tanks (oil, gas, etc.): metal plate

(G-7052)
UNITED SILICONE INC
4471 Walden Ave (14086-9778)
PHONE..................716 681-8222
Donato Curcio, *President*
Robert Le Posa, *Vice Pres*
Don Fink, *Opers Mgr*
David Loos, *Purch Agent*
Kevin Vincent, *Accounting Mgr*
◆ **EMP:** 81
SQ FT: 80,000
SALES (est): 14.3MM **Privately Held**
SIC: 3953 Pads, inking & stamping

(G-7053)
W N R PATTERN & TOOL INC
21 Pavement Rd (14086-9595)
PHONE..................716 681-9334
Gary Machniak, *President*
Jeffrey Tucker, *Vice Pres*
EMP: 6
SQ FT: 6,000
SALES (est): 360K **Privately Held**
SIC: 3544 3543 Industrial molds; forms (molds), for foundry & plastics working machinery; industrial patterns

(G-7054)
WEB-TECH PACKAGING INC
500 Commerce Pkwy (14086-1793)
PHONE..................716 684-4520
David C Rost, *President*
Kevin Kelly, *Shareholder*
William Rost, *Shareholder*
Kathleen Visciano, *Shareholder*
EMP: 16
SQ FT: 10,000
SALES (est): 3.3MM **Privately Held**
SIC: 2679 Labels, paper: made from purchased material

Lansing
Tompkins County

(G-7055)
CAYUGA CRUSHED STONE INC
87 Portland Point Rd (14882)
P.O. Box 41 (14882-0041)
PHONE..................607 533-4273
Thomas Besemer, *President*
Matthew Besemer, *Vice Pres*
EMP: 20
SQ FT: 1,200
SALES (est): 3.3MM **Privately Held**
SIC: 1422 Crushed & broken limestone

(G-7056)
METAL IMPROVEMENT COMPANY LLC
Also Called: IMR Test Labs
131 Woodsedge Dr (14882-8940)
PHONE..................607 533-7000
Peter Damian, *Branch Mgr*
EMP: 69
SALES (corp-wide): 2.2B **Publicly Held**
SIC: 3398 Shot peening (treating steel to reduce fatigue)
HQ: Metal Improvement Company, Llc
80 E Rte 4 Ste 310
Paramus NJ 07652
201 843-7800

Larchmont
Westchester County

(G-7057)
INTERNATIONAL ROBOTICS INC
2001 Palmer Ave Ste LI1 (10538-2420)
P.O. Box 11474, Naples FL (34101-1474)
PHONE..................914 630-1060
Robert Doornic, *CEO*
EMP: 10
SALES (est): 1.1MM **Privately Held**
SIC: 3535 Robotic conveyors

(G-7058)
MAGIC REED
723 Larchmont Acres Apt D (10538-7363)
PHONE..................914 630-4006
Kathy Sheinhouse, *Principal*
EMP: 11
SALES (est): 1.4MM **Privately Held**
SIC: 3931 Musical instruments

(G-7059)
SOGGY DOGGY PRODUCTIONS LLC
50 Chestnut Ave (10538-3534)
PHONE..................877 504-4811
Joanna Rein, *Mng Member*
▲ **EMP:** 4
SALES: 2MM **Privately Held**
SIC: 3999 Pet supplies

(G-7060)
WEB-COTE INDUSTRIES
19 Avon Rd (10538-1420)
P.O. Box 239 (10538-0239)
PHONE..................914 630-1600
Leslie Cowen, *CEO*
EMP: 25 **EST:** 2012
SALES (est): 1.8MM **Privately Held**
SIC: 2891 Adhesives

Latham
Albany County

(G-7061)
AB ENGINE
4a Northway Ln (12110-4809)
PHONE..................518 557-3510
Alexander Bakharev, *Principal*
EMP: 8
SALES (est): 370K **Privately Held**
SIC: 3519 Internal combustion engines

(G-7062)
ACCUMETRICS ASSOCIATES INC
6 British American Blvd # 100 (12110-1476)
PHONE..................518 393-2200
John M Reschovsky, *President*
Sandra Reschovsky, *Director*
EMP: 17
SQ FT: 5,000
SALES (est): 2.9MM **Privately Held**
WEB: www.accumetrix.com
SIC: 3674 Semiconductors & related devices

(G-7063)
ANGIODYNAMICS INC (PA)
14 Plaza Dr (12110-2166)
PHONE..................518 795-1400
Howard W Donnelly, *Ch of Bd*
James C Clemmer, *President*
Brent J Boucher, *Senior VP*
Chad T Campbell, *Senior VP*
Heather J Daniels-Cariveau, *Senior VP*
EMP: 277
SQ FT: 55,000
SALES: 344.2MM **Publicly Held**
WEB: www.angiodynamics.com
SIC: 3841 Surgical & medical instruments

(G-7064)
BAJAN GROUP INC
950 New Loudon Rd Ste 280 (12110-2111)
PHONE..................518 464-2884
Anthony Lombordo, *President*
EMP: 8 **Privately Held**
WEB: www.bajangroup.com
SIC: 2752 Commercial printing, offset
PA: The Bajan Group Inc
950 New Loudon Rd Ste 280
Latham NY 12110

(G-7065)
BRITISH AMERICAN PUBLISHING
19 British American Blvd (12110-6405)
PHONE..................518 786-6000
Bernard F Conners, *Chairman*
Francis Coughlin, *Treasurer*
John T De Graff, *Admin Sec*
EMP: 60
SALES (est): 17MM **Privately Held**
WEB: www.bapublish.com
SIC: 2731 Books: publishing only

(G-7066)
BULLOCK BOYS LLC
400 Old Loudon Rd (12110-2908)
PHONE..................518 783-6161
James Morrell, *CEO*
EMP: 15
SQ FT: 25,500
SALES (est): 858.3K **Privately Held**
SIC: 2599 Bar, restaurant & cafeteria furniture

(G-7067)
BUSINESS FIRST OF NEW YORK
Also Called: Business Review
40 British American Blvd (12110-1421)
PHONE..................518 640-6800
Carolyn Jones, *Publisher*
Caroline Jones, *General Mgr*
EMP: 23
SALES (corp-wide): 1.4B **Privately Held**
SIC: 2711 Newspapers: publishing only, not printed on site
HQ: Business First Of New York Inc
465 Main St Ste 100
Buffalo NY 14203
716 854-5822

(G-7068)
CALLANAN INDUSTRIES INC
Also Called: Clemente Latham Concrete
9 Fonda Rd (12110)
PHONE..................518 785-5666
Mark Clemente, *Manager*
EMP: 8
SALES (corp-wide): 29.7B **Privately Held**
WEB: www.callanan.com
SIC: 3272 Concrete products, precast

HQ: Callanan Industries, Inc.
8 Southwoods Blvd Ste 4
Albany NY 12211
518 374-2222

(G-7069)
CARR MANUFACTURING JEWELERS
Also Called: Carr Jewelers
22 West Ln (12110-5320)
PHONE 518 783-6093
W James Dix, *President*
James E Dix, *Vice Pres*
Gloria Dix, *Treasurer*
EMP: 5
SALES (est): 347.1K Privately Held
SIC: 3911 7621 5944 Jewelry, precious metal; jewelry repair services; jewelry stores

(G-7070)
D & W DIESEL INC
51 Sicker Rd Ste 3 (12110-1505)
PHONE 518 437-1300
Jeffrey Hartgraves, *Manager*
EMP: 12
SALES (corp-wide): 117.2MM Privately Held
WEB: www.dwdiesel.com
SIC: 3519 Diesel engine rebuilding
PA: D & W Diesel, Inc.
1503 Clark Street Rd
Auburn NY 13021
315 253-5300

(G-7071)
EAZYLIFT ALBANY LLC
836 Troy Schenectady Rd (12110-2424)
P.O. Box 340 (12110-0340)
PHONE 518 452-6929
Theresa Farrigan,
▲ EMP: 5
SALES (est): 950K Privately Held
SIC: 3534 Elevators & moving stairways

(G-7072)
EMERGENT POWER INC (HQ)
968 Albany Shaker Rd (12110-1401)
PHONE 201 441-3590
Andrew Marsh, *President*
EMP: 5
SALES (est): 17.8MM
SALES (corp-wide): 103.2MM Publicly Held
SIC: 2679 Fuel cell forms, cardboard: made from purchased material
PA: Plug Power Inc.
968 Albany Shaker Rd
Latham NY 12110
518 782-7700

(G-7073)
G AND G SERVICE
21 Nelson Ave (12110-1805)
PHONE 518 785-9247
Greg Gilbert,
EMP: 5
SALES (est): 336.9K Privately Held
SIC: 3089 8999 Plastics products; services

(G-7074)
HOWMEDICA OSTEONICS CORP
2 Northway Ln (12110-4820)
PHONE 518 783-1880
Steve Bulger, *Branch Mgr*
EMP: 9
SALES (corp-wide): 12.4B Publicly Held
SIC: 3842 Surgical appliances & supplies
HQ: Howmedica Osteonics Corp.
325 Corporate Dr
Mahwah NJ 07430
201 831-5000

(G-7075)
IMPERIAL POOLS INC (PA)
33 Wade Rd (12110-2613)
PHONE 518 786-1200
William Churchman, *CEO*
John V Maiuccoro, *President*
Katie Maiuccoro, *Principal*
Gary Maiuccoro, *Vice Pres*
Earl Cromie, *Prdtn Mgr*
◆ EMP: 123 EST: 1966
SQ FT: 100,000
SALES (est): 70.3MM Privately Held
WEB: www.imperialpools.com
SIC: 3949 5091 Swimming pools, except plastic; swimming pools, equipment & supplies

(G-7076)
JUNIOR ACHEVEMENT OF EASTRN NY
8 Stanley Cir Ste 8 # 8 (12110-2606)
PHONE 518 783-4336
Ed Murray, *President*
EMP: 5
SALES: 580.1K Privately Held
SIC: 3613 Distribution cutouts

(G-7077)
KAFKO (US) CORP
787 Watervliet Shaker Rd (12110-2211)
PHONE 877 721-7665
Mark Laven, *President*
EMP: 5
SALES (est): 403K
SALES (corp-wide): 197MM Privately Held
SIC: 3999 Manufacturing industries
PA: Latham International, Inc.
787 Watervliet Shaker Rd
Latham NY 12110
518 783-7776

(G-7078)
KJCKD INC (PA)
Also Called: Camelot Print & Copy Centers
630 Columbia St Ext Ste 2 (12110-3063)
PHONE 518 435-9696
John Derboghossian, *CEO*
Cristene Derboghossian, *COO*
EMP: 3 EST: 2015
SQ FT: 20,000
SALES (est): 1.2MM Privately Held
SIC: 2752 7334 7374 7336 Photo-offset printing; photocopying & duplicating services; optical scanning data service; commercial art & graphic design; posters: publishing & printing

(G-7079)
KOVATCH MOBILE EQUIPMENT CORP
Walter Truck Division
68 Sicker Rd (12110-1560)
PHONE 518 785-0900
John Kovatch, *President*
EMP: 12
SQ FT: 31,000 Publicly Held
SIC: 3711 Fire department vehicles (motor vehicles), assembly of; snow plows (motor vehicles), assembly of
HQ: Kovatch Mobile Equipment Corp.
1 Industrial Complex
Nesquehoning PA 18240
570 669-9461

(G-7080)
LATHAM INTERNATIONAL INC (PA)
787 Watervliet Shaker Rd (12110-2211)
PHONE 518 783-7776
Mark Laven, *President*
Gary Whitcher, *VP Opers*
Tom Correll, *Plant Mgr*
Harold Brooks, *Engineer*
Ed Urbanczyk, *Controller*
◆ EMP: 1 EST: 2004
SQ FT: 90,000
SALES (est): 197MM Privately Held
WEB: www.pacificpools.com
SIC: 3086 3081 Plastics foam products; vinyl film & sheet

(G-7081)
LATHAM INTERNATIONAL MFG CORP
Also Called: Latham Pool Products
787 Watervliet Shaker Rd (12110-2211)
PHONE 800 833-3800
Scott Rajeski, *CEO*
EMP: 500
SALES (est): 115.6MM Privately Held
SIC: 3949 Swimming pools, except plastic

(G-7082)
LATHAM POOL PRODUCTS INC (PA)
787 Watervliet Shaker Rd (12110-2211)
P.O. Box 550, Jane Lew WV (26378-0550)
PHONE 518 951-1000
Mark Laven, *President*
Ed Kriz, *Business Mgr*
Tim Golden, *Vice Pres*
John McGough, *Vice Pres*
Richard Piontkowski, *Vice Pres*
◆ EMP: 172
SQ FT: 25,000
SALES (est): 159.6MM Privately Held
SIC: 3949 Swimming pools, except plastic

(G-7083)
LATHAM POOL PRODUCTS INC
Also Called: Latham Manufacturing
787 Watervliet Shaker Rd (12110-2211)
PHONE 260 432-8731
Kristen Hladik, *Buyer*
Matt Geyman, *Branch Mgr*
EMP: 44 Privately Held
SIC: 3086 Plastics foam products
PA: Latham Pool Products, Inc.
787 Watervliet Shaker Rd
Latham NY 12110

(G-7084)
LATHAM SOFTWARE SCIENCES INC
678 Troy Schenectady Rd # 104 (12110-2502)
PHONE 518 785-1100
Michael Dellavilla, *President*
John D Miller, *Vice Pres*
EMP: 12
SALES (est): 840K Privately Held
SIC: 7372 Prepackaged software

(G-7085)
LATORRE ORTHOPEDIC LABORATORY
960 Troy Schenectady Rd (12110-1609)
PHONE 518 786-8655
Timothy Lacy, *President*
EMP: 15
SALES (est): 930K Privately Held
SIC: 3842 Orthopedic appliances; prosthetic appliances

(G-7086)
LINDEN MEYR MUNROE INC
20 Hemlock St (12110-2217)
PHONE 518 471-5111
▲ EMP: 11
SALES (est): 2.7MM Privately Held
SIC: 2621 Paper mills

(G-7087)
MARKTECH INTERNATIONAL CORP (PA)
Also Called: Marktech Optoelectronics
3 Northway Ln N Ste 1 (12110-2232)
PHONE 518 956-2980
Mark G Campito, *Ch of Bd*
Clive A Sofe, *President*
Joseph Andrascik, *Vice Pres*
▲ EMP: 25
SALES (est): 3MM Privately Held
WEB: www.marktechopto.com
SIC: 3674 Semiconductors & related devices

(G-7088)
PEPSI BEVERAGES CO
Also Called: Pepsico
421 Old Niskayuna Rd (12110-1566)
PHONE 518 782-2150
EMP: 7
SALES (est): 718.5K Privately Held
SIC: 2086 Carbonated soft drinks, bottled & canned

(G-7089)
PHILIPS MEDICAL SYSTEMS MR (DH)
Also Called: Philips Healthcare
450 Old Niskayuna Rd (12110-1569)
PHONE 518 782-1122
Stephen H Rusckowski, *CEO*
Leo Blecher, *President*
Richard Stevens, *President*
Thomas J O'Brien, *Exec VP*
Gerard Van Spaenbonck, *CFO*
◆ EMP: 400
SQ FT: 146,000
SALES (est): 206MM
SALES (corp-wide): 20.9B Privately Held
SIC: 3674 3679 3845 Integrated circuits, semiconductor networks, etc.; cryogenic cooling devices for infrared detectors, masers; cores, magnetic; magnetic resonance imaging device, nuclear

(G-7090)
PIP INC
Also Called: PIP Printing
968 Albany Shaker Rd (12110-1401)
PHONE 518 861-0133
Allan Piper, *Ch of Bd*
EMP: 6 EST: 1994
SALES (est): 750.7K Privately Held
SIC: 2752 Commercial printing, offset

(G-7091)
PLUG POWER INC (PA)
968 Albany Shaker Rd (12110-1428)
PHONE 518 782-7700
George C McNamee, *Ch of Bd*
Andrew Marsh, *President*
Keith C Schmid, *COO*
Gerard L Conway Jr, *Senior VP*
Jose Luis Crespo, *Vice Pres*
▲ EMP: 277 EST: 1997
SQ FT: 140,000
SALES: 103.2MM Publicly Held
WEB: www.plugpower.com
SIC: 3674 2679 Fuel cells, solid state; fuel cell forms, cardboard: made from purchased material

(G-7092)
RESPONSELINK INC
Also Called: Responselink of Albany
31 Dussault Dr (12110-2303)
PHONE 518 424-7776
Jason Kutey, *President*
EMP: 6
SALES (est): 381.5K Privately Held
SIC: 3841 Surgical & medical instruments

(G-7093)
TIRE CONVERSION TECH INC
874 Albany Shaker Rd (12110-1416)
PHONE 518 372-1600
Garen Szablewski, *CEO*
Jeff Henry, *Vice Pres*
▲ EMP: 25
SQ FT: 10,000
SALES (est): 4.2MM Privately Held
WEB: www.tire-conversion.com
SIC: 3069 Custom compounding of rubber materials

(G-7094)
TRANE US INC
301 Old Niskayuna Rd # 1 (12110-2276)
PHONE 518 785-1315
William Seward, *Branch Mgr*
EMP: 35 Privately Held
SIC: 3585 Refrigeration & heating equipment
HQ: Trane U.S. Inc.
3600 Pammel Creek Rd
La Crosse WI 54601
608 787-2000

(G-7095)
TRANSTECH SYSTEMS INC (PA)
900 Albany Shaker Rd (12110-1416)
PHONE 518 370-5558
David Apkarian, *CEO*
Jaret C Morse, *Vice Pres*
Adam Cartner, *Manager*
David Dussault, *Director*
Kevin Lynch, *Director*
▼ EMP: 21
SQ FT: 14,000
SALES: 3.9MM Privately Held
WEB: www.transtechsys.com
SIC: 3823 8731 Industrial instrmnts msrmnt display/control process variable; commercial physical research

Latham - Albany County

(G-7096)
UL INFORMATION & INSIGHTS INC (DH)
23 British American Blvd # 2 (12110-1429)
PHONE..................................518 640-9200
Lou Desorbo, *President*
Gabriel Guzman, *Project Mgr*
Dave Spore, *Project Mgr*
Emily Swartz, *Project Mgr*
Gabriel Valentin-Ramos, *Sr Project Mgr*
EMP: 39
SALES (est): 9.5MM
SALES (corp-wide): 728MM **Privately Held**
WEB: www.thewercs.com
SIC: 7372 8748 Business oriented computer software; business consulting
HQ: Ul Llc
  333 Pfingsten Rd
  Northbrook IL 60062
  847 272-8800

(G-7097)
VINYL WORKS INC
33 Wade Rd (12110-2613)
PHONE..................................518 786-1200
John Maiuccoro, *President*
EMP: 50 EST: 1971
SALES (est): 4.1MM **Privately Held**
WEB: www.thevinylworks.com
SIC: 2394 Liners & covers, fabric: made from purchased materials

(G-7098)
WILLIAM BOYD PRINTING CO INC
Also Called: Boyd Printing Company
4 Weed Rd Ste 1 (12110-2939)
PHONE..................................518 339-5832
Henry R Bosselman, *Ch of Bd*
Jane Q Carey, *President*
Stacey Dunning, *Principal*
Carl R Johnson, *Vice Pres*
Marion Quellmalz, *Vice Pres*
EMP: 120 EST: 1889
SQ FT: 81,000
SALES (est): 4.9MM **Privately Held**
SIC: 2711 2752 Commercial printing & newspaper publishing combined; commercial printing, lithographic

Laurelton
Queens County

(G-7099)
EPIC PHARMA LLC
22715 N Conduit Ave (11413-3134)
PHONE..................................718 276-8600
Aqeel Fatmi, *Senior VP*
Paul Cook, *Engineer*
Dharmesh Patel, *Engineer*
Tarachand Sookram, *Engineer*
Jeanne Stefaniak, *Human Res Mgr*
▲ EMP: 160
SQ FT: 110,000
SALES (est): 67.1MM **Privately Held**
SIC: 2834 Pharmaceutical preparations

(G-7100)
NOVARTIS CORPORATION
22715 N Conduit Ave (11413-3134)
PHONE..................................718 276-8600
Kumar Rathnam, *Vice Pres*
EMP: 56
SALES (corp-wide): 49.1B **Privately Held**
WEB: www.novartis.com
SIC: 2834 Pharmaceutical preparations
HQ: Novartis Corporation
  1 S Ridgedale Ave
  East Hanover NJ 07936
  212 307-1122

(G-7101)
NOVARTIS PHARMACEUTICALS CORP
22715 N Conduit Ave (11413-3134)
PHONE..................................718 276-8600
EMP: 8
SALES (est): 2.2MM
SALES (corp-wide): 49.4B **Privately Held**
SIC: 2834 Pharmaceutical Preparations

PA: Novartis Ag
  Lichtstrasse 35
  Basel BS 4056
  613 241-111

Lawrence
Nassau County

(G-7102)
ATLAZ INTERNATIONAL LTD
298 Lawrence Ave Unit 1 (11559-1268)
PHONE..................................516 239-1854
Loretta Zalta, *President*
Adam Zalta, *Vice Pres*
Andre Zalta, *Vice Pres*
EMP: 11
SQ FT: 3,000
SALES (est): 2.6MM **Privately Held**
WEB: www.atlaz.com
SIC: 3577 5045 5112 Computer peripheral equipment; computer peripheral equipment; stationery & office supplies

(G-7103)
JOHN J RICHARDSON
Also Called: Gad Systems
12 Bernard St (11559-1245)
PHONE..................................516 538-6339
John J Richardson, *Owner*
EMP: 15
SQ FT: 4,000
SALES: 900K **Privately Held**
SIC: 3695 Computer software tape & disks: blank, rigid & floppy

(G-7104)
LAST STRAW INC
Also Called: Zenith Promotions
22 Lawrence Ln Unit 1 (11559-1137)
P.O. Box 960177, Inwood (11096-0177)
PHONE..................................516 371-2727
Sharon Hecht, *President*
Maria Lafichi, *Shareholder*
▲ EMP: 40 EST: 1995
SQ FT: 9,000
SALES (est): 6.5MM **Privately Held**
WEB: www.zenithpromotions.com
SIC: 2656 5092 Straws, drinking: made from purchased material; toys & games

(G-7105)
M W MICROWAVE CORP
45 Auerbach Ln (11559-2529)
PHONE..................................516 295-1814
Mariam Wiesenfeld, *President*
EMP: 12 EST: 1970
SQ FT: 10,000
SALES (est): 1MM **Privately Held**
SIC: 3679 Waveguides & fittings; microwave components

(G-7106)
MEDITUB INCORPORATED
11 Wedgewood Ln (11559-1427)
P.O. Box 668 (11559-0668)
PHONE..................................866 633-4882
Joseph Swartz, *President*
EMP: 17
SALES (est): 621.6K **Privately Held**
SIC: 3272 Bathtubs, concrete
PA: Spa World Corporation
  1 Oakwood Blvd Ste 200
  Hollywood FL 33020

(G-7107)
PREMIER SKIRTING PRODUCTS INC
Also Called: Premier Skrting Tblecloths Too
241 Mill St (11559-1209)
PHONE..................................516 239-6581
Ross Yudin, *CEO*
Beth Yudin, *President*
Linda Ehrlich, *Corp Secy*
EMP: 16
SQ FT: 8,500
SALES (est): 1.5MM **Privately Held**
WEB: www.premierskirting.com
SIC: 2392 Tablecloths: made from purchased materials; napkins, fabric & nonwoven: made from purchased materials

(G-7108)
RICHNER COMMUNICATIONS INC
Also Called: Oceanside-Island Park Herald
379 Central Ave (11559-1607)
PHONE..................................516 569-4000
Rhonda Glickman, *Vice Pres*
Cliff Richner, *Branch Mgr*
EMP: 5
SALES (corp-wide): 14.2MM **Privately Held**
SIC: 2711 Newspapers: publishing only, not printed on site
PA: Richner Communications, Inc.
  2 Endo Blvd
  Garden City NY 11530
  516 569-4000

(G-7109)
SEVILLE CENTRAL MIX CORP
101 Johnson Rd (11559)
PHONE..................................516 239-8333
Peter Buck, *Manager*
EMP: 30
SALES (corp-wide): 12.3MM **Privately Held**
WEB: www.sevillecentralmix.com
SIC: 3273 Ready-mixed concrete
PA: Seville Central Mix Corp.
  157 Albany Ave
  Freeport NY 11520
  516 868-3000

(G-7110)
TG PEPPE INC
Also Called: Doery Awning Co
299 Rockaway Tpke Unit B (11559-1269)
PHONE..................................516 239-7852
Thomas Peppe, *President*
Gregory Peppe, *Vice Pres*
EMP: 8
SQ FT: 6,000
SALES (est): 985K **Privately Held**
SIC: 2394 7699 Awnings, fabric: made from purchased materials; awning repair shop

(G-7111)
VILLAGE HERALD
379 Central Ave (11559-1607)
PHONE..................................516 569-4403
Nathan Rodriguez, *Executive*
EMP: 5
SALES (est): 165.6K **Privately Held**
SIC: 2711 Newspapers, publishing & printing

Le Roy
Genesee County

(G-7112)
ALUMINUM INJECTION MOLD CO LLC
8741 Lake Street Rd Ste 4 (14482-9381)
PHONE..................................585 502-6087
Gerald Ayers, *Vice Pres*
Don Taylor, *Manager*
Tom Bergman,
EMP: 8
SQ FT: 12,000
SALES (est): 1.5MM **Privately Held**
WEB: www.aluminumjnjectionmold.com
SIC: 3089 Injection molded finished plastic products; injection molding of plastics

(G-7113)
BATAVIA LEGAL PRINTING INC
7 Bank St (14482-1413)
P.O. Box 57, Stafford (14143-0057)
PHONE..................................585 768-2100
Susan Duyssen, *President*
EMP: 5
SQ FT: 4,000
SALES: 350K **Privately Held**
WEB: www.batavialegal.com
SIC: 2759 Laser printing

(G-7114)
CK COATINGS
57 North St Ste 150 (14482-1143)
P.O. Box 203 (14482-0203)
PHONE..................................585 502-0425
Linda Wright, *Owner*

EMP: 5
SALES (est): 487.6K **Privately Held**
SIC: 3827 Optical instruments & lenses

(G-7115)
DOLOMITE PRODUCTS COMPANY INC
8250 Golf Rd (14482)
PHONE..................................585 768-7295
Matt McCormick, *Manager*
EMP: 12
SQ FT: 9,122
SALES (corp-wide): 29.7B **Privately Held**
WEB: www.dolomitegroup.com
SIC: 2951 Paving mixtures
HQ: Dolomite Products Company Inc.
  1150 Penfield Rd
  Rochester NY 14625
  315 524-1998

(G-7116)
DRAY ENTERPRISES INC
Also Called: Le Roy Pennysaver
1 Church St (14482-1017)
P.O. Box 190 (14482-0190)
PHONE..................................585 768-2201
David J Grayson Jr, *President*
Danette L Grayson, *Admin Sec*
EMP: 14
SQ FT: 16,000
SALES (est): 1MM **Privately Held**
WEB: www.leroyny.com
SIC: 2711 7389 Newspapers: publishing only, not printed on site; embroidering of advertising on shirts, etc.

(G-7117)
DUZMOR PAINTING INC
Also Called: Finishing Line, The
7959 E Main Rd (14482-9726)
P.O. Box 135 (14482-0135)
PHONE..................................585 768-4760
Peter Mc Quillen, *President*
Judy Mc Quillen, *Vice Pres*
EMP: 6
SQ FT: 10,000
SALES (est): 757.8K **Privately Held**
WEB: www.thefinishinglineco.com
SIC: 3479 Painting of metal products

(G-7118)
HELIOJET CLEANING TECH INC
57 North St Ste 120 (14482-1143)
PHONE..................................585 768-8710
Russell Knisel Jr, *President*
Scott Meurer, *Vice Pres*
EMP: 12 EST: 1980
SQ FT: 11,640
SALES (est): 1.1MM **Privately Held**
WEB: www.heliojet.com
SIC: 3589 High pressure cleaning equipment

(G-7119)
ICON DESIGN LLC
9 Lent Ave (14482-1009)
PHONE..................................585 768-6040
Wendell Castle,
EMP: 25
SALES (est): 2.8MM **Privately Held**
WEB: www.icondesign.com
SIC: 2511 Wood household furniture

(G-7120)
J & L PRECISION CO INC
9222 Summit Street Rd (14482-8950)
PHONE..................................585 768-6388
James Lytle, *President*
Laurita Lytle, *Corp Secy*
EMP: 8
SQ FT: 6,500
SALES (est): 720K **Privately Held**
SIC: 3599 Machine shop, jobbing & repair; electrical discharge machining (EDM)

(G-7121)
LEROY PLASTICS INC
20 Lent Ave (14482-1010)
PHONE..................................585 768-8158
Ernest Truax, *President*
◆ EMP: 61 EST: 1971
SQ FT: 62,305
SALES: 7.4MM **Privately Held**
WEB: www.leroyplastics.com
SIC: 3498 Fabricated pipe & fittings

(G-7122)
MARMACH MACHINE INC
11 Lent Ave (14482)
PHONE.................................585 768-8800
John M Lynch, *President*
EMP: 6
SALES (est): 940.3K **Privately Held**
SIC: 3451 Screw machine products

(G-7123)
MOFFITT FAN CORPORATION
54 Church St (14482-1037)
PHONE.................................585 768-7010
Terence R Wirth II, *President*
EMP: 40
SQ FT: 50,000
SALES (est): 9.1MM **Privately Held**
SIC: 3564 Blowers & fans

(G-7124)
PFISTERER LAPP LLC
130 Gilbert St (14482-1352)
PHONE.................................585 768-6221
Bernhard Kahl, *CEO*
Geoff Buell, *General Mgr*
Rob Johnson, *COO*
Tom Zembsch, *Project Mgr*
Gary Carnahan, *Engineer*
◆ **EMP:** 125
SQ FT: 651,000
SALES (est): 26.7MM **Privately Held**
WEB: www.lappinsulator.com
SIC: 3264 3644 Insulators, electrical: porcelain; noncurrent-carrying wiring services; insulators & insulation materials, electrical

(G-7125)
T S P CORP
Also Called: Thom McGinnes Excavating Plbg
78 One Half Lake St (14482)
PHONE.................................585 768-6769
Thomas W McGinnis, *President*
EMP: 10
SQ FT: 1,000
SALES: 550K **Privately Held**
SIC: 3531 Plows: construction, excavating & grading

Leicester
Livingston County

(G-7126)
CPAC INC (DH)
Also Called: Stanley Home Products
2364 State Route 20a (14481-9734)
P.O. Box 175 (14481-0175)
PHONE.................................585 382-3223
Thomas N Hendrickson, *Principal*
Jos J Coronas, *Director*
◆ **EMP:** 50
SQ FT: 31,262
SALES: 49.1MM
SALES (corp-wide): 81.8MM **Privately Held**
SIC: 3991 2392 2841 2844 Brooms & brushes; mops, floor & dust; soap & other detergents; shampoos, rinses, conditioners: hair; cosmetic preparations; photographic equipment & supplies; sensitized film, cloth & paper; photographic processing chemicals; specialty cleaning preparations

(G-7127)
CPAC EQUIPMENT INC
2364 State Route 20a (14481-9734)
P.O. Box 175 (14481-0175)
PHONE.................................585 382-3223
Thomas Weldgen, *CEO*
Natalie Gayton, *Controller*
EMP: 16
SQ FT: 15,000
SALES (est): 2.3MM **Privately Held**
WEB: www.cpacequipment.com
SIC: 3843 Sterilizers, dental; dental equipment; glue, dental
PA: Integrated Medical Technologies, Inc.
2422 E Washington St # 103
Bloomington IL 61704
309 662-3614

(G-7128)
FISHERS STORAGE SHEDS
7854 Alverson Rd (14481-9617)
PHONE.................................585 382-9580
Wayne Fisher, *Partner*
Jesse Fisher, *Partner*
Leon Fisher, *Partner*
EMP: 6
SALES: 566.4K **Privately Held**
WEB: www.fishers-storage-sheds.com
SIC: 2452 Prefabricated wood buildings

(G-7129)
SENECA FOODS CORPORATION
Also Called: Comstock Food
5705 Rte 36 (14481)
P.O. Box 278 (14481-0278)
PHONE.................................585 658-2211
Gary Ellis, *Plant Mgr*
Michael Hanchette, *Plant Mgr*
Cameron Ellis, *Warehouse Mgr*
Michael Mallaber, *Purch Mgr*
Flo Mullen, *QC Mgr*
EMP: 40
SALES (corp-wide): 1.3B **Publicly Held**
SIC: 2033 Vegetables: packaged in cans, jars, etc.
PA: Seneca Foods Corporation
3736 S Main St
Marion NY 14505
315 926-8100

Levittown
Nassau County

(G-7130)
APOGEE RETAIL NY
3041 Hempstead Tpke (11756-1332)
PHONE.................................516 731-1727
EMP: 5 **EST:** 2010
SALES (est): 379.5K **Privately Held**
SIC: 2329 Men's & boys' clothing

(G-7131)
BEYOND BEAUTY BASICS LLC
3359 Hempstead Tpke (11756-1310)
PHONE.................................516 731-7100
Claudie Oslian, *Mng Member*
EMP: 15
SALES (est): 1.7MM **Privately Held**
SIC: 2899 Core wash or wax

(G-7132)
CCZ READY MIX CONCRETE CORP
2 Loring Rd (11756-1516)
PHONE.................................516 579-7352
Michael Zampini, *President*
EMP: 5
SALES (est): 531.3K **Privately Held**
SIC: 3273 Ready-mixed concrete

(G-7133)
DEUNALL CORPORATION
147 Blacksmith Rd E (11756-3127)
PHONE.................................516 667-8875
Kevin Park, *President*
Steve Yoon, *Vice Pres*
Myeoan Kim, *Shareholder*
Russell Lin, *Shareholder*
Hugh Thung, *Shareholder*
EMP: 205
SQ FT: 2,800
SALES (est): 4MM **Privately Held**
SIC: 2342 Foundation garments, women's

(G-7134)
GLITNIR TICKETING INC
Also Called: Glitner Ticketing
3 Snapdragon Ln (11756-3315)
PHONE.................................516 390-5168
Gordon Krstacic, *CEO*
EMP: 5
SALES (est): 488.9K **Privately Held**
WEB: www.glitnir.com
SIC: 7372 Prepackaged software

(G-7135)
KB MILLWORK INC
36 Grey Ln (11756-4411)
P.O. Box 395 (11756-0395)
PHONE.................................516 280-2183
Kenneth Wright, *President*
EMP: 5
SQ FT: 1,200
SALES: 1.5MM **Privately Held**
SIC: 2431 Millwork

(G-7136)
UNIVERSAL ARMOR SYSTEMS CORP
Also Called: 2nd Skin Armor
9 Tanners Ln (11756-4703)
PHONE.................................631 838-1836
Stephen Moran, *CEO*
EMP: 26
SALES (est): 1.9MM **Privately Held**
SIC: 3728 9711 Aircraft parts & equipment; national security

Lewis
Essex County

(G-7137)
UPSTONE MATERIALS INC
Also Called: Lewis Sand & Gravel
Rr 9 (12950)
PHONE.................................518 873-2275
Ron Haugh, *Manager*
EMP: 9
SALES (corp-wide): 95.5MM **Privately Held**
WEB: www.graymont-ab.com
SIC: 2951 3273 3272 3241 Asphalt paving mixtures & blocks; ready-mixed concrete; concrete products; cement, hydraulic
HQ: Upstone Materials Inc.
111 Quarry Rd
Plattsburgh NY 12901
518 561-5321

Lewiston
Niagara County

(G-7138)
450 RIDGE ST INC
Also Called: Mellen Pressroom & Bindery
450 Ridge St (14092-1206)
PHONE.................................716 754-2789
Ruth Koheil, *President*
EMP: 7
SQ FT: 1,488
SALES (est): 656.1K **Privately Held**
SIC: 2731 2752 2732 Books: publishing & printing; commercial printing, lithographic; book printing

(G-7139)
EASTON PHARMACEUTICALS INC
736 Center St Ste 5 (14092-1706)
PHONE.................................347 284-0192
Joseph Slechta, *President*
Peter Rothbart, *Treasurer*
EMP: 6 **EST:** 1998
SALES (est): 173.3K **Privately Held**
SIC: 2834 8731 Ointments; commercial physical research; commercial research laboratory; medical research, commercial

(G-7140)
EDWIN MELLEN PRESS INC
442 Center St (14092-1604)
PHONE.................................716 754-2796
Herbert Richardson, *President*
EMP: 38
SALES (est): 1.6MM **Privately Held**
SIC: 2731 Books-Publishing/Printing

(G-7141)
PROTOCASE INCORPORATED
210 S 8th St (14092-1702)
PHONE.................................866 849-3911
Steve Lilley, *President*
Doug Milburn, *Vice Pres*
Patricia McCann, *Controller*
Shirley Evely, *Accounts Mgr*
Alex Milburn, *Accounts Mgr*
EMP: 138
SALES: 8.6MM **Privately Held**
WEB: www.protocase.com
SIC: 3499 3466 Furniture parts, metal; crowns & closures

(G-7142)
PSR PRESS LTD
Also Called: Mellen Press, The
415 Ridge St (14092-1205)
P.O. Box 450 (14092-0450)
PHONE.................................716 754-2266
Herbert Richardson, *CEO*
EMP: 12
SQ FT: 2,000
SALES (est): 1.2MM **Privately Held**
WEB: www.mellenpress.com
SIC: 2731 Books: publishing only

Liberty
Sullivan County

(G-7143)
CRANESVILLE BLOCK CO INC
Also Called: Cranesville Concrete Co
1794 State Route 52 (12754-8304)
PHONE.................................845 292-1585
Stephen Miller, *Manager*
EMP: 10
SALES (corp-wide): 45.6MM **Privately Held**
SIC: 3273 Ready-mixed concrete
PA: Cranesville Block Co., Inc.
1250 Riverfront Ctr
Amsterdam NY 12010
518 684-6154

(G-7144)
IDEAL SNACKS CORPORATION
89 Mill St (12754-2038)
PHONE.................................845 292-7000
Zeke Alenick, *President*
Steven Van Poucke, *Vice Pres*
◆ **EMP:** 200
SQ FT: 250,000
SALES (est): 55.5MM **Privately Held**
WEB: www.idealsnacks.com
SIC: 2096 Potato chips & similar snacks

(G-7145)
MAJOR-IPC INC
53 Webster Ave (12754-2005)
P.O. Box 350 (12754-0350)
PHONE.................................845 292-2200
David Feldman, *President*
▲ **EMP:** 5 **EST:** 1976
SQ FT: 9,800
SALES (est): 825.3K **Privately Held**
SIC: 3089 3441 Plastic processing; fabricated structural metal

(G-7146)
NEVERSINK STEEL CORP
Also Called: Liberty Iron Works
12 Asthalter Rd (12754-2617)
PHONE.................................845 292-4611
Barbara Siegel, *President*
Joseph G Siegel, *Vice Pres*
EMP: 8
SALES (est): 1.7MM **Privately Held**
SIC: 3441 7389 1791 Fabricated structural metal; crane & aerial lift service; iron work, structural

Lido Beach
Nassau County

(G-7147)
AIRLINE CONTAINER SERVICES
Also Called: Airline Container Svces
354 Harbor Dr (11561-4907)
PHONE.................................516 371-4125
R Dino Persaud, *President*
Gomattie Persaud, *Vice Pres*
▲ **EMP:** 7
SALES (est): 1.1MM **Privately Held**
SIC: 2448 Cargo containers, wood & wood with metal

Lido Beach - Nassau County

(G-7148)
MARVEL DAIRY WHIP INC
258 Lido Blvd (11561-5024)
PHONE 516 889-4232
Pauline Seremetis, *President*
EMP: 5
SALES (est): 312.6K **Privately Held**
SIC: 2024 5451 Ice cream, bulk; ice cream (packaged)

Lima
Livingston County

(G-7149)
BEARS MANAGEMENT GROUP INC
Also Called: Bears Playgrounds
7577 E Main St (14485-9735)
PHONE 585 624-5694
C Daniel Bears, *President*
Marcie Bears, *Vice Pres*
Marcye Bears, *Executive*
EMP: 9
SQ FT: 2,000
SALES (est): 1.2MM **Privately Held**
WEB: www.bearsplaygrounds.com
SIC: 3949 Playground equipment

(G-7150)
CORNEAL DESIGN CORPORATION
3288 Plank Rd (14485-9408)
PHONE 301 670-7076
Daniel L Bell, *President*
Linda Adkins, *Manager*
EMP: 10
SQ FT: 4,000
SALES (est): 1.3MM **Privately Held**
SIC: 3851 Contact lenses

(G-7151)
EAST MAIN ASSOCIATES
Also Called: Lakelands Concrete
7520 E Main St (14485-9731)
PHONE 585 624-1990
Todd Clarke, *President*
EMP: 60
SQ FT: 28,720
SALES: 270K **Privately Held**
SIC: 3272 Concrete products, precast

(G-7152)
LAKELANDS CONCRETE PDTS INC
7520 E Main St (14485-9731)
PHONE 585 624-1990
Todd Clarke, *President*
Geoff Lawrence, *Engineer*
Gina Lathan, *Sales Mgr*
Jennifer French, *Office Mgr*
EMP: 49
SQ FT: 40,000
SALES (est): 9.3MM **Privately Held**
WEB: www.lakelandsconcrete.com
SIC: 3272 Concrete products, precast

(G-7153)
NORTHEAST CONVEYORS INC
7620 Evergreen St (14485-9727)
P.O. Box 55, Le Roy (14482-0055)
PHONE 585 768-8912
Paul Hastings, *Ch of Bd*
Guy Bianchi, *Vice Pres*
Michael Schaffer, *Vice Pres*
Beth Bartz, *Treasurer*
Ed Milligan, *Sales Staff*
EMP: 17
SQ FT: 8,024
SALES (est): 5.4MM **Privately Held**
WEB: www.neind.com
SIC: 3535 Conveyors & conveying equipment
PA: Northeast Industrial Technologies, Inc.
7115 W Main Rd Ste 2
Le Roy NY 14482

(G-7154)
P & H THERMOTECH INC
1883 Heath Markham Rd (14485-9529)
PHONE 585 624-1310
Dave Howes, *CEO*
Ray Platt, *President*
EMP: 5
SALES (est): 463.7K **Privately Held**
SIC: 2796 Platemaking services

(G-7155)
SMIDGENS INC
7336 Community Dr (14485-9772)
PHONE 585 624-1486
Rita Villa, *President*
Gary Villa, *Vice Pres*
EMP: 8
SQ FT: 3,000
SALES (est): 1.1MM **Privately Held**
WEB: www.smidgens.com
SIC: 3599 Machine shop, jobbing & repair

(G-7156)
SUPERIOR WALLS UPSTATE NY INC
7574 E Main St (14485-9731)
PHONE 585 624-9390
Gary T Hess, *President*
EMP: 90
SQ FT: 200,000
SALES (est): 19.4MM **Privately Held**
SIC: 3272 Precast terrazo or concrete products

Limestone
Cattaraugus County

(G-7157)
CASE BROTHERS INC
370 Quinn Rd (14753-9713)
P.O. Box 181 (14753-0181)
PHONE 716 925-7172
Thomas A Case, *President*
EMP: 9
SALES (est): 949.7K **Privately Held**
SIC: 1389 Oil & gas field services

(G-7158)
JAY LITTLE OIL WELL SERVI
5460 Nichols Run (14753-9774)
PHONE 716 925-8905
Jay Little, *Principal*
EMP: 5
SALES (est): 333.2K **Privately Held**
SIC: 1389 Well logging

Lindenhurst
Suffolk County

(G-7159)
ALRAJS INC (PA)
Also Called: Yohay Baking Company
146 Albany Ave (11757-3628)
PHONE 631 225-0300
Mike Solomon, *President*
Lew Solomon, *Chairman*
Mitch Margolis, *Vice Pres*
▲ EMP: 27 EST: 1948
SQ FT: 15,000
SALES (est): 6.4MM **Privately Held**
WEB: www.yohay.com
SIC: 2051 2052 2064 Pastries, e.g. danish: except frozen; cones, ice cream; fudge (candy)

(G-7160)
ALRO MACHINE TOOL & DIE CO INC
Also Called: Alro Machine Company
585 W Hoffman Ave (11757-4032)
PHONE 631 226-5020
Steven Young, *President*
Ronald Young, *Founder*
Elizabeth Young, *Corp Secy*
EMP: 15 EST: 1960
SQ FT: 22,000
SALES (est): 3.1MM **Privately Held**
SIC: 3599 Machine shop, jobbing & repair

(G-7161)
ANTHONY MANUFACTURING INC
34 Gear Ave (11757-1005)
PHONE 631 957-9424
Jon Hatz, *President*
Benjamin Hatz, *Shareholder*
Melanie Hatz, *Shareholder*
Sandy Hatz, *Shareholder*
Kevin Jampolis, *Shareholder*
EMP: 9
SQ FT: 12,000
SALES (est): 1.2MM **Privately Held**
WEB: www.keithmachinery.com
SIC: 3547 5084 Rolling mill machinery; industrial machinery & equipment

(G-7162)
AUTO BODY SERVICES LLC
400 W Hoffman Ave (11757-4038)
PHONE 631 431-4640
Michael Moretti, *Officer*
EMP: 12
SALES (est): 5MM **Privately Held**
SIC: 3563 3444 5013 Spraying outfits: metals, paints & chemicals (compressor); booths, spray: prefabricated sheet metal; body repair or paint shop supplies, automotive

(G-7163)
AUTODYNE MANUFACTURING CO INC
200 N Strong Ave (11757-3629)
PHONE 631 957-5858
Lindsay Howe, *Ch of Bd*
Shari Kramberg, *Treasurer*
EMP: 10
SALES (est): 2MM **Privately Held**
WEB: www.autodyne.com
SIC: 3674 Solid state electronic devices

(G-7164)
BUXTON MEDICAL EQUIPMENT CORP
1178 Route 109 (11757-1004)
PHONE 631 957-4500
Carl Newman, *President*
▲ EMP: 30
SALES (est): 5.3MM **Privately Held**
WEB: www.buxtonmed.com
SIC: 3841 Surgical & medical instruments

(G-7165)
CANFIELD ELECTRONICS INC (PA)
6 Burton Pl (11757-1812)
PHONE 631 585-4100
Lynn Zaun, *President*
▲ EMP: 18
SQ FT: 15,000
SALES (est): 3.1MM **Privately Held**
WEB: www.canfieldelectronics.com
SIC: 3679 5065 Electronic circuits; electronic parts & equipment

(G-7166)
CAROB INDUSTRIES INC
215 W Hoffman Ave (11757-4096)
PHONE 631 225-0900
Robert A Levey, *President*
EMP: 10
SQ FT: 8,000
SALES (est): 1.2MM **Privately Held**
SIC: 2431 Millwork

(G-7167)
CRYSTAL FUSION TECH INC
185 W Montauk Hwy (11757-5654)
PHONE 631 253-9800
Ray Doran, *President*
Tony Seara, *Sales Staff*
Gary Locicero, *Manager*
EMP: 19
SALES (est): 3.2MM **Privately Held**
SIC: 2899 Water treating compounds

(G-7168)
DELANEY MACHINE PRODUCTS LTD
150 S Alleghany Ave Ste A (11757-5062)
PHONE 631 225-1032
Bob Delaney, *President*
Sharon Delaney, *Vice Pres*
EMP: 6
SQ FT: 10,000
SALES: 850K **Privately Held**
SIC: 3599 Machine shop, jobbing & repair

(G-7169)
DERMATECH LABS INC
165 S 10th St (11757-4505)
PHONE 631 225-1700
Dan Bryle, *President*
▲ EMP: 10
SQ FT: 11,000
SALES (est): 940K **Privately Held**
SIC: 2844 5122 Cosmetic preparations; cosmetics

(G-7170)
DINE RITE SEATING PRODUCTS INC
165 E Hoffman Ave Unit 3 (11757-5036)
PHONE 631 226-8899
Phil Driesen, *President*
EMP: 20
SALES (est): 3.6MM **Privately Held**
SIC: 2599 7641 Restaurant furniture, wood or metal; upholstery work

(G-7171)
DULCETTE TECHNOLOGIES LLC
2 Hicks St (11757-1007)
PHONE 631 752-8700
Luke Verdet, *Director*
Mel Blum,
Eric Saltsberg,
Ashish Tandakar,
EMP: 7
SQ FT: 1,500
SALES (est): 641.2K
SALES (corp-wide): 47.8MM **Privately Held**
WEB: www.dulcettetech.com
SIC: 2869 Sweeteners, synthetic
PA: Camlin Fine Sciences Limited
Plot No.F/11 & F/12, Opp.Seepz Main Gate,
Mumbai MH 40009
226 700-1000

(G-7172)
ELITE SEMI CONDUCTOR PRODUCTS
860 N Richmond Ave (11757-3007)
PHONE 631 884-8400
Robert Kravitz, *President*
Edward Kravitz, *Vice Pres*
Joan Kravitz, *Vice Pres*
EMP: 8
SQ FT: 5,000
SALES (est): 1.2MM **Privately Held**
WEB: www.elitesemi.com
SIC: 3674 Integrated circuits, semiconductor networks, etc.

(G-7173)
JOHNNY MICA INC
116 E Hoffman Ave (11757-5029)
PHONE 631 225-5213
John Desimini, *President*
Karla Desimini, *Corp Secy*
EMP: 5
SALES (est): 692.6K **Privately Held**
WEB: www.johnnymica.com
SIC: 2541 5031 1799 1751 Cabinets, except refrigerated: show, display, etc.: wood; kitchen cabinets; counter top installation; cabinet & finish carpentry

(G-7174)
LINDENHURST FABRICATORS INC
117 S 13th St (11757-4546)
PHONE 631 226-3737
Charles Rogers, *President*
EMP: 8
SQ FT: 17,500
SALES (est): 1.6MM **Privately Held**
SIC: 3441 Fabricated structural metal

(G-7175)
LINEAR SIGNS INC
Also Called: Vista Visual Group
275 W Hoffman Ave Ste 1 (11757-4081)
PHONE 631 532-5330
Mike Shroff, *President*
Sohel Vakil, *Vice Pres*
Mobin Shroff, *Marketing Staff*
Judy Minaya, *Consultant*
EMP: 15
SQ FT: 7,000

GEOGRAPHIC SECTION

SALES (est): 2.3MM **Privately Held**
SIC: 3993 Signs, not made in custom sign painting shops

(G-7176)
LONGO COMMERCIAL CABINETS INC
Also Called: Longo Cabinets
829 N Richmond Ave (11757-3008)
PHONE 631 225-4290
Robert Longo, *President*
Sandy Giuffrida, *Purch Mgr*
EMP: 50 **EST:** 1966
SQ FT: 22,000
SALES (est): 5.9MM **Privately Held**
SIC: 2541 2521 2434 Store fixtures, wood; wood office furniture; wood kitchen cabinets

(G-7177)
MAR-A-THON FILTERS INC
369 41st St (11757-2713)
PHONE 631 957-4774
John Reinbold, *President*
Sean Boyle, *General Mgr*
Thomas Cornell, *Corp Secy*
EMP: 6
SQ FT: 7,000
SALES (est): 846.7K **Privately Held**
SIC: 3364 3599 5046 Nonferrous die-castings except aluminum; machine & other job shop work; commercial cooking & food service equipment

(G-7178)
MARIA DIONISIO WELDING INC
71 W Montauk Hwy (11757-5751)
PHONE 631 956-0815
Maria Dionisio, *President*
EMP: 5
SALES (est): 118.1K **Privately Held**
SIC: 7692 Welding repair

(G-7179)
MATTHEW-LEE CORPORATION
149 Pennsylvania Ave (11757-5052)
PHONE 631 226-0100
John Ferrigno, *President*
Matthew Ferrigno, *Corp Secy*
EMP: 10
SQ FT: 13,000
SALES (est): 638K **Privately Held**
WEB: www.mattlee.com
SIC: 2759 Screen printing

(G-7180)
MIDDLEBY CORPORATION
Also Called: Marsal & Sons
175 E Hoffman Ave (11757-5013)
PHONE 631 226-6688
Carl Ferrara, *Treasurer*
Joseph Ferrera, *Branch Mgr*
EMP: 33
SALES (corp-wide): 2.3B **Publicly Held**
SIC: 3444 Restaurant sheet metalwork
PA: The Middleby Corporation
1400 Toastmaster Dr
Elgin IL 60120
847 741-3300

(G-7181)
MODERN CRAFT BAR REST EQUIP
Also Called: Modern Craft Bar Rest Equip
165 E Hoffman Ave Unit 3 (11757-5036)
PHONE 631 226-5647
John Venticinque, *President*
Heidee Venticinque, *Admin Sec*
EMP: 7
SALES (est): 959.7K **Privately Held**
WEB: www.moderncraft.com
SIC: 2599 5046 2542 Bar, restaurant & cafeteria furniture; commercial cooking & food service equipment; bar fixtures, except wood

(G-7182)
NAS-TRA AUTOMOTIVE INDS INC
Also Called: Nastra Automotive
3 Sidney Ct (11757-1011)
PHONE 631 225-1225
James Lambert, *Ch of Bd*
Americo De Rocchis, *President*
Antonio Abbatiello, *Corp Secy*
Tim Nolan, *VP Opers*
Ramesh Lakshmanan, *Prdtn Mgr*
▲ **EMP:** 150 **EST:** 1978
SQ FT: 60,000
SALES (est): 24.1MM **Privately Held**
WEB: www.nastra.com
SIC: 3714 3694 3625 Motor vehicle parts & accessories; engine electrical equipment; relays & industrial controls

(G-7183)
NEW FINE CHEMICALS INC
35 W Hoffman Ave (11757-4012)
PHONE 631 321-8151
Jim Haseez, *Director*
EMP: 7 **EST:** 2017
SALES (est): 304.1K **Privately Held**
SIC: 2899 Chemical preparations

(G-7184)
NEXGEN ENVIRO SYSTEMS INC
190 E Hoffman Ave Ste D (11757-5017)
PHONE 631 226-2930
Michael Robbins, *President*
Jason Robbins, *Vice Pres*
▲ **EMP:** 3
SALES: 1.1MM **Privately Held**
WEB: www.nexgenenviro.com
SIC: 3826 Environmental testing equipment

(G-7185)
NICOLIA CONCRETE PRODUCTS INC
Also Called: Nicolia of Long Island
640 Muncy St (11757-4318)
P.O. Box 1120, West Babylon (11704-0120)
PHONE 631 669-0700
R Glenn Schroeder, *Principal*
Robert Nicolia, *Chairman*
Antonio Nicolia, *Vice Pres*
Gian Nicolia, *Vice Pres*
Franco Nicolia, *Treasurer*
▲ **EMP:** 53
SQ FT: 22,000
SALES (est): 6.3MM **Privately Held**
SIC: 3271 3272 2951 5211 Paving blocks, concrete; concrete products; asphalt paving mixtures & blocks; masonry materials & supplies

(G-7186)
NICOLIA READY MIX INC (PA)
615 Cord Ave (11757-4314)
P.O. Box 1065, West Babylon (11704-0065)
PHONE 631 669-7000
Robert Nicolia, *Ch of Bd*
Antonio Nicolia, *President*
Frank Nicolia, *Vice Pres*
Gian Pierro Nicolia, *Vice Pres*
Sandy Nicolia, *Vice Pres*
EMP: 80 **EST:** 1980
SQ FT: 5,500
SALES (est): 17.6MM **Privately Held**
WEB: www.nicoliareadymix.com
SIC: 3273 Ready-mixed concrete

(G-7187)
NICOLIA READY MIX INC
615 Cord Ave (11757-4314)
PHONE 631 669-7000
Antonio L Nicolia, *President*
EMP: 30
SALES (corp-wide): 17.6MM **Privately Held**
WEB: www.nicoliareadymix.com
SIC: 3273 Ready-mixed concrete
PA: Nicolia Ready Mix, Inc.
615 Cord Ave
Lindenhurst NY 11757
631 669-7000

(G-7188)
NICOLOCK PAVING STONES LLC (HQ)
612 Muncy St (11757-4318)
PHONE 631 669-0700
Robert Nicolia, *President*
Nino Nicolia, *President*
Craig Luna, *Project Mgr*
Greg Adams, *CFO*
Jason Georgevich, *Regl Sales Mgr*
▲ **EMP:** 59
SALES: 35.4MM
SALES (corp-wide): 35.6MM **Privately Held**
SIC: 3272 Concrete products
PA: Nicolia Industries, Inc.
615 Cord Ave
Lindenhurst NY 11757
631 888-2200

(G-7189)
PACE UP PHARMACEUTICALS LLC
200 Bangor St (11757-3644)
PHONE 631 450-4495
Ming Yang,
EMP: 9
SALES (est): 1.3MM **Privately Held**
SIC: 2834 Druggists' preparations (pharmaceuticals)

(G-7190)
PRIDE LINES LTD
651 W Hoffman Ave (11757-4034)
PHONE 631 225-0033
Fax: 631 225-0099
EMP: 8
SQ FT: 8,000
SALES (est): 720K **Privately Held**
SIC: 3944 Manufactures Toy Trains

(G-7191)
RUSSELL PLASTICS TECH CO INC
521 W Hoffman Ave (11757-4052)
PHONE 631 963-8602
Alexander Bozza, *Ch of Bd*
EMP: 110
SQ FT: 58,000
SALES (est): 18.8MM
SALES (corp-wide): 1.9B **Privately Held**
WEB: www.russellplastics.com
SIC: 3089 Injection molding of plastics
HQ: Vaupell Holdings, Inc.
1144 Nw 53rd St
Seattle WA 98107

(G-7192)
SIMS STEEL CORPORATION
650 Muncy St (11757-4396)
PHONE 631 587-8670
William Sims, *President*
EMP: 25
SQ FT: 4,000
SALES (est): 6.3MM **Privately Held**
WEB: www.simssteel.com
SIC: 3449 Miscellaneous metalwork

(G-7193)
STEELFLEX ELECTRO CORP
145 S 13th St (11757-4546)
P.O. Box 515 (11757-0515)
PHONE 516 226-4466
Philip Rine, *President*
Anthony Rine, *Vice Pres*
EMP: 60
SQ FT: 25,000
SALES (est): 7.6MM **Privately Held**
SIC: 3357 Nonferrous wiredrawing & insulating

(G-7194)
STEINWAY PASTA & GELATI INC
146 Albany Ave (11757-3628)
PHONE 718 246-5414
Vincenzo Arpaia, *President*
▲ **EMP:** 15
SALES (est): 2.1MM **Privately Held**
SIC: 2099 5149 Packaged combination products: pasta, rice & potato; pasta & rice

(G-7195)
STJ ORTHOTIC SERVICES INC (PA)
Also Called: S T J Orthotic Svces
920 Wellwood Ave Ste B (11757-1246)
PHONE 631 956-0181
James De Francisco, *President*
Steve Goldring, *General Mgr*
Steven Levitz, *Vice Pres*
EMP: 12
SQ FT: 14,000
SALES: 3.5MM **Privately Held**
WEB: www.stjorthotic.com
SIC: 3842 Orthopedic appliances

(G-7196)
STRUX CORP
Also Called: Art Foam
100 Montauk Hwy (11757-5835)
PHONE 516 768-3969
Robert Kjeldsen, *President*
EMP: 25 **EST:** 1970
SQ FT: 30,000
SALES (est): 2.1MM **Privately Held**
WEB: www.strux.com
SIC: 3083 3675 3086 Laminated plastics plate & sheet; electronic capacitors; plastics foam products

(G-7197)
SUFFOLK GRANITE MANUFACTURING
Also Called: Suffolk Monument Mfg
25 Gear Ave (11757-1006)
PHONE 631 226-4774
Martin Solomon, *President*
EMP: 20
SQ FT: 17,500
SALES (est): 2.1MM **Privately Held**
WEB: www.uk-engineering.net
SIC: 3281 1423 1411 Monuments, cut stone (not finishing or lettering only); crushed & broken granite; dimension stone

(G-7198)
SUPERBOATS INC
694 Roosevelt Ave (11757-5820)
PHONE 631 226-1761
John H Coen, *President*
EMP: 6
SQ FT: 10,000
SALES: 600K **Privately Held**
SIC: 3732 5551 7699 Boats, fiberglass: building & repairing; boat dealers; boat repair

(G-7199)
SUPERIOR AGGREGATES SUPPLY LLC
612 Muncy St (11757-4318)
PHONE 516 333-2923
Robert Nicolia,
Antonio L Nicolia,
Franco A Nicolia,
Gian P Nicolia,
Sandy H Nicolia,
EMP: 30
SALES: 2.9MM **Privately Held**
SIC: 3272 Precast terrazo or concrete products

(G-7200)
SUPREME STEEL INC
690 N Jefferson Ave (11757-2902)
PHONE 631 884-1320
Jay Shikora, *President*
Vincent Caravana, *Vice Pres*
EMP: 12
SQ FT: 10,000
SALES (est): 1.7MM **Privately Held**
WEB: www.supremesteelinc.com
SIC: 3441 5051 Fabricated structural metal; structural shapes, iron or steel

(G-7201)
TENTINA WINDOW FASHIONS INC
1186 Route 109 (11757-1088)
P.O. Box 617 (11757-0617)
PHONE 631 957-9585
Frank J Miritello, *CEO*
Andrea Miritello, *President*
Jeffery Miritello, *Vice Pres*
Neil Miritello, *Treasurer*
Stephanie Miritello, *Admin Sec*
EMP: 105
SQ FT: 40,000
SALES (est): 11.4MM **Privately Held**
WEB: www.tentina.com
SIC: 2591 Window blinds; window shades

(G-7202)
VELIS ASSOCIATES INC (PA)
151 S 14th St (11757-4432)
PHONE 631 225-4220
Suriya Khan, *Chairman*
Brian Mastoberti, *Vice Pres*
EMP: 3

Linderhurst - Suffolk County (G-7203)

SALES (est): 5.3MM **Privately Held**
SIC: 3534 Elevators & equipment

(G-7203)
VIKING ATHLETICS LTD
80 Montauk Hwy Ste 1 (11757-5800)
PHONE.................................631 957-8000
David C Kjeldsen, *CEO*
Jerry Ehrlich, *CIO*
▲ **EMP:** 40 **EST:** 1995
SQ FT: 28,000
SALES (est): 4.1MM **Privately Held**
WEB: www.vikingathletics.com
SIC: 3949 5949 2759 Sporting & athletic goods; needlework goods & supplies; screen printing

(G-7204)
VIKING TECHNOLOGIES LTD
80 E Montauk Hwy (11757)
PHONE.................................631 957-8000
David Kjeldsen, *President*
EMP: 45 **EST:** 1959
SQ FT: 35,000
SALES: 10MM **Privately Held**
WEB: www.cardwellcondenser.com
SIC: 3629 3674 3675 Condensers, fixed or variable; semiconductors & related devices; electronic capacitors

(G-7205)
VILLAGE LANTERN BAKING CORP
155 N Wellwood Ave (11757-4085)
PHONE.................................631 225-1690
Linda Gramer, *Principal*
EMP: 8
SALES (est): 655.7K **Privately Held**
SIC: 2051 Bread, cake & related products

(G-7206)
VISUAL CITI INC (PA)
305 Henry St (11757-4315)
PHONE.................................631 482-3030
Abbas Devji, *President*
Fazle Abbas Deyjiyani, *Chairman*
Samina Devji, *Vice Pres*
Rene Rangel, *Project Mgr*
Deloar Khan, *Prdtn Mgr*
▲ **EMP:** 125
SQ FT: 28,000
SALES (est): 38.5MM **Privately Held**
WEB: www.visualciti.com
SIC: 3993 Displays & cutouts, window & lobby

Lindley
Steuben County

(G-7207)
LINDLEY WOOD WORKS INC
9625 Morgan Creek Rd (14858-9780)
P.O. Box 5 (14858-0005)
PHONE.................................607 523-7786
Peter McIntosh, *President*
Peter Mc Intosh, *President*
Keith Mc Intosh, *Vice Pres*
Mary Mc Intosh, *Admin Sec*
EMP: 15
SQ FT: 10,000
SALES (est): 2.3MM **Privately Held**
SIC: 2448 Pallets, wood

Little Falls
Herkimer County

(G-7208)
BURROWS PAPER CORPORATION
Also Called: Burrows Paper Mill
730 E Mill St (13365)
PHONE.................................315 823-2300
Fred Scarano, *Manager*
EMP: 70
SALES (corp-wide): 182.9MM **Privately Held**
WEB: www.burrowspaper.com
SIC: 2621 Paper mills
PA: Burrows Paper Corporation
501 W Main St Ste 1
Little Falls NY 13365
800 272-7122

(G-7209)
BURROWS PAPER CORPORATION
Also Called: Mohawk Valley Mill
489 W Main St (13365)
PHONE.................................315 823-2300
Duane Judd, *Manager*
EMP: 66
SALES (corp-wide): 182.9MM **Privately Held**
WEB: www.burrowspaper.com
SIC: 2621 Tissue paper; specialty papers
PA: Burrows Paper Corporation
501 W Main St Ste 1
Little Falls NY 13365
800 272-7122

(G-7210)
IDEAL WOOD PRODUCTS INC
Also Called: Ideal Stair Parts
225 W Main St (13365-1800)
PHONE.................................315 823-1124
Bruce Mang, *President*
Doug Plourde, *Controller*
▲ **EMP:** 40
SQ FT: 14,000
SALES (est): 6.1MM **Privately Held**
WEB: www.idealstairparts.com
SIC: 2431 Staircases & stairs, wood

(G-7211)
PEMS TOOL & MACHINE INC
125 Southern Ave (13365-1906)
PHONE.................................315 823-3595
Isabella Stone, *Ch of Bd*
Roger Schulze, *Engineer*
EMP: 31
SQ FT: 17,500
SALES (est): 7.5MM **Privately Held**
WEB: www.pemstoolandmachine.com
SIC: 3599 3549 Machine shop, jobbing & repair; metalworking machinery

(G-7212)
PRETTY FUEL INC
29 W Lansing St (13365-1317)
PHONE.................................315 823-4063
Gamdur Narain, *Principal*
EMP: 5
SALES (est): 360.6K **Privately Held**
SIC: 2869 Fuels

(G-7213)
R D S MOUNTAIN VIEW TRUCKING
Also Called: R D Drive and Shop
1600 State Route 5s (13365-5405)
P.O. Box 924 (13365-0924)
PHONE.................................315 823-4265
Randall Dawley, *Owner*
EMP: 7 **EST:** 2000
SALES (est): 745.9K **Privately Held**
SIC: 2611 Soda pulp

(G-7214)
SUNBELT INDUSTRIES INC (PA)
540 E Mill St (13365-2027)
P.O. Box 584 (13365-0584)
PHONE.................................315 823-2947
Earl Mannion, *President*
EMP: 10
SQ FT: 36,000
SALES (est): 1.2MM **Privately Held**
SIC: 3291 5085 Abrasive grains; abrasives

(G-7215)
TWIN RIVERS PAPER COMPANY LLC
501 W Main St (13365-1829)
PHONE.................................315 823-2300
EMP: 279 **Privately Held**
SIC: 2621 Paper mills
PA: Twin Rivers Paper Company Llc
82 Bridge Ave
Madawaska ME 04756

(G-7216)
VINCENT MANUFACTURING CO INC
560 E Mill St (13365-2027)
P.O. Box 306 (13365-0306)
PHONE.................................315 823-0280
Todd R Vincent, *President*
Alan N Vincent, *President*
Todd Vincent, *President*
Linda B Vincent, *Vice Pres*
EMP: 11 **EST:** 1892
SQ FT: 50,000
SALES: 800K **Privately Held**
SIC: 2299 5169 Batts & batting: cotton mill waste & related material; polyurethane products

Little Neck
Queens County

(G-7217)
ANGEL TIPS NAIL SALON
25473 Horace Harding Expy (11362-1816)
PHONE.................................718 225-8300
Sun Kim, *Owner*
EMP: 6
SALES (est): 542.8K **Privately Held**
SIC: 2844 7231 Manicure preparations; manicurist, pedicurist

(G-7218)
E GLUCK CORPORATION (PA)
Also Called: Armitron Watch Div
6015 Little Neck Pkwy (11362-2500)
PHONE.................................718 784-0700
Eugen Gluck, *President*
Rachel Fredman, *Partner*
Stanislav Kravets, *Editor*
Jerry Dikowitz, *Vice Pres*
Michael Feagan, *Vice Pres*
▲ **EMP:** 122 **EST:** 1957
SQ FT: 200,000
SALES (est): 68.9MM **Privately Held**
WEB: www.egluck.com
SIC: 3873 5094 Watches & parts, except crystals & jewels; clocks, assembly of; watches & parts; clocks

(G-7219)
RECON CONSTRUCTION CORP
1108 Shore Rd (11363-1054)
PHONE.................................718 939-1305
Gloria Kemper, *President*
EMP: 30
SQ FT: 5,000
SALES: 3.5MM **Privately Held**
SIC: 3312 Stainless steel

(G-7220)
RENEWABLE ENERGY INC
6 Cornell Ln (11363-1939)
PHONE.................................718 690-2691
EMP: 6
SALES (est): 518.5K **Privately Held**
SIC: 3674 Mfg Semiconductors/Related Devices

Little Valley
Cattaraugus County

(G-7221)
LITTLE VALLEY SAND & GRAVEL
8984 New Albion Rd (14755)
PHONE.................................716 938-6676
John R Charlesworth, *President*
Jay Charlesworth, *Treasurer*
Mary Charlesworth, *Admin Sec*
EMP: 7
SQ FT: 5,000
SALES (est): 624.6K **Privately Held**
SIC: 1442 4212 Construction sand mining; gravel mining; local trucking, without storage

Liverpool
Onondaga County

(G-7222)
BARRETT PAVING MATERIALS INC
4530 Wetzel Rd (13090-2517)
PHONE.................................315 652-4585
Frank Costanzo, *Project Engr*
Chris Winter, *Controller*
Frank Simmons, *Finance*
Heather Schmidtka, *Human Res Mgr*
EMP: 30
SQ FT: 12,368
SALES (corp-wide): 95.5MM **Privately Held**
WEB: www.barrettpaving.com
SIC: 2951 Asphalt paving mixtures & blocks
HQ: Barrett Paving Materials Inc.
3 Becker Farm Rd Ste 307
Roseland NJ 07068
973 533-1001

(G-7223)
BELLOTTI PACKAGING INC
Also Called: Bell-Pac
5089 Constitution Ln (13088-5871)
PHONE.................................315 433-0131
Louis Bellotti Jr, *President*
Kathlyn Bellotti, *Vice Pres*
EMP: 13
SQ FT: 26,100
SALES (est): 2.5MM **Privately Held**
WEB: www.bell-pak.com
SIC: 2653 Boxes, corrugated: made from purchased materials

(G-7224)
BODYCOTE SYRACUSE HEAT TREATIN
4629 Crossroads Park Dr (13088-3515)
PHONE.................................315 451-0000
John H Mac Allister, *Ch of Bd*
George Stupp, *Vice Pres*
EMP: 23 **EST:** 1932
SQ FT: 30,000
SALES (est): 5.6MM
SALES (corp-wide): 911.9MM **Privately Held**
WEB: www.syracuseheatreating.com
SIC: 3398 Brazing (hardening) of metal
HQ: Bodycote Usa, Inc.
12700 Park Central Dr # 700
Dallas TX 75251
214 904-2420

(G-7225)
BRANNOCK DEVICE CO INC
116 Luther Ave (13088-6726)
PHONE.................................315 475-9862
Salvatore A Leonardi Jr, *President*
Tim Follett, *Vice Pres*
EMP: 20 **EST:** 1929
SQ FT: 10,000
SALES (est): 2.5MM **Privately Held**
WEB: www.brannock.com
SIC: 3842 Foot appliances, orthopedic

(G-7226)
C & G VIDEO SYSTEMS INC (PA)
7778 Tirrell Hill Cir (13090-2508)
P.O. Box 2476, Syracuse (13220-2476)
PHONE.................................315 452-1490
Charles F Bisesi, *President*
Gail Bisesi, *Vice Pres*
EMP: 5
SQ FT: 3,600
SALES: 1MM **Privately Held**
SIC: 3699 1731 Security control equipment & systems; electrical welding equipment; electrical work

(G-7227)
C SPEED LLC
316 Commerce Blvd (13088-4511)
PHONE.................................315 453-1043
David Lysack, *President*
Michael Lesmerises, *Project Mgr*
Brian D Sherry -, *Engineer*
Kevin Francis -, *Engineer*
Pat McHenry, *Engineer*
EMP: 32

SQ FT: 5,000
SALES (est): 6.9MM **Privately Held**
WEB: www.cspeed.com
SIC: **3812** 8711 3825 Search & navigation equipment; electrical or electronic engineering; instruments to measure electricity

(G-7228)
CARGILL INCORPORATED
7700 Maltage Dr (13090-2513)
PHONE.................................315 622-3533
Hugh Fordyce, *Branch Mgr*
EMP: 25
SQ FT: 27,466
SALES (corp-wide): 51.2B **Privately Held**
WEB: www.cargill.com
SIC: **2048** Prepared feeds
PA: Cargill, Incorporated
  15407 Mcginty Rd W
  Wayzata MN 55391
  952 742-7575

(G-7229)
CASCADE HELMETS HOLDINGS INC
4697 Crssrads Pk Dr Ste 1 (13088)
PHONE.................................315 453-3073
Bill Brine, *CEO*
Steve Moore, *COO*
EMP: 8
SALES (est): 2.7MM **Privately Held**
SIC: **3949** Helmets, athletic

(G-7230)
CAYUGA PRESS CORTLAND INC
4707 Dey Rd (13088-3510)
PHONE.................................888 229-8421
Thomas Quartier, *President*
Joe Shelton, *Accounts Exec*
EMP: 32 **EST: 2011**
SALES (est): 342K **Privately Held**
SIC: **2752** 2741 Commercial printing, offset; miscellaneous publishing

(G-7231)
CREATIVE COSTUME CO
3804 Rivers Pointe Way (13090-4917)
PHONE.................................212 564-5552
Susan Handler, *Partner*
Linda Carcaci, *Partner*
EMP: 7
SALES (est): 877.3K **Privately Held**
WEB: www.creativecostume.com
SIC: **2389** Costumes

(G-7232)
EAGLE COMTRONICS INC
7665 Henry Clay Blvd (13088-3507)
P.O. Box 2457, Syracuse (13220-2457)
PHONE.................................315 451-3313
William Devendorf, *CEO*
Timothy Devendorf, *President*
Gary Clark, *Engineer*
Glenn Sparling, *CFO*
▲ EMP: 200 **EST: 1975**
SQ FT: 100,000
SALES (est): 38.8MM **Privately Held**
WEB: www.eaglecomtronics.com
SIC: **3663** Cable television equipment

(G-7233)
FAYETTE STREET COATINGS INC
1 Burr Dr (13088)
PHONE.................................315 488-5401
Bill Udovich, *Branch Mgr*
EMP: 11
SALES (corp-wide): 35.1MM **Publicly Held**
SIC: **2851** Paints & allied products
HQ: Fayette Street Coatings, Inc.
  11917 Cutten Rd
  Houston TX 77066
  315 488-5401

(G-7234)
HEARTH CABINETS AND MORE LTD
4483 Buckley Rd (13088-2506)
P.O. Box 2700 (13089-2700)
PHONE.................................315 641-1197
Richard D Hovey, *President*
Chris Yager, *Consultant*
EMP: 2
SALES (est): 2.3MM **Privately Held**
SIC: **2434** Wood kitchen cabinets

(G-7235)
HSM PACKAGING CORPORATION
4529 Crown Rd (13090-3541)
PHONE.................................315 476-7996
Sheila M Martin, *CEO*
Homer S Martin III, *COO*
Jessica T Pletka, *CFO*
Sheila Martin, *Executive*
▲ EMP: 58
SQ FT: 30,000
SALES (est): 13.8MM **Privately Held**
WEB: www.hsmpackaging.com
SIC: **2657** Folding paperboard boxes

(G-7236)
INFIMED INC (PA)
Also Called: Varian Medical Systems
121 Metropolitan Park Dr (13088-5335)
PHONE.................................315 453-4545
Robert Kluge, *President*
Norman Shoenfeld, *Ch of Bd*
Amy L Ryan, *President*
▲ EMP: 64
SQ FT: 26,000
SALES (est): 8.3MM **Privately Held**
WEB: www.digitalxrayimages.com
SIC: **3845** Electromedical equipment

(G-7237)
INFO QUICK SOLUTIONS
7460 Morgan Rd (13090-3979)
PHONE.................................315 463-1400
Bernie Owens, *President*
Christine Lohr, *Opers Staff*
Dennis Owens, *Sales Staff*
Tedd Kehoe, *Manager*
Tony Tabone, *Database Admin*
EMP: 50
SALES (est): 4.9MM **Privately Held**
SIC: **7372** Prepackaged software

(G-7238)
INTEGRATED MEDICAL DEVICES
549 Electronics Pkwy # 200 (13088-4391)
PHONE.................................315 457-4200
Stephen L Esposito, *President*
EMP: 7
SQ FT: 4,400
SALES (est): 650K **Privately Held**
WEB: www.qrstech.com
SIC: **3845** Electrocardiographs

(G-7239)
IRONSHORE HOLDINGS INC
Also Called: Lipe Automation
290 Elwood Davis Rd (13088-2100)
PHONE.................................315 457-1052
Robert Offley, *CEO*
Jay Lacey, *President*
Campbell McIntire, *Shareholder*
EMP: 16
SQ FT: 27,000
SALES (est): 1.3MM **Privately Held**
SIC: **3599** Machine shop, jobbing & repair

(G-7240)
JOHN MEZZALINGUA ASSOC LLC (PA)
Also Called: Jma Wireless
7645 Henry Clay Blvd (13088-3512)
P.O. Box 678 (13088-0678)
PHONE.................................315 431-7100
Darlene Braunschweig, *President*
Eli Fischer, *President*
Dadrian Carrington, *Vice Pres*
Brian Foley, *Vice Pres*
Ray Hild, *Vice Pres*
▲ EMP: 645
SALES (est): 224.9MM **Privately Held**
SIC: **3663** Antennas, transmitting & communications; airborne radio communications equipment

(G-7241)
JT SYSTEMS INC
8132 Oswego Rd (13090-1500)
P.O. Box 2575 (13089-2575)
PHONE.................................315 622-1980
Jit Turakhia, *Ch of Bd*
Manda Turakhia, *Admin Sec*
EMP: 10
SQ FT: 1,700
SALES (est): 2.5MM **Privately Held**
WEB: www.jtsystemsinc.com
SIC: **3564** Air purification equipment; ventilating fans: industrial or commercial

(G-7242)
LOCKHEED MARTIN CORPORATION
497 Electronics Pkwy # 5 (13088-5394)
P.O. Box 4840, Syracuse (13221-4840)
PHONE.................................315 456-0123
T S Kires, *Principal*
Luanne Vendetti, *COO*
Ronald Bailey, *QC Mgr*
Rich Brown, *Engineer*
Paul Dehm, *Engineer*
EMP: 2200 **Publicly Held**
WEB: www.lockheedmartin.com
SIC: **3761** 3812 Rockets, space & military, complete; navigational systems & instruments
PA: Lockheed Martin Corporation
  6801 Rockledge Dr
  Bethesda MD 20817

(G-7243)
LOCKHEED MARTIN GLOBAL INC (HQ)
Also Called: Lmgi
497 Electronics Pkwy # 5 (13088-5394)
PHONE.................................315 456-2982
Dale M Johnson, *President*
Zachary Parmely, *General Mgr*
Karen Barrett, *Admin Sec*
EMP: 30
SALES (est): 537.8MM **Publicly Held**
SIC: **3812** Search & navigation equipment

(G-7244)
LOCKHEED MARTIN OVERSEAS
497 Electronics Pkwy # 7 (13088-5394)
P.O. Box 4840, Syracuse (13221-4840)
PHONE.................................315 456-0123
Kwame Otieku, *Principal*
Ralph Heath, *Exec VP*
Kaz Kushida, *Design Engr*
Linda Raymond, *Branch Mgr*
EMP: 14 **Publicly Held**
SIC: **3812** Sonar systems & equipment; radar systems & equipment
HQ: Lockheed Martin Overseas Services Corporation
  6801 Rockledge Dr
  Bethesda MD 20817

(G-7245)
MCAULIFFE PAPER INC
100 Commerce Blvd (13088-4500)
PHONE.................................315 453-2222
Charles Thiaville, *President*
Mary Y Maltbie, *Vice Pres*
Amy Caldeira, *VP Sales*
Mary Maltbie, *Admin Sec*
EMP: 35 **EST: 1920**
SQ FT: 40,000
SALES (est): 3.5MM **Privately Held**
WEB: www.mcauliffepad.com
SIC: **2759** Business forms: printing

(G-7246)
MERCER MILLING CO
4698 Crossroads Park Dr (13088-3598)
PHONE.................................315 701-1334
Bill Colten, *President*
Scott Lyndaker, *Opers Staff*
▲ EMP: 36 **EST: 1829**
SQ FT: 60,000
SALES (est): 16.3MM **Privately Held**
SIC: **2834** 2833 Intravenous solutions; botanical products, medicinal: ground, graded or milled

(G-7247)
MIDSTATE PRINTING CORP
4707 Dey Rd (13088-3510)
PHONE.................................315 475-4101
John Williams Iii, *President*
Bob Williams, *Vice Pres*
Robert Williams, *Vice Pres*
Thomas Keehfus, *CFO*
Richard Fedeli, *Sales Staff*
EMP: 49
SQ FT: 28,000
SALES (est): 1.3MM **Privately Held**
SALES (corp-wide): 52.9K **Privately Held**
WEB: www.midstateprinting.com
SIC: **2752** Commercial printing, offset
PA: Qpc-Mpc Consolidation, Inc.
  4707 Dey Rd
  Liverpool NY 13088
  315 475-4101

(G-7248)
MODERN DECAL CO
8146 Soule Rd (13090-1536)
PHONE.................................315 622-2778
William J Hitchcock, *Owner*
Kathleen Hitchcock, *Co-Owner*
EMP: 6
SALES (est): 220K **Privately Held**
SIC: **2759** 3993 Decals: printing; name plates: except engraved, etched, etc.: metal

(G-7249)
NANOPV CORPORATION
7526 Morgan Rd (13090-3502)
PHONE.................................609 851-3666
Anna Selvan John, *President*
Carlos Pozo, *Accountant*
EMP: 188 **Privately Held**
SIC: **3433** Solar heaters & collectors
PA: Nanopv Corporation
  122 Mountainview Rd
  Ewing NJ 08560

(G-7250)
O BRIEN GERE MFG INC
7600 Morgan Rd Ste 1 (13090-4128)
PHONE.................................315 437-6100
Terry Brown, *Owner*
EMP: 8 **EST: 2011**
SALES (est): 862.9K **Privately Held**
SIC: **3999** Manufacturing industries

(G-7251)
PACKAGING CORPORATION AMERICA
Also Called: Pca/Syracuse, 384
4471 Steelway Blvd S (13090-3508)
P.O. Box 584 (13088-0584)
PHONE.................................315 457-6780
Joseph Armentrout, *General Mgr*
Julie Clark, *Controller*
Kevin Ryan, *Mktg Dir*
Joe Schwind, *Marketing Staff*
Teresa Bashore, *Branch Mgr*
EMP: 130
SQ FT: 144,672
SALES (corp-wide): 6.4B **Publicly Held**
WEB: www.packagingcorp.com
SIC: **2653** Boxes, corrugated: made from purchased materials
PA: Packaging Corporation Of America
  1955 W Field Ct
  Lake Forest IL 60045
  847 482-3000

(G-7252)
PACTIV LLC
4471 Steelway Blvd S (13090-3517)
P.O. Box 584 (13088-0584)
PHONE.................................315 457-6780
Teresa J Bashore, *Manager*
EMP: 130 **Privately Held**
WEB: www.pactiv.com
SIC: **2653** Boxes, corrugated: made from purchased materials; boxes, solid fiber: made from purchased materials
HQ: Pactiv Llc
  1900 W Field Ct
  Lake Forest IL 60045
  847 482-2000

(G-7253)
PAUL DE LIMA COMPANY INC (PA)
Also Called: Paul De Lima Coffee Company
7546 Morgan Rd Ste 1 (13090-3532)
PHONE.................................315 457-3725
Paul W Delima Jr, *CEO*
William J Drescher Jr, *Ch of Bd*
Michael Drescher, *Vice Pres*
Peter Miller, *Vice Pres*
Lisa Priest, *Purch Mgr*
▲ EMP: 55
SQ FT: 15,000

Liverpool - Onondaga County (G-7254)

SALES (est): 14.9MM **Privately Held**
WEB: www.delimacoffee.com
SIC: 2095 5149 Coffee roasting (except by wholesale grocers); coffee, green or roasted

(G-7254)
PERFORMANCE LACROSSE GROUP INC (HQ)
4697 Crossroads Park Dr (13088-3515)
PHONE 315 453-3073
Stephen Moore, *President*
▲ EMP: 8
SALES (est): 1.2MM
SALES (corp-wide): 166.2MM **Privately Held**
WEB: www.sporthelmets.com
SIC: 3949 Helmets, athletic
PA: Old Bh Inc.
   100 Domain Dr
   Exeter NH 03833
   603 430-2111

(G-7255)
POINTWISE INFORMATION SERVICE
223 1st St (13088-5140)
P.O. Box 11457, Syracuse (13218-1457)
PHONE 315 457-4111
Richard C Jaquin, *Owner*
EMP: 10
SQ FT: 1,000
SALES (est): 837.2K **Privately Held**
SIC: 2721 Periodicals: publishing only

(G-7256)
PRAXAIR DISTRIBUTION INC
4560 Morgan Pl (13090-3522)
PHONE 315 457-5821
Todd Saumier, *Principal*
EMP: 7
SALES (corp-wide): 11.4B **Privately Held**
SIC: 2813 5984 5169 Oxygen, compressed or liquefied; nitrogen; liquefied petroleum gas dealers; oxygen; industrial gases; acetylene
HQ: Praxair Distribution, Inc.
   10 Riverview Dr
   Danbury CT 06810
   203 837-2000

(G-7257)
PRECISION SYSTEMS MFG INC
4855 Executive Dr (13088-5378)
PHONE 315 451-3480
Theodore Jeske, *President*
EMP: 48
SQ FT: 40,000
SALES (est): 11MM **Privately Held**
WEB: www.psmi.org
SIC: 3599 3444 7389 3549 Machine shop, jobbing & repair; sheet metalwork; design, commercial & industrial; metalworking machinery; special dies, tools, jigs & fixtures

(G-7258)
PRINT SOLUTIONS PLUS INC
7325 Oswego Rd (13090-3717)
PHONE 315 234-3801
Darren Petragnani, *President*
EMP: 6
SALES (est): 772.3K **Privately Held**
SIC: 2752 Commercial printing, offset

(G-7259)
QRS TECHNOLOGIES INC
549 Electronics Pkwy (13088-6059)
PHONE 315 457-5300
Steve Esposito, *Owner*
EMP: 5
SALES (est): 329.1K **Privately Held**
SIC: 3845 Electromedical apparatus

(G-7260)
ROBERTS OFFICE FURN CNCPTS INC
7327 Henry Clay Blvd (13088-3529)
PHONE 315 451-9185
Robert L Barcza, *CEO*
R Scott Barcza, *President*
Dave Straub, *Accounting Mgr*
EMP: 25
SQ FT: 76,000
SALES (est): 4.8MM **Privately Held**
WEB: www.robertsofc.com
SIC: 2522 7641 Office furniture, except wood; office furniture repair & maintenance

(G-7261)
SCAPA NORTH AMERICA
Also Called: Great Lakes Technologies
1111 Vine St (13088-5301)
PHONE 315 413-1111
Ace Baylon, *Engineer*
Stuart Ganslaw,
Angelo Labbadia,
Steve Lennon,
▲ EMP: 20
SQ FT: 70,000
SALES (est): 10.5MM
SALES (corp-wide): 408.3MM **Privately Held**
WEB: www.greatlakestechnologies.com
SIC: 3081 Unsupported plastics film & sheet
HQ: Scapa Tapes North America Llc
   111 Great Pond Dr
   Windsor CT 06095
   860 688-8000

(G-7262)
SOLENIS LLC
Also Called: Ashland Water Technologies
911 Old Liverpool Rd (13088-1504)
PHONE 315 461-4730
EMP: 9
SALES (corp-wide): 667.2MM **Privately Held**
SIC: 2899 Water treating compounds
HQ: Solenis Llc
   3 Beaver Valley Rd # 500
   Wilmington DE 19803
   866 337-1533

(G-7263)
STALLION TECHNOLOGIES INC
4324 Loveland Dr (13090-6862)
PHONE 315 622-1176
Marshall MA, *President*
EMP: 8
SALES (est): 520K **Privately Held**
WEB: www.stalliontech.com
SIC: 3861 Photographic equipment & supplies

(G-7264)
STAMPCRETE INTERNATIONAL LTD
Also Called: Stampcrete Decorative Concrete
325 Commerce Blvd (13088-4595)
PHONE 315 451-2837
Karen Reith, *President*
Bob Williams, *Vice Pres*
▼ EMP: 20
SQ FT: 10,000
SALES (est): 7MM **Privately Held**
SIC: 3469 Metal stampings

(G-7265)
SYRACUSE PLASTICS LLC
7400 Morgan Rd (13090-3902)
PHONE 315 637-9881
Thomas Falcone,
Joseph R Falcone Sr,
Joseph R Falcone Jr,
Thomas R Falcone,
▲ EMP: 150 EST: 1953
SQ FT: 55,000
SALES (est): 34.7MM **Privately Held**
SIC: 3089 Injection molding of plastics

(G-7266)
TACTAIR FLUID CONTROLS INC
4806 W Taft Rd (13088-4810)
PHONE 315 451-3928
Dudley D Johnson, *Ch of Bd*
Peter Kaido, *President*
Michael Yates, *President*
Tony Ilacqua, *Senior Buyer*
Theresa Beard, *Buyer*
EMP: 240
SQ FT: 70,000
SALES (est): 50.9MM
SALES (corp-wide): 3.5B **Publicly Held**
WEB: www.tactair.com
SIC: 3492 3593 Fluid power valves for aircraft; fluid power actuators, hydraulic or pneumatic
HQ: Young & Franklin, Inc.
   942 Old Liverpool Rd
   Liverpool NY 13088
   315 457-3110

(G-7267)
THERMO CIDTEC INC
Also Called: Cid Technologies
101 Commerce Blvd (13088-4507)
PHONE 315 451-9410
Seth H Hoogasian, *Ch of Bd*
Mike Pilon, *General Mgr*
Jon Miles, *Mfg Mgr*
Mark Ptaszek, *Purchasing*
Steve Van Gorden, *Engineer*
EMP: 30
SQ FT: 14,000
SALES (est): 10MM
SALES (corp-wide): 20.9B **Publicly Held**
SIC: 3861 3674 Photographic equipment & supplies; solid state electronic devices
HQ: Thermo Vision Corp
   8 Forge Pkwy Ste 4
   Franklin MA 02038

(G-7268)
VANSANTIS DEVELOPMENT INC
4595 Morgan Pl (13090-3521)
PHONE 315 461-0113
Bill Vanauken, *President*
EMP: 40
SQ FT: 16,356
SALES (est): 5.6MM **Privately Held**
SIC: 2448 Pallets, wood

(G-7269)
VAREX IMAGING CORPORATION
Also Called: Infimed
121 Metropolitan Dr (13088-5335)
PHONE 315 234-6853
EMP: 703
SALES (corp-wide): 698.1MM **Publicly Held**
SIC: 3844 X-ray apparatus & tubes
PA: Varex Imaging Corporation
   1678 S Pioneer Rd
   Salt Lake City UT 84104
   801 972-5000

(G-7270)
WARD STEEL COMPANY INC
4591 Morgan Pl (13090-3511)
P.O. Box 628 (13088-0628)
PHONE 315 451-4566
John E Ward, *President*
Terrance Ward, *Vice Pres*
EMP: 25
SQ FT: 28,000
SALES (est): 7MM **Privately Held**
SIC: 3441 Building components, structural steel

(G-7271)
WARNER ENERGY LLC (PA)
7526 Morgan Rd (13090-3502)
PHONE 315 457-3828
Zach Drescher, *Vice Pres*
Steven Toomey, *Administration*
EMP: 8
SALES (est): 3.8MM **Privately Held**
SIC: 3674 Solar cells

(G-7272)
WHITACRE ENGINEERING COMPANY
4522 Wetzel Rd (13090-2548)
PHONE 315 622-1075
Samuel Conley, *Branch Mgr*
EMP: 7
SQ FT: 48,359
SALES (corp-wide): 10MM **Privately Held**
SIC: 3441 Fabricated structural metal
PA: Whitacre Engineering Company
   4645 Rebar Ave Ne
   Canton OH 44705
   330 455-8505

(G-7273)
XTO INCORPORATED (PA)
110 Wrentham Dr (13088-4503)
PHONE 315 451-7807
Donald G Kreiger, *CEO*
Ric Sill, *President*
D Keith Krieger, *Vice Pres*
Don Knoop, *Purch Mgr*
Keith Hughes, *VP Sales*
▲ EMP: 65
SQ FT: 38,000
SALES (est): 14.9MM **Privately Held**
WEB: www.xtoinc.com
SIC: 3053 5085 3549 Gaskets & sealing devices; adhesives, tape & plasters; seals, industrial; metalworking machinery

(G-7274)
YOUNG & FRANKLIN INC (HQ)
942 Old Liverpool Rd (13088-5596)
PHONE 315 457-3110
Peter Kaido, *Vice Pres*
Chuck Roberts, *Purch Mgr*
James Sterio, *Engrg Mgr*
Francis Bouziden, *Engineer*
Richard Passero, *Engineer*
EMP: 100 EST: 1918
SQ FT: 70,000
SALES: 73MM
SALES (corp-wide): 3.5B **Publicly Held**
SIC: 3492 3625 3728 3593 Control valves, aircraft: hydraulic & pneumatic; control valves, fluid power: hydraulic & pneumatic; actuators, industrial; aircraft parts & equipment; fluid power cylinders & actuators
PA: Transdigm Group Incorporated
   1301 E 9th St Ste 3000
   Cleveland OH 44114
   216 706-2960

Livingston
Columbia County

(G-7275)
F H STICKLES & SON INC
2590 Rr 9 (12541)
PHONE 518 851-9048
Bernard F Stickles Jr, *President*
EMP: 15 EST: 1928
SQ FT: 1,000
SALES (est): 2.2MM **Privately Held**
SIC: 3273 5032 Ready-mixed concrete; sand, construction; gravel

Livingston Manor
Sullivan County

(G-7276)
FLOUR POWER BAKERY CAFE
87 Debruce Rd (12758-2001)
PHONE 917 747-6895
Rowley, *President*
Denise Rowley, *Admin Sec*
EMP: 5
SALES (est): 275K **Privately Held**
SIC: 2051 Bakery: wholesale or wholesale/retail combined

Livonia
Livingston County

(G-7277)
AG BIOTECH INC
3578 Shoreline Dr (14487-9645)
P.O. Box 636, Lakeville (14480-0636)
PHONE 585 346-0020
Robert Hudack, *President*
Patti Hudack, *Vice Pres*
◆ EMP: 8
SALES: 2MM **Privately Held**
SIC: 2836 Biological products, except diagnostic

(G-7278)
FINGER LAKES TIMBER CO INC
6274 Decker Rd (14487)
PHONE 585 346-2990
Ronald Munson, *President*
Aaron Munson, *Vice Pres*
EMP: 6
SQ FT: 1,000
SALES (est): 907.2K **Privately Held**
SIC: 2411 Logging

GEOGRAPHIC SECTION

Lloyd Harbor
Suffolk County

(G-7279)
DILLNER PRECAST INC (PA)
14 Meadow Ln (11743-9721)
PHONE......................631 421-9130
John Dillner, *President*
Maureen Dillner, *Corp Secy*
EMP: 5
SALES: 1MM **Privately Held**
SIC: 3272 Concrete products, precast

(G-7280)
KANNALIFE SCIENCES INC
4 Knoll Ct (11743-9731)
PHONE......................516 669-3219
EMP: 5
SALES (est): 514.4K **Privately Held**
SIC: 2834 2833 2835 Mfg Pharmaceutical Preparations Mfg Medicinal/Botanical Products Mfg Diagnostic Substances

Locke
Cayuga County

(G-7281)
COTE HARDWOOD PRODUCTS INC (PA)
Also Called: Cote Wood Products
4725 Cat Path Rd (13092-4135)
PHONE......................607 898-5737
Pierre Cote, *President*
Carl Cote, *Vice Pres*
Paulette Cote, *Treasurer*
EMP: 11
SALES: 950K **Privately Held**
SIC: 2421 Sawmills & planing mills, general

Lockport
Niagara County

(G-7282)
6478 RIDGE ROAD LLC (PA)
6251 S Transit Rd (14094-6332)
PHONE......................716 625-8400
Somers G Sherman, *President*
EMP: 8
SALES (est): 1.4MM **Privately Held**
SIC: 3281 Granite, cut & shaped

(G-7283)
6478 RIDGE ROAD LLC
Also Called: International Stone Gallery
6478 Ridge Rd (14094-1015)
PHONE......................716 625-8400
EMP: 16
SALES (corp-wide): 1.4MM **Privately Held**
SIC: 3281 Granite, cut & shaped
PA: 6478 Ridge Road, Llc
  6251 S Transit Rd
  Lockport NY 14094
  716 625-8400

(G-7284)
ALLVAC
695 Ohio St (14094-4221)
PHONE......................716 433-4411
Reginald C Buri, *Principal*
▲ **EMP:** 11 **EST:** 2012
SALES (est): 2.3MM **Privately Held**
SIC: 3312 Stainless steel

(G-7285)
ARROWHEAD SPRING VINEYARDS LLC
4746 Townline Rd (14094-9604)
PHONE......................716 434-8030
Duncan Ross,
EMP: 5
SALES (est): 441K **Privately Held**
WEB: www.duncanrossphoto.com
SIC: 2084 Wines

(G-7286)
BARRY STEEL FABRICATION INC (PA)
30 Simonds St (14094-4111)
P.O. Box 579 (14095-0579)
PHONE......................716 433-2144
Steven R Barry, *President*
Jody Barry, *Vice Pres*
Randy Allen, *Project Mgr*
Herb Asbach, *Project Mgr*
EMP: 34
SQ FT: 8,400
SALES (est): 11.6MM **Privately Held**
WEB: www.barrysteel.com
SIC: 3441 1791 Fabricated structural metal; structural steel erection

(G-7287)
BISON BAG CO INC
5404 Crown Dr (14094-1850)
PHONE......................716 434-4380
James Streacher, *Ch of Bd*
Scott J Zgoda, *Ch of Bd*
Bruce Zgoda, *President*
Jim Streicher, *President*
Mark Smith, *Vice Pres*
▲ **EMP:** 55
SQ FT: 50,000
SALES (est): 14MM **Privately Held**
WEB: www.bisonbag.com
SIC: 2673 Plastic bags: made from purchased materials

(G-7288)
BUFFALO MACHINE TLS OF NIAGARA
4935 Lockport Rd (14094-9630)
PHONE......................716 201-1310
Theresa Silva, *President*
Joseph Silva, *Vice Pres*
EMP: 11
SQ FT: 25,000
SALES: 500K **Privately Held**
WEB: www.bmt-usa.com
SIC: 3542 Machine tools, metal forming type

(G-7289)
CANDLELIGHT CABINETRY INC
Also Called: Renaissance Import
24 Michigan St (14094-2628)
PHONE......................716 434-2114
Robert Sanderson, *Ch of Bd*
John Yakich, *President*
EMP: 210
SQ FT: 40,000
SALES (est): 26.6MM **Privately Held**
WEB: www.candlelightcab.com
SIC: 2434 Wood kitchen cabinets

(G-7290)
CHAMELEON COLOR CARDS LTD
6530 S Transit Rd (14094-6334)
PHONE......................716 625-9452
Phyllis Duha, *President*
Emeric J Duha, *Corp Secy*
Tricia Haney, *Production*
Sherrie Campbell, *MIS Dir*
▲ **EMP:** 55
SQ FT: 16,000
SALES (est): 10.4MM **Privately Held**
WEB: www.duhagroup.com
SIC: 3993 Displays, paint process
PA: Duha Color Services Limited
  750 Bradford St
  Winnipeg MB R3H 0
  204 786-8961

(G-7291)
CNHI LLC
Also Called: Union Sun & Journal
135 Main St Ste 1 (14094-3728)
PHONE......................716 439-9222
Denise Young, *Branch Mgr*
EMP: 33 **Privately Held**
SIC: 2711 Newspapers: publishing only, not printed on site
HQ: Cnhi, Llc
  445 Dexter Ave
  Montgomery AL 36104

(G-7292)
CUSTOM LASER INC (PA)
6747 Akron Rd (14094-5316)
P.O. Box 962 (14095-0962)
PHONE......................716 434-8600
Gary Brockman, *President*
Carol Cambell, *Human Res Dir*
Jason Walling, *Sales Staff*
Ken Hammond, *Manager*
EMP: 30
SQ FT: 9,000
SALES (est): 4.5MM **Privately Held**
WEB: www.customlaserinc.com
SIC: 7692 3479 Welding repair; etching & engraving

(G-7293)
DELPHI THERMAL SYSTEMS
350 Upper Mountain Rd (14094-1861)
PHONE......................716 439-2454
EMP: 11 **EST:** 2014
SALES (est): 1.6MM **Privately Held**
SIC: 3714 Mfg Motor Vehicle Parts/Accessories

(G-7294)
DERN MOORE MACHINE COMPANY INC
151 S Niagara St (14094-1907)
PHONE......................716 433-6243
Ken Moore, *President*
Sally J Moore, *Vice Pres*
EMP: 9
SQ FT: 10,000
SALES (est): 840K **Privately Held**
WEB: www.moorewashsystems.com
SIC: 3599 Machine shop, jobbing & repair

(G-7295)
DOBRIN INDUSTRIES INC (PA)
210 Walnut St Ste 22 (14094-3713)
PHONE......................800 353-2229
Paul Dobrin, *President*
EMP: 5
SQ FT: 5,000
SALES (est): 853.1K **Privately Held**
WEB: www.time-frames.com
SIC: 3499 Picture frames, metal

(G-7296)
E & R MACHINE INC
211 Grand St (14094-2198)
P.O. Box 499 (14095-0499)
PHONE......................716 434-6639
Garry E Sauls, *Ch of Bd*
Linda Penwright, *Office Mgr*
Doug Betts, *Manager*
EMP: 30 **EST:** 1961
SALES (est): 5.5MM **Privately Held**
WEB: www.er-machine.com
SIC: 3599 Machine shop, jobbing & repair

(G-7297)
E Z ENTRY DOORS INC
5299 Enterprise Dr (14094-1853)
PHONE......................716 434-3440
Roger W Grear, *President*
Patricia R Grear, *Vice Pres*
EMP: 12
SQ FT: 5,000
SALES (est): 2.2MM **Privately Held**
WEB: www.ezentrydoors.com
SIC: 3534 Elevators & equipment

(G-7298)
EMPRO NIAGARA INC
5027 Ridge Rd (14094-8948)
PHONE......................716 433-2769
Willa L Hand, *President*
Willa Hand, *President*
Will Hand, *Principal*
Melissa Hand, *Vice Pres*
EMP: 6
SALES: 500K **Privately Held**
WEB: www.emproniagara.com
SIC: 3441 Fabricated structural metal

(G-7299)
ENTERTRON INDUSTRIES INC
99 Robinson Pl (14094-4617)
PHONE......................716 772-7216
Stephen Luft, *President*
EMP: 24 **EST:** 1979
SQ FT: 6,000
SALES (est): 220.5K **Privately Held**
WEB: www.entertron.com
SIC: 3625 3672 Electric controls & control accessories, industrial; printed circuit boards

(G-7300)
F W ROBERTS MFG CO INC
73 Lock St (14094-2891)
P.O. Box 408, Mountville PA (17554-0408)
PHONE......................716 434-3555
Sherri Sczepczenski, *Admin Sec*
▲ **EMP:** 13
SQ FT: 13,363
SALES (est): 2.2MM **Privately Held**
SIC: 3554 3545 Paper mill machinery: plating, slitting, waxing, etc.; machine tool accessories

(G-7301)
FISHING VALLEY LLC
7217 N Canal Rd (14094-9411)
PHONE......................716 523-6158
Anna Zhalyalotdinova,
EMP: 5
SALES (est): 175.5K **Privately Held**
SIC: 3949 Bait, artificial; fishing

(G-7302)
FREEDOM RUN WINERY INC
5138 Lower Mountain Rd (14094-9767)
PHONE......................716 433-4136
Larry Manning, *Manager*
EMP: 7
SALES (est): 715.8K **Privately Held**
SIC: 2084 Wines

(G-7303)
GLOBAL ABRASIVE PRODUCTS INC (PA)
62 Mill St (14094-2460)
PHONE......................716 438-0047
John Sidebottom, *President*
John T Sidebottom, *President*
Laurie J Sidebottom, *Vice Pres*
Laurie Sidebottom, *Vice Pres*
Carolyn Payne, *Executive Asst*
EMP: 40
SALES (est): 5MM **Privately Held**
WEB: www.preson.com
SIC: 3291 Coated abrasive products; sandpaper

(G-7304)
GM COMPONENTS HOLDINGS LLC
Also Called: Gmch Lockport Ptc
200 Upper Mountain Rd (14094-1819)
PHONE......................716 439-2237
Pat Murtha, *Branch Mgr*
EMP: 209 **Publicly Held**
SIC: 3714 Air conditioner parts, motor vehicle; defrosters, motor vehicle; heaters, motor vehicle; radiators & radiator shells & cores, motor vehicle
HQ: Gm Components Holdings, Llc
  300 Renaissance Ctr
  Detroit MI 48243

(G-7305)
GM COMPONENTS HOLDINGS LLC
Also Called: Gmch Lockport
200 Upper Mountain Rd (14094-1819)
PHONE......................716 439-2463
Ronald Pirtle, *Branch Mgr*
EMP: 350 **Publicly Held**
SIC: 3629 3714 3585 3563 Condensers, for motors or generators; motor vehicle parts & accessories; refrigeration & heating equipment; air & gas compressors
HQ: Gm Components Holdings, Llc
  300 Renaissance Ctr
  Detroit MI 48243

(G-7306)
GM COMPONENTS HOLDINGS LLC
Also Called: General Mtr Cmponents Holdings
200 Upper Mountain Rd # 7 (14094-1819)
PHONE......................716 439-2011
Anita Mullen, *Branch Mgr*
EMP: 300 **Publicly Held**

Lockport - Niagara County (G-7307)

SIC: 3629 3714 3585 3563 Condensers, for motors or generators; motor vehicle parts & accessories; refrigeration & heating equipment; air & gas compressors
HQ: Gm Components Holdings, Llc
　　300 Renaissance Ctr
　　Detroit MI 48243

(G-7307)
GM COMPONENTS HOLDINGS LLC
Also Called: Integrated Indus Resources
200 Upper Mountain Rd # 10 (14094-1819)
PHONE...................................716 439-2402
Mark Inchiosa, *Branch Mgr*
EMP: 75 **Publicly Held**
WEB: www.delphiauto.com
SIC: 3053 Gaskets & sealing devices
HQ: Gm Components Holdings, Llc
　　300 Renaissance Ctr
　　Detroit MI 48243

(G-7308)
GOODING CO INC
Also Called: Insert Outsert Experts, The
5568 Davison Rd (14094-9090)
PHONE...................................716 266-6252
Gerald J Hace, *President*
▼ EMP: 34 EST: 1957
SQ FT: 26,500
SALES: 6.4MM
SALES (corp-wide): 312.6MM **Privately Held**
WEB: www.goodingcoinc.com
SIC: 2679 2752 2621 Tags & labels, paper; commercial printing, offset; wrapping & packaging papers; packaging paper
HQ: Nosco, Inc
　　2199 N Delany Rd
　　Gurnee IL 60031
　　847 336-4200

(G-7309)
HTI RECYCLING LLC (PA)
Also Called: Manufacturing
490 Ohio St (14094-4220)
PHONE...................................716 433-9294
Derek Martin,
EMP: 22
SALES (est): 8MM **Privately Held**
SIC: 3069 Reclaimed rubber (reworked by manufacturing processes)

(G-7310)
J M CANTY INC
6100 Donner Rd (14094-9227)
PHONE...................................716 625-4227
Thomas Canty, *Ch of Bd*
Jean Canty, *Vice Pres*
EMP: 30
SQ FT: 38,000
SALES (est): 8MM **Privately Held**
WEB: www.jmcanty.com
SIC: 3443 3648 2891 Vessels, process or storage (from boiler shops): metal plate; lighting equipment; sealants

(G-7311)
JACK J FLORIO JR
Also Called: Micro Graphics
36b Main St (14094-3607)
PHONE...................................716 434-9123
Jack J Florio Jr, *Owner*
EMP: 5
SALES (est): 462.6K **Privately Held**
SIC: 2752 2754 2759 2791 Commercial printing, offset; commercial printing, gravure; commercial printing; typesetting; bookbinding & related work; automotive & apparel trimmings

(G-7312)
JONATHAN BROSE
Also Called: Steamworks
51 Canal St (14094-2817)
PHONE...................................716 417-8978
Jonathan Brose, *Mng Member*
EMP: 8
SALES: 160K **Privately Held**
SIC: 2095 5812 Roasted coffee; coffee shop

(G-7313)
LAFARGE NORTH AMERICA INC
400 Hinman Rd (14094-9276)
PHONE...................................716 772-2621
Courtland Hess, *Plant Mgr*
Harry McCormick, *Manager*
Matthew Stoll, *Director*
EMP: 30
SQ FT: 47,480
SALES (corp-wide): 26.4B **Privately Held**
WEB: www.lafargenorthamerica.com
SIC: 3241 Cement, hydraulic
HQ: Lafarge North America Inc.
　　8700 W Bryn Mawr Ave
　　Chicago IL 60631
　　773 372-1000

(G-7314)
MAHLE BEHR USA INC
Also Called: Delphi Thrmal Lckport Model Sp
350 Upper Mountain Rd (14094-1861)
PHONE...................................716 439-2011
Dave Patterson, *Branch Mgr*
EMP: 450 **Privately Held**
SIC: 3714 Motor vehicle parts & accessories
HQ: Mahle Behr Usa Inc.
　　2700 Daley Dr
　　Troy MI 48083
　　248 743-3700

(G-7315)
MERRITT MACHINERY LLC
10 Simonds St (14094-4111)
PHONE...................................716 434-5558
Anna McCann,
◆ EMP: 20 EST: 1977
SQ FT: 30,000
SALES (est): 4.6MM **Privately Held**
WEB: www.merrittpmi.com
SIC: 3553 Woodworking machinery

(G-7316)
METAL CLADDING INC
230 S Niagara St (14094-1927)
PHONE...................................716 434-5513
Alexander F Robb, *CEO*
Raymond S Adornetto, *CFO*
Deborah Reimer, *Admin Sec*
▲ EMP: 87 EST: 1945
SQ FT: 70,000
SALES (est): 14.5MM **Privately Held**
WEB: www.metalcladding.com
SIC: 3479 3089 Coating of metals with plastic or resins; coating, rust preventive; plastic hardware & building products; plastic & fiberglass tanks

(G-7317)
METRO GROUP INC
Also Called: Retailer
8 South St (14094-4412)
PHONE...................................716 434-4055
Bernard Bradpiece, *President*
EMP: 5 EST: 1948
SQ FT: 1,500
SALES (est): 246K **Privately Held**
SIC: 2741 Guides: publishing only, not printed on site; shopping news: publishing only, not printed on site

(G-7318)
MILWARD ALLOYS INC
500 Mill St (14094-1712)
PHONE...................................716 434-5536
Johanna Van De Mark, *President*
Allen Van De Mark, *Vice Pres*
John Starr, *Vice Pres*
Johanna V Mark, *Plant Mgr*
David Summerlee, *Plant Mgr*
◆ EMP: 37
SQ FT: 60,000
SALES: 5MM **Privately Held**
WEB: www.milward.com
SIC: 3351 3365 Bands, copper & copper alloy; aluminum & aluminum-based alloy castings

(G-7319)
MODERN-TEC MANUFACTURING INC
4935 Lockport Rd (14094-9630)
PHONE...................................716 625-8700
Christopher Matyas, *President*
EMP: 5
SQ FT: 11,000

SALES (est): 654K **Privately Held**
SIC: 3599 Air intake filters, internal combustion engine, except auto; machine shop, jobbing & repair

(G-7320)
MOLEY MAGNETICS INC
5202 Commerce Dr (14094-1862)
PHONE...................................716 434-4023
John S Moley, *CEO*
Ronald Slaby, *Vice Pres*
Nick Moley, *Opers Staff*
Susan Davis, *Purch Agent*
Brandon Darnell, *Engineer*
▲ EMP: 12
SALES (est): 1.2MM **Privately Held**
SIC: 3621 Electric motor & generator parts

(G-7321)
NIAGARA COOLER INC
6605 Slyton Settlement Rd (14094-1144)
PHONE...................................716 434-1235
Joseph Loiacano, *President*
EMP: 7
SQ FT: 5,000
SALES: 1MM **Privately Held**
WEB: www.niagaracooler.com
SIC: 3443 Fabricated plate work (boiler shop)

(G-7322)
NIAGARA FIBERBOARD INC
140 Van Buren St (14094-2437)
P.O. Box 520 (14095-0520)
PHONE...................................716 434-8881
Stephen W Halas, *Ch of Bd*
Kevin Cain, *Vice Pres*
EMP: 23
SQ FT: 60,000
SALES (est): 3.9MM **Privately Held**
WEB: www.niagarafiberboard.com
SIC: 2493 2631 Fiberboard, other vegetable pulp; paperboard mills

(G-7323)
NIAGARA PRECISION INC
233 Market St (14094-2917)
PHONE...................................716 439-0956
Roger Hood, *President*
Dennis Hood, *Vice Pres*
Barbara Hood, *Admin Sec*
EMP: 24
SQ FT: 12,000
SALES (est): 4MM **Privately Held**
WEB: www.niagaraprecision.net
SIC: 3599 Machine shop, jobbing & repair

(G-7324)
NORTON PULPSTONES INCORPORATED
120 Church St (14094-2825)
P.O. Box 408, Mountville PA (17554-0408)
PHONE...................................716 433-9400
Glen Smith, *Branch Mgr*
EMP: 8
SALES (corp-wide): 1.1MM **Privately Held**
SIC: 2611 Mechanical pulp, including groundwood & thermomechanical
PA: Norton Pulpstones Incorporated
　　604 Lindsay Cir
　　Villanova PA 19085
　　610 964-0544

(G-7325)
ONTARIO LABEL GRAPHICS INC
6444 Ridge Rd (14094-1015)
PHONE...................................716 434-8505
Richard E Verheyn, *President*
Rose M Verheyn, *Vice Pres*
EMP: 12
SQ FT: 9,000
SALES (est): 1.5MM **Privately Held**
SIC: 2759 Labels & seals: printing

(G-7326)
PIVOT PUNCH CORPORATION
6550 Campbell Blvd (14094-9228)
PHONE...................................716 625-8000
Robert H King Jr, *CEO*
Christopher C King, *President*
Robert H King, *Chairman*
Christopher King, *Vice Pres*
▲ EMP: 87 EST: 1945
SQ FT: 32,500

SALES: 7.2MM **Privately Held**
WEB: www.pivotpunch.com
SIC: 3544 Punches, forming & stamping

(G-7327)
PRECISE PUNCH CORPORATION
6550 Campbell Blvd (14094-9210)
PHONE...................................716 625-8000
Robert H King Jr, *President*
Christopher King, *Vice Pres*
Joseph La Monto, *Accounting Mgr*
EMP: 11
SQ FT: 3,000
SALES (est): 1.1MM **Privately Held**
SIC: 3544 Punches, forming & stamping

(G-7328)
ROSS JC INC
6722 Lincoln Ave (14094-6220)
PHONE...................................716 439-1161
John Ross, *President*
Natalie Ross, *Vice Pres*
EMP: 5
SQ FT: 5,452
SALES: 400K **Privately Held**
SIC: 3545 Machine tool accessories

(G-7329)
ROYALTON MILLWORK & DESIGN
7526 Tonawanda Creek Rd (14094-9350)
PHONE...................................716 439-4092
Thomas Herberger, *President*
EMP: 5
SQ FT: 10,000
SALES (est): 743.3K **Privately Held**
SIC: 2431 Doors & door parts & trim, wood; windows & window parts & trim, wood; moldings & baseboards, ornamental & trim; staircases, stairs & railings

(G-7330)
RUBBERFORM RECYCLED PDTS LLC
75 Michigan St (14094-2629)
PHONE...................................716 478-0404
Bill Robbins, *CEO*
Roberta Callaghan, *Sales Staff*
Jamie Rexinger, *Marketing Staff*
Kristin Gugino, *Manager*
Deborah A Robbins,
▼ EMP: 14
SQ FT: 30,000
SALES (est): 3.4MM **Privately Held**
WEB: www.rubberform.com
SIC: 3069 Reclaimed rubber (reworked by manufacturing processes)

(G-7331)
SENTRY METAL BLAST INC
Also Called: Sentry Metal Services
553 West Ave (14094-4116)
P.O. Box 160 (14095-0160)
PHONE...................................716 285-5241
Gary D Verost, *President*
James Verost, *Vice Pres*
Mark Verost, *Vice Pres*
EMP: 30
SQ FT: 47,000
SALES (est): 7.1MM **Privately Held**
WEB: www.sentrymetal.com
SIC: 3441 3479 Fabricated structural metal; coating of metals & formed products

(G-7332)
SUMMIT MSP LLC
6042 Old Beattie Rd (14094-7943)
PHONE...................................716 433-1014
John Butcher, *General Mgr*
Rose Butcher, *Mng Member*
EMP: 8
SQ FT: 1,500
SALES: 767K **Privately Held**
SIC: 2752 Commercial printing, offset

(G-7333)
SUMMIT PRINT & MAIL LLC
6042 Old Beattie Rd (14094-7943)
PHONE...................................716 433-1014
J Butcher, *Mng Member*
John Butcher, *Mng Member*
Cookie Butcher,
EMP: 7

GEOGRAPHIC SECTION

SALES (est): 809.6K **Privately Held**
WEB: www.summitprintmail.com
SIC: 2752 Commercial printing, offset

(G-7334)
TDY INDUSTRIES LLC
Also Called: ATI Specialty Materials
695 Ohio St (14094-4221)
PHONE 716 433-4411
Anthony Santini, *Engineer*
H Dalton, *Branch Mgr*
EMP: 35
SQ FT: 438 **Publicly Held**
WEB: www.alleghenyludlum.com
SIC: 3312 3339 Stainless steel; primary nonferrous metals
HQ: Tdy Industries, Llc
1000 Six Ppg Pl
Pittsburgh PA 15222
412 394-2896

(G-7335)
TED WESTBROOK
Also Called: Westbrook Machinery
4736 Mapleton Rd (14094-9621)
PHONE 716 625-4443
Ted Westbrook, *Owner*
EMP: 1 **EST:** 1995
SALES: 1MM **Privately Held**
SIC: 3599 Machine shop, jobbing & repair

(G-7336)
TITANIUM DEM REMEDIATION GROUP
4907 I D A Park Dr (14094-1833)
P.O. Box 471 (14095-0471)
PHONE 716 433-4100
Angela M Bodami, *Principal*
EMP: 12
SALES (est): 4.6MM **Privately Held**
SIC: 3356 Nonferrous Rolling/Drawing

(G-7337)
TORRENT EMS LLC
190 Walnut St (14094-3710)
PHONE 716 312-4099
Michael Dehn, *CEO*
Louise Cadwalader, *Treasurer*
EMP: 16
SALES (est): 4.3MM
SALES (corp-wide): 13.8MM **Privately Held**
SIC: 3577 Computer peripheral equipment
PA: Trek, Inc.
190 Walnut St
Lockport NY 14094
716 438-7555

(G-7338)
TREK INC (PA)
190 Walnut St (14094-3710)
PHONE 716 438-7555
Toshio Uehara, *CEO*
Mike Dehn, *President*
Louise Cadwalader, *VP Finance*
Bruce T Williams, *Director*
John Carney, *Admin Sec*
EMP: 16
SQ FT: 30,330
SALES: 13.8MM **Privately Held**
SIC: 3825 Instruments to measure electricity

(G-7339)
TWIN LAKE CHEMICAL INC
520 Mill St (14094-1794)
P.O. Box 411 (14095-0411)
PHONE 716 433-3824
James J Hodan, *President*
William Caswell, *Engineer*
▲ **EMP:** 18
SQ FT: 10,000
SALES (est): 3.9MM **Privately Held**
WEB: www.twinlakechemical.com
SIC: 2869 Industrial organic chemicals

(G-7340)
ULRICH SIGN CO INC
177 Oakhurst St (14094-1920)
PHONE 716 434-0167
C McCaffrey, *President*
Christopher McCaffrey, *President*
EMP: 21 **EST:** 1939
SQ FT: 6,000

SALES (est): 2MM **Privately Held**
WEB: www.ulrichsigns.com
SIC: 3993 Neon signs; signs, not made in custom sign painting shops

(G-7341)
VANCHLOR COMPANY INC (PA)
45 Main St (14094-2838)
PHONE 716 434-2624
Richard G Shotell, *Ch of Bd*
Dirk A Van De Mark, *Vice Pres*
Bill Streams, *Plant Mgr*
◆ **EMP:** 12 **EST:** 1960
SALES (est): 2.7MM **Privately Held**
WEB: www.vanchlor.com
SIC: 2819 Aluminum chloride

(G-7342)
VANCHLOR COMPANY INC
555 W Jackson St (14094-1744)
PHONE 716 434-2624
Richard Shotell, *Branch Mgr*
EMP: 16
SQ FT: 30,839
SALES (corp-wide): 2.7MM **Privately Held**
WEB: www.vanchlor.com
SIC: 2819 Aluminum chloride
PA: Vanchlor Company, Inc.
45 Main St
Lockport NY 14094
716 434-2624

(G-7343)
VANDEMARK CHEMICAL INC (PA)
1 N Transit Rd (14094-2323)
PHONE 716 433-6764
Michael Kucharski, *CEO*
Paul Ameis, *COO*
Paul Ameb, *Exec VP*
Brian Law, *Senior VP*
Bill Thompson, *Warehouse Mgr*
◆ **EMP:** 85 **EST:** 1951
SQ FT: 13,770
SALES (est): 28.5MM **Privately Held**
WEB: www.vdmchemical.com
SIC: 2819 Industrial inorganic chemicals

Lockwood
Tioga County

(G-7344)
H F CARY & SONS
70 Reniff Rd (14859-9753)
PHONE 607 598-2563
Lewis A Cary, *Owner*
EMP: 5
SALES: 250K **Privately Held**
SIC: 3272 Septic tanks, concrete

Locust Valley
Nassau County

(G-7345)
ALPHA 6 DISTRIBUTIONS LLC
Also Called: Arctix
11 Oyster Bay Rd (11560-2322)
PHONE 516 801-8290
Judy Ward, *CFO*
Matthew Bruderman, *Mng Member*
▲ **EMP:** 12
SQ FT: 3,000
SALES (est): 30MM **Privately Held**
SIC: 2329 5137 2339 Athletic (warmup, sweat & jogging) suits: men's & boys'; women's & children's clothing; women's & misses' athletic clothing & sportswear

(G-7346)
FERA PHARMACEUTICALS LLC
134 Birch Hill Rd (11560-1833)
PHONE 516 277-1449
Marc Tokars, *Vice Pres*
Frank J Dellafer,
Janet Dellafera,
EMP: 12
SQ FT: 800
SALES (est): 2.8MM **Privately Held**
SIC: 2834 Pharmaceutical preparations

(G-7347)
FILESTREAM INC
257 Buckram Rd (11560-1906)
P.O. Box 93, Glen Head (11545-0093)
PHONE 516 759-4100
Yao Chu, *President*
EMP: 10
SQ FT: 1,200
SALES: 2MM **Privately Held**
WEB: www.filestream.com
SIC: 7372 Application computer software; business oriented computer software; educational computer software

(G-7348)
FOREST IRON WORKS INC
3 Elm St Ste A (11560-2149)
PHONE 516 671-4229
Mario Gallo, *President*
EMP: 8
SQ FT: 13,000
SALES (est): 1.4MM **Privately Held**
SIC: 3446 Architectural metalwork

(G-7349)
HENRY DESIGN STUDIOS INC
129 Birch Hill Rd Ste 2 (11560-1841)
PHONE 516 801-2760
Henry Perlstein, *President*
Henri Rayski, *Vice Pres*
Elka Perlstein, *Treasurer*
EMP: 7
SQ FT: 1,400
SALES: 1MM **Privately Held**
SIC: 3911 Jewelry, precious metal

(G-7350)
JK MANUFACTURING INC
115 Forest Ave Unit 22 (11560-4001)
PHONE 212 683-3535
Joe Rubens, *Owner*
EMP: 9
SALES (est): 809K **Privately Held**
SIC: 3911 Jewelry, precious metal

(G-7351)
STANDARD BOTS COMPANY
33 Wellington Rd (11560-2415)
PHONE 646 876-2687
Evan Beard, *CEO*
▲ **EMP:** 6
SQ FT: 2,000
SALES (est): 263.9K **Privately Held**
SIC: 3549 Assembly machines, including robotic

(G-7352)
T G S INC
6 Wildwood Ct (11560-1108)
PHONE 516 629-6905
Rajesh Raichoudhury, *CEO*
EMP: 5
SALES (est): 285.9K **Privately Held**
WEB: www.tgs.com
SIC: 2731 Books: publishing & printing

Lodi
Seneca County

(G-7353)
LAMOREAUX LANDING WI
Also Called: Wagner Farms
9224 State Route 414 (14860-9641)
PHONE 607 582-6162
Michele Harris, *Mktg Dir*
Brenda Clawson, *Office Mgr*
Mark Wagner,
EMP: 70
SQ FT: 4,070
SALES (est): 5.2MM **Privately Held**
WEB: www.lamoreauxwine.com
SIC: 2084 Wines

(G-7354)
WAGNER VINEYARDS LLC
9322 State Route 414 (14860-9641)
PHONE 607 582-6976
John Wagner, *General Mgr*
Katie Roller, *Director*
EMP: 5
SALES: 900K **Privately Held**
SIC: 2084 Wines

(G-7355)
WAGNER VINEYARDS & BREWING CO
Also Called: Ginny Lee Cafe
9322 State Route 414 (14860-9641)
PHONE 607 582-6574
Stanley Wagner, *Owner*
Brent Wojnowski, *Manager*
EMP: 30
SQ FT: 1,200
SALES (est): 3MM **Privately Held**
WEB: www.wagnervineyards.com
SIC: 2084 0172 2082 Wines; grapes; malt beverages

Long Beach
Nassau County

(G-7356)
AIR TITE MANUFACTURING INC
Also Called: Focus Point Windows & Doors
724 Park Pl Ste B (11561-2158)
P.O. Box 149 (11561-0149)
PHONE 516 897-0295
Fax: 516 897-0299
EMP: 120
SQ FT: 40,000
SALES (est): 1.6MM **Privately Held**
SIC: 3442 Mfg Storm Doors & Windows Metal

(G-7357)
BARRIER BREWING COMPANY LLC
612 W Walnut St (11561-2919)
PHONE 516 316-4429
Evan Klein, *Administration*
EMP: 5 **EST:** 2012
SALES (est): 335K **Privately Held**
SIC: 2082 Malt beverages

(G-7358)
ECHO APPELLATE PRESS INC
30 W Park Ave Ste 200 (11561-2018)
PHONE 516 432-3601
Stuart Davis, *President*
Joyce Davis, *Corp Secy*
EMP: 7
SQ FT: 4,500
SALES: 763K **Privately Held**
WEB: www.echoappellate.com
SIC: 2752 Commercial printing, offset

(G-7359)
INNOVATION IN MOTION INC
Also Called: Iim Global
780 Long Beach Blvd (11561-2238)
PHONE 407 878-7561
David Jones, *CEO*
Thomas Szoke, *COO*
Daniel Fovzati, *Director*
Andrash Vago, *Director*
▼ **EMP:** 6
SQ FT: 10,000
SALES (est): 460.9K
SALES (corp-wide): 2.3MM **Publicly Held**
SIC: 3663 7371 3559 Mobile communication equipment; computer software development & applications; screening equipment, electric
PA: Ipsidy Inc.
780 Long Beach Blvd
Long Beach NY 11561
407 951-8640

(G-7360)
IPSIDY INC (PA)
780 Long Beach Blvd (11561-2238)
PHONE 407 951-8640
Philip D Beck, *Ch of Bd*
Douglas Solomon, *COO*
Charles Albanese, *CFO*
Stuart Stoller, *CFO*
Thomas Szoke, *CTO*
EMP: 12
SALES: 2.3MM **Publicly Held**
SIC: 7372 7371 Prepackaged software; computer software development & applications

Long Eddy
Sullivan County

(G-7361)
DEDECO INTERNATIONAL SALES INC (PA)
11617 State Route 97 (12760-5603)
PHONE..................845 887-4840
Steven M Antler, *President*
▲ **EMP:** 35
SALES (est): 7.5MM **Privately Held**
WEB: www.dedeco.com
SIC: 3291 3843 Abrasive products; dental equipment & supplies

Long Island City
Queens County

(G-7362)
21ST CENTURY OPTICS INC (DH)
Also Called: S&G Optical
4700 33rd St Ste 1r (11101-2401)
PHONE..................347 527-1079
Ralph Woythaler, *President*
Bernard Woythaler, *Vice Pres*
Michael Woythaler, *Vice Pres*
Hy Kislak, *Inv Control Mgr*
Nicholas Cacace, *Manager*
EMP: 28 **EST:** 1967
SQ FT: 22,000
SALES (est): 6MM **Privately Held**
WEB: www.21stcenturyoptics.com
SIC: 3851 5048 3827 Ophthalmic goods; ophthalmic goods; lenses, ophthalmic; lenses, optical: all types except ophthalmic
HQ: Essilor Laboratories Of America Holding Co., Inc.
13555 N Stemmons Fwy
Dallas TX 75234
214 496-4141

(G-7363)
A W R GROUP INC
3715 Hunters Point Ave (11101-1913)
PHONE..................718 729-0412
Mark Schinderman, *President*
EMP: 10
SALES (est): 1.1MM **Privately Held**
SIC: 2385 7699 Waterproof outerwear; antique repair & restoration, except furniture, automobiles

(G-7364)
AAAA YORK INC
Also Called: York Ladders
3720 12th St (11101-6009)
PHONE..................718 784-6666
Kenneth Buettner, *President*
▲ **EMP:** 10
SQ FT: 5,000
SALES (est): 1.3MM **Privately Held**
SIC: 3531 Construction machinery

(G-7365)
ABBOT & ABBOT BOX CORP
Also Called: Abbot & Abbot Packing Service
3711 10th St (11101-6043)
PHONE..................888 930-5972
Stuart Gleiber, *President*
Douglas Gleiber, *Vice Pres*
EMP: 17 **EST:** 1888
SQ FT: 40,000
SALES (est): 3.3MM **Privately Held**
WEB: www.abbotbox.com
SIC: 2441 2448 2449 3412 Boxes, wood; pallets, wood; skids, wood; wood containers; metal barrels, drums & pails; folding paperboard boxes

(G-7366)
ABLE STEEL EQUIPMENT CO INC
5002 23rd St (11101-4595)
PHONE..................718 361-9240
Bonnie S Tarkenton, *President*
Ed Morgan, *Treasurer*
EMP: 15 **EST:** 1935
SQ FT: 30,000
SALES (est): 1.6MM **Privately Held**
WEB: www.ablesteelequipment.com
SIC: 2542 1799 2531 2522 Cabinets: show, display or storage: except wood; partitions for floor attachment, prefabricated: except wood; shelving, office & store: except wood; demountable partition installation; public building & related furniture; office furniture, except wood

(G-7367)
ACTION TECHNOLOGIES INC
Also Called: Active Business Systems
3809 33rd St Apt 1 (11101-2230)
PHONE..................718 278-1000
Francine Amendola, *President*
EMP: 5
SALES (est): 232.9K **Privately Held**
SIC: 3579 Canceling machinery, post office

(G-7368)
ADVERTISING LITHOGRAPHERS
2812 41st Ave (11101-3706)
PHONE..................212 966-7771
Randolph Hafter, *President*
Robert Hafter, *Vice Pres*
EMP: 10
SQ FT: 11,250
SALES (est): 1.3MM **Privately Held**
SIC: 2752 Commercial printing, lithographic

(G-7369)
AIR LOUVER & DAMPER INC (PA)
2121 44th Rd (11101-5010)
PHONE..................718 392-3232
Joseph Chalpin, *President*
EMP: 12
SQ FT: 20,000
SALES (est): 2.4MM **Privately Held**
SIC: 3822 3444 Damper operators: pneumatic, thermostatic, electric; metal ventilating equipment

(G-7370)
ALFRED MAINZER INC (PA)
2708 40th Ave (11101-3725)
PHONE..................718 392-4200
Ronald Mainzer, *President*
Barry Mainzer, *Vice Pres*
Brad Packer, *Treasurer*
Sari Mainzer, *Admin Sec*
▼ **EMP:** 50 **EST:** 1938
SQ FT: 40,000
SALES (est): 4MM **Privately Held**
WEB: www.alfredmainzer.com
SIC: 2741 Miscellaneous publishing

(G-7371)
ALL CITY SWITCHBOARD CORP
3541 11th St (11106-5013)
PHONE..................718 956-7244
Peter Tsimoyianis, *President*
Efstratios Kountouris, *Treasurer*
EMP: 26
SALES (est): 8.9MM **Privately Held**
WEB: www.allcityswbd.com
SIC: 3613 Switchgear & switchboard apparatus

(G-7372)
ALLSTATEBANNERSCOM CORPORATION
Also Called: Allstate Banners
3511 9th St (11106-5103)
PHONE..................718 300-1256
Panagiotis Panagi, *President*
Alexander Phioukas, *Vice Pres*
EMP: 9
SQ FT: 2,000
SALES (est): 1.5MM **Privately Held**
SIC: 2752 Commercial printing, offset

(G-7373)
ALP STONE INC
2520 50th Ave Fl 2 (11101-4421)
PHONE..................718 706-6166
Yunus Bickici, *President*
Hakton Bor, *Vice Pres*
▲ **EMP:** 15
SALES (est): 4MM **Privately Held**
WEB: www.alpstone.com
SIC: 3272 1743 Stone, cast concrete; tile installation, ceramic

(G-7374)
ALPHA PACKAGING INDUSTRIES INC
2004 33rd St (11105-2010)
PHONE..................718 267-4115
David Zaret, *President*
Steven Zaret, *Corp Secy*
Michael Zaret, *Vice Pres*
EMP: 35
SQ FT: 25,000
SALES (est): 12MM **Privately Held**
SIC: 2657 Folding paperboard boxes

(G-7375)
AMBRAS FINE JEWELRY INC
Also Called: Ambras Fjc
3100 47th Ave Unit 3 (11101-3010)
PHONE..................718 784-5252
Morris Dweck, *Ch of Bd*
EMP: 50
SQ FT: 9,000
SALES (est): 5.3MM **Privately Held**
SIC: 3911 Jewelry, precious metal

(G-7376)
AMCI LTD
3302 48th Ave (11101-2418)
PHONE..................718 937-5858
Justo Lorenzotti, *President*
Luis Lorenzotti, *Vice Pres*
Mike Gover, *Accounts Mgr*
Nicole Bouverie, *Program Mgr*
▲ **EMP:** 60
SQ FT: 25,000
SALES (est): 5.9MM **Privately Held**
SIC: 2499 Picture frame molding, finished; picture & mirror frames, wood

(G-7377)
AMERICAN WAX COMPANY INC
Also Called: American Cleaning Solutions
3930 Review Ave (11101-2020)
P.O. Box 1943 (11101-0943)
PHONE..................718 392-8080
Alan Winik, *CEO*
Ronald Ingber, *President*
EMP: 50
SQ FT: 65,000
SALES (est): 10.6MM **Privately Held**
WEB: www.cleaning-solutions.com
SIC: 2842 Cleaning or polishing preparations

(G-7378)
AMERICAN WOODS & VENEERS WORKS
4735 27th St (11101-4410)
PHONE..................718 937-2195
Chingyu Peng, *President*
Dianna Serro, *Manager*
EMP: 30
SQ FT: 11,000
SALES (est): 4.7MM **Privately Held**
SIC: 2499 Furniture inlays (veneers); veneer work, inlaid

(G-7379)
ANIMA MUNDI HERBALS LLC
Also Called: Rainforest Apothecary
2323 Borden Ave (11101-4508)
PHONE..................415 279-5727
Adriana Ayales, *CEO*
EMP: 6
SQ FT: 1,000
SALES (est): 556K **Privately Held**
SIC: 2834 Vitamin, nutrient & hematinic preparations for human use

(G-7380)
ANTHONY LAWRENCE OF NEW YORK
Also Called: Belfair Draperies
3233 47th Ave (11101-2426)
PHONE..................212 206-8820
Joseph Calagna, *Ch of Bd*
Anthony Lawrence, *Owner*
EMP: 20
SALES (est): 3.1MM **Privately Held**
WEB: www.anthonylawrence.com
SIC: 2391 7641 2511 Draperies, plastic & textile: from purchased materials; reupholstery; wood household furniture

(G-7381)
APPLE ENTERPRISES INC
Also Called: Apple Digital Printing
1308 43rd Ave (11101-6833)
PHONE..................718 361-2200
Howard N Sturm, *CEO*
Howard Sturm, *CEO*
Adam Sturm, *President*
EMP: 30 **EST:** 1995
SALES (est): 5.7MM **Privately Held**
WEB: www.applevisualgraphics.com
SIC: 2759 7389 Commercial printing; advertising, promotional & trade show services

(G-7382)
APPLE HEALING & RELAXATION
3114 Broadway (11106-2585)
PHONE..................718 278-1089
EMP: 5
SALES (est): 468.5K **Privately Held**
SIC: 3571 Mfg Electronic Computers

(G-7383)
APPLIED SAFETY LLC
4349 10th St Ste 311 (11101-6941)
PHONE..................718 608-6292
Jose Hernandez,
EMP: 8
SALES (est): 200K **Privately Held**
SIC: 3564 Blowers & fans

(G-7384)
ARC REMANUFACTURING INC
1940 42nd St (11105-1113)
PHONE..................718 728-0701
William P Hayes, *President*
John Hayes, *Site Mgr*
▲ **EMP:** 60
SQ FT: 150,000
SALES (est): 9.5MM **Privately Held**
WEB: www.arcparts.com
SIC: 3714 Motor vehicle engines & parts; power steering equipment, motor vehicle; windshield wiper systems, motor vehicle; motor vehicle brake systems & parts

(G-7385)
ARCHAELOGY MAGAZINE
3636 33rd St Ste 301 (11106-2329)
PHONE..................718 472-3050
Phyliss Katz, *President*
EMP: 20
SALES (est): 1.3MM **Privately Held**
WEB: www.archaeology.org
SIC: 2721 Periodicals

(G-7386)
ARGO ENVELOPE CORP
4310 21st St (11101-5002)
PHONE..................718 729-2700
Lawrence Chait, *President*
Eric Chait, *Vice Pres*
EMP: 60 **EST:** 1946
SQ FT: 50,000
SALES (est): 6.3MM **Privately Held**
WEB: www.argoenvelope.com
SIC: 2759 2752 Envelopes: printing; commercial printing, lithographic

(G-7387)
ARGO GENERAL MACHINE WORK INC
3816 11th St (11101-6114)
PHONE..................718 392-4605
Frank Scaduto, *President*
Ignazio Scaduto, *Vice Pres*
EMP: 7
SQ FT: 2,400
SALES (est): 883K **Privately Held**
SIC: 3599 Machine shop, jobbing & repair

(G-7388)
ARGO LITHOGRAPHERS INC
4310 21st St (11101-5002)
PHONE..................718 729-2700
Lawrence Chait, *President*
Eric Chait, *Vice Pres*
EMP: 25
SQ FT: 5,000
SALES: 4MM **Privately Held**
WEB: www.argoenvelope.com
SIC: 2752 5112 5111 2789 Commercial printing, offset; stationery & office supplies; printing & writing paper; bookbinding & related work; commercial printing

▲ = Import ▼ = Export
◆ = Import/Export

GEOGRAPHIC SECTION

Long Island City - Queens County (G-7419)

(G-7389)
ASCO CASTINGS INC (PA)
3100 47th Ave Ste G (11101-3013)
PHONE.....................212 719-9800
Barry Smith, *General Mgr*
EMP: 6
SQ FT: 4,000
SALES (est): 1MM **Privately Held**
WEB: www.ascocasting.com
SIC: 3915 Jewelers' castings

(G-7390)
ASIAN GLOBAL TRADING CORP
3613 36th Ave Ste 2 (11106-1306)
PHONE.....................718 786-0998
Chau Pei Hsu, *President*
▲ **EMP:** 10
SALES (est): 1MM **Privately Held**
SIC: 2253 Knit outerwear mills

(G-7391)
ASTRON CANDLE MANUFACTURING CO
1125 30th Ave (11102-4098)
PHONE.....................718 728-3330
Menelaos G Tzelios, *President*
◆ **EMP:** 7
SQ FT: 7,000
SALES (est): 733.7K **Privately Held**
SIC: 3999 Candles

(G-7392)
ASTUCCI US LTD
4369 9th St (11101-6907)
PHONE.....................718 752-9700
Dan Benmoshe, *Branch Mgr*
EMP: 18 **Privately Held**
SIC: 3172 Mfg Personal Leather Goods
PA: Astucci, U.S., Ltd.
385 5th Ave Rm 1100
New York NY 10016

(G-7393)
ASUR JEWELRY INC
4709 30th St Ste 403 (11101-3400)
PHONE.....................718 472-1687
Aydin Barka, *President*
EMP: 6
SQ FT: 2,500
SALES: 700K **Privately Held**
SIC: 3915 Jewelers' castings

(G-7394)
ATLANTIC PRECIOUS METAL CAST
4132 27th St (11101-3825)
PHONE.....................718 937-7100
Ricky Barbieri, *Principal*
EMP: 9
SALES (est): 630K **Privately Held**
SIC: 3911 Jewelry, precious metal

(G-7395)
AUGUST STUDIOS
Also Called: Augusta Studios
4008 22nd St Fl 3 (11101-4826)
PHONE.....................718 706-6487
August Helbling, *Owner*
EMP: 8
SALES (est): 390K **Privately Held**
SIC: 2512 7641 Upholstered household furniture; upholstery work

(G-7396)
B & B SHEET METAL INC
2540 50th Ave (11101-4421)
PHONE.....................718 433-2501
Robert Baschnagel, *President*
Robert Baschnagel III, *President*
Peter Barry, *Engineer*
Voitek Emerling, *Sales Staff*
Thomas Hessler, *Director*
◆ **EMP:** 50
SALES (est): 10.4MM **Privately Held**
SIC: 3444 Sheet metal specialties, not stamped

(G-7397)
BANGLA PATRIKA INC
3806 31st St 2 (11101-2719)
PHONE.....................718 482-9923
Mahabubur Rahman, *President*
EMP: 9
SQ FT: 1,250
SALES: 32K **Privately Held**
SIC: 2711 Newspapers

(G-7398)
BARGOLD STORAGE SYSTEMS LLC
4141 38th St (11101-1708)
PHONE.....................718 247-7000
Gerald Goldman, *Mng Member*
Alan Goldman, *Mng Member*
Jordan Goldman, *Mng Member*
Joshua Goldman, *Mng Member*
EMP: 40
SQ FT: 3,000
SALES (est): 8.6MM **Privately Held**
WEB: www.bargoldstorage.com
SIC: 3444 1796 Sheet metalwork; installing building equipment

(G-7399)
BENLEE ENTERPRISES LLC
3100 47th Ave Unit 2 (11101-3068)
PHONE.....................212 730-7330
Daniel Dabakarov, *President*
Josh Dabakarov, *Principal*
EMP: 13
SALES (est): 952K **Privately Held**
SIC: 3911 Jewelry, precious metal

(G-7400)
BIRCH GUYS LLC
Also Called: Birch Coffee
4035 23rd St (11101)
P.O. Box 287507, New York (10128-0026)
PHONE.....................917 763-0751
Paul Schlader,
EMP: 8
SALES (est): 396K **Privately Held**
SIC: 2095 Roasted coffee

(G-7401)
BLATT SEARLE & COMPANY LTD (PA)
4121 28th St (11101-3757)
PHONE.....................212 730-7717
Searle Blatt, *President*
Alice Blatt, *Exec VP*
▲ **EMP:** 20
SALES (est): 4.3MM **Privately Held**
WEB: www.momao.com
SIC: 2337 Suits: women's, misses' & juniors'; skirts, separate: women's, misses' & juniors'; women's & misses' capes & jackets

(G-7402)
BLEECKER PASTRY TARTUFO INC
3722 13th St (11101-6025)
PHONE.....................718 937-9830
Fax: 718 392-5965
EMP: 7
SQ FT: 7,500
SALES (est): 400K **Privately Held**
SIC: 2024 5451 Mfg Ice Cream/Frozen Desert Ret Dairy Products

(G-7403)
BRIDGE PRINTING INC
4710 32nd Pl Fl 2 (11101-2415)
PHONE.....................212 243-5390
Fax: 718 361-9123
EMP: 5
SQ FT: 8,000
SALES: 1MM **Privately Held**
SIC: 2752 Lithographic Commercial Printing

(G-7404)
CABINET SHAPES CORP
3721 12th St (11101-6008)
PHONE.....................718 784-6255
Fax: 718 392-4282
EMP: 15
SALES: 1.2MM **Privately Held**
SIC: 2434 2499 1751 Mfg Wood Kitchen Cabinets Mfg Wood Products Carpentry Contractor

(G-7405)
CAMA GRAPHICS INC
Also Called: Altum Press
3200 Skillman Ave Ste B (11101-2308)
PHONE.....................718 707-9747
Anthony Cappuccio, *President*
EMP: 12
SQ FT: 4,800
SALES (est): 830K **Privately Held**
WEB: www.camagraphics.com
SIC: 2759 Commercial printing

(G-7406)
CASSINELLI FOOD PRODUCTS INC
3112 23rd Ave (11105-2407)
PHONE.....................718 274-4881
Anthony Bonfigli, *President*
Nella Costella, *Treasurer*
EMP: 6 **EST:** 1973
SQ FT: 3,000
SALES: 700K **Privately Held**
SIC: 2098 5411 Macaroni & spaghetti; delicatessens

(G-7407)
CENTRAL TIME CLOCK INC
Also Called: Discountclocks.com
523 50th Ave (11101-5711)
PHONE.....................718 784-4900
Sheldon Reinhardt, *President*
JP Altenau, *Managing Dir*
Hal Reinhardt, *Vice Pres*
Mathew Reinhardt, *Vice Pres*
Mat Reinhardt, *VP Sales*
EMP: 10 **EST:** 1931
SQ FT: 4,000
SALES (est): 1.4MM **Privately Held**
WEB: www.centraltimeclock.com
SIC: 3579 Time clocks & time recording devices

(G-7408)
CHOCOMIZE INC
3010 41st Ave (11101-2814)
PHONE.....................631 506-6085
Fabian Kaempfer, *CEO*
Frank Mueller, *Accounts Mgr*
▲ **EMP:** 10
SQ FT: 5,000
SALES (est): 904.1K **Privately Held**
SIC: 2066 Chocolate bars, solid

(G-7409)
CIVIL SVC RTRED EMPLOYEES ASSN
Also Called: Csrea
3427 Steinway St Ste 1 (11101-8602)
PHONE.....................718 937-0290
Kjell Kjellberg, *Editor*
EMP: 12
SALES (est): 560K **Privately Held**
SIC: 2721 Magazines: publishing & printing

(G-7410)
CLADDAGH ELECTRONICS LTD
1032 47th Rd (11101-5514)
PHONE.....................718 784-0571
William J Casey, *President*
Angelo Mottola, *Vice Pres*
EMP: 20
SQ FT: 3,000
SALES (est): 3.4MM **Privately Held**
WEB: www.claddaghelectronics.com
SIC: 3613 5065 Panelboards & distribution boards, electric; electronic parts & equipment

(G-7411)
CNC MANUFACTURING CORP
Also Called: Gt Machine & Tool
3214 49th St (11103-1403)
PHONE.....................718 728-6800
Dean Theotos, *President*
EMP: 25
SALES (est): 154.6K **Privately Held**
SIC: 3599 Machine shop, jobbing & repair

(G-7412)
COE DISPLAYS INC
4301 22nd St Ste 603 (11101-5031)
P.O. Box 3203, Fort Lee NJ (07024-9203)
PHONE.....................718 937-5658
Joel Sgroe, *CEO*
Masimo Russo, *Co-Owner*
EMP: 5 **EST:** 1960
SQ FT: 10,000
SALES (est): 691.6K **Privately Held**
SIC: 2752 3993 2396 Commercial printing, offset; signs & advertising specialties; automotive & apparel trimmings

(G-7413)
COLOR INDUSTRIES LLC
3002 48th Ave Ste H (11101-3401)
PHONE.....................718 392-8301
Edward Tikkanen, *Mng Member*
EMP: 8
SALES (est): 1MM **Privately Held**
SIC: 2754 Commercial printing, gravure

(G-7414)
COLUMBIA DENTOFORM CORPORATION (PA)
3110 37th Ave Ste 307 (11101-2112)
PHONE.....................718 482-1569
Jeffrey E Perelman, *CEO*
Carl Bredco, *President*
Penelope Bichardo, *Vice Pres*
EMP: 55
SQ FT: 25,000
SALES (est): 6.2MM **Privately Held**
WEB: www.columbiadentoform.com
SIC: 3843 3842 3999 3544 Dental equipment & supplies; models, anatomical; mannequins; special dies, tools, jigs & fixtures

(G-7415)
COOPERFRIEDMAN ELC SUP CO INC
2219 41st Ave (11101-4835)
PHONE.....................718 269-4906
EMP: 7
SALES (corp-wide): 12.2MM **Privately Held**
SIC: 3699 1731 Electrical equipment & supplies; electrical work
HQ: Cooperfriedman Electric Supply Co., Inc.
1 Matrix Dr
Monroe Township NJ 08831
732 747-2233

(G-7416)
COSMOS COMMUNICATIONS INC
1105 44th Dr (11101-7027)
PHONE.....................718 482-1800
Jack Weiss, *Ch of Bd*
Arnold Weiss, *President*
Gerald Weiss, *Corp Secy*
Richard Quarto, *Vice Pres*
Frank Ferraro, *Production*
EMP: 105 **EST:** 1933
SQ FT: 54,000
SALES (est): 26.7MM **Privately Held**
WEB: www.cosmosinc.net
SIC: 2752 2791 2789 Commercial printing, offset; typesetting; bookbinding & related work

(G-7417)
CRISADA INC
3913 23rd St (11101-4816)
PHONE.....................718 729-9730
Chris Kole, *President*
EMP: 5
SALES: 1.2MM **Privately Held**
WEB: www.crisada.com
SIC: 2335 2311 Gowns, formal; tailored suits & formal jackets

(G-7418)
CUSTOM CAS INC
2631 1st St (11102-4124)
PHONE.....................718 726-3575
Yiota Yerolemuo, *President*
Tasos Yerolemuo, *Vice Pres*
EMP: 20
SQ FT: 10,000
SALES (est): 2.4MM **Privately Held**
WEB: www.customcas.com
SIC: 2434 Wood kitchen cabinets

(G-7419)
CW METALS INC
3421 Greenpoint Ave (11101-2013)
PHONE.....................917 416-7906
Caesar Witek, *President*
EMP: 20
SALES: 1MM **Privately Held**
SIC: 3444 Sheet metalwork

(G-7420)
D3 REPRO GROUP
3401 38th Ave (11101-2223)
PHONE..................347 507-1075
EMP: 7 **EST:** 2011
SALES (est): 30.4K **Privately Held**
SIC: 2759 Commercial printing

(G-7421)
DAVID FLATT FURNITURE LTD
3842 Review Ave Ste 2 (11101-2045)
PHONE..................718 937-7944
David Flatt, *President*
▲ **EMP:** 10
SQ FT: 11,000
SALES (est): 943.2K **Privately Held**
SIC: 2541 Display fixtures, wood

(G-7422)
DELTA SHEET METAL CORP
3935 Skillman Ave (11104-3706)
PHONE..................718 429-5805
Peter J Pappas, *President*
Eva Georgopoulos, *Vice Pres*
EMP: 202
SQ FT: 25,000
SALES (est): 31.6MM **Privately Held**
SIC: 3444 Ducts, sheet metal

(G-7423)
DEPENDABLE LITHOGRAPHERS INC
3200 Skillman Ave (11101-2309)
PHONE..................718 472-4200
Fax: 718 472-5260
EMP: 15
SQ FT: 15,000
SALES (est): 1.5MM **Privately Held**
SIC: 2752 2789 Lithographic Commercial Printing Bookbinding/Related Work

(G-7424)
DEPP GLASS INC
4140 38th St (11101-1709)
PHONE..................718 784-8500
Wesley R Depp, *President*
Judy Depp, *Admin Sec*
▲ **EMP:** 12 **EST:** 1923
SQ FT: 14,000
SALES (est): 1.7MM **Privately Held**
WEB: www.deppglass.com
SIC: 3229 3231 Lamp parts & shades, glass; mirrored glass

(G-7425)
DI FIORE AND SONS CUSTOM WDWKG
4202 Astoria Blvd (11103-2504)
PHONE..................718 278-1663
Santino Di Fiore, *President*
Maria T Di Fiore, *Vice Pres*
EMP: 5
SQ FT: 8,000
SALES (est): 596.4K **Privately Held**
SIC: 2434 5712 5031 2499 Wood kitchen cabinets; cabinet work, custom; kitchen cabinets; decorative wood & woodwork; kitchen & bathroom remodeling; single-family home remodeling, additions & repairs

(G-7426)
DIMENSION DEVELOPMENT CORP
3630 37th St Fl 1 (11101-1606)
PHONE..................718 361-8825
Wiston A Williams, *President*
George Chung, *Managing Dir*
Jeanette M Pineda, *Administration*
EMP: 9
SALES: 256K **Privately Held**
SIC: 1389 Testing, measuring, surveying & analysis services

(G-7427)
DRILLCO EQUIPMENT CO INC
3452 11th St (11106-5012)
PHONE..................718 777-5986
Gus Neos, *Treasurer*
Angelo Neos, *Treasurer*
▲ **EMP:** 25
SALES (est): 4.6MM **Privately Held**
SIC: 3532 Drills, bits & similar equipment

(G-7428)
DRILLCO NATIONAL GROUP INC (PA)
2432 44th St (11103-2002)
P.O. Box 2182 (11102-0182)
PHONE..................718 726-9801
Patrick Lacey, *President*
Jim Wieder, *Corp Secy*
Nicholas Lacey, *Vice Pres*
EMP: 36
SALES (est): 5.9MM **Privately Held**
SIC: 3531 Drags, road (construction & road maintenance equipment)

(G-7429)
DURA ENGRAVING CORPORATION
Also Called: Dura Architectural Signage
4815 32nd Pl (11101-2538)
PHONE..................718 706-6400
Eva Forst, *CEO*
Ark Forst, *President*
Dan Forst, *Accountant*
Art Forst, *Sales Executive*
EMP: 25 **EST:** 1941
SQ FT: 20,000
SALES (est): 2MM **Privately Held**
WEB: www.duracorp.com
SIC: 3993 Signs, not made in custom sign painting shops; name plates: except engraved, etched, etc.: metal

(G-7430)
DURAL DOOR COMPANY INC
3128 Greenpoint Ave (11101-2006)
PHONE..................718 729-1333
Peter Macari, *President*
Louis Vella, *Vice Pres*
EMP: 13 **EST:** 1945
SQ FT: 2,500
SALES (est): 1.2MM **Privately Held**
SIC: 3534 3442 Elevators & equipment; metal doors, sash & trim

(G-7431)
DWM INTERNATIONAL INC
Also Called: Society Awards
37-18 Nthrn Blvd Ste 516 (11101)
PHONE..................646 290-7448
David Moritz, *President*
Larry Maloney, *COO*
Clark Leoppard, *Prdtn Mgr*
Jason Garcia, *Accounts Mgr*
▲ **EMP:** 15
SQ FT: 3,000
SALES (est): 1.2MM **Privately Held**
SIC: 3914 7336 Trophies; art design services

(G-7432)
E & T PLASTIC MFG CO INC (PA)
Also Called: E&T Plastics
4545 37th St (11101-1801)
PHONE..................718 729-6226
Gary Thal, *President*
Mark Elowsky, *Vice Pres*
Shahid Bacchus, *Controller*
Tom Paluch, *Sales Staff*
Daniel Sanchez, *Sales Staff*
◆ **EMP:** 40 **EST:** 1946
SQ FT: 15,000
SALES: 75MM **Privately Held**
SIC: 3089 Extruded finished plastic products; plastic processing

(G-7433)
EDISON PRICE LIGHTING INC (PA)
Also Called: Epl
4150 22nd St (11101-4815)
PHONE..................718 685-0700
Emma Price, *President*
Rick Shaver, *Exec VP*
Joel Siegel, *Exec VP*
Gregory Mortman, *Vice Pres*
Mary Romano, *Vice Pres*
▲ **EMP:** 120 **EST:** 1952
SQ FT: 40,000
SALES (est): 27MM **Privately Held**
SIC: 3646 Commercial indusl & institutional electric lighting fixtures

(G-7434)
EDISON PRICE LIGHTING INC
4105 21st St (11101-6102)
PHONE..................718 685-0700
Fulgencio Bengochea, *Branch Mgr*
James Vizzini, *MIS Dir*
EMP: 80
SALES (est): 8.6MM
SALES (corp-wide): 27MM **Privately Held**
SIC: 3646 5063 Commercial indusl & institutional electric lighting fixtures; electrical apparatus & equipment
PA: Edison Price Lighting, Inc.
4150 22nd St
Long Island City NY 11101
718 685-0700

(G-7435)
EFAM ENTERPRISES LLC
Also Called: Finestar
3731 29th St (11101-2611)
PHONE..................718 204-1760
Toll Free:..................888 -
Jeff Aronowitz, *Accounting Mgr*
Shai Bivas, *Mng Member*
EMP: 20
SQ FT: 12,000
SALES (est): 2.7MM **Privately Held**
SIC: 3861 5045 7699 Toners, prepared photographic (not made in chemical plants); computers, peripherals & software; printing trades machinery & equipment repair

(G-7436)
EFRON DESIGNS LTD
2121 41st Ave Ste 5b (11101-4828)
PHONE..................718 482-8440
Daniel Efron, *President*
Jill Efron, *Vice Pres*
EMP: 8
SALES (est): 1MM **Privately Held**
SIC: 3911 Jewelry apparel

(G-7437)
ELENIS NYC INC (PA)
Also Called: Eleni's Cookies
4725 34th St Ste 305 (11101-2442)
PHONE..................718 361-8136
Eleni Gianopulos, *CEO*
Randall Gianopulos, *President*
Matthew Gilson, *Controller*
▲ **EMP:** 32
SQ FT: 4,000
SALES (est): 4MM **Privately Held**
SIC: 2052 Cookies

(G-7438)
ENDEAVOR PRINTING LLC
3704 29th St (11101-2612)
PHONE..................718 570-2720
Brian Baltes,
EMP: 5
SQ FT: 2,000
SALES: 650K **Privately Held**
SIC: 2752 Commercial printing, lithographic

(G-7439)
ESENSE LLC
4402 23rd St Ste 114 (11101-5027)
PHONE..................718 887-9779
Brad Beckerman, *Managing Prtnr*
▲ **EMP:** 10
SALES (est): 1.3MM **Privately Held**
SIC: 2087 Extracts, flavoring

(G-7440)
EUROPADISK LLC
2402 Queens Plz S (11101-4602)
PHONE..................718 407-7300
James P Shelton, *President*
Vince Sbarra, *CFO*
EMP: 50
SQ FT: 75,000
SALES: 6MM **Privately Held**
SIC: 3652 Phonograph record blanks; magnetic tape (audio): prerecorded; compact laser discs, prerecorded

(G-7441)
EXHIBIT CORPORATION AMERICA
Also Called: Exhibit Portables
4623 Crane St Ste 3 (11101)
PHONE..................718 937-2600
Gregory Abbate, *President*
Ronald A Abbate Jr, *Chairman*
Lorraine Pasieka, *Treasurer*
Giannina Abbate, *Admin Sec*
EMP: 30 **EST:** 1965
SQ FT: 50,000
SALES: 100K **Privately Held**
SIC: 3993 7389 2522 2521 Signs & advertising specialties; interior designer; office furniture, except wood; wood office furniture

(G-7442)
EXPERT MACHINE SERVICES INC
3944a 28th St (11101-3729)
PHONE..................718 786-1200
Stuart Fischer, *President*
EMP: 5
SALES (est): 500.6K **Privately Held**
SIC: 3599 Machine shop, jobbing & repair

(G-7443)
EXPERT METAL SLITTERS CORP
3740 12th St (11101-6009)
PHONE..................718 361-2735
Kent Derossi, *President*
▲ **EMP:** 6
SQ FT: 22,000
SALES (est): 1.3MM **Privately Held**
SIC: 3549 Cutting & slitting machinery

(G-7444)
FALCON PERSPECTIVES INC
28 Vernon Blvd Ste 45 (11101)
PHONE..................718 706-9168
Elizabeth Toma, *President*
Frank Marrazzo, *Manager*
EMP: 8
SQ FT: 14,000
SALES (est): 1MM **Privately Held**
SIC: 3498 Coils, pipe: fabricated from purchased pipe

(G-7445)
FASHION RIBBON CO INC (PA)
Also Called: Pascale Madonna
3401 38th Ave (11101-2223)
PHONE..................718 482-0100
William Rosenzweig, *Ch of Bd*
Jeffrey Rosenzweig, *President*
Donald Rubin, *President*
▲ **EMP:** 35 **EST:** 1949
SQ FT: 28,000
SALES (est): 1.6MM **Privately Held**
WEB: www.fashionribbon.com
SIC: 2241 Ribbons

(G-7446)
FELDMAN MANUFACTURING CORP
3010 41st Ave Ste 3fl (11101-2814)
PHONE..................718 433-1700
Richard Feldman, *President*
▲ **EMP:** 93
SALES (est): 5.4MM **Privately Held**
WEB: www.ebathingsuit.com
SIC: 2339 Bathing suits: women's, misses' & juniors'

(G-7447)
FINE ARTS FURNITURE INC
3872 13th St (11101-6120)
PHONE..................212 744-9139
Robert Longo Sr, *President*
Michelle Longo, *Corp Secy*
Robert Longo Jr, *Vice Pres*
EMP: 7
SQ FT: 12,500
SALES (est): 747.5K **Privately Held**
SIC: 2511 Wood household furniture

(G-7448)
FIREFIGHTERS JOURNAL
2420 Jackson Ave (11101-4323)
PHONE..................718 391-0283
Tony Coretto, *Officer*
EMP: 25

SALES (est): 513.7K Privately Held
SIC: 2711 Newspapers-Publishing/Printing

(G-7449)
FIRST DISPLAYS INC
2415 43rd Ave Fl 2 (11101-4623)
PHONE.................................347 642-5972
Philip Wong, Owner
▲ EMP: 10
SALES (est): 991.3K Privately Held
SIC: 2752 Advertising posters, lithographed

(G-7450)
FISONIC CORP
4402 23rd St (11101-5000)
PHONE.................................212 732-3777
Robert Kremer, CEO
EMP: 8
SQ FT: 4,000 Privately Held
SIC: 3561 3433 Industrial pumps & parts; heating equipment, except electric
PA: Fisonic Corp
 31-00 47th Ave Ste 106
 New York NY 10023

(G-7451)
FOO YUAN FOOD PRODUCTS CO INC
2301 Borden Ave (11101-4517)
PHONE.................................212 925-2840
George Chuang, President
▲ EMP: 9 EST: 1979
SQ FT: 1,200
SALES (est): 805.2K Privately Held
SIC: 2092 Fish, fresh; prepared

(G-7452)
FREEDA VITAMINS INC (PA)
4725 34th St Ste 303 (11101-2436)
PHONE.................................718 433-4337
Philip W Zimmerman, President
Sylvia Zimmerman, Vice Pres
M Kaganoff, Treasurer
Eli Zimmerman, Treasurer
Samuel Zimmerman, Treasurer
EMP: 25
SQ FT: 3,600
SALES (est): 2.2MM Privately Held
SIC: 2834 Vitamin, nutrient & hematinic preparations for human use

(G-7453)
GAILER STAMPING DIECUTTING LLC
3718 Nthrn Blvd 324 Fl 3 (11101)
PHONE.................................212 243-5662
Dennis Dourgarian, Mng Member
EMP: 12 EST: 2000
SQ FT: 12,000
SALES: 2MM Privately Held
SIC: 2759 3554 Embossing on paper; die cutting & stamping machinery, paper converting

(G-7454)
GALAS FRAMING SERVICES
4224 Orchard St Fl 4 (11101-2936)
PHONE.................................718 706-0007
Fax: 718 706-0731
EMP: 15
SQ FT: 10,000
SALES: 750K Privately Held
SIC: 2499 5023 7699 Mfg Wood Products Whol Homefurnishings Repair Services

(G-7455)
GALMER LTD
Also Called: Galmer Silversmiths
4301 21st St Ste 130b (11101-5082)
PHONE.................................718 392-4609
Michael Izrael, Ch of Bd
EMP: 9
SQ FT: 10,000
SALES (est): 770K Privately Held
SIC: 3499 3471 Novelties & giftware, including trophies; plating of metals or formed products

(G-7456)
GEM METAL SPINNING & STAMPING
517 47th Rd (11101-5592)
PHONE.................................718 729-7014
Stephen Sloop, President
EMP: 5
SQ FT: 12,500
SALES: 175K Privately Held
SIC: 3469 Spinning metal for the trade; stamping metal for the trade

(G-7457)
GN PRINTING
4216 34th Ave (11101-1110)
PHONE.................................718 784-1713
Tony Barsamin, President
EMP: 20
SALES (est): 933K Privately Held
SIC: 2752 Commercial printing, offset

(G-7458)
GNOSIS CHOCOLATE INC
4003 27th St (11101-3814)
PHONE.................................646 688-5549
Vanessa Barg, CEO
EMP: 8
SALES (est): 657.5K Privately Held
SIC: 2066 Chocolate & cocoa products

(G-7459)
GRADUAL LLC
1040 46th Ave Fl 2 (11101-5217)
PHONE.................................347 293-0974
EMP: 10
SALES (est): 460K Privately Held
SIC: 3579 Time clocks & time recording devices

(G-7460)
GRAND MERIDIAN PRINTING INC
Also Called: GM Printing
3116 Hunters Point Ave (11101-3131)
PHONE.................................718 937-3888
K Y Chow, President
Carol Chiu, Vice Pres
EMP: 20
SQ FT: 1,500
SALES (est): 3.4MM Privately Held
SIC: 2752 2759 Commercial printing, offset; commercial printing

(G-7461)
GRAPHICS 247 CORP
4402 23rd St Ste 113 (11101-5027)
PHONE.................................718 729-2470
George Ibanez, President
EMP: 7
SALES (est): 625.5K Privately Held
WEB: www.graphics247.com
SIC: 2759 Publication printing

(G-7462)
GRAPHICS SERVICE BUREAU INC (PA)
Also Called: Gsb Digital
3030 47th Ave (11101-3433)
PHONE.................................212 684-3600
Stephan Steiner, President
Troy E Steiner, Vice Pres
EMP: 12
SQ FT: 5,000
SALES (est): 9.6MM Privately Held
WEB: www.gsbinc.net
SIC: 2759 Commercial printing

(G-7463)
GREAT WALL CORP
4727 36th St (11101-1823)
PHONE.................................212 704-4372
Ping Nen Lin, Ch of Bd
George Lin, President
▲ EMP: 120
SQ FT: 86,000
SALES (est): 9.6MM Privately Held
SIC: 2339 Athletic clothing: women's, misses' & juniors'

(G-7464)
GUARANTEED PRINTING SVC CO INC
4710 33rd St (11101-2408)
PHONE.................................212 929-2410
Bob Cohen, President
EMP: 20 EST: 1931
SQ FT: 3,000
SALES: 3MM Privately Held
SIC: 2752 Commercial printing, lithographic

(G-7465)
H K TECHNOLOGIES INC
4332 22nd St Ste 405 (11101-5079)
PHONE.................................718 255-1898
Rie Fechita, Ch of Bd
Atsu Karino, Manager
Taisuke Hamada, Administration
Hiroto Kinoshita, Administration
EMP: 4
SQ FT: 800
SALES (est): 1.1MM Privately Held
WEB: www.hktechnologies.com
SIC: 3674 Semiconductors & related devices

(G-7466)
HANNA ALTINIS CO INC
3601 48th Ave (11101-1815)
PHONE.................................718 706-1134
Kenny Altinis, President
John Acello, Accountant
EMP: 50
SQ FT: 10,000
SALES (est): 4.9MM Privately Held
WEB: www.altunis.com
SIC: 3911 Jewelry, precious metal

(G-7467)
HEALTHY BRAND OIL CORP (PA)
5215 11th St Ste A (11101-5830)
PHONE.................................718 937-0806
Bradly Green, Chairman
Jason Thomas, Vice Pres
Kim Glockner, Administration
▲ EMP: 20
SQ FT: 1,000
SALES (est): 86.1MM Privately Held
SIC: 2079 Cooking oils, except corn: vegetable refined

(G-7468)
HERBERT JAFFE INC
4011 Skillman Ave (11104-3203)
P.O. Box 4189 (11104-0189)
PHONE.................................718 392-1956
Herbert Jaffe, President
Henny Jaffe, Treasurer
EMP: 5
SQ FT: 5,000
SALES: 350K Privately Held
SIC: 3559 Sewing machines & attachments, industrial

(G-7469)
HERSCO-ORTHOTIC LABS CORP
Also Called: Hersco-Arch Products
3928 Crescent St (11101-3802)
PHONE.................................718 391-0416
James Kennedy, President
Cathal Kennedy, Executive
EMP: 20 EST: 1939
SQ FT: 3,000
SALES (est): 1.5MM Privately Held
WEB: www.hersco.com
SIC: 3842 Orthopedic appliances; foot appliances, orthopedic

(G-7470)
HOLA PUBLISHING CO
Also Called: Spanish Tele Dirctry Hola 912
2932 Northern Blvd (11101-4013)
PHONE.................................718 424-3129
Hernando Solano, President
EMP: 5 EST: 1977
SALES (est): 190K Privately Held
SIC: 2741 Directories, telephone: publishing only, not printed on site

(G-7471)
HUMBOLDT WOODWORKING
3836 11th St (11101-6114)
PHONE.................................718 707-0022
Moshe Granit, CEO
EMP: 5
SALES (est): 507.5K Privately Held
SIC: 2431 Millwork

(G-7472)
I 2 PRINT INC
3819 24th St (11101-3619)
PHONE.................................718 937-8800
Shulan Leong, President
EMP: 10

SALES (est): 1.8MM Privately Held
WEB: www.i2print.com
SIC: 2752 Commercial printing, offset

(G-7473)
IMPORT-EXPORT CORPORATION
Also Called: Wilda
3814 30th St (11101-2792)
PHONE.................................718 707-0880
William Wu, President
▲ EMP: 15
SQ FT: 2,500
SALES: 7.5MM Privately Held
SIC: 3199 Equestrian related leather articles

(G-7474)
IN TOON AMKOR FASHIONS INC
Also Called: Galaxy Knitting Mills
4809 34th St (11101-2515)
PHONE.................................718 937-4546
Albert Plant, President
EMP: 30 EST: 1985
SQ FT: 50,000
SALES (est): 1.9MM Privately Held
SIC: 2254 Mfg Underwear

(G-7475)
INNOVATIVE INDUSTRIES LLC
4322 22nd St Ste 205 (11101-5004)
P.O. Box 92, Westernville (13486-0092)
PHONE.................................718 784-7300
EMP: 7
SALES (est): 854.5K Privately Held
SIC: 3999 Barber & beauty shop equipment

(G-7476)
INTERIORS-PFT INC
Also Called: Props For Today
3200 Skillman Ave Fl 3 (11101-2308)
PHONE.................................212 244-9600
Dyann Klein, President
EMP: 48
SALES (est): 4.8MM Privately Held
SIC: 2599 Factory furniture & fixtures

(G-7477)
J J CREATIONS INC
4742 37th St (11101-1804)
PHONE.................................718 392-2828
John Thor, President
EMP: 50
SALES: 22MM Privately Held
WEB: www.jjcreations.com
SIC: 3911 3961 Costume jewelry; earrings, precious metal

(G-7478)
JADO SEWING MACHINES INC
4008 22nd St (11101-4826)
PHONE.................................718 784-2314
Onik Balian, President
Alexander Saks, Vice Pres
Anneke Stern, Vice Pres
EMP: 20 EST: 1978
SQ FT: 14,000
SALES: 2.5MM Privately Held
WEB: www.jadosewingmachine.com
SIC: 3559 Sewing machines & hat & zipper making machinery

(G-7479)
JIM HENSON COMPANY INC
Also Called: Jim Henson Productions
3718 Northern Blvd # 400 (11101-1636)
PHONE.................................212 794-2400
Howard Sharp, Branch Mgr
EMP: 50
SALES (est): 4.8MM
SALES (corp-wide): 12MM Privately Held
WEB: www.farscape.com
SIC: 2399 Emblems, badges & insignia
PA: The Jim Henson Company Inc
 1416 N La Brea Ave
 Los Angeles CA 90028
 323 856-6680

(G-7480)
JOHN GAILER INC
3718 Northern Blvd Ste 3 (11101-1631)
PHONE.................................212 243-5662
Steven Dourgarian, President
Dennis Dourgarian, Vice Pres

Long Island City - Queens County (G-7481)

EMP: 30
SALES (est): 2.2MM Privately Held
WEB: www.gailer.com
SIC: 3999 3111 Gold stamping, except books; die-cutting of leather

(G-7481)
JOHN R ROBINSON INC
3805 30th St (11101-2716)
PHONE..................718 786-6088
Frank V Cunningham, *President*
Albert Jackson, *General Mgr*
Sharon Racette, *Vice Pres*
EMP: 20
SQ FT: 5,000
SALES (est): 4MM Privately Held
SIC: 3443 Heat exchangers, condensers & components

(G-7482)
JULIAN FREIRICH COMPANY INC (PA)
4601 5th St (11101-5369)
PHONE..................718 361-9111
Paul Dardiens, *President*
Jeff Freirich, *President*
Jerry Freirich, *Chairman*
Digna Freirich, *Admin Sec*
EMP: 30 EST: 1923
SQ FT: 25,000
SALES (est): 4.8MM Privately Held
WEB: www.freirich.com
SIC: 2013 Prepared beef products from purchased meat; corned beef from purchased meat; pastrami from purchased meat; roast beef from purchased meat

(G-7483)
JURIST COMPANY INC
1105 44th Dr (11101-5107)
PHONE..................212 243-8008
Joseph Jurist, *President*
David Shushansky, *Exec VP*
EMP: 7
SQ FT: 13,000
SALES (est): 1.4MM Privately Held
WEB: www.juristprinting.com
SIC: 2752 Commercial printing, offset

(G-7484)
JUSTA COMPANY
3464 9th St (11106-5102)
PHONE..................718 932-6139
Janechai Sayananon, *Owner*
EMP: 8
SQ FT: 4,000
SALES: 900K Privately Held
WEB: www.justacompany.com
SIC: 3873 5199 Watches, clocks, watchcases & parts; gifts & novelties

(G-7485)
JUSTIN ASHLEY DESIGNS INC
4301 21st St Ste 212a (11101-5049)
PHONE..................718 707-0200
Scott Barcvi, *President*
▲ EMP: 6
SALES (est): 540K Privately Held
SIC: 3911 Jewelry, precious metal

(G-7486)
KAITERY FURS LTD
2529 49th St (11103-1120)
PHONE..................718 204-1396
Jimmy Kaitery, *President*
◆ EMP: 6
SQ FT: 7,500
SALES (est): 837.3K Privately Held
SIC: 2371 Hats, fur; apparel, fur

(G-7487)
KARR GRAPHICS CORP
2219 41st Ave Ste 2a (11101-4807)
PHONE..................212 645-6000
Larry Karr, *President*
Myron Karr, *Vice Pres*
EMP: 20
SQ FT: 25,000
SALES (est): 2.9MM Privately Held
SIC: 2752 2759 2796 2754 Commercial printing, lithographic; thermography; platemaking services; stationery: gravure printing

(G-7488)
KERNS MANUFACTURING CORP (PA)
3714 29th St (11101-2690)
PHONE..................718 784-4044
Simon Srybnik, *Ch of Bd*
Louis Srybnik, *President*
Robert Arrighi, *General Mgr*
Naldo Pena, *QC Dir*
Ben Movaseghi, *CFO*
▲ EMP: 125
SQ FT: 60,000
SALES (est): 19MM Privately Held
WEB: www.kernsmfg.com
SIC: 3469 3724 3812 3714 Electronic enclosures, stamped or pressed metal; aircraft engines & engine parts; search & navigation equipment; motor vehicle parts & accessories

(G-7489)
KOENIG IRON WORKS INC
814 37th Ave (11101-6011)
PHONE..................718 433-0900
Barry Leistner, *President*
Jane Ross, *President*
Norman Rosenbaum, *Vice Pres*
Richard Velting, *Vice Pres*
Mike Bock, *Project Mgr*
EMP: 50
SQ FT: 35,000
SALES (est): 12.3MM Privately Held
WEB: www.koenigironworks.com
SIC: 3441 3446 Fabricated structural metal; ornamental metalwork

(G-7490)
KONG KEE FOOD CORP
4831 Van Dam St (11101-3101)
PHONE..................718 937-2746
Ip Kong, *President*
▲ EMP: 45
SQ FT: 18,000
SALES (est): 5.8MM Privately Held
SIC: 2026 5141 Fermented & cultured milk products; groceries, general line

(G-7491)
KOREA CENTRAL DAILY NEWS INC (HQ)
4327 36th St (11101-1703)
PHONE..................718 361-7700
Byoungsoo Sohn, *CEO*
Wanseob Kong, *Publisher*
Seok J Kim, *General Mgr*
Sangmook Lee, *CFO*
Sangmuk Lee, *CFO*
▲ EMP: 58
SQ FT: 10,000
SALES (est): 9.2MM
SALES (corp-wide): 244.9MM Privately Held
SIC: 2711 Newspapers, publishing & printing
PA: Joongang Ilbo
100 Seosomun-Ro, Jung-Gu
Seoul 04513
822 751-9114

(G-7492)
KOREA TIMES NEW YORK INC (HQ)
3710 Skillman Ave (11101-1731)
PHONE..................718 784-4526
Jae Min Chang, *CEO*
Hak Shin, *President*
▲ EMP: 80 EST: 1967
SQ FT: 16,000
SALES (est): 16MM
SALES (corp-wide): 83.9MM Privately Held
SIC: 2711 Newspapers: publishing only, not printed on site; newspapers, publishing & printing
PA: The Korea Times Los Angeles Inc
3731 Wilshire Blvd
Los Angeles CA 90010
323 692-2000

(G-7493)
KOREA TIMES NEW YORK INC
3710 Skillman Ave (11101-1731)
PHONE..................718 729-5555
Jae Min Chang, *Branch Mgr*
EMP: 8

SALES (corp-wide): 83.9MM Privately Held
SIC: 2711 Newspapers, publishing & printing
HQ: The Korea Times New York Inc
3710 Skillman Ave
Long Island City NY 11101
718 784-4526

(G-7494)
L & L OVERHEAD GARAGE DOORS (PA)
3125 45th St (11103-1620)
PHONE..................718 721-2518
Louis Lauri Jr, *President*
EMP: 9
SQ FT: 5,000
SALES (est): 783.8K Privately Held
SIC: 3442 5211 Garage doors, overhead: metal; garage doors, sale & installation

(G-7495)
LARKIN ANYA LTD
4310 23rd St Ste 2b (11101-5020)
PHONE..................718 361-1827
Anya Larkin, *President*
EMP: 9 EST: 1981
SQ FT: 4,000
SALES (est): 1.7MM Privately Held
WEB: www.anyalarkin.com
SIC: 2679 Wallpaper

(G-7496)
LARTE DEL GELATO GRUPPO INC
3100 47th Ave (11101-3013)
PHONE..................718 383-6600
Francesco Realmuto, *Principal*
▲ EMP: 10
SALES (est): 1MM Privately Held
SIC: 2024 2053 Ice cream & frozen desserts; cakes, bakery: frozen

(G-7497)
LESIEUR CRISTAL INC
1034 44th Dr Fl 2 (11101-7001)
PHONE..................646 604-4314
Nizar Azarkane, *Managing Dir*
EMP: 5
SALES (est): 139.9K Privately Held
SIC: 2079 Olive oil

(G-7498)
LIFFEY SHEET METAL CORP
4555 36th St (11101-1821)
PHONE..................347 381-1134
Michael Freeman, *President*
Francisco Piscitelly, *Principal*
Priscilla Freeman, *Shareholder*
Bridgette Piscitelli, *Shareholder*
EMP: 14
SALES (est): 2.7MM Privately Held
SIC: 3444 1711 Ducts, sheet metal; ventilation & duct work contractor

(G-7499)
LINCO PRINTING INC
5022 23rd St (11101-4502)
PHONE..................718 937-5141
Yu-Ou Lin, *President*
Sandy Lin, *Vice Pres*
Sherry Mao, *Manager*
EMP: 40 EST: 1975
SQ FT: 34,000
SALES (est): 4.6MM Privately Held
WEB: www.lincoprinting.com
SIC: 2759 Letterpress printing

(G-7500)
LINEAR LIGHTING CORPORATION
3130 Hunters Point Ave (11101-3132)
PHONE..................718 361-7552
Stanley Deutsch, *President*
Larry Deutsch, *Principal*
Fred Jona, *Purch Dir*
Lois Shoor, *Human Res Mgr*
Michael Deutsch, *VP Sales*
▲ EMP: 150
SQ FT: 85,000
SALES (est): 27.1MM Privately Held
WEB: www.linearlighting.com
SIC: 3646 5063 Commercial indusl & institutional electric lighting fixtures; electrical apparatus & equipment

(G-7501)
LIQUID KNITS INC
3200 Skillman Ave Fl 2 (11101-2308)
PHONE..................718 706-6600
Jeffrey Schechter, *President*
▲ EMP: 18
SQ FT: 35,000
SALES (est): 2.7MM Privately Held
WEB: www.liquidknits.com
SIC: 2339 Women's & misses' athletic clothing & sportswear

(G-7502)
LITELAB CORP
540 54th Ave (11101-5925)
PHONE..................718 361-6829
Rafael Ramirez, *Manager*
Edgar Alvarado, *Supervisor*
EMP: 6
SALES (corp-wide): 25.7MM Privately Held
WEB: www.litelab.com
SIC: 3646 Commercial indusl & institutional electric lighting fixtures
PA: Litelab Corp.
251 Elm St
Buffalo NY 14203
716 856-4300

(G-7503)
LOCKWOOD TRADE JOURNAL CO INC
Also Called: Tea & Coffee Trade Journal
3743 Crescent St Fl 2 (11101-3516)
PHONE..................212 391-2060
George E Lockwood Jr, *President*
Frederick Lockwood, *Publisher*
Robert Lockwood Sr, *Vice Pres*
▲ EMP: 20 EST: 1872
SQ FT: 4,000
SALES (est): 1.9MM Privately Held
WEB: www.lockwoodpublications.com
SIC: 2721 Trade journals: publishing & printing

(G-7504)
LONG ISLAND BRAND BEVS LLC
3788 Review Ave (11101-2052)
PHONE..................855 542-2832
Philip Thomas, *CEO*
EMP: 100
SQ FT: 25,000
SALES (est): 22.1MM
SALES (corp-wide): 4.4MM Privately Held
SIC: 2086 Iced tea & fruit drinks, bottled & canned
PA: Long Blockchain Corp.
12 Dubon Ct Ste 1
Farmingdale NY 11735
855 542-2832

(G-7505)
LUCINAS GOURMET FOOD INC
3646 37th St (11101-1606)
PHONE..................646 835-9784
Desmond Morais, *President*
Pauline Morais, *Vice Pres*
EMP: 6
SQ FT: 500
SALES: 18.5K Privately Held
SIC: 2035 Pickles, sauces & salad dressings

(G-7506)
LUKAS LIGHTING INC
4020 22nd St Ste 11 (11101-4814)
PHONE..................800 841-4011
Craig Corona, *CEO*
Ida Gold, *Purch Mgr*
David Haiderzad, *Manager*
▲ EMP: 30
SALES (est): 7.1MM Privately Held
SIC: 3646 Commercial indusl & institutional electric lighting fixtures

(G-7507)
LUXERDAME CO INC
4315 Queens St Ste A (11101-2923)
PHONE..................718 752-9800
Leonard Finkel, *President*
EMP: 20 EST: 1933

GEOGRAPHIC SECTION

Long Island City - Queens County (G-7534)

SALES (est): 1.4MM **Privately Held**
SIC: **2341** 2342 Mfg Women's/Youth Underwear Mfg Bras/Girdles

(G-7508)
M A R A METALS LTD
2520 40th Ave (11101-3810)
PHONE..................718 786-7868
Andreas Fiorentino, *President*
Andreas Vassiliou, *Vice Pres*
EMP: 6
SQ FT: 600
SALES (est): 500K **Privately Held**
SIC: **3911** Jewelry, precious metal

(G-7509)
MAC CRETE CORPORATION
Also Called: Mac Donuts of New York
3412 10th St (11106-5108)
PHONE..................718 932-1803
Georga Papadopoulos, *President*
EMP: 10
SALES (est): 1.6MM **Privately Held**
SIC: **2051** 5149 Cakes, pies & pastries; bakery products

(G-7510)
MANA PRODUCTS INC (PA)
Also Called: Your Name Professional Brand
3202 Queens Blvd Fl 6 (11101-2341)
PHONE..................718 361-2550
Nikos Mouyiaris, *Chairman*
Jerry Bisram, *Vice Pres*
Susannah Carney, *Vice Pres*
David Chan, *Vice Pres*
Edward Ewankov, *Vice Pres*
◆ EMP: 276
SALES (est): 284.9MM **Privately Held**
WEB: www.manaproducts.com
SIC: **2844** 5122 Cosmetic preparations; cosmetics

(G-7511)
MANA PRODUCTS INC
Esthetic Research Group
3202 Queens Blvd Fl 6 (11101-2341)
PHONE..................718 361-5204
Necos Mouyiaris, *Branch Mgr*
EMP: 500
SALES (corp-wide): 284.9MM **Privately Held**
SIC: **2844** Toilet preparations
PA: Mana Products, Inc.
3202 Queens Blvd Fl 6
Long Island City NY 11101
718 361-2550

(G-7512)
MANE ENTERPRISES INC
4929 30th Pl (11101-3116)
PHONE..................718 472-4955
Bill Mountain, *CEO*
Nicholas Sackett, *President*
John Mountain, *Vice Pres*
▲ EMP: 55
SQ FT: 12,000
SALES (est): 5.2MM **Privately Held**
SIC: **2323** Men's & boys' neckwear

(G-7513)
MANHATTAN COOLING TOWERS INC
1142 46th Rd (11101-5322)
PHONE..................212 279-1045
Richard Silver, *President*
EMP: 15
SQ FT: 10,400
SALES (est): 1.8MM **Privately Held**
SIC: **3443** Cooling towers, metal plate

(G-7514)
MANHATTAN DISPLAY INC
1215 Jackson Ave Ste B (11101-5551)
PHONE..................718 392-1365
John Petursson, *President*
EMP: 6
SQ FT: 1,500
SALES (est): 697.4K **Privately Held**
WEB: www.manhattandisplay.com
SIC: **2542** 5046 Office & store showcases & display fixtures; store fixtures & display equipment

(G-7515)
MARITIME BROADBAND INC
1143 47th Ave (11101-5465)
PHONE..................347 404-6041
Mary Ellen Kramer, *President*
Zebi Kramer, *Admin Sec*
▲ EMP: 27
SALES (est): 5.9MM **Privately Held**
SIC: **3663** Marine radio communications equipment

(G-7516)
MASPETH STEEL FABRICATORS INC
5215 11th St Ste 21 (11101-5844)
PHONE..................718 361-9192
Dominick Lofaso, *Ch of Bd*
EMP: 7
SALES (est): 1.1MM **Privately Held**
SIC: **3441** Fabricated structural metal

(G-7517)
MASTERCRAFT MANUFACTURING CO
3715 11th St (11101-6006)
PHONE..................718 729-5620
Peter Borsits, *President*
EMP: 5 EST: 1960
SALES (est): 310K **Privately Held**
SIC: **3993** Advertising novelties

(G-7518)
MATOV INDUSTRIES INC
Also Called: Roxter Lighting
1011 40th Ave (11101-6105)
PHONE..................718 392-5060
Alan Hochster, *President*
EMP: 20
SQ FT: 15,000
SALES (est): 3.4MM **Privately Held**
SIC: **3645** 3469 3646 5063 Residential lighting fixtures; metal stampings; commercial indusl & institutional electric lighting fixtures; lighting fixtures

(G-7519)
MECHO SYSTEMS
3708 34th St (11101-2213)
PHONE..................718 729-8373
Anthony Gryak, *Manager*
EMP: 15
SALES (corp-wide): 15.8MM **Privately Held**
WEB: www.stretchwall.com
SIC: **3296** Acoustical board & tile, mineral wool
HQ: Mecho Systems
4203 35th St
Long Island City NY 11101
718 729-8376

(G-7520)
MECHOSHADE SYSTEMS INC (DH)
4203 35th St (11101-2301)
PHONE..................718 729-2020
Jan Berman, *President*
Norman Rathfelder, *CFO*
Florin Baicu, *Accountant*
◆ EMP: 200
SQ FT: 45,000
SALES (est): 107.4MM
SALES (corp-wide): 2.6B **Privately Held**
WEB: www.soleilshades.com
SIC: **2591** Window shades
HQ: Springs Window Fashions, Llc
7549 Graber Rd
Middleton WI 53562
608 836-1011

(G-7521)
MEDITERREAN DYRO COMPANY
1102 38th Ave (11101-6041)
PHONE..................718 786-4888
Jimmy Austin, *President*
Amalia Malamis, *Principal*
▲ EMP: 40
SALES (est): 2.1MM **Privately Held**
SIC: **2099** Food preparations

(G-7522)
METRO DUCT SYSTEMS INC
1219 Astoria Blvd Apt 2 (11102-4478)
PHONE..................718 278-4294
Orson Arroyo, *President*

EMP: 11
SALES (est): 1.2MM **Privately Held**
SIC: **3444** 1711 Sheet metalwork; mechanical contractor

(G-7523)
METRO GROUP INC (PA)
Also Called: Metro Grouping
5023 23rd St (11101-4501)
PHONE..................718 729-7200
Bernard Bradpiece, *CEO*
Robert H Seidman, *President*
Krista Pasfield, *Opers Staff*
Gary Ho, *Engineer*
M Jackson, *Engineer*
EMP: 74 EST: 1925
SQ FT: 15,000
SALES (est): 20.7MM **Privately Held**
WEB: www.metrogroupinc.com
SIC: **3589** 1389 Water treatment equipment, industrial; chemically treating wells

(G-7524)
MICHAEL FELDMAN INC
3010 41st Ave Ste 3 (11101-2817)
PHONE..................718 433-1700
Richard Feldman, *President*
Grace Feldman, *Treasurer*
EMP: 95 EST: 1964
SQ FT: 20,000
SALES (est): 6.6MM **Privately Held**
WEB: www.permanentfoliage.com
SIC: **2339** Bathing suits: women's, misses' & juniors'

(G-7525)
MING PAO (NEW YORK) INC
Also Called: Ming Pao Daily News, New York
4331 33rd St Fl 2 (11101-2316)
PHONE..................718 786-2888
Stephanie Liu, *CEO*
EMP: 20
SALES (corp-wide): 302.5MM **Privately Held**
SIC: **2711** Newspapers
HQ: Ming Pao (New York), Inc
4331 33rd St
Long Island City NY 11101

(G-7526)
MING PAO (NEW YORK) INC (HQ)
Also Called: Ming Pay N Y
4331 33rd St Fl 2 (11101-2316)
PHONE..................718 786-2888
Ryan Low, *President*
Francis Tiong, *President*
Leon Cai, *Comp Tech*
EMP: 70
SQ FT: 21,000
SALES (est): 4.6MM
SALES (corp-wide): 302.5MM **Privately Held**
WEB: www.mingpaousa.com
SIC: **2711** Commercial printing & newspaper publishing combined
PA: Media Chinese International Limited
15/F Ming Pao Indl Ctr Blk A
Chai Wan HK
259 531-11

(G-7527)
MISSION CRANE SERVICE INC (PA)
4700 33rd St (11101-2419)
PHONE..................718 937-3333
David Chazen, *President*
EMP: 60
SQ FT: 30,000
SALES (est): 4.5MM **Privately Held**
SIC: **3999** 7993 Coin-operated amusement machines; game machines

(G-7528)
MODUTANK INC
4104 35th Ave (11101-1410)
PHONE..................718 392-1112
John Reed Margulis, *President*
Thomas G Carren, *Vice Pres*
EMP: 10
SQ FT: 15,000
SALES (est): 2.6MM **Privately Held**
WEB: www.modutank.com
SIC: **3443** Tanks, lined: metal plate

(G-7529)
MONGRU NECKWEAR INC
1010 44th Ave Fl 2 (11101-7032)
PHONE..................718 706-0406
Ramdihal Mongru, *President*
EMP: 40
SQ FT: 10,580
SALES (est): 4.4MM **Privately Held**
SIC: **2253** 2323 5136 Neckties, knit; men's & boys' neckwear; neckwear, men's & boys'

(G-7530)
MUTUAL SALES CORP
Also Called: Mutual Harware
545 49th Ave (11101-5610)
PHONE..................718 361-8373
Mary Piotrowski, *President*
Vincent Marmallardi, *Vice Pres*
Maria Stewart, *Treasurer*
Jacob Hyzer, *Director*
Maret Asaro, *Shareholder*
▲ EMP: 23
SQ FT: 10,000
SALES (est): 8.4MM **Privately Held**
SIC: **2391** 7922 5131 Curtains & draperies; equipment rental, theatrical; textiles, woven

(G-7531)
MZB ACCESSORIES LLC
2976 Northern Blvd Fl 4 (11101-2829)
PHONE..................718 472-7500
AMI Alterin, *Mng Member*
▲ EMP: 100
SALES (est): 20MM
SALES (corp-wide): 68.4MM **Privately Held**
SIC: **2844** Toilet preparations; cosmetic preparations; deodorants, personal; lotions, shaving
PA: M.Z. Berger & Co. Inc.
2976 Northern Blvd Fl 4
Long Island City NY 11101
718 472-7500

(G-7532)
N A ALUMIL CORPORATION
Also Called: Alumil NA Fabrication
4401 21st St Ste 203 (11101-5009)
PHONE..................718 355-9393
Kyprianos Bazehika, *Ch of Bd*
John McElroy, *Vice Pres*
Eric Tan, *Engineer*
John Lombardi, *Sr Project Mgr*
▲ EMP: 8
SALES (est): 2.7MM
SALES (corp-wide): 151.2MM **Privately Held**
SIC: **3355** Aluminum rolling & drawing
PA: Alumil Aluminium Industry S.A.
Industrial Area, Stavrochori, P.O. Box 37
Kilkis 61100
234 107-9300

(G-7533)
NATIONAL HERALD INC
Also Called: Greek Nat Hrald Dily Nwsppr In
3710 30th St (11101-2614)
PHONE..................718 784-5255
Anthony H Diamataris, *President*
Andy Dabilis, *Editor*
Vasilis Magalios, *Editor*
Victoria Diamataris, *Corp Secy*
▲ EMP: 35 EST: 1915
SQ FT: 4,200
SALES (est): 2.6MM **Privately Held**
WEB: www.nationalherald.com
SIC: **2711** Newspapers: publishing only, not printed on site

(G-7534)
NAZIM IZZAK INC
Also Called: N I Boutique
4402 23rd St Ste 517 (11101-5072)
PHONE..................212 920-5546
Nazim I Guity, *President*
EMP: 6
SQ FT: 2,800
SALES (est): 494.4K **Privately Held**
SIC: **2231** 5632 Apparel & outerwear broadwoven fabrics; apparel accessories

---

(PA)=Parent Co (HQ)=Headquarters (DH)=Div Headquarters
✪ = New Business established in last 2 years

2019 Harris
New York Manufacturers Directory

Long Island City - Queens County (G-7535)

(G-7535)
NECESSARY OBJECTS LTD (PA)
3030 47th Ave Fl 6 (11101-3433)
PHONE..................212 334-9888
Ady Gluck Frankel, *Ch of Bd*
Bill Kauffman, *CFO*
▲ EMP: 50
SALES (est): 12.6MM Privately Held
WEB: www.necessaryobjects.com
SIC: 2335 2339 2331 Women's, juniors' & misses' dresses; slacks: women's, misses' & juniors'; blouses, women's & juniors': made from purchased material

(G-7536)
NEPENTHES AMERICA INC
2219 41st Ave 401 (11101-4835)
PHONE..................212 343-4262
Keizo Shimizu, *President*
Daiki Suzuki, *Corp Secy*
Akiko Shimizu, *Vice Pres*
Angelo F Urrutia, *Sales Staff*
▲ EMP: 8 EST: 1996
SQ FT: 1,500
SALES (est): 1.7MM Privately Held
WEB: www.nepenthesny.com
SIC: 2329 Men's & boys' athletic uniforms

(G-7537)
NEW CLASSIC INC
4143 37th St (11101-1723)
PHONE..................718 609-1100
Simon Yiu, *President*
Rachel Yiu, *Vice Pres*
Alex Quinones, *Sales Mgr*
▲ EMP: 14
SQ FT: 20,000
SALES (est): 1.5MM Privately Held
WEB: www.newclassic.net
SIC: 2387 5136 5137 Apparel belts; apparel belts, men's & boys'; apparel belts, women's & children's

(G-7538)
NEW SENSOR CORPORATION (PA)
Also Called: ELECTRO-HARMONIX
5501 2nd St (11101-5908)
PHONE..................718 937-8300
Michael Matthews, *President*
Laura Ho, *Purch Agent*
John Pisani, *Senior Engr*
Matthias Raabe, *Controller*
Kevin Jolly, *Marketing Staff*
◆ EMP: 55
SQ FT: 89,886
SALES (est): 30.8MM Privately Held
WEB: www.newsensor.com
SIC: 3931 3671 5065 Musical instruments, electric & electronic; vacuum tubes; electronic parts & equipment

(G-7539)
NEW YORK BINDING CO INC
2121 41st Ave Ste A (11101-4833)
PHONE..................718 729-2454
Roger Levin, *President*
Linda Van Dine, *Manager*
EMP: 40
SQ FT: 15,000
SALES (est): 4.5MM Privately Held
WEB: www.newyorkbindingco.com
SIC: 2241 2396 Bindings, textile; trimmings, textile; automotive & apparel trimmings

(G-7540)
NOVELTY CRYSTAL CORP (PA)
3015 48th Ave (11101-3419)
PHONE..................718 458-6700
Rivka Michaeli, *President*
Ed Coslett, *COO*
Asher Michaeli, *Exec VP*
Jason Michaeli, *Assistant VP*
Daniel Weatherly, *Plant Mgr*
▲ EMP: 100 EST: 1961
SQ FT: 50,000
SALES (est): 15.2MM Privately Held
WEB: www.noveltycrystal.com
SIC: 3089 3421 Plastic kitchenware, tableware & houseware; kitchenware, plastic; cutlery

(G-7541)
NY IRON INC
3131 48th Ave Ste 2 (11101-3022)
PHONE..................718 302-9000
Todd Devito, *Ch of Bd*
EMP: 15
SALES (est): 955.7K Privately Held
SIC: 7692 Welding repair

(G-7542)
ODEGARD INC
3030 47th Ave Ste 700 (11101-3492)
PHONE..................212 545-0069
John Nihoul, *Manager*
EMP: 12
SALES (corp-wide): 7.4MM Privately Held
WEB: www.odegardinc.com
SIC: 2273 Carpets & rugs
PA: Odegard, Inc.
   200 Lexington Ave Rm 1206
   New York NY 10016
   212 545-0205

(G-7543)
OUGRA INC
3100 47th Ave Unit 4 (11101-3068)
PHONE..................646 342-4575
Phillip Soliman, *President*
EMP: 4
SALES (est): 2MM Privately Held
SIC: 7372 Business oriented computer software

(G-7544)
P C RFRS RADIOLOGY
Also Called: Radiology Film Reading Svcs
3630 37th St Frnt (11101-1606)
PHONE..................212 586-5700
Joseph Gottesman, *President*
Joseph J Gottesman, *Med Doctor*
EMP: 8
SQ FT: 1,000
SALES (est): 874.1K Privately Held
WEB: www.radiologyreadings.com
SIC: 3577 Film reader devices

(G-7545)
P-RYTON CORP
Also Called: Skin Dynamic
504 50th Ave (11101-5712)
PHONE..................718 937-7052
Joseph Palumbo Jr, *President*
Sergio Palumbo, *Vice Pres*
Joseph Palumbo Sr, *Shareholder*
Linda Palumbo, *Admin Sec*
▲ EMP: 11
SQ FT: 6,000
SALES (est): 1.9MM Privately Held
WEB: www.p-ryton.com
SIC: 3841 Surgical & medical instruments

(G-7546)
PACIFIC POLY PRODUCT CORP
3934 Crescent St (11101-3802)
PHONE..................718 786-7129
Henry Ly, *President*
▲ EMP: 10
SQ FT: 10,000
SALES: 1MM Privately Held
SIC: 2673 Plastic bags: made from purchased materials; garment bags (plastic film): made from purchased materials

(G-7547)
PADDY LEE FASHIONS INC
4709 36th St Fl 2nd (11101-1823)
PHONE..................718 786-6020
Ralph Covelli Jr, *CEO*
John Covelli, *Exec VP*
EMP: 15 EST: 1955
SQ FT: 46,000
SALES (est): 3MM Privately Held
WEB: www.paddylee.com
SIC: 2339 2331 Slacks: women's, misses' & juniors'; blouses, women's & juniors': made from purchased material

(G-7548)
PARKMATIC CAR PRKG SYSTEMS LLC (PA)
47-10 A 32nd Pl (11101)
PHONE..................516 224-7700
Max Wassef, *President*
Elza Wassef, *Vice Pres*
EMP: 3 EST: 2016
SQ FT: 2,000
SALES: 3.5MM Privately Held
SIC: 3559 1799 Parking facility equipment & supplies; parking facility equipment installation

(G-7549)
PARSONS-MEARES LTD
2107 41st Ave Ste 1l (11101-4802)
PHONE..................212 242-3378
James Mears, *President*
Sally Ann Parsons, *Vice Pres*
EMP: 60
SQ FT: 12,000
SALES (est): 4.8MM Privately Held
WEB: www.parsons-meares.com
SIC: 2389 Theatrical costumes

(G-7550)
PASS EM-ENTRIES INC (PA)
3914 Crescent St (11101-3802)
PHONE..................718 392-0100
Joseph Stegmayer, *President*
John La Salle, *Vice Pres*
EMP: 18
SALES (est): 1.1MM Privately Held
SIC: 2395 Pleating & stitching

(G-7551)
PEACHTREE ENTERPRISES INC
2219 41st Ave Ste 4a (11101-4807)
PHONE..................212 989-3445
Robert Sussman, *President*
Jeffrey Alpert, *Vice Pres*
Jonathan Bortey, *Production*
Bart Sussman, *Treasurer*
EMP: 38 EST: 1976
SALES (est): 6.4MM Privately Held
WEB: www.peachtree-printingnyc.com
SIC: 2752 Commercial printing, offset

(G-7552)
PELICAN BAY LTD
Also Called: Ravioli Store, The
3901 22nd St (11101-4809)
PHONE..................718 729-9300
Donna Nasoff, *Principal*
Michael Nasoff, *Principal*
EMP: 12
SALES (est): 990K Privately Held
SIC: 2099 Food preparations

(G-7553)
PENN & FLETCHER INC
2107 41st Ave Fl 5 (11101-4802)
PHONE..................212 239-6868
Ernie Smith, *President*
EMP: 15
SQ FT: 4,500
SALES (est): 1.1MM Privately Held
SIC: 2395 5131 Embroidery products, except schiffli machine; lace fabrics; trimmings, apparel

(G-7554)
PETCAP PRESS CORPORATION
3200 Skillman Ave Ste F (11101-2308)
PHONE..................718 609-0910
Joan Caputo, *President*
Peter Caputo, *Vice Pres*
EMP: 10
SALES (est): 1.1MM Privately Held
SIC: 2752 Commercial printing, offset

(G-7555)
PHEONIX CUSTOM FURNITURE LTD
2107 41st Ave Fl 2 (11101-4802)
PHONE..................212 727-2648
John J Clarke, *Principal*
Vito D'Alessandro, *Vice Pres*
EMP: 20
SQ FT: 10,000
SALES: 2MM Privately Held
SIC: 2512 2521 Upholstered household furniture; wood office furniture

(G-7556)
PILOT PRODUCTS INC
2413 46th St (11103-1007)
P.O. Box 3221 (11103-0221)
PHONE..................718 728-2141
Carolyn J Hebel, *President*
Herbert Hebel, *President*
Elizabeth Hammell, *Vice Pres*
EMP: 13
SQ FT: 17,000
SALES (est): 1.9MM Privately Held
SIC: 3061 Mechanical rubber goods

(G-7557)
PLATINUM SALES PROMOTION INC
Also Called: The Spirited Shipper
3514a Crescent St (11106-3920)
PHONE..................718 361-0200
Bruce Cappels, *President*
▲ EMP: 7
SQ FT: 12,000
SALES: 1.4MM Privately Held
WEB: www.spiritedshipper.com
SIC: 3993 4225 8743 4213 Displays & cutouts, window & lobby; general warehousing; sales promotion; trucking, except local

(G-7558)
PRESTONE PRESS LLC
Also Called: Prestone Printing Company
4750 30th St (11101-3404)
PHONE..................347 468-7900
Margaret Horn, *Accounts Mgr*
Alan Wechsler, *Sales Executive*
Barbara Padovano, *Technology*
Robert Adler,
Steven Amoroso,
EMP: 113
SALES: 24MM Privately Held
SIC: 2752 Commercial printing, offset

(G-7559)
PRIME ELECTRIC MOTORS INC
4850 33rd St (11101-2514)
P.O. Box 1374 (11101-0374)
PHONE..................718 784-1124
Gul Zaman, *President*
EMP: 9
SALES (est): 820K Privately Held
SIC: 7694 Electric motor repair

(G-7560)
PRIMO COAT CORP
Also Called: Ciccarelli Custom Taylor
4315 Queens St Fl 3 (11101-2947)
PHONE..................718 349-2070
Rocco Ciccarelli, *President*
EMP: 35 EST: 1963
SQ FT: 13,500
SALES: 1MM Privately Held
SIC: 2311 2337 2339 2325 Suits, men's & boys': made from purchased materials; suits: women's, misses' & juniors'; women's & misses' outerwear; men's & boys' trousers & slacks

(G-7561)
PROMETHEUS INTERNATIONAL INC
4502 11th St (11101-5206)
PHONE..................718 472-0700
Sayedd Rabb, *President*
Monjur Hossain, *Manager*
EMP: 16 EST: 1989
SALES (est): 630.3K Privately Held
SIC: 2711 Commercial printing & newspaper publishing combined

(G-7562)
PULSAR TECHNOLOGY SYSTEMS INC
2720 42nd Rd (11101-4112)
PHONE..................718 361-9292
Rudolph Robinson, *President*
Joann Pitcher, *Manager*
EMP: 9
SQ FT: 3,750
SALES: 1.3MM Privately Held
WEB: www.taxi-meters.com
SIC: 3825 Test equipment for electronic & electrical circuits; meters: electric, pocket, portable, panelboard, etc.

(G-7563)
PURA FRUTA LLC
2323 Borden Ave (11101-4508)
PHONE..................415 279-5727
Mark Fridman, *Prdtn Mgr*
Adriana Ayales,
EMP: 12

▲ = Import ▼ = Export
◆ = Import/Export

SALES (est): 1.3MM **Privately Held**
SIC: 2037 Fruit juices

(G-7564)
QPBC INC
1306 38th Ave (11101-6034)
PHONE..............................718 685-1900
Kenneth Maurer, *Ch of Bd*
EMP: 40 EST: 2014
SQ FT: 20,000
SALES (est): 4.2MM **Privately Held**
SIC: 3465 5013 Body parts, automobile: stamped metal; automotive supplies & parts

(G-7565)
QUADLOGIC CONTROLS CORPORATION
Also Called: Qlc
3300 Northern Blvd Fl 2 (11101-2215)
PHONE..............................212 930-9300
Sayre Swarztrauber, *Ch of Bd*
Doron Shafrir, *President*
Phil Fram, *Vice Pres*
Jordon Herzog, *Technical Mgr*
Stanley Lo, *Engineer*
▲ EMP: 75
SQ FT: 36,000
SALES (est): 17MM **Privately Held**
SIC: 3825 7389 Electrical energy measuring equipment; meters: electric, pocket, portable, panelboard, etc.; meter readers, remote

(G-7566)
QUALITY CASTINGS INC
3100 47th Ave Ste 2120b (11101-3023)
PHONE..............................732 409-3203
Carl Morfino, *President*
Frank Bono, *General Mgr*
EMP: 50
SQ FT: 3,200
SALES (est): 7.2MM **Privately Held**
WEB: www.qualitycasting.com
SIC: 3369 3324 Castings, except die-castings, precision; steel investment foundries

(G-7567)
QUALITY IMPRESSIONS INC
4334 32nd Pl Ste 3 (11101-2313)
PHONE..............................646 613-0002
Brennan Ganga, *President*
EMP: 6
SALES: 600K **Privately Held**
SIC: 2759 Commercial printing

(G-7568)
QUALITY OFFSET LLC
4750 30th St (11101-3404)
PHONE..............................347 342-4660
Steve Wong,
EMP: 7
SQ FT: 2,000
SALES (est): 752.8K **Privately Held**
SIC: 2759 Commercial printing

(G-7569)
QUATTRO FRAMEWORKS INC
4310 23rd St Ste 307 (11101-4604)
PHONE..............................718 361-2620
Sebastian Ramundo, *President*
EMP: 11
SALES (est): 567K **Privately Held**
SIC: 2499 Picture frame molding, finished

(G-7570)
RAGOZIN DATA
Also Called: Sheets, The
4402 11th St Ste 613 (11101-5184)
PHONE..............................212 674-3123
Len Ragozin, *Owner*
EMP: 20
SQ FT: 2,000
SALES (est): 1.4MM **Privately Held**
WEB: www.thesheets.com
SIC: 2721 Magazines: publishing & printing

(G-7571)
RAPID FAN & BLOWER INC
2314 39th Ave (11101-3612)
PHONE..............................718 786-2060
George J Rogner Jr, *President*
George Rogner, *Purchasing*
EMP: 10 EST: 1956
SQ FT: 15,000
SALES (est): 2.1MM **Privately Held**
WEB: www.rapidfan.com
SIC: 3564 5084 Blowing fans: industrial or commercial; turbo-blowers, industrial; industrial machinery & equipment

(G-7572)
RAVIOLI STORE INC
4344 21st St (11101-5002)
PHONE..............................718 729-9300
Michael Nasoss, *Manager*
EMP: 5
SALES (est): 500K **Privately Held**
WEB: www.raviolistore.com
SIC: 2098 5411 Macaroni & spaghetti; grocery stores

(G-7573)
RAYANA DESIGNS INC
2520 40th Ave (11101-3810)
PHONE..............................718 786-2040
Andreas Vassiliou, *President*
Andreas Fiorentino, *Corp Secy*
Mihran Panossian, *Vice Pres*
Dennis Fiorentino, *Admin Sec*
EMP: 20 EST: 1979
SQ FT: 5,000
SALES (est): 2.8MM **Privately Held**
WEB: www.rayanadesigns.com
SIC: 3479 Engraving jewelry silverware, or metal

(G-7574)
RELIANCE MACHINING INC
4335 Vernon Blvd (11101-6911)
PHONE..............................718 784-0314
Lloyd Larsen, *President*
EMP: 30
SQ FT: 15,000
SALES: 3MM **Privately Held**
SIC: 3599 Machine shop, jobbing & repair

(G-7575)
RENCO MANUFACTURING INC
1040 45th Ave Fl 2 (11101-7094)
PHONE..............................718 392-8877
AVI Shaul, *President*
EMP: 32
SQ FT: 15,000
SALES: 660K **Privately Held**
SIC: 3915 Jewelers' findings & materials

(G-7576)
ROBERT MILLER ASSOCIATES LLC
2219 41st Ave Ste 505 (11101-4841)
PHONE..............................718 392-1640
Robert Miller, *Mng Member*
EMP: 15
SALES: 1MM **Privately Held**
SIC: 2389 Men's miscellaneous accessories

(G-7577)
ROLLHAUS SEATING PRODUCTS INC
4310 21st Ave (11101-5002)
PHONE..............................718 729-9111
Michael Rollhaus, *President*
EMP: 13 EST: 1945
SQ FT: 28,000
SALES (est): 1.8MM **Privately Held**
WEB: www.seatingproducts.com
SIC: 2599 Restaurant furniture, wood or metal; bar furniture

(G-7578)
RONBAR LABORATORIES INC
5202 Van Dam St (11101-3221)
PHONE..............................718 937-6755
Sheldon Borgen, *President*
Barry Borgen, *Vice Pres*
EMP: 11
SQ FT: 12,000
SALES: 2MM **Privately Held**
SIC: 2841 7699 Detergents, synthetic organic or inorganic alkaline; restaurant equipment repair

(G-7579)
RONER INC (PA)
3553 24th St (11106-4416)
P.O. Box 6077 (11106-0077)
PHONE..............................718 392-6020
Ron Meltsner, *President*
Eric Spar, *Vice Pres*
Henry Meltsner, *Treasurer*
Harold Spar, *President*
▲ EMP: 5 EST: 1959
SQ FT: 20,000
SALES (est): 14.7MM **Privately Held**
SIC: 3842 5047 Hearing aids; medical & hospital equipment

(G-7580)
RONER INC
1433 31st Ave (11106-4536)
PHONE..............................718 392-6020
Marge Weber, *Branch Mgr*
EMP: 150
SALES (corp-wide): 14.7MM **Privately Held**
SIC: 3842 Hearing aids
PA: Roner, Inc.
  3553 24th St
  Long Island City NY 11106
  718 392-6020

(G-7581)
RUBINSTEIN JEWELRY MFG CO
3100 47th Ave (11101-3013)
PHONE..............................718 784-8650
Fax: 718 784-8893
EMP: 12 EST: 1956
SQ FT: 5,000
SALES (est): 74.5K **Privately Held**
SIC: 3911 Mfg Gold Jewelry

(G-7582)
S & B FASHION INC
4315 Queens St Ste B (11101-2923)
PHONE..............................718 482-1386
Tony Song, *President*
▲ EMP: 5 EST: 2000
SALES (est): 279.4K **Privately Held**
SIC: 2389 Apparel & accessories

(G-7583)
S BROOME AND CO INC
Also Called: Samuel Broome Uniform ACC
3300 47th Ave Fl 1 (11101-2428)
PHONE..............................718 663-6800
Michael Broome, *President*
Daniel Broome, *Vice Pres*
David Schaffer, *Treasurer*
ARI Wilker, *MIS Dir*
Kathy Broome, *Info Tech Mgr*
▲ EMP: 80 EST: 1917
SQ FT: 27,000
SALES (est): 7.8MM **Privately Held**
WEB: www.sbroome.com
SIC: 2339 2323 Neckwear & ties: women's, misses' & juniors'; men's & boys' neckwear

(G-7584)
SADOWSKY GUITARS LTD
2107 41st Ave Fl 4 (11101-4802)
PHONE..............................718 433-1990
Roger Sadowsky, *President*
Robin Phillips, *Shareholder*
▲ EMP: 10
SQ FT: 4,100
SALES (est): 1.3MM **Privately Held**
WEB: www.sadowsky.com
SIC: 3931 7699 String instruments & parts; musical instrument repair services

(G-7585)
SCOTTI GRAPHICS INC
3200 Skillman Ave Fl 1 (11101-2308)
PHONE..............................212 367-9602
Richard J Scotti, *President*
EMP: 50
SQ FT: 8,000
SALES (est): 6.4MM **Privately Held**
WEB: www.scottigraphics.com
SIC: 2752 2791 2759 Commercial printing, offset; typesetting; letterpress printing

(G-7586)
SCREEN TEAM INC
3402c Review Ave (11101-3242)
PHONE..............................718 786-2424
Richard Grubman, *President*
EMP: 10
SQ FT: 10,000
SALES: 1.5MM **Privately Held**
WEB: www.screenteam.com
SIC: 3552 Silk screens for textile industry

(G-7587)
SELECT JEWELRY INC
4728 37th St Fl 3 (11101-1809)
PHONE..............................718 784-3626
Nissim Seliktar, *Ch of Bd*
Ronny Seliktar, *President*
▲ EMP: 60
SQ FT: 40,000
SALES (est): 14.5MM **Privately Held**
SIC: 3911 5094 Jewelry, precious metal; jewelry

(G-7588)
SERVICE ADVERTISING GROUP INC
Also Called: Western Queens Gazette
4216 34th Ave (11101-1110)
PHONE..............................718 361-6161
Tony Barsamian, *President*
EMP: 15
SQ FT: 2,118
SALES (est): 804.2K **Privately Held**
WEB: www.qgazette.com
SIC: 2711 2741 7311 7313 Commercial printing & newspaper publishing combined; shopping news: publishing only, not printed on site; advertising agencies; newspaper advertising representative

(G-7589)
SHAPEWAYS INC
3002 48th Ave Ste 2 (11101-3401)
PHONE..............................646 470-3576
Gregory Kress, *CEO*
EMP: 7
SALES (est): 730.2K **Privately Held**
SALES (corp-wide): 40.4MM **Privately Held**
SIC: 2759 Commercial printing
PA: Shapeways, Inc.
  419 Park Ave S Fl 9
  New York NY 10016
  914 356-5816

(G-7590)
SIGN DESIGN GROUP NEW YORK INC
3326 Northern Blvd (11101-2224)
PHONE..............................718 392-0779
Mazher Khalfan, *Ch of Bd*
Muhammad Mohsin, *Opers Staff*
Sid Walli, *Manager*
Gavinder Dhillon, *Art Dir*
Shan Khalfan, *Admin Sec*
▲ EMP: 18
SALES (est): 2.7MM **Privately Held**
WEB: www.sdgny.com
SIC: 3993 Electric signs

(G-7591)
SIMS GROUP USA HOLDINGS CORP
Sims Metal
3027 Greenpoint Ave (11101-2009)
PHONE..............................718 786-6031
Thomas Ferretti, *Opers-Prdtn-Mfg*
EMP: 66 **Privately Held**
SIC: 3312 3341 Stainless steel; secondary nonferrous metals
HQ: Sims Group Usa Holdings Corp
  16 W 22nd St Fl 10
  New York NY 10010
  212 604-0710

(G-7592)
SIXTHSCENTS PAPER PRODUCTS LTD
Also Called: Sixthscents Products
37-18 Nthrn Blvd Ste 418 (11101)
PHONE..............................212 627-5066
Kristine Ferrara, *CEO*
Warren Pugach, *President*
EMP: 8 EST: 2009
SQ FT: 2,000
SALES: 450K **Privately Held**
SIC: 2844 Perfumes & colognes

(G-7593)
SIZZAL LLC
Also Called: Influence Graphics
1105 44th Rd Fl 2 (11101)
PHONE..............................212 354-6123
Bill Reeve, *Vice Pres*
Paul Gonzalez, *Prdtn Mgr*
Al Weiss, *Mng Member*

Ron Sizemore,
EMP: 28
SALES (est): 2.6MM **Privately Held**
SIC: 2752 Commercial printing, offset

(G-7594)
SLYDE INC
474 48th Ave Apt 18a (11109-5711)
PHONE.................................917 331-2114
Jason Peltz, *CEO*
Edward Ludvigsen, *Principal*
Kai Blache, *CFO*
EMP: 15
SALES (est): 587.4K **Privately Held**
SIC: 7372 7389 Prepackaged software;

(G-7595)
SPANJER CORP
Also Called: Spanjer Signs
3856 11th St (11101-6114)
PHONE.................................347 448-8033
Steve Silverberg, *President*
Alissa Silverberg, *Vice Pres*
Rose Silverberg, *Admin Sec*
EMP: 6 **EST:** 1908
SQ FT: 5,000
SALES: 446K **Privately Held**
SIC: 3993 Signs & advertising specialties

(G-7596)
STALLION INC (PA)
3620 34th St (11106-1902)
PHONE.................................718 706-0111
John Georgiades, *Ch of Bd*
Ioannis Georgiades, *President*
James Charles, *CFO*
Achilleas Georgiades, *Admin Sec*
▲ **EMP:** 26
SQ FT: 30,000
SALES (est): 37.5MM **Privately Held**
SIC: 2371 5621 Coats, fur; ready-to-wear apparel, women's

(G-7597)
STAMP RITE TOOL & DIE INC
4311 35th St (11101-2303)
PHONE.................................718 752-0334
EMP: 5
SQ FT: 1,000
SALES: 200K **Privately Held**
SIC: 3544 Manufacturer Of Tools

(G-7598)
STANDARD MOTOR PRODUCTS INC (PA)
3718 Northern Blvd # 600 (11101-1637)
PHONE.................................718 392-0200
Lawrence I Sills, *Ch of Bd*
Eric P Sills, *President*
Carmine J Broccole, *Senior VP*
James J Burke, *CFO*
Dale Burks, *Ch Credit Ofcr*
EMP: 500 **EST:** 1919
SQ FT: 75,800
SALES: 1.1B **Publicly Held**
WEB: www.smpcorp.com
SIC: 3714 3694 3585 3564 Motor vehicle engines & parts; fuel systems & parts, motor vehicle; air conditioner parts, motor vehicle; motor vehicle electrical equipment; ignition systems, high frequency; harness wiring sets, internal combustion engines; battery cable wiring sets for internal combustion engines; compressors for refrigeration & air conditioning equipment; parts for heating, cooling & refrigerating equipment; air conditioning equipment, complete; blowers & fans; rubber & plastics hose & beltings

(G-7599)
STANLEY CREATIONS INC
Also Called: Sgg
3100 47th Ave Ste 4105 (11101-3068)
PHONE.................................718 361-6100
David Lowy, *Branch Mgr*
EMP: 111
SALES (corp-wide): 12.7MM **Privately Held**
SIC: 3911 Jewelry, precious metal
PA: Stanley Creations, Inc.
1414 Willow Ave
Elkins Park PA 19027
215 635-6200

(G-7600)
STARCRAFT PRESS INC
4402 11th St Ste 311 (11101-5150)
PHONE.................................718 383-6700
Robert Glickman, *President*
Jeff Glickman, *Vice Pres*
EMP: 8
SALES (est): 1.1MM **Privately Held**
SIC: 2759 Letterpress printing

(G-7601)
STEINWAY INC (DH)
Also Called: Steinway Hall
1 Steinway Pl (11105-1033)
PHONE.................................718 721-2600
Ronald Losby, *CEO*
Kyle R Kirkland, *Exec VP*
▲ **EMP:** 575
SQ FT: 449,000
SALES (est): 133.3MM
SALES (corp-wide): 318.4MM **Privately Held**
WEB: www.steinway.com
SIC: 3931 5736 Pianos, all types: vertical, grand, spinet, player, etc.; pianos

(G-7602)
STEINWAY AND SONS (DH)
1 Steinway Pl (11105-1033)
PHONE.................................718 721-2600
Michael Sweeney, *Ch of Bd*
Kyle R Kirkland, *President*
Ronald Losby, *President*
Dana D Messina, *Exec VP*
Amy Nenner, *Senior VP*
◆ **EMP:** 101
SQ FT: 450,000
SALES (est): 108.6MM
SALES (corp-wide): 318.4MM **Privately Held**
WEB: www.steinwaypiano.net
SIC: 3931 5736 Pianos, all types: vertical, grand, spinet, player, etc.; pianos

(G-7603)
STELLAR PRINTING INC
3838 9th St (11101-6110)
PHONE.................................718 361-1600
Dirk Anthonis, *President*
Fred Newton, *President*
Bill Ednie, *General Mgr*
EMP: 100
SQ FT: 35,000
SALES (est): 15.7MM
SALES (corp-wide): 582.7MM **Privately Held**
WEB: www.americasnewspaper.com
SIC: 2759 Newspapers: printing
HQ: News World Communications, Inc.
3600 New York Ave Ne
Washington DC 20002
202 636-3000

(G-7604)
STEVEN MADDEN LTD (PA)
Also Called: STEVE MADDEN
5216 Barnett Ave (11104-1018)
PHONE.................................718 446-1800
Edward R Rosenfeld, *Ch of Bd*
Amelia Newton Varela, *President*
Mia Edwards, *District Mgr*
Angela Aviles, *Area Mgr*
Colleen Donovan, *Business Mgr*
EMP: 265
SQ FT: 90,000
SALES: 1.5B **Publicly Held**
WEB: www.mypinecastle.com
SIC: 3143 3144 3149 5632 Men's footwear, except athletic; women's footwear, except athletic; children's footwear, except athletic; handbags; apparel accessories

(G-7605)
STONE & TERRAZZO WORLD INC
5132 35th St (11101-3257)
PHONE.................................718 361-6899
Konstadinos Hagias, *President*
Mary Hagias, *Admin Sec*
EMP: 5
SQ FT: 3,500
SALES (est): 540.8K **Privately Held**
SIC: 3281 5032 Curbing, granite or stone; marble building stone

(G-7606)
STUART-DEAN CO INC
4350 10th St (11101-6910)
PHONE.................................718 472-1326
Kristen Rice, *Branch Mgr*
EMP: 13
SALES (corp-wide): 65.4MM **Privately Held**
SIC: 3479 1741 1752 Etching & engraving; stone masonry; wood floor installation & refinishing
PA: Stuart-Dean Co. Inc.
450 Fashion Ave Ste 3800
New York NY 10123
212 273-6900

(G-7607)
SUBSTRATE LLC
539 46th Ave (11101-5214)
PHONE.................................212 913-9600
James Wegner, *Partner*
EMP: 24 **EST:** 2016
SALES (est): 225.6K **Privately Held**
SIC: 3993 Displays & cutouts, window & lobby

(G-7608)
SUMMIT AEROSPACE INC
4301 21st St Ste 203 (11101-5039)
PHONE.................................718 433-1326
Moon K Lee, *President*
EMP: 7
SQ FT: 4,000
SALES: 1.2MM **Privately Held**
SIC: 3369 Aerospace castings, nonferrous: except aluminum

(G-7609)
SUPERIOR METALS & PROCESSING
Also Called: Super Stud Building Products
801 26th Ave (11102)
PHONE.................................718 545-7500
Raymond Frobosilo, *President*
John Conneely, *Info Tech Mgr*
▲ **EMP:** 6
SQ FT: 20,500
SALES (est): 340K **Privately Held**
SIC: 3479 Sherardizing of metals or metal products

(G-7610)
SUPREME POULTRY INC
3788 Review Ave (11101-2052)
PHONE.................................718 472-0300
Nasrullah Kamran, *President*
▲ **EMP:** 5 **EST:** 2015
SALES (est): 1.2MM **Privately Held**
SIC: 3089 Tableware, plastic

(G-7611)
SUSSMAN-AUTOMATIC CORPORATION (PA)
Also Called: Mr Steam
4320 34th St (11101-2321)
PHONE.................................347 609-7652
Jay Wilsker, *Ch of Bd*
Richard Sussman, *Ch of Bd*
Martha Orellana, *President*
Mike Pinkus, *President*
Dan Reinert, *President*
▲ **EMP:** 73 **EST:** 1944
SQ FT: 60,000
SALES: 30MM **Privately Held**
WEB: www.sussmanelectricboilers.com
SIC: 3569 Generators: steam, liquid oxygen or nitrogen

(G-7612)
TAYLOR COMMUNICATIONS INC
Also Called: Vectra Visual
3200 Skillman Ave Fl 3 (11101-2308)
PHONE.................................718 361-1000
EMP: 6
SALES (corp-wide): 3.5B **Privately Held**
SIC: 2752 Lithographic Commercial Printing
HQ: Taylor Communications, Inc.
4205 S 96th St
Omaha NE 68127
402 898-6422

(G-7613)
TEMPTU INC
522 46th Ave Ste B (11101-5204)
PHONE.................................718 937-9503
Steven Gary, *Manager*
EMP: 5
SALES (corp-wide): 5.6MM **Privately Held**
WEB: www.temptu.com
SIC: 2844 Cosmetic preparations
PA: Temptu Inc.
26 W 17th St Rm 302
New York NY 10011
212 675-4000

(G-7614)
THEODOSIOU INC
Also Called: G T Machine & Tool
3214 49th St (11103-1403)
PHONE.................................718 728-6800
Dean Theodos, *President*
Harry Theodos, *President*
Vj Sukhu, *Manager*
EMP: 8 **EST:** 1971
SQ FT: 7,500
SALES (est): 1.6MM **Privately Held**
WEB: www.gtmachine.com
SIC: 3599 Machine shop, jobbing & repair

(G-7615)
THOMAS C WILSON LLC
Also Called: Thomas C Wilson
2111 44th Ave (11101-5007)
PHONE.................................718 729-3360
Stephen Hanley, *Ch of Bd*
David Hanley, *Opers Mgr*
Moses Vidal, *Purchasing*
Tony Perez, *Engineer*
Sugelis Gonzalez, *Supervisor*
▼ **EMP:** 42 **EST:** 2009
SQ FT: 45,600
SALES (est): 12.6MM **Privately Held**
WEB: www.tcwilson.com
SIC: 3546 Power-driven handtools

(G-7616)
THOMSON PRESS (INDIA) LIMITED
Also Called: Living Media
4 Court Sq Fl 3rm2 (11101-4327)
PHONE.................................646 318-0369
Anup Uniyal, *Branch Mgr*
EMP: 5 **Privately Held**
SIC: 2759 Commercial printing
HQ: Thomson Press India Limited
18/35, Thomson Press Building,
Faridabad HR 12100
129 228-5524

(G-7617)
TOTAL SOLUTION GRAPHICS INC
2511 49th Ave (11101-4429)
PHONE.................................718 706-1540
Ricki Noto, *President*
EMP: 3
SALES: 3MM **Privately Held**
SIC: 2759 Commercial Printing

(G-7618)
TOWERIQ INC
Also Called: NAMSNET
37-18 Nthrn Blvd Ste 421 (11101)
PHONE.................................844 626-7638
Connor Crowley, *CEO*
Douglas Baena, *Vice Pres*
EMP: 18
SQ FT: 11,000
SALES: 1.5MM **Privately Held**
SIC: 3669 Fire alarm apparatus, electric

(G-7619)
TOWNE HOUSE RESTORATIONS INC
4309 Vernon Blvd (11101-6831)
PHONE.................................718 497-9200
Ivan Cerina, *Principal*
EMP: 5 **EST:** 2011
SALES (est): 681.9K **Privately Held**
SIC: 3272 Concrete products

(G-7620)
TRANE US INC
4518 Court Sq Ste 100 (11101-4341)
PHONE.................................718 721-8844

GEOGRAPHIC SECTION

Lowville - Lewis County (G-7649)

James Barrus, *General Mgr*
Jason Dively, *General Mgr*
Dave Palty, *Business Mgr*
Laura Rygielski, *Vice Pres*
Ronald Swanson, *Vice Pres*
EMP: 70 **Privately Held**
SIC: 3585 Refrigeration & heating equipment
HQ: Trane U.S. Inc.
3600 Pammel Creek Rd
La Crosse WI 54601
608 787-2000

(G-7621)
TRIBORO IRON WORKS INC
3830 31st St (11101-2719)
PHONE 718 361-9600
Salvatore Gulino, *President*
EMP: 9
SQ FT: 2,500
SALES (est): 1.7MM **Privately Held**
SIC: 3441 1799 1791 Fabricated structural metal; fire escape installation; iron work, structural

(G-7622)
UNIQUE MBL GRAN ORGNZTION CORP
3831 9th St (11101-6109)
PHONE 718 482-0440
John Manassakis, *President*
▲ **EMP:** 5
SALES (est): 436.5K **Privately Held**
SIC: 3281 Marble, building: cut & shaped; granite, cut & shaped

(G-7623)
UNITED PRINT GROUP INC
Also Called: United Business Forms
3636 33rd St Ste 303 (11106-2329)
P.O. Box 1430 (11101-0430)
PHONE 718 392-4242
Robert Sanchez, *Ch of Bd*
Henry Morales, *Vice Pres*
Norma Sanchez, *Treasurer*
EMP: 16
SQ FT: 6,200
SALES (est): 2.6MM **Privately Held**
WEB: www.unitedpg.com
SIC: 2759 3993 Business forms: printing; advertising artwork

(G-7624)
UNITED SHEET METAL CORP
4602 28th St (11101)
PHONE 718 482-1197
Joseph Grgas, *President*
Siraj Bora, *Vice Pres*
Bhadresh Shah, *Vice Pres*
Alex Fiks, *Project Mgr*
EMP: 50
SQ FT: 4,000
SALES (est): 4.7MM **Privately Held**
SIC: 3444 Ducts, sheet metal

(G-7625)
UNIVERSAL DESIGNS INC
3517 31st St (11106-2320)
PHONE 718 721-1111
Panos Adamopoulos, *President*
Silvia Adamopoulos, *Vice Pres*
EMP: 6
SQ FT: 8,000
SALES: 700K **Privately Held**
SIC: 2511 2521 2541 5712 Wood household furniture; wood office furniture; wood partitions & fixtures; unfinished furniture

(G-7626)
USA HALAL FOODS INC
4700 Northern Blvd (11101-1013)
PHONE 718 291-9111
Kashif Saeed, *President*
EMP: 7
SALES (est): 724.7K **Privately Held**
SIC: 2011 Meat by-products from meat slaughtered on site

(G-7627)
VANDAM INC
1111 44th Rd Fl 403 (11101-5115)
PHONE 212 929-0416
Stephan Muth Vandam, *President*
Jacob Benjamin, *Editor*
Jessy Cerda, *Opers Staff*
Bob Troast, *VP Sales*

Gail Grant, *Corp Comm Staff*
▲ **EMP:** 12
SQ FT: 2,500
SALES: 2MM **Privately Held**
SIC: 2741 2731 6794 Maps: publishing only, not printed on site; books: publishing only; patent buying, licensing, leasing

(G-7628)
VANILLA SKY LLC
3318 Broadway (11106-1806)
PHONE 347 738-4195
EMP: 5
SALES (est): 276.8K **Privately Held**
SIC: 2024 Ice cream & ice milk

(G-7629)
VENUE GRAPHICS SUPPLY INC
1120 46th Rd (11101-5322)
PHONE 718 361-1690
EMP: 13
SQ FT: 10,000
SALES: 1.2MM **Privately Held**
SIC: 2899 Mfr Industrial Chemical Solutions

(G-7630)
VERNON WINE & LIQUOR INC
5006 Vernon Blvd (11101-5702)
PHONE 718 784-5096
Adrian Bettencourt, *Manager*
EMP: 5
SALES (est): 275.4K **Privately Held**
SIC: 2082 Malt liquors

(G-7631)
VERSAILLES DRAPERY UPHOLSTERY
4709 30th St Ste 200 (11101-3400)
PHONE 212 533-2059
Jorge Loayza, *President*
Ricardo Loayza, *Treasurer*
EMP: 11
SQ FT: 20,000
SALES: 1MM **Privately Held**
SIC: 2512 5714 2211 Upholstered household furniture; draperies; draperies & drapery fabrics, cotton

(G-7632)
VITOBOB FURNITURE INC
3879 13th St (11101-6119)
PHONE 516 676-1696
Robert Longo, *President*
Michele Longo, *Admin Sec*
EMP: 5
SQ FT: 5,000
SALES (est): 490K **Privately Held**
SIC: 2426 Frames for upholstered furniture, wood

(G-7633)
WALNUT PRINTING INC
2812 41st Ave (11101-3706)
PHONE 718 707-0100
Gerald Paul Pont, *President*
EMP: 5
SQ FT: 3,500
SALES (est): 637.6K **Privately Held**
WEB: www.walnutprinting.com
SIC: 2752 Commercial printing, offset

(G-7634)
WARREN PRINTING INC
3718 Northern Blvd # 418 (11101-1636)
PHONE 212 627-5000
Warren Pugach, *President*
Priscilla Pugach, *Corp Secy*
Seymour Pugach, *Vice Pres*
John Rubbinaccio, *Opers Staff*
EMP: 10
SQ FT: 7,500
SALES (est): 1.8MM **Privately Held**
SIC: 2752 Commercial printing, offset

(G-7635)
WATCHCRAFT INC
2214 40th Ave Ste 4 (11101-4830)
PHONE 347 531-0382
Eduardo Milieris, *President*
▲ **EMP:** 5
SALES (est): 742.5K **Privately Held**
SIC: 3873 5094 Watches, clocks, watchcases & parts; clocks, watches & parts

(G-7636)
WESTMORE LITHO CORP
Also Called: Westmore Litho Printing Co
4017 22nd St (11101-4834)
PHONE 718 361-9403
Spike Kalashian, *President*
EMP: 8
SQ FT: 10,000
SALES (est): 901.9K **Privately Held**
SIC: 2752 Commercial Printing Lithographic

(G-7637)
WILLIAM E WILLIAM VALVE CORP
3852 Review Ave (11101-2019)
PHONE 718 392-1660
Sherman Richard, *Owner*
EMP: 22
SALES (est): 4.1MM **Privately Held**
SIC: 3494 Valves & pipe fittings

(G-7638)
WILLIAM E WILLIAMS VALVE CORP
3850 Review Ave (11101-2019)
P.O. Box 1190 (11101-0190)
PHONE 718 392-1660
Richard Sherman, *President*
◆ **EMP:** 23
SQ FT: 60,000
SALES (est): 6.1MM **Privately Held**
SIC: 3494 3491 Valves & pipe fittings; industrial valves

(G-7639)
WILLIAM H JACKSON COMPANY
3629 23rd St (11106-4405)
PHONE 718 784-4482
Eric Nelson, *Manager*
EMP: 7
SQ FT: 4,800
SALES (corp-wide): 1.5MM **Privately Held**
WEB: www.bumrails.com
SIC: 3429 Fireplace equipment, hardware: andirons, grates, screens
PA: William H Jackson Company
18 E 17th St Frnt 1
New York NY 10003
212 753-9400

(G-7640)
WINNER PRESS INC
4331 33rd St 1 (11101-2316)
PHONE 718 937-7715
Hermi Fu, *President*
Ya Tang Fu, *Principal*
Marissa Santiago, *Admin Sec*
EMP: 25
SQ FT: 20,000
SALES (est): 3.2MM **Privately Held**
WEB: www.winnerpress.com
SIC: 2752 Commercial printing, offset

(G-7641)
WINSON SURNAMER INC
4402 11th St Ste 601 (11101-5149)
PHONE 718 729-8787
Gary Levinson, *President*
Lawrence Levinson, *Treasurer*
Robert Levinson, *Admin Sec*
EMP: 5
SQ FT: 40,000
SALES (est): 702.1K **Privately Held**
SIC: 2752 Commercial printing, offset

(G-7642)
WONTON FOOD INC
5210 37th St (11101-2001)
PHONE 718 784-8178
Norman Wong, *Vice Chairman*
Foo Kam Wong, *Manager*
EMP: 20
SQ FT: 5,320
SALES (corp-wide): 76.5MM **Privately Held**
WEB: www.wontonfood.com
SIC: 2099 2052 Noodles, fried (Chinese); cracker meal & crumbs
PA: Wonton Food Inc.
220 Moore St 222
Brooklyn NY 11206
718 628-6868

(G-7643)
X BRAND EDITIONS
4020 22nd St Ste 1 (11101-4814)
PHONE 718 482-7646
Robert Blanton, *President*
EMP: 8 **EST:** 2010
SALES (est): 1.1MM **Privately Held**
SIC: 3577 Printers & plotters

(G-7644)
XANIA LABS INC
3202 Queens Blvd Fl 6 (11101-2332)
PHONE 718 361-2550
Nikos Mouyiaris, *President*
Brenda Gallagher, *Sales Dir*
EMP: 5
SALES (est): 411.1K
SALES (corp-wide): 284.9MM **Privately Held**
SIC: 2844 5122 Cosmetic preparations; cosmetics
PA: Mana Products, Inc.
3202 Queens Blvd Fl 6
Long Island City NY 11101
718 361-2550

(G-7645)
YORK INTERNATIONAL CORPORATION
1130 45th Rd (11101-5832)
PHONE 718 389-4152
Ben Cohen, *Branch Mgr*
EMP: 94 **Privately Held**
SIC: 3585 Refrigeration & heating equipment
HQ: York International Corporation
631 S Richland Ave
York PA 17403
717 771-7890

(G-7646)
YORK LADDER INC
3720 12th St (11101-6098)
PHONE 718 784-6666
Kenneth J Buettner, *President*
Daniel Buettner, *General Mgr*
John Ottulich, *Sales Staff*
David Caro, *Manager*
Tammy Wood, *Admin Asst*
▲ **EMP:** 10
SALES (est): 891K **Privately Held**
SIC: 2499 Ladders & stepladders, wood

(G-7647)
ZELMAN & FRIEDMAN JWLY MFG CO
4722 37th St (11101-1804)
P.O. Box 547, Woodbury (11797-0547)
PHONE 718 349-3400
Irwin Friedman, *President*
Morris Zelman, *Treasurer*
Gary Zelman, *Asst Treas*
Alan Zelman, *Shareholder*
EMP: 25 **EST:** 1951
SQ FT: 5,000
SALES (est): 2.3MM **Privately Held**
SIC: 3911 Jewelry, precious metal

(G-7648)
ZENITH COLOR COMM GROUP INC (PA)
4710 33rd St (11101-2408)
PHONE 212 989-4400
Peter D Savitt, *President*
EMP: 20
SALES (est): 4MM **Privately Held**
SIC: 2711 Commercial printing & newspaper publishing combined

Lowville
Lewis County

(G-7649)
CLIMAX PACKAGING INC
7840 State Route 26 (13367-2926)
PHONE 315 376-8000
Patrick Purdy, *President*
Mary Wuest, *CFO*
EMP: 105
SQ FT: 110,000

Lowville - Lewis County (G-7650)

SALES (est): 14.1MM **Privately Held**
WEB: www.stjpkg.com
SIC: **3993** 2657 Signs & advertising specialties; folding paperboard boxes

(G-7650)
FARNEY LUMBER CORPORATION
7194 Brewery Rd (13367-2524)
PHONE.................315 346-6013
Duane Farney, *President*
Terry Farney, *Vice Pres*
Todd Farney, *Vice Pres*
Karen Farney, *Admin Sec*
EMP: 17
SQ FT: 20,000
SALES: 2MM **Privately Held**
SIC: **2421** Sawmills & planing mills, general

(G-7651)
KRAFT HEINZ FOODS COMPANY
7388 Utica Blvd (13367-9503)
PHONE.................315 376-6575
Gary Schantz, *Production*
Tim Regan, *Branch Mgr*
EMP: 335
SQ FT: 460
SALES (corp-wide): 26.2B **Publicly Held**
WEB: www.kraftfoods.com
SIC: **2022** Cheese, natural & processed
HQ: Kraft Heinz Foods Company
1 Ppg Pl Ste 3200
Pittsburgh PA 15222
412 456-5700

(G-7652)
LOWVILLE FARMERS COOP INC
5500 Shady Ave (13367-1698)
PHONE.................315 376-6587
John Williams, *President*
Mark Karelus, *Vice Pres*
Tim Smithling, *CFO*
Stanley Szalch, *Treasurer*
Glen Beller, *Admin Sec*
EMP: 37
SQ FT: 20,000
SALES: 10MM **Privately Held**
SIC: **2048** 5999 5251 5211 Prepared feeds; feed & farm supply; hardware; lumber products

(G-7653)
LOWVILLE NEWSPAPER CORPORATION
Also Called: Journal and Republican
7567 S State St (13367-1512)
PHONE.................315 376-3525
Cindy Aucter, *Business Mgr*
Jeremiah Papineau, *Manager*
Adam Atkinson, *Manager*
EMP: 7
SQ FT: 2,000
SALES (est): 442.3K
SALES (corp-wide): 32MM **Privately Held**
WEB: www.ogd.com
SIC: **2711** Commercial printing & newspaper publishing combined; newspapers, publishing & printing
PA: Johnson Newspaper Corporation
260 Washington St
Watertown NY
315 782-1000

(G-7654)
NEENAH NORTHEAST LLC
5492 Bostwick St (13367)
PHONE.................315 376-3571
Brandon Stinebrickner, *Engineer*
Larry Kieffer, *Branch Mgr*
EMP: 179
SALES (corp-wide): 979.9MM **Publicly Held**
WEB: www.fibermark.com
SIC: **2672** Coated & laminated paper
HQ: Neenah Northeast, Llc
70 Front St
West Springfield MA 01089
413 533-0699

(G-7655)
QUBICAAMF WORLDWIDE LLC
Also Called: Pins and Lanes
7412 Utica Blvd (13367-9572)
PHONE.................315 376-6541
Wayne White, *General Mgr*
EMP: 150
SALES (corp-wide): 22.7MM **Privately Held**
SIC: **3949** Bowling pins
HQ: Qubicaamf Worldwide, Llc
8100 Amf Dr
Mechanicsville VA 23111
804 569-1000

(G-7656)
ROYAL CUSTOM CABINETS
6149 Patty St (13367-4206)
PHONE.................315 376-6042
David Lapp, *Owner*
EMP: 8
SALES (est): 760K **Privately Held**
SIC: **2434** Wood kitchen cabinets

(G-7657)
TUG HILL VINEYARDS
4051 Yancey Rd (13367-4710)
PHONE.................315 376-4336
Susan Maring, *Owner*
Michael Maring, *Co-Owner*
EMP: 5 **EST**: 1981
SQ FT: 3,500
SALES (est): 350.5K **Privately Held**
SIC: **2084** Wines

Lynbrook
Nassau County

(G-7658)
ADVANCE BIOFACTORES CORP
35 Wilbur St (11563-2358)
PHONE.................516 593-7000
Edwin Wegman, *President*
Thomas Wegman, *Senior VP*
Larry Dobross, *Admin Sec*
EMP: 20 **EST**: 1957
SQ FT: 15,000
SALES (est): 1.4MM
SALES (corp-wide): 27.4MM **Publicly Held**
WEB: www.biospecifics.com
SIC: **2836** 8731 Biological products, except diagnostic; biological research
PA: Biospecifics Technologies Corp.
35 Wilbur St
Lynbrook NY 11563
516 593-7000

(G-7659)
ALL METRO EMRGNCY RESPONSE SYS
50 Broadway (11563-2519)
PHONE.................516 750-9100
Irving Edwards, *President*
EMP: 6
SALES (est): 460K **Privately Held**
WEB: www.amerslifeline.com
SIC: **3669** Emergency alarms

(G-7660)
ALLOY MACHINE & TOOL CO INC
169 Vincent Ave (11563-2607)
P.O. Box 708 (11563-0708)
PHONE.................516 593-3445
Paul R Will, *President*
Gary Will, *Vice Pres*
EMP: 8 **EST**: 1967
SQ FT: 8,000
SALES: 900K **Privately Held**
SIC: **3679** Electronic circuits

(G-7661)
BIMBO BAKERIES USA INC
669 Sunrise Hwy Spc 4 (11563-3246)
PHONE.................516 887-1024
George Weston, *Branch Mgr*
EMP: 18 **Privately Held**
SIC: **2051** Bakery: wholesale or wholesale/retail combined
HQ: Bimbo Bakeries Usa, Inc
255 Business Center Dr # 200
Horsham PA 19044
215 347-5500

(G-7662)
BIOSPECIFICS TECHNOLOGIES CORP (PA)
35 Wilbur St (11563-2358)
PHONE.................516 593-7000
Thomas L Wegman, *President*
Ron Law, *Senior VP*
James Goris, *Controller*
Helen Piazza, *Human Res Dir*
Bo Yu, *Director*
▲ EMP: 5
SALES: 27.4MM **Publicly Held**
WEB: www.biospecifics.com
SIC: **2834** Pharmaceutical preparations

(G-7663)
CASCADE TECHNICAL SERVICES LLC (DH)
30 N Prospect Ave (11563-1313)
PHONE.................516 596-6300
Tim Smith, *CEO*
Gary Crueger, *Vice Pres*
Tyler Kopet, *CFO*
EMP: 17
SQ FT: 6,400
SALES: 5.3MM
SALES (corp-wide): 874.5MM **Privately Held**
SIC: **3822** Auto controls regulating residntl & coml environmt & applncs

(G-7664)
DOAR INC
170 Earle Ave (11563-2642)
PHONE.................516 872-8140
Paul Neale, *Manager*
EMP: 8
SALES (corp-wide): 19.8MM **Privately Held**
WEB: www.doar.com
SIC: **3571** 3575 7371 5045 Electronic computers; computer terminals; custom computer programming services; computer peripheral equipment; computer software; motion picture equipment; business consulting
PA: Doar, Inc.
1370 Broadway Fl 15l
New York NY 10018
212 235-2700

(G-7665)
ISH PRECISION MACHINE CORP (PA)
190 Earle Ave (11563-2627)
PHONE.................718 436-8858
Issac Sheran, *President*
EMP: 10
SALES: 1.5MM **Privately Held**
SIC: **3599** Machine shop, jobbing & repair

(G-7666)
JANEL CORPORATION (PA)
303 Merrick Rd Ste 400 (11563-2521)
PHONE.................516 256-8143
David Gardner, *Opers Mgr*
EMP: 2
SQ FT: 6,800
SALES: 77.7MM **Publicly Held**
WEB: www.janelgroup.net
SIC: **3556** 4731 Cutting, chopping, grinding, mixing & similar machinery; freight forwarding

(G-7667)
LABGRAFIX PRINTING INC
43 Rocklyn Ave Unit B (11563-2752)
PHONE.................516 280-8300
Lev Galkin, *President*
EMP: 6 **EST**: 2010
SALES: 1MM **Privately Held**
SIC: **3861** 7384 Photographic equipment & supplies; photographic services

(G-7668)
MASTER CRAFT JEWELRY CO INC
Also Called: L'Etoile Jewelers
150 Vincent Ave (11563-2608)
PHONE.................516 599-1012
Robert Sharaby, *President*
EMP: 55 **EST**: 1945
SQ FT: 10,000
SALES (est): 5.1MM **Privately Held**
WEB: www.mastercraftjewelry.net
SIC: **3911** Bracelets, precious metal

(G-7669)
ND LABS INC
Also Called: Nutritional Designs
202 Merrick Rd (11563-2622)
PHONE.................516 612-4900
Beth Beller, *Ch of Bd*
Diane Altos, *President*
Elisa Gross, *Office Mgr*
EMP: 10
SQ FT: 10,000
SALES (est): 1.7MM **Privately Held**
WEB: www.ndlabs.com
SIC: **2834** Vitamin, nutrient & hematinic preparations for human use

(G-7670)
PRO PRINTING
Also Called: PIP Printing
359 Merrick Rd (11563-2517)
PHONE.................516 561-9700
Raymond Kenney Sr, *Partner*
Raymond Kenney Jr, *Partner*
EMP: 5
SQ FT: 1,000
SALES (est): 370K **Privately Held**
SIC: **2752** 2791 2789 Commercial printing, offset; typesetting; bookbinding & related work

(G-7671)
RAYDON PRECISION BEARING CO
75 Merrick Rd (11563-2713)
P.O. Box 679 (11563-0679)
PHONE.................516 887-2582
Dominick Pinto, *President*
Barbara Pinto, *Treasurer*
EMP: 6 **EST**: 1965
SQ FT: 1,000
SALES (est): 972.4K **Privately Held**
SIC: **3562** 5085 Ball & roller bearings; bearings

(G-7672)
REGENCE PICTURE FRAMES INC
12 Cherry Ln (11563-4120)
PHONE.................718 779-0888
Cecilia Litzak, *President*
EMP: 25
SQ FT: 7,500
SALES: 1MM **Privately Held**
WEB: www.regencepictureframes.com
SIC: **2499** Picture & mirror frames, wood

(G-7673)
RUSSELL INDUSTRIES INC
Also Called: Conco Division
40 Horton Ave (11563-2333)
P.O. Box 807 (11563-0807)
PHONE.................516 536-5000
Adam Russell, *President*
▲ EMP: 7 **EST**: 1965
SQ FT: 20,000
SALES (est): 1.4MM **Privately Held**
SIC: **3679** 3675 Antennas, receiving; electronic capacitors

(G-7674)
SIGNS OF SUCCESS LTD
247 Merrick Rd Ste 101 (11563-2641)
PHONE.................516 295-6000
Steven Cohen, *President*
EMP: 17
SQ FT: 4,500
SALES: 700K **Privately Held**
WEB: www.signs-of-success.com
SIC: **3993** Signs, not made in custom sign painting shops

(G-7675)
SWIFT FULFILLMENT SERVICES
290 Broadway (11563-3293)
PHONE.................516 593-1198
Barbara Fiegas, *President*
Preston D Theiber, *Vice Pres*
EMP: 7
SQ FT: 5,000
SALES: 999K **Privately Held**
SIC: **2721** 5192 Periodicals: publishing only; books

GEOGRAPHIC SECTION

Macedon - Wayne County (G-7701)

(G-7676)
TOP FORTUNE USA LTD
100 Atlantic Ave Ste 2 (11563-3471)
PHONE..................516 608-2694
Elan Oved, *CEO*
▲ EMP: 6
SALES: 1,000K **Privately Held**
SIC: 2385 Waterproof outerwear

(G-7677)
VALLEY STREAM SPORTING GDS INC
Also Called: Arrowear Athletic Apparel
325 Hendrickson Ave (11563-1055)
PHONE..................516 593-7800
Robert J Heller, *Ch of Bd*
EMP: 25
SQ FT: 16,000
SALES (est): 3.3MM **Privately Held**
WEB: www.arrowear.com
SIC: 2329 2262 Mfg Men's/Boy's Clothing Manmade Fiber & Silk Finishing Plant

(G-7678)
ZEBRA ENVIRONMENTAL CORP (PA)
30 N Prospect Ave (11563-1398)
PHONE..................516 596-6300
Fax: 516 596-4422
EMP: 17
SQ FT: 6,400
SALES (est): 5.2MM **Privately Held**
SIC: 3822 Mfg Environmental Controls

Lyndonville
Orleans County

(G-7679)
ANDROS BOWMAN PRODUCTS LLC
151 West Ave (14098-9744)
PHONE..................540 217-4100
Jon Corscer, *Branch Mgr*
EMP: 5 **Privately Held**
SIC: 2033 2099 Fruits: packaged in cans, jars, etc.; food preparations
HQ: Bowman Andros Products, Llc
10119 Old Valley Pike
Mount Jackson VA 22842
540 217-4100

(G-7680)
MIZKAN AMERICA INC
Also Called: Nakano Foods
247 West Ave (14098-9744)
PHONE..................585 765-9171
Steven Gardepe, *Principal*
Steve Gardepe, *Plant Mgr*
Dave Carpenter, *Safety Mgr*
EMP: 70
SQ FT: 82,000 **Privately Held**
SIC: 2033 2099 2035 Fruit juices: packaged in cans, jars, etc.; food preparations; pickles, sauces & salad dressings
HQ: Mizkan America, Inc.
1661 Feehanville Dr # 200
Mount Prospect IL 60056
847 590-0059

(G-7681)
SHORELINE FRUIT LLC
Also Called: Atwater Foods
10190 Route 18 (14098-9785)
PHONE..................585 765-2639
Fax: 585 765-9443
EMP: 70
SALES (corp-wide): 43.3MM **Privately Held**
SIC: 2034 Processor Of Fruit Products
PA: Shoreline Fruit, Llc
10850 E Traverse Hwy # 4001
Traverse City MI 49684
231 941-4336

Lyons
Wayne County

(G-7682)
CASWELL INC
7696 State Route 31 (14489-9116)
PHONE..................315 946-1213
Lance Caswell, *President*
Carol Caswell, *Vice Pres*
Mike Caswell, *Shareholder*
◆ EMP: 10
SQ FT: 8,000
SALES (est): 2MM **Privately Held**
WEB: www.caswellplating.net
SIC: 3559 5169 Electroplating machinery & equipment; chemicals & allied products

(G-7683)
CONNEX GRINDING & MACHINING
65 Clyde Rd (14489-9364)
PHONE..................315 946-4340
Carlton J Collins Jr, *President*
Barbara A Collins, *Treasurer*
EMP: 5 EST: 1979
SQ FT: 2,400
SALES (est): 503.8K **Privately Held**
SIC: 3541 Grinding machines, metalworking

(G-7684)
DELOKA LLC
150 Dunn Rd (14489-9772)
PHONE..................315 946-6910
Scott Lord,
Dercy Gordner, *Admin Asst*
Mike Kunes,
Roger Westerman,
EMP: 5
SQ FT: 21,000
SALES (est): 730.3K **Privately Held**
WEB: www.deloka.com
SIC: 3479 Coating of metals & formed products

(G-7685)
LAGASSE WORKS INC
5 Old State Route 31 (14489-9214)
PHONE..................315 946-9202
Daniel Lagasse, *President*
Dan Lagasse, *Manager*
▲ EMP: 6
SQ FT: 10,000
SALES (est): 1.4MM **Privately Held**
WEB: www.lagasseworks.com
SIC: 7692 3599 Welding repair; machine shop, jobbing & repair

(G-7686)
PENN CAN EQUIPMENT CORPORATION
Also Called: Penn Can Asphalt Materials
300 Cole Rd (14489-9602)
PHONE..................315 378-0337
EMP: 7
SALES (corp-wide): 1.1MM **Privately Held**
SIC: 3531 Mfg Construction Machinery
PA: Penn Can Equipment Corporation
555 State Fair Blvd
Syracuse NY
315 637-3168

(G-7687)
SILGAN CONTAINERS MFG CORP
8673 Lyons Marengo Rd (14489-9726)
PHONE..................315 946-4826
Tom Kaczynski, *Manager*
EMP: 150
SALES (corp-wide): 4B **Publicly Held**
WEB: www.silgancontainers.com
SIC: 3411 Food containers, metal
HQ: Silgan Containers Manufacturing Corporation
21600 Oxnard St Ste 1600
Woodland Hills CA 91367

(G-7688)
TIM CRETIN LOGGING & SAWMILL
3607 Wayne Center Rd (14489-9321)
PHONE..................315 946-4476
Tim Cretin, *President*
EMP: 11
SQ FT: 1,961
SALES: 2MM **Privately Held**
SIC: 2411 Logging

Lyons Falls
Lewis County

(G-7689)
OTIS PRODUCTS INC (PA)
Also Called: Otis Technology
6987 Laura St (13368-1802)
P.O. Box 582 (13368-0582)
PHONE..................315 348-4300
Doreen Garrett, *CEO*
Larry Williams, *VP Mfg*
Mike Tuttle, *Opers Mgr*
Harold Philbrick, *Opers Staff*
Patricia Wright, *Purch Mgr*
▲ EMP: 122
SQ FT: 12,000
SALES (est): 20.7MM **Privately Held**
WEB: www.otisgun.com
SIC: 3949 Shooting equipment & supplies, general

(G-7690)
TWIN RIVERS PAPER COMPANY LLC
Lyonsdale Rd (13368)
PHONE..................315 348-8491
Dennis Gigliotti, *Branch Mgr*
EMP: 37
SQ FT: 67,484 **Privately Held**
WEB: www.burrowspaper.com
SIC: 2621 Tissue paper
PA: Twin Rivers Paper Company Llc
82 Bridge Ave
Madawaska ME 04756

Macedon
Wayne County

(G-7691)
A&M MODEL MAKERS LLC
1675 Wayneport Rd Ste 1 (14502-8770)
PHONE..................626 813-9661
Derek Backus,
EMP: 6
SALES: 350K **Privately Held**
SIC: 3999 Manufacturing industries

(G-7692)
ANKOM DEVELOPMENT LLC
2052 Oneil Rd (14502-8953)
PHONE..................315 986-1937
Andrew Komarek,
EMP: 5 EST: 2006
SALES (est): 625.9K **Privately Held**
SIC: 3534 Elevators & moving stairways

(G-7693)
ANKOM TECHNOLOGY CORP
2052 Oneil Rd (14502-8953)
PHONE..................315 986-8090
Andrew Komarek, *President*
Christopher Kelley, *Vice Pres*
Ron Komarek, *Vice Pres*
Ronald Komarek, *Vice Pres*
Shawn Ritchie, *Vice Pres*
EMP: 30
SQ FT: 50,000
SALES (est): 6.7MM **Privately Held**
WEB: www.ankom.com
SIC: 3821 5049 Laboratory equipment: fume hoods, distillation racks, etc.; laboratory equipment, except medical or dental

(G-7694)
AUBURN BEARING & MFG INC
4 State Route 350 (14502-9177)
PHONE..................315 986-7600
Peter Schroth, *CEO*

EMP: 8
SQ FT: 1,280
SALES (est): 888.5K **Privately Held**
SIC: 3714 3599 Motor vehicle transmissions, drive assemblies & parts; custom machinery

(G-7695)
BALDWIN RICHARDSON FOODS CO
3268 Blue Heron Dr (14502-9337)
PHONE..................315 986-2727
Matt Igler, *Production*
Jake Neis, *Buyer*
Nick Severino, *Info Tech Dir*
Mike Davis, *Director*
EMP: 142
SALES (est): 55.4MM **Privately Held**
SIC: 2035 2099 2087 Pickles, sauces & salad dressings; mustard, prepared (wet); food preparations; extracts, flavoring
PA: Baldwin Richardson Foods Company
1 Tower Ln
Oakbrook Terrace IL 60181

(G-7696)
BERRY GLOBAL INC
112 Main St (14502-8996)
PHONE..................315 986-2161
Richard Leone, *Branch Mgr*
EMP: 200 **Publicly Held**
WEB: www.6sens.com
SIC: 3089 3081 2673 Bottle caps, molded plastic; unsupported plastics film & sheet; bags: plastic, laminated & coated
HQ: Berry Global, Inc.
101 Oakley St
Evansville IN 47710
812 424-2904

(G-7697)
BERRY PLASTICS CORPORATION
200 Main St (14502-8977)
PHONE..................315 986-6270
EMP: 400
SALES (corp-wide): 4.8B **Publicly Held**
SIC: 3081 3086 2671 Mfg Unsupported Plastic Film/Sheet Mfg Plastic Foam Products Mfg Packaging Paper/Film
HQ: Berry Plastics Corporation
101 Oakley St
Evansville IN 47710
812 424-2904

(G-7698)
CLAD INDUSTRIES LLC
1704 Wayneport Rd Ste 1 (14502-9181)
PHONE..................585 413-4359
Alan Brown,
EMP: 7
SQ FT: 1,200
SALES (est): 1.5MM **Privately Held**
SIC: 3499 Fire- or burglary-resistive products

(G-7699)
FB SALE LLC
1688 Wayneport Rd (14502-8765)
PHONE..................315 986-9999
Marc Fleischer,
EMP: 8 EST: 1974
SQ FT: 42,000
SALES (est): 1MM **Privately Held**
WEB: www.fleischersbagels.com
SIC: 2051 Bagels, fresh or frozen

(G-7700)
KTK THERMAL TECHNOLOGIES INC
1657 E Park Dr (14502-8892)
PHONE..................585 678-9025
Kevin Kreger, *President*
Gary Turkovich, *Controller*
Michael Kulzer, *VP Sales*
◆ EMP: 45
SQ FT: 35,000
SALES: 6.5MM **Privately Held**
SIC: 3823 Thermal conductivity instruments, industrial process type

(G-7701)
LAWSON M WHITING INC
15 State Route 350 (14502-9177)
PHONE..................315 986-3064

Macedon - Wayne County (G-7702)

Jay D Whiting, *President*
Lawson M Whiting, *Shareholder*
EMP: 8 **EST:** 1973
SQ FT: 14,000
SALES (est): 1.4MM **Privately Held**
WEB: www.rockcrusher.com
SIC: 3532 Crushing, pulverizing & screening equipment

(G-7702)
PENTA-TECH COATED PRODUCTS LLC
1610 Commons Pkwy (14502-9190)
PHONE..............................315 986-4098
Robert Debruin, *Branch Mgr*
EMP: 12
SALES (est): 2.5MM
SALES (corp-wide): 6.6MM **Privately Held**
WEB: www.ptcp.net
SIC: 2671 Packaging paper & plastics film, coated & laminated
PA: Penta-Tech Coated Products Llc
58 Main Rd N
Hampden ME 04444
207 862-3105

(G-7703)
PLIANT LLC
200 Main St (14502-8977)
PHONE..............................315 986-6286
Kim Kirby, *Manager*
EMP: 400
SALES (est): 48.5MM **Publicly Held**
SIC: 3081 3086 2671 Unsupported plastics film & sheet; plastics foam products; packaging paper & plastics film, coated & laminated
HQ: Berry Global, Inc.
101 Oakley St
Evansville IN 47710
812 424-2904

(G-7704)
SHORT JJ ASSOCIATES INC (PA)
1645 Wayneport Rd (14502-9110)
P.O. Box 183, Fairport (14450-0183)
PHONE..............................315 986-3511
John Short Jr, *President*
John J Short Jr, *President*
Peter J Short, *CFO*
EMP: 11
SQ FT: 12,500
SALES: 750K **Privately Held**
WEB: www.jjshort.com
SIC: 3069 Molded rubber products

(G-7705)
WATER TECHNOLOGIES INC (PA)
Also Called: Columbia
1635 Commons Pkwy (14502-9191)
PHONE..............................315 986-0000
Joe Cupido, *President*
Bruce Dan, *Vice Pres*
▲ **EMP:** 5
SALES (est): 6.1MM **Privately Held**
SIC: 3589 Water filters & softeners, household type

Machias
Cattaraugus County

(G-7706)
MACHIAS FURNITURE FACTORY INC (PA)
3638 Route 242 (14101-9727)
PHONE..............................716 353-8687
Charles I Horning, *President*
Cindy Horning, *Vice Pres*
EMP: 9
SQ FT: 25,000
SALES (est): 473.1K **Privately Held**
SIC: 2511 Wood desks, bookcases & magazine racks

Mahopac
Putnam County

(G-7707)
ADVANCED TCHNCAL SOLUTIONS INC
Also Called: Ats
8 Lupi Plz (10541-3766)
P.O. Box 28, Yorktown Heights (10598-0028)
PHONE..............................914 214-8230
Joe Yaniv, *President*
David Wright, *VP Opers*
▲ **EMP:** 10
SQ FT: 2,000
SALES (est): 5MM **Privately Held**
SIC: 3569 5049 Lubrication equipment, industrial; engineers' equipment & supplies

(G-7708)
MICHAEL BENALT INC
100 Buckshollow Rd (10541-3756)
PHONE..............................845 628-1008
Michael Benalt, *President*
Kevin Grieger, *Sales Executive*
Gary Lewis, *Office Mgr*
EMP: 25 **EST:** 1975
SQ FT: 37,000
SALES (est): 665.5K **Privately Held**
WEB: www.michaelbenaltinc.com
SIC: 3559 Pharmaceutical machinery

(G-7709)
MORTECH INDUSTRIES INC
961 Route 6 (10541-1796)
P.O. Box 962 (10541-0962)
PHONE..............................845 628-6138
Anthony Morando, *President*
EMP: 8 **EST:** 1945
SQ FT: 12,000
SALES: 1.5MM **Privately Held**
SIC: 3541 5999 Grinding, polishing, buffing, lapping & honing machines; buffing & polishing machines; cleaning equipment & supplies

(G-7710)
NORTHEAST DOULAS
23 Hilltop Dr (10541-2815)
PHONE..............................845 621-0654
Debbie Aglietti, *Principal*
EMP: 5
SALES (est): 667K **Privately Held**
SIC: 2835 Pregnancy test kits

(G-7711)
RICHS STTCHES EMB SCREENPRINT
407 Route 6 (10541-3783)
PHONE..............................845 621-2175
Rich Schnetzinger, *Owner*
EMP: 5
SALES: 210K **Privately Held**
SIC: 2759 Screen printing

(G-7712)
RMD HOLDING INC
Also Called: X-Press Printing & Office Sup
593 Route 6 (10541-1682)
PHONE..............................845 628-0030
Richard De Cola, *President*
Marie De Cola, *Vice Pres*
EMP: 8
SQ FT: 2,500
SALES (est): 1.1MM **Privately Held**
SIC: 2752 5943 2791 2789 Commercial printing, offset; office forms & supplies; typesetting; bookbinding & related work

(G-7713)
STEERING COLUMNS GALORE INC
8 Vine Rd (10541-5429)
PHONE..............................845 278-5762
William Lanza, *President*
Rick Lanza, *Vice Pres*
EMP: 5
SALES: 414K **Privately Held**
WEB: www.columnsgalore.com
SIC: 3714 Steering mechanisms, motor vehicle

(G-7714)
T JN ELECTRIC
116 Cortlandt Rd (10541-3620)
PHONE..............................917 560-0981
Tina Giustino, *Owner*
EMP: 12
SALES (est): 1.5MM **Privately Held**
SIC: 3699 Electrical equipment & supplies

(G-7715)
T JN ELECTRIC INC
901 Route 6 (10541-1717)
PHONE..............................845 628-6970
Tina Giustino, *President*
EMP: 5
SALES (est): 398.7K **Privately Held**
SIC: 3699 Electrical equipment & supplies

(G-7716)
WALSH & SONS MACHINE INC
15 Secor Rd Ste 5 (10541-2078)
PHONE..............................845 526-0301
Frank Walsh, *President*
EMP: 6 **EST:** 1997
SALES (est): 652.7K **Privately Held**
SIC: 3599 Machine shop, jobbing & repair

Malone
Franklin County

(G-7717)
ADIRONDACK ICE & AIR INC
Also Called: Adirondex
26 Railroad St (12953-1014)
PHONE..............................518 483-4340
James McKee, *Ch of Bd*
Tim Boyea, *Vice Pres*
Molly Mc Kee, *Admin Sec*
EMP: 14 **EST:** 1968
SQ FT: 4,800
SALES (est): 1.6MM **Privately Held**
SIC: 2097 4222 5499 7389 Manufactured ice; storage, frozen or refrigerated goods; water: distilled mineral or spring; coffee service

(G-7718)
ADIRONDACK POWER SPORTS
5378 State Route 37 (12953-4114)
P.O. Box 390 (12953-0390)
PHONE..............................518 481-6269
John Waters, *General Mgr*
EMP: 8 **EST:** 2013
SQ FT: 5,000
SALES (est): 905.7K **Privately Held**
SIC: 3799 5012 Recreational vehicles; recreation vehicles, all-terrain

(G-7719)
ASEPT PAK INC
64 West St (12953-1118)
PHONE..............................518 651-2026
Gary L Hanley, *Ch of Bd*
EMP: 23 **EST:** 2004
SALES (est): 5.4MM **Privately Held**
SIC: 2833 Organic medicinal chemicals: bulk, uncompounded

(G-7720)
COCA-COLA BOTTLING COMPANY
15 Ida Pkwy (12953)
PHONE..............................518 483-0422
Ron Lavalley, *Branch Mgr*
EMP: 28
SALES (corp-wide): 16.6B **Privately Held**
SIC: 2086 Bottled & canned soft drinks
HQ: The Coca-Cola Bottling Company Of Northern New England Inc
1 Executive Park Dr # 330
Bedford NH 03110
603 627-7871

(G-7721)
FASPRINT
20 Finney Blvd (12953-1039)
P.O. Box 832 (12953-0832)
PHONE..............................518 483-4631
Tammi M Dupont, *Owner*
EMP: 6
SQ FT: 2,000
SALES (est): 705.7K **Privately Held**
SIC: 2752 Commercial printing, offset

(G-7722)
JOHNSON NEWSPAPER CORPORATION
Also Called: Malone News
469 E Main St Ste 2 (12953-2128)
PHONE..............................518 483-4700
Karen Carre, *Advt Staff*
Chuck Kelly, *Manager*
EMP: 20
SALES (corp-wide): 32MM **Privately Held**
WEB: www.ogd.com
SIC: 2711 Newspapers: publishing only, not printed on site
PA: Johnson Newspaper Corporation
260 Washington St
Watertown NY
315 782-1000

(G-7723)
LOMIR INC
Also Called: Lomir Biomedical Inc
213 W Main St (12953-9577)
P.O. Box 778 (12953-0778)
PHONE..............................518 483-7697
Teresa Price, *CEO*
Teresa Woodger, *President*
Karen Coles, *General Mgr*
Mr Tom Long, *Chairman*
EMP: 16
SQ FT: 10,000
SALES (est): 1.8MM **Privately Held**
WEB: www.lomir.com
SIC: 3821 Laboratory equipment: fume hoods, distillation racks, etc.
PA: Lomir Biomedical Inc
95 Rue Huot
Notre-Dame-De-L'Ile-Perrot QC J7V 7
514 425-3604

(G-7724)
MALONE INDUSTRIAL PRESS INC
10 Stevens St (12953-1634)
P.O. Box 267 (12953-0267)
PHONE..............................518 483-5880
Bernard Desnoyers, *President*
EMP: 6 **EST:** 1939
SQ FT: 3,000
SALES: 725K **Privately Held**
SIC: 2752 5111 2759 Commercial printing, offset; printing paper; letterpress printing

(G-7725)
SCOTTS FEED INC
Also Called: Collins Pet & Garden Center
245 Elm St (12953-1541)
PHONE..............................518 483-3110
Scott Collins, *President*
EMP: 23
SQ FT: 6,000
SALES (est): 4.9MM **Privately Held**
SIC: 2048 5191 Prepared feeds; animal feeds

(G-7726)
SEAWAY MATS INC
Also Called: Sea Mats
252 Park St (12953-1234)
P.O. Box 407 (12953-0407)
PHONE..............................518 483-2560
Roy Hamilton, *CEO*
Diane Hamilton, *Vice Pres*
EMP: 7
SALES (est): 851.3K **Privately Held**
SIC: 3069 3949 3089 2391 Mats or matting, rubber; nets: badminton, volleyball, tennis, etc.; composition stone, plastic; doors, folding: plastic or plastic coated fabric; curtains & draperies
PA: Seaway Plastics Ltd
270 Boul Saint-Joseph
Lachine QC H8S 2
514 637-2323

(G-7727)
SIGNS INC
2 Boyer Ave (12953-1628)
P.O. Box 185 (12953-0185)
PHONE..............................518 483-4759
Judy Sousie, *President*
Shannon Niles, *Treasurer*
EMP: 5

SALES (est): 444.7K **Privately Held**
SIC: 3993 Signs & advertising specialties

(G-7728)
TITUS MOUNTAIN SAND & GRAV LLC
17 Junction Rd (12953-4217)
P.O. Box 390 (12953-0390)
PHONE.................................518 483-3740
William Hewitt, *Mng Member*
EMP: 6
SALES (est): 920.8K **Privately Held**
SIC: 1442 Construction sand & gravel

(G-7729)
UPSTONE MATERIALS INC
Also Called: Malone Concrete Products Div
359 Elm St (12953-1500)
P.O. Box 457, North Bangor (12966-0457)
PHONE.................................518 483-2671
Jim Odis, *Manager*
EMP: 6
SALES (corp-wide): 95.5MM **Privately Held**
WEB: www.graymont-ab.com
SIC: 3272 Concrete products
HQ: Upstone Materials Inc.
   111 Quarry Rd
   Plattsburgh NY 12901
   518 561-5321

Malta
Saratoga County

(G-7730)
GLOBALFOUNDRIES US INC
400 Stone Break Rd Ext (12020)
PHONE.................................518 305-9013
Norm Armour, *Vice Pres*
Bill Barrett, *Vice Pres*
John Kent, *Vice Pres*
Pruthvi Anekal, *Engineer*
Sanggil Bae, *Engineer*
EMP: 95
SALES (corp-wide): 8.5B **Privately Held**
SIC: 3369 3572 Nonferrous foundries; computer disk & drum drives & components
HQ: Globalfoundries U.S. Inc.
   2600 Great America Way
   Santa Clara CA 95054

(G-7731)
GOLUB CORPORATION
Also Called: Price Chopper Pharmacy 184
3 Hemphill Pl Ste 116 (12020-4419)
PHONE.................................518 899-6063
Rob Russell, *Branch Mgr*
EMP: 28
SALES (corp-wide): 3.3B **Privately Held**
SIC: 3751 Motorcycles & related parts
PA: The Golub Corporation
   461 Nott St
   Schenectady NY 12308
   518 355-5000

(G-7732)
TOKYO ELECTRON AMERICA INC
2 Bayberry Dr (12020-6352)
PHONE.................................518 289-3100
Tetsuo Tsuneishi, *Branch Mgr*
EMP: 6
SALES (corp-wide): 10.6B **Privately Held**
SIC: 3674 Semiconductors & related devices
HQ: Tokyo Electron America, Inc.
   2400 Grove Blvd
   Austin TX 78741
   512 424-1000

(G-7733)
WIRED COFFEE AND BAGEL INC
Rr 9 (12020)
PHONE.................................518 506-3194
Matthew J Michele, *President*
EMP: 12
SALES (est): 1MM **Privately Held**
SIC: 3556 5812 Roasting machinery: coffee, peanut, etc.; lunchrooms & cafeterias

Mamaroneck
Westchester County

(G-7734)
AUTOMATED BUILDING CONTROLS
629 N Barry Ave (10543-1608)
PHONE.................................914 381-2860
Barry Novick, *President*
Mary Ellen Keefer, *Office Mgr*
Maryellen Kiefas, *Manager*
EMP: 8
SQ FT: 400
SALES: 800K **Privately Held**
SIC: 3822 Temperature controls, automatic

(G-7735)
BRANDS WITHIN REACH LLC
Also Called: AMI Brands
141 Halstead Ave Ste 201 (10543-2652)
PHONE.................................847 720-9090
Kyle Caffero, *District Mgr*
Jady Conboy, *Business Mgr*
Jessie James, *Opers Mgr*
Tim Irwin, *Opers Staff*
Wayne Minott, *Opers Staff*
▲ **EMP:** 24
SQ FT: 2,500
SALES (est): 5MM **Privately Held**
SIC: 2086 Bottled & canned soft drinks

(G-7736)
CARPET FABRICATIONS INTL
628 Waverly Ave Ste 1 (10543-2259)
PHONE.................................914 381-6060
Thomas L Budetti, *President*
Edward Soto, *Vice Pres*
▲ **EMP:** 23
SQ FT: 15,000
SALES (est): 2.3MM **Privately Held**
SIC: 2273 5023 Carpets & rugs; floor coverings

(G-7737)
CATHOLIC NEWS PUBLISHING CO
Also Called: School Guide Publications
420 Railroad Way (10543-2257)
PHONE.................................914 632-7771
Myles A Ridder, *President*
Joseph Ridder, *Treasurer*
EMP: 15 **EST:** 1886
SQ FT: 5,500
SALES: 3MM **Privately Held**
WEB: www.schoolguides.com
SIC: 2741 7372 Directories: publishing only, not printed on site; publishers' computer software

(G-7738)
CHOCOLATIONS LLC
607 E Boston Post Rd (10543-3742)
PHONE.................................914 777-3600
Maria Valente,
EMP: 5
SALES: 200K **Privately Held**
SIC: 2064 Candy & other confectionery products

(G-7739)
COLDSTREAM GROUP INC (PA)
Also Called: Nessen Lighting, The
420 Railroad Way (10543-2257)
P.O. Box 187 (10543-0187)
PHONE.................................914 698-5959
Bob Henderson, *President*
Ralph Izzi, *Controller*
▲ **EMP:** 19
SALES (est): 7MM **Privately Held**
SIC: 3646 Commercial indusl & institutional electric lighting fixtures

(G-7740)
CORIUM CORPORATION (PA)
Also Called: Cromwell Group
147 Palmer Ave (10543-3632)
PHONE.................................914 381-0100
Thomas Fleisch, *President*
Rick Derr, *Treasurer*
▲ **EMP:** 18
SALES (est): 5.6MM **Privately Held**
WEB: www.coriumcorp.com
SIC: 3111 Leather tanning & finishing

(G-7741)
CULIN/COLELLA INC
632 Center Ave (10543-2206)
PHONE.................................914 698-7727
Raynsford Culin, *President*
Janice Colella Culin, *Corp Secy*
EMP: 9 **EST:** 1975
SQ FT: 10,000
SALES: 1.1MM **Privately Held**
WEB: www.culincolella.com
SIC: 2519 2521 Household furniture, except wood or metal: upholstered; cabinets, office: wood

(G-7742)
DIVISION DEN-BAR ENTERPRISES
Also Called: Arborn Printing & Graphics
745 W Boston Post Rd (10543-3320)
PHONE.................................914 381-2220
Barry Arborn, *President*
Denise Arborn, *Vice Pres*
EMP: 5
SQ FT: 1,000
SALES: 650K **Privately Held**
SIC: 2759 2789 Commercial printing; bookbinding & related work

(G-7743)
ENCORE RETAIL SYSTEMS INC (PA)
180 E Prospect Ave (10543-3709)
PHONE.................................718 385-3443
Louis Fusaro, *President*
Stephen Cain, *Vice Pres*
EMP: 10
SQ FT: 10,000
SALES (est): 1.9MM **Privately Held**
SIC: 2499 2541 Display forms, boot & shoes; wood partitions & fixtures

(G-7744)
FAMILY PUBLISHING GROUP INC
Also Called: New York Familypublications
141 Halstead Ave (10543-2607)
PHONE.................................914 381-7474
Fax: 914 381-7672
EMP: 20
SQ FT: 1,200
SALES (est): 1.8MM **Privately Held**
SIC: 2721 2731 Periodicals-Publishing/Printing Books-Publishing/Printing

(G-7745)
GANNETT STLLITE INFO NTWRK LLC
Also Called: Gannett Suburban Newspapers
700 Waverly Ave (10543-2262)
PHONE.................................914 381-3400
Larry James, *Manager*
EMP: 16
SQ FT: 6,000
SALES (corp-wide): 3.1B **Publicly Held**
WEB: www.usatoday.com
SIC: 2711 Newspapers, publishing & printing
HQ: Gannett Satellite Information Network, Llc
   7950 Jones Branch Dr
   Mc Lean VA 22102
   703 854-6000

(G-7746)
INFLATION SYSTEMS INC
500 Ogden Ave (10543-2227)
PHONE.................................914 381-8070
Sandra Goldman, *President*
Robert Goldman, *Vice Pres*
EMP: 20
SQ FT: 7,500
SALES: 3.4MM **Privately Held**
SIC: 3069 Valves, hard rubber; hard rubber & molded rubber products

(G-7747)
MARINE & INDUS HYDRAULICS INC
329 Center Ave (10543-2304)
PHONE.................................914 698-2036
John J Wright, *President*
Brooks Wright, *Vice Pres*
▲ **EMP:** 10
SQ FT: 10,000
SALES (est): 2.1MM **Privately Held**
SIC: 3625 Actuators, industrial

(G-7748)
MARVAL INDUSTRIES INC
Also Called: M I I
315 Hoyt Ave (10543-1899)
PHONE.................................914 381-2400
Alan Zimmerman, *CEO*
Thomas Zimmerman, *Ch of Bd*
Emil Kocur, *President*
Logan Osberg, *Opers Mgr*
Manuela Blossy, *Controller*
▲ **EMP:** 70 **EST:** 1956
SQ FT: 54,000
SALES (est): 39.6MM **Privately Held**
WEB: www.marvalindustries.com
SIC: 2869 5162 3089 3087 Industrial organic chemicals; plastics materials; thermoformed finished plastic products; custom compound purchased resins

(G-7749)
MDJ SALES ASSOCIATES INC
27 Doris Rd (10543-1009)
PHONE.................................914 420-5897
Michael Aaronson, *CEO*
EMP: 5
SALES: 750K **Privately Held**
SIC: 2253 Knit outerwear mills

(G-7750)
ON THE JOB EMBROIDERY & AP
154 E Boston Post Rd # 1 (10543-3755)
PHONE.................................914 381-3556
Michael Federici, *President*
Joseph Bilotto, *Vice Pres*
EMP: 5
SALES (est): 320K **Privately Held**
SIC: 2395 Embroidery products, except schiffli machine

(G-7751)
ORTHO RITE INC
434 Waverly Ave (10543-2232)
PHONE.................................914 235-9100
Gregory Sands, *President*
EMP: 28
SQ FT: 4,000
SALES: 3.2MM **Privately Held**
WEB: www.ortho-rite.com
SIC: 3842 Suspensories

(G-7752)
PALETERIA FERNANDEZ INC
350 Mamaroneck Ave (10543-2608)
PHONE.................................914 315-1598
Ignacio Fernandez, *CEO*
EMP: 12 **Privately Held**
SIC: 2024 Ice cream, bulk
PA: Paleteria Fernandez Inc.
   33 N Main St
   Port Chester NY 10573

(G-7753)
PICONE MEAT SPECIALTIES LTD
Also Called: Picone's Sausage
180 Jefferson Ave (10543-1912)
PHONE.................................914 381-3002
Frank Picone, *President*
Anthony Picone, *Vice Pres*
EMP: 8
SQ FT: 6,600
SALES (est): 2.4MM **Privately Held**
SIC: 2013 Sausages & other prepared meats

(G-7754)
POLKADOT USA INC
33 Country Rd (10543-1108)
PHONE.................................914 835-3697
Debra Schoenau, *President*
Howard Friedman, *Vice Pres*
EMP: 2
SQ FT: 6,000
SALES: 2MM **Privately Held**
WEB: www.polkadotusa.com
SIC: 2396 Apparel & other linings, except millinery

Mamaroneck - Westchester County (G-7755)

(G-7755)
RICHARD ENGDAL BAKING CORP
Also Called: Hudson Valley Baking Co
421 Waverly Ave (10543-2233)
PHONE..................914 777-9600
Richard Cuozzo, *President*
EMP: 10
SQ FT: 4,000
SALES (est): 1.1MM **Privately Held**
SIC: 2051 Bakery: wholesale or wholesale/retail combined

(G-7756)
ROBERT E DERECKTOR INC
Also Called: Derecktor Shipyards
311 E Boston Post Rd (10543-3738)
PHONE..................914 698-0962
Eric P Derecktor, *Ch of Bd*
E Paul Derecktor, *Ch of Bd*
Peter Smykowski, *CFO*
Thomas Derecktor, *Shareholder*
▲ EMP: 80 EST: 1947
SQ FT: 64,000
SALES (est): 15.5MM **Privately Held**
SIC: 3731 4493 7699 3444 Ferryboats, building & repairing; boat yards, storage & incidental repair; boat repair; sheet metalwork; fabricated structural metal; fishing boats: lobster, crab, oyster, etc.: small

(G-7757)
SHORE LINE MONOGRAMMING INC
Also Called: Shore Line Momogramming & EMB
115 Hoyt Ave (10543-1891)
PHONE..................914 698-8000
John Moller, *President*
Andrew Moller, *President*
EMP: 12
SQ FT: 18,000
SALES (est): 1.3MM **Privately Held**
SIC: 2759 5941 Screen printing; sporting goods & bicycle shops

(G-7758)
TOM & JERRY PRINTCRAFT FORMS (PA)
960 Mamaroneck Ave (10543-1631)
P.O. Box 743 (10543-0743)
PHONE..................914 777-7468
Thomas La Guidice, *President*
Phil Caragine, *Treasurer*
EMP: 25
SQ FT: 5,000
SALES (est): 3.9MM **Privately Held**
WEB: www.printcraftny.com
SIC: 2752 2791 2789 Commercial printing, offset; typesetting; bookbinding & related work

(G-7759)
TRIDENT VALVE ACTUATOR CO
329 Center Ave (10543-2304)
PHONE..................914 698-2650
John Cermanski, *General Mgr*
John Wright, *Principal*
Kathleen Wright, *Treasurer*
Brooks Wright, *VP Finance*
EMP: 12
SQ FT: 10,000
SALES (est): 1.1MM **Privately Held**
SIC: 3625 5085 Actuators, industrial; valves & fittings

Manchester
Ontario County

(G-7760)
ELITE MACHINE INC
3 Merrick Cir (14504-9740)
P.O. Box 8 (14504-0008)
PHONE..................585 289-4733
Steve Hawkins, *President*
EMP: 5
SQ FT: 5,304
SALES (est): 451K **Privately Held**
SIC: 3599 Machine shop, jobbing & repair

(G-7761)
ROCHESTER INSULATED GLASS INC
73 Merrick Cir (14504-9740)
P.O. Box 168 (14504-0168)
PHONE..................585 289-3611
Richard S Wolk, *President*
Gretchen Wolk, *Corp Secy*
Tyler Wolk, *Vice Pres*
◆ EMP: 55
SALES (est): 13.6MM **Privately Held**
WEB: www.rochesterinsulatedglass.com
SIC: 3231 Insulating glass: made from purchased glass; safety glass: made from purchased glass

(G-7762)
SIDCO FILTER CORPORATION
58 North Ave (14504-9769)
PHONE..................585 289-3100
Sidney T Cutt, *Ch of Bd*
Andrea Fitzgerald, *President*
Bill Florance, *Sales Dir*
Kathy Shattuck, *Cust Svc Mgr*
EMP: 27
SQ FT: 20,000
SALES (est): 5.8MM **Privately Held**
WEB: www.sidcofilter.com
SIC: 3569 Filters, general line: industrial

Manhasset
Nassau County

(G-7763)
ADVANCED PROSTHETICS ORTHOTICS
Also Called: Joyce Center
50 Maple Pl (11030-1927)
PHONE..................516 365-7225
Michael A Joyce, *President*
Cheryl Caruso, *Manager*
EMP: 10
SALES (est): 1.5MM **Privately Held**
SIC: 3842 Prosthetic appliances; orthopedic appliances

(G-7764)
CABINETRY BY TBR INC
1492 Northern Blvd (11030-3006)
PHONE..................516 365-8500
Basiliki Ypsilantis, *Principal*
EMP: 8
SALES (est): 760.3K **Privately Held**
SIC: 2434 Wood kitchen cabinets

(G-7765)
CALIBRATED INSTRUMENTS INC
306 Aerie Ct (11030-4053)
PHONE..................914 741-5700
John B Shroyer, *President*
Bruce Gallit, *Manager*
▲ EMP: 10 EST: 1954
SALES (est): 1.6MM **Privately Held**
SIC: 3823 On-stream gas/liquid analysis instruments, industrial

(G-7766)
DOHNSCO INC
19 Gracewood Dr (11030-3931)
PHONE..................516 773-4800
EMP: 5
SQ FT: 2,100
SALES (est): 310K **Privately Held**
SIC: 2741 7379 Misc Publishing Computer Related Services

(G-7767)
FRAME SHOPPE & ART GALLERY
Also Called: Frame Shoppe & Gallery
447 Plandome Rd (11030-1942)
PHONE..................516 365-6014
Demitri Kazianis, *Partner*
Thomas Walsh, *Partner*
Elaine Karton, *Manager*
EMP: 6
SALES (est): 429.6K **Privately Held**
SIC: 2499 3499 7699 5999 Picture frame molding, finished; picture frames, metal; picture framing, custom; art dealers; gift shop

(G-7768)
GOLF DIRECTORIES USA INC
39 Orchard St Ste 7 (11030-1969)
PHONE..................516 365-5351
Ray Cyrgalis, *President*
EMP: 5
SQ FT: 1,000
SALES (est): 274.8K **Privately Held**
SIC: 2741 Telephone & other directory publishing

(G-7769)
MDR PRINTING CORP
Also Called: Minuteman Press
125 Plandome Rd (11030-2331)
PHONE..................516 627-3221
Les Forrai, *President*
EMP: 5
SQ FT: 1,200
SALES (est): 749.5K **Privately Held**
WEB: www.manhassetminuteman.com
SIC: 2752 Commercial printing, lithographic

(G-7770)
NATIONAL SECURITY SYSTEMS INC
511 Manhasset Woods Rd (11030-1663)
PHONE..................516 627-2222
Jay Baron, *President*
John W Walter, *Chairman*
William T Walter, *Vice Pres*
Joan Walter, *Admin Sec*
EMP: 26
SQ FT: 3,200
SALES (est): 34.6MM **Privately Held**
WEB: www.plazaconstruction.com
SIC: 3699 Security control equipment & systems

(G-7771)
PRISCILLA QUART CO FIRTS
160 Plandome Rd Fl 2 (11030-2326)
PHONE..................516 365-2755
EMP: 6
SALES (est): 278.8K **Privately Held**
SIC: 3131 Quarters

(G-7772)
SUPERIOR FURS INC
1697 Northern Blvd (11030-3026)
PHONE..................516 365-4123
Tom Djoganopoulos, *President*
EMP: 13
SQ FT: 1,000
SALES (est): 1.1MM **Privately Held**
SIC: 2371 5632 Apparel, fur; furriers

(G-7773)
TEA LIFE LLC
73 Plandome Rd (11030-2330)
PHONE..................516 365-7711
Linda Villano,
EMP: 8
SQ FT: 3,000
SALES (est): 284.7K **Privately Held**
SIC: 2099 Tea blending

Manlius
Onondaga County

(G-7774)
BASILEUS COMPANY LLC
8104 Cazenovia Rd (13104-6700)
PHONE..................315 963-3516
Gerald E Wilson, *Mng Member*
◆ EMP: 10
SQ FT: 2,215
SALES (est): 940K **Privately Held**
SIC: 2211 Apparel & outerwear fabrics, cotton

(G-7775)
CARPENTER MANUFACTURING CO
110 Fairgrounds Dr (13104-2481)
P.O. Box 188 (13104-0188)
PHONE..................315 682-9176
Thomas Carpenter, *President*
Susan C Sorensen, *Vice Pres*
Kenneth Carpenter, *Shareholder*
EMP: 20 EST: 1955
SQ FT: 14,500
SALES (est): 4.5MM **Privately Held**
WEB: www.carpentermfg.com
SIC: 3549 Wiredrawing & fabricating machinery & equipment, ex. die; cutting & slitting machinery

(G-7776)
CREATIVE YARD DESIGNS INC
8329 Us Route 20 (13104-9536)
PHONE..................315 706-6143
Ron King, *Manager*
EMP: 5
SALES (est): 377.6K **Privately Held**
SIC: 3271 Blocks, concrete: landscape or retaining wall

(G-7777)
FILTER TECH INC (PA)
113 Fairgrounds Dr (13104-2497)
P.O. Box 527 (13104-0527)
PHONE..................315 682-8815
Joseph F Scalise, *President*
Ahmad El-Hindi, *Principal*
Joseph El-Hindi, *Vice Pres*
Elizabeth Elhindi, *Vice Pres*
Mehdi Meghezzi, *Electrical Engi*
▲ EMP: 59
SQ FT: 10,000
SALES (est): 12.2MM **Privately Held**
WEB: www.filtertech.com
SIC: 3569 Filters, general line: industrial; lubricating systems, centralized

(G-7778)
GLOBAL INSTRUMENTATION LLC
8104 Cazenovia Rd Ste 2/3 (13104-6700)
PHONE..................315 682-0272
James Demaso, *Mng Member*
Scott Meyers,
Craig Sellers,
EMP: 10
SALES (est): 1.9MM **Privately Held**
WEB: www.globalinstrumentation.com
SIC: 3845 Ultrasonic scanning devices, medical

(G-7779)
L& JG STICKLEY INCORPORATED (PA)
1 Stickley Dr (13104-2485)
P.O. Box 480 (13104-0480)
PHONE..................315 682-5500
Aminy I Audi, *Ch of Bd*
Edward Audi, *President*
James Torres, *General Mgr*
Paul Terwilliger, *VP Opers*
Steve D'Amico, *Opers Mgr*
▲ EMP: 900 EST: 1895
SQ FT: 400,000
SALES (est): 252MM **Privately Held**
WEB: www.stickley.com
SIC: 2511 2519 Wood household furniture; household furniture, except wood or metal: upholstered

(G-7780)
MAYBERRY SHOE COMPANY INC
Also Called: Kangaroo Crossing
131 W Seneca St Ste B (13104-2444)
PHONE..................315 692-4086
Bruce Mayberry, *President*
EMP: 5
SQ FT: 500
SALES (est): 776K **Privately Held**
SIC: 3149 2329 2339 Athletic shoes, except rubber or plastic; men's & boys' athletic uniforms; uniforms, athletic: women's, misses' & juniors'

(G-7781)
VOSS SIGNS LLC
112 Fairgrounds Dr Ste 2 (13104-2437)
P.O. Box 553 (13104-0553)
PHONE..................315 682-6418
Jim Menter, *General Mgr*
James Menter, *CFO*
Jeff Woodworth, *VP Mktg*
Thomas Tenerovicz, *Mktg Dir*
Nicholas Diamond, *Marketing Mgr*
EMP: 25
SQ FT: 31,000

▲ = Import ▼=Export
◆ =Import/Export

SALES (est): 3.8MM Privately Held
WEB: www.vosssigns.com
SIC: 2759 3993 2791 Screen printing; signs & advertising specialties; typesetting

Manorville
Suffolk County

(G-7782)
B&K PRECISION CORPORATION
31 Oakwood Dr (11949-1211)
PHONE..................................631 369-2665
Ray Kreiger, *Branch Mgr*
EMP: 5 Privately Held
WEB: www.bkprecision.com
SIC: 3559 Automotive related machinery
PA: B&K Precision Corporation
       22820 Savi Ranch Pkwy
       Yorba Linda CA 92887

(G-7783)
COVERGRIP CORPORATION
16 Douglas Ln (11949-2016)
P.O. Box 304, Holderness NH (03245-0304)
PHONE..................................855 268-3747
John Barry, *President*
▲ **EMP:** 5 EST: 2011
SALES: 800K Privately Held
WEB: www.covergrip.com
SIC: 2394 Canvas covers & drop cloths

(G-7784)
CPI INDUSTRIES INC
275 Dayton Ave (11949-2029)
PHONE..................................631 909-3434
Ciro Intini, *President*
Denise Intini, *Opers Mgr*
EMP: 55
SALES: 4MM Privately Held
SIC: 3444 Sheet metalwork

(G-7785)
SAS INDUSTRIES INC
939 Wading River Manor Rd (11949)
P.O. Box 245 (11949-0245)
PHONE..................................631 727-1441
Steve Steckis, *President*
A Steckis, *Manager*
Mitchell Steckis, *Info Tech Mgr*
▲ **EMP:** 15 EST: 1973
SQ FT: 10,000
SALES (est): 3.3MM Privately Held
WEB: www.sasindustries.com
SIC: 3053 5085 Gaskets, all materials; industrial supplies

(G-7786)
SPLICE TECHNOLOGIES INC
625 North St (11949-2055)
P.O. Box 644 (11949-0644)
PHONE..................................631 924-8108
Robert P Auteri, *President*
Nannette M Auteri, *Admin Sec*
▼ **EMP:** 8
SQ FT: 2,000
SALES: 1.2MM Privately Held
WEB: www.splicetechnologies.com
SIC: 3661 Fiber optics communications equipment

(G-7787)
VULCAN IRON WORKS INC
190 Weeks Ave (11949-2034)
PHONE..................................631 395-6846
Carl Forster, *President*
EMP: 4 EST: 1926
SQ FT: 1,800
SALES (est): 2MM Privately Held
WEB: www.vulcanironworks.com
SIC: 3441 Fabricated structural metal

Marathon
Cortland County

(G-7788)
AUTOMATED BIOMASS SYSTEMS LLC
2235 Clarks Corners Rd (13803-1528)
PHONE..................................607 849-7800
Timmins Karl Matthieu, *Principal*
Matthew Dubitzky, *Mktg Dir*
EMP: 18
SALES (est): 5.1MM Privately Held
SIC: 3535 Conveyors & conveying equipment

(G-7789)
GALLERY OF MACHINES LLC
Also Called: DH Machine Tool Services
20 Front St (13803-7705)
P.O. Box 460 (13803-0460)
PHONE..................................607 849-6028
Derrick Hartman,
EMP: 4
SQ FT: 46,000
SALES: 1MM¹ Privately Held
WEB: www.galleryofmachines.com
SIC: 3541 Machine tools, metal cutting type

(G-7790)
KURTZ TRUCK EQUIPMENT INC
1085 Mcgraw Marathon Rd (13803-2806)
PHONE..................................607 849-3468
Mellisa Slack, *President*
Roger Smith, *Sales Staff*
Chuck Winters, *Sales Staff*
EMP: 18 EST: 1960
SQ FT: 4,000
SALES (est): 3.8MM Privately Held
SIC: 3713 3599 3714 Specialty motor vehicle bodies; machine shop, jobbing & repair; propane conversion equipment, motor vehicle

(G-7791)
MARATHON BOAT GROUP INC
1 Grumman Way (13803-3030)
P.O. Box 549 (13803-0549)
PHONE..................................607 849-3211
Doug Potter, *President*
Greg Harvey, *Treasurer*
▼ **EMP:** 15
SQ FT: 24,050
SALES (est): 1.3MM Privately Held
WEB: www.marathonboat.com
SIC: 3732 5551 Motorized boat, building & repairing; canoes, building & repairing; boat dealers

Marcellus
Onondaga County

(G-7792)
ARMSTRONG TRANSMITTER CORP
4835 N Street Rd (13108-9715)
PHONE..................................315 673-1269
Sinan Mimaroglu, *President*
Ernie Belanger, *Mktg Dir*
Kevin Smith, *Marketing Staff*
▲ **EMP:** 10
SQ FT: 40,000
SALES (est): 1.2MM Privately Held
WEB: www.armstrongtx.com
SIC: 3663 Transmitting apparatus, radio or television

(G-7793)
CHOCOLATE PIZZA COMPANY INC
3774 Lee Mulroy Rd (13108-9814)
PHONE..................................315 673-4098
Ryan Novak, *Ch of Bd*
EMP: 18
SQ FT: 7,000
SALES (est): 3.3MM Privately Held
WEB: www.chocolatepizza.com
SIC: 2066 2064 5149 Chocolate candy, solid; chocolate candy, except solid chocolate; chocolate

(G-7794)
QUIKRETE COMPANIES LLC
4993 Limeledge Rd Ste 560 (13108-9798)
PHONE..................................315 673-2020
Greg Breen, *Branch Mgr*
EMP: 20 Privately Held
SIC: 3272 Concrete products
HQ: The Quikrete Companies Llc
       5 Concourse Pkwy Ste 1900
       Atlanta GA 30328
       404 634-9100

(G-7795)
SMITH SAND & GRAVEL INC
4782 Shepard Rd (13108-9745)
P.O. Box 166 (13108-0166)
PHONE..................................315 673-4124
David J Smith, *Ch of Bd*
Chelsea Smith, *Office Mgr*
EMP: 9 EST: 2005
SALES (est): 1.6MM Privately Held
SIC: 1442 Common sand mining

Marcy
Oneida County

(G-7796)
DEANS PAVING INC
6002 Cavanaugh Rd (13403-2411)
PHONE..................................315 736-7601
James J Dean, *Principal*
EMP: 6
SALES: 700K Privately Held
WEB: www.deanspaving.com
SIC: 2951 4959 0782 7521 Asphalt paving mixtures & blocks; sweeping service: road, airport, parking lot, etc.; snow-plowing; lawn services; parking lots

(G-7797)
PRAXAIR DISTRIBUTION INC
9432 State Route 49 (13403-2342)
PHONE..................................315 735-6153
Ron Marson, *Manager*
EMP: 11
SALES (corp-wide): 11.4B Privately Held
SIC: 2813 Oxygen, compressed or liquefied; nitrogen; acetylene
HQ: Praxair Distribution, Inc.
       10 Riverview Dr
       Danbury CT 06810
       203 837-2000

Margaretville
Delaware County

(G-7798)
HUBBELL INC
46124 State Highway 30 # 2 (12455-3111)
P.O. Box 664 (12455-0664)
PHONE..................................845 586-2707
Joseph Rudd Hubbell, *President*
Bill Dietz, *Design Engr*
Robert Hubbell, *Info Tech Mgr*
EMP: 21
SQ FT: 5,000
SALES (est): 3.6MM Privately Held
SIC: 3643 Current-carrying wiring devices

(G-7799)
ROBERT GREENBURG (PA)
Cross Rd (12455)
PHONE..................................845 586-2226
Robert Greenburg, *President*
Robert Kane, *Vice Pres*
Al Bates, *Manager*
EMP: 5
SQ FT: 2,000
SALES (est): 898.5K Privately Held
SIC: 2851 Epoxy coatings; polyurethane coatings

Marion
Wayne County

(G-7800)
DUNLAP MACHINE LLC
4205 Sunset Dr (14505-9556)
PHONE..................................315 926-1013
Roger Dunlap, *Mng Member*
EMP: 12
SQ FT: 5,000
SALES (est): 355K Privately Held
SIC: 3599 3541 3542 Machine shop, jobbing & repair; machine tools, metal cutting type; machine tools, metal forming type

(G-7801)
GREEN VALLEY FOODS LLC
3736 S Main St (14505-9751)
PHONE..................................315 926-4280
Kraig H Kayser,
Timothy Benjamin,
Paul Palmby,
Jeffrey Van Riper,
EMP: 7
SQ FT: 348,000
SALES (est): 291.3K
SALES (corp-wide): 1.3B Publicly Held
SIC: 2033 Vegetables: packaged in cans, jars, etc.; fruits: packaged in cans, jars, etc.
PA: Seneca Foods Corporation
       3736 S Main St
       Marion NY 14505
       315 926-8100

(G-7802)
HADLEYS FAB-WELD INC
4202 Sunset Dr (14505-9538)
PHONE..................................315 926-5101
Alan Hadley, *President*
Adriana Hadley, *Vice Pres*
EMP: 9
SQ FT: 5,800
SALES (est): 1.1MM Privately Held
WEB: www.hadleyfabweld.com
SIC: 7692 Welding repair

(G-7803)
J & G MACHINE & TOOL CO INC
4510 Smith Rd (14505-9509)
PHONE..................................315 310-7130
Gary Prutsman, *President*
Jody Prutsman, *Office Admin*
EMP: 14
SQ FT: 15,000
SALES: 1.5MM Privately Held
SIC: 3599 Machine shop, jobbing & repair

(G-7804)
PARKER-HANNIFIN CORPORATION
Also Called: Engineered Polymer Systems Div
3967 Buffalo St (14505-9616)
P.O. Box 6 (14505-0006)
PHONE..................................315 926-4211
Mathias Bischoping, *QC Mgr*
Sue Remmel, *Personnel*
Robson Veruti, *Manager*
EMP: 30
SALES (corp-wide): 12B Publicly Held
WEB: www.parker.com
SIC: 2821 Plastics materials & resins
PA: Parker-Hannifin Corporation
       6035 Parkland Blvd
       Cleveland OH 44124
       216 896-3000

(G-7805)
PETER C HERMAN INC
5395 Skinner Rd (14505-9406)
PHONE..................................315 926-4100
Matthew Herman, *President*
Joseph Herman, *Vice Pres*
EMP: 50
SQ FT: 2,000
SALES (est): 7.8MM Privately Held
SIC: 2448 Pallets, wood

(G-7806)
SENECA FOODS CORPORATION (PA)
3736 S Main St (14505-9751)
PHONE..................................315 926-8100
Arthur S Wolcott, *Ch of Bd*
Kraig H Kayser, *President*
Paul L Palmby, *COO*
Timothy Benjamin, *Vice Pres*
Jeffrey L Van Riper, *Vice Pres*
EMP: 50
SQ FT: 348,000
SALES: 1.3B **Publicly Held**
SIC: 2033 2037 Vegetables: packaged in cans, jars, etc.; fruits: packaged in cans, jars, etc.; vegetables, quick frozen & cold pack, excl. potato products; fruits, quick frozen & cold pack (frozen); fruit juices, frozen

(G-7807)
SENECA FOODS CORPORATION
3709 Mill St (14505-9602)
PHONE..................................315 926-0531
Patricia East, *Accounting Dir*
Mike Hanchette, *Manager*
Ken Lohmann, *Supervisor*
EMP: 66
SQ FT: 544
SALES (corp-wide): 1.3B **Publicly Held**
SIC: 3411 Metal cans
PA: Seneca Foods Corporation
   3736 S Main St
   Marion NY 14505
   315 926-8100

(G-7808)
SENECA FOODS CORPORATION
Also Called: Vegetable Operations
3732 S Main St (14505-9751)
P.O. Box 996 (14505-0996)
PHONE..................................315 926-4277
Dan Janke, *Manager*
Ben Scherwitz, *Admin Sec*
EMP: 18
SALES (corp-wide): 1.3B **Publicly Held**
SIC: 2033 Vegetables: packaged in cans, jars, etc.
PA: Seneca Foods Corporation
   3736 S Main St
   Marion NY 14505
   315 926-8100

(G-7809)
TEC GLASS & INST LLC
Also Called: Thomas R Schul TEC GL & Inst
4211 Sunset Dr (14505-9556)
PHONE..................................315 926-7639
Thomas Schul, *Mng Member*
Hope Schul
EMP: 7
SQ FT: 3,000
SALES: 150K **Privately Held**
WEB: www.tecglass.biz
SIC: 3231 5049 Laboratory glassware; laboratory equipment, except medical or dental

(G-7810)
VERNS MACHINE CO INC
4929 Steel Point Rd (14505-9552)
PHONE..................................315 926-4223
Al Visingard, *President*
EMP: 28 **EST:** 1975
SQ FT: 8,000
SALES (est): 3.6MM **Privately Held**
SIC: 3541 3599 3451 Machine tools, metal cutting type; machine & other job shop work; screw machine products

(G-7811)
WESSIE MACHINE INC
5229 Steel Point Rd (14505-9534)
PHONE..................................315 926-4060
Alan Wessie, *President*
EMP: 7
SALES (est): 1.1MM **Privately Held**
SIC: 3469 Machine parts, stamped or pressed metal

Marlboro
Ulster County

(G-7812)
CIGAR BOX STUDIOS INC
24 Riverview Dr (12542-5310)
PHONE..................................845 236-9283
Gary Rausenberger, *President*
Scott Rausenberger, *Vice Pres*
Nick Rausenberger, *VP Prdtn*
Gary Tercasio, *Project Mgr*
Rob Macdonald, *Purch Mgr*
▲ **EMP:** 14
SQ FT: 20,000
SALES (est): 3.6MM **Privately Held**
WEB: www.cigarboxstudios.com
SIC: 3443 Fabricated plate work (boiler shop)

(G-7813)
ROYAL WINE CORPORATION
Also Called: Royal Kedem Wine
1519 Route 9w (12542-5420)
PHONE..................................845 236-4000
Michael Herzog, *Branch Mgr*
Tara-Joy Coupart, *Manager*
EMP: 15
SALES (corp-wide): 44MM **Privately Held**
SIC: 2084 5182 Wines; wine; liquor
PA: Royal Wine Corporation
   63 Lefante Dr
   Bayonne NJ 07002
   718 384-2400

Masonville
Delaware County

(G-7814)
AXTELL BRADTKE LUMBER CO
113 Beals Pond Rd (13804-2031)
PHONE..................................607 265-3850
Stuart Axtell, *Partner*
EMP: 6
SALES (est): 554.1K **Privately Held**
SIC: 2421 5211 Sawmills & planing mills, general; lumber products

(G-7815)
MASONVILLE STONE INCORPORATED
12999 State Highway 8 (13804-2119)
PHONE..................................607 265-3597
David Barnes, *President*
Douglas Barnes, *Vice Pres*
EMP: 8
SQ FT: 7,800
SALES (est): 937.4K **Privately Held**
SIC: 3281 Cut stone & stone products

Maspeth
Queens County

(G-7816)
AGL INDUSTRIES INC
5912 57th St (11378-3112)
PHONE..................................718 326-7597
Frank Lofaso, *President*
EMP: 50 **EST:** 2012
SQ FT: 4,500
SALES (est): 10.3MM **Privately Held**
SIC: 3449 Bars, concrete reinforcing: fabricated steel

(G-7817)
ALL-CITY METAL INC
5435 46th St (11378-1035)
PHONE..................................718 937-3975
Frank J Buccola, *Ch of Bd*
Roni Lifshitz, *Vice Pres*
Clark Buccola, *Opers Staff*
John Majowka, *Controller*
Mark Pukhovich, *Manager*
EMP: 40
SQ FT: 2,000
SALES (est): 11MM **Privately Held**
SIC: 3441 1711 Fabricated structural metal; mechanical contractor

(G-7818)
ALLE PROCESSING CORP
Also Called: Amazing Meals
5620 59th St (11378-2314)
PHONE..................................718 894-2000
Sam Hollander, *Ch of Bd*
Albert Weinstock, *President*
Ehud Bassis, *Vice Pres*
Zevi Wienstock, *Purch Mgr*
Yoely Ehrenfeld, *Purchasing*
◆ **EMP:** 250 **EST:** 1954
SQ FT: 75,000
SALES (est): 51.9MM **Privately Held**
WEB: www.alleprocessing.com
SIC: 2015 2038 2013 Poultry slaughtering & processing; dinners, frozen & packaged; prepared beef products from purchased beef

(G-7819)
AMAX PRINTING INC
6417 Grand Ave (11378-2421)
PHONE..................................718 384-8600
Anton Chan, *President*
Fanny Fang, *Vice Pres*
EMP: 15
SQ FT: 8,000
SALES (est): 2.3MM **Privately Held**
WEB: www.amaxprinting.com
SIC: 2759 2752 Letterpress printing; commercial printing, lithographic

(G-7820)
AMERICA NY RI WANG FD GROUP CO
5885 58th Ave (11378-2721)
PHONE..................................718 628-8999
Lian You Ye, *President*
Eddie Leung, *Senior Mgr*
▲ **EMP:** 50 **EST:** 2009
SQ FT: 40,000
SALES (est): 5MM **Privately Held**
SIC: 2038 Ethnic foods, frozen

(G-7821)
ANDIKE MILLWORK INC (PA)
Also Called: A & M Home Improvement
5818 64th St Fl 2 (11378-2817)
PHONE..................................718 894-1796
Andrew La Russa, *President*
Mike Machalski, *Vice Pres*
EMP: 3
SQ FT: 6,500
SALES (est): 1MM **Privately Held**
WEB: www.amhomeimprovement.com
SIC: 2434 5211 2499 1521 Wood kitchen cabinets; millwork & lumber; decorative wood & woodwork; single-family home remodeling, additions & repairs

(G-7822)
APEXX OMNI-GRAPHICS INC
5829 64th St (11378-2836)
PHONE..................................718 326-3330
Larry A Peters, *Ch of Bd*
Patricio Corella, *VP Mfg*
Louis Gonzalez, *Engineer*
Diran Avedissian, *Sales Staff*
Luis Arroyo, *Info Tech Mgr*
EMP: 55 **EST:** 1963
SQ FT: 40,000
SALES (est): 10.3MM **Privately Held**
WEB: www.apexxog.com
SIC: 3555 2656 3861 3089 Plates, offset; plates, paper: made from purchased material; plates, photographic (sensitized); plates, plastic; labels, paper: made from purchased material; packaging paper & plastics film, coated & laminated

(G-7823)
ARISTA COFFEE INC
5901 55th St (11378-3103)
PHONE..................................347 531-0813
Stephen Vouvoudakis, *Ch of Bd*
EMP: 15
SALES (est): 665.7K **Privately Held**
SIC: 3589 2095 Coffee brewing equipment; roasted coffee

(G-7824)
ASN INC
Also Called: Tri Star
6020 59th Pl Ste 2 (11378-3349)
PHONE..................................718 894-0800
Albert Nawroth, *Ch of Bd*
Rudy Bove, *Vice Pres*
EMP: 40
SALES (est): 1.5MM **Privately Held**
SIC: 2759 2752 Commercial printing; commercial printing, lithographic

(G-7825)
AUCAPINA CABINETS INC
5737 58th Dr (11378-2229)
PHONE..................................718 609-9054
Pedro Aucapina, *President*
EMP: 8
SALES (est): 134.8K **Privately Held**
SIC: 2434 Mfg Wood Kitchen Cabinets

(G-7826)
BG BINDERY INC
5877 57th St (11378-3125)
PHONE..................................631 767-4242
Barbara Michael, *CEO*
EMP: 5 **EST:** 2011
SALES (est): 593.6K **Privately Held**
SIC: 2789 Bookbinding & related work

(G-7827)
BIG GEYSER INC (PA)
5765 48th St (11378-2015)
PHONE..................................718 821-2200
Lewis Hershkowitz, *CEO*
Irving Hershkowitz, *President*
Harold Baron, *Principal*
Jerry Reda, *COO*
Carl Galio, *Vice Pres*
▲ **EMP:** 200
SQ FT: 125,000
SALES (est): 103.7MM **Privately Held**
WEB: www.biggeyser.com
SIC: 2086 Bottled & canned soft drinks

(G-7828)
BIMBO BAKERIES USA INC
Also Called: Stroehmann Bakeries 33
5754 Page Pl (11378-2236)
PHONE..................................718 463-6300
Steven Hartley, *Branch Mgr*
EMP: 117 **Privately Held**
SIC: 2051 5149 Bread, all types (white, wheat, rye, etc): fresh or frozen; groceries & related products
HQ: Bimbo Bakeries Usa, Inc
   255 Business Center Dr # 200
   Horsham PA 19044
   215 347-5500

(G-7829)
CASCADES NEW YORK INC
5515 Grand Ave (11378-3113)
PHONE..................................718 340-2100
Robert Sattelberg, *Manager*
EMP: 100
SALES (corp-wide): 3.3B **Privately Held**
SIC: 2652 Setup paperboard boxes
HQ: Cascades New York Inc.
   1845 Emerson St
   Rochester NY 14606
   585 527-8110

(G-7830)
COCA-COLA BTLG CO OF NY INC
5840 Borden Ave (11378-1106)
PHONE..................................718 416-7575
Sharon Smith, *Manager*
EMP: 20
SALES (corp-wide): 35.4B **Publicly Held**
SIC: 2086 Bottled & canned soft drinks
HQ: The Coca-Cola Bottling Company Of New York Inc
   2500 Windy Ridge Pkwy Se
   Atlanta GA 30339
   770 989-3000

(G-7831)
CRAFT CUSTOM WOODWORK CO INC
5949 56th Ave (11378-2324)
PHONE..................................718 821-2162
Yakov Roitman, *President*
▼ **EMP:** 10
SQ FT: 3,500
SALES: 600K **Privately Held**
SIC: 2434 2521 Wood kitchen cabinets; cabinets, office: wood

▲ = Import ▼ = Export
◆ = Import/Export

GEOGRAPHIC SECTION

Maspeth - Queens County (G-7860)

(G-7832)
CRAFTSMEN WOODWORKERS LTD
5865 Maspeth Ave (11378-2728)
PHONE..................718 326-3350
Joseph Finocchiaro, *Principal*
EMP: 25
SQ FT: 13,000
SALES (est): 3.8MM **Privately Held**
WEB: www.craftsmenwoodworkers.com
SIC: 2431 Millwork

(G-7833)
D & G SHEET METAL CO INC
5400 Grand Ave (11378-3006)
PHONE..................718 326-9111
Frank Doka, *President*
EMP: 12
SQ FT: 12,400
SALES (est): 1.3MM **Privately Held**
SIC: 3444 Sheet metalwork

(G-7834)
DAL-TILE CORPORATION
5840 55th Dr (11378-1152)
PHONE..................718 894-9574
Gary Guarascio, *Manager*
EMP: 6
SALES (corp-wide): 9.4B **Publicly Held**
WEB: www.mohawk.com
SIC: 2824 5032 Organic fibers, noncellulosic; ceramic wall & floor tile
HQ: Dal-Tile Corporation
7834 C F Hawn Fwy
Dallas TX 75217
214 398-1411

(G-7835)
DAYLIGHT TECHNOLOGY USA INC
5971 59th St (11378-3229)
PHONE..................973 255-8100
Reawei Lee, *President*
▲ **EMP:** 5 **EST:** 2013
SQ FT: 2,000
SALES (est): 2MM **Privately Held**
SIC: 3229 Bulbs for electric lights

(G-7836)
DIAMOND CORING & CUTTING INC
5919 55th St (11378-3103)
PHONE..................718 381-4545
David Obbink, *President*
EMP: 5
SALES: 80K **Privately Held**
SIC: 3531 Construction machinery

(G-7837)
DSI GROUP INC
Also Called: Ovation Instore
5713 49th St (11378-2020)
PHONE..................800 553-2202
Benjamin S Weshler, *Ch of Bd*
Robert Gray, *Vice Pres*
Jonathan Palmer, *Vice Pres*
Emily Pelton, *Vice Pres*
Frishta Yaqubie, *Project Mgr*
▲ **EMP:** 200
SQ FT: 130,000
SALES (est): 47.7MM **Privately Held**
SIC: 3993 Displays & cutouts, window & lobby

(G-7838)
DURA FOAM INC
6302 59th Ave (11378-2808)
PHONE..................718 894-2488
Antony Fontana, *President*
EMP: 35 **EST:** 1977
SQ FT: 50,000
SALES (est): 4.2MM **Privately Held**
SIC: 3086 Plastics foam products

(G-7839)
DYNASTY STAINLESS STEEL & META
5985 Maurice Ave (11378-1236)
PHONE..................718 205-6623
Peter Liou, *President*
EMP: 30
SQ FT: 120,000
SALES (est): 6.3MM **Privately Held**
SIC: 3444 1542 Sheet metalwork; nonresidential construction

(G-7840)
EAST CAST ENVLOPE GRAPHICS LLC
5615 55th Dr (11378-1108)
PHONE..................718 326-2424
Leslie Stern, *President*
Alfred Wilkowski, *COO*
Maribel Corchado, *Vice Pres*
Patrick Nunziante, *CFO*
EMP: 41
SQ FT: 78,000
SALES: 8MM **Privately Held**
WEB: www.interstate-envelope.com
SIC: 2677 Envelopes

(G-7841)
EAST COAST INTL TIRE INC
5746 Flushing Ave Bldg C (11378-3136)
PHONE..................718 386-9088
EMP: 10
SALES (est): 1.2MM **Privately Held**
SIC: 3011 Tires & inner tubes
PA: Qingdao Taining Industry Co., Ltd.
No.247, 308 National Highway, Hai'er Industrial Zone, Laoshan Di
Qingdao
532 886-0033

(G-7842)
ELDORADO COFFEE ROASTERS LTD
Also Called: Eldorado Coffee Distributors
5675 49th St (11378-2012)
PHONE..................718 418-4100
Segundo Martin, *President*
Andres Martin, *Vice Pres*
Juan Martin, *Vice Pres*
Albert Valdes, *Vice Pres*
Robert Magan, *Sales Dir*
▲ **EMP:** 80 **EST:** 1980
SQ FT: 54,000
SALES (est): 18.3MM **Privately Held**
WEB: www.eldoradocoffee.com
SIC: 2095 Coffee extracts; coffee roasting (except by wholesale grocers)

(G-7843)
EXTREME SPICES INC (PA)
Also Called: Sanaa Spices
5634 56th St Ste 36 (11378-1132)
PHONE..................917 496-4081
Marc Salih, *President*
▲ **EMP:** 2
SQ FT: 8,000
SALES (est): 1.3MM **Privately Held**
SIC: 2099 Spices, including grinding

(G-7844)
FALLON INC
5930 56th Rd (11378-2330)
PHONE..................718 326-7226
Steven Rosenblatt, *President*
EMP: 20
SQ FT: 27,000
SALES (est): 1.6MM **Privately Held**
WEB: www.structuralprocessing.com
SIC: 3471 Anodizing (plating) of metals or formed products

(G-7845)
FINAL DIMENSION INC
57-401 59th St Fl 1 Flr 1 (11378)
PHONE..................718 786-0100
Labros Magoutas, *President*
EMP: 5
SQ FT: 3,000
SALES: 500K **Privately Held**
SIC: 2511 Wood household furniture

(G-7846)
FORMOSA POLYMER CORPORATION
5641 55th Ave (11378-1104)
PHONE..................718 326-1769
Su Sheng Shyoung, *Ch of Bd*
▲ **EMP:** 6
SALES (est): 891.4K **Privately Held**
SIC: 2822 Ethylene-propylene rubbers, EPDM polymers

(G-7847)
FRANKS CUSHIONS INC
6302 59th Ave (11378-2808)
PHONE..................718 848-1216
Anthony Fontana, *President*
Maryann Fontana, *Bookkeeper*
▲ **EMP:** 15 **EST:** 1930
SQ FT: 10,000
SALES (est): 1.3MM **Privately Held**
WEB: www.frankscushions.com
SIC: 2392 Cushions & pillows

(G-7848)
GOTHIC CABINET CRAFT INC (PA)
5877 57th St (11378-3125)
PHONE..................347 881-1420
Theo Zaharopoulos, *President*
Greg Vassilakos, *Vice Pres*
EMP: 80
SQ FT: 100,000
SALES (est): 12.6MM **Privately Held**
WEB: www.gothiccabinetcraft.com
SIC: 2522 5712 2521 Cabinets, office: except wood; furniture stores; cabinets, office: wood

(G-7849)
GREAT AMERICAN DESSERT CO LLC
5842 Maurice Ave (11378-2333)
PHONE..................718 894-3494
Mike Goodman,
EMP: 55 **EST:** 1998
SALES (est): 7.6MM **Privately Held**
SIC: 2051 Cakes, bakery: except frozen

(G-7850)
GYM STORE INC
Also Called: GYM STORE.COM
5889 57th St (11378-3125)
PHONE..................718 366-7804
Christopher Kelly, *President*
▼ **EMP:** 5
SQ FT: 10,000
SALES: 2MM **Privately Held**
SIC: 3949 Exercise equipment; dumbbells & other weightlifting equipment; treadmills; gymnasium equipment

(G-7851)
HERGO ERGONOMIC SUPPORT (PA)
5601 55th Ave (11378-1104)
PHONE..................718 894-0639
Eli E Hertz, *CEO*
Barry J Goldsammler, *Senior VP*
Albert Hirschson, *Senior VP*
I Marilyn Hertz, *Vice Pres*
Kristen Speranza-Diamond, *Vice Pres*
◆ **EMP:** 40
SQ FT: 42,000
SALES (est): 5.6MM **Privately Held**
WEB: www.hergo.com
SIC: 3577 3699 3444 2542 Computer peripheral equipment; electrical equipment & supplies; sheet metalwork; partitions & fixtures, except wood; office furniture, except wood

(G-7852)
HI-TECH METALS INC
5920 56th Ave (11378-2325)
PHONE..................718 894-1212
Manny Tzilzelis, *President*
Menelaos Tzilvelis, *President*
Chris Christodoulou, *Vice Pres*
Jim Sculco, *Vice Pres*
Tom Robinson, *Project Mgr*
EMP: 50
SQ FT: 10,000
SALES (est): 14.9MM **Privately Held**
WEB: www.hi-techmetals.com
SIC: 3446 Architectural metalwork

(G-7853)
J & R UNIQUE GIFTWARE
5863 56th St (11378-3105)
PHONE..................718 821-0398
John Daidone, *Owner*
EMP: 20 **EST:** 2008
SALES (est): 930K **Privately Held**
SIC: 3999 Manufacturing industries

(G-7854)
JACK LUCKNER STEEL SHELVING CO
Also Called: Kart
5454 43rd St (11378-1028)
PHONE..................718 363-0500
Burton J Gold, *President*
Scott Mair, *Purchasing*
Alan Sheldon, *Controller*
Gardenia McCray, *Credit Mgr*
Gold Adam, *Manager*
EMP: 75 **EST:** 1947
SQ FT: 12,000
SALES (est): 7.4MM
SALES (corp-wide): 21.7MM **Privately Held**
WEB: www.karpinc.com
SIC: 2542 Shelving, office & store: except wood
PA: Karp Associates Inc.
260 Spagnoli Rd
Melville NY 11747
631 768-8300

(G-7855)
JAG LIGHTING
6105 56th Dr (11378-2407)
PHONE..................917 226-3575
Jerzy Golonka, *Principal*
EMP: 5
SALES (est): 379.9K **Privately Held**
SIC: 3648 Lighting equipment

(G-7856)
KARP OVERSEAS CORPORATION
5454 43rd St (11378-1028)
PHONE..................718 784-2105
Burton J Gold, *President*
EMP: 40
SQ FT: 30,000
SALES: 500K
SALES (corp-wide): 21.7MM **Privately Held**
WEB: www.karpinc.com
SIC: 3965 8742 Straight pins: steel or brass; sales (including sales management) consultant
PA: Karp Associates Inc.
260 Spagnoli Rd
Melville NY 11747
631 768-8300

(G-7857)
MASPETH PRESS INC
6620 Grand Ave (11378-2531)
PHONE..................718 429-2363
Frederick F Strobel, *President*
Frederick J Strobel, *President*
Linda Strobel, *Vice Pres*
EMP: 5
SQ FT: 2,000
SALES (est): 698.8K **Privately Held**
SIC: 2759 Letterpress printing

(G-7858)
MASPETH WELDING INC
5930 54th St (11378-3004)
PHONE..................718 497-5430
Jeffrey Anschlowar, *Ch of Bd*
Mike Aylward, *Project Mgr*
Lou Javier, *Project Mgr*
Vera Galvez, *Opers Staff*
Evelyn Agnoli, *VP Finance*
EMP: 40 **EST:** 1977
SQ FT: 48,000
SALES (est): 11.9MM **Privately Held**
WEB: www.maspethwelding.com
SIC: 3441 7692 Fabricated structural metal; welding repair

(G-7859)
MAXSUN CORPORATION (PA)
Also Called: Maxsun Furnishings
5711 49th St (11378-2020)
PHONE..................718 418-6800
Johnny Song Lin, *Ch of Bd*
Stephen Lin, *Manager*
▲ **EMP:** 17
SALES (est): 867.1K **Privately Held**
SIC: 2599 5719 Restaurant furniture, wood or metal; bar furniture; bar, restaurant & cafeteria furniture; lighting fixtures

(G-7860)
N Y CONTRACT SEATING INC
5560 60th St (11378-2338)
PHONE..................718 417-9298
John Glantzis, *President*
EMP: 7
SQ FT: 2,100

Maspeth - Queens County (G-7861)

SALES (est): 738.1K **Privately Held**
SIC: 2211 Upholstery fabrics, cotton

(G-7861)
NE & WS INC
6085 60th St (11378-3550)
PHONE..................................718 326-4699
Edward Nowakowski, *President*
Margaret Nowakowski, *Admin Sec*
EMP: 9
SQ FT: 4,900
SALES: 950K **Privately Held**
SIC: 2431 Staircases & stairs, wood; staircases, stairs & railings

(G-7862)
NELSON AIR DEVICE CORPORATION
Also Called: C W Sheet Metal
4628 54th Ave (11378-1012)
PHONE..................................718 729-3801
Nelson Blitz Jr, *President*
Thomas Howard, *COO*
Michael Doff, *Vice Pres*
Peter Unrath, *Vice Pres*
Mike Tedesco, *Project Mgr*
EMP: 200 **EST:** 1938
SQ FT: 20,000
SALES (est): 83.2MM **Privately Held**
WEB: www.nadcw.com
SIC: 3444 1711 Ducts, sheet metal; heating & air conditioning contractors

(G-7863)
NORAMPAC NEW YORK CITY INC
5515 Grand Ave (11378-3113)
PHONE..................................718 340-2100
Marc Andre Depin, *Ch of Bd*
EMP: 160 **EST:** 1906
SQ FT: 340,000
SALES (est): 34.8MM
SALES (corp-wide): 3.3B **Privately Held**
SIC: 2653 3993 2675 Boxes, corrugated: made from purchased materials; display items, corrugated: made from purchased materials; signs & advertising specialties; die-cut paper & board
PA: Cascades Inc
    404 Boul Marie-Victorin
    Kingsey Falls QC J0A 1
    819 363-5100

(G-7864)
NY TEMPERING LLC
6021 Flushing Ave (11378-3220)
PHONE..................................718 326-8989
Tim LI, *Manager*
▲ **EMP:** 5 **EST:** 2012
SALES (est): 838.7K **Privately Held**
SIC: 3272 Concrete products

(G-7865)
OWAYNE ENTERPRISES INC
4901 Maspeth Ave (11378-2219)
PHONE..................................718 326-2200
Owen M Mester, *President*
Wayne Wattenberg, *Vice Pres*
EMP: 38
SQ FT: 30,000
SALES (est): 7.1MM **Privately Held**
SIC: 2051 Cakes, pies & pastries; cakes, bakery: except frozen

(G-7866)
P & F INDUSTRIES OF NY CORP
Also Called: P and F Machine Industries
6006 55th Dr (11378-2351)
PHONE..................................718 894-3501
Frank Passantino, *President*
▲ **EMP:** 6
SQ FT: 7,000
SALES (est): 440K **Privately Held**
SIC: 3599 Machine shop, jobbing & repair

(G-7867)
PATCO TAPES INC
Also Called: Patco Group
5927 56th St (11378-3395)
PHONE..................................718 497-1527
Michael Rosenberg, *Corp Secy*
Joel Rosenberg, *Vice Pres*
EMP: 8 **EST:** 1973
SQ FT: 30,000
SALES: 2.5MM **Privately Held**
WEB: www.patcogroup.com
SIC: 2672 2671 5199 Gummed tape, cloth or paper base: from purchased materials; paper coated or laminated for packaging; packaging materials

(G-7868)
PURVI ENTERPRISES INCORPORATED
Also Called: Sinnara
5556 44th St (11378-2024)
PHONE..................................347 808-9448
Harshi Patel, *President*
▲ **EMP:** 7
SALES (est): 616.1K **Privately Held**
SIC: 3556 Dehydrating equipment, food processing

(G-7869)
QUEENS LDGR/GRENPOINT STAR INC
6960 Grand Ave Fl 2 (11378-1828)
P.O. Box 780376 (11378-0376)
PHONE..................................718 639-7000
Walter Sanchez, *President*
Tammy Sanchez, *General Mgr*
Benjamin Fang, *Safety Mgr*
EMP: 15
SALES (est): 587.6K **Privately Held**
SIC: 2711 Newspapers, publishing & printing

(G-7870)
RISA MANAGEMENT CORP
Also Called: Risa's
5501 43rd St Fl 3 (11378-2023)
PHONE..................................718 361-2606
D Savi Prashad, *CEO*
▲ **EMP:** 25
SQ FT: 50,000
SALES (est): 9.1MM **Privately Held**
WEB: www.risacorp.com
SIC: 3449 3441 Miscellaneous metalwork; fabricated structural metal

(G-7871)
ROCKMILLS STEEL PRODUCTS CORP
5912 54th St (11378-3004)
P.O. Box 234838, Great Neck (11023-4838)
PHONE..................................718 366-8300
Ann O'Brien, *President*
Daniel Obrien, *Shareholder*
Mary Obrien, *Shareholder*
EMP: 15
SQ FT: 25,200
SALES (est): 4MM **Privately Held**
WEB: www.rockmillsboilers.com
SIC: 3433 Boilers, low-pressure heating: steam or hot water

(G-7872)
T&B BAKERY CORP
5870 56th St (11378-3106)
PHONE..................................646 642-4300
Tomasz Eider, *President*
EMP: 6
SQ FT: 6,000
SALES: 2.8MM **Privately Held**
SIC: 2051 Bakery products, partially cooked (except frozen)

(G-7873)
TRI-STAR OFFSET CORP
6020 59th Pl Ste 3 (11378-3349)
PHONE..................................718 894-5555
Brian Nawroth, *CEO*
Al Nawroth, *President*
Mark Serwetz, *Vice Pres*
Nanette Roman, *Office Mgr*
EMP: 25 **EST:** 1977
SALES (est): 5.7MM **Privately Held**
SIC: 2752 Commercial printing, offset

(G-7874)
US ALLEGRO INC
5430 44th St (11378-1034)
PHONE..................................347 408-6601
Yuriy Bogutskiy, *President*
Marty McMahon, *Vice Pres*
EMP: 30
SQ FT: 10,000

SALES: 4MM **Privately Held**
SIC: 1442 Construction sand & gravel

(G-7875)
VALENTINE PACKAGING CORP
6020 59th Pl Ste 7 (11378-3349)
PHONE..................................718 418-6000
Daniel Suchow, *Vice Pres*
Richard Suchow, *Vice Pres*
Steven Suchow, *Vice Pres*
EMP: 18 **EST:** 1953
SQ FT: 25,000
SALES (est): 4.9MM **Privately Held**
SIC: 2653 7389 Sheets, corrugated: made from purchased materials; packaging & labeling services

Massapequa
Nassau County

(G-7876)
A & M APPEL DISTRIBUTING INC
500 N Atlanta Ave (11758-2000)
PHONE..................................516 735-1172
Michael Appel, *Principal*
EMP: 5
SALES (est): 320.4K **Privately Held**
SIC: 2051 5149 Bread, cake & related products; bakery products

(G-7877)
ACRAN SPILL CONTAINMENT INC (PA)
898 N Broadway Ste 1 (11758-2307)
PHONE..................................631 841-2300
John Deangelo, *President*
EMP: 11
SALES (est): 1.7MM **Privately Held**
SIC: 2655 Containers, liquid tight fiber: from purchased material

(G-7878)
ADAMS INTERIOR FABRICATIONS
8 Iroquois Pl (11758-7622)
PHONE..................................631 249-8282
Anthony E Adams, *President*
EMP: 11
SALES (est): 1.4MM **Privately Held**
SIC: 2431 2499 Millwork; decorative wood & woodwork

(G-7879)
CANOPY BOOKS LLC (PA)
28 N Wisconsin Ave 2-1 (11758-1705)
PHONE..................................516 354-4888
Clifford Brechner, *CEO*
EMP: 4
SALES (est): 1.7MM **Privately Held**
SIC: 2731 Book publishing

(G-7880)
HUNTINGTON SERVICES INC
Also Called: Vox Systems
727 N Broadway Ste A4 (11758-2348)
PHONE..................................516 795-8500
Richard Vience, *President*
Chris Vience, *Network Enginr*
Angel Larocca, *Executive*
EMP: 6
SQ FT: 1,200
SALES (est): 833.1K **Privately Held**
WEB: www.hsi4service.com
SIC: 7372 Prepackaged software

(G-7881)
LIGHT DENTAL LABS INC
250 N Syracuse Ave (11758-2026)
PHONE..................................516 785-7730
Frank Tomasino, *President*
EMP: 5
SALES: 750K **Privately Held**
SIC: 3843 Dental equipment & supplies

(G-7882)
PLURA BROADCAST INC (PA)
67 Grand Ave (11758-4947)
PHONE..................................516 997-5675
Ray Kalo, *Owner*
Azucena Soto, *Sales Mgr*
Leslie Brock, *Manager*
EMP: 7

SALES (est): 3MM **Privately Held**
SIC: 3679 Liquid crystal displays (LCD)

(G-7883)
PRINT IT HERE
185 Jerusalem Ave (11758-3308)
PHONE..................................516 308-7785
Shari Levine, *CEO*
EMP: 5
SALES (est): 342K **Privately Held**
SIC: 2752 Commercial printing, lithographic

(G-7884)
R KLEIN JEWELRY CO INC
Also Called: Klein & Company
39 Brockmeyer Dr (11758-7804)
PHONE..................................516 482-3260
Richard Klein, *President*
EMP: 55
SQ FT: 30,000
SALES (est): 4.7MM **Privately Held**
WEB: www.kleinjewelry.com
SIC: 3911 Jewelry, precious metal

(G-7885)
S SCHARF INC
278 N Richmond Ave (11758-3231)
PHONE..................................516 541-9552
Irwin Scharf, *President*
Jesse Scharf, *Treasurer*
EMP: 13 **EST:** 1935
SQ FT: 5,000
SALES (est): 1.2MM **Privately Held**
SIC: 3911 Jewelry, precious metal

(G-7886)
SUNRISE JEWELERS OF NY INC
1220 Sunrise Hwy (11758)
PHONE..................................516 541-1302
EMP: 8
SALES (est): 930K **Privately Held**
SIC: 3911 Mfg Precious Metal Jewelry

(G-7887)
SWIRLS TWIRLS INCORPORATED
4116 Sunrise Hwy (11758-5301)
PHONE..................................516 541-9400
EMP: 5 **EST:** 2011
SALES (est): 252.6K **Privately Held**
SIC: 2026 Yogurt

(G-7888)
WOODS KNIFE CORPORATION
19 Brooklyn Ave (11758-4855)
PHONE..................................516 798-4972
James S Woods, *President*
Ann Woods, *Vice Pres*
EMP: 24 **EST:** 1916
SQ FT: 2,600
SALES (est): 2.4MM **Privately Held**
SIC: 3423 3421 Knives, agricultural or industrial; cutlery

Massapequa Park
Nassau County

(G-7889)
CUSTOM MIX INC
31 Clark Blvd (11762-2609)
PHONE..................................516 797-7090
Matthew Lott, *Principal*
EMP: 9
SALES (est): 933.8K **Privately Held**
SIC: 3273 Ready-mixed concrete

(G-7890)
GENERAL DIE AND DIE CUTNG INC
11 Finch Ct (11762-3915)
PHONE..................................516 665-3584
Peter Vallone Sr, *CEO*
Peter Vallone Jr, *President*
Louann Vallone Pepi, *Vice Pres*
Richard Vallone, *Treasurer*
▲ **EMP:** 55 **EST:** 1961
SQ FT: 30,000

GEOGRAPHIC SECTION

Mattituck - Suffolk County (G-7917)

SALES (est): 52.4K **Privately Held**
WEB: www.gendiecut.com
SIC: **2653** 2675 3544 Display items, corrugated: made from purchased materials; boxes, corrugated: made from purchased materials; corrugated boxes, partitions, display items, sheets & pad; die-cut paper & board; special dies, tools, jigs & fixtures

(G-7891)
IMAGE SALES & MARKETING INC
106 Thornwood Rd (11762-4023)
PHONE..................................516 238-7023
Francine Walk, *President*
Steven Walk, *Vice Pres*
EMP: 2
SQ FT: 3,000
SALES: 4MM **Privately Held**
WEB: www.imagesalesny.com
SIC: **2754** Commercial printing, gravure

(G-7892)
INNOVATIVE SYSTEMS OF NEW YORK
201 Rose St (11762-1022)
PHONE..................................516 541-7410
Joseph Esposito, *President*
EMP: 5
SALES (est): 310.1K **Privately Held**
SIC: **3577** 7373 7378 Computer peripheral equipment; computer integrated systems design; computer maintenance & repair

(G-7393)
MASSAPEQUA POST
Also Called: Acj Communications
1045b Park Blvd (11762-2764)
PHONE..................................516 798-5100
Alfred James, *President*
Carolyn James, *Vice Pres*
EMP: 21
SALES (est): 475.6K **Privately Held**
WEB: www.massapequapost.com
SIC: **2711** Newspapers: publishing only, not printed on site

(G-7894)
PRINT COTTAGE LLC
1138 Lakeshore Dr (11762-2054)
PHONE..................................516 369-1749
James Altadonna, *Mng Member*
EMP: 10
SQ FT: 1,000
SALES: 4MM **Privately Held**
SIC: **2752** Commercial printing, lithographic

(G-7895)
TVI IMPORTS LLC
178 Abbey St (11762-3430)
PHONE..................................631 793-3077
Anthony Tisi, *Mng Member*
▲ EMP: 6
SQ FT: 2,500
SALES: 19MM **Privately Held**
SIC: **3089** Flower pots, plastic

(G-7896)
WORLD BUSINESS MEDIA LLC
Also Called: Gsn Government Security News
4770 Sunrise Hwy Ste 105 (11762-2911)
PHONE..................................212 344-0759
EMP: 12
SQ FT: 2,000
SALES: 2MM **Privately Held**
SIC: **2721** 7313 7382 Periodicals-Publishing/Printing Advertising Representative Security Systems Services

Massena
St. Lawrence County

(G-7897)
ALCOA CORPORATION
45 County Route 42 (13662-4249)
P.O. Box 5278 (13662-5278)
PHONE..................................412 315-2900
EMP: 480
SALES (corp-wide): 11.6B **Publicly Held**
SIC: **3355** Aluminum rolling & drawing
PA: Alcoa Corporation
 201 Isabella St Ste 500
 Pittsburgh PA 15212
 412 315-2900

(G-7898)
ALCOA USA CORP
45 County Route 42 (13662-4249)
PHONE..................................315 764-4011
EMP: 6
SALES (corp-wide): 11.6B **Publicly Held**
SIC: **3334** Primary aluminum
HQ: Alcoa Usa Corp.
 201 Isabella St Ste 500
 Pittsburgh PA 15212
 212 518-5400

(G-7899)
ALCOA USA CORP
1814 State Highway 131 (13662-4210)
P.O. Box 5278 (13662-5278)
PHONE..................................315 764-4106
Kevin Condlin, *Engineer*
Bryan Eggleston, *Info Tech Mgr*
EMP: 33
SALES (corp-wide): 11.6B **Publicly Held**
SIC: **3353** Aluminum sheet, plate & foil
HQ: Alcoa Usa Corp.
 201 Isabella St Ste 500
 Pittsburgh PA 15212
 212 518-5400

(G-7900)
ARCONIC INC
45 County Route 42 (13662-4249)
PHONE..................................315 764-4011
Bryan Murphy, *Manager*
EMP: 7
SALES (corp-wide): 12.9B **Publicly Held**
SIC: **3355** 3353 3354 3463 Aluminum rolling & drawing; aluminum sheet & strip; aluminum extruded products; aluminum forgings
PA: Arconic Inc.
 390 Park Ave Fl 12
 New York NY 10022
 212 836-2758

(G-7901)
CURRAN RENEWABLE ENERGY LLC
20 Commerce Dr (13662-2576)
PHONE..................................315 769-2000
Patrick Curran, *Mng Member*
▲ EMP: 30
SALES (est): 19.1MM **Privately Held**
SIC: **2421** Sawmills & planing mills, general

(G-7902)
GENERAL MOTORS LLC
56 Chevrolet Rd (13662-1378)
PHONE..................................315 764-2000
Scott Wifniewski, *Branch Mgr*
Dan Flores, *Manager*
EMP: 500 **Publicly Held**
SIC: **3369** 3714 Castings, except die-castings, precision; motor vehicle parts & accessories
HQ: General Motors Llc
 300 Renaissance Ctr L1
 Detroit MI 48243

(G-7903)
HANYAN & HIGGINS COMPANY INC
9772 State Highway 56 (13662-3416)
PHONE..................................315 769-8838
Donald Walters, *CEO*
EMP: 5
SALES (est): 268.2K **Privately Held**
SIC: **3297** Castable refractories, nonclay

(G-7904)
KINGSTON PHARMA LLC
Also Called: Kingston Pharmaceuticals
5 County Route 42 (13662-1569)
PHONE..................................315 705-4019
Venkat Kakani, *CEO*
Sridhar Thyagarajan, *Controller*
EMP: 82
SQ FT: 32,778
SALES: 875K **Privately Held**
SIC: **2834** Druggists' preparations (pharmaceuticals)

(G-7905)
MASSENA METALS INC
86 S Racquette River Rd (13662-4318)
P.O. Box 5282 (13662-5282)
PHONE..................................315 769-3846
J Goldstein, *President*
Lawrence Leibo, *Corp Secy*
Gary Master, *Vice Pres*
EMP: 15
SQ FT: 10,000
SALES (est): 1.7MM **Privately Held**
SIC: **3365** 5093 5051 Aluminum foundries; ferrous metal scrap & waste; steel

(G-7906)
MUSTARD TIN
6100 Saint Lawrence Ctr (13662-3214)
PHONE..................................315 769-8409
EMP: 5 **EST:** 2012
SALES (est): 318.7K **Privately Held**
SIC: **3356** Tin

(G-7907)
PURINEPHARMA LLC
5 County Route 42 (13662-1569)
PHONE..................................732 485-1400
Venkat Kakani, *Manager*
EMP: 5
SALES (est): 592.3K **Privately Held**
SIC: **2834** Pharmaceutical preparations

(G-7908)
SEAWAY TIMBER HARVESTING INC (PA)
15121 State Highway 37 (13662-6194)
PHONE..................................315 769-5970
Patrick Curran, *President*
Tim Curran, *Vice Pres*
Tricia Terry, *Manager*
Lee Curran, *Admin Sec*
EMP: 59
SQ FT: 15,000
SALES (est): 11.9MM **Privately Held**
SIC: **2411** 4789 Logging; log loading & unloading

(G-7909)
STUBBS PRINTING INC
271 E Orvis St Ste B (13662-2352)
P.O. Box 110 (13662-0110)
PHONE..................................315 769-8641
Karen Stubbs, *President*
Robert T Stubbs, *Vice Pres*
EMP: 5
SQ FT: 2,000
SALES (est): 390K **Privately Held**
SIC: **2752** Commercial printing, offset

(G-7910)
UPSTONE MATERIALS INC
Also Called: Massena Ready Mix
539 S Main St (13662-2537)
P.O. Box 825, Plattsburgh (12901)
PHONE..................................315 764-0251
James Otis, *District Mgr*
EMP: 5
SQ FT: 9,608
SALES (corp-wide): 95.5MM **Privately Held**
WEB: www.graymont-ab.com
SIC: **3273** Ready-mixed concrete
HQ: Upstone Materials Inc.
 111 Quarry Rd
 Plattsburgh NY 12901
 518 561-5321

Mastic
Suffolk County

(G-7911)
EAST END SIGN DESIGN INC
1425 Montauk Hwy (11950-2916)
PHONE..................................631 399-2574
Joseph Colucci, *President*
John Dugan, *Manager*
Mike Powell, *Manager*
EMP: 5
SALES (est): 580.6K **Privately Held**
SIC: **3993** Signs, not made in custom sign painting shops

Mastic Beach
Suffolk County

(G-7912)
VINCENT GENOVESE
Also Called: Long Island Radiant Heat
19 Woodmere Dr (11951-2016)
PHONE..................................631 281-8170
Vincent Genovese, *Owner*
EMP: 6
SALES (est): 674.5K **Privately Held**
SIC: **3634** 5074 8711 1711 Heating units, electric (radiant heat): baseboard or wall; heating equipment & panels, solar; heating & ventilation engineering; heating & air conditioning contractors; industrial furnaces & ovens; heating equipment, except electric

Mattituck
Suffolk County

(G-7913)
AMEREON LTD
800 Wickham Ave (11952-1684)
P.O. Box 1200 (11952-0921)
PHONE..................................631 298-5100
Joanna Paulsen, *President*
John Clauss, *Vice Pres*
EMP: 5
SQ FT: 30,000
SALES (est): 594.3K **Privately Held**
WEB: www.amereon.com
SIC: **2731** Books: publishing only

(G-7914)
LIEB CELLARS LLC
Also Called: Lieb Cellars Tasting Room
35 Cox Neck Rd (11952-1458)
P.O. Box 907, Cutchogue (11935-0907)
PHONE..................................631 298-1942
Gary Madden, *General Mgr*
EMP: 20
SALES (est): 1.2MM **Privately Held**
WEB: www.liebcellars.com
SIC: **2084** Wines
PA: Lieb Cellars Llc
 13050 Oregon Rd
 Cutchogue NY 11935

(G-7915)
NORTH FORK WOOD WORKS INC
5175 Route 48 (11952-3260)
P.O. Box 1407, Southold (11971-0938)
PHONE..................................631 255-4028
Scott Edgett, *CEO*
Rachel Terry, *Office Mgr*
EMP: 9
SALES (est): 1.1MM **Privately Held**
SIC: **2431** Millwork

(G-7916)
PREMIUM WINE GROUP LLC
35 Cox Neck Rd (11952-1458)
PHONE..................................631 298-1900
Russell Hearn, *Principal*
John Leo, *Principal*
▲ EMP: 22 **EST:** 2001
SALES (est): 3.5MM **Privately Held**
WEB: www.premiumwinegroup.com
SIC: **2084** Wines

(G-7917)
SHINN WINERY LLC
Also Called: Shinn Vineyard
2000 Oregon Rd (11952-1762)
PHONE..................................631 804-0367
Robert Rudko, *General Mgr*
Andi Parks, *Exec VP*
Barbara Shinn,
▲ EMP: 7
SALES (est): 660K **Privately Held**
SIC: **2084** Wines

Mattituck - Suffolk County (G-7918)

(G-7918)
TIMES REVIEW NEWSPAPER CORP
Also Called: News Review, The
7780 Main Rd (11952-1539)
PHONE..................631 354-8031
Troy Gustavson, *President*
Laura Huber, *Editor*
Joe Werkmeister, *Editor*
Karen Cullen, *Manager*
Mary Joe Wrynn, *Manager*
EMP: 33
SQ FT: 6,000
SALES (est): 3.2MM **Privately Held**
WEB: www.timesreview.com
SIC: 2711 2791 Newspapers: publishing only, not printed on site; typesetting

Mayfield
Fulton County

(G-7919)
BART OSTRANDER TRCKG LOG CORP
1556 State Highway 30 (12117-3755)
PHONE..................518 661-6535
Bart D Ostrander, *President*
Evette Ostrander, *Admin Sec*
EMP: 9
SALES (est): 1.2MM **Privately Held**
SIC: 2411 4789 7389 Logging; log loading & unloading;

Mayville
Chautauqua County

(G-7920)
EMPIRE DEVLEOPMENT
5889 Magnolia Stedman Rd (14757-9420)
PHONE..................716 789-2097
Micah Meredith, *Principal*
EMP: 8 EST: 2007
SALES (est): 996.7K **Privately Held**
SIC: 3423 Jewelers' hand tools

(G-7921)
KLEINFELDER JOHN
Also Called: Chautauqua Iron Works
5239 W Lake Rd (14757-9507)
PHONE..................716 753-3163
John Kleinfelder, *Owner*
EMP: 5
SQ FT: 990
SALES (est): 467.8K **Privately Held**
SIC: 3441 3446 5947 4491 Fabricated structural metal; ornamental metalwork; artcraft & carvings; docks, incl. buildings & facilities: operation & maintenance; boat lifts; welding on site

(G-7922)
LYN JO ENTERPRISES LTD
Also Called: Standard Portable
Rr 394 Box 147 (14757)
PHONE..................716 753-2776
Julie Baraniewicz, *President*
EMP: 7
SQ FT: 288
SALES: 750K **Privately Held**
WEB: www.standardportable.com
SIC: 3496 3699 Lamp frames, wire; trouble lights

(G-7923)
RANGE RSURCES - APPALACHIA LLC
Also Called: Lomak Petroleum
100 E Chautauqua St (14757-1040)
P.O. Box 187 (14757-0187)
PHONE..................716 753-3385
Doug Stebbins, *Manager*
EMP: 30
SALES (corp-wide): 2.6B **Publicly Held**
WEB: www.gl-energy.com
SIC: 1382 Oil & gas exploration services
HQ: Range Resources - Appalachia, Llc.
3000 Town Center Blvd
Canonsburg PA 15317
724 743-6700

(G-7924)
STEDMAN ENERGY INC
4411 Canterbury Dr (14757-9610)
P.O. Box 1006, Chautauqua (14722-1006)
PHONE..................716 789-3018
Kevin E McChesney, *President*
EMP: 7
SALES: 100K **Privately Held**
SIC: 1311 Crude petroleum production; natural gas production

Mc Connellsville
Oneida County

(G-7925)
HARDEN FURNITURE LLC (PA)
8550 Mill Pond Way (13401-1844)
PHONE..................315 675-3600
Gregory Harden, *President*
Mike Allen, *Superintendent*
Andrew Clark, *Vice Pres*
Pete Raynford, *Vice Pres*
Ryan Dust, *Project Engr*
◆ **EMP:** 183
SQ FT: 400,000
SALES: 19.7MM **Privately Held**
WEB: www.cnywinter.com
SIC: 2512 2521 5021 2511 Upholstered household furniture; living room furniture: upholstered on wood frames; wood office furniture; desks, office: wood; bookcases, office: wood; furniture; dining room furniture: wood

Mc Graw
Cortland County

(G-7926)
COUTURE TIMBER HARVESTING
2760 Phelps Rd (13101-9561)
P.O. Box 66, Cortland (13045-0066)
PHONE..................607 836-4719
EMP: 7
SALES (est): 653.5K **Privately Held**
SIC: 2411 Logging

(G-7927)
HIGGINS SUPPLY COMPANY INC
Also Called: Higgins Supl Co
18-25 South St (13101)
PHONE..................607 836-6474
Terri Maxson, *Ch of Bd*
Cathy Gregg, *President*
Glenn Doran, *Vice Pres*
Terri L Gutchess, *Vice Pres*
EMP: 65 EST: 1921
SQ FT: 30,000
SALES (est): 9.4MM **Privately Held**
SIC: 3842 2342 Orthopedic appliances; corset accessories: clasps, stays, etc.

(G-7928)
MCGRAW WOOD PRODUCTS LLC (PA)
1 Charles St (13101-9190)
P.O. Box 652 (13101-0652)
PHONE..................607 836-6465
Harold J Ousby III, *Mng Member*
EMP: 30 EST: 2006
SQ FT: 100,000
SALES (est): 5.7MM **Privately Held**
WEB: www.mcgrawwoodproducts.com
SIC: 2511 2499 2441 2434 Silverware chests: wood; decorative wood & woodwork; nailed wood boxes & shook; wood kitchen cabinets

Mechanicville
Saratoga County

(G-7929)
ALABU INC
Also Called: Alabu Skin Care
30 Graves Rd (12118-3218)
PHONE..................518 665-0411
Mary Claire, *President*
Dean Mayes, *President*
Hal Mayes, *COO*
EMP: 7
SALES (est): 1MM **Privately Held**
WEB: www.alabu.com
SIC: 2844 Toilet preparations

(G-7930)
ALONZO FIRE WORKS DISPLAY INC (PA)
12 County Route 75 (12118-3357)
PHONE..................518 664-9994
Jeff Alonzo, *President*
▲ **EMP:** 8
SALES (est): 654K **Privately Held**
WEB: www.alonzofireworks.com
SIC: 2899 7999 Fireworks; fireworks display service

(G-7931)
GLAXOSMITHKLINE LLC
108 Woodfield Blvd (12118-3038)
PHONE..................518 852-9637
EMP: 27
SALES (corp-wide): 39.8B **Privately Held**
SIC: 2834 Pharmaceutical preparations
HQ: Glaxosmithkline Llc
5 Crescent Dr
Philadelphia PA 19112
215 751-4000

(G-7932)
POLYSET COMPANY INC
65 Hudson Ave (12118-4517)
P.O. Box 111 (12118-0111)
PHONE..................518 664-6000
Niladri Ghoshal, *President*
April Mullen, *Purchasing*
Tom Meacham, *Engineer*
Rajat Ghoshal, *Treasurer*
Terry Eck, *Regl Sales Mgr*
◆ **EMP:** 37
SQ FT: 40,000
SALES (est): 16MM **Privately Held**
WEB: www.polyset.com
SIC: 2819 3087 2952 2891 Industrial inorganic chemicals; custom compound purchased resins; coating compounds, tar; adhesives & sealants

(G-7933)
RALOID TOOL CO INC
Hc 146 (12118)
P.O. Box 551 (12118-0551)
PHONE..................518 664-4261
Ronald Brownell, *President*
David Brownell, *Vice Pres*
Stephen Shafts, *Project Mgr*
Molly Montanye, *Info Tech Mgr*
EMP: 19 EST: 1945
SQ FT: 23,200
SALES (est): 3.5MM **Privately Held**
WEB: www.raloidtool.com
SIC: 3544 3542 Special dies & tools; die casting & extruding machines

(G-7934)
ST SILICONES INC
95 N Central Ave (12118-1543)
PHONE..................518 664-0745
David A Scagnelli, *President*
EMP: 5
SQ FT: 3,500
SALES: 500K **Privately Held**
WEB: www.st-silicones.com
SIC: 1446 Silica mining

(G-7935)
VOICES FOR ALL LLC
29 Moreland Dr (12118-3630)
PHONE..................518 261-1664
Paul Benedetti,
Stan Denis,
EMP: 8
SALES (est): 858.1K **Privately Held**
SIC: 3679 Voice controls

Medford
Suffolk County

(G-7936)
ACCUVEIN INC
3243 Route 112 Ste 2 (11763-1438)
P.O. Box 1303, Huntington (11743-0657)
PHONE..................816 997-9400
Ron Goldman, *Ch of Bd*
David Beahm, *Area Mgr*
Daniel Delaney, *COO*
Heidi Siegel, *COO*
Jeff Schou, *Vice Pres*
EMP: 53
SQ FT: 5,000
SALES (est): 11MM **Privately Held**
SIC: 3829 Thermometers, including digital: clinical

(G-7937)
AMERICAN AVIONIC TECH CORP
Also Called: Aatc
25 Industrial Blvd (11763-2243)
PHONE..................631 924-8200
Amin J Khoury, *Ch of Bd*
Werner Lieberherr, *Ch of Bd*
Salvatore F Scilingo, *President*
David Eckland, *CFO*
EMP: 60
SQ FT: 12,000
SALES (est): 17.6MM **Publicly Held**
WEB: www.aatcorp.com
SIC: 3699 8711 Electrical equipment & supplies; engineering services
HQ: Tsi Group, Inc.
94 Tide Mill Rd
Hampton NH 03842

(G-7938)
B & R INDUSTRIES INC
Also Called: Manifold Center, The
12 Commercial Blvd (11763-1523)
PHONE..................631 736-2275
Christian P Burian, *President*
EMP: 12
SQ FT: 64,000
SALES (est): 2.2MM **Privately Held**
WEB: www.bnrindustries.com
SIC: 3599 Machine shop, jobbing & repair

(G-7939)
BLAIR INDUSTRIES INC (PA)
3671 Horseblock Rd (11763-2240)
PHONE..................631 924-6600
William R Lehmann Jr, *Ch of Bd*
John Andrucci, *QC Dir*
Gabrielle Piazza, *Manager*
▲ **EMP:** 50
SQ FT: 8,000
SALES (est): 7.9MM **Privately Held**
WEB: www.blair-hsm.com
SIC: 3728 Aircraft landing assemblies & brakes

(G-7940)
BOILERMATIC WELDING INDS INC (PA)
17 Peconic Ave (11763-3295)
PHONE..................631 654-1341
Shasho Pole, *Ch of Bd*
John Wojnowski, *Vice Pres*
Anthony Sala, *Safety Dir*
Tom Slattery, *Project Mgr*
Joe Vorraro, *Purch Agent*
EMP: 34
SQ FT: 3,200
SALES (est): 20.2MM **Privately Held**
WEB: www.boilermatic.com
SIC: 7692 Welding repair

(G-7941)
CHEMBIO DIAGNOSTIC SYSTEMS INC
3661 Horseblock Rd Ste A (11763-2244)
PHONE..................631 924-1135
Javan Esfandiari, *Senior VP*
Tom Ippolito, *Vice Pres*
Michael Steele, *Vice Pres*
Karen Keskinen, *Research*
Richard Larkin, *CFO*
▲ **EMP:** 105
SQ FT: 14,000

GEOGRAPHIC SECTION

Medford - Suffolk County (G-7968)

SALES (est): 20.4MM
SALES (corp-wide): 24MM **Publicly Held**
WEB: www.chembio.com
SIC: 2835 In vitro & in vivo diagnostic substances
PA: Chembio Diagnostics, Inc.
3661 Horseblock Rd Ste C
Medford NY 11763
631 924-1135

(G-7942)
CHEMBIO DIAGNOSTICS INC (PA)
3661 Horseblock Rd Ste C (11763-2225)
PHONE.................................631 924-1135
Sharon Klugewicz, *CEO*
Katherine L Davis, *Ch of Bd*
Robert Passas, *President*
John J Sperzel III, *President*
Javan Esfandiari, *Exec VP*
▲ EMP: 131
SQ FT: 39,660
SALES: 24MM **Publicly Held**
WEB: www.chembio.com
SIC: 2835 In vitro & in vivo diagnostic substances

(G-7943)
CHROMA COMMUNICATIONS INC
2030 Route 112 (11763-3644)
P.O. Box 340, Bohemia (11716-0340)
PHONE.................................631 289-8871
Peter Gulyas, *President*
EMP: 5
SALES (est): 310K **Privately Held**
SIC: 2759 Commercial printing

(G-7944)
CLARKE HESS COMMUNICATION RES
3243 Route 112 Ste 1 (11763-1438)
PHONE.................................631 698-3350
Kenneth Salz, *President*
Doante Alessi, *Vice Pres*
EMP: 8
SQ FT: 4,500
SALES (est): 1.6MM **Privately Held**
WEB: www.clarke-hess.com
SIC: 3825 Test equipment for electronic & electrical circuits

(G-7945)
DATA FLOW INC
6 Balsam Dr (11763-4304)
PHONE.................................631 436-9200
Timothy Stead, *President*
Joseph Crook, *Vice Pres*
EMP: 8
SQ FT: 8,500
SALES: 1.7MM **Privately Held**
WEB: www.printtomail.com
SIC: 2759 Commercial printing

(G-7946)
ENECON CORPORATION (PA)
Also Called: High Prfmce Plymr Cmposits Div
6 Platinum Ct (11763-2251)
PHONE.................................516 349-0022
Andrew A Janczik, *Ch of Bd*
Andrew A Janczak, *President*
John McDonough, *District Mgr*
Michael Tedesco, *Exec VP*
Matt Goldberg, *Vice Pres*
◆ EMP: 56
SQ FT: 30,000
SALES (est): 10.7MM **Privately Held**
WEB: www.enecon.com
SIC: 2851 Coating, air curing

(G-7947)
ENEFLUX ARMTEK MAGNETICS INC (HQ)
6 Platinum Ct (11763-2251)
PHONE.................................516 576-3434
Tony Mantella, *President*
Andrew Janczak, *Exec VP*
Edward Krensel, *Treasurer*
Deann Dambrosio, *Accounts Mgr*
EMP: 4 EST: 1997
SQ FT: 20,000

SALES (est): 3.1MM
SALES (corp-wide): 10.7MM **Privately Held**
WEB: www.eamagnetics.com
SIC: 3264 Magnets, permanent: ceramic or ferrite
PA: Enecon Corporation
6 Platinum Ct
Medford NY 11763
516 349-0022

(G-7948)
GLOBAL TISSUE GROUP INC (PA)
870 Expressway Dr S (11763-2027)
PHONE.................................631 924-3019
Meir Elnekaveh, *CEO*
Freydoun Elhekaveh, *Ch of Bd*
David Shaoul, *President*
Philip Shaoul, *COO*
Daniel David, *Exec VP*
◆ EMP: 50
SQ FT: 90,000
SALES (est): 14.1MM **Privately Held**
WEB: www.gtgtissue.com
SIC: 2621 Paper mills

(G-7949)
H B MILLWORK INC (PA)
500 Long Island Ave (11763-2510)
PHONE.................................631 289-8086
Timothy Hollowell, *President*
Michael Hollowell, *Vice Pres*
EMP: 21
SQ FT: 6,000
SALES (est): 2.8MM **Privately Held**
WEB: www.hbmillwork.com
SIC: 2431 2436 2426 Millwork; softwood veneer & plywood; hardwood dimension & flooring mills

(G-7950)
HAMPTON ART LLC
19 Scouting Blvd (11763-2220)
PHONE.................................631 924-1335
Ronald T Gallagher,
Kevin T Gallagher,
Steven G Gallagher,
▲ EMP: 44
SQ FT: 13,500
SALES: 5.6MM **Privately Held**
WEB: www.hamptonart.com
SIC: 3069 3953 Stationers' rubber sundries; marking devices

(G-7951)
HAMPTON TECHNOLOGIES LLC
19 Scouting Blvd (11763-2220)
PHONE.................................631 924-1335
Joseph Sowinski, *Manager*
Ron Gallagher,
Ronald Gallagher, *Administration*
Kevin Gallagher,
Steven Gallagher,
▲ EMP: 30
SQ FT: 13,500
SALES (est): 6.1MM **Privately Held**
WEB: www.hamptonsecurity.com
SIC: 3699 Security devices

(G-7952)
HEALTHY BASEMENT SYSTEMS LLC
79 Cedarhurst Ave (11763-1503)
PHONE.................................516 650-9046
William Simone,
EMP: 14
SALES (est): 1.4MM **Privately Held**
WEB: www.healthybasementsystems.com
SIC: 3272 Areaways, basement window: concrete

(G-7953)
HSM MACHINE WORKS INC (PA)
Also Called: Blair-Hsm
3671 Horseblock Rd (11763-2295)
PHONE.................................631 924-6600
William R Lehmann Jr, *Ch of Bd*
Kevin Dembinski, *President*
Bill Lehmann, *President*
Scott Wigley, *General Mgr*
Rex Betita, *QC Mgr*
▲ EMP: 39 EST: 1951
SQ FT: 30,000

SALES (est): 8.2MM **Privately Held**
SIC: 3599 3728 Machine shop, jobbing & repair; aircraft parts & equipment

(G-7954)
ISLAND CUSTOM STAIRS INC
23 Scouting Blvd Unit C (11763-2245)
PHONE.................................631 205-5335
Christopher L Brett, *President*
Carol Hodosky, *Treasurer*
EMP: 7
SQ FT: 5,800
SALES: 900K **Privately Held**
SIC: 3534 Elevators & moving stairways

(G-7955)
JACOBI TOOL & DIE MFG INC
Also Called: Jacobi Industries
131 Middle Island Rd (11763-1517)
P.O. Box 50 (11763-0050)
PHONE.................................631 736-5394
Roger Jacobi, *Principal*
EMP: 6
SQ FT: 10,000
SALES (est): 907.4K **Privately Held**
WEB: www.jacobiindustries.com
SIC: 3599 Machine shop, jobbing & repair

(G-7956)
K DYMOND INDUSTRIES INC
16 Commercial Blvd (11763-1523)
PHONE.................................631 828-0826
EMP: 11
SALES (est): 1.3MM **Privately Held**
SIC: 3999 Manufacturing industries

(G-7957)
L VII RESILIENT LLC
108 Cherry Ln (11763-4022)
PHONE.................................631 987-5819
John Scelsi, *Mng Member*
EMP: 12 EST: 2012
SALES (est): 1MM **Privately Held**
SIC: 2676 7389 Tampons, sanitary: made from purchased paper;

(G-7958)
LIVING DOORS INC
22 Scouting Blvd Ste 3 (11763-2260)
P.O. Box 95, Yaphank (11980-0095)
PHONE.................................631 924-5393
Don Plante, *President*
EMP: 10
SQ FT: 4,000
SALES: 700K **Privately Held**
WEB: www.livingdoors.com
SIC: 2431 Doors, wood

(G-7959)
MACHOONJDGROUP
18 Victorian Ln (11763-2574)
PHONE.................................856 345-4689
Alphajour Ahmed Bah III, *Principal*
Chierno Bah, *Administration*
EMP: 5
SALES (est): 145K **Privately Held**
SIC: 2046 Starch

(G-7960)
MACROLINK INC
25 Scouting Blvd Ste 1 (11763-2243)
PHONE.................................631 924-8200
Mark Cordivari, *CEO*
EMP: 50 EST: 1975
SQ FT: 30,000
SALES (est): 17.1MM **Publicly Held**
WEB: www.macrolink.com
SIC: 3823 3577 Computer interface equipment for industrial process control; computer peripheral equipment
HQ: B/E Aerospace, Inc.
1400 Corporate Center Way
Wellington FL 33414
561 791-5000

(G-7961)
MICRO CONTRACT MANUFACTURING
27 Scouting Blvd Unit E (11763-2286)
PHONE.................................631 738-7874
Michael L Matula, *President*
Thomas Degasperi, *President*
Josephine Matula, *Corp Secy*
EMP: 90
SQ FT: 12,000

SALES (est): 16MM **Privately Held**
WEB: www.microcontractmfg.com
SIC: 3674 Semiconductors & related devices

(G-7962)
MTK ELECTRONICS INC
1 National Blvd (11763-2252)
PHONE.................................631 924-7666
David Radford, *President*
Lorraine Coloprisco, *Purch Mgr*
George Scheriff, *Manager*
▲ EMP: 35
SQ FT: 15,000
SALES (est): 8.1MM **Privately Held**
WEB: www.mtkelec.com
SIC: 3677 3675 Filtration devices, electronic; electronic capacitors

(G-7963)
PHYMETRIX INC
28 Scouting Blvd Ste C (11763-2250)
PHONE.................................631 627-3950
Bedros Bedrossian, *President*
Ani Omer, *Vice Pres*
EMP: 9
SQ FT: 10,000
SALES: 3MM **Privately Held**
SIC: 3826 8734 Moisture analyzers; calibration & certification

(G-7964)
POSIMECH INC
15 Scouting Blvd Unit 3 (11763-2254)
PHONE.................................631 924-5959
Steven R Fazio, *President*
Steven Fazio, *President*
Dan George, *VP Mfg*
Stephanie Giglio, *Bookkeeper*
▼ EMP: 22
SQ FT: 12,236
SALES (est): 3.6MM **Privately Held**
WEB: www.posimech.com
SIC: 3599 3728 Machine shop, jobbing & repair; aircraft assemblies, subassemblies & parts

(G-7965)
SAYEDA MANUFACTURING CORP
20 Scouting Blvd (11763-2221)
PHONE.................................631 345-2525
Ali Khan, *President*
EMP: 10
SQ FT: 5,000
SALES (est): 810K **Privately Held**
WEB: www.sayeda.com
SIC: 3679 Harness assemblies for electronic use: wire or cable

(G-7966)
STAR READY MIX INC
172 Peconic Ave (11763-3244)
P.O. Box 371 (11763-0371)
PHONE.................................631 289-8787
Joseph A Di Silva, *President*
Frank Otero, *Vice Pres*
Thomas Hess, *Treasurer*
EMP: 13
SQ FT: 1,000
SALES (est): 1.6MM **Privately Held**
SIC: 3273 Ready-mixed concrete

(G-7967)
TINT WORLD
3165 Route 112 (11763-1407)
PHONE.................................631 458-1999
Timothy Kjaer, *Principal*
EMP: 5
SALES (est): 484.7K **Privately Held**
SIC: 3089 5013 Automotive parts, plastic; automotive supplies & parts

(G-7968)
WAVERLY IRON CORP
25 Commercial Blvd (11763-1531)
PHONE.................................631 732-2800
Anthony Pizzichemi, *President*
Joseph Pizzichemi, *Project Mgr*
EMP: 21
SQ FT: 7,000
SALES (est): 5.3MM **Privately Held**
WEB: www.waverlyiron.com
SIC: 3441 Fabricated structural metal

Medford - Suffolk County (G-7969)

(G-7969)
WOOD INNOVATIONS OF SUFFOLK
266 Middle Island Rd # 8 (11763-1525)
PHONE.................................631 698-2345
Gino Genna, *President*
Mary Weiss, *Treasurer*
EMP: 6
SQ FT: 3,000
SALES (est): 856.3K **Privately Held**
WEB: www.woodin.com
SIC: 2431 2499 5712 1799 Interior & ornamental woodwork & trim; exterior & ornamental woodwork & trim; decorative wood & woodwork; outdoor & garden furniture; fence construction

Medina
Orleans County

(G-7970)
ASSOCIATED BRANDS INC
4001 Salt Works Rd (14103-9578)
PHONE.................................585 798-3475
Scott Greenwood, *President*
Paul Kerr, *Opers Mgr*
Derek Briffett, *CFO*
Marylou Porter, *Executive*
◆ **EMP:** 266
SQ FT: 340,000
SALES (est): 54.6MM
SALES (corp-wide): 6.3B **Publicly Held**
WEB: www.associatedbrands.com
SIC: 2034 2043 2066 2099 Fruits, dried or dehydrated, except freeze-dried; vegetables, dried or dehydrated (except freeze-dried); cereal breakfast foods; chocolate & cocoa products; food preparations
HQ: Associated Brands Inc
944 Highway 8
Stoney Creek ON L8E 5
905 643-1211

(G-7971)
BARNES METAL FINISHING INC
3932 Salt Works Rd (14103-9546)
P.O. Box 517 (14103-0517)
PHONE.................................585 798-4817
Wilfred Barnes, *President*
Darrel Barnes, *Vice Pres*
EMP: 14
SQ FT: 6,000
SALES: 800K **Privately Held**
SIC: 3471 Polishing, metals or formed products

(G-7972)
BAXTER HEALTHCARE CORPORATION
711 Park Ave (14103-1078)
PHONE.................................800 356-3454
Christopher Peticca, *Accounts Mgr*
Nelson Tatterson, *Branch Mgr*
EMP: 380
SALES (corp-wide): 10.5B **Publicly Held**
SIC: 2834 Pharmaceutical preparations
HQ: Baxter Healthcare Corporation
1 Baxter Pkwy
Deerfield IL 60015
224 948-2000

(G-7973)
BMP AMERICA INC
Also Called: B M P
11625 Maple Ridge Rd (14103-9710)
PHONE.................................585 798-0950
Edward D Andrew, *CEO*
Peter Milicia, *President*
Peter Rodrigue, *Business Mgr*
Jason Gillard, *Vice Pres*
Alan Lebold, *Vice Pres*
▲ **EMP:** 112
SQ FT: 40,000
SALES (est): 26.3MM
SALES (corp-wide): 95.6MM **Privately Held**
SIC: 3555 Sticks, printers'
PA: Andrew Industries Limited
Walton House
Accrington LANCS BB5 5
128 277-8022

(G-7974)
BRUNNER INTERNATIONAL INC
3959 Bates Rd (14103-9705)
P.O. Box 111 (14103-0111)
PHONE.................................585 798-6000
Peter Brunner, *Ch of Bd*
Lynn Pietkiewicz, *QC Mgr*
Bob Baker, *Engineer*
Roy Wagner, *Senior Engr*
Jim Carlson, *Controller*
▲ **EMP:** 122
SALES (est): 35.7MM **Privately Held**
SIC: 3713 Truck bodies & parts

(G-7975)
CNHI LLC
Also Called: Medina Journal Register
541-543 Main St (14103)
PHONE.................................585 798-1400
Mark Francis, *Publisher*
EMP: 38
SQ FT: 14,301 **Privately Held**
WEB: www.clintonnc.com
SIC: 2711 Newspapers: publishing only, not printed on site
HQ: Cnhi, Llc
445 Dexter Ave
Montgomery AL 36104

(G-7976)
D & W ENTERPRISES LLC
10775 W Shelby Rd (14103-9584)
PHONE.................................585 590-6727
Darrel Barnes,
EMP: 17
SALES (est): 960K **Privately Held**
SIC: 3471 Finishing, metals or formed products

(G-7977)
F & H METAL FINISHING CO INC
Also Called: Fearby Enterprises
700 Genesee St (14103-1504)
P.O. Box 486 (14103-0486)
PHONE.................................585 798-2151
Timothy Fearby, *President*
Patricia Caleb, *Corp Secy*
Kim Stevens, *Vice Pres*
EMP: 18
SQ FT: 10,000
SALES: 800K **Privately Held**
SIC: 3479 3471 Enameling, including porcelain, of metal products; lacquering of metal products; varnishing of metal products; painting of metal products; cleaning, polishing & finishing; buffing for the trade; finishing, metals or formed products; polishing, metals or formed products

(G-7978)
GANNETT STLLITE INFO NTWRK INC
Also Called: Greater Niagara Newspaper
413 Main St (14103-1416)
PHONE.................................585 798-1400
Dan Caswell, *Director*
EMP: 88
SALES (corp-wide): 3.1B **Publicly Held**
WEB: www.usatoday.com
SIC: 2711 Newspapers, publishing & printing
HQ: Gannett Satellite Information Network, Llc
7950 Jones Branch Dr
Mc Lean VA 22102
703 854-6000

(G-7979)
GEOPUMP INC
213 State St (14103-1337)
PHONE.................................585 798-6666
James Mirand, *President*
Paul Fox, *Vice Pres*
EMP: 5
SQ FT: 1,500
SALES (est): 650.2K **Privately Held**
WEB: www.geopump.com
SIC: 3561 Pumps, domestic: water or sump

(G-7980)
HANSON AGGREGATES EAST LLC
Glenwood Ave (14103)
PHONE.................................585 798-0762
EMP: 15
SALES (corp-wide): 18.7B **Privately Held**
SIC: 3273 Mfg Ready-Mixed Concrete
HQ: Hanson Aggregates East Llc
2300 Gateway Centre Blvd
Morrisville NC 27560
919 380-2500

(G-7981)
HINSPERGERS POLY INDUSTRIES
430 W Oak Orchard St (14103-1551)
PHONE.................................585 798-6625
Bill Thompson, *Sales Mgr*
Greg Budd, *Manager*
EMP: 27 **Privately Held**
WEB: www.hinspergers.com
SIC: 3949 Swimming pools, plastic
PA: Hinspergers Poly Industries Ltd
645 Needham Lane
Mississauga ON L5A 1
905 272-0144

(G-7982)
LEONARD OAKES ESTATE WINERY
10609 Ridge Rd (14103-9431)
PHONE.................................585 318-4418
Wendy Wilson, *Principal*
EMP: 5
SALES (est): 346.4K **Privately Held**
SIC: 2084 Wines

(G-7983)
MEDINA MILLWORKS LLC
10694 Ridge Rd (14103-9406)
PHONE.................................585 798-2969
Matt Graber,
Jerome Graber,
Philip Graber,
Steven Graber,
EMP: 8
SQ FT: 960
SALES (est): 1MM **Privately Held**
WEB: www.medinamillworks.com
SIC: 2431 Millwork

(G-7984)
MILLERS BULK FOOD AND BAKERY
10858 Ridge Rd (14103-9432)
PHONE.................................585 798-9700
Steven Miller, *Principal*
EMP: 8
SALES (est): 744.2K **Privately Held**
SIC: 2051 Bakery: wholesale or wholesale/retail combined

(G-7985)
MIZKAN AMERICA INC
Also Called: Nakano Foods
711 Park Ave (14103-1078)
PHONE.................................585 798-5720
Craig Smith, *President*
EMP: 18 **Privately Held**
SIC: 2099 2035 Vinegar; dressings, salad: raw & cooked (except dry mixes)
HQ: Mizkan America, Inc.
1661 Feehanville Dr # 200
Mount Prospect IL 60056
847 590-0059

(G-7986)
PRIDE PAK INC
11531 Maple Ridge Rd (14103-9765)
PHONE.................................905 828-2149
Steve Carr, *CEO*
Mauro Lorusso, *Vice Pres*
EMP: 75 EST: 2015
SALES (est): 12.2MM **Privately Held**
SIC: 2099 Salads, fresh or refrigerated

(G-7987)
QUORUM GROUP LLC
Also Called: Takeform Archtectural Graphics
11601 Maple Ridge Rd (14103-9710)
PHONE.................................585 798-8888
William Hungerford, *President*
Skip Dahlmann, *Regional Mgr*
Dee Ann Courcy, *CFO*
Jenn Twitchell, *Accounts Mgr*
Ashleigh Heffernan, *Sales Staff*
EMP: 52
SQ FT: 35,000
SALES: 6.3MM **Privately Held**
WEB: www.takeform.net
SIC: 3993 Signs, not made in custom sign painting shops

(G-7988)
S B WHISTLER & SONS INC
11023 W Center Street Ext (14103-9557)
P.O. Box 270 (14103-0270)
PHONE.................................585 798-3000
Brendan Whistler, *Owner*
Larry Massey, *CFO*
Cliff Fuller, *Manager*
Sandra Whistler, *Consultant*
EMP: 46
SQ FT: 25,000
SALES (est): 14.4MM **Privately Held**
WEB: www.phinneytool.com
SIC: 3544 Special dies & tools

(G-7989)
SHELBY CRUSHED STONE INC
10830 Blair Rd (14103-9590)
PHONE.................................585 798-4501
Thomas S Biamonte, *CEO*
April Biamonte, *Controller*
EMP: 32
SALES (est): 2.8MM **Privately Held**
SIC: 1429 1442 1422 Sandstone, crushed & broken-quarrying; gravel mining; crushed & broken limestone

(G-7990)
SIGMA INTL GEN MED APPRTUS LLC
711 Park Ave (14103-1078)
PHONE.................................585 798-3901
Nelson Tatterson, *President*
Lisa Testa, *Supervisor*
Roger Hungerford,
Gary Colister,
Greg Dipuccio,
▼ **EMP:** 500
SQ FT: 40,000
SALES (est): 219.5MM
SALES (corp-wide): 10.5B **Publicly Held**
WEB: www.sigmapumps.com
SIC: 3841 IV transfusion apparatus
PA: Baxter International Inc.
1 Baxter Pkwy
Deerfield IL 60015
224 948-2000

(G-7991)
VIVUS TECHNOLOGIES LLC
591 Mahar St (14103-1612)
PHONE.................................585 798-6658
David Cooper,
EMP: 9
SQ FT: 20,000
SALES (est): 223.5K **Privately Held**
SIC: 3821 Autoclaves, laboratory

(G-7992)
WESTERN NEW YORK ENERGY LLC
4141 Bates Rd (14103-9706)
P.O. Box 191 (14103-0191)
PHONE.................................585 798-9693
Isaiah Schoolcraft, *Plant Mgr*
Mike Makarevic, *Plant Engr*
Michelle Kingdollar, *Accountant*
Mike Langdon, *Lab Dir*
John Sawyer,
EMP: 40
SALES (est): 17.6MM **Privately Held**
WEB: www.wnyenergy.com
SIC: 2869 Ethanolamines

Medusa
Albany County

(G-7993)
DEGENNARO FUEL SERVICE LLC
242 County Route 357 (12120-2005)
PHONE.................................518 239-6350
Million Ow, *Owner*
EMP: 10
SALES (est): 647.9K **Privately Held**
SIC: 2869 Fuels

Melville
Suffolk County

(G-7994)
110 SAND COMPANY (PA)
136 Spagnoli Rd (11747-3502)
PHONE................................631 694-2822
Chester Broman, *Partner*
EMP: 50
SQ FT: 20,000
SALES (est): 5.8MM **Privately Held**
SIC: 1442 Construction sand & gravel

(G-7995)
18 ROCKS LLC
102 Marcus Dr (11747-4212)
PHONE................................631 465-9990
Michael Schatten, *Mng Member*
EMP: 21
SQ FT: 3,000
SALES (est): 1.7MM
SALES (corp-wide): 1.2MM **Privately Held**
SIC: 2335 2331 Women's, juniors' & misses' dresses; blouses, women's & juniors': made from purchased material
PA: Melwood Partners, Inc.
100 Qentin Roosevelt Blvd
Garden City NY

(G-7996)
A K ALLEN CO INC
Also Called: Allen Air
1860 Walt Whitman Rd # 900 (11747-3098)
PHONE................................516 747-5450
Ronald Buttner, *President*
Tim Byrnes, *General Mgr*
Steve Werlinitsch, *Plant Mgr*
Sylvia C Allen, *Treasurer*
Linda Johansen, *Financial Exec*
▲ EMP: 120 EST: 1945
SQ FT: 150,000
SALES (est): 15.7MM **Privately Held**
SIC: 3679 3443 3822 3593 Electronic circuits; cylinders, pressure: metal plate; pneumatic relays, air-conditioning type; fluid power cylinders & actuators; valves & pipe fittings; fluid power valves & hose fittings

(G-7997)
ADVANTAGE PLUS DIAGNOSTICS INC
200 Broadhollow Rd (11747-4846)
PHONE................................631 393-5044
Jason Damianio, *President*
Anthony Rollo, *Admin Sec*
EMP: 5
SALES (est): 304.1K **Privately Held**
SIC: 3841 Diagnostic apparatus, medical

(G-7998)
AERO-VISION TECHNOLOGIES INC (PA)
7 Round Tree Dr (11747-3314)
PHONE................................631 643-8349
Donald P Burkhardt, *President*
EMP: 8
SQ FT: 6,200
SALES (est): 2MM **Privately Held**
WEB: www.aero-vision.com
SIC: 3577 Computer peripheral equipment

(G-7999)
AIP PUBLISHING LLC
1305 Walt Whitman Rd # 300 (11747-4300)
PHONE................................516 576-2200
John Haynes, *CEO*
Roy Levenson, *CFO*
Madeline Babtiste, *Human Res Dir*
Christine Dipasca, *Manager*
EMP: 125 EST: 2013
SALES: 48.9MM
SALES (corp-wide): 14.7MM **Privately Held**
SIC: 2731 Books: publishing only
PA: American Institute Of Physics Incorporated
1 Physics Ellipse
College Park MD 20740
301 209-3100

(G-8000)
AIR TECHNIQUES INC (HQ)
1295 Walt Whitman Rd (11747-3062)
PHONE................................516 433-7676
Christoph Roeer, *CEO*
Theresa Hamilton, *General Mgr*
Lou Guellnitz, *Vice Pres*
Robert Nordquist, *Vice Pres*
Dominic Giordano, *Plant Mgr*
▲ EMP: 326
SQ FT: 92,000
SALES (est): 59.1MM
SALES (corp-wide): 248.9MM **Privately Held**
WEB: www.airtechniques.com
SIC: 3861 3563 3821 3844 Photographic processing equipment & chemicals; air & gas compressors including vacuum pumps; laboratory equipment: fume hoods, distillation racks, etc.; X-ray apparatus & tubes; dental equipment & supplies; pumps & pumping equipment
PA: DUrr Dental Se
Hopfigheimer Str. 17
Bietigheim-Bissingen 74321
714 270-50

(G-8001)
ALL-PRO IMAGING CORP
1295 Walt Whitman Rd (11747-3070)
PHONE................................516 433-7676
Louis E Brooks, *Ch of Bd*
Frank Bader, *President*
Mark S Brooks, *Vice Pres*
Fredrick Fischer, *Vice Pres*
Joanne Iannacone, *Human Res Dir*
▲ EMP: 20
SQ FT: 10,000
SALES (est): 2.2MM **Privately Held**
WEB: www.allproimaging.com
SIC: 3861 Processing equipment, photographic

(G-8002)
AMERICAN INSTITUTE PHYSICS INC
Hntngton Qad Ste 1n1-2 (11747)
PHONE................................516 576-2410
Doris Lewis, *Branch Mgr*
EMP: 250
SALES (corp-wide): 14.7MM **Privately Held**
SIC: 2721 2731 8733 Trade journals: publishing only, not printed on site; books: publishing only; noncommercial research organizations
PA: American Institute Of Physics Incorporated
1 Physics Ellipse
College Park MD 20740
301 209-3100

(G-8003)
AN GROUP INC
17 Scott Dr (11747-1013)
P.O. Box 895 (11747-0895)
PHONE................................631 549-4090
Steve Hopfenmuller, *President*
Steven Hopfenmuller, *President*
Jill Hopfenmuller, *Vice Pres*
EMP: 5
SALES (est): 283.2K **Privately Held**
WEB: www.smbiz.com
SIC: 2741 Business service newsletters: publishing & printing

(G-8004)
BANNER TRANSMISSION & ENG CO
Also Called: Banner Transmissions
4 Cabriolet Ln (11747-1922)
PHONE................................516 221-9459
Clifforddwin Hettinger, *President*
Christopher B Sweeny, *Admin Sec*
EMP: 10 EST: 1963
SQ FT: 4,500
SALES (est): 1.2MM **Privately Held**
WEB: www.bannertransmission.com
SIC: 3714 7539 Transmissions, motor vehicle; automotive repair shops

(G-8005)
BZ MEDIA LLC
Also Called: SD Times
225 Broadhollow Rd 211e (11747-4807)
PHONE................................631 421-4158
Ted Bahr, *President*
H Ted Bahr, *President*
Alan L Zeichick, *Exec VP*
Caroline Seiter, *Opers Staff*
Viena Ludewig, *Controller*
EMP: 18 EST: 1999
SQ FT: 4,000
SALES: 5.5MM **Privately Held**
WEB: www.bzmedia.com
SIC: 2721 Magazines: publishing & printing

(G-8006)
CAPY MACHINE SHOP INC (PA)
114 Spagnoli Rd (11747-3502)
PHONE................................631 694-6916
Salvatore Capacchione, *CEO*
Rosemary Capacchione, *Shareholder*
▲ EMP: 40
SQ FT: 7,500
SALES (est): 7.6MM **Privately Held**
SIC: 3599 Machine shop, jobbing & repair

(G-8007)
CHROMAGRAPHICS PRESS INC
3 Martha Dr (11747-1906)
PHONE................................631 367-6160
Frank Cuoco, *President*
Irene Cuoco, *Vice Pres*
Thomas Cuoco, *Vice Pres*
EMP: 5
SALES (est): 480K **Privately Held**
WEB: www.chromagraphicspress.com
SIC: 2752 8748 Commercial printing, lithographic; business consulting

(G-8008)
CHYRONHEGO CORPORATION (HQ)
5 Hub Dr (11747-3523)
PHONE................................631 845-2000
Marco Lopez, *CEO*
Johan Apel, *Chairman*
Neil Foster, *COO*
Rickard Ohrn, *COO*
Aldo Campisi, *Vice Pres*
EMP: 104
SQ FT: 47,000
SALES (est): 40MM **Privately Held**
WEB: www.chyron.com
SIC: 3663 Radio & TV communications equipment

(G-8009)
COMAX AROMATICS CORPORATION
130 Baylis Rd (11747-3808)
PHONE................................631 249-0505
Peter J Calabretta, *President*
Norman Katz, *Vice Pres*
Francis J Keppel, *Admin Sec*
EMP: 50
SQ FT: 40,000
SALES (est): 4.1MM **Privately Held**
SIC: 2869 Flavors or flavoring materials, synthetic

(G-8010)
COMAX MANUFACTURING CORP (PA)
Also Called: Comax Flavors
130 Baylis Rd (11747-3808)
PHONE................................631 249-0505
Peter J Calabretta Jr, *Ch of Bd*
Paul Calabretta, *Vice Pres*
◆ EMP: 55
SQ FT: 40,000
SALES (est): 10.9MM **Privately Held**
SIC: 2087 Flavoring extracts & syrups

(G-8011)
COMTECH PST CORP (HQ)
105 Baylis Rd (11747-3833)
PHONE................................631 777-8900
Dr Stan Sloane, *CEO*
Jim Heick, *Managing Dir*
Michael Kellerman, *Manager*
Barry Gross, *CIO*
J Preston Windus Jr, *Admin Sec*
▲ EMP: 120
SQ FT: 46,000
SALES (est): 223.3MM
SALES (corp-wide): 570.5MM **Publicly Held**
WEB: www.comtechpst.com
SIC: 3663 3825 Microwave communication equipment; amplifiers, RF power & IF; test equipment for electronic & electric measurement
PA: Comtech Telecommunications Corp.
68 S Service Rd Ste 230
Melville NY 11747
631 962-7000

(G-8012)
COMTECH TELECOM CORP (PA)
68 S Service Rd Ste 230 (11747-2350)
PHONE................................631 962-7000
Fred Kornberg, *Ch of Bd*
Michael D Porcelain, *COO*
John Branscum Jr, *Senior VP*
Richard L Burt, *Senior VP*
Michael Bondi, *CFO*
◆ EMP: 146
SQ FT: 9,600
SALES: 570.5MM **Publicly Held**
WEB: www.comtechtel.com
SIC: 3663 Microwave communication equipment; amplifiers, RF power & IF; mobile communication equipment

(G-8013)
CROWN NOVELTY WORKS INC
42 Elkland Rd (11747-3302)
PHONE................................631 253-0949
EMP: 7 EST: 1909
SQ FT: 10,000
SALES: 1.2MM **Privately Held**
SIC: 3364 Mfg Lead Curtain Weights

(G-8014)
DADDARIO & COMPANY INC
99 Marcus Dr (11747-4209)
PHONE................................631 439-3300
EMP: 67
SALES (corp-wide): 193.1MM **Privately Held**
SIC: 3931 String instruments & parts
PA: D'addario & Company, Inc.
595 Smith St
Farmingdale NY 11735
631 439-3300

(G-8015)
DESIGNER EPOXY FINISHES INC
445 Broadhollow Rd Ste 25 (11747-3645)
PHONE................................646 943-6044
Justin Palladino, *President*
EMP: 6 EST: 2007
SALES (est): 885.2K **Privately Held**
SIC: 2851 1752 Epoxy coatings; floor laying & floor work

(G-8016)
DISTINCTION MAGAZINE INC
Also Called: Island Publications
235 Pinelawn Rd (11747-4226)
PHONE................................631 843-3522
Madelyn Roberts, *CEO*
Patrice Golde, *President*
EMP: 25
SALES (est): 2.4MM **Privately Held**
SIC: 2721 Magazines: publishing & printing

(G-8017)
DORIS PANOS DESIGNS LTD
130 Old East Neck Rd (11747-3209)
PHONE................................631 245-0580
Doris Panos, *President*
EMP: 6
SQ FT: 250
SALES (est): 710K **Privately Held**
SIC: 3911 Jewelry, precious metal

(G-8018)
E-Z-EM INC (DH)
155 Pinelawn Rd Ste 230n (11747-3249)
PHONE................................609 524-2864
Vittorio Puppo, *CEO*
◆ EMP: 32
SALES (est): 11MM **Privately Held**
WEB: www.ezem.com
SIC: 2835 3841 In vitro & in vivo diagnostic substances; diagnostic apparatus, medical

Melville - Suffolk County (G-8019)

(G-8019)
EQUAL OPPRTNITY PBLCATIONS INC
Also Called: Careers and The Disabled
445 Broadhollow Rd # 425 (11747-3669)
PHONE.....................631 421-9421
John R Miller III, *Ch of Bd*
Tamara Dreyfuss, *Publisher*
John Miller, *Publisher*
Barbara Loehr, *Editor*
Debra Kahn, *Business Mgr*
EMP: 12
SQ FT: 3,000
SALES (est): 2.1MM **Privately Held**
WEB: www.eop.com
SIC: 2721 7361 Magazines: publishing & printing; employment agencies

(G-8020)
ESTEE LAUDER COMPANIES INC
80 Ruland Rd Ste 3 (11747-4211)
PHONE.....................631 694-2601
Kulbhushan Sharma, *Manager*
Raymond Haller, *Consultant*
Lisa Mankin, *Consultant*
John Sands, *Exec Dir*
EMP: 82 **Publicly Held**
SIC: 2844 Toilet preparations
PA: The Estee Lauder Companies Inc
   767 5th Ave Fl 1
   New York NY 10153

(G-8021)
ESTEE LAUDER COMPANIES INC
7 Corporate Center Dr (11747-3115)
PHONE.....................212 572-4200
John Capotosto, *Director*
Larry Marotta, *Director*
EMP: 504 **Publicly Held**
WEB: www.elcompanies.com
SIC: 2844 Toilet preparations
PA: The Estee Lauder Companies Inc
   767 5th Ave Fl 1
   New York NY 10153

(G-8022)
ESTEE LAUDER INC
125 Pinelawn Rd (11747-3135)
PHONE.....................631 531-1000
Ken Marenus, *Senior VP*
Johannes Hartmann, *Vice Pres*
Gavin Kaplan, *Vice Pres*
Daniel Kelly, *Vice Pres*
Louis Schapiro, *Vice Pres*
EMP: 100 **Publicly Held**
WEB: www.esteelauder.com
SIC: 2844 5999 5122 Perfumes & colognes; toiletries, cosmetics & perfumes; cosmetics; perfumes & colognes; drugs, proprietaries & sundries
HQ: Estee Lauder Inc.
   767 5th Ave Fl 1
   New York NY 10153
   212 572-4200

(G-8023)
FALCONSTOR SOFTWARE INC (PA)
2 Huntington Quadrangle (11747-4503)
PHONE.....................631 777-5188
Todd Brooks, *CEO*
Eli Oxenhorn, *Ch of Bd*
Gary Quinn, *President*
Alan Komet, *Exec VP*
Ernest Wan, *Exec VP*
EMP: 106
SQ FT: 55,000
SALES: 25.1MM **Publicly Held**
WEB: www.falconstor.com
SIC: 7372 7371 Computer software development; computer software systems analysis & design, custom; application computer software

(G-8024)
FILMPAK EXTRUSION LLC
125 Spagnoli Rd (11747-3518)
PHONE.....................631 293-6767
Peter Levy, *President*
EMP: 60
SQ FT: 100,000
SALES: 20MM **Privately Held**
SIC: 2673 Plastic bags: made from purchased materials

(G-8025)
FONAR CORPORATION (PA)
110 Marcus Dr (11747-4292)
PHONE.....................631 694-2929
Raymond V Damadian, *Ch of Bd*
Timothy R Damadian, *President*
Luciano B Bonanni, *COO*
Claudette J V Chan, *Admin Sec*
EMP: 137
SQ FT: 78,000
SALES: 81.5MM **Publicly Held**
WEB: www.fonar.com
SIC: 3845 8741 Electromedical equipment; management services

(G-8026)
FOUGERA PHARMACEUTICALS INC (DH)
Also Called: Pharmaderm
60 Baylis Rd (11747-3838)
P.O. Box 2006 (11747-0103)
PHONE.....................631 454-7677
Brian A Markison, *CEO*
Donald Degolyer, *Ch of Bd*
Jeff Bailey, *COO*
Chris Klein, *Senior VP*
George Schwab, *Vice Pres*
▲ **EMP:** 250 **EST:** 1963
SQ FT: 190,000
SALES (est): 315.9MM
SALES (corp-wide): 49.1B **Privately Held**
WEB: www.altanapharma-us.com
SIC: 2834 2851 2821 3479 Druggists' preparations (pharmaceutical); ointments; paints & paint additives; plasticizer/additive based plastic materials; painting, coating & hot dipping; measuring & controlling devices
HQ: Sandoz Inc.
   100 College Rd W
   Princeton NJ 08540
   609 627-8500

(G-8027)
GPC INTERNATIONAL INC (PA)
510 Broadhollow Rd # 205 (11747-3606)
PHONE.....................631 752-9600
Steven Roth, *President*
Don Fleisheiar, *CFO*
EMP: 117
SQ FT: 2,500
SALES (est): 13MM **Privately Held**
SIC: 3861 Graphic arts plates, sensitized

(G-8028)
GRAPHIC IMAGE ASSOCIATES LLC
305 Spagnoli Rd (11747-3506)
PHONE.....................631 249-9600
EMP: 100
SQ FT: 8,500
SALES (est): 8.5MM **Privately Held**
SIC: 3111 Leather Tanning/Finishing

(G-8029)
GUIDANCE GROUP INC
Also Called: Child's Work-Child's Play
1 Huntington Quad 1n03 (11747-4466)
PHONE.....................631 756-4618
Jon D Werz, *CEO*
Carmine Russo, *CFO*
Chase Conatser, *Graphic Designe*
EMP: 12
SALES (est): 946.8K **Privately Held**
SIC: 2711 Newspapers, publishing & printing

(G-8030)
HENRY SCHEIN FINCL SVCS LLC (HQ)
Also Called: Henry Schein International Inc
135 Duryea Rd (11747-3834)
PHONE.....................631 843-5500
Stanley Bergman, *CEO*
James Piombino, *Regional Mgr*
Steven Paladino, *CFO*
EMP: 9
SALES (est): 966.7K
SALES (corp-wide): 12.4B **Publicly Held**
SIC: 3843 Dental equipment & supplies
PA: Henry Schein, Inc.
   135 Duryea Rd
   Melville NY 11747
   631 843-5500

(G-8031)
HONEYWELL INTERNATIONAL INC
2 Corporate Center Dr # 100 (11747-3269)
P.O. Box 1353 (11747-0353)
PHONE.....................516 577-2661
EMP: 19
SALES (corp-wide): 40.5B **Publicly Held**
WEB: www.honeywell.com
SIC: 3724 Aircraft engines & engine parts
PA: Honeywell International Inc.
   115 Tabor Rd
   Morris Plains NJ 07950
   973 455-2000

(G-8032)
HONEYWELL INTERNATIONAL INC
2 Corporate Center Dr # 100 (11747-3269)
PHONE.....................516 577-2000
Jim Dodd, *Exec Dir*
EMP: 23
SALES (corp-wide): 40.5B **Publicly Held**
SIC: 3724 Aircraft engines & engine parts
PA: Honeywell International Inc.
   115 Tabor Rd
   Morris Plains NJ 07950
   973 455-2000

(G-8033)
HONEYWELL INTERNATIONAL INC
2 Corporate Center Dr # 100 (11747-3269)
PHONE.....................516 577-2813
Roger Fradin, *Principal*
EMP: 11
SALES (corp-wide): 40.5B **Publicly Held**
SIC: 3724 Aircraft engines & engine parts
PA: Honeywell International Inc.
   115 Tabor Rd
   Morris Plains NJ 07950
   973 455-2000

(G-8034)
HONEYWELL INTERNATIONAL INC
263 Old Country Rd (11747-2712)
P.O. Box 22324, Brooklyn (11202-2324)
PHONE.....................212 964-5111
EMP: 657
SALES (corp-wide): 38.5B **Publicly Held**
SIC: 3724 Aircraft Engines And Engine Parts
PA: Honeywell International Inc.
   115 Tabor Rd
   Morris Plains NJ 07950
   973 455-2000

(G-8035)
HONEYWELL INTERNATIONAL INC
2 Corporate Center Dr # 100 (11747-3269)
PHONE.....................516 577-2000
Ron Rothman, *President*
EMP: 400
SALES (corp-wide): 40.5B **Publicly Held**
WEB: www.honeywell.com
SIC: 3724 Aircraft engines & engine parts
PA: Honeywell International Inc.
   115 Tabor Rd
   Morris Plains NJ 07950
   973 455-2000

(G-8036)
I W INDUSTRIES INC (PA)
Also Called: Concinnity Division
35 Melville Park Rd (11747-3104)
PHONE.....................631 293-9494
Jerome Warshawsky, *President*
Murray Cohen, *Vice Pres*
ARI Warshawsky, *Vice Pres*
Marc Warshawsky, *Admin Sec*
▲ **EMP:** 230
SQ FT: 110,000
SALES (est): 11.2MM **Privately Held**
WEB: www.iwindustries.com
SIC: 3451 3471 3432 Screw machine products; finishing, metals or formed products; faucets & spigots, metal & plastic

(G-8037)
INTELLICHECK INC (PA)
535 Broadhollow Rd B51 (11747-3720)
PHONE.....................516 992-1900
Bill White, *CEO*
Michael D Malone, *Ch of Bd*
Russell T Embry, *Senior VP*
Jack Davis, *Bd of Directors*
Guy Smith, *Bd of Directors*
EMP: 29
SQ FT: 9,233
SALES: 3.6MM **Publicly Held**
WEB: www.intellicheck.com
SIC: 3699 Security devices

(G-8038)
INTERDGITAL COMMUNICATIONS LLC
2 Huntington Quad Ste 4s (11747-4508)
PHONE.....................631 622-4000
Gary Lomp, *Manager*
EMP: 125 **Publicly Held**
WEB: www.interdigital.com
SIC: 3661 8731 Telephone & telegraph apparatus; commercial physical research
HQ: Interdigital Communications, Inc.
   200 Bellevue Pkwy Ste 300
   Wilmington DE 19809
   610 878-7800

(G-8039)
INTERNATIONAL METALS TRDG LLC
25 Melville Park Rd # 114 (11747-3175)
PHONE.....................866 923-0182
Ian Parker, *CEO*
Joseph Kalinowski, *Principal*
Bret Bedges, *COO*
EMP: 5 **EST:** 2013
SALES: 20MM **Privately Held**
SIC: 3441 Building components, structural steel

(G-8040)
ISINE INC (PA)
105 Maxess Rd Ste 124 (11747-3821)
PHONE.....................631 913-4400
Jeffrey Remmers, *President*
Louis J Morales, *Chairman*
Barry Eckstein, *Vice Pres*
Helen Schneider, *Research*
Robert Gross, *Senior Engr*
▲ **EMP:** 23
SQ FT: 3,000
SALES (est): 3.2MM **Privately Held**
WEB: www.isine.com
SIC: 3672 3674 Printed circuit boards; semiconductors & related devices

(G-8041)
KARP ASSOCIATES INC (PA)
Also Called: Adjustable Shelving
260 Spagnoli Rd (11747-3505)
PHONE.....................631 768-8300
Adam Gold, *Chairman*
Augustine Lopez, *Safety Mgr*
Ronnit Kessler, *Engineer*
Ronnie Peterson, *Controller*
Lawrence Mass, *VP Sales*
▲ **EMP:** 95 **EST:** 1956
SALES (est): 21.7MM **Privately Held**
WEB: www.karpinc.com
SIC: 3442 2541 Metal doors; shelving, office & store, wood

(G-8042)
KNICKERBOCKER PARTITION CORP (PA)
260 Spagnoli Rd (11747-3505)
P.O. Box 690, Freeport (11520-0690)
PHONE.....................516 546-0550
Stewart Markbreiter, *President*
Albert Giorgianni, *Vice Pres*
Mark Reiss, *VP Opers*
Andrew Kennedy, *Treasurer*
Ted Williams, *Sales Associate*
▲ **EMP:** 115
SQ FT: 60,000
SALES: 18.2MM **Privately Held**
WEB: www.knickerbockerpartition.com
SIC: 2542 Partitions for floor attachment, prefabricated: except wood

GEOGRAPHIC SECTION

Melville - Suffolk County (G-8068)

(G-8043)
LEVITON MANUFACTURING CO INC (PA)
201 N Service Rd (11747-3138)
P.O. Box 10600 (11747-0056)
PHONE.................631 812-6000
Stephen Sokolow, *Vice Ch Bd*
Donald J Hendler, *President*
Bruno Filio, *President*
Daryoush Larizadeh, *President*
Mark Baydarian, *CFO*
◆ **EMP:** 450 **EST:** 1906
SALES (est): 1.7B **Privately Held**
WEB: www.leviton.com
SIC: 3613 3357 3674 3694 Fuses, electric; nonferrous wiredrawing & insulating; building wire & cable, nonferrous; diodes, solid state (germanium, silicon, etc.); transistors; engine electrical equipment; electronic connectors: caps & plugs, electric: attachment

(G-8044)
LSI COMPUTER SYSTEMS
1235 Walt Whitman Rd (11747-3086)
PHONE.................631 271-0400
Alfred Musto, *CEO*
Attila Tetik, *President*
Alvin Kaplan, *Corp Secy*
Sethu Madhvan, *Engineer*
Hassan Syed, *Engineer*
▼ **EMP:** 35 **EST:** 1969
SQ FT: 13,500
SALES (est): 4.6MM **Privately Held**
WEB: www.lsicsi.com
SIC: 3674 Integrated circuits, semiconductor networks, etc.; metal oxide silicon (MOS) devices

(G-8045)
MELWOOD PARTNERS INC
102 Marcus Dr (11747-4212)
PHONE.................631 923-0134
Brian Wasserman, *Ch of Bd*
Richard Cotler, *Partner*
EMP: 15
SQ FT: 6,000
SALES: 10MM **Privately Held**
SIC: 2211 Apparel & outerwear fabrics, cotton

(G-8046)
MEYCO PRODUCTS INC (PA)
1225 Walt Whitman Rd (11747-3093)
PHONE.................631 421-9800
David W Weissner, *CEO*
John Ciniglio, *President*
Donnie Griffin, *Vice Pres*
Patricia K Weissner, *Admin Sec*
▼ **EMP:** 30 **EST:** 1898
SQ FT: 70,000
SALES (est): 21.5MM **Privately Held**
WEB: www.meycoproducts.com
SIC: 2394 Liners & covers, fabric: made from purchased materials

(G-8047)
MILITARY PARTS EXCHANGE LLC
Also Called: M P X
145 Pinelawn Rd Ste 240n (11747-3161)
PHONE.................631 243-1700
EMP: 15 **Privately Held**
SIC: 3728 Aircraft parts & equipment
PA: Military Parts Exchange Llc
701 Nw 57th Pl
Fort Lauderdale FL 33309

(G-8048)
MITSUBISHI ELC PWR PDTS INC
55 Marcus Dr (11747-4209)
PHONE.................516 962-2813
Nicole Allison, *Production*
Todd Charles, *Production*
Kayla Fisher, *Engineer*
Joseph Prudente, *Regl Sales Mgr*
Paul Bell, *Manager*
EMP: 7
SALES (corp-wide): 41.5B **Privately Held**
SIC: 3699 1731 Electrical equipment & supplies; electrical work
HQ: Mitsubishi Electric Power Products, Inc.
530 Keystone Dr
Warrendale PA 15086
724 772-2555

(G-8049)
NEW DIMENSIONS RESEARCH CORP
260 Spagnoli Rd (11747-3593)
PHONE.................631 694-1356
Timothy L Mason, *Ch of Bd*
Jeffrey Mason, *President*
▲ **EMP:** 125 **EST:** 1957
SQ FT: 155,000
SALES (est): 30.7MM **Privately Held**
WEB: www.ndrc.com
SIC: 3993 7389 Signs & advertising specialties; design, commercial & industrial

(G-8050)
NEWSDAY LLC (PA)
Also Called: Newsday Media Group
235 Pinelawn Rd (11747-4250)
PHONE.................631 843-4050
Patrick Dolan, *President*
Karen Bailis, *Editor*
Diane Daniels, *Editor*
William Perlman, *Editor*
Judy Raia, *Editor*
EMP: 400 **EST:** 1940
SALES (est): 288.8MM **Privately Held**
SIC: 2711 Commercial printing & newspaper publishing combined; newspapers, publishing & printing

(G-8051)
NEWSDAY LLC
25 Deshon Dr (11747-4221)
PHONE.................631 843-3135
Raymond Jansen, *Branch Mgr*
EMP: 150
SALES (corp-wide): 288.8MM **Privately Held**
SIC: 2711 Newspapers, publishing & printing
PA: Newsday Llc
235 Pinelawn Rd
Melville NY 11747
631 843-4050

(G-8052)
NIKON INSTRUMENTS INC (DH)
1300 Walt Whitman Rd Fl 2 (11747-3064)
PHONE.................631 547-4200
Yoshinobu Ishikawa, *Ch of Bd*
Toshiaki Nagano, *President*
Keiko Gluss, *Chief*
James Hamlin, *Vice Pres*
Eric Kozerski, *Opers Staff*
◆ **EMP:** 75
SALES (est): 42.2MM
SALES (corp-wide): 6.7B **Privately Held**
WEB: www.nikonusa.com
SIC: 3826 Analytical instruments

(G-8053)
OLYMPIC SOFTWARE & CONSULTING
290 Broadhollow Rd 130e (11747-4852)
PHONE.................631 351-0655
Chris McLean, *Owner*
EMP: 7 **EST:** 2001
SALES (est): 596.9K **Privately Held**
SIC: 7372 Prepackaged software

(G-8054)
OPUS TECHNOLOGY CORPORATION
10 Gwynne Rd (11747-1414)
PHONE.................631 271-1883
James Startin, *President*
EMP: 10
SALES (est): 1.1MM **Privately Held**
SIC: 3679 Electronic circuits

(G-8055)
P & F INDUSTRIES INC (PA)
Also Called: P&F
445 Broadhollow Rd # 100 (11747-3615)
PHONE.................631 694-9800
Richard A Horowitz, *Ch of Bd*
Joseph A Molino Jr, *COO*
◆ **EMP:** 38 **EST:** 1963
SQ FT: 5,000
SALES: 58.9MM **Publicly Held**
WEB: www.pfina.com
SIC: 3429 3714 3546 Manufactured hardware (general); filters: oil, fuel & air, motor vehicle; grinders, portable: electric or pneumatic

(G-8056)
PARK ELECTROCHEMICAL CORP (PA)
48 S Service Rd Ste 300 (11747-2335)
PHONE.................631 465-3600
Brian E Shore, *Ch of Bd*
Christopher T Mastrogiacomo, *President*
Christopher Mastrogiacomo, *COO*
Stephen E Gilhuley, *Exec VP*
Mark A Esquivel, *Senior VP*
▲ **EMP:** 97
SQ FT: 8,000
SALES: 111.2MM **Publicly Held**
WEB: www.parkelectro.com
SIC: 3672 3674 Printed circuit boards; microcircuits, integrated (semiconductor)

(G-8057)
POLY-PAK INDUSTRIES INC (PA)
Also Called: Colorpak
125 Spagnoli Rd (11747-3518)
PHONE.................631 293-6767
Peter Levy, *Ch of Bd*
Leonard Levy, *Chairman*
Doug Kiesel, *Vice Pres*
Adam Kugler, *Vice Pres*
Sy Miller, *Vice Pres*
◆ **EMP:** 280
SQ FT: 150,000
SALES (est): 81.9MM **Privately Held**
WEB: www.poly-pak.com
SIC: 2673 2677 Plastic bags: made from purchased materials; envelopes

(G-8058)
PRECISION PHARMA SERVICES INC
155 Duryea Rd (11747-3894)
PHONE.................631 752-7314
Jim Moose, *President*
June Heck, *CFO*
EMP: 125
SQ FT: 100,000
SALES (est): 24.5MM **Privately Held**
WEB: www.precisionpharma.com
SIC: 2834 Pharmaceutical preparations

(G-8059)
PUBLISHERS CLEARING HOUSE LLC
265 Spagnoli Rd Ste 1 (11747-3508)
PHONE.................516 249-4063
EMP: 32
SALES (corp-wide): 116.4MM **Privately Held**
SIC: 2741 Miscellaneous publishing
PA: Publishers Clearing House Llc
300 Jericho Quadrangle # 300
Jericho NY 11753
516 883-5432

(G-8060)
QUADRANGLE QUICKPRINTS LTD
Also Called: Quadrangle Quick Print
1 Huntington Quad Ll04 (11747-4401)
P.O. Box 2753, North Babylon (11703-0753)
PHONE.................631 694-4464
Henry Schaja, *Owner*
EMP: 6
SQ FT: 1,000
SALES (est): 757.1K **Privately Held**
WEB: www.cardsandstationery.com
SIC: 2752 Commercial printing, offset

(G-8061)
RINGLEAD INC
200 Broadhollow Rd # 400 (11747-4806)
PHONE.................310 906-0545
Jaime Muirhead, *Senior VP*
Gregg Thaler, *Officer*
EMP: 10 **EST:** 2016
SALES (est): 357.3K **Privately Held**
SIC: 7372 Business oriented computer software

(G-8062)
ROSS COMMUNICATIONS ASSOCIATES
200 Broadhollow Rd # 207 (11747-4846)
PHONE.................631 393-5089
Robert Ross, *President*
Jodie Ross, *Vice Pres*
EMP: 10
SALES (est): 4.8MM **Privately Held**
SIC: 2721 Magazines: publishing & printing

(G-8063)
SIEMENS PRODUCT LIFE MGMT SFTW
Also Called: Analysis & Design Aplicat Co
60 Broadhollow Rd (11747-2504)
PHONE.................631 549-2300
Cedomir Kralj, *Project Mgr*
Somee Lee, *Engineer*
Kshitij Neroorkar, *Engineer*
Matt McCullum, *Accounts Exec*
Zhilei Wu, *Manager*
EMP: 319
SALES (corp-wide): 97.7B **Privately Held**
SIC: 7372 Prepackaged software
HQ: Siemens Product Lifecycle Management Software Inc.
5800 Granite Pkwy Ste 600
Plano TX 75024
972 987-3000

(G-8064)
SIMPLY AMAZING ENTERPRISES INC
68 S Service Rd Ste 1 (11747-2354)
PHONE.................631 503-6452
EMP: 7 **EST:** 2014
SALES: 390K **Privately Held**
SIC: 2842 Mfg Polish/Sanitation Goods

(G-8065)
STAR COMMUNITY PUBLISHING
Also Called: Star Community Pubg Group LLC
235 Pinelawn Rd (11747-4226)
PHONE.................631 843-4050
Michael Gates, *VP Sales*
EMP: 194
SALES: 45MM
SALES (corp-wide): 288.8MM **Privately Held**
WEB: www.tribune.com
SIC: 2711 Newspapers, publishing & printing
PA: Newsday Llc
235 Pinelawn Rd
Melville NY 11747
631 843-4050

(G-8066)
STERIS CORPORATION
Also Called: Vts Medical Systems
40 Melville Park Rd Ste 1 (11747-3173)
PHONE.................877 887-1788
EMP: 6
SALES (corp-wide): 2.6B **Privately Held**
SIC: 3842 Surgical appliances & supplies
HQ: Steris Corporation
5960 Heisley Rd
Mentor OH 44060
440 354-2600

(G-8067)
SUTTON PLACE SOFTWARE INC
13 Tappen Dr (11747-1019)
PHONE.................631 421-1737
Steve J Sutton, *President*
EMP: 5 **EST:** 1982
SALES (est): 290.2K **Privately Held**
SIC: 7372 Prepackaged software

(G-8068)
SYSTEMS TRADING INC
48 S Svc Rd Ste Ll90 (11747)
PHONE.................718 261-8900
Harold Schwartz, *Ch of Bd*
EMP: 7
SQ FT: 1,650
SALES: 8MM **Privately Held**
WEB: www.btn.net
SIC: 7372 7377 Prepackaged software; computer rental & leasing

Melville - Suffolk County (G-8069)

(G-8069)
TAYLOR COMMUNICATIONS INC
155 Pinelawn Rd Ste 120s (11747-3252)
PHONE.................................937 221-1303
Bob Paradise, *Branch Mgr*
EMP: 10
SALES (corp-wide): 3.4B **Privately Held**
WEB: www.stdreg.com
SIC: 2761 Manifold business forms
HQ: Taylor Communications, Inc.
4205 S 96th St
Omaha NE 68127
402 898-6422

(G-8070)
TECH SOFTWARE LLC
Also Called: BEC Acquisition Co
270 Spagnoli Rd Ste 102 (11747-3515)
PHONE.................................516 986-3050
Walden Leverich,
EMP: 6
SALES (est): 376.2K **Privately Held**
SIC: 7372 Business oriented computer software

(G-8071)
TEL TECH INTERNATIONAL
200 Broadhollow Rd # 207 (11747-4846)
PHONE.................................516 393-5174
Donald Wuerfl, *Manager*
EMP: 40
SALES (est): 1.1MM **Privately Held**
SIC: 7372 Prepackaged software

(G-8072)
TOPTEC PRODUCTS LLC
1225 Walt Whitman Rd (11747-3010)
PHONE.................................631 421-9800
John Ciniglio, *President*
EMP: 14
SALES (est): 1.5MM **Privately Held**
SIC: 2394 Tents: made from purchased materials

(G-8073)
VERINT AMERICAS INC
175 Broadhollow Rd # 100 (11747-4911)
PHONE.................................631 962-9334
EMP: 12 **EST:** 2016
SALES (est): 1.6MM **Publicly Held**
SIC: 7372 Prepackaged software
PA: Verint Systems Inc.
175 Broadhollow Rd # 100
Melville NY 11747

(G-8074)
VERINT SEC INTELLIGENCE INC
Also Called: Vsii
175 Broadhollow Rd # 100 (11747-4911)
PHONE.................................631 962-9300
Dan Bodner, *CEO*
EMP: 100
SQ FT: 49,000
SALES: 50MM **Publicly Held**
SIC: 7372 Prepackaged software
PA: Verint Systems Inc.
175 Broadhollow Rd # 100
Melville NY 11747

(G-8075)
VERINT SYSTEMS INC (PA)
175 Broadhollow Rd # 100 (11747-4910)
PHONE.................................631 962-9600
Dan Bodner, *Ch of Bd*
Elan Moriah, *President*
Missy Brant, *Managing Dir*
Lauren Buckley, *Vice Pres*
Dean Godfrey, *Vice Pres*
EMP: 125
SQ FT: 49,000
SALES: 1.1B **Publicly Held**
WEB: www.verintsystems.com
SIC: 7372 7382 7373 Prepackaged software; security systems services; systems software development services

Memphis
Onondaga County

(G-8076)
MATTESSICH IRON LLC
1484 New State Route 31 (13112-8719)
PHONE.................................315 409-8496
Michael Mattessich, *Principal*
EMP: 5 **EST:** 2010
SQ FT: 4,000
SALES: 500K **Privately Held**
SIC: 3462 Iron & steel forgings

Menands
Albany County

(G-8077)
A M & J DIGITAL
800 N Pearl St Ste 5 (12204-1893)
PHONE.................................518 434-2579
Alan Brand, *Accounts Mgr*
Nell Fodera, *Accounts Mgr*
Lori Squadere,
Beth Cipperly, *Graphic Designe*
EMP: 8
SALES (est): 1.1MM **Privately Held**
SIC: 2752 Commercial printing, lithographic

(G-8078)
ACKROYD METAL FABRICATORS INC
966 Broadway Ste 2 (12204-2521)
PHONE.................................518 434-1281
Paul Zabinski, *President*
EMP: 12
SQ FT: 40,000
SALES: 1.5MM **Privately Held**
SIC: 3441 Fabricated structural metal

(G-8079)
ALBANY INTERNATIONAL CORP
Appleton Wire Division
1373 Broadway (12204-2697)
PHONE.................................518 445-2230
Tony Ferguson, *President*
Chris Spraggins, *Vice Pres*
Stacey Smith, *Export Mgr*
Steven Maye, *Opers-Prdtn-Mfg*
Lisa Fontanella, *Purch Mgr*
EMP: 150
SALES (corp-wide): 863.7MM **Publicly Held**
WEB: www.albint.com
SIC: 2621 2296 Paper mills; tire cord & fabrics
PA: Albany International Corp.
216 Airport Dr
Rochester NH 03867
603 330-5850

(G-8080)
ALBANY INTERNATIONAL CORP
Dryer Fabrics Division
1373 Broadway (12204-2697)
P.O. Box 1907, Albany (12201-1907)
PHONE.................................518 447-6400
Al Drinkwater, *Manager*
EMP: 100
SALES (corp-wide): 863.7MM **Publicly Held**
WEB: www.albint.com
SIC: 2672 Cloth lined paper: made from purchased paper
PA: Albany International Corp.
216 Airport Dr
Rochester NH 03867
603 330-5850

(G-8081)
ARCADIA MFG GROUP INC
1032 Broadway (12204-2506)
PHONE.................................518 434-6213
William T Sumner, *Ch of Bd*
EMP: 6
SALES (corp-wide): 10.8MM **Privately Held**
SIC: 3498 3446 3444 3999 Fabricated pipe & fittings; ornamental metalwork; sheet metalwork; cigar lighters, except precious metal
PA: Arcadia Manufacturing Group, Inc.
80 Cohoes Ave
Green Island NY 12183
518 434-6213

(G-8082)
ATLANTIC STATES DISTRIBUTING
Also Called: Atlantic States Kitchens Baths
1325 Broadway (12204-2652)
PHONE.................................518 427-6364
Philip Crane, *President*
James Flood, *Vice Pres*
EMP: 8 **EST:** 1959
SALES (est): 1.7MM **Privately Held**
WEB: www.atlanticstateskitchens.com
SIC: 2434 Wood kitchen cabinets

(G-8083)
BLASCH PRECISION CERAMICS INC (PA)
580 Broadway Ste 1 (12204-2896)
PHONE.................................518 436-1263
Robert A Baker, *Ch of Bd*
David W Bobrek, *Ch of Bd*
John Parrish, *Exec VP*
Edwin Collins, *Vice Pres*
Ted Collins, *VP Sls/Mktg*
▲ **EMP:** 98
SALES: 18MM **Privately Held**
WEB: www.powermaterials.com
SIC: 3297 Graphite refractories: carbon bond or ceramic bond

(G-8084)
DYNASTY CHEMICAL CORP
444 N Pearl St (12204-1511)
PHONE.................................518 463-1146
Jane Waldman, *President*
Mel R Waldman, *Vice Pres*
Michael Waldman, *Manager*
▲ **EMP:** 48
SQ FT: 109,000
SALES (est): 14.8MM **Privately Held**
SIC: 2819 5169 Industrial inorganic chemicals; industrial chemicals

(G-8085)
GEROME TECHNOLOGIES INC
85 Broadway Ste 1 (12204-2791)
PHONE.................................518 463-1324
Mark Smisloff, *President*
Justyna Zieba, *Design Engr*
Grace Smisloff, *Sales Staff*
▲ **EMP:** 54
SQ FT: 54,000
SALES (est): 17.7MM **Privately Held**
SIC: 3644 3699 7539 Insulators & insulation materials, electrical; electrical equipment & supplies; electrical services

(G-8086)
LEXIS PUBLISHING
Also Called: Lexis Nexis Mathew Bender
1275 Broadway (12204-2638)
PHONE.................................518 487-3000
Lou Androzzi, *President*
Mark Osbourne, *Info Tech Dir*
EMP: 102 **EST:** 2001
SALES (est): 8.4MM **Privately Held**
SIC: 2731 Book publishing

(G-8087)
MCALLISTERS PRECISION WLDG INC
Also Called: Precision Co.
47 Broadway (12204-2767)
PHONE.................................518 221-3455
April McCallister, *President*
Jason McCallister, *Vice Pres*
EMP: 15
SQ FT: 12,000
SALES (est): 1.2MM **Privately Held**
SIC: 3446 3548 Fences or posts, ornamental iron or steel; welding & cutting apparatus & accessories

(G-8088)
MCCARTHY TIRE SVC CO NY INC
Also Called: McCarthy Tire and Auto Ctr
980 Broadway (12204-2504)
PHONE.................................518 449-5185
Rick Beckman, *Principal*
EMP: 15
SQ FT: 7,140
SALES (corp-wide): 308.9MM **Privately Held**
SIC: 3011 Automobile tires, pneumatic
HQ: McCarthy Tire Service Company Of New York, Inc.
340 Kidder St
Wilkes Barre PA 18702

(G-8089)
MIDLAND FARMS INC (PA)
375 Broadway (12204-2708)
PHONE.................................518 436-7038
Demetrios E Haseotes, *CEO*
Bob Walton, *Manager*
EMP: 51
SALES (est): 14.5MM **Privately Held**
WEB: www.midlandfarms.com
SIC: 2026 Milk processing (pasteurizing, homogenizing, bottling)

(G-8090)
NEW YORK LEGAL PUBLISHING
120 Broadway Ste 1a (12204-2722)
PHONE.................................518 459-1100
Ernest Barvoets, *President*
Edward M Neiles Jr, *Vice Pres*
Suzanne Barvoets, *Sales Staff*
EMP: 7
SALES: 1.2MM **Privately Held**
WEB: www.nylp.com
SIC: 2741 2759 2731 Miscellaneous publishing; commercial printing; book publishing

(G-8091)
SIMMONS MACHINE TOOL CORP (PA)
Also Called: Nsh
1700 Broadway (12204-2701)
PHONE.................................518 462-5431
John O Naumann, *CEO*
Hans J Naumann, *Ch of Bd*
David William Davis, *President*
Roger Collen, *Vice Pres*
Andrew Healey, *Project Mgr*
▲ **EMP:** 104
SQ FT: 145,000
SALES (est): 19.4MM **Privately Held**
WEB: www.smtgroup.com
SIC: 3541 5084 Machine tools, metal cutting type; industrial machinery & equipment

(G-8092)
T LEMME MECHANICAL INC
Selby & Smith
1074 Broadway (12204-2507)
PHONE.................................518 436-4136
Bill Mattfeld, *Opers Mgr*
EMP: 40 **Privately Held**
SIC: 3444 Sheet metalwork
PA: T. Lemme Mechanical, Inc.
67 Erie Blvd
Menands NY 12204

Mendon
Monroe County

(G-8093)
N Y B P INC
Also Called: New York Blood Pressure
1355 Pittsford Mendon Rd (14506-9733)
P.O. Box 471 (14506-0471)
PHONE.................................585 624-2541
Gregory J Sarkis, *President*
EMP: 3
SALES: 1MM **Privately Held**
SIC: 3841 Blood pressure apparatus

(G-8094)
SAXBY IMPLEMENT CORP (PA)
Also Called: Kubota Authorized Dealer
180 Mendon Victor Rd (14506)
P.O. Box 333 (14506-0333)
PHONE.................................585 624-2938
Marvin E Hogan, *President*
Teri H Maxwell, *Vice Pres*
Randall Hogan, *Treasurer*
Joanne Hogan, *Admin Sec*
EMP: 10
SQ FT: 9,400
SALES (est): 1.2MM **Privately Held**
SIC: 3524 5083 Lawn & garden tractors & equipment; farm & garden machinery

Merrick
Nassau County

(G-8095)
CREATIVE MAGAZINE INC
31 Merrick Ave Ste 60 (11566-3499)
PHONE..................................516 378-0800
David Flasterstein, *President*
Lisa Flasterstein, *Assoc Editor*
EMP: 5 **EST:** 2008
SALES (est): 83.6K **Privately Held**
SIC: 2721 Periodicals: publishing only

(G-8096)
D G M GRAPHICS INC
Also Called: Printing Emporium
55 Merrick Ave (11566-3415)
P.O. Box 121 (11566-0121)
PHONE..................................516 223-2220
Douglas G Mills, *President*
EMP: 11
SQ FT: 3,300
SALES (est): 1.1MM **Privately Held**
WEB: www.printingemporium.com
SIC: 2752 2791 2789 2759 Photo-offset printing; typesetting; bookbinding & related work; commercial printing

(G-8097)
E J MANUFACTURING INC
2935 Charlotte Dr (11566-5301)
PHONE..................................516 313-9380
Elliot S Negrin, *President*
Jeff Negrin, *Vice Pres*
▲ **EMP:** 2
SQ FT: 8,000
SALES: 3MM **Privately Held**
SIC: 2326 Men's & boys' work clothing

(G-8098)
FUEL SOUL
188 Merrick Rd (11566-4532)
PHONE..................................516 379-0810
Gregory Fine, *CEO*
EMP: 5
SALES (est): 392.7K **Privately Held**
SIC: 2869 Fuels

(G-8099)
JON LYN INK INC
Also Called: Minuteman Press
255 Sunrise Hwy Ste 1 (11566-3700)
PHONE..................................516 546-2312
John Jutt, *President*
EMP: 6
SQ FT: 1,200
SALES (est): 918.8K **Privately Held**
SIC: 2752 7334 2759 2791 Commercial printing, offset; photocopying & duplicating services; invitation & stationery printing & engraving; typesetting; bookbinding & related work

(G-8100)
L I C SCREEN PRINTING INC
2949 Joyce Ln (11566-5209)
PHONE..................................516 546-7289
Edward Rosenblum, *President*
EMP: 25
SQ FT: 15,000
SALES (est): 1.9MM **Privately Held**
WEB: www.licscreenprinting.com
SIC: 2759 3089 3993 2396 Letterpress & screen printing; screen printing; plastic processing; signs & advertising specialties; automotive & apparel trimmings

(G-8101)
LEADER PRINTING INC
Also Called: Print-O-Rama Copy Center
2272 Babylon Tpke (11566-3829)
PHONE..................................516 546-1544
Steve Leads, *President*
EMP: 10 **EST:** 1969
SALES (est): 737.7K **Privately Held**
SIC: 2752 7334 Photo-offset printing; photocopying & duplicating services

(G-8102)
LEGAL STRATEGIES INC
1795 Harvard Ave (11566-4413)
PHONE..................................516 377-3940
Steven Mitchell Sack, *President*
EMP: 7
SALES (est): 519.4K **Privately Held**
SIC: 2731 Book publishing

(G-8103)
MEGA SOURCING INC (PA)
Also Called: Mega Apparel International
1929 Edward Ln (11566-4922)
PHONE..................................646 682-0304
Mandy Sciortino, *President*
Michael Sciortino, *Vice Pres*
▲ **EMP:** 2 **EST:** 2006
SALES: 1MM **Privately Held**
SIC: 2331 2321 5621 5611 Women's & misses' blouses & shirts; men's & boys' furnishings; women's clothing stores; ready-to-wear apparel, women's; men's & boys' clothing stores

(G-8104)
NORTHEAST WINDOWS USA INC
1 Kees Pl (11566-3642)
P.O. Box 159 (11566-0159)
PHONE..................................516 378-6577
Jill Kaiserman, *President*
Jeffrey Kaiserman, *Vice Pres*
Steven Kaiserman, *Sales Dir*
Phil Reid, *Sales Executive*
▲ **EMP:** 48
SQ FT: 35,000
SALES: 8MM **Privately Held**
SIC: 3089 Windows, plastic

(G-8105)
PRESTIGE ENVELOPE & LITHOGRAPH
Also Called: Prestige Litho & Graphics
1745 Merrick Ave Ste 2 (11566-2700)
PHONE..................................631 521-7043
Gary Gingo, *CEO*
Angel Irimia, *President*
Gregory Catanese, *Office Mgr*
Joe Nieves, *Admin Sec*
EMP: 12
SQ FT: 30,000
SALES (est): 2.1MM **Privately Held**
WEB: www.prestigelg.com
SIC: 2752 2791 2789 7389 Commercial printing, offset; typesetting; bookbinding & related work; printing broker; envelopes

(G-8106)
QUALITY LINEALS USA INC (PA)
Also Called: Quality Fence
1 Kees Pl (11566-3642)
P.O. Box 159 (11566-0159)
PHONE..................................516 378-6577
Jill Kaiserman, *President*
Jeffrey Kaiserman, *Vice Pres*
EMP: 55
SALES: 16MM **Privately Held**
SIC: 3089 Billfold inserts, plastic

(G-8107)
WORLDWIDE TICKET CRAFT
1390 Jerusalem Ave (11566-1364)
PHONE..................................516 538-6200
Eric Colts, *President*
EMP: 60
SALES (est): 4.4MM **Privately Held**
WEB: www.ticketcraft.com
SIC: 2752 2791 2759 Tickets, lithographed; typesetting; commercial printing

Mexico
Oswego County

(G-8108)
GRANDMA BROWNS BEANS INC
5837 Scenic Ave (13114-3481)
P.O. Box 230 (13114-0230)
PHONE..................................315 963-7221
Sandra L Brown, *President*
EMP: 15 **EST:** 1938
SQ FT: 35,000
SALES: 19.7K **Privately Held**
SIC: 2032 Canned specialties

Middle Granville
Washington County

(G-8109)
EVERGREEN SLATE COMPANY INC
2027 County Route 23 (12849-4901)
P.O. Box 248, Granville (12832-0248)
PHONE..................................518 642-2530
Fred Whitridge, *President*
Shannon Humphrey, *General Mgr*
Ray Loomis, *Vice Pres*
Jan Edwards, *Sales Staff*
Mike Flower, *Sales Staff*
◆ **EMP:** 70 **EST:** 1916
SQ FT: 1,000
SALES (est): 9.9MM **Privately Held**
WEB: www.evergreenslate.com
SIC: 3281 Slate products

(G-8110)
HILLTOP SLATE INC
Rr 22 Box A (12849)
PHONE..................................518 642-1453
David Thomas, *President*
David Lundy, *Manager*
▲ **EMP:** 30 **EST:** 1948
SQ FT: 50,000
SALES (est): 3.3MM **Privately Held**
WEB: www.hilltopslate.com
SIC: 3281 Cut stone & stone products

(G-8111)
K-D STONE INC
Rr 22 (12849)
PHONE..................................518 642-2082
Nelson Dunster, *President*
Kimberly Dunster, *Vice Pres*
EMP: 12
SALES (est): 1.8MM **Privately Held**
SIC: 2952 Roof cement: asphalt, fibrous or plastic

(G-8112)
SHELDON SLATE PRODUCTS CO INC
Fox Rd (12849)
PHONE..................................518 642-1280
John Tatko Jr, *President*
EMP: 50 **EST:** 1924
SQ FT: 1,200
SALES (est): 5.3MM **Privately Held**
SIC: 3281 2952 2951 Slate products; asphalt felts & coatings; asphalt paving mixtures & blocks

(G-8113)
VERMONT MULTICOLOR SLATE
146 State Route 22a (12849-5431)
P.O. Box 202 (12849-0202)
PHONE..................................518 642-2400
William Enny, *President*
Renold Tang, *CFO*
EMP: 9
SQ FT: 10,000
SALES (est): 447.1K **Privately Held**
SIC: 1411 Slate, dimension-quarrying

(G-8114)
VERMONT NATURAL STONEWORKS
Also Called: Ritchie Brothers Slate Co
146 State Route 22a (12849)
PHONE..................................518 642-2460
Bonnie Pratt, *President*
EMP: 30
SALES (est): 2.1MM **Privately Held**
SIC: 3281 Slate products

Middle Grove
Saratoga County

(G-8115)
CUCCIO-ZANETTI INC
Also Called: Zanetti Millwork
455 Middle Grove Rd (12850-1107)
PHONE..................................518 587-1363
John Zanetti, *President*
EMP: 8
SQ FT: 9,000
SALES (est): 1.1MM **Privately Held**
SIC: 2431 Doors, wood

Middle Island
Suffolk County

(G-8116)
AFCO PRECAST SALES CORP
Also Called: Old Castle Precast
114 Rocky Point Rd (11953-1216)
PHONE..................................631 924-7114
Richard Affenita, *Ch of Bd*
Peter Kaplin, *President*
▲ **EMP:** 75
SQ FT: 1,560
SALES (est): 10.7MM **Privately Held**
SIC: 3272 5211 Concrete products, precast; masonry materials & supplies

(G-8117)
ALLEY CAT SIGNS INC
506 Middle Country Rd (11953-2521)
PHONE..................................631 924-7446
Albert Borsella, *President*
EMP: 12
SALES (est): 1.3MM **Privately Held**
SIC: 3993 1799 5999 Electric signs; sign installation & maintenance; awnings

(G-8118)
MID ENTERPRISE INC
809 Middle Country Rd (11953-2511)
PHONE..................................631 924-3933
Shahid Ali Khan, *Principal*
EMP: 5
SALES (est): 541.5K **Privately Held**
SIC: 3578 Automatic teller machines (ATM)

Middle Village
Queens County

(G-8119)
ACCURATE SPECIALTY METAL FABRI
6420 Admiral Ave (11379-1614)
PHONE..................................718 418-6895
Ronald Palmerick, *Ch of Bd*
Gene Griffin, *Manager*
EMP: 35
SQ FT: 30,000
SALES: 7.2MM
SALES (corp-wide): 51.2MM **Privately Held**
WEB: www.asm-mech.com
SIC: 3444 Ducts, sheet metal
PA: Aabco Sheet Metal Co., Inc.
   47 40 Metropolitan Ave
   Ridgewood NY 11385
   718 821-1166

(G-8120)
AGLIKA TRADE LLC
5905 74th St (11379-5216)
PHONE..................................727 424-1944
Maya Petkova,
EMP: 10
SALES (est): 599.5K **Privately Held**
SIC: 3552 Textile machinery

(G-8121)
GOLDMONT ENTERPRISES INC
Also Called: Superior Model Form Co
7603 Caldwell Ave (11379-5233)
PHONE..................................212 947-3633
Vito Montalto, *President*
EMP: 15 **EST:** 1940
SQ FT: 7,000
SALES: 1MM **Privately Held**
WEB: www.superiormodel.com
SIC: 3999 Forms: display, dress & show

(G-8122)
J M R PLASTICS CORPORATION
5847 78th St (11379-5305)
PHONE..................................718 898-9825
John Daidone, *President*
Selina Daidone, *Corp Secy*
EMP: 8
SQ FT: 10,000

Middle Village - Queens County (G-8123)

SALES: 2MM *Privately Held*
SIC: 3089 Plastic kitchenware, tableware & houseware; plastic processing

(G-8123)
JONATHAN DAVID PUBLISHERS INC
6822 Eliot Ave (11379-1131)
PHONE ....(718) 456-8611
Alfred J Kolatch, *President*
Thelma Kolatch, *Corp Secy*
Carol Zelezny, *Accounting Mgr*
▲ **EMP:** 10 **EST:** 1949
SQ FT: 2,400
SALES (est): 860K *Privately Held*
WEB: www.jdbooks.com
SIC: 2731 Books: publishing only

(G-8124)
JUNIPER ELBOW CO INC (PA)
Also Called: Juniper Industries
7215 Metropolitan Ave (11379-2198)
P.O. Box 148 (11379-0148)
PHONE 718 326-2546
Jesse L Wiener, *CEO*
Celia Wiener, *Vice Pres*
Elliot Wiener, *Vice Pres*
▲ **EMP:** 185 **EST:** 1929
SQ FT: 100,000
SALES (est): 24.8MM *Privately Held*
WEB: www.juniperind.com
SIC: 3444 3498 3433 3312 Elbows, for air ducts, stovepipes, etc.: sheet metal; ventilators, sheet metal; metal ventilating equipment; fabricated pipe & fittings; heating equipment, except electric; blast furnaces & steel mills

(G-8125)
JUNIPER INDUSTRIES FLORIDA INC
7215 Metropolitan Ave (11379-2107)
PHONE 718 326-2546
▲ **EMP:** 5
SALES (est): 384.6K *Privately Held*
SIC: 3498 Mfg Fabricated Pipe/Fittings

(G-8126)
PATDAN FUEL CORPORATION
7803 68th Rd (11379-2836)
PHONE 718 326-3668
EMP: 6
SALES (est): 743.4K *Privately Held*
SIC: 2869 Fuels

(G-8127)
SILVER BELL BAKING CO
6406 Admiral Ave (11379-1614)
PHONE 718 335-9539
Dalia Radziunas, *Owner*
EMP: 8
SQ FT: 6,000
SALES (est): 361.4K *Privately Held*
SIC: 2051 Bread, cake & related products

(G-8128)
WETHERALL CONTRACTING NY INC
8312 Penelope Ave Ste 101 (11379-2321)
PHONE 718 894-7011
Bryan Wetherall, *President*
EMP: 5
SALES (est): 695.2K *Privately Held*
SIC: 2323 Men's & boys' neckwear

Middleburgh
Schoharie County

(G-8129)
DR REDDYS LABORATORIES NY INC
1974 State Route 145 (12122-5315)
PHONE 518 827-7702
Alok Sonig, *President*
Swaninathan Chandrasekaran, *Corp Secy*
Sunil Kumar Chebrolu, *Finance*
Gv Prasad, *Director*
Satish Reddy, *Director*
EMP: 30
SALES (est): 3MM *Privately Held*
SIC: 2834 Pharmaceutical preparations
HQ: Dr. Reddy's Laboratories, Inc.
107 College Rd E Ste 100
Princeton NJ 08540

(G-8130)
URREY LUMBER
663 Clauverwie Rd (12122-3411)
PHONE 518 827-4851
Allan Urrey, *Partner*
Jeff Urrey, *Partner*
Toni Urrey, *Partner*
EMP: 9
SALES: 2.1MM *Privately Held*
SIC: 2421 Sawmills & planing mills, general

Middleport
Niagara County

(G-8131)
BIRCH MACHINE & TOOL INC
80 Telegraph Rd (14105-9638)
PHONE 716 735-9802
Jerry Stadelman, *President*
Mary Stadelman, *Vice Pres*
EMP: 7
SQ FT: 1,500
SALES (est): 550K *Privately Held*
SIC: 3599 Machine & other job shop work; machine shop, jobbing & repair

(G-8132)
FMC CORPORATION
Also Called: F M C Aricultural Chem Group
100 Niagara St (14105-1398)
PHONE 716 735-3761
Stewart Throop, *Plant Mgr*
John Velletta, *Engineer*
Jessica Morton, *Sales Mgr*
Roger L Krough, *Branch Mgr*
EMP: 50
SALES (corp-wide): 2.8B *Publicly Held*
WEB: www.fmc.com
SIC: 2879 2819 Agricultural chemicals; industrial inorganic chemicals
PA: Fmc Corporation
2929 Walnut St
Philadelphia PA 19104
215 299-6000

(G-8133)
PERFORMANCE MFG INC
90 Telegraph Rd (14105-9638)
PHONE 716 735-3500
Jody P Herriven, *President*
Tim Worth, *Vice Pres*
EMP: 15
SALES (est): 2.2MM *Privately Held*
WEB: www.pmikartparts.com
SIC: 3599 Machine shop, jobbing & repair

(G-8134)
SIGMAMOTOR INC
3 N Main St (14105-1005)
P.O. Box 298 (14105-0298)
PHONE 716 735-3115
Donald Heschke Jr, *President*
Shari Heschke, *Corp Secy*
EMP: 22 **EST:** 1951
SQ FT: 6,500
SALES (est): 6MM *Privately Held*
SIC: 3599 3494 Machine shop, jobbing & repair; valves & pipe fittings

Middletown
Orange County

(G-8135)
209 DISCOUNT OIL
10 Sands Station Rd (10940-4415)
PHONE 845 386-2090
Steve Cortese, *Principal*
EMP: 20
SALES (est): 1.6MM *Privately Held*
SIC: 2911 Oils, fuel

(G-8136)
ADVANCED ENTERPRISES INC
Also Called: Wonder Products
366 Highland Ave Ext (10940-4454)
PHONE 845 342-1009
Eugene Polanish, *President*
Christian Al, *Principal*
▲ **EMP:** 10
SQ FT: 100
SALES (est): 1.5MM *Privately Held*
SIC: 3842 Cotton & cotton applicators

(G-8137)
ARCHITECTURAL ENHANCEMENTS INC
135 Crotty Rd (10941-4070)
P.O. Box 4680 (10941-8680)
PHONE 845 343-9663
Philip Cohen, *President*
Chaim Cohen, *Exec VP*
EMP: 10 **EST:** 1962
SQ FT: 31,000
SALES (est): 1.5MM *Privately Held*
SIC: 2431 Millwork

(G-8138)
BALL METAL BEVERAGE CONT CORP
Also Called: Ball Metal Beverage Cont Div
95 Ballard Rd (10941-3013)
PHONE 845 692-3800
Terree Angerame, *Principal*
Robert Chapin, *Principal*
Noreen Dellay, *Principal*
Mark Chandler, *Prdtn Mgr*
Thomas Young, *Prdtn Mgr*
EMP: 175
SALES (corp-wide): 10.9B *Publicly Held*
SIC: 3411 Aluminum cans
HQ: Ball Metal Beverage Container Corp.
9300 W 108th Cir
Westminster CO 80021

(G-8139)
BRAGA WOODWORKS
19 Montgomery St (10940-5115)
PHONE 845 342-4636
Leo Braga, *Owner*
EMP: 5
SALES (est): 410.6K *Privately Held*
SIC: 2431 Millwork

(G-8140)
BRAIDED OAK SPIRITS LLC
12 Roberts St (10940-5007)
PHONE 845 381-1525
Peter J Matos,
Peter Matos,
EMP: 17
SALES: 5.2MM *Privately Held*
SIC: 2085 Distilled & blended liquors

(G-8141)
CHROMALLOY GAS TURBINE LLC
Also Called: Chromalloy Middletown
105 Tower Dr (10941-2034)
PHONE 845 692-8912
Kenneth Martin, *Opers Mgr*
Matt Wilson, *Branch Mgr*
EMP: 28
SALES (corp-wide): 3.6B *Publicly Held*
WEB: www.chromalloysatx.com
SIC: 3479 3724 Painting, coating & hot dipping; aircraft engines & engine parts
HQ: Chromalloy Gas Turbine Llc
3999 Rca Blvd
Palm Beach Gardens FL 33410
561 935-3571

(G-8142)
CLASSIC HOSIERY INC
33 Mulberry St Ste 4 (10940-6359)
PHONE 845 342-6661
Tuvia Brach, *President*
▲ **EMP:** 35 **EST:** 1980
SQ FT: 18,000
SALES (est): 5.1MM *Privately Held*
SIC: 2251 Panty hose

(G-8143)
COMMERCIAL COMMUNICATIONS LLC
Also Called: Msdivisions
14 Montgomery St (10940-5116)
PHONE 845 343-9078
Steven Rosenblatt,
EMP:
SALES (est): 881.8K *Privately Held*
WEB: www.msdspring.com
SIC: 3495 Wire springs

(G-8144)
COUNTY DRAPERIES INC
64 Genung St (10940-5317)
PHONE 845 342-9009
Sara Markowitz, *CEO*
Carl Markowitz, *President*
David C Markowitz, *Vice Pres*
Krystal Bell, *Project Mgr*
Devi Heyer, *Project Mgr*
◆ **EMP:** 45
SQ FT: 50,000
SALES (est): 9.5MM *Privately Held*
WEB: www.drape.com
SIC: 2391 2392 Draperies, plastic & textile: from purchased materials; curtains, window: made from purchased materials; bedspreads & bed sets: made from purchased materials

(G-8145)
CROWN CORK & SEAL USA INC
21 Industrial Pl (10940)
PHONE 845 343-9586
EMP: 118
SALES (corp-wide): 8.7B *Publicly Held*
WEB: www.crowncork.com
SIC: 3411 Metal cans
HQ: Crown Cork & Seal Usa, Inc.
770 Township Line Rd # 100
Yardley PA 19067
215 698-5100

(G-8146)
D & W DESIGN INC (PA)
62 Industrial Pl (10940-3609)
PHONE 845 343-3366
Mariam Weiss, *President*
David Weiss, *Vice Pres*
Simon Kraus, *Manager*
Mike Toplamos, *Admin Sec*
▲ **EMP:** 26
SQ FT: 50,000
SALES: 3MM *Privately Held*
WEB: www.dustinwdesign.com
SIC: 2511 2514 5712 Wood household furniture; metal household furniture; furniture stores

(G-8147)
DELFORD INDUSTRIES INC
82 Washington St 84 (10940-4268)
P.O. Box 863 (10940-0863)
PHONE 845 342-3901
Robert L Reach Jr, *President*
Eric McCaffrey, *Opers Staff*
EMP: 80 **EST:** 1983
SQ FT: 55,000
SALES: 2MM *Privately Held*
WEB: www.delford-industries.com
SIC: 3061 Mechanical rubber goods

(G-8148)
E TETZ & SONS INC (PA)
130 Crotty Rd (10941-4059)
PHONE 845 692-4486
Edward Tetz Jr, *Ch of Bd*
Bob Weber, *Info Tech Mgr*
Denise Tetz, *Admin Sec*
EMP: 55 **EST:** 1979
SQ FT: 3,000
SALES (est): 22.8MM *Privately Held*
WEB: www.etetz-sons.com
SIC: 3273 1442 Ready-mixed concrete; construction sand & gravel

(G-8149)
EAD CASES
43 Smith St (10940-3710)
P.O. Box 957 (10940-0957)
PHONE 845 343-2111
Julio Diaz, *President*
EMP: 10
SALES (est): 975.1K *Privately Held*
SIC: 3161 Cases, carrying

(G-8150)
ECO-BAT AMERICA LLC
Also Called: RSR
65 Ballard Rd (10941-3013)
PHONE 845 692-4414
Dan Demercurio, *Branch Mgr*
EMP: 183

▲ = Import ▼=Export
◆ =Import/Export

GEOGRAPHIC SECTION

Middletown - Orange County (G-8175)

SQ FT: 20,000
SALES (corp-wide): 6.3MM Privately Held
SIC: 3356 3339 3341 Nonferrous rolling & drawing; precious metals; lead smelting & refining (secondary)
HQ: Eco-Bat America Llc
2777 N Stemmons Fwy # 1800
Dallas TX 75207
214 688-4000

(G-8151)
EQUILIBRIUM BREWERY LLC
22 Henry St (10940)
PHONE......................201 245-0292
Ricardo Petroni, CEO
Peter Oates, COO
EMP: 5
SQ FT: 6,800
SALES (est): 700K Privately Held
SIC: 2082 Malt beverages

(G-8152)
FAIRBANKS MFG LLC
79 Industrial Pl (10940-3608)
PHONE......................845 341-0002
Michael Ruppel, CFO
Zeke Alenick, Mng Member
◆ EMP: 145 EST: 2011
SQ FT: 100,000
SALES (est): 34.5MM Privately Held
SIC: 2064 Candy & other confectionery products

(G-8153)
FUEL DATA SYSTEMS INC
772 Greenville Tpke (10940-7125)
PHONE......................800 447-7870
Steve Michalek, President
EMP: 6 EST: 1989
SALES (est): 457.1K Privately Held
WEB: www.fueldatasystems.com
SIC: 7372 7371 Prepackaged software; custom computer programming services

(G-8154)
GENPAK INDUSTRIES INC
26 Republic Plz (10940-6543)
P.O. Box 727, Glens Falls (12801-0727)
PHONE......................518 798-9511
Jim Riley, President
EMP: 50
SALES (est): 9.4MM Privately Held
SIC: 2657 Food containers, folding: made from purchased material
HQ: Great Pacific Enterprises (U.S.) Inc.
10601 Westlake Dr
Charlotte NC 28273
518 761-2593

(G-8155)
GENPAK LLC
Republic Plz (10940)
PHONE......................845 343-7971
Betty Hager, Opers-Prdtn-Mfg
Jeff Cole, Marketing Mgr
James Cunningham, Manager
Bill Gentes, Facilities
EMP: 200
SQ FT: 150,000 Privately Held
WEB: www.genpak.com
SIC: 3089 5046 Plastic processing; commercial cooking & food service equipment
HQ: Genpak Llc
10601 Westlake Dr
Charlotte NC 28273
980 256-7729

(G-8156)
GERITREX LLC
40 Commercial Ave (10941-1444)
PHONE......................914 668-4003
Boyd Relac, President
Tim Sawyer, Chairman
John Francis, Exec VP
David Gershen, CFO
▲ EMP: 40
SQ FT: 47,500
SALES: 10.1MM Privately Held
WEB: www.geritrex.com
SIC: 2834 Pharmaceutical preparations

(G-8157)
GOLUB CORPORATION
Also Called: Price Chopper Pharmacy
511 Schutt Road Ext (10940-2569)
PHONE......................845 344-0327
EMP: 28
SALES (corp-wide): 3.3B Privately Held
SIC: 3751 Motorcycles & related parts
PA: The Golub Corporation
461 Nott St
Schenectady NY 12308
518 355-5000

(G-8158)
HONEYWELL INTERNATIONAL INC
13 Bedford Ave (10940-6401)
PHONE......................845 342-4400
EMP: 673
SALES (corp-wide): 40.5B Publicly Held
SIC: 3724 Aircraft engines & engine parts
PA: Honeywell International Inc.
115 Tabor Rd
Morris Plains NJ 07950
973 455-2000

(G-8159)
LOCAL MEDIA GROUP INC
Orange County Publications
40 Mulberry St (10940-6302)
P.C. Box 2046 (10940-0558)
PHONE......................845 341-1100
Dick Bayne, Editor
Shaniquah Gabino, Editor
Beth Kalet, Editor
Eric Stutz, Editor
Paul Woodruff, Plant Mgr
EMP: 290
SALES (corp-wide): 1.3B Publicly Held
WEB: www.ottaway.com
SIC: 2711 Newspapers: publishing only, not printed on site
HQ: Local Media Group, Inc.
40 Mulberry St
Middletown NY 10940
845 341-1100

(G-8160)
LOCAL MEDIA GROUP INC (DH)
40 Mulberry St (10940-6302)
P.O. Box 580 (10940-0580)
PHONE......................845 341-1100
John Wilcox, President
Patrick Purcell, Chairman
William T Kennedy, COO
Kurt Lozier, Senior VP
Patricia Gatto, Vice Pres
EMP: 50 EST: 1936
SQ FT: 10,000
SALES (est): 527.2MM
SALES (corp-wide): 1.3B Publicly Held
WEB: www.ottaway.com
SIC: 2711 7313 Newspapers: publishing only, not printed on site; newspaper advertising representative
HQ: Local Media Group Holdings, Llc
175 Sullys Trl Ste 300
Pittsford NY 14534
585 598-0030

(G-8161)
LOCAL MEDIA GROUP INC
Also Called: Times Herald-Record
60 Brookline Ave (10940)
PHONE......................845 341-1100
Andy Mark, Branch Mgr
EMP: 68
SALES (corp-wide): 1.3B Publicly Held
WEB: www.ottaway.com
SIC: 2711 Commercial printing & newspaper publishing combined
HQ: Local Media Group, Inc.
40 Mulberry St
Middletown NY 10940
845 341-1100

(G-8162)
MANDARIN SOY SAUCE INC
Also Called: Wan Ja Shan
4 Sands Station Rd (10940-4415)
PHONE......................845 343-1505
Michael Wu, Ch of Bd
▲ EMP: 25 EST: 1974
SQ FT: 85,000
SALES (est): 4.1MM Privately Held
WEB: www.wanjashan.com
SIC: 2035 5149 Seasonings & sauces, except tomato & dry; soy sauce; groceries & related products
PA: Wan Ja Shan Brewery Co., Ltd.
5f-6, 9, Dehui St.,
Taipei City TAP
266 180-101

(G-8163)
MEDLINE INDUSTRIES INC
3301 Route 6 (10940-6992)
PHONE......................845 344-3301
George Vargulish, Surgery Dir
EMP: 276
SALES (corp-wide): 5.6B Privately Held
SIC: 3842 3841 2326 2392 Surgical appliances & supplies; surgical & medical instruments; men's & boys' work clothing; household furnishings; surgical fabrics, cotton; scrub cloths; surgical equipment & supplies; hospital equipment & supplies; hospital furniture
PA: Medline Industries, Inc.
3 Lakes Dr
Northfield IL 60093
847 949-5500

(G-8164)
MIDDLETOWN PRESS (PA)
20 W Main St 26 (10940-5716)
PHONE......................845 343-1895
Jo Cover, Owner
EMP: 5
SQ FT: 2,800
SALES (est): 401.6K Privately Held
WEB: www.mtprintandpromote.com
SIC: 2752 7311 7336 5199 Commercial printing, offset; advertising agencies; graphic arts & related design; advertising specialties; commercial printing

(G-8165)
MIX N MAC LLC
280 Route 211 E (10940-3109)
PHONE......................845 381-5536
EMP: 5 EST: 2011
SALES (est): 413.6K Privately Held
SIC: 3273 Ready-mixed concrete

(G-8166)
MONROE CABLE COMPANY INC
14 Commercial Ave (10941-1444)
PHONE......................845 692-2800
Isaac Wieder, President
▲ EMP: 104 EST: 1978
SQ FT: 95,000
SALES (est): 39.3MM Privately Held
SIC: 3357 Shipboard cable, nonferrous; coaxial cable, nonferrous

(G-8167)
NEW DYNAMICS CORPORATION
15 Fortune Rd W (10941-1625)
PHONE......................845 692-0022
James Destefano, President
Walter Pawlowski, Vice Pres
EMP: 20
SQ FT: 35,000
SALES: 5MM Privately Held
WEB: www.newdynamics.net
SIC: 3842 5963 7349 Ear plugs; food services, direct sales; janitorial service, contract basis

(G-8168)
NEW YORK CUTTING & GUMMING CO
265 Ballard Rd (10941-3034)
PHONE......................212 563-4146
Jack Siegel, President
Richard Deteresa, Principal
Robert Siegel, Vice Pres
EMP: 45 EST: 1914
SQ FT: 44,000
SALES (est): 4.2MM Privately Held
SIC: 3089 2295 2675 2672 Laminating of plastic; laminating of fabrics; die-cut paper & board; coated & laminated paper

(G-8169)
OTTAWAY NEWSPAPERS INC
40 Mulberry St (10940-6302)
PHONE......................845 343-2181
Joe Vanderhoof, Principal

Kelly Walsh, Accounts Exec
EMP: 9 EST: 2010
SALES (est): 597.5K Privately Held
SIC: 2711 Newspapers, publishing & printing

(G-8170)
PILLER POWER SYSTEMS INC (DH)
45 Wes Warren Dr (10941-1772)
PHONE......................845 695-6658
Dean Richards, President
Mark Nuelle, Vice Pres
Charles Daling, Project Mgr
Eric Forman, Engineer
Frank Illemann, Engineer
▲ EMP: 40
SQ FT: 20,000
SALES: 65MM
SALES (corp-wide): 1B Privately Held
WEB: www.piller.com
SIC: 3699 3612 Electrical equipment & supplies; transformers, except electric
HQ: Piller Group Gmbh
Abgunst 24
Osterode Am Harz 37520
552 231-10

(G-8171)
PRESIDENT CONT GROUP II LLC
Also Called: Manufacturing Facility
290 Ballard Rd (10941-3035)
PHONE......................845 516-1600
John Parella, Manager
Sabrina Washington, Manager
EMP: 29
SALES: 7.9MM
SALES (corp-wide): 203.8MM Privately Held
SIC: 2653 Boxes, corrugated: made from purchased materials; sheets, corrugated: made from purchased materials; display items, corrugated: made from purchased materials
PA: President Container Group Ii, Llc
200 W Commercial Ave
Moonachie NJ 07074
201 933-7500

(G-8172)
PRINCETON UPHOLSTERY CO INC (PA)
Also Called: Bright Chair Co
51 Railroad Ave (10940-5117)
P.O. Box 269 (10940-0269)
PHONE......................845 343-2196
Stan Gottlieb, Ch of Bd
Roxanne Beacon, Human Res Mgr
Jody Gottlieb, Admin Sec
◆ EMP: 100
SQ FT: 100,000
SALES (est): 12.6MM Privately Held
WEB: www.brightchair.com
SIC: 2521 2512 Wood office furniture; upholstered household furniture

(G-8173)
RIJ PHARMACEUTICAL CORPORATION
40 Commercial Ave (10941-1444)
PHONE......................845 692-5799
Hassan Zaidi, CEO
Brij Gupta, President
EMP: 20
SQ FT: 52,000
SALES (est): 5.3MM Privately Held
WEB: www.rijpharm.com
SIC: 2834 Pharmaceutical preparations

(G-8174)
RIMS LIKE NEW INC
507 Union School Rd (10941-5018)
PHONE......................845 537-0396
Manuel P Heredia Jr, Owner
EMP: 10
SALES (est): 630K Privately Held
SIC: 3479 Painting of metal products

(G-8175)
S R & R INDUSTRIES INC
45 Enterprise Pl (10941-2043)
PHONE......................845 692-8329
Paul Rosanelli, President
EMP: 6
SQ FT: 10,000

Middletown - Orange County (G-8176)

SALES: 450K **Privately Held**
SIC: 3531 3462 3599 Rollers, sheepsfoot & vibratory; gears, forged steel; machine shop, jobbing & repair

(G-8176)
STAFFORD LABS ORTHOTICS/PROSTH
189 Monhagen Ave (10940-6020)
P.O. Box 1004, Goshen (10924-8004)
PHONE..................845 692-5227
Kimberly Thompson, *President*
EMP: 15
SALES (est): 1.2MM **Privately Held**
WEB: www.staffordlabsoandp.com
SIC: 3842 Limbs, artificial

(G-8177)
STERLING MOLDED PRODUCTS INC
9-17 Oliver Ave (10940-6095)
PHONE..................845 344-4546
Stephen Crescimanno, *Ch of Bd*
▲ EMP: 40
SALES (est): 7.2MM **Privately Held**
SIC: 3089 Injection molded finished plastic products; injection molding of plastics

(G-8178)
SURVING STUDIOS
17 Millsburg Rd (10940-8497)
PHONE..................845 355-1430
Natalie Surving, *Owner*
EMP: 10
SALES (est): 1.2MM **Privately Held**
SIC: 3469 8999 Tile, floor or wall: stamped metal; sculptor's studio

(G-8179)
TPI INDUSTRIES LLC (HQ)
265 Ballard Rd (10941-3034)
PHONE..................845 692-2820
John Bowe, *President*
▲ EMP: 42 EST: 1978
SQ FT: 50,000
SALES (est): 82.1MM
SALES (corp-wide): 184.2MM **Privately Held**
WEB: www.darlexx.com
SIC: 2295 Laminating of fabrics
PA: Shawmut Llc
208 Manley St
West Bridgewater MA 02379
508 588-3300

(G-8180)
TRIAD PRINTING INC
Also Called: Chester Printing Service
7 Prospect St (10940-4809)
PHONE..................845 343-2722
Joseph Stewart, *President*
Ralph Carr, *Corp Secy*
Michelle Francis, *Diabetes*
EMP: 5
SALES (est): 861.6K **Privately Held**
SIC: 2752 Commercial printing, offset

(G-8181)
TURBINE ARFOIL CATING REPR LLC
Also Called: Tacr
105 Tower Dr (10941-2034)
PHONE..................845 692-8912
Marc Lafontaine, *CFO*
Gerard Milidantri,
▲ EMP: 250
SQ FT: 65,000
SALES (est): 20.6MM **Privately Held**
SIC: 3479 Painting, coating & hot dipping

(G-8182)
UNIQUE QUALITY FABRICS INC
115 Wisner Ave (10940-3635)
PHONE..................845 343-3070
Henry Klein, *President*
◆ EMP: 7 EST: 1980
SQ FT: 13,000
SALES (est): 977.2K **Privately Held**
WEB: www.uniquequalityfabrics.com
SIC: 2221 Draperies & drapery fabrics, manmade fiber & silk

(G-8183)
WANJASHAN INTERNATIONAL LLC
4 Sands Station Rd (10940-4415)
PHONE..................845 343-1505
Michael Wu, *President*
◆ EMP: 17
SALES (est): 2.9MM **Privately Held**
SIC: 2035 Soy sauce

(G-8184)
WATEC AMERICA CORPORATION
720 Route 17m Ste 4 (10940-4350)
PHONE..................702 434-6111
Chia L Liu, *President*
EMP: 50
SALES (est): 4.3MM **Privately Held**
SIC: 3861 Cameras & related equipment

(G-8185)
ZENITH AUTOPARTS CORP
20 Industrial Pl (10940-3609)
PHONE..................845 344-1382
Moses Goldstein, *President*
Joel Goldstein, *Vice Pres*
▲ EMP: 25
SQ FT: 38,000
SALES: 5MM **Privately Held**
SIC: 3694 Ignition systems, high frequency

Middleville
Herkimer County

(G-8186)
E J WILLIS COMPANY INC
37 N Main St (13406)
PHONE..................315 891-7602
Evelyn Reile, *President*
EMP: 15
SQ FT: 75,000
SALES (est): 1MM **Privately Held**
SIC: 3599 Machine shop, jobbing & repair

Millbrook
Dutchess County

(G-8187)
ALICIA ADAMS ALPACA INC
3262 Franklin Ave (12545-5918)
P.O. Box 1455 (12545-1455)
PHONE..................845 868-3366
Alicaia Adams, *Ch of Bd*
Daniel Adams, *Principal*
EMP: 8
SALES (est): 700.2K **Privately Held**
SIC: 2231 2337 Alpacas, mohair: woven; women's & misses' capes & jackets

(G-8188)
GORDON S ANDERSON MFG CO
215 N Mabbettsville Rd (12545-5358)
P.O. Box 1459 (12545-1459)
PHONE..................845 677-3304
Stewart Anderson, *President*
Christine Horihan, *Vice Pres*
EMP: 7 EST: 1946
SQ FT: 7,000
SALES (est): 505.6K **Privately Held**
SIC: 3648 3559 Lighting equipment; pharmaceutical machinery

(G-8189)
MICRO SYSTEMS SPECIALISTS INC
Also Called: Mssi
3280 Franklin Ave Fl 2 (12545-5975)
P.O. Box 347 (12545-0347)
PHONE..................845 677-6150
Catherine Culkin, *President*
Dawn Roeller, *Vice Pres*
Eileen Sunderland, *Treasurer*
Judy Bruning, *Admin Sec*
EMP: 5
SQ FT: 2,000
SALES (est): 431K **Privately Held**
SIC: 7372 Business oriented computer software

(G-8190)
MILLBROOK WINERY INC
Also Called: Millbrook Vineyard
26 Wing Rd (12545-5017)
PHONE..................845 677-8383
John Dyson, *President*
John Graziano, *Vice Pres*
Jaclyn Wisniewski, *Manager*
▲ EMP: 12
SQ FT: 960
SALES (est): 1.7MM **Privately Held**
WEB: www.millbrookwine.com
SIC: 2084 Wines

Miller Place
Suffolk County

(G-8191)
MILLER PLACE PRINTING INC
451 Route 25a Unit 11 (11764-2500)
PHONE..................631 473-1158
Leah G Casey, *Ch of Bd*
EMP: 9
SALES (est): 1.1MM **Privately Held**
SIC: 2759 2752 Laser printing; business form & card printing, lithographic

Millerton
Dutchess County

(G-8192)
ASSOCIATED LIGHTNING ROD CO
6020 Route 22 (12546-4537)
P.O. Box 529 (12546-0529)
PHONE..................845 373-8309
Robert J Cooper, *President*
EMP: 18
SALES (est): 3.2MM **Privately Held**
WEB: www.alrci.com
SIC: 3643 Current-carrying wiring devices

(G-8193)
HARNEY & SONS TEA CORP (PA)
5723 Route 22 (12546-4521)
PHONE..................518 789-2100
Michael Harney, *Vice Pres*
Paul Harney, *Vice Pres*
Naomi Santana, *Opers Mgr*
Christopher McKenna, *Prdtn Mgr*
Elvira Cardenas, *Purchasing*
◆ EMP: 150
SQ FT: 90,000
SALES (est): 44.8MM **Privately Held**
WEB: www.harney.com
SIC: 2099 5149 5499 Tea blending; tea; tea

(G-8194)
ILLINOIS TOOL WORKS INC
5979 N Elm Ave (12546-4525)
PHONE..................860 435-2574
EMP: 89
SALES (corp-wide): 14.3B **Publicly Held**
SIC: 3089 Injection molding of plastics
PA: Illinois Tool Works Inc.
155 Harlem Ave
Glenview IL 60025
847 724-7500

Millport
Chemung County

(G-8195)
BLUE MANUFACTURING CO INC
3852 Watkins Rd (14864-9782)
PHONE..................607 796-2463
Teresa K Liston, *President*
Marlene Liston, *Vice Pres*
EMP: 6
SQ FT: 4,800
SALES (est): 733K **Privately Held**
WEB: www.bluemoonmanufacturing.com
SIC: 3599 Grease cups, metal

Milton
Ulster County

(G-8196)
PRAGMATICS TECHNOLOGY INC
14 Old Indian Trl (12547-5114)
PHONE..................845 795-5071
Chris Mack, *President*
EMP: 8 EST: 2000
SQ FT: 700
SALES (est): 1.4MM **Privately Held**
WEB: www.pragmaticstech.com
SIC: 3825 Semiconductor test equipment

(G-8197)
SONO-TEK CORPORATION (PA)
2012 Route 9w Stop 3 (12547-5034)
PHONE..................845 795-2020
Christopher L Coccio, *Ch of Bd*
R Stephen Harshbarger, *President*
Bennett D Bruntil, *Vice Pres*
Robb W Engle, *Vice Pres*
Shane Ketcham, *Engineer*
▲ EMP: 64 EST: 1975
SQ FT: 50,000
SALES: 11MM **Publicly Held**
WEB: www.sprayfluxing.com
SIC: 3499 Nozzles, spray: aerosol, paint or insecticide

(G-8198)
SUNDANCE INDUSTRIES INC
36 Greentree Ln (12547-5437)
PHONE..................845 795-5809
Alden Link, *President*
Carol Link, *Treasurer*
EMP: 5
SQ FT: 10,000
SALES: 1.5MM **Privately Held**
WEB: www.sundanceind.com
SIC: 3634 Juice extractors, electric

Mineola
Nassau County

(G-8199)
A & M STEEL STAMPS INC
55 Windsor Ave (11501-1923)
PHONE..................516 741-6223
Paul Argendorf, *President*
EMP: 5
SQ FT: 2,000
SALES: 500K **Privately Held**
SIC: 3953 Embossing seals & hand stamps

(G-8200)
AERO TRADES MFG CORP
65 Jericho Tpke (11501-2991)
PHONE..................516 746-3360
Jeffrey E Love, *President*
John Niebuhr, *Vice Pres*
EMP: 33 EST: 1931
SQ FT: 60,000
SALES (est): 6.6MM **Privately Held**
WEB: www.aerotrades.com
SIC: 3728 3444 Aircraft assemblies, sub-assemblies & parts; sheet metalwork

(G-8201)
AERODUCT INC
134 Herricks Rd (11501-2205)
PHONE..................516 248-9550
Alvin Soffler, *President*
Blanche Soffler, *Corp Secy*
Glen Soffler, *Vice Pres*
Glenn Soffler, *Vice Pres*
EMP: 20 EST: 1967
SQ FT: 3,500
SALES (est): 2.6MM **Privately Held**
WEB: www.aeroduct.com
SIC: 3444 1711 Sheet metalwork; ventilation & duct work contractor

(G-8202)
AGRECOLOR INC (PA)
400 Sagamore Ave (11501-1987)
PHONE..................516 741-8700
Anthony Greco, *President*

Donnie Superville, *Production*
Doreen Greco, *Treasurer*
EMP: 18
SQ FT: 15,000
SALES (est): 2.4MM **Privately Held**
WEB: www.agrecolor.com
SIC: 2752 2791 2789 Commercial printing, offset; typesetting; bookbinding & related work

(G-8203)
ALLEN AVIONICS INC
255 E 2nd St (11501-3524)
P.O. Box 350 (11501-0350)
PHONE..................................516 248-8080
Alton K Allen, *President*
Sylvia G Allen, *Vice Pres*
▲ **EMP:** 50
SQ FT: 80,000
SALES (est): 7.4MM **Privately Held**
WEB: www.allenavionics.com
SIC: 3677 3679 Filtration devices, electronic; delay lines

(G-8204)
AQUIFER DRILLING & TESTING INC (HQ)
Also Called: A D T
75 E 2nd St (11501-3503)
PHONE..................................516 616-6026
H Leonard Rexrode Jr, *Ch of Bd*
▲ **EMP:** 60
SQ FT: 22,000
SALES (est): 24MM **Privately Held**
SIC: 1382 7375 1711 Geological exploration, oil & gas field; information retrieval services; plumbing contractors
PA: Cascade Drilling, L.P.
9406 Massillon Rd
Dundee OH 44624
330 359-0079

(G-8205)
ARISTA INNOVATIONS INC
Also Called: Arista Printing
131 Liberty Ave (11501-3510)
PHONE..................................516 746-2262
Edward Sikorski, *President*
Eleanor Sikorski, *Corp Secy*
Leonard Sikorski, *Vice Pres*
Raymond Sikorski, *Vice Pres*
EMP: 30
SQ FT: 25,000
SALES (est): 3.8MM **Privately Held**
WEB: www.aristaprinters.com
SIC: 2752 2791 2789 2759 Commercial printing, offset; typesetting; bookbinding & related work; commercial printing

(G-8206)
BEARDSLEE REALTY
290 E Jericho Tpke (11501-2197)
PHONE..................................516 747-5557
Kan McDowbll, *Manager*
EMP: 6
SALES (corp-wide): 757.3K **Privately Held**
SIC: 2326 6519 Industrial garments, men's & boys'; real property lessors
PA: Beardslee Realty
27 To 22 Jackson Ave
Long Island City NY 11101
718 784-4100

(G-8207)
BIMBO BAKERIES USA INC
12 E Jericho Tpke (11501-3141)
PHONE..................................516 877-2850
EMP: 25
SALES (corp-wide): 13.7B **Privately Held**
SIC: 2051 Mfg Bread/Related Products
HQ: Bimbo Bakeries Usa, inc
255 Business Center Dr # 300
Horsham PA 19044
215 347-5500

(G-8208)
BLC TEXTILES INC
330 Old Country Rd # 201 (11501-4187)
P.O. Box 5485, New Hyde Park (11042-5485)
PHONE..................................844 500-7900
Mark Lichter, *CEO*
EMP: 26

SALES (est): 2.5MM **Privately Held**
SIC: 2299 Towels & towelings, linen & linen-and-cotton mixtures

(G-8209)
CANVAS PRODUCTS COMPANY INC
234 Herricks Rd (11501-2208)
PHONE..................................516 742-1058
Edwin E Youngstrom, *President*
EMP: 10
SQ FT: 1,500
SALES (est): 1MM **Privately Held**
SIC: 2394 Awnings, fabric: made from purchased materials

(G-8210)
CAROL PERETZ
Also Called: Carol Peretz Workshop
49 Windsor Ave Ste 103 (11501-1933)
PHONE..................................516 248-6300
Carol Peretz, *Owner*
EMP: 18
SQ FT: 4,000
SALES (est): 1.1MM **Privately Held**
WEB: www.carolperetz.com
SIC: 2335 Dresses, paper: cut & sewn

(G-8211)
CAST-ALL CORPORATION (PA)
229 Liberty Ave (11501-3575)
P.O. Box 271 (11501-0271)
PHONE..................................516 741-4025
Jack Mandell, *President*
Rose Mandell, *Corp Secy*
Chaim Mandell, *Vice Pres*
Theodore Mandell, *Vice Pres*
EMP: 35 **EST:** 1962
SALES (est): 3.6MM **Privately Held**
WEB: www.cast-all.com
SIC: 3089 3364 3429 3369 Injection molding of plastics; zinc & zinc-base alloy die-castings; manufactured hardware (general); nonferrous foundries

(G-8212)
CAST-ALL CORPORATION
229 Liberty Ave (11501-3575)
P.O. Box 271 (11501-0271)
PHONE..................................516 741-4025
Jack Mandell, *President*
EMP: 25
SALES (corp-wide): 3.6MM **Privately Held**
WEB: www.cast-all.com
SIC: 3364 3089 Zinc & zinc-base alloy die-castings; injection molding of plastics
PA: Cast-All Corporation
229 Liberty Ave
Mineola NY 11501
516 741-4025

(G-8213)
COMMON SENSE MARKETING INC
100 Herricks Rd (11501-3637)
PHONE..................................516 282-1214
Avishay Levanovsky, *CEO*
Amir Karp, *COO*
EMP: 4
SQ FT: 5,000
SALES: 6MM **Privately Held**
SIC: 3841 Diagnostic apparatus, medical; diagnostic equipment, medical
PA: Common Sense Ltd.
7 Haeshel
Caesarea
462 771-01

(G-8214)
COMPETICION MOWER REPAIR
75 Windsor Ave (11501-1983)
PHONE..................................516 280-6584
Christopher Sideris, *Owner*
EMP: 5
SALES (est): 495.7K **Privately Held**
SIC: 7692 Welding repair

(G-8215)
DCL FURNITURE MANUFACTURING
96 Windsor Ave (11501-1922)
PHONE..................................516 248-2683
Domingos Lopes, *President*
Carlos Lopes, *Manager*

EMP: 20
SQ FT: 2,000
SALES (est): 2.2MM **Privately Held**
WEB: www.dclfurniture.com
SIC: 2511 2522 2521 Wood household furniture; office furniture, except wood; wood office furniture

(G-8216)
DONMAR PRINTING CO
90 2nd St Ste 2 (11501-3060)
PHONE..................................516 280-2239
Sanford Scharf, *President*
EMP: 10
SALES (est): 251.8K **Privately Held**
SIC: 2752 Commercial printing, offset

(G-8217)
ELIAS ARTMETAL INC
70 E 2nd St (11501-3505)
P.O. Box 1872 (11501-0909)
PHONE..................................516 873-7501
Constantine Elias, *President*
Ruth Elias, *Vice Pres*
EMP: 19 **EST:** 1976
SQ FT: 9,000
SALES (est): 1MM **Privately Held**
WEB: www.eliasartmetal.com
SIC: 3499 Picture frames, metal; novelties & specialties, metal

(G-8218)
ENVIRONMENTAL TEMP SYSTEMS LLC
Also Called: Ets
111 Roosevelt Ave Ste C (11501-3056)
P.O. Box 701 (11501-0701)
PHONE..................................516 640-5818
Wayman Lee, *Mng Member*
Kwon Chan,
Joseph D'Alessio,
EMP: 5
SALES (est): 1.2MM **Privately Held**
SIC: 3585 Refrigeration & heating equipment

(G-8219)
EPS IRON WORKS INC
38 Windsor Ave Ste 101 (11501-1932)
PHONE..................................516 294-5840
Edward Strocchia, *President*
Philip Strocchia, *Vice Pres*
EMP: 8
SQ FT: 2,000
SALES (est): 1.7MM **Privately Held**
SIC: 3441 Fabricated structural metal

(G-8220)
ERICEIRA INC
Also Called: Bakers of All Nations
54 E Jericho Tpke (11501-3141)
PHONE..................................516 294-4034
Paula Rego, *President*
Joao Malheiro, *Treasurer*
EMP: 7
SALES (est): 540K **Privately Held**
WEB: www.ericeira.com
SIC: 2051 Bakery: wholesale or wholesale/retail combined

(G-8221)
EXTREME AUTO ACCESSORIES CORP (PA)
Also Called: Rennen International
235 Liberty Ave (11501-3513)
PHONE..................................718 978-6722
Takang Lee, *Ch of Bd*
Weizrung Lee, *COO*
Rich Sha, *Vice Pres*
▲ **EMP:** 15
SQ FT: 15,000
SALES (est): 3.9MM **Privately Held**
WEB: www.renneninternational.com
SIC: 3714 5013 Wheel rims, motor vehicle; automotive supplies

(G-8222)
F J REMEY CO INC
121 Willis Ave (11501-2612)
P.O. Box 589 (11501-0589)
PHONE..................................516 741-5112
Richard A Haas, *President*
EMP: 40
SQ FT: 20,000

SALES (est): 5.7MM **Privately Held**
WEB: www.fjremey.com
SIC: 2752 5112 Commercial printing, offset; stationery

(G-8223)
GENERAL LED CORP
206 E Jericho Tpke (11501-2034)
PHONE..................................516 280-2854
George Geffen, *President*
EMP: 6
SALES (est): 251.5K **Privately Held**
SIC: 3648 Lighting equipment

(G-8224)
GEOTECHNICAL DRILLING INC
Also Called: Environmental Closures
75 E 2nd St (11501-3503)
PHONE..................................516 616-6055
H L Rexrode Jr, *Ch of Bd*
William Poupis, *Vice Pres*
Rebecca Silber, *Admin Asst*
EMP: 85
SQ FT: 1,250
SALES (est): 3.2MM **Privately Held**
SIC: 1381 Drilling oil & gas wells

(G-8225)
H KLEIN & SONS INC
95 Searing Ave Ste 2 (11501-3046)
P.O. Box 349 (11501-0349)
PHONE..................................516 746-0163
Douglas Klein, *President*
Peter Klein, *Admin Sec*
EMP: 26 **EST:** 1902
SQ FT: 15,000
SALES (est): 4.7MM **Privately Held**
SIC: 3444 1761 Sheet metalwork; roofing contractor; sheet metalwork

(G-8226)
H R INDUSTRIES
393 Jericho Tpke (11501-1200)
PHONE..................................516 487-3825
EMP: 5
SALES (est): 324K **Privately Held**
SIC: 3088 Plastics plumbing fixtures

(G-8227)
HMS PRODUCTIONS LLC (PA)
72 Jericho Tpke (11501-1822)
PHONE..................................212 719-9190
Thomas Stanziale,
Dennis Belline Jr,
EMP: 5
SALES (est): 786.8K **Privately Held**
WEB: www.cousinfungus.com
SIC: 2399 Hand woven & crocheted products

(G-8228)
HYGRADE FUEL INC
260 Columbus Pkwy (11501-3137)
PHONE..................................516 741-0723
R Grieco, *Principal*
EMP: 5
SALES (est): 490.2K **Privately Held**
SIC: 2911 Oils, fuel

(G-8229)
ISLAND MARKETING CORP
95 Searing Ave Ste 2 (11501-3046)
PHONE..................................516 739-0500
Frank Scarangella, *President*
EMP: 5
SALES: 400K **Privately Held**
SIC: 2879 8742 Insecticides, agricultural or household; sales (including sales management) consultant

(G-8230)
ISLAND ORDNANCE SYSTEMS LLC
267 E Jericho Tpke Ste 2 (11501-2100)
PHONE..................................516 746-2100
Amnon Parizat, *President*
Anne Parizat, *Treasurer*
Linda Aguilo, *Controller*
◆ **EMP:** 13
SQ FT: 3,000
SALES (est): 2.3MM **Privately Held**
WEB: www.islandgroup.com
SIC: 3489 5099 5169 Ordnance & accessories; firearms & ammunition, except sporting; explosives

Mineola - Nassau County

(G-8231)
ISLAND PYROCHEMICAL INDS CORP (PA)
267 E Jericho Tpke Ste 2 (11501-2100)
PHONE..................................516 746-2100
Amnon Parizat, *President*
Robert Massey, *Business Mgr*
Claudia Orjuela, *Vice Pres*
Anne Parizat, *Vice Pres*
William Solomon, *VP Sls/Mktg*
◆ **EMP:** 215 **EST:** 1982
SQ FT: 6,000
SALES (est): 38.3MM **Privately Held**
WEB: www.worldvoi.com
SIC: 3081 2899 5169 Film base, cellulose acetate or nitrocellulose plastic; pyrotechnic ammunition: flares, signals, rockets, etc.; chemicals & allied products

(G-8232)
KHK USA INC
259 Elm Pl Ste 2 (11501-2960)
PHONE..................................516 248-3850
Toshiharu Kohara, *President*
Naoji Kohara, *Corp Secy*
EMP: 5 **EST:** 2015
SQ FT: 5,000
SALES: 1MM **Privately Held**
SIC: 3566 5084 5085 Gears, power transmission, except automotive; industrial machinery & equipment; gears

(G-8233)
LI COMMUNITY NEWSPAPERS INC
132 E 2nd St (11501-3533)
PHONE..................................516 747-8282
Angela Anton, *Publisher*
Julia Abreu, *Accounts Exec*
EMP: 5
SALES (est): 260.6K **Privately Held**
SIC: 2711 Commercial printing & newspaper publishing combined; newspapers, publishing & printing

(G-8234)
LIBERTY PIPE INCORPORATED
128 Liberty Ave (11501-3509)
PHONE..................................516 747-2472
John Kritis, *President*
EMP: 5
SALES (est): 516.5K **Privately Held**
SIC: 3317 Steel pipe & tubes

(G-8235)
LONG ISLAND CMNTY NWSPPERS INC (PA)
Also Called: Anton Community Newspapers
132 E 2nd St (11501-3522)
PHONE..................................516 482-4490
Angela Anton, *President*
EMP: 99
SALES (est): 7.4MM **Privately Held**
WEB: www.antonnews.com
SIC: 2711 7313 Commercial printing & newspaper publishing combined; newspaper advertising representative

(G-8236)
MAXIM HYGIENE PRODUCTS INC (PA)
Also Called: Organic Peak
121 E Jericho Tpke (11501-2031)
PHONE..................................516 621-3323
Kenneth Alvandi, *Ch of Bd*
▲ **EMP:** 15
SALES (est): 1.9MM **Privately Held**
SIC: 2676 Feminine hygiene paper products

(G-8237)
MEDIPOINT INC
Also Called: Medipoint International,
72 E 2nd St (11501-3591)
PHONE..................................516 294-8822
Peter Gollobin, *President*
EMP: 12
SQ FT: 7,200
SALES (est): 1.7MM **Privately Held**
SIC: 3841 Surgical instruments & apparatus; medical instruments & equipment, blood & bone work

(G-8238)
NASSAU CHROMIUM PLATING CO INC
122 2nd St (11501-3054)
PHONE..................................516 746-6666
George Waring, *President*
Shirley Waring, *Corp Secy*
EMP: 45 **EST:** 1929
SQ FT: 10,000
SALES (est): 4.6MM **Privately Held**
WEB: www.nassaufdrant.com
SIC: 3471 Plating of metals or formed products

(G-8239)
NORTH SHORE FARMS TWO LTD
330 E Jericho Tpke (11501-2111)
PHONE..................................516 280-6880
Jose Juan, *Store Mgr*
EMP: 8
SALES (est): 325.1K **Privately Held**
SIC: 2099 Food preparations

(G-8240)
NORTHEAST HARDWARE SPECIALTIES
393 Jericho Tpke Ste 103 (11501-1213)
PHONE..................................516 487-6868
Wayne A Reed Jr, *Owner*
EMP: 10
SALES: 174.6K **Privately Held**
SIC: 3599 Industrial machinery

(G-8241)
NORWOOD SCREW MACHINE PARTS
200 E 2nd St Ste 2 (11501-3519)
PHONE..................................516 481-6644
Gary Prchal, *President*
EMP: 10
SQ FT: 10,000
SALES: 1.5MM **Privately Held**
WEB: www.norwoodscrewmachine.com
SIC: 3451 Screw machine products

(G-8242)
NOVITA FABRICS FURNISHING CORP
207 Elm Pl Ste 2 (11501-2948)
PHONE..................................516 299-4500
David Rahimi, *President*
EMP: 12 **EST:** 2014
SQ FT: 12,000
SALES: 2.5MM **Privately Held**
SIC: 2299 Linen fabrics

(G-8243)
ORIGIN PRESS INC
131 Liberty Ave (11501-3510)
PHONE..................................516 746-2262
Ray Sikorski, *President*
EMP: 5
SQ FT: 3,000
SALES (est): 415.3K **Privately Held**
WEB: www.originpress.com
SIC: 2731 Book publishing

(G-8244)
RA NEWHOUSE INC (PA)
110 Liberty Ave (11501-3509)
P.O. Box 791 (11501-0791)
PHONE..................................516 248-6670
Richard A Newhouse Jr, *President*
EMP: 60 **EST:** 1955
SQ FT: 20,000
SALES (est): 7.5MM **Privately Held**
SIC: 2389 Uniforms & vestments; academic vestments (caps & gowns)

(G-8245)
RAYTECH CORP ASBESTOS PERSONAL
190 Willis Ave (11501-2672)
PHONE..................................516 747-0300
Richard A Lippe, *Mng Trustee*
EMP: 1710
SALES (est): 98.9MM **Privately Held**
SIC: 3499 Friction material, made from powdered metal

(G-8246)
REIS D FURNITURE MFG
327 Sagamore Ave Ste 2 (11501-1944)
PHONE..................................516 248-5676
Domingos Reis, *President*
Candida C Reis, *Corp Secy*
▼ **EMP:** 45
SQ FT: 15,000
SALES (est): 6.3MM **Privately Held**
WEB: www.mineolachamber.com
SIC: 2511 Wood household furniture

(G-8247)
RUBBER STAMPS INC
174 Herricks Rd (11501-2206)
PHONE..................................212 675-1180
Robert A Kowalsky, *President*
Abel Kowalsky, *Vice Pres*
Dorothy Kowalsky, *Admin Sec*
EMP: 25
SALES (est): 3MM **Privately Held**
WEB: www.rubberstampsinc.com
SIC: 3953 3555 2791 3069 Postmark stamps, hand: rubber or metal; printing plates; typographic composition, for the printing trade; stationers' rubber sundries

(G-8248)
S & V CUSTOM FURNITURE MFG
75 Windsor Ave Unit E (11501-1935)
PHONE..................................516 746-8299
Carlos Silva, *President*
Norman Kurtz, *Vice Pres*
George Valente, *Treasurer*
EMP: 10
SQ FT: 2,800
SALES (est): 1.2MM **Privately Held**
SIC: 2434 Wood kitchen cabinets

(G-8249)
SCHAEFER MACHINE CO INC
100 Hudson St (11501-3581)
PHONE..................................516 248-6880
Peter G Walter, *President*
Paul Rubilotta, *Vice Pres*
Paul Walter, *Vice Pres*
EMP: 22 **EST:** 1907
SQ FT: 15,000
SALES (est): 2.8MM **Privately Held**
WEB: www.schaeferco.com
SIC: 3542 3452 Machine tools, metal forming type; bolts, nuts, rivets & washers

(G-8250)
STANDARD DIVERSIFIED INC (HQ)
155 Mineola Blvd (11501-3920)
PHONE..................................302 824-7062
Gregory H A Baxter, *Ch of Bd*
Ian W Estus, *President*
Deborah Barbara, *VP Bus Dvlpt*
Edward J Sweeney, *CFO*
Michael Jones, *Manager*
EMP: 3
SALES: 285.8MM
SALES (corp-wide): 285.7MM **Publicly Held**
WEB: www.sdix.com
SIC: 2131 Chewing & smoking tobacco
PA: Turning Point Brands, Inc.
5201 Interchange Way
Louisville KY 40229
502 778-4421

(G-8251)
VISUAL ID SOURCE INC
65 E 2nd St (11501-3503)
PHONE..................................516 307-9759
Fayaz Khalfan, *Ch of Bd*
Adam ID, *Director*
EMP: 15
SQ FT: 20,000
SALES (est): 1.5MM **Privately Held**
SIC: 3993 Signs & advertising specialties

(G-8252)
WESTBURY TIMES
Also Called: Three Village Times
132 E 2nd St (11501-3522)
PHONE..................................516 747-8282
Angela Anton, *Owner*
EMP: 75
SALES (est): 1.7MM **Privately Held**
WEB: www.westburytimes.com
SIC: 2711 Newspapers, publishing & printing

Mineville
Essex County

(G-8253)
ESSEX INDUSTRIES
17 Pilfershire Rd (12956-1092)
P.O. Box 374 (12956-0374)
PHONE..................................518 942-6671
John Anello, *Manager*
EMP: 8
SALES (est): 849.4K **Privately Held**
SIC: 3999 Manufacturing industries

(G-8254)
PRE-TECH PLASTICS INC
3085 Plank Rd (12956-1050)
P.O. Box 370 (12956-0370)
PHONE..................................518 942-5950
Mike Cave, *Branch Mgr*
EMP: 30
SALES (corp-wide): 11.9MM **Privately Held**
WEB: www.pretechplastics.com
SIC: 3599 Machine shop, jobbing & repair
PA: Pre-Tech Plastics, Inc.
209 Blair Park Rd
Williston VT 05495
802 879-9441

Mohawk
Herkimer County

(G-8255)
MARY F MORSE
Also Called: Kwik Kut Manufacturing Co
125 Columbia St Ste 1 (13407-1527)
P.O. Box 116 (13407-0116)
PHONE..................................315 866-2741
Mary Morse, *Owner*
EMP: 8 **EST:** 1954
SQ FT: 3,600
SALES (est): 888.1K **Privately Held**
WEB: www.kwik-kut.com
SIC: 3556 Choppers, commercial, food

(G-8256)
R D R INDUSTRIES INC
146 W Main St (13407-1085)
PHONE..................................315 866-5020
Mark Rushton, *President*
EMP: 17
SQ FT: 22,000
SALES (est): 2.9MM **Privately Held**
SIC: 3444 Metal housings, enclosures, casings & other containers

Mohegan Lake
Westchester County

(G-8257)
BARONE OFFSET PRINTING CORP
89 Lake Ridge Cv (10547-1222)
PHONE..................................212 989-5500
Sandra Barone, *President*
EMP: 5
SALES (est): 541.3K **Privately Held**
WEB: www.baronepress.com
SIC: 2752 Commercial printing, offset

(G-8258)
ICON ENTERPRISES INTL INC
Also Called: Icon-TV
2653 Stony St (10547-2009)
PHONE..................................718 752-9764
Claudio Laraia, *President*
Moe Belin, *Vice Pres*
▲ **EMP:** 23
SQ FT: 7,000
SALES (est): 4.2MM **Privately Held**
WEB: www.icon-tv.org
SIC: 3663 Satellites, communications; television monitors; radio broadcasting & communications equipment; television broadcasting & communications equipment

GEOGRAPHIC SECTION

Monsey - Rockland County (G-8290)

(G-8259)
SHOPPING CENTER WINE & LIQUOR
Also Called: Kimbri Liquor
3008 E Main St (10547)
PHONE..................914 528-1600
Cathereen Lebleu, *Owner*
EMP: 5
SALES (est): 176.1K **Privately Held**
SIC: 2086 Bottled & canned soft drinks

(G-8260)
SOHO EDITIONS INC
2641 Deer St (10547-2019)
PHONE..................914 591-5100
Elliot Burns, *CEO*
Nicole Mone, *Vice Pres*
EMP: 25
SALES (est): 2.1MM **Privately Held**
WEB: www.sohoeditions.com
SIC: 2741 Art copy: publishing & printing

Moira
Franklin County

(G-8261)
MOIRA NEW HOPE FOOD PANTRY
2341 County Route 5 (12957)
PHONE..................518 529-6524
Joanne Deno, *Director*
EMP: 20
SALES (est): 1MM **Privately Held**
SIC: 2099 Food preparations

Monroe
Orange County

(G-8262)
6TH AVE GOURMET INC
51 Forest Rd Unit 116 (10950-2948)
PHONE..................845 782-9067
Clara Perl, *President*
EMP: 8
SQ FT: 4,000
SALES (est): 678.7K **Privately Held**
SIC: 2092 Fresh or frozen packaged fish

(G-8263)
ASSOCIATED DRAPERY & EQUIPMENT
Also Called: Novelty Scenic Studios Inc
3 Kosnitz Dr Unit 111 (10950-1163)
PHONE..................516 671-5245
Feivel Weiss, *Principal*
Howard Kessler, *Corp Secy*
Leslie Kessler, *Vice Pres*
EMP: 10 **EST:** 1968
SQ FT: 19,000
SALES (est): 838.6K
SALES (corp-wide): 1.1MM **Privately Held**
SIC: 2391 Curtains & draperies
PA: Novelty Scenic Studios Inc
3 Kosnitz Dr Unit 111
Monroe NY
516 671-5940

(G-8264)
B & H ELECTRONICS CORP
308 Museum Village Rd (10950-1638)
PHONE..................845 782-5000
Harvey Horowitz, *President*
Bernard Horowitz, *Vice Pres*
EMP: 25
SQ FT: 7,300
SALES (est): 2.3MM **Privately Held**
WEB: www.bhelectronicscorp.com
SIC: 3663 8734 3651 3699 Amplifiers, RF power & IF; testing laboratories; household audio & video equipment; electrical equipment & supplies

(G-8265)
BLOOMING GROVE STAIR CO (PA)
1 Stair Way (10950-1642)
PHONE..................845 783-4245
Glen Durant, *President*
Serena Aglaff, *Co-Owner*
EMP: 11
SALES (est): 1.1MM **Privately Held**
SIC: 2431 Stair railings, wood

(G-8266)
C T A DIGITAL INC (PA)
Also Called: Sol Markowitz
326 State Route 208 (10950-2874)
PHONE..................845 513-0433
Joseph Markowitz, *Ch of Bd*
Leo Markowitz, *President*
Eli Treitel, *Bookkeeper*
Steve Stern, *Sales Mgr*
Al Hoffman, *Director*
▲ **EMP:** 25
SALES (est): 12.7K **Privately Held**
WEB: www.ctadigital.com
SIC: 3944 Video game machines, except coin-operated

(G-8267)
CHECK-O-MATIC INC
13 D A Weider Blvd # 101 (10950-6124)
P.O. Box 2141 (10949-7141)
PHONE..................845 781-7675
Chaim Ellenbogen, *President*
Pearl Gruber, *Admin Sec*
EMP: 7
SQ FT: 2,500
SALES (est): 1.3MM **Privately Held**
WEB: www.checkomatic.com
SIC: 2759 Publication printing

(G-8268)
DER BLATT INC
6 Taitch Ct Unit 112 (10950-2195)
PHONE..................845 783-1148
Aron Muller, *Principal*
EMP: 11
SALES (est): 1.6MM **Privately Held**
SIC: 2711 Newspapers, publishing & printing

(G-8269)
FIVE STAR CREATIONS INC
4 Preshburg Blvd Unit 302 (10950-2968)
PHONE..................845 783-1187
Baruch Weiss, *President*
EMP: 20
SQ FT: 1,500
SALES (est): 1.7MM **Privately Held**
SIC: 3961 3999 3911 Costume jewelry; bric-a-brac; jewelry, precious metal

(G-8270)
G & M CLEARVIEW INC
Also Called: Clearview Glass & Mirror
112 Spring St (10950-3679)
PHONE..................845 781-4877
Chaim Weisberg, *President*
EMP: 6
SALES (est): 436.7K **Privately Held**
SIC: 3231 Mirrored glass

(G-8271)
H&F PRODUCTS INC
51 Forest Rd Ste 360 (10950-2938)
PHONE..................845 651-6100
Rivkah Brach, *Ch of Bd*
EMP: 6
SALES (est): 522K **Privately Held**
SIC: 2037 Frozen fruits & vegetables

(G-8272)
HOUSE OF STONE INC
1015 State Route 17m (10950-1626)
PHONE..................845 782-7271
Raymond Krok Sr, *President*
EMP: 6
SALES (est): 695.6K **Privately Held**
SIC: 3281 Granite, cut & shaped

(G-8273)
JOEL KIRYAS MEAT MARKET CORP
Also Called: Kirays & Joel Meat Market
51 Forest Rd Ste 345 (10950-2939)
PHONE..................845 782-9194
Harry Polatchek, *President*
Moses Mewman, *Vice Pres*
EMP: 14
SQ FT: 3,000
SALES (est): 1.8MM **Privately Held**
SIC: 2011 Meat by-products from meat slaughtered on site

(G-8274)
JW CONSULTING INC
Also Called: KJ MEAT DIRECT
20 Chevron Rd Unit 201 (10950-7432)
PHONE..................845 325-7070
Joel Weiss, *President*
EMP: 2 **EST:** 1987
SQ FT: 1,000
SALES (est): 4MM **Privately Held**
SIC: 2015 Poultry slaughtering & processing

(G-8275)
LASER PRINTER CHECKS CORP
7 Vayoel Moshe Ct # 101 (10950-6387)
PHONE..................845 782-5837
Solomon Klagsbrun, *President*
▼ **EMP:** 6
SALES (est): 696.5K **Privately Held**
SIC: 2752 Commercial printing, lithographic

(G-8276)
MARKOWITZ JEWELRY CO INC
53 Forest Rd Ste 104 (10950-2903)
PHONE..................845 774-1175
Isaac Markowitz, *President*
Baruch Markowitz, *Vice Pres*
EMP: 30
SQ FT: 10,000
SALES (est): 4.4MM **Privately Held**
WEB: www.markowitzjewelry.com
SIC: 3911 Jewelry, precious metal

(G-8277)
MEDEK LABORATORIES INC
63 First Ave (10950-2063)
PHONE..................845 943-4988
Isaac Schwartz, *COO*
EMP: 27
SALES (est): 1.3MM **Privately Held**
SIC: 2834 Solutions, pharmaceutical

(G-8278)
MONROE STAIR PRODUCTS INC (PA)
1 Stair Way (10950-1642)
PHONE..................845 783-4245
Glen T Durant, *President*
Jesse J Kehoe, *Vice Pres*
Paul Graham, *Treasurer*
EMP: 29
SQ FT: 21,500
SALES (est): 3MM **Privately Held**
WEB: www.bloominggrovestair.com
SIC: 2431 Staircases & stairs, wood

(G-8279)
PRIMA SATCHEL INC
51 Forest Rd Ste 302 (10950-2938)
PHONE..................929 367-7770
Joachim Feldman, *President*
EMP: 6
SQ FT: 2,000
SALES (est): 500K **Privately Held**
SIC: 2393 Textile bags

(G-8280)
REB LYBSS INC
44 Virginia Ave (10950-2214)
PHONE..................845 238-5633
Mendel Rosenberg, *President*
EMP: 4
SALES (est): 3MM **Privately Held**
SIC: 2844 Toilet preparations

(G-8281)
STOP ENTERTAINMENT INC
408 Rye Hill Rd (10950-4509)
PHONE..................212 242-7867
EMP: 15
SQ FT: 1,500
SALES (est): 1.1MM **Privately Held**
SIC: 2732 7311 Book Printing Advertising Agency

(G-8282)
TRI COUNTY CUSTOM VACUUM
653 State Route 17m (10950-3309)
PHONE..................845 774-7595
Mike Zahra, *Partner*
EMP: 5
SALES: 200K **Privately Held**
SIC: 3635 Household vacuum cleaners

Monsey
Rockland County

(G-8283)
A&B CONSERVATION LLC
12 Maple Leaf Rd (10952-3030)
PHONE..................845 282-7272
Baruch Tabak, *General Mgr*
Dovber Tabak, *Manager*
Judah Rominek,
EMP: 7
SQ FT: 1,000
SALES (est): 499.6K **Privately Held**
SIC: 3295 Pumice, ground or otherwise treated

(G-8284)
AMERTAC HOLDINGS INC (PA)
25 Robert Pitt Dr (10952-3365)
PHONE..................610 336-1330
Charles Peifer, *Ch of Bd*
John Cooper, *President*
Peter Hermann, *Vice Pres*
EMP: 6
SALES (est): 29.7MM **Privately Held**
SIC: 3699 3429 5063 5072 Electrical equipment & supplies; manufactured hardware (general); metal fasteners; electrical apparatus & equipment; hardware; tacks

(G-8285)
ARONOWITZ METAL WORKS
5 Edwin Ln (10952-3102)
PHONE..................845 356-1660
Avigdor Aronowitz, *Owner*
Sal Hurst CPA, *Accountant*
EMP: 5
SQ FT: 2,900
SALES (est): 293.7K **Privately Held**
SIC: 2522 Office furniture, except wood

(G-8286)
ATLANTIC SPECIALTY CO INC
20 Jeffrey Pl (10952-2703)
PHONE..................845 356-2502
Mark Srulowitz, *President*
Seung Lee, *Treasurer*
EMP: 20 **EST:** 1908
SQ FT: 5,000
SALES (est): 2MM **Privately Held**
SIC: 3161 3172 Luggage; key cases

(G-8287)
DJS NYC INC
Also Called: Deejays
15 S Remsen St (10952-2807)
PHONE..................845 445-8618
Chaim Einhorn, *President*
Sarah Koenig, *Admin Sec*
EMP: 8
SALES: 1.6MM **Privately Held**
SIC: 3674 Solid state electronic devices

(G-8288)
DVASH FOODS INC
2 Brewer Rd (10952-4001)
PHONE..................845 578-1959
Mel Gertner, *President*
▲ **EMP:** 10 **EST:** 2008
SALES (est): 2.4MM **Privately Held**
SIC: 2038 Frozen specialties

(G-8289)
MAGCREST PACKAGING INC
Also Called: Wally Packaging
5 Highview Rd (10952-2943)
PHONE..................845 425-0451
Aaron Rubinson, *President*
Gitty Rubinson, *Vice Pres*
◆ **EMP:** 6
SALES (est): 1.3MM **Privately Held**
WEB: www.magcrest.com
SIC: 2673 7389 Plastic bags: made from purchased materials;

(G-8290)
MAVIANO CORP
21 Robert Pitt Dr Ste 207 (10952-5305)
PHONE..................845 494-2598
Brenda Falk, *President*
EMP: 7

Monsey - Rockland County (G-8291)

SALES (est): 549.3K **Privately Held**
SIC: 2821 Plastics materials & resins

(G-8291)
NAVY PLUM LLC
47 Plum Rd (10952-1525)
PHONE..................845 641-7441
Jonathan Joseph,
▲ EMP: 3
SQ FT: 2,500
SALES: 40MM **Privately Held**
SIC: 2299 5199 Fabrics: linen, jute, hemp, ramie; yarn: flax, jute, hemp & ramie; fabrics, yarns & knit goods

(G-8292)
NYAHB INC
161 Route 59 Ste 101 (10952-7817)
P.O. Box 448, Spring Valley (10977-0448)
PHONE..................845 352-5300
Alexander D Kranz, *President*
Evette Kranz, *Vice Pres*
Tara J Collazo, *Director*
Gary Bondi, *Shareholder*
▲ EMP: 3
SALES (est): 1.5MM **Privately Held**
WEB: www.galex.net
SIC: 3354 Aluminum extruded products

(G-8293)
PLASTICWARE LLC (PA)
13 Wilsher Dr (10952-2328)
PHONE..................845 267-0790
Sam Meth, *Mng Member*
EMP: 16
SQ FT: 10,000
SALES (est): 6.3MM **Privately Held**
SIC: 3089 Plastic containers, except foam

(G-8294)
PRINT IT INC
59 Route 59 Ste 141 (10952-3543)
PHONE..................845 371-2227
EMP: 7
SALES (est): 163.5K **Privately Held**
SIC: 2752 Commercial printing, lithographic

(G-8295)
S B MANUFACTURING LLC
161 Route 59 (10952-7819)
PHONE..................845 352-3700
Michael Bloch, *President*
Ralph Heidings, *CFO*
EMP: 14
SALES (est): 1.9MM **Privately Held**
SIC: 3999 Barber & beauty shop equipment

(G-8296)
SAFE-DENT ENTERPRISES LLC
4 Orchard Hill Dr (10952-1503)
PHONE..................845 362-0141
Hedy Worch, *Mng Member*
EMP: 5
SQ FT: 20,000
SALES (est): 442K **Privately Held**
SIC: 3843 Dental materials

(G-8297)
SB MOLDS LLC
161 Route 59 Ste 203a (10952-7817)
PHONE..................845 352-3700
Michael Bloch, *Mng Member*
EMP: 80
SALES (est): 3.3MM **Privately Held**
SIC: 3544 Industrial molds

(G-8298)
SUNRISE SNACKS ROCKLAND INC (PA)
3 Sunrise Dr (10952)
PHONE..................845 352-2676
Moshe A Singer, *President*
Rivka Singer, *Sales Staff*
EMP: 15 EST: 2008
SQ FT: 22,000
SALES: 1.4MM **Privately Held**
SIC: 2099 Popcorn, packaged: except already popped

(G-8299)
SZ - DESIGN & PRINT INC
Also Called: S Z Design & Prints
33 Rita Ave (10952-2699)
PHONE..................845 659-2273
Shlomo Zeibe, *President*
EMP: 13
SALES (est): 2MM **Privately Held**
SIC: 2752 Commercial printing, lithographic

(G-8300)
TA CHEN INTERNATIONAL INC
Also Called: Galax
17 Main St Ste 217 (10952-3707)
PHONE..................845 352-5300
Alex Kranz, *Branch Mgr*
EMP: 10
SALES (corp-wide): 2.1B **Privately Held**
SIC: 3452 5051 Bolts, nuts, rivets & washers; steel
HQ: Ta Chen International, Inc.
 5855 Obispo Ave
 Long Beach CA 90805
 562 808-8000

(G-8301)
TAMI GREAT FOOD CORP
22 Briarcliff Dr (10952-2503)
PHONE..................845 352-7901
David Rosenberg, *President*
Martin Rosenberg, *President*
Renee Rosenberg, *Vice Pres*
EMP: 8
SQ FT: 6,000
SALES (est): 585.6K **Privately Held**
SIC: 2037 2038 Vegetables, quick frozen & cold pack, excl. potato products; frozen specialties

(G-8302)
TELE-PAK INC
Also Called: Card Printing.us
421 Route 59 Ste 7 (10952-2847)
P.O. Box 430 (10952-0430)
PHONE..................845 426-2300
Jack Steinmetz, *Ch of Bd*
Al Zowada, *Production*
Abraham Joseph, *Accountant*
Isaac Adler, *Sales Dir*
Ben Steinmetz, *Sales Mgr*
◆ EMP: 42
SQ FT: 7,000
SALES (est): 8.8MM **Privately Held**
WEB: www.tele-pak.com
SIC: 2754 2759 2752 7929 Commercial printing, gravure; commercial printing; cards, lithographed; entertainers & entertainment groups

(G-8303)
YATED NEEMAN INC
53 Olympia Ln (10952-2829)
PHONE..................845 369-1600
Pinchos Lipschutz, *President*
▲ EMP: 12
SALES (est): 687K **Privately Held**
WEB: www.yated.com
SIC: 2711 Newspapers: publishing only, not printed on site

Montauk
Suffolk County

(G-8304)
JESSE JOECKEL
Also Called: Whalebone Creative
65 Tuthill Rd (11954-5460)
PHONE..................631 668-2772
Jesse Joeckel, *Owner*
EMP: 5
SQ FT: 600
SALES (est): 385.5K **Privately Held**
SIC: 2339 Women's & misses' outerwear

(G-8305)
MONTAUK BREWING COMPANY INC
62 S Erie Ave (11954-5370)
P.O. Box 1079 (11954-0802)
PHONE..................631 668-8471
Vaughan Cutillo, *Vice Pres*
EMP: 10

SALES (est): 25.9K **Privately Held**
SIC: 2082 Beer (alcoholic beverage)

(G-8306)
MONTAUK INLET SEAFOOD INC
E Lake Dr Ste 540-541 (11954)
P.O. Box 2148 (11954-0905)
PHONE..................631 668-3419
Charles S Weimar, *President*
David Aripocth, *Owner*
Kevin Maguire, *Owner*
William Grimm, *Vice Pres*
Richard Jones, *Treasurer*
EMP: 3
SQ FT: 5,000
SALES (est): 1MM **Privately Held**
SIC: 2092 5146 5983 Fish, fresh: prepared; fish, fresh; fuel oil dealers

(G-8307)
NYEMAC INC
Also Called: On Montauk
Paradise Ln (11954)
P.O. Box 2087 (11954-0903)
PHONE..................631 668-1303
Joseph Nye, *President*
Carol Macdonald-Nye, *President*
EMP: 8 EST: 1990
SQ FT: 1,200
SALES (est): 690K **Privately Held**
SIC: 2721 4813 Magazines: publishing only, not printed on site;

Montgomery
Orange County

(G-8308)
BAXTER INTERNATIONAL INC
500 Neelytown Rd (12549-2828)
PHONE..................845 457-9370
EMP: 5
SALES (corp-wide): 10.5B **Publicly Held**
SIC: 2834 Pharmaceutical preparations
PA: Baxter International Inc.
 1 Baxter Pkwy
 Deerfield IL 60015
 224 948-2000

(G-8309)
CALLANAN INDUSTRIES INC
215 Montgomery Rd (12549-2814)
P.O. Box 505, Maybrook (12543-0505)
PHONE..................845 457-3158
Charlie Tady, *Opers Mgr*
Kevin Schuler, *Manager*
EMP: 25
SALES (corp-wide): 29.7B **Privately Held**
WEB: www.callanan.com
SIC: 2951 5032 2952 Asphalt & asphaltic paving mixtures (not from refineries); stone, crushed or broken; asphalt felts & coatings
HQ: Callanan Industries, Inc.
 8 Southwoods Blvd Ste 4
 Albany NY 12211
 518 374-2222

(G-8310)
CARLISLE CONSTRUCTION MTLS LLC
9 Hudson Crossing Dr (12549-2854)
PHONE..................386 753-0786
Scott Pearson, *Manager*
EMP: 65
SALES (corp-wide): 4B **Publicly Held**
WEB: www.hpanels.com
SIC: 3086 Insulation or cushioning material, foamed plastic
HQ: Carlisle Construction Materials, Llc
 1285 Ritner Hwy
 Carlisle PA 17013

(G-8311)
GLAXOSMITHKLINE LLC
3 Tyler St (12549-1609)
PHONE..................845 341-7590
EMP: 26
SALES (corp-wide): 39.8B **Privately Held**
SIC: 2834 Pharmaceutical preparations
HQ: Glaxosmithkline Llc
 5 Crescent Dr
 Philadelphia PA 19112
 215 751-4000

(G-8312)
GROSSO MATERIALS INC
90 Collabar Rd (12549-1805)
PHONE..................845 361-5211
Allan Grosso, *President*
EMP: 10
SQ FT: 300
SALES (est): 1.7MM **Privately Held**
SIC: 1459 5261 5032 Shale (common) quarrying; top soil; stone, crushed or broken

(G-8313)
JOHN WILEY & SONS INC
46 Wavey Willow Ln (12549-1501)
PHONE..................845 457-6250
Kalli Schultea, *Editor*
Victoria Angus, *Information Mgr*
EMP: 65
SALES (corp-wide): 1.8B **Publicly Held**
SIC: 2731 Textbooks: publishing only, not printed on site
PA: John Wiley & Sons, Inc.
 111 River St Ste 2000
 Hoboken NJ 07030
 201 748-6000

(G-8314)
NORTHEAST CNSTR INDS INC
Also Called: Nci Panel Systems
657 Rte 17 K S St Ste 2 (12549)
PHONE..................845 565-1000
Robert Schroeder, *President*
EMP: 10 EST: 1999
SQ FT: 12,000
SALES: 630K **Privately Held**
SIC: 3316 Cold finishing of steel shapes

(G-8315)
ORANGE COUNTY IRONWORKS LLC
36 Maybrook Rd (12549-2815)
PHONE..................845 769-3000
Todd Cicardo, *Project Mgr*
Matthew Haaksma, *Project Mgr*
Shawn Quill, *Project Mgr*
John Villielm, *Project Mgr*
Steve Michael, *Prdtn Mgr*
EMP: 44
SQ FT: 65,000
SALES: 61.3MM **Privately Held**
SIC: 3449 3441 1541 Miscellaneous metalwork; fabricated structural metal; industrial buildings, new construction

(G-8316)
QUICK ROLL LEAF MFG CO INC (PA)
118 Bracken Rd (12549-2600)
P.O. Box 53, Middletown (10940-0053)
PHONE..................845 457-1500
Charles E Quick, *Ch of Bd*
Edward Quick Jr, *President*
William Crowley, *Vice Pres*
Solena Quick-Porras, *Manager*
EMP: 48
SQ FT: 80,000
SALES (est): 33.8MM **Privately Held**
SIC: 3497 Metal foil & leaf

(G-8317)
REUTER PALLET PKG SYS INC
272 Neelytown Rd (12549-2840)
PHONE..................845 457-9937
Joseph A Carfizzi Sr, *President*
George Reuter Jr, *Vice Pres*
EMP: 9
SQ FT: 10,000
SALES (est): 920.4K **Privately Held**
SIC: 2448 2441 Wood pallets & skids; nailed wood boxes & shook

(G-8318)
TILCON NEW YORK INC
Also Called: Maybrook Asphalt
215 Montgomery Rd (12549-2814)
PHONE..................845 457-3158
Ciaran Brennan, *Principal*
EMP: 63
SALES (corp-wide): 29.7B **Privately Held**
SIC: 1429 Dolomitic marble, crushed & broken-quarrying

GEOGRAPHIC SECTION

Mount Kisco - Westchester County (G-8342)

HQ: Tilcon New York Inc.
9 Entin Rd
Parsippany NJ 07054
800 789-7625

(G-8319)
VALAD ELECTRIC HEATING CORP
65 Leonards Dr (12549-2643)
PHONE..................888 509-4927
Arthur Cecchini, *Ch of Bd*
Lauren Cecchini, *Corp Secy*
Arthur Cecchini Jr, *Vice Pres*
Lauren Cecchini Janes, *Treasurer*
Lauren James, *Manager*
EMP: 12 **EST:** 1941
SQ FT: 35,000
SALES (est): 3.3MM **Privately Held**
WEB: www.valadelectric.com
SIC: 3634 Heaters, space electric; electric household cooking appliances

Monticello
Sullivan County

(G-8320)
BLOOMING GROVE STAIR CO
309 E Broadway (12701-8839)
PHONE..................845 791-4016
Glen Durant, *Principal*
EMP: 7 **Privately Held**
SIC: 2431 Stair railings, wood
PA: Blooming Grove Stair Co
1 Stair Way
Monroe NY 10950

(G-8321)
LOCAL MEDIA GROUP INC
Also Called: Times Herald-Record
479 Broadway (12701-1756)
PHONE..................845 794-3712
EMP: 10
SALES (corp-wide): 610.2MM **Publicly Held**
SIC: 2711 Newspapers-Publishing/Printing
HQ: Local Media Group, Inc.
40 Mulberry St
Middletown NY 10940
845 294-8181

(G-8322)
MONROE STAIR PRODUCTS INC
309 E Broadway (12701-8839)
PHONE..................845 791-4016
Glen Durant, *Manager*
EMP: 5
SALES (corp-wide): 3MM **Privately Held**
WEB: www.bloominggrovestair.com
SIC: 2431 Staircases & stairs, wood
PA: Monroe Stair Products Inc.
1 Stair Way
Monroe NY 10950
845 783-4245

(G-8323)
PATRICK ROHAN
Also Called: Wadadda.com
9 Green St (12701-1307)
PHONE..................718 781-2573
Rohan Patrick, *Owner*
EMP: 5
SALES (est): 211.9K **Privately Held**
SIC: 2396 2759 7336 7389 Printing & embossing on plastics fabric articles; woodcuts for use in printing illustrations, posters, etc.; commercial art & graphic design; commercial art & illustration;

(G-8324)
WYDE LUMBER
419 State Route 17b (12701-3525)
PHONE..................845 513-5571
Wallace Madnick, *Owner*
EMP: 12
SALES (est): 760K **Privately Held**
SIC: 2421 Lumber: rough, sawed or planed

Montour Falls
Schuyler County

(G-8325)
CHICONE BUILDERS LLC
Chicone Cabinetmakers
302 W South St (14865-9743)
PHONE..................607 535-6540
David H Chicone,
EMP: 5 **Privately Held**
SIC: 2521 2434 Cabinets, office: wood; wood kitchen cabinets
PA: Chicone Builders Llc
302 W South St
Montour Falls NY 14865

(G-8326)
MALINA MANAGEMENT COMPANY INC
Also Called: Castel Grisch Winery
3620 County Road 16 (14865-9708)
PHONE..................607 535-9614
Thomas Malina, *President*
Barbara A Malina, *Treasurer*
Scott Wachter, *Admin Sec*
EMP: 22
SQ FT: 1,250
SALES (est): 2.6MM **Privately Held**
SIC: 2084 5812 7011 Wines; eating places; bed & breakfast inn

(G-8327)
ROBERT M BROWN
Also Called: Malone Welding
150 Mill St (14865-9734)
PHONE..................607 426-6250
Robert M Brown, *Owner*
EMP: 11
SALES (est): 368.3K **Privately Held**
WEB: www.empiregp.com
SIC: 7692 Welding repair

(G-8328)
TAYLOR PRECISION MACHINING
3921 Dug Rd (14865-9722)
P.O. Box 396 (14865-0396)
PHONE..................607 535-3101
Mickey Taylor, *Owner*
EMP: 7
SQ FT: 1,056
SALES (est): 1MM **Privately Held**
SIC: 3599 Machine shop, jobbing & repair

Montrose
Westchester County

(G-8329)
QUALITY CIRCLE PRODUCTS INC
2108 Albany Post Rd (10548-1431)
P.O. Box 36 (10548-0036)
PHONE..................914 736-6600
Gary Flaum, *President*
Anthony Cenname, *Vice Pres*
▲ **EMP:** 70
SQ FT: 32,500
SALES (est): 14.3MM **Privately Held**
WEB: www.qualitycircle.com
SIC: 2679 2671 Labels, paper: made from purchased material; tags, paper (unprinted): made from purchased paper; packaging paper & plastics film, coated & laminated

Mooers
Clinton County

(G-8330)
ACME ENGINEERING PRODUCTS INC
2330 State Route 11 (12958-3725)
PHONE..................518 236-5659
G S Presser, *President*
Robert Presser, *Vice Pres*
Julie Hawa, *Finance*
Leon Karanfil, *Manager*
EMP: 25
SALES (est): 4MM **Privately Held**
WEB: www.acmeprod.com
SIC: 3564 8711 3569 Air cleaning systems; engineering services; filters

Mooers Forks
Clinton County

(G-8331)
NORTHERN TIER CNC INC (PA)
733 Woods Falls Rd (12959)
PHONE..................518 236-4702
Jerry Meseck, *President*
Jamie Meseck, *Treasurer*
EMP: 9
SQ FT: 4,000
SALES (est): 1.2MM **Privately Held**
SIC: 3599 Custom machinery

Moravia
Cayuga County

(G-8332)
BROOKSIDE LUMBER INC
4191 Duryea St (13118-2500)
PHONE..................315 497-0937
William Millier, *President*
Katherine Millier, *Shareholder*
EMP: 17
SQ FT: 10,000
SALES (est): 2.4MM **Privately Held**
SIC: 2421 Lumber: rough, sawed or planed

(G-8333)
CROSS FILTRATION LTD LBLTY CO
87 W Cayuga St (13118-3000)
P.O. Box 1082 (13118-1082)
PHONE..................315 412-1539
Joanne Cross, *Mng Member*
John Ramirez, *Manager*
◆ **EMP:** 9
SALES (est): 360.5K **Privately Held**
SIC: 3569 Filters, general line: industrial

(G-8334)
REPUBLICAN REGISTRAR INC
Also Called: Community Newspapers
6 Central St (13118-3609)
P.O. Box 591 (13118-0591)
PHONE..................315 497-1551
Bernard McGuerty III, *President*
EMP: 8
SALES (est): 620.2K **Privately Held**
SIC: 2759 Newspapers: printing

Morris
Otsego County

(G-8335)
H W NAYLOR CO INC
121 Main St (13808-6920)
P.O. Box 190 (13808-0190)
PHONE..................607 263-5145
David Lucas, *President*
Jennifer Wynn, *Sales Staff*
▲ **EMP:** 12 **EST:** 1926
SQ FT: 10,000
SALES (est): 1.3MM **Privately Held**
WEB: www.drnaylor.com
SIC: 2834 Veterinary pharmaceutical preparations

Morrisville
Madison County

(G-8336)
COPESETIC INC
62 E Main St (13408-7731)
P.O. Box 1119 (13408-1119)
PHONE..................315 684-7780
Eric Beyer, *President*
Anthony Lee, *Vice Pres*
David Lee, *VP Opers*
Shannon Cook, *Office Mgr*
EMP: 15
SQ FT: 10,000
SALES (est): 1.7MM **Privately Held**
WEB: www.copeseticinc.com
SIC: 3999 Models, except toy

Mount Kisco
Westchester County

(G-8337)
ACCEL PRINTING & GRAPHICS
128 Radio Circle Dr Ste 2 (10549-2640)
PHONE..................914 241-3369
Bill Harden, *President*
Anna Harden, *Vice Pres*
EMP: 9
SQ FT: 2,200
SALES: 625K **Privately Held**
WEB: www.accelprinting.com
SIC: 2759 Commercial printing; banners, pennants & flags

(G-8338)
BROOKS WOODWORKING INC
15 Kensico Dr (10549-1003)
PHONE..................914 666-2029
Richard Brooks, *President*
Kevin Wright, *Vice Pres*
Richard Track, *Sales Mgr*
▲ **EMP:** 14
SQ FT: 5,000
SALES: 1.1MM **Privately Held**
SIC: 2499 Decorative wood & woodwork

(G-8339)
CURTIS INSTRUMENTS INC (PA)
Also Called: Curtis PMC Division
200 Kisco Ave (10549-1400)
PHONE..................914 666-2971
Stuart Marwell, *Ch of Bd*
Eugene Finger, *President*
Wang Jinghui, *General Mgr*
Randy Miller, *Business Mgr*
Jim Byrnes, *Vice Pres*
▲ **EMP:** 150 **EST:** 1960
SQ FT: 35,000
SALES (est): 301.5MM **Privately Held**
SIC: 3825 3824 3629 Elapsed time meters, electronic; speed indicators & recorders, vehicle; electronic generation equipment

(G-8340)
D C I PLASMA CENTER INC (PA)
71 S Bedford Rd (10549-3407)
PHONE..................914 241-1646
Martin Silver, *President*
Perry Ciarrletta, *Treasurer*
EMP: 3
SQ FT: 700
SALES (est): 1.9MM **Privately Held**
SIC: 2836 Plasmas

(G-8341)
DATALINK COMPUTER PRODUCTS
165 E Main St 175 (10549-2923)
PHONE..................914 666-2358
Vickram Bedi, *President*
Chhaya Bedi, *Vice Pres*
EMP: 10
SALES: 2.4MM **Privately Held**
SIC: 3572 7374 Mfg Computer Storage Devices Data Processing/Preparation

(G-8342)
ENTERMARKET
280 N Bedford Rd Ste 305 (10549-1148)
PHONE..................914 437-7268
Jeff Tong, *Owner*
Mark Matich, *Director*
EMP: 5
SALES (est): 608.2K **Privately Held**
WEB: www.entermarket.com
SIC: 2752 Commercial printing, lithographic

Mount Kisco - Westchester County (G-8343)

(G-8343)
IAT INTERACTIVE LLC
Also Called: It's About Time
333 N Bedford Rd Ste 110 (10549-1161)
P.O. Box 7862, Greenwich CT (06836-7862)
PHONE..................914 273-2233
Chuck Criss, Accounts Exec
Thomas Laster, Shareholder
Laurie Kreindler, Shareholder
EMP: 37
SQ FT: 574,600
SALES (est): 3.4MM Privately Held
SIC: 2731 Textbooks: publishing & printing

(G-8344)
INTERDYNAMICS
100 S Bedford Rd Ste 300 (10549-3444)
PHONE..................914 241-1423
Ken Motush, Principal
▲ EMP: 14
SALES (est): 2.3MM Privately Held
SIC: 2992 Lubricating oils & greases

(G-8345)
JEROME LEVY FORECASTING CENTER
Also Called: Industry Forecast
69 S Moger Ave Ste 202 (10549-2222)
PHONE..................914 244-8617
David Levy, Principal
EMP: 5
SALES (est): 384.4K Privately Held
SIC: 2721 Periodicals

(G-8346)
JT ROSELLE LIGHTING & SUP INC
333 N Bedford Rd Ste 120 (10549-1158)
PHONE..................914 666-3700
EMP: 14
SALES (est): 3.1MM Privately Held
SIC: 3648 Lighting equipment

(G-8347)
KIDZ TOYZ INC
280 N Bedford Rd Ste 203 (10549-1147)
PHONE..................914 261-4453
Scott Spiegel, President
EMP: 2
SALES: 2MM Privately Held
SIC: 3944 Electronic games & toys

(G-8348)
KOHLBERG SPORTS GROUP INC (HQ)
111 Radio Circle Dr (10549-2609)
PHONE..................914 241-7430
Walter W Farley,
EMP: 5
SALES (est): 1.1MM
SALES (corp-wide): 5.6B Privately Held
SIC: 3949 Hockey equipment & supplies, general
PA: Kohlberg & Co., L.L.C.
111 Radio Circle Dr
Mount Kisco NY 10549
914 241-7430

(G-8349)
LAURTOM INC
Also Called: It's About Time Publishing
333 N Bedford Rd Ste 100 (10549-1160)
PHONE..................914 273-2233
Laurie Kreindler, CEO
Cheryl Deese, Vice Pres
Sal Marottoli, Vice Pres
John Nordland, Director
Dana Turner, Director
EMP: 35
SQ FT: 4,000
SALES (est): 3.8MM
SALES (corp-wide): 1.1B Privately Held
WEB: www.its-about-time.com
SIC: 2721 Periodicals
HQ: Herff Jones, Llc
4501 W 62nd St
Indianapolis IN 46268
800 419-5462

(G-8350)
MOUNT KISCO TRANSFER STN INC
10 Lincoln Pl (10549-2614)
PHONE..................914 666-6350
Anthony Orlando, CEO
EMP: 7
SALES (est): 576.9K
SALES (corp-wide): 1.7B Publicly Held
SIC: 3443 4953 5722 Mfg Fabricated Plate Work Refuse System Ret Household Appliances
HQ: Covanta Energy, Llc
445 South St
Morristown NJ 07960
862 345-5000

(G-8351)
NATIONWIDE COILS INC (PA)
24 Foxwood Cir (10549-1127)
PHONE..................914 277-7396
Ross Stephens, President
Stephen Barzelatto, Vice Pres
Debra Stephens, Accounts Mgr
Justin Campanello, Sales Staff
▼ EMP: 4
SQ FT: 1,000
SALES (est): 1.3MM Privately Held
WEB: www.nationwidecoils.com
SIC: 3585 Refrigeration & heating equipment

(G-8352)
NORCORP INC
Also Called: NORTHERN WESTCHESTER HOSPITAL
400 E Main St (10549-3417)
PHONE..................914 666-1310
Joel Seligman, President
John Partenza, Treasurer
EMP: 27
SALES: 186.1K
SALES (corp-wide): 266.6MM Privately Held
SIC: 2326 8062 Medical & hospital uniforms, men's; general medical & surgical hospitals
PA: Northern Westchester Hospital Association
400 E Main St
Mount Kisco NY 10549
914 666-1200

(G-8353)
ORBIT INDUSTRIES LLC
116 Radio Circle Dr # 302 (10549-2631)
PHONE..................914 244-1500
Marc Shur,
John Katz,
EMP: 14
SALES (est): 2.7MM Privately Held
SIC: 2258 Lace & lace products

(G-8354)
PECKER IRON WORKS LLC
137 Ruxton Rd (10549-4025)
PHONE..................914 665-0100
Elliott Pecker, Mng Member
EMP: 4
SQ FT: 1,000
SALES (est): 1.2MM Privately Held
SIC: 3441 Fabricated structural metal

(G-8355)
PLASTIC & RECONSTRUCTIVE SVCS
Also Called: Spa Sciara
333 N Bedford Rd (10549-1158)
PHONE..................914 584-5605
Sharon Dechiara, President
EMP: 5 EST: 2010
SQ FT: 1,800
SALES: 1.2MM Privately Held
SIC: 2844 Cosmetic preparations

(G-8356)
R L C ELECTRONICS INC
83 Radio Circle Dr (10549-2622)
PHONE..................914 241-1334
Charles Alan Borck, CEO
Doug Borck, President
EMP: 65 EST: 1959
SQ FT: 20,000
SALES (est): 12.8MM Privately Held
WEB: www.rlcelectronics.com
SIC: 3679 Electronic circuits; microwave components

(G-8357)
RDI INC (PA)
Also Called: Rdi Electronics
333 N Bedford Rd Ste 135 (10549-1160)
PHONE..................914 773-1000
James Diamond, Ch of Bd
Barry Miller, President
Greg Mozingo, Regional Mgr
John Horl, CFO
David Del Monte, Controller
▲ EMP: 18
SQ FT: 10,000
SALES: 38.9MM Privately Held
WEB: www.rdiusa.com
SIC: 3679 3678 3677 3577 Electronic circuits; electronic connectors; electronic coils, transformers & other inductors; computer peripheral equipment; nonferrous wiredrawing & insulating

(G-8358)
RPB DISTRIBUTORS LLC
Also Called: Protec Friction Supply
45 Kensico Dr (10549-1025)
PHONE..................914 244-3600
Roy Landesberg, President
Parker Silzer, Vice Pres
Jer Thompson, Engineer
▲ EMP: 8
SALES (est): 1.2MM Privately Held
WEB: www.protecfriction.com
SIC: 3714 5084 5013 Motor vehicle brake systems & parts; industrial machine parts; clutches

(G-8359)
WESTCHESTER SIGNS INC
Also Called: Sign-A-Rama
145 Kisco Ave (10549-1418)
PHONE..................914 666-7446
Karl Theile, President
EMP: 5
SALES (est): 339.2K Privately Held
SIC: 3993 Signs & advertising specialties

(G-8360)
XELEUM LIGHTING LLC
333 N Bedford Rd Ste 135 (10549-1160)
PHONE..................954 617-8170
Jon Cooper, Branch Mgr
EMP: 11
SALES: 1.8MM
SALES (corp-wide): 6.2MM Privately Held
SIC: 3646 Commercial indusl & institutional electric lighting fixtures
PA: Xeleum Lighting, Llc
3430 Quantum Blvd
Boynton Beach FL 33426
914 773-6250

(G-8361)
ZIERICK MANUFACTURING CORP (PA)
131 Radio Circle Dr (10549-2623)
PHONE..................800 882-8020
Gretchen Zierick, President
Russell Zierick, President
Frank Lynster, Plant Mgr
Fred Ackerman, QC Dir
Bill Searles, Engineer
▲ EMP: 80 EST: 1919
SQ FT: 47,500
SALES (est): 12.5MM Privately Held
WEB: www.zierick.com
SIC: 3643 3452 3644 3694 Connectors & terminals for electrical devices; solderless connectors (electric wiring devices); nuts, metal; noncurrent-carrying wiring services; terminal boards; ignition apparatus, internal combustion engines; machinery castings, nonferrous: ex. alum., copper, die, etc.

(G-8362)
ZUMBACH ELECTRONICS CORP
Also Called: Elvo
140 Kisco Ave (10549-1412)
PHONE..................914 241-7080
Bruno Zumbach, Ch of Bd
Rainer Zumbach, President
Daleo James, COO
Sven Naegeli, Vice Pres
James Fox, Project Mgr
▲ EMP: 55
SQ FT: 15,000
SALES (est): 10.9MM Privately Held
SIC: 3825 Instruments to measure electricity

Mount Marion
Ulster County

(G-8363)
LAIRD TELEMEDIA
2000 Sterling Rd (12456)
PHONE..................845 339-9555
Mark Braunstein, CEO
Vincent Bruno, Vice Pres
EMP: 110
SALES (est): 8.5MM Privately Held
WEB: www.lairdtelemedia.com
SIC: 3651 7812 Household audio & video equipment; motion picture & video production

(G-8364)
METHODS TOOLING & MFG INC
635 Glasco Tpke (12456)
P.O. Box 400 (12456-0400)
PHONE..................845 246-7100
Keith Michaels, President
Michael Allen, Vice Pres
EMP: 31
SQ FT: 30,000
SALES (est): 5.2MM Privately Held
WEB: www.methodstooling.com
SIC: 3545 3444 3648 2514 Tools & accessories for machine tools; sheet metalwork; stage lighting equipment; kitchen cabinets: metal; fabricated plate work (boiler shop); wood kitchen cabinets

(G-8365)
NORTHEAST SOLITE CORPORATION
962 Kings Hwy (12456)
PHONE..................845 246-2177
Gary Green, Branch Mgr
EMP: 40
SALES (corp-wide): 16.2MM Privately Held
WEB: www.nesolite.com
SIC: 3295 1442 3281 Minerals, ground or treated; construction sand & gravel; slate products
PA: Northeast Solite Corporation
1135 Kings Hwy
Saugerties NY 12477
845 246-2646

Mount Morris
Livingston County

(G-8366)
ELAM MATERIALS INC
1 Conlon Ave (14510-1038)
P.O. Box 337 (14510-0337)
PHONE..................585 658-2248
David Spallina, President
EMP: 12
SALES (est): 1.7MM Privately Held
SIC: 3273 Ready-mixed concrete

(G-8367)
MT MORRIS SHOPPER INC
85 N Main St (14510-1023)
PHONE..................585 658-3520
Jerry W Rolison, President
Evelyn C Rolison, Corp Secy
EMP: 6
SQ FT: 1,800
SALES (est): 606.5K Privately Held
WEB: www.mtmorrisshopper.com
SIC: 2741 Guides: publishing only, not printed on site; shopping news: publishing only, not printed on site

Mount Sinai
Suffolk County

(G-8368)
KENDALL CIRCUITS INC
5507-10 Nesconset Hwy 105 (11766)
PHONE.................................631 473-3636
Danielle Seaford, *President*
EMP: 37
SALES (est): 4.7MM **Privately Held**
WEB: www.wordcircuits.com
SIC: 3672 Circuit boards, television & radio printed

(G-8369)
OSPREY BOAT
96 Mount Sinai Ave (11766-2311)
P.O. Box 331, Port Jefferson (11777-0331)
PHONE.................................631 331-4153
Amanda Cash, *Owner*
EMP: 5 **EST:** 2010
SALES (est): 448.2K **Privately Held**
SIC: 2399 Fishing nets

(G-8370)
TRANSPORTGISTICS INC
28 N Country Rd Ste 103 (11766-1518)
PHONE.................................631 567-4100
Alan Miller, *President*
Stewart Miller, *Senior VP*
Kerry Loudenback, *Vice Pres*
Robert Munro, *Vice Pres*
EMP: 12 **EST:** 2001
SQ FT: 3,000
SALES (est): 2.3MM **Privately Held**
WEB: www.transportgistics.com
SIC: 7372 Business oriented computer software

Mount Upton
Chenango County

(G-8371)
LILAC QUARRIES LLC
1702 State Highway 8 (13809-4103)
PHONE.................................607 867-4016
Russell Heath,
EMP: 6
SALES (est): 245.9K **Privately Held**
SIC: 1422 Crushed & broken limestone

Mount Vernon
Westchester County

(G-8372)
AARON GROUP LLC
Also Called: Diamond Dimensions
115 S Macquesten Pkwy (10550-1724)
PHONE.................................718 392-5454
Robert Kempler, *President*
Richard Katz, *COO*
Harry Schnitzer, *Sales Staff*
Jeff Steinberg, *Sales Staff*
Cindy Chen, *Manager*
EMP: 100
SALES: 9MM
SALES (corp-wide): 242.1B **Publicly Held**
WEB: www.saaron.com
SIC: 3911 5094 5944 Jewelry, precious metal; jewelry; jewelry, precious stones & precious metals
HQ: Richline Group, Inc.
1385 Broadway Fl 12
New York NY 10018

(G-8373)
ABALON PRECISION MFG CORP (PA)
717 S 3rd Ave (10550-4905)
PHONE.................................914 665-7700
Norman Orenstein, *President*
EMP: 30 **EST:** 1945
SQ FT: 9,000
SALES: 5.6MM **Privately Held**
SIC: 3441 Fabricated structural metal

(G-8374)
ABALON PRECISION MFG CORP
717 S 3rd Ave (10550-4905)
PHONE.................................718 589-5682
Norman Orent, *Manager*
EMP: 15
SALES (corp-wide): 5.6MM **Privately Held**
SIC: 3441 Fabricated structural metal
PA: Abalon Precision Mfg Corp
717 S 3rd Ave
Mount Vernon NY 10550
914 665-7700

(G-8375)
ACCURATE METAL WEATHER STRIP
725 S Fulton Ave (10550-5086)
PHONE.................................914 668-6042
Fred O Kammerer, *President*
Ronald R Kammerer, *Corp Secy*
EMP: 7 **EST:** 1898
SQ FT: 15,000
SALES: 17.5MM **Privately Held**
SIC: 3442 3449 Weather strip, metal; miscellaneous metalwork

(G-8376)
ALBERT AUGUSTINE LTD
161 S Macquesten Pkwy (10550-1724)
PHONE.................................718 913-9635
Stephen Griesgraber, *President*
EMP: 55 **EST:** 1945
SQ FT: 10,500
SALES (est): 648.1K **Privately Held**
WEB: www.albertaugustine.com
SIC: 3931 5736 Strings, musical instrument; musical instrument stores

(G-8377)
APPLE MED URGENT CARE PC
504 Gramatan Ave (10552-3009)
PHONE.................................914 523-5965
Jeannine Raciti, *Owner*
EMP: 5
SALES (est): 237.2K **Privately Held**
SIC: 3571 Freestanding emergency medical center

(G-8378)
ARIESUN INC
160 W 3rd St (10550-3750)
PHONE.................................866 274-3049
Donny McPaggart, *President*
EMP: 50
SQ FT: 10,000
SALES (est): 330K **Privately Held**
SIC: 2086 Pasteurized & mineral waters, bottled & canned; mineral water, carbonated: packaged in cans, bottles, etc.

(G-8379)
BALL CHAIN MFG CO INC (PA)
Also Called: BCM
741 S Fulton Ave (10550-5085)
PHONE.................................914 664-7500
Valentine Taubner Jr, *President*
Valentine J Taubner III, *Vice Pres*
Steven Kapuch, *Safety Mgr*
James Taubner, *Treasurer*
Teresa Dejesus, *Asst Controller*
▲ **EMP:** 90 **EST:** 1938
SQ FT: 35,000
SALES (est): 14.5MM **Privately Held**
WEB: www.ballchain.com
SIC: 3462 Gear & chain forgings

(G-8380)
BARRETT BRONZE INC
115 Miller Pl (10550-4728)
PHONE.................................914 699-6060
Eli Ross, *President*
Jamie Ross, *Principal*
Jeff Hirshon, *Prdtn Mgr*
▲ **EMP:** 20
SALES (est): 2.1MM **Privately Held**
WEB: www.barrettbronze.com
SIC: 3299 2821 Statuary: gypsum, clay, papier mache, metal, etc.; plastics materials & resins

(G-8381)
BEACON ADHESIVES INC
Also Called: Beacon Chemical
125 S Macquesten Pkwy (10550-1724)
PHONE.................................914 699-3400
Milton Meshirer, *CEO*
David Meshirer, *President*
Debbie Meshirer-Wojcik, *Vice Pres*
Barbara Meshirer, *Treasurer*
Ryan Pet, *Sales Dir*
◆ **EMP:** 30
SQ FT: 20,000
SALES (est): 7.3MM **Privately Held**
WEB: www.beacon1.com
SIC: 2891 Adhesives

(G-8382)
BRIDGE METAL INDUSTRIES LLC
717 S 3rd Ave (10550-4905)
PHONE.................................914 663-9200
Alan Cowen, *Mng Member*
▲ **EMP:** 130
SQ FT: 8,000
SALES (est): 16.4MM **Privately Held**
SIC: 2542 Partitions & fixtures, except wood

(G-8383)
BRONX WSTCHESTER TEMPERING INC
160 S Macquesten Pkwy (10550-1705)
PHONE.................................914 663-9400
Miles Kiho, *President*
▲ **EMP:** 26
SALES (est): 4.4MM **Privately Held**
SIC: 3229 Art, decorative & novelty glassware

(G-8384)
CANAL ASPHALT INC
645 S Columbus Ave (10550-4730)
PHONE.................................914 667-8500
August M Nigro, *President*
EMP: 10
SALES (est): 2.9MM **Privately Held**
SIC: 2951 Asphalt paving mixtures & blocks

(G-8385)
CASTOLEUM CORPORATION
240 E 7th St (10550-4615)
P.O. Box 41, Yonkers (10710-0041)
PHONE.................................914 664-5877
S V Goldrich, *President*
Leslie Schwebel, *Corp Secy*
Steve Neil, *Vice Pres*
EMP: 15
SQ FT: 25,000
SALES (est): 2.8MM **Privately Held**
WEB: www.sterifab.com
SIC: 2992 2842 5169 Lubricating oils & greases; disinfectants, household or industrial plant; coal tar products, primary & intermediate; gum & wood chemicals

(G-8386)
CHESTER WEST COUNTY PRESS
29 W 4th St (10550-4108)
P.O. Box 152, White Plains (10602-0152)
PHONE.................................914 684-0006
EMP: 6 **EST:** 1959
SALES (est): 280.2K **Privately Held**
SIC: 2711 Newspapers-Publishing/Printing

(G-8387)
CINE MAGNETICS INC
F R Chemical Division
524 S Columbus Ave (10550-4712)
PHONE.................................914 667-6707
EMP: 25
SALES (corp-wide): 18.9MM **Privately Held**
SIC: 3861 Mfg Processing Chemicals For X-Ray & Micrographics
PA: Cine Magnetics, Inc.
9 W Broad St Ste 250
Stamford CT 06902
914 273-7600

(G-8388)
CLASSIC MEDALLICS INC
520 S Fulton Ave (10550-5010)
PHONE.................................718 392-5410
Gerald Singer, *President*
Mario Singer, *Vice Pres*
Ruth Cavaliere, *Cust Mgr*
Kevin Fink, *Office Mgr*
REO Gutierrez, *Info Tech Mgr*
▲ **EMP:** 50 **EST:** 1941
SALES (est): 9.7MM **Privately Held**
SIC: 3499 5094 Trophies, metal, except silver; jewelry

(G-8389)
COLD MIX MANUFACTURING CORP
65 Edison Ave (10550-5003)
PHONE.................................718 463-1444
Dario Amicucci, *President*
Mark Pugliese, *Plant Mgr*
David Waters, *Marketing Staff*
Laura Trotta,
EMP: 17
SQ FT: 2,000
SALES (est): 4.5MM **Privately Held**
SIC: 2951 Asphalt paving mixtures & blocks

(G-8390)
CON-TEES CUSTOM PRINTING LTD
Also Called: Print Masters
514 Union Ave (10550-4536)
P.O. Box 3020 (10553-3020)
PHONE.................................914 664-0251
Michael Conti, *Ch of Bd*
Joseph Conti, *President*
EMP: 6
SQ FT: 10,000
SALES (est): 914.9K **Privately Held**
WEB: www.contees.com
SIC: 2759 Screen printing

(G-8391)
COVENTRY MANUFACTURING CO INC (PA)
115 E 3rd St (10550-3606)
PHONE.................................914 668-2212
Myron S Gorel, *President*
Edward R Gorel, *Vice Pres*
Phyllis Gorel, *Admin Sec*
EMP: 31 **EST:** 1953
SQ FT: 26,000
SALES (est): 2.9MM **Privately Held**
WEB: www.trulytubular.com
SIC: 3498 3317 3312 Tube fabricating (contract bending & shaping); steel pipe & tubes; blast furnaces & steel mills

(G-8392)
CROWN DIE CASTING CORP
268 W Lincoln Ave (10550-2509)
PHONE.................................914 667-5400
Sam Strober, *President*
Bill Gutwein, *Vice Pres*
EMP: 28
SQ FT: 17,000
SALES (est): 6MM **Privately Held**
WEB: www.crowndiecasting.com
SIC: 3364 3643 3444 3369 Nonferrous die-castings except aluminum; connectors, electric cord; sheet metalwork; non-ferrous foundries; aluminum foundries; aluminum die-castings

(G-8393)
CROWN SIGN SYSTEMS INC
2 South St (10550-1708)
PHONE.................................914 375-2118
Michelle Strum, *President*
Justin Coltun, *Marketing Staff*
Carolyn Cohen, *Office Mgr*
▲ **EMP:** 11
SALES (est): 1.9MM **Privately Held**
SIC: 3993 Signs, not made in custom sign painting shops

(G-8394)
DAB-O-MATIC CORP (PA)
896 S Columbus Ave (10550-5074)
P.O. Box 3839 (10553-3839)
PHONE.................................914 699-7070
Gerard Magaletti, *Ch of Bd*
James P Bell, *President*
Jim Bell, *General Mgr*
Scott Bell, *Purchasing*
Daphne Maurrasse, *Manager*
EMP: 97

Mount Vernon - Westchester County (G-8395)

SQ FT: 29,000
SALES: 11.9MM **Privately Held**
WEB: www.dabomatic.com
SIC: 3953 Pads, inking & stamping

(G-8395)
DRG NEW YORK HOLDINGS CORP (PA)
700 S Fulton Ave (10550-5014)
PHONE..................................914 668-9000
Montague Wolfson, *Ch of Bd*
Stephen Bardfield, *Corp Secy*
◆ EMP: 132
SQ FT: 40,000
SALES (est): 19MM **Privately Held**
WEB: www.wolfsoncasing.com
SIC: 2011 5149 Meat packing plants; sausage casings

(G-8396)
DUNCAN & SON CARPENTRY INC
1 W Prospect Ave (10550-2008)
PHONE..................................914 664-4311
EMP: 21
SQ FT: 10,000
SALES (est): 2.2MM **Privately Held**
SIC: 2431 Carpentry Contractor

(G-8397)
DUNLEA WHL GL & MIRROR INC
Also Called: J&T Macquesten Realty
147 S Macquesten Pkwy (10550-1724)
PHONE..................................914 664-5277
Timothy Dunlea, *President*
John Arminio, *Vice Pres*
Alex Puranbuda, *Vice Pres*
EMP: 6
SQ FT: 7,000
SALES (est): 837.3K **Privately Held**
SIC: 3231 Insulating glass: made from purchased glass

(G-8398)
FINA CABINET CORP
20 N Macquesten Pkwy (10550-1841)
PHONE..................................718 409-2900
Annette Alberti, *President*
John Albertti, *Vice Pres*
EMP: 5
SALES (est): 764.8K **Privately Held**
SIC: 2521 2434 2541 Cabinets, office: wood; wood kitchen cabinets; wood partitions & fixtures

(G-8399)
GERITREX HOLDINGS INC (PA)
144 E Kingsbridge Rd (10550-4909)
PHONE..................................914 668-4003
Mitch Blashinsky, *CEO*
EMP: 4
SALES (est): 1.5MM **Privately Held**
SIC: 2834 6719 Pharmaceutical preparations; investment holding companies, except banks

(G-8400)
GIAGNI ENTERPRISES LLC
Also Called: Qmi
550 S Columbus Ave (10550-4712)
PHONE..................................914 699-6500
Vincent Giagni, *Mng Member*
EMP: 5
SALES (est): 582.9K **Privately Held**
SIC: 3432 Faucets & spigots, metal & plastic

(G-8401)
GIAGNI INTERNATIONAL CORP
548 S Columbus Ave (10550-4712)
PHONE..................................914 699-6500
Vincent Giagni, *President*
EMP: 5
SALES (est): 417.4K **Privately Held**
SIC: 3432 Faucets & spigots, metal & plastic

(G-8402)
GRACE RYAN & MAGNUS MLLWK LLC
17 N Bleeker St (10550-1801)
PHONE..................................914 665-0902
Joseph Grace, *Mng Member*
Thor Magnus,
Eamonn Ryan,
EMP: 70
SQ FT: 10,000
SALES (est): 7.4MM **Privately Held**
SIC: 2431 Millwork

(G-8403)
GRANITE TOPS INC
716 S Columbus Ave (10550-4717)
PHONE..................................914 699-2909
Christopher Sanzaro, *President*
EMP: 40
SQ FT: 11,000
SALES (est): 3.2MM **Privately Held**
SIC: 3281 Granite, cut & shaped

(G-8404)
H & S EDIBLE PRODUCTS CORP
119 Fulton Ln (10550-4607)
PHONE..................................914 413-3489
Mari P Sweeney, *President*
Peter J Rowan, *Vice Pres*
EMP: 30
SQ FT: 13,000
SALES (est): 3.2MM **Privately Held**
SIC: 2099 2051 Bread crumbs, not made in bakeries; bread, cake & related products

(G-8405)
HAMLET PRODUCTS INC
221 N Macquesten Pkwy (10550-1005)
PHONE..................................914 665-0307
Russ Hamlet, *President*
Marlo Barreto, *Vice Pres*
Randy Hamlet, *Vice Pres*
▲ EMP: 12
SQ FT: 12,000
SALES (est): 1.7MM **Privately Held**
WEB: www.hamletproducts.com
SIC: 2542 3089 5046 2541 Fixtures, store: except wood; cases, plastic; commercial equipment; wood partitions & fixtures

(G-8406)
HI SPEED ENVELOPE CO INC
560 S 3rd Ave Ste 1 (10550-4568)
PHONE..................................718 617-1600
Charles Romeo, *President*
Mary Romeo-Springman, *Corp Secy*
Anthony Romeo, *Director*
Fortunato C Romeo, *Director*
Jim Romeo, *Director*
EMP: 16 EST: 1939
SQ FT: 26,000
SALES (est): 1.9MM **Privately Held**
WEB: www.hispeedprinting.com
SIC: 2752 2759 Commercial printing, offset; letterpress printing

(G-8407)
HI-TECH CNC MACHINING CORP
13 Elm Ave (10550-2305)
PHONE..................................914 668-5090
Karl Hormann, *President*
Karl Hormann Jr, *Vice Pres*
EMP: 5 EST: 1970
SQ FT: 7,000
SALES (est): 1.2MM **Privately Held**
SIC: 3599 Machine shop, jobbing & repair

(G-8408)
ICE AIR LLC
80 Hartford Ave (10553-1327)
PHONE..................................914 668-4700
Anthony Gili, *Project Mgr*
Fredric Nadel,
Moshe Siegel,
▲ EMP: 20
SQ FT: 26,000
SALES (est): 7.5MM **Privately Held**
SIC: 3585 Air conditioning units, complete: domestic or industrial

(G-8409)
INTERNATIONAL MDSE SVCS INC
336 S Fulton Ave Fl 1 (10553-1748)
PHONE..................................914 699-4000
Johnny Peralta, *President*
EMP: 5
SALES (est): 639.4K **Privately Held**
SIC: 3578 Automatic teller machines (ATM)

(G-8410)
ISO PLASTICS CORP
160 E 1st St (10550-3435)
PHONE..................................914 663-8300
Raul Silva, *President*
Jim Coughlin, *Vice Pres*
Fred Squitire, *Treasurer*
▲ EMP: 65 EST: 1996
SQ FT: 43,000
SALES (est): 11.1MM **Privately Held**
WEB: www.isoplastics.com
SIC: 3089 3599 Molding primary plastic; machine & other job shop work

(G-8411)
J-K PROSTHETICS & ORTHOTICS
699 N Macquesten Pkwy (10552-2121)
PHONE..................................914 699-2077
Jack Caputo, *President*
Kathleen Caputo, *Corp Secy*
EMP: 22 EST: 1974
SALES (est): 3MM **Privately Held**
WEB: www.trishare.com
SIC: 3842 Limbs, artificial; prosthetic appliances

(G-8412)
K & B STAMPING CO INC
Also Called: K & B Signs
29 Mount Vernon Ave (10550-2492)
PHONE..................................914 664-8555
Albert Aghabekian, *President*
Elaine Dechiara, *Manager*
EMP: 7 EST: 1946
SQ FT: 4,500
SALES (est): 1MM **Privately Held**
WEB: www.kbsign.com
SIC: 2759 3993 Plateless engraving; screen printing; neon signs; displays & cutouts, window & lobby

(G-8413)
KEY DIGITAL SYSTEMS INC
521 E 3rd St (10553-1606)
PHONE..................................914 667-9700
Mikhail Tsingberg, *President*
Dwayne Husbands, *Business Mgr*
Greg Sam, *Engineer*
Edison Yu, *Engineer*
Farisa Pepic, *Accountant*
▲ EMP: 20
SQ FT: 24,000
SALES (est): 6.2MM **Privately Held**
WEB: www.keydigital.com
SIC: 3651 Household audio & video equipment

(G-8414)
KING LITHOGRAPHERS INC (PA)
245 S 4th Ave (10550-3804)
PHONE..................................914 667-4200
Martin Rego, *President*
Joseph A Rego, *Treasurer*
EMP: 35 EST: 1956
SQ FT: 55,000
SALES (est): 4.4MM **Privately Held**
WEB: www.kinglitho.com
SIC: 2752 2789 Commercial printing, lithographic; bookbinding & related work

(G-8415)
KINGSTON BUILDING PRODUCTS LLC
Also Called: Century Awning Concepts
11 Brookdale Pl Ste 101 (10550-3505)
PHONE..................................914 665-0707
John Kingston, *President*
EMP: 9
SALES (est): 403.7K **Privately Held**
SIC: 2394 Canvas awnings & canopies; shades, canvas: made from purchased materials

(G-8416)
LAMPARTS CO INC
160 E 3rd St Ste 2 (10550-3694)
PHONE..................................914 723-8986
Anthony Sorbaro Jr, *President*
EMP: 10 EST: 1948
SQ FT: 30,000
SALES (est): 1.5MM **Privately Held**
SIC: 3648 3469 Lighting equipment; metal stampings

(G-8417)
LEONARDO PRINTING CORP
Also Called: Leonardo Prntng
529 E 3rd St (10553-1606)
PHONE..................................914 664-7890
Frank Leonardo Jr, *President*
Mark Leonardo, *Vice Pres*
Steven Leonardo, *Admin Sec*
EMP: 5 EST: 1947
SALES (est): 691K **Privately Held**
SIC: 2754 Job printing, gravure

(G-8418)
LGN MATERIALS & SOLUTIONS
149 Esplanade (10553-1116)
PHONE..................................888 414-0005
Maria Nonni, *President*
EMP: 12
SALES (est): 414.1K **Privately Held**
SIC: 2796 Steel line engraving for the printing trade

(G-8419)
LUMINATTA INC
Also Called: Apollo Lighting and Hasco Ltg
717 S 3rd Ave (10550-4905)
PHONE..................................914 664-3600
Joseph Sagona, *President*
Paul Verkleij, *Vice Pres*
EMP: 8 EST: 1947
SQ FT: 14,000
SALES (est): 1.5MM **Privately Held**
WEB: www.apollolighting.com
SIC: 3646 Mfg Commercial Lighting Fixtures

(G-8420)
M&F STRINGING LLC
2 Cortlandt St (10550-2706)
PHONE..................................914 664-1600
Kenneth Jacobs, *Mng Member*
EMP: 20 EST: 1953
SQ FT: 8,000
SALES (est): 2MM **Privately Held**
WEB: www.mfstringing.com
SIC: 2631 Cardboard, tagboard & strawboard

(G-8421)
METAL MAN RESTORATION
254 E 3rd St Fl 1 (10553-5115)
PHONE..................................914 662-4218
Anthony Bugliomo, *Principal*
EMP: 10
SALES (est): 770K **Privately Held**
SIC: 3471 Plating of metals or formed products

(G-8422)
MITCHELL ELECTRONICS CORP
85 W Grand St (10552-2108)
PHONE..................................914 699-3800
Nancy Lerner, *President*
Jonathan Lerner, *Corp Secy*
EMP: 25 EST: 1956
SQ FT: 5,000
SALES: 2.5MM **Privately Held**
WEB: www.mitchellxfmr.com
SIC: 3677 3612 Electronic coils, transformers & other inductors; specialty transformers

(G-8423)
MOUNT VERNON IRON WORKS INC
130 Miller Pl (10550-4706)
P.O. Box 3009 (10553-3009)
PHONE..................................914 668-7064
Joeseph Lividini, *President*
Peter M Lividini, *Vice Pres*
Grace Lividini, *Treasurer*
EMP: 7 EST: 1945
SQ FT: 2,000
SALES (est): 1.4MM **Privately Held**
SIC: 3441 Expansion joints (structural shapes), iron or steel

(G-8424)
MUNN WORKS LLC
150 N Macquesten Pkwy (10550-1836)
PHONE..................................914 665-6100
Max Munn, *Mng Member*
◆ EMP: 23

SALES: 4.7MM *Privately Held*
SIC: 3231 3211 Framed mirrors; antique glass

(G-8425)
NOBLE PINE PRODUCTS CO INC
240 E 7th St (10550-4615)
P.O. Box 41, Yonkers (10710-0041)
PHONE..................914 664-5877
Sylvia Goldrich, *President*
Leslie Schwebel, *Corp Secy*
Steven Goldrich, *Vice Pres*
Steve Neil, *Vice Pres*
EMP: 12
SQ FT: 12,000
SALES (est): 2.2MM *Privately Held*
SIC: 2842 2879 Disinfectants, household or industrial plant; insecticides, agricultural or household

(G-8426)
NSI INDUSTRIES LLC
Tork Division
50 S Macquesten Pkwy (10550-1741)
PHONE..................800 841-2505
R Sam Shankar, *Division Pres*
EMP: 200
SALES (est): 17.5MM *Privately Held*
WEB: www.nsipolaris.com
SIC: 3625 3674 Light sensitive devices; switches, electric power
PA: Nsi Industries, Llc
   9730 Northcross Center Ct
   Huntersville NC 28078

(G-8427)
OWN INSTRUMENT INC
250 E 7th St (10550-4615)
PHONE..................914 668-6546
Gerald Chapins, *President*
Patricia Chapins, *Treasurer*
EMP: 13 **EST:** 1957
SQ FT: 5,000
SALES (est): 2.1MM *Privately Held*
WEB: www.owninstrument.com
SIC: 3492 Fluid power valves & hose fittings

(G-8428)
PCI INDUSTRIES CORP
550 Franklin Ave (10550-4516)
PHONE..................914 662-2700
Richard Persico, *President*
EMP: 22
SALES (est): 3.5MM *Privately Held*
SIC: 3999 Barber & beauty shop equipment

(G-8429)
PEPSI-COLA BOTTLING CO NY INC
601 S Fulton Ave (10550-5094)
PHONE..................914 699-2600
Mike Freeman, *Sales Executive*
Jim Perry, *Technology*
EMP: 107
SALES (corp-wide): 500MM *Privately Held*
SIC: 2086 Soft drinks: packaged in cans, bottles, etc.
PA: Pepsi-Cola Bottling Company Of New York, Inc.
   11202 15th Ave
   College Point NY 11356
   718 392-1000

(G-8430)
PERFECT SHOULDER COMPANY INC
2 Cortlandt St (10550-2706)
PHONE..................914 699-8100
Harold Greenberg, *President*
▲ **EMP:** 25 **EST:** 1938
SQ FT: 35,000
SALES (est): 2.8MM *Privately Held*
SIC: 2396 Pads, shoulder: for coats, suits, etc.

(G-8431)
PRECISION COSMETICS MFG CO
519 S 5th Ave Ste 6 (10550-4476)
PHONE..................914 667-1200
Aubrey Fenton Sr, *President*
Aubrey Fenton Jr, *Treasurer*
EMP: 5
SQ FT: 5,000
SALES: 50K *Privately Held*
SIC: 2844 Lipsticks

(G-8432)
PREMIER BRANDS AMERICA INC (PA)
31 South St Ste 2s1 (10550-1748)
PHONE..................914 667-6200
Steven D Corsun, *Ch of Bd*
Glenn Livi, *VP Opers*
Osvaldo Cruz, *Prdtn Mgr*
Alex Corsun, *Purch Agent*
Jessica Ferreira, *Purchasing*
▲ **EMP:** 148
SQ FT: 75,000
SALES (est): 34.6MM *Privately Held*
WEB: www.premier-brands.com
SIC: 3842 3131 2842 Surgical appliances & supplies; orthopedic appliances; footwear cut stock; shoe polish or cleaner

(G-8433)
PREMIER BRANDS OF AMERICA INC
120 Pearl St (10550-1725)
PHONE..................718 325-3000
Vinnie Gioffre, *VP Sales*
Pat O'Brien, *Technology*
EMP: 25
SALES (est): 4.5MM
SALES (corp-wide): 34.6MM *Privately Held*
SIC: 2842 2865 Shoe polish or cleaner; polishing preparations & related products; cyclic crudes & intermediates
PA: Premier Brands Of America Inc.
   31 South St Ste 2s1
   Mount Vernon NY 10550
   914 667-6200

(G-8434)
PRO-LINE SOLUTIONS INC
Also Called: Pry Care Products
18 Sargent Pl (10550-4727)
P.O. Box 651, Bronx (10465-0617)
PHONE..................914 664-0002
Alex Lodato, *President*
EMP: 7
SQ FT: 10,000
SALES (est): 957.1K *Privately Held*
SIC: 2841 Soap & other detergents

(G-8435)
PROACTIVE MEDICAL PRODUCTS LLC
270 Washington St (10553-1017)
PHONE..................845 205-6004
Mordecai Light, *President*
Brian Goldstein, *VP Sales*
▲ **EMP:** 8 **EST:** 2012
SQ FT: 20,000
SALES: 7MM *Privately Held*
SIC: 3841 Diagnostic apparatus, medical

(G-8436)
PURINE PHARMA LLC
144 E Kingsbridge Rd (10550-4909)
PHONE..................315 705-4030
Mount Vernon,
EMP: 25
SQ FT: 32,778
SALES (est): 162.6K
SALES (corp-wide): 1.5MM *Privately Held*
SIC: 2834 Cough medicines; analgesics; vitamin preparations
PA: Geritrex Holdings, Inc.
   144 E Kingsbridge Rd
   Mount Vernon NY 10550
   914 668-4003

(G-8437)
R I R COMMUNICATIONS SYSTEMS
20 Nuvern Ave (10550-4819)
PHONE..................718 706-9957
Ralph Robinson, *Manager*
EMP: 20
SALES (corp-wide): 1.8MM *Privately Held*
SIC: 3661 Mfg Voice & Data Communications

PA: R I R Communications Systems Inc
   20 Nuvern Ave
   Mount Vernon NY 10550
   718 706-9957

(G-8438)
R V H ESTATES INC
138 Mount Vernon Ave (10550-1719)
PHONE..................914 664-9888
Robert Belluzzi, *President*
Vincent Belluzzi, *Vice Pres*
EMP: 6
SALES: 390K *Privately Held*
SIC: 2599 Bar, restaurant & cafeteria furniture

(G-8439)
RELIABLE ELEC MT VERNON INC
519 S 5th Ave (10550-4498)
PHONE..................914 668-4440
Jay Friedman, *President*
EMP: 23
SQ FT: 8,000
SALES: 75K *Privately Held*
WEB: www.reliableelectronics.net
SIC: 3577 Computer peripheral equipment

(G-8440)
ROHLFS STINED LEADED GL STUDIO
783 S 3rd Ave (10550-4946)
PHONE..................914 699-4848
Peter A Rohlf, *CEO*
Gregory Rohlf, *Vice Pres*
EMP: 25
SQ FT: 10,000
SALES (est): 3.1MM *Privately Held*
WEB: www.rohlfstudio.com
SIC: 3231 3442 Stained glass: made from purchased glass; leaded glass; casements, aluminum

(G-8441)
SECS INC (PA)
550 S Columbus Ave (10550-4712)
PHONE..................914 667-5600
Vincent Giagni, *Ch of Bd*
Leonora Giagni, *Ch of Bd*
Stephen Giagni, *President*
Anthony Palattella, *Med Doctor*
▲ **EMP:** 20
SQ FT: 15,000
SALES (est): 6.4MM *Privately Held*
WEB: www.prosecs.com
SIC: 3462 Gears, forged steel

(G-8442)
SECS INC
550 S Columbus Ave (10550-4712)
PHONE..................914 667-5600
Nichoas Bianculli, *Principal*
EMP: 30
SALES (corp-wide): 6.4MM *Privately Held*
WEB: www.prosecs.com
SIC: 3679 3462 Electronic switches; gears, forged steel
PA: Secs, Inc.
   550 S Columbus Ave
   Mount Vernon NY 10550
   914 667-5600

(G-8443)
SIGMUND COHN CORP
121 S Columbus Ave (10553-1324)
PHONE..................914 664-5300
Thomas Cohn, *President*
George Pilke, *CFO*
EMP: 55 **EST:** 1901
SQ FT: 72,000
SALES (est): 12.7MM *Privately Held*
SIC: 3496 3339 3315 3356 Miscellaneous fabricated wire products; primary nonferrous metals; steel wire & related products; precious metals

(G-8444)
TAPE SYSTEMS INC
630 S Columbus Ave (10550-4734)
P.O. Box 8612, Pelham (10803-8612)
PHONE..................914 668-3700
Aniello Scotti, *President*
▲ **EMP:** 10
SQ FT: 30,000

SALES (est): 2.2MM *Privately Held*
SIC: 3842 Adhesive tape & plasters, medicated or non-medicated

(G-8445)
TENNYSON MACHINE CO INC
535 S 5th Ave (10550-4483)
PHONE..................914 668-5468
Lawrence A Castiglia, *President*
Larry Castiglia, *MIS Mgr*
EMP: 16 **EST:** 1961
SQ FT: 10,000
SALES: 1.2MM *Privately Held*
SIC: 3599 Machine shop, jobbing & repair

(G-8446)
TORK INC (PA)
50 S Macquesten Pkwy (10550-1738)
PHONE..................914 664-3542
Victoria White, *Ch of Bd*
R Sam Shankar, *President*
Leonard Caponigro, *Vice Pres*
Nicholas Murlo, *Vice Pres*
Marie Napoli, *Human Res Mgr*
▲ **EMP:** 100
SQ FT: 40,000
SALES (est): 11.3MM *Privately Held*
WEB: www.tork.com
SIC: 3674 3625 Light sensitive devices; switches, electric power

(G-8447)
TRAC REGULATORS INC
160 S Terrace Ave (10550-2408)
PHONE..................914 699-9352
Adelmo Costantini, *President*
Cynthia La Sorsa, *Corp Secy*
Tom Notaro, *Vice Pres*
George Witzel, *Shareholder*
EMP: 20
SQ FT: 10,000
SALES (est): 3.4MM *Privately Held*
SIC: 3613 3491 Regulators, power; industrial valves

(G-8448)
TRI STAR LABEL INC
630 S Columbus Ave (10550-4734)
PHONE..................914 237-4800
Dan Mesisco, *President*
Neil Scotti, *Vice Pres*
▲ **EMP:** 7
SQ FT: 8,000
SALES: 900K *Privately Held*
SIC: 2759 Labels & seals: printing

(G-8449)
TRI-TECHNOLOGIES INC
40 Hartford Ave (10553-5119)
PHONE..................914 699-2001
David Hirsch, *CEO*
Dennis Di Donato, *President*
▲ **EMP:** 48
SQ FT: 25,000
SALES (est): 10.2MM *Privately Held*
SIC: 3484 3451 3444 3469 Small arms; screw machine products; sheet metalwork; metal stampings

(G-8450)
TRULY TUBULAR FITTING CORP
115 E 3rd St (10550-3606)
P.O. Box 1160 (10551-1160)
PHONE..................914 664-8686
Myron S Gorel, *President*
Edward Gorel, *Vice Pres*
Phyllis Gorel, *Admin Sec*
EMP: 19
SQ FT: 26,000
SALES (est): 880K
SALES (corp-wide): 2.9MM *Privately Held*
WEB: www.trulytubular.com
SIC: 3498 Fabricated pipe & fittings
PA: Coventry Manufacturing Company, Inc.
   115 E 3rd St
   Mount Vernon NY 10550
   914 668-2212

(G-8451)
TURBOFIL PACKAGING MCHS LLC
30 Beach St (10550-1702)
PHONE..................914 239-3878
Eli Uriel, *Branch Mgr*
Deborah Smook, *Mng Member*

Mount Vernon - Westchester County (G-8452)

Elaine Epps, *Director*
▲ EMP: 10
SQ FT: 7,000
SALES (est): 2MM **Privately Held**
WEB: www.turbofil.com
SIC: 3565 Packing & wrapping machinery

(G-8452)
UFS INDUSTRIES INC
Also Called: Sally Sherman Foods
300 N Macquesten Pkwy (10550-1008)
PHONE...................718 822-1100
  Thomas Recine, *President*
  Felix Endico, *COO*
  Debbie Gentile, *Sales Staff*
  Sherine Robinson, *Assistant*
EMP: 100 EST: 1930
SQ FT: 50,000
SALES (est): 24.3MM **Privately Held**
SIC: 2099 Cole slaw, in bulk

(G-8453)
UNITED IRON INC
6 Roslyn Pl (10550-4540)
PHONE...................914 667-5700
  Randall Rifelli, *President*
  Matt Affek, *Project Mgr*
  Ted Valev, *Project Mgr*
  Cecil Bernard, *Safety Mgr*
  Luigi Saturnino, *Purch Mgr*
EMP: 30 EST: 1922
SQ FT: 27,000
SALES (est): 7.3MM **Privately Held**
SIC: 3449 3441 3446 Miscellaneous metalwork; fabricated structural metal; architectural metalwork

(G-8454)
YOUR WAY CUSTOM CABINETS INC
20 N Macquesten Pkwy (10550-1841)
PHONE...................914 371-1870
  Annette Alberti, *President*
EMP: 7
SALES (est): 915.7K **Privately Held**
SIC: 2434 Wood kitchen cabinets

Mountainville
Orange County

(G-8455)
GLUTEN FREE BAKE SHOP INC
Also Called: Katz Gluten Free
19 Industry Dr (10953)
P.O. Box 58, Monroe (10949-0058)
PHONE...................845 782-5307
  Rachel Jacobowitz, *President*
  Mordche Jacobowitz, *Vice Pres*
▼ EMP: 50
SQ FT: 13,000
SALES (est): 9.3MM **Privately Held**
SIC: 2051 Bakery: wholesale or wholesale/retail combined

(G-8456)
JP FILLING INC
20 Industry Dr (10953)
PHONE...................845 534-4793
  Joel Polatsek, *President*
▲ EMP: 65
SQ FT: 3,000
SALES (est): 3.2MM **Privately Held**
SIC: 2844 Perfumes & colognes

Munnsville
Madison County

(G-8457)
BRIGGS & STRATTON CORPORATION
5375 N Main St (13409-4003)
PHONE...................315 495-0100
  Kevin Kiehn, *Plant Mgr*
  Kurt Shea, *Safety Mgr*
  William Mills, *Production*
  Robert Laurin, *Design Engr*
  William Shea, *VP Sales*
EMP: 175

SALES (corp-wide): 1.8B **Publicly Held**
WEB: www.briggsandstratton.com
SIC: 3519 3524 Internal combustion engines; lawn & garden equipment
PA: Briggs & Stratton Corporation
  12301 W Wirth St
  Wauwatosa WI 53222
  414 259-5333

(G-8458)
CUSTOM WOODCRAFT LLC
2525 Perry Schumaker Rd (13409-3620)
PHONE...................315 843-4234
  Daniel Stoltzfus,
EMP: 12
SQ FT: 11,000
SALES (est): 1.3MM **Privately Held**
SIC: 2434 5712 2511 Wood kitchen cabinets; cabinet work, custom; wood household furniture

Nanuet
Rockland County

(G-8459)
BRIGADOON SOFTWARE INC (PA)
119 Rockland Ctr 250 (10954-2956)
PHONE...................845 624-0909
  Terrance Kawles, *President*
  Martin Moran, *Vice Pres*
  Frank Jones, *Sls & Mktg Exec*
  Tim Albright, *VP Sales*
EMP: 2
SALES (est): 1.4MM **Privately Held**
WEB: www.brigadoonsoftware.com
SIC: 7372 Prepackaged software

(G-8460)
BRUNO & CANIO LTD
130 Blauvelt Rd (10954-3602)
PHONE...................845 624-3060
EMP: 37
SQ FT: 6,500
SALES (est): 1MM **Privately Held**
SIC: 2325 2337 Contract Manufacturer Men's Separate Trousers & Women's Skirts

(G-8461)
CITIZEN PUBLISHING CORP
Also Called: Rockland County Times
119 Main St Ste 2 (10954-2883)
PHONE...................845 627-1414
  Armand Miele, *Manager*
EMP: 10
SALES (est): 477.5K **Privately Held**
WEB: www.rocklandcountytimes.com
SIC: 2711 Newspapers, publishing & printing

(G-8462)
CROWN MILL WORK CORP
33 Murray Hill Dr (10954-5941)
PHONE...................845 371-2200
  Benzion Lebovits, *Ch of Bd*
EMP: 5
SQ FT: 15,500
SALES (est): 1.2MM **Privately Held**
SIC: 2431 Millwork

(G-8463)
DENMAR ELECTRIC
202 Main St (10954-3324)
PHONE...................845 624-4430
  Dennis Maher, *Owner*
EMP: 17
SALES (est): 3.7MM **Privately Held**
SIC: 3699 Electrical equipment & supplies

(G-8464)
JAR METALS INC
50 2nd Ave (10954-4405)
PHONE...................845 425-8901
  Andrew Gallina, *President*
  John Shepitka, *Vice Pres*
EMP: 15
SQ FT: 10,000
SALES (est): 322.1K **Privately Held**
SIC: 3444 5085 Sheet metalwork; industrial supplies

(G-8465)
JESCAR ENTERPRISES INC
Also Called: Mazerna USA
213 Airport Executive Par (10954-5252)
PHONE...................845 352-5850
  Jeff Silver, *President*
  Jeff L Silver, *President*
▲ EMP: 5
SQ FT: 3,100
SALES (est): 1MM **Privately Held**
WEB: www.jescar.com
SIC: 2842 Automobile polish

(G-8466)
MINUTEMAN PRESS INC
121 W Nyack Rd Ste 3 (10954-2962)
PHONE...................845 623-2277
  Brian H Gunn, *President*
EMP: 5
SQ FT: 2,000
SALES (est): 611.9K **Privately Held**
SIC: 2752 Commercial printing, lithographic

(G-8467)
PHILIPP FELDHEIM INC (PA)
Also Called: Feldheim Publishers
208 Airport Executive Par (10954-5262)
PHONE...................845 356-2282
  Yitzchak Feldheim, *President*
  Elia Hollander, *Managing Dir*
  Mirian Mendlowitz, *Treasurer*
  Suzanne Brandt, *Sales Mgr*
  Moshe Grossman, *Sales Mgr*
▲ EMP: 9 EST: 1939
SALES (est): 607.3K **Privately Held**
WEB: www.feldheim.com
SIC: 2731 Books: publishing only

(G-8468)
WENDYS AUTO EXPRESS INC
121 Main St (10954-2800)
PHONE...................845 624-6100
  Wendy Winnick, *President*
  Cindy Cherny, *Manager*
EMP: 6
SALES (est): 523.1K **Privately Held**
SIC: 3711 Chassis, motor vehicle

(G-8469)
WR SMITH & SONS INC
121 W Nyack Rd (10954-2939)
P.O. Box 225, West Nyack (10994-0225)
PHONE...................845 620-9400
  William Smith, *Principal*
EMP: 7
SQ FT: 1,500
SALES (est): 914.6K **Privately Held**
SIC: 2821 3469 Plastics materials & resins; metal stampings

Naples
Ontario County

(G-8470)
BAKER LOGGING & FIREWOOD
8781 Grlnghuse Atlanta Rd (14512-9247)
PHONE...................585 374-5733
  Richard Baker, *Owner*
EMP: 9
SALES (est): 489.5K **Privately Held**
SIC: 2411 Logging camps & contractors

(G-8471)
L & D ACQUISITION LLC
1 Lake Niagara Ln (14512-9770)
PHONE...................585 531-9000
  Doug Hazlitt, *Principal*
EMP: 16
SALES (est): 1MM **Privately Held**
SIC: 2084 Wines

(G-8472)
LAKE COUNTRY WOODWORKERS LTD
12 Clark St (14512-9535)
P.O. Box 400 (14512-0400)
PHONE...................585 374-6353
  Donna Fargo, *President*
  Karen Wood, *President*
  Chris Cooney, *Project Mgr*
  Brad Reigelsperger, *Engineer*
  Sarah Wood, *Admin Asst*

▲ EMP: 40 EST: 1976
SQ FT: 30,000
SALES (est): 7.1MM **Privately Held**
WEB: www.lcww.com
SIC: 2521 Wood office furniture

(G-8473)
NAPLES VLY MRGERS ACQSTONS LLC
Also Called: Angelic Gourmet
154 N Main St (14512-9156)
P.O. Box 39 (14512-0039)
PHONE...................585 490-1339
  Donna Nichols, *Mng Member*
▼ EMP: 9 EST: 2011
SQ FT: 6,000
SALES (est): 500K **Privately Held**
SIC: 2064 Cake ornaments, confectionery

Narrowsburg
Sullivan County

(G-8474)
NARROWSBURG FEED & GRAIN CO
Also Called: Honor Brand Feeds
Fifth And Main St (12764)
PHONE...................845 252-3936
  Raymond Villeneuve, *President*
  Roy G Morris, *General Mgr*
  Patrick C Brown, *Treasurer*
EMP: 16 EST: 1970
SQ FT: 20,000
SALES (est): 2.2MM **Privately Held**
WEB: www.narrowsburg.org
SIC: 2048 Poultry feeds

(G-8475)
STUART COMMUNICATIONS INC
Also Called: The River Reporter
93 Erie Ave (12764-6423)
P.O. Box 150 (12764-0150)
PHONE...................845 252-7414
  Laura Stuart, *President*
  Tanya Hubbert, *Sales Mgr*
EMP: 13
SALES (est): 879.3K **Privately Held**
WEB: www.riverreporter.com
SIC: 2711 Newspapers: publishing only, not printed on site

Nassau
Rensselaer County

(G-8476)
CAPITAL SAWMILL SERVICE
4119 Us Highway 20 (12123-1904)
PHONE...................518 479-0729
  Steven Daniels,
  Teresa Eddy,
EMP: 9
SALES (est): 907.8K **Privately Held**
WEB: www.capitalsawmill.com
SIC: 2421 Sawmills & planing mills, general

(G-8477)
COPELAND COATING COMPANY INC
3600 Us Highway 20 (12123-1934)
P.O. Box 595 (12123-0595)
PHONE...................518 766-2932
  John R Copeland, *Ch of Bd*
  Steven W Hinding, *Vice Pres*
  Matthew Mitchell, *CFO*
  Lawrence G Copeland, *Shareholder*
▲ EMP: 15 EST: 1945
SQ FT: 10,000
SALES (est): 4.3MM **Privately Held**
WEB: www.copelandcoating.com
SIC: 3272 Paving materials, prefabricated concrete

GEOGRAPHIC SECTION

New Hartford - Oneida County (G-8502)

Nedrow
Onondaga County

(G-8478)
BOWEN PRODUCTS CORPORATION
5084 S Onondaga Rd (13120-9702)
PHONE..................315 498-4481
Charles D Smith, *President*
Louise M Smith, *Vice Pres*
EMP: 9 **EST:** 1896
SQ FT: 18,000
SALES (est): 1.1MM **Privately Held**
SIC: 3469 3569 Metal stampings; lubricating equipment

(G-8479)
ONONDAGA NATION
Onondaga Nation Factory
3951 State Route 11 (13120-8655)
PHONE..................315 469-3230
Duane Williams, *Manager*
EMP: 7 **Privately Held**
SIC: 2111 Cigarettes
PA: Onondaga Nation
    4040 Route 11
    Nedrow NY 13120
    315 469-0302

(G-8480)
W F SAUNDERS & SONS INC (PA)
5126 S Onondaga Rd (13120-9789)
P.O. Box A (13120-0129)
PHONE..................315 469-3217
Sherman V Saunders Jr, *President*
Michael Saunders, *Treasurer*
EMP: 15 **EST:** 1891
SQ FT: 5,000
SALES (est): 7.7MM **Privately Held**
SIC: 3273 3281 Ready-mixed concrete; cut stone & stone products

Nelliston
Montgomery County

(G-8481)
BIMBO BAKERIES USA INC
Also Called: Freihofer's Bakery Outlet
And Dygert Rd Rr 5 (13410)
P.O. Box 67 (13410-0067)
PHONE..................518 993-3300
Steve Hastings, *Manager*
EMP: 20 **Privately Held**
SIC: 2051 Bread, cake & related products
HQ: Bimbo Bakeries Usa, Inc
    255 Business Center Dr # 200
    Horsham PA 19044
    215 347-5500

(G-8482)
FUCCILLO FORD NELLISTON INC
6500 State Hwy 5 (13410)
PHONE..................518 993-5555
William B Fuccillo, *CEO*
Shawn Sponable, *Sales Mgr*
EMP: 7
SALES (est): 208.1K **Privately Held**
SIC: 3429 5511 Motor vehicle hardware; new & used car dealers

Nesconset
Suffolk County

(G-8483)
C D A INC
66 Southern Blvd Ste A (11767-1092)
PHONE..................631 473-1595
Robert Tuniewicz, *President*
Gilbert D Talamo, *Vice Pres*
Gil Talamo, *Sales Engr*
▲ **EMP:** 9 **EST:** 1996
SQ FT: 2,000
SALES (est): 1.1MM **Privately Held**
SIC: 3625 Industrial electrical relays & switches

(G-8484)
HUM LIMITED LIABILITY CORP
70 Deer Valley Dr (11767-1568)
PHONE..................631 525-2174
Richard Blumenfeld, *Principal*
EMP: 6
SALES (est): 185.1K **Privately Held**
SIC: 2051 7389 Bakery: wholesale or wholesale/retail combined;

(G-8485)
KEY HIGH VACUUM PRODUCTS INC
36 Southern Blvd (11767-1097)
PHONE..................631 584-5959
Anthony Kozyrski, *President*
Elizabeth Kozyrski, *Corp Secy*
Patricia Abrilz, *Office Mgr*
▲ **EMP:** 30
SQ FT: 15,000
SALES (est): 5.7MM **Privately Held**
WEB: www.keyhigh.com
SIC: 3589 3494 3492 3429 Vacuum cleaners & sweepers, electric: industrial; valves & pipe fittings; fluid power valves & hose fittings; manufactured hardware (general)

(G-8486)
PERFECT POLY INC
1 Gina Ct (11767-2058)
PHONE..................631 265-0539
Malke Gelbstein, *President*
EMP: 20
SALES (est): 3.5MM **Privately Held**
SIC: 2821 Polyesters

New Berlin
Chenango County

(G-8487)
CHOBANI LLC
669 County Road 25 (13411-4403)
PHONE..................607 847-6181
Al Dejewski, *Vice Pres*
Grace Simmons, *Vice Pres*
Hector Yzquierdo, *Opers Mgr*
Carl Guntle, *Safety Mgr*
Pradeep Narayanan, *Research*
EMP: 8
SALES (corp-wide): 235.5MM **Privately Held**
SIC: 2026 Yogurt
HQ: Chobani, Llc
    147 State Highway 320
    Norwich NY 13815

(G-8488)
GOLDEN ARTIST COLORS INC
188 Bell Rd (13411-3616)
PHONE..................607 847-6154
Mark Golden, *Ch of Bd*
Barbara J Schindler, *President*
Scott Turner, *Opers Staff*
Jeremiah Micklas, *Buyer*
Dean Hubbard, *Purchasing*
◆ **EMP:** 125
SQ FT: 60,000
SALES (est): 30.6MM **Privately Held**
WEB: www.goldenpaint.com
SIC: 3952 Paints, except gold & bronze: artists'; paints, gold or bronze: artists'

New City
Rockland County

(G-8489)
A TRADITION OF EXCELLENCE INC
85b Maple Ave (10956)
PHONE..................845 638-4595
Tom Sullivan, *President*
John Cusick, *Vice Pres*
EMP: 5
SALES (est): 499.1K **Privately Held**
SIC: 2759 Screen printing

(G-8490)
DARK STAR LITHOGRAPH CORP
9 Perth Ln (10956-5808)
P.O. Box 9074, Bardonia (10954-9074)
PHONE..................845 634-3780
Richard Suben, *President*
EMP: 5
SALES (est): 510K **Privately Held**
SIC: 2752 Commercial printing, lithographic

(G-8491)
DOCTOROW COMMUNICATIONS INC
Also Called: Home Lighting & Accessories
180 Phillips Hill Rd # 5 (10956-4132)
P.O. Box 293 (10956-0293)
PHONE..................845 708-5166
Jeffrey Doctorow, *President*
EMP: 12
SALES (est): 1.5MM **Privately Held**
WEB: www.contractlighting.net
SIC: 2721 Magazines: publishing only, not printed on site

(G-8492)
E L SMITH PRINTING CO INC
3 Lisa Ct (10956-2605)
P.O. Box 6567, Carlstadt NJ (07072-0567)
PHONE..................201 373-0111
Hilton I Kaufman, *President*
Beverly Kaufman, *Admin Sec*
EMP: 20 **EST:** 1929
SALES (est): 2.5MM **Privately Held**
SIC: 2752 2789 Commercial printing, offset; bookbinding & related work

(G-8493)
EASTERN INDUSTRIAL STEEL CORP (PA)
4 Fringe Ct (10956-6802)
P.O. Box 132, Blauvelt (10913-0132)
PHONE..................845 639-9749
Peter Lacombe, *President*
EMP: 15
SALES: 1MM **Privately Held**
WEB: www.easternindustrialsteel.com
SIC: 3325 3089 Steel foundries; extruded finished plastic products

(G-8494)
MSI INC
329 Strawtown Rd (10956-6634)
PHONE..................845 639-6683
Murray Steinfink, *President*
EMP: 10
SALES (est): 880K **Privately Held**
SIC: 3081 Unsupported plastics film & sheet

(G-8495)
SHINING CREATIONS INC
Also Called: Strawtown Jewerly
40 S Main St Ste 1 (10956-3533)
PHONE..................845 358-4911
Ellen Arkin, *President*
Glenn Arkin, *Vice Pres*
EMP: 5
SALES: 200K **Privately Held**
SIC: 3911 5944 Jewelry mountings & trimmings; jewelry, precious stones & precious metals

(G-8496)
YELLOW PAGES INC (PA)
222 N Main St (10956-5302)
PHONE..................845 639-6060
Robert Gazzetta, *Ch of Bd*
EMP: 4
SALES (est): 6.6MM **Privately Held**
WEB: www.ypinc.net
SIC: 2741 Telephone & other directory publishing

New Hampton
Orange County

(G-8497)
BALCHEM CORPORATION (PA)
52 Sunrise Park Rd (10958-4703)
P.O. Box 600 (10958-0600)
PHONE..................845 326-5600
Theodore L Harris, *Ch of Bd*
David F Ludwig, *Vice Pres*
Mary Theresa Coelho, *CFO*
William A Backus,
Mark A Stach, *Admin Sec*
EMP: 277
SQ FT: 20,000
SALES (est): 594.7MM **Publicly Held**
WEB: www.balchem.com
SIC: 2899 2869 Chemical preparations; methyl alcohol, synthetic methanol

(G-8498)
BCP INGREDIENTS INC (HQ)
52 Sunrise Park Rd (10958-4703)
PHONE..................845 326-5600
Dino A Rossi, *Ch of Bd*
Richard Bendure, *COO*
John E Kuehner, *Vice Pres*
David F Ludwig, *Vice Pres*
Dana Putnam, *Vice Pres*
▼ **EMP:** 54
SALES (est): 18.2MM
SALES (corp-wide): 594.7MM **Publicly Held**
SIC: 2899 Chemical preparations
PA: Balchem Corporation
    52 Sunrise Park Rd
    New Hampton NY 10958
    845 326-5600

(G-8499)
DICKS CONCRETE CO INC (PA)
1053 County Route 37 (10958-4811)
PHONE..................845 374-5966
Richard Penaluna Jr, *President*
Barbara Penaluna, *Vice Pres*
Jan Dodd, *CFO*
EMP: 40
SQ FT: 5,000
SALES (est): 11.5MM **Privately Held**
WEB: www.dicksconcrete.com
SIC: 1442 5032 3273 3271 Sand mining; gravel mining; cement; ready-mixed concrete; concrete block & brick

(G-8500)
EAST COAST SPRING MIX INC
211 Lynch Ave (10958-4504)
PHONE..................845 355-1215
Richard Minkus Jr, *President*
EMP: 7
SALES (est): 885.2K **Privately Held**
SIC: 3273 Ready-mixed concrete

New Hartford
Oneida County

(G-8501)
B & D ENTERPRISES OF UTICA (PA)
Also Called: Hemstrought's Bakeries
2 Campion Rd Ste 7 (13413-1647)
PHONE..................315 735-3311
Thomas R Batters, *President*
Michael J Denz, *Vice Pres*
Mary Denz, *Treasurer*
Paul Remizowski, *Shareholder*
EMP: 75
SQ FT: 20,000
SALES (est): 10.9MM **Privately Held**
SIC: 2051 5461 5149 Bakery: wholesale or wholesale/retail combined; bakeries; bakery products

(G-8502)
DARTCOM INCORPORATED
Also Called: Dart Communications
2 Oxford Xing Ste 1 (13413-3246)
PHONE..................315 790-5456
Michael Baldwin, *President*
Jamie Powell, *General Mgr*

New Hartford - Oneida County (G-8503)

Don Lawrence, *Software Dev*
Nick Baldwin, *Administration*
EMP: 4
SQ FT: 7,500
SALES (est): 1.3MM **Privately Held**
WEB: www.dart.com
SIC: 7372 Business oriented computer software

(G-8503)
ELM GRAPHICS INC
9694 Mallory Rd (13413-3618)
PHONE...............................315 737-5984
Stanley Lebiednik, *President*
Gerald Eischen, *Vice Pres*
EMP: 5
SQ FT: 1,200
SALES (est): 532.6K **Privately Held**
SIC: 2759 Commercial printing

(G-8504)
FASTER-FORM CORP
Also Called: Lifesake Division
1 Faster Form Cir Ste 1 # 1 (13413-9564)
P.O. Box 825 (13413-0825)
PHONE...............................800 327-3676
J C Waszkiewicz III, *President*
Lawrence P Ulrich, *Vice Pres*
J C Waszkiewicz II, *Treasurer*
Carolyn Kearney, *Manager*
▲ **EMP:** 85 **EST:** 1959
SQ FT: 200,000
SALES (est): 8.5MM **Privately Held**
WEB: www.vincenzaflowers.com
SIC: 3999 3993 Flowers, artificial & preserved; bric-a-brac; displays, paint process

(G-8505)
GAN KAVOD INC
2050 Tilden Ave (13413-3613)
P.O. Box 1000 (13413-0709)
PHONE...............................315 797-3114
Patricia A Hays, *Principal*
EMP: 2
SALES: 5.7MM **Privately Held**
SIC: 3843 Enamels, dentists'

(G-8506)
HARTFORD HWY DEPT
Also Called: Hartford Town Park System
Rr 12 (13413)
PHONE...............................315 724-0654
John Cunningham, *Director*
EMP: 7 **Privately Held**
SIC: 2531 9111 Picnic tables or benches, park; mayors' offices
PA: Town Of Hartford
165 Cr 23
Hartford NY 12838
518 632-5255

(G-8507)
LOCKHEED MARTIN CORPORATION
8373 Seneca Tpke (13413-4957)
PHONE...............................315 793-5800
Cassaundra Wilkerson, *Business Anlyst*
Richard Kahler, *Manager*
Wayne Jenne, *Admin Asst*
Charles Huntington,
EMP: 80 **Publicly Held**
WEB: www.lockheedmartin.com
SIC: 3721 7371 Aircraft; custom computer programming services
PA: Lockheed Martin Corporation
6801 Rockledge Dr
Bethesda MD 20817

(G-8508)
PAR TECHNOLOGY CORPORATION (PA)
8383 Seneca Tpke Ste 2 (13413-4991)
PHONE...............................315 738-0600
Donald H Foley, *President*
Bryan A Menar, *CFO*
EMP: 99 **EST:** 1968
SQ FT: 180,200
SALES: 232.6MM **Publicly Held**
WEB: www.partech.com
SIC: 7372 7382 Prepackaged software; confinement surveillance systems maintenance & monitoring

(G-8509)
PARTECH INC (HQ)
8383 Seneca Tpke Ste 2 (13413-4991)
PHONE...............................315 738-0600
Ronald J Casciano, *CEO*
Karen E Sammon, *President*
Charles Constantino, *Director*
Karen Sammon, *Bd of Directors*
Gregory Cortese, *Admin Sec*
▲ **EMP:** 250
SQ FT: 99,400
SALES (est): 106.3MM
SALES (corp-wide): 232.6MM **Publicly Held**
SIC: 3571 Mainframe computers
PA: Par Technology Corporation
8383 Seneca Tpke Ste 2
New Hartford NY 13413
315 738-0600

(G-8510)
RIVERHAWK COMPANY LP
Also Called: Indikon Company
215 Clinton Rd (13413-5306)
PHONE...............................315 624-7171
Allen Williams, *Manager*
EMP: 32 **Privately Held**
WEB: www.indikon.com
SIC: 3823 3829 3674 Industrial process measurement equipment; measuring & controlling devices; semiconductors & related devices
PA: Riverhawk Company L.P.
215 Clinton Rd
New Hartford NY 13413

(G-8511)
SAES SMART MATERIALS INC
Also Called: Saes Memry
4355 Middle Settlement Rd (13413-5317)
PHONE...............................315 266-2026
Richard Lafond, *CEO*
Giorgio Vergani, *Ch of Bd*
John Schosser, *CFO*
Steve Dayton, *Treasurer*
▲ **EMP:** 27
SALES (est): 7MM
SALES (corp-wide): 62.1MM **Privately Held**
SIC: 3339 Titanium metal, sponge & granules
PA: Saes Getters Spa
Viale Italia 77
Lainate MI 20020
029 317-81

(G-8512)
SPECIAL METALS CORPORATION
4317 Middle Settlement Rd (13413-5392)
PHONE...............................315 798-2900
EMP: 300
SALES (corp-wide): 242.1B **Publicly Held**
SIC: 3356 Nickel & nickel alloy: rolling, drawing or extruding
HQ: Special Metals Corporation
4832 Richmond Rd Ste 100
Warrensville Heights OH 44128
216 755-3030

(G-8513)
WESTROCK CP LLC
45 Campion Rd (13413-1601)
PHONE...............................770 448-2193
William Ross, *Manager*
EMP: 147
SALES (corp-wide): 14.8B **Publicly Held**
SIC: 2653 Boxes, corrugated: made from purchased materials
HQ: Westrock Cp, Llc
504 Thrasher St
Norcross GA 30071

New Hyde Park
Nassau County

(G-8514)
ALLIED BOLT PRODUCTS LLC
3000 Marcus Ave Ste 3e09 (11042-1041)
PHONE...............................516 512-7600
Glen Malin, *Mng Member*
EMP: 14
SALES (est): 1.9MM
SALES (corp-wide): 15.7MM **Privately Held**
SIC: 3452 Bolts, nuts, rivets & washers
PA: Allied Bolt, Inc.
3000 Marcus Ave Ste 3e09
New Hyde Park NY 11042
516 512-7600

(G-8515)
AMERICAN CHALLENGE ENTERPRISES
1804 Plaza Ave Ste 6 (11040-4937)
PHONE...............................631 595-7171
Robert Laker Sr, *Ch of Bd*
Robert J Laker Jr, *President*
Bruce Laker, *Vice Pres*
▲ **EMP:** 6
SALES (est): 864.6K **Privately Held**
SIC: 2329 2339 Men's & boys' athletic uniforms; uniforms; athletic: women's, misses' & juniors'

(G-8516)
APPLE COMMUTER INC
54 Lake Dr (11040-1125)
PHONE...............................917 299-0066
Shah Biren, *Principal*
EMP: 6
SALES (est): 689.5K **Privately Held**
SIC: 3571 Mfg Electronic Computers

(G-8517)
ARNOUSE DIGITAL DEVICES CORP
Also Called: Biodigitalpc
1983 Marcus Ave Ste 104 (11042-2002)
PHONE...............................516 673-4444
Michael Arnouse, *President*
Daniel Dellick, *COO*
Rich Tackels, *Vice Pres*
Frank Marano, *CFO*
Cherh-Lin Chen, *Director*
EMP: 62
SQ FT: 4,963
SALES (est): 5.6MM **Privately Held**
SIC: 3571 Electronic computers

(G-8518)
ATLANTIC ER INC
180 Atlantic Ave (11040-5028)
P.O. Box 6077, Astoria (11106-0077)
PHONE...............................516 294-3200
Ronald Meltsner, *President*
Eric Spar, *Vice Pres*
Harold Spar, *Treasurer*
Henry Meltsner, *Admin Sec*
▲ **EMP:** 50 **EST:** 1946
SQ FT: 20,000
SALES (est): 7.9MM **Privately Held**
WEB: www.halhen.com
SIC: 3842 Hearing aids

(G-8519)
BARC USA INC
5 Delaware Dr Ste 2 (11042-1100)
PHONE...............................516 719-1052
Joseph Jonckheere, *CEO*
▲ **EMP:** 34
SQ FT: 17,500
SALES (est): 11.2MM
SALES (corp-wide): 75.8K **Privately Held**
WEB: www.barclab.com
SIC: 2834 Pharmaceutical preparations
HQ: Bio Analytical Research Corporation Nv
Industriepark-Zwijnaarde 3
Gent 9052
932 923-26

(G-8520)
BILLANTI CASTING CO INC
Also Called: Billanti Jewelry Casting
299 S 11th St (11040-5558)
P.O. Box 1117 (11040-7117)
PHONE...............................516 775-4800
Rosemarie Billanti, *Exec Officer*
EMP: 30 **EST:** 1955
SALES (est): 4.3MM **Privately Held**
WEB: www.billanticasting.com
SIC: 3911 3339 Mfg Precious Metal Jewelry Primary Nonferrous Metal Producer

(G-8521)
CAMBRIDGE MANUFACTURING LLC
1700 Jericho Tpke (11040-4742)
PHONE...............................516 326-1350
Vittoria McNevin, *Manager*
Peter Negri,
EMP: 8
SALES (est): 1.1MM **Privately Held**
SIC: 3826 Laser scientific & engineering instruments

(G-8522)
CHEMICOLLOID LABORATORIES INC
55 Herricks Rd (11040-5340)
P.O. Box 14094, Hauppauge (11788-0789)
PHONE...............................516 747-2666
Geo Ryder, *President*
▲ **EMP:** 19 **EST:** 1920
SQ FT: 10,000
SALES (est): 2.9MM **Privately Held**
SIC: 3556 2099 Dairy & milk machinery; emulsifiers, food

(G-8523)
COLORS IN OPTICS LTD
Also Called: Ic Optics
120 Broadway G (11040-5301)
PHONE...............................718 845-0300
Gabe Tusk, *Branch Mgr*
EMP: 80
SQ FT: 10,000
SALES (corp-wide): 14.4MM **Privately Held**
SIC: 3851 Eyeglasses, lenses & frames
PA: Colors In Optics, Ltd.
366 5th Ave Rm 804
New York NY
212 465-1200

(G-8524)
COMPUCOLOR ASSOCIATES INC
2200 Marcus Ave Ste C (11042-1043)
PHONE...............................516 358-0000
Thomas Weitzmann, *President*
Mark Rosner, *Admin Sec*
▲ **EMP:** 45
SQ FT: 22,000
SALES (est): 4.9MM **Privately Held**
WEB: www.compucolor.
SIC: 2752 Commercial printing, offset

(G-8525)
CONTINENTAL QUILTING CO INC
3000 Marcus Ave Ste 3e6 (11042-1006)
PHONE...............................718 499-9100
Alfred G Sayegh, *President*
Stephen Sayegh, *Vice Pres*
▲ **EMP:** 50 **EST:** 1919
SQ FT: 40,000
SALES (est): 4.4MM **Privately Held**
SIC: 2392 Mattress pads; mattress protectors, except rubber; comforters & quilts: made from purchased materials

(G-8526)
CORA MATERIALS CORP
Also Called: Cora Matrls
30 Nassau Terminal Rd (11040-4928)
PHONE...............................516 488-6300
Robert Raths, *President*
Christine Goldfuss, *Marketing Mgr*
Elissa Raths, *Admin Sec*
EMP: 10
SQ FT: 10,000
SALES (est): 1.5MM **Privately Held**
WEB: www.corarefining.com
SIC: 3341 Secondary nonferrous metals

(G-8527)
DISPLAY TECHNOLOGIES LLC (DH)
1111 Marcus Ave Ste M68 (11042-2041)
PHONE...............................718 321-3100
Marshall Goldberg, *President*
Bruce Gommermann, *Vice Pres*
Jon Noce, *Vice Pres*
Diogo Pereira, *Vice Pres*
Anthony Puglisi, *CFO*
▲ **EMP:** 53
SQ FT: 30,000

▲ = Import ▼ = Export
◆ = Import/Export

GEOGRAPHIC SECTION

New Hyde Park - Nassau County (G-8553)

SALES: 76.1MM
SALES (corp-wide): 242.1B **Publicly Held**
WEB: www.display-technologies.com
SIC: 2542 Fixtures: display, office or store: except wood

(G-8528)
DOREEN INTERIORS LTD
76 Nottingham Rd (11040-2214)
PHONE..................212 255-9008
Shalom Sharoni, *President*
Boaz Sharoni, *Vice Pres*
Yoav Sharoni, *Vice Pres*
Yona Sharoni, *Treasurer*
EMP: 24
SQ FT: 40,000
SALES (est): 2.5MM **Privately Held**
WEB: www.doreeninteriors.com
SIC: 2512 Upholstered household furniture

(G-8529)
DYNASTY BELTS INC
161 Railroad Ave (11040-5016)
PHONE..................516 625-6280
Harbans Lal Chandihok, *President*
Rajinder K Chandihok, *Vice Pres*
EMP: 35
SQ FT: 8,000
SALES (est): 1.4MM **Privately Held**
SIC: 2387 5136 Apparel belts; apparel belts, men's & boys'

(G-8530)
EASTERN FINDING CORP
116 County Courthouse Rd (11040-5342)
PHONE..................516 747-6640
Paul Posner, *President*
Anthony Millaci, *Partner*
Sylvia Posner, *Treasurer*
▲ EMP: 10
SQ FT: 5,000
SALES (est): 1.3MM **Privately Held**
WEB: www.easternfindings.com
SIC: 3366 Brass foundry

(G-8531)
ELECTRIC SWTCHBARD SLTIONS LLC
270 Park Ave (11040-5318)
PHONE..................718 643-1105
Jerry Dicunzolo,
EMP: 8 EST: 2006
SQ FT: 25,000
SALES (est): 1.6MM
SALES (corp-wide): 51.8MM **Privately Held**
SIC: 3613 Switchboards & parts, power
PA: Power-Flo Technologies, Inc.
270 Park Ave
New Hyde Park NY 11040
516 812-6800

(G-8532)
ELI LILLY AND COMPANY
Also Called: Elanco Animal Health
1979 Marcus Ave (11042-1076)
PHONE..................516 622-2244
James Sweeny, *Manager*
EMP: 14
SALES (corp-wide): 22.8B **Publicly Held**
WEB: www.lilly.com
SIC: 2834 Pharmaceutical preparations
PA: Eli Lilly And Company
Lilly Corporate Ctr
Indianapolis IN 46285
317 276-2000

(G-8533)
EON LABS INC (DH)
1999 Marcus Ave Ste 300 (11042-1020)
PHONE..................516 478-9700
Thomas Strungmann, *Ch of Bd*
Bernhard Hampl, *President*
Pranab Bhattacharyya, *Vice Pres*
Sadie Ciganek, *Vice Pres*
William F Holt, *Vice Pres*
EMP: 19
SQ FT: 25,000
SALES (est): 29.9MM
SALES (corp-wide): 49.1B **Privately Held**
WEB: www.sandoz.com
SIC: 2834 Pharmaceutical preparations

HQ: Sandoz Inc.
100 College Rd W
Princeton NJ 08540
609 627-8500

(G-8534)
FAR EAST INDUSTRIES INC (PA)
118 Stephan Marc Ln (11040-1811)
PHONE..................718 687-2482
Yong Xiang Cui, *Ch of Bd*
EMP: 4
SQ FT: 1,200
SALES: 6.5MM **Privately Held**
SIC: 2326 Men's & boys' work clothing

(G-8535)
FERGUSON ENTERPRISES INC
Also Called: Pollardwater
200 Atlantic Ave (11040-5057)
PHONE..................800 437-1146
Thomas Towler, *Principal*
Ed Sadowski, *Purch Mgr*
Paul Alleman, *Marketing Staff*
Mark Bevans, *Technical Staff*
EMP: 30
SALES (est): 1.3MM **Privately Held**
SIC: 3589 Sewage & water treatment equipment

(G-8536)
GENERAL FIBRE PRODUCTS CORP
170 Nassau Terminal Rd (11040-4940)
PHONE..................516 358-7500
Stuart Shrode, *CEO*
James Miller, *President*
Michael Petti, *Vice Pres*
Frank Anthony, *Plant Mgr*
Ruth Cartegena, *QC Mgr*
◆ EMP: 70
SQ FT: 52,000
SALES (est): 21.2MM **Privately Held**
WEB: www.generalfibre.com
SIC: 2553 2671 2675 2679 Boxes, corrugated: made from purchased materials; packaging paper & plastics film, coated & laminated; die-cut paper & board; corrugated paper: made from purchased material

(G-8537)
HAIN BLUEPRINT INC
1111 Marcus Ave Ste 100 (11042-2033)
PHONE..................212 414-5741
EMP: 19
SALES (est): 5.7MM **Publicly Held**
SIC: 2037 Fruit juices
PA: The Hain Celestial Group Inc
1111 Marcus Ave Ste 100
New Hyde Park NY 11042

(G-8538)
HAIN CELESTIAL GROUP INC (PA)
1111 Marcus Ave Ste 100 (11042-2033)
PHONE..................516 587-5000
John Carroll, *CEO*
Gary W Tickle, *CEO*
Irwin D Simon, *Ch of Bd*
Connor McKim, *Business Mgr*
Mark Osinoff, *Business Mgr*
◆ EMP: 130
SQ FT: 86,000
SALES (est): 2.4B **Publicly Held**
WEB: www.hain-celestial.com
SIC: 2023 2034 2096 2086 Dried & powdered milk & milk products; dried milk preparations; dietary supplements, dairy & non-dairy based; vegetable flour, meal & powder; potato chips & similar snacks; iced tea & fruit drinks, bottled & canned; toilet preparations

(G-8539)
HAIN REFRIGERATED FOODS INC
1111 Marcus Ave Ste 100 (11042-2033)
PHONE..................425 485-2476
Basel Nassar, *COO*
EMP: 10
SALES (est): 781.6K **Privately Held**
SIC: 2038 Ethnic foods, frozen

(G-8540)
HARBORS MAINE LOBSTER LLC
969 Lakeville Rd (11040-3008)
PHONE..................516 775-2400
Christian Limbereg,
Peter Cardone,
William Kienke,
EMP: 48 EST: 2015
SALES: 250K **Privately Held**
SIC: 2091 Seafood products: packaged in cans, jars, etc.

(G-8541)
HASCO COMPONETS
906 Jericho Tpke (11040-4604)
PHONE..................516 328-9292
Tom Marcus, *President*
Wayne Hauser, *Exec VP*
Warren Pritzker, *Sales Executive*
▲ EMP: 20
SALES: 11MM **Privately Held**
SIC: 3625 Relays, for electronic use

(G-8542)
INTERNTNAL BUS CMMNCATIONS INC (PA)
Also Called: IBC/ Worldwide
1981 Marcus Ave Ste C105 (11042-2028)
PHONE..................516 352-4505
Norman Kay, *President*
Philip Schoonmaker, *Exec VP*
Diane Banks, *Admin Asst*
▲ EMP: 25
SQ FT: 53,000
SALES (est): 23.4MM **Privately Held**
WEB: www.ibcshell.com
SIC: 3086 2679 Packaging & shipping materials, foamed plastic; pressed fiber & molded pulp products except food products

(G-8543)
IVER PRINTING INC
124 N 12th St (11040-4265)
PHONE..................718 275-2070
William Iverson, *President*
Ann Iverson, *Vice Pres*
Martin Iverson, *Treasurer*
John Iverson, *Admin Sec*
EMP: 5 EST: 1979
SQ FT: 900
SALES: 400K **Privately Held**
WEB: www.iverprinting.com
SIC: 2752 Commercial printing, offset

(G-8544)
JOSEPH STRUHL CO INC
Also Called: Super Moderna/Magic Master
195 Atlantic Ave (11040-5027)
PHONE..................516 741-3660
Clifford Struhl, *President*
Harriet Struhl, *Corp Secy*
Joseph Struhl, *Vice Pres*
EMP: 14
SQ FT: 13,000
SALES (est): 1.9MM **Privately Held**
WEB: www.magicmaster.com
SIC: 3993 Displays & cutouts, window & lobby

(G-8545)
JSM VINYL PRODUCTS INC
44 Orchid Ln (11040-1918)
PHONE..................516 775-4520
Fax: 516 239-2879
EMP: 15
SQ FT: 26,000
SALES: 4MM **Privately Held**
SIC: 3089 Mfg Plastic Products

(G-8546)
KEYSTONE ELECTRONICS CORP (PA)
2040 Jericho Tpke (11040-4741)
PHONE..................516 328-7500
Richard David, *President*
Thomas Voytac, *President*
Joe Roosenblum, *General Mgr*
Joe Schmalzried, *Regional Mgr*
Mike Gibbs, *Prdtn Mgr*
▲ EMP: 126
SQ FT: 40,000

SALES (est): 33.1MM **Privately Held**
WEB: www.keyelco.com
SIC: 3678 Electronic connectors

(G-8547)
LAFAYETTE MIRROR & GLASS CO
2300 Marcus Ave (11042-1058)
PHONE..................718 768-0660
Micheal Chuisano, *President*
Anthony Garaufis, *Technology*
▲ EMP: 7 EST: 1910
SQ FT: 7,000
SALES (est): 881.2K **Privately Held**
SIC: 3211 3231 1793 Plate glass, polished & rough; mirrored glass; glass & glazing work

(G-8548)
LIQUID MANAGEMENT PARTNERS LLC
3000 Marcus Ave Ste 1w9 (11042-1027)
PHONE..................516 775-5050
Michael H Lam,
▲ EMP: 11
SQ FT: 3,000
SALES (est): 2.1MM **Privately Held**
SIC: 2086 5182 Carbonated beverages, nonalcoholic: bottled & canned; wine & distilled beverages

(G-8549)
MARLOU GARMENTS INC
2115 Jericho Tpke (11040-4703)
P.O. Box 407, West Hempstead (11552-0407)
PHONE..................516 739-7100
Louis De Angelo, *Ch of Bd*
Rose De Angelo, *Admin Sec*
▲ EMP: 15 EST: 1952
SQ FT: 19,200
SALES (est): 1.4MM **Privately Held**
WEB: www.marlou.com
SIC: 2337 Uniforms, except athletic: women's, misses' & juniors'

(G-8550)
MASON CONTRACT PRODUCTS LLC
85 Denton Ave (11040-4002)
P.O. Box 609, Port Washington (11050-0609)
PHONE..................516 328-6900
Leonard Horowitz,
Lisa Horowitz,
▼ EMP: 80
SQ FT: 100,000
SALES (est): 5.9MM **Privately Held**
SIC: 2391 2211 Curtains & draperies; bedspreads, cotton

(G-8551)
NATURAL E CREATIVE LLC
Also Called: Be The Media
1110 Jericho Tpke (11040-4606)
PHONE..................516 488-1143
David Mathison,
Eric Mathison,
Peter Mathison,
EMP: 11
SALES (est): 75K **Privately Held**
WEB: www.bethemedia.com
SIC: 2731 Books: publishing & printing

(G-8552)
NEW YORK PACKAGING CORP
Also Called: Redi-Bag USA
135 Fulton Ave (11040-5305)
P.O. Box 1039 (11040-7039)
PHONE..................516 746-0600
Jeffrey Rabiea, *President*
▲ EMP: 90
SQ FT: 50,000
SALES (est): 25MM **Privately Held**
WEB: www.newyorkpackaging.com
SIC: 2673 Plastic bags: made from purchased materials

(G-8553)
NEW YORK RAVIOLI PASTA CO INC
12 Denton Ave S (11040-4904)
PHONE..................516 270-2852
David Creo, *President*
Paul Moncada, *Corp Secy*

New Hyde Park - Nassau County (G-8554)

EMP: 20
SQ FT: 20,000
SALES (est): 3.6MM **Privately Held**
WEB: www.nyravioli.com
SIC: **2099** 5499 5149 Packaged combination products: pasta, rice & potato; gourmet food stores; pasta & rice

(G-8554)
NY 1 ART GALLERY INC
32 3rd St (11040-4438)
PHONE...................917 698-0626
Faisal Sheikh, *President*
EMP: 4
SALES: 1MM **Privately Held**
SIC: **2389** Men's miscellaneous accessories

(G-8555)
OCALA GROUP LLC
1981 Marcus Ave Ste 227 (11042-1055)
PHONE...................516 233-2750
◆ EMP: 17
SALES (est): 2.6MM **Privately Held**
SIC: **3841** 3089 Surgical & medical instruments; plastic kitchenware, tableware & houseware

(G-8556)
OVERNIGHT MOUNTINGS INC
1400 Plaza Ave (11040-4921)
PHONE...................516 865-3000
Morris Adwar, *CEO*
Jeffery Adwar, *President*
Matthew Roth, *Vice Pres*
EMP: 55
SQ FT: 550,000
SALES (est): 7.7MM **Privately Held**
WEB: www.overnightmountings.com
SIC: **3911** Jewelry, precious metal

(G-8557)
P J D PUBLICATIONS LTD
1315 Jericho Tpke (11040-4613)
P.O. Box 966, Westbury (11590-0966)
PHONE...................516 626-0650
Siva Sankar, *CEO*
Douglas Sankar, *Vice Pres*
Jason Sankar, *Vice Pres*
Priscilla Wong,
EMP: 5
SALES (est): 330K **Privately Held**
WEB: www.pjdonline.com
SIC: **2731** 5045 Books: publishing only; computers, peripherals & software

(G-8558)
PROVISIONS 5 CORP
119 S 3rd St Ste D201 (11040-4836)
PHONE...................718 809-5292
Hemlata Aidasani, *President*
EMP: 2
SQ FT: 1,000
SALES (est): 1.2MM **Privately Held**
SIC: **2844** Toilet preparations

(G-8559)
QUALITY READY MIX INC
1824 Gilford Ave (11040-4031)
PHONE...................516 437-0100
Eugene Messina, *President*
EMP: 15
SALES (est): 2.3MM **Privately Held**
SIC: **3273** Ready-mixed concrete

(G-8560)
QUANTUM LOGIC CORP
91 5th Ave (11040-5005)
PHONE...................516 746-1380
John Carbone, *Ch of Bd*
EMP: 9 EST: 2002
SALES (est): 1.1MM **Privately Held**
SIC: **3572** Mfg Computer Storage Devices

(G-8561)
SATCO CASTINGS SERVICE INC
Also Called: Plaza Bracelette Mounting
1400 Plaza Ave (11040-4921)
P.O. Box 1068 (11040-1068)
PHONE...................516 354-1500
Steven Feld, *President*
EMP: 45
SQ FT: 18,000
SALES (est): 7MM **Privately Held**
WEB: www.satcocasting.com
SIC: **3915** 3911 Jewelers' castings; jewelry, precious metal

(G-8562)
SHELL CONTAINERS INC (NY)
1981 Marcus Ave Ste C105 (11042-2028)
PHONE...................516 352-4505
Norman Kay, *President*
Philip Schoonmaker, *Vice Pres*
▲ EMP: 20
SQ FT: 19,000
SALES (est): 2.8MM
SALES (corp-wide): 23.4MM **Privately Held**
WEB: www.shellcontainers.com
SIC: **3086** 2679 Packaging & shipping materials, foamed plastic; building, insulating & packaging paperboard
PA: International Business Communications, Inc.
1981 Marcus Ave Ste C105
New Hyde Park NY 11042
516 352-4505

(G-8563)
SNOW CRAFT CO INC
200 Fulton Ave (11040-5306)
P.O. Box 829 (11040-0829)
PHONE...................516 739-1399
Kirk Guyton, *President*
Robert Farina, *Vice Pres*
William Hess, *Admin Sec*
EMP: 28 EST: 1954
SQ FT: 22,500
SALES (est): 3.8MM **Privately Held**
SIC: **3086** Packaging & shipping materials, foamed plastic

(G-8564)
SONOMED INC
Also Called: Sonomed Escalon
1979 Marcus Ave Ste C105 (11042-1002)
PHONE...................516 354-0900
Barry Durante, *President*
Ronald Hueneke, *COO*
EMP: 30
SQ FT: 11,000
SALES (est): 5.4MM
SALES (corp-wide): 11.4MM **Privately Held**
WEB: www.sonomedinc.com
SIC: **3845** 3841 Electromedical equipment; ophthalmic instruments & apparatus
PA: Escalon Medical Corp.
435 Devon Park Dr Ste 100
Wayne PA 19087
610 688-6830

(G-8565)
SPECIAL CIRCLE INC
123 Shelter Rock Rd (11040-1328)
PHONE...................516 595-9988
Lawrence Lin, *Principal*
Kathleen Loftus, *Co-Owner*
Phoebe Lin, *COO*
Selena Zhang, *COO*
Darren Yang, *Chief Engr*
EMP: 12
SALES (est): 281.6K **Privately Held**
SIC: **7372** 7389 Educational computer software;

(G-8566)
TEXAS HOME SECURITY INC (PA)
Also Called: Medallion Security Door & Win
50 Rose Pl (11040-5312)
PHONE...................516 747-2100
Gregory E Falgoust, *President*
Brian S Falgoust, *Vice Pres*
Alexis Cohen, *Assistant*
EMP: 50
SALES (est): 6.5MM **Privately Held**
WEB: www.medalliondoors.com
SIC: **3442** 1521 Storm doors or windows, metal; general remodeling, single-family houses

(G-8567)
THREE GEMS INC
Also Called: Sign-A-Rama
2201 Hillside Ave (11040-2714)
PHONE...................516 248-0388
Sal Italiano, *President*
Jane Italiano, *Vice Pres*
EMP: 5
SQ FT: 1,200
SALES (est): 646.9K **Privately Held**
WEB: www.threegems.com
SIC: **3993** Signs & advertising specialties

(G-8568)
UBM LLC (HQ)
Also Called: Ubm Tech
1983 Marcus Ave Ste 250 (11042-2000)
PHONE...................516 562-7800
Scott D Schulman, *CEO*
Atif Malik, *President*
Marco Pardi, *Managing Dir*
Liza Haar, *Editor*
Simon Carless, *Exec VP*
EMP: 60
SQ FT: 230,000
SALES (est): 317.7MM
SALES (corp-wide): 1B **Privately Held**
WEB: www.cmp.com
SIC: **2721** 2711 7319 7389 Periodicals: publishing only; newspapers; media buying service; decoration service for special events
PA: Ubm Plc
240 Blackfriars Road
London SE1 8
207 921-8029

(G-8569)
UNITED METAL INDUSTRIES INC
1008 3rd Ave (11040-5529)
PHONE...................516 354-6800
Richard M Meyers, *President*
Robert S Meyers, *Vice Pres*
▲ EMP: 8 EST: 1912
SQ FT: 8,000
SALES (est): 1MM **Privately Held**
WEB: www.unitedmetal.net
SIC: **3429** Clamps & couplings, hose

(G-8570)
UNITED STTES BRNZE SIGN OF FLA
811 2nd Ave (11040-4869)
PHONE...................516 352-5155
George Barbeosch, *President*
Alan Kasten, *Vice Pres*
EMP: 25 EST: 1927
SQ FT: 10,000
SALES (est): 2.6MM **Privately Held**
WEB: www.usbronze.com
SIC: **3993** 3953 Signs & advertising specialties; marking devices

(G-8571)
UNIVERSAL READY MIX INC
197 Atlantic Ave (11040-5048)
PHONE...................516 746-4535
Guilio Viti, *President*
Anthony Logiudice, *Vice Pres*
Rocco Viti, *Admin Sec*
EMP: 5 EST: 1997
SALES (est): 877.9K **Privately Held**
WEB: www.universalreadymix.com
SIC: **2951** Asphalt paving mixtures & blocks

(G-8572)
USE ACQUISITION LLC
Also Called: US Energy Group
270 Park Ave (11040-5318)
PHONE...................516 812-6800
Gregory Dinome, *Engineer*
Gerald Dicunzolo,
EMP: 10
SALES (est): 1.4MM **Privately Held**
SIC: **3822** Temperature controls, automatic

(G-8573)
WINDOWTEX INC
Also Called: Wt Shade
77 2nd Ave (11040-5030)
PHONE...................877 294-3580
Joseph J Daniels, *President*
Bill Coutz, *COO*
Chuck Raible, *Vice Pres*
David Lin, *Opers Mgr*
Fang Lin, *Design Engr*
EMP: 12
SALES (est): 146.9K **Privately Held**
SIC: **2591** Window shade rollers & fittings

New Lebanon
Columbia County

(G-8574)
WASTEQUIP MANUFACTURING CO LLC
Also Called: Wastequip - Consolidated
1079 State Route 20 (12125-3206)
PHONE...................800 235-0734
Paul Fitzgerald, *Branch Mgr*
EMP: 33
SALES (corp-wide): 574.7MM **Privately Held**
WEB: www.rayfo.com
SIC: **3443** Dumpsters, garbage
HQ: Wastequip Manufacturing Company Llc
1901 Roxborough Rd # 300
Charlotte NC 28211

New Paltz
Ulster County

(G-8575)
BIMBO BAKERIES USA INC
Also Called: Freihofer's Bakery Outlet
27 N Putt Corners Rd (12561-3408)
PHONE...................845 255-4345
Mike Croce, *Manager*
EMP: 10
SQ FT: 21,413 **Privately Held**
SIC: **2051** Bread, cake & related products
HQ: Bimbo Bakeries Usa, Inc
255 Business Center Dr # 200
Horsham PA 19044
215 347-5500

(G-8576)
BRUYNSWICK SALES INC
14 Bruynswick Rd (12561-4106)
PHONE...................845 789-2049
Wayne Elliot, *President*
EMP: 12
SALES (est): 564.3K **Privately Held**
SIC: **3949** Lures, fishing: artificial

(G-8577)
GILDED OTTER BREWING CO
3 Main St (12561-1742)
P.O. Box 57 (12561-0057)
PHONE...................845 256-1700
Rick Rauch, *President*
EMP: 70 EST: 1996
SQ FT: 10,000
SALES (est): 6.8MM **Privately Held**
WEB: www.gildedotter.com
SIC: **2082** 5812 Beer (alcoholic beverage); eating places

(G-8578)
KEVCO INDUSTRIES
Also Called: Engineering Educational Eqp Co
6 Millbrook Rd (12561-1315)
PHONE...................845 255-7407
Peter C Bowers, *Owner*
Pete Bower, *MIS Staff*
EMP: 7
SALES (est): 480K **Privately Held**
WEB: www.eeeco.com
SIC: **3999** Education aids, devices & supplies

(G-8579)
LYOPHILIZATION SYSTEMS INC
14 Hickory Hill Rd (12561-3104)
PHONE...................845 338-0456
Marc Thompson, *President*
Roger W Grange, *Opers Mgr*
EMP: 5
SQ FT: 6,000
SALES (est): 540K **Privately Held**
WEB: www.lyogroup.com
SIC: **3556** Food products machinery

(G-8580)
PDQ SHIPPING SERVICES
Also Called: PDQ Printing
8 New Paltz Plz 299 (12561-1616)
PHONE...................845 255-5500
Craig Shinkles, *Owner*

▲ = Import ▼ = Export
◆ = Import/Export

GEOGRAPHIC SECTION

EMP: 8
SALES (est): 340K **Privately Held**
SIC: 2759 7331 Promotional printing; mailing service

(G-8581)
TOTAL WEBCASTING INC
8 Bruce St (12561-2101)
P.O. Box 665 (12561-0665)
PHONE..................................845 883-0909
Robert Feldman, *President*
EMP: 6
SQ FT: 3,000
SALES: 700K **Privately Held**
SIC: 2741

(G-8582)
ULSTER COUNTY IRON WORKS LLC
64 N Putt Corners Rd (12561-3405)
PHONE..................................845 255-0003
Steven Vasalka, *President*
EMP: 8
SQ FT: 5,000
SALES (est): 825K **Privately Held**
SIC: 3499 Mfg Misc Fabricated Metal Products

(G-8583)
ULSTER PUBLISHING CO INC
Also Called: New Paltz Times
29 S Chestnut St Ste 101 (12561-1949)
PHONE..................................845 255-7005
Debbie Alexsa, *Principal*
EMP: 10
SALES (corp-wide): 3.5MM **Privately Held**
WEB: www.ulsterpublishing.com
SIC: 2711 Newspapers: publishing only, not printed on site
PA: Ulster Publishing Co Inc
322 Wall St Fl 1
Kingston NY 12401
845 334-8205

(G-8584)
VIKING INDUSTRIES INC
89 S Ohioville Rd (12561-4012)
P.O. Box 249 (12561-0249)
PHONE..................................845 883-6325
Richard Croce, *President*
Rich Croce, *Vice Pres*
Michael Cozzolino, *Plant Mgr*
Mark Nowak, *Controller*
Cindy Brooks, *Finance*
EMP: 55
SQ FT: 50,000
SALES (est): 12.3MM **Privately Held**
WEB: www.vikingindustries.net
SIC: 2657 Folding paperboard boxes

New Rochelle
Westchester County

(G-8585)
A & T IRON WORKS INC
25 Cliff St (10801-6803)
PHONE..................................914 632-8992
Gessie Tassone, *President*
▲ **EMP:** 28
SQ FT: 20,000
SALES (est): 5.6MM **Privately Held**
WEB: www.atironworks.com
SIC: 3446 5211 3441 Architectural metalwork; fencing; fabricated structural metal

(G-8586)
ABSOLUTE COATINGS INC
38 Portman Rd (10801-2103)
PHONE..................................914 636-0700
Brian A Demkowicz, *Principal*
EMP: 35
SQ FT: 40,000
SALES (est): 1.4MM
SALES (corp-wide): 49.9MM **Privately Held**
SIC: 2851 Polyurethane coatings
PA: Valentus Specialty Chemicals, Inc.
1999 Elizabeth St
North Brunswick NJ 08902
732 821-3200

(G-8587)
ALEXANDRA FERGUSON LLC
180 Davenport Ave (10805-2105)
PHONE..................................718 788-7768
Alexandra Ferguson, *Mng Member*
EMP: 8
SALES (est): 641.2K **Privately Held**
SIC: 2392 Cushions & pillows

(G-8588)
ALICIAS BAKERY INC
498 Main St Ste A (10801-6326)
PHONE..................................914 235-4689
Alicia Zapien, *President*
EMP: 5
SALES (est): 416.5K **Privately Held**
SIC: 2051 Doughnuts, except frozen

(G-8589)
ALLIED CONVERTERS INC
64 Drake Ave (10805-1598)
P.O. Box 548 (10802-0548)
PHONE..................................914 235-1585
Richard E Ellenbogen, *President*
Wilma J Ellenbogen, *Corp Secy*
▲ **EMP:** 30 **EST:** 1954
SQ FT: 50,000
SALES (est): 6.7MM **Privately Held**
WEB: www.garb-o-liner.com
SIC: 2673 2671 2679 Plastic bags: made from purchased materials; plastic film, coated or laminated for packaging; paperboard products, converted

(G-8590)
APPLE INTERCOM AND ELEC INC
Also Called: Apple Security Solutions
271 North Ave Ste A2 (10801-5121)
PHONE..................................914 633-5101
Robert Moriarty, *Owner*
Mason Wilson, *Consultant*
EMP: 5
SALES (est): 163K **Privately Held**
SIC: 3571 Security systems services

(G-8591)
BAKERS PRIDE OVEN CO INC
145 Huguenot St Ste Mz1 (10801-6997)
PHONE..................................914 576-0200
Hylton Jones, *CEO*
Howard Kraines, *Vice Pres*
Brian Rosenbloom, *Vice Pres*
Don Wall, *CFO*
Lawrence Rosenbloom, *Admin Sec*
EMP: 150 **EST:** 1995
SQ FT: 120,000
SALES (est): 22MM
SALES (corp-wide): 868.3MM **Publicly Held**
WEB: www.associatedamericanindustries.com
SIC: 3589 3631 3556 Commercial cooking & foodwarming equipment; cooking equipment, commercial; household cooking equipment; food products machinery
HQ: Associated American Industries, Inc.
1307 N Watters Rd
Allen TX 75013

(G-8592)
BENCHMARK EDUCATION CO LLC (PA)
145 Huguenot St Fl 8 (10801-5233)
PHONE..................................914 637-7200
Wainright Samuel, *President*
Elaine Caughlan, *Editor*
Susan Rivers, *Senior VP*
Barbara Andrews, *Finance*
Jennifer Kays, *Human Resources*
▲ **EMP:** 75
SALES (est): 19.8MM **Privately Held**
WEB: www.benchmarkeducation.com
SIC: 2731 Book publishing

(G-8593)
BREAD FACTORY LLC
30 Grove Ave (10801-6207)
PHONE..................................914 637-8150
Jean Yves Lebris, *Partner*
Anthony Orza, *Partner*
EMP: 24 **EST:** 2000
SQ FT: 10,000
SALES (est): 1.4MM **Privately Held**
SIC: 2051 Bread, cake & related products

(G-8594)
BRIDGE RECORDS INC
200 Clinton Ave (10801-1525)
PHONE..................................914 654-9270
David Starobin, *President*
Becky Starobin, *Vice Pres*
Allegra Starobin, *Associate Dir*
Casey Siu, *Graphic Designe*
EMP: 5
SQ FT: 2,000
SALES (est): 709.1K **Privately Held**
SIC: 3652 Master records or tapes, preparation of

(G-8595)
CASTEK INC (HQ)
20 Jones St (10801-6000)
PHONE..................................914 636-1000
Arthur M Dinitz, *President*
Mike Stento, *Vice Pres*
Robert J Welsh, *Treasurer*
▲ **EMP:** 3
SQ FT: 42,000
SALES (est): 3.1MM
SALES (corp-wide): 7.4MM **Privately Held**
WEB: www.castek.net
SIC: 3272 Concrete products, precast
PA: Transpo Industries, Inc.
20 Jones St Ste 3
New Rochelle NY 10801
914 636-1000

(G-8596)
CERAMICA VARM (PA)
Also Called: Ceramica V. A. R. M.
479 5th Ave (10801-2212)
PHONE..................................914 381-6215
Fax: 914 381-3785
EMP: 9
SQ FT: 4,000
SALES: 7.5MM **Privately Held**
SIC: 3263 Mfg Of Ceramic Earthenware-Italy

(G-8597)
CUFFS PLANNING & MODELS LTD
317 Beechmont Dr (10804-4601)
PHONE..................................914 632-1883
David K Combs, *President*
David Combs, *President*
Sandra Kirkendall, *Vice Pres*
EMP: 8
SALES (est): 520K **Privately Held**
WEB: www.cuffs88.com
SIC: 7372 Business oriented computer software

(G-8598)
DERAFFELE MFG CO INC
2525 Palmer Ave Ste 4 (10801-4476)
PHONE..................................914 636-6850
Philip De Raffele Jr, *President*
Stephen De Raffele, *Treasurer*
Stephen D Raffele, *Treasurer*
Joseph De Raffele, *Admin Sec*
EMP: 25 **EST:** 1933
SQ FT: 30,000
SALES (est): 5.7MM **Privately Held**
SIC: 3448 Prefabricated metal buildings

(G-8599)
DISPLAY PRODUCERS INC
40 Winding Brook Rd (10804-2008)
PHONE..................................718 904-1200
Joseph A Laurite, *President*
Arthur E Landi, *President*
Richard Tevere, *Corp Secy*
Chris Asmussen, *Director*
▲ **EMP:** 250
SQ FT: 150,000
SALES (est): 22.5MM **Privately Held**
WEB: www.displayproducersinc.com
SIC: 3993 Displays & cutouts, window & lobby

(G-8600)
EMERGENCY BEACON CORP
15 River St (10801-4354)
PHONE..................................914 576-2700
Joan Goodman, *President*
George Ramos, *Vice Pres*
Patricia Wyllie, *Vice Pres*
EMP: 15
SQ FT: 12,000
SALES: 1MM **Privately Held**
WEB: www.emergencybeaconcorp.com
SIC: 3812 Aircraft/aerospace flight instruments & guidance systems

(G-8601)
ENTERPRISE TECH GROUP INC
3 Church St (10801-6301)
PHONE..................................914 588-0327
Liza Zaneri, *President*
EMP: 12
SALES: 950K **Privately Held**
SIC: 7372 Prepackaged software

(G-8602)
ERIC S TURNER & COMPANY INC
Also Called: Turner Plating
3335 Centre Ave (10801)
PHONE..................................914 235-7114
Kenneth Turner, *President*
William Vernon Turner, *Vice Pres*
EMP: 12 **EST:** 1931
SQ FT: 10,000
SALES: 900K **Privately Held**
WEB: www.turnerplating.com
SIC: 3471 2851 Electroplating of metals or formed products; finishing, metals or formed products; polishing, metals or formed products; paints & allied products

(G-8603)
FORMCRAFT DISPLAY PRODUCTS
42 Beverly Rd (10804-1703)
PHONE..................................914 632-1410
George Bartoli, *President*
Joanne Bartoli, *Vice Pres*
EMP: 5
SQ FT: 5,000
SALES (est): 330K **Privately Held**
SIC: 3229 Christmas tree ornaments, from glass produced on-site

(G-8604)
FORREST ENGRAVING CO INC
Also Called: Forrest Engravg
92 1st St (10801-6121)
P.O. Box 1240, Carmel (10512-8240)
PHONE..................................845 228-0200
Tom Giordano, *President*
EMP: 11
SQ FT: 3,000
SALES (est): 1MM **Privately Held**
SIC: 3993 Signs & advertising specialties

(G-8605)
FRADAN MANUFACTURING CORP
499 5th Ave (10801-2212)
PHONE..................................914 632-3653
Frank De Bartolo, *President*
EMP: 15
SQ FT: 12,000
SALES (est): 2MM **Privately Held**
SIC: 3524 Lawn & garden equipment

(G-8606)
GANNETT CO INC
Also Called: Bronxville Review
92 North Ave (10801-7413)
PHONE..................................914 278-9315
Jerry McKinstry, *Principal*
EMP: 20
SALES (corp-wide): 3.1B **Publicly Held**
WEB: www.gannett.com
SIC: 2711 Newspapers, publishing & printing
PA: Gannett Co., Inc.
7950 Jones Branch Dr
Mc Lean VA 22102
703 854-6000

(G-8607)
GARB-O-LINER INC
64 Drake Ave (10805-1598)
P.O. Box 548 (10802-0548)
PHONE..................................914 235-1585
Richard Ellenbogen, *President*
Richard E Ellenbogen, *President*
Wilma Ellenbogen, *Treasurer*
EMP: 7 **EST:** 1986

New Rochelle - Westchester County (G-8608)

SALES (est): 1MM **Privately Held**
SIC: 2673 5113 Trash bags (plastic film): made from purchased materials; bags, paper & disposable plastic

(G-8608)
GEN PUBLISHING INC
Also Called: Genetic Engineering News
140 Huguenot St Fl 3 (10801-5215)
PHONE.................914 834-3880
Mary Ann Liebert, *President*
Alex Philippidis, *Editor*
Sharon Spitz, *Sales Mgr*
Julie Chauca, *Manager*
Randi Hernandez, *Manager*
EMP: 99
SALES: 950K **Privately Held**
WEB: www.genengnews.com
SIC: 2741 Miscellaneous publishing

(G-8609)
HAGEDORN COMMUNICATIONS INC (PA)
Also Called: Co-Op City News
662 Main St Ste 1 (10801-7145)
P.O. Box 680 (10802-0680)
PHONE.................914 636-7400
Christopher Hagedorn, *President*
Richard Kondub, *General Mgr*
▲ EMP: 70
SQ FT: 20,000
SALES (est): 10.5MM **Privately Held**
WEB: www.rew-online.com
SIC: 2711 Newspapers: publishing only, not printed on site

(G-8610)
HAITIAN TIMES INC
80 Lakeside Dr (10801-3130)
PHONE.................718 230-8700
Garry P Pierre, *President*
EMP: 5
SQ FT: 1,200
SALES (est): 300K **Privately Held**
WEB: www.haitiantimes.com
SIC: 2711 Newspapers

(G-8611)
HALPERN TOOL CORP (PA)
Also Called: Vernon Devices
111 Plain Ave (10801-2206)
PHONE.................914 633-0038
David Newmark, *President*
Marlene Werner, *Vice Pres*
EMP: 16
SQ FT: 12,500
SALES (est): 500K **Privately Held**
SIC: 3541 5084 Machine tools, metal cutting type; industrial machinery & equipment

(G-8612)
HARBOR ELC FABRICATION TLS INC
Also Called: Hefti
29 Portman Rd (10801-2104)
PHONE.................914 636-4400
Jerry Schiff, *President*
EMP: 25
SALES (est): 5.2MM **Privately Held**
SIC: 3444 Metal housings, enclosures, casings & other containers

(G-8613)
HB ATHLETIC INC (PA)
Also Called: Globe-Tex
56 Harrison St Ste 305 (10801-6561)
PHONE.................914 560-8422
Robert Hurvitz, *Ch of Bd*
Stuart Hurvitz, *President*
Arthur Trujillo, *Production*
Jaymee Kahn, *Legal Staff*
▲ EMP: 15
SQ FT: 4,500
SALES (est): 1.8MM **Privately Held**
SIC: 2339 2389 Athletic clothing: women's, misses' & juniors'; uniforms, athletic: women's, misses' & juniors'; women's & misses' athletic clothing & sportswear; disposable garments & accessories

(G-8614)
HIGHLANDER REALTY INC
Also Called: Seaboard Electronics
70 Church St (10805-3204)
PHONE.................914 235-8073
Jerrold Hacker, *President*
Dorothy Hacker, *Treasurer*
Amy Gibson, *Bookkeeper*
EMP: 35 EST: 1993
SQ FT: 15,000
SALES (est): 3.9MM **Privately Held**
WEB: www.highlanderrealty.com
SIC: 3699 Security devices

(G-8615)
HOMEGROWN FOR GOOD LLC
29 Beechwood Ave (10801-6818)
PHONE.................857 540-6361
Timothy Gibb, *CEO*
Thomas Gibb,
EMP: 10
SALES (est): 1.5MM **Privately Held**
SIC: 3021 Rubber & plastics footwear

(G-8616)
IVY CLASSIC INDUSTRIES INC
40 Plain Ave (10801-2205)
PHONE.................914 632-8200
Anthony Schwartz, *President*
Greg Schwartz, *Vice Pres*
Justin Schwartz, *Vice Pres*
Stanley Schwartz, *Treasurer*
◆ EMP: 30
SQ FT: 30,000
SALES (est): 4.7MM **Privately Held**
SIC: 3423 3546 3547 Hand & edge tools; power-driven handtools; rolling mill machinery

(G-8617)
J P INSTALLATIONS WAREHOUSE
29 Portman Rd (10801-2104)
PHONE.................914 576-3188
John Pompi, *President*
EMP: 10
SALES (est): 1.1MM **Privately Held**
SIC: 2599 Factory furniture & fixtures

(G-8618)
JOHNS RAVIOLI COMPANY INC
15 Drake Ave (10805-1506)
PHONE.................914 576-7030
Robert Guarnero, *President*
Lee Key, *Bookkeeper*
▲ EMP: 15
SQ FT: 8,800
SALES (est): 2.5MM **Privately Held**
SIC: 2099 5499 Pasta, uncooked: packaged with other ingredients; gourmet food stores

(G-8619)
KORING BROS INC
30 Pine St (10801-6906)
PHONE.................888 233-1292
EMP: 4
SQ FT: 5,000
SALES (est): 2MM **Privately Held**
SIC: 2399 Mfg Fabricated Textile Products

(G-8620)
MARY ANN LIEBERT INC
140 Huguenot St Fl 3 (10801-5215)
PHONE.................914 740-2100
Mary Ann Liebert, *President*
Gerry Williams, *Partner*
Durland Fish PH, *Editor*
John Sterling, *Chief*
Ruth Maysonet, *Vice Pres*
EMP: 70
SQ FT: 4,500
SALES (est): 11.7MM **Privately Held**
WEB: www.mmsionline.com
SIC: 2721 2731 2741 Trade journals: publishing only, not printed on site; books: publishing only; miscellaneous publishing

(G-8621)
PAINT OVER RUST PRODUCTS INC
Also Called: Last N Last
38 Portman Rd (10801-2103)
PHONE.................914 636-0700
David Sherman, *CEO*

◆ EMP: 35 EST: 1923
SQ FT: 40,000
SALES (est): 14.5MM **Privately Held**
WEB: www.absolutecoatings.com
SIC: 2851 Polyurethane coatings; varnishes

(G-8622)
PLASTIC WORKS
26 Garden St (10801-4204)
P.O. Box 51, Crompond (10517-0051)
PHONE.................914 576-2050
David J Jeskie, *Owner*
EMP: 8 EST: 1978
SALES (est): 800K **Privately Held**
SIC: 3089 Molding primary plastic; plastic processing

(G-8623)
PREMCO INC
11 Beechwood Ave (10801-6818)
P.O. Box 266 (10802-0266)
PHONE.................914 636-7095
Harold Jacobs, *Ch of Bd*
EMP: 18
SQ FT: 22,000
SALES (est): 3.9MM **Privately Held**
SIC: 3621 7694 Motors & generators; motor repair services

(G-8624)
RAM TRANSFORMER TECHNOLOGIES
11 Beechwood Ave (10801-6818)
P.O. Box 266 (10802-0266)
PHONE.................914 632-3988
Harold Jacobs, *President*
EMP: 10
SQ FT: 7,600
SALES (est): 990K **Privately Held**
SIC: 3612 Transformers, except electric

(G-8625)
REINO MANUFACTURING CO INC
34 Circuit Rd (10805-1930)
PHONE.................914 636-8990
Florence Reino, *President*
Linda Reino, *Corp Secy*
EMP: 10 EST: 1945
SALES (est): 554.3K **Privately Held**
SIC: 3961 Costume jewelry

(G-8626)
REPUBLIC CONSTRUCTION CO INC
305 North Ave (10801-4169)
PHONE.................914 235-3654
Joeseph Pogostin, *President*
EMP: 6 EST: 1985
SALES (est): 480.9K **Privately Held**
SIC: 1442 Construction sand & gravel

(G-8627)
SCEPTER PUBLISHERS INC
56 Harrison St Ste 401 (10801-6560)
P.O. Box 360694, Strongsville OH (44136-0012)
PHONE.................212 354-0670
Robert Singerline, *President*
John Powers, *Sales Mgr*
Violet Sukdeo, *Manager*
◆ EMP: 5
SALES (est): 840.1K **Privately Held**
SIC: 2741 Miscellaneous publishing

(G-8628)
SHANGHAI HARMONY AP INTL LLC
3 Wykagyl Ter (10804-3206)
PHONE.................646 569-5680
Robert Wang, *Mng Member*
EMP: 21
SALES (est): 763.3K **Privately Held**
SIC: 2326 2339 Men's & boys' work clothing; women's & misses' athletic clothing & sportswear

(G-8629)
TOWSE PUBLISHING CO
Also Called: Furniture World
1333a North Ave (10804-2120)
PHONE.................914 235-3095
Russell Bienenstock, *President*
Mark Testa, *Sales Mgr*

Barbara Bienenstock, *Director*
EMP: 11
SALES: 1MM **Privately Held**
WEB: www.furnitureworldmagazine.com
SIC: 2721 Magazines: publishing & printing

(G-8630)
TRANSPO INDUSTRIES INC (PA)
20 Jones St Ste 3 (10801-6098)
PHONE.................914 636-1000
Arthur M Dinitz, *Ch of Bd*
Michael S Stenko, *President*
Robert Welsh, *Vice Pres*
Lewis Kruger, *Admin Sec*
▲ EMP: 38
SQ FT: 33,000
SALES (est): 7.4MM **Privately Held**
WEB: www.transpo.com
SIC: 3089 3272 2821 Plastic hardware & building products; hardware, plastic; concrete products, precast; plastics materials & resins

(G-8631)
VIC-GINA PRINTING COMPANY INC
Also Called: Adrean Printing
1299 North Ave (10804-2642)
PHONE.................914 636-0200
Victor Diede, *President*
Louise Diede, *Admin Sec*
EMP: 5
SQ FT: 2,500
SALES (est): 619K **Privately Held**
SIC: 2752 Commercial printing, lithographic

New Windsor
Orange County

(G-8632)
24 SEVEN ENTERPRISES INC
1073 State Route 94 Ste 9 (12553-6822)
PHONE.................845 563-9033
John Cerven, *Vice Pres*
EMP: 9
SALES (est): 1.4MM **Privately Held**
SIC: 3086 Packaging & shipping materials, foamed plastic

(G-8633)
A & R CONCRETE PRODUCTS LLC
7 Ruscitti Rd (12553-6205)
PHONE.................845 562-0640
Jay Nannini, *President*
EMP: 25 EST: 2013
SALES (est): 2MM **Privately Held**
SIC: 3272 Concrete products, precast

(G-8634)
AIGNER LABEL HOLDER CORP
Also Called: Aigner Index
218 Mac Arthur Ave (12553-7011)
PHONE.................845 562-4510
Mark Aigner, *President*
Lisa Arestin, *Accounts Mgr*
Lisa Cirig, *Sales Staff*
▲ EMP: 11 EST: 1930
SALES (est): 2.5MM **Privately Held**
WEB: www.aignerindex.com
SIC: 2679 Paper products, converted

(G-8635)
AMERICAN FELT & FILTER CO INC
Also Called: Affco
361 Walsh Ave (12553-6727)
PHONE.................845 561-3560
Wilson H Pryne, *Ch of Bd*
▲ EMP: 60
SQ FT: 230,000
SALES (est): 25.1MM **Privately Held**
WEB: www.affco.com
SIC: 3569 Filters, general line: industrial

(G-8636)
BELSITO COMMUNICATIONS INC
Also Called: 1st Responder Newspaper
1 Ardmore St (12553-8303)
PHONE.................845 534-9700

GEOGRAPHIC SECTION

New Windsor - Orange County (G-8663)

Joseph P Belsito, *President*
Jim Stankiewicz, *General Mgr*
Wanda Rogers, *Sales Staff*
Michelle Belsito, *Office Mgr*
EMP: 12 **EST:** 1997
SQ FT: 2,000
SALES (est): 1MM **Privately Held**
SIC: 2711 7374 Newspapers: publishing only, not printed on site; computer graphics service

(G-8637)
BLEND SMOOTHIE BAR
25 Creamery Dr (12553-8011)
PHONE 845 568-7366
EMP: 5
SALES (est): 337.8K **Privately Held**
SIC: 2037 Frozen fruits & vegetables

(G-8638)
CAFE SPICE GCT INC
Also Called: Zaika Flavors of India
677 Little Britain Rd (12553-6152)
PHONE 845 863-0910
Sushil Malhotra, *CEO*
Sameer Malhotra, *Vice Pres*
EMP: 200
SALES (est): 47.2MM **Privately Held**
SIC: 2099 Food preparations

(G-8639)
CENTER LINE STUDIOS INC
261 Otterkill Rd (12553-8842)
PHONE 845 534-7143
Roger P Gray, *President*
Roger Gray, *Branch Mgr*
EMP: 6
SALES (est): 869.1K
SALES (corp-wide): 1.6MM **Privately Held**
SIC: 3999 Theatrical scenery
PA: Center Line Studios, Inc.
112 Forge Hill Rd
New Windsor NY 12553
845 534-7143

(G-8640)
CENTER LINE STUDIOS INC (PA)
112 Forge Hill Rd (12553-8061)
PHONE 845 534-7143
Roger Gray, *President*
Shelley Gray, *Managing Dir*
Jeff Chrzczon, *Exec VP*
Prokosch Poni, *Human Resources*
Alexis Gray, *Sales Staff*
▲ **EMP:** 15
SQ FT: 30,000
SALES: 1.6MM **Privately Held**
WEB: www.centerlinestudios.com
SIC: 3999 Theatrical scenery

(G-8641)
CLASSIC TOOL DESIGN INC
31 Walnut St (12553-7021)
PHONE 845 562-8700
Ralph Edwards, *President*
Marge Edwards, *Vice Pres*
EMP: 20
SQ FT: 22,000
SALES (est): 1.2MM **Privately Held**
WEB: www.ctd4ac.com
SIC: 3423 Mechanics' hand tools

(G-8642)
COCA-COLA BTLG CO OF NY INC
10 Heampstead Rd (12553-5501)
PHONE 845 562-3037
John Lacey, *Manager*
EMP: 15
SQ FT: 15,000
SALES (corp-wide): 35.4B **Publicly Held**
SIC: 2086 Bottled & canned soft drinks
HQ: The Coca-Cola Bottling Company Of New York Inc
2500 Windy Ridge Pkwy Se
Atlanta GA 30239
770 989-3000

(G-8643)
E W SMITH PUBLISHING CO
Also Called: Sentinel, The
36 Meriline Ave (12553-6520)
P.O. Box 406, Vails Gate (12584-0406)
PHONE 845 562-1218
Everett W Smith, *President*
Michael Smith, *Vice Pres*
Steven Smith, *Vice Pres*
EMP: 11
SALES (est): 804.8K **Privately Held**
WEB: www.ewsmithpublishing.com
SIC: 2711 2752 Commercial printing & newspaper publishing combined; commercial printing, lithographic

(G-8644)
FIFTY DOOR PARTNERS LLC (PA)
Also Called: AJW Architectural Products
509 Temple Hill Rd (12553-5532)
PHONE 845 562-3332
Hurley Gordon, *General Mgr*
Sean Quin, *COO*
Chris Duran, *VP Mfg*
Keith Gallagher, *Senior Mgr*
Christopher Hansen,
▲ **EMP:** 20
SALES (est): 5.8MM **Privately Held**
SIC: 2541 2542 Cabinets, lockers & shelving; partitions & fixtures, except wood; office & store showcases & display fixtures

(G-8645)
GAMMA PRODUCTS INC
Also Called: A & J Washroom Accessories
509 Temple Hill Rd (12553-5532)
P.O. Box 4569 (12553-0569)
PHONE 845 562-3332
Anthony Granuzzo, *Ch of Bd*
Richard Rebusmen, *President*
Jayne F Granuzzo, *Exec VP*
Marilyn Walsh, *Accounting Mgr*
Tom Butler, *Info Tech Mgr*
▲ **EMP:** 70
SQ FT: 50,000
SALES (est): 10.7MM **Privately Held**
WEB: www.ajwashroom.com
SIC: 3261 Bathroom accessories/fittings, vitreous china or earthenware

(G-8646)
HI-TECH PACKG WORLD-WIDE LLC
110 Corporate Dr (12553-6952)
P.O. Box 4232 (12553-0232)
PHONE 845 947-1912
Robert Trimble, *Owner*
EMP: 2
SQ FT: 10,000
SALES: 1.1MM **Privately Held**
SIC: 2759 Commercial printing

(G-8647)
JUST WOOD PALLETS INC
78 Vails Gate Heights Dr (12553-8514)
PHONE 718 644-7013
Carlos Garcia, *Principal*
EMP: 8 **EST:** 2010
SALES (est): 980.5K **Privately Held**
SIC: 2448 Pallets, wood & wood with metal

(G-8648)
LARCENT ENTERPRISES INC
Also Called: Angie Washroom
509 Temple Hill Rd (12553-5532)
P.O. Box 4569 (12553-0569)
PHONE 845 562-3332
Anthony J Granuzzo, *Ch of Bd*
▲ **EMP:** 50
SALES (est): 6.4MM **Privately Held**
SIC: 3261 Bathroom accessories/fittings, vitreous china or earthenware

(G-8649)
LSI LIGHTRON INC
500 Hudson Valley Ave (12553-4744)
P.O. Box 4270 (12553-0270)
PHONE 845 562-5500
Gene Littman, *CEO*
Barry White, *President*
Glenn Reinheimer, *Plant Mgr*
▲ **EMP:** 1000
SQ FT: 170,000
SALES (est): 184.5MM
SALES (corp-wide): 342MM **Publicly Held**
WEB: www.lsilightron.com
SIC: 3646 5063 Commercial indusl & institutional electric lighting fixtures; electrical apparatus & equipment
PA: Lsi Industries Inc.
10000 Alliance Rd
Blue Ash OH 45242
513 793-3200

(G-8650)
METAL CONTAINER CORPORATION
1000 Breunig Rd (12553-8438)
PHONE 845 567-1500
Mark Stafford, *Branch Mgr*
EMP: 200
SALES (corp-wide): 1.9B **Privately Held**
SIC: 3411 Metal cans
HQ: Metal Container Corporation
3636 S Geyer Rd Ste 100
Saint Louis MO 63127
314 577-2000

(G-8651)
NEW WINDSOR WASTE WATER PLANT
145 Caesars Ln (12553-7742)
P.O. Box 4653 (12553-0653)
PHONE 845 561-2550
John Egitto, *Manager*
EMP: 10
SALES (est): 778.8K **Privately Held**
SIC: 3589 Water treatment equipment, industrial

(G-8652)
NEWBURGH DISTRIBUTION CORP (PA)
463 Temple Hill Rd (12553-5527)
PHONE 845 561-6330
Donald Harkness, *President*
Sharon Harkness, *Vice Pres*
▲ **EMP:** 3
SALES (est): 47.6MM **Privately Held**
WEB: www.baricosmetics.com
SIC: 2844 Cosmetic preparations

(G-8653)
NEWLINE PRODUCTS INC
509 Temple Hill Rd (12553-5532)
PHONE 972 881-3318
Kevin Wang, *CEO*
Chris Bradford, *President*
William Bowers, *CFO*
▲ **EMP:** 195
SQ FT: 30,000
SALES (est): 15MM **Privately Held**
WEB: www.newlineproduct.com
SIC: 3993 Displays & cutouts, window & lobby

(G-8654)
PATTERSON MATERIALS CORP
322 Walsh Ave (12553-6748)
P.O. Box 800, Wingdale (12594-0800)
PHONE 845 832-6000
John Peckham, *Manager*
EMP: 20
SQ FT: 6,171
SALES (corp-wide): 200.6MM **Privately Held**
SIC: 1422 Crushed & broken limestone
HQ: Patterson Materials Corp
20 Haarlem Ave
White Plains NY 10603
914 949-2000

(G-8655)
PRODUCTION RESOURCE GROUP LLC
539 Temple Hill Rd (12553-5533)
PHONE 845 567-5700
Jerry Harris, *President*
Richard Mc Donald, *Business Mgr*
EMP: 50 **Privately Held**
SIC: 3999 7922 Theatrical scenery; equipment rental, theatrical
PA: Production Resource Group Llc
200 Business Park Dr # 109
Armonk NY 10504

(G-8656)
PVH CORP
Also Called: Van Heusen
1073 State Route 94 (12553-6821)
PHONE 845 561-0233
Lenore Dunn, *Branch Mgr*
EMP: 9
SALES (corp-wide): 8.9B **Publicly Held**
SIC: 2321 Men's & boys' dress shirts
PA: Pvh Corp.
200 Madison Ave Bsmt 1
New York NY 10016
212 381-3500

(G-8657)
REGE INC
110 Corporate Dr (12553-6952)
P.O. Box 4417 (12553-0417)
PHONE 845 565-7772
Cheskel Smilowitz, *CEO*
Ramon Echevarria, *President*
▲ **EMP:** 18
SQ FT: 30,000
SALES (est): 5.6MM **Privately Held**
WEB: www.polyworksinc.com
SIC: 2673 Plastic bags: made from purchased materials

(G-8658)
SALKO KITCHENS INC
256 Walsh Ave (12553-5752)
PHONE 845 565-4420
Aron Sandel, *President*
▲ **EMP:** 19
SALES: 1.5MM **Privately Held**
WEB: www.salkokitchens.com
SIC: 2434 Wood kitchen cabinets

(G-8659)
SCREEN GEMS INC
41 Windsor Hwy (12553-6225)
PHONE 845 561-0036
Carl Friedwall, *President*
EMP: 5
SQ FT: 3,600
SALES (est): 752.7K **Privately Held**
WEB: www.screengemsny.com
SIC: 2262 2395 Screen printing: man-made fiber & silk broadwoven fabrics; embroidery & art needlework

(G-8660)
SENTINEL PRINTING SERVICES INC
Also Called: Smith, E W Publishing
36 Meriline Ave (12553-6520)
P.O. Box 406, Vails Gate (12584-0406)
PHONE 845 562-1218
Everett Smith, *President*
Michael Smith, *Vice Pres*
Steve Smith, *Vice Pres*
EMP: 55
SQ FT: 4,000
SALES (est): 4.2MM **Privately Held**
SIC: 2741 Catalogs: publishing & printing

(G-8661)
SIMCHA CANDLE CO INC
244 Mac Arthur Ave (12553-7011)
P.O. Box 309, Monroe (10949-0309)
PHONE 845 783-0406
Samuel Marcus, *President*
▲ **EMP:** 6
SQ FT: 15,000
SALES (est): 626.5K **Privately Held**
WEB: www.simchacandle.com
SIC: 3999 Candles

(G-8662)
USA ILLUMINATION INC
Also Called: Usai
1126 River Rd (12553-6728)
PHONE 845 565-8500
Bonnie Littman, *Principal*
Sean Gaydos, *Senior VP*
Ann Schiffers, *Senior VP*
Donald Wray, *VP Engrg*
Oriana Starr, *Engineer*
▲ **EMP:** 35
SQ FT: 40,000
SALES (est): 16.5MM **Privately Held**
WEB: www.usaillumination.com
SIC: 3648 Public lighting fixtures

(G-8663)
VERLA INTERNATIONAL LTD
463 Temple Hill Rd (12553-5527)
PHONE 845 561-2440
Mario F Maffei, *President*
Robert R Roth, *Vice Pres*
▲ **EMP:** 400
SQ FT: 60,000

New York
New York County

SALES (est): 107.7MM **Privately Held**
SIC: 2844 Cosmetic preparations

(G-8664)
1 ATELIER LLC
347 W 36th St (10018-6406)
PHONE.....................917 916-2968
Stephanie Sarka, *CEO*
EMP: 8 EST: 2014
SALES (est): 275.5K **Privately Held**
SIC: 2339 5632 7389 Women's & misses' accessories; women's accessory & specialty stores; design services

(G-8665)
1510 ASSOCIATES LLC
1500 Lexington Ave (10029-7349)
PHONE.....................212 828-8720
EMP: 6
SALES (est): 498.4K **Privately Held**
SIC: 2211 Cotton Broadwoven Fabric Mill

(G-8666)
180S LLC (HQ)
1 Liberty Plz Rm 3500 (10006-1421)
PHONE.....................410 534-6320
Helen Rockey, *CEO*
Lester C Lee, *CEO*
Brian Le Gette, *President*
Shelley Foland, *Vice Pres*
Flor Andres, *CFO*
▲ EMP: 35
SQ FT: 45,000
SALES (est): 5.5MM **Privately Held**
SIC: 2253 Scarves & mufflers, knit
PA: 180s, Inc.
 700 S Caroline St
 New York NY 10006
 410 534-6320

(G-8667)
2 1 2 POSTCARDS INC
121 Varick St Frnt B (10013-1408)
PHONE.....................212 767-8227
Jiff Wed Work, *Manager*
EMP: 25
SALES (est): 2.9MM **Privately Held**
SIC: 2759 2752 Commercial printing; commercial printing, lithographic

(G-8668)
2 X 4 INC
180 Varick St Rm 1610 (10014-5861)
PHONE.....................212 647-1170
Georgie Stout, *President*
Michael Rock, *Partner*
Gala Delmont-Benatar, *Project Mgr*
Jie Yu, *Production*
Doug Freedman, *CFO*
EMP: 22
SQ FT: 2,000
SALES (est): 3.7MM **Privately Held**
WEB: www.2x4.org
SIC: 2752 Commercial printing, lithographic

(G-8669)
212 BIZ LLC (PA)
525 Fashion Ave Rm 2301 (10018-4923)
PHONE.....................212 391-4444
Ira Levinas,
▲ EMP: 9 EST: 2007
SQ FT: 2,000
SALES: 12MM **Privately Held**
SIC: 3161 Clothing & apparel carrying cases

(G-8670)
212 DB CORP
Also Called: Gig-It
30 W 22nd St Fl 6 (10010-5892)
PHONE.....................212 652-5600
John Acunto, *CEO*
EMP: 40
SALES (est): 2.8MM **Privately Held**
SIC: 3944 Electronic games & toys

(G-8671)
212 MEDIA LLC
460 Park Ave S Fl 4 (10016-7561)
PHONE.....................212 710-3092
Rishi Malhotra, *Managing Prtnr*
Inesha Singh, *Sales Mgr*
Neal Shenoy, *Mng Member*
Brian Litvack, *Business Dir*
▲ EMP: 40
SALES (est): 2.9MM **Privately Held**
WEB: www.212media.com
SIC: 2741 Miscellaneous publishing

(G-8672)
21ST CENTURY FOX AMERICA INC
1185 Av Of The Americas (10036-2601)
PHONE.....................212 782-8000
Sandra Childers, *Area Mgr*
Maria Delgado, *Area Mgr*
Liz Jones, *Area Mgr*
Kathy Kelley, *Area Mgr*
Kate McCombs, *Area Mgr*
EMP: 8
SALES (corp-wide): 30.4B **Publicly Held**
SIC: 2711 Newspapers, publishing & printing
HQ: 21st Century Fox America, Inc.
 1211 Ave Of The Americas
 New York NY 10036
 212 852-7000

(G-8673)
21ST CENTURY FOX AMERICA INC (HQ)
1211 Ave Of The Americas (10036-8701)
PHONE.....................212 852-7000
James Murdoch, *CEO*
John Nallen, *CFO*
EMP: 60
SQ FT: 40,000
SALES (est): 2.1B
SALES (corp-wide): 30.4B **Publicly Held**
SIC: 2752 4833 7812 2721 Promotional printing, lithographic; television broadcasting stations; motion picture production & distribution; magazines: publishing only, not printed on site
PA: Twenty-First Century Fox, Inc.
 1211 Ave Of The Americas
 New York NY 10036
 212 852-7000

(G-8674)
21ST CENTURY FOX AMERICA INC
Mirabella Magazine
200 Madison Ave Fl 8 (10016-3908)
PHONE.....................212 447-4600
Grace Mirabella, *Director*
EMP: 85
SALES (corp-wide): 30.4B **Publicly Held**
SIC: 2721 Periodicals
HQ: 21st Century Fox America, Inc.
 1211 Ave Of The Americas
 New York NY 10036
 212 852-7000

(G-8675)
2K INC
622 Broadway Fl 6 (10012-2600)
PHONE.....................646 536-3007
Strauss Zelnick, *CEO*
Lainie Goldstein, *CFO*
EMP: 6 EST: 2013
SALES (est): 392.7K **Publicly Held**
SIC: 7372 Prepackaged software
PA: Take-Two Interactive Software, Inc.
 110 W 44th St
 New York NY 10036

(G-8676)
30DC INC (PA)
80 Broad St Fl 5 (10004-2257)
PHONE.....................212 962-4400
Henry Pinskier, *Ch of Bd*
Theodore A Greenberg, *CFO*
EMP: 11
SALES (est): 738.1K **Privately Held**
SIC: 7372 Prepackaged software

(G-8677)
30DC INC
80 Broad St Fl 5 (10004-2257)
PHONE.....................212 962-4400
Teodore A Greenbird, *CFO*
Greg Laborde, *Director*
EMP: 12
SQ FT: 3,000
SALES: 1MM **Privately Held**
SIC: 7372 Application computer software

(G-8678)
31 PHILLIP LIM LLC (PA)
304 Hudson St Fl 8 (10013-1015)
PHONE.....................212 354-6540
Priscilla Camacho, *Sales Dir*
Wen Zhou,
Melissa Lee,
Phillip Lim,
▲ EMP: 40
SQ FT: 2,000
SALES (est): 9.8MM **Privately Held**
WEB: www.31phillipim.com
SIC: 2339 Sportswear, women's

(G-8679)
3835 LEBRON REST EQP & SUP INC (PA)
Also Called: Lebron Equipment Supply
3835 9th Ave (10034-3740)
PHONE.....................212 942-8258
Catalina Lebron, *Ch of Bd*
Manuel Lebron, *President*
Edward Perez, *Director*
EMP: 20
SQ FT: 400
SALES (est): 2.9MM **Privately Held**
SIC: 3679 Power supplies, all types: static

(G-8680)
4BUMPERS LLC
285 New Wstmnster End Ave (10023)
PHONE.....................212 721-9600
Jeffrey Levine,
Alan Levine,
EMP: 10
SALES (est): 596.8K **Privately Held**
SIC: 3714 Bumpers & bumperettes, motor vehicle

(G-8681)
5 STAR APPAREL LLC
Also Called: Enyce
31 W 34th St Fl 7 (10001-3031)
PHONE.....................212 563-1233
Albert Pardo, *Division Mgr*
EMP: 6
SALES (corp-wide): 56.3MM **Privately Held**
SIC: 2326 Men's & boys' work clothing
HQ: 5 Star Apparel L.L.C.
 31 W 34th St Fl 4
 New York NY 10001
 212 563-1233

(G-8682)
525 AMERICA LLC (PA)
525 7th Ave Rm 1000 (10018-4910)
PHONE.....................212 921-5688
Seena Addeo, *Accounts Exec*
EMP: 7
SALES (est): 9.3MM **Privately Held**
SIC: 2339 Women's & misses' outerwear

(G-8683)
6 SHORE ROAD LLC
54 Thompson St Fl 5 (10012-4308)
PHONE.....................212 274-9666
Pooja Kharbanda, *Mng Member*
EMP: 5 EST: 2007
SALES (est): 279.4K **Privately Held**
SIC: 2369 5621 Bathing suits & swimwear: girls', children's & infants'; women's clothing stores

(G-8684)
6TH AVENUE SHOWCASE INC
Also Called: Tempo Paris
241 W 37th St Frnt 2 (10018-6797)
PHONE.....................212 382-0400
Shawn Assil, *President*
▲ EMP: 6
SQ FT: 5,300
SALES (est): 1.1MM **Privately Held**
SIC: 2339 Women's & misses' outerwear

(G-8685)
79 METRO LTD (PA)
265 W 37th St Rm 205 (10018-5031)
PHONE.....................212 944-4030
Nancy Bossio Hutnick, *President*
EMP: 1
SQ FT: 8,500
SALES (est): 1.1MM **Privately Held**
SIC: 2337 2253 2331 Women's & misses' suits & coats; sweaters & sweater coats, knit; blouses, women's & juniors': made from purchased material

(G-8686)
99CENT WORLD AND VARIETY CORP
4242 Broadway (10033-3708)
PHONE.....................212 740-0010
Gamal Alsaidi, *CEO*
EMP: 5
SALES (est): 294.3K **Privately Held**
SIC: 3643 Mfg Conductive Wiring Devices

(G-8687)
A & M LLC
Also Called: H and B Digital
29 W 46th St (10036-4104)
PHONE.....................212 354-1341
Dan Murdock, *Mktg Dir*
Tony Aama, *Mng Member*
EMP: 6
SQ FT: 3,000
SALES (est): 7MM **Privately Held**
SIC: 3634 Electric housewares & fans

(G-8688)
A & M ROSENTHAL ENTPS INC (PA)
Also Called: Dessy Creations
8 W 38th St Fl 4 (10018-0154)
PHONE.....................646 638-9600
Alan Dessy, *President*
Ronnie Dey, *Purchasing*
Vivian G Diamond, *Treasurer*
Nancy Vargas, *Supervisor*
Karla Sanchez, *Director*
◆ EMP: 45 EST: 1963
SQ FT: 18,400
SALES (est): 5.4MM **Privately Held**
SIC: 2335 Wedding gowns & dresses

(G-8689)
A & V CASTINGS INC
257 W 39th St Fl 16w (10018-3106)
PHONE.....................212 997-0042
Alex Kvitko, *President*
EMP: 8
SALES: 1MM **Privately Held**
SIC: 3325 3911 Alloy steel castings, except investment; jewelry, precious metal

(G-8690)
A AND J APPAREL CORP
Also Called: Forwear
209 W 38th St Rm 1207 (10018-4498)
PHONE.....................212 398-8899
Mahin Azizian, *President*
EMP: 9
SALES (est): 1.1MM **Privately Held**
SIC: 2211 Apparel & outerwear fabrics, cotton

(G-8691)
A ESTEBAN & COMPANY INC (PA)
132 W 36th St Rm 1000 (10018-8819)
PHONE.....................212 989-7000
Alphonso C Esteban, *Ch of Bd*
Carl Bednarz, *General Mgr*
Michelle Wikoff, *Sales Staff*
Greta Esteban, *Technology*
Basil Fraser, *Technology*
▲ EMP: 25
SALES (est): 5.6MM **Privately Held**
WEB: www.esteban.com
SIC: 2752 7334 Commercial printing, offset; blueprinting service

(G-8692)
A ESTEBAN & COMPANY INC
132 W 36th St Rm 1000 (10018-8819)
PHONE.....................212 714-2227
Tim Gibbaid, *Manager*
EMP: 25
SALES (corp-wide): 5.6MM **Privately Held**
WEB: www.esteban.com
SIC: 2752 Commercial printing, lithographic

New York - New York County (G-8718)

PA: A. Esteban & Company, Inc.
132 W 36th St Rm 1000
New York NY 10018
212 989-7000

(G-8693)
A FLEISIG PAPER BOX CORP
1751 2nd Ave Apt 10a (10128-5371)
PHONE.................................212 226-7490
Robert Fleisig, *President*
EMP: 10 **EST:** 1999
SALES: 1MM **Privately Held**
WEB: www.afleisig.com
SIC: 2652 Setup paperboard boxes

(G-8694)
A GRAPHIC PRINTING INC
49 Market St Frnt 2 (10002-7229)
PHONE.................................212 233-9696
M Siam, *President*
▲ **EMP:** 7
SALES (est): 596.6K **Privately Held**
SIC: 2759 Commercial printing

(G-8695)
A GUIDEPOSTS CHURCH CORP
16 E 34th St Fl 21 (10016-4328)
PHONE.................................212 251-8100
Kevin Eans, *Editor*
Carolina Bhagirathy, *Marketing Staff*
Adam Hunter, *Manager*
Meg Belviso, *Manager*
EMP: 180
SALES (est): 12.3MM
SALES (corp-wide): 31.6MM **Privately Held**
SIC: 2721 Magazines: publishing only, not printed on site
PA: A Guideposts Church Corp
39 Old Ridgebury Rd # 27
Danbury CT 06810
203 749-0203

(G-8696)
A J C JEWELRY CONTRACTING INC
247 W 30th St Fl 3 (10001-2824)
PHONE.................................212 594-3703
Dion Smith, *Owner*
EMP: 6 **EST:** 1993
SALES (est): 525.2K **Privately Held**
SIC: 3915 Jewel preparing: instruments, tools, watches & jewelry

(G-8697)
A JAFFE INC
Also Called: Sandberg & Sikorski
592 5th Ave Fl 3 (10036-4707)
PHONE.................................212 843-7464
Mihir Bhansali, *CEO*
Stanley Sikorski, *President*
Samuel Sandberg, *Chairman*
Salvin Dixon, *Accounts Exec*
Bruce Watson, *Accounts Exec*
EMP: 175
SQ FT: 30,000
SALES (est): 28.4MM **Privately Held**
WEB: www.ajaffe.com
SIC: 3911 Jewelry, precious metal

(G-8698)
A THOUSAND CRANES INC
Also Called: Knitty City
208 W 79th St Apt 2 (10024-6269)
PHONE.................................212 724-9596
Pearl Chin, *President*
Arvin Chin, *Vice Pres*
EMP: 10
SALES (est): 1.1MM **Privately Held**
WEB: www.knittycity.com
SIC: 2299 Yarns, specialty & novelty

(G-8699)
A TO Z MEDIA INC (PA)
243 W 30th St Fl 6 (10001-2812)
PHONE.................................212 260-0237
Sarah Robertson, *CEO*
Scott Pollack, *President*
Stacy Karp, *VP Prdtn*
Anastassia Douchinova, *Controller*
Barbara Coates, *Bookkeeper*
▲ **EMP:** 20
SALES (est): 10.7MM **Privately Held**
WEB: www.atozmedia.com
SIC: 3652 7389 Compact laser discs, prerecorded; magnetic tape (audio): prerecorded; design services

(G-8700)
A2IA CORP
24 W 40th St Fl 3 (10018-1856)
PHONE.................................917 237-0390
Jean-Louis Fages, *President*
Olivier Baret, *Senior VP*
Nikolai Gorski, *Research*
Jeremy Benattar, *Sales Dir*
Bob Degliuomini, *Accounts Mgr*
EMP: 8
SALES (est): 1.2MM
SALES (corp-wide): 45.3MM **Publicly Held**
SIC: 7372 Prepackaged software
HQ: Analyse Image Intelli Artific
37 Au 39
Paris 75008

(G-8701)
A3 APPAREL LLC
1407 Broadway Rm 716a (10018-5293)
PHONE.................................888 403-9669
Peter Regondo, *CEO*
EMP: 7 **EST:** 2014
SQ FT: 1,200
SALES: 8MM **Privately Held**
SIC: 2211 Apparel & outerwear fabrics, cotton

(G-8702)
AAA AMERCN FLAG DCTG CO INC
36 W 37th St Rm 409 (10018-7452)
PHONE.................................212 279-3524
Ian Flamm, *President*
Marian Watson, *Vice Pres*
EMP: 4 **EST:** 1946
SQ FT: 2,500
SALES: 1MM **Privately Held**
SIC: 2399 Flags, fabric; banners, made from fabric

(G-8703)
AAA NOODLE PRODUCTS MFG
102 Bowery (10013-4727)
PHONE.................................212 431-4090
David Ho, *Vice Pres*
EMP: 5
SQ FT: 10,800
SALES: 1MM **Privately Held**
SIC: 2098 2052 Noodles (e.g. egg, plain & water), dry; cookies

(G-8704)
ABACUS LABS INC
14 E 38th St Fl 9 (10016-0632)
PHONE.................................917 426-6642
Omar Qari, *President*
Stephanie Walsh, *Vice Pres*
Julia Broder, *Consultant*
Josh Halickman, *CTO*
Ted Power, *Officer*
EMP: 30
SALES (est): 156.4K
SALES (corp-wide): 14.5MM **Privately Held**
SIC: 7372 Business oriented computer software
PA: Certify, Inc.
20 York St Ste 201
Portland ME 04101
207 773-6100

(G-8705)
ABALENE DECORATING SERVICES
315 W 39th St Rm 611 (10018-4035)
PHONE.................................718 782-2000
Moseha Goldman, *President*
Kalmen Weiss, *President*
Miriam Weiss, *Vice Pres*
EMP: 21
SQ FT: 18,000
SALES: 1.8MM **Privately Held**
SIC: 2591 2391 7216 Drapery hardware & blinds & shades; curtains & draperies; curtain cleaning & repair

(G-8706)
ABBEVILLE PRESS INC
Also Called: Abbeville Publishing Group
116 W 23rd St Fl 5 (10011-2599)
PHONE.................................212 366-5585
Robert E Abrams, *Ch of Bd*
Robert Abrams, *Publisher*
Louise Kurtz, *Prdtn Dir*
Nadine Winns, *Marketing Mgr*
Carolina Ortiz, *Marketing Staff*
▲ **EMP:** 33
SALES (est): 3.6MM **Privately Held**
WEB: www.abbeville.com
SIC: 2731 Books: publishing only

(G-8707)
ABC PEANUT BUTTER LLC
295 Madison Ave Ste 1618 (10017-6434)
PHONE.................................212 661-6886
H J Warden, *Mng Member*
EMP: 355
SALES (est): 23.4MM **Privately Held**
SIC: 2099 Peanut butter

(G-8708)
ABEL NOSER SOLUTIONS LLC
1 Battery Park Plz # 601 (10004-1446)
PHONE.................................646 432-4000
Ted Morgan, *CEO*
Peter Weiler, *President*
EMP: 20
SALES: 4MM
SALES (corp-wide): 1.2MM **Privately Held**
SIC: 7372 Business oriented computer software
PA: Abel Noser Holdings, L.L.C.
24 Whitehall St Fl 6 Flr 6
New York NY 10004
646 432-4000

(G-8709)
ABEONA THERAPEUTICS INC (PA)
1330 Avenue Of Americas Flr 33 (10019)
PHONE.................................646 813-4712
Frank Carsten Thiel, *CEO*
Steven H Rouhandeh, *Ch of Bd*
Timothy J Miller, *President*
Jeffrey B Davis, *COO*
Stephen B Thompson, *Treasurer*
EMP: 42 **EST:** 1974
SQ FT: 5,730
SALES: 837K **Publicly Held**
WEB: www.ampex.com
SIC: 2834 Pharmaceutical preparations

(G-8710)
ABKCO MUSIC & RECORDS INC (PA)
85 5th Ave Fl 11 (10003-3019)
PHONE.................................212 399-0300
Allen Klein, *President*
Alan E Horowitz, *Vice Pres*
Peter J Howard, *Vice Pres*
Peter Howard, *Vice Pres*
Iris W Keitel, *Vice Pres*
EMP: 20 **EST:** 1961
SQ FT: 11,000
SALES (est): 8.4MM **Privately Held**
SIC: 3652 6794 2741 7922 Phonograph records, prerecorded; magnetic tape (audio); prerecorded; compact laser discs, prerecorded; copyright buying & licensing; music, sheet: publishing only, not printed on site; legitimate live theater producers; motion picture production

(G-8711)
ABLETON INC
36 W Colo Blvd Ste 300 (10013)
PHONE.................................646 723-4586
Jesse Terry, *Partner*
Mads Lindgren, *Principal*
Maggie Tang, *Design Engr*
Luca Iacomino, *Sales Mgr*
Tony McCall, *Director*
EMP: 8
SALES (est): 423.4K **Privately Held**
SIC: 7372 Prepackaged software

(G-8712)
ABP INTERNATIONAL INC
1466 Broadway Ste 910 (10036-7309)
PHONE.................................212 490-3999
Bill Schnirring, *Ch of Bd*
Joseph Pramberger, *President*
Domenic Mucchetti, *COO*
Adam Santiago, *Prdtn Mgr*
Sylvia Ruiz, *Human Res Mgr*
EMP: 40 **EST:** 1975
SQ FT: 11,000
SALES (est): 5.1MM **Privately Held**
WEB: www.emhartcontest.com
SIC: 2721 Magazines: publishing only, not printed on site

(G-8713)
ABRAHAM JWLY DESIGNERS & MFRS
71 W 47th St Ste 905 (10036-2865)
PHONE.................................212 944-1149
Can Akdemir, *Partner*
Ibrahim Akdemir, *Partner*
Iskender Akdemir, *Partner*
EMP: 16
SALES (est): 1.6MM **Privately Held**
SIC: 3911 Jewelry, precious metal

(G-8714)
ABRIMIAN BROS CORP
48 W 48th St Ste 805 (10036-1713)
PHONE.................................212 382-1106
Marty Abrimian, *President*
EMP: 10
SALES (est): 860.2K **Privately Held**
SIC: 3911 Jewelry, precious metal

(G-8715)
ABSOLUTE COLOR CORPORATION
109 W 27th St Frnt 2 (10001-6208)
PHONE.................................212 868-0404
Daniel Shil, *President*
Peter Gordon, *Vice Pres*
EMP: 8
SQ FT: 2,500
SALES (est): 1MM **Privately Held**
WEB: www.absolutcolor.com
SIC: 2796 2741 Color separations for printing; miscellaneous publishing

(G-8716)
ACADEMY OF POLITICAL SCIENCE
Also Called: POLITICAL SCIENCE QUARTERLY
475 Riverside Dr Ste 1274 (10115-1298)
PHONE.................................212 870-2500
Demetrios Caraley, *President*
Virgil Conway, *Principal*
Diana Murray, *Vice Pres*
Loren Kando, *Manager*
EMP: 6
SQ FT: 2,309
SALES: 1MM **Privately Held**
WEB: www.psqonline.org
SIC: 2721 Periodicals: publishing only

(G-8717)
ACAI OF AMERICA INC
225 W 34th St Fl 9 (10122-0901)
PHONE.................................862 205-9334
Will Anderson, *Principal*
EMP: 8
SALES (est): 1MM **Privately Held**
SIC: 3556 Juice extractors, fruit & vegetable: commercial type

(G-8718)
ACCELIFY SOLUTIONS LLC
16 W 36th St Rm 902 (10018-9748)
PHONE.................................888 922-2354
Alex Brecher, *CEO*
Joe Jacobs, *President*
Leonid Shum, *CTO*
EMP: 25
SQ FT: 3,000
SALES (est): 2.7MM **Privately Held**
SIC: 7372 Educational computer software

New York - New York County (G-8719) **GEOGRAPHIC SECTION**

(G-8719)
ACCESS INTELLIGENCE LLC
Also Called: Pbi Media Inc.
249 W 17th St (10011-5390)
PHONE..................212 204-4269
John French, *President*
Andrea Persily, *COO*
EMP: 950
SALES (est): 35.7MM
SALES (corp-wide): 82.6MM **Privately Held**
SIC: 2721 Trade journals: publishing only, not printed on site
PA: Access Intelligence Llc
9211 Corp Blvd Fl 4 Flr 4
Rockville MD 20850
301 354-2000

(G-8720)
ACCESSORY PLAYS LLC
29 W 36th St (10018-7907)
PHONE..................212 564-7301
Richard Dauplaise, *President*
EMP: 50
SQ FT: 5,000
SALES (est): 1.5MM **Privately Held**
SIC: 3961 Costume jewelry, ex. precious metal & semiprecious stones

(G-8721)
ACCESSORY STREET LLC
1370 Broadway (10018-7302)
PHONE..................212 686-8990
Andrew Pizzo,
Mitchell Grossman,
▲ **EMP:** 12
SALES (est): 685.8K **Privately Held**
SIC: 2339 Women's & misses' outerwear

(G-8722)
ACCESSRIES DIRECT INTL USA INC
1450 Broadway Fl 22 (10018-2222)
PHONE..................646 448-8200
Alberto Rosenthal, *CEO*
Rody Moreira, *President*
▲ **EMP:** 23
SALES: 12.1MM **Privately Held**
SIC: 2389 2331 2339 5137 Men's miscellaneous accessories; women's & misses' blouses & shirts; women's & misses' accessories; handbags

(G-8723)
ACCUTRAK INC
432 Washington St Ste 113 (10013-1721)
PHONE..................212 925-5330
Eli Camhi, *President*
Stanford Silverman, *Vice Pres*
EMP: 15
SALES (est): 1MM **Privately Held**
SIC: 3812 Electronic detection systems (aeronautical)

(G-8724)
ACE BANNER & FLAG COMPANY
Also Called: Ace Banner Flag & Graphics
107 W 27th St (10001-6213)
PHONE..................212 620-9111
Carl Calo, *President*
Elizabeth Calo, *Treasurer*
Leah Segarra, *Manager*
EMP: 12 **EST:** 1916
SQ FT: 10,000
SALES: 1MM **Privately Held**
WEB: www.acebanner.com
SIC: 2399 Banners, made from fabric; flags, fabric

(G-8725)
ACE DIAMOND CORP
30 W 47th St Ste 808r (10036-8665)
PHONE..................212 730-8231
Herman Witriol, *President*
Margaret Witriol, *Treasurer*
EMP: 3 **EST:** 1975
SALES: 1MM **Privately Held**
SIC: 3915 5094 Diamond cutting & polishing; jewelry & precious stones; diamonds (gems)

(G-8726)
ACF INDUSTRIES HOLDING LLC (DH)
767 5th Ave (10153-0023)
PHONE..................212 702-4363
Keith Cozza, *CEO*
Carl C Icahn, *President*
Richard T Buonato, *Vice Pres*
EMP: 2
SALES (est): 219.6MM
SALES (corp-wide): 955MM **Privately Held**
SIC: 3743 4741 4789 6799 Freight cars & equipment; tank freight cars & car equipment; railroad equipment, except locomotives; rental of railroad cars; railroad car repair; real estate speculators for own account
HQ: Highcrest Investors Llc
445 Hamilton Ave Ste 1210
New York NY 10153
212 702-4323

(G-8727)
ACKER & LI MILLS CORPORATION
44 W 62nd St Apt 3b (10023-7009)
PHONE..................212 307-7247
Daniel Feder, *President*
EMP: 5
SALES: 2MM **Privately Held**
SIC: 2231 Broadwoven fabric mills, wool

(G-8728)
ACOLYTE TECHNOLOGIES CORP
44 E 32nd St Rm 901 (10016-5508)
PHONE..................212 629-3239
Marvin Figenbaum, *CEO*
Salvatore Guerrieri, *President*
Abel Gonzalez, *Sales Staff*
Sam Fischer, *Manager*
▲ **EMP:** 13
SALES (est): 1.8MM **Privately Held**
SIC: 3674 Light emitting diodes

(G-8729)
ACS CUSTOM USA LLC
Also Called: Advanced Comm Solutions Ltd
520 W 25th St (10001-5502)
PHONE..................646 559-5642
Adam Rhodes, *Director*
EMP: 8
SALES (est): 729.2K
SALES (corp-wide): 551.4K **Privately Held**
SIC: 3842 Surgical appliances & supplies
PA: Advanced Communication Solutions Limited
Unit 22 - 23
Banbury OXON OX16
129 526-6665

(G-8730)
ACTINIUM PHARMACEUTICALS INC (PA)
275 Madison Ave Ste 702 (10016-1154)
PHONE..................646 677-3870
Sandesh Seth, *Ch of Bd*
Nitya Ray, *Exec VP*
Robert N Daly, *Vice Pres*
Vijay Reddy, *Vice Pres*
Mark S Berger, *Chief Mktg Ofcr*
EMP: 23 **EST:** 1997
SALES (est): 3.2MM **Publicly Held**
SIC: 2834 8069 Pharmaceutical preparations; cancer hospital

(G-8731)
ADA GEMS CORP
Also Called: Mordechai Collection
10 W 47th St Ste 707 (10036-3301)
PHONE..................212 719-0100
Daniel Mor, *Treasurer*
▲ **EMP:** 5
SALES (est): 457.3K **Privately Held**
SIC: 3172 Cases, jewelry

(G-8732)
ADAM SCOTT DESIGNS INC
118 E 25th St Fl 11 (10010-2966)
PHONE..................212 420-8866
Steven Dubler, *President*
▲ **EMP:** 20
SQ FT: 8,000
SALES (est): 3.6MM **Privately Held**
WEB: www.scottadamdesigns.com
SIC: 3111 3161 3069 5199 Accessory products, leather; upholstery leather; luggage; bags, rubber or rubberized fabric; bags, textile; polyvinyl chloride resins (PVC); umbrellas, men's & boys'; hats, men's & boys'; robes, men's & boys'; men's & boys' outerwear

(G-8733)
ADAMOR INC
Also Called: Izi Creations
17 E 48th St Rm 901 (10017-1010)
PHONE..................212 688-8885
Izidor Kamhi, *President*
EMP: 7
SALES (est): 1.1MM **Privately Held**
WEB: www.adamor.com
SIC: 3911 Jewelry, precious metal

(G-8734)
ADC DOLLS INC
112 W 34th St Ste 1207 (10120-1207)
PHONE..................212 244-4500
Herbert E Brown, *Ch of Bd*
Gale Jarvis, *President*
Rob Porell, *CFO*
William J Beckett, *Admin Sec*
◆ **EMP:** 163
SQ FT: 90,000
SALES (est): 10.5MM **Privately Held**
WEB: www.alexdoll.com
SIC: 3942 Dolls, except stuffed toy animals

(G-8735)
ADESSO INC (PA)
353 W 39th St Fl 2 (10018-1645)
PHONE..................212 736-4440
Lee Schaak, *President*
Barney Wenograd, *Vice Pres*
Cherolyn L Shawe-Stratton, *Credit Staff*
Paul Berk, *VP Sales*
Lia Barbery, *Sales Staff*
◆ **EMP:** 32
SQ FT: 5,000
SALES (est): 5.2MM **Privately Held**
SIC: 3645 Floor lamps; table lamps

(G-8736)
ADFIN SOLUTIONS INC
25 W 31st St Fl 4 (10001-4413)
PHONE..................650 464-0742
Tyler Liebowitz, *Vice Pres*
Bobby Shethia, *Controller*
Milosz Tanski, *CTO*
EMP: 15 **EST:** 2011
SALES (est): 1.1MM **Privately Held**
SIC: 7372 Business oriented computer software

(G-8737)
ADGORITHMICS LLC (PA)
260 Madison Ave Fl 8 (10016-2418)
PHONE..................646 277-8728
Michael Kim, *CEO*
EMP: 4
SALES (est): 1.7MM **Privately Held**
SIC: 7372 Business oriented computer software

(G-8738)
ADITIANY INC
37 W 39th St Rm 1100 (10018-0579)
PHONE..................212 997-8440
Nita K Shah, *President*
EMP: 2
SALES: 1.5MM **Privately Held**
SIC: 2395 Embroidery products, except schiffli machine

(G-8739)
ADOBE SYSTEMS INC
1540 Broadway Fl 17 (10036-4039)
PHONE..................212 471-0904
Fax: 212 471-0990
EMP: 20
SALES (est): 1.9MM **Privately Held**
SIC: 7372 Prepackaged Software Services

(G-8740)
ADOBE SYSTEMS INCORPORATED
Also Called: Behance
100 5th Ave Fl 5 (10011-6903)
PHONE..................212 592-1400
Scott Belsky, *Branch Mgr*
Levi Van Veluw,
EMP: 250
SALES (corp-wide): 7.3B **Publicly Held**
SIC: 7372 Prepackaged software
PA: Adobe Inc.
345 Park Ave
San Jose CA 95110
408 536-6000

(G-8741)
ADOBE SYSTEMS INCORPORATED
8 W 40th St Fl 8 # 8 (10018-2275)
PHONE..................212 471-0904
Bruce Chizen, *Manager*
EMP: 32
SALES (corp-wide): 7.3B **Publicly Held**
WEB: www.adobe.com
SIC: 7372 Application computer software
PA: Adobe Inc.
345 Park Ave
San Jose CA 95110
408 536-6000

(G-8742)
ADRIENNE LANDAU DESIGNS INC
519 8th Ave Fl 21 (10018-4573)
PHONE..................212 695-8362
Adrienne Landau, *CEO*
EMP: 15
SQ FT: 12,000
SALES (est): 1.7MM **Privately Held**
WEB: www.adriennelandau.com
SIC: 2337 Capes, except fur or rubber: women's, misses' & juniors'

(G-8743)
ADSTREAM AMERICA LLC (DH)
345 7th Ave Fl 6 (10001-5053)
PHONE..................212 804-8498
Michael Palmer, *Mng Member*
EMP: 20
SALES (est): 4.8MM
SALES (corp-wide): 73.2MM **Privately Held**
SIC: 3993 Advertising artwork
HQ: Adstream (Uk) Limited
7th Floor, Berkshire House
London WC1V
207 539-8400

(G-8744)
ADTECH US INC
770 Broadway Fl 4 (10003-9558)
PHONE..................212 402-4840
Will Schmahl, *Vice Pres*
Peter Meyer, *Vice Pres*
EMP: 125
SALES (est): 5.2MM
SALES (corp-wide): 126B **Publicly Held**
SIC: 7372 Prepackaged software
HQ: Adtech Gmbh
Robert-Bosch-Str. 32
Dreieich 63303
610 357-150

(G-8745)
ADVANCE APPAREL INTL INC
265 W 37th St Rm 906 (10018-5728)
PHONE..................212 944-0984
Charles Hu, *President*
Eugene Hu, *Vice Pres*
▲ **EMP:** 5
SALES (est): 621.2K **Privately Held**
SIC: 2311 Men's & boys' suits & coats

(G-8746)
ADVANCE FINANCE GROUP LLC
101 Park Ave Frnt (10178-0399)
PHONE..................212 630-5900
Tom Summer, *CFO*
Christina Cruz, *Senior Mgr*
Richard Marerro, *President*
EMP: 100
SALES (est): 768.3K **Privately Held**
SIC: 2759 8721 Publication printing; auditing services

▲ = Import ▼ = Export
◆ = Import/Export

GEOGRAPHIC SECTION

New York - New York County (G-8773)

(G-8747)
ADVANCE MAGAZINE PUBLS INC (HQ)
Also Called: Conde Nast Publications
1 World Trade Ctr Fl 43 (10007-0090)
PHONE.................................212 286-2860
S I Newhouse Jr, *Ch of Bd*
Robert A Sauerberg Jr, *President*
Charles Townsend, *President*
Susan Falletta, *Publisher*
Grace Coddington, *Principal*
▲ **EMP**: 2200
SALES (est): 1.2B
SALES (corp-wide): 5.6B **Privately Held**
WEB: www.condenast.com
SIC: 2721 Magazines: publishing & printing
PA: Advance Publications, Inc.
   950 W Fingerboard Rd
   Staten Island NY 10305
   718 981-1234

(G-8748)
ADVANCE MAGAZINE PUBLS INC
Also Called: Conde Nast Publications Div
1 World Trade Ctr Fl 20 (10007-0090)
PHONE.................................212 790-4422
Kevin Hurley, *Prdtn Dir*
James Condrat, *Purchasing*
Ryan Brown, *Adv Dir*
Christina Ramdawar, *Marketing Staff*
Josephine Zagari, *Marketing Staff*
EMP: 64
SALES (corp-wide): 5.6B **Privately Held**
WEB: www.condenast.com
SIC: 2721 Magazines: publishing & printing
HQ: Advance Magazine Publishers Inc.
   1 World Trade Ctr Fl 43
   New York NY 10007
   212 286-2860

(G-8749)
ADVANCE MAGAZINE PUBLS INC
1166 Ave Of The Amrcs 1 (10036-2708)
PHONE.................................212 286-2860
Alexandra Walsh, *Branch Mgr*
EMP: 64
SALES (corp-wide): 5.6B **Privately Held**
WEB: www.condenast.com
SIC: 2721 Magazines: publishing & printing
HQ: Advance Magazine Publishers Inc.
   1 World Trade Ctr Fl 43
   New York NY 10007
   212 286-2860

(G-8750)
ADVANCE MAGAZINE PUBLS INC
Parade Publications
711 3rd Ave Rm 700 (10017-9210)
PHONE.................................212 450-7000
John J Beni, *Vice Chairman*
John Garvey, *Senior VP*
Lee Kravitz, *Senior VP*
Marcel Schloss, *Vice Pres*
Carol Unger, *Vice Pres*
EMP: 195
SALES (corp-wide): 5.6B **Privately Held**
SIC: 2721 2711 Periodicals-Publishing/Printing Newspapers-Publishing/Printing
HQ: Advance Magazine Publishers Inc.
   1 World Trade Ctr Fl 43
   New York NY 10007
   212 286-2860

(G-8751)
ADVANCE MAGAZINE PUBLS INC
Also Called: Vogue China
750 3rd Ave Frnt G (10017-2728)
PHONE.................................212 697-0126
Alexandra Wolfe, *Branch Mgr*
Cari Wolfert, *Assoc Editor*
EMP: 64
SALES (corp-wide): 5.6B **Privately Held**
SIC: 2721 Magazines: publishing & printing
HQ: Advance Magazine Publishers Inc.
   1 World Trade Ctr Fl 43
   New York NY 10007
   212 286-2860

(G-8752)
ADVANCED BIOMEDICAL TECH INC
350 5th Ave Fl 59 (10118-5999)
PHONE.................................718 766-7898
Chiming Yu, *President*
EMP: 5
SALES (est): 110.4K **Privately Held**
SIC: 1081 8731 Metal mining exploration & development services; commercial physical research

(G-8753)
ADVANCED BUSINESS GROUP INC
266 W 37th St Fl 15 (10018-6615)
PHONE.................................212 398-1010
Michael J Mulligan, *President*
EMP: 15
SQ FT: 7,000
SALES (est): 3.1MM **Privately Held**
SIC: 2752 Commercial printing, lithographic

(G-8754)
ADVANCED DIGITAL PRINTING LLC
65 W 36th St Fl 11 (10018-7936)
PHONE.................................718 649-1500
Aaron Menche, *Mng Member*
EMP: 35 **EST**: 2005
SQ FT: 85,000
SALES (est): 3.7MM **Privately Held**
SIC: 2752 Commercial printing, lithographic

(G-8755)
ADVANCED FASHIONS TECHNOLOGY
110 W 40th St Rm 1100 (10018-8529)
PHONE.................................212 221-0606
EMP: 8
SALES (est): 580K **Privately Held**
SIC: 2211 Cotton Broadwoven Fabric Mill

(G-8756)
ADVANCED PRINTING NEW YORK INC
263 W 38th St (10018-4483)
PHONE.................................212 840-8108
Carlos Cruz, *President*
EMP: 8
SALES (est): 1.1MM **Privately Held**
WEB: www.apnyc.com
SIC: 2752 Commercial printing, offset

(G-8757)
ADVANCED RESPONSE CORPORATION
345 W 58th Ave Apt 11a (10019-1140)
P.O. Box 2213 (10019)
PHONE.................................212 459-0887
Inge Rothenberg, *President*
P G Woog, *Owner*
Lionel Woog, *Director*
▲ **EMP**: 5
SALES (est): 555.4K **Privately Held**
WEB: www.broxo.com
SIC: 3634 Massage machines, electric, except for beauty/barber shops

(G-8758)
ADVANTAGE QUICK PRINT INC
Also Called: Hampshire Lithographers
30 E 33rd St Frnt B (10016-5337)
PHONE.................................212 989-5644
Stuart Menkes, *President*
▲ **EMP**: 6
SQ FT: 6,000
SALES (est): 350K **Privately Held**
SIC: 2752 Commercial printing, offset

(G-8759)
ADVD HEART PHYS & SURGS
130 E 77th St Fl 4 (10075-1851)
PHONE.................................212 434-3000
Michael Gorman, *Principal*
EMP: 10
SALES (est): 613.4K **Privately Held**
SIC: 3845 Surgical support systems: heart-lung machine, exc. iron lung

(G-8760)
ADVENTURE PUBLISHING GROUP
307 7th Ave Rm 1601 (10001-6042)
PHONE.................................212 575-4510
Laurie Schacht, *President*
Bill Reese, *Prdtn Mgr*
Lori Rubin, *Controller*
Joseph Ibraham, *Art Dir*
EMP: 20
SALES (est): 2.6MM **Privately Held**
WEB: www.adventurepub.com
SIC: 2721 Magazines: publishing only, not printed on site

(G-8761)
ADVERTISER PERCEPTIONS INC
1120 Ave Of The Americas (10036-6700)
PHONE.................................212 626-6683
Ken Pearl, *Principal*
Tedd Speck, *Exec VP*
Karen Cramp, *Research*
Janine Mitrano, *Research*
Doug Houghton, *Director*
EMP: 9
SALES (est): 50.8K **Privately Held**
SIC: 2711 Newspapers

(G-8762)
AEGIS OIL LIMITED VENTURES LLC
14 Wall St Fl 20 (10005-2123)
PHONE.................................646 233-4900
James Freiman, *Manager*
EMP: 11
SALES (est): 561.7K
SALES (corp-wide): 955.3K **Privately Held**
SIC: 1382 Oil & gas exploration services
PA: Aegis Oil Limited Ventures Llc
   100 Crescent Ct Ste 700
   Dallas TX 75201
   214 431-5201

(G-8763)
AES ELECTRONICS INC
135 E 54th St Apt 10j (10022-4511)
PHONE.................................212 371-8120
Abraham E Schenfeld, *President*
Ruth Schenfeld, *Treasurer*
EMP: 7
SQ FT: 1,200
SALES (est): 430K **Privately Held**
SIC: 3633 5065 Household laundry equipment; communication equipment

(G-8764)
AF DESIGN INC
1239 Broadway Ste 310 (10001-4438)
PHONE.................................347 548-5273
Ali Ahmad, *CEO*
Behroz Ahmad, *Shareholder*
EMP: 2
SQ FT: 3,000
SALES: 3.5MM **Privately Held**
SIC: 3911 5094 Jewel settings & mountings, precious metal; jewelry

(G-8765)
AFFORDABLE LUXURY GROUP INC
Also Called: Aimee Kestenberg
10 W 33rd St Rm 615 (10001-3348)
PHONE.................................631 523-9266
Adam Protass, *COO*
▲ **EMP**: 9
SALES (est): 237.9K **Privately Held**
SIC: 3171 Women's handbags & purses

(G-8766)
AFFYMAX INC
630 5th Ave Ste 2260 (10111-2291)
PHONE.................................650 812-8700
Jonathan M Couchman, *President*
John A Orwin, *Principal*
Christine Conroy, *Vice Pres*
Mark G Thompson, *CFO*
Brett Norman, *Manager*
▲ **EMP**: 6
SQ FT: 1,500
SALES (est): 1.4MM **Privately Held**
WEB: www.affymax.com
SIC: 2834 Pharmaceutical preparations

(G-8767)
AG NEOVO PROFESSIONAL INC
Also Called: Agn Professional
156 5th Ave Ste 434 (10010-7002)
PHONE.................................212 647-9080
Minson Chen, *President*
EMP: 5
SQ FT: 1,900
SALES (est): 1.3MM **Privately Held**
WEB: www.agnpro.com
SIC: 3575 Computer terminals

(G-8768)
AGI BROOKS PRODUCTION CO INC (PA)
7 E 14th St Apt 615 (10003-3130)
PHONE.................................212 268-1533
Agi Brooks, *President*
Don Mc Lean, *Vice Pres*
EMP: 11
SQ FT: 5,000
SALES (est): 1.4MM **Privately Held**
WEB: www.agibrooks.com
SIC: 2337 2331 2335 Suits: women's, misses' & juniors'; blouses, women's & juniors': made from purchased material; women's, juniors' & misses' dresses

(G-8769)
AGILENT TECHNOLOGIES INC
399 Park Ave (10022-4614)
PHONE.................................877 424-4536
EMP: 2498
SALES (corp-wide): 4.4B **Publicly Held**
SIC: 3825 Instruments to measure electricity
PA: Agilent Technologies, Inc.
   5301 Stevens Creek Blvd
   Santa Clara CA 95051
   408 345-8886

(G-8770)
AGNOVOS HEALTHCARE LLC
140 Broadway Fl 46 (10005-1155)
PHONE.................................646 502-5860
David Mackey, *CFO*
Dana Krayeski, *Manager*
EMP: 10
SALES (est): 1.2MM
SALES (corp-wide): 9.3MM **Privately Held**
SIC: 3842 Implants, surgical
PA: Agnovos Healthcare Usa, Llc
   7301 Calhoun Pl Ste 100
   Rockville MD 20855
   240 753-6500

(G-8771)
AGUILAR AMPLIFICATION LLC
599 Broadway Fl 7 (10012-3371)
PHONE.................................212 431-9109
Dave Avenius, *CEO*
David Boonshoft, *CEO*
Alexander Aguilar, *President*
Conor Montgomery, *Production*
Marco Passarelli, *Marketing Mgr*
▲ **EMP**: 10
SQ FT: 10,000
SALES (est): 1.9MM **Privately Held**
WEB: www.aguilaramp.com
SIC: 3651 Amplifiers: radio, public address or musical instrument

(G-8772)
AHHMIGO LLC
120 Cent Park S Rm 7c (10019)
PHONE.................................212 315-1818
Yaacob Dabah, *Manager*
Yaacov Dabah, *Manager*
EMP: 12
SALES (est): 820K **Privately Held**
SIC: 2099 Food preparations

(G-8773)
AHQ LLC
Also Called: Accesory Headquarters
10 W 33rd St Rm 306 (10001-3340)
PHONE.................................212 328-1560
Abe Chehebar, *Mng Member*
▲ **EMP**: 40 **EST**: 2012
SALES: 20MM **Privately Held**
SIC: 3171 Women's handbags & purses

New York - New York County (G-8774)

(G-8774)
AI ENTERTAINMENT HOLDINGS LLC (HQ)
730 5th Ave Fl 20 (10019-4105)
PHONE.................................212 247-6400
Lincoln Benet, *President*
EMP: 15
SALES (est): 3.5B **Privately Held**
SIC: 2731 Book music: publishing & printing

(G-8775)
AI MEDIA GROUP INC
1359 Broadway Fl 5 (10018-7747)
PHONE.................................212 660-2400
Andy Fenster, *CEO*
John Bernbach, *Ch of Bd*
Sergio Alvarez, *COO*
Krista Dibiccari, *Marketing Staff*
Krista Lewis, *Marketing Staff*
EMP: 16
SQ FT: 2,500
SALES: 9.6MM **Privately Held**
SIC: 2741

(G-8776)
AIMSUN INC
Also Called: Tss-Transport Simulation
20 W 22nd St Ste 612 (10010-6067)
PHONE.................................917 267-8534
Alex Gerodimos, *President*
Alejandro Molina, *Managing Dir*
Nadia Feddo, *Officer*
EMP: 5
SALES (est): 485.1K
SALES (corp-wide): 97.7B **Privately Held**
SIC: 7372 Application computer software
HQ: Aimsun S.L.
  Ronda Universitat, 22 - B At
  Barcelona 08007

(G-8777)
AIP MC HOLDINGS LLC (PA)
330 Madison Ave Fl 28 (10017-5018)
PHONE.................................212 627-2360
Kim Marvin, *Partner*
Nikhil Bodade, *Partner*
Danny Davis, *Partner*
Rich Dennis, *Partner*
Ben Derosa, *Partner*
EMP: 5
SALES (est): 92.9MM **Privately Held**
SIC: 3399 Aluminum atomized powder; brads: aluminum, brass or other nonferrous metal or wire; metal fasteners; staples, nonferrous metal or wire

(G-8778)
AIR SKATE & AIR JUMP CORP
1385 Broadway (10018-6001)
PHONE.................................212 967-1201
Patrick Denihan, *Branch Mgr*
EMP: 5
SALES (corp-wide): 6.2MM **Privately Held**
SIC: 3143 5139 Men's footwear, except athletic; footwear, athletic
PA: Air Skate & Air Jump Corp.
  2208 E 5th St
  Brooklyn NY 11223
  212 967-1201

(G-8779)
AKARI THERAPEUTICS PLC
24 W 40th St Fl 8 (10018-1028)
PHONE.................................646 350-0702
Gur Aroshwalb, *CEO*
EMP: 11 **EST:** 2015
SALES (est): 193K **Privately Held**
SIC: 2834 Druggists' preparations (pharmaceuticals)

(G-8780)
AKH GROUP LLC
Also Called: Marchesa Accesories
601 W 26th St Rm M228 (10001-1129)
PHONE.................................646 320-8720
Debra Torres, *CFO*
Anneli Hofstrom,
Ashley Kennedy,
Lou Wood Kennedy,
EMP: 6 **EST:** 2015
SQ FT: 1,272

SALES (est): 800K **Privately Held**
SIC: 3144 3171 Women's footwear, except athletic; women's handbags & purses

(G-8781)
ALADDIN MANUFACTURING CORP
295 5th Ave Ste 1412 (10016-7124)
PHONE.................................212 561-8715
Dennis Fein, *Manager*
EMP: 187
SALES (corp-wide): 9.4B **Publicly Held**
SIC: 2273 Carpets & rugs
HQ: Aladdin Manufacturing Corporation
  160 S Industrial Blvd
  Calhoun GA 30701
  706 629-7721

(G-8782)
ALART INC
578 5th Ave Unit 33 (10036-4836)
PHONE.................................212 840-1508
Alan Becer, *President*
Arthur Becer, *Vice Pres*
Artie Becer, *Vice Pres*
Vivian Becer, *Treasurer*
EMP: 3
SALES (est): 2MM **Privately Held**
SIC: 3911 3281 Jewelry, precious metal; cut stone & stone products

(G-8783)
ALBALUZ FILMS LLC
954 Lexington Ave (10021-5055)
PHONE.................................347 613-2321
Carols Plasencia, *CEO*
EMP: 1
SALES: 1MM **Privately Held**
SIC: 3312 Blast furnaces & steel mills

(G-8784)
ALBEA COSMETICS AMERICA INC (DH)
595 Madison Ave Fl 10 (10022-1955)
PHONE.................................212 371-5100
Jean P Imbert, *President*
Tina Sukapdjo, *Controller*
Laurent Clausse, *Finance*
Steve Granwehr, *Manager*
Robert Pelliciari, *Director*
◆ **EMP:** 25
SALES (est): 252.9MM **Privately Held**
SIC: 3089 3911 5162 5051 Plastic containers, except foam; precious metal cases; plastics products; metals service centers & offices
HQ: Albea Services
  Zac Des Barbanniers Le Signac
  Gennevilliers 92230
  181 932-000

(G-8785)
ALBION COSMETICS AMERICA INC
1350 Avenue Of The (10019)
PHONE.................................212 869-1052
Yusuke Kobayaski, *President*
Etsuko Onuma, *Accountant*
▲ **EMP:** 7
SQ FT: 1,500
SALES (est): 1.1MM
SALES (corp-wide): 2.8B **Privately Held**
SIC: 2844 Cosmetic preparations
HQ: Albion Co., Ltd.
  1-7-10, Ginza
  Chuo-Ku TKY 104-0
  355 241-711

(G-8786)
ALCHEMY SIMYA INC
Also Called: Birthstone Enterprises
161 Avnue Of The Americas (10013-1205)
PHONE.................................646 230-1122
Feonia Tilly, *President*
EMP: 30 **EST:** 2004
SALES (est): 2.3MM **Privately Held**
SIC: 3911 Jewelry, precious metal

(G-8787)
ALCOHOLICS ANONYMOUS GRAPEVINE (PA)
475 Riverside Dr Ste 1264 (10115-0052)
PHONE.................................212 870-3400
Robin Bromley, *CEO*

Arnold Bros, *Ch of Bd*
John Skillton, *Treasurer*
Eugene O' Brien, *Controller*
Valerie Thomas, *Finance*
▲ **EMP:** 15
SQ FT: 4,000
SALES: 2.9MM **Privately Held**
SIC: 2721 Periodicals: publishing only

(G-8788)
ALDINE INC (NY)
150 Varick St Fl 5 (10013-1218)
PHONE.................................212 226-2870
Alan Zuniss, *President*
EMP: 62
SQ FT: 23,000
SALES (est): 12MM **Privately Held**
WEB: www.aldine.com
SIC: 2752 2796 2759 Commercial printing, offset; embossing plates for printing; engraving

(G-8789)
ALE VIOLA LLC
Also Called: Ippolita
259 W 30th St Fl 9th10th (10001-2809)
PHONE.................................212 868-3808
Ippolita Rostagno, *President*
Diego McDonald, *COO*
John Siedel, *Senior VP*
◆ **EMP:** 100
SALES (est): 90.2K **Privately Held**
SIC: 3911 Jewelry apparel

(G-8790)
ALEN SANDS YORK ASSOCIATES LTD
Also Called: Stellar Alliance
236 W 26th St Rm 801 (10001-6882)
PHONE.................................212 563-6305
Alen S York, *President*
Joshua Rosen, *Vice Pres*
▲ **EMP:** 10
SALES (est): 790K **Privately Held**
SIC: 2392 Comforters & quilts: made from purchased materials

(G-8791)
ALEX ARCHER DESIGNS LTD
594 Broadway Rm 306 (10012-3234)
PHONE.................................212 219-8664
Temple Carr, *CEO*
Paul S Engler, *Ch of Bd*
Frank Trent, *CFO*
Dora Maddux, *Sales Staff*
EMP: 1
SQ FT: 3,000
SALES: 9MM **Privately Held**
WEB: www.templestclair.com
SIC: 3911 Jewelry, precious metal

(G-8792)
ALEX SEPKUS INC
42 W 48th St Ste 501 (10036-1701)
PHONE.................................212 391-8466
Alex Sepkus, *President*
Jeffrey D Feero, *Vice Pres*
EMP: 13
SALES (est): 1.7MM **Privately Held**
SIC: 3911 Bracelets, precious metal

(G-8793)
ALEXANDER PRIMAK JEWELRY INC
Also Called: Platina
529 5th Ave Fl 15 (10017-4674)
PHONE.................................212 398-0287
Alexander Primak, *President*
EMP: 59
SQ FT: 8,000
SALES (est): 11.3MM **Privately Held**
WEB: www.platinacasting.com
SIC: 3911 Jewelry, precious metal

(G-8794)
ALEXANDER WANG INCORPORATED (PA)
386 Broadway Fl 3 (10013-6021)
PHONE.................................212 532-3103
Aimie Wang, *CEO*
Rodrigo Bazan, *President*
Felita Harris, *Vice Pres*
Jessica Kipp, *Vice Pres*
Melissa Wong, *Marketing Staff*
▲ **EMP:** 66

SALES (est): 51.8MM **Privately Held**
SIC: 2331 2329 Blouses, women's & juniors': made from purchased material; shirt & slack suits: men's, youths' & boys'

(G-8795)
ALFRED DUNNER INC (PA)
Also Called: Skye's The Limit
1333 Broadway Fl 11 (10018-1064)
PHONE.................................212 478-4300
Peter Aresty, *President*
Joseph Aresty, *Chairman*
Jerome Aresty, *Vice Pres*
Linda Gold, *Prdtn Mgr*
Ray Barrick, *CFO*
▲ **EMP:** 275 **EST:** 1946
SQ FT: 10,000
SALES (est): 70.5MM **Privately Held**
WEB: www.alfreddunner.com
SIC: 2337 2331 2339 Skirts, separate: women's, misses' & juniors'; jackets & vests, except fur & leather: women's; T-shirts & tops, women's: made from purchased materials; slacks: women's, misses' & juniors'; shorts (outerwear): women's, misses' & juniors'

(G-8796)
ALLAN JOHN COMPANY
611 5th Ave Fl 7 (10022-6813)
PHONE.................................212 940-2210
John Allan Meing, *CEO*
Clare Ludvigsen, *CFO*
Richard Macary, *Treasurer*
▲ **EMP:** 10
SALES (est): 706K
SALES (corp-wide): 1.6MM **Privately Held**
WEB: www.johnallans.com
SIC: 2844 Toilet preparations
PA: The John Allan Company Llc
  46 E 46th St
  New York NY

(G-8797)
ALLEY MUSIC CORP
126 E 38th St (10016-2602)
PHONE.................................212 779-7977
Caroline Bienstock, *President*
EMP: 25
SALES (est): 1.2MM **Privately Held**
SIC: 2741 Music books: publishing & printing

(G-8798)
ALLIED BRONZE CORP (DEL CORP)
32 Avenue Of The Americas (10013-2473)
PHONE.................................646 421-6400
Herbert Koenig, *President*
Susan Mc Cormick, *Manager*
▲ **EMP:** 40
SQ FT: 55,000
SALES (est): 4.1MM **Privately Held**
WEB: www.alliedbronze.com
SIC: 3446 Ornamental metalwork

(G-8799)
ALLIED REPRODUCTIONS INC
70 W 36th St Rm 500 (10018-8050)
PHONE.................................212 255-2472
Peter Bird, *President*
EMP: 20
SALES (est): 2MM **Privately Held**
SIC: 2752 Commercial printing, offset

(G-8800)
ALLISON CHE FASHION INC (PA)
1400 Broadway Lbby 5 (10018-5300)
PHONE.................................212 391-1433
Barbara Weiner, *President*
Edith Fisher, *Treasurer*
EMP: 12
SALES (est): 957.8K **Privately Held**
SIC: 2335 Women's, juniors' & misses' dresses

(G-8801)
ALLSTAR CASTING CORPORATION
240 W 37th St Frnt 7 (10018-5091)
PHONE.................................212 563-0909
Robert Winters, *President*
Phyllis Vulcano, *Vice Pres*
Denise Winters, *Vice Pres*
EMP: 40

GEOGRAPHIC SECTION

New York - New York County (G-8827)

SQ FT: 2,200
SALES: 2.5MM **Privately Held**
SIC: **3915** 3369 Mfg Jewelers' Materials Nonferrous Metal Foundry

(G-8802)
ALLURE JEWELRY AND ACC LLC (PA)
15 W 36th St Fl 12 (10018-7113)
P.O. Box 41305, Plymouth MN (55441-0305)
PHONE..................646 226-8057
Amy Bohaty,
Arlene Tourville,
◆ EMP: 11
SQ FT: 5,000
SALES (est): 3.2MM **Privately Held**
SIC: **3961** Costume jewelry

(G-8803)
ALLWORTH COMMUNICATIONS INC
Also Called: Allworth Press
10 E 23rd St Ste 510 (10010-4459)
PHONE..................212 777-8395
Tad Crawford, *President*
▲ EMP: 12
SALES (est): 930K **Privately Held**
WEB: www.allworth.com
SIC: **2731** Textbooks: publishing only, not printed on site

(G-8804)
ALLY NYC CORP
230 W 39th St Rm 525 (10018-4933)
PHONE..................212 447-7277
Jenny Chen, *President*
EMP: 7 EST: 2017
SQ FT: 25,000
SALES: 15MM **Privately Held**
SIC: **2339** Women's & misses' outerwear

(G-8805)
ALM MEDIA LLC (HQ)
Also Called: New York Law Journal
150 E 42nd St (10017-5612)
PHONE..................212 457-9400
Bill Carter, *CEO*
Mark Fried, *President*
Mayra Sinchi, *Partner*
Tashawna Rodwell, *Publisher*
Paul Bubny, *Editor*
EMP: 350
SQ FT: 31,000
SALES (est): 175.5MM
SALES (corp-wide): 177.1MM **Privately Held**
WEB: www.alm.com
SIC: **2721** 2711 2741 2731 Magazines: publishing only, not printed on site; newspapers: publishing only, not printed on site; newsletter publishing; book publishing; trade show arrangement
PA: Alm Media Holdings, Inc.
120 Broadway Fl 5
New York NY 10271
212 457-9400

(G-8806)
ALM MEDIA HOLDINGS INC (PA)
120 Broadway Fl 5 (10271-1100)
PHONE..................212 457-9400
William L Pollak, *President*
Andrew Neblett, *President*
Sherry Costello, *General Mgr*
Jack Berkowitz, *Senior VP*
Anup Bagaria, *Vice Pres*
EMP: 400
SQ FT: 31,000
SALES (est): 177.1MM **Privately Held**
SIC: **2721** 2711 2741 2731 Magazines: publishing only, not printed on site; newspapers: publishing only, not printed on site; newsletter publishing; book publishing; trade show arrangement

(G-8807)
ALPARGATAS USA INC
Also Called: Havaianas
33 E 33rd St Rm 501 (10016-5335)
PHONE..................646 277-7171
Marcio Moura, *CEO*
Afonso Fugiyama, *President*
Michele Kearns, *Marketing Staff*
◆ EMP: 30
SQ FT: 7,500
SALES (est): 7.3MM **Privately Held**
SIC: **3144** Women's footwear, except athletic
PA: Alpargatas S/A
Av. Doutor Cardoso De Melo 1.336
Sao Paulo SP 04548

(G-8808)
ALPHA MEDIA GROUP INC (PA)
415 Madison Ave Fl 4 (10017-7945)
PHONE..................212 302-2626
Kent Brownridge, *CEO*
Felix Dennis, *Ch of Bd*
Stephen Duggan, *COO*
Robert Bartner, *Shareholder*
Peter Godfrey, *Shareholder*
▲ EMP: 300
SALES (est): 40MM **Privately Held**
WEB: www.stuffmagazine.com
SIC: **2721** Magazines: publishing & printing

(G-8809)
ALPHONSE LDUC - RBERT KING INC
Also Called: Robert King Music
180 Madison Ave 24 (10016-5267)
PHONE..................508 238-8118
Francois Leduc, *Principal*
EMP: 6
SALES (est): 367.3K **Privately Held**
SIC: **2741** Music book & sheet music publishing

(G-8810)
ALPINA COLOR GRAPHICS INC
27 Cliff St Rm 502 (10038-2850)
PHONE..................212 285-2700
Harish Sawhney, *President*
EMP: 7
SALES: 800K **Privately Held**
WEB: www.alpinaonline.com
SIC: **2752** Commercial printing, offset

(G-8811)
ALPINA COPYWORLD INC (PA)
Also Called: Alpina Digital
134 E 28th St (10016-8299)
PHONE..................212 683-3511
Harish Sawhney, *CEO*
Naveen Sawhney, *President*
Ram Pokharel, *Sales Executive*
EMP: 15
SQ FT: 7,000
SALES: 6MM **Privately Held**
WEB: www.alpina.net
SIC: **2759** 2752 Commercial printing; commercial printing, lithographic

(G-8812)
ALP!NE BUSINESS GROUP INC (PA)
Also Called: Alpine Creative Group
30 E 33rd St Frnt A (10016-5337)
PHONE..................212 989-4198
Steve Paster, *President*
Laura Leigh, *Vice Pres*
Angie Bhow, *Accountant*
Samantha Goldman, *Sales Staff*
Molly Bea, *Comms Mgr*
EMP: 10
SALES (est): 1.6MM **Privately Held**
WEB: www.alpinecreativegroup.com
SIC: **2759** 2752 Invitations: printing; commercial printing, lithographic

(G-8813)
ALPINE CREATIONS LTD
Also Called: TS Manufacturing
17 E 48th St Fl 6 (10017-1010)
PHONE..................212 308-9353
Samy Sanar, *President*
Zack Sanar, *Vice Pres*
▲ EMP: 6
SQ FT: 2,000
SALES (est): 731.9K **Privately Held**
WEB: www.alpineweddingbands.com
SIC: **3911** Jewelry, precious metal

(G-8814)
ALVINA VLENTA COUTURE COLLECTN
525 Fashion Ave Rm 1703 (10018-4935)
PHONE..................212 921-7058
Joe Murphy, *President*
Jim Hjelm, *Principal*
Joe O'Grady, *Admin Sec*
EMP: 10
SALES (est): 802.4K
SALES (corp-wide): 11.7MM **Publicly Held**
WEB: www.jimhelmcouture.com
SIC: **2335** Wedding gowns & dresses
PA: Jlm Couture, Inc.
225 W 37th St Fl 14
New York NY 10018
212 921-7058

(G-8815)
ALYK INC
Also Called: Lola
440 Park Ave S Fl 14 (10016-8012)
PHONE..................917 968-2552
Jordana Kier, *CEO*
Alexandra Friedman, *President*
▲ EMP: 13
SALES (est): 2.8MM **Privately Held**
SIC: **2676** Tampons, sanitary: made from purchased paper

(G-8816)
AMARANTUS BSCENCE HOLDINGS INC (PA)
110 Wall St (10005-3801)
PHONE..................917 686-5317
Gerald E Commissiong, *President*
Barney Monte, *COO*
Elise Brownell, *Senior VP*
John W Commissiong, *Security Dir*
John Commissiong, *Officer*
EMP: 12
SALES (est): 3.1MM **Publicly Held**
SIC: **2834** 3829 Pharmaceutical preparations; medical diagnostic systems, nuclear

(G-8817)
AMCOM SOFTWARE INC
256 W 38th St Fl 8 (10018-9123)
PHONE..................212 951-7600
EMP: 5
SALES (corp-wide): 171.1MM **Publicly Held**
WEB: www.amcomsoft.com
SIC: **7372** 7371 Application computer software; computer software development & applications
HQ: Amcom Software, Inc.
10400 Yellow Circle Dr # 100
Eden Prairie MN 55343
952 230-5200

(G-8818)
AMENITY ANALYTICS INC
387 Park Ave S Fl 9 (10016-8810)
PHONE..................646 786-8316
Nathaniel Storch, *President*
EMP: 24
SALES: 600K **Privately Held**
SIC: **7372** Prepackaged software

(G-8819)
AMEREX CORPORATION
512 7th Ave Fl 9 (10018-0861)
PHONE..................212 221-3151
Renee McGovern, *Manager*
EMP: 7
SALES (corp-wide): 1.3B **Privately Held**
WEB: www.amerex-fire.com
SIC: **2331** Blouses, women's & juniors': made from purchased material
HQ: Amerex Corporation
7595 Gadsden Hwy
Trussville AL 35173
205 655-3271

(G-8820)
AMERICA CAPITAL ENERGY CORP
Also Called: Acec
405 Lexington Ave Fl 65 (10174-6301)
P.O. Box 849 (10163-0849)
PHONE..................212 983-8316
Min Zhaing, *Ch of Bd*
Zhilin Feng, *President*
EMP: 5
SQ FT: 7,289
SALES (est): 402.7K **Privately Held**
SIC: **1382** Oil & gas exploration services

(G-8821)
AMERICA HEALTH CORP
708 3rd Ave Ste 600 (10017-4201)
PHONE..................800 860-1868
Jeff Law, *President*
EMP: 5 EST: 2017
SALES (est): 139.9K **Privately Held**
SIC: **2023** Dietary supplements, dairy & non-dairy based

(G-8822)
AMERICA PRESS INC (PA)
Also Called: National Catholic Wkly Review
1212 Ave Of The Americas (10036-3314)
PHONE..................212 581-4640
Thomas Reese, *President*
EMP: 33 EST: 1909
SQ FT: 36,674
SALES (est): 4.7MM **Privately Held**
SIC: **2721** Magazines: publishing only, not printed on site

(G-8823)
AMERICAN APPAREL TRADING CORP (PA)
Also Called: Vertical Apparel
209 W 38th St Rm 1004 (10018-0391)
PHONE..................212 764-5990
Peter Marsella, *President*
Ellen Barry, *Vice Pres*
EMP: 3 EST: 2003
SALES (est): 1.4MM **Privately Held**
SIC: **2339** Sportswear, women's

(G-8824)
AMERICAN BPTST CHRCHES MTRO NY
Flemister Housing Services
527 W 22nd St (10011-1179)
PHONE..................212 870-3195
James D Stallings, *Principal*
EMP: 8
SALES (corp-wide): 762.2K **Privately Held**
WEB: www.abcmny.org
SIC: **2531** Church furniture
PA: American Baptist Churches Of Metropolitan New York
475 Riverside Dr Ste 432
New York NY 10115
212 870-3195

(G-8825)
AMERICAN COMFORT DIRECT LLC
708 3rd Ave Fl 6 (10017-4119)
PHONE..................201 364-8309
Benzvi Cohen, *CEO*
Timothy Enarson, *Vice Pres*
EMP: 25
SALES (est): 1.7MM **Privately Held**
SIC: **3433** 3634 3635 3589 Space heaters, except electric; electric household fans, heaters & humidifiers; household vacuum cleaners; carpet sweepers, except household electric vacuum sweepers; automotive air conditioners;

(G-8826)
AMERICAN DSPLAY DIE CTTERS INC
121 Varick St Rm 301 (10013-1408)
PHONE..................212 645-1274
Juan Leon, *President*
Christa Leon, *Treasurer*
EMP: 30
SQ FT: 20,000
SALES (est): 269.4K **Privately Held**
SIC: **2675** 3544 Die-cut paper & board; dies & die holders for metal cutting, forming, die casting

(G-8827)
AMERICAN GRAPHIC DESIGN AWARDS
Also Called: Graphic Design U S A
89 5th Ave Ste 901 (10003-3046)
PHONE..................212 696-4380
Gordon Kaye, *CEO*
EMP: 5
SALES (est): 430K **Privately Held**
WEB: www.graphicdesignusa.com
SIC: **2721** Magazines: publishing & printing

New York - New York County (G-8828)

(G-8828)
AMERICAN HEALTHCARE SUPPLY INC
304 Park Ave S (10010-4301)
PHONE.................................212 674-3636
P H Lee, *President*
▲ **EMP:** 12
SQ FT: 4,000
SALES (est): 948.2K **Privately Held**
SIC: 3841 5047 Surgical & medical instruments; medical equipment & supplies

(G-8829)
AMERICAN HOME MFG LLC (HQ)
302 5th Ave Fl 5 (10001-3604)
PHONE.................................212 643-0680
Nathan Accad, *President*
Isaac Ades, *COO*
Benjamin Akkad, *Vice Pres*
◆ **EMP:** 3 **EST:** 2014
SALES (est): 3.7MM
SALES (corp-wide): 93.9MM **Privately Held**
SIC: 2299 Pillow fillings: curled hair, cotton waste, moss, hemp tow
PA: Idea Nuova Inc
302 5th Ave Fl 5
New York NY 10001
212 643-0680

(G-8830)
AMERICAN INST CHEM ENGINEERS (PA)
Also Called: Aiche
120 Wall St Fl 23 (10005-5991)
PHONE.................................646 495-1355
William Grieco, *CEO*
Shami Nayak, *Business Mgr*
Rich Sarnie, *Project Dir*
Gina Gatto, *Engineer*
Lucia Matthew, *Controller*
▲ **EMP:** 75
SQ FT: 18,400
SALES: 35.2MM **Privately Held**
WEB: www.naache.net
SIC: 2721 8621 2731 Magazines: publishing only, not printed on site; engineering association; book publishing

(G-8831)
AMERICAN JEWISH COMMITTEE
Also Called: Commentary Magazine
561 Fashion Ave Fl 16 (10018-1816)
PHONE.................................212 891-1400
Davi Birnstein, *Manager*
Michael Winograd, *Asst Director*
EMP: 8
SALES (corp-wide): 69.8MM **Privately Held**
WEB: www.projectinterchange.org
SIC: 2721 Magazines: publishing only, not printed on site
PA: American Jewish Committee
165 E 56th St
New York NY 10022
212 751-4000

(G-8832)
AMERICAN JEWISH CONGRESS INC (PA)
Also Called: A J Congress
825 3rd Ave Fl 181800 (10022-7519)
PHONE.................................212 879-4500
David Haberman, *Vice Chairman*
Neil Goldstein, *Director*
EMP: 20 **EST:** 1918
SQ FT: 9,000
SALES (est): 2.7MM **Privately Held**
SIC: 2721 8661 Magazines: publishing & printing; religious organizations

(G-8833)
AMERICAN JUICE COMPANY LLC
224 W 35th St Fl 11 (10001-2533)
PHONE.................................347 620-0252
Chris Wirth,
EMP: 7 **EST:** 2013
SQ FT: 400
SALES (est): 856.1K **Privately Held**
SIC: 2087 Cocktail mixes, nonalcoholic

(G-8834)
AMERICAN MINERALS INC (DH)
Also Called: Prince Minerals
21 W 46th St Fl 14 (10036-4119)
PHONE.................................646 747-4222
Willson Ropp, *President*
Roderik Alewijnse, *CFO*
Kevin St Germaine, *CFO*
Bin Zhou, *Manager*
Anthony Weiss, *Admin Sec*
◆ **EMP:** 14 **EST:** 1963
SQ FT: 3,000
SALES (est): 39.2MM
SALES (corp-wide): 1.5MM **Privately Held**
WEB: www.princeminerals.com
SIC: 1446 Silica mining; silica sand mining
HQ: Prince Minerals Llc
15311 Vantage Pkwy W
Houston TX 77032
646 747-4222

(G-8835)
AMERICAN ORIGINALS CORPORATION
Also Called: Gotham Diamonds
1156 Avenue Of The Americ (10036-2784)
PHONE.................................212 836-4155
Saumil Parikh, *President*
EMP: 9
SALES (est): 1.3MM **Privately Held**
SIC: 3911 5094 Jewelry, precious metal; jewelry

(G-8836)
AMERICAN REFRIGERATION INC (HQ)
142 W 57th St Fl 17 (10019-3300)
PHONE.................................212 699-4000
Stephen Presser, *President*
EMP: 4
SALES (est): 38.1MM **Privately Held**
SIC: 3585 Refrigeration equipment, complete

(G-8837)
AMERICAN SPRAY-ON CORP
5 Hanover Sq Fl 5 # 5 (10004-2614)
PHONE.................................212 929-2100
Steven Alessio, *President*
Steve Alessio, *President*
Marvin Sweet, *Chairman*
Micheal Boone, *Treasurer*
EMP: 30
SALES (est): 4.5MM **Privately Held**
SIC: 2396 2262 Automotive & apparel trimmings; fire resistance finishing: man-made & silk broadwoven

(G-8838)
AMERICAN T SHIRTS INC
Also Called: Premium Shirts Lerma Mexico
225 W 39th St Fl 6 (10018-3103)
PHONE.................................212 563-7125
Nasser Mokhtar, *President*
American T-Shirt Group, *Shareholder*
EMP: 5
SALES: 5MM **Privately Held**
WEB: www.americantshirts.com
SIC: 2253 T-shirts & tops, knit

(G-8839)
AMERICAN VINTAGE WINE BISCUIT
409 E 74th St Apt 1a (10021-3946)
PHONE.................................718 361-1003
Mary-Lynn Mondich, *President*
EMP: 7
SQ FT: 2,500
SALES (est): 464.5K **Privately Held**
WEB: www.americanvintage.com
SIC: 2051 Bread, cake & related products

(G-8840)
AMERICO GROUP INC
498 7th Ave Fl 8 (10018-6944)
PHONE.................................212 563-2700
Tom Miller, *Manager*
EMP: 33 **Privately Held**
SIC: 2321 Men's & boys' dress shirts
PA: Americo Group Inc.
1411 Broadway Fl 2
New York NY 10018

(G-8841)
AMERICO GROUP INC (PA)
Also Called: Joseph's Cloak
1411 Broadway Fl 2 (10018-3420)
PHONE.................................212 563-2700
Eli Harari, *Ch of Bd*
Susan Feigenson, *Vice Pres*
Marc Lieber, *Vice Pres*
Joel Weisinger, *CFO*
Marc Becker, *Manager*
▲ **EMP:** 42
SQ FT: 30,000
SALES (est): 10.2MM **Privately Held**
WEB: www.josephscloak.com
SIC: 2321 Men's & boys' dress shirts

(G-8842)
AMERIKOM GROUP INC
247 W 30th St Rm 6w (10001-2808)
PHONE.................................212 675-1329
Yaron Ben-Horin, *COO*
Nitsan Ben-Horin, *Vice Pres*
Derekh Cohen, *Vice Pres*
EMP: 80
SQ FT: 50,000
SALES (est): 10MM **Privately Held**
WEB: www.amerikom.com
SIC: 2759 Commercial printing

(G-8843)
AMG JV LLC (HQ)
Also Called: AMG Global LLC
15 W 34th St Fl 8 (10001-3015)
PHONE.................................212 602-1818
Aharon Franco, *Vice Pres*
◆ **EMP:** 5
SQ FT: 5,000
SALES (est): 1.4MM
SALES (corp-wide): 63.1MM **Privately Held**
SIC: 3261 Bathroom accessories/fittings, vitreous china or earthenware
PA: Enchante Accessories Inc.
16 E 34th St Fl 16 # 16
New York NY 10016
646 887-1442

(G-8844)
AMNEWS CORPORATION
2340 Frdrick Duglass Blvd (10027)
PHONE.................................212 932-7400
Elinor Tatum, *CEO*
EMP: 27 **EST:** 2003
SALES (est): 36.9K **Privately Held**
WEB: www.amsterdamnews.com
SIC: 2711 Newspapers, publishing & printing

(G-8845)
AMNEWYORK
330 W 34th St Fl 17 (10001-2406)
PHONE.................................212 239-5555
Paul Turcotte, *General Mgr*
EMP: 66
SALES (est): 438.7K
SALES (corp-wide): 288.8MM **Privately Held**
SIC: 2711 Commercial printing & newspaper publishing combined; newspapers, publishing & printing
PA: Newsday Llc
235 Pinelawn Rd
Melville NY 11747
631 843-4050

(G-8846)
AMOSEASTERN APPAREL INC (PA)
49 W 38th St Fl 7 (10018-1936)
PHONE.................................212 921-1859
Yanling Zhang, *Administration*
▲ **EMP:** 15
SALES (est): 2MM **Privately Held**
SIC: 2396 Apparel & other linings, except millinery

(G-8847)
AMPEX CASTING CORPORATION
23 W 47th St Unit 3 (10036-2826)
PHONE.................................212 719-1318
Joseph Ipek, *President*
EMP: 19
SQ FT: 3,000
SALES (est): 1.3MM **Privately Held**
SIC: 3915 Jewelers' castings

(G-8848)
AMPLIENCE INC
135 W 29th St Rm 404 (10001-5184)
PHONE.................................917 410-7189
James Brooke, *CEO*
Brian K Walker, *Security Dir*
Michael Jones, *Risk Mgmt Dir*
EMP: 6
SALES (est): 222K
SALES (corp-wide): 166.1K **Privately Held**
SIC: 7372 Business oriented computer software
PA: Icc Managed Services Limited
2 Sandbeck Lane
Wetherby
845 302-1922

(G-8849)
AMSCO SCHOOL PUBLICATIONS INC
315 Hudson St Fl 5 (10013-1009)
PHONE.................................212 886-6500
Henry Brun, *President*
Irene Rubin, *Vice Pres*
Laurence Beller, *Treasurer*
Inna Kushnir, *Supervisor*
Iris L Beller, *Admin Sec*
▼ **EMP:** 80 **EST:** 1935
SQ FT: 20,000
SALES (est): 6.9MM **Privately Held**
WEB: www.amscopub.com
SIC: 2731 Textbooks: publishing only, not printed on site

(G-8850)
AMSTEAD PRESS CORP
225 W 37th St Fl 16 (10018-6637)
PHONE.................................347 416-2373
EMP: 5
SALES (est): 125K **Privately Held**
SIC: 2759 Commercial Printing

(G-8851)
ANACOR PHARMACEUTICALS INC (HQ)
235 E 42nd St (10017-5703)
PHONE.................................212 733-2323
Douglas E Giordano, *President*
Margaret M Madden, *Vice Pres*
Donnie W Owens, *Manager*
EMP: 21
SALES: 82.3MM
SALES (corp-wide): 52.5B **Publicly Held**
WEB: www.anacor.com
SIC: 2834 Pharmaceutical preparations
PA: Pfizer Inc.
235 E 42nd St
New York NY 10017
212 733-2323

(G-8852)
ANAGE INC
530 Fashion Ave Frnt 5 (10018-4878)
PHONE.................................212 944-6533
Kenneth Berkowitz, *President*
Fred Heiser, *Vice Pres*
▲ **EMP:** 15
SALES (est): 1.1MM **Privately Held**
SIC: 2371 Jackets, fur

(G-8853)
ANALYSTS IN MEDIA (AIM) INC
55 Broad St Fl 9 (10004-2501)
PHONE.................................212 488-1777
Garry M Chocky, *Controller*
EMP: 50
SALES (est): 4.8MM **Privately Held**
SIC: 2721 Magazines: publishing only, not printed on site

(G-8854)
ANANDAMALI INC
35 N Moore St (10013-5711)
PHONE.................................212 343-8964
Cheryl Hazan, *President*
EMP: 10
SQ FT: 2,900
SALES (est): 800K **Privately Held**
SIC: 2519 Garden furniture, except wood, metal, stone or concrete

▲ = Import ▼ = Export
◆ = Import/Export

GEOGRAPHIC SECTION

New York - New York County (G-8883)

(G-8855)
ANASTASIA FURS INTERNATIONAL (PA)
Also Called: Alexandros
224 W 30th St Rm 204 (10001-4938)
PHONE..................212 868-9241
Anastasia Dimitriades, *President*
Tommy Dimitriades, *Vice Pres*
Alex Dimitriades, *Admin Sec*
EMP: 5
SQ FT: 7,000
SALES (est): 1MM **Privately Held**
SIC: 2371 5632 7219 Fur goods; furriers; fur garment cleaning, repairing & storage

(G-8856)
ANDES GOLD CORPORATION
405 Lexington Ave (10174-0002)
PHONE..................212 541-2495
Alejandro Diaz, *CEO*
EMP: 95
SALES (est): 2.3MM
SALES (corp-wide): 9MM **Privately Held**
SIC: 1041 Gold ores mining
PA: New World Gold Corporation
350 Camino Gardens Blvd
Boca Raton FL 33432
561 962-4139

(G-8857)
ANDIGO NEW MEDIA INC
150 W 25th St Rm 900 (10001-7458)
PHONE..................212 727-8445
Andrew Schulkind, *President*
EMP: 5
SALES (est): 508.1K **Privately Held**
WEB: www.andigo.com
SIC: 7372 Business oriented computer software

(G-8858)
ANDREA STRONGWATER
Also Called: A Strongwater Designs
465 W End Ave (10024-4926)
PHONE..................212 873-0905
Andrea Strongwater, *Owner*
EMP: 5
SALES (est): 229.9K **Privately Held**
SIC: 2253 Knit outerwear mills

(G-8859)
ANDREAS PROTEIN CAKERY INC
229 E 85th St Unit 332 (10028-9614)
PHONE..................646 801-9826
Andra Marchese, *Principal*
EMP: 5
SALES (est): 345.9K **Privately Held**
SIC: 2051 Bakery: wholesale or wholesale/retail combined

(G-8860)
ANDREW M SCHWARTZ LLC
Also Called: Sam NY
71 Gansevoort St Ste 2a (10014-1411)
PHONE..................212 391-7070
Andrew M Schwartz, *Mng Member*
Kathy Kirwin, *Manager*
Suzanne Schwartz,
▲ EMP: 9
SALES (est): 1MM **Privately Held**
SIC: 2386 Coats & jackets, leather & sheep-lined

(G-8861)
ANDY & EVAN INDUSTRIES INC
Also Called: Andy & Evan Shirt Co., The
1071 Ave Of The Amer # 804 (10018-3749)
PHONE..................212 967-7908
Evan Hakalir, *President*
Ariella Zeitlin, *COO*
Isaac Maleh, *Exec VP*
A Jonathan Perl, *Vice Pres*
Davida Graber, *Cust Svc Dir*
▲ EMP: 9
SALES: 4MM **Privately Held**
SIC: 2361 2321 Girls' & children's dresses, blouses & shirts; men's & boys' furnishings

(G-8862)
ANGEL TEXTILES INC
519 8th Ave Fl 21 (10018-4573)
P.O. Box 1169, New Paltz (12561-7169)
PHONE..................212 532-0900
Michael Nist, *CEO*
Helen Prior, *Principal*
EMP: 8
SQ FT: 1,000
SALES (est): 1.2MM **Privately Held**
WEB: www.angelnyc.com
SIC: 3552 2396 Silk screens for textile industry; automotive & apparel trimmings

(G-8863)
ANGEL-MADE IN HEAVEN INC (PA)
525 Fashion Ave Rm 1710 (10018-0440)
PHONE..................212 869-5678
Morris Dahan, *President*
▲ EMP: 12 EST: 1998
SQ FT: 1,000
SALES (est): 1.3MM **Privately Held**
WEB: www.angelmih.com
SIC: 2339 Sportswear, women's

(G-8864)
ANGIOGENEX INC (PA)
Also Called: (A DEVELOPMENT STAGE COMPANY)
425 Madison Ave Ste 902 (10017-1110)
PHONE..................347 468-6799
William A Garland PHD, *CEO*
Richard A Salvador PHD, *President*
Robert Benezra PHD, *Chief*
Michael M Strage, *Vice Pres*
EMP: 5
SQ FT: 700
SALES (est): 547K **Publicly Held**
SIC: 2834 Pharmaceutical preparations

(G-8865)
ANHEUSER-BUSCH LLC
250 Park Ave Fl 2 (10177-0299)
PHONE..................212 573-8800
Carlos Brito, *Branch Mgr*
EMP: 162
SALES (corp-wide): 1.9B **Privately Held**
SIC: 2082 Beer (alcoholic beverage)
HQ: Anheuser-Busch, Llc
1 Busch Pl
Saint Louis MO 63118
314 632-6777

(G-8866)
ANHEUSER-BUSCH INBEV FIN INC
250 Park Ave (10177-0001)
PHONE..................212 573-8800
Carlos Brito, *CEO*
Marianne Amssoms, *Vice Pres*
Brent Dial, *Vice Pres*
Robert Golden, *Vice Pres*
Josh Halpern, *Vice Pres*
EMP: 10
SALES (est): 1.1MM **Privately Held**
SIC: 2082 Beer (alcoholic beverage)

(G-8867)
ANHEUSER-BUSCH INBEV SVCS LLC
250 Park Ave Fl 2 (10177-0299)
PHONE..................314 765-4729
Fabio Mazza, *Director*
EMP: 7
SALES (est): 674.3K **Privately Held**
SIC: 2082 Malt beverages

(G-8868)
ANIMA GROUP LLC
Also Called: 1884 Collection
435 E 79th St Ph H (10075-1079)
PHONE..................917 913-2053
Alberto Petochi,
▲ EMP: 7
SALES (est): 967.4K **Privately Held**
SIC: 3911 Jewelry, precious metal

(G-8869)
ANIMAL FAIR MEDIA INC
545 8th Ave Rm 401 (10018-4341)
PHONE..................212 629-0392
Wendy Diamond, *President*
EMP: 12
SQ FT: 1,200
SALES (est): 1.2MM **Privately Held**
WEB: www.animalfair.com
SIC: 2721 Magazines: publishing only, not printed on site

(G-8870)
ANJU SYLOGENT LLC (HQ)
251 W 19th St (10011-4039)
PHONE..................480 326-2358
Kurien Jacob, *CEO*
Rebecca Barr, *Finance*
Elizabeth Whinnie, *Officer*
EMP: 15
SALES (est): 305.2K
SALES (corp-wide): 3MM **Privately Held**
SIC: 7372 Prepackaged software
PA: Anju Software, Inc.
251 W 19th St
New York NY 10011
480 326-2358

(G-8871)
ANN GISH INC (PA)
4 W 20th St (10011-4203)
PHONE..................212 969-9200
Ann P Gish Phillips, *CEO*
David Phillips, *CFO*
▲ EMP: 1
SQ FT: 2,000
SALES (est): 2.5MM **Privately Held**
WEB: www.anngish.com
SIC: 2211 2341 2392 2262 Broadwoven fabric mills, cotton; nightgowns & negligees: women's & children's; household furnishings; blankets, comforters & beddings; finishing plants, manmade fiber & silk fabrics; interior design services

(G-8872)
ANNA B INC
55 Great Jones St Apt 6 (10012-1140)
PHONE..................516 680-6609
Anna Blumenfeld, *President*
EMP: 5
SALES: 250K **Privately Held**
SIC: 2335 Bridal & formal gowns

(G-8873)
ANNA SUI CORP (PA)
484 Broome St (10013-2253)
PHONE..................212 941-8406
Anna Sui, *Ch of Bd*
Bob Sui, *President*
Heidi Poon, *Prdtn Mgr*
Katelyn Lair, *Production*
Wen Liao, *Production*
▲ EMP: 40
SQ FT: 3,000
SALES (est): 5.5MM **Privately Held**
WEB: www.annasui.com
SIC: 2331 2339 2335 2337 Blouses, women's & juniors': made from purchased material; women's & misses' athletic clothing & sportswear; slacks: women's, misses & juniors'; women's, juniors' & misses' dresses; skirts, separate: women's, misses' & juniors'; jackets & vests, except fur & leather: women's

(G-8874)
ANNUALS PUBLISHING CO INC
Also Called: Madison Square Press
10 E 23rd St Ste 510 (10010-4459)
PHONE..................212 505-0950
Fax: 212 979-2207
EMP: 3
SQ FT: 1,000
SALES: 1.5MM **Privately Held**
SIC: 2731 Books-Publishing/Printing

(G-8875)
ANSWER PRINTING INC
Also Called: Answer Company, The
505 8th Ave Rm 1101 (10018-4540)
P.O. Box 3442 (10163-3442)
PHONE..................212 922-2922
Larry Dunne, *President*
Joanne Cohen, *Sales Staff*
Billy Rodriguez, *Sales Staff*
Brian Dunne, *Marketing Staff*
EMP: 15
SQ FT: 3,800
SALES (est): 2.1MM **Privately Held**
WEB: www.answerprinting.com
SIC: 2741 2752 Business service newsletters: publishing & printing; commercial printing, lithographic

(G-8876)
ANTERIOS INC
60 E 42nd St Ste 1160 (10165-6206)
PHONE..................212 303-1683
Jon Edelson MD, *President*
Fabian Tenenbaum, *CFO*
Klaus Theobald MD, *Osteopathy*
EMP: 6
SALES (est): 870.6K **Privately Held**
SIC: 2834 Pharmaceutical preparations
PA: Allergan Public Limited Company
Euro House
Cork

(G-8877)
ANTHONY L & S LLC (PA)
Also Called: Anthony L&S Footwear Group
500 Fashion Ave Fl 16b (10018-0810)
PHONE..................212 386-7245
Joy Krooks, *Manager*
Anthony Loconte,
▲ EMP: 6
SQ FT: 6,000
SALES (est): 3.4MM **Privately Held**
WEB: www.anthonyls.com
SIC: 3021 5139 Rubber & plastics footwear; shoes

(G-8878)
ANTIMONY NEW YORK LLC
120 E 34th St Apt 7g (10016-4625)
PHONE..................917 232-1836
Jason Shelowitz,
Rachel Shelowitz,
EMP: 2 EST: 2017
SALES: 5MM **Privately Held**
SIC: 2844 Toilet preparations

(G-8879)
ANTWERP DIAMOND DISTRIBUTORS
581 5th Ave Fl 5 (10017-8824)
PHONE..................212 319-3300
Phyllis Lisker, *President*
EMP: 15 EST: 1955
SQ FT: 4,000
SALES (est): 1.5MM **Privately Held**
WEB: www.antwerpdistributors.com
SIC: 3915 5094 Diamond cutting & polishing; diamonds (gems)

(G-8880)
ANTWERP SALES INTL INC
Also Called: A.S.I. Fancies Ltd
576 5th Ave (10036-4807)
PHONE..................212 354-6515
Norbert May, *President*
Danny Klugman, *Vice Pres*
EMP: 18
SQ FT: 3,500
SALES (est): 2.9MM **Privately Held**
SIC: 3915 Diamond cutting & polishing

(G-8881)
ANYVISION US INC
152 Madison Ave Fl 20 (10016-5424)
PHONE..................606 901-4894
Maximilian Constant, *COO*
Nisha Dunston, *Director*
EMP: 14
SALES: 3MM **Privately Held**
SIC: 7372 Prepackaged software

(G-8882)
APEC PAPER INDUSTRIES LTD
Also Called: American Printing & Envelope
189 W 89th St Apt 5w (10024-1962)
PHONE..................212 730-0088
Justin Koplin, *President*
EMP: 5 EST: 1935
SQ FT: 900
SALES: 2.4MM **Privately Held**
SIC: 2677 5112 Envelopes; envelopes

(G-8883)
APEX TEXICON INC (PA)
295 Madison Ave (10017-6434)
P.O. Box 960670, Inwood (11096-0670)
PHONE..................516 239-4400
Edward Schlussel, *President*
John Kurz, *Vice Pres*
David Kurz, *Treasurer*
EMP: 24 EST: 1943
SQ FT: 9,000

New York - New York County (G-8884) **GEOGRAPHIC SECTION**

SALES: 1.7MM **Privately Held**
SIC: **2221** 2258 2257 Broadwoven fabric mills, manmade; net & netting products; tricot fabrics; weft knit fabric mills

(G-8884)
APICELLA JEWELERS INC
40 W 39th St Fl 4 (10018-2142)
PHONE.....................212 840-2024
John Apicella, *President*
Anthony Apicella, *Vice Pres*
EMP: 30 **EST:** 1946
SQ FT: 2,500
SALES (est): 3.1MM **Privately Held**
SIC: **3911** Jewelry, precious metal

(G-8885)
APOLLO APPAREL GROUP LLC
Also Called: Apollo Jeans
1407 Brdway Ste 2000-200 (10018)
PHONE.....................212 398-6585
Salim Mann, *Mng Member*
▲ **EMP:** 10
SALES (est): 2.2MM **Privately Held**
SIC: **2211** 2389 Jean fabrics; men's miscellaneous accessories

(G-8886)
APOLLO INVESTMENT FUND VII LP
9 W 57th St Fl 43 (10019-2700)
PHONE.....................212 515-3200
Martin Kelly, *CFO*
Leon Black,
Laurence Berg,
EMP: 7
SALES (est): 741.7K **Privately Held**
SIC: **2731** Books: publishing & printing

(G-8887)
APPARATUS STUDIO
122 W 30th St Fl 4 (10001-4009)
PHONE.....................646 527-9732
Jeremy Anderson, *Mng Member*
Alex Smith, *Manager*
Gabriel Hendifar,
▲ **EMP:** 42
SQ FT: 12,000
SALES (est): 4.3MM **Privately Held**
SIC: **3646** Commercial indusl & institutional electric lighting fixtures

(G-8888)
APPAREL GROUP LTD
Thyme
35 W 36th St Rm 10w (10018-7652)
PHONE.....................212 328-1200
Thomas Bietrich, *President*
EMP: 40 **Privately Held**
SIC: **2331** Women's & misses' blouses & shirts
HQ: The Apparel Group Ltd
883 Trinity Dr
Lewisville TX 75056
214 469-3300

(G-8889)
APPAREL PARTNERSHIP GROUP LLC
250 W 39th St Rm 701 (10018-4719)
PHONE.....................212 302-7722
Matthew Healy, *Mng Member*
▲ **EMP:** 5
SALES (est): 451.8K **Privately Held**
SIC: **2322** 2341 5136 5137 Men's & boys' underwear & nightwear; women's & children's undergarments; underwear, men's & boys'; women's & children's lingerie & undergarments

(G-8890)
APPAREL PRODUCTION INC
270 W 39th St Rm 1701 (10018-0330)
PHONE.....................212 278-8362
Theodore Sadaka, *President*
▲ **EMP:** 50
SALES (est): 570.3K **Privately Held**
SIC: **3949** Sporting & athletic goods

(G-8891)
APPFIGURES INC
133 Chrystie St Fl 3 (10002-2810)
PHONE.....................212 343-7900
Eliahu Michaeli, *President*
Alex Weiss, *Accounts Mgr*
Ashley Flores, *Office Admin*
Jorge Vargas, *Administration*
EMP: 14
SALES (est): 925.8K **Privately Held**
SIC: **7372** Business oriented computer software

(G-8892)
APPLICATION SECURITY INC (DH)
55 Broad St Rm 10a (10004-2509)
PHONE.....................212 912-4100
Jack Hembrough, *President*
Madhuri Kulkarni, *QA Dir*
Peter Schwartz, *CFO*
Wing Lui, *Technology*
Jun Wang, *Software Engr*
EMP: 75
SALES: 1.6MM
SALES (corp-wide): 13.3B **Privately Held**
WEB: www.appsecinc.com
SIC: **7372** Business oriented computer software
HQ: Trustwave Holdings, Inc.
70 W Madison St Ste 600
Chicago IL 60602
312 750-0950

(G-8893)
APRIL PRINTING CO INC
1201 Broadway Ste 711 (10001-5656)
PHONE.....................212 685-7455
Brad April, *President*
Muriel April, *Vice Pres*
EMP: 12
SQ FT: 2,500
SALES (est): 1.4MM **Privately Held**
WEB: www.aprilprinting.com
SIC: **2759** Commercial printing

(G-8894)
APS AMERICAN POLYMERS SVCS INC
104 W 40th St Rm 500 (10018-3770)
PHONE.....................212 362-7711
Gustavo Sampaio De Souza, *CEO*
◆ **EMP:** 2 **EST:** 2017
SQ FT: 120
SALES: 4MM **Privately Held**
SIC: **2821** Polyethylene resins; polypropylene resins; polystyrene resins

(G-8895)
AR & AR JEWELRY INC
31 W 47th St Fl 15 (10036-2808)
PHONE.....................212 764-7916
Aras Tirtirian, *President*
Aras Tirtir, *Vice Pres*
▲ **EMP:** 40 **EST:** 1996
SALES (est): 4.9MM **Privately Held**
SIC: **3911** Jewelry, precious metal

(G-8896)
AR PUBLISHING COMPANY INC
55 Broad St Rm 20b (10004-2589)
PHONE.....................212 482-0303
Helen Brusilovsky, *President*
EMP: 10
SALES (est): 479.6K **Privately Held**
WEB: www.vnsnews.com
SIC: **2711** Newspapers, publishing & printing

(G-8897)
ARABELLA TEXTILES LLC
Also Called: Deborah Connolly & Associates
303 5th Ave Rm 1402 (10016-6601)
PHONE.....................212 679-0611
Deborah Connolly, *Mng Member*
▲ **EMP:** 5
SALES (est): 464.3K **Privately Held**
WEB: www.deborahconnolly.com
SIC: **2299** Batting, wadding, padding & fillings

(G-8898)
ARBEIT BROS INC
345 7th Ave Fl 20 (10001-5034)
PHONE.....................212 736-9761
Sam Arbeit, *President*
EMP: 5 **EST:** 1948
SQ FT: 2,000
SALES (est): 390K **Privately Held**
SIC: **2371** Apparel, fur

(G-8899)
ARCANGEL INC
Also Called: Catherine Deane
209 W 38th St Rm 1001 (10018-4465)
PHONE.....................347 771-0789
Catherine Deane, *CEO*
Kathryn Hayman, *Director*
EMP: 2
SQ FT: 2,000
SALES: 1MM
SALES (corp-wide): 628.2K **Privately Held**
SIC: **2335** Wedding gowns & dresses
HQ: Atelier Arcangel Limited
1st Floor
London

(G-8900)
ARCHITECTS NEWSPAPER LLC
Also Called: Bd Projects
21 Murray St Fl 5 (10007-2244)
PHONE.....................212 966-0630
Dionne Darling, *Publisher*
Sukjong Hong, *Editor*
Olivia Martin, *Editor*
Matthew Messner, *Editor*
Antonio Pacheco, *Editor*
EMP: 12
SALES (est): 840K **Privately Held**
WEB: www.archpaper.com
SIC: **2711** Newspapers: publishing only, not printed on site

(G-8901)
ARCHITECTURAL TEXTILES USA INC
Also Called: Architex International
36 E 23rd St Ste F (10010-4409)
PHONE.....................212 213-6972
EMP: 35
SALES (est): 2MM
SALES (corp-wide): 61.6MM **Privately Held**
WEB: www.architex-ljh.com
SIC: **2299** 5087 Broadwoven fabrics: linen, jute, hemp & ramie; service establishment equipment
PA: Architectural Textiles U.S.A., Inc.
3333 Commercial Ave
Northbrook IL 60062
847 205-1333

(G-8902)
ARCHIVE360 INC
165 Broadway Fl 23 (10006-1404)
P.O. Box 291, Rutherford NJ (07070-0291)
PHONE.....................212 731-2438
Robert Desteno, *CEO*
Tiberiu Popp, *CTO*
EMP: 45
SQ FT: 1,000
SALES: 15MM **Privately Held**
SIC: **7372** Prepackaged software

(G-8903)
ARCONIC INC (PA)
390 Park Ave Fl 12 (10022-4608)
PHONE.....................212 836-2758
Charles Blankenship, *CEO*
John C Plant, *Ch of Bd*
Timothy D Myers, *President*
Raymond Kilmer, *Exec VP*
Mark J Krakowiak, *Exec VP*
◆ **EMP:** 100 **EST:** 1888
SALES: 12.9B **Publicly Held**
SIC: **3355** 3353 3354 3463 Aluminum rolling & drawing; aluminum sheet & strip; coils, sheet aluminum; foil, aluminum; plates, aluminum; aluminum extruded products; aluminum forgings

(G-8904)
AREA INC
Also Called: Area Warehouse
58 E 11th St Fl 2 (10003-6019)
PHONE.....................212 924-7084
Anki Spets, *President*
▲ **EMP:** 9
SQ FT: 6,000
SALES (est): 1MM **Privately Held**
WEB: www.lundstrom-id.com
SIC: **2392** Household furnishings

(G-8905)
ARGEE AMERICA INC
Also Called: Argee Sportswear
1410 Broadway Rm 1204 (10018-9352)
PHONE.....................212 768-9840
Roshan L Gera, *President*
Shyama Gera, *Vice Pres*
▲ **EMP:** 8
SALES (est): 1.6MM **Privately Held**
SIC: **2339** 5137 Sportswear, women's; sportswear, women's & children's

(G-8906)
ARGOSY COMPOSITE ADVANCED MATE
225 W 34th St Ste 1106 (10122-1106)
PHONE.....................212 268-0003
Michael Kaufman, *Controller*
Richard Rocco, *Mng Member*
Crissy Tecerini, *Administration*
EMP: 12
SALES (est): 791.3K **Privately Held**
SIC: **3299** Ceramic fiber

(G-8907)
ARIELA AND ASSOCIATES INTL LLC (PA)
1359 Broadway Fl 21 (10018-7824)
PHONE.....................212 683-4131
Ariela Balk, *President*
Leann Williams, *Sales Associate*
▲ **EMP:** 140
SQ FT: 27,741
SALES (est): 28.8MM **Privately Held**
WEB: www.ariela-alpha.com
SIC: **2341** Women's & children's undergarments

(G-8908)
ARLEE HOME FASHIONS INC (PA)
Also Called: Arlee Group
36 E 31st St Rm 800 (10016-6917)
PHONE.....................212 689-0020
David Frankel, *CEO*
Marsha Caparelli, *Vice Pres*
Alan Mandell, *CFO*
▲ **EMP:** 60 **EST:** 1976
SQ FT: 15,805
SALES (est): 132.6MM **Privately Held**
SIC: **2392** Pillows, bed: made from purchased materials; chair covers & pads: made from purchased materials

(G-8909)
ARMACEL ARMOR CORPORATION
745 5th Ave Fl 7 (10151-0802)
PHONE.....................805 384-1144
Asia Fernandez, *President*
David Fernandez, *Vice Pres*
EMP: 35
SALES (est): 4.6MM **Privately Held**
WEB: www.armacelarmorcorp.com
SIC: **3728** Military aircraft equipment & armament

(G-8910)
ARPER USA INC
476 Broadway Ste 2f (10013-2641)
P.O. Box 1683 (10013-0870)
PHONE.....................212 647-8900
Emanuele Corvo, *President*
Emanuele Corvo, *Managing Dir*
Carmela Puleo, *Cust Mgr*
Simone Passon, *Sales Staff*
Angela Bartolotta, *Planning*
▲ **EMP:** 6
SALES (est): 1.2MM **Privately Held**
SIC: **2599** Factory furniture & fixtures
HQ: Arper Spa
Via Lombardia 16
Monastier Di Treviso TV 31050
042 279-18

(G-8911)
ARRAY MARKETING GROUP INC (HQ)
200 Madison Ave Ste 2121 (10016-4000)
PHONE.....................212 750-3367
Tom Hendren, *CEO*
Mike Caron, *Vice Pres*
Kevin Pattrick, *CFO*
▲ **EMP:** 21

SALES (est): 5.4MM Privately Held
WEB: www.arraymarketing.com
SIC: 2541 Store & office display cases & fixtures
PA: Array Canada Inc
45 Progress Ave
Scarborough ON M1P 2
416 299-4865

(G-8912)
ARSENAL HOLDINGS LLC (PA)
885 3rd Ave Rm 2403 (10022-4834)
PHONE..................212 398-9139
Mike Healy, Mng Member
EMP: 9 EST: 2013
SALES (est): 81.4MM Privately Held
SIC: 3812 Acceleration indicators & systems components, aerospace

(G-8913)
ART ASIAPACIFIC PUBLISHING LLC
410 W 24th St Apt 14a (10011-1356)
PHONE..................212 255-6003
Elaine Ng,
EMP: 8 EST: 2005
SALES: 800K Privately Held
SIC: 2741 Miscellaneous publishing

(G-8914)
ART INDUSTRIES OF NEW YORK
601 W 26th St Rm 1425 (10001-1160)
PHONE..................212 633-9200
Steve Kaitz, President
Neal H Klein, Vice Pres
EMP: 50 EST: 1949
SQ FT: 80,000
SALES (est): 6.4MM Privately Held
WEB: www.salinesolutions.com
SIC: 2675 Die-cut paper & board

(G-8915)
ART PEOPLE INC
594 Broadway Rm 1102 (10012-3289)
PHONE..................212 431-4865
Gary Golkin, President
Carrie Golkin, Treasurer
EMP: 8 EST: 1975
SQ FT: 10,000
SALES (est): 798.4K Privately Held
SIC: 2221 Wall covering fabrics, manmade fiber & silk; upholstery fabrics, manmade fiber & silk

(G-8916)
ART RESOURCES TRANSFER INC
526 W 26th St Rm 614 (10001-5522)
PHONE..................212 255-2919
Yael Meridan Schori, President
Bill Bartman, Exec Dir
Jennifer Seass, Director
▲ EMP: 5
SQ FT: 4,000
SALES: 786.8K Privately Held
WEB: www.artretran.com
SIC: 2791 Typesetting

(G-8917)
ART SCROLL PRINTING CORP
230 W 41st St Bsmt 1 (10036-7207)
PHONE..................212 929-2413
Elliot Schwartz, President
EMP: 13
SALES (est): 1.8MM Privately Held
SIC: 2752 Commercial printing, offset

(G-8918)
ART-TEC JEWELRY DESIGNS LTD (PA)
48 W 48th St Ste 401 (10036-1727)
PHONE..................212 719-2941
Edward Zylka, President
EMP: 20
SQ FT: 5,000
SALES (est): 4.1MM Privately Held
SIC: 3911 Jewelry, precious metal

(G-8919)
ARTICULATE GLOBAL INC
244 5th Ave Ste 2960 (10001-7604)
PHONE..................800 861-4880
Adam Schwartz, CEO
Lucy Suros, Exec VP
Megan C Niedenthal, Opers Staff

Patrick Eakin, QA Dir
Christine Hendrickson, QA Dir
EMP: 130
SQ FT: 20,000
SALES (est): 19.2MM Privately Held
WEB: www.articulate.com
SIC: 7372 Business oriented computer software

(G-8920)
ARTIFEX PRESS LLC
109 W 27th St (10001-6208)
PHONE..................212 414-1482
David Groz, President
Sara Davidson, Editor
Carina Evangelista, Editor
Marianne Stockebrand, Editor
Hannah Barton, Research
EMP: 15
SALES (est): 554.4K Privately Held
SIC: 2721 Periodicals: publishing & printing

(G-8921)
ARTISTIC FRAME CORP (PA)
979 3rd Ave Ste 1705 (10022-3804)
PHONE..................212 289-2100
David Stevens, President
Mark Rosenman, General Mgr
Joe Weldon, Manager
Yossi Dilmani, Info Tech Mgr
Mike Diaz, Technology
◆ EMP: 110
SQ FT: 400,000
SALES (est): 97.5MM Privately Held
SIC: 2426 5021 Frames for upholstered furniture, wood; office furniture

(G-8922)
ARTISTIC RIBBON NOVELTY CO INC
22 W 21st St Fl 3 (10010-6948)
P.O. Box 126, Hillsdale NJ (07642-0126)
PHONE..................212 255-4224
Kenneth Hanz, President
Kenneth Handz, President
Steve Eigner, Corp Secy
▲ EMP: 20 EST: 1928
SQ FT: 15,000
SALES (est): 2.7MM Privately Held
WEB: www.artisticribbon.com
SIC: 2396 5131 Ribbons & bows, cut & sewed; sewing supplies & notions; ribbons

(G-8923)
ARTISTIC TYPOGRAPHY CORP (PA)
Also Called: Artistic Group, The
151 W 30th St Fl 8 (10001-4026)
PHONE..................212 463-8880
Paul J Weinstein, President
▲ EMP: 15 EST: 1959
SQ FT: 7,500
SALES (est): 2.1MM Privately Held
WEB: www.tagimage.com
SIC: 2759 2791 Commercial printing; typographic composition, for the printing trade

(G-8924)
ARTKRAFT STRAUSS LLC
Also Called: Artkraft Sign
130 W 57th St Apt 5e (10019-3314)
PHONE..................212 265-5155
Tama Starr, President
Robert Jackowitz, Admin Sec
EMP: 30 EST: 1935
SQ FT: 1,500
SALES (est): 3.8MM Privately Held
WEB: www.artkraft.com
SIC: 3993 7312 Electric signs; outdoor advertising services

(G-8925)
ARTNEWS LTD (PA)
Also Called: Artnewsletter
110 Greene St Ph 2 (10012-3824)
PHONE..................212 398-1690
Peter M Brant, Principal
Barbara Macadam, Editor
Sarah Douglas, Chief
Nicole De George, Assistant
Jeff Mac Donald, Assistant
▲ EMP: 18 EST: 1902
SQ FT: 12,000

SALES (est): 2.9MM Privately Held
WEB: www.artnews.com
SIC: 2721 Magazines: publishing & printing

(G-8926)
ARTSCROLL PRINTING CORP (PA)
53 W 23rd St Fl 4 (10010-4239)
PHONE..................212 929-2413
Elliot Schwartz, President
David Schwartz, Corp Secy
EMP: 22
SALES (est): 4.3MM Privately Held
SIC: 2759 2791 2752 7336 Screen printing; thermography; typesetting; commercial printing, lithographic; commercial art & graphic design; signs & advertising specialties

(G-8927)
ARUBA NETWORKS INC
556 W 22nd St (10011-1108)
PHONE..................732 343-1305
EMP: 5
SALES (corp-wide): 28.8B Publicly Held
SIC: 3577 Computer peripheral equipment
HQ: Aruba Networks, Inc.
3333 Scott Blvd
Santa Clara CA 95054
408 227-4500

(G-8928)
ARUVIL INTERNATIONAL INC (PA)
185 Madison Ave Rm 1701 (10016-7711)
PHONE..................212 447-5020
Vilas Kulkarni, President
Russell Jenkins, Vice Pres
Elia Cordova, Branch Mgr
▲ EMP: 5
SQ FT: 2,800
SALES (est): 6.6MM Privately Held
WEB: www.aruvil.com
SIC: 3315 Fence gates posts & fittings: steel

(G-8929)
ASAHI SHIMBUN AMERICA INC
620 8th Ave (10018-1618)
PHONE..................212 398-0257
Erika Toh, Principal
Ko Tanaka, Administration
EMP: 15
SALES (est): 1.1MM Privately Held
SIC: 2711 Newspapers, publishing & printing

(G-8930)
ASENCE INC
65 Broadway Fl 7 (10006-2536)
PHONE..................347 335-2606
Fax: 212 430-6501
EMP: 21
SALES: 3MM Privately Held
SIC: 2834 Pharmaceutical Preparations

(G-8931)
ASHKO GROUP LLC
Also Called: Wholesale
10 W 33rd St Rm 1019 (10001-3306)
PHONE..................212 594-6050
Jack Ashkenazi, President
Charles Ashkenazi, COO
Candy Chu, Production
David Braha, CFO
Antonia Collado, Sales Dir
▲ EMP: 18
SQ FT: 1,500
SALES (est): 3.6MM Privately Held
SIC: 2252 5139 Socks; footwear

(G-8932)
ASI SIGN SYSTEMS INC
192 Lexington Ave Rm 1002 (10016-6823)
PHONE..................646 742-1320
EMP: 7
SALES (corp-wide): 20.7MM Privately Held
SIC: 3993 Signs & advertising specialties
PA: Asi Sign Systems, Inc.
8181 Jetstar Dr Ste 110
Irving TX 75063
214 352-9140

(G-8933)
ASITE LLC
245 W 29th St Rm 1601 (10001-5216)
PHONE..................203 545-3089
Gordon Ashworth, Principal
EMP: 60
SALES (est): 2.2MM Privately Held
SIC: 7372 Prepackaged software

(G-8934)
ASM USA INC
73 Spring St Rm 309 (10012-5801)
PHONE..................212 925-2906
EMP: 12
SALES (est): 1MM
SALES (corp-wide): 188.1K Privately Held
SIC: 3444 5051 Sheet metal specialties, not stamped; steel
HQ: Approche Sur Mesure (A.S.M.)
63 Rue Edouard Vaillant
Levallois Perret 92300
147 481-020

(G-8935)
ASPEN RESEARCH GROUP LTD
17 State St Fl 15 (10004-1532)
PHONE..................212 425-9588
Mike Neff, Manager
EMP: 7
SALES (est): 306.4K Privately Held
SIC: 7372 Business oriented computer software
PA: Aspen Research Group Ltd
802 Grand Ave Ste 120
Glenwood Springs CO 81601

(G-8936)
ASPEX INCORPORATED
161 Hudson St Apt 1a (10013-2145)
PHONE..................212 966-0410
Gerald Henrici, President
James M Herriman, Principal
John Strohbeen, Principal
Jesus Chico, Engineer
EMP: 20
SALES (est): 3.9MM Privately Held
SIC: 3823 3829 Computer interface equipment for industrial process control; measuring & controlling devices

(G-8937)
ASSESSMENT TECHNOLOGIES INC
1350 Ave Of The Americas (10019-4702)
PHONE..................646 530-8666
Michael Hirsh, President
EMP: 5
SALES (est): 254.1K Privately Held
SIC: 7372 Educational computer software

(G-8938)
ASSOCIATION FOR CMPT MCHY INC (PA)
Also Called: ACM
2 Penn Plz Rm 701 (10121-0799)
P.O. Box 30777 (10087-0777)
PHONE..................212 869-7440
John R White, CEO
Vinton Cerf, President
Wendy Hall, President
Joshua Horowitz, General Mgr
Vicki Hanson, Corp Secy
EMP: 72
SQ FT: 30,000
SALES: 70.1MM Privately Held
SIC: 2721 8621 Periodicals: publishing only; scientific membership association

(G-8939)
ASSOULINE PUBLISHING INC (PA)
3 Park Ave Fl 27 (10016-5902)
PHONE..................212 989-6769
Prosper Assouline, President
Yaffa Assouline, Vice Pres
Eduard De Lange, Vice Pres
Stephanie Labeille, Vice Pres
Nicole Ziomek, Sales Staff
▲ EMP: 12
SQ FT: 3,000
SALES (est): 2.6MM Privately Held
WEB: www.assouline.com
SIC: 2731 Book publishing

New York - New York County (G-8940) — GEOGRAPHIC SECTION

(G-8940)
ASTON LEATHER INC
153 W 27th St Ste 406 (10001-6258)
PHONE..................................212 481-2760
Metin Adam, *Ch of Bd*
▲ EMP: 6
SALES (est): 600K **Privately Held**
SIC: 3111 Leather tanning & finishing

(G-8941)
ASTUCCI US LTD (PA)
385 5th Ave Rm 1100 (10016-3340)
PHONE..................................212 725-3171
Dan Benmoshe, *President*
Hanna Levy, *Vice Pres*
Ivy Lee, *Technical Mgr*
▲ EMP: 8
SQ FT: 3,000
SALES: 15MM **Privately Held**
SIC: 3172 Cases, jewelry; cases, glasses

(G-8942)
AT&T CORP
Also Called: Sherwin Commerce
767 5th Ave Fl 12a (10153-0023)
PHONE..................................212 317-7048
Debra Surrette, *Manager*
EMP: 15
SALES (corp-wide): 160.5B **Publicly Held**
WEB: www.swbell.com
SIC: 7372 Prepackaged software
HQ: At&t Corp.
 1 At&T Way
 Bedminster NJ 07921
 800 403-3302

(G-8943)
ATC PLASTICS LLC
Also Called: Heller Performance Polymers
555 Madison Ave Fl 5 (10022-3410)
PHONE..................................212 375-2515
Herbert Heller, *President*
EMP: 39
SALES (corp-wide): 7.9MM **Privately Held**
SIC: 3087 3643 2851 2821 Custom compound purchased resins; current-carrying wiring devices; paints & allied products; plastics materials & resins
PA: Atc Plastics, Llc
 8425 Woodfield Crossing B
 Indianapolis IN 46240
 317 469-7552

(G-8944)
ATELIERS TAMALET CORP
Also Called: Les Ateliers Tamalet
349 5th Ave (10016-5019)
PHONE..................................929 325-7976
David Benayoun, *President*
EMP: 20
SALES (est): 724.2K **Privately Held**
SIC: 3911 Jewelry apparel

(G-8945)
ATERET LLC
22 W 48th St (10036-1803)
PHONE..................................212 819-0777
Khodahbaksh Levy,
Samuel Levy,
EMP: 5
SALES (est): 410K **Privately Held**
WEB: www.ateret.com
SIC: 3911 Jewelry, precious metal

(G-8946)
ATERIAN INVESTMENT PARTNERS LP (PA)
11 E 44th St Rm 1803 (10017-3670)
PHONE..................................212 547-2806
Michael Fieldstone, *Partner*
Eric Dieckman, *Partner*
EMP: 23
SALES (est): 136.4MM **Privately Held**
SIC: 3398 Metal heat treating

(G-8947)
ATERRA EXPLORATION LLC
230 W 56th St Apt 53d (10019-0077)
PHONE..................................212 315-0030
David G Sepiashvili, *President*
▲ EMP: 20
SALES (est): 893.1K **Privately Held**
SIC: 1382 Geological exploration, oil & gas field

(G-8948)
ATHALON SPORTGEAR INC
10 W 33rd St Rm 1012 (10001-3317)
PHONE..................................212 268-8070
Andrew Nitkin, *Ch of Bd*
Robert Goldener, *President*
Justin Maged, *Marketing Staff*
Brian E Sullen, *Manager*
Mike McLoughlin, *Director*
▲ EMP: 7
SALES (est): 1.1MM **Privately Held**
WEB: www.athalonskyvalet.com
SIC: 3949 Bags, golf

(G-8949)
ATHLON SPT COMMUNICATIONS INC
60 E 42nd St Ste 820 (10165-0820)
PHONE..................................212 478-1910
Tracey Altman, *President*
Irene Broderick, *Hlthcr Dir*
EMP: 28
SALES (corp-wide): 31.1MM **Privately Held**
SIC: 2721 Periodicals: publishing only
PA: Athlon Sports Communications, Inc.
 2451 Atrium Way Ste 320
 Nashville TN 37214
 615 327-0747

(G-8950)
ATLANTIC MONTHLY GROUP INC
Also Called: Atlantic, The
60 Madison Ave (10010-1600)
PHONE..................................202 266-7000
Katie Storrs, *Principal*
Hadley Haut, *Associate Dir*
Michael Proffitt, *Associate Dir*
Anna Sadler, *Sr Associate*
EMP: 25
SALES (corp-wide): 11.9MM **Privately Held**
WEB: www.theatlantic.com
SIC: 2721 Magazines: publishing only, not printed on site
PA: The Atlantic Monthly Group Inc
 600 New Hampshire Ave Nw # 4
 Washington DC 20037
 202 266-7000

(G-8951)
ATLANTIC RECORDING CORP (DH)
Also Called: Atlantic Records
1633 Broadway Lowr 2c1 (10019-6708)
PHONE..................................212 707-2000
Craig Kauman, *Ch of Bd*
Ahmet M Ertegun, *Ch of Bd*
Julie Geenwald, *President*
Greg Kallman, *President*
David Saslow, *General Mgr*
EMP: 325
SQ FT: 133,000
SALES (est): 96.8MM **Privately Held**
WEB: www.ledzep.com
SIC: 3652 Compact laser discs, prerecorded; master records or tapes, preparation of; phonograph record blanks
HQ: Warner Music Group Corp.
 1633 Broadway
 New York NY 10019
 212 275-2000

(G-8952)
ATLANTIC TROPHY CO INC
866 Avenue Of The America (10001-4168)
PHONE..................................212 684-6020
Arthur Schneider, *President*
EMP: 6
SQ FT: 1,000
SALES (est): 758.9K **Privately Held**
SIC: 3914 Trophies, silver; trophies, nickel silver; trophies, pewter; trophies, plated (all metals)

(G-8953)
ATLAS & COMPANY LLC
355 Lexington Ave Fl 6 (10017-6603)
PHONE..................................212 234-3100
James Atlas, *President*
David Barker, *Manager*
Peter Desrochers, *Manager*
Ulla Schnell, *Director*
EMP: 6
SALES (est): 500K **Privately Held**
SIC: 2731 Book publishing

(G-8954)
ATLAS MUSIC PUBLISHING LLC (PA)
6 E 39th St Ste 1104 (10016-0116)
PHONE..................................646 502-5170
Richard Stumpf, *CEO*
Doug Heinle, *Manager*
EMP: 9
SQ FT: 3,000
SALES (est): 941K **Privately Held**
SIC: 2741 Music books: publishing & printing; music, sheet: publishing only, not printed on site

(G-8955)
ATLAS PRINT SOLUTIONS INC
589 8th Ave Fl 4 (10018-3092)
PHONE..................................212 949-8775
Patrick Fardella, *Prdtn Mgr*
Mike Sorrentino, *Opers Staff*
Kathleen Tan, *Finance*
Mark Paulvin, *Accounts Mgr*
Fran Lupo, *Accounts Exec*
EMP: 25
SALES (est): 4MM **Privately Held**
SIC: 2752 Commercial printing, offset

(G-8956)
ATLAS RECYCLING LLC
Also Called: Pep Realty
25 Howard St Fl 2 (10013-3164)
PHONE..................................212 925-3280
John Pasquale, *CEO*
J Pasqual, *General Mgr*
Luke Lee, *Office Mgr*
Amer Radoncic, *Property Mgr*
EMP: 5
SALES (est): 446.3K **Privately Held**
SIC: 2621 Paper mills

(G-8957)
ATR JEWELRY INC
71 W 47th St Ste 402 (10036-2819)
PHONE..................................212 819-0075
Aron Aranbaev, *President*
EMP: 10
SALES (est): 1.1MM **Privately Held**
WEB: www.atrjewelry.com
SIC: 3911 5944 Jewelry, precious metal; jewelry, precious stones & precious metals

(G-8958)
ATTENDS HEALTHCARE INC
200 Park Ave (10166-0005)
PHONE..................................212 338-5100
Michael Fagan, *CEO*
Sara Weintraub, *Assistant*
EMP: 651
SALES (est): 29.7MM
SALES (corp-wide): 5.1B **Privately Held**
SIC: 2676 Sanitary paper products
PA: Domtar Corporation
 395 Boul De Maisonneuve O Bureau 200
 Montreal QC H3A 1
 514 848-5555

(G-8959)
ATTITUDES FOOTWEAR INC
1040 1st Ave Ste 232 (10022-2991)
PHONE..................................212 754-9113
Paul Mayer, *President*
Levy Jeff, *Exec VP*
Jeff Levy, *Vice Pres*
EMP: 3
SALES (est): 2MM **Privately Held**
SIC: 3144 Dress shoes, women's

(G-8960)
AUGURY INC
263 W 38th St Fl 16 (10018-0483)
PHONE..................................866 432-0976
Saar Yoskovitz, *CEO*
Emery Rosansky, *Vice Pres*
Eric Epstein, *Opers Staff*
Issana Raudnitz, *CFO*
Brian Charles, *Accounts Exec*
EMP: 24
SALES (est): 512.6K **Privately Held**
SIC: 7372 Business oriented computer software

(G-8961)
AUGUST SILK INC (PA)
499 7th Ave Fl 5s (10018-6868)
PHONE..................................212 643-2400
Benedict Chen, *Ch of Bd*
Fritz Penwell, *President*
Ron Petraglia, *Credit Staff*
Lauren Cafasso, *Accounts Exec*
Francine Shane, *Manager*
▲ EMP: 23
SQ FT: 83,000
SALES (est): 30MM **Privately Held**
SIC: 2321 2331 2335 2392 Men's & boys' furnishings; women's & misses' blouses & shirts; women's, juniors' & misses' dresses; household furnishings

(G-8962)
AUGUST SILK INC
H F G Design
499 7th Ave Fl 5s (10018-6868)
PHONE..................................212 643-2400
Fritz Penwell, *President*
EMP: 7 **Privately Held**
SIC: 2321 2331 2335 2392 Men's & boys' furnishings; women's & misses' blouses & shirts; women's, juniors' & misses' dresses; household furnishings
PA: August Silk Inc.
 499 7th Ave Fl 5s
 New York NY 10018

(G-8963)
AURASPACE INC
41 E 11th St Fl 6 (10003-4654)
PHONE..................................212 905-6100
Maximus Yaney, *President*
EMP: 8
SALES: 10MM **Privately Held**
SIC: 3699 Security control equipment & systems

(G-8964)
AURATIC INC
41 Madison Ave Ste 1402 (10010-2245)
PHONE..................................914 413-8154
Lewis Wong, *President*
▲ EMP: 6
SALES (est): 380.7K **Privately Held**
SIC: 2541 Counter & sink tops

(G-8965)
AUSTIN NICHOLS & CO INC (DH)
Also Called: Wild Turkey
250 Park Ave (10177-0001)
PHONE..................................519 561-5225
Paul Duffy, *CEO*
EMP: 23
SALES (est): 6.2MM **Privately Held**
SIC: 2086 2085 5182 2084 Soft drinks: packaged in cans, bottles, etc.; distilled & blended liquors; liquor; wines, brandy & brandy spirits
HQ: Campari America Llc
 40 E 34th St Rm 1504
 New York NY 10016
 415 315-8000

(G-8966)
AUTHENTIC BRANDS GROUP LLC (PA)
Also Called: Jones New York
1411 Broadway Fl 4 (10018-3460)
PHONE..................................212 760-2410
James Salter, *CEO*
Nicholas Woodhouse, *President*
Bridgette Fitzpatrick, *Counsel*
Serena Godwin, *Vice Pres*
Marc Rosen, *Vice Pres*
EMP: 150
SALES (est): 1.2B **Privately Held**
SIC: 2339 2384 5137 5611 Women's & misses' accessories; robes & dressing gowns; bathrobes, men's & women's: made from purchased materials; women's & children's lingerie & undergarments; clothing, sportswear, men's & boys'; franchises, selling or licensing

New York - New York County (G-8995)

(G-8967)
AUTOMOTIVE ACCESSORIES GROUP
505 8th Ave Rm 12a05 (10018-6581)
PHONE..................................212 736-8100
Allan J Marrus, *President*
Stephen Delman, *Admin Sec*
EMP: 300
SALES (est): 16.1MM **Privately Held**
SIC: 3714 Steering mechanisms, motor vehicle

(G-8968)
AUVEN THERAPEUTICS MGT LP
1325 Avenue Of The Americ (10019-6043)
PHONE..................................212 616-4000
Peter B Corr, *General Ptnr*
Stephen Evans-Freke, *General Ptnr*
EMP: 10
SALES (est): 1.6MM **Privately Held**
SIC: 2834 Pharmaceutical preparations

(G-8969)
AV THERAPEUTICS INC
Also Called: A V T
20 E 68th St Ste 204 (10065-5836)
PHONE..................................917 497-5523
Robert Pollock, *President*
EMP: 25 EST: 2007
SALES (est): 1.8MM **Privately Held**
SIC: 2836 Vaccines

(G-8970)
AVALANCHE STUDIOS NEW YORK INC
536 Broadway (10012-3915)
PHONE..................................212 993-6447
David Grijns, *Ch of Bd*
Arnaldo Espinal, *Technology*
EMP: 60
SALES (est): 4.8MM
SALES (corp-wide): 64.9MM **Privately Held**
SIC: 7372 Home entertainment computer software
HQ: Fatalist Holdings Ab
    Stockholm 100 6
    844 276-70

(G-8971)
AVALIN LLC
221 W 37th St Fl 3 (10018-5782)
PHONE..................................212 842-2286
Zoheir Aghravi, *President*
Matt Cohen, *Vice Pres*
Dawn Smith, *Sales Staff*
▲ EMP: 14
SQ FT: 10,000
SALES (est): 1.6MM **Privately Held**
WEB: www.avalinknits.com
SIC: 2339 Women's & misses' athletic clothing & sportswear

(G-8972)
AVANTI PRESS INC
6 W 18th St Ste 6l (10011-4630)
PHONE..................................212 414-1025
Frederic Ruffner III, *Branch Mgr*
EMP: 25
SALES (corp-wide): 14.2MM **Privately Held**
SIC: 2771 Greeting cards
PA: Avanti Press, Inc.
    155 W Congress St Ste 200
    Detroit MI 48226
    800 228-2684

(G-8973)
AVAYA SERVICES INC
2 Penn Plz Rm 702 (10121-1000)
PHONE..................................866 462-8292
Michael Sisselman, *Senior Mgr*
EMP: 7
SALES (est): 468.9K **Publicly Held**
SIC: 3661 Telephones & telephone apparatus
HQ: Avaya Inc.
    4655 Great America Pkwy
    Santa Clara CA 95054
    908 953-6000

(G-8974)
AVENUE MOSAIC COMPANY (PA)
307 W 38th St Unit Ph-21 (10018-2913)
P.O. Box 578, Libertyville IL (60048-0578)
PHONE..................................216 245-6306
Micheal Golden, *Owner*
Michael Golden, *Owner*
◆ EMP: 3 EST: 2016
SQ FT: 1,000
SALES: 1MM **Privately Held**
SIC: 3253 3231 Mosaic tile, glazed & unglazed: ceramic; mosaics, glass: made from purchased glass

(G-8975)
AVENUE THERAPEUTICS INC
2 Gansevoort St Fl 9 (10014-1667)
PHONE..................................781 652-4500
Lindsay A Rosenwald, *Ch of Bd*
Lucy Lu, *President*
Joseph Vazzano, *Vice Pres*
David Horin, *CFO*
Scott A Reines, *Chief Mktg Ofcr*
EMP: 4
SALES (est): 1.9MM **Publicly Held**
SIC: 2834 Pharmaceutical preparations
PA: Fortress Biotech, Inc.
    2 Gansevoort St Fl 9
    New York NY 10014

(G-8976)
AVERY DENNISON CORPORATION
218 W 40th St Fl 8 (10018-1758)
PHONE..................................626 304-2000
Peter Gunshon, *Manager*
EMP: 115
SALES (corp-wide): 6.6B **Publicly Held**
SIC: 2672 Adhesive backed films, foams & foils
PA: Avery Dennison Corporation
    207 N Goode Ave Ste 500
    Glendale CA 91203
    626 304-2000

(G-8977)
AVI-SPL EMPLOYEE
8 W 38th St Rm 1101 (10018-6244)
PHONE..................................212 840-4801
EMP: 350
SALES (corp-wide): 596.9MM **Privately Held**
SIC: 3669 3861 3663 3651 Mfg Communications Equip Mfg Photo Equip/Supplies Mfg Radio/Tv Comm Equip Mfg Home Audio/Video Eqp Whol Photo Equip/Supply
HQ: Avi-Spl Employee Emergency Relief Fund, Inc.
    6301 Benjamin Rd Ste 101
    Tampa FL 33634
    813 884-7168

(G-8978)
AVID TECHNOLOGY INC
90 Park Ave (10016-1301)
PHONE..................................212 983-2424
Adam Taylor, *Branch Mgr*
EMP: 22
SALES (corp-wide): 419MM **Publicly Held**
WEB: www.avid.com
SIC: 3861 Editing equipment, motion picture: viewers, splicers, etc.
PA: Avid Technology, Inc.
    75 Network Dr
    Burlington MA 01803
    978 640-6789

(G-8979)
AVITTO LEATHER GOODS INC
424 W Broadway Frnt A (10012-3796)
PHONE..................................212 219-7501
AVI Sharifi, *President*
EMP: 7
SALES (est): 560K **Privately Held**
SIC: 2211 Shoe fabrics

(G-8980)
AVM SOFTWARE INC (HQ)
Also Called: Paltalk
122 E 42nd St Rm 2600 (10168-2699)
P.O. Box 3454 (10008-3454)
PHONE..................................646 381-2468
Jason Katz, *CEO*
Wilson Kriegel, *President*
Adam Zalko, *Manager*
Jeremy McPherson, *Sr Software Eng*
EMP: 17
SQ FT: 5,000
SALES (est): 5MM **Publicly Held**
WEB: www.mpath.com
SIC: 7372 Prepackaged software

(G-8981)
AVS GEM STONE CORP
48 W 48th St Ste 1010 (10036-1713)
PHONE..................................212 944-6380
Antonio Santos, *President*
EMP: 5
SALES (est): 305.5K **Privately Held**
SIC: 1499 Gemstone & industrial diamond mining

(G-8982)
AWARD PUBLISHING LIMITED
40 W 55th St Apt 9b (10019-5376)
PHONE..................................212 246-0405
Iris Dodge, *Principal*
EMP: 9
SALES (est): 601.8K **Privately Held**
SIC: 2741 Miscellaneous publishing

(G-8983)
AXIM BIOTECHNOLOGIES INC
5 Rockefeller Plz Fl 20 Flr 20 (10111)
PHONE..................................212 751-0001
George E Anastassov, *Ch of Bd*
Robert Malasek, *CFO*
Philip A Van Damme, *Chief Mktg Ofcr*
Lekhram Changoer, *CTO*
EMP: 10 EST: 2010
SALES: 47.5K **Privately Held**
SIC: 2834 Pharmaceutical preparations

(G-8984)
AXIS NA LLC (PA)
Also Called: Axis Denim
70 W 40th St Fl 11 (10018-2619)
PHONE..................................212 840-4005
Ling Kwok,
Leigh Martin,
▲ EMP: 10
SALES (est): 1.2MM **Privately Held**
SIC: 2211 Denims

(G-8985)
AZ YASHIR BAPAZ INC
Also Called: A Yashir Bapa
134 W 37th St (10018-6911)
PHONE..................................212 947-7357
Rasael Yaghoubian, *President*
EMP: 5
SALES (est): 630K **Privately Held**
SIC: 2339 Sportswear, women's

(G-8986)
AZIBI LTD
Also Called: Luna Luz
270 W 39th St Rm 1501 (10018-4415)
PHONE..................................212 869-6550
Michael Samuels, *President*
Dennis Tilden, *Vice Pres*
EMP: 10
SQ FT: 8,000
SALES (est): 1MM **Privately Held**
WEB: www.azibi.com
SIC: 3949 Sporting & athletic goods

(G-8987)
B & F ARCHITECTURAL SUPPORT GR
Also Called: Advance Construction Group
450 7th Ave Ste 307 (10123-0307)
PHONE..................................212 279-6488
Stewart Ratzker, *President*
EMP: 30
SALES (est): 2MM **Privately Held**
SIC: 2851 8712 Paints & allied products; architectural services

(G-8988)
B & R PROMOTIONAL PRODUCTS
Also Called: Beal Blocks
34 W 120th St Apt 1 (10027-6478)
PHONE..................................212 563-0040
Gary Bimblick, *President*
Miriam Del Valle, *Admin Sec*
EMP: 6 EST: 1963
SQ FT: 5,000
SALES (est): 743.4K **Privately Held**
SIC: 3299 3999 Plaques: clay, plaster or papier mache; plaques, picture, laminated; badges, metal: policemen, firemen, etc.

(G-8989)
B K JEWELRY CONTRACTOR INC
71 W 47th St Fl 11 (10036-2819)
PHONE..................................212 398-9093
Jacob Solomon, *President*
Rachel Solomon, *Admin Sec*
EMP: 20
SQ FT: 5,000
SALES: 1MM **Privately Held**
SIC: 3911 Jewelry, precious metal

(G-8990)
B S J LIMITED
1400 Broadway Ste 1702 (10018-5300)
PHONE..................................212 764-4600
Shari Levine, *President*
EMP: 24
SQ FT: 10,000
SALES (est): 3.7MM **Privately Held**
SIC: 2335 5621 Bridal & formal gowns; women's specialty clothing stores
PA: B S J Limited
    1375 Broadway Rm 507
    New York NY 10018

(G-8991)
B S J LIMITED (PA)
1375 Broadway Rm 507 (10018-7197)
PHONE..................................212 221-8403
Shari Levine, *Ch of Bd*
Mike Mann, *President*
▲ EMP: 30
SALES (est): 5.3MM **Privately Held**
SIC: 2335 Bridal & formal gowns

(G-8992)
B SMITH FURS INC
224 W 30th St Rm 402 (10001-0406)
PHONE..................................212 967-5290
Gary Smith, *President*
Michael Hennessey, *Vice Pres*
Hennessey International, *Shareholder*
EMP: 10
SQ FT: 4,000
SALES (est): 980K **Privately Held**
SIC: 2371 Fur goods

(G-8993)
B TWEEN LLC
Also Called: Btween US
1412 Broadway Rm 1400 (10018-9836)
PHONE..................................212 819-9040
Robert Terzi, *President*
Jack Terzi, *Vice Pres*
Rochelle Terzi, *Vice Pres*
▲ EMP: 12
SQ FT: 3,000
SALES (est): 1.3MM **Privately Held**
SIC: 2339 Women's & misses' athletic clothing & sportswear

(G-8994)
B-REEL FILMS INC
401 Broadway Fl 24 (10013-3007)
PHONE..................................917 388-3836
Anders Wahlquist, *President*
Alistair Campbell, *Managing Dir*
Andy Williams, *Managing Dir*
Katie Flynn, *Production*
Aneisa Hagen, *Production*
EMP: 24
SALES (est): 5.2MM **Privately Held**
SIC: 3571 Computers, digital, analog or hybrid

(G-8995)
B601 V2 INC
315 5th Ave Rm 903 (10016-6588)
PHONE..................................646 391-6431
Steven Cohn, *CEO*
EMP: 5
SALES (est): 141.8K **Privately Held**
SIC: 7372 Business oriented computer software

New York - New York County

(G-8996)
BABY SIGNATURE INC (PA)
Also Called: Dainty Home
251 5th Ave Fl 2l (10016-6515)
PHONE.................212 686-1700
Hassib Baghdadi, *President*
◆ **EMP:** 1
SQ FT: 5,000
SALES: 5MM **Privately Held**
SIC: 2391 2392 5023 Curtains & draperies; placemats, plastic or textile; shower curtains: made from purchased materials; curtains

(G-8997)
BABYFAIR INC
Also Called: Diversify Apparel
34 W 33rd St Rm 818 (10001-3304)
PHONE.................212 736-7989
Maurice Shamah, *Ch of Bd*
Ralph Shamah, *Vice Pres*
◆ **EMP:** 35 **EST:** 1971
SQ FT: 8,000
SALES (est): 5.2MM **Privately Held**
WEB: www.babyfair.com
SIC: 2369 Play suits: girls', children's & infants'; rompers: infants'

(G-8998)
BACKTECH INC
2 Peter Cooper Rd Apt Mf (10010-6733)
PHONE.................973 279-0838
Eier Rystedt, *President*
EMP: 2
SALES: 1MM **Privately Held**
SIC: 3842 Surgical appliances & supplies

(G-8999)
BADGLEY MISCHKA LICENSING LLC
Also Called: Jsc Design
550 7th Ave Fl 22 (10018-3223)
PHONE.................212 921-1585
Neil Cole, *Mng Member*
James Mischka, *Pres*
EMP: 29
SQ FT: 3,000
SALES (est): 2.9MM
SALES (corp-wide): 225.8MM **Publicly Held**
WEB: www.badgleymischka.com
SIC: 2326 Men's & boys' work clothing
PA: Iconix Brand Group, Inc.
1450 Broadway Fl 3
New York NY 10018
212 730-0030

(G-9000)
BAG ARTS LTD
20 W 36th St Rm 5r (10018-9790)
PHONE.................212 684-7020
Steve Zagha, *President*
Isaac Cohen, *Vice Pres*
▲ **EMP:** 7
SQ FT: 7,000
SALES (est): 896.6K **Privately Held**
WEB: www.bagarts.com
SIC: 3053 Packing materials

(G-9001)
BAG ARTS THE ART PACKAGING LLC
20 W 36th St Fl 5 (10018-8005)
PHONE.................212 684-7020
Steve Zagha, *President*
▲ **EMP:** 6
SQ FT: 7,000
SALES (est): 548.4K **Privately Held**
SIC: 2673 2674 Food storage & trash bags (plastic); grocers' bags: made from purchased materials

(G-9002)
BAG BAZAAR LTD
Metro Accessories
1 E 33rd St Fl 6 (10016-5099)
PHONE.................212 689-3508
Joey Shames, *Branch Mgr*
EMP: 25
SALES (corp-wide): 43.1MM **Privately Held**
WEB: www.aeny.com
SIC: 2339 Women's & misses' accessories
PA: Bag Bazaar Ltd.
1 E 33rd St Fl 6
New York NY 10016
212 689-3508

(G-9003)
BAGZNYC CORP
Also Called: Kids
19 W 34th St Rm 318 (10001-0055)
PHONE.................212 643-8202
Jeff Goldstein, *President*
Larry Zakarin, *Vice Pres*
▲ **EMP:** 18
SQ FT: 5,300
SALES (est): 1.2MM **Privately Held**
SIC: 2339 3171 Women's & misses' outerwear; women's handbags & purses

(G-9004)
BAIKAL INC (PA)
341 W 38th St Fl 3 (10018-9694)
PHONE.................212 239-4650
Josef Itskovich, *President*
Richard Itskovich, *Vice Pres*
▲ **EMP:** 70
SQ FT: 5,000
SALES (est): 5MM **Privately Held**
WEB: www.baikal.com
SIC: 3171 Handbags, women's

(G-9005)
BAINBRIDGE & KNIGHT LLC
801 2nd Ave Fl 19 (10017-8618)
PHONE.................212 986-5100
Carl Ruderman, *President*
Steven Schwartz, *Mng Member*
EMP: 50
SQ FT: 12,000
SALES (est): 5.2MM **Privately Held**
SIC: 2099 Food preparations

(G-9006)
BALAJEE ENTERPRISES INC
Also Called: Digitech Printers
150 W 30th St Frnt 2 (10001-4161)
PHONE.................212 629-6150
Shul Khalfan, *President*
EMP: 8
SQ FT: 2,500
SALES (est): 1MM **Privately Held**
WEB: www.digitechprinters.com
SIC: 2759 Commercial printing

(G-9007)
BALANCED TECH CORP
Also Called: New Balance Underwear
37 W 37th St Fl 10 (10018-6354)
PHONE.................212 768-8330
Ezra Jack Cattan, *Ch of Bd*
Judah Cattan, *President*
▲ **EMP:** 20
SALES (est): 1.2MM **Privately Held**
WEB: www.newbalanceunderwear.com
SIC: 2254 Underwear, knit

(G-9008)
BALTICARE INC (PA)
501 Fashion Ave Rm 414 (10018-8608)
PHONE.................646 380-9470
Chris Ioannides, *Engineer*
Al Rivera, *Engineer*
Hugh D Reitmeyer, *Director*
EMP: 10 **EST:** 2007
SALES (est): 2.6MM **Privately Held**
SIC: 3585 Air conditioning units, complete: domestic or industrial

(G-9009)
BAM SALES LLC (PA)
1407 Broadway Rm 2018 (10018-2863)
PHONE.................212 781-3000
Marc Moyal,
Alan Cohen,
Scott Danziger,
Nicole Hausman,
Robert Klein,
EMP: 3
SALES (est): 1.2MM **Privately Held**
SIC: 2339 Women's & misses' athletic clothing & sportswear

(G-9010)
BAMBOO GLOBAL INDUSTRIES
339 E 58th St Apt 7e (10022-2268)
PHONE.................973 943-1878
Matthew Renov, *Principal*
EMP: 5
SALES (est): 347.7K **Privately Held**
SIC: 2869 Industrial organic chemicals

(G-9011)
BANDIER CORP
960 Park Ave Apt 11b (10028-0325)
PHONE.................212 242-5400
Jeff Peterson, *President*
Ashleigh Hults, *Mktg Dir*
Nicole Marconi, *Asst Mgr*
Jacqueline Stoner, *Relations*
EMP: 8 **EST:** 2013
SALES (est): 1.5MM **Privately Held**
SIC: 2211 5661 2339 Apparel & outerwear fabrics, cotton; shoes, custom; women's & misses' athletic clothing & sportswear

(G-9012)
BARBARA MATERA LTD
890 Broadway Fl 5 (10003-1211)
PHONE.................212 475-5006
Jared Aswegan, *President*
Larry Feinman, *CFO*
EMP: 100 **EST:** 1967
SQ FT: 8,500
SALES (est): 5.5MM **Privately Held**
SIC: 2389 Theatrical costumes

(G-9013)
BARBER BROTHERS JEWELRY MFG
Also Called: B & B Jewelry Mfg Co
580 5th Ave Ste 725 (10036-4724)
PHONE.................212 819-0666
Abraham Barber, *President*
Simon Barber, *Vice Pres*
EMP: 15 **EST:** 1963
SQ FT: 2,200
SALES (est): 1.5MM **Privately Held**
SIC: 3911 Jewelry, precious metal

(G-9014)
BARDWIL INDUSTRIES INC (PA)
Also Called: Bardwil Linens
4 Bryant Park Fl 4 Flr 4 (10018)
PHONE.................212 944-1870
George Bardwil, *CEO*
▲ **EMP:** 185 **EST:** 1906
SQ FT: 12,000
SALES (est): 19MM **Privately Held**
WEB: www.beyondmarketing.com
SIC: 2392 2241 Napkins, fabric & nonwoven: made from purchased materials; placemats, plastic or textile; tablecloths: made from purchased materials; chair covers & pads: made from purchased materials; trimmings, textile

(G-9015)
BARE BEAUTY LASER HAIR REMOVAL
5 E 57th St Fl 6 (10022-2553)
PHONE.................718 278-2273
Debbie Patadopoulas, *Owner*
EMP: 6
SALES (est): 71.5K **Privately Held**
SIC: 3699 Laser systems & equipment

(G-9016)
BARE ESCENTUALS INC
Also Called: Bare Minerals
1140 3rd Ave (10065)
PHONE.................646 537-0070
Melissa Colom, *Manager*
EMP: 7
SALES (corp-wide): 8.9B **Privately Held**
SIC: 2844 5122 Cosmetic preparations; toilet preparations
HQ: Bare Escentuals, Inc.
900 3rd Ave Fl 28
New York NY 10022
201 337-3750

(G-9017)
BARI ENGINEERING CORP
240 Bowery (10012-3501)
PHONE.................212 966-2080
Frank Bari, *President*
EMP: 24
SQ FT: 51,000
SALES (est): 2.8MM **Privately Held**
WEB: www.bariequipment.com
SIC: 3556 5046 Food products machinery; restaurant equipment & supplies

(G-9018)
BARI-JAY FASHIONS INC (PA)
230 W 38th St Fl 12 (10018-5729)
PHONE.................212 921-1551
Bruce Cohen, *President*
EMP: 20
SQ FT: 20,000
SALES (est): 5.4MM **Privately Held**
WEB: www.barijay.com
SIC: 2335 Gowns, formal; wedding gowns & dresses

(G-9019)
BAROKA CREATIONS INC
36 W 47th St Ste 1402 (10036-8601)
P.O. Box 290744, Brooklyn (11229-0744)
PHONE.................212 768-0527
Rami Bareket, *President*
Nftali Rockah, *Vice Pres*
EMP: 7
SQ FT: 11,000
SALES (est): 4MM **Privately Held**
WEB: www.baroka.com
SIC: 3911 3915 Jewelry, precious metal; diamond cutting & polishing

(G-9020)
BARRAGE
401 W 47th St Frnt A (10036-2306)
PHONE.................212 586-9390
Tom Johnson, *Owner*
EMP: 20
SALES (est): 2.2MM **Privately Held**
WEB: www.barrage.com
SIC: 3639 Major kitchen appliances, except refrigerators & stoves

(G-9021)
BARRERA JOSE & MARIA CO LTD
29 W 36th St Fl 8 (10018-7668)
PHONE.................212 239-1994
Jose Barrera, *Owner*
Maria Barrera, *Co-Owner*
EMP: 28
SQ FT: 3,000
SALES (est): 1.9MM **Privately Held**
SIC: 2387 3961 Apparel belts; costume jewelry, ex. precious metal & semi-precious stones

(G-9022)
BARRY INDUSTRIES INC
Also Called: Barry Supply Co Div
36 W 17th St Frnt 1 (10011-5731)
PHONE.................212 242-5200
Barry Weinberger, *President*
William Wein, *Manager*
EMP: 15
SQ FT: 4,000
SALES (est): 1.1MM **Privately Held**
SIC: 3429 5072 Manufactured hardware (general); hardware

(G-9023)
BARTHOLOMEW MAZZA LTD INC
22 W 48th St Ste 805 (10036-1803)
P.O. Box 231444 (10023-0025)
PHONE.................212 935-4530
Hugo Mazza, *President*
Diane Mazza, *Treasurer*
EMP: 50
SQ FT: 4,000
SALES (est): 5.5MM **Privately Held**
WEB: www.mazzabartholomew.com
SIC: 3911 Jewelry, precious metal

(G-9024)
BASIL S KADHIM
Also Called: Eton International
280 Madison Ave Rm 912 (10016-0801)
PHONE.................888 520-5192
Basil S Kadhim, *Owner*
Julie A Seward, *Manager*
EMP: 8
SQ FT: 1,000
SALES (est): 1.1MM **Privately Held**
WEB: www.etoninternational.com
SIC: 3663 5045 7382 5047 Television broadcasting & communications equipment; computers, peripherals & software; protective devices, security; medical equipment & supplies

▲ = Import ▼ = Export
◆ = Import/Export

GEOGRAPHIC SECTION

(G-9025)
BASILOFF LLC
179 Bennett Ave Apt 7f (10040-4059)
PHONE.....................................646 671-0353
Dmitri Vassiliev, *President*
EMP: 6 EST: 2014
SALES (est): 330K **Privately Held**
SIC: 2261 Sponging cotton broadwoven cloth for the trade

(G-9026)
BASIN HOLDINGS LLC (PA)
200 Park Ave Fl 58b (10166-5899)
PHONE.....................................212 695-7376
John Fitzgibbons, *CEO*
Gail Coleman, *Exec VP*
Hadley Hosea, *Vice Pres*
Steve Waters, *Marketing Staff*
Nigeria Savoy, *Senior Mgr*
EMP: 21 EST: 2011
SALES (est): 149MM **Privately Held**
SIC: 3533 Oil & gas field machinery

(G-9027)
BAUBLE BAR INC
16 Madison Sq W Fl 5 (10010-1630)
PHONE.....................................646 846-2044
Amy Jain, *CEO*
Rotimi Akinyemiju, *COO*
Miriam Gassel, *Vice Pres*
Amy McDowell, *Vice Pres*
Jennifer May, *Prdtn Mgr*
▲ **EMP:** 50
SALES (est): 19.7MM **Privately Held**
SIC: 3172 Cases, jewelry

(G-9028)
BAUSCH & LOMB HOLDINGS INC (DH)
450 Lexington Ave (10017-3904)
PHONE.....................................585 338-6000
Brent L Saunders, *CEO*
Gerald M Ostrov, *Ch of Bd*
EMP: 9
SALES (est): 2.4B
SALES (corp-wide): 8.7B **Privately Held**
SIC: 3851 2834 Ophthalmic goods; pharmaceutical preparations
HQ: Valeant Pharmaceuticals International
400 Somerset Corp Blvd
Bridgewater NJ 08807
908 927-1400

(G-9029)
BAZAAR
300 W 57th St Fl 25 (10019-3741)
PHONE.....................................212 903-5497
Linda Crowley, *Principal*
Diana Kaufman, *Bd of Directors*
▲ **EMP:** 5
SALES (est): 250.6K **Privately Held**
SIC: 2721 Magazines: publishing & printing

(G-9030)
BDG MEDIA INC
Also Called: Bustle Digital Group
315 Park Ave S Fl 12 (10010-3625)
PHONE.....................................917 551-6510
Bryan Goldberg, *CEO*
Chip Krueger, *Accounts Exec*
Richard Maier, *Project Leader*
EMP: 250
SQ FT: 51,000
SALES (est): 611K **Privately Held**
SIC: 2741

(G-9031)
BEAR PORT PUBLISHING COMPANY
45 W 21st St 3b (10010-6865)
PHONE.....................................877 337-8577
Ken Goin, *President*
Kenn Goin, *Publisher*
Kathryn Camisa, *Marketing Staff*
Joyce Tavolacci, *Senior Editor*
EMP: 11
SQ FT: 3,000
SALES: 3MM
SALES (corp-wide): 116.3MM **Privately Held**
WEB: www.bearportpublishing.com
SIC: 2741 Miscellaneous publishing

PA: Woongjin Co., Ltd.
Jongro Place Bldg.
Seoul 03130
822 207-6470

(G-9032)
BEAUTY FASHION INC
Also Called: Astor-Honor Division
8 W 38th St Frnt 2 (10018-0133)
PHONE.....................................212 840-8800
John G Ledes, *Ch of Bd*
George M Ledes, *President*
EMP: 20
SALES (est): 1.8MM **Privately Held**
WEB: www.astorhonor.com
SIC: 2731 2721 Book publishing; magazines: publishing only, not printed on site

(G-9033)
BECCA INC
Also Called: Becca Cosmetics
142 W 36th St Fl 15 (10018-8785)
PHONE.....................................646 568-6250
▲ **EMP:** 100 EST: 2001
SALES (est): 4.1MM **Publicly Held**
SIC: 2844 Mfg Toilet Preparations
PA: The Estee Lauder Companies Inc
767 5th Ave Fl 1
New York NY 10153

(G-9034)
BEDFORD FREEMAN & WORTH (DH)
Also Called: Scientific American Library
1 New York Plz Ste 4500 (10004-1562)
PHONE.....................................212 576-9400
Elizabeth A Widdicombe, *Senior VP*
Lawrence Jankovic, *CFO*
Michael Ross, *Treasurer*
Cindy Rabinowitz, *Sales Staff*
Matthew Weaver, *Marketing Staff*
EMP: 192
SQ FT: 36,000
SALES (est): 82.7MM
SALES (corp-wide): 1.7B **Privately Held**
WEB: www.bfwpub.com
SIC: 2759 2732 2721 2731 Commercial printing; book printing; periodicals; textbooks: publishing only, not printed on site

(G-9035)
BEDFORD FREEMAN & WORTH
Also Called: Saint Martins Press
1 New York Plz Ste 4500 (10004-1562)
PHONE.....................................212 375-7000
Joan Feinberg, *President*
Cathy Shin, *Project Mgr*
EMP: 70
SALES (corp-wide): 1.7B **Privately Held**
WEB: www.bfwpub.com
SIC: 2731 Textbooks: publishing only, not printed on site
HQ: Bedford, Freeman & Worth Publishing Group, Llc
1 New York Plz Ste 4500
New York NY 10004
212 576-9400

(G-9036)
BEDFORD COMMUNICATIONS INC
1410 Broadway Frnt 2 (10018-9302)
PHONE.....................................212 807-8220
Edward D Brown, *President*
EMP: 30
SALES (est): 3.9MM **Privately Held**
WEB: www.bedfordcommunications.com
SIC: 2721 Magazines: publishing only, not printed on site

(G-9037)
BEDROCK COMMUNICATIONS
Also Called: Facilities
152 Madison Ave Rm 802 (10016-5476)
PHONE.....................................212 532-4150
Susan Wexner, *President*
Michael Caffin, *Editor*
Michael Casffin, *Vice Pres*
David Korn, *Senior Mgr*
George Seli, *Director*
EMP: 5
SQ FT: 3,500
SALES (est): 479.4K **Privately Held**
WEB: www.facilitiesonline.com
SIC: 2731 Book publishing

(G-9038)
BEILA GROUP INC
Also Called: City Hats
285 Mott St (10012-3430)
PHONE.....................................212 260-1948
Alexandra Tiouleneva, *CEO*
EMP: 12
SALES (est): 1MM **Privately Held**
SIC: 3942 Hats, doll

(G-9039)
BELLATAIRE DIAMONDS INC
19 W 44th St Fl 15 (10036-6101)
PHONE.....................................212 687-8881
Bill Moryto, *CFO*
Charles A Meyer, *Exec Dir*
EMP: 10
SALES (est): 840K **Privately Held**
WEB: www.bellatairediamonds.com
SIC: 3911 Jewelry, precious metal

(G-9040)
BELLEROPHON PUBLICATIONS INC
Also Called: Metropolis Magazine
205 Lexington Ave Fl 17 (10016-6022)
PHONE.....................................212 627-9977
Horace Havemeyer III, *President*
Tamara Stout, *General Mgr*
Mikki Brammer, *Editor*
Samuel Medina, *Editor*
Helene Silverman, *Editor*
EMP: 35
SQ FT: 4,000
SALES (est): 4.6MM **Privately Held**
WEB: www.metropolismag.com
SIC: 2721 Magazines: publishing only, not printed on site

(G-9041)
BELUGA INC (PA)
Also Called: Adjmi Apparel Group
463 7th Ave Fl 4 (10018-8725)
PHONE.....................................212 594-5511
Eric Adjmi, *Ch of Bd*
Mark Adjmi, *Vice Pres*
Gerard Agoglia, *CFO*
Jessica Fuller, *Human Resources*
Joey Dwek, *Info Tech Mgr*
▲ **EMP:** 40
SQ FT: 15,000
SALES (est): 6.8MM **Privately Held**
WEB: www.beluga.com
SIC: 2329 Men's & boys' sportswear & athletic clothing

(G-9042)
BEN-SAK TEXTILE INC
Also Called: Bensak
307 W 38th St Frnt 9 (10018-9501)
PHONE.....................................212 279-5122
Benhour Ahdout, *CEO*
David Ahdout, *Vice Pres*
Ned Saki, *CFO*
EMP: 7
SQ FT: 550
SALES (est): 960K **Privately Held**
WEB: www.getinkjet.com
SIC: 2269 Finishing plants

(G-9043)
BENARTEX LLC
132 W 36th St Rm 401 (10018-8837)
PHONE.....................................212 840-3250
David Lochner, *President*
Susan Neill, *Vice Pres*
Jeremy Jeffries, *Sales Executive*
Yudith Holguin, *Manager*
Susan Kemler, *Manager*
▲ **EMP:** 25
SQ FT: 7,000
SALES (est): 4MM **Privately Held**
WEB: www.benartex.com
SIC: 2211 Apparel & outerwear fabrics, cotton

(G-9044)
BENCHMARK GRAPHICS LTD
9 E 37th St Fl 5 (10016-2894)
PHONE.....................................212 683-1711
Fax: 212 889-1927
EMP: 15
SQ FT: 5,000
SALES (est): 1.8MM **Privately Held**
SIC: 2752 Lithographic Commercial Printing

(G-9045)
BENETTON TRADING USA INC (PA)
601 5th Ave Fl 4 (10017-8258)
P.O. Box 6020, Somerset NJ (08875-6020)
PHONE.....................................212 593-0290
ARI Hoffman, *Principal*
Diane Mravcak, *VP Finance*
◆ **EMP:** 7
SALES (est): 985.6K **Privately Held**
SIC: 2329 Men's & boys' sportswear & athletic clothing

(G-9046)
BENSON INDUSTRIES INC
192 Lexington Ave Rm 502 (10016-6912)
PHONE.....................................212 779-3230
John Frank, *Manager*
EMP: 10
SALES (corp-wide): 242.1B **Publicly Held**
SIC: 3231 1793 5031 Products of purchased glass; glass & glazing work; lumber, plywood & millwork
HQ: Benson Industries, Inc.
1650 Nw Naito Pkwy # 250
Portland OR 97209
503 226-7611

(G-9047)
BENTLEY MANUFACTURING INC (PA)
10 W 33rd St Rm 220 (10001-3306)
PHONE.....................................212 714-1800
Victor Braha, *President*
Ralph Braha, *CFO*
Eli Braha, *Admin Sec*
◆ **EMP:** 7
SQ FT: 5,200
SALES (est): 2MM **Privately Held**
SIC: 2676 Diapers, paper (disposable): made from purchased paper; napkins, sanitary: made from purchased paper

(G-9048)
BENTLEY MILLS INC
91 5th Ave Rm 800 (10003-3035)
PHONE.....................................212 463-0606
Beth Schoshan, *Manager*
Lori Rounsavall, *Manager*
Wendy Jorgensen, *Executive*
EMP: 9
SALES (corp-wide): 218.1MM **Privately Held**
SIC: 2273 Carpets & rugs
PA: Bentley Mills, Inc.
14641 Don Julian Rd
City Of Industry CA 91746
626 333-4585

(G-9049)
BEOWAWE BINARY LLC
1095 Avenue Of The Ave (10036)
PHONE.....................................646 829-3900
James Pagano,
James R Pagano,
EMP: 30
SALES: 500K **Privately Held**
SIC: 3511 Turbines & turbine generator sets

(G-9050)
BERGER & WILD LLC
Also Called: Last Magazine, The
401 Broadway Ste 302 (10013-3005)
PHONE.....................................646 415-8459
Tenzen Wild, *Partner*
Migus Berger, *Partner*
Tenzen Wilt, *Partner*
Zachary Sniderman, *Assoc Editor*
▲ **EMP:** 5
SALES (est): 436.2K **Privately Held**
SIC: 2721 Periodicals

(G-9051)
BERNARD CHAUS INC (DH)
530 7th Ave Fl 18 (10018-4855)
PHONE.....................................212 354-1280
Ariel Chaus, *CEO*
Judith Leech, *Vice Pres*
William P Runge, *CFO*
Jackie Muldowney, *VP Merchandise*
Donna Poach, *Mktg Dir*
▲ **EMP:** 76
SQ FT: 33,000

New York - New York County (G-9052)

SALES (est): 68.6MM
SALES (corp-wide): 287.1MM Privately Held
SIC: 2339 2331 Sportswear, women's; slacks: women's, misses' & juniors'; shorts (outerwear): women's, misses' & juniors'; women's & misses' blouses & shirts

(G-9052)
BERNARD CHAUS INC
Also Called: Cynthia Steffe
515 7th Ave Ste 18 (10018-5902)
PHONE.................646 562-4700
Tina Cardell, Branch Mgr
EMP: 200
SALES (corp-wide): 287.1MM Privately Held
SIC: 2339 2331 Sportswear, women's; slacks: women's, misses' & juniors'; shorts (outerwear): women's, misses' & juniors'; women's & misses' blouses & shirts
HQ: Bernard Chaus, Inc.
530 7th Ave Fl 18
New York NY 10018
212 354-1280

(G-9053)
BERNETTE APPAREL LLC
42 W 39th St Fl 2 (10018-3895)
PHONE.................212 279-5526
Adam Siskind,
Jeff Siskind,
EMP: 16
SQ FT: 7,000
SALES (est): 1.1MM Privately Held
WEB: www.btexusa.com
SIC: 2329 Sweaters & sweater jackets: men's & boys'

(G-9054)
BERNHARD ARNOLD & COMPANY INC (PA)
551 5th Ave Fl 3 (10176-2800)
PHONE.................212 907-1500
Howard Brecher, Vice Pres
David Henigson, Vice Pres
EMP: 3
SQ FT: 70,000
SALES: 36MM Publicly Held
WEB: www.valueline.com
SIC: 2721 6282 Periodicals: publishing only; investment advice

(G-9055)
BERTELSMANN INC (DH)
1745 Broadway Fl 20 (10019-4651)
PHONE.................212 782-1000
Jaroslaw Gabor, CEO
Thomas Rabe, Ch of Bd
Joshua Kraus, President
Immanuel Hermreck, Exec VP
William Tung, Vice Pres
▲ EMP: 30
SALES (est): 1.7B
SALES (corp-wide): 82.3MM Privately Held
WEB: www.bertelsmann.com
SIC: 2731 2721 7819 3652 Books: publishing & printing; magazines: publishing & printing; trade journals: publishing & printing; video tape or disk reproduction; compact laser discs, prerecorded; commercial & industrial building operation
HQ: Bertelsmann Se & Co. Kgaa
Carl-Bertelsmann-Str. 270
Gutersloh 33335
524 180-0

(G-9056)
BERTELSMANN PUBG GROUP INC (DH)
1540 Broadway Fl 24 (10036-4039)
PHONE.................212 782-1000
Thomas Middelhoff, CEO
Robert J Sorrentino, CEO
Hans-Martin Sorge, Ch of Bd
Peter Olson, President
Bernhard U Derlath, Treasurer
EMP: 1000
SQ FT: 710,000

SALES (est): 89.8MM
SALES (corp-wide): 82.3MM Privately Held
SIC: 2731 2721 Books: publishing only; magazines: publishing only, not printed on site
HQ: Bertelsmann, Inc.
1745 Broadway Fl 20
New York NY 10019
212 782-1000

(G-9057)
BEST BRANDS CONSUMER PDTS INC (PA)
20 W 33rd St Fl 5 (10001-3305)
PHONE.................212 684-7456
Peter Felberbaum, President
Meyer Kassin, Vice Pres
Albert Kassin, Treasurer
Isaac Kassin, Admin Sec
▲ EMP: 8
SQ FT: 26,000
SALES (est): 1.7MM Privately Held
SIC: 2369 2371 Headwear: girls', children's & infants'; hats, fur

(G-9058)
BESTYPE DIGITAL IMAGING LLC
285 W Broadway Frnt A (10013-2246)
PHONE.................212 966-6886
John W Lam, Mng Member
Chick Lam,
EMP: 10
SQ FT: 3,000
SALES: 1MM Privately Held
SIC: 2759 Commercial printing

(G-9059)
BETH KOBLINER COMPANY LLC
1995 Broadway Ste 1800 (10023-5857)
PHONE.................212 501-8407
Beth Kobliner,
EMP: 5
SALES (est): 274.6K Privately Held
SIC: 2711 Newspapers, publishing & printing

(G-9060)
BETH WARD STUDIOS LLC
133 W 25th St Rm 8e (10001-7281)
PHONE.................646 922-7575
Beth Ward, Mng Member
EMP: 10
SALES: 3.4MM Privately Held
SIC: 3961 Costume jewelry

(G-9061)
BETSY & ADAM LTD (PA)
525 Fashion Ave Fl 21 (10018-4921)
PHONE.................212 302-3750
Martin Sklar, Owner
▲ EMP: 50
SQ FT: 12,000
SALES (est): 17MM Privately Held
WEB: www.betsyandadam.com
SIC: 2253 Dresses & skirts

(G-9062)
BETTERTEX INC
Also Called: Bettertex Interioirs
450 Broadway (10013-5822)
PHONE.................212 431-3373
Raymond Nakash, President
EMP: 15 EST: 2008
SALES (est): 1.5MM Privately Held
SIC: 2391 7641 Curtains & draperies; upholstery work

(G-9063)
BEVERAGE MEDIA GROUP INC (PA)
152 Madison Ave Rm 600 (10016-5471)
PHONE.................212 571-3232
Mike Roth, President
Kristen Wolfe, Editor
Marlena Hoffman, Comms Mgr
James Laurenti, Manager
▲ EMP: 10
SQ FT: 13,300
SALES (est): 1.8MM Privately Held
WEB: www.bevmedia.com
SIC: 2721 Magazines: publishing only, not printed on site

(G-9064)
BEYOND LOOM INC (PA)
Also Called: Franetta
262 W 38th St Rm 203 (10018-5881)
P.O. Box 105 (10150-0105)
PHONE.................212 575-3100
Joanne Satin, President
▲ EMP: 6 EST: 1991
SQ FT: 4,000
SALES (est): 607.3K Privately Held
WEB: www.beyondtheloom.com
SIC: 2211 2221 2231 Cotton broad woven goods; silk broadwoven fabrics; fabric finishing: wool, mohair or similar fibers

(G-9065)
BEYONDLY INC
Also Called: Everplans
20 W 20th St Ste 1004 (10011-9252)
PHONE.................646 658-3665
Abby Schneiderman, President
Adam Seifer, President
Gene Newman, Director
EMP: 22
SQ FT: 1,700
SALES (est): 1.3MM Privately Held
SIC: 7372 Business oriented computer software

(G-9066)
BEYONDSPRING INC
28 Liberty St Fl 39 (10005-1451)
PHONE.................646 305-6387
Lan Huang, Ch of Bd
Richard J Daly, COO
Ramon Mohanlal, Vice Pres
Edward Dongheng Liu, CFO
G Kenneth Lloyd, Officer
EMP: 24
SALES (est): 1.7MM Privately Held
SIC: 2834 Pharmaceutical preparations

(G-9067)
BEYONDSPRING PHRMCEUTICALS INC
28 Liberty St Fl 39 (10005-1451)
PHONE.................646 305-6387
Lan Huang, CEO
G Kenneth Lloyd, COO
Steven D Reich, Vice Pres
Robert Dickey IV, CFO
Gloria Lee, Chief Mktg Ofcr
EMP: 11
SALES (est): 1.2MM Privately Held
SIC: 2834 Pharmaceutical preparations

(G-9068)
BH BRAND INC
10 W 33rd St Rm 218 (10001-3306)
PHONE.................212 239-1635
Kenny Harari, CEO
Morris Harari, President
▲ EMP: 25
SQ FT: 4,500
SALES: 10.8MM Privately Held
SIC: 2389 2339 Men's miscellaneous accessories; women's & misses' accessories

(G-9069)
BH MULTI COM CORP (PA)
15 W 46th St Fl 6 (10036-4196)
PHONE.................212 944-0020
Fatolah Hematian, Ch of Bd
Effy Hematian, President
David Bassalalli, Corp Secy
Hertsel Akhavan, Vice Pres
▲ EMP: 47
SQ FT: 6,000
SALES (est): 6.9MM Privately Held
WEB: www.bhmulti.com
SIC: 3911 Jewelry, precious metal

(G-9070)
BIANCA GROUP LTD
244 W 39th St Fl 4 (10018-4413)
PHONE.................212 768-3011
Ricardo Garcia, President
EMP: 5
SQ FT: 2,200
SALES: 200K Privately Held
SIC: 3953 3543 Marking devices; industrial patterns

(G-9071)
BIBO INTERNATIONAL LLC
130 Water St Apt 4g (10005-1614)
P.O. Box 492, Newport RI (02840-0492)
PHONE.................617 304-2242
Mark Lester, Mng Member
EMP: 18 EST: 2011
SALES: 1.6MM Privately Held
SIC: 2084 Wines, brandy & brandy spirits

(G-9072)
BICKER INC
Also Called: Holiday House Publishing
50 Broad St Ste 301 (10004-2826)
PHONE.................212 688-0085
John H Briggs Jr, President
Kate Briggs, Vice Pres
Mary Cash, Vice Pres
Terry Borzumato-Green, VP Mktg
Kerry Martin, Director
▲ EMP: 15 EST: 1935
SQ FT: 2,000
SALES (est): 2.3MM Privately Held
WEB: www.holidayhouse.com
SIC: 2731 Books: publishing only

(G-9073)
BIDPRESS LLC
659 Washington St Apt 5r (10014-2874)
P.O. Box 351, Asheville NC (28802-0351)
PHONE.................267 973-8876
Anthony Wavering, CEO
EMP: 5 EST: 2013
SQ FT: 1,000
SALES (est): 189.8K Privately Held
SIC: 2759 Screen printing

(G-9074)
BIELKA INC
141 E 56th St Apt 6f (10022-2713)
PHONE.................212 980-6841
Robert Bruce Bielka, President
Regina Suzanne Eros, Vice Pres
EMP: 5
SQ FT: 1,200
SALES (est): 504K Privately Held
WEB: www.bielkajewelry.com
SIC: 3911 Jewelry, precious metal

(G-9075)
BIG APPLE ELEVTR SRV & CONSULT
247 W 30th St (10001-2824)
PHONE.................212 279-0700
Jaclyn Hanning, CEO
Joseph Hanning, President
EMP: 8
SALES (est): 454.4K Privately Held
SIC: 3534 Elevators & equipment

(G-9076)
BIG APPLE SIGN CORP (PA)
Also Called: BIG APPLE VISUAL GROUP
247 W 35th St Rm 400 (10001-1925)
PHONE.................212 629-3650
Amir Khalfan, Ch of Bd
Richi Shah, CFO
Maria B Varga, Consultant
Mehul Dharia, Administration
▲ EMP: 93
SQ FT: 40,000
SALES: 18.2MM Privately Held
WEB: www.bigapplegroup.com
SIC: 2399 2759 3993 Banners, made from fabric; commercial printing; signs, not made in custom sign painting shops; displays & cutouts, window & lobby

(G-9077)
BIG FISH ENTERTAINMENT LLC
1411 Broadway Fl 16 (10018-3471)
PHONE.................646 797-4955
Crystal Kaufman, Production
Daniel Cesareo, Mng Member
EMP: 200
SALES: 25.7MM Privately Held
SIC: 3663 Studio equipment, radio & television broadcasting

(G-9078)
BIG IDEA BRANDS LLC
Also Called: Flow Society
1410 Broadway Frnt 4 (10018-9343)
PHONE.................212 938-0270
Mark Elenowitz, CEO

GEOGRAPHIC SECTION

Anthony Ottimo, *President*
Brian Frank, *Principal*
Carlos Vazquez, *COO*
Larry Fihma, *Senior VP*
▲ **EMP:** 10
SQ FT: 4,000
SALES (est): 857.6K **Privately Held**
SIC: 2329 Athletic (warmup, sweat & jogging) suits: men's & boys'

(G-9079)
BIG WHITE WALL HOLDING INC
41 E 11th St Fl 11 (10003-4602)
PHONE 917 281-2649
Tina Trenkler, *CEO*
EMP: 15 **EST:** 2013
SQ FT: 1,200
SALES: 250K
SALES (corp-wide): 32.3K **Privately Held**
SIC: 7372 Application computer software
HQ: Bigwhitewall Limited
Evergreen House Grafton Place
London NW1 2

(G-9080)
BIGNAY INC
315 E 86th St Apt 21ge (10028-4867)
PHONE 786 346-1673
Lucas Toledo, *CEO*
Gabriel Nudel, *COO*
Eric Sevillia, *CFO*
Emanuel Ravera, *CTO*
EMP: 8 **EST:** 2014
SALES (est): 924K **Privately Held**
SIC: 3751 5571 5941 Bicycles & related parts; bicycles, motorized; bicycle & bicycle parts

(G-9081)
BILCO INDUSTRIES INC
214 W 39th St Rm 301 (10018-8311)
PHONE 917 783-5008
Billy Chen, *President*
Jerry Lau, *Vice Pres*
EMP: 16 **EST:** 2013
SALES: 30MM **Privately Held**
SIC: 2329 2339 5136 5137 Men's & boys' sportswear & athletic clothing; women's & misses' athletic clothing & sportswear; men's & boys' sportswear & work clothing; work clothing, men's & boys'; women's & children's clothing

(G-9082)
BILLION TOWER INTL LLC
Also Called: Machine Clothing Company
989 6th Ave Fl 8 (10018-0871)
PHONE 212 220-0608
Joeson Ko Cho Shun,
▲ **EMP:** 15
SQ FT: 3,000
SALES: 122MM **Privately Held**
SIC: 2326 5136 Men's & boys' work clothing; men's & boys' clothing

(G-9083)
BILLION TOWER USA LLC
989 Avenue Of The America (10018-0871)
PHONE 212 220-0608
Joeson Cho Shun Ko,
EMP: 5
SALES: 5MM **Privately Held**
SIC: 2329 Men's & boys' sportswear & athletic clothing

(G-9084)
BILLY BEEZ USA LLC (PA)
3 W 35th St Fl 3 (10001-2237)
PHONE 646 606-2249
Ron Palerico, *General Mgr*
Mark Bain, *Sales Staff*
EMP: 15
SALES (est): 15.6MM **Privately Held**
SIC: 3949 5137 7999 Playground equipment; women's & children's dresses, suits, skirts & blouses; amusement ride

(G-9085)
BINO PRODUCTS LLC
236 5th Ave Fl 8 (10001-7989)
PHONE 212 689-6008
EMP: 22
SALES (est): 3.8MM **Privately Held**
SIC: 3634 Housewares, excluding cooking appliances & utensils

(G-9086)
BIOCONTINUUM GROUP INC
116 Chambers St (10007-1336)
PHONE 212 406-1060
John M Dimor, *President*
EMP: 5
SQ FT: 1,200
SALES (est): 290K **Privately Held**
WEB: www.bioc.net
SIC: 3999 Education aids, devices & supplies

(G-9087)
BIOFEEDBACK INSTRUMENT CORP
Also Called: Allied Products
255 W 98th St Apt 3d (10025-5596)
PHONE 212 222-5665
Philip Brotman, *President*
▲ **EMP:** 8
SQ FT: 1,000
SALES: 800K **Privately Held**
WEB: www.biof.com
SIC: 3845 5045 5734 Electromedical apparatus; computers, peripherals & software; computer peripheral equipment; computer & software stores

(G-9088)
BIOLITEC INC
110 E 42nd St Rm 1800 (10017-5648)
PHONE 413 525-0600
Wolfgang Neuberger, *CEO*
EMP: 50
SQ FT: 16,000
SALES (est): 5.1MM
SALES (corp-wide): 42.2MM **Privately Held**
WEB: www.biolitec-us.com
SIC: 3229 Fiber optics strands
HQ: Biolitec Biomedical Technology Gmbh
Otto-Schott-Str. 15
Jena 07745
364 151-9530

(G-9089)
BIRDSIGNS INC
16 W 19th St Apt 3e (10011-4336)
PHONE 201 388-7613
Zvetan Dragulev, *CEO*
EMP: 5
SALES (est): 117.2K **Privately Held**
SIC: 7372 7389 Application computer software;

(G-9090)
BIRNBAUM & BULLOCK LTD
151 W 25th St Rm 2a (10001-7262)
PHONE 212 242-2914
Robert Bullock, *CEO*
Steven Birnbaum, *President*
EMP: 8
SQ FT: 1,500
SALES (est): 1.1MM **Privately Held**
SIC: 2335 Wedding gowns & dresses

(G-9091)
BISLEY INC
Also Called: Bisley North America
1140 Broadway Rm 902 (10001-7504)
PHONE 212 675-3055
Garth Fielding, *Managing Dir*
Jean-Francis Vellozzo, *Accounts Mgr*
▲ **EMP:** 6
SALES (est): 389.8K **Privately Held**
SIC: 2522 Office furniture, except wood

(G-9092)
BISTATE OIL MANAGEMENT CORP
10 E 40th St Rm 2710 (10016-0301)
PHONE 212 935-4110
Richard D Siegal, *President*
Maria Scibelli, *Principal*
Paul H Howard, *Vice Pres*
EMP: 10
SQ FT: 4,500
SALES (est): 2.8MM **Privately Held**
SIC: 1382 Oil & gas exploration services

(G-9093)
BIZBASH MEDIA INC (PA)
Also Called: Bizbash Masterplanner
115 W 27th St Fl 8 (10001-6217)
PHONE 646 638-3602

David Adler, *CEO*
Richard Aaron, *President*
Simon Butler, *Editor*
Beth Kormanik, *Editor*
Michele Laufik, *Editor*
EMP: 55
SQ FT: 5,000
SALES (est): 11.9MM **Privately Held**
WEB: www.bizbash.com
SIC: 2759 2721 Advertising literature: printing; periodicals: publishing & printing

(G-9094)
BJ MAGAZINES INC
200 Varick St (10014-4810)
PHONE 212 367-9705
Renu Hooda, *President*
EMP: 5
SALES (est): 530K **Privately Held**
SIC: 2721 Periodicals

(G-9095)
BJG SERVICES LLC
237 W 35th St Ste 505 (10001-1905)
PHONE 516 592-5692
Isaac Newmann, *CEO*
Ben Neuberg, *President*
EMP: 25
SQ FT: 1,600
SALES (est): 6.3MM **Privately Held**
SIC: 3911 Jewelry, precious metal

(G-9096)
BLACK BOOK PHOTOGRAPHY INC
Also Called: Black Book, The
740 Broadway Ste 202 (10003-9518)
PHONE 212 979-6700
Ted Rubin, *President*
Kelly Landress, *Sales Staff*
Brian Clegg, *Manager*
Ron Lawson, *Manager*
▲ **EMP:** 19 **EST:** 1970
SALES (est): 1.3MM
SALES (corp-wide): 3.3MM **Privately Held**
WEB: www.modernholdings.com
SIC: 2741 Directories: publishing only, not printed on site
PA: Modern Holding Company
601 Lexington Ave Rm 5900
New York NY

(G-9097)
BLACKBOOK MEDIA CORP
32 Union Sq E Ste 4l (10003-3209)
PHONE 212 334-1800
Robert Hoff, *CEO*
Joseph Landry, *President*
EMP: 21
SQ FT: 1,500
SALES (est): 2.4MM **Privately Held**
SIC: 2721 Magazines: publishing & printing

(G-9098)
BLADES
659 Broadway (10012-2302)
PHONE 212 477-1059
George Pohntes, *Manager*
▼ **EMP:** 10
SALES (est): 783.8K **Privately Held**
SIC: 3949 Skateboards

(G-9099)
BLANCHE P FIELD LLC
155 E 56th St Ph (10022-2718)
PHONE 212 355-6616
Blanche Field, *President*
EMP: 25 **EST:** 1942
SQ FT: 3,000
SALES (est): 1.5MM **Privately Held**
SIC: 3999 5932 Shades, lamp or candle; antiques

(G-9100)
BLISS FOODS INC
Also Called: Yorganic
275 Greenwich St Frnt 2 (10007-3824)
PHONE 212 732-8888
Sung Kim, *President*
Shawn Reilly, *Vice Pres*
EMP: 5
SALES (est): 466.3K **Privately Held**
SIC: 2026 Yogurt

(G-9101)
BLISS FOODS INC
Also Called: Yorganic
275 Greenwich St Frnt 2 (10007-3824)
PHONE 212 732-8888
EMP: 11 **Privately Held**
SIC: 2026 Mfg Fluid Milk

(G-9102)
BLISS-POSTON THE SECOND WIND
928 Broadway Ste 403 (10010-8151)
PHONE 212 481-1055
Marcia Poston, *Vice Pres*
John Bliss, *Exec Dir*
EMP: 6
SALES (est): 522.9K **Privately Held**
SIC: 2011 Lard from carcasses slaughtered on site

(G-9103)
BLOOMSBURG CARPET INDS INC
Also Called: Silver Creek Carpet
11 E 26th St Frnt (10010-1431)
PHONE 212 688-7447
Thomas J Habib, *Branch Mgr*
EMP: 6
SALES (corp-wide): 50MM **Privately Held**
SIC: 2273 Carpets & rugs
PA: Bloomsburg Carpet Industries, Inc.
4999 Columbia Blvd
Bloomsburg PA 17815
800 233-8773

(G-9104)
BLOOMSBURY PUBLISHING INC
Also Called: Bloomsbury USA
1385 Brdwy Fl 5 Flr 5 (10018)
PHONE 212 419-5300
Nigel Newton, *President*
George Gibson, *Publisher*
Doug White, *Principal*
Wendy Fuller, *Editor*
Edie Weinberg, *Editor*
▲ **EMP:** 100
SALES (est): 18.3MM
SALES (corp-wide): 225.2MM **Privately Held**
WEB: www.bloomsburyusa.com
SIC: 2731 Books: publishing only
PA: Bloomsbury Publishing Plc
50 Bedford Square
London WC1B
207 631-5600

(G-9105)
BLU SAND LLC
333 W 39th St Rm 704 (10018-1556)
PHONE 212 564-1147
Eddie Shomer, *Vice Pres*
Morris Sitt,
▲ **EMP:** 9
SQ FT: 2,000
SALES (est): 1.1MM **Privately Held**
WEB: www.blusand.com
SIC: 2211 Towels & toweling, cotton

(G-9106)
BLUE AND WHITE PUBLISHING INC
Also Called: Bwog
425 Riverside Dr Apt 3c (10025-7724)
PHONE 215 431-3339
Jake Hershman, *CEO*
EMP: 10 **EST:** 2013
SALES (est): 504.7K **Privately Held**
SIC: 2711 Newspapers: publishing only, not printed on site

(G-9107)
BLUE DUCK TRADING LTD
463 7th Ave Rm 806 (10018-8712)
PHONE 212 268-3122
Barry Novick, *President*
▲ **EMP:** 8
SQ FT: 4,500
SALES: 3MM **Privately Held**
WEB: www.blueduckshearling.com
SIC: 2339 2311 Women's & misses' jackets & coats, except sportswear; coats, tailored, men's & boys': from purchased materials

New York - New York County (G-9108)

(G-9108)
BLUE HORIZON MEDIA INC (PA)
11 Park Pl Rm 1508 (10007-2816)
PHONE..................212 661-7878
Geoffrey D Lurie, *COO*
David Bernstein, *CFO*
EMP: 16
SQ FT: 16,000
SALES (est): 3MM **Privately Held**
WEB: www.bluehrzn.com
SIC: 2721 Magazines: publishing only, not printed on site

(G-9109)
BLUE TEE CORP (PA)
387 Park Ave S Fl 5 (10016-1495)
PHONE..................212 598-0880
David P Alldian, *Ch of Bd*
William M Kelly, *President*
Annette Marino D'Arienzo, *Exec Dir*
◆ **EMP:** 7
SQ FT: 2,500
SALES (est): 124.4MM **Privately Held**
SIC: 3533 3589 5093 3715 Water well drilling equipment; garbage disposers & compactors, commercial; ferrous metal scrap & waste; semitrailers for truck tractors; water quality monitoring & control systems; structural shapes, iron or steel

(G-9110)
BLUE WOLF GROUP LLC (HQ)
11 E 26th St Fl 21 (10010-1413)
PHONE..................866 455-9653
Tim Anderson, *Principal*
Eric Berridge, *Mng Member*
Michael Kirven,
EMP: 100
SQ FT: 5,000
SALES (est): 80.4MM
SALES (corp-wide): 79.1B **Publicly Held**
WEB: www.bluewolfgroup.com
SIC: 7372 Business oriented computer software
PA: International Business Machines Corporation
1 New Orchard Rd Ste 1 # 1
Armonk NY 10504
914 499-1900

(G-9111)
BLUESOHO (PA)
160 Varick St Fl 2 (10013-1251)
PHONE..................646 805-2583
Jennifer Bergin, *Managing Prtnr*
Tom Galbreath, *Managing Prtnr*
John Puterbaugh, *Managing Prtnr*
Stephanie Stanton, *Managing Prtnr*
Janine Crowley, *Opers Mgr*
EMP: 10
SALES (est): 2.7MM **Privately Held**
SIC: 2752 Commercial printing, lithographic

(G-9112)
BLUM & FINK INC
Also Called: Fleurette
158 W 29th St Fl 12 (10001-5300)
PHONE..................212 695-2606
Stanley Blum, *President*
▲ **EMP:** 12 **EST:** 1961
SQ FT: 10,000
SALES (est): 1.7MM **Privately Held**
SIC: 2371 5137 Fur coats & other fur apparel; fur clothing, women's & children's

(G-9113)
BMG RIGHTS MANAGEMENT (US) LLC (DH)
Also Called: Bmg Chrysalis
1 Park Ave Fl 18 (10016-5818)
PHONE..................212 561-3000
Hartwig Masuch, *CEO*
Jon Cohen, *Exec VP*
Claribel Caraballo, *Vice Pres*
Steve Redmond, *Vice Pres*
Dan Rosenbaum, *Vice Pres*
EMP: 20
SALES (est): 3.6MM
SALES (corp-wide): 82.3MM **Privately Held**
SIC: 2731 Books: publishing only
HQ: Bertelsmann Se & Co. Kgaa
Carl-Bertelsmann-Str. 270
Gutersloh 33330
524 180-0

(G-9114)
BNNS CO INC
71 W 47th St Ste 600-601 (10036-2866)
PHONE..................212 302-1844
Nick Barhnakov, *President*
Simon Nikhamin, *Vice Pres*
EMP: 8
SALES (est): 510K **Privately Held**
WEB: www.bnnsco.com
SIC: 3961 Costume jewelry

(G-9115)
BOARDMAN SIMONS PUBLISHING (PA)
Also Called: Davidson Publishing
55 Broad St Fl 26 (10004-2580)
PHONE..................212 620-7200
Arthur J McGinnis Jr, *President*
EMP: 40
SQ FT: 12,000
SALES (est): 8.8MM **Privately Held**
WEB: www.sbpub.com
SIC: 2721 2731 8249 Periodicals: publishing only; books: publishing only; correspondence school

(G-9116)
BOCK FAMILY HOLDINGS INC (HQ)
Also Called: 525 America
525 Fashion Ave Rm 1000 (10018-4910)
PHONE..................212 921-5688
Robert Bock, *Ch of Bd*
▲ **EMP:** 28
SQ FT: 1,700
SALES (est): 2.9MM
SALES (corp-wide): 9.3MM **Privately Held**
WEB: www.525america.com
SIC: 2339 2253 5137 Women's & misses' outerwear; knit outerwear mills; sweaters, women's & children's
PA: 525 America Llc
525 7th Ave Rm 1000
New York NY 10018
212 921-5688

(G-9117)
BOEING COMPANY
304 Park Ave S (10010-4301)
PHONE..................201 259-9400
Donald Boeing, *Branch Mgr*
EMP: 897
SALES (corp-wide): 93.3B **Publicly Held**
SIC: 3721 Airplanes, fixed or rotary wing
PA: The Boeing Company
100 N Riverside Plz
Chicago IL 60606
312 544-2000

(G-9118)
BOLLMAN HAT COMPANY
Also Called: Betmar
411 5th Ave Fl 2 (10016-2276)
PHONE..................212 981-9836
Florentino Apostadero, *Vice Pres*
Alice Gallant, *Manager*
Paula Calvert, *Creative Dir*
EMP: 6
SALES (corp-wide): 291.8MM **Privately Held**
WEB: www.bollmanhats.com
SIC: 2353 Hats, caps & millinery
PA: Bollman Hat Company
110 E Main St
Adamstown PA 19501
717 484-4361

(G-9119)
BONELLI FOODS LLC
139 Fulton St Rm 314 (10038-2537)
PHONE..................212 346-0942
Tommaso Asaro, *Mng Member*
▲ **EMP:** 1
SQ FT: 1,000
SALES: 1.4MM **Privately Held**
SIC: 2079 Olive oil

(G-9120)
BONNIER PUBLISHING USA INC
251 Park Ave S Fl 12 (10010-7302)
PHONE..................212 321-0237
Shimul Tolia, *President*
Thomas Morgan, *Finance Dir*
EMP: 40
SQ FT: 4,000
SALES (est): 1.3MM
SALES (corp-wide): 3.1B **Privately Held**
SIC: 2731 Books: publishing only
HQ: Bonnier Ab
Kungsgatan 49
Stockholm 111 2
873 640-00

(G-9121)
BOOM LLC
Also Called: Boom Creative Development
800 3rd Ave Fl 2 (10022-7683)
PHONE..................646 218-0752
Art Degaetano, *President*
Glenn Marks, *COO*
Rick Barr, *Vice Pres*
◆ **EMP:** 35
SQ FT: 12,000
SALES (est): 5.8MM **Privately Held**
WEB: www.boomllc.com
SIC: 3999 5122 Atomizers, toiletry; cosmetics, perfumes & hair products

(G-9122)
BOOSEY AND HAWKES INC (PA)
229 W 28th St Fl 11 (10001-5915)
PHONE..................212 358-5300
Steven Lankenau, *Vice Pres*
Holly Mentzer, *Manager*
Rachel Peters, *Director*
▲ **EMP:** 20
SALES (est): 3MM **Privately Held**
WEB: www.christopherrouse.com
SIC: 2741 7389 Music book & sheet music publishing; music copying service; music distribution systems

(G-9123)
BORGHESE INC (PA)
Also Called: Princess Marcella Borghese
3 E 54th St Fl 20 (10022-3130)
PHONE..................212 659-5318
Georgette Mosbacher, *President*
Christopher Stephen West, *President*
Frank Palladino, *CFO*
Michael Tugetman, *Treasurer*
▲ **EMP:** 25
SQ FT: 10,000
SALES (est): 7.6MM **Privately Held**
WEB: www.chateauxdemeures.com
SIC: 2844 5122 5961 5999 Toilet preparations; cosmetics; cosmetics & perfumes, mail order; cosmetics

(G-9124)
BOTIFY CORPORATION
119 W 24th St (10011-1913)
PHONE..................617 576-2005
Adrien Menard, *President*
Raphael D Roubin, *Accountant*
EMP: 8 **EST:** 2015
SALES (est): 204.7K
SALES (corp-wide): 247.3K **Privately Held**
SIC: 7372 Business oriented computer software
PA: Botify
22 Rue Royale
Paris 75002
183 629-078

(G-9125)
BOTKIER NY LLC
19 W 34th St Fl 7 (10001-0055)
PHONE..................212 343-2782
David Seamon,
EMP: 8
SALES (est): 604.8K **Privately Held**
SIC: 2339 Women's & misses' accessories
PA: Trebbianno, Llc
19 W 34th St Fl 7
New York NY 10001

(G-9126)
BOUCHERON JOAILLERIE USA INC
Also Called: Parfums Boucheron Jewelry
460 Park Ave Fl 12 (10022-1906)
PHONE..................212 715-7330
Thomas Indermuhle, *Ch of Bd*
EMP: 8
SALES (est): 571.7K
SALES (corp-wide): 212.2MM **Privately Held**
SIC: 3423 3915 Jewelers' hand tools; jewelers' findings & materials
HQ: Boucheron Holding
26 Place Vendome
Paris 75001
142 444-244

(G-9127)
BOULEVARD ARTS INC
1133 Broadway Ste 1523 (10010-7927)
PHONE..................917 968-8693
Elizabeth Reede, *CEO*
Chelsea Menzies, *Vice Pres*
Robert Knowles, *Surgery Dir*
EMP: 6 **EST:** 2013
SALES (est): 300K **Privately Held**
SIC: 7372 Home entertainment computer software

(G-9128)
BOUNDLESS SPATIAL INC
222 Broadway Fl 19 (10038-2550)
PHONE..................646 831-5531
Andy Dearing, *CEO*
Robert Huffman, *Partner*
Brody Stout, *COO*
Elliott Ferguson, *Vice Pres*
David Hemphill, *Vice Pres*
EMP: 35 **EST:** 2012
SALES (est): 4.5MM **Privately Held**
SIC: 7372 Business oriented computer software

(G-9129)
BOURNE MUSIC PUBLISHERS
Also Called: Bourne Co
35 W 45th St Fl 2 (10036-4918)
PHONE..................212 391-4300
Mary Elizabeth Bourne, *Owner*
EMP: 19
SQ FT: 6,500
SALES (est): 974.7K **Privately Held**
WEB: www.bournemusic.com
SIC: 2741 Music, sheet: publishing only, not printed on site

(G-9130)
BOYLAN BOTTLING CO INC
6 E 43rd St Fl 18 (10017-4657)
PHONE..................800 289-7978
Ronald C Fiorina, *President*
Mark Fiorina, *Vice Pres*
▲ **EMP:** 30 **EST:** 1891
SQ FT: 25,000
SALES (est): 6.3MM **Privately Held**
WEB: www.boylanbottling.com
SIC: 2086 2087 Soft drinks: packaged in cans, bottles, etc.; beverage bases, concentrates, syrups, powders & mixes

(G-9131)
BPE STUDIO INC
270 W 38th St Rm 702 (10018-1520)
PHONE..................212 868-9896
Dan Ping Zhang, *President*
EMP: 5
SALES (est): 410K **Privately Held**
SIC: 2396 Linings, apparel: made from purchased materials

(G-9132)
BRADLEY MARKETING GROUP INC
1431 Broadway Fl 12 (10018-1912)
PHONE..................212 967-6100
James Lemmo, *Principal*
Edward Brucia, *Vice Pres*
Kathy Reccardi, *Vice Pres*
Adam Perry, *VP Sales*
Jackie Sneyers, *Executive Asst*
EMP: 6
SALES (corp-wide): 20.1MM **Privately Held**
WEB: www.bradleymg.com
SIC: 2759 Commercial printing
PA: Bradley Marketing Group, Inc.
170 Wilbur Pl Ste 700
Bohemia NY 11716
631 231-9200

New York - New York County

(G-9133)
BRAINPOP L LC
Also Called: Brainpop Group
71 W 23rd St Fl 17 (10010-4183)
PHONE 212 574-6017
Ilana Kurizki, *CEO*
Richard Ho, *Editor*
Raffi Kahana, *Senior VP*
Mike Watanabe, *Senior VP*
Daniel Donohue, *Vice Pres*
EMP: 50
SALES (est): 6MM **Privately Held**
SIC: 7372 Educational computer software

(G-9134)
BRAL NADER FINE JEWELRY INC
576 5th Ave (10036-4807)
PHONE 800 493-1222
Nader Bral, *President*
EMP: 5
SALES: 3MM **Privately Held**
SIC: 3911 Mfg Fine Jewelry

(G-9135)
BRANNKEY INC (PA)
Also Called: Honora
1385 Broadway Fl 14 (10018-6001)
PHONE 212 371-1515
Joel Schechter, *Ch of Bd*
Roberta Schechter, *Vice Pres*
▲ **EMP:** 52 **EST:** 1969
SQ FT: 6,500
SALES (est): 10.6MM **Privately Held**
WEB: www.honora.com
SIC: 3911 Jewelry, precious metal

(G-9136)
BRASILANS PRESS PBLCATIONS INC
60 W 46th St Rm 302 (10036)
P.O. Box 985 (10185-0985)
PHONE 212 764-6161
EMP: 40
SALES (est): 2.1MM **Privately Held**
SIC: 2711 Newspapers-Publishing/Printing

(G-9137)
BRAZE INC
318 W 39th St Fl 5 (10018-1655)
PHONE 504 327-7269
William Magnuson, *CEO*
Myles Kleeger, *President*
Oliver Bell, *Treasurer*
Lauren Teixeira, *Marketing Mgr*
Jon Hyman, *CTO*
EMP: 34 **EST:** 2011
SALES: 28.3MM **Privately Held**
SIC: 7372 Application computer software

(G-9138)
BREWER-CANTELMO CO INC
Also Called: Script-Master Div
55 W 39th St Rm 205 (10018-0573)
PHONE 212 244-4600
Stephen Kirschenbaum, *President*
David Kirschenbaum, *Vice Pres*
Elissa Christian, *Sales Staff*
Danny Kirschenbaum, *Sales Staff*
Steve Kirschenbaum, *Sales Executive*
EMP: 23 **EST:** 1928
SQ FT: 9,000
SALES (est): 2.7MM **Privately Held**
WEB: www.brewer-cantelmo.com
SIC: 2782 Looseleaf binders & devices

(G-9139)
BRIGANTINE INC
225 W 37th St (10018-5703)
PHONE 212 354-8550
Isidore Friedman, *Ch of Bd*
Mark Friedman, *President*
Paul Friedman, *President*
William Fuchs, *Treasurer*
EMP: 5
SQ FT: 10,000
SALES (est): 654K
SALES (corp-wide): 8MM **Privately Held**
WEB: www.brigantine.com
SIC: 2329 2339 Men's & boys' leather, wool & down-filled outerwear; women's & misses' jackets & coats, except sportswear
PA: S. Rothschild & Co., Inc.
1407 Broadway Fl 10
New York NY 10018
212 354-8550

(G-9140)
BRIGHT KIDS NYC INC
225 Broadway Ste 1504 (10007-3704)
PHONE 917 539-4575
Bige Doruk, *CEO*
Keyosha Murray, *Manager*
▲ **EMP:** 40 **EST:** 2009
SALES: 0 **Privately Held**
SIC: 2731 8299 8748 Textbooks: publishing & printing; tutoring school; testing service, educational or personnel

(G-9141)
BRIGHTLINE VENTURES I LLC
1120 Avenue Of The Americ (10036-6700)
PHONE 212 626-6829
EMP: 26
SALES (est): 1.5MM **Privately Held**
SIC: 2099 Food preparations

(G-9142)
BRILLIANT JEWELERS/MJJ INC
Also Called: Mjj Brilliant
902 Broadway Fl 18 (10010-6038)
PHONE 212 353-2326
Nicolay Yakubovich, *Ch of Bd*
Robert Schwartz, *COO*
AVI Levy, *Vice Pres*
Jason Yakubovich, *Opers Staff*
Albert Kvint, *Production*
EMP: 120
SALES (est): 19.7MM **Privately Held**
WEB: www.mjjbrilliant.com
SIC: 3911 Jewelry, precious metal

(G-9143)
BRISTOL SEAMLESS RING CORP
209 W 86th St Apt 817 (10024-3337)
PHONE 212 874-2645
Irving Skydell, *President*
EMP: 16 **EST:** 1910
SALES (est): 173.1K **Privately Held**
SIC: 3911 Jewelry, precious metal

(G-9144)
BRISTOL-MYERS SQUIBB COMPANY (PA)
430 E 29th St Fl 14 (10016-8367)
PHONE 212 546-4000
Giovanni Caforio, *Ch of Bd*
Sandra Leung, *Exec VP*
Thomas J Lynch, *Exec VP*
Joseph C Caldarella, *Senior VP*
Mathias Hukkelhoven, *Vice Pres*
EMP: 1200 **EST:** 1887
SALES: 20.7B **Publicly Held**
WEB: www.bms.com
SIC: 2834 Drugs acting on the cardiovascular system, except diagnostic

(G-9145)
BROADCAST MANAGER INC
Also Called: Promosuite
65 Broadway Ste 602 (10006-2519)
PHONE 212 509-1200
Rocco Macri, *CEO*
Christopher Bungo, *President*
Craig Zimmerman, *President*
Matthew Jacobson, *Opers Mgr*
Rachel Field, *VP Sales*
EMP: 8
SALES (est): 890K **Privately Held**
WEB: www.broadcastmanager.org
SIC: 3651 Amplifiers: radio, public address or musical instrument

(G-9146)
BROADWAY TECHNOLOGY LLC (PA)
28 Liberty St Fl 50 (10005)
PHONE 646 912-6450
Jonathan Fieldman, *COO*
Andy Browning, *Vice Pres*
Daniel Flax, *Vice Pres*
Preston Mesick, *Accounts Mgr*
Lindsay Young, *Office Mgr*
EMP: 20
SALES: 1MM **Privately Held**
WEB: www.broadwaytechnology.com
SIC: 7372 Business oriented computer software

(G-9147)
BROKEN THREADS INC
147 W 35th St Ste 501 (10001-0070)
PHONE 212 730-4351
Rohan Shah, *Ch of Bd*
▲ **EMP:** 2 **EST:** 2007
SQ FT: 500
SALES (est): 5.1MM **Privately Held**
SIC: 2329 Men's & boys' sportswear & athletic clothing

(G-9148)
BROOKE MAYA INC
124 W 36th St Fl 7 (10018-8845)
PHONE 212 268-2626
Allen Hakimian, *President*
◆ **EMP:** 35
SQ FT: 11,000
SALES (est): 2.7MM **Privately Held**
SIC: 2361 Dresses: girls', children's & infants'

(G-9149)
BROWN PRINTING COMPANY
1500 Broadway Ste 505 (10036-4055)
PHONE 212 782-7800
Volker Peterson, *President*
EMP: 25 **EST:** 2010
SALES (est): 2.3MM **Privately Held**
SIC: 2752 Commercial printing, offset

(G-9150)
BROWN PUBLISHING NETWORK INC
122 E 42nd St Rm 2810 (10168-2893)
PHONE 212 682-3330
Marie Brown, *Branch Mgr*
EMP: 5
SALES (corp-wide): 7.2MM **Privately Held**
WEB: www.brownpubnet.com
SIC: 2731 Textbooks: publishing only, not printed on site
PA: Brown Publishing Network, Inc.
10 City Sq Ste 3
Charlestown MA 02129
781 547-7600

(G-9151)
BROWNSTONE PUBLISHERS INC
149 5th Ave Fl 10 (10010-6832)
PHONE 212 473-8200
John Striker, *President*
Andrew Shapiro, *Vice Pres*
Robert Ditosto, *Director*
John L Page, *Director*
EMP: 46
SQ FT: 10,000
SALES (est): 3.4MM **Privately Held**
SIC: 2721 2741 Periodicals: publishing only; miscellaneous publishing

(G-9152)
BRUMIS IMPORTS INC
Also Called: Core Bamboo
42 W 39th St Fl 4 (10018-3841)
PHONE 646 845-6000
Alan Bram, *President*
Steven Bram, *Vice Pres*
Yana Shum, *Controller*
Rebecca Prentice, *Natl Sales Mgr*
Rich Gonzalez, *Accounts Mgr*
▲ **EMP:** 60
SALES (est): 500MM **Privately Held**
SIC: 3634 Housewares, excluding cooking appliances & utensils

(G-9153)
BSO ENERGY CORP
125 Park Ave Ste 2507 (10017-5529)
PHONE 212 520-1827
Sergio S Correa, *President*
Roberto A Santos, *Director*
EMP: 10
SALES (est): 1.3MM **Privately Held**
SIC: 2821 Thermoplastic materials

(G-9154)
BUCKSENSE INC
140 West St Fl 2 (10007-2141)
PHONE 877 710-2825
Claudio Carnevale, *President*
Geetha Chandra, *Treasurer*
Cristian Carnevale, *Admin Sec*
EMP: 30 **EST:** 2011
SALES: 25.3MM
SALES (corp-wide): 3.1MM **Privately Held**
SIC: 2741 Miscellaneous publishing
PA: Acotel Group Spa
Via Della Valle Dei Fontanili 29/37
Roma RM 00168
066 114-1000

(G-9155)
BULKLEY DUNTON (DH)
1 Penn Plz Ste 2814 (10119-2814)
PHONE 212 863-1800
Doehner George, *President*
Bill Duggan, *Executive*
EMP: 34
SALES (est): 44.7MM
SALES (corp-wide): 8.3B **Publicly Held**
SIC: 2741 Miscellaneous publishing
HQ: Veritiv Operating Company
1000 Abernathy Rd
Atlanta GA 30328
770 391-8200

(G-9156)
BULL STREET LLC
Also Called: Supdates
19 W 69th St Apt 201 (10023-4750)
PHONE 212 495-9855
Jared Gettinger,
EMP: 5
SALES (est): 266K **Privately Held**
SIC: 7372 Application computer software

(G-9157)
BULLETT MEDIA LLC
419 Lafayette St Fl 6 (10003-7033)
PHONE 212 242-2123
Jack Becht,
EMP: 14
SALES (est): 125.2K **Privately Held**
SIC: 2721 Magazines: publishing & printing

(G-9158)
BUREAU OF NATIONAL AFFAIRS INC
25 W 43rd St Ste 1007 (10036-7410)
PHONE 212 687-4530
John Herzfeld, *Manager*
EMP: 23
SALES (corp-wide): 1.9B **Privately Held**
SIC: 2711 Newspapers
HQ: The Bureau Of National Affairs Inc
1801 S Bell St Ste Cn110
Arlington VA 22202
703 341-3000

(G-9159)
BURLEN CORP
6 E 32nd St Fl 10 (10016-5415)
PHONE 212 684-0052
Steve Klein, *President*
EMP: 12
SALES (corp-wide): 1.3B **Privately Held**
SIC: 2342 Girdles & panty girdles
HQ: Burlen Corp.
1904 Mccormick Dr
Tifton GA 31793
229 382-4100

(G-9160)
BURNS ARCHIVE PHOTOGRAPHIC DIS
140 E 38th St Frnt 1 (10016-2686)
PHONE 212 889-1938
Stanley Burns MD, *Owner*
▼ **EMP:** 4
SQ FT: 4,000
SALES: 1MM **Privately Held**
WEB: www.burnsarchive.com
SIC: 2731 8099 Book publishing; medical photography & art

(G-9161)
BUSINESS EXPERT PRESS LLC
222 E 46th St Rm 203 (10017-2906)
PHONE 212 661-8810

New York - New York County (G-9162)   GEOGRAPHIC SECTION

Sean Kaneski, *Editor*
Charlene Kronstedt, *Opers Staff*
Scott Isenberg, *Executive*
Rob Zwettler, *Executive*
Michael Dupler,
EMP: 15
SALES (est): 6.7K **Privately Held**
SIC: 2741 Miscellaneous publishing

(G-9162)
BUSINESS INTEGRITY INC (DH)
79 Madison Ave Fl 2 (10016-7805)
PHONE.................................718 238-2008
Tim Allen, *President*
Thomas Mule, *COO*
Mark Winders, *Vice Pres*
Lucia Sandin, *Marketing Staff*
EMP: 6
SQ FT: 3,000
SALES (est): 895K **Privately Held**
WEB: www.business-integrity.com
SIC: 7372 Business oriented computer software

(G-9163)
BUSINESS JOURNALS
1166 Ave Of The America (10036-2708)
PHONE.................................212 790-5100
Keith Edwards, *Manager*
EMP: 11
SALES (corp-wide): 1.4B **Privately Held**
SIC: 2711 Newspapers
HQ: The Business Journals
    120 W Morehead St Ste 420
    Charlotte NC 28202
    704 371-3248

(G-9164)
BUTTONS & TRIMCOM INC
519 8th Ave Rm 26 (10018-5275)
PHONE.................................212 868-1971
Peter Frankel, *President*
Susan Frankel, *Vice Pres*
EMP: 13
SQ FT: 2,200
SALES (est): 1.5MM **Privately Held**
SIC: 3965 3089 3499 Buttons & parts; buckles & buckle parts; novelties, plastic; novelties & specialties, metal

(G-9165)
BY ROBERT JAMES
74 Orchard St (10002-4515)
PHONE.................................212 253-2121
Robert Loomis, *Principal*
Michelle Lindsay, *Mktg Dir*
EMP: 5
SALES (est): 658.9K **Privately Held**
SIC: 2329 5611 Men's & boys' clothing; men's & boys' clothing stores

(G-9166)
BYELOCORP SCIENTIFIC INC (PA)
76 Perry St (10014-3238)
PHONE.................................212 785-2580
Lowell A Mintz, *Ch of Bd*
William Begell, *President*
Kathleen Kent, *Vice Pres*
EMP: 27
SALES (est): 1.6MM **Privately Held**
SIC: 3491 3443 Industrial valves; industrial vessels, tanks & containers

(G-9167)
BYER CALIFORNIA
1407 Broadway Rm 807 (10018-5149)
PHONE.................................212 944-8989
Martin Bernstein, *Manager*
EMP: 7
SALES (corp-wide): 372.3MM **Privately Held**
WEB: www.byer.com
SIC: 3842 Surgical appliances & supplies
PA: Byer California
    66 Potrero Ave
    San Francisco CA 94110
    415 626-7844

(G-9168)
BYLINER INC
27 W 24th St Ste 202 (10010-3299)
PHONE.................................415 680-3608
John Tayman, *CEO*
Deanna Brown, *President*
Theodore Barnett, *COO*
EMP: 20 **EST:** 2010
SALES (est): 1.4MM **Privately Held**
SIC: 2731 2741 Book publishing;

(G-9169)
BYTE CONSULTING INC
295 Madison Ave Fl 35 (10017-6414)
PHONE.................................646 500-8606
Rak Chugh, *President*
Dan Costin, *Director*
Thomas Loop, *Bd of Directors*
Kai Chuang, *Executive Asst*
EMP: 8
SALES (est): 943.6K **Privately Held**
WEB: www.byteconsulting.com
SIC: 7372 Prepackaged software

(G-9170)
C O P R A INC
Also Called: Copra
215 E Broadway Apt 2r (10002-5518)
PHONE.................................917 224-1727
Benjamin Minges, *President*
EMP: 5
SQ FT: 1,900
SALES (est): 153.8K **Privately Held**
SIC: 2037 Frozen fruits & vegetables

(G-9171)
CA INC (HQ)
520 Madison Ave Fl 22 (10022-4327)
PHONE.................................800 225-5224
Michael P Gregoire, *CEO*
Dayton Semerjian, *General Mgr*
Ava M Hahn, *Exec VP*
Kevin Gard, *Vice Pres*
James Kokoszynski, *Vice Pres*
EMP: 1500 **EST:** 1974
SALES: 4.2B
SALES (corp-wide): 17.6B **Publicly Held**
WEB: www.cai.com
SIC: 7372 8742 Business oriented computer software; application computer software; management consulting services
PA: Broadcom Inc.
    1320 Ridder Park Dr
    San Jose CA 95131
    408 433-8000

(G-9172)
CABBA PRINTING INCORPORATED
Also Called: Copyright Reprographics
133 E 55th St (10022-3502)
P.O. Box 3444 (10163-3444)
PHONE.................................212 319-4747
Carol L Schor, *President*
William F Bloxham, *Admin Sec*
EMP: 5
SQ FT: 590
SALES (est): 528K **Privately Held**
WEB: www.copyrightreprographics.com
SIC: 2752 Commercial printing, offset

(G-9173)
CABLES AND CHIPS INC (PA)
121 Fulton St Fl 4 (10038-2795)
PHONE.................................212 619-3132
Howard Feinstein, *CEO*
Susan Feinstein, *President*
Rick Scherer, *Shareholder*
EMP: 27
SQ FT: 5,500
SALES (est): 3MM **Privately Held**
WEB: www.cablesandchipsinc.com
SIC: 2298 3644 5734 5063 Cable, fiber; switch boxes, electric; computer peripheral equipment; electronic wire & cable; connectors, electronic; local area network (LAN) systems integrator

(G-9174)
CABRIOLE DESIGNS INC
315 E 91st St Ste 3 (10128-5938)
PHONE.................................212 593-4528
Louis Tonna, *President*
EMP: 6
SALES (est): 476.2K **Privately Held**
WEB: www.cabrioledesign.com
SIC: 2391 Curtains & draperies

(G-9175)
CACHET INDUSTRIES INC
463 Fashion Ave Rm 601 (10018-8720)
PHONE.................................212 944-2188
David Darouvar, *President*

Mark Naim, *Admin Sec*
▲ **EMP:** 30
SQ FT: 12,000
SALES (est): 4.8MM **Privately Held**
SIC: 2335 Wedding gowns & dresses

(G-9176)
CAI INC (PA)
Also Called: Copen International Limited
430 E 56th St (10022-4171)
PHONE.................................212 819-0008
Carin Trundle, *CEO*
Barry Emmanuel, *President*
◆ **EMP:** 35
SQ FT: 2,300
SALES (est): 4.8MM **Privately Held**
WEB: www.midsouthmfg.com
SIC: 2211 2396 Pocketing twill, cotton; waistbands, trouser

(G-9177)
CAI DESIGN INC
240 W 37th St Rm 303 (10018-2419)
PHONE.................................212 401-9973
Yiming Cai, *Partner*
Yisei Cai, *Partner*
▲ **EMP:** 14
SALES (est): 554.9K **Privately Held**
SIC: 2339 Sportswear, women's

(G-9178)
CAITHNESS EQUITIES CORPORATION (PA)
Also Called: Shepherds Flat
565 5th Ave Fl 29 (10017-2478)
PHONE.................................212 599-2112
James D Bishop Jr, *Ch of Bd*
James C Sullivan, *Senior VP*
Christopher T Mc Callion, *Vice Pres*
Gail Conboy, *Admin Sec*
EMP: 23
SALES (est): 36.1MM **Privately Held**
WEB: www.caithnessenergy.com
SIC: 3491 4911 4961 6162 Compressed gas cylinder valves; generation, electric power; steam supply systems, including geothermal; mortgage bankers

(G-9179)
CALIFORNIA PETRO TRNSPT CORP
114 W 47th St (10036-1510)
PHONE.................................212 302-5151
Frank Bilotta, *President*
EMP: 2
SALES (est): 1.9MM **Privately Held**
SIC: 2911 Petroleum refining

(G-9180)
CALIFORNIA US HOLDINGS INC
417 5th Ave Lbby 7th (10016-3380)
PHONE.................................212 726-6500
Bruno Bonnell, *President*
EMP: 564
SQ FT: 90,000
SALES (est): 28.4MM
SALES (corp-wide): 3.2MM **Privately Held**
SIC: 7372 5045 Prepackaged software; computers, peripherals & software
PA: Atari Sa
    Atari
    Paris 75009
    972 335-791

(G-9181)
CALLAWAY ARTS & ENTRMT INC
41 Union Sq W Ste 1101 (10003-3253)
PHONE.................................646 465-4667
John Lee, *CEO*
Nicholas Callaway, *President*
EMP: 11
SALES (est): 618.1K **Privately Held**
SIC: 2731 Books: publishing & printing

(G-9182)
CALLAWAY DIGITAL ARTS INC
41 Union Sq W Ste 1101 (10003-3253)
PHONE.................................212 675-3050
Rex Ishibashi, *CEO*
John Lee, *President*
Nicholas Callaway, *Officer*
EMP: 30

SALES (est): 1.8MM **Privately Held**
SIC: 7372 Application computer software

(G-9183)
CALLIDUS SOFTWARE INC
152 W 57th St Fl 8 (10019-3310)
PHONE.................................212 554-7300
Leslie Stretch, *CEO*
Robert H Youngjohns, *Ch of Bd*
Bryan Burkhart, *Vice Pres*
Richey Gupta, *Client Mgr*
Chris Dobbertin, *Accounts Exec*
EMP: 15
SALES (est): 1.1MM **Privately Held**
SIC: 7372 Business oriented computer software

(G-9184)
CALVIN KLEIN INC
654 Madison Ave (10065-8445)
PHONE.................................212 292-9000
Fax: 212 292-9001
EMP: 50
SALES (corp-wide): 8.2B **Publicly Held**
SIC: 3161 Mfg Luggage
HQ: Calvin Klein, Inc.
    205 W 39th St Lbby 2
    New York NY 10018
    212 719-2600

(G-9185)
CAMBRIDGE INFO GROUP INC (PA)
Also Called: C I G
888 7th Ave Ste 1701 (10106-1799)
PHONE.................................301 961-6700
Andrew M Snyder, *CEO*
Robert Snyder, *Chairman*
Michael K Chung, *COO*
Barbara Inkellis, *Senior VP*
Larisa Avner Trainor, *Senior VP*
EMP: 12
SQ FT: 24,000
SALES (est): 375.1MM **Privately Held**
WEB: www.csa.com
SIC: 2741 Technical manual & paper publishing

(G-9186)
CAMBRIDGE UNIVERSITY PRESS
165 Broadway Fl 20 (10006-1435)
PHONE.................................212 337-5000
Jeffrey Zingle, *Sales Staff*
Tania Saiz, *Mktg Dir*
Richard Ziemacki, *Manager*
Dieynaba Sall, *Education*
EMP: 80
SALES (corp-wide): 443.4MM **Privately Held**
SIC: 2731 2721 4226 Books: publishing only; periodicals; special warehousing & storage
PA: Cambridge University Press
    University Printing House
    Cambridge CAMBS CB2 8
    122 335-8331

(G-9187)
CAMINUS CORPORATION (DH)
340 Madison Ave Fl 8 (10173-0899)
PHONE.................................212 515-3600
John A Andrus, *President*
EMP: 65 **EST:** 1999
SALES (est): 11.7MM
SALES (corp-wide): 9.1B **Publicly Held**
SIC: 7372 7379 Business oriented computer software; computer related consulting services
HQ: Fis Data Systems Inc.
    200 Campus Dr
    Collegeville PA 19426
    484 582-2000

(G-9188)
CAMPBELL ALLIANCE GROUP INC
335 Madison Ave Fl 17 (10017-4677)
PHONE.................................212 377-2740
EMP: 24 **EST:** 1997
SQ FT: 50
SALES (est): 3MM **Privately Held**
SIC: 2834 Mfg Pharmaceutical Preparations

▲ = Import ▼=Export
◆ =Import/Export

New York - New York County

(G-9189)
CANADA GOOSE INC
601 W 26th St Rm 1745 (10001-1141)
PHONE..................................888 276-6297
EMP: 5 **Privately Held**
SIC: 2339 Uniforms, athletic: women's, misses' & juniors'
PA: Canada Goose Inc
250 Bowie Ave
Toronto ON M6E 4
416 780-9850

(G-9190)
CANADA GOOSE INC
601 W 26th St Rm 1745 (10001-1141)
PHONE..................................888 668-0625
EMP: 7 **Privately Held**
SIC: 2339 Women's & misses' outerwear
PA: Canada Goose Inc
250 Bowie Ave
Toronto ON M6E 4
416 780-9850

(G-9191)
CANALI USA INC (DH)
415 W 13th St Fl 2 (10014-1114)
PHONE..................................212 767-0205
Paolo Canali, *CEO*
Georgio Canali, *Vice Pres*
Carmine Noce, *Controller*
Alyssa Lund, *Accounts Exec*
Joel O Cardona, *Director*
▲ **EMP:** 37
SALES (est): 1.9MM **Privately Held**
SIC: 2311 Suits, men's & boys': made from purchased materials
HQ: Canali Spa
Via Lombardia 17
Sovico 20845
039 201-4226

(G-9192)
CANARY CONNECT INC
222 Broadway Fl 19 (10038-2550)
PHONE..................................212 390-8576
Adam Sager, *CEO*
Jon Troutman, *Ch Credit Ofcr*
Chris Rill, *CTO*
EMP: 120 **EST:** 2013
SALES (est): 1.7MM **Privately Held**
SIC: 3699 Security devices

(G-9193)
CANDEX SOLUTIONS INC
420 Lexington Ave Rm 300 (10170-0399)
PHONE..................................215 650-3214
Jeremy Lappin, *CEO*
Mark Steinke, *President*
Marianna Suckova, *Vice Pres*
Shani Vaza, *Vice Pres*
EMP: 5
SALES (est): 843.6K **Privately Held**
SIC: 7372 Business oriented computer software

(G-9194)
CANDLESTICKS INC
112 W 34th St Fl 18 (10120-0911)
PHONE..................................212 947-8900
Leonard Bernstein, *President*
Jay Bernstein, *Vice Pres*
Laura Bernstein, *Vice Pres*
Lawrence Bernstein, *Vice Pres*
▲ **EMP:** 10
SQ FT: 5,500
SALES (est): 1.2MM **Privately Held**
WEB: www.candlesticks.com
SIC: 2341 2369 2339 2322 Mfg Clothing

(G-9195)
CANE SUGAR LLC
Also Called: Cane Simple
950 3rd Ave Ste 2200 (10022-2773)
PHONE..................................212 329-2695
Reid Chase, *Mng Member*
EMP: 6
SALES: 230K **Privately Held**
SIC: 2062 Cane syrup from purchased raw sugar

(G-9196)
CANOPY CANOPY CANOPY INC
Also Called: TRIPLE CANOPY
264 Canal St Ste 3w (10013-3592)
PHONE..................................347 529-5182
Peter Russo, *Principal*
Bidita Choudhury, *Editor*
Seth Erickson, *Editor*
Allison Tepper, *Asst Director*
Franklin Bruno, *Author*
EMP: 1
SALES: 1.1MM **Privately Held**
SIC: 2721 Periodicals: publishing & printing

(G-9197)
CANT LIVE WITHOUT IT LLC
Also Called: S'Well Bottle
28 W 23rd St Fl 5 (10010-5259)
PHONE..................................844 517-9355
Sarah Kauss, *CEO*
Katie Garbis, *Mktg Dir*
▲ **EMP:** 100
SQ FT: 25,000
SALES (est): 40.9MM **Privately Held**
SIC: 3429 Vacuum bottles or jugs

(G-9198)
CANTON NOODLE CORPORATION
101 Mott St (10013-5093)
PHONE..................................212 226-3276
James Eng, *Principal*
EMP: 8 **EST:** 1951
SQ FT: 4,000
SALES (est): 600K **Privately Held**
SIC: 2098 Noodles (e.g. egg, plain & water), dry

(G-9199)
CANYON PUBLISHING INC
55 John St Ste 6 (10038-3752)
PHONE..................................212 334-0227
Sandra Vasceannie, *President*
EMP: 10
SALES (est): 880K **Privately Held**
SIC: 2752 Publishing Firm

(G-9200)
CAP USA JERSEYMAN HARLEM INC (PA)
112 W 125th St (10027-4403)
PHONE..................................212 222-7942
Sung R Park, *Ch of Bd*
EMP: 5
SALES (est): 401.6K **Privately Held**
SIC: 2257 Jersey cloth

(G-9201)
CAPCO WAI SHING LLC
132 W 36th St Rm 509 (10018-8843)
PHONE..................................212 268-1976
Jim Capuano, *Mng Member*
EMP: 8
SALES (est): 921.4K **Privately Held**
SIC: 3089 Clothes hangers, plastic

(G-9202)
CAPITAL E FINANCIAL GROUP
Also Called: Victoire Latam Asset MGT LLC
598 Madison Ave Fl 9 (10022-1668)
PHONE..................................212 319-6550
Nadim Razzouck, *Chairman*
EMP: 10
SALES (est): 1.2MM **Privately Held**
SIC: 3524 6799 Hedge trimmers, electric; venture capital companies
PA: Sindicatum Holdings Limited
Suite 225 10 Greycoat Place
London

(G-9203)
CAPITAL GOLD CORPORATION (PA)
601 Lexington Ave Fl 36 (10022-4611)
PHONE..................................212 668-0842
▲ **EMP:** 8
SALES (est): 15.1MM **Privately Held**
SIC: 1041 1499 Gold And Mineral Exploration

(G-9204)
CAPITAL PROGRAMS INC
Also Called: CPI
420 Lexington Ave Lbby 6 (10170-0624)
PHONE..................................212 842-4640
Sabi Kanaan, *CEO*
EMP: 7
SQ FT: 1,000
SALES (est): 590K **Privately Held**
SIC: 7372 Application computer software

(G-9205)
CARAVAN INTERNATIONAL CORP
641 Lexington Ave Fl 13 (10022-4503)
PHONE..................................212 223-7190
Ursula Cernuschi, *President*
Dennis Friedman, *Vice Pres*
EMP: 6 **EST:** 1963
SQ FT: 32,000
SALES: 2.5MM **Privately Held**
WEB: www.caravan-ny.com
SIC: 3728 5065 Aircraft parts & equipment; communication equipment

(G-9206)
CARBERT MUSIC INC
126 E 38th St (10016-2692)
PHONE..................................212 725-9277
Freddy Bienstock, *President*
EMP: 30
SQ FT: 8,000
SALES (est): 1.3MM **Privately Held**
SIC: 2741 Music book & sheet music publishing

(G-9207)
CARIBBEAN FASHION GROUP INC
Also Called: Cfg Group
1410 Broadway Rm 3202 (10018-9314)
PHONE..................................212 706-8851
Andy Tie, *President*
Marc Friedland, *President*
▲ **EMP:** 8
SQ FT: 1,200
SALES: 10MM **Privately Held**
SIC: 2329 2339 5621 Men's & boys' sportswear & athletic clothing; athletic (warmup, sweat & jogging) suits: men's & boys'; down-filled clothing: men's & boys'; women's & misses' athletic clothing & sportswear; athletic clothing: women's, misses' & juniors'; maternity clothing; women's clothing stores

(G-9208)
CARL FISCHER LLC (PA)
48 Wall St 28 (10005-2903)
PHONE..................................212 777-0900
Hayden Connor, *CEO*
Denise Eaton, *Editor*
Jessie Eppelheimer, *Mktg Coord*
Sabrina Juetting, *Office Mgr*
Shira Flescher, *Manager*
EMP: 20 **EST:** 1872
SALES (est): 2.9MM **Privately Held**
WEB: www.carlfischer.com
SIC: 2741 5736 5099 5199 Music, sheet: publishing & printing; musical instrument stores; sheet music; musical instruments parts & accessories; sheet music

(G-9209)
CARLO MONTE DESIGNS INC
17 E 48th St Fl 8 (10017-1010)
PHONE..................................212 935-5611
Karnik Garipian, *President*
Haci Garipian, *President*
EMP: 6
SQ FT: 2,400
SALES: 2.5MM **Privately Held**
WEB: www.montecarlodesigns.com
SIC: 3911 Jewelry, precious metal

(G-9210)
CARODA INC
254 W 35th St (10001-2504)
PHONE..................................212 630-9986
Ida Leigh M Law, *CEO*
EMP: 30 **EST:** 2009
SALES (est): 1.2MM **Privately Held**
SIC: 2329 Athletic (warmup, sweat & jogging) suits: men's & boys'

(G-9211)
CAROL FOR EVA GRAHAM INC
366 5th Ave Rm 815 (10001-2211)
PHONE..................................212 889-8686
Carol Graham, *President*
Eva C Graham, *Vice Pres*
EMP: 12
SQ FT: 10,000
SALES (est): 2.2MM **Privately Held**
SIC: 3961 Costume jewelry, ex. precious metal & semiprecious stones

(G-9212)
CAROL GROUP LTD
Also Called: Habitat Magazine
150 W 30th St Rm 902 (10001-4125)
PHONE..................................212 505-2030
Carol Ott, *President*
Paul Ukena, *Partner*
Ivis Fundichely, *Opers Mgr*
Chad Townsend, *Art Dir*
EMP: 7
SQ FT: 1,000
SALES: 891K **Privately Held**
WEB: www.habitatmag.com
SIC: 2721 Magazines: publishing only, not printed on site

(G-9213)
CAROLINA AMATO INC
270 W 38th St Rm 902 (10018-1759)
PHONE..................................212 768-9095
Carolina Amato, *President*
▲ **EMP:** 6 **EST:** 1977
SALES: 1.5MM **Privately Held**
WEB: www.carolinaamato.com
SIC: 2339 Women's & misses' accessories

(G-9214)
CAROLINA HERRERA LTD (HQ)
501 Fashion Ave Fl 17 (10018-5911)
PHONE..................................212 944-5757
Claudia Thomas, *President*
Carolina Herrera, *Principal*
Nate Rosenberg, *CFO*
▼ **EMP:** 45
SALES (est): 19.3MM
SALES (corp-wide): 174.2K **Privately Held**
WEB: www.carolinaherrera.com
SIC: 2337 2339 Skirts, separate: women's, misses' & juniors'; women's & misses' outerwear
PA: Equipamientos Puig Sl
Calle Lardero, 3 - Bj
Logrono
941 202-026

(G-9215)
CARRERA CASTING CORP
64 W 48th St Fl 2 (10036-1708)
PHONE..................................212 382-3296
Eric Schwartz, *Ch of Bd*
Owen Schwartz, *President*
Dean Schwartz, *Dean*
Joel Weiss, *Vice Pres*
Joseph Sorrentino, *Draft/Design*
EMP: 160
SQ FT: 8,000
SALES (est): 41.9MM **Privately Held**
WEB: www.carreracasting.net
SIC: 3915 3369 Jewelers' castings; non-ferrous foundries

(G-9216)
CARRY HOT INC
545 W 45th St Rm 501 (10036-3409)
PHONE..................................212 279-7535
Sanford Plotkin, *President*
Elizabeth Werner, *Info Tech Dir*
EMP: 10
SALES (est): 1.1MM **Privately Held**
WEB: www.carryhot.com
SIC: 2393 Bags & containers, except sleeping bags: textile

(G-9217)
CARTIHEAL INC
575 5th Ave Fl 14 (10017-2452)
PHONE..................................917 703-6992
Nir Altschuler, *CEO*
EMP: 6
SALES (est): 279.1K **Privately Held**
SIC: 3827 Optical instruments & lenses

(G-9218)
CARVART GLASS INC (PA)
1441 Broadway Fl 28 (10018-1905)
PHONE..................................212 675-0030
Antoly Geyman, *President*
Edward Geyman, *Vice Pres*
EMP: 25
SQ FT: 17,000
SALES: 5.6MM **Privately Held**
WEB: www.carvart.com
SIC: 3231 Art glass: made from purchased glass

New York - New York County (G-9219)

(G-9219)
CARVIN FRENCH JEWELERS INC
515 Madison Ave Rm 5c (10022-5439)
PHONE.................................212 755-6474
Andre Chervin, *President*
Grafinka Chunov, *Controller*
EMP: 20 **EST:** 1954
SQ FT: 4,000
SALES (est): 2.1MM **Privately Held**
SIC: 3911 3961 Jewelry, precious metal; costume jewelry

(G-9220)
CAS BIOSCIENCES LLC
1501 Broadway Fl 12 (10036-5505)
PHONE.................................844 227-2467
Steven Seltzer,
EMP: 250
SQ FT: 1,000
SALES (est): 16.2MM **Privately Held**
SIC: 2834 Pharmaceutical preparations

(G-9221)
CASABLANCA FOODS LLC
1617 3rd Ave Unit 287447 (10128-9468)
P.O. Box 287447 (10128-0025)
PHONE.................................212 317-1111
Maryam Kallamn, *Manager*
Mina Kallamni,
Fouad Kallamni,
EMP: 5
SALES (est): 900K **Privately Held**
SIC: 2099 Sauces: dry mixes; seasonings & spices; spices, including grinding; sauces: gravy, dressing & dip mixes

(G-9222)
CASSINI PARFUMS LTD
3 W 57th St Fl 8 (10019-3407)
PHONE.................................212 753-7540
EMP: 8
SQ FT: 8,000
SALES (est): 797.6K **Privately Held**
SIC: 2844 Mfg Fragrances

(G-9223)
CASTLE BRANDS INC (PA)
122 E 42nd St Rm 5000 (10168-4700)
PHONE.................................646 356-0200
Mark E Andrews III, *Ch of Bd*
Richard J Lampen, *President*
Jason Barlow, *Editor*
John S Glover, *COO*
Alejandra Pena, *Senior VP*
▲ **EMP:** 42
SQ FT: 5,000
SALES: 89.9MM **Publicly Held**
WEB: www.castlebrandsinc.com
SIC: 2085 2082 Rum (alcoholic beverage); scotch whiskey; vodka (alcoholic beverage); malt liquors

(G-9224)
CASTLE CONNOLLY MEDICAL LTD
42 W 24th St Fl 2 (10010-3201)
PHONE.................................212 367-8400
John K Castle, *Ch of Bd*
Dr John J Connolly, *President*
Mark McGinty, *President*
William Liss-Levinson, *COO*
Nicki Hughes, *Comms Mgr*
EMP: 25
SQ FT: 500
SALES (est): 3.1MM **Privately Held**
WEB: www.eldercareliving.com
SIC: 2731 2741 Books: publishing only; miscellaneous publishing

(G-9225)
CASUALS ETC INC
Also Called: E T C
16 E 52nd St Fl 4 (10022-5306)
PHONE.................................212 838-1319
William Rondina, *President*
Steven Steinberg, *CFO*
EMP: 100
SALES (est): 5MM **Privately Held**
SIC: 2339 5137 Women's & misses' athletic clothing & sportswear; sportswear, women's & children's

(G-9226)
CATALYST GROUP INC
Also Called: Catalyst Group Design
345 7th Ave Rm 1100 (10001-5165)
PHONE.................................212 243-7777
Nicholas Gould, *CEO*
Jon Mysel, *President*
Peter Hughes, *Admin Sec*
EMP: 6
SQ FT: 2,000
SALES (est): 860.7K **Privately Held**
WEB: www.catalystgroupdesign.com
SIC: 7372 Application computer software

(G-9227)
CATAPULT
1140 Broadway Rm 704 (10001-7504)
PHONE.................................323 839-6204
Russell Hunter, *Principal*
EMP: 5
SALES (est): 135.2K **Privately Held**
SIC: 3599 Catapults

(G-9228)
CATCH VENTURES INC
30 W 63rd St Apt 14o (10023-7173)
PHONE.................................347 620-4351
Scott Graulich, *President*
EMP: 10
SALES (est): 252.5K **Privately Held**
SIC: 7372 7389 Application computer software;

(G-9229)
CATHAY HOME INC (PA)
230 5th Ave Ste 215 (10001-7914)
PHONE.................................212 213-0988
Zhiming Qian, *Ch of Bd*
▲ **EMP:** 23
SQ FT: 10,000
SALES (est): 40MM **Privately Held**
SIC: 2392 Blankets, comforters & beddings

(G-9230)
CATHERINE STEIN DESIGNS INC
411 5th Ave Rm 600 (10016-2270)
PHONE.................................212 840-1188
Catherine Stein, *President*
Sharon Goldberg, *Vice Pres*
Donna Bair, *Accounts Exec*
EMP: 30
SQ FT: 10,000
SALES (est): 2MM **Privately Held**
WEB: www.csteindesigns.com
SIC: 3961 Costume jewelry, ex. precious metal & semiprecious stones

(G-9231)
CATHY DANIELS LTD (PA)
Also Called: Ecco Bay Sportswear
501 Fashion Ave Rm 400 (10018-8602)
PHONE.................................212 354-8000
Herb Chestler, *Ch of Bd*
Steven Chestler, *President*
Elizabeth Go, *Controller*
◆ **EMP:** 50
SQ FT: 20,000
SALES (est): 5.9MM **Privately Held**
WEB: www.cathydaniels.com
SIC: 2339 Sportswear, women's

(G-9232)
CAVA SPILIADIS USA
200 W 57th St Ste 908 (10019-3211)
PHONE.................................212 247-8214
Martha Tsapanos, *Principal*
▲ **EMP:** 20 **EST:** 2007
SALES (est): 205.3K **Privately Held**
SIC: 2084 Wines

(G-9233)
CCT INC
Also Called: Committee For Color & Trends
60 Madison Ave Ste 1209 (10010-1635)
P.O. Box 1621 (10159-1621)
PHONE.................................212 532-3355
Ellen Campuzano, *President*
EMP: 6
SQ FT: 1,500
SALES (est): 471.9K **Privately Held**
SIC: 2732 Books: printing only

(G-9234)
CEGID CORPORATION
274 Madison Ave Rm 1400 (10016-0701)
PHONE.................................212 757-9038
Mary Andren, *Accounts Mgr*
Lyndsey McIntosh, *Marketing Mgr*
Arnaud Coste, *Manager*
EMP: 16
SALES (est): 2MM **Privately Held**
SIC: 7372 Word processing computer software
HQ: Cegid Group
52 Quai Paul Sedallian
Lyon 69009
426 295-051

(G-9235)
CELLECTIS INC
430 E 29th St Ste 810 (10016-8367)
PHONE.................................347 809-5980
Stefan Scherer, *Senior VP*
Arjan Roozen, *Vice Pres*
Sabrina Cogoni, *QC Mgr*
Sonal Temburni, *Research*
Mathieu Simon, *Chief Mktg Ofcr*
EMP: 10
SALES (est): 1.6MM
SALES (corp-wide): 31MM **Publicly Held**
SIC: 2834 Pharmaceutical preparations
PA: Cellectis
8 Rue De La Croix Jarry
Paris 75013

(G-9236)
CEMENTEX LATEX CORP
121 Varick St Frnt 2 (10013-1408)
PHONE.................................212 741-1770
Arthur Gononsky, *President*
Susan Gononsky, *Corp Secy*
Jeff Gonosky, *Vice Pres*
▼ **EMP:** 10 **EST:** 1936
SQ FT: 12,000
SALES (est): 850K **Privately Held**
WEB: www.cementex.com
SIC: 3089 3069 5084 Plastic hardware & building products; reclaimed rubber & specialty rubber compounds; machine tools & accessories

(G-9237)
CEMEX CEMENT INC
590 Madison Ave Fl 41 (10022-2524)
PHONE.................................212 317-6000
Javier Garcia, *President*
EMP: 78 **Privately Held**
SIC: 3273 Ready-mixed concrete
HQ: Cemex Cement, Inc.
10100 Katy Fwy Ste 300
Houston TX 77043
713 650-6200

(G-9238)
CEMOI INC (PA)
5 Penn Plz Ste 2325 (10001-1810)
PHONE.................................212 583-4920
Thierry Beaujeon, *CEO*
▲ **EMP:** 2
SALES (est): 4.3MM **Privately Held**
SIC: 2066 Chocolate bars, solid

(G-9239)
CENIBRA INC
1251 Ave Of The Americas (10020-1104)
PHONE.................................212 818-8242
Yoshida Kazuhiro, *President*
▲ **EMP:** 6
SALES: 1B **Privately Held**
SIC: 2611 5159 Pulp mills; bristles

(G-9240)
CENTENNIAL MEDIA LLC
10th Floor 40 Worth St Flr 10 (10013)
PHONE.................................646 527-7320
Sebastiano Raatz, *Partner*
Benjamin Harris, *Partner*
▼ **EMP:** 15 **EST:** 2017
SALES (est): 12MM **Privately Held**
SIC: 2721 Magazines: publishing only, not printed on site

(G-9241)
CENTINEL SPINE LLC (PA)
505 Park Ave Fl 14 (10022-1106)
PHONE.................................212 583-9700
John J Viscogliosi, *CEO*
Michael Will, *President*
Wayne Malcolm, *Controller*
Daniel Levy, *VP Sales*
EMP: 5
SALES (est): 4.2MM **Privately Held**
SIC: 3842 Surgical appliances & supplies

(G-9242)
CENTRAL APPAREL GROUP LTD
Also Called: Central Park Active Wear
16 W 36th St Rm 1202 (10018-9751)
PHONE.................................212 868-6505
Shalom Asher, *CEO*
Steve Goldfarb, *President*
◆ **EMP:** 18
SQ FT: 900
SALES (est): 10MM **Privately Held**
SIC: 2339 5621 Sportswear, women's; women's sportswear

(G-9243)
CENTRAL CNFRNCE OF AMRCN RBBIS
355 Lexington Ave Fl 18 (10017-6603)
PHONE.................................212 972-3636
Jonathan A Stein, *President*
Hara Person, *Publisher*
Steven Fox, *Rabbi*
Rex Perlmeter, *Rabbi*
Walter Jacob, *Vice Pres*
▲ **EMP:** 16
SALES (est): 2.5MM **Privately Held**
WEB: www.ccarnet.org
SIC: 2731 Books: publishing only; pamphlets: publishing only, not printed on site

(G-9244)
CENTRAL MILLS INC
Also Called: Freeze Divisional Centl Mills
1400 Broadway Rm 1605 (10018-5200)
PHONE.................................212 764-9011
Solomon Shalam, *Branch Mgr*
EMP: 110
SALES (est): 16.8MM
SALES (corp-wide): 79.1MM **Privately Held**
SIC: 2329 2339 2253 Men's & boys' sportswear & athletic clothing; women's & misses' outerwear; T-shirts & tops, knit
PA: Central Mills, Inc.
473 Ridge Rd
Dayton NJ 08810
732 329-2009

(G-9245)
CENTRAL TEXTILES INC
Also Called: Cotswolt Industries
10 E 40th St Rm 3410 (10016-0301)
PHONE.................................212 213-8740
Steve Rosenberg, *Sales Staff*
James McKinnon, *Manager*
EMP: 15
SALES (corp-wide): 48.7MM **Privately Held**
WEB: www.ctextiles.com
SIC: 2261 2262 Finishing plants, cotton; finishing plants, manmade fiber & silk fabrics
PA: Central Textiles, Inc.
237 Mill Ave
Central SC 29630
864 639-2491

(G-9246)
CENTRIC BRANDS INC (PA)
350 5th Ave Lbby 6 (10118-0224)
PHONE.................................323 890-1800
Jason Rabin, *CEO*
Anurup Pruthi, *CFO*
EMP: 80
SQ FT: 30,915
SALES: 164MM **Publicly Held**
WEB: www.innovogroup.com
SIC: 2337 2339 2311 2325 Jeans: women's, misses' & juniors'; men's & boys' suits & coats; jeans: men's, youths' & boys'; accessory products, leather; handbag leather; shoe leather; apparel belts; women's & misses' suits & skirts

(G-9247)
CENTRIC DENIM USA LLC (DH)
Also Called: Gbg Denim Usa, LLC
350 5th Ave Lbby 9 (10118-0109)
PHONE.................................646 839-7000
Bruce Philip Rockowitz, *CEO*

GEOGRAPHIC SECTION

New York - New York County (G-9275)

EMP: 15
SALES (est): 4.5MM **Privately Held**
SIC: 2325 2339 5651 Jeans: men's, youths' & boys'; jeans: women's, misses' & juniors'; jeans stores
HQ: Gbg Usa Inc.
350 5th Ave Lbby 11
New York NY 10118
646 839-7000

(G-9248)
CENTRIC WEST LLC (HQ)
Also Called: Joes Jeans
350 5th Ave Fl 5 (10118-0110)
PHONE..................................646 839-7000
Suzy Biszantz, *CEO*
Elena Pickett, *Senior VP*
EMP: 110
SQ FT: 150,000
SALES (est): 54.5MM
SALES (corp-wide): 164MM **Publicly Held**
SIC: 2339 Jeans: women's, misses' & juniors'
PA: Centric Brands Inc.
350 5th Ave Lbby 6
New York NY 10118
323 890-1800

(G-9249)
CENTRO INC
841 Broadway Fl 6 (10003-4704)
P.O. Box 13464, Chicago IL (60613-0426)
PHONE..................................212 791-9450
EMP: 265
SALES (corp-wide): 23.6MM **Privately Held**
SIC: 3089 Plastic processing
PA: Centro, Inc.
11 E Madison St Ste 300
Chicago IL 60602
312 642-7348

(G-9250)
CENTURY GRAND INC
Also Called: Century Pharmacy Three
302 Grand St (10002-4465)
PHONE..................................212 925-3838
Steven T Ho, *Principal*
EMP: 10
SALES (est): 1.3MM **Privately Held**
SIC: 2834 Druggists' preparations (pharmaceuticals)

(G-9251)
CEO CAST INC
211 E 43rd St Rm 400 (10017-8620)
PHONE..................................212 732-4300
Kenneth Sgro, *President*
Jim Fallon, *Managing Prtnr*
EMP: 18
SQ FT: 25,000
SALES (est): 1.3MM **Privately Held**
WEB: www.ceocast.com
SIC: 2741 Business service newsletters: publishing & printing

(G-9252)
CEROS INC (PA)
40 W 25th St Fl 12 (10010-2759)
PHONE..................................347 744-9250
Simon Burg, *CEO*
Noelle Tassey, *Opers Staff*
Aaron Wood, *QA Dir*
Kaity Ng, *Controller*
Elina Strizhak, *Human Resources*
EMP: 30 EST: 2007
SALES (est): 4.3MM **Privately Held**
SIC: 7372 Publishers' computer software

(G-9253)
CFO PUBLISHING LLC (PA)
50 Broad St Frnt (10004-2354)
PHONE..................................212 459-3004
Alan Glass, *President*
Richard Rivera, *President*
EMP: 42
SQ FT: 7,500
SALES (est): 8MM **Privately Held**
SIC: 2721 Magazines: publishing only, not printed on site

(G-9254)
CGI TECHNOLOGIES SOLUTIONS INC
655 3rd Ave Ste 700 (10017-9124)
PHONE..................................212 682-7411
Don O'Brien, *Principal*
EMP: 15
SALES (corp-wide): 8.6B **Privately Held**
SIC: 7372 5045 7379 Prepackaged software; computer software; computer related consulting services
HQ: Cgi Technologies And Solutions Inc.
11325 Random Hills Rd
Fairfax VA 22030
703 267-8000

(G-9255)
CHAIN STORE AGE MAGAZINE
425 Park Ave (10022-3506)
PHONE..................................212 756-5000
EMP: 5
SQ FT: 30,000
SALES (est): 402.6K
SALES (corp-wide): 122.5MM **Privately Held**
SIC: 2731 Book Publisher
PA: Lebhar-Friedman, Inc.
150 W 30th St Fl 19
New York NY 33610
212 756-5000

(G-9256)
CHAINDOM ENTERPRISES INC
48 W 48th St Ste 200 (10036-1779)
PHONE..................................212 719-4778
Fikri Akdemir, *President*
Steve Pinkin, *Treasurer*
EMP: 6
SQ FT: 2,500
SALES (est): 533.5K **Privately Held**
SIC: 3911 Jewelry, precious metal

(G-9257)
CHAM COLD BREW LLC
300 Park Ave Fl 12 (10022-7419)
PHONE..................................646 926-0206
Niko Nikolaou, *CEO*
Georgia Masouras, *CFO*
EMP: 5
SALES (est): 124.5K **Privately Held**
SIC: 2086 5149 Iced tea & fruit drinks, bottled & canned; coffee & tea

(G-9258)
CHAMPION ZIPPER CORP
Also Called: Sew True
447 W 36th St Fl 2 (10018-6300)
PHONE..................................212 239-0414
Steven Silberberg, *President*
Chris Roldan, *Principal*
EMP: 6
SQ FT: 5,000
SALES (est): 1.3MM **Privately Held**
WEB: www.sewtrue.com
SIC: 3965 2241 Zipper; trimmings, textile

(G-9259)
CHANSE PETROLEUM CORPORATION (PA)
828 5th Ave Apt 1f (10065-7272)
PHONE..................................212 682-3789
Kai Chang, *President*
EMP: 3 EST: 1972
SQ FT: 1,000
SALES (est): 1.5MM **Privately Held**
SIC: 1311 Crude petroleum production; natural gas production

(G-9260)
CHARING CROSS MUSIC INC
3 Columbus Cir Ste 1720 (10019-8708)
PHONE..................................212 541-7571
Paul Simon, *President*
EMP: 6
SQ FT: 1,000
SALES (est): 410K **Privately Held**
SIC: 2741 Music, sheet: publishing only, not printed on site

(G-9261)
CHARIS & MAE INC
31 W 34th St Fl 8 (10001-3030)
PHONE..................................212 641-0816
Yi Shan Su, *President*
EMP: 5

SALES (est): 239.4K **Privately Held**
SIC: 3911 Jewelry, precious metal

(G-9262)
CHARLES HENRICKS INC
Also Called: Starkey & Henricks
70 W 36th St Rm 500 (10018-8050)
PHONE..................................212 243-5800
Peter Bird, *President*
EMP: 15
SALES (est): 1.6MM **Privately Held**
SIC: 2796 Gravure printing plates or cylinders, preparation of

(G-9263)
CHARLES KRYPELL INC
22 W 48th St Ste 801-803 (10036-1819)
PHONE..................................212 752-3313
Charles Krypell, *President*
Debbie Krypell, *Vice Pres*
Brian Krypell, *Sales Mgr*
Evan Krypell, *Sales Mgr*
Judy Loew, *Accounts Exec*
EMP: 20 EST: 1989
SALES (est): 499.5K **Privately Held**
WEB: www.charleskrypell.com
SIC: 3911 Jewelry, precious metal

(G-9264)
CHARLES P ROGERS BRASS BEDS (PA)
Also Called: Charles P Rogers Brass Ir Bed
26 W 17th St (10011-5710)
PHONE..................................212 675-4400
Linda Klein, *President*
David Klein, *Vice Pres*
Donnie Ray, *Vice Pres*
William Mardorf, *Sales Staff*
Chung Wan, *Webmaster*
◆ **EMP:** 15 EST: 1979
SQ FT: 9,000
SALES (est): 3.9MM **Privately Held**
SIC: 2514 5712 5961 Beds, including folding & cabinet, household: metal; beds & accessories; furniture & furnishings, mail order

(G-9265)
CHARLES VAILLANT INC
37 W 57th St Ste 803 (10019-3411)
PHONE..................................212 752-4832
Thomas Renna, *President*
Kenneth Danielsson, *Admin Sec*
▲ **EMP:** 7
SALES (est): 705.3K **Privately Held**
SIC: 3911 Jewelry, precious metal

(G-9266)
CHARMING FASHION INC
247 W 38th St Rm 1400 (10018-0230)
PHONE..................................212 730-2872
Charles Kim, *President*
EMP: 5
SALES (est): 261K **Privately Held**
SIC: 2211 Apparel & outerwear fabrics, cotton

(G-9267)
CHARTER VENTURES LLC
135 W 36th St Rm 1800 (10018-6951)
PHONE..................................212 868-0222
Jennifer Lai,
Howard Cohen,
▲ **EMP:** 10 EST: 2000
SQ FT: 4,838
SALES (est): 1.5MM
SALES (corp-wide): 100MM **Privately Held**
SIC: 2253 Sweaters & sweater coats, knit
PA: Charter Ventures Limited
6a/F Chiap Luen Indl Bldg
Kwai Chung NT
221 106-07

(G-9268)
CHECK GROUP LLC
1385 Broadway Fl 16 (10018-6041)
PHONE..................................212 221-4700
Lawrence Jemal,
Richard Tan, *Admin Sec*
▲ **EMP:** 100 EST: 1999

SALES (est): 6.8MM **Privately Held**
WEB: www.checkgroup.com
SIC: 2311 2321 2322 2325 Men's & boys' suits & coats; men's & boys' furnishings; underwear, men's & boys': made from purchased materials; men's & boys' trousers & slacks

(G-9269)
CHELSEA PLASTICS INC
200 Lexington Ave Rm 914 (10016-6255)
PHONE..................................212 924-4530
George Frechter, *President*
EMP: 12
SQ FT: 7,000
SALES (est): 1.5MM **Privately Held**
WEB: www.chelseaplastics.com
SIC: 3082 Unsupported plastics profile shapes

(G-9270)
CHERI MON BABY LLC
1412 Broadway Rm 1608 (10018-9270)
PHONE..................................212 354-5511
Ralph Kassin, *President*
▲ **EMP:** 6
SQ FT: 1,500
SALES (est): 605.9K **Privately Held**
SIC: 2361 Girls' & children's blouses & shirts

(G-9271)
CHERRY LANE MAGAZINE LLC
1745 Broadway 19 (10019-4640)
PHONE..................................212 561-3000
Peter Primont, *Mng Member*
EMP: 80
SQ FT: 30,000
SALES (est): 4.9MM **Privately Held**
SIC: 2741 Miscellaneous publishing

(G-9272)
CHESKY RECORDS INC
1650 Broadway Ste 900 (10019-6965)
PHONE..................................212 586-7799
Norman Chesky, *President*
David Chesky, *Vice Pres*
Jeff Lanier, *Manager*
EMP: 12
SQ FT: 6,000
SALES (est): 1.2MM **Privately Held**
SIC: 3652 Phonograph record blanks; compact laser discs, prerecorded

(G-9273)
CHF INDUSTRIES INC (PA)
1 Park Ave Fl 9 (10016-5803)
P.O. Box 410727, Charlotte NC (28241-0727)
PHONE..................................212 951-7800
Frank Foley, *President*
Spencer Foley, *Vice Pres*
Donald Harwood, *Vice Pres*
Don Harwood, *CFO*
Kelly Dennis, *Credit Mgr*
▲ **EMP:** 30
SQ FT: 50,000
SALES (est): 99.4MM **Privately Held**
SIC: 2221 5023 Bedding, manmade or silk fabric; window covering parts & accessories; linens & towels

(G-9274)
CHIA USA LLC
Also Called: Chia Company
379 W Broadway (10012-5121)
PHONE..................................212 226-7512
John Foss, *CEO*
April Helliwell, *COO*
EMP: 1 EST: 2014
SQ FT: 3,000
SALES (est): 18MM
SALES (corp-wide): 26MM **Privately Held**
SIC: 2043 5153 Cereal breakfast foods; grains; barley
PA: Chia Inc.
379 W Broadway
New York NY 10012
212 226-7512

(G-9275)
CHILD NUTRITION PROG DEPT ED
1011 1st Ave Fl 6 (10022-4112)
PHONE..................................212 371-1000

Thomas Smith, *President*
Christine Plantamura, *Admin Asst*
EMP: 99
SALES (est): 3.6MM Privately Held
SIC: 2099 Food preparations

(G-9276)
CHILDRENS PROGRESS INC
108 W 39th St Rm 1305 (10018-8258)
PHONE..................212 730-0905
Kevin Greaney, *President*
Pat Santo, *Business Mgr*
EMP: 20
SQ FT: 1,700
SALES (est): 1.5MM Privately Held
WEB: www.childrensprogress.com
SIC: 7372 Educational computer software

(G-9277)
CHINA DAILY DISTRIBUTION CORP (HQ)
1500 Broadway Ste 2800 (10036-4097)
PHONE..................212 537-8888
Larry Lee, *CEO*
Leshuo Dong, *General Mgr*
Kenny Zheng, *Graphic Designe*
Davis Chris Wes, *Instructor*
EMP: 20
SALES (est): 1.2MM Privately Held
SIC: 2711 Newspapers
PA: China Daily
No.15, Huixin East Street, Chaoyang District
Beijing
106 499-5969

(G-9278)
CHINA HUAREN ORGANIC PDTS INC
100 Wall St Fl 15 (10005-3701)
PHONE..................212 232-0120
Cao Yushu, *CEO*
▲ EMP: 3
SALES: 7.4MM Privately Held
WEB: www.ultradatasystems.com
SIC: 2099 2844 Food preparations; toilet preparations; cosmetic preparations

(G-9279)
CHINA INDUSTRIAL STEEL INC
110 Wall St Fl 11 (10005-3834)
PHONE..................646 328-1502
Shenghong Liu, *Principal*
EMP: 2
SALES: 649.3MM Privately Held
SIC: 3312 Blast furnaces & steel mills

(G-9280)
CHINA LITHIUM TECHNOLOGIES (PA)
15 W 39th St Fl 14 (10018-0626)
PHONE..................212 391-2688
EMP: 9
SQ FT: 215
SALES: 15.7MM Privately Held
SIC: 3691 3629 Mfg Storage Batteries Mfg Electrical Industrial Apparatus

(G-9281)
CHINA N E PETRO HOLDINGS LTD
445 Park Ave (10022-2606)
PHONE..................212 307-3568
Jingfu LI, *CEO*
Shaohui Chen, *CFO*
EMP: 715
SALES: 99.5MM Privately Held
WEB: www.cnepetroleum.com
SIC: 1311 Crude petroleum production

(G-9282)
CHINA NEWSWEEK CORPORATION
15 E 40th St Fl 11 (10016-0463)
PHONE..................212 481-2510
WEI Xiang Peng, *Ch of Bd*
Fred Teng, *Exec Dir*
EMP: 10
SALES (est): 440K Privately Held
SIC: 2711 Newspapers

(G-9283)
CHINA TING FASHION GROUP (USA) (HQ)
525 7th Ave Rm 1606 (10018-0401)
PHONE..................212 716-1600
Ren Shen, *President*
▲ EMP: 7
SALES: 8.5MM
SALES (corp-wide): 12.4MM Privately Held
SIC: 2269 2335 2339 Linen fabrics: dyeing, finishing & printing; dresses, paper: cut & sewn; ensemble dresses: women's, misses' & juniors'; women's & misses' outerwear
PA: Zhejiang China Ting Group Co., Ltd.
No.56, Beisha East Road, Yuhang District
Hangzhou 31119
571 862-5918

(G-9284)
CHINA XD PLASTICS COMPANY LTD
500 5th Ave Ste 938 (10110-0008)
PHONE..................212 747-1118
Taylor Zhang, *CEO*
EMP: 6
SALES (est): 594.4K Privately Held
SIC: 3086 Plastics foam products
PA: China Xd Plastics Company Limited
11 Broadway Ste 1004
New York NY

(G-9285)
CHLOE INTERNATIONAL INC
525 Fashion Ave Rm 1601 (10018-0545)
PHONE..................212 730-6661
Leon Hedvat, *CEO*
Faramarz Hedvat, *Ch of Bd*
Behrooz Hedvat, *President*
▲ EMP: 15
SALES (est): 2.4MM Privately Held
SIC: 2339 Service apparel, washable: women's

(G-9286)
CHOCNYC LLC
4996 Broadway (10034-1635)
PHONE..................917 804-4848
Jemal Edwards, *Principal*
Brad Jon Doles, *Principal*
Dewayne Jemal Edwards, *Principal*
EMP: 6
SALES (est): 246.3K Privately Held
SIC: 2051 Cakes, bakery: except frozen

(G-9287)
CHOCOLAT MODERNE LLC
27 W 20th St Ste 904 (10011-3725)
PHONE..................212 229-4797
Joan Coukos, *Mng Member*
▲ EMP: 5
SQ FT: 950
SALES (est): 250K Privately Held
WEB: www.chocolatmoderne.com
SIC: 2064 5145 5961 Candy & other confectionery products; candy; mail order house

(G-9288)
CHOPT CREATIVE SALAD CO LLC (PA)
853 Broadway Ste 606 (10003-4723)
PHONE..................646 233-2923
Guillermo Flores, *General Mgr*
Cole Thomas, *General Mgr*
Laura Parada, *District Mgr*
Tom Kelleher, *Vice Pres*
Erica Retblatt, *Vice Pres*
EMP: 10
SALES (est): 31.5MM Privately Held
SIC: 2099 Ready-to-eat meals, salads & sandwiches

(G-9289)
CHRISTIAN CASEY LLC (PA)
Also Called: Sean John
1440 Broadway Frnt 3 (10018-2301)
PHONE..................212 500-2200
Dawn Robertson,
Sean John,
▲ EMP: 40
SQ FT: 5,000
SALES (est): 20.3MM Privately Held
SIC: 2325 2322 2321 2311 Men's & boys' trousers & slacks; men's & boys' underwear & nightwear; men's & boys' furnishings; men's & boys' suits & coats

(G-9290)
CHRISTIAN CASEY LLC
Also Called: Sean John Clothing
1440 Broadway Frnt 3 (10018-2301)
PHONE..................212 500-2200
Kevin Lowney, *Branch Mgr*
EMP: 37
SALES (corp-wide): 20.3MM Privately Held
SIC: 2325 2322 2321 2311 Men's & boys' trousers & slacks; men's & boys' underwear & nightwear; men's & boys' furnishings; men's & boys' suits & coats
PA: Christian Casey Llc
1440 Broadway Frnt 3
New York NY 10018
212 500-2200

(G-9291)
CHRISTIAN DIOR PERFUMES LLC (DH)
19 E 57th St (10022-2506)
PHONE..................212 931-2200
Pamela Baxter, *CEO*
Scott Johnson, *COO*
Joanna Grillo, *Vice Pres*
Diana Miles, *Vice Pres*
Pertrand Tesra, *Vice Pres*
◆ EMP: 35
SALES: 34.2MM
SALES (corp-wide): 315.2MM Privately Held
WEB: www.saniflo.com
SIC: 2844 3999 Perfumes, natural or synthetic; cosmetic preparations; atomizers, toiletry
HQ: Parfums Christian Dior
33 Avenue Hoche
Paris 75008
153 423-600

(G-9292)
CHRISTIAN SIRIANO HOLDINGS LLC
5 W 54th St (10019-5404)
PHONE..................212 695-5494
Christian Siriano, *Managing Dir*
EMP: 9
SQ FT: 3,000
SALES (est): 1.2MM Privately Held
SIC: 2335 Women's, juniors' & misses' dresses

(G-9293)
CHRISTINA SALES INC
1441 Broadway (10018-1905)
PHONE..................212 391-0710
Joey Schwebel, *President*
▲ EMP: 10
SQ FT: 5,000
SALES (est): 1.2MM Privately Held
SIC: 2339 5137 Bathing suits: women's, misses' & juniors'; swimsuits: women's, children's & infants'

(G-9294)
CHRISTOPHER DESIGNS INC
50 W 47th St Ste 1507 (10036-8687)
PHONE..................212 382-1013
Christopher Slowinski, *President*
Ewa Slowinski, *Vice Pres*
Barbara Oleksiak, *Production*
Kuba Lipien, *Technology*
Ursula Piekut, *Director*
▲ EMP: 27
SQ FT: 3,800
SALES (est): 4MM Privately Held
WEB: www.christopherdesigns.com
SIC: 3915 3911 Jewelers' materials & lapidary work; jewelry, precious metal

(G-9295)
CHRISTOS INC
318 W 39th St Fl 12 (10018-1484)
PHONE..................212 921-0025
Christos Yiannakou, *President*
Michael Decuollo, *Vice Pres*
▲ EMP: 37
SQ FT: 7,500
SALES (est): 2.4MM Privately Held
WEB: www.christosbridal.com
SIC: 2335 Wedding gowns & dresses

(G-9296)
CHURCH PUBLISHING INCORPORATED (HQ)
Also Called: Morehouse Publishing
445 5th Ave Frnt 1 (10016-0133)
PHONE..................212 592-1800
Alan F Blanchard, *President*
▼ EMP: 8
SALES (est): 1MM
SALES (corp-wide): 337.6MM Privately Held
WEB: www.preparingforsunday.com
SIC: 2731 Books: publishing only
PA: Church Pension Group Services Corporation
19 E 34th St
New York NY 10016
212 592-1800

(G-9297)
CINCH TECHNOLOGIES INC
7 World Trade Ctr (10007-2140)
PHONE..................212 266-0022
Maya Komerov, *CEO*
EMP: 6 EST: 2017
SALES: 100K Privately Held
SIC: 7372 Prepackaged software

(G-9298)
CINDERELLA PRESS LTD
327 Canal St 3 (10013-2513)
PHONE..................212 431-3130
Robert Cenedella, *President*
Peter Nashel, *Mktg Dir*
EMP: 6
SALES (est): 548.5K Privately Held
SIC: 2731 Books: publishing only

(G-9299)
CINE DESIGN GROUP LLC
Also Called: Cinedeck
15 Park Row Lbby L (10038-2321)
PHONE..................646 747-0734
Charles Dautremont,
EMP: 8
SQ FT: 5,000
SALES (est): 737.2K Privately Held
SIC: 3575 Cathode ray tube (CRT), computer terminal

(G-9300)
CINEDIGM SOFTWARE
45 W 36th St Fl 7 (10018-7634)
PHONE..................212 206-9001
Dan Sherlock, *President*
Jill Calcaterra, *Principal*
Diane Anselmo, *Vice Pres*
Dan Coyle, *Vice Pres*
Tom Hassell, *Vice Pres*
EMP: 5
SALES (est): 303.4K Privately Held
SIC: 7372 Prepackaged software

(G-9301)
CINER MANUFACTURING CO INC
20 W 37th St Fl 10 (10018-7484)
PHONE..................212 947-3770
David Hill, *President*
Patricia Ciner Hill, *Vice Pres*
EMP: 28
SQ FT: 6,000
SALES (est): 3.7MM Privately Held
SIC: 3961 Costume jewelry, ex. precious metal & semiprecious stones

(G-9302)
CIRCLE PEAK CAPITAL MGT LLC (PA)
1325 Ave Of The Americas (10019-6026)
PHONE..................646 230-8812
R Adam Smith, *CEO*
James H Clippard, *Principal*
Holbrook M Forusz, *Principal*
John R Jonge Poerink,
▲ EMP: 30
SALES (est): 733.9MM Privately Held
SIC: 2053 6799 Pies, bakery: frozen; venture capital companies

GEOGRAPHIC SECTION

New York - New York County (G-9330)

(G-9303)
CIRCLE PRESS INC (PA)
Also Called: Press Room New York Division
121 Varick St Fl 4 (10013-1408)
PHONE................................212 924-4277
Richard T Springer, *President*
Lawrence Lembo, *Vice Pres*
Benjamin Caringal, *Treasurer*
Gary Lacinski, *Business Dir*
EMP: 53
SQ FT: 30,000
SALES (est): 5.6MM **Privately Held**
SIC: 2752 2796 Commercial printing, lithographic; platemaking services

(G-9304)
CISCO SYSTEMS INC
1 Penn Plz Ste 3306 (10119-3306)
PHONE................................212 714-4000
Carl Demarco, *Partner*
Chuck Scheifele, *Partner*
Cliff Thomas, *Managing Dir*
Christopher Augenstein, *Regional Mgr*
Adam Pasieka, *Regional Mgr*
EMP: 250
SALES (corp-wide): 49.3B **Publicly Held**
WEB: www.cisco.com
SIC: 3577 7373 Data conversion equipment, media-to-media: computer; computer integrated systems design
PA: Cisco Systems, Inc.
170 W Tasman Dr
San Jose CA 95134
408 526-4000

(G-9305)
CIT AEROSPACE LLC
11 W 42nd St (10036-8002)
PHONE................................212 461-5200
EMP: 5
SALES (est): 103K **Privately Held**
SIC: 3812 Search & navigation equipment
PA: Hkac Holdings (Ireland) Limited
5th Floor
Dun Laoghaire

(G-9306)
CITIGROUP INC
388 Greenwich St (10013-2375)
PHONE................................212 816-6000
Michael Carpenter, *CEO*
ARI Glazer, *President*
Barbara Tasiounis, *President*
Peter Charles, *Managing Dir*
Jack Jared, *Managing Dir*
EMP: 97
SALES (corp-wide): 71.4B **Publicly Held**
SIC: 2621 Parchment, securites & bank note papers
PA: Citigroup Inc.
388 Greenwich St
New York NY 10013
212 559-1000

(G-9307)
CITISOURCE INDUSTRIES INC
244 5th Ave Ste 229 (10001-7604)
PHONE................................212 683-1033
◆ **EMP:** 30
SALES (est): 3.9MM **Privately Held**
SIC: 2231 5131 Wool Broadwoven Fabric Mill Whol Piece Goods/Notions

(G-9308)
CITIXSYS TECHNOLOGIES INC
1 Rockefeller Plz Fl 11 (10020-2073)
PHONE................................212 745-1365
Kamal Karmakar, *CEO*
Pankaj Mathur, *COO*
Paula Da Silva, *Senior VP*
Paula Dasilva, *Senior VP*
Ajay Mamgain, *Vice Pres*
EMP: 8
SALES (est): 974.8K **Privately Held**
SIC: 7372 Prepackaged software

(G-9309)
CITY AND STATE NY LLC
Also Called: Think Tank
61 Broadway Rm 1315 (10006-2721)
PHONE................................212 268-0442
Tom Allon, *CEO*
Lissa Blake, *Publisher*
Kelly Murphy, *Publisher*
Jim Katocin, *Vice Pres*
Dawn M Rubino, *Manager*

EMP: 27 **EST:** 2012
SALES (est): 1.3MM **Privately Held**
SIC: 2721 Magazines: publishing & printing

(G-9310)
CITY BAKERY INC (PA)
Also Called: Maury's Cookie Dough
3 W 18th St Frnt 1 (10011-4610)
PHONE................................212 366-1414
Maury Rubin, *President*
Cheryl Winnicki, *Admin Asst*
EMP: 30
SQ FT: 2,000
SALES (est): 3MM **Privately Held**
SIC: 2051 Bakery: wholesale or wholesale/retail combined

(G-9311)
CITY CASTING CORP
151 W 46th St Fl 5 (10036-8512)
PHONE................................212 938-0511
Luis Ontiveros, *CEO*
EMP: 7
SALES (est): 946.3K **Privately Held**
SIC: 3369 White metal castings (lead, tin, antimony), except die

(G-9312)
CITY SPORTS INC
64 W 48th St Frnt B (10036-1708)
PHONE................................212 730-2009
EMP: 6
SALES (corp-wide): 135.8MM **Privately Held**
SIC: 3949 Mfg Sporting/Athletic Goods
PA: City Sports, Inc.
77 N Washington St # 500
Boston MA 02114
617 391-9100

(G-9313)
CITY SPORTS IMAGING INC
20 E 46th St Rm 200 (10017-9287)
PHONE................................212 481-3600
Lawrence Silverberg, *President*
EMP: 20
SALES (est): 1.2MM **Privately Held**
SIC: 3845 Magnetic resonance imaging device, nuclear

(G-9314)
CITYSCAPE OB/GYN PLLC
38 E 32nd St Fl 4 (10016-5567)
PHONE................................212 683-3595
Heidi S Rosenberg, *Principal*
EMP: 19
SALES (est): 2.7MM **Privately Held**
SIC: 3842 Gynecological supplies & appliances

(G-9315)
CITYWIRE LLC
Also Called: Citywire Americas
1350 Ave Of The Am Frnt 4 (10019)
PHONE................................646 503-2216
Michelle Abrego, *Editor*
Atholl Simpson, *Editor*
Marissa Lewis, *Mng Member*
Samantha Muratori, *Manager*
Crystelle Tap, *Manager*
EMP: 13
SALES (est): 1.5MM
SALES (corp-wide): 45.7MM **Privately Held**
SIC: 2711 Newspapers
HQ: Citywire Financial Publishers Ltd
87 Vauxhall Walk
London SE11
207 840-2250

(G-9316)
CJ JEWELRY INC
2 W 47th St Ste 1106 (10036-3318)
PHONE................................212 719-2464
Chaim Fischman, *President*
▲ **EMP:** 12
SALES (est): 1.3MM **Privately Held**
WEB: www.cjjewelry.com
SIC: 3911 Jewelry apparel

(G-9317)
CLARKSON N POTTER INC
1745 Broadway (10019-4640)
PHONE................................212 782-9000
Lauren Shakely, *Director*
▲ **EMP:** 17

SALES (est): 654.7K
SALES (corp-wide): 82.3MM **Privately Held**
WEB: www.anchorbooks.com
SIC: 2731 Books: publishing only
HQ: Penguin Random House Llc
1745 Broadway
New York NY 10019
212 782-9000

(G-9318)
CLASSIC BUSINESS SOLUTIONS
42 W 38th St Rm 1204 (10018-0054)
PHONE................................212 563-9100
David Beck, *President*
David Wiley, *Mktg Coord*
Michael Yoon, *Graphic Designe*
▲ **EMP:** 5
SALES (est): 789.8K **Privately Held**
WEB: www.classicbusinesssolutions.com
SIC: 2752 Commercial printing, lithographic

(G-9319)
CLASSIC DESIGNER WORKSHOP INC
265 W 37th St Rm 703 (10018-5929)
PHONE................................212 730-8480
Keith Lin, *General Mgr*
EMP: 8
SALES (est): 631.2K **Privately Held**
SIC: 2326 2341 Industrial garments, men's & boys'; women's & children's undergarments

(G-9320)
CLASSIC FLAVORS FRAGRANCES INC
878 W End Ave Apt 12b (10025-4957)
PHONE................................212 777-0004
George Ivolin, *CEO*
EMP: 6
SQ FT: 750
SALES (est): 836K **Privately Held**
SIC: 2869 2899 5122 5169 Flavors or flavoring materials, synthetic; perfumes, flavorings & food additives; chemical preparations: essential oils; cosmetics, perfumes & hair products; aromatic chemicals; chemical additives; essential oils

(G-9321)
CLASSIC SOFA LTD
130 E 63rd St Ph B (10065-7340)
PHONE................................212 620-0485
Jeffrey Stone, *President*
Maurice Stone, *Shareholder*
▲ **EMP:** 55
SQ FT: 15,000
SALES (est): 6.2MM **Privately Held**
SIC: 2512 5712 Couches, sofas & davenports: upholstered on wood frames; furniture stores

(G-9322)
CLASSPASS INC (PA)
275 7th Ave Fl 11 (10001-6708)
PHONE................................888 493-5953
Kristina Baker, *Partner*
Claire Goodill, *Partner*
Jen Burke, *General Mgr*
Valerie Meyer, *General Mgr*
Payal Kadakia, *Principal*
EMP: 29
SALES (est): 7.6MM **Privately Held**
SIC: 2741

(G-9323)
CLASSROOM INC
245 5th Ave Fl 20 (10016-8728)
PHONE................................212 545-8400
Lisa Holton, *President*
EMP: 25
SALES: 5MM **Privately Held**
SIC: 7372 7379 Educational computer software; computer related consulting services

(G-9324)
CLAYTON DUBILIER & RICE FUN (PA)
375 Park Ave Fl 18 (10152-0144)
PHONE................................212 407-5200
Joseph L Rice III, *Ch of Bd*

Donald J Gogel, *President*
▲ **EMP:** 50 **EST:** 1985
SALES: 3.1MM **Privately Held**
SIC: 3825 3661 3812 3577 Test equipment for electronic & electric measurement; digital test equipment, electronic & electrical circuits; telephone & telegraph apparatus; switching equipment, telephone; headsets, telephone; search & navigation equipment; computer peripheral equipment; computer terminals; prepackaged software

(G-9325)
CLEAN BEAUTY COLLECTIVE INC
Also Called: Fusion Brands America Inc.
45 W 45th St Fl 2 (10036-4607)
PHONE................................212 269-1387
Gregory Black, *President*
EMP: 25
SQ FT: 8,500
SALES (est): 18MM **Privately Held**
WEB: www.fusionbrandscorp.com
SIC: 2844 5122 Cosmetic preparations; cosmetics
PA: Fusion Brands Inc
40 St Clair Ave W Suite 200
Toronto ON M4V 1
800 261-9110

(G-9326)
CLEVER GOATS MEDIA LLC
40 Exchange Pl Ste 1602 (10005-2727)
PHONE................................917 512-0340
Lionel Crear,
EMP: 5
SALES (est): 312.6K **Privately Held**
SIC: 7372 Home entertainment computer software

(G-9327)
CLINIQUE LABORATORIES LLC (DH)
Also Called: Clinique Laboratories, Inc.
767 5th Ave Fl 41 (10153-0023)
PHONE................................212 572-4200
Daniel J Brestle, *CEO*
William P Lauder, *Ch of Bd*
Mary Armas, *Vice Pres*
Jenny Belknap, *Vice Pres*
Carol Thornton, *Opers Staff*
▲ **EMP:** 2
SQ FT: 20,000
SALES (est): 2.4MM **Publicly Held**
WEB: www.clinique.com
SIC: 2844 5122 Cosmetic preparations; cosmetics
HQ: Estee Lauder Inc.
767 5th Ave Fl 1
New York NY 10153
212 572-4200

(G-9328)
CLINIQUE SERVICES INC (DH)
767 5th Ave Fl Conc6 (10153-0003)
PHONE................................212 572-4200
Lynne Greene, *Ch of Bd*
William P Lauder, *President*
Caitlyn Wunsch, *Business Mgr*
Melissa Knapp, *Senior VP*
Goullin Arnaud, *Vice Pres*
EMP: 9
SALES (est): 2.4MM **Publicly Held**
SIC: 2844 Cosmetic preparations
HQ: Clinique Laboratories, Llc
767 5th Ave Fl 41
New York NY 10153
212 572-4200

(G-9329)
CLO-SHURE INTL INC (PA)
224 W 35th St Ste 1000 (10001-2533)
PHONE................................212 268-5029
Cory Liner, *Principal*
▲ **EMP:** 8
SALES (est): 832.6K **Privately Held**
SIC: 3965 Fasteners, buttons, needles & pins

(G-9330)
CLOPAY AMES TRUE TEMPER (HQ)
712 5th Ave (10019-4108)
PHONE................................212 957-5096

New York - New York County (G-9331)

Ronald J Kramer, *CEO*
James Stansberry, *Director*
EMP: 11
SALES (est): 404.9MM
SALES (corp-wide): 1.5B **Publicly Held**
SIC: 3423 3799 3524 Garden & farm tools, including shovels; shovels, spades (hand tools); wheelbarrows; lawn & garden equipment
PA: Griffon Corporation
  712 5th Ave Fl 18
  New York NY 10019
  212 957-5000

(G-9331)
CLOUD PRINTING
66 W Broadway Frnt E (10007-2113)
PHONE..................212 775-0888
Vivian Lin, *Owner*
EMP: 7
SALES (est): 148.6K **Privately Held**
SIC: 2752 Commercial printing, lithographic

(G-9332)
CLOUDPARC INC
122 W 27th St Fl 10 (10001-6227)
PHONE..................954 665-5962
Mike Critelli, *CEO*
Dana Klein, *Vice Pres*
Steven Neyaroff, *Vice Pres*
EMP: 5
SALES (est): 141.8K **Privately Held**
SIC: 7372 Application computer software

(G-9333)
CLOUDSENSE INC
1325 Avenue Of The Flr 28 (10019)
PHONE..................917 880-6195
Jonathan Douglas, *Exec VP*
Rowley Douglas, *Exec VP*
David Hawkes, *Sales Engr*
Seth Gross, *Technology*
Fawzi Fares, *Director*
EMP: 6
SALES (est): 663.8K
SALES (corp-wide): 9.1MM **Privately Held**
SIC: 7372 Prepackaged software
HQ: Cloudsense Ltd
  Moray House 23-31
  London W1W 7
  207 580-6685

(G-9334)
CLP HOLDINGS LLC (PA)
575 Madison Ave Ste 1006 (10022-8511)
P.O. Box 20627 (10021-0072)
PHONE..................917 846-5094
Cesar Pereira, *Mng Member*
EMP: 5
SQ FT: 1,500
SALES (est): 105MM **Privately Held**
SIC: 2672 Coated & laminated paper

(G-9335)
CLP PB LLC (PA)
Also Called: Perseus Books Group
1290 Ave Of The Amrcas (10104-0101)
PHONE..................212 340-8100
Joe Mangan, *COO*
Charles Gallagher, *CFO*
David Steinberger,
▲ **EMP:** 40
SQ FT: 16,800
SALES (est): 173.4MM **Privately Held**
WEB: www.perseusbooks.com
SIC: 2721 Comic books: publishing only, not printed on site

(G-9336)
CLYDE DUNEIER INC (PA)
415 Madison Ave Fl 6 (10017-7929)
PHONE..................212 398-1122
Dana Duneier, *CEO*
Mark Duneier, *President*
Clyde Duneier, *Corp Secy*
Rebecca Walis, *Merchandising*
▲ **EMP:** 100
SQ FT: 12,000
SALES (est): 13.6MM **Privately Held**
SIC: 3911 5094 Pearl jewelry, natural or cultured; rings, finger: precious metal; jewelry & precious stones

(G-9337)
CMNTY CORPORATION
228 E 45th St Ste 9e (10017-3303)
PHONE..................646 712-9949
Zach Katagiri, *Principal*
EMP: 5
SALES (est): 407.6K **Privately Held**
SIC: 7372 Prepackaged software

(G-9338)
CMX MEDIA LLC
Also Called: Complex Magazine
1271 Av Of The Americas (10020-1300)
PHONE..................917 793-5831
Rich Antoniello, *CEO*
Scott Cherkin, *Exec VP*
Moksha Fitzgibbons, *Exec VP*
Aleksey Baksheyev, *Vice Pres*
Edgar Hernandez, *Vice Pres*
▲ **EMP:** 20
SALES (est): 4.7MM **Privately Held**
WEB: www.complex.com
SIC: 2721 Magazines: publishing & printing

(G-9339)
COACH LEATHERWARE INTL
516 W 34th St Bsmt 5 (10001-1394)
PHONE..................212 594-1850
EMP: 5
SALES (est): 845.6K
SALES (corp-wide): 5.8B **Publicly Held**
WEB: www.coach.com
SIC: 3171 Handbags, women's
PA: Tapestry, Inc.
  10 Hudson Yards
  New York NY 10001
  212 594-1850

(G-9340)
COACH SERVICES INC
10 Hudson Yards (10001-2157)
PHONE..................212 594-1850
EMP: 5
SALES (est): 779.4K
SALES (corp-wide): 5.8B **Publicly Held**
SIC: 3171 Handbags, women's
PA: Tapestry, Inc.
  10 Hudson Yards
  New York NY 10001
  212 594-1850

(G-9341)
COALITION ON POSITIVE HEALTH
1751 Park Ave Fl 4 (10035-2809)
PHONE..................212 633-2500
Gloria Searson, *Director*
EMP: 14
SALES: 591K **Privately Held**
SIC: 7372 Educational computer software

(G-9342)
COBICO PRODUCTIONS INC
344 E 50th St Apt 1b (10022-7963)
PHONE..................347 417-5883
Jacob Babchuk, *President*
EMP: 5
SALES (est): 34K **Privately Held**
SIC: 2752 7335 Commercial printing, lithographic; commercial photography

(G-9343)
COCKPIT USA INC
15 W 39th St Fl 12 (10018-0628)
PHONE..................212 575-1616
Jacky Clyman, *Branch Mgr*
EMP: 12
SALES (corp-wide): 10.5MM **Privately Held**
WEB: www.avirex.com
SIC: 2386 5136 5611 5961 Coats & jackets, leather & sheep-lined; sportswear, men's & boys'; clothing, sportswear, men's & boys'; clothing, mail order (except women's)
PA: Cockpit Usa, Inc.
  15 W 39th St Fl 12
  New York NY 10018
  212 575-1616

(G-9344)
COCKPIT USA INC
15 W 39th St Fl 12 (10018-0628)
PHONE..................908 558-9704
Andrew Baljeet, *Manager*

EMP: 10
SALES (corp-wide): 10.5MM **Privately Held**
WEB: www.avirex.com
SIC: 2386 Leather & sheep-lined clothing
PA: Cockpit Usa, Inc.
  15 W 39th St Fl 12
  New York NY 10018
  212 575-1616

(G-9345)
CODA MEDIA INC
Also Called: Coda Story
108 W 39th St Rm 1000 (10018-8267)
PHONE..................917 478-2565
Greenberg Ilan, *Principal*
EMP: 5 **EST:** 2016
SALES (est): 171.1K **Privately Held**
SIC: 2721 Magazines: publishing only, not printed on site

(G-9346)
CODESTERS INC
900 Broadway Ste 903 (10003-1223)
PHONE..................646 232-1025
Gordon Smith, *CEO*
Thomas Juarez, *Opers Mgr*
Manesh Patel, *Treasurer*
Kimberly Sauter, *Manager*
Juan Farfan, *Web Dvlpr*
EMP: 8
SQ FT: 4,500
SALES: 600K **Privately Held**
SIC: 2731 8299 Textbooks: publishing & printing; schools & educational service

(G-9347)
COGNOTION INC
1407 Broadway Fl 24 (10018-5101)
PHONE..................347 692-0640
Joanna Schneier, *CEO*
Jonathan Dariyanani, *President*
Michael Goldberg, *CFO*
EMP: 4
SQ FT: 1,000
SALES: 8MM **Privately Held**
SIC: 7372 Educational computer software

(G-9348)
COLGAT-PLMOLIVE CENTL AMER INC (HQ)
300 Park Ave (10022-7402)
PHONE..................212 310-2000
Ian Cook, *Ch of Bd*
EMP: 9
SALES (est): 8MM
SALES (corp-wide): 15.4B **Publicly Held**
SIC: 2844 Toothpastes or powders, dentifrices
PA: Colgate-Palmolive Company
  300 Park Ave Fl 3
  New York NY 10022
  212 310-2000

(G-9349)
COLGATE-PALMOLIVE COMPANY (PA)
300 Park Ave Fl 3 (10022-7499)
PHONE..................212 310-2000
Ian Cook, *Ch of Bd*
Noel R Wallace, *President*
P Justin Skala, *Exec VP*
Philip G Shotts, *Vice Pres*
Henning Jakobsen, *CFO*
EMP: 3000
SALES: 15.4B **Publicly Held**
WEB: www.colgate.com
SIC: 2844 3991 2841 2842 Toothpastes or powders, dentifrices; mouthwashes; deodorants, personal; shaving preparations; toothbrushes, except electric; soap & other detergents; detergents, synthetic organic or inorganic alkaline; dishwashing compounds; soap: granulated, liquid, cake, flaked or chip; specialty cleaning, polishes & sanitation goods; fabric softeners; bleaches, household: dry or liquid; dog & cat food

(G-9350)
COLGATE-PALMOLIVE NJ INC
300 Park Ave Fl 8 (10022-7499)
PHONE..................212 310-2000
Bill Shanahan, *President*
EMP: 20

SALES (est): 3.1MM
SALES (corp-wide): 15.4B **Publicly Held**
WEB: www.colgate.com
SIC: 2841 Soap & other detergents
PA: Colgate-Palmolive Company
  300 Park Ave Fl 3
  New York NY 10022
  212 310-2000

(G-9351)
COLLECTION XIIX LTD (PA)
1370 Broadway Fl 17 (10018-7764)
PHONE..................212 686-8990
Andrew Pizzo, *President*
Ron Dangelo, *Senior VP*
Ralph Bergman, *CFO*
Rae LI Piec, *Bookkeeper*
Viji Thomas, *Manager*
▲ **EMP:** 10
SQ FT: 14,000
SALES (est): 22.9MM **Privately Held**
WEB: www.collection18.com
SIC: 2339 Women's & misses' accessories

(G-9352)
COLONY HOLDINGS INTL LLC
131 W 35th St Fl 6 (10001-2111)
PHONE..................212 868-2800
Douglas Chan, *CEO*
EMP: 10
SALES: 950K **Privately Held**
SIC: 2321 Men's & boys' furnishings

(G-9353)
COLOR UNLIMITED INC
244 5th Ave Frnt (10001-7604)
PHONE..................212 802-7547
Henri Boll, *Principal*
EMP: 5
SQ FT: 1,200
SALES: 100K **Privately Held**
WEB: www.go2museum.com
SIC: 2741 Art copy: publishing & printing

(G-9354)
COLORFAST
121 Varick St Fl 9 (10013-1408)
PHONE..................212 929-2440
John R Arbucci, *President*
Ira Schwidel, *Vice Pres*
EMP: 15
SALES (est): 1MM **Privately Held**
WEB: www.vividcolorinternational.com
SIC: 2752 Commercial printing, offset

(G-9355)
COLORTEX INC
1202 Lexington Ave 115 (10028-1439)
P.O. Box 115 (10028-0015)
PHONE..................212 564-2000
Steven Usdan, *President*
▲ **EMP:** 5
SQ FT: 10,000
SALES (est): 412.8K **Privately Held**
SIC: 2281 5199 Yarn spinning mills; yarns

(G-9356)
COLUMBIA DAILY SPECTATOR
2875 Broadway Ste 303 (10025-7846)
PHONE..................212 854-9550
Natan Belchikov, *Editor*
J Chan, *Editor*
Tiffany Fang, *Editor*
Daniel Radov, *Editor*
Veronica Taleon, *Editor*
EMP: 20
SALES: 287.6K **Privately Held**
WEB: www.columbiaspectator.com
SIC: 2711 Newspapers, publishing & printing

(G-9357)
COLUMBIA RECORDS INC
25 Madison Ave Fl 19 (10010-8601)
PHONE..................212 833-8000
Ron Perry, *CEO*
James Grosso, *Manager*
EMP: 13
SALES (est): 1.7MM
SALES (corp-wide): 80.1B **Privately Held**
SIC: 3652 Pre-recorded records & tapes
HQ: Sony Music Entertainment
  25 Madison Ave Fl 19
  New York NY 10010

GEOGRAPHIC SECTION

New York - New York County (G-9384)

(G-9358)
COLUMBIA UNIVERSITY PRESS (HQ)
61 W 62nd St Fl 3 (10023-7015)
PHONE..................................212 459-0600
Wendy Lochner, *Publisher*
Greg Lara, *Info Tech Mgr*
Jennifer Crewe, *Director*
▲ **EMP:** 23
SQ FT: 31,500
SALES: 9.4MM
SALES (corp-wide): 3.8B **Privately Held**
SIC: 2731 Books: publishing only; pamphlets: publishing only, not printed on site
PA: The Trustees Of Columbia University In The City Of New York
116th And Bdwy Way
New York NY 10027
212 854-9970

(G-9359)
COLUMBIA UNIVERSITY PRESS
61 W 62nd St Fl 3 (10023-7015)
PHONE..................................212 459-0600
EMP: 37
SALES (corp-wide): 3.8B **Privately Held**
SIC: 2731 Books: publishing only
HQ: Columbia University Press
61 W 62nd St Fl 3
New York NY 10023
212 459-0600

(G-9360)
COLUMBIA UNIVERSITY PRESS
61 W 62nd St Fl 3 (10023-7015)
PHONE..................................212 459-0600
Angela Ajayi, *Branch Mgr*
EMP: 50
SALES (corp-wide): 3.8B **Privately Held**
SIC: 2731 5192 Books: publishing only; pamphlets: publishing only, not printed on site; books
HQ: Columbia University Press
61 W 62nd St Fl 3
New York NY 10023
212 459-0600

(G-9361)
COLUMBUS TRADING CORP
Also Called: Columbus Accessories
120 W 31st St Rm 600 (10001-3407)
PHONE..................................212 564-1780
Chin C S Kim, *President*
▲ **EMP:** 15
SALES (est): 1.4MM **Privately Held**
SIC: 3961 Costume jewelry

(G-9362)
COMELY INTERNATIONAL TRDG INC
303 5th Ave Rm 1903 (10016-6658)
PHONE..................................212 683-1240
Qinghe Liu, *President*
Xu Sue Wang, *Vice Pres*
▲ **EMP:** 5
SQ FT: 1,800
SALES (est): 2.4MM **Privately Held**
WEB: www.comelyinternational.com
SIC: 2519 Furniture, household: glass, fiberglass & plastic

(G-9363)
COMINT APPAREL GROUP LLC (PA)
Also Called: Sebby Clothing
463 7th Ave Fl 4 (10018-8725)
P.O. Box 630, Englewood NJ (07631-0630)
PHONE..................................212 947-7474
Carlos Donzis, *Mng Member*
Graciela Donzis,
▲ **EMP:** 10
SQ FT: 4,000
SALES (est): 3.4MM **Privately Held**
WEB: www.comintapparel.com
SIC: 2339 Women's & misses' outerwear

(G-9364)
COMMENTARY INC
165 E 56th St Fl 16 (10022-2709)
PHONE..................................212 891-1400
Davi Birnstein, *Publisher*
EMP: 10
SALES: 2.9MM **Privately Held**
SIC: 2721 Magazines: publishing & printing

(G-9365)
COMMERCIAL GASKETS NEW YORK
247 W 38th St Rm 409 (10018-1047)
PHONE..................................212 244-8130
Stewart Shabman, *Principal*
EMP: 11
SALES (est): 1.3MM **Privately Held**
SIC: 3053 Packing, metallic

(G-9366)
COMMONWEAL FOUNDATION INC
Also Called: COMMONWEAL MAGAZINE
475 Riverside Dr Rm 405 (10115-0433)
PHONE..................................212 662-4200
Thomas Baker, *President*
James Hannan, *Vice Pres*
Steven Aubrey, *Manager*
Matthew Boudway, *Assoc Editor*
Tiina Aleman, *Art Dir*
EMP: 10 **EST:** 1924
SALES: 2MM **Privately Held**
WEB: www.catholicsinpublicsquare.org
SIC: 2721 Magazines: publishing only, not printed on site

(G-9367)
COMMONWEALTH TOY NOVELTY INC (PA)
980 Ave Of The Amer # 301 (10018-7958)
PHONE..................................212 242-4070
Steven Greenfield, *Ch of Bd*
Lee Schneider, *President*
◆ **EMP:** 45 **EST:** 1934
SQ FT: 16,000
SALES (est): 6.7MM **Privately Held**
SIC: 3942 Stuffed toys, including animals

(G-9368)
COMMUNITY MEDIA LLC
Also Called: Downtown Express Newspaper
515 Canal St Fl 1 (10013-1330)
PHONE..................................212 229-1890
John Sutter,
EMP: 20
SALES (est): 1MM **Privately Held**
WEB: www.communitymediallc.com
SIC: 2711 2752 Newspapers, publishing & printing; commercial printing, lithographic

(G-9369)
COMPAR MANUFACTURING CORP
308 Dyckman St (10034-5351)
PHONE..................................212 304-2777
Alex Neuburger, *President*
Steven Neuburger, *Vice Pres*
EMP: 50
SALES (est): 3.2MM
SALES (corp-wide): 10MM **Privately Held**
SIC: 3496 3469 Miscellaneous fabricated wire products; metal stampings
PA: Magic Novelty Co., Inc.
308 Dyckman St
New York NY 10034
212 304-2777

(G-9370)
COMPLETE PUBLISHING SOLUTIONS
Also Called: CPS Creative
350 W 51st St Apt 13b (10019-6445)
PHONE..................................212 242-7321
James Hohl, *Mng Member*
EMP: 5
SQ FT: 900
SALES (est): 337.6K **Privately Held**
WEB: www.cpspress.com
SIC: 2741 Miscellaneous publishing

(G-9371)
COMPLEX MEDIA INC (PA)
229 W 43rd St Fl 10 (10036-3982)
PHONE..................................917 793-5831
Richard Antoniello, *President*
Brian Kelley, *Admin Sec*
EMP: 45
SALES (est): 9.2MM **Privately Held**
SIC: 2721 Magazines: publishing & printing

(G-9372)
CONCEPTS NYC INC
20 W 33rd St Fl 9 (10001-3305)
PHONE..................................212 244-1033
Joseph Bibi, *President*
Reuben J Bibi, *Principal*
Elliott J Bibi, *Vice Pres*
▲ **EMP:** 25
SALES (est): 3.1MM **Privately Held**
SIC: 2221 Apparel & outerwear fabric, manmade fiber or silk

(G-9373)
CONCORD JEWELRY MFG CO LLC
Also Called: Concord Jwlry Mfrs
64 W 48th St Ste 1004 (10036-1708)
PHONE..................................212 719-4030
Ann Seregi, *President*
EMP: 25 **EST:** 1951
SALES (est): 1.8MM **Privately Held**
SIC: 3911 Jewelry, precious metal

(G-9374)
CONCORDE APPAREL COMPANY LLC (PA)
55 W 39th St Fl 11 (10018-3803)
PHONE..................................212 307-7848
Lee Wattenburg,
Paul Wattenburg,
▲ **EMP:** 5
SALES: 20.7MM **Privately Held**
SIC: 2311 Men's & boys' suits & coats

(G-9375)
CONDE NAST ENTERTAINMENT LLC
Also Called: Teen Vogue
1 World Trade Ctr (10007-0089)
PHONE..................................212 286-2860
Robert Sauerberg Jr, *President*
Susan Plagemann, *Publisher*
Heddy Sams-Pierson, *Publisher*
Gina Sanders, *Publisher*
Edward Barsamian, *Editor*
EMP: 1145 **EST:** 2013
SALES (est): 191.8MM
SALES (corp-wide): 5.6B **Privately Held**
SIC: 2721 Magazines: publishing & printing
PA: Advance Publications, Inc.
950 W Fingerboard Rd
Staten Island NY 10305
718 981-1234

(G-9376)
CONDECO SOFTWARE INC
1350 Broadway Rm 1712 (10018-0900)
PHONE..................................408 508-7330
Martin Brooker, *COO*
EMP: 25
SALES (corp-wide): 29.3MM **Privately Held**
SIC: 7372 Business oriented computer software
HQ: Condeco Software, Inc.
2105 S Bascom Ave Ste 150
Campbell CA 95008
917 677-7600

(G-9377)
CONFERENCE BOARD INC (PA)
845 3rd Ave Fl 2 (10022-6600)
PHONE..................................212 759-0900
Jonathan Spector, *President*
Francisco G Rodr Guez, *Trustee*
James H Slamp, *Exec VP*
Amanda Spears, *Manager*
Carolyn Brancato, *Director*
EMP: 180
SQ FT: 49,750
SALES (est): 25.4MM **Privately Held**
WEB: www.conference-board.org
SIC: 2721 8299 Periodicals: publishing only; educational service, nondegree granting: continuing educ.

(G-9378)
CONFIANT INC
833 Broadway Apt 2 (10003-4700)
PHONE..................................646 397-4198
Louis-David Mangin, *CEO*
Jerome Dangu, *CTO*
EMP: 12

SALES (est): 209K **Privately Held**
SIC: 7372 Business oriented computer software

(G-9379)
CONGRESS FOR JEWISH CULTURE
Also Called: DI ZUKUNFT
1133 Broadway Ste 1019 (10010-7996)
P.O. Box 1590 (10159-1590)
PHONE..................................212 505-8040
Barnett Zumoff, *President*
Shane Baker, *Exec Dir*
EMP: 5
SQ FT: 800
SALES: 94.8K **Privately Held**
SIC: 2731 2721 7922 Book music: publishing only, not printed on site; periodicals: publishing only; theatrical producers & services; theatrical producers

(G-9380)
CONNECTIVA SYSTEMS INC (PA)
19 W 44th St Ste 611 (10036-5900)
PHONE..................................646 722-8741
AVI Basu, *President*
EMP: 18
SALES (est): 23.8MM **Privately Held**
WEB: www.connectivasystems.com
SIC: 3695 Computer software tape & disks: blank, rigid & floppy

(G-9381)
CONSOLIDATED CHILDRENS AP INC (HQ)
Also Called: Bonjour For Kids
100 W 33rd St Ste 1105 (10001-2990)
PHONE..................................212 239-8615
Mark Adjmi, *President*
Jack Adjmi, *Chairman*
Joy Mahana, *Treasurer*
▲ **EMP:** 3
SALES (est): 6.9MM
SALES (corp-wide): 27.5MM **Privately Held**
SIC: 2361 Dresses: girls', children's & infants'
PA: Adjmi Apparel Group Llc
463 7th Ave
New York NY 10018
212 594-5511

(G-9382)
CONSOLIDATED COLOR PRESS INC
307 7th Ave Rm 607 (10001-6082)
PHONE..................................212 929-8197
William D Sommers Jr, *President*
Richard M Sommers, *Vice Pres*
Richard Sommers, *Vice Pres*
EMP: 12
SQ FT: 10,000
SALES (est): 1.5MM **Privately Held**
SIC: 2752 2791 Commercial printing, offset; typesetting

(G-9383)
CONSOLIDATED FASHION CORP
225 W 39th St Fl 12 (10018-3129)
PHONE..................................212 719-3000
Steven Sall, *President*
Angela Sall, *Corp Secy*
EMP: 6
SALES (est): 710K **Privately Held**
SIC: 2339 Women's & misses' outerwear

(G-9384)
CONSOLIDATED LOOSE LEAF INC (PA)
989 Avnue Of The Americas (10018-5410)
PHONE..................................212 924-5800
Sol Kleinman, *President*
Martin Schneider, *Corp Secy*
EMP: 45 **EST:** 1943
SQ FT: 32,000
SALES (est): 3MM **Privately Held**
SIC: 2782 Looseleaf binders & devices; library binders, looseleaf

New York - New York County (G-9385) GEOGRAPHIC SECTION

(G-9385)
CONSTELLATION BRANDS SMO LLC
111 8th Ave (10011-5201)
PHONE..................................585 396-7161
EMP: 5
SALES (est): 250.5K
SALES (corp-wide): 7.5B **Publicly Held**
SIC: 2084 Wines, brandy & brandy spirits
PA: Constellation Brands, Inc.
   207 High Point Dr # 100
   Victor NY 14564
   585 678-7100

(G-9386)
CONSTELLIUM
830 3rd Ave Rm 901 (10022-6504)
PHONE..................................212 675-5087
Richard B Evans, *Chairman*
Rina Tran, *COO*
Didier Fontaine, *CFO*
Pierre Vareille, *Director*
EMP: 50 EST: 2015
SALES (est): 19.2MM
SALES (corp-wide): 6.1B **Privately Held**
SIC: 3354 Aluminum extruded products
PA: Constellium N.V.
   Tupolevlaan 41
   Schiphol-Rijk
   206 549-780

(G-9387)
CONTACTIVE INC
137 Varick St Ste 605 (10013-1105)
PHONE..................................646 476-9059
Inaki Berenguer, *CEO*
Julio Viera, *President*
EMP: 50
SALES (est): 2.2MM
SALES (corp-wide): 110.8MM **Privately Held**
SIC: 7372 Application computer software
PA: Fuze, Inc.
   2 Copley Pl Ste 700
   Boston MA 02116
   800 890-1553

(G-9388)
CONTINUITY PUBLISHING INC
15 W 39th St Fl 9 (10018-0631)
PHONE..................................212 869-4170
Neil Adams, *President*
Kristine Adams, *Vice Pres*
Marilyn Adams, *Vice Pres*
EMP: 12
SQ FT: 4,000
SALES (est): 750K **Privately Held**
SIC: 2721 Comic books: publishing only, not printed on site

(G-9389)
CONTINUITY SOFTWARE INC
5 Penn Plz Fl 23 (10001-1810)
PHONE..................................646 216-8628
Gil Hecht, *CEO*
Giza Venture Fund, *Shareholder*
EMP: 40
SALES (est): 2.1MM **Privately Held**
SIC: 7372 Business oriented computer software

(G-9390)
CONTINUUM INTL PUBG GROUP INC
15 W 26th St Fl 8 (10010-1065)
PHONE..................................646 649-4215
Fax: 212 953-5944
EMP: 12
SALES (corp-wide): 173.2MM **Privately Held**
SIC: 2731 Book Publishers
HQ: The Continuum International Publishing Group Inc
   175 5th Ave Lbby 5
   New York NY

(G-9391)
CONVENIENCE STORE NEWS
770 Broadway Fl 5 (10003-9554)
PHONE..................................214 217-7800
Maureen Arzato, *Principal*
Don Longo, *Director*
EMP: 5

SALES (est): 309.3K **Privately Held**
WEB: www.csnews.com
SIC: 2721 Magazines: publishing & printing

(G-9392)
CONVERSION LABS INC (PA)
1460 Broadway (10036-7329)
PHONE..................................866 351-5907
John R Strawn Jr, *Ch of Bd*
Justin Schreiber, *President*
Stefan Galluppi, *COO*
Robert Kalkstein, *CFO*
Joseph Ditrolio, *Chief Mktg Ofcr*
EMP: 11 EST: 1987
SALES: 5MM **Publicly Held**
SIC: 2833 Medicinals & botanicals

(G-9393)
COOKIES INC
Also Called: Carnival
1 E 33rd St Fl 6 (10016-5011)
PHONE..................................646 452-5552
Charles Dweck, *President*
Mitch Melamed, *Director*
▲ EMP: 575
SALES (est): 31MM **Privately Held**
SIC: 2353 5947 Hats, trimmed: women's, misses' & children's; gift, novelty & souvenir shop

(G-9394)
COOKS INTL LTD LBLTY CO
7 World Trade Ctr Fl 46 (10007-2337)
PHONE..................................212 741-4407
Henry Mandil,
◆ EMP: 5
SQ FT: 1,500
SALES (est): 270K **Privately Held**
SIC: 2999 3567 Fuel briquettes or boulets: made with petroleum binder; metal melting furnaces, industrial: electric

(G-9395)
COPEN UNITED LLC
37 W 39th St Fl 6 (10018-3886)
PHONE..................................212 819-0008
◆ EMP: 8 EST: 2012
SALES (est): 844.1K
SALES (corp-wide): 30MM **Privately Held**
SIC: 2299 Ramie yarn, thread, roving & textiles
PA: Selecta International Limited
   Rm 11-13 16/F One Midtown
   Tsuen Wan NT
   279 992-80

(G-9396)
COPIA INTERACTIVE LLC
105 Madison Ave (10016-7418)
PHONE..................................212 481-0520
Uday Mahtani, *Partner*
Michael Schluter, *Partner*
Nathan Cayzer, *Senior VP*
Seth Kaufman, *Vice Pres*
Rafi Blumenthal, *Sales Staff*
EMP: 16
SALES (est): 1.1MM **Privately Held**
SIC: 2711 Newspapers, publishing & printing

(G-9397)
COPY ROOM INC
885 3rd Ave Lowr 2ll (10022-4804)
PHONE..................................212 371-8600
George Dispigno, *President*
EMP: 12
SQ FT: 4,000
SALES: 2.5MM **Privately Held**
WEB: www.nydmv.com
SIC: 2759 2789 7389 Commercial printing; magazines, binding; laminating service

(G-9398)
COPY4LES INC
146 W 29th St Rm 9w (10001-8207)
PHONE..................................212 487-9778
Davesham Walter Panagoda, *CEO*
EMP: 11
SALES (est): 2MM **Privately Held**
SIC: 3555 Copy holders, printers'

(G-9399)
CORBERTEX LLC
1412 Broadway Rm 1100 (10018-3320)
PHONE..................................212 971-0008
Howard Corber,
EMP: 5
SALES (est): 310K **Privately Held**
SIC: 3552 Textile machinery

(G-9400)
COREMET TRADING INC
160 Brdwy Ste 1107 (10038)
PHONE..................................212 964-3600
Leo Horowitz, *Ch of Bd*
M Elliott Czermak, *Vice Pres*
Warren Katzman, *Treasurer*
◆ EMP: 5
SQ FT: 800
SALES (est): 1.1MM **Privately Held**
SIC: 1081 Metal mining exploration & development services

(G-9401)
CORINNE MCCORMACK INC
7 W 36th St Fl 9 (10018-7158)
PHONE..................................212 868-7919
Corinne McCormack, *President*
▲ EMP: 10
SALES (est): 1.1MM **Privately Held**
WEB: www.corinnemccormack.com
SIC: 3851 Eyeglasses, lenses & frames
HQ: Fgx International Inc.
   500 George Washington Hwy
   Smithfield RI 02917
   401 231-3800

(G-9402)
CORNING INCORPORATED
767 5th Ave Ste 2301 (10153-0012)
PHONE..................................646 521-9600
Karen Nelson, *Branch Mgr*
EMP: 5
SALES (corp-wide): 10.1B **Publicly Held**
WEB: www.corning.com
SIC: 3229 Pressed & blown glass
PA: Corning Incorporated
   1 Riverfront Plz
   Corning NY 14831
   607 974-9000

(G-9403)
COSMOPOLITAN MAGAZINE
300 W 57th St Fl 38 (10019-3299)
PHONE..................................212 649-2000
EMP: 5
SALES (est): 352K **Privately Held**
SIC: 2721 Magazines: publishing & printing

(G-9404)
COTY INC
350 5th Ave Ste 2700 (10118-2700)
PHONE..................................212 389-7000
Dr Peter Harf, *Ch of Bd*
Romain Ritter, *General Mgr*
Rich Garzon, *Principal*
Lori Rosario, *Counsel*
Jay Clarke, *Vice Pres*
EMP: 113
SALES (est): 52.3MM **Privately Held**
SIC: 2844 Toilet preparations

(G-9405)
COTY INC (PA)
350 5th Ave Ste 2700 (10118-2700)
PHONE..................................212 389-7300
Pierre Laubies, *CEO*
Lambertus J H Becht, *Ch of Bd*
Edgar Huber, *President*
Laurent Kleitman, *President*
Sylvie Moreau, *President*
◆ EMP: 60
SALES: 9.4B **Publicly Held**
WEB: www.cotyshop.com
SIC: 2844 Perfumes & colognes

(G-9406)
COTY US LLC (HQ)
Also Called: Private Portfolio
350 5th Ave (10118-0110)
PHONE..................................212 389-7000
Bart Becht, *CEO*
Patrice De Talhout, *Exec VP*
Camillo Pane, *Exec VP*
Mario Reis, *Exec VP*
Jules Kaufman, *Senior VP*
▲ EMP: 130

SALES (est): 513.4MM **Publicly Held**
WEB: www.cotyinc.com
SIC: 2844 Perfumes & colognes; cosmetic preparations

(G-9407)
COUNTER EVOLUTION
37 W 17th St (10011-5503)
PHONE..................................212 647-7505
Jim Malone, *Owner*
EMP: 6
SALES (est): 808.5K **Privately Held**
SIC: 3131 Counters

(G-9408)
COUNTESS CORPORATION
Also Called: Terani Couture
225 W 37th St Fl 12 (10018-5726)
PHONE..................................212 869-7070
Daryoush Peter Tehrant, *President*
Joyce Hatoum, *Accounts Exec*
▲ EMP: 8
SQ FT: 10,000
SALES (est): 1.7MM **Privately Held**
SIC: 2337 Women's & misses' suits & coats

(G-9409)
COUNTESS MARA INC
120 W 45th St Fl 37 (10036-4195)
PHONE..................................212 768-7300
Ross Gershkowitz, *President*
EMP: 6
SQ FT: 3,000
SALES (est): 358.6K
SALES (corp-wide): 151.7MM **Privately Held**
WEB: www.randacorp.com
SIC: 2323 Neckties, men's & boys': made from purchased materials
HQ: Randa Corporation
   417 5th Ave Fl 11
   New York NY 10016
   212 768-8800

(G-9410)
COURTAULDS TEXTILES LTD
Also Called: Sara Lee Courtaulds USA
358 5th Ave Fl 6 (10001-2209)
PHONE..................................212 946-8000
Shannon McKeen, *Branch Mgr*
EMP: 14
SALES (corp-wide): 6.8B **Privately Held**
SIC: 2299 Batting, wadding, padding & fillings; felts & felt products; yarns & thread, made from non-fabric materials
HQ: Courtaulds Textiles Limited
   225 Bath Road
   Slough BERKS

(G-9411)
COUTURE INC
16 W 37th St Frnt 1 (10018-7404)
PHONE..................................212 921-1166
Catherine Ansel, *Principal*
▲ EMP: 5 EST: 2007
SALES (est): 470K **Privately Held**
SIC: 2335 Wedding gowns & dresses

(G-9412)
COUTURE PRESS
200 Park Ave (10166-0005)
PHONE..................................310 734-4831
Dorita Porter, *President*
EMP: 15
SALES (est): 588.2K **Privately Held**
SIC: 2741 Miscellaneous publishing

(G-9413)
COVE POINT HOLDINGS LLC (PA)
60 E 42nd St Rm 3210 (10165-0056)
PHONE..................................212 599-3388
William C Morris, *Chairman*
EMP: 20
SALES: 26.5K **Privately Held**
SIC: 2671 2672 Paper coated or laminated for packaging; adhesive papers, labels or tapes: from purchased material

(G-9414)
CPT USA LLC (PA)
Also Called: Captain USA
15 W 39th St Fl 12 (10018-0628)
PHONE..................................212 575-1616
Jeffrey Clyman,

GEOGRAPHIC SECTION

New York - New York County (G-9442)

▲ EMP: 27
SQ FT: 4,200
SALES (est): 2.4MM Privately Held
SIC: 2371 Apparel, fur

(G-9415)
CRABTREE PUBLISHING INC
350 5th Ave Ste 3304 (10118-3304)
PHONE..................212 496-5040
John Siemens, *Branch Mgr*
EMP: 27 Privately Held
WEB: www.crabtreebooks.com
SIC: 2731 Books: publishing & printing
PA: Crabtree Publishing Company Limited
    616 Welland Ave
    St Catharines ON L2M 5
    905 682-5221

(G-9416)
CRAFT CLERICAL CLOTHES INC
Also Called: Craft Robe Co.
247 W 37th St Rm 1700 (10018-5051)
PHONE..................212 764-6122
Marvin Goldman, *President*
EMP: 8
SQ FT: 3,000
SALES: 1MM Privately Held
SIC: 2389 5699 Uniforms & vestments; academic vestments (caps & gowns); clergymen's vestments; uniforms; caps & gowns (academic vestments); clergy vestments

(G-9417)
CRAFTATLANTIC LLC
Also Called: Craft Atlantic
115 Greenwich Ave (10014-1915)
PHONE..................646 726-4205
Pierre Mordacq, *Mng Member*
EMP: 13
SALES (est): 1.2MM Privately Held
SIC: 2329 Knickers, dress (separate): men's & boys'

(G-9418)
CRAIN COMMUNICATIONS INC
Business Insurance
685 3rd Ave (10017-4024)
PHONE..................212 210-0100
Martin Ross, *Principal*
Tom Fetters, *Editor*
Omari Gardner, *Editor*
Irene Bar-AM, *Adv Dir*
EMP: 200
SALES (corp-wide): 225MM Privately Held
WEB: www.crainsnewyork.com
SIC: 2721 7812 Magazines: publishing only, not printed on site; motion picture & video production
PA: Crain Communications, Inc.
    1155 Gratiot Ave
    Detroit MI 48207
    313 446-6000

(G-9419)
CRAINS NEW YORK BUSINESS
711 3rd Ave (10017-4014)
PHONE..................212 210-0250
Jill Kaplan, *Owner*
EMP: 30 EST: 2012
SALES (est): 2.6MM Privately Held
SIC: 2721 Magazines: publishing only, not printed on site

(G-9420)
CREATIVE FORMS INC
80 Varick St Apt 10a (10013-1945)
P.O. Box 1485 (10013-0878)
PHONE..................212 431-7540
Donald Macpherson, *President*
EMP: 5
SALES (est): 450K Privately Held
SIC: 2752 Commercial printing, offset

(G-9421)
CREATIVE PRINTING CORP
Also Called: Creative Prntng
70 W 36th St Rm 500 (10018-8050)
PHONE..................212 226-3870
Mark Jackson, *President*
Candice Jackson, *Corp Secy*
Dave Bird, *Vice Pres*
Doug Bird, *Vice Pres*
EMP: 7
SQ FT: 6,000
SALES (est): 560K Privately Held
WEB: www.starkey-henricks.com
SIC: 2752 Commercial printing, offset

(G-9422)
CREATIVE TOOLS & SUPPLY INC
Also Called: All Craft Jewelry Supply
135 W 29th St Rm 205 (10001-5191)
PHONE..................212 279-7077
Tevel Herbstman, *President*
▲ EMP: 9
SQ FT: 2,000
SALES (est): 1.3MM Privately Held
SIC: 3915 Jewelers' materials & lapidary work

(G-9423)
CREDIT UNION JOURNAL INC (PA)
Also Called: Source Media
1 State St Fl 26 (10004-1561)
PHONE..................212 803-8200
Sean Kron, *CFO*
Lisa Freeman, *Manager*
Allison Adams, *Security Dir*
EMP: 5
SALES (est): 485.9K Privately Held
WEB: www.cujournal.com
SIC: 2721 Magazines: publishing & printing

(G-9424)
CROWD MEDIA INC
245 5th Ave Rm 1102 (10016-8717)
PHONE..................212 497-1100
Anton Pertsel, *CEO*
EMP: 1 EST: 2017
SALES: 1.2MM Privately Held
SIC: 7372 Application computer software

(G-9425)
CROWLEY TAR PRODUCTS CO INC (PA)
305 Madison Ave Ste 1035 (10165-1036)
PHONE..................212 682-1200
William A Callaman, *CEO*
William Jennings, *Principal*
▲ EMP: 7
SQ FT: 10,000
SALES (est): 3.2MM Privately Held
WEB: www.crowleychemical.com
SIC: 2865 Cyclic crudes, coal tar; tar

(G-9426)
CROWN JEWELERS INTL INC
168 7th Ave S (10014-2727)
PHONE..................212 420-7800
Neryo Shimunov, *Ch of Bd*
EMP: 5
SALES (est): 494.9K Privately Held
SIC: 3911 5094 Jewelry, precious metal; jewelry

(G-9427)
CRUNCHED INC
41 E 11th St (10003-4602)
PHONE..................415 484-9909
Sean Black, *CEO*
Roger Billerey-Mosier, *Engineer*
EMP: 7
SALES (est): 340.3K
SALES (corp-wide): 128.6MM Privately Held
SIC: 7372 Business oriented computer software
HQ: Clearslide, Inc.
    45 Fremont St Fl 32
    San Francisco CA 94105
    877 360-3366

(G-9428)
CRUZIN MANAGEMENT INC (DH)
401 Park Ave S Fl 7 (10016-8808)
PHONE..................212 641-8700
Jay S Maltby, *President*
Thomas A Valdes, *Exec VP*
D Chris Mitchell, *Senior VP*
Ousik Yu, *Senior VP*
Ezra Shashoua, *CFO*
▼ EMP: 50
SQ FT: 250,000
SALES (est): 31.4MM
SALES (corp-wide): 182.4MM Privately Held
WEB: www.cruzanrum.com
SIC: 2085 2084 5182 Rum (alcoholic beverage); brandy; wines; liquor; wine; brandy & brandy spirits
HQ: The Absolut Spirits Company Inc
    250 Park Ave 17
    New York NY 10177
    914 848-4800

(G-9429)
CSCO LLC
1407 Broadway Rm 1503 (10018-5100)
PHONE..................212 375-6180
David Apperman, *CEO*
Salomon Murciano, *Vice Pres*
Penelope Savinon, *Admin Sec*
▲ EMP: 22 EST: 2014
SALES (est): 545.7K Privately Held
SIC: 2335 Women's, juniors' & misses' dresses

(G-9430)
CTS LLC
Also Called: Costello Tagliapietra
211 E 18th St Apt 4d (10003-3624)
PHONE..................212 278-0058
Aby Saltiel,
Jeffrey Costello,
Regino Nieves,
Robert Tagliapietra,
EMP: 5
SQ FT: 5,000
SALES (est): 382.4K Privately Held
SIC: 2335 Women's, juniors' & misses' dresses

(G-9431)
CUBIC TRNSP SYSTEMS INC
245 W 17th St Fl 8 (10011-5373)
PHONE..................212 255-1810
Richard Trenery, *Branch Mgr*
EMP: 15
SALES (corp-wide): 1.4B Publicly Held
SIC: 3829 3714 3581 Fare registers for street cars, buses, etc.; motor vehicle parts & accessories; automatic vending machines
HQ: Cubic Transportation Systems, Inc.
    5650 Kearny Mesa Rd
    San Diego CA 92111
    858 268-3100

(G-9432)
CULT RECORDS LLC
263 Bowery Apt 3 (10002-5656)
PHONE..................718 395-2077
Julian Casablancas, *Co-Owner*
EMP: 5
SALES (est): 261.4K Privately Held
SIC: 3652 Pre-recorded records & tapes

(G-9433)
CULTUREIQ INC (PA)
7 Penn Plz Ste 1112 (10001-3390)
PHONE..................212 755-8633
Gregory Besner, *CEO*
Jeremy Hamel, *Marketing Staff*
Andrew McKenna, *Software Dev*
Krissy Buongiorno, *Associate*
EMP: 50
SQ FT: 4,500
SALES (est): 4.4MM Privately Held
SIC: 7372 Prepackaged software

(G-9434)
CUPID FOUNDATIONS INC (PA)
Also Called: CUPID INTIMATES
475 Park Ave S Manhattan (10022)
PHONE..................212 686-6224
David Welsch, *President*
Marilyn Welsch, *Corp Secy*
Ken Langston, *VP Opers*
Monica Meyer, *Sales Executive*
Matt Miller, *Manager*
▲ EMP: 200 EST: 1943
SQ FT: 5,000
SALES: 63.5MM Privately Held
WEB: www.cshape.com
SIC: 2342 Brassieres; girdles & panty girdles

(G-9435)
CUREATR INC
222 Broadway Fl 20 (10038-2510)
PHONE..................212 203-3927
Richard Resnick, *CEO*
James Bradley, *Ch of Bd*
Mary Stuyvesant, *President*
Oleksiy Khomenko, *COO*
Julia Pulzone, *CFO*
EMP: 25 EST: 2011
SQ FT: 300
SALES (est): 1.4MM Privately Held
SIC: 7372 Business oriented computer software

(G-9436)
CUSTOM SPORTS LAB INC
Also Called: U S Orthotic Center
515 Madison Ave Rm 1204 (10022-5484)
PHONE..................212 832-1648
Jeff Rich, *President*
EMP: 5
SALES: 500K Privately Held
SIC: 3149 3842 8734 Athletic shoes, except rubber or plastic; orthopedic appliances; product testing laboratory, safety or performance

(G-9437)
CUSTOMIZE ELITE SOCKS LLC
156 2nd Ave Apt 2c (10003-5759)
PHONE..................212 533-8551
Roger Cheng, *Principal*
EMP: 5
SALES (est): 463.6K Privately Held
SIC: 2252 Socks

(G-9438)
CUSTOMSHOW INC
216 E 45th St Fl 17 (10017-3304)
PHONE..................800 255-5303
Paul Shapiro, *CEO*
George Chevalier, *Ch of Bd*
EMP: 8
SQ FT: 3,000
SALES (est): 353.8K Privately Held
SIC: 7372 Application computer software

(G-9439)
CW FASTENERS & ZIPPERS CORP
142 W 36th St Fl 5 (10018-8796)
PHONE..................212 594-3203
Suk Chun Wong, *Principal*
Stella Wong, *Info Tech Dir*
EMP: 13
SALES (est): 1.5MM Privately Held
SIC: 3965 Fasteners; zipper

(G-9440)
CY FASHION CORP
525 7th Ave Rm 811 (10018-0988)
PHONE..................212 730-8600
Irene Cho, *CEO*
Barkin Eren, *President*
EMP: 3
SQ FT: 1,100
SALES: 2MM Privately Held
SIC: 2211 Apparel & outerwear fabrics, cotton

(G-9441)
CYBERLIMIT INC
257 W 38th St Fl 6 (10018-4457)
PHONE..................212 840-9597
David MEI, *President*
EMP: 10
SQ FT: 2,000
SALES: 210K Privately Held
SIC: 2331 2321 Women's & misses' blouses & shirts; men's & boys' furnishings

(G-9442)
CYGNET STUDIO INC
251 W 39th St Fl 17 (10018-3117)
PHONE..................646 450-4550
Daniel Ehrenard, *General Mgr*
Daniel Ehrenbard, *Managing Dir*
EMP: 12
SALES (est): 943.4K Privately Held
SIC: 2389 Costumes

(G-9443)
CYNTHIA ROWLEY INC (PA)
376 Bleecker St (10014-3210)
PHONE..................212 242-3803
Cynthia Rowley, *Ch of Bd*
Peter Arnold, *President*
Chelsey Wayte, *Vice Pres*
Zoe Saunders, *Pub Rel Mgr*
Robert Shaw, *CFO*
▲ **EMP:** 12
SQ FT: 7,000
SALES (est): 1.9MM **Privately Held**
SIC: 2331 2335 2339 Women's & misses' blouses & shirts; women's, juniors' & misses' dresses; women's & misses' outerwear; women's & misses' accessories; women's & misses' athletic clothing & sportswear

(G-9444)
CYPRESS BIOSCIENCE INC
110 E 59th St Fl 33 (10022-1315)
PHONE..................858 452-2323
Jay D Kranzler PHD, *Ch of Bd*
Sabrina Martucci Johnson, *COO*
Sharon Kay Cochran, *Manager*
R Michael Gendreau PHD, *Officer*
Srinivas G RAO PHD, *Officer*
EMP: 16
SQ FT: 5,700
SALES (est): 3.3MM **Privately Held**
WEB: www.cypressbio.com
SIC: 2836 Biological products, except diagnostic

(G-9445)
D & A OFFSET SERVICES INC
185 Varick St Ste 3 (10014-4607)
PHONE..................212 924-0612
Carmine D'Elia, *President*
Al D'Elia, *President*
Henny D'Elia, *Corp Secy*
Vincent D'Elia, *Vice Pres*
EMP: 14
SQ FT: 11,000
SALES (est): 1.4MM **Privately Held**
SIC: 2796 Engraving platemaking services

(G-9446)
D & D WINDOW TECH INC (PA)
979 3rd Ave Lbby 132 (10022-1298)
PHONE..................212 308-2822
Amos Regev, *President*
EMP: 5
SQ FT: 250
SALES (est): 401.6K **Privately Held**
SIC: 2591 5023 Window blinds; window shades; venetian blinds; vertical blinds; window shades

(G-9447)
D J NIGHT LTD
225 W 37th St Fl 6 (10018-6741)
PHONE..................212 302-9050
Roholah Simhaee, *President*
EMP: 30
SALES (est): 2.4MM **Privately Held**
SIC: 2335 Gowns, formal

(G-9448)
D M J CASTING INC
62 W 47th St Ste 508 (10036-3270)
PHONE..................212 719-1951
David Green, *President*
EMP: 5
SALES: 310K **Privately Held**
SIC: 3915 Jewelers' castings

(G-9449)
D R S INC (PA)
Also Called: Dason Company Div
64 W 48th St Ste 1302 (10036-1708)
PHONE..................212 819-0237
Peter Susser, *President*
Joseph Borella, *Vice Pres*
Robert Galiardo, *Manager*
▲ **EMP:** 30 **EST:** 1946
SQ FT: 4,000
SALES (est): 2.5MM **Privately Held**
WEB: www.drsny.com
SIC: 3911 5094 Rings, finger: precious metal; jewelers' findings

(G-9450)
D R S WATCH MATERIALS
64 W 48th St Ste 1302 (10036-1708)
PHONE..................212 819-0470
Joseph Borella, *Vice Pres*
EMP: 40 **EST:** 1980
SALES (est): 1.7MM **Privately Held**
SIC: 3915 Jewel preparing: instruments, tools, watches & jewelry

(G-9451)
D3 LED LLC
Also Called: D3 NY
566 7th Ave Rm 504 (10018-1866)
PHONE..................917 757-9671
George Pappas, *Mng Member*
EMP: 22 **Privately Held**
SIC: 3999 Advertising display products
PA: D3 Led, Llc
  11370 Sunrise Park Dr
  Rancho Cordova CA 95742

(G-9452)
DABBY-REID LTD
347 W 36th St Rm 701 (10018-7225)
PHONE..................212 356-0040
Ida Reid, *President*
EMP: 15
SALES: 165.6K **Privately Held**
SIC: 3961 5094 Costume jewelry, ex. precious metal & semiprecious stones; jewelry & precious stones

(G-9453)
DAHESHIST PUBLISHING CO LTD
1775 Broadway 501 (10019-1903)
PHONE..................212 581-8360
Mervat Zahid, *President*
EMP: 10
SQ FT: 2,500
SALES (est): 867.9K **Privately Held**
WEB: www.daheshheritage.org
SIC: 2731 Books: publishing only

(G-9454)
DAILY BEAST COMPANY LLC (HQ)
7 Hanover Sq (10004-2616)
PHONE..................212 445-4600
Baba Shetty, *Mng Member*
Justin Miller, *Senior Editor*
Thomas E Ascheim,
Joseph Galarneau,
Sidney Harman,
▲ **EMP:** 31 **EST:** 1936
SQ FT: 203,000
SALES (est): 68.4MM
SALES (corp-wide): 3.3B **Publicly Held**
WEB: www.newsweek.com
SIC: 2721 Magazines: publishing only, not printed on site
PA: Iac/Interactivecorp
  555 W 18th St
  New York NY 10011
  212 314-7300

(G-9455)
DAILY NEWS LP (DH)
Also Called: New York Daily News
4 New York Plz Fl 6 (10004-2828)
PHONE..................212 210-2100
William D Holiber, *President*
Bruce Diamond, *Editor*
Dan Good, *Editor*
Alyssa Katz, *Editor*
Michael Nam, *Editor*
▲ **EMP:** 600
SQ FT: 150,000
SALES (est): 331.9MM
SALES (corp-wide): 1.5B **Publicly Held**
WEB: www.nydailynews.com
SIC: 2711 Commercial printing & newspaper publishing combined
HQ: Trx Pubco, Llc
  435 N Michigan Ave
  Chicago IL 60611
  312 222-9100

(G-9456)
DAILY RACING FORM INC (HQ)
708 3rd Ave Fl 12 (10017-4129)
PHONE..................212 366-7600
Steven Crist, *President*
Irwin Cohen, *Vice Pres*
Charles Hayward, *Vice Pres*
Michael Kravchenko, *Vice Pres*
Richard Rosenbush, *Vice Pres*
▼ **EMP:** 140 **EST:** 1894
SQ FT: 34,000
SALES (est): 41.1MM
SALES (corp-wide): 244.6MM **Privately Held**
WEB: www.drf.com
SIC: 2711 Newspapers, publishing & printing
PA: Arlington Capital Partners, L.P.
  5425 Wisconsin Ave # 200
  Chevy Chase MD 20815
  202 337-7500

(G-9457)
DAILY RACING FORM LLC
75 Broad St (10004-2415)
PHONE..................212 514-2180
Mandy Minger, *VP Mktg*
EMP: 12
SALES (corp-wide): 244.6MM **Privately Held**
SIC: 2711 Newspapers, publishing & printing
HQ: Daily Racing Form Llc
  708 3rd Ave Fl 12
  New York NY 10017
  212 366-7600

(G-9458)
DAILY WORLD PRESS INC
Also Called: Daily Sun New York
228 E 45th St Rm 700 (10017-3336)
PHONE..................212 922-9201
Yoshida Gin, *President*
EMP: 10
SALES (est): 591.9K **Privately Held**
SIC: 2711 Commercial printing & newspaper publishing combined; newspapers, publishing & printing

(G-9459)
DAILYCANDY INC
584 Broadway Rm 510 (10012-5244)
PHONE..................646 230-8719
Danielle Levy, *Ch of Bd*
Catherine Levene, *COO*
Peter A Sheinbaum, *COO*
EMP: 23
SQ FT: 6,100
SALES (est): 2.7MM **Privately Held**
WEB: www.dailycandy.com
SIC: 2741 Miscellaneous publishing

(G-9460)
DAKOTT LLC
244 Madison Ave Ste 211 (10016-2817)
PHONE..................888 805-6795
Michael Etedgi, *CEO*
Joshua Martin, *Exec VP*
Vera A Etedgi, *CFO*
▲ **EMP:** 5
SQ FT: 2,500
SALES: 1MM **Privately Held**
SIC: 3944 Scooters, children's

(G-9461)
DAMPITS INTERNATIONAL INC
425 W 57th St (10019-1764)
P.O. Box 493 (10019)
PHONE..................212 581-3047
David Hollander, *President*
Tair Hollander, *Vice Pres*
EMP: 5 **EST:** 1966
SALES (est): 480K **Privately Held**
SIC: 3634 Humidifiers, electric: household

(G-9462)
DAN KANE PLATING CO INC
357 W 36th St (10018-6455)
PHONE..................212 675-4947
Jack Zwas, *Owner*
EMP: 16
SQ FT: 5,000
SALES (est): 1.4MM **Privately Held**
SIC: 3471 Electroplating of metals or formed products

(G-9463)
DANA MICHELE LLC
3 E 84th St (10028-0447)
PHONE..................917 757-7777
Dana Schiavo, *President*
EMP: 1
SQ FT: 5,000
SALES: 2MM **Privately Held**
SIC: 3942 3944 2339 Dolls & stuffed toys; games, toys & children's vehicles; women's & misses' outerwear

(G-9464)
DANAHER CORPORATION
445 E 14th St Apt 3f (10009-2805)
PHONE..................516 443-9432
EMP: 186
SALES (corp-wide): 18.3B **Publicly Held**
SIC: 3823 Water quality monitoring & control systems
PA: Danaher Corporation
  2200 Penn Ave Nw Ste 800w
  Washington DC 20037
  202 828-0850

(G-9465)
DANHIER CO LLC
Also Called: Christophe Danhier
380 Rector Pl Apt 3d (10280-1442)
PHONE..................212 563-7683
Christophe Danhier,
EMP: 14
SQ FT: 1,200
SALES (est): 1.5MM **Privately Held**
WEB: www.danhier.com
SIC: 3915 Jewelers' materials & lapidary work

(G-9466)
DANI II INC (PA)
231 W 39th St Rm 1002 (10018-3167)
PHONE..................212 869-5999
Kirat Singh, *CEO*
▲ **EMP:** 14
SALES (est): 1.3MM **Privately Held**
SIC: 2339 Women's & misses' outerwear

(G-9467)
DANICE STORES INC
305 W 125th St (10027-3620)
PHONE..................212 665-0389
Barry Group, *Manager*
EMP: 12
SALES (corp-wide): 50.5MM **Privately Held**
SIC: 2339 5137 Sportswear, women's; sportswear, women's & children's
PA: Danice Stores, Inc.
  525 Fashion Ave Rm 507
  New York NY 10018
  212 776-1001

(G-9468)
DANIEL M FRIEDMAN & ASSOC INC
19 W 34th St Fl 4 (10001-3006)
PHONE..................212 695-5545
Daniel M Friedman, *President*
▲ **EMP:** 30
SQ FT: 5,000
SALES (est): 4.5MM **Publicly Held**
WEB: www.dmfassociates.com
SIC: 2387 Apparel belts
PA: Steven Madden, Ltd.
  5216 Barnett Ave
  Long Island City NY 11104

(G-9469)
DANNY MACAROONS INC
2191 3rd Ave Ste 3 (10035-3520)
PHONE..................260 622-8463
Daniel Cohen, *President*
EMP: 6 **EST:** 2010
SALES (est): 512.4K **Privately Held**
SIC: 2052 Cookies & crackers

(G-9470)
DANRAY TEXTILES CORP (PA)
Also Called: Dantex Trimming & Textile Co
270 W 39th St Fl 5 (10018-4409)
PHONE..................212 354-5213
Daniel Bergstein, *President*
Danny Bergstein, *Branch Mgr*
▲ **EMP:** 13
SQ FT: 2,000
SALES (est): 915.3K **Privately Held**
SIC: 2241 Trimmings, textile

(G-9471)
DARCY PRINTING AND LITHOG
121 Varick St Fl 9 (10013-1408)
PHONE..................212 924-1554

James Tsiropinas, *President*
EMP: 8
SALES (est): 590K **Privately Held**
SIC: 2759 Commercial printing

(G-9472)
DASH PRINTING INC
153 W 27th St (10001-6203)
PHONE..................212 643-8534
David Ashendorf, *President*
Rachel Feiner, *Exec VP*
EMP: 5
SQ FT: 1,100
SALES (est): 457.1K **Privately Held**
WEB: www.dashprinting.com
SIC: 2759 Commercial printing

(G-9473)
DASHLANE INC
156 5th Ave Ste 504 (10010-7757)
PHONE..................212 596-7510
Emmanuel Schalit, *CEO*
Alexandre Barreira, *President*
David Sawin, *Partner*
Alexis Fogel, *Vice Pres*
Guillaume Maron, *Vice Pres*
EMP: 45
SALES (est): 3.2MM **Privately Held**
SIC: 7372 Prepackaged software

(G-9474)
DATA IMPLEMENTATION INC
5 E 22nd St Apt 14t (10010-5325)
PHONE..................212 979-2015
Gerald A Goldstein, *President*
William F Hahn, *Vice Pres*
Diana Goldstein, *Treasurer*
Debra Hahn, *Admin Sec*
EMP: 5
SALES (est): 410K **Privately Held**
SIC: 7372 Prepackaged software

(G-9475)
DATADOG INC (PA)
620 8th Ave Fl 45 (10018-1741)
PHONE..................866 329-4466
Olivier Promel, *CEO*
Alexis Le-Quoc, *President*
David Obstler, *CFO*
Adam Gentile, *Accounts Exec*
Alex Rosemblat, *Mktg Dir*
EMP: 43
SQ FT: 7,000
SALES (est): 15.7MM **Privately Held**
SIC: 7372 Publishers' computer software

(G-9476)
DATAMAX INTERNATIONAL INC
Also Called: Data Max
132 Nassau St Rm 511 (10038-2433)
PHONE..................212 693-0933
Saul Wasser, *CEO*
Max Wasser, *Treasurer*
Richard Dawkins, *Executive Asst*
▲ EMP: 45
SQ FT: 15,000
SALES (est): 4.2MM **Privately Held**
WEB: www.datamaxplanners.com
SIC: 2782 3172 Checkbooks; diaries; personal leather goods

(G-9477)
DAVE & JOHNNY LTD
225 W 37th St Fl 6 (10018-6741)
PHONE..................212 302-9050
Roholah Simhaee, *President*
▲ EMP: 25
SQ FT: 9,000
SALES (est): 2.2MM **Privately Held**
WEB: www.daveandjohnny.com
SIC: 2335 Women's, juniors' & misses' dresses

(G-9478)
DAVES ELECTRIC MOTORS & PUMPS
282 E 7th St Apt 1 (10009-6027)
PHONE..................212 982-2930
Yefim Vinokur, *President*
EMP: 5
SQ FT: 5,600
SALES (est): 769.9K **Privately Held**
SIC: 7694 7699 Electric motor repair; pumps & pumping equipment repair

(G-9479)
DAVID & YOUNG CO INC
366 5th Ave Rm 707 (10001-2211)
PHONE..................212 594-6034
John Yoo, *President*
Jesus Arriola, *Vice Pres*
EMP: 6 EST: 2005
SALES (est): 494.7K **Privately Held**
SIC: 2389 Apparel & accessories

(G-9480)
DAVID FRIEDMAN CHAIN CO INC
Also Called: David Friedman and Sons
10 E 33rd St Fl 6 (10016-0014)
PHONE..................212 684-1760
Peter Banyasz, *President*
Matthew Friedman, *Vice Pres*
EMP: 15 EST: 1913
SQ FT: 5,000
SALES (est): 1.4MM **Privately Held**
SIC: 3911 Jewelry, precious metal

(G-9481)
DAVID ISSEKS & SONS INC
298 Broome St (10002-3704)
PHONE..................212 966-8694
David Hackhauser, *President*
Joyce Hockhauser, *Exec VP*
EMP: 22
SQ FT: 5,000
SALES (est): 1.6MM **Privately Held**
SIC: 3443 7699 2449 Water tanks, metal plate; tank repair; wood containers

(G-9482)
DAVID KING LINEN INC
295 5th Ave Ste 1202 (10016-7110)
PHONE..................718 241-7298
Abraham Aosi, *Ch of Bd*
◆ EMP: 15
SQ FT: 8,000
SALES (est): 1.6MM **Privately Held**
SIC: 2299 5023 Linen fabrics; linens & towels

(G-9483)
DAVID PEYSER SPORTSWEAR INC
Also Called: 30 Degrees Weatherproof
4 Bryant Park Fl 12 Flr 12 (10018)
PHONE..................212 695-7716
Eliot Peyser, *Branch Mgr*
EMP: 40
SALES (corp-wide): 54.7MM **Privately Held**
WEB: www.mvsport.com
SIC: 2329 5651 Men's & boys' sportswear & athletic clothing; unisex clothing stores
PA: David Peyser Sportswear, Inc.
90 Spence St
Bay Shore NY 11706
631 231-7788

(G-9484)
DAVID S DIAMONDS INC
546 5th Ave Fl 7 (10036-5000)
PHONE..................212 921-8029
David So, *Chairman*
Joan So, *Vice Pres*
▲ EMP: 15
SQ FT: 350
SALES (est): 2.3MM **Privately Held**
WEB: www.davidsdiamonds.com
SIC: 3911 5944 Jewelry, precious metal; jewelry, precious stones & precious metals

(G-9485)
DAVID SUTHERLAND SHOWROOMS - N (PA)
D&D Building 979 3rd (10022)
PHONE..................212 871-9717
Thomas William, *Principal*
EMP: 5
SALES (est): 366.1K **Privately Held**
SIC: 2511 Wood household furniture

(G-9486)
DAVID WEEKS STUDIO
38 Walker St Frnt 1 (10013-3589)
PHONE..................212 966-3433
David Weeks, *President*
▲ EMP: 18

SALES (est): 2.5MM **Privately Held**
SIC: 3645 5719 Residential lighting fixtures; lighting fixtures

(G-9487)
DAVID WEISZ & SONS USA LLC
20 W 47th St Ste 601 (10036-3768)
PHONE..................212 840-4747
David Weisz, *Ch of Bd*
EMP: 8
SALES (est): 1.2MM **Privately Held**
SIC: 3911 5094 Jewelry, precious metal; diamonds (gems)

(G-9488)
DAVID YURMAN ENTERPRISES LLC (PA)
Also Called: Yurman Retail
24 Vestry St (10013-1903)
PHONE..................212 896-1550
Gabriella Forte, *CEO*
Guillaume Boutry, *Vice Pres*
Tracy Cotton, *Vice Pres*
Kate Harrison, *Vice Pres*
Tom O'Rourke, *Vice Pres*
◆ EMP: 300
SQ FT: 75,000
SALES (est): 268.5MM **Privately Held**
SIC: 3911 Jewelry, precious metal

(G-9489)
DAVID YURMAN RETAIL LLC
712 Madison Ave (10065-7207)
PHONE..................877 226-1400
EMP: 7
SALES (est): 881.6K
SALES (corp-wide): 275MM **Privately Held**
SIC: 3911 Mfg Precious Metal Jewelry
PA: David Yurman Enterprises Llc
24 Vestry St
New York NY 10013
212 896-1550

(G-9490)
DAVLER MEDIA GROUP LLC (PA)
213 W 35th St Rm 1201 (10001-1916)
PHONE..................212 315-0800
Bethany Braun, *Editor*
Whitney Harris, *Editor*
Griffin Miller, *Editor*
Linda Sheridan, *Editor*
Emma Steven, *Editor*
EMP: 30
SALES (est): 4.8MM **Privately Held**
WEB: www.davlermedia.com
SIC: 2721 Magazines: publishing & printing

(G-9491)
DAVOS BRANDS LLC
381 Park Ave S Rm 1015 (10016-8827)
PHONE..................212 779-1911
Andrew Chrisomaois, *CEO*
Blake Bond, *COO*
Sean Hartnell, *Vice Pres*
Kenrik Mannion, *Vice Pres*
Janelle Basa, *Manager*
◆ EMP: 10
SALES (est): 311.7K **Privately Held**
SIC: 2084 Neutral spirits, fruit

(G-9492)
DAXOR CORPORATION (PA)
350 5th Ave Ste 4740 (10118-0002)
PHONE..................212 330-8500
Michael Feldschuh, *Ch of Bd*
Romeo Mendoza, *COO*
Robert J Michel, *CFO*
John Wilkens, *CFO*
Edward Feuer, *Bd of Directors*
EMP: 12 EST: 1971
SALES (est): 1.6MM **Publicly Held**
WEB: www.daxor.com
SIC: 3841 8099 Surgical & medical instruments; sperm bank; blood bank

(G-9493)
DE MEO BROTHERS INC (PA)
Also Called: De Meo Brothers Hair
129 W 29th St Fl 5 (10001-5105)
PHONE..................212 268-1400
Gabriel Klugmann, *President*
▲ EMP: 7
SQ FT: 6,000

SALES (est): 928.8K **Privately Held**
SIC: 3999 6221 Hair & hair-based products; commodity traders, contracts

(G-9494)
DEBMAR-MERCURY
75 Rockefeller Plz # 1600 (10019-6908)
PHONE..................212 669-5025
Ira Bernstein, *President*
Karen Bonck, *Senior VP*
Alexandra Jewett, *Senior VP*
Jim Kramer, *Senior VP*
Tresha Marshall, *Senior VP*
EMP: 9
SALES (est): 721.7K **Privately Held**
SIC: 2836 Culture media

(G-9495)
DEFINITION PRESS INC
141 Greene St (10012-3201)
PHONE..................212 777-4490
Margot Carpenter, *Exec Dir*
Ellen Reiss, *Director*
EMP: 10 EST: 1954
SQ FT: 2,210
SALES (est): 780K **Privately Held**
WEB: www.definitionpress.com
SIC: 2731 Books: publishing only

(G-9496)
DEFRAN SYSTEMS INC
1 Penn Plz Ste 1700 (10119-1700)
PHONE..................212 727-8342
Fran L Turso, *President*
Ron Aceto, *Vice Pres*
Deborah Huyer, *Vice Pres*
Boris Kagan, *Vice Pres*
Greg Travis, *Vice Pres*
EMP: 35
SALES (est): 2.3MM **Privately Held**
WEB: www.defran.com
SIC: 7372 7371 Prepackaged software; custom computer programming services
PA: Netsmart Technologies, Inc.
4950 College Blvd
Overland Park KS 66211

(G-9497)
DELCATH SYSTEMS INC (PA)
1633 Broadway Fl 22c (10019-6708)
PHONE..................212 489-2100
Roger G Stoll, *Ch of Bd*
Jennifer K Simpson, *President*
John Purpura, *Exec VP*
Barbra C Keck, *CFO*
Jennifer Simpson, *Director*
EMP: 46
SQ FT: 6,877
SALES: 2.7MM **Privately Held**
WEB: www.delcath.com
SIC: 3841 2834 Surgical & medical instruments; catheters; pharmaceutical preparations

(G-9498)
DELL COMMUNICATIONS INC
Also Called: Dell Graphics
109 W 27th St Frnt 2 (10001-6208)
PHONE..................212 989-3434
Steve Dell, *President*
Trg Aguiar, *Production*
EMP: 5
SQ FT: 5,000
SALES (est): 784.8K **Privately Held**
WEB: www.dellgraphics.com
SIC: 2752 Commercial printing, offset

(G-9499)
DEMOS MEDICAL PUBLISHING LLC
11 W 42nd St Ste 15c (10036-8002)
PHONE..................516 889-1791
Phyllis Gold, *President*
EMP: 10
SQ FT: 1,600
SALES (est): 970K **Privately Held**
WEB: www.demosmedpub.com
SIC: 2731 2721 Books: publishing only; trade journals: publishing only, not printed on site

New York - New York County (G-9500)

(G-9500)
DENIZ INFORMATION SYSTEMS
Also Called: Dis
208 E 51st St Ste 129 (10022-6557)
P.O. Box 841 (10150-0841)
PHONE..................212 750-5199
Haluk Deniz, *Ch of Bd*
Nihat Ozkaya, *VP Opers*
Karen Emer, *VP Mktg*
EMP: 9
SQ FT: 600
SALES (est): 527.2K **Privately Held**
SIC: 7372 5045 Prepackaged software; computers, peripherals & software

(G-9501)
DENNIS BASSO COUTURE INC
Also Called: Dennis Basso Furs
825 Madison Ave (10065-5042)
PHONE..................212 794-4500
Dennis Basso, *President*
▲ **EMP:** 12
SALES (est): 1.2MM **Privately Held**
SIC: 2371 Fur goods

(G-9502)
DENNIS PUBLISHING INC
Also Called: Week Publications, The
55 W 39th St Fl 5 (10018-3850)
P.O. Box 111 (10018-0002)
PHONE..................646 717-9500
Steven Kotok, *CEO*
Marc Ambinder, *Editor*
Alexis Boncy, *Editor*
Harold Maass, *Editor*
Loren Talbot, *Editor*
EMP: 100
SALES (est): 22.5MM
SALES (corp-wide): 142.3MM **Privately Held**
SIC: 2721 Magazines: publishing only, not printed on site
HQ: Dennis Publishing Limited
2nd Floor,
London W2 3R
203 890-3890

(G-9503)
DENTAL TRIBUNE AMERICA LLC
116 W 23rd St Ste 500 (10011-2599)
PHONE..................212 244-7181
Daniel Zimmermann, *Editor*
Nadine Dehmel, *Vice Pres*
Anna Kataoka, *Research*
Humberto Estrada, *Sales Staff*
Grzegorz Rosiak, *Sales Staff*
EMP: 14
SQ FT: 4,000
SALES (est): 3MM **Privately Held**
SIC: 2759 Publication printing

(G-9504)
DESIGN ARCHIVES INC
1460 Broadway (10036-7329)
PHONE..................212 768-0617
Veena Advani, *President*
EMP: 5
SQ FT: 2,000
SALES (est): 415.5K **Privately Held**
SIC: 2395 5137 Embroidery & art needlework; women's & children's clothing

(G-9505)
DESIGN LITHOGRAPHERS INC
519 8th Ave Ste 3 (10018-6506)
PHONE..................212 645-8900
Daniel Green, *President*
Dan Green, *Officer*
EMP: 12
SALES (est): 1.1MM **Privately Held**
WEB: www.designlitho.com
SIC: 2752 Commercial printing, offset

(G-9506)
DESIGN RESEARCH LTD
Also Called: Tom Dixon
243 Centre St (10013-3224)
PHONE..................212 228-7675
Alex Wisnioski, *Mng Member*
▲ **EMP:** 150
SQ FT: 2,000
SALES (est): 4.1MM **Privately Held**
SIC: 3299 Non-metallic mineral statuary & other decorative products

(G-9507)
DESIGN SOURCE BY LG INC
115 Bowery Frnt 1 (10002-4933)
PHONE..................212 274-0022
Leo Greisman, *CEO*
Daniel Olejnik, *Manager*
▲ **EMP:** 23 **EST:** 1968
SQ FT: 1,000
SALES (est): 3MM **Privately Held**
SIC: 3423 Plumbers' hand tools

(G-9508)
DESIGNLOGOCOM INC
Also Called: Impressions Prtg & Graphics
15 W 37th St Lbby A (10018-5317)
PHONE..................212 564-0200
Arif Jacksi, *Chairman*
Balkrishna Mehta, *Controller*
EMP: 6
SALES (est): 825.8K **Privately Held**
WEB: www.designlogo.com
SIC: 2752 Commercial printing, lithographic

(G-9509)
DESIGNWAY LTD
27 E 21st St Fl 7 (10010-6249)
PHONE..................212 254-2220
Joan Morgan, *President*
EMP: 6
SALES: 1MM **Privately Held**
SIC: 2211 5712 Draperies & drapery fabrics, cotton; custom made furniture, except cabinets

(G-9510)
DESSIN/FOURNIR INC
Also Called: Rose Cumming
232 E 59th St Fl 2 (10022-1464)
PHONE..................212 758-0844
Jay Shemwell, *Sales Mgr*
Ashley Dopita, *General Counsel*
EMP: 18
SALES (corp-wide): 8.4MM **Privately Held**
WEB: www.dessinfournir.com
SIC: 2511 Wood household furniture
HQ: Dessin/Fournir, Inc.
308 W Mill St
Plainville KS 67663

(G-9511)
DETNY FOOTWEAR INC
Also Called: Shane & Shawn
1 River Pl Apt 1224 (10036-4369)
PHONE..................212 423-1040
Shane Ward, *CEO*
Shawn J Ward, *President*
▲ **EMP:** 8
SQ FT: 1,800
SALES: 1MM **Privately Held**
WEB: www.detny.com
SIC: 3143 3144 3021 Men's footwear, except athletic; women's footwear, except athletic; rubber & plastics footwear

(G-9512)
DETOUR APPAREL INC (PA)
Also Called: Chula Girls
530 7th Ave Rm 608 (10018-4888)
PHONE..................212 221-3265
Lisa Medina, *President*
EMP: 46 **EST:** 2003
SQ FT: 3,000
SALES (est): 1.9MM **Privately Held**
SIC: 2369 Jackets: girls', children's & infants'

(G-9513)
DEUX LUX INC
37 W 20th St Ste 1204 (10011-3712)
PHONE..................212 620-0801
Sarah Jones, *General Mgr*
EMP: 5
SALES (est): 340.2K
SALES (corp-wide): 2.1MM **Privately Held**
SIC: 3171 Handbags, women's
PA: Deux Lux Inc.
11609 Vanowen St Ste B
North Hollywood CA 91605
213 746-7040

(G-9514)
DEVA CONCEPTS LLC
Also Called: Devacurl
75 Spring St Fl 8 (10012-4071)
PHONE..................212 343-0344
Samantha Mellone, *Relations*
EMP: 50
SALES (est): 7.4MM **Privately Held**
SIC: 3999 Atomizers, toiletry

(G-9515)
DEW GRAPHICS INC
Also Called: Dew Graphics
519 8th Ave Fl 18 (10018-4577)
PHONE..................212 727-8820
Elaine Weisbrot, *President*
Don Weisbrot, *Vice Pres*
Brian Demars, *Chief Engr*
EMP: 35
SQ FT: 17,000
SALES (est): 2.9MM **Privately Held**
SIC: 2759 Screen printing

(G-9516)
DEZAWY LLC
Also Called: Thewritedeal
55 W 116th St Ste 327 (10026-2508)
PHONE..................917 436-8820
Yves Sorokobi, *Mng Member*
EMP: 6
SALES (est): 70K **Privately Held**
SIC: 2741 7389 Miscellaneous publishing;

(G-9517)
DFA NEW YORK LLC
318 W 39th St Fl 10 (10018-1486)
PHONE..................212 523-0021
Alan Madoff, *Mng Member*
Jeff Zwiebel, *Mng Member*
▲ **EMP:** 21
SALES (est): 2.1MM **Privately Held**
SIC: 2339 Women's & misses' accessories

(G-9518)
DIA
535 W 22nd St Fl 4 (10011-1119)
PHONE..................212 675-4097
Nathalie De Gunzburg, *Principal*
EMP: 1
SALES (est): 13.3MM **Privately Held**
SIC: 2675 Die-cut paper & board

(G-9519)
DIALASE INC
36 W 47th St Ste 709 (10036-8601)
PHONE..................212 575-8833
Isace Landerer, *President*
EMP: 5
SQ FT: 1,200
SALES (est): 330K **Privately Held**
SIC: 3915 Diamond cutting & polishing

(G-9520)
DIAMEX INC
580 5th Ave Ste 625 (10036-4725)
PHONE..................212 575-8145
David Steinmetz, *President*
Ronald Vanderlinden, *Vice Pres*
EMP: 5
SQ FT: 1,200
SALES (est): 590.4K **Privately Held**
SIC: 3915 5094 Diamond cutting & polishing; diamonds (gems)

(G-9521)
DIAMOND CONSTELLATION CORP
37 W 47th St Ste 506 (10036-2809)
P.O. Box 650466, Fresh Meadows (11365-0466)
PHONE..................212 819-0324
Fax: 212 944-9245
EMP: 6 **EST:** 1959
SQ FT: 2,500
SALES (est): 470K **Privately Held**
SIC: 3915 5094 Diamond Cutting & Whol Of Precious Diamonds

(G-9522)
DIAMOND DISTRIBUTORS INC (PA)
608 5th Ave Fl 10 (10020-2303)
PHONE..................212 921-9188
EMP: 8

SALES (est): 1.7MM **Privately Held**
SIC: 3911 Jewelry, precious metal

(G-9523)
DIAMOND INSCRIPTION TECH
36 W 47th St Ste 1008 (10036-8601)
PHONE..................646 366-7944
Jacob Dresdner, *Owner*
EMP: 10
SALES (est): 913.2K **Privately Held**
WEB: www.dresdiam.com
SIC: 2759 7389 Laser printing; business services

(G-9524)
DIANOS KATHRYN DESIGNS
376 Broadway Apt 13b (10013-3943)
PHONE..................212 267-1584
Kathryn Dianos, *Owner*
EMP: 5
SALES (est): 520K **Privately Held**
SIC: 2339 7389 Women's & misses' athletic clothing & sportswear; apparel designers, commercial

(G-9525)
DIGIFAB SYSTEMS INC
1412 Broadway Ste 2100 (10018-9228)
PHONE..................212 944-9882
Avedik Izmirlian, *Branch Mgr*
EMP: 5
SALES (est): 387.8K **Privately Held**
SIC: 3663 Digital encoders
PA: Digifab Systems, Inc.
5015 Pacific Blvd
Vernon CA 90058

(G-9526)
DIGITAL COLOR CONCEPTS INC (PA)
Also Called: D C C
30 W 21st St Fl 5 (10010-6961)
PHONE..................212 989-4888
Stephen Pandolfi, *CEO*
Donald Terwilliger, *Exec VP*
Bret Hesler, *Vice Pres*
Doug Simmons, *Vice Pres*
Jim D'Alessandro, *VP Mfg*
EMP: 24
SQ FT: 15,000
SALES (est): 15.7MM **Privately Held**
WEB: www.dccnyc.com
SIC: 2752 2791 Commercial printing, lithographic; photocomposition, for the printing trade

(G-9527)
DIGITAL EVOLUTION INC (PA)
200 N End Ave Apt 20e (10282-7018)
PHONE..................212 732-2722
Eric Pulier, *CEO*
Dominic Giordano, *President*
Nicholas Giordano, *Vice Pres*
EMP: 23 **EST:** 2000
SQ FT: 5,000
SALES (est): 4.2MM **Privately Held**
WEB: www.digitalevolution.com
SIC: 2759 7336 7384 Commercial printing; commercial art & graphic design; graphic arts & related design; photofinish laboratories; photograph developing & retouching

(G-9528)
DILIGENT BOARD MEMBER SVCS LLC
310 5th Ave Fl 7 (10001-3605)
PHONE..................212 741-8181
Warren Allen, *Counsel*
Bryan Zwahlen, *Vice Pres*
Matthew Evangelisti, *Engineer*
Danielle Nathanson, *Marketing Staff*
Tricia Burke, *Manager*
EMP: 20
SQ FT: 8,000
SALES (est): 1.4MM **Privately Held**
SIC: 7372 Prepackaged software

(G-9529)
DILIGENT CORPORATION (PA)
1385 Brdwy Fl 19 Flr 19 (10018)
PHONE..................212 741-8181
Brian Stafford, *President*
Michael Flickman, *Exec VP*
Jeff Hilk, *Exec VP*
Thomas N Tartaro, *Exec VP*

▲ = Import ▼=Export
◆ =Import/Export

GEOGRAPHIC SECTION

Marco Morsella, *Senior VP*
EMP: 122
SALES (est): 79.4MM **Privately Held**
SIC: 7372 Business oriented computer software

(G-9530)
DIMODA DESIGNS INC
48 W 48th St Ste 403 (10036-1713)
PHONE..................212 355-8166
Karabet Koroglu, *CEO*
Hayk Ogulluk, *President*
Garo Koroglu, *Vice Pres*
Mardik Marachlian, *Accountant*
EMP: 25
SALES (est): 2.1MM **Privately Held**
WEB: www.dimoda.com
SIC: 3911 Jewelry, precious metal

(G-9531)
DIRECT MKTG EDCTL FNDATION INC
Also Called: DMEF/EDGE
1333 Broadway Rm 301 (10018-1170)
PHONE..................212 790-1512
Terri L Bartlett, *President*
John Taborosi, *COO*
Linda High, *Exec VP*
Marie Adolphe, *Vice Pres*
Gina Scala, *Vice Pres*
EMP: 8
SALES: 1.5MM **Privately Held**
WEB: www.the-dmef.com
SIC: 2721 Trade journals: publishing only, not printed on site

(G-9532)
DIRECT PRINT INC (PA)
77 E 125th St (10035-1622)
PHONE..................212 987-6003
Kevin Williams, *President*
EMP: 10
SALES (est): 1.9MM **Privately Held**
SIC: 2759 Commercial printing

(G-9533)
DIRTY LEMON BEVERAGES LLC (PA)
95 Grand St Apt 5 (10013-5902)
PHONE..................877 897-7784
Zak Normantin, *CEO*
EMP: 9 **EST:** 2015
SALES (est): 2MM **Privately Held**
SIC: 2086 Lemonade: packaged in cans, bottles, etc.

(G-9534)
DISCOVER CASTING INC
17 W 45th St Ste 701 (10036-4907)
PHONE..................212 302-5060
Yanneth Perlaza, *President*
Louis Perlaza, *Vice Pres*
EMP: 10
SQ FT: 1,900
SALES: 3.4MM **Privately Held**
SIC: 3366 3089 Castings (except die): brass; casting of plastic

(G-9535)
DISCOVER MEDIA LLC
Also Called: Discover Magazine
90 5th Ave Ste 1100 (10011-2051)
PHONE..................212 624-4800
Henry Donahue, *CEO*
Bob Guccione, *Ch of Bd*
Ernie Mastroianni, *Editor*
Jeniene Lossowski, *Marketing Staff*
April Reese, *Assoc Editor*
EMP: 35
SQ FT: 11,500
SALES (est): 3.2MM **Privately Held**
WEB: www.discovermedia.net
SIC: 2721 Periodicals Printing & Publishing

(G-9536)
DISPATCH GRAPHICS INC
Also Called: Dispatch Letter Service
344 W 38th St Fl 4r (10018-6432)
PHONE..................212 307-5943
Paul A Grech, *President*
Stephen Grech, *Exec VP*
EMP: 10
SQ FT: 8,000

SALES (est): 1.2MM **Privately Held**
SIC: 2752 7331 2791 2789 Commercial printing, offset; mailing service; typesetting; bookbinding & related work

(G-9537)
DISPLAY SHOP INC (PA)
261 Madison Ave Fl 9 (10016-2311)
PHONE..................646 202-9494
Manuel Rodrigues, *Owner*
EMP: 13
SALES (est): 4.2MM **Privately Held**
SIC: 2542 Fixtures: display, office or store: except wood

(G-9538)
DISSENT MAGAZINE
120 Wall St Fl 31 (10005-4007)
PHONE..................212 316-3120
Michael Walder, *President*
EMP: 10
SALES (est): 789.6K **Privately Held**
SIC: 2721 Magazines: publishing only, not printed on site

(G-9539)
DISTINCTIVE PRINTING INC
225 W 37th St Fl 16 (10018-6637)
PHONE..................212 727-3000
Fax: 212 727-3004
EMP: 6
SQ FT: 5,000
SALES (est): 866.2K **Privately Held**
SIC: 2752 Lithographic Commercial Printing

(G-9540)
DISTRIBIO USA LLC
Also Called: Biologique Recherche
261 5th Ave Rm 2000 (10016-7701)
PHONE..................212 989-6077
Philippe Allouche,
EMP: 5
SALES (est): 1MM **Privately Held**
WEB: www.biologiquerecherche.com
SIC: 2844 Face creams or lotions

(G-9541)
DK PUBLISHING
345 Hudson St (10014-4502)
PHONE..................212 366-2000
Gary June, *CEO*
Tom Korman, *Vice Pres*
Thomas Leddy, *Prdtn Mgr*
Stephanie Kull, *Sales Staff*
Alice Monteverdi, *Sales Associate*
▲ **EMP:** 18 **EST:** 2009
SALES (est): 1.8MM **Privately Held**
SIC: 2741 Miscellaneous publishing

(G-9542)
DM2 MEDIA LLC
Also Called: Digiday
1 Liberty Plz Fl 8 (10006-1431)
PHONE..................646 419-4357
Newton J Friese, *CEO*
Brian Morrissey, *President*
Nancy Picker, *Exec VP*
Elaine Mershon, *Vice Pres*
Andrea Sontz, *Vice Pres*
EMP: 40
SALES (est): 708.5K **Privately Held**
SIC: 3695 Magnetic & optical recording media

(G-9543)
DNP ELECTRONICS AMERICA LLC
Also Called: Deal
335 Madison Ave Fl 3 (10017-4616)
PHONE..................212 503-1060
Masaru Suzuki, *President*
Kaoru Kando, *CFO*
▲ **EMP:** 60
SALES (est): 6.4MM
SALES (corp-wide): 13.2B **Privately Held**
SIC: 3861 Screens, projection
HQ: Dnp Corporation Usa
335 Madison Ave Fl 3
New York NY 10017

(G-9544)
DOCUMENT JOURNAL INC
264 Canal St (10013-3529)
PHONE..................646 586-3099
Joshua Glass, *Manager*

▲ **EMP:** 8
SALES (est): 399.5K **Privately Held**
SIC: 2711 Newspapers, publishing & printing

(G-9545)
DOG GOOD PRODUCTS LLC
Also Called: Victoria Stilwell Positively
1407 Broadway Fl 41 (10018-2348)
PHONE..................212 789-7000
David Cayre,
Sandy Menichelli,
EMP: 6
SQ FT: 20,000
SALES (est): 563.5K **Privately Held**
SIC: 3199 2047 Dog furnishings: collars, leashes, muzzles, etc.: leather; dog food

(G-9546)
DOLBY LABORATORIES INC
1350 6th Ave Fl 28 (10019-4702)
PHONE..................212 767-1700
Bill Allen, *Manager*
EMP: 15
SALES (corp-wide): 1.1B **Publicly Held**
WEB: www.dolby.com
SIC: 3861 Motion picture film
PA: Dolby Laboratories, Inc.
1275 Market St
San Francisco CA 94103
415 558-0200

(G-9547)
DONALD BRUHNKE
Also Called: Chicago Watermark Company
455 W 37th St Apt 1018 (10018-4785)
PHONE..................212 600-1260
Donald Bruhnke, *Owner*
EMP: 10
SQ FT: 1,200
SALES: 1MM **Privately Held**
SIC: 2759 Commercial printing

(G-9548)
DONNA DISTEFANO LTD (PA)
37 W 20th St Ste 1106 (10011-3713)
PHONE..................212 594-3757
Donna Distefano, *President*
EMP: 9
SALES (est): 820.8K **Privately Held**
SIC: 3911 Jewelry, precious metal

(G-9549)
DONNA KARAN COMPANY LLC
Also Called: Dkny Jeans
240 W 40th St Bsmt 2 (10018-1533)
PHONE..................212 372-6500
Mark Webber, *Branch Mgr*
EMP: 12
SALES (corp-wide): 2.8B **Publicly Held**
WEB: www.donnakaran.com
SIC: 2337 Women's & misses' suits & coats
HQ: The Donna Karan Company Llc
240 W 40th St
New York NY 10018
212 789-1500

(G-9550)
DONNA KARAN COMPANY LLC
240 W 40th St Bsmt (10018-1533)
PHONE..................212 789-1500
Carol Knouse, *Senior VP*
EMP: 157
SALES (corp-wide): 2.8B **Publicly Held**
WEB: www.dkny.com
SIC: 2335 2337 2331 2339 Women's, juniors' & misses' dresses: suits: women's, misses' & juniors'; skirts, separate: women's, misses' & juniors'; pantsuits: women's, misses' & juniors'; blouses, women's & juniors': made from purchased material; women's & misses' jackets & coats, except sportswear; suits, men's & boys': made from purchased materials; coats, tailored, men's & boys': from purchased materials; slacks, dress: men's, youths' & boys'
HQ: The Donna Karan Company Llc
240 W 40th St
New York NY 10018
212 789-1500

(G-9551)
DONNA KARAN COMPANY LLC (DH)
Also Called: Dkny
240 W 40th St (10018-1533)
PHONE..................212 789-1500
Donna Karan, *CEO*
Carolyn Mariani, *President*
Fred Wilson, *Manager*
Louis Praino,
Stephen Ruzow,
◆ **EMP:** 300 **EST:** 1984
SQ FT: 67,000
SALES (est): 355.3MM
SALES (corp-wide): 2.8B **Publicly Held**
WEB: www.dkny.com
SIC: 2335 2337 2331 2339 Women's, juniors' & misses' dresses; suits: women's, misses' & juniors'; skirts, separate: women's, misses' & juniors'; pantsuits: women's, misses' & juniors'; blouses, women's & juniors': made from purchased material; women's & misses' jackets & coats, except sportswear; suits, men's & boys': made from purchased materials; coats, tailored, men's & boys': from purchased materials; slacks, dress: men's, youths' & boys'
HQ: Donna Karan International Inc.
240 W 40th St
New York NY 10018
212 789-1500

(G-9552)
DONNA KARAN INTERNATIONAL INC (HQ)
240 W 40th St (10018-1533)
PHONE..................212 789-1500
Patricia F Kalberer, *CFO*
◆ **EMP:** 10 **EST:** 1996
SQ FT: 80,000
SALES (est): 394.8MM
SALES (corp-wide): 2.8B **Publicly Held**
WEB: www.donnakaran.com
SIC: 2335 2337 2331 2339 Women's, juniors' & misses' dresses; jackets & vests, except fur & leather: women's; skirts, separate: women's, misses' & juniors'; suits: women's, misses' & juniors'; blouses, women's & juniors': made from purchased material; shirts, women's & juniors': made from purchased materials; women's & misses' outerwear; slacks: women's, misses' & juniors'; jeans: women's, misses' & juniors'; athletic clothing: women's, misses' & juniors'; men's & boys' furnishings; slacks, dress: men's, youths' & boys'; jeans: men's, youths' & boys'
PA: G-Iii Apparel Group, Ltd.
512 7th Ave Fl 35
New York NY 10018
212 403-0500

(G-9553)
DONNA KARAN INTERNATIONAL INC
240 W 40th St Bsmt (10018-1533)
PHONE..................212 768-5800
Fred Wilson, *Manager*
EMP: 8
SALES (corp-wide): 2.8B **Publicly Held**
WEB: www.donnakaran.com
SIC: 2335 2337 2331 2339 Women's, juniors' & misses' dresses; jackets & vests, except fur & leather: women's; blouses, women's & juniors': made from purchased material; women's & misses' outerwear; men's & boys' furnishings; slacks, dress: men's, youths' & boys'
HQ: Donna Karan International Inc.
240 W 40th St
New York NY 10018
212 789-1500

(G-9554)
DONNA MORGAN LLC
Also Called: Ali Ro
132 W 36th St Rm 801 (10018-8824)
PHONE..................212 575-2550
Haley Moss, *Production*
Kathleen Mc Feeters,
Donna Annunziata,
Milton Cahn,
Larry Lefkowitz,
EMP: 25

New York - New York County (G-9555)

SALES (est): 3.8MM **Privately Held**
WEB: www.donnamorgan.com
SIC: 3161 Clothing & apparel carrying cases

(G-9555)
DONNELLEY FINANCIAL LLC (HQ)
Also Called: Bowne Enterprise Solutions
55 Water St Fl 11 (10041-0022)
PHONE..................................212 425-0298
Thomas J Quinlan III, *CEO*
William P Penders, *President*
Scott L Spitzer, *Senior VP*
Tim Maclean, *Vice Pres*
John J Walker, *CFO*
▲ EMP: 420
SQ FT: 143,000
SALES (est): 781.5MM
SALES (corp-wide): 1B **Publicly Held**
WEB: www.bowne.com
SIC: 2752 Commercial printing, lithographic; business forms, lithographed
PA: Donnelley Financial Solutions, Inc.
35 W Wacker Dr
Chicago IL 60601
312 326-8000

(G-9556)
DONNELLEY FINANCIAL LLC
Also Called: Bowne Business Solutions
555 5th Ave Fl 4 (10017-9271)
PHONE..................................212 351-9000
Susan Fenwick, *Vice Pres*
EMP: 60
SALES (corp-wide): 1B **Publicly Held**
SIC: 2752 Commercial printing, lithographic
HQ: Donnelley Financial, Llc
55 Water St Fl 11
New York NY 10041
212 425-0298

(G-9557)
DONORWALL INC
125 Maiden Ln Rm 205 (10038-5099)
P.O. Box 1005 (10272-1005)
PHONE..................................212 766-9670
Barry Silverberg, *President*
EMP: 16
SALES (est): 1.3MM **Privately Held**
WEB: www.donorwall.com
SIC: 3999 Plaques, picture, laminated

(G-9558)
DORAL APPAREL GROUP INC
498 Fashion Ave Fl 10 (10018-6957)
PHONE..................................917 208-5652
Martin Ehrlich, *President*
EMP: 9 EST: 1999
SQ FT: 5,000
SALES (est): 1.1MM **Privately Held**
SIC: 2339 2326 Women's & misses' athletic clothing & sportswear; men's & boys' work clothing

(G-9559)
DOREMUS FP LLC
228 E 45th St Fl 10 (10017-3331)
PHONE..................................212 366-3800
Dave Wade, *President*
Jed Dorney, *General Mgr*
James Bonilla, *Vice Pres*
Carlos Rodriguez, *Production*
Edmond Sorg, *CFO*
EMP: 47
SQ FT: 13,800
SALES (est): 6.9MM **Privately Held**
WEB: www.doremusfp.com
SIC: 2759 Financial note & certificate printing & engraving

(G-9560)
DORLING KINDERSLEY PUBLISHING
375 Hudson St (10014-3658)
PHONE..................................212 213-4800
Peter Kindersley, *Ch of Bd*
Nakul Bhatnagar, *Sales Mgr*
Ebony Lazare, *Sales Staff*
Wade Ivan, *Manager*
Sheila Phelan, *Director*
▲ EMP: 60
SQ FT: 5,000
SALES (est): 5.1MM
SALES (corp-wide): 82.3MM **Privately Held**
SIC: 2731 3652 Books: publishing only; pre-recorded records & tapes
HQ: Dorling Kindersley Limited
Shell Mex House
London WC2R
207 010-3000

(G-9561)
DOUBLE TAKE FASHIONS INC
1407 Broadway Rm 712 (10018-5293)
PHONE..................................718 832-9000
Michael Mizrahi, *President*
Jeanette Mizrahi, *Vice Pres*
Daniel Marchese, *Production*
EMP: 18
SQ FT: 5,000
SALES (est): 1.5MM **Privately Held**
WEB: www.doubletakefashions.com
SIC: 2339 Sportswear, women's

(G-9562)
DOVER GLOBAL HOLDINGS INC (HQ)
280 Park Ave (10017-1274)
PHONE..................................212 922-1640
Robert A Livingston, *President*
Annette Della Penna, *Analyst*
◆ EMP: 18
SALES (est): 3.6MM
SALES (corp-wide): 7.8B **Publicly Held**
SIC: 3531 3542 3565 3534 Construction machinery; machine tools, metal forming type; packaging machinery; elevators & moving stairways
PA: Dover Corporation
3005 Highland Pkwy # 200
Downers Grove IL 60515
630 541-1540

(G-9563)
DOW JONES & COMPANY INC (HQ)
1211 Avenue Of The Americ (10036-8711)
P.O. Box 300, Princeton NJ (08543-0300)
PHONE..................................609 627-2999
William Lewis, *CEO*
Edwin Finn Jr, *President*
Will Wilkinson, *General Mgr*
Linda Shockley, *Managing Dir*
John Bussey, *Editor*
▲ EMP: 500 EST: 1882
SALES (est): 2.4B
SALES (corp-wide): 9B **Publicly Held**
SIC: 2711 2721 Newspapers, publishing & printing; magazines: publishing & printing
PA: News Corporation
1211 Ave Of The Americas
New York NY 10036
212 416-3400

(G-9564)
DOW JONES & COMPANY INC
1211 Avenue Of The Americ (10036-8711)
PHONE..................................212 597-5983
Adrian Delucca, *Editor*
Edwin Finn, *Branch Mgr*
Dorothy Gelormino, *Manager*
Patricia Kasner, *Exec Dir*
EMP: 46
SALES (corp-wide): 9B **Publicly Held**
SIC: 2711 2721 6289 7383 Newspapers, publishing & printing; magazines: publishing only, not printed on site; statistical reports (periodicals): publishing & printing; financial reporting; stock quotation service; news reporting services for newspapers & periodicals; business oriented computer software
HQ: Dow Jones & Company, Inc.
1211 Avenue Of The Americ
New York NY 10036
609 627-2999

(G-9565)
DOW JONES AER COMPANY INC
1211 Av Of The Am Lwr C3r (10036)
PHONE..................................212 416-2000
Alice Chai, *President*
Gail Griffin, *General Mgr*
Sharon Terlep, *General Mgr*
Teresa Vozzo, *General Mgr*
Frederick Schuler, *Managing Dir*
EMP: 701
SALES (est): 125.7MM
SALES (corp-wide): 9B **Publicly Held**
WEB: www.opinionjournal.com
SIC: 2721 Periodicals
HQ: Dow Jones & Company, Inc.
1211 Avenue Of The Americ
New York NY 10036
609 627-2999

(G-9566)
DOWA INTERNATIONAL CORP
370 Lexington Ave Rm 1002 (10017-6586)
PHONE..................................212 697-3217
Junichi Nagao, *President*
Wataru Okuda, *Marketing Mgr*
Akihisa Yamaguchi, *Marketing Mgr*
EMP: 13
SALES (corp-wide): 4.2B **Privately Held**
WEB: www.dicny.com
SIC: 1241 8732 Coal mining services; research services, except laboratory
PA: Dowa Holdings Co.,Ltd.
4-14-1, Sotokanda
Chiyoda-Ku TKY 101-0
368 471-106

(G-9567)
DOWNTOWN INTERIORS INC
250 Hudson St Lbby 1 (10013-1413)
PHONE..................................212 337-0230
Hertzel Abraham, *President*
Nicole Rowars, *Bookkeeper*
EMP: 12
SQ FT: 3,600
SALES (est): 1MM **Privately Held**
SIC: 3553 Furniture makers' machinery, woodworking

(G-9568)
DOWNTOWN MEDIA GROUP LLC
Also Called: Tokion Magazine
12 W 27th St Ste 1000 (10001-6903)
PHONE..................................646 723-4510
Larry Rosenblum,
Isam Walji,
EMP: 15
SALES (est): 1.4MM **Privately Held**
SIC: 2721 Periodicals

(G-9569)
DOWNTOWN MUSIC LLC
485 Broadway Fl 3 (10013-3071)
PHONE..................................212 625-2980
EMP: 9 EST: 2008
SALES (est): 1MM **Privately Held**
SIC: 2741 Misc Publishing

(G-9570)
DOYLE & ROTH MFG CO INC (PA)
39 Broad St Ste 710 (10004-2513)
PHONE..................................212 269-7840
Mary Ann Avella, *President*
Rohit Patel, *Vice Pres*
Kathy Troise, *Buyer*
George Hahn, *Treasurer*
EMP: 64 EST: 1932
SQ FT: 3,200
SALES (est): 12.6MM **Privately Held**
WEB: www.doyleroth.com
SIC: 3443 3491 Heat exchangers, condensers & components; pressure valves & regulators, industrial

(G-9571)
DR JAYSCOM
853 Broadway Ste 1900 (10003-4703)
PHONE..................................888 437-5297
▼ EMP: 9
SALES (est): 1.1MM **Privately Held**
SIC: 2339 Women's & misses' athletic clothing & sportswear

(G-9572)
DRAGON TRADING INC
Also Called: Dragon Steel Products
211 E 70th St Apt 20d (10021-5209)
PHONE..................................212 717-1496
James Steindecker, *President*
Chen Tan, *Manager*
◆ EMP: 9
SQ FT: 800
SALES (est): 13.1MM **Privately Held**
SIC: 3315 3731 3321 3462 Cable, steel: insulated or armored; marine rigging; cast iron pipe & fittings; chains, forged steel

(G-9573)
DRAPER ASSOCIATES INCORPORATED
121 Varick St Rm 203 (10013-1455)
P.O. Box 393 (10014-0393)
PHONE..................................212 255-2727
Joseph Disomma, *President*
EMP: 15
SQ FT: 1,200
SALES (est): 179K **Privately Held**
WEB: www.draperassociates.com
SIC: 2741 2791 Miscellaneous publishing; typesetting

(G-9574)
DREAMWAVE LLC
34 W 33rd St Fl 2 (10001-3304)
PHONE..................................212 594-4250
George Saade, *Controller*
Jakey Dweck, *VP Sales*
David Grazi, *Mng Member*
▲ EMP: 26
SQ FT: 13,000
SALES (est): 2.7MM **Privately Held**
SIC: 2389 Men's miscellaneous accessories

(G-9575)
DRESDIAM INC
Also Called: Jacob Dresdner Co
36 W 47th St Ste 1008 (10036-8601)
PHONE..................................212 819-2217
Jacob Dresdner, *President*
EMP: 40
SQ FT: 3,000
SALES (est): 3.4MM **Privately Held**
SIC: 3915 Diamond cutting & polishing

(G-9576)
DRESSY TESSY INC (PA)
Also Called: Dt Industry
1410 Broadway Rm 502 (10018-9373)
PHONE..................................212 869-0750
Kitty Koo, *President*
▲ EMP: 9
SQ FT: 5,000
SALES (est): 702.6K **Privately Held**
SIC: 2253 Knit outerwear mills

(G-9577)
DREW PHILIPS CORP (PA)
Also Called: Supply & Demand
231 W 39th St (10018-1070)
PHONE..................................212 354-0095
Andrew Cohen, *President*
▲ EMP: 7
SALES (est): 3.9MM **Privately Held**
WEB: www.supplydemand.com
SIC: 2339 Sportswear, women's

(G-9578)
DREYFUS ASHBY INC (HQ)
630 3rd Ave Fl 15 (10017-6939)
PHONE..................................212 818-0770
Chris Ryan, *President*
Micheal Katz, *President*
William Welch, *Regional Mgr*
Daniel Schmalen, *Vice Pres*
Patrick Sere, *Vice Pres*
▲ EMP: 34
SQ FT: 3,000
SALES (est): 5.9MM
SALES (corp-wide): 47.3MM **Privately Held**
WEB: www.dreyfusashby.com
SIC: 3646 2084 3645 Commercial indusl & institutional electric lighting fixtures; wines, brandy & brandy spirits; lamp & light shades
PA: Sa Maison Joseph Drouhin
7 Rue D Enfer
Beaune 21200
380 246-888

(G-9579)
DROPCAR OPERATING COMPANY INC (HQ)
1412 Broadway Ste 2100 (10018-9228)
PHONE..................................646 342-1595
Michael Richardson, *CEO*
Jon Collins, *President*
Paul Commons, *CFO*
EMP: 7

SALES (est): 1.4MM
SALES (corp-wide): 22.4MM **Publicly Held**
SIC: 7372 Business oriented computer software
PA: Dropcar, Inc.
1412 Broadway Ste 2105
New York NY 10018
646 342-1595

(G-9580)
DRUMMOND FRAMING INC
38 W 21st St Fl 10 (10010-6969)
PHONE.................................212 647-1701
Donald Delli Paoli, *Owner*
Mariko Frost, *Office Mgr*
EMP: 14
SQ FT: 2,300
SALES (est): 2MM **Privately Held**
WEB: www.drummondframing.com
SIC: 2499 Picture frame molding, finished

(G-9581)
DU MONDE TRADING INC
Also Called: Up Country
1407 Brrdwy Rm 1905 (10018)
PHONE.................................212 944-1306
Donald Eatz, *President*
Dale Trienekens, *COO*
▲ EMP: 50
SQ FT: 4,500
SALES (est): 6.5MM **Privately Held**
SIC: 2339 2326 Women's & misses' jackets & coats, except sportswear; men's & boys' work clothing

(G-9582)
DUCDUC LLC (PA)
Also Called: Ducduc Nyc
200 Lexington Ave Rm 715 (10016-6101)
PHONE.................................212 226-1868
Lelia Byrne, *Mktg Dir*
Philip Eidles, *Mng Member*
Brady Wilcox, *Officer*
EMP: 15
SALES (est): 2.7MM **Privately Held**
SIC: 2511 Children's wood furniture

(G-9583)
DUCK RIVER TEXTILES INC (PA)
295 5th Ave (10016-7103)
PHONE.................................212 679-2980
Eili Alhakim, *President*
Raymond Cohen, *COO*
Oury Alhakim, *Vice Pres*
Jack Cohen, *Sales Mgr*
Joel Bren, *VP Mktg*
▲ EMP: 18 EST: 1997
SQ FT: 50,000
SALES (est): 3.7MM **Privately Held**
WEB: www.duckrivertextile.com
SIC: 2269 Linen fabrics: dyeing, finishing & printing

(G-9584)
DUCON TECHNOLOGIES INC (PA)
5 Penn Plz Ste 2403 (10001-1848)
PHONE.................................631 694-1700
Aron Govil, *Chairman*
William Papa, *Chairman*
Renato Delarama, *Vice Pres*
Bob Gupta, *Vice Pres*
◆ EMP: 15
SQ FT: 35,000
SALES: 479.4MM **Privately Held**
WEB: www.ducon.com
SIC: 3564 3537 1629 1623 Blowers & fans; industrial trucks & tractors; power plant construction; communication line & transmission tower construction; road construction & maintenance machinery

(G-9585)
DUNE INC
200 Lexington Ave Rm 200 # 200 (10016-6103)
PHONE.................................212 925-6171
Richard Shemtov, *President*
Aaron Shemtov, *Vice Pres*
Marthy Soliven, *Production*
Timothy Houser, *Manager*
▲ EMP: 5
SQ FT: 12,000
SALES (est): 794.6K **Privately Held**
WEB: www.dune-ny.com
SIC: 2511 Wood household furniture

(G-9586)
DURAN JEWELRY INC
36 W 47th St Ste 1205 (10036-8637)
PHONE.................................212 431-1959
Erol Civi, *President*
Arlet Tknezi, *Manager*
▲ EMP: 6
SQ FT: 1,000
SALES (est): 460K **Privately Held**
SIC: 3911 Jewelry, precious metal

(G-9587)
DURATA THERAPEUTICS INC
7 Times Sq Ste 3502 (10036-6540)
PHONE.................................646 871-6400
Paul R Edick, *CEO*
Richard U De Schutter, *Ch of Bd*
Corey N Fishman, *COO*
Michael Dunne, *Officer*
John P Shannon, *Officer*
EMP: 5
SQ FT: 9,000
SALES (est): 386.3K **Privately Held**
SIC: 2834 8731 Antibiotics, packaged; commercial physical research

(G-9588)
DUXIANA DUX BED
235 E 58th St (10022-1201)
PHONE.................................212 755-2600
Bo Gustafsson, *Principal*
EMP: 6
SALES (est): 529K **Privately Held**
SIC: 2515 5712 5719 Mattresses & bedsprings; beds & accessories; beddings & linens

(G-9589)
DVF STUDIO LLC (PA)
Also Called: Diane Von Furstenberg The Shop
440 W 14th St (10014-1004)
PHONE.................................212 741-6607
Robert McCormick, *COO*
Paul Aberasturi, *CFO*
Amy Bobrow, *Controller*
Diane Von Furstenberg, *Mng Member*
Jennifer Crawford, *Manager*
▲ EMP: 75
SALES (est): 29.2MM **Privately Held**
WEB: www.dvf.com
SIC: 3199 2389 5621 Leather garments; disposable garments & accessories; women's specialty clothing stores

(G-9590)
DVF STUDIO LLC (PA)
252 W 37th St Fl 14 (10018-6636)
PHONE.................................646 576-8009
Diane Furstenber, *Branch Mgr*
EMP: 6
SALES (est): 2.5MM **Privately Held**
SIC: 3199 2389 5621 Leather garments; disposable garments & accessories; women's specialty clothing stores

(G-9591)
DWELL LIFE INC
Also Called: Dwell Store The
60 Broad St Fl 24 (10004-2342)
PHONE.................................212 382-2010
Regina Flynn, *Office Mgr*
EMP: 25
SALES (corp-wide): 20MM **Privately Held**
SIC: 2741 Miscellaneous publishing
PA: Dwell Life, Inc.
595 Pacific Ave 4
San Francisco CA 94133
415 373-5100

(G-9592)
DWNLD INC
601394 Broadway Fl 6 Flr 6 (10013)
PHONE.................................484 483-6572
Aj Framk, *CEO*
Alexandra Keating, *CEO*
EMP: 28
SALES (est): 663.9K **Privately Held**
SIC: 7372 Application computer software

(G-9593)
DYENAMIX INC
359 Broadway Frnt 2 (10013-3932)
PHONE.................................212 941-6642
Raylene Marasco, *President*
EMP: 7
SALES (est): 250K **Privately Held**
SIC: 2261 2262 2752 Dyeing cotton broadwoven fabrics; screen printing of cotton broadwoven fabrics; screen printing: manmade fiber & silk broadwoven fabrics; commercial printing, lithographic

(G-9594)
DYNAMICA INC
930 5th Ave Apt 3f (10021-2680)
PHONE.................................212 818-1900
Daniel Schwartz, *President*
▲ EMP: 10
SALES (est): 1.1MM **Privately Held**
SIC: 3821 Laboratory apparatus & furniture

(G-9595)
DYNAMO DEVELOPMENT INC
860 Broadway Fl 5 (10003-1228)
PHONE.................................212 385-1552
Dmitry I Grinberg, *President*
EMP: 6
SALES (est): 2.2MM **Privately Held**
WEB: www.dynamodevelopment.com
SIC: 7372 Prepackaged software

(G-9596)
E P SEWING PLEATING INC
327 W 36th St Frnt 2 (10018-6405)
PHONE.................................212 967-2575
EMP: 20 EST: 1998
SALES (est): 820K **Privately Held**
SIC: 2342 Mfg Bras/Girdles

(G-9597)
E SCHREIBER INC
580 5th Ave Fl 32a (10036-4716)
PHONE.................................212 382-0280
Norbert Steinmetz, *President*
Ben Moller, *Vice Pres*
▲ EMP: 22
SQ FT: 5,000
SALES (est): 2MM **Privately Held**
WEB: www.eschreiber.com
SIC: 3915 5094 Diamond cutting & polishing; diamonds (gems)

(G-9598)
E W WILLIAMS PUBLICATIONS
Also Called: LDB Interior Textiles
370 Lexington Ave Rm 1409 (10017-6583)
PHONE.................................212 661-1516
Aleksandra Ilnicki, *Editor*
Wanda Jankowski, *Editor*
Jenny George, *Sales Staff*
Philippa Hochschild, *Manager*
EMP: 9
SALES (corp-wide): 42.3MM **Privately Held**
WEB: www.williamspublications.com
SIC: 2721 2731 Magazines: publishing only, not printed on site; textbooks: publishing only, not printed on site
HQ: E W Williams Publications
2125 Center Ave Ste 305
Fort Lee NJ 07024

(G-9599)
E&I PRINTING
145 W 55th St Apt 12a (10019-5354)
PHONE.................................212 206-0506
Eric Eisenberg, *President*
EMP: 15
SALES: 5MM **Privately Held**
WEB: www.eiprints.com
SIC: 2759 Commercial printing

(G-9600)
E-PLAY BRANDS LLC
25 W 39th St Lbby A (10018-4199)
PHONE.................................212 563-2646
Joseph Esses,
EMP: 6
SALES (est): 288.5K **Privately Held**
SIC: 2361 2369 Shirts: girls', children's & infants'; dresses: girls', children's & infants'; coat & legging sets: girls' & children's

(G-9601)
E-WON INDUSTRIAL CO INC
Also Called: New York Trading Co
625 Main St Apt 1532 (10044-0036)
PHONE.................................212 750-9610
▲ EMP: 37
SQ FT: 1,000
SALES (est): 4MM **Privately Held**
SIC: 3965 Mfg Buttons

(G-9602)
EAGLE ART PUBLISHING INC
475 Park Ave S Rm 2800 (10016-6901)
PHONE.................................212 685-7411
Samuel J Lurie, *President*
EMP: 5
SALES (est): 330K **Privately Held**
SIC: 2731 Book publishing

(G-9603)
EAGLE LACE DYEING CORP
335 W 35th St Fl 2 (10001-1726)
PHONE.................................212 947-2712
Leonard Shally, *President*
EMP: 10
SALES (est): 620K **Privately Held**
SIC: 2258 2396 Dyeing & finishing lace goods & warp knit fabric; automotive & apparel trimmings

(G-9604)
EAGLES NEST HOLDINGS LLC (PA)
Also Called: Sabin Robbins
455 E 86th St (10028-6400)
PHONE.................................513 874-5270
Wayne Penrod,
Joseph Hardiman,
EMP: 32
SQ FT: 6,000
SALES (est): 13.3MM **Privately Held**
SIC: 2679 Paper products, converted

(G-9605)
EARL G GRAVES PUBG CO INC (HQ)
Also Called: Black Enterprise
260 Madison Ave Ste 11 (10016-2413)
PHONE.................................212 242-8000
Earl G Graves Sr, *CEO*
Earl Butch Graves Jr, *CEO*
Jacques Jiha, *Principal*
Dirk J Caldwell, *Senior VP*
Angela Mitchell, *Vice Pres*
EMP: 83
SQ FT: 22,000
SALES (est): 8.4MM
SALES (corp-wide): 20.2MM **Privately Held**
SIC: 2721 Magazines: publishing only, not printed on site
PA: Earl G. Graves, Ltd.
260 Madison Ave Ste 11
New York NY 10016
212 242-8000

(G-9606)
EARRING KING JEWELRY MFG INC
62 W 47th St Ste 1202 (10036-3230)
PHONE.................................718 544-7947
Kowk Mok, *President*
Jane Mok, *Vice Pres*
EMP: 7
SALES (est): 630K **Privately Held**
SIC: 3911 Jewelry, precious metal

(G-9607)
EARTH ENTERPRISES INC
Also Called: Green Earth Enterprise
250 W 40th St Fl 15 (10018-4601)
PHONE.................................212 741-3999
Susan Hort, *President*
Usman Shaikh, *Business Mgr*
Micheal Hort, *Vice Pres*
Penelope Hort, *Treasurer*
Chris Mullin, *VP Sales*
EMP: 25
SQ FT: 40,000
SALES (est): 6.5MM **Privately Held**
SIC: 2752 Commercial printing, lithographic

New York - New York County (G-9608)

(G-9608)
EAST COAST ORTHOIC & PROS COR
3927 Broadway (10032-1538)
PHONE..............................212 923-2161
Lawrence Benenati, *Branch Mgr*
EMP: 14
SALES (corp-wide): 12.7MM **Privately Held**
SIC: 3842 Orthopedic appliances
PA: East Coast Orthotic & Prosthetic Corp.
75 Burt Dr
Deer Park NY 11729
516 248-5566

(G-9609)
EAST MEET EAST INC
32 W 39th St Fl 4 (10018-2166)
PHONE..............................646 481-0033
Mariko Tokioka, *Ch of Bd*
Kentaro Ejima, *Admin Sec*
EMP: 7 EST: 2014
SALES (est): 299.1K **Privately Held**
SIC: 2741

(G-9610)
EASTERN JEWELRY MFG CO INC
48 W 48th St Ste 707 (10036-1714)
PHONE..............................212 840-0001
Soloman Witriol, *President*
EMP: 50
SQ FT: 16,000
SALES (est): 3.4MM **Privately Held**
SIC: 3911 Jewelry apparel; bracelets, precious metal; earrings, precious metal; rosaries or other small religious articles, precious metal

(G-9611)
EASTERN SILK MILLS INC
148 W 37th St Fl 3 (10018-6987)
PHONE..............................212 730-1300
Andy Ryu, *Controller*
EMP: 9
SALES (corp-wide): 4.4MM **Privately Held**
SIC: 2262 2221 Dyeing: manmade fiber & silk broadwoven fabrics; broadwoven fabric mills, manmade
PA: Eastern Silk Mills Inc.
212 Catherine St
Elizabeth NJ

(G-9612)
EASTERN STRATEGIC MATERIALS
45 Rockefeller Plz # 2000 (10111-0100)
PHONE..............................212 332-1619
Kai Wong, *President*
Matthew Harris, *Vice Pres*
EMP: 41
SALES (est): 4MM **Privately Held**
SIC: 3365 3812 3822 Aerospace castings, aluminum; defense systems & equipment; space vehicle guidance systems & equipment; energy cutoff controls, residential or commercial types

(G-9613)
EASTNETS AMERICAS CORP
450 7th Ave Ste 1509 (10123-1509)
PHONE..............................212 631-0666
Hazem Mulhim, *President*
Paul W Chin, *General Mgr*
Mohamed E Bakkali, *CFO*
Olivier Denis, *Manager*
Hazem Kharbat, *Manager*
EMP: 10
SALES (est): 1.3MM **Privately Held**
SIC: 7372 Prepackaged software

(G-9614)
EB ACQUISITIONS LLC
444 Madison Ave Ste 501 (10022-6974)
PHONE..............................212 355-3310
Nachum Stein,
EMP: 100
SALES (est): 5.7MM **Privately Held**
SIC: 3643 3315 Connectors, electric cord; wire & fabricated wire products

(G-9615)
EB COUTURE LTD
Also Called: Elie Balleh Couture
110 W 34th St Rm 1002 (10001-2128)
PHONE..............................212 912-0190
Mari Mineh, *Post Master*
▲ EMP: 20
SALES (est): 179.8K **Privately Held**
SIC: 2389 2329 5137 Apparel for handicapped; knickers, dress (separate): men's & boys'; women's & children's clothing

(G-9616)
EBM CARE INC
317 Madison Ave (10017-5201)
PHONE..............................212 500-5000
Jack Fitzgibbons, *President*
EMP: 7
SALES (est): 327.8K **Privately Held**
SIC: 7372 Business oriented computer software

(G-9617)
EBNER PUBLISHING INTERNATIONAL
Also Called: Watchtime Magazine
37 W 26th St Rm 412 (10010-1077)
PHONE..............................646 742-0740
Wolfgang Blum, *President*
Mark Bernardo, *Editor*
Sara Orlando, *Sls & Mktg Exec*
Steve Brown, *Office Mgr*
EMP: 5
SALES (est): 45.7K **Privately Held**
WEB: www.watchtime.com
SIC: 2721 Magazines: publishing & printing

(G-9618)
EBREVIA INC
12 E 49th St Fl 11 (10017-1012)
PHONE..............................203 870-3000
Ned Gannon, *CEO*
Jacob Mundt, *Principal*
Adam Nguyen, *COO*
Alessia Bell, *Vice Pres*
Stacy Lettie, *Director*
EMP: 20
SQ FT: 30,000
SALES (est): 560.4K **Privately Held**
SIC: 7372 Business oriented computer software

(G-9619)
ECCELLA CORPORATION
75 Broad St Rm 2900 (10004-2475)
PHONE..............................718 612-0451
Meitav Harpaz, *CEO*
Gil Rosen, *President*
EMP: 8
SQ FT: 2,960
SALES (est): 509.1K
SALES (corp-wide): 34.3K **Privately Held**
SIC: 7372 7389 Business oriented computer software;
PA: Ngdata Nv
Sluisweg 2, Internal Postal Box 10
Gent
933 882-20

(G-9620)
ECCLESIASTICAL COMMUNICATIONS
Also Called: Catholic New York
1011 1st Ave Fl 6 (10022-4112)
PHONE..............................212 688-2399
Bishop Robert A Brucato, *President*
Mary Gregory, *Accountant*
John Woods, *Manager*
Matthew Schiller, *Manager*
EMP: 13
SALES (est): 750K **Privately Held**
SIC: 2711 Newspapers: publishing only, not printed on site

(G-9621)
ECHO GROUP INC
62 W 39th St Ste 1005 (10018-3818)
PHONE..............................917 608-7440
Fax: 212 382-2490
EMP: 15
SALES (est): 980K **Privately Held**
SIC: 3911 Mfg Precious Metal Jewelry

(G-9622)
ECLECTIC CNTRACT FURN INDS INC
450 Fashion Ave Ste 2710 (10123-2710)
PHONE..............................212 967-5504
Alex Marc, *President*
▲ EMP: 14
SQ FT: 1,000
SALES (est): 2MM **Privately Held**
WEB: www.eclecticcontract.com
SIC: 2511 Wood household furniture

(G-9623)
ECLIPSE COLLECTION JEWELERS (PA)
7 W 45th St Rm 1401 (10036-4905)
PHONE..............................212 764-6883
Vatcag Aghjayan, *President*
EMP: 7
SALES (est): 1MM **Privately Held**
SIC: 3911 Jewelry, precious metal

(G-9624)
ECONOMIST INTELLIGENCE UNIT NA
750 3rd Ave Fl 5 (10017-2723)
PHONE..............................212 554-0600
Chris Stibbs, *Ch of Bd*
David Cox, *Senior VP*
Paul Rossi, *Senior VP*
EMP: 68
SQ FT: 18,000
SALES (est): 11.8MM
SALES (corp-wide): 513.5MM **Privately Held**
WEB: www.eiu.com
SIC: 2721 8732 Periodicals: publishing only; business analysis
HQ: The Economist Newspaper Group Incorporated
750 3rd Ave Fl 5
New York NY 10017
212 541-0500

(G-9625)
ECONOMIST NEWSPAPER NA INC (DH)
Also Called: Economist Magazine, The
750 3rd Ave Fl 5 (10017-2723)
PHONE..............................212 554-0676
Chris Stibbs, *CEO*
Samantha Weinberg, *Editor*
Paul Rossi, *Exec VP*
Leila Berkeley, *Senior VP*
Jessica Martinson, *Opers Staff*
EMP: 22
SQ FT: 28,900
SALES (est): 17.7MM
SALES (corp-wide): 513.5MM **Privately Held**
SIC: 2711 5192 Newspapers; magazines
HQ: The Economist Newspaper Group Incorporated
750 3rd Ave Fl 5
New York NY 10017
212 541-0500

(G-9626)
EDESIA WORLD WIDE LLC
1485 5th Ave (10035-2772)
PHONE..............................646 705-3505
Sabbia Auriti,
Antonia Ricco,
EMP: 2
SALES: 2MM **Privately Held**
SIC: 2032 7389 Italian foods: packaged in cans, jars, etc.;

(G-9627)
EDITH LANCES CORP
247 W 35th St Fl 2 (10001-1927)
PHONE..............................212 683-1990
Jay S Gingold, *President*
Marsha Gingold, *Vice Pres*
EMP: 20 EST: 1935
SQ FT: 3,000
SALES (est): 748K **Privately Held**
SIC: 2342 Brassieres

(G-9628)
EDITIONS DE PRFUMS MADISON LLC (HQ)
654 Madison Ave Rm 1609 (10065-8430)
PHONE..............................646 666-0527
Frederic Malle, *General Mgr*
EMP: 18
SALES (est): 1.4MM **Publicly Held**
SIC: 2844 Perfumes & colognes

(G-9629)
EDRINGTON GROUP USA LLC (PA)
27 W 23rd St Fl 4 (10010-4216)
PHONE..............................212 352-6000
Michael Misiorski, *COO*
Chris Spalding, *Vice Pres*
Michael Schutzbank, *Opers Dir*
Nadege Dethy, *Human Res Dir*
Karin Wilkins, *Human Res Mgr*
EMP: 31
SALES (est): 12.3MM **Privately Held**
SIC: 2084 Wines, brandy & brandy spirits

(G-9630)
EDSIM LEATHER CO INC (PA)
131 W 35th St Fl 14 (10001-2111)
PHONE..............................212 695-8500
Simone Kamali, *President*
Edmond Kamali, *Vice Pres*
Edmond R Kamali, *Vice Pres*
Suren Lall, *Controller*
Daniel Kamali, *Sales Mgr*
▲ EMP: 20
SQ FT: 7,000
SALES: 37MM **Privately Held**
WEB: www.hinet.net
SIC: 3111 Leather tanning & finishing

(G-9631)
EDUCATIONAL NETWORKS INC
104 W 40th St Rm 1810 (10018-3758)
PHONE..............................866 526-0200
Erica Fields, *Vice Pres*
Robert Corbi, *Sales Staff*
Oliver Diaz-Neda, *Marketing Staff*
Liz Milivio, *Office Mgr*
Justin Jensen, *Manager*
EMP: 7
SALES (corp-wide): 3.3MM **Privately Held**
SIC: 7372 Educational computer software
PA: Educational Networks, Inc
901 Ponce De Leon Blvd # 508
Coral Gables FL 33134
866 526-0200

(G-9632)
EEBOO CORPORATION
170 W 74th St Apt 102 (10023-2351)
PHONE..............................212 222-0823
Maria Galison, *President*
Grace Choi, *Prdtn Mgr*
Grace Giessel, *Opers Staff*
Christine Hooker, *Cust Mgr*
Alex Nunes, *Sales Staff*
▲ EMP: 14
SQ FT: 1,000
SALES (est): 2.3MM **Privately Held**
WEB: www.eeboo.com
SIC: 3944 Board games, puzzles & models, except electronic; puzzles

(G-9633)
EFRONT FINANCIAL SOLUTIONS INC
Also Called: E-Front
11 E 44th St Fl 15 (10017-3608)
PHONE..............................212 220-0660
Eric Bernstein, *COO*
Francisco Braganza, *Info Tech Mgr*
EMP: 25
SALES (corp-wide): 25.5MM **Privately Held**
SIC: 7372 Business oriented computer software
HQ: E-Front
2 4
Paris 75116
149 964-060

(G-9634)
EFT ANALYTICS INC
350 5th Ave Ste 4810 (10118-4810)
PHONE..............................212 290-2300
Brent Youngers, *President*
Craig Ennis, *CTO*
EMP: 8
SALES (est): 1.1MM
SALES (corp-wide): 42.9B **Privately Held**
SIC: 7372 Application computer software

▲ = Import ▼ = Export
◆ = Import/Export

GEOGRAPHIC SECTION

New York - New York County (G-9661)

PA: Koch Industries, Inc.
4111 E 37th St N
Wichita KS 67220
316 828-5500

(G-9635)
EGMONT US INC
443 Park Ave S Rm 806 (10016-7322)
PHONE..................212 685-0102
▲ EMP: 8
SALES (est): 615K
SALES (corp-wide): 1.6B **Privately Held**
SIC: 2731 Books-Publishing/Printing
HQ: Egmont Uk Limited
The Yellow Building
London W11 4
203 220-0400

(G-9636)
EIDOSMEDIA INC
14 Wall St Ste 6c (10005-2170)
PHONE..................646 795-2100
Steven Ball, *CEO*
EMP: 22
SALES (est): 2.8MM **Privately Held**
SIC: 2721 Periodicals: publishing & printing
HQ: Eidosmedia Spa
Corso Vercelli 40
Milano MI 20145
023 673-2000

(G-9637)
EILEENS SPECIAL CHEESECAKE
17 Cleveland Pl Frnt A (10012-4052)
PHONE..................212 966-5585
Eileen Avezzano, *President*
EMP: 6
SQ FT: 600
SALES (est): 310K **Privately Held**
WEB: www.eileenscheesecake.com
SIC: 2051 Bakery: wholesale or wholesale/retail combined; cakes, bakery: except frozen

(G-9638)
EL-LA DESIGN INC
Also Called: My Apparel
209 W 38th St Rm 901 (10018-4558)
PHONE..................212 382-1080
Elaine Lai, *President*
EMP: 5
SALES (est): 590K **Privately Held**
SIC: 2339 Sportswear, women's

(G-9639)
ELANA LADEROS LTD
Also Called: Joanna Mastroianni
230 W 38th St Fl 15 (10018-9026)
PHONE..................212 764-0840
Joanna Mastroianni, *President*
EMP: 10
SQ FT: 3,500
SALES (est): 1.6MM **Privately Held**
WEB: www.joannamastroianni.com
SIC: 2335 Wedding gowns & dresses

(G-9640)
ELECTRIC LIGHTING AGENCIES (PA)
Also Called: Ela
36 W 25th St Fl 6 (10010-2757)
PHONE..................212 645-4580
EMP: 22
SALES (est): 3.8MM **Privately Held**
SIC: 3646 Mfg Commercial Lighting Fixtures

(G-9641)
ELECTRONIC ARTS INC
1515 Broadway Rm 3601 (10036-8901)
PHONE..................212 672-0722
Barbara Gallacher, *Vice Pres*
EMP: 7
SALES (corp-wide): 5.1B **Publicly Held**
WEB: www.ea.com
SIC: 7372 Prepackaged software
PA: Electronic Arts, Inc.
209 Redwood Shores Pkwy
Redwood City CA 94065
650 628-1500

(G-9642)
ELEGANT HEADWEAR CO INC
Also Called: ABG Accessories
10 W 33rd St Rm 1122 (10001-3306)
PHONE..................212 695-8520
Chris Moccia, *VP Sales*
Michael Brett, *Branch Mgr*
EMP: 8
SALES (est): 652.1K
SALES (corp-wide): 28.5MM **Privately Held**
WEB: www.elegantheadwear.com
SIC: 2253 T-shirts & tops, knit
PA: Elegant Headwear Co. Inc.
1000 Jefferson Ave
Elizabeth NJ 07201
908 558-1200

(G-9643)
ELEGANT JEWELERS MFG CO INC
31 W 47th St Ste 301 (10036-2888)
PHONE..................212 869-4951
Sandy Petropoulos, *President*
Nick Seretis, *Vice Pres*
EMP: 12
SQ FT: 1,500
SALES (est): 1.1MM **Privately Held**
WEB: www.elegantsilverjewellery.net
SIC: 3911 Jewelry, precious metal

(G-9644)
ELEVONDATA LABS INC
1350 Ave Of The Amrcs 2nd (10019-4702)
PHONE..................470 222-5438
Rohit Tandon, *CEO*
EMP: 50
SALES (est): 4MM **Privately Held**
SIC: 7372 Prepackaged software

(G-9645)
ELIE TAHARI LTD
501 5th Ave Fl 2 (10017-7825)
PHONE..................212 398-2622
Elie Tahari, *Principal*
EMP: 8
SALES (corp-wide): 178.6MM **Privately Held**
SIC: 2331 2339 2337 5621 Blouses, women's & juniors': made from purchased material; slacks: women's, misses' & juniors'; suits: women's, misses' & juniors'; jackets & vests, except fur & leather: women's; women's clothing stores; men's & boys' clothing stores
PA: Elie Tahari Ltd.
16 Bleeker St
Millburn NJ 07041
973 671-6300

(G-9646)
ELIE TAHARI LTD
510 5th Ave Fl 3 (10036-7507)
PHONE..................212 398-2622
David Elron, *Branch Mgr*
EMP: 75
SALES (corp-wide): 178.6MM **Privately Held**
SIC: 2337 8741 2339 Suits: women's, misses' & juniors'; management services; women's & misses' outerwear
PA: Elie Tahari Ltd.
16 Bleeker St
Millburn NJ 07041
973 671-6300

(G-9647)
ELIE TAHARI LTD
1114 Ave Of The Americas (10036-7703)
PHONE..................212 763-2000
Arthur S Levine, *Branch Mgr*
EMP: 60
SALES (corp-wide): 178.6MM **Privately Held**
SIC: 2331 2337 Blouses, women's & juniors': made from purchased material; uniforms, except athletic: women's, misses' & juniors'
PA: Elie Tahari Ltd.
16 Bleeker St
Millburn NJ 07041
973 671-6300

(G-9648)
ELIE TAHARI LTD
510 5th Ave Lbby A (10036-7507)
PHONE..................973 671-6300
Lisanne Kolligs, *President*
Susan Kellogg, *Manager*
EMP: 75
SALES (corp-wide): 178.6MM **Privately Held**
SIC: 2337 Suits: women's, misses' & juniors'
PA: Elie Tahari Ltd.
16 Bleeker St
Millburn NJ 07041
973 671-6300

(G-9649)
ELIS BREAD (ELI ZABAR) INC (PA)
1064 Madison Ave Apt 5 (10028-0252)
PHONE..................212 772-2011
Eli Zabar, *President*
Robert Shaloff, *VP Opers*
Andy Tsavides, *Purchasing*
Wayne Ponemon, *Manager*
Natalie Stettner, *Manager*
EMP: 10
SALES (est): 15.9MM **Privately Held**
WEB: www.elisbread.com
SIC: 2045 Bread & bread type roll mixes: from purchased flour

(G-9650)
ELITE DAILY INC
53 W 23rd St Fl 12 (10010-4313)
PHONE..................212 402-9097
Martin Clarke, *President*
EMP: 15
SALES (est): 14.4MM **Privately Held**
SIC: 2741

(G-9651)
ELITE PARFUMS LTD (HQ)
551 5th Ave Rm 1500 (10176-1599)
PHONE..................212 983-2640
Jean Madar, *President*
Philippe Benacin, *President*
Bruce Elbelia, *Exec VP*
Wayne C Hamerling, *Exec VP*
Russell Greenberg, *CFO*
▲ EMP: 57
SQ FT: 12,000
SALES (est): 4MM
SALES (corp-wide): 591.2MM **Publicly Held**
SIC: 2844 5122 Toilet preparations; perfumes; toiletries
PA: Inter Parfums, Inc.
551 5th Ave
New York NY 10176
212 983-2640

(G-9652)
ELITE TRAVELER LLC
441 Lexington Ave Fl 3 (10017-3950)
PHONE..................646 430-7900
Kat Czarnecki, *Business Mgr*
Lorraine Cousland, *Senior VP*
Lorraine Chu, *Production*
Lindsey Sole, *Mktg Coord*
Randy Silverman, *Director*
EMP: 11
SALES (est): 806.6K **Privately Held**
SIC: 2721 Magazines: publishing & printing

(G-9653)
ELIZABETH EAKINS INC (PA)
654 Madison Ave Rm 1409 (10065-8432)
PHONE..................212 628-1950
Elizabeth Eakins, *President*
Scott Lethbridge, *Vice Pres*
▲ EMP: 10
SQ FT: 4,000
SALES (est): 2.9MM **Privately Held**
WEB: www.elizabetheakins.com
SIC: 2273 5713 5023 Carpets, hand & machine made; carpets; carpets

(G-9654)
ELIZABETH FILLMORE LLC
27 W 20th St Ste 705 (10011-3727)
PHONE..................212 647-0863
Thomas Allen, *Vice Pres*
Elizabeth Fillmore,
EMP: 7
SQ FT: 1,900
SALES (est): 818.7K **Privately Held**
WEB: www.elizabethfillmorebridal.com
SIC: 2335 Gowns, formal

(G-9655)
ELIZABETH GILLETT LTD
Also Called: Elizabeth Gillett Designs
260 W 36th St Rm 802 (10018-8992)
PHONE..................212 629-7993
Elizabeth Gillett, *President*
Tarafawn Marek, *Exec VP*
J'Ne Brathwaite, *Production*
◆ EMP: 6
SQ FT: 1,500
SALES (est): 2.2MM **Privately Held**
WEB: www.egillett.com
SIC: 2339 Scarves, hoods, headbands, etc.: women's

(G-9656)
ELLIOT MANN NYC INC
324 E 9th St Frnt A (10003-7929)
PHONE..................212 260-0658
Lisa Paul, *Principal*
EMP: 6
SALES (est): 838.9K **Privately Held**
SIC: 2339 Women's & misses' accessories

(G-9657)
ELMGANG ENTERPRISES I INC
Also Called: Espostos Fnest Qlty Ssage Pdts
354 W 38th St Frnt (10018-2954)
PHONE..................212 868-4142
David Samuels, *President*
EMP: 10
SQ FT: 5,000
SALES (est): 1.6MM **Privately Held**
WEB: www.espositosausage.com
SIC: 2013 5147 Sausages & related products, from purchased meat; meats & meat products

(G-9658)
ELODINA INC
222 Broadway Fl 19 (10038-2550)
PHONE..................646 402-5202
Paul Reinitz, *President*
EMP: 5
SALES (est): 156K **Privately Held**
SIC: 7372 Business oriented computer software

(G-9659)
ELSEVIER INC (DH)
230 Park Ave Fl 8 (10169-0123)
PHONE..................212 989-5800
Ron Mobed, *CEO*
Hajo Oltmanns, *President*
Mj Janse, *Editor*
Youngsuk CHI, *Chairman*
Gavin Howe, *Exec VP*
◆ EMP: 277 EST: 1962
SQ FT: 65,000
SALES (est): 178.5MM
SALES (corp-wide): 9.7B **Privately Held**
WEB: www.elsevierfoundation.org
SIC: 2741 Technical manuals: publishing only, not printed on site
HQ: Elsevier B.V.
Radarweg 29
Amsterdam
204 853-911

(G-9660)
ELUMINOCITY US INC
80 Pine St Fl 24 (10005-1732)
PHONE..................651 528-1165
Sebastian Jagsch, *CEO*
Mike Rockwood Jr, *Sales Staff*
EMP: 2 EST: 2015
SQ FT: 200
SALES: 1.8MM **Privately Held**
SIC: 3648 3694 3629 Street lighting fixtures; battery charging generators, automobile & aircraft; battery chargers, rectifying or nonrotating

(G-9661)
ELY BEACH SOLAR LLC
5030 Broadway Ste 819 (10034-1670)
PHONE..................718 796-9400
Alison Karmel, *Vice Pres*
EMP: 7
SALES (est): 642.4K **Privately Held**
SIC: 3674 Solar cells

New York - New York County (G-9662) GEOGRAPHIC SECTION

(G-9662)
EMA JEWELRY INC
246 W 38th St Fl 6 (10018-5854)
PHONE..................................212 575-8989
Michael Weiss, *CEO*
Edward Weiss, *Vice Pres*
Alex Weiss, *Treasurer*
▼ **EMP:** 65
SQ FT: 7,500
SALES (est): 8.9MM **Privately Held**
WEB: www.emajewelry.com
SIC: 3911 3961 Jewelry, precious metal; costume jewelry

(G-9663)
EMBASSY APPAREL INC
37 W 37th St Fl 10 (10018-6354)
PHONE..................................212 768-8330
Ezra Cattan, *President*
Jack Cattan, *Vice Pres*
Judah Cattan, *Vice Pres*
EMP: 18
SQ FT: 10,000
SALES (est): 950.8K **Privately Held**
SIC: 2331 5136 5137 Women's & misses' blouses & shirts; men's & boys' furnishings; women's & children's accessories

(G-9664)
EMBER MEDIA CORPORATION
224 W 35th St 1502 (10001-2507)
PHONE..................................212 695-1919
Clayton A Banks, *President*
Andi Fehr, *Vice Pres*
EMP: 10
SQ FT: 2,500
SALES (est): 920K **Privately Held**
WEB: www.embermedia.com
SIC: 3695 Magnetic & optical recording media

(G-9665)
EMBLAZE SYSTEMS INC (HQ)
Also Called: Geo Publishing
424 Madison Ave Fl 16 (10017-1137)
PHONE..................................212 371-1100
Bruce Edwards, *President*
Joe Budenholzer, *President*
Brad Grob, *Vice Pres*
Lydia Edward, *Treasurer*
Marc Honorof, *Admin Sec*
EMP: 120
SQ FT: 7,000
SALES (est): 7MM
SALES (corp-wide): 58.5MM **Privately Held**
SIC: 7372 Prepackaged software
PA: B.S.D Crown Ltd
7 Begin Menachem Rd
Ramat Gan 52681
374 017-70

(G-9666)
EMC CORPORATION
2 Penn Plz Fl 24 (10121-2600)
PHONE..................................212 564-6866
Tony Picciuti, *Engineer*
Vincent Fiore, *Sales Mgr*
Ed Bowen, *Accounts Mgr*
Chris Byrne, *Accounts Mgr*
Brad Hirsch, *Accounts Mgr*
EMP: 200
SALES (corp-wide): 78.6B **Publicly Held**
WEB: www.emc.com
SIC: 3572 Computer storage devices
HQ: Emc Corporation
176 South St
Hopkinton MA 01748
508 435-1000

(G-9667)
EMCO ELECTRIC SERVICES LLC
526 W 26th St Rm 1012 (10001-5541)
PHONE..................................212 420-9766
Meziar Ghavidel, *Mng Member*
Mehr Mansuri, *Mng Member*
EMP: 5 **EST:** 2013
SALES: 170K **Privately Held**
SIC: 3699 1731 Electrical equipment & supplies; electronic controls installation

(G-9668)
EMERSON ELECTRIC CO
1250 Broadway Ste 2300 (10001-3726)
PHONE..................................212 244-2490
Jennifer Nichols, *Principal*
EMP: 23
SALES (corp-wide): 15.2B **Publicly Held**
WEB: www.gotoemerson.com
SIC: 3823 Industrial instrmnts msrmnt display/control process variable
PA: Emerson Electric Co.
8000 West Florissant Ave
Saint Louis MO 63136
314 553-2000

(G-9669)
EMSARU USA CORP
Also Called: Hampshire Jewels
608 5th Ave Ste 500 (10020-2303)
PHONE..................................212 459-9355
Harry Molhan, *President*
EMP: 5
SALES (est): 430K **Privately Held**
SIC: 3911 Jewelry, precious metal

(G-9670)
EMSIG MANUFACTURING CORP (PA)
263 W 38th St Fl 5 (10018-0291)
PHONE..................................718 784-7717
Lawrence Jacobs, *President*
John Lerner, *Vice Pres*
Samantha Morgan, *Accounts Mgr*
Paula Muster, *Software Dev*
Arthur Klein, *Admin Sec*
◆ **EMP:** 15 **EST:** 1965
SQ FT: 19,000
SALES (est): 25.5MM **Privately Held**
SIC: 3965 Buttons & parts

(G-9671)
EMSIG MANUFACTURING CORP
263 W 38th St Fl 5 (10018-0291)
PHONE..................................718 784-7717
Lawrence Jacobs, *President*
EMP: 20
SALES (corp-wide): 25.5MM **Privately Held**
SIC: 3965 Buttons & parts
PA: Emsig Manufacturing Corp.
263 W 38th St Fl 5
New York NY 10018
718 784-7717

(G-9672)
EMUSICCOM INC (PA)
215 Lexington Ave Fl 18 (10016-6023)
PHONE..................................212 201-9240
Peter Chapman, *CEO*
Daniel Stein, *Ch of Bd*
David Packman, *President*
Leann Rampulla, *Counsel*
Randy McKelvey, *Vice Pres*
EMP: 49
SALES (est): 10.3MM **Privately Held**
WEB: www.emusic.com
SIC: 3652 Pre-recorded records & tapes

(G-9673)
ENCHANTE LITES LLC (HQ)
Also Called: AMG Global
15 W 34th St Fl 8 (10001-3015)
PHONE..................................212 602-1818
Ezra Erani, *President*
Abraham Weinberger, *CFO*
▲ **EMP:** 8
SALES (est): 2.7MM
SALES (corp-wide): 63.1MM **Privately Held**
SIC: 3648 Decorative area lighting fixtures
PA: Enchante Accessories Inc.
16 E 34th St Fl 16 # 16
New York NY 10016
646 887-1442

(G-9674)
ENCYSIVE PHARMACEUTICALS INC (HQ)
235 E 42nd St (10017-5703)
PHONE..................................212 733-2323
John M Pietruski, *Ch of Bd*
Bruce D Given, *President*
Richard A F Dixon, *Senior VP*
Paul S Manierre, *Vice Pres*
Thierry A Plouvier, *Opers Staff*
▲ **EMP:** 35
SQ FT: 40,730
SALES (est): 13.9MM
SALES (corp-wide): 52.5B **Publicly Held**
SIC: 2834 8733 Pharmaceutical preparations; medical research
PA: Pfizer Inc.
235 E 42nd St
New York NY 10017
212 733-2323

(G-9675)
ENDAVA INC (HQ)
441 Lexington Ave Rm 702 (10017-3922)
PHONE..................................212 920-7240
Dan Sullivan, *President*
Nicholas Zakrzewski, *Marketing Staff*
EMP: 12
SQ FT: 2,000
SALES (est): 24MM
SALES (corp-wide): 291.8MM **Privately Held**
SIC: 7372 7371 7375 Business oriented computer software; custom computer programming services; on-line data base information retrieval
PA: Endava Plc
125 Old Broad Street
London EC2N
207 367-1000

(G-9676)
ENDOVOR INC
1330 1st Ave Apt 1119 (10021-4792)
PHONE..................................214 679-7385
Derek Carroll, *CEO*
EMP: 5
SALES (est): 198.4K **Privately Held**
SIC: 3841 Surgical & medical instruments

(G-9677)
ENDOVOR LLC
525 E 68th St A1027 (10065-4870)
PHONE..................................214 679-7385
Derek Carroll, *Opers Staff*
EMP: 8
SALES (est): 293.5K **Privately Held**
SIC: 3841 Surgical & medical instruments

(G-9678)
ENDURANCE LLC
530 7th Ave Rm 902 (10018-4874)
PHONE..................................212 719-2500
Athanasios Nastos,
Renjie Luo,
Daidai Ni,
Qiwen Zhao,
▲ **EMP:** 20
SALES (est): 1.9MM **Privately Held**
SIC: 2329 Men's & boys' sportswear & athletic clothing

(G-9679)
ENDURART INC
Also Called: Quality Embedments Mfg Co
132 Nassau St Rm 1100 (10038-2430)
PHONE..................................212 473-7000
Stuart Levine, *President*
Henry Richmond, *Executive*
EMP: 30
SQ FT: 18,000
SALES (est): 2.4MM **Privately Held**
SIC: 3914 2821 Trophies; plastics materials & resins

(G-9680)
ENERGY BRANDS INC (HQ)
Also Called: Glaceau
260 Madison Ave Fl 10 (10016-2417)
PHONE..................................212 545-6000
J Darius Bikoff, *CEO*
Michael Repole, *President*
Carol Dollard, *COO*
Michael Venuti, *CFO*
▼ **EMP:** 50
SQ FT: 15,000
SALES (est): 30.2MM
SALES (corp-wide): 35.4B **Publicly Held**
WEB: www.energybrands.com
SIC: 2086 Soft drinks; packaged in cans, bottles, etc.
PA: The Coca-Cola Company
1 Coca Cola Plz Nw
Atlanta GA 30313
404 676-2121

(G-9681)
ENERGY INTELLIGENCE GROUP INC (PA)
270 Madison Ave Fl 19 (10016-0601)
PHONE..................................212 532-1112
David Kirsch, *Managing Dir*
David Knapp, *Managing Dir*
Jason Fargo, *Editor*
Tom Haywood, *Editor*
Jill Junnola, *Editor*
EMP: 90
SQ FT: 7,000
SALES (est): 10.7MM **Privately Held**
SIC: 2741 Newsletter publishing

(G-9682)
ENERTIV INC
320 W 37th St Ste 1500 (10018-4232)
PHONE..................................646 350-3525
Connell McGill, *Ch of Bd*
Sharad Shankar, *Senior Engr*
EMP: 6
SALES (est): 1MM **Privately Held**
SIC: 3825 Instruments to measure electricity

(G-9683)
ENGELACK GEM CORPORATION
36 W 47th St Ste 601 (10036-8636)
PHONE..................................212 719-3094
Imre England, *President*
Herman Ackerman, *Vice Pres*
EMP: 2
SALES: 1MM **Privately Held**
SIC: 3915 Lapidary work & diamond cutting & polishing

(G-9684)
ENHANCE A COLOUR CORP
211 E 43rd St Rm 700 (10017-4821)
PHONE..................................212 490-3620
Kevin O'Connor, *President*
EMP: 43
SALES (corp-wide): 9.8MM **Privately Held**
SIC: 2741 Misc Publishing
PA: Enhance A Colour Corp.
15 Old Newtown Rd
Danbury CT 06810
203 748-5111

(G-9685)
ENLIGHTEN AIR INC
23 E 81st St Apt 10 (10028-0225)
P.O. Box 3111, Sag Harbor (11963-0405)
PHONE..................................917 656-1248
William O'Boyle, *CEO*
EMP: 5
SALES: 392MM **Privately Held**
SIC: 3728 Target drones

(G-9686)
ENPLAS AMERICA INC
299 Park Ave Fl 41a (10171-3808)
PHONE..................................646 892-7811
EMP: 8
SALES (est): 1MM
SALES (corp-wide): 312.4MM **Privately Held**
SIC: 3714 5065 3827 Gears, motor vehicle; semiconductor devices; lenses, optical: all types except ophthalmic
PA: Enplas Corporation
2-30-1, Namiki
Kawaguchi STM 332-0
482 533-131

(G-9687)
ENTERPRISE PRESS INC
627 Greenwich St (10014-3327)
PHONE..................................212 741-2111
Robert Hort, *Ch of Bd*
Benjamin Hort, *President*
Michael Rabinowitz, *President*
Michael Hort, *Principal*
Andrew Hort, *Treasurer*
EMP: 145 **EST:** 1915
SQ FT: 85,000
SALES (est): 12.5MM **Privately Held**
SIC: 2759 2752 Commercial printing; commercial printing, lithographic

(G-9688)
ENTERTAINMENT WEEKLY INC (DH)
135 W 50th St Frnt 3 (10020-1201)
PHONE..................................212 522-5600
Andy Sareyan, *President*
Rick Tetzeli, *Manager*
Diana Bernal, *Associate Dir*
▲ **EMP:** 135

▲ = Import ▼ = Export
◆ = Import/Export

SQ FT: 50,000
SALES (est): 17.2MM
SALES (corp-wide): 2.2B **Publicly Held**
SIC: **2731** 7812 Book publishing; motion picture & video production; television film production; motion picture production
HQ: Time Inc.
225 Liberty St Ste C2
New York NY 10281
212 522-1212

(G-9689)
ENTRAINANT INC
Also Called: Stylesprit
1 World Trade Ctr Fl 85 (10007-0103)
PHONE..................................212 946-4724
Ihsan Ugurlu, *President*
EMP: 6
SALES (est): 256.7K **Privately Held**
SIC: **2741**

(G-9690)
ENUMERAL BIOMEDICAL CORP
1370 Broadway Fl 5 (10018-7350)
PHONE..................................347 227-4787
Arthur H Tinkelenberg, *CEO*
Kevin Sarney, *Vice Pres*
EMP: 6
SALES (est): 1.3MM
SALES (corp-wide): 2.4MM **Privately Held**
SIC: **2834** Pharmaceutical preparations
PA: Enumeral Biomedical Holdings, Inc.
200 Cambridge St
Cambridge MA 02141
617 945-9146

(G-9691)
ENVY PUBLISHING GROUP INC
Also Called: N V Magazine
118 E 25th St Bsmt Ll (10010-2915)
PHONE..................................212 253-9874
Kyle Donovan, *CEO*
Maria Gordian, *President*
Christopher Chaney, *Adv Dir*
EMP: 6
SQ FT: 3,000
SALES: 500K **Privately Held**
WEB: www.nvmagazine.com
SIC: **2721** 6282 Periodicals; investment advice

(G-9692)
EON COLLECTIONS
247 W 35th St Rm 401 (10001-1962)
PHONE..................................212 695-1263
Alex Andropoulos, *Owner*
EMP: 20
SALES (est): 769K **Privately Held**
SIC: **2329** Men's & boys' clothing

(G-9693)
EPIC BEAUTY CO LLC
929 Park Ave 5 (10028-0211)
PHONE..................................212 327-3059
Annette McCoy, *Mng Member*
Maggie G Wedemeyer,
EMP: 2
SQ FT: 500
SALES (est): 1MM **Privately Held**
SIC: **2844** 7991 Cosmetic preparations; spas

(G-9694)
EPOST INTERNATIONAL INC
483 10th Ave (10018-1118)
PHONE..................................212 352-9390
Justine Brown, *President*
EMP: 5
SALES: 1MM **Privately Held**
SIC: **2741**

(G-9695)
EQUILEND HOLDINGS LLC (PA)
225 Liberty St Fl 10 (10281-1049)
PHONE..................................212 901-2200
Brian Lamb, *CEO*
Chris Benedict, *Vice Pres*
Sally Chu, *Vice Pres*
Gregory Shulman, *Vice Pres*
Dow Veeranarong, *Vice Pres*
EMP: 30
SQ FT: 5,500

SALES (est): 8.2MM **Privately Held**
WEB: www.equilend.com
SIC: **7372** Business oriented computer software

(G-9696)
EQUINOX AEGIS LLC
80 Riverside Blvd (10069-0301)
PHONE..................................212 316-9078
Jennifer C Bresnan, *Principal*
Alex Vorobeychik, *Vice Pres*
EMP: 5
SALES (est): 496.7K **Privately Held**
SIC: **2834** Pharmaceutical preparations

(G-9697)
EQUIPMENT APPAREL LLC
19 W 34th St Fl 8 (10001-3006)
PHONE..................................212 502-1890
Lisa Armstrong, *Credit Mgr*
Gila Dweck,
▲ EMP: 100
SALES (est): 7.7MM **Privately Held**
SIC: **2211** Apparel & outerwear fabrics, cotton

(G-9698)
EQUIVITAL INC
19 W 34th St Rm 1018 (10001-3006)
PHONE..................................646 513-4169
Anmol Sood, *CEO*
Anand Vasudev, *Vice Pres*
EMP: 22
SALES (est): 1.7MM **Privately Held**
SIC: **3845** Patient monitoring apparatus

(G-9699)
ER BUTLER & CO INC (PA)
55 Prince St Frnt A (10012-3472)
P.O. Box 272 (10012-0005)
PHONE..................................212 925-3565
Edward R Butler, *CEO*
▲ EMP: 25
SQ FT: 11,000
SALES (est): 5.2MM **Privately Held**
WEB: www.erbutler.com
SIC: **3429** 5072 8742 7699 Manufactured hardware (general); builders' hardware; industry specialist consultants; miscellaneous building item repair services; plumbing fixture fittings & trim; residential lighting fixtures

(G-9700)
ERIC WINTERLING INC
Also Called: Winterling, Eric Costumes
20 W 20th St Fl 5 (10011-9257)
PHONE..................................212 629-7686
Eric Winterling, *President*
EMP: 50
SALES (est): 4.8MM **Privately Held**
SIC: **2389** Costumes

(G-9701)
ERICKSON BEAMON LTD
498 Fashion Ave Rm 2406 (10018-6798)
PHONE..................................212 643-4810
Karen Foster Erickson, *President*
Eric Erickson, *Vice Pres*
EMP: 15
SQ FT: 7,500
SALES (est): 2MM **Privately Held**
WEB: www.ericksonbeamon.com
SIC: **3961** Costume jewelry, ex. precious metal & semiprecious stones

(G-9702)
ERIKA T SCHWARTZ MD PC
724 5th Ave Fl 10 (10019-4106)
PHONE..................................212 873-3420
Erika T Schwartz, *President*
Joshua Trutt, *Vice Pres*
EMP: 6
SALES (est): 1.3MM **Privately Held**
SIC: **2834** 8011 Hormone preparations; specialized medical practitioners, except internal

(G-9703)
ERIN SNOW LTD
140 E 56th St Apt 3a (10022-3624)
PHONE..................................212 675-7762
Erin Isakov, *President*
Sari Schwarz, *Prdtn Mgr*
Michael Isakov, *CFO*
▲ EMP: 5

SQ FT: 1,000
SALES (est): 500K **Privately Held**
WEB: www.erinsnow.com
SIC: **2211** Apparel & outerwear fabrics, cotton

(G-9704)
ESCHEN PROSTHETIC & ORTHOTIC L
510 E 73rd St Ste 201 (10021-4010)
PHONE..................................212 606-1262
Andrew Meyers, *President*
EMP: 20
SQ FT: 6,000
SALES (est): 2.7MM **Privately Held**
SIC: **3842** Braces, orthopedic; prosthetic appliances

(G-9705)
ESI CASES & ACCESSORIES INC
44 E 32nd St Rm 601 (10016-5557)
PHONE..................................212 883-8838
Elliot Azoulay, *Ch of Bd*
Karen Kuchta, *Vice Pres*
▲ EMP: 38 EST: 1993
SQ FT: 10,000
SALES (est): 10.1MM **Privately Held**
WEB: www.esicellular.com
SIC: **3661** Telephone & telegraph apparatus

(G-9706)
ESSAR AMERICAS
277 Park Ave 47th (10172-0003)
PHONE..................................212 292-2600
EMP: 5
SALES (est): 348.8K **Privately Held**
SIC: **1389** Oil & gas field services

(G-9707)
ESSAR STEEL MINNESOTA LLC (PA)
150 E 52nd St Fl 27 (10022-6017)
PHONE..................................212 292-2600
Carola Almonte, *Administration*
▲ EMP: 18
SALES (est): 7.7MM **Privately Held**
SIC: **1011** Iron ore mining

(G-9708)
ESSENCE VENTURES LLC
225 Liberty St Fl 9 (10281-1088)
PHONE..................................212 522-1212
Ed Lewis, *CEO*
EMP: 165
SALES (est): 3.3MM **Privately Held**
SIC: **2721** Magazines: publishing only, not printed on site

(G-9709)
ESSENTIAL PUBLICATIONS US LLC
Also Called: Essential Homme Magazine
14 E 4th St Rm 604 (10012-1141)
PHONE..................................646 707-0898
Roger Antin, *Publisher*
Algis Puidokas, *Principal*
EMP: 5 EST: 2009
SALES (est): 255.6K **Privately Held**
SIC: **2721** Magazines: publishing & printing

(G-9710)
ESSENTIAL RIBBONS INC
53 W 36th St Rm 405 (10018-7623)
PHONE..................................212 967-4173
Jie Lin, *Ch of Bd*
▲ EMP: 7
SALES (est): 620.2K **Privately Held**
SIC: **2241** Ribbons

(G-9711)
ESSEQUATTRO USA INC
1 Little West 12th St (10014-1302)
PHONE..................................917 862-0005
Giovanni De Santis, *Principal*
EMP: 6
SALES (est): 553.7K **Privately Held**
SIC: **2426** Carvings, furniture: wood

(G-9712)
ESSEX MANUFACTURING INC
Also Called: Baum Essex
350 5th Ave Ste 2400 (10118-0128)
P.O. Box 190, Washington GA (30673-0190)
PHONE..................................212 239-0080
William Baum, *CEO*
Myron Baum, *Ch of Bd*
Charles J Baum, *President*
Peter Baum, *COO*
◆ EMP: 75 EST: 1961
SQ FT: 85,300
SALES (est): 9.1MM **Privately Held**
SIC: **3999** 3171 2385 Umbrellas, canes & parts; women's handbags & purses; raincoats, except vulcanized rubber: purchased materials

(G-9713)
ESSIE COSMETICS LTD
575 5th Ave (10017-2422)
PHONE..................................212 818-1500
Esther Weingarten, *President*
Blanche Weingarten, *Treasurer*
◆ EMP: 75
SQ FT: 25,000
SALES (est): 16.8MM
SALES (corp-wide): 4.2B **Privately Held**
WEB: www.essie.com
SIC: **2844** 5122 Manicure preparations; toilet preparations; cosmetics
HQ: L'oreal Usa, Inc.
10 Hudson Yards Fl 30
New York NY 10001
212 818-1500

(G-9714)
ESTEE LAUDER COMPANIES INC
9 W 22nd St (10010-5101)
PHONE..................................917 606-3240
EMP: 504 **Publicly Held**
SIC: **2844** Toilet preparations
PA: The Estee Lauder Companies Inc
767 5th Ave Fl 1
New York NY 10153

(G-9715)
ESTEE LAUDER COMPANIES INC
110 E 59th St Fl 37 (10022-1600)
PHONE..................................212 572-4200
Seth E Herbert, *Counsel*
John Downey, *Vice Pres*
Marielle Hemschot, *Executive*
Desiree Thayer, *Education*
EMP: 21 **Publicly Held**
SIC: **2844** Cosmetic preparations
PA: The Estee Lauder Companies Inc
767 5th Ave Fl 1
New York NY 10153

(G-9716)
ESTEE LAUDER COMPANIES INC
655 Madison Ave Fl 15 (10065-8043)
PHONE..................................212 756-4800
Shanna Weinblatt, *Director*
EMP: 7 **Publicly Held**
SIC: **2844** Cosmetic preparations
PA: The Estee Lauder Companies Inc
767 5th Ave Fl 1
New York NY 10153

(G-9717)
ESTEE LAUDER COMPANIES INC
28 W 23rd St (10010-5204)
PHONE..................................646 762-7718
EMP: 14 **Publicly Held**
SIC: **2844** Toilet preparations
PA: The Estee Lauder Companies Inc
767 5th Ave Fl 1
New York NY 10153

(G-9718)
ESTEE LAUDER COMPANIES INC (PA)
767 5th Ave Fl 1 (10153-0003)
PHONE..................................212 572-4200
William P Lauder, *Ch of Bd*
Fabrizio Freda, *President*
John Demsey, *President*

Carl Haney, *Exec VP*
Sara E Moss, *Exec VP*
◆ **EMP:** 1000
SALES: 13.6B **Publicly Held**
WEB: www.elcompanies.com
SIC: 2844 Cosmetic preparations

(G-9719)
ESTEE LAUDER COMPANIES INC
65 Bleecker St Frnt 1 (10012-2420)
PHONE..................................646 602-7590
EMP: 504 **Publicly Held**
SIC: 2844 Toilet preparations
PA: The Estee Lauder Companies Inc
767 5th Ave Fl 1
New York NY 10153

(G-9720)
ESTEE LAUDER INTERNATIONAL INC (DH)
767 5th Ave Fl Conc6 (10153-0003)
PHONE..................................212 572-4200
Patrick Bousquet-Chavanne, *President*
Joel Bramble, *President*
Sara Moss, *Exec VP*
Sara Beaney, *Vice Pres*
Herve Bouix, *Vice Pres*
▲ **EMP:** 7
SALES (est): 366.2MM **Publicly Held**
SIC: 2844 Face creams or lotions
HQ: Estee Lauder Inc.
767 5th Ave Fl 1
New York NY 10153
212 572-4200

(G-9721)
ETERNAL FORTUNE FASHION LLC (PA)
Also Called: Profile
135 W 36th St Fl 3 (10018-6900)
PHONE..................................212 965-5322
Bill Ingoglia, *Sales Mgr*
Ed Rzonca, *Accounts Exec*
Roy Zou, *Mng Member*
Candice Wong,
◆ **EMP:** 1
SQ FT: 5,600
SALES (est): 2MM **Privately Held**
SIC: 2329 Men's & boys' sportswear & athletic clothing

(G-9722)
ETNA PRODUCTS CO INC (PA)
99 Madison Ave Fl 11 (10016-7419)
PHONE..................................212 989-7591
Raymond Trinh, *Ch of Bd*
Jeffrey Snyder, *Ch of Bd*
Paula Snyder, *Admin Sec*
▲ **EMP:** 19 **EST:** 1957
SQ FT: 15,000
SALES (est): 3.4MM **Privately Held**
WEB: www.etna.com
SIC: 3089 5021 Plastic kitchenware, tableware & houseware; furniture

(G-9723)
ETNA TOOL & DIE CORPORATION
42 Bond St Frnt A (10012-2476)
PHONE..................................212 475-4350
Keranus Galuppo, *President*
James Galuppo, *Admin Sec*
EMP: 12 **EST:** 1946
SQ FT: 14,000
SALES (est): 1.3MM **Privately Held**
WEB: www.etnatoolanddie.com
SIC: 3599 3544 7692 Machine shop, jobbing & repair; special dies & tools; welding repair

(G-9724)
ETON INSTITUTE
1 Rockefeller Plz Fl 11 (10020-2073)
PHONE..................................855 334-3688
EMP: 10
SALES (est): 710K **Privately Held**
SIC: 3999 Mfg Misc Products

(G-9725)
EU DESIGN LLC
73 Spring St Rm 506 (10012-5802)
PHONE..................................212 420-7788
Roberto Berardi, *President*
Leonardo Caraffini, *Accounts Mgr*
Alyssa Miller, *Accounts Mgr*
Lizzie Reeves, *Manager*
Susan Wong, *Manager*
▲ **EMP:** 7 **EST:** 1999
SALES (est): 948K
SALES (corp-wide): 7.7MM **Privately Held**
WEB: www.eu-design.com
SIC: 3965 3961 5131 Buttons & parts; costume jewelry; piece goods & other fabrics; ribbons
PA: Eu Design, Hk Limited
Rm 301-302 3/F Tins Enterprises Ctr
Cheung Sha Wan KLN
342 115-54

(G-9726)
EUGENE BIRO CORP
581 5th Ave Fl 3 (10017-8826)
PHONE..................................212 997-0146
Eugene Biro, *President*
Ety Biro, *Vice Pres*
Anne J Fox, *Vice Pres*
Jack Ko, *Info Tech Dir*
EMP: 30 **EST:** 1975
SQ FT: 15,000
SALES (est): 3.7MM **Privately Held**
WEB: www.eugenebiro.com
SIC: 3915 5094 Diamond cutting & polishing; diamonds (gems)

(G-9727)
EUPHORBIA PRODUCTIONS LTD
632 Broadway Fl 9 (10012-2614)
PHONE..................................212 533-1700
Philip Glass, *President*
Kurt Munkaisi, *Officer*
EMP: 6
SALES (est): 483K **Privately Held**
WEB: www.euphorbia.com
SIC: 2741 7389 Music books: publishing only, not printed on site; music recording producer

(G-9728)
EURO BANDS INC
247 W 37th St Ste 700 (10018-5706)
PHONE..................................212 719-9777
Zbigniew Jarosh, *President*
EMP: 16
SALES (est): 500K **Privately Held**
WEB: www.e-bands.net
SIC: 3911 Jewelry, precious metal

(G-9729)
EURO PACIFIC PRECIOUS METALS
152 Madison Ave Rm 1003 (10016-5414)
PHONE..................................212 481-0310
Peter Schiff, *Principal*
EMP: 6 **EST:** 2010
SALES (est): 697.5K **Privately Held**
SIC: 3339 Precious metals

(G-9730)
EUROCO COSTUMES INC
254 W 35th St Fl 15 (10001-2504)
PHONE..................................212 629-9665
Janet Bloor, *President*
▼ **EMP:** 9
SQ FT: 3,000
SALES (est): 1MM **Privately Held**
SIC: 2389 Theatrical costumes

(G-9731)
EUROPROJECTS INTL INC
Also Called: Adotta America
152 W 25th St Fl 8b (10001-7402)
PHONE..................................917 262-0795
Luigi Zannier, *President*
EMP: 11
SALES (corp-wide): 13MM **Privately Held**
SIC: 3211 Structural glass
PA: Europrojects Int'l Inc
500 Nordhoff Pl Ste 5
Englewood NJ 07631
201 408-5215

(G-9732)
EV-BOX NORTH AMERICA INC
335 Madison Ave Fl 4 (10017-4675)
PHONE..................................646 930-6305
Nicholas Lalli, *Director*
EMP: 5
SQ FT: 12,000
SALES (est): 237.6K **Privately Held**
SIC: 3694 Automotive electrical equipment

(G-9733)
EVADO FILIP
159 Bleecker St (10012-1457)
PHONE..................................917 774-8666
Craig Gainsboro, *CFO*
EMP: 12 **EST:** 2013
SQ FT: 2,000
SALES (est): 819.2K **Privately Held**
SIC: 3663

(G-9734)
EVERBLOCK SYSTEMS LLC (PA)
790 Madison Ave Rm 506 (10065-6124)
PHONE..................................844 422-5625
Arnon Rosan,
EMP: 7 **EST:** 2015
SALES (est): 4.4MM **Privately Held**
SIC: 3271 3251 3299 3089 Blocks, concrete: landscape or retaining wall; structural brick & blocks; blocks & brick, sand lime; injection molded finished plastic products

(G-9735)
EVERCORE PARTNERS SVCS E LLC
55 E 52nd St (10055-0002)
PHONE..................................212 857-3100
Roger Altman,
David Ossensend,
EMP: 2214
SALES (est): 132.9MM **Publicly Held**
SIC: 2711 Newspapers, publishing & printing
PA: Evercore Inc.
55 E 52nd St Fl 36
New York NY 10055

(G-9736)
EVEREST BBN INC
42 Broadway Ste 1736 (10004-3853)
PHONE..................................212 268-7979
Ruth Shelling, *Principal*
Paul Stamoulis, *Exec VP*
EMP: 11 **EST:** 2011
SALES (est): 1.7MM **Privately Held**
SIC: 3825 Mfg Electrical Measuring Instruments

(G-9737)
EVERLAST SPORTS MFG CORP (DH)
42 W 39th St (10018-3809)
PHONE..................................212 239-0990
Neil Morton, *CEO*
▲ **EMP:** 41 **EST:** 1945
SQ FT: 300,000
SALES (est): 12.9MM
SALES (corp-wide): 4.7B **Privately Held**
SIC: 3949 5091 Sporting & athletic goods; sporting & recreation goods

(G-9738)
EVERLAST WORLDWIDE INC (DH)
42 W 39th St Fl 3 (10018-3832)
PHONE..................................212 239-0990
Mark Hunter, *CFO*
Sixto Montalvo, *Director*
EMP: 40
SQ FT: 12,087
SALES: 70MM
SALES (corp-wide): 4.7B **Privately Held**
SIC: 3949 8049 3144 3149 Boxing equipment & supplies, general; gloves, sport & athletic: boxing, handball, etc.; nutritionist; women's footwear, except athletic; children's footwear, except athletic

(G-9739)
EVERSTONE INDUSTRIES LLC
242 W 122nd St Apt 4b (10027-5468)
PHONE..................................347 777-8150
Everstone Adams, *Principal*
EMP: 25
SALES (est): 686K **Privately Held**
SIC: 3999 Manufacturing industries

(G-9740)
EVIDON INC (HQ)
Also Called: Digital Governance Division
10 E 39th St Fl 8 (10016-0111)
PHONE..................................917 262-2530
Scott Meyer, *CEO*
Mark Rudolph, *COO*
Todd Ruback, *Vice Pres*
Meagan Kelly, *Mktg Coord*
William Littman, *Corp Counsel*
EMP: 55 **EST:** 2009
SALES (est): 12.4MM
SALES (corp-wide): 13MM **Privately Held**
SIC: 7372 Application computer software
PA: Crownpeak Technology, Inc.
707 17th St Ste 3800
Denver CO 80202
310 841-5920

(G-9741)
EVOCATE MEDIA LLC
100 W 139th St Apt 34a (10030-2217)
PHONE..................................646 361-3014
Parveez Syed, *Mng Member*
EMP: 10
SALES: 0 **Privately Held**
SIC: 7372 7389 Application computer software;

(G-9742)
EVOLUTION SPIRITS INC
Also Called: Monkey Rum
401 Park Ave S (10016-8808)
PHONE..................................917 543-7880
Ian Crystal, *President*
EMP: 7
SALES (est): 589.8K **Privately Held**
SIC: 2085 Rum (alcoholic beverage)

(G-9743)
EWATCHFACTORY CORP (PA)
Also Called: Pacific Concepts
390 5th Ave Rm 910 (10018-8111)
PHONE..................................212 564-8318
Remi Chabrat, *CEO*
Andy Yeung, *Parts Mgr*
Jaffy Ng, *Accountant*
Vanessa Ramirez, *Manager*
Barbara A Rizzo, *Manager*
▲ **EMP:** 5
SQ FT: 1,200
SALES (est): 531.9K **Privately Held**
WEB: www.watchfactory.com
SIC: 3873 Watches, clocks, watchcases & parts

(G-9744)
EWT HOLDINGS III CORP (HQ)
666 5th Ave Fl 36 (10103-3102)
PHONE..................................212 644-5900
EMP: 11
SALES (est): 1.4B
SALES (corp-wide): 1.1B **Publicly Held**
SIC: 3589 3823 3826 4941 Sewage & water treatment equipment; water treatment equipment, industrial; sewage treatment equipment; water purification equipment, household type; water quality monitoring & control systems; water testing apparatus; water supply; iron & steel (ferrous) products; cast iron pipe; piling, iron & steel
PA: Evoqua Water Technologies Corp.
210 6th Ave Ste 3300
Pittsburgh PA 15222
724 772-0044

(G-9745)
EX EL ENTERPRISES LTD
630 Fort Washington Ave (10040-3900)
PHONE..................................212 489-4500
Henry Lehman, *President*
EMP: 11
SQ FT: 1,900
SALES (est): 960K **Privately Held**
WEB: www.ex-el.com
SIC: 7372 7373 Prepackaged software; systems software development services

(G-9746)
EX-IT MEDICAL DEVICES INC
1330 Ave Of The Americas (10019-5400)
PHONE..................................212 653-0637
Shlomo Shopen, *CEO*
EMP: 3

SALES: 10MM **Privately Held**
SIC: **2844** Cosmetic preparations
PA: Ex-It Medical Devices Limited
3/F Jonsim Place
Wan Chai HK

(G-9747)
EXACT SOLUTIONS INC
139 Fulton St Rm 511 (10038-2535)
PHONE..................................212 707-8627
Hardev Deindsa, *President*
Narvinder Matharu, *Sales Engr*
Ruchir Garg, *CTO*
EMP: 11
SALES (est): 1MM **Privately Held**
WEB: www.exact-solutions.com
SIC: **7372** Business oriented computer software

(G-9748)
EXCEL GRAPHICS SERVICES INC
519 8th Ave Fl 18 (10018-4577)
PHONE..................................212 929-2183
Joseph Risola, *President*
Anthony Fazio III, *Vice Pres*
EMP: 12 EST: 1997
SQ FT: 16,500
SALES (est): 1.7MM **Privately Held**
SIC: **2752** Commercial printing, offset

(G-9749)
EXCEL TECHNOLOGY INC
780 3rd Ave (10017-2024)
PHONE..................................212 355-3400
Donald Hill, *CEO*
EMP: 15 **Publicly Held**
WEB: www.exceltechinc.com
SIC: **3845** Electromedical equipment
HQ: Excel Technology, Inc.
125 Middlesex Tpke
Bedford MA 01730
781 266-5700

(G-9750)
EXCELLED SHEEPSKIN & LEA COAT (PA)
Also Called: RG Apparel Group
1359 Broadway Fl 9 (10018-7190)
P.O. Box 659, Carteret NJ (07008-0659)
PHONE..................................212 594-5843
William Goldman, *President*
Myron Goldman, *Chairman*
Michael Holzberg, *Vice Pres*
Ken Walton, *CFO*
Carol Goldman, *Manager*
▲ EMP: 12 EST: 1927
SQ FT: 50,000
SALES (est): 72.8MM **Privately Held**
WEB: www.leathercoatsetc.com
SIC: **2386** 3172 2337 2311 Coats & jackets, leather & sheep-lined; personal leather goods; women's & misses' suits & coats; men's & boys' suits & coats

(G-9751)
EXCELSIOR GRAPHICS INC
485 Madison Ave Fl 13 (10022-5820)
PHONE..................................212 730-6200
Harold Siegel, *President*
EMP: 5
SQ FT: 8,000
SALES (est): 450K **Privately Held**
SIC: **2752** Commercial printing, offset

(G-9752)
EXECUTIVE SIGN CORPORATION
347 W 36th St Rm 902 (10018-6491)
PHONE..................................212 397-4050
Isaac Goldman, *President*
Kelle Hankins, *Vice Pres*
EMP: 6
SQ FT: 1,800
SALES: 600K **Privately Held**
SIC: **3993** Signs, not made in custom sign painting shops

(G-9753)
EXOTIC PRINT AND PAPER INC
Also Called: Arthur Invitation
15 E 13th St (10003-4405)
PHONE..................................212 807-0465
Arfa Rejaei, *Ch of Bd*
Arthur Rajaei, *President*

EMP: 11
SQ FT: 1,800
SALES (est): 1.1MM **Privately Held**
SIC: **2759** 5947 Commercial printing; gift shop

(G-9754)
EXPERIMENT LLC
260 5th Ave Fl 3 (10001-6408)
PHONE..................................212 889-1659
Matthew Lore,
Peter Burri,
▲ EMP: 5
SALES (est): 517.5K **Privately Held**
SIC: **2732** Book printing

(G-9755)
EXPERIMENT PUBLISHING LLC
220 E 23rd St Ste 600 (10010-4658)
PHONE..................................212 889-1273
Matthew Lore, *Mng Member*
▲ EMP: 9
SALES (est): 902.6K **Privately Held**
SIC: **2741** Miscellaneous publishing

(G-9756)
EXPRESS CHECKOUT LLC
110 E 1st St Apt 20 (10009-7977)
PHONE..................................646 512-2068
William Hogben,
EMP: 6
SQ FT: 300
SALES (est): 313.4K **Privately Held**
SIC: **7372** Application computer software

(G-9757)
EXTREME GROUP HOLDINGS LLC (DH)
550 Madison Ave Fl 6 (10022-3211)
PHONE..................................212 833-8000
▲ EMP: 12
SALES (est): 1.8MM
SALES (corp-wide): 80.1B **Privately Held**
SIC: **3652** Pre-recorded records & tapes
HQ: Sony/Atv Music Publishing Llc
25 Madison Ave Fl 24
New York NY 10010
212 833-7730

(G-9758)
EYELOCK CORPORATION
321 W 44th St Ste 702 (10036-5468)
PHONE..................................855 393-5625
Amy Romeo, *CFO*
Chris Ream, *Security Dir*
EMP: 19
SALES: 3.8MM
SALES (corp-wide): 507MM **Publicly Held**
SIC: **3699** Security control equipment & systems
HQ: Eyelock Llc
321 W 44th St Ste 702
New York NY 10036
855 393-5625

(G-9759)
EYELOCK LLC (HQ)
321 W 44th St Ste 702 (10036-5468)
PHONE..................................855 393-5625
Jeff Carter, *CEO*
Sarvesh Makthal, *President*
Michael Petrov, *VP Engrg*
Anthony Antolino,
Samuel Carter,
EMP: 10 EST: 2015
SALES (est): 10.2MM
SALES (corp-wide): 507MM **Publicly Held**
SIC: **3699** Security control equipment & systems
PA: Voxx International Corporation
2351 J Lawson Blvd
Orlando FL 32824
800 645-7750

(G-9760)
EYENOVIA INC
501 5th Ave Rm 1404 (10017-7863)
PHONE..................................917 289-1117
Fred Eshelman, *Ch of Bd*
Jennifer Clasby, *Vice Pres*
Luke Clauson, *Vice Pres*
John Gandolfo, *CFO*
Tsontcho Ianchulev, *Chief Mktg Ofcr*
EMP: 5

SALES (est): 496.4K **Privately Held**
SIC: **2834** 8731 Pharmaceutical preparations; biological research

(G-9761)
F & J DESIGNS INC
Also Called: Thalian
526 Fashion Ave Fl 8 (10018-4822)
PHONE..................................212 302-8755
Franklin Bergman, *President*
Joan Mendlinger, *Admin Sec*
▲ EMP: 9
SQ FT: 5,000
SALES (est): 1.3MM **Privately Held**
WEB: www.fjdesigns.com
SIC: **2339** 5137 Mfg Women's/Misses' Outerwear Whol Women's/Child's Clothing

(G-9762)
F P H COMMUNICATIONS
225 Broadway Ste 2008 (10007-3737)
PHONE..................................212 528-1728
Steve Young, *President*
EMP: 2
SQ FT: 2,100
SALES (est): 3.5MM **Privately Held**
SIC: **2731** Book publishing

(G-9763)
F&M ORNAMENTAL DESIGNS LLC
Also Called: Desiron
200 Lexington Ave Rm 702 (10016-6123)
PHONE..................................212 353-2600
Frank J Carfaro, *Owner*
EMP: 6 **Privately Held**
SIC: **2514** Metal household furniture
PA: F&M Ornamental Designs L.L.C.
200 Lexington Ave Rm 702
New York NY 10016

(G-9764)
F&M ORNAMENTAL DESIGNS LLC (PA)
Also Called: Desiron
200 Lexington Ave Rm 702 (10016-6123)
PHONE..................................908 241-7776
Frank J Carfaro, *Mng Member*
▲ EMP: 17
SQ FT: 20,000
SALES (est): 5.4MM **Privately Held**
SIC: **2514** Metal household furniture

(G-9765)
F+W MEDIA INC
1140 Broadway Fl 14 (10001-7504)
PHONE..................................212 447-1400
Megan Fitzpatrick, *Editor*
Chuck Sambuchino, *Editor*
Phil Graham, *Vice Pres*
Stephanie Adams, *Marketing Staff*
David Nussbaum, *Branch Mgr*
EMP: 8
SALES (corp-wide): 266.2MM **Privately Held**
SIC: **2741** Miscellaneous publishing
HQ: F+W Media, Inc.
10151 Carver Rd Ste 200
Blue Ash OH 45242
513 531-2690

(G-9766)
F-O-R SOFTWARE LLC
Also Called: Two-Four Software
757 3rd Ave Fl 20 (10017-2046)
PHONE..................................212 231-9506
Steve Davis, *Branch Mgr*
EMP: 15
SALES (corp-wide): 3.1MM **Privately Held**
SIC: **7372** Prepackaged software
PA: F-O-R Software Llc
10 Bank St Ste 880
White Plains NY 10606
914 220-8800

(G-9767)
F-O-R SOFTWARE LLC
100 Park Ave Rm 1600 (10017-5538)
PHONE..................................212 724-3920
Chris Davis, *Manager*
EMP: 9
SALES (corp-wide): 3.1MM **Privately Held**
SIC: **7372** Prepackaged software

PA: F-O-R Software Llc
10 Bank St Ste 880
White Plains NY 10606
914 220-8800

(G-9768)
F5 NETWORKS INC
600 Lexington Ave Fl 5 (10022-7634)
PHONE..................................888 882-7535
James Reardon, *Principal*
Maxim Zavodchik, *Engineer*
EMP: 6 **Publicly Held**
SIC: **2752** Commercial printing, lithographic
PA: F5 Networks, Inc.
401 Elliott Ave W Ste 500
Seattle WA 98119

(G-9769)
FABBIAN USA CORP
307 W 38th St Rm 1103 (10018-2946)
PHONE..................................973 882-3824
Vincenzo Tersigni, *Vice Pres*
▲ EMP: 6
SQ FT: 33,000
SALES (est): 953.5K **Privately Held**
SIC: **3648** Lighting equipment

(G-9770)
FACSIMILE CMMNCATIONS INDS INC (PA)
Also Called: Atlantic Business Products
134 W 26th St Fl 3 (10001-6803)
PHONE..................................212 741-6400
Larry Weiss, *Ch of Bd*
Austin Eric, *Vice Pres*
Bill Green, *Vice Pres*
Rob Habeeb, *Vice Pres*
Jonathan Elson, *Project Mgr*
EMP: 75
SQ FT: 12,000
SALES (est): 47.9MM **Privately Held**
WEB: www.tomorrowsoffice.com
SIC: **3861** 3571 Photocopy machines; computers, digital, analog or hybrid

(G-9771)
FADER INC
71 W 23rd St Ste 1300 (10010-3540)
PHONE..................................212 741-7100
Jon Cohen, *President*
EMP: 14
SALES (est): 1.4MM **Privately Held**
SIC: **2721** Magazines: publishing only, not printed on site

(G-9772)
FAHRENHEIT NY INC
315 W 39th St Rm 803 (10018-1492)
PHONE..................................212 354-6554
Connie Bates, *President*
Christine Bates, *Admin Sec*
EMP: 7
SQ FT: 2,200
SALES (est): 908.9K **Privately Held**
SIC: **3199** 3172 Leather belting & strapping; personal leather goods

(G-9773)
FAIRCHILD PUBLICATIONS INC (DH)
Also Called: Womens Wear Daily
475 5th Ave (10017-6220)
PHONE..................................212 630-4000
Charles H Townsend, *President*
Richard Baylef, *President*
Michael Coady, *President*
Donald E Newhouse, *Vice Pres*
John Balendo, *CFO*
▲ EMP: 600
SQ FT: 150,000
SALES (est): 146.8MM
SALES (corp-wide): 5.6B **Privately Held**
WEB: www.fairchildbooks.com
SIC: **2721** 2711 2731 Periodicals; newspapers; book publishing
HQ: Advance Magazine Publishers Inc.
1 World Trade Ctr Fl 43
New York NY 10007
212 286-2860

(G-9774)
FAIRCHILD PUBLISHING LLC
4 Times Sq Fl 17 (10036-6518)
PHONE..................................212 286-3897
EMP: 8

New York - New York County (G-9775)　　GEOGRAPHIC SECTION

SALES (est): 803K Privately Held
SIC: 2721 Periodicals

(G-9775)
FAIRMOUNT PRESS
70 W 36th St Rm 500 (10018-8050)
PHONE....................................212 255-2300
Peter Bird, President
EMP: 6
SALES (est): 510.1K Privately Held
SIC: 2759 7334 Letterpress printing; photocopying & duplicating services

(G-9776)
FAIT USA INC
350 5th Ave Fl 41 (10118-4100)
PHONE....................................215 674-5310
Massimo Bassi, President
Alessandro Bronzini, Vice Pres
▲ EMP: 4
SQ FT: 8,000
SALES: 1MM
SALES (corp-wide): 30.4MM Privately Held
SIC: 3568 Shafts, flexible
PA: Fait Group Spa
Via Raffaello Scarpettini 367/369
Montemurlo PO 59013
057 468-121

(G-9777)
FAM CREATIONS
7 W 45th St Ste 1404 (10036-4905)
PHONE....................................212 869-4833
Mario Scimaca, President
EMP: 20
SALES (est): 1.6MM Privately Held
SIC: 3911 Jewelry Manufacturer

(G-9778)
FAMILY PUBLICATIONS LTD
325 W 38th St Rm 804 (10018-9623)
PHONE....................................212 947-2177
Gail Granet-Velez, President
EMP: 12
SALES (est): 1.2MM Privately Held
WEB: www.familypublications.com
SIC: 2741 7999 Guides: publishing only, not printed on site; exposition operation

(G-9779)
FANCY FLAMINGO LLC
450 W 17th St Apt 528 (10011-5846)
PHONE....................................516 209-7306
Sanchali Sundaram, CEO
Senthil Sundaram, COO
EMP: 6 EST: 2011
SALES (est): 407.5K Privately Held
SIC: 2086 Bottled & canned soft drinks

(G-9780)
FANSHAWE FOODS LLC
5 Columbus Cir (10019-1412)
PHONE....................................212 757-3130
Lee Zalben, President
EMP: 10
SALES (est): 564.3K Privately Held
SIC: 2099 5149 Food preparations; specialty food items

(G-9781)
FANTASIA JEWELRY INC
42 W 39th St Fl 14 (10018-2082)
PHONE....................................212 921-9590
Sebastian De Serio, President
Joseph De Serio, Vice Pres
Edward Deserio, Treasurer
Jennifer Deserio, Marketing Mgr
EMP: 42
SQ FT: 7,000
SALES (est): 3.2MM Privately Held
WEB: www.fantasiajewelry.com
SIC: 3961 3911 Costume jewelry, ex. precious metal & semiprecious stones; jewelry, precious metal

(G-9782)
FANTASY SPORTS MEDIA GROUP INC
Also Called: Fantasy Sports Network
27 W 20th St Ste 900 (10011-3725)
PHONE....................................416 917-6002
Leonard Asper, President
EMP: 20
SALES (est): 2.5MM Privately Held
SIC: 2741 Miscellaneous publishing

(G-9783)
FANVISION ENTERTAINMENT LLC (PA)
33 W 17th St Ste 901 (10011-5520)
PHONE....................................917 297-7428
Andrew Daines, CEO
EMP: 3
SALES (est): 21.2MM Privately Held
SIC: 3861 Cameras & related equipment

(G-9784)
FASHION ACCENTS LLC
366 5th Ave Rm 802 (10001-2231)
PHONE....................................401 331-6626
EMP: 13
SALES (corp-wide): 3.4MM Privately Held
SIC: 3961 Earrings, except precious metal
PA: Fashion Accents, Llc
100 Nashua St
Providence RI 02904
401 331-6626

(G-9785)
FASHION AVE SWEATER KNITS LLC
525 7th Ave Fl 4 (10018-4940)
PHONE....................................212 302-8282
Melvyn Weiss, President
Austin Mallis, Vice Pres
EMP: 100
SQ FT: 18,000
SALES (est): 6.4MM Privately Held
SIC: 2339 Service apparel, washable: women's

(G-9786)
FASHION AVENUE KNITS INC
Also Called: Its Our Time
1400 Broadway Rm 2401 (10018-5300)
PHONE....................................718 456-9000
Mel Weiss, Manager
EMP: 10
SALES (est): 1MM
SALES (corp-wide): 46.3MM Privately Held
WEB: www.fashionavenueknits.com
SIC: 2253 Knit outerwear mills
PA: Fashion Avenue Knits Inc.
525 Fashion Ave Fl 4
New York NY 10018
718 456-9000

(G-9787)
FASHION CALENDAR INTERNATIONAL
153 E 87th St Apt 6a (10128-2705)
PHONE....................................212 289-0420
Ruth Finley, Owner
EMP: 7 EST: 1939
SALES (est): 665.9K Privately Held
WEB: www.fashioncalendar.net
SIC: 2721 Periodicals

(G-9788)
FASHIONDEX INC
153 W 27th St Ste 701 (10001-6255)
PHONE....................................914 271-6121
Andrea Kennedy, President
Max Andrews, Vice Pres
▲ EMP: 6
SALES: 150K Privately Held
WEB: www.fashiondex.com
SIC: 2741 5192 Telephone & other directory publishing; books, periodicals & newspapers

(G-9789)
FAVIANA INTERNATIONAL INC (PA)
320 W 37th St Fl 10 (10018-4675)
PHONE....................................212 594-4422
Parviz Pourmoradi, President
Omid Pourmoradi, Vice Pres
Shala Pourmoradi, Treasurer
▲ EMP: 31
SQ FT: 32,000
SALES (est): 7.8MM Privately Held
WEB: www.faviana.com
SIC: 2335 Women's, juniors' & misses' dresses

(G-9790)
FEDERAL ENVELOPE INC
22 W 32nd St (10001-3807)
PHONE....................................212 243-8380
Fax: 212 691-8076
EMP: 10 EST: 1953
SQ FT: 10,000
SALES (est): 730K Privately Held
SIC: 2759 2752 Printer Of Printing Envelopes Letterpress & An Offset Printing Service

(G-9791)
FEDERAL PUMP CORPORATION
250 E 73rd St Apt 18c (10021-4314)
PHONE....................................718 451-2000
Christopher Murtagh, President
Jeff Mayzus, General Mgr
Jake Burns, Engineer
Tony Tsang, Engineer
Julian Verdeguer, Engineer
▲ EMP: 45 EST: 1935
SQ FT: 53,000
SALES (est): 18.3MM
SALES (corp-wide): 4.4MM Privately Held
SIC: 3561 Industrial pumps & parts
PA: Pumpman Holdings, Llc
600 Madison Ave
New York NY 10022
626 939-0300

(G-9792)
FELDMAN COMPANY INC
Also Called: Ango Home
241 W 37th St Rm 1001 (10018-7072)
PHONE....................................212 966-1303
Alfred Feldman, President
Hershel Feldman, Vice Pres
Eli Jeidel, Vice Pres
▲ EMP: 13
SQ FT: 6,000
SALES (est): 2.5MM Privately Held
WEB: www.feldmanco.com
SIC: 2299 5023 Fabrics: linen, jute, hemp, ramie; home furnishings

(G-9793)
FELLUSS RECORDING
36 E 23rd St Rm 9l (10010-4417)
PHONE....................................212 727-8055
Andrew Fellus, Owner
EMP: 6
SALES (est): 320K Privately Held
SIC: 3679 Recording heads, speech & musical equipment

(G-9794)
FEMINIST PRESS INC
365 5th Ave Ste 5406 (10016-4309)
PHONE....................................212 817-7915
Lauren Hook, Editor
David Olan, Dean
Yamberlie Tavarez, Development
John Flaherty, Security Mgr
Hannah Goodwin, Admin Mgr
EMP: 9
SQ FT: 2,000
SALES: 878.4K Privately Held
SIC: 2731 Book publishing

(G-9795)
FERRARA BAKERY & CAFE INC (PA)
195 Grand St (10013-3717)
PHONE....................................212 226-6150
Ernest Lepore, Ch of Bd
Peter Lepore, President
Josie Olah, General Mgr
Jose Torres, General Mgr
Anthony Sessa, Opers Staff
▲ EMP: 95 EST: 1892
SALES (est): 10.8MM Privately Held
WEB: www.ferraracafe.com
SIC: 2051 5461 Cakes, bakery: except frozen; pastries, e.g. danish: except frozen; bakeries; cakes; pastries

(G-9796)
FERRIS USA LLC
18 W 108th St Apt 4a (10025-8918)
PHONE....................................617 895-8102
Taylor Conlin, Mng Member
EMP: 8

SALES: 150K Privately Held
SIC: 2326 2329 5621 Men's & boys' work clothing; men's & boys' sportswear & athletic clothing; field jackets, military; ready-to-wear apparel, women's

(G-9797)
FIBER-SEAL OF NEW YORK INC (PA)
979 3rd Ave Ste 903 (10022-3802)
PHONE....................................212 888-5580
Steven Mittman, President
Roberta Mittman, Corp Secy
▲ EMP: 160 EST: 1954
SALES (est): 15MM Privately Held
WEB: www.lewismittman.com
SIC: 2512 2511 Upholstered household furniture; wood bedroom furniture

(G-9798)
FIBRE CASE & NOVELTY CO INC (PA)
270 Lafayette St Ste 1510 (10012-3377)
PHONE....................................212 254-6060
Elliot Kozer, President
Richard Rubin, Treasurer
EMP: 4 EST: 1956
SALES (est): 2.4MM Privately Held
SIC: 3161 Sample cases; trunks

(G-9799)
FIDELUS TECHNOLOGIES LLC
240 W 35th St Fl 6 (10001-2506)
PHONE....................................212 616-7800
Ron Rosansky, President
Don Harloff, Vice Pres
Nancee Pronsati, Vice Pres
Ruben Delgado, Opers Staff
Eric Nelson, CFO
EMP: 51
SQ FT: 25,000
SALES (est): 15MM Privately Held
WEB: www.fidelus.com
SIC: 7372 Prepackaged software

(G-9800)
FIDESA US CORPORATION
17 State St Unit 122 (10004-1501)
PHONE....................................212 269-9000
Robert Thompson, Principal
Joy Rosenstein, Exec VP
Camillo Amato, Vice Pres
Michael Begic, Vice Pres
Nigel Holmes-Mitchell, Vice Pres
EMP: 400
SALES (est): 20.5MM
SALES (corp-wide): 467.6MM Privately Held
WEB: www.royalbluefinancial.com
SIC: 7372 7371 Prepackaged software; custom computer programming services
PA: Fidessa Group Holdings Limited
2nd Floor Concourse 2
Belfast BT3 9
289 046-3000

(G-9801)
FIERCE FUN TOYS LLC
100 Riverside Dr Ste 2 (10024-4822)
P.O. Box 905 (10024-0546)
PHONE....................................646 322-7172
Angela Larson, Mng Member
EMP: 7
SALES (est): 447.2K Privately Held
SIC: 3942 5092 Stuffed toys, including animals; toys & hobby goods & supplies

(G-9802)
FINDMINE INC
137 Varick St Fl 2 (10013-1110)
PHONE....................................925 787-6181
Michelle Bacharach, CEO
Devon Safran, Vice Pres
EMP: 15 EST: 2014
SALES (est): 305.2K Privately Held
SIC: 7372 Business oriented computer software

(G-9803)
FINE CUT DIAMONDS CORPORATION
580 5th Ave Ste 709 (10036-4728)
PHONE....................................212 575-8780
Michael Deutsch, President
EMP: 5 EST: 1967

GEOGRAPHIC SECTION

SQ FT: 1,100
SALES (est): 395.9K Privately Held
SIC: 3915 5094 Diamond cutting & polishing; diamonds (gems)

(G-9804)
FINE SHEER INDUSTRIES INC (PA)
350 5th Ave Ste 4710 (10118-4710)
PHONE...................212 594-4224
Grace Franco, President
Isaac Franco, President
▲ EMP: 18
SQ FT: 6,000
SALES (est): 275.1K Privately Held
SIC: 2252 2251 2369 Socks; panty hose; leggings; girls', children's & infants'

(G-9805)
FINE SOUNDS GROUP INC (PA)
Also Called: World of McIntosh
214 Lafayette St (10012-4079)
PHONE...................212 364-0219
Charles Randall, CEO
Mauro Grange, Ch of Bd
Giovanni Palacardo, CFO
EMP: 12
SALES (est): 25.9MM Privately Held
SIC: 3679 Recording heads, speech & musical equipment; recording & playback heads, magnetic; recording & playback apparatus, including phonograph

(G-9806)
FIRST CHOICE NEWS INC
639 1/2 Broadway (10012)
PHONE...................212 477-2044
Raffie Hadibhai, Ch of Bd
EMP: 6
SALES (est): 229K Privately Held
SIC: 2711 5311 Newspapers, publishing & printing; department stores, discount

(G-9807)
FIRST GAMES PUBLR NETWRK INC
Also Called: 1gpn
420 Lexington Ave Rm 412 (10170-0499)
PHONE...................212 983-0501
EMP: 100
SALES: 1,000K Privately Held
SIC: 2741 Developer & Publisher Mmog

(G-9808)
FIRST LOVE FASHIONS LLC
1407 Broadway Rm 2010 (10018-2718)
PHONE...................212 256-1089
Joseph Hamadani, President
EMP: 10
SALES (est): 1.2MM Privately Held
SIC: 2339 Women's & misses' athletic clothing & sportswear

(G-9809)
FIRST2PRINT INC
494 8th Ave Fl 12 (10001-2578)
PHONE...................212 868-6886
Neil Brasleau, CEO
EMP: 7 EST: 2000
SALES (est): 937.2K Privately Held
WEB: www.first2print.com
SIC: 2759 Screen printing

(G-9810)
FISCHER DIAMONDS INC
1212 Avenue Of The Americ (10036-1622)
PHONE...................212 869-1990
Jeffrey H Fisher, President
EMP: 10
SQ FT: 5,000
SALES (est): 1.1MM Privately Held
WEB: www.fischerdiamonds.com
SIC: 3915 Lapidary work & diamond cutting & polishing

(G-9811)
FISCHLER DIAMONDS INC
580 5th Ave Ste 3100 (10036-4701)
PHONE...................212 921-8196
Serge Fischler, Ch of Bd
Marcella Fischler, Vice Pres
▲ EMP: 5

SALES (est): 518.7K Privately Held
WEB: www.fischlerdiamonds.com
SIC: 3915 5094 Diamond cutting & polishing; diamonds (gems)

(G-9812)
FISCHLER HOCKEY SERVICE
200 W 109th St Apt C5 (10025-2252)
PHONE...................212 749-4152
Stan Fischler, Owner
EMP: 10
SALES (est): 438.9K Privately Held
SIC: 2741 Misc Publishing

(G-9813)
FISH & CROWN LTD (PA)
42 W 39th St (10018-3809)
PHONE...................212 707-9603
Bergljot Wathne, President
Thorunn Wathne, Corp Secy
Soffia Wathne, Vice Pres
Thomas Faivre, CFO
◆ EMP: 100
SQ FT: 14,350
SALES (est): 8.9MM Privately Held
WEB: www.wathne.com
SIC: 3161 3999 Luggage; novelties, bric-a-brac & hobby kits

(G-9814)
FISONIC CORP (PA)
Also Called: Fisonic Technology
31-00 47th Ave Ste 106 (10023)
PHONE...................716 763-0295
Robert Kremer, CEO
Professor Vladimir Fisenko, Ch of Bd
Joe Hoose, President
▲ EMP: 10
SQ FT: 1,000
SALES: 1.8MM Privately Held
WEB: www.fisonic.com
SIC: 3561 3433 Pumps & pumping equipment; heating equipment, except electric

(G-9815)
FIVE STAR PRTG & MAILING SVCS
225 W 37th St Fl 16 (10018-6637)
PHONE...................212 929-0300
Judith Magnus, President
Steven Magnus, Vice Pres
▲ EMP: 13
SQ FT: 4,800
SALES: 2MM Privately Held
SIC: 2752 7331 3993 Commercial printing, offset; mailing service; signs & advertising specialties

(G-9816)
FLAVORS HOLDINGS INC (DH)
35 E 62nd St (10065-8014)
PHONE...................212 572-8677
Albert Mazone, CEO
EMP: 10 EST: 2015
SALES (est): 188.1MM Privately Held
SIC: 2869 6712 Sweeteners, synthetic; bank holding companies
HQ: Macandrews & Forbes Inc.
38 E 63rd St
New York NY 10065
212 688-9000

(G-9817)
FLIK INTERNATIONAL/COMPASS
450 Lexington Ave (10017-3904)
PHONE...................212 450-4750
Chris Sarell, Director
EMP: 50
SALES (est): 3.3MM Privately Held
SIC: 2099 Food preparations

(G-9818)
FLYCELL INC
80 Pine St Fl 29 (10005-1714)
PHONE...................212 400-1212
Cristian Carnevale, CEO
Gita Kapur, Controller
Michele Berardi, Network Mgr
EMP: 57
SQ FT: 2,000
SALES (est): 5.9MM
SALES (corp-wide): 3.1MM Privately Held
WEB: www.flycell.com
SIC: 3663 Mobile communication equipment

PA: Acotel Group Spa
Via Della Valle Dei Fontanili 29/37
Roma RM 00168
066 114-1000

(G-9819)
FLYNNS INC (PA)
Also Called: Flynn's Xerox
115 W 30th St (10001-4010)
PHONE...................212 339-8700
Martin Lerner, Ch of Bd
Arthur Cantor, President
Brian Cantor, Vice Pres
Eric Roberts, Sales Staff
Tony Tutura, Manager
▲ EMP: 35
SQ FT: 4,200
SALES (est): 6.1MM Privately Held
WEB: www.lorraineflynn.com
SIC: 2752 5943 Commercial printing, lithographic; stationery stores

(G-9820)
FOG CREEK SOFTWARE INC
75 Broad St Fl 19 (10004-2491)
PHONE...................866 364-2733
Joel Spolsky, CEO
Jordan Harris, VP Sales
Kate Dunn, Accounts Exec
Jude Allred, Technical Staff
EMP: 5
SALES (est): 1MM Privately Held
WEB: www.fogcreek.com
SIC: 7372 7371 Prepackaged software; custom computer programming services

(G-9821)
FOLIA WATER INC
175 Varick St (10014-4604)
PHONE...................412 802-5083
Jonathan Levine, CEO
Theresa Dankovich, Ch of Bd
Juliet Martinez, Principal
Cantwell Carson, COO
John Rossmiller, CFO
EMP: 8 EST: 2016
SALES (est): 384.2K Privately Held
SIC: 2679 8731 Filter paper: made from purchased material; biological research

(G-9822)
FOREST LABORATORIES LLC (HQ)
909 3rd Ave Fl 23 (10022-4748)
PHONE...................212 421-7850
R Todd Joyce, President
Donald Robertson, President
Benjamin Gober, Principal
Robert Stewart, COO
Francis I Perier Jr, Exec VP
▲ EMP: 227
SQ FT: 169,000
SALES (est): 1.2B Privately Held
WEB: www.frx.com
SIC: 2834 5122 Pharmaceutical preparations; pharmaceuticals

(G-9823)
FOREVER GROWN DIAMONDS INC
22 W 48th St Ste 402 (10036-1818)
PHONE...................212 354-2827
Kinish Shah, President
EMP: 2
SQ FT: 480
SALES: 3MM Privately Held
SIC: 3915 5094 Diamond cutting & polishing; diamonds (gems)

(G-9824)
FORMART CORP
Also Called: Bellini Collections
312 5th Ave Fl 6 (10001-3603)
PHONE...................212 819-1819
Sheung MEI Liu, President
EMP: 12
SQ FT: 2,100
SALES (est): 1.5MM Privately Held
WEB: www.cancerpins.com
SIC: 3171 5094 5137 3961 Purses, women's; jewelry; watches & parts; purses; costume jewelry

(G-9825)
FORTRESS BIOTECH INC (PA)
2 Gansevoort St Fl 9 (10014-1667)
PHONE...................781 652-4500
Lindsay A Rosenwald, Ch of Bd
Eric K Rowinsky, Ch of Bd
George Avgerinos, Senior VP
Andrew Scott, VP Bus Dvlpt
Robyn M Hunter, CFO
EMP: 36
SALES: 187.5MM Publicly Held
SIC: 2834 Pharmaceutical preparations

(G-9826)
FOUNDATION CENTER INC (PA)
1 Financial Sq Fl 24 (10005-3076)
PHONE...................212 620-4230
Bradford K Smith, President
Monisha De Quadros, Vice Pres
Tushar Deshpande, Vice Pres
Loretta Ferrari, Vice Pres
Lisa Philp, Vice Pres
▲ EMP: 125
SQ FT: 150,000
SALES: 24.1MM Privately Held
WEB: www.fdncenter.net
SIC: 2741 8231 Directories: publishing only, not printed on site; libraries

(G-9827)
FOUNDTION FOR A MNDFUL SOC INC (PA)
228 Park Ave S (10003-1502)
PHONE...................902 431-8062
Andrew Karr, Treasurer
Ken Swick, Controller
James Gimian, Exec Dir
EMP: 5
SALES: 2.5MM Privately Held
SIC: 2721 Magazines: publishing & printing

(G-9828)
FOUR M STUDIOS
125 Park Ave Fl 20 (10017-8545)
PHONE...................212 557-6600
Andrea Gingold, Branch Mgr
EMP: 250
SALES (corp-wide): 2.2B Publicly Held
WEB: www.meredith.com
SIC: 2721 Magazines: publishing & printing
PA: Meredith Corporation
1716 Locust St
Des Moines IA 50309
515 284-3000

(G-9829)
FOUR M STUDIOS
125 Park Ave Fl 20 (10017-8545)
PHONE...................212 557-6600
EMP: 96
SALES (corp-wide): 1.7B Publicly Held
WEB: www.meredith.com
SIC: 2721 Periodicals
PA: Meredith Corporation
1716 Locust St
Des Moines IA 50309
515 284-3000

(G-9830)
FOUR M STUDIOS
Also Called: Meredith Corporate Solutions
805 3rd Ave Fl 22 (10022-7541)
PHONE...................212 499-2000
Brett Gilman, Managing Dir
Pete Moran, Vice Pres
Lynn Balik, Research
Julia Corbett, Accounts Exec
Neale Desousa, Sr Project Mgr
EMP: 17
SALES (corp-wide): 1.7B Publicly Held
WEB: www.meredith.com
SIC: 2721 Magazines: publishing only, not printed on site
PA: Meredith Corporation
1716 Locust St
Des Moines IA 50309
515 284-3000

(G-9831)
FOUR M STUDIOS
Also Called: Meredith Hispanic Ventures
805 3rd Ave Fl 29 (10022-7541)
PHONE...................515 284-2157
Mike Lovell, Branch Mgr
EMP: 96

New York - New York County (G-9832) — GEOGRAPHIC SECTION

SALES (corp-wide): 2.2B **Publicly Held**
SIC: 2721 2731 Magazines: publishing & printing; books: publishing only
PA: Meredith Corporation
1716 Locust St
Des Moines IA 50309
515 284-3000

(G-9832)
FOUR SEASONS FASHION MFG INC
270 W 39th St Fl 12 (10018-0338)
PHONE....................212 947-6820
Mohan Singh, *President*
Sandra Gonsalzes, *Administration*
EMP: 45
SALES (est): 3.3MM **Privately Held**
SIC: 2335 2339 2337 Women's, juniors' & misses' dresses; women's & misses' outerwear; women's & misses' suits & coats

(G-9833)
FOURTYS NY INC
231 W 39th St Rm 806 (10018-0734)
PHONE....................212 382-0301
Dawn Mayo, *President*
EMP: 10
SQ FT: 4,000
SALES: 900K **Privately Held**
SIC: 2331 Women's & misses' blouses & shirts

(G-9834)
FOWNES BROTHERS & CO INC (PA)
16 E 34th St Fl 5 (10016-4370)
PHONE....................212 683-0150
Thomas Gluckman, *Ch of Bd*
Chris Giattino, *Exec VP*
Helmuth Dosch, *Vice Pres*
Bruna Maney, *Vice Pres*
Howard Samuels, *Vice Pres*
◆ **EMP:** 50 EST: 1887
SQ FT: 18,000
SALES (est): 76.1MM **Privately Held**
SIC: 3151 2381 5136 5137 Gloves, leather: dress or semidress; gloves, woven or knit: made from purchased materials; gloves, men's & boys'; gloves, women's & children's; gloves, sport & athletic: boxing, handball, etc.

(G-9835)
FOX UNLIMITED INC
345 7th Ave Rm 2b (10001-5058)
PHONE....................212 736-3071
Marvin Levenson, *President*
Natalya Bogatyuk, *Prdtn Mgr*
EMP: 5
SQ FT: 4,000
SALES (est): 694.1K **Privately Held**
WEB: www.foxunlimited.com
SIC: 2371 Apparel, fur

(G-9836)
FOXHILL PRESS INC
37 E 7th St Ste 2 (10003-8027)
PHONE....................212 995-9620
▲ **EMP:** 20
SQ FT: 1,600
SALES (est): 1.1MM
SALES (corp-wide): 35.2MM **Privately Held**
SIC: 2731 Books-Publishing/Printing
PA: Mcevoy Properties Llc
85 2nd St Fl 6
San Francisco CA 94107

(G-9837)
FRANCEPRESS LLC (PA)
115 E 57th St Fl 11 (10022-2120)
PHONE....................646 202-9828
Hana Mataillet, *Marketing Staff*
Louis Kyle, *Mng Member*
▲ **EMP:** 4
SQ FT: 1,800
SALES (est): 1.1MM **Privately Held**
SIC: 2711 Newspapers, publishing & printing

(G-9838)
FRANCIS EMORY FITCH INC (HQ)
Also Called: Fitch Group
229 W 28th St (10001-5915)
PHONE....................212 619-3800
William Contessa, *CEO*
Joe Barrett, *Exec VP*
Carl Corsi, *Prdtn Mgr*
Frank Riina, *Sales Staff*
EMP: 23 EST: 1886
SQ FT: 25,000
SALES (est): 2.8MM **Privately Held**
WEB: www.fitchgroup.com
SIC: 2721 2752 Periodicals: publishing only; commercial printing, offset
PA: Topside Advisors, Llc
84 Rockledge Rd
Bronxville NY 10708
212 619-3800

(G-9839)
FRANCO APPAREL GROUP INC
Also Called: Franco Apparel Group Team
1407 Broadway (10018-5100)
PHONE....................212 967-7272
Ike Franco, *Ch of Bd*
▲ **EMP:** 100
SQ FT: 15,000
SALES (est): 8.9MM **Privately Held**
WEB: www.francoapparel.com
SIC: 2369 Girls' & children's outerwear

(G-9840)
FRANK BILLANTI CASTING CO INC
42 W 38th St Rm 204 (10018-6220)
PHONE....................212 221-0440
Frank L Billanti, *President*
Kristin N Billanti, *Principal*
Katherine O Billanti, *Vice Pres*
Kathy Billanti, *Director*
Frank J Billanti, *Administration*
EMP: 16
SALES: 1MM **Privately Held**
SIC: 3915 Jewelers' castings

(G-9841)
FRANK BLANCATO INC
64 W 48th St Fl 16 (10036-1708)
PHONE....................212 768-1495
Frank Blancato, *President*
EMP: 10
SALES (est): 4MM **Privately Held**
WEB: www.fblancato.com
SIC: 3911 Jewelry, precious metal

(G-9842)
FRANK WINES INC
Also Called: HI Wines
345 E 80th St Apt 8b (10075-0688)
PHONE....................646 765-6637
Olivier Pasquini, *Ch of Bd*
EMP: 5
SALES (est): 203.8K **Privately Held**
SIC: 2084 Wines

(G-9843)
FRANKLIN REPORT LLC
201 E 69th St Apt 14j (10021-5470)
PHONE....................212 639-9100
Elizabeth Franklin, *Owner*
Josh Maio, *Editor*
Fred Nicolaus, *Manager*
EMP: 8
SALES (est): 600K **Privately Held**
WEB: www.franklinreport.com
SIC: 2731 Book publishing

(G-9844)
FREEDOM RAINS INC
Also Called: Northern Goose Polar Project
230 W 39th St Fl 7 (10018-4977)
PHONE....................646 710-4512
Bobby Reiger, *CEO*
Steven Zellman, *President*
Nick Grazione, *COO*
▲ **EMP:** 8
SQ FT: 3,500
SALES: 12MM **Privately Held**
SIC: 2253 Jackets, knit; sweaters & sweater coats, knit

(G-9845)
FRENCH ACCNT RUGS & TAPESTRIES
36 E 31st St Frnt B (10016-6821)
PHONE....................212 686-6097
Kevin Rahmanan, *President*
▲ **EMP:** 6
SQ FT: 10,000
SALES (est): 774.6K **Privately Held**
WEB: www.farugs.com
SIC: 2211 Upholstery, tapestry & wall coverings: cotton; casement cloth, cotton; tapestry fabrics, cotton

(G-9846)
FRENCH ATMOSPHERE INC (PA)
Also Called: Urban Rose
421 7th Ave 525 (10001-2002)
PHONE....................516 371-9100
Lawrence Kessler, *President*
Benjamin Kessler, *Vice Pres*
▲ **EMP:** 15
SQ FT: 1,350
SALES (est): 1MM **Privately Held**
SIC: 2339 Sportswear, women's

(G-9847)
FRENCH MORNING LLC
27 W 20th St Ste 800 (10011-3726)
PHONE....................646 290-7463
Emmanuel Saint-Martin, *President*
David Treussard, *Managing Prtnr*
EMP: 6
SQ FT: 1,200
SALES (est): 258.9K **Privately Held**
SIC: 2711 Newspapers: publishing only, not printed on site

(G-9848)
FRESH PRINTS LLC
134 E 70th St (10021-5035)
PHONE....................917 826-2752
Jacob Goodman,
Josh Arbit,
EMP: 40
SALES (est): 2MM **Privately Held**
SIC: 2759 7389 Screen printing;

(G-9849)
FRESHLY INC (PA)
Also Called: F3 Foods
115 E 23rd St Fl 7 (10010-4561)
PHONE....................844 373-7459
Michael Wystrach, *CEO*
Carter Comstock, *Admin Sec*
EMP: 25 EST: 2015
SALES (est): 87.7MM **Privately Held**
SIC: 2099 Ready-to-eat meals, salads & sandwiches

(G-9850)
FRIDGE MAGAZINE INC
108 W 39th St Fl 4 (10018-3614)
PHONE....................212 997-7673
Jonathon Levine, *President*
EMP: 5
SALES (est): 410K **Privately Held**
WEB: www.fridgemagazine.com
SIC: 2721 Magazines: publishing only, not printed on site

(G-9851)
FROEBE GROUP LLC
154 W 27th St Rm 4 (10001-6215)
PHONE....................646 649-2150
Troy Froebe, *Mng Member*
Sabrina Parys, *Executive*
EMP: 8
SALES: 800K **Privately Held**
SIC: 2741 Business service newsletters: publishing & printing

(G-9852)
FROZEN FOOD DIGEST INC
Also Called: Quick Frzen Foods Annual Prcss
271 Madison Ave Ste 805 (10016-1005)
PHONE....................212 557-8600
Saul Beck, *President*
Audrey Beck, *Publisher*
Anna Beck, *Vice Pres*
▲ **EMP:** 6
SALES (est): 510K **Privately Held**
SIC: 2721 Magazines: publishing only, not printed on site

(G-9853)
FRP APPAREL GROUP LLC
110 W 40th St 26 (10018-3626)
PHONE....................212 695-8000
Johann Cooke,
Edwin Herman,
▲ **EMP:** 9
SALES (est): 620K **Privately Held**
SIC: 2221 Upholstery, tapestry & wall covering fabrics

(G-9854)
FRUIT ST HLTH PUB BENEFT CORP
85 Broad St Fl 18 (10004-2783)
PHONE....................347 960-6400
Laurence Girard, *CEO*
Christopher Meatto, *CFO*
Asif Ali, *VP Sales*
EMP: 5
SALES (est): 401.3K **Privately Held**
SIC: 7372 Prepackaged software

(G-9855)
FSR BEAUTY LTD
411 5th Ave Rm 804 (10016-2264)
PHONE....................212 447-0036
Jerrold Rauchwerger, *President*
Maxine Rauchwerger, *Vice Pres*
Falen Rauchwerger, *Marketing Staff*
▲ **EMP:** 6
SQ FT: 1,300
SALES (est): 752.4K **Privately Held**
SIC: 2844 Face creams or lotions; lipsticks

(G-9856)
FT PUBLICATIONS INC (HQ)
Also Called: Financial Times, The
330 Hudson St (10013-1046)
PHONE....................212 641-6500
Loredana Beg, *Ch of Bd*
David Bell, *President*
Scheherazade Daneshkhu, *Editor*
Michael Tamburri, *Marketing Staff*
Lisa Tanner, *Office Mgr*
▲ **EMP:** 80
SQ FT: 40,000
SALES (est): 18.8MM
SALES (corp-wide): 3.2B **Privately Held**
SIC: 2711 Newspapers, publishing & printing
PA: Nikkei Inc.
1-3-7, Otemachi
Chiyoda-Ku TKY 100-0
332 700-251

(G-9857)
FT PUBLICATIONS INC
Also Called: Financial Times Newspaper
330 Hudson St (10013-1046)
PHONE....................212 641-2420
EMP: 46
SALES (corp-wide): 3.2B **Privately Held**
SIC: 2711 Newspapers: publishing only, not printed on site
HQ: F.T. Publications Inc.
330 Hudson St
New York NY 10013
212 641-6500

(G-9858)
FUDA GROUP (USA) CORPORATION
48 Wall St Fl 11 (10005-2887)
PHONE....................646 751-7488
Benjamin Wu, *CEO*
Robert Rash,
EMP: 7
SALES (est): 299.2K **Privately Held**
SIC: 1041 Gold recovery from tailings

(G-9859)
FULCRUM PROMOTIONS & PRTG LLC
Also Called: Fulcrum Promos
135 W 41st St (10036-7303)
PHONE....................203 909-6362
Gia-Marie Vacca, *Partner*
Vincent Miceli,
Anthony Monaco,
EMP: 4 EST: 2010
SQ FT: 700

New York - New York County (G-9884)

SALES: 1MM **Privately Held**
SIC: 2759 7389 Promotional printing; advertising, promotional & trade show services

(G-9860)
FULL CIRCLE HOME LLC
131 W 35th St Fl 8 (10001-2111)
PHONE..................212 432-0001
Tal Chitayat, *CEO*
David Chitayat, *Managing Dir*
Heather Kauffman, *COO*
▲ EMP: 9
SALES: 1.5MM **Privately Held**
SIC: 3991 5199 Brooms & brushes; gifts & novelties

(G-9861)
FUN MEDIA INC
1001 Ave Of The Americas (10018-5460)
PHONE..................646 472-0135
Joseph Giarraputo, *President*
A Basodan, *Principal*
P Panerai, *Chairman*
Francesco Librio, *Admin Sec*
EMP: 25
SQ FT: 7,500
SALES (est): 2.6MM
SALES (corp-wide): 6.9MM **Privately Held**
WEB: www.classeditori.com
SIC: 2721 7319 Magazines: publishing only, not printed on site; transit advertising services
PA: Class Editori Spa
    Via Marco Burigozzo 5
    Milano MI 20122
    025 821-91

(G-9862)
FUNG WONG BAKERY INC
Also Called: Fung Wong Bakery Shop
30 Mott St Frnt (10013-5037)
PHONE..................212 267-4037
Sherwin Choy, *President*
Eberline P Choy, *Corp Secy*
EMP: 20
SQ FT: 600
SALES (est): 1.7MM **Privately Held**
SIC: 2051 Mfg Bread/Related Products

(G-9863)
FUSION CONNECT INC (PA)
420 Lexington Ave Rm 1718 (10170-1707)
PHONE..................212 201-2400
Matthew D Rosen, *Ch of Bd*
Holcombe T Green Jr, *Vice Ch Bd*
Gordon Hutchins Jr, *President*
Russell P Markman, *President*
James P Prenetta Jr, *Exec VP*
EMP: 119
SQ FT: 9,956
SALES: 150.5MM **Publicly Held**
WEB: www.fusiontel.com
SIC: 7372 4813 Prepackaged software; business oriented computer software; telephone communication, except radio;

(G-9864)
FUSION PRO PERFORMANCE LTD
Also Called: Ki Pro Performance
16 W 36th St Rm 1205 (10018-9754)
PHONE..................917 833-0761
Steven Goldfarb, *President*
EMP: 16 EST: 2014
SQ FT: 2,000
SALES (est): 11.8MM **Privately Held**
SIC: 2339 Athletic clothing: women's, misses' & juniors'

(G-9865)
FX INC
Also Called: Facilities Exchange
1 Penn Plz Ste 6238 (10119-0002)
PHONE..................212 244-2240
Martin Friedman, *President*
Charles Valva, *Corp Secy*
EMP: 18
SQ FT: 15,000
SALES (est): 1.5MM **Privately Held**
SIC: 2522 7641 1799 5712 Office furniture, except wood; furniture refinishing; counter top installation; office furniture

(G-9866)
G & P PRINTING INC
142 Baxter St (10013-3605)
PHONE..................212 274-8092
Stanley Chen, *President*
EMP: 5 EST: 1998
SALES (est): 477.7K **Privately Held**
WEB: www.gpprinting.com
SIC: 2752 Commercial printing, offset

(G-9867)
G I CERTIFIED INC
623 W 51st St (10019-5008)
PHONE..................212 397-1945
Michael Borrico, *Ch of Bd*
C Russonello, *Director*
Charlie Rucinelli, *Director*
EMP: 6
SALES: 500K **Privately Held**
WEB: www.certifiedny.com
SIC: 3993 Signs & advertising specialties

(G-9868)
G SCHIRMER INC (HQ)
Also Called: Music Sales
180 Madison Ave Ste 2400 (10016-5241)
PHONE..................212 254-2100
Barrie Edwards, *President*
John Castaldo, *Controller*
Greg Legaz, *Librarian*
Jessica Hobbs, *Manager*
Ed Matthew, *Manager*
▲ EMP: 4
SALES (est): 5.9MM
SALES (corp-wide): 13.6MM **Privately Held**
WEB: www.schirmer.com
SIC: 2741 7929 Music books: publishing only, not printed on site; entertainers & entertainment groups
PA: Music Sales Corporation
    180 Madison Ave Ste 2400
    New York NY 10016
    212 254-2100

(G-9869)
G-III APPAREL GROUP LTD (PA)
512 7th Ave Fl 35 (10018-0832)
PHONE..................212 403-0500
Morris Goldfarb, *Ch of Bd*
Sammy Aaron, *Vice Chairman*
Wayne S Miller, *COO*
Jeffrey Goldfarb, *Exec VP*
Neal S Nackman, *CFO*
▲ EMP: 277
SQ FT: 220,000
SALES: 2.8B **Publicly Held**
WEB: www.g-iii.com
SIC: 2337 2339 2311 2329 Women's & misses' suits & coats; women's & misses' outerwear; men's & boys' suits & coats; coats, overcoats & vests; jackets (suede, leatherette, etc.), sport: men's & boys'; garments, leather; coats & jackets, leather & sheep-lined; pants, leather; men's & boys' clothing

(G-9870)
G-III APPAREL GROUP LTD
Jessica Howard
512 Fashion Ave Fl 35 (10018-0832)
PHONE..................212 403-0500
Karol Gass, *Branch Mgr*
EMP: 50
SALES (corp-wide): 2.8B **Publicly Held**
SIC: 2335 Women's, juniors' & misses' dresses
PA: G-Iii Apparel Group, Ltd.
    512 7th Ave Fl 35
    New York NY 10018
    212 403-0500

(G-9871)
G-III APPAREL GROUP LTD
Jl Colebrook Cloth Div
512 7th Ave Fl 35 (10018-0832)
PHONE..................212 840-7272
EMP: 10
SALES (corp-wide): 2.8B **Publicly Held**
SIC: 2311 Mfg Men's/Boy's Suits/Coats
PA: G-Iii Apparel Group, Ltd.
    512 7th Ave Fl 35
    New York NY 10018
    212 403-0500

(G-9872)
G-III LEATHER FASHIONS INC
Also Called: G-III Apparel Group
512 7th Ave Fl 35 (10018-0832)
PHONE..................212 403-0500
EMP: 20
SALES (corp-wide): 2.8B **Publicly Held**
SIC: 2386 2337 2339 Leather & sheep-lined clothing; women's & misses' suits & coats; women's & misses' outerwear
HQ: G-Iii Leather Fashions, Inc.
    512 Fashion Ave Fl 35
    New York NY 10018
    212 403-0500

(G-9873)
G18 CORPORATION
215 W 40th St Fl 9 (10018-1575)
PHONE..................212 869-0010
Laurence Goldfarb, *President*
EMP: 2
SQ FT: 2,500
SALES: 7MM **Privately Held**
SIC: 2337 Women's & misses' suits & coats

(G-9874)
GABRIELLA IMPORTERS INC
305 W 87th St (10024-2602)
PHONE..................212 579-3945
Jacques Azoulay, *President*
EMP: 11
SALES (corp-wide): 5MM **Privately Held**
SIC: 2084 Wines
PA: Gabriella Importers, Inc.
    305 W 87th St
    New York NY 10024
    212 579-3945

(G-9875)
GABRIELLE ANDRA
305 W 21st St (10011-3073)
PHONE..................212 366-9624
Andra Gabrielle, *Owner*
EMP: 5
SALES (est): 220K **Privately Held**
SIC: 2331 Blouses, women's & juniors': made from purchased material

(G-9876)
GALISON PUBLISHING LLC
Also Called: Mudpuppy
70 W 36th St Fl 11 (10018-1249)
PHONE..................212 354-8840
Bill Miller, *CEO*
Laura L Greaves, *Production*
Clairissa McLaurin, *Production*
Gillian Moran, *Production*
Sam Minnitti, *CFO*
▲ EMP: 20
SQ FT: 7,500
SALES (est): 2.8MM
SALES (corp-wide): 30.2MM **Privately Held**
SIC: 2741 Miscellaneous publishing
PA: The Mcevoy Group Llc
    680 2nd St
    San Francisco CA 94107
    415 537-4200

(G-9877)
GALLERY 57 DENTAL
24 W 57th St Ste 701 (10019-3949)
PHONE..................212 246-8700
Andrew Koenigsberg DDS, *Partner*
Valentina Henriquez, *Internal Med*
EMP: 20
SALES (est): 2.2MM **Privately Held**
SIC: 3843 Enamels, dentists'

(G-9878)
GALT INDUSTRIES INC
121 E 71st St Frnt A (10021-4275)
PHONE..................212 758-0770
George T Votis, *Ch of Bd*
▲ EMP: 9
SQ FT: 2,000
SALES (est): 1.3MM **Privately Held**
SIC: 3089 Injection molding of plastics

(G-9879)
GAME TIME LLC
1407 Broadway Rm 400 (10018-3843)
PHONE..................914 557-9662
Adam Pennington, *Mng Member*
Patrick McGeough,
▲ EMP: 17
SQ FT: 30,000
SALES: 3.5MM **Privately Held**
SIC: 3873 Watches, clocks, watchcases & parts

(G-9880)
GAMECLUB INC
46 W 65th St Apt 1a (10023-6621)
PHONE..................415 359-5742
Daniel Sherman, *CEO*
EMP: 2
SALES: 1MM **Privately Held**
SIC: 7372 Prepackaged software

(G-9881)
GAMES FOR CHANGE INC
205 E 42nd St Fl 20 (10017-5706)
PHONE..................212 242-4922
Susanna Pollack, *President*
Erik Huey, *Vice Pres*
Sara Cornish, *Project Dir*
Ling Lu, *Controller*
Tania Hack, *Senior Mgr*
EMP: 1 EST: 2004
SALES: 1.7MM **Privately Held**
SIC: 7372 Prepackaged software

(G-9882)
GARAN INCORPORATED (HQ)
200 Madison Ave Fl 4 (10016-3905)
PHONE..................212 563-1292
Seymour Lichtenstein, *CEO*
Jerald Kamiel, *President*
Marvin S Robinson, *Vice Pres*
David M Fligel, *CFO*
◆ EMP: 120 EST: 1957
SQ FT: 38,500
SALES (est): 601.3MM
SALES (corp-wide): 242.1B **Publicly Held**
WEB: www.garanimals.com
SIC: 2361 2369 2331 2339 T-shirts & tops: girls', children's & infants'; slacks: girls' & children's; T-shirts & tops, women's: made from purchased materials; shirts, women's & juniors': made from purchased materials; jeans: women's, misses' & juniors'; men's & boys' furnishings; sport shirts, men's & boys': from purchased materials
PA: Berkshire Hathaway Inc.
    3555 Farnam St Ste 1140
    Omaha NE 68131
    402 346-1400

(G-9883)
GARAN MANUFACTURING CORP (DH)
200 Madison Ave Fl 4 (10016-3905)
PHONE..................212 563-2000
Seymour Lichtenstein, *CEO*
Ron Dutta, *President*
Jerald Kamiel, *President*
David M Fligel, *Vice Pres*
▼ EMP: 1
SALES (est): 21.2MM
SALES (corp-wide): 242.1B **Publicly Held**
SIC: 2361 2369 2331 2339 T-shirts & tops: girls', children's & infants'; slacks: girls' & children's; T-shirts & tops, women's: made from purchased materials; shirts, women's & juniors': made from purchased materials; jeans: women's, misses' & juniors'; men's & boys' furnishings; sport shirts, men's & boys': from purchased materials
HQ: Garan, Incorporated
    200 Madison Ave Fl 4
    New York NY 10016
    212 563-1292

(G-9884)
GARYS LOFT
28 W 36th St (10018-1284)
PHONE..................212 244-0970
Rob Tuttle, *Office Mgr*
Roger Wingfield, *Manager*
EMP: 6
SALES (est): 764K **Privately Held**
SIC: 3861 Photographic equipment & supplies

New York - New York County (G-9885) — GEOGRAPHIC SECTION

(G-9885)
GB GROUP INC
Umpire State Bldg 1808 (10021)
PHONE 212 594-3748
Howard Zhanz, *President*
EMP: 8
SALES (est): 548.4K **Privately Held**
WEB: www.crystalsland.com
SIC: 3699 Laser systems & equipment

(G-9886)
GBG NATIONAL BRANDS GROUP LLC
350 5th Ave Lbby 9 (10118-0109)
PHONE 646 839-7000
Bruce Philip Rockowitz, *CEO*
Dow Peter Famulak, *President*
Ronald Ventricelli, *CFO*
Jason Andrew Rabin, *Chief Mktg Ofcr*
EMP: 6
SALES (est): 402.9K **Privately Held**
SIC: 2321 Men's & boys' furnishings
HQ: Fung Holdings (1937) Limited
    11/F Lifung Twr
    Cheung Sha Wan KLN
    230 023-00

(G-9887)
GBG SOCKS LLC
350 5th Ave Lbby 9 (10118-0109)
PHONE 646 839-7000
Dow Famulak, *Mng Member*
EMP: 25
SALES (est): 1.2MM **Privately Held**
SIC: 2252 Socks

(G-9888)
GBG USA INC
350 5th Ave Fl 7 (10118-0701)
PHONE 646 839-7083
EMP: 93 **Privately Held**
SIC: 2387 Apparel belts
HQ: Gbg Usa Inc.
    350 5th Ave Lbby 11
    New York NY 10118
    646 839-7000

(G-9889)
GBG USA INC
Lf USA Accessories
261 W 35th St Fl 15 (10001-1902)
PHONE 212 615-3400
Steven Kahn, *Branch Mgr*
EMP: 50 **Privately Held**
SIC: 2387 Apparel belts
HQ: Gbg Usa Inc.
    350 5th Ave Lbby 11
    New York NY 10118
    646 839-7000

(G-9890)
GCE INTERNATIONAL INC (PA)
Also Called: Great China Empire
1385 Broadway Fl 21 (10018-6022)
PHONE 212 704-4800
Donald Oberfield, *President*
John Hoffman, *General Mgr*
Peter Markson, *Chairman*
Martin J Kelly, *Treasurer*
Alfredo Bermejo, *Manager*
▲ EMP: 100 EST: 1920
SQ FT: 40,000
SALES (est): 176.8MM **Privately Held**
WEB: www.parisaccessories.com
SIC: 2253 2389 2331 5137 Hats & headwear, knit; scarves & mufflers, knit; handkerchiefs, except paper; T-shirts & tops, women's: made from purchased materials; blouses, women's & juniors': made from purchased material; scarves, women's & children's; gloves, women's & children's; scarves, men's & boys'; gloves, men's & boys'

(G-9891)
GCE INTERNATIONAL INC
Also Called: Baar & Beards
350 5th Ave Ste 616 (10118-0110)
PHONE 212 868-0500
Martin Kelly, *Manager*
EMP: 12
SALES (corp-wide): 176.8MM **Privately Held**
WEB: www.parisaccessories.com
SIC: 2353 2361 2381 Hats, caps & millinery; girls' & children's dresses, blouses & shirts; fabric dress & work gloves
PA: Gce International, Inc.
    1385 Broadway Fl 21
    New York NY 10018
    212 704-4800

(G-9892)
GCE INTERNATIONAL INC
Also Called: Capital Mercury Shirtmakers Co
1359 Broadway Rm 2000 (10018-7841)
PHONE 773 263-1210
Peter Markson, *CEO*
EMP: 60
SALES (corp-wide): 176.8MM **Privately Held**
WEB: www.parisaccessories.com
SIC: 2321 Men's & boys' dress shirts
PA: Gce International, Inc.
    1385 Broadway Fl 21
    New York NY 10018
    212 704-4800

(G-9893)
GDS PUBLISHING INC
40 Wall St Fl 5 (10005-1472)
PHONE 212 796-2000
Dave Cullinane, *Principal*
EMP: 14
SALES (est): 1.4MM
SALES (corp-wide): 34.4MM **Privately Held**
SIC: 2741
HQ: Gds Publishing Limited
    Queen Square House
    Bristol BS1 4
    117 921-4000

(G-9894)
GE HEALTHCARE FINCL SVCS INC
299 Park Ave Fl 3 (10171-0022)
PHONE 212 713-2000
Batcrio Buyo, *Branch Mgr*
EMP: 5 **Publicly Held**
SIC: 2759 Commercial printing
HQ: Ge Healthcare Financial Services, Inc.
    500 W Monroe St Fl 19
    Chicago IL 60661
    312 697-3999

(G-9895)
GELIKO LLC
1601 3rd Ave Apt 16a (10128-3455)
PHONE 212 876-5620
Zach Rubin, *Mng Member*
▲ EMP: 20
SALES (est): 2.6MM **Privately Held**
SIC: 2899 Gelatin

(G-9896)
GEMORO INC
48 W 48th St Ste 1102 (10036-1703)
PHONE 212 768-8844
Dennis Hakim, *President*
EMP: 5
SALES (est): 530K **Privately Held**
WEB: www.gemoro.com
SIC: 3911 5094 Jewelry, precious metal; jewelry & precious stones

(G-9897)
GEMPRINT CORPORATION
580 5th Ave Bsmt Ll05 (10036-4726)
PHONE 212 997-0007
Angelo Palmieri, *President*
EMP: 20
SQ FT: 5,500
SALES (est): 1.1MM **Privately Held**
SIC: 3826 Laser scientific & engineering instruments

(G-9898)
GEMVETO JEWELRY COMPANY INC
18 E 48th St Rm 501 (10017-1014)
PHONE 212 755-2522
Jean Vitau, *President*
Irene Vitau, *Corp Secy*
EMP: 20
SQ FT: 3,500
SALES (est): 2.6MM **Privately Held**
WEB: www.gems-online.org
SIC: 3911 Jewelry, precious metal

(G-9899)
GENERAL ART COMPANY INC
Also Called: General Art Framing
14 E 38th St Fl 6 (10016-0636)
PHONE 212 255-1298
Jen Chan, *President*
EMP: 10
SQ FT: 4,000
SALES (est): 1MM **Privately Held**
SIC: 2499 5023 Picture frame molding, finished; frames & framing, picture & mirror

(G-9900)
GENERAL LED HOLDINGS LLC
Also Called: Acolyte Industries
19 W 36th St Fl 6 (10018-7943)
PHONE 212 629-6830
EMP: 15
SALES (est): 560.7K
SALES (corp-wide): 970.6K **Privately Held**
SIC: 3674 Light emitting diodes
PA: General Led Holdings, Llc
    1074 Arion Cir Ste 116
    San Antonio TX 78216
    210 360-1444

(G-9901)
GENERAL MEDIA STRATEGIES INC
Also Called: African American Observer
521 5th Ave Fl 17 (10175-1799)
PHONE 212 586-4141
Steve Mallory, *President*
EMP: 8 EST: 2001
SALES (est): 250K **Privately Held**
SIC: 2711 Newspapers

(G-9902)
GENERAL SPORTWEAR COMPANY INC (PA)
230 W 38th St Fl 4 (10018-9085)
P.O. Box 588, Ellenville (12428-0588)
PHONE 212 764-5820
Herbert Rosenstock, *Ch of Bd*
Jeffrey Rosenstock, *President*
David Rosenstock, *Corp Secy*
Michael Brickner, *Plant Mgr*
Tony Shannahan, *Human Res Mgr*
◆ EMP: 120 EST: 1927
SQ FT: 20,000
SALES (est): 24.9MM **Privately Held**
WEB: www.generalsportwear.com
SIC: 2361 2369 2329 T-shirts & tops: girls', children's & infants'; jeans: girls', children's & infants'; men's & boys' sportswear & athletic clothing

(G-9903)
GENESIS MANNEQUINS USA II INC
151 W 25th St Fl 4 (10001-7204)
PHONE 212 505-6600
Joseph Klinow, *President*
▲ EMP: 8
SQ FT: 3,500
SALES (est): 2.8MM **Privately Held**
SIC: 3999 Mannequins

(G-9904)
GENEVA WATCH COMPANY INC (DH)
1407 Broadway Rm 400 (10018-3843)
PHONE 212 221-1177
▲ EMP: 20
SQ FT: 15,000
SALES (est): 6.1MM
SALES (corp-wide): 98.7K **Privately Held**
SIC: 3873 Mfg Watches/Clocks/Parts
HQ: Awc Liquidating Co.
    1407 Broadway Rm 400
    New York NY 10018
    212 221-1177

(G-9905)
GENIE INSTANT PRINTING CO INC
Also Called: Genie Instant Printing Center
37 W 43rd St (10036-7403)
PHONE 212 575-8258
Sal Cohen, *President*
Ronnie Cohen, *Vice Pres*
EMP: 10
SALES (est): 1MM **Privately Held**
SIC: 2759 2752 Commercial printing; photo-offset printing

(G-9906)
GENOMEWEB LLC
Also Called: Bioinformatics Publishing
40 Fulton St Rm 1002 (10038-5057)
P.O. Box 998 (10272-0998)
PHONE 212 651-5636
Dennis Waters,
Harry Greenwald,
EMP: 17
SQ FT: 3,600
SALES (est): 2.4MM **Privately Held**
SIC: 2721 Magazines: publishing only, not printed on site

(G-9907)
GENZYME CORPORATION
Also Called: Genzyme Genetics
521 W 57th St Fl 5 (10019-2916)
PHONE 212 698-0300
Martha Weinstein, *QC Mgr*
Kevin Byrne, *Controller*
Jim Luisi, *Human Res Dir*
Robert Barclay, *Manager*
Michael B Broscius, *Pathologist*
EMP: 67
SALES (corp-wide): 609.6MM **Privately Held**
SIC: 2834 Pharmaceutical preparations
HQ: Genzyme Corporation
    50 Binney St
    Cambridge MA 02142
    617 252-7500

(G-9908)
GEOFFREY BEENE INC
37 W 57th St Frnt 2 (10019-3410)
PHONE 212 371-5570
Geoffrey Beene, *President*
G Thompson Hutton, *President*
Russell Nardozza, *COO*
EMP: 20
SALES (est): 1.6MM **Privately Held**
WEB: www.geoffreybeene.com
SIC: 2335 2337 2331 2339 Women's, juniors' & misses' dresses; skirts, separate: women's, misses' & juniors'; jackets & vests, except fur & leather: women's; blouses, women's & juniors': made from purchased material; slacks: women's, misses' & juniors'

(G-9909)
GEONEX INTERNATIONAL CORP
200 Park Ave S Ste 920 (10003-1509)
PHONE 212 473-4555
George Nikiforov, *President*
EMP: 6
SQ FT: 1,000
SALES (est): 720K **Privately Held**
SIC: 2435 Hardwood plywood, prefinished

(G-9910)
GEORGE KNITTING MILLS CORP
116 W 23rd St Fl 4 (10011-2599)
PHONE 212 242-3300
Lawrence Aibel, *President*
Richard Aibel, *Vice Pres*
EMP: 5 EST: 1958
SQ FT: 10,000
SALES (est): 738.7K **Privately Held**
SIC: 2258 Pile fabrics, warp or flat knit

(G-9911)
GEORGE LEDERMAN INC
515 Madison Ave Rm 1218 (10022-5452)
PHONE 212 753-4556
Serge Lederman, *President*
Adrienne Lederman, *Vice Pres*
Janine Lederman, *Admin Sec*
EMP: 5 EST: 1937
SQ FT: 800
SALES (est): 567.7K **Privately Held**
WEB: www.glederman.com
SIC: 3911 Jewelry, precious metal

▲ = Import ▼ = Export
◆ = Import/Export

GEOGRAPHIC SECTION

(G-9912)
GEORGY CREATIVE FASHIONS INC
Also Called: Georgie Kaye
249 W 29th St (10001-5211)
PHONE..................212 279-4885
George Kambouris, *President*
EMP: 6
SQ FT: 3,000
SALES (est): 484.9K **Privately Held**
SIC: 2371 5136 5137 2386 Fur goods; fur clothing, men's & boys'; fur clothing, women's & children's; garments, leather

(G-9913)
GERLI & CO INC
Also Called: American Silk Mills
41 Madison Ave Ste 4101 (10010-2203)
PHONE..................212 213-1919
Robin L Slough, *President*
Cynthia Douthit, *Vice Pres*
John M Sullivan Jr, *Vice Pres*
James Harowicz, *CFO*
Mac Lane, *Sales Dir*
◆ **EMP:** 270
SQ FT: 7,500
SALES (est): 22.8MM **Privately Held**
SIC: 2211 2221 Cotton broad woven goods; broadwoven fabric mills, man-made; rayon broadwoven fabrics; silk broadwoven fabrics

(G-9914)
GERSON & GERSON INC (PA)
100 W 33rd St Ste 911 (10001-2913)
PHONE..................212 244-6775
Matthew Gerson, *Ch of Bd*
Jessica Gerson, *Vice Pres*
Larry Jones, *Prdtn Mgr*
Shelley Striar, *Prdtn Mgr*
Anita Shih, *Production*
◆ **EMP:** 120 **EST:** 1933
SQ FT: 13,000
SALES (est): 21.7MM **Privately Held**
WEB: www.gersonandgerson.com
SIC: 2369 2361 Girls' & children's outerwear; dresses; girls', children's & infants'

(G-9915)
GFB FASHIONS LTD
Also Called: Jonathan Michael Coats
463 Fashion Ave Rm 1502 (10018-7596)
PHONE..................212 239-9230
Paul Cohen, *President*
▲ **EMP:** 12
SALES (est): 1.1MM **Privately Held**
SIC: 2339 Women's & misses' jackets & coats, except sportswear

(G-9916)
GG DESIGN AND PRINTING
93 Henry St Frnt 1 (10002-7035)
PHONE..................718 321-3220
Allan Yin, *President*
▲ **EMP:** 9
SQ FT: 3,500
SALES: 1MM **Privately Held**
SIC: 2791 7336 Typesetting; graphic arts & related design

(G-9917)
GH BASS & CO (DH)
512 7th Ave Fl 28 (10018-0845)
PHONE..................646 768-4600
John Gietl, *President*
▲ **EMP:** 50 **EST:** 1987
SALES (est): 81.1MM
SALES (corp-wide): 2.8B **Publicly Held**
WEB: www.ghbass.com
SIC: 3144 3143 3149 5661 Women's footwear, except athletic; men's footwear, except athletic; children's footwear, except athletic; shoe stores

(G-9918)
GIFTS SOFTWARE INC
360 Lexington Ave Rm 601 (10017-6562)
PHONE..................904 438-6000
Jawaid M Khan, *CEO*
EMP: 35
SQ FT: 10,000
SALES (est): 1.5MM
SALES (corp-wide): 9.1B **Publicly Held**
WEB: www.giftssoft.com
SIC: 7372 Business oriented computer software

PA: Fidelity National Information Services, Inc.
601 Riverside Ave
Jacksonville FL 32204
904 438-6000

(G-9919)
GILDAN APPAREL USA INC (DH)
Also Called: Anvil Knitwear, Inc.
48 W 38th St Fl 8 (10018-0043)
PHONE..................212 476-0341
Anthony Corsano, *Ch of Bd*
Jacob Hollander, *Exec VP*
▲ **EMP:** 65
SALES (est): 534.1MM
SALES (corp-wide): 2.7B **Privately Held**
WEB: www.anvilknitwear.com
SIC: 2253 2331 Knit outerwear mills; women's & misses' blouses & shirts

(G-9920)
GILIBERTO DESIGNS INC
142 W 36th St Fl 8 (10018-8792)
PHONE..................212 695-0216
Rosario Giliberto Jr, *President*
Anthony Giliberto, *Vice Pres*
EMP: 23
SQ FT: 6,500
SALES (est): 2.3MM **Privately Held**
WEB: www.gilibertodesigns.com
SIC: 2311 5611 Men's & boys' suits & coats; clothing accessories: men's & boys'

(G-9921)
GILMORES SOUND ADVICE INC
599 11th Ave Fl 5 (10036-2110)
PHONE..................212 265-4445
Edward Gilmore, *President*
EMP: 12
SALES (est): 1.6MM **Privately Held**
SIC: 3651 Audio electronic systems

(G-9922)
GINA GROUP LLC
Also Called: Gina Hosiery
10 W 33rd St Ph 3 (10001-3317)
PHONE..................212 947-2445
Edmond Harary, *Mng Member*
Raymond Dayan,
Jack J Gindi,
◆ **EMP:** 35
SQ FT: 10,500
SALES (est): 8.1MM **Privately Held**
WEB: www.ginagroup.com
SIC: 2251 2252 Women's hosiery, except socks; socks

(G-9923)
GIOVANE LTD
Also Called: Giovane Piranesi
592 5th Ave Ste L (10036-4707)
PHONE..................212 332-7373
Sami Hajibay, *President*
Mishel H H Piranesi, *Vice Pres*
EMP: 22
SQ FT: 8,500
SALES (est): 3.2MM **Privately Held**
SIC: 3911 Jewelry, precious metal

(G-9924)
GIOVANNI BAKERY CORP
Also Called: Trio French Bakery
476 9th Ave (10018-5603)
P.O. Box 50057, Staten Island (10305-0057)
PHONE..................212 695-4296
Mario De Giovanni, *President*
Romona De Giovanni, *Corp Secy*
John De Giovanni, *Vice Pres*
EMP: 13 **EST:** 1953
SALES (est): 40.3K **Privately Held**
SIC: 2051 5461 Bread, all types (white, wheat, rye, etc): fresh or frozen; rolls, bread type: fresh or frozen; bread

(G-9925)
GIVAUDAN FRAGRANCES CORP
40 W 57th St Fl 11 (10019-4001)
PHONE..................212 649-8800
Jeanine Szweda, *Vice Pres*
Haley Rutkowski, *Buyer*
Gwen Gonzalez, *Research*
Lauren Bitet, *Accounts Exec*
Claudia Tascon, *Accounts Exec*
EMP: 130

SALES (corp-wide): 5.1B **Privately Held**
SIC: 2869 Perfume materials, synthetic; flavors or flavoring materials, synthetic
HQ: Givaudan Fragrances Corporation
1199 Edison Dr Ste 1-2
Cincinnati OH 45216
513 948-3428

(G-9926)
GIVI INC
16 W 56th St Fl 4 (10019-3872)
PHONE..................212 586-5029
Mario Fabris, *President*
EMP: 12
SALES (est): 1.1MM
SALES (corp-wide): 149.7K **Privately Held**
SIC: 3111 5661 3999 Bag leather; shoe stores; atomizers, toiletry
PA: Givi Holding Spa
Via Alessandro Manzoni 38
Milano MI
027 600-8529

(G-9927)
GLACEE SKINCARE LLC
611 W 136th St Apt 4 (10031-8137)
PHONE..................212 690-7632
Jose De La Cruz,
EMP: 6 **EST:** 2015
SALES (est): 280.4K **Privately Held**
SIC: 2844 Lotions, shaving; cosmetic preparations

(G-9928)
GLAMOUR MAGAZINE
4 Times Sq Fl 16 (10036-6625)
PHONE..................212 286-2860
Wendy Naugle, *Editor*
Genevieve Roth, *Editor*
Bill Wackermann, *Vice Pres*
EMP: 5
SALES (est): 472.3K **Privately Held**
SIC: 2721 Magazines: publishing & printing

(G-9929)
GLAMOURPUSS NYC LLC
1305 Madison Ave (10128-1327)
PHONE..................212 722-1370
Gigi Mortimer, *Principal*
Courtney Moss, *Principal*
EMP: 9
SALES (est): 874K **Privately Held**
SIC: 2331 Women's & misses' blouses & shirts

(G-9930)
GLASS APPS LLC (PA)
11 Times Sq Ste 15 (10036-6606)
PHONE..................310 987-1536
Thomas Lee,
EMP: 10
SQ FT: 1,200
SALES (est): 3.7MM **Privately Held**
SIC: 3211 Laminated glass

(G-9931)
GLASSBOX US INC
234 5th Ave Ste 207 (10001-7607)
PHONE..................917 378-2933
Yaron Morgenstern, *CEO*
Steve Dieugenio, *Human Res Mgr*
Yifat Golan, *Director*
EMP: 61
SALES (est): 1MM **Privately Held**
SIC: 7372 Business oriented computer software

(G-9932)
GLASSES USA LLC
Also Called: Glassesusa.com
954 Lexington Ave Ste 537 (10021-5055)
PHONE..................212 784-6094
Daniel Rothman, *CEO*
Jay Engelmayer, *President*
Eldad Rothman, *COO*
Roy Yamner, *CTO*
Brett Rudolph, *Director*
EMP: 15
SALES (est): 2.5MM **Privately Held**
SIC: 3851 Glasses, sun or glare

(G-9933)
GLASSVIEW LLC (PA)
25 E 67th St Ph A (10065-5871)
PHONE..................646 844-4922

James Brooks, *Mng Member*
Michael Goefron, *Security Dir*
EMP: 40
SALES: 51MM **Privately Held**
SIC: 2741 Miscellaneous publishing

(G-9934)
GLENN HOROWITZ BOOKSELLER INC
20 W 55th St Ph (10019-0026)
PHONE..................212 691-9100
Glenn Horowitz, *President*
EMP: 9
SALES (est): 1.2MM **Privately Held**
SIC: 2759 5932 Publication printing; rare books

(G-9935)
GLOBAL ALLIANCE FOR TB
40 Wall St Fl 24 (10005-1338)
PHONE..................212 227-7540
Melvin K Spigelman, *President*
Maarten Van Cleeff, *President*
Robert C Lorette, *Senior VP*
Bradley Jensen, *Finance Dir*
Melvin Spigelman, *Director*
EMP: 27
SQ FT: 8,500
SALES: 53MM **Privately Held**
WEB: www.tballiance.org
SIC: 2834 Druggists' preparations (pharmaceuticals)

(G-9936)
GLOBAL ALUMINA SERVICES CO
277 Park Ave Fl 40 (10172-2902)
PHONE..................212 309-8060
EMP: 500
SQ FT: 15,400
SALES: 25.8MM
SALES (corp-wide): 26MM **Privately Held**
SIC: 3297 Mfg Nonclay Refractories
PA: Global Alumina Corporation
277 Park Ave Fl 40
New York NY
212 351-0000

(G-9937)
GLOBAL APPLCTIONS SOLUTION LLC
125 Park Ave Fl 25 (10017-5550)
PHONE..................212 741-9595
EMP: 8
SALES: 125.1K **Privately Held**
SIC: 7372 7379 Prepackaged Software Services Computer Related Services

(G-9938)
GLOBAL FINANCE MAGAZINE
Also Called: Global Finance Magazine.
7 E 20th St (10003-1106)
PHONE..................212 524-3223
Susan Berger, *Managing Dir*
Josepy Giarraputo, *Principal*
Denise Bedell, *Editor*
Andrea Fiano, *Editor*
Peter McManus, *Vice Pres*
EMP: 5
SALES (est): 705.1K **Privately Held**
WEB: www.gfmag.com
SIC: 2721 Periodicals

(G-9939)
GLOBAL FINANCE MEDIA INC
Also Called: Global Finance Magazine.
7 E 20th St Fl 2 (10003-1106)
PHONE..................212 447-7900
Andrew Spindler, *CEO*
EMP: 12
SALES (est): 1.3MM **Privately Held**
SIC: 2721 5192 Periodicals; magazines

(G-9940)
GLOBAL FIRE CORPORATION
244 5th Ave Ste 2238 (10001-7604)
PHONE..................888 320-1799
Daniel Olszanski, *President*
◆ **EMP:** 21
SALES: 4.8MM **Privately Held**
WEB: www.globalfirecorp.com
SIC: 3711 Fire department vehicles (motor vehicles), assembly of

New York - New York County (G-9941)

(G-9941)
GLOBAL GEM CORPORATION
Also Called: Global Creations
425 Madison Ave Rm 400 (10017-1141)
PHONE.................................212 350-9936
Moosa Ebrahimian, *President*
Robert Ebrahimian, *Vice Pres*
Steve Ebrahimian, *Manager*
EMP: 5
SQ FT: 1,100
SALES (est): 400K **Privately Held**
WEB: www.globalcreations.com
SIC: 3911 5094 Jewelry, precious metal; diamonds (gems)

(G-9942)
GLOBAL GOLD INC (PA)
1410 Broadway Fl 8 (10018-9362)
PHONE.................................212 239-4657
John Bang, *CEO*
Bruce Fisher, *President*
Jeffrey Fischer, *Vice Pres*
Jeff Fisher, *Vice Pres*
Richard Fleet, *Vice Pres*
▲ **EMP:** 15
SALES (est): 7.6MM **Privately Held**
SIC: 2337 Women's & misses' suits & coats

(G-9943)
GLOBAL GRIND DIGITAL
512 Fashion Ave Fl 42 (10018-4603)
PHONE.................................212 840-9399
Osman Eralt, *CEO*
Tricia Clarke-Stone, *Principal*
EMP: 30
SALES (est): 2MM **Privately Held**
SIC: 2741 Miscellaneous publishing

(G-9944)
GLOBAL PLASTICS LP
21 Downing St Frnt 1 (10014-0836)
PHONE.................................800 417-4605
EMP: 33 **Privately Held**
SIC: 2821 Plastics materials & resins
PA: Global Plastics, Lp
  99 Middle St Ste 1
  Manchester NH 03101

(G-9945)
GLOBAL RESOURCES SG INC
Also Called: Milli Home
267 5th Ave Rm 506 (10016-7503)
PHONE.................................212 686-1411
Anil Nayar, *President*
Pavan Uttam, *Exec VP*
Marsha Cutler, *Director*
▲ **EMP:** 12
SQ FT: 800
SALES (est): 1.5MM **Privately Held**
SIC: 2299 3635 Mfg Textile Goods Mfg Home Vacuum Cleaners

(G-9946)
GLORIA APPAREL INC
500 Fashion Ave 8 (10018-4502)
PHONE.................................212 947-0869
Young H Lee, *President*
◆ **EMP:** 10
SQ FT: 3,500
SALES (est): 36MM **Privately Held**
WEB: www.gloria-texteis.com
SIC: 2339 Women's & misses' outerwear

(G-9947)
GLUCK ORGELBAU INC
170 Park Row Apt 20a (10038-1156)
PHONE.................................212 233-2684
Sebastian M Gluck, *President*
Albert Jensenmoulton, *General Mgr*
EMP: 5 **EST:** 1985
SALES (est): 370K **Privately Held**
SIC: 3931 Organs, all types: pipe, reed, hand, electronic, etc.

(G-9948)
GMC MERCANTILE CORP
231 W 39th St Rm 612 (10018-3109)
PHONE.................................212 498-9488
Garrick Chan, *President*
Sherman Chan, *Vice Pres*
Agean Chen, *CFO*
▲ **EMP:** 18
SALES (est): 1.8MM **Privately Held**
SIC: 2339 Service apparel, washable: women's

(G-9949)
GNCC CAPITAL INC (PA)
244 5th Ave Ste 2525 (10001-7604)
PHONE.................................702 951-9793
Peter Voss, *CEO*
Ronald Lowenthal, *Ch of Bd*
EMP: 4
SALES (est): 1.2MM **Privately Held**
SIC: 1041 Gold ores

(G-9950)
GODIVA CHOCOLATIER INC (DH)
333 W 34th St Fl 6 (10001-2566)
PHONE.................................212 984-5900
Jim Goldman, *President*
Joy Bagnato, *General Mgr*
Charles Adams, *District Mgr*
Brett Barnello, *Vice Pres*
Kaan Dagalti, *Vice Pres*
▲ **EMP:** 35
SQ FT: 15,000
SALES (est): 849MM **Privately Held**
WEB: www.godiva.com
SIC: 2066 5149 5441 2064 Chocolate candy, solid; chocolate; candy; candy & other confectionery products
HQ: Yildiz Holding Anonim Sirketi
  No.6/1 Kisikli Mahallesi
  Istanbul (Anatolia) 34692
  216 524-2900

(G-9951)
GOLDARAMA COMPANY INC
Also Called: Silvertique Fine Jewelry
56 W 45th St Ste 1504 (10036-4206)
PHONE.................................212 730-7299
Ernie Golan, *President*
Hagay Golan, *Vice Pres*
EMP: 7
SALES (est): 660K **Privately Held**
SIC: 3911 Jewelry, precious metal

(G-9952)
GOLDBERGER COMPANY LLC (PA)
Also Called: Goldberger International
36 W 25th St Fl 14 (10010-2749)
PHONE.................................212 924-1194
Jeffrey Holtzman, *Mng Member*
Lawrence Doppelt,
Michael Pietrafesa,
▲ **EMP:** 16 **EST:** 1916
SQ FT: 10,000
SALES (est): 2MM **Privately Held**
WEB: www.goldbergerdoll.com
SIC: 3942 Dolls & doll clothing; stuffed toys, including animals

(G-9953)
GOLDEN ARGOSY LLC (PA)
225 W 34th St Ste 1106 (10122-1106)
PHONE.................................212 268-0003
Paul Marks, *CEO*
Richard Rocco, *President*
EMP: 2
SALES (est): 120MM **Privately Held**
SIC: 3353 5199 Aluminum sheet, plate & foil; foil, aluminum: household

(G-9954)
GOLDEN EAGLE MARKETING LLC
244 5th Ave (10001-7604)
PHONE.................................212 726-1242
Monika Sylvester,
EMP: 5 **EST:** 2009
SALES (est): 217.8K **Privately Held**
SIC: 2741

(G-9955)
GOLDEN INTEGRITY INC
Also Called: B K Integrity
37 W 47th St Ste 1601 (10036-3069)
PHONE.................................212 764-6753
Darek Schwartz, *President*
Khris Kornezi, *Vice Pres*
EMP: 20
SALES (est): 150K **Privately Held**
WEB: www.goldenintegrity.com
SIC: 3911 5944 Jewel settings & mountings, precious metal; jewelry stores

(G-9956)
GOLDSTAR LIGHTING LLC
1407 Broadway Fl 30 (10018-2480)
PHONE.................................646 543-6811
EMP: 18
SQ FT: 18,000
SALES (est): 1.3MM **Privately Held**
SIC: 3641 Mfg Electric Lamps

(G-9957)
GOOD HOME CO INC
132 W 24th St (10011-1981)
PHONE.................................212 352-1509
Christine Dimmick, *President*
Arni Halling, *CFO*
EMP: 6
SQ FT: 1,800
SALES (est): 1.2MM **Privately Held**
WEB: www.thegoodhomecompany.com
SIC: 2844 Oral preparations

(G-9958)
GOOD SHOW SPORTWEAR INC
Also Called: Good Show Sportswear
132 Mulberry St 3 (10013-5551)
PHONE.................................212 334-8751
Danny Tsui, *Owner*
EMP: 11
SALES (est): 350K **Privately Held**
SIC: 3949 Sporting & athletic goods

(G-9959)
GORGA FEHREN FINE JEWELRY LLC
Also Called: Eva Fehren
153 E 88th St (10128-2270)
PHONE.................................646 861-3595
Ann Gorga, *CEO*
EMP: 6
SALES (est): 0 **Privately Held**
SIC: 3911 7389 Jewelry, precious metal;

(G-9960)
GOTHAM ENERGY 360 LLC
48 Wall St Fl 5 (10005-2911)
PHONE.................................917 338-1023
Jennifer Kearney, *Mng Member*
EMP: 10 **EST:** 2008
SALES (est): 546.5K **Privately Held**
SIC: 1389 8748 Oil consultants; energy conservation consultant

(G-9961)
GOTHAM VETERINARY CENTER PC
700 Columbus Ave Frnt 5 (10025-6662)
PHONE.................................212 222-1900
Bonnie Brown, *President*
Dwight Edwards, *Business Mgr*
EMP: 20
SALES (est): 4MM **Privately Held**
SIC: 2835 Veterinary diagnostic substances

(G-9962)
GOTTLIEB & SONS INC
Also Called: Gottlieb Jewelery Mfg
21 W 47th St Fl 4 (10036-2825)
PHONE.................................212 575-1907
Allen Gottlieb, *Owner*
EMP: 25
SALES (corp-wide): 8.7MM **Privately Held**
WEB: www.gottlieb-sons.com
SIC: 3911 Jewelry, precious metal
PA: Gottlieb & Sons, Inc.
  1100 Superior Ave E # 2050
  Cleveland OH 44114
  216 771-4785

(G-9963)
GOYARD INC (HQ)
Also Called: Goyard US
20 E 63rd St (10065-7210)
PHONE.................................212 813-0005
Deborah Ruiz, *Manager*
EMP: 6
SALES (est): 2.1MM
SALES (corp-wide): 55.2MM **Privately Held**
SIC: 3161 5137 Wardrobe bags (luggage); handbags
PA: Goyard St Honore
  16 Place Vendome
  Paris 75001
  142 601-881

(G-9964)
GOYARD MIAMI LLC (DH)
Also Called: Maison Goyard
20 E 63rd St (10065-7210)
PHONE.................................212 813-0005
Deborah Ruiz,
EMP: 6 **EST:** 2015
SALES (est): 1MM
SALES (corp-wide): 55.2MM **Privately Held**
SIC: 3161 5137 Wardrobe bags (luggage); handbags
HQ: Goyard, Inc.
  20 E 63rd St
  New York NY 10065
  212 813-0005

(G-9965)
GOYARD NM BEVERLY HILLS LLC
20 E 63rd St (10065-7210)
PHONE.................................212 355-3872
▲ **EMP:** 6 **EST:** 2014
SALES (est): 750K **Privately Held**
SIC: 3161 Luggage

(G-9966)
GQ MAGAZINE
4 Times Sq Fl 9 (10036-6518)
PHONE.................................212 286-2860
Charles Townsend, *CEO*
Damien Nunes, *Editor*
Daniel Riley, *Editor*
Giulio Capua, *Vice Pres*
Peter Hunsinger, *Vice Pres*
EMP: 8
SALES (est): 570K **Privately Held**
SIC: 2731 Book publishing

(G-9967)
GRADIAN HEALTH SYSTEMS INC
915 Broadway Ste 1001 (10010-8268)
PHONE.................................212 537-0340
Stephen M Rudy, *CEO*
Stephen Rudy, *CEO*
Erica Frenkel, *Vice Pres*
Lina Sayed, *Vice Pres*
Adam Lewis, *Marketing Mgr*
EMP: 7
SQ FT: 3,400
SALES (est): 786.5K **Privately Held**
SIC: 3841 Anesthesia apparatus

(G-9968)
GRAFCONECT CORP
575 8th Ave Rm 1902 (10018-3023)
PHONE.................................212 714-1795
Carl Odhner, *President*
Maggie Yeoh, *Manager*
EMP: 6 **EST:** 2012
SQ FT: 2,000
SALES: 1.9MM **Privately Held**
SIC: 2752 Commercial printing, lithographic

(G-9969)
GRAMERCY JEWELRY MFG CORP
35 W 45th St Fl 5 (10036-4903)
PHONE.................................212 268-0461
Danny Lai, *President*
Peter Law, *Vice Pres*
▲ **EMP:** 50
SQ FT: 13,000
SALES (est): 6.8MM **Privately Held**
WEB: www.gramercyjewelry.com
SIC: 3911 Jewelry apparel

(G-9970)
GRAND CENTRAL PUBLISHING (DH)
1290 Ave Of The Americas (10104-0101)
PHONE.................................212 364-1200
David Young, *Ch of Bd*
Beth Ford, *Principal*
Lawrence Kirshbaum, *Principal*
Lew Barnes, *Technology*
Elizabeth Connor, *Art Dir*
EMP: 240 **EST:** 1960

SQ FT: 140,000
SALES (est): 33.4MM
SALES (corp-wide): 70.7MM Privately Held
WEB: www.biggamesmallworld.com
SIC: 2731 Books: publishing only
HQ: Hachette Book Group, Inc.
1290 Ave Of The Americas
New York NY 10104
800 759-0190

(G-9971)
GRAND SLAM HOLDINGS LLC (DH)
Also Called: Blackstone Group
345 Park Ave Bsmt Lb4 (10154-0004)
PHONE..................................212 583-5000
Stephen A Schwarzman, CEO
EMP: 29
SALES (est): 1.5B
SALES (corp-wide): 7.1B Publicly Held
WEB: www.backstone-gro.com
SIC: 3842 Surgical appliances & supplies; implants, surgical

(G-9972)
GRANDEUR CREATIONS INC
146 W 29th St Rm 9e (10001-8207)
PHONE..................................212 643-1277
Jal Billimoria, President
Meherukh Billimoria, Treasurer
EMP: 6
SQ FT: 2,450
SALES (est): 531.2K Privately Held
WEB: www.grandeurcreations.com
SIC: 3911 Rings, finger: precious metal; bracelets, precious metal

(G-9973)
GRANDMA MAES CNTRY NTURALS LLC
340 E 93rd St Apt 30h (10128-5556)
PHONE..................................212 348-8171
Barry Berman, Mng Member
EMP: 5
SALES (est): 740K Privately Held
SIC: 2048 Canned pet food (except dog & cat); dry pet food (except dog & cat); frozen pet food (except dog & cat)

(G-9974)
GRANTOO LLC
60 Broad St Ste 3502 (10004-2356)
PHONE..................................646 356-0460
Tamer Ossama Hassanein, Vice Pres
EMP: 5
SALES (est): 205.7K Privately Held
SIC: 7372 Application computer software

(G-9975)
GRANTS FINANCIAL PUBLISHING
Also Called: Grant's Interest Rate Observer
2 Wall St Ste 603 (10005-2000)
PHONE..................................212 809-7994
James Grant, President
Philip Grant, Publisher
Katherine Messenger, Editor
Eric Whitehead, Controller
John D'Alberto, Marketing Staff
EMP: 10
SALES (est): 1.7MM Privately Held
WEB: www.grantspub.com
SIC: 2721 Magazines: publishing only, not printed on site

(G-9976)
GRAPHIC LAB INC
228 E 45th St Fl 4 (10017-3303)
PHONE..................................212 682-1815
Richard Campisi, President
Carmine Campisi Jr, Vice Pres
Robert Campisi, Treasurer
Jeannette Duran, Controller
Albert Mahoney, Accounts Exec
EMP: 34
SQ FT: 7,600
SALES (est): 5.6MM Privately Held
WEB: www.gocdp.com
SIC: 2759 Commercial printing

(G-9977)
GRAPHICS FOR INDUSTRY INC
Also Called: Graphic For Industry
307 W 36th St Fl 10 (10018-6474)
PHONE..................................212 889-6202
Mark Palmer, President
EMP: 10 EST: 1973
SQ FT: 5,000
SALES (est): 1MM Privately Held
SIC: 2759 Screen printing

(G-9978)
GRAPHIS INC
389 5th Ave Rm 1105 (10016-3350)
PHONE..................................212 532-9387
B Martin Pedersen, President
Arna Pedersen, Bookkeeper
▲ EMP: 10
SQ FT: 5,000
SALES (est): 1.5MM Privately Held
WEB: www.graphis.com
SIC: 2721 2731 Magazines: publishing only, not printed on site; books: publishing only

(G-9979)
GRAVITY EAST VILLAGE INC
515 E 5th St (10009-6703)
PHONE..................................212 388-9788
Michael J Perrine, Chairman
EMP: 7
SALES (est): 746.1K Privately Held
SIC: 3845 Colonoscopes, electromedical

(G-9980)
GRAYERS AMERICA INC
304 Bleecker St (10014-3400)
PHONE..................................310 953-2742
EMP: 6
SALES (corp-wide): 848.3K Privately Held
SIC: 2321 Men's & boys' furnishings
PA: Grayers America, Inc.
10 E 53rd St Fl 14
New York NY 10022
310 953-2742

(G-9981)
GREAT JONES LUMBER CORP
45 Great Jones St (10012-1627)
PHONE..................................212 254-5560
Joseph Lauto, President
Anthony Lauto, Vice Pres
EMP: 15
SALES (est): 1.3MM Privately Held
SIC: 2421 Lumber: rough, sawed or planed; fuelwood, from mill waste

(G-9982)
GREAT UNIVERSAL CORP
Also Called: ATW Group
1441 Broadway Ste 6066 (10018-1905)
PHONE..................................917 302-0065
Grace Lu, President
◆ EMP: 20
SQ FT: 1,000
SALES (est): 8.1MM Privately Held
SIC: 2361 2321 Girls' & children's dresses, blouses & shirts; men's & boys' dress shirts

(G-9983)
GREEN GIRL PRTG & MSGNR INC
44 W 39th St (10018-3802)
PHONE..................................212 575-0357
Alice Harford, President
EMP: 6
SALES (est): 400K Privately Held
SIC: 2752 Commercial printing, lithographic

(G-9984)
GREENBEADS LLC
Also Called: Emily and Ashley
220 E 72nd St Apt 17d (10021-4531)
PHONE..................................212 327-2765
Emily Green, Partner
Ashley Green, Partner
EMP: 5
SALES (est): 350K Privately Held
WEB: www.greenbeads.com
SIC: 3961 Costume jewelry

(G-9985)
GRESHAM TECHNOLOGIES (US) INC
Also Called: Gresham Computing
11 Park Pl Frnt 3 (10007-2841)
PHONE..................................646 943-5955
Ian Manocha, CEO
Tom Mullan, CFO
Christopher Young, Director
EMP: 15
SALES (est): 5MM Privately Held
SIC: 7372 Application computer software

(G-9986)
GREY STATE APPAREL LLC
305 7th Ave Ste 13a (10001-6008)
PHONE..................................212 255-4216
Saima Chowdhury, CEO
EMP: 23 EST: 2015
SALES (est): 848.1K Privately Held
SIC: 2331 Women's & misses' blouses & shirts

(G-9987)
GRID TYPOGRAPHIC SERVICES INC
Also Called: Grid Typographic Svces
27 W 24th St Ste 9c (10010-3290)
PHONE..................................212 627-0303
Donald Davidson, President
John Duffy, Treasurer
Sy Schwartz, Admin Sec
EMP: 10
SQ FT: 3,300
SALES (est): 1.6MM Privately Held
WEB: www.gridtypography.com
SIC: 2791 Typesetting

(G-9988)
GRIFFON CORPORATION (PA)
712 5th Ave Fl 18 (10019-4108)
PHONE..................................212 957-5000
Ronald J Kramer, CEO
Harvey R Blau, Ch of Bd
Robert F Mehmel, President
Seth L Kaplan, Senior VP
Thomas Gibbons, Vice Pres
◆ EMP: 20 EST: 1959
SQ FT: 20,000
SALES: 1.5B Publicly Held
WEB: www.griffoncorp.com
SIC: 3442 2431 1751 1799 Garage doors, overhead: metal; garage doors, overhead: wood; garage door, installation or erection; home/office interiors finishing, furnishing & remodeling; prefabricated fireplace installation; laminated plastics plate & sheet; laminated plastic sheets; radio & TV communications equipment

(G-9989)
GRILLBOT LLC
1562 1st Ave Ste 251 (10028-4004)
PHONE..................................646 258-5639
Ethan Woods, Vice Pres
Shawn Dickerson, Creative Dir
EMP: 5
SALES (est): 788K Privately Held
SIC: 2842 Cleaning or polishing preparations

(G-9990)
GRIND
1216 Broadway Fl 2 (10001-4482)
PHONE..................................646 558-3250
EMP: 7
SALES (est): 749.1K Privately Held
SIC: 3599 Mfg Industrial Machinery

(G-9991)
GRINNELL DESIGNS LTD
260 W 39th St Rm 302 (10018-4434)
PHONE..................................212 391-5277
Francis De Ocampo, President
Larry Holliday, Vice Pres
Patricia Hudson, Vice Pres
EMP: 20
SQ FT: 4,000
SALES (est): 2.5MM Privately Held
WEB: www.grinnelldesigns.com
SIC: 3911 Jewelry, precious metal

(G-9992)
GRIT ENERGY SERVICES INC (PA)
100 Wall St Fl 11 (10005-3763)
PHONE..................................212 701-4500
Steven Baffico, CEO
Jerry Baftian, COO
Jennifer Wilson, CFO
EMP: 5 EST: 2017
SALES (est): 1.3MM Privately Held
SIC: 1389 Oil field services

(G-9993)
GROHE AMERICA INC
160 5th Ave Fl 4 (10010-7065)
PHONE..................................212 206-8820
Ivana Molzen MBA, Manager
Allison Wu, Manager
EMP: 7 Privately Held
SIC: 2499 Laundry products, wood
HQ: Grohe America, Inc.
200 N Gary Ave Ste G
Roselle IL 60172
630 582-7711

(G-9994)
GROLIER INTERNATIONAL INC (HQ)
557 Broadway (10012-3962)
PHONE..................................212 343-6100
Lisa Tarsi, Principal
EMP: 4
SALES (est): 2.3MM
SALES (corp-wide): 1.6B Publicly Held
SIC: 2731 Book publishing
PA: Scholastic Corporation
557 Broadway Lbby 1
New York NY 10012
212 343-6100

(G-9995)
GROM COLUMBUS LLC
1796 Broadway (10019-1400)
PHONE..................................212 974-3444
Eran Keren, Principal
▲ EMP: 6 EST: 2010
SALES (est): 456.9K
SALES (corp-wide): 63B Privately Held
SIC: 2024 Ice cream, bulk
PA: Unilever Plc
Unilever House
London EC4Y
207 822-5252

(G-9996)
GROUP COMMERCE INC (PA)
902 Broadway Fl 6 (10010-6039)
PHONE..................................646 346-0598
Jonty Kelt, CEO
David Lebow, President
Andrew Glenn, CTO
EMP: 13
SALES (est): 2.9MM Privately Held
SIC: 7372 Prepackaged software

(G-9997)
GROUP ENTERAINMENT LLC
115 W 29th St Rm 1102 (10001-5106)
PHONE..................................212 868-5233
Gill Holland,
EMP: 6
SALES (est): 552.6K Privately Held
SIC: 3571 Computers, digital, analog or hybrid

(G-9998)
GROUPE 16SUR20 LLC (PA)
Also Called: Seize Sur Vingt
198 Bowery (10012-4203)
P.O. Box 2280, Lenox MA (01240-5280)
PHONE..................................212 625-1620
James Jurney Jr, Mng Member
EMP: 15
SQ FT: 2,000
SALES (est): 1.6MM Privately Held
SIC: 2329 2321 2325 Men's & boys' sportswear & athletic clothing; men's & boys' furnishings; men's & boys' trousers & slacks

(G-9999)
GROWNBEANS INC
110 Bank St Apt 2j (10014-2164)
PHONE..................................212 989-3486
Karen Groner, President

New York - New York County (G-10000)

EMP: 5
SQ FT: 2,400
SALES (est): 412.3K **Privately Held**
SIC: 3172 Personal leather goods

(G-10000)
GRUNER + JAHR PRTG & PUBG CO
Also Called: New York Times Co Mag Group
110 5th Ave Fl 7 (10011-5632)
PHONE................................212 463-1000
John Heins, *Manager*
EMP: 160
SALES (corp-wide): 588.8MM **Privately Held**
WEB: www.gjusa.com
SIC: 2721 7311 Magazines: publishing only, not printed on site; advertising agencies
PA: Gruner + Jahr Usa Group, Inc.
1745 Broadway Fl 16
New York NY 10019
866 323-9336

(G-10001)
GRUNER + JAHR USA GROUP INC (PA)
Also Called: Gruner Jahr USA Publishing Div
1745 Broadway Fl 16 (10019-4640)
PHONE................................866 323-9336
Mike Amundson, *President*
Gregg Black, *Exec VP*
Larry Hawkey, *Exec VP*
Dan Nitz, *Exec VP*
◆ EMP: 500
SQ FT: 173,000
SALES (est): 588.8MM **Privately Held**
WEB: www.gjusa.com
SIC: 2721 2754 Periodicals: publishing & printing; magazines: publishing & printing; commercial printing, gravure

(G-10002)
GRUNT APPAREL INC
105 Duane St Apt 7c (10007-3603)
PHONE................................646 878-6171
Wendy Cheung, *President*
Bill Ng, *Vice Pres*
▲ EMP: 7
SQ FT: 1,000
SALES: 500K **Privately Held**
SIC: 2321 5611 5136 Men's & boys' sports & polo shirts; men's & boys' clothing stores; caps, men's & boys'

(G-10003)
GSCP EMAX ACQUISITION LLC
85 Broad St (10004-2434)
PHONE................................212 902-1000
Henry M Paulson Jr, *CEO*
Michael Marsh, *Vice Pres*
EMP: 5
SALES (est): 454.4K **Privately Held**
SIC: 3442 Metal doors, sash & trim

(G-10004)
GUARDIAN NEWS & MEDIA LLC
315 W 36th St Fl 8 (10018-6624)
PHONE................................917 900-4663
Eamonn Store,
Rajesh Gupta, *Professor*
Scott Klemmer, *Assoc Prof*
EMP: 48
SALES (est): 3.8MM
SALES (corp-wide): 304.6MM **Privately Held**
SIC: 2711 Newspapers, publishing & printing
HQ: Guardian News & Media Limited
Kings Place
London N1 9G
203 353-2000

(G-10005)
GUEST INFORMAT LLC
Also Called: Quick Guide
110 E 42nd St Rm 1714 (10017-5611)
PHONE................................212 557-3010
Lisa Nusynowitz, *Principal*
EMP: 13 **Privately Held**
SIC: 2741 Miscellaneous publishing
HQ: Guest Informat, L.L.C.
21200 Erwin St
Woodland Hills CA
818 716-7484

(G-10006)
GUEST OF A GUEST INC
113 Jane St (10014-1700)
PHONE................................212 206-0397
Victoria Eisner, *CEO*
Christie Grimm, *Mktg Dir*
Mackenzie Johnson, *Marketing Staff*
Stephanie Maida, *Manager*
EMP: 6 EST: 2013
SALES (est): 262.9K **Privately Held**
SIC: 2711 Newspapers: publishing only, not printed on site

(G-10007)
GUILD DIAMOND PRODUCTS INC (PA)
1212 Avenue Of The Americ (10036-1600)
PHONE................................212 871-0007
Jacques H Elion, *President*
Douglas Panker, *Corp Secy*
▲ EMP: 13
SQ FT: 7,000
SALES (est): 1.4MM **Privately Held**
SIC: 3911 3915 Jewelry, precious metal; diamond cutting & polishing

(G-10008)
GUILFORD PUBLICATIONS INC
Also Called: Guilford Press
7 Penn Plz Ste 1200 (10001-1020)
PHONE................................212 431-9800
Robert Matloff, *President*
Martin Coleman, *Editor*
Judith Grauman, *Editor*
Anna Nelson, *Editor*
Seymour Weingarten, *Corp Secy*
EMP: 75 EST: 1973
SQ FT: 10,000
SALES (est): 8.6MM **Privately Held**
WEB: www.guilford.com
SIC: 2741 2731 2721 7812 Miscellaneous publishing; books: publishing only; trade journals: publishing & printing; audio-visual program production

(G-10009)
GUILFORD PUBLICATIONS INC
Also Called: Guilford Press
370 7th Ave Ste 1200 (10001-1020)
PHONE................................800 365-7006
Robert Matloff, *President*
Carolyn Graham, *Editor*
Laura Patchkofsky, *Editor*
Vernita Hurston, *Credit Mgr*
Axel Davieau, *Marketing Staff*
EMP: 7
SALES (est): 66.5K **Privately Held**
SIC: 2741 2731 Miscellaneous publishing; book publishing

(G-10010)
GUOSA LIFE SCIENCES INC
708 3rd Ave Fl 6 (10017-4119)
PHONE................................718 813-7806
Charles Oviawe, *Principal*
Edema Oviawe,
EMP: 12 EST: 2012
SALES (est): 887.1K **Privately Held**
SIC: 2834 8999 Solutions, pharmaceutical; tablets, pharmaceutical; scientific consulting

(G-10011)
GW ACQUISITION LLC
Also Called: G&W Industries
1370 Broadway Rm 1100 (10018-7774)
PHONE................................212 736-4848
Michael Marinoff, *Mng Member*
◆ EMP: 34
SALES: 100MM **Privately Held**
SIC: 2361 2369 Girls' & children's blouses & shirts; girls' & children's outerwear

(G-10012)
H & T GOLDMAN CORPORATION
2 W 46th St Ste 607 (10036-4566)
PHONE................................800 822-0272
Nathan Goldman, *President*
EMP: 5
SQ FT: 1,200
SALES (est): 477.6K **Privately Held**
SIC: 3911 Jewelry, precious metal

(G-10013)
H BEST LTD
Moret Time
1411 Broadway Fl 8 (10018-3565)
PHONE................................212 354-2400
Morris Chabott, *Director*
EMP: 10 **Privately Held**
SIC: 3873 Watches, clocks, watchcases & parts
PA: H. Best, Ltd.
1411 Broadway Fl 8
New York NY 10018

(G-10014)
H C KIONKA & CO INC
Also Called: Kimberley Diamond
15 Maiden Ln Ste 908 (10038-5118)
PHONE................................212 227-3155
Mark Levy, *President*
Mark Baum, *Vice Pres*
Elizabeth Ozog-Osewski, *Accounting Mgr*
EMP: 13
SQ FT: 2,500
SALES (est): 8MM **Privately Held**
WEB: www.kimberleydiamond.com
SIC: 3911 Jewelry apparel

(G-10015)
H GROUP LLC
462 7th Ave Fl 9 (10018-7436)
PHONE................................212 719-5500
Joe Dahan, *President*
EMP: 15 EST: 2004
SALES (est): 173.7K **Privately Held**
SIC: 2211 Apparel & outerwear fabrics, cotton

(G-10016)
HACHETTE BOOK GROUP INC (DH)
1290 Ave Of The Americas (10104-0101)
PHONE................................800 759-0190
David Young, *Ch of Bd*
Kim Sayle, *Publisher*
Anthony Goff, *Editor*
Benjamin Greenberg, *Editor*
Kurt Hassler, *Editor*
◆ EMP: 350
SALES (est): 412.7MM
SALES (corp-wide): 70.7MM **Privately Held**
SIC: 2731 5192 Books: publishing only; books, periodicals & newspapers
HQ: Hachette Livre
Istra Gecri Hachette Jeunesse
Vanves 92170
143 923-000

(G-10017)
HACHETTE BOOK GROUP USA
237 Park Ave (10017-3140)
PHONE................................212 364-1200
Mark Kent, *Vice Pres*
Jaime Leifer, *Vice Pres*
Stephen Mubarek, *Vice Pres*
Bob Babbin, *Opers Mgr*
Mitch Kelly, *Opers Staff*
EMP: 20
SALES (est): 1.1MM **Privately Held**
SIC: 2731 Books: publishing only

(G-10018)
HADDAD BROS INC (PA)
Also Called: Madonna
28 W 36th St Rm 1026 (10018-1290)
PHONE................................212 563-2117
Alan Haddad, *President*
Mac Haddad, *Chairman*
▲ EMP: 12
SQ FT: 3,500
SALES (est): 7.2MM **Privately Held**
WEB: www.haddadbros.com
SIC: 2321 2361 Men's & boys' furnishings; girls' & children's dresses, blouses & shirts

(G-10019)
HADDAD HOSIERY LLC
34 W 33rd St Rm 401 (10001-3342)
PHONE................................212 251-0022
Jack Haddad, *President*
▲ EMP: 5 EST: 2000
SALES (est): 431.3K **Privately Held**
SIC: 2252 Hosiery

(G-10020)
HAGEDORN COMMUNICATIONS INC
20 W 22nd St Ste 906 (10010-5862)
PHONE................................914 636-7400
Chris Vivion, *Manager*
EMP: 5
SALES (corp-wide): 10.5MM **Privately Held**
WEB: www.fouke.com
SIC: 2711 2741 Newspapers; miscellaneous publishing
PA: Hagedorn Communications Inc
662 Main St Ste 1
New Rochelle NY 10801
914 636-7400

(G-10021)
HAILO NETWORK USA INC
568 Broadway Fl 11 (10012-3374)
PHONE................................646 561-8552
EMP: 5 EST: 2012
SALES (est): 470K **Privately Held**
SIC: 7372 Prepackaged Software Services

(G-10022)
HALEYS COMET SEAFOOD CORP
605 3rd Ave Fl 34 (10158-3499)
PHONE................................212 571-1828
Robert Leone, *President*
EMP: 45
SALES: 1.5MM **Privately Held**
SIC: 2211 Long cloth, cotton

(G-10023)
HALMODE APPAREL INC
Also Called: Halmode Petite Div
1400 Brdwy 11th & Fl 16 (10018)
PHONE................................212 819-9114
Jay Diamond, *CEO*
Bea Myerson, *Exec VP*
Michael M Saunders, *Vice Pres*
▲ EMP: 600
SQ FT: 240,000
SALES (est): 34.9MM
SALES (corp-wide): 350.8MM **Privately Held**
SIC: 2339 2335 5137 Sportswear, women's; uniforms, athletic: women's, misses & juniors'; maternity clothing; women's, juniors' & misses' dresses; women's & children's clothing
PA: Kellwood Company, Llc
600 Kellwood Pkwy Ste 200
Chesterfield MO 63017
314 576-3100

(G-10024)
HALO ASSOCIATES
289 Bleecker St Fl 5 (10014-4106)
PHONE................................212 691-9549
EMP: 6
SQ FT: 7,000
SALES: 500K **Privately Held**
SIC: 3299 8999 Art Related Services

(G-10025)
HAMIL AMERICA INC
42 W 39th St Fl 15 (10018-2081)
PHONE................................212 244-2645
Jerry Miller, *President*
▲ EMP: 16
SALES (est): 1.4MM **Privately Held**
WEB: www.algo.com
SIC: 2253 Knit outerwear mills
PA: Groupe Algo Inc
5555 Rue Cypihot
Saint-Laurent QC H4S 1
514 388-8888

(G-10026)
HAMMERMAN BROS INC
Also Called: H2 At Hammerman
50 W 57th St Fl 12 (10019-3914)
PHONE................................212 956-2800
Brett Hammerman, *President*
Darcy Hammerman, *Vice Pres*
Rose Dennis, *Controller*
EMP: 9
SQ FT: 10,000

SALES (est): 1.7MM **Privately Held**
WEB: www.hammermanbrothers.com
SIC: 3911 3873 Bracelets, precious metal; earrings, precious metal; necklaces, precious metal; rings, finger: precious metal; watches, clocks, watchcases & parts

(G-10027)
HAMPSHIRE SUB II INC (HQ)
114 W 41st St Fl 5 (10036-7308)
PHONE..................................631 321-0923
Martin Axman, *President*
Mark Abramson, *VP Sales*
◆ EMP: 70
SQ FT: 7,000
SALES (est): 8.4MM
SALES (corp-wide): 91.4MM **Publicly Held**
WEB: www.item-eyes.com
SIC: 2337 2339 5137 Skirts, separate: women's, misses' & juniors'; jackets & vests, except fur & leather: women's; slacks: women's, misses' & juniors'; women's & children's clothing
PA: Hampshire Group, Limited
    1924 Pearman Dairy Rd
    Anderson SC 29625
    212 540-5666

(G-10028)
HAMPTON PRESS INCORPORATED
307 7th Ave Rm 506 (10001-6079)
PHONE..................................646 638-3800
Barbara Bernstein, *Owner*
EMP: 9
SALES (est): 689.9K **Privately Held**
SIC: 2741 Miscellaneous publishing

(G-10029)
HANDCRAFT MANUFACTURING CORP (PA)
34 W 33rd St Rm 401 (10001-3342)
PHONE..................................212 251-0022
Isaac Mizrahi, *President*
Myla Mirasol, *Production*
Marshall Mizrahi, *Treasurer*
Betsy Cowan, *Financial Analy*
Joe Mizrahi, *Sales Staff*
▲ EMP: 150
SQ FT: 11,000
SALES (est): 17.1MM **Privately Held**
WEB: www.handcraftmfg.com
SIC: 2341 Women's & children's undergarments

(G-10030)
HANDSOME DANS LLC (PA)
186 1st Ave (10009-4002)
PHONE..................................917 965-2499
EMP: 5 EST: 2012
SALES (est): 1.5MM **Privately Held**
SIC: 2064 Candy & other confectionery products

(G-10031)
HANDY & HARMAN LTD (DH)
Also Called: Hnh
590 Madison Ave Rm 3202 (10022-8536)
PHONE..................................212 520-2300
Jack L Howard, *CEO*
Warren G Lichtenstein, *Ch of Bd*
William T Fejes Jr, *Senior VP*
James F McCabe Jr, *Senior VP*
Douglas B Woodworth, *CFO*
▼ EMP: 799
SALES: 828.3MM
SALES (corp-wide): 1.3B **Publicly Held**
WEB: www.whxcorp.com
SIC: 3339 3011 3312 Precious metals; tire & inner tube materials & related products; wire products, steel or iron
HQ: Sph Group Holdings Llc
    590 Madison Ave Fl 32
    New York NY 10022
    212 520-2300

(G-10032)
HANESBRANDS INC
260 Madison Ave Fl 6 (10016-2406)
PHONE..................................212 576-9300
Kimberly Sorrano, *Office Mgr*
EMP: 9

SALES (corp-wide): 6.4B **Publicly Held**
WEB: www.hanesbrands.com
SIC: 2211 5699 Apparel & outerwear fabrics, cotton; sports apparel
PA: Hanesbrands Inc.
    1000 E Hanes Mill Rd
    Winston Salem NC 27105
    336 519-8080

(G-10033)
HANIA BY ANYA COLE LLC
16 W 56th St Fl 4 (10019-3872)
PHONE..................................212 302-3550
Anya Cole, *Mng Member*
EMP: 8
SALES (est): 1MM **Privately Held**
SIC: 2253 Knit outerwear mills

(G-10034)
HANSA USA LLC
18 E 48th St Fl 3 (10017-1014)
PHONE..................................646 412-6407
Hansa Styles, *Technology*
Andrew Fox, *Software Dev*
Eric Hu, *Director*
▲ EMP: 20
SALES (est): 3.4MM **Privately Held**
SIC: 3911 Jewelry, precious metal

(G-10035)
HANSAE CO LTD
501 Fashion Ave Rm 208 (10018-8611)
PHONE..................................212 354-6690
Aesun Kim, *Mng Member*
EMP: 9
SALES (est): 871.2K
SALES (corp-wide): 1.2B **Privately Held**
SIC: 2329 2331 Men's & boys' sportswear & athletic clothing; T-shirts & tops, women's: made from purchased materials
PA: Hansae Co., Ltd.
    5/F Jeongwoo Bldg.
    Seoul 07238
    822 377-9077

(G-10036)
HARD TEN CLOTHING INC
231 W 39th St Rm 606 (10018-0745)
PHONE..................................212 302-1321
Jesse Battino, *Principal*
EMP: 5
SALES: 5MM **Privately Held**
SIC: 2361 5136 Shirts: girls', children's & infants'; shirts, men's & boys'

(G-10037)
HARPERCOLLINS
195 Broadway (10007-3100)
PHONE..................................212 207-7000
Brian Murray, *President*
EMP: 12 EST: 2012
SALES (est): 204.3K
SALES (corp-wide): 9B **Publicly Held**
SIC: 2731 Books: publishing only
PA: News Corporation
    1211 Ave Of The Americas
    New York NY 10036
    212 416-3400

(G-10038)
HARPERCOLLINS PUBLISHERS LLC (HQ)
Also Called: William Morrow Publishing
195 Broadway Fl 2 (10007-3132)
PHONE..................................212 207-7000
Brian Murray, *CEO*
David Steinberger, *President*
Mary Sasso, *Marketing Staff*
Thomas Callan, *Analyst*
Janet Gervasio,
▲ EMP: 600 EST: 1817
SQ FT: 260,000
SALES (est): 737MM
SALES (corp-wide): 9B **Publicly Held**
WEB: www.harpercollins.com
SIC: 2731 Books: publishing only
PA: News Corporation
    1211 Ave Of The Americas
    New York NY 10036
    212 416-3400

(G-10039)
HARPERCOLLINS PUBLISHERS LLC
Harlequin & Silhouette Books
233 Broadway Rm 1001 (10279-1099)
PHONE..................................212 553-4200
Eisbell Swift, *Branch Mgr*
EMP: 43
SALES (corp-wide): 9B **Publicly Held**
SIC: 2731 Book publishing
HQ: Harpercollins Publishers L.L.C.
    195 Broadway Fl 2
    New York NY 10007
    212 207-7000

(G-10040)
HARPERS MAGAZINE FOUNDATION
666 Broadway Fl 11 (10012-2394)
PHONE..................................212 420-5720
John Macarthur, *President*
John R Mc Arthur, *President*
Andrew Cockburn, *Editor*
North Intern, *Editor*
Adrian Kneubuhl, *Editor*
EMP: 28 EST: 1982
SQ FT: 7,800
SALES: 6.9MM **Privately Held**
SIC: 2721 Magazines: publishing only, not printed on site

(G-10041)
HARRISON SPORTSWEAR INC
Also Called: Eric Signature
260 W 39th St Fl 7 (10018-4410)
PHONE..................................212 391-1051
Eric Makofsky, *President*
Lemuel Shiuh, *Vice Pres*
Xie Ai Yi, *Vice Pres*
▲ EMP: 12
SQ FT: 3,000
SALES (est): 1.4MM **Privately Held**
WEB: www.randykemper.com
SIC: 2337 Pantsuits: women's, misses' & juniors'; skirts, separate: women's, misses' & juniors'; jackets & vests, except fur & leather: women's

(G-10042)
HARRY N ABRAMS INCORPORATED
Also Called: Stewart Tobori & Chang Div
195 Broadway Fl 9 (10007-3122)
PHONE..................................212 206-7715
Herve De La Martiniere, *Ch of Bd*
Michael Jacobs, *Ch of Bd*
Shawna Mullen, *Publisher*
Erin Barnett, *Editor*
Tamar Brazis, *Editor*
▲ EMP: 94 EST: 1949
SQ FT: 30,000
SALES (est): 32.7MM
SALES (corp-wide): 408.6K **Privately Held**
WEB: www.hnabooks.com
SIC: 2731 Books: publishing only
PA: La Martiniere Groupe
    La Martiniere Media Participations
    Paris
    153 263-335

(G-10043)
HARRY WINSTON INC (DH)
717 5th Ave Fl 9 (10022-8132)
PHONE..................................212 399-1000
Nayla Hayek, *CEO*
Jennifer Liu, *Managing Dir*
Gwen Halsted-Horne, *Vice Pres*
Michael Moser, *Vice Pres*
Harry Winston, *Vice Pres*
▲ EMP: 110 EST: 1932
SQ FT: 18,000
SALES (est): 60.8MM
SALES (corp-wide): 8B **Privately Held**
SIC: 3911 5944 Jewelry, precious metal; jewelry, precious stones & precious metals; watches
HQ: Hw Holdings, Inc.
    718 5th Ave
    New York NY 10019
    212 399-1000

(G-10044)
HARRYS INC (PA)
Also Called: Harry's Razor Company
75 Varick St Fl 9 (10013-1917)
PHONE..................................888 212-6855
Andy Katz-Mayfield, *CEO*
Jeffrey Raider, *Corp Secy*
Brittania Boey, *Senior VP*
Ryan Dougherty, *Prdtn Mgr*
Tyler Sgro, *Buyer*
▲ EMP: 87
SALES (est): 24.9MM **Privately Held**
SIC: 3634 Razors, electric

(G-10045)
HART ENERGY PUBLISHING LLLP
110 William St Fl 18 (10038-3954)
PHONE..................................212 621-4621
EMP: 5
SALES (corp-wide): 49.3MM **Privately Held**
SIC: 2721 2741 Magaziine/Newsletter Publisher
PA: Hart Energy Llc
    1616 S Voss Rd Ste 1000
    Houston TX 77057
    713 993-9320

(G-10046)
HART REPRODUCTION SERVICES
Also Called: Nyc Thermography
242 W 36th St Rm 801 (10018-8960)
PHONE..................................212 704-0556
Brett Greer, *President*
EMP: 5
SQ FT: 7,400
SALES: 800K **Privately Held**
WEB: www.hartrepro.com
SIC: 2759 7331 Stationery: printing; mailing service

(G-10047)
HARVARD UNIVERSITY PRESS
150 5th Ave Ste 632 (10011-4311)
PHONE..................................212 337-0280
Joyce Seltzer, *Director*
EMP: 100
SALES (est): 5.7MM **Privately Held**
SIC: 2731 Book publishing

(G-10048)
HASKELL JEWELS LTD (PA)
390 5th Ave Fl 2 (10018-8162)
PHONE..................................212 764-3332
Linda Fialkoss, *Principal*
▲ EMP: 50
SALES (est): 3.4MM **Privately Held**
SIC: 3911 Jewelry, precious metal

(G-10049)
HAUTE BY BLAIR STANLEY LLC
330 E 38th St Apt 23e (10016-2780)
PHONE..................................212 557-7868
EMP: 5
SQ FT: 1,000
SALES: 375K **Privately Held**
SIC: 2335 Mfg Women's/Misses' Dresses

(G-10050)
HAYMAN-CHAFFEY DESIGNS INC
137 E 25th St (10010-2314)
PHONE..................................212 889-7771
Charles R Hayman Chaffey, *President*
EMP: 10
SQ FT: 10,000
SALES (est): 700K **Privately Held**
SIC: 2511 Wood household furniture

(G-10051)
HAYMARKET GROUP LTD
Also Called: Chocolatier Magazine
12 W 37th St 9 (10018-7480)
PHONE..................................212 239-0855
Fax: 212 967-4184
EMP: 12
SQ FT: 3,000
SALES (est): 950K **Privately Held**
SIC: 2721 Magazine Publishers

New York - New York County (G-10052) — GEOGRAPHIC SECTION

(G-10052)
HAYMARKET MEDIA INC (DH)
Also Called: Prweek/Prescribing Reference
275 7th Ave Fl 10 (10001-6756)
PHONE..................646 638-6000
Kevin Costello, *CEO*
Amey Bordikar, *President*
Dominic Barone, *Publisher*
Chad Holloway, *Publisher*
Karmen Maurer, *Publisher*
▲ **EMP:** 130
SQ FT: 27,000
SALES (est): 76.6MM
SALES (corp-wide): 223.6MM **Privately Held**
SIC: 2721 Magazines: publishing only, not printed on site

(G-10053)
HAYNES ROBERTS INC
601 W 26th St Rm 1655 (10001-1151)
PHONE..................212 989-1901
Timothy Haynes, *Owner*
Vanessa Lacson, *Project Mgr*
Esteban Arboleda, *Manager*
Agustin Reynoso, *Technology*
Michael Silva, *Associate*
▲ **EMP:** 15
SALES (est): 1.9MM **Privately Held**
SIC: 3679 Electronic components

(G-10054)
HC CONTRACTING INC
Also Called: Ferrara Manufacturing Company
318 W 39th St Fl 4 (10018-1493)
PHONE..................212 643-9292
Carolyn Ferrara, *President*
Joseph Ferrara, *Vice Pres*
Daniel Littell, *Manager*
Patrick McHale, *Manager*
Eddy Molina, *Software Dev*
◆ **EMP:** 60 **EST:** 1987
SQ FT: 25,000
SALES: 5MM **Privately Held**
WEB: www.ferraramfg.com
SIC: 2339 2326 Service apparel, washable: women's; service apparel (baker, barber, lab, etc.), washable: men's

(G-10055)
HEARST BUS COMMUNICATIONS INC (PA)
300 W 57th St Fl 2 (10019-3741)
PHONE..................212 649-2000
Richard P Malloch, *President*
Barry J Green, *Vice Pres*
Peter Rowlinson, *Vice Pres*
Robert D Wilbanks, *Treasurer*
David L Kors, *Asst Treas*
EMP: 7 **EST:** 1980
SALES (est): 367.3K **Privately Held**
SIC: 2721 Magazines: publishing only, not printed on site

(G-10056)
HEARST BUSINESS MEDIA CORP
300 W 57th St Fl 2 (10019-3741)
PHONE..................631 650-4441
Richard P Malloch, *President*
Gregory Dorn MD MPH, *Exec VP*
Steven A Hobbs, *Exec VP*
Donna Yeager, *Manager*
EMP: 10
SALES (est): 245K
SALES (corp-wide): 6.6B **Privately Held**
SIC: 2721 2731 2711 4832 Magazines: publishing only, not printed on site; books: publishing only; newspapers, publishing & printing; newspapers: publishing only, not printed on site; radio broadcasting stations; television broadcasting stations; news feature syndicate
PA: The Hearst Corporation
300 W 57th St Fl 42
New York NY 10019
212 649-2000

(G-10057)
HEARST BUSINESS PUBLISHING INC
Also Called: Diversion Magazine
888 7th Ave Fl 2 (10106-0001)
PHONE..................212 969-7500
Cathy Cavender, *Principal*
EMP: 16
SALES (corp-wide): 6.6B **Privately Held**
SIC: 2721 Magazines: publishing only, not printed on site
HQ: Hearst Business Publishing, Inc.
300 W 57th St Fl 2
New York NY 10019
704 348-8614

(G-10058)
HEARST COMMUNICATIONS INC (DH)
Also Called: San Francisco Chronicle
300 W 57th St (10019-3741)
PHONE..................212 649-2000
Steven R Swartz, *CEO*
Mark E Aldam, *President*
Mark Flinn, *General Mgr*
Jennifer Condon, *Editor*
Kari Costas, *Editor*
▲ **EMP:** 1100
SQ FT: 100,000
SALES (est): 327.2MM
SALES (corp-wide): 6.6B **Privately Held**
WEB: www.telegram.com
SIC: 2711 Newspapers, publishing & printing
HQ: Hearst Holdings Inc
300 W 57th St
New York NY 10019
212 649-2000

(G-10059)
HEARST COMMUNICATIONS INC
828 9th Ave (10019-5587)
PHONE..................212 247-1014
EMP: 6
SALES (corp-wide): 6.6B **Privately Held**
SIC: 2741 Miscellaneous publishing
HQ: Hearst Communications, Inc.
300 W 57th St
New York NY 10019
212 649-2000

(G-10060)
HEARST COMMUNICATIONS INC (DH)
Also Called: Hearst Interactive Media
300 W 57th St (10019-3741)
PHONE..................212 649-2000
Steven R Swartz, *CEO*
Mark E Aldam, *President*
Roberta Kowalishin, *President*
Darren Nichols, *Managing Dir*
Alison Caporimo, *Editor*
EMP: 156
SALES (est): 20.7MM
SALES (corp-wide): 6.6B **Privately Held**
SIC: 2721 Magazines: publishing only, not printed on site
HQ: Hearst Holdings Inc
300 W 57th St
New York NY 10019
212 649-2000

(G-10061)
HEARST CORPORATION (PA)
Also Called: Hearst Enterprises
300 W 57th St Fl 42 (10019-3790)
PHONE..................212 649-2000
Steven R Swartz, *President*
Mark E Aldam, *President*
Kevin Martinez, *Publisher*
Kevin O'Malley, *Publisher*
William R Hearst III, *Chairman*
▲ **EMP:** 2500
SQ FT: 166,612
SALES (est): 6.6B **Privately Held**
WEB: www.hearstcorp.com
SIC: 2721 2731 2711 4832 Magazines: publishing only, not printed on site; books: publishing only; newspapers, publishing & printing; newspapers: publishing only, not printed on site; radio broadcasting stations; television broadcasting stations; news feature syndicate

(G-10062)
HEARST CORPORATION
Seventeen Magazine
300 W 57th St Fl 29 (10019-3741)
PHONE..................212 649-3100
Joanna Saltz, *Editor*
Glenn Haygood, *Sales Mgr*
EMP: 50
SALES (corp-wide): 6.6B **Privately Held**
SIC: 2721 Magazines: publishing only, not printed on site
PA: The Hearst Corporation
300 W 57th St Fl 42
New York NY 10019
212 649-2000

(G-10063)
HEARST CORPORATION
Also Called: Oprah Magazine
224 W 57th St Frnt 1 (10019-3212)
PHONE..................212 903-5366
Amy Gross, *Principal*
Helen G Brown, *Principal*
Alicia Bridgewater, *Editor*
Lauren Crespo, *Research*
Mamie Healey, *Manager*
EMP: 35
SALES (corp-wide): 6.6B **Privately Held**
WEB: www.hearstcorp.com
SIC: 2721 Magazines: publishing only, not printed on site
PA: The Hearst Corporation
300 W 57th St Fl 42
New York NY 10019
212 649-2000

(G-10064)
HEARST CORPORATION
Also Called: Elle Magazine
1633 Broadway Fl 44 (10019-6708)
PHONE..................212 767-5800
Laurie Abraham, *Principal*
Diane Arlotta, *Prdtn Dir*
Anna Araman, *Adv Dir*
John Howley, *Manager*
Marianne Fiorito, *Director*
EMP: 300
SALES (corp-wide): 6.6B **Privately Held**
WEB: www.popphoto.com
SIC: 2721 Magazines: publishing only, not printed on site
PA: The Hearst Corporation
300 W 57th St Fl 42
New York NY 10019
212 649-2000

(G-10065)
HEARST CORPORATION
Also Called: Popular Mechanics
810 7th Ave (10019-5818)
PHONE..................516 382-4580
Sarah Deem, *Editor*
James Joyce, *Vice Pres*
Donna Lagani, *Vice Pres*
Greg Lindsay, *Vice Pres*
Kevin Malley, *Vice Pres*
EMP: 60
SALES (corp-wide): 6.6B **Privately Held**
WEB: www.hearstcorp.com
SIC: 2721 Magazines: publishing only, not printed on site
PA: The Hearst Corporation
300 W 57th St Fl 42
New York NY 10019
212 649-2000

(G-10066)
HEARST CORPORATION
Also Called: Esquire Magazine
300 W 57th St Fl 21 (10019-3741)
PHONE..................212 649-4271
Jack Essig, *Vice Pres*
EMP: 70
SALES (corp-wide): 6.6B **Privately Held**
SIC: 2721 Magazines: publishing only, not printed on site
PA: The Hearst Corporation
300 W 57th St Fl 42
New York NY 10019
212 649-2000

(G-10067)
HEARST CORPORATION
Also Called: Seventeen Magazine
1440 Broadway Fl 13 (10018-2301)
PHONE..................212 204-4300
Sabrina Weill, *Editor*
Howard Grier, *Associate*
EMP: 100
SALES (corp-wide): 6.6B **Privately Held**
WEB: www.hearstcorp.com
SIC: 2721 Magazines: publishing only, not printed on site
PA: The Hearst Corporation
300 W 57th St Fl 42
New York NY 10019
212 649-2000

(G-10068)
HEARST CORPORATION
Also Called: Harper's Bazaar
300 W 57th St Fl 42 (10019-3790)
PHONE..................212 903-5000
Jennifer Bruno, *Publisher*
Pamela Fiori, *Editor*
Victoria Pedersen, *Editor*
Robert Rufino, *Editor*
Liz Sgroi, *Editor*
EMP: 65
SALES (corp-wide): 6.6B **Privately Held**
WEB: www.hearstcorp.com
SIC: 2721 Magazines: publishing & printing
PA: The Hearst Corporation
300 W 57th St Fl 42
New York NY 10019
212 649-2000

(G-10069)
HEARST CORPORATION
Also Called: Country Living
300 W 57th St Fl 32 (10019-3741)
PHONE..................212 649-3204
Rachel Barrett, *Editor*
Nancy Soriano, *Manager*
EMP: 100
SALES (corp-wide): 6.6B **Privately Held**
WEB: www.hearstcorp.com
SIC: 2721 Magazines: publishing only, not printed on site
PA: The Hearst Corporation
300 W 57th St Fl 42
New York NY 10019
212 649-2000

(G-10070)
HEARST CORPORATION
Hearst Magazines International
300 W 57th St Fl 42 (10019-3790)
PHONE..................212 649-2275
Vicki Wellington, *Branch Mgr*
Alexander Karpodinis, *Technical Staff*
EMP: 50
SALES (corp-wide): 6.6B **Privately Held**
SIC: 2721 2731 2711 Magazines: publishing only, not printed on site; books: publishing only; newspapers, publishing & printing; newspapers: publishing only, not printed on site
PA: The Hearst Corporation
300 W 57th St Fl 42
New York NY 10019
212 649-2000

(G-10071)
HEARST DIGITAL STUDIOS INC
Also Called: Hearst Entertainment
300 W 57th St (10019-3741)
PHONE..................212 969-7552
Neeraj Khemlani, *Ch of Bd*
Kate Doherty, *Editor*
Mike Bachmann, *CFO*
EMP: 40
SQ FT: 2,500
SALES (est): 1.2MM **Privately Held**
SIC: 2741 7371 ; computer software development & applications

(G-10072)
HEARST HOLDINGS INC (HQ)
300 W 57th St (10019-3741)
PHONE..................212 649-2000
George R Hearst Jr, *Ch of Bd*
Cathleen P Black, *Senior VP*
John G Conomikes, *Senior VP*
George B Irish, *Senior VP*
Raymond E Joslin, *Senior VP*
▲ **EMP:** 10
SALES (est): 676MM
SALES (corp-wide): 6.6B **Privately Held**
SIC: 2721 4841 Magazines: publishing only, not printed on site; cable television services
PA: The Hearst Corporation
300 W 57th St Fl 42
New York NY 10019
212 649-2000

▲ = Import ▼ = Export
◆ = Import/Export

GEOGRAPHIC SECTION

New York - New York County (G-10097)

(G-10073)
HEART OF TEA
419 Lafayette St Fl 2f (10003-7033)
PHONE..................917 725-3164
Gerami Masoud, *CEO*
EMP: 10 EST: 2014
SALES (est): 1.1MM Privately Held
SIC: 2086 Iced tea & fruit drinks, bottled & canned

(G-10074)
HEARTS OF PALM LLC
Also Called: Ruby Road
1411 Broadway Fl 23 (10018-3471)
PHONE..................212 944-6660
Peter Aresty
EMP: 45 Privately Held
SIC: 2339 Women's & misses' athletic clothing & sportswear
PA: Hearts Of Palm, Llc
1411 Broadway Fl 25
New York NY 10018

(G-10075)
HEARTS OF PALM LLC (PA)
Also Called: Ruby Road
1411 Broadway Fl 25 (10018-3496)
PHONE..................212 944-6660
Raymond Barrick, *CFO*
Peter Aresty
EMP: 55
SQ FT: 25,000
SALES (est): 8.3MM Privately Held
SIC: 2339 Women's & misses' athletic clothing & sportswear

(G-10076)
HEAT USA II LLC
35 E 21st St (10010-6212)
PHONE..................212 564-4328
Mark Kohan, *Director*
EMP: 22
SALES (corp-wide): 3.4MM Privately Held
SIC: 2911 Oils, fuel
PA: Heat Usa Ii Llc
11902 23rd Ave
College Point NY 11356
212 254-4328

(G-10077)
HEED LLC
462 Fashion Ave Fl 5 (10018-7852)
PHONE..................646 708-7111
EMP: 25
SALES (est): 1.3MM Privately Held
SIC: 2741

(G-10078)
HELIUM MEDIA INC
Also Called: Heleo.com
165 Duane St Apt 7b (10013-3348)
PHONE..................917 596-4081
Rufus Griscom, *CEO*
EMP: 5
SALES (est): 173.7K Privately Held
SIC: 2741 Miscellaneous publishing

(G-10079)
HELVETICA PRESS INCORPORATED
Also Called: Vendome Press
244 5th Ave (10001-7604)
PHONE..................212 737-1857
Mark Magowan, *President*
Alexis Gregory, *Chairman*
▲ EMP: 5
SQ FT: 3,000
SALES: 31.4K Privately Held
WEB: www.vendomepress.com
SIC: 2741 Miscellaneous publishing

(G-10080)
HENRY DUNAY DESIGNS INC
10 W 46th St Ste 1200 (10036-9312)
PHONE..................212 768-9700
Henry Dunay, *President*
EMP: 30
SQ FT: 6,000
SALES (est): 3.8MM Privately Held
WEB: www.henrydunay.com
SIC: 3911 5944 Jewelry, precious metal; jewelry stores

(G-10081)
HENRY HOLT AND COMPANY LLC
Also Called: Owl Books Div
175 5th Ave Ste 400 (10010-7726)
PHONE..................646 307-5095
Sara Bershtel, *Publisher*
Gillian Blake, *Editor*
Barbara Jones, *Editor*
Rachel Murray, *Editor*
Maggie Richards, *Vice Pres*
▲ EMP: 80
SQ FT: 30,000
SALES (est): 15.9MM
SALES (corp-wide): 1.7B Privately Held
WEB: www.henryholt.com
SIC: 2731 Books: publishing only
HQ: Macmillan Holdings, Llc
175 5th Ave
New York NY 10010

(G-10082)
HERALD PUBLISHING COMPANY LLC
4 Times Sq Fl 23 (10036-6518)
PHONE..................315 470-2022
EMP: 6 EST: 2013
SALES (est): 281.8K Privately Held
SIC: 2711 Newspapers, publishing & printing

(G-10083)
HERMAN KAY COMPANY LTD
Also Called: Michael Kors
463 7th Ave Fl 12 (10018-7499)
PHONE..................212 239-2025
Richard Kringstein, *Ch of Bd*
Barry Kringstein, *President*
▼ EMP: 250 EST: 2009
SALES (est): 18.5MM
SALES (corp-wide): 183.5MM Privately Held
SIC: 2337 2339 2329 Women's & misses' suits & coats; women's & misses' outerwear; men's & boys' leather, wool & down-filled outerwear
PA: Mystic Inc.
463 7th Ave Fl 12
New York NY 10018
212 239-2025

(G-10084)
HERSHEL HOROWITZ CORP
50 W 47th St Ste 2011 (10036-8687)
PHONE..................212 719-1710
Leibish Horowitz, *President*
Rachel Horowitz, *Treasurer*
Chaya Dachner, *Admin Sec*
EMP: 7
SQ FT: 1,300
SALES (est): 2.3MM Privately Held
SIC: 3915 Diamond cutting & polishing

(G-10085)
HESS CORPORATION (PA)
1185 Ave Of The Amer (10036-2601)
PHONE..................212 997-8500
John B Hess, *CEO*
James H Quigley, *Ch of Bd*
Steve Hendel, *Managing Dir*
Gregory P Hill, *COO*
Timothy B Goodell, *Senior VP*
EMP: 254 EST: 1920
SALES: 5.4B Publicly Held
WEB: www.hess.com
SIC: 1311 2911 5171 5541 Crude petroleum production; natural gas production; petroleum bulk stations; petroleum terminals; filling stations, gasoline; transmission, electric power

(G-10086)
HESS ENERGY EXPLORATION LTD (HQ)
1185 Ave Of The Americas (10036-2601)
PHONE..................732 750-6500
Kevin B Wilcox, *Vice Pres*
Timothy B Goodell, *Vice Pres*
John P Reilly, *Vice Pres*
EMP: 3
SALES (est): 2MM
SALES (corp-wide): 5.4B Publicly Held
SIC: 1382 1311 Oil & gas exploration services; crude petroleum & natural gas production
PA: Hess Corporation
1185 Ave Of The Amer
New York NY 10036
212 997-8500

(G-10087)
HESS EXPLRTION PROD HLDNGS LTD (DH)
1185 Ave Of The Americas (10036-2601)
PHONE..................732 750-6000
John P Rielly, *Vice Pres*
Kevin B Wilcox, *Vice Pres*
EMP: 3
SALES (est): 1.2MM
SALES (corp-wide): 5.4B Publicly Held
SIC: 1382 1311 Oil & gas exploration services; crude petroleum & natural gas production
HQ: Hess Energy Exploration Limited
1185 Ave Of The Americas
New York NY 10036
732 750-6500

(G-10088)
HESS OIL VIRGIN ISLAND CORP
1185 Ave Of The Amer 39 (10036-2603)
PHONE..................212 997-8500
John Hess, *Ch of Bd*
Walt Davenport, *Engineer*
Roy Chisum, *Manager*
Kahlid Mahmood, *Manager*
Doug Cohan, *Officer*
EMP: 3000
SALES (est): 228.8MM
SALES (corp-wide): 5.4B Publicly Held
WEB: www.hess.com
SIC: 2911 Petroleum refining
PA: Hess Corporation
1185 Ave Of The Amer
New York NY 10036
212 997-8500

(G-10089)
HESS PIPELINE CORPORATION
1185 Ave Of The Amer 39 (10036-2603)
PHONE..................212 997-8500
John Hess, *CEO*
Timothy B Goodell, *Principal*
EMP: 197
SALES (est): 22.5MM
SALES (corp-wide): 5.4B Publicly Held
WEB: www.hess.com
SIC: 1311 2911 Crude petroleum production; natural gas production; petroleum refining
PA: Hess Corporation
1185 Ave Of The Amer
New York NY 10036
212 997-8500

(G-10090)
HF MFG CORP (PA)
Also Called: Happy Fella
1460 Broadway (10036-7329)
P.O. Box 318, Hewlett (11557-0318)
PHONE..................212 594-9142
Bruce Tucker, *President*
Michael Tucker, *Vice Pres*
◆ EMP: 60 EST: 1963
SQ FT: 2,000
SALES (est): 6.2MM Privately Held
WEB: www.hfmfgcorp.com
SIC: 2329 Men's & boys' sportswear & athletic clothing

(G-10091)
HFC PRESTIGE INTL US LLC
350 5th Ave (10118-0110)
PHONE..................212 389-7800
Patrice De Talhouet, *President*
Kevin Monaco
Michelle Garcia, *Asst Sec*
EMP: 3000 EST: 2015
SALES: 30MM Publicly Held
SIC: 2844 2676 3421 2842 Toilet preparations, towels, napkins & tissue paper products; razor blades & razors; specialty cleaning preparations; soap: granulated, liquid, cake, flaked or chip
PA: Coty Inc.
350 5th Ave Ste 2700
New York NY 10118

(G-10092)
HH LIQUIDATING CORP
Also Called: Zinc Corporation America Div
110 E 59th St Fl 34 (10022-1308)
PHONE..................646 282-2500
William E Flaherty, *Ch of Bd*
Robert D Scherich, *Vice Pres*
Louis Martin, *Technician*
EMP: 843
SALES (est): 86MM Privately Held
SIC: 3624 2999 3356 3339 Carbon & graphite products; electrodes, thermal & electrolytic uses: carbon, graphite; carbon specialties for electrical use; coke, calcined petroleum: made from purchased materials; coke (not from refineries), petroleum; lead & zinc; zinc refining (primary), including slabs & dust

(G-10093)
HHS PHARMACEUTICALS INC
107 Hamilton Pl (10031-6821)
PHONE..................347 674-1670
Richard Moreno, *CEO*
Wendy Chin, *COO*
EMP: 10
SALES (est): 409.5K Privately Held
SIC: 2899 2834 7389 Gelatin: edible, technical, photographic or pharmaceutical; lozenges, pharmaceutical; tinctures, pharmaceutical;

(G-10094)
HIGH POINT DESIGN LLC
1411 Broadway Fl 8 (10018-3565)
PHONE..................212 354-2400
Mark Lopiparo, *CFO*
Daniel Chrem, *Sales Staff*
▲ EMP: 15
SQ FT: 20,000
SALES (est): 1.9MM Privately Held
SIC: 2252 Hosiery

(G-10095)
HIGH QUALITY VIDEO INC (PA)
12 W 27th St Fl 7 (10001-6903)
PHONE..................212 686-9534
Hirofumy Imoto, *President*
EMP: 10
SALES (est): 1.1MM Privately Held
SIC: 3652 Pre-recorded records & tapes

(G-10096)
HIGHCREST INVESTORS LLC (HQ)
445 Hamilton Ave Ste 1210 (10153)
PHONE..................212 702-4323
Carl C Icahn, *Ch of Bd*
EMP: 80
SQ FT: 25,000
SALES (est): 219.6MM
SALES (corp-wide): 955MM Privately Held
SIC: 3743 4741 4789 4813 Freight cars & equipment; rental of railroad cars; railroad car repair; local telephone communications; long distance telephone communications;
PA: Starfire Holding Corporation
767 5th Ave Fl 47
New York NY 10153
914 614-7000

(G-10097)
HIGHLINE MEDIA LLC
375 Park Ave (10152-3804)
PHONE..................859 692-2100
Andrew Goodenough, *President*
Thomas Flynn, *CFO*
EMP: 250
SALES (est): 7.4MM Privately Held
WEB: www.highlinemedia.com
SIC: 2731 2711 2721 2741 Books: publishing only; pamphlets: publishing only, not printed on site; newspapers: publishing only, not printed on site; periodicals: publishing only; directories: publishing only, not printed on site
PA: Summit Business Media Holding Company
4157 Olympic Blvd Ste 225
Erlanger KY 41018

(G-10098)
HIGHSIDE INC
531 W 143rd St Apt 3c (10031-6028)
PHONE...........................917 525-3340
Brendan Diaz, *CEO*
Andy Johnson, *Production*
Jonathan Warren, *Chief Engr*
EMP: 10 **EST:** 2015
SALES (est): 94.6K **Privately Held**
SIC: 7372 7389 Business oriented computer software;

(G-10099)
HILLARY MERCHANT INC
2 Wall St Ste 807 (10005-2001)
PHONE...........................646 575-9242
Zhaoxiong Zhang, *President*
EMP: 8 **EST:** 2012
SQ FT: 500
SALES: 1MM **Privately Held**
SIC: 2326 5621 Men's & boys' work clothing; ready-to-wear apparel, women's

(G-10100)
HILLS PET PRODUCTS INC (DH)
300 Park Ave (10022-7402)
PHONE...........................212 310-2000
N Thompson, *Principal*
EMP: 7
SALES (est): 5.8MM
SALES (corp-wide): 15.4B **Publicly Held**
SIC: 2047 Dog & cat food
HQ: Hill's Pet Nutrition, Inc.
  400 Sw 8th Ave Ste 101
  Topeka KS 66603
  800 255-0449

(G-10101)
HIMATSINGKA AMERICA INC (DH)
261 5th Ave Rm 1400 (10016-7707)
PHONE...........................212 824-2949
David Greenstein, *CEO*
Steve Zaffos, *President*
Ashutosh Halbe, *CFO*
Tricia Burgess, *Human Res Dir*
Simon Fennell, *Marketing Staff*
▲ **EMP:** 24 **EST:** 1998
SQ FT: 10,600
SALES (est): 53.1MM
SALES (corp-wide): 228.4MM **Privately Held**
WEB: www.dwholdings.com
SIC: 2392 Bedspreads & bed sets: made from purchased materials

(G-10102)
HIMATSINGKA AMERICA INC
Also Called: Global Textile
261 5th Ave Rm 501 (10016-0036)
PHONE...........................212 252-0802
EMP: 22
SALES (corp-wide): 228.4MM **Privately Held**
WEB: www.divatex.com
SIC: 2221 Silk broadwoven fabrics
HQ: Himatsingka America Inc.
  261 5th Ave Rm 1400
  New York NY 10016
  212 824-2949

(G-10103)
HINGE INC
137 5th Ave Fl 5 (10010-7145)
PHONE...........................502 445-3111
Justin McLeod, *President*
Tim Macgougan, *Manager*
Sam Levy, *Director*
Jean-Marie McGrath, *Administration*
EMP: 14
SALES (est): 1.1MM
SALES (corp-wide): 3.3B **Publicly Held**
SIC: 7372 Prepackaged software
HQ: The Match Group Inc
  8750 N Cntl Expy Ste 1400
  Dallas TX 75231
  214 576-9352

(G-10104)
HIPPOCRENE BOOKS INC (PA)
171 Madison Ave Rm 1605 (10016-5113)
PHONE...........................212 685-4371
George Blagowidow, *President*
▲ **EMP:** 6
SQ FT: 1,200
SALES (est): 908.5K **Privately Held**
WEB: www.hippocrenebooks.com
SIC: 2731 Textbooks: publishing only, not printed on site

(G-10105)
HIS PRODUCTIONS USA INC
Also Called: Kingstreet Sounds
15 Broad St Apt 3030 (10005-1992)
PHONE...........................212 594-3737
Hisanao Ishioka, *President*
EMP: 7
SALES (est): 1.1MM **Privately Held**
WEB: www.kingstreetsounds.com
SIC: 3652 5084 Pre-recorded records & tapes; recording instruments & accessories

(G-10106)
HISTORIC TW INC (DH)
75 Rockefeller Plz (10019-6908)
PHONE...........................212 484-8000
RE Turner, *Vice Ch Bd*
Richard D Parsons, *President*
Christopher P Bogart, *Exec VP*
Carl F Dill Jr, *Vice Pres*
Joseph Ripp, *CFO*
▲ **EMP:** 38
SQ FT: 451,000
SALES (est): 2.7B
SALES (corp-wide): 160.5B **Publicly Held**
SIC: 3652 6794 2741 7812 Compact laser discs, prerecorded; magnetic tape (audio): prerecorded; music licensing to radio stations; performance rights, publishing & licensing; music royalties, sheet & record; music, sheet: publishing only, not printed on site; music books: publishing only, not printed on site; motion picture production & distribution; television film production; motion picture production & distribution, television; video tape production; cable television services; magazines: publishing only, not printed on site

(G-10107)
HJN INC (PA)
Also Called: Bentones Enterprises
16 W 46th St Fl 9 (10036-4503)
PHONE...........................212 398-9564
Joel Namdar, *Ch of Bd*
I Raj, *President*
Benny Namdar, *Vice Pres*
Effy Namdar, *Vice Pres*
H J Namdar, *Vice Pres*
▲ **EMP:** 15
SALES (est): 2.1MM **Privately Held**
SIC: 3911 Rings, finger: precious metal

(G-10108)
HK METAL TRADING LTD
450 Fashion Ave Ste 2300 (10123-2300)
PHONE...........................212 868-3333
Kenny Chen, *Partner*
▼ **EMP:** 6
SQ FT: 350
SALES: 3MM **Privately Held**
SIC: 3399 Metal powders, pastes & flakes

(G-10109)
HKS PRINTING COMPANY INC
Also Called: Official Press, The
115 E 27th St (10016-8945)
PHONE...........................212 675-2529
Inhyung You, *President*
Sue You, *Corp Secy*
EMP: 10
SALES (est): 940K **Privately Held**
SIC: 2752 2791 Lithographing on metal; typesetting

(G-10110)
HNI CORPORATION
200 Lexington Ave Rm 1112 (10016-6219)
PHONE...........................212 683-2232
Tom Talon, *President*
EMP: 226
SALES (corp-wide): 2.1B **Publicly Held**
WEB: www.honi.com
SIC: 2521 Wood office furniture
PA: Hni Corporation
  600 E 2nd St
  Muscatine IA 52761
  563 272-7400

(G-10111)
HOFFMANN-LA ROCHE INC
430 E 29th St (10016-8367)
PHONE...........................973 890-2291
Eileen Kelly, *Branch Mgr*
EMP: 6
SALES (corp-wide): 53.9B **Privately Held**
SIC: 2834 Pharmaceutical preparations
HQ: Hoffmann-La Roche Inc.
  150 Clove Rd Ste 88th
  Little Falls NJ 07424
  973 890-2268

(G-10112)
HOGAN FLAVORS & FRAGRANCES
Also Called: Hogan Fragrances International
130 E 18th St Frnt (10003-2416)
PHONE...........................212 598-4310
Ray Hogan, *Ch of Bd*
Cory Warner, *Vice Pres*
Sean Hogan, *VP Sales*
EMP: 35
SQ FT: 3,000
SALES (est): 4.3MM **Privately Held**
WEB: www.hoganff.com
SIC: 2844 Perfumes & colognes

(G-10113)
HOLBROOKE INC
Also Called: Holbrooke By Sberry
444 E 20th St Apt 1b (10009-8142)
PHONE...........................646 397-4674
EMP: 5
SALES (est): 309.8K **Privately Held**
SIC: 3961 Costume jewelry

(G-10114)
HOLDENS SCREEN SUPPLY CORP
121 Varick St (10013-1408)
PHONE...........................212 627-2727
Arthur I Gononsky, *President*
EMP: 7
SALES (est): 319.8K **Privately Held**
SIC: 2711 Commercial printing & newspaper publishing combined

(G-10115)
HOLLAND & SHERRY INC (PA)
Also Called: Holland & Sherry Intr Design
330 E 59th St Ph (10022-1537)
PHONE...........................212 542-8410
Sergio Casalena, *Ch of Bd*
Bryan Dicker, *President*
Daniel Waldron, *Vice Pres*
Helen Shannon, *Opers Staff*
Ashley Walker, *Purchasing*
▲ **EMP:** 29
SQ FT: 4,700
SALES (est): 18.9MM **Privately Held**
WEB: www.hollandandsherry.com
SIC: 2395 7389 2519 5021 Embroidery & art needlework; design services; garden furniture, except wood, metal, stone or concrete; furniture

(G-10116)
HOLLANDER HM FSHONS HLDNGS LLC
440 Park Ave S Fl 10 (10016-8012)
PHONE...........................212 575-0400
Jeff Hollander, *President*
EMP: 10
SALES (corp-wide): 197.2MM **Privately Held**
WEB: www.hollander.com
SIC: 2392 Pillows, bed: made from purchased materials
PA: Hollander Home Fashions Holdings, Llc
  6501 Congress Ave Ste 300
  Boca Raton FL 33487
  212 302-6571

(G-10117)
HOLLANDER SLEEP PRODUCTS LLC
440 Park Ave S (10016-8012)
PHONE...........................212 575-0400
Donald Kelly, *Branch Mgr*
EMP: 79
SALES (corp-wide): 943.4MM **Privately Held**
SIC: 2392 Cushions & pillows
PA: Hollander Sleep Products, Llc
  6501 Congress Ave Ste 300
  Boca Raton FL 33487
  561 997-6900

(G-10118)
HOLMES GROUP THE INC
271 W 47th St Apt 23a (10036-1447)
PHONE...........................212 333-2300
Paul Holmes, *President*
Greg Druey, *President*
EMP: 6
SALES (est): 610.8K **Privately Held**
WEB: www.holmesreport.com
SIC: 2741 8748 Miscellaneous publishing; business consulting

(G-10119)
HOME FASHIONS INTL LLC (PA)
295 5th Ave Ste 1520 (10016-7126)
PHONE...........................212 689-3579
Tom Goldstein, *Controller*
David LI, *Mng Member*
▲ **EMP:** 39
SQ FT: 3,600
SALES (corp-wide): 19MM **Privately Held**
SIC: 2392 Pillows, bed: made from purchased materials

(G-10120)
HOME FASHIONS INTL LLC
Also Called: Hfi
295 5th Ave Ste 1520 (10016-7126)
PHONE...........................212 684-0091
Tom Goldstein, *Controller*
EMP: 15
SALES (corp-wide): 19MM **Privately Held**
SIC: 2392 Pillows, bed: made from purchased materials
PA: Home Fashions International, Llc
  295 5th Ave Ste 1520
  New York NY 10016
  212 689-3579

(G-10121)
HOOEK PRODUKTION INC
147 W 26th St Fl 6 (10001-6817)
PHONE...........................212 367-9111
Joseph Primiano, *President*
Lew Cohen, *Sales Staff*
▲ **EMP:** 7
SQ FT: 2,000
SALES (est): 1.1MM **Privately Held**
SIC: 2752 Commercial printing, lithographic

(G-10122)
HOPE INTERNATIONAL PRODUCTIONS
315 W 57th St Apt 6h (10019-3145)
P.O. Box 237078 (10023-0029)
PHONE...........................212 247-3188
David King, *Ch of Bd*
Hope King, *President*
EMP: 18
SQ FT: 1,800
SALES (est): 1.3MM **Privately Held**
SIC: 3652 3651 5099 1531 Phonograph records, prerecorded; magnetic tape (audio): prerecorded; video cassette recorders/players & accessories; phonograph records; tapes & cassettes, prerecorded; video cassettes, accessories & supplies; operative builders

(G-10123)
HORIZON FLOORS I LLC
11 Broadway Lbby 5 (10004-1330)
PHONE...........................212 509-9686
Alex Shaoulpour, *President*
EMP: 1
SALES (est): 4MM **Privately Held**
SIC: 2426 Hardwood dimension & flooring mills

(G-10124)
HORO CREATIONS LLC
Also Called: Designs By Hc
71 W 47th St Ste 404 (10036-2865)
PHONE...........................212 719-4818
Suresh Krishnani, *President*
Vinay Krishnani,
EMP: 6
SALES (est): 618.8K **Privately Held**
SIC: 3911 Jewelry, precious metal

GEOGRAPHIC SECTION

(G-10125)
HOSEL & ACKERSON INC (PA)
570 Fashion Ave Rm 805 (10018-1603)
PHONE.....................212 575-1490
Monte Braverman, *President*
EMP: 8 **EST:** 1944
SALES (est): 553.2K **Privately Held**
SIC: 2258 2395 2269 Lace, knit; embroidery products, except schiffli machine; finishing plants

(G-10126)
HOSPITALITY GRAPHIC SYSTEMS
500 10th Ave (10018-1180)
PHONE.....................212 563-9334
Joyce Healy, *CFO*
Akshay Kulkarni, *Info Tech Mgr*
Richard M Seider, *Director*
EMP: 11
SALES (est): 1.1MM **Privately Held**
SIC: 3993 Mfg Signs/Advertising Specialties

(G-10127)
HOSPITALITY GRAPHICS INC
545 8th Ave Rm 401 (10018-4341)
PHONE.....................212 643-6700
Louis Melito, *President*
Marshall Silverman, *Treasurer*
EMP: 9
SQ FT: 3,500
SALES (est): 1.5MM **Privately Held**
WEB: www.hg!nyc.com
SIC: 2752 Commercial printing, offset

(G-10128)
HOSPITALITY INC
247 W 35th St 4 (10001-1908)
PHONE.....................212 268-1930
Howard Pitler, *President*
EMP: 22
SALES (est): 1.1MM **Privately Held**
SIC: 2759 6513 Commercial printing; apartment building operators

(G-10129)
HOT KISS INC
1407 Brdwy Ste 2000 (10018)
PHONE.....................212 730-0404
Moshe Tsabag, *President*
EMP: 6
SALES (est): 551.8K **Privately Held**
SIC: 2325 Jeans: men's, youths' & boys'

(G-10130)
HOT SOX COMPANY INCORPORATED (PA)
Also Called: Polo Ralph Lauren Hosiery Div
95 Madison Ave Fl 15 (10016-7801)
PHONE.....................212 957-2000
Gary Wolkowitz, *President*
Mark Gordon, *Senior VP*
Sarah Wolkowitz, *Treasurer*
Josephine Cordero, *Controller*
Eugene Merkushen, *Info Tech Dir*
▼ **EMP:** 40
SQ FT: 18,000
SALES (est): 6.4MM **Privately Held**
SIC: 2252 2251 Men's, boys' & girls' hosiery; women's hosiery, except socks

(G-10131)
HOUGHTON MIFFLIN HARCOURT PUBG
Also Called: Houghton Mifflin Clarion Books
3 Park Ave Fl 18 (10016-5902)
PHONE.....................212 420-5800
Ann Healy, *Manager*
EMP: 40
SALES (corp-wide): 1.4B **Publicly Held**
WEB: www.hmco.com
SIC: 2731 Textbooks: publishing only, not printed on site
HQ: Houghton Mifflin Harcourt Publishing Company
125 High St Ste 900
Boston MA 02110
617 351-5000

(G-10132)
HOULES USA INC
979 3rd Ave Ste 1200 (10022-1234)
PHONE.....................212 935-3900
Philippe Dasilva, *Manager*
EMP: 5
SALES (corp-wide): 1.3MM **Privately Held**
WEB: www.houlesusa.com
SIC: 3911 Trimmings for canes, umbrellas, etc.: precious metal
HQ: Houles Usa Inc
8687 Melrose Ave Ste B617
West Hollywood CA 90069
310 652-6171

(G-10133)
HOUND & GATOS PET FOODS CORP
14 Wa'l St Fl 20 (10005-2123)
P.O. Box 11750, Atlanta GA (30355-1750)
PHONE.....................212 618-1917
Will Post, *President*
EMP: 8
SQ FT: 25,000
SALES: 1.4MM **Privately Held**
WEB: www.houndgatos.com
SIC: 2047 Dog & cat food

(G-10134)
HOURGLASS INTERACTIVE LLC
1 Union Sq S Apt 20j (10003-4192)
PHONE.....................954 254-2853
David Scott, *Mng Member*
EMP: 12 **EST:** 2016
SALES: 150K **Privately Held**
SIC: 7372 7389 Prepackaged software;

(G-10135)
HOUSE OF HEYDENRYK JR INC
Also Called: House of Heydenryk The
601 W 26th St Rm 305 (10001-1159)
PHONE.....................212 206-9611
Charles Schreiber, *President*
David Mandel, *Chairman*
Rigmor Heydenryk, *Admin Sec*
EMP: 18 **EST:** 1935
SQ FT: 5,000
SALES (est): 2.2MM **Privately Held**
WEB: www.heydenryk.com
SIC: 2499 Picture & mirror frames, wood

(G-10136)
HOUSE OF PORTFOLIOS CO INC (PA)
37 W 26th St Rm 305 (10010-1047)
PHONE.....................212 206-7323
Thomas Lombardo, *President*
EMP: 22
SQ FT: 900
SALES (est): 2.8MM **Privately Held**
WEB: www.houseofportfolios.com
SIC: 3172 5948 Personal leather goods; leather goods, except luggage & shoes

(G-10137)
HOUSE OF PORTFOLIOS CO INC
48 W 21st St (10010-6907)
PHONE.....................212 206-7323
Thomas Lombardo, *Branch Mgr*
EMP: 17 **Privately Held**
WEB: www.houseofportfolios.com
SIC: 3172 Personal leather goods
PA: The House Of Portfolios Co Inc
37 W 26th St Rm 305
New York NY 10010

(G-10138)
HOUSE PEARL FASHIONS (US) LTD
1410 Broadway Rm 1501 (10018-9834)
PHONE.....................212 840-3183
Mehesh Seth, *President*
EMP: 10
SQ FT: 4,000 **Privately Held**
SIC: 2329 2339 Coats (oiled fabric, leatherette, etc.): men's & boys'; women's & misses' outerwear; women's & misses' accessories
PA: House Of Pearl Fashions (Us) Ltd.
300-2 D&E Rr 17
Lodi NJ 07644

(G-10139)
HOVEE INC
722 Saint Nicholas Ave (10031-4002)
PHONE.....................646 249-6200
Paul Kogan, *CEO*
EMP: 10

SALES (est): 593.6K **Privately Held**
SIC: 7372 7389 Business oriented computer software;

(G-10140)
HP INC
556 W 22nd St Fl 8 (10011-1108)
PHONE.....................650 857-1501
Kris Gordon, *Vice Pres*
Kevin Romero, *Engineer*
Steven Flanagan, *Finance*
Esther Balestrieri, *Marketing Staff*
Rafael Solano, *Marketing Staff*
EMP: 10
SALES (corp-wide): 52B **Publicly Held**
SIC: 3571 Personal computers (microcomputers)
PA: Hp Inc.
1501 Page Mill Rd
Palo Alto CA 94304
650 857-1501

(G-10141)
HS HOMEWORX LLC
18 E 74th St Fl 5 (10021-2612)
PHONE.....................646 870-0406
Yvonne Franco, *Controller*
Harry Slatkin, *Mng Member*
EMP: 5
SALES (est): 355.8K **Privately Held**
SIC: 3999 7389 Candles;

(G-10142)
HUDSON ENVELOPE CORPORATION (PA)
Also Called: Jam Paper
135 3rd Ave (10003-2543)
PHONE.....................212 473-6666
Michael Jacobs, *President*
Steve Levine, *Marketing Mgr*
▲ **EMP:** 25
SQ FT: 7,000
SALES (est): 4.4MM **Privately Held**
SIC: 2752 2759 Commercial printing, offset; envelopes: printing

(G-10143)
HUDSON NEWS INC
250 Greenwich St (10007-2140)
PHONE.....................212 971-6800
EMP: 6 **EST:** 2011
SALES (est): 233K **Privately Held**
SIC: 2711 Newspapers, publishing & printing

(G-10144)
HUDSON PARK PRESS INC
232 Madison Ave Rm 1400 (10016-2918)
P.O. Box 774, Pine Plains (12567-0774)
PHONE.....................212 929-8898
Gilman Park, *Ch of Bd*
▲ **EMP:** 5
SALES (est): 398.4K **Privately Held**
SIC: 2752 2731 Publication printing, lithographic; books: publishing only

(G-10145)
HUDSON PRINTING CO INC
747 3rd Ave Lbby 3 (10017-2810)
PHONE.....................718 937-8600
Robert Bergman, *President*
Alan Bergman, *Admin Sec*
EMP: 25 **EST:** 1923
SQ FT: 33,000
SALES (est): 3.1MM **Privately Held**
WEB: www.hudsonprints.com
SIC: 2752 2789 Commercial printing, offset; bookbinding & related work

(G-10146)
HUGO BOSS USA INC (HQ)
55 Water St Fl 48 (10041-3204)
PHONE.....................212 940-0600
Andre Maeder, *CEO*
Anthony Lucia, *President*
Gretchen Ruoillard, *President*
Mark Brashear, *Managing Dir*
JD Perez, *Area Mgr*
◆ **EMP:** 75
SQ FT: 100,000

SALES (est): 293.9MM
SALES (corp-wide): 3.2B **Privately Held**
WEB: www.hugoboss.com
SIC: 2311 2325 2337 5136 Men's & boys' suits & coats; men's & boys' trousers & slacks; men's & misses' suits & coats; suits: women's, misses' & juniors'; skirts, separate: women's, misses' & juniors'; jackets & vests, except fur & leather: women's; men's & boys' suits & trousers; men's & boys' sportswear & work clothing; men's & boys' outerwear; men's & boys' clothing stores; franchises, selling or licensing
PA: Hugo Boss Ag
Dieselstr. 12
Metzingen 72555
712 394-0

(G-10147)
HUMAN CONDITION SAFETY INC
61 Broadway Fl 31 (10006-2803)
PHONE.....................646 867-0644
Alexander R Baugh, *Ch of Bd*
Greg Wolyniec, *President*
Robert Price, *CFO*
Gary Foreman, *CTO*
Adam Bellin, *Director*
EMP: 10
SALES (est): 1.7MM **Privately Held**
SIC: 7372 5099 Prepackaged software; safety equipment & supplies

(G-10148)
HUMAN LIFE FOUNDATION INC
271 Madison Ave Ste 1005 (10016-1006)
PHONE.....................212 685-5210
Maria McFadden, *President*
Faith McFadden, *Vice Pres*
Ann Conlon, *Admin Sec*
EMP: 5 **EST:** 1974
SQ FT: 500
SALES: 658.4K **Privately Held**
WEB: www.humanlifereview.com
SIC: 2721 8399 8733 Periodicals: publishing only; social service information exchange; noncommercial research organizations

(G-10149)
HUMANA PRESS INC
233 Spring St Fl 6 (10013-1522)
PHONE.....................212 460-1500
Thomas Lanigan Jr, *President*
Julia Lanigan, *Vice Pres*
▲ **EMP:** 40
SQ FT: 8,500
SALES (est): 2.1MM
SALES (corp-wide): 1.7B **Privately Held**
WEB: www.humanapr.com
SIC: 2741 2731 2721 Technical papers: publishing only, not printed on site; book clubs: publishing only, not printed on site; trade journals: publishing only, not printed on site
HQ: Springer Science + Business Media, Llc
233 Spring St Fl 6
New York NY 10013
212 460-1500

(G-10150)
HUMANSCALE CORPORATION (PA)
1114 Ave Of Americas 15 (10036)
PHONE.....................212 725-4749
Robert King, *CEO*
Heather Fennimore, *President*
Paul Levy, *President*
Steve McManama, *District Mgr*
Sean Resch, *District Mgr*
◆ **EMP:** 32
SQ FT: 10,000
SALES (est): 132.7MM **Privately Held**
SIC: 3577 2521 Computer peripheral equipment; wood office furniture

(G-10151)
HUMOR RAINBOW INC
Also Called: Okcupid
555 W 18th St (10011-2822)
PHONE.....................646 402-9113
Michael Maxim, *President*
EMP: 43

New York - New York County (G-10152)   GEOGRAPHIC SECTION

SALES (est): 2MM
SALES (corp-wide): 3.3B **Publicly Held**
SIC: 2741 Miscellaneous publishing
PA: Iac/Interactivecorp
 555 W 18th St
 New York NY 10011
 212 314-7300

(G-10152)
HUNTER DOUGLAS INC
979 3rd Ave (10022-1234)
PHONE...........................212 588-0564
 David Shmil, *Branch Mgr*
EMP: 191 **Privately Held**
SIC: 2591 Window blinds
HQ: Hunter Douglas Inc.
 1 Blue Hill Plz Ste 1569
 Pearl River NY 10965
 845 664-7000

(G-10153)
HW HOLDINGS INC (DH)
718 5th Ave (10019-4102)
PHONE...........................212 399-1000
 Nayla Hayek, *CEO*
EMP: 4
SALES (est): 59.9MM
SALES (corp-wide): 8B **Privately Held**
SIC: 3911 5944 6719 Jewelry, precious metal; jewelry, precious stones & precious metals; watches; investment holding companies, except banks
HQ: The Swatch Group Far East Distribution Ltd
 Seevorstadt 6
 Biel-Bienne BE 2502
 323 436-811

(G-10154)
HYDROGEN TECHNOLOGY CORP
915 Broadway Ste 801 (10010-7139)
PHONE...........................800 315-9554
 Matthew Kane, *Vice Pres*
EMP: 27 **EST:** 2017
SALES: 3MM **Privately Held**
SIC: 7372 Application computer software

(G-10155)
HYPERLAW INC
17 W 70th St Apt 4 (10023-4544)
PHONE...........................212 873-6982
 Alan D Sugarman, *President*
EMP: 10
SALES (est): 830K **Privately Held**
WEB: www.hyperlaw.com
SIC: 7372 Publishers' computer software

(G-10156)
HYPOXICO INC
50 Lexington Ave Ste 249 (10010-2935)
PHONE...........................212 972-1009
 Gary Kotliar, *President*
 Yulia Soukhanova, *Vice Pres*
 Brian Oe Strike, *Vice Pres*
 Brian Bilius, *Manager*
 Matt Formato, *Director*
 ▲ **EMP:** 6
SQ FT: 3,000
SALES (est): 500K **Privately Held**
WEB: www.hypoxico.com
SIC: 3949 Exercise equipment

(G-10157)
HYS LLC (HQ)
Also Called: Hudsonyards Studios LLC
80 Broad St (10004-2209)
PHONE...........................212 716-6600
 Diane Romano, *President*
EMP: 10 **EST:** 2014
SALES (est): 1MM
SALES (corp-wide): 3.6B **Publicly Held**
SIC: 2732 Book printing
PA: Lsc Communications, Inc.
 191 N Wacker Dr Ste 1400
 Chicago IL 60606
 773 272-9200

(G-10158)
I LOVE ACCESSORIES INC
10 W 33rd St Rm 210 (10001-3326)
PHONE...........................212 239-1875
 Daren Malles, *President*
 ▲ **EMP:** 5
SQ FT: 1,200
SALES: 5MM **Privately Held**
SIC: 3961 Costume jewelry

(G-10159)
I N K T INC
250 W 54th St Fl 9 (10019-5515)
PHONE...........................212 957-2700
 Gary Winnick, *CEO*
 Scott Jacobson, *COO*
 Ed Ickowski, *Senior VP*
 Jim Vickers, *Senior VP*
 Saurabh Suri, *Vice Pres*
 ▲ **EMP:** 10
SALES (est): 1.6MM **Privately Held**
WEB: www.t-ink.com
SIC: 2759 5085 Commercial printing; ink, printers'

(G-10160)
I S C A CORP (PA)
Also Called: Elliot Lauren
512 7th Ave Fl 7 (10018-0862)
PHONE...........................212 719-5123
 Elliot Grosovsky, *Ch of Bd*
 ▲ **EMP:** 16
SQ FT: 4,200
SALES (est): 4.7MM **Privately Held**
SIC: 2335 Women's, juniors' & misses' dresses

(G-10161)
I SHALOM & CO INC
411 5th Ave Fl 4 (10016-2272)
PHONE...........................212 532-7911
 Isaac Shalom, *Ch of Bd*
 Albert Bhojwani, *Traffic Mgr*
 A Koven, *Traffic Mgr*
 Valerie Shalom, *Treasurer*
 Edward Kurzawa, *Controller*
EMP: 150 **EST:** 1919
SQ FT: 9,000
SALES (est): 20.4K **Privately Held**
SIC: 2389 2339 Men's miscellaneous accessories; women's & misses' accessories

(G-10162)
I SPIEWAK & SONS INC
225 W 37th St Fl 15l (10018-6667)
PHONE...........................212 695-1620
 Roy J Spiewak, *Ch of Bd*
 ▲ **EMP:** 35 **EST:** 1904
SQ FT: 10,000
SALES (est): 6.5MM **Privately Held**
SIC: 2329 Men's & boys' leather, wool & down-filled outerwear; field jackets, military; down-filled clothing: men's & boys'

(G-10163)
IAC SEARCH LLC (HQ)
555 W 18th St (10011-2822)
PHONE...........................212 314-7300
 Barry Diller, *Chairman*
 Roman Degtyur, *Vice Pres*
 Paul Scribano, *Vice Pres*
 Stacy Simpson, *Vice Pres*
 Shaun Duncan, *Manager*
EMP: 37
SALES (est): 6.6MM
SALES (corp-wide): 3.3B **Publicly Held**
SIC: 7372 7375 Prepackaged software; information retrieval services; on-line data base information retrieval
PA: Iac/Interactivecorp
 555 W 18th St
 New York NY 10011
 212 314-7300

(G-10164)
IAC/INTERACTIVECORP (PA)
555 W 18th St (10011-2822)
PHONE...........................212 314-7300
 Joseph Levin, *CEO*
 Barry Diller, *Ch of Bd*
 Victor A Kaufman, *Vice Ch Bd*
 Mark Stein, *Exec VP*
 Gregg Winiarski, *Exec VP*
EMP: 3300
SQ FT: 202,500
SALES: 3.3B **Publicly Held**
WEB: www.usanetworks.com
SIC: 7372 7375 5961 Prepackaged software; information retrieval services; on-line data base information retrieval; catalog & mail-order houses

(G-10165)
IBIO INC
600 Madison Ave Ste 1601 (10022-1737)
PHONE...........................302 355-0650
 Robert B Kay, *Ch of Bd*
 Robert L Erwin, *President*
 James P Mullaney, *CFO*
 James Mullaney, *CFO*
 Glenn Chang, *Bd of Directors*
EMP: 43 **EST:** 2008
SALES: 444K **Privately Held**
SIC: 2834 Pharmaceutical preparations

(G-10166)
IBRANDS INTERNATIONAL LLC
230 W 39th St (10018-4411)
PHONE...........................212 354-1330
 Marc Garson, *Chairman*
EMP: 16 **EST:** 2014
SQ FT: 4,200
SALES (est): 585.6K **Privately Held**
SIC: 2321 Polo shirts, men's & boys': made from purchased materials

(G-10167)
ICARUS ENTERPRISES INC
568 Broadway Fl 11 (10012-3374)
PHONE...........................917 969-4461
 Nicholas Hubbard, *President*
EMP: 5
SALES: 500K **Privately Held**
SIC: 2721 Magazines: publishing & printing

(G-10168)
ICER SCRUBS LLC
Also Called: Crocs Medical Apparel
1385 Broadway Fl 16 (10018-6041)
PHONE...........................212 221-4700
 Lawrence Jemal, *Mng Member*
 ▲ **EMP:** 10
SQ FT: 2,000
SALES (est): 532.1K **Privately Held**
SIC: 2335 Women's, juniors' & misses' dresses

(G-10169)
ICER SPORTS LLC
1385 Broadway Fl 16 (10018-6041)
PHONE...........................212 221-4700
 Iven Sandler, *Mng Member*
EMP: 10
SALES (est): 480K **Privately Held**
SIC: 2329 2331 Men's & boys' sportswear & athletic clothing; women's & misses' blouses & shirts

(G-10170)
IDALIA SOLAR TECHNOLOGIES LLC
270 Lafayette St Ste 1402 (10012-3364)
PHONE...........................212 792-3913
 Marc Dee,
 Eric Laufer,
EMP: 9
SQ FT: 2,500
SALES: 500K **Privately Held**
SIC: 3674 Solar cells

(G-10171)
IDEAL CREATIONS INC
10 W 33rd St Rm 708 (10001-3306)
PHONE...........................212 563-5928
 Moses Grunbaum, *President*
 ▲ **EMP:** 20
SALES (est): 1.4MM **Privately Held**
WEB: www.idealcreations.net
SIC: 2369 5136 Headwear: girls', children's & infants'; hats, men's & boys'

(G-10172)
IDEAL FASTENER CORPORATION
Also Called: Ideal Accessories
246 W 38th St Rm 502 (10018-9074)
PHONE...........................212 244-0260
 Ralph Gut, *President*
 Steven Gut, *Director*
EMP: 122
SALES (corp-wide): 47.3MM **Privately Held**
WEB: www.idealfastener.com
SIC: 3965 Fasteners, buttons, needles & pins

PA: Ideal Fastener Corporation
 603 W Industry Dr
 Oxford NC 27565
 919 693-3115

(G-10173)
IDENTIFYCOM INC
120 W 45th St Ste 2701 (10036-4041)
PHONE...........................212 235-0000
 Debra Brown, *General Mgr*
 Alexander Valcic, *Manager*
EMP: 8
SQ FT: 3,171
SALES (est): 609.5K **Privately Held**
SIC: 7372 Application computer software

(G-10174)
IDESCO CORP
37 W 26th St Fl 10 (10010-1097)
PHONE...........................212 889-2530
 Andrew Schonzeit, *President*
EMP: 15
SALES (corp-wide): 19.9MM **Privately Held**
WEB: www.idesco.com
SIC: 2671 Packaging paper & plastics film, coated & laminated
PA: Idesco Corp.
 37 W 26th St Fl 10
 New York NY 10010
 212 889-2530

(G-10175)
IEP ENERGY HOLDING LLC
767 5th Ave Ste 4600 (10153-0023)
PHONE...........................212 702-4300
EMP: 2415
SALES (est): 109.8K
SALES (corp-wide): 21.7B **Publicly Held**
SIC: 2911 Petroleum refining
HQ: Icahn Enterprises Holdings L.P.
 767 5th Ave Fl 17
 New York NY 10153
 212 702-4300

(G-10176)
IFG CORP
1372 Brdwy 12ae 12 Ae (10018)
PHONE...........................212 629-9600
EMP: 159
SALES (corp-wide): 30.6MM **Privately Held**
SIC: 2329 2339 Athletic (warmup, sweat & jogging) suits: men's & boys'; athletic clothing: women's, misses' & juniors'
PA: Ifg Corp.
 1400 Broadway Rm 2202
 New York NY 10018
 212 629-9600

(G-10177)
IFG CORP
463 7th Ave Fl 4 (10018-8725)
PHONE...........................212 239-8615
 Ronald Adjmi, *President*
EMP: 5
SALES (corp-wide): 30.6MM **Privately Held**
SIC: 2329 Athletic (warmup, sweat & jogging) suits: men's & boys'
PA: Ifg Corp.
 1400 Broadway Rm 2202
 New York NY 10018
 212 629-9600

(G-10178)
IHEARTCOMMUNICATIONS INC
Also Called: Lite FM Radio
1133 Ave Americas Fl 34 (10036-6710)
PHONE...........................212 603-4660
 Robert Williams, *President*
EMP: 50 **Publicly Held**
SIC: 3663 Radio receiver networks
HQ: Iheartcommunications, Inc.
 20880 Stone Oak Pkwy
 San Antonio TX 78258
 210 822-2828

(G-10179)
IHI INC (HQ)
150 E 52nd St Fl 24 (10022-6246)
PHONE...........................212 599-8100
 Masato Kawaguchi, *CEO*
 ◆ **EMP:** 27

SALES (est): 372.3MM
SALES (corp-wide): 14.9B **Privately Held**
WEB: www.ihiinc.ihi.co.jp
SIC: 3812 1731 Acceleration indicators & systems components, aerospace; energy management controls
PA: Ihi Corporation
3-1-1, Toyosu
Koto-Ku TKY 135-0
362 047-800

(G-10180)
IKEDDI ENTERPRISES INC (PA)
1407 Brdwy Ste 2900 (10018)
PHONE 212 302-7644
Raymond Salem, *Ch of Bd*
David Salem, *Vice Pres*
Monique Burth, *Production*
Bruce Cotter, *CFO*
▲ **EMP:** 18
SQ FT: 28,000
SALES (est): 3.2MM **Privately Held**
SIC: 2339 Sportswear, women's

(G-10181)
IKEDDI ENTERPRISES INC
1407 Broadway Rm 1805 (10018-2764)
PHONE 212 302-7644
Raymond Salem, *Manager*
EMP: 6 **Privately Held**
SIC: 2339 Sportswear, women's
PA: Ikeddi Enterprises Inc.
1407 Brdwy Ste 2900
New York NY 10018

(G-10182)
ILES FORMULA INC (PA)
40 Harrison St Apt 17h (10013-2722)
PHONE 315 834-2478
Jeacques Masi, *CEO*
Wendy Iles, *President*
EMP: 6 **EST:** 2013
SALES: 700K **Privately Held**
SIC: 2844 Toilet preparations

(G-10183)
IMEK MEDIA LLC
32 Broadway Ste 511 (10004-1665)
PHONE 212 422-9000
Kemi Osukoya,
EMP: 20 **EST:** 2012
SALES (est): 1.5MM **Privately Held**
SIC: 2721 Magazines: publishing only, not printed on site

(G-10184)
IMENA JEWELRY MANUFACTURER INC
2 W 45th St Ste 1000 (10036-4252)
PHONE 212 827-0073
Paul Yan, *President*
Cindy Yan, *Office Mgr*
EMP: 15
SALES (est): 1.7MM **Privately Held**
SIC: 3911 Jewelry, precious metal

(G-10185)
IMG THE DAILY
432 W 45th St Fl 5 (10036-3503)
PHONE 212 541-5640
George Maier, *Principal*
Justin Clements, *Consultant*
EMP: 5
SALES (est): 345.5K **Privately Held**
SIC: 2711 Newspapers, publishing & printing

(G-10186)
IMPERIAL-HARVARD LABEL CO
Also Called: Harvard Woven Label
236 W 40th St Fl 3 (10018-1692)
PHONE 212 736-8420
Ira I Altfeder, *President*
Larry Saputo, *Treasurer*
EMP: 10
SQ FT: 3,000
SALES (est): 1.2MM **Privately Held**
SIC: 2241 Labels, woven

(G-10187)
IMPERIUM PARTNERS GROUP LLC (PA)
509 Madison Ave (10022-5501)
PHONE 212 433-1360
Maurice Hryshko, *Accountant*

John Michaelson,
EMP: 135
SALES (est): 14.4MM **Privately Held**
SIC: 3674 Microcircuits, integrated (semiconductor)

(G-10188)
IMPRESSIONS INC
36 W 37th St Rm 400 (10018-7497)
PHONE 212 594-5954
John Baise, *Principal*
EMP: 5
SALES (est): 732.2K **Privately Held**
SIC: 2721 Periodicals: publishing only

(G-10189)
IMPRINT BRANDED CONTENT LLC
34 W 27th St Rm 501 (10001-6996)
PHONE 212 888-8073
Andy Seibert, *Mng Member*
EMP: 7
SALES (est): 378.3K **Privately Held**
SIC: 2759 Imprinting
PA: Sullivan & Company Marketing Collateral, Inc.
450 W 14th St Fl 12
New York NY

(G-10190)
IN MOCEAN GROUP LLC (PA)
463 Fashion Ave Fl 21 (10018-7595)
PHONE 212 944-0317
Max Anteby, *Exec VP*
Angelina De Simone, *Vice Pres*
Joy Pescaru, *Production*
Sal Azzinnari, *CFO*
Monica Astalus, *Human Resources*
▲ **EMP:** 95 **EST:** 2000
SQ FT: 12,000
SALES (est): 14.6MM **Privately Held**
SIC: 2369 Bathing suits & swimwear: girls', children's & infants'

(G-10191)
IN-STEP MARKETING INC (PA)
Also Called: Z Card North America
39 Broadway Fl 32 (10006-3047)
PHONE 212 797-3450
Tim Kunhardt, *President*
EMP: 15
SQ FT: 6,600
SALES (est): 1.5MM **Privately Held**
WEB: www.zcardna.com
SIC: 2752 5199 8742 Promotional printing, lithographic; advertising specialties; marketing consulting services

(G-10192)
INCITEC PIVOT LIMITED
120 Broadway Fl 32 (10271-3299)
PHONE 212 238-3010
EMP: 5
SALES (est): 383.5K **Privately Held**
SIC: 2819 Chemicals, high purity: refined from technical grade

(G-10193)
INCON GEMS INC
Also Called: Jeypore Group
2 W 46th St Ste 603 (10036-4561)
PHONE 212 221-8560
Raju Gupta, *President*
EMP: 15
SQ FT: 2,000
SALES (est): 1.6MM **Privately Held**
SIC: 3911 5094 Jewelry, precious metal; precious stones (gems)

(G-10194)
INCRO MARKETING USA CORP (PA)
157 Columbus Ave (10023-6082)
PHONE 917 365-5552
Rachel Braha, *President*
EMP: 1
SALES: 1MM **Privately Held**
SIC: 2091 8742 Canned & cured fish & seafoods; marketing consulting services

(G-10195)
INCYCLE SOFTWARE CORP (PA)
1120 Ave Of The Americas (10036-6700)
PHONE 212 626-2608
Martin Rajotte, *President*

Julie Beaulieu, *CFO*
EMP: 10
SALES (est): 1.5MM **Privately Held**
SIC: 7372 Application computer software

(G-10196)
INDEGY INC
1460 Broadway (10036-7329)
PHONE 866 801-5394
Barak Perelman, *CEO*
Todd Warwick, *Vice Pres*
Joe Scotto, *Chief Mktg Ofcr*
EMP: 30
SALES (est): 700.9K **Privately Held**
SIC: 7372 7382 Prepackaged software; security systems services

(G-10197)
INDEX MAGAZINE
526 W 26th St Rm 920 (10001-5540)
PHONE 212 243-1428
Peter Halley, *Owner*
EMP: 6
SALES (est): 300K **Privately Held**
WEB: www.indexmagazine.com
SIC: 2721 Magazines: publishing & printing

(G-10198)
INDIA ABROAD PUBLICATIONS INC
102 Madison Ave Frnt B (10016-7592)
PHONE 212 929-1727
Ajit Balakrishnan, *President*
Geeta Singh, *Sales Executive*
EMP: 59
SQ FT: 6,500
SALES (est): 4.5MM **Privately Held**
SIC: 2711 Newspapers: publishing only, not printed on site

(G-10199)
INDIGO HOME INC
230 5th Ave Ste 1916 (10001-7730)
PHONE 212 684-4146
Taniya Kapoor, *Ch of Bd*
◆ **EMP:** 6
SALES (est): 725.5K **Privately Held**
WEB: www.indigohome.com
SIC: 2392 Blankets, comforters & beddings

(G-10200)
INDONESIAN IMPORTS INC (PA)
Also Called: Elliot Lucca
339 5th Ave Fl 2 (10016-5016)
PHONE 888 800-5899
Mark A Talucchi, *CEO*
Todd Elliott, *President*
Kristin Wilcox, *VP Human Res*
▲ **EMP:** 30
SQ FT: 52,000
SALES (est): 11.4MM **Privately Held**
WEB: www.elliottlucca.com
SIC: 3911 5961 Earrings, precious metal; jewelry, mail order

(G-10201)
INDULGE DESSERTS HOLDINGS LLC (PA)
666 5th Ave Fl 27 (10103-0001)
PHONE 212 231-8600
Andy Unanue, *Mng Member*
EMP: 2
SALES (est): 2.4MM **Privately Held**
SIC: 2051 2024 Cakes, pies & pastries; dairy based frozen desserts

(G-10202)
INDUSTRIAL RAW MATERIALS LLC
112 W 56th St (10019-3841)
PHONE 212 688-8080
Keith Aufhauser,
EMP: 8 **EST:** 2011
SALES (est): 782.3K **Privately Held**
SIC: 2999 Waxes, petroleum: not produced in petroleum refineries

(G-10203)
INFINITY AUGMENTED REALITY INC
228 Park Ave S 61130 (10003-1502)
PHONE 917 677-2084
Motti Kushnir, *CEO*
Moshe Hogeg, *Ch of Bd*
Enon Landenberg, *President*

Ortal Zanzuri, *CFO*
EMP: 6
SALES (est): 179.5K **Privately Held**
SIC: 7372 7371 Prepackaged software; custom computer programming services; computer software development & applications

(G-10204)
INFINITY SOURCING SERVICES LLC
224 W 35th St Ste 902 (10001-2534)
PHONE 212 868-2900
Ray Kim, *Mng Member*
EMP: 8
SALES: 22MM **Privately Held**
SIC: 2335 Women's, juniors' & misses' dresses

(G-10205)
INFIRMARY NYC
1720 2nd Ave (10128-4411)
PHONE 504 606-6280
James Cottingham, *Principal*
EMP: 5
SALES (est): 134.7K **Privately Held**
SIC: 2085 Cordials & premixed alcoholic cocktails

(G-10206)
INFOBASE HOLDINGS INC (HQ)
Also Called: Learn360
132 W 31st St Fl 17 (10001-3406)
PHONE 212 967-8800
Mark D McDonnell, *President*
Eleanor Jaekel, *Business Mgr*
James Housley, *CFO*
Olga Kovalchuk, *Controller*
Liz Clarke, *Human Res Dir*
▲ **EMP:** 54 **EST:** 1940
SALES (est): 15.3MM **Privately Held**
WEB: www.factsonfile.com
SIC: 2731 7372 Books: publishing only; prepackaged software
PA: Infobase Publishing Company
132 W 31st St Fl 17
New York NY 10001
212 967-8800

(G-10207)
INFOBASE PUBLISHING COMPANY (PA)
Also Called: Films Media Group
132 W 31st St Fl 17 (10001-3406)
PHONE 212 967-8800
Mark D McDonnell, *Ch of Bd*
James Chambers, *Editor*
David Giuffre, *Editor*
Kayla Harrington, *Editor*
Jonathan Leith, *Editor*
EMP: 1
SALES (est): 15.3MM **Privately Held**
SIC: 2731 7372 Books: publishing only; prepackaged software

(G-10208)
INFOR GLOBAL SOLUTIONS INC (DH)
641 Avenue Of Americas (10011)
PHONE 646 336-1700
James Schaper, *CEO*
Bill Ellis, *Vice Pres*
Shahriar Rafimayeri, *Vice Pres*
Song Lip Tan, *Project Mgr*
Tony Johnson, *Sales Staff*
EMP: 94
SALES: 39.5MM
SALES (corp-wide): 3.1B **Privately Held**
SIC: 7372 Prepackaged software
HQ: Infor (Us), Inc.
13560 Morris Rd Ste 4100
Alpharetta GA 30004
678 319-8000

(G-10209)
INFORMA BUSINESS MEDIA INC (DH)
Also Called: Penton Information Services
605 3rd Ave (10158-0180)
PHONE 212 204-4200
Patrick Martell, *CEO*
Richard White, *Business Mgr*
EMP: 211 **EST:** 1989
SQ FT: 83,000

New York - New York County (G-10210)
GEOGRAPHIC SECTION

SALES (est): 250.1MM **Privately Held**
WEB: www.primediabusiness.com
SIC: 2721 Magazines: publishing only, not printed on site
HQ: Informa Plc
  Mortimer House
  London W1T 3
  207 017-5000

(G-10210)
INFORMA MEDIA INC (DH)
Also Called: Penton Media - Aviation Week
605 3rd Ave Fl 22 (10158-0007)
PHONE..................................212 204-4200
David Kieselstein, *Ch of Bd*
Sandi Brown, *President*
Paul Miller, *President*
Francine Brasseur, *Publisher*
Geoff Belz, *Principal*
▲ EMP: 500 EST: 1976
SQ FT: 189,000
SALES (est): 183.7MM **Privately Held**
WEB: www.penton.com
SIC: 2721 7389 7313 7375 Magazines: publishing only, not printed on site; periodicals: publishing & printing; magazines: publishing & printing; advertising, promotional & trade show services; printed media advertising representatives; on-line data base information retrieval
HQ: Informa Business Media, Inc.
  605 3rd Ave
  New York NY 10158
  212 204-4200

(G-10211)
INFORMA MEDIA INC
Also Called: Used Equipment Directory
1166 Ave Of The Americas (10036-2708)
PHONE..................................212 204-4200
James Mack, *Principal*
Brian Rubin, *Director*
EMP: 9 **Privately Held**
WEB: www.penton.com
SIC: 2721 Magazines: publishing & printing
HQ: Informa Media, Inc.
  605 3rd Ave Fl 22
  New York NY 10158
  212 204-4200

(G-10212)
INFORMA SOLUTIONS INC
Also Called: Analytics Intell
45 Rockefeller Plz # 2000 (10111-0100)
PHONE..................................516 543-3733
David Bissainthe, *President*
EMP: 48 EST: 2015
SQ FT: 200
SALES (est): 1.1MM **Privately Held**
SIC: 7372 7373 7374 Prepackaged software; computer integrated systems design; data processing & preparation; data processing service

(G-10213)
INFORMA UK LTD
Lloyd's List Intelligence
52 Vanderbilt Ave Fl 7 (10017-3846)
PHONE..................................646 957-8966
Kieran Brown, *Branch Mgr*
EMP: 5 **Privately Held**
SIC: 2711 Newspapers
HQ: Informa Uk Limited
  5 Howick Place
  London SW1P
  207 017-6242

(G-10214)
INFORMATICA LLC
810 7th Ave Ste 1100c (10019-7597)
PHONE..................................212 845-7650
Maryanne Cotrone, *Partner*
Michael Warthen, *Sales Staff*
Alistair Duguid, *Manager*
Ron Reichenbach, *Manager*
Mike Pickart, *Consultant*
EMP: 11
SALES (corp-wide): 1B **Privately Held**
SIC: 7372 Prepackaged software
HQ: Informatica Llc
  2100 Seaport Blvd
  Redwood City CA 94063

(G-10215)
INFORMERLY INC
35 Essex St (10002-4712)
PHONE..................................646 238-7137
Ranjan Roy, *CEO*
Emily Moss, *President*
EMP: 5
SALES (est): 270K **Privately Held**
SIC: 7372 Prepackaged software

(G-10216)
INKKAS LLC
38 E 29th St Rm 6r (10016-7963)
PHONE..................................646 845-9803
Daniel Ben-Mun, *Mng Member*
EMP: 6
SALES (est): 698K **Privately Held**
SIC: 3021 Canvas shoes, rubber soled

(G-10217)
INNOFUN DIGITAL ENTRMT LLC
19 W 34th St Rm 1018 (10001-3006)
PHONE..................................347 708-0078
Wang Shiqiang, *CEO*
EMP: 15
SALES (est): 500K **Privately Held**
SIC: 7372 Application computer software

(G-10218)
INNOVANT INC
37 W 20th St Ste 1101 (10011-3713)
PHONE..................................212 929-4883
Juan Argueta, *Manager*
EMP: 6
SALES (corp-wide): 48MM **Privately Held**
WEB: www.innovant.com
SIC: 2511 Kitchen & dining room furniture
PA: Innovant, Inc.
  135 Oval Dr
  Islandia NY 11749
  631 348-1900

(G-10219)
INNOVATIVE DESIGNS LLC
141 W 36th St Fl 8 (10018-6980)
PHONE..................................212 695-0892
Douglas Haber, *Mng Member*
▲ EMP: 34
SQ FT: 8,000
SALES (est): 54MM **Privately Held**
SIC: 2678 3944 Stationery products; craft & hobby kits & sets

(G-10220)
INNROAD INC
519 8th Ave Fl 15 (10018-4765)
PHONE..................................631 458-1437
Murat Ozsu, *CEO*
Cecilia Horton-Williams, *Controller*
EMP: 30 EST: 2000
SALES (est): 1.5MM **Privately Held**
SIC: 7372 Business oriented computer software
PA: Innroad Software Development Services Private Limited
  B Wing, 1st Floor Software Building 2
  Hyderabad TS

(G-10221)
INO-TEX LLC
135 W 36th St Fl 6 (10018-9482)
PHONE..................................212 400-2205
Yongjun Yu, *Director*
EMP: 6
SALES (est): 406K
SALES (corp-wide): 604.2MM **Privately Held**
SIC: 2299 Batts & batting: cotton mill waste & related material; ramie yarn, thread, roving & textiles
PA: Jiangsu Lianfa Textile Co., Ltd.
  No.88 Henglian Road, Chengdong Town, Haian County
  Nantong 22660
  513 888-6906

(G-10222)
INOLIFE TCHNLGIES OPRTIONS INC
11 E 86th St Ste 19b (10028-0501)
PHONE..................................212 386-5575
Mark Corrao, *Officer*
EMP: 6
SALES (corp-wide): 543.7K **Privately Held**
SIC: 2834 2835 Veterinary pharmaceutical preparations; pregnancy test kits
HQ: Inolife Technologies Operations, Inc.
  2401 Nowata Pl A
  Bartlesville OK 74006
  212 386-5575

(G-10223)
INORI JEWELS
580 5th Ave (10036-4701)
PHONE..................................347 703-5078
Guy Israeli, *Owner*
EMP: 10 EST: 2014
SALES (est): 748.5K **Privately Held**
SIC: 3911 Jewelry, precious metal

(G-10224)
INPROTOPIA CORPORATION
401 W 110th St Apt 2001 (10025-2445)
PHONE..................................917 338-7501
Souyun Lee, *CEO*
WEI-Yeh Lee, *Co-Owner*
EMP: 11 EST: 2011
SALES (est): 616.4K **Privately Held**
SIC: 7372 7373 7371 Business oriented computer software; systems software development services; computer software systems analysis & design, custom

(G-10225)
INSIGHT VENTURE PARTNERS IV
1114 Avenue Of The Americ (10036-7703)
PHONE..................................212 230-9200
Alex Crisses, *Partner*
EMP: 150
SALES (est): 120.2K **Privately Held**
SIC: 7372 Prepackaged software

(G-10226)
INSPIRED ENTERTAINMENT INC (PA)
250 W 57th St Ste 2223 (10107-0013)
PHONE..................................646 565-3861
A Lorne Weil, *Ch of Bd*
Luke L Alvarez, *President*
Brooks Pierce, *President*
Daniel B Silvers, *Exec VP*
Daniel Silvers, *Exec VP*
EMP: 14
SALES: 122.5MM **Publicly Held**
SIC: 7372 7993 7999 Prepackaged software; arcades; gambling & lottery services

(G-10227)
INSTANT STREAM INC
Also Called: Stream Police
1271 Ave Of The Americas (10020-1300)
PHONE..................................917 438-7182
Michael Daly III, *CEO*
EMP: 32
SALES (est): 2.3MM **Privately Held**
SIC: 2752 Commercial printing, lithographic

(G-10228)
INSTITUTE OF ELECTRICAL AND EL
Ieee Communications Society
3 Park Ave Fl 17 (10016-5902)
PHONE..................................212 705-8900
Christina Zarrello, *Editor*
David Bell, *Commander*
Marc Apter, *Vice Pres*
Kerrieanne Sullivan, *Project Mgr*
Paula Dunne, *Opers Staff*
EMP: 25
SALES (corp-wide): 496.6MM **Privately Held**
SIC: 2721 Trade journals: publishing & printing
PA: The Institute Of Electrical And Electronics Engineers Incorporated
  445 Hoes Ln
  Piscataway NJ 08854
  212 419-7900

(G-10229)
INT TRADING USA LLC
261 W 35th St Ste 1100 (10001-1900)
PHONE..................................212 760-2338
Sung Pak,

▲ EMP: 230 EST: 2004
SALES (est): 33.5MM **Privately Held**
SIC: 2325 2339 Men's & boys' trousers & slacks; women's & misses' outerwear

(G-10230)
INTEGRATED COPYRIGHT GROUP
Also Called: Evergreen
1745 Broadway 19 (10019-4640)
PHONE..................................615 329-3999
John Barker, *President*
EMP: 22
SALES (est): 1.4MM **Privately Held**
SIC: 2741 Music, sheet: publishing only, not printed on site

(G-10231)
INTEGRATED GRAPHICS INC (PA)
Also Called: I C S
7 W 36th St Fl 12 (10018-7154)
PHONE..................................212 592-5600
James Kearns, *President*
Jay Beber, *Vice Pres*
EMP: 5
SALES (est): 3.3MM **Privately Held**
WEB: www.integratedgraphics.com
SIC: 2759 8748 Commercial printing; business consulting

(G-10232)
INTELLIGNC THE FTR CMPTNG NWSL
Also Called: Intelligence Newsletter
360 Central Park W (10025-6541)
P.O. Box 20008 (10025-1510)
PHONE..................................212 222-1123
Edward Rosenfeld, *Owner*
EMP: 10
SALES (est): 445.4K **Privately Held**
WEB: www.eintelligence.com
SIC: 2721 Magazines: publishing only, not printed on site

(G-10233)
INTELLITRAVEL MEDIA INC (DH)
530 Fashion Ave Rm 201 (10018-4821)
PHONE..................................646 695-6700
Nancy Telliho, *Ch of Bd*
Harold Shain, *President*
EMP: 8
SALES (est): 782.3K
SALES (corp-wide): 3.3B **Publicly Held**
SIC: 2721 Magazines: publishing only, not printed on site
HQ: The Daily Beast Company Llc
  7 Hanover Sq
  New York NY 10004
  212 445-4600

(G-10234)
INTER PARFUMS INC (PA)
551 5th Ave (10176-0001)
PHONE..................................212 983-2640
Jean Madar, *Ch of Bd*
Philippe Benacin, *President*
Frederic Garcia-Pelayo, *COO*
Russell Greenberg, *CFO*
Philippe Santi, *CFO*
▲ EMP: 83
SQ FT: 16,800
SALES: 591.2MM **Publicly Held**
WEB: www.interparfumsinc.com
SIC: 2844 Cosmetic preparations; perfumes & colognes

(G-10235)
INTER PARFUMS USA LLC
551 5th Ave Rm 1500 (10176-1599)
PHONE..................................212 983-2640
Jean Madar, *Ch of Bd*
Russell Greenberg, *CFO*
EMP: 7
SALES (est): 595.7K
SALES (corp-wide): 591.2MM **Publicly Held**
SIC: 2844 Concentrates, perfume
PA: Inter Parfums, Inc.
  551 5th Ave
  New York NY 10176
  212 983-2640

GEOGRAPHIC SECTION
New York - New York County (G-10262)

(G-10236)
INTERAXISSOURCINGCOM INC
41 E 11th St Fl 11 (10003-4602)
PHONE..................................212 905-6001
Donald Taffurelli, *President*
▲ EMP: 50
SQ FT: 1,000
SALES (est): 4.6MM Privately Held
SIC: 2231 Apparel & outerwear broadwoven fabrics

(G-10237)
INTERBRAND LLC
1 W 37th St Fl 9 (10018-5354)
PHONE..................................212 840-9595
Bob McMeekin, *President*
EMP: 9
SALES (corp-wide): 9MM Privately Held
WEB: www.interbrandllc.com
SIC: 2321 Men's & boys' furnishings
PA: Interbrand Llc
225 Dupont St Ste 2
Plainview NY 11803
516 349-5884

(G-10238)
INTERCEPT PHARMACEUTICALS INC (PA)
10 Hudson Yards Fl 37 (10001-2160)
PHONE..................................646 747-1000
Paolo Fundaro, *Ch of Bd*
Mark Pruzanski, *President*
Jerome B Durso, *COO*
Christian Weyer, *Exec VP*
Richard Kim, *Senior VP*
EMP: 72
SQ FT: 45,500
SALES: 130.9MM Publicly Held
SIC: 2834 Pharmaceutical preparations

(G-10239)
INTERCOTTGN COMPANY INC
888 7th Ave Fl 29 (10106-2899)
PHONE..................................212 265-3809
Herman Landman, *President*
EMP: 3
SALES: 8.9MM Privately Held
SIC: 2389 Men's miscellaneous accessories

(G-10240)
INTERFACEFLOR LLC
330 5th Ave Fl 12 (10001-3213)
PHONE..................................212 686-8284
Pete Waldron, *Manager*
EMP: 25
SALES (corp-wide): 996.4MM Publicly Held
WEB: www.ca.interfaceinc.com
SIC: 2273 Finishers of tufted carpets & rugs
HQ: Interfaceflor, Llc
1503 Orchard Hill Rd
Lagrange GA 30240
706 882-1891

(G-10241)
INTERHELLENIC PUBLISHING INC
Also Called: Estiator
421 7th Ave Ste 810 (10001-2002)
PHONE..................................212 967-5016
Peter Makrias, *President*
EMP: 7
SQ FT: 1,500
SALES: 1.2MM Privately Held
WEB: www.estiator.com
SIC: 2721 Magazines: publishing only, not printed on site

(G-10242)
INTERNATIONAL AIDS VCCNE INTTV (PA)
125 Broad St Fl 9th (10004-2400)
PHONE..................................212 847-1111
Alex Godwin Coutinho, *Ch of Bd*
Margaret McGlynn, *President*
Thomas P Monath, *Partner*
David N Cook, *COO*
Lynn Doren, *Senior VP*
EMP: 95
SQ FT: 32,000
SALES: 72.3MM Privately Held
WEB: www.iavi.org
SIC: 2836 8731 Vaccines; commercial physical research

(G-10243)
INTERNATIONAL BUS MCHS CORP
Also Called: IBM
55 Broad St Fl 27 (10004-2563)
PHONE..................................212 324-5000
Jim Hertzig, *Software Engr*
Carol Moore, *Director*
EMP: 40
SALES (corp-wide): 79.1B Publicly Held
WEB: www.ibm.com
SIC: 3674 Computer logic modules
PA: International Business Machines Corporation
1 New Orchard Rd Ste 1 # 1
Armonk NY 10504
914 499-1900

(G-10244)
INTERNATIONAL DATA GROUP INC
Also Called: Idg Technetwork
117 E 55th St Ste 204 (10022-3502)
PHONE..................................212 331-7883
EMP: 30
SALES (corp-wide): 3.5B Privately Held
SIC: 2721 8732 7389 Periodicals-Publishing/Printing Commercial Nonphysical Research Business Services
PA: International Data Group, Inc.
1 Exeter Plz Fl 15
Boston MA 02116
617 534-1200

(G-10245)
INTERNATIONAL DESIGN ASSOC LTD
Also Called: Life Plus Style
747 3rd Ave Rm 218 (10017-2878)
PHONE..................................212 687-0333
Robin Nedboy, *President*
Steven Kletz, *Vice Pres*
Victoria Carrion, *Bookkeeper*
▲ EMP: 8
SQ FT: 3,500
SALES (est): 3.2MM Privately Held
SIC: 2678 3999 5999 Stationery products; candles; toiletries, cosmetics & perfumes

(G-10246)
INTERNATIONAL DIRECT GROUP INC
Also Called: Idg
525 7th Ave Rm 208 (10018-5280)
PHONE..................................212 921-9036
Haynes Holding, *CEO*
Toby Williams, *General Mgr*
Joel Ratner, *Exec VP*
Wesley Matthews, *CFO*
Elysia Tietjen, *Accounts Exec*
▲ EMP: 30
SALES (est): 5.9MM Privately Held
WEB: www.internationaldg.com
SIC: 2331 7389 Blouses, women's & juniors': made from purchased material; design services

(G-10247)
INTERNATIONAL INSPIRATIONS LTD (PA)
Also Called: Lux Accessories
358 5th Ave Rm 501 (10001-2228)
PHONE..................................212 465-8500
Saul Shaya Reiter, *CEO*
Maninder Kaur, *Controller*
▲ EMP: 61
SQ FT: 1,000
SALES (est): 10.6MM Privately Held
SIC: 3961 Costume jewelry

(G-10248)
INTERNATIONAL MGT NETWRK
445 Park Ave Fl 9 (10022-8606)
PHONE..................................646 401-0032
Jeff Krantz, *President*
EMP: 15
SALES: 950K Privately Held
SIC: 7372 Prepackaged software

(G-10249)
INTERNATIONAL OFFICE
110 Greene St Ste 1206 (10012-4319)
PHONE..................................212 334-4617
Marcello Pepori, *President*
Pratima Raichur, *Director*
▲ EMP: 5
SALES (est): 226.5K Privately Held
SIC: 2522 Office furniture, except wood

(G-10250)
INTERNATIONL STUDIOS INC
108 W 39th St Rm 1300 (10018-3614)
PHONE..................................212 819-1616
Alan S Ginsberg, *President*
EMP: 5
SALES (est): 360K Privately Held
SIC: 2211 Apparel & outerwear fabrics, cotton

(G-10251)
INTERNTNAL FLVORS FRGRNCES INC (PA)
Also Called: Iff
521 W 57th St (10019-2929)
PHONE..................................212 765-5500
Andreas Fibig, *Ch of Bd*
Anne Chwat, *Exec VP*
Francisco Fortanet, *Exec VP*
Gregory Yep, *Exec VP*
Richard A O'Leary, *CFO*
EMP: 180
SALES: 3.4B Publicly Held
WEB: www.iff.com
SIC: 2869 2844 2087 Flavors or flavoring materials, synthetic; perfume materials, synthetic; toilet preparations; flavoring extracts & syrups

(G-10252)
INTERNTNL PUBLCATNS MEDIA GRUP
Also Called: Interntnal Pblctons Mdia Group
708 3rd Ave 145 (10017-4201)
P.O. Box 2412 (10163-2412)
PHONE..................................917 604-9602
Francois Wilson, *CEO*
EMP: 7
SQ FT: 400
SALES: 269.4K Privately Held
SIC: 2731 5112 5085 2721 Books: publishing & printing; laserjet supplies; ink, printers'; comic books: publishing only, not printed on site; computer software; film processing, editing & titling: motion picture

(G-10253)
INTERTEX USA INC
Also Called: B C America
131 W 35th St Fl 10 (10001-2111)
PHONE..................................212 279-3601
Yong Lee, *President*
EMP: 15
SQ FT: 6,500
SALES (est): 1MM Privately Held
SIC: 2221 2262 Specialty broadwoven fabrics, including twisted weaves; screen printing: manmade fiber & silk broadwoven fabrics

(G-10254)
INTERVIEW NEW YORK
77 Bleecker St (10012-1547)
PHONE..................................857 928-4120
Russell Cameron, *Principal*
EMP: 5
SALES (est): 219.5K Privately Held
SIC: 2721 Magazines: publishing only, not printed on site

(G-10255)
INTEVA PRODUCTS LLC
30 Rockefeller Plz (10112-0015)
PHONE..................................248 655-8886
Lon Offenbacher, *Branch Mgr*
EMP: 300
SALES (corp-wide): 3.8B Privately Held
SIC: 3089 Injection molding of plastics
HQ: Inteva Products, Llc
1401 Crooks Rd
Troy MI 48084

(G-10256)
INTIMATECO LLC
Also Called: Inteco Intimates
463 7th Ave Rm 602 (10018-8719)
PHONE..................................212 239-4411
Gaby Sutton,
Eli Levy,
◆ EMP: 8 EST: 2008
SALES (est): 3.9MM Privately Held
SIC: 2341 Women's & children's underwear

(G-10257)
INTRA-CELLULAR THERAPIES INC (PA)
430 E 29th St Ste 900 (10016-8367)
PHONE..................................646 440-9333
Sharon Mates, *Ch of Bd*
Robert E Davis, *Senior VP*
Suresh Durgam, *Senior VP*
Michael I Halstead, *Senior VP*
Michael Olchaskey, *Senior VP*
▲ EMP: 42
SQ FT: 16,753
SALES: 330.7K Publicly Held
WEB: www.intracellulartherapies.com
SIC: 2834 8732 Pharmaceutical preparations; research services, except laboratory

(G-10258)
INTRALINKS HOLDINGS INC (HQ)
150 E 42nd St Fl 8 (10017-5626)
PHONE..................................212 543-7700
Leif Oleary, *CEO*
Nitai Agrawal, *Engineer*
Carlos Cueva, *Engineer*
Krishna Bolineni, *Senior Engr*
Shay Gonen, *CFO*
EMP: 31
SQ FT: 43,304
SALES: 276.1MM
SALES (corp-wide): 28.8MM Privately Held
SIC: 7372 7382 Prepackaged software; security systems services
PA: Impala Private Holdings Ii, Llc
601 Lexington Ave Fl 59
New York NY 10022
212 231-0095

(G-10259)
INTRAWORLDS INC
222 Broadway Fl 19 (10038-2550)
PHONE..................................631 602-5333
Stephan Herrlich, *President*
EMP: 5
SALES (est): 117.2K Privately Held
SIC: 7372 Application computer software

(G-10260)
INTRIGUING THREADS APPAREL INC (PA)
552 Fashion Ave Rm 603 (10018-3211)
PHONE..................................212 768-8733
Alayne Weinstein, *President*
Frederick Demario, *Corp Secy*
Lori Kamhi, *Vice Pres*
▲ EMP: 17
SQ FT: 2,500
SALES (est): 1.9MM Privately Held
SIC: 2339 Sportswear, women's

(G-10261)
INTSTRUX LLC
Also Called: Pixacore
15 W 39th St Fl 13 (10018-0627)
PHONE..................................646 688-2782
Sanjiv Mody, *President*
Dhaval Parikh, *Exec VP*
Thom Graves, *Vice Pres*
Azim Aghil, *Director*
Elizabeth Taurisani, *Director*
EMP: 25
SQ FT: 7,500
SALES: 6.5MM Privately Held
SIC: 2834 Digitalis pharmaceutical preparations

(G-10262)
INTUITION PUBLISHING LIMITED
40 E 34th St Rm 1101 (10016-4501)
PHONE..................................212 838-7115
David Harrison, *Manager*

New York - New York County (G-10263)

Francis McKeagney, *Officer*
EMP: 8
SALES (corp-wide): 105.9K **Privately Held**
SIC: 2741 Miscellaneous publishing
HQ: Intuition Publishing Limited
I F S C House
Dublin
353 160-5430

(G-10263)
INVESTMENT NEWS
711 3rd Ave Fl 3 (10017-9214)
PHONE.................................212 210-0100
Mary B Franklin, *Editor*
Frederick Gabriel, *Editor*
Andrew Leigh, *Regional Mgr*
Suzanne Siracuse, *Vice Pres*
Simone Pryce, *Prdtn Dir*
EMP: 50
SALES (est): 2.5MM **Privately Held**
WEB: www.investmentnews.net
SIC: 2711 Newspapers, publishing & printing

(G-10264)
INVESTORS BUSINESS DAILY INC
140 E 45th St Ste 19b (10017-7143)
PHONE.................................212 626-7676
Janice Janendo, *Branch Mgr*
EMP: 18
SALES (corp-wide): 231.5MM **Privately Held**
WEB: www.investors.com
SIC: 2711 6282 Newspapers, publishing & printing; investment advice
HQ: Investor's Business Daily, Inc.
12655 Beatrice St
Los Angeles CA 90066
310 448-6000

(G-10265)
INVISION INC (HQ)
25 W 43rd St Ste 609 (10036-7422)
PHONE.................................212 557-5554
Steve Marshall, *CEO*
Teresa Taveras, *Partner*
Kami Ragsdale, *COO*
Travis Howe, *Senior VP*
Ryan Burke, *Vice Pres*
EMP: 5
SALES (est): 1MM
SALES (corp-wide): 101MM **Privately Held**
SIC: 7372 Prepackaged software
PA: Mediaocean Llc
45 W 18th St
New York NY 10011
212 633-8100

(G-10266)
IPC/RAZOR LLC (PA)
277 Park Ave Fl 39 (10172-2901)
PHONE.................................212 551-4500
Douglas Korn, *Mng Member*
Douglas R Korn, *Mng Member*
EMP: 60 **EST:** 2010
SALES (est): 64.4MM **Privately Held**
SIC: 3541 Machine tools, metal cutting type

(G-10267)
IR MEDIA GROUP (USA) INC
25 Broadway Fl 9 (10004-1058)
PHONE.................................212 425-9649
Ian Richman, *Ch of Bd*
Candice Monts-Petit, *Editor*
Andrea Pion, *Sales Staff*
Brigitte Toledano, *Sales Staff*
Kathleen Hennessy, *Manager*
EMP: 30 **EST:** 1995
SALES (est): 1.7MM
SALES (corp-wide): 4MM **Privately Held**
WEB: www.irmag.com
SIC: 2731 Books: publishing only
HQ: Cross-Border Publishing (London) Limited
111-113 Great Titchfield Street
London W1W 6

(G-10268)
IRADJ MOINI COUTURE LTD
403 W 46th St (10036-3510)
PHONE.................................212 594-9242
Iradj Moini, *President*

EMP: 12
SQ FT: 800
SALES: 500K **Privately Held**
SIC: 3911 Jewelry, precious metal

(G-10269)
IRIDESSE INC
600 Madison Ave Fl 5 (10022-1615)
PHONE.................................212 230-6000
Patrick B Dorsey, *President*
Daniel Wright, *General Mgr*
Judith A Baldissard, *Principal*
Michael W Connolly, *Principal*
James N Fernandez, *Principal*
EMP: 15
SALES (est): 1.9MM **Privately Held**
SIC: 3911 Necklaces, precious metal

(G-10270)
IRISH AMERICA INC
Also Called: Irish America Magazine
875 Americas Rm 2100 (10001-3586)
PHONE.................................212 725-2993
Niall O'Dowd, *Publisher*
Brendon Maclua, *Shareholder*
EMP: 20
SQ FT: 3,000
SALES (est): 1.7MM **Privately Held**
WEB: www.smurfitkappa.com
SIC: 2721 Magazines: publishing only, not printed on site
HQ: Smurfit Kappa Packaging Limited
Beech Hill
Dublin 4

(G-10271)
IRISH ECHO NEWSPAPER CORP
165 Madison Ave Rm 302 (10016-5431)
PHONE.................................212 482-4818
Peter Quinn, *Ch of Bd*
EMP: 19 **EST:** 1928
SQ FT: 3,000
SALES (est): 1.3MM **Privately Held**
WEB: www.irishecho.com
SIC: 2711 Newspapers: publishing only, not printed on site

(G-10272)
IRISH TRIBUNE INC
Also Called: Irish Voice Newspaper
875 Avenue Of The Amerrm2 Rm 2100 (10001)
PHONE.................................212 684-3366
Niell O'Dowd, *President*
Robert S Bennett, *Partner*
Sean E Crowley, *Partner*
Ann Marie Zito, *Opers Mgr*
EMP: 14
SALES (est): 864.5K **Privately Held**
WEB: www.smurfitkappa.com
SIC: 2711 Newspapers, publishing & printing
HQ: Smurfit Kappa Packaging Limited
Beech Hill
Dublin 4

(G-10273)
IRV INC
Also Called: Warshaw Jacobson Group
475 Park Ave S Fl 11 (10016-6901)
PHONE.................................212 334-4507
Steve Warshaw, *President*
Sal Mercadante, *President*
Jay Warshaw, *Vice Pres*
EMP: 23
SALES (est): 1.2MM **Privately Held**
SIC: 7372 7371 Prepackaged software; custom computer programming services

(G-10274)
IRVING FARM COFFEE CO INC (PA)
151 W 19th St Fl 6 (10011-4158)
PHONE.................................212 206-0707
David Elwell, *President*
Chad Freilino, *COO*
Daniel Streetman, *Vice Pres*
Mario Cortes, *Accountant*
Clyde Miller, *Director*
EMP: 4
SALES (est): 3.1MM **Privately Held**
WEB: www.irvingfarm.com
SIC: 2095 Roasted coffee

(G-10275)
ISFEL CO INC (PA)
Also Called: Top Stuff
110 W 34th St Rm 1101 (10001-2115)
PHONE.................................212 736-6216
Joseph Feldman, *President*
▲ **EMP:** 8 **EST:** 1948
SQ FT: 2,000
SALES (est): 3.1MM **Privately Held**
WEB: www.topstuff.com
SIC: 2369 Girls' & children's outerwear

(G-10276)
ISISNET LLC
Also Called: Isis/Koppermann
53 W 36th St Rm 502 (10018-7993)
PHONE.................................212 239-1205
Michael Dematteis,
Wolfgang Koppermann,
Andreas Lachner,
EMP: 6
SQ FT: 1,200
SALES: 1MM **Privately Held**
SIC: 7372 Prepackaged software

(G-10277)
ISONICS CORPORATION
535 8th Ave Fl 3 (10018-4305)
PHONE.................................212 356-7400
EMP: 4
SALES: 22.1MM **Privately Held**
SIC: 2819 3674 Mfg Industrial Inorganic Chemicals Mfg Semiconductors/Related Devices

(G-10278)
ITC MFG GROUP INC
109 W 38th St Rm 701 (10018-3673)
PHONE.................................212 684-3696
Anthony Dadika, *President*
Irwin Jaeger, *Vice Pres*
EMP: 10
SQ FT: 6,000
SALES (est): 1.4MM **Privately Held**
SIC: 2241 3965 2759 Labels, woven; fasteners, buttons, needles & pins; tags: printing

(G-10279)
IZQUIERDO STUDIOS LTD
34 W 28th St 6 (10001-4201)
PHONE.................................212 807-9757
Martin Izquierdo, *President*
EMP: 13
SQ FT: 2,000
SALES (est): 1.3MM **Privately Held**
SIC: 2389 Theatrical costumes

(G-10280)
IZUN PHARMACEUTICALS CORP (PA)
1 Rockefeller Plz Fl 11 (10020-2073)
PHONE.................................212 618-6357
William Levine, *CEO*
Ronald Stern, *President*
William Levine, *Executive*
EMP: 12
SALES (est): 1.5MM **Privately Held**
WEB: www.izunpharma.com
SIC: 2834 Pharmaceutical preparations

(G-10281)
J & H CREATIONS INC
19 W 36th St Fl 3 (10018-7103)
PHONE.................................212 465-0962
Jay Baek, *President*
▲ **EMP:** 20
SQ FT: 2,000
SALES (est): 2.6MM **Privately Held**
WEB: www.jhcreation.com
SIC: 3961 5094 Costume jewelry, ex. precious metal & semiprecious stones; jewelry

(G-10282)
J & M TEXTILE CO INC
505 8th Ave Rm 701 (10018-4552)
PHONE.................................212 268-8000
Maria Wiesiolek, *President*
▲ **EMP:** 11
SQ FT: 7,000
SALES (est): 1.1MM **Privately Held**
SIC: 2241 5131 Narrow Fabric Mill Whol Piece Goods/Notions

(G-10283)
J & X PRODUCTION INC
327 W 36th St 7f (10018-6405)
PHONE.................................718 200-1228
Guo Jun Lin, *President*
EMP: 10
SALES (est): 127K **Privately Held**
SIC: 2311 Men's & boys' suits & coats

(G-10284)
J A G DIAMOND MANUFACTURERS
580 5th Ave Ste 905b (10036-4733)
PHONE.................................212 575-0660
Volf Goldrath, *President*
Sharon Fink,
EMP: 7
SALES (est): 587.5K **Privately Held**
SIC: 3915 Diamond cutting & polishing

(G-10285)
J EDLIN INTERIORS LTD
122 W 27th St Fl 2 (10001-6274)
PHONE.................................212 243-2111
Jeffrey Edlin, *President*
Joyse Edlin, *Vice Pres*
▲ **EMP:** 10
SALES (est): 1MM **Privately Held**
WEB: www.reisner.net
SIC: 2391 Curtains & draperies

(G-10286)
J PERCY FOR MRVIN RCHARDS LTD (HQ)
512 Fashion Ave (10018-4603)
PHONE.................................212 944-5300
Morris Goldfarb, *Ch of Bd*
Sammy Aaron, *President*
Andrew Reid, *Vice Pres*
Allan Inger, *CFO*
Lee Lipton, *Admin Sec*
◆ **EMP:** 40
SQ FT: 12,000
SALES: 4.4MM
SALES (corp-wide): 2.8B **Publicly Held**
SIC: 2386 2371 2337 2339 Coats & jackets, leather & sheep-lined; fur coats & other fur apparel; women's & misses' suits & coats; women's & misses' jackets & coats, except sportswear
PA: G-lii Apparel Group, Ltd.
512 7th Ave Fl 35
New York NY 10018
212 403-0500

(G-10287)
J R GOLD DESIGNS LTD
555 5th Ave Fl 19 (10017-2416)
PHONE.................................212 922-9292
Rami Uziel, *President*
Rina Uziel, *Principal*
EMP: 10
SQ FT: 2,500
SALES: 10MM **Privately Held**
WEB: www.rinalimor.com
SIC: 3911 5094 Jewelry, precious metal; jewelry

(G-10288)
J R NITES (PA)
1400 Broadway Rm 601 (10018-0728)
PHONE.................................212 354-9670
John Klein, *Principal*
EMP: 8
SALES (est): 1MM **Privately Held**
SIC: 2335 Women's, juniors' & misses' dresses

(G-10289)
J9 TECHNOLOGIES INC
25 Broadway Fl 9 (10004-1058)
PHONE.................................412 586-5038
Alan Wasserberger, *President*
Robert C Roach, *CTO*
EMP: 20
SALES (est): 2.7MM **Privately Held**
SIC: 7372 Operating systems computer software

(G-10290)
JAC USA INC
45 Broadway Ste 1810 (10006-3710)
PHONE.................................212 841-7430
Kazunari Okuda, *Ch of Bd*
Sinji Naka, *President*

GEOGRAPHIC SECTION

Mary Bailey, *Manager*
EMP: 5
SQ FT: 1,400
SALES (est): 3.1MM
SALES (corp-wide): 51.7B **Privately Held**
WEB: www.jacusa.com
SIC: 3728 Aircraft parts & equipment
HQ: Japan Aerospace Corporation
1-1-1, Minamiaoyama
Minato-Ku TKY 107-0
357 855-970

(G-10291)
JACKEL INC
Also Called: Jackel International
1359 Broadway Fl 17 (10018-7117)
PHONE..............................908 359-2039
Gerard Raymond, *President*
Sebastien Williams, *Sales Executive*
April Wasnick, *Manager*
Scott Pestyner, *Admin Sec*
▲ **EMP:** 30
SQ FT: 11,800
SALES (est): 12.7MM **Privately Held**
WEB: www.jackelus.com
SIC: 2844 Cosmetic preparations

(G-10292)
JACKS AND JOKERS 52 LLC
215 E 68th St Apt 5o (10065-5720)
PHONE..............................917 740-2595
Scot Lerner,
EMP: 5
SALES (est): 631.3K **Privately Held**
SIC: 2321 Blouses, boys': made from purchased materials

(G-10293)
JACKSON DAKOTA INC
979 3rd Ave Ste 501 (10022-1393)
PHONE..............................718 786-8600
Ross Conn, *Manager*
EMP: 15
SALES (est): 1.8MM
SALES (corp-wide): 6.1MM **Privately Held**
WEB: www.dakotajackson.com
SIC: 2512 Wood upholstered chairs & couches
PA: Jackson Dakota Inc
979 3rd Ave Ste 503
New York NY 10022
212 838-9444

(G-10294)
JACKSON DAKOTA INC (PA)
979 3rd Ave Ste 503 (10022-1393)
PHONE..............................212 838-9444
Dakota Jackson, *President*
Gwyneth Perrott, *Manager*
▲ **EMP:** 2
SQ FT: 5,500
SALES (est): 6.1MM **Privately Held**
WEB: www.dakotajackson.com
SIC: 2512 Upholstered household furniture

(G-10295)
JACLYN INC
Also Called: Lindsay Lyn Accessories Div
330 5th Ave Rm 1305 (10001-3101)
PHONE..............................212 736-5657
Howard Rucker, *Division Mgr*
EMP: 10
SALES (corp-wide): 34.6MM **Publicly Held**
WEB: www.jaclyninc.com
SIC: 2335 Dresses, paper: cut & sewn
HQ: Jaclyn Llc
197 W Spring Valley Ave # 101
Maywood NJ 07607
201 909-6000

(G-10296)
JACMEL JEWELRY INC (PA)
1385 Broadway Fl 8 (10018-2102)
PHONE..............................718 349-4300
Jack Rahmey, *President*
Morris Dweck, *Vice Pres*
Evan Barkley, *Treasurer*
Thomas Milillo, *Admin Sec*
Nathan Dweck, *Asst Sec*
▲ **EMP:** 113 **EST:** 1977
SQ FT: 60,000
SALES: 100MM **Privately Held**
WEB: www.jacmel.com
SIC: 3911 Medals, precious or semiprecious metal

(G-10297)
JACOB HIDARY FOUNDATION INC
10 W 33rd St Rm 900 (10001-3317)
PHONE..............................212 736-6540
Abe Hidary, *President*
Jack A Hidary, *Vice Pres*
EMP: 10
SALES: 123.4K **Privately Held**
SIC: 2329 Men's & boys' sportswear & athletic clothing

(G-10298)
JACOBS & COHEN INC
Also Called: Sun Source
255 W 36th St Fl 9 (10018-7583)
PHONE..............................212 714-2702
Benjamin Cohen, *Ch of Bd*
Edward Jacobs, *President*
EMP: 25
SALES (est): 20.4K **Privately Held**
WEB: www.sunsourcejewelry.com
SIC: 3911 Jewelry, precious metal

(G-10299)
JAG FOOTWEAR ACC & RET CORP
1411 Broadway Fl 20 (10018-3471)
PHONE..............................800 999-1877
EMP: 6000
SALES (corp-wide): 287.1MM **Privately Held**
SIC: 3171 5661 5632 5139 Women's handbags & purses; handbags, women's; purses, women's; shoe stores; women's shoes; women's boots; apparel accessories; handbags; footwear; boots, canvas or leather: women's
HQ: Jag Footwear, Accessories And Retail Corporation
411 W Putnam Ave Fl 3
Greenwich CT 06830
239 301-3001

(G-10300)
JAGUAR CASTING CO INC
100 United Nations Plz 38a (10017-1713)
PHONE..............................212 869-0197
Puzant Khatchadourian, *President*
Jean Khatchadourian, *Vice Pres*
EMP: 25
SQ FT: 5,000
SALES (est): 2.9MM **Privately Held**
SIC: 3915 3911 Jewelers' castings; jewelry, precious metal

(G-10301)
JAGUAR JEWELRY CASTING NY INC
48 W 48th St Ste 500 (10036-1713)
PHONE..............................212 768-4848
Hovig Kajajian, *President*
Kevork Vekerejian, *Owner*
Jack Hallak, *Vice Pres*
Jospeh Nakashian, *Info Tech Mgr*
EMP: 9
SQ FT: 2,500
SALES (est): 2MM **Privately Held**
SIC: 3911 Jewelry apparel

(G-10302)
JAKOB SCHLAEPFER INC
37 W 26th St Rm 208 (10010-1150)
PHONE..............................212 221-2323
Peter Anderegg, *President*
Shkendie Kaziu, *Vice Pres*
EMP: 3
SQ FT: 1,000
SALES (est): 1.3MM **Privately Held**
WEB: www.jakobschlaepfer.com
SIC: 2221 2241 Broadwoven fabric mills, manmade; trimmings, textile

(G-10303)
JAMES MORGAN PUBLISHING (PA)
5 Penn Plz Ste 2300 (10001-1821)
PHONE..............................212 655-5470
Tiffany Gibson, *Editor*
David L Hancock, *Chairman*
Cindy Sauer, *Vice Pres*
Nickcole Watkins, *Marketing Staff*
Bethany Marshall, *Asst Director*
EMP: 1
SALES: 2MM **Privately Held**
SIC: 2731 Books: publishing & printing

(G-10304)
JAMES THOMPSON & COMPANY INC (PA)
463 7th Ave Rm 1603 (10018-7421)
PHONE..............................212 686-4242
Nicholas Griseto, *President*
Joseph Atarien, *General Mgr*
Barry Garr, *Vice Pres*
Terry Schultz, *Manager*
▲ **EMP:** 42 **EST:** 1860
SALES (est): 12.9MM **Privately Held**
WEB: www.jamesthompson.com
SIC: 2299 Burlap, jute

(G-10305)
JANE BOHAN INC
611 Broadway (10012-2608)
PHONE..............................212 529-6090
Jane Bohan, *President*
Laura Bothfeld, *Vice Pres*
▲ **EMP:** 6
SQ FT: 300
SALES: 970K **Privately Held**
SIC: 3911 Jewelry, precious metal

(G-10306)
JANES DESIGNER YRN PTTRNS INC
Also Called: Jane Knitting Kit
1745 Broadway Ste 1750 (10019-4640)
PHONE..............................347 260-3071
Jane Klein, *Principal*
EMP: 6
SQ FT: 50
SALES: 6K **Privately Held**
SIC: 2282 5949 Knitting yarn: twisting, winding or spooling; sewing, needlework & piece goods

(G-10307)
JANICE MOSES REPRESENTS
99 Battery Pl Apt 10d (10280-1324)
PHONE..............................212 898-4898
Janice Moses, *Principal*
EMP: 5
SALES (est): 354.1K **Privately Held**
SIC: 2672 Coated paper, except photographic, carbon or abrasive

(G-10308)
JAPAN PRINTING & GRAPHICS INC
160 Broadway Lbby D (10038-4201)
PHONE..............................212 406-2905
Hiroshi Ono, *President*
EMP: 7
SALES: 500K **Privately Held**
WEB: www.japanprint.com
SIC: 2759 2752 Commercial printing; commercial printing, lithographic

(G-10309)
JARVIK HEART INC
333 W 52nd St Ste 700 (10019-6238)
PHONE..............................212 397-3911
Robert Jarvik MD, *President*
Dave Perry, *Vice Pres*
Pamela Whitehead, *Purch Mgr*
John Teal, *Research*
Marilyn Vos Savant, *CFO*
EMP: 36
SALES (est): 6.6MM **Privately Held**
WEB: www.jarvikheart.com
SIC: 3845 Surgical support systems: heart-lung machine, exc. iron lung

(G-10310)
JASANI DESIGNS USA INC
25 W 43rd St Ste 1014 (10036-7431)
PHONE..............................212 257-2465
Ameya Joshi, *President*
EMP: 8
SALES (est): 2.4MM **Privately Held**
SIC: 3911 Jewelry, precious metal
PA: Jasani
Hw - 6010, 6th Floor,
Mumbai MH

(G-10311)
JAX COCO USA LLC
5 Penn Plz Ste 2300 (10001-1821)
PHONE..............................347 688-8198
Jason Gonzales, *Sales Mgr*
Joel McMinn, *Sales Mgr*
John Craig,
▲ **EMP:** 5 **EST:** 2013
SALES: 300K **Privately Held**
SIC: 2076 Coconut oil

(G-10312)
JAY STRONGWATER HOLDINGS LLC (HQ)
12 W 21st St Fl 11 (10010-7097)
PHONE..............................646 657-0558
John J Ling, *CEO*
Brenda Jordan, *Accounts Exec*
▲ **EMP:** 1000
SALES (est): 140.6MM
SALES (corp-wide): 165.4MM **Privately Held**
SIC: 3499 3911 3471 3229 Picture frames, metal; jewelry, precious metal; jewelry apparel; decorative plating & finishing of formed products; glassware, art or decorative
PA: Rauch Industries, Inc.
3800a Little Mountain Rd
Gastonia NC 28056
704 867-5333

(G-10313)
JAYA APPAREL GROUP LLC
1384 Broadway Fl 18 (10018-6122)
PHONE..............................212 764-4980
Don Lewis, *Branch Mgr*
EMP: 20
SALES (corp-wide): 23.8MM **Privately Held**
SIC: 2339 Women's & misses' athletic clothing & sportswear
PA: Jaya Apparel Group Llc
5175 S Soto St
Vernon CA 90058
323 584-3500

(G-10314)
JAYDEN STAR LLC
385 5th Ave Rm 507 (10016-3346)
PHONE..............................212 686-0400
Maurice Mandelbaum, *Vice Pres*
Winnie Fung, *Accounts Mgr*
Jason Mandelbaum, *Mng Member*
Steven Tam, *Info Tech Dir*
EMP: 30
SQ FT: 5,000
SALES (est): 1.5MM **Privately Held**
SIC: 3911 5094 Jewelry apparel; jewelry & precious stones

(G-10315)
JAYMAR JEWELRY CO INC
69 5th Ave Apt 8d (10003-3008)
PHONE..............................212 564-4788
Jayson Levy, *President*
EMP: 5
SQ FT: 3,000
SALES (est): 551.2K **Privately Held**
SIC: 3961 Costume jewelry, ex. precious metal & semiprecious stones

(G-10316)
JBL TRADING LLC
Also Called: Crest Mills
3 W 35th St Fl 5 (10001-2204)
PHONE..............................347 394-5592
Joey Levy, *Mng Member*
EMP: 8
SALES (est): 614.8K **Privately Held**
SIC: 2273 Carpets & rugs
PA: Jbl Trading Llc
43 W 33rd St Rm 201
New York NY 10001

(G-10317)
JC CALIFORNIA INC
359 Broadway Fl 3 (10013-3932)
PHONE..............................212 334-4380
Hayati Banastey, *President*
EMP: 5
SALES (est): 186.2K **Privately Held**
SIC: 2389 Apparel & accessories

New York - New York County (G-10318) **GEOGRAPHIC SECTION**

(G-10318)
JC CRYSTAL INC
260 W 35th St Fl 10 (10001-2528)
PHONE 212 594-0858
Jimmy Ping Chong Loh, *President*
Lana Hertel, *Sales Dir*
▲ **EMP:** 50
SQ FT: 5,000
SALES: 5.8MM **Privately Held**
SIC: 3911 Jewelry apparel

(G-10319)
JCDECAUX MALLSCAPE LLC (DH)
350 5th Ave Fl 73 (10118-7401)
PHONE 646 834-1200
Bernard Pariost,
Jean-Luc Decaux,
EMP: 11
SALES (est): 1.6MM
SALES (corp-wide): 10.2MM **Privately Held**
SIC: 2531 Benches for public buildings
HQ: Jcdecaux North America, Inc.
350 5th Ave Fl 73
New York NY 10118
646 834-1200

(G-10320)
JDS GRAPHICS INC
Also Called: Jds Graphics
226 W 37th St Fl 10 (10018-9016)
PHONE 973 330-3300
Debra Yuran, *President*
Sheryl Heller, *Vice Pres*
Jeffery Kirschenbaum, *Vice Pres*
EMP: 12
SQ FT: 2,500
SALES (est): 1.1MM **Privately Held**
WEB: www.jdsgraphics.com
SIC: 2752 Commercial printing, offset

(G-10321)
JDT INTERNATIONAL LLC
276 5th Ave Rm 704 (10001-4527)
PHONE 212 400-7570
Tariq Osman, *Branch Mgr*
EMP: 8
SALES (corp-wide): 1.7MM **Privately Held**
SIC: 2392 5021 Blankets, comforters & beddings; beds & bedding
PA: Jdt International, Llc
3532 Tonkawood Rd
Minnetonka MN 55345
952 933-2558

(G-10322)
JEAN PHILIPPE FRAGRANCES LLC
551 5th Ave Rm 1500 (10176-1599)
PHONE 212 983-2640
Jean Madar,
Russell Greenberg,
◆ **EMP:** 57
SQ FT: 7,000
SALES (est): 9.9MM
SALES (corp-wide): 591.2MM **Publicly Held**
WEB: www.interparfumsinc.com
SIC: 2844 Perfumes & colognes
PA: Inter Parfums, Inc.
551 5th Ave
New York NY 10176
212 983-2640

(G-10323)
JEANJER LLC
Also Called: Just For Men Div
1400 Broadway Fl 15 (10018-5300)
PHONE 212 944-1370
Joe Nakash, *President*
AVI Naakash, *Vice Pres*
Ralph Nakash, *Treasurer*
John Banevicius 6463838123, *Manager*
▲ **EMP:** 3000
SALES (est): 105.7MM **Privately Held**
SIC: 2331 2337 2339 2369 Blouses, women's & juniors': made from purchased material; suits: women's, juniors'; slacks: women's, misses' & juniors'; girls' & children's outerwear

(G-10324)
JEANS INC
1357 Broadway Ste 411 (10018-7101)
PHONE 646 223-1122
Deepak Ramchandani, *CEO*
Paul Maulucci, *Controller*
EMP: 9 **EST:** 2012
SALES (est): 377.5K **Privately Held**
SIC: 2399 5136 Hand woven apparel; men's & boys' clothing

(G-10325)
JEMCAP SERVICING LLC
360 Madison Ave Rm 1902 (10017-7158)
PHONE 212 213-9353
Marsh Peter, *Principal*
EMP: 5
SALES (est): 278.6K **Privately Held**
SIC: 1389 Roustabout service

(G-10326)
JENALEX CREATIVE MARKETING INC
116 E 57th St Fl 3 (10022-2613)
PHONE 212 935-2266
Alexandra Grondahl, *President*
Ludwig J Cserhat, *Corp Secy*
▲ **EMP:** 7
SQ FT: 2,000
SALES (est): 800.2K **Privately Held**
WEB: www.jenalex.com
SIC: 3999 Boutiquing: decorating gift items with sequins, fruit, etc.

(G-10327)
JENVIE SPORT INC
241 W 37th St Rm 1007 (10018-6786)
P.O. Box 856, Bethpage (11714-0017)
PHONE 212 967-2322
Eli Goldstein, *President*
Linda Swobe, *Vice Pres*
Steven Goldstein, *Admin Sec*
▲ **EMP:** 7
SALES (est): 965.2K **Privately Held**
WEB: www.jenvie.com
SIC: 2339 Sportswear, women's

(G-10328)
JERRY SORBARA FURS INC
39 W 32nd St Rm 1400 (10001-3841)
PHONE 212 594-3897
Jerry Sorbara, *President*
Sal Sorbara, *Vice Pres*
Catherine Wilson, *Treasurer*
EMP: 11
SQ FT: 4,500
SALES: 2MM **Privately Held**
SIC: 2371 Apparel, fur

(G-10329)
JEWELRY ARTS MANUFACTURING
151 W 46th St Fl 12 (10036-8512)
PHONE 212 382-3583
Alberto Tapia, *CEO*
Ligia Tapia, *Vice Pres*
EMP: 40
SALES (est): 2.3MM **Privately Held**
WEB: www.jewelartjewelers.com
SIC: 3915 3961 3911 Jewelers' castings; jewelry polishing for the trade; jewelry soldering for the trade; costume jewelry; jewelry, precious metal

(G-10330)
JEWELS BY STAR LTD
Also Called: JB Star
555 5th Ave Fl 7 (10017-9267)
PHONE 212 308-3490
Yehuda Fouzailoff, *President*
Yehuda Feodailoff, *Vice Pres*
Rafael Fouzailoff, *Vice Pres*
EMP: 20
SQ FT: 2,000
SALES (est): 2.6MM **Privately Held**
WEB: www.jewelsbystar.com
SIC: 3911 Jewelry, precious metal

(G-10331)
JEWELTEX MFG CORP
48 W 48th St Ste 507 (10036-1713)
PHONE 212 921-8188
Barry Rosenfeld, *President*
Joe Itzkowitx, *Admin Sec*
EMP: 13

SQ FT: 1,500
SALES (est): 2.3MM **Privately Held**
SIC: 3911 Jewelry, precious metal

(G-10332)
JEWISH WEEK INC (PA)
1501 Broadway Ste 505 (10036-5504)
PHONE 212 921-7822
Richard Waloff, *Publisher*
Gary Rosenblatt, *Principal*
Robert Goldblum, *Editor*
Robert Glassman, *Accounts Exec*
Stephanie Leone, *Accounts Exec*
EMP: 35 **EST:** 1970
SQ FT: 6,000
SALES (est): 7MM **Privately Held**
WEB: www.thejewishweek.com
SIC: 2711 Newspapers: publishing only, not printed on site

(G-10333)
JFE ENGINEERING CORPORATION
350 Park Ave Fl 27th (10022-6022)
PHONE 212 310-9320
Hedenori Tawaza, *Branch Mgr*
EMP: 10
SALES (corp-wide): 34.5B **Privately Held**
SIC: 3312 Sheet or strip, steel, hot-rolled
HQ: Jfe Engineering Corporation
1-8-1, Marunouchi
Chiyoda-Ku TKY 100-0
362 120-800

(G-10334)
JFE STEEL AMERICA INC (HQ)
600 3rd Ave Fl 12 (10016-1921)
PHONE 212 310-9320
Kaoru Okamoto, *President*
EMP: 7
SALES (est): 2.2MM
SALES (corp-wide): 34.5B **Privately Held**
SIC: 3312 Sheet or strip, steel, hot-rolled; sheet or strip, steel, cold-rolled: own hot-rolled; tinplate; iron & steel: galvanized, pipes, plates, sheets, etc.
PA: Jfe Holdings, Inc.
2-2-3, Uchisaiwaicho
Chiyoda-Ku TKY 100-0
335 974-321

(G-10335)
JFS INC
Also Called: Joe Fresh
531 W 26th St Unit 531 # 531 (10001-5514)
PHONE 646 264-1200
Mario Grauso, *President*
Ciaran Parr, *Director*
EMP: 19 **EST:** 2010
SALES (est): 3.7MM
SALES (corp-wide): 37.8B **Privately Held**
SIC: 2253 T-shirts & tops, knit
HQ: Loblaw Companies Limited
1 Presidents Choice Cir
Brampton ON L6Y 5
905 459-2500

(G-10336)
JGX LLC
1407 Broadway Rm 1416 (10018-2842)
PHONE 212 575-1244
Nouri Jaradeh, *Vice Pres*
Jack Grazi, *Vice Pres*
EMP: 5
SQ FT: 3,000
SALES (est): 87K **Privately Held**
SIC: 2369 Leggings: girls', children's & infants'

(G-10337)
JILL FAGIN ENTERPRISES INC (PA)
Also Called: Jillery
39 E 12th St Apt 612 (10003-4621)
PHONE 212 674-9383
Jill Fagin, *President*
EMP: 8
SALES (est): 670K **Privately Held**
SIC: 3961 3262 Costume jewelry; vitreous china table & kitchenware

(G-10338)
JIM WACHTLER INC
1212 Avenue Of The (10036)
PHONE 212 755-4367

James Wachtler, *President*
EMP: 3
SALES: 3MM **Privately Held**
SIC: 3915 5094 5944 Gems, real & imitation: preparation for settings; diamond cutting & polishing; precious stones (gems); jewelry, precious stones & precious metals

(G-10339)
JIMEALE INCORPORATED
130 Church St Ste 163 (10007-2226)
P.O. Box 841, Southport CT (06890-0841)
PHONE 917 686-5383
▲ **EMP:** 6
SALES (est): 692.9K **Privately Held**
SIC: 2389 Mfg Accessories

(G-10340)
JIMMY CRYSTAL NEW YORK CO LTD
47 W 37th St Fl 3 (10018-6294)
PHONE 212 594-0858
Ping Chong Loh, *Ch of Bd*
Alice Chui, *Vice Pres*
Tracy Liao, *Buyer*
▲ **EMP:** 32
SQ FT: 13,500
SALES (est): 3.4MM **Privately Held**
SIC: 3231 3911 Watch crystals, glass; jewelry, precious metal

(G-10341)
JIRANIMO INDUSTRIES LTD
Also Called: Long Paige
49a W 37th St (10018-6202)
PHONE 212 921-5106
Parviz Shirian, *President*
Aaron Ostad, *President*
Adam Ostad, *Vice Pres*
Shamouiel Ostad, *Treasurer*
▲ **EMP:** 12
SQ FT: 17,500
SALES (est): 1.3MM **Privately Held**
SIC: 2335 Women's, juniors' & misses' dresses

(G-10342)
JJ BASICS LLC (PA)
525 7th Ave Rm 307 (10018-4930)
PHONE 212 768-4779
Steven Bensadigh, *President*
Vivian Zhao, *Vice Pres*
Taylor Zhao, *Production*
Erika Kwon, *Design Engr*
Subhash Parikh, *Controller*
▲ **EMP:** 21
SQ FT: 5,400
SALES (est): 2.4MM **Privately Held**
SIC: 2253 Sweaters & sweater coats, knit

(G-10343)
JJ FANTASIA INC
38 W 32nd St (10001-3816)
PHONE 212 868-1198
Cheng Hsuan Wu, *Ch of Bd*
EMP: 7
SALES (est): 630.1K **Privately Held**
SIC: 3961 Jewelry apparel, non-precious metals

(G-10344)
JM MANUFACTURER INC
241 W 37th St Rm 924 (10018-6970)
PHONE 212 869-0626
Liuchu Jia, *Principal*
EMP: 3
SQ FT: 700
SALES (est): 4.1MM **Privately Held**
SIC: 2221 Apparel & outerwear fabric, manmade fiber or silk

(G-10345)
JM STUDIO INC
247 W 35th St Fl 3 (10001-1926)
PHONE 646 546-5514
Yim Lan Dong, *CEO*
▲ **EMP:** 15
SQ FT: 6,000
SALES (est): 1.7MM **Privately Held**
SIC: 2389 5699 Uniforms & vestments; sports apparel

▲ = Import ▼ = Export
◆ = Import/Export

(G-10346)
JOAN BOYCE LTD (PA)
19 W 44th St Ste 417 (10036-5900)
PHONE..................................212 867-7474
Joan Boyce, *President*
Allen Boyce, *Vice Pres*
EMP: 4
SQ FT: 1,100
SALES: 7MM **Privately Held**
WEB: www.joanboyce.com
SIC: 3911 5944 Jewelry, precious metal; jewelry stores

(G-10347)
JOBSON MEDICAL INFORMATION LLC (PA)
440 9th Ave Fl 14 (10001-1629)
PHONE..................................212 274-7000
Michael Tansey, *CEO*
Peter Skinner, *Exec VP*
John Orr, *CFO*
Jeff Macdonald, *Mng Member*
Michael R Lemon, *Mng Member*
▲ **EMP:** 120 **EST:** 1958
SALES (est): 87.5MM **Privately Held**
WEB: www.revoptom.com
SIC: 2721 2741 Magazines: publishing & printing; miscellaneous publishing

(G-10348)
JOCKEY INTERNATIONAL INC
Also Called: Jockey Store
1411 Broadway Rm 1010 (10018-3560)
PHONE..................................212 840-4900
Janine Forgie, *Branch Mgr*
EMP: 30
SALES (corp-wide): 209.4MM **Privately Held**
SIC: 2254 Knit underwear mills
PA: Jockey International, Inc.
2300 60th St
Kenosha WI 53140
262 658-8111

(G-10349)
JOE BENBASSET INC (PA)
213 W 35th St Fl 11 (10001-1903)
PHONE..................................212 594-8440
Murray Benbasset, *President*
◆ **EMP:** 30 **EST:** 1948
SQ FT: 10,000
SALES (est): 8.2MM **Privately Held**
SIC: 2339 Sportswear, women's

(G-10350)
JOED PRESS
242 W 36th St Fl 8 (10018-7542)
PHONE..................................212 243-3620
Angela Vann, *General Mgr*
EMP: 5 **EST:** 2010
SALES (est): 268.1K **Privately Held**
SIC: 2759 Commercial printing

(G-10351)
JOHN KOCHIS CUSTOM DESIGNS
237 W 35th St Ste 502 (10001-1905)
PHONE..................................212 244-6046
John Kochis, *Owner*
EMP: 7
SALES: 300K **Privately Held**
SIC: 2311 Tailored suits & formal jackets

(G-10352)
JOHN KRISTIANSEN NEW YORK INC
665 Broadway Frnt (10012-2300)
PHONE..................................212 388-1097
John Kristiansen, *President*
EMP: 10
SALES (est): 953.1K **Privately Held**
SIC: 2389 Costumes

(G-10353)
JOHN N FEHLINGER CO INC (PA)
20 Vesey St Rm 1000 (10007-4225)
PHONE..................................212 233-5656
Kevin Arcuri, *President*
John Capuano, *Treasurer*
Thomas Lautenschlager, *Sales Engr*
James Talerico, *Manager*
Sheree Pelmen, *Admin Sec*
▲ **EMP:** 15 **EST:** 1945
SQ FT: 4,000
SALES (est): 5MM **Privately Held**
WEB: www.fehlingerco.com
SIC: 3491 3561 5084 5085 Steam traps; pumps & pumping equipment; industrial pumps & parts; industrial machinery & equipment; water pumps (industrial); valves & fittings

(G-10354)
JOHN SZOKE GRAPHICS INC
Also Called: John Szoke Editions
24 W 57th St Ste 304 (10019-3918)
PHONE..................................212 219-8300
John Szoke, *President*
▲ **EMP:** 8
SQ FT: 10,000
SALES (est): 520K **Privately Held**
WEB: www.johnszokeeditions.com
SIC: 2741 Miscellaneous publishing

(G-10355)
JOHNNY BIENSTOCK MUSIC
126 E 38th St (10016-2602)
PHONE..................................212 779-7977
John Bienstock, *Owner*
EMP: 25
SALES (est): 1.3MM **Privately Held**
SIC: 2741 Music books: publishing & printing

(G-10356)
JOLIBE ATELIER LLC
325 W 38th St Studio (10018)
PHONE..................................917 319-5908
EMP: 10 **EST:** 2007
SALES: 917K **Privately Held**
SIC: 2389 Men's miscellaneous accessories

(G-10357)
JON TERI SPORTS INC (PA)
241 W 37th St Frnt 2 (10018-6797)
PHONE..................................212 398-0657
Rickie Freeman, *President*
Leora Platt, *Sales Staff*
▲ **EMP:** 35 **EST:** 1981
SQ FT: 6,000
SALES (est): 4.9MM **Privately Held**
SIC: 2335 2337 Women's, juniors' & misses' dresses; suits: women's, misses' & juniors'

(G-10358)
JONATHAN MEIZLER LLC
Also Called: Title of Work
57 Orchard St (10002-5414)
PHONE..................................212 213-2977
Jonathan Meizler, *Mfg Staff*
EMP: 7
SQ FT: 1,500
SALES (est): 418K **Privately Held**
SIC: 2389 Men's miscellaneous accessories

(G-10359)
JONATHAN MICHAEL COAT CORP
463 Fashion Ave Rm 1502 (10018-7596)
PHONE..................................212 239-9230
Bruce Heart, *President*
Nathan Printz, *Corp Secy*
▲ **EMP:** 7
SQ FT: 1,500
SALES (est): 840.5K **Privately Held**
SIC: 2339 Women's & misses' jackets & coats, except sportswear

(G-10360)
JORDACHE ENTERPRISES INC
Fubu Jeans By Je Sport Co Div
1400 Broadway Rm 1415 (10018-5336)
PHONE..................................212 944-1330
Ezri Sirveb, *Branch Mgr*
EMP: 100
SALES (corp-wide): 1.4B **Privately Held**
WEB: www.jordache.com
SIC: 2339 2325 2369 2331 Slacks: women's, misses' & juniors'; men's & boys' trousers & slacks; slacks: girls' & children's; jackets: girls', children's & infants'; shirts, women's & juniors': made from purchased materials; men's & boys' furnishings; shirts: girls', children's & infants'
PA: Jordache Enterprises Inc.
1400 Broadway Rm 1400 # 1400
New York NY 10018
212 643-8400

(G-10361)
JORDACHE ENTERPRISES INC (PA)
1400 Broadway Rm 1400 # 1400 (10018-5336)
PHONE..................................212 643-8400
Joe Nakash, *CEO*
Jonathan Bennett, *Managing Dir*
Ralph Nakash, *Corp Secy*
Eddie Benaderet, *Exec VP*
Albert Braha, *Vice Pres*
▲ **EMP:** 145
SALES (est): 1.4B **Privately Held**
WEB: www.jordache.com
SIC: 2339 2325 2369 2331 Slacks: women's, misses' & juniors'; men's & boys' trousers & slacks; slacks: girls' & children's; jackets: girls', children's & infants'; shirts, women's & juniors': made from purchased materials; men's & boys' furnishings; shirts: girls', children's & infants'

(G-10362)
JORDAN SCOTT DESIGNS LTD
Also Called: Plaza Group Creation
25 W 36th St Fl 12 (10018-7677)
PHONE..................................212 947-4250
Edward Schantz, *CEO*
EMP: 25
SQ FT: 4,500
SALES (est): 2.4MM **Privately Held**
SIC: 3911 Jewelry, precious metal

(G-10363)
JOSEPH (UK) INC
1061 Madison Ave Grnd (10028-0239)
PHONE..................................212 570-0077
Hiroaki Sumi, *Ch of Bd*
Louis Loketch, *Principal*
EMP: 5
SALES (est): 527.5K **Privately Held**
SIC: 2329 5621 5651 Men's & boys' sportswear & athletic clothing; women's clothing stores; jeans stores

(G-10364)
JOSEPH INDUSTRIES INC (PA)
Also Called: Color Fx
1410 Broadway Rm 1201 (10018-9348)
PHONE..................................212 764-0010
Prakash Joseph, *President*
▲ **EMP:** 50
SQ FT: 5,000
SALES (est): 4.6MM **Privately Held**
SIC: 2389 Men's miscellaneous accessories

(G-10365)
JOSEPH TREU SUCCESSORS INC
104 W 27th St Rm 5b (10001-6210)
PHONE..................................212 691-7026
Harvey Schreibman, *President*
Arlene Schreibman, *Corp Secy*
EMP: 5
SQ FT: 3,000
SALES: 700K **Privately Held**
SIC: 3953 Embossing seals & hand stamps

(G-10366)
JOSIE ACCESSORIES INC
Also Called: Elrene Home Fashions
261 5th Ave Fl 10 (10016-7701)
PHONE..................................212 889-6376
Bryan Siegel, *Ch of Bd*
Craig Siegel, *Vice Pres*
Frank Giacomini, *CFO*
Richard Orent, *CFO*
▲ **EMP:** 90 **EST:** 1945
SQ FT: 20,000
SALES (est): 10.9MM **Privately Held**
SIC: 2392 Tablecloths: made from purchased materials; placemats, plastic or textile

(G-10367)
JOTALY INC
Also Called: Andin International Inc.
1385 Broadway Fl 12 (10018-6118)
PHONE..................................212 886-6000
Ofer Azrielant, *Ch of Bd*
John C Esposito, *Vice Pres*
Leeann Nunnery, *Accounts Mgr*
Isaac E Drucker, *Asst Sec*
▲ **EMP:** 750
SQ FT: 48,000
SALES (est): 87.8MM
SALES (corp-wide): 242.1B **Publicly Held**
WEB: www.andin.com
SIC: 3911 Jewelry, precious metal
HQ: Richline Group, Inc.
1385 Broadway Fl 12
New York NY 10018

(G-10368)
JOURNAL REGISTER COMPANY (PA)
5 Hanover Sq Fl 25 (10004-4008)
PHONE..................................212 257-7212
John Paton, *CEO*
James W Hall, *Ch of Bd*
Paul Provost, *President*
William J Higginson, *Senior VP*
Edward J Yocum Jr, *Senior VP*
EMP: 40
SQ FT: 36,443
SALES (est): 661.2MM **Privately Held**
WEB: www.journalregister.com
SIC: 2711 Newspapers, publishing & printing

(G-10369)
JOVANI FASHION LTD
1370 Broadway Fl 4 (10018-7786)
PHONE..................................212 279-0222
Saul Maslavi, *President*
Abraham Maslavi, *Vice Pres*
◆ **EMP:** 30
SQ FT: 8,000
SALES (est): 3.8MM **Privately Held**
WEB: www.jovani.com
SIC: 2335 Gowns, formal

(G-10370)
JOYCE TRIMMING INC
109 W 38th St (10018-3615)
PHONE..................................212 719-3110
Hwe Young Lee, *President*
▲ **EMP:** 8
SQ FT: 2,000
SALES: 2MM **Privately Held**
WEB: www.ejoyce.com
SIC: 3965 Buttons & parts

(G-10371)
JPL DESIGNS LTD
343 E 30th St Apt 3k (10016-6409)
PHONE..................................212 689-7096
John Leveroni, *Ch of Bd*
EMP: 8
SALES (est): 686.9K **Privately Held**
SIC: 3449 Miscellaneous metalwork

(G-10372)
JRG APPAREL GROUP COMPANY LTD
Also Called: Indigo Rein
1407 Broadway Rm 817 (10018-3287)
PHONE..................................212 997-0900
Jay Gorman, *Ch of Bd*
▲ **EMP:** 24
SQ FT: 3,300
SALES (est): 30MM **Privately Held**
SIC: 2211 Denims

(G-10373)
JS BLANK & CO INC
112 Madison Ave Fl 7 (10016-7484)
PHONE..................................212 689-4835
Joseph S Blank, *CEO*
Barbara Blank, *Vice Pres*
EMP: 25
SQ FT: 7,500
SALES (est): 2.6MM **Privately Held**
SIC: 2323 Men's & boys' neckwear

New York - New York County (G-10374) GEOGRAPHIC SECTION

(G-10374)
JSC DESIGNS LTD
550 Fashion Ave Fl 22 (10018-3223)
PHONE.................................212 302-1001
Mitchell Hops, *President*
Alicia Moscovitch, *Accounts Mgr*
▲ **EMP:** 20
SQ FT: 8,000
SALES (est): 2MM **Privately Held**
SIC: 2339 Service apparel, washable: women's

(G-10375)
JUDYS GROUP INC
226 W 37th St Fl 7 (10018-0659)
PHONE.................................212 921-0515
Howard Schlossberg, *President*
Michele Tepper, *Exec VP*
Stefan Ciobanescu, *Prdtn Mgr*
Michelle Pepper, *CFO*
▲ **EMP:** 50
SQ FT: 11,000
SALES (est): 10.5MM **Privately Held**
WEB: www.judysgroup.com
SIC: 2337 2339 2335 Suits: women's, misses' & juniors'; athletic clothing: women's, misses' & juniors'; women's, juniors' & misses' dresses

(G-10376)
JULIUS KLEIN GROUP
580 5th Ave Ste 500 (10036-4727)
PHONE.................................212 719-1811
Julius Klein, *Owner*
Pearl Rothman, *COO*
Moshe Klein, *Sales Dir*
Steve Berger, *Sales Staff*
Sidney Mandel, *Sales Executive*
▲ **EMP:** 50
SALES (est): 4.1MM **Privately Held**
SIC: 3915 Diamond cutting & polishing

(G-10377)
JULIUS LOWY FRAME RESTORING CO
232 E 59th St 4fn (10022-1464)
PHONE.................................212 861-8585
Lawrence A Shar, *President*
Patty Tan, *Human Resources*
Lisa Wyer, *VP Sales*
Michael Tramis, *Manager*
Adam Sperling, *Technician*
EMP: 35
SQ FT: 20,000
SALES (est): 4.2MM **Privately Held**
WEB: www.lowyonline.com
SIC: 2499 8999 Picture frame molding, finished; art restoration

(G-10378)
JUMP DESIGN GROUP INC
Also Called: Jump Design Group, The
1400 Broadway Fl 2 (10018-1075)
PHONE.................................212 869-3300
Glenn Schlossberg, *Ch of Bd*
Terry Friedman, *President*
Peter Gabbe, *Principal*
Jodie Mendoza, *Vice Pres*
Joann Abellar, *Project Mgr*
▲ **EMP:** 140
SQ FT: 18,000
SALES (est): 30.7MM **Privately Held**
WEB: www.jumpapparel.com
SIC: 2335 Women's, juniors' & misses' dresses

(G-10379)
JUMP RAMP GAMES INC
307 W 38th St Rm 1101 (10018-9528)
PHONE.................................212 500-1456
Dan Kim, *President*
Tony Vartanian, *Principal*
Alexander Betancur, *Chairman*
Jeremy Strauser, *Vice Pres*
Ryan Safarian, *Engineer*
EMP: 45
SALES (est): 336.4K **Privately Held**
SIC: 7372 Application computer software

(G-10380)
JUMPROPE INC
121 W 27th St Ste 1204 (10001-6261)
P.O. Box 1616 (10113-1616)
PHONE.................................347 927-5867
Jesse Olsen, *CEO*
Justin Meyer, *COO*
Nathan Patton, *Engineer*
EMP: 9
SQ FT: 500
SALES (est): 580K **Privately Held**
SIC: 7372 Educational computer software

(G-10381)
JUNE JACOBS LABS LLC
460 Park Ave Fl 16 (10022-1829)
PHONE.................................212 471-4830
Tiffany Cavallaro, *Vice Pres*
Elisabeth Gil, *Sales Staff*
Jessica Khani, *Marketing Mgr*
Vanessa Gonzalez, *Marketing Staff*
Tamara Ramos, *Marketing Staff*
EMP: 65
SALES (corp-wide): 16.4MM **Privately Held**
SIC: 2844 Cosmetic preparations
PA: June Jacobs Labs, Llc
  46 Graphic Pl
  Moonachie NJ 07074
  201 329-9100

(G-10382)
JUPITER CREATIONS INC
330 7th Ave Ste 901 (10001-5010)
PHONE.................................917 493-9393
Michael Katina, *President*
◆ **EMP:** 2
SQ FT: 1,000
SALES (est): 3MM **Privately Held**
SIC: 3942 3944 Dolls & stuffed toys; airplanes, toy

(G-10383)
JUST BOTTOMS & TOPS INC (PA)
Also Called: Hot Cashews
1412 Broadway Rm 1808 (10018-9228)
PHONE.................................212 564-3202
Mickey Mait, *President*
Sanders Acker, *Vice Pres*
Mitch Levy, *Vice Pres*
Aaron Feder, *Treasurer*
Jerry Hymowitz, *Admin Sec*
EMP: 10
SQ FT: 3,900
SALES (est): 915.3K **Privately Held**
SIC: 2329 2339 Sweaters & sweater jackets: men's & boys'; women's & misses' outerwear

(G-10384)
JUST BRASS INC
215 W 90th St Apt 9a (10024-1224)
PHONE.................................212 724-5447
Ronald Zabinski, *President*
EMP: 5
SALES (est): 150K **Privately Held**
SIC: 3172 5136 2321 Personal leather goods; shirts, men's & boys'; men's & boys' furnishings

(G-10385)
JUST GOODS INC
311 W 43rd St Fl 12 (10036-6004)
PHONE.................................917 294-0043
Ira Laufer, *CEO*
Dan Danai, *CFO*
EMP: 14 **EST:** 2013
SALES (est): 887.3K **Privately Held**
SIC: 2086 Water, pasteurized: packaged in cans, bottles, etc.

(G-10386)
JUSTPERFECTMSP LTD
48 W 48th St Ste 401 (10036-1727)
PHONE.................................877 201-0005
Edward Zylka, *President*
Shirley Glumer, *Exec VP*
Ewa Zylka, *Director*
▲ **EMP:** 45 **EST:** 1994
SQ FT: 5,000
SALES (est): 1.9MM **Privately Held**
SIC: 3911 5094 Jewelry, precious metal; jewelry & precious stones
PA: Art-Tec Jewelry Designs Ltd
  48 W 48th St Ste 401
  New York NY 10036

(G-10387)
JUSTYNA KAMINSKA NY INC
1261 Broadway Rm 406 (10001-3631)
PHONE.................................917 423-5527
J Kaminska Cabbad, *President*
Justyna Kaminska Cabbad, *President*
▲ **EMP:** 1
SALES: 800
SALES (est): 1MM **Privately Held**
SIC: 3911 Jewelry, precious metal

(G-10388)
JUVLY AESTHETICS INC
18 E 41st St Rm 406 (10017-6269)
PHONE.................................614 686-3627
Justin Harper, *Principal*
EMP: 100
SALES (est): 3.1MM **Privately Held**
SIC: 3845 Laser systems & equipment, medical

(G-10389)
JVL VENTURES LLC
Also Called: Softcard
230 Park Ave Rm 2829 (10169-2801)
PHONE.................................212 365-7555
Michael Abbott, *CEO*
EMP: 100
SQ FT: 9,000
SALES (est): 16.4MM **Privately Held**
SIC: 7372 Application computer software

(G-10390)
K ROAD POWER MANAGEMENT LLC (PA)
330 Madison Ave Fl 25 (10017-5022)
PHONE.................................212 351-0535
William Kriegel, *CEO*
Mathew Sachs, *Vice Pres*
Carl Weatherley-White, *CFO*
Amine Alami, *Director*
Armelle Buvron, *Executive Asst*
EMP: 9
SALES (est): 1.2MM **Privately Held**
SIC: 3612 Transformers, except electric

(G-10391)
K T P DESIGN CO INC
118 E 28th St Rm 707 (10016-8448)
PHONE.................................212 481-6613
Patrick Walsh, *President*
▼ **EMP:** 15 **EST:** 1998
SALES (est): 1.6MM **Privately Held**
WEB: www.customtie.com
SIC: 2339 Neckwear & ties: women's, misses' & juniors'

(G-10392)
K2 INTERNATIONAL CORP
22 W 32nd St Fl 9 (10001-3807)
PHONE.................................212 947-1734
John Hyun Kim, *President*
▲ **EMP:** 5
SQ FT: 7,000
SALES (est): 390K **Privately Held**
SIC: 3961 Costume jewelry

(G-10393)
KADMON CORPORATION LLC (PA)
450 E 29th St Fl 5 (10016-8367)
PHONE.................................212 308-6000
Harlan Waksal, *CEO*
Samuel D Waksal, *Chairman*
Larry Cohen, *Exec VP*
John Ryan, *Exec VP*
Zhenping Zhu, *Exec VP*
EMP: 10
SALES (est): 26.2MM **Privately Held**
SIC: 2834 Pharmaceutical preparations

(G-10394)
KADMON HOLDINGS INC
450 E 29th St (10016-8367)
PHONE.................................212 308-6000
Bart M Schwartz, *Ch of Bd*
Harlan W Waksal, *President*
Konstantin Poukalov, *Exec VP*
John Ryan, *Chief Mktg Ofcr*
Eugene Bauer, *Bd of Directors*
EMP: 58
SALES: 12.2MM **Privately Held**
SIC: 2836 2834 Biological products, except diagnostic; pharmaceutical preparations

(G-10395)
KAHN-LUCAS-LANCASTER INC
112 W 34th St Ste 600 (10120-0700)
PHONE.................................212 239-2407
Maria Rizzolo, *Vice Pres*
Jenny Lin, *Prdtn Mgr*
Yuliya Akopova, *Production*
Susan Ashcroft, *Controller*
Howard Kahn, *Branch Mgr*
EMP: 80
SALES (corp-wide): 44.5MM **Privately Held**
WEB: www.kahnlucas.com
SIC: 2369 Mfg Girl/Youth Outerwear
PA: Kahn-Lucas-Lancaster, Inc.
  306 Primrose Ln
  Mountville PA 17554
  717 537-4140

(G-10396)
KALEIDOSCOPE IMAGING INC
251 W 39th St Fl 4 (10018-3143)
PHONE.................................212 631-9947
Garo Ksparian, *Partner*
EMP: 30
SALES (est): 4.7MM
SALES (corp-wide): 14.4MM **Privately Held**
SIC: 2752 Commercial printing, lithographic
PA: Kaleidoscope Imaging, Inc.
  700 N Sacramento Blvd # 2
  Chicago IL 60612
  773 722-9300

(G-10397)
KALEKO BROS
62 W 47th St Ste 1504 (10036-3249)
PHONE.................................212 819-0100
Jerome Kaleko, *Partner*
EMP: 5 **EST:** 1948
SQ FT: 2,000
SALES (est): 304.2K **Privately Held**
SIC: 3915 Diamond cutting & polishing

(G-10398)
KALIKOW BROTHERS LP
34 W 33rd St Fl 4n (10001-3304)
PHONE.................................212 643-0315
Marc Kalikow, *President*
Paul Levine, *Vice Pres*
EMP: 30 **EST:** 1929
SQ FT: 8,000
SALES (est): 1.8MM **Privately Held**
WEB: www.fishmantobin.com
SIC: 2325 Trousers, dress (separate): men's, youths' & boys'
HQ: F&T Apparel Llc
  4000 Chemical Rd Ste 500
  Plymouth Meeting PA 19462
  610 828-8400

(G-10399)
KALLEN CORP
Also Called: Capstone Printing
99 Hudson St (10013-2815)
P.O. Box 516 (10014-0516)
PHONE.................................212 242-1470
Alan Finkelstein, *President*
EMP: 5
SQ FT: 3,000
SALES (est): 801.6K **Privately Held**
SIC: 2759 Commercial printing

(G-10400)
KALTEX AMERICA INC
350 5th Ave Ste 7100 (10118-7120)
PHONE.................................212 971-0575
Hebe Schecter, *CEO*
Rafael M Kalach, *Ch of Bd*
Jennifer Mason, *CFO*
EMP: 18 **EST:** 1987
SQ FT: 1,000
SALES: 161MM **Privately Held**
SIC: 2339 2325 Jeans: women's, misses' & juniors'; jeans: men's, youths' & boys'
HQ: Kaltex North America, Inc.
  350 5th Ave Ste 7100
  New York NY 10118
  212 894-3200

(G-10401)
KALTEX NORTH AMERICA INC (HQ)
350 5th Ave Ste 7100 (10118-7120)
PHONE.................................212 894-3200
Rafael Kalach, *Ch of Bd*
Moises Kalach, *Senior VP*
James Blaine, *IT/INT Sup*
Travis Spicer, *Internal Med*

GEOGRAPHIC SECTION

Haleen Zweifel, *Regional*
▲ **EMP:** 10
SALES (est): 196MM **Privately Held**
WEB: www.kaltexhome.com
SIC: 2392 Comforters & quilts: made from purchased materials

(G-10402)
KAMWO MERIDIAN HERBS LLC
211 Grand St (10013-4223)
PHONE 212 966-6370
Thomas N Leung,
EMP: 48
SALES (est): 1.7MM **Privately Held**
SIC: 2833 Drugs & herbs: grading, grinding & milling

(G-10403)
KANE-M INC
Also Called: Morito/Kane-M
135 W 29th St Rm 1003 (10001-5162)
PHONE 973 777-2797
Ken Egawa, *CEO*
EMP: 7
SQ FT: 10,000
SALES (est): 490.9K
SALES (corp-wide): 364MM **Privately Held**
SIC: 3965 Fasteners, buttons, needles & pins
PA: Morito Co., Ltd.
4-2-4, Minamihonmachi, Chuo-Ku
Osaka OSK 541-0
662 523-551

(G-10404)
KANEKA AMERICA LLC
546 5th Ave Fl 21 (10036-5000)
PHONE 212 705-4340
Yasushi Kawasumi, *Controller*
Kazuo Kuruma,
EMP: 73 **EST:** 1972
SALES (est): 10.9MM
SALES (corp-wide): 5.6B **Privately Held**
WEB: www.kanecaron.com
SIC: 2295 2834 2099 3089 Resin or plastic coated fabrics; pharmaceutical preparations; food preparations; synthetic resin finished products; chemical preparations
HQ: Kaneka Americas Holding, Inc.
6250 Underwood Rd
Pasadena TX 77507
281 474-7084

(G-10405)
KAPLAN INC
Kaplan Interactive
444 Madison Ave Ste 803 (10022-6903)
PHONE 212 752-1840
Robert Greenburg, *Manager*
EMP: 35
SALES (corp-wide): 2.5B **Publicly Held**
WEB: www.kaplan.com
SIC: 2731 Software Book Publishers
HQ: Kaplan, Inc.
750 3rd Ave Fl 7
New York NY 10017
212 492-5800

(G-10406)
KAPRIELIAN ENTERPRISES INC
Also Called: Concord Settings
207 W 25th St Fl 8 (10001-7158)
PHONE 212 645-6623
Hratch Kaprielian, *President*
Linda Carlsen, *Sales Staff*
Ray Mercurius, *Sales Executive*
Timothy Kilburn, *Manager*
▲ **EMP:** 70
SQ FT: 6,000
SALES (est): 9.7MM **Privately Held**
WEB: www.kaprielian.com
SIC: 3911 3015 Jewel settings & mountings, precious metal; jewelers' materials & lapidary work

(G-10407)
KARBRA COMPANY
460 Park Ave Rm 401 (10022-1848)
PHONE 212 736-9300
Sing Ming Liu, *Partner*
Carole Roth, *Partner*
Peter Roth, *Partner*
Fiam Ildiko Roth, *Vice Pres*
George Barna, *MIS Dir*

EMP: 140 **EST:** 1940
SQ FT: 10,000
SALES (est): 11.5MM **Privately Held**
WEB: www.karbra.com
SIC: 3915 3911 3369 3341 Jewelers' castings; jewelry, precious metal; nonferrous foundries; secondary nonferrous metals

(G-10408)
KAREN KANE INC
1441 Broadway Fl 33 (10018-1905)
PHONE 212 827-0980
Becky Blair, *Manager*
EMP: 12
SALES (corp-wide): 58MM **Privately Held**
SIC: 2339 Sportswear, women's
PA: Karen Kane, Inc.
2275 E 37th St
Vernon CA 90058
323 588-0000

(G-10409)
KARTELL US INC
39 Greene St (10013-2605)
PHONE 212 966-6665
◆ **EMP:** 6
SALES (est): 130.3K **Privately Held**
SIC: 2392 Household furnishings

(G-10410)
KAS-RAY INDUSTRIES INC
Also Called: Kay-Ray Industries
122 W 26th St (10001-6804)
PHONE 212 620-3144
Tony Petrizzo, *President*
EMP: 10
SQ FT: 10,000
SALES (est): 1.9MM **Privately Held**
WEB: www.kasray.com
SIC: 2752 5112 5021 Commercial printing, offset; stationery & office supplies; office furniture

(G-10411)
KASEYA US SALES LLC
26 W 17th St Fl 9 (10011-5710)
PHONE 415 694-5700
Fred Voccola, *Mng Member*
Isaac Itenberg,
EMP: 99
SALES (est): 16.2MM **Privately Held**
SIC: 7372 Prepackaged software

(G-10412)
KASISTO INC
43 W 24th St Rm 8b (10010-3530)
PHONE 917 734-4750
Zor Gorelov, *CEO*
William Mark, *Principal*
Jeffrey Seltzer, *Principal*
Rich Ciapala, *Senior VP*
Ruth Brown, *Vice Pres*
EMP: 40 **EST:** 2013
SQ FT: 150
SALES (est): 396.7K **Privately Held**
SIC: 7372 Business oriented computer software

(G-10413)
KASPER GROUP LLC (HQ)
1412 Broadway Fl 5 (10018-3330)
PHONE 212 354-4311
EMP: 15
SALES (est): 1.7MM
SALES (corp-wide): 244.7MM **Privately Held**
SIC: 2339 Mfg Women's/Misses' Outerwear
PA: Jones Holdings Llc
1411 Brdwy
New York NY
215 785-4000

(G-10414)
KASPER GROUP LLC
1412 Broadway (10018-9228)
PHONE 212 354-4311
Gregg I Marks, *CEO*
Irene Koumendouros, *President*
Daniel Fishman, *COO*
Nikki Palma, *Exec VP*
◆ **EMP:** 250

SALES (est): 229.6MM
SALES (corp-wide): 2.2B **Privately Held**
SIC: 2335 Women's, juniors' & misses' dresses
HQ: Nine West Holdings, Inc.
180 Rittenhouse Cir
Bristol PA 19007
215 785-4000

(G-10415)
KATE SPADE & COMPANY LLC (HQ)
2 Park Ave Fl 8 (10016-5613)
PHONE 212 354-4900
George M Carrara, *President*
Sarah Jaxheimer *Exec VP*
Timothy F Michno, *Senior VP*
Linda Yanussi, *Senior VP*
Marissa Andrada, *Vice Pres*
◆ **EMP:** 420
SQ FT: 135,000
SALES: 1.3B
SALES (corp-wide): 5.8B **Publicly Held**
WEB: www.lizclaiborne.com
SIC: 2331 5651 5136 5137 Women's & misses' blouses & shirts; family clothing stores; unisex clothing stores; men's & boys' clothing; women's & children's clothing; catalog & mail-order houses
PA: Tapestry, Inc.
10 Hudson Yards
New York NY 10001
212 594-1850

(G-10416)
KATES PAPERIE LTD
188 Lafayette St Frnt A (10013-3200)
PHONE 212 966-3904
Leonard Flax, *Manager*
▲ **EMP:** 6
SALES (est): 330K **Privately Held**
SIC: 2759 Announcements: engraved

(G-10417)
KATHMANDO VALLEY PRESERVATION
Also Called: H THEOPHILE
36 W 25th St Fl 17 (10010-2706)
PHONE 212 727-0074
Erich Theophile, *Owner*
EMP: 10
SALES: 491.4K **Privately Held**
SIC: 3851 Temples & fronts, ophthalmic

(G-10418)
KATZ MARTELL FASHION TRDG INTL
1385 Broadway Rm 1401 (10018-6057)
PHONE 212 840-0070
Debbie Martell, *President*
Bonnie Katz, *Vice Pres*
▲ **EMP:** 7 **LST:** 1998
SQ FT: 2,500
SALES (est): 424.5K **Privately Held**
SIC: 2339 Women's & misses' athletic clothing & sportswear

(G-10419)
KAUFMAN BROTHERS PRINTING
327 W 36th St Rm 403 (10018-6971)
PHONE 212 563-1854
Harvey Kaufman, *Owner*
EMP: 5
SQ FT: 2,000
SALES (est): 1.8MM **Privately Held**
SIC: 2752 2759 2789 Commercial printing, offset; letterpress printing; bookbinding & related work

(G-10420)
KAWASHO FOODS USA INC
45 Broadway Fl 18 (10006-3007)
PHONE 212 841-7400
Tatsuya Ito, *President*
EMP: 11
SALES: 52MM
SALES (corp-wide): 34.5B **Privately Held**
SIC: 2032 Canned specialties
HQ: Kawasho Foods Corporation
2-7-1, Otemachi
Chiyoda-Ku TKY 100-0
352 031-028

(G-10421)
KAY SEE DENTAL MFG CO
777 Avenue Of The (10001)
PHONE 816 842-2817
Yachiyo Smith, *President*
Clark Y Smith, *Vice Pres*
EMP: 12 **EST:** 1947
SQ FT: 15,000
SALES (est): 1.4MM **Privately Held**
WEB: www.hydrocast.com
SIC: 3843 Dental equipment; dental materials

(G-10422)
KAYMIL PRINTING COMPANY INC
Also Called: Kaymil Ticket Company
140 W 30th St Frnt (10001-4005)
PHONE 212 594-3718
Richwar Warner, *President*
EMP: 5 **EST:** 1961
SQ FT: 6,000
SALES (est): 248.2K **Privately Held**
WEB: www.kaymil.com
SIC: 2759 2752 Letterpress printing; screen printing; offset & photolithographic printing

(G-10423)
KAYO OF CALIFORNIA
525 Fashion Ave Rm 309 (10018-0485)
PHONE 212 354-6336
Jesse Vasquez, *Office Mgr*
Steven Berman, *Manager*
EMP: 5
SALES (corp-wide): 7.6MM **Privately Held**
WEB: www.kayo.com
SIC: 2337 2339 Skirts, separate: women's, misses' & juniors'; sportswear, women's; shorts (outerwear): women's, misses' & juniors'; slacks: women's, misses' & juniors'
PA: Kayo Of California
161 W 39th St
Los Angeles CA 90037
323 233-6107

(G-10424)
KBL HEALTHCARE LP
757 3rd Ave Fl 20 (10017-2046)
PHONE 212 319-5555
Dr Marlene Krauss, *Manager*
EMP: 7
SALES (est): 563.6K **Privately Held**
SIC: 2834 Pharmaceutical preparations

(G-10425)
KBS COMMUNICATIONS LLC
Also Called: Mystery Scene Magazine
331 W 57th St Ste 148 (10019-3101)
PHONE 212 765-7124
Kathleen M Stine, *Mng Member*
Brian Skupin,
EMP: 12
SALES (est): 950.6K **Privately Held**
WEB: www.mysteryscenemag.com
SIC: 2721 Magazines: publishing & printing

(G-10426)
KCP HOLDCO INC (PA)
603 W 50th St (10019-7029)
PHONE 212 265-1500
Paul Blum, *CEO*
EMP: 13
SALES (est): 576.7MM **Privately Held**
SIC: 3143 3171 5661 5632 Men's footwear, except athletic; handbags, women's; purses, women's; shoe stores; women's boots; men's shoes; women's accessory & specialty stores; apparel accessories; costume jewelry; handbags; men's & boys' clothing stores

(G-10427)
KEARNEY-NATIONAL INC (HQ)
Also Called: Coto Technology
565 5th Ave Fl 4 (10017-2424)
PHONE 212 661-4600
Robert R Dyson, *Ch of Bd*
Marc Feldman, *Vice Pres*
John Fitzsimons, *Admin Sec*
◆ **EMP:** 10 **EST:** 1988

New York - New York County (G-10428)

SALES (est): 196.1MM
SALES (corp-wide): 465.2MM **Privately Held**
WEB: www.cotorelay.com
SIC: 3679 3694 3714 3625 Electronic switches; engine electrical equipment; fuel systems & parts, motor vehicle; relays & industrial controls
PA: The Dyson-Kissner-Moran Corporation
2515 South Rd Ste 5
Poughkeepsie NY 12601
212 661-4600

(G-10428)
KELLY GRACE CORP (PA)
Also Called: Danny & Nicole
49 W 37th St Fl 10 (10018-0180)
PHONE..............................212 704-9603
Jamshid Zar, *Ch of Bd*
Daniel Zar, *President*
Esshagh Zar, *Vice Pres*
Korosh Zar, *Vice Pres*
▲ **EMP:** 110
SQ FT: 16,000
SALES (est): 16.4MM **Privately Held**
WEB: www.dannyandnicole.com
SIC: 2335 Wedding gowns & dresses

(G-10429)
KEMP TECHNOLOGIES INC (PA)
1540 Broadway Fl 23 (10036-4039)
PHONE..............................631 345-5292
John Becker, *Ch of Bd*
Raymond Downes, *President*
Melanie Straschydlo, *Chairman*
Peter Melerud, *COO*
Lexie Liu, *Accountant*
▲ **EMP:** 50
SQ FT: 15,000
SALES (est): 10.1MM **Privately Held**
WEB: www.kemptechnologies.com
SIC: 3571 Electronic computers

(G-10430)
KENNETH COLE PRODUCTIONS LP (DH)
603 W 50th St (10019-7051)
PHONE..............................212 265-1500
Kenneth Cole, *Chairman*
EMP: 22
SALES (est): 4.1MM
SALES (corp-wide): 576.7MM **Privately Held**
SIC: 3143 Men's footwear, except athletic
HQ: Kenneth Cole Productions, Inc.
603 W 50th St
New York NY 10019
212 265-1500

(G-10431)
KENNETH COLE PRODUCTIONS INC (HQ)
603 W 50th St (10019-7051)
PHONE..............................212 265-1500
Marc Schneider, *CEO*
Mia Dellosso-Caputo, *President*
Chris Nakatani, *President*
Joshua Schulman, *President*
Scott Williamson, *President*
▲ **EMP:** 277
SQ FT: 119,000
SALES (est): 576.5MM
SALES (corp-wide): 576.7MM **Privately Held**
WEB: www.kennethcole.com
SIC: 3143 3144 3171 5661 Men's footwear, except athletic; women's footwear, except athletic; women's handbags, women's; purses, women's; shoe stores; women's boots; men's shoes; women's accessory & specialty stores; apparel accessories; costume jewelry; handbags; men's & boys' clothing stores
PA: Kcp Holdco, Inc.
603 W 50th St
New York NY 10019
212 265-1500

(G-10432)
KENNETH J LANE INC
20 W 37th St Fl 9 (10018-7367)
PHONE..............................212 868-1780
Kenneth J Lane, *President*
EMP: 15
SQ FT: 5,500
SALES (est): 1.6MM **Privately Held**
SIC: 3961 Jewelry apparel, non-precious metals

(G-10433)
KENSINGTON & SONS LLC
Also Called: Sir Kensington's
270 Lafayette St Ste 200 (10012-3376)
PHONE..............................646 430-8298
Sami Freeman, *Division Mgr*
Zachary Gazzaniga, *COO*
Laura Villevieille, *Sales Staff*
Yan Sim, *Marketing Staff*
Mark Ramadan, *Mng Member*
EMP: 30
SALES (est): 2.1MM **Privately Held**
SIC: 2035 2033 5149 Mayonnaise; mustard, prepared (wet); catsup: packaged in cans, jars, etc.; condiments

(G-10434)
KENSINGTON PUBLISHING CORP
Also Called: Zebra Books
119 W 40th St Fl 21 (10018-2522)
PHONE..............................212 407-1500
Steven Zacharius, *CEO*
Tracy Marx, *Chief*
Laurie Parkin, *Vice Pres*
Robin Cook, *Production*
Susanna Gruninger, *Pub Rel Mgr*
EMP: 81
SQ FT: 25,000
SALES (est): 10.5MM **Privately Held**
WEB: www.kensingtonbooks.com
SIC: 2731 5192 Books: publishing only; books

(G-10435)
KENT ASSOCIATES INC
99 Battery Pl Apt 11p (10280-1324)
PHONE..............................212 675-0722
Herman Lederfarb, *President*
EMP: 8 **EST:** 1947
SQ FT: 4,000
SALES (est): 870K **Privately Held**
SIC: 2752 Commercial printing, offset

(G-10436)
KENT CHEMICAL CORPORATION
460 Park Ave Fl 7 (10022-1841)
PHONE..............................212 521-1700
John Farber, *Ch of Bd*
John Oram, *President*
Susan Aibinder, *Treasurer*
Maya Farber, *Director*
Paul Sailick, *Admin Sec*
◆ **EMP:** 25 **EST:** 1983
SQ FT: 15,000
SALES (est): 3.9MM
SALES (corp-wide): 1.2B **Privately Held**
SIC: 2821 2869 2911 2899 Polyvinyl chloride resins (PVC); flavors or flavoring materials, synthetic; perfume materials, synthetic; paraffin wax; fire retardant chemicals; unsupported plastics film & sheet; solutions, pharmaceutical
PA: Icc Industries Inc.
460 Park Ave Fl 7
New York NY 10022
212 521-1700

(G-10437)
KEY BRAND ENTERTAINMENT INC
104 Franklin St (10013-2923)
PHONE..............................212 966-5400
EMP: 121
SALES (corp-wide): 473K **Privately Held**
SIC: 2752 Lithographic Commercial Printing
PA: Key Brand Entertainment, Inc.
1619 Broadway Fl 9
New York NY 10019
917 421-5400

(G-10438)
KEY COMPUTER SVCS OF CHELSEA
227 E 56th St (10022-3754)
PHONE..............................212 206-8060
Paco Valeez, *President*
EMP: 60

SALES (est): 3.5MM **Privately Held**
SIC: 2759 7377 7372 7338 Commercial printing; computer rental & leasing; prepackaged software; resume writing service; facsimile transmission services; telephone communication, except radio

(G-10439)
KIDS DISCOVER LLC
192 Lexington Ave Rm 1003 (10016-6913)
PHONE..............................212 677-4457
Theodore Levine, *Mng Member*
EMP: 6
SALES (est): 256.1K **Privately Held**
SIC: 2721 Magazines: publishing only, not printed on site

(G-10440)
KIDTELLECT INC
222 Broadway Level19 (10038-2510)
PHONE..............................617 803-1456
Phylaktis Georgiou, *President*
Charles Bart Clareman, *COO*
Azadeh Jamalian, *Officer*
▲ **EMP:** 5
SALES (est): 372.3K **Privately Held**
SIC: 3944 Games, toys & children's vehicles

(G-10441)
KIDZ CONCEPTS LLC
Also Called: One Step Up Kids
1412 Broadway Fl 3 (10018-3372)
PHONE..............................212 398-1110
Harry Adjmi,
Irwin Gindi,
▲ **EMP:** 52
SQ FT: 15,000
SALES (est): 10.2MM **Privately Held**
WEB: www.kidzconcepts.com
SIC: 2389 5137 Costumes; women's & children's sportswear & swimsuits

(G-10442)
KIDZ WORLD INC
Also Called: High Energy U. S. A.
226 W 37th St Fl 12 (10018-9850)
PHONE..............................212 563-4949
Vittorio Dana, *President*
Victor Hara, *Vice Pres*
▲ **EMP:** 15
SQ FT: 2,172
SALES (est): 165.1K **Privately Held**
SIC: 2329 Men's & boys' sportswear & athletic clothing

(G-10443)
KIK US INC
Also Called: Kinecosystem
161 Bowery Apt 6 (10002-2846)
PHONE..............................519 505-7616
Edward Livingston, *CEO*
Peter Heinke, *CFO*
Brandon Brunet, *Controller*
EMP: 12
SALES: 500K **Privately Held**
SIC: 7372 Application computer software
PA: Kik Interactive Inc.
420 Weber St N Suite I
Waterloo ON
226 868-0056

(G-10444)
KIM EUGENIA INC
347 W 36th St Rm 502 (10018-7262)
PHONE..............................212 674-1345
Eugenia Kim, *President*
▲ **EMP:** 8
SQ FT: 1,400
SALES (est): 1.6MM **Privately Held**
WEB: www.eugeniakim.com
SIC: 2353 Hats, caps & millinery

(G-10445)
KIM SEYBERT INC (PA)
37 W 37th St Fl 9 (10018-6219)
PHONE..............................212 564-7850
Kim Seybert, *President*
◆ **EMP:** 16
SQ FT: 10,000
SALES: 5MM **Privately Held**
WEB: www.kimseybert.com
SIC: 2392 Household furnishings

(G-10446)
KIMBALL OFFICE INC
215 Park Ave S Fl 3 (10003-1616)
PHONE..............................212 753-6161
Michael Donahue, *Vice Pres*
Thomas P Mitchell, *Manager*
EMP: 30
SALES (corp-wide): 685.6MM **Publicly Held**
SIC: 2521 Wood office furniture
HQ: Kimball Office Inc.
1600 Royal St
Jasper IN 47549

(G-10447)
KIMBERLY-CLARK CORPORATION
1285 Ave Of The Americas (10019-6031)
PHONE..............................212 554-4252
Guy Zbonack, *Principal*
EMP: 83
SALES (corp-wide): 18.2B **Publicly Held**
WEB: www.kimberly-clark.com
SIC: 2621 2676 Sanitary tissue paper; infant & baby paper products
PA: Kimberly-Clark Corporation
351 Phelps Dr
Irving TX 75038
972 281-1200

(G-10448)
KIND GROUP LLC (PA)
19 W 44th St Ste 811 (10036-5901)
PHONE..............................212 645-0800
Jonathan Teller, *Mng Member*
Katie Braswell, *Manager*
Adrian Adamson, *Associate*
EMP: 2
SQ FT: 3,000
SALES (est): 28.5MM **Privately Held**
WEB: www.20-10.com
SIC: 2844 Toilet preparations

(G-10449)
KINDLING INC
440 Park Ave S Fl 14 (10016-8012)
PHONE..............................212 400-6296
Timothy Meaney, *CEO*
Daniel Summa, *President*
Alaina Jones, *Accounts Mgr*
Richard Ziade, *Admin Sec*
EMP: 17
SALES (est): 1MM **Privately Held**
SIC: 7372 Business oriented computer software

(G-10450)
KINETIC MARKETING INC
1133 Broadway Ste 221 (10010-8197)
PHONE..............................212 620-0600
Charles Y Beyda, *Vice Pres*
▲ **EMP:** 7
SQ FT: 2,000
SALES (est): 901K **Privately Held**
WEB: www.kineticmarketing.net
SIC: 3699 5065 Household electrical equipment; electronic parts & equipment

(G-10451)
KING DISPLAYS INC
333 W 52nd St (10019-6238)
PHONE..............................212 629-8455
Wayne Sapper, *President*
Joel Benton, *Prdtn Mgr*
Julie Rivkin, *Accountant*
Scott McAloon, *Manager*
Mirella Vargas,
EMP: 14
SQ FT: 7,500
SALES (est): 1.8MM **Privately Held**
WEB: www.kingdisplays.com
SIC: 3999 3993 Theatrical scenery; displays & cutouts, window & lobby

(G-10452)
KINGBOARD HOLDINGS LIMITED
120 Broadway Fl 32 (10271-3299)
PHONE..............................705 844-1993
EMP: 600
SALES (est): 12.1MM **Privately Held**
SIC: 3672 7371 Printed circuit boards; computer software development & applications

▲ = Import ▼=Export
◆ =Import/Export

(G-10453) KITON BUILDING CORP
4 E 54th St (10022-4203)
PHONE 212 486-3224
Antonio De Matteis, *Ch of Bd*
Ciro Paone, *President*
EMP: 20
SQ FT: 18,077
SALES (est): 2.2MM **Privately Held**
SIC: 2389 Costumes

(G-10454) KKR MILLENNIUM GP LLC
9 W 57th St Ste 4150 (10019-2701)
PHONE 212 750-8300
Lawrence J Rogers, *President*
EMP: 4850
SALES (est): 13.4B **Publicly Held**
SIC: 2515 Mattresses, innerspring or box spring
PA: Kkr & Co. Inc.
9 W 57th St Ste 4200
New York NY 10019

(G-10455) KKR NTRAL RSOURCES FUND I-A LP
9 W 57th St Ste 4200 (10019-2707)
PHONE 212 750-8300
David J Sorkin, *General Counsel*
EMP: 6
SALES (est): 362.9MM **Publicly Held**
SIC: 1382 Oil & gas exploration services
PA: Kkr & Co. Inc.
9 W 57th St Ste 4200
New York NY 10019

(G-10456) KLARA TECHNOLOGIES INC
1 State St Fl 25 (10004-1729)
PHONE 844 215-5272
Simon Bolz, *CEO*
Vivek Nanda, *Mktg Dir*
EMP: 17
SALES (est): 407.5K
SALES (corp-wide): 592K **Privately Held**
SIC: 7372 Business oriented computer software
PA: Klara Holdings, Inc.
1 State St Fl 25
New York NY 10004
844 215-5272

(G-10457) KLAUBER BROTHERS INC (PA)
253 W 35th St Fl 11 (10001-1907)
PHONE 212 686-2531
Roger Klauber, *President*
Mark Klauber, *Vice Pres*
Jay Marcus, *Vice Pres*
Andy Larivee, *Prdtn Mgr*
Gordon Klauber, *Treasurer*
▲ **EMP:** 35 **EST:** 1942
SQ FT: 11,000
SALES: 133K **Privately Held**
WEB: www.klauberlace.com
SIC: 2258 5131 Lace, knit; warp & flat knit products; textile converters

(G-10458) KLUTZ (HQ)
Also Called: Klutz Store
568 Broadway Rm 503 (10012-3264)
PHONE 650 687-2600
Richard Robinson, *CEO of Purch*
Dewitt Durham, *Vice Pres*
▲ **EMP:** 23
SALES (est): 9MM
SALES (corp-wide): 1.6B **Publicly Held**
WEB: www.klutz.com
SIC: 2731 Books: publishing & printing
PA: Scholastic Corporation
557 Broadway Lbby 1
New York NY 10012
212 343-6100

(G-10459) KNIT RESOURCE CENTER LTD
250 W 39th St Rm 207 (10018-4742)
PHONE 212 221-1990
Joseph Katz, *President*
EMP: 7
SQ FT: 2,500
SALES (est): 646.5K
SALES (corp-wide): 295.4MM **Privately Held**
SIC: 2253 Sweaters & sweater coats, knit
HQ: Stoll America Knitting Machinery Inc
250 W 39th St Frnt 1
New York NY 10018
212 398-3869

(G-10460) KNOLL INC
Also Called: Knoll Textile
1330 Ave Of The A (10019)
PHONE 212 343-4124
Benjamin A Pardo, *Exec VP*
Liz Needle, *VP Finance*
Leah Kalotay, *Marketing Staff*
Amy Dara, *Manager*
Nicole Pedersen, *Manager*
EMP: 100 **Publicly Held**
WEB: www.knoll.com
SIC: 2521 2522 2511 Wood office furniture; panel systems & partitions, office: except wood; wood household furniture
PA: Knoll, Inc.
1235 Water St
East Greenville PA 18041

(G-10461) KOBALT MUSIC PUBG AMER INC (HQ)
2 Gansevoort St Fl 6 (10014-1667)
PHONE 212 247-6204
Willard Ahdritz, *CEO*
Pete Dodge, *General Mgr*
Nestor Casonu, *Managing Dir*
Jim Arnay, *Vice Pres*
Jeannette Perez, *Vice Pres*
EMP: 70
SALES (est): 23.6MM
SALES (corp-wide): 320.9MM **Privately Held**
WEB: www.kobaltmusic.com
SIC: 2731 Book music: publishing & printing
PA: Kobalt Music Group Limited
1 Cousin Lane
London EC4R
207 401-5500

(G-10462) KOBE STEEL USA HOLDINGS INC (HQ)
535 Madison Ave Fl 5 (10022-4214)
PHONE 212 751-9400
Hiroya Kawasaki, *President*
◆ **EMP:** 8
SQ FT: 5,697
SALES (est): 215.5MM
SALES (corp-wide): 17.6B **Privately Held**
WEB: www.kobelco.com
SIC: 3542 3089 Extruding machines (machine tools), metal; injection molding of plastics
PA: Kobe Steel, Ltd.
2-2-4, Wakinohamakaigandori, Chuo-Ku
Kobe HYO 651-0
782 615-111

(G-10463) KOCH SUPPLY & TRADING LP
667 Madison Ave Fl 22 (10065-8051)
PHONE 212 319-4895
EMP: 5
SALES (corp-wide): 42.9B **Privately Held**
SIC: 2911 Petroleum refining
HQ: Koch Supply & Trading, Lp
4111 E 37th St N
Wichita KS 67220
316 828-5500

(G-10464) KODANSHA USA INC
451 Park Ave S Fl 7 (10016-7390)
PHONE 917 322-6200
Sawako Noma, *Ch of Bd*
Yoichi Kiyata, *Sr Exec VP*
▲ **EMP:** 9
SQ FT: 7,000
SALES (est): 3.6MM **Privately Held**
SIC: 2731 5192 Books: publishing only; books

(G-10465) KOKIN INC
247 W 38th St Rm 701 (10018-4470)
PHONE 212 643-8225
Steven Kokin, *President*
Audrey Kokin, *Corp Secy*
Gary Kokin, *Vice Pres*
▲ **EMP:** 30
SQ FT: 6,800
SALES (est): 3.9MM **Privately Held**
SIC: 2353 2341 Hats, caps & millinery; women's & children's nightwear

(G-10466) KOLLAGE WORK TOO LTD
261 W 35th St Ste 302 (10001-1902)
PHONE 212 695-1821
Maria Meunier,
EMP: 7
SALES (est): 398.8K **Privately Held**
SIC: 2326 Men's & boys' work clothing

(G-10467) KOMAR LAYERING LLC (HQ)
Also Called: O'Bryan Bros
16 E 34th St Fl 10 (10016-4360)
PHONE 212 725-1500
Charlie Komar, *President*
David Komar, *Principal*
Allen R Bartine, *CFO*
▲ **EMP:** 40
SQ FT: 13,000
SALES (est): 11MM
SALES (corp-wide): 310.7MM **Privately Held**
WEB: www.cuddlduds.com
SIC: 2341 Nightgowns & negligees: women's & children's; pajamas & bed-jackets: women's & children's; slips: women's, misses', children's & infants'; panties: women's, misses', children's & infants'
PA: Charles Komar & Sons, Inc.
90 Hudson St Fl 9
Jersey City NJ 07302
212 725-1500

(G-10468) KOMAR LUXURY BRANDS
16 E 34th St Fl 10 (10016-4360)
PHONE 646 472-0060
Charles Komar, *President*
Harry Gaffney, *CFO*
▲ **EMP:** 8
SALES (est): 887.6K
SALES (corp-wide): 310.7MM **Privately Held**
SIC: 2341 2384 5137 2329 Women's & children's nightwear; robes & dressing gowns; nightwear: women's, children's & infants'; sweaters & sweater jackets: men's & boys'
PA: Charles Komar & Sons, Inc.
90 Hudson St Fl 9
Jersey City NJ 07302
212 725-1500

(G-10469) KOPPERS CHOCLAT SPECIALTY INC
501 Madison Ave Rm 402 (10022-5635)
PHONE 917 834-2290
Lorie Alexander, *Principal*
EMP: 7
SALES (est): 576.7K **Privately Held**
SIC: 2064 Candy & other confectionery products

(G-10470) KORANGY PUBLISHING INC (PA)
Also Called: Real Deal, The
450 W 31st St Fl 4 (10001-4613)
PHONE 212 260-1332
Amir Korangy, *CEO*
Hannah Miet, *Editor*
Heidi Patalano, *Editor*
Richard Bailey, *Assistant VP*
Sean Stewart-Muniz, *Producer*
EMP: 120
SALES (est): 14.1MM **Privately Held**
SIC: 2741 Miscellaneous publishing

(G-10471) KORIN JAPANESE TRADING CORP
57 Warren St Frnt A (10007-1018)
PHONE 212 587-7021
Saori Kawano, *President*
John Wong, *CFO*
Sally Cen, *Asst Controller*
Joy Zhou, *Natl Sales Mgr*
Mitsuko Muramatsu, *Sales Associate*
◆ **EMP:** 32
SQ FT: 8,000
SALES (est): 4.8MM **Privately Held**
WEB: www.korin.com
SIC: 3469 3262 3263 3421 Utensils, household: metal, except cast; vitreous china table & kitchenware; commercial tableware or kitchen articles, fine earthenware; cutlery; commercial cooking & food-warming equipment; barbecues, grills & braziers (outdoor cooking)

(G-10472) KOSSARS ON GRAND LLC
367 Grand St (10002-3951)
PHONE 212 473-4810
Evan Giniger, *CEO*
EMP: 10
SALES (est): 728.3K **Privately Held**
SIC: 2051 Rolls, bread type: fresh or frozen

(G-10473) KOTEL IMPORTERS INC
22 W 48th St Ste 607 (10036-1803)
PHONE 212 245-6200
Raphel Dagan, *President*
EMP: 12
SQ FT: 1,200
SALES (est): 1.1MM **Privately Held**
SIC: 1499 Gemstone & industrial diamond mining

(G-10474) KOWA AMERICAN CORPORATION (DH)
55 E 59th St Fl 19 (10022-1112)
PHONE 212 303-7800
Reid C Anthony, *Ch of Bd*
Takashi Mamemura, *Ch of Bd*
Kanako Fujimoto, *Accounting Mgr*
Noriko Nagamoto, *Accountant*
Lina Skripskaite, *Sales Staff*
◆ **EMP:** 20
SQ FT: 6,400
SALES (est): 4.5MM
SALES (corp-wide): 4B **Privately Held**
SIC: 2819 5032 5131 Industrial inorganic chemicals; tile, clay or other ceramic, excluding refractory; textiles, woven

(G-10475) KOZINN+SONS MERCHANT TAILORS
Also Called: Saint Laurie
150 W 55th St 4c (10019-5586)
PHONE 212 643-1916
Andrew Kozinn, *CEO*
▲ **EMP:** 26
SQ FT: 7,500
SALES (est): 3.4MM **Privately Held**
WEB: www.saintlaurie.com
SIC: 2311 2337 5611 5621 Suits, men's & boys': made from purchased materials; suits: women's, misses' & juniors'; suits, men's; women's clothing stores

(G-10476) KPS CAPITAL PARTNERS LP (PA)
485 Lexington Ave Fl 31 (10017-2641)
PHONE 212 338-5100
Michael G Psaros, *Managing Prtnr*
Jay Bernstein, *Partner*
Raquel Palmer, *Partner*
David Shapiro, *Partner*
◆ **EMP:** 40
SQ FT: 6,000
SALES (est): 2.1B **Privately Held**
SIC: 3541 6722 3545 5084 Machine tools, metal cutting type; management investment, open-end; machine tool accessories; industrial machinery & equipment

New York - New York County (G-10477)

(G-10477)
KRAINZ CREATIONS INC
589 5th Ave (10017-1923)
PHONE 212 583-1555
Roland Krainz, *President*
Frank Gannon, *Foreman/Supr*
Paola Parra, *Manager*
EMP: 35
SALES (est): 3.6MM **Privately Held**
SIC: 3911 Jewelry, precious metal

(G-10478)
KRAMAN IRON WORKS INC
410 E 10th St (10009-4203)
PHONE 212 460-8400
Richard Kraman, *President*
EMP: 11 **EST:** 1913
SQ FT: 3,600
SALES: 1.6MM **Privately Held**
SIC: 3449 Miscellaneous metalwork

(G-10479)
KRASNER GROUP INC (PA)
40 W 37th St Ph A (10018-7415)
PHONE 212 268-4100
Al Cerbo, *Vice Pres*
Barry Ort, *Vice Pres*
David Pardington, *CFO*
▼ **EMP:** 1
SQ FT: 4,500
SALES (est): 8.2MM **Privately Held**
SIC: 3911 2339 2331 2335 Jewelry, precious metal; women's & misses' accessories; women's & misses' blouses & shirts; women's, juniors' & misses' dresses

(G-10480)
KRAUS & SONS INC
355 S End Ave Apt 10j (10280-1056)
PHONE 212 620-0408
Paul Schneider, *President*
Mildred Schneider, *Treasurer*
EMP: 15 **EST:** 1886
SQ FT: 5,000
SALES (est): 1.4MM **Privately Held**
WEB: www.krausbanners.com
SIC: 2399 3993 2394 3965 Banners, made from fabric; signs & advertising specialties; tents: made from purchased materials; buttons & parts

(G-10481)
KRAUS ORGANIZATION LIMITED (PA)
Also Called: Bernan Associates
181 Hudson St Ste 2a (10013-1812)
PHONE 212 686-5411
Frank Cermak, *President*
Herbert Gstalder, *Chairman*
Steven Gstalder, *Vice Pres*
EMP: 80
SALES (est): 8.2MM **Privately Held**
WEB: www.krausorgltd.com
SIC: 2741 7383 7389 Miscellaneous publishing; news pictures, gathering & distributing; photographic library service

(G-10482)
KRAVITZ DESIGN INC (PA)
13 Crosby St Rm 401 (10013-3145)
PHONE 212 625-1644
Lenny Kravitz, *Ch of Bd*
Laura Lukens, *Bookkeeper*
Richard Feldstein, *Admin Sec*
▲ **EMP:** 8
SALES (est): 1.1MM **Privately Held**
SIC: 2732 Books: printing only

(G-10483)
KSE SPORTSMAN MEDIA INC (PA)
1040 Ave Of The Americas (10018-3703)
PHONE 212 852-6600
David Koff, *CEO*
Peter Kern, *Chairman*
Jeff Paro, *Chairman*
Michael Carney, *Vice Pres*
Andy Goldstein, *CFO*
EMP: 59
SALES (est): 38.6MM **Privately Held**
SIC: 2326 5045 Industrial garments, men's & boys'; computer software

(G-10484)
KSK INTERNATIONAL INC (PA)
Also Called: Easel
450 Park Ave Ste 2703 (10022-2668)
PHONE 212 354-7770
Neil Weiss, *CEO*
EMP: 25
SQ FT: 10,335
SALES (est): 1.8MM **Privately Held**
SIC: 2331 2339 Women's & misses' blouses & shirts; women's & misses' accessories

(G-10485)
KT GROUP INC
13 W 36th St Fl 3 (10018-7139)
PHONE 212 760-2500
Eugene Huh, *President*
Yujin Huh, *Chairman*
▲ **EMP:** 8
SALES (est): 954K **Privately Held**
SIC: 2321 Sport shirts, men's & boys': from purchased materials

(G-10486)
KURARAY AMERICA INC
33 Maiden Ln Fl 6 (10038-5152)
PHONE 212 986-2230
John Dennis, *Research*
Corey Mays, *Engineer*
Kelley Sturm, *Engineer*
Michelle Denny, *Regl Sales Mgr*
Gary Wooddell, *Mktg Dir*
EMP: 17
SALES (corp-wide): 4.6B **Privately Held**
SIC: 2821 Plastics materials & resins
HQ: Kuraray America, Inc.
2625 Bay Area Blvd # 600
Houston TX 77058

(G-10487)
KURT GAUM INC
Also Called: Soper Designs
580 5th Ave Ste 303 (10036-4724)
PHONE 212 719-2836
Blake Soper, *President*
Peter Boutsas, *Vice Pres*
EMP: 13 **EST:** 1954
SQ FT: 1,250
SALES (est): 1.6MM **Privately Held**
WEB: www.kurtgaum.com
SIC: 3911 Jewelry, precious metal

(G-10488)
KWW PRODUCTIONS CORP
Also Called: American Attitude
1410 Broadway Fl 24 (10018-5007)
PHONE 212 398-8181
Izzy Pnini, *President*
EMP: 10
SALES (corp-wide): 5.7MM **Privately Held**
WEB: www.knitwork.com
SIC: 2389 Apparel for handicapped
PA: Kww Productions Corp.
1639 Centre St
Ridgewood NY 11385
718 821-2201

(G-10489)
KYBOD GROUP LLC
Also Called: Sriracha2go
305 E 40th St Apt 5k (10016-2017)
PHONE 408 306-1657
Kyle Lewis,
Farbod Deylamian,
EMP: 2
SALES (est): 1.5MM **Privately Held**
SIC: 3085 Plastics bottles

(G-10490)
KYLE EDITING LLC
48 W 25th St Fl 5 (10010-2767)
PHONE 212 675-3464
Sarah Farrand, *Producer*
Jackie Sparks, *Info Tech Mgr*
Michael McKenna, *Creative Dir*
Tina Mintus,
EMP: 9 **EST:** 2010
SALES (est): 1.1MM **Privately Held**
WEB: www.kyleedit.com
SIC: 3861 Editing equipment, motion picture: viewers, splicers, etc.

(G-10491)
L & M OPTICAL DISC LLC
Also Called: L & M West
65 W 36th St Fl 11 (10018-7936)
PHONE 718 649-3500
Aaron Menche,
▲ **EMP:** 100
SALES (est): 12.7MM **Privately Held**
WEB: www.dxbind.com
SIC: 3695 Optical disks & tape, blank

(G-10492)
L A BURDICK CHOCOLATES
5 E 20th St (10003-1103)
PHONE 212 796-0143
Larry Burdick, *Branch Mgr*
EMP: 5
SALES (est): 269.6K **Privately Held**
SIC: 2064 Candy & other confectionery products
PA: L A Burdick Chocolates
47 Main St Unit 1
Walpole NH 03608

(G-10493)
L D WEISS INC (PA)
Also Called: Bandaroos
320 E 42nd St Apt 3106 (10017-5990)
P.O. Box 14, Skaneateles (13152-0014)
PHONE 212 697-3023
Lawrence D Weiss, *President*
Katharine Weiss, *Vice Pres*
John Weiss, *Admin Sec*
▲ **EMP:** 6
SQ FT: 3,000
SALES (est): 448.4K **Privately Held**
WEB: www.linescale.com
SIC: 2339 2389 8742 Women's & misses' accessories; men's miscellaneous accessories; new products & services consultants

(G-10494)
L F FASHION ORIENT INTL CO LTD
32 W 40th St Apt 2l (10018-3839)
PHONE 917 667-3398
Lisa LI, *President*
▲ **EMP:** 5
SALES (est): 350.1K **Privately Held**
SIC: 2311 2335 Men's & boys' suits & coats; women's, juniors' & misses' dresses

(G-10495)
L F INTERNATIONAL INC
Also Called: Labhar - Freidman
425 Park Ave Fl 5 (10022-3506)
PHONE 212 756-5000
J Roger Friedman, *President*
▼ **EMP:** 90
SALES (est): 3.8MM
SALES (corp-wide): 101.7MM **Privately Held**
WEB: www.lf.com
SIC: 2721 Periodicals
PA: Lebhar-Friedman, Inc.
4508 Oak Fair Blvd # 108
Tampa FL 33610
212 756-5000

(G-10496)
L-3 CMMNCTONS NTRONIX HOLDINGS
600 3rd Ave Fl 34 (10016-2001)
PHONE 212 697-1111
Michael T Strianese, *President*
Steven M Post, *Senior VP*
Curtis Brunson, *Vice Pres*
Ralph G D'Ambrosio, *CFO*
Jane Jurgensen, *Senior Mgr*
EMP: 65
SALES (est): 18.2MM
SALES (corp-wide): 9.5B **Publicly Held**
SIC: 3625 3699 8711 Marine & navy auxiliary controls; underwater sound equipment; marine engineering
PA: L3 Technologies, Inc.
600 3rd Ave Fl 34
New York NY 10016
212 697-1111

(G-10497)
L3 FOREIGN HOLDINGS INC (HQ)
Also Called: L3 Communication
600 3rd Ave Fl 32 (10016-2001)
PHONE 212 697-1111
Jim Parker, *President*
Brian Pope, *President*
Larry Riddle, *President*
Elissa Seidenglanz, *President*
Michael T Strianese, *Principal*
▲ **EMP:** 81
SALES (est): 57.3MM
SALES (corp-wide): 9.5B **Publicly Held**
SIC: 3663 3669 3679 3812 Telemetering equipment, electronic; receiver-transmitter units (transceiver); amplifiers, RF power & IF; signaling apparatus, electric; intercommunication systems, electric; microwave components; search & navigation equipment; guided missile & space vehicle parts & auxiliary equipment
PA: L3 Technologies, Inc.
600 3rd Ave Fl 34
New York NY 10016
212 697-1111

(G-10498)
L3 TECHNOLOGIES INC (PA)
600 3rd Ave Fl 34 (10016-2001)
PHONE 212 697-1111
Michael T Strianese, *Ch of Bd*
Christopher E Kubasik, *President*
Sean J Stackley, *President*
Richard A Cody, *Senior VP*
Ann D Davidson, *Senior VP*
EMP: 277 **EST:** 1997
SALES: 9.5B **Publicly Held**
SIC: 3812 3663 3669 3679 Search & navigation equipment; aircraft control systems, electronic; telemetering equipment, electronic; receiver-transmitter units (transceiver); amplifiers, RF power & IF; signaling apparatus, electric; intercommunication systems, electric; microwave components; guided missile & space vehicle parts & auxiliary equipment

(G-10499)
LA COLA 1 INC
529 W 42nd St Apt 5b (10036-6228)
PHONE 917 509-6669
Thomas Dugal, *Principal*
EMP: 5
SALES (est): 270.6K **Privately Held**
SIC: 2086 Soft drinks: packaged in cans, bottles, etc.

(G-10500)
LA CREMERIA
178 Mulberry St (10012-4556)
PHONE 212 226-6758
Alessandro Tiodesam, *Managing Prtnr*
Elena Tiodesam, *Partner*
EMP: 6
SALES (est): 234.8K **Privately Held**
SIC: 2024 Ice cream, bulk

(G-10501)
LA FINA DESIGN INC
42 W 38th St Rm 1200 (10018-6212)
PHONE 212 689-6725
Chol Choi, *President*
Peter Choi, *President*
▲ **EMP:** 7
SALES (est): 952.7K **Privately Held**
SIC: 3911 Jewelry, precious metal

(G-10502)
LA LAME INC
Also Called: La Lame Importers
215 W 40th St Fl 5 (10018-1602)
PHONE 212 921-9770
Benjamin Schneer, *CEO*
Edward Schneer, *Principal*
Glen Schneer, *Principal*
Billy Pellegrini, *Sales Staff*
▲ **EMP:** 8 **EST:** 1958
SQ FT: 7,500

GEOGRAPHIC SECTION

SALES (est): 1.3MM **Privately Held**
WEB: www.lalame.com
SIC: 2299 2241 2282 2221 Yarns, specialty & novelty; fabrics: linen, jute, hemp, ramie; braids, textile; embroidery yarn: twisting, winding or spooling; spandex broadwoven fabrics; brocade, cotton; textile converters

(G-10503)
LABEL SOURCE INC
321 W 35th St (10001-1739)
PHONE.................................212 244-1403
Stuart Rosen, *President*
EMP: 6
SQ FT: 2,000
SALES: 1.2MM **Privately Held**
SIC: 2241 Labels, woven

(G-10504)
LABELS INTER-GLOBAL INC
Also Called: Labels I-G
109 W 38th St Rm 701 (10018-3673)
PHONE.................................212 398-0006
Steve Ziangos, *President*
Effie Ziangos, *Vice Pres*
Juan Fernandez, *Manager*
Rosena Rasheed, *Technology*
Steve Sellinger, *Technology*
▲ EMP: 14
SQ FT: 3,400
SALES (est): 2.2MM **Privately Held**
WEB: www.labelsig.com
SIC: 2759 5112 2241 Labels & seals: printing; stationery & office supplies; labels, woven

(G-10505)
LABELTEX MILLS INC
1430 Broadway Rm 1510 (10018-3368)
PHONE.................................212 279-6165
Raphaela Penn, *Vice Pres*
Ian Kantor, *Manager*
EMP: 7 **Privately Held**
WEB: www.labeltexmills.com
SIC: 2241 Narrow fabric mills
PA: Labeltex Mills, Inc.
   6100 Wilmington Ave
   Los Angeles CA 90001

(G-10506)
LADY ESTER LINGERIE CORP
Also Called: Sliperfection
33 E 33rd St Rm 800 (10016-5335)
PHONE.................................212 689-1729
Robert T Sadock, *President*
M William Sadock, *President*
Karen L Sadock, *Exec VP*
Greg Strahn, *CFO*
EMP: 45 EST: 1929
SQ FT: 15,000
SALES (est): 4.4MM **Privately Held**
SIC: 2384 2341 Robes & dressing gowns; chemises, camisoles & teddies: women's & children's

(G-10507)
LAFAYETTE PUB INC
Also Called: Temple Bar
332 Lafayette St (10012-2739)
PHONE.................................212 925-4242
George Schwartz, *President*
EMP: 25
SALES (est): 1.4MM **Privately Held**
WEB: www.templebarnyc.com
SIC: 2599 5813 Bar, restaurant & cafeteria furniture; drinking places

(G-10508)
LAGARDERE NORTH AMERICA INC (DH)
60 E 42nd St Ste 1940 (10165-6201)
PHONE.................................212 477-7373
David Leckey, *Senior VP*
Richard Rabinowitz, *Vice Pres*
EMP: 21
SALES (est): 161.8MM
SALES (corp-wide): 70.7MM **Privately Held**
SIC: 2721 Magazines: publishing only, not printed on site
HQ: Lagardere Media
   4 Rue De Presbourg
   Paris 75116
   140 691-600

(G-10509)
LAI APPAREL DESIGN INC
Also Called: Ella Design
209 W 38th St Rm 901 (10018-4558)
PHONE.................................212 382-1075
Elaine Lai, *President*
▲ EMP: 21
SQ FT: 7,000
SALES (est): 3.5MM **Privately Held**
SIC: 2339 Women's & misses' athletic clothing & sportswear

(G-10510)
LAKESTAR SEMI INC (PA)
888 7th Ave Ste 3300 (10106-3402)
PHONE.................................212 974-6254
Sailesh Chittipeddi, *President*
Shiva Gowni, *President*
Phillip E Pompa, *Senior VP*
Kevin V Strong, *Senior VP*
Dennis E O Reilly, *Vice Pres*
▲ EMP: 14
SALES (est): 62.8MM **Privately Held**
WEB: www.conexant.com
SIC: 3674 5065 Mfg Semiconductors/Related Devices Whol Electronic Parts/Equipment

(G-10511)
LALI JEWELRY INC
Also Called: Lali Jewels
50 W 47th St Ste 1610 (10036-8734)
PHONE.................................212 944-2277
Arun Bassalali, *President*
Adam Bassalali, *Vice Pres*
EMP: 4 EST: 2015
SQ FT: 1,000
SALES: 1MM **Privately Held**
SIC: 3911 Pearl jewelry, natural or cultured

(G-10512)
LALIQUE NORTH AMERICA INC
Also Called: Lalique Boutique
609 Madison Ave (10022-1901)
PHONE.................................212 355-6550
Maggie WEI, *Marketing Staff*
Marya Samawi, *Branch Mgr*
EMP: 20 **Privately Held**
SIC: 3231 5719 Watch crystals, glass; kitchenware
HQ: Lalique North America, Inc.
   133 5th Ave Fl 3
   New York NY 10003
   212 355-8536

(G-10513)
LAND N SEA INC (PA)
1375 Broadway Fl 2 (10018-7073)
PHONE.................................212 444-6000
Robert Sobel, *Ch of Bd*
Kirk Gellin, *Ch of Bd*
Heather Smith, *Opers Mgr*
Brenda Torres, *Purch Mgr*
Fred Mandato, *CFO*
◆ EMP: 100 EST: 1958
SQ FT: 21,000
SALES (est): 48.8MM **Privately Held**
SIC: 2361 2331 2339 Blouses: girls', children's & infants'; blouses, women's & juniors': made from purchased material; girls' & children's outerwear; women's & misses' outerwear; family clothing stores

(G-10514)
LANDLORD GUARD INC
1 Maiden Ln Fl 7 (10038-5168)
PHONE.................................212 695-6505
Christine Mathis, *President*
Tamar Ojalvo, *Manager*
EMP: 10
SALES (est): 780K **Privately Held**
SIC: 2759 Advertising literature: printing

(G-10515)
LANES FLR CVRNGS INTRIORS INC
30 W 26th St Fl 11r (10010-2065)
PHONE.................................212 532-5200
Lane Brettschneider, *Ch of Bd*
Gary Ragin, *Sales Staff*
Umberto Aponte, *Manager*
Kwasi Pecou, *Manager*
EMP: 25 EST: 1965
SQ FT: 9,000
SALES (est): 5MM **Privately Held**
WEB: www.lanes-carpets.com
SIC: 2273 Carpets & rugs

(G-10516)
LANGUAGE AND GRAPHICS INC
350 W 57th St Apt 14i (10019-3762)
PHONE.................................212 315-5266
Margaret Keppler, *President*
Patricia Encinosa, *Vice Pres*
Michael Keppler, *Treasurer*
EMP: 5
SALES (est): 317.1K **Privately Held**
SIC: 2741 7389 Miscellaneous publishing; translation services

(G-10517)
LAREGENCE INC
34 W 27th St Fl 2 (10001-6901)
PHONE.................................212 736-2548
Jay Perlstein, *President*
Kathy Jones, *Treasurer*
Lily Lau, *Office Mgr*
▼ EMP: 20
SALES (est): 2.6MM **Privately Held**
SIC: 2221 2391 Upholstery, tapestry & wall covering fabrics; curtains & draperies

(G-10518)
LARGO MUSIC INC
425 Park Ave Ste 501 (10022-3519)
PHONE.................................212 756-5080
Jay Roger Friedman, *President*
EMP: 7
SQ FT: 10,000
SALES (est): 311.1K
SALES (corp-wide): 101.7MM **Privately Held**
WEB: www.largomusic.com
SIC: 2741 Music books: publishing only, not printed on site
PA: Lebhar-Friedman, Inc.
   4508 Oak Fair Blvd # 108
   Tampa FL 33610
   212 756-5000

(G-10519)
LARTE DEL GELATO INC
75 9th Ave Frnt 38 (10011-4730)
PHONE.................................212 366-0570
Francisco Realmuto, *Owner*
Marco Cattaneo, *General Mgr*
Luciano Boron, *Production*
▲ EMP: 9
SALES (est): 738K **Privately Held**
SIC: 2052 2099 Cones, ice cream; jelly, corncob (gelatin)

(G-10520)
LASER & ELECTRON BEAM INC
77 7th Ave Apt 3h (10011-6612)
PHONE.................................603 626-6080
EMP: 6
SQ FT: 4,800
SALES (est): 65.9K **Privately Held**
SIC: 3599 8734 8711 Operates As A Machine Shop Testing Laboratory & Consulting Service For Hi-Tech Equipment

(G-10521)
LATCHABLE INC
450 W 33rd St Fl 12 (10001-2610)
PHONE.................................646 833-0604
Luke Schoenfelder, *CEO*
Ryan Agran, *Opers Staff*
Ivan Almaral, *Director*
EMP: 25 EST: 2014
SALES (est): 267.2K **Privately Held**
SIC: 7372 7389 Business oriented computer software;

(G-10522)
LATINA MEDIA VENTURES LLC (PA)
625 Madison Ave Frnt 3 (10022-1801)
PHONE.................................212 642-0200
Edward Lewis, *Ch of Bd*
Peter Glusker, *Mng Member*
Asten Morgan, *Exec Dir*
Robyn Moreno, *Director*
Priscilla Rodriguez, *Senior Editor*
▲ EMP: 46
SQ FT: 11,000
SALES (est): 15.8MM **Privately Held**
WEB: www.latinapromotions.com
SIC: 2721 Magazines: publishing & printing

(G-10523)
LAUFER WIND GROUP LLC
270 Lafayette St Ste 1402 (10012-3364)
PHONE.................................212 792-3912
Eric Laufer, *Mng Member*
EMP: 15
SALES (est): 2.5MM **Privately Held**
SIC: 3812 Radar systems & equipment

(G-10524)
LAUNDRESS INC
247 W 30th St Ste 7l (10001-2824)
PHONE.................................212 209-0074
Gwen Whiting, *President*
Lindsey Wieber Boyd, *Vice Pres*
Emily Herzig, *Manager*
▲ EMP: 10
SALES (est): 2MM **Privately Held**
SIC: 2842 Laundry cleaning preparations

(G-10525)
LAZARE KAPLAN INTL INC (PA)
19 W 44th St Fl 16 (10036-6101)
PHONE.................................212 972-9700
Maurice Tempelsman, *Ch of Bd*
Leon Tempelsman, *Vice Chairman*
Jeff Edelstein, *Vice Pres*
Charlie Rosario, *Vice Pres*
William H Moryto, *CFO*
EMP: 56 EST: 1903
SQ FT: 17,351
SALES (est): 10.8MM **Privately Held**
WEB: www.lazarediamonds.com
SIC: 3915 Diamond cutting & polishing

(G-10526)
LE BOOK PUBLISHING INC (HQ)
580 Broadway Rm 1001 (10012-3295)
PHONE.................................212 334-5252
Veronique Kolasa, *President*
Michael Kazam, *Vice Pres*
Ajay Seechurn, *Accountant*
Fabien Duverneuil, *Associate Dir*
▲ EMP: 9
SQ FT: 2,500
SALES (est): 1MM **Privately Held**
WEB: www.lebook.com
SIC: 2731 Books: publishing only

(G-10527)
LE PAVEH LTD
23 W 47th St Ste 501 (10036-2826)
PHONE.................................212 736-6110
John H Naghshbandi, *CEO*
EMP: 10
SALES (est): 924.7K **Privately Held**
SIC: 3911 Jewelry, precious metal

(G-10528)
LE VIAN CORP
10 W 46th St (10036-4515)
PHONE.................................516 466-7200
Louis Ebrani, *President*
EMP: 36
SALES (corp-wide): 32.1MM **Privately Held**
SIC: 3911 Jewelry, precious metal
PA: Le Vian Corp.
   235 Great Neck Rd
   Great Neck NY 11021
   516 466-7200

(G-10529)
LEA & VIOLA INC
525 Fashion Ave Rm 1401 (10018-4914)
PHONE.................................646 918-6866
Minji Kim, *President*
EMP: 6
SQ FT: 4,000
SALES (est): 810K **Privately Held**
SIC: 2331 Women's & misses' blouses & shirts

(G-10530)
LEADERSHIP DIRECTORIES INC (PA)
Also Called: Leadership Connect
1407 Broadway Rm 318 (10018-3853)
PHONE.................................212 627-4140
Gretchen G Teichgraeber, *CEO*
William W Cressey, *Chairman*
Sanja Klima, *Vice Pres*
Shai Tzach, *Controller*
Ed Faas, *Sales Mgr*
EMP: 70

New York - New York County (G-10531)   **GEOGRAPHIC SECTION**

SQ FT: 11,400
SALES (est): 10.8MM **Privately Held**
SIC: 2721 2741 Periodicals: publishing only; directories: publishing only, not printed on site

(G-10531)
LEADERTEX INTL INC
Also Called: Leadertex Group
135 W 36th St Fl 12 (10018-6981)
PHONE..................212 563-2242
Joseph Delijani, *President*
▲ **EMP:** 20
SALES (est): 1.7MM **Privately Held**
SIC: 2252 Men's, boys' & girls' hosiery

(G-10532)
LEARNINGEXPRESS LLC
224 W 29th St Fl 3 (10001-5204)
PHONE..................646 274-6454
Barry Lippman, *CEO*
Kheil McIntyre, *COO*
Ilsa Halpern, *Vice Pres*
Steve Nolan, *Vice Pres*
EMP: 35
SALES (est): 5.7MM **Privately Held**
WEB: www.learningexpressllc.com
SIC: 2731 Book publishing

(G-10533)
LEBLON HOLDINGS LLC
33 Irving Pl Fl 3 (10003-2332)
PHONE..................212 741-2675
Jim Myers, *CFO*
Steven Luttmann,
▲ **EMP:** 35
SQ FT: 3,000
SALES (est): 3.8MM **Privately Held**
SIC: 2085 Rum (alcoholic beverage)
PA: Bacardi Limited
65 Pitts Bay Road
Hamilton

(G-10534)
LEBLON LLC
Also Called: Leblon Cachaca
33 Irving Pl Fl 3 (10003-2332)
PHONE..................954 649-0148
Eric Goldman, *President*
Rosa Gar, *Manager*
▲ **EMP:** 11 **EST:** 2005
SALES (est): 1.2MM **Privately Held**
SIC: 2085 Distilled & blended liquors

(G-10535)
LEBLON LLC
266 W 26th St Ste 801 (10001-6722)
PHONE..................786 281-5672
Thomas Bonney, *CFO*
Steve Luttmann, *Mng Member*
Gerrard Schweitzer,
▲ **EMP:** 40
SALES (est): 2.9MM **Privately Held**
SIC: 2085 Distilled & blended liquors

(G-10536)
LEDES GROUP INC
Also Called: Cosmetic World
85 5th Ave Fl 12 (10003-3019)
PHONE..................212 840-8800
George M Ledes, *President*
John Ledes, *Publisher*
Joseph Garces, *Vice Pres*
Sally C Ledes, *Vice Pres*
Hasu Shah, *Treasurer*
EMP: 18
SQ FT: 7,000
SALES: 25.4K **Privately Held**
WEB: www.cosmeticworld.com
SIC: 2741 Newsletter publishing

(G-10537)
LEE & LOW BOOKS INCORPORATED
Also Called: Bebop Books
95 Madison Ave Rm 1205 (10016-7808)
PHONE..................212 779-4400
Thomas Low, *President*
Jessica Echeverria, *Editor*
Emily Hazel, *Editor*
Craig Low, *Vice Pres*
Randy Eng, *Opers Spvr*
▲ **EMP:** 14
SQ FT: 4,500
SALES (est): 1.6MM **Privately Held**
WEB: www.leeandlow.com
SIC: 2731 Books: publishing only

(G-10538)
LEE WORLD INDUSTRIES LLC (PA)
150 Broadway Ste 1608 (10038-4381)
PHONE..................212 265-8866
James Lee, *President*
Lisa Lee, *Vice Pres*
▲ **EMP:** 13
SQ FT: 14,500
SALES: 4MM **Privately Held**
WEB: www.leeworld.com
SIC: 3714 Motor vehicle parts & accessories

(G-10539)
LEE YUEN FUNG TRADING CO INC (PA)
125 W 29th St Fl 5 (10001-5780)
PHONE..................212 594-9595
Moon Tong Fok, *President*
EMP: 14
SQ FT: 4,000
SALES: 8MM **Privately Held**
SIC: 2833 5149 Drugs & herbs: grading, grinding & milling; seasonings, sauces & extracts

(G-10540)
LEFRAK ENTERTAINMENT CO LTD
Also Called: L M R
40 W 57th St Fl 4 (10019-4001)
PHONE..................212 586-3600
Samuel J Lefrak, *Ch of Bd*
Richard S Lefrak, *Vice Ch Bd*
Herbert Moelis, *President*
EMP: 9
SALES (est): 660K **Privately Held**
SIC: 2741 3652 Music book & sheet music publishing; pre-recorded records & tapes

(G-10541)
LEGGIADRO INTERNATIONAL INC (PA)
8 W 36th St Fl 9 (10018-9772)
PHONE..................212 997-8766
Brooks Ross, *President*
Ann Ross, *Corp Secy*
Karen Degand, *Controller*
◆ **EMP:** 50
SQ FT: 6,000
SALES (est): 8.5MM **Privately Held**
SIC: 2339 Sportswear, women's

(G-10542)
LEHMANN PRINTING COMPANY INC
247 W 37th St Rm 2a (10018-5066)
PHONE..................212 929-2395
David Lehmann, *President*
Ruth Lehmann, *Manager*
EMP: 5
SQ FT: 10,000
SALES (est): 763.5K **Privately Held**
WEB: www.lehmannprinting.com
SIC: 2752 Commercial printing, offset

(G-10543)
LEMETRIC HAIR CENTERS INC
124 E 40th St Rm 601 (10016-1769)
PHONE..................212 986-5620
Elline Surianello, *President*
Marvin Blender, *Vice Pres*
EMP: 15
SALES (est): 1.2MM **Privately Held**
WEB: www.lemetric.com
SIC: 3999 7231 Hairpin mountings; beauty shops

(G-10544)
LENDING TRIMMING CO INC
179 Christopher St (10014-2815)
PHONE..................212 242-7502
John Benis, *President*
William Jarblum, *Admin Sec*
EMP: 80 **EST:** 1944
SQ FT: 7,000
SALES (est): 4.6MM **Privately Held**
SIC: 2396 Trimming, fabric

(G-10545)
LENG UNIVERSAL INC
Also Called: Emoji
530 7th Ave Rm 1101 (10018-4868)
PHONE..................212 398-6800
Chun Pao Pleng, *CEO*
EMP: 12
SQ FT: 3,800
SALES (est): 1.2MM **Privately Held**
SIC: 2369 2339 2325 Mfg Girl/Youth Outerwear Mfg Women's/Misses' Outerwear Mfg Men's/Boy's Trousers

(G-10546)
LENON MODELS INC
236 W 27th St Rm 900 (10001-5906)
PHONE..................212 229-1581
Elise Hubsher, *President*
EMP: 5
SQ FT: 2,000
SALES (est): 480.2K **Privately Held**
SIC: 3259 Architectural clay products

(G-10547)
LENORE MARSHALL INC
231 W 29th St Frnt 1 (10001-5209)
PHONE..................212 947-5945
Leo Marshall, *President*
John Petkanas, *President*
▲ **EMP:** 5 **EST:** 1957
SALES (est): 390K **Privately Held**
SIC: 2353 Millinery

(G-10548)
LEO D BERNSTEIN & SONS INC (PA)
Also Called: Bernstein Display
151 W 25th St Frnt 1 (10001-7204)
PHONE..................212 337-9578
Roger Friedman, *Ch of Bd*
Anthony Tripoli, *President*
Edmund Bernstein, *Chairman*
Mitchell Bernstein, *COO*
▲ **EMP:** 20 **EST:** 1965
SQ FT: 192,000
SALES (est): 18.8MM **Privately Held**
WEB: www.bernsteindisplay.com
SIC: 3999 2541 5046 7389 Forms: display, dress & show; store & office display cases & fixtures; store fixtures; store equipment; design services

(G-10549)
LEO INGWER INC
62 W 47th St Ste 1004 (10036-3286)
PHONE..................212 719-1342
Kenneth Ingwer, *President*
Danielle I Cohen, *Vice Pres*
Rochelle Ingwer-Levine, *Vice Pres*
Matt Selig, *VP Sales*
Ashley Ingwer, *Sales Staff*
▲ **EMP:** 42 **EST:** 1941
SQ FT: 3,500
SALES (est): 5.8MM **Privately Held**
WEB: www.leoingwer.com
SIC: 3911 Mountings, gold or silver: pens, leather goods, etc.

(G-10550)
LEO PAPER INC
286 5th Ave Fl 6 (10001-4512)
PHONE..................917 305-0708
Bijan Pakzada, *President*
EMP: 7
SALES (est): 426.5K **Privately Held**
SIC: 2759 Commercial printing

(G-10551)
LEO SCHACHTER & CO INC
529 5th Ave (10017-4608)
PHONE..................212 688-2000
Michael Metz, *CEO*
Sandy Marks, *VP Sales*
EMP: 100
SALES (est): 3.6MM **Privately Held**
SIC: 3911 5094 Jewelry apparel; diamonds (gems)

(G-10552)
LEO SCHACHTER DIAMONDS LLC
Also Called: Leo Diamond, The
50 W 47th St Ste 2100 (10036-8687)
PHONE..................212 688-2000
Eric Austein, *Partner*
Andrew Doenias, *Accountant*
Jennifer Pleva, *Human Resources*
Shimrit Adika, *Accounts Mgr*
Lenny Kramer, *Sales Staff*
EMP: 100 **EST:** 1981
SQ FT: 11,335
SALES (est): 15.7MM **Privately Held**
WEB: www.leoschachter.com
SIC: 3915 5094 Jewelers' materials & lapidary work; jewelry & precious stones
PA: Leo Schachter Diamonds Ltd
Bezalel
Ramat Gan
357 662-23

(G-10553)
LEON MEGE INC
Also Called: Art of Platinum, The
151 W 46th St Ste 901 (10036-8512)
PHONE..................212 768-3868
Leon Mege, *Owner*
EMP: 12
SQ FT: 4,500
SALES (est): 118.8K **Privately Held**
WEB: www.artofplatinum.com
SIC: 3911 Medals, precious or semi-precious metal

(G-10554)
LESILU PRODUCTIONS INC
Also Called: Hey Doll
60 W 38th St Rm 302 (10018-0281)
PHONE..................212 947-6419
Steven Sunshine, *CEO*
Lesli Sunshine, *President*
Luanne Trovato, *Corp Secy*
▲ **EMP:** 6 **EST:** 2000
SQ FT: 650
SALES (est): 1.1MM **Privately Held**
SIC: 3961 Costume jewelry, ex. precious metal & semiprecious stones

(G-10555)
LESLIE STUART CO INC
Also Called: Donna Degan
149 W 36th St Fl 8 (10018-9474)
PHONE..................212 629-4551
Gene Fobarty, *President*
Donna Degan, *Vice Pres*
Heshy Feldman, *Sales Mgr*
Eugene Fogarty, *Director*
▲ **EMP:** 17
SQ FT: 4,000
SALES (est): 2.2MM **Privately Held**
WEB: www.donnadegnan.com
SIC: 2339 Women's & misses' athletic clothing & sportswear

(G-10556)
LEVI SHABTAI
1 W 47th St (10036-4785)
PHONE..................212 302-7393
Levi Shabtai, *Owner*
EMP: 5
SALES (est): 208.6K **Privately Held**
SIC: 3915 Diamond cutting & polishing

(G-10557)
LEVY GROUP INC (PA)
Also Called: Liz Claiborne Coats
1333 Broadway Fl 9 (10018-1064)
PHONE..................212 398-0707
Jack Arthur Levy, *Ch of Bd*
Donald Levy, *Chairman*
Lawrence Levy, *Vice Pres*
Richard Levy, *Vice Pres*
▲ **EMP:** 150 **EST:** 1995
SQ FT: 27,000
SALES (est): 77.7MM **Privately Held**
WEB: www.oasisfarm.com
SIC: 2385 2337 Raincoats, except vulcanized rubber: purchased materials; jackets & vests, except fur & leather: women's

(G-10558)
LF OUTERWEAR LLC
463 7th Ave Fl 12 (10018-7499)
PHONE..................212 239-2025
Richard Kringstein,
Barry Kringstein,
▲ **EMP:** 80
SALES (est): 3.4MM **Privately Held**
SIC: 2337 Women's & misses' suits & coats

GEOGRAPHIC SECTION

New York - New York County (G-10588)

(G-10559)
LGB INC
Also Called: J Valdi
1410 Broadway Rm 3205 (10018-9633)
PHONE..................212 278-8280
Eduardo Snider, *President*
Peter Reidell, *Corp Secy*
EMP: 20
SALES (est): 836.8K **Privately Held**
SIC: 2339 Women's & misses' outerwear

(G-10560)
LIBERTY APPAREL COMPANY INC (PA)
1407 Broadway Rm 1500 (10018-2836)
PHONE..................718 625-4000
Hagai Laniado, *President*
Albert Negri, *Principal*
Bryan Lattmen, *Vice Pres*
Jeffrey Wine, *CFO*
▲ EMP: 50
SQ FT: 38,000
SALES (est): 4MM **Privately Held**
WEB: www.libertyapparel.com
SIC: 2331 2339 2369 Women's & misses' blouses & shirts; women's & misses' outerwear; girls' & children's outerwear

(G-10561)
LICENDERS (PA)
939 8th Ave (10019-4264)
PHONE..................212 759-5200
Adie Horowitz, *Principal*
EMP: 9 EST: 2010
SALES (est): 1.2MM **Privately Held**
SIC: 3647 5087 Headlights (fixtures), vehicular; service establishment equipment

(G-10562)
LIFE EARTH COMPANY
200 W 113th St Apt 2d (10026-3303)
PHONE..................310 751-0627
Reginald Askew, *CEO*
EMP: 2
SALES: 7.5MM **Privately Held**
SIC: 2013 2086 Frozen meats from purchased meat; soft drinks: packaged in cans, bottles, etc.

(G-10563)
LIFE ON EARTH INC (PA)
Also Called: HISPANICA INTERNATIONAL DELIGH
575 Lexington Ave Fl 4 (10022-6146)
PHONE..................866 928-5070
Fernando Oswaldo Leonzo, *Ch of Bd*
John Romagosa, *President*
Robert Gunther, *COO*
Randy Berholtz, *Exec VP*
EMP: 11 EST: 2013
SALES: 3.2MM **Publicly Held**
SIC: 2087 Beverage bases

(G-10564)
LIFE STYLE DESIGN GROUP
Also Called: Sag Harbor
1441 Broadway Fl 7 (10018-1905)
PHONE..................212 391-8666
EMP: 35
SQ FT: 12,000
SALES (est): 2.6MM
SALES (corp-wide): 350.8MM **Privately Held**
WEB: www.kellwoodco.com
SIC: 2339 Sportswear, women's
PA: Kellwood Company, Llc
   600 Kellwood Pkwy Ste 200
   Chesterfield MO 63017
   314 576-3100

(G-10565)
LIFESTYLE DESIGN USA LTD
Also Called: Cyber Knit
315 W 39th St Rm 1400 (10018-4063)
PHONE..................212 279-9400
Daniel Honig, *President*
Janine Girardi, *Director*
▲ EMP: 6
SQ FT: 1,000
SALES (est): 1.2MM **Privately Held**
SIC: 2257 Dyeing & finishing circular knit fabrics

(G-10566)
LIFTFORWARD INC (PA)
180 Maiden Ln Fl 10 (10038-5178)
PHONE..................917 693-4993
Jeffrey Rogers, *President*
Barbara Steinberg, *Controller*
Susan Kraft, *Human Res Mgr*
Anthony Galan, *Underwriter*
Geoff Miller, *Exec Dir*
EMP: 20
SALES: 25MM **Privately Held**
SIC: 7372 Business oriented computer software

(G-10567)
LIGHT HOUSE HILL MARKETING
Also Called: Signatures
38 W 39th St Fl 4l (10018-2150)
PHONE..................212 354-1338
Donald Schmidt, *President*
▲ EMP: 16
SQ FT: 2,900
SALES (est): 1.5MM **Privately Held**
WEB: www.signaturespromo.com
SIC: 2231 Apparel & outerwear broadwoven fabrics

(G-10568)
LIGHT INC
530 Fashion Ave Rm 1002 (10018-4869)
PHONE..................212 629-3255
Alice Sim, *President*
▲ EMP: 6 EST: 1993
SALES (est): 881.5K **Privately Held**
WEB: www.light.com
SIC: 2339 Women's & misses' outerwear

(G-10569)
LIGHTBULB PRESS INC
39 W 28th St (10001-4203)
PHONE..................212 485-8800
Kenneth Morris, *Ch of Bd*
Delphine Leymarie, *Office Mgr*
Rickie Kowlessar, *Info Tech Mgr*
Mavis Wright, *Director*
Kara Hatch, *Art Dir*
EMP: 30
SQ FT: 7,500
SALES (est): 2.7MM **Privately Held**
WEB: www.lightbulbpress.net
SIC: 2741 Miscellaneous publishing

(G-10570)
LIGHTHOUSE COMPONENTS
14 Wall St (10005-2101)
PHONE..................917 993-6820
Maurice Gaete, *CEO*
EMP: 25
SALES (est): 944.2K **Privately Held**
SIC: 3679 Electronic components

(G-10571)
LILY & TAYLOR INC
Also Called: Lilly Collection
247 W 37th St Frnt 6 (10018-5042)
PHONE..................212 564-5459
Sohail Elyaszadeh, *President*
Morris Elyaszadeh, *Manager*
◆ EMP: 15
SQ FT: 3,500
SALES: 6MM **Privately Held**
WEB: www.lilyandtaylor.com
SIC: 2335 2337 2339 Gowns, formal; suits: women's, misses' & juniors'; skirts, separate: women's, misses' & juniors'; slacks: women's, misses' & juniors'

(G-10572)
LINDER NEW YORK LLC
195 Chrystie St Rm 900 (10002-1230)
PHONE..................646 678-5819
Sam Linder, *Mng Member*
EMP: 11 EST: 2007
SALES (est): 1.3MM **Privately Held**
SIC: 2329 2389 Athletic (warmup, sweat & jogging) suits: men's & boys'; men's miscellaneous accessories

(G-10573)
LINRICH DESIGNS INC
Also Called: Linda Richards
256 W 38th St Fl 8 (10018-9123)
PHONE..................212 382-2257
Linda Breatti, *Owner*
Frank Bretti, *Marketing Staff*
EMP: 5
SALES (corp-wide): 699.3K **Privately Held**
WEB: www.lindarichards.com
SIC: 2339 2337 Women's & misses' jackets & coats, except sportswear; suits: women's, misses' & juniors'; skirts, separate: women's, misses' & juniors'
PA: Linrich Designs Inc
   256 W 38th St Fl 8
   New York NY
   212 382-2257

(G-10574)
LINTEX LINENS INC
295 5th Ave Ste 1703 (10016-7130)
PHONE..................212 679-8046
Kurt Hamburger, *President*
Rae Ellen Blum, *Vice Pres*
▲ EMP: 500
SQ FT: 6,000
SALES (est): 40.5MM **Privately Held**
SIC: 2299 5023 Fabrics: linen, jute, hemp, ramie; linens, table

(G-10575)
LIONEL HABAS ASSOCIATES INC
1601 3rd Ave Apt 22d (10128-0028)
PHONE..................212 860-8454
Lionel Habas, *President*
EMP: 10
SQ FT: 200
SALES (est): 840K **Privately Held**
SIC: 2652 Mfg Setup Paperboard Boxes

(G-10576)
LIPPINCOTT MASSIE MCQUILKIN L
27 W 20th St Ste 305 (10011-3731)
PHONE..................212 352-2055
Rob McQuilkin, *Mng Member*
Kent Wolf, *Agent*
Martin Lemelman, *Professor*
EMP: 10
SALES (est): 896.1K **Privately Held**
SIC: 2731 Books: publishing only

(G-10577)
LIST & BEISLER GMBH
311 W 43rd St Fl 12 (10036-6004)
PHONE..................646 866-6960
Samuel Grigg, *Director*
EMP: 30
SALES (est): 942.1K **Privately Held**
SIC: 2095 Roasted coffee

(G-10578)
LITERARY CLASSICS OF US
Also Called: LIBRARY OF AMERICA
14 E 60th St Ste 1101 (10022-7115)
PHONE..................212 308-3360
Cheryl Hurley, *President*
Trish Hoard, *Editor*
Geoffrey G Obrien, *Editor*
Daniel Baker, *CFO*
Benjamin Ordover, *Treasurer*
▲ EMP: 16
SQ FT: 4,000
SALES: 6MM **Privately Held**
SIC: 2731 2732 Books: publishing only; book printing

(G-10579)
LITHOMATIC BUSINESS FORMS INC
233 W 18th St Frnt A (10011-4570)
PHONE..................212 255-6700
Irwin Ostrega, *President*
EMP: 3 EST: 1971
SQ FT: 5,000
SALES: 1.5MM **Privately Held**
SIC: 2752 Commercial printing, offset

(G-10580)
LITTLE ERIC SHOES ON MADISON
1118 Madison Ave (10028-0406)
PHONE..................212 717-1513
Robert Pansinkoff, *President*
Robert Pasinkoff, *President*
EMP: 6
SALES (est): 904.7K **Privately Held**
SIC: 3021 Canvas shoes, rubber soled

(G-10581)
LITTLE WOLF CABINET SHOP INC
1583 1st Ave Frnt 1 (10028-4273)
PHONE..................212 734-1116
John Wolf, *President*
Maureen Fritsch, *Corp Secy*
John Fritsch, *Vice Pres*
EMP: 20
SQ FT: 2,500
SALES (est): 2.8MM **Privately Held**
SIC: 2511 5712 Wood household furniture; furniture stores

(G-10582)
LITTLEBITS ELECTRONICS INC (PA)
601 W 26th St Rm M274 (10001-1129)
PHONE..................917 464-4577
Aya Bdeir, *CEO*
EMP: 47
SQ FT: 18,000
SALES (est): 12.1MM **Privately Held**
SIC: 3944 Electronic toys

(G-10583)
LIVE VOTE II INC
105 W 86th St 322 (10024-3412)
PHONE..................646 343-9053
Michael Fellmeth, *COO*
EMP: 5 EST: 2017
SALES (est): 142.2K **Privately Held**
SIC: 7372 7371 Prepackaged Software Services Custom Computer Programing

(G-10584)
LIVERIGHT PUBLISHING CORP
Also Called: Norton, Ww & Company,
500 5th Ave Fl 6 (10110-0699)
PHONE..................212 354-5500
Drake McSeely, *President*
Victor Schmalzer, *General Mgr*
John G Benedict, *Vice Pres*
Star Lawrence, *Vice Pres*
Angela Der Lippe, *Manager*
EMP: 9
SQ FT: 3,000
SALES (est): 888.2K
SALES (corp-wide): 185.1MM **Privately Held**
WEB: www.wwnorton.com
SIC: 2731 Books: publishing only
PA: W. W. Norton & Company, Inc.
   500 5th Ave Fl 6
   New York NY 10110
   212 354-5500

(G-10585)
LIVETILES CORP (PA)
60 Madison Ave Fl 8 (10010-1676)
PHONE..................917 472-7887
Jonathan Green, *Finance Dir*
EMP: 17
SQ FT: 100
SALES (est): 3.7MM **Privately Held**
SIC: 7372 Business oriented computer software

(G-10586)
LLC MAJOR MAJOR
1407 Broadway Fl 10 (10018-3271)
PHONE..................212 354-8550
Claudia Polon, *Credit Staff*
EMP: 50
SALES (est): 1MM **Privately Held**
SIC: 2326 Men's & boys' work clothing

(G-10587)
LMR GROUP INC
463 7th Ave Fl 4 (10018-8725)
PHONE..................212 730-9221
Linlin Fang, *Principal*
Robi Hagooli, *Principal*
Steven Stuppler, *Director*
EMP: 5 EST: 2016
SALES (est): 247.8K **Privately Held**
SIC: 2335 Women's, juniors' & misses' dresses

(G-10588)
LOAR GROUP INC (PA)
450 Lexington Ave Fl 31 (10017-3925)
PHONE..................212 210-9348
Jim Mullen, *President*
Glenn Dalessandro, *CFO*

New York - New York County (G-10589)   **GEOGRAPHIC SECTION**

EMP: 144
SALES (est): 20MM **Privately Held**
SIC: 3728 Aircraft parts & equipment

(G-10589)
LOCATIONS MAGAZINE
124 E 79th St (10075-0353)
PHONE................................212 288-4745
Joel Scher, *Owner*
EMP: 5
SALES (est): 290K **Privately Held**
SIC: 2721 Magazines: publishing only, not printed on site

(G-10590)
LOCKHEED MARTIN CORPORATION
420 Lexington Ave Rm 2601 (10170-2602)
PHONE................................212 953-1510
Ellen Strauss, *Manager*
EMP: 8 **Publicly Held**
WEB: www.lockheedmartin.com
SIC: 3812 Search & navigation equipment
PA: Lockheed Martin Corporation
6801 Rockledge Dr
Bethesda MD 20817

(G-10591)
LOCKHEED MARTIN CORPORATION
600 3rd Ave Fl 35 (10016-2001)
PHONE................................212 697-1105
Brad Kaminsky, *Mfg Staff*
Brook Awoke, *Engineer*
Daniel Butash, *Engineer*
Lisa McMeekin, *Branch Mgr*
EMP: 85 **Publicly Held**
WEB: www.lockheedmartin.com
SIC: 3812 Search & navigation equipment
PA: Lockheed Martin Corporation
6801 Rockledge Dr
Bethesda MD 20817

(G-10592)
LOGO
1515 Broadway (10036-8901)
PHONE................................212 846-2568
EMP: 6 **EST:** 2008
SALES (est): 542.4K **Privately Held**
SIC: 2869 Fuels

(G-10593)
LOIS KITCHEN LLC
206 Avenue A Apt 2a (10009-3405)
PHONE................................216 308-9375
Nora O'Malley,
EMP: 5
SALES (est): 165.7K **Privately Held**
SIC: 3999 Manufacturing industries

(G-10594)
LOKAI HOLDINGS LLC
36 E 31st St Rm 602 (10016-6918)
PHONE................................646 979-3474
Steven Izen, *CEO*
Andrew Actman, *CFO*
Elyse McAvoy, *Accounts Exec*
Jenna Stangl, *Sales Staff*
Kyle Hunte, *Marketing Staff*
▲ **EMP:** 10
SQ FT: 3,000
SALES: 13MM **Privately Held**
SIC: 3911 5199 Bracelets, precious metal; general merchandise, non-durable

(G-10595)
LOLLYTOGS LTD (PA)
Also Called: Lt Apparel Group
100 W 33rd St Ste 1012 (10001-2984)
PHONE................................212 502-6000
Richard Sutton, *CEO*
Morris Sutton, *President*
Joseph Sutton, *Vice Pres*
Jeffery Sutton, *Treasurer*
Jeffrey Sutton, *Treasurer*
◆ **EMP:** 80 **EST:** 1958
SQ FT: 40,000
SALES (est): 2.6MM **Privately Held**
SIC: 2369 5137 Girls' & children's outerwear; sportswear, women's & children's

(G-10596)
LONDON THEATER NEWS LTD
12 E 86th St Apt 620 (10028-0511)
PHONE................................212 517-8608
Roger Harris, *President*
EMP: 19
SALES (est): 130K **Privately Held**
SIC: 2741 7922 Newsletter publishing; ticket agency, theatrical

(G-10597)
LONGO NEW YORK INC
444 W 17th St (10011-5893)
P.O. Box 511, Wharton NJ (07885-0511)
PHONE................................212 929-7128
Joe M Longo, *President*
EMP: 10
SALES (est): 530.5K **Privately Held**
SIC: 7694 Armature Rewinding

(G-10598)
LONGTAIL STUDIOS INC
180 Varick St Rm 820 (10014-5419)
PHONE................................646 443-8146
Gerard Guillemot, *President*
Claude Guillemot, *Vice Pres*
Michelle Guillemot, *Vice Pres*
Yves Guillemot, *Vice Pres*
Christian Guillemot, *Admin Sec*
EMP: 26
SQ FT: 4,000
SALES (est): 3.3MM **Privately Held**
WEB: www.longtailstudios.com
SIC: 3695 Computer software tape & disks: blank, rigid & floppy

(G-10599)
LOOK BY M INC
838 Avenue Of The America (10001-4194)
PHONE................................212 213-4019
Youjung Kim, *President*
▲ **EMP:** 5
SALES (est): 398.4K **Privately Held**
SIC: 2252 Tights & leg warmers

(G-10600)
LOOKBOOKS MEDIA INC
208 W 30th St Rm 802 (10001-0883)
PHONE................................646 737-3360
Manny Serrano, *Vice Pres*
Emmanuel Serrano, *VP Finance*
Adam Helfgott, *CTO*
EMP: 15
SALES (est): 1.1MM **Privately Held**
SIC: 7372 Application computer software

(G-10601)
LOOM CONCEPTS LLC
767 Lexington Ave Rm 405 (10065-8553)
PHONE................................212 813-9586
▲ **EMP:** 2
SQ FT: 500
SALES (est): 1.8MM **Privately Held**
SIC: 2273 Mfg Carpets/Rugs

(G-10602)
LOOMSTATE LLC
270 Bowery Fl 3 (10012-3674)
PHONE................................212 219-2300
Annie Graziani, *General Mgr*
Valerie Bleza, *Controller*
Art Ryan, *Mng Member*
Courtney Hoctor, *Manager*
Aishwarya Mahulikar, *Manager*
▲ **EMP:** 25
SALES (est): 3.7MM **Privately Held**
SIC: 2231 Weaving mill, broadwoven fabrics: wool or similar fabric

(G-10603)
LORAL SPACE & COMMNCTNS HOLDNG
600 5th Ave Fl 16 (10020-2324)
PHONE................................212 697-1105
EMP: 30
SALES (est): 1.6MM **Publicly Held**
SIC: 3663 Satellites, communications
HQ: Loral Spacecom Corporation
565 5th Ave Fl 19
New York NY 10017
212 697-1105

(G-10604)
LORAL SPACE COMMUNICATIONS INC (PA)
600 5th Ave Fl 16 (10020-2324)
PHONE................................212 697-1105
Mark H Rachesky, *Ch of Bd*
Michael B Targoff, *Vice Ch Bd*
AVI Katz, *President*
Michael Targoff, *Vice Chairman*
Harvey Rein, *Vice Pres*
EMP: 22
SQ FT: 9,000
SALES (est): 869.9MM **Publicly Held**
WEB: www.ssloral.com
SIC: 3663 4899 Satellites, communications; satellite earth stations; data communication services

(G-10605)
LORAL SPACECOM CORPORATION (HQ)
565 5th Ave Fl 19 (10017-2431)
PHONE................................212 697-1105
Michael Targoff, *CEO*
Stephen Hartland, *Project Mgr*
Randy Simons, *Opers Mgr*
Richard Mastoloni, *Treasurer*
Richard P Mastoloni, *Treasurer*
EMP: 30
SALES (est): 869.4MM **Publicly Held**
WEB: www.hq.loral.com
SIC: 3663 Satellites, communications

(G-10606)
LOREAL USA INC
Biotherm
575 5th Ave Bsmt (10017-2446)
PHONE................................212 818-1500
Matt Fluck, *President*
Dan Miller, *President*
Malay Parikh, *President*
Robert J Cassou, *Senior VP*
Roger Dolden, *Senior VP*
EMP: 470
SALES (corp-wide): 4.2B **Privately Held**
WEB: www.lorealparisusa.com
SIC: 2844 Hair preparations, including shampoos; cosmetic preparations; perfumes & colognes
HQ: L'oreal Usa, Inc.
10 Hudson Yards Fl 30
New York NY 10001
212 818-1500

(G-10607)
LOREAL USA INC
435 Hudson St (10014-3941)
PHONE................................917 606-9554
Lindsay Atha, *Manager*
EMP: 373
SALES (corp-wide): 4.2B **Privately Held**
WEB: www.lorealparisusa.com
SIC: 2844 5122 Toilet preparations; cosmetics, perfumes & hair products
HQ: L'oreal Usa, Inc.
10 Hudson Yards Fl 30
New York NY 10001
212 818-1500

(G-10608)
LOREAL USA INC
10 Hudson Yards Fl 27 (10001-2159)
PHONE................................212 389-4201
Karen Czajkowski, *Branch Mgr*
EMP: 30
SALES (corp-wide): 4.2B **Privately Held**
WEB: www.lorealparisusa.com
SIC: 2844 Depilatories (cosmetic); shampoos, rinses, conditioners: hair; face creams or lotions; hair coloring preparations
HQ: L'oreal Usa, Inc.
10 Hudson Yards Fl 30
New York NY 10001
212 818-1500

(G-10609)
LOREAL USA PRODUCTS INC (DH)
10 Hudson Yards (10001-2157)
PHONE................................212 818-1500
Frederic Roze, *President*
Rebecca McFadden, *President*
Ryan Stevenson, *President*
Rebecca Caruso, *Exec VP*
Kevin Mason, *Vice Pres*
▲ **EMP:** 5
SALES (est): 9.9MM
SALES (corp-wide): 4.2B **Privately Held**
SIC: 2844 Hair coloring preparations; shaving preparations; cosmetic preparations; toilet preparations

HQ: L'oreal Usa, Inc.
10 Hudson Yards Fl 30
New York NY 10001
212 818-1500

(G-10610)
LORELEI ORTHOTICS PROSTHETICS
30 E 40th St Rm 905 (10016-1231)
PHONE................................212 727-2011
Brian Kilcommons, *President*
Alene Chase, *Vice Pres*
EMP: 6
SQ FT: 5,000
SALES (est): 839.6K **Privately Held**
SIC: 3842 Braces, orthopedic; prosthetic appliances

(G-10611)
LORNAMEAD INC (DH)
1359 Broadway Fl 17 (10018-7117)
PHONE................................716 874-7190
Randy Sloan, *CEO*
Brian Bradley, *President*
Jeff Lokken, *Vice Pres*
James Carney, *VP Opers*
Alex Stugis, *Opers Mgr*
◆ **EMP:** 90
SQ FT: 66,000
SALES (est): 19MM **Privately Held**
WEB: www.lornameadna.com
SIC: 2844 3843 Cosmetic preparations; compounds, dental

(G-10612)
LOS ANGLES TMES CMMNCTIONS LLC
780 3rd Ave Fl 40 (10017-2024)
PHONE................................212 418-9600
Bonnie Sherer-Herrera, *Vice Pres*
Virginia Moncada, *Manager*
EMP: 35
SALES (corp-wide): 769.2MM **Privately Held**
SIC: 2711 Newspapers, publishing & printing
PA: Los Angeles Times Communications, Llc
2300 E Imperial Hwy
El Segundo CA 90245
213 237-5000

(G-10613)
LOST WORLDS INC
920 Riverside Dr Apt 68 (10032-5468)
PHONE................................212 923-3423
Stuart Clurman, *President*
EMP: 9
SALES (est): 670K **Privately Held**
SIC: 2386 5699 Coats & jackets, leather & sheep-lined; leather garments

(G-10614)
LOTTA LUV BEAUTY LLC
1359 Broadway Fl 17 (10018-7117)
PHONE................................646 786-2847
Elizabeth Alli,
▲ **EMP:** 10
SQ FT: 20,000
SALES (est): 1MM **Privately Held**
SIC: 2834 5122 Lip balms; cosmetics
PA: Li & Fung Limited
C/O Estera Management (Bermuda) Limited
Hamilton

(G-10615)
LOU SALLY FASHIONS CORP (DH)
Also Called: S L Fashions Group
1400 Broadway Rm 601 (10018-0728)
PHONE................................212 354-9670
Mitchell Grabow, *President*
▲ **EMP:** 31
SQ FT: 5,500
SALES: 35MM **Privately Held**
SIC: 2335 Women's, juniors' & misses' dresses
HQ: Alex Apparel Group, Inc.
1407 Broadway Rm 1500
New York NY 10018
212 549-8510

GEOGRAPHIC SECTION

New York - New York County (G-10645)

(G-10616)
LOU SALLY FASHIONS CORP
1400 Broadway Frnt 3 (10018-5367)
PHONE................................212 354-1283
Tony Porni, *Vice Pres*
EMP: 40 **Privately Held**
SIC: 2335 Women's, juniors' & misses' dresses
HQ: Lou Sally Fashions Corp
  1400 Broadway Rm 601
  New York NY 10018
  212 354-9670

(G-10617)
LOUIS VUITTON NORTH AMER INC
1000 3rd Ave (10022-1230)
PHONE................................212 644-2574
George Daco, *Opers Mgr*
Susan Chandler, *Store Mgr*
Michael Chavez, *Store Mgr*
Laura Knaub, *Store Mgr*
Francine Lin, *Store Mgr*
EMP: 9
SALES (corp-wide): 315.2MM **Privately Held**
SIC: 2711 Newspapers, publishing & printing
HQ: Louis Vuitton North America, Inc.
  1 E 57th St
  New York NY 10022
  212 758-8877

(G-10618)
LOUNGEHOUSE LLC
34 W 33rd St Fl 11 (10001-3304)
PHONE................................646 524-2965
Irving Safdieh, *Mng Member*
EMP: 20
SQ FT: 10,000
SALES (est): 856.7K **Privately Held**
SIC: 2341 Nightgowns & negligees: women's & children's; women's accessory & specialty stores; family clothing stores

(G-10619)
LOVEE DOLL & TOY CO INC
39 W 38th St Rm 4w (10018-5540)
PHONE................................212 242-1545
Sam Horowitz, *President*
◆ **EMP:** 5 **EST:** 1962
SQ FT: 40,000
SALES (est): 896.2K **Privately Held**
SIC: 3942 Dolls, except stuffed toy animals

(G-10620)
LR ACQUISITION LLC
1407 Broadway Rm 1207 (10018-2899)
PHONE................................212 301-8765
Sammy Catton, *CEO*
Harry Catton, *CFO*
Wayne Lederman, *Sales Executive*
EMP: 10 **EST:** 2017
SALES (est): 1.1MM **Privately Held**
SIC: 2252 Hosiery

(G-10621)
LR PARIS LLC (PA)
Also Called: Lr Paris
345 7th Ave Fl 7 (10001-5052)
PHONE................................212 634-9372
Charles Dolige, *Mng Member*
Mariemma Dolige,
▲ **EMP:** 15
SALES (est): 1.2MM **Privately Held**
WEB: www.lrparis.com
SIC: 2389 3499 5947 5137 Masquerade costumes; giftware, brass goods; gift, novelty & souvenir shop; scarves, women's & children's; cloth cutting, bolting or winding; fabrics: linen, jute, hemp, ramie

(G-10622)
LS POWER EQUITY PARTNERS LP (PA)
1700 Broadway Fl 35 (10019-5905)
PHONE................................212 615-3456
Mike Segal, *Ch of Bd*
Mark Brennan, *Exec VP*
Shimon Edelstein, *Exec VP*
John King, *Exec VP*
David Nanus, *Exec VP*
EMP: 1

SALES (est): 108.2MM **Privately Held**
WEB: www.ziccardi.com
SIC: 3568 1796 Power transmission equipment; power generating equipment installation

(G-10623)
LT2 LLC
Also Called: Letigre
250 Park Ave S Fl 10 (10003-1402)
PHONE................................212 684-1510
Ryan O'Sullivan,
EMP: 25
SQ FT: 1,500
SALES: 25MM **Privately Held**
WEB: www.lt2.com
SIC: 2321 2331 Men's & boys' furnishings; women's & misses' blouses & shirts

(G-10624)
LTB MEDIA (USA) INC
Also Called: Louise Blouin Media
77 Water St Ste 702 (10005-4416)
PHONE................................212 447-9555
Louise B Macbain, *President*
Rochelle Stolzenberg, *Sales Dir*
Ronald Gutierrez, *Manager*
Mariette Moore, *Manager*
Scott Indrisek, *Senior Editor*
EMP: 100
SQ FT: 10,000
SALES (est): 12.7MM **Privately Held**
SIC: 2721 Magazines: publishing & printing

(G-10625)
LUCKY MAGAZINE
4 Times Sq Fl 22 (10036-6518)
PHONE................................212 286-6220
EMP: 15
SALES (est): 1.2MM **Privately Held**
SIC: 2721 Periodicals-Publishing/Printing

(G-10626)
LUCKY PEACH LLC
60 E 11th St Fl 5 (10003-6009)
PHONE................................212 228-0031
Narie Chung, *Finance*
Susan Wright,
EMP: 7
SALES (est): 762.6K **Privately Held**
SIC: 2741 Miscellaneous publishing

(G-10627)
LUDLOW MUSIC INC
266 W 37th St Fl 17 (10018-6655)
PHONE................................212 594-9795
Larry Richmond, *President*
Allen Brackerman, *General Mgr*
Bernard Gartler, *Vice Pres*
EMP: 14 **EST:** 1949
SALES (est): 655.3K **Privately Held**
SIC: 2741 Music, sheet: publishing only, not printed on site

(G-10628)
LUKOIL AMERICAS CORPORATION (HQ)
505 5th Ave Fl 9 (10017-4921)
PHONE................................212 421-4141
Robert Ferluga, *CEO*
Vadim Guzman, *Ch of Bd*
EMP: 125 **EST:** 1997
SALES: 128.1MM
SALES (corp-wide): 3.7B **Privately Held**
SIC: 1311 Crude petroleum & natural gas
PA: Lukoil, Pao
  11 Bulvar Sretenski
  Moscow 10100
  495 627-4444

(G-10629)
LUKOIL NORTH AMERICA LLC (DH)
505 5th Ave Fl 9 (10017-4921)
PHONE................................212 421-4141
Vadim Gulzman, *CEO*
EMP: 23
SALES (est): 19.1MM
SALES (corp-wide): 3.7B **Privately Held**
SIC: 1381 5541 Drilling oil & gas wells; filling stations, gasoline
HQ: Lukoil-Volgogradenergo, Ooo
  17 Ul. Im Motsarta
  Volgograd 40002
  844 225-2769

(G-10630)
LULUVISE INC
229 W 116th St Apt 5a (10026-2799)
PHONE................................914 309-7812
Kewhyun Kelly-Yuoh, *CFO*
EMP: 25 **EST:** 2011
SQ FT: 1,000
SALES (est): 1.4MM **Privately Held**
SIC: 7372 Application computer software

(G-10631)
LUXCORE NETWORKS INC (PA)
14 Wall St Fl 20 (10005-2123)
PHONE................................212 618-1724
Gerald Ramdeen, *CEO*
Richard B Black, *COO*
Nick Lefkaditis, *Vice Pres*
Dr Marcus W Shute, *Vice Pres*
Tamer Yacoub, *Vice Pres*
EMP: 12
SALES (est): 2.4MM **Privately Held**
SIC: 3661 Telephones & telephone apparatus

(G-10632)
LUXE IMAGINE CONSULTING LLC
261 W 35th St Ste 404 (10001-1906)
PHONE................................212 273-9770
EMP: 5
SALES (est): 270K **Privately Held**
SIC: 2329 2339 Mfg Mens Children & Women's Apparel

(G-10633)
LVL XIII BRANDS INC
315 W 39th St Rm 1201 (10018-3928)
PHONE................................646 530-2795
Antonio Brown, *CEO*
EMP: 10
SQ FT: 600
SALES: 962K **Privately Held**
SIC: 2311 Men's & boys' suits & coats

(G-10634)
M & S QUALITY CO LTD
26 W 47th St Ste 502 (10036-8603)
PHONE................................212 302-8757
Michael Saks, *President*
EMP: 10
SALES (est): 969.5K **Privately Held**
SIC: 3911 Jewelry, precious metal

(G-10635)
M & S SCHMALBERG INC
242 W 36th St Rm 700 (10018-8965)
PHONE................................212 244-2090
Warren Brand, *President*
Deborah Brand, *Vice Pres*
EMP: 10 **EST:** 1947
SQ FT: 2,500
SALES (est): 700K **Privately Held**
SIC: 3999 5992 Flowers, artificial & preserved; florists

(G-10636)
M G NEW YORK INC
14 E 60th St Ste 400 (10022-7146)
PHONE................................212 371-5566
Marlyse Gros, *President*
◆ **EMP:** 10
SQ FT: 1,665
SALES (est): 25.9MM **Privately Held**
SIC: 3172 Cosmetic bags

(G-10637)
M H MANUFACTURING INCORPORATED
50 W 47th St (10036-8621)
P.O. Box 1743 (10163-1743)
PHONE................................212 461-6900
Judah Poupko, *Vice Pres*
EMP: 9 **EST:** 2009
SALES (est): 1.2MM **Privately Held**
WEB: www.mhdco.com
SIC: 3911 Pins (jewelry), precious metal

(G-10638)
M HESKIA COMPANY INC
98 Cutter Rd Ste 125 (10036)
PHONE................................212 768-1845
EMP: 5
SALES (est): 450K **Privately Held**
SIC: 3911 Mfg Jewelry

(G-10639)
M HIDARY & CO INC
10 W 33rd St Rm 900 (10001-3317)
PHONE................................212 736-6540
Morris Hidary, *Chairman*
Richard Levine, *CFO*
David Hidary, *Treasurer*
Jennifer Okeefe, *Credit Mgr*
Alan Handel, *VP Sales*
▲ **EMP:** 100 **EST:** 1948
SQ FT: 20,000
SALES (est): 17.3MM **Privately Held**
SIC: 2369 2311 2325 2329 Girls' & children's outerwear; men's & boys' suits & coats; men's & boys' trousers & slacks; men's & boys' sportswear & athletic clothing; men's & boys' clothing; women's & children's clothing

(G-10640)
M I T POLY-CART CORP
211 Central Park W (10024-6020)
PHONE................................212 724-7290
Dan Moss, *President*
Isaac Rinkewich, *Vice Pres*
Tova Moss, *Treasurer*
EMP: 5
SQ FT: 1,000
SALES (est): 300K **Privately Held**
WEB: www.mitpolycart.com
SIC: 3089 Plastic containers, except foam

(G-10641)
M L DESIGN INC (PA)
77 Ludlow St Frnt 1 (10002-3898)
PHONE................................212 233-0213
Tommy Lam, *President*
▲ **EMP:** 10
SALES (est): 946.1K **Privately Held**
SIC: 2752 Commercial printing, offset

(G-10642)
M S B INTERNATIONAL LTD (PA)
Also Called: Nyc Design Co
1412 Broadway Rm 1210 (10018-9228)
PHONE................................212 302-5551
Maia Chait, *President*
Robert Guttenberg, *President*
Sunny Leigh, *Vice Pres*
▲ **EMP:** 15
SALES (est): 2.6MM **Privately Held**
SIC: 2331 2321 2325 Women's & misses' blouses & shirts; men's & boys' furnishings; men's & boys' trousers & slacks

(G-10643)
M S RIVIERA INC
Also Called: Rfg
42 W 48th St Fl 4 (10036-1706)
PHONE................................212 391-0206
Michael Palmeri, *President*
Steven Donadio, *Opers Mgr*
EMP: 21
SALES (est): 1.2MM **Privately Held**
SIC: 3911 Jewelry, precious metal

(G-10644)
M SHANKEN COMMUNICATIONS INC (PA)
825 8th Ave Fl 33 (10019-8872)
PHONE................................212 684-4224
Marvin R Shanken, *Ch of Bd*
Michael Moaba, *Vice Ch Bd*
Kimberly Carmichael, *Editor*
Blake Droesch, *Editor*
Owen Dugan, *Editor*
EMP: 125
SQ FT: 15,000
SALES (est): 26.6MM **Privately Held**
SIC: 2721 Magazines: publishing & printing

(G-10645)
M2 FASHION GROUP HOLDINGS INC
Also Called: M2 Apparel
153 E 87th St Apt 10d (10128-2708)
PHONE................................917 208-2948
Ming Lee Wilcox, *President*
EMP: 6
SQ FT: 1,000
SALES (est): 2MM **Privately Held**
SIC: 2389 Apparel for handicapped

New York - New York County (G-10646) — GEOGRAPHIC SECTION

(G-10646)
MAC SWED INC
20 W 36th St Rm 5l (10018-9811)
PHONE.....................212 684-7730
Marc Shams, *President*
▲ EMP: 15
SQ FT: 15,000
SALES (est): 539.6K **Privately Held**
SIC: 3949 Bowling equipment & supplies

(G-10647)
MACFADDEN CMMNCTIONS GROUP LLC
Also Called: HSN
333 7th Ave Fl 11 (10001-5824)
PHONE.....................212 979-4800
Peter Callahan, *Managing Prtnr*
Jess Schesser, *Partner*
Brian Moy, *Business Mgr*
Jean Yannes, *Accounting Mgr*
Nora Cunningham, *Human Res Dir*
▲ EMP: 105
SQ FT: 33,000
SALES (est): 14MM **Privately Held**
SIC: 2721 Magazines: publishing only, not printed on site

(G-10648)
MACMILLAN AUDIO
175 5th Ave (10010-7703)
PHONE.....................646 600-7856
Ken Michaels, *COO*
Gareth Hancock, *Vice Pres*
Laura Wilson, *Production*
Cheryl Carpenter, *Sales Staff*
Michelle Merlo, *Sales Staff*
EMP: 6
SALES (est): 124.2K **Privately Held**
SIC: 2731 Book publishing

(G-10649)
MACMILLAN COLLEGE PUBG CO INC
866 3rd Ave Frnt 2 (10022-6221)
PHONE.....................212 702-2000
John Bender, *Manager*
EMP: 10
SALES (corp-wide): 1.7B **Privately Held**
SIC: 2731 Book publishing
HQ: Springer Nature (Uk) Limited
20 New Wharf Road
London N1 9R
203 192-2030

(G-10650)
MACMILLAN HOLDINGS LLC
1 New York Plz Ste 4500 (10004-1562)
PHONE.....................212 576-9428
Fritz Foy, *Principal*
Andrew Crenshaw, *Director*
EMP: 12
SALES (corp-wide): 1.7B **Privately Held**
SIC: 2721 Magazines: publishing only, not printed on site
HQ: Macmillan Holdings, Llc
175 5th Ave
New York NY 10010

(G-10651)
MACMILLAN PUBLISHERS INC
175 5th Ave Ste 400 (10010-7726)
PHONE.....................646 307-5151
John Sargent, *CEO*
Rose Hilliard, *Editor*
Daniela Rapp, *Editor*
Charles Spicer, *Editor*
Liz Szabla, *Editor*
▲ EMP: 1200
SALES (est): 103.3MM
SALES (corp-wide): 1.7B **Privately Held**
SIC: 2731 5192 Books: publishing only; books
HQ: Springer Nature (Uk) Limited
20 New Wharf Road
London N1 9R
203 192-2030

(G-10652)
MACMILLAN PUBLISHING GROUP LLC (DH)
Also Called: Palagrave Macmillan
175 5th Ave (10010-7703)
PHONE.....................212 674-5145
Sally Richardson, *President*
Marta Fleming, *Publisher*
Lisa Senz, *Publisher*
Nichole Argyres, *Editor*
Hope Dellon, *Editor*
◆ EMP: 361
SQ FT: 81,000
SALES (est): 117.3MM
SALES (corp-wide): 1.7B **Privately Held**
WEB: www.stmartins.com
SIC: 2731 5192 Books: publishing only; books

(G-10653)
MADAME ALEXANDER DOLL 2018 LLC
600 3rd Ave Fl 2 (10016-1919)
PHONE.....................917 576-8381
Noam Welfer, *Vice Pres*
Yuen Kwan Cheung, *Manager*
EMP: 6
SQ FT: 500
SALES (est): 203.3K **Privately Held**
SIC: 3942 Dolls, except stuffed toy animals

(G-10654)
MADAME ALEXANDER DOLL CO LLC
112 W 34th St Ste 1207 (10120-1207)
PHONE.....................212 244-4500
Adolfo Reynoso, *Branch Mgr*
EMP: 100
SALES (corp-wide): 44.5MM **Privately Held**
SIC: 3942 Dolls, except stuffed toy animals
HQ: Madame Alexander Doll Company, Llc
306 Primrose Ln
Mountville PA 17554
717 537-4140

(G-10655)
MADE FRESH DAILY
226 Front St (10038-2009)
PHONE.....................212 285-2253
Jackie Moran, *Manager*
EMP: 7
SALES (est): 373.7K **Privately Held**
SIC: 2711 Newspapers, publishing & printing

(G-10656)
MADHAT INC
149 Sullivan St Apt 3e (10012-3041)
PHONE.....................518 947-0732
Jude Anasta, *CEO*
EMP: 5 EST: 2015
SALES (est): 149.4K **Privately Held**
SIC: 7372 Application computer software

(G-10657)
MADISON LIFESTYLE NY LLC (PA)
1412 Broadway Rm 1610 (10018-9270)
PHONE.....................212 725-4002
Adriana Cerrato, *General Mgr*
Moshe Levy,
EMP: 3
SQ FT: 1,800
SALES: 11MM **Privately Held**
SIC: 3089 5023 Plastic kitchenware, tableware & housewares; kitchenware; glassware

(G-10658)
MADOFF ENERGY III LLC
319 Lafayette St (10012-2711)
PHONE.....................212 744-1918
Andy Madoff, *Mng Member*
EMP: 8
SQ FT: 3,000
SALES: 29.4K **Privately Held**
SIC: 1382 Oil & gas exploration services

(G-10659)
MAFCO CONSOLIDATED GROUP INC (HQ)
35 E 62nd St (10065-8014)
PHONE.....................212 572-8600
Ronald O Perelman, *Ch of Bd*
EMP: 10
SALES (est): 287.7MM **Privately Held**
SIC: 2121 2131 2869 Cigars; smoking tobacco; flavors or flavoring materials, synthetic

(G-10660)
MAG BRANDS LLC
Also Called: Babydoll
463 7th Ave Fl 4 (10018-8725)
PHONE.....................212 629-9600
Raymond A Dayan, *CEO*
Gerard Agoglia, *CFO*
Michael Nagurka, *Controller*
Mark Adjmi,
▲ EMP: 55
SALES (est): 6.2MM **Privately Held**
SIC: 2339 Service apparel, washable: women's

(G-10661)
MAGAZINE I SPECTRUM E
Also Called: I Triple E Spectrum
3 Park Ave Fl 17 (10016-5902)
PHONE.....................212 419-7555
James Vick, *Principal*
EMP: 38 EST: 2001
SALES (est): 1.6MM **Privately Held**
SIC: 2721 Periodicals

(G-10662)
MAGEBA USA LLC
575 Lexington Ave Fl 4 (10022-6146)
PHONE.....................212 317-1991
Thomas Spuler, *CEO*
Jim Hatch, *President*
Gianni Moor, *COO*
James Hatch, *Vice Pres*
Robert Bradley, *Project Mgr*
▲ EMP: 20 EST: 2011
SALES (est): 12.2MM **Privately Held**
SIC: 3441 3562 Expansion joints (structural shapes), iron or steel; ball bearings & parts

(G-10663)
MAGER & GOUGELMAN INC (PA)
345 E 37th St Rm 316 (10016-3256)
PHONE.....................212 661-3939
Henry P Gougelman, *President*
EMP: 7
SALES (est): 855.4K **Privately Held**
WEB: www.artificial-eyes.com
SIC: 3851 Eyes, glass & plastic

(G-10664)
MAGGY BOUTIQUE LTD
Also Called: Maggy London
530 Fashion Ave Fl 6 (10018-4878)
PHONE.....................212 997-5222
Larry Lefkowitz, *President*
Lisa Leavy, *President*
Jerry Sholtz, *CFO*
▲ EMP: 50
SQ FT: 5,000
SALES (est): 4.7MM **Privately Held**
SIC: 2339 5137 2337 Women's & misses' outerwear; women's & children's clothing; women's & misses' suits & coats

(G-10665)
MAGGY LONDON INTERNATIONAL LTD (PA)
Also Called: Maggy London Blouse Div
530 Fashion Ave Fl 16 (10018-4896)
PHONE.....................212 944-7199
Larry Lefkowitz, *Ch of Bd*
Milton Cahn, *Chairman*
Devin Fitzpatrick, *Vice Pres*
Barb Schwaner, *Vice Pres*
Lisa West, *Vice Pres*
▲ EMP: 225
SQ FT: 18,000
SALES (est): 28.8MM **Privately Held**
SIC: 2331 Women's & misses' blouses & shirts

(G-10666)
MAGIC BRANDS INTERNATIONAL LLC
31 W 34th St Rm 401 (10001-3036)
PHONE.....................212 563-4999
Edward J Falack,
Albert Pardo,
▲ EMP: 10
SALES (est): 1.1MM **Privately Held**
SIC: 2211 Apparel & outerwear fabrics, cotton

(G-10667)
MAGIC NOVELTY CO INC (PA)
308 Dyckman St (10034-5397)
PHONE.....................212 304-2777
Alex Neuburger, *President*
David Neuburger, *Vice Pres*
Steve Neuburger, *Vice Pres*
Steven Neuburger, *Vice Pres*
Wendy Torres, *Controller*
▲ EMP: 50 EST: 1940
SQ FT: 40,000
SALES (est): 10MM **Privately Held**
SIC: 3961 5094 3915 3469 Costume jewelry, ex. precious metal & semi-precious stones; jewelry; jewelers' materials & lapidary work; metal stampings; miscellaneous fabricated wire products

(G-10668)
MAGIC NUMBERS INC
Also Called: Glitter
29 Little West 12th St (10014-1393)
PHONE.....................646 839-8578
EMP: 5 EST: 2015
SQ FT: 16,000
SALES (est): 280K **Privately Held**
SIC: 7372 Prepackaged Software Services

(G-10669)
MAGIC TANK LLC
80 Maiden Ln Rm 2204 (10038-4815)
PHONE.....................877 646-2442
Steve Distritzky, *President*
EMP: 3
SQ FT: 8,000
SALES: 5MM **Privately Held**
SIC: 2865 Cyclic organic crudes

(G-10670)
MAGIC TOUCH ICEWARES INTL
220 E 72nd St Apt 11g (10021-4527)
PHONE.....................212 794-2852
Susan Gitelson, *President*
◆ EMP: 6
SQ FT: 3,000
SALES (est): 824.7K **Privately Held**
SIC: 3069 5049 Laboratory sundries: cases, covers, funnels, cups, etc.; laboratory equipment, except medical or dental

(G-10671)
MAGNUM CREATION INC
23 W 47th St Fl 5 (10036-2826)
PHONE.....................212 642-0993
Nathan Cohen, *President*
Mira Cohen, *Vice Pres*
EMP: 13
SQ FT: 5,500
SALES (est): 1.4MM **Privately Held**
SIC: 3911 Jewelry, precious metal

(G-10672)
MAIDENFORM LLC
260 Madison Ave Fl 6 (10016-2406)
PHONE.....................201 436-9200
Maurice Reznik, *Branch Mgr*
EMP: 10
SALES (corp-wide): 6.4B **Publicly Held**
WEB: www.maidenform.com
SIC: 2259 2254 Girdles & other foundation garments, knit; knit underwear mills
HQ: Maidenform Llc
1000 E Hanes Mill Rd
Winston Salem NC 27105
336 519-8080

(G-10673)
MAILERS-PBLSHER WLFARE TR FUND
1501 Broadway (10036-5601)
PHONE.....................212 869-5986
EMP: 1
SALES: 2.6MM **Privately Held**
SIC: 2741 Miscellaneous publishing

(G-10674)
MAIYET INC
16 Crosby St Apt Corp (10013-3108)
PHONE.....................212 343-9999
Paul Van Zyl, *Ch of Bd*
Andy Childs, *Director*
Stev Nguyen Cfa, *Officer*
Rochelle Gordon, *Assistant*
EMP: 5

SALES (est): 1MM **Privately Held**
SIC: 2329 2339 Men's & boys' leather, wool & down-filled outerwear; women's & misses' outerwear

(G-10675)
MAJESTIC RAYON CORPORATION
116 W 23rd St Fl 4 (10011-2498)
PHONE..................212 929-6443
Lawrence Aibel, *President*
Richard Aibel, *Vice Pres*
▲ **EMP:** 25 **EST:** 1930
SQ FT: 60,000
SALES (est): 4MM **Privately Held**
SIC: 2282 2269 Twisting yarn; winding yarn; finishing plants

(G-10676)
MAJESTY BRANDS LLC
469 7th Ave Rm 1301 (10018-7616)
PHONE..................212 283-3400
Jack Safdeye, *CEO*
▲ **EMP:** 5
SALES (est): 221.4K **Privately Held**
SIC: 2252 Socks

(G-10677)
MALER TECHNOLOGIES INC
337 E 81st St Bsmt (10028-4068)
PHONE..................212 391-2070
Stanley Vashovsky, *Ch of Bd*
EMP: 2
SQ FT: 13,617
SALES (est): 7.2MM **Privately Held**
WEB: www.healthsystemssolutions.com
SIC: 7372 Prepackaged software

(G-10678)
MALIN + GOETZ INC (PA)
330 7th Ave Ste 2100 (10001-5236)
PHONE..................212 244-7771
Matthew Malin, *Ch of Bd*
Andrew Goetz, *President*
Dan Avery, *Accounts Exec*
Amanda Michaud, *Marketing Mgr*
Ashima Jain, *Director*
EMP: 12
SQ FT: 600
SALES (est): 2.6MM **Privately Held**
WEB: www.malinandgoetz.com
SIC: 2844 5999 Cosmetic preparations; cosmetics

(G-10679)
MALLORY & CHURCH LLC
552 Fashion Ave Rm 202 (10018-3247)
PHONE..................212 868-7888
Paul Weiss, *Mng Member*
EMP: 9
SALES (est): 22.2K **Privately Held**
SIC: 2323 Neckties, men's & boys': made from purchased materials

(G-10680)
MALOUF COLETTE INC
594 Broadway Rm 1216 (10012-3289)
PHONE..................212 941-9588
Colette Malouf, *President*
Lee Tam, *Prdtn Mgr*
April Klavins, *Finance*
EMP: 14
SQ FT: 2,200
SALES (est): 1.3MM **Privately Held**
WEB: www.colettemalouf.com
SIC: 3999 Hair & hair-based products

(G-10681)
MAN OF WORLD
25 W 39th St Fl 5 (10018-4075)
PHONE..................212 915-0017
Alan Maleh, *Principal*
EMP: 5
SALES (est): 847.3K **Privately Held**
SIC: 2836 Culture media

(G-10682)
MANCHU NEW YORK INC
530 Fashion Ave Rm 1906 (10018-4853)
PHONE..................212 921-5050
▲ **EMP:** 8
SQ FT: 5,100
SALES (est): 705.4K **Privately Held**
SIC: 2361 2339 2311 Manufacturer's Rep Of Garment Manufacturer

(G-10683)
MANCHU TIMES FASHION INC
530 Sventh Ave Ste 1906 (10018)
PHONE..................212 921-5050
Michael Durbin, *CEO*
Jay Goldman, *Administration*
▲ **EMP:** 8 **EST:** 2014
SQ FT: 2,300
SALES (est): 831.7K
SALES (corp-wide): 226.6MM **Privately Held**
SIC: 2339 Women's & misses' outerwear
HQ: Manchu Times Fashion Limited
Rm 1102-03 Ginza Plz
Mongkok KLN
278 161-88

(G-10684)
MANHATTAN CABINETS INC
1349 2nd Ave (10021-4504)
PHONE..................212 548-2436
Zaheer Akber, *President*
EMP: 3
SQ FT: 1,300
SALES (est): 1.7MM **Privately Held**
SIC: 2514 1751 Kitchen cabinets: metal; cabinet building & installation

(G-10685)
MANHATTAN EASTSIDE DEV CORP
Also Called: Eastside Orthotics Prosthetics
622 W 168th St Ste Vc333 (10032-3720)
PHONE..................212 305-3275
Matt D Flynn, *CEO*
Matt Flynn, *President*
EMP: 10 **EST:** 2011
SALES (est): 537.6K **Privately Held**
SIC: 3841 Medical instruments & equipment, blood & bone work

(G-10686)
MANHATTAN MEDIA LLC (PA)
Also Called: Avenue Magazine
535 5th Ave Fl 23 (10017-3678)
PHONE..................212 268-8600
Joanne Harras, *CEO*
Thomas Allon, *President*
Alex Schweitzer, *Publisher*
Kate Walsh, *Publisher*
Lauren Kaplan, *Human Res Dir*
EMP: 19
SQ FT: 7,500
SALES (est): 10.9MM **Privately Held**
SIC: 2711 2721 Newspapers: publishing only, not printed on site; magazines: publishing only, not printed on site

(G-10687)
MANHATTAN NEON SIGN CORP
640 W 28th St Fl 2 (10001-1118)
PHONE..................212 714-0430
Marylin Tomasso, *President*
Pat Tomasso, *Vice Pres*
Debra Martinez, *Bookkeeper*
Chris O'Shea, *Technology*
EMP: 13
SQ FT: 7,500
SALES (est): 1.9MM **Privately Held**
SIC: 3993 Neon signs

(G-10688)
MANHATTAN SCIENTIFICS INC (PA)
405 Lexington Ave Fl 26 (10174-2699)
PHONE..................212 541-2405
Emmanuel Tsoupanarias, *Ch of Bd*
Leonard Friedman, *Admin Sec*
EMP: 11
SQ FT: 300
SALES (est): 142K **Publicly Held**
SIC: 3699 Electrical equipment & supplies

(G-10689)
MANHATTAN TIMES INC
5030 Broadway Ste 801 (10034-1666)
PHONE..................212 569-5800
Mike Fitelson, *Publisher*
Luis Miranda, *Chairman*
EMP: 15
SALES (est): 662.1K **Privately Held**
SIC: 2711 Newspapers: publishing only, not printed on site

(G-10690)
MANN PUBLICATIONS INC
450 Fashion Ave Ste 2306 (10123-2306)
PHONE..................212 840-6266
Jeffrey Mann, *President*
Barbara Machtiger, *Editor*
Alexis McDonell, *Assoc Editor*
Douglas Elliman, *Assistant*
EMP: 20
SQ FT: 4,000
SALES (est): 2.5MM **Privately Held**
SIC: 2721 Magazines: publishing only, not printed on site

(G-10691)
MANNESMANN CORPORATION
601 Lexington Ave Fl 56 (10022-4611)
PHONE..................212 258-4000
Peter Prinz Wittgenstein, *President*
Dr Manfred Becker, *Exec VP*
Joseph E Innamorati, *Vice Pres*
Olaf Klinger, *Treasurer*
▲ **EMP:** 100
SALES (est): 20.6MM
SALES (corp-wide): 97.7B **Privately Held**
SIC: 3536 3544 3511 3547 Hoists; cranes, industrial plant; cranes, overhead traveling; special dies, tools, jigs & fixtures; industrial molds; turbo-generators; hydraulic turbines; rolling mill machinery; steel rolling machinery; pumps & pumping equipment; internal combustion engines
HQ: Siemens Corporation
300 New Jersey Ave Nw # 10
Washington DC 20001
202 434-4800

(G-10692)
MANNY GRUNBERG INC
62 W 47th St Ste 703 (10036-3185)
PHONE..................212 302-6173
Manny Grunberg, *President*
▲ **EMP:** 33 **EST:** 1952
SQ FT: 2,000
SALES (est): 2.4MM **Privately Held**
SIC: 3911 Mfg Precious Jewelry

(G-10693)
MANRICO USA INC
Also Called: Manrico Cashmere
922 Madison Ave (10021-3576)
PHONE..................212 794-4200
Virgile Verellen, *Branch Mgr*
EMP: 5
SALES (corp-wide): 8.2MM **Privately Held**
SIC: 2253 Sweaters & sweater coats, knit
PA: Manrico Usa, Inc.
922 Madison Ave
New York NY 10021
212 794-4200

(G-10694)
MANRICO USA INC (PA)
922 Madison Ave (10021-3576)
PHONE..................212 794-4200
Manrico Calzoni, *President*
▲ **EMP:** 5
SQ FT: 750
SALES (est): 8.2MM **Privately Held**
SIC: 2299 Upholstery filling, textile

(G-10695)
MANSFIELD PRESS INC
599 11th Ave Fl 3 (10036-2110)
PHONE..................212 265-5411
Stanley J Friedman, *President*
Marc Friedman, *Exec VP*
Frank J Ephraim, *Vice Pres*
▲ **EMP:** 15 **EST:** 1935
SALES (est): 1.9MM **Privately Held**
SIC: 2752 Lithographing on metal

(G-10696)
MANSUETO VENTURES LLC
Also Called: Fast Company Magazine
7 World Trade Ctr Fl 29 (10007-2174)
PHONE..................212 389-5300
Jennifer Henkus, *Publisher*
Jane Hazel, *Principal*
Abigail Baron, *Editor*
Tim Crino, *Editor*
Colleen Debaise, *Editor*
EMP: 225

SALES (est): 60.9MM **Privately Held**
SIC: 2721 Magazines: publishing only, not printed on site

(G-10697)
MARCASIANO INC
296 Elizabeth St Apt 2f (10012-3590)
PHONE..................212 614-9412
Mary Jane Marcasiano, *President*
▲ **EMP:** 5 **EST:** 1977
SQ FT: 3,000
SALES (est): 501.4K **Privately Held**
SIC: 2339 Sportswear, women's

(G-10698)
MARCO HI-TECH JV LLC (PA)
475 Park Ave S Fl 10 (10016-6930)
PHONE..................212 798-8100
Reuben Seltzer,
David Garner,
Alan Kestenbaum,
Mark Levitt,
▲ **EMP:** 8
SQ FT: 4,000
SALES (est): 1.4MM **Privately Held**
WEB: www.marcohi-tech.com
SIC: 2834 Vitamin, nutrient & hematinic preparations for human use

(G-10699)
MARCONI INTL USA CO LTD
214 W 39th St Rm 703 (10018-5566)
PHONE..................212 391-2626
Lilian Ching, *President*
▲ **EMP:** 9
SQ FT: 2,500
SALES (est): 1.3MM **Privately Held**
SIC: 2339 Women's & misses' athletic clothing & sportswear

(G-10700)
MARCUS GOLDMAN INC
Also Called: Run It Systems
37 W 39th St Rm 1201 (10018-0577)
PHONE..................212 431-0707
Robert Marcus, *President*
Walter Crespin, *Technical Mgr*
Tamar Markowitz, *Marketing Staff*
Steven Treiber, *Manager*
Mark Schmidt, *Technical Staff*
EMP: 14
SQ FT: 5,000
SALES (est): 1.7MM **Privately Held**
WEB: www.runit.com
SIC: 7372 Application computer software

(G-10701)
MARI STRINGS INC
14 W 71st St (10023-4209)
PHONE..................212 799-6781
Daniel Mari, *President*
▲ **EMP:** 15
SQ FT: 1,600
SALES: 400K **Privately Held**
SIC: 3931 Strings, musical instrument

(G-10702)
MARIE CLAIRE USA
Also Called: Marie Claire Magazine
300 W 57th St Fl 34 (10019-1497)
PHONE..................212 841-8493
Anne Fulenwider, *Editor*
Chris Moore, *Editor*
Nancy Berger, *Vice Pres*
Amanda Hearst, *Associate*
▲ **EMP:** 100
SALES (est): 924.1K **Privately Held**
SIC: 2721 Magazines: publishing & printing

(G-10703)
MARINA JEWELRY CO INC
Also Called: Jn Marina
42 W 48th St Ste 804 (10036-1712)
PHONE..................212 354-5027
Joseph Fontana, *President*
Anthony Barona, *Partner*
EMP: 6
SQ FT: 1,200
SALES (est): 540K **Privately Held**
WEB: www.marina-jewellery.com
SIC: 3911 3339 Jewelry, precious metal; primary nonferrous metals

New York - New York County (G-10704)

GEOGRAPHIC SECTION

(G-10704)
MARITIME ACTIVITY REPORTS (PA)
118 E 25th St Fl 2 (10010-2994)
PHONE..................212 477-6700
John C O'Malley, *Vice Pres*
Esther Rothenberger, *Opers Mgr*
Jocelyn Redfern, *Marketing Mgr*
EMP: 28
SQ FT: 2,500
SALES (est): 1.8MM **Privately Held**
SIC: 2721 Magazines: publishing only, not printed on site

(G-10705)
MARK KING JEWELRY INC
62 W 47th St Ste 310r (10036-3245)
PHONE..................212 921-0746
Mark Beznicki, *President*
EMP: 8
SQ FT: 1,000
SALES (est): 1MM **Privately Held**
SIC: 3911 5094 Jewelry, precious metal; jewelry & precious stones

(G-10706)
MARK LEVINE
Also Called: Kids Discover
149 5th Ave Fl 10 (10010-6832)
PHONE..................212 677-4457
Mark Levine, *Owner*
▲ **EMP:** 11
SQ FT: 2,500
SALES (est): 810K **Privately Held**
SIC: 2721 Magazines: publishing only, not printed on site

(G-10707)
MARK NELSON DESIGNS LLC
404 E 55th St Fl 4 (10022-5136)
PHONE..................646 422-7020
Mark Nelson, *Mng Member*
▲ **EMP:** 10
SALES (est): 1.3MM **Privately Held**
SIC: 2273 Rugs, hand & machine made

(G-10708)
MARK ROBINSON INC
18 E 48th St Rm 1102 (10017-1059)
PHONE..................212 223-3515
Mark Robinson, *President*
EMP: 9
SQ FT: 200
SALES (est): 1.5MM **Privately Held**
WEB: www.markrobinson.net
SIC: 3911 Jewelry, precious metal

(G-10709)
MARKET FACTORY INC
45 W 27th St Frnt 1 (10001-6916)
PHONE..................212 625-9988
James Sinclair, *CEO*
Darren Jer, *COO*
Julia Mantel, *Project Mgr*
Tom Guilfoyle, *Sales Staff*
Ashley Binford, *Marketing Staff*
EMP: 19
SQ FT: 3,000
SALES (est): 5.3MM **Privately Held**
SIC: 7372 Business oriented computer software

(G-10710)
MARKET LOGIC SOFTWARE INC
80 Pine St Fl 24 (10005-1732)
PHONE..................646 405-1041
Kay Iversen, *Director*
Phillip Chambers, *Executive*
EMP: 19
SALES (est): 182.1K **Privately Held**
SIC: 7372 Prepackaged software

(G-10711)
MARKET PARTNERS INTERNATIONAL
Also Called: Publishing Trends
232 Madison Ave Rm 1400 (10016-2918)
PHONE..................212 447-0855
Lorraine Shanley, *President*
Constance Sayre, *Director*
EMP: 5
SQ FT: 1,300
SALES (est): 379.1K **Privately Held**
WEB: www.marketpartnersinternational.com
SIC: 2741 Miscellaneous publishing

(G-10712)
MARKETING ACTION XECUTIVES INC
50 W 96th St Apt 7b (10025-6529)
P.O. Box 20356 (10025-1519)
PHONE..................212 971-9155
Karen Korman, *President*
Barry Steinman, *Vice Pres*
EMP: 5
SALES: 2MM **Privately Held**
WEB: www.mactionx.com
SIC: 2241 Trimmings, textile

(G-10713)
MARKETRESEARCHCOM INC
641 Ave Of The America (10011-2014)
PHONE..................212 807-2600
Rocco Distefano, *Branch Mgr*
EMP: 15
SALES (corp-wide): 33.6MM **Privately Held**
WEB: www.marketresearch.com
SIC: 2741 Miscellaneous publishing
PA: Marketresearch.Com, Inc.
11200 Rockville Pike # 504
Rockville MD 20852
240 747-3000

(G-10714)
MARLEY SPOON INC
Also Called: Martha & Marley Spoon
601 W 26th St Rm 900 (10001-1143)
PHONE..................646 934-6970
Fabian Siegel, *President*
Michelle Lumino, *Opers Mgr*
Maurice John, *Manager*
EMP: 140
SALES (est): 1MM
SALES (corp-wide): 2.7MM **Privately Held**
SIC: 3411 8742 Food & beverage containers; food & beverage consultant
PA: Marley Spoon Ag
Paul-Lincke-Ufer 39/-40
Berlin
302 084-8051

(G-10715)
MARNIER-LAPOSTOLLE INC
Also Called: GRAND MARNIER
183 Madison Ave (10016-4501)
PHONE..................212 207-4350
Elise Seignolle, *Finance Dir*
Justin Cochren,
▲ **EMP:** 54
SALES: 439.6K **Privately Held**
WEB: www.grandmarnier.com
SIC: 2082 5182 2085 Malt liquors; liquor; distilled & blended liquors

(G-10716)
MARRETTI USA INC
101 Ave Of The Am Fl 9 (10013)
PHONE..................212 255-5565
Marzia Marzi, *President*
EMP: 8 **EST:** 2008
SQ FT: 600
SALES (est): 513.9K **Privately Held**
SIC: 2431 5021 Staircases, stairs & railings; furniture

(G-10717)
MARTHA STEWART LIVING (HQ)
601 W 26th St Rm 900 (10001-1143)
PHONE..................212 827-8000
Daniel W Dienst, *CEO*
Zaki Kamandy, *President*
Jacqueline Landaeta, *President*
Naomi Demanana, *Editor*
Maureen Farago, *Editor*
▲ **EMP:** 120
SQ FT: 176,550
SALES (est): 167.4MM **Publicly Held**
WEB: www.marthastewart.com
SIC: 2721 2731 4813 7812 Magazines: publishing only, not printed on site; book publishing; ; motion picture production & distribution, television
PA: Sequential Brands Group, Inc.
601 W 26th St 9
New York NY 10001
646 564-2577

(G-10718)
MARTHA STEWART LIVING OMNI LLC
20 W 43rd St (10036-7400)
PHONE..................212 827-8000
Robin Marino, *CEO*
Anthony Luscia, *Editor*
Betsy Perreten, *Counsel*
Melissa Stemple, *Mktg Dir*
Jeffrey W Ubben, *Bd of Directors*
▲ **EMP:** 350 **EST:** 1997
SALES (est): 28.1MM
SALES (corp-wide): 167.4MM **Publicly Held**
WEB: www.msliving.com
SIC: 2721 Magazines: publishing only, not printed on site
HQ: Martha Stewart Living Omnimedia, Inc.
601 W 26th St Rm 900
New York NY 10001
212 827-8000

(G-10719)
MARVEL ENTERTAINMENT LLC (HQ)
135 W 50th St Fl 7 (10020-1201)
P.O. Box 1527, Long Island City (11101-0527)
PHONE..................212 576-4000
Isaac Perlmutter, *CEO*
Michael Helfant, *President*
Timothy E Rothwell, *President*
David Maisel, *Exec VP*
John Turitzin, *Exec VP*
▲ **EMP:** 164
SQ FT: 65,253
SALES (est): 115.6MM **Publicly Held**
SIC: 2721 6794 3944 7929 Comic books: publishing only, not printed on site; magazines: publishing only, not printed on site; patent buying, licensing, leasing; electronic games & toys; entertainment service

(G-10720)
MARVELLISSIMA INTL LTD
333 E 46th St Apt 20a (10017-7431)
PHONE..................212 682-7306
Marvel Perilla, *President*
Shanez Kollnescher, *Vice Pres*
Ellen Stutzer, *Vice Pres*
Abba Kyari, *Shareholder*
Lola Osunsade, *Shareholder*
EMP: 6
SALES (est): 615.2K **Privately Held**
SIC: 2844 5122 Toilet preparations; cosmetics

(G-10721)
MARY BRIGHT INC
269 E 10th St Apt 7 (10009-4849)
PHONE..................212 677-1970
David Paskin, *President*
Mary Bright, *President*
EMP: 6
SALES (est): 367K **Privately Held**
WEB: www.marybright.com
SIC: 2258 Curtains & curtain fabrics, lace

(G-10722)
MAS CUTTING INC
257 W 39th St Rm 11e (10018-3228)
PHONE..................212 869-0826
Kitman MA, *President*
EMP: 6
SALES (est): 350K **Privately Held**
SIC: 2396 Apparel findings & trimmings

(G-10723)
MASQUERADE LLC
Also Called: Holloween Adventures
104 4th Ave (10003-5232)
PHONE..................212 673-4546
Tony Bianchi, *Manager*
EMP: 16
SQ FT: 20,000
SALES (corp-wide): 9.3MM **Privately Held**
WEB: www.halloweenadventure.com
SIC: 2389 Masquerade costumes
PA: Masquerade, Llc
450 Rritan Ctr Pkwy Ste I
Edison NJ 08837
516 732-7242

(G-10724)
MATA FASHIONS LLC
222 W 37th St Fl 4 (10018-9158)
PHONE..................917 716-7894
Maria Maglaras, *Treasurer*
Dona Elias,
EMP: 2 **EST:** 2014
SQ FT: 1,200
SALES: 1MM **Privately Held**
SIC: 2384 Dressing gowns, men's & women's: from purchased materials

(G-10725)
MATACI INC
Also Called: Lazo Setter Company
247 W 35th St Fl 15 (10001-1915)
PHONE..................212 502-1899
Adrianna Chico, *President*
▲ **EMP:** 60
SALES (est): 6.1MM **Privately Held**
SIC: 3961 Costume jewelry

(G-10726)
MATEL LLC
90 Park Ave Fl 18 (10016-1322)
PHONE..................646 825-6760
EMP: 5
SALES (est): 365.8K **Privately Held**
SIC: 3944 Games, toys & children's vehicles

(G-10727)
MATERNE NORTH AMERICA CORP (DH)
Also Called: Gogo Squeez
20 W 22nd St Fl 12 (10010-5843)
PHONE..................212 675-7881
Michel Larroche, *CEO*
William Graham, *President*
Carole Larson, *CFO*
◆ **EMP:** 277
SALES: 162K
SALES (corp-wide): 7.6MM **Privately Held**
SIC: 2035 5145 Pickles, sauces & salad dressings; snack foods
HQ: Materne
45 Chemin Des Peupliers
Dardilly 69570
478 663-232

(G-10728)
MATHISEN VENTURES INC
Also Called: Cruise Industry News
441 Lexington Ave Rm 809 (10017-3935)
PHONE..................212 986-1025
Oivind Mathisen, *President*
Angela Mathisen, *Publisher*
Monty Mathisen, *Technical Staff*
EMP: 6
SALES (est): 628.9K **Privately Held**
WEB: www.cruiseindustrynews.com
SIC: 2731 2721 2741 Book publishing; periodicals: publishing only; magazines: publishing only, not printed on site; newsletter publishing

(G-10729)
MATRIXCARE INC
Also Called: Sigmacare
575 8th Ave Fl 15 (10018-3175)
PHONE..................518 583-6400
EMP: 7 **Privately Held**
SIC: 7372 7371 Prepackaged software; custom computer programming services
HQ: Matrixcare, Inc.
10900 Hampshire Ave S # 100
Bloomington MN 55438
952 995-9800

(G-10730)
MAURICE MAX INC
Also Called: Roxanne Assoulin
49 W 27th St Fl 5 (10001-6936)
PHONE..................212 334-6573
Roxanne Assoulin, *President*
Meyer Assoulin, *Vice Pres*
EMP: 34
SALES (est): 5.1MM **Privately Held**
WEB: www.leeangel.com
SIC: 3961 Costume jewelry

▲ = Import ▼=Export
◆ =Import/Export

(G-10731)
MAVEN MARKETING LLC (PA)
Also Called: Golf Odyssey
349 5th Ave Fl 8 (10016-5019)
PHONE..................................615 510-3248
Justin Tapper, *CEO*
Ryan Klockner, *President*
Dean Strickler, *Exec Dir*
Wayne Caparas,
EMP: 6 **EST:** 2008
SALES (est): 3.3MM **Privately Held**
SIC: 7372 7371 8742 Educational computer software; software programming applications; marketing consulting services

(G-10732)
MAVERIK LACROSSE LLC
535 W 24th St Fl 5 (10011-1140)
PHONE..................................516 213-3050
John Gagliardi,
▲ **EMP:** 5022
SALES (est): 373.4K
SALES (corp-wide): 5.6B **Privately Held**
SIC: 3949 Lacrosse equipment & supplies, general
HQ: Kohlberg Sports Group, Inc.
111 Radio Circle Dr
Mount Kisco NY 10549

(G-10733)
MAX BRENNER UNION SQUARE LLC
841 Broadway (10003-4704)
PHONE..................................646 467-8803
Ever M Elivo, *Principal*
▲ **EMP:** 5
SALES (est): 585.6K **Privately Held**
SIC: 2066 Chocolate bars, solid

(G-10734)
MAX KAHAN INC
20 W 47th St Ste 300 (10036-3303)
PHONE..................................212 575-4646
Max Kahan, *President*
David Gluck, *Vice Pres*
Abraham Grossman, *Treasurer*
EMP: 10
SQ FT: 3,000
SALES (est): 980K **Privately Held**
SIC: 3915 Jewelers' materials & lapidary work

(G-10735)
MAYBELLINE INC
575 5th Ave Bsmt Fl (10017-2446)
PHONE..................................212 885-1310
Robert N Hiatt, *Ch of Bd*
John R Wendt, *President*
Gerald C Beddall, *President*
Jack J Bucher, *President*
Daniel J Coffey Jr, *President*
EMP: 4118 **EST:** 1915
SALES (est): 66K
SALES (corp-wide): 4.2B **Privately Held**
WEB: www.maybelline.com
SIC: 2841 2844 Soap: granulated, liquid, cake, flaked or chip; cosmetic preparations
HQ: L'oreal Usa, Inc.
10 Hudson Yards Fl 30
New York NY 10001
212 818-1500

(G-10736)
MAZ SYSTEMS INC (PA)
127 W 26th St Ste 500 (10001-6808)
PHONE..................................855 629-3444
Paul Canetti, *CEO*
Michael Ram, *President*
Paul Shouvik, *President*
Shikha Arora, *Principal*
Simon Baumer, *Principal*
EMP: 10
SALES (est): 2.7MM **Privately Held**
SIC: 7372 Publishers' computer software

(G-10737)
MBNY LLC (PA)
260 5th Ave Fl 9 (10001-6408)
PHONE..................................646 467-8810
Yaniv Shtanger, *Mng Member*
EMP: 10
SALES (est): 1.2MM **Privately Held**
SIC: 2066 Chocolate bars, solid

(G-10738)
MC SQUARED NYC INC
Also Called: Mancum Graphics
121 Varick St Frnt B (10013-1408)
PHONE..................................212 947-2260
Robert Copjec, *President*
EMP: 10
SQ FT: 2,000
SALES (est): 1.7MM **Privately Held**
SIC: 2752 Commercial printing, offset

(G-10739)
MCCALL PATTERN COMPANY (HQ)
Also Called: Butterck McCall Vogue Pattern
120 Broadway Fl 34 (10271-3499)
P.O. Box 3755, Manhattan KS (66505-8502)
PHONE..................................212 465-6800
Frank J Rizzo, *Ch of Bd*
Robin Davies, *President*
Kathleen Klausner, *Senior VP*
Nancy Dicocco, *Vice Pres*
Gail Hamilton, *Vice Pres*
▲ **EMP:** 200
SQ FT: 62,600
SALES (est): 52.2MM
SALES (corp-wide): 361.9MM **Publicly Held**
WEB: www.mccallpattern.com
SIC: 2335 Dresses, paper: cut & sewn; ensemble dresses: women's, misses' & juniors'
PA: Css Industries, Inc.
450 Plymouth Rd Ste 300
Plymouth Meeting PA 19462
610 729-3959

(G-10740)
MCCARTHY LLC
Also Called: Blackbook
32 Union Sq E (10003-3209)
PHONE..................................646 862-5354
Jonathan Bond,
EMP: 10
SALES (est): 787.6K **Privately Held**
SIC: 2721 Periodicals: publishing only

(G-10741)
MCGRAW-HILL EDUCATION INC (PA)
2 Penn Plz Fl 20 (10121-2100)
PHONE..................................646 766-2000
Lloyd Waterhouse, *CEO*
Scott Grillo, *President*
Willian Glass, *Managing Dir*
Cheryl Ringer, *President*
James Shanahan, *Editor*
EMP: 63
SALES (est): 20.4MM **Privately Held**
SIC: 2731 Books: publishing only

(G-10742)
MCGRAW-HILL SCHOOL EDUCATION H (PA)
2 Penn Plz Fl 20 (10121-2100)
PHONE..................................646 766-2000
David Levin, *President*
Teresa Martin-Retortillo, *Senior VP*
David B Stafford, *Senior VP*
Maryellen Valaitis, *Senior VP*
Patrick Milano, *CFO*
EMP: 500
SALES (est): 750MM **Privately Held**
SIC: 2731 Books: publishing only

(G-10743)
MCGRAW-HILL SCHOOL EDUCATN LLC
2 Penn Plz Fl 20 (10121-2100)
PHONE..................................646 766-2060
David Levin, *President*
Teresa Martin-Retortillo, *Senior VP*
Maryellen Valaitis, *Senior VP*
Patrick Milano, *CFO*
David Wright, *CIO*
EMP: 599 **EST:** 2013
SALES (est): 116.8MM
SALES (corp-wide): 750MM **Privately Held**
SIC: 2731 Books: publishing & printing
PA: Mcgraw-Hill School Education Holdings, Llc
2 Penn Plz Fl 20
New York NY 10121
646 766-2000

(G-10744)
MCM PRODUCTS USA INC (PA)
681 5th Ave Fl 10 (10022-4306)
PHONE..................................646 756-4090
Michael R Callahan, *CEO*
Paolo Fontanelli, *CEO*
Sung-Joo Kim, *Ch of Bd*
Patrick Valeo, *President*
EMP: 50 **EST:** 2007
SALES (est): 26.2MM **Privately Held**
SIC: 3171 3149 3199 Women's handbags & purses; athletic shoes, except rubber or plastic; belt laces, leather

(G-10745)
MCMAHON GROUP LLC (PA)
Also Called: McMahon Publishing Group
545 W 45th St (10036-3409)
PHONE..................................212 957-5300
Raymond E McMahon, *CEO*
Van N Velle, *President*
Cynthia Gordon, *Editor*
Frank Tagarello, *Vice Pres*
Rose Anne McMahon, *Treasurer*
EMP: 72
SALES: 18.5MM **Privately Held**
SIC: 2721 Trade journals: publishing only, not printed on site

(G-10746)
MCPC INC
Also Called: McArdle Solutions
731 Lexington Ave (10022-1331)
PHONE..................................212 583-6000
Lisa Arsenault, *President*
EMP: 100 **EST:** 1947
SQ FT: 350,000
SALES: 7MM
SALES (corp-wide): 1.9B **Privately Held**
WEB: www.mcardleprinting.com
SIC: 2752 Commercial printing, offset
HQ: The Bureau Of National Affairs Inc
1801 S Bell St Ste Cn110
Arlington VA 22202
703 341-3000

(G-10747)
MDI HOLDINGS LLC
Also Called: C/O Court Sq Capitl Partners
399 Park Ave Fl 14 (10022-4614)
PHONE..................................212 559-1127
Joseph M Silvestri, *President*
EMP: 2900
SALES (est): 187.9MM **Privately Held**
SIC: 2842 2874 2992 2752 Cleaning or polishing preparations; phosphates; lubricating oils; offset & photolithographic printing; printers & plotters; plating compounds

(G-10748)
ME & RO INC (PA)
241 Elizabeth St Frnt A (10012-3544)
PHONE..................................212 431-8744
Robin Renzi, *CEO*
EMP: 7
SQ FT: 4,000
SALES (est): 2.4MM **Privately Held**
WEB: www.meandrojewelry.com
SIC: 3911 3915 Jewelry, precious metal; jewelers' materials & lapidary work

(G-10749)
MEALPLAN CORP
203 E 4th St Apt 6 (10009-7281)
PHONE..................................909 706-8398
Kevin Carter, *President*
Daniel Mao, *Vice Pres*
Vinh Thai, *Treasurer*
Helal Saleh, *Sales Mgr*
Michelle Chen, *Admin Sec*
EMP: 5
SALES (est): 141.8K **Privately Held**
SIC: 7372 Prepackaged software

(G-10750)
MED REVIEWS LLC
1370 Broadway Fl 5 (10018-7350)
PHONE..................................212 239-5860
Charles Benaiah,
Miichael Brawer,
Diane Gern,
Herbert Lepor,
Norman Lepor,
EMP: 27 **EST:** 1998
SQ FT: 10,000
SALES (est): 3.6MM **Privately Held**
WEB: www.medreviews.com
SIC: 2721 Publishers Of Medical Journals

(G-10751)
MEDALLION ASSOCIATES INC
37 W 20th St Fl 4 (10011-3791)
PHONE..................................212 929-9130
Donna Peters, *Principal*
Judy Melioli, *Personnel Exec*
▲ **EMP:** 50
SALES (est): 5.3MM **Privately Held**
WEB: www.medallionltd.com
SIC: 2752 2759 2791 Commercial printing, offset; promotional printing; typesetting

(G-10752)
MEDIA PRESS CORP
55 John St 520 (10038-3752)
PHONE..................................212 791-6347
Givi Topchishvili, *President*
EMP: 20
SALES (est): 1MM **Privately Held**
WEB: www.skullman.com
SIC: 2721 Periodicals-Publishing/Printing

(G-10753)
MEDIA TRANSCRIPTS INC
41 W 83rd St Apt 2b (10024-5247)
PHONE..................................212 362-1481
Pat King, *President*
Pat Podell, *Administration*
▲ **EMP:** 24
SALES (est): 1.7MM **Privately Held**
WEB: www.mediatranscripts.com
SIC: 2741 Miscellaneous publishing

(G-10754)
MEDIA TRUST LLC (PA)
404 Park Ave S Fl 2 (10016-8404)
PHONE..................................212 802-1162
Peter Bordes, *CEO*
Keith Cohn, *President*
Trevor Thomas, *Officer*
EMP: 5
SALES (est): 4MM **Privately Held**
SIC: 2741 7311 ; advertising agencies

(G-10755)
MEDIAPLANET PUBLISHING HSE INC (DH)
350 7th Ave Fl 18 (10001-5013)
PHONE..................................646 922-1400
Luciana Olson, *Managing Dir*
Timothy Rossi, *Finance Mgr*
Ramin Amili, *Accountant*
EMP: 32
SALES (est): 10.5MM
SALES (corp-wide): 8.7MM **Privately Held**
SIC: 2731 Book publishing
HQ: Mediaplanet Limited
Gate House
London EC1M
203 642-0737

(G-10756)
MEDIAPOST COMMUNICATIONS LLC
1460 Broadway Fl 12 (10036-7306)
PHONE..................................212 204-2000
Ken Fadner, *CEO*
Jeff Loechner, *President*
Kenneth Fadner, *Publisher*
Phyllis Fine, *Editor*
Wayne Friedman, *Editor*
EMP: 50
SALES (est): 5.3MM **Privately Held**
WEB: www.mediapost.com
SIC: 7372 Publishers' computer software

(G-10757)
MEDICAL DAILY INC
7 Hanover Sq Fl 6 (10004-2702)
PHONE..................................646 867-7100
Johnathan Davis, *President*
Dong-Chan Kim, *Principal*
Etienne Uzac, *Treasurer*
EMP: 30

New York - New York County (G-10758) GEOGRAPHIC SECTION

SALES (est): 1.7MM **Privately Held**
SIC: 2741

(G-10758)
MEDIDATA SOLUTIONS INC (PA)
350 Hudson St Fl 9 (10014-4535)
PHONE.....................212 918-1800
Tarek A Sherif, *Ch of Bd*
Glen M De Vries, *President*
Michael L Capone, *COO*
Michael I Otner, *Exec VP*
Michael Otner, *Exec VP*
EMP: 432
SQ FT: 137,535
SALES: 545.5MM **Publicly Held**
WEB: www.mdsol.com
SIC: 7372 Application computer software

(G-10759)
MEDIKIDZ USA INC
Also Called: Jumo
205 Lexington Ave Rm 1601 (10016-6022)
PHONE.....................646 895-9319
Kevin Aniskovich, *CEO*
Kate Hersov, *Founder*
Mitzie Garland, *CFO*
EMP: 7 EST: 2013
SQ FT: 1,000
SALES (est): 2.9MM **Privately Held**
SIC: 2721 2731 Comic books: publishing & printing; books: publishing only

(G-10760)
MEDIUS SOFTWARE INC
Also Called: Medius North America
12 E 49th St Fl 11 (10017-1012)
PHONE.....................877 295-0058
EMP: 17
SALES (est): 205.4K **Privately Held**
SIC: 7372 Prepackaged Software Services

(G-10761)
MEDIZINE OPERATING LLC (PA)
Also Called: Remedy Intelligent Staffing
750 3rd Ave Fl 6 (10017-2703)
PHONE.....................212 695-2223
Michael Cunnion, *CEO*
Jim Curtis, *President*
Don Vergara, *Publisher*
Michael Collins, *Exec VP*
Lindsey Guenther, *Exec VP*
EMP: 58
SQ FT: 7,000
SALES (est): 28MM **Privately Held**
WEB: www.remedyhealthmedia.com
SIC: 2721 7319 Magazines: publishing & printing; media buying service

(G-10762)
MEE ACCESSORIES LLC (PA)
Also Called: Mark Ecko Enterprises
475 10th Ave Fl 9 (10018-9718)
PHONE.....................917 262-1000
Mark Ecko, *CEO*
Seth Gerszberg, *President*
Greg Lucci, *Vice Pres*
Andy Cousin, *Manager*
Elliot Brown, *Legal Staff*
▲ EMP: 350
SQ FT: 30,000
SALES (est): 30.2MM **Privately Held**
WEB: www.phys-sci.com
SIC: 2329 5136 5621 5611 Men's & boys' sportswear & athletic clothing; sportswear, men's & boys'; women's clothing stores; men's & boys' clothing stores

(G-10763)
MEEGENIUS INC
151 W 25th St Fl 3 (10001-7228)
P.O. Box 287434 (10128-0024)
PHONE.....................212 283-7285
David K Park, *CEO*
EMP: 5
SALES: 60K **Privately Held**
SIC: 2731 Book publishing

(G-10764)
MEGA POWER SPORTS CORPORATION
1123 Broadway Ph (10010-2084)
PHONE.....................212 627-3380
EMP: 6 EST: 1995
SALES (est): 360K **Privately Held**
SIC: 2353 5136 5137 Mfg & Whol Hats

(G-10765)
MEIRAGTX HOLDINGS PLC (PA)
430 E 29th St Fl 10 (10016-8367)
PHONE.....................646 490-2965
Keith R Harris, *Ch of Bd*
Alexandria Forbes, *President*
Richard Giroux, *COO*
Katherine Breedis, *CFO*
EMP: 20
SQ FT: 5,887
SALES (est): 6.6MM **Publicly Held**
SIC: 2836 Biological products, except diagnostic

(G-10766)
MEJ BEATS LLC
Also Called: Me-J
180 E 64th St (10065-7478)
PHONE.....................516 707-6655
Stephen Dabah, *Principal*
EMP: 6 EST: 2017
SALES (est): 221.6K **Privately Held**
SIC: 7372 Application computer software

(G-10767)
MEKANISM INC
80 Broad St Fl 35 (10004-2216)
PHONE.....................212 226-2772
Laura Peguero, *Branch Mgr*
EMP: 40
SALES (corp-wide): 21.8MM **Privately Held**
SIC: 3993 Signs & advertising specialties
PA: Mekanism, Inc.
640 2nd St Fl 3
San Francisco CA 94107
415 908-4000

(G-10768)
MEL BERNIE AND COMPANY INC
Also Called: 1928 Jewelry Co
384 5th Ave Fl 4 (10018-8140)
PHONE.....................212 889-8570
Mel Bernie, *President*
EMP: 5
SALES (corp-wide): 55.6MM **Privately Held**
WEB: www.1928.com
SIC: 3961 Costume jewelry
PA: Mel Bernie And Company, Inc.
3000 W Empire Ave
Burbank CA 91504
818 841-1928

(G-10769)
MELCHER MEDIA INC
124 W 13th St (10011-7802)
PHONE.....................212 727-2322
Charles Melcher, *President*
Karl Daum, *Editor*
Bonnie Eldon, *VP Opers*
Susan Lynch, *Prdtn Mgr*
Kurt Andrews, *Opers Staff*
▲ EMP: 11
SQ FT: 1,500
SALES (est): 1.8MM **Privately Held**
WEB: www.melcher.com
SIC: 2731 2789 Books: publishing only; bookbinding & related work

(G-10770)
MEMORY MD INC
205 E 42nd St Fl 14 (10017-5752)
PHONE.....................917 318-0215
Boris Goldstein, *Ch of Bd*
Yuriy Shirokikh, *CFO*
EMP: 5 EST: 2015
SALES (est): 240K **Privately Held**
SIC: 3841 5047 Diagnostic apparatus, medical; diagnostic equipment, medical

(G-10771)
MENS JOURNAL LLC
1290 Ave Of The Americas (10104-0295)
PHONE.....................212 484-1616
Greg Emmanuel, *Ch Credit Ofcr*
Jay Gallagher, *Risk Mgmt Dir*
EMP: 9
SALES (est): 6MM
SALES (corp-wide): 300MM **Privately Held**
SIC: 2741 Miscellaneous publishing

PA: American Media, Inc.
1350 E Newport
Deerfield Beach FL 33442
212 545-4800

(G-10772)
MER GEMS CORP
Also Called: Romir Enterprises
62 W 47th St Ste 614 (10036-3201)
PHONE.....................212 714-9129
Roshel Mirzakanzov, *President*
Nelly Mirzakanzov, *Vice Pres*
◆ EMP: 5 EST: 1998
SQ FT: 800
SALES (est): 1MM **Privately Held**
SIC: 3911 Jewelry, precious metal

(G-10773)
MERGENT INC
444 Madison Ave Ste 502 (10022-6976)
PHONE.....................212 413-7700
Jonathan Worral, *CEO*
Mike Winn, *Managing Dir*
Greg Collins, *Vice Pres*
Charles E Miller Jr, *CFO*
Colleen Beamon, *Manager*
EMP: 300
SALES (est): 16.5MM **Privately Held**
SIC: 2721 Magazines: publishing only, not printed on site

(G-10774)
MERIDIAN ADHESIVES GROUP LLC (PA)
100 Park Ave Fl 31 (10017-5584)
PHONE.....................212 771-1717
Dan Pelton, *CEO*
EMP: 2
SALES (est): 18.1MM **Privately Held**
SIC: 2891 Adhesives & sealants

(G-10775)
MERRILL COMMUNICATIONS LLC
1345 Ave Of The Amrcs 1 (10105-0199)
PHONE.....................212 620-5600
EMP: 7
SALES (corp-wide): 566.6MM **Privately Held**
SIC: 2759 Commercial printing
HQ: Merrill Communications Llc
1 Merrill Cir
Saint Paul MN 55108
651 646-4501

(G-10776)
MERRILL CORPORATION
25 W 45th St Ste 900 (10036-4902)
PHONE.....................917 934-7300
Peter Jordan, *Branch Mgr*
EMP: 87
SALES (corp-wide): 566.6MM **Privately Held**
WEB: www.merrillcorp.com
SIC: 2759 Commercial printing
PA: Merrill Corporation
1 Merrill Cir
Saint Paul MN 55108
651 646-4501

(G-10777)
MERRILL CORPORATION
1345 Ave Of The Ave Fl 17 Flr 17 (10105)
PHONE.....................212 620-5600
Susan Kindya, *Sales Dir*
Mike James, *Manager*
Kathy Riewe, *Office Admin*
Shelle Martin, *Director*
EMP: 100
SALES (corp-wide): 566.6MM **Privately Held**
WEB: www.merrillcorp.com
SIC: 2741 Miscellaneous publishing
PA: Merrill Corporation
1 Merrill Cir
Saint Paul MN 55108
651 646-4501

(G-10778)
MERRILL NEW YORK COMPANY INC
Also Called: Merrill Communications
246 W 54th St (10019-5502)
PHONE.....................212 229-6500
Tod Albright, *President*

EMP: 200
SALES (est): 11.9MM
SALES (corp-wide): 566.6MM **Privately Held**
WEB: www.merrillcorp.com
SIC: 2759 2752 Financial note & certificate printing & engraving; commercial printing, lithographic
PA: Merrill Corporation
1 Merrill Cir
Saint Paul MN 55108
651 646-4501

(G-10779)
MERYL DIAMOND LTD (PA)
Also Called: M D L
1375 Broadway Fl 9 (10018-7052)
PHONE.....................212 730-0333
Meryl Diamond, *President*
Kim Reinle, *Financial Exec*
▲ EMP: 60
SQ FT: 13,000
SALES (est): 101.1MM **Privately Held**
SIC: 2339 2389 Sportswear, women's; men's miscellaneous accessories

(G-10780)
MESH LLC
350 5th Ave Lbby 9 (10118-0109)
PHONE.....................646 839-7000
Richard Darling,
▲ EMP: 30
SALES (est): 1.6MM **Privately Held**
SIC: 2326 Men's & boys' work clothing
HQ: Gbg Usa Inc.
350 5th Ave Lbby 11
New York NY 10118
646 839-7000

(G-10781)
MESOBLAST INC
505 5th Ave Fl 3 (10017-4910)
PHONE.....................212 880-2060
Silviu Itescu, *CEO*
John McMannis, *Exec VP*
Daniel Devine, *Senior VP*
Christopher James, *Vice Pres*
John Picciano, *Vice Pres*
EMP: 8
SALES (est): 4.5MM **Privately Held**
SIC: 2834 Drugs acting on the cardiovascular system, except diagnostic
PA: Mesoblast Limited
55 Collins St
Melbourne VIC 3000

(G-10782)
MESSEX GROUP INC
244 5th Ave Ste D256 (10001-7604)
PHONE.....................646 229-2582
Tom Carmody, *President*
Diana Popescu, *Vice Pres*
EMP: 4 EST: 2011
SQ FT: 1,000
SALES: 2MM **Privately Held**
SIC: 2325 Men's & boys' jeans & dungarees

(G-10783)
METALSIGMA USA INC
350 5th Ave (10118-0110)
PHONE.....................212 731-4346
Carlo Geddo, *President*
EMP: 3
SQ FT: 400
SALES: 8MM
SALES (corp-wide): 37.6MM **Privately Held**
SIC: 3449 Curtain wall, metal
PA: Metalsigma Tunesi Spa
Via Vicinale Galdina S.P. 34
Arluno MI 20010
029 015-762

(G-10784)
METRO CREATIVE GRAPHICS INC (PA)
519 8th Ave Fl 18 (10018-4577)
PHONE.....................212 947-5100
Robert Zimmerman, *CEO*
Andrew Shapiro, *Ch of Bd*
Darrell Davis, *Vice Pres*
Benjamin Sandoval, *Controller*
EMP: 38
SQ FT: 22,000

GEOGRAPHIC SECTION

New York - New York County (G-10812)

SALES (est): 6.4MM Privately Held
WEB: www.metroeditorialservices.com
SIC: 2731 2759 Books: publishing & printing; screen printing

(G-10785)
METRO FUEL LLC
800 3rd Ave Fl 28 (10022-7604)
PHONE..................................212 836-9608
EMP: 209 EST: 2010
SALES (est): 523.6K
SALES (corp-wide): 1.5B Publicly Held
SIC: 2869 Fuels
PA: Outfront Media Inc.
  405 Lexington Ave Fl 17
  New York NY 10174
  212 297-6400

(G-10786)
METROSOURCE PUBLISHING INC
498 Fashion Ave Fl 10 (10018-6957)
PHONE..................................212 691-5127
Rob Davis, *President*
EMP: 12
SALES (est): 1.4MM
SALES (corp-wide): 4.8MM Privately Held
SIC: 2721 Magazines: publishing & printing; magazines: publishing only, not printed on site
PA: Davler Media Group Llc
  213 W 35th St Rm 1201
  New York NY 10001
  212 315-0800

(G-10787)
MG IMAGING
229 W 28th St Rm 300 (10001-5915)
PHONE..................................212 704-4073
Mario Gambuzza, *President*
EMP: 5
SALES (est): 773.3K Privately Held
SIC: 3577 Printers & plotters

(G-10788)
MGK GROUP INC
Also Called: Lamontage
979 3rd Ave Ste 1811 (10022-3804)
PHONE..................................212 989-2732
Liora Manne, *President*
EMP: 30
SQ FT: 10,000
SALES (est): 4MM Privately Held
WEB: www.lamontage.com
SIC: 2273 2211 2221 2392 Rugs, hand & machine made; upholstery fabrics, cotton; tapestry fabrics, cotton; wall covering fabrics, manmade fiber & silk; household furnishings; textile bags; nonwoven fabrics

(G-10789)
MIAMI MEDIA LLC (HQ)
72 Madison Ave Fl 11 (10016-8731)
PHONE..................................212 268-8600
Thomas Allon, *Mng Member*
EMP: 13
SALES (est): 1.6MM
SALES (corp-wide): 10.9MM Privately Held
SIC: 2711 2721 Newspapers: publishing only, not printed on site; magazines: publishing only, not printed on site
PA: Manhattan Media, Llc
  535 5th Ave Fl 23
  New York NY 10017
  212 268-8600

(G-10790)
MICHAEL ANDREWS LLC
Also Called: Michael Andrews Bespoke
680 Broadway Fl Mezz (10012-2322)
PHONE..................................212 677-1755
Michael Mantegna, *CEO*
Cory Sylvester, *VP Opers*
▲ EMP: 16
SALES (est): 933.4K Privately Held
SIC: 2311 5611 Suits, men's & boys': made from purchased materials; men's & boys' clothing stores

(G-10791)
MICHAEL BONDANZA INC
10 E 38th St Fl 6 (10016-0619)
PHONE..................................212 869-0043
Michael Bondanza, *President*

Geri Bondanza, *Vice Pres*
EMP: 26
SQ FT: 2,500
SALES (est): 3.3MM Privately Held
WEB: www.bondanza.com
SIC: 3911 5094 Jewelry, precious metal; jewelry

(G-10792)
MICHAEL KARP MUSIC INC
Also Called: 39th Street Music-Div
59 W 71st St Apt 7a (10023-4115)
PHONE..................................212 840-3285
Michael Karp, *President*
EMP: 6
SQ FT: 5,500
SALES (est): 490K Privately Held
WEB: www.michaelkarpmusic.com
SIC: 2741 7389 Music, sheet: publishing only, not printed on site; music & broadcasting services

(G-10793)
MICHAELIAN & KOHLBERG INC
225 E 59th St (10022-1403)
PHONE..................................212 431-9009
EMP: 9
SALES (corp-wide): 4.2MM Privately Held
SIC: 2273 Mfg Carpets/Rugs
PA: Michaelian & Kohlberg, Inc.
  5216 Brevard Rd
  Horse Shoe NC 28742
  828 891-8511

(G-10794)
MICKELBERRY COMMUNICATIONS INC (PA)
405 Park Ave (10022-4405)
PHONE..................................212 832-0303
James C Marlas, *Ch of Bd*
Gregory J Garville, *President*
EMP: 8
SQ FT: 4,000
SALES (est): 46.5MM Privately Held
WEB: www.mickelberry.com
SIC: 2752 7311 Commercial printing, lithographic; advertising agencies

(G-10795)
MICRO PUBLISHING INC
Also Called: Micropage
71 W 23rd St Lbby A (10010-3521)
PHONE..................................212 533-9180
Kevin Boyajian, *President*
Brian Boyajian, *Admin Sec*
EMP: 5
SQ FT: 9,000
SALES (est): 3MM Privately Held
WEB: www.micropage.com
SIC: 2731 2796 Book-Publishing/Printing Platemaking Services

(G-10796)
MICRO SEMICDTR RESEARCHES LLC (PA)
310 W 52nd St Apt 12b (10019-6292)
PHONE..................................646 863-6070
Seiji Yamashita, *Principal*
▲ EMP: 4
SALES (est): 1.7MM Privately Held
SIC: 3674 8748 Semiconductors & related devices; test development & evaluation service

(G-10797)
MICROMEM TECHNOLOGIES
245 Park Ave Fl 24 (10167-2699)
PHONE..................................212 672-1806
Steven Van Fleet, *Principal*
EMP: 10
SALES (est): 545.8K Privately Held
SIC: 3674 Semiconductors & related devices

(G-10798)
MICROSOFT CORPORATION
11 Times Sq Fl 9 (10036-6619)
PHONE..................................212 245-2100
Dwayne Johnson, *Managing Dir*
Matt O'Donnell, *Business Mgr*
Scott Velechko, *Business Mgr*
Nicole Jones, *Senior VP*
Nancy John, *Store Mgr*
EMP: 10

SALES (corp-wide): 110.3B Publicly Held
WEB: www.microsoft.com
SIC: 7372 Application computer software
PA: Microsoft Corporation
  1 Microsoft Way
  Redmond WA 98052
  425 882-8080

(G-10799)
MICROSTRATEGY INCORPORATED
5 Penn Plz Ste 901 (10001-1837)
PHONE..................................888 537-8135
John Larkin, *CEO*
Stephen Goodson, *Technical Staff*
EMP: 15
SALES (corp-wide): 504.5MM Publicly Held
WEB: www.microstrategy.com
SIC: 7372 Application computer software
PA: Microstrategy Incorporated
  1850 Towers Crescent Plz # 700
  Tysons Corner VA 22182
  703 848-8600

(G-10800)
MIDAS MDICI GROUP HOLDINGS INC (PA)
445 Park Ave Frnt 5 (10022-8603)
PHONE..................................212 792-0920
Nana Baffour, *Ch of Bd*
Johnson M Kachidza, *President*
Robert F McCarthy, *Exec VP*
Frank Asante-Kissi, *Officer*
EMP: 4
SALES (est): 80.7MM Privately Held
SIC: 7372 Prepackaged software

(G-10801)
MIDURA JEWELS INC
36 W 47th St Ste 809i (10036-8601)
PHONE..................................213 265-8090
EMP: 2 EST: 2013
SALES: 1MM Privately Held
SIC: 3911 5094 5944 Mfg Precious Metal Jewelry Whol Jewelry/Precious Stones Ret Jewelry

(G-10802)
MIGHTY QUINNS BARBEQUE LLC
103 2nd Ave Frnt 1 (10003-8336)
PHONE..................................973 777-8340
Christos Gourmos, *Managing Prtnr*
EMP: 160
SQ FT: 3,000
SALES: 10MM Privately Held
SIC: 2099 Food preparations

(G-10803)
MIGUELINA INC
325 W 37th St Fl 2 (10018-4817)
PHONE..................................212 925-0320
Miguelina Ganbiccini, *President*
Miguelina C Ganbiccini, *President*
Riccardo Ganbiccini, *Vice Pres*
EMP: 10
SQ FT: 6,500
SALES (est): 1.2MM Privately Held
WEB: www.miguelina.com
SIC: 2339 Women's & misses' outerwear

(G-10804)
MIKAEL AGHAL LLC
49 W 38th St Fl 4 (10018-1913)
PHONE..................................212 596-4010
Michael Hakimi,
Albert Aghalarian,
◆ EMP: 11
SQ FT: 5,000
SALES (est): 786K Privately Held
WEB: www.mikaelaghal.com
SIC: 2339 Athletic clothing: women's, misses' & juniors'; women's & misses' athletic clothing & sportswear

(G-10805)
MIKAM GRAPHICS LLC
1440 Broadway Fl 22 (10018-3041)
PHONE..................................212 684-9393
Donald Pesce, *Vice Pres*
Jeff Getelman, *Mng Member*
EMP: 100
SQ FT: 5,000

SALES (est): 10MM
SALES (corp-wide): 1.1B Publicly Held
WEB: www.mikam.com
SIC: 2752 Commercial printing, offset
PA: Innerworkings, Inc.
  600 W Chicago Ave Ste 850
  Chicago IL 60654
  312 642-3700

(G-10806)
MILAAYA INC
Also Called: Milaaya Embroideries
147 W 35th St Ste 602 (10001-0118)
PHONE..................................212 764-6386
Gayatri Khanna, *President*
EMP: 4
SALES: 1.2MM Privately Held
SIC: 2395 Embroidery products, except schiffli machine

(G-10807)
MILLENNIUM MEDICAL PUBLISHING
611 Broadway Rm 310 (10012-2654)
PHONE..................................212 995-2211
Steve Kurlander, *CEO*
EMP: 18
SQ FT: 3,000
SALES: 6MM Privately Held
SIC: 2741 Miscellaneous publishing

(G-10808)
MILLENNIUM PRODUCTIONS INC
Also Called: Alice & Trixie
265 W 37th St 11 (10018-5707)
PHONE..................................212 944-6203
Andrew Oshrin, *President*
Lynn Harechmak, *Bookkeeper*
Malise Collins, *Sales Staff*
▲ EMP: 12
SQ FT: 2,000
SALES (est): 1.3MM Privately Held
WEB: www.aliceandtrixie.com
SIC: 2335 2339 Housedresses; sportswear, women's

(G-10809)
MILLER & BERKOWITZ LTD
345 7th Ave Fl 20 (10001-5034)
PHONE..................................212 244-5459
Nathan Berkowitz, *President*
EMP: 13 EST: 1949
SQ FT: 13,500
SALES (est): 780K Privately Held
SIC: 2371 Fur goods

(G-10810)
MILLER & VEIT INC
22 W 48th St Ste 703 (10036-1820)
PHONE..................................212 247-2275
Edward Ludel, *President*
Edward E Ludel, *Vice Pres*
Barbara Ludel, *Admin Sec*
EMP: 10
SQ FT: 1,566
SALES (est): 1MM Privately Held
SIC: 3915 5094 Diamond cutting & polishing; diamonds (gems)

(G-10811)
MILLIORE FASHION INC
250 W 39th St Rm 506 (10018-8332)
PHONE..................................212 302-0001
Ws Min, *President*
◆ EMP: 4
SALES (est): 7.3MM Privately Held
SIC: 2335 Women's, juniors' & misses' dresses

(G-10812)
MILTON MERL & ASSOCIATES INC
647 W 174th St Bsmt B (10033-7716)
PHONE..................................212 634-9292
Milton Merl, *President*
Bob Langelius, *Engineer*
Charles Houghton, *Creative Dir*
▲ EMP: 5
SQ FT: 2,000
SALES (est): 725.2K Privately Held
WEB: www.miltonmerl.com
SIC: 2542 Partitions & fixtures, except wood

New York - New York County (G-10813)

GEOGRAPHIC SECTION

(G-10813)
MILTONS OF NEW YORK INC
110 W 40th St Rm 1001 (10018-8535)
PHONE................212 997-3359
Kerman Minbatiwalla, *President*
Shalini Amersey, *Vice Pres*
EMP: 9
SQ FT: 600
SALES (est): 1.1MM **Privately Held**
WEB: www.miltonsny.com
SIC: 2339 2321 2325 2369 Women's & misses' outerwear; men's & boys' furnishings; men's & boys' trousers & slacks; girls' & children's outerwear

(G-10814)
MIMEOCOM INC (PA)
3 Park Ave Fl 22 (10016-5909)
P.O. Box 654018, Dallas TX (75265-4018)
PHONE................212 847-3000
Adam Slutsky, *CEO*
John Delbridge, *COO*
Nicole P Haughey, *COO*
Mike Barker, *Vice Pres*
Ryan Deitch, *Vice Pres*
EMP: 277
SQ FT: 145,000
SALES (est): 215MM **Privately Held**
WEB: www.mimeo.com
SIC: 2759 Commercial printing

(G-10815)
MIMI SO INTERNATIONAL LLC
Also Called: Mimi So New York
22 W 48th St Ste 902 (10036-1803)
PHONE................212 300-8600
Gregory Wong, *Controller*
Molly Conlin, *Marketing Mgr*
Karissa Basile, *Marketing Staff*
Mimi So, *Mng Member*
Stephanie Preville, *Director*
EMP: 20
SALES (est): 3.3MM **Privately Held**
SIC: 3911 5944 5094 Jewelry, precious metal; jewelry stores; jewelry

(G-10816)
MIN HO DESIGNS INC
425 Madison Ave Rm 1703 (10017-1150)
PHONE................212 838-3667
Fax: 212 838-3689
EMP: 9
SQ FT: 1,600
SALES (est): 740K **Privately Held**
SIC: 3911 Mfg Jewelry

(G-10817)
MINERALS TECHNOLOGIES INC (PA)
Also Called: MTI
622 3rd Ave Rm 3800 (10017-6729)
PHONE................212 878-1800
Douglas T Dietrich, *CEO*
Duane R Dunham, *Ch of Bd*
Jonathan Hastings, *President*
Ramanathan Chandran, *Managing Dir*
D J Monagle III, *COO*
▲ **EMP:** 50
SALES: 1.6B **Publicly Held**
WEB: www.mineralstech.com
SIC: 2819 3274 1411 3281 Calcium compounds & salts, inorganic; quicklime; limestone & marble dimension stone; limestone, cut & shaped; limestone; minerals, ground or otherwise treated

(G-10818)
MING PAO (NEW YORK) INC
265 Canal St Ste 403 (10013-6010)
PHONE................212 334-2220
EMP: 10
SALES (corp-wide): 429.1MM **Privately Held**
SIC: 2711 Printing & Circulation Of Newspaper
HQ: Ming Pao (New York), Inc
4331 33rd St
Long Island City NY 11101

(G-10819)
MINK MART INC
345 7th Ave Fl 9 (10001-5049)
PHONE................212 868-2785
George J Haralabatos, *President*
EMP: 7 **EST:** 1960
SQ FT: 7,200
SALES (est): 680K **Privately Held**
SIC: 2371 Apparel, fur

(G-10820)
MINY GROUP INC
148 Lafayette St Fl 2 (10013-3115)
PHONE................212 925-6722
Shun Yen Siu, *President*
Harvey Lock, *Vice Pres*
Deirdre Quinn, *Vice Pres*
Anita Wong, *Vice Pres*
EMP: 70
SALES (est): 3.1MM **Privately Held**
SIC: 2337 Women's & misses' suits & coats

(G-10821)
MINYANVILLE MEDIA INC
708 3rd Ave Fl 6 (10017-4119)
PHONE................212 991-6200
Todd Harrison, *CEO*
Kevin Wassong, *President*
Bradford Campeau-Laurion, *CTO*
EMP: 23
SQ FT: 6,000
SALES (est): 1.5MM **Privately Held**
SIC: 2741 Miscellaneous publishing

(G-10822)
MISS GROUP (PA)
1410 Broadway Rm 703 (10018-9365)
PHONE................212 391-2535
▲ **EMP:** 9
SALES (est): 5MM **Privately Held**
SIC: 2329 Mens And Boys Clothing, Nec, Nsk

(G-10823)
MISS JESSIES LLC
Also Called: Miss Jessies Products
441 Broadway Fl 2 (10013-2592)
PHONE................718 643-9016
Jasmine Major, *Mktg Coord*
Dionne Cargill, *Marketing Staff*
Miko Branch, *Mng Member*
Piti Branch, *Mng Member*
Furner Marquis, *Technology*
EMP: 8
SQ FT: 3,000
SALES (est): 1.3MM **Privately Held**
SIC: 3999 Hair & hair-based products

(G-10824)
MISTDODA INC (DH)
Also Called: Croscill Home Fashions
261 5th Ave Fl 25 (10016-7601)
PHONE................919 735-7111
Douglas Kahn, *CEO*
Marc Navarre, *President*
Eliana Cuevas, *Vice Pres*
Ken Hedrick, *Vice Pres*
Leonard Soifer, *Vice Pres*
▲ **EMP:** 50 **EST:** 1925
SQ FT: 35,000
SALES (est): 85MM
SALES (corp-wide): 4.1B **Privately Held**
WEB: www.croscill.com
SIC: 2391 5023 Curtains & draperies; decorative home furnishings & supplies

(G-10825)
MITSUBISHI CHEMICAL AMER INC (PA)
Also Called: Composite Materials Division
655 3rd Ave Fl 15 (10017-9135)
PHONE................212 223-3043
John Canfield, *President*
Carolyn Orner, *Human Resources*
EMP: 23
SALES (est): 5MM **Privately Held**
SIC: 3355 3444 3443 2893 Aluminum rolling & drawing; sheet metalwork; fabricated plate work (boiler shop); printing ink

(G-10826)
MJM JEWELRY CORP (PA)
Also Called: Berry Jewelry Company
29 W 38th St Rm 1601 (10018-5504)
PHONE................212 354-5014
Martha Berry, *President*
▲ **EMP:** 80
SQ FT: 10,000
SALES (est): 14.6MM **Privately Held**
WEB: www.berryjewelry.com
SIC: 3911 Jewelry, precious metal

(G-10827)
MKSF INC
Also Called: Marc Kaufman Furs
212 W 30th St (10001-4901)
PHONE................212 563-3877
Marc Kaufman, *CEO*
EMP: 10
SALES (est): 479K **Privately Held**
SIC: 2371 Fur coats & other fur apparel

(G-10828)
MOBO SYSTEMS INC
Also Called: Go Mobo
26 Broadway Fl 24 (10004-1840)
PHONE................212 260-0895
Noah H Glass, *CEO*
Jamar Parris, *District Mgr*
Matt Tucker, *COO*
Matthew Tucker, *COO*
David Fellows, *Vice Pres*
EMP: 86
SQ FT: 400
SALES (est): 12MM **Privately Held**
SIC: 7372 Business oriented computer software

(G-10829)
MODERN LANGUAGE ASSN AMER INC
Also Called: M L A
85 Broad St Fl 5 (10004-1789)
PHONE................646 576-5000
Margaret W Ferguson, *President*
Kwame Anthony Appiah, *Vice Pres*
Roland Greene, *Vice Pres*
Sara Pastel, *Assoc Editor*
Rosemary G Feal, *Exec Dir*
EMP: 110 **EST:** 1883
SQ FT: 37,500
SALES: 16.3MM **Privately Held**
SIC: 2731 8641 Books: publishing only; educator's association

(G-10830)
MODO RETAIL LLC
Also Called: Modo Eyewear
252 Mott St (10012-3436)
PHONE................212 965-4900
Sue Ng, *Controller*
Monti Blazevich, *Manager*
Alex Lenaro,
EMP: 40
SALES (est): 3.2MM **Privately Held**
SIC: 3851 Spectacles

(G-10831)
MODULEX NEW YORK INC
Also Called: Asi Sign Systems
192 Lexington Ave Rm 1002 (10016-6823)
PHONE................646 742-1320
Selwyn Josset, *President*
John Jackson, *Sales Associate*
Lauren Corrigan, *Office Mgr*
EMP: 8
SQ FT: 2,200
SALES: 2.1MM **Privately Held**
SIC: 3993 Signs, not made in custom sign painting shops

(G-10832)
MODULIGHTOR INC
246 E 58th St (10022-2011)
PHONE................212 371-0336
Ernest Wagner, *President*
▲ **EMP:** 12
SQ FT: 7,000
SALES (est): 1.5MM **Privately Held**
WEB: www.Modulightor.com
SIC: 3646 3645 Commercial indusl & institutional electric lighting fixtures; residential lighting fixtures

(G-10833)
MOLABS INC
32 Little West 12th St (10014-1303)
PHONE................310 721-6828
James Payne, *CEO*
EMP: 6 **EST:** 2015
SALES (est): 163.7K **Privately Held**
SIC: 7372 Application computer software

(G-10834)
MOM DAD PUBLISHING INC
Also Called: C/O Pdell Ndell Fine Winberger
59 Maiden Ln Fl 27 (10038-4647)
PHONE................646 476-9170
Bert Padell, *President*
EMP: 30
SALES (est): 2.4MM **Privately Held**
SIC: 2741 Music, sheet: publishing only, not printed on site

(G-10835)
MOMOFUKU 171 FIRST AVENUE LLC
171 1st Ave (10003-2949)
PHONE................212 777-7773
Ryan Schuler, *General Mgr*
David Chang, *Mng Member*
Richard Hargreave, *Director*
Matthew Rudofker, *Director*
Sean Gray, *Executive*
EMP: 52 **EST:** 2007
SALES (est): 5.8MM **Privately Held**
SIC: 2098 Noodles (e.g. egg, plain & water), dry

(G-10836)
MONACELLI PRESS LLC
236 W 27th St Rm 4a (10001-5906)
PHONE................212 229-9925
Gianfranco Monacelli, *President*
Victoria Craven, *Editor*
Michael Vagnetti, *Prdtn Mgr*
Susan Enochs, *Pub Rel Dir*
Sarah Herda, *Marketing Staff*
▲ **EMP:** 8
SALES (est): 1MM **Privately Held**
WEB: www.monacellipress.com
SIC: 2731 Books: publishing only

(G-10837)
MONDO PUBLISHING INC (PA)
980 Avenue Of The America (10018-7810)
PHONE................212 268-3560
Mark Vineis, *President*
Ellen Ungaro, *Editor*
Sallye Drinkard, *Prdtn Mgr*
Charles Arasi, *Manager*
Marina Maurici, *Graphic Designe*
▲ **EMP:** 20
SALES (est): 2.1MM **Privately Held**
WEB: www.mondopub.com
SIC: 2731 Books: publishing only

(G-10838)
MONELLE JEWELRY
608 5th Ave Ste 504 (10020-2303)
PHONE................212 977-9535
Avis Swed, *Owner*
EMP: 3
SQ FT: 600
SALES (est): 1.1MM **Privately Held**
WEB: www.monellejewelry.com
SIC: 3911 Jewelry, precious metal

(G-10839)
MONGODB INC (PA)
1633 Broadway Fl 38 (10019-6763)
PHONE................646 727-4092
Kevin Ryan, *Ch of Bd*
Dev Ittycheria, *President*
Michael Gordon, *CFO*
Meagen Eisenberg, *Chief Mktg Ofcr*
Eliot Horowitz, *CTO*
EMP: 120
SQ FT: 106,230
SALES: 154.5MM **Publicly Held**
SIC: 7372 Prepackaged software

(G-10840)
MONTHLY GIFT INC
Also Called: Montly Gift
401 Park Ave S (10016-8808)
PHONE................888 444-9661
Lisamarie Scotti, *Vice Pres*
EMP: 6
SQ FT: 350
SALES: 500K **Privately Held**
SIC: 2676 Sanitary paper products

(G-10841)
MORELLE PRODUCTS LTD
Also Called: Philippe Adec Paris
211 E 18th St Apt 4d (10003-3624)
PHONE................212 391-8070

GEOGRAPHIC SECTION

New York - New York County (G-10869)

Aby Saltiel, *President*
Alexander Fronimos, *Vice Pres*
EMP: 17
SQ FT: 13,500
SALES (est): 1.4MM **Privately Held**
WEB: www.philippeadec.com
SIC: 2339 5137 Mfg Women's/Misses' Outerwear Whol Women's/Child's Clothing

(G-10842)
MORGIK METAL DESIGNS
145 Hudson St Frnt 4 (10013-2122)
P.O. Box 213, Elmwood Park NJ (07407-0213)
PHONE.................212 463-0304
Larry Kaufman, *President*
Joe Kaufman, *Admin Sec*
EMP: 18
SQ FT: 4,000
SALES (est): 2.5MM **Privately Held**
WEB: www.morgik.com
SIC: 3446 1761 3429 Architectural metalwork; architectural sheet metal work; furniture builders' & other household hardware

(G-10843)
MORRIS BROTHERS SIGN SVC INC
37 W 20th St Ste 708 (10011-3717)
PHONE.................212 675-9130
Peter V Bellantone, *President*
Michael Bellantone, *General Mgr*
EMP: 3
SQ FT: 2,000
SALES: 1MM **Privately Held**
WEB: www.morrisbrotherssigns.com
SIC: 3993 Signs & advertising specialties

(G-10844)
MOSBY HOLDINGS CORP (DH)
125 Park Ave (10017-5529)
PHONE.................212 309-8100
Ron Mobed, *President*
EMP: 6
SALES (est): 82.3MM
SALES (corp-wide): 9.7B **Privately Held**
SIC: 2741 8999 Technical manuals: publishing only, not printed on site; writing for publication
HQ: Relx Inc.
    230 Park Ave Ste 700
    New York NY 10169
    212 309-8100

(G-10845)
MOSCHOS FURS INC
345 7th Ave Rm 1501 (10001-5042)
PHONE.................212 244-0255
George Moschos, *President*
Patricia Moschos, *Corp Secy*
EMP: 5
SQ FT: 4,000
SALES (est): 350K **Privately Held**
SIC: 2371 Fur coats & other fur apparel

(G-10846)
MOSCOT WHOLESALE CORP
69 W 14th St Fl 2 (10011-7417)
PHONE.................212 647-1550
Dr Harvey Moscot, *President*
Tess Destefano, *Bookkeeper*
Zack Moscot, *Senior Mgr*
Kenny Moscot, *Shareholder*
▲ **EMP:** 6
SQ FT: 2,000
SALES (est): 847.8K **Privately Held**
SIC: 3851 5049 Frames, lenses & parts, eyeglass & spectacle; optical goods

(G-10847)
MOTEMA MUSIC LLC
8 W 127th St Apt 2 (10027-3949)
PHONE.................212 860-6969
Jana Herzen,
Wayne More,
EMP: 7
SQ FT: 600
SALES: 700K **Privately Held**
SIC: 2782 5735 Record albums; records

(G-10848)
MOUNTAIN AND ISLES LLC
525 7th Ave Fl 22 (10018-0428)
PHONE.................212 354-1890

Marie Huftel,
Victor Rousso,
EMP: 11
SALES (est): 488.9K **Privately Held**
SIC: 2389 Men's miscellaneous accessories

(G-10849)
MP STUDIO INC
147 W 35th St Ste 1603 (10001-2100)
PHONE.................212 302-5666
EMP: 5 **EST:** 2013
SALES (est): 300K **Privately Held**
SIC: 2337 Mfg Women's/Misses' Suits/Coats

(G-10850)
MPDRAW LLC
109 Ludlow St (10002-3240)
PHONE.................212 228-8383
EMP: 25
SALES (est): 1.6MM **Privately Held**
SIC: 3421 Table & food cutlery, including butchers'

(G-10851)
MPDW INC (PA)
158 W 29th St Fl 12 (10001-5300)
PHONE.................925 631-6878
Sharon Huebschwerlen, *CEO*
▲ **EMP:** 7
SQ FT: 7,000
SALES (est): 952.9K **Privately Held**
WEB: www.mycrapac.com
SIC: 2385 Raincoats, except vulcanized rubber: purchased materials

(G-10852)
MRINALINI INC
Also Called: M & R Design
469 7th Ave Rm 1254 (10018-7605)
PHONE.................646 510-2747
Mrinalini Kumari, *President*
EMP: 6
SALES (est): 41.4K **Privately Held**
SIC: 2395 Embroidery & art needlework

(G-10853)
MRS JOHN L STRONG & CO LLC
Also Called: Strong Ventures
699 Madison Ave Fl 5 (10065-8039)
PHONE.................212 838-3775
Joe Lewis, *President*
Nanette Brown,
EMP: 14
SALES (est): 1.5MM **Privately Held**
WEB: www.mrsstrong.com
SIC: 2754 Stationery: gravure printing

(G-10854)
MRT TEXTILE INC
350 5th Ave (10118-0110)
PHONE.................800 674-1073
Ibrahim Eyidemir, *President*
David Davitoglu, *Vice Pres*
EMP: 3
SQ FT: 7,000
SALES: 4MM **Privately Held**
SIC: 2341 5137 Chemises, camisoles & teddies: women's & children's; women's & children's lingerie & undergarments

(G-10855)
MTM PUBLISHING INC
435 W 23rd St (10011-1402)
PHONE.................212 242-6930
Valerie Tomaselli, *President*
EMP: 6
SALES (est): 507K **Privately Held**
SIC: 2741 Miscellaneous publishing

(G-10856)
MUD PUDDLE BOOKS INC
36 W 25th St Fl 5 (10010-2718)
PHONE.................212 647-9168
Gregory Boehm, *President*
Nelly Duran, *Office Mgr*
▲ **EMP:** 5
SQ FT: 3,000
SALES (est): 603K **Privately Held**
WEB: www.mudpuddlebooks.com
SIC: 2731 Books: publishing only

(G-10857)
MULITEX USA INC
215 W 40th St Fl 7 (10018-1575)
PHONE.................212 398-0440
Harry Mohinani, *CEO*
Sivaprakasham Rajakkal, *President*
Vijay Mohinani, *Director*
▲ **EMP:** 6
SQ FT: 2,000
SALES: 7.1MM
SALES (corp-wide): 110MM **Privately Held**
WEB: www.mulitex.com
SIC: 2321 2325 2331 Men's & boys' furnishings; men's & boys' trousers & slacks; women's & misses' blouses & shirts
PA: Mulitex (Exports) Limited
    9/F Angel Twr
    Lai Chi Kok KLN
    225 110-00

(G-10858)
MULTI PACKAGING SOLUTIONS INC (DH)
150 E 52nd St Fl 28 (10022-6017)
PHONE.................646 885-0005
Marc Shore, *CEO*
Dennis Kaltman, *President*
Betsy Meschke, *Business Mgr*
Arthur Kern, *Exec VP*
Rick Smith, *Exec VP*
◆ **EMP:** 20
SALES (est): 805.5MM
SALES (corp-wide): 14.8B **Publicly Held**
WEB: www.ivyhill-wms.com
SIC: 2731 2761 3089 5092 Books: publishing & printing; continuous forms, office & business; identification cards, plastic; arts & crafts equipment & supplies; packaging paper & plastics film, coated & laminated; screen printing
HQ: Multi Packaging Solutions International Limited
    885 3rd Ave Fl 28
    New York NY 10022
    646 885-0005

(G-10859)
MULTI PACKG SOLUTIONS INTL LTD (HQ)
885 3rd Ave Fl 28 (10022-4834)
PHONE.................646 885-0005
Marc Shore, *President*
Kevin Kain, *President*
Dennis Kaltman, *Exec VP*
Rick Smith, *Exec VP*
Mark Wenham, *Exec VP*
EMP: 19 **EST:** 2005
SQ FT: 9,772
SALES: 1.6B
SALES (corp-wide): 14.8B **Publicly Held**
SIC: 2657 Folding paperboard boxes
PA: Westrock Company
    1000 Abernathy Rd Ste 125
    Atlanta GA 30328
    770 448-2193

(G-10860)
MULTIMEDIA PLUS INC
853 Broadway Ste 1605 (10003-4714)
PHONE.................212 982-3229
David Harouche, *President*
Jodi Harouche, *Admin Sec*
EMP: 15
SQ FT: 5,000
SALES (est): 2.7MM **Privately Held**
WEB: www.multimediaplus.com
SIC: 7372 Educational computer software

(G-10861)
MUSIC SALES CORPORATION (PA)
Also Called: Acorn
180 Madison Ave Ste 2400 (10016-5241)
PHONE.................212 254-2100
Barrie Edwards, *President*
Susan Feder, *Exec VP*
Bob Knight, *Vice Pres*
Robert Wise, *Vice Pres*
Steven Wilson, *VP Bus Dvlpt*
▲ **EMP:** 6
SQ FT: 6,800

SALES (est): 13.6MM **Privately Held**
WEB: www.msc-catalog.com
SIC: 2741 Music books: publishing only, not printed on site; music, sheet: publishing only, not printed on site

(G-10862)
MUSTANG BIO INC
2 Gansevoort St Fl 9 (10014-1667)
PHONE.................781 652-4500
Michael S Weiss, *Ch of Bd*
Manuel Litchman, *President*
Martina A Sersch, *Chief Mktg Ofcr*
Knut Niss, *CTO*
Neil Herskowitz, *Bd of Directors*
EMP: 5
SALES (est): 282.6K **Publicly Held**
SIC: 2834 Pharmaceutical preparations
PA: Fortress Biotech, Inc.
    2 Gansevoort St Fl 9
    New York NY 10014

(G-10863)
MX SOLAR USA LLC
100 Wall St Ste 1000 (10005-3727)
PHONE.................732 356-7300
◆ **EMP:** 150
SALES (est): 10.1MM **Privately Held**
SIC: 3433 Mfg Heating Equipment-Non-electric

(G-10864)
MY MOST FAVORITE FOOD
247 W 72nd St Frnt 1 (10023-2723)
PHONE.................212 580-5130
Scott A Magram, *Principal*
EMP: 5
SALES (est): 271.8K **Privately Held**
SIC: 2052 2024 Bakery products, dry; ices, flavored (frozen dessert)

(G-10865)
MY PUBLISHER INC
845 3rd Ave Rm 1410 (10022-6619)
PHONE.................212 935-5215
Katherine Lewis, *President*
EMP: 8
SALES (est): 7.3MM
SALES (corp-wide): 1.1B **Publicly Held**
SIC: 2741 Miscellaneous publishing
PA: Shutterfly, Inc.
    2800 Bridge Pkwy Ste 100
    Redwood City CA 94065
    650 610-5200

(G-10866)
MYERS GROUP LLC (PA)
Also Called: Sogimex
257 W 38th St (10018-4457)
PHONE.................973 761-6414
Jay Myers,
◆ **EMP:** 9
SQ FT: 3,200
SALES (est): 87MM **Privately Held**
SIC: 3111 Tanneries, leather

(G-10867)
MYLAN HEALTH MANAGEMENT LLC
405 Lexington Ave (10174-0002)
PHONE.................917 262-2950
Adele Gulfo, *Principal*
EMP: 9 **EST:** 2016
SALES (est): 1MM **Privately Held**
SIC: 2834 Pharmaceutical preparations

(G-10868)
MYMEE INC
110 E 25th St (10010-2913)
PHONE.................917 476-4122
Mette Dyhrberg, *President*
Daniel Rothman, *COO*
EMP: 10
SALES (est): 338.4K **Privately Held**
SIC: 7372 Prepackaged software

(G-10869)
MYSTIC INC (PA)
Also Called: Herman Kay
463 7th Ave Fl 12 (10018-7499)
PHONE.................212 239-2025
Richard Kringstein, *President*
Barry Kringstein, *Vice Pres*
Sara Lee, *Prdtn Mgr*
Kim Reid, *VP Sales*
Anna Kim, *Director*

New York - New York County (G-10870) GEOGRAPHIC SECTION

▲ EMP: 108
SQ FT: 35,000
SALES: 183.5MM **Privately Held**
WEB: www.mystic.com
SIC: 2339 Women's & misses' outerwear

(G-10870)
N Y WINSTONS INC
Also Called: Eko-Blu
5 W 86th St Apt 9e (10024-3664)
PHONE.................................212 665-3166
Lauren Swoszowski, *CEO*
EMP: 5
SALES (est): 212.9K **Privately Held**
SIC: 2086 Bottled & canned soft drinks

(G-10871)
NAGLE FUEL CORPORATION
265 Nagle Ave (10034-3573)
PHONE.................................212 304-4618
Johnny Arais, *Manager*
EMP: 5 EST: 2011
SALES (est): 312.9K **Privately Held**
SIC: 2869 Fuels

(G-10872)
NAME BASE INC
172 Lexington Ave Apt 1 (10016-7481)
PHONE.................................212 545-1400
James Singer, *President*
Margaret Wolfson, *Creative Dir*
EMP: 9
SALES (est): 598.3K **Privately Held**
WEB: www.namebase.com
SIC: 3953 Irons, marking or branding

(G-10873)
NANZ CUSTOM HARDWARE INC (PA)
Also Called: Nanz Company, The
20 Vandam St Fl 5l (10013-1277)
PHONE.................................212 367-7000
Carl Sorenson, *CEO*
Samuel Michaelson, *COO*
Kate Spota, *Project Mgr*
Alex Berlingieri, *Engineer*
Maritza Osorio, *Human Res Dir*
◆ EMP: 35
SQ FT: 7,500
SALES (est): 28.3MM **Privately Held**
WEB: www.nanz.com
SIC: 3429 5031 Door opening & closing devices, except electrical; building materials, interior

(G-10874)
NAPEAN LLC
Also Called: Luxury Daily
401 Broadway Ste 1408 (10013-3022)
PHONE.................................917 968-6757
Sophie Doran, *Chief*
Mir Maqbool Alam Khan,
EMP: 8
SALES (est): 850K **Privately Held**
SIC: 2741

(G-10875)
NASSERATI INC
Also Called: Lotus Thread
225 W 39th St Fl 6 (10018-3103)
PHONE.................................212 947-8100
Nasser Mokhtarzadeh, *CEO*
Maribel Diaz, *President*
▲ EMP: 7 EST: 2011
SQ FT: 5,000
SALES: 1.8MM **Privately Held**
SIC: 2335 Bridal & formal gowns

(G-10876)
NAT NAST COMPANY INC (PA)
1370 Broadway Rm 900 (10018-7309)
PHONE.................................212 575-1186
Sonny Haddad, *President*
Lawrence Deparis, *President*
▲ EMP: 22
SALES (est): 1.5MM **Privately Held**
WEB: www.natnast.com
SIC: 2321 Blouses, boys': made from purchased materials

(G-10877)
NATHAN LOVE LLC
407 Broome St Rm 6r (10013-3213)
PHONE.................................212 925-7111
James Elio, *Production*
Anca Risca, *Creative Dir*
Joe Burrascano,
EMP: 10
SALES: 1.6MM **Privately Held**
SIC: 3931 Musical instruments

(G-10878)
NATION COMPANY LLC
Also Called: Nation, The
520 8th Ave Rm 2100 (10018-4164)
PHONE.................................212 209-5400
Scott Klein, *President*
Sky Barsch, *Adv Dir*
Teresa Stack, *Mng Member*
Debra Eliezer, *Manager*
Katrina Vanden Heuvel,
EMP: 30 EST: 1865
SQ FT: 11,000
SALES (est): 5.6MM **Privately Held**
SIC: 2721 Magazines: publishing only, not printed on site

(G-10879)
NATION MAGAZINE
33 Irving Pl Fl 8 (10003-2307)
PHONE.................................212 209-5400
Victor Navasky, *Publisher*
EMP: 40 EST: 2008
SALES (est): 572.3K **Privately Held**
SIC: 2721 Magazines: publishing only, not printed on site

(G-10880)
NATIONAL ADVERTISING & PRTG
231 W 29th St Rm 1408 (10001-5589)
P.O. Box 1775 (10001)
PHONE.................................212 629-7650
Scott Damashek, *President*
Tiffany Moy, *Partner*
James Ricciardella, *VP Mktg*
EMP: 5
SALES (est): 701.7K **Privately Held**
SIC: 3993 2679 Advertising novelties; novelties, paper: made from purchased material

(G-10881)
NATIONAL CONTRACT INDUSTRIES
Also Called: Nci
510 E 86th St Apt 16b (10028-7508)
P.O. Box 671 (10028-0044)
PHONE.................................212 249-0045
Maxwell J Moss, *President*
EMP: 5
SQ FT: 1,000
SALES (est): 1.5MM **Privately Held**
WEB: www.ncionline.com
SIC: 2221 Wall covering fabrics, manmade fiber & silk

(G-10882)
NATIONAL FLAG & DISPLAY CO INC (PA)
30 E 21st St Apt 2b (10010-7217)
PHONE.................................212 228-6600
Howard J Siegel, *President*
Alan R Siegel, *Vice Pres*
▲ EMP: 20
SQ FT: 8,500
SALES (est): 7.4MM **Privately Held**
WEB: www.nationalflag.com
SIC: 2399 Flags, fabric

(G-10883)
NATIONAL GGRAPHIC PARTNERS LLC
485 Lexington Ave Fl 3 (10017-2651)
PHONE.................................212 656-0726
Amori Langstaff, *Director*
EMP: 5
SALES (est): 324.4K **Privately Held**
SIC: 2721 Magazines: publishing & printing

(G-10884)
NATIONAL REPRODUCTIONS INC
229 W 28th St Fl 9 (10001-5915)
PHONE.................................212 619-3800
George Pavoides, *CEO*
John K Fitch III, *President*
EMP: 30 EST: 1946
SQ FT: 5,000
SALES (est): 2.6MM
SALES (corp-wide): 2.8MM **Privately Held**
WEB: www.fitchgroup.com
SIC: 2752 7334 Photo-offset printing; photocopying & duplicating services
HQ: Francis Emory Fitch Inc
229 W 28th St
New York NY 10001
212 619-3800

(G-10885)
NATIONAL REVIEW INC (PA)
Also Called: NATIONAL REVIEW ONLINE
19 W 44th St Ste 1701 (10036-6101)
PHONE.................................212 679-7330
Thomas L Rhodes, *President*
James Kilbridge, *CFO*
Rose Demaio, *Treasurer*
Lynn Gibson, *Manager*
Aaron Robinow, *Manager*
EMP: 30 EST: 1955
SQ FT: 17,000
SALES: 5.6MM **Privately Held**
WEB: www.nationalreview.com
SIC: 2721 Magazines: publishing only, not printed on site; periodicals: publishing only

(G-10886)
NATIONAL SPINNING CO INC
Also Called: Caron Distribution Center
1212 Ave Of The Americ St (10036-1602)
PHONE.................................212 382-6400
Todd Browder, *Principal*
Morgan Miller, *Vice Chairman*
Bob Miller, *Exec VP*
Paula Boyd, *Technical Mgr*
Sherri Thomas, *Credit Staff*
EMP: 25
SALES (corp-wide): 204.3MM **Privately Held**
WEB: www.natspin.com
SIC: 2281 2269 5199 Yarn spinning mills; finishing plants; yarns
PA: National Spinning Co., Inc.
1481 W 2nd St Ste 103
Washington NC 27889
252 975-7111

(G-10887)
NATIONAL TIME RECORDING EQP CO
64 Reade St Fl 2 (10007-1870)
PHONE.................................212 227-3310
Stanley A Akivis, *President*
Richard Akivis, *Vice Pres*
Ethel Akivis, *Treasurer*
EMP: 10 EST: 1932
SQ FT: 10,000
SALES: 1,000K **Privately Held**
WEB: www.national-pinkpages.com
SIC: 3579 7629 3873 3625 Dating & numbering devices; business machine repair, electric; watches, clocks, watchcases & parts; relays & industrial controls

(G-10888)
NATIONAL TOBACCO COMPANY LP
Also Called: North Atlantic Trading Co
257 Park Ave S Fl 7 (10010-7304)
PHONE.................................212 253-8185
Thomas Holmes, *Chairman*
EMP: 10
SALES (corp-wide): 285.7MM **Publicly Held**
SIC: 2131 Chewing tobacco
HQ: National Tobacco Company, L.P.
5201 Interchange Way
Louisville KY 40229
800 579-0975

(G-10889)
NATIVE TEXTILES INC (PA)
411 5th Ave Rm 901 (10016-2259)
PHONE.................................212 951-5100
John Gunyan, *President*
Carl Andersen, *Vice Pres*
EMP: 6 EST: 1975
SQ FT: 7,000
SALES (est): 12.1MM **Privately Held**
SIC: 2253 2254 Knit outerwear mills; knit underwear mills

(G-10890)
NATORI COMPANY INCORPORATED (PA)
180 Madison Ave Fl 18 (10016-5267)
PHONE.................................212 532-7796
Josie Natori, *Ch of Bd*
Kathleen Olivieri, *Vice Pres*
Elizabeth Yee, *Vice Pres*
Blair Boyer, *Prdtn Mgr*
Pamela Stengel, *Opers Staff*
▲ EMP: 60
SQ FT: 10,500
SALES (est): 38.5MM **Privately Held**
SIC: 2384 2341 Bathrobes, men's & women's: made from purchased materials; women's & children's nightwear

(G-10891)
NATORI COMPANY INCORPORATED
Also Called: Natori Company, The
180 Madison Ave Fl 19 (10016-5267)
PHONE.................................212 532-7796
Efren Lota, *Manager*
EMP: 40
SALES (corp-wide): 38.5MM **Privately Held**
SIC: 2341 Women's & children's underwear
PA: The Natori Company Incorporated
180 Madison Ave Fl 18
New York NY 10016
212 532-7796

(G-10892)
NATURAL MATTERS INC
300 W 12th St (10014-1939)
PHONE.................................212 337-3077
John J Castro, *Ch of Bd*
EMP: 6
SALES (est): 370.4K **Privately Held**
SIC: 2099 Food preparations

(G-10893)
NATURE AMERICA INC (DH)
Also Called: Nature Publishing Group
1 New York Plz Ste 4500 (10004-1562)
PHONE.................................212 726-9200
Steven Inchcoombe, *President*
Matt Hansen, *Publisher*
Kyle Vogan, *Publisher*
Muctar Ibrahim, *General Mgr*
Roxanne Khamsi, *Editor*
▼ EMP: 380
SQ FT: 66,000
SALES: 300MM
SALES (corp-wide): 1.7B **Privately Held**
WEB: www.nature.com
SIC: 2721 Magazines: publishing only, not printed on site
HQ: Springer Nature Limited
Cromwell Place
Basingstoke HANTS RG24
125 632-9242

(G-10894)
NATURE PUBLISHING CO
345 Park Ave S (10010-1707)
PHONE.................................212 726-9200
Rebecca Walton, *President*
Myles Axton, *Editor*
Simon Fenwick, *Editor*
Ursula Hofer, *Editor*
Katie Kingwell, *Editor*
EMP: 5
SALES (est): 136.5K **Privately Held**
SIC: 2741 Miscellaneous publishing

(G-10895)
NAUTICA INTERNATIONAL INC (DH)
40 W 57th St (10019-4001)
PHONE.................................212 541-5757
Karen Murray, *President*
Sarah A Deckey, *President*
Harvey Sanders, *Exec VP*
Matt Puckett, *CFO*
▲ EMP: 100
SALES (est): 34.8MM **Privately Held**
SIC: 2329 Men's & boys' sportswear & athletic clothing; men's & boys' leather, wool & down-filled outerwear

HQ: Nautica Opco Llc
40 W 57th St Fl 3
New York NY 10019
212 541-5757

(G-10896)
NAUTICA OPCO LLC (HQ)
Also Called: Nautica Vf
40 W 57th St Fl 3 (10019-4001)
PHONE..................212 541-5757
Karen Murray, *Ch of Bd*
Christopher H Heyn, *President*
Paulette McCready, *President*
Tord Hellbing Von Dyrssen, *Managing Dir*
John Varvatos, *Senior VP*
◆ **EMP:** 500
SQ FT: 63,000
SALES (est): 928.2MM **Privately Held**
WEB: www.nautica.com
SIC: 2329 2384 5136 5137 Men's & boys' sportswear & athletic clothing; robes & dressing gowns; bathrobes, men's & women's; made from purchased materials; men's & boys' sportswear & work clothing; men's & boys' robes, nightwear & undergarments; women's & children's lingerie & undergarments; clothing, sportswear, men's & boys'; franchises, selling or licensing

(G-10897)
NAUTILUSTHINK INC
360 W 36th St Apt 7s (10018-6496)
PHONE..................646 239-6858
John Steele, *President*
EMP: 7 **EST:** 2014
SALES: 1.3MM **Privately Held**
SIC: 2721 Magazines: publishing & printing

(G-10898)
NAVAS DESIGNS INC
200 E 58th St Apt 17b (10022-2035)
PHONE..................818 988-9050
EMP: 25
SQ FT: 4,000
SALES (est): 1.7MM **Privately Held**
SIC: 2211 Cotton Broadwoven Fabric Mill

(G-10899)
NAVATAR GROUP INC (HQ)
90 Broad St Ste 1703 (10004-2373)
PHONE..................212 863-9655
Alok Misra, *President*
Bill McMonagle, *Senior VP*
Ketan Khandkar, *Vice Pres*
Allan Siegert, *VP Sales*
Laura Llano, *Accounts Mgr*
EMP: 40
SALES (est): 12.7MM **Privately Held**
WEB: www.navatargroup.com
SIC: 7372 Business oriented computer software

(G-10900)
NBM PUBLISHING INC
Also Called: Nantier Ball Minoustchine Pubg
160 Brdway Ste 700 E Wing (10038)
PHONE..................646 559-4681
Terry Nantier, *President*
Mart Minoustchine, *Vice Pres*
Chris Beall, *Admin Sec*
▲ **EMP:** 5
SQ FT: 1,200
SALES: 600K **Privately Held**
WEB: www.nbmpub.com
SIC: 2731 Book publishing

(G-10901)
NC AUDIENCE EXCHANGE LLC
1211 Ave Of The Americas (10036-8701)
PHONE..................212 416-3400
EMP: 15
SALES (est): 301K
SALES (corp-wide): 9B **Publicly Held**
SIC: 2731 2711 Book publishing, newspapers, publishing & printing
PA: News Corporation
1211 Ave Of The Americas
New York NY 10036
212 416-3400

(G-10902)
NCM PUBLISHERS INC
200 Varick St Rm 608 (10014-7486)
PHONE..................212 691-9100
Michael Zemeck, *President*

EMP: 8
SQ FT: 10,000
SALES: 1MM **Privately Held**
SIC: 2721 7812 Trade journals: publishing only, not printed on site; video tape production

(G-10903)
NEIL SAVALIA INC
15 W 47th St Ste 903 (10036-5715)
PHONE..................212 869-0123
Neil Savalia, *President*
EMP: 10
SQ FT: 1,000
SALES: 2MM **Privately Held**
SIC: 3911 5944 5094 Jewelry, precious metal; jewelry stores; jewelry & precious stones

(G-10904)
NEMARIS INC
475 Park Ave S Fl 11 (10016-6901)
PHONE..................646 794-8648
Frank Schwab, *CEO*
Stephen Schwab, *COO*
Virginie Lafage, *Info Tech Mgr*
EMP: 20
SALES (est): 1.3MM **Privately Held**
SIC: 7372 Educational computer software

(G-10905)
NEON
1400 Broadway Rm 300 (10018-1078)
PHONE..................212 727-5628
Julie Tripi, *Senior VP*
Sabrina Prince, *Vice Pres*
Sherman Yee, *Vice Pres*
Tom Ozga, *Production*
Ashley Holbrook, *Supervisor*
EMP: 11
SALES (est): 2MM **Privately Held*
SIC: 2813 Neon

(G-10906)
NERVECOM INC
199 Lafayette St Apt 3b (10012-4279)
PHONE..................212 625-9914
Rufus Griscom, *CEO*
EMP: 12
SQ FT: 5,000
SALES (est): 1.4MM **Privately Held**
WEB: www.nerve.com
SIC: 2721 Magazines: publishing only, not printed on site

(G-10907)
NERVVE TECHNOLOGIES INC (PA)
450 Park Ave Fl 30 (10022-2637)
PHONE..................716 800-2250
Thomas Slowe, *CEO*
Jose Cecin, *COO*
Jacob Goellner, *CTO*
EMP: 22
SALES (est): 3.7MM **Privately Held**
SIC: 7372 8711 Application computer software; electrical or electronic engineering

(G-10908)
NES JEWELRY INC (PA)
Also Called: Nes Costume
10 W 33rd St Fl 9 (10001-3306)
PHONE..................212 502-0025
Nemo Gindi, *President*
Heather Goldstein, *Vice Pres*
Jack Yedid, *Vice Pres*
Kenia Ceballos, *Prdtn Mgr*
Deanna Christian, *Production*
▲ **EMP:** 70
SQ FT: 14,000
SALES (est): 31.1MM **Privately Held**
SIC: 3961 Costume jewelry

(G-10909)
NESHER PRINTING INC
30 E 33rd St Frnt A (10016-5337)
PHONE..................212 760-2521
Sheldon Wrotslavsky, *President*
EMP: 6 **EST:** 1971
SQ FT: 3,500
SALES: 1MM **Privately Held**
WEB: www.nesherprinting.com
SIC: 2752 Commercial printing, offset

(G-10910)
NESTLE USA INC
Also Called: Perugina Div
520 Madison Ave (10022-4213)
PHONE..................212 688-2490
Rosa Dimaggio, *Manager*
EMP: 139
SALES (corp-wide): 90.8B **Privately Held**
WEB: www.nestleusa.com
SIC: 2023 Evaporated milk
HQ: Nestle Usa, Inc.
1812 N Moore St
Rosslyn VA 22209
818 549-6000

(G-10911)
NETOLOGIC INC
Also Called: Investars
17 State St Fl 38 (10004-1537)
PHONE..................212 269-3796
Kei Kianpoor, *CEO*
John Eagleton, *President*
Lars Heimsath, *Marketing Staff*
William Eagleton,
Anna Aunon, *Associate*
EMP: 45
SQ FT: 1,900
SALES (est): 3.1MM **Privately Held**
WEB: www.aidworks.com
SIC: 7372 Prepackaged software

(G-10912)
NETSUITE INC
8 W 40th St 5f (10018-3902)
PHONE..................646 652-5700
Zachary Nelson, *CEO*
EMP: 9
SALES (corp-wide): 39.8B **Publicly Held**
SIC: 7372 Prepackaged software
HQ: Netsuite Inc.
2955 Campus Dr Ste 100
San Mateo CA 94403
650 627-1000

(G-10913)
NETWORK INFRSTRUCTURE TECH INC
Also Called: N I T
90 John St Fl 7 (10038-3202)
PHONE..................212 404-7340
Lior Blik, *President*
Craig Calafiore, *Exec VP*
Garry Chocky, *Finance*
Sharon Schedra, *Human Res Dir*
Brian Crowley, *Manager*
EMP: 2
SQ FT: 3,900
SALES (est): 5.3MM
SALES (corp-wide): 9MM **Privately Held**
WEB: www.nitconnect.com
SIC: 7372 Business oriented computer software
PA: Exzac, Inc.
Harborside Financial Ctr
Jersey City NJ 07311
201 204-5300

(G-10914)
NEUMANN JUTTA NEW YORK INC
355 E 4th St (10009-8513)
PHONE..................212 982-7048
Jutta Neumann, *President*
▲ **EMP:** 10
SQ FT: 750
SALES: 800K **Privately Held**
SIC: 3143 3144 3172 Sandals, men's; sandals, women's; personal leather goods

(G-10915)
NEUROTROPE INC
205 E 42nd St Fl 17 (10017-5751)
PHONE..................973 242-0005
Charles S Ryan, *CEO*
Joshua N Silverman, *Ch of Bd*
William S Singer, *Vice Ch Bd*
Daniel L Alkon, *President*
Robert Weinstein, *CFO*
EMP: 5 **EST:** 2011
SALES (est): 603.3K **Privately Held**
SIC: 2834 8731 Pharmaceutical preparations; biological research

(G-10916)
NEVERWARE INC (PA)
112 W 27th St Ste 201 (10001-6242)
PHONE..................516 302-3223
Jonathan Hefter, *CEO*
Andrew Bauer, *COO*
Jesse Pierce, *Opers Staff*
Emily Roiter, *Opers Staff*
Emily Esposito, *Accounts Mgr*
EMP: 12 **EST:** 2011
SQ FT: 2,000
SALES (est): 2.9MM **Privately Held**
SIC: 7372 Business oriented computer software

(G-10917)
NEW AUDIO LLC
Also Called: Master & Dynamics
132 W 31st St Rm 701 (10001-3478)
PHONE..................212 213-6060
Jonathan Levine, *CEO*
Viggo Olsen, *Officer*
EMP: 30
SQ FT: 10,000
SALES: 6MM **Privately Held**
SIC: 3651 Microphones

(G-10918)
NEW AVON LLC (HQ)
1 Liberty Plz Fl 25 (10006-1430)
PHONE..................212 282-6000
Betty Palm, *President*
Anjana Srivastava, *President*
Steven Bosson, *Mng Member*
Helene F Rutledge, *CIO*
Ginny Edwards,
▲ **EMP:** 277
SQ FT: 100,000
SALES (est): 1.6B
SALES (corp-wide): 31.2B **Privately Held**
SIC: 2844 5122 5999 Cosmetic preparations; cosmetics; cosmetics
PA: Cerberus Capital Management, L.P.
875 3rd Ave
New York NY 10022
212 891-2100

(G-10919)
NEW DEAL PRINTING CORP (PA)
Also Called: Altro Business Forms Div
420 E 55th St Apt Grdp (10022-5149)
PHONE..................718 729-5800
David Ruzal, *President*
Doreen Beynders, *Corp Secy*
▲ **EMP:** 7
SALES: 9MM **Privately Held**
WEB: www.narcainus.com
SIC: 2759 Commercial printing

(G-10920)
NEW DIRECTIONS PUBLISHING
80 8th Ave Fl 19 (10011-7146)
PHONE..................212 255-0230
Peggy Fox, *President*
Christopher Wait, *Editor*
Jeffrey Yang, *Editor*
Jeff Clapper, *Prgrmr*
Declan Spring, *Senior Editor*
EMP: 10 **EST:** 1936
SQ FT: 2,800
SALES (est): 1.2MM **Privately Held**
WEB: www.ndpublishing.com
SIC: 2731 Books: publishing only

(G-10921)
NEW ENERGY SYSTEMS GROUP
116 W 23rd St Fl 5 (10011-2599)
PHONE..................917 573-0302
Weihe Yu, *Ch of Bd*
Jufeng Chen, *CFO*
EMP: 214
SALES (est): 10.4MM **Privately Held**
SIC: 3691 3433 Storage batteries; solar heaters & collectors; space heaters, except electric

(G-10922)
NEW ENGLAND ORTHOTIC & PROST
235 E 38th St (10016-2709)
PHONE..................212 682-9313
Ryan Murphy, *Manager*
EMP: 5

New York - New York County (G-10923)   **GEOGRAPHIC SECTION**

SALES (corp-wide): 23.7MM **Privately Held**
WEB: www.neops.com
SIC: 3842 Limbs, artificial; prosthetic appliances
PA: New England Orthotic And Prosthetic Systems, Llc
16 Commercial St
Branford CT 06405
203 483-8488

(G-10923)
NEW GENERATION LIGHTING INC
144 Bowery Frnt 1 (10013-4288)
PHONE.................................212 966-0328
Tony Chu, *Manager*
EMP: 10
SALES (est): 880K **Privately Held**
WEB: www.newgenerationlighting.com
SIC: 3645 Residential lighting fixtures

(G-10924)
NEW GOLDSTAR 1 PRINTING CORP
63 Orchard St (10002-5414)
PHONE.................................212 343-3909
Xue Hua Xie, *President*
EMP: 8
SALES (est): 502.6K **Privately Held**
SIC: 2752 Commercial printing, lithographic

(G-10925)
NEW HAMPTON CREATIONS INC
237 W 35th St Ste 502 (10001-1905)
PHONE.................................212 244-7474
Victor Hoffman, *President*
David P Hoffman, *Corp Secy*
EMP: 5
SQ FT: 1,000
SALES (est): 522.3K **Privately Held**
WEB: www.nyshose.com
SIC: 2252 Socks

(G-10926)
NEW HOPE MEDIA LLC
Also Called: Additude Magazine
108 W 39th St Rm 805 (10018-8277)
PHONE.................................646 366-0830
Eve Gilman, *General Mgr*
Marie Dolfi, *Bd of Directors*
Susan Caughman,
EMP: 6
SALES (est): 630.3K **Privately Held**
SIC: 2721 Magazines: publishing & printing

(G-10927)
NEW MEDIA INVESTMENT GROUP INC (PA)
1345 Avenue Of The Americ (10105-0014)
PHONE.................................212 479-3160
Michael E Reed, *CEO*
Wesley R Edens, *Ch of Bd*
Gregory W Freiberg, *CFO*
Theodore Janulis, *Bd of Directors*
Kevin Sheehan, *Bd of Directors*
EMP: 300
SALES: 1.3B **Publicly Held**
SIC: 2711 7373 Newspapers, publishing & printing; systems integration services

(G-10928)
NEW PRESS
120 Wall St Fl 31 (10005-4007)
PHONE.................................212 629-8802
Ellen Adler, *Publisher*
Julie Enszer, *Editor*
Emily Albarillo, *Production*
Phillip Pascascio, *Accounting Mgr*
Paris Williams, *Human Resources*
EMP: 20
SQ FT: 3,500
SALES: 5MM **Privately Held**
WEB: www.thenewpress.com
SIC: 2731 Books: publishing only

(G-10929)
NEW REPUBLIC
1 Union Sq W (10003-3303)
PHONE.................................212 989-8200
EMP: 5 EST: 2015
SALES (est): 371K **Privately Held**
SIC: 2711 Newspapers, publishing & printing

(G-10930)
NEW STYLE SIGNS LIMITED INC
171 Madison Ave Rm 204 (10016-5110)
PHONE.................................212 242-7848
Joseph Fleischer, *President*
Anna Vershinskaya, *Manager*
Lisa Feder, *Administration*
EMP: 10
SALES (est): 1.3MM **Privately Held**
SIC: 3993 Displays & cutouts, window & lobby; signs, not made in custom sign painting shops

(G-10931)
NEW TRIAD FOR COLLABORATIVE
205 W 86th St Apt 911 (10024-3344)
PHONE.................................212 873-9610
EMP: 24
SALES (est): 90.1K **Privately Held**
SIC: 7372 Prepackaged software

(G-10932)
NEW YORK ACCESSORY GROUP INC (PA)
411 5th Ave Fl 4 (10016-2272)
PHONE.................................212 532-7911
Isaac Shallom, *CEO*
Joseph Tawil, *President*
Leslie Shalom, *COO*
Bill Paganini, *CFO*
▲ EMP: 50
SALES (est): 12.3MM **Privately Held**
SIC: 2389 2339 Men's miscellaneous accessories; women's & misses' accessories

(G-10933)
NEW YORK CT LOC246 SEIU WEL BF
217 Broadway (10007-2909)
PHONE.................................212 233-0616
Branka Stijovic, *Principal*
EMP: 4
SALES: 2.9MM **Privately Held**
SIC: 3011 Tires & inner tubes

(G-10934)
NEW YORK CVL SRVC EMPLYS PBLSH
Also Called: Chief, The
277 Broadway Ste 1506 (10007-2008)
PHONE.................................212 962-2690
Edward Prial, *President*
EMP: 12
SALES (est): 680K **Privately Held**
SIC: 2711 Newspapers: publishing only, not printed on site

(G-10935)
NEW YORK DAILY NEWS
4 New York Plz Fl 6 (10004-2473)
PHONE.................................212 248-2100
Nikhil Rele, *Principal*
EMP: 5
SALES (est): 371.8K **Privately Held**
SIC: 2711 Newspapers, publishing & printing

(G-10936)
NEW YORK ELEGANCE ENTPS INC
385 5th Ave Rm 709 (10016-3344)
PHONE.................................212 685-3088
Wing CHI Chung, *President*
Andrew Lupo, *Vice Pres*
▲ EMP: 15
SQ FT: 2,000
SALES (est): 1.3MM **Privately Held**
SIC: 2342 Brassieres

(G-10937)
NEW YORK ENRGY SYNTHETICS INC
375 Park Ave Ste 2607 (10152-2600)
PHONE.................................212 634-4787
EMP: 6
SALES (est): 450K **Privately Held**
SIC: 3825 3229 Mfg Electrical Measuring Instruments Mfg Pressed/Blown Glass

(G-10938)
NEW YORK FINDINGS CORP
70 Bowery Unit 8 (10013-4607)
PHONE.................................212 925-5745
Cheryl Kerber, *President*
Mel Kerber, *Treasurer*
EMP: 15 EST: 1953
SQ FT: 3,000
SALES (est): 1.5MM **Privately Held**
WEB: www.newyorkfindings.com
SIC: 3915 5094 Jewelers' findings & materials; jewelers' findings

(G-10939)
NEW YORK FSHION WEEK GUIDE LLC
387 Park Ave S Fl 5 (10016-8810)
PHONE.................................646 757-9119
Lanzer Robinson,
EMP: 15
SALES (est): 453.4K **Privately Held**
SIC: 2721 Magazines: publishing & printing

(G-10940)
NEW YORK MEDIA LLC
75 Varick St Ste 1404 (10013-1917)
PHONE.................................212 508-0700
Michael Silberman, *General Mgr*
Joe Adalian, *Editor*
Steve Fishman, *Editor*
Wendy Goodman, *Editor*
Stacey Hunt, *Editor*
EMP: 250
SQ FT: 73,000
SALES (est): 78.5MM **Privately Held**
SIC: 2721 Magazines: publishing only, not printed on site

(G-10941)
NEW YORK PRESS INC
72 Madison Ave Fl 11 (10016-8731)
PHONE.................................212 268-8600
Russ Smith, *President*
Stephanie Musso, *Adv Dir*
Brooke Schuldt, *Assoc Editor*
Holly Morrison, *Art Dir*
EMP: 50
SQ FT: 10,000
SALES (est): 3.8MM **Privately Held**
WEB: www.nypress.com
SIC: 2711 Newspapers, publishing & printing

(G-10942)
NEW YORK SPRING WATER INC
517 W 36th St (10018-1100)
PHONE.................................212 777-4649
Richard Zakka, *President*
▲ EMP: 28
SQ FT: 200,000
SALES (est): 37.5K **Privately Held**
SIC: 2086 Mineral water, carbonated: packaged in cans, bottles, etc.

(G-10943)
NEW YORK SWEATER COMPANY INC
141 W 36th St Rm 17 (10018-9489)
PHONE.................................845 629-9533
Leonard Keff, *President*
EMP: 30
SALES (est): 2.1MM **Privately Held**
SIC: 2253 Sweaters & sweater coats, knit

(G-10944)
NEW YORK TIMES COMPANY (PA)
620 8th Ave (10018-1618)
PHONE.................................212 556-1234
Arthur Sulzberger Jr, *Ch of Bd*
Mark Thompson, *President*
Meredith Kopit Levien, *COO*
Diane Brayton, *Exec VP*
Roland A Caputo, *CFO*
EMP: 277
SQ FT: 828,000
SALES: 1.6B **Publicly Held**
WEB: www.nytco.com
SIC: 2711 4832 4833 7383 Newspapers, publishing & printing; radio broadcasting stations; television broadcasting stations; news feature syndicate; information retrieval services

(G-10945)
NEW YORK TIMES COMPANY
Also Called: Timesdigest
620 8th Ave Fl 9 (10018-1618)
PHONE.................................212 556-1200
Tom Brady, *Branch Mgr*
EMP: 7
SALES (corp-wide): 1.6B **Publicly Held**
SIC: 2741 Miscellaneous publishing
PA: The New York Times Company
620 8th Ave
New York NY 10018
212 556-1234

(G-10946)
NEW YORK TIMES COMPANY
Also Called: Times Center, The
620 8th Ave Bsmt 1 (10018-1604)
PHONE.................................212 556-4300
Melanie Masserant, *Branch Mgr*
EMP: 12
SALES (corp-wide): 1.6B **Publicly Held**
SIC: 2711 Newspapers, publishing & printing
PA: The New York Times Company
620 8th Ave
New York NY 10018
212 556-1234

(G-10947)
NEW YORK UNIVERSITY
Also Called: Washington Square News
7 E 12th St Ste 800 (10003-4475)
PHONE.................................212 998-4300
David Cosgrove, *General Mgr*
Billie Gastic, *Dean*
Jasmina Husovic, *Facilities Mgr*
Sage Morison, *Research*
Christopher Nightingale, *Research*
EMP: 25
SQ FT: 7,410
SALES (corp-wide): 8.5B **Privately Held**
WEB: www.nyu.edu
SIC: 2711 8221 Newspapers, publishing & printing; university
PA: New York University
70 Washington Sq S
New York NY 10012
212 998-1212

(G-10948)
NEW YORK1 NEWS OPERATIONS
75 9th Ave Frnt 6 (10011-7033)
PHONE.................................212 379-3311
Steve Paulus, *CEO*
EMP: 12
SALES (est): 724.1K **Privately Held**
SIC: 2711 Newspapers, publishing & printing

(G-10949)
NEWBAY MEDIA LLC (HQ)
28 E 28th St Fl 12 (10016-7959)
PHONE.................................212 378-0400
Steve Palm, *CEO*
Sarah Jones, *Editor*
Garen Sahagian, *Editor*
Adam Goldstein, *Exec VP*
Carmel King, *Exec VP*
EMP: 75
SALES (est): 64.2MM
SALES (corp-wide): 108.3MM **Privately Held**
WEB: www.nbmedia.com
SIC: 2741 Miscellaneous publishing
PA: Future Plc
Quay House
Bath BA1 1
122 544-2244

(G-10950)
NEWPORT GRAPHICS INC
121 Varick St Rm 302 (10013-1408)
PHONE.................................212 924-2600
John Di Somma, *President*
Michael Paulmasano, *Vice Pres*
EMP: 30 EST: 1971
SQ FT: 10,000
SALES (est): 3MM **Privately Held**
WEB: www.newportgraphics.com
SIC: 2752 2789 Commercial printing, offset; bookbinding & related work

▲ = Import ▼ = Export
◆ = Import/Export

GEOGRAPHIC SECTION

New York - New York County (G-10975)

(G-10951)
NEWS COMMUNICATIONS INC (PA)
501 Madison Ave Fl 23 (10022-5608)
PHONE.................................212 689-2500
James A Finkelstein, *Ch of Bd*
Jerry A Finkelstein, *Ch of Bd*
E Paul Leishman, *CFO*
EMP: 11
SQ FT: 2,900
SALES (est): 8.9MM **Privately Held**
WEB: www.thehill.com
SIC: 2711 Newspapers: publishing only, not printed on site

(G-10952)
NEWS CORPORATION (PA)
1211 Ave Of The Americas (10036-8701)
PHONE.................................212 416-3400
Robert J Thomson, *CEO*
K Rupert Murdoch, *Ch of Bd*
Lachlan K Murdoch, *Ch of Bd*
Susan Panuccio, *CFO*
David B Pitofsky, *Ch Credit Ofcr*
EMP: 217
SALES: 9B **Publicly Held**
SIC: 2731 7375 2711 Book publishing; on-line data base information retrieval; newspapers, publishing & printing

(G-10953)
NEWS INDIA USA LLC
Also Called: News India Times
37 W 20th St Ste 1109 (10011-3749)
PHONE.................................212 675-7515
Shomik Chaudhuri, *Adv Dir*
Dr Sudhir Parikh,
EMP: 8
SALES: 600K **Privately Held**
SIC: 2711 Commercial printing & newspaper publishing combined

(G-10954)
NEWS INDIA USA INC
Also Called: News India Times
37 W 20th St Ste 1109 (10011-3749)
PHONE.................................212 675-7515
Veena Merchant, *President*
Prakash Parekh, *Mktg Dir*
Vikram Chatwal, *Director*
Dr Bhupendra Patel, *Director*
EMP: 15
SQ FT: 6,000
SALES: 720K **Privately Held**
SIC: 2711 2731 2791 Newspapers, publishing & printing; books: publishing & printing; typesetting

(G-10955)
NEWS/SPRTS MICROWAVE RENTL INC
Also Called: NSM Surveillance
415 Madison Ave Fl 11 (10017-7930)
PHONE.................................619 670-0572
Andrew R Berdy, *President*
Carlos Arnero, *COO*
EMP: 35
SQ FT: 10,000
SALES (est): 5MM **Privately Held**
WEB: www.nsmsurveillance.com
SIC: 3699 Security devices; security control equipment & systems
PA: Solutionpoint International, Inc.
415 Madison Ave Fl 11
New York NY 10017

(G-10956)
NEWSWEEK LLC
7 Hanover Sq Fl 5 (10004-2636)
PHONE.................................646 867-7100
Etienne Uzac, *President*
Malcolm Magri, *Comptroller*
Mark Lappin, *Comms Dir*
Bill Powell, *Software Engr*
Sarah Hayes, *Director*
EMP: 6 **EST:** 2013
SALES (est): 92.2K **Privately Held**
SIC: 2711 Newspapers: publishing only, not printed on site

(G-10957)
NEWSWEEK MEDIA GROUP INC (PA)
Also Called: International Business Times
7 Hanover Sq Fl 5 (10004-2636)
PHONE.................................646 867-7100
Etienne Uzac, *President*
Alan Press, *President*
Mitchell Caplan, *Chief Mktg Ofcr*
EMP: 46
SQ FT: 50,000
SALES (est): 27MM **Privately Held**
SIC: 2741

(G-10958)
NEXT BIG SOUND INC
125 Park Ave Fl 19 (10017-8545)
PHONE.................................646 657-9837
Alex White, *CEO*
David Hoffman, *Founder*
Samir Rayani, *Founder*
Yu-Ting Lin, *VP Finance*
Jay Troop, *Analyst*
EMP: 6 **EST:** 2008
SALES (est): 1MM **Privately Held**
SIC: 3695 Magnetic & optical recording media

(G-10959)
NEXT POTENTIAL LLC
Also Called: Nextpotential
278 E 10th St Apt 5b (10009-4868)
PHONE.................................401 742-5190
Jack Blanchette, *President*
John Blanchette, *Principal*
EMP: 6
SALES (est): 466.8K **Privately Held**
SIC: 2819 Catalysts, chemical

(G-10960)
NFE MANAGEMENT LLC
1345 Ave Of The Americas (10105-0302)
PHONE.................................212 798-6100
Joseph Adams Jr, *President*
Demetrios Tserpelis, *Principal*
Kenneth Nicholson, *COO*
Cameron Macdougall, *Admin Sec*
Rosario Lualhati, *Administration*
EMP: 15
SQ FT: 2,038,200
SALES (est): 1MM **Privately Held**
SIC: 1321 Natural gas liquids

(G-10961)
NICHE MEDIA HOLDINGS LLC (HQ)
Also Called: Greengale Publishing
257 Park Ave S Fl 5 (10010-7304)
PHONE.................................702 990-2500
Jonathan Kushnir, *CFO*
EMP: 26
SALES (est): 27.9MM
SALES (corp-wide): 41MM **Privately Held**
SIC: 2721 Magazines: publishing & printing
PA: Dickey Publishing, Inc.
3280 Peachtree Rd Ne S
Atlanta GA 30305
404 949-0700

(G-10962)
NICHOLAS KIRKWOOD LLC (PA)
807 Washington St (10014-1557)
PHONE.................................646 559-5239
Marell Battle, *Manager*
EMP: 8
SALES (est): 21.3MM **Privately Held**
SIC: 3144 3143 Women's footwear, except athletic; men's footwear, except athletic

(G-10963)
NICK LUGO INC
Also Called: La Voz Hispana
159 E 116th St Fl 2 (10029-1399)
PHONE.................................212 348-2100
Nick Lugo, *President*
EMP: 12
SALES (est): 449.4K **Privately Held**
SIC: 2711 Newspapers

(G-10964)
NICKELODEON MAGAZINES INC (HQ)
1633 Broadway Fl 7 (10019-7637)
PHONE.................................212 541-1949
Herb Scannell, *President*
Brian Robbins, *President*
Jeff Dunn, *COO*
Dan Sullivan, *Senior VP*
Martha Ribeiro, *Director*
EMP: 3
SALES (est): 4.2MM
SALES (corp-wide): 13.2B **Publicly Held**
SIC: 2721 Magazines: publishing, not printed on site
PA: Viacom Inc.
1515 Broadway
New York NY 10036
212 258-6000

(G-10965)
NICOLO RAINERI
Also Called: Nicolo Raineri Jeweler
82 Bowery (10013-4656)
PHONE.................................212 925-6128
Nicolo Raineri, *Owner*
Daniel Levi, *IT/INT Sup*
▲ **EMP:** 6
SQ FT: 3,000
SALES (est): 623.4K **Privately Held**
WEB: www.rainerijewelers.com
SIC: 3911 5944 Jewelry, precious metal; jewelry, precious stones & precious metals

(G-10966)
NIGHTINGALE FOOD ENTPS INC
2306 1st Ave (10035-4304)
PHONE.................................347 577-1630
Constantinos Kotjias, *Ch of Bd*
▼ **EMP:** 4
SALES: 1.5MM **Privately Held**
SIC: 2051 Bread, cake & related products

(G-10967)
NIKE INC
21 Mercer St Frnt A (10013-2771)
PHONE.................................212 226-5433
Wil Whitney, *Branch Mgr*
Darah Ross, *Manager*
EMP: 38
SALES (corp-wide): 36.4B **Publicly Held**
WEB: www.nike.com
SIC: 3021 Rubber & plastics footwear
PA: Nike, Inc.
1 Sw Bowerman Dr
Beaverton OR 97005
503 671-6453

(G-10968)
NIKKEI AMERICA INC (HQ)
1325 Avenue Of The Americ (10019-6055)
PHONE.................................212 261-6200
Hisao Tonedachi, *President*
Hiro Aki Honda, *Exec VP*
Yihsuan Wu, *Asst Mgr*
EMP: 40
SQ FT: 33,000
SALES (est): 6.9MM
SALES (corp-wide): 3.2B **Privately Held**
WEB: www.nikkeius.com
SIC: 2711 Newspapers: publishing & printing
PA: Nikkei Inc.
1-3-7, Otemachi
Chiyoda-Ku TKY 100-0
332 700-251

(G-10969)
NIKKEI AMERICA HOLDINGS INC (HQ)
1325 Avenue Of The Americ (10019-6055)
PHONE.................................212 261-6200
Kiyoshi Hasegawa, *President*
Fumiko Tanaka, *Vice Pres*
EMP: 60
SQ FT: 33,000
SALES: 27MM
SALES (corp-wide): 3.2B **Privately Held**
WEB: www.nikkei.com
SIC: 2711 Newspapers, publishing & printing
PA: Nikkei Inc.
1-3-7, Otemachi
Chiyoda-Ku TKY 100-0
332 700-251

(G-10970)
NIMBLETV INC
450 Fashion Ave Fl 43 (10123-4399)
PHONE.................................646 502-7010
Anand Subramanian, *CEO*
Peter Von Schlossberg, *President*
Paul George, *CTO*
EMP: 12
SALES (est): 831.1K
SALES (corp-wide): 140MM **Publicly Held**
SIC: 2741
PA: Synacor, Inc.
40 La Riviere Dr Ste 300
Buffalo NY 14202
716 853-1362

(G-10971)
NINE WEST HOLDINGS INC
Jones New York
1411 Broadway Fl 38 (10018-3409)
PHONE.................................212 642-3860
Gail Onorato, *Principal*
Christine Bender, *Vice Pres*
Andy Cho, *Vice Pres*
Steffie Kirschner, *Vice Pres*
Gary Mansfield, *Vice Pres*
EMP: 6
SALES (corp-wide): 2.2B **Privately Held**
WEB: www.jny.com
SIC: 2339 Sportswear, women's
HQ: Nine West Holdings, Inc.
180 Rittenhouse Cir
Bristol PA 19007
215 785-4000

(G-10972)
NINE WEST HOLDINGS INC
1411 Broadway (10018-3496)
PHONE.................................212 642-3860
Wesley Card, *Branch Mgr*
EMP: 120
SALES (corp-wide): 2.2B **Privately Held**
SIC: 2337 Women's & misses' suits & coats
HQ: Nine West Holdings, Inc.
180 Rittenhouse Cir
Bristol PA 19007
215 785-4000

(G-10973)
NINE WEST HOLDINGS INC
1411 Broadway Fl 15 (10018-3471)
PHONE.................................212 391-5000
Chris Zimmer, *Branch Mgr*
EMP: 6
SALES (corp-wide): 2.2B **Privately Held**
WEB: www.ninewest.com
SIC: 2335 Retail Womens Apparel
HQ: Nine West Holdings, Inc.
180 Rittenhouse Cir
Bristol PA 19007
215 785-4000

(G-10974)
NINE WEST HOLDINGS INC
Jones New York
1411 Broadway Fl 38 (10018-3409)
PHONE.................................212 221-6376
Lynne Fish, *Manager*
EMP: 7
SALES (corp-wide): 2.2B **Privately Held**
WEB: www.jny.com
SIC: 2339 Women's & misses' athletic clothing & sportswear
HQ: Nine West Holdings, Inc.
180 Rittenhouse Cir
Bristol PA 19007
215 785-4000

(G-10975)
NINE WEST HOLDINGS INC
Also Called: Jones New York
1441 Broadway Fl 20 (10018-1905)
PHONE.................................212 575-2571
Jack Gross, *Branch Mgr*
EMP: 7

New York - New York County (G-10976)

SALES (corp-wide): 2.2B Privately Held
WEB: www.jny.com
SIC: 2329 2339 Men's & boys' sportswear & athletic clothing; women's & misses' athletic clothing & sportswear
HQ: Nine West Holdings, Inc.
180 Rittenhouse Cir
Bristol PA 19007
215 785-4000

(G-10976)
NINE WEST HOLDINGS INC
1411 Broadway Fl 15 (10018-3471)
PHONE..................212 642-3860
Carla Del, Branch Mgr
EMP: 6
SALES (corp-wide): 2.2B Privately Held
SIC: 3144 Women's footwear, except athletic
HQ: Nine West Holdings, Inc.
180 Rittenhouse Cir
Bristol PA 19007
215 785-4000

(G-10977)
NINE WEST HOLDINGS INC
Also Called: Jones New York
575 Fashion Ave Frnt 1 (10018-1886)
PHONE..................212 642-3860
Charles Hostepler, President
Lisa Garson, Branch Mgr
EMP: 22
SALES (corp-wide): 2.2B Privately Held
WEB: www.jny.com
SIC: 2339 Sportswear, women's
HQ: Nine West Holdings, Inc.
180 Rittenhouse Cir
Bristol PA 19007
215 785-4000

(G-10978)
NINE WEST HOLDINGS INC
Jones New York
1441 Broadway (10018-1905)
PHONE..................212 822-1300
EMP: 22
SALES (corp-wide): 2.2B Privately Held
SIC: 2339 Jeans: women's, misses' & juniors'
HQ: Nine West Holdings, Inc.
180 Rittenhouse Cir
Bristol PA 19007
215 785-4000

(G-10979)
NINE WEST HOLDINGS INC
Also Called: Jones New York
1441 Broadway Fl 10 (10018-1905)
PHONE..................215 785-4000
EMP: 22
SALES (corp-wide): 2.2B Privately Held
SIC: 2339 Women's & misses' athletic clothing & sportswear
HQ: Nine West Holdings, Inc.
180 Rittenhouse Cir
Bristol PA 19007
215 785-4000

(G-10980)
NLR COUNTER TOPS LLC
902 E 92nd St (10128)
PHONE..................347 295-0410
AVI Harel, Mng Member
EMP: 5
SALES (est): 467.8K Privately Held
SIC: 2541 5211 5084 Counter & sink tops; counter tops; countersinks

(G-10981)
NO LONGER EMPTY INC
122 W 27th St Fl 10 (10001-6227)
PHONE..................202 413-4262
Carol Stakenas, Exec Dir
Naomi Ringskog, Exec Dir
EMP: 6 EST: 2012
SALES: 680.6K Privately Held
SIC: 3812 Aircraft/aerospace flight instruments & guidance systems

(G-10982)
NOAH ENTERPRISES LTD (PA)
520 8th Ave Lbby 2 (10018-6590)
PHONE..................212 736-2888
Sam Noah, President
▲ EMP: 20
SQ FT: 12,000
SALES (est): 1.3MM Privately Held
WEB: www.noahenterprises.com
SIC: 2339 5137 Sportswear, women's; sportswear, women's & children's

(G-10983)
NOCHAIRS INC
325 W 38th St Rm 310 (10018-9664)
PHONE..................917 748-8731
Anthony Lilore, President
Celeste Lilore, Vice Pres
EMP: 2
SQ FT: 1,100
SALES: 1MM Privately Held
SIC: 2211 2259 5199 Bags & bagging, cotton; bags & bagging, knit; bags, textile

(G-10984)
NOETIC PARTNERS INC
445 Park Ave Frnt 1 (10022-8600)
PHONE..................212 836-4351
Justin Magruder, President
Tracy Sennett, Business Mgr
Azmat Mohammed, Consultant
EMP: 15
SQ FT: 300
SALES: 2.7MM Privately Held
SIC: 7372 5734 Business oriented computer software; software, business & non-game

(G-10985)
NOHO HEALTH INC
Also Called: Care/of
9 Great Jones St Apt 4 (10012-1164)
PHONE..................877 227-3631
David Elbert, CEO
EMP: 48 EST: 2015
SALES (est): 1.9MM Privately Held
SIC: 2834 Pharmaceutical preparations

(G-10986)
NOIR JEWELRY LLC
358 5th Ave Rm 501 (10001-2228)
PHONE..................212 465-8500
Shaya Reiter, CEO
EMP: 6
SQ FT: 10,000
SALES: 580.2K
SALES (corp-wide): 14.3MM Privately Held
SIC: 3961 Costume jewelry
PA: International Inspirations, Ltd.
358 5th Ave Rm 501
New York NY 10001
212 465-8500

(G-10987)
NOODLE EDUCATION INC
59 Charles St Suite200 (10014-2625)
PHONE..................646 289-7800
John Katzman, CEO
Gregory O'Brien, COO
Aryeh Morris, Vice Pres
Mindy Sinyak, Vice Pres
Jason Isaacs, Opers Staff
EMP: 20
SALES (est): 3.2MM Privately Held
SIC: 2098 Noodles (e.g. egg, plain & water), dry

(G-10988)
NORDIC PRESS INC
243 E 34th St (10016-4852)
PHONE..................212 686-3356
Denis Mets, President
Kart Ulman, Editor
Anne Karu, Administration
EMP: 5
SALES (est): 210K Privately Held
WEB: www.metronome.com
SIC: 2711 Newspapers: publishing only, not printed on site

(G-10989)
NORFALCO LLC
330 Madison Ave Fl 7 (10017-5040)
PHONE..................416 775-1431
Paul Shaw, President
◆ EMP: 10
SALES: 119.8MM
SALES (corp-wide): 205.4B Privately Held
SIC: 2819 Sulfuric acid, oleum

HQ: Glencore Ltd.
330 Madison Ave
New York NY 10017
646 949-2500

(G-10990)
NORTH AMERICAN BEAR CO INC
1261 Broadway Rm 815 (10001-3532)
PHONE..................212 388-0700
Barbara Iserberg, Sales/Mktg Mgr
EMP: 10
SALES (corp-wide): 3.9MM Privately Held
WEB: www.nabear.com
SIC: 3942 Stuffed toys, including animals
PA: North American Bear Co., Inc.
1200 W 35th St
Chicago IL 60609
773 376-3457

(G-10991)
NORTH AMERICAN GRAPHICS INC
150 Varick St Rm 303 (10013-1218)
PHONE..................212 725-2200
Arthur Ascher, President
EMP: 10
SQ FT: 2,500
SALES (est): 1.2MM Privately Held
SIC: 2759 7336 Commercial printing; graphic arts & related design

(G-10992)
NORTH AMERICAN MILLS INC
Also Called: Chams
1370 Broadway Rm 1101 (10018-7826)
PHONE..................212 695-6146
▲ EMP: 15
SQ FT: 6,600
SALES (est): 1MM Privately Held
SIC: 2329 Mfg Men's/Boy's Clothing

(G-10993)
NORTH EASTERN FABRICATORS INC
Also Called: Great Gates Etc
910 Park Ave Ph Ph (10075-0277)
PHONE..................718 542-0450
Gerald Cohen, President
John Fisher, Vice Pres
▲ EMP: 20 EST: 1932
SQ FT: 10,000
SALES (est): 3.4MM Privately Held
SIC: 3441 Fabricated structural metal

(G-10994)
NORTH SIX INC
159 Bleecker St Frnt A (10012-1457)
PHONE..................212 463-7227
Oliver Hicks, President
EMP: 12
SALES (est): 10.5MM Privately Held
SIC: 2759 7812 Commercial printing; motion picture & video production

(G-10995)
NORTH-SOUTH BOOKS INC
600 3rd Ave Fl 2 (10016-1919)
PHONE..................212 706-4545
Davy Sidjanski, CEO
David Reuther, President
▲ EMP: 25
SQ FT: 11,000
SALES (est): 1.5MM Privately Held
WEB: www.northsouth.com
SIC: 2731 5192 Books: publishing only; books

(G-10996)
NORTHPOINT DIGITAL LLC
1540 Broadway Fl 41 (10036-4039)
PHONE..................212 819-1700
Richard Cooley, Managing Prtnr
Jeffrey Penner, Partner
Andree Engelhardt, Business Mgr
Edwin Pacheco, Human Res Mgr
Arwin Holmes, Sr Project Mgr
EMP: 8 EST: 2015
SALES (est): 191.4K Privately Held
SIC: 3571 Computers, digital, analog or hybrid

(G-10997)
NORTHPOINT TRADING INC (PA)
347 5th Ave (10016-5010)
PHONE..................212 481-8001
Abe Kassin, President
Isaac Kassin, Vice Pres
Jacob Kassin, Regl Sales Mgr
◆ EMP: 10
SQ FT: 4,000
SALES (est): 28.6MM Privately Held
SIC: 2273 2211 2392 6512 Carpets & rugs; handkerchief fabrics, cotton; blankets, comforters & beddings; shopping center, property operation only

(G-10998)
NORTHWEST URGENT CARE
2628 Broadway (10025-5005)
PHONE..................646 870-6406
EMP: 8
SALES (corp-wide): 4.1MM Privately Held
SIC: 3131 Uppers
PA: Northwest Urgent Care Phase Ii Llc
5555 Glenridge Connector # 700
Atlanta GA 30342
360 799-3912

(G-10999)
NOVA INC
362 5th Ave Ste 1001 (10001-2251)
PHONE..................212 967-1139
Vinod Jain, CEO
Berry Nooj, President
▲ EMP: 8
SQ FT: 1,300
SALES (est): 680.5K Privately Held
SIC: 2752 7389 Offset & photolithographic printing; automobile recovery service

(G-11000)
NOVARTIS PHARMACEUTICALS CORP
230 Park Ave (10169-0005)
PHONE..................888 669-6682
Richard Pulik, Vice Pres
Marcus Calendrillo, Marketing Staff
Jaclyn Feeley, Branch Mgr
EMP: 5
SALES (corp-wide): 49.1B Privately Held
SIC: 2834 Pharmaceutical preparations
HQ: Novartis Pharmaceuticals Corporation
1 Health Plz
East Hanover NJ 07936
862 778-8300

(G-11001)
NOVEN PHARMACEUTICALS INC
350 5th Ave Ste 3700 (10118-3799)
PHONE..................212 682-4420
Jeffrey F Eisenberg, CEO
Saima Siddiqui, Project Mgr
EMP: 32
SQ FT: 25,000
SALES (corp-wide): 1.3B Privately Held
SIC: 2834 Pharmaceutical preparations
HQ: Noven Pharmaceuticals, Inc.
11960 Sw 144th St
Miami FL 33186
305 964-3393

(G-11002)
NR FRAGRANCES & COSMETICS INC
1220 Broadway Rm 700 (10001-4312)
PHONE..................212 686-4006
Khalid Raja, President
EMP: 2
SALES (est): 3.8MM Privately Held
SIC: 2844 Concentrates, perfume

(G-11003)
NSGV INC
90 5th Ave (10011-7629)
PHONE..................212 367-3167
Malcolm Forbes, Branch Mgr
Josh Robinson, Director
EMP: 20

SALES (corp-wide): 181.1MM **Privately Held**
WEB: www.forbes.com
SIC: 2721 6282 6552 Magazines: publishing only, not printed on site; investment advisory service; subdividers & developers
HQ: Nsgv Inc.
499 Washington Blvd Fl 9
Jersey City NJ 07310
212 620-2200

(G-11004)
NSGV INC
Also Called: American Heritage Magazine
90 5th Ave (10011-7629)
PHONE.....................212 367-3100
Malcolm S Forbes Jr, *Ch of Bd*
Jeff Reilly, *Branch Mgr*
EMP: 50
SALES (corp-wide): 181.1MM **Privately Held**
WEB: www.forbes.com
SIC: 2721 Magazines: publishing only, not printed on site
HQ: Nsgv Inc.
499 Washington Blvd Fl 9
Jersey City NJ 07310
212 620-2200

(G-11005)
NUCARE PHARMACY INC
Also Called: Nucare Pharmacy & Surgical
1789 1st Ave (10128-6901)
PHONE.....................212 426-9300
Harry Wivietsky, *President*
Russell Shvartsshteyn, *Vice Pres*
EMP: 14
SQ FT: 2,100
SALES (est): 3MM **Privately Held**
WEB: www.mynucare.com
SIC: 3842 5912 Surgical appliances & supplies; drug stores & proprietary stores

(G-11006)
NUCARE PHARMACY WEST LLC
Also Called: Nucare Pharmacy & Surgical
250 9th Ave (10001-6602)
PHONE.....................212 462-2525
Robert Marchini, *Mng Member*
Rob Marchini, *Mng Member*
Russell Shavartsshtyn,
Harry Wivietsky,
EMP: 11
SALES (est): 1.5MM **Privately Held**
WEB: www.mynucare.com
SIC: 3842 5912 Surgical appliances & supplies; drug stores & proprietary stores

(G-11007)
NUMERIX LLC (PA)
99 Park Ave Fl 5 (10016-1360)
PHONE.....................212 302-2220
Steven R O'Hanlon, *CEO*
Gregory Whitten, *Chairman*
EMP: 90
SQ FT: 31,650
SALES: 67.3MM **Privately Held**
SIC: 7372 Business oriented computer software

(G-11008)
NUTRACEUTICAL WELLNESS LLC
Also Called: Nutrafol
28 W 27th St Fl 2 (10001-6941)
PHONE.....................888 454-3320
Giorgos Tsetis, *CEO*
Roland Peralta, *President*
EMP: 8
SQ FT: 1,000
SALES (est): 900K **Privately Held**
SIC: 2834 Vitamin preparations

(G-11009)
NUTRAQUEEN LLC
138 E 34th St Apt 2f (10016-4773)
PHONE.....................347 368-6568
Silvia Demeter, *CEO*
EMP: 12
SALES (est): 909.2K **Privately Held**
WEB: www.nutraqueen.com
SIC: 2833 Vitamins, natural or synthetic: bulk, uncompounded

(G-11010)
NUTRIFAST LLC
244 5th Ave Ste W249 (10001-7604)
PHONE.....................347 671-3181
Andres Ballares,
EMP: 10 EST: 2013
SALES (est): 548.4K **Privately Held**
SIC: 2024 Ice cream & frozen desserts

(G-11011)
NY DENIM INC
1407 Broadway Rm 1021 (10018-3256)
PHONE.....................212 764-6668
EMP: 10
SALES (est): 720K **Privately Held**
SIC: 2253 Knit Outerwear Mills

(G-11012)
NYC DISTRICT COUNCIL UBCJA
395 Hudson St Lbby 3 (10014-7450)
PHONE.....................212 366-7500
Michael Forde, *Principal*
EMP: 2
SALES: 27.9MM **Privately Held**
SIC: 3423 Carpenters' hand tools, except saws: levels, chisels, etc.

(G-11013)
NYC IDOL APPAREL INC
214 W 39th St Rm 807 (10018-4455)
PHONE.....................212 997-9797
David Shaaya, *President*
▲ EMP: 4 EST: 2008
SQ FT: 700
SALES: 2MM **Privately Held**
SIC: 2329 2337 Down-filled clothing: men's & boys'; skirts, separate: women's, misses' & juniors'

(G-11014)
NYC KNITWEAR INC
525 Fashion Ave Rm 701 (10018-0473)
PHONE.....................212 840-1313
Jian Guo, *Chairman*
▲ EMP: 22
SQ FT: 13,000
SALES (est): 2.4MM **Privately Held**
SIC: 2331 Women's & misses' blouses & shirts

(G-11015)
NYLON LLC
Also Called: Nylon Magazine
110 Greene St Ste 607 (10012-3838)
PHONE.....................212 226-6454
Ben Barna, *Editor*
Yasmeen Gharnit, *Editor*
Sydney Gore, *Editor*
Keryce Henry, *Editor*
Marissa Smith, *Editor*
EMP: 20
SALES (est): 3.7MM **Privately Held**
WEB: www.nylonmag.com
SIC: 2721 Magazines: publishing only, not printed on site

(G-11016)
NYLON MEDIA INC (PA)
Also Called: Nylonshop
110 Greene St Ste 607 (10012-3838)
PHONE.....................212 226-6454
Paul Greenberg, *CEO*
Marc Luzzatto, *Ch of Bd*
Jamie Elden, *President*
Carrie S Reynolds, *President*
Melissa Giannini, *Editor*
EMP: 16
SALES (est): 5.8MM **Privately Held**
SIC: 2721 Magazines: publishing & printing

(G-11017)
NYMAN JEWELRY INC (PA)
66 W 9th St (10011-8972)
PHONE.....................212 944-1976
Corc Aydin, *President*
EMP: 6
SQ FT: 2,000
SALES (est): 558.2K **Privately Held**
SIC: 3915 5944 Gems, real & imitation: preparation for settings; jewelry stores

(G-11018)
NYP HOLDINGS INC (DH)
Also Called: New York Post
1211 Ave Of The Americas (10036-8790)
PHONE.....................212 997-9722
K Rupert Murdoch, *President*
Amanda Greenfield, *Vice Pres*
▲ EMP: 540
SALES (est): 170MM
SALES (corp-wide): 9B **Publicly Held**
WEB: www.nypost.com
SIC: 2711 Commercial printing & newspaper publishing combined
HQ: News Preferred Holdings Inc
20 Westport Rd
Wilton CT 06897
203 563-6483

(G-11019)
NYREV INC
Also Called: New York Review of Books
435 Hudson St Rm 300 (10014-3949)
P.O. Box 9310, Big Sandy TX (75755-3316)
PHONE.....................212 757-8070
Rae S Hederman, *Ch of Bd*
EMP: 35
SQ FT: 12,000
SALES: 93K **Privately Held**
WEB: www.nybooks.com
SIC: 2721 Magazines: publishing only, not printed on site

(G-11020)
NYS NYU-CNTR INTL COOPERATION
418 Lafayette St (10003-6947)
PHONE.....................212 998-3680
Chris Jones, *Director*
Noah Gall, *Assistant*
EMP: 30
SALES (est): 1.6MM **Privately Held**
SIC: 2759 Publication printing

(G-11021)
NYT CAPITAL LLC (HQ)
620 8th Ave (10018-1618)
PHONE.....................212 556-1234
Dave Frank, *Vice Pres*
EMP: 18
SALES: 43.2K
SALES (corp-wide): 1.6B **Publicly Held**
SIC: 2711 5192 5963 7322 Newspapers, publishing & printing; commercial printing & newspaper publishing combined; newspapers; newspapers, home delivery, not by printers or publishers: collection agency, except real estate; credit reporting services
PA: The New York Times Company
620 8th Ave
New York NY 10018
212 556-1234

(G-11022)
NYTIMES CORPORATE
620 8th Ave Fl 17 (10018-1618)
PHONE.....................212 556-1234
Ben Schott, *Principal*
Nick Dandrea, *Systems Dir*
EMP: 6 EST: 2009
SALES (est): 265.8K **Privately Held**
SIC: 2711 Newspapers, publishing & printing

(G-11023)
O VAL NICK MUSIC CO INC
254 W 72nd St Apt 1a (10023-2851)
PHONE.....................212 873-2179
Nicholas Ashford, *President*
EMP: 5
SALES (est): 231.8K **Privately Held**
SIC: 2741 Miscellaneous publishing

(G-11024)
OAKHURST PARTNERS LLC
Also Called: Amicale Cashmere
148 Madison Ave Fl 13 (10016-6772)
PHONE.....................212 502-3220
Boris Shlomm, *Mng Member*
Alexander Shlomm,
Daniel Shlomm,
▲ EMP: 5
SQ FT: 5,000
SALES (est): 822.1K **Privately Held**
SIC: 2231 Apparel & outerwear broadwoven fabrics

(G-11025)
OBSERVER MEDIA LLC
1 Whitehall St Fl 7 (10004-2109)
PHONE.....................212 755-2400
Joseph Meyer, *Principal*
Dan Entin, *Vice Pres*
Lauren Russell, *Marketing Mgr*
EMP: 22
SALES (est): 1.5MM **Privately Held**
SIC: 2711 Newspapers, publishing & printing

(G-11026)
OCCIDENTAL ENERGY MKTG INC
1230 Av Of The Amrcs 80 (10020-1513)
PHONE.....................212 632-4950
Francis Sheridan, *Manager*
EMP: 5
SALES (corp-wide): 13.2B **Publicly Held**
SIC: 1382 Oil & gas exploration services
HQ: Occidental Energy Marketing, Inc.
5 Greenway Plz Ste 110
Houston TX 77046
713 215-7000

(G-11027)
OCEAN WAVES SWIM LLC
19 W 34th St Fl 11 (10001-3075)
PHONE.....................212 967-4481
Eli Seruya,
Lisa Bailey,
▲ EMP: 7
SQ FT: 1,600
SALES (est): 507.5K **Privately Held**
SIC: 2339 Bathing suits: women's, misses' & juniors

(G-11028)
OCEANCONNECT MARINE INC (HQ)
330 Madison Ave (10017-5001)
PHONE.....................203 328-3117
Charles Badurski, *CEO*
EMP: 3 EST: 2010
SALES (est): 2.2MM
SALES (corp-wide): 205.4B **Privately Held**
SIC: 2869 Fuels
PA: Glencore Plc
Queensway House
Jersey JE1 1
870 707-4040

(G-11029)
OCI USA INC (PA)
660 Madison Ave Fl 19 (10065-8415)
PHONE.....................646 589-6180
Kevin Struve, *President*
▲ EMP: 8 EST: 2013
SALES (est): 2MM **Privately Held**
SIC: 2873 2861 Ammonium nitrate, ammonium sulfate; methanol, natural (wood alcohol)

(G-11030)
OCIP HOLDING LLC (PA)
660 Madison Ave Fl 19 (10065-8415)
PHONE.....................646 589-6180
Kevin Struve, *Manager*
EMP: 4 EST: 2014
SALES (est): 343.3MM **Privately Held**
SIC: 2861 2873 Methanol, natural (wood alcohol); ammonium nitrate, amrnonium sulfate

(G-11031)
OCTAVE MUSIC GROUP INC (DH)
850 3rd Ave Ste 15th (10022-6222)
PHONE.....................212 991-6540
Ross Honey, *President*
EMP: 2
SALES (est): 63.9MM
SALES (corp-wide): 95.2MM **Privately Held**
SIC: 3651 Household audio & video equipment

(G-11032)
ODY ACCESSORIES INC
1239 Broadway (10001-4311)
PHONE.....................212 239-0580
Michael Weiss, *President*
▲ EMP: 27

New York - New York County (G-11033)　　　　　　　　　　　　　　　　　　　　　　　　　　**GEOGRAPHIC SECTION**

SQ FT: 12,000
SALES (est): 3.6MM **Privately Held**
SIC: 2339 Women's & misses' accessories

(G-11033)
ODYSSEY MAG PUBG GROUP INC
4 New York Plz (10004-2413)
PHONE.................................212 545-4800
David J Pecker, *Principal*
EMP: 1
SALES (est): 2.8MM
SALES (corp-wide): 300MM **Privately Held**
SIC: 2721 Magazines: publishing & printing
PA: American Media, Inc.
　　1350 E Newport
　　Deerfield Beach FL 33442
　　212 545-4800

(G-11034)
OKEY ENTERPRISES INC
347 5th Ave Rm 1005 (10016-5033)
PHONE.................................212 213-2640
Felek Ozdemir Sitkiye, *Principal*
EMP: 9
SALES (est): 967K **Privately Held**
SIC: 2759 Screen printing

(G-11035)
OKRA ENERGY LLC
99 Jane St Apt 5d (10014-7230)
PHONE.................................206 495-7574
Louis Ravenet, *CEO*
Andrea Ravenet, *COO*
Donald Gongaware, *CTO*
EMP: 8
SALES (est): 1MM **Privately Held**
SIC: 1321 Natural gas liquids

(G-11036)
OLDCASTLE BUILDING ENVELOPE (HQ)
1350 Ave Of The Americas (10019-4702)
PHONE.................................212 957-5400
Melissa Wood, *Assistant*
EMP: 13 EST: 2014
SALES (est): 4.9MM
SALES (corp-wide): 29.7B **Privately Held**
SIC: 3231 Products of purchased glass
PA: Crh Public Limited Company
　　Stonemasons Way
　　Dublin 14
　　140 410-00

(G-11037)
OLYMPIC JEWELRY INC
62 W 47th St Ste 509 (10036-3201)
PHONE.................................212 768-7004
Roberto Ganz, *President*
Mike Genuth, *Vice Pres*
EMP: 4
SALES (est): 1.2MM **Privately Held**
SIC: 3873 5094 Watches, clocks, watchcases & parts; clocks, watches & parts

(G-11038)
OLYMPIC PRESS INC
950 3rd Ave Fl 7 (10022-2788)
PHONE.................................212 242-4934
Howard Bau, *President*
EMP: 15 EST: 1929
SALES (est): 1.5MM **Privately Held**
SIC: 2752 Commercial printing, offset

(G-11039)
OMRIX BIOPHARMACEUTICALS INC
1 Rckfller Ctr Ste 2322 (10020)
PHONE.................................908 218-0707
Robert Taub, *CEO*
Larry Ellberger, *Ch of Bd*
Nissim Mashiach, *President*
V Marc Droppert, *Exec VP*
Nanci Prado, *Vice Pres*
EMP: 212
SQ FT: 8,945
SALES (est): 13.7MM
SALES (corp-wide): 76.4B **Publicly Held**
WEB: www.omrix.com
SIC: 2836 Biological products, except diagnostic

HQ: Ethicon Inc.
　　Us Route 22
　　Somerville NJ 08876
　　732 524-0400

(G-11040)
OMX (US) INC
Also Called: Nasdaq Omx
140 Broadway Fl 25 (10005-1142)
PHONE.................................646 428-2800
Roland Tibell, *President*
Andrew Lacatena, *Opers Staff*
Diana Antuna, *Manager*
Lisa Carroll, *Associate Dir*
EMP: 1500
SQ FT: 50,000
SALES (est): 58.4MM **Privately Held**
SIC: 7372 Application computer software

(G-11041)
ON DEMAND BOOKS LLC
939 Lexington Ave (10065-5771)
PHONE.................................212 966-2222
Dane Neller,
Herbert Krippner,
EMP: 5
SALES (est): 923.8K **Privately Held**
WEB: www.ondemandbooks.com
SIC: 7372 Publishers' computer software

(G-11042)
ONE JEANSWEAR GROUP INC (DH)
Also Called: Jones Jeanswear Group
1441 Broadway (10018-1905)
PHONE.................................212 575-2571
Jack N Gross, *CEO*
Jeanise Vazquez, *Production*
Ira Margulies, *CFO*
Christopher R Cade, *Admin Sec*
▲ EMP: 300
SALES (est): 57.8MM
SALES (corp-wide): 2.2B **Privately Held**
WEB: www.jny.com
SIC: 2339 2325 Jeans: women's, misses' & juniors'; men's & boys' jeans & dungarees
HQ: Nine West Holdings, Inc.
　　180 Rittenhouse Cir
　　Bristol PA 19007
　　215 785-4000

(G-11043)
ONE STEP UP LTD (PA)
1412 Broadway Fl 3 (10018-3372)
PHONE.................................212 398-1110
Harry Adjmi, *President*
Tom Wentley, *Vice Pres*
Sandy Gewercman, *CFO*
▲ EMP: 81
SALES (est): 30.3MM **Privately Held**
SIC: 2339 2329 Women's & misses' athletic clothing & sportswear; men's & boys' sportswear & athletic clothing

(G-11044)
ONE-BLUE LLC
1350 Broadway Rm 1406 (10018-0926)
PHONE.................................212 223-4380
Roel Kramer, *CEO*
Tom Chen, *CFO*
William Lenihan, *Director*
Ashley Teitelbaum, *Executive Asst*
EMP: 7
SALES (est): 676.5K **Privately Held**
SIC: 7372 Application computer software

(G-11045)
ONIA LLC (PA)
10 E 40th St Fl 37 (10016-0301)
PHONE.................................646 701-0008
Kelly Sullivan, *Opers Staff*
Corey English, *Accounts Exec*
Allie Mintz, *Sales Staff*
Carl Cunow, *Mng Member*
Nathan Romano, *Mng Member*
▲ EMP: 20
SQ FT: 1,200
SALES (est): 3.1MM **Privately Held**
SIC: 2389 5136 5137 5139 Men's miscellaneous accessories; men's & boys' clothing; women's & children's clothing; shoes

(G-11046)
ONLY HEARTS LTD (PA)
134 W 37th St Fl 9 (10018-6946)
PHONE.................................212 268-0886
Jonathan Stewart, *President*
Tina Vito, *Opers Staff*
Carol Ottavino, *Bookkeeper*
Keili Leahy, *Accounts Exec*
EMP: 43
SQ FT: 4,000
SALES (est): 4.4MM **Privately Held**
SIC: 2341 5137 2339 Women's & children's underwear; women's & children's clothing; lingerie; women's & children's accessories; women's & misses' outerwear

(G-11047)
ONYX SOLAR GROUP LLC
79 Madison Ave Fl 8 (10016-7810)
PHONE.................................917 951-9732
David Mann, *Principal*
Diego Cuevas, *Vice Pres*
▲ EMP: 8
SALES (est): 960.8K **Privately Held**
SIC: 3674 Photovoltaic devices, solid state

(G-11048)
OPENFIN INC
25 Broadway Fl 9 (10004-1058)
PHONE.................................917 450-8822
Mazy Dar, *CEO*
Adam Toms, *CEO*
Fred Doerr, *President*
Chuck Doerr, *COO*
Steve Greenblatt, *Sales Staff*
EMP: 9
SQ FT: 1,500
SALES (est): 855.4K **Privately Held**
SIC: 7372 7371 Prepackaged software; custom computer programming services

(G-11049)
OPENROAD INTEGRATED MEDIA INC
180 Maiden Ln Ste 2803 (10038-4988)
PHONE.................................212 691-0900
Paul Slavin, *CEO*
Jane Friedman, *Ch of Bd*
Laura Ferguson, *Senior VP*
Jennifer Jackson, *Vice Pres*
Daniel Shemesh, *CFO*
EMP: 23
SALES (est): 2.8MM **Privately Held**
SIC: 2741 Miscellaneous publishing

(G-11050)
OPERATIVE MEDIA INC (DH)
6 E 32nd St Fl 3 (10016-5415)
PHONE.................................212 994-8930
Lorne Brown, *President*
Venugopal Goteti, *President*
Michael Leo, *Principal*
Paul Kind, *Vice Pres*
Kristina Kiki Burton, *Opers Staff*
EMP: 79
SALES (est): 49.4MM **Privately Held**
WEB: www.operative.com
SIC: 7372 Business oriented computer software
HQ: Sintec Media Ltd
　　21 Hefetzdi Nachum
　　Jerusalem
　　265 151-22

(G-11051)
OPHTHOTECH CORPORATION
1 Penn Plz Ste 3520 (10119-3501)
PHONE.................................212 845-8200
David R Guyer, *Ch of Bd*
Glenn P Sblendorio, *President*
Keith Westby, *COO*
Barbara A Wood, *Senior VP*
Tom Biancardi, *Vice Pres*
EMP: 156
SQ FT: 22,400
SALES (est): 50.9MM **Privately Held**
SIC: 2834 Pharmaceutical preparations

(G-11052)
OPPOSUITS USA INC
228 E 45th St Ste 9e (10017-3303)
PHONE.................................917 438-8878
Jelle Van Der Zwet, *President*
Manon Lisbet, *CFO*
EMP: 25

SALES: 6MM **Privately Held**
SIC: 2311 2337 Men's & boys' suits & coats; women's & misses' suits & skirts

(G-11053)
ORACLE CORPORATION
120 Park Ave Fl 26 (10017-5511)
PHONE.................................212 508-7700
Rob Bushell, *Manager*
Elena Bond, *Analyst*
EMP: 250
SALES (corp-wide): 39.8B **Publicly Held**
WEB: www.forcecapital.com
SIC: 7372 Business oriented computer software
PA: Oracle Corporation
　　500 Oracle Pkwy
　　Redwood City CA 94065
　　650 506-7000

(G-11054)
ORANGENIUS INC
79 Madison Ave Fl 4 (10016-7805)
PHONE.................................631 742-0648
Grace Cho, *CEO*
Chris Reed, *Counsel*
Nicole Martinez, *Manager*
Robert Schlackman, *CTO*
EMP: 16 EST: 2015
SALES (est): 552.3K **Privately Held**
SIC: 7372 Business oriented computer software

(G-11055)
ORBIS BRYNMORE LITHOGRAPHICS
1735 2nd Ave Frnt 1 (10128-3516)
PHONE.................................212 987-2100
Ceasar Romero, *President*
Anna Romero, *Admin Sec*
EMP: 8 EST: 1932
SALES (est): 1.1MM **Privately Held**
SIC: 2752 Commercial printing, offset

(G-11056)
ORCAM INC
16 Madison Sq W Fl 11 (10010-1629)
PHONE.................................800 713-3741
Rhys Filmer, *President*
Carlos Rodriguez, *Area Mgr*
Yonatan Wexler, *Exec VP*
Rami Yehuda, *Vice Pres*
Efrat Bartov, *Engineer*
EMP: 10
SALES (est): 685.5K **Privately Held**
SIC: 3842 Technical aids for the handicapped

(G-11057)
ORCHARD APPAREL GROUP LTD
212 W 35th St Fl 7 (10001-2508)
PHONE.................................212 268-8701
Robert Fox, *President*
EMP: 5
SALES (est): 349.1K
SALES (corp-wide): 51.2MM **Privately Held**
WEB: www.robertfox.com
SIC: 2331 Blouses, women's & juniors': made from purchased material
PA: Robert Fox Inc.
　　79 Main St
　　Mineola NY 11501
　　516 294-4873

(G-11058)
ORCHARD PLATFORM ADVISORS LLC
55 W 21st St Fl 2 (10010-6813)
PHONE.................................888 217-2718
Sarah Masters, *Mng Member*
EMP: 26
SALES (est): 1.2MM **Privately Held**
SIC: 7372 Prepackaged software

(G-11059)
ORCHID MANUFACTURING CO INC
Also Called: Jessica Michelle
77 W 55th St Apt 4k (10019-4920)
PHONE.................................212 840-5700
Michael Laufer, *Ch of Bd*
Michael H Laufer, *President*
Richard Weiss, *Controller*

GEOGRAPHIC SECTION

New York - New York County (G-11085)

EMP: 10 EST: 1983
SALES (est): 980K Privately Held
SIC: 2331 Women's & misses' blouses & shirts

(G-11060)
ORDERGROOVE INC
75 Broad St Fl 23 (10004-2487)
PHONE..................866 253-1261
Greg Alvo, *CEO*
Andrew Magne, *Partner*
Erin Rucker, *COO*
Dave Frechette, *Senior VP*
Stephanie Chan, *Vice Pres*
EMP: 25 EST: 2011
SALES (est): 3.2MM Privately Held
SIC: 7372 Business oriented computer software

(G-11061)
ORENS DAILY ROAST INC (PA)
12 E 46th St Fl 6 (10017-2418)
PHONE..................212 348-5400
Oren Bloostein, *President*
▲ EMP: 7
SQ FT: 400
SALES (est): 14.1MM Privately Held
SIC: 2095 5149 5499 Instant coffee; coffee, green or roasted; coffee

(G-11062)
ORPHEO USA CORP
315 Madison Ave Rm 2601 (10017-5410)
PHONE..................212 464-8255
Alain Eisenstein, *CEO*
Danelle Downer, *Train & Dev Mgr*
EMP: 5
SALES (est): 692.3K Privately Held
SIC: 3695 7371 Audio range tape, blank; computer software development & applications

(G-11063)
ORTHO MEDICAL PRODUCTS (PA)
315 E 83rd St (10028-4301)
P.O. Box 847617, Dallas TX (75284-7617)
PHONE..................212 879-3700
Jane Wilde, *President*
EMP: 22 EST: 1944
SQ FT: 7,500
SALES (est): 2.3MM Privately Held
SIC: 3841 3842 5999 Surgical & medical instruments; orthopedic appliances; orthopedic & prosthesis applications

(G-11064)
OS33 INC
16 W 22nd St Fl 6 (10010-5969)
PHONE..................708 336-3466
Jacob Kazakevich, *President*
Paul Angelides, *Vice Pres*
Aron Derstine, *Vice Pres*
Matt Haynes, *VP Opers*
Jennifer Schule, *Executive Asst*
EMP: 6
SALES (est): 4.3MM Privately Held
SIC: 7372 7371 Prepackaged software; computer software development; computer software development & applications; computer software systems analysis & design, custom
PA: Os33 Services Corp.
120 Wood Ave S Ste 505
Iselin NJ 08830
866 796-0310

(G-11065)
OSCAR HEYMAN & BROS INC (PA)
501 Madison Ave Fl 15 (10022-5676)
PHONE..................212 593-0400
Marvin Heyman, *President*
Adam Heyman, *Vice Pres*
Paul Howie, *Buyer*
Thomas Heyman, *Treasurer*
Whitney Wenk, *Sales Staff*
EMP: 50 EST: 1912
SQ FT: 12,000
SALES (est): 7MM Privately Held
WEB: www.oscarheyman.com
SIC: 3911 Jewelry, precious metal

(G-11066)
OSNAT GAD INC
Also Called: Ogi Limited
608 5th Ave Ste 609 (10020-2303)
PHONE..................212 957-0535
Osnat Gad, *President*
EMP: 7
SQ FT: 1,450
SALES (est): 955.1K Privately Held
WEB: www.ogi-ltd.com
SIC: 3911 Jewelry, precious metal

(G-11067)
OSPREY PUBLISHING INC
1385 Broadway Fl 5 (10018-6050)
PHONE..................212 419-5300
Rebecca Smart, *Principal*
▲ EMP: 9
SALES (est): 518K Privately Held
SIC: 2741 Miscellaneous publishing

(G-11068)
OTHER PRESS LLC
267 5th Ave Fl 6 (10016-7508)
PHONE..................212 414-0054
Judith Gurewich, *CEO*
Paul Kozlowski, *Publisher*
Bill Foo, *CFO*
Ed Sokolowski, *Controller*
Mindy Okura, *Marketing Mgr*
EMP: 8
SALES (est): 1.2MM Privately Held
WEB: www.otherpress.com
SIC: 2731 Books: publishing only

(G-11069)
OTIS ELEVATOR COMPANY
1 Penn Plz Ste 410 (10119-0499)
PHONE..................917 339-9600
Ben Petruzella, *Manager*
EMP: 33
SALES (corp-wide): 59.8B Publicly Held
SIC: 3534 1796 7699 Elevators & equipment; escalators, passenger & freight; walkways, moving; installing building equipment; elevator installation & conversion; miscellaneous building item repair services; elevators: inspection, service & repair
HQ: Otis Elevator Company
1 Carrier Pl
Farmington CT 06032
860 674-3000

(G-11070)
OVED MENS LLC
31 W 34th St Fl 4 (10001-3009)
PHONE..................212 563-4999
Isaac Oved, *Principal*
EMP: 20
SALES: 2MM Privately Held
SIC: 2321 Men's & boys' sports & polo shirts

(G-11071)
OVERTURE MEDIA INC
411 Lafayette St Ste 638 (10003-7032)
PHONE..................917 446-7455
Jared Weiss, *CEO*
EMP: 7 EST: 2014
SQ FT: 153
SALES (est): 345.4K Privately Held
SIC: 7372 Prepackaged software

(G-11072)
OVID THERAPEUTICS INC
1460 Broadway Fl 4 (10036-7328)
PHONE..................646 661-7661
Jeremy M Levin, *Ch of Bd*
Matthew During, *President*
Amit Rakhit, *Chief*
Timothy Daly, *Senior VP*
Dirk Haasner, *Senior VP*
EMP: 43
SALES (est): 6.9MM Privately Held
SIC: 2834 Pharmaceutical preparations

(G-11073)
OWENS TABLE MIXERS LLC
250 Mercer St Apt C616 (10012-6123)
PHONE..................650 303-7342
Tyler Holland, *CEO*
EMP: 5
SALES (est): 359.2K Privately Held
SIC: 2086 Bottled & canned soft drinks

(G-11074)
OXFORD BOOK COMPANY INC
9 Pine St (10005-4701)
PHONE..................212 227-2120
William Dinger, *President*
EMP: 150
SALES (est): 5.2MM
SALES (corp-wide): 61.1MM Privately Held
WEB: www.sadlier.com
SIC: 2731 Textbooks: publishing only, not printed on site
PA: William H. Sadlier, Inc.
9 Pine St
New York NY 10005
212 233-3646

(G-11075)
OXFORD CLEANERS
847 Lexington Ave Frnt (10065-6636)
PHONE..................212 734-0006
Joong Lee, *Owner*
EMP: 5
SALES (est): 280K Privately Held
SIC: 3589 7215 Commercial cleaning equipment; coin-operated laundries & cleaning

(G-11076)
OXFORD INDUSTRIES INC
Also Called: Lanier Clothes
600 5th Ave Fl 12 (10020-2325)
PHONE..................212 247-7712
Greg Love, *Vice Pres*
Tracy Hunt, *Accounting Mgr*
Alan Rubin, *Branch Mgr*
Tim Brown, *Manager*
Elissa Golub, *Admin Asst*
EMP: 25
SALES (corp-wide): 1B Publicly Held
SIC: 2329 Athletic (warmup, sweat & jogging) suits: men's & boys'
PA: Oxford Industries, Inc.
999 Peachtree St Ne # 688
Atlanta GA 30309
404 659-2424

(G-11077)
OXFORD INDUSTRIES INC
25 W 39th St (10018-3805)
PHONE..................212 840-2288
Fran Hicks, *Manager*
EMP: 14
SALES (corp-wide): 1B Publicly Held
WEB: www.oxm.com
SIC: 2321 Men's & boys' furnishings
PA: Oxford Industries, Inc.
999 Peachtree St Ne # 688
Atlanta GA 30309
404 659-2424

(G-11078)
OXFORD UNIVERSITY PRESS LLC (HQ)
Also Called: Oxford University Press USA
198 Madison Ave Fl 8 (10016-4308)
PHONE..................212 726-6000
Niko Pfund, *President*
Joan Bossert, *Publisher*
Vineeta Gupta, *Publisher*
Sharon Sargent, *Publisher*
Laura Pearson, *General Mgr*
◆ EMP: 265 EST: 1973
SQ FT: 145,000
SALES (est): 140.9MM
SALES (corp-wide): 1.5B Privately Held
SIC: 2731 5961 Books: publishing only; book & record clubs
PA: University Of Oxford
University Offices
Oxford OXON OX1 2
186 527-0000

(G-11079)
OXFORD UNIVERSITY PRESS LLC
Chancellor Masters & Scholrs
198 Madison Ave Fl 8 (10016-4308)
PHONE..................212 726-6000
Giles Kerr, *Finance*
EMP: 8
SALES (corp-wide): 1.5B Privately Held
SIC: 2731 5961 Book publishing; book & record clubs

HQ: Oxford University Press, Llc
198 Madison Ave Fl 8
New York NY 10016
212 726-6000

(G-11080)
OXO INTERNATIONAL INC
601 W 26th St Rm 1050 (10001-1148)
PHONE..................212 242-3333
Alex Lee, *President*
Michael Delevante, *Vice Pres*
Tiffany Chen, *Engineer*
Jeff Doong, *Engineer*
Mark Drayer, *Engineer*
▲ EMP: 110
SQ FT: 2,500
SALES (est): 14MM Privately Held
SIC: 3631 3469 5099 Household cooking equipment; household cooking & kitchen utensils, metal; baby carriages, strollers & related products
PA: Helen Of Troy Limited
C/O Conyers, Dill & Pearman
Hamilton HM 11

(G-11081)
OZMODYL LTD
Also Called: Soho and Tribeca Map
233 Broadway Rm 707 (10279-0705)
PHONE..................212 226-0622
EMP: 5
SALES (est): 550K Privately Held
SIC: 2731 Publish A Map And Guide Book Of The Soho And Tribeca Area

(G-11082)
P & I SPORTSWEAR INC
384 5th Ave (10018-8103)
PHONE..................718 934-4587
Ignacio Bursztyn, *President*
Flora Bursztyn, *Vice Pres*
EMP: 5
SALES (est): 1.2MM Privately Held
SIC: 2339 2329 Women's & misses' athletic clothing & sportswear; men's & boys' sportswear & athletic clothing

(G-11083)
P & W PRESS INC
20 W 22nd St Ste 710 (10010-5877)
PHONE..................646 486-3417
Philip Foxman, *President*
Keith Foxman, *Vice Pres*
EMP: 20
SQ FT: 3,000
SALES (est): 1.8MM Privately Held
WEB: www.pwpress.com
SIC: 2752 2759 Commercial printing, offset; letterpress printing

(G-11084)
P E GUERIN (PA)
23 Jane St (10014-1999)
PHONE..................212 243-5270
Andrew F Ward, *President*
Martin Grubman, *General Mgr*
Kendall Davis, *Technology*
Lila Tublin, *Admin Asst*
◆ EMP: 69 EST: 1857
SALES (est): 6.5MM Privately Held
WEB: www.peguerin.com
SIC: 3429 5072 3432 5074 Door locks, bolts & checks; builders' hardware; plumbing fixture fittings & trim; plumbing fittings & supplies; drapery hardware & blinds & shades; window covering parts & accessories

(G-11085)
PACE EDITIONS INC (PA)
Also Called: Pace Prints
32 E 57th St Fl 3 (10022-8573)
PHONE..................212 421-3237
Richard H Solomon, *President*
Kristin Heming, *Director*
Donald Traver, *Director*
Chantal Salomon-Lee, *Associate Dir*
Jacob Lewis, *Asst Director*
EMP: 21
SQ FT: 10,000
SALES (est): 2.3MM Privately Held
WEB: www.paceprints.com
SIC: 2741 7999 Art copy & poster publishing; art gallery, commercial

New York - New York County (G-11086) — GEOGRAPHIC SECTION

(G-11086)
PACE EDITIONS INC
44 W 18th St Fl 5 (10011-4644)
PHONE......................................212 675-7431
Richard Soloman, *President*
EMP: 5
SALES (corp-wide): 2.3MM **Privately Held**
WEB: www.paceprints.com
SIC: 2752 2759 2741 Commercial printing, lithographic; commercial printing; miscellaneous publishing
PA: Pace Editions, Inc.
32 E 57th St Fl 3
New York NY 10022
212 421-3237

(G-11087)
PACHANGA INC
Also Called: Fika
824 10th Ave (10019-5040)
PHONE......................................212 832-0022
Lars Akerlund, *Ch of Bd*
EMP: 13
SALES (est): 2MM **Privately Held**
SIC: 2064 Candy & other confectionery products

(G-11088)
PACIFIC ALLIANCE USA INC
350 5th Ave Lbby 9 (10118-0109)
PHONE......................................336 500-8184
Bruce P Rockowitz, *Branch Mgr*
EMP: 6 **Privately Held**
SIC: 2339 Women's & misses' outerwear
HQ: Pacific Alliance Usa, Inc.
1450 Broadway Fl 21
New York NY 10018

(G-11089)
PACIFIC ALLIANCE USA INC (DH)
1450 Broadway Fl 21 (10018-2221)
PHONE......................................646 839-7000
Bruce Philip Rockowitz, *CEO*
Dow Famulak, *President*
Richard Darling, *Principal*
Ron Ventricelli, *COO*
▲ **EMP:** 53
SALES (est): 27.6MM **Privately Held**
SIC: 2339 Women's & misses' outerwear
HQ: Gbg Usa Inc.
350 5th Ave Lbby 11
New York NY 10118
646 839-7000

(G-11090)
PACIFIC CITY INTERNATIONAL
265 W 37th St (10018-5707)
PHONE......................................646 309-1250
Feng Tao, *President*
EMP: 11
SQ FT: 3,000
SALES (est): 7MM **Privately Held**
SIC: 2211 Apparel & outerwear fabrics, cotton

(G-11091)
PACIFIC WORLDWIDE INC
20 W 33rd St Fl 11 (10001-3305)
PHONE......................................212 502-3360
Martin Terzian, *President*
Ronald J Herro, *Vice Pres*
▲ **EMP:** 15
SALES (est): 2.1MM **Privately Held**
SIC: 3111 Leather Tanning/Finishing

(G-11092)
PACK AMERICA CORP (HQ)
108 W 39th St Fl 16 (10018-8255)
PHONE......................................212 508-6666
Hisao Ueda, *President*
Haruyuki Kochi, *Vice Pres*
▲ **EMP:** 4
SQ FT: 3,100
SALES (est): 6.5MM
SALES (corp-wide): 806MM **Privately Held**
WEB: www.packdash.com
SIC: 2673 2679 Plastic bags: made from purchased materials; paper products, converted
PA: The Pack Corporation
2-9-9, Higashiobase, Higashinari-Ku
Osaka OSK 537-0
669 721-221

(G-11093)
PAGEANT MEDIA US LIMITED
200 Park Ave S Fl 16 (10003-1503)
PHONE......................................646 891-2110
Charlie Kerr, *CEO*
EMP: 45
SALES (est): 3.7MM
SALES (corp-wide): 18.3MM **Privately Held**
SIC: 2721 Trade journals: publishing & printing
PA: Pageant Media Holdings Limited
1 London Wall
London EC2Y
207 832-6500

(G-11094)
PALETOT LTD
Also Called: Patricia Underwood
499 Fashion Ave Rm 25s (10018-6847)
PHONE......................................212 268-3774
Judy Hummel, *President*
Patricia Underwood, *Chairman*
EMP: 11
SQ FT: 1,500
SALES (est): 670K **Privately Held**
SIC: 2353 Hats & caps; millinery

(G-11095)
PALGRAVE MACMILLAN LTD
175 5th Ave Frnt 4 (10010-7728)
PHONE......................................646 307-5028
Grace Jackson, *Editor*
Andy Williams, *Opers Dir*
Iris Elam, *Marketing Staff*
Marit Vagstad, *Associate Dir*
Jessie Wheeler, *Assistant*
▲ **EMP:** 9
SALES (est): 952.8K
SALES (corp-wide): 1.7B **Privately Held**
WEB: www.palgrave-usa.com
SIC: 2731 Books: publishing only
HQ: Springer Nature Limited
Cromwell Place
Basingstoke HANTS RG24
125 632-9242

(G-11096)
PALLADIA INC
105 W 17th St (10011-5432)
PHONE......................................212 206-3669
Corinne Workman, *Manager*
EMP: 116
SALES (corp-wide): 36.6MM **Privately Held**
SIC: 3421 Table & food cutlery, including butchers'
PA: Palladia, Inc.
305 7th Ave Fl 10
New York NY 10001

(G-11097)
PAN AMERICAN LEATHERS INC (PA)
347 W 36th St Rm 1204 (10018-6480)
PHONE......................................978 741-4150
Mark Mendal, *President*
Abram Mendal, *Vice Pres*
▲ **EMP:** 3
SQ FT: 3,000
SALES (est): 1.4MM **Privately Held**
WEB: www.panamleathers.com
SIC: 3111 5199 Finishing of leather; leather goods, except footwear, gloves, luggage, belting

(G-11098)
PANGEA BRANDS LLC (PA)
6 W 20th St Fl 3 (10011-9270)
PHONE......................................617 638-0001
Joshua Fink, *Mng Member*
Michael London,
Dan Miller,
▲ **EMP:** 10
SQ FT: 5,000
SALES (est): 1.5MM **Privately Held**
SIC: 2396 Apparel & other linings, except millinery

(G-11099)
PANGEA BRANDS LLC
6 W 20th St Fl 3 (10011-9270)
PHONE......................................617 638-0001
Joshua Fink, *Branch Mgr*
EMP: 6

SALES (corp-wide): 1.5MM **Privately Held**
SIC: 2396 Apparel & other linings, except millinery
PA: Pangea Brands, Llc
6 W 20th St Fl 3
New York NY 10011
617 638-0001

(G-11100)
PAPA BUBBLE
380 Broome St Frnt A (10013-3799)
PHONE......................................212 966-2599
Ryan Grassi, *Owner*
EMP: 7
SALES (est): 496.8K **Privately Held**
SIC: 2064 Mfg Candy/Confectionery

(G-11101)
PAPER BOX CORP
Also Called: Aaaaaa Creative Designs
1751 2nd Ave Apt 10a (10128-5377)
PHONE......................................212 226-7490
Robert Fleisig, *President*
EMP: 70
SALES (est): 6.1MM **Privately Held**
SIC: 2631 2657 Folding boxboard; setup boxboard; folding paperboard boxes

(G-11102)
PAPER MAGIC GROUP INC
345 7th Ave Fl 6 (10001-5053)
PHONE......................................631 521-3682
Nathan Caldwell, *Manager*
EMP: 450
SALES (corp-wide): 361.9MM **Publicly Held**
WEB: www.papermagic.com
SIC: 2771 2678 Greeting cards; stationery products
HQ: Paper Magic Group Inc.
54 Glenmra Ntl Blvd
Moosic PA 18507
570 961-3863

(G-11103)
PAPER PUBLISHING COMPANY INC
Also Called: Paper Magazine
15 E 32nd St (10016-5423)
PHONE......................................212 226-4405
David Hershkovits, *President*
Kim Hastreiter, *Treasurer*
EMP: 27
SQ FT: 3,000
SALES (est): 3.5MM **Privately Held**
WEB: www.papermag.com
SIC: 2721 Magazines: publishing only, not printed on site

(G-11104)
PAPERCUTZ INC
160 Broadway Rm 700e (10038-4241)
PHONE......................................646 559-4681
Terry Nantier, *President*
Jim Salicrup, *Vice Pres*
Sasha Kimiatek, *Production*
Jeffrey Whitman, *Production*
Sven Larsen, *VP Mktg*
▲ **EMP:** 5
SALES (est): 2.2MM **Privately Held**
SIC: 2731 Books: publishing only

(G-11105)
PARACE BIONICS LLC
100 Park Ave Rm 1600 (10017-5538)
PHONE......................................877 727-2231
Vandette Carter, *Mng Member*
EMP: 5
SALES (est): 345.8K **Privately Held**
SIC: 3841 Surgical & medical instruments

(G-11106)
PARACHUTE PUBLISHING LLC
322 8th Ave Ste 702 (10001-6791)
PHONE......................................212 337-6743
Joan Waricha,
Jane Stine,
▲ **EMP:** 30
SALES (est): 2.9MM **Privately Held**
WEB: www.parachuteproperties.com
SIC: 2731 Books: publishing only

(G-11107)
PARADE PUBLICATIONS INC (DH)
Also Called: Parade Magazine
711 3rd Ave (10017-4014)
PHONE......................................212 450-7000
Carlo Vittorini, *CEO*
Susan Ollinick, *President*
EMP: 37
SALES (est): 5.9MM
SALES (corp-wide): 5.6B **Privately Held**
SIC: 2721 Magazines: publishing only, not printed on site
HQ: The Herald Newspapers Company Inc
220 S Warren St
Syracuse NY 13202
315 470-0011

(G-11108)
PARADIGM SPINE LLC
505 Park Ave Fl 14 (10022-1106)
PHONE......................................888 273-9897
Marc Viscigliosi, *CEO*
Gutmar Eisen, *President*
Jeremy Laynor, *President*
Gerry Marini, *President*
Catherine Higbee, *Business Mgr*
EMP: 23
SQ FT: 1,500
SALES (est): 7.6MM **Privately Held**
SIC: 3842 Implants, surgical

(G-11109)
PARAMOUNT TEXTILES INC
34 Walker St (10013-3514)
PHONE......................................212 966-1040
Steven Katz, *CEO*
Estate J Katz, *President*
Ronald Katz, *Vice Pres*
Alan Katz, *Admin Sec*
EMP: 10 **EST:** 1940
SQ FT: 15,000
SALES (est): 1.2MM **Privately Held**
WEB: www.paramounttextile.com
SIC: 2392 5023 5047 Household furnishings; linens & towels; linens, table; surgical equipment & supplies

(G-11110)
PARENTS GUIDE NETWORK CORP
Also Called: P G Media
419 Park Ave S Rm 505 (10016-8410)
PHONE......................................212 213-8840
Steve Elgort, *President*
Donald McDermott, *Editor*
Margaret Baldauf, *Art Dir*
Howard Baum, *Executive*
EMP: 25
SALES (est): 2.4MM **Privately Held**
WEB: www.parentguidenews.com
SIC: 2721 8351 Magazines: publishing only, not printed on site; child day care services

(G-11111)
PARETEUM CORPORATION (PA)
1185 Ave Of The Americas (10036-2601)
PHONE......................................212 984-1096
Victor Bozzo, *CEO*
Vic Bozzo, *CEO*
Robert H Turner, *Ch of Bd*
Denis McCarthy, *President*
David Hess, *Vice Pres*
EMP: 15
SALES: 13.5MM **Publicly Held**
SIC: 7372 Prepackaged software

(G-11112)
PARIJAT JEWELS INC
15 W 47th St Ste 1811 (10036-5700)
PHONE......................................212 302-2549
Ramesh Vaje, *President*
EMP: 7
SALES: 2.5MM **Privately Held**
SIC: 3911 Jewelry, precious metal

(G-11113)
PARIS REVIEW FOUNDATION INC
544 W 27th St Fl 3 (10001-5537)
PHONE......................................212 343-1333
Robert T McDonell, *Ch of Bd*
Jessica Calderon, *General Mgr*
Emily Cole-Kelly, *Principal*

▲ = Import ▼ = Export
◆ = Import/Export

GEOGRAPHIC SECTION

New York - New York County (G-11139)

Nadja Spiegelman, *Editor*
Andrew Jimenez, *Manager*
EMP: 7
SALES: 2.4MM **Privately Held**
SIC: 2721 Periodicals

(G-11114)
PARIS WEDDING CENTER CORP
45 E Broadway Fl 2 (10002-6804)
PHONE.................212 267-8088
Yuki Lin, *Branch Mgr*
EMP: 26
SALES (corp-wide): 888.6K **Privately Held**
SIC: 2335 Wedding gowns & dresses
PA: Paris Wedding Center Corp.
    42-53 42 55 Main St
    Flushing NY 11355
    347 368-4085

(G-11115)
PARK ASSIST LLC
57 W 38th St Fl 11 (10018-1296)
PHONE.................646 666-7525
Gary Nef, *Mng Member*
Gary Nef, *Mng Member*
Andrew Eisen,
Joshua Eisen,
▲ **EMP:** 70
SALES (est): 1.2MM **Privately Held**
WEB: www.parkassist.com
SIC: 3559 Parking facility equipment & supplies

(G-11116)
PARK WEST JEWELERY INC
565 W End Ave Apt 8b (10024-2734)
PHONE.................646 329-6145
Dale Bearman, *President*
EMP: 6
SQ FT: 900
SALES (est): 490K **Privately Held**
SIC: 3911 Jewelry apparel

(G-11117)
PARKER WARBY RETAIL INC (PA)
Also Called: Warby Parker Eyewear
161 Ave Of The Amer Fl 6f (10013-1205)
PHONE.................646 517-5223
Neil Blumenthal, *CEO*
Dave Gilboa, *CEO*
Andy Hunt, *Partner*
▲ **EMP:** 41
SALES (est): 19.9MM **Privately Held**
SIC: 3851 5995 Eyeglasses, lenses & frames; optical goods stores

(G-11118)
PARLOR LABS INC
Also Called: Ponder
515 W 19th St (10011-2872)
PHONE.................866 801-7323
Alexander Selkirk, *President*
EMP: 5
SALES (est): 236K **Privately Held**
SIC: 7372 8748 Educational computer software; systems engineering consultant, ex. computer or professional

(G-11119)
PASABAHCE USA
41 Madison Ave Fl 7 (10010-2202)
PHONE.................212 683-1600
Neil M Orzeck, *Manager*
Martin Anderson, *Director*
▲ **EMP:** 4
SALES (est): 25MM **Privately Held**
SIC: 3229 Art, decorative & novelty glassware

(G-11120)
PASSPORT BRANDS INC (PA)
240 Madison Ave Fl 8 (10016-2878)
PHONE.................646 459-2625
Robert S Stec, *CEO*
Robert Arnot, *President*
Ernest K Jacquet, *Director*
◆ **EMP:** 35
SQ FT: 13,500
SALES (est): 7.7MM **Publicly Held**
WEB: www.icisaacs.com
SIC: 2325 2339 Jeans: men's, youths' & boys'; slacks, dress: men's, youths' & boys'; shorts (outerwear): men's, youths' & boys'; jeans: women's, misses' & juniors'; slacks: women's, misses' & juniors'; shorts (outerwear): women's, misses' & juniors'

(G-11121)
PAT & ROSE DRESS INC
327 W 36th St Rm 3a (10018-7014)
PHONE.................212 279-1357
Rosalia Panebianco, *President*
Pat Capolupo, *Manager*
EMP: 60
SQ FT: 5,000
SALES (est): 3.6MM **Privately Held**
SIC: 2335 2331 2337 2339 Women's, juniors' & misses' dresses; blouses, women's & juniors': made from purchased material; skirts, separate: women's, misses' & juniors'; women's & misses' outerwear; men's & boys' trousers & slacks; men's & boys' suits & coats

(G-11122)
PATMIAN LLC
655 Madison Ave Fl 24 (10065-8043)
PHONE.................212 758-0770
George Botis, *Chairman*
EMP: 350
SALES (est): 19.9MM **Privately Held**
SIC: 3089 3544 Plastic processing; injection molded finished plastic products; special dies, tools, jigs & fixtures

(G-11123)
PAUL DAVID ENTERPRISES INC
19 W 34th St Rm 1018 (10001-3006)
PHONE.................646 667-5530
Daniel Korolev, *Vice Pres*
EMP: 9 **EST:** 2013
SALES (est): 356.2K **Privately Held**
SIC: 2431 Jalousies, glass, wood frame

(G-11124)
PAULA DORF COSMETICS INC
850 7th Ave Ste 801 (10019-5446)
PHONE.................212 582-0073
Sandy Dekovnick, *CEO*
Sandy De Kovnick, *CEO*
Paula Dorf, *President*
▲ **EMP:** 30
SALES (est): 4.2MM **Privately Held**
WEB: www.pauladorf.com
SIC: 2844 5122 Toilet preparations; cosmetics, perfumes & hair products

(G-11125)
PAULA VARSALONA LTD
552 Fashion Ave Rm 602 (10018-3239)
PHONE.................212 570-9100
Paula Varsalona, *President*
EMP: 15
SQ FT: 5,000
SALES (est): 1.3MM **Privately Held**
WEB: www.paulavarsalona.com
SIC: 2335 2396 Wedding gowns & dresses; veils & veiling: bridal, funeral, etc.

(G-11126)
PAVANA USA INC
10 W 33rd St Rm 408 (10001-3306)
P.O. Box 237191 (10023-0033)
PHONE.................646 833-8811
Avisha Uttamchandani, *President*
◆ **EMP:** 5
SALES (est): 1MM **Privately Held**
SIC: 3873 Watches, clocks, watchcases & parts

(G-11127)
PAVMED INC
60 E 42nd St Fl 46 (10165-0043)
PHONE.................212 401-1951
Dennis M McGrath, *CFO*
EMP: 5
SALES (est): 616.6K **Privately Held**
SIC: 3841 Surgical & medical instruments

(G-11128)
PEANUT BUTTER & CO INC
119 W 57th St Ste 300 (10019-2302)
P.O. Box 2000 (10101-2000)
PHONE.................212 757-3130
Lee E Zalben, *President*
▲ **EMP:** 25
SALES (est): 5.5MM **Privately Held**
WEB: www.ilovepeanutbutter.com
SIC: 2099 Peanut butter

(G-11129)
PEARL ERWIN INC (PA)
389 5th Ave Rm 1100 (10016-3350)
PHONE.................212 889-7410
Erwin Pearl, *President*
Michael Elswit, *Vice Pres*
Joel Weinstein, *CFO*
Mark Grodin, *Controller*
Lorraine Robson, *Executive Asst*
EMP: 30
SALES (est): 33.8MM **Privately Held**
SIC: 3961 3911 Costume jewelry; jewelry, precious metal

(G-11130)
PEARSON EDUCATION INC
1185 Avenu Of The Americ (10036-2601)
PHONE.................212 782-3337
Roth Wilkofsky, *President*
EMP: 16
SALES (corp-wide): 5.9B **Privately Held**
WEB: www.phgenit.com
SIC: 2731 Book publishing
HQ: Pearson Education, Inc.
    221 River St
    Hoboken NJ 07030
    201 236-7000

(G-11131)
PEARSON EDUCATION INC
375 Hudson St (10014-3658)
PHONE.................212 366-2000
Tom Altier, *Branch Mgr*
EMP: 27
SALES (corp-wide): 5.9B **Privately Held**
WEB: www.phgenit.com
SIC: 2731 Book publishing
HQ: Pearson Education, Inc.
    221 River St
    Hoboken NJ 07030
    201 236-7000

(G-11132)
PEARSON EDUCATION HOLDINGS INC (HQ)
330 Hudson St Fl 9 (10013-1048)
PHONE.................201 236-6716
Will Ethridge, *President*
Bill Triant, *President*
Michelle West, *Editor*
Sharon K Young, *District Mgr*
Donna Nielsen, *Business Mgr*
▲ **EMP:** 2000 **EST:** 1998
SQ FT: 475,000
SALES (est): 5.2B
SALES (corp-wide): 5.9B **Privately Held**
WEB: www.pearsoned.com
SIC: 2731 Textbooks: publishing & printing
PA: Pearson Plc
    Shell Mex House
    London WC2R
    207 010-2000

(G-11133)
PEARSON INC (HQ)
1330 Hudson St (10013)
PHONE.................212 641-2400
John Fallon, *CEO*
Boone Novy, *Principal*
Glen Moreno, *Chairman*
Michael Fortini, *Vice Pres*
Megan Johnson, *Vice Pres*
◆ **EMP:** 58
SALES (est): 2.4B
SALES (corp-wide): 5.9B **Privately Held**
SIC: 2711 2731 Newspapers; books: publishing & printing; textbooks: publishing & printing
PA: Pearson Plc
    Shell Mex House
    London WC2R
    207 010-2000

(G-11134)
PEARSON LONGMAN LLC
51 Madison Ave Fl 27 (10010-1609)
PHONE.................917 981-2200
Bruce Styron, *Facilities Mgr*
Roth Wilkofsky, *Manager*
EMP: 120
SALES (corp-wide): 5.9B **Privately Held**
SIC: 2731 Books: publishing & printing
HQ: Pearson Longman Llc
    10 Bank St Ste 1030
    White Plains NY 10606
    212 641-2400

(G-11135)
PEEK A BOO USA INC
Also Called: Beaba USA
555 8th Ave Rm 403 (10018-4383)
PHONE.................201 533-8700
Lisa Speransky, *CEO*
▲ **EMP:** 5
SQ FT: 1,200
SALES (est): 712K
SALES (corp-wide): 114.2K **Privately Held**
SIC: 3089 3634 Plastic kitchenware, tableware & houseware; electric household cooking appliances
HQ: Beaba
    31 Avenue De L Opera
    Paris 75001
    474 120-910

(G-11136)
PEER INTERNATIONAL CORP (HQ)
Also Called: 3239603400 La Head Quarters
152 W 57th St Fl 10 (10019-3340)
PHONE.................212 265-3910
Ralph Peer II, *President*
Elizabeth W Peer, *Vice Pres*
Cecile Russo, *Vice Pres*
Kathryn Spanberger, *Vice Pres*
Todd Vunderink, *Vice Pres*
▲ **EMP:** 30
SALES (est): 2.8MM
SALES (corp-wide): 9.8MM **Privately Held**
SIC: 2741 Music books: publishing only, not printed on site
PA: Southern Music Publishing Co., Inc.
    810 7th Ave Fl 36
    New York NY 10019
    212 265-3910

(G-11137)
PEER-SOUTHERN PRODUCTIONS INC (HQ)
152 W 57th St Fl 10 (10019-3340)
PHONE.................212 265-3910
Ralph Peer II, *President*
Marilyn La Vine, *Admin Sec*
EMP: 30 **EST:** 1961
SALES (est): 1.8MM
SALES (corp-wide): 9.8MM **Privately Held**
SIC: 3652 Master records or tapes, preparation of
PA: Southern Music Publishing Co., Inc.
    810 7th Ave Fl 36
    New York NY 10019
    212 265-3910

(G-11138)
PEERMUSIC III LTD (PA)
152 W 57th St Fl 10 (10019-3340)
PHONE.................212 265-3910
EMP: 14 **EST:** 2013
SALES (est): 6.1MM **Privately Held**
SIC: 2741 Music books: publishing only, not printed on site

(G-11139)
PEERMUSIC LTD (HQ)
152 W 57th St Fl 10 (10019-3340)
PHONE.................212 265-3910
Ralph Peer II, *President*
Elizabeth W Peer, *Vice Pres*
Cecile Russo, *Vice Pres*
Katheryn Spanberger, *Vice Pres*
Craig Currier, *Director*
EMP: 12

New York - New York County (G-11140) — GEOGRAPHIC SECTION

SALES (est): 3.3MM
SALES (corp-wide): 9.8MM **Privately Held**
WEB: www.digitalpressure.com
SIC: 2741 7922 Music books: publishing only, not printed on site; theatrical producers & services
PA: Southern Music Publishing Co., Inc.
  810 7th Ave Fl 36
  New York NY 10019
  212 265-3910

(G-11140)
PEGASUS BOOKS NY LTD
148 W 37th St Fl 13 (10018-6976)
PHONE................................646 343-9502
EMP: 5
SALES: 500K **Privately Held**
SIC: 2731 Book publishing

(G-11141)
PEGASYSTEMS INC
1120 Ave Of The Americas (10036-6700)
PHONE................................212 626-6550
Beth Saperstein, *Branch Mgr*
EMP: 25
SALES (corp-wide): 840.5MM **Publicly Held**
WEB: www.pega.com
SIC: 7372 7379 Business oriented computer software; computer related consulting services
PA: Pegasystems Inc.
  1 Rogers St
  Cambridge MA 02142
  617 374-9600

(G-11142)
PELOTON INTERACTIVE INC
140 W 23rd St Frnt 1 (10011-9404)
PHONE................................866 679-9129
Lindsay Yatrakis, *Vice Pres*
Blair Friley, *Store Mgr*
Ted Dekams, *Sales Associate*
EMP: 11
SALES (corp-wide): 28.5MM **Privately Held**
SIC: 3949 Gymnasium equipment
PA: Peloton Interactive, Inc.
  125 W 25th St Fl 11
  New York NY 10001
  866 650-1996

(G-11143)
PELOTON INTERACTIVE INC (PA)
125 W 25th St Fl 11 (10001-7213)
PHONE................................866 650-1996
John Foley, *CEO*
William Lynch, *President*
Graham Stanton, *President*
Thomas Cortese, *COO*
Carolyn Blodgett, *Vice Pres*
◆ EMP: 50
SQ FT: 9,000
SALES (est): 28.5MM **Privately Held**
SIC: 3949 Gymnasium equipment

(G-11144)
PENGUIN PUTNAM INC
375 Hudson St Bsmt 1 (10014-3672)
P.O. Box 20998, Floral Park (11002-0998)
PHONE................................212 366-2000
John Fagan, *Principal*
◆ EMP: 8
SALES (est): 1.4MM **Privately Held**
SIC: 2731 Books: publishing only

(G-11145)
PENGUIN RANDOM HOUSE LLC
1540 Broadway (10036-4039)
PHONE................................212 782-1000
Markus Dohle, *CEO*
Henrik Pahls, *Senior VP*
Jacqueline Chasey, *Vice Pres*
Mara Davis, *Project Mgr*
Freddie Helrich, *Human Res Mgr*
EMP: 25
SALES (corp-wide): 82.3MM **Privately Held**
SIC: 2731 Books: publishing only
HQ: Penguin Random House Llc
  1745 Broadway
  New York NY 10019
  212 782-9000

(G-11146)
PENGUIN RANDOM HOUSE LLC (DH)
1745 Broadway (10019-4640)
PHONE................................212 782-9000
Markus Dohle, *CEO*
Madeline McIntosh, *President*
Claire Von Schilling, *Exec VP*
Jacqueline Updike, *Senior VP*
Leigh Marchant, *Vice Pres*
▲ EMP: 277
SALES (est): 1.4B
SALES (corp-wide): 82.3MM **Privately Held**
SIC: 2731 Books: publishing only
HQ: Bertelsmann Se & Co. Kgaa
  Carl-Bertelsmann-Str. 270
  Gutersloh 33335
  524 180-0

(G-11147)
PENGUIN RANDOM HOUSE LLC
1745 Broadway Frnt 3 (10019-4641)
PHONE................................212 572-6162
Markus Dohle, *CEO*
EMP: 513
SALES (corp-wide): 82.3MM **Privately Held**
SIC: 2731 5942 Books: publishing only; book stores
HQ: Penguin Random House Llc
  1745 Broadway
  New York NY 10019
  212 782-9000

(G-11148)
PENGUIN RANDOM HOUSE LLC
1745 Broadway Frnt 3 (10019-4641)
PHONE................................212 782-9000
Markus Dohle, *CEO*
EMP: 1000
SALES (corp-wide): 82.3MM **Privately Held**
SIC: 2731 Books: publishing only
HQ: Penguin Random House Llc
  1745 Broadway
  New York NY 10019
  212 782-9000

(G-11149)
PENHOUSE MEDIA GROUP INC (PA)
11 Penn Plz Fl 12 (10001-2027)
PHONE................................212 702-6000
John Prebich, *President*
Claude Bertin, *Exec VP*
Nina Guccione, *Exec VP*
Hope Brick, *Vice Pres*
Larry Sutter, *Admin Sec*
▲ EMP: 150
SALES (est): 11.5MM **Privately Held**
SIC: 2721 5999 6512 6794 Magazines: publishing only, not printed on site; art dealers; commercial & industrial building operation; copyright buying & licensing

(G-11150)
PENSIONS & INVESTMENTS
Also Called: P&I, Pper P I Daily P I People
711 3rd Ave (10017-4014)
PHONE................................212 210-0763
William T Bisson Jr, *Principal*
EMP: 43
SALES (est): 3.7MM **Privately Held**
SIC: 2721 Magazines: publishing & printing

(G-11151)
PEPE CREATIONS INC
2 W 45th St Ste 1003 (10036-4212)
PHONE................................212 391-1514
Frank Gomez, *President*
EMP: 12
SALES: 1.5MM **Privately Held**
WEB: www.pepecreations.com
SIC: 3961 Costume jewelry

(G-11152)
PER ANNUM INC
555 8th Ave Rm 202 (10018-4386)
PHONE................................212 647-8700
Alicia Settle, *President*
Tom Settle, *Corp Secy*
▲ EMP: 25
SQ FT: 14,000
SALES (est): 2MM **Privately Held**
WEB: www.perannum.com
SIC: 2741 Miscellaneous publishing

(G-11153)
PEREGRINE INDUSTRIES INC
40 Wall St (10005-1304)
PHONE................................631 838-2870
Richard Rubin, *CEO*
Amir Uziel, *Director*
EMP: 5
SALES (est): 471.7K
SALES (corp-wide): 2.1MM **Privately Held**
SIC: 3569 Filters
PA: Dolomite Holdings Ltd
  8 Hamanofim
  Herzliya 46725
  722 220-930

(G-11154)
PEREIRA & ODELL LLC
5 Crosby St Rm 5h (10013-3154)
PHONE................................212 897-1000
Cory Berger, *Director*
Rory Hill, *Director*
EMP: 8
SALES (est): 890.6K
SALES (corp-wide): 18MM **Privately Held**
SIC: 3993 Advertising artwork
PA: Pereira & O'dell Llc
  215 2nd St Ste 100
  San Francisco CA 94105
  415 284-9916

(G-11155)
PERFUME AMRCANA WHLESALERS INC
11 W 30th St Betwe Broad Between (10001)
PHONE................................212 683-8029
Mukhtar S Cheema, *President*
Bharati Cheema, *President*
▼ EMP: 10
SALES (est): 1.2MM **Privately Held**
SIC: 2844 Perfumes & colognes

(G-11156)
PERFUMERS WORKSHOP INTL LTD (PA)
350 7th Ave Rm 802 (10001-1941)
PHONE................................212 644-8950
Donald G Bauchner, *President*
Steven Levenson, *Exec VP*
▲ EMP: 8
SQ FT: 1,800
SALES (est): 1MM **Privately Held**
SIC: 2844 Perfumes & colognes

(G-11157)
PERIMONDO LLC
331 W 84th St Apt 2 (10024-4215)
P.O. Box 200 (10024-0200)
PHONE................................212 749-0721
Matthias Rebmann, *Mng Member*
▲ EMP: 6
SALES (est): 1.1MM **Privately Held**
SIC: 2074 Lecithin, cottonseed

(G-11158)
PERMA GLOW LTD INC
48 W 48th St Ste 301 (10036-1713)
PHONE................................212 575-9677
Richard Scandaglia, *President*
Joseph Scandaglia, *Vice Pres*
▲ EMP: 15
SQ FT: 2,000
SALES: 400K **Privately Held**
SIC: 3915 Jewel cutting, drilling, polishing, recutting or setting

(G-11159)
PERMANENT OBSERVER MISSION
320 E 51st St (10022-7803)
PHONE................................212 883-0140
Iyad Ameen Madani, *Principal*
EMP: 5 EST: 2016
SALES (est): 124.6K **Privately Held**
SIC: 2711 Newspapers, publishing & printing

(G-11160)
PERRY ELLIS INTERNATIONAL INC
1126 Avenue Of The Americ (10036)
PHONE................................212 536-5400
John Griffin, *Branch Mgr*
EMP: 12
SALES (corp-wide): 874.8MM **Privately Held**
SIC: 2321 2325 6794 Men's & boys' sports & polo shirts; men's & boys' trousers & slacks; trousers, dress (separate): men's, youths' & boys'; shorts (outerwear): men's, youths' & boys'; franchises, selling or licensing
HQ: Perry Ellis International Inc
  3000 Nw 107th Ave
  Doral FL 33172
  305 592-2830

(G-11161)
PERRY ELLIS INTERNATIONAL INC
42 W 39th St Fl 4 (10018-3841)
PHONE................................212 536-5499
Hope Wright, *VP Finance*
Kevin Kiley, *Branch Mgr*
Angela Hyndman, *Manager*
EMP: 9
SALES (corp-wide): 874.8MM **Privately Held**
WEB: www.cubabera.com
SIC: 2321 Men's & boys' sports & polo shirts
HQ: Perry Ellis International Inc
  3000 Nw 107th Ave
  Doral FL 33172
  305 592-2830

(G-11162)
PERRY ELLIS MENSWEAR LLC (DH)
Also Called: Perry Ellis America
1120 Avenue Of The Americ (10036-6700)
PHONE................................212 221-7500
Doug Jakubowski, *Ch of Bd*
Awadhesh K Sinha, *COO*
Brian Root, *Vice Pres*
Linda Nash Merker, *VP Human Res*
Andrea Lawrence, *Technology*
◆ EMP: 150 EST: 1893
SQ FT: 27,000
SALES (est): 106.1MM
SALES (corp-wide): 874.8MM **Privately Held**
WEB: www.perryellis.com
SIC: 2325 5611 2321 2387 Slacks, dress: men's, youths' & boys'; jeans: men's, youths' & boys'; men's & boys' clothing stores; men's & boys' furnishings; apparel belts; suspenders; neckties, men's & boys': made from purchased materials
HQ: Perry Ellis International Inc
  3000 Nw 107th Ave
  Doral FL 33172
  305 592-2830

(G-11163)
PERRY STREET SOFTWARE INC
489 5th Ave Rm 2900 (10017-6115)
PHONE................................415 935-1429
John Skandros, *President*
Eric Silverberg, *Admin Sec*
EMP: 5 EST: 2011
SALES (est): 430K **Privately Held**
SIC: 7372 Prepackaged software

(G-11164)
PERSISTENT SYSTEMS LLC
303 5th Ave Rm 306 (10016-6635)
PHONE................................212 561-5895
Herbert B Rubens, *CEO*
Charles Yoo, *Purch Agent*
Phil Furmato, *Project Engr*
Matthew Fricke, *Controller*
Kai Fletcher, *Finance Mgr*
EMP: 50
SQ FT: 5,000
SALES (est): 23.1MM **Privately Held**
SIC: 3663 Radio broadcasting & communications equipment

▲ = Import ▼ = Export
◆ = Import/Export

(G-11165)
PESSELNIK & COHEN INC
82 Bowery Unit 10 (10013-4656)
PHONE.................................212 925-0287
Salvatore Diadema, *President*
Stephen De Angelo, *Admin Sec*
EMP: 7
SALES (est): 550K **Privately Held**
SIC: 3911 5094 Jewelry, precious metal; jewelry; watches & parts

(G-11166)
PET PROTEINS LLC
347 W 36th St Rm 1204 (10018-6480)
PHONE.................................888 293-1029
Steven Mendal,
Jayme Mendal,
Mark Mendal,
◆ **EMP:** 7
SQ FT: 500
SALES: 1MM **Privately Held**
SIC: 2047 Dog & cat food

(G-11167)
PETER ATMAN INC
6 E 45th St Rm 1100 (10017-2475)
PHONE.................................212 644-8882
Peter Philipakos, *Ch of Bd*
Peter Phillips, *President*
EMP: 10 **EST:** 1977
SALES (est): 1.3MM **Privately Held**
WEB: www.peteratman.com
SIC: 3911 5944 Jewelry, precious metal; jewelry, precious stones & precious metals

(G-11168)
PETER LANG PUBLISHING INC (DH)
29 Broadway Rm 1800 (10006-3221)
PHONE.................................212 647-7700
Alessandra Anzani, *Editor*
Elisabeth Hanuschkin, *Editor*
Susanne Hoeves, *Editor*
Laurel Plapp, *Editor*
Christabel Scaife, *Editor*
EMP: 12
SQ FT: 8,000
SALES (est): 1.3MM
SALES (corp-wide): 274.9K **Privately Held**
WEB: www.peterlangusa.com
SIC: 2731 Textbooks: publishing only, not printed on site
HQ: Peter Lang Ag Internationaler Verlag
   Der Wissenschaften
   Wabernstrasse 40
   Bern BE
   313 061-717

(G-11169)
PETER MAYER PUBLISHERS INC
Also Called: Overlook Press, The
141 Wooster St Fl 4 (10012-3163)
PHONE.................................212 673-2210
Peter Mayer, *President*
George Davidson, *Production*
Michael Goldsmith, *Analyst*
▲ **EMP:** 13
SQ FT: 5,000
SALES: 1MM **Privately Held**
WEB: www.overlookpress.com
SIC: 2731 Books: publishing only

(G-11170)
PETER THOMAS ROTH LABS LLC (PA)
Also Called: Naturally Serious
460 Park Ave Fl 16 (10022-1829)
PHONE.................................212 581-5800
June Jacobs,
Peter Roth,
▲ **EMP:** 40
SQ FT: 5,500
SALES (est): 28.2MM **Privately Held**
SIC: 2844 Cosmetic preparations

(G-11171)
PETNET SOLUTIONS INC
660 1st Ave Rm 140 (10016-3295)
PHONE.................................865 218-2000
Barry Scott, *CEO*
EMP: 6
SALES (corp-wide): 97.7B **Privately Held**
SIC: 2835 In vitro & in vivo diagnostic substances
HQ: Petnet Solutions, Inc.
   810 Innovation Dr
   Knoxville TN 37932
   865 218-2000

(G-11172)
PEXIP INC (HQ)
240 W 35th St Ste 300 (10001-2506)
PHONE.................................703 338-3544
Adam Marlin, *Vice Pres*
Richard Coder, *Vice Pres*
Rik Coder, *Vice Pres*
Matt Hansen, *VP Opers*
Danny Dunn, *Director*
EMP: 40 **EST:** 2012
SQ FT: 3,000
SALES (est): 2.6MM
SALES (corp-wide): 17.4MM **Privately Held**
SIC: 7372 Application computer software
PA: Pexip As
   Fornebuveien 42
   Lysaker
   215 561-00

(G-11173)
PFIZER HCP CORPORATION (HQ)
235 E 42nd St (10017-5703)
PHONE.................................212 733-2323
Ian C Read, *CEO*
Geno Germano, *President*
Kaha Kvachatadze, *Counsel*
Jeff Mastracchio, *Counsel*
Frank D'Amelio, *Exec VP*
▲ **EMP:** 12
SALES (est): 4.4MM
SALES (corp-wide): 52.5B **Publicly Held**
WEB: www.pfizer.com
SIC: 2834 Pharmaceutical preparations
PA: Pfizer Inc.
   235 E 42nd St
   New York NY 10017
   212 733-2323

(G-11174)
PFIZER INC (PA)
235 E 42nd St (10017-5703)
PHONE.................................212 733-2323
Ian C Read, *Ch of Bd*
Albert Bourla, *COO*
Douglas M Lankler, *Exec VP*
Alexander R Mackenzie, *Exec VP*
Robert Bagdorf, *Vice Pres*
EMP: 2500 **EST:** 1942
SALES: 52.5B **Publicly Held**
WEB: www.pfizer.com
SIC: 2833 2834 Antibiotics; drugs acting on the cardiovascular system, except diagnostic

(G-11175)
PFIZER INC
150 E 42nd St Fl 38 (10017-5612)
PHONE.................................937 746-3603
Daniel Reardon, *Principal*
Tim Anderson, *District Mgr*
Markus Green, *Counsel*
John Hong, *Counsel*
Feng Shao, *Counsel*
EMP: 214
SALES (corp-wide): 52.5B **Publicly Held**
SIC: 2834 Pharmaceutical preparations
PA: Pfizer Inc.
   235 E 42nd St
   New York NY 10017
   212 733-2323

(G-11176)
PFIZER INC
150 E 42nd St Bsmt 2 (10017-5612)
PHONE.................................212 733-6276
Joy Allette, *Marketing Mgr*
Ira Stoler, *Manager*
Rafael Rivera, *Manager*
Andrew Clair, *Director*
Kevin Dillon, *Director*
EMP: 70
SALES (corp-wide): 52.5B **Publicly Held**
WEB: www.pfizer.com
SIC: 2834 Pharmaceutical preparations

(G-11177)
PFIZER INC
235 E 42nd St (10017-5703)
PHONE.................................212 733-2323
EMP: 146
SALES (corp-wide): 52.5B **Publicly Held**
SIC: 2834 Pharmaceutical preparations
PA: Pfizer Inc.
   235 E 42nd St
   New York NY 10017
   212 733-2323

(G-11178)
PFIZER OVERSEAS LLC
235 E 42nd St (10017-5703)
PHONE.................................212 733-2323
Ian C Read, *Ch of Bd*
Mikael Dolsten, *President*
Frank D'Amelio, *Exec VP*
Chuck Hill, *Exec VP*
Rady Johnson, *Exec VP*
EMP: 8
SALES (est): 484.5K
SALES (corp-wide): 52.5B **Publicly Held**
SIC: 2834 2833 Pharmaceutical preparations; antibiotics
PA: Pfizer Inc.
   235 E 42nd St
   New York NY 10017
   212 733-2323

(G-11179)
PHAIDON PRESS INC
65 Bleecker St Fl 8 (10012-2420)
PHONE.................................212 652-5400
Keith Fox, *CEO*
Bridget McCarthy, *Editor*
Philip Ruppel, *COO*
Deborah Aaronson, *Vice Pres*
Andrew Price, *Vice Pres*
▲ **EMP:** 20
SALES (est): 2.6MM
SALES (corp-wide): 33.2MM **Privately Held**
SIC: 2731 Books: publishing only
HQ: Phaidon Press Limited
   Regent's Wharf
   London N1 9P
   207 843-1000

(G-11180)
PHC RESTORATION HOLDINGS LLC
Also Called: Philip Crangi
147 W 29th St Ste 4e (10001-4265)
PHONE.................................212 643-0517
Courtney Crangi, *Mng Member*
Jeffry Aronsson,
Philip Crangi,
EMP: 10
SQ FT: 2,000
SALES: 1.5MM
SALES (corp-wide): 745.6K **Privately Held**
SIC: 3911 Jewelry, precious metal
PA: Phc Restoration, Inc.
   147 W 29th St Ste 4e
   New York NY 10001
   212 643-0517

(G-11181)
PHILIP MORRIS INTL INC (PA)
120 Park Ave Fl 6 (10017-5592)
PHONE.................................917 663-2000
Andre Calantzopoulos, *CEO*
Louis C Camilleri, *Ch of Bd*
Drago Azinovic, *President*
Frederic De Wilde, *President*
Marc S Firestone, *President*
EMP: 88
SALES: 78.1B **Publicly Held**
SIC: 2111 Cigarettes

(G-11182)
PHILIPS LIGHTING N AMER CORP
267 5th Ave (10016-7503)
PHONE.................................646 265-7170
Jeffrey Cassis, *CEO*
EMP: 190
SALES (corp-wide): 20.9B **Privately Held**
SIC: 3646 Commercial indusl & institutional electric lighting fixtures
HQ: Philips Lighting North America Corporation
   3 Burlington Woods Dr # 4
   Burlington MA 01803
   617 423-9999

(G-11183)
PHILLIPS-VAN HEUSEN EUROPE
Also Called: Pvh Europe
200 Madison Ave Bsmt 1 (10016-3913)
PHONE.................................212 381-3500
Ellen Constantinides, *President*
Carlos Heredia, *Project Mgr*
Reji Thomas, *Project Mgr*
Warren Gerber, *Finance*
Christopher Daly, *HR Admin*
EMP: 12
SALES: 20MM
SALES (corp-wide): 8.9B **Publicly Held**
SIC: 2321 2331 2253 3143 Men's & boys' dress shirts; blouses, women's & juniors': made from purchased material; sweaters & sweater coats, knit; men's footwear, except athletic; ready-to-wear apparel, women's; men's & boys' clothing stores
PA: Pvh Corp.
   200 Madison Ave Bsmt 1
   New York NY 10016
   212 381-3500

(G-11184)
PHOENIX USA LLC
315 W 33rd St Apt 30h (10001-2795)
PHONE.................................646 351-6598
Roger Garcia,
▲ **EMP:** 2
SALES (est): 4.5MM **Privately Held**
SIC: 2211 7389 Apparel & outerwear fabrics, cotton;

(G-11185)
PHOENIX VENTURE FUND LLC
70 E 55th St Fl 10 (10022-3334)
PHONE.................................212 759-1909
Philip S Sassower, *Ch of Bd*
EMP: 21
SALES (est): 1.8MM **Privately Held**
SIC: 3577 Computer peripheral equipment

(G-11186)
PHYSICALMIND INSTITUTE
84 Wooster St Ste 605 (10012-4363)
PHONE.................................212 343-2150
Joan Breibart, *General Mgr*
▲ **EMP:** 10
SALES (est): 1MM **Privately Held**
SIC: 3949 7812 8621 Exercise equipment; video tape production; professional membership organizations

(G-11187)
PIAGGIO GROUP AMERICAS INC
257 Park Ave S Fl 4 (10010-7304)
PHONE.................................212 380-4400
Mario Di Maria, *President*
Roland Delongoria, *Regl Sales Mgr*
◆ **EMP:** 35
SALES (est): 8MM
SALES (corp-wide): 5.2MM **Privately Held**
WEB: www.piaggiousa.com
SIC: 3751 Motor scooters & parts
PA: Immsi Spa
   Piazza Vilfredo Pareto 3
   Mantova MN 46100
   027 621-261

(G-11188)
PIANO SOFTWARE INC
1 World Trade Ctr Ste 46d (10007-0092)
PHONE.................................646 350-1999
Kweli Washington, *COO*
Alex Franta, *CFO*
Meghan Wright, *Sales Staff*
Allison Munro, *Chief Mktg Ofcr*
EMP: 100
SALES (est): 1.4MM **Privately Held**
SIC: 7372 Application computer software

New York - New York County (G-11189)

(G-11189)
PICADOR USA
175 5th Ave (10010-7703)
PHONE..................646 307-5629
Frances Coady, *Vice Pres*
EMP: 12
SALES (est): 825.6K
SALES (corp-wide): 1.7B **Privately Held**
SIC: 2731 Books: publishing only
HQ: Macmillan Holdings, Llc
175 5th Ave
New York NY 10010

(G-11190)
PICTOURE INC
110 Wall St (10005-3801)
PHONE..................212 641-0098
Lamese Bakhsh, *CEO*
EMP: 5
SALES (est): 130.5K **Privately Held**
SIC: 2741

(G-11191)
PIDYON CONTROLS INC (PA)
141 W 24th St Apt 4 (10011-1958)
PHONE..................212 683-9523
Yochi Cohen, *CEO*
EMP: 16
SQ FT: 10,000
SALES: 10MM **Privately Held**
SIC: 3944 Child restraint seats, automotive

(G-11192)
PIEMONTE HOME MADE RAVIOLI CO
190 Grand St (10013-3712)
PHONE..................212 226-0475
Mario Bertorelli, *President*
EMP: 6
SALES (corp-wide): 1.7MM **Privately Held**
WEB: www.piemonteravioli.com
SIC: 2098 Noodles (e.g. egg, plain & water), dry
PA: Piemonte Home Made Ravioli Co, Inc
3436 65th St
Woodside NY 11377
718 429-1972

(G-11193)
PILOT INC (PA)
421 W 24th St Apt 4c (10011-1244)
PHONE..................212 951-1133
Ben Brooks, *President*
EMP: 8
SALES (est): 483K **Privately Held**
SIC: 7372 7389 Business oriented computer software;

(G-11194)
PILOT INC
110 E 25th St (10010-2913)
PHONE..................212 951-1133
Ben Brooks, *Manager*
EMP: 8
SALES (corp-wide): 483K **Privately Held**
SIC: 7372 7389 Business oriented computer software;
PA: Pilot, Inc.
421 W 24th St Apt 4c
New York NY 10011
212 951-1133

(G-11195)
PIN PHARMA INC
3960 Broadway Fl 2 (10032-1543)
PHONE..................212 543-2583
Hestaline Reynolds, *Principal*
EMP: 8
SALES (est): 894.3K **Privately Held**
SIC: 3452 Pins

(G-11196)
PINGMD INC
136 Madison Ave Fl 6 (10016-6795)
PHONE..................212 632-2665
Susan Driscoll, *CEO*
Lawrence Sosnow, *Ch of Bd*
Joshua Pokotilow, *VP Engrg*
Kevin Easley, *Manager*
EMP: 6 EST: 2009
SALES (est): 491.7K **Privately Held**
SIC: 7372 Application computer software

(G-11197)
PINK INC
23 E 10th St Apt 1b (10003-6114)
PHONE..................212 352-8282
Debra Roth, *President*
EMP: 22
SQ FT: 2,000
SALES (est): 1.6MM **Privately Held**
WEB: www.pinkinc.org
SIC: 2395 Quilted fabrics or cloth

(G-11198)
PINK CRUSH LLC
1410 Broadway Rm 1002 (10018-9359)
PHONE..................718 788-6978
Rori Nadrich, *President*
Raymond Kassin, *Vice Pres*
EMP: 4
SQ FT: 1,800
SALES: 2MM **Privately Held**
SIC: 2369 Girls' & children's outerwear

(G-11199)
PINS N NEEDLES
1045 Lexington Ave Apt 2n (10021-3254)
PHONE..................212 535-6222
Rachel Low, *CEO*
EMP: 10
SALES (est): 1.1MM **Privately Held**
SIC: 3452 Pins

(G-11200)
PITNEY BOWES INC
637 W 27th St Fl 8 (10001-1019)
PHONE..................212 564-7548
Joe Mackin, *Branch Mgr*
EMP: 35
SALES (corp-wide): 3.5B **Publicly Held**
SIC: 3579 7359 Postage meters; business machine & electronic equipment rental services
PA: Pitney Bowes Inc.
3001 Summer St Ste 3
Stamford CT 06905
203 356-5000

(G-11201)
PITNEY BOWES INC
90 Park Ave Rm 1110 (10016-1301)
PHONE..................203 356-5000
Michael Levitan, *Principal*
EMP: 35
SALES (corp-wide): 3.5B **Publicly Held**
SIC: 3579 7359 Postage meters; business machine & electronic equipment rental services
PA: Pitney Bowes Inc.
3001 Summer St Ste 3
Stamford CT 06905
203 356-5000

(G-11202)
PIWIK PRO LLC
222 Broadway Fl 19 (10038-2550)
PHONE..................888 444-0049
Maiciej Zawadski, *CEO*
EMP: 30
SALES (est): 987.2K **Privately Held**
SIC: 7372 Application computer software

(G-11203)
PJ DESIGNS INC
Also Called: Peggy Jennings Designs
100 E 50th St Ste 38a (10022-6844)
PHONE..................212 355-3100
Herbert Kosterlitz, *Manager*
EMP: 40
SALES (corp-wide): 5.1MM **Privately Held**
SIC: 2335 Dresses, paper: cut & sewn
PA: P.J. Designs, Inc.
2830 46th Ave N
Saint Petersburg FL 33714
727 525-0599

(G-11204)
PKG GROUP
560 Broadway Rm 406 (10012-3938)
PHONE..................212 965-0112
Mallory Wood, *Accounts Exec*
Edward Csaszar, *Manager*
EMP: 7
SALES (est): 679.7K **Privately Held**
SIC: 2631 Container, packaging & boxboard

(G-11205)
PLACE VENDOME HOLDING CO INC
Also Called: R & F Marketing
230 5th Ave Ste 1107 (10001-7823)
PHONE..................212 696-0765
Rhonda Finkelstein, *Ch of Bd*
Arnold Finkelstein, *President*
Mark Engel, *Vice Pres*
◆ EMP: 110
SQ FT: 3,500
SALES (est): 14.5MM **Privately Held**
WEB: www.rfmarketing.com
SIC: 2392 Pillows, bed: made from purchased materials

(G-11206)
PLASCOLINE INC
275 Madison Ave Fl 14th (10016-1101)
PHONE..................917 410-5754
EMP: 18
SQ FT: 2,000
SALES: 7MM **Privately Held**
SIC: 3089 Mfg Plastic Products

(G-11207)
PLAYBILL INCORPORATED (PA)
729 7th Ave Fl 4 (10019-6827)
PHONE..................212 557-5757
Philip S Birsh, *President*
Arthur T Birsh, *Chairman*
Mark Peikert, *Chief*
Joan Alleman-Birsh, *Exec VP*
Alex Birsh, *Vice Pres*
EMP: 135 EST: 1882
SQ FT: 4,500
SALES (est): 18.5MM **Privately Held**
SIC: 2721 Magazines: publishing & printing

(G-11208)
PLAYLIFE LLC
297 Church St Fl 5 (10013-5716)
PHONE..................646 207-9082
Mattias Stanghed,
EMP: 5
SALES (est): 250K **Privately Held**
SIC: 2741 7389 ;

(G-11209)
PLEASURE CHEST SALES LTD
156 7th Ave S (10014-2727)
PHONE..................212 242-2158
Brian Robinson, *President*
EMP: 10
SALES (est): 83.8K **Privately Held**
WEB: www.pleasurewipes.com
SIC: 3089 Novelties, plastic

(G-11210)
PLECTICA LLC
175 Varick St (10014-4604)
PHONE..................917 304-7052
Adam Riggs, *Partner*
Derek Cabrera, *Partner*
Laura Cabrera, *Partner*
EMP: 9
SQ FT: 300
SALES (est): 236.6K **Privately Held**
SIC: 7372 Application computer software

(G-11211)
PLEXI CRAFT QUALITY PRODUCTS
200 Lexington Ave Rm 914 (10016-6255)
PHONE..................212 924-3244
George Frechter, *President*
EMP: 15
SQ FT: 10,000
SALES (est): 2.4MM **Privately Held**
WEB: www.plexi-craft.com
SIC: 2511 Wood household furniture

(G-11212)
PLUGG LLC
Also Called: Coliseum
1410 Broadway Frnt 2 (10018-9302)
PHONE..................212 840-6655
John Kiplani, *Branch Mgr*
EMP: 10
SALES (est): 1.1MM
SALES (corp-wide): 6MM **Privately Held**
WEB: www.coliseum.com
SIC: 2331 2335 2339 Women's & misses' blouses & shirts; women's, juniors' & misses' dresses; slacks: women's, misses' & juniors'
PA: Plugg Llc
250 Moonachie Rd Ste 204
Moonachie NJ 07074
201 662-8200

(G-11213)
PMI GLOBAL SERVICES INC
120 Park Ave Fl 6 (10017-5579)
PHONE..................917 663-2000
James R Mortensen, *President*
Patrick Murphy, *Analyst*
EMP: 23
SALES (est): 4.8MM
SALES (corp-wide): 78.1B **Publicly Held**
SIC: 2111 Cigarettes
PA: Philip Morris International Inc.
120 Park Ave Fl 6
New York NY 10017
917 663-2000

(G-11214)
PODRAVKA INTERNATIONAL USA
420 Lexington Ave Rm 2034 (10170-0012)
PHONE..................212 661-0125
Domagoj Kero, *President*
Milka Jacvic, *Administration*
▲ EMP: 12
SALES (est): 1.9MM **Privately Held**
SIC: 3631 Barbecues, grills & braziers (outdoor cooking)

(G-11215)
POETS HOUSE INC
10 River Ter (10282-1240)
PHONE..................212 431-7920
Margo Viscusi, *President*
Frank Platt, *Vice Pres*
Martin Gomez, *Treasurer*
Jane Preston, *Exec Dir*
Fredric Hugue, *Admin Sec*
EMP: 14 EST: 1985
SALES: 1.3MM **Privately Held**
SIC: 2731 8231 Book publishing; libraries

(G-11216)
POLLACK GRAPHICS INC
601 W 26th St Ste M204 (10001-1101)
PHONE..................212 727-8400
Glenn Pollack, *President*
EMP: 5
SQ FT: 1,600
SALES (est): 450K **Privately Held**
SIC: 2752 Commercial printing, offset

(G-11217)
POLYMER SLUTIONS GROUP FIN LLC (PA)
100 Park Ave Fl 31 (10017-5584)
PHONE..................212 771-1717
Mike Ivany, *CEO*
EMP: 4 EST: 2015
SALES (est): 40.4MM **Privately Held**
SIC: 2869 Industrial organic chemicals

(G-11218)
POPNYC 1 LLC
Also Called: Pop Nyc
75 Saint Nicholas Pl 2e (10032-8030)
PHONE..................646 684-4600
Gina Panella, *Mng Member*
Joseph Peraino,
▲ EMP: 5
SQ FT: 1,000
SALES: 2MM **Privately Held**
SIC: 2339 Women's & misses' accessories

(G-11219)
POPPIN INC
Also Called: Www.poppin.com
16 Madison Sq W Fl 3 (10010-1630)
PHONE..................212 391-7200
Randy Nicolau, *CEO*
Andrew Benoit, *COO*
Jimmy Abbott, *Vice Pres*
Len Wierzbicki, *Vice Pres*
Erica Stokes, *Opers Staff*
◆ EMP: 52

GEOGRAPHIC SECTION

New York - New York County (G-11246)

SALES (est): 17.9MM **Privately Held**
SIC: 2521 2522 Cabinets, office: wood; tables, office: wood; chairs, office: padded or plain, except wood

(G-11220)
PORTFOLIO DECISIONWARE INC
235 W 48th St (10036-1404)
PHONE..................212 947-1326
Jeff Hewitt, *President*
David Sim, *Marketing Staff*
EMP: 30
SALES (est): 1.9MM **Privately Held**
SIC: 7372 Prepackaged software

(G-11221)
PORTFOLIO MEDIA INC
Also Called: Law360
111 W 19th St Fl 5 (10011-4166)
PHONE..................646 783-7100
Scott Roberts, *CEO*
Patricia Cole, *Editor*
Kelly Duncan, *Editor*
Richard McVay, *Editor*
Anthony Finelli, *Natl Sales Mgr*
EMP: 200
SQ FT: 46,000
SALES (est): 17.8MM
SALES (corp-wide): 9.7B **Privately Held**
WEB: www.portfoliomedia.com
SIC: 2741 Business service newsletters: publishing & printing
HQ: Relx Inc.
230 Park Ave Ste 700
New York NY 10169
212 309-8100

(G-11222)
PORTWARE LLC (HQ)
233 Broadway Fl 24 (10279-2502)
PHONE..................212 425-5233
Alfred Eskandar, *CEO*
Scott Depetris, *President*
Eric Goldberg, *Founder*
Ary Khatchikian, *Founder*
Jason La, *Engineer*
EMP: 70
SALES (est): 15.2MM
SALES (corp-wide): 1.3B **Publicly Held**
SIC: 7372 Prepackaged software
PA: Factset Research Systems Inc.
601 Merritt 7
Norwalk CT 06851
203 810-1000

(G-11223)
POSITIVE PRINT LITHO OFFSET
121 Varick St Rm 204 (10013-1408)
PHONE..................212 431-4850
Garry Koppel, *President*
EMP: 8
SQ FT: 2,000
SALES (est): 1MM **Privately Held**
SIC: 2752 Commercial printing, offset

(G-11224)
POST ROAD
101 E 16th St Apt 4b (10003-2150)
PHONE..................203 545-2122
David Ryan, *President*
John Todd, *Managing Prtnr*
EMP: 14
SALES (est): 833.3K **Privately Held**
SIC: 2752 7371 Publication printing, lithographic; computer software development & applications

(G-11225)
POWA TECHNOLOGIES INC
1 Bryant Park Ste 39 (10036-6747)
PHONE..................347 344-7848
EMP: 40
SQ FT: 10,000
SALES (est): 3.8MM
SALES (corp-wide): 328.1K **Privately Held**
SIC: 7372 3578 Prepackaged Software Services Mfg Calculating Equipment
HQ: Powa Technologies Group Plc
Heron Tower 35th Floor
London EC2N

(G-11226)
PRAGER METIS CPAS LLC
225 W 34th St Ste 1800 (10122-1800)
PHONE..................212 972-7555
Amy Joyce, *Partner*
Richard Miller, *Partner*
Thomas Smith, *Partner*
Maria Lopez, *Accountant*
Ralph Anderson, *CPA*
EMP: 12
SALES (corp-wide): 40.9MM **Privately Held**
SIC: 3661 Communication headgear, telephone
HQ: Prager Metis Cpas, Llc
14 Penn Plz Ste 1800
New York NY 10122
212 643-0099

(G-11227)
PRC LIQUIDATING COMPANY
Also Called: New York Running Co
10 Columbus Cir (10019-1158)
PHONE..................212 823-9626
Eugene Mitchell, *Bd of Directors*
EMP: 30
SALES (corp-wide): 4.4B **Privately Held**
SIC: 3949 Sporting & athletic goods
HQ: Prc Liquidating Company
632 Overhill Rd
Ardmore PA 19003
610 649-1876

(G-11228)
PRECISION CUSTOM COATINGS LLC
Also Called: PRECISION CUSTOM COATINGS LLC
234 W 39th St (10018-4412)
PHONE..................212 868-5770
Peter Longo, *Branch Mgr*
EMP: 242
SALES (corp-wide): 130.1MM **Privately Held**
SIC: 2295 Coated fabrics, not rubberized
PA: Precision Textiles Llc
200 Maltese Dr
Totowa NJ 07512
973 890-3873

(G-11229)
PRECISION INTERNATIONAL CO INC
Also Called: Cenere
201 E 28th St 9n (10016-8538)
PHONE..................212 268-9090
Michelle Kim, *President*
▲ EMP: 6
SQ FT: 4,200
SALES (est): 754.9K **Privately Held**
SIC: 3873 5094 Watches, clocks, watchcases & parts; jewelry & precious stones

(G-11230)
PREMIER JEWELRY DESIGNS LLC
25 W 45th St Ste 305 (10036-4902)
PHONE..................212 391-8778
Larry Gordon, *Mng Member*
▲ EMP: 7
SQ FT: 1,500
SALES (est): 2.7MM **Privately Held**
SIC: 3911 Jewelry, precious metal

(G-11231)
PREMIUM 5 KIDS LLC
Also Called: AG Kids
31 W 34th St (10001-3009)
PHONE..................212 563-4999
Albert Pardo,
EMP: 15
SALES (est): 526K **Privately Held**
SIC: 2211 Apparel & outerwear fabrics, cotton

(G-11232)
PREPLAY INC
33 W 17th St Ste 901 (10011-5520)
PHONE..................917 297-7428
Andrew Daines, *CEO*
Scott Neff, *Admin Sec*
EMP: 8

SALES (est): 548.4K
SALES (corp-wide): 21.2MM **Privately Held**
SIC: 7372 Application computer software
PA: Fanvision Entertainment Llc
33 W 17th St Ste 901
New York NY 10011
917 297-7428

(G-11233)
PRESCRIBING REFERENCE INC
275 7th Ave Fl 10 (10001-6756)
PHONE..................646 638-6000
William Pecover, *Ch of Bd*
Lee Maniscalco, *President*
Ian Griggs, *Editor*
John Harrington, *Editor*
Sam James, *Editor*
EMP: 85
SQ FT: 18,000
SALES (est): 3.5MM
SALES (corp-wide): 223.6MM **Privately Held**
SIC: 2721 Magazines: publishing only, not printed on site
HQ: Haymarket Media, Inc.
275 7th Ave Fl 10
New York NY 10001
646 638-6000

(G-11234)
PRESCRIPTIVES INC (DH)
Also Called: Estee Lauder
767 5th Ave (10153-0023)
PHONE..................212 572-4400
Pamela Baxter, *President*
EMP: 7
SALES (est): 1.2MM **Publicly Held**
WEB: www.prescriptives.com
SIC: 2844 Toilet preparations
HQ: Estee Lauder Inc.
767 5th Ave Fl 1
New York NY 10153
212 572-4200

(G-11235)
PRESS GLASS NA INC (PA)
1345 Ave Of The Flr 2 (10105)
PHONE..................212 631-3044
EMP: 3
SALES (est): 17.8MM **Privately Held**
SIC: 3231 Insulating glass: made from purchased glass; art glass: made from purchased glass

(G-11236)
PRESTEL PUBLISHING LLC
900 Broadway Ste 603 (10003-1237)
PHONE..................212 995-2720
Raya Thoma, *Marketing Staff*
Stephen Hulburt,
▲ EMP: 8
SQ FT: 1,620
SALES (est): 1MM
SALES (corp-wide): 82.3MM **Privately Held**
SIC: 2731 Books: publishing only
HQ: Verlagsgruppe Random House Gmbh
Carl-Bertelsmann-Str. 270
Gutersloh 33335
894 136-0

(G-11237)
PRESTIGE GLOBAL NY SLS CORP
102 W 38th St Fl 8 (10018-3685)
PHONE..................212 776-4322
Linda Tencek, *President*
Catherine Sierra, *Office Mgr*
EMP: 7 EST: 2015
SALES (est): 271.1K **Privately Held**
SIC: 2329 Riding clothes:, men's, youths' & boys'

(G-11238)
PRICING ENGINE INC
175 Varick St Fl 4 (10014-7412)
P.O. Box 221 (10276-0221)
PHONE..................917 549-3289
Jeremy Kagan, *CEO*
Yagmur Coker, *CTO*
EMP: 10
SALES (est): 268.4K **Privately Held**
SIC: 7372 Business oriented computer software

(G-11239)
PRIDE & JOYS INC
Also Called: OLIVEA MATHEWS
1400 Broadway Rm 503 (10018-1044)
PHONE..................212 594-9820
Eli Rousso, *Ch of Bd*
Rochelle Reis, *Corp Secy*
Neil Rousso, *Vice Pres*
EMP: 15
SQ FT: 4,000
SALES (est): 7.4MM **Privately Held**
SIC: 2339 2329 Sportswear, women's; knickers, dress (separate): men's & boys'

(G-11240)
PRIMARY WAVE PUBLISHING LLC
116 E 16th St Fl 9 (10003-2123)
PHONE..................212 661-6990
Seth Faber, *Partner*
Justin Shukat, *Partner*
Winston Simone, *Principal*
Robert Dippold, *VP Sls/Mktg*
Erica Emerson, *Controller*
EMP: 9
SALES (est): 660K **Privately Held**
SIC: 2741 Miscellaneous publishing

(G-11241)
PRIME PACK LLC
Also Called: Prime Pharmaceutical
303 5th Ave Rm 1007 (10016-6681)
PHONE..................732 253-7734
Sreedara Nagarajan, *Mng Member*
Amrita Gupta,
Lakshmi Nagarajan,
▲ EMP: 10
SQ FT: 13,598
SALES (est): 1.2MM **Privately Held**
SIC: 2834 Pharmaceutical preparations

(G-11242)
PRIME VIEW USA INC
36 W 44th St Ste 812 (10036-8105)
PHONE..................212 730-4905
Shay Giuili, *CEO*
Chanan Averbuch, *Exec VP*
Michael Green, *Sales Staff*
Elinor Bayen, *Office Mgr*
David Delaplain, *Director*
▲ EMP: 5
SALES (est): 2MM **Privately Held**
SIC: 3663 Television broadcasting & communications equipment

(G-11243)
PRINCESS MUSIC PUBLISHING CO
1650 Broadway Ste 701 (10019-6966)
PHONE..................212 586-0240
Hal Webman, *Owner*
EMP: 20
SALES (est): 1MM **Privately Held**
SIC: 2741 Music books: publishing & printing

(G-11244)
PRINCIPIA PARTNERS LLC
140 Broadway Fl 46 (10005-1155)
PHONE..................212 480-2270
Theresa Adams, *Mng Member*
Suzanne Brower, *Sr Software Eng*
Brian Donnally,
Woodward Hoffman,
EMP: 55
SALES (est): 4.5MM **Privately Held**
WEB: www.ppllc.com
SIC: 7372 8742 Business oriented computer software; financial consultant

(G-11245)
PRINT BY PREMIER LLC
Also Called: Premier Supplies
470 Fashion Ave Fl 8 (10018-7850)
PHONE..................212 947-1365
Sheldon Lehman, *Mng Member*
EMP: 5
SALES (est): 1.5MM **Privately Held**
SIC: 2752 Publication printing, lithographic

(G-11246)
PRINT CITY CORP
165 W 29th St (10001-5101)
PHONE..................212 487-9778
Anna Wadolowska-Panagoda, *Ch of Bd*

New York - New York County (G-11247)

Walter Panagoda, *President*
Buck Benik, *Executive*
EMP: 16
SALES (est): 545K **Privately Held**
SIC: 2759 Commercial printing

(G-11247)
PRINT MANAGEMENT GROUP INC
33 E 33rd St Fl 3 (10016-5335)
PHONE..................212 213-1555
John Scalli, *President*
Helen Marsh, *Technology*
EMP: 7
SALES (est): 1.4MM **Privately Held**
SIC: 2752 Commercial printing, lithographic

(G-11248)
PRINT MEDIA INC
350 7th Ave Fl 12 (10001-5013)
PHONE..................212 563-4040
Jordan H Wachtell, *Ch of Bd*
Jeffrey Burgazzoli, *Exec VP*
▲ **EMP:** 100
SQ FT: 2,000
SALES (est): 11MM **Privately Held**
SIC: 2752 Commercial printing, offset

(G-11249)
PRINTECH BUSINESS SYSTEMS INC
519 8th Ave Fl 3 (10018-4594)
PHONE..................212 290-2542
Frank Passantino, *President*
Marc Zaransky, *Vice Pres*
Sue Teraghty, *Office Mgr*
EMP: 18
SQ FT: 15,000
SALES (est): 3.2MM **Privately Held**
WEB: www.printechny.com
SIC: 2789 2752 7374 2759 Binding only: books, pamphlets, magazines, etc.; commercial printing, lithographic; commercial printing, offset; optical scanning data service; promotional printing

(G-11250)
PRINTFACILITY INC
225 Broadway Fl 3 (10007-3001)
PHONE..................212 349-4009
Farah Khan, *CEO*
EMP: 8
SQ FT: 2,000
SALES (est): 670K **Privately Held**
WEB: www.printfacility.com
SIC: 2759 Commercial printing

(G-11251)
PRINTINGHOUSE PRESS LTD
10 E 39th St Rm 700 (10016-0111)
PHONE..................212 719-0990
Myron Schonfeld, *Chairman*
Sean Leary, *Production*
EMP: 6
SALES (est): 1MM **Privately Held**
WEB: www.phpny.com
SIC: 2752 Commercial printing, offset

(G-11252)
PRO DRONES USA LLC
115 E 57th St Fl 11 (10022-2120)
PHONE..................718 530-3558
Vivien Heriard Dubreuil,
EMP: 12 **EST:** 2015
SALES (est): 590.2K **Privately Held**
SIC: 3721 Aircraft

(G-11253)
PRO PUBLICA INC
155 Ave Of The Americas (10013-1507)
PHONE..................212 514-5250
Richard Tofel, *President*
Rachel Glickhouse, *Partner*
Stephen Engelberg, *Editor*
Terry Parris, *Editor*
Debby Goldberg, *Vice Pres*
EMP: 52
SALES: 14.5MM **Privately Held**
SIC: 2741

(G-11254)
PROCTER & GAMBLE COMPANY
120 W 45th St Fl 3 (10036-4041)
PHONE..................646 885-4201
Brandon Lane, *Treasurer*
Jie Zhang, *Accountant*
Nancy Medici, *Branch Mgr*
EMP: 150
SALES (corp-wide): 66.8B **Publicly Held**
SIC: 2844 Deodorants, personal
PA: The Procter & Gamble Company
1 Procter And Gamble Plz
Cincinnati OH 45202
513 983-1100

(G-11255)
PRODUCT DEVELOPMENT INTL LLC
215 W 40th St Fl 8 (10018-1575)
PHONE..................212 279-6170
Donald L Foss, *Mng Member*
Eric Chu,
▲ **EMP:** 9
SQ FT: 5,000
SALES (est): 1MM **Privately Held**
SIC: 2335 Women's, juniors' & misses' dresses

(G-11256)
PROFESSNL SPT PBLICATIONS INC (PA)
Also Called: Touchdown
519 8th Ave (10018-6506)
PHONE..................212 697-1460
Mitchell Zeifman, *President*
Julie Wong, *Exec VP*
Mark Craig, *Vice Pres*
Paul Michaels, *Vice Pres*
Cheng Ju, *Production*
EMP: 70
SALES (est): 22.6MM **Privately Held**
WEB: www.pspsports.com
SIC: 2721 7941 Magazines: publishing only, not printed on site; sports promotion

(G-11257)
PROGENICS PHARMACEUTICALS INC (PA)
1 World Trade Ctr Fl 47s (10007-0089)
PHONE..................646 975-2500
Mark R Baker, *CEO*
Peter J Crowley, *Ch of Bd*
Vivien Wong, *Exec VP*
Benedict Osorio, *Senior VP*
Jeffrey D Summer, *Senior VP*
EMP: 64
SQ FT: 26,000
SALES: 11.7MM **Publicly Held**
WEB: www.progenics.com
SIC: 2834 Pharmaceutical preparations

(G-11258)
PROGRESSIVE FIBRE PRODUCTS CO
160 Broadway Rm 1105 (10038-4212)
PHONE..................212 566-2720
Elliot Kozer, *President*
EMP: 40
SALES (est): 3.7MM **Privately Held**
WEB: www.fibrecase.com
SIC: 3161 Sample cases

(G-11259)
PROLINK INDUSTRIES INC
1407 Broadway Rm 3605 (10018-2364)
PHONE..................212 354-5690
▲ **EMP:** 10
SALES (est): 1.1MM **Privately Held**
SIC: 2389 Mfg Apparel/Accessories

(G-11260)
PROMOTIONAL SALES BOOKS LLC
30 W 26th St Frnt (10010-2011)
PHONE..................212 675-0364
EMP: 5
SQ FT: 2,500
SALES (est): 410K **Privately Held**
SIC: 2732 Publisher

(G-11261)
PROMPT BINDERY CO INC
350 W 38th St (10018-5206)
PHONE..................212 675-5181
Louis Levine, *President*
EMP: 12 **EST:** 1946
SQ FT: 5,800
SALES (est): 687.6K **Privately Held**
SIC: 2789 Bookbinding/Related Work

(G-11262)
PRONOVIAS USA INC
14 E 52nd St (10022-5308)
PHONE..................212 897-6393
Alberto Palatchi, *Ch of Bd*
Joseluis Perez Herrero, *President*
Jordi Morral, *Exec VP*
Nicole Vega, *Manager*
▲ **EMP:** 30
SQ FT: 20,000
SALES (est): 4.5MM **Privately Held**
WEB: www.pronoviasusa.com
SIC: 2335 Gowns, formal
PA: Galma Grupo Corporativo S.L.
Calle Del Camino De Hoyarrasa (La Moraleja) 48
Alcobendas
938 135-286

(G-11263)
PRONTO JEWELRY INC
23 W 47th St (10036-2826)
PHONE..................212 719-9455
Misak Terjinian, *President*
EMP: 23
SALES (est): 1.8MM **Privately Held**
SIC: 3911 Jewelry, precious metal

(G-11264)
PROOF 7 LTD
121 Varick St Rm 301 (10013-1408)
PHONE..................212 680-1843
EMP: 10
SQ FT: 3,000
SALES (est): 1.1MM **Privately Held**
SIC: 2759 7336 7299 Commercial Printing Coml Art/Graphic Design

(G-11265)
PROPER CLOTH LLC
495 Broadway Fl 6 (10012-4457)
PHONE..................646 964-4221
Joseph Skerritt, *Mng Member*
EMP: 8
SQ FT: 3,000
SALES (est): 856.9K **Privately Held**
SIC: 2311 Men's & boys' suits & coats

(G-11266)
PROPS DISPLAYS & INTERIORS
Also Called: Pdi
132 W 18th St (10011-5403)
PHONE..................212 620-3840
Stephen Sebbane, *President*
Wendy Isaacson, *President*
EMP: 15
SALES (est): 1.3MM **Privately Held**
SIC: 3993 3999 2431 Displays, paint process; stage hardware & equipment, except lighting; interior & ornamental woodwork & trim

(G-11267)
PROSPECT NEWS INC
6 Maiden Ln Fl 9 (10038-5134)
PHONE..................212 374-2800
Bernard Dankowski, *President*
Susanna Moon, *Editor*
Zhaniece Springer, *Admin Asst*
EMP: 13 **EST:** 2007
SALES (est): 582.6K **Privately Held**
SIC: 2711 Newspapers, publishing & printing

(G-11268)
PS38 LLC
Also Called: Public School
209 W 38th St Fl 5 (10018-4405)
PHONE..................212 302-1108
EMP: 7 **EST:** 2012
SALES (est): 301.2K **Privately Held**
SIC: 2311 2337 Men's & boys' suits & coats; suits: women's, misses' & juniors'

(G-11269)
PS38 LLC
Also Called: Public School
545 8th Ave Rm 350 (10018-4647)
PHONE..................212 819-1123
Alan Mak,
EMP: 12 **EST:** 2012
SALES (est): 837.9K **Privately Held**
SIC: 2329 Men's & boys' sportswear & athletic clothing

(G-11270)
PSYCHONOMIC SOCIETY INC
233 Spring St Fl 7 (10013-1522)
PHONE..................512 381-1494
EMP: 26
SQ FT: 6,000
SALES: 954.7K **Privately Held**
SIC: 2721 2789 2752 Periodical-Publish/Print Bookbinding/Related Work Lithographic Coml Print

(G-11271)
PTI-PACIFIC INC
166 5th Ave Fl 4t (10010-5909)
PHONE..................212 414-8495
Simon Chong, *President*
▲ **EMP:** 5 **EST:** 2009
SQ FT: 2,000
SALES (est): 10MM **Privately Held**
SIC: 2329 2339 2369 Men's & boys' athletic uniforms; women's & misses' outerwear; girls' & children's outerwear

(G-11272)
PTS FINANCIAL TECHNOLOGY LLC
1001 Ave Of The Americas (10018-5460)
PHONE..................844 825-7634
Farid Naib, *CEO*
EMP: 40 **EST:** 1999
SALES (est): 1MM **Privately Held**
SIC: 7372 Application computer software

(G-11273)
PUBLIC RELATIONS SOC AMER INC (PA)
Also Called: Prsa
120 Wall St Fl 21 (10005-4024)
PHONE..................212 460-1400
Joseph P Truncale, *CEO*
William Murray, *President*
Jeffrey P Julin, *Principal*
Mary Derning Barber, *Director*
Chris Duncan, *Director*
EMP: 50
SQ FT: 22,000
SALES: 11.6MM **Privately Held**
WEB: www.newyorkcity.com
SIC: 2721 8621 Trade journals: publishing only, not printed on site; professional membership organizations

(G-11274)
PUBLISHING GROUP AMERICA INC
Also Called: American Profile Magazine
60 E 42nd St Ste 1146 (10165-1146)
PHONE..................646 658-0550
Peggy Bosco, *Branch Mgr*
EMP: 18
SALES (corp-wide): 5.8MM **Privately Held**
WEB: www.pubgroupofamerica.com
SIC: 2711 Newspapers: publishing only, not printed on site
PA: Publishing Group Of America, Inc.
1200 Clinton St Ste 219
Nashville TN 37203
615 468-6000

(G-11275)
PUBLISHING SYNTHESIS LTD
39 Crosby St Apt 2n (10013-3254)
PHONE..................212 219-0135
Otto H Barz, *Partner*
George Ernsberger, *Manager*
EMP: 6 **EST:** 1975
SQ FT: 1,000
SALES (est): 420K **Privately Held**
WEB: www.pubsyn.com
SIC: 2791 Typesetting

(G-11276)
PURE TRADE US INC
347 5th Ave Rm 604 (10016-5031)
PHONE..................212 256-1600
Stefane Ladous, *CEO*
▲ **EMP:** 40
SALES (est): 3.2MM **Privately Held**
SIC: 2652 3171 Setup paperboard boxes; women's handbags & purses

GEOGRAPHIC SECTION

New York - New York County (G-11302)

(G-11277)
PUREBASE NETWORKS INC
37 Wall St Apt 9a (10005-2019)
PHONE..................................646 670-8964
Steven Ridder, *CEO*
EMP: 8
SALES (est): 204.7K **Privately Held**
SIC: 7372 Business oriented computer software

(G-11278)
PURELY MAPLE LLC
902 Broadway Fl 6 (10010-6039)
P.O. Box 20784 (10025-1523)
PHONE..................................203 997-9309
ARI Tolwin, *CEO*
EMP: 15 **EST:** 2013
SALES (est): 936.4K **Privately Held**
SIC: 2086 Fruit drinks (less than 100% juice): packaged in cans, etc.

(G-11279)
PUREOLOGY RESEARCH LLC
565 5th Ave (10017-2413)
PHONE..................................212 984-4360
Pat Parenty, *General Mgr*
EMP: 18
SALES (est): 1.5MM
SALES (corp-wide): 4.2B **Privately Held**
WEB: www.pureology.com
SIC: 2844 Hair preparations, including shampoos
HQ: L'oreal Usa, Inc.
10 Hudson Yards Fl 30
New York NY 10001
212 818-1500

(G-11280)
PUTNAM ROLLING LADDER CO INC (PA)
32 Howard St (10013-3112)
P.O. Box 111, Hoboken NJ (07030-0111)
PHONE..................................212 226-5147
Warren R Monsees, *President*
K Laura Monsees, *Director*
Gregg Monsees, *Admin Sec*
▲ **EMP:** 15 **EST:** 1897
SQ FT: 45,000
SALES (est): 3.4MM **Privately Held**
WEB: www.putnamrollingladder.com
SIC: 2499 5084 Ladders, wood; woodworking machinery

(G-11281)
PVH CORP (PA)
200 Madison Ave Bsmt 1 (10016-3913)
P.O. Box 64945, Saint Paul MN (55164-0945)
PHONE..................................212 381-3500
Francis K Duane, *CEO*
Emanuel Chirico, *Ch of Bd*
Michael A Shaffer, *COO*
Mark D Fischer, *Exec VP*
David F Kozel, *Officer*
◆ **EMP:** 100 **EST:** 1881
SQ FT: 209,000
SALES: 8.9B **Publicly Held**
WEB: www.pvh.com
SIC: 2321 2331 2253 3143 Men's & boys' dress shirts; sport shirts, men's & boys': from purchased materials; blouses, women's & juniors': made from purchased material; shirts, women's & juniors': made from purchased materials; sweaters & sweater coats, knit; shirts (outerwear), knit; men's footwear, except athletic; ready-to-wear apparel, women's; men's & boys' clothing stores

(G-11282)
PVH CORP
Also Called: Tommy Hilfiger
285 Madison Ave Fl 2 (10017-6437)
PHONE..................................212 549-6000
Kelly Brush, *District Mgr*
Victor Capper, *District Mgr*
Kelly Molloy, *District Mgr*
Karen Sanchez, *District Mgr*
Bradley Burchfield, *Vice Pres*
EMP: 5
SALES (corp-wide): 8.9B **Publicly Held**
SIC: 2321 2331 2253 3143 Men's & boys' dress shirts; sport shirts, men's & boys': from purchased materials; blouses, women's & juniors': made from purchased material; shirts, women's & juniors': made from purchased materials; sweaters & sweater coats, knit; shirts (outerwear), knit; men's footwear, except athletic; ready-to-wear apparel, women's; men's & boys' clothing stores
PA: Pvh Corp.
200 Madison Ave Bsmt 1
New York NY 10016
212 381-3500

(G-11283)
PVH CORP
Van Heusen
200 Madison Ave Bsmt 1 (10016-3913)
PHONE..................................212 381-3800
Ken Duane, *Branch Mgr*
Daniel Mackey, *Manager*
Jillian Smith, *Director*
Yahaira Keeler, *Executive Asst*
EMP: 7
SALES (corp-wide): 8.9B **Publicly Held**
WEB: www.pvh.com
SIC: 2329 2339 Men's & boys' sportswear & athletic clothing; sportswear, women's
PA: Pvh Corp.
200 Madison Ave Bsmt 1
New York NY 10016
212 381-3500

(G-11284)
PVH CORP
Also Called: Van Heusen
404 5th Ave Fl 4 (10018-7566)
PHONE..................................212 502-6300
Allain Russo, *President*
EMP: 60
SALES (corp-wide): 8.9B **Publicly Held**
WEB: www.pvh.com
SIC: 2339 Women's & misses' outerwear
PA: Pvh Corp.
200 Madison Ave Bsmt 1
New York NY 10016
212 381-3500

(G-11285)
PVH CORP
Also Called: Van Heusen
205 W 39th St Fl 4 (10018-3102)
PHONE..................................212 719-2600
Jeffrey Hui, *COO*
Lauren Kinder, *Vice Pres*
Shawn Ricker, *Vice Pres*
Armando Sosa, *Controller*
Brian Chamish, *Accountant*
EMP: 9
SALES (corp-wide): 8.9B **Publicly Held**
SIC: 2321 2331 Men's & boys' dress shirts; sport shirts, men's & boys': from purchased materials; blouses, women's & juniors': made from purchased material; shirts, women's & juniors': made from purchased materials
PA: Pvh Corp.
200 Madison Ave Bsmt 1
New York NY 10016
212 381-3500

(G-11286)
PVI SOLAR INC
599 11th Ave Bby (10036-2110)
PHONE..................................212 280-2100
Paul Mladineo, *COO*
Ted Hasenstaub, *Exec VP*
Ed Shenker, *Exec VP*
EMP: 8
SALES (est): 642.1K **Privately Held**
SIC: 3674 3679 Integrated circuits, semiconductor networks, etc.; electronic loads & power supplies

(G-11287)
PWXYZ LLC
Also Called: Publishers Weekly
71 W 23rd St Ste 1608 (10010-4186)
PHONE..................................212 377-5500
George W Slowik Jr, *President*
Carl Pritzkat, *President*
Andrew Albanese, *Editor*
Gabe Habash, *Editor*
Calvin Reid, *Editor*
EMP: 50
SALES (est): 952.8K **Privately Held**
SIC: 2741 Miscellaneous publishing

(G-11288)
Q COMMUNICATIONS INC
Also Called: Passport Magazine
247 W 35th St Rm 1200 (10001-1917)
PHONE..................................212 594-6520
Don Tuthill, *President*
Robert Adams, *Treasurer*
EMP: 7
SALES (est): 890K **Privately Held**
WEB: www.passportmagazine.net
SIC: 2721 Magazines: publishing only, not printed on site

(G-11289)
Q ED CREATIONS
Also Called: Savoritefactory
2 W 46th St Ste 1408 (10036-4502)
PHONE..................................212 391-1155
Ariel Assaf, *Owner*
Daniel Assaf, *Co-Owner*
◆ **EMP:** 1
SQ FT: 1,400
SALES: 3.7MM **Privately Held**
SIC: 3911 5094 Jewelry, precious metal; jewelry

(G-11290)
Q SQUARED DESIGN LLC
1133 Broadway Ste 1424 (10010-7941)
P.O. Box 1550, Sanibel FL (33957-1550)
PHONE..................................212 686-8860
Karen Scanlon, *COO*
Nancy Mosny, *Mng Member*
Rudolf Mosny,
▲ **EMP:** 25 **EST:** 2008
SALES (est): 2.9MM **Privately Held**
SIC: 3089 2392 Tableware, plastic; household furnishings

(G-11291)
QHI GROUP INCORPORATED
40 Wall St Ste 2866 (10005-1304)
PHONE..................................646 512-5727
Steven Quinn, *President*
EMP: 5 **EST:** 2010
SALES (est): 658.5K **Privately Held**
SIC: 3829 Thermometers & temperature sensors

(G-11292)
QLOGIX ENTERTAINMENT LLC
600 W 113th St 7b4 (10025-7952)
PHONE..................................215 459-6315
Shyno Mathew, *CEO*
Jennifer Appawu, *President*
EMP: 5
SALES (est): 125.8K **Privately Held**
SIC: 7372 7371 Educational computer software; custom computer programming services

(G-11293)
QTALK PUBLISHING LLC
1 E Broadway Fl 4 (10038-1113)
PHONE..................................877 549-1841
Maurice Hazan, *Principal*
EMP: 7
SALES (est): 193.9K **Privately Held**
SIC: 2741 Miscellaneous publishing

(G-11294)
QUAD/GRAPHICS INC
135 W 50th St Fl 8 (10020-1201)
PHONE..................................212 672-1300
Matilda Isabella, *Opers Dir*
Caleb Uhe, *Technical Mgr*
Lawrence Kennedy, *Sales Staff*
Steve Stoma, *Manager*
EMP: 120
SALES (corp-wide): 4.1B **Publicly Held**
SIC: 2752 Commercial printing, offset
PA: Quad/Graphics Inc.
N61w23044 Harrys Way
Sussex WI 53089
414 566-6000

(G-11295)
QUAD/GRAPHICS INC
60 5th Ave Lowr Level (10011-8868)
PHONE..................................212 206-5535
EMP: 509
SALES (corp-wide): 4.1B **Publicly Held**
SIC: 2752 Commercial printing, offset
PA: Quad/Graphics Inc.
N61w23044 Harrys Way
Sussex WI 53089
414 566-6000

(G-11296)
QUAD/GRAPHICS INC
375 Hudson St (10014-3658)
PHONE..................................212 741-1001
Mike Horton, *Branch Mgr*
EMP: 509
SALES (corp-wide): 4.1B **Publicly Held**
SIC: 2752 Commercial printing, offset
PA: Quad/Graphics Inc.
N61w23044 Harrys Way
Sussex WI 53089
414 566-6000

(G-11297)
QUALITY PATTERNS INC
246 W 38th St Fl 9 (10018-9076)
PHONE..................................212 704-0355
Mario Lipari, *President*
Joe Lipari, *Vice Pres*
EMP: 70
SQ FT: 14,000
SALES (est): 5.8MM **Privately Held**
WEB: www.qualitypatterns.com
SIC: 2335 2741 Women's, juniors' & misses' dresses; miscellaneous publishing

(G-11298)
QUARTET FINANCIAL SYSTEMS INC (PA)
1412 Broadway Rm 2300 (10018-9240)
PHONE..................................845 358-6071
Kathleen Perrotte, *President*
Xavier Bellouard, *Managing Dir*
Kathy Perrotte, *Managing Dir*
Allen Whipple, *Managing Dir*
Antoine Chambille, *Research*
EMP: 14
SALES (est): 5.9MM **Privately Held**
SIC: 7372 Prepackaged software

(G-11299)
QUARTO GROUP INC (HQ)
276 5th Ave Rm 205 (10001-8308)
PHONE..................................212 779-0700
Lawrence Orbach, *Chairman*
▲ **EMP:** 30
SALES: 59.2MM
SALES (corp-wide): 152.5MM **Privately Held**
WEB: www.quarto.com
SIC: 2731 Books: publishing only
PA: Quarto Group Inc(The)
The Old Brewery
London N7 9B
207 700-6700

(G-11300)
QUEST BEAD & CAST INC
Also Called: Quest Beads
49 W 37th St Fl 16 (10018-6226)
PHONE..................................212 354-1737
Marcelle Rosenstrauch, *President*
▼ **EMP:** 8
SQ FT: 2,000
SALES (est): 510K **Privately Held**
WEB: www.questbeads.com
SIC: 3914 Pewter ware

(G-11301)
QUEST MEDIA LLC
Also Called: Quest Magazine
920 3rd Ave Fl 6 (10022-3627)
PHONE..................................646 840-3404
James Stoffel, *Editor*
Valerie Fox, *Production*
Tykiscba Jacobs, *Production*
Brooke Kelly, *Assoc Editor*
Christopher Meigher,
EMP: 19
SQ FT: 9,000
SALES (est): 2.6MM **Privately Held**
SIC: 2721 Magazines: publishing only, not printed on site

(G-11302)
QUILTED KOALA LTD
1384 Broadway Ste 15 (10018-6108)
PHONE..................................800 223-5678

New York - New York County (G-11303) GEOGRAPHIC SECTION

Stephanie Oppenheim, *CEO*
David Weinstein, *President*
EMP: 11
SALES (est): 148.2K **Privately Held**
SIC: 3171 5137 5632 Women's handbags & purses; handbags; handbags

(G-11303)
QUINN AND CO OF NY LTD
48 W 38th St Ph (10018-6248)
PHONE.............................212 868-1900
Florence Quinn, *President*
Morgan Painvin, *Exec VP*
John Frazier, *Officer*
EMP: 70
SALES: 10MM **Privately Held**
SIC: 2084 5141 7011 4724 Wines, brandy & brandy spirits; food brokers; resort hotel; travel agencies

(G-11304)
QUOGUE CAPITAL LLC
1285 Ave Of The Ave Fl 35 Flr 35 (10019)
PHONE.............................212 554-4475
Wayne Rothbaum, *Mng Member*
EMP: 5 **EST:** 2001
SALES (est): 406.8K **Privately Held**
SIC: 2834 Pharmaceutical preparations

(G-11305)
QUOTABLE CARDS INC
611 Broadway Rm 615 (10012-2650)
PHONE.............................212 420-7552
Gillian Simon, *CEO*
Lauren Dopkin, *Sales Mgr*
Carol Monte, *Director*
Kris Ohlsen, *Director*
▲ **EMP:** 6
SALES (est): 500K **Privately Held**
WEB: www.quotablecards.com
SIC: 2771 2782 Greeting cards; memorandum books, printed

(G-11306)
QUVA PHARMA INC
135 Central Park W (10023-2413)
PHONE.............................973 224-7795
Stuart Hinchen, *President*
EMP: 5
SALES (est): 355K **Privately Held**
SIC: 2834 Pharmaceutical preparations

(G-11307)
QWORLDSTAR INC
200 Park Ave S Fl 8 (10003-1526)
PHONE.............................212 768-4500
EMP: 8 **EST:** 2013
SALES (est): 470.7K **Privately Held**
SIC: 2741 Internet Publishing And Broadcasting

(G-11308)
R & M GRAPHICS OF NEW YORK
121 Varick St Fl 9 (10013-1408)
PHONE.............................212 929-0294
Mario Balzano, *President*
Ron Balzano, *Vice Pres*
EMP: 15 **EST:** 1991
SQ FT: 10,000
SALES: 1.5MM **Privately Held**
SIC: 2759 Commercial printing

(G-11309)
R & M INDUSTRIES INC
111 Broadway Rm 1112 (10006-1933)
PHONE.............................212 366-6414
Erik Van Kreuninger, *CEO*
Metje Saffir, *Principal*
Robert Van Kreuninger, *Vice Pres*
▲ **EMP:** 14
SQ FT: 198,000
SALES (est): 1MM **Privately Held**
SIC: 2392 Pillows, bed: made from purchased materials; tablecloths: made from purchased materials

(G-11310)
R & M RICHARDS INC (PA)
1400 Broadway Fl 9 (10018-5300)
PHONE.............................212 921-8820
Mario Dellanno, *CEO*
Richard Dellanno, *President*
Robert Dellanno, *Vice Pres*
Robert Dellano, *Vice Pres*
Stephanie Louis, *Production*
▲ **EMP:** 65

SQ FT: 19,000
SALES (est): 33.1MM **Privately Held**
WEB: www.rmrich.com
SIC: 2337 2335 Women's & misses' suits & skirts; women's, juniors' & misses' dresses

(G-11311)
R & R GROSBARD INC
1156 Avenue Of The Amrcs (10036-2702)
PHONE.............................212 575-0077
Robert Grosbard, *Ch of Bd*
Amish Shah, *COO*
Lloyd Pasach, *Opers Dir*
Glendy Harinarain, *Controller*
EMP: 30
SALES (est): 3.3MM **Privately Held**
SIC: 3911 Jewelry apparel

(G-11312)
R R DONNELLEY & SONS COMPANY
Also Called: Studio 26
250 W 26th St Rm 402 (10001-6737)
PHONE.............................646 755-8125
Jennifer Gnall, *Sales Staff*
Andrea Robinson, *Sales Staff*
Barry Weinstein, *Sales Staff*
Michael White, *Sales Staff*
Mike James, *Manager*
EMP: 8
SALES (corp-wide): 6.9B **Publicly Held**
WEB: www.rrdonnelley.com
SIC: 2759 Commercial printing
PA: R. R. Donnelley & Sons Company
35 W Wacker Dr Ste 3650
Chicago IL 60601
312 326-8000

(G-11313)
R-PAC INTERNATIONAL CORP (PA)
132 W 36th St Fl 7 (10018-8825)
PHONE.............................212 465-1818
Daniel Teitelbaum, *CEO*
Michael Teitelbaum, *President*
Peter D Amico, *CFO*
Marian Brass, *Admin Asst*
▲ **EMP:** 50
SQ FT: 15,000
SALES (est): 9.9MM **Privately Held**
SIC: 2241 Labels, woven

(G-11314)
R-S RESTAURANT EQP MFG CORP (PA)
Also Called: Preferred Wholesale
272 Bowery (10012-3674)
PHONE.............................212 925-0335
Chekee Ho, *President*
▲ **EMP:** 10
SQ FT: 2,500
SALES (est): 1.8MM **Privately Held**
SIC: 3589 5046 Commercial cooking & foodwarming equipment; restaurant equipment & supplies

(G-11315)
RADICLE FARM LLC
Also Called: Radicle Farm Company
394 Broadway Fl 5 (10013-6023)
P.O. Box 7361, Newark NJ (07107-0361)
PHONE.............................315 226-3294
Christopher Washington, *CEO*
Jenna Blumenfeld, *Principal*
Tony Gibbons, *Principal*
Silvia Huerta, *Principal*
James Livengood, *Principal*
EMP: 5
SALES (est): 183K **Privately Held**
SIC: 2099 Salads, fresh or refrigerated

(G-11316)
RAG & BONE INDUSTRIES LLC (PA)
425 W 13th St Fl 3 (10014-1123)
PHONE.............................212 278-8214
Miles Freeland, *Vice Pres*
Marissa Kraxberger, *Vice Pres*
Jennie E McCormick, *Vice Pres*
Gabriel Saca, *Vice Pres*
Lucia Contreras, *Store Mgr*
▲ **EMP:** 70
SALES (est): 51.9MM **Privately Held**
SIC: 2326 Men's & boys' work clothing

(G-11317)
RAILWORKS TRANSIT SYSTEMS INC (DH)
5 Penn Plz (10001-1810)
PHONE.............................212 502-7900
Jeffrey M Levy, *President*
Daniel Brown, *Principal*
Gene Cellini, *Senior VP*
John August, *Vice Pres*
Geane Jospeh Celoini, *Vice Pres*
EMP: 21
SALES (est): 70.3MM
SALES (corp-wide): 1.5B **Privately Held**
SIC: 3531 Railway track equipment
HQ: Railworks Corporation
5 Penn Plz
New York NY 10001
212 502-7900

(G-11318)
RAINFOREST APPAREL LLC
1385 Broadway Fl 24 (10018-6009)
PHONE.............................212 840-0880
Jack Wo, *President*
▲ **EMP:** 8
SALES (est): 513.4K **Privately Held**
SIC: 2389 Disposable garments & accessories

(G-11319)
RAINFOREST INC
Also Called: Rft
54 W 40th St (10018-2602)
PHONE.............................212 575-7620
Jack Wu, *Ch of Bd*
Daisy Wu, *CFO*
▲ **EMP:** 10
SQ FT: 11,850
SALES (est): 2.7MM **Privately Held**
SIC: 2329 8742 6794 Men's & boys' leather, wool & down-filled outerwear; down-filled clothing: men's & boys'; jackets (suede, leatherette, etc.), sport: men's & boys'; marketing consulting services; patent owners & lessors

(G-11320)
RALEIGH AND DRAKE PBC
110 E 25th St Fl 3 (10010-2913)
PHONE.............................212 625-8212
Patrick Sarkissian, *CEO*
Gilad Goren,
EMP: 15
SALES (est): 860K **Privately Held**
SIC: 7372 Application computer software

(G-11321)
RALPH LAUREN CORPORATION (PA)
650 Madison Ave Fl C1 (10022-1070)
PHONE.............................212 318-7000
Ralph Lauren, *Ch of Bd*
David Lauren, *Vice Ch Bd*
Patrice Louvet, *President*
Christian Tookes, *Publisher*
Stavros Garger, *Vice Pres*
EMP: 500 **EST:** 1967
SQ FT: 270,000
SALES: 6.1B **Publicly Held**
WEB: www.polo.com
SIC: 2325 2321 2253 2323 Men's & boys' trousers & slacks; men's & boys' dress shirts; men's & boys' sports & polo shirts; shirts (outerwear), knit; sweaters & sweater coats, knit; ties, handsewn: made from purchased materials; topcoats, men's & boys': made from purchased materials; men's & boys' sportswear & athletic clothing; sweaters & sweater jackets: men's & boys'

(G-11322)
RAMSBURY PROPERTY US INC (DH)
Also Called: Benetton Services
601 5th Ave Fl 4 (10017-8258)
P.O. Box 6020, Somerset NJ (08875-6020)
PHONE.............................212 223-6250
Carlo Tunioli, *Vice Pres*
Diane Mravcak, *Vice Pres*
Ruslan Malich, *Manager*
▲ **EMP:** 13
SQ FT: 10,000

SALES (est): 4.4MM **Privately Held**
SIC: 2329 2339 5651 8742 Men's & boys' sportswear & athletic clothing; sportswear, women's; family clothing stores; marketing consulting services
HQ: Benetton Group Srl
Via Villa Minelli 1
Ponzano Veneto TV 31050
042 251-9111

(G-11323)
RAMSEY SOLUTIONS LLC
228 Park Ave S Ste 29075 (10003-1502)
PHONE.............................888 329-1055
Travis Ramsey, *CEO*
Carlos Ali, *COO*
Aldo Fernandez, *CTO*
EMP: 12
SALES (est): 80K
SALES (corp-wide): 1.8MM **Privately Held**
SIC: 7372 Prepackaged software
PA: Config Consultants Corporation
6800 Koll Center Pkwy # 160
Pleasanton CA 94566
408 512-1583

(G-11324)
RAMY BROOK LLC
231 W 39th St Rm 720 (10018-1089)
PHONE.............................212 744-2789
Ira Rosenfeld, *COO*
George Moody, *Opers Mgr*
Nellie Roch, *Opers Mgr*
Richie Bucello, *Store Mgr*
Cory Cole, *Engineer*
▲ **EMP:** 30
SQ FT: 5,000
SALES (est): 4.4MM **Privately Held**
SIC: 2331 Women's & misses' blouses & shirts

(G-11325)
RANDA ACCESSORIES LEA GDS LLC
417 5th Ave Fl 11 (10016-2238)
PHONE.............................212 354-5100
John Hastings, *Branch Mgr*
EMP: 100
SALES (corp-wide): 151.7MM **Privately Held**
SIC: 2387 3161 3172 2389 Apparel belts; attache cases; briefcases; suitcases; wallets; suspenders; neckties, men's & boys': made from purchased materials
PA: Randa Accessories Leather Goods Llc
5600 N River Rd Ste 500
Rosemont IL 60018
847 292-8300

(G-11326)
RANDALL LOEFFLER INC
588 Broadway Rm 1203 (10012-5237)
PHONE.............................212 226-8787
Brian Murphy, *CEO*
Amanda Thomas, *COO*
Jessica L Randall, *Creative Dir*
▲ **EMP:** 30
SQ FT: 2,500
SALES (est): 5.1MM **Privately Held**
SIC: 3131 7371 5699 Boot & shoe accessories; computer software development & applications; designers, apparel

(G-11327)
RASCO GRAPHICS INC
519 8th Ave Fl 18 (10018-4577)
PHONE.............................212 206-0447
Howard Frank, *President*
EMP: 6
SQ FT: 2,000
SALES (est): 570K **Privately Held**
SIC: 2752 Commercial printing, offset

(G-11328)
RAVEN NEW YORK LLC
450 W 15th St (10011-7097)
PHONE.............................212 584-9690
Fax: 212 466-1808
▲ **EMP:** 6
SQ FT: 2,500
SALES (est): 710K **Privately Held**
SIC: 2331 2335 Womens And Misses Blouses And Shirts, Nsk

GEOGRAPHIC SECTION

New York - New York County (G-11357)

(G-11329)
RAXON FABRICS CORP (HQ)
261 5th Ave (10016-7701)
PHONE 212 532-6816
Joe Berasi, *President*
Ruud Avcrson, *President*
Harry Ellis, *Vice Pres*
Kevin Michael, *Plant Mgr*
Connie Loftis, *QA Dir*
▲ **EMP:** 13 EST: 1947
SQ FT: 7,400
SALES (est): 4.8MM **Privately Held**
WEB: www.raxon.com
SIC: 2262 Silk broadwoven fabric finishing
PA: Vescom B.V.
  V Diepenheim Scheltusln 32
  Leusden
  334 944-010

(G-11330)
RAY GRIFFITHS INC
303 5th Ave Rm 1901 (10016-6658)
PHONE 212 689-7209
Ray Griffiths, *Principal*
Arielle Singman, *Prdtn Mgr*
Kirsten Geary, *Marketing Staff*
EMP: 7
SALES (est): 457.8K **Privately Held**
SIC: 1499 Gem stones (natural) mining

(G-11331)
RAY MEDICA INC
505 Park Ave Ste 1400 (10022-9315)
PHONE 952 885-0500
Mary Fuller, *CFO*
EMP: 45
SALES (est): 1.9MM **Privately Held**
SIC: 3845 Electromedical equipment

(G-11332)
RAY THETA INC
31 W 34th St Fl 7 (10001-3031)
PHONE 646 757-4956
Mark Gazit, *CEO*
Joel Kandy, *Business Dir*
EMP: 7
SALES (est): 45K **Privately Held**
SIC: 7372 Business oriented computer software
PA: Theta Ray Ltd
  8 Hanagar
  Hod Hasharon
  722 287-777

(G-11333)
RAYDOOR INC
134 W 29th St Rm 909 (10001-5304)
PHONE 212 421-0641
Luke Sigel, *President*
Craig Weidhorn, *General Mgr*
Theodore Fotopoulos, *Opers Mgr*
Dhruv Patel, *Prdtn Mgr*
Maciek Serafin, *Mfg Mgr*
EMP: 6
SALES (est): 1MM **Privately Held**
WEB: www.raydoor.com
SIC: 3442 Metal doors, sash & trim

(G-11334)
RB DIAMOND INC
22 W 48th St Ste 904 (10036-1803)
PHONE 212 398-4560
Rafael Inoyatov, *Principal*
EMP: 5
SALES (est): 396.3K **Privately Held**
SIC: 3356 Gold & gold alloy bars, sheets, strip, etc.

(G-11335)
RD INTRNTNL STYLE
275 W 39th St Fl 7 (10018-0748)
PHONE 212 382-2360
Kenneth Hollinger, *Ch of Bd*
▲ **EMP:** 8
SALES (est): 839.3K **Privately Held**
SIC: 2339 Women's & misses' outerwear

(G-11336)
RDA HOLDING CO (PA)
Also Called: Rittlewood Holding Co
750 3rd Ave (10017-2703)
PHONE 914 238-1000
Harvey Golub, *CEO*
Fredric G Reynolds, *Ch of Bd*
Bonnie Kintzer, *President*
Randall Curran, *Chairman*
Albert L Perruzza, *Exec VP*
EMP: 22
SQ FT: 445,193
SALES (est): 1.3B **Privately Held**
SIC: 2721 2731 5961 2741 Periodicals; book publishing; catalog & mail-order houses; miscellaneous publishing

(G-11337)
RDD PHARMA INC
3 Columbus Cir Fl 15 (10019-8716)
PHONE 302 319-9970
Mark Sirgo, *Ch of Bd*
Nir Barak, *Principal*
Arie Giniger,
EMP: 5
SQ FT: 150
SALES (est): 254.6K **Privately Held**
SIC: 3841 Surgical & medical instruments

(G-11338)
READERS DIGEST ASSN INC THE
16 E 34th St Fl 14 (10016-4360)
PHONE 414 423-0100
Diane Jones, *Branch Mgr*
EMP: 16 **Privately Held**
WEB: www.rd.com
SIC: 2721 Magazines: publishing only, not printed on site
HQ: Trusted Media Brands, Inc.
  750 3rd Ave Fl 3
  New York NY 10017
  914 238-1000

(G-11339)
REAL ESTATE MEDIA INC
120 Broadway Fl 5 (10271-1100)
PHONE 212 929-6976
Jonathan Schein, *President*
EMP: 45
SALES (est): 3.9MM **Privately Held**
SIC: 2721 Periodicals-Publishing/Printing

(G-11340)
REALITY ANALYTICS INC (PA)
Also Called: Reality Ai
157 Columbus Ave (10023-6082)
PHONE 347 363-2200
Stuart Feffer, *CEO*
Jeff Sieracki, *CTO*
EMP: 3 EST: 2015
SALES (est): 2MM **Privately Held**
SIC: 7372 Business oriented computer software

(G-11341)
REASON SOFTWARE COMPANY INC
228 Park Ave S Unit 74122 (10003-1502)
PHONE 646 664-1038
Andrew Newman, *CEO*
EMP: 10
SQ FT: 2,000
SALES (est): 324.8K **Privately Held**
SIC: 7372 Operating systems computer software

(G-11342)
REDBOOK MAGAZINE
224 W 57th St Lbby Fl22 (10019-3212)
PHONE 212 649-3331
Daniel Zucchi, *Principal*
EMP: 12
SALES (est): 1.4MM **Privately Held**
SIC: 2721 7313 Magazines: publishing & printing; radio, television, publisher representatives

(G-11343)
REDKEN 5TH AVENUE NYC LLC
575 5th Ave Fl 23 (10017-2430)
PHONE 212 818-1500
Roger Dolden, *COO*
Carolyn O'Connor, *Assistant VP*
Kevin Bauman, *Controller*
Suzie Manofsky, *Marketing Staff*
Ashley Giannetto, *Manager*
▼ **EMP:** 134
SALES (est): 18.1MM
SALES (corp-wide): 4.2B **Privately Held**
WEB: www.redken.com
SIC: 2844 Cosmetic preparations
HQ: L'oreal Usa, Inc.
  10 Hudson Yards Fl 30
  New York NY 10001
  212 818-1500

(G-11344)
REDKEN 5TH AVENUE NYC LLC
565 5th Ave (10017-2413)
PHONE 212 984-5113
Sheri Doss, *Vice Pres*
Monet Colbert, *Sales Staff*
Claire Buxton, *Director*
EMP: 7
SALES (est): 1MM **Privately Held**
SIC: 2844 Cosmetic preparations

(G-11345)
REENTRY GAMES INC
215 E 5th St (10003-8563)
PHONE 646 421-0080
Andrew Kutruff, *President*
EMP: 5
SALES (est): 235.3K **Privately Held**
SIC: 7372 Home entertainment computer software

(G-11346)
REFINERY 29 INC (PA)
225 Broadway Fl 23 (10007-3728)
PHONE 212 966-3112
Philippe Von Borrios, *Principal*
Christene Barberich, *Principal*
Piera Gelardi, *Principal*
Melissa Goidel, *Principal*
Justin Stesano, *Principal*
EMP: 80
SALES (est): 5MM **Privately Held**
SIC: 2741 Miscellaneous publishing

(G-11347)
REGAL EMBLEM CO INC
250 W Broadway Fl 2 (10013-2431)
P.O. Box 230695 (10023-0012)
PHONE 212 925-8833
Judith Nadelson, *President*
Michael Bottino, *Vice Pres*
EMP: 15 EST: 1931
SQ FT: 5,000
SALES (est): 1.7MM **Privately Held**
SIC: 2399 Emblems, badges & insignia: from purchased materials

(G-11348)
REGAL JEWELRY INC
39 W 32nd St Rm 1004 (10001-3842)
PHONE 212 382-1695
Isaac Fraiwa, *President*
▲ **EMP:** 6
SQ FT: 10,000
SALES (est): 6MM **Privately Held**
SIC: 3911 Jewelry, precious metal

(G-11349)
REGAN ARTS LLC
65 Bleecker St Fl 8 (10012-2420)
PHONE 646 488-6610
Judith Regan, *CEO*
Clarke Bowling, *Marketing Staff*
EMP: 13
SALES (est): 1.6MM
SALES (corp-wide): 33.2MM **Privately Held**
SIC: 2741 Miscellaneous publishing
HQ: Phaidon Press Limited
  Regent's Wharf
  London N1 9P
  207 843-1000

(G-11350)
REGENLAB USA LLC
575 Madison Ave Ste 1006 (10022-8511)
PHONE 800 220-9082
Edward Von Horstein, *Principal*
EMP: 8
SALES (est): 1MM **Privately Held**
SIC: 2834 Pharmaceutical preparations

(G-11351)
REINHOLD BROTHERS INC
799 Park Ave (10021-3275)
PHONE 212 867-8310
John Reinhold, *President*
EMP: 20
SALES (est): 1.5MM **Privately Held**
SIC: 3911 5944 Jewel settings & mountings, precious metal; pearl jewelry, natural or cultured; jewelry, precious stones & precious metals

(G-11352)
RELAVIS CORPORATION
40 Wall St Ste 3300 (10005-1463)
PHONE 212 995-2900
Robert De Maio, *President*
Michael Baum, *President*
Jean-Pierre Ducondi, *Vice Pres*
EMP: 45
SQ FT: 2,500
SALES (est): 3MM **Privately Held**
SIC: 7372 Business oriented computer software

(G-11353)
RELIANT SECURITY
450 Fashion Ave Ste 503 (10123-0591)
PHONE 917 338-2200
Richard Newman, *CEO*
Mark Weiner, *Principal*
Tom Juliani, *Info Tech Dir*
Sam Akiba, *Executive*
EMP: 23
SALES: 2.8MM **Privately Held**
SIC: 7372 Prepackaged software

(G-11354)
RELMADA THERAPEUTICS INC
750 3rd Ave Fl 9 (10017-2718)
PHONE 646 677-3853
Sergio Traversa, *CEO*
Danny KAO, *Senior VP*
Ottavio Vitolo, *Senior VP*
Michael Becker, *Vice Pres*
Michael D Becker, *CFO*
EMP: 17 EST: 2007
SALES (est): 3.2MM **Privately Held**
SIC: 2834 Pharmaceutical preparations

(G-11355)
RELX INC (DH)
Also Called: Reed Business Information
230 Park Ave Ste 700 (10169-0005)
PHONE 212 309-8100
Mark Kelsey, *CEO*
Dominic Feltham, *President*
Nicholas Luff, *President*
Mark Armour, *Principal*
Erik Engstrom, *Principal*
◆ **EMP:** 40
SQ FT: 30,000
SALES (est): 5.8B
SALES (corp-wide): 9.7B **Privately Held**
WEB: www.lexis-nexis.com
SIC: 2721 2731 7389 7374 Trade journals: publishing only, not printed on site; books: publishing only; trade show arrangement; data processing & preparation; systems analysis or design
HQ: Reed Elsevier Us Holdings, Inc.
  1105 N Market St Ste 501
  Wilmington DE 19801
  302 427-2672

(G-11356)
RELX INC
249 W 17th St (10011-5390)
PHONE 212 463-6644
Cheryl Miller, *Manager*
EMP: 35
SALES (corp-wide): 9.7B **Privately Held**
WEB: www.lexis-nexis.com
SIC: 2721 Magazines: publishing only, not printed on site
HQ: Relx Inc.
  230 Park Ave Ste 700
  New York NY 10169
  212 309-8100

(G-11357)
RELX INC
655 6th Ave (10010-5107)
PHONE 212 633-3900
Russell White, *President*
EMP: 260
SALES (corp-wide): 9.7B **Privately Held**
WEB: www.lexis-nexis.com
SIC: 2721 Periodicals

New York - New York County (G-11358)

HQ: Relx Inc.
230 Park Ave Ste 700
New York NY 10169
212 309-8100

(G-11358)
REMAINS LIGHTING
130 W 28th St Frnt 1 (10001-6151)
PHONE..................................212 675-8051
David Calligeros, *Owner*
Jimmy Kaston, *General Mgr*
Lauren Stacy, *Opers Staff*
Katie Brennan, *Sales Dir*
Clay Wright, *Sales Dir*
EMP: 20
SQ FT: 1,500
SALES (est): 2.5MM **Privately Held**
SIC: 3646 3645 Commercial indusl & institutional electric lighting fixtures; residential lighting fixtures

(G-11359)
RENAISSANCE BIJOU LTD
20 W 47th St Ste 18 (10036-3303)
PHONE..................................212 869-1969
Elias Theodoropoulos, *President*
EMP: 8
SQ FT: 3,000
SALES (est): 680K **Privately Held**
SIC: 3911 Jewelry, precious metal

(G-11360)
RENAISSNCE CRPT TAPESTRIES INC
Also Called: Renaissance Global
200 Lexington Ave Rm 1006 (10016-6255)
PHONE..................................212 696-0080
Jan Soleimani, *President*
Jeffrey Soleimani, *Vice Pres*
Bergi Andonian, *Admin Sec*
◆ **EMP:** 12
SQ FT: 7,000
SALES (est): 1.5MM **Privately Held**
SIC: 2273 2211 Rugs, hand & machine made; tapestry fabrics, cotton

(G-11361)
RENCO GROUP INC (PA)
Also Called: Renco Group of Companies, Inc.
1 Rockefeller Plz Fl 29 (10020-2021)
PHONE..................................212 541-6000
Ira Leon Rennert, *President*
ARI Rennert, *Chairman*
Marvin Koenig, *Exec VP*
Roger L Fay, *Vice Pres*
John Siegel, *Vice Pres*
◆ **EMP:** 4
SQ FT: 10,000
SALES (est): 3.8B **Privately Held**
WEB: www.rencogroup.net
SIC: 3312 3316 2514 2511 Sheet or strip, steel, cold-rolled: own hot-rolled; corrugating iron & steel, cold-rolled; metal kitchen & dining room furniture; wood household furniture; kitchen & dining room furniture; handbags, women's; cages, wire

(G-11362)
RENEGADE NATION LTD
434 Av Of The Amercs Fl 6 (10011-8411)
PHONE..................................212 868-9000
Jerry Eisner, *Principal*
Louis Arzonico, *Art Dir*
EMP: 15 **EST:** 1993
SQ FT: 4,400
SALES (est): 1.4MM **Privately Held**
WEB: www.renegadenation.com
SIC: 2782 Record albums

(G-11363)
RENEGADE NATION ONLINE LLC
434 Ave Of The Americas # 6 (10011-8411)
PHONE..................................212 868-9000
Jerome Eisner, *Accountant*
EMP: 8
SQ FT: 2,400
SALES (est): 265K **Privately Held**
SIC: 2741

(G-11364)
REPERTOIRE INTERNATIONAL DE LI
Also Called: RILM
365 5th Ave Fl 3 (10016-4309)
PHONE..................................212 817-1990
Yun Fan, *Editor*
Jason Oakes, *Editor*
Lori Rothstein, *Editor*
Martha Samuel, *Editor*
Michele Smith, *Editor*
EMP: 25
SALES: 3.3MM **Privately Held**
SIC: 2731 2741 Book publishing; miscellaneous publishing

(G-11365)
REPUBLIC CLOTHING CORPORATION
Also Called: Republic Clothing Group
1411 Broadway Fl 37 (10018-3413)
PHONE..................................212 719-3000
Steven M Sall, *Ch of Bd*
Michael Warner, *President*
Betty Yeung, *Technical Staff*
▲ **EMP:** 30
SQ FT: 7,500
SALES (est): 10.6MM **Privately Held**
SIC: 2339 Women's & misses' outerwear

(G-11366)
REPUBLIC CLOTHING GROUP INC
1411 Broadway Fl 37 (10018-3413)
PHONE..................................212 719-3000
Michael Warner, *President*
Steven M Sall, *Chairman*
EMP: 150
SQ FT: 7,500
SALES (est): 2MM **Privately Held**
SIC: 2339 Aprons, except rubber or plastic: women's, misses', juniors'

(G-11367)
RESERVOIR MEDIA MANAGEMENT INC (PA)
225 Varick St Fl 6 (10014-4388)
PHONE..................................212 675-0541
Golnar Khosrowshahi, *CEO*
Rell Lafargue, *COO*
Donna Caseine, *Vice Pres*
Faith Newman, *Vice Pres*
Steven Storch, *CFO*
EMP: 12
SQ FT: 8,000
SALES (est): 1.2MM **Privately Held**
SIC: 2741 Music book & sheet music publishing

(G-11368)
RESONANT LEGAL MEDIA LLC
1040 Av Of The Amrcs 18 (10018-3703)
PHONE..................................212 687-7100
Patrick Swart, *Branch Mgr*
EMP: 20 **Privately Held**
SIC: 2752 7336 8748 Commercial printing, lithographic; commercial art & graphic design; business consulting
PA: Resonant Legal Media, Llc
1 Penn Plz Ste 1514
New York NY 10119

(G-11369)
RESONANT LEGAL MEDIA LLC (PA)
Also Called: Trialgraphix
1 Penn Plz Ste 1514 (10119-1514)
PHONE..................................800 781-3591
Richard S Pennell, *CEO*
Steven Stolberg, *President*
Luis E Otero, *Vice Pres*
Patrick Paulin, *Vice Pres*
Ana Miguel, *Admin Sec*
EMP: 90
SQ FT: 35,000
SALES (est): 31.4MM **Privately Held**
SIC: 2752 7336 3993 2761 Commercial printing, offset; graphic arts & related design; signs & advertising specialties; manifold business forms

(G-11370)
RESOURCE PTRLM&PTROCHMCL INTL
3 Columbus Cir Fl 15 (10019-8716)
PHONE..................................212 537-3856
Damon Lee, *Ch of Bd*
Daunette Lee, *Vice Pres*
Akpan Ekpo, *Director*
EMP: 20
SALES (est): 384.9K **Privately Held**
SIC: 1311 Crude petroleum production

(G-11371)
RESTAURANT 570 8TH AVENUE LLC
Also Called: Wok To Walk
213 W 40th St Fl 3 (10018-1627)
PHONE..................................646 722-8191
Aviv Schwietzer,
EMP: 15
SALES (est): 1.5MM **Privately Held**
SIC: 2599 Food wagons, restaurant

(G-11372)
RESTORSEA LLC
641 Lexington Ave Fl 27 (10022-4503)
PHONE..................................212 828-8878
EMP: 7 **EST:** 2012
SALES (est): 1.2MM **Privately Held**
SIC: 2844 Mfg Toilet Preparations

(G-11373)
RETROPHIN LLC
777 3rd Ave Fl 22 (10017-1401)
PHONE..................................646 564-3680
Martin Shkreli, *CEO*
Elizabeth Reed, *Vice Pres*
Bryan Selby, *Vice Pres*
Jesse Shefferman, *Vice Pres*
Andrew Martinez, *Opers Staff*
EMP: 8
SALES (est): 832.1K **Privately Held**
SIC: 2834 Pharmaceutical preparations

(G-11374)
REUTERS LOAN PRICING CORP
3 Times Sq Fl 3 # 3 (10036-6533)
PHONE..................................212 833-9200
Arthur P Davis, *President*
EMP: 100
SALES (est): 3.8MM **Publicly Held**
WEB: www.loanpricing.com
SIC: 2741 7375 Miscellaneous publishing; data base information retrieval
HQ: Thomson Reuters Corporation
3 Times Sq
New York NY 10036
646 223-4000

(G-11375)
REVIVAL SASH & DOOR LLC (PA)
135 E 57th St Bldg 15125 (10022-2050)
PHONE..................................973 500-4242
Mike Canizales, *Mng Member*
EMP: 6 **EST:** 2017
SALES (est): 2.1MM **Privately Held**
SIC: 3442 Sash, door or window: metal

(G-11376)
REVLON INC (PA)
1 New York Plz (10004-1901)
PHONE..................................212 527-4000
Paul M Meister, *CEO*
Ronald O Perelman, *Ch of Bd*
Martin Flaherty, *General Mgr*
Debra G Perelman, *COO*
Christopher H Peterson, *COO*
▲ **EMP:** 277
SQ FT: 107,000
SALES: 2.6B **Publicly Held**
WEB: www.revlon.com
SIC: 2844 Cosmetic preparations; perfumes & colognes; deodorants, personal; hair coloring preparations

(G-11377)
REVLON CONSUMER PRODUCTS CORP (HQ)
1 New York Plz (10004-1901)
PHONE..................................212 527-4000
Ronald O Perelman, *Ch of Bd*
Gianni Pieraccioni, *COO*
Juan R Figuereo, *CFO*
▲ **EMP:** 277
SQ FT: 91,000
SALES: 2.6B **Publicly Held**
SIC: 3421 2844 Clippers, fingernail & toenail; scissors, hand; cosmetic preparations

(G-11378)
REVMAN INTERNATIONAL INC (DH)
350 5th Ave 70th (10118-0110)
PHONE..................................212 894-3100
Richard Roman, *President*
Normand Savaria, *Senior VP*
Brad Comisar, *Vice Pres*
Renee Jones, *Opers Staff*
Hebe Schetcher, *CFO*
◆ **EMP:** 40
SQ FT: 20,000
SALES (est): 35MM **Privately Held**
WEB: www.revman.com
SIC: 2391 2392 Draperies, plastic & textile: from purchased materials; comforters & quilts: made from purchased materials
HQ: Kaltex North America, Inc.
350 5th Ave Ste 7100
New York NY 10118
212 894-3200

(G-11379)
REVOLUTIONWEAR INC
1745 Broadway Fl 17 (10019-4642)
PHONE..................................617 669-9191
Mathias Ingvarsson, *President*
▲ **EMP:** 5
SALES (est): 368.2K **Privately Held**
SIC: 2322 Men's & boys' underwear & nightwear

(G-11380)
REYNOLDS METALS COMPANY LLC (HQ)
390 Park Ave (10022-4608)
PHONE..................................212 518-5400
Tomas Mar Sigurdsson, *President*
Francesco Bassoli, *Vice Pres*
Robert Bear, *Vice Pres*
Amador Cardenas, *Vice Pres*
John Kenna, *Vice Pres*
◆ **EMP:** 1 **EST:** 1928
SALES (est): 1.3B
SALES (corp-wide): 11.6B **Publicly Held**
SIC: 3411 Aluminum cans; beverage cans, metal: except beer; beer cans, metal; food containers, metal
PA: Alcoa Corporation
201 Isabella St Ste 500
Pittsburgh PA 15212
412 315-2900

(G-11381)
RFP LLC
Also Called: Bridal Guide
228 E 45th St Fl 11 (10017-3345)
PHONE..................................212 838-7733
Barry Rosenbloom, *Partner*
Jeremy Bucovetsky, *Partner*
Yelena Malinovskaya, *Partner*
Mike Rosenbloom, *Partner*
Jeff Hendlin, *Publisher*
EMP: 35
SQ FT: 11,000
SALES (est): 5.3MM **Privately Held**
WEB: www.bridalguide.com
SIC: 2721 4724 Magazines: publishing only, not printed on site; travel agencies

(G-11382)
RG BARRY CORPORATION
Also Called: Dearfoams Div
9 E 37th St Fl 11 (10016-2822)
PHONE..................................212 244-3145
Howard Eisenberg, *Manager*
EMP: 10
SALES (corp-wide): 94.2MM **Privately Held**
WEB: www.rgbarry.com
SIC: 3142 House slippers
HQ: R.G. Barry Corporation
13405 Yarmouth Rd Nw
Pickerington OH 43147
614 864-6400

▲ = Import ▼ = Export
◆ = Import/Export

GEOGRAPHIC SECTION
New York - New York County (G-11408)

(G-11383)
RG GLASS CREATIONS INC
Also Called: R G Glass
1441 Broadway Ste 28 (10018-1905)
PHONE...................212 675-0030
Edward Geyman, *President*
Joseph Laporta, *Controller*
Maria Roman, *Administration*
EMP: 38
SALES (est): 7.8MM **Privately Held**
SIC: 3211 Construction glass

(G-11384)
RHODA LEE INC
77 W 55th St Apt 4k (10019-4920)
PHONE...................212 840-5700
Michael Laufer, *President*
Henry Alcalay, *Vice Pres*
Audrey Laufer, *Vice Pres*
▲ **EMP:** 75 **EST:** 1947
SQ FT: 11,000
SALES (est): 6.2MM **Privately Held**
SIC: 2331 2337 2339 Blouses, women's & juniors': made from purchased material; skirts, separate: women's, misses' & juniors'; slacks: women's, misses' & juniors'

(G-11385)
RIBZ LLC
1407 Broadway Rm 1402 (10018-2838)
PHONE...................212 764-9595
EMP: 5
SALES (est): 330K **Privately Held**
SIC: 2389 Mfg Apparel/Accessories

(G-11386)
RiCHEMONT NORTH AMERICA INC
Also Called: Iwc New York Btq
535 Madison Ave (10022-4214)
PHONE...................212 355-7052
Schellmoser Andrea, *Branch Mgr*
EMP: 5
SALES (corp-wide): 13.6B **Privately Held**
SIC: 3873 Watches, clocks, watchcases & parts
HQ: Richemont North America, Inc.
645 5th Ave Fl 5
New York NY 10022
212 891-2440

(G-11387)
RICHEMONT NORTH AMERICA INC
Also Called: Vacheron New York Btq
729 Madison Ave (10065-8003)
PHONE...................212 644-9500
EMP: 5
SALES (corp-wide): 13.6B **Privately Held**
SIC: 3873 Watches, clocks, watchcases & parts
HQ: Richemont North America, Inc.
645 5th Ave Fl 5
New York NY 10022
212 891-2440

(G-11388)
RICHLINE GROUP INC
Eclipse Design Div
245 W 29th St Rm 900 (10001-5396)
PHONE...................212 643-2908
Eric Frid, *Branch Mgr*
EMP: 45
SALES (corp-wide): 242.1B **Publicly Held**
WEB: www.aurafin.net
SIC: 3911 Earrings, precious metal
HQ: Richline Group, Inc.
1385 Broadway Fl 12
New York NY 10018

(G-11389)
RICHLINE GROUP INC
1385 Broadway Fl 12 (10018-6118)
PHONE...................212 764-8454
EMP: 194
SALES (corp-wide): 194.6B **Publicly Held**
SIC: 3911 5094 Mfg Precious Metal Jewelry Whol Jewelry/Precious Stones
HQ: Richline Group, Inc.
1385 Broadway Fl 12
New York NY 10018
212 886-6000

(G-11390)
RICHLINE GROUP INC
Also Called: Aurafin Oroamerica
1385 Broadway Fl 12 (10018-6118)
PHONE...................914 699-0000
EMP: 177
SALES (corp-wide): 194.6B **Publicly Held**
SIC: 3911 Mfg Precious Metal Jewelry
HQ: Richline Group, Inc.
1385 Broadway Fl 12
New York NY 10018
212 886-6000

(G-11391)
RICHLOOM FABRICS CORP (PA)
261 5th Ave Fl 12 (10016-7794)
PHONE...................212 685-5400
James Richman, *Ch of Bd*
Fred M Richman, *President*
Ralph Geller, *Vice Pres*
Marvin Karp, *CFO*
Sidney J Silverman, *Admin Sec*
◆ **EMP:** 10
SQ FT: 12,000
SALES (est): 30.3MM **Privately Held**
SIC: 2391 5131 2392 Curtains & draperies; drapery material, woven; household furnishings

(G-11392)
RICHLOOM FABRICS GROUP INC (PA)
Also Called: Berkshire Weaving
261 5th Ave Fl 12 (10016-7794)
PHONE...................212 685-5400
Great Neck Richman, *CEO*
James Richman, *Ch of Bd*
Sean Prouty, *Vice Pres*
Amy Tezak, *Director*
Sidney Silverman, *Admin Sec*
▲ **EMP:** 5
SQ FT: 1,500
SALES (est): 2MM **Privately Held**
SIC: 2392 2391 Blankets, comforters & beddings; curtains & draperies

(G-11393)
RINGS WIRE INC
Also Called: Rome Fastener
246 W 38th St Rm 501 (10018-9089)
PHONE...................212 741-9779
Dr Stanley Reiter, *President*
EMP: 5
SALES (corp-wide): 2.4MM **Privately Held**
SIC: 3965 Fasteners, snap; buckles & buckle parts
PA: Rings Wire Inc
257 Depot Rd
Milford CT 06460
203 874-6719

(G-11394)
RIRI USA INC
350 5th Ave Ste 6700 (10118-6704)
PHONE...................212 268-3866
L Benjamin Howell II, *Ch of Bd*
Mitch Kupinsky, *Regional Mgr*
Mark Teel, *Vice Pres*
▲ **EMP:** 6
SQ FT: 5,000
SALES (est): 553.9K **Privately Held**
SIC: 3965 Zipper
HQ: Riri Sa
Via Della Regione Veneto 3
Padova PD
049 899-6611

(G-11395)
RISION INC
306 E 78th St Apt 1b (10075-2243)
PHONE...................212 987-2628
Kate Cornick, *CEO*
Earle Harper, *COO*
Ryan O'Donnell, *Vice Pres*
EMP: 7 **EST:** 2015
SALES (est): 299.7K **Privately Held**
SIC: 7372 7389 Business oriented computer software;

(G-11396)
RISK SOCIETY MANAGEMENT PUBG
Also Called: Risk Management Magazine
655 3rd Ave Fl 2 (10017-9130)
PHONE...................212 286-9364
Jack Hampton, *Exec Dir*
Colin Ferenbach, *Administration*
EMP: 43
SALES (est): 1.7MM
SALES (corp-wide): 15.3MM **Privately Held**
SIC: 2721 Magazines: publishing only, not printed on site
PA: Risk And Insurance Management Society, Inc.
1407 Broadway Fl 29
New York NY 10018
212 655-6030

(G-11397)
RITCHIE CORP
263 W 38th St Fl 13 (10018-0280)
PHONE...................212 768-0083
Lynn Ritchie, *President*
Andre Tirenin, *Design Engr*
▲ **EMP:** 16 **EST:** 1990
SQ FT: 3,000
SALES (est): 1.4MM **Privately Held**
WEB: www.lynn-ritchie.com
SIC: 2339 Sportswear, women's

(G-11398)
RIZZOLI INTL PUBLICATIONS INC (DH)
300 Park Ave S Fl 4 (10010-5399)
PHONE...................212 387-3400
Antonio Polito, *President*
Caitlin Leffel, *Editor*
Anthony Petrillose, *Editor*
Allison Power, *Editor*
Julie Schumacher, *Editor*
◆ **EMP:** 40
SALES (est): 15.9MM
SALES (corp-wide): 212.1K **Privately Held**
WEB: www.rizzoliusa.com
SIC: 2731 5192 5942 5961 Books: publishing only; books; book stores; books, mail order (except book clubs)
HQ: Rizzoli Education Spa
Via Arnoldo Mondadori 1
Segrate MI 20090
028 470-71

(G-11399)
RIZZOLI INTL PUBLICATIONS INC
Also Called: Universe Publishing
300 Park Ave S Fl 3 (10010-5399)
PHONE...................212 387-3572
Antonio Polito, *President*
EMP: 15
SALES (corp-wide): 212.1K **Privately Held**
SIC: 2731 Book publishing
HQ: Rizzoli International Publications, Inc.
300 Park Ave S Fl 4
New York NY 10010
212 387-3400

(G-11400)
RIZZOLI INTL PUBLICATIONS INC
Also Called: Amica Magazine
300 Park Ave Frnt 4 (10022-7404)
PHONE...................212 308-2000
Imma Vaccaro, *Manager*
EMP: 12
SALES (corp-wide): 212.1K **Privately Held**
SIC: 2711 Newspapers
HQ: Rizzoli International Publications, Inc.
300 Park Ave S Fl 4
New York NY 10010
212 387-3400

(G-11401)
RJM2 LTD
241 W 37th St Rm 926 (10018-6963)
PHONE...................212 944-1660
Richard Weinsieder, *President*
Meryl Weinsieder, *Vice Pres*
▲ **EMP:** 5
SALES (est): 487.2K **Privately Held**
WEB: www.rjm2ltd.com
SIC: 2389 Men's miscellaneous accessories

(G-11402)
RLE INDUSTRIES LLC
Also Called: Robert Lighting & Energy
1175 York Ave Apt 15e (10065-7175)
PHONE...................973 276-1444
Scott Koenig, *CEO*
Louis A Bani, *President*
Marvin Koenig, *Chairman*
◆ **EMP:** 35
SQ FT: 20,000
SALES (est): 13.2MM **Privately Held**
WEB: www.rleindustries.com
SIC: 3646 8748 Ornamental lighting fixtures, commercial; energy conservation consultant

(G-11403)
RND ENTERPRISES INC
Also Called: Next Magazine
446 W 33rd St (10001-2601)
PHONE...................212 627-0165
David Moyal, *President*
EMP: 4
SALES (est): 1MM **Privately Held**
SIC: 2721 Magazines: publishing & printing

(G-11404)
ROADRUNNER RECORDS INC (PA)
1290 Avenue Of The Americ (10104-0101)
PHONE...................212 274-7500
Jones Nachsin, *President*
Phil Kaso, *Regional*
EMP: 35
SQ FT: 8,000
SALES (est): 2.9MM **Privately Held**
WEB: www.roadrunnerrecords.com
SIC: 3652 Magnetic tape (audio): prerecorded

(G-11405)
ROBELL RESEARCH INC
Also Called: Supersmile
635 Madison Ave Fl 13 (10022-1009)
PHONE...................212 755-6577
Irwin Smigel, *CEO*
Lucia Smigel, *President*
Joel Levy, *COO*
Phil Mussman, *Sales Dir*
Ashley Vargas, *Marketing Staff*
▲ **EMP:** 8
SQ FT: 1,500
SALES (est): 1.8MM **Privately Held**
SIC: 2844 5122 Oral preparations; mouthwashes; toiletries

(G-11406)
ROBERT DANES DANES INC (PA)
481 Greenwich St Apt 5b (10013-1398)
PHONE...................212 226-1351
Rachel Danes, *President*
Robert Danes, *Treasurer*
EMP: 4
SQ FT: 1,500
SALES (est): 1.6MM **Privately Held**
WEB: www.robertdanes.com
SIC: 2331 Women's & misses' blouses & shirts

(G-11407)
ROBERT EHRLICH
Also Called: Blackswirl
75 Saint Marks Pl (10003-7944)
PHONE...................516 353-4617
Robert Ehrlich, *Owner*
EMP: 5
SALES (est): 174.7K **Privately Held**
SIC: 7372 Application computer software

(G-11408)
ROBERT J DELUCA ASSOCIATES
Also Called: Rjd Associates
260 Riverside Dr Apt 8a (10025-5259)
PHONE...................845 357-3212
Robert J Deluca, *President*
EMP: 1 **EST:** 1996
SQ FT: 500

New York - New York County (G-11409)

GEOGRAPHIC SECTION

SALES (est): 1.8MM **Privately Held**
SIC: 3399 Iron ore recovery from open hearth slag

(G-11409)
ROBESPIERRE INC
Also Called: Nanette Lepore Showroom
214 W 39th St Ph Ste 602 (10018-4404)
PHONE.................212 764-8810
Megan Darling, *Manager*
EMP: 8
SALES (corp-wide): 15.9MM **Privately Held**
WEB: www.nanettelepore.com
SIC: 2339 Sportswear, women's
PA: Robespierre, Inc.
   225 W 35th St Ste 801
   New York NY 10001
   212 594-0012

(G-11410)
ROBESPIERRE INC (PA)
Also Called: Nanette Lepore
225 W 35th St Ste 801 (10001-1904)
PHONE.................212 594-0012
Robert Savage, *President*
Nanette Lepore, *Vice Pres*
Paul Genlar, *Controller*
▲ EMP: 115
SQ FT: 39,000
SALES (est): 15.9MM **Privately Held**
WEB: www.nanettelepore.com
SIC: 2339 Sportswear, women's

(G-11411)
ROBIN STANLEY INC
Also Called: Pearltek
1212 Avenue Of The Americ (10036-1600)
PHONE.................212 871-0007
Stanley Robin, *President*
EMP: 6 EST: 1975
SALES (est): 510K **Privately Held**
SIC: 3911 Pearl jewelry, natural or cultured

(G-11412)
ROBLY DIGITAL MARKETING LLC
93 Leonard St Apt 6 (10013-3459)
PHONE.................917 238-0730
Adam Robinson, *Mng Member*
Jesse Jimison, *Business Dir*
EMP: 40
SALES (est): 966.9K **Privately Held**
SIC: 7372 Prepackaged software

(G-11413)
ROCCO BORMIOLI GLASS CO INC (PA)
41 Madison Ave Ste 1603 (10010-2236)
PHONE.................212 719-0606
Davide Sereni, *Ch of Bd*
Rocco Bormioli, *President*
Jose Perez, *Vice Pres*
Michael Marchitto, *Opers Staff*
Maurizio Amari, *Treasurer*
▲ EMP: 20 EST: 1978
SALES (est): 3MM **Privately Held**
SIC: 3221 Glass containers

(G-11414)
ROCHE TCRC INC
420 E 29th St Fl 15 Flr 15 (10016)
PHONE.................800 626-3553
Judith Dunn, *CEO*
Marcie Seiler, *Manager*
EMP: 7 EST: 2012
SALES (est): 758.6K **Privately Held**
SIC: 2834 Pharmaceutical preparations

(G-11415)
ROCKET FUEL INC
401 Park Ave S Fl 5 (10016-8808)
PHONE.................212 594-8888
Nick Sagginario, *Accounts Mgr*
Alison Horlander, *Sales Staff*
Peter Sulick, *Manager*
Timothy Obryan, *Sr Software Eng*
Fred Decaro, *Director*
EMP: 15
SALES (corp-wide): 509MM **Privately Held**
SIC: 3993 Advertising artwork
HQ: Rocket Fuel Inc.
   2000 Seaport Blvd Ste 400
   Redwood City CA 94063

(G-11416)
ROCKPORT PA LLC
505 5th Ave Fl 26 (10017-4910)
PHONE.................212 482-8580
Jeremy Getz, *Managing Dir*
William Trepp, *Principal*
Ashish Patel, *QA Dir*
Manoj Abraham, *Technical Staff*
EMP: 10
SALES (est): 913.9K **Privately Held**
SIC: 7372 Prepackaged software

(G-11417)
RODALE INC
Also Called: Women's Health Magazine
733 3rd Ave Fl 15 (10017-3293)
PHONE.................212 697-2040
Karen Kunkelman, *Marketing Staff*
Thomas Bair, *Manager*
Patten Alexis, *Director*
Eric Bizzak, *Director*
Melissa Bizzak, *Director*
EMP: 300
SALES (corp-wide): 374.8MM **Privately Held**
WEB: www.rodale.com
SIC: 2721 Magazines: publishing & printing
PA: Rodale Inc.
   400 S 10th St
   Emmaus PA 18049

(G-11418)
RODEM INCORPORATED
Also Called: Galian Handbags
120 W 29th St Frnt A (10001-5596)
PHONE.................212 779-7122
John Woo, *General Mgr*
▲ EMP: 10
SALES (est): 765.6K **Privately Held**
SIC: 3171 Women's handbags & purses

(G-11419)
ROFFE ACCESSORIES INC
833 Broadway Apt 4 (10003-4700)
PHONE.................212 213-1440
Murray Roffe, *Ch of Bd*
Andy Carter, *Exec VP*
Mark Ptak, *Vice Pres*
Arati Lakhani, *Production*
Mark Vesseur, *Director*
▲ EMP: 30
SQ FT: 50,000
SALES (est): 3MM **Privately Held**
SIC: 2321 2323 5136 Men's & boys' furnishings; men's & boys' neckwear; neckwear, men's & boys'

(G-11420)
ROGAN LLC
330 Bowery (10012-2414)
PHONE.................212 680-1407
Kevin Ryan, *Branch Mgr*
EMP: 5
SALES (corp-wide): 2.4MM **Privately Held**
WEB: www.roganandcompany.com
SIC: 2335 Women's, juniors' & misses' dresses
PA: Rogan, Llc
   270 Bowery 3
   New York NY 10012
   646 496-9339

(G-11421)
ROGAN LLC (PA)
270 Bowery 3 (10012-3674)
PHONE.................646 496-9339
Kylea Vignovich, *Prdtn Mgr*
Kevin Ryan,
Roger Gregory,
▲ EMP: 25
SALES (est): 2.4MM **Privately Held**
WEB: www.roganandcompany.com
SIC: 2335 Women's, juniors' & misses' dresses

(G-11422)
ROGER & SONS INC (PA)
268 Bowery Frnt 6 (10012-3992)
PHONE.................212 226-4734
Carl Saitta, *Ch of Bd*
Anthony Saitta, *Ch of Bd*
Maria Saitta, *President*
Joe Cirone, *Vice Pres*
EMP: 8
SQ FT: 15,000
SALES (est): 2.1MM **Privately Held**
SIC: 3589 5046 5719 Commercial cooking & foodwarming equipment; restaurant equipment & supplies; kitchenware

(G-11423)
ROGERS GROUP INC
Also Called: Ferrara Manufacturing
318 W 39th St Fl 4 (10018-1493)
PHONE.................212 643-9292
Joe Ferrara, *Ch of Bd*
Carolyn Ferrara, *President*
Joseph Ferrara, *Vice Pres*
Doug Jones, *Director*
Jason White, *Administration*
EMP: 50
SQ FT: 25,000
SALES (est): 4MM **Privately Held**
SIC: 2369 2339 Girls' & children's outerwear; women's & misses' outerwear

(G-11424)
ROLI USA INC
100 5th Ave (10011-6903)
PHONE.................412 600-4840
Danny Siger, *Manager*
EMP: 15 EST: 2015
SALES (est): 689.4K **Privately Held**
SIC: 3931 Musical instruments

(G-11425)
ROLLING STONE MAGAZINE
1290 Ave Of The Amer Fl 2 (10104-0295)
PHONE.................212 484-1616
R Brownridge, *Principal*
EMP: 9
SALES (est): 832.5K **Privately Held**
WEB: www.rollingstone.com
SIC: 2741 2721 Miscellaneous publishing; periodicals

(G-11426)
ROMA INDUSTRIES LLC
12 W 37th St Fl 10 (10018-7379)
PHONE.................212 268-0723
Paul Aglietti, *Vice Pres*
Kristin Franz, *Manager*
Adam Aglietti, *Manager*
Lynda Keehan, *Asst Mgr*
Howard Baum, *Director*
EMP: 8
SALES (corp-wide): 44.5MM **Privately Held**
WEB: www.watchstraps.com
SIC: 3172 Watch straps, except metal
PA: Roma Industries Llc
   12821 Starkey Rd Ste 4500
   Largo FL 33773
   727 545-9009

(G-11427)
ROMANCE & CO INC
2 W 47th St Ste 1111 (10036)
PHONE.................212 382-0337
Uriel Kaykov, *CEO*
EMP: 6
SALES (est): 305.4K **Privately Held**
SIC: 1499 5094 Diamond mining, industrial; diamonds (gems)

(G-11428)
ROME FASTENER SALES CORP (PA)
246 W 38th St Rm 501 (10018-9089)
PHONE.................212 741-9779
Stanley F Reiter, *President*
Howard J Reiter, *Vice Pres*
EMP: 36 EST: 1957
SALES (est): 2.9MM **Privately Held**
SIC: 3965 Fasteners, buttons, needles & pins

(G-11429)
RONNI NICOLE GROUP LLC
1400 Broadway Rm 2102 (10018-0649)
PHONE.................212 764-1000
Ronnie Russell, *President*
David Brokman, *Prdtn Mgr*
Ale Barbera, *Production*
Andy Hilowitz, *VP Human Res*
Merrill Bernstein,
◆ EMP: 35
SQ FT: 2,500
SALES (est): 4.1MM **Privately Held**
SIC: 2335 Women's, juniors' & misses' dresses

(G-11430)
ROSEMONT PRESS INCORPORATED (PA)
253 Church St Apt 2 (10013-3438)
PHONE.................212 239-4770
James J Reardon, *Ch of Bd*
James Reardon, *Principal*
Patricia Reardon, *Manager*
▲ EMP: 48 EST: 1963
SQ FT: 12,800
SALES (est): 8.2MM **Privately Held**
WEB: www.rosemontpress.com
SIC: 2752 2789 Commercial printing, offset; bookbinding & related work

(G-11431)
ROSEN MANDELL & IMMERMAN INC
Also Called: Rmi Printing
121 Varick St Rm 301 (10013-1408)
PHONE.................212 691-2277
Steve Visoky, *President*
EMP: 24
SQ FT: 3,500
SALES (est): 2.8MM **Privately Held**
WEB: www.rmiprinting.com
SIC: 2789 2752 Bookbinding & related work; commercial printing, lithographic

(G-11432)
ROSEN PUBLISHING GROUP INC
29 E 21st St Fl 2 (10010-6256)
P.O. Box 29278 (10087-9278)
PHONE.................212 777-3017
Roger C Rosen, *President*
Gina Hayn, *Vice Pres*
▲ EMP: 150
SQ FT: 12,000
SALES (est): 40.9MM **Privately Held**
WEB: www.rosenpublishing.com
SIC: 2731 Books: publishing only

(G-11433)
ROSENAU BECK INC
135 W 36th St Rm 10l (10018-9473)
PHONE.................212 279-6202
Thomas Rosenau, *President*
Dominique Kurzawa, *Prdtn Mgr*
Joan Krasnow, *Accounts Exec*
EMP: 12
SALES (corp-wide): 2.5MM **Privately Held**
SIC: 2361 Dresses: girls', children's & infants'
PA: Beck Rosenau Inc
   1310 Industrial Blvd # 201
   Southampton PA 18966
   215 364-1714

(G-11434)
ROSETTI HANDBAGS AND ACC (DH)
350 5th Ave Lbby 9 (10118-0109)
PHONE.................646 839-7945
Jane Thompson, *President*
▲ EMP: 45
SQ FT: 4,000
SALES (est): 6.4MM **Privately Held**
SIC: 2389 Men's miscellaneous accessories
HQ: Gbg Usa Inc.
   350 5th Ave Lbby 11
   New York NY 10118
   646 839-7000

(G-11435)
ROSY BLUE INC (HQ)
529 5th Ave Fl 12 (10017-4676)
PHONE.................212 687-8838
Aashish Jhaveri, *Ch of Bd*
Dipu Mehta, *Ch of Bd*
Shyam Jagirdar, *Vice Pres*
EMP: 35
SQ FT: 9,000
SALES (est): 4.8MM **Privately Held**
WEB: www.rosyblue.com
SIC: 3911 5094 Jewelry, precious metal; diamonds (gems)

GEOGRAPHIC SECTION

New York - New York County (G-11465)

(G-11436)
ROUGH DRAFT PUBLISHING LLC
Also Called: Proof Magazine
1916 Old Chelsea Sta (10113)
PHONE 212 741-4773
Stephen Davis,
EMP: 15
SALES (est): 1.1MM Privately Held
SIC: 2721 Magazines: publishing only, not printed on site

(G-11437)
ROUGH GUIDES US LTD
345 Hudson St Fl 4 (10014-4536)
PHONE 212 414-3635
Martin Dunford, *Exec Dir*
▲ EMP: 75
SALES (est): 3.9MM Privately Held
WEB: www.roughguides.com
SIC: 2741 Miscellaneous publishing

(G-11438)
ROYAL MIRACLE CORP
2 W 46th St Rm 9209 (10036-4811)
PHONE 212 921-5797
Edmond Elyassian, *President*
EMP: 30
SQ FT: 5,000
SALES (est): 22.5MM Privately Held
WEB: www.royalmiracle.com
SIC: 3911 Jewelry, precious metal

(G-11439)
ROYAL NEWS CORP
Also Called: Royal Media Group
8 W 38th St Rm 901 (10018-6239)
PHONE 212 564-8972
Jonathan Hornblass, *President*
Rakib Mohiuddin, *Controller*
Jason Rosen, *Sales Staff*
Tatjana Kulkarni, *Assoc Editor*
EMP: 12
SQ FT: 2,000
SALES (est): 1.2MM Privately Held
WEB: www.momentic.com
SIC: 2711 Newspapers, publishing & printing

(G-11440)
ROYAL PROMOTION GROUP INC
Also Called: Rpg
119 W 57th St Ste 906 (10019-2401)
PHONE 212 246-3780
Bruce E Teitelbaum, *CEO*
Ellen L Friedman, *Exec VP*
Andrea Millner, *Exec VP*
Eric Williams, *Exec VP*
Ajay Khanna, *CFO*
▲ EMP: 60
SQ FT: 20,000
SALES (est): 9.8MM Privately Held
WEB: www.royalpromo.com
SIC: 3993 Displays & cutouts, window & lobby

(G-11441)
ROYALTY NETWORK INC (PA)
224 W 30th St Rm 1007 (10001-1077)
PHONE 212 967-4300
Frank Liwall, *President*
Renato Olivari, *Vice Pres*
EMP: 7
SQ FT: 2,500
SALES (est): 754.9K Privately Held
WEB: www.roynet.com
SIC: 2741 Patterns, paper: publishing & printing

(G-11442)
RP55 INC
230 W 39th St Fl 7 (10018-4977)
PHONE 212 840-4035
Lisa Blumenthal, *Vice Pres*
Sabai Burnett, *VP Mktg*
Ron Poisson, *Manager*
EMP: 6
SALES (corp-wide): 9.1MM Privately Held
SIC: 2329 Men's & boys' sportswear & athletic clothing

PA: Rp55, Inc.
520 Viking Dr
Virginia Beach VA 23452
757 428-0300

(G-11443)
RSL MEDIA LLC
Also Called: New York Enterprise Report
1001 Ave Of The Ave Fl 11 Flr 11 (10018)
PHONE 212 307-6760
Robert Lebin,
EMP: 9
SALES (est): 1MM Privately Held
SIC: 2721 2741 Magazines: publishing only, not printed on site; miscellaneous publishing

(G-11444)
RTR BAG & CO LTD
27 W 20th St (10011-3707)
PHONE 212 620-0011
Ron Raznick, *President*
▲ EMP: 7
SALES (est): 503.4K Privately Held
SIC: 2673 2674 Plastic bags: made from purchased materials; shopping bags: made from purchased materials

(G-11445)
RUBY NEWCO LLC
1211 Ave Of The Americas (10036-8701)
PHONE 212 852-7000
Keith Rupert Murdoch, *CEO*
EMP: 6
SALES (est): 228.2K
SALES (corp-wide): 9B Publicly Held
SIC: 2711 2721 6289 Newspapers, publishing & printing; magazines: publishing only, not printed on site; statistical reports (periodicals): publishing & printing; financial reporting; stock quotation service
HQ: News Preferred Holdings Inc
20 Westport Rd
Wilton CT 06897
203 563-6483

(G-11446)
RUDOLF FRIEDMAN INC
42 W 48th St Ste 1102 (10036-1701)
PHONE 212 869-5070
Alexander Nadaner, *President*
Glenn Nadaner, *Vice Pres*
Fay Nadaner, *Treasurer*
Helen Forman, *Office Admin*
Celena Hecht, *Admin Sec*
EMP: 12 EST: 1946
SQ FT: 1,200
SALES (est): 940K Privately Held
WEB: www.rudolffriedmann.com
SIC: 3911 Jewelry, precious metal

(G-11447)
RUMSON ACQUISITION LLC (PA)
Also Called: Stephen Dweck
1385 Broadway Fl 9 (10018-6001)
PHONE 718 349-4300
Jack Rahmey, *President*
EMP: 8
SQ FT: 4,500
SALES: 3MM Privately Held
SIC: 3911 Jewelry, precious metal

(G-11448)
RUNS CAPITAL INC ✪
14 Wall St Fl 203420 (10005-2101)
PHONE 212 618-1201
Giri Devanur, *CEO*
Artit Wangperawong, *CTO*
EMP: 50 EST: 2018
SALES (est): 787.2K Privately Held
SIC: 7372 5961 Application computer software;

(G-11449)
RUNS INC
14 Wall St Fl 203420 (10005-2101)
PHONE 212 618-1201
EMP: 50
SALES (est): 787.2K Privately Held
SIC: 7372 Prepackaged Software Services

(G-11450)
RUSSIAN STANDARD VODKA USA INC (PA)
Also Called: Roust USA
232 Madison Ave Fl 16 (10016-2909)
PHONE 212 679-1894
Leonid Yangarber, *CEO*
John Palatella, *President*
Michael Stoner, *President*
Giulio Bertozzi, *General Mgr*
Nelia Nuriakhmetova, *Principal*
◆ EMP: 5
SALES (est): 1.6MM Privately Held
SIC: 2085 Vodka (alcoholic beverage)

(G-11451)
RVC ENTERPRISES LLC (PA)
Also Called: Dereon/24 K Style
1384 Broadway Fl 17 (10018-0508)
P.O. Box 607 (10150-0607)
PHONE 212 391-4600
Victor Azrak, *Mng Member*
Charles Azrak,
Reuben Azrak,
▲ EMP: 29
SALES (est): 8.3MM Privately Held
SIC: 2339 Women's & misses' outerwear

(G-11452)
RYAN GEMS INC
20 E 46th St Rm 200 (10017-9287)
PHONE 212 697-0149
Edison Akhavan, *President*
Khin Chit, *Accounts Mgr*
Simon Eliassi, *Sales Staff*
▲ EMP: 38
SQ FT: 4,500
SALES (est): 9MM Privately Held
WEB: www.ryangems.com
SIC: 3911 Jewelry, precious metal

(G-11453)
RYLAND PETERS & SMALL INC
341 E 116th St (10029-1502)
PHONE 646 791-5410
David Peters, *President*
▲ EMP: 6
SALES (est): 586.9K Privately Held
WEB: www.rylandpeters.com
SIC: 2731 Books: publishing only

(G-11454)
S & C BRIDAL LLC (PA)
1407 Broadway Fl 41 (10018-2348)
PHONE 212 789-7000
Stanley Cayre,
Amin Cayre,
Hank Shalom,
▲ EMP: 12
SQ FT: 10,000
SALES (est): 5.2MM Privately Held
WEB: www.usangels.com
SIC: 2361 5641 Girls' & children's dresses, blouses & shirts; children's wear

(G-11455)
S & C BRIDALS LLC
Also Called: US Angels
1407 Broadway Fl 41 (10018-2348)
PHONE 213 624-4777
David Gardner, *Branch Mgr*
EMP: 8
SALES (corp-wide): 5.2MM Privately Held
SIC: 2361 5641 Girls' & children's dresses, blouses & shirts; children's wear
PA: S & C Bridal Llc
1407 Broadway Fl 41
New York NY 10018
212 789-7000

(G-11456)
S & S MANUFACTURING CO INC (PA)
1375 Broadway Fl 2 (10018-7073)
PHONE 212 444-6000
Kirk Gellin, *Co-President*
Robert Sobel, *Co-President*
Robert Frederick, *Vice Pres*
▲ EMP: 75
SQ FT: 21,000
SALES (est): 5.7MM Privately Held
SIC: 2331 2339 Blouses, women's & juniors': made from purchased material; sportswear, women's

(G-11457)
S G I
40 E 52nd St Frnt A (10022-5911)
PHONE 917 386-0385
Richard L Miller, *Principal*
EMP: 5
SALES (est): 401.4K Privately Held
SIC: 3577 Computer peripheral equipment

(G-11458)
S P BOOKS INC
99 Spring St Fl 3 (10012-3929)
PHONE 212 431-5011
Pearson Allen, *President*
EMP: 6
SALES (est): 1.5MM Privately Held
WEB: www.spibooks.com
SIC: 2731 5192 Book publishing; books

(G-11459)
S ROTHSCHILD & CO INC (PA)
Also Called: RCM Design Division
1407 Broadway Fl 10 (10018-3271)
PHONE 212 354-8550
Isidore Friedman, *CEO*
Mark Friedman, *President*
William Mitchell, *CFO*
◆ EMP: 110 EST: 1881
SQ FT: 50,000
SALES (est): 8MM Privately Held
SIC: 2369 Girls' & children's outerwear

(G-11460)
S1 BIOPHARMA INC
7 World Trade Ctr 250g (10007-2140)
PHONE 201 839-0941
John Kaufmann, *CFO*
Peter Jain, *CFO*
EMP: 6 EST: 2013
SALES (est): 536.4K Privately Held
SIC: 2834 Pharmaceutical preparations

(G-11461)
SAAD COLLECTION INC (PA)
1165 Broadway Ste 305 (10001-7450)
PHONE 212 937-0341
Farzana Younus, *President*
EMP: 9
SALES (est): 1.3MM Privately Held
SIC: 2321 2331 Men's & boys' furnishings; women's & misses' blouses & shirts

(G-11462)
SABIN ROBBINS PAPER COMPANY
455 E 86th St (10028-6400)
PHONE 513 874-5270
Thomas Roberts, *President*
EMP: 30
SALES (est): 10.4MM Privately Held
SIC: 2621 Building paper, sheathing

(G-11463)
SACKS AND COMPANY NEW YORK (PA)
119 W 57th St Ste 512 (10019-2302)
PHONE 212 741-1000
Carla Sacks, *President*
Reid Kutrow, *Pub Rel Mgr*
Krista Williams, *Sales Staff*
Samantha Tillman, *Director*
Ethan Stuber, *Personnel Assit*
EMP: 9
SALES (est): 849.8K Privately Held
SIC: 2741 Miscellaneous publishing

(G-11464)
SAFE SKIES LLC (PA)
Also Called: TSA Luggage Locks
954 3rd Ave Ste 504 (10022-2013)
PHONE 888 632-5027
David Tropp, *Mng Member*
▲ EMP: 9
SQ FT: 70,000
SALES (est): 106.4MM Privately Held
SIC: 3429 Locks or lock sets

(G-11465)
SAGE AUDIO VIDEO TECH LLC
53 W 36th St Rm 605 (10018-7991)
PHONE 212 213-1523
EMP: 42
SALES (est): 1.3MM Privately Held
SIC: 3651 Household audio & video equipment

New York - New York County (G-11466) — GEOGRAPHIC SECTION

(G-11466)
SAKONNET TECHNOLOGY LLC
11 E 44th St Fl 1000 (10017-0058)
PHONE..................212 849-9267
Alarik Myrin, *Partner*
Melanie Penachio, *Vice Pres*
EMP: 30
SALES (est): 2.5MM **Privately Held**
WEB: www.sknt.com
SIC: 7372 Business oriented computer software

(G-11467)
SALE 121 CORP
1324 Lexington Ave # 111 (10128-1145)
PHONE..................240 855-8998
Mohammad Naz, *Branch Mgr*
EMP: 99
SALES (corp-wide): 3.5MM **Privately Held**
SIC: 3572 8748 7371 7373 Disk drives, computer; systems engineering consultant, ex. computer or professional; computer software development; systems software development services
PA: Sale 121 Corp
1467 68th Ave
Sacramento CA 95822
888 233-7667

(G-11468)
SALENTICA CORP
245 Park Ave Fl 39 (10167-4000)
PHONE..................212 672-1777
William Stone, *CEO*
EMP: 30 **EST:** 2008
SALES (est): 1.1MM
SALES (corp-wide): 1.6B **Publicly Held**
SIC: 7372 Prepackaged software
PA: Ss&C Technologies Holdings, Inc.
80 Lamberton Rd
Windsor CT 06095
860 298-4500

(G-11469)
SALES HACKER INC
505 E 14th St Apt 5h (10009-2904)
P.O. Box 503, Armonk (10504-0503)
PHONE..................516 660-2836
Max Altschuler, *CEO*
Amy Weicker, *Marketing Staff*
EMP: 6 **EST:** 2014
SALES (est): 139K
SALES (corp-wide): 8.7MM **Privately Held**
SIC: 7372 8742 Business oriented computer software; marketing consulting services
PA: Outreach Corporation
1441 N 34th St Ste 100
Seattle WA 98103
206 235-3672

(G-11470)
SALES TAX ASSET RCEIVABLE CORP
255 Greenwich St Fl 6 (10007-2422)
PHONE..................212 788-5874
Allan Anders, *President*
Jay Olson, *Treasurer*
EMP: 3
SALES: 170.4MM **Privately Held**
SIC: 3953 Embossing seals, corporate & official

(G-11471)
SALMCO JEWELRY CORP
Also Called: Bay Sales Company
22 W 32nd St Fl 16 (10001-1698)
PHONE..................212 695-8792
Errol Salm, *President*
Morton Salm, *Principal*
Lance Salm, *Manager*
▲ **EMP:** 17
SQ FT: 6,000
SALES (est): 2.6MM **Privately Held**
WEB: www.baysalesinc.com
SIC: 3961 Costume jewelry, ex. precious metal & semiprecious stones

(G-11472)
SALONCLICK LLC
Also Called: Min New York
117 Crosby St (10012-3301)
PHONE..................718 643-6793
Chad Muranczyk,
EMP: 12
SQ FT: 2,000
SALES (est): 2MM **Privately Held**
SIC: 2844 Hair coloring preparations; hair preparations, including shampoos

(G-11473)
SALUTEM GROUP LLC
44 Wall St Fl 12 (10005-2433)
PHONE..................347 620-2640
Mikhail Abarshalin, *Principal*
EMP: 6
SALES (est): 655.2K **Privately Held**
SIC: 2834 Pharmaceutical preparations

(G-11474)
SAM HEE INTERNATIONAL INC
213 W 35th St Ste 503 (10001-1903)
PHONE..................212 594-7815
Hoon Lee, *CEO*
▲ **EMP:** 7
SQ FT: 3,000
SALES (est): 1.6MM **Privately Held**
SIC: 2339 Athletic clothing: women's, misses' & juniors'

(G-11475)
SAM SALEM & SON LLC
302 5th Ave Fl 4 (10001-3604)
PHONE..................212 695-6020
Amit Nanda, *Vice Pres*
Jesse Salem, *Mng Member*
Sam Salem,
Carey Sutton,
▲ **EMP:** 13
SQ FT: 1,800
SALES (est): 3.7MM **Privately Held**
SIC: 2299 Linen fabrics

(G-11476)
SAMOSS GROUP LTD (PA)
Also Called: Samuel H Moss
213 W 35th St Rm 1301 (10001)
PHONE..................212 239-6677
Julius Hirsch, *President*
Ranning Marks, *Vice Pres*
Humberto Estrada, *Manager*
EMP: 30
SQ FT: 9,000
SALES (est): 1.7MM **Privately Held**
WEB: www.thesamossgrp.com
SIC: 3953 Marking devices

(G-11477)
SAMUEL FRENCH INC (PA)
235 Park Ave S Fl 5 (10003-1405)
PHONE..................212 206-8990
Nathan Collins, *Ch of Bd*
Charles Nostrand, *President*
Merle Cosgrove, *Vice Pres*
Casey McLain, *Opers Staff*
Charles Graytok, *Treasurer*
EMP: 45 **EST:** 1830
SQ FT: 17,000
SALES (est): 6.7MM **Privately Held**
WEB: www.samuelfrench.com
SIC: 2731 5942 5192 Books: publishing & printing; book stores; books

(G-11478)
SAMUEL SCHULMAN FURS INC
Also Called: Alexandre Furs
150 W 30th St Fl 13 (10001-4185)
PHONE..................212 736-5550
Edwin L Schulman, *President*
Larry Schulman, *Vice Pres*
Stanley R Schulman, *Treasurer*
EMP: 25 **EST:** 1940
SQ FT: 12,000
SALES (est): 1.4MM **Privately Held**
SIC: 2371 Fur coats & other fur apparel; jackets, fur

(G-11479)
SANCTUARY BRANDS LLC (PA)
Also Called: Tailorbyrd
70 W 40th St Fl 5 (10018-2626)
PHONE..................212 704-4014
Traci Young, *President*
Eva Yue, *Production*
Larry Stemerman,
EMP: 6
SALES (est): 699.8K **Privately Held**
SIC: 2329 5136 5611 Riding clothes:, men's, youths' & boys'; men's & boys' clothing; men's & boys' clothing stores

(G-11480)
SANDBOX BRANDS INC
26 W 17th St Lbby (10011-5710)
PHONE..................212 647-8877
David Barber, *President*
Tom Hubben, *Vice Pres*
EMP: 7 **EST:** 1997
SALES: 490K **Privately Held**
WEB: www.sandboxbrands.com
SIC: 3944 Games, toys & children's vehicles

(G-11481)
SANDOW MEDIA LLC
101 Park Ave Fl 4 (10178-0300)
PHONE..................646 805-0200
Robyn Fingerman, *Vice Pres*
Karlee Linman, *Sales Staff*
William Kirkland, *Branch Mgr*
Chad Simpson, *Info Tech Dir*
EMP: 10
SALES (corp-wide): 108.8MM **Privately Held**
SIC: 2721 Magazines: publishing only, not printed on site
PA: Sandow Media, Llc
3651 Nw 8th Ave Ste 200
Boca Raton FL 33431
561 961-7700

(G-11482)
SANDY DALAL LTD
220 Central Park S 10f (10019-1417)
PHONE..................212 532-5822
Michael Agashiwala, *President*
Loma Agashiwala, *Admin Sec*
EMP: 5
SQ FT: 1,200
SALES (est): 330K **Privately Held**
WEB: www.sandydalal.com
SIC: 2329 Men's & boys' sportswear & athletic clothing

(G-11483)
SANGUINE GAS EXPLORATION LLC
152 W 57th St Fl 4100 (10019-3322)
PHONE..................212 582-8555
Randy Nelson, *Branch Mgr*
EMP: 26
SALES (est): 1.1MM
SALES (corp-wide): 115.9MM **Privately Held**
SIC: 1382 Oil & gas exploration services
PA: Sanguine Gas Exploration, L.L.C.
110 W 7th St Ste 2700
Tulsa OK 74119
918 494-6070

(G-11484)
SANOY INC
Also Called: Bonnie J
19 W 36th St Fl 11 (10018-7699)
PHONE..................212 695-6384
Larry Jonas, *President*
Bonnie Jonas, *Vice Pres*
EMP: 28
SQ FT: 5,000
SALES (est): 4.1MM **Privately Held**
SIC: 3911 3961 Jewelry, precious metal; costume jewelry

(G-11485)
SANTEE PRINT WORKS (PA)
58 W 40th St Fl 11 (10018-2638)
PHONE..................212 997-1570
Martin Barocas, *Chairman*
Leon Barocas, *Vice Pres*
▲ **EMP:** 500 **EST:** 1949
SQ FT: 1,500,000
SALES (est): 102MM **Privately Held**
WEB: www.classiccottons.com
SIC: 2261 Screen printing of cotton broadwoven fabrics; printing of cotton broadwoven fabrics

(G-11486)
SAPPHIRE SYSTEMS INC (HQ)
405 Lexington Ave Fl 49 (10174-0002)
PHONE..................212 905-0100
Clare Howard, *Business Mgr*
Greg Smith, *Business Mgr*
Uys Moller, *Vice Pres*
Lorenzo Zecca, *Vice Pres*
Donna Jones, *Project Mgr*
EMP: 10
SALES (est): 1.5MM
SALES (corp-wide): 35.3MM **Privately Held**
SIC: 7372 Business oriented computer software
PA: Sapphire Systems Limited
32 London Bridge Street
London SE1 9
207 648-2000

(G-11487)
SARATOGA LIGHTING HOLDINGS LLC
535 Madison Ave Fl 4 (10022-4291)
PHONE..................212 906-7800
Christian L Oberbeck,
Damon H Ball,
Richard A Petrocelli,
▲ **EMP:** 1483
SALES (est): 75MM **Privately Held**
SIC: 3641 3645 3646 3648 Electric lamps & parts for generalized applications; residential lighting fixtures; commercial indusl & institutional electric lighting fixtures; lighting equipment

(G-11488)
SARGENT MANUFACTURING INC
120 E 124th St (10035-1933)
P.O. Box 740607, Bronx (10474-9425)
PHONE..................212 722-7000
Richard Oswald, *President*
Robert Oswald, *Vice Pres*
Andrew Geraci, *Engineer*
Jacqueline Bacha, *Manager*
Chris Maslowski, *Manager*
EMP: 2
SQ FT: 5,000
SALES: 1.4MM
SALES (corp-wide): 3.4MM **Privately Held**
SIC: 3443 Chutes & troughs
PA: H. C. Oswald Supply Co., Inc.
725 Whittier St
Bronx NY 10474
718 620-1400

(G-11489)
SARGENTO FOODS INC
498 7th Ave (10018-6798)
PHONE..................920 893-8484
EMP: 108
SALES (corp-wide): 1.8B **Privately Held**
SIC: 2022 Natural cheese; processed cheese
PA: Sargento Foods Inc.
1 Persnickety Pl
Plymouth WI 53073
920 893-8484

(G-11490)
SARINA ACCESSORIES LLC
15 W 36th St Fl 5 (10018-7130)
PHONE..................212 239-8106
Marc Faham, *Mng Member*
▲ **EMP:** 12
SQ FT: 4,000
SALES (est): 2.8MM **Privately Held**
SIC: 3961 2339 3873 Costume jewelry; scarves, hoods, headbands, etc.: women's; watches, clocks, watchcases & parts

(G-11491)
SARKISIANS JEWELRY CO
17 W 45th St Ste 201 (10036-4922)
PHONE..................212 869-1060
Vazgen Sarkisian, *President*
EMP: 5
SALES (est): 360K **Privately Held**
WEB: www.sarkisiansjewelry.com
SIC: 3911 Medals, precious or semiprecious metal

(G-11492)
SATELLITE INCORPORATED
43 W 46th St Ste 503 (10036-4121)
PHONE..................212 221-6687
Paula STA Cruz, *General Mgr*
EMP: 5
SALES (est): 316.3K **Privately Held**
SIC: 3911 Jewelry, precious metal

▲ = Import ▼ = Export
◆ = Import/Export

GEOGRAPHIC SECTION

New York - New York County (G-11517)

(G-11493)
SAVEUR MAGAZINE
304 Park Ave S Fl 8 (10010-4310)
PHONE..................212 219-7400
Coleman Andrews, *Manager*
Stefanie McNamara, *Associate Dir*
EMP: 32
SALES (est): 2MM **Privately Held**
SIC: 2721 Magazines: publishing & printing

(G-11494)
SAVWATT USA INC (PA)
475 Park Ave S Fl 30 (10016-6901)
PHONE..................646 478-2676
Michael Haug, *CEO*
Isaac H Sutton, *Ch of Bd*
EMP: 8
SQ FT: 2,000
SALES (est): 715.8K **Publicly Held**
SIC: 3646 3645 Commercial indusl & institutional electric lighting fixtures; residential lighting fixtures

(G-11495)
SB CORPORATION
114 W 41st St Fl 4 (10036-7308)
PHONE..................212 822-3166
Rob Cohen, *Principal*
▼ **EMP:** 5
SALES (est): 360K **Privately Held**
SIC: 2329 Men's & boys' sportswear & athletic clothing

(G-11496)
SB NEW YORK INC (HQ)
Also Called: Metro New York
120 Broadway (10271-0002)
PHONE..................212 457-7790
Joseph Lauletta, *General Mgr*
Eva Kis, *Editor*
Jennifer Logue, *Editor*
Oskar Bjorner, *CFO*
Michele Earl, *Accounting Dir*
EMP: 57
SALES (est): 10.2MM **Privately Held**
WEB: www.metronewyork.com
SIC: 2711 Newspapers, publishing & printing

(G-11497)
SC BUILDING SOLUTIONS LLC
53 W 23rd St Fl 12 (10010-4313)
PHONE..................800 564-1152
Ross Goldenberg,
Jason Griffith,
EMP: 80
SALES (est): 2.6MM **Privately Held**
SIC: 7372 8742 Application computer software; real estate consultant

(G-11498)
SC SUPPLY CHAIN MANAGEMENT LLC
Also Called: SCM
90 Broad St Ste 1504 (10004-2276)
PHONE..................212 344-3322
Anan Bishara, *Mng Member*
▲ **EMP:** 6
SQ FT: 2,600
SALES: 3MM **Privately Held**
SIC: 3569 Filters

(G-11499)
SCALAMANDRE SILKS INC (PA)
979 3rd Ave Ste 202 (10022-1294)
PHONE..................212 980-3888
▲ **EMP:** 65 **EST:** 1927
SALES (est): 62.1MM **Privately Held**
SIC: 2221 2241 5131 2273 Manmad Brdwv Fabric Mill Narrow Fabric Mill Whol Piece Goods/Notions

(G-11500)
SCH DPX CORPORATION
22 W 21st St Ste 700 (10010-6982)
PHONE..................917 405-5377
Joe Schoenfelder, *President*
EMP: 7
SALES (est): 510K **Privately Held**
WEB: www.schoenfelder.com
SIC: 2369 Girls' & children's outerwear

(G-11501)
SCHALLER MANUFACTURING CORP (PA)
Also Called: Schaller & Weber
1654 2nd Ave Apt 2n (10028-3109)
PHONE..................718 721-5480
Ralph Schaller, *Ch of Bd*
Marianne Schaller, *Vice Pres*
Harald Nagel, *Manager*
Jesse Denes, *Director*
Jeremy Schaller, *Director*
EMP: 70 **EST:** 1937
SQ FT: 16,000
SALES (est): 8.8MM **Privately Held**
WEB: www.schallerweber.com
SIC: 2013 5421 Prepared pork products from purchased pork; meat & fish markets

(G-11502)
SCHALLER MANUFACTURING CORP
Also Called: Schaller & Webber
1654 2nd Ave Apt 2n (10028-3109)
PHONE..................212 879-3047
Chris Cunningham, *Manager*
EMP: 12
SALES (est): 1.1MM
SALES (corp-wide): 8.8MM **Privately Held**
WEB: www.schallerweber.com
SIC: 2013 Sausages & other prepared meats
PA: Schaller Manufacturing Corp.
1654 2nd Ave Apt 2n
New York NY 10028
718 721-5480

(G-11503)
SCHINDLER ELEVATOR CORPORATION
620 12th Ave Fl 4 (10036-1016)
PHONE..................212 708-1000
Michael Joseph, *Project Mgr*
Jack Walsh, *Manager*
EMP: 250
SALES (corp-wide): 10.3B **Privately Held**
WEB: www.us.schindler.com
SIC: 3534 1796 Elevators & equipment; installing building equipment
HQ: Schindler Elevator Corporation
20 Whippany Rd
Morristown NJ 07960
973 397-6500

(G-11504)
SCHINDLER ELEVATOR CORPORATION
1211 6th Ave Ste 2950 (10036-8705)
PHONE..................800 225-3123
James Iannaccone, *Manager*
EMP: 30
SALES (corp-wide): 10.3B **Privately Held**
WEB: www.us.schindler.com
SIC: 3534 1796 Elevators & equipment; elevator installation & conversion
HQ: Schindler Elevator Corporation
20 Whippany Rd
Morristown NJ 07960
973 397-6500

(G-11505)
SCHLUMBERGER FOUNDATION INC
601 Lexington Ave Fl 57 (10022-4627)
PHONE..................212 350-9400
Anissa Abbas, *Partner*
Terry Keller, *Opers Mgr*
EMP: 3
SALES: 1MM **Privately Held**
SIC: 1389 Oil field services

(G-11506)
SCHNEEMAN STUDIO LIMITED
330 W 38th St Rm 505 (10018-8639)
PHONE..................212 244-3330
John Schneeman, *President*
EMP: 5
SQ FT: 2,000
SALES: 500K **Privately Held**
SIC: 2389 Theatrical costumes

(G-11507)
SCHNEIDER AMAL CO INC
600 3rd Ave Fl 2 (10016-1919)
PHONE..................917 470-9674
Thomas Schneider, *CEO*
EMP: 10
SQ FT: 3,500
SALES (est): 515.8K **Privately Held**
SIC: 1381 1389 6792 Drilling oil & gas wells; oil field services; oil royalty traders; oil leases, buying & selling on own account

(G-11508)
SCHNEIDER ELC SYSTEMS USA INC
7 E 8th St (10003-5901)
PHONE..................214 527-3099
EMP: 10
SALES (corp-wide): 200.4K **Privately Held**
SIC: 3823 Flow instruments, industrial process type
HQ: Schneider Electric Systems Usa, Inc.
38 Neponset Ave
Foxboro MA 02035
508 543-8750

(G-11509)
SCHNEIDER ELECTRIC IT CORP
Also Called: APC-Mge
520 8th Ave Rm 2103 (10018-6507)
PHONE..................646 335-0216
Brian Goffe, *Engineer*
Ralph Antonetti, *Sales Engr*
George Chappas, *Manager*
EMP: 10
SALES (corp-wide): 200.4K **Privately Held**
WEB: www.apcc.com
SIC: 3612 Power & distribution transformers
HQ: Schneider Electric It Corporation
132 Fairgrounds Rd
West Kingston RI 02892
401 789-5735

(G-11510)
SCHNEIDER ELECTRIC USA INC
112 W 34th St Ste 908 (10120-0999)
PHONE..................646 335-0220
James Montemarano, *Principal*
Evan Vogel, *Director*
EMP: 136
SALES (corp-wide): 200.4K **Privately Held**
SIC: 3613 Switchgear & switchboard apparatus
HQ: Schneider Electric Usa, Inc.
800 Federal St
Andover MA 01810
978 975-9600

(G-11511)
SCHNEIDER MILLS INC
Also Called: Wilkesboro Road
1430 Broadway Rm 1202 (10018-3390)
P.O. Box 519, Taylorsville NC (28681-0519)
PHONE..................828 632-0801
Emmett Pruett, *Manager*
EMP: 250
SALES (est): 37.6MM
SALES: 54.9MM **Privately Held**
SIC: 2211 2221 Broadwoven fabric mills, cotton; broadwoven fabric mills, manmade
PA: Schneider Mills, Inc.
1170 Nc Highway 16 N
Taylorsville NC 28681
828 632-8181

(G-11512)
SCHOEN TRIMMING & CORD CO INC
151 W 25th St Fl 10 (10001-7250)
PHONE..................212 255-3949
Martin Silver, *President*
▲ **EMP:** 17
SQ FT: 6,000
SALES: 2.6MM **Privately Held**
SIC: 2241 Cords, fabric

(G-11513)
SCHOLASTIC CORPORATION (PA)
557 Broadway Lbby 1 (10012-3999)
PHONE..................212 343-6100
Richard Robinson, *Ch of Bd*
Satbir Bedi, *Exec VP*
Andrew S Hedden, *Exec VP*
Iole Lucchese, *Exec VP*
Judith A Newman, *Exec VP*
▲ **EMP:** 9
SQ FT: 500,000
SALES: 1.6B **Publicly Held**
WEB: www.scholastic.com
SIC: 2731 2721 7372 7812 Books: publishing only; textbooks: publishing only, not printed on site; magazines: publishing only, not printed on site; educational computer software; non-theatrical motion picture production, television; video production; motion picture production; copyright buying & licensing; advertising agencies

(G-11514)
SCHOLASTIC INC (HQ)
Also Called: Scholastic U.S.A.
557 Broadway Lbby 1 (10012-3999)
PHONE..................800 724-6527
Richard Robinson, *Ch of Bd*
Janice Behrens, *Editor*
Judy Goldberg, *Editor*
Ellie Berger, *Exec VP*
Deborah A Forte, *Exec VP*
◆ **EMP:** 2000 **EST:** 1920
SQ FT: 300,000
SALES (est): 1.4B
SALES (corp-wide): 1.6B **Publicly Held**
WEB: www.scholasticdealer.com
SIC: 2731 2721 7372 7812 Books: publishing only; textbooks: publishing only, not printed on site; magazines: publishing only, not printed on site; statistical reports (periodicals): publishing only; educational computer software; video production; television film production; motion picture production & distribution
PA: Scholastic Corporation
557 Broadway Lbby 1
New York NY 10012
212 343-6100

(G-11515)
SCHOLASTIC INC
Also Called: Scholastic Copy Center
557 Broadway Lbby 1 (10012-3999)
PHONE..................212 343-6100
Abigail McAden, *Publisher*
Jenne Abramowitz, *Editor*
Katie Brickner, *Editor*
Elizabeth Carney, *Editor*
Mackenzie Carro, *Editor*
EMP: 25
SALES (corp-wide): 1.6B **Publicly Held**
WEB: www.scholasticdealer.com
SIC: 2731 Book publishing
HQ: Scholastic Inc.
557 Broadway Lbby 1
New York NY 10012
800 724-6527

(G-11516)
SCHOLASTIC INC
568 Broadway Rm 809 (10012-3253)
PHONE..................212 343-7100
Seth Radwell, *Branch Mgr*
Leticia Stewart, *Admin Asst*
EMP: 100
SALES (corp-wide): 1.6B **Publicly Held**
WEB: www.scholasticdealer.com
SIC: 2741 Business service newsletters: publishing & printing
HQ: Scholastic Inc.
557 Broadway Lbby 1
New York NY 10012
800 724-6527

(G-11517)
SCHOOLNET INC (DH)
525 Fashion Ave Fl 4 (10018-4940)
PHONE..................646 496-9000
Jonathan D Harber, *CEO*
Mark Chernis, *President*
Susan Aspey, *Vice Pres*
Andy Brenner, *Vice Pres*
Marsha Spanswick, *Project Mgr*

New York - New York County (G-11518) GEOGRAPHIC SECTION

EMP: 116
SQ FT: 11,500
SALES (est): 10.4MM
SALES (corp-wide): 5.9B Privately Held
WEB: www.schoolnet.com
SIC: 7372 7373 Educational computer software; systems software development services
HQ: Pearson Education, Inc.
221 River St
Hoboken NJ 07030
201 236-7000

(G-11518)
SCI BORE INC
70 Irving Pl Apt 5c (10003-2218)
PHONE..............................212 674-7128
Robert Olsen, *Partner*
Nadiya D Jinnah, *Partner*
EMP: 7
SALES (est): 550K Privately Held
SIC: 3496 Miscellaneous fabricated wire products

(G-11519)
SCIENTIFIC PLASTICS INC
243 W 30th St Fl 8 (10001-2812)
PHONE..............................212 967-1199
Steven Stegman, *President*
Jeffrey Stegman, *Vice Pres*
EMP: 12 EST: 1940
SALES (est): 1.1MM Privately Held
WEB: www.scientificplastics.com
SIC: 3842 Surgical appliances & supplies

(G-11520)
SCITERRA LLC
244 5th Ave Ste L280 (10001-7604)
PHONE..............................646 883-3724
Alexandra Litvinov, *CEO*
Astrid Androsch, *COO*
EMP: 5
SALES: 200K Privately Held
SIC: 7372 Prepackaged Software Services

(G-11521)
SCOOPS R US INCORPORATED
1514 Broadway (10036-4002)
PHONE..............................212 730-7959
EMP: 8
SALES (est): 652.9K Privately Held
SIC: 2024 Mfg Ice Cream/Frozen Desert

(G-11522)
SCOTT SILVERSTEIN LLC
242 W 38th St (10018-5804)
PHONE..............................212 781-1818
Scott Silverstein, *Mng Member*
EMP: 8 EST: 2016
SALES (est): 628K Privately Held
SIC: 3144 Dress shoes, women's

(G-11523)
SCREEN GEMS-EMI MUSIC INC (DH)
Also Called: EMI Music Publishing
150 5th Ave Fl 7 (10011-4372)
PHONE..............................212 786-8000
Martin Bandier, *CEO*
Santiago Men Ndez-Pidal, *Managing Dir*
Joanne Boris, *Exec VP*
EMP: 60
SQ FT: 45,000
SALES (est): 47.6MM
SALES (corp-wide): 3.2MM Privately Held
SIC: 2741 Music, sheet: publishing only, not printed on site

(G-11524)
SCROLL MEDIA INC
235 W 102nd St Apt 14i (10025-8432)
PHONE..............................617 395-8904
Samir Patil, *President*
EMP: 5 EST: 2013
SALES (est): 660K Privately Held
SIC: 3577 Data conversion equipment, media-to-media: computer

(G-11525)
SEABAY MEDIA HOLDINGS LLC (PA)
Also Called: Metro Nespaper
120 Broadway Fl 6 (10271-0034)
PHONE..............................212 457-7790
Pelle Tornberg, *CEO*
Lenyon Whitaker, *Editor*
EMP: 1
SALES (est): 15.3MM Privately Held
SIC: 2711 2741 Newspapers, publishing & printing; miscellaneous publishing

(G-11526)
SEAN JOHN CLOTHING INC
1710 Broadway Frnt 1 (10019-5254)
PHONE..............................212 500-2200
Sean John, *Manager*
EMP: 30 Privately Held
SIC: 2325 Men's & boys' trousers & slacks
PA: Sean John Clothing, Inc.
1440 Broadway Frnt 3
New York NY 10018

(G-11527)
SEAN JOHN CLOTHING INC (PA)
1440 Broadway Frnt 3 (10018-2301)
PHONE..............................212 500-2200
Jeff Tweedy, *President*
Sean John, *Manager*
EMP: 23
SALES (est): 6.4MM Privately Held
SIC: 2325 Men's & boys' trousers & slacks

(G-11528)
SECRET CELEBRITY LICENSING LLC
1431 Broadway Fl 10 (10018-1910)
PHONE..............................212 812-9277
Kathryn Sio, *Mng Member*
EMP: 5
SALES (est): 930.2K Privately Held
SIC: 3648 5023 Decorative area lighting fixtures; decorative home furnishings & supplies

(G-11529)
SECURED SERVICES INC (PA)
110 William St Fl 14 (10038-3901)
PHONE..............................866 419-3900
King T Moore, *President*
EMP: 4
SALES (est): 3.2MM Privately Held
WEB: www.secured-services.com
SIC: 7372 Prepackaged software

(G-11530)
SECURITIES DATA PUBLISHING INC (PA)
Also Called: Venture Economics
11 Penn Plz Fl 17 (10001-2006)
PHONE..............................212 631-1411
Bruce Morris, *President*
Wendi Winshall, *Vice Pres*
William Johnston, *CFO*
▲ EMP: 4
SALES (est): 16.8MM Privately Held
SIC: 2721 Magazines: publishing & printing

(G-11531)
SECURITY LETTER
166 E 96th St Apt 3b (10128-2512)
PHONE..............................212 348-1553
Robert McCrie, *Owner*
EMP: 5 EST: 1970
SALES (est): 270K Privately Held
SIC: 2721 8742 Trade journals: publishing only, not printed on site; business consultant

(G-11532)
SEEDLNGS LF SCNCE VENTURES LLC
230 E 15th St Apt 1a (10003-3941)
PHONE..............................917 913-8511
Keith Rubin, *CEO*
Ken Solovay,
EMP: 7
SALES (est): 541.3K Privately Held
SIC: 3841 Surgical & medical instruments

(G-11533)
SEFAIRA INC
135 E 57th St Fl 6 (10022-2185)
PHONE..............................855 733-2472
Mads Jensen, *CEO*
Fabian Metz, *Editor*
Nick Obrien, *Counsel*
Craig Macdonald, *Purch Mgr*
Stephen Grist, *CFO*
EMP: 35
SALES (est): 2.6MM Privately Held
SIC: 7372 Business oriented computer software
HQ: Sefaira Limited
Sefaira Uk Ltd, Queens House, 55-56
London
207 269-8500

(G-11534)
SEGOVIA TECHNOLOGY CO
33 Irving Pl Fl 7 (10003-2332)
PHONE..............................212 868-4412
Michael Faye, *CEO*
Liana Paris, *Manager*
EMP: 10
SQ FT: 1,500
SALES (est): 696.7K Privately Held
SIC: 7372 Prepackaged software

(G-11535)
SEIDLIN CONSULTING
580 W End Ave (10024-1723)
PHONE..............................212 496-2043
Mindell Seidlin, *Owner*
EMP: 1
SALES: 1MM Privately Held
SIC: 2834 Pharmaceutical preparations

(G-11536)
SEKAS INTERNATIONAL LTD
345 7th Ave Fl 9 (10001-5049)
PHONE..............................212 629-6095
Nicholas Sekas, *President*
Gus Sekas, *Director*
Athina Orthodoxou, *Admin Sec*
EMP: 10
SQ FT: 2,500
SALES (est): 3.1MM Privately Held
SIC: 2371 Fur goods

(G-11537)
SELECT INDUSTRIES NEW YORK INC
450 Fashion Ave Ste 3002 (10123-3002)
PHONE..............................800 723-5333
Jerry Friedman, *Principal*
Rachel Shatz, *Vice Pres*
Monique Le Gendre, *Project Mgr*
Emma Miran, *Project Mgr*
Edwina Telemaque, *Project Mgr*
▲ EMP: 13 EST: 2011
SALES (est): 2.2MM Privately Held
SIC: 3999 Manufacturing industries

(G-11538)
SELECT INFORMATION EXCHANGE
175 W 79th St 3a (10024-6450)
PHONE..............................212 496-6435
George H Wein, *Owner*
Terri Chiodo, *Director*
EMP: 18
SQ FT: 2,200
SALES (est): 1.1MM Privately Held
WEB: www.siecom.com
SIC: 2741 7331 Catalogs: publishing only, not printed on site; mailing list compilers

(G-11539)
SELECTIVE BEAUTY CORPORATION
315 Bleecker St 109 (10014-3427)
PHONE..............................585 336-7600
Sylvie Ganter, *President*
EMP: 10
SALES (est): 980K Privately Held
WEB: www.selective-beauty.com
SIC: 2844 Perfumes & colognes

(G-11540)
SELLAS LIFE SCIENCES GROUP INC (PA)
15 W 38th St Fl 10 (10018)
PHONE..............................917 438-4353
Jane Wasman, *Ch of Bd*
Angelos M Stergiou, *President*
Barbara A Wood, *Exec VP*
Gene Mack, *CFO*
Nicholas J Sarlis, *Chief Mktg Ofcr*
EMP: 11
SQ FT: 3,700
SALES (est): 2.5MM Publicly Held
SIC: 2834 Pharmaceutical preparations

(G-11541)
SEMI-LINEAR INC
1123 Broadway Ste 718 (10010-2097)
PHONE..............................212 243-2108
Linda Holliday, *CEO*
EMP: 5
SALES (est): 526.6K Privately Held
SIC: 3599 Industrial machinery

(G-11542)
SENDYNE CORP
250 W Broadway Fl 6 (10013-2431)
PHONE..............................212 966-0663
John Milios, *CEO*
Aakar Patel, *Vice Pres*
Victor Marten, *Engineer*
Marcin Ziemianowicz, *Engineer*
Ellen Gooch, *Marketing Staff*
EMP: 6
SALES (est): 550K Privately Held
SIC: 3674 Semiconductors & related devices

(G-11543)
SENSATIONAL COLLECTION INC (PA)
1410 Broadway Rm 505 (10018-9372)
PHONE..............................212 840-7388
Azar Kada, *Owner*
Jeff Matalon, *Vice Pres*
▲ EMP: 3
SQ FT: 5,600
SALES (est): 3.8MM Privately Held
SIC: 2339 5137 Women's & misses' athletic clothing & sportswear; women's & children's sportswear & swimsuits

(G-11544)
SENSUAL INC
Also Called: Icy Hot Lingerie
463 7th Ave (10018-7448)
PHONE..............................212 869-1450
Sami Souid, *CEO*
Avraham Cohen, *Accountant*
EMP: 20
SQ FT: 4,000
SALES (est): 2.3MM
SALES (corp-wide): 2.4MM Privately Held
SIC: 2342 Bras, girdles & allied garments
PA: Usa Apparel Group Inc
463 7th Ave Rm 1101
New York NY 10018
212 869-1450

(G-11545)
SERRAVIEW AMERICA INC
2 Wall St Fl 10 (10005-2004)
PHONE..............................800 903-3716
Stephen Macnee, *CEO*
Ian Morley, *Principal*
EMP: 70
SQ FT: 1,000
SALES (est): 1.2MM Privately Held
SIC: 7372 Business oriented computer software

(G-11546)
SERVICENOW INC
60 E 42nd St Ste 1230 (10165-1203)
PHONE..............................914 318-1168
Tom Moore, *Branch Mgr*
EMP: 10
SALES (corp-wide): 1.9B Publicly Held
SIC: 7372 Business oriented computer software
PA: Servicenow, Inc.
2225 Lawson Ln
Santa Clara CA 95054
408 501-8550

(G-11547)
SEVEN STORIES PRESS INC
140 Watts St (10013-1738)
PHONE..............................212 226-8760
Daniel Simon, *President*
Dan Simon, *Publisher*
Dennis Loo, *COO*
Jon Gilbert, *Sls & Mktg Exec*
Charlie Winton, *Shareholder*
▲ EMP: 7
SQ FT: 2,500
SALES (est): 1.1MM Privately Held
WEB: www.sevenstories.com
SIC: 2731 Books: publishing only

(G-11548)
SG NYC LLC
28 W 27th St Fl 12 (10001-6906)
PHONE.............................310 210-1837
Daniel Chiu, *Managing Prtnr*
Stephanie Garcia, *Managing Prtnr*
Tiffany Chang, *Manager*
EMP: 20
SQ FT: 4,000
SALES: 4.2MM **Privately Held**
SIC: 2335 Women's, juniors' & misses' dresses

(G-11549)
SGD NORTH AMERICA
900 3rd Ave Fl 4 (10022-4998)
PHONE.............................212 753-4200
Peter Acerra, *President*
▲ **EMP:** 33 **EST:** 2007
SALES (est): 3.5MM **Privately Held**
SIC: 3221 Glass containers

(G-11550)
SGD PHARMA PACKAGING INC
900 3rd Ave Fl 4 (10022-4998)
PHONE.............................212 223-7100
Nadir Lahneur, *President*
EMP: 9
SQ FT: 2,500
SALES (est): 134.2K **Privately Held**
SIC: 3221 Glass containers
HQ: Sgd S.A.
14 B Terrasse Bellini
Puteaux 92800
140 903-600

(G-11551)
SHADAL LLC
Also Called: Sermoneta Gloves
609 Madison Ave Ste 611 (10022-1901)
PHONE.............................212 319-5946
Aldo Sermonetta, *Manager*
EMP: 6
SALES (est): 18.1K **Privately Held**
SIC: 3111 Glove leather

(G-11552)
SHADOWTV INC
630 9th Ave Ste 202 (10036-4752)
PHONE.............................212 445-2540
Joachim Kim, *President*
Carl Rischar, *President*
Tracy Fred, *Bookkeeper*
Phil Gove, *Director*
EMP: 6
SALES (est): 855K **Privately Held**
WEB: www.shadowtv.com
SIC: 3575 Computer terminals, monitors & components

(G-11553)
SHAH DIAMONDS INC
Also Called: Venus
22 W 48th St Ste 600 (10036-1820)
PHONE.............................212 888-9393
Natwar Shah, *President*
Harshit Shah, *Sales Staff*
Gita Shah, *Admin Sec*
▲ **EMP:** 19
SQ FT: 4,000
SALES (est): 3.2MM **Privately Held**
WEB: www.hoc.com
SIC: 3911 3915 5094 Jewelry, precious metal; diamond cutting & polishing; jewelry; diamonds (gems)

(G-11554)
SHAHIN DESIGNS LTD
766 Madison Ave Fl 3 (10065-6563)
PHONE.............................212 737-7225
Samouhi Shahin, *President*
EMP: 5
SALES (est): 390K **Privately Held**
SIC: 2211 Apparel & outerwear fabrics, cotton

(G-11555)
SHAKE INC
175 Varick St Fl 4 (10014-7412)
PHONE.............................650 544-5479
Abraham Geiger, *CEO*
Amanda Wild, *Manager*
EMP: 13 **EST:** 2012
SQ FT: 1,000
SALES (est): 936.8K **Privately Held**
SIC: 7372 Business oriented computer software

(G-11556)
SHANU GEMS INC
1212 Ave Of The Americas (10036-1602)
P.O. Box 680, New City (10956-0680)
PHONE.............................212 921-4470
Pramod Agrawal, *President*
Manensha Agrawal, *Vice Pres*
EMP: 10
SALES (est): 840K **Privately Held**
WEB: www.shanugems.com
SIC: 3911 5094 Jewelry, precious metal; jewelry

(G-11557)
SHAPEWAYS INC (PA)
419 Park Ave S Fl 9 (10016-8409)
PHONE.............................914 356-5816
Gregory Kress, *CEO*
Peter Weijmarshausen, *CEO*
Pieter Limburg, *President*
Elizabeth New, *Production*
Martin Meyer, *CFO*
EMP: 188
SALES (est): 40.4MM **Privately Held**
SIC: 2759 Commercial printing

(G-11558)
SHAPIRO BERNSTEIN & CO INC
488 Madison Ave Fl 1201 (10022-5708)
PHONE.............................212 588-0878
Micheal Brettler, *President*
▲ **EMP:** 12
SALES (est): 850K **Privately Held**
WEB: www.shapirobernstein.com
SIC: 2741 Music, sheet: publishing only, not printed on site

(G-11559)
SHAREDBOOK INC
110 William St Fl 30 (10038-3901)
PHONE.............................646 442-8840
Caroline Vanderlip, *CEO*
Josef Hollander, *President*
EMP: 30
SQ FT: 8,000
SALES (est): 397.5K **Privately Held**
WEB: www.sharedbook.com
SIC: 2741 5942 Miscellaneous publishing; book stores

(G-11560)
SHAWMUT WOODWORKING & SUP INC
Also Called: Shawmutdesign and Construction
3 E 54th St Fl 8 (10022-3141)
PHONE.............................212 920-8900
Jack Fickes, *Superintendent*
Randy Shelly, *Vice Pres*
Michael Simon, *Branch Mgr*
Kenneth H Scott, *Business Dir*
Jessica Dejoy, *Executive Asst*
EMP: 185
SALES (corp-wide): 1.1B **Privately Held**
WEB: www.shawmut.com
SIC: 2431 Millwork
PA: Shawmut Woodworking & Supply, Inc.
560 Harrison Ave Ste 200
Boston MA 02118
617 622-7000

(G-11561)
SHELL PIPE LINE CORPORATION
4116 Broadway (10033-3703)
PHONE.............................212 740-8786
Nabe Ragan, *Branch Mgr*
EMP: 5
SALES (corp-wide): 305.1B **Privately Held**
SIC: 2911 Gasoline
HQ: Shell Pipe Line Corporation
2 Shell Plz Ste 1160
Houston TX 77002
713 241-6161

(G-11562)
SHELLEY PROMOTIONS INC
87 5th Ave (10003)
PHONE.............................212 924-4987
James Scott Shelley, *President*
EMP: 5
SALES (est): 370K **Privately Held**
SIC: 3861 Photographic film, plate & paper holders

(G-11563)
SHENGKUN NORTH AMERICA INC
262 W 38th St Rm 903 (10018-9173)
PHONE.............................212 217-2460
Wen Ming MA, *CEO*
Mia Kang, *Project Mgr*
EMP: 10 **EST:** 2015
SQ FT: 1,200
SALES: 3.2MM **Privately Held**
SIC: 2221 5131 5949 Textile mills, broadwoven: silk & manmade, also glass; textiles, woven; fabric stores piece goods

(G-11564)
SHENNONG PHARMACEUTICALS INC
110 Wall St (10005-3801)
PHONE.............................347 422-2200
Jason Frankovich, *Manager*
EMP: 20
SALES (est): 846.9K **Privately Held**
SIC: 2834 Pharmaceutical preparations

(G-11565)
SHIELD PRESS INC
9 Lispenard St Fl 1 (10013-2290)
PHONE.............................212 431-7489
Bryan Shield, *President*
Stephen Shield, *Treasurer*
Ellen Shield, *Admin Sec*
EMP: 6 **EST:** 1940
SQ FT: 1,500
SALES: 750K **Privately Held**
SIC: 2752 7389 Commercial printing, offset; printers' services: folding, collating

(G-11566)
SHIMADA SHOJI (HK) LIMITED
165 W 46th St Ste 709 (10036-2519)
PHONE.............................212 268-0465
Toshio Shimada, *Branch Mgr*
EMP: 9
SALES (corp-wide): 1.9MM **Privately Held**
SIC: 3965 Buttons & parts
HQ: Shimada Shoji (H.K.) Limited
Rm 507-11 5/F Cheung Sha Wan Plz Twr 1
Cheung Sha Wan KLN
273 933-19

(G-11567)
SHINDO USA INC
162 W 36th St (10018-6901)
PHONE.............................212 868-9311
Tadashi Shindo, *CEO*
Shingo Nagai, *Principal*
Matthew Schechter, *Sales Mgr*
Junichiro Tanaka, *Regl Sales Mgr*
Viviana Velasquez, *Sales Staff*
EMP: 7
SALES (est): 429.3K **Privately Held**
SIC: 2211 Stretch fabrics, cotton

(G-11568)
SHIRA ACCESSORIES LTD
28 W 36th St Fl 6 (10018-8006)
PHONE.............................212 594-4455
Barry Shapiro, *President*
EMP: 15
SQ FT: 2,000
SALES (est): 1.8MM **Privately Held**
SIC: 3961 Costume jewelry

(G-11569)
SHIRO LIMITED
928 Broadway Ste 806 (10010-8128)
PHONE.............................212 780-0007
Gary Mandel, *President*
▲ **EMP:** 5
SQ FT: 2,000
SALES (est): 390.8K **Privately Held**
SIC: 3911 Jewelry, precious metal

(G-11570)
SHISEIDO AMERICAS CORPORATION (HQ)
Also Called: Shiseido Cosmetics
900 3rd Ave Fl 15 (10022-4792)
PHONE.............................212 805-2300
Marc Rey, *President*
Edward W Klause, *Vice Pres*
Tatsuya Toda, *Vice Pres*
George Grossi Jr, *CFO*
Pankaj Gupta, *CFO*
◆ **EMP:** 7
SQ FT: 108,000
SALES (est): 504.8MM
SALES (corp-wide): 8.9B **Privately Held**
SIC: 2844 5122 Cosmetic preparations; toilet preparations; cosmetics; toilet preparations
PA: Shiseido Company, Limited
7-5-5, Ginza
Chuo-Ku TKY 104-0
335 725-111

(G-11571)
SHRINEETA PHARMACY
1749 Amsterdam Ave Frnt (10031-4618)
PHONE.............................212 234-7959
Robby Annamaneni, *Principal*
EMP: 5
SALES (est): 812.6K **Privately Held**
SIC: 2834 Pharmaceutical preparations

(G-11572)
SHRINEETA PHARMACY INC
Also Called: Amsterdam Pharmacy
1743 Amsterdam Ave (10031-4614)
PHONE.............................212 234-7959
Sreenivasa R Gade, *Ch of Bd*
Ravinder Annamaneni, *Director*
EMP: 21
SQ FT: 1,600
SALES (est): 7.2MM **Privately Held**
SIC: 2834 Pharmaceutical preparations

(G-11573)
SHYAM AHUJA LIMITED
201 E 56th St Frnt A (10022-3724)
PHONE.............................212 644-5910
Azmina Merali, *Branch Mgr*
EMP: 7
SALES (corp-wide): 965.8K **Privately Held**
WEB: www.shyamahujahome.com
SIC: 2391 2273 3999 Curtains & draperies; carpets & rugs; atomizers, toiletry
PA: Shyam Ahuja Private Limited
A - 6 Poonam Appartment
Mumbai MH 40001
226 524-6967

(G-11574)
SHYK INTERNATIONAL CORP
258 Riverside Dr Apt 7b (10025-6160)
PHONE.............................212 663-3302
Steven Kline, *President*
EMP: 2
SQ FT: 2,500
SALES: 75MM **Privately Held**
SIC: 3651 Home entertainment equipment, electronic

(G-11575)
SIDE HUSTLE MUSIC GROUP LLC
600 3rd Ave Fl 2 (10016-1919)
PHONE.............................800 219-4003
Fabian Cummings, *Prgrmr*
EMP: 10
SQ FT: 10,000
SALES (est): 1.7MM **Privately Held**
WEB: www.sidehustlemusicgroup.com
SIC: 3652 Pre-recorded records & tapes

(G-11576)
SIEGEL & STOCKMAN INC
126 W 25th St Frnt 1 (10001-7413)
PHONE.............................212 633-1508
Chris Israel, *President*
Tess Tobias, *Comptroller*
▲ **EMP:** 5
SALES (est): 374.2K **Privately Held**
SIC: 3999 Mannequins

(G-11577)
SIEMENS CORPORATION
527 Madison Ave Fl 8 (10022-4376)
PHONE.............................202 434-7800
Steve Kachlik, *Regl Sales Mgr*
Bruce Tucker, *Manager*
Michael Panigel, *Director*
Mark Henning, *Director*

New York - New York County (G-11578) — GEOGRAPHIC SECTION

EMP: 10
SALES (corp-wide): 97.7B Privately Held
SIC: 3661 3641 3844 3612 Telephones & telephone apparatus; electric lamps; radiographic X-ray apparatus & tubes; distribution transformers, electric; voltage regulators, transmission & distribution; nonferrous wiredrawing & insulating
HQ: Siemens Corporation
300 New Jersey Ave Nw # 10
Washington DC 20001
202 434-4800

(G-11578)
SIEMENS ELECTRO INDUSTRIAL SA
527 Madison Ave Fl 8 (10022-4376)
PHONE....................212 258-4000
James Harris, General Mgr
Jim W White, General Mgr
Steffen Meyer, Principal
Craig Johnson, Vice Pres
Andreas Hilmer, Project Mgr
EMP: 785
SALES (est): 63.5MM
SALES (corp-wide): 97.7B Privately Held
SIC: 3648 Lighting equipment
PA: Siemens Ag
Werner-Von-Siemens-Str. 1
Munchen 80333
896 360-0

(G-11579)
SIEMENS MOBILITY INC (HQ)
1 Penn Plz Frnt 11 (10119-0207)
PHONE....................916 717-8174
Matthaeus Decker, Manager
EMP: 7 EST: 2017
SALES (est): 239MM
SALES (corp-wide): 97.7B Privately Held
SIC: 3711 3743 Motor vehicles & car bodies; railway motor cars
PA: Siemens Ag
Werner-Von-Siemens-Str. 1
Munchen 80333
896 360-0

(G-11580)
SIEMENS USA HOLDINGS INC
527 Madison Ave Fl 8 (10022-4376)
PHONE....................212 258-4000
George C Nolan, President
Ashish Bhat, General Mgr
Tim Grigg, Business Mgr
Bas Idzenga, Business Mgr
Praveen Muniyappa, Business Mgr
EMP: 300
SALES (est): 40MM
SALES (corp-wide): 97.7B Privately Held
SIC: 3612 3844 3641 3357 Distribution transformers, electric; voltage regulators, transmission & distribution; radiographic X-ray apparatus & tubes; electric lamps; nonferrous wiredrawing & insulating; telephones & telephone apparatus
PA: Siemens Ag
Werner-Von-Siemens-Str. 1
Munchen 80333
896 360-0

(G-11581)
SIFONYA INC
Also Called: Cego Custom Shirts
303 Park Ave S Frnt 2 (10010-3677)
PHONE....................212 620-4512
Carl Goldberg, President
EMP: 6
SQ FT: 300
SALES: 600K Privately Held
WEB: www.cego.com
SIC: 2321 5131 Men's & boys' furnishings; piece goods & other fabrics

(G-11582)
SIGA TECHNOLOGIES INC (PA)
31 E 62nd St (10065-8014)
PHONE....................212 672-9100
Phillip L Gomez, CEO
Eric A Rose, Ch of Bd
Dennis E Hruby, Vice Pres
Daniel Luckshire, CFO
Annie Offutt, Human Res Mgr
EMP: 37
SQ FT: 3,200
SALES: 12.2MM Publicly Held
WEB: www.siga.com
SIC: 2834 2836 Pharmaceutical preparations; vaccines & other immunizing products

(G-11583)
SIGMA WORLDWIDE LLC (PA)
65 W 83rd St Apt 5 (10024-5237)
PHONE....................646 217-0629
Jeffrey Muti, CEO
Peter Devries, Opers Staff
EMP: 8
SALES: 15MM Privately Held
SIC: 3161 5099 3089 Cases, carrying; cases, carrying; cases, plastic

(G-11584)
SIGN CENTER INC
Also Called: Sign Company, The
15 W 39th St Fl 7 (10018-0633)
PHONE....................212 967-2113
Mark Dressman, President
James Kelly, Vice Pres
EMP: 10
SQ FT: 2,000
SALES (est): 897.7K Privately Held
SIC: 3993 Signs, not made in custom sign painting shops; displays & cutouts, window & lobby

(G-11585)
SIGN COMPANY
Also Called: Sjm Interface
15 W 39th St Fl 7 (10018-0633)
PHONE....................212 967-2113
EMP: 9
SALES (est): 544.6K Privately Held
SIC: 3993 5812 Mfg Signs/Advertising Specialties Eating Place

(G-11586)
SIGNA CHEMISTRY INC (PA)
400 Madison Ave Fl 21 (10017-8901)
PHONE....................212 933-4101
Michael Lefenfeld, President
Michael Alt, Vice Pres
Paul Krumrine, Research
Nidhi Wahi, Human Res Mgr
Kate Carney, Marketing Staff
EMP: 14
SQ FT: 7,000
SALES (est): 7.6MM Privately Held
WEB: www.signachem.com
SIC: 2819 3511 Catalysts, chemical; hydraulic turbine generator set units, complete

(G-11587)
SIGNATURE DIAMOND ENTPS LLC
15 W 47th St Ste 203 (10036-5708)
PHONE....................212 869-5115
Jeremy S Hill,
EMP: 40
SQ FT: 3,000
SALES (est): 3.2MM Privately Held
SIC: 1499 Diamond mining, industrial

(G-11588)
SIGNEXPO ENTERPRISES INC (PA)
Also Called: Sign Expo
127 W 26th St Rm 401 (10001-6870)
PHONE....................212 925-8585
Offer Sharaby, CEO
Frayda Sharaby, Ch of Bd
Michelle Shapiro, General Mgr
Keren Harris, Controller
EMP: 14
SALES (est): 1.5MM Privately Held
SIC: 3993 Signs & advertising specialties

(G-11589)
SIGNPOST INC
127 W 26th St Fl 2 (10001-6881)
PHONE....................877 334-2837
Stuart Wall, CEO
Seth Purcell, President
John Buchanan, Founder
Christopher Depatria, Vice Pres
Reid Erardy, Accountant
EMP: 250
SALES (est): 2.2MM Privately Held
SIC: 7372 Application computer software

(G-11590)
SILVATRIM CORP
Also Called: Silvatrim Corporation America
324 W 22nd St (10011-2602)
PHONE....................212 675-0933
William Shanok, President
Daniel Shanock, Vice Pres
Frederick Shanok, Vice Pres
Victor Shanok, Treasurer
EMP: 120 EST: 1931
SQ FT: 120,000
SALES (est): 8MM Privately Held
SIC: 3089 Plastic processing; molding primary plastic

(G-11591)
SILVERLIGHT DIGITAL LLC
15 E 32nd St Fl 3 (10016-5570)
PHONE....................646 650-5330
Lori Goldberg, CEO
Michael Ackerman, Business Mgr
Benjamin Friedman, Vice Pres
Anthony Frisina, Asst Controller
Nick Rane, Director
EMP: 5
SALES (est): 289K Privately Held
SIC: 3663 7319 Digital encoders; media buying service

(G-11592)
SIMILARWEB INC
50 W 17th St Fl 9 (10011-5702)
PHONE....................347 685-5422
Jason Schwartz, CFO
Dan Valach, VP Human Res
EMP: 18
SALES (est): 468.9K Privately Held
SIC: 7372 Prepackaged software

(G-11593)
SIMKA DIAMOND CORP
580 5th Ave Ste 709 (10036-4728)
PHONE....................212 921-4420
Philip Katz, President
Isaac Friedman, Vice Pres
Surie Friedman, Admin Sec
Raizel Katz, Admin Sec
EMP: 15
SQ FT: 3,000
SALES (est): 1.4MM Privately Held
WEB: www.simkadiamond.com
SIC: 3911 Jewelry, precious metal

(G-11594)
SIMMONS-BOARDMAN PUBG CORP (HQ)
55 Broad St Fl 26 (10004-2580)
PHONE....................212 620-7200
Arthur J Mc Ginnis Jr, President
EMP: 50 EST: 1928
SQ FT: 10,000
SALES (est): 8.6MM Privately Held
WEB: www.marinelog.com
SIC: 2721 2731 8249 Magazines: publishing only, not printed on site; book music: publishing only, not printed on site; correspondence school

(G-11595)
SIMON & SCHUSTER INC
Pocket Books
1230 Ave Of The Americas (10020-1586)
PHONE....................212 698-7000
Carolyn Kroll Reidy, Branch Mgr
EMP: 51
SALES (corp-wide): 13.7B Publicly Held
SIC: 2731 Books: publishing only
HQ: Simon & Schuster, Inc.
1230 Ave Of The Americas
New York NY 10020
212 698-7000

(G-11596)
SIMON & SIMON LLC
Also Called: Magic Maestro Music
1745 Broadway Fl 17 (10019-4642)
PHONE....................202 419-0490
Bonnie Simon, Mng Member
Stephen Simon,
EMP: 5
SALES: 10K Privately Held
SIC: 2782 Record albums

(G-11597)
SIMON SCHUSTER DIGITAL SLS INC
51 W 52d St (10019)
PHONE....................212 698-4391
Carolyn Reidy, Chairman
Robert Riger, Vice Pres
Michael Grant, Marketing Mgr
EMP: 53
SALES (est): 3.2MM
SALES (corp-wide): 13.7B Publicly Held
SIC: 2731 Book publishing
HQ: Simon & Schuster, Inc.
1230 Ave Of The Americas
New York NY 10020
212 698-7000

(G-11598)
SING TAO NEWSPAPERS NY LTD (PA)
Also Called: Sing Tao Daily
188 Lafayette St (10013-3200)
PHONE....................212 699-3800
Robin Mui, CEO
Rick Ho, General Mgr
Alice Lee, Corp Secy
Celia Wong, Sales Mgr
Peter Yan, Sales Staff
▲ EMP: 20
SALES: 22.5MM Privately Held
WEB: www.nysingtao.com
SIC: 2711 2741 Newspapers: publishing only, not printed on site; miscellaneous publishing

(G-11599)
SING TRIX
118 W 22nd St Fl 3 (10011-2416)
PHONE....................212 352-1500
Al Roque, Principal
John Devecka, Vice Pres
Eric Berkowitz, Mng Member
EMP: 10
SALES (est): 893.1K Privately Held
SIC: 3651 Home entertainment equipment, electronic

(G-11600)
SINO PRINTING INC
30 Allen St Frnt A (10002-5363)
PHONE....................212 334-6896
Craig Marsden, Principal
◆ EMP: 15
SALES (est): 1.1MM Privately Held
SIC: 2759 Screen printing

(G-11601)
SISKIND GROUP INC
1385 Broadway Fl 24 (10018-6009)
PHONE....................212 840-0880
Jon Siskind, President
Richard L Siskind, Vice Pres
EMP: 15
SALES (est): 2.5MM Privately Held
SIC: 2329 2339 Men's & boys' sportswear & athletic clothing; sportswear, women's

(G-11602)
SISTER SISTER INC (PA)
463 7th Ave Fl 4 (10018-8725)
PHONE....................212 629-9600
Jack Adjmi, Ch of Bd
Joseph Dwek, President
Joseph Dweck, President
Mark Adjmi, Vice Pres
Terry Dwek, Vice Pres
▲ EMP: 6
SQ FT: 15,000
SALES (est): 4.9MM Privately Held
SIC: 2369 2329 Headwear: girls', children's & infants'; men's & boys' sportswear & athletic clothing

(G-11603)
SIXTEEN MARKETS INC
110 Wall St Ste 1502 (10005-3801)
PHONE....................347 759-1024
Minjin Chen, Director
EMP: 10
SALES: 800K Privately Held
SIC: 7372 7389 Business oriented computer software; financial services

GEOGRAPHIC SECTION

New York - New York County (G-11632)

(G-11604)
SK CAPITAL PARTNERS II LP (PA)
400 Park Ave Ste 820 (10022-9481)
PHONE.....................212 826-2700
Jack Norris, *Managing Dir*
Barry Siadat,
EMP: 19
SALES (est): 1.2B **Privately Held**
SIC: **2821** 2299 Nylon resins; batting, wadding, padding & fillings

(G-11605)
SK TITAN HOLDINGS LLC (HQ)
400 Park Ave (10022-4406)
PHONE.....................212 826-2700
Barry Siadat, *Mng Member*
EMP: 6
SALES (est): 1.2B **Privately Held**
SIC: **2821** 2299 Nylon resins; batting, wadding, padding & fillings
PA: Sk Capital Partners Ii, L.P.
   400 Park Ave Ste 820
   New York NY 10022
   212 826-2700

(G-11606)
SKAFFLES GROUP LLC
1400 Broadway Fl 26 (10018-5396)
PHONE.....................212 944-9494
Steven Shwekey, *Mng Member*
EMP: 18 **Privately Held**
SIC: **3999** Pet supplies
PA: Skaffles Group Llc
   115 Kennedy Dr
   Sayreville NJ 08872

(G-11607)
SKETCH STUDIO TRADING INC
221 W 37th St Ste 600 (10018-5782)
PHONE.....................212 244-2875
ARI Merabi, *President*
Isaac Merabi, *Manager*
EMP: 3
SQ FT: 2,500
SALES (est): 9MM **Privately Held**
SIC: **2384** Bathrobes, men's & women's: made from purchased materials

(G-11608)
SKILLS ALLIANCE INC
135 W 29th St Rm 201 (10001-5188)
PHONE.....................646 492-5300
Joseph Wolf CPA, *Principal*
EMP: 8
SALES (est): 896.2K **Privately Held**
SIC: **2834** Pharmaceutical preparations

(G-11609)
SKINCARE PRODUCTS INC
118 E 57th St (10022-2663)
PHONE.....................917 837-5255
Allan Vanhoven, *CEO*
EMP: 9
SALES: 900K **Privately Held**
SIC: **2834** 7991 7389 Dermatologicals; spas; design services

(G-11610)
SKIP HOP INC
50 W 23rd St Fl 10 (10010-5270)
PHONE.....................646 902-9874
Michael Damant, *CEO*
Michael Damiant, *CEO*
Ellen Damiant, *COO*
Janet Villano, *Vice Pres*
Michael Fox, *CFO*
◆ EMP: 40
SALES (est): 28MM
SALES (corp-wide): 3.4B **Publicly Held**
WEB: www.skiphop.com
SIC: **2361** 3942 2676 Girls' & children's dresses, blouses & shirts; stuffed toys, including animals; infant & baby paper products
HQ: Skip Hop Holdings, Inc.
   50 W 23rd St Fl 10
   New York NY 10010
   212 868-9850

(G-11611)
SKIP HOP HOLDINGS INC (HQ)
50 W 23rd St Fl 10 (10010-5270)
PHONE.....................212 868-9850
Michael Diamant, *CEO*
EMP: 3
SALES (est): 28MM
SALES (corp-wide): 3.4B **Publicly Held**
SIC: **2361** 3942 2676 6719 Girls' & children's dresses, blouses & shirts; stuffed toys, including animals; infant & baby paper products; investment holding companies, except banks
PA: Carter's, Inc.
   3438 Peachtree Rd Ne # 1800
   Atlanta GA 30326
   678 791-1000

(G-11612)
SKY ART MEDIA INC
Also Called: Whitewall Magazine
114 E 25th St Fl 11 (10010-2979)
PHONE.....................917 355-9022
Michael Klug, *President*
Katy Donoghue, *Editor*
Ashley A Clairmont, *Mktg Dir*
Margaux Cerruti, *Manager*
EMP: 7
SALES (est): 1.1MM **Privately Held**
SIC: **2721** Periodicals: publishing & printing

(G-11613)
SKY FRAME & ART INC (PA)
Also Called: Pop A2z
141 W 28th St Fl 12 (10001-6115)
PHONE.....................212 925-7856
Robert Benrimon, *President*
Sheila Benrimon, *Vice Pres*
Stephanie Rich, *Vice Pres*
Meagan Long, *Sales Staff*
EMP: 45
SQ FT: 7,000
SALES (est): 5.5MM **Privately Held**
SIC: **2499** Picture frame molding, finished

(G-11614)
SKYHORSE PUBLISHING INC (PA)
Also Called: All Worth Press
307 W 36th St Fl 11 (10018-6592)
PHONE.....................212 643-6816
Tony Lyons, *President*
Niels Aaboe, *Editor*
Julia Abramoff, *Editor*
Cory Allyn, *Editor*
Chelsey Emmelhainz, *Editor*
▲ EMP: 50
SALES: 35MM **Privately Held**
WEB: www.skyhorsepublishing.com
SIC: **2731** Books: publishing only

(G-11615)
SKYLER BRAND VENTURES LLC
590 Madison Ave Fl 19 (10022-2544)
PHONE.....................646 979-5904
Betsy Schmalz Ferguson, *President*
Paul Wahlgren, *Managing Dir*
Konstantinos M Lahanas, *Vice Pres*
Jules Zecchino, *Officer*
EMP: 5 EST: 2013
SALES: 1MM **Privately Held**
SIC: **3841** Skin grafting equipment

(G-11616)
SKYSTEM LLC
100 W 92nd St Apt 20d (10025-7504)
PHONE.....................877 778-3320
Shagun Malhotra, *CEO*
EMP: 5
SALES (est): 251.4K **Privately Held**
SIC: **7372** Business oriented computer software

(G-11617)
SLEEPABLE SOFAS LTD
Also Called: Lodi Down & Feather
600 3rd Ave Fl 15 (10016-1928)
PHONE.....................973 546-4502
Donna De Matteo, *President*
EMP: 80
SQ FT: 28,000
SALES (est): 12.2MM
SALES (corp-wide): 15.4MM **Privately Held**
WEB: www.sleepablesofas.com
SIC: **2515** 2512 2392 Sofa beds (convertible sofas); wood upholstered chairs & couches; household furnishings; comforters & quilts: made from purchased materials
PA: Carlyle Custom Convertibles Ltd
   6 Empire Blvd
   Moonachie NJ 07074
   973 546-4502

(G-11618)
SLEEPWEAR HOLDINGS INC
Also Called: Knothe Apparel Group
1372 Broadway Fl 18 (10018-6107)
PHONE.....................516 466-4738
Brian Minkoff, *CEO*
Richard N Bern, *Ch of Bd*
Maria Zoccoli, *President*
David Ford, *Vice Pres*
Richard Bern, *CFO*
▲ EMP: 125
SQ FT: 11,500
SALES (est): 89.8K **Privately Held**
WEB: www.knothe.com
SIC: **2322** 2341 Nightwear, men's & boys': from purchased materials; pajamas & bedjackets: women's & children's

(G-11619)
SLIDEBEAN INCORPORATED
25 Broadway (10004-1010)
PHONE.....................866 365-0588
Jose Cayasso, *CEO*
EMP: 15
SALES: 500K **Privately Held**
SIC: **7372** Prepackaged software

(G-11620)
SM NEWS PLUS INCORPORATED
346 E 59th St Frnt 1 (10022-1527)
PHONE.....................212 888-0153
M Faraq, *President*
EMP: 5
SALES (est): 170.8K **Privately Held**
SIC: **2711** Newspapers

(G-11621)
SMART & STRONG LLC
Also Called: Poz Publishing
212 W 35th St Fl 8 (10001-2508)
PHONE.....................212 938-2051
Brad Peebles, *Partner*
Sean O'Brien Strub, *Founder*
Dennis Daniel, *Finance Dir*
EMP: 25
SALES (est): 2.6MM **Privately Held**
WEB: www.poz.com
SIC: **2721** Magazines: publishing only, not printed on site

(G-11622)
SMART SPACE PRODUCTS LLC (PA)
244 5th Ave Ste 2487 (10001-7604)
PHONE.....................877 777-2441
Adam Rozen, *Mng Member*
EMP: 5
SQ FT: 1,200
SALES: 1MM **Privately Held**
SIC: **2599** 5712 Hotel furniture; furniture stores

(G-11623)
SMILE SPECIALISTS
236 E 36th St (10016-3777)
PHONE.....................877 337-6135
Marvin Lagstein, *Principal*
EMP: 9
SALES (est): 1.3MM **Privately Held**
SIC: **3843** Cutting instruments, dental

(G-11624)
SMITH & WATSON
200 Lexington Ave Rm 805 (10016-6111)
PHONE.....................212 686-6444
Robert Ryan, *President*
John P Ryan, *Chairman*
Barbara R Pilcher, *Vice Pres*
▲ EMP: 20 EST: 1907
SQ FT: 8,000
SALES: 2MM **Privately Held**
WEB: www.smith-watson.com
SIC: **2512** Upholstered household furniture

(G-11625)
SMITH INTERNATIONAL INC
601 Lexington Ave Fl 57 (10022-4627)
PHONE.....................212 350-9400
Ann Marie Copo, *Office Mgr*
EMP: 89 **Publicly Held**
SIC: **1382** 1389 Geophysical exploration, oil & gas field; well logging
HQ: Smith International, Inc.
   1310 Rankin Rd
   Houston TX 77073
   281 443-3370

(G-11626)
SML USA INC (PA)
5 Penn Plz Ste 1500 (10001-1810)
PHONE.....................212 736-8800
Paul Gnieser, *CEO*
Thomas Blaze, *Manager*
▲ EMP: 50
SQ FT: 16,000
SALES (est): 12.8MM **Privately Held**
SIC: **2679** 2241 2269 5131 Tags & labels, paper; building, insulating & packaging paper; labels, woven; labels, cotton: printed; labels; textile machinery & equipment

(G-11627)
SMM - NORTH AMERICA TRADE CORP
Also Called: Sims Metal Management
16 W 22nd St Fl 10 (10010-5967)
PHONE.....................212 604-0710
Robert A Kelman, *President*
Michael S Collins, *Vice Pres*
EMP: 5
SALES (est): 1.2MM **Privately Held**
SIC: **3291** Grit, steel

(G-11628)
SMOOTH INDUSTRIES INCORPORATED
1411 Broadway Rm 3000 (10018-3496)
PHONE.....................212 869-1080
Celeste Chan, *President*
▲ EMP: 25
SQ FT: 7,000
SALES (est): 1.9MM **Privately Held**
WEB: www.smoothny.com
SIC: **2339** Women's & misses' outerwear

(G-11629)
SMOOTH MAGAZINE
55 John St Ste 800 (10038-3752)
PHONE.....................212 925-1150
Sandra Vasceannie, *President*
EMP: 10
SALES (est): 724K **Privately Held**
SIC: **2721** Magazines: publishing only, not printed on site

(G-11630)
SNEAKER NEWS INC
41 Elizabeth St Ste 301 (10013-4637)
PHONE.....................347 687-1588
Yu-Ming Wu, *President*
EMP: 9
SALES: 1.8MM **Privately Held**
SIC: **2741** Shopping news: publishing only, not printed on site

(G-11631)
SNEAKERS SOFTWARE INC
Also Called: Dvmax
519 8th Ave Rm 812 (10018-4588)
PHONE.....................800 877-9221
Paul R Greenman, *CEO*
Paul S Greenman, *Engineer*
Kathie Stecher, *Office Mgr*
EMP: 18
SQ FT: 800
SALES: 3MM **Privately Held**
WEB: www.DVMAX.com
SIC: **7372** Prepackaged software

(G-11632)
SNOWMAN
404 5th Ave Fl 7 (10018-7447)
PHONE.....................212 239-8818
Jennifer Suh, *Vice Pres*

New York - New York County (G-11633) — GEOGRAPHIC SECTION

Baekkyu Suh, *Mng Member*
EMP: 5
SALES (est): 576.8K **Privately Held**
SIC: 2339 Sportswear, women's

(G-11633)
SOCIAL REGISTER ASSOCIATION
14 Wall St Ste 3f (10005-2141)
PHONE 646 612-7314
Matthew Campbell, *President*
EMP: 18
SALES (est): 92.8K **Privately Held**
WEB: www.socialregisterassociation.com
SIC: 2731 Books: publishing only

(G-11634)
SOCIETY FOR THE STUDY
Also Called: PARABOLA
20 W 20th St Fl 2 (10011-9260)
PHONE 212 822-8806
Steven Schiff, *President*
Jeff Zaleski, *Publisher*
EMP: 7
SQ FT: 1,500
SALES: 428.8K **Privately Held**
SIC: 2721 5735 5942 Magazines: publishing only, not printed on site; video tapes, prerecorded; audio tapes, prerecorded; book stores

(G-11635)
SOFT SHEEN PRODUCTS INC (DH)
575 5th Ave (10017-2422)
PHONE 212 818-1500
Patricia Cumberland, *President*
Candace Matthews, *Principal*
Sanjay Devi, *Senior VP*
Steve Hofemann, *Assistant VP*
Barbara Kline, *Vice Pres*
▼ **EMP:** 1
SALES (est): 4MM
SALES (corp-wide): 4.2B **Privately Held**
WEB: www.softsheen-carson.com
SIC: 2844 Shampoos, rinses, conditioners: hair
HQ: L'oreal Usa, Inc.
10 Hudson Yards Fl 30
New York NY 10001
212 818-1500

(G-11636)
SOHO APPAREL LTD
Also Called: Flirtatious
525 Fashion Ave Fl 6 (10018-4960)
PHONE 212 840-1109
Nikou Achouri, *President*
Jeffrey Stein, *Exec VP*
EMP: 5
SQ FT: 3,140
SALES (est): 550.2K **Privately Held**
SIC: 2331 5137 Women's & misses' blouses & shirts; women's & children's clothing

(G-11637)
SOHO PRESS INC
853 Broadway Ste 1402 (10003-4716)
PHONE 212 260-1900
Juris Jurjevics, *President*
Bronwen Hruska, *Publisher*
Mark Doten, *Editor*
Juliet Grames, *Editor*
Amara Hoshijo, *Editor*
EMP: 5
SQ FT: 1,250
SALES (est): 510K **Privately Held**
WEB: www.sohopress.com
SIC: 2731 5942 Books: publishing only; book stores

(G-11638)
SOLABIA USA INC
28 W 44th St (10036-7406)
PHONE 212 847-2397
Michael J Conti, *President*
▲ **EMP:** 7
SQ FT: 1,100
SALES (est): 6.6MM **Privately Held**
SIC: 2844 Cosmetic preparations

(G-11639)
SOLARPATH INC
Also Called: Solarpath Sun Solutions
415 Madison Ave Fl 14 (10017-7935)
PHONE 201 490-4499
Ori Aldubi, *CEO*
Amir Warshazsky, *President*
EMP: 6
SQ FT: 5,000
SALES (est): 900.6K **Privately Held**
SIC: 3646 Commercial indusl & institutional electric lighting fixtures

(G-11640)
SOLSTARS INC
Also Called: Solstarny
575 Madison Ave Ste 1006 (10022-8511)
PHONE 212 605-0430
Haim Hassin, *President*
▲ **EMP:** 7
SALES (est): 706.4K **Privately Held**
SIC: 2084 Wine cellars, bonded: engaged in blending wines

(G-11641)
SOLSTISS INC
561 Fashion Ave Fl 16 (10018-1816)
PHONE 212 719-9194
Francois Damide, *President*
Sandrine Bernard, *Exec VP*
Sara Harris, *Marketing Mgr*
EMP: 6
SQ FT: 3,500
SALES (est): 624.7K **Privately Held**
SIC: 2241 2258 Silk narrow fabrics; lace & lace products

(G-11642)
SOLUDOS LLC
520 Broadway Fl 5 (10012-4436)
PHONE 212 219-1101
Brigid Foster, *COO*
Danielle Marmorale, *Prdtn Mgr*
Ardit Keqi, *Accountant*
Catherine Leavitt, *VP Sales*
Meredith Hamilton, *Accounts Exec*
▲ **EMP:** 13 **EST:** 2010
SALES (est): 1.9MM **Privately Held**
SIC: 3021 7389 Shoes, rubber or plastic molded to fabric; shoe designers

(G-11643)
SOLUTIA BUSINESS ENTPS INC
111 8th Ave (10011-5201)
PHONE 314 674-1000
Timothy J Spihlman, *Ch of Bd*
EMP: 15
SALES (est): 1MM **Publicly Held**
SIC: 2824 Organic fibers, noncellulosic
HQ: Solutia Inc.
575 Maryville Centre Dr
Saint Louis MO 63141
423 229-2000

(G-11644)
SONY BROADBAND ENTERTAINMENT (DH)
550 Madison Ave Fl 6 (10022-3211)
PHONE 212 833-6800
Howard Stringer, *Ch of Bd*
Nobuyuki Idei, *Vice Chairman*
Robert Wiesenthal, *CFO*
▲ **EMP:** 12
SQ FT: 20,000
SALES (est): 1B
SALES (corp-wide): 80.1B **Privately Held**
SIC: 3652 7812 5734 7832 Pre-recorded records & tapes; motion picture production & distribution; motion picture production & distribution, television; software, computer games; motion picture theaters, except drive-in; video discs & tapes, prerecorded
HQ: Sony Corporation Of America
25 Madison Ave Fl 27
New York NY 10010
212 833-8000

(G-11645)
SONY CORPORATION OF AMERICA (HQ)
Also Called: Sony Music Entertainment
25 Madison Ave Fl 27 (10010-8601)
PHONE 212 833-8000
Kazuo Hirai, *Ch of Bd*
Howard Stringer, *President*
Nicole Seligman, *Exec VP*
Mary Jo V Green, *Senior VP*
Steven E Kober, *CFO*
◆ **EMP:** 250
SQ FT: 20,000
SALES (est): 9.4B
SALES (corp-wide): 80.1B **Privately Held**
WEB: www.sony.com
SIC: 3695 3652 3651 3577 Optical disks & tape, blank; compact laser discs, prerecorded; household audio & video equipment; computer peripheral equipment; computer storage devices
PA: Sony Corporation
1-7-1, Konan
Minato-Ku TKY 108-0
367 482-111

(G-11646)
SONY DADC US INC
Also Called: Sony Style
550 Madison Ave (10022-3211)
PHONE 212 833-8800
Steve Hodges, *Exec VP*
John Zarling, *Exec VP*
Shane Allen, *Vice Pres*
Mark Arrington, *Vice Pres*
Matthias Wagner, *Sales Staff*
EMP: 386
SALES (corp-wide): 80.1B **Privately Held**
SIC: 3695 Optical disks & tape, blank
HQ: Sony Dadc Us Inc.
1800 N Fruitridge Ave
Terre Haute IN 47804
812 462-8100

(G-11647)
SONY MUSIC ENTERTAINMENT
Also Called: Sony Music Holdings
25 Madison Ave Fl 19 (10010-8601)
PHONE 212 833-8000
Thomas Mottola, *CEO*
Kevin Kiernan, *Director*
EMP: 2000
SALES (corp-wide): 80.1B **Privately Held**
WEB: www.sonymusic.com
SIC: 3652 Pre-recorded records & tapes
HQ: Sony Music Entertainment
25 Madison Ave Fl 19
New York NY 10010

(G-11648)
SONY MUSIC ENTERTAINMENT INC
Tristar Music
79 5th Ave Fl 16 (10003-3034)
PHONE 212 833-5057
Rich Isaacson, *President*
EMP: 45
SALES (corp-wide): 80.1B **Privately Held**
WEB: www.sonymusic.com
SIC: 3652 Pre-recorded records & tapes
HQ: Sony Music Entertainment
25 Madison Ave Fl 19
New York NY 10010

(G-11649)
SONY MUSIC HOLDINGS INC (DH)
Also Called: Sony Music Entertainment
25 Madison Ave Fl 26 (10010-8601)
PHONE 212 833-8000
Douglas P Morris, *CEO*
Steven E Kober, *President*
Charles Goldstuck, *President*
Richard Griffiths, *President*
Robert Jamieson, *President*
◆ **EMP:** 800
SQ FT: 300,000
SALES (est): 465.3MM
SALES (corp-wide): 80.1B **Privately Held**
WEB: www.bmgentertainment.com
SIC: 3652 5099 2741 Pre-recorded records & tapes; phonograph records; tapes & cassettes, prerecorded; compact discs; miscellaneous publishing
HQ: Sony Corporation Of America
25 Madison Ave Fl 27
New York NY 10010
212 833-8000

(G-11650)
SONY/ATV MUSIC PUBLISHING LLC (DH)
25 Madison Ave Fl 24 (10010-8601)
PHONE 212 833-7730
Martin N Bandier, *CEO*
Paul Martin, *Vice Pres*
Nicolas Barendson, *Marketing Staff*
Nick Barker, *Manager*
▲ **EMP:** 20 **EST:** 1995
SALES (est): 23MM
SALES (corp-wide): 80.1B **Privately Held**
SIC: 2741 Music book & sheet music publishing
HQ: Sony Corporation Of America
25 Madison Ave Fl 27
New York NY 10010
212 833-8000

(G-11651)
SOS INTERNATIONAL LLC
426 W Broadway Apt 6a (10012-3773)
PHONE 212 742-2410
EMP: 353
SALES (corp-wide): 93.7MM **Privately Held**
SIC: 3724 Aircraft engines & engine parts
PA: Sos International Llc
1881 Campus Commons Dr
Reston VA 20191
703 391-9680

(G-11652)
SOTERIX MEDICAL INC
Also Called: Soterix Medical Technologies
237 W 35th St Ste 1401 (10001-1950)
PHONE 888 990-8327
Lucas Parra, *President*
Chris Thomas, *Research*
Pragya Bista, *Engineer*
Nitish Shrestha, *Design Engr*
Kamran Nazim, *Manager*
▲ **EMP:** 12
SALES (est): 655.5K **Privately Held**
SIC: 3845 Electromedical equipment

(G-11653)
SOURCE MEDIA LLC (HQ)
1 State St Fl 27 (10004-1561)
PHONE 212 803-8200
Douglas J Manoni, *CEO*
Benjamin Felix, *General Mgr*
Victor Kuo, *General Mgr*
Allison Bisbey, *Editor*
Carrie Burns, *Editor*
▲ **EMP:** 205
SQ FT: 60,000
SALES (est): 194.2MM **Privately Held**
WEB: www.sourcemedia.com/
SIC: 2721 Magazines: publishing & printing

(G-11654)
SOUTH BRIDGE PRESS INC
122 W 26th St Fl 3 (10001-6804)
PHONE 212 233-4047
Mitch Nochlin, *President*
EMP: 8
SALES (est): 946.9K **Privately Held**
SIC: 2752 Commercial printing, offset

(G-11655)
SOUTINE INC
104 W 70th St Frnt 1 (10023-4454)
PHONE 212 496-1450
Madge Rosenberg, *President*
Barry Rosenberg, *Vice Pres*
EMP: 6
SQ FT: 600
SALES (est): 497.2K **Privately Held**
WEB: www.soutine.com
SIC: 2051 5812 Bakery: wholesale or wholesale/retail combined; caterers

(G-11656)
SOVEREIGN BRANDS LLC (PA)
81 Greene St Apt 2 (10012-5349)
PHONE 212 343-8366
Brett R Berish, *CEO*
Brett Berish, *Managing Prtnr*
Brandon Jones, *Area Mgr*
Amelia Salafrio, *Area Mgr*
Scott Cohen, *VP Opers*
▲ **EMP:** 6
SQ FT: 1,800

GEOGRAPHIC SECTION
New York - New York County (G-11684)

SALES (est): 1MM **Privately Held**
WEB: www.sovereignbrands.com
SIC: 2085 Distilled & blended liquors

(G-11657)
SPARK CREATIONS INC
10 W 46th St Fl 9 (10036-4515)
PHONE.................................212 575-8385
Eli Aviram, *President*
Benjamin Aviram, *Vice Pres*
▲ EMP: 17
SQ FT: 4,000
SALES (est): 1.8MM **Privately Held**
WEB: www.sparkcreations.com
SIC: 3911 Jewelry, precious metal

(G-11658)
SPARTA COMMERCIAL SERVICES INC (PA)
555 5th Ave Fl 14 (10017-9257)
PHONE.................................212 239-2666
Anthony L Havens, *Ch of Bd*
Richard P Trotter, *COO*
Sandra L Ahman, *Vice Pres*
Sandra Ahman, *Vice Pres*
Jan Karim, *Human Res Dir*
EMP: 11
SQ FT: 3,000
SALES: 604.8K **Publicly Held**
WEB: www.spartacommercial.com
SIC: 7372 7375 Prepackaged software; on-line data base information retrieval

(G-11659)
SPARTACIST PUBLISHING CO
48 Warren St (10007-1017)
P.O. Box 1377 (10116-1377)
PHONE.................................212 732-7860
Elizabeth R Gordis, *CEO*
James M Robertson, *President*
A Robinson Hunt, *Treasurer*
EMP: 20
SALES (est): 1.8MM **Privately Held**
SIC: 2731 2711 Pamphlets: publishing only, not printed on site; newspapers: publishing only, not printed on site

(G-11660)
SPARTAN BRANDS INC (PA)
451 Park Ave S Fl 5 (10016-7390)
PHONE.................................212 340-0320
Gary Grey, *President*
Eli Motovich, *CFO*
◆ EMP: 12 EST: 1946
SQ FT: 2,500
SALES (est): 12.7MM **Privately Held**
WEB: www.spartanbrands.com
SIC: 3999 Hair & hair-based products

(G-11661)
SPECIALTY MINERALS INC (HQ)
Also Called: S M I
622 3rd Ave Fl 38 (10017-6707)
PHONE.................................212 878-1800
Paul R Saueracker, *Ch of Bd*
Dj Monagle, *Principal*
Kenneth Mueller, *Business Mgr*
◆ EMP: 50
SQ FT: 42,000
SALES (est): 925MM **Publicly Held**
WEB: www.specialtyminerals.com
SIC: 2819 5032 1422 5169 Lime building products; crushed & broken limestone; chemical additives; chemical preparations; calcium carbide

(G-11662)
SPECIALTY SIGNS CO INC
15 W 39th St Fl 7 (10018-0633)
PHONE.................................212 243-8521
Marc Frankel, *President*
Edna Batounis, *Project Mgr*
EMP: 13 EST: 1971
SQ FT: 6,000
SALES: 850K **Privately Held**
SIC: 3993 Signs & advertising specialties

(G-11663)
SPECILTY BUS MCHS HOLDINGS LLC
260 W 35th St Fl 11 (10001-2528)
PHONE.................................212 587-9600
Steven Schaps, *Mng Member*
EMP: 26
SALES (est): 3.6MM **Privately Held**
SIC: 3555 Printing trades machinery

(G-11664)
SPECTRUM APPAREL INC
463 Fashion Ave Fl 12 (10018-7499)
PHONE.................................212 239-2025
Richard Kringstein, *President*
EMP: 85
SALES (est): 5.7MM **Privately Held**
SIC: 2339 Women's & misses' jackets & coats, except sportswear

(G-11665)
SPECTRUM PRTG LITHOGRAPHY INC
Also Called: Earth Spectrum
505 8th Ave Rm 1802 (10018-4707)
PHONE.................................212 255-3131
Peter Mandelkern, *President*
Karen Targrove, *Vice Pres*
EMP: 26
SQ FT: 5,000
SALES (est): 2.3MM **Privately Held**
SIC: 2752 2789 2759 2675 Color lithography; bookbinding & related work; commercial printing; die-cut paper & board

(G-11666)
SPEKTRIX INC
115 W 30th St Rm 501 (10001-4071)
PHONE.................................646 741-5110
Steven Walsh, *Project Mgr*
Joanne Stewart, *CFO*
David Ciano, *Accounts Exec*
Rebecca Kahn, *Mng Member*
Alexandra Shepherd, *Manager*
EMP: 6
SQ FT: 1,200
SALES (est): 163.7K **Privately Held**
SIC: 7372 Publishers' computer software

(G-11667)
SPENCER AB INC
265 W 37th St Rm 2388 (10018-5757)
PHONE.................................646 831-3728
Tommy Tsui, *President*
Joel Glentz, *VP Sales*
EMP: 7
SALES (est): 1.5MM **Privately Held**
SIC: 2335 2331 Women's, juniors' & misses' dresses; women's & misses' blouses & shirts

(G-11668)
SPF HOLDINGS II LLC (HQ)
9 W 57th St Ste 4200 (10019-2707)
PHONE.................................212 750-8300
Dave West, *President*
EMP: 9
SALES (est): 2.1B
SALES (corp-wide): 7.3B **Publicly Held**
SIC: 2033 5149 6719 2099 Fruits & fruit products in cans, jars, etc.; vegetables & vegetable products in cans, jars, etc.; tomato products: packaged in cans, jars, etc.; canned goods: fruit, vegetables, seafood, meats, etc.; pet foods; personal holding companies, except banks; syrups, frosting, ready-to-use; sandwiches, assembled & packaged: for wholesale market; peanut butter
PA: The J M Smucker Company
1 Strawberry Ln
Orrville OH 44667
330 682-3000

(G-11669)
SPH GROUP HOLDINGS LLC (HQ)
590 Madison Ave Fl 32 (10022-2524)
PHONE.................................212 520-2300
Jack L Howard, *CEO*
EMP: 14 EST: 2013
SALES (est): 828.3MM
SALES (corp-wide): 1.3B **Publicly Held**
SIC: 3339 3011 3312 Precious metals; tire & inner tube materials & related products; wire products, steel or iron
PA: Steel Partners Holdings L.P.
590 Madison Ave Rm 3202
New York NY 10022
212 520-2300

(G-11670)
SPIN MAGAZINE MEDIA
276 5th Ave Rm 800 (10001-4509)
PHONE.................................212 231-7400
Nion McEvoy, *CEO*
Jack Jensen, *President*
Tom Fernald, *Vice Pres*
EMP: 20
SALES (est): 218.2K
SALES (corp-wide): 3.2MM **Privately Held**
WEB: www.spinmag.com
SIC: 2721 Magazines: publishing only, not printed on site
PA: Buzz Media Inc.
6464 W Sunset Blvd # 650
Los Angeles CA 90028
213 252-8999

(G-11671)
SPIRIT MUSIC GROUP INC (HQ)
235 W 23rd St Fl 4 (10011-2371)
PHONE.................................212 533-7672
Mark Fried, *President*
David Renzer, *Chairman*
EMP: 20
SALES (est): 1.6MM **Publicly Held**
WEB: www.spiritmusicgroup.com
SIC: 2741 Music books: publishing & printing

(G-11672)
SPLACER INC
33 W 17th St Fl 6 (10011-5511)
PHONE.................................646 853-9789
ADI Biran, *CEO*
Gabi Peles, *COO*
EMP: 6
SALES (est): 350K **Privately Held**
SIC: 7372 Application computer software

(G-11673)
SPORT ATHLEISURE LTD
16 W 36th St Rm 1205 (10018-9754)
PHONE.................................212 868-6505
Shalom Asher, *President*
Steven Goldfarb, *Vice Pres*
EMP: 10 EST: 2017
SQ FT: 2,100
SALES (est): 12MM **Privately Held**
SIC: 2339 2329 Women's & misses' athletic clothing & sportswear; men's & boys' sportswear & athletic clothing

(G-11674)
SPORTS ILLUSTRATED FOR KIDS
1271 Ave Of The Americas (10020-1300)
PHONE.................................212 522-1212
Don Logan, *CEO*
Diane Oshin, *Publisher*
Maureen Shelly, *General Mgr*
Joe Ripp, *Principal*
Tina Jordan, *Editor*
▲ EMP: 50
SALES (est): 5.3MM
SALES (corp-wide): 2.2B **Publicly Held**
WEB: www.siphoto.com
SIC: 2721 Magazines: publishing only, not printed on site
HQ: Time Inc.
225 Liberty St Ste C2
New York NY 10281
212 522-1212

(G-11675)
SPORTS PBLICATIONS PROD NY LLC
708 3rd Ave Fl 12 (10017-4129)
PHONE.................................212 366-7700
Brent Diamond,
EMP: 80
SALES (est): 2.3MM **Privately Held**
SIC: 2711 Newspapers, publishing & printing

(G-11676)
SPORTS PRODUCTS AMERICA LLC
Popsicle Playwear
34 W 33rd St Fl 2 (10001-3304)
PHONE.................................212 594-5511
Ezra Haber, *QC Dir*
Richard Adjmi, *Sales Associate*
EMP: 50
SALES (corp-wide): 27.5MM **Privately Held**
SIC: 2361 Girls' & children's blouses & shirts
HQ: Sports Products Of America Llc
463 7th Ave
New York NY 10018
212 629-9600

(G-11677)
SPORTS REPORTER INC
527 3rd Ave Ste 327 (10016-4168)
PHONE.................................212 737-2750
Lindsay Hamilton, *President*
EMP: 6
SALES (est): 280K **Privately Held**
WEB: www.sportsreporter.com
SIC: 2711 Newspapers, publishing & printing

(G-11678)
SPORTSGRID INC
404 5th Ave Fl 3 (10018-7510)
PHONE.................................646 849-4085
Jeremy Stein, *CEO*
Alexander Dubin, *Shareholder*
Louis Maione, *Shareholder*
EMP: 10
SALES: 1MM **Privately Held**
SIC: 2741

(G-11679)
SPRAY MORET LLC
Also Called: Sprayground
1411 Broadway Fl 8 (10018-3565)
PHONE.................................917 213-9592
David Ben-David,
EMP: 5
SALES (est): 117.2K **Privately Held**
SIC: 2393 Canvas bags

(G-11680)
SPRING INC
41 E 11th St Fl 11 (10003-4602)
PHONE.................................646 732-0323
Ofer Leidner, *President*
EMP: 6
SALES (est): 468.2K **Privately Held**
SIC: 7372 Application computer software

(G-11681)
SPRINGER ADIS US LLC (DH)
233 Spring St Fl 6 (10013-1522)
PHONE.................................212 460-1500
Derk Haank, *CEO*
EMP: 16
SALES (est): 3.3MM
SALES (corp-wide): 1.7B **Privately Held**
SIC: 2721 2731 Trade journals: publishing only, not printed on site; magazines: publishing only, not printed on site; books: publishing only
HQ: Springer Science + Business Media, Llc
233 Spring St Fl 6
New York NY 10013
212 460-1500

(G-11682)
SPRINGER CUSTOMER SVC CTR LLC
233 Spring St Fl 6 (10013-1522)
PHONE.................................212 460-1500
Edward Woods, *CFO*
EMP: 400
SQ FT: 80,000
SALES (est): 26MM
SALES (corp-wide): 1.7B **Privately Held**
SIC: 2731 Book publishing
HQ: Springer Nature Customer Service Center Gmbh
Tiergartenstr. 15-17
Heidelberg 69121
622 134-50

(G-11683)
SPRINGER HEALTHCARE LLC
233 Spring St Fl 6 (10013-1522)
PHONE.................................212 460-1500
Rick Werdann, *Principal*
Jan De Boer, *Exec VP*
EMP: 25
SALES: 950K **Privately Held**
SIC: 2721 Periodicals

(G-11684)
SPRINGER PUBLISHING CO LLC
11 W 42nd St Ste 15a (10036-8007)
PHONE.................................212 431-4370
Ursula Springer, *President*

New York - New York County (G-11685)   **GEOGRAPHIC SECTION**

Christina Morgan, *Editor*
Joanne Jay, *Vice Pres*
Jason Roth, *Vice Pres*
Pascal Schwarzer, *Vice Pres*
EMP: 38 **EST:** 1950
SQ FT: 9,000
SALES (est): 7.1MM **Privately Held**
WEB: www.springerpub.com
SIC: 2731 2721 Books: publishing only; trade journals: publishing only, not printed on site

(G-11685)
SPRINGER SCNCE + BUS MEDIA LLC (DH)
Also Called: Springer Business Media
233 Spring St Fl 6 (10013-1522)
PHONE.................212 460-1500
Miguel Quesada, *General Mgr*
Sean Beppler, *Editor*
Mayra Castro, *Editor*
Herma Drees, *Editor*
Jennifer Evans, *Editor*
◆ **EMP:** 76 **EST:** 1964
SQ FT: 40,000
SALES (est): 102.7MM
SALES (corp-wide): 1.7B **Privately Held**
WEB: www.telospub.com
SIC: 2721 2731 Trade journals: publishing only, not printed on site; books: publishing only
HQ: Springer Nature Three Gmbh
    Heidelberger Platz 3
    Berlin 14197
    308 278-70

(G-11686)
SPUTNICK 84 LLC
Also Called: Out of Print
1745 Broadway Frnt 3 (10019-4641)
PHONE.................844 667-7468
Todd Lawton, *Principal*
Jeffrey Leblanc, *Principal*
EMP: 7
SALES (est): 658.2K
SALES (corp-wide): 82.3MM **Privately Held**
SIC: 2752 Commercial printing, lithographic
HQ: Penguin Random House Llc
    1745 Broadway
    New York NY 10019
    212 782-9000

(G-11687)
SRP APPAREL GROUP INC
525 7th Ave Rm 1808 (10018-5274)
PHONE.................212 764-4810
Scott Pianin, *President*
▲ **EMP:** 5
SALES (est): 905.3K **Privately Held**
SIC: 2339 Women's & misses' outerwear

(G-11688)
SSA TRADING LTD
226 W 37th St Fl 6 (10018-9020)
PHONE.................646 465-9500
Gary Cohen, *President*
Robert Klein, *CFO*
Marc Klein, *Treasurer*
EMP: 12
SQ FT: 5,000
SALES (est): 1.4MM **Privately Held**
SIC: 2339 Sportswear, women's

(G-11689)
SSG FASHIONS LTD
27 E 37th St Frnt 1 (10016-3004)
PHONE.................212 221-0933
William Seng, *President*
▲ **EMP:** 6
SQ FT: 3,000
SALES (est): 966.2K **Privately Held**
WEB: www.ssgfashions.com
SIC: 2339 2335 Sportswear, women's; women's, juniors' & misses' dresses

(G-11690)
ST TROPEZ INC
530 Broadway Fl 10 (10012-3920)
PHONE.................800 366-6383
Isaac Naim, *President*
EMP: 6
SQ FT: 4,300

SALES (est): 300K
SALES (corp-wide): 1B **Privately Held**
SIC: 2844 Suntan lotions & oils
PA: Pz Cussons Plc
    3500 Aviator Way Manchester Business Park
    Manchester M22 5
    161 435-1000

(G-11691)
STANDARD ANALYTICS IO INC
7 World Trade Ctr 46th (10007-2140)
PHONE.................917 882-5422
Tiffany Bogich, *COO*
EMP: 6
SALES (est): 219.1K **Privately Held**
SIC: 2721 2741 7371 7374 Periodicals; ; computer software development; data processing & preparation; distribution channels consultant

(G-11692)
STANDARD INDUSTRIES INC (PA)
9 W 57th St Fl 30 (10019-2701)
PHONE.................212 821-1600
David Millstone, *CEO*
David Winter, *Co-CEO*
EMP: 6
SALES (est): 2MM **Privately Held**
SIC: 3272 Building materials, except block or brick: concrete

(G-11693)
STANDARD SCREEN SUPPLY CORP (PA)
Also Called: Active Process Supply
121 Varick St Rm 200 (10013-1408)
PHONE.................212 627-2727
Arthur Gononsky, *President*
Susan Gononsky, *Treasurer*
▼ **EMP:** 11 **EST:** 1951
SALES (est): 1.2MM **Privately Held**
WEB: www.standardscreen.com
SIC: 2893 Screen process ink

(G-11694)
STANMARK JEWELRY INC
64 W 48th St Ste 1303 (10036-1708)
PHONE.................212 730-2557
Stanley Krukowski, *President*
EMP: 6
SQ FT: 10,000
SALES (est): 510K **Privately Held**
WEB: www.stanmark.com
SIC: 3911 5944 Jewelry, precious metal; jewelry stores

(G-11695)
STAR CHILDRENS DRESS CO INC (PA)
Also Called: Rare Editions
1250 Broadway Fl 18 (10001-3749)
PHONE.................212 279-1524
Edward Rosen, *Ch of Bd*
Dominique Carter, *Production*
Josie Chumney, *Supervisor*
Ken Dippold, *Info Tech Mgr*
▲ **EMP:** 60
SQ FT: 12,000
SALES (est): 42.9MM **Privately Held**
WEB: www.rareeditions.com
SIC: 2361 Dresses: girls', children's & infants'

(G-11696)
STAR WIRE MESH FABRICATORS
518 E 119th St (10035-4432)
P.O. Box 678 (10035-0678)
PHONE.................212 831-4133
Alex Pavur, *President*
Anistasia Pavur, *Treasurer*
EMP: 5
SQ FT: 2,500
SALES (est): 510K **Privately Held**
WEB: www.starwiremesh.com
SIC: 3496 Screening, woven wire: made from purchased wire; mesh, made from purchased wire

(G-11697)
STARFIRE HOLDING CORPORATION (PA)
767 5th Ave Fl 47 (10153-0023)
PHONE.................914 614-7000
Carl Celian Icahn, *Ch of Bd*
Keith Cozza, *Vice Pres*
EMP: 50
SALES (est): 955MM **Privately Held**
SIC: 3743 4741 4789 Freight cars & equipment; rental of railroad cars; railroad car repair

(G-11698)
STARLITE MEDIA LLC (PA)
118 E 28th St Rm 601 (10016-8447)
PHONE.................212 909-7700
Harold Lueken, *CEO*
Oscar Martinez, *Managing Dir*
Tim Daly,
Karen Jolicoeur,
Bruce Seidel,
EMP: 4
SQ FT: 1,000
SALES (est): 3.7MM **Privately Held**
WEB: www.starlitemedia.com
SIC: 3993 Signs & advertising specialties

(G-11699)
STEEL PARTNERS HOLDINGS LP (PA)
590 Madison Ave Rm 3202 (10022-8536)
PHONE.................212 520-2300
Jack L Howard, *President*
Warren G Lichtenstein, *Chairman*
Douglas B Woodworth, *CFO*
Alejandra Hillman, *Asst Controller*
James Hedges, *Chief Mktg Ofcr*
EMP: 51
SALES: 1.3B **Publicly Held**
SIC: 3479 3497 1381 6141 Etching & engraving; copper foil; gold foil or leaf; nickel foil; silver foil or leaf; drilling oil & gas wells; consumer finance companies

(G-11700)
STEEZYS LLC
80 8th Ave 202 (10011-5126)
PHONE.................646 276-5333
Robert Lebowitz, *Mng Member*
Edina Sultanik,
EMP: 7
SALES (est): 592.2K **Privately Held**
SIC: 3961 Costume jewelry, ex. precious metal & semiprecious stones

(G-11701)
STEFAN FURS INC
150 W 30th St Fl 15 (10001-4138)
PHONE.................212 594-2788
Alex Amanatides, *President*
EMP: 5
SQ FT: 800
SALES (est): 382.1K **Privately Held**
SIC: 2371 Fur goods

(G-11702)
STEINWAY MUSICAL INSTRS INC (HQ)
1133 Avenue Of The Americ (10036-6710)
PHONE.................781 894-9770
Michael T Sweeney, *President*
Ron Losby, *President*
John Stoner Jr, *President*
Donna M Lucente, *Vice Pres*
Dennis M Hanson, *Treasurer*
◆ **EMP:** 40
SALES (est): 316.2MM
SALES (corp-wide): 318.4MM **Privately Held**
WEB: www.steinwaymusical.com
SIC: 3931 Musical instruments; pianos, all types: vertical, grand, spinet, player, etc.; string instruments & parts; woodwind instruments & parts
PA: Paulson & Co. Inc.
    1133 Ave Of The Americas
    New York NY 10036
    212 956-2221

(G-11703)
STEMLINE THERAPEUTICS INC
750 Lexington Ave Fl 11 (10022-9817)
PHONE.................646 502-2311
Ivan Bergstein, *Ch of Bd*

Kenneth Hoberman, *COO*
David G Gionco, *CFO*
Ron Bentsur, *Bd of Directors*
Eric Dobmeier, *Bd of Directors*
EMP: 29
SALES (est): 898.2K **Privately Held**
WEB: www.stemline.com
SIC: 2834 Pharmaceutical preparations

(G-11704)
STENSUL INC (PA)
150 W 25th St Fl 3 (10001-7404)
PHONE.................212 380-8620
Noah Dinkin, *CEO*
Gabriel Sosa, *Vice Pres*
Jonathan Travin, *Vice Pres*
Michael Zusel, *Consultant*
EMP: 6
SQ FT: 5,500
SALES (est): 3.6MM **Privately Held**
SIC: 7372 Prepackaged software

(G-11705)
STEPHAN & COMPANY ACC LTD (PA)
10 E 38th St Fl 9 (10016-0616)
PHONE.................212 481-3888
Stephan Rubin, *President*
▲ **EMP:** 20
SQ FT: 2,400
SALES (est): 3.5MM **Privately Held**
WEB: www.stephanco.com
SIC: 3961 Costume jewelry, ex. precious metal & semiprecious stones

(G-11706)
STEPHEN SINGER PATTERN CO INC
Also Called: Popular Pattern
340 W 39th St Fl 4 (10018-1345)
PHONE.................212 947-2902
Stephen Singer, *President*
EMP: 12
SQ FT: 7,000
SALES (est): 1.9MM **Privately Held**
SIC: 2621 2741 Pattern tissue; miscellaneous publishing

(G-11707)
STERLING POSSESSIONS LTD
251 W 39th St (10018-3105)
PHONE.................212 594-0418
William Callaghan, *Ch of Bd*
Richard Castagna, *President*
▲ **EMP:** 8
SQ FT: 3,000
SALES (est): 740K **Privately Held**
WEB: www.sterlingposs.com
SIC: 3911 5094 2329 2339 Jewelry apparel; jewelry; men's & boys' sportswear & athletic clothing; sportswear, women's; sportswear, men's & boys'; sportswear, women's & children's

(G-11708)
STERLING SOUND INC
88 10th Ave Frnt 6 (10011-4745)
PHONE.................212 604-9433
Murat Aktar, *President*
EMP: 30
SALES (est): 4.7MM **Privately Held**
SIC: 3652 Master records or tapes, preparation of

(G-11709)
STEVEN MADDEN LTD
Also Called: Madden Zone
19 W 34th St Fl 4 (10001-3006)
PHONE.................212 695-5545
Jeff Goldstein, *Branch Mgr*
EMP: 75 **Publicly Held**
SIC: 3144 Boots, canvas or leather: women's
PA: Steven Madden, Ltd.
    5216 Barnett Ave
    Long Island City NY 11104

(G-11710)
STEVENS BANDES GRAPHICS CORP
333 Hudson St Fl 3 (10013-1006)
PHONE.................212 675-1128
Stephen Kilduff, *President*
Kevin Roach, *Admin Sec*
EMP: 10

GEOGRAPHIC SECTION

New York - New York County (G-11738)

SQ FT: 2,500
SALES: 1.5MM **Privately Held**
WEB: www.stevensbandes.com
SIC: 2752 Commercial printing, offset

(G-11711)
STEVES ORIGINAL FURS INC
345 7th Ave Fl 9 (10001-5049)
PHONE.....................212 967-8007
Steve Panaretos, *President*
Aspasia Panaretos, *Admin Sec*
EMP: 20
SALES (est): 2MM **Privately Held**
WEB: www.stevesoriginalfurs.com
SIC: 2371 Fur finishers & liners for the fur goods trade

(G-11712)
STICKY SOCKS LLC
200 W 60th St Apt 7g (10023-8504)
PHONE.....................212 541-5927
Eva Di Nardo, *President*
EMP: 5
SALES (est): 309K **Privately Held**
SIC: 2252 Socks

(G-11713)
STITCH & COUTURE INC (PA)
Also Called: Lela Rose
224 W 30th St Fl 14 (10001-1493)
PHONE.....................212 947-9204
Lela Rose, *Ch of Bd*
Betsy Kilough, *Vice Pres*
Amy Park, *Prdtn Mgr*
Chanelle Smith, *Production*
Erin Anderson, *Controller*
EMP: 25
SQ FT: 3,000
SALES (est): 11MM **Privately Held**
WEB: www.lelarose.com
SIC: 2331 2335 Blouses, women's & juniors': made from purchased material; shirts, women's & juniors': made from purchased materials; bridal & formal gowns

(G-11714)
STONE HOUSE ASSOCIATES INC
37 W 47th St Ste 910 (10036-2809)
PHONE.....................212 221-7447
Elaine Wong, *President*
EMP: 5
SALES: 450K **Privately Held**
WEB: www.theidea-network.com
SIC: 3911 Jewelry, precious metal

(G-11715)
STONESONG PRESS LLC
270 W 39th St Rm 201 (10018-0137)
PHONE.....................212 929-4600
Emmanuelle Morgen, *Principal*
Madelyn Burt, *Editor*
Katherine Latshaw, *Editor*
Judy Linden, *Exec VP*
Alyssa Jennette, *Production*
EMP: 6 EST: 1978
SALES (est): 450K **Privately Held**
SIC: 2731 Book publishing

(G-11716)
STONY APPAREL CORP
Also Called: Eye Shadow
1407 Broadway Rm 3300 (10018-2395)
PHONE.....................212 391-0022
Shaun Jackson, *Manager*
EMP: 5 **Privately Held**
SIC: 2339 Women's & misses' athletic clothing & sportswear
PA: Stony Apparel Corp.
  1500 S Evergreen Ave
  Los Angeles CA 90023

(G-11717)
STRAIGHT ARROW PUBLISHING CO
Also Called: Mens Journal
1290 Ave Of The Amer Fl 2 (10104-0298)
PHONE.....................212 484-1616
John Gruber, *CFO*
EMP: 200
SALES (est): 12.2MM
SALES (corp-wide): 63.3MM **Privately Held**
WEB: www.mensjournal.com
SIC: 2741 Miscellaneous publishing
PA: Wenner Media Llc
  1290 Ave Of The Amer Fl 2
  New York NY 10104
  212 484-1616

(G-11718)
STRATCONGLOBAL INC
685 3rd Ave Fl 4 (10017-8408)
PHONE.....................212 989-2355
Joanna Peters, *Principal*
EMP: 5
SALES (est): 215.4K **Privately Held**
SIC: 2711 Newspapers

(G-11719)
STREET KING LLC
Also Called: Sk Energy Shots
575 Madison Ave Fl 24 (10022-8538)
PHONE.....................212 400-2200
Sabrina Peterson, *President*
EMP: 8
SALES: 1MM **Privately Held**
SIC: 2086 Bottled & canned soft drinks

(G-11720)
STREET SMART DESIGNS INC
29 W 35th St Fl 6 (10001-2299)
PHONE.....................646 865-0056
Richard H Bienen, *Ch of Bd*
▲ EMP: 6
SALES (est): 977.6K **Privately Held**
WEB: www.streetsmartdesigns.com
SIC: 3111 5137 Handbag leather; handbags

(G-11721)
STREETCRED NYC LLC
1006 6th Ave Fl 3 (10018-0283)
PHONE.....................646 675-0073
Tomislav Markovski, *CEO*
EMP: 5
SALES: 950K **Privately Held**
SIC: 7372 7389 Application computer software; business services

(G-11722)
STRIATA INC
48 Wall St Ste 1100 (10005-2903)
PHONE.....................212 918-4677
Michael Wright, *President*
Mia Papanicolaou, *COO*
Garin Toren, *COO*
Natasha Felski, *Project Mgr*
Renee Hart, *Project Mgr*
EMP: 85
SQ FT: 6,000
SALES (est): 6.3MM **Privately Held**
WEB: www.striata.com
SIC: 7372 Application computer software

(G-11723)
STRIDER GLOBAL LLC
261 W 28th St Apt 6a (10001-5936)
PHONE.....................212 726-1302
EMP: 5
SALES: 100K **Privately Held**
SIC: 3648 Mfg Lighting Equipment

(G-11724)
STRUCTURED RETAIL PRODUCTS
Also Called: SRP
225 Park Ave S Fl 8 (10003-1604)
PHONE.....................212 224-3692
Sunny Singh, *Principal*
Joe Burris, *Principal*
EMP: 5
SQ FT: 60,000
SALES (est): 233.8K
SALES (corp-wide): 496.5MM **Privately Held**
SIC: 7372 Business oriented computer software
HQ: Euromoney Global Limited
  6-8 Bouverie Street
  London EC4Y
  207 779-8888

(G-11725)
STRUCTUREDWEB INC
20 W 20th St Ste 402 (10011-9258)
PHONE.....................201 325-3110
Daniel Nissan, *President*
Mauricio Fernandes, *Partner*
Yotam Hadass, *Vice Pres*
Michael Coscetta, *VP Sales*
Sam Oliff, *Sales Staff*
EMP: 40
SQ FT: 7,500
SALES (est): 5.1MM **Privately Held**
WEB: www.structuredweb.com
SIC: 7372 7371 Business oriented computer software; computer software development; software programming applications

(G-11726)
STUDIO 22 PRINT
20 Park Ave (10016-3840)
PHONE.....................212 679-2656
E J Rosenberger, *Principal*
EMP: 8
SALES (est): 786.5K **Privately Held**
SIC: 2752 Commercial printing, lithographic

(G-11727)
STUDIO ASSOCIATES OF NEW YORK
242 W 30th St Rm 604 (10001-4913)
P.O. Box 4306 (10163-4306)
PHONE.....................212 268-1163
Edward Jenner, *President*
Joseph Perilla, *Corp Secy*
EMP: 6
SALES (est): 450K **Privately Held**
WEB: www.sanylaser.com
SIC: 3299 Architectural sculptures: gypsum, clay, papier mache, etc.

(G-11728)
STUDIO ONE LEATHER DESIGN INC
270 W 39th St Rm 505 (10018-0334)
PHONE.....................212 760-1701
Arthur Coines, *President*
Ken Sackheim, *Editor*
EMP: 12
SQ FT: 2,500
SALES (est): 3.5MM **Privately Held**
SIC: 2386 3543 3111 Garments, leather; foundry patternmaking; leather tanning & finishing

(G-11729)
STUFF MAGAZINE
1040 Ave Of The Amrcas (10018-3703)
PHONE.....................212 302-2626
Steven Collvin, *President*
EMP: 5
SALES (est): 500K **Privately Held**
SIC: 2721 Magazines: publishing & printing

(G-11730)
STYLECLICK INC (HQ)
810 7th Ave Fl 18 (10019-5879)
PHONE.....................212 329-0300
Lisa Brown, *CEO*
Robert Halper, *President*
Bruce Goldstein, *Exec VP*
Barry W Hall, *CFO*
EMP: 52
SALES: 3.6MM
SALES (corp-wide): 3.3B **Publicly Held**
WEB: www.styleclick.com
SIC: 7372 Business oriented computer software
PA: Iac/Interactivecorp
  555 W 18th St
  New York NY 10011
  212 314-7300

(G-11731)
STYLISTIC PRESS INC
99 Battery Pl Apt 11p (10280-1324)
PHONE.....................212 675-0797
Jeff Lederfarb, *President*
EMP: 15
SQ FT: 2,500
SALES (est): 1.4MM **Privately Held**
SIC: 2752 Commercial printing, offset

(G-11732)
SUBE INC
Also Called: Satya Jewelry
146 W 29th St Rm 4e (10001-0057)
PHONE.....................212 243-6930
Satya Scainetti, *President*
Faneeza Allie, *CFO*
Faneeza Allie-Cruz, *CFO*
Ron Sosely, *Director*
Mamasa Dukureh, *Assistant*
◆ EMP: 30
SQ FT: 6,000
SALES (est): 4.6MM **Privately Held**
WEB: www.satyajewelry.com
SIC: 3911 Jewelry, precious metal

(G-11733)
SUCCESS APPAREL LLC
19 W 34th St Fl 7 (10001-0055)
PHONE.....................212 502-1890
Gila Goodman, *CEO*
Ewan Mendis, *Admin Sec*
EMP: 6 EST: 2015
SALES (est): 237.1K **Privately Held**
SIC: 2211 Apparel & outerwear fabrics, cotton

(G-11734)
SUGAR FOODS CORPORATION (PA)
950 3rd Ave Fl 21 (10022-2786)
PHONE.....................212 753-6900
Donald G Tober, *Ch of Bd*
Marty Wilson, *President*
Stephen Odell, *President*
Myron Stein, *Vice Pres*
Jack Vivinetto, *CFO*
◆ EMP: 34
SQ FT: 10,000
SALES (est): 286.3MM **Privately Held**
WEB: www.sugarfoods.com
SIC: 2869 2023 2099 2068 Sweeteners, synthetic; cream substitutes; sugar; seasonings & spices; packaged combination products: pasta, rice & potato; bread crumbs, not made in bakeries; salted & roasted nuts & seeds; packaging & labeling services

(G-11735)
SULLIVAN ST BKY - HLLS KIT INC
533 W 47th St (10036-7903)
PHONE.....................212 265-5580
James Lahey, *Principal*
▲ EMP: 29
SALES (est): 4.4MM **Privately Held**
SIC: 2051 Bread, cake & related products

(G-11736)
SUMA INDUSTRIES INC
345 E 52nd St Apt 9d (10022-6344)
PHONE.....................646 436-5202
Arthur Forst, *President*
Bob Katz, *Exec VP*
Robert Katz, *Exec VP*
Christopher Patterson, *Vice Pres*
Myra Hyman, *Executive*
EMP: 5
SALES (est): 420K **Privately Held**
WEB: www.sumaindustries.com
SIC: 3993 Signs, not made in custom sign painting shops

(G-11737)
SUMER GOLD LTD
33 W 46th St Fl 4 (10036-4103)
PHONE.....................212 354-8677
Juan Merchan, *President*
Suzanna Merchan, *Treasurer*
EMP: 6
SQ FT: 700
SALES (est): 634.5K **Privately Held**
SIC: 3911 Jewelry, precious metal

(G-11738)
SUMITOMO ELC USA HOLDINGS INC (HQ)
600 5th Ave Fl 18 (10020-2320)
PHONE.....................212 490-6610
Yoshitomo Kasui, *President*
Shuji Nosaka, *Treasurer*
▲ EMP: 8
SALES: 46MM
SALES (corp-wide): 28.9B **Privately Held**
WEB: www.engsin.com
SIC: 3674 Semiconductors & related devices
PA: Sumitomo Electric Industries, Ltd.
  4-5-33, Kitahama, Chuo-Ku
  Osaka OSK 541-0
  662 204-141

New York - New York County (G-11739) GEOGRAPHIC SECTION

(G-11739)
SUMMIT FINCL DISCLOSURE LLC
216 E 45th St Fl 15 (10017-3304)
PHONE 212 913-0510
James W Palmiter, *Owner*
Kenneth M McClure, *Owner*
Scott Damico, *COO*
EMP: 40
SQ FT: 15,000
SALES (est): 8MM
SALES (corp-wide): 4.3B **Publicly Held**
SIC: 2621 Printing paper
PA: Broadridge Financial Solutions, Inc.
5 Dakota Dr Ste 300
New Hyde Park NY 11042
516 472-5400

(G-11740)
SUMMIT PROFESSIONAL NETWORKS
469 Fashion Ave Fl 10 (10018-7640)
PHONE 212 557-7480
Joyce Coots, *Education*
EMP: 60
SALES (corp-wide): 177.1MM **Privately Held**
SIC: 2721 Magazines: publishing & printing
HQ: Summit Professional Networks
4157 Olympic Blvd Ste 225
Erlanger KY 41018
859 692-2100

(G-11741)
SUNA BROS INC
10 W 46th St Fl 5 (10036-4515)
PHONE 212 869-5670
Aron Suna, *President*
Jonathan Suna, *Vice Pres*
Wendy Schwartz, *Cust Mgr*
EMP: 30 **EST:** 1934
SQ FT: 5,000
SALES (est): 4.2MM **Privately Held**
WEB: www.sunabros.com
SIC: 3911 5944 Jewelry, precious metal; jewelry stores

(G-11742)
SUNHAM HOME FASHIONS LLC (PA)
136 Madison Ave Fl 16 (10016-6786)
PHONE 212 695-1218
Howard Yung, *CEO*
Jane Bognacki, *President*
Arthur Coubanou, *COO*
Richard Landis, *Vice Pres*
Susan Wojewoda, *Vice Pres*
◆ **EMP:** 58
SQ FT: 15,000
SALES (est): 37.7MM **Privately Held**
WEB: www.sunham.com
SIC: 2392 Blankets, comforters & beddings

(G-11743)
SUNNY SCUBA INC (PA)
Also Called: Sunny Sports
454 9th Ave (10018-5617)
PHONE 212 333-4915
Leo Kline, *Manager*
EMP: 2
SALES (est): 1.1MM **Privately Held**
SIC: 3949 Skin diving equipment, scuba type; camping equipment & supplies

(G-11744)
SUNSHINE DIAMOND CUTTER INC
38 W 48th St Ste 905 (10036-1805)
PHONE 212 221-1028
Manglaben Dhanani, *President*
EMP: 7
SALES (est): 532.4K **Privately Held**
SIC: 3915 Lapidary work & diamond cutting & polishing

(G-11745)
SUNWIN GLOBAL INDUSTRY INC
295 5th Ave Ste 515 (10016-7103)
PHONE 646 370-6196
Sophie Cheng, *President*
EMP: 5
SQ FT: 850

SALES: 423.6K
SALES (corp-wide): 125.1MM **Privately Held**
SIC: 2258 5137 Lace & warp knit fabric mills; baby goods; apparel belts, women's & children's
PA: Shanghai Sunwin Investment Holding Group Co., Ltd.
Rm. 04, 3/F, Building 11, 688 Lane, Hengnan Rd., Minhang Dist.
Shanghai 20111
216 036-0260

(G-11746)
SUNYNAMS FASHIONS LTD
Also Called: Sunny Names
270 W 38th St Fl 2 (10018-1563)
PHONE 212 268-5200
Sunny Neman, *President*
▲ **EMP:** 7
SQ FT: 5,000
SALES (est): 1.3MM **Privately Held**
SIC: 2339 Women's & misses' outerwear

(G-11747)
SUPER-TRIM INC
30 W 24th St Fl 4 (10010-3558)
PHONE 212 255-2370
Daniel Noy, *President*
EMP: 20
SQ FT: 5,000
SALES (est): 1.1MM **Privately Held**
WEB: www.supertrim.com
SIC: 2258 5131 Lace & lace products; lace fabrics

(G-11748)
SUPERMEDIA LLC
Also Called: Verizon
2 Penn Plz Fl 22 (10121-2299)
PHONE 212 513-9700
Jeanne Ryans, *Manager*
EMP: 100
SALES (corp-wide): 1.8B **Privately Held**
WEB: www.verizon.superpages.com
SIC: 2741 8741 Publishing only, not printed on site; administrative management
HQ: Supermedia Llc
2200 W Airfield Dr
Dfw Airport TX 75261
972 453-7000

(G-11749)
SURE FIT INC
58 W 40th St Rm 2a (10018-2658)
PHONE 212 395-9340
Dean Smith, *Opers Staff*
EMP: 25 **Privately Held**
SIC: 2392 Mfg Household Furnishings
HQ: Sure Fit Home Products, Llc
8000 Quarry Rd Ste C
Alburtis PA 18011
610 264-7300

(G-11750)
SUREPURE INC
405 Lexington Ave Fl 25 (10174-0002)
PHONE 917 368-8480
Guy Kebble, *President*
Stephen Robinson, *CFO*
EMP: 6
SALES: 1.2MM **Privately Held**
SIC: 3559 Chemical machinery & equipment; refinery, chemical processing & similar machinery

(G-11751)
SURFACE MAGAZINE
Also Called: Surface Publishing
134 W 26th St Frnt 1 (10001-6803)
PHONE 646 805-0200
Richard Klein, *Owner*
Lance Crapo, *Principal*
Dani Vernon, *Editor*
Spencer Bailey, *Chief*
Miles Bingham, *Controller*
EMP: 25
SALES (est): 1.9MM **Privately Held**
SIC: 2721 Periodicals

(G-11752)
SUSSEX PUBLISHERS LLC (PA)
Also Called: Psychology Today
115 E 23rd St Fl 9 (10010-4559)
PHONE 212 260-7210

John P Colman, *President*
EMP: 20
SQ FT: 7,400
SALES (est): 3.3MM **Privately Held**
WEB: www.blues-buster.com
SIC: 2721 Magazines: publishing & printing

(G-11753)
SWANK INC
90 Park Ave Rm 1302 (10016-1395)
PHONE 212 867-2600
John A Tulin, *Ch of Bd*
Eric P Luft, *President*
Paul Duckett, *Senior VP*
James E Tulin, *Senior VP*
Christophe Wolf, *Senior VP*
▲ **EMP:** 256 **EST:** 1936
SQ FT: 242,000
SALES (est): 388.2K
SALES (corp-wide): 151.7MM **Privately Held**
WEB: www.swankaccessories.com
SIC: 2389 5611 Men's miscellaneous accessories; clothing accessories: men's & boys'
PA: Randa Accessories Leather Goods Llc
5600 N River Rd Ste 500
Rosemont IL 60018
847 292-8300

(G-11754)
SWAPS MONITOR PUBLICATIONS INC
29 Broadway Rm 1315 (10006-3252)
PHONE 212 742-8550
Paul Spraos, *President*
EMP: 10
SALES (est): 1.2MM **Privately Held**
WEB: www.financialcalendar.com
SIC: 2721 6282 Periodicals; investment advice

(G-11755)
SWAROVSKI NORTH AMERICA LTD
1 Penn Plz Frnt 4 (10119-0202)
PHONE 212 695-1502
EMP: 7
SALES (corp-wide): 3.7B **Privately Held**
SIC: 3961 Costume jewelry
HQ: Swarovski North America Limited
1 Kenney Dr
Cranston RI 02920
401 463-6400

(G-11756)
SWATFAME INC
530 Fashion Ave Rm 1204 (10018-4862)
PHONE 212 944-8022
Marcy Olin, *Branch Mgr*
EMP: 6
SALES (corp-wide): 188.8MM **Privately Held**
WEB: www.swatfame.com
SIC: 2339 2369 Women's & misses' athletic clothing & sportswear; girls' & children's outerwear
PA: Swat.Fame, Inc.
16425 Gale Ave
City Of Industry CA 91745
626 961-7928

(G-11757)
SWEET MOUTH INC
244 5th Ave Ste L243 (10001-7604)
PHONE 800 433-7758
Lucas Dawson, *President*
EMP: 20
SQ FT: 2,000
SALES (est): 720.6K **Privately Held**
SIC: 2731 Book publishing

(G-11758)
SYMANTEC CORPORATION
1 Penn Plz Ste 5420 (10119-5420)
PHONE 646 487-6000
Ken Lowe, *Manager*
EMP: 65
SALES (corp-wide): 4.8B **Publicly Held**
WEB: www.symantec.com
SIC: 7372 Prepackaged software
PA: Symantec Corporation
350 Ellis St
Mountain View CA 94043
650 527-8000

(G-11759)
SYMPHONY TALENT LLC (PA)
19 W 34th St Rm 1000 (10001-3006)
PHONE 212 999-9000
Roopesh Nair, *CEO*
Ryan Kellogg, *Vice Pres*
Obrien Tim, *Vice Pres*
Carl Calarco, *CFO*
Stephen Henkenmeier,
EMP: 75 **EST:** 2007
SALES: 50MM **Privately Held**
SIC: 7372 7361 Business oriented computer software; employment agencies

(G-11760)
SYMRISE INC
505 Park Ave Fl 15 (10022-9333)
PHONE 646 459-5000
Sara Garofalo, *Research*
Marianne Romans, *Sales Staff*
Achim Daub, *Branch Mgr*
Kevin Dailey, *Corp Counsel*
Asiye Hanoglu, *Manager*
EMP: 25
SALES (corp-wide): 3.5B **Privately Held**
WEB: www.symriseinc.com
SIC: 2869 Perfume materials, synthetic; flavors or flavoring materials, synthetic
HQ: Symrise Inc.
300 North St
Teterboro NJ 07608
201 288-3200

(G-11761)
SYNCED INC
120 Walker St Ste 4 (10013-4117)
PHONE 917 565-5591
Andrew Ferenci, *CEO*
Scott Paladini, *COO*
Michael Paladini, *Risk Mgmt Dir*
EMP: 5
SALES: 5MM **Privately Held**
SIC: 7372 Application computer software

(G-11762)
SYNCO TECHNOLOGIES INC
54 W 21st St Rm 602 (10010-7347)
P.O. Box 976 (10113-0976)
PHONE 212 255-2031
John Rau, *President*
Terry Cook, *Vice Pres*
EMP: 6
SQ FT: 1,250
SALES: 1MM **Privately Held**
WEB: www.syncotec.com
SIC: 7372 Prepackaged software

(G-11763)
SYNERGY PHARMACEUTICALS INC (HQ)
420 Lexington Ave Rm 2500 (10170-0020)
PHONE 212 227-8611
EMP: 6
SQ FT: 1,750
SALES (est): 992.3K **Publicly Held**
SIC: 2836 8731 Mfg Biological Products Commercial Physical Research

(G-11764)
SYNERGY PHARMACEUTICALS INC (PA)
420 Lexington Ave Rm 2012 (10170-2099)
PHONE 212 297-0020
Troy Hamilton, *CEO*
Gary S Jacob, *Ch of Bd*
Marino Garcia, *Exec VP*
Paul Eng, *Vice Pres*
Gem Hopkins, *Vice Pres*
EMP: 313
SALES: 16.8MM **Publicly Held**
SIC: 2834 Pharmaceutical preparations

(G-11765)
SYNTEL INC
1 Exchange Plz Ste 2001 (10006-3736)
PHONE 212 785-9810
Bhares Bissa, *President*
EMP: 14
SALES (corp-wide): 384.7K **Privately Held**
SIC: 7372 8748 Business oriented computer software; systems analysis & engineering consulting services

▲ = Import ▼=Export
◆ =Import/Export

HQ: Syntel, Inc.
525 E Big Beaver Rd # 300
Troy MI 48083
248 619-2800

(G-11766)
T & M PLATING INC
357 W 36th St Fl 7 (10018-6455)
PHONE 212 967-1110
Joseph AMI, *President*
EMP: 30
SQ FT: 24,000
SALES (est): 3.2MM **Privately Held**
SIC: 3471 Electroplating of metals or formed products; polishing, metals or formed products

(G-11767)
T & R KNITTING MILLS INC
Also Called: Direct Alliance
214 W 39th St (10018-4404)
PHONE 212 840-8665
Rocco Marini, *Branch Mgr*
EMP: 16
SALES (corp-wide): 20MM **Privately Held**
SIC: 2253 Knit outerwear mills
PA: T & R Knitting Mills Inc.
8000 Cooper Ave Ste 6
Glendale NY 11385
718 497-4017

(G-11768)
T L DIAMOND & COMPANY INC (PA)
Also Called: Eagle Zinc Co Div
116 E 68th St Apt 5a (10065-5995)
PHONE 212 249-6660
Theodore L Diamond, *President*
C W Diamond, *Corp Secy*
EMP: 9 **EST:** 1950
SQ FT: 5,000
SALES (est): 6.7MM **Privately Held**
SIC: 3356 Lead & zinc

(G-11769)
T M W DIAMONDS MFG CO (PA)
15 W 47th St Ste 302 (10036-3442)
PHONE 212 869-8444
Leibis Morgenstern, *President*
Jonah Morgenstern, *Vice Pres*
EMP: 9
SALES (est): 1.5MM **Privately Held**
SIC: 3915 5094 Diamond cutting & polishing; diamonds (gems)

(G-11770)
T O DEY SERVICE CORP
Also Called: To Dey
151 W 46th St Fl 3 (10036-8512)
PHONE 212 683-6300
Rose Bifulco, *President*
Thomas Bifulco, *Vice Pres*
Ciro Bifulco, *Treasurer*
EMP: 16
SQ FT: 6,700
SALES (est): 1.7MM **Privately Held**
SIC: 3144 3143 Orthopedic shoes, women's; men's footwear, except athletic

(G-11771)
T O GRONLUND COMPANY INC
200 Lexington Ave Rm 1515 (10016-6112)
PHONE 212 679-3535
Robert L Gronlund, *President*
Brooks Grounlund, *Corp Secy*
EMP: 18
SQ FT: 3,600
SALES (est): 2.1MM **Privately Held**
SIC: 2599 Cabinets, factory

(G-11772)
T V TRADE MEDIA INC
Also Called: TV Executive
216 E 75th St Apt 1w (10021-2921)
PHONE 212 288-3933
Dom Serafini, *President*
EMP: 12
SQ FT: 2,000
SALES (est): 890K **Privately Held**
SIC: 2721 Magazines: publishing & printing

(G-11773)
TABRISSE COLLECTIONS INC
Also Called: Oberon
1412 Broadway (10018-9228)
PHONE 212 921-1014
Mark Naim, *President*
Ebi Shaer, *Vice Pres*
Sam Naim, *Treasurer*
EMP: 10
SQ FT: 5,500
SALES (est): 644.5K **Privately Held**
SIC: 2335 Women's, juniors' & misses' dresses

(G-11774)
TACTICA INTERNATIONAL INC (PA)
11 W 42nd St (10036-8002)
PHONE 212 575-0500
Prem Ramchandani, *President*
Kurt Streams, *CFO*
AVI Sivan, *Director*
Paul Greenfield, *Admin Sec*
▲ **EMP:** 28
SQ FT: 11,500
SALES (est): 3MM **Privately Held**
SIC: 3634 3999 Electric housewares & fans; hair & hair-based products

(G-11775)
TAHARI ASL LLC
Also Called: Tahari Arthur S Levine
1114 Ave Of The Americas (10036-7703)
PHONE 212 763-2800
Lester Schreiber, *Manager*
EMP: 309
SALES (corp-wide): 85.1MM **Privately Held**
SIC: 2331 2335 2339 Blouses, women's & juniors': made from purchased material; women's, juniors' & misses' dresses; slacks: women's, misses' & juniors'
PA: Tahari A.S.L. Llc
16 Bleeker St
Millburn NJ 07041
888 734-7459

(G-11776)
TAILORED SPORTSMAN LLC
Also Called: Ogulnick Uniforms
230 W 38th St Fl 6 (10018-9058)
PHONE 646 366-8733
Peter Loferfo, *General Mgr*
Van Isaacs, *Info Tech Mgr*
▲ **EMP:** 12
SALES (est): 1.8MM **Privately Held**
WEB: www.thetailoredsportsman.com
SIC: 2339 Neckwear & ties: women's, misses' & juniors'; riding habits: women's, misses' & juniors'

(G-11777)
TALISMAN INDUSTRIES LLC
237 Flatbush Ave Apt 3 (10007)
PHONE 908 433-7116
Gregory Kremler,
EMP: 5
SALES (est): 179.9K **Privately Held**
SIC: 3999 Manufacturing industries

(G-11778)
TAMBETTI INC
48 W 48th St Ste 501 (10036-1713)
PHONE 212 751-9584
Dvora Horvitz, *President*
Joseph Segal, *Corp Secy*
EMP: 5
SQ FT: 1,612
SALES (est): 340K **Privately Held**
SIC: 3911 Jewelry, precious metal

(G-11779)
TAMSEN Z LLC
350 Park Ave Fl 4 (10022-6067)
PHONE 212 292-6412
Tamsen Ziff, *Mng Member*
Victoria Wallace, *Manager*
EMP: 5
SALES (est): 348.3K **Privately Held**
SIC: 3911 Jewelry, precious metal

(G-11780)
TANAGRO JEWELRY CORP
36 W 44th St Ste 1101 (10036-8104)
PHONE 212 753-2817
Pietro Dibenedetto, *President*
Antonio Dibenedetto, *Vice Pres*
EMP: 20
SQ FT: 2,200
SALES: 4.3MM **Privately Held**
WEB: www.tanagro.com
SIC: 3911 Jewelry, precious metal

(G-11781)
TAO GROUP LLC
355 W 16th St (10011-5902)
PHONE 646 625-4818
EMP: 6
SALES (est): 132.4K **Privately Held**
SIC: 2599 5963 Food wagons, restaurant; beverage services, direct sales

(G-11782)
TAP2PLAY LLC
110 W 40th St Rm 1902 (10018-3699)
PHONE 914 960-6232
Ilya Nikolayev, *CEO*
EMP: 5 **EST:** 2017
SALES (est): 128.9K **Privately Held**
SIC: 7372 Prepackaged software

(G-11783)
TAPESTRY INC
515 W 33rd St (10001-1302)
PHONE 212 615-2082
EMP: 9
SALES (corp-wide): 5.8B **Publicly Held**
SIC: 3171 Handbags, women's
PA: Tapestry, Inc.
10 Hudson Yards
New York NY 10001
212 594-1850

(G-11784)
TAPESTRY INC (PA)
10 Hudson Yards (10001-2157)
PHONE 212 594-1850
Victor Luis, *CEO*
Jide Zeitlin, *Ch of Bd*
Kevin Wills, *CFO*
Sarah Dunn, *Officer*
Todd Kahn,
◆ **EMP:** 277
SQ FT: 695,000
SALES: 5.8B **Publicly Held**
WEB: www.coach.com
SIC: 3172 2387 3143 3144 Personal leather goods; apparel belts; men's footwear, except athletic; women's footwear, except athletic; handbags, women's

(G-11785)
TARSIER LTD
1365 York Ave Apt 23e (10021-4036)
PHONE 646 880-8680
Isaac H Sutton, *Ch of Bd*
EMP: 106
SALES (est): 8.1MM **Privately Held**
SIC: 3645 3674 3648 Residential lighting fixtures; light emitting diodes; public lighting fixtures

(G-11786)
TAYLOR & FRANCIS GROUP LLC
52 Vanderbilt Ave Fl 11 (10017-3839)
PHONE 212 216-7800
Len Cornacchia, *Principal*
Hilary Lafoe, *Editor*
Denise Schanck, *Vice Pres*
Dave Miniaci, *Production*
Juliana Peluso, *Production*
EMP: 133 **Privately Held**
SIC: 2731 Book publishing
HQ: Taylor & Francis Group, Llc
6000 Broken Sound Pkwy Nw # 300
Boca Raton FL 33487
561 994-0555

(G-11787)
TBHL INTERNATIONAL LLC
Also Called: Globe-Tex Apparal
252 W 38th St Fl 11 (10018-5806)
PHONE 212 799-2007
Stuart Hurvitz, *Principal*
Jodi Gallagher, *Production*
Robert Hurvitz,
Joel Limenes,
EMP: 10 **EST:** 1995
SQ FT: 1,400

SALES (est): 1MM **Privately Held**
SIC: 2329 2339 Men's & boys' sportswear & athletic clothing; women's & misses' outerwear

(G-11788)
TC TRANSCONTINENTAL USA INC
Also Called: Transcontinental Ross-Ellis
67 Irving Pl Fl 2 (10003-2202)
PHONE 818 993-4767
Nina Sheldon, *Director*
EMP: 6
SALES (corp-wide): 1.6B **Privately Held**
SIC: 2759 Commercial printing
HQ: Tc Transcontinental U.S.A. Inc.
8550 Balboa Blvd Ste 240
Northridge CA 91325
818 993-4767

(G-11789)
TDG OPERATIONS LLC
200 Lexington Ave Rm 1314 (10016-6201)
PHONE 212 779-4300
Mark Nestler, *Owner*
EMP: 9
SALES (corp-wide): 412.4MM **Publicly Held**
SIC: 2273 Carpets & rugs
HQ: Tdg Operations, Llc
716 Bill Myles Dr
Saraland AL 36571
251 675-9080

(G-11790)
TE NEUES PUBLISHING COMPANY (PA)
350 7th Ave Rm 301 (10001-1957)
PHONE 212 627-9090
Hendrik Te Neues, *Partner*
Sebastian Te Neues, *Partner*
Harold Thiec, *Managing Dir*
Allison Stern, *Vice Pres*
Audrey Barr, *Sales Staff*
▲ **EMP:** 11
SQ FT: 5,000
SALES (est): 1.3MM **Privately Held**
WEB: www.teneues-usa.com
SIC: 2741 5192 Miscellaneous publishing; books

(G-11791)
TEACHERGAMING LLC
809 W 181st St 231 (10033-4516)
PHONE 866 644-9323
Joel Levin, *Principal*
Santeri Koivisto, *Principal*
Carl Syren, *Principal*
Jannika Aalto, *COO*
EMP: 12 **EST:** 2012
SQ FT: 200
SALES (est): 309.8K **Privately Held**
SIC: 7372 Educational computer software

(G-11792)
TEACHLEY LLC
25 Broadway Fl 13 (10004-1081)
PHONE 347 552-1272
Rachael Labrecque, *Partner*
Kara Carpenter, *Partner*
Dana Pagar, *Partner*
EMP: 6
SALES (est): 480.2K **Privately Held**
SIC: 7372 Educational computer software

(G-11793)
TECHGRASS
77 Water St (10005-4401)
PHONE 646 719-2000
Susan Aexander, *Mng Member*
EMP: 10
SALES (est): 580.6K **Privately Held**
SIC: 3999 Grasses, artificial & preserved

(G-11794)
TECHNOLOGY DESKING INC
39 Broadway Rm 1640 (10006-3057)
PHONE 212 257-6998
Lee Markwick, *President*
▲ **EMP:** 26
SQ FT: 6,100
SALES: 4.1MM **Privately Held**
SIC: 2521 Wood office furniture

New York - New York County (G-11795) GEOGRAPHIC SECTION

(G-11795)
TECTONIC FLOORING USA LLC
1140 1st Ave Frnt 1 (10065-7961)
PHONE..................212 686-2700
Mondo Pallon,
Rupert Dowd,
▲ EMP: 4
SQ FT: 2,100
SALES: 7MM **Privately Held**
SIC: 2426 Flooring, hardwood

(G-11796)
TELEPHONE SALES & SERVICE CO (PA)
132 W Broadway (10013-3396)
PHONE..................212 233-8505
William Bradley, *President*
Neil Bradley, *Vice Pres*
James Woods, *Engineer*
EMP: 23
SQ FT: 4,000
SALES (est): 3MM **Privately Held**
SIC: 3612 1731 Transmission & distribution voltage regulators; sound equipment specialization

(G-11797)
TELESCA-HEYMAN INC
304 E 94th St 6 (10128-5688)
PHONE..................212 534-3442
Mario Dire, *President*
Remo Dire, *Vice Pres*
EMP: 15 EST: 1958
SQ FT: 14,500
SALES (est): 805.2K **Privately Held**
SIC: 2541 7641 Cabinets, except refrigerated: show, display, etc.: wood; furniture refinishing; antique furniture repair & restoration

(G-11798)
TELMAR INFORMATION SERVICES (PA)
711 3rd Ave Rm 1500 (10017-9201)
PHONE..................212 725-3000
Stanley Federman, *Ch of Bd*
Corey V Panno, *President*
Corey Panno, *President*
Susan Lanzetta, *Exec VP*
EMP: 30 EST: 1968
SQ FT: 4,400
SALES (est): 19.1MM **Privately Held**
WEB: www.telmar.com
SIC: 7372 Business oriented computer software

(G-11799)
TEMPLE ST CLAIR LLC
594 Broadway Rm 306 (10012-3234)
PHONE..................212 219-8664
Paul Engler, *COO*
Rekha-Leigh Punch, *Vice Pres*
Kimberly Rainone, *Vice Pres*
Deborah Spirio, *Vice Pres*
Phyllis Mahabir, *Prdtn Mgr*
▲ EMP: 27
SALES: 13MM **Privately Held**
SIC: 3911 Jewelry, precious metal

(G-11800)
TENBY LLC
344 W 38th St Fl 3 (10018-8414)
PHONE..................646 863-5890
EMP: 101 EST: 2016
SALES (est): 2.3MM
SALES (corp-wide): 189.6MM **Privately Held**
SIC: 2337 Skirts, separate: women's, misses' & juniors'
PA: The Kittrich Corporation
1585 W Mission Blvd
Pomona CA 91766
714 736-1000

(G-11801)
TERRA ENRGY RESOURCE TECH INC (PA)
99 Park Ave Ph A (10016-1340)
PHONE..................212 286-9197
Dmitry Vilbaum, *CEO*
Alexandre Agaian PHD, *Ch of Bd*
EMP: 10

SALES (est): 3.3MM **Publicly Held**
WEB: www.terrainsight.com
SIC: 1389 Testing, measuring, surveying & analysis services

(G-11802)
TERRANUA US CORP
535 5th Ave Fl 4 (10017-8020)
PHONE..................212 852-9028
Brian Fahey, *CEO*
EMP: 16
SALES (est): 2.1MM **Privately Held**
SIC: 7372 Prepackaged software
PA: Terranua Limited
Unit 2c
Dublin

(G-11803)
TESLA MOTORS INC
10 Columbus Cir Ste 102d (10019-1215)
PHONE..................212 206-1204
EMP: 663
SALES (corp-wide): 4B **Publicly Held**
SIC: 3711 3714 Mfg Motor Vehicle/Car Bodies & Components
PA: Tesla Motors, Inc.
3500 Deer Creek Rd
Palo Alto CA 94304
650 681-500

(G-11804)
TEVA PHARMACEUTICALS USA INC
145 W 57th St (10019-2220)
PHONE..................212 259-2030
Scott Allan, *Manager*
Kim Mylan, *Executive Asst*
EMP: 8
SALES (corp-wide): 22.3B **Privately Held**
SIC: 2834 Pharmaceutical preparations
HQ: Teva Pharmaceuticals Usa, Inc.
1090 Horsham Rd
North Wales PA 19454
215 591-3000

(G-11805)
TEXPORT FABRICS CORP
Also Called: Rose-Ann Division
495 Broadway Fl 7 (10012-4457)
PHONE..................212 226-6066
Sonia Essebag, *President*
▲ EMP: 10
SQ FT: 48,000
SALES (est): 1.1MM **Privately Held**
SIC: 2335 Women's, juniors' & misses' dresses

(G-11806)
TG THERAPEUTICS INC
2 Gansevoort St Fl 9 (10014-1667)
PHONE..................212 554-4484
Michael S Weiss, *Ch of Bd*
Robert Niecestro, *Exec VP*
Sean A Power, *CFO*
Christian Mayorga, *Controller*
Adam Waldman, *Ch Credit Ofcr*
EMP: 64
SALES (est): 152.3K **Privately Held**
WEB: www.manhattanpharma.com
SIC: 2834 Pharmaceutical preparations

(G-11807)
TGP FLYING CLOUD HOLDINGS LLC
565 5th Ave Fl 27 (10017-2478)
PHONE..................646 829-3900
James Pagano, *Principal*
Ashlynn Smith, *Principal*
EMP: 25
SALES: 500K **Privately Held**
SIC: 3511 Turbines & turbine generator sets

(G-11808)
THE DESIGN GROUP INC
Also Called: J.hoaglund
240 Madison Ave Fl 8 (10016-2878)
PHONE..................212 681-1548
Robert Rosen, *President*
Daniel Cohen, *Chairman*
▲ EMP: 10
SALES: 3MM **Privately Held**
SIC: 2339 Women's & misses' outerwear

(G-11809)
THEHUFFINGTONPOSTCOM INC (DH)
Also Called: Huffington Post, The
770 Broadway Fl 4 (10003-9558)
PHONE..................212 245-7844
Eric Hippeau, *CEO*
Sara Boboltz, *Editor*
Caroline Bologna, *Editor*
Angelina Chapin, *Editor*
Ron Dicker, *Editor*
EMP: 33
SALES (est): 4.9MM
SALES (corp-wide): 126B **Publicly Held**
SIC: 2741

(G-11810)
THEIRAPP LLC
Also Called: Apprise Mobile
950 3rd Ave Ste 190 (10022-2705)
PHONE..................212 896-1255
Ben Gholian, *Partner*
Doug Pierce, *COO*
Jeffrey Corbin, *Mng Member*
EMP: 35
SALES (est): 2.1MM
SALES (corp-wide): 5.5MM **Privately Held**
SIC: 7372 Application computer software
PA: Kanan, Corbin, Schupak & Aronow, Inc.
420 5th Ave Rm 300
New York NY 10018
212 682-6300

(G-11811)
THEORY LLC
1114 Avenue Of The Americ (10036-7703)
PHONE..................212 762-2300
Andrew Rosen, *Manager*
EMP: 100
SALES (corp-wide): 19.1B **Privately Held**
SIC: 2337 Suits: women's, misses' & juniors'
HQ: Theory Llc
38 Gansevoort St
New York NY 10014
212 300-0800

(G-11812)
THEORY LLC
1157 Madison Ave (10028-0409)
PHONE..................212 879-0265
Sylke Cunha, *Branch Mgr*
EMP: 7
SALES (corp-wide): 19.1B **Privately Held**
SIC: 2337 Suits: women's, misses' & juniors'
HQ: Theory Llc
38 Gansevoort St
New York NY 10014
212 300-0800

(G-11813)
THESKIMM INC
50 W 23rd St Ste 501 (10010-5278)
PHONE..................646 213-4754
Carly Zakin, *CEO*
EMP: 15
SQ FT: 1,500
SALES (est): 1.4MM **Privately Held**
SIC: 2741

(G-11814)
THESTREET INC (PA)
14 Wall St Fl 15 (10005-2139)
PHONE..................212 321-5000
Lawrence S Kramer, *Ch of Bd*
David Callaway, *President*
Jeffrey Davis, *President*
Margaret De Luna, *President*
Rachelle Zorn, *President*
EMP: 72
SALES: 62.4MM **Publicly Held**
WEB: www.thestreet.com
SIC: 2711 2721 Newspapers: publishing only, not printed on site; periodicals: publishing only

(G-11815)
THING DAEMON INC
Also Called: Fancy
57 Bond St (10012-2483)
PHONE..................917 746-9895
Joseph Einhorn, *CEO*
Jack Einhorn, *President*
Gilah Elul, *Partner*

Michael Silverman, *COO*
Kevin Siewert, *Vice Pres*
EMP: 25 EST: 2010
SALES (est): 4MM **Privately Held**
SIC: 7372 Application computer software

(G-11816)
THINKTREK INC
Also Called: Complystream
420 Lexington Ave Rm 300 (10170-0399)
PHONE..................212 884-8399
Jyoti Prasanna, *Principal*
Tridib Majumder, *Director*
Prasanna Kumar, *Director*
EMP: 10
SQ FT: 1,000
SALES (est): 385.8K **Privately Held**
SIC: 7372 Business oriented computer software

(G-11817)
THOMAS GROUP INC
Also Called: Thomas Group, The
131 Varick St Rm 1016 (10013-1417)
PHONE..................212 947-6400
Jamie H Tomashoff, *President*
EMP: 10
SQ FT: 18,000
SALES (est): 2.2MM **Privately Held**
WEB: www.thethomasgroup.com
SIC: 2752 2791 2789 Commercial printing, offset; typesetting; bookbinding & related work

(G-11818)
THOMAS PUBLISHING COMPANY LLC (PA)
Also Called: Thomas Enterprise Solutions
5 Penn Plz Fl 9 (10001-1860)
PHONE..................212 695-0500
Jos E Andrade, *Ch of Bd*
Tony Uphoff, *President*
Sandra Hanzlik, *Partner*
Heather Holst-Knudsen, *Publisher*
Grace James, *Project Mgr*
EMP: 300 EST: 1898
SQ FT: 100,000
SALES (est): 167MM **Privately Held**
WEB: www.inboundlogistics.com
SIC: 2741 2721 7331 Directories: publishing only, not printed on site; catalogs: publishing only, not printed on site; trade journals: publishing only, not printed on site; data processing service; direct mail advertising services

(G-11819)
THOMAS PUBLISHING COMPANY LLC
5 Penn Plz Fl 9 (10001-1860)
PHONE..................212 695-0500
EMP: 70
SALES (corp-wide): 167MM **Privately Held**
WEB: www.inboundlogistics.com
SIC: 2741 Misc Publishing
PA: Thomas Publishing Company Llc
5 Penn Plz Fl 9
New York NY 10001
212 695-0500

(G-11820)
THOMAS PUBLISHING COMPANY LLC
Also Called: Magazine Group
5 Penn Plz Fl 8 (10001-1851)
PHONE..................212 695-0500
Ralph Richardson, *Manager*
EMP: 9
SALES (corp-wide): 167MM **Privately Held**
WEB: www.inboundlogistics.com
SIC: 2721 Magazines: publishing only, not printed on site
PA: Thomas Publishing Company Llc
5 Penn Plz Fl 9
New York NY 10001
212 695-0500

(G-11821)
THOMAS PUBLISHING COMPANY LLC
Managing Automation Magazine
5 Penn Plz Fl 9 (10001-1860)
PHONE..................212 695-0500

Margret Bresto, *Manager*
EMP: 9
SALES (corp-wide): 167MM **Privately Held**
WEB: www.inboundlogistics.com
SIC: 2721 Magazines: publishing & printing
PA: Thomas Publishing Company Llc
5 Penn Plz Fl 9
New York NY 10001
212 695-0500

(G-11822)
THOMAS SASSON CO INC
555 5th Ave Rm 1900 (10017-9250)
PHONE.................212 697-4998
Jeffery Thomas, *President*
Lois Dianne Sasson, *Vice Pres*
EMP: 2
SQ FT: 1,000
SALES: 1MM **Privately Held**
SIC: 3911 Jewelry apparel

(G-11823)
THOMPSON FERRIER LLC
230 5th Ave Ste 1004 (10001-7834)
PHONE.................212 244-2212
Raffi Arslanian,
Pauline Dana,
▲ EMP: 9 EST: 2011
SQ FT: 2,000
SALES (est): 1.2MM **Privately Held**
SIC: 3999 2844 Candles; concentrates, perfume

(G-11824)
THOMSON REUTERS CORPORATION
500 Pearl St (10007-1316)
PHONE.................212 393-9461
Gail Appleson, *Principal*
EMP: 15 **Publicly Held**
SIC: 2741 Miscellaneous publishing
HQ: Thomson Reuters Corporation
3 Times Sq
New York NY 10036
646 223-4000

(G-11825)
THOMSON REUTERS CORPORATION (DH)
3 Times Sq (10036-6564)
PHONE.................646 223-4000
David Thomson, *Ch of Bd*
James C Smith, *President*
David W Craig, *President*
Gonzalo Lissarrague, *President*
Susan Taylor Martin, *President*
▲ EMP: 4219
SQ FT: 555,500
SALES: 11.3B **Publicly Held**
WEB: www.thomsonreuters.com
SIC: 2741 8111 7372 7383 Miscellaneous publishing; legal services; prepackaged software; news syndicates
HQ: Woodbridge Company Limited, The
65 Queen St W Suite 2400
Toronto ON M5H 2
416 364-8700

(G-11826)
THORNWILLOW PRESS LTD
57 W 58th St Ste 11e (10019-1630)
P.O. Box 1202 (10028-0048)
PHONE.................212 980-0738
Luke Pontifell, *President*
EMP: 5
SALES: 1MM **Privately Held**
WEB: www.thornwillow.com
SIC: 2731 5942 Book publishing; book stores

(G-11827)
THREAD LLC (PA)
26 W 17th St Rm 301 (10011-5730)
PHONE.................212 414-8844
Beth Blake,
Melissa Akey,
▲ EMP: 5 EST: 1999
SALES (est): 482.1K **Privately Held**
WEB: www.threaddesign.com
SIC: 2335 Bridal & formal gowns

(G-11828)
THREE FIVE III-V MATERIALS INC
19 W 21st St Rm 203 (10010-6866)
PHONE.................212 213-8290
Thomas Guan, *President*
EMP: 10
SALES (est): 919.2K **Privately Held**
SIC: 3679 Electronic loads & power supplies

(G-11829)
THYSSENKRUPP MATERIALS NA INC
Thyssnkrupp MtlIrgcal Pdts USA
489 5th Ave Fl 20 (10017-6125)
PHONE.................212 972-8800
Herr Thorsten Sorje, *Branch Mgr*
EMP: 11
SALES (corp-wide): 48.7B **Privately Held**
SIC: 3499 3313 Fire- or burglary-resistive products; ferroalloys
HQ: Thyssenkrupp Materials Na, Inc.
22355 W 11 Mile Rd
Southfield MI 48033
248 233-5600

(G-11830)
TIBCO SOFTWARE INC
120 W 45th St Fl 18 (10036-4041)
PHONE.................646 495-2600
M Williams, *Branch Mgr*
Geordie TSE, *Manager*
Pankaj Sharma, *Consultant*
EMP: 9
SALES (corp-wide): 4.4B **Privately Held**
SIC: 7372 Prepackaged software
HQ: Tibco Software Inc.
3307 Hillview Ave
Palo Alto CA 94304

(G-11831)
TIE KING INC
Jimmy's Sales
42 W 38th St Rm 1200 (10018-6212)
PHONE.................212 714-9611
Jimmy Azizo, *President*
EMP: 5
SALES (corp-wide): 5.6MM **Privately Held**
WEB: www.thetieking.com
SIC: 2323 Ties, handsewn: made from purchased materials
PA: The Tie King Inc
243 44th St
Brooklyn NY 11232
718 768-8484

(G-11832)
TIGER 21 LLC
1995 Broadway Fl 6 (10023-5882)
PHONE.................212 360-1700
Michael Sonnenfeldt, *Principal*
EMP: 7
SALES (est): 1.7MM **Privately Held**
SIC: 2273 Carpets & rugs

(G-11833)
TIGER J LLC
1430 Broadway Rm 1900 (10018-3308)
PHONE.................212 465-9300
Jeffrey Steinberg, *Ch of Bd*
Mark Locks, *President*
Jeff Wark, *Vice Pres*
Arnold Brodsky, *CFO*
Andrew Steinberg, *Info Tech Dir*
▲ EMP: 49
SQ FT: 15,600
SALES (est): 35.5MM **Privately Held**
WEB: www.terrytiger.com
SIC: 2337 2339 Jackets & vests, except fur & leather: women's & misses' suits & skirts; skirts, separate: women's, misses' & juniors'; sportswear, women's

(G-11834)
TIKA MOBILE INC (PA)
Also Called: Tikamobile
902 Broadway Fl 6 (10010-6039)
PHONE.................646 650-5545
Anthony Bowden, *Principal*
Manish Sharma, *Principal*
Cliona Barry, *Analyst*
EMP: 7

SQ FT: 500
SALES (est): 1.5MM **Privately Held**
SIC: 7372 Business oriented computer software

(G-11835)
TILLSONBURG COMPANY USA INC
37 W 39th St Rm 1101 (10018-3894)
PHONE.................267 994-8096
Tony Cooper, *CEO*
Ramaswamy Arakoni, *Ch of Bd*
Sandy Jabaly, *Director*
Alex Lam, *Director*
Jai Waney, *Director*
▲ EMP: 50
SQ FT: 3,000
SALES (est): 5MM **Privately Held**
SIC: 2339 2329 Women's & misses' athletic clothing & sportswear: men's & boys' sportswear & athletic clothing
PA: Tillsonburg Company Limited
18/F Corporation Sq
Kowloon Bay KLN
233 138-84

(G-11836)
TIME HOME ENTERTAINMENT INC
1271 Ave Of The Americas (10020-1300)
PHONE.................212 522-1212
Jim Childs, *Publisher*
EMP: 32
SALES (est): 2.4MM
SALES (corp-wide): 1.7B **Publicly Held**
SIC: 2731 Book publishing
HQ: Time Inc.
225 Liberty St Ste C2
New York NY 10281
212 522-1212

(G-11837)
TIME INC
Sports Illustrated Magazine
1271 Avenue Of The Americ (10020-1300)
PHONE.................212 522-1212
William Gasperoni, *Publisher*
Greg McCastle, *Managing Dir*
Bradford Wallick, *Principal*
Katherine Cobbs, *Editor*
Jennifer M Richards, *Editor*
EMP: 34
SALES (corp-wide): 2.2B **Publicly Held**
SIC: 2721 2731 Magazines: publishing & printing; book publishing
HQ: Time Inc.
225 Liberty St Ste C2
New York NY 10281
212 522-1212

(G-11838)
TIME INC (HQ)
Also Called: Four M Studios
225 Liberty St Ste C2 (10281-1088)
P.O. Box 231035 (10023-0018)
PHONE.................212 522-1212
Joseph Ceryanec, *President*
Armando Correa, *Editor*
Jamie Ldn, *Editor*
Elizabeth Murray, *Editor*
Brittany Robins, *Editor*
◆ EMP: 2800
SQ FT: 696,000
SALES: 3B
SALES (corp-wide): 2.2B **Publicly Held**
WEB: www.timeinc.com
SIC: 2721 Magazines: publishing only, not printed on site
PA: Meredith Corporation
1716 Locust St
Des Moines IA 50309
515 284-3000

(G-11839)
TIME INC
Time/Fortune Money Group
1271 Ave Of The Amer Sb7 (10020-1302)
PHONE.................212 522-0361
Ann Moore, *CEO*
EMP: 28
SALES (corp-wide): 2.2B **Publicly Held**
SIC: 2721 Magazines: publishing only, not printed on site

HQ: Time Inc.
225 Liberty St Ste C2
New York NY 10281
212 522-1212

(G-11840)
TIME INC AFFLUENT MEDIA GROUP (DH)
Also Called: American Express Publishing
1120 Ave Of The Americas (10036-6700)
PHONE.................212 382-5600
Edward F Kelly Jr, *President*
Dana Cowin, *Senior VP*
Michael Crotty, *Senior VP*
Nikki Upshaw, *Senior VP*
Darla Vaugh, *Vice Pres*
▲ EMP: 300 EST: 1938
SALES (est): 34.4MM
SALES (corp-wide): 2.2B **Publicly Held**
WEB: www.fwmediakit.com
SIC: 2721 Magazines: publishing only, not printed on site
HQ: Time Inc.
225 Liberty St Ste C2
New York NY 10281
212 522-1212

(G-11841)
TIME INC AFFLUENT MEDIA GROUP (DH)
Also Called: Travel Leisure Magazine
1120 Ave Of The Americas (10036-6700)
PHONE.................212 382-5600
Ted Kelly, *President*
EMP: 5
SALES (est): 461.2K
SALES (corp-wide): 2.2B **Publicly Held**
SIC: 2721 7389 Magazines: publishing only, not printed on site; subscription fulfillment services: magazine, newspaper, etc.
HQ: Southern Progress Corporation
2100 Lakeshore Dr
Birmingham AL 35209
205 445-6000

(G-11842)
TIME OUT AMERICA LLC
1540 Broadway Fl 42 (10036-4039)
PHONE.................646 432-3000
Jason Catlett, *Editor*
Andrew Zimmer, *Editor*
Mark Davies, *Sales Dir*
Kristine Peterson, *Mng Member*
Adam Jones, *Manager*
EMP: 200 EST: 2011
SALES (est): 5.4MM
SALES (corp-wide): 58.6MM **Privately Held**
SIC: 2721 Magazines: publishing & printing
PA: Time Out Group Plc
77 Wicklow Street
London WC1X
207 813-3000

(G-11843)
TIME OUT NEW YORK PARTNERS LP
475 10th Ave Fl 12 (10018-1175)
PHONE.................646 432-3000
Alison Tocci, *President*
Tony Elliott, *Partner*
Marisa Fari A, *Publisher*
Michael Freidson, *Principal*
Justin Etheridge, *Exec VP*
▲ EMP: 91
SALES (est): 17.8MM
SALES (corp-wide): 58.6MM **Privately Held**
SIC: 2721 Periodicals
HQ: Time Out Digital Limited
4th Floor
London W1T 7
207 813-3000

(G-11844)
TIME TO KNOW INC
655 3rd Ave Fl 21 (10017-5621)
PHONE.................212 230-1210
Yonit Tzadok, *CFO*
Jamie Iesner, *Director*
Lawrence Malkin, *Director*
EMP: 10
SALES (est): 875K **Privately Held**
SIC: 7372 Educational computer software

New York - New York County (G-11845)

(G-11845)
TIME WARNER COMPANIES INC (DH)
1 Time Warner Ctr Bsmt B (10019-6010)
PHONE..................................212 484-8000
Jeff Bewkes, *Ch of Bd*
Howard M Averill, *Exec VP*
Paul T Cappuccio, *Exec VP*
Gary L Ginsberg, *Exec VP*
Karen Magee, *Exec VP*
EMP: 87
SQ FT: 451,000
SALES (est): 62.1MM
SALES (corp-wide): 160.5B **Publicly Held**
SIC: 3652 6794 2741 7812 Compact laser discs, prerecorded; magnetic tape (audio): prerecorded; music licensing to radio stations; performance rights, publishing & licensing; music royalties, sheet & record; music, sheet: publishing only, not printed on site; music books: publishing only, not printed on site; motion picture production & distribution; television film production; motion picture production & distribution, television; video tape production; cable television services; magazines: publishing only, not printed on site

(G-11846)
TIMELESS FASHIONS LLC
100 United Nations Plz (10017-1753)
PHONE..................................212 730-9328
Navin Mahtani, *Mng Member*
Ravi Datwani,
▲ **EMP:** 7
SQ FT: 2,900
SALES: 10MM **Privately Held**
SIC: 2389 Apparel for handicapped

(G-11847)
TIMES SQUARE STUDIOS LTD
Also Called: ABC Television Network
1500 Broadway Fl 2 (10036-4055)
PHONE..................................212 930-7720
Ruth Anne Alsop, *Senior VP*
Jeff Hartnett, *Manager*
EMP: 200 **EST:** 1999
SALES (est): 30.9MM **Publicly Held**
WEB: www.go.com
SIC: 3663 Studio equipment, radio & television broadcasting
PA: The Walt Disney Company
500 S Buena Vista St
Burbank CA 91521

(G-11848)
TIMING GROUP LLC
237 W 37th St Ste 1100 (10018-6770)
P.O. Box 275, Tallman (10982-0275)
PHONE..................................646 878-2600
AVI Schwebel, *Mng Member*
Alan Friedman,
▲ **EMP:** 15
SALES (est): 1.7MM **Privately Held**
SIC: 3021 Rubber & plastics footwear

(G-11849)
TIO FOODS LLC
Also Called: Tio Gazpacho
120 E 23rd St Fl 5 (10010-4519)
PHONE..................................917 946-1160
Theo Kalogerakis, *Opers Mgr*
Austin V Allan, *Mng Member*
EMP: 10 **EST:** 2013
SQ FT: 150
SALES (est): 500K **Privately Held**
SIC: 3411 Food & beverage containers

(G-11850)
TITAN CONTROLS INC
122 W 27th St Fl 5 (10001-6227)
PHONE..................................516 358-2407
Paul Deronde, *President*
Gary Sefcheck, *Vice Pres*
EMP: 11
SQ FT: 2,000
SALES (est): 820K **Privately Held**
WEB: www.titancontrols.com
SIC: 3829 Temperature sensors, except industrial process & aircraft

(G-11851)
TIZIANA THERAPEUTICS INC
420 Lexington Ave # 2525 (10170-0002)
PHONE..................................646 396-4970
Kunwar Shailubhai, *Principal*
EMP: 8
SALES (est): 281.7K **Privately Held**
SIC: 2835 Microbiology & virology diagnostic products
PA: Tiziana Life Sciences Plc
3rd Floor, 11-12 St. James's Square
London
207 495-2379

(G-11852)
TLC-LC INC (PA)
115 E 57th St Bsmt (10022-2090)
PHONE..................................212 756-8900
Loida Nicolas Lewis, *Ch of Bd*
Reynaldo P Glover, *President*
▲ **EMP:** 27
SQ FT: 2,500
SALES (est): 62.1MM **Privately Held**
SIC: 2024 2096 5149 5411 Ice cream & ice milk; dairy based frozen desserts; potato chips & similar snacks; potato chips & other potato-based snacks; beverages, except coffee & tea; grocery stores

(G-11853)
TM MUSIC INC
Also Called: Casablanca Records
9 E 63rd St Apt 2-3 (10065-7236)
PHONE..................................212 471-4000
Thomas Mottola, *President*
EMP: 10
SQ FT: 12,000
SALES: 5MM **Privately Held**
SIC: 2782 Record albums

(G-11854)
TMS STRUCTURES INC
1745 Broadway Fl 17 (10019-4642)
PHONE..................................646 740-7646
Gilbert Roy, *CEO*
EMP: 150
SALES (est): 4.6MM **Privately Held**
SIC: 3441 Fabricated structural metal

(G-11855)
TOHO COMPANY LIMITED
1501 Broadway Ste 2005 (10036-5600)
PHONE..................................212 391-9058
Darryl Pitt, *Manager*
EMP: 6
SALES (corp-wide): 1.8B **Privately Held**
SIC: 3999 Stringing beads
PA: Toho Co.,Ltd.
5-9, Koyochonishi, Higashinada-Ku
Kobe HYO 658-0
788 452-400

(G-11856)
TOHO SHOJI (NEW YORK) INC
990 Avenue Of The America (10018-5419)
PHONE..................................212 868-7466
T Mishide, *President*
▲ **EMP:** 15
SALES (est): 1.1MM
SALES (corp-wide): 22.3MM **Privately Held**
SIC: 3961 Costume jewelry
PA: Toho Shoji Co., Ltd.
5-29-8, Asakusabashi
Taito-Ku TKY 111-0
338 613-274

(G-11857)
TOLTEC FABRICS INC
437 5th Ave Fl 10 (10016-2205)
PHONE..................................212 706-9310
Barbara Nymark, *President*
EMP: 155
SQ FT: 6,000
SALES (est): 8.2MM **Privately Held**
WEB: www.interfacefabricsgroup.com
SIC: 2221 2262 Broadwoven fabric mills, manmade; decorative finishing of man-made broadwoven fabrics
HQ: Duvaltex (Us), Inc.
9 Oak St
Guilford ME 04443
207 873-3331

(G-11858)
TOM & LINDA PLATT INC
55 W 39th St Rm 1701 (10018-0540)
PHONE..................................212 221-7208
Linda Platt, *President*
Tom Platt, *Treasurer*
Andrew Scott, *Sales Staff*
EMP: 13
SALES (est): 1.3MM **Privately Held**
WEB: www.tomandlindaplatt.com
SIC: 2335 Women's, juniors' & misses' dresses

(G-11859)
TOM DOHERTY ASSOCIATES INC
Also Called: Tor Books
175 5th Ave Frnt 1 (10010-7704)
PHONE..................................212 388-0100
Tom Doherty, *President*
Roy Gainsburg, *Exec VP*
Philip Schwartz, *Exec VP*
EMP: 44
SQ FT: 7,000
SALES (est): 9.3MM
SALES (corp-wide): 1.7B **Privately Held**
WEB: www.stmartins.com
SIC: 2731 Books: publishing only
HQ: Macmillan Holdings, Llc
175 5th Ave
New York NY 10010

(G-11860)
TOM JAMES COMPANY
717 5th Ave (10022-8101)
PHONE..................................212 593-0204
George Mattos, *Branch Mgr*
EMP: 10
SALES (corp-wide): 618.7MM **Privately Held**
WEB: www.englishamericanco.com
SIC: 2311 Suits, men's & boys': made from purchased materials
PA: Tom James Company
263 Seaboard Ln
Franklin TN 37067
615 771-1122

(G-11861)
TOMAS MAIER
956 Madison Ave Frnt 1 (10021-2635)
PHONE..................................212 988-8686
Tomas Maier, *Owner*
EMP: 7
SALES (est): 511K **Privately Held**
SIC: 2253 Bathing suits & swimwear, knit; jerseys, knit
HQ: B.V. Servizi Srl
Localita' Conti Maltraverso 1
Montebello Vicentino VI 36054

(G-11862)
TOMIA BEAUTY BRANDS LLC
Also Called: Tomia Beauty Supply
38 W 21st St (10010-6906)
PHONE..................................917 301-0125
Jack Bensason,
▲ **EMP:** 5 **EST:** 2014
SALES (est): 131.8K **Privately Held**
SIC: 2844 Toilet preparations

(G-11863)
TOMMY BOY ENTERTAINMENT LLC
220 E 23rd St Ste 400 (10010-4669)
PHONE..................................212 388-8300
Thomas Silverman,
EMP: 12
SQ FT: 5,500
SALES (est): 1.3MM **Privately Held**
WEB: www.tommyboy.com
SIC: 2782 Record albums

(G-11864)
TOMMY JOHN INC
100 Broadway Ste 1101 (10005-4504)
PHONE..................................800 708-3490
Thomas J Patterson, *President*
John Wu, *COO*
Ronnie Boadi, *Vice Pres*
Al Valdes, *Vice Pres*
Margaret Breitton, *Opers Staff*
▲ **EMP:** 50
SQ FT: 17,500
SALES (est): 22.6MM **Privately Held**
SIC: 2322 Men's & boys' underwear & nightwear

(G-11865)
TONIX PHARMACEUTICALS INC (HQ)
509 Madison Ave Rm 306 (10022-5583)
PHONE..................................212 980-9155
Seth Lederman, *President*
EMP: 6
SALES (est): 691.1K **Publicly Held**
SIC: 2834 Pharmaceutical preparations

(G-11866)
TONIX PHRMCEUTICALS HOLDG CORP (PA)
509 Madison Ave Rm 306 (10022-5583)
PHONE..................................212 980-9155
Seth Lederman, *Ch of Bd*
Jessica Morris, *COO*
Bradley Saenger, *CFO*
Gregory Sullivan, *Chief Mktg Ofcr*
John Rhodes, *Director*
EMP: 12
SQ FT: 4,800
SALES (est): 2MM **Publicly Held**
SIC: 2834 Pharmaceutical preparations

(G-11867)
TOPPAN VINTAGE INC (DH)
747 3rd Ave Fl 7 (10017-2821)
PHONE..................................212 596-7747
Jeff Riback, *President*
Glen Buchbaum, *Senior VP*
Edward Vaccaro, *Vice Pres*
EMP: 80
SALES (est): 23.5MM
SALES (corp-wide): 13.6B **Privately Held**
SIC: 2759 8732 Commercial printing; merger, acquisition & reorganization research
HQ: Toppan Leefung Pte. Ltd.
1 Kim Seng Promenade
Singapore 23799
682 696-00

(G-11868)
TORAY HOLDING (USA) INC (HQ)
461 5th Ave Fl 9 (10017-7730)
PHONE..................................212 697-8150
Akihiro Nikkaku, *President*
Yasuke Orito, *Principal*
◆ **EMP:** 50
SALES (est): 558.7MM
SALES (corp-wide): 20.6B **Privately Held**
SIC: 2821 Plastics materials & resins
PA: Toray Industries,Inc.
2-1-1, Nihombashimuromachi
Chuo-Ku TKY 103-0
332 455-111

(G-11869)
TORAY INDUSTRIES INC
600 3rd Ave Fl 5 (10016-1919)
PHONE..................................212 697-8150
Yvette Kosar, *Branch Mgr*
EMP: 8
SALES (corp-wide): 20.6B **Privately Held**
WEB: www.toray.co.jp
SIC: 2221 2821 3089 3081 Broadwoven fabric mills, manmade; plastics materials & resins; plastic processing; unsupported plastics film & sheet
PA: Toray Industries,Inc.
2-1-1, Nihombashimuromachi
Chuo-Ku TKY 103-0
332 455-111

(G-11870)
TORRE PRODUCTS CO INC
479 Washington St (10013-1381)
PHONE..................................212 925-8989
Liberty F Raho, *President*
Peter N Raho, *Treasurer*
Philip Raho, *Admin Sec*
EMP: 9 **EST:** 1917
SALES (est): 1MM **Privately Held**
SIC: 2899 2087 Essential oils; flavoring extracts & syrups

(G-11871)
TOSHIBA AMER INFO SYSTEMS INC (DH)
1251 Ave Of The (10020)
P.O. Box 19724, Irvine CA (92623-9724)
PHONE..................................949 583-3000
Mark Simons, *CEO*

▲ = Import ▼=Export
◆ =Import/Export

GEOGRAPHIC SECTION

New York - New York County (G-11896)

Ted Flati, *Vice Pres*
▲ **EMP:** 277
SQ FT: 446,000
SALES (est): 287.4MM
SALES (corp-wide): 37B Privately Held
WEB: www.toshiba-components.com
SIC: 3571 3577 3572 3661 Electronic computers; computer peripheral equipment; disk drives, computer; telephones & telephone apparatus; facsimile equipment; computers, peripherals & software
HQ: Toshiba America Inc
 1251 Ave Of Ameri
 New York NY 10020
 212 596-0600

(G-11872)
TOSHIBA AMERICA INC (HQ)
1251 Ave Of Ameri (10020)
PHONE 212 596-0600
Hideo Ito, *CEO*
Takeshi Okatomi, *Ch of Bd*
Hiromitsu Igarashi, *President*
Hisashi Izumi, *President*
Toru Uchiike, *President*
◆ **EMP:** 28
SALES (est): 4.1B
SALES (corp-wide): 37B Privately Held
SIC: 3651 3631 5064 5075 Television receiving sets; video cassette recorders/players & accessories; microwave ovens, including portable; household; video cassette recorders & accessories; high fidelity equipment; compressors, air conditioning; personal computers (microcomputers); multiplex equipment, telephone & telegraph
PA: Toshiba Corporation
 1-1-1, Shibaura
 Minato-Ku TKY 105-0
 334 574-511

(G-11873)
TOTAL CONCEPT GRAPHIC INC
519 8th Ave Rm 805a (10018-5182)
PHONE 212 229-2626
Joe Ferrara, *President*
John Chessa, *Vice Pres*
EMP: 4
SQ FT: 500
SALES: 2MM Privately Held
SIC: 2752 Commercial printing, offset

(G-11874)
TOTO USA INC
20 W 22nd St Frnt 2 (10010-5887)
PHONE 917 237-0665
Kazuo Sako, *Principal*
Lori Peterson, *Human Res Mgr*
Ivette Cardenas, *Sales Staff*
EMP: 5
SALES (corp-wide): 5.5B Privately Held
SIC: 3432 Plumbing fixture fittings & trim
HQ: Toto U.S.A., Inc.
 1155 Southern Rd
 Morrow GA 30260

(G-11875)
TOUCHCARE P LLC
111 W 19th St Fl 8 (10011-4315)
PHONE 646 824-5373
Joel Kristoferson, *CEO*
Matthew Roth, *Controller*
EMP: 17
SALES (est): 802.9K Privately Held
SIC: 7372 Business oriented computer software

(G-11876)
TOUCHTUNES MUSIC CORPORATION (HQ)
Also Called: Touch Tunes
850 3rd Ave Ste 15c (10022-7263)
PHONE 847 419-3300
Charles Goldstuck, *CEO*
Ross Honey, *President*
Marc Felsen, *Senior VP*
Vicki Saunders, *Senior VP*
Pam Schoenfeld, *Senior VP*
EMP: 60
SALES (est): 71.8MM
SALES (corp-wide): 95.2MM Privately Held
SIC: 3651 Household audio & video equipment; audio electronic systems

PA: Searchlight Capital Partners, L.P.
 745 5th Ave Fl 27
 New York NY 10151
 212 293-3730

(G-11877)
TOWNLEY INC
Also Called: Townley Cosmetics
10 W 33rd St Rm 418 (10001-3324)
PHONE 212 779-0544
Abraham Safdieh, *President*
Joe Gindi, *Vice Pres*
Felena Jagarnauth, *Vice Pres*
Stan Cliett, *Manager*
▲ **EMP:** 30
SQ FT: 9,000
SALES (est): 5.6MM Privately Held
SIC: 3915 Jewelers' materials & lapidary work

(G-11878)
TOYMAX INC (DH)
Also Called: Candy Planet Division
200 5th Ave (10010-3302)
PHONE 212 633-6611
David Ki Kwan Chu, *Ch of Bd*
Steven Lebensfeld, *President*
Carmine Russo, *COO*
Harvey Goldberg, *Exec VP*
Kenneth Price, *Senior VP*
EMP: 8
SQ FT: 30,000
SALES (est): 3.6MM Publicly Held
WEB: www.toymax.com
SIC: 3944 5092 Games, toys & children's vehicles; toys

(G-11879)
TPHG 419 LTD
Also Called: Bread & Butter
419 Park Ave S Frnt A (10016-8410)
PHONE 212 683-0444
Byung IL Park, *President*
▲ **EMP:** 13
SALES (est): 1.7MM Privately Held
SIC: 2051 Bread, cake & related products

(G-11880)
TR APPAREL LLC
609 Greenwich St Fl 3 (10014-3610)
PHONE 310 595-4337
Andrew Wong, *Branch Mgr*
EMP: 40
SALES (corp-wide): 9.7MM Privately Held
SIC: 2389 Academic vestments (caps & gowns)
HQ: Tr Apparel, Llc
 609 Greenwich St Fl 3
 New York NY 10014

(G-11881)
TR APPAREL LLC (HQ)
Also Called: Row, The
609 Greenwich St Fl 3 (10014-3610)
PHONE 646 358-3888
Francois Kress, *President*
Ashley Olsen, *Owner*
Mary Kate Olsen, *Owner*
Catherine Dueck, *Vice Pres*
Kimberly Kennedy, *Opers Staff*
EMP: 9
SALES (est): 9.7MM Privately Held
WEB: www.therow.com
SIC: 2389 5632 Academic vestments (caps & gowns); women's accessory & specialty stores

(G-11882)
TR DESIGNS INC
Also Called: Tracy Reese
260 W 39th St Fl 19 (10018-0360)
PHONE 212 398-9300
ADI Kandel, *President*
Tracy Reese, *Principal*
Om Batheja, *Vice Pres*
Yasmin Batista, *Prdtn Mgr*
Alyssa Jones, *Comms Dir*
▲ **EMP:** 32
SQ FT: 11,000
SALES (est): 4.1MM Privately Held
SIC: 2339 Sportswear, women's

(G-11883)
TRADER JOES COMPANY
Also Called: Trader Joe's 541
138 E 14th St (10003-4170)
PHONE 212 529-6326
John Martinelli, *Manager*
EMP: 40
SALES (corp-wide): 1.3B Privately Held
SIC: 2084 Wines
PA: Trader Joe's Company
 800 S Shamrock Ave
 Monrovia CA 91016
 626 599-3700

(G-11884)
TRADING SERVICES INTERNATIONAL
Also Called: Tsi Technologies
133 W 72nd St Rm 601 (10023-3236)
PHONE 212 501-0142
Joel Darr, *President*
Judy Darr, *Vice Pres*
▲ **EMP:** 14
SQ FT: 2,000
SALES (est): 24MM Privately Held
WEB: www.tsitec.com
SIC: 3679 5013 Electronic circuits; motor vehicle supplies & new parts

(G-11885)
TRAFALGAR COMPANY LLC (HQ)
417 5th Ave Fl 11 (10016-2238)
PHONE 212 768-8800
Jeffrey Spiegel, *Mng Member*
John Hastings,
▲ **EMP:** 5 **EST:** 2003
SQ FT: 6,500
SALES (est): 680K
SALES (corp-wide): 151.7MM Privately Held
WEB: www.ghurka.com
SIC: 2387 3172 3161 2389 Apparel belts; wallets; attache cases; briefcases; suitcases; suspenders
PA: Randa Accessories Leather Goods Llc
 5600 N River Rd Ste 500
 Rosemont IL 60018
 847 292-8300

(G-11886)
TRANS-HIGH CORPORATION
250 W 57th St Ste 920 (10107-0003)
PHONE 212 387-0500
Mary McCvoy, *Principal*
EMP: 22 **EST:** 2013
SALES (est): 2.6MM Privately Held
SIC: 2721 Periodicals-Publishing/Printing

(G-11887)
TRANS-LUX CORPORATION (PA)
135 E 57th St Unt 100 (10022-2172)
PHONE 800 243-5544
George W Schiele, *Ch of Bd*
Jean-Marc Allain, *President*
Alberto Shaio, *COO*
Alexandro Gomez, *Senior VP*
Todd Dupee, *Vice Pres*
EMP: 80
SQ FT: 268,000
SALES: 24.4MM Publicly Held
WEB: www.trans-lux.com
SIC: 3993 Electric signs

(G-11888)
TRASH AND VAUDEVILLE INC
96 E 7th St Frnt A (10009-8042)
PHONE 212 777-1727
Diana Otoole, *Manager*
EMP: 6
SALES (corp-wide): 1MM Privately Held
SIC: 2389 Men's miscellaneous accessories
PA: Trash And Vaudeville, Inc.
 5200 W Side Ave
 North Bergen NJ 07047
 201 520-0420

(G-11889)
TREAUU INC
60 E 120th St Fl 2 (10035-3571)
PHONE 703 731-0196
Tahira White, *Principal*
Marcus Scott, *Principal*
EMP: 6

SALES (est): 340K Privately Held
SIC: 7372 7389 Application computer software;

(G-11890)
TREND POT INC
40 Exchange Pl Ste 1902 (10005-2711)
PHONE 212 431-9970
Tetsuji Shintani, *Ch of Bd*
▲ **EMP:** 25
SQ FT: 2,000
SALES: 2.5MM Privately Held
WEB: www.trendpot.com
SIC: 2721 Periodicals

(G-11891)
TRENDSFORMERS LTD LIABILITY CO
Also Called: Trendsformers
150 W 56th St Apt 6406 (10019-3848)
PHONE 888 700-2423
David Klar,
EMP: 4
SQ FT: 5,000
SALES: 2MM Privately Held
SIC: 3999 8748 Atomizers, toiletry; business consulting

(G-11892)
TRI-FORCE SALES LLC
767 3rd Ave Rm 35b (10017-2082)
PHONE 732 261-5507
Robert Bracebic, *President*
Scp Crusader LLC, *Principal*
Matthew Marone, *Vice Pres*
Hemang Mehta, *Vice Pres*
▼ **EMP:** 24 **EST:** 2008
SQ FT: 5,500
SALES: 12MM Privately Held
SIC: 3999 8742 Models, except toy; marketing consulting services

(G-11893)
TRI-LON CLOR LITHOGRAPHERS LTD
Also Called: Trilon Color Lithographers
233 Spring St Frnt 9th (10013-1522)
PHONE 212 255-6140
Marc Strickler, *President*
David Strickler, *Chairman*
Esther Strickler, *Corp Secy*
EMP: 26 **EST:** 1964
SQ FT: 10,000
SALES: 3.2MM Privately Held
SIC: 2752 2791 2789 2759 Commercial printing, offset; typesetting; bookbinding & related work; commercial printing

(G-11894)
TRI-PLEX PACKAGING CORPORATION
307 5th Ave Fl 7 (10016-6574)
PHONE 212 481-6070
Ken Golden, *President*
Barry Walsh, *Opers Staff*
Adam Caraher, *Director*
▲ **EMP:** 26
SALES: 10MM Privately Held
WEB: www.lieberman-nyc.com
SIC: 3999 2671 Advertising display products; paper coated or laminated for packaging

(G-11895)
TRI-STATE BRICK & STONE NY INC (PA)
333 7th Ave Fl 5 (10001-5829)
PHONE 212 366-0300
Robert Turzilli, *President*
Michael Falcone, *Vice Pres*
Vincent Falcone, *Vice Pres*
Louis J Formica, *Vice Pres*
▲ **EMP:** 60
SQ FT: 6,500
SALES (est): 26.8MM Privately Held
SIC: 2421 5031 Building & structural materials, wood; building materials, exterior

(G-11896)
TRIANON COLLECTION INC
16 W 46th St Fl 10 (10036-4503)
PHONE 212 921-9450
Anthony Hopenka JM, *CEO*
Joseph Bauer, *President*
Anthony Hopenhajm, *Vice Pres*

New York - New York County (G-11897) — GEOGRAPHIC SECTION

Anthony JM, *Sales Mgr*
Manwant Walia, *Manager*
▲ **EMP:** 24
SQ FT: 3,390
SALES (est): 3MM **Privately Held**
WEB: www.trianonnet.com
SIC: 3911 Jewelry, precious metal
PA: Banisa Corporation
21860 Masters Cir
Estero FL 33928
239 949-2309

(G-11897)
TRIBUNE ENTERTAINMENT CO DEL
220 E 42nd St Fl 26 (10017-5806)
PHONE..................203 866-2204
EMP: 40
SALES (corp-wide): 1.8B **Publicly Held**
SIC: 2711 2741 4833 Newspapers, publishing & printing; miscellaneous publishing; television broadcasting stations
HQ: Tribune Entertainment Company (Del)
435 N Michigan Ave Fl 19
Chicago IL 60611
312 222-4441

(G-11898)
TRICYCLE FOUNDATION INC
89 5th Ave Ste 301 (10003-3020)
PHONE..................800 873-9871
Elizabeth Lees, *President*
Emma Varvaloucas, *Editor*
Alyssa Snow, *Controller*
Joellen Sommer, *Controller*
Phil Ryan, *Webmaster*
EMP: 9
SQ FT: 2,500
SALES: 1.5MM **Privately Held**
SIC: 2711 Newspapers: publishing only, not printed on site

(G-11899)
TRIMASTER/HTECH HOLDING LLC (HQ)
590 Madison Ave Fl 27 (10022-2544)
PHONE..................212 257-6772
EMP: 4
SALES (est): 18.7MM **Privately Held**
SIC: 3544 3545 Special dies, tools, jigs & fixtures; precision tools, machinists'

(G-11900)
TRIMFIT INC (PA)
Also Called: Trimfit Global
463 7th Ave Rm 1501 (10018-7596)
PHONE..................215 245-1122
Martin Kramer, *Ch of Bd*
Arnold A Kramer, *President*
▲ **EMP:** 40 **EST:** 1921
SQ FT: 12,000
SALES (est): 50.4MM **Privately Held**
WEB: www.trimfit.com
SIC: 2252 2251 Socks; tights & leg warmers; women's hosiery, except socks

(G-11901)
TRIUMPH APPAREL CORPORATION (PA)
530 Fashion Ave Ste M1 (10018-4878)
PHONE..................212 302-2606
Carol Hockman, *President*
Donald Schupak, *Principal*
John A Sarto, *CFO*
▲ **EMP:** 42
SALES (est): 87.8MM **Privately Held**
WEB: www.danskin.com
SIC: 2331 Women's & misses' blouses & shirts

(G-11902)
TRIUMPH LEARNING LLC (DH)
Also Called: Options Publishing
212 W 35th St Fl 2 (10001-2508)
PHONE..................212 652-0200
Rick Noble, *President*
Thomas Emrick, *President*
Brad Peters, *President*
Amy Goodale, *Editor*
Jack Beers, *Vice Pres*
▲ **EMP:** 50 **EST:** 1963
SALES (est): 23.1MM
SALES (corp-wide): 83.8MM **Privately Held**
SIC: 2741 Miscellaneous publishing

(G-11903)
TROPP PRINTING CORP
Also Called: Tropp Prntng
181 Broadway Fl 3 (10007-3129)
PHONE..................212 233-4519
Lee Tropp, *President*
William Tropp, *Vice Pres*
EMP: 6
SQ FT: 4,000
SALES (est): 757.5K **Privately Held**
SIC: 2752 Commercial printing, offset; lithographing on metal

(G-11904)
TRUEEX LLC
162 5th Ave Ste 900 (10010-5972)
PHONE..................646 786-8526
Sunil Hirani, *CEO*
Karen O'Connor, *COO*
Karen L O'Connor, *COO*
Tu-Lien Nguyen, *Project Dir*
Christina Landry, *Project Mgr*
EMP: 48
SALES (est): 462.1K **Privately Held**
SIC: 7372 Business oriented computer software

(G-11905)
TRUNK & TROLLEY LLC
15 W 34th St (10001-3015)
PHONE..................212 947-9001
Sammy Sitt,
Steven Russo,
▲ **EMP:** 5
SQ FT: 25,000
SALES (est): 290K **Privately Held**
SIC: 3161 Luggage

(G-11906)
TRUST OF COLUM UNIVE IN THE CI
Also Called: Columbia Univ Publications
2929 Broadway Fl 3 (10025-7819)
PHONE..................212 854-2793
Sandy Kaufman, *Director*
EMP: 19
SALES (corp-wide): 3.8B **Privately Held**
WEB: www.columbia.edu
SIC: 2754 8221 Labels: gravure printing; letter, circular & form: gravure printing; university
PA: The Trustees Of Columbia University In The City Of New York
116th And Bdwy Way
New York NY 10027
212 854-9970

(G-11907)
TRUSTED MEDIA BRANDS INC (HQ)
Also Called: Reader's Digest
750 3rd Ave Fl 3 (10017-2723)
PHONE..................914 238-1000
Randall Curran, *Ch of Bd*
Bonnie Kintzer, *President*
Rebecca Steele, *Editor*
Howard Halligan, *COO*
Brian Kennedy, *COO*
◆ **EMP:** 1100 **EST:** 1922
SQ FT: 445,193
SALES (est): 1.3B **Privately Held**
WEB: www.rd.com
SIC: 2721 2731 5961 2741 Magazines: publishing only, not printed on site; books: publishing only; books, mail order (except book clubs); record &/or tape (music or video) club, mail order; miscellaneous publishing

(G-11908)
TRYP TIMES SQUARE
234 W 48th St (10036-1540)
PHONE..................212 246-8800
EMP: 6
SALES (est): 122.7K **Privately Held**
SIC: 2711 Newspapers

(G-11909)
TSAR USA LLC
99 Madison Ave Fl 5 (10016-7419)
PHONE..................646 415-7968
Lucy Tupu, *General Mgr*
David Sharpley, *Mng Member*
▲ **EMP:** 12 **EST:** 2011

SALES (est): 1.4MM **Privately Held**
SIC: 2273 Carpets, hand & machine made
PA: Dakee Australia Pty. Ltd.
3 Wellington St
St Kilda VIC 3182

(G-11910)
TTG LLC
Also Called: Titan Technology Group
115 W 30th St Rm 209 (10001-4218)
PHONE..................917 777-0959
Mark Liebmam, *Mng Member*
Tom Skovran, *Manager*
Mark Liebman, *Info Tech Dir*
Danny Keren,
EMP: 9
SQ FT: 1,600
SALES (est): 968.9K **Privately Held**
WEB: www.titantechgroup.com
SIC: 7372 Prepackaged software

(G-11911)
TUCANO USA INC
77 Bleecker St Apt C212 (10012-1586)
PHONE..................212 966-9211
Franco Luini, *President*
Sergio Musati, *Exec VP*
◆ **EMP:** 6
SQ FT: 1,200
SALES (est): 4.8MM **Privately Held**
SIC: 3199 Leather garments

(G-11912)
TUDOR ELECTRICAL SUPPLY CO INC
137 W 24th St (10011-1901)
PHONE..................212 867-7550
Jay Wittner, *President*
Steve Kramer, *Vice Pres*
EMP: 8
SQ FT: 8,500
SALES (est): 1.4MM **Privately Held**
SIC: 3645 5063 Residential lighting fixtures; electrical supplies

(G-11913)
TURN ON PRODUCTS INC (PA)
Also Called: Almost Famous Clothing
270 W 38th St Rm 1200 (10018-1573)
PHONE..................212 764-2121
Peter Kossoy, *President*
Robert Regina, *Vice Pres*
Marc Wasserman, *CFO*
▲ **EMP:** 80 **EST:** 1974
SQ FT: 20,000
SALES (est): 100.3MM **Privately Held**
WEB: www.youniqueclothing.com
SIC: 2339 2331 Sportswear, women's; women's & misses' blouses & shirts

(G-11914)
TURN ON PRODUCTS INC
Also Called: Younique Clothing
525 7th Ave Rm 1403 (10018-4967)
PHONE..................212 764-4545
Peter Kossoy, *President*
EMP: 12
SALES (corp-wide): 100.3MM **Privately Held**
WEB: www.youniqueclothing.com
SIC: 2321 2339 2337 2335 Blouses, women's & juniors': made from purchased material; slacks: women's, misses' & juniors'; skirts, separate: women's, misses' & juniors'; women's, juniors' & misses' dresses
PA: Turn On Products Inc.
270 W 38th St Rm 1200
New York NY 10018
212 764-2121

(G-11915)
TV GUIDE MAGAZINE LLC (HQ)
50 Rockefeller Plz Fl 14 (10020-1617)
PHONE..................800 866-1400
David J Fishman, *CEO*
Michell Lindquist, *CFO*
Richard Steele, *Human Res Mgr*
Michael Clayton,
Mark Fernberg,
EMP: 5
SALES (est): 97.2MM
SALES (corp-wide): 99.5MM **Privately Held**
SIC: 2721 Magazines: publishing & printing

PA: Ntvb Media, Inc.
213 Park Dr
Troy MI 48083
248 583-4190

(G-11916)
TV GUIDE MAGAZINE GROUP INC (DH)
1211 Ave Of The Americas (10036-8701)
PHONE..................212 852-7500
John Loughlin, *CEO*
Michael Clayton, *Vice Pres*
Richard Steele, *CFO*
▲ **EMP:** 100
SQ FT: 40,000
SALES (est): 10.1MM
SALES (corp-wide): 99.5MM **Privately Held**
SIC: 2721 Magazines: publishing only, not printed on site; television schedules: publishing only, not printed on site

(G-11917)
TWCC PRODUCT AND SALES
122 5th Ave (10011-5605)
PHONE..................212 614-9364
Katrina Hanritty, *Vice Pres*
EMP: 50
SALES (est): 2.7MM **Privately Held**
SIC: 2389 7389 Apparel & accessories; design services

(G-11918)
TWIST INTIMATE GROUP LLC (PA)
Also Called: Twist Intimate Apparel
35 W 35th St Rm 903 (10001-2238)
PHONE..................212 695-5990
Jack Sardar, *Sales Staff*
Jack Saldar, *Mng Member*
David Sutone,
◆ **EMP:** 7
SQ FT: 5,000
SALES (est): 1.1MM **Privately Held**
SIC: 2322 Underwear, men's & boys': made from purchased materials

(G-11919)
TWO PALMS PRESS INC
476 Broadway Ste 3f (10013-2641)
PHONE..................212 965-8598
David Lasry, *President*
Abelan Lasry, *Co-Owner*
EMP: 10
SALES: 950K **Privately Held**
WEB: www.twopalmspress.com
SIC: 2741 Miscellaneous publishing

(G-11920)
TWO WORLDS ARTS LTD (PA)
122 W 18th St (10011-5403)
PHONE..................212 929-2210
Jean Chau, *President*
Frank Chau, *Vice Pres*
EMP: 6
SQ FT: 5,000
SALES (est): 931.1K **Privately Held**
SIC: 3645 2519 5099 5021 Table lamps; household furniture, except wood or metal: upholstered; antiques; household furniture

(G-11921)
TWP AMERICA INC (DH)
Also Called: Tien Wah Press
299 Broadway Ste 720 (10007-1987)
PHONE..................212 274-8090
Gary Watson, *Manager*
Yoichi Sanada, *Director*
◆ **EMP:** 7
SQ FT: 4,500
SALES (est): 559.7K
SALES (corp-wide): 13.2B **Privately Held**
WEB: www.twpny.com
SIC: 2732 Books: printing only
HQ: Tien Wah Press (Pte.) Limited
4 Pandan Crescent
Singapore 12847
646 662-22

(G-11922)
TYCOON INTERNATIONAL INC
3436 W 32nd St Fl 4 Flr 4 (10001)
PHONE..................212 563-7107
Young Eun Kin, *President*
▲ **EMP:** 6

▲ = Import ▼ = Export
◆ = Import/Export

SALES (est): 682.8K Privately Held
SIC: 3961 Costume jewelry

(G-11923)
TYME GLOBAL TECHNOLOGIES LLC
Also Called: Hotelexpert
60 W 66th St Apt 15a (10023-6288)
PHONE.................................212 796-1950
David Cristescu, *CFO*
Ryan Levin,
EMP: 21
SALES (est): 481.3K Privately Held
SIC: 7372 Business oriented computer software

(G-11924)
TYME INC
48 Wall St Ste 1100 (10005-2903)
PHONE.................................646 205-1603
Steven Hoffman, *CEO*
Michael Demurjian, *COO*
Robert Dickey IV, *CFO*
EMP: 6 EST: 2013
SALES (est): 104.6K
SALES (corp-wide): 1.6MM Publicly Held
SIC: 2834 Pharmaceutical preparations
PA: Tyme Technologies, Inc.
    17 State St Fl 7
    New York NY 10004
    212 461-2315

(G-11925)
TYME TECHNOLOGIES INC (PA)
17 State St Fl 7 (10004-1585)
PHONE.................................212 461-2315
Steve Hoffman, *CEO*
Ben R Taylor, *President*
Michele Korfin, *Ch Credit Ofcr*
Giuseppe Del Priore, *Chief Mktg Ofcr*
James Biehl, *Officer*
EMP: 11
SQ FT: 4,752
SALES (est): 1.6MM Publicly Held
SIC: 2834 Pharmaceutical preparations

(G-11926)
U S JAPAN PUBLICATION NY INC
147 W 35th St Ste 1705 (10001-2100)
PHONE.................................212 252-8833
Nobuo Ijichi, *Ch of Bd*
Naoki Hishida, *Art Dir*
▲ EMP: 7
SQ FT: 2,500
SALES (est): 750K Privately Held
SIC: 2721 Magazines: publishing only, not printed on site

(G-11927)
U SERVE BRANDS INC
Also Called: Insomnia Cookies On The Hill
345 7th Ave Rm 501 (10001-5054)
PHONE.................................877 632-6354
Seth Berkowitz, *Chairman*
EMP: 12
SALES (est): 1.3MM Privately Held
SIC: 2052 Cookies & crackers

(G-11928)
UBEES INC
575 5th Ave 21 (10017-2422)
PHONE.................................916 505-8470
Arnaud Lacourt, *Principal*
Laurence Bouju, *Principal*
JC Morisseau, *Principal*
EMP: 12
SALES (est): 329.6K Privately Held
SIC: 3999 Smokers, bee (beekeepers' supplies)

(G-11929)
UBM INC
2 Penn Plz (10121-0101)
PHONE.................................212 600-3000
David Levin, *CEO*
Thomas Claburn, *Editor*
Tim Wilson, *Editor*
Marilyn Cohodas, *Chief*
Christopher Fischer, *Business Mgr*
EMP: 3500
SALES (est): 228.8MM
SALES (corp-wide): 1B Privately Held
WEB: www.unm.com
SIC: 2721 2711 8732 2741 Periodicals; newspapers; commercial nonphysical research; business research service; business service newsletters: publishing & printing
PA: Ubm Plc
    240 Blackfriars Road
    London SE1 8
    207 921-8029

(G-11930)
UBM LLC
Also Called: Cmp Media
2 Penn Plz Fl 15 (10121-1700)
PHONE.................................516 562-5000
Jim Donahue, *Editor*
Laurianne McLaughlin, *Chief*
Albert Sabbah, *Business Mgr*
Annmarie Fowler, *Assistant VP*
Robert Demarzo, *Vice Pres*
EMP: 10
SALES (corp-wide): 1B Privately Held
WEB: www.cmp.com
SIC: 2711 2721 Commercial printing & newspaper publishing combined; magazines: publishing & printing
HQ: Ubm, Llc
    1983 Marcus Ave Ste 250
    New Hyde Park NY 11042
    516 562-7800

(G-11931)
UDISENSE INC
Also Called: Nanit
315 W 36th St Fl 2 (10018-6643)
PHONE.................................866 696-2648
Assaf Glazer, *CEO*
Abraham Spitz, *President*
EMP: 13
SQ FT: 600
SALES (est): 811.8K Privately Held
SIC: 7372 Home entertainment computer software

(G-11932)
UFO CONTEMPORARY INC
42 W 38th St Rm 1204 (10018-0054)
P.O. Box 20505 (10017-0005)
PHONE.................................212 226-5400
Lorna Brody, *President*
▲ EMP: 10
SALES (est): 1.1MM Privately Held
WEB: www.ufojeans.com
SIC: 2389 Men's miscellaneous accessories

(G-11933)
UFX HOLDING I CORPORATION (HQ)
55 E 52nd St Fl 35 (10055-0002)
PHONE.................................212 644-5900
Vincent MAI, *Principal*
▲ EMP: 1
SALES (est): 61.3MM
SALES (corp-wide): 2.6B Privately Held
SIC: 3299 Ceramic fiber
PA: Aea Investors Lp
    666 5th Ave Fl 36
    New York NY 10103
    212 644-5900

(G-11934)
UFX HOLDING II CORPORATION (DH)
55 E 52nd St Fl 35 (10055-0002)
PHONE.................................212 644-5900
Vincent MAI, *Principal*
EMP: 1
SALES (est): 61.3MM
SALES (corp-wide): 2.6B Privately Held
SIC: 3299 Ceramic fiber

(G-11935)
ULLINK INC (HQ)
11 Times Sq Ste 31d (10036-6622)
PHONE.................................646 565-6675
Torben Munch, *President*
Bill Torpey, *Managing Dir*
Nicolas Rodriguez, *Project Mgr*
Narendhar Vemulapalli, *Project Mgr*
William Wong, *Production*
EMP: 10
SALES (est): 10.7MM
SALES (corp-wide): 46MM Privately Held
SIC: 7372 Business oriented computer software
PA: Ullink
    21 Boulevard Haussmann
    Paris
    144 502-500

(G-11936)
UNCHARTED POWER INC
527 W 125th St (10027-3402)
PHONE.................................646 675-7783
Jessica O Matthews, *Ch of Bd*
Christopher Strunk, *Finance*
Nicholas Navarro, *Director*
▲ EMP: 25
SALES (est): 3.7MM Privately Held
SIC: 3699 Generators, ultrasonic

(G-11937)
UNDERLINE COMMUNICATIONS LLC
12 W 27th St Fl 14 (10001-6903)
PHONE.................................212 994-4340
Kathryn Whitenight, *Partner*
Nikki Woods, *Partner*
Michelle Duda, *Director*
Erik Wennerod, *Director*
Ashley Paterson, *Art Dir*
EMP: 10
SALES (est): 1.3MM Privately Held
WEB: www.underlinecom.com
SIC: 2741 Miscellaneous publishing

(G-11938)
UNI JEWELRY INC
48 W 48th St Ste 1401 (10036-1718)
PHONE.................................212 398-1818
Frank Lee, *President*
▲ EMP: 7
SQ FT: 1,000
SALES (est): 540K Privately Held
SIC: 3911 5094 Jewelry, precious metal; jewelry

(G-11939)
UNIFIED INC IED
35 W 36th St (10018-7906)
PHONE.................................646 370-4650
EMP: 10
SALES (est): 500K Privately Held
SIC: 2389 Mfg Apparel/Accessories

(G-11940)
UNIFIED MEDIA INC
180 Madison Ave Lbby L (10016-5267)
PHONE.................................917 595-2710
Sheldon Owen, *CEO*
Michel Owen, *Vice Pres*
Amanda Baldauf, *Accounts Mgr*
Derek Webb, *Sales Staff*
James Errico, *Manager*
EMP: 19
SALES (est): 1.2MM Privately Held
SIC: 2711 Newspapers, publishing & printing

(G-11941)
UNIFOR INC
149 5th Ave Ste 3r (10010-6899)
PHONE.................................212 673-3434
Gianfranco Marinelli, *President*
Angela Dispensa, *COO*
Mersiha Makota, *Project Mgr*
▲ EMP: 19
SALES (est): 3MM Privately Held
SIC: 2531 Public building & related furniture

(G-11942)
UNIFORMED FIRE OFFICER ASSOIAT
125 Maiden Ln (10038-4912)
PHONE.................................212 293-9300
Richard D Brower, *President*
John Corr, *Vice Pres*
Arthur Parrinello, *Treasurer*
James M Slevin, *Admin Sec*
EMP: 17
SQ FT: 1,870
SALES: 6.9MM Privately Held
SIC: 1389 Fire fighting, oil & gas field

(G-11943)
UNIFRAX HOLDING CO (DH)
55 E 52nd St Fl 35 (10055-0002)
PHONE.................................212 644-5900
Vincent MAI, *Principal*
EMP: 1
SALES (est): 61.3MM
SALES (corp-wide): 2.6B Privately Held
SIC: 3299 Ceramic fiber

(G-11944)
UNILEVER UNITED STATES INC
390 Park Ave (10022-4608)
PHONE.................................212 546-0200
EMP: 9
SALES (corp-wide): 63B Privately Held
SIC: 2035 2086 2024 2038 Bottled & canned soft drinks; ice cream & frozen desserts; frozen specialties; toilet preparations; toothpastes or powders, dentifrices; hair preparations, including shampoos; cosmetic preparations; detergents, synthetic organic or inorganic alkaline; dishwashing compounds; soap: granulated, liquid, cake, flaked or chip; dressings, salad: raw & cooked (except dry mixes)
HQ: Unilever United States, Inc.
    700 Sylvan Ave
    Englewood Cliffs NJ 07632
    201 894-4000

(G-11945)
UNILEVER UNITED STATES INC
Also Called: Elizabeth Arden
663 5th Ave Fl 8 (10022-5328)
PHONE.................................212 546-0200
Teresa McKee, *Manager*
EMP: 250
SALES (corp-wide): 63B Privately Held
WEB: www.unilever.com
SIC: 2035 2086 2024 2038 Bottled & canned soft drinks; ice cream & frozen desserts; frozen specialties; toilet preparations; toothpastes or powders, dentifrices; hair preparations, including shampoos; cosmetic preparations; detergents, synthetic organic or inorganic alkaline; dishwashing compounds; soap: granulated, liquid, cake, flaked or chip; dressings, salad: raw & cooked (except dry mixes)
HQ: Unilever United States, Inc.
    700 Sylvan Ave
    Englewood Cliffs NJ 07632
    201 894-4000

(G-11946)
UNIMEX CORPORATION (PA)
Also Called: Lee Spring Company Div
54 E 64th St (10065-7306)
PHONE.................................212 755-8800
Arthur L Carter, *Ch of Bd*
Tom Scheinman, *President*
Vincent A Bohn Jr, *Vice Pres*
Brian G Kempner, *Vice Pres*
Ezra Berger, *Treasurer*
EMP: 100
SQ FT: 10,000
SALES (est): 45.3MM Privately Held
SIC: 3495 Wire springs

(G-11947)
UNIPHARM INC
350 5th Ave Ste 6701 (10118-6708)
PHONE.................................212 594-3260
Victor Sapritsky, *President*
Robert D Sires, *President*
Chris Adamo, *General Mgr*
Lou Cordova, *Controller*
Tatiana Pehanicova, *Controller*
▼ EMP: 100
SALES (est): 30.1MM Privately Held
WEB: www.unipharmus.com
SIC: 2834 5122 Vitamin preparations; vitamins & minerals

(G-11948)
UNIQLO USA LLC
546 Broadway (10012-3912)
PHONE.................................877 486-4756
Andrew Rosen, *Mng Member*
▲ EMP: 17

New York - New York County (G-11949) — GEOGRAPHIC SECTION

SALES (est): 1.9MM
SALES (corp-wide): 19.1B **Privately Held**
SIC: 2329 2337 5621 Sweaters & sweater jackets: men's & boys'; women's & misses' capes & jackets; women's clothing stores
PA: Fast Retailing Co., Ltd.
9-7-1, Akasaka
Minato-Ku TKY 107-0
368 650-050

(G-11949)
UNIQUE DESIGNS INC
521 5th Ave Rm 820 (10175-0800)
PHONE..................................212 575-7701
Tejas Shah, *CEO*
Ben Yep, *President*
Chai Lin, *Vice Pres*
Karen Lin, *Controller*
EMP: 19
SQ FT: 1,000
SALES: 147.5MM
SALES (corp-wide): 1.3B **Privately Held**
WEB: www.uniquedesigns.com
SIC: 3911 Jewelry, precious metal
PA: Kiran Gems Private Limited
Fe-5011, G Block, Bandra Kurla Complex,
Mumbai MH 40005
224 050-4444

(G-11950)
UNIQUE PETZ LLC
10 W 33rd St Rm 220 (10001-3306)
PHONE..................................212 714-1800
Adam Ash, *President*
▲ EMP: 25
SALES: 20MM **Privately Held**
SIC: 3999 Pet supplies

(G-11951)
UNISYSTEMS INC (PA)
Also Called: Modern Publishing
155 E 55th St Apt 203 (10022-4051)
PHONE..................................212 826-0850
Larry Steinberg, *Ch of Bd*
Andrew Steinberg, *President*
Warren Cohen, *Exec VP*
▲ EMP: 34
SQ FT: 8,200
SALES (est): 3.6MM **Privately Held**
WEB: www.modernpublishing.com
SIC: 2731 Books: publishing only

(G-11952)
UNITED BROTHERS JEWELRY INC
Also Called: U B J
48 W 48th St Ste 700 (10036-1703)
PHONE..................................212 921-2558
Gabriel Nisanov, *CEO*
Roman Nisanov, *Vice Pres*
Israel Nisanov, *Treasurer*
Israel Maximof, *Admin Sec*
EMP: 20
SQ FT: 6,000
SALES (est): 4.2MM **Privately Held**
SIC: 3911 Jewelry, precious metal

(G-11953)
UNITED KNITWEAR INTERNATIONAL (PA)
1384 Broadway Rm 1210 (10018-0509)
PHONE..................................212 354-2920
Carlos Hausner, *President*
▲ EMP: 3
SQ FT: 860
SALES (est): 4.4MM **Privately Held**
WEB: www.unitedknitwear.com
SIC: 2253 5136 5137 Sweaters & sweater coats, knit; men's & boys' clothing; women's & children's clothing

(G-11954)
UNITED RETAIL II
Also Called: Happy Sock
436 W Broadway (10012-3752)
PHONE..................................212 966-9692
EMP: 6 EST: 2013
SALES (est): 400.9K **Privately Held**
SIC: 2252 Socks

(G-11955)
UNITED STRUCTURE SOLUTION INC
240 W 65th St Apt 26c (10023-6412)
PHONE..................................347 227-7526
Ying Lu, *President*
EMP: 15 EST: 2010
SALES: 2MM **Privately Held**
SIC: 3441 Fabricated structural metal

(G-11956)
UNITED SYNGGUE CNSRVTIVE JDISM (PA)
120 Broadway Ste 1540 (10271-0032)
PHONE..................................212 533-7800
Rabbi Steven Wernick, *CEO*
Rabbi Jerome Epstein, *Exec VP*
Abe Fried-Tanzer, *Project Dir*
Melissa Marans, *Project Mgr*
Jennifer Stofman, *Manager*
▲ EMP: 50
SQ FT: 50,000
SALES (est): 15.4MM **Privately Held**
WEB: www.uscj.org
SIC: 2731 8661 Books: publishing only; religious organizations

(G-11957)
UNITONE COMMUNICATION SYSTEMS
220 E 23rd St Ste 411 (10010-4659)
PHONE..................................212 777-9090
Lucien Bohbot, *President*
EMP: 6
SALES (est): 983.4K **Privately Held**
WEB: www.unitonecom.com
SIC: 3669 7622 Burglar alarm apparatus, electric; fire alarm apparatus, electric; intercommunication systems, electric; communication equipment repair

(G-11958)
UNIVERSAL CMMNCATIONS OF MIAMI
Also Called: Elite Traveler Magazine
801 2nd Ave Lbby (10017-4706)
PHONE..................................212 986-5100
Geoffrey Lurie, *CEO*
Carl Reuderman, *Ch of Bd*
Douglas Gollan, *President*
Thea Halstead, *Editor*
Kristen Shirley, *Editor*
EMP: 125
SALES (est): 10.7MM **Privately Held**
SIC: 2721 Magazines: publishing & printing

(G-11959)
UNIVERSAL EDITION INC
Also Called: Ue Music
331 W 57th St Ste 380 (10019-3101)
PHONE..................................917 213-2177
Robert Thompson, *President*
▲ EMP: 65
SQ FT: 5,000
SALES: 8MM **Privately Held**
WEB: www.roxannapanufnik.com
SIC: 2741 Music books: publishing & printing

(G-11960)
UNIVERSAL ELLIOT CORP
327 W 36th St Rm 700 (10018-6929)
PHONE..................................212 736-8877
Mike Gadh, *President*
Ush Gadh, *Vice Pres*
Gurpal Gadh, *Admin Sec*
EMP: 9
SALES (est): 605K **Privately Held**
SIC: 2387 Apparel belts

(G-11961)
UNIVERSAL MUS GROUP HLDNGS INC (DH)
1755 Broadway Fl 6 (10019-3743)
PHONE..................................212 333-8000
Alain Levy, *Principal*
▲ EMP: 23
SALES (est): 37.5MM
SALES (corp-wide): 78.4MM **Privately Held**
SIC: 3652 5099 6794 8742 Magnetic tape (audio): prerecorded; master records or tapes, preparation of; phonograph records, prerecorded; compact discs; phonograph records; tapes & cassettes, prerecorded; video cassettes, accessories & supplies; copyright buying & licensing; music licensing & royalties; business consultant; men's & boys' clothing; women's & children's clothing
HQ: Universal Music Group, Inc.
2220 Colorado Ave
Santa Monica CA 90404
310 865-4000

(G-11962)
UNIVERSAL MUSIC GROUP INC
825 8th Ave Fl C2b (10019-7472)
PHONE..................................212 333-8237
Bill Evans, *Regional Mgr*
Marc Cimino, *COO*
Holly Adams, *Vice Pres*
Nick Allen, *Vice Pres*
Jason Boyd, *Vice Pres*
EMP: 11
SALES (corp-wide): 78.4MM **Privately Held**
SIC: 3652 Pre-recorded records & tapes
HQ: Universal Music Group, Inc.
2220 Colorado Ave
Santa Monica CA 90404
310 865-4000

(G-11963)
UNQORK INC
85 5th Ave Fl 6 (10003-3019)
PHONE..................................844 486-7675
Gary Hoberman, *CEO*
EMP: 25
SQ FT: 10,000
SALES (est): 456.2K **Privately Held**
SIC: 7372 Business oriented computer software

(G-11964)
UNTITLED MEDIA
Also Called: Indira Cesarine
45 Lispenard St Apt 1w (10013-2530)
PHONE..................................212 780-0960
Indira Cesarine, *President*
EMP: 45
SALES (est): 3.1MM **Privately Held**
SIC: 2721 7335 Magazines: publishing only, not printed on site; commercial photography

(G-11965)
UNTUCKIT LLC (PA)
110 Greene St Ste 400 (10012-3832)
PHONE..................................201 214-9054
Chris Riccobono, *CEO*
Aaron Sanandres, *Co-CEO*
Deepshika RAO, *Manager*
Sabrielle Lezeau, *Director*
Bjorn Bengtsson, *Officer*
▲ EMP: 38
SALES (est): 66.9MM **Privately Held**
SIC: 2326 2339 Men's & boys' work clothing; athletic clothing: women's, misses' & juniors'

(G-11966)
UNTUCKIT LLC
379 W Broadway Fl 2 (10012-5125)
PHONE..................................646 724-1857
EMP: 132
SALES (corp-wide): 66.9MM **Privately Held**
SIC: 2326 2339 Men's & boys' work clothing; athletic clothing: women's, misses' & juniors'
PA: Untuckit, Llc
110 Greene St Ste 400
New York NY 10012
201 214-9054

(G-11967)
UPTOWN MEDIA GROUP LLC
113 E 125th St Frnt 1 (10035-1661)
PHONE..................................212 360-5073
Brett Wright,
Leonard Burnett,
EMP: 36

SALES (est): 4MM **Privately Held**
SIC: 2721 Publishing & Printing Magazines

(G-11968)
URBAN APPAREL GROUP INC
226 W 37th St Fl 17 (10018-9011)
PHONE..................................212 947-7009
Karen Camporeale, *President*
Noreen Camporeale, *Vice Pres*
Dave Dulinski, *CFO*
David A Dulinski, *CFO*
▲ EMP: 37
SQ FT: 9,000
SALES (est): 4.5MM **Privately Held**
WEB: www.urbanapparel.com
SIC: 2339 Sportswear, women's

(G-11969)
URBAN MAPPING INC
Also Called: Umi
295 Madison Ave Rm 1010 (10017-6340)
PHONE..................................415 946-8170
Ian White, *President*
John Marshall, *CTO*
Amy Ocasio, *Admin Sec*
EMP: 11
SALES (est): 1.1MM **Privately Held**
WEB: www.urbanmapping.com
SIC: 2741 Atlas, map & guide publishing

(G-11970)
URBAN TEXTILES INC
Also Called: Forest Uniforms
254 W 35th St Unit 13 (10001-2517)
PHONE..................................212 777-1900
Michael Schackett, *President*
▲ EMP: 10
SQ FT: 5,000
SALES (est): 1.5MM **Privately Held**
SIC: 2311 Men's & boys' uniforms

(G-11971)
URBANDADDY INC
900 Broadway Ste 1003 (10003-1215)
P.O. Box 1050 (10276-1050)
PHONE..................................212 929-7905
Lance Broumand, *CEO*
Kelly Larson, *Editor*
Geoff Rynex, *Editor*
Hadley Tomicki, *Editor*
Lebaron Meyer, *Vice Pres*
EMP: 14
SALES (est): 3.2MM **Privately Held**
SIC: 2721 Magazines: publishing & printing

(G-11972)
URTHWORX INC
320 W 106th St Apt 2f (10025-3470)
PHONE..................................646 373-7535
Michael Fox, *CEO*
EMP: 5 EST: 2014
SALES (est): 304.8K **Privately Held**
SIC: 7372 7389 Home entertainment computer software;

(G-11973)
US CHINA MAGAZINE
200 W 95th St Apt 21 (10025-6315)
PHONE..................................212 663-4333
Zhong Vhan, *President*
Angila Chan, *Vice Pres*
Andrew Jee, *Director*
EMP: 25 EST: 1994
SALES: 500K **Privately Held**
SIC: 2721 Periodicals

(G-11974)
US DESIGN GROUP LTD
Also Called: Request Jeans
1385 Broadway Rm 1905 (10018-6001)
PHONE..................................212 354-4070
Frank Jbara, *President*
Frank Jebara, *President*
Assad Charles Jebara, *Vice Pres*
Imad Jebara, *Admin Sec*
▲ EMP: 18
SQ FT: 10,000
SALES (est): 1.2MM **Privately Held**
SIC: 2211 Apparel & outerwear fabrics, cotton

(G-11975)
US DIAGNOSTICS INC
Also Called: Vertaloc
711 3rd Ave Rm 1502 (10017-9200)
PHONE..................................866 216-5308

GEOGRAPHIC SECTION

New York - New York County (G-12002)

Edward Letko, *President*
▲ **EMP:** 20
SALES (est): 3.2MM **Privately Held**
SIC: 2835 In vitro & in vivo diagnostic substances

(G-11976)
US FRONTLINE NEWS INC
228 E 45th St Rm 700 (10017-3336)
PHONE.................212 922-9090
Fax: 212 922-9119
EMP: 30
SQ FT: 5,000
SALES (est): 3.5MM **Privately Held**
SIC: 2721 Periodicals-Publishing/Printing

(G-11977)
US HOME TEXTILES GROUP LLC
1400 Broadway Fl 18 (10018-5300)
PHONE.................212 768-3030
▲ **EMP:** 6
SALES (est): 570K **Privately Held**
SIC: 2221 Manmade Broadwoven Fabric Mill

(G-11978)
US NEWS & WORLD REPORT INC (PA)
120 5th Ave Fl 7 (10011-5637)
PHONE.................212 716-6800
Mortimer B Zuckerman, *CEO*
Arthur Young-Spivey, *Partner*
Brian Duffy, *Editor*
Jessie Sholl, *Editor*
Cody Trotter, *Editor*
▲ **EMP:** 150
SQ FT: 100,000
SALES (est): 108.3MM **Privately Held**
WEB: www.usnews.com
SIC: 2721 Magazines: publishing & printing

(G-11979)
US WEEKLY LLC
1290 Ave Of The Americas (10104-0295)
PHONE.................212 484-1616
David J Pecker, *CEO*
Emily Longeretta, *Editor*
Sharon Tharp, *Editor*
Amy Van Etten, *Director*
Victoria Lasdon, *Officer*
EMP: 75
SQ FT: 15,000
SALES (est): 10.3MM
SALES (corp-wide): 300MM **Privately Held**
WEB: www.usweekly.com
SIC: 2721 Magazines: publishing only, not printed on site
PA: American Media, Inc.
    1350 E Newport
    Deerfield Beach FL 33442
    212 545-4800

(G-11980)
USA TODAY INTERNATIONAL CORP
535 Madison Ave Fl 27 (10022-4216)
PHONE.................703 854-3400
David Mazzarella, *Manager*
EMP: 8
SALES (corp-wide): 3.1B **Publicly Held**
SIC: 2711 Newspapers
HQ: Usa Today International Corp
    7950 Jones Branch Dr
    Mc Lean VA 22102

(G-11981)
USPA ACCESSORIES LLC
Also Called: Concept One Accessories
1411 Broadway Fl 7 (10018-3401)
PHONE.................212 868-2590
Debra Medley, *President*
Margaret Close, *Vice Pres*
Kim White, *Vice Pres*
Paul Pierce, *Engineer*
Bernie Hafif, *CFO*
▲ **EMP:** 150
SQ FT: 38,000
SALES (est): 22MM **Privately Held**
SIC: 2339 Women's & misses' accessories

(G-11982)
USQ GROUP LLC
222 Broadway Fl 19 (10038-2550)
PHONE.................212 777-7751
Shanto Goswami, *CEO*
EMP: 5
SALES (est): 198.3K **Privately Held**
SIC: 7372 Application computer software; home entertainment computer software

(G-11983)
UXC ECLIPSE (USA) INC
Also Called: Uxc Eclipse USA
200 W 41st St Fl 15 (10036-7220)
PHONE.................212 965-6400
Bradley Stroop, *CEO*
Andrew Devitt, *Partner*
Ryan Grant, *Business Mgr*
Cyndi Whitehead, *Business Mgr*
Nathan Miller, *COO*
EMP: 65
SQ FT: 20,000
SALES (est): 10.6MM
SALES (corp-wide): 10.6MM **Privately Held**
SIC: 7372 Prepackaged software
PA: Eclipse Intelligent Solutions Usa
    250 Monroe Ave Nw Ste 400
    Grand Rapids MI 49503
    616 735-2010

(G-11984)
VALENTIN & KALICH JWLY MFG LTD
Also Called: Valentin Magro
42 W 48th St Ste 903 (10036-1712)
PHONE.................212 575-9044
Valente Magro, *President*
Terry Magro, *Vice Pres*
EMP: 24
SALES (est): 3.1MM **Privately Held**
SIC: 3911 Jewelry, precious metal

(G-11985)
VALENTINE JEWELRY MFG CO INC
31 W 47th St Ste 602 (10036-2833)
PHONE.................212 382-0606
Emil Feiger, *President*
EMP: 20 **EST:** 1969
SQ FT: 2,000
SALES (est): 1.9MM **Privately Held**
SIC: 3911 Jewelry, precious metal

(G-11986)
VALIANT ENTERTAINMENT LLC
350 7th Ave Rm 300 (10001-1957)
PHONE.................212 972-0361
Russell Brown, *President*
Fred Pierce, *Publisher*
Warren Simons, *Editor*
Peter Stern, *Opers Mgr*
Jeff Walker, *Production*
EMP: 20
SQ FT: 4,000
SALES: 5MM
SALES (corp-wide): 1.8MM **Privately Held**
SIC: 2721 Comic books: publishing only, not printed on site
HQ: Dmg Entertainment, Inc.
    9290 Civic Center Dr
    Beverly Hills CA 90210
    310 275-3750

(G-11987)
VALMONT INC (PA)
1 W 34th St Rm 303 (10001-3011)
PHONE.................212 685-1653
Nicholas Vales, *President*
Nicholas Vale, *President*
Nick Vale, *VP Opers*
David Klein, *Accountant*
▲ **EMP:** 15 **EST:** 1944
SQ FT: 1,000
SALES (est): 3.1MM **Privately Held**
SIC: 2342 5961 Brassieres; catalog & mail-order houses

(G-11988)
VALUE LINE INC (HQ)
551 5th Ave Fl 3 (10176-2800)
PHONE.................212 907-1500
Howard A Brecher, *Ch of Bd*
Stephen R Anastasio, *CFO*
Mary Bernstein, *Accountant*
EMP: 68
SQ FT: 24,726
SALES: 35.8MM
SALES (corp-wide): 36MM **Publicly Held**
SIC: 2721 6282 2741 Magazines: publishing only, not printed on site; investment advisory service; miscellaneous publishing
PA: Bernhard Arnold & Company Inc
    551 5th Ave Fl 3
    New York NY 10176
    212 907-1500

(G-11989)
VALUE LINE PUBLISHING LLC
551 5th Ave Fl 3 (10176-2800)
PHONE.................201 842-8054
Howard Brether, *CEO*
EMP: 175
SQ FT: 80,000
SALES (est): 36.7MM
SALES (corp-wide): 36MM **Publicly Held**
SIC: 2721 Periodicals: publishing only
HQ: Value Line, Inc.
    551 5th Ave Fl 3
    New York NY 10176
    212 907-1500

(G-11990)
VANDER HEYDEN WOODWORKING
Also Called: Tapestries Etc
151 W 25th St Fl 8 (10001-7204)
PHONE.................212 242-0525
Marcia Vander Heyden, *President*
EMP: 6
SQ FT: 3,000
SALES (est): 480K **Privately Held**
WEB: www.metookids.com
SIC: 2431 0742 Interior & ornamental woodwork & trim; veterinary services, specialties

(G-11991)
VANITY FAIR
4 Times Sq Bsmt C1b (10036-6518)
PHONE.................212 286-6052
Graydon Carter, *Chief*
Ron Ferraz, *Art Dir*
◆ **EMP:** 15
SALES (est): 1.9MM **Privately Held**
WEB: www.vf.com
SIC: 2721 Magazines: publishing & printing

(G-11992)
VANITY FAIR BRANDS LP
25 W 39th St (10018-3805)
PHONE.................212 548-1548
Pat Lager, *Manager*
EMP: 250
SALES (corp-wide): 242.1B **Publicly Held**
SIC: 2341 Nightgowns & negligees: women's & children's
HQ: Vanity Fair Brands, Lp
    1 Fruit Of The Loom Dr
    Bowling Green KY 42103
    270 781-6400

(G-11993)
VANITY ROOM INC
Also Called: Four Star
230 W 39th St Rm 900 (10018-4438)
PHONE.................212 921-7154
Geneva Goldsmith, *President*
EMP: 10
SALES (est): 2.8MM **Privately Held**
SIC: 2331 2335 Women's & misses' blouses & shirts; women's, juniors' & misses' dresses

(G-11994)
VARIABLE GRAPHICS LLC
15 W 36th St Rm 601 (10018-7122)
PHONE.................212 691-2323
Keneth Ratskin,
Arthur Raskin,
Kenneth Ratskin,
▲ **EMP:** 6
SALES (est): 773.8K **Privately Held**
WEB: www.variablegraphics.com
SIC: 2752 Commercial printing, offset

(G-11995)
VARICK STREET LITHO INC
149 W 27th St Fl 4 (10001-6279)
PHONE.................646 843-0800
EMP: 6
SALES (est): 718.9K **Privately Held**
SIC: 2759 Commercial printing

(G-11996)
VARNISH SOFTWARE INC
85 Broad St Fl 18 (10004-2783)
PHONE.................201 857-2832
Lars Larsson, *President*
Lina Gunhamre, *Finance Mgr*
Daniel Jacobs, *Sales Mgr*
Alexandra Lehner, *Marketing Staff*
EMP: 5
SALES (est): 146.4K **Privately Held**
SIC: 7372 Business oriented computer software

(G-11997)
VARONIS SYSTEMS INC (PA)
1250 Broadway Fl 29 (10001-3720)
PHONE.................877 292-8767
Yakov Faitelson, *Ch of Bd*
Eric Mann, *COO*
James O'Boyle, *Senior VP*
Seth Gerson, *Vice Pres*
Ken Spinner, *Vice Pres*
EMP: 94
SQ FT: 31,000
SALES: 217.3MM **Publicly Held**
SIC: 7372 Business oriented computer software

(G-11998)
VARSITY MONITOR LLC
50 5th Ave Fl 3 Flr 3 (10011)
PHONE.................212 691-6292
Sam Carnahan, *Managing Prtnr*
Farrah Carnahan, *Managing Dir*
EMP: 9
SALES (est): 470K **Privately Held**
SIC: 7372 Business oriented computer software

(G-11999)
VASQUEZ TITO
Also Called: Tito Moldmaker Co
36 W 47th St Ste 206 (10036-8636)
PHONE.................212 944-0441
Tito Vasquez, *Owner*
EMP: 10
SALES (est): 868.9K **Privately Held**
SIC: 2822 Silicone rubbers

(G-12000)
VAUGHAN DESIGNS INC (HQ)
979 3rd Ave Ste 1511 (10022-3804)
PHONE.................212 319-7070
Michael Vaughan, *President*
▲ **EMP:** 13
SQ FT: 1,700
SALES (est): 1.9MM
SALES (corp-wide): 17.3MM **Privately Held**
WEB: www.vaughandesigns.com
SIC: 3645 5021 Residential lighting fixtures; tables, occasional
PA: Vaughan Limited
    Unit 1 Chelsea Harbour Design Centre, Chelsea Harbour
    London SW10
    207 349-4600

(G-12001)
VAULTCOM INC (PA)
Also Called: Vault.com, Vault Media
132 W 31st St Rm 1501 (10001-3406)
PHONE.................212 366-4212
Eric Ober, *President*
Matt Moody, *Editor*
Phil Stott, *Editor*
Samer Hamadeh, *Chairman*
Hussam Hamadeh, *Vice Pres*
EMP: 33 **EST:** 1992
SALES (est): 5.7MM **Privately Held**
WEB: www.vaultmatch.com
SIC: 2731 7361 Books: publishing only; employment agencies

(G-12002)
VECTOR GROUP LTD
712 5th Ave (10019-4108)
PHONE.................212 409-2800

New York - New York County (G-12003) — GEOGRAPHIC SECTION

Ellen Jorgenson, *Manager*
EMP: 259
SALES (corp-wide): 1.6B **Publicly Held**
SIC: 2111 Cigarettes
PA: Vector Group Ltd.
    4400 Biscayne Blvd Fl 10
    Miami FL 33137
    305 579-8000

(G-12003)
VEGA COFFEE INC
325 N End Ave Apt 4b (10282-1027)
PHONE.................................415 881-7969
William Deluca, *Co-Owner*
Noushin Ketabi, *Co-Owner*
Robert Terenzi, *Co-Owner*
EMP: 5
SALES (est): 204.8K **Privately Held**
SIC: 2095 Roasted coffee

(G-12004)
VENDOME GROUP LLC
237 W 35th St Fl 16 (10001-1905)
PHONE.................................646 795-3899
Jane Butler, *CEO*
Mark Fried, *President*
Gary Enos, *Editor*
Charlene Marietti, *Chief*
Julie Miller, *Chief*
EMP: 89
SQ FT: 10,000
SALES (est): 14.6MM **Privately Held**
SIC: 2741 Miscellaneous publishing

(G-12005)
VENTRUS BIOSCIENCES INC
99 Hudson St (10013-2815)
PHONE.................................646 706-5208
John Gunderson, *Counsel*
JP Benya, *Vice Pres*
Elizabeth Lacy, *Vice Pres*
Melissa Fiacco, *Accounting Mgr*
Steve Cockrill, *Director*
EMP: 7 EST: 2017
SALES (est): 709.3K **Privately Held**
SIC: 2834 Pharmaceutical preparations

(G-12006)
VENTURA ENTERPRISE CO INC
512 Fashion Ave Fl 38 (10018-0827)
PHONE.................................212 391-0170
Saul Tawil, *Ch of Bd*
Shelley Rindner, *Exec VP*
Henry Dweck, *Vice Pres*
Phil Horowitz, *VP Sales*
Anne King, *Director*
▲ **EMP:** 40
SQ FT: 8,000
SALES (est): 4.3MM **Privately Held**
SIC: 2326 2331 Men's & boys' work clothing; women's & misses' blouses & shirts

(G-12007)
VERA WANG GROUP LLC (PA)
Also Called: V E W
15 E 26th St Fl 4 (10010-1536)
PHONE.................................212 575-6400
Vera W Becker, *Ch of Bd*
▲ **EMP:** 200 EST: 2004
SQ FT: 14,000
SALES (est): 28.8MM **Privately Held**
WEB: www.verawang.com
SIC: 2335 5621 Bridal & formal gowns; wedding gowns & dresses; gowns, formal; bridal shops; dress shops

(G-12008)
VERANDA PUBLICATIONS INC
Also Called: Veranda Magazine
300 W 57th St Fl 28 (10019-5288)
PHONE.................................212 903-5206
Lisa Newsom, *President*
Katie Brockman, *Publisher*
EMP: 8
SALES (est): 510.1K
SALES (corp-wide): 6.6B **Privately Held**
WEB: www.hearstcorp.com
SIC: 2721 Magazines: publishing only, not printed on site
PA: The Hearst Corporation
    300 W 57th St Fl 42
    New York NY 10019
    212 649-2000

(G-12009)
VERATEX INC (PA)
254 5th Ave Fl 3 (10001-6406)
P.O. Box 682 (10108-0682)
PHONE.................................212 683-9300
Claude Simon, *President*
John Simon, *Vice Pres*
▲ **EMP:** 10
SQ FT: 2,500
SALES (est): 2MM **Privately Held**
SIC: 2258 Tricot fabrics

(G-12010)
VERDONETTE INC
270 W 39th St Fl 5 (10018-4409)
PHONE.................................212 719-2003
EMP: 5
SALES (est): 310K **Privately Held**
SIC: 2395 Pleating/Stitching Services

(G-12011)
VERILED INC
100 Church St Ste 871 (10007-2601)
PHONE.................................877 521-5520
Michael Handerhan, *CEO*
EMP: 6
SQ FT: 2,000
SALES (est): 922.5K **Privately Held**
SIC: 3674 Light emitting diodes

(G-12012)
VERRIS INC
99 Wall St Unit 236 (10005-4301)
PHONE.................................201 565-1648
John Paris, *CEO*
Scott Berchin, *Senior VP*
EMP: 2 EST: 2017
SALES (est): 2MM **Privately Held**
SIC: 7372 7389 Prepackaged software;

(G-12013)
VERSAILLES INDUSTRIES LLC
485 Fashion Ave Rm 500 (10018-6804)
PHONE.................................212 792-9615
Freddy Hamra, *Mng Member*
▲ **EMP:** 6
SALES (est): 579.6K **Privately Held**
SIC: 2329 Riding clothes:, men's, youths' & boys'

(G-12014)
VERSO CORPORATION
370 Lexington Ave Rm 802 (10017-6510)
PHONE.................................212 599-2700
Gerhard Nussbaumer, *Principal*
EMP: 400 **Publicly Held**
SIC: 2621 3554 Paper mills; paper industries machinery
PA: Verso Corporation
    8540 Gander Creek Dr
    Miamisburg OH 45342

(G-12015)
VERSO PAPER MANAGEMENT LP
370 Lexington Ave Rm 802 (10017-6510)
PHONE.................................781 320-8660
Alvin Smart, *Branch Mgr*
EMP: 580 **Publicly Held**
SIC: 2621 Paper mills
PA: Verso Paper Management Lp
    60 W 42nd Ste 1942
    New York NY 10165

(G-12016)
VERSO PAPER MANAGEMENT LP (PA)
60 W 42nd Ste 1942 (10165)
PHONE.................................212 599-2700
Michael A Jackson, *President*
EMP: 3
SALES (est): 735.6MM **Privately Held**
SIC: 2621 Paper mills

(G-12017)
VERTANA GROUP LLC (PA)
Also Called: Killer Motor Sports
450 Lexington Ave Fl 4 (10017-3912)
PHONE.................................646 430-8226
Emmanuel Tesone, *President*
EMP: 5 EST: 2012
SALES (est): 2.5MM **Privately Held**
SIC: 7372 Prepackaged software

(G-12018)
VERTICAL RESEARCH PARTNERS LLC
52 Vanderbilt Ave Rm 200 (10017-3860)
PHONE.................................212 257-6499
EMP: 18
SALES (corp-wide): 4.4MM **Privately Held**
SIC: 2591 Drapery Hardware And Blinds And Shades
PA: Vertical Research Partners Llc
    1 Landmark Sq Fl 4
    Stamford CT 06901
    203 276-5680

(G-12019)
VETROELITE INC
115 W 30th St Rm 402 (10001-4179)
PHONE.................................925 724-7900
Daniele Feletto, *Ch of Bd*
▲ **EMP:** 6
SALES (est): 547.1K **Privately Held**
SIC: 3565 Packing & wrapping machinery

(G-12020)
VETTA JEWELRY INC (PA)
Also Called: Spring Street Design Group
989 Avenue Of The America (10018-0875)
PHONE.................................212 564-8250
Edwin Peissis, *Ch of Bd*
Mary Walsh, *President*
▲ **EMP:** 20
SALES (est): 4MM **Privately Held**
WEB: www.cosmotronics.com
SIC: 3961 Costume jewelry

(G-12021)
VEXOS INC (HQ)
60 E 42nd St Ste 1250 (10165-1299)
PHONE.................................855 711-3227
Paul Jona, *CEO*
Christopher Gallion, *Engineer*
Rory Kirkpatrick, *CFO*
Ken Lau, *Treasurer*
EMP: 27
SALES (est): 150MM **Privately Held**
SIC: 3672 Printed circuit boards

(G-12022)
VF SERVICES LLC
25 W 39th St (10018-3805)
P.O. Box 4307 (10163-4307)
PHONE.................................212 575-7820
Nina Flood, *VP Mktg*
EMP: 5
SALES (corp-wide): 11.8B **Publicly Held**
SIC: 2211 Apparel & outerwear fabrics, cotton
HQ: Vf Services, Llc
    105 Corporate Center Blvd
    Greensboro NC 27408
    336 424-6000

(G-12023)
VGG HOLDING LLC
590 Madison Ave Fl 41 (10022-2524)
PHONE.................................212 415-6700
EMP: 5
SALES (est): 587.8K **Privately Held**
SIC: 3674 Semiconductors & related devices

(G-12024)
VHX CORPORATION
555 W 18th St (10011-2822)
PHONE.................................347 689-1446
Jamie Wilkinson, *CEO*
Kevin Sheurs, *CTO*
EMP: 13 EST: 2013
SALES (est): 1.1MM
SALES (corp-wide): 3.3B **Publicly Held**
SIC: 7372 Application computer software
PA: Iac/Interactivecorp
    555 W 18th St
    New York NY 10011
    212 314-7300

(G-12025)
VIA AMERICA FINE JEWELRY INC
578 5th Ave Unit 26 (10036-4836)
PHONE.................................212 302-1218
Mary Yogurtcu, *President*
Sadik Yogurtco, *Vice Pres*
Harutyn Temurco, *Admin Sec*
EMP: 5
SQ FT: 3,000
SALES (est): 420K **Privately Held**
SIC: 3915 Jewelers' materials & lapidary work

(G-12026)
VIBE MEDIA GROUP LLC
Also Called: Vibe Magazine
120 Wall St Fl 21 (10005-4024)
P.O. Box 618180, Chicago IL (60661-8171)
PHONE.................................212 448-7300
Shenequa Golding, *Editor*
Danyel Smith, *Vice Pres*
Gary R Lewis, *Officer*
Steve Aaron,
EMP: 65
SALES (est): 3.9MM **Privately Held**
SIC: 2721 Periodicals

(G-12027)
VICKERS STOCK RESEARCH CORP (HQ)
61 Broadway Rm 1910 (10006-2761)
PHONE.................................212 425-7500
Fern Dorsey, *President*
EMP: 40
SQ FT: 5,000
SALES (est): 2.8MM
SALES (corp-wide): 12MM **Privately Held**
WEB: www.vickers-stock.com
SIC: 2721 Periodicals
PA: Argus Research Group Inc Del
    61 Broadway Rm 1702
    New York NY 10006
    212 425-7500

(G-12028)
VICTORIA ALBI INTERNATIONAL
Also Called: Makari
1178 Broadway Fl 5 (10001-5404)
PHONE.................................212 689-2600
Raquel Aini, *CEO*
Leah Hollender, *Sales Executive*
▲ **EMP:** 10
SALES (est): 1.7MM **Privately Held**
SIC: 2844 Cosmetic preparations

(G-12029)
VICTORY GARDEN
31 Carmine St Frnt A (10014-4427)
PHONE.................................212 206-7273
Sophia Brittain, *Owner*
EMP: 7 EST: 2011
SALES (est): 423.8K **Privately Held**
SIC: 2024 Ice cream, bulk

(G-12030)
VIDAL CANDIES USA INC
845 3rd Ave Fl 6 (10022-6630)
PHONE.................................609 781-8169
Mitchell Bernstein, *Sales Staff*
▲ **EMP:** 9
SALES (est): 988.2K
SALES (corp-wide): 93.8MM **Privately Held**
SIC: 2064 Candy & other confectionery products
PA: Vidal Golosinas Sa
    Avenida Gutierrez Mellado, S/N
    Molina De Segura 30500
    968 647-100

(G-12031)
VIEW COLLECTIONS INC
265 W 37th St Rm 5w (10018-5750)
PHONE.................................212 944-4030
David Shavolian, *President*
Nathan Shavolian, *Chairman*
EMP: 12
SQ FT: 6,000
SALES (est): 1.2MM **Privately Held**
SIC: 2337 Suits: women's, misses' & juniors'

(G-12032)
VIEWFINDER INC
Also Called: First View
101 W 23rd St Ste 2303 (10011-2490)
PHONE.................................212 831-0939
Donald Asbey, *President*
Marcio Moraes, *Vice Pres*
EMP: 5 EST: 1995

GEOGRAPHIC SECTION

New York - New York County (G-12063)

SALES (est): 574.9K **Privately Held**
WEB: www.firstview.com
SIC: 2741 Miscellaneous publishing

(G-12033)
VIKTOR GOLD ENTERPRISE CORP
58 W 47th St Unit 36 (10036-8610)
PHONE..................................212 768-8885
Boris Yakutilov, *Principal*
EMP: 3 EST: 1996
SALES: 1MM **Privately Held**
SIC: 3911 Jewelry, precious metal

(G-12034)
VILEBREQUIN
160 Varick St Fl 2 (10013-1251)
PHONE..................................212 546-9220
Emily Unale, *Principal*
Jeffery Lamb, *Area Mgr*
Stacey Bell, *Store Mgr*
Marie Gloria, *Engineer*
Joysree Sharma, *Accountant*
EMP: 7
SALES (est): 51.7K **Privately Held**
SIC: 2253 Bathing suits & swimwear, knit

(G-12035)
VILLEROY & BOCH USA INC
41 Madison Ave Ste 1801 (10010-2226)
PHONE..................................212 213-8149
EMP: 11
SALES (corp-wide): 986.4MM **Privately Held**
SIC: 3089 Plastic kitchenware, tableware & houseware
HQ: Villeroy & Boch Usa, Inc.
3a S Middlesex Ave
Monroe Township NJ 08831
800 536-2284

(G-12036)
VINOUS GROUP LLC
Also Called: Delectable
54 W 40th St (10018-2602)
PHONE..................................917 275-5184
EMP: 6 EST: 2016
SQ FT: 100
SALES (est): 170.5K **Privately Held**
SIC: 2741 Internet Publishing And Broadcasting

(G-12037)
VIRGIL MOUNTAIN INC (PA)
1 E 28th St Fl 4 (10016-7432)
PHONE..................................212 378-0007
Stephen Dignam, *President*
Edmund Mandrala, *Corp Secy*
Gerard Glenn, *Vice Pres*
▲ EMP: 8
SQ FT: 5,000
SALES (est): 1MM **Privately Held**
SIC: 2752 Commercial printing, lithographic

(G-12038)
VIRIDIS LEARNING INC
2 Gold St Apt 4005 (10038-4862)
PHONE..................................347 420-9181
Felix Ortiz, *CEO*
Felix W Ortiz III, *Principal*
Alex Carstens, *COO*
EMP: 6
SALES (est): 33.2K **Privately Held**
SIC: 7372 Prepackaged software

(G-12039)
VIROPRO INC
49 W 38th St Fl 11 (10018-1933)
PHONE..................................650 300-5190
Bruce A Cohen, *Ch of Bd*
Joseph J Vallner, *President*
Scott M Brown, *Security Dir*
EMP: 34
SALES (est): 1.8MM **Privately Held**
SIC: 2834 Pharmaceutical preparations

(G-12040)
VIRTUAL FRAMEWORKS INC
115 5th Ave Frnt 2 (10003-1004)
PHONE..................................646 690-8207
Tomer Benami, *Vice Pres*
EMP: 16
SALES (est): 470.1K **Privately Held**
SIC: 7372 Application computer software

(G-12041)
VIRTUAL SUPER LLC
116 E 27th St Fl 3 (10016-8942)
PHONE..................................212 685-6400
Joshua Smith,
EMP: 5
SALES (est): 50K **Privately Held**
SIC: 3822 Building services monitoring controls, automatic

(G-12042)
VISION LOGIC INC
300 Park Ave Fl 12 (10022-7419)
PHONE..................................212 729-4606
Lou Bivona, *President*
John Walsh, *Principal*
Graham Conran, *COO*
Rick Urban, *Vice Pres*
EMP: 5 EST: 2016
SALES (est): 500K **Privately Held**
SIC: 7372 7373 Application computer software; value-added resellers, computer systems

(G-12043)
VISIONAIRE PUBLISHING LLC
Also Called: V Magazine
30 W 24th St (10010-3207)
PHONE..................................646 434-6091
William Defebaugh, *Editor*
Donald Hearn, *Prdtn Dir*
Ivana Williams, *Asst Controller*
Lars Petersen, *Director*
Stephen Gan,
▲ EMP: 20
SALES (est): 3.1MM **Privately Held**
WEB: www.visionaireworld.com
SIC: 2721 Magazines: publishing only, not printed on site

(G-12044)
VITAFEDE (PA)
25 W 26th St Fl 5 (10010-1039)
PHONE..................................213 488-0136
▲ EMP: 10
SALES (est): 4.9MM **Privately Held**
SIC: 3961 Mfg Costume Jewelry

(G-12045)
VITALIS LLC
902 Broadway Fl 6 (10010-6039)
PHONE..................................646 831-7338
Joseph Habboushe,
EMP: 5 EST: 2012
SALES (est): 58.7K **Privately Held**
SIC: 2834 Pharmaceutical preparations

(G-12046)
VITALIZE LABS LLC
Also Called: Eboost
134 Spring St Ste 502 (10012-3886)
PHONE..................................212 966-6130
Malijian Sjam, *CFO*
Thomas Ortis, *Marketing Staff*
John McDonald, *Associate Dir*
Josh Taekman,
EMP: 5
SQ FT: 1,000
SALES: 3MM **Privately Held**
SIC: 2833 Vitamins, natural or synthetic: bulk, uncompounded

(G-12047)
VITRA INC (DH)
10 Gansevoort St (10014)
PHONE..................................212 463-5700
Rolf Fehlbaum, *CEO*
Agneta Ferdfelt, *Sales Staff*
Claudette Marasigan, *Manager*
◆ EMP: 16
SALES (est): 15.3MM **Privately Held**
SIC: 2522 Chairs, office: padded or plain, except wood
HQ: Vitra Collections Ag
Klunenfeldstrasse 22
Muttenz BL
418 111-327

(G-12048)
VIZBEE INC
120 E 23rd St Fl 5 (10010-4519)
PHONE..................................650 787-1424
Darren Feher, *CEO*
Prashanth Pappu, *Principal*
EMP: 8

SALES (est): 200K **Privately Held**
SIC: 7372 7371 Home entertainment computer software; computer software systems analysis & design, custom

(G-12049)
VIZIO MEDICAL DEVICES LLC
200 Chambers St Apt 28a (10007-1350)
PHONE..................................646 845-7382
EMP: 10
SALES (est): 600K **Privately Held**
SIC: 3841 Mfg Surgical/Medical Instruments

(G-12050)
VNOVOM SVETE
55 Broad St Fl 20 (10004-2501)
PHONE..................................212 302-9480
Helen Brusilovski, *Principal*
EMP: 9 EST: 2012
SALES (est): 318.5K **Privately Held**
SIC: 2711 Commercial printing & newspaper publishing combined

(G-12051)
VOGEL APPLIED TECHNOLOGIES
Also Called: Brainwave Toys-New York
36 E 12th St Fl 7 (10003-4604)
PHONE..................................212 677-3136
David Vogel, *President*
EMP: 1
SQ FT: 500
SALES: 1MM **Privately Held**
WEB: www.brainwavetoys.com
SIC: 3944 Games, toys & children's vehicles

(G-12052)
VOGUE TOO PLTING STITCHING EMB
265 W 37th St Fl 14 (10018-5707)
PHONE..................................212 354-1022
Larry Geffner, *President*
EMP: 13 EST: 2001
SALES (est): 1.1MM **Privately Held**
SIC: 2395 Pleating & tucking, for the trade

(G-12053)
VON MUSULIN PATRICIA
148 W 24th St Fl 10 (10011-1951)
PHONE..................................212 206-8345
Patricia Von Musulin, *President*
EMP: 8
SALES (est): 610K **Privately Held**
SIC: 3911 3961 Jewelry, precious metal; jewelry apparel, non-precious metals

(G-12054)
VON POK & CHANG NEW YORK INC
4 E 43rd St Fl 7 (10017-4607)
PHONE..................................212 599-0556
Omega Chang, *President*
▲ EMP: 6
SQ FT: 1,000
SALES (est): 4.8MM **Privately Held**
WEB: www.vonpok.com
SIC: 3993 Advertising novelties

(G-12055)
VONDOM LLC
979 3rd Ave Ste 1532 (10022-3806)
PHONE..................................212 207-3252
Olga Tomas, *CFO*
Antonio Esteve,
▲ EMP: 4
SALES: 1.6MM **Privately Held**
SIC: 2519 Furniture, household: glass, fiberglass & plastic

(G-12056)
VOSS USA INC
236 W 30th St Rm 900 (10001-0900)
PHONE..................................212 995-2255
Jack Baelsito, *CEO*
Antoinette Borromeo, *Regional Mgr*
Joe Bayern, *COO*
Mark Zettle, *Vice Pres*
Tuula Vartiainen, *Opers Mgr*
◆ EMP: 150
SQ FT: 1,000
SALES (est): 36MM **Privately Held**
SIC: 3561 Pumps & pumping equipment

HQ: Voss Of Norway As
Vatnestrom Industriomrade 5
Vatnestrom 4730
231 316-16

(G-12057)
VSM INVESTORS LLC (PA)
245 Park Ave Fl 41 (10167-0002)
PHONE..................................212 351-1600
◆ EMP: 1 EST: 2000
SALES (est): 402.8MM **Privately Held**
SIC: 3842 2599 2515 Wheelchairs; personal safety equipment; respirators; hospital beds; hospital furniture, except beds; mattresses & foundations

(G-12058)
VVS INTERNATIONAL INC
2 W 46th St (10036-4811)
PHONE..................................212 302-5410
EMP: 5
SALES (est): 252.8K **Privately Held**
SIC: 2834 Pharmaceutical preparations

(G-12059)
VYERA PHARMACEUTICALS LLC
600 3rd Ave Fl 10 (10016-1923)
PHONE..................................646 356-5577
Kevin Mulleady, *CEO*
Eliseo Salinas, *President*
Howard L Dorfman, *Senior VP*
Nicholas Pelliccione, *Vice Pres*
Michael Harrison, *CFO*
EMP: 25
SALES (est): 10.1MM
SALES (corp-wide): 1.1MM **Privately Held**
SIC: 2836 5122 Biological products, except diagnostic; pharmaceuticals
PA: Phoenixus Ag
Haldenstrasse 5
Baar ZG 6340
417 602-424

(G-12060)
W B BOW TIE CORP
Also Called: Bentley Cravats
521 W 26th St Fl 6 (10001-5531)
PHONE..................................212 683-6130
Walter Schick, *President*
Marion Schick, *Admin Sec*
EMP: 10 EST: 1948
SQ FT: 10,000
SALES (est): 514.9K **Privately Held**
SIC: 2323 Neckties, men's & boys': made from purchased materials

(G-12061)
W W NORTON & COMPANY INC (PA)
500 5th Ave Fl 6 (10110-0054)
PHONE..................................212 354-5500
W Drake McFeely, *President*
Amber Watkins, *Publisher*
Katie Adams, *Editor*
Katherine Brayton, *Editor*
John Elliott, *Editor*
▲ EMP: 130 EST: 1923
SQ FT: 30,000
SALES (est): 185.1MM **Privately Held**
WEB: www.wwnorton.com
SIC: 2731 5192 Textbooks: publishing only, not printed on site; books: publishing only; books

(G-12062)
W W NORTON & COMPANY INC
Countryman Press, The
500 5th Ave Lbby 1 (10110-0105)
PHONE..................................212 354-5500
Ann Treistman, *Branch Mgr*
EMP: 8
SALES (corp-wide): 185.1MM **Privately Held**
SIC: 2731 Book publishing
PA: W. W. Norton & Company, Inc.
500 5th Ave Fl 6
New York NY 10110
212 354-5500

(G-12063)
WACOAL AMERICA INC
Also Called: Dkny Underwear
136 Madison Ave Fl 15 (10016-6787)
PHONE..................................212 743-9600

New York - New York County (G-12064)   **GEOGRAPHIC SECTION**

Virginia Grudichak, *Sales Staff*
Rich Murray, *Branch Mgr*
Margarita Yagudayeva, *Manager*
Sandra Lopez, *Consultant*
Kenneth Gonzalez, *Programmer Anys*
EMP: 30
SALES (corp-wide): 1.8B **Privately Held**
WEB: www.wacoal-america.com
SIC: 2342 Bras, girdles & allied garments
HQ: Wacoal America, Inc.
1 Wacoal Plz
Lyndhurst NJ 07071
201 933-8400

(G-12064)
WACOAL INTERNATIONAL CORP
136 Madison Ave Fl 15 (10016-6787)
PHONE..................212 532-6100
Richard C Murray, *President*
EMP: 100
SALES (corp-wide): 1.8B **Privately Held**
SIC: 2341 Women's & children's undergarments
HQ: Wacoal International Corp
1 Wacoal Plz
Lyndhurst NJ 07071
201 933-8400

(G-12065)
WALDMAN ALEXANDER M DIAMOND CO
Also Called: Waldman Diamond Company
30 W 47th St Ste 805 (10036-8644)
PHONE..................212 921-8098
Alexander M Waldman, *President*
Leon Waldman, *Admin Sec*
EMP: 35
SQ FT: 3,500
SALES (est): 4.6MM **Privately Held**
WEB: www.wdcgroup.com
SIC: 3915 5094 Diamond cutting & polishing; diamonds (gems)

(G-12066)
WALDMAN PUBLISHING CORPORATION (PA)
570 Fashion Ave Rm 800 (10018-1603)
P.O. Box 1587 (10028-0013)
PHONE..................212 730-9590
Rachel Waldman, *Ch of Bd*
▲ **EMP:** 10 **EST:** 1961
SQ FT: 3,200
SALES (est): 2.4MM **Privately Held**
SIC: 2731 Textbooks: publishing only, not printed on site

(G-12067)
WALL STREET REPORTER MAGAZINE
419 Lafayette St Fl 2 (10003-7033)
PHONE..................212 363-2600
Jack Marks, *President*
Alan Wolski, *Treasurer*
EMP: 62 **EST:** 1993
SQ FT: 9,000
SALES: 4MM **Privately Held**
WEB: www.wallstreetreporter.com
SIC: 2721 Magazines: publishing & printing

(G-12068)
WALLACE REFINERS INC
15 W 47th St Ste 808 (10036-5703)
PHONE..................212 391-2649
EMP: 5
SQ FT: 1,500
SALES (est): 510K **Privately Held**
SIC: 3339 5094 Refine Buys And Wholesales Precious Metals

(G-12069)
WARM
181 Mott St Frnt 1 (10012-4581)
PHONE..................212 925-1200
Rob Magnotta, *Principal*
EMP: 10 **EST:** 2014
SALES (est): 427K **Privately Held**
SIC: 2253 Warm weather knit outerwear, including beachwear

(G-12070)
WARNACO GROUP INC (HQ)
501 Fashion Ave (10018-5903)
PHONE..................212 287-8000
Helen McCluskey, *CEO*

James B Gerson, *President*
Joanne Kaye, *President*
Martha Olson, *President*
Michael Prendergast, *President*
◆ **EMP:** 30
SALES: 794.2MM
SALES (corp-wide): 8.9B **Publicly Held**
SIC: 2322 2329 2339 2369 Underwear, men's & boys': made from purchased materials; men's & boys' sportswear & athletic clothing; women's & misses' outerwear; bathing suits: women's, misses' & juniors'; beachwear: women's, misses' & juniors'; children's bathing suits & beachwear; bras, girdles & allied garments; brassieres; girdles & panty girdles; panties: women's, misses', children's & infants'; women's & children's nightwear
PA: Pvh Corp.
200 Madison Ave Bsmt 1
New York NY 10016
212 381-3500

(G-12071)
WARNACO INC (DH)
Also Called: Warner S
501 Fashion Ave Fl 14 (10018-5942)
PHONE..................212 287-8000
Joseph R Gromek, *Ch of Bd*
Charles R Perrin, *Ch of Bd*
Helen McCluskey, *President*
Les Hall, *President*
Larry Rutkowski, *Exec VP*
◆ **EMP:** 300 **EST:** 1874
SQ FT: 25,000
SALES (est): 670.5MM
SALES (corp-wide): 8.9B **Publicly Held**
WEB: www.warnaco.com
SIC: 2341 2321 2329 2322 Panties: women's, misses', children's & infants'; women's & children's nightwear; men's & boys' dress shirts; men's & boys' sportswear & athletic clothing; underwear, men's & boys': made from purchased materials; men's & boys' neckwear; brassieres
HQ: The Warnaco Group Inc
501 Fashion Ave
New York NY 10018
212 287-8000

(G-12072)
WARNER MUSIC GROUP CORP (DH)
1633 Broadway (10019-6708)
PHONE..................212 275-2000
Stu Bergen, *CEO*
Stephen Cooper, *CEO*
Cameron Strang, *CEO*
Len Blavatnik, *Vice Ch Bd*
Maria Osherova, *Exec VP*
EMP: 255
SALES: 3.5B **Privately Held**
SIC: 3652 6794 Pre-recorded records & tapes; music licensing & royalties

(G-12073)
WARNER MUSIC INC (DH)
1633 Broadway (10019-6708)
PHONE..................212 275-2000
Paul Rene' Albertini, *President*
Howie Singer, *President*
Scott Hendricks, *Exec VP*
David H Johnson, *Exec VP*
Dale Hecker, *Senior VP*
▼ **EMP:** 100
SQ FT: 333,500
SALES (est): 780.2MM **Privately Held**
SIC: 2741 3652 Music, sheet: publishing & printing; phonograph records, prerecorded
HQ: Wmg Acquisition Corp.
75 Rockefeller Plz
New York NY 10019
212 275-2000

(G-12074)
WARREN CORPORATION (DH)
711 5th Ave Fl 11 (10022-3113)
PHONE..................917 379-3434
Pier Guerci, *President*
Guy Birkhead, *Senior VP*
Lisa Cornish, *Vice Pres*
Richard Anderman, *Admin Sec*
◆ **EMP:** 180 **EST:** 1853
SQ FT: 330,000

SALES (est): 21MM **Privately Held**
WEB: www.warrencorp.com
SIC: 2231 Overcoatings: wool, mohair or similar fibers; suitings: wool, mohair or similar fibers
HQ: Loro Piana Spa
Corso Pietro Rolandi 10
Quarona VC 13017
016 320-1111

(G-12075)
WARREN ENERGY SERVICES LLC
1114 Ave Of The Americas (10036-7703)
PHONE..................212 697-9660
Gonzalo Bucio, *Production*
Donny Arnold, *Manager*
Greg Fox, *Manager*
Allen Veith, *Supervisor*
James A Watt,
EMP: 10
SQ FT: 4,200
SALES (est): 409.7K **Publicly Held**
SIC: 1382 Oil & gas exploration services
PA: Warren Resources, Inc.
5420 Lbj Fwy Ste 600
Dallas TX 75240

(G-12076)
WASTECORP PUMPS LLC (PA)
345 W 85th St Apt 23 (10024-3834)
P.O. Box 70, Grand Island (14072-0070)
PHONE..................888 829-2783
Marc Johnson, *Engineer*
Dan Starr,
◆ **EMP:** 10
SQ FT: 2,000,000
SALES (est): 1.3MM **Privately Held**
SIC: 3561 Pumps & pumping equipment

(G-12077)
WATCH JOURNAL LLC
110 E 25th St Fl 4 (10010-2913)
PHONE..................212 229-1500
John Clarkin, *Publisher*
Marc Lotenberg,
EMP: 6
SALES (est): 1.7MM **Privately Held**
SIC: 2721 Magazines: publishing & printing

(G-12078)
WATCHANISH LLC
1 Rockefeller Plz Fl 11 (10020-2073)
PHONE..................917 558-0404
Anish Bhatt, *Principal*
EMP: 10
SALES (est): 249.7K **Privately Held**
SIC: 2741 Miscellaneous publishing

(G-12079)
WATER ENERGY SYSTEMS LLC
1 Maiden Ln (10038-4015)
PHONE..................844 822-7665
EMP: 8 **EST:** 2015
SALES (est): 431K **Privately Held**
SIC: 3589 Mfg Service Industry Machinery

(G-12080)
WATERBURY GARMENT LLC
Also Called: Jackie's Girls
16 E 34th St Fl 10 (10016-4360)
PHONE..................212 725-1500
Daniel Livingston, *President*
Harry Gaffney, *CFO*
▲ **EMP:** 30 **EST:** 1921
SQ FT: 19,000
SALES (est): 1.6MM
SALES (corp-wide): 310.7MM **Privately Held**
WEB: www.waterburygarment.com
SIC: 2341 2369 2322 Women's & children's nightwear; children's robes & housecoats; men's & boys' underwear & nightwear
HQ: Komar Kids, L.L.C.
90 Hudson St
Jersey City NJ 07302
212 725-1500

(G-12081)
WATSON ADVENTURES LLC
330 W 38th St Rm 407 (10018-8307)
PHONE..................212 564-8293
Daniel Maranon, *Principal*
Eileen Gribbon, *Accounts Mgr*
Tara Melvin, *Accounts Mgr*

Corin Coyle, *Sales Staff*
EMP: 6
SALES (est): 550.2K **Privately Held**
SIC: 3949 Sporting & athletic goods

(G-12082)
WAY OUT TOYS INC
230 5th Ave Ste 800 (10001-7851)
PHONE..................212 689-9094
Eddie Mishan, *President*
Al Mishan, *Vice Pres*
Jeffrey Mishan, *Vice Pres*
Steven Mishan, *Vice Pres*
EMP: 6
SALES (est): 660K **Privately Held**
SIC: 3944 5092 Games, toys & children's vehicles; toys & games

(G-12083)
WE WORK
1 Little West 12th St (10014-1302)
PHONE..................877 673-6628
EMP: 7
SALES (est): 454.2K **Privately Held**
SIC: 2011 Meat packing plants

(G-12084)
WEA INTERNATIONAL INC (DH)
75 Rockefeller Plz (10019-6908)
PHONE..................212 275-1300
Tom Shaheen, *President*
Keith Bruce, *Senior VP*
EMP: 100
SQ FT: 3,500
SALES (est): 127.9MM **Privately Held**
SIC: 3652 Master records or tapes, preparation of

(G-12085)
WEAR ABOUTS APPAREL INC
260 W 36th St Rm 602 (10018-7603)
PHONE..................212 827-0888
Kim Yu, *President*
Sandy Wu, *Production*
▲ **EMP:** 12 **EST:** 1998
SQ FT: 4,500
SALES (est): 4.1MM **Privately Held**
SIC: 2335 Women's, juniors' & misses' dresses

(G-12086)
WEEKLY BUSINESS NEWS CORP
274 Madison Ave Rm 1101 (10016-0700)
PHONE..................212 689-5888
Yoshiaki Takahashi, *President*
EMP: 6
SALES (est): 222.5K **Privately Held**
SIC: 2711 Newspapers, publishing & printing

(G-12087)
WEIDER PUBLICATIONS LLC
Also Called: A M I
1 Park Ave Fl 10 (10016-5818)
PHONE..................212 545-4800
Mirel Ketchiff, *Editor*
Beverly Levy, *Branch Mgr*
EMP: 200
SALES (corp-wide): 300MM **Privately Held**
WEB: www.fitnessonline.com
SIC: 2721 Magazines: publishing only, not printed on site
HQ: Weider Publications, Llc
3699 Wilshire Blvd # 1220
Los Angeles CA 90010

(G-12088)
WEISCO INC
246 W 38th St Fl 6 (10018-5854)
PHONE..................212 575-8989
Alex Weiss, *President*
Edward Weiss, *Vice Pres*
Peter Weiss, *Treasurer*
EMP: 15
SQ FT: 7,000
SALES (est): 1.5MM **Privately Held**
WEB: www.weisco.com
SIC: 3911 Jewelry, precious metal

GEOGRAPHIC SECTION

New York - New York County (G-12117)

(G-12089)
WELCOME RAIN PUBLISHERS LLC
Also Called: South Brooklyn Book Company
230 5th Ave (10001-7704)
PHONE..................212 686-1909
John Weber,
EMP: 2
SALES: 1.5MM Privately Held
SIC: 2741 Miscellaneous publishing

(G-12090)
WELDING CHAPTER OF NEW YORK
44 W 28th St Fl 12 (10001-4212)
PHONE..................212 481-1496
Ray Hopkins, President
EMP: 5
SALES (est): 379.6K Privately Held
SIC: 7692 Welding repair

(G-12091)
WELLQUEST INTERNATIONAL INC (PA)
230 5th Ave Ste 800 (10001-7851)
PHONE..................212 689-9094
Eddie Mishan, President
Al Mishan, Vice Pres
Isaac Mishan, Vice Pres
Morris Mishan, Vice Pres
▲ EMP: 6
SQ FT: 2,000
SALES (est): 847.4K Privately Held
WEB: www.wellquestinternational.com
SIC: 2833 5122 Vitamins, natural or synthetic: bulk, uncompounded; vitamins & minerals

(G-12092)
WELLSPRING CORP (PA)
54a Ludlow St (10002-5410)
PHONE..................212 529-5454
Yon K Lai, Ch of Bd
Danny Lai, President
EMP: 5
SQ FT: 1,000
SALES (est): 741.4K Privately Held
WEB: www.wellspringcorp.com
SIC: 2064 5149 Candy & other confectionery products; groceries & related products; chocolate; mineral or spring water bottling; crackers, cookies & bakery products

(G-12093)
WELLSPRING OMNI HOLDINGS CORP
390 Park Ave (10022-4608)
PHONE..................212 318-9800
William F Dawson Jr, President
Joshua C Cascade, Corp Secy
EMP: 950
SALES (est): 12.1MM Privately Held
SIC: 1382 1389 7349 Seismograph surveys; lease tanks, oil field: erecting, cleaning & repairing; cleaning service, industrial or commercial

(G-12094)
WENNER MEDIA LLC (PA)
Also Called: Rolling Stone
1290 Ave Of The Amer Fl 2 (10104-0295)
P.O. Box 30895 (10087-0895)
PHONE..................212 484-1616
Hugh Scogin, CEO
Dana L Fields, Publisher
Steven Schwartz, Chairman
Katey Distefano, COO
Amber Mundinger, Senior VP
▲ EMP: 250
SQ FT: 75,000
SALES (est): 63.3MM Privately Held
SIC: 2721 Magazines: publishing & printing

(G-12095)
WEST INTERNET TRADING COMPANY
Also Called: Idonethis
47 Great Jones St Fl 5 (10012-1196)
PHONE..................415 484-5848
EMP: 6
SALES (est): 320K Privately Held
SIC: 7372 Prepackaged Software Services

(G-12096)
WESTPOINT HOME LLC (HQ)
28 E 28th St Cncrse Level (10016)
PHONE..................212 930-2000
Jud Lusk, Vice Pres
Justin Coffey, Opers Mgr
Cindy Norman, Senior Buyer
Mike Smith, VP Human Res
Jen Gulley, Sales Staff
◆ EMP: 800
SALES (est): 784MM
SALES (corp-wide): 21.7B Publicly Held
SIC: 2221 2211 Bedding, manmade or silk fabric; sheets, bedding & table cloths: cotton
PA: Icahn Enterprises L.P.
767 5th Ave Ste 4700
New York NY 10153
212 702-4300

(G-12097)
WESTROCK MWV LLC
299 Park Ave Fl 13 (10171-3800)
PHONE..................212 688-5000
Luke John, Trustee
Jeff Jensen, Vice Pres
Tony Milikin, Vice Pres
John Cherry, Sales Staff
John A Luke, Branch Mgr
EMP: 227
SALES (corp-wide): 14.8B Publicly Held
WEB: www.meadwestvaco.com
SIC: 2631 2671 2678 2677 Linerboard; packaging paper & plastics film, coated & laminated; stationery products; envelopes; gum & wood chemicals
HQ: Westrock Mwv, Llc
501 S 5th St
Richmond VA 23219
804 444-1000

(G-12098)
WETPAINTCOM INC
Also Called: Wet Paint
45 W 89th St Apt 4a (10024-2078)
PHONE..................206 859-6300
Ben Elowitz, CEO
Bert Hogue, CFO
EMP: 38
SALES (est): 3MM
SALES (corp-wide): 4.5MM Publicly Held
WEB: www.wetpaint.com
SIC: 7372 7371 Prepackaged software; custom computer programming services
PA: X Function Inc
45 W 89th St Apt 4a
New York NY 10024
212 231-0092

(G-12099)
WEY INC
21 W 39th St Fl 6 (10018-0614)
PHONE..................212 532-3299
Matt Zierdniewski, President
EMP: 7
SALES (est): 645.5K Privately Held
SIC: 3575 Keyboards, computer, office machine

(G-12100)
WHENTECH LLC (DH)
55 E 52nd St Fl 40 (10055-0005)
PHONE..................212 571-0042
David Wender,
EMP: 10
SALES (est): 2.8MM
SALES (corp-wide): 4.6B Publicly Held
WEB: www.whentech.com
SIC: 7372 Business oriented computer software

(G-12101)
WHISPR GROUP INC
6 Saint Johns Ln (10013-2115)
PHONE..................212 924-3979
Joakim Leijon, President
Katy Haas, Manager
EMP: 13 EST: 2009
SQ FT: 4,000
SALES (est): 1MM Privately Held
SIC: 3993 5199 7389 7311 Advertising artwork; advertising specialties; ; advertising consultant

(G-12102)
WHITE GATE HOLDINGS INC (PA)
22 W 38th St Fl 6 (10018-0107)
PHONE..................212 564-3266
Michael Nolan, President
Kevin Joss, Vice Pres
Stephi Ruben, Vice Pres
Ellen Lipkin, CFO
▲ EMP: 20
SALES (est): 4.6MM Privately Held
WEB: www.nolanglove.com
SIC: 2339 Women's & misses' accessories

(G-12103)
WHITE LABEL PARTNERS LLC
250 Mercer St Apt B1205 (10012-6125)
PHONE..................917 445-6650
Mark Kaplan,
EMP: 5
SALES (est): 286.6K Privately Held
SIC: 7372 Application computer software

(G-12104)
WHITE WORKROOM INC
40 W 27th St Fl 11 (10001-6944)
PHONE..................212 941-5910
Vivian White, Partner
Gary Weisner, Partner
EMP: 6
SQ FT: 1,000
SALES (est): 280K Privately Held
SIC: 2391 Curtains & draperies

(G-12105)
WHITEBOARD VENTURES INC
Also Called: Xpand
315 W 36th St Fl 10 (10018-6527)
PHONE..................855 972-6346
Deb Bardhan, CEO
Kalyan Anumula, President
EMP: 16
SALES (est): 51.6K Privately Held
SIC: 7372 Application computer software

(G-12106)
WHITTALL & SHON (PA)
1201 Broadway Ste 904a (10001-5656)
PHONE..................212 594-2626
Elliot Whittall, President
Richard Shon, Vice Pres
EMP: 3
SALES (est): 14.2MM Privately Held
SIC: 2353 2321 Hats: cloth, straw & felt; millinery; men's & boys' furnishings

(G-12107)
WICKED SPOON INC
127 W 24th St Fl 6 (10011-1943)
PHONE..................646 335-2890
Alex Rozhitsky, President
EMP: 11
SALES: 750K Privately Held
SIC: 2024 Ice cream & frozen desserts

(G-12108)
WIDMER TIME RECORDER COMPANY
27 Park Pl Rm 219 (10007-2526)
PHONE..................212 227-0405
Robert Widmer, President
James Carney, Administration
EMP: 10
SALES (corp-wide): 8.8MM Privately Held
WEB: www.widmertime.com
SIC: 3579 Time clocks & time recording devices
PA: Widmer Time Recorder Company Inc
228 Park St
Hackensack NJ 07601
201 489-3810

(G-12109)
WILLCO FINE ART LTD
145 Nassau St Apt 9c (10038-1514)
PHONE..................718 935-9567
William Wolod, President
EMP: 10
SALES: 700K Privately Held
SIC: 2759 Commercial printing

(G-12110)
WILLIAM GOLDBERG DIAMOND CORP
589 5th Ave Fl 14 (10017-7293)
PHONE..................212 980-4343
Saul Goldberg, Ch of Bd
Benjamin Goldberg, President
Eve Goldberg, Vice Pres
Lili Goldberg, CFO
EMP: 20 EST: 1954
SQ FT: 6,000
SALES (est): 4.6MM Privately Held
SIC: 3915 3911 5094 Diamond cutting or polishing; jewelry, precious metal; jewelry & precious stones

(G-12111)
WILLIAM H SADLIER INC (PA)
9 Pine St (10005-4701)
P.O. Box 5685, Hicksville (11802-5685)
PHONE..................212 233-3646
Frank S Dinger, Ch of Bd
Ray Fagan, President
William S Dinger, President
Suzan Larroquette, Division Mgr
Rosemary Calicchio, Exec VP
◆ EMP: 111 EST: 1928
SQ FT: 56,000
SALES (est): 61.1MM Privately Held
WEB: www.sadlier.com
SIC: 2731 Books: publishing only

(G-12112)
WILLIAM H SHAPIRO
Also Called: Shapiro Wliam NY Univ Med Ctr
530 1st Ave Ste 3e (10016-6402)
PHONE..................212 263-7037
William H Shapiro, Owner
EMP: 5 EST: 1999
SALES (est): 424.9K Privately Held
SIC: 3842 Hearing aids

(G-12113)
WILLIAM SOMERVILLE MAINTENANCE
129 E 124th St (10035-1934)
PHONE..................212 534-4600
Merna Miller, President
EMP: 68
SQ FT: 40,000
SALES (est): 5.2MM Privately Held
SIC: 2511 Wood household furniture

(G-12114)
WILLIAMS-SONOMA STORES INC
Also Called: Williams-Sonoma Store 154
110 7th Ave (10011-1801)
PHONE..................212 633-2203
Donnie Cassell, Manager
EMP: 13
SALES (corp-wide): 5.2B Publicly Held
SIC: 3263 Cookware, fine earthenware
HQ: Williams-Sonoma Stores, Inc.
3250 Van Ness Ave
San Francisco CA 94109
415 421-7900

(G-12115)
WILLIS MC DONALD CO INC
44 W 62nd St Ph A (10023-7039)
PHONE..................212 366-1526
Jerry Dennehy, President
EMP: 15
SQ FT: 10,000
SALES: 1.3MM Privately Held
SIC: 2759 2732 Periodicals: printing; pamphlets: printing only, not published on site

(G-12116)
WILMAX USA LLC
315 5th Ave Rm 505 (10016-6592)
PHONE..................917 388-2790
Maksym Kyrylov,
EMP: 15
SQ FT: 1,500
SALES (est): 1MM Privately Held
SIC: 3469 Cooking ware, porcelain enameled

(G-12117)
WINDIAM USA INC
580 5th Ave Ste 2907 (10036-4724)
PHONE..................212 542-0949
Sacha Zaidman, CEO

New York - New York County (G-12118)   GEOGRAPHIC SECTION

EMP: 6
SALES (est): 19.3K **Privately Held**
SIC: 3915 Diamond cutting & polishing

(G-12118)
WINE & SPIRITS MAGAZINE INC (PA)
2 W 32nd St Ste 601 (10001-3834)
PHONE.................................212 695-4660
Joshua Greene, *President*
Marcy Crimmins, *Vice Pres*
Roy Schneider, *Finance Dir*
EMP: 6
SQ FT: 2,300
SALES (est): 1MM **Privately Held**
WEB: www.wineandspiritsmagazine.com
SIC: 2721 Magazines: publishing only, not printed on site

(G-12119)
WING HEUNG NOODLE INC
144 Baxter St (10013-3605)
PHONE.................................212 966-7496
Ng Shoong Kwong, *Ch of Bd*
EMP: 13
SQ FT: 2,000
SALES (est): 910K **Privately Held**
WEB: www.chicago-chinatown.com
SIC: 2098 Noodles (e.g. egg, plain & water), dry

(G-12120)
WING KEI NOODLE INC
102 Canal St (10002-6004)
PHONE.................................212 226-1644
Yik Pui Kong, *Ch of Bd*
EMP: 17
SQ FT: 1,200
SALES (est): 1.5MM **Privately Held**
SIC: 2098 Macaroni products (e.g. alphabets, rings & shells), dry

(G-12121)
WINK INC
606 W 28th St Fl 6 (10001-1108)
PHONE.................................212 389-1382
EMP: 45 **EST:** 2013
SALES (est): 2.2MM
SALES (corp-wide): 19.5MM **Privately Held**
SIC: 7372 5961 Prepackaged Software Services Ret Mail-Order House
PA: Quirky, Inc.
    606 W 28th St Fl 7
    New York NY 10001
    212 389-4759

(G-12122)
WINK LABS INC (DH)
Also Called: Wink Acquisition Corp.
606 W 28th St Fl 7 (10001-1177)
PHONE.................................916 717-0437
Nathan Smith, *President*
EMP: 30
SQ FT: 6,000
SALES (est): 14.2MM
SALES (corp-wide): 23.8B **Privately Held**
SIC: 7372 Application computer software

(G-12123)
WINSIGHT LLC
90 Broad St Ste 402 (10004-3312)
PHONE.................................646 708-7309
EMP: 7
SALES (est): 473K
SALES (corp-wide): 15.9MM **Privately Held**
SIC: 2721 Periodicals
HQ: Winsight, Llc
    300 S Riverside Plz # 1600
    Chicago IL 60606
    312 876-0004

(G-12124)
WINTERWHEAT CORP
11 Wall St (10005-1905)
PHONE.................................212 203-2064
Robert Dailor, *Ch of Bd*
EMP: 8
SALES (est): 216.7K **Privately Held**
SIC: 2741

(G-12125)
WIZQ INC
307 5th Ave Fl 8 (10016-6573)
PHONE.................................586 381-9048
Marcus Kay, *CEO*
Wing Tung LI, *Controller*
EMP: 10 **EST:** 2011
SQ FT: 3,000
SALES (est): 358.3K **Privately Held**
SIC: 7372 Prepackaged software

(G-12126)
WMG ACQUISITION CORP (DH)
75 Rockefeller Plz (10019-6908)
PHONE.................................212 275-2000
Stephen F Cooper, *President*
Mark Ansorge, *Exec VP*
Paul M Robinson, *Exec VP*
Will Tanous, *Exec VP*
Steven Macri, *CFO*
EMP: 17
SALES (est): 813.2MM **Privately Held**
SIC: 2782 2741 7929 Record albums; music books: publishing & printing; music, sheet: publishing & printing; musical entertainers
HQ: Warner Music Group Corp.
    1633 Broadway
    New York NY 10019
    212 275-2000

(G-12127)
WOBBLEWORKS INC (PA)
Also Called: 3doodler
89 5th Ave Ste 802 (10003-3020)
PHONE.................................718 618-9904
Maxwell Bogue, *CEO*
Daniel Cowen, *COO*
Peter Dilworth, *CTO*
EMP: 22
SALES (est): 2.7MM **Privately Held**
SIC: 3944 Electronic toys

(G-12128)
WOCHIT INC (PA)
12 E 33rd St Fl 4 (10016-5090)
PHONE.................................212 979-8343
Dror Ginzberg, *CEO*
Christoph Pleitgen, *Senior VP*
Drew Berkowitz, *Vice Pres*
Elizabeth Hellman, *Vice Pres*
Joachim Schmaltz, *Vice Pres*
EMP: 9
SALES (est): 3.7MM **Privately Held**
SIC: 7372 7812 Business oriented computer software; publishers' computer software; video production

(G-12129)
WOLTERS KLUWER US INC
111 8th Ave Fl 13 (10011-5213)
PHONE.................................212 894-8920
Holly Greenwood, *Editor*
Gloria Moran, *Editor*
Christopher Glenn, *Business Mgr*
Tom Basiliere, *Vice Pres*
Jennifer Brogan, *Vice Pres*
EMP: 12
SALES (corp-wide): 5.2B **Privately Held**
SIC: 2731 Books: publishing only
HQ: Wolters Kluwer United States Inc.
    2700 Lake Cook Rd
    Riverwoods IL 60015
    847 580-5000

(G-12130)
WOMENS E NEWS INC
6 Barclay St Fl 6 # 6 (10007-2721)
PHONE.................................212 244-1720
Rita Henley Jensen, *President*
Angie Alvarado, *Senior Editor*
Lori Sokol, *Assistant*
EMP: 7
SALES (est): 840.9K **Privately Held**
WEB: www.womensenews.org
SIC: 2721 Magazines: publishing only, not printed on site

(G-12131)
WONTON FOOD INC
183 E Broadway (10002)
PHONE.................................212 677-8865
Chan Wai, *Principal*
EMP: 15
SALES (corp-wide): 76.5MM **Privately Held**
WEB: www.wontonfood.com
SIC: 2099 2098 Noodles, fried (Chinese); noodles (e.g. egg, plain & water), dry
PA: Wonton Food Inc.
    220 Moore St 222
    Brooklyn NY 11206
    718 628-6868

(G-12132)
WOOD FLOOR EXPO INC
Also Called: Scerri Quality Wood Floors
426 E 73rd St Frnt 1 (10021-3866)
PHONE.................................212 472-0671
Joseph Scerri, *President*
Edward Laboy, *Vice Pres*
Peter Palagian, *Controller*
EMP: 5
SALES (est): 510K **Privately Held**
WEB: www.woodfloorexpo.com
SIC: 2426 Flooring, hardwood

(G-12133)
WOOLMARK AMERICAS INC
Also Called: Woolmark Company, The
110 E 25th St Fl 3 (10010-2913)
PHONE.................................347 767-3160
Velma George, *Principal*
EMP: 1
SALES (est): 2.6MM **Privately Held**
SIC: 2231 Cloth, wool: mending

(G-12134)
WORKING MOTHER MEDIA INC
Also Called: Diversity Best Practices
2 Park Ave Fl 10 (10016-5604)
PHONE.................................212 351-6400
Carol Evans, *President*
Olivia Kopchik, *Publisher*
Joan Labarge, *Publisher*
Meredith Bogdas, *Chief*
Nancy Colter, *CFO*
EMP: 51 **EST:** 2001
SQ FT: 15,000
SALES (est): 5.1MM
SALES (corp-wide): 3.1B **Privately Held**
WEB: www.workingmother.com
SIC: 2721 4813 Magazines: publishing only, not printed on site;
HQ: Bonnier Corporation
    460 N Orlando Ave Ste 200
    Winter Park FL 32789

(G-12135)
WORKMAN PUBLISHING CO INC (PA)
Also Called: Algonquin Books Chapel Hl Div
225 Varick St Fl 9 (10014-4381)
PHONE.................................212 254-5900
Dan Reynolds, *CEO*
Chuck Adams, *Editor*
Margot Herrera, *Editor*
Kate Karol, *Editor*
Mary Oneill, *Editor*
◆ **EMP:** 200
SQ FT: 57,000
SALES (est): 92.7MM **Privately Held**
WEB: www.pageaday.com
SIC: 2731 Books: publishing only

(G-12136)
WORKMAN PUBLISHING CO INC
Artisan House Div
708 Broadway Fl 6 (10003-9508)
PHONE.................................212 254-5900
Richard Petry, *Controller*
EMP: 150
SALES (corp-wide): 92.7MM **Privately Held**
WEB: www.pageaday.com
SIC: 2731 Books: publishing only
PA: Workman Publishing Co. Inc.
    225 Varick St Fl 9
    New York NY 10014
    212 254-5900

(G-12137)
WORLD GUIDE PUBLISHING
1271 Ave Of The Americas (10020-1300)
PHONE.................................800 331-7840
Tina Threston, *CEO*
EMP: 40
SQ FT: 600
SALES (est): 1.5MM **Privately Held**
SIC: 2721 Magazines: publishing only, not printed on site

(G-12138)
WORLD MARITIME NEWS
118 E 25th St Fl 2 (10010-2977)
PHONE.................................212 477-6700
John Omalley, *President*
Frank Covella, *Advt Staff*
Mitch Engel, *Advt Staff*
EMP: 5 **EST:** 2013
SALES (est): 260.6K **Privately Held**
SIC: 3731 Shipbuilding & repairing

(G-12139)
WORTH COLLECTION LTD (PA)
520 8th Ave Rm 2301 (10018-4108)
PHONE.................................212 268-0312
Francine Della Badia, *CEO*
David Defeo, *CEO*
Kathy Bonner, *Exec VP*
Alain Tiangco, *VP Prdtn*
Lucy Haynes, *Sales Associate*
▲ **EMP:** 50
SQ FT: 8,000
SALES (est): 44.9MM **Privately Held**
WEB: www.worthny.com
SIC: 2335 Women's, juniors' & misses' dresses

(G-12140)
WORTH PUBLISHERS INC
1 New York Plz Ste 4500 (10004-1562)
PHONE.................................212 475-6000
Elizabeth Widdicombe, *President*
Marc Edwards, *Sales Staff*
Sara Crites, *Consultant*
Jacqueline Seltzer, *Info Tech Dir*
Lawrence Jankovic, *Officer*
EMP: 110
SQ FT: 14,000
SALES (est): 23.2MM
SALES (corp-wide): 1.7B **Privately Held**
WEB: www.hbpubny.com
SIC: 2731 Textbooks: publishing only, not printed on site
HQ: Macmillan Holdings, Llc
    175 5th Ave
    New York NY 10010

(G-12141)
WORZALLA PUBLISHING COMPANY
222 W 37th St Fl 10 (10018-9001)
PHONE.................................212 967-7909
Lynn Carroll, *Branch Mgr*
EMP: 190
SALES (corp-wide): 144.4MM **Privately Held**
SIC: 2732 Book printing
PA: Worzalla Publishing Company
    3535 Jefferson St
    Stevens Point WI 54481
    715 344-9600

(G-12142)
WP COMPANY LLC
Also Called: Washington Post Advg Sls Ofc
395 Hudson St Lbby 1 (10014-3669)
PHONE.................................212 445-5050
Rick Tippett, *Director*
EMP: 5 **Privately Held**
SIC: 2711 Newspapers, publishing & printing
HQ: Wp Company Llc
    1301 K St Nw
    Washington DC 20071

(G-12143)
WP LAVORI USA INC (DH)
597 Broadway Fl 2 (10012-3211)
PHONE.................................212 244-6074
Cristina Calori, *President*
Ethem Gungor, *Vice Pres*
▲ **EMP:** 5
SALES (est): 1.2MM **Privately Held**
SIC: 2311 5136 Men's & boys' suits & coats; men's & boys' clothing

(G-12144)
WR DESIGN CORP
Also Called: Wr9000
230 W 39th St Fl 5f (10018-4933)
PHONE.................................212 354-9000
Sunny Lam, *President*
EMP: 20
SALES: 8.4MM **Privately Held**
SIC: 2253 Sweaters & sweater coats, knit

▲ = Import ▼ = Export
◆ = Import/Export

GEOGRAPHIC SECTION

New York - New York County (G-12173)

(G-12145)
WSN INC
Also Called: World Screen News
1123 Broadway Ste 1207 (10010-2007)
PHONE 212 924-7620
Ricardo Guise, *President*
Mansha Daswani, *Publisher*
Nathalie Jaspar, *Vice Pres*
Victor Cuevas, *Production*
Matt Rippetoe, *Production*
EMP: 6
SQ FT: 500
SALES (est): 540K **Privately Held**
WEB: www.worldscreen.com
SIC: 2721 Magazines: publishing only, not printed on site

(G-12146)
WYETH LLC (HQ)
235 E 42nd St (10017-5703)
PHONE 973 660-5000
Ian Reid, *CEO*
Etienne N Attar, *President*
Richard R Deluca, *President*
Michael Kamarck, *President*
Joseph Mahady, *President*
◆ **EMP:** 850 **EST:** 1926
SALES (est): 4.6B
SALES (corp-wide): 52.5B **Publicly Held**
WEB: www.wyeth.com
SIC: 2834 2836 Analgesics; cough medicines; veterinary pharmaceutical preparations; biological products, except diagnostic; allergens, allergenic extracts; vaccines; veterinary biological products
PA: Pfizer Inc.
235 E 42nd St
New York NY 10017
212 733-2323

(G-12147)
X FUNCTION INC (PA)
45 W 89th St Apt 4a (10024-2078)
PHONE 212 231-0092
Frank E Barnes III, *CEO*
Michelle Lanken, *CFO*
EMP: 21
SQ FT: 16,500
SALES: 4.5MM **Publicly Held**
SIC: 7372 7371 Prepackaged software; custom computer programming services

(G-12148)
X MYLES MAR INC
Also Called: Marx Myles Graphic Services
875 Av Of The Americas (10001-3507)
PHONE 212 683-2015
Arthur Marx, *President*
Sheldon Marx, *Vice Pres*
Nancy Lupton, *Controller*
Barry Heaney, *Sales Dir*
Craig Liebowitz, *Accounts Exec*
EMP: 40
SQ FT: 7,000
SALES (est): 6.1MM **Privately Held**
WEB: www.marxmyles.com
SIC: 2759 2791 2789 2752 Commercial printing; typesetting; bookbinding & related work; commercial printing, lithographic

(G-12149)
XANADU
150 W 30th St Rm 702 (10001-4155)
PHONE 212 465-0580
Gus Xanthoudakis, *Owner*
EMP: 5
SQ FT: 5,000
SALES: 750K **Privately Held**
SIC: 2371 Apparel, fur

(G-12150)
XEROX CORPORATION
485 Lexington Ave Fl 10 (10017-2652)
PHONE 212 330-1386
David Miller, *Med Doctor*
Ramyar Rastan, *Consultant*
Ying Zhou, *Consultant*
Christine Henry, *Prgrmr*
Sharon Chernitsky, *Director*
EMP: 80
SALES (corp-wide): 10.2B **Publicly Held**
SIC: 3861 Photocopy machines
PA: Xerox Corporation
201 Merritt 7
Norwalk CT 06851
203 968-3000

(G-12151)
XING LIN USA INTL CORP
1410 Broadway Rm 3201 (10018-9313)
PHONE 212 947-4846
Wen Y Wu, *President*
Richard Jacobs, *General Mgr*
Maggie Yeoh, *Opers Mgr*
Glenn Barnett, *VP Sales*
▲ **EMP:** 5
SQ FT: 900
SALES (est): 6.5MM **Privately Held**
SIC: 2211 Denims

(G-12152)
XINYA INTERNATIONAL TRADING CO
Also Called: Polly Treating
115 W 30th St Rm 1109 (10001-4056)
PHONE 212 216-9681
Peng Sen Liu, *President*
EMP: 6 **EST:** 1996
SALES: 700K **Privately Held**
SIC: 2387 3851 Apparel belts; glasses, sun or glare

(G-12153)
XL GRAPHICS INC
121 Varick St Rm 300 (10013-1408)
PHONE 212 929-8700
Jeff Baltimore, *Ch of Bd*
EMP: 5
SQ FT: 4,000
SALES (est): 610.9K **Privately Held**
SIC: 2759 Commercial printing

(G-12154)
XOMOX JEWELRY INC
151 W 46th St Fl 15 (10036-8512)
PHONE 212 944-8428
Mark Bugnacki, *President*
EMP: 7
SQ FT: 1,200
SALES (est): 850K **Privately Held**
WEB: www.xomoxjewelry.com
SIC: 3911 Jewelry, precious metal

(G-12155)
XSTELOS HOLDINGS INC
630 5th Ave Ste 2600 (10111-2697)
PHONE 212 729-4962
Jonathan M Couchman, *President*
EMP: 3
SALES: 28.7MM **Privately Held**
SIC: 2834 Pharmaceutical preparations

(G-12156)
Y-MABS THERAPEUTICS INC (PA)
230 Park Ave Fl 33 (10169-0005)
PHONE 917 817-2992
Claus Juan Moller San Pedro, *CEO*
Thomas Gad, *Ch of Bd*
Joris Wiel Jan Wilms, *COO*
Torben Lund-Hansen, *Senior VP*
Bo Kruse, *CFO*
EMP: 10
SQ FT: 4,312
SALES (est): 2.6MM **Publicly Held**
SIC: 2834 Pharmaceutical preparations

(G-12157)
YACOUBIAN JEWELERS INC
2 W 45th St Ste 1104 (10036-4248)
PHONE 212 302-6729
Mike Yacoubian, *President*
EMP: 30
SALES (est): 2.7MM **Privately Held**
SIC: 3961 Costume jewelry

(G-12158)
YALE ROBBINS INC
Also Called: Manhattan Map Co
205 Lexington Ave Fl 12 (10016-6022)
PHONE 212 683-5700
Yale Robbins, *President*
Henry Robbins, *Vice Pres*
Ian Goodwin, *Research*
Victor Marcos, *Research*
Sofia Sapeg, *Research*
EMP: 60
SQ FT: 4,000
SALES (est): 8.9MM **Privately Held**
WEB: www.yalerobbins.com
SIC: 2721 8742 6531 Periodicals: publishing & printing; business consultant; real estate brokers & agents

(G-12159)
YAM TV LLC
144 W 23rd St Apt 8e (10011-9403)
PHONE 917 932-5418
Matan Koren,
EMP: 2
SALES: 5MM **Privately Held**
SIC: 2741 7819 Miscellaneous publishing; services allied to motion pictures

(G-12160)
YARNZ INTERNATIONAL INC
260 W 36th St Rm 201 (10018-7524)
PHONE 212 868-5883
Mujadid Shah, *Chairman*
▲ **EMP:** 6 **EST:** 2000
SALES (est): 686.3K **Privately Held**
WEB: www.yarnz.com
SIC: 2231 Apparel & outerwear broadwoven fabrics

(G-12161)
YEOHLEE INC
12 W 29th St (10001-4516)
PHONE 212 631-8099
Yeohlee Teng, *President*
EMP: 13 **EST:** 1975
SQ FT: 6,000
SALES (est): 1.5MM **Privately Held**
WEB: www.yeohlee.com
SIC: 2331 2335 2337 Women's & misses' blouses & shirts; women's, juniors' & misses' dresses; women's & misses' suits & coats

(G-12162)
YIGAL-AZROUEL INC (PA)
500 7th Ave Fl 8 (10018-4502)
PHONE 212 302-1194
Yigal Azrouel, *President*
Flora Cervantes, *Principal*
Danielle B Smotrich, *Executive Asst*
EMP: 30
SALES (est): 3.2MM **Privately Held**
WEB: www.yigal-azrouel.com
SIC: 2369 2339 Girls' & children's outerwear; women's & misses' outerwear

(G-12163)
YIWEN USA INC
60 E 42nd St Ste 1030 (10165-1030)
PHONE 212 370-0828
You Chang, *President*
EMP: 10
SALES (est): 1.3MM **Privately Held**
SIC: 2899 Chemical preparations

(G-12164)
YOMIURI INTERNATIONAL INC
747 3rd Ave Fl 28 (10017-2832)
PHONE 212 752-2196
Michiro Okamoto, *Principal*
EMP: 7
SALES (est): 693.8K
SALES (corp-wide): 19.3MM **Privately Held**
SIC: 3714 Motor vehicle parts & accessories
HQ: Yomiuri Shinbun, The
1-7-1, Otemachi
Chiyoda-Ku TKY 100-0
332 421-111

(G-12165)
YOU AND ME LEGWEAR LLC
10 W 33rd St Rm 300 (10001-3306)
PHONE 212 279-9292
Albert Cohen,
▲ **EMP:** 18
SQ FT: 5,000
SALES (est): 6.7MM **Privately Held**
SIC: 2252 Hosiery

(G-12166)
YS PUBLISHING CO INC
228 E 45th St Rm 700 (10017-3336)
PHONE 212 682-9360
Hitoshi Yoshida, *President*
Eri Sano, *Editor*
Ayako Ueda, *Editor*
Shintaro Torii, *Exec VP*
Miyuki Hanakoshi, *Accountant*
▲ **EMP:** 9
SALES (est): 1.1MM **Privately Held**
WEB: www.us-benricho.com
SIC: 2731 Books: publishing only

(G-12167)
Z-PLY CORP
Also Called: Texray
213 W 35th St Ste 5w (10001)
PHONE 212 398-7011
Timothy Chung, *Ch of Bd*
J J Hou, *Exec VP*
Sam Chang, *CFO*
▲ **EMP:** 40
SQ FT: 5,000
SALES (est): 5.1MM **Privately Held**
WEB: www.z-ply.com
SIC: 2339 2369 Women's & misses' athletic clothing & sportswear; girls' & children's outerwear

(G-12168)
ZAK JEWELRY TOOLS INC
55 W 47th St Fl 2 (10036-2812)
PHONE 212 768-8122
Roman Zak, *President*
Robert Zak, *Vice Pres*
◆ **EMP:** 14
SQ FT: 7,500
SALES (est): 1.7MM **Privately Held**
SIC: 3915 5251 Jewel preparing: instruments, tools, watches & jewelry; tools

(G-12169)
ZAR GROUP LLC (PA)
Also Called: Zar Apparel Group
1450 Broadway Fl 17 (10018-2217)
PHONE 212 944-2510
Bobby Zar, *CEO*
Bruce Bond, *President*
Mansour Zar, *Chairman*
Michael Namdar, *Director*
Vicky Skevofelix, *Officer*
▼ **EMP:** 9
SALES: 100MM **Privately Held**
SIC: 2339 Women's & misses' outerwear

(G-12170)
ZAZOOM LLC (PA)
Also Called: Zazoom Media Group
1 Exchange Plz Ste 801 (10006-3008)
PHONE 212 321-2100
Tim Minton, *CEO*
Chris Green, *Editor*
Steve Charlier, *Vice Pres*
Troy Frisby, *Producer*
EMP: 17
SALES (est): 1.6MM **Privately Held**
SIC: 2741

(G-12171)
ZEDGE INC
22 Cortlandt St Fl 11 (10007-3171)
PHONE 330 577-3424
Tom Arnoy, *CEO*
Michael Jonas, *Ch of Bd*
Howard S Jonas, *Vice Ch Bd*
Jonathan Reich, *COO*
EMP: 64
SQ FT: 500
SALES: 10.8MM **Privately Held**
SIC: 7372 Prepackaged software

(G-12172)
ZEEBA JEWELRY MFG INC
Also Called: Zeeba Jewelry Manufacturing
36 W 47th St Ste 902 (10036-8641)
PHONE 212 997-1009
Fred Navi, *President*
Ray Lavi, *Vice Pres*
EMP: 3
SQ FT: 2,000
SALES: 1MM **Privately Held**
SIC: 3911 Jewelry, precious metal

(G-12173)
ZENITH ENERGY US LOGISTICS (PA)
725 5th Ave Fl 19 (10022-2519)
PHONE 212 993-1280
Jeff Armstrong, *CEO*
EMP: 1

New York - New York County (G-12174)

SALES (est): 9.8MM **Privately Held**
SIC: **1311** Crude petroleum & natural gas

(G-12174)
ZETEK CORPORATION
Also Called: Zeteck
13 E 37th St Ste 701 (10016-2841)
PHONE.................................212 668-1485
Bertrand Dorfman, *President*
Bertand Dorfman, *IT/INT Sup*
Raymond McKee, *Director*
EMP: 10
SQ FT: 1,500
SALES (est): 1.1MM **Privately Held**
WEB: www.zetek.com
SIC: **3663** 3669 7622 7629 Radio & TV communications equipment; fire detection systems, electric; communication equipment repair; electrical equipment repair services

(G-12175)
ZG APPAREL GROUP LLC
1450 Broadway Fl 17 (10018-2217)
PHONE.................................212 944-2510
Mansour Zar,
Babak Zar,
◆ EMP: 40 EST: 2014
SQ FT: 20,000
SALES (est): 21.8MM **Privately Held**
SIC: **2339** Women's & misses' athletic clothing & sportswear; athletic clothing: women's, misses' & juniors'

(G-12176)
ZIA POWER INC
116 E 27th St (10016-8942)
PHONE.................................845 661-8388
Nathaniel Thompkins, *President*
EMP: 36
SQ FT: 2,000
SALES (est): 1.4MM **Privately Held**
SIC: **2339** Women's & misses' outerwear

(G-12177)
ZIFF DAVIS PUBLISHING LLC (DH)
Also Called: Ziff-Davis Publishing
28 E 28th St Fl 10 (10016-7939)
PHONE.................................212 503-3500
Michelle Dwyer, *Partner*
James Whitehead, *General Mgr*
Geoff Inns, *Managing Dir*
Tom McGrade, *Exec VP*
Michael J Miller, *Exec VP*
▲ EMP: 100
SQ FT: 310,000
SALES (est): 94.3MM
SALES (corp-wide): 1.1B **Publicly Held**
WEB: www.zdnet.com
SIC: **2721** 2731 7371 Periodicals; book publishing; custom computer programming services

(G-12178)
ZINEPAK LLC
349 5th Ave (10016-5019)
PHONE.................................212 706-8621
Brittney Hodak, *Mng Member*
Brittany Hodak, *Mng Member*
Abby Downing, *Creative Dir*
EMP: 10
SALES: 2.9MM **Privately Held**
SIC: **2731** Book publishing

(G-12179)
ZIRCONIA CREATIONS INTL
134 W 29th St Rm 801 (10001-0107)
PHONE.................................212 239-3730
Michael Halpert, *President*
Yisha Weber, *Vice Pres*
EMP: 8
SQ FT: 3,000
SALES: 1.1MM **Privately Held**
SIC: **3915** Jewelers' materials & lapidary work

(G-12180)
ZITOMER LLC
969 Madison Ave Fl 1 (10021-2763)
PHONE.................................212 737-5560
Thanh Tran, *Principal*
Sharmin Rai, *Marketing Mgr*
Sallie Aorta, *Manager*
▲ EMP: 9 EST: 1997

SALES (est): 1.5MM **Privately Held**
SIC: **2834** Solutions, pharmaceutical

(G-12181)
ZOE SAKOUTIS LLC
Also Called: Blueprint Cleanse
135 W 29th St Rm 704 (10001-5172)
PHONE.................................212 414-5741
Zoe Sakoutis, *Principal*
Erica Huss, *Principal*
EMP: 15
SALES (est): 2.4MM **Publicly Held**
SIC: **2037** Mfg Frozen Fruits/Vegetables
PA: The Hain Celestial Group Inc
1111 Marcus Ave Ste 100
New Hyde Park NY 11042

(G-12182)
ZOGRAPHOS DESIGNS LTD
300 E 33rd St Apt 9m (10016-9412)
PHONE.................................212 545-0227
Nicos Zographos, *President*
EMP: 8
SQ FT: 2,250
SALES (est): 961.6K **Privately Held**
WEB: www.zographos.com
SIC: **2521** 2522 Wood office furniture; office furniture, except wood

(G-12183)
ZOOMIFIER CORPORATION
216 E 45th St Fl 17 (10017-3304)
PHONE.................................800 255-5303
Chetan Saiya, *CEO*
EMP: 100
SALES (corp-wide): 13.9MM **Privately Held**
SIC: **7372** Business oriented computer software
PA: Zoomifier Corporation
870 Market St Ste 919
San Francisco CA 94102
800 255-5303

(G-12184)
ZORLU USA INC (PA)
295 5th Ave Ste 503 (10016-7103)
PHONE.................................212 689-4622
Vedat Aydin, *President*
Sevket Celikkanat, *Vice Pres*
Filiz Ozpicak, *Vice Pres*
Leonardo Gulkok, *Production*
Alihan Altunbas, *Controller*
▲ EMP: 65
SALES (est): 9.6MM **Privately Held**
WEB: www.zorluusa.com
SIC: **2221** 5131 Textile mills, broadwoven: silk & manmade, also glass; textiles, woven

New York Mills
Oneida County

(G-12185)
DI HIGHWAY SIGN STRUCTURE CORP
40 Greenman Ave (13417-1004)
P.O. Box 123 (13417-0123)
PHONE.................................315 736-8312
Steven Mulvihill, *General Mgr*
Jane Mulvihill, *Principal*
Jeff Welch, *Production*
Joel Sims, *QC Mgr*
Noreen Sheridan, *Controller*
EMP: 40
SQ FT: 35,000
SALES (est): 12.8MM **Privately Held**
SIC: **3499** Metal household articles; trophies, metal, except silver

(G-12186)
FOUNTAINHEAD GROUP INC (PA)
Also Called: Burgess Products Division
23 Garden St (13417-1318)
PHONE.................................315 736-0037
John F Romano, *CEO*
John O'Toole, *President*
George Mitchell, *Vice Pres*
Jackie Romano, *Vice Pres*
Linda E Romano, *Vice Pres*
◆ EMP: 150 EST: 1973
SQ FT: 40,000

SALES (est): 33MM **Privately Held**
WEB: www.thefountainheadgroup.com
SIC: **3563** 3523 3569 Spraying outfits: metals, paints & chemicals (compressor); sprayers & spraying machines, agricultural; fertilizing, spraying, dusting & irrigation machinery; firefighting apparatus

(G-12187)
FOUNTAINHEAD GROUP INC
Bridgeview Aerosol
3 Graden St (13417)
PHONE.................................708 598-7100
Jack Young, *COO*
EMP: 170
SALES (corp-wide): 33MM **Privately Held**
SIC: **3563** 2813 Spraying outfits: metals, paints & chemicals (compressor); aerosols
PA: The Fountainhead Group Inc
23 Garden St
New York Mills NY 13417
315 736-0037

(G-12188)
HERMOSA CORP
102 Main St (13417-1103)
P.O. Box 274 (13417-0274)
PHONE.................................315 768-4320
Steven Mulvihill, *President*
Michael Sheridan Pe, *Vice Pres*
Joann Western, *Office Mgr*
David Bintz, *Asst Mgr*
Daniel M Hubbell, *Shareholder*
EMP: 20
SQ FT: 40,000
SALES (est): 3.4MM **Privately Held**
WEB: www.hermosacorp.com
SIC: **3993** Signs, not made in custom sign painting shops

(G-12189)
MOHAWK VALLEY KNT MCHY CO INC
561 Main St (13417-1431)
P.O. Box 120 (13417-0120)
PHONE.................................315 736-3038
Thomas P Firsching, *President*
EMP: 19
SQ FT: 40,000
SALES (est): 3.6MM **Privately Held**
SIC: **3552** Textile machinery

(G-12190)
QUALITY MACHINING SERVICE INC
70 Sauquoit St (13417-1018)
PHONE.................................315 736-5774
Tom Ostrander, *President*
EMP: 5
SQ FT: 3,000
SALES: 150K **Privately Held**
SIC: **3599** Machine shop, jobbing & repair

Newark
Wayne County

(G-12191)
ADDEX INC
251 Murray St (14513-1216)
PHONE.................................315 331-7700
Barb Cree, *Owner*
EMP: 9 **Privately Held**
WEB: www.addexinc.com
SIC: **3625** Control equipment, electric
PA: Addex, Inc.
251 Murray St
Newark NY 14513

(G-12192)
ADDEX INC (PA)
251 Murray St (14513-1216)
PHONE.................................781 344-5800
Rudiger Von Kraus, *President*
Robert E Cree, *Exec VP*
Mary Cree, *Executive Asst*
▲ EMP: 5
SQ FT: 10,000
SALES (est): 1.6MM **Privately Held**
WEB: www.addexinc.com
SIC: **3559** Plastics working machinery

(G-12193)
C&C AUTOMATICS INC
127 W Shore Blvd (14513-1259)
PHONE.................................315 331-1436
Craig T Parsons, *President*
Craig Halstead, *Vice Pres*
EMP: 20
SQ FT: 9,000
SALES (est): 2.3MM **Privately Held**
WEB: www.ccautomatics.com
SIC: **3451** Screw machine products

(G-12194)
CELMET CO
105 Norton St (14513-1218)
P.O. Box 271 (14513-0271)
PHONE.................................585 647-1760
Jeffrey T Schlarbaum, *Principal*
EMP: 5
SALES (est): 624.5K **Privately Held**
SIC: **3679** Electronic circuits

(G-12195)
HALLAGAN MANUFACTURING CO INC
500 Hoffman St (14513-1858)
P.O. Box 268 (14513-0268)
PHONE.................................315 331-4640
Charles W Hallagan, *Ch of Bd*
Stephen Hallagan, *President*
Walter Hallagan, *Vice Pres*
EMP: 80
SQ FT: 97,000
SALES (est): 10.3MM **Privately Held**
SIC: **2512** Living room furniture: upholstered on wood frames

(G-12196)
IEC ELECTRONICS CORP (PA)
105 Norton St (14513-1298)
PHONE.................................315 331-7742
Jeremy R Nowak, *Ch of Bd*
Jeffrey T Schlarbaum, *President*
Jens Hauvn, *Senior VP*
Thomas L Barbato, *CFO*
Michael T Williams, *CFO*
▲ EMP: 277 EST: 1966
SQ FT: 235,000
SALES: 96.4MM **Publicly Held**
WEB: www.iec-electronics.com
SIC: **3672** 3679 Printed circuit boards; electronic circuits

(G-12197)
IEC ELECTRONICS WIRE CABLE INC
105 Norton St (14513-1218)
P.O. Box 271 (14513-0271)
PHONE.................................585 924-9010
Jeffrey T Schlarbaum, *President*
Donald S Doody, *Vice Pres*
Vincent Leo, *CFO*
EMP: 100
SQ FT: 19,000
SALES (est): 11.6MM
SALES (corp-wide): 96.4MM **Publicly Held**
WEB: www.val-u-tech.com
SIC: **3672** Printed circuit boards
PA: Iec Electronics Corp.
105 Norton St
Newark NY 14513
315 331-7742

(G-12198)
LEGENDARY AUTO INTERIORS LTD
121 W Shore Blvd (14513-1259)
PHONE.................................315 331-1212
Martin J Beckenbach, *Ch of Bd*
▲ EMP: 40
SQ FT: 12,000
SALES (est): 5.5MM **Privately Held**
WEB: www.legendaryautointeriors.com
SIC: **2396** 5013 5531 3429 Automotive trimmings, fabric; automotive trim; automotive accessories; manufactured hardware (general); leather tanning & finishing; nonwoven fabrics

(G-12199)
MACO BAG CORPORATION
412 Van Buren St (14513-9205)
PHONE.................................315 226-1000
J Scott Miller, *Ch of Bd*

Craig Miller, *President*
Susan Miller, *Corp Secy*
Bob Finley, *Safety Dir*
Steve Crysler, *Opers Mgr*
▲ **EMP:** 140 **EST:** 1929
SQ FT: 60,000
SALES (est): 38MM **Privately Held**
WEB: www.macobag.com
SIC: 3081 2673 Plastic film & sheet; plastic & pliofilm bags

(G-12200)
MCDOWELL RESEARCH CO INC (HQ)
2000 Technology Pkwy (14513-2175)
PHONE..............................315 332-7100
John D Kavazanjian, *President*
Julius Cirin, *Vice Pres*
Dede Emery, *Senior Buyer*
Jeff Luke, *Chief Mktg Ofcr*
Edward Knauf, *Marketing Staff*
▲ **EMP:** 100
SQ FT: 54,000
SALES (est): 78.8MM
SALES (corp-wide): 85.5MM **Publicly Held**
WEB: www.mrc-power.com
SIC: 3669 Intercommunication systems, electric
PA: Ultralife Corporation
2000 Technology Pkwy
Newark NY 14513
315 332-7100

(G-12201)
MICRO-TECH MACHINE INC
301 W Shore Blvd (14513-1261)
PHONE..............................315 331-6671
Michael R Davis, *President*
Amy Davis, *CFO*
EMP: 44
SQ FT: 13,000
SALES (est): 7.4MM **Privately Held**
WEB: www.microtechmachine.com
SIC: 3599 Machine shop, jobbing & repair

(G-12202)
MOOSEBERRY SOAP CO LLC
513 W Union St Ste B (14513-1365)
PHONE..............................315 332-8913
Mary Bartolotta, *Mng Member*
EMP: 7 **EST:** 2011
SQ FT: 5,000
SALES (est): 896.5K **Privately Held**
SIC: 2841 Manufactures Oragnic Soap

(G-12203)
NORTH AMERICAN FILTER CORP (PA)
Also Called: Nafco
200 W Shore Blvd (14513-1258)
PHONE..............................800 265-8943
Steve Taylor, *President*
▼ **EMP:** 74
SQ FT: 75,000
SALES (est): 14.3MM **Privately Held**
WEB: www.nafcoinc.com
SIC: 3569 3564 Filters, general line: industrial; blowers & fans

(G-12204)
P V C MOLDING TECHNOLOGIES
122 W Shore Blvd (14513-1258)
PHONE..............................315 331-1212
Martin Beckenbach, *President*
EMP: 12
SQ FT: 14,198
SALES (est): 1MM **Privately Held**
SIC: 3089 Molding primary plastic

(G-12205)
PROGRESSIVE GRAPHICS & PRTG
1171 E Union St (14513-9529)
P.O. Box 492 (14513-0492)
PHONE..............................315 331-3635
Robert Kelly, *President*
Dennis Chasse, *Vice Pres*
EMP: 6
SQ FT: 10,000
SALES (est): 418K **Privately Held**
SIC: 2752 2791 2789 Commercial printing, offset; typesetting; bookbinding & related work

(G-12206)
SMITH METAL WORKS NEWARK INC
1000 E Union St (14513-1643)
PHONE..............................315 331-1651
Wayne F Smith, *President*
Barbara Shear, *General Mgr*
Janice Smith, *Treasurer*
Gail Rosann Tack, *Human Res Mgr*
John C Cornwell, *Manager*
EMP: 27 **EST:** 1942
SQ FT: 5,000
SALES (est): 7.5MM **Privately Held**
WEB: www.smithspreaders.com
SIC: 3714 3599 Sanders, motor vehicle safety; machine shop, jobbing & repair; custom machinery

(G-12207)
SPINCO METAL PRODUCTS INC
1 Country Club Dr (14513-1250)
PHONE..............................315 331-6285
C Robert Straubing Jr, *Ch of Bd*
John Bulger, *Admin Sec*
▲ **EMP:** 80
SQ FT: 48,000
SALES (est): 24MM **Privately Held**
WEB: www.spincometal.com
SIC: 3498 Tube fabricating (contract bending & shaping)

(G-12208)
SUPERGEN PRODUCTS LLC
320 Hoffman St (14513-1830)
PHONE..............................315 573-7887
Paul Cole, *Mng Member*
EMP: 9
SALES (est): 140K **Privately Held**
SIC: 3621 Motors & generators

(G-12209)
ULTRALIFE CORPORATION (PA)
2000 Technology Pkwy (14513-2175)
PHONE..............................315 332-7100
Bradford T Whitmore, *Ch of Bd*
Michael D Popielec, *President*
Isabelle Melody, *Counsel*
Ken Bird, *Vice Pres*
Peter Comerford, *Vice Pres*
▲ **EMP:** 272
SQ FT: 250,000
SALES: 85.5MM **Publicly Held**
WEB: www.ulbi.com
SIC: 3679 3691 Electronic loads & power supplies; harness assemblies for electronic use: wire or cable; parametric amplifiers; alkaline cell storage batteries

(G-12210)
UPSTATE REFRACTORY SVCS INC
100 Erie Blvd (14513-1163)
PHONE..............................315 331-2955
David Wetmore, *President*
Diane Wetmore, *Vice Pres*
Bryan Wetmore, *Warehouse Mgr*
Bill Wilck, *Senior Engr*
Mike Parker, *Sales Executive*
EMP: 29
SQ FT: 18,000
SALES (est): 5.5MM **Privately Held**
WEB: www.upstaterefractoryservices.com
SIC: 3255 5085 Clay refractories; refractory material

(G-12211)
VAN LAEKEN RICHARD
Also Called: Harris Machine
2680 Parker Rd (14513-9750)
PHONE..............................315 331-0289
Richard Van Laeken, *Owner*
EMP: 5 **EST:** 1995
SQ FT: 2,600
SALES (est): 450K **Privately Held**
SIC: 3599 Machine shop, jobbing & repair

Newburgh
Orange County

(G-12212)
ALUMIL FABRICATION INC
1900 Corporate Blvd (12550-6412)
PHONE..............................845 469-2874
Kyt Bazenikas, *Ch of Bd*
▲ **EMP:** 15
SALES (est): 3.2MM **Privately Held**
SIC: 3442 Screens, window, metal

(G-12213)
AMERICAN ICON INDUSTRIES INC
392 N Montgomery St Ste 2 (12550-6802)
PHONE..............................845 561-1299
Robert Kucharek, *CEO*
Gary Rausenberger, *Principal*
EMP: 6
SALES (est): 991.4K **Privately Held**
SIC: 2752 Commercial printing, lithographic

(G-12214)
AMSCAN INC
Kookaburra
108 Route 17k (12550-5010)
PHONE..............................845 782-0490
Walter Thompson, *Manager*
EMP: 49
SALES (corp-wide): 2.3B **Publicly Held**
SIC: 2656 Plates, paper: made from purchased material
HQ: Amscan Inc.
80 Grasslands Rd Ste 3
Elmsford NY 10523
914 345-2020

(G-12215)
ARCTIC GLACIER NEWBURGH INC (DH)
225 Lake St (12550-5242)
PHONE..............................845 561-0549
Robert Nagy, *President*
Keith McMahon, *Vice Pres*
Hugh Adams, *Admin Sec*
EMP: 15
SQ FT: 40,000
SALES (est): 3.4MM
SALES (corp-wide): 3.6B **Publicly Held**
SIC: 2097 Manufactured ice
HQ: Agi Ccaa Inc
625 Henry Ave
Winnipeg MB R3A 0
204 772-2473

(G-12216)
BIG SHINE WORLDWIDE INC
Also Called: Big Shine Energy
300 Corporate Blvd (12550-6402)
PHONE..............................845 444-5255
Dong IL Lee, *CEO*
Bong Hee Lee Kim, *Admin Sec*
EMP: 6
SALES: 30MM **Privately Held**
SIC: 3646 Commercial indusl & institutional electric lighting fixtures

(G-12217)
BIMBO BAKERIES USA INC
98 Scobie Dr (12550-3257)
PHONE..............................845 568-0943
Michael D'Adamo, *Director*
EMP: 53 **Privately Held**
SIC: 2051 Bakery: wholesale or wholesale/retail combined
HQ: Bimbo Bakeries Usa, Inc
255 Business Center Dr # 200
Horsham PA 19044
215 347-5500

(G-12218)
COMMODORE CHOCOLATIER USA INC
482 Broadway (12550-5333)
PHONE..............................845 561-3960
John Courtsunis, *President*
EMP: 10 **EST:** 1935
SQ FT: 5,000
SALES: 1MM **Privately Held**
SIC: 2066 5149 5441 Chocolate; chocolate; candy

(G-12219)
CONSOLIDATED SPRING LLC
Also Called: Atlas Industries
11 Spring St (12550-5511)
PHONE..............................845 391-8855
EMP: 10
SALES (est): 821.9K **Privately Held**
SIC: 3999 Manufacturing industries

(G-12220)
E & O MARI INC
Also Called: La Bella Strings
256 Broadway (12550-5487)
P.O. Box 869 (12551-0869)
PHONE..............................845 562-4400
Richard Cocco Jr, *President*
Lorenza Cocco, *Director*
▲ **EMP:** 89 **EST:** 1915
SQ FT: 29,000
SALES (est): 12.8MM **Privately Held**
SIC: 3931 Strings, musical instrument

(G-12221)
EMPIRE BUSINESS FORMS INC (PA)
Also Called: Forms For You Division
128 S Robinson Ave 2 (12550-5822)
P.O. Box 3480, Poughkeepsie (12603-0480)
PHONE..............................845 562-7780
John Vincent Rice, *President*
Louise Rice, *Corp Secy*
EMP: 12
SQ FT: 10,000
SALES (est): 2MM **Privately Held**
SIC: 2759 5112 Business forms: printing; business forms

(G-12222)
FRAGRANCE ACQUISITIONS LLC
Also Called: Preferred Fragrance
1900 Corporate Blvd (12550-6412)
PHONE..............................845 534-9172
Glenn Palmer, *Partner*
▲ **EMP:** 70 **EST:** 2011
SALES (est): 11.2MM **Privately Held**
SIC: 2844 Perfumes & colognes

(G-12223)
GASOFT EQUIPMENT INC
231 Dubois St (12550-3410)
PHONE..............................845 863-1010
Tony M Colandrea, *President*
Nick Gurlakis, *Vice Pres*
◆ **EMP:** 14
SQ FT: 5,000
SALES: 5.6MM **Privately Held**
SIC: 3577 5045 Computer peripheral equipment; computers, peripherals & software

(G-12224)
GLASBAU HAHN AMERICA LLC
15 Little Brook Ln Ste 2 (12550-1687)
PHONE..............................845 566-3331
Jamie Ponton, *Principal*
Cathy Lima, *Manager*
▲ **EMP:** 5
SALES (est): 390K **Privately Held**
SIC: 2542 Counters or counter display cases: except wood

(G-12225)
GTI GRAPHIC TECHNOLOGY INC (PA)
211 Dupont Ave (12550-4019)
P.O. Box 3138 (12550-0651)
PHONE..............................845 562-7066
Robert Mc Curdy, *President*
Louis Chappo, *Vice Pres*
Robert McCurdy, *Vice Pres*
Barry Petrillo, *Engineer*
Elizabeth Mc Curdy, *Treasurer*
EMP: 32
SQ FT: 35,000
SALES: 4.9MM **Privately Held**
WEB: www.graphiclite.com
SIC: 3648 Lighting equipment

(G-12226)
HUDSON VALLEY BLACK PRESS
343 Broadway (12550-5301)
P.O. Box 2160 (12550-0332)
PHONE..............................845 562-1313
Charles Stewart, *President*
John Callahan, *Accounts Exec*
EMP: 7
SQ FT: 4,000
SALES (est): 378.6K **Privately Held**
SIC: 2711 Newspapers: publishing only, not printed on site

Newburgh - Orange County

(G-12227)
HUDSON VALLEY OFFICE FURN INC
7 Wisner Ave (12550-5133)
PHONE.................................845 565-6673
Tom Chickery, Owner
EMP: 8
SALES (corp-wide): 2MM Privately Held
WEB: www.thewowguys.com
SIC: 2522 Office furniture, except wood
PA: Hudson Valley Office Furniture, Inc.
375 Main St
Poughkeepsie NY 12601
845 471-7910

(G-12228)
HUDSON VALLEY PAPER WORKS INC
8 Lander St 15 (12550-4938)
PHONE.................................845 569-8883
Luke Pontifell, President
▲ EMP: 15
SALES (est): 1.2MM Privately Held
SIC: 2732 Book printing

(G-12229)
HUDSON VALLEY STEEL PRODUCTS
5231 Route 9w (12550-1483)
PHONE.................................845 565-2270
EMP: 5
SALES (est): 328.8K Privately Held
SIC: 3312 Hot-rolled iron & steel products

(G-12230)
LA ESCONDIDA INC
129 Lake St (12550-5242)
PHONE.................................845 562-1387
Andres Garcia, President
Emigdio Carrera, Vice Pres
EMP: 8
SQ FT: 2,000
SALES (est): 850.5K Privately Held
WEB: www.laescondida.com
SIC: 2099 Tortillas, fresh or refrigerated

(G-12231)
MAGNETIC AIDS INC
201 Ann St (12550-5417)
P.O. Box 2502 (12550-0610)
PHONE.................................845 863-1400
Joe Formoso, President
Eve Formoso, Manager
▲ EMP: 8 EST: 1958
SQ FT: 12,000
SALES: 550K Privately Held
WEB: www.magneticaids.com
SIC: 3499 Magnets, permanent: metallic

(G-12232)
MIXTURE SCREEN PRINTING
1607 Route 300 100 (12550-1738)
PHONE.................................845 561-2857
Christopher D Fahrbach, Owner
EMP: 8
SALES (est): 515.6K Privately Held
SIC: 2759 3993 5099 Screen printing; signs & advertising specialties; signs, except electric

(G-12233)
MOKAI MANUFACTURING INC
13 Jeanne Dr (12550-1788)
PHONE.................................845 566-8287
Rick Murray, President
Justin Bruyn, Design Engr
EMP: 6
SALES (est): 1MM Privately Held
WEB: www.mokai.com
SIC: 3732 Boat building & repairing

(G-12234)
MONDELEZ GLOBAL LLC
Also Called: Nabisco
800 Corporate Blvd (12550-6407)
PHONE.................................845 567-4701
Patrick Sherman, General Mgr
EMP: 6 Publicly Held
SIC: 2022 Cheese, natural & processed
HQ: Mondelez Global Llc
3 N Pkwy Ste 300
Deerfield IL 60015
847 943-4000

(G-12235)
NEWBURGH BREWING COMPANY LLC
88 S Colden St (12550-5640)
Rural Route 72, Salisbury Mills (12577)
PHONE.................................845 569-2337
Paul Halayko, President
EMP: 14 EST: 2012
SALES (est): 2.2MM Privately Held
SIC: 2082 Beer (alcoholic beverage)

(G-12236)
NEWBURGH ENVELOPE CORP
1720 Route 300 (12550-8930)
PHONE.................................845 566-4211
Carl Stillwaggon, President
Stuart Stillwaggon, Vice Pres
EMP: 7
SQ FT: 1,800
SALES (est): 640K Privately Held
SIC: 2752 Commercial printing, offset

(G-12237)
ORANGE COUNTY CHOPPERS INC
Also Called: O C Choppers
14 Crossroads Ct (12550-5064)
PHONE.................................845 522-5200
Paul Teutul Sr, President
Kelvin Cordero, Opers Staff
Jim Quinn, Engineer
Rosie Meyers, VP Bus Dvlpt
Jon Randazzo, Human Resources
EMP: 6
SALES: 1MM Privately Held
SIC: 3751 Motorcycles & related parts

(G-12238)
ORANGE DIE CUTTING CORP
Also Called: Orange Packaging
1 Favoriti Ave (12550-4015)
P.O. Box 2295 (12550-0441)
PHONE.................................845 562-0900
Anthony Esposito Sr, Ch of Bd
Anthony Esposito Jr, President
Hector Torres, General Mgr
Joe Gobosack, Foreman/Supr
Brenda Benevides, Sales Staff
▲ EMP: 120 EST: 1950
SQ FT: 40,000
SALES (est): 27.8MM Privately Held
SIC: 2653 Corrugated & solid fiber boxes

(G-12239)
ORNAMETAL INC
216 S William St (12550-5845)
PHONE.................................845 562-5151
Richard Cohen, Owner
EMP: 5
SALES (est): 387K Privately Held
SIC: 3446 Stairs, staircases, stair treads: prefabricated metal

(G-12240)
PECKHAM MATERIALS CORP
322 Walsh Ave (12553-6748)
P.O. Box 4074, New Windsor (12553-0074)
PHONE.................................845 562-5370
EMP: 5
SALES (corp-wide): 200.6MM Privately Held
SIC: 2951 Asphalt & asphaltic paving mixtures (not from refineries)
HQ: Peckham Materials Corp
20 Haarlem Ave Ste 200
White Plains NY 10603
914 686-2045

(G-12241)
PEPSI-COLA NEWBURGH BTLG INC
Also Called: Pepsico
1 Pepsi Way (12550-3921)
PHONE.................................845 562-5400
Charles T Tenney Jr, President
John Croce, Division Mgr
Mike Travis, Division Mgr
Tom Strahle, COO
James Lynch, Vice Pres
EMP: 150 EST: 1939
SALES (est): 28.9MM Privately Held
SIC: 2086 Carbonated soft drinks, bottled & canned

(G-12242)
PRISMATIC DYEING & FINSHG INC
40 Wisner Ave (12550-5132)
P.O. Box 2456 (12550-0732)
PHONE.................................845 561-1800
Gary Innocenti, President
Deborah Emerick, Manager
EMP: 60 EST: 1997
SQ FT: 110,000
SALES (est): 11.7MM Privately Held
WEB: www.prismaticdyeing.com
SIC: 2861 2269 2262 2261 Dyeing materials, natural; finishing plants; finishing plants, manmade fiber & silk fabrics; finishing plants, cotton

(G-12243)
PROKOSCH AND SONN SHEET METAL
772 South St (12550-4149)
PHONE.................................845 562-4211
Alfred Prokosch Jr, Ch of Bd
Annunciata Prokosch, President
John F Prokosch, Vice Pres
EMP: 21
SQ FT: 2,400
SALES (est): 4.1MM Privately Held
SIC: 3444 1711 Sheet metal specialties, not stamped; heating & air conditioning contractors

(G-12244)
PROSTHETIC REHABILITATION CTR (PA)
2 Winding Ln (12550-2223)
PHONE.................................845 565-8255
Andrew Carubia, President
Carol Hatcher, Admin Sec
EMP: 8
SALES (est): 750.9K Privately Held
SIC: 3842 5999 Limbs, artificial; artificial limbs

(G-12245)
SANDY LITTMAN INC
Also Called: American Glass Light
420 N Montgomery St (12550-3680)
P.O. Box 11089, Greenwich CT (06831-1089)
PHONE.................................845 562-1112
Sandy Littman, President
John Soltes, Manager
EMP: 6
SQ FT: 800
SALES (est): 1.2MM Privately Held
WEB: www.americanglasslight.com
SIC: 3646 3645 Commercial indusl & institutional electric lighting fixtures; residential lighting fixtures

(G-12246)
STEELWAYS INC
Also Called: Steelways Shipyard
401 S Water St (12553-6038)
PHONE.................................845 562-0860
David Plotkins, Ch of Bd
Brian Plotkins, Exec VP
Steve Laker, CFO
EMP: 29
SQ FT: 15,000
SALES (est): 6.8MM Privately Held
WEB: www.steelwaysinc.com
SIC: 3731 3443 Commercial cargo ships, building & repairing; tanks, standard or custom fabricated: metal plate
PA: Steelways Holdings Group, Inc.
401 S Water St
Newburgh NY 12553

(G-12247)
TELECHEMISCHE INC
222 Dupont Ave (12550-4060)
PHONE.................................845 561-3237
Mary Mallavarapu, Ch of Bd
Leo Mallavarapu PHD, President
Anita Soares, Admin Sec
EMP: 6
SALES: 100K Privately Held
WEB: www.telechemische.en.ecplaza.net
SIC: 2821 2869 Plastics materials & resins; industrial organic chemicals

(G-12248)
UNICO SPECIAL PRODUCTS INC
25 Renwick St (12550-6029)
PHONE.................................845 562-9255
Joseph Guarneri Jr, President
Edward Guarneri, Corp Secy
Michael Guarneri, Vice Pres
▲ EMP: 50
SQ FT: 44,000
SALES: 250K Privately Held
SIC: 3083 Plastic finished products, laminated

(G-12249)
UNIVERSAL THIN FILM LAB CORP
232 N Plank Rd (12550-1775)
PHONE.................................845 562-0601
Carmelo Comito, President
Jordan Comito, Prdtn Mgr
Christopher Infante, Engineer
Mike Middleton, Engineer
Alison Comito, Treasurer
EMP: 7 EST: 1997
SQ FT: 3,000
SALES: 1MM Privately Held
SIC: 3559 Optical lens machinery

(G-12250)
WAGNER TECHNICAL SERVICES INC
1658 Route 300 (12550-1757)
PHONE.................................845 566-4018
Gerald L Wagner, President
Gerald Wagner, President
Laurie Wagner, Vice Pres
David Cappelli, Info Tech Mgr
EMP: 17
SALES: 3.4MM Privately Held
WEB: www.wagnertech.com
SIC: 7372 Utility computer software

(G-12251)
WALLKILL VALLEY PUBLICATIONS
Also Called: Wallkill Valley Times
300 Stony Brook Ct Ste B (12550-6535)
PHONE.................................845 561-0170
Carl Aiello, President
EMP: 20
SQ FT: 1,500
SALES (est): 1.1MM Privately Held
WEB: www.tcnewspapers.com
SIC: 2711 2791 2752 2721 Newspapers: publishing only, not printed on site; typesetting; commercial printing, lithographic; periodicals

Newfane
Niagara County

(G-12252)
KSM GROUP LTD
2905 Beebe Rd (14108-9655)
PHONE.................................716 751-6006
Daniel King, President
Judith M King, Vice Pres
EMP: 5
SQ FT: 18,000
SALES (est): 430K Privately Held
WEB: www.ksmgroup.org
SIC: 3444 Sheet metalwork

(G-12253)
SAVACO INC
2905 Beebe Rd (14108-9655)
PHONE.................................716 751-9455
Judith King, President
Kevin King, Opers Mgr
Brad Few, Info Tech Mgr
EMP: 7
SQ FT: 18,000
SALES: 500K Privately Held
WEB: www.savacoinc.com
SIC: 3441 Fabricated structural metal

(G-12254)
VANTE INC
Also Called: Plasticweld Systems
3600 Coomer Rd (14108-9651)
PHONE.................................716 778-7691
Brian Strini, CEO

Norman Strobel, *President*
▲ **EMP:** 10
SQ FT: 4,800
SALES (est): 1.9MM
SALES (corp-wide): 17.9MM **Privately Held**
WEB: www.plasticweldsystems.com
SIC: 3841 3548 Catheters; welding apparatus
PA: Machine Solutions, Inc.
2951 W Shamrell Blvd # 107
Flagstaff AZ 86005
928 556-3109

Newport
Herkimer County

(G-12255)
FULLER TOOL INCORPORATED
225 Platform Rd (13416-2217)
PHONE.................................315 891-3183
Rodney Fuller, *CEO*
EMP: 10
SQ FT: 2,800
SALES: 500K **Privately Held**
WEB: www.fullertool.com
SIC: 3312 3544 Tool & die steel & alloys; special dies, tools, jigs & fixtures

(G-12256)
REYNOLDS DRAPERY SERVICE INC
Also Called: Country Coin-Op
7440 Main St (13416-7707)
PHONE.................................315 845-8632
Richard Reynolds, *President*
Michael Moody, *Vice Pres*
EMP: 10 **EST:** 1964
SQ FT: 6,500
SALES (est): 964.8K **Privately Held**
SIC: 2391 5023 5714 7216 Draperies, plastic & textile: from purchased materials; draperies; draperies; curtain cleaning & repair; fire resistance finishing of cotton broadwoven fabrics; laundry, coin-operated

Niagara Falls
Niagara County

(G-12257)
AAVID NIAGARA LLC (DH)
3315 Haseley Dr (14304-1460)
PHONE.................................716 297-0652
Barry Heckman, *CEO*
Alan Wong, *President*
Scott Mowry, *Vice Pres*
Mark Parisi, *Vice Pres*
Ken Norwich, *Design Engr*
▲ **EMP:** 45
SQ FT: 45,000
SALES (est): 29.5MM
SALES (corp-wide): 874.5MM **Privately Held**
WEB: www.niagarathermal.com
SIC: 3443 5084 Heat exchangers, condensers & components; heat exchange equipment, industrial
HQ: Aavid Thermalloy, Llc
1 Aavid Cir
Laconia NH 03246
603 528-3400

(G-12258)
ADVANTAGE MACHINING INC
6421 Wendt Dr (14304-1100)
PHONE.................................716 731-6418
Scott Ranney, *President*
EMP: 10
SALES (est): 1MM **Privately Held**
SIC: 3441 Fabricated structural metal

(G-12259)
AMERICARB INC
6100 Niagara Falls Blvd (14304-1534)
PHONE.................................419 281-5800
Matt Reineke, *President*
Leland P Reineke, *Chairman*
Ajit Sane, *Vice Pres*
Tim Barrett, *CFO*
Brian Guido, *VP Sales*
▲ **EMP:** 75
SQ FT: 140,000
SALES (est): 18.5MM **Privately Held**
SIC: 3624 Carbon & graphite products

(G-12260)
AMERICARB INTERNATIONAL CORP
6100 Niagara Falls Blvd (14304-1534)
PHONE.................................419 281-5800
Matt Reineke, *CEO*
Lee Reineke, *Chairman*
Brian Guido, *Vice Pres*
Rick Mellino, *Vice Pres*
Eugene Cabonor, *CFO*
EMP: 7 **EST:** 2010
SALES (est): 635K **Privately Held**
SIC: 3624 Carbon & graphite products

(G-12261)
AMTEK RESEARCH LLC
1711 Cudaback Ave # 3865 (14303-1709)
PHONE.................................416 400-2906
Ajay Misra, *Branch Mgr*
EMP: 23
SALES (corp-wide): 134.6K **Privately Held**
SIC: 2819 2899 Industrial inorganic chemicals; fuel tank or engine cleaning chemicals
PA: Amtek Research, Llc
705 Killarney Dr Nw
Huntsville AL

(G-12262)
AMTEK RESEARCH LLC
1711 Cudaback Ave # 3865 (14303-1709)
PHONE.................................212 537-6462
Ajay Misra, *Mng Member*
EMP: 23
SQ FT: 4,700
SALES (est): 2.3MM **Privately Held**
SIC: 2819 Industrial inorganic chemicals

(G-12263)
ANGUS CHEMICAL COMPANY
Also Called: Angus Buffers & Biochemicals
2236 Liberty Dr (14304-3756)
PHONE.................................716 283-1434
Mark Deuble, *Manager*
EMP: 23
SALES (corp-wide): 10.6B **Privately Held**
SIC: 2836 Culture media
HQ: Angus Chemical Company
1500 E Lake Cook Rd
Buffalo Grove IL 60089
847 215-8600

(G-12264)
APOLLO STEEL CORPORATION
4800 Tomson Ave (14304-2150)
PHONE.................................716 283-8758
George J Merkling III, *President*
EMP: 16
SQ FT: 15,000
SALES (est): 5.7MM **Privately Held**
SIC: 3441 Bridge sections, prefabricated highway; bridge sections, prefabricated railway; expansion joints (structural shapes), iron or steel; floor jacks, metal

(G-12265)
BRAUN HORTICULTURE INC
3302 Highland Ave (14305-2013)
P.O. Box 260 (14305-0260)
PHONE.................................716 282-6101
Peter Braun, *President*
▲ **EMP:** 7
SQ FT: 31,500
SALES (est): 1.3MM **Privately Held**
WEB: www.braungroup.com
SIC: 3315 Baskets, steel wire
HQ: Braun Nursery Limited
2004 Glancaster Rd
Mount Hope ON L0R 1
905 648-1911

(G-12266)
BRODA MACHINE CO INC
8745 Packard Rd (14304-1497)
PHONE.................................716 297-3221
Matthew Broda, *President*
Thomas J Broda, *President*
Lillian Broda, *Corp Secy*
Mark Broda, *Vice Pres*
Jeff Kilroy, *Plant Mgr*
EMP: 13
SQ FT: 10,000
SALES (est): 3.6MM **Privately Held**
WEB: www.brodamachine.com
SIC: 3451 Screw machine products

(G-12267)
CALSPAN CORPORATION
Also Called: Calspan Flight Research Center
2041 Niagara Falls Blvd (14304-1617)
PHONE.................................716 236-1040
Paul Nafziger, *Branch Mgr*
EMP: 11
SALES (corp-wide): 79.2MM **Privately Held**
WEB: www.windtunnel.com
SIC: 3721 Research & development on aircraft by the manufacturer
HQ: Calspan Corporation
4455 Genesee St
Buffalo NY 14225
716 631-6955

(G-12268)
CASCADES NEW YORK INC
4001 Packard Rd (14303-2202)
PHONE.................................716 285-3681
Craig Griffith, *General Mgr*
Harry Garton, *Sales Staff*
Mary Malone, *Manager*
EMP: 115
SALES (corp-wide): 3.3B **Privately Held**
SIC: 2631 Linerboard
HQ: Cascades New York Inc.
1845 Emerson St
Rochester NY 14606
585 527-8110

(G-12269)
CCT (US) INC
2221 Niagara Falls Blvd # 5 (14304-5709)
PHONE.................................716 297-7509
Yves Therrien, *President*
Jacques Chevrette, *Admin Sec*
▲ **EMP:** 15
SQ FT: 20,000
SALES (est): 595.4K **Privately Held**
SIC: 2679 Building, insulating & packaging paper; building, insulating & packaging paperboard
PA: Papiers C.C.T. Inc
830 Rue Saint-Viateur
Berthierville QC J0K 1
450 836-3846

(G-12270)
CENTRE DE CONFORMITE ICC INC
2150 Liberty Dr Ste 1 (14304-3780)
PHONE.................................716 283-0002
Shirley Coles, *Office Mgr*
EMP: 28 **Privately Held**
SIC: 2673 Bags: plastic, laminated & coated
PA: Centre De Conformite Icc Inc
88 Av Lindsay
Dorval QC H9P 2
514 636-8146

(G-12271)
CHEMOURS COMPANY FC LLC
3181 Buffalo Ave (14303-2158)
P.O. Box 787 (14302-0787)
PHONE.................................716 278-5100
Tim Reece, *Manager*
Esther Lorence, *Director*
EMP: 50
SALES (corp-wide): 6.1B **Publicly Held**
WEB: www.dupont.com
SIC: 2819 2865 2812 Industrial inorganic chemicals; cyclic crudes & intermediates; alkalies & chlorine
HQ: The Chemours Company Fc Llc
1007 Market St
Wilmington DE 19898
302 773-1000

(G-12272)
CNHI LLC
Also Called: Tonawanda News
473 3rd St Ste 201 (14301-1500)
PHONE.................................716 693-1000
Wayne Lowman, *Branch Mgr*
EMP: 100
SQ FT: 21,892 **Privately Held**
WEB: www.clintonnc.com
SIC: 2711 Newspapers: publishing only, not printed on site
HQ: Cnhi, Llc
445 Dexter Ave
Montgomery AL 36104

(G-12273)
CNHI LLC
Also Called: Niagara Gazette
473 3rd St Ste 201 (14301-1500)
PHONE.................................716 282-2311
Steve Braver, *Principal*
EMP: 55
SQ FT: 21,534 **Privately Held**
WEB: www.clintonnc.com
SIC: 2711 2741 Newspapers: publishing only, not printed on site; miscellaneous publishing
HQ: Cnhi, Llc
445 Dexter Ave
Montgomery AL 36104

(G-12274)
COSTANZOS WELDING INC (PA)
Also Called: Cataract Steel Industries
22nd Allen St (14302)
P.O. Box 862 (14302-0862)
PHONE.................................716 282-0845
Scott Costanzo, *President*
Thomas Costanzo, *Vice Pres*
Jim Willett, *Manager*
▼ **EMP:** 49
SQ FT: 100,000
SALES (est): 8MM **Privately Held**
WEB: www.cataractsteel.com
SIC: 3443 Heat exchangers, plate type

(G-12275)
CRYSTAL CERES INDUSTRIES INC
2250 Liberty Dr (14304-3756)
PHONE.................................716 283-0445
Michael Lynch, *Vice Pres*
▲ **EMP:** 58
SALES (est): 8.2MM **Privately Held**
WEB: www.cerescrystal.com
SIC: 1481 7631 Nonmetallic mineral services; diamond setter

(G-12276)
CSI INTERNATIONAL INC
1001 Main St (14301-1111)
PHONE.................................800 441-2895
Steven Brown, *President*
CAM Mackenzie, *General Mgr*
Jorge Garcia, *Area Mgr*
Erika Lorange, *Opers Mgr*
Lillian Starr, *Prdtn Mgr*
▲ **EMP:** 40
SQ FT: 37,000
SALES (est): 7MM **Privately Held**
SIC: 3911 3914 5947 Jewelry, precious metal; trophies, plated (all metals); gift shop

(G-12277)
DELFINGEN US-NEW YORK INC
Also Called: Sofanou
2221 Niagara Falls Blvd # 12 (14304-5709)
PHONE.................................716 215-0300
Bernard Streit, *President*
Olivier Mathieu, *General Mgr*
David Streit, *Vice Pres*
Mark Blanke, *Treasurer*
Emmanuel Klinklin, *Admin Sec*
▲ **EMP:** 25
SALES (est): 5.9MM
SALES (corp-wide): 3.8MM **Privately Held**
SIC: 3643 Caps & plugs, electric: attachment
HQ: Delfingen Us, Inc.
3985 W Hamlin Rd
Rochester Hills MI 48309

(G-12278)
DONNA KARAN COMPANY LLC
1900 Military Rd (14304-1737)
PHONE.................................716 297-0752
Elizabeth Carroll, *Branch Mgr*
EMP: 157
SALES (corp-wide): 2.8B **Publicly Held**
SIC: 2335 Women's, juniors' & misses' dresses

Niagara Falls - Niagara County (G-12279) GEOGRAPHIC SECTION

HQ: The Donna Karan Company Llc
    240 W 40th St
    New York NY 10018
    212 789-1500

(G-12279)
DUREZ CORPORATION
5000 Packard Rd (14304-1510)
PHONE..................................716 286-0100
John W Fisher, *CEO*
EMP: 15
SALES (corp-wide): 1.9B **Privately Held**
SIC: 2865 2821 Cyclic crudes & intermediates; plastics materials & resins
HQ: Durez Corporation
    46820 Magellan Dr Ste C
    Novi MI 48377
    248 313-7000

(G-12280)
EASTERN MACHINE AND ELECTRIC
1041 Niagara Ave (14305-2639)
PHONE..................................716 284-8271
Louis Destino, *President*
Daniel Destino, *Corp Secy*
EMP: 6 **EST:** 1957
SQ FT: 7,200
SALES (est): 514.2K **Privately Held**
SIC: 3599 Machine shop, jobbing & repair

(G-12281)
ENSIL TECHNICAL SERVICES INC
1901 Maryland Ave (14305-1722)
PHONE..................................716 282-1020
Farsad Kiani, *President*
Louis Koikas, *Principal*
EMP: 50
SALES (est): 7.3MM **Privately Held**
SIC: 3728 Aircraft parts & equipment

(G-12282)
EUROTEX INC
Also Called: Eurotex North America
4600 Witmer Rd (14305-1217)
PHONE..................................716 205-8861
Sasha Mitic, *President*
▲ **EMP:** 12
SALES (est): 1.3MM **Privately Held**
SIC: 2295 Coated fabrics, not rubberized

(G-12283)
FELICETTI CONCRETE PRODUCTS
4129 Hyde Park Blvd (14305-1711)
PHONE..................................716 284-5740
Gene Felicetti, *Corp Secy*
Henry Felicetti, *Vice Pres*
Frank M Felicetti, *Shareholder*
Phillip Felicetti, *Shareholder*
Richard B Felicetti, *Shareholder*
EMP: 7
SQ FT: 1,750
SALES (est): 1.2MM **Privately Held**
SIC: 3271 Blocks, concrete or cinder: standard; brick, concrete

(G-12284)
FELTON MACHINE CO INC
2221 Niagara Falls Blvd (14304-5709)
P.O. Box 239 (14304-0239)
PHONE..................................716 215-9001
Robert J Schroeder, *President*
Jeff Gorney, *Mfg Staff*
Bridget M Schroeder, *Treasurer*
Mike Schroder, *Info Tech Mgr*
Kay Spatorico, *Technology*
EMP: 38
SQ FT: 42,000
SALES (est): 6.3MM **Privately Held**
WEB: www.feltonmachine.com
SIC: 3599 Machine shop, jobbing & repair

(G-12285)
FERRO ELECTRONICS MATERIALS
4511 Hyde Park Blvd (14305-1215)
PHONE..................................716 278-9400
Lyndon La Brake, *Branch Mgr*
EMP: 180
SALES (corp-wide): 1.4B **Publicly Held**
SIC: 3264 2819 Porcelain electrical supplies; industrial inorganic chemicals

HQ: Ferro Electronics Materials Inc
    1789 Transelco Dr
    Penn Yan NY 14527
    315 536-3357

(G-12286)
FLAME CONTROL COATINGS LLC
4120 Hyde Park Blvd (14305-1793)
PHONE..................................716 282-1399
Pamela Allen, *Production*
Tim Lockhart, *Marketing Mgr*
Jeff Fallon,
Jonathan Hatch,
▼ **EMP:** 26 **EST:** 1976
SQ FT: 26,000
SALES (est): 7.3MM **Privately Held**
WEB: www.flamecontrol.com
SIC: 2899 Fire retardant chemicals

(G-12287)
FROSS INDUSTRIES INC
Also Called: Niagara Development & Mfg Div
3315 Haseley Dr (14304-1460)
PHONE..................................716 297-0652
Silvio Derubeis, *President*
Robert Schultz, *Vice Pres*
Donald H Smith, *Treasurer*
Gordon Smith, *Admin Sec*
EMP: 50 **EST:** 1981
SQ FT: 16,000
SALES (est): 6.2MM **Privately Held**
SIC: 3443 3599 Heat exchangers, plate type; machine shop, jobbing & repair

(G-12288)
GLOBE METALLURGICAL INC
Also Called: Globe Specialty Metals
3807 Highland Ave (14305-1723)
PHONE..................................716 804-0862
Steven Dorszynski, *Production*
Paul Kwapiszeski, *Branch Mgr*
EMP: 90
SALES (corp-wide): 1.7B **Privately Held**
WEB: www.globemetallurgical.com
SIC: 3339 3313 Silicon refining (primary, over 99% pure); ferromanganese, not made in blast furnaces
HQ: Globe Metallurgical Inc.
    Co Rd 32
    Waterford OH 45786
    740 984-2361

(G-12289)
GRAPHICOMM INC
Also Called: Insty-Prints
7703 Niagara Falls Blvd (14304-1739)
P.O. Box 543, Grand Island (14072-0543)
PHONE..................................716 283-0830
John Jones, *President*
Stephen Perry, *Prdtn Mgr*
EMP: 5
SQ FT: 2,200
SALES (est): 696.8K **Privately Held**
SIC: 2752 7334 2791 2789 Commercial printing, offset; photocopying & duplicating services; typesetting; bookbinding & related work

(G-12290)
GREATER NIAGARA BLDG CTR INC
9540 Niagara Falls Blvd (14304-4909)
PHONE..................................716 299-0543
Bill Burg, *CEO*
EMP: 12
SALES (est): 2.1MM **Privately Held**
SIC: 2421 Building & structural materials, wood

(G-12291)
GREENPAC MILL LLC (DH)
4400 Royal Ave (14303-2128)
PHONE..................................716 299-0560
Luc Nadeau,
▲ **EMP:** 110 **EST:** 2010
SALES (est): 47.6MM
SALES (corp-wide): 3.3B **Privately Held**
SIC: 2631 Linerboard
HQ: Cascades New York Inc.
    1845 Emerson St
    Rochester NY 14606
    585 527-8110

(G-12292)
GUESS INC
1826 Military Rd Spc 113 (14304-1772)
PHONE..................................716 298-3561
Danielle Guetta, *Manager*
EMP: 25
SALES (corp-wide): 2.3B **Publicly Held**
WEB: www.guess.com
SIC: 2325 Men's & boys' jeans & dungarees
PA: Guess , Inc.
    1444 S Alameda St
    Los Angeles CA 90021
    213 765-3100

(G-12293)
HELMEL ENGINEERING PDTS INC
6520 Lockport Rd (14305-3512)
PHONE..................................716 297-8644
Erwin Helmel, *President*
Dora Helmel, *Admin Sec*
▲ **EMP:** 22
SQ FT: 23,000
SALES (est): 2.7MM **Privately Held**
WEB: www.helmel.com
SIC: 3545 Machine tool accessories

(G-12294)
IMBITIVE TECH AMER CORP
Also Called: Imbtec America
1623 Military Rd Ste 1011 (14304-1745)
PHONE..................................888 843-2323
John Brinkman, *President*
Bruno Iafrate, *Vice Pres*
EMP: 5
SALES: 254K
SALES (corp-wide): 4.5MM **Privately Held**
SIC: 2821 5162 Plastics materials & resins; plastics materials & basic shapes
PA: Imbitive Technologies Corporation
    1623 Military Rd Ste 1011
    Niagara Falls NY 14304
    888 843-2323

(G-12295)
IMBITIVE TECHNOLOGIES CORP (PA)
1623 Military Rd Ste 1011 (14304-1745)
PHONE..................................888 843-2323
John Brinkman, *President*
Richard Hall, *Vice Pres*
Nick Flor, *CFO*
Richard Halinda, *Treasurer*
EMP: 4
SALES (est): 4.5MM **Privately Held**
SIC: 2821 5162 Plastics materials & resins; plastics materials & basic shapes

(G-12296)
IMERYS FSED MNRL NGARA FLS INC
4901 Hyde Park Blvd (14305-1224)
P.O. Box 1438 (14302-1438)
PHONE..................................716 286-1250
Dave Gratz, *Manager*
EMP: 9
SALES (corp-wide): 2.6MM **Privately Held**
SIC: 3291 Abrasive products
HQ: Imerys Fused Minerals Niagara Falls, Inc.
    2000 College Ave
    Niagara Falls NY 14305

(G-12297)
IMERYS FSED MNRL NGARA FLS INC (DH)
2000 College Ave (14305-1734)
P.O. Box 1438 (14302-1438)
PHONE..................................716 286-1250
Christian Pfeifer, *CEO*
▲ **EMP:** 35
SQ FT: 4,950
SALES (est): 7.9MM
SALES (corp-wide): 2.6MM **Privately Held**
SIC: 3291 Abrasive products
HQ: Imerys Usa, Inc.
    100 Mansell Ct E Ste 300
    Roswell GA 30076
    770 645-3300

(G-12298)
IMERYS STEELCASTING USA INC (DH)
4111 Witmer Rd (14305-1720)
P.O. Box 368 (14302-0368)
PHONE..................................716 278-1634
Gilles Michel, *CEO*
Jurgen Sardemann, *Ch of Bd*
Manfred Beck, *President*
Tim Wilson, *Part Secy*
Michael Monberg, *Vice Pres*
▲ **EMP:** 66
SALES (est): 18.2MM
SALES (corp-wide): 2.6MM **Privately Held**
WEB: www.stollberg.com
SIC: 3399 Powder, metal
HQ: Imerys Metalcasting Germany Gmbh
    Duisburger Str. 69-73
    Oberhausen 46049
    208 850-0500

(G-12299)
INDUSTRIAL SERVICES OF WNY
7221 Niagara Falls Blvd (14305-1715)
PHONE..................................716 799-7788
Georgena Dinieri, *Owner*
EMP: 5
SALES (est): 239K **Privately Held**
SIC: 3599 Machine & other job shop work

(G-12300)
J D CALATO MANUFACTURING CO (PA)
Also Called: Regal Tip
4501 Hyde Park Blvd (14305-1215)
PHONE..................................716 285-3546
Carol Calato, *CEO*
Joseph D Calato, *CEO*
Catherine Calato, *Vice Pres*
Sharon Schaal, *Purch Agent*
Matthew Carrier, *QC Dir*
EMP: 35 **EST:** 1961
SQ FT: 17,000
SALES (est): 4.1MM **Privately Held**
WEB: www.calato.com
SIC: 3931 Guitars & parts, electric & non-electric; drums, parts & accessories (musical instruments)

(G-12301)
JOHNNIE RYAN CO INC
3084 Niagara St (14303-2030)
PHONE..................................716 282-1606
Paul Janik, *Vice Pres*
EMP: 15
SQ FT: 10,000
SALES (est): 2.1MM **Privately Held**
WEB: www.johnnieryan.com
SIC: 2086 Soft drinks: packaged in cans, bottles, etc.

(G-12302)
KINTEX INC
Also Called: Niagara Thermo Products
3315 Haseley Dr (14304-1460)
PHONE..................................716 297-0652
Barry Heckman, *Owner*
Donald Hall, *Engineer*
Frank Yang, *Manager*
EMP: 90
SALES (est): 6.3MM **Privately Held**
SIC: 3443 Heat exchangers, condensers & components

(G-12303)
KITTREDGE & SONS INC
3315 Haseley Dr (14304-1460)
PHONE..................................978 567-0998
Peter Rolla, *President*
James L Kittredge, *Treasurer*
John Shea, *Admin Sec*
EMP: 65
SQ FT: 45,000
SALES (est): 9.8MM
SALES (corp-wide): 874.5MM **Privately Held**
WEB: www.jkittredge.com
SIC: 3599 7692 3398 3471 Machine shop, jobbing & repair; brazing; metal heat treating; plating & polishing; sheet metalwork

▲ = Import ▼ = Export
◆ = Import/Export

GEOGRAPHIC SECTION

Niagara Falls - Niagara County (G-12329)

HQ: Aavid Thermalloy, Llc
1 Aavid Cir
Laconia NH 03246
603 528-3400

(G-12304)
L A R ELECTRONICS CORP
2733 Niagara St (14303-2027)
PHONE..................716 285-0555
Lawrence Kutner, *President*
EMP: 7 **EST:** 1980
SQ FT: 3,500
SALES: 150K **Privately Held**
WEB: www.laraudio.com
SIC: 3651 5065 1731 Speaker systems; sound equipment, electronic; sound equipment specialization

(G-12305)
LIDDELL CORPORATION
4600 Witmer Ind Est 5 (14305-1364)
PHONE..................716 297-8557
Lon Flick, *President*
EMP: 14
SALES: 1.3MM **Privately Held**
WEB: www.nicel.com
SIC: 2844 Cosmetic preparations

(G-12306)
LIQUID INDUSTRIES INC
7219 New Jersey Ave (14305)
PHONE..................716 628-2999
Hamish Shaw, *President*
EMP: 6
SALES (est): 694.3K **Privately Held**
SIC: 3589 Car washing machinery

(G-12307)
LOCKHEED MARTIN CORPORATION
2221 Niagara Falls Blvd (14304-5709)
PHONE..................716 297-1000
Mike Davis, *Safety Mgr*
Donald Kellner, *QC Mgr*
David Savini, *Engineer*
Nate Phillips, *Electrical Engi*
Matthew McGrath, *Manager*
EMP: 40 **Publicly Held**
WEB: www.lockheedmartin.com
SIC: 3721 3812 3769 Motorized aircraft; search & navigation equipment; guided missile & space vehicle parts & auxiliary equipment
PA: Lockheed Martin Corporation
6801 Rockledge Dr
Bethesda MD 20817

(G-12308)
MARIPHARM LABORATORIES
2045 Niagara Falls Blvd (14304-1675)
PHONE..................716 984-6520
Christopher Dean, *Owner*
EMP: 10
SALES (est): 564.9K **Privately Held**
SIC: 3821 Laboratory apparatus & furniture

(G-12309)
METAL PRODUCTS INTL LLC
7510 Porter Rd Ste 4 (14304-1692)
PHONE..................716 215-1930
Thomas Fleckestien,
Kenneth Koedinger,
▲ **EMP:** 5
SALES: 12MM **Privately Held**
WEB: www.metalproducts.com
SIC: 3449 Miscellaneous metalwork

(G-12310)
METRO MATTRESS CORP
2212 Military Rd (14304-1760)
PHONE..................716 205-2300
Randy Pegan, *Branch Mgr*
EMP: 28
SALES (corp-wide): 42.3MM **Privately Held**
SIC: 2515 5712 5719 Mattresses & bedsprings; beds & accessories; beddings & linens
PA: Metro Mattress Corp.
3545 John Glenn Blvd
Syracuse NY 13209
315 218-1200

(G-12311)
MOOG INC
Also Called: Moog - Isp
6686 Walmore Rd (14304-1638)
PHONE..................716 731-6300
Donna Lough, *Accountant*
Jerry Fritz, *Branch Mgr*
Thomas Donnelly, *Manager*
Cheryl Gray, *Manager*
EMP: 100
SALES (corp-wide): 2.7B **Publicly Held**
SIC: 2819 Industrial inorganic chemicals
PA: Moog Inc.
400 Jamison Rd
Elma NY 14059
716 652-2000

(G-12312)
NATIONAL MAINT CONTG CORP
Also Called: Nmcc
5600 Niagara Falls Blvd (14304-1532)
P.O. Box 258 (14304-0258)
PHONE..................716 285-1583
Samuel D Lehr, *President*
EMP: 54
SALES (est): 5MM **Privately Held**
SIC: 3499 Welding tips, heat resistant: metal

(G-12313)
NIAGARA SAMPLE BOOK CO INC
1717 Mackenna Ave (14303-1715)
PHONE..................716 284-6151
Joseph P Pinzotti, *President*
Marsha A Pinzotti, *Vice Pres*
Mary B Pinzotti, *Treasurer*
Marcella Pinzotti, *Admin Sec*
EMP: 15 **EST:** 1945
SQ FT: 20,000
SALES (est): 1.3MM **Privately Held**
WEB: www.niagarasample.com
SIC: 2782 2759 Sample books; commercial printing

(G-12314)
NIKE INC
1886 Military Rd (14304-1772)
PHONE..................716 298-5615
EMP: 7
SALES (corp-wide): 36.4B **Publicly Held**
SIC: 3021 Rubber & plastics footwear
PA: Nike, Inc.
1 Sw Bowerman Dr
Beaverton OR 97005
503 671-6453

(G-12315)
NORTH AMERICAN HOGANAS INC
5950 Packard Rd (14304-1584)
P.O. Box 310 (14304-0310)
PHONE..................716 285-3451
Avinash Gore, *President*
Terry Heinrich, *Corp Secy*
George Gillespie, *Vice Pres*
Nagarjuna Nandivada, *Vice Pres*
Eric Reynolds, *Accountant*
◆ **EMP:** 41
SALES (est): 14MM
SALES (corp-wide): 974.4MM **Privately Held**
SIC: 2819 Iron (ferric/ferrous) compounds or salts
HQ: North American Hoganas Holdings, Inc.
111 Hoganas Way
Hollsopple PA 15935
814 479-2551

(G-12316)
NORTHKNIGHT LOGISTICS INC
7724 Buffalo Ave (14304-4134)
PHONE..................716 283-3090
John Rendle, *CEO*
◆ **EMP:** 15 **EST:** 2007
SQ FT: 14,000
SALES (est): 2MM **Privately Held**
SIC: 3429 Builders' hardware

(G-12317)
NUTTALL GEAR L L C (HQ)
Also Called: Delroyd Worm Gear
2221 Niagara Falls Blvd # 17 (14304-5710)
PHONE..................716 298-4100
Michael Hurt, *CEO*
Scott Jimbroni, *General Mgr*
Denis Hadden, *QC Mgr*
Steve Szychowski, *Engineer*
Mark Rawls, *Controller*
▲ **EMP:** 45
SQ FT: 107,000
SALES (est): 15MM
SALES (corp-wide): 876.7MM **Publicly Held**
WEB: www.nuttallgear.com
SIC: 3566 Gears, power transmission, except automotive
PA: Altra Industrial Motion Corp.
300 Granite St Ste 201
Braintree MA 02184
781 917-0600

(G-12318)
OCCIDENTAL CHEMICAL CORP
4700 Buffalo Ave (14304-3821)
P.O. Box 344 (14304-0344)
PHONE..................716 278-7795
Joseph Guzzetta, *Engineer*
Tom Feeney, *Branch Mgr*
Nancy McDonell, *Administration*
EMP: 35
SALES (corp-wide): 13.2B **Publicly Held**
WEB: www.oxychem.com
SIC: 2812 Alkalies & chlorine
HQ: Occidental Chemical Corporation
5005 Lyndon B Johnson Fwy
Dallas TX 75244
972 404-3800

(G-12319)
OCCIDENTAL CHEMICAL CORP
56 Street & Energy Blvd (14302)
P.O. Box 344 (14302-0344)
PHONE..................716 278-7794
Herb Jones, *General Mgr*
EMP: 200
SALES (corp-wide): 13.2B **Publicly Held**
SIC: 2812 2874 Phosphatic fertilizers; chlorine, compressed or liquefied
HQ: Occidental Chemical Corporation
5005 Lyndon B Johnson Fwy
Dallas TX 75244
972 404-3800

(G-12320)
OLIN CHLOR ALKALI LOGISTICS
Also Called: Chlor Alkali Products & Vinyls
2400 Buffalo Ave (14303-1959)
P.O. Box 748 (14302-0748)
PHONE..................716 278-6411
Tom Tirabassi, *Manager*
Rick Mac Donell, *Administration*
EMP: 150
SALES (corp-wide): 6.2B **Publicly Held**
WEB: www.olin.com
SIC: 2812 2842 Alkalies & chlorine; specialty cleaning, polishes & sanitation goods
HQ: Olin Chlor Alkali Logistics Inc
490 Stuart Rd Ne
Cleveland TN 37312
423 336-4850

(G-12321)
OXAIR LTD
8320 Quarry Rd (14304-1068)
P.O. Box 4039 (14304-8039)
PHONE..................716 298-8288
Flavio Zeni, *President*
◆ **EMP:** 5
SQ FT: 10,000
SALES (est): 886.4K **Privately Held**
WEB: www.oxair.com
SIC: 2813 Oxygen, compressed or liquefied

(G-12322)
PENETRADAR CORPORATION
2509 Niagara Falls Blvd (14304-4518)
PHONE..................716 731-2629
Anthony J Alongi, *President*
Anthony Stang, *Electrical Engi*
Carol Eames, *CIO*
EMP: 15
SQ FT: 15,000
SALES (est): 2.1MM **Privately Held**
WEB: www.penetradar.com
SIC: 3812 Radar systems & equipment

(G-12323)
PLIOTRON COMPANY AMERICA LLC
4650 Witmer Indus Est (14305-1360)
PHONE..................716 298-4457
Robert Leiathton, *Plant Mgr*
Albert E Matthews,
Linda Matthews,
EMP: 5 **EST:** 1962
SQ FT: 8,125
SALES (est): 363K **Privately Held**
WEB: www.pliotron.com
SIC: 3564 Filters, air: furnaces, air conditioning equipment, etc.

(G-12324)
PRAXAIR INC
4501 Royal Ave (14303-2121)
PHONE..................716 286-4600
Brian McKie, *Branch Mgr*
EMP: 50
SALES (corp-wide): 11.4B **Privately Held**
SIC: 2813 Industrial gases
PA: Praxair, Inc.
10 Riverview Dr
Danbury CT 06810
203 837-2000

(G-12325)
PRECIOUS PLATE INC
2124 Liberty Dr (14304-3799)
PHONE..................716 283-0690
David R Hurst, *President*
William Copping, *Vice Pres*
Scott Law, *Vice Pres*
David Miller, *Vice Pres*
Ken Russell, *Safety Mgr*
▲ **EMP:** 75
SQ FT: 65,000
SALES (est): 16.8MM **Privately Held**
SIC: 3471 Electroplating of metals or formed products

(G-12326)
PRECISION ELCTRO MNRL PMCO INC
150 Portage Rd (14303-1535)
P.O. Box 8 (14302-0008)
PHONE..................716 284-2484
Abdul Labi, *President*
EMP: 25
SQ FT: 40,000
SALES (est): 2MM **Privately Held**
WEB: www.pemco-niagara.com
SIC: 2819 3291 1446 Mfg Industrial Inorganic Chemicals Mfg Abrasive Products Industrial Sand Mining

(G-12327)
PRECISION PROCESS INC (PA)
2111 Liberty Dr (14304-3744)
PHONE..................716 731-1587
David Hurst, *CEO*
Bill Copping, *Vice Pres*
Matthew Velez, *Engineer*
Joe Hoyt, *VP Finance*
John Bondi, *Sales Mgr*
▲ **EMP:** 83
SQ FT: 65,000
SALES (est): 17.3MM **Privately Held**
WEB: www.precisionprocess.com
SIC: 3559 Electroplating machinery & equipment

(G-12328)
RANNEY PRECISION
Also Called: Ranney Precision Machining
6421 Wendt Dr (14304-1100)
PHONE..................716 731-6418
David Ranney, *Owner*
Joanne Ranney, *Co-Owner*
EMP: 17
SQ FT: 10,000
SALES (est): 1.3MM **Privately Held**
WEB: www.ranneyprecision.com
SIC: 3451 Screw machine products

(G-12329)
RELIANCE FLUID TECH LLC
3943 Buffalo Ave (14303-2136)
PHONE..................716 332-0988
John Garguiolo, *President*
EMP: 40
SALES (est): 2MM **Privately Held**
SIC: 2899 Corrosion preventive lubricant

Niagara Falls - Niagara County (G-12330)

(G-12330)
RT MACHINED SPECIALTIES
2221 Niagara Falls Blvd (14304-5709)
PHONE....................................716 731-2055
Rebecca Christie, *President*
EMP: 5
SALES: 300K **Privately Held**
SIC: 3599 Machine shop, jobbing & repair

(G-12331)
RUS INDUSTRIES INC
3255 Lockport Rd (14305-2398)
PHONE....................................716 284-7828
Alice G Carlson, *Ch of Bd*
James A Ryding, *Vice Pres*
Greg Robinson, *VP Sales*
Dave Hogrewe, *Manager*
Pat Johnson, *Manager*
▲ **EMP:** 32
SQ FT: 29,000
SALES (est): 4.8MM **Privately Held**
WEB: www.rusindustries.com
SIC: 3441 3661 Fabricated structural metal; communication headgear, telephone

(G-12332)
SAINT GOBAIN GRAINS & POWDERS
6600 Walmore Rd (14304-1638)
PHONE....................................716 731-8200
Tom Vincent, *Principal*
▲ **EMP:** 1015
SALES (est): 74.7MM
SALES (corp-wide): 213.5MM **Privately Held**
SIC: 3269 2891 3221 Laboratory & industrial pottery; chemical porcelain; adhesives; adhesives, plastic; cement, except linoleum & tile; epoxy adhesives; food containers, glass
HQ: Saint-Gobain Corporation
20 Moores Rd
Malvern PA 19355

(G-12333)
SAINT-GBAIN ADVNCED CRMICS LLC (HQ)
Also Called: Structural Ceramics Division
23 Acheson Dr (14303-1555)
PHONE....................................716 278-6066
Ron Lambright, *CEO*
Jean Louis Beffa, *Ch of Bd*
Curtis Schmit, *General Mgr*
Diana Tierney, *Human Res Mgr*
Joseph Cannavo, *Technology*
▲ **EMP:** 150
SQ FT: 1,064
SALES (est): 29.2MM
SALES (corp-wide): 213.5MM **Privately Held**
WEB: www.hexoloy.com
SIC: 3269 Laboratory & industrial pottery
PA: Compagnie De Saint-Gobain
La Defense 3 Tour Les Miroirs
Courbevoie 92400
147 623-000

(G-12334)
SAINT-GOBAIN DYNAMICS INC
Also Called: Structural Ceramics Group
23 Acheson Dr (14303-1555)
PHONE....................................716 278-6007
Curtis M Schmit, *President*
EMP: 10
SALES (est): 1MM **Privately Held**
SIC: 3297 Nonclay refractories

(G-12335)
SAINT-GOBAIN STRL CERAMICS
23 Acheson Dr (14303-1555)
PHONE....................................716 278-6233
John T Crowe, *CEO*
◆ **EMP:** 1720
SALES (est): 139.8MM
SALES (corp-wide): 213.5MM **Privately Held**
SIC: 3255 Brick, clay refractory
HQ: Saint-Gobain Corporation
20 Moores Rd
Malvern PA 19355

(G-12336)
SHIPMAN PRINTING INDS INC
Also Called: Shipman Print Solutions
2424 Niagara Falls Blvd (14304-4562)
P.O. Box 357 (14304-0357)
PHONE....................................716 504-7700
Gary Blum, *Ch of Bd*
Richard Faiola, *Exec VP*
Randy Duncan, *Vice Pres*
Michael Fiore, *Vice Pres*
Diane Donner, *Accounts Mgr*
EMP: 34 **EST:** 1905
SQ FT: 20,000
SALES (est): 6.8MM **Privately Held**
WEB: www.shipmanprint.com
SIC: 2752 2789 2759 Commercial printing, offset; bookbinding & related work; envelopes: printing

(G-12337)
SILIPOS HOLDING LLC (PA)
7049 Williams Rd (14304-3731)
PHONE....................................716 283-0700
Richard Margolis, *President*
◆ **EMP:** 7 **EST:** 2015
SQ FT: 35,000
SALES (est): 34.6MM **Privately Held**
SIC: 3842 Surgical appliances & supplies

(G-12338)
STEPHENSON CUSTOM CASE COMPANY
Also Called: Portequip Work Stations
1623 Military Rd (14304-1745)
PHONE....................................905 542-8762
John Stephenson, *Owner*
EMP: 30
SALES: 950K **Privately Held**
SIC: 3949 Sporting & athletic goods

(G-12339)
SWISSMAR INC
6391 Walmore Rd (14304-1613)
PHONE....................................905 764-1121
Daniel Oehy, *President*
George Hobson, *VP Finance*
EMP: 8 **EST:** 1990
SQ FT: 15,000
SALES (est): 917.4K **Privately Held**
SIC: 3262 5719 China cookware; housewares

(G-12340)
TAM CERAMICS GROUP OF NY LLC
4511 Hyde Park Blvd (14305-1298)
PHONE....................................716 278-9400
George Bilkey, *President*
Mike Chu,
EMP: 62
SQ FT: 3,750
SALES: 30MM **Privately Held**
SIC: 3399 Powder, metal

(G-12341)
TAM CERAMICS LLC
4511 Hyde Park Blvd (14305-1298)
PHONE....................................716 278-9480
Eric Hanson, *Vice Pres*
Robert Difranco, *Purchasing*
Shamus Crean, *Engineer*
John Hess, *Engineer*
Matthew Szarleta, *Engineer*
▲ **EMP:** 52
SQ FT: 373,593
SALES (est): 18.1MM **Privately Held**
SIC: 2899 Chemical preparations
PA: All American Holdings, Llc
3714 W End Ave
Nashville TN 37205

(G-12342)
TECMOTIV (USA) INC
1500 James Ave (14305-1222)
PHONE....................................905 669-5911
Arthur Hayden, *President*
Gary Sheedy, *Vice Pres*
Tony Blazek, *Engineer*
Sally L Yan, *CFO*
◆ **EMP:** 35
SQ FT: 27,000
SALES (est): 9MM
SALES (corp-wide): 3.5MM **Privately Held**
WEB: www.tecmotiv.com
SIC: 3795 Tanks & tank components
PA: Tecmotiv Corporation
131 Saramia Cres 2nd Fl
Concord ON L4K 4
905 669-5911

(G-12343)
TRANSCEDAR INDUSTRIES LTD
Also Called: Motorad of America
6292 Walmore Rd (14304-5703)
PHONE....................................716 731-6442
Christy Etheridge, *Site Mgr*
Kelly Runkle, *Branch Mgr*
Brandon Kight, *Director*
EMP: 5 **Privately Held**
SIC: 3714 Air conditioner parts, motor vehicle
PA: Transcedar Industries Ltd
120 Silver Star Blvd Unit A
Scarborough ON M1V 4
416 293-4420

(G-12344)
TULIP MOLDED PLASTICS CORP
Also Called: Niagara Falls Plant
3123 Highland Ave (14305-2051)
PHONE....................................716 282-1261
James Carter, *Vice Pres*
Steve Shoecraft, *Engineer*
John Signore, *Manager*
EMP: 80 **Privately Held**
WEB: www.tulipcorp.com
SIC: 3089 Injection molding of plastics
HQ: Tulip Molded Plastics Corporation
714 E Keefe Ave
Milwaukee WI 53212
414 963-3120

(G-12345)
UNIFRAX CORPORATION
2351 Whirlpool St (14305-2413)
PHONE....................................716 278-3800
Matt W Colbert, *Vice Pres*
Paul Viola, *Vice Pres*
Elton Frazier, *Mfg Spvr*
Digvijay Chauhan, *Engineer*
Brian Mellett, *Engineer*
EMP: 34
SALES (est): 5MM **Privately Held**
SIC: 3296 Mineral wool insulation products

(G-12346)
US DRIVES INC
2221 Niagara Falls Blvd # 41 (14304-5711)
P.O. Box 281 (14304-0281)
PHONE....................................716 731-1606
Kader Laroussi, *President*
Dick Torbenson, *President*
James S Grisante, *Vice Pres*
Paul Wizner, *VP Prdtn*
Theodore G Nuding, *VP Finance*
EMP: 60
SQ FT: 70,000
SALES (est): 9.6MM **Privately Held**
WEB: www.usdrivesinc.com
SIC: 3625 Motor controls, electric

(G-12347)
VIOLA CABINET CORPORATION
Also Called: Viola Construction
4205 Hyde Park Blvd (14305-1709)
PHONE....................................716 284-6327
Pat Viola, *President*
EMP: 6
SQ FT: 3,500
SALES: 1MM **Privately Held**
SIC: 2434 Wood kitchen cabinets

(G-12348)
VISHAY THIN FILM LLC
2160 Liberty Dr (14304-3727)
PHONE....................................716 283-4025
Dr Felix Zandman, *President*
Robert A Freece, *Treasurer*
William Spires, *Admin Sec*
▲ **EMP:** 154
SQ FT: 33,000
SALES (est): 23.9MM
SALES (corp-wide): 2.6B **Publicly Held**
SIC: 3676 3861 3577 Electronic resistors; photographic equipment & supplies; computer peripheral equipment
HQ: Dale Vishay Electronics Llc
1122 23rd St
Columbus NE 68601
605 665-9301

(G-12349)
WASHINGTOM MILLS ELEC MNRLS (HQ)
1801 Buffalo Ave (14303-1528)
P.O. Box 423 (14302-0423)
PHONE....................................716 278-6600
Don McLeod, *President*
Ron Campbell, *COO*
Anne Williams, *Exec VP*
Kurt Owanisian, *Safety Dir*
Armand Ladage, *Plant Mgr*
◆ **EMP:** 100
SALES (est): 28.2MM
SALES (corp-wide): 171.9MM **Privately Held**
WEB: www.washingtonmills.com
SIC: 3291 2819 Abrasive grains; industrial inorganic chemicals
PA: Washington Mills Group, Inc.
20 N Main St
North Grafton MA 01536
508 839-6511

(G-12350)
YORKVILLE SOUND INC
4625 Witmer Indus Est (14305-1390)
PHONE....................................716 297-2920
Steven Long, *Owner*
Jack Long, *Founder*
Shahin Etemadzadeh, *Design Engr*
Tim Marshall, *Marketing Mgr*
Todd Michael, *Manager*
▲ **EMP:** 7
SALES (est): 1.3MM **Privately Held**
SIC: 3651 Audio electronic systems

Nichols
Tioga County

(G-12351)
WOODS MACHINE AND TOOL LLC
150 Howell St (13812-2146)
PHONE....................................607 699-3253
Ricky E Woods,
Michael Woods,
Richard Woods,
EMP: 16
SQ FT: 2,400
SALES (est): 1.4MM **Privately Held**
SIC: 3599 Machine shop, jobbing & repair

Niskayuna
Schenectady County

(G-12352)
ADC ACQUISITION COMPANY
Also Called: Automated Dynamics
2 Commerce Park Rd (12309-3545)
PHONE....................................518 377-6471
Robert Langone, *President*
Robert Becker, *Opers Staff*
Dave Hauber, *Engineer*
Raymond Johnston, *Treasurer*
Ralph Marcario, *Marketing Staff*
▼ **EMP:** 34
SQ FT: 30,000
SALES: 5.7MM
SALES (corp-wide): 3.7B **Privately Held**
WEB: www.automateddynamics.com
SIC: 3083 Thermoplastic laminates: rods, tubes, plates & sheet
HQ: Trelleborg Coated Systems Us, Inc.
715 Railroad Ave
Rutherfordton NC 28139
864 576-1210

(G-12353)
GE GLOBAL RESEARCH
1 Research Cir (12309-1027)
PHONE....................................518 387-5000

▲ = Import ▼ = Export
◆ = Import/Export

Victor R Abate, *Senior VP*
Anil Duggal, *Vice Pres*
Xianglei Chen, *Research*
John Deaton, *Research*
David Esler, *Engineer*
EMP: 1200 **EST:** 2016
SALES (est): 342.4MM
SALES (corp-wide): 122B **Publicly Held**
SIC: 3511 8742 Turbines & turbine generator sets; industrial consultant
PA: General Electric Company
    41 Farnsworth St
    Boston MA 02210
    617 443-3000

(G-12354)
GENERAL ELECTRIC COMPANY
2690 Balltown Rd Bldg 600 (12309-1004)
PHONE 518 385-7620
Doug Wood, *Branch Mgr*
EMP: 50
SALES (corp-wide): 122B **Publicly Held**
SIC: 3511 3612 3724 Steam turbines; gas turbines, mechanical drive; autotransformers, electric (power transformers); research & development on aircraft engines & parts
PA: General Electric Company
    41 Farnsworth St
    Boston MA 02210
    617 443-3000

(G-12355)
KINEMATIC TECHNOLOGIES INC
Also Called: Kinatek
1129 Glenmeadow Ct (12309-2511)
PHONE 518 346-7686
Peter Nickel, *President*
Patricia Nickel, *Vice Pres*
EMP: 5 **EST:** 1999
SALES (est): 766.9K **Privately Held**
WEB: www.kinatek.com
SIC: 3535 Conveyors & conveying equipment

Norfolk
St. Lawrence County

(G-12356)
APC PAPER COMPANY INC
100 Remington Ave (13667-4136)
P.O. Box 756 (13667-0756)
PHONE 315 384-4225
Al Ames, *Manager*
EMP: 55 **Privately Held**
WEB: www.apcpaper.com
SIC: 2621 4953 2674 2611 Kraft paper; refuse systems; bags: uncoated paper & multiwall; pulp mills
PA: Apc Paper Company, Inc.
    130 Sullivan St
    Claremont NH 03743

(G-12357)
CRANESVILLE BLOCK CO INC
Also Called: Cranesville Concrete
8405 State Highway 56 (13667-4221)
PHONE 315 384-4000
Randy Braul, *Manager*
EMP: 6
SALES (corp-wide): 45.6MM **Privately Held**
SIC: 3273 5211 Ready-mixed concrete; masonry materials & supplies
PA: Cranesville Block Co., Inc.
    1250 Riverfront Dr
    Amsterdam NY 12010
    518 684-6154

(G-12358)
LENCORE ACOUSTICS CORP
1 S Main St (13667-3111)
P.O. Box 616 (13667-0616)
PHONE 315 384-9114
Brian Leonard, *Branch Mgr*
EMP: 10
SALES (corp-wide): 5.6MM **Privately Held**
WEB: www.lencore.com
SIC: 3296 Acoustical board & tile, mineral wool

PA: Lencore Acoustics Corp.
    1 Crossways Park Dr W
    Woodbury NY 11797
    516 682-9292

(G-12359)
NORTHERN MACHINING INC
2a N Main St (13667-4154)
PHONE 315 384-3189
Ted Ashley, *President*
Kathie Ashley, *Vice Pres*
EMP: 10
SQ FT: 7,000
SALES: 1.1MM **Privately Held**
WEB: www.northernmachininginc.com
SIC: 3599 Machine shop, jobbing & repair

North Babylon
Suffolk County

(G-12360)
GO BLUE TECHNOLOGIES LTD
325 August Rd (11703-1014)
PHONE 631 404-6285
Carlo Drago, *CEO*
EMP: 1
SALES: 1MM **Privately Held**
SIC: 3624 3842 Carbon & graphite products; gas masks

(G-12361)
QUALITY FUEL 1 CORPORATION
1235 Deer Park Ave (11703-3112)
PHONE 631 392-4090
EMP: 6
SALES (est): 664.8K **Privately Held**
SIC: 2869 Fuels

North Baldwin
Nassau County

(G-12362)
DURA SPEC INC
Also Called: Jamaica Electroplating
1239 Village Ct (11510-1138)
PHONE 718 526-3053
Fax: 718 657-8867
EMP: 18
SQ FT: 5,000
SALES (est): 1.5MM **Privately Held**
SIC: 3471 Electroplating Of Metals

(G-12363)
GENESIS MACHINING CORP
725 Brooklyn Ave (11510-2708)
PHONE 516 377-1197
Michael A Chin, *President*
EMP: 12
SQ FT: 4,000
SALES (est): 1.9MM **Privately Held**
SIC: 3599 Machine shop, jobbing & repair

(G-12364)
HUBRAY INC
Also Called: Stu-Art Supplies
2045 Grand Ave (11510-2915)
PHONE 800 645-2855
Lisa Hubley, *President*
Andrew Ray, *Vice Pres*
EMP: 12
SQ FT: 10,000
SALES: 1MM **Privately Held**
WEB: www.stu-artsupplies.com
SIC: 2675 2499 5961 Panels, cardboard, die-cut: made from purchased materials; picture & mirror frames, wood; mail order house

(G-12365)
NOTICIA HISPANOAMERICANA INC
636 Seaman Ave (11510-2646)
PHONE 516 223-5678
Cinthia Diaz, *Owner*
Silvana Diaz, *Publisher*
Jeovanny Mata, *Director*
▲ **EMP:** 30
SALES (est): 885.3K **Privately Held**
SIC: 2711 Newspapers

(G-12366)
SANDY DUFTLER DESIGNS LTD
775 Brooklyn Ave Ste 105 (11510-2948)
PHONE 516 379-3084
Irwin Duftler, *CEO*
Sandra Duftler, *Ch of Bd*
Gregg Duftler, *President*
EMP: 12
SALES (est): 1.2MM **Privately Held**
SIC: 2387 Apparel belts

(G-12367)
SPLIT SYSTEMS CORP (PA)
Also Called: Johnson Contrls Authorized Dlr
1593 Grand Ave (11510-1849)
PHONE 516 223-5511
Charles Solon, *President*
Mike Solon, *Vice Pres*
EMP: 1
SALES (est): 1.8MM **Privately Held**
SIC: 3585 5075 Air conditioning equipment, complete; refrigeration equipment, complete; warm air heating & air conditioning

(G-12368)
SWIRL BLISS LLC
1777 Grand Ave (11510-2429)
PHONE 516 867-9475
Jeanette Reed,
EMP: 5
SALES (est): 331.9K **Privately Held**
SIC: 2024 Yogurt desserts, frozen

(G-12369)
V C N GROUP LTD INC
1 Clifton St (11510-2114)
PHONE 516 223-4812
Florence Abate, *President*
Vincent Abate, *Vice Pres*
Anthony Abate, *Admin Sec*
EMP: 5
SQ FT: 500
SALES (est): 523.6K **Privately Held**
SIC: 2752 Advertising posters, lithographed

(G-12370)
VORTEX VENTURES INC
857 Newton Ave (11510-2826)
PHONE 516 946-8345
Kevin Walters, *President*
EMP: 5
SALES (est): 193.4K **Privately Held**
SIC: 7372 7389 Publishers' computer software;

(G-12371)
W & B MAZZA & SONS INC
Also Called: Mazza Co, The
2145 Marion Pl (11510-2921)
PHONE 516 379-4130
William Mazza Sr, *President*
William Mazza Jr, *Treasurer*
Steven Mazza, *VP Mktg*
Jeffrey Mazza, *Admin Sec*
EMP: 28
SQ FT: 8,000
SALES (est): 3MM **Privately Held**
WEB: www.mazzajewelry.com
SIC: 3911 Rings, finger: precious metal

North Bellmore
Nassau County

(G-12372)
21ST CENTURY FINISHES INC
1353 Newbridge Rd Unit A (11710-1661)
P.O. Box 471, Bellmore (11710-0471)
PHONE 516 221-7000
Al Doerbecker, *President*
EMP: 14
SALES (est): 1.4MM **Privately Held**
SIC: 3471 Finishing, metals or formed products

(G-12373)
CAPITOL RESTORATION CORP
2473 Belmond Ave (11710-1205)
PHONE 516 783-1425
Seeme Rizvi, *President*
EMP: 6

SALES (est): 672.2K **Privately Held**
SIC: 3297 1771 1521 Brick refractories; concrete repair; new construction, single-family houses

(G-12374)
CHANGDU TECHNOLOGY (USA) CO
1417 Horseshoe Dr (11710-2458)
PHONE 917 340-1976
Chunlan Wang, *President*
Kevin Qiu, *Manager*
EMP: 15
SALES (est): 1MM **Privately Held**
SIC: 2731 Book publishing

(G-12375)
COSTANZA READY MIX INC
1345 Newbridge Rd (11710-1629)
PHONE 516 783-4444
Frank Costanza, *President*
EMP: 5
SALES (est): 540.3K **Privately Held**
SIC: 3273 Ready-mixed concrete

(G-12376)
CUPCAKE CONTESSAS CORPORATION
1242 Julia Ln (11710-1925)
PHONE 516 307-1222
Laura Andreacchi, *Chairman*
EMP: 6
SALES (est): 412K **Privately Held**
SIC: 2051 Cakes, bakery: except frozen

(G-12377)
CUSTOM DISPLAY MANUFACTURE
1686 Logan St (11710-2528)
PHONE 516 783-6491
Paul Kassbaum, *President*
EMP: 5
SQ FT: 8,000
SALES (est): 440K **Privately Held**
SIC: 2511 3993 Chairs, household, except upholstered: wood; signs & advertising specialties

(G-12378)
GEORGE BASCH CO INC
1554 Peapond Rd (11710-2925)
P.O. Box 188, Freeport (11520-0188)
PHONE 516 378-8100
Laurie Basch-Levy, *President*
Mildred Basch, *Treasurer*
Rhonda Ax, *Admin Sec*
EMP: 10 **EST:** 1929
SQ FT: 6,800
SALES (est): 1MM **Privately Held**
WEB: www.nevrdull.com
SIC: 2842 Cleaning or polishing preparations

(G-12379)
KP INDUSTRIES INC
Also Called: K P Signs
2481 Charles Ct Ste 1 (11710-2761)
P.O. Box 1000, Bethpage (11714-0019)
PHONE 516 679-3161
Karen A Puchacz, *President*
Dee Smith, *Admin Sec*
EMP: 11 **EST:** 1997
SQ FT: 3,600
SALES (est): 1.5MM **Privately Held**
SIC: 3993 Mfg Signs & Advertising Specialties

(G-12380)
NASSAU AUTO REMANUFACTURER
Also Called: Nassau Auto Remanufacturers
2477 Charles Ct (11710-2733)
PHONE 516 485-4500
Dorothy Pontrelli, *President*
EMP: 8
SQ FT: 9,000
SALES: 500K **Privately Held**
SIC: 3714 Motor vehicle electrical equipment

North Chili
Monroe County

(G-12381)
ALBERT GATES INC
3434 Union St (14514-9731)
PHONE.....................585 594-9401
Andrew J Laniak, *Ch of Bd*
Robert J Brinkman, *President*
Dan Ferries, *General Mgr*
James Adams, *Vice Pres*
Dan Helfrich, *QC Mgr*
EMP: 75
SQ FT: 26,000
SALES (est): 17.4MM
SALES (corp-wide): 106.6MM Privately Held
WEB: www.gatesalbert.com
SIC: 3451 Screw machine products
PA: Brinkman International Group, Inc.
  167 Ames St
  Rochester NY 14611
  585 429-5000

(G-12382)
P TOOL & DIE CO INC
3535 Union St (14514-9709)
P.O. Box 369 (14514-0369)
PHONE.....................585 889-1340
Michael J Sucese, *President*
John Hall, *Project Mgr*
Mike Carr, *Department Mgr*
EMP: 22
SQ FT: 18,000
SALES (est): 4.6MM Privately Held
SIC: 3544 Special dies & tools

North Collins
Erie County

(G-12383)
AMERICAN WIRE TIE INC (PA)
2073 Franklin St (14111-9636)
P.O. Box 696 (14111-0696)
PHONE.....................716 337-2412
James W Smith, *President*
Ronald Lehnortt, *Sales Staff*
Leslie Oleary, *Sales Staff*
Amelia Jarzynski, *Sales Associate*
Gregory C Mumbach, *Admin Sec*
▲ **EMP:** 30
SQ FT: 54,000
SALES (est): 12.4MM Privately Held
WEB: www.americanwiretie.com
SIC: 3599 3496 3315 2631 Ties, form: metal; miscellaneous fabricated wire products; steel wire & related products; paperboard mills

(G-12384)
CRESCENT MARKETING INC (PA)
Also Called: Crescent Manufacturing
10285 Eagle Dr (14111)
P.O. Box 1500 (14111-1500)
PHONE.....................716 337-0145
Richard Frazer Jr, *President*
Rick Taber, *Plant Mgr*
Karen Frazer, *CFO*
▲ **EMP:** 123
SQ FT: 110,000
SALES (est): 34.7MM Privately Held
SIC: 2842 Specialty cleaning preparations

(G-12385)
E & D SPECIALTY STANDS INC
2081 Franklin St (14111-9636)
P.O. Box 700 (14111-0700)
PHONE.....................716 337-0161
David A Metzger, *President*
Doug Bigelow, *Vice Pres*
Gerald Paul Sullivan, *Purch Mgr*
Dean Metzger, *CFO*
John Williams, *Sales Mgr*
EMP: 50 **EST:** 1956
SQ FT: 85,000
SALES (est): 9MM Privately Held
WEB: www.edstands.com
SIC: 2531 Bleacher seating, portable

(G-12386)
NITRO MANUFACTURING LLC
440 Shirley Rd (14111)
PHONE.....................716 646-9900
Christine Frascella, *Mng Member*
Tim Frascella,
William Frascella,
Dave Kota,
EMP: 5
SALES (est): 630.1K Privately Held
SIC: 3599 Machine shop, jobbing & repair

(G-12387)
NITRO WHEELS INC
4440 Shirley Rd (14111-9783)
PHONE.....................716 337-0709
Louis Frascella, *Principal*
EMP: 10
SALES (est): 1MM Privately Held
SIC: 3312 Wheels, locomotive & car: iron & steel

(G-12388)
RENALDOS SALES & SERVICE CTR
1770 Milestrip Rd (14111-9753)
P.O. Box 820 (14111-0820)
PHONE.....................716 337-3760
James V Renaldo, *President*
Joan E Renaldo, *Vice Pres*
EMP: 8
SQ FT: 3,800
SALES (est): 4.8MM Privately Held
SIC: 3523 3713 Trailers & wagons, farm; planting machines, agricultural; truck bodies (motor vehicles)

(G-12389)
TIMBERBUILT INC
10821 Schaffstall Dr (14111)
P.O. Box 940 (14111-0940)
PHONE.....................716 337-0012
George Klemens, *President*
Adam Lincoln, *Opers Mgr*
EMP: 10
SQ FT: 10,200
SALES (est): 1.4MM Privately Held
WEB: www.timberbuilt.com
SIC: 2452 Log cabins, prefabricated, wood

(G-12390)
WINTERS RAILROAD SERVICE INC
11309 Sisson Hwy (14111-9729)
PHONE.....................716 337-2668
David Winter, *President*
Michael Winter, *Corp Secy*
EMP: 6
SQ FT: 15,000
SALES: 530K Privately Held
SIC: 3423 3441 Hand & edge tools; fabricated structural metal

North Creek
Warren County

(G-12391)
CREATIVE STAGE LIGHTING CO INC
Also Called: C S L
149 State Route 28n (12853-2707)
P.O. Box 567 (12853-0567)
PHONE.....................518 251-3302
George B Studnicky III, *President*
Jason Lemery, *CFO*
Phil Heid, *Sales Staff*
Ashley Oconnor, *Sales Staff*
Susan Baker, *Sales Associate*
♦ **EMP:** 43
SQ FT: 32,000
SALES: 8MM Privately Held
WEB: www.creativestagelighting.com
SIC: 3648 5063 7922 Lighting equipment; lighting fixtures, commercial & industrial; lighting, theatrical

North Java
Wyoming County

(G-12392)
SELECT INTERIOR DOOR LTD
Also Called: Select Door
2074 Perry Rd (14113-9722)
P.O. Box 178 (14113-0178)
PHONE.....................585 535-9900
John Angelbeck, *President*
Maureen Ronan, *CFO*
EMP: 40
SQ FT: 25,000
SALES (est): 5.7MM Privately Held
WEB: www.sidl.com
SIC: 2431 3231 Doors, wood; products of purchased glass

North Lawrence
St. Lawrence County

(G-12393)
UPSTATE NIAGARA COOP INC
Also Called: North Country Dairy
22 County Route 52 (12967-9539)
PHONE.....................315 389-5111
Tim Gominiack, *Branch Mgr*
EMP: 59
SALES (corp-wide): 893.9MM Privately Held
SIC: 2026 Milk & cream, except fermented, cultured & flavored
PA: Upstate Niagara Cooperative, Inc.
  25 Anderson Rd
  Buffalo NY 14225
  716 892-3156

North Rose
Wayne County

(G-12394)
FLEISCHMANNS VINEGAR CO INC
Also Called: Fleischman Vinegar
4754 State Route 414 (14516-9704)
PHONE.....................315 587-4414
John Wilson, *Manager*
EMP: 20
SALES (corp-wide): 3.6B Publicly Held
WEB: www.breadworld.com
SIC: 2099 Vinegar
HQ: Fleischmann's Vinegar Company, Inc.
  12604 Hiddencreek Way A
  Cerritos CA 90703
  562 483-4619

(G-12395)
GARGRAVES TRACKAGE CORPORATION (PA)
Also Called: Gardner The Train Doctor
8967 Ridge Rd (14516-9753)
PHONE.....................315 483-6577
Michael Roder, *President*
Thomas Roder, *Vice Pres*
EMP: 5
SQ FT: 5,000
SALES: 500K Privately Held
WEB: www.gargraves.com
SIC: 3944 5945 Trains & equipment, toy: electric & mechanical; hobby, toy & game shops

(G-12396)
OLMSTEAD MACHINE INC
10399 Warehouse Ave (14516-9537)
P.O. Box 331 (14516-0331)
PHONE.....................315 587-9864
Dale Liechti, *President*
EMP: 10
SQ FT: 10,000
SALES (est): 1.5MM Privately Held
SIC: 3599 Machine shop, jobbing & repair

North Salem
Westchester County

(G-12397)
TOTAL ENERGY FABRICATION CORP
2 Hardscrabble Rd (10560-1014)
PHONE.....................580 363-1500
Robert Armentano, *CEO*
Gary Harvey, *Principal*
Frank Kovacs, *Principal*
▲ **EMP:** 6
SALES (est): 1.3MM Privately Held
SIC: 3491 Pressure valves & regulators, industrial

North Syracuse
Onondaga County

(G-12398)
CLEANROOM SYSTEMS INC
7000 Performance Dr (13212-3439)
PHONE.....................315 452-7400
Larry Wetzel, *President*
Bruce Meissner, *Engineer*
Deb Emery, *CFO*
Jeffrey Brewster, *Marketing Staff*
EMP: 42
SQ FT: 48,378
SALES: 191.9K
SALES (corp-wide): 8.9MM Privately Held
WEB: www.cleanroomsystems.com
SIC: 3585 Refrigeration equipment, complete
PA: Air Innovations, Inc.
  7000 Performance Dr
  North Syracuse NY 13212
  315 452-7400

(G-12399)
DISPLAYS BY RIOUX INC
6090 E Taft Rd (13212-3303)
PHONE.....................315 458-3639
Robert A Rioux Jr, *President*
EMP: 7
SQ FT: 12,200
SALES (est): 875.2K Privately Held
WEB: www.displaysbyrioux.com
SIC: 3083 3089 Mfg Laminated Plastic Plate/Sheet Mfg Plastic Products

(G-12400)
DL MANUFACTURING INC
340 Gateway Park Dr (13212-3758)
PHONE.....................315 432-8977
Donald L Metz, *Ch of Bd*
EMP: 30
SQ FT: 22,000
SALES: 12MM Privately Held
WEB: www.dlmanufacturing.com
SIC: 3537 5084 5031 5075 Loading docks: portable, adjustable & hydraulic; industrial machinery & equipment; doors; ventilating equipment & supplies

(G-12401)
G A BRAUN INC (PA)
79 General Irwin Blvd (13212-5279)
P.O. Box 3029, Syracuse (13220-3029)
PHONE.....................315 475-3123
JB Werner, *Ch of Bd*
Joe Gudenburr, *President*
David Welsh, *General Mgr*
David Clark, *Vice Pres*
Mark Kirby, *Plant Mgr*
▲ **EMP:** 150
SQ FT: 75,000
SALES (est): 45.1MM Privately Held
WEB: www.gabraun.com
SIC: 3582 5087 Washing machines, laundry: commercial, incl. coin-operated; laundry equipment & supplies

(G-12402)
GAYLORD BROS INC
Also Called: Gaylord Archival
7282 William Barry Blvd (13212-3347)
P.O. Box 4901, Syracuse (13221-4901)
PHONE.....................315 457-5070

GEOGRAPHIC SECTION

North Tonawanda - Niagara County (G-12427)

R Keith George, *CEO*
Keith George, *VP Opers*
Joseph Faiola, *Finance*
Jon Moretti, *Sales Staff*
Maria Wilson, *Marketing Staff*
◆ **EMP:** 60
SQ FT: 80,000
SALES (est): 17.7MM
SALES (corp-wide): 115.2MM **Privately Held**
WEB: www.gaylord.com
SIC: 2679 2657 2542 Adding machine rolls, paper; made from purchased material; folding paperboard boxes; fixtures: display, office or store; except wood
PA: Demco, Inc.
  4810 Forest Run Rd
  Madison WI 53704
  800 356-1200

(G-12403)
GEDDES BAKERY CO INC
421 S Main St (13212-2800)
PHONE 315 437-8084
Vasilios Pappas, *President*
EMP: 24
SQ FT: 5,600
SALES (est): 3.3MM **Privately Held**
WEB: www.geddesbakery.com
SIC: 2051 5461 Bakery: wholesale or wholesale/retail combined; bakeries

(G-12404)
GRYPHON SENSORS LLC
5801 E Taft Rd (13212-3291)
PHONE 315 452-8882
Anthony Albanese, *President*
Adam Helak, *Engineer*
Michael Pecoraro, *Engineer*
EMP: 15
SQ FT: 1,000
SALES (est): 2.9MM **Privately Held**
SIC: 3812 Antennas, radar or communications

(G-12405)
ICM CONTROLS CORP
7313 William Barry Blvd (13212-3384)
PHONE 315 233-5266
Hassan B Kadah, *Ch of Bd*
Andrew Kadah, *President*
Laurie Kadah, *Treasurer*
▲ **EMP:** 18
SALES (est): 3.2MM
SALES (corp-wide): 50MM **Privately Held**
SIC: 3625 Electric controls & control accessories, industrial
PA: International Controls & Measurements Corp.
  7313 William Barry Blvd
  North Syracuse NY 13212
  315 233-5266

(G-12406)
INTERNTNAL CNTRLS MSRMNTS CORP (PA)
Also Called: ICM
7313 William Barry Blvd (13212-3384)
PHONE 315 233-5266
Hassan B Kadah, *Ch of Bd*
Andrew Kadah, *President*
Laurie Kadah, *Treasurer*
Charles Hunt, *MIS Staff*
▲ **EMP:** 194
SQ FT: 85,000
SALES: 50MM **Privately Held**
WEB: www.icmcontrols.com
SIC: 3625 Electric controls & control accessories, industrial

(G-12407)
JADAK TECHNOLOGIES INC
7279 William Barry Blvd (13212-3349)
PHONE 315 701-0678
Janie Goddard, *President*
Jennifer Cruse, *Purch Mgr*
Jim Parker, *Research*
Michael Desocio, *Engineer*
Aron Pomerleau, *Engineer*
EMP: 165
SALES (est): 28.3MM **Publicly Held**
WEB: www.jadaktech.com
SIC: 3577 Bar code (magnetic ink) printers

HQ: Novanta Corporation
  125 Middlesex Tpke
  Bedford MA 01730
  781 266-5700

(G-12408)
NORTHERN READY MIX LLC (HQ)
Also Called: Northern Ready-Mix Inc
6131 E Taft Rd (13212-2525)
PHONE 315 336-7900
Joseph F Riccelli, *CEO*
Richard J Riccelli Sr, *President*
EMP: 15
SALES (est): 6.2MM **Privately Held**
WEB: www.northerncompanies.com
SIC: 3273 Ready-mixed concrete

North Tonawanda
Niagara County

(G-12409)
369 RIVER ROAD INC
369 River Rd (14120-7108)
PHONE 716 694-5001
Michael Deakin, *President*
EMP: 25
SQ FT: 25,000
SALES (est): 1MM **Privately Held**
SIC: 3496 Miscellaneous fabricated wire products

(G-12410)
AMERI-CUT TOOL GRINDING INC
Also Called: Superior Tool Company
1020 Oliver St (14120-2710)
PHONE 716 692-3900
Todd Brosius Jr, *President*
EMP: 5
SQ FT: 10,000
SALES: 500K **Privately Held**
WEB: www.superiortoolllc.com
SIC: 3545 Cutting tools for machine tools

(G-12411)
AN-COR INDUSTRIAL PLASTICS INC
900 Niagara Falls Blvd (14120-2096)
PHONE 716 695-3141
Merrill W Arthur, *President*
Howard Merrill, *Engineer*
Kevin Sweeney, *Design Engr*
Paul Biondi, *CFO*
Ronald Hughes, *Sales Mgr*
EMP: 83
SQ FT: 96,000
SALES (est): 24MM **Privately Held**
WEB: www.an-cor.com
SIC: 3089 3088 Plastic & fiberglass tanks; plastics plumbing fixtures

(G-12412)
ARMSTRONG PUMPS INC
93 East Ave (14120-6594)
PHONE 716 693-8813
J A C Armstrong, *CEO*
Bruce Van Nus, *Managing Dir*
Cathie Yanulevich, *Controller*
Catherine Holesko, *Human Res Mgr*
Scott Davignon, *Manager*
◆ **EMP:** 100
SQ FT: 150,000
SALES (est): 49.4MM **Privately Held**
WEB: www.armstrongpumps.com
SIC: 3561 Industrial pumps & parts
PA: S. A. Armstrong Limited
  23 Bertrand Ave
  Scarborough ON M1L 2
  416 755-2291

(G-12413)
ASCENSION INDUSTRIES INC (PA)
1254 Erie Ave (14120-3036)
PHONE 716 693-9381
Jack Kopczynski Jr, *Ch of Bd*
Donald Naab, *President*
Cliff Post, *VP Opers*
Chris Slipko, *Project Mgr*
Richard Tomczak, *Project Mgr*
▲ **EMP:** 120 **EST:** 2000

SQ FT: 140,000
SALES (est): 25.5MM **Privately Held**
WEB: www.asmfab.com
SIC: 3544 3541 3444 Special dies, tools, jigs & fixtures; machine tools, metal cutting type; sheet metalwork

(G-12414)
AUDUBON MACHINERY CORPORATION (PA)
Also Called: Oxygen Generating Systems Intl
814 Wurlitzer Dr (14120-3042)
PHONE 716 564-5165
Joseph M McMahon, *President*
Robert Schlehr, *Vice Pres*
Bob Schlehr, *VP Sls/Mktg*
Timothy Blach, *CFO*
◆ **EMP:** 60
SQ FT: 40,000
SALES (est): 13.7MM **Privately Held**
WEB: www.ogsi.com
SIC: 3569 Gas producers, generators & other gas related equipment

(G-12415)
BAKER TOOL & DIE
48 Industrial Dr (14120-3244)
PHONE 716 694-2025
Jon C Olstad, *President*
EMP: 8
SALES (est): 690K **Privately Held**
SIC: 3312 Blast furnaces & steel mills

(G-12416)
BAKER TOOL & DIE & DIE
48 Industrial Dr (14120-3244)
PHONE 716 694-2025
Jon C Olstad, *President*
EMP: 6
SQ FT: 6,000
SALES (est): 480K **Privately Held**
SIC: 3312 Tool & die steel

(G-12417)
BATTENFELD GREASE OIL CORP NY
1174 Erie Ave (14120-3036)
P.O. Box 728 (14120-0728)
PHONE 716 695-2100
Barbara A Bellanti, *Ch of Bd*
John A Bellanti, *President*
▲ **EMP:** 39
SALES (est): 11.8MM **Privately Held**
SIC: 2992 Oils & greases, blending & compounding

(G-12418)
BROADWAY KNITTING MILLS INC
1333 Strad Ave Ste 216 (14120-3061)
PHONE 716 692-4421
Craig Boyce, *President*
Russell Boyce, *Vice Pres*
Susan Boyce, *Treasurer*
Molly Boyce, *Admin Sec*
EMP: 5
SQ FT: 8,400
SALES: 210K **Privately Held**
WEB: www.broadwayknitting.com
SIC: 2329 5611 2326 Jackets (suede, leatherette, etc.), sport; men's & boys'; clothing accessories: men's & boys'; men's & boys' work clothing

(G-12419)
BUFFALO ABRASIVES INC (PA)
960 Erie Ave (14120-3503)
PHONE 716 693-3856
Arthur A Russ Jr, *President*
Jeffrey J Binkley, *Chairman*
Tim Wagner, *Vice Pres*
Fred Williams, *Vice Pres*
Frank Pawlik, *Safety Mgr*
▲ **EMP:** 45
SQ FT: 65,000
SALES (est): 13.4MM **Privately Held**
WEB: www.buffaloabrasives.com
SIC: 3291 Abrasive products

(G-12420)
BUFFALO PUMPS INC (HQ)
Also Called: A Division A & Liquid Systems
874 Oliver St (14120-3298)
PHONE 716 693-1850
Robert Paul, *Ch of Bd*

Charles Kistner, *President*
Christopher Marlow, *Engineer*
Scott Richter, *Engineer*
Terrence Kenny, *Treasurer*
▲ **EMP:** 109
SQ FT: 140,000
SALES (est): 35.6MM
SALES (corp-wide): 432.4MM **Publicly Held**
WEB: www.buffalopumps.com
SIC: 3561 Industrial pumps & parts
PA: Ampco-Pittsburgh Corporation
  726 Bell Ave Ste 301
  Carnegie PA 15106
  412 456-4400

(G-12421)
CALGON CARBON CORPORATION
830 River Rd (14120-6557)
PHONE 716 531-9113
EMP: 8
SALES (est): 1.2MM **Privately Held**
SIC: 2819 Charcoal (carbon), activated

(G-12422)
COMMERCIAL FABRICS INC
908 Niagara Falls Blvd (14120-2019)
PHONE 716 694-0641
Michel Senecal, *President*
James Senecal, *Corp Secy*
EMP: 15
SQ FT: 30,000
SALES (est): 1.7MM **Privately Held**
WEB: www.commercialfabrics.com
SIC: 3999 Hot tub & spa covers

(G-12423)
CONFER PLASTICS INC
97 Witmer Rd (14120-2421)
PHONE 800 635-3213
Douglas C Confer, *President*
Bob Confer, *Vice Pres*
Pete Miller, *Plant Mgr*
Dave Lipnianski, *Engineer*
Dave Lipniarski, *Engineer*
◆ **EMP:** 130 **EST:** 1973
SQ FT: 100,000
SALES (est): 37.1MM **Privately Held**
WEB: www.conferladders.com
SIC: 3089 Blow molded finished plastic products

(G-12424)
COOPERSURGICAL INC
825 Wurlitzer Dr (14120-3041)
PHONE 716 693-6230
Jennifer Gates, *Branch Mgr*
EMP: 17
SALES (corp-wide): 2.1B **Publicly Held**
WEB: www.barrlabs.com
SIC: 2834 Pharmaceutical preparations
HQ: Coopersurgical, Inc.
  95 Corporate Dr
  Trumbull CT 06611

(G-12425)
DMIC INC
Also Called: Delaware Manufacturing Inds
3776 Commerce Ct (14120-2024)
PHONE 716 743-4360
Chuck Wolski, *Principal*
EMP: 9
SALES (est): 1.3MM **Privately Held**
SIC: 3492 3714 Fluid power valves for aircraft; motor vehicle parts & accessories

(G-12426)
EXPEDIENT HEAT TREATING CORP
61 Dale Dr (14120-4201)
PHONE 716 433-1177
Paul Waild, *President*
EMP: 5 **EST:** 1979
SQ FT: 2,000
SALES (est): 400K **Privately Held**
SIC: 3398 Metal heat treating

(G-12427)
FEI PRODUCTS LLC (PA)
825 Wurlitzer Dr (14120-3041)
PHONE 716 693-6230
Charles S Craig, *President*
Paul Wasielewski, *Opers Staff*
EMP: 35
SQ FT: 23,500

North Tonawanda - Niagara County (G-12428)

SALES (est): 5.2MM Privately Held
SIC: 3089 Plastic processing

(G-12428)
FREY CONCRETE INC
Also Called: Frey Sand & Gravel
3949 Frest Pk Way Ste 400 (14120)
PHONE..................716 213-5832
Martin L Segarra, *President*
EMP: 9
SALES (est): 1MM Privately Held
SIC: 3273 Ready-mixed concrete

(G-12429)
GARDEI INDUSTRIES LLC (PA)
Also Called: F K Williams Division
1087 Erie Ave (14120-3532)
PHONE..................716 693-7100
Lori Ferraraccio, *Mng Member*
Jordon Lizy,
▲ EMP: 17 EST: 1936
SQ FT: 25,000
SALES (est): 1.6MM Privately Held
WEB: www.gardei.net
SIC: 2679 3545 Paper products, converted; machine tool accessories

(G-12430)
GLI-DEX SALES CORP
Also Called: Glidden Machine & Tool
855 Wurlitzer Dr (14120-3041)
PHONE..................716 692-6501
James Gerace, *President*
Marcia Gerace, *Corp Secy*
Robert Gerace, *Vice Pres*
EMP: 35 EST: 1946
SQ FT: 12,000
SALES (est): 2.5MM Privately Held
WEB: www.glidex.biz
SIC: 3599 Machine shop, jobbing & repair

(G-12431)
GRIFFIN CHEMICAL COMPANY LLC
Also Called: W.O.w Brand Products
889 Erie Ave Ste 1 (14120-3533)
PHONE..................716 693-2465
Elyse Robinson, *Mktg Dir*
Gregory Robinson, *Mng Member*
Bernard Zysman,
EMP: 9
SQ FT: 15,000
SALES: 500K Privately Held
SIC: 2842 Specialty cleaning preparations

(G-12432)
IMPRESSIVE IMPRINTS
601 Division St (14120-4461)
PHONE..................716 692-0905
Robert Albert, *Owner*
Jason Cefaly, *Sales Mgr*
Cathy Piciulo, *Accounts Exec*
EMP: 12
SQ FT: 3,000
SALES (est): 1.1MM Privately Held
SIC: 2759 Screen printing

(G-12433)
INTERNATIONAL FIBER CORP
50 Bridge St (14120-6842)
PHONE..................716 693-4040
Jit Ang, *Exec VP*
Peter Vogt, *Vice Pres*
Lawrence A McKee, *Vice Pres*
Deep Parmar, *VP Finance*
Jason Khayat, *Sales Engr*
EMP: 34
SALES (est): 7.4MM Privately Held
SIC: 2823 Cellulosic manmade fibers

(G-12434)
ISLAND STREET LUMBER CO INC
11 Felton St (14120-6503)
PHONE..................716 692-4127
James Le Blanc, *President*
Joan Le Blanc, *Vice Pres*
EMP: 5
SQ FT: 11,500
SALES (est): 641.1K Privately Held
SIC: 2431 5211 Millwork; millwork & lumber

(G-12435)
ISOLATION SYSTEMS INC
889 Erie Ave Ste 1 (14120-3533)
PHONE..................716 694-6390
Ted Arts, *President*
Theodore Arts, *Sales Staff*
EMP: 10
SQ FT: 98,000
SALES (est): 2.3MM Privately Held
WEB: www.isolation-systems.com
SIC: 3564 Filters, air: furnaces, air conditioning equipment, etc.

(G-12436)
L & S METALS INC
111 Witmer Rd (14120-2443)
PHONE..................716 692-6865
Gary Schade, *President*
Becky Beutel, *Manager*
EMP: 23 EST: 1978
SQ FT: 17,000
SALES (est): 4MM Privately Held
WEB: www.ls-metals.com
SIC: 3599 7692 Machine shop, jobbing & repair; welding repair

(G-12437)
LISTON MANUFACTURING INC
421 Payne Ave (14120-6987)
P.O. Box 178 (14120-0178)
PHONE..................716 695-2111
Theodore Pyrak, *Ch of Bd*
Joseph Laduca, *Vice Pres*
Russell Laduca, *Vice Pres*
Charles E Pyrak, *Treasurer*
Edward Pyrak, *Treasurer*
EMP: 50 EST: 1954
SQ FT: 60,000
SALES (est): 10.7MM Privately Held
WEB: www.listonmfg.com
SIC: 3568 Bearings, bushings & blocks

(G-12438)
MODU-CRAFT INC
337 Payne Ave (14120-7236)
PHONE..................716 694-0709
Kenneth Babka, *President*
EMP: 7
SALES (corp-wide): 1MM Privately Held
SIC: 2599 3821 Factory furniture & fixtures; laboratory furniture
PA: Modu-Craft Inc
  276 Creekside Dr
  Tonawanda NY 14150
  716 694-0709

(G-12439)
NIAGARA SHEETS LLC
7393 Shawnee Rd (14120-1325)
PHONE..................716 692-1129
John Bolender, *President*
Skip Polowy, *Vice Pres*
Steve Lisicki, *Controller*
Mona Macfarlane, *HR Admin*
Greg Sommer, *Sales Executive*
▲ EMP: 75 EST: 2007
SALES (est): 35MM
SALES (corp-wide): 148.3MM Privately Held
SIC: 2653 Boxes, corrugated: made from purchased materials
PA: Jamestown Container Corp
  14 Deming Dr
  Falconer NY 14733
  716 665-4623

(G-12440)
OCCIDENTAL CHEMICAL CORP
3780 Commerce Ct Ste 600 (14120-2025)
PHONE..................716 694-3827
Rose Zenturin, *General Mgr*
EMP: 5
SALES (corp-wide): 13.2B Publicly Held
WEB: www.oxychem.com
SIC: 2812 Alkalies & chlorine
HQ: Occidental Chemical Corporation
  5005 Lyndon B Johnson Fwy
  Dallas TX 75244
  972 404-3800

(G-12441)
PELLETS LLC
63 Industrial Dr Ste 3 (14120-3248)
PHONE..................716 693-1750
Mike Deakin, *President*
Kevin Deakin, *Vice Pres*
Kevin Walters, *Technical Staff*
Kathy Reitz, *Admin Asst*
▲ EMP: 6 EST: 1948
SQ FT: 7,500
SALES (est): 1MM
SALES (corp-wide): 2.7MM Privately Held
WEB: www.pelletsllc.com
SIC: 3291 Abrasive metal & steel products
PA: Val-Kro, Inc.
  369 River Rd
  North Tonawanda NY
  716 694-5001

(G-12442)
PIONEER PRINTERS INC
Also Called: Gardei Manufacturing
1087 Erie Ave (14120-3532)
PHONE..................716 693-7100
Carl Hoover, *CEO*
EMP: 16
SQ FT: 7,000
SALES (est): 2.7MM Privately Held
WEB: www.pioneerprinters.com
SIC: 2752 Commercial printing, offset

(G-12443)
PROTOTYPE MANUFACTURING CORP
836 Wurlitzer Dr (14120-3042)
PHONE..................716 695-1700
Richard A Christie, *President*
Timothy G Christie, *Vice Pres*
EMP: 10
SQ FT: 8,000
SALES (est): 1.5MM Privately Held
SIC: 3599 Machine shop, jobbing & repair

(G-12444)
RAVE INC
940 River Rd (14120-6555)
PHONE..................716 695-1110
Albert Bluemle, *President*
EMP: 64
SALES (est): 5.2MM Privately Held
SIC: 3999 Education aids, devices & supplies

(G-12445)
RECORD ADVERTISER
435 River Rd (14120-6809)
P.O. Box 668 (14120-0668)
PHONE..................716 693-1000
Wayne Lowman, *President*
EMP: 40
SALES (est): 1.1MM Privately Held
SIC: 2711 Newspapers

(G-12446)
RILEY GEAR CORPORATION
61 Felton St (14120-6598)
PHONE..................716 694-0900
Donn Neffke, *Manager*
EMP: 20
SALES (est): 3.5MM
SALES (corp-wide): 27.5MM Privately Held
WEB: www.rileygear.com
SIC: 3462 Gears, forged steel
PA: Riley Gear Corporation
  1 Precision Dr
  Saint Augustine FL 32092
  904 829-5652

(G-12447)
RIVERFRONT COSTUME DESIGN
Also Called: A D M
200 River Rd (14120-5708)
PHONE..................716 693-2501
Paul Tucker, *President*
Barbara Tucker, *Vice Pres*
EMP: 9
SQ FT: 12,500
SALES (est): 1MM Privately Held
SIC: 2521 2522 Cabinets, office: wood; cabinets, office: except wood

(G-12448)
ROEMAC INDUSTRIAL SALES INC
Also Called: Buffalo Snowmelter
27 Fredericka St (14120-6590)
PHONE..................716 692-7332
Mitchell Roemer, *President*
Greg Roemer, *Corp Secy*
Nicholas B Roemer, *Vice Pres*
EMP: 9 EST: 1947
SQ FT: 7,000
SALES: 900K Privately Held
WEB: www.roemac.com
SIC: 3443 3585 Fabricated plate work (boiler shop); evaporative condensers, heat transfer equipment

(G-12449)
ROGER L URBAN INC (PA)
Also Called: Platter's Chocolates
908 Niagara Falls Blvd # 107 (14120-2021)
PHONE..................716 693-5391
Joseph Urban, *President*
Sherry Di Guiseppe, *Vice Pres*
Sherry Diguiseppe, *Vice Pres*
Sherry Guiseppe, *Comms Dir*
Michael Urban, *Shareholder*
EMP: 21
SQ FT: 11,000
SALES (est): 2.7MM Privately Held
WEB: www.platterschocolate.com
SIC: 2066 5441 5145 2064 Chocolate candy, solid; candy; confectionery; candy & other confectionery products

(G-12450)
SHANNON ENTPS WSTN NY INC
Also Called: Insultech
75 Main St (14120-5903)
P.O. Box 199 (14120-0199)
PHONE..................716 693-7954
Frank Kovacs, *President*
Scott Shafer, *Project Mgr*
Chad Snopkowski, *Project Mgr*
Joseph Moran, *Sales Dir*
Bill Moss, *Sales Associate*
▼ EMP: 58
SQ FT: 20,000
SALES (est): 6.7MM Privately Held
WEB: www.corian-countertop.com
SIC: 2299 Insulating felts

(G-12451)
SOLID SURFACE ACRYLICS LLC
800 Walck Rd Ste 14 (14120-3500)
PHONE..................716 743-1870
Jack Tillotsom,
Merrill Arthur,
EMP: 16
SQ FT: 76,000
SALES (est): 3.8MM Privately Held
WEB: www.ssacrylics.com
SIC: 2824 Acrylic fibers

(G-12452)
SOLIVAIRA SPECIALTIES INC
4 Detroit St (14120-6843)
PHONE..................716 693-4009
Jerry Bianchi, *Manager*
EMP: 58
SALES (corp-wide): 112.3MM Privately Held
WEB: www.ifcfiber.com
SIC: 2023 2299 2823 Dry, condensed, evaporated dairy products; flock (recovered textile fibers); cellulosic manmade fibers
PA: Solvaira Specialties Inc.
  50 Bridge St
  North Tonawanda NY 14120
  716 693-4040

(G-12453)
SOLVAIRA SPECIALTIES INC (PA)
50 Bridge St (14120-6842)
PHONE..................716 693-4040
L J Baillargeon, *CEO*
Ron Evans, *Senior VP*
Jit Ang, *Vice Pres*
Peter Vogt, *Vice Pres*
Ronald Rich, *Controller*
◆ EMP: 110 EST: 1917
SQ FT: 270,000
SALES (est): 112.3MM Privately Held
WEB: www.ifcfiber.com
SIC: 2823 2299 Cellulosic manmade fibers; flock (recovered textile fibers)

GEOGRAPHIC SECTION

(G-12454)
SOLVAIRA SPECIALTY LP (PA)
50 Bridge St (14120-6842)
PHONE.....................716 693-4040
Thorsten Willman, *CEO*
Thorsten Willmann, *CEO*
Jit Ang, *General Mgr*
Josef Rettenmaier Holding USA, *Ltd Ptnr*
EMP: 23
SALES (est): 43.3MM **Privately Held**
SIC: 2823 2299 Cellulosic manmade fibers; flock (recovered textile fibers)

(G-12455)
SOLVAIRA SPECIALTY LP
50 Bridge St (14120-6842)
PHONE.....................716 693-4040
EMP: 51
SALES (corp-wide): 43.3MM **Privately Held**
SIC: 2823 2299 Cellulosic manmade fibers; flock (recovered textile fibers)
PA: Solvaira Specialty L.P.
50 Bridge St
North Tonawanda NY 14120
716 693-4040

(G-12456)
STRASSBURG MEDICAL LLC
525 Wheatfield St (14120-7034)
P.O. Box 1213, Lockport (14095-1213)
PHONE.....................716 433-9368
David Strassburg,
Amanda Bunn,
EMP: 4
SALES: 1.3MM **Privately Held**
WEB: www.thesock.com
SIC: 2252 Socks

(G-12457)
T-S-K ELECTRONICS INC
908 Niagara Falls Blvd # 201 (14120-2021)
PHONE.....................716 693-3916
Kevin Kedzierski, *President*
Michael Kedzierski, *Vice Pres*
EMP: 5 EST: 1958
SQ FT: 15,000
SALES (est): 727.7K **Privately Held**
SIC: 3679 Electronic circuits

(G-12458)
TABER ACQUISITION CORP
Also Called: Taber Industries
455 Bryant St (14120-7043)
PHONE.....................716 694-4000
Daniel Slawson, *Ch of Bd*
Martin Slawson, *President*
Lori Anderson, *Vice Pres*
John Bertola, *Purch Mgr*
Christopher Schultz, *Engineer*
EMP: 60
SQ FT: 72,000
SALES (est): 18.5MM **Privately Held**
WEB: www.taberindustries.com
SIC: 3823 Pressure measurement instruments, industrial

(G-12459)
TAYLOR DEVICES INC (PA)
90 Taylor Dr (14120-6894)
P.O. Box 748 (14120-0748)
PHONE.....................716 694-0800
Alan R Klembczyk, *President*
Richard G Hill, *Vice Pres*
Mark V McDonough, *CFO*
▲ **EMP:** 110 EST: 1955
SALES: 24.3MM **Publicly Held**
WEB: www.taylordevices.com
SIC: 3569 Industrial shock absorbers

(G-12460)
TRINITY TOOLS INC
261 Main St (14120-7106)
PHONE.....................716 694-1111
Mitchell Banas, *President*
Chris Wein, *Vice Pres*
Michael Ostrowski, *Admin Sec*
EMP: 20
SQ FT: 18,000
SALES (est): 2.2MM **Privately Held**
WEB: www.trinitytoolrentals.com
SIC: 3544 3545 Special dies & tools; jigs & fixtures; gauges (machine tool accessories)

(G-12461)
UNITED MATERIALS LLC (PA)
3949 Frest Pk Way Ste 400 (14120)
PHONE.....................716 683-1432
Ross Eckert, *Ch of Bd*
Peter Romano, *President*
Jim Kirkland, *Project Mgr*
Roger Ball, *CFO*
EMP: 57
SQ FT: 15,000
SALES (est): 17.3MM **Privately Held**
SIC: 3273 Ready-mixed concrete

(G-12462)
WESTROCK CP LLC
51 Robinson St (14120-6805)
PHONE.....................716 692-6510
Mike McGugan, *Branch Mgr*
EMP: 101
SALES (corp-wide): 14.8B **Publicly Held**
WEB: www.smurfit-stone.com
SIC: 2653 Boxes, corrugated: made from purchased materials
HQ: Westrock Cp, Llc
504 Thrasher St
Norcross GA 30071

(G-12463)
WESTROCK CP LLC
51 Robinson St (14120-6805)
PHONE.....................716 694-1000
Mark Savre, *Manager*
EMP: 165
SALES (corp-wide): 14.8B **Publicly Held**
WEB: www.sto.com
SIC: 2653 3412 Boxes, corrugated: made from purchased materials; metal barrels, drums & pails
HQ: Westrock Cp, Llc
504 Thrasher St
Norcross GA 30071

Northport
Suffolk County

(G-12464)
BIO-CHEM BARRIER SYSTEMS LLC
11 W Scudder Pl (11768-3040)
PHONE.....................631 261-2682
Patricia J Maloney,
Raymond Maloney,
EMP: 8
SQ FT: 1,200
SALES: 1.6MM **Privately Held**
WEB: www.bio-chembarriersystemllc.com
SIC: 3842 Personal safety equipment

(G-12465)
CADDELL BURNS MANUFACTURING CO
247 Asharoken Ave (11768-1120)
PHONE.....................631 757-1772
Vincent Burns, *President*
Caryl Burns, *Vice Pres*
EMP: 20
SQ FT: 14,000
SALES (est): 2.6MM **Privately Held**
WEB: www.caddell-burns.com
SIC: 3677 3612 Coil windings, electronic; transformers, except electric

(G-12466)
CHASE CORPORATION
Also Called: Chase Partners
7 Harbour Point Dr (11768-1556)
PHONE.....................631 827-0476
EMP: 11
SALES (corp-wide): 252.5MM **Publicly Held**
SIC: 3644 Noncurrent-carrying wiring services
PA: Chase Corporation
295 University Ave
Westwood MA 02090
781 332-0700

(G-12467)
CYPRESS SEMICONDUCTOR CORP
Also Called: Sales Office
34 Rowley Dr (11768-3246)
PHONE.....................631 261-1358
Carl Finke, *Branch Mgr*
EMP: 14
SALES (corp-wide): 2.3B **Publicly Held**
WEB: www.cypress.com
SIC: 3674 5065 Semiconductors & related devices; electronic parts & equipment
PA: Cypress Semiconductor Corporation
198 Champion Ct
San Jose CA 95134
408 943-2600

(G-12468)
FRANKLIN PACKAGING INC (PA)
96 Sea Cove Rd (11768-1847)
PHONE.....................631 582-8900
Steven Lincon, *CEO*
Joan Lincoln, *Treasurer*
EMP: 6
SQ FT: 1,500
SALES: 800K **Privately Held**
SIC: 2759 Labels & seals: printing

(G-12469)
KEEP HEALTHY INC
1019 Fort Salonga Rd (11768-2270)
PHONE.....................631 651-9090
Ronald Sowa, *President*
EMP: 12 EST: 2014
SALES (est): 500K **Privately Held**
SIC: 2064 Breakfast bars

(G-12470)
LEDAN INC
Also Called: Ledan Design Group
6 Annetta Ave (11768-1802)
PHONE.....................631 239-1226
Daniel Leo Sr, *CEO*
Steven Leo, *President*
Dan Leo Jr, *Vice Pres*
EMP: 25 EST: 1955
SQ FT: 20,000
SALES (est): 3.1MM **Privately Held**
WEB: www.ledan.com
SIC: 2542 Office & store showcases & display fixtures

(G-12471)
LIK LLC
6 Bluff Point Rd (11768-1516)
PHONE.....................516 848-5135
Laura Kampa, *President*
EMP: 10
SALES (est): 761.8K **Privately Held**
SIC: 3669 Communications equipment

(G-12472)
MARKETING GROUP INTERNATIONAL
Also Called: Mgi
1 Stargazer Ct (11768-1054)
PHONE.....................631 754-8095
Bruce Chautin, *Partner*
Linda Kupcewicz, *Partner*
▲ **EMP:** 7
SALES (est): 1.1MM **Privately Held**
SIC: 2679 Paper products, converted

(G-12473)
NIKISH SOFTWARE CORP
12 Whispering Fields Dr (11768-2866)
PHONE.....................631 754-1618
Kishin Bharwani, *President*
Nitsha Bharwani, *Vice Pres*
EMP: 6
SALES (est): 566.6K **Privately Held**
WEB: www.nikish.com
SIC: 7372 Business oriented computer software

(G-12474)
WACF ENTERPRISE INC
275 Asharoken Ave (11768-1120)
PHONE.....................631 745-5841
Richard Orofino, *Owner*
EMP: 50
SQ FT: 4,000
SALES (est): 5.2MM **Privately Held**
SIC: 2833 Botanical products, medicinal: ground, graded or milled

(G-12475)
X-GEN PHARMACEUTICALS INC
4 York Ct (11768-3346)
P.O. Box 150 (11768-0150)
PHONE.....................631 261-8188
Susan Badia, *Branch Mgr*
EMP: 30
SALES (corp-wide): 4MM **Privately Held**
SIC: 2834 Pharmaceutical preparations
PA: X-Gen Pharmaceuticals, Inc.
300 Daniel Zenker Dr
Big Flats NY 14814
607 562-2700

Northville
Fulton County

(G-12476)
BEST TINSMITH SUPPLY INC
4 Zetta Dr (12134-5322)
PHONE.....................518 863-2541
John Crawford Jr, *President*
Claudia Hutchins, *Treasurer*
EMP: 5
SQ FT: 6,000
SALES: 507.1K **Privately Held**
SIC: 3444 Sheet metalwork

Norwich
Chenango County

(G-12477)
BYTHEWAY PUBLISHING SERVICES
365 Follett Hill Rd (13815-3378)
PHONE.....................607 334-8365
Betty Bytheway, *Owner*
Lori Holland, *Office Mgr*
EMP: 17
SALES (est): 1.4MM **Privately Held**
WEB: www.bytheway.com
SIC: 2791 Typesetting

(G-12478)
CHENANGO CONCRETE CORP
Also Called: Boeing Medcl Trtmnt Mltry Arcr
County Rd 32 E River Rd (13815)
PHONE.....................607 334-2545
Mike Dwyer, *Director*
EMP: 10
SQ FT: 3,264
SALES (corp-wide): 5.9MM **Privately Held**
SIC: 3271 Concrete block & brick
PA: Chenango Concrete Corp.
145 Podpadic Rd
Richmondville NY 12149
518 294-9964

(G-12479)
CHENANGO UNION PRINTING INC
15 American Ave (13815-1834)
P.O. Box 149 (13815-0149)
PHONE.....................607 334-2112
Andrew Phelps, *President*
David Phelps, *Shareholder*
EMP: 8
SALES (est): 1.2MM **Privately Held**
WEB: www.chenangounion.com
SIC: 2759 2752 Letterpress printing; commercial printing, offset

(G-12480)
CHENTRONICS CORPORATION
115 County Rd 45 (13815)
PHONE.....................607 334-5531
John Killean, *President*
Stephen Biviano, *Vice Pres*
Allen Pardon, *Admin Sec*
▲ **EMP:** 22
SALES (est): 4.5MM
SALES (corp-wide): 42.9B **Privately Held**
WEB: www.chentronics.com
SIC: 3433 Heating equipment, except electric

Norwich - Chenango County (G-12481)   GEOGRAPHIC SECTION

PA: Koch Industries, Inc.
4111 E 37th St N
Wichita KS 67220
316 828-5500

(G-12481)
CHOBANI LLC (HQ)
147 State Highway 320 (13815-3561)
PHONE..................607 337-1246
Hamdi Ulukaya, *CEO*
Tim Brown, *President*
Michael Gonda, *President*
Ravi Babu, *General Mgr*
John Casey, *General Mgr*
◆ **EMP:** 120
SQ FT: 60,000
SALES (est): 1B
SALES (corp-wide): 235.5MM **Privately Held**
SIC: 2026 Yogurt
PA: Chobani Global Holdings, Llc
147 State Highway 320
Norwich NY 13815
607 847-6181

(G-12482)
CHOBANI IDAHO LLC
147 State Highway 320 (13815-3561)
PHONE..................208 432-2248
Aaron Ash, *Maint Spvr*
Jose Trelles, *Manager*
Randy Sabin, *Supervisor*
Emily Acee, *Administration*
EMP: 7
SALES (est): 110.5K
SALES (corp-wide): 235.5MM **Privately Held**
SIC: 2024 Dairy based frozen desserts
HQ: Chobani, Llc
147 State Highway 320
Norwich NY 13815

(G-12483)
COMMERCIAL DISPLAY DESIGN LLC
120 Kemper Ln (13815-3579)
PHONE..................607 336-7353
W Russell Hurd,
Thomas G Naughton,
Gregory C Yungbluth,
EMP: 15
SALES (est): 100K
SALES (corp-wide): 19.6MM **Privately Held**
SIC: 2521 Cabinets, office: wood
PA: Burt Rigid Box, Inc.
58 Browne St
Oneonta NY 13820
607 433-2510

(G-12484)
DAN WESSON CORP
Also Called: Cz USA Dwf Dan Wesson Firearm
65 Borden Ave (13815)
PHONE..................607 336-1174
Robert W Serva, *President*
EMP: 18
SQ FT: 24,000
SALES (est): 1.4MM **Privately Held**
WEB: www.danwessonfirearms.com
SIC: 3484 Small arms

(G-12485)
ELECTRON COIL INC
Also Called: Eci
141 Barr Rd (13815)
P.O. Box 71 (13815-0071)
PHONE..................607 336-7414
Douglas Marchant, *CEO*
John Barnett, *General Mgr*
Richard Marchant, *Vice Pres*
Paula McCall, *Purch Agent*
Jeff Cola, *QC Mgr*
EMP: 55
SQ FT: 10,000
SALES (est): 10.7MM **Privately Held**
WEB: www.electroncoil.com
SIC: 3621 3612 3675 3677 Coils, for electric motors or generators; power & distribution transformers; electronic capacitors; electronic coils, transformers & other inductors

(G-12486)
GOLUB CORPORATION
Also Called: Price Chopper Pharmacy
5631 State Highway 12 (13815-3205)
PHONE..................607 336-2588
Vincent Mainella, *Branch Mgr*
EMP: 21
SALES (corp-wide): 3.3B **Privately Held**
SIC: 3751 Motorcycles & related parts
PA: The Golub Corporation
461 Nott St
Schenectady NY 12308
518 355-5000

(G-12487)
HANGER PRSTHETCS & ORTHO INC
6142 State Highway 12 # 14 (13815-3719)
PHONE..................607 334-3320
Shawna Smith, *Office Mgr*
Florent Berger, *Manager*
EMP: 5
SALES (corp-wide): 1B **Publicly Held**
SIC: 3842 Surgical appliances & supplies
HQ: Hanger Prosthetics & Orthotics, Inc.
10910 Domain Dr Ste 300
Austin TX 78758
512 777-3800

(G-12488)
KERRY BFNCTNAL INGREDIENTS INC (DH)
Also Called: Kerry Bio-Science
158 State Highway 320 (13815-3561)
PHONE..................608 363-1200
Stan McCarthy, *CEO*
Michael O'Neill, *President*
Gerry Behan, *Chairman*
◆ **EMP:** 80
SQ FT: 127,353
SALES (est): 18.3MM **Privately Held**
SIC: 2079 2023 2099 Edible fats & oils; dry, condensed, evaporated dairy products; seasonings: dry mixes
HQ: Kerry Inc.
3330 Millrington Rd
Beloit WI 53511
608 363-1200

(G-12489)
LABEL GALLERY INC
1 Lee Ave 11 (13815-1108)
PHONE..................607 334-3244
Christopher Ulatowski, *President*
Anna Ulatowski, *Vice Pres*
Michael Gladstone, *Plant Mgr*
Walt Reid, *Opers Staff*
Gail Lawrence, *Human Res Dir*
EMP: 30
SQ FT: 15,000
SALES (est): 6.5MM **Privately Held**
WEB: www.labelgallery.net
SIC: 2672 2752 Labels (unprinted), gummed: made from purchased materials; commercial printing, lithographic

(G-12490)
NORWICH PHARMACEUTICALS INC
Also Called: Norwich Pharma Services
6826 State Highway 12 (13815-3335)
PHONE..................607 335-3000
Chris Calhoun, *President*
Darren Alkins, *President*
Lisa Graver, *Exec VP*
Kevin Bain, *CFO*
▲ **EMP:** 375
SQ FT: 375,000
SALES (est): 66.5MM **Privately Held**
SIC: 2834 Pharmaceutical preparations
PA: Alvogen Group, Inc.
10 Bloomfield Ave
Pine Brook NJ 07058

(G-12491)
PRECISION BUILT TOPS LLC
89 Borden Ave (13815-1105)
PHONE..................607 336-5417
Steven Serafan,
EMP: 6
SALES (est): 654.5K **Privately Held**
WEB: www.precisionbuilttops.com
SIC: 2541 Counter & sink tops

(G-12492)
PRIME TOOL & DIE LLC
6277 County Road 32 (13815-3560)
P.O. Box 83 (13815-0083)
PHONE..................607 334-5435
George H Prime Jr, *Mng Member*
EMP: 6
SALES: 400K **Privately Held**
SIC: 3544 Jigs & fixtures

(G-12493)
SUN PRINTING INCORPORATED
57 Borden Ave 65 (13815-1105)
P.O. Box 151 (13815-0151)
PHONE..................607 337-3034
Bradford R Dick, *Principal*
EMP: 29 **EST:** 2001
SALES (est): 2.5MM **Privately Held**
SIC: 2752 Commercial printing, lithographic

(G-12494)
UNISON INDUSTRIES LLC
5345 State Highway 12 (13815-1246)
P.O. Box 310 (13815-0310)
PHONE..................607 335-5000
Gary Cummings, *Opers Staff*
Mike Terzo, *Engineer*
Herbert Allen, *Supervisor*
EMP: 350
SALES (corp-wide): 122B **Publicly Held**
WEB: www.unisonindustries.com
SIC: 3679 3769 Electronic circuits; guided missile & space vehicle parts & auxiliary equipment
HQ: Unison Industries, Llc
7575 Baymeadows Way
Jacksonville FL 32256
904 739-4000

Norwood
St. Lawrence County

(G-12495)
BARRETT PAVING MATERIALS INC
Also Called: Norwood Quar Btmnous Con Plnts
Rr 56 (13668)
P.O. Box 203 (13668-0203)
PHONE..................315 353-6611
David R Wright, *Superintendent*
EMP: 25
SALES (corp-wide): 95.5MM **Privately Held**
WEB: www.barrettpaving.com
SIC: 2951 5032 1611 2952 Concrete, bituminous; paving materials; surfacing & paving; asphalt felts & coatings
HQ: Barrett Paving Materials Inc.
3 Becker Farm Rd Ste 307
Roseland NJ 07068
973 533-1001

(G-12496)
POTTERS INDUSTRIES LLC
56 Reynolds Rd (13668-4131)
PHONE..................315 265-4920
Andy Gray, *Manager*
Andrew Gray, *Manager*
EMP: 40
SALES (corp-wide): 1.4B **Publicly Held**
WEB: www.flexolite.com
SIC: 3231 Reflector glass beads, for highway signs or reflectors
HQ: Potters Industries, Llc
300 Lindenwood Dr
Malvern PA 19355
610 651-4700

Nunda
Livingston County

(G-12497)
ONCE AGAIN NUT BUTTER COLLECTV (PA)
12 S State St (14517)
P.O. Box 429 (14517-0429)
PHONE..................585 468-2535
Robert Gelser, *President*
Amy Snyder, *Transportation*
Franklin Lew, *Production*
Lawrence Filipski, *CFO*
Gael Orr, *Comms Mgr*
▲ **EMP:** 64
SQ FT: 20,000
SALES: 55.9MM **Privately Held**
WEB: www.onceagainnutbutter.com
SIC: 2099 Peanut butter; almond pastes; honey, strained & bottled

(G-12498)
SEATING INC
60 N State St (14517)
P.O. Box 898 (14517-0898)
PHONE..................800 468-2475
Judy Hart, *President*
Doug Hart, *Vice Pres*
EMP: 31
SQ FT: 65,000
SALES (est): 3.7MM **Privately Held**
WEB: www.seatinginc.com
SIC: 2522 2531 Office chairs, benches & stools, except wood; public building & related furniture

Nyack
Rockland County

(G-12499)
AMS STAR STRUCTURES INC
453 S Broadway (10960-4807)
PHONE..................914 584-0898
Wade Petty, *President*
Robert Schroeder, *Principal*
EMP: 2
SALES: 1MM **Privately Held**
SIC: 2394 Tents: made from purchased materials

(G-12500)
BECTON DICKINSON AND COMPANY
Also Called: Bd Initiative-Hlthcare Wrkr SA
1 Main St Apt 3307 (10960-3236)
PHONE..................845 353-3371
Jill Garnette, *Manager*
EMP: 379
SALES (corp-wide): 12B **Publicly Held**
SIC: 3841 Diagnostic apparatus, medical
PA: Becton, Dickinson And Company
1 Becton Dr
Franklin Lakes NJ 07417
201 847-6800

(G-12501)
BERRY INDUSTRIAL GROUP INC (PA)
30 Main St (10960-3202)
PHONE..................845 353-8338
Debra Berry, *CEO*
Peter Berry, *President*
EMP: 8
SQ FT: 1,800
SALES (est): 1.5MM **Privately Held**
WEB: www.berryindustrial.com
SIC: 2448 5031 Pallets, wood; lumber: rough, dressed & finished

(G-12502)
CHARLES PERRELLA INC
78 S Broadway (10960-6802)
PHONE..................845 348-4777
Marie Somos, *President*
Richard Townsend, *Corp Secy*
Phyllis Townsend, *Vice Pres*
EMP: 20
SQ FT: 7,500
SALES (est): 1.5MM **Privately Held**
WEB: www.perrellainc.com
SIC: 3911 5944 Jewelry, precious metal; jewelry stores

(G-12503)
CONCEPT PRINTING INC
Also Called: Concept Printing and Promotion
40 Lydecker St (10960-2104)
PHONE..................845 353-4040
Kerry Gaughan Monahan, *President*
▲ **EMP:** 4

SALES: 1.3MM **Privately Held**
WEB: www.conceptprintinginc.com
SIC: 2752 5199 Commercial printing, offset; advertising specialties

(G-12504)
DESIGNPLEX LLC
107 Cedar Hill Ave (10960-3705)
PHONE..................................845 358-6647
Loren Bloom, *President*
EMP: 5
SQ FT: 1,500
SALES: 200K **Privately Held**
WEB: www.designplex.org
SIC: 3993 Signs & advertising specialties

(G-12505)
DIRECTORY MAJOR MALLS INC
20 N Broadway Ste 2 (10960-2644)
P.O. Box 837 (10960-0837)
PHONE..................................845 348-7000
Tama J Shor, *President*
EMP: 8
SALES (est): 794.1K **Privately Held**
WEB: www.directoryofmajormalls.com
SIC: 2741 6531 Atlases: publishing only, not printed on site; real estate agents & managers

(G-12506)
EASTERN PRECISION MFG
76 S Franklin St 78 (10960-3734)
PHONE..................................845 358-1951
Harold Hill, *President*
EMP: 6 **EST:** 1973
SQ FT: 600
SALES (est): 410.3K **Privately Held**
SIC: 3569 Firefighting apparatus

(G-12507)
EDROY PRODUCTS CO INC
245 N Midland Ave (10960-1949)
P.O. Box 998 (10960-0998)
PHONE..................................845 358-6600
Steven Stoltze, *President*
EMP: 7 **EST:** 1937
SQ FT: 4,700
SALES: 606.2K **Privately Held**
WEB: www.edroyproducts.com
SIC: 3851 Magnifiers (readers & simple magnifiers)

(G-12508)
GLOBAL BRANDS INC
1031 Route 9w S (10960-4907)
PHONE..................................845 358-1212
Ralph Ferrante, *CEO*
Herbert M Paul, *President*
EMP: 8
SQ FT: 1,250
SALES (est): 802.1K **Privately Held**
SIC: 2086 Mineral water, carbonated: packaged in cans, bottles, etc.

(G-12509)
LUGO NUTRITION INC
51 N Broadway Ste 2 (10960-2639)
PHONE..................................302 573-2503
Richard Lugo, *President*
Nicholas Lugo, *Vice Pres*
Karen Logu, *CFO*
EMP: 6
SALES (est): 348.4K **Privately Held**
SIC: 2099 Food preparations

(G-12510)
SARAVAL INDUSTRIES
348 N Midland Ave (10960-1531)
PHONE..................................516 768-9033
Dave Schwartz, *Owner*
EMP: 9
SALES (est): 480K **Privately Held**
SIC: 2521 Wood office furniture

(G-12511)
TANDY LEATHER FACTORY INC
298 Main St (10960-2418)
PHONE..................................845 480-3588
Kelly Per.ni, *Manager*
EMP: 5
SALES (corp-wide): 82.3MM **Publicly Held**
SIC: 3111 5199 5948 Accessory products, leather; lace leather; leather, leather goods & furs; leather goods, except luggage & shoes
PA: Tandy Leather Factory, Inc.
1900 Se Loop 820
Fort Worth TX 76140
817 872-3200

(G-12512)
TEKA PRECISION INC
251 Mountainview Ave (10960-1700)
PHONE..................................845 753-1900
Helen Roderick, *President*
EMP: 7
SQ FT: 1,500
SALES (est): 660K **Privately Held**
SIC: 3496 3541 3495 3452 Miscellaneous fabricated wire products; machine tools, metal cutting type; wire springs; bolts, nuts, rivets & washers

(G-12513)
WIRELESS COMMUNICATIONS INC
4 Chemong Ct (10960-2307)
PHONE..................................845 353-5921
Robert H Colten, *Owner*
EMP: 5
SALES (est): 317.7K **Privately Held**
SIC: 3663 Radio broadcasting & communications equipment

Oakdale
Suffolk County

(G-12514)
CJ COMPONENT PRODUCTS LLC
624 Tower Mews (11769-2449)
PHONE..................................631 567-3733
David Howe, *CEO*
Kevin Lee, *Vice Pres*
▼ **EMP:** 5
SQ FT: 880
SALES (est): 770.5K **Privately Held**
WEB: www.cjcomponents.com
SIC: 3663 Radio & TV communications equipment

(G-12515)
DARK STORM INDUSTRIES LLC
4116 Sunrise Hwy (11769-1013)
PHONE..................................631 967-3170
EMP: 5
SALES (est): 371.9K **Privately Held**
SIC: 3999 Manufacturing industries

(G-12516)
GALAXY SOFTWARE LLC
927 Montauk Hwy Unit 229 (11769-3011)
P.O. Box 229 (11769-0229)
PHONE..................................631 244-8405
Andrew Cohen, *Sales Executive*
Cathline Cohen,
EMP: 8
SALES (est): 727.3K **Privately Held**
WEB: www.galaxy-software.com
SIC: 7372 7371 Application computer software; software programming applications

(G-12517)
GSA UPSTATE NY (PA)
755 Montauk Hwy (11769-1801)
PHONE..................................631 244-5744
John Beaver, *CEO*
Chris Biava, *Engineer*
EMP: 2
SQ FT: 1,000
SALES (est): 5.4MM **Privately Held**
WEB: www.gsasales.com
SIC: 3699 Electrical equipment & supplies

(G-12518)
MODERN ITLN BKY OF W BABYLON
301 Locust Ave (11769-1652)
PHONE..................................631 589-7300
James Turco, *Principal*
Ken Burke, *Vice Pres*
Bridgette Johnston, *Controller*
Mike Sable, *Controller*
Jerry Yllanes, *Persnl Mgr*
EMP: 170
SQ FT: 54,000
SALES (est): 43.9MM **Privately Held**
WEB: www.modernbakedprod.com
SIC: 2051 5142 5149 Bread, all types (white, wheat, rye, etc): fresh or frozen; bakery products, frozen; bakery products

(G-12519)
MORELAND HOSE & BELTING CORP
4118 Sunrise Hwy (11769-1013)
PHONE..................................631 563-7071
William Delmore, *Manager*
EMP: 8
SALES (est): 1MM
SALES (corp-wide): 6.4MM **Privately Held**
WEB: www.morelandhose.com
SIC: 3052 Hose, pneumatic: rubber or rubberized fabric
PA: Moreland Hose & Belting Corp
135 Adams Ave
Hempstead NY 11550
516 485-9898

(G-12520)
SPECIALTY FABRICATORS
4120 Sunrise Hwy (11769-1079)
PHONE..................................631 256-6982
EMP: 10
SALES (est): 1.1MM **Privately Held**
SIC: 3399 Mfg Primary Metal Products

(G-12521)
SPEEDZONE INC
Also Called: Speedzone Raceway Hobbies
937 Montauk Hwy (11769-1733)
PHONE..................................631 750-1973
EMP: 6 **EST:** 2007
SALES (est): 70.8K **Privately Held**
SIC: 3644 Raceways

(G-12522)
STEEL-BRITE LTD
Also Called: September Associates
2 Dawn Dr (11769-1624)
PHONE..................................631 589-4044
Marilyn Cohen, *President*
Susan McCarthy, *Managing Dir*
EMP: 10
SQ FT: 2,500
SALES (est): 770K **Privately Held**
SIC: 3993 5072 Displays & cutouts, window & lobby; hardware

Oakfield
Genesee County

(G-12523)
BONDUELLE USA INC
40 Stevens St (14125-1227)
PHONE..................................585 948-5252
Daniel Vielfaure, *CEO*
EMP: 29
SALES (est): 9.3MM **Privately Held**
SIC: 3556 Smokers, food processing equipment

(G-12524)
KEEBLER COMPANY
2999 Judge Rd (14125-9771)
PHONE..................................585 948-8010
Ed Watson, *Manager*
EMP: 17
SALES (corp-wide): 12.9B **Publicly Held**
WEB: www.keebler.com
SIC: 2052 Cookies
HQ: Keebler Company
1 Kellogg Sq
Battle Creek MI 49017
269 961-2000

(G-12525)
UNITED STATES GYPSUM COMPANY
2750 Maple Ave (14125-9722)
PHONE..................................585 948-5221
James Perry, *Plant Mgr*
Jim Roz, *Opers Staff*
Ray Tamblin, *Plant Engr*
Ray Dunlevy, *Personnel*
Gregg Diefenbacher, *Branch Mgr*
EMP: 123
SALES (corp-wide): 3.2B **Publicly Held**
WEB: www.usg.com
SIC: 3275 Gypsum products
HQ: United States Gypsum Company
550 W Adams St Ste 1300
Chicago IL 60661
312 606-4000

Oakland Gardens
Queens County

(G-12526)
SLIMS BAGELS UNLIMITED INC (PA)
22118 Horace Harding Expy (11364-2390)
P.O. Box 640206 (11364-0206)
PHONE..................................718 229-1140
Joseph Dvir, *President*
David Katz, *Vice Pres*
EMP: 27 **EST:** 1999
SQ FT: 5,000
SALES (est): 1.5MM **Privately Held**
SIC: 2051 5641 Bakery: wholesale or wholesale/retail combined; children's & infants' wear stores

Oaks Corners
Ontario County

(G-12527)
ELDERLEE INCORPORATED (HQ)
729 Cross Rd (14518)
P.O. Box 10 (14518-0010)
PHONE..................................315 789-6670
Basil A Shorb III, *Ch of Bd*
William J Shorb, *President*
David Dejohn, *Vice Pres*
Robert Rook, *Vice Pres*
Paul R Strain, *Vice Pres*
EMP: 120
SQ FT: 240,000
SALES (est): 45.5MM
SALES (corp-wide): 78.7MM **Privately Held**
WEB: www.elderlee.com
SIC: 3312 1611 3444 3993 Iron & steel: galvanized, pipes, plates, sheets, etc.; guardrail construction, highways; guard rails, highway: sheet metal; signs & advertising specialties; concrete products
PA: Reh Holdings, Inc
150 S Sumner St
York PA 17404
717 843-0021

(G-12528)
HANSON AGGREGATES PA LLC
2026 County Rd Ste 6 (14518)
PHONE..................................315 789-6202
Kenny Thurston, *Opers-Prdtn-Mfg*
EMP: 25
SALES (corp-wide): 20.3B **Privately Held**
SIC: 1442 3281 1422 Gravel mining; stone, quarrying & processing of own stone products; crushed & broken limestone
HQ: Hanson Aggregates Pennsylvania, Llc
7660 Imperial Way
Allentown PA 18195
610 366-4626

Oceanside
Nassau County

(G-12529)
3KRF LLC
3516 Hargale Rd (11572-5820)
PHONE..................................516 208-6824
Timothy Hopper, *Managing Prtnr*
Mark Gruenspecht, *Mng Member*
EMP: 5
SALES (est): 410K **Privately Held**
SIC: 3699 Electrical welding equipment

Oceanside - Nassau County (G-12530)

(G-12530)
ADF ACCESSORIES INC
Also Called: Todaysgentleman.com
3539 Lawson Blvd (11572-4993)
PHONE......................516 450-5755
Jack Fischman, *President*
Chanie Manheimer, *Vice Pres*
▲ EMP: 5
SALES (est): 628.9K **Privately Held**
WEB: www.todaysgentleman.com
SIC: 2389 Men's miscellaneous accessories

(G-12531)
AHW PRINTING CORP
Also Called: PIP Printing
2920 Long Beach Rd (11572-3114)
PHONE......................516 536-3600
Alan Waldman, *President*
Harriet Waldman, *Treasurer*
EMP: 11
SQ FT: 1,900
SALES (est): 1.8MM **Privately Held**
SIC: 2752 Commercial printing, offset

(G-12532)
ASTRODYNE INC
18 Neil Ct (11572-5816)
P.O. Box 354, Rockville Centre (11571-0354)
PHONE......................516 536-5755
David J Salwen, *CEO*
Ira M Salwen, *President*
Barbara Salwen, *Admin Sec*
EMP: 6
SQ FT: 5,000
SALES (est): 931.1K **Privately Held**
SIC: 3861 5045 5734 Photographic equipment & supplies; computers, peripherals & software; computer software; computer & software stores; computer software & accessories

(G-12533)
CHUDNOW MANUFACTURING CO INC
3055 New St (11572-2743)
PHONE......................516 593-4222
Richard B Cohen, *President*
Gary Clausen, *Sales Mgr*
EMP: 45 EST: 1934
SQ FT: 28,000
SALES: 5MM **Privately Held**
SIC: 3585 Soda fountain & beverage dispensing equipment & parts; soda fountains, parts & accessories

(G-12534)
D & M CUSTOM CABINETS INC
2994 Long Beach Rd (11572-3205)
P.O. Box 37 (11572-0037)
PHONE......................516 678-2818
Fax: 516 678-0042
EMP: 12
SQ FT: 7,500
SALES (est): 1.3MM **Privately Held**
SIC: 2434 Mfg Wood Kitchen Cabinet Doors

(G-12535)
DDC TECHNOLOGIES INC
311 Woods Ave (11572-2128)
PHONE......................516 594-1533
Dimitri Donskoy, *President*
Donskoy Dmitry, *Manager*
EMP: 5
SALES (est): 872.9K **Privately Held**
WEB: www.ddctech.com
SIC: 3845 Laser systems & equipment, medical

(G-12536)
EAST COAST MOLDERS INC
3001 New St Ste F (11572-2747)
PHONE......................516 240-6000
EMP: 225
SQ FT: 7,000
SALES (est): 9.5MM **Privately Held**
SIC: 2342 Mfg Bras/Girdles

(G-12537)
EXPRESS BUILDING SUPPLY INC
Also Called: Wholesale Window Warehouse
3550 Lawson Blvd (11572-4908)
PHONE......................516 608-0379
Robert Freedman, *President*
Justin Freedman, *Vice Pres*
EMP: 25 EST: 1996
SQ FT: 9,000
SALES: 2.5MM **Privately Held**
SIC: 3211 5031 5211 Window glass, clear & colored; windows; windows, storm: wood or metal

(G-12538)
FIRST MANUFACTURING CO INC (HQ)
Also Called: FMC Fashion Division
3800 Oceanside Rd W (11572-5904)
PHONE......................516 763-0400
Ajmal Cheema, *Ch of Bd*
Mushtaq Cheema, *President*
Amir Mukhtar, *Production*
Patrick Curran, *Credit Mgr*
Nafar Ali, *Manager*
▲ EMP: 36
SQ FT: 80,000
SALES (est): 8.4MM
SALES (corp-wide): 32.6MM **Privately Held**
SIC: 3199 3172 Leather garments; personal leather goods
PA: Leather Field (Pvt) Limited.
Cheema Square, Capital Road
Sialkot
523 556-272

(G-12539)
FIVE BORO DOORS MOULDINGS INC
3569 Maple Ct (11572-4821)
PHONE......................718 865-9371
Usher Krasne, *Principal*
EMP: 8
SALES (est): 157.6K **Privately Held**
SIC: 3442 Metal doors, sash & trim

(G-12540)
HENNIG CUSTOM WOODWORK CORP
Also Called: Hennig Custom Woodworking
2497 Long Beach Rd (11572-1321)
PHONE......................516 536-3460
James Hennig, *President*
EMP: 5
SALES: 500K **Privately Held**
SIC: 2421 7389 5031 2499 Furniture dimension stock, softwood; laminating service; kitchen cabinets; decorative wood & woodwork; cabinet & finish carpentry

(G-12541)
IP MED INC
3571 Hargale Rd (11572-5821)
PHONE......................516 766-3800
Judah Isaacs, *President*
EMP: 7
SALES (est): 346K **Privately Held**
SIC: 2836 3841 2834 5122 Bacterial vaccines; inhalators, surgical & medical; proprietary drug products; drugs & drug proprietaries

(G-12542)
JONDEN MANUFACTURING CO INC
3069 Lawson Blvd (11572-2939)
P.O. Box 401, Hewlett (11557-0401)
PHONE......................516 442-4895
Linda Smilowitz, *CEO*
Jon Smilowitz, *President*
Linda Leal, *Principal*
John Smilowitz, *Chairman*
Denise Smilowitz, *Exec VP*
▲ EMP: 18
SALES (est): 3.3MM **Privately Held**
WEB: www.jonden.com
SIC: 2339 Sportswear, women's

(G-12543)
JQ WOODWORKING INC
3085 New St (11572-2743)
PHONE......................516 766-3424
John Quinn, *Ch of Bd*
EMP: 5
SQ FT: 10,000
SALES: 1MM **Privately Held**
SIC: 3259 1751 Architectural clay products; cabinet & finish carpentry

(G-12544)
KANTEK INC
Also Called: Spectrum
3460a Hampton Rd (11572-4803)
PHONE......................516 594-4600
Herman Kappel, *President*
AVI Kappel, *General Mgr*
Nancy Pollack,
▲ EMP: 30
SQ FT: 25,000
SALES (est): 12.1MM **Privately Held**
WEB: www.kantek.com
SIC: 3577 5045 Computer peripheral equipment; computers, peripherals & software

(G-12545)
L N D INCORPORATED
Also Called: Lnd
3230 Lawson Blvd (11572-3796)
PHONE......................516 678-6141
Peter T Neyland, *President*
Spencer B Neyland, *Vice Pres*
Robert Sierzputowski, *Purch Mgr*
William Chatfield, *Controller*
William J Lehnert, *VP Sales*
EMP: 45 EST: 1964
SQ FT: 14,000
SALES (est): 10.7MM **Privately Held**
WEB: www.lndinc.com
SIC: 3829 Nuclear radiation & testing apparatus

(G-12546)
LOVE BRIGHT JEWELRY INC
Also Called: Lovebrightjewelry.com
3446 Frederick St (11572-4713)
PHONE......................516 620-2509
Bhupen Kapadia, *President*
EMP: 25
SQ FT: 2,000
SALES (est): 1.4MM **Privately Held**
SIC: 3911 5094 5944 Jewelry apparel; jewelry; jewelry stores

(G-12547)
MARK PERI INTERNATIONAL
3516 Hargale Rd (11572-5820)
PHONE......................516 208-6824
Mark Gruenspecht, *Director*
EMP: 10
SALES (est): 797.8K **Privately Held**
SIC: 3663 Radio & TV communications equipment

(G-12548)
MARKPERICOM
3516 Hargale Rd (11572-5820)
PHONE......................516 208-6824
Mark Gruenstpecht, *President*
EMP: 9
SALES (est): 711.8K **Privately Held**
SIC: 3569 General industrial machinery

(G-12549)
ONLY NATURAL INC
Also Called: Bio Nutrition
3580 Oceanside Rd Unit 5 (11572-5825)
PHONE......................516 897-7001
Robert Lomaccio, *President*
◆ EMP: 15
SQ FT: 3,600
SALES (est): 2.6MM **Privately Held**
WEB: www.onlynaturalinc.com
SIC: 2833 5499 Vitamins, natural or synthetic: bulk, uncompounded; health & dietetic food stores

(G-12550)
PIER-TECH INC
7 Hampton Rd (11572-4838)
PHONE......................516 442-5420
Robert Sackaris, *Ch of Bd*
EMP: 42
SALES (est): 8.8MM **Privately Held**
SIC: 3531 Construction machinery

(G-12551)
POETRY MAILING LIST MARSH HAWK
2823 Rockaway Ave (11572-1018)
P.O. Box 206, East Rockaway (11518-0206)
PHONE......................516 766-1891
Jane Augustine, *President*
EMP: 5
SALES: 45.4K **Privately Held**
SIC: 2731 Book publishing

(G-12552)
RADIANT PRO LTD
245 Merrick Rd (11572-1428)
PHONE......................516 763-5678
John Cioento, *Owner*
EMP: 7
SALES (est): 719.8K **Privately Held**
SIC: 3567 Radiant heating systems, industrial process

(G-12553)
RALPHS ICES OF LEVITTOWN
3831 Carrel Blvd (11572-5912)
PHONE......................516 520-0618
Cindy Roch, *Owner*
Cindy Toch, *Owner*
EMP: 10
SALES (est): 622.6K **Privately Held**
SIC: 2024 Ice cream & frozen desserts

(G-12554)
ROSE TRUNK MFG CO INC
3935 Sally Ln (11572-5934)
PHONE......................516 766-6686
Melvin Lapidus, *President*
Mark Lapidus, *Vice Pres*
◆ EMP: 15 EST: 1945
SQ FT: 15,000
SALES (est): 1.8MM **Privately Held**
WEB: www.rosetrunk.com
SIC: 3161 Trunks

(G-12555)
ROYAL MARBLE & GRANITE INC
3295 Royal Ave (11572-3625)
PHONE......................516 536-5900
Richard Tafuri, *President*
Anthony Tafuri, *Vice Pres*
▲ EMP: 8
SQ FT: 8,000
SALES (est): 893.4K **Privately Held**
SIC: 3281 3272 Granite, cut & shaped; art marble, concrete

(G-12556)
SEA WAVES INC (PA)
2425 Long Beach Rd (11572-1320)
PHONE......................516 766-4201
Brian Corhan, *President*
Harold Corhan, *Vice Pres*
▲ EMP: 5
SQ FT: 2,000
SALES (est): 660.1K **Privately Held**
SIC: 2339 Bathing suits: women's, misses' & juniors'; beachwear: women's, misses' & juniors'

(G-12557)
SIGELOCK SYSTEMS LLC (PA)
3205 Lawson Blvd (11572-3703)
PHONE......................888 744-3562
George Sigelakis, *President*
Scott Horak, *Exec VP*
Ira Wender, *Senior VP*
Larry Davis, *Vice Pres*
Michelle Sigelakis, *Vice Pres*
EMP: 4
SALES (est): 1.1MM **Privately Held**
SIC: 3569 4971 Firefighting apparatus & related equipment; water distribution or supply systems for irrigation

(G-12558)
STRONG GROUP INC
222 Atlantic Ave Unit B (11572-2045)
PHONE......................516 766-6300
Walter Bistrong, *President*
Ann Sigel, *Corp Secy*
EMP: 8
SALES (est): 605K **Privately Held**
SIC: 2311 Manufacture Police Equipment

GEOGRAPHIC SECTION

(G-12559)
STYLES MANUFACTURING CORP
3571 Hargale Rd (11572-5821)
PHONE.................................516 763-5303
Louis Fuchs, *President*
Ron Keyes, *Vice Pres*
▲ **EMP:** 5
SALES (est): 5MM **Privately Held**
SIC: 3315 Hangers (garment), wire

(G-12560)
TAG FLANGE & MACHINING INC
3375 Royal Ave (11572-4812)
PHONE.................................516 536-1300
Theodore A Gallucci III, *President*
Sean F Gallucci, *Vice Pres*
EMP: 6
SQ FT: 10,000
SALES (est): 500K **Privately Held**
SIC: 3498 Fabricated pipe & fittings

(G-12561)
THE NUGENT ORGANIZATION INC
Also Called: Nugent Printing Company
3433 Ocean Harbor Dr (11572-3516)
PHONE.................................212 645-6600
Antonino Longo, *President*
Vincent Longo, *Vice Pres*
EMP: 18
SQ FT: 10,000
SALES (est): 2.3MM **Privately Held**
WEB: www.nugentprint.com
SIC: 2752 7331 2732 Commercial printing, offset; mailing service; book printing

(G-12562)
UNITED THREAD MILLS CORP (PA)
3530 Lawson Blvd Gf (11572-4908)
P.O. Box 766, Rockville Centre (11571-0766)
PHONE.................................516 536-3900
Ira Henkus, *President*
▼ **EMP:** 6 **EST:** 1948
SQ FT: 66,000
SALES (est): 54.2MM **Privately Held**
SIC: 2284 2281 Thread mills; yarn spinning mills

(G-12563)
VENEER ONE INC
3415 Hampton Rd (11572-4835)
PHONE.................................516 536-6480
Victor Giaime, *Ch of Bd*
Arnold Lanzillotta, *President*
Steve Horan, *Admin Sec*
▲ **EMP:** 28 **EST:** 2000
SQ FT: 19,000
SALES (est): 4.5MM **Privately Held**
WEB: www.veneer1.com
SIC: 2435 Hardwood veneer & plywood

(G-12564)
VIANA SIGNS CORP
3520 Lawson Blvd (11572-4908)
PHONE.................................516 887-2000
Leo Viana, *President*
EMP: 10
SALES (est): 750K **Privately Held**
SIC: 3993 Signs & advertising specialties

(G-12565)
WESTRON CORPORATION
Also Called: Westron Lighting
18 Neil Ct (11572-5816)
PHONE.................................516 678-2300
Irving Allerhand, *Ch of Bd*
Hershel Allerhand, *President*
▲ **EMP:** 50
SQ FT: 25,000
SALES (est): 5.4MM **Privately Held**
WEB: www.westronlighting.com
SIC: 3641 Electric lamps

(G-12566)
YALE TROUSER CORPORATION
Also Called: Smokey Joes
3670 Oceanside Rd W Ste 6 (11572-5961)
PHONE.................................516 255-0700
Arnold Bloom, *President*
Gary Bloom, *Vice Pres*
EMP: 10 **EST:** 1950
SALES (est): 1.1MM **Privately Held**
WEB: www.yaletrouser.com
SIC: 2325 2321 Slacks, dress: men's, youths' & boys'; trousers, dress (separate): men's, youths' & boys'; men's & boys' furnishings

Odessa
Schuyler County

(G-12567)
FINGER LAKES CHEESE TRAIL
4970 County Road 14 (14869-9730)
PHONE.................................607 857-5726
Carmella Hoffman, *Treasurer*
EMP: 13
SALES (est): 718.6K **Privately Held**
SIC: 2026 Fluid milk

Ogdensburg
St. Lawrence County

(G-12568)
ACCO BRANDS USA LLC
Also Called: Acco North America
941 Acco Way (13669-4438)
PHONE.................................847 541-9500
Jeffery Almasian, *Director*
Lisa Toola, *Administration*
EMP: 120
SALES (corp-wide): 1.9B **Publicly Held**
WEB: www.accobrands.com
SIC: 2782 Looseleaf binders & devices
HQ: Acco Brands Usa Llc
4 Corporate Dr
Lake Zurich IL 60047
800 222-6462

(G-12569)
ALGONQUIN POWER
19 Mill St (13669-1304)
PHONE.................................315 393-5595
Walter Bracy, *Manager*
EMP: 7
SALES (est): 886.8K **Privately Held**
SIC: 3634 Electric housewares & fans

(G-12570)
ANSEN CORPORATION (PA)
100 Chimney Point Dr (13669-2206)
PHONE.................................315 393-3573
James Kingman, *CEO*
Jerry W Slusser, *President*
Kenneth Emter, *Corp Secy*
Rodney Bush, *Branch Mgr*
Jason W Slusser, *Director*
▲ **EMP:** 1
SQ FT: 72,000
SALES (est): 97MM **Privately Held**
WEB: www.ansencorp.com
SIC: 3672 Printed circuit boards

(G-12571)
ANSEN CORPORATION
100 Chimney Point Dr (13669-2206)
PHONE.................................315 393-3573
Rodney Bush, *Branch Mgr*
EMP: 110
SQ FT: 71,000
SALES (corp-wide): 97MM **Privately Held**
WEB: www.ansencorp.com
SIC: 3672 Printed circuit boards
PA: Ansen Corporation
100 Chimney Point Dr
Ogdensburg NY 13669
315 393-3573

(G-12572)
CANARM LTD
808 Commerce Park Dr (13669-2208)
PHONE.................................800 267-4427
David Beatty, *CEO*
James Cooper, *President*
▲ **EMP:** 2
SQ FT: 1,500
SALES (est): 75MM **Privately Held**
SIC: 3564 3645 3646 5064 Blowing fans: industrial or commercial; exhaust fans: industrial or commercial; ventilating fans: industrial or commercial; residential lighting fixtures; commercial indusl & institutional electric lighting fixtures; fans, household: electric; fans, industrial: lighting fixtures, commercial & industrial; lighting fixtures, residential
PA: Canarm Ltd
2157 Parkedale Ave
Brockville ON K6V 0
613 342-5424

(G-12573)
DEFELSKO CORPORATION
800 Proctor Ave (13669-2205)
PHONE.................................315 393-4450
Frank Koch, *President*
Terry Larue, *General Mgr*
David Beamish, *Chairman*
Linda K Beamish, *Vice Pres*
Linda Beamish, *Vice Pres*
◆ **EMP:** 60
SQ FT: 15,000
SALES (est): 17.5MM **Privately Held**
WEB: www.defelsko.com
SIC: 3823 3829 Industrial instrmnts msrmnt display/control process variable; measuring & controlling devices

(G-12574)
HANSON AGGREGATES PA LLC
701 Cedar St (13669-3000)
P.O. Box 250 (13669-0250)
PHONE.................................315 393-3743
Daniel O'Connor, *Manager*
EMP: 14
SQ FT: 2,196
SALES (corp-wide): 20.3B **Privately Held**
SIC: 1429 1422 Grits mining (crushed stone); limestones, ground
HQ: Hanson Aggregates Pennsylvania, Llc
7660 Imperial Way
Allentown PA 18195
610 366-4626

(G-12575)
HOOSIER MAGNETICS INC
110 Denny St (13669-1797)
PHONE.................................315 323-5832
B Thomas Shirk, *President*
Andy Blaine, *Plant Mgr*
Mary Alice Shirk, *Admin Sec*
Lori Hill, *Admin Asst*
◆ **EMP:** 50
SQ FT: 30,000
SALES (est): 8.7MM **Privately Held**
WEB: www.hoosiermagnetics.com
SIC: 3264 Ferrite & ferrite parts

(G-12576)
LAWTONS ELECTRIC MOTOR SERVICE
Also Called: Lawton Electric Co
148 Cemetery Rd (13669-4179)
PHONE.................................315 393-2728
Bernard Lawton, *Partner*
Timothy Lawton, *Partner*
EMP: 7 **EST:** 1968
SALES (est): 500K **Privately Held**
SIC: 7694 Electric motor repair

(G-12577)
MED-ENG LLC
103 Tulloch Dr (13669-2215)
PHONE.................................315 713-0103
Scott Obrien, *CEO*
Dennis Morris, *President*
Maureen Mackie, *Info Tech Mgr*
EMP: 40
SALES (est): 3.6MM
SALES (corp-wide): 875.1MM **Privately Held**
WEB: www.allen-vanguard.com
SIC: 2311 Mfg Men's/Boy's Suits/Coats
HQ: Safariland, Llc
13386 International Pkwy
Jacksonville FL 32218
904 741-5400

(G-12578)
QUEENAIRE TECHNOLOGIES INC
9483 State Highway 37 (13669-4467)
PHONE.................................315 393-5454
Susan Duffy, *President*
Richard Luscombe-Mills, *Research*
Nicole Plumley, *Finance Dir*
Tom Coplen, *Sales Staff*
▼ **EMP:** 6
SQ FT: 6,600
SALES (est): 1.3MM **Privately Held**
SIC: 3559 Ozone machines

(G-12579)
T-BASE COMMUNICATIONS USA INC
806 Commerce Park Dr (13669-2208)
PHONE.................................315 713-0013
Sharylyn Ayotte, *President*
Bruce Moszcelt, *Managing Dir*
Mike Hadfield, *Opers Staff*
Kayla Monahan, *Production*
Christine Roy, *Human Res Dir*
EMP: 40
SALES (est): 3.2MM **Privately Held**
SIC: 2759 Commercial printing

(G-12580)
TULMAR MANUFACTURING INC
101 Tulloch Dr (13669-2215)
PHONE.................................315 393-7191
Manna Doyle, *President*
EMP: 8
SQ FT: 7,700
SALES: 900K **Privately Held**
SIC: 2399 Military insignia, textile
PA: Tulmar Safety Systems Inc
1123 Cameron St
Hawkesbury ON K6A 2
613 632-1282

Old Bethpage
Nassau County

(G-12581)
ALJO PRECISION PRODUCTS INC
205 Bethpge Sweet Holw (11804-1309)
PHONE.................................516 420-4419
John Adelmann, *President*
Albert Adelmann, *Vice Pres*
Michael Mattern, *Vice Pres*
Robert Zerebak, *Sales Mgr*
Marilyn Platz, *Office Mgr*
EMP: 35 **EST:** 1953
SQ FT: 24,000
SALES (est): 5MM **Privately Held**
WEB: www.aljogefa.com
SIC: 3599 Machine shop, jobbing & repair

(G-12582)
ALJO-GEFA PRECISION MFG LLC
205 Bethpage Sweet Holw (11804-1309)
PHONE.................................516 420-4419
John Addleman, *Partner*
Michael Mattern, *General Mgr*
Albert Adelmann, *Senior VP*
Gregory Nasta, *QC Mgr*
Suanne Hippner, *Office Mgr*
EMP: 33 **EST:** 1999
SQ FT: 26,000
SALES (est): 5.9MM **Privately Held**
SIC: 3599 Machine shop, jobbing & repair

(G-12583)
BARSON COMPOSITES CORPORATION (PA)
Also Called: Hitemco
160 Bethpage Sweet (11804)
PHONE.................................516 752-7882
Terrell Barnard, *CEO*
Edwin Garofalo, *Vice Pres*
Dana Barnard, *CFO*
Kristen Larson, *Supervisor*
EMP: 50
SQ FT: 32,500

Old Bethpage - Nassau County (G-12584)

SALES (est): 14.4MM Privately Held
WEB: www.hitemco.com
SIC: 3479 2899 2851 Coating of metals & formed products; chemical preparations; paints & allied products

(G-12584)
GEFA INSTRUMENT CORP
205 Bethpage Sweet (11804)
PHONE................516 420-4419
Gunther Faas, President
Tyrone Faas, Treasurer
Collette Faas, Shareholder
EMP: 12 EST: 1966
SQ FT: 10,000
SALES (est): 1.2MM Privately Held
SIC: 3599 Machine shop, jobbing & repair

(G-12585)
HITEMCO MED APPLICATIONS INC
Also Called: Hi-Med
160 Sweet Hollow Rd (11804-1315)
PHONE................516 752-7882
Edwin Garofalo, President
John Legeros, Director
Bruce McCormick, Director
EMP: 134
SQ FT: 5,000
SALES (est): 13.1MM
SALES (corp-wide): 14.4MM Privately Held
WEB: www.hitemco.com
SIC: 3479 Painting, coating & hot dipping
PA: Barson Composites Corporation
160 Bethpage Sweet
Old Bethpage NY 11804
516 752-7882

(G-12586)
INTELLIGEN POWER SYSTEMS LLC
301 Winding Rd (11804-1322)
PHONE................212 750-0373
David H Lesser,
Stephen Bellone,
EMP: 8
SALES (est): 990K Privately Held
SIC: 3621 Power generators

(G-12587)
SEVILLE CENTRAL MIX CORP
495 Wining Rd (11804)
PHONE................516 293-6190
Peter Buck, Branch Mgr
EMP: 60
SALES (corp-wide): 12.3MM Privately Held
WEB: www.sevillecentralmix.com
SIC: 3273 3531 Ready-mixed concrete; concrete plants
PA: Seville Central Mix Corp.
157 Albany Ave
Freeport NY 11520
516 868-3000

(G-12588)
STASI INDUSTRIES INC
501 Winding Rd (11804-1336)
PHONE................516 334-2742
Crescenzo Stasi, President
EMP: 6
SALES (est): 209.4K Privately Held
SIC: 3999 Manufacturing industries

Old Forge
Herkimer County

(G-12589)
ADIRONDACK OUTDOOR CENTER LLC (PA)
2839 State Route 28 (13420)
P.O. Box 1146 (13420-1146)
PHONE................315 369-2300
John Nemjo,
EMP: 8
SALES (est): 2.3MM Privately Held
SIC: 3949 5091 Camping equipment & supplies; camping equipment & supplies

Old Westbury
Nassau County

(G-12590)
DE ORIGINALS LTD
22 Laurel Ln (11568-1544)
PHONE................516 474-6544
Daniel Kalu, President
EMP: 8 EST: 2016
SQ FT: 2,000
SALES: 6MM Privately Held
SIC: 2821 Polyvinyl chloride resins (PVC)

(G-12591)
NU LIFE RESTORATIONS OF L I
Also Called: Nu-Life Long Island
51 Valley Rd (11568-1015)
PHONE................516 489-5200
Mark Marinbach, President
EMP: 84
SQ FT: 8,500
SALES (est): 10.2MM Privately Held
WEB: www.nulifeli.com
SIC: 3843 Dental laboratory equipment

Olean
Cattaraugus County

(G-12592)
AVX CORPORATION
Also Called: Olean Advanced Products
1695 Seneca Ave (14760-9532)
PHONE................716 372-6611
Philip Ghent, General Mgr
Samantha White, Buyer
Stanley Cygan, Engineer
John Monhan, Branch Mgr
Paul Bohn, Info Tech Mgr
EMP: 95
SALES (corp-wide): 14.8B Publicly Held
WEB: www.avxcorp.com
SIC: 3675 5065 Mfg Electronic Capacitors Whol Electronic Parts/Equipment
HQ: Avx Corporation
1 Avx Blvd
Fountain Inn SC 29644
864 967-2150

(G-12593)
BIMBO BAKERIES USA INC
Also Called: Stroehmann Bakeries 56
111 N 2nd St (14760-2501)
PHONE................716 372-8444
Nancy Fox, Human Res Dir
Ted Lipeowski, Branch Mgr
EMP: 140 Privately Held
SIC: 2051 Bakery: wholesale or wholesale/retail combined
HQ: Bimbo Bakeries Usa, Inc
255 Business Center Dr # 200
Horsham PA 19044
215 347-5500

(G-12594)
BRADFORD PUBLICATIONS INC
Also Called: Times Herald, The
639 W Norton Dr (14760-1402)
PHONE................716 373-2500
Lori Coffman, Manager
Patrick Vecchio, Manager
EMP: 130
SQ FT: 22,300
SALES (est): 7MM Privately Held
WEB: www.oleantimesherald.com
SIC: 2711 7313 Newspapers, publishing & printing; newspaper advertising representative
HQ: Bradford Publishing Company
43 Main St
Bradford PA 16701
814 368-3173

(G-12595)
CITY OF OLEAN
Also Called: Olean Waste Water Treatment
174 S 19th St (14760-3326)
PHONE................716 376-5694
William Aiello, Mayor
Jeremy Meerdink, Manager
John Anastasia, Hlthcr Dir
Jim Bennett,
EMP: 9
SQ FT: 1,080 Privately Held
SIC: 3589 9111 Water treatment equipment, industrial; mayors' offices
PA: City Of Olean
101 E State St Ste 1
Olean NY 14760
716 376-5683

(G-12596)
CONCRETE MIXER SUPPLYCOM INC (PA)
1721 Cornell Dr (14760-9753)
PHONE................716 375-5565
Audrey D Pavia, President
◆ EMP: 9
SQ FT: 3,000
SALES (est): 1.6MM Privately Held
SIC: 3713 Truck bodies & parts

(G-12597)
COOPER POWER SYSTEMS LLC
1648 Dugan Rd (14760-9527)
PHONE................716 375-7100
Cindy Peterson, Buyer
Herce Alcocer, Engineer
Mark Schubel, Branch Mgr
Jennifer Noll, Supervisor
Jim Lee, Prgrmr
EMP: 300 Privately Held
WEB: www.cooperpower.com
SIC: 3612 3699 3674 3643 Transformers, except electric; electrical equipment & supplies; semiconductors & related devices; current-carrying wiring devices; switchgear & switchboard apparatus
HQ: Cooper Power Systems, Llc
2300 Badger Dr
Waukesha WI 53188
262 896-2400

(G-12598)
CYTEC INDUSTRIES INC
Also Called: Cytec Solvay Group
1405 Buffalo St (14760-1197)
PHONE................716 372-9650
Jeff Maley, Site Mgr
David Lilley, Branch Mgr
Mary Isaman, Info Tech Mgr
Maureen Dearmitt, Technology
Rick Jordan, Technical Staff
EMP: 66
SALES (corp-wide): 10MM Privately Held
SIC: 2899 2821 2672 2851 Water treating compounds; plastics materials & resins; adhesive backed films, foams & foils; paints & allied products; cellulosic manmade fibers
HQ: Cytec Industries Inc.
250 Pehle Ave Ste 306
Saddle Brook NJ 07663

(G-12599)
DRESSER-RAND GROUP INC
500 Paul Clark Dr (14760-9560)
PHONE................716 375-3000
Michael Jeannerette, Project Mgr
Timothy Sciortino, Opers Mgr
Mike Johnson, Facilities Mgr
Glenn Grosso, Technical Mgr
Job Barboza, Engineer
EMP: 66
SALES (corp-wide): 97.7B Privately Held
SIC: 3563 3511 Air & gas compressors; turbines & turbine generator sets
HQ: Dresser-Rand Group Inc.
15375 Memorial Dr Ste 600
Houston TX 77079
713 354-6100

(G-12600)
DYNAMIC SEALING TECH INC
Also Called: Scott Rotary Seals
301 W Franklin St (14760-1211)
PHONE................716 376-0708
Jeffrey Meister, Branch Mgr
EMP: 8
SQ FT: 15,000
SALES (corp-wide): 12.5MM Privately Held
SIC: 3492 Control valves, fluid power: hydraulic & pneumatic
PA: Dynamic Sealing Technologies, Inc.
13829 Jay St Nw
Andover MN 55304
763 786-3758

(G-12601)
DZ9 POWER LLC
408 Wayne St (14760-2462)
P.O. Box 862 (14760-0862)
PHONE................877 533-5530
Brian Benka, President
EMP: 7 EST: 2015
SALES (est): 358.3K Privately Held
SIC: 3499 Target drones, for use by ships: metal

(G-12602)
ELANTAS PDG INC
1405 Buffalo St (14760-1139)
PHONE................716 372-9650
EMP: 9 Privately Held
SIC: 2851 Lacquers, varnishes, enamels & other coatings
HQ: Elantas Pdg, Inc.
5200 N 2nd St
Saint Louis MO 63147
314 621-5700

(G-12603)
KAMERYS WHOLESALE MEATS INC
322 E Riverside Dr (14760-3964)
PHONE................716 372-6756
David A Kamery, President
EMP: 6
SALES (est): 572.6K Privately Held
SIC: 2011 5147 Meat packing plants; meats, fresh

(G-12604)
L AMERICAN LTD
Also Called: Swatt Baking Co
222 Homer St (14760-1132)
PHONE................716 372-9480
Leonard Anzivine, President
Lee Anzivine, Vice Pres
EMP: 16
SQ FT: 9,400
SALES (est): 2MM Privately Held
WEB: www.lamerican.com
SIC: 2051 5461 Bread, all types (white, wheat, rye, etc): fresh or frozen; rolls, bread type: fresh or frozen; bakeries

(G-12605)
NES BEARING COMPANY INC
1601 Johnson St (14760-1127)
PHONE................716 372-6532
Christopher Napoleon, President
Melissa Curran, Opers Mgr
Jim Hardy, QC Mgr
Jeremy Martin, Engineer
Heather Franz-Piatt, Office Mgr
▲ EMP: 48
SALES (est): 13.6MM Privately Held
WEB: www.nesbearings.com
SIC: 3562 8711 Ball bearings & parts; sanitary engineers

(G-12606)
PIERCE STEEL FABRICATORS
430 N 7th St (14760-2330)
P.O. Box 504 (14760-0504)
PHONE................716 372-7652
Michael Derose, President
Daniel Derose, Vice Pres
Larry Hinman, Sales Staff
EMP: 11
SQ FT: 20,000
SALES (est): 2.6MM Privately Held
WEB: www.piercesteel.com
SIC: 3441 Fabricated structural metal

(G-12607)
SOLEPOXY INC
211 W Franklin St (14760-1211)
PHONE................716 372-6300
Jeff Belt, Ch of Bd
Robert Groele, President
Robert Perkins, Plant Supt
Kaitlyn Penston, QC Mgr
Chiffon Stewart, Manager
◆ EMP: 55 EST: 2010
SQ FT: 250,000
SALES (est): 12.8MM Privately Held
SIC: 2821 Plastics materials & resins

GEOGRAPHIC SECTION
Oneonta - Otsego County (G-12632)

(G-12608)
TOTAL PIPING SOLUTIONS INC
1760 Haskell Rd (14760-9756)
P.O. Box 525 (14760-0525)
PHONE 716 372-0160
Daryl Piontek, *President*
Mark Langenhan, *President*
▲ EMP: 10
SQ FT: 35,000
SALES (est): 2.4MM Privately Held
WEB: www.tps.us
SIC: 3498 Fabricated pipe & fittings

Oneida
Madison County

(G-12609)
GOLUB CORPORATION
Also Called: Price Chopper Pharmacy
142 Genesee St (13421-2704)
PHONE 315 363-0679
Nena Crowne, *Branch Mgr*
EMP: 28
SALES (corp-wide): 3.3B Privately Held
SIC: 3751 Motorcycles & related parts
PA: The Golub Corporation
    461 Nott St
    Schenectady NY 12308
    518 355-5000

(G-12610)
HARTMAN ENTERPRISES INC
455 Elizabeth St (13421-2438)
P.O. Box 360 (13421-0360)
PHONE 315 363-7300
Robert E Sweet Jr, *CEO*
Bob Sweep, *President*
EMP: 55
SQ FT: 18,000
SALES (est): 9.2MM Privately Held
WEB: www.hartmanenterprisesinc.com
SIC: 3599 7692 Machine shop, jobbing & repair; welding repair

(G-12611)
HP HOOD LLC
252 Genesee St (13421-2709)
P.O. Box 491 (13421-0491)
PHONE 315 363-3870
Brandon Cook, *Warehouse Mgr*
James Davis, *Purch Mgr*
Ross Hasty, *Engineer*
Steve Pelky, *Manager*
EMP: 200
SALES (corp-wide): 2.1B Privately Held
WEB: www.hphood.com
SIC: 2026 5143 Fluid milk; dairy products, except dried or canned
PA: Hp Hood Llc
    6 Kimball Ln Ste 400
    Lynnfield MA 01940
    617 887-8441

(G-12612)
M M WELDING
558 Lenox Ave (13421-1522)
PHONE 315 363-3980
Michael Marley, *Owner*
Denice Marley, *Partner*
EMP: 20
SALES (est): 428.9K Privately Held
SIC: 7692 Welding repair

(G-12613)
NUTECH BIOSCIENCES INC
537 Fitch St (13421-1515)
PHONE 315 505-6500
Pratap Reddy, *President*
EMP: 15
SQ FT: 2,000
SALES: 2MM Privately Held
SIC: 3295 Minerals, ground or otherwise treated

(G-12614)
ONEIDA FOUNDRIES INC
559 Fitch St (13421-1515)
PHONE 315 363-4570
John Albanse, *President*
Harry Hood, *Vice Pres*
EMP: 20 EST: 1900
SQ FT: 30,000
SALES (est): 5.4MM Privately Held
SIC: 3321 Gray iron castings

(G-12615)
ONEIDA INTERNATIONAL INC
163-181 Kenwood Ave (13421)
PHONE 315 361-3000
Terry G Westbrook, *President*
EMP: 6
SALES (est): 301.7K
SALES (corp-wide): 598MM Privately Held
WEB: www.oneida.net
SIC: 3262 3231 3914 3421 Vitreous china table & kitchenware; ornamental glass: cut, engraved or otherwise decorated; silverware & plated ware; cutlery
HQ: Oneida Ltd.
    163 Kenwood Ave Ste 181
    Oneida NY 13421
    315 361-3000

(G-12616)
ONEIDA MOLDED PLASTICS LLC (PA)
104 S Warner St (13421-1510)
PHONE 315 363-7980
Barry Uber, *Ch of Bd*
Kevin McGreevy, *President*
David Power, *Business Mgr*
Steve Thalmann, *COO*
Richard Harrington, *Plant Mgr*
▲ EMP: 130 EST: 2006
SQ FT: 82,000
SALES (est): 36.4MM Privately Held
WEB: oneidamoldedplastics.com
SIC: 3089 Injection molding of plastics

(G-12617)
ONEIDA MOLDED PLASTICS LLC
104 S Warner St (13421-1510)
PHONE 315 363-7980
Joe Kiah, *CEO*
David Harrington, *President*
Tim Mc Cullough, *Vice Pres*
EMP: 72
SQ FT: 41,000
SALES (est): 4.5MM
SALES (corp-wide): 36.4MM Privately Held
SIC: 3089 Plastic containers, except foam
PA: Oneida Molded Plastics, Llc
    104 S Warner St
    Oneida NY 13421
    315 363-7980

(G-12618)
ONEIDA PUBLICATIONS INC
Also Called: Oneida Dispatch
730 Lenox Ave (13421-1513)
PHONE 315 363-5100
Phil Austin, *CEO*
Kyle Mennig, *Editor*
Janice Collins, *Sales Staff*
Bradley Markowski, *Sales Staff*
Jim Vanburen, *Sales Staff*
EMP: 40 EST: 1851
SQ FT: 10,000
SALES (est): 2.1MM Privately Held
SIC: 2711 Newspapers, publishing & printing

(G-12619)
ONEIDA SILVERSMITHS INC
163 Kenwood Ave 181 (13421-2829)
PHONE 315 361-3000
James E Joseph, *Ch of Bd*
EMP: 7
SALES (est): 705.1K
SALES (corp-wide): 598MM Privately Held
WEB: www.oneida.net
SIC: 3262 3231 3914 3421 Vitreous china table & kitchenware; ornamental glass: cut, engraved or otherwise decorated; silverware & plated ware; cutlery
HQ: Oneida Ltd.
    163 Kenwood Ave Ste 181
    Oneida NY 13421
    315 361-3000

(G-12620)
PATHFINDER 103 INC
229 Park Ave (13421-2021)
PHONE 315 363-4260
Larry Manser, *President*
EMP: 8
SALES (est): 961.4K Privately Held
SIC: 3589 Sewer cleaning equipment, power

(G-12621)
SHIRL-LYNN OF NEW YORK (PA)
266 Wilson St (13421)
PHONE 315 363-5898
Shirley Thurston, *Partner*
Mary Blau, *Partner*
EMP: 12
SQ FT: 4,300
SALES: 1MM Privately Held
SIC: 2339 5699 5632 Women's & misses' athletic clothing & sportswear; bathing suits: women's, misses' & juniors'; bathing suits; sports apparel; costumes, masquerade or theatrical; dancewear

(G-12622)
V & J GRAPHICS INC
153 Phelps St (13421-1708)
PHONE 315 363-1933
Vernon Waters, *President*
Janice Waters, *Treasurer*
Sandy Harrison,
EMP: 8
SQ FT: 4,960
SALES (est): 989.5K Privately Held
SIC: 2752 Commercial printing, offset

(G-12623)
VISIBLE SYSTEMS CORPORATION (PA)
248 Main St Ste 2 (13421-2100)
PHONE 508 628-1510
George Cagliuso, *President*
Michael Paul, *Vice Pres*
Ellen Shoner, *CFO*
EMP: 20
SQ FT: 6,000
SALES (est): 4MM Privately Held
SIC: 7372 5045 8748 Prepackaged software; computer software; systems analysis or design

Oneonta
Otsego County

(G-12624)
AMERICAN BLADE MFG LLC (PA)
Also Called: G C Casting
138 Roundhouse Rd (13820-1200)
PHONE 607 432-4518
Raymond Harvey,
EMP: 12 EST: 1946
SQ FT: 1,500
SALES (est): 1.3MM Privately Held
WEB: www.charleslay.com
SIC: 3365 3366 Aluminum foundries; bronze foundry

(G-12625)
ARNAN DEVELOPMENT CORP (PA)
Also Called: PICKETT BUILDING MATERIALS
6459 State Highway 23 (13820-6542)
PHONE 607 432-8391
Robert A Harlem Jr, *Ch of Bd*
Rebecca Lloyd, *Vice Pres*
Kevin Curnalia, *Store Mgr*
Tom Ballard, *Sales Staff*
Brant Conover, *Sales Staff*
EMP: 52
SQ FT: 40,000
SALES (est): 14.9MM Privately Held
WEB: www.oneontablock.com
SIC: 3271 3272 5082 5211 Architectural concrete: block, split, fluted, screen, etc.; concrete products; septic tanks, concrete; masonry equipment & supplies; lumber & other building materials; management services

(G-12626)
BK ASSOCIATES INTL INC
127 Commerce Rd (13820-3539)
P.O. Box 1238 (13820-5238)
PHONE 607 432-1499
Paul Karabinis, *President*
Steve Palmer, *General Mgr*
Eugene Bettiol Sr, *Treasurer*
EMP: 15
SQ FT: 20,000
SALES (est): 2.1MM Privately Held
SIC: 2095 Coffee roasting (except by wholesale grocers)

(G-12627)
BROOKS BOTTLING CO LLC
5560 State Highway 7 (13820-3699)
PHONE 607 432-1782
Ryan Brooks, *Mng Member*
EMP: 10
SALES (est): 1.4MM Privately Held
SIC: 3565 Bottling machinery: filling, capping, labeling

(G-12628)
BURT RIGID BOX INC
58 Browne St (13820-1092)
PHONE 607 433-2510
Dave Van Pelt, *Purch Agent*
Ron Blaird, *Manager*
EMP: 52
SQ FT: 77,280
SALES (est): 4.9MM
SALES (corp-wide): 19.6MM Privately Held
WEB: www.burtbox.com
SIC: 2653 2657 2652 Boxes, solid fiber: made from purchased materials; folding paperboard boxes; setup paperboard boxes
PA: Burt Rigid Box, Inc.
    58 Browne St
    Oneonta NY 13820
    607 433-2510

(G-12629)
BURT RIGID BOX INC (PA)
58 Browne St (13820-1092)
P.O. Box 1883, Buffalo (14225-8883)
PHONE 607 433-2510
W Russell Hurd, *President*
William Howard, *Vice Pres*
Greg Ward, *Opers Mgr*
Bill Howard, *Safety Mgr*
Laura Hurd, *Treasurer*
▲ EMP: 10
SQ FT: 500,000
SALES (est): 19.6MM Privately Held
WEB: www.burtbox.com
SIC: 2631 Folding boxboard; setup boxboard

(G-12630)
CITY OF ONEONTA
Also Called: Oneonta City Wtr Trtmnt Plant
110 East St (13820-1304)
PHONE 607 433-3470
Stanley Shaffer, *Manager*
EMP: 5 Privately Held
SIC: 3589 9111 Water treatment equipment, industrial; mayors' offices
PA: City Of Oneonta
    258 Main St Ste 1
    Oneonta NY 13820
    607 432-6450

(G-12631)
CO-OPTICS AMERICA LAB INC
Also Called: Co-Optics Groups, The
297 River Street Svc Rd Service (13820)
PHONE 607 432-0557
Paul Strenn, *President*
Israel Soto, *Vice Pres*
EMP: 20
SQ FT: 3,300
SALES (est): 3MM Privately Held
WEB: www.co-optics.com
SIC: 3851 3229 Lenses, ophthalmic; pressed & blown glass

(G-12632)
COBLESKILL STONE PRODUCTS INC
Also Called: Oneonta Asphalt
57 Ceperley Ave (13820)
PHONE 607 432-8321
Lennie Goodspeed, *Branch Mgr*
EMP: 10
SQ FT: 1,353

Oneonta - Otsego County (G-12633)

SALES (est): 1MM
SALES (corp-wide): 115.2MM **Privately Held**
WEB: www.cobleskillstone.com
SIC: 2951 Asphalt & asphaltic paving mixtures (not from refineries)
PA: Cobleskill Stone Products, Inc.
112 Rock Rd
Cobleskill NY 12043
518 234-0221

(G-12633)
COMMUNITY NEWSPAPER GROUP LLC
Daily Star, The
102 Chestnut St (13820-2584)
P.O. Box 250 (13820-0250)
PHONE 607 432-1000
Fred Scheller, *Branch Mgr*
EMP: 19 **Privately Held**
WEB: www.clintonnc.com
SIC: 2711 2752 Newspapers: publishing only, not printed on site; commercial printing, lithographic
HQ: Community Newspaper Group, Llc
3500 Colonnade Pkwy # 600
Birmingham AL 35243

(G-12634)
COOPERSTOWN BREWING CO LLC
41 Browne St (13820-1472)
PHONE 607 286-9330
Dennis Haeley, *Partner*
Jewel Hall, *Partner*
Stanley Hall,
EMP: 5
SQ FT: 5,000
SALES (est): 413.7K **Privately Held**
WEB: www.cooperstownbrewing.com
SIC: 2082 Beer (alcoholic beverage)

(G-12635)
CORNING INCORPORATED
275 River St (13820-2299)
PHONE 607 433-3100
Marla Kelly, *Engineer*
Mark Maroz, *Engineer*
Steven Swanberry, *Engineer*
Teri Mauk, *Engnr/R&D Mgr*
EMP: 25
SQ FT: 20,106
SALES (corp-wide): 10.1B **Publicly Held**
WEB: www.corning.com
SIC: 3229 Pressed & blown glass
PA: Corning Incorporated
1 Riverfront Plz
Corning NY 14831
607 974-9000

(G-12636)
CREATIVE ORTHOTICS PROSTHETICS
Also Called: Hanger Clinic
37 Associate Dr (13820-2266)
PHONE 607 431-2526
Chris German, *Manager*
EMP: 7
SALES (corp-wide): 1B **Publicly Held**
WEB: www.creativeoandp.com
SIC: 3842 Surgical appliances & supplies
HQ: Creative Orthotics & Prosthetics, Inc.
1300 College Ave Ste 1
Elmira NY 14901
607 734-7215

(G-12637)
CUSTOM ELECTRONICS INC
Also Called: Cei
87 Browne St (13820-1096)
PHONE 607 432-3880
Michael Pentaris, *President*
Carol Brower, *Vice Pres*
Carroll Brower, *Vice Pres*
Jonathan Dokuchitz, *VP Opers*
Anthony Berwin, *Engineer*
▲ **EMP:** 80 **EST:** 1964
SQ FT: 27,500
SALES: 8MM **Privately Held**
WEB: www.customelec.com
SIC: 3675 Electronic capacitors

(G-12638)
FOTIS ONEONTA ITALIAN BAKERY
42 River St (13820-4320)
PHONE 607 432-3871
James Tomaino, *Owner*
EMP: 6
SALES (est): 508.7K **Privately Held**
SIC: 2051 Bakery: wholesale or wholesale/retail combined

(G-12639)
MAM MOLDING INC
147 River St (13820-2239)
PHONE 607 433-2121
Siro Vergari, *Principal*
EMP: 5
SALES (est): 460.8K **Privately Held**
SIC: 3089 Injection molding of plastics

(G-12640)
MEDICAL COACHES INCORPORATED (PA)
399 County Highway 58 (13820-3422)
P.O. Box 129 (13820-0129)
PHONE 607 432-1333
Geoffrey A Smith, *President*
Leonard W Marsh, *COO*
Jim Brownell, *Vice Pres*
Kathy Caffery, *Purch Agent*
Tony Quinones, *Engineer*
◆ **EMP:** 50 **EST:** 1952
SQ FT: 100,000
SALES: 10MM **Privately Held**
WEB: www.medcoach.com
SIC: 3711 Automobile assembly, including specialty automobiles

(G-12641)
MOLD-A-MATIC CORPORATION
Also Called: Mamco
147 River St (13820-2276)
PHONE 607 433-2121
Siro Vergari, *Ch of Bd*
Mark Vergari, *Vice Pres*
▲ **EMP:** 45 **EST:** 1964
SQ FT: 31,000
SALES: 4MM **Privately Held**
WEB: www.mamcomolding.com
SIC: 3549 3089 Assembly machines, including robotic; plastic processing

(G-12642)
ONEONTA FENCE
2 Washburn St (13820-2721)
PHONE 607 433-6707
EMP: 6
SALES (est): 506.7K **Privately Held**
SIC: 3089 3315 Fences, gates & accessories: plastic; fence gates posts & fittings: steel

(G-12643)
OTSEGO READY MIX INC
2 Wells Ave (13820-2723)
PHONE 607 432-3400
Robert Harlem Jr, *President*
EMP: 16
SQ FT: 8,000
SALES: 3.9MM **Privately Held**
SIC: 3273 Ready-mixed concrete

(G-12644)
PONY FARM PRESS & GRAPHICS
Also Called: Village Print Room
330 Pony Farm Rd (13820-3591)
PHONE 607 432-9020
Edward May, *President*
EMP: 7
SQ FT: 12,000
SALES (est): 594.5K **Privately Held**
WEB: www.ponyfarmpress.com
SIC: 2759 Commercial printing

(G-12645)
RJ MILLWORKERS INC
12 Lewis St (13820-2652)
PHONE 607 433-0525
Randy J Morley, *President*
Ellen Morley, *Vice Pres*
Christy Parish, *Opers Mgr*
Andy Lowenthal, *Manager*
EMP: 20
SALES (est): 3.7MM **Privately Held**
WEB: www.rjmillworkers.com
SIC: 2431 Doors, wood

(G-12646)
T S PINK CORP
Also Called: TS Pink
139 Pony Farm Rd (13820-3537)
PHONE 607 432-1100
Todd Pink, *President*
Diana Colone, *Vice Pres*
Jennifer Hamilton, *Sales Staff*
▲ **EMP:** 16
SQ FT: 15,000
SALES (est): 2.6MM **Privately Held**
WEB: www.tspink.com
SIC: 2841 Textile soap

Ontario
Wayne County

(G-12647)
ARIEL OPTICS INC
261 David Pkwy (14519-8955)
PHONE 585 265-4820
Frederick Koch, *President*
EMP: 8
SALES (est): 525K **Privately Held**
WEB: www.arieloptics.com
SIC: 3827 Prisms, optical

(G-12648)
AVALANCHE FABRICATION INC
6314 Dean Pkwy (14519-9011)
PHONE 585 545-4000
Paul Duerr, *President*
Thad Spaulding, *Vice Pres*
EMP: 14 **EST:** 1998
SQ FT: 5,500
SALES (est): 1.1MM **Privately Held**
WEB: www.afinc.biz
SIC: 3444 Sheet metal specialties, not stamped

(G-12649)
CNC SYSTEMS 2000 INC
6368 Dean Pkwy (14519-8970)
PHONE 585 265-0160
Michael Bechtold, *Ch of Bd*
▲ **EMP:** 38
SQ FT: 15,000
SALES (est): 312.8K **Privately Held**
SALES (corp-wide): 5.8MM **Privately Held**
WEB: www.websterny.com
SIC: 3471 3827 Polishing, metals or formed products; lens grinding equipment, except ophthalmic
PA: Vi Manufacturing, Inc.
164 Orchard St
Webster NY 14580
585 872-5650

(G-12650)
CS AUTOMATION INC
Also Called: C S Welding
518 Berg Rd (14519-9376)
PHONE 315 524-5123
Craig Schieven, *Principal*
EMP: 10
SALES (est): 480K **Privately Held**
SIC: 7692 7389 8742 Welding repair; inspection & testing services; automation & robotics consultant

(G-12651)
DATA CONTROL INC
277 David Pkwy (14519-8955)
PHONE 585 265-2980
Lori Ferguson, *President*
EMP: 4
SQ FT: 12,712
SALES: 1MM **Privately Held**
WEB: www.datacontrolinc.com
SIC: 2542 Fixtures: display, office or store: except wood

(G-12652)
DJ ACQUISITION MANAGEMENT CORP
Also Called: Weco Metal Products
6364 Dean Pkwy (14519-8970)
PHONE 585 265-3000
Donald Cornwell, *President*
John R Gillan, *Vice Pres*
John Gillan, *Marketing Staff*
▲ **EMP:** 75
SQ FT: 55,000
SALES (est): 18MM **Privately Held**
WEB: www.wecometal.com
SIC: 3444 Sheet metalwork

(G-12653)
FRED A NUDD CORPORATION (PA)
1743 State Route 104 (14519-8935)
P.O. Box 577 (14519-0577)
PHONE 315 524-2531
Thomas Nudd, *President*
Frederick Nudd, *Vice Pres*
Bonnie Judware, *Accountant*
Lyle Nudd, *Manager*
Lance Palmisano,
EMP: 52
SQ FT: 40,000
SALES (est): 8.5MM **Privately Held**
WEB: www.nuddtowers.com
SIC: 3444 3441 1799 1622 Sheet metalwork; tower sections, radio & television transmission; antenna installation; bridge, tunnel & elevated highway

(G-12654)
HARBEC INC
358 Timothy Ln (14519-9012)
PHONE 585 265-0010
Robert Bechtold, *President*
Brad Miller, *Project Mgr*
John Hoefen, *Production*
Keith Harbec, *Engineer*
Doug McKnight, *Engineer*
EMP: 100
SQ FT: 15,000
SALES (est): 24MM **Privately Held**
WEB: www.harbec.com
SIC: 3089 Injection molded finished plastic products; injection molding of plastics

(G-12655)
INTEGRITY TOOL INCORPORATED
6485 Furnace Rd (14519-8920)
PHONE 315 524-4409
Mike Freidler, *President*
Les Saiers, *Plant Mgr*
EMP: 13 **EST:** 1996
SQ FT: 6,000
SALES (est): 2MM **Privately Held**
SIC: 3599 Machine shop, jobbing & repair

(G-12656)
LAKE IMMUNOGENICS INC
348 Berg Rd (14519-9374)
PHONE 585 265-1973
James Bowman, *President*
Barbara Bowman, *Vice Pres*
Ginger Sullivan, *Manager*
EMP: 15
SQ FT: 8,000
SALES (est): 3.1MM **Privately Held**
WEB: www.lakeimmunogenics.com
SIC: 2836 Plasmas; veterinary biological products

(G-12657)
NORTHERN BIODIESEL INC
317 State Route 104 (14519-8958)
PHONE 585 545-4534
Jason Masters, *Ch of Bd*
Robert Bethold, *Vice Pres*
Jeff Frank, *Technician*
EMP: 5
SALES (est): 690K **Privately Held**
WEB: www.northernbiodiesel.com
SIC: 2911 Diesel fuels

(G-12658)
OPTIMAX SYSTEMS INC (PA)
6367 Dean Pkwy (14519-8939)
PHONE 585 265-1020
Rick Plympton, *CEO*
Michael P Mandina, *Ch of Bd*
Richard Plympton, *Vice Pres*
John Rohrbaugh, *Facilities Mgr*
Joe Serio, *Mfg Staff*
EMP: 133
SQ FT: 40,000

▲ = Import ▼ = Export
◆ = Import/Export

GEOGRAPHIC SECTION

Orangeburg - Rockland County (G-12681)

SALES (est): 35.8MM **Privately Held**
WEB: www.optimaxsi.com
SIC: 3827 Lenses, optical: all types except ophthalmic; prisms, optical

(G-12659)
OPTIPRO SYSTEMS LLC
6368 Dean Pkwy (14519-8970)
PHONE.................................585 265-0160
Mike Bechtold, *Mng Member*
◆ EMP: 54
SQ FT: 20,000
SALES (est): 13.8MM
SALES (corp-wide): 10.5MM **Privately Held**
WEB: www.optipro.com
SIC: 3559 3827 Optical lens machinery; optical instruments & lenses
PA: Brightside 09 Inc.
6368 Dean Pkwy
Ontario NY 14519
585 265-0160

(G-12660)
PHOTON GEAR INC
245 David Pkwy (14519-8955)
PHONE.................................585 265-3360
Gary Blough, *President*
EMP: 11
SQ FT: 5,400
SALES (est): 2.4MM **Privately Held**
WEB: www.photongear.com
SIC: 3827 8711 Optical elements & assemblies, except ophthalmic; engineering services

(G-12661)
R C KOLSTAD WATER CORP
73 Lake Rd (14519-9311)
PHONE.................................585 216-2230
William Kolstad, *President*
EMP: 5
SALES: 2MM **Privately Held**
SIC: 3589 Water treatment equipment, industrial

(G-12662)
RANGER DESIGN US INC
6377 Dean Pkwy (14519-8939)
PHONE.................................800 565-5321
Derek Cowie, *President*
Randal Cowie, *Chairman*
Braden Harper, *Vice Pres*
Katie Stearns, *Human Resources*
Ray Hewines, *Manager*
▲ EMP: 20
SQ FT: 80,000
SALES (est): 3.6MM **Privately Held**
SIC: 3711 Motor vehicles & car bodies

(G-12663)
ROCHESTER INDUSTRIAL CTRL INC (PA)
6400 Furnace Rd (14519-9744)
PHONE.................................315 524-4555
Anthony J Mastrodonato, *CEO*
Donna Perry, *Purch Mgr*
Robin Cook, *QC Mgr*
Tammy Johnson, *QC Mgr*
Zachary Pond, *Engineer*
▲ EMP: 99
SQ FT: 23,600
SALES: 10MM **Privately Held**
SIC: 3625 3679 3672 Relays & industrial controls; electronic circuits; printed circuit boards

(G-12664)
ROCHESTER INDUSTRIAL CTRL INC
Also Called: R I C
6345 Furnace Rd (14519-9744)
PHONE.................................315 524-4555
Eric Albert, *President*
EMP: 100
SQ FT: 8,050
SALES (corp-wide): 10MM **Privately Held**
SIC: 3679 Electronic circuits
PA: Rochester Industrial Control, Inc.
6400 Furnace Rd
Ontario NY 14519
315 524-4555

(G-12665)
SCIENTIFIC POLYMER PRODUCTS
6265 Dean Pkwy (14519-8997)
PHONE.................................585 265-0413
Bret Vanzo, *Ch of Bd*
Leslie Twist, *Manager*
EMP: 5
SQ FT: 10,000
SALES (est): 1.2MM **Privately Held**
WEB: www.scientificpolymer.com
SIC: 2819 Industrial inorganic chemicals

(G-12666)
SMITH INTERNATIONAL INC
Also Called: Smith Service Corps
1915 Lake Rd (14519-9792)
PHONE.................................585 265-2330
Drew Smith, *Principal*
EMP: 12 **Publicly Held**
WEB: www.smith-intl.com
SIC: 3533 Oil & gas field machinery
HQ: Smith International, Inc.
1310 Rankin Rd
Houston TX 77073
281 443-3370

Orangeburg
Rockland County

(G-12667)
AALBORG INSTRS & CONTRLS INC
20 Corporate Dr (10962-2616)
PHONE.................................845 398-3160
T J Baan, *CEO*
Karen Baan, *Admin Sec*
EMP: 54
SQ FT: 33,000
SALES (est): 11.4MM **Privately Held**
WEB: www.aalborg.com
SIC: 3823 3824 3577 3494 Primary elements for process flow measurement; fluid meters & counting devices; computer peripheral equipment; valves & pipe fittings; fluid power valves & hose fittings

(G-12668)
API INDUSTRIES INC (PA)
Also Called: Aluf Plastics Division
2 Glenshaw St (10962-1207)
PHONE.................................845 365-2200
Susan Rosenberg, *CEO*
Reuven Rosenberg, *President*
Avalon Pierre, *Editor*
David Anderson, *Vice Pres*
Greg Kampschroer, *Vice Pres*
▲ EMP: 310
SQ FT: 300,000
SALES (est): 148.6MM **Privately Held**
SIC: 2673 3081 Plastic bags: made from purchased materials; unsupported plastics film & sheet

(G-12669)
API INDUSTRIES INC
Base Plastics
2 Glenshaw St (10962-1207)
PHONE.................................845 365-2200
Susan Rosenberg, *CEO*
EMP: 125
SALES (corp-wide): 148.6MM **Privately Held**
SIC: 2673 3081 Plastic bags: made from purchased materials; unsupported plastics film & sheet
PA: Api Industries, Inc.
2 Glenshaw St
Orangeburg NY 10962
845 365-2200

(G-12670)
ARON STREIT INC
Also Called: Streit Matzoh Co
171 Route 303 (10962-2209)
PHONE.................................212 475-7000
Aron S Yagoda, *Ch of Bd*
Isabella Dinatale, *Exec VP*
Alan Adler, *Vice Pres*
Malka Kubersky, *Controller*
Carmine V Minichino, *Controller*
▲ EMP: 45
SQ FT: 100,000
SALES (est): 7.9MM **Privately Held**
WEB: www.streitsmatzos.com
SIC: 2052 5149 Matzos; bakery products

(G-12671)
CEROVENE INC
10 Corporate Dr (10962-2614)
PHONE.................................845 359-1101
Manish Shah, *President*
EMP: 10 **Privately Held**
SIC: 2834 Pharmaceutical preparations
PA: Cerovene Inc.
612 Corporate Way Ste 10
Valley Cottage NY 10989

(G-12672)
CHROMALLOY AMERICAN LLC (DH)
330 Blaisdell Rd (10962-2510)
PHONE.................................845 230-7355
Armand F Lauzon Jr, *CEO*
EMP: 24 EST: 1986
SALES (est): 26.2MM
SALES (corp-wide): 3.6B **Publicly Held**
SIC: 3724 7699 Aircraft engines & engine parts; engine repair & replacement, non-automotive
HQ: Chromalloy Gas Turbine Llc
3999 Rca Blvd
Palm Beach Gardens FL 33410
561 935-3571

(G-12673)
CHROMALLOY GAS TURBINE LLC
Also Called: Chromalloy New York
330 Blaisdell Rd (10962-2510)
PHONE.................................845 359-2462
Anthony Licciardi, *President*
Dennis Walsh, *President*
Zenon Piatnyczka, *General Mgr*
Michael Sieber, *Production*
Anthony Lombardi, *Controller*
EMP: 200
SALES (corp-wide): 3.6B **Publicly Held**
WEB: www.chromalloysatx.com
SIC: 3724 Aircraft engines & engine parts
HQ: Chromalloy Gas Turbine Llc
3999 Rca Blvd
Palm Beach Gardens FL 33410
561 935-3571

(G-12674)
DHS SYSTEMS LLC (HQ)
560 Route 303 Ste 206 (10962-1329)
PHONE.................................845 359-6066
Samuel R Marrone, *CEO*
A Jon Prusmack, *President*
Chuck Gregory, *Vice Pres*
Mike Hall, *Prdtn Mgr*
Ed Hughes, *Prdtn Mgr*
▲ EMP: 15
SQ FT: 75,000
SALES: 80MM **Privately Held**
WEB: www.drash.com
SIC: 2394 Tents: made from purchased materials

(G-12675)
EMMI USA INC
100 Dutch Hill Rd Ste 220 (10962-2198)
PHONE.................................845 268-9990
Steven Millard, *President*
Paul Schilt, *President*
Mattaias Kinz, *Chairman*
Carol Nicolay, *Manager*
▲ EMP: 19
SQ FT: 12,000
SALES (est): 3.7MM
SALES (corp-wide): 251.6MM **Privately Held**
WEB: www.emmiusa.com
SIC: 2096 Cheese curls & puffs
HQ: Emmi International Ag
Landenbergstrasse 1
Luzern LU 6005

(G-12676)
ESSILOR LABORATORIES AMER INC
Also Called: Nova Optical
165 Route 303 (10962-2209)
PHONE.................................845 365-6700
EMP: 50

SALES (corp-wide): 100.9MM **Privately Held**
SIC: 3851 Mfg Ophthalmic Goods
HQ: Essilor Laboratories Of America, Inc.
13515 N Stemmons Fwy
Dallas TX 75234
972 241-4141

(G-12677)
EUROMED INC
25 Corporate Dr (10962-2615)
PHONE.................................845 359-4039
Richard Wildnauer, *Ch of Bd*
Thomas E Gardner, *President*
Stephen Powell, *COO*
Brian Coughlin, *Vice Pres*
Ravi Ramjit, *Vice Pres*
◆ EMP: 95
SQ FT: 42,000
SALES (est): 22.8MM
SALES (corp-wide): 408.3MM **Privately Held**
WEB: www.euromedinc.com
SIC: 3842 Bandages & dressings
PA: Scapa Group Public Limited Company
994 Manchester Road
Ashton-Under-Lyne LANCS OL7 0
161 301-7400

(G-12678)
FERRO MACHINE CO INC
70 S Greenbush Rd (10962-1323)
PHONE.................................845 398-3641
John Ferrogari, *President*
Susan Ferrogari, *Vice Pres*
EMP: 5
SQ FT: 4,500
SALES (est): 490K **Privately Held**
SIC: 3599 Machine shop, jobbing & repair

(G-12679)
INERTIA SWITCH INC
70 S Greenbush Rd (10962-1323)
PHONE.................................845 359-8300
Ruth Fischer, *President*
Nadine Nodhturft, *Controller*
Brian Digirolamo, *Officer*
EMP: 25 EST: 1959
SQ FT: 9,500
SALES (est): 5.4MM **Privately Held**
WEB: www.inertiaswitch.com
SIC: 3625 3812 3643 3613 Control circuit devices, magnet & solid state; acceleration indicators & systems components, aerospace; current-carrying wiring devices; switchgear & switchboard apparatus

(G-12680)
INNOVATIVE PLASTICS CORP (PA)
400 Route 303 (10962-1340)
PHONE.................................845 359-7500
Judith Hershaft, *Ch of Bd*
Steve Fairbanks, *Regional Mgr*
Stephen Hershaft, *Vice Pres*
Rick Colton, *VP Opers*
Andy Fraga, *Prdtn Mgr*
▼ EMP: 150 EST: 1982
SQ FT: 100,000
SALES: 40.4MM **Privately Held**
WEB: www.innovative-plastics.com
SIC: 3089 Injection molding of plastics; thermoformed finished plastic products; molding primary plastic

(G-12681)
INSTRUMENTATION LABORATORY CO
526 Route 303 (10962-1309)
PHONE.................................845 680-0028
Doug Ward, *General Mgr*
Poliana Pagulayan, *Engineer*
Christopher Leong, *Design Engr*
Pamela Hawkins, *Manager*
Jim Ryan, *Supervisor*
EMP: 180
SQ FT: 54,883
SALES (corp-wide): 157.1MM **Privately Held**
WEB: www.ilww.com
SIC: 2836 3842 3821 2899 Blood derivatives; surgical appliances & supplies; laboratory apparatus & furniture; chemical preparations

Orangeburg - Rockland County (G-12682)

HQ: Instrumentation Laboratory Company
180 Hartwell Rd
Bedford MA 01730
781 861-0710

(G-12682)
LTS INC
37 Ramland Rd 2 (10962-2606)
PHONE..................845 494-2940
Hirak Aarmaker, *President*
Slava Kogan, *Treasurer*
▲ **EMP:** 12
SQ FT: 1,400
SALES (est): 1.5MM **Privately Held**
WEB: www.ltschem.com
SIC: 2865 Chemical indicators

(G-12683)
MACHIDA INCORPORATED
Also Called: Vision-Sciences
40 Ramland Rd S Ste 1 (10962-2698)
PHONE..................845 365-0600
Ron Hadani, *CEO*
Yoav M Cohen, *CFO*
EMP: 7
SQ FT: 10,000
SALES (est): 1.9MM
SALES (corp-wide): 56.3MM **Privately Held**
WEB: www.visionscopes.com
SIC: 3827 Boroscopes
HQ: Cogentix Medical, Inc.
5420 Feltl Rd
Minnetonka MN 55343

(G-12684)
NICE-PAK PRODUCTS INC (PA)
2 Nice Pak Park (10962-1376)
PHONE..................845 365-2772
Robert Julius, *President*
John Culligan, *President*
Jon Kupperman, *President*
William E Dwan, *Senior VP*
Kim Babusik, *Vice Pres*
◆ **EMP:** 400
SQ FT: 168,000
SALES (est): 428.1MM **Privately Held**
WEB: www.nicepak.com
SIC: 2621 7389 2676 Towels, tissues & napkins: paper & stock; sanitary tissue paper; packaging & labeling services; sanitary paper products

(G-12685)
PICCINI INDUSTRIES LTD
37 Ramland Rd (10962-2606)
PHONE..................845 365-0614
John Piccininni, *Ch of Bd*
EMP: 30
SQ FT: 23,000
SALES (est): 3.2MM **Privately Held**
WEB: www.piccini.net
SIC: 2421 2522 2521 2511 Sawmills & planing mills, general; office furniture, except wood; wood office furniture; wood household furniture; wood kitchen cabinets; millwork

(G-12686)
PRAXAIR INC
542 Route 303 (10962-1309)
PHONE..................845 359-4200
Mark Murphy, *President*
Paul Gilman, *Info Tech Dir*
David Strauss, *Director*
EMP: 150
SALES (corp-wide): 11.4B **Privately Held**
SIC: 2813 Industrial gases
PA: Praxair, Inc.
10 Riverview Dr
Danbury CT 06810
203 837-2000

(G-12687)
PRAXAIR SURFACE TECH INC
560 Route 303 (10962-1329)
PHONE..................845 398-8322
Nicole Mitchell, *Human Res Dir*
David Strauff, *Manager*
Mark Nestle, *Director*
Stewart Bennion, *Maintence Staff*
EMP: 160
SALES (corp-wide): 11.4B **Privately Held**
SIC: 3471 Plating & polishing

HQ: Praxair Surface Technologies, Inc.
1500 Polco St
Indianapolis IN 46202
317 240-2500

(G-12688)
PRODUCTO ELECTRIC CORP
Also Called: Peco Conduit Fittings
11 Kings Hwy (10962-1897)
PHONE..................845 359-4900
Arthur Lemay, *President*
John Fischer, *Vice Pres*
◆ **EMP:** 30 **EST:** 1935
SQ FT: 54,000
SALES (est): 5.1MM **Privately Held**
WEB: www.pecoelect.com
SIC: 3644 Electric conduits & fittings

(G-12689)
PROFESSIONAL DISPOSABLES INC
2 Nice Pak Park (10962-1317)
PHONE..................845 365-1700
Robert P Julius, *President*
William E Dwan, *Senior VP*
Ron Kraus, *Natl Sales Mgr*
Al Betz, *Manager*
Roza Gandelman, *Manager*
◆ **EMP:** 590
SALES (est): 157.1MM **Privately Held**
SIC: 2676 7389 2621 Sanitary paper products; packaging & labeling services; towels, tissues & napkins: paper & stock; sanitary tissue paper

(G-12690)
RADIANCY INC (DH)
40 Ramland Rd S Ste 200 (10962-2623)
PHONE..................845 398-1647
Dolev Rafaeli, *CEO*
Giora Fishman, *Vice Pres*
AVI Hanin, *Controller*
Megi Devolli, *Accountant*
Miki Van Soest, *Office Mgr*
▲ **EMP:** 10
SQ FT: 5,000
SALES (est): 1.7MM
SALES (corp-wide): 31.4MM **Publicly Held**
WEB: www.radiancy.com
SIC: 3845 Electromedical equipment
HQ: Ictv Holdings, Inc.
489 Devon Park Dr Ste 315
Wayne PA 19087
484 598-2300

(G-12691)
SENSORMATIC ELECTRONICS LLC
10 Corporate Dr (10962-2614)
PHONE..................845 365-3125
Per-Olof Loof, *President*
EMP: 15 **Privately Held**
WEB: www.sensormatic.com
SIC: 3812 Detection apparatus: electronic/magnetic field, light/heat
HQ: Sensormatic Electronics, Llc
6600 Congress Ave
Boca Raton FL 33487
561 912-6000

(G-12692)
SEQUA CORPORATION
330 Blaisdell Rd (10962-2510)
PHONE..................201 343-1122
John Lansdale, *President*
Donna Costello, *Controller*
Gary Begeman, *Exec Dir*
Gary Palomba, *Director*
Cynthia Trow, *Assistant*
EMP: 50
SQ FT: 367,000
SALES (corp-wide): 3.6B **Publicly Held**
WEB: www.sequa.com
SIC: 3479 Coating of metals & formed products
HQ: Sequa Corporation
3999 Rca Blvd
Palm Beach Gardens FL 33410
561 935-3571

(G-12693)
ZACKS ENTERPRISES INC
Also Called: Zagwear
33 Corporate Dr (10962-2615)
PHONE..................800 366-4924

Toby Zacks, *CEO*
Judd Karofsky, *President*
Lenny Polakoff, *Exec VP*
Bob Hay, *Senior VP*
Nate Jacobs, *Senior VP*
▲ **EMP:** 50
SQ FT: 48,000
SALES (est): 14.1MM **Privately Held**
SIC: 2759 8742 Screen printing; marketing consulting services

Orchard Park
Erie County

(G-12694)
303 CONTRACTING INC (HQ)
5486 Powers Rd (14127-3111)
P.O. Box 831, Buffalo (14240-0831)
PHONE..................716 896-2122
Edward Janowski, *Ch of Bd*
Henry Van Mollenberg, *President*
Joseph Kilijanski, *Exec VP*
James P Camarre, *CFO*
EMP: 20
SQ FT: 10,000
SALES (est): 2.4MM
SALES (corp-wide): 52.7MM **Privately Held**
SIC: 3444 1799 7692 3699 Welding on site; welding repair; electrical equipment & supplies; ducts, sheet metal
PA: Mollenberg-Betz Holdings Llc
300 Scott St
Buffalo NY 14204
716 614-7473

(G-12695)
A LUNT DESIGN INC
5755 Big Tree Rd (14127-4115)
P.O. Box 247 (14127-0247)
PHONE..................716 662-0781
Audrey Lunt, *President*
Thomas Lunt, *Vice Pres*
Robert Kresse, *Shareholder*
▲ **EMP:** 16
SQ FT: 15,000
SALES (est): 1.4MM **Privately Held**
WEB: www.alunt.com
SIC: 2389 Disposable garments & accessories

(G-12696)
A TITAN INSTRUMENTS INC
10 Centere Dr (14127)
PHONE..................716 667-9211
Michael Tuber, *President*
Christopher Mahle, *Vice Pres*
Emily Hawkins, *Opers Mgr*
Kevin Ernst, *Opers Staff*
Dan Ettipio, *Engineer*
▲ **EMP:** 15
SQ FT: 3,000
SALES (est): 3.1MM **Privately Held**
WEB: www.atitan.com
SIC: 3841 Surgical & medical instruments

(G-12697)
ACCIPITER RADAR CORPORATION
40 Centre Dr Ste 3 (14127-4100)
PHONE..................716 508-4432
Dr Tim Nohara, *President*
Darryl Nohara, *Vice Pres*
Jeffrey Ogden, *Vice Pres*
Gerry Key, *Marketing Staff*
EMP: 5
SALES (est): 509.1K **Privately Held**
SIC: 3812 Search & navigation equipment
HQ: Accipiter Radar Technologies Inc
576 Hwy 20
Fenwick ON L0S 1
905 228-6888

(G-12698)
ADVAN-TECH MANUFACTURING INC
3645 California Rd (14127-1715)
PHONE..................716 667-1500
Peter Munschauer, *President*
Mathew Weierheiser, *QC Mgr*
Denise Dietz, *Manager*
EMP: 23
SQ FT: 7,750

SALES (est): 3.7MM **Privately Held**
SIC: 3599 Machine shop, jobbing & repair

(G-12699)
AURORA INDUS MACHINING INC
3380 N Benzing Rd (14127-1538)
PHONE..................716 826-7911
Robert T Hesse, *President*
Mary C Hesse, *Vice Pres*
John Breen, *Treasurer*
EMP: 25
SQ FT: 20,000
SALES (est): 4.5MM
SALES (corp-wide): 39.8MM **Privately Held**
WEB: www.auroraheatexchangers.com
SIC: 3443 Heat exchangers, condensers & components; vessels, process or storage (from boiler shops); metal plate
PA: Hesse Industrial Sales, Inc.
3370 N Benzing Rd
Orchard Park NY 14127
716 827-4951

(G-12700)
BOS-HATTEN INC
Also Called: Ipe
50 Cobham Dr (14127-4121)
PHONE..................716 662-7030
Warner G Martin, *Ch of Bd*
Anthony Paliwoda, *Vice Pres*
Shirley Martin, *Admin Sec*
EMP: 10
SQ FT: 5,500
SALES (est): 747.9K
SALES (corp-wide): 345MM **Publicly Held**
WEB: www.bos-hatten.com
SIC: 3443 Mfg Fabricated Plate Work
HQ: Peerless Mfg. Co.
14651 Dallas Pkwy Ste 500
Dallas TX 75254
214 357-6181

(G-12701)
BOSTON VALLEY POTTERY INC (PA)
Also Called: Boston Valley Terra Cotta
6860 S Abbott Rd (14127-4707)
PHONE..................716 649-7490
John B Krouse, *Principal*
Gretchen E Krouse, *Vice Pres*
Richard O Krouse, *Vice Pres*
William D Krouse, *Vice Pres*
Mark Cansdale, *Prdtn Mgr*
▲ **EMP:** 95
SQ FT: 95,300
SALES (est): 52.2MM **Privately Held**
SIC: 3259 Architectural terra cotta; roofing tile, clay

(G-12702)
BUCKLEY QC FASTENERS INC
3874 California Rd (14127-2262)
PHONE..................716 662-1490
Ruth M Kohl, *General Mgr*
Kris Furjanic, *Sales Staff*
EMP: 32
SQ FT: 11,000
SALES (est): 4MM **Privately Held**
SIC: 3452 Nuts, metal; bolts, metal; screws, metal

(G-12703)
BUFFALO CIRCUITS INC
105 Mid County Dr (14127-1773)
PHONE..................716 662-2113
Peter Messina Jr, *President*
Liz Bever, *Manager*
EMP: 7
SQ FT: 4,920
SALES (est): 1MM **Privately Held**
SIC: 3672 7336 Circuit boards, television & radio printed; silk screen design

(G-12704)
BURGESS-MANNING INC (DH)
Also Called: Skimovex USA
50 Cobham Dr (14127-4121)
PHONE..................716 662-6540
Warner G Martin, *Ch of Bd*
Robert Sherman, *President*
Anthony Paliwoda, *VP Finance*
Shirley Martin, *Admin Sec*
▲ **EMP:** 60
SQ FT: 5,500

▲ = Import ▼ = Export
◆ = Import/Export

GEOGRAPHIC SECTION

Orchard Park - Erie County (G-12729)

SALES (est): 19.4MM
SALES (corp-wide): 345MM **Publicly Held**
WEB: www.burgessmanning.com
SIC: 3625 Noise control equipment
HQ: Peerless Mfg. Co.
  14651 Dallas Pkwy Ste 500
  Dallas TX 75254
  214 357-6181

(G-12705)
CARBON ACTIVATED CORPORATION
336 Stonehenge Dr (14127-2841)
PHONE 716 662-2005
Chris Allen, *Branch Mgr*
EMP: 8 **Privately Held**
WEB: www.carbonactivatedcorp.com
SIC: 2819 Charcoal (carbon), activated
PA: Carbon Activated Corporation
  2250 S Central Ave
  Compton CA 90220

(G-12706)
CARLETON TECHNOLOGIES INC (HQ)
10 Cobham Dr (14127-4195)
PHONE 716 662-0006
Kenneth Kota, *Ch of Bd*
Kelly Coffield, *President*
Nicholas Dziama, *General Mgr*
Kenneth A Kota, *General Mgr*
Jim Hatcher, *Project Mgr*
EMP: 277
SQ FT: 93,000
SALES (est): 228.8MM
SALES (corp-wide): 2.7B **Privately Held**
SIC: 3728 Aircraft parts & equipment
PA: Cobham Plc
  Brook Road
  Wimborne BH21
  120 288-2020

(G-12707)
COBHAM HOLDINGS (US) INC
10 Cobham Dr (14127-4121)
PHONE 716 662-0006
Betty Bible, *President*
Bob Murphy, *Principal*
EMP: 3700
SALES (est): 228.8MM
SALES (corp-wide): 2.7B **Privately Held**
SIC: 3679 3812 Microwave components; acceleration indicators & systems components, aerospace
HQ: Lockman Investments Limited
  Brook Road
  Wimborne

(G-12708)
COBHAM HOLDINGS INC (DH)
10 Cobham Dr (14127-4121)
PHONE 716 662-0006
Kelly Coffield, *President*
Rob Schaeffer, *Business Mgr*
Steven Cochran, *Accounts Mgr*
Robert Atkins, *Manager*
Ken Kota, *Manager*
EMP: 22
SALES (est): 945.2MM
SALES (corp-wide): 2.7B **Privately Held**
SIC: 3812 3679 Acceleration indicators & systems components, aerospace; microwave components

(G-12709)
COBHAM MANAGEMENT SERVICES INC
Also Called: Cobham Mission Systems Div
10 Centre Dr (14127-2280)
PHONE 716 662-0006
Warren Tucker, *President*
James Tuttle, *Engineer*
Betty Bible, *Treasurer*
Erica Forcucci, *Manager*
◆ EMP: 2650
SALES (est): 228.8MM
SALES (corp-wide): 2.7B **Privately Held**
SIC: 3812 Search & navigation equipment
HQ: Cobham Holdings Inc.
  10 Cobham Dr
  Orchard Park NY 14127
  716 662-0006

(G-12710)
CONTECH ENGNERED SOLUTIONS LLC
34 Birdsong Pkwy (14127-3067)
PHONE 716 870-9091
Gene Majchrzack, *Principal*
EMP: 12 **Privately Held**
SIC: 3443 Fabricated plate work (boiler shop)
HQ: Contech Engineered Solutions Llc
  9025 Centre Pointe Dr # 400
  West Chester OH 45069
  513 645-7000

(G-12711)
CURBELL MEDICAL PRODUCTS INC
20 Centre Dr (14127-4102)
PHONE 716 667-2520
Stephanie Booker, *Mfg Mgr*
Rick Crandall, *Engineer*
Thomas Rutherford, *Engineer*
Mary Deibel, *Marketing Staff*
Dave Zavah, *Branch Mgr*
EMP: 12
SALES (corp-wide): 200.6MM **Privately Held**
SIC: 3669 Intercommunication systems, electric
HQ: Curbell Medical Products, Inc.
  7 Cobham Dr
  Orchard Park NY 14127

(G-12712)
CURBELL MEDICAL PRODUCTS INC (HQ)
7 Cobham Dr (14127-4180)
PHONE 716 667-2520
Thomas E Leone, *Ch of Bd*
Christine L Sabuda, *Vice Ch Bd*
Abdulkadir Sarac, *President*
Doug Rockwood, *Exec VP*
Don Gibson, *Vice Pres*
▲ EMP: 152
SALES (est): 49.7MM
SALES (corp-wide): 200.6MM **Privately Held**
WEB: www.curbell.com
SIC: 3669 Intercommunication systems, electric
PA: Curbell, Inc.
  7 Cobham Dr
  Orchard Park NY 14127
  716 667-3377

(G-12713)
DESMI-AFTI INC
227 Thorn Ave Bldg C (14127-2600)
P.O. Box 575 (14127-0575)
PHONE 716 662-0632
Peter Lane, *President*
Charlene Cousineau, *Accountant*
Carole Lane, *Admin Sec*
▼ EMP: 20
SQ FT: 26,131
SALES (est): 5MM **Privately Held**
WEB: www.afti.com
SIC: 3533 3535 Oil field machinery & equipment; belt conveyor systems, general industrial use

(G-12714)
FLOW-SAFE INC
3865 Taylor Rd (14127-2297)
PHONE 716 662-2585
Warner Martin, *Ch of Bd*
Kevin Martin, *President*
John Ostroot, *Engineer*
Sharon Ruggiero,
▲ EMP: 40
SQ FT: 25,000
SALES (est): 8.5MM **Privately Held**
SIC: 3491 5074 Industrial valves; plumbing & heating valves

(G-12715)
GAYMAR INDUSTRIES INC
10 Centre Dr (14127-2280)
PHONE 800 828-7341
Bradford L Saar, *CEO*
Kent J Davies, *Principal*
▲ EMP: 350 **EST:** 1956
SQ FT: 110,000
SALES (est): 45.1MM
SALES (corp-wide): 12.4B **Publicly Held**
WEB: www.gaymar.com
SIC: 3841 Surgical & medical instruments
PA: Stryker Corporation
  2825 Airview Blvd
  Portage MI 49002
  269 385-2600

(G-12716)
GOODNATURE PRODUCTS INC (PA)
3860 California Rd (14127-2262)
PHONE 716 855-3325
Dale Wettlaufer, *President*
Eric Wettlaufer, *Engineer*
Charles Wettlaufer, *VP Sls/Mktg*
Lori Sonnenfeld, *Human Res Mgr*
Pete Whitehead, *VP Sales*
EMP: 30
SQ FT: 18,000
SALES (est): 5MM **Privately Held**
WEB: www.goodnature.com
SIC: 3634 3556 Juice extractors, electric; pasteurizing equipment, dairy machinery

(G-12717)
GRASERS DENTAL CERAMICS
5020 Armor Duells Rd # 2 (14127-4441)
PHONE 716 649-5100
Thomas John Graser Jr, *Owner*
EMP: 6
SQ FT: 600
SALES (est): 60K **Privately Held**
SIC: 3843 Dental materials

(G-12718)
IMPACT JOURNALS LLC
Also Called: Publishing Medical Journals
6666 E Quaker St Ste 1 (14127-2547)
PHONE 800 922-0957
Zoya Demidenko, *Mng Member*
Bert Vogelstein, *Professor*
EMP: 8
SALES (est): 100K **Privately Held**
SIC: 2721 Periodicals: publishing & printing

(G-12719)
ITT CORP
7 Centre Dr (14127-2281)
PHONE 716 662-1900
Michael Siino, *President*
Scott Shular, *Opers Staff*
Matthew Calipari, *Buyer*
Justin Reese, *Buyer*
Mark Ott, *Engineer*
EMP: 20
SALES (est): 3.2MM **Privately Held**
SIC: 3625 Control equipment, electric

(G-12720)
ITT ENIDINE INC (DH)
Also Called: Enivate - Aerospace Division
7 Centre Dr (14127-2281)
PHONE 716 662-1900
Dennise Ramos, *CEO*
Munish Nanda, *Ch of Bd*
Dennis Schully, *President*
David Snowberger, *Business Mgr*
Dan Claycomb, *Plant Mgr*
▲ EMP: 275
SQ FT: 85,000
SALES (est): 122.2MM
SALES (corp-wide): 2.5B **Publicly Held**
WEB: www.enidine.com
SIC: 3724 3714 3593 Aircraft engines & engine parts; motor vehicle parts & accessories; fluid power cylinders & actuators
HQ: Itt Llc
  1133 Westchester Ave N-100
  White Plains NY 10604
  914 641-2000

(G-12721)
J H BUSCHER INC
227 Thorn Ave Ste 30 (14127-2671)
PHONE 716 667-2003
John H Buscher, *President*
Margaret G Buscher, *Vice Pres*
EMP: 5
SQ FT: 3,000
SALES: 700K **Privately Held**
WEB: www.jhbi.com
SIC: 3491 Industrial valves

(G-12722)
JARACZ JR JOSEPH PAUL
64 Ferndale Dr (14127-1644)
PHONE 716 533-1377
Joseph Paul Jaracz Jr, *Owner*
Kyle Gooding, *CFO*
EMP: 8
SALES (est): 293.5K **Privately Held**
SIC: 3845 3841 Electromedical equipment; surgical & medical instruments

(G-12723)
KELSON PRODUCTS INC
3300 N Benzing Rd (14127-1538)
PHONE 716 825-2585
Joseph P Merz, *President*
EMP: 7
SQ FT: 10,864
SALES (est): 700K **Privately Held**
WEB: www.kelsonproducts.com
SIC: 3069 Rubberized fabrics

(G-12724)
KINEDYNE INC
Also Called: Engineered Lifting Tech
3566 S Benzing Rd (14127-1703)
PHONE 716 667-6833
William Hanes, *President*
Andrew Reardon, *VP Opers*
Jeremy Inda, *Design Engr*
Sue Sherry, *Office Mgr*
EMP: 18
SQ FT: 17,000
SALES (est): 4.3MM **Privately Held**
SIC: 3531 Cranes

(G-12725)
LAKE REGION MEDICAL INC
3902 California Rd (14127-2275)
P.O. Box 637 (14127-0637)
PHONE 716 662-5025
Michael Ekstrum, *Opers Staff*
Michael Clayback, *Director*
EMP: 110
SALES (corp-wide): 1.4B **Publicly Held**
SIC: 3841 Surgical instruments & apparatus; medical instruments & equipment, blood & bone work
HQ: Lake Region Medical, Inc.
  100 Fordham Rd Ste 3
  Wilmington MA 01887

(G-12726)
LD MCCAULEY LLC
3875 California Rd (14127-2239)
PHONE 716 662-6744
Durham McCauley, *President*
Peter McCauley, *Vice Pres*
David Powers, *Vice Pres*
EMP: 120
SALES (est): 15.5MM **Privately Held**
SIC: 3452 Bolts, nuts, rivets & washers

(G-12727)
MANZELLA KNITTING
3345 N Benzing Rd (14127-1539)
PHONE 716 825-0808
Ed Masanovic, *Owner*
▲ EMP: 7
SALES (est): 608.3K **Privately Held**
SIC: 2381 Gloves, work: woven or knit, made from purchased materials

(G-12728)
MARATHON ROOFING PRODUCTS INC
3310 N Benzing Rd (14127-1538)
PHONE 716 685-3340
Tod Cislo, *President*
◆ EMP: 10
SQ FT: 30,000
SALES (est): 3MM **Privately Held**
WEB: www.marathondrains.com
SIC: 2952 5033 Roofing materials; roofing & siding materials

(G-12729)
MEDSOURCE TECHNOLOGIES LLC
3902 California Rd (14127-2275)
PHONE 716 662-5025
Jim Clark, *Manager*
EMP: 100

(PA)=Parent Co (HQ)=Headquarters (DH)=Div Headquarters
✪ = New Business established in last 2 years

Orchard Park - Erie County (G-12730)

SALES (corp-wide): 1.4B **Publicly Held**
WEB: www.medsourcetech.com
SIC: 3841 Surgical & medical instruments
HQ: Medsource Technologies, Llc
100 Fordham Rd Ste 1
Wilmington MA 01887
978 570-6900

(G-12730)
MENTHOLATUM COMPANY (DH)
707 Sterling Dr (14127-1587)
PHONE.................................716 677-2500
Akiyoshi Yoshida PHD, *CEO*
Kunio Yamada, *President*
Barbara Regan, *Regional Mgr*
David Moore, *Sr Corp Ofcr*
Francis Chan, *Vice Pres*
◆ **EMP:** 34 **EST:** 1889
SQ FT: 102,000
SALES (est): 63.9MM
SALES (corp-wide): 1.3B **Privately Held**
WEB: www.mentholatum.com
SIC: 2844 2834 Toilet preparations; analgesics
HQ: Rohto Usa Inc
707 Sterling Dr
Orchard Park NY 14127
716 677-2500

(G-12731)
MRP SUPPORTS LLC
3310 N Benzing Rd (14127-1538)
PHONE.................................716 332-7673
Tod Cislo, *Mng Member*
▲ **EMP:** 15
SQ FT: 37,000
SALES (est): 1.5MM **Privately Held**
SIC: 2541 Pedestals & statuary, wood

(G-12732)
NITRAM ENERGY INC
Also Called: Alco Products Div
50 Cobham Dr (14127-4121)
PHONE.................................716 662-6540
Peter J Burlage, *CEO*
Robert Sherman, *President*
Shirley Martin, *Admin Sec*
EMP: 50 **EST:** 1979
SQ FT: 5,500
SALES (est): 4.5MM
SALES (corp-wide): 345MM **Publicly Held**
SIC: 3625 3443 Control equipment, electric; heat exchangers: coolers (after, inter), condensers, etc.
HQ: Peerless Mfg. Co.
14651 Dallas Pkwy Ste 500
Dallas TX 75254
214 357-6181

(G-12733)
P M PLASTICS INC
1 Bank St Ste 1 # 1 (14127-2997)
PHONE.................................716 662-1255
Paul Sparks, *President*
Mark Zybert, *Corp Secy*
EMP: 25
SQ FT: 46,000
SALES: 3.5MM **Privately Held**
SIC: 3089 Injection molding of plastics

(G-12734)
PANAGRAPHICS INC
Also Called: Polish American Journal
30 Quail Run (14127-4611)
P.O. Box 198, Bowmansville, (14026-0198)
PHONE.................................716 312-8088
Mark A Cohan, *President*
Christopher Misztal, *Vice Pres*
Caroline Szczepanski, *Treasurer*
EMP: 5
SQ FT: 1,200
SALES (est): 462K **Privately Held**
SIC: 2791 2711 Typesetting; newspapers

(G-12735)
PARATUS INDUSTRIES INC
6659 E Quaker St (14127-2503)
PHONE.................................716 826-2000
Stephen Idziur, *President*
Thomas Zimmermann, *Vice Pres*
EMP: 30
SQ FT: 20,000
SALES (est): 4.8MM **Privately Held**
WEB: www.paratusindustries.com
SIC: 3999 Barber & beauty shop equipment

(G-12736)
PEERLESS MFG CO
Also Called: Alco Products USA
50 Cobham Dr (14127-4121)
PHONE.................................716 539-7400
Peter J Burlage, *Branch Mgr*
EMP: 40
SALES (corp-wide): 345MM **Publicly Held**
WEB: www.peerlessmfg.com
SIC: 3569 Separators for steam, gas, vapor or air (machinery)
HQ: Peerless Mfg. Co.
14651 Dallas Pkwy Ste 500
Dallas TX 75254
214 357-6181

(G-12737)
POLYMER CONVERSIONS INC
5732 Big Tree Rd (14127-4196)
PHONE.................................716 662-8550
Jack E Bertsch, *CEO*
Joan Bertsch, *Corp Secy*
Benjamin Harp, *COO*
Tom Rybicki, *Opers Staff*
Richard Baumann, *QA Dir*
EMP: 70
SQ FT: 35,000
SALES (est): 18.7MM **Privately Held**
WEB: www.polymerconversions.com
SIC: 3089 Molding primary plastic; injection molding of plastics

(G-12738)
PRECISION ABRASIVES CORP
3176 Abbott Rd (14127-1069)
PHONE.................................716 826-5833
Kevin Wyckoff, *President*
Pam Vogel, *Exec VP*
Craig Young, *Prdtn Mgr*
Stacey Coyne, *Purch Agent*
David Menzer, *Treasurer*
▲ **EMP:** 50
SQ FT: 25,000
SALES (est): 6.9MM
SALES (corp-wide): 11MM **Privately Held**
WEB: www.wesand.com
SIC: 3291 Coated abrasive products
PA: Sopark Corp.
3300 S Park Ave
Buffalo NY 14218
716 822-0434

(G-12739)
PUMPCRETE CORPORATION
7126 Ellicott Rd (14127-3438)
PHONE.................................716 667-7867
George Culp, *President*
Melissa Williams, *General Ptnr*
Lisa Pickard, *Manager*
EMP: 8
SQ FT: 3,500
SALES: 1.8MM **Privately Held**
SIC: 3561 Pumps & pumping equipment

(G-12740)
QUAKER BOY INC (PA)
Also Called: Quaker Boy Turkey Calls
5455 Webster Rd (14127-1742)
PHONE.................................716 662-3979
Richard C Kirby, *President*
▲ **EMP:** 50
SQ FT: 13,000
SALES (est): 5.4MM **Privately Held**
WEB: www.quakerboy.com
SIC: 3949 5961 Game calls; hunting equipment; mail order house

(G-12741)
QUAKER MILLWORK & LUMBER INC
77 S Davis St (14127-2684)
PHONE.................................716 662-3388
Robert J Raber, *President*
EMP: 40
SQ FT: 36,000
SALES (est): 6.7MM **Privately Held**
WEB: www.quakermills.com
SIC: 2431 Doors & door parts & trim, wood

(G-12742)
QUALITY INDUSTRIAL SERVICES
Also Called: Bws Specialty Fabrication
75 Bank St (14127-2908)
PHONE.................................716 667-7703
John E Sisson, *CEO*
EMP: 14
SQ FT: 52,800
SALES (est): 2.9MM **Privately Held**
SIC: 3496 7692 Miscellaneous fabricated wire products; welding repair

(G-12743)
S & K COUNTER TOPS INC
4708 Duerr Rd (14127-3141)
PHONE.................................716 662-7986
Bob Hayes, *President*
Tim Huwes, *Vice Pres*
EMP: 7
SQ FT: 2,400
SALES: 500K **Privately Held**
SIC: 2542 5211 Cabinets: show, display or storage: except wood; counters or counter display cases: except wood; cabinets, kitchen; counter tops

(G-12744)
STI-CO INDUSTRIES INC
11 Cobham Dr Ste A (14127-4187)
PHONE.................................716 662-2680
Antoinette Kaiser, *President*
Antoinette P Kaiser, *CEO*
Kyle Sawiat, *President*
Joseph Collura, *Prdtn Mgr*
Michael King, *Production*
EMP: 48
SQ FT: 10,000
SALES (est): 12.2MM **Privately Held**
WEB: www.sti-co.com
SIC: 3663 Antennas, transmitting & communications

(G-12745)
TAYLOR METALWORKS INC
3925 California Rd (14127-2276)
PHONE.................................716 662-3113
Peter G Taylor, *President*
Jason Taylor, *Vice Pres*
EMP: 110
SQ FT: 37,000
SALES (est): 21.8MM **Privately Held**
WEB: www.taylorcnc.com
SIC: 3451 3365 Screw machine products; aluminum & aluminum-based alloy castings

(G-12746)
TRANSPORT NATIONAL DEV INC (PA)
Also Called: North American Carbide
5720 Ellis Rd (14127-2223)
PHONE.................................716 662-0270
Robert A Gralke, *President*
Robert Gralke Jr, *Sales Mgr*
Brian Mroz, *Sales Staff*
Cindy Donnelly, *Office Mgr*
Marsha Gralke, *Admin Sec*
EMP: 50
SQ FT: 30,000
SALES (est): 17MM **Privately Held**
SIC: 3541 Machine tools, metal cutting type

(G-12747)
TRANSPORT NATIONAL DEV INC
Also Called: North American Carbide of NY
5720 Ellis Rd (14127-2223)
PHONE.................................716 662-0270
Robert Gralke, *Engnr/R&D Mgr*
EMP: 50
SALES (corp-wide): 17MM **Privately Held**
SIC: 2819 3545 Carbides; machine tool accessories
PA: Transport National Development, Inc.
5720 Ellis Rd
Orchard Park NY 14127
716 662-0270

(G-12748)
UNITED MATERIALS LLC
Also Called: Frey Concrete Incoporated
75 Bank St (14127-2908)
PHONE.................................716 662-0564
EMP: 6
SALES (corp-wide): 19.2MM **Privately Held**
SIC: 3273 1442 Mfg Ready-Mixed Concrete Construction Sand/Gravel
PA: United Materials, L.L.C.
3949 Frest Pk Way Ste 400
North Tonawanda NY 14120
716 683-1432

(G-12749)
VIBRATION & NOISE ENGRG CORP
Also Called: Vanec
3374 N Benzing Rd (14127-1538)
PHONE.................................716 827-4959
Art Cagney, *President*
Thomas Love, *President*
Doug Wittkowsky, *Engineer*
EMP: 3
SQ FT: 2,000
SALES (est): 1.6MM **Privately Held**
WEB: www.vanec.com
SIC: 3625 5084 Noise control equipment; industrial machinery & equipment

Oriskany
Oneida County

(G-12750)
ALFRED PUBLISHING CO INC
Also Called: Alfred Music
123 Dry Rd (13424-4312)
PHONE.................................315 736-1572
Michelle Major, *General Mgr*
Daniel Mayack, *Branch Mgr*
Brian Simpson, *Info Tech Mgr*
EMP: 70
SALES (corp-wide): 59.1MM **Privately Held**
WEB: www.alfred.com
SIC: 2731 5192 Book music: publishing & printing; books, periodicals & newspapers
PA: The Full Void 2 Inc
16320 Roscoe Blvd Ste 100
Van Nuys CA 91406
818 891-5999

(G-12751)
BONIDE PRODUCTS INC
6301 Sutliff Rd (13424-4326)
PHONE.................................315 736-8231
James J Wurz, *CEO*
Edward T Wurz, *Vice Pres*
Brenda Adcock, *Sales Staff*
Richard Celentano, *Sales Staff*
Tom Combs, *Sales Staff*
◆ **EMP:** 200
SQ FT: 27,000
SALES (est): 65.4MM **Privately Held**
WEB: www.bonideproducts.com
SIC: 2899 Chemical preparations

(G-12752)
CALDWELL BENNETT INC
Also Called: C B I
6152 County Seat Rd (13424-4308)
P.O. Box 610, Rome (13442-0610)
PHONE.................................315 337-8540
Douglas Brazinski, *President*
Brian Brazinski, *Vice Pres*
Joan Brazinski, *Vice Pres*
Paul Brazinski, *Vice Pres*
Laura Niemetz, *Purch Agent*
EMP: 45
SQ FT: 40,000
SALES (est): 9.1MM **Privately Held**
WEB: www.cbicables.com
SIC: 3357 Communication wire

(G-12753)
COVENTYA INC (DH)
132 Clear Rd (13424-4300)
PHONE.................................216 351-1500
Erik Weyls, *CEO*
◆ **EMP:** 70
SQ FT: 51,000

SALES (est): 13.2MM
SALES (corp-wide): 24.4MM **Privately Held**
WEB: www.taskem.com
SIC: 2899 Water treating compounds
HQ: Coventya
7 Rue Du Cdt D Estienne D Orves
Villeneuve La Garenne 92390
147 157-300

(G-12754)
COVENTYA INC
132 Clear Rd (13424-4300)
PHONE.................................315 768-6635
EMP: 11
SALES (corp-wide): 24.4MM **Privately Held**
WEB: www.sirius-tech.com
SIC: 2899 Plating compounds
HQ: Coventya, Inc.
132 Clear Rd
Oriskany NY 13424
216 351-1500

(G-12755)
CPP - STEEL TREATERS
100 Furnace St (13424-4816)
PHONE.................................315 736-3081
Joseph Weber, *President*
Jennifer Landry, *Manager*
David Stopera, *Manager*
EMP: 29 EST: 1957
SQ FT: 4,000
SALES (est): 6.1MM
SALES (corp-wide): 6.3B **Privately Held**
SIC: 3398 Metal heat treating
HQ: Cpp-Syracuse, Inc.
901 E Genesee St
Chittenango NY 13037
315 687-0014

(G-12756)
DAIMLER BUSES NORTH AMER INC
165 Base Rd (13424)
P.O. Box 748 (13424-0748)
PHONE.................................315 768-8101
Bernd Voigt, *Ch of Bd*
Andreas Strecker, *President*
Harry Rendel, *CFO*
▲ EMP: 560
SQ FT: 40,000
SALES (est): 68.3MM
SALES (corp-wide): 193.7B **Privately Held**
WEB: www.orionbus.com
SIC: 3713 3711 Truck & bus bodies; motor buses, except trackless trollies, assembly of
HQ: Daimler Trucks North America Llc
4555 N Channel Ave
Portland OR 97217
503 745-8000

(G-12757)
FIBER INSTRUMENT SALES INC (PA)
Also Called: F I S
161 Clear Rd (13424-4339)
PHONE.................................315 736-2206
Frank Giotto, *President*
Susan Grabinsky, *President*
Kirk Donley, *Senior VP*
Valerie Sitler, *Senior VP*
John Bruno, *Vice Pres*
◆ EMP: 220
SQ FT: 90,000
SALES (est): 108.6MM **Privately Held**
WEB: www.fisfiber.com
SIC: 3661 3643 2298 3699 Fiber optics communications equipment; connectors & terminals for electrical devices; cable, fiber; security devices

(G-12758)
GOLD MEDAL PACKING INC
8301 Old River Rd (13424)
PHONE.................................315 337-1911
Joseph Rocco III, *President*
Nancy Stilwell, *Controller*
Liz Shapano, *Admin Sec*
EMP: 60
SQ FT: 10,000
SALES (est): 9MM **Privately Held**
WEB: www.goldmedalpacking.com
SIC: 2011 Meat packing plants

(G-12759)
INDUSTRIAL OIL TANK SERVICE
120 Dry Rd (13424-4311)
PHONE.................................315 736-6080
John E Hitchings Jr, *President*
John E Hitchings Sr, *Admin Sec*
EMP: 10
SQ FT: 11,580
SALES (est): 1.8MM **Privately Held**
SIC: 2992 Re-refining lubricating oils & greases

(G-12760)
ORISKANY ARMS INC
175 Clear Rd (13424-4301)
PHONE.................................315 737-2196
Frank Giotto, *CEO*
Jim Rabbia, *President*
EMP: 13
SQ FT: 10,000
SALES (est): 4MM **Privately Held**
SIC: 3484 Guns (firearms) or gun parts, 30 mm. & below

(G-12761)
SEIFERT GRAPHICS INC
Also Called: Seifert Transit Graphics
6133 Judd Rd (13424-4220)
PHONE.................................315 736-2744
Karen M Seifert, *President*
Emmett Seifert, *Accounts Exec*
Todd Stern, *Manager*
EMP: 15
SQ FT: 20,000
SALES (est): 3.1MM **Privately Held**
WEB: www.seifertgraphics.com
SIC: 2752 Commercial printing, lithographic

(G-12762)
SQUARE ONE COATING SYSTEMS LLC
170 Base Rd (13424-4204)
PHONE.................................315 790-5921
Jody McRedmond, *Manager*
EMP: 10 EST: 2013
SALES (est): 1.2MM **Privately Held**
SIC: 3471 Plating & polishing

(G-12763)
SUIT-KOTE CORPORATION
Also Called: Central Asphalt
191 Dry Rd (13424-4312)
PHONE.................................315 735-8501
Lee Wall, *Branch Mgr*
EMP: 13
SALES (corp-wide): 234.8MM **Privately Held**
WEB: www.suit-kote.com
SIC: 2951 Asphalt paving mixtures & blocks
PA: Suit-Kote Corporation
1911 Lorings Crossing Rd
Cortland NY 13045
607 753-1100

(G-12764)
SUMAX CYCLE PRODUCTS INC
122 Clear Rd (13424-4300)
PHONE.................................315 768-1058
Linda Van Scoten, *President*
Kirk Van Scotten, *Vice Pres*
EMP: 16
SQ FT: 11,000
SALES: 611.4K **Privately Held**
WEB: www.sumax.com
SIC: 3751 Motorcycles & related parts; motorcycle accessories

(G-12765)
TERAHERTZ TECHNOLOGIES INC
Also Called: T T I
169 Clear Rd (13424-4301)
PHONE.................................315 736-3642
John Gentile, *President*
Donald Biron, *Director*
Donna Gentile, *Admin Sec*
EMP: 6
SQ FT: 28,000
SALES: 1.8MM **Privately Held**
WEB: www.terahertztechnologies.com
SIC: 3661 8742 8731 Fiber optics communications equipment; industrial & labor consulting services; electronic research

(G-12766)
TLC-THE LIGHT CONNECTION INC
132 Base Rd (13424-4204)
PHONE.................................315 736-7384
Brian Mohar, *President*
Brain Mohar, *President*
Fritz Barns, *Principal*
Doug Rouse, *Principal*
Keith Vanderzell, *Principal*
EMP: 70
SQ FT: 19,500
SALES: 19.5MM
SALES (corp-wide): 108.6MM **Privately Held**
WEB: www.thelightconnection.com
SIC: 3357 Fiber optic cable (insulated)
PA: Fiber Instrument Sales, Inc.
161 Clear Rd
Oriskany NY 13424
315 736-2206

Oriskany Falls
Oneida County

(G-12767)
HANSON AGGREGATES PA LLC
1780 State Route 12b (13425)
PHONE.................................315 821-7222
Donald Henings, *Manager*
EMP: 15
SALES (corp-wide): 20.3B **Privately Held**
SIC: 1442 1429 1422 Common sand mining; grits mining (crushed stone); crushed & broken limestone
HQ: Hanson Aggregates Pennsylvania, Llc
7660 Imperial Way
Allentown PA 18195
610 366-4626

(G-12768)
ZIELINSKIS ASPHALT INC
4989 State Route 12b (13425-4541)
PHONE.................................315 306-4057
Kevin J Zielinski, *Principal*
EMP: 12
SALES (est): 2.4MM **Privately Held**
SIC: 2951 Asphalt paving mixtures & blocks

Ossining
Westchester County

(G-12769)
CATARACT HOSE CO
Also Called: Cataract Hose Co No 2
6 Waller Ave (10562-4711)
PHONE.................................914 941-9019
Louie Diloreto, *President*
EMP: 40
SALES (est): 2.7MM **Privately Held**
SIC: 3052 Fire hose, rubber

(G-12770)
CLEAR CAST TECHNOLOGIES INC (PA)
99 N Water St (10562-3255)
PHONE.................................914 945-0848
Peter Goldstein, *President*
Jerry Brown, *General Mgr*
Chris Beigie, *Vice Pres*
Janice McAlevy, *Accounts Mgr*
Larry Thomas, *Maintence Staff*
▲ EMP: 30
SQ FT: 28,000
SALES (est): 5.8MM **Privately Held**
WEB: www.clearcasttech.com
SIC: 3083 Plastic finished products, laminated

(G-12771)
METALLIZED CARBON CORPORATION (PA)
Also Called: Metcar Products
19 S Water St (10562-4633)
PHONE.................................914 941-3738
Matt Brennan, *Ch of Bd*
Frank Puentes, *Opers Staff*
Jeri Lacari, *Buyer*
Theresa Maniscalco, *Buyer*
Chris Dipaolo, *Engineer*
EMP: 140 EST: 1945
SQ FT: 50,000
SALES (est): 32.6MM **Privately Held**
WEB: www.carbongraphite.net
SIC: 3624 3568 Electric carbons; carbon specialties for electrical use; fibers, carbon & graphite; power transmission equipment

(G-12772)
OSSINING BAKERY LMP INC
50 N Highland Ave (10562-3432)
PHONE.................................914 941-2654
Tony Martins, *President*
EMP: 7 EST: 1973
SQ FT: 3,000
SALES: 490K **Privately Held**
SIC: 2051 Bread, cake & related products

(G-12773)
OSSINING VILLAGE OF INC
Also Called: Indian Water Treatment Plant
25 Fowler Ave (10562-1919)
P.O. Box 1166 (10562-0996)
PHONE.................................914 202-9668
George Gibson, *Chief*
EMP: 5 **Privately Held**
SIC: 3589 Water treatment equipment, industrial
PA: Ossining, Village Of Inc
16 Croton Ave Ste 2
Ossining NY 10562
914 941-3554

(G-12774)
PAN AMERICAN ROLLER INC
5 Broad Ave (10562-4601)
P.O. Box 1225 (10562-0057)
PHONE.................................914 762-8700
Gertrude Wolf, *Corp Secy*
Michael Wolf, *Vice Pres*
EMP: 10
SQ FT: 15,000
SALES: 1MM **Privately Held**
SIC: 3991 Paint rollers

Oswego
Oswego County

(G-12775)
BATTERY RESEARCH AND TSTG INC
1313 County Route 1 (13126-5999)
PHONE.................................315 342-2373
Patricia I Demar, *CEO*
Edward Demar, *Vice Pres*
Petter Demar, *Vice Pres*
Dennis Barber, *Natl Sales Mgr*
Pam Shatrau, *Executive*
EMP: 10
SQ FT: 3,600
SALES: 2MM **Privately Held**
WEB: www.batteryresearch.com
SIC: 3691 Storage batteries

(G-12776)
DOTTO WAGNER
Also Called: Local News
185 E Seneca St (13126-1600)
P.O. Box 276 (13126-0276)
PHONE.................................315 342-8020
Wagner Dotto, *Owner*
EMP: 6
SALES (est): 723.7K **Privately Held**
WEB: www.cnyfall.com
SIC: 2721 Magazines: publishing only, not printed on site

(G-12777)
ENERGY NUCLEAR OPERATIONS
Also Called: Chemistry Department
268 Lake Rd (13126-6325)
P.O. Box 110, Lycoming (13093-0110)
PHONE.................................315 342-0055
Ted Sullivan, *Vice Pres*
EMP: 30
SALES (est): 8.6MM **Privately Held**
SIC: 3443 Nuclear reactors, military or industrial

Oswego - Oswego County (G-12778)

(G-12778)
HEALTHWAY PRODUCTS COMPANY
249a Mitchell St (13126-1279)
PHONE..................................315 207-1410
William O'Hara, *President*
Michael Daly, *Vice Pres*
EMP: 25
SQ FT: 33,000
SALES (est): 3.8MM **Privately Held**
SIC: 3564 3585 Blowers & fans; refrigeration & heating equipment

(G-12779)
INDUSTRIAL PRECISION PDTS INC
350 Mitchell St (13126-1270)
PHONE..................................315 343-4421
William J Gallagher, *Chairman*
EMP: 20 EST: 1951
SQ FT: 26,000
SALES: 1.7MM **Privately Held**
WEB: www.indprecision.com
SIC: 3599 Machine shop, jobbing & repair; custom machinery

(G-12780)
LAZAREK INC
209 Erie St (13126)
PHONE..................................315 343-1242
Walter Lazarek Jr, *President*
Stanley Lazarek, *Admin Sec*
EMP: 5 EST: 1936
SQ FT: 950
SALES (est): 710.8K **Privately Held**
SIC: 3273 5032 1442 Ready-mixed concrete; concrete & cinder block; construction sand mining; gravel mining

(G-12781)
MITCHELL PRTG & MAILING INC (PA)
1 Burkle St (13126-3261)
P.O. Box 815 (13126-0815)
PHONE..................................315 343-3531
John Henry, *President*
Kathleen Henry, *Vice Pres*
EMP: 10 EST: 1930
SQ FT: 2,112
SALES: 400K **Privately Held**
WEB: www.mpcny.com
SIC: 2752 Commercial printing, offset

(G-12782)
NORTHLAND FILTER INTL LLC
249a Mitchell St (13126-1279)
PHONE..................................315 207-1410
Gilles Morin,
◆ EMP: 20
SALES (est): 4.4MM **Privately Held**
WEB: www.northlandfilter.com
SIC: 3564 Filters, air: furnaces, air conditioning equipment, etc.

(G-12783)
NOVELIS CORPORATION
448 County Route 1a (13126-5962)
P.O. Box 28 (13126-0028)
PHONE..................................315 342-1036
Thomas Walpole, *Engineer*
EMP: 300
SALES (corp-wide): 6.5B **Privately Held**
SIC: 3353 Aluminum sheet, plate & foil
HQ: Novelis Corporation
3560 Lenox Rd Ne Ste 2000
Atlanta GA 30326
404 760-4000

(G-12784)
NOVELIS CORPORATION
72 Alcan W Entrance Rd (13126)
P.O. Box 28 (13126-0028)
PHONE..................................315 349-0121
Jack Morrison, *Principal*
EMP: 300
SALES (corp-wide): 6.5B **Privately Held**
SIC: 3353 Aluminum sheet, plate & foil
HQ: Novelis Corporation
3560 Lenox Rd Ne Ste 2000
Atlanta GA 30326
404 760-4000

(G-12785)
NOVELIS INC
448 County Route 1a (13126-5963)
P.O. Box 28 (13126-0028)
PHONE..................................315 349-0121
Steve Fisher, *CEO*
Philip Robert Martens, *Ch of Bd*
Dick Delaney, *Safety Dir*
Chris Smith, *Plant Mgr*
Michael Herron, *Purch Mgr*
EMP: 25
SALES (est): 3.4MM **Privately Held**
SIC: 3355 Aluminum ingot

(G-12786)
PATRICK KRAFT (PA)
Also Called: Kraftees
262 W Seneca St (13126-1820)
PHONE..................................315 343-9376
Patrick Kraft, *Owner*
Terry Peck, *Manager*
EMP: 6
SQ FT: 1,500
SALES (est): 921K **Privately Held**
WEB: www.kraftees.com
SIC: 2759 5942 Screen printing; college book stores

(G-12787)
SAMPLE NEWS GROUP LLC
Also Called: Palladium Times
140 W 1st St (13126-1514)
PHONE..................................315 343-3800
Sarah McCrobie, *Editor*
John Spalding, *Manager*
EMP: 55
SQ FT: 9,620
SALES (corp-wide): 8MM **Privately Held**
WEB: www.gatehousemedia.com
SIC: 2711 2752 Newspapers; commercial printing, lithographic
PA: Sample News Group, L.L.C.
28 W South St
Corry PA 16407
814 665-8291

(G-12788)
SPEEDWAY PRESS INC (HQ)
Also Called: Mitchell's Speedway Press
1 Burkle St (13126-3271)
P.O. Box 2006 (13126-0606)
PHONE..................................315 343-3531
George Caruso Jr, *President*
Romeo Caruso, *Corp Secy*
Douglas Caruso, *Vice Pres*
Kathy Henry, *VP Sales*
EMP: 9
SQ FT: 9,000
SALES: 360K
SALES (corp-wide): 400K **Privately Held**
WEB: www.speedwaypress.com
SIC: 2752 Commercial printing, offset
PA: Mitchell Printing & Mailing, Inc.
1 Burkle St
Oswego NY 13126
315 343-3531

(G-12789)
STONES HOMEMADE CANDIES INC
145 W Bridge St (13126-1440)
PHONE..................................315 343-8401
Margaret Stanchowicz, *President*
Margaret Stachowicz, *President*
EMP: 7 EST: 1946
SQ FT: 3,000
SALES (est): 650.3K **Privately Held**
SIC: 2064 Candy & other confectionery products

Ovid
Seneca County

(G-12790)
CROSSWINDS FARM & CREAMERY
6762 Log City Rd (14521-9789)
PHONE..................................607 327-0363
Sarah B Vanorden, *Owner*
EMP: 5
SALES (est): 236.8K **Privately Held**
SIC: 2022 5451 Natural cheese; dairy products stores

(G-12791)
HOSMER INC
Also Called: Hosmer's Winery
6999 State Route 89 (14521-9569)
PHONE..................................888 467-9463
Cameron Hosmer, *President*
Maren Hosmer, *Vice Pres*
EMP: 15
SALES: 500K **Privately Held**
WEB: www.hosmerwinery.com
SIC: 2084 Wines

(G-12792)
SENECA COUNTY AREA SHOPPER
1885 State Route 96a (14521-9712)
PHONE..................................607 532-4333
Joan E Hendrix, *Principal*
EMP: 6
SALES (est): 290.3K **Privately Held**
SIC: 2711 Commercial printing & newspaper publishing combined; newspapers, publishing & printing

(G-12793)
SHELDRAKE POINT VINEYARD LLC
Also Called: Sheldrake Point Winery
7448 County Road 153 (14521-9564)
PHONE..................................607 532-8967
Chuck Tauck, *Managing Prtnr*
Robert Madill, *General Mgr*
EMP: 10
SQ FT: 4,063
SALES: 800K **Privately Held**
SIC: 2084 Wines

(G-12794)
THIRSTY OWL WINE COMPANY
6861 State Route 89 (14521-9599)
PHONE..................................607 869-5805
Jonathan C Cupp, *President*
John Cupp, *President*
EMP: 7
SALES (est): 759.8K **Privately Held**
WEB: www.thirstyowl.com
SIC: 2084 Wines

Owego
Tioga County

(G-12795)
APPLIED TECHNOLOGY MFG CORP
71 Temple St (13827-1338)
P.O. Box 189 (13827-0189)
PHONE..................................607 687-2200
Stephen M Lounsberry III, *President*
Peter C Lounsberry, *Vice Pres*
Steve Bean, *Manager*
EMP: 30 EST: 1927
SQ FT: 25,000
SALES (est): 7.9MM **Privately Held**
WEB: www.appliedtechmfg.com
SIC: 3531 3599 Railway track equipment; railroad related equipment; machine & other job shop work

(G-12796)
C & C READY-MIX CORPORATION
3818 Rt 17 C (13827)
P.O. Box 174 (13827-0174)
PHONE..................................607 687-1690
Andy Cerretani, *Enginr/R&D Mgr*
EMP: 10
SALES (corp-wide): 5.3MM **Privately Held**
WEB: www.ccreadymix.com
SIC: 3273 2951 Ready-mixed concrete; asphalt paving mixtures & blocks
PA: C & C Ready-Mix Corporation
3112 Vestal Rd
Vestal NY 13850
607 797-5108

(G-12797)
INDUSTRIAL PAINT SERVICES CORP
60 W Main St 62 (13827-1537)
PHONE..................................607 687-0107
Jean Chapman, *President*
EMP: 17
SQ FT: 20,000
SALES (est): 1.7MM **Privately Held**
WEB: www.ipsowego.com
SIC: 3479 Painting of metal products

(G-12798)
KYOCERA PRECISION TOOLS INC
Also Called: New York Division
1436 Taylor Rd (13827-1833)
PHONE..................................607 687-0012
Stephen Hansen, *Branch Mgr*
EMP: 14
SALES (corp-wide): 14.8B **Publicly Held**
WEB: www.tycom.com
SIC: 3541 Machine tools, metal cutting type
HQ: Kyocera Precision Tools, Inc
102 Industrial Park Rd
Hendersonville NC 28792
800 823-7284

(G-12799)
LOCKHEED MARTIN CORPORATION
1801 State Route 17 (13827)
PHONE..................................607 751-2000
Dustin Vantassel, *Engineer*
Bryan Ruskavich, *Mktg Dir*
Joseph Trench, *Manager*
Michael McNeil, *Manager*
Martin Patchett, *Manager*
EMP: 1261 **Publicly Held**
WEB: www.lockheedmartin.com
SIC: 3812 3761 Search & navigation equipment; guided missiles & space vehicles
PA: Lockheed Martin Corporation
6801 Rockledge Dr
Bethesda MD 20817

(G-12800)
NATIONAL PAPER CONVERTING INC
207 Corporate Dr (13827-3249)
PHONE..................................607 687-6049
Eric Kretzmer, *President*
EMP: 5
SQ FT: 8,000
SALES (est): 837.5K **Privately Held**
WEB: www.nationaladh.com
SIC: 2621 Absorbent paper

(G-12801)
NORWESCO INC
263 Corporate Dr (13827-3249)
PHONE..................................607 687-8081
Rich Barto, *Manager*
EMP: 11
SALES (corp-wide): 44.1MM **Privately Held**
WEB: www.ncmmolding.com
SIC: 3089 Plastic & fiberglass tanks
PA: Norwesco, Inc.
4365 Steiner St
Saint Bonifacius MN 55375
952 446-1945

(G-12802)
OWEGO PENNYSAVER PRESS INC
181 Front St (13827-1520)
PHONE..................................607 687-2434
George V Lynett, *President*
EMP: 10
SALES (est): 509.9K
SALES (corp-wide): 12MM **Privately Held**
WEB: www.sundayreview.com
SIC: 2711 Commercial printing & newspaper publishing combined; newspapers, publishing & printing
PA: Towanda Printing Co Inc
116 N Main St
Towanda PA 18848
570 265-2151

(G-12803)
SANMINA CORPORATION
1200 Taylor Rd (13827-1292)
PHONE..................................607 689-5000
Dennis Young, *President*
Mark Gable, *Vice Pres*
Brian Barber, *Purch Mgr*

Todd Thrasher, *Software Engr*
EMP: 500 **Publicly Held**
WEB: www.sanmina.com
SIC: 3672 Circuit boards, television & radio printed
PA: Sanmina Corporation
2700 N 1st St
San Jose CA 95134

(G-12804)
TIOGA COUNTY COURIER
59 Church St (13827-1439)
PHONE.................607 687-0108
Mary Jones, *Owner*
EMP: 5
SALES (est): 204.6K **Privately Held**
SIC: 2711 Newspapers: publishing only, not printed on site

(G-12805)
WAGNER MILLWORK INC
Also Called: Wagner Lumber
4060 Gaskill Rd (13827-4741)
PHONE.................607 687-5362
Steven Schaeffer, *Vice Pres*
Steve Houseknecht, *Sales Staff*
▼ **EMP:** 70
SQ FT: 60,000
SALES (est): 21.5MM **Privately Held**
WEB: www.wagnerlumber.com
SIC: 2421 2431 2426 Sawmills & planing mills, general; millwork; hardwood dimension & flooring mills

(G-12806)
WHOLESALE MULCH & SAWDUST INC
Also Called: Tioga County Waste Wood Recycl
3711 Waverly Rd (13827-2860)
PHONE.................607 687-2637
Philip Nestor, *President*
Cynthia Nestor, *Vice Pres*
EMP: 5
SQ FT: 1,624
SALES (est): 460K **Privately Held**
SIC: 2499 Mulch or sawdust products, wood

Oxford
Chenango County

(G-12807)
AUTOMECHA INTERNATIONAL LTD (PA)
48 S Canal St (13830-4318)
P.O. Box 660 (13830-0660)
PHONE.................607 843-2235
Kenneth E St John, *President*
Kevin Gates, *Controller*
Mike Sawyer, *Manager*
Sonjia Strobach, *Admin Sec*
EMP: 28
SQ FT: 23,000
SALES (est): 4.8MM **Privately Held**
WEB: www.asmarc.com
SIC: 3579 5044 3565 3554 Addressing machines, plates & plate embossers; address labeling machines; mailing, letter handling & addressing machines; office equipment; packaging machinery; paper industries machinery

(G-12808)
RAPID REPRODUCTIONS LLC
4511 State Hwy 12 (13830)
PHONE.................607 843-2221
Bryant Latourette,
EMP: 8
SQ FT: 11,000
SALES: 680K **Privately Held**
SIC: 2752 Commercial printing, offset

Oyster Bay
Nassau County

(G-12809)
AMERICAN TRANS-COIL CORP
Also Called: A T C
69 Hamilton Ave Ste 3 (11771-1573)
P.O. Box 629 (11771-0629)
PHONE.................516 922-9640
Mark Masin, *President*
William Rogers, *Principal*
EMP: 15 **EST:** 1960
SQ FT: 5,000
SALES (est): 2.2MM **Privately Held**
WEB: www.atc-us.com
SIC: 3677 Electronic coils, transformers & other inductors

(G-12810)
APOTHECUS PHARMACEUTICAL CORP (PA)
220 Townsend Sq (11771-2339)
PHONE.................516 624-8200
Thomas Leon, *Ch of Bd*
Daniel Leon, *President*
Jonathan Leon, *Vice Pres*
Paul Gabel, *VP Opers*
Michael Lesser, *CFO*
EMP: 14
SQ FT: 7,000
SALES (est): 4.6MM **Privately Held**
WEB: www.apothecus.com
SIC: 2834 5122 Pharmaceutical preparations; proprietary (patent) medicines

(G-12811)
CIRCO FILE CORP
69 Hamilton Ave Ste 1 (11771-1573)
PHONE.................516 922-1848
Thomas Carrella, *President*
Ralph Carrella, *Shareholder*
EMP: 7 **EST:** 1955
SQ FT: 2,000
SALES (est): 1MM **Privately Held**
WEB: www.circofile.com
SIC: 3545 Machine tool accessories

(G-12812)
COMANDER TERMINALS LLC
1 Commander Sq (11771-1536)
PHONE.................516 922-7600
Abrham Prznaski, *President*
EMP: 14
SALES (est): 1.6MM **Privately Held**
SIC: 2843 Oils & greases

(G-12813)
ENGINEERING MAINT PDTS INC
Also Called: Hippo Industries
250 Berry Hill Rd (11771-3121)
P.O. Box 548 (11771-0548)
PHONE.................516 624-9774
Ansuya Dave, *President*
Peter Dave, *Vice Pres*
Shashidhar H Dave, *Vice Pres*
EMP: 14
SQ FT: 4,000
SALES (est): 3.6MM **Privately Held**
SIC: 2899 5169 Corrosion preventive lubricant; anti-corrosion products

(G-12814)
IMREX LLC (PA)
55 Sandy Hill Rd (11771-3110)
P.O. Box 154 (11771-0154)
PHONE.................516 479-3675
Jacob Armon, *Mng Member*
Harry Armon,
Alan J Weiss,
EMP: 350
SQ FT: 32,000
SALES (est): 53.5MM **Privately Held**
WEB: www.imrex.com
SIC: 3679 Electronic circuits

(G-12815)
MILL-MAX MFG CORP
190 Pine Hollow Rd (11771-4711)
P.O. Box 300 (11771-0300)
PHONE.................516 922-6000
Roger L Bahnik, *Ch of Bd*
James W Litke, *President*
Claude A Bahnik, *Vice Pres*
Bradley E Kuczinski, *Vice Pres*
Peter Simicic, *Technology*
▲ **EMP:** 190 **EST:** 1971
SQ FT: 135,000
SALES: 56.8MM **Privately Held**
WEB: www.mil-max.com
SIC: 3678 5065 Electronic connectors; electronic parts & equipment

(G-12816)
MIRODDI IMAGING INC (PA)
Also Called: M Squared Graphics
27 Centre View Dr (11771-2815)
PHONE.................516 624-6898
Cherrise Miroddi, *Ch of Bd*
EMP: 2
SQ FT: 8,000
SALES (est): 1MM **Privately Held**
WEB: www.msquaredgraphics.com
SIC: 2796 Gravure printing plates or cylinders, preparation of

(G-12817)
OYSTER BAY BREWING COMPANY
36 Audrey Ave (11771-1548)
PHONE.................516 802-5546
Gabriel Haim, *Ch of Bd*
Gabe Haim, *Sales Executive*
EMP: 11 **EST:** 2012
SQ FT: 6,000
SALES (est): 1MM **Privately Held**
SIC: 2082 Beer (alcoholic beverage)

(G-12818)
PRINTERY
Also Called: Printing House of W S Miller
43 W Main St (11771-2215)
PHONE.................516 922-3250
William Miller, *President*
Mary Albene, *Vice Pres*
EMP: 5 **EST:** 1973
SALES (est): 533.5K **Privately Held**
SIC: 2759 2791 Card printing & engraving, except greeting; typesetting

(G-12819)
PURE GREEN LLC
439 Centre Island Rd (11771-5012)
PHONE.................800 306-9122
Brigitte Stetson, *Principal*
EMP: 5 **EST:** 2007
SALES (est): 888.9K **Privately Held**
SIC: 2842 Specialty cleaning, polishes & sanitation goods

(G-12820)
R F GIARDINA CO
200 Lexington Ave Apt 3a (11771-2114)
P.O. Box 562 (11771-0562)
PHONE.................516 922-1364
Robert Giardina, *President*
EMP: 10
SALES (est): 763.7K **Privately Held**
WEB: www.rfgco.com
SIC: 3944 Craft & hobby kits & sets

Ozone Park
Queens County

(G-12821)
ABIGAL PRESS INC
9735 133rd Ave (11417-2119)
P.O. Box 170704 (11417-0704)
PHONE.................718 641-5350
Salvatore Stratis, *CEO*
Jeff Gaines, *President*
Jeffrey Gaines, *President*
Lois Berl, *Vice Pres*
Michael O'Connor, *CFO*
◆ **EMP:** 98 **EST:** 1956
SQ FT: 30,000
SALES (est): 13.9MM **Privately Held**
WEB: www.abigal.com
SIC: 2759 Card printing & engraving, except greeting

(G-12822)
CENTRE INTERIORS WDWKG CO INC
10001 103rd Ave (11417-1712)
PHONE.................718 323-1343
Alex Lee, *President*
EMP: 20
SALES (est): 3.5MM **Privately Held**
SIC: 2521 Wood office desks & tables

(G-12823)
COIL CRAFT INC (PA)
10324 99th St (11417-1639)
PHONE.................718 369-1210
Roy Henry, *President*
Rohal Henry, *COO*
EMP: 5
SQ FT: 4,300
SALES: 900K **Privately Held**
SIC: 3585 Heating equipment, complete

(G-12824)
ELEVATOR VENTURES CORPORATION
Also Called: Ver-Tech Elevator
9720 99th St (11416-2602)
PHONE.................212 375-1900
Don Gelestino, *Owner*
EMP: 99
SALES (est): 10.2MM **Privately Held**
SIC: 3534 Elevators & moving stairways

(G-12825)
FASTENER DIMENSIONS INC
9403 104th St (11416-1723)
PHONE.................718 847-6321
Darryl A Hinkle, *President*
Debbie Blizzard, *Manager*
EMP: 35
SQ FT: 24,000
SALES (est): 3.2MM **Privately Held**
WEB: www.fastdim.com
SIC: 3429 5085 5088 3452 Aircraft hardware; fasteners, industrial: nuts, bolts, screws, etc.; aircraft equipment & supplies; bolts, nuts, rivets & washers

(G-12826)
FOOD GEMS LTD
8423 Rockaway Blvd (11416-1249)
PHONE.................718 296-7788
Bradley Stroll, *President*
Frank Kurt, *Vice Pres*
EMP: 24
SQ FT: 10,000
SALES (est): 2.7MM **Privately Held**
WEB: www.foodgems.com
SIC: 2051 5812 Bakery: wholesale or wholesale/retail combined; eating places

(G-12827)
JOLDESON ONE AEROSPACE INDS
Also Called: Joldeson One Aerospace Inds
10002 103rd Ave (11417-1713)
PHONE.................718 848-7396
Ecatarina Joldeson, *President*
George Joldeson, *Vice Pres*
Richard Joldeson, *Admin Sec*
EMP: 93
SALES: 8.5MM **Privately Held**
SIC: 3728 3496 3812 3643 Aircraft parts & equipment; woven wire products; search & navigation equipment; current-carrying wiring devices; conveyors & conveying equipment; partitions & fixtures, except wood

(G-12828)
JULIA KNIT INC
8050 Pitkin Ave (11211-1211)
PHONE.................718 848-1900
Avraham Lip, *President*
▲ **EMP:** 6
SALES (est): 1.3MM **Privately Held**
SIC: 2253 Sweaters & sweater coats, knit

(G-12829)
KW DISTRIBUTORS GROUP INC
Also Called: Kw Kitchen Design
9018 Liberty Ave (11417-1350)
PHONE.................718 843-3500
Vito Altesi, *President*
Daniel Altesi, *Corp Secy*
Riccardo Altesi, *Vice Pres*
▲ **EMP:** 10
SQ FT: 3,600
SALES (est): 1MM **Privately Held**
SIC: 2434 Wood kitchen cabinets

Ozone Park - Queens County (G-12830)

(G-12830)
MAMITAS ICES LTD
10411 100th St (11417-2206)
PHONE..................................718 738-3238
Javier Morel, *Partner*
◆ **EMP:** 10
SALES: 780K **Privately Held**
SIC: 2097 Manufactured ice

(G-12831)
PREMIER KNITS LTD
9735 133rd Ave (11417-2119)
PHONE..................................718 323-8264
Panta Ardeljan, *President*
Petar Ardeljan Jr, *Vice Pres*
EMP: 10
SQ FT: 35,000
SALES (est): 610K **Privately Held**
WEB: www.premierknits.com
SIC: 2253 5199 Sweaters & sweater coats, knit; knit goods

(G-12832)
ROBERT COHEN
Also Called: Allied Orthopedics
10540 Rockaway Blvd Ste A (11417-2304)
PHONE..................................718 789-0996
Robert F Cohen, *Owner*
EMP: 6
SQ FT: 4,000
SALES (est): 587.9K **Privately Held**
SIC: 3842 Limbs, artificial; braces, orthopedic

(G-12833)
WALL TOOL & TAPE CORP
Also Called: Wall Tool Manufacturing
8111 101st Ave (11416-2008)
P.O. Box 20637, Floral Park (11002-0637)
PHONE..................................718 641-6813
Dorothy Kaliades, *President*
Steven Kaliades, *Vice Pres*
EMP: 20
SQ FT: 12,000
SALES (est): 3.2MM **Privately Held**
SIC: 3423 Mfg Hand/Edge Tools

(G-12834)
ZONE FABRICATORS INC
10780 101st St (11417-2609)
PHONE..................................718 272-0200
Peter Scaminaci, *President*
Frances Hultin, *Vice Pres*
EMP: 16
SQ FT: 8,000
SALES (est): 1.7MM **Privately Held**
WEB: www.zonefabinc.com
SIC: 3089 3443 Plastic processing; metal parts

Painted Post
Steuben County

(G-12835)
AUTOMATED CELLS & EQP INC
9699 Enterprise Dr (14870-9166)
PHONE..................................607 936-1341
James Morris, *President*
Dylan Kephart, *Engineer*
Mindi McCann, *Controller*
Melinda McCann, *Persnl Dir*
Jerry North, *Regl Sales Mgr*
EMP: 38
SQ FT: 27,000
SALES (est): 10.9MM **Privately Held**
WEB: www.autocells.com
SIC: 3569 5084 Robots, assembly line: industrial & commercial; robots, industrial

(G-12836)
CORNING INCORPORATED
905 Addison Rd (14870-9726)
PHONE..................................607 974-1274
Dipak Chowdhury, *Division VP*
Ji Wang, *Project Mgr*
Chris Hoaglin, *Opers Staff*
Vince Haduck, *Buyer*
Doug Allan, *Research*
EMP: 50
SALES (corp-wide): 10.1B **Publicly Held**
WEB: www.corning.com
SIC: 3229 3264 Glass fiber products; porcelain electrical supplies

PA: Corning Incorporated
1 Riverfront Plz
Corning NY 14831
607 974-9000

(G-12837)
CORNING INCORPORATED
9261 Addison Rd (14870-9650)
PHONE..................................607 974-6729
Jim Blade, *Principal*
Thomas Moag, *Engineer*
EMP: 5
SALES (corp-wide): 10.1B **Publicly Held**
WEB: www.corning.com
SIC: 3357 3661 3211 3229 Fiber optic cable (insulated); telephone & telegraph apparatus; flat glass; pressed & blown glass; semiconductors & related devices; analytical instruments
PA: Corning Incorporated
1 Riverfront Plz
Corning NY 14831
607 974-9000

(G-12838)
CORNING INCORPORATED
103 Canada Rd (14870)
PHONE..................................607 962-6036
Keith Emig, *Manager*
Richard Clark, *Director*
EMP: 15
SALES (corp-wide): 10.1B **Publicly Held**
WEB: www.corning.com
SIC: 3229 Pressed & blown glass
PA: Corning Incorporated
1 Riverfront Plz
Corning NY 14831
607 974-9000

(G-12839)
DRESSER-RAND (DELAWARE) LLC (DH)
100 E Chemung St (14870-1377)
PHONE..................................607 937-2011
Malcolm Cliff, *Engineer*
Anthony Gioffredi,
EMP: 1
SALES (est): 15.8MM
SALES (corp-wide): 97.7B **Privately Held**
SIC: 3563 Air & gas compressors
HQ: Dresser-Rand Company
500 Paul Clark Dr
Olean NY 14760
716 375-3000

(G-12840)
SCHULER-HAAS ELECTRIC CORP
598 Ritas Way (14870-8546)
PHONE..................................607 936-3514
EMP: 7
SALES (est): 778.5K
SALES (corp-wide): 21MM **Privately Held**
SIC: 3699 1731 Electrical equipment & supplies; electrical work
PA: Schuler-Haas Electric Corp.
240 Commerce Dr
Rochester NY 14623
585 325-1060

(G-12841)
SIRIANNI HARDWOODS INC
912 Addison Rd (14870-9729)
PHONE..................................607 962-4688
James Sirianni, *CEO*
Tom Armentano, *Purch Agent*
Mary Sirianni, *Treasurer*
EMP: 24
SQ FT: 69,024
SALES (est): 3.5MM **Privately Held**
WEB: www.siriannihardwoods.com
SIC: 2421 Sawmills & planing mills, general

Palatine Bridge
Montgomery County

(G-12842)
LEE NEWSPAPERS INC
6113 State Highway 5 (13428)
PHONE..................................518 673-3237
Fred Lee, *Principal*
EMP: 12
SALES (est): 807.4K **Privately Held**
SIC: 2711 Newspapers, publishing & printing

(G-12843)
LEE PUBLICATIONS INC (PA)
Also Called: Waste Management
6113 State Highway 5 (13428-2809)
P.O. Box 121 (13428-0121)
PHONE..................................518 673-3237
Fred Lee, *President*
Janet Lee Button, *Treasurer*
Mark Lee, *Admin Sec*
EMP: 99
SQ FT: 25,000
SALES (est): 11.9MM **Privately Held**
WEB: www.leepub.com
SIC: 2711 Newspapers, publishing & printing

Palenville
Greene County

(G-12844)
NATIONAL PARACHUTE INDUSTRIES
Also Called: National Parachute Industry
78 White Rd Extensio (12463)
P.O. Box 245 (12463-0245)
PHONE..................................908 782-1646
Larry Krueger, *President*
Jeanette Krueger, *Admin Sec*
EMP: 20 **EST:** 1976
SQ FT: 6,000
SALES (est): 1.2MM **Privately Held**
SIC: 2399 Parachutes

(G-12845)
PRECISION TOOL AND MFG
314 Pennsylvania Ave (12463-2615)
P.O. Box 160 (12463-0160)
PHONE..................................518 678-3130
Alan Schneck, *President*
EMP: 27
SALES (est): 3.2MM **Privately Held**
SIC: 3599 Machine shop, jobbing & repair

Palisades
Rockland County

(G-12846)
HISTORY PUBLISHING COMPANY LLC
173 Route 9w (10964-1616)
P.O. Box 700 (10964-0700)
PHONE..................................845 398-8161
Don Bracken, *Mng Member*
EMP: 6
SALES (est): 462.2K **Privately Held**
WEB: www.historypublishingco.com
SIC: 2741 Posters: publishing only, not printed on site

(G-12847)
SKAE POWER SOLUTIONS LLC (PA)
348 Route 9w (10964-1200)
P.O. Box 615 (10964-0615)
PHONE..................................845 365-9103
Jason Ketcham, *Engineer*
Michael Patrizio, *Engineer*
Anthony Russo, *Engineer*
Russ Mykytyn, *Accounts Exec*
Andrew Asfendis, *Info Tech Mgr*
EMP: 30
SQ FT: 6,000
SALES (est): 7.9MM **Privately Held**
WEB: www.skaepower.com
SIC: 3699 8711 Electrical equipment & supplies; consulting engineer

(G-12848)
TRI VALLEY IRON INC
700 Oak Tree Rd (10964-1533)
P.O. Box 234 (10964-0234)
PHONE..................................845 365-1013
Nancy Bucciarelli, *President*
James McCarthy, *Vice Pres*
EMP: 15
SALES: 1.5MM **Privately Held**
SIC: 3312 Bars, iron: made in steel mills

(G-12849)
VELL COMPANY INC
700 Oak Tree Rd (10964-1533)
P.O. Box 622 (10964-0622)
PHONE..................................845 365-1013
Larry Bucciarelli, *Principal*
EMP: 8
SALES (est): 1MM **Privately Held**
SIC: 3312 Bars & bar shapes, steel, hot-rolled

Palmyra
Wayne County

(G-12850)
FAIRBANKS MORSE ENGINE
1666 Division St (14522-9383)
PHONE..................................608 364-8465
EMP: 6
SALES (est): 1.4MM **Privately Held**
SIC: 3694 Engine electrical equipment

(G-12851)
FARADYNE MOTORS LLC
Also Called: Juan Motors
2077 Division St (14522-9211)
PHONE..................................315 331-5985
Mellisa Kidd, *Mng Member*
Juan Lugo, *Mng Member*
Colin R Sabol, *Director*
▲ **EMP:** 14
SQ FT: 28,000
SALES (est): 4.2MM **Publicly Held**
WEB: www.faradynemotors.com
SIC: 3621 Motors, electric
PA: Xylem Inc.
1 International Dr
Rye Brook NY 10573

(G-12852)
FINZER HOLDING LLC
Also Called: Finzer Roller New York
2085 Division St (14522-9211)
PHONE..................................315 597-1147
David Finzer, *President*
Kevin Byer, *Plant Mgr*
EMP: 27
SALES (corp-wide): 12.7MM **Privately Held**
SIC: 3069 3061 Roll coverings, rubber; mechanical rubber goods
PA: Finzer Holding Llc
129 Rawls Rd
Des Plaines IL 60018
847 390-6200

(G-12853)
GARLOCK SEALING TECH LLC
1666 Division St (14522-9350)
PHONE..................................315 597-4811
Paul Baldetti, *President*
EMP: 950
SALES (corp-wide): 1.3B **Publicly Held**
SIC: 3053 Gaskets, packing & sealing devices
HQ: Garlock Sealing Technologies Llc
1666 Division St
Palmyra NY 14522
315 597-4811

(G-12854)
GENTNER PRECISION COMPONENTS
406 Stafford Rd (14522-9426)
PHONE..................................315 597-5734
Richard Genter, *President*
John E Gentner Jr, *Principal*
EMP: 5
SALES (est): 438.4K **Privately Held**
SIC: 3599 Machine shop, jobbing & repair

(G-12855)
JRLON INC
4344 Fox Rd (14522-9423)
P.O. Box 244 (14522-0244)
PHONE..................................315 597-4067
James F Redmond, *President*
Lindsey Redmond, *Corp Secy*
Jerry Sprague, *Engineer*
Douglas Camp, *Sales Staff*

▲ = Import ▼=Export
◆ =Import/Export

Brandon Redmond, *Marketing Mgr*
▲ **EMP:** 80 **EST:** 1981
SQ FT: 60,000
SALES (est): 18.1MM **Privately Held**
WEB: www.jrlon.com
SIC: 2821 3566 3479 3462 Molding compounds, plastics; gears, power transmission, except automotive; painting, coating & hot dipping; iron & steel forgings; paints & allied products

(G-12856)
KYLE R LAWRENCE ELECTRIC INC
101 Hyde Pkwy (14522-1209)
PHONE.................315 502-4181
Kyle R Lawrence, *Ch of Bd*
EMP: 5
SALES (est): 397.8K **Privately Held**
SIC: 3699 Electrical equipment & supplies

(G-12857)
LABCO OF PALMYRA INC
904 Canandaigua Rd (14522-9701)
P.O. Box 216 (14522-0216)
PHONE.................315 597-5202
Gary Laberge, *President*
Lynette McTigue, *Vice Pres*
Sharyl Digiovanni, *Treasurer*
Marybeth Laberge, *Admin Sec*
EMP: 12
SQ FT: 7,800
SALES (est): 1.8MM **Privately Held**
WEB: www.labco-ny.com
SIC: 3599 Machine shop, jobbing & repair

(G-12858)
MODERN COATING AND RESEARCH
400 E Main St (14522-1132)
PHONE.................315 597-3517
James Deagman, *President*
Jae Chatfield, *Office Mgr*
James Hollingsworth, *Shareholder*
Kevin Marvin, *Administration*
EMP: 11
SQ FT: 26,000
SALES (est): 700K **Privately Held**
WEB: www.moderncoatings.com
SIC: 3479 Coating of metals & formed products

(G-12859)
PAUL T FREUND CORPORATION (PA)
216 Park Dr (14522-1114)
P.O. Box 475 (14522-0475)
PHONE.................315 597-4873
Dennis Baron, *President*
Paul T Freund Jr, *Corp Secy*
Thomas Farnham, *Vice Pres*
▲ **EMP:** 85
SQ FT: 126,000
SALES (est): 7.2MM **Privately Held**
WEB: www.freundcarton.com
SIC: 2652 Filing boxes, paperboard: made from purchased materials

Parish
Oswego County

(G-12860)
BIOSPHERIX LTD
Also Called: Biospherix Medical
25 Union St (13131)
PHONE.................315 387-3414
Sue Lavere, *Purchasing*
Rich Ruffos, *Research*
Ray Gould, *Sales Mgr*
Mike Brownell, *Sales Staff*
Peter Yerden, *Sales Staff*
EMP: 50
SQ FT: 30,000
SALES (est): 10.6MM **Privately Held**
WEB: www.biospherix.com
SIC: 3821 Laboratory equipment: fume hoods, distillation racks, etc.

Patchogue
Suffolk County

(G-12861)
BAKERY INNOVATIVE TECH CORP
139 N Ocean Ave (11772-2018)
PHONE.................631 758-3081
Robert White, *President*
Robert Andersen, *Engineer*
EMP: 15
SQ FT: 8,000
SALES (est): 1.5MM **Privately Held**
WEB: www.bit-corp.com
SIC: 3625 Motor control accessories, including overload relays

(G-12862)
BAYSHORE ELECTRIC MOTORS
Also Called: Bayshore Motors
33 Suffolk Ave (11772-1651)
PHONE.................631 475-1397
Paul Phillips, *Owner*
EMP: 5
SALES (est): 220.1K **Privately Held**
SIC: 7694 Electric motor repair

(G-12863)
CLASSIC LABELS INC
217 River Ave (11772-3312)
PHONE.................631 467-2300
John Orta, *President*
EMP: 21 **EST:** 1978
SQ FT: 29,000
SALES (est): 2MM **Privately Held**
WEB: www.classiclabels.com
SIC: 2759 2891 2672 2671 Labels & seals: printing; adhesives & sealants; coated & laminated paper; packaging paper & plastics film, coated & laminated

(G-12864)
DEPOT LABEL COMPANY INC
Also Called: Colonial Label
217 River Ave (11772-3312)
PHONE.................631 467-2952
Mike Juliano, *President*
EMP: 8
SALES (est): 1.9MM **Privately Held**
SIC: 2679 5013 2671 2241 Tags & labels, paper; automotive supplies & parts; packaging paper & plastics film, coated & laminated; narrow fabric mills

(G-12865)
EQUICHECK LLC
20 Medford Ave Ste 7 (11772-1220)
PHONE.................631 987-6356
Warren Rothstein, *Owner*
Rob Visalli, *Case Mgr*
EMP: 5
SALES (est): 300K **Privately Held**
WEB: www.equicheck.com
SIC: 3851 Lens coating, ophthalmic

(G-12866)
HOPTRON BREWTIQUE
22 W Main St Ste 11 (11772-3007)
PHONE.................631 438-0296
Amanda Danielsen, *Owner*
EMP: 8
SALES (est): 578.5K **Privately Held**
SIC: 2082 5182 Beer (alcoholic beverage); wine coolers, alcoholic

(G-12867)
JABO AGRICULTURAL INC
9 Northwood Ln (11772-2228)
PHONE.................631 475-1800
Robert Muchnick, *CEO*
Jacob Gurewich, *President*
EMP: 5
SQ FT: 1,000
SALES (est): 226.8K **Privately Held**
SIC: 2452 Farm & agricultural buildings, prefabricated wood

(G-12868)
JOHN LOR PUBLISHING LTD
Also Called: Islip Bulletin
20 Medford Ave Ste 1 (11772-1220)
P.O. Box 780 (11772-0780)
PHONE.................631 475-1000
John Tuthill III, *President*
Lorerir Mary Lou Cohalon, *Vice Pres*
EMP: 20 **EST:** 1950
SALES (est): 981.7K **Privately Held**
WEB: www.islipbulletin.net
SIC: 2711 Newspapers: publishing only, not printed on site

(G-12869)
KEVIN FREEMAN
Also Called: Rf Inter Science Co
414 S Service Rd Ste 119 (11772-2254)
PHONE.................631 447-5321
Kevin Freeman, *President*
EMP: 5
SALES (est): 399.6K **Privately Held**
SIC: 3827 Optical instruments & apparatus

(G-12870)
L3 TECHNOLOGIES INC
L3 Communications Narda - Atm
49 Rider Ave (11772-3915)
PHONE.................631 289-0363
Dirk Aubram, *Facilities Mgr*
Geoffrey Smith, *Branch Mgr*
EMP: 50
SALES (corp-wide): 9.5B **Publicly Held**
SIC: 3679 Microwave components
PA: L3 Technologies, Inc.
  600 3rd Ave Fl 34
  New York NY 10016
  212 697-1111

(G-12871)
NEW LIVING INC
99 Waverly Ave Apt 6d (11772-1922)
PHONE.................631 751-8819
Christine Harvey, *Principal*
EMP: 8
SALES (est): 293.7K **Privately Held**
SIC: 2711 Newspapers, publishing & printing

(G-12872)
PARIS ART LABEL CO INC
217 River Ave (11772-3312)
PHONE.................631 467-2300
Ronald P Tarantino, *Ch of Bd*
▲ **EMP:** 100 **EST:** 1925
SQ FT: 20,000
SALES (est): 21.2MM
SALES (corp-wide): 14.8B **Publicly Held**
WEB: www.parisartlabel.com
SIC: 2759 Commercial printing
HQ: Multi Packaging Solutions International Limited
  885 3rd Ave Fl 28
  New York NY 10022
  646 885-0005

(G-12873)
PATCHOGUE ADVANCE INC
Also Called: Long Island Advance
20 Medford Ave Ste 1 (11772-1220)
PHONE.................631 475-1000
John T Tuthill III, *President*
Lorelei T Tuthill, *Admin Sec*
EMP: 35 **EST:** 1821
SQ FT: 7,000
SALES (est): 1.8MM **Privately Held**
WEB: www.longislandadvance.net
SIC: 2711 Newspapers: publishing only, not printed on site

(G-12874)
PEPSI BOTTLING VENTURES LLC
Also Called: Pepsi-Cola
4141 Parklane Ave Ste 600 (11772)
PHONE.................631 772-6144
Theresa Dunton, *Manager*
EMP: 53
SALES (corp-wide): 76.5MM **Privately Held**
SIC: 2086 Carbonated soft drinks, bottled & canned
HQ: Pepsi Bottling Ventures Llc
  4141 Parklake Ave Ste 600
  Raleigh NC 27612
  919 865-2300

(G-12875)
PRINCETON LABEL & PACKAGING
217 River Ave (11772-3312)
PHONE.................609 490-0800
Donald J Guli, *President*
EMP: 35
SQ FT: 7,800
SALES (est): 6.4MM **Privately Held**
WEB: www.princetonlabel.com
SIC: 2672 7389 Coated & laminated paper; packaging & labeling services

(G-12876)
RELIABLE WELDING & FABRICATION
214 W Main St (11772-3004)
PHONE.................631 758-2637
EMP: 7
SALES (est): 490K **Privately Held**
SIC: 7692 5051 5021 1799 Welding Repair Metals Service Center Whol Furniture Special Trade Contractor

(G-12877)
SUFFOLK MCHY & PWR TL CORP (PA)
Also Called: Gschwind Group
12 Waverly Ave (11772-1902)
PHONE.................631 289-7153
Arthur F Gschwind Sr, *President*
Debbie Freyre, *General Mgr*
Tom Davies, *Director*
▼ **EMP:** 3
SQ FT: 4,000
SALES (est): 1.2MM **Privately Held**
WEB: www.timberwolf1.com
SIC: 3425 Saw blades & handsaws

(G-12878)
T & SMOOTHIE INC
499 N Service Rd Ste 83 (11772-2290)
PHONE.................631 804-6653
Tiffany Wirth, *Principal*
EMP: 6
SALES (est): 316.5K **Privately Held**
SIC: 2037 Frozen fruits & vegetables

(G-12879)
YOMAN MADEO FANO
1 S Ocean Ave (11772-3738)
PHONE.................631 438-0246
EMP: 7
SALES (est): 653.7K **Privately Held**
SIC: 2759 Business forms: printing
PA: Yoman Madeo Fano
  299 Broadway Ste 810
  New York NY

Patterson
Putnam County

(G-12880)
DICAMILLO MARBLE AND GRANITE
20 Jon Barrett Rd (12563-2164)
PHONE.................845 878-0078
Fax: 845 878-2250
EMP: 20 **EST:** 1991
SALES (est): 1.6MM **Privately Held**
SIC: 3281 Mfg Cut Stone/Products

(G-12881)
EAST HUDSON WATERSHED CORP
2 Route 164 (12563-2813)
PHONE.................845 319-6349
Peter Parsons, *President*
EMP: 5
SQ FT: 1,000
SALES: 2.2MM **Privately Held**
SIC: 3822 Auto controls regulating residntl & coml environmt & applncs

(G-12882)
GOLDEN GROUP INTERNATIONAL LTD
305 Quaker Rd (12563-2191)
P.O. Box 407, Brewster (10509-0407)
PHONE.................845 440-1025
Jacqueline Transue, *President*
Kevin Hanna, *Info Tech Mgr*
EMP: 6

SALES (est): 530K **Privately Held**
SIC: 2673 5113 3444 5199 Trash bags (plastic film); made from purchased materials; food storage & trash bags (plastic); bags, paper & disposable plastic; bins, prefabricated sheet metal; art goods & supplies

(G-12883)
JRS PHARMA LP (DH)
2981 Route 22 Ste 1 (12563-2359)
PHONE.....................845 878-8300
Josef Rettenmaier, *Partner*
J Rettenmaier America, *Partner*
Josef Otto Rettenmaier, *Partner*
J Rettenmaier Holding USA, *Partner*
Antony Gerardi, *Safety Mgr*
◆ **EMP:** 48
SQ FT: 46,000
SALES (est): 22.6MM **Privately Held**
SIC: 2834 Druggists' preparations (pharmaceuticals)
HQ: Jrs Pharma Gmbh & Co. Kg
   Holzmuhle 1
   Rosenberg 73494
   796 715-2312

(G-12884)
REELEX PACKAGING SOLUTIONS INC
39 Jon Barrett Rd (12563-2165)
PHONE.....................845 878-7878
Thomas R Copp, *President*
Frank Kotzur, *Vice Pres*
Ronald Zajac, *Vice Pres*
Thomas Briggs, *Opers Mgr*
Crystal Newman, *Purchasing*
▲ **EMP:** 40
SQ FT: 50,000
SALES (est): 9.2MM **Privately Held**
SIC: 3549 6794 Metalworking machinery; patent buying, licensing, leasing
PA: Da Capo Al Fine Ltd
   81 Stone Crop Ln
   Cold Spring NY 10516
   845 265-2011

(G-12885)
SPANISH ARTISAN WINE GROUP LLC
Also Called: Spanish Artisan Wine Group Ltd
370 Cushman Rd (12563-2638)
PHONE.....................914 414-6982
Gerry Dawes, *Principal*
Gerald Dawes, *Mng Member*
EMP: 5
SALES (est): 1MM **Privately Held**
SIC: 2084 5182 7389 Wines; neutral spirits; brokers, business: buying & selling business enterprises

(G-12886)
TAUMEL METALFORMING CORP
Also Called: Taumel Assembly Systems
25 Jon Barrett Rd (12563-2165)
PHONE.....................845 878-3100
Ernest Bodmer, *President*
Tony A Huber, *Vice Pres*
Werner Stutz, *Vice Pres*
Peter Bodmer, *Treasurer*
Phil Huber, *Manager*
EMP: 8
SQ FT: 10,000
SALES (est): 839.7K **Privately Held**
WEB: www.taumel.com
SIC: 3542 Machine tools, metal forming type

(G-12887)
WERLATONE INC
17 Jon Barrett Rd (12563-2165)
P.O. Box 47, Brewster (10509-0047)
PHONE.....................845 278-2220
Glen C Werlau, *Ch of Bd*
Austin Kile, *Corp Secy*
Werner Schuster, *Mfg Spvr*
Jim Kakadeles, *Purch Mgr*
Giny Coleman, *Purchasing*
EMP: 38 **EST:** 1965
SQ FT: 7,000
SALES (est): 7.5MM **Privately Held**
WEB: www.werlatone.com
SIC: 3679 Microwave components; electronic circuits

Pattersonville
Schenectady County

(G-12888)
DJ PIRRONE INDUSTRIES INC
8865 Mariaville Rd (12137-3007)
PHONE.....................518 864-5496
David Pirrone, *Principal*
EMP: 5
SALES (est): 234.2K **Privately Held**
SIC: 3999 Manufacturing industries

Pavilion
Genesee County

(G-12889)
HANSON AGGREGATES NEW YORK LLC
6895 Ellicott Street Rd (14525-9614)
PHONE.....................585 638-5841
Daniel M Meehan, *Principal*
Scott Wheaton, *Plant Mgr*
Dennis Dolan, *Controller*
Doug Fuess, *VP Sales*
EMP: 15
SALES (corp-wide): 20.3B **Privately Held**
SIC: 3273 Ready-mixed concrete
HQ: Hanson Aggregates New York Llc
   8505 Freport Pkwy Ste 500
   Irving TX 75063

(G-12890)
WNY CHEESE ENTERPRISE LLC
Also Called: Craigs Station Cheese
1842 Craig Rd (14525-9200)
PHONE.....................585 243-6516
Gordon Lafferty, *General Mgr*
EMP: 20
SALES (est): 671.8K
SALES (corp-wide): 14.6B **Privately Held**
SIC: 2022 Cheese, natural & processed
PA: Dairy Farmers Of America, Inc.
   1405 N 98th St
   Kansas City KS 66111
   816 801-6455

(G-12891)
WNY ENTERPRISE LLC
1840 Craig Rd (14525-9200)
PHONE.....................585 243-6514
Brian Paris, *General Mgr*
EMP: 20
SALES (est): 6.6MM
SALES (corp-wide): 14.6B **Privately Held**
SIC: 2026 Milk processing (pasteurizing, homogenizing, bottling)
PA: Dairy Farmers Of America, Inc.
   1405 N 98th St
   Kansas City KS 66111
   816 801-6455

Pawling
Dutchess County

(G-12892)
JOE PIETRYKA INCORPORATED (PA)
85 Charles Colman Blvd (12564-1160)
PHONE.....................845 855-1201
Joseph W Pietryka, *Ch of Bd*
EMP: 49
SQ FT: 65,000
SALES (est): 13.1MM **Privately Held**
WEB: www.dwconcepts.net
SIC: 3089 Injection molded finished plastic products

(G-12893)
PAWLING CORPORATION (PA)
Also Called: Pawling Engineered Products
157 Charles Colman Blvd (12564-1188)
PHONE.....................845 855-1000
Craig Busby, *President*
Roger W Smith, *Chairman*
John Rickert, *COO*
Gregory S Holen, *Vice Pres*
John C Rickert, *Vice Pres*
▼ **EMP:** 180
SQ FT: 250,000
SALES (est): 44MM **Privately Held**
WEB: www.pawling.com
SIC: 3061 3069 3089 2821 Mechanical rubber goods; custom compounding of rubber materials; rubber floor coverings, mats & wallcoverings; mats or matting, rubber; molding primary plastic; extruded finished plastic products; silicone resins

(G-12894)
PAWLING ENGINEERED PDTS INC
157 Charles Colman Blvd (12564-1121)
PHONE.....................845 855-1000
Craig Busby, *President*
John Rickert, *Vice Pres*
EMP: 120
SQ FT: 250,000
SALES (est): 9.5MM **Privately Held**
SIC: 3061 3089 Mechanical rubber goods; extruded finished plastic products

Pearl River
Rockland County

(G-12895)
C B MANAGEMENT SERVICES INC
Also Called: Beitals Aquarium Sales & Svc
73 S Pearl St (10965-2235)
PHONE.....................845 735-2300
Craig Beital, *President*
Creig Beital, *President*
EMP: 13
SQ FT: 5,000
SALES (est): 970K **Privately Held**
WEB: www.cbmanagementservices.com
SIC: 3231 5999 7389 Aquariums & reflectors, glass; aquarium supplies; aquarium design & maintenance

(G-12896)
FIVE STAR MILLWORK LLC
6 E Dexter Plz (10965-2360)
PHONE.....................845 920-0247
Marco Santos,
Dario Fonseca,
Tiago Fonseca,
EMP: 12
SQ FT: 15,000
SALES (est): 4MM **Privately Held**
SIC: 2431 Millwork

(G-12897)
FUJITSU NTWRK CMMNICATIONS INC
2 Blue Hill Plz Ste 1609 (10965-3115)
PHONE.....................845 731-2000
Alexandre Attal, *Exec VP*
Bob Demarco, *Manager*
EMP: 18
SALES (corp-wide): 38.4B **Privately Held**
WEB: www.fnc.fujitsu.com
SIC: 3661 8731 3663 Fiber optics communications equipment; commercial physical research; radio & TV communications equipment
HQ: Fujitsu Network Communications, Inc.
   2801 Telecom Pkwy
   Richardson TX 75082

(G-12898)
HEARTLAND COMMERCE INC
Also Called: Pcamerica
1 Blue Hill Plz Ste 16 (10965-3100)
PHONE.....................845 920-0800
David J Gosman, *CEO*
EMP: 21
SALES (corp-wide): 3.9B **Publicly Held**
SIC: 7372 Business oriented computer software
HQ: Heartland Commerce, Inc.
   90 Nassau St Fl 2
   Princeton NJ 08542
   609 683-3831

(G-12899)
HNST MOLD INSPECTIONS LLC (PA)
87 S Nauraushaun Rd (10965-2919)
PHONE.....................845 215-9258
John Skelly, *Mng Member*
EMP: 4 **EST:** 2010
SALES (est): 1.6MM **Privately Held**
SIC: 3544 Industrial molds

(G-12900)
HUDSON TECHNOLOGIES COMPANY (HQ)
1 Blue Hill Plz Ste 1541 (10965-3110)
PHONE.....................845 735-6000
Kevin Zugibe, *Ch of Bd*
Briann Coleman, *President*
Stephen Mandracchia, *Vice Pres*
EMP: 48
SQ FT: 4,500
SALES: 48.6MM **Publicly Held**
SIC: 2869 Fluorinated hydrocarbon gases

(G-12901)
HUNTER DOUGLAS INC (DH)
1 Blue Hill Plz Ste 1569 (10965-6101)
PHONE.....................845 664-7000
Ralph Sonnenberg, *Ch of Bd*
Marvin B Hopkins, *President*
David H Sonnenberg, *President*
Marko H Sonnenberg, *President*
Ron Rice, *General Mgr*
▲ **EMP:** 100
SQ FT: 32,000
SALES (est): 2.7B **Privately Held**
WEB: www.hunterdouglas.com
SIC: 2591 3444 5084 Window blinds; window shades; venetian blinds; sheet metalwork; industrial machinery & equipment
HQ: Hunter Douglas N.V.
   Piekstraat 2
   Rotterdam 3071
   104 869-911

(G-12902)
HUNTS POINT CLEAN ENERGY LLC
Also Called: Hpce
401 N Middletown Rd (10965-1298)
PHONE.....................203 451-5143
Alfredo Forte,
Steven Switzen,
EMP: 6
SQ FT: 63,000
SALES (est): 267.4K **Privately Held**
SIC: 2869 Methyl alcohol, synthetic methanol

(G-12903)
JANE BAKES INC
40 S Main St (10965-2425)
PHONE.....................845 920-1100
Jane Carroll, *Principal*
EMP: 5
SALES (est): 150K **Privately Held**
SIC: 2051 Bakery: wholesale or wholesale/retail combined

(G-12904)
KRAFT HAT MANUFACTURERS INC
7 Veterans Pkwy (10965-1328)
PHONE.....................845 735-6200
Israel Rosenzweig, *President*
Steven Rosenzweig, *Corp Secy*
Lawrence Rosenzweig, *Vice Pres*
▲ **EMP:** 100
SQ FT: 34,000
SALES (est): 9.4MM **Privately Held**
WEB: www.krafthat.com
SIC: 2353 Hats & caps; millinery

(G-12905)
LEVOLOR INC (DH)
Also Called: Levolor Window Furnishings Inc
1 Blue Hill Plz (10965-3104)
PHONE.....................845 664-7000
Marvin B Hopkins, *President*
▲ **EMP:** 300
SALES (est): 55.3MM **Privately Held**
SIC: 2591 Window blinds; blinds vertical
HQ: Hunter Douglas Inc.
   1 Blue Hill Plz Ste 1569
   Pearl River NY 10965
   845 664-7000

GEOGRAPHIC SECTION

Pelham - Westchester County (G-12933)

(G-12906)
LUST FOR LIFE FOOTWEAR LLC
48 S Main St (10965-2427)
PHONE 646 732-9742
Steven Berend, *Branch Mgr*
EMP: 10
SALES (corp-wide): 2.4MM **Privately Held**
SIC: 3021 5139 Protective footwear, rubber or plastic; footwear
PA: Lust For Life Footwear, Llc
   1086 Teaneck Rd Ste 3d
   Teaneck NJ 07666
   646 732-9742

(G-12907)
PIEZO ELECTRONICS RESEARCH
Also Called: Peri
30 Walter St (10965-1722)
PHONE 845 735-9349
David Marsh, *President*
EMP: 12 EST: 1946
SQ FT: 3,000
SALES: 1MM **Privately Held**
SIC: 3674 7389 Solid state electronic devices; packaging & labeling services

(G-12908)
PROTEIN SCIENCES CORPORATION
401 N Middletown Rd (10965-1298)
PHONE 203 686-0800
Bill Edsall, *Project Mgr*
Manon M J Cox, *Branch Mgr*
Joseph Revello, *Director*
EMP: 27
SALES (corp-wide): 24.5MM **Privately Held**
SIC: 2834 Pharmaceutical preparations
PA: Protein Sciences Corporation
   1000 Research Pkwy
   Meriden CT 06450
   203 686-0800

(G-12909)
QUALITY GRAPHICS TRI STATE
171 Center St (10965-1630)
PHONE 845 735-2523
Phyllis Schweizer, *President*
Bruce Schweizer, *Vice Pres*
EMP: 5
SALES (est): 788.6K **Privately Held**
SIC: 2752 Commercial printing, offset

(G-12910)
RK PHARMA INC
401 Milltown Rd Bldg (10965)
PHONE 646 884-3765
George Roby Thomas, *CEO*
Ravishanker Kovi, *Chairman*
Michael Chang, *Director*
EMP: 5
SALES: 2MM **Privately Held**
SIC: 2834 Pharmaceutical preparations

(G-12911)
SKIN PRINTS INC
63 Walter St (10965-1723)
PHONE 845 920-8756
Diane Kaufman, *President*
EMP: 3
SQ FT: 10,000
SALES (est): 1.2MM **Privately Held**
SIC: 2269 Finishing plants

(G-12912)
UTILITY ENGINEERING CO
40 Walter St (10965-1795)
PHONE 845 735-8900
George Huston, *President*
EMP: 10
SQ FT: 7,400
SALES (est): 620K **Privately Held**
WEB: www.utilitydisplays.com
SIC: 3496 Miscellaneous fabricated wire products

(G-12913)
WYETH HOLDINGS LLC
Also Called: Wyeth Pharmaceutical Division
401 N Middletown Rd (10965-1298)
PHONE 845 602-5000
David Zisa, *Principal*
James S Morrissey, *Project Leader*
EMP: 100
SALES (corp-wide): 52.5B **Publicly Held**
SIC: 2834 2836 3842 3841 Pharmaceutical preparations; biological products, except diagnostic; surgical appliances & supplies; surgical & medical instruments; ophthalmic goods; chemical preparations
HQ: Wyeth Holdings Llc
   5 Giralda Farms
   Madison NJ 07940

Peconic
Suffolk County

(G-12914)
DORSET FARMS INC
Also Called: Lenz
38355 Main Rd (11958-1515)
P.O. Box 28 (11958-0028)
PHONE 631 734-6010
Peter Carroll, *President*
Deborah Carroll, *Vice Pres*
▲ EMP: 10
SALES (est): 1.1MM **Privately Held**
SIC: 2084 Wines

(G-12915)
J PETROCELLI WINE CELLARS LLC
Also Called: Raphael
39390 Route 25 (11958-1501)
P.O. Box 17 (11958-0017)
PHONE 631 765-1100
Chip Cheek, *Sales Mgr*
Joann Deangelo, *Sales Staff*
Jack Petrocelli, *Mng Member*
▲ EMP: 25
SALES: 450K **Privately Held**
SIC: 2084 5921 Wines; wine

(G-12916)
PINDAR VINEYARDS LLC
37645 Route 25 (11958-1514)
P.O. Box 332 (11958-0332)
PHONE 631 734-6200
Herdotes Damianos, *Mng Member*
EMP: 20
SQ FT: 5,000
SALES (est): 2.2MM **Privately Held**
WEB: www.pindar.net
SIC: 2084 Wines

Peekskill
Westchester County

(G-12917)
BASF CORPORATION
1057 Lower South St (10566-5302)
PHONE 914 737-2554
Daniel S Gulley, *Branch Mgr*
EMP: 344
SALES (corp-wide): 76B **Privately Held**
WEB: www.basf.com
SIC: 2869 Industrial organic chemicals
HQ: Basf Corporation
   100 Park Ave
   Florham Park NJ 07932
   973 245-6000

(G-12918)
CANDLES BY FOSTER
810 South St (10566-3431)
P.O. Box 89 (10566-0089)
PHONE 914 739-9226
Donald Foster, *Owner*
EMP: 6
SQ FT: 6,500
SALES (est): 355.5K **Privately Held**
SIC: 3999 5999 Candles; candle shops

(G-12919)
ELEVATOR ACCESSORIES MFG
Also Called: Paxton Metal Craft Division
1035 Howard St 37 (10566-2819)
P.O. Box 430 (10566-0430)
PHONE 914 739-7004
Alan Messing, *President*
Tracey Johnson, *General Mgr*
John Johnson, *Vice Pres*
Vicki Messing, *Admin Sec*
EMP: 12
SALES (est): 2.2MM **Privately Held**
SIC: 3534 3441 3446 3444 Elevators & equipment; fabricated structural metal; architectural metalwork; sheet metalwork

(G-12920)
GIULIANTE MACHINE TOOL INC
12 John Walsh Blvd (10566-5323)
PHONE 914 835-0008
Martha Giuliante, *President*
Armando Giuliante, *Vice Pres*
Marcelo Giuliante, *Vice Pres*
EMP: 25
SQ FT: 27,000
SALES: 4.5MM **Privately Held**
WEB: www.gmtgear.com
SIC: 3599 Machine shop, jobbing & repair

(G-12921)
HAT FACTORY FURNITURE CO
Also Called: Hudson Cabinetry Design
1000 N Division St Ste 8 (10566-1830)
PHONE 914 788-6288
Douglas Bialor, *Owner*
EMP: 6 EST: 1998
SALES (est): 119.7K **Privately Held**
SIC: 3553 Cabinet makers' machinery

(G-12922)
HUDSON MIRROR LLC
Also Called: Mirrorlite Superscript
710 Washington St (10566-5418)
PHONE 914 930-8906
Dwayne Reith, *Vice Pres*
Gary Reith,
EMP: 25
SQ FT: 2,000
SALES: 4MM **Privately Held**
SIC: 3827 Mirrors, optical

(G-12923)
RESCUESTUFF INC
962 Washington St (10566-5816)
PHONE 718 318-7570
Greg Grimaldi, *President*
Seth Porter, *CFO*
EMP: 5
SQ FT: 2,000
SALES: 250K **Privately Held**
WEB: www.rescuestuff.net
SIC: 2395 2262 Embroidery products, except schiffli machine; screen printing: manmade fiber & silk broadwoven fabrics

(G-12924)
RMS PACKAGING INC
Also Called: Aurora Sef
1050 Lower South St (10566-5313)
PHONE 914 205-2070
Sheldon Rosenberg, *President*
▲ EMP: 16
SALES (est): 4.4MM **Privately Held**
SIC: 2671 Plastic film, coated or laminated for packaging

(G-12925)
SD CHRISTIE ASSOCIATES INC
424 Central Ave Ste 5 (10566-2056)
P.O. Box 5158, Cary NC (27512-5158)
PHONE 914 734-1800
Thomas Christie, *President*
EMP: 5
SALES (est): 503.9K **Privately Held**
SIC: 3069 5085 Molded rubber products; mattress protectors, rubber; fasteners, industrial: nuts, bolts, screws, etc.; rubber goods, mechanical

(G-12926)
VIVID RGB LIGHTING LLC
824 Main St Ste 1 (10566-2052)
PHONE 718 635-0817
Brian Fassett, *Managing Dir*
EMP: 7
SQ FT: 3,000
SALES (est): 770.9K **Privately Held**
SIC: 3648 Lighting equipment

(G-12927)
W DESIGNE INC
Also Called: Wood Design
5 John Walsh Blvd (10566-5307)
PHONE 914 736-1058
Alex Bernabo, *President*
Gladys Pagan, *Manager*
▲ EMP: 20
SQ FT: 25,000
SALES (est): 3.1MM **Privately Held**
SIC: 2434 2517 Wood kitchen cabinets; wood television & radio cabinets

(G-12928)
WALTER G LEGGE COMPANY INC
Also Called: Legge System
444 Central Ave (10566-2003)
PHONE 914 737-5040
Elizabeth Bauer, *President*
Jane Fejes, *General Mgr*
▲ EMP: 9 EST: 1936
SQ FT: 10,000
SALES (est): 1.6MM **Privately Held**
WEB: www.leggesystems.com
SIC: 2842 3272 3679 Sanitation preparations, disinfectants & deodorants; tile, precast terrazzo or concrete; power supplies, all types: static

(G-12929)
WESTCHESTER TECHNOLOGIES INC
8 John Walsh Blvd Ste 311 (10566-5347)
PHONE 914 736-1034
Roger Prahl, *CEO*
EMP: 23
SQ FT: 4,000
SALES: 4.1MM **Privately Held**
WEB: www.microoptics.com
SIC: 3827 Optical instruments & apparatus

(G-12930)
WESTYPO PRINTERS INC
540 Harrison Ave (10566-2318)
PHONE 914 737-7394
Mike Mc Guggart, *President*
Teri Mc Guggart, *Treasurer*
EMP: 6 EST: 1964
SQ FT: 8,000
SALES (est): 535.1K **Privately Held**
SIC: 2752 2759 Commercial printing, offset; commercial printing

(G-12931)
WHITE PLAINS COAT APRON CO INC
Also Called: White Plains Linen
4 John Walsh Blvd (10566-5323)
PHONE 914 736-2610
Allan Botchman, *Ch of Bd*
Bruce Botchman, *President*
Keith Botchman, *Vice Pres*
Len Labonia, *Vice Pres*
Thomas Moscati, *VP Sales*
EMP: 7
SQ FT: 30,000
SALES (est): 2.3MM **Privately Held**
SIC: 2389 7213 Uniforms & vestments; apron supply

Pelham
Westchester County

(G-12932)
ARCHIE COMIC PUBLICATIONS INC
Also Called: Archie Comics Publishers
629 Fifth Ave Ste 100 (10803-3714)
PHONE 914 381-5155
Michael Silberkleit, *Chairman*
Steve Mooar, *Vice Pres*
Paul Kaminski, *Exec Dir*
Alex Segura, *Exec Dir*
Jonathan Betancourt, *Director*
EMP: 75 EST: 1939
SQ FT: 10,000
SALES (est): 12.1MM **Privately Held**
WEB: www.archiecomics.com
SIC: 2721 Comic books: publishing only, not printed on site

(G-12933)
BANK-MILLER CO INC
333 Fifth Ave (10803-1203)
PHONE 914 227-9357
Steven Bank, *President*
▲ EMP: 20
SQ FT: 5,500

Pelham - Westchester County (G-12934)

SALES (est): 2.6MM Privately Held
WEB: www.bankmiller.com
SIC: 2259 2339 5131 Convertors, knit goods; women's & misses' outerwear; textile converters

(G-12934)
EASTCO MANUFACTURING CORP
Also Called: K & S & East
323 Fifth Ave (10803-1203)
PHONE..................914 738-5667
Jack Koff, *President*
Philip Schwartzman, *Vice Pres*
EMP: 12
SQ FT: 5,000
SALES (est): 2.3MM Privately Held
SIC: 3699 Electrical equipment & supplies

(G-12935)
ENVENT SYSTEMS INC
62 Harmon Ave (10803-1708)
PHONE..................646 294-6980
Michael Curtin, *President*
EMP: 6
SALES: 2MM Privately Held
SIC: 3571 7389 Electronic computers;

(G-12936)
IMPERIA MASONRY SUPPLY CORP (PA)
57 Canal Rd (10803-2706)
PHONE..................914 738-0900
Joseph Imperia, *President*
Lisa Carabello, *Admin Sec*
▲ EMP: 32 EST: 1927
SQ FT: 8,400
SALES (est): 3.2MM Privately Held
WEB: www.imperiabros.com
SIC: 3271 5031 5032 5211 Blocks, concrete or cinder: standard; lumber, plywood & millwork; brick, stone & related material; brick, except refractory; stone, crushed or broken; lumber & other building materials; lumber products; brick; masonry materials & supplies

(G-12937)
MANACRAFT PRECISION INC
945 Spring Rd (10803-2714)
PHONE..................914 654-0967
Richard Osterer, *President*
EMP: 10 EST: 1946
SQ FT: 3,000
SALES (est): 1.2MM Privately Held
SIC: 3451 Screw machine products

(G-12938)
SHORELINE PUBLISHING INC
629 Fifth Ave Ste B01 (10803-3708)
PHONE..................914 738-7869
Edward Shapiro, *President*
EMP: 7
SQ FT: 1,000
SALES (est): 941.3K Privately Held
WEB: www.shorelinepub.com
SIC: 2721 2752 Magazines: publishing only, not printed on site; commercial printing, offset

Penfield
Monroe County

(G-12939)
ALUMI-TECH LLC
1640 Harris Rd (14526-1816)
PHONE..................585 663-7010
James Putnam,
EMP: 8
SQ FT: 2,500
SALES (est): 103.5K Privately Held
WEB: www.saddlestackers.com
SIC: 3354 Aluminum extruded products

(G-12940)
DOLOMITE PRODUCTS COMPANY INC
746 Whalen Rd (14526-1022)
PHONE..................585 586-2568
Pat Tooley, *Branch Mgr*
EMP: 20
SQ FT: 2,280
SALES (corp-wide): 29.7B Privately Held
WEB: www.dolomitegroup.com
SIC: 1429 Trap rock, crushed & broken-quarrying
HQ: Dolomite Products Company Inc.
1150 Penfield Rd
Rochester NY 14625
315 524-1998

(G-12941)
IRPENSCOM
4 Katsura Ct (14526-2612)
PHONE..................585 507-7997
Sabatino Agnitti Jr, *Owner*
EMP: 5
SALES (est): 343.2K Privately Held
SIC: 3571 Electronic computers

(G-12942)
NIFTY BAR GRINDING & CUTTING
450 Whitney Rd (14526-2326)
PHONE..................585 381-0450
John Raimondi, *President*
EMP: 23 EST: 1967
SQ FT: 24,000
SALES (est): 5MM Privately Held
WEB: www.niftybar.com
SIC: 3541 Machine tools, metal cutting type

(G-12943)
RANGE REPAIR WAREHOUSE
421 Penbrooke Dr Ste 2 (14526-2045)
PHONE..................585 235-0980
Paul V Ciminelli, *Owner*
EMP: 5
SALES (est): 274.5K Privately Held
SIC: 3499 Fabricated metal products

(G-12944)
ROBINSON TOOLS LLC
Also Called: Garco
477 Whitney Rd (14526-2328)
PHONE..................585 586-5432
James D Keppel, *President*
EMP: 7 EST: 1836
SQ FT: 5,000
SALES (est): 650K Privately Held
WEB: www.robinsontools.com
SIC: 3423 Hand & edge tools

(G-12945)
SCHNEIDER ELECTRIC USA INC
441 Penbrooke Dr Ste 9 (14526-2046)
PHONE..................585 377-1313
Brian Hoffman, *Manager*
EMP: 11
SALES (corp-wide): 200.4K Privately Held
WEB: www.squared.com
SIC: 3612 Transformers, except electric
HQ: Schneider Electric Usa, Inc.
800 Federal St
Andover MA 01810
978 975-9600

(G-12946)
THERMO FISHER SCIENTIFIC INC
1935 Penfield Rd (14526-1434)
PHONE..................585 899-7780
EMP: 47
SALES (corp-wide): 20.9B Publicly Held
SIC: 3826 Analytical instruments
PA: Thermo Fisher Scientific Inc.
168 3rd Ave
Waltham MA 02451
781 622-1000

(G-12947)
VIEWSPORT INTERNATIONAL INC
11 Feathery Cir (14526-2816)
PHONE..................585 259-1562
Benjamin Wood, *President*
EMP: 3
SALES: 5.7MM Privately Held
SIC: 2396 7389 Screen printing on fabric articles;

Penn Yan
Yates County

(G-12948)
ANTHONY ROAD WINE CO INC
1020 Anthony Rd (14527-9632)
PHONE..................315 536-2182
John Martini, *President*
Sarah Eighmey, *General Mgr*
Ann Martini, *Vice Pres*
Elizabeth Castner, *Manager*
EMP: 15
SQ FT: 3,800
SALES (est): 1.8MM Privately Held
WEB: www.anthonyroadwine.com
SIC: 2084 Wines

(G-12949)
BIRKETT MILLS (PA)
163 Main St Ste 2 (14527-1284)
PHONE..................315 536-3311
Wayne W Wagner, *President*
Jeffrey S Gifford, *Exec VP*
Cliff Orr, *Sls & Mktg Exec*
Brian McFetridge, *CFO*
Wayne Agner, *Manager*
◆ EMP: 5 EST: 1797
SQ FT: 12,018
SALES (est): 7.8MM Privately Held
WEB: www.thebirkettmills.com
SIC: 2041 5999 5261 Flour & other grain mill products; farm equipment & supplies; nurseries & garden centers; lawn & garden supplies

(G-12950)
BIRKETT MILLS
163 Main St Ste 3 (14527-1284)
PHONE..................315 536-4112
Jeff Gifford, *Manager*
EMP: 32
SQ FT: 60,455
SALES (corp-wide): 7.8MM Privately Held
WEB: www.thebirkettmills.com
SIC: 2041 Flour & other grain mill products
PA: The Birkett Mills
163 Main St Ste 2
Penn Yan NY 14527
315 536-3311

(G-12951)
CHRONICLE EXPRESS
138 Main St (14527-1299)
PHONE..................315 536-4422
George Barnes, *President*
Irene Vanderlinder, *Sales/Mktg Mgr*
Robert Corey, *Manager*
Michael Hansen, *Graphic Designe*
EMP: 15
SALES (est): 704K Privately Held
WEB: www.chronicleexpress.com
SIC: 2711 5994 Newspapers, publishing & printing; news dealers & newsstands

(G-12952)
DAVID F DE MARCO
Also Called: De Marco Vineyards
929 Davy Rd (14527-9644)
P.O. Box 551 (14527-0551)
PHONE..................315 536-0882
David F De Marco, *Owner*
EMP: 2
SQ FT: 4,500
SALES: 240K Privately Held
WEB: www.daviddemarco.com
SIC: 2084 Wines

(G-12953)
FERRO CORPORATION
1789 Transelco Dr (14527-9752)
PHONE..................315 536-3357
Hector Ortino, *Branch Mgr*
EMP: 200
SALES (corp-wide): 1.4B Publicly Held
WEB: www.ferro.com
SIC: 2819 Industrial inorganic chemicals
PA: Ferro Corporation
6060 Parkland Blvd # 250
Mayfield Heights OH 44124
216 875-5600

(G-12954)
FERRO ELECTRONICS MATERIALS (HQ)
Also Called: Ferro Electronic Mtl Systems
1789 Transelco Dr (14527-9752)
PHONE..................315 536-3357
Lyn Labrake, *Manager*
◆ EMP: 2
SALES (est): 17MM
SALES (corp-wide): 1.4B Publicly Held
SIC: 3264 Porcelain electrical supplies
PA: Ferro Corporation
6060 Parkland Blvd # 250
Mayfield Heights OH 44124
216 875-5600

(G-12955)
FERRO ELECTRONICS MATERIALS
Also Called: Ferro Electronic Mtl Systems
1789 Transelco Dr (14527-9752)
PHONE..................315 536-3357
EMP: 101
SALES (corp-wide): 1.4B Publicly Held
SIC: 3264 Porcelain electrical supplies
HQ: Ferro Electronics Materials Inc
1789 Transelco Dr
Penn Yan NY 14527
315 536-3357

(G-12956)
FOX RUN VINEYARDS INC
670 State Route 14 (14527-9622)
PHONE..................315 536-4616
Scott Osbourne, *President*
Ruth Osborn, *Vice Pres*
Dan Mitchell, *Sales Mgr*
Marisa Indelicato, *Marketing Staff*
EMP: 12
SQ FT: 8,000
SALES (est): 3.7MM Privately Held
WEB: www.foxrunvineyards.com
SIC: 2084 Wines

(G-12957)
HANSON AGGREGATES EAST LLC
131 Garfield Ave (14527-1655)
P.O. Box 168 (14527-0168)
PHONE..................315 536-9391
Kenny Thurston, *Manager*
EMP: 6
SALES (corp-wide): 20.3B Privately Held
WEB: www.hansonaggeast.com
SIC: 1442 Common sand mining
HQ: Hanson Aggregates East Llc
3131 Rdu Center Dr
Morrisville NC 27560
919 380-2500

(G-12958)
HOFFMAN & HOFFMAN
Also Called: Rooster Hill Vineyards
489 State Route 54 (14527-9595)
P.O. Box 11 (14527-0011)
PHONE..................315 536-4773
David W Hoffman, *Partner*
Amy E Hoffman, *Partner*
EMP: 7
SALES (est): 574.1K Privately Held
WEB: www.roosterhill.com
SIC: 2084 Wines

(G-12959)
IVAN HORNING
Also Called: Horning Greenhouses
848 State Route 14a (14527-9189)
PHONE..................315 536-3028
Ivan Horning, *Owner*
Mason Horning, *Asst Mgr*
EMP: 6
SALES: 450K Privately Held
SIC: 2499 0181 Decorative wood & woodwork; flowers: grown under cover (e.g. greenhouse production)

(G-12960)
JASPER TRANSPORT LLC
1680 Flat St (14527-9024)
P.O. Box 441 (14527-0441)
PHONE..................315 729-5760
Ross Newcomb,
EMP: 6

GEOGRAPHIC SECTION

Philadelphia - Jefferson County (G-12985)

SALES (est): 570K Privately Held
SIC: 3537 Trucks, tractors, loaders, carriers & similar equipment

(G-12961)
KAN PAK LLC
105 Horizon Park Dr (14527-8764)
PHONE 620 440-2319
EMP: 5
SALES (corp-wide): 1.3B Privately Held
SIC: 2024 Ice cream & frozen desserts
HQ: Kan. Pak, Llc
1016 S Summit St
Arkansas City KS 67005
620 442-6820

(G-12962)
PREJEAN WINERY INC
2634 State Route 14 (14527-9735)
PHONE 315 536-7524
Elizabeth Prejean, President
Thomas Prejean, Vice Pres
EMP: 11
SQ FT: 6,000
SALES (est): 1.2MM Privately Held
WEB: www.prejeanwinery.com
SIC: 2084 Wines

(G-12963)
RED TAIL RIDGE INC
Also Called: Red Tail Ridge Winery
846 State Route 14 (14527-9622)
PHONE 315 536-4580
Mike Schnelle, President
Nancy Irelan, Principal
EMP: 15
SALES (est): 485.2K Privately Held
SIC: 2084 Wines

(G-12964)
RIBBLE LUMBER INC
249 1/2 Lake St (14527-1812)
PHONE 315 536-6221
Roger C Ribble, President
Roger A Ribble Sr, Corp Secy
EMP: 5
SALES (est): 360K Privately Held
SIC: 2434 1794 4212 Wood kitchen cabinets; excavation work; dump truck haulage

(G-12965)
ROTO SALT COMPANY INC
118 Monell St (14527-1404)
PHONE 315 536-3742
Brett M Oakes, President
Susan Ettinger, Vice Pres
Ann Olney, Office Mgr
EMP: 32
SQ FT: 20,000
SALES (est): 7.8MM Privately Held
SIC: 2899 3281 Salt; building stone products

(G-12966)
SILGAN PLASTICS LLC
40 Powell Ln (14527-1072)
PHONE 315 536-5690
Aksel Jensen, Engineer
Rodney Olevnik, Senior Engr
Diana Brown, HR Admin
Joseph Pollhein, Manager
Stacy Fisher, Manager
EMP: 250
SQ FT: 100,000
SALES (corp-wide): 4B Publicly Held
WEB: www.silganplastics.com
SIC: 3089 Plastic containers, except foam
HQ: Silgan Plastics Llc
14515 North Outer 40 Rd # 210
Chesterfield MO 63017
800 274-5426

Perry
Wyoming County

(G-12967)
CREATIVE FOOD INGREDIENTS INC
Also Called: CFI
1 Lincoln Ave (14530-1605)
PHONE 585 237-2213
Andrew W O'Flaherty, CEO
Jeffrey Arcand, CFO
◆ EMP: 140
SALES (est): 25.4MM Privately Held
SIC: 2052 Bakery products, dry

(G-12968)
EAST HILL CREAMERY LLC
346 Main St S (14530-9551)
PHONE 585 237-3622
Gary Burley, Mng Member
EMP: 6
SALES (est): 203.6K Privately Held
SIC: 2022 Cheese spreads, dips, pastes & other cheese products

(G-12969)
J N WHITE ASSOCIATES INC
Also Called: J.N. White Designs
129 N Center St (14530-9701)
P.O. Box 219 (14530-0219)
PHONE 585 237-5191
Randy White, President
Ken Boss, Vice Pres
Mary Patrick-Grabows, Vice Pres
John Steff, Vice Pres
Susan C White, Vice Pres
EMP: 95
SQ FT: 25,000
SALES (est): 17.5MM Privately Held
WEB: www.jnwhitedesigns.com
SIC: 2759 7389 Screen printing; printed circuitry graphic layout

(G-12970)
R J LIEBE ATHLETIC COMPANY
Also Called: Liebe NY
200 Main St N (14530-1211)
PHONE 585 237-6111
Jim Liebe, Mng Member
Rob Knoll,
EMP: 95
SQ FT: 200,000
SALES (est): 6.8MM Privately Held
WEB: www.americanclassicoutfitters.com
SIC: 2329 Men's & boys' athletic uniforms

(G-12971)
SIGN LANGUAGE INC
Also Called: Sign Language Custom WD Signs
6491 State Route 20a (14530-9758)
PHONE 585 237-2620
Dave Caito, President
Jeff Fitch, Corp Secy
Mike Fitch, Exec VP
EMP: 8
SQ FT: 3,000
SALES (est): 1.2MM Privately Held
WEB: www.signlanguageinc.com
SIC: 3993 Signs, not made in custom sign painting shops

Peru
Clinton County

(G-12972)
ROBERT W BUTTS LOGGING CO
420 Mannix Rd (12972-4529)
PHONE 518 643-2897
Robert Butts, Owner
EMP: 6
SALES (est): 625.6K Privately Held
SIC: 2411 Logging camps & contractors

Petersburg
Rensselaer County

(G-12973)
TONOGA INC (PA)
Also Called: Taconic
95-136 Coonbrook Rd (12138)
P.O. Box 69 (12138-0069)
PHONE 518 658-3202
Andrew G Russell, Chairman
Lawrence Carroll, Exec VP
Sharon Goodermote, Vice Pres
Manfred Huschka, Vice Pres
Scott Schulz, Vice Pres
◆ EMP: 180 EST: 1961
SQ FT: 150,000
SALES (est): 129.5MM Privately Held
WEB: www.taconic-afd.com
SIC: 2295 3629 Resin or plastic coated fabrics; electronic generation equipment

Phelps
Ontario County

(G-12974)
AMERICAN CRMIC PROCESS RES LLC
835 Mcivor Rd (14532-9535)
P.O. Box 213 (14532-0213)
PHONE 315 828-6268
Jesse Sheckler,
EMP: 6
SQ FT: 18,670
SALES (est): 259.3K Privately Held
SIC: 3299 Nonmetallic mineral products

(G-12975)
BENEMY WELDING & FABRICATION
8 Pleasant Ave (14532-1100)
PHONE 315 548-8500
Dave Suhr, President
Christine Suhr, Vice Pres
EMP: 6
SQ FT: 1,852
SALES (est): 675.2K Privately Held
SIC: 7692 Welding repair

(G-12976)
DORGAN WELDING SERVICE
1378 White Rd (14532-9502)
PHONE 315 462-9030
Bob Dorgan, Owner
EMP: 5
SQ FT: 7,000
SALES: 450K Privately Held
SIC: 7692 1799 Welding repair; welding on site

(G-12977)
GW LISK COMPANY INC
Also Called: Lisk Coils
1369 Phelps Junction Rd (14532-9747)
PHONE 315 548-2165
EMP: 40
SALES (corp-wide): 113.1MM Privately Held
SIC: 3629 Mfg Electrical Industrial Apparatus
PA: G.W. Lisk Company, Inc.
2 South St
Clifton Springs NY 14432
315 462-2611

(G-12978)
MAGNUS PRECISION MFG INC
1912 State Route 96 (14532-9705)
PHONE 315 548-8032
Thomas Shepard, Principal
Steve Strauss, Purch Agent
Eric Galens, QC Mgr
Steve Johnston, Engineer
John Schwenzer, Engineer
EMP: 68
SQ FT: 55,000
SALES (est): 13.6MM
SALES (corp-wide): 61MM Privately Held
WEB: www.magnuscnc.com
SIC: 3625 3544 Relays & industrial controls; special dies & tools
PA: Floturn, Inc.
4236 Thunderbird Ln
West Chester OH 45014
513 860-8040

(G-12979)
PHELPS CEMENT PRODUCTS INC
5 S Newark St (14532-9708)
P.O. Box 40 (14532-0040)
PHONE 315 548-9415
Gerald Haers, Ch of Bd
Michael Haers, President
Gerry Haers, Admin Sec
EMP: 23
SQ FT: 4,000
SALES (est): 4.9MM Privately Held
WEB: www.phelpscement.com
SIC: 3271 5211 5032 Blocks, concrete or cinder: standard; lumber & other building materials; brick, stone & related material

(G-12980)
SENECA CERAMICS CORP
835 Mcivor Rd (14532-9535)
P.O. Box 213 (14532-0213)
PHONE 315 781-0100
Chad Scheckler, President
Howard Hersey, Treasurer
Larisa Scheckler, Admin Sec
EMP: 6
SALES (est): 300K Privately Held
SIC: 3469 Utensils, household: porcelain enameled

(G-12981)
SHEPPARD GRAIN ENTERPRISES LLC
1615 Maryland Rd (14532-9507)
PHONE 315 548-9271
Steve Sheppard, Mng Member
◆ EMP: 35
SQ FT: 3,600
SALES: 40MM Privately Held
SIC: 2041 Flour & other grain mill products

(G-12982)
TRIPLETT MACHINE INC
1374 Phelps Junction Rd (14532-9747)
PHONE 315 548-3198
Douglas A Triplett Jr, CEO
Greg Triplett, Plant Mgr
Grant Abrams, Engineer
Paula Triplett, VP Sls/Mktg
Jeffrey Triplett, Treasurer
EMP: 65
SQ FT: 30,000
SALES (est): 14.9MM Privately Held
WEB: www.triplettmachine.com
SIC: 3599 Machine shop, jobbing & repair

(G-12983)
VALVETECH INC
1391 Phelps Junction Rd (14532-9747)
P.O. Box 118 (14532-0118)
PHONE 315 548-4551
Michael Mullally, President
Jeff Merkel, Opers Mgr
Michelle Smith, Purch Mgr
Jeff Pullano, Chief Engr
Brice Shipley, Engineer
EMP: 35
SQ FT: 1,000
SALES (est): 7.1MM
SALES (corp-wide): 165.7MM Privately Held
WEB: www.valvetech.net
SIC: 3592 Valves, aircraft
PA: G.W. Lisk Company, Inc.
2 South St
Clifton Springs NY 14432
315 462-2611

(G-12984)
Z-AXIS INC
Also Called: Boundless Technologies
1916 State Route 96 (14532-9705)
PHONE 315 548-5000
Michael Allen, President
Bob Sparlin, Purch Mgr
Wendy German, Purchasing
▲ EMP: 72
SQ FT: 30,000
SALES (est): 16.5MM Privately Held
WEB: www.zaxis.net
SIC: 3699 3577 3845 Electrical equipment & supplies; computer peripheral equipment; electromedical equipment

Philadelphia
Jefferson County

(G-12985)
NATURES WAREHOUSE
55 Main St (13673-4189)
P.O. Box 221, Kidron OH (44636-0221)
PHONE 800 215-4372
Cari L Laudon, Partner
Daniel Laudon, Partner

Philmont - Columbia County (G-12986) — GEOGRAPHIC SECTION

EMP: 10
SALES (est): 1.3MM **Privately Held**
SIC: 2899 2841 5499 Essential oils; soap & other detergents; vitamin food stores

Philmont
Columbia County

(G-12986)
FALLS MANUFACTURING INC (PA)
95 Main St (12565)
P.O. Box 798 (12565-0798)
PHONE.................518 672-7189
Frederick A Meyer, *President*
EMP: 8
SQ FT: 4,800
SALES (est): 2.3MM **Privately Held**
SIC: 2381 2339 Fabric dress & work gloves; women's & misses' outerwear

(G-12987)
PVC CONTAINER CORPORATION
Also Called: Nova Pack
370 Stevers Crossing Rd (12565)
PHONE.................518 672-7721
Edna Hover, *Manager*
EMP: 160
SALES (corp-wide): 141MM **Privately Held**
WEB: www.airopak.com
SIC: 3085 3089 Plastics bottles; molding primary plastic
HQ: Pvc Container Corporation
15450 South Outer 40 Rd # 120
Chesterfield MO 63017

Phoenix
Oswego County

(G-12988)
AMERICAN MATERIAL PROCESSING
126 Bankrupt Rd (13135-2193)
P.O. Box 643, Newark (14513-0643)
PHONE.................315 318-0017
Lawson Whiting, *President*
Matthew Eddy, *COO*
Jason McKinney, *Vice Pres*
EMP: 11 **EST:** 2013
SQ FT: 800
SALES (est): 1.2MM **Privately Held**
SIC: 3532 3569 5082 3535 Crushing, pulverizing & screening equipment; feeders, ore & aggregate; ice crushers (machinery); crushing, pulverizing & screening machinery; belt conveyor systems, general industrial use; bulk handling conveyor systems

(G-12989)
LOCK 1 DISTILLING COMPANY LLC
17 Culvert St (13135)
PHONE.................315 934-4376
Stephen Dates, *Mng Member*
Brendan Backus,
Kevin Dates,
EMP: 5
SQ FT: 7,000
SALES: 150K **Privately Held**
SIC: 2082 Beer (alcoholic beverage)

(G-12990)
MAJESTIC MOLD & TOOL INC
177 Volney St (13135-3116)
PHONE.................315 695-2079
Timothy King, *President*
Dennis Lyons, *CFO*
Stephen Corsette, *Treasurer*
Pam Najdul, *Manager*
EMP: 16
SQ FT: 8,000
SALES (est): 3.6MM **Privately Held**
WEB: www.majesticmold.com
SIC: 2821 Molding compounds, plastics

(G-12991)
NUTRATECH LABS INC
406 State Route 264 (13135-2124)
PHONE.................315 695-2256
Philip R Stone, *Ch of Bd*
EMP: 5 **EST:** 2017
SALES (est): 676.5K **Privately Held**
SIC: 2834 Pharmaceutical preparations

(G-12992)
PHOENIX WELDING & FABG INC
Also Called: Phoenix Material Handling
10 County Route 6 (13135-2118)
PHONE.................315 695-2223
Brian D Dates, *Ch of Bd*
EMP: 5
SQ FT: 2,500
SALES (est): 970.3K **Privately Held**
SIC: 7692 Welding repair

(G-12993)
SOUTHERN GRAPHIC SYSTEMS LLC
Also Called: SGS
67 County Route 59 (13135-2116)
PHONE.................315 695-7079
Jennifer Shutts-Leblanc, *Manager*
Jennifer Shutts, *Technology*
Vic Baranowski,
Jim Chlebus, *Admin Sec*
EMP: 27
SALES (corp-wide): 395.8MM **Privately Held**
SIC: 3555 Printing trades machinery
PA: Southern Graphic Systems, Llc
626 W Main St Ste 500
Louisville KY 40202
502 637-5443

Piermont
Rockland County

(G-12994)
ROCKLAND COLLOID CORP (PA)
Also Called: Rockaloid
44 Franklin St (10968-1010)
P.O. Box 3120, Oregon City OR (97045-0306)
PHONE.................845 359-5559
Robert Cone, *President*
Francis Cooper, *Corp Secy*
Robert Cone Jr, *Vice Pres*
EMP: 5 **EST:** 1966
SQ FT: 3,000
SALES (est): 697.4K **Privately Held**
WEB: www.rockloid.com
SIC: 3861 5043 Photographic equipment & supplies; photographic equipment & supplies

Piffard
Livingston County

(G-12995)
ARKEMA INC
Also Called: Genesee Plant
3289 Genesee St (14533-9745)
PHONE.................585 243-6359
Catherine Amber, *Buyer*
Martin Foess, *Branch Mgr*
James Linz, *Manager*
Eileen Maher, *Manager*
Susan Wilson, *Technician*
EMP: 170
SALES (corp-wide): 77.8MM **Privately Held**
SIC: 2869 2819 Industrial organic chemicals; industrial inorganic chemicals
HQ: Arkema Inc.
900 First Ave
King Of Prussia PA 19406
610 205-7000

(G-12996)
EXXELIA-RAF TABTRONICS LLC
2854 Genesee St (14533-9749)
P.O. Box 128, Geneseo (14454-0128)
PHONE.................585 243-4331
James Charles Tabbi, *Manager*
EMP: 43
SALES (corp-wide): 16MM **Privately Held**
SIC: 3677 3643 3612 Electronic transformers; coil windings, electronic; current-carrying wiring devices; transformers, except electric
PA: Exxelia-Raf Tabtronics, Llc
1221 N Us Highway 17 92
Longwood FL 32750
386 736-1698

Pine Bush
Orange County

(G-12997)
MOBILE MEDIA INC (PA)
24 Center St (12566-6004)
P.O. Box 177 (12566-0177)
PHONE.................845 744-8080
Lance Pennington, *Principal*
Nancy Pennington, *Vice Pres*
▲ **EMP:** 23
SQ FT: 31,000
SALES (est): 10.9MM **Privately Held**
WEB: www.rolleasy.com
SIC: 2542 Partitions & fixtures, except wood

(G-12998)
P & B WOODWORKING INC
2415 State Route 52 (12566-7041)
P.O. Box 225 (12566-0225)
PHONE.................845 744-2508
Jake Donnell, *President*
Steven Reinhardt, *Vice Pres*
EMP: 10
SQ FT: 11,000
SALES: 1.1MM **Privately Held**
SIC: 2541 Cabinets, lockers & shelving

Pine City
Chemung County

(G-12999)
DALRYMPLE GRAV & CONTG CO INC (HQ)
2105 S Broadway (14871-9700)
PHONE.................607 739-0391
David J Dalrymple, *Ch of Bd*
Robert H Dalrymple, *President*
Thomas Farmer, *General Mgr*
Edward C Dalrymple Jr, *Vice Pres*
Brian Adams, *Plant Supt*
EMP: 18 **EST:** 1890
SQ FT: 10,000
SALES (est): 45MM
SALES (corp-wide): 105.9MM **Privately Held**
SIC: 1442 3273 Construction sand & gravel; ready-mixed concrete
PA: Dalrymple Holding Corp
2105 S Broadway
Pine City NY 14871
607 737-6200

(G-13000)
DALRYMPLE HOLDING CORP (PA)
2105 S Broadway (14871-9700)
PHONE.................607 737-6200
David J Dalrymple, *President*
Edward C Dalrymple Jr, *Vice Pres*
Sue Knighton, *Director*
Robert H Dalrymple, *Admin Sec*
EMP: 20
SQ FT: 5,000
SALES (est): 105.9MM **Privately Held**
SIC: 3273 1611 1442 1622 Ready-mixed concrete; highway & street construction; construction sand & gravel; bridge construction; stone, quarrying & processing of own stone products

(G-13001)
SENECA STONE CORPORATION (HQ)
2105 S Broadway (14871-9700)
PHONE.................607 737-6200
David J Dalrymple, *President*
Sandy Strong, *General Mgr*
Edward C Dalrymple Jr, *Vice Pres*
Robert H Dalrymple, *Vice Pres*
Edward C Dalrymple Sr, *Treasurer*
EMP: 4
SQ FT: 800
SALES (est): 1.7MM
SALES (corp-wide): 105.9MM **Privately Held**
SIC: 3281 1771 1442 Cut stone & stone products; concrete work; construction sand & gravel
PA: Dalrymple Holding Corp
2105 S Broadway
Pine City NY 14871
607 737-6200

Pine Island
Orange County

(G-13002)
REELCOLOGY INC
39 Transport Ln (10969-1223)
P.O. Box 305 (10969-0305)
PHONE.................845 258-1880
Kenneth H Smith, *President*
EMP: 15
SQ FT: 7,000
SALES (est): 1.8MM **Privately Held**
SIC: 3496 3499 Cable, uninsulated wire: made from purchased wire; reels, cable: metal

(G-13003)
SABILA CORP (PA)
480 Liberty Corners Rd (10969-1918)
P.O. Box 691 (10969-0691)
PHONE.................845 981-7128
Kenan Porter, *CEO*
EMP: 9 **EST:** 2010
SALES (est): 7.1MM **Privately Held**
SIC: 2087 Concentrates, drink

Pine Plains
Dutchess County

(G-13004)
ABRA MEDIA INC
Also Called: Live Oak Media
2773 W Church St (12567-5421)
P.O. Box 652 (12567-0652)
PHONE.................518 398-1010
Arnold Cardillo, *President*
Debra Cardillo, *Admin Sec*
EMP: 6
SALES (est): 480K **Privately Held**
WEB: www.liveoakmedia.com
SIC: 2741 7812 Miscellaneous publishing; audio-visual program production

(G-13005)
DUTCH SPIRITS LLC
Also Called: Dutch's Spirits
98 Ryan Rd (12567-5022)
PHONE.................518 398-1022
Ariel Schlein, *Mng Member*
John Adams,
Ronit Schlein,
▲ **EMP:** 17
SQ FT: 7,424,000
SALES: 250K **Privately Held**
SIC: 2084 5999 2085 Neutral spirits, fruit; alcoholic beverage making equipment & supplies; cocktails, alcoholic

Pine Valley
Chemung County

(G-13006)
AMES COMPANIES INC
114 Smith Rd (14872)
P.O. Box 126 (14872-0126)
PHONE.................607 739-4544
John Stoner, *Owner*
Mark Schrage, *Manager*
EMP: 20
SQ FT: 13,235

Pittsford
Monroe County

(G-13007)
AD PUBLICATIONS INC
8 Greenwood Park (14534-2912)
PHONE..................585 248-2888
Donald Stahl, *President*
Cheryl Stahl, *Vice Pres*
Patricia Stahl, *Admin Sec*
EMP: 10
SQ FT: 450
SALES (est): 786.8K **Privately Held**
SIC: 2759 Coupons: printing

(G-13008)
AMERICAN-SWISS PRODUCTS CO INC
1987 W Jefferson Rd (14534-1041)
PHONE..................585 292-1720
Rebecca J Luce, *President*
Zahl Cama, *QC Mgr*
Douglas Bell, *Sales Staff*
Robert Latore, *Manager*
EMP: 6
SQ FT: 7,000
SALES (est): 1.2MM **Privately Held**
WEB: www.americanswiss.com
SIC: 3451 Screw machine products

(G-13009)
BRIGHT LINE ETING SLUTIONS LLC
41 Lake Lacoma Dr (14534-3954)
PHONE..................585 245-2956
Julia Harold,
EMP: 26
SALES: 6MM **Privately Held**
SIC: 2741

(G-13010)
EASTMAN KODAK COMPANY
1818 W Jefferson Rd (14534-1033)
PHONE..................585 722-9695
Dawn Schweitze, *Principal*
EMP: 67
SALES (corp-wide): 1.5B **Publicly Held**
SIC: 3861 Film, sensitized motion picture, X-ray, still camera, etc.
PA: Eastman Kodak Company
343 State St
Rochester NY 14650
585 724-4000

(G-13011)
EMPHASCIENCE
115 Sullys Trl Ste 6 (14534-4571)
PHONE..................585 348-9415
EMP: 5
SALES (est): 639.6K **Privately Held**
SIC: 2834 Pharmaceutical preparations

(G-13012)
FLUOROLOGIC INC
33 Bishops Ct (14534-2882)
PHONE..................585 248-2796
Laura Weller-Brophy, *CEO*
EMP: 7
SALES (est): 407K **Privately Held**
SIC: 3841 Surgical & medical instruments

(G-13013)
GATEHOUSE MEDIA LLC (HQ)
175 Sullys Trl Ste 300 (14534-4560)
PHONE..................585 598-0030
Kirk Davis, *CEO*
Rick Daniels, *President*
Peter Newton, *President*
Paul Ameden, *Principal*
Brad Dennison, *Senior VP*
▲ EMP: 277
SQ FT: 15,000
SALES (est): 709.1MM
SALES (corp-wide): 1.3B **Publicly Held**
WEB: www.gatehousemedia.com
SIC: 2711 7311 2759 Newspapers, publishing & printing; advertising agencies; commercial printing
PA: New Media Investment Group Inc.
1345 Avenue Of The Americ
New York NY 10105
212 479-3160

(G-13014)
GATEHUSE MEDIA PA HOLDINGS INC (HQ)
175 Sullys Trl Fl 3 (14534-4560)
PHONE..................585 598-0030
Kirk Davis, *CEO*
EMP: 45
SALES (est): 9.9MM
SALES (corp-wide): 1.3B **Publicly Held**
SIC: 2711 Commercial printing & newspaper publishing combined
PA: New Media Investment Group Inc.
1345 Avenue Of The Americ
New York NY 10105
212 479-3160

(G-13015)
IMAGINANT INC
Also Called: Jsr Ultrasonics Division
3800 Monroe Ave Ste 29 (14534-1330)
PHONE..................585 264-0480
Todd Jackson, *CEO*
Samuel Rosenberg, *President*
Robert Hibbard, *Corp Secy*
Steve Smith, *Engineer*
Sam Rosenberg, *Program Mgr*
EMP: 32
SQ FT: 10,000
SALES (est): 5.9MM **Privately Held**
WEB: www.jsrultrasonics.com
SIC: 3829 Measuring & controlling devices

(G-13016)
INFIMED INC
15 Fisher Rd (14534-9544)
PHONE..................585 383-1710
Pat Rox, *Branch Mgr*
EMP: 7
SALES (corp-wide): 8.3MM **Privately Held**
SIC: 3845 Mfg Electromedical Equipment
PA: Infimed, Inc.
121 Metropolitan Park Dr
Liverpool NY 13088
315 453-4545

(G-13017)
KERNOW NORTH AMERICA
5 Park Forest Dr (14534-3557)
PHONE..................585 586-3590
Bosy Colak, *President*
Craig Surette, *Info Tech Mgr*
EMP: 11
SALES (est): 1.1MM **Privately Held**
SIC: 3089 Mfg Plastic Products

(G-13018)
LIFE JUICE BRANDS LLC
115 Brook Rd (14534-1144)
PHONE..................585 944-7982
Peter Schulick, *CEO*
EMP: 4
SQ FT: 1,400
SALES: 1.7MM **Privately Held**
SIC: 2033 Vegetable juices: packaged in cans, jars, etc.

(G-13019)
LOCAL MEDIA GROUP HOLDINGS LLC (DH)
175 Sullys Trl Ste 300 (14534-4560)
PHONE..................585 598-0030
Kirk Davis, *CEO*
EMP: 3
SALES (est): 527.2MM
SALES (corp-wide): 1.3B **Publicly Held**
SIC: 2711 Commercial printing & newspaper publishing combined
HQ: Gatehouse Media, Llc
175 Sullys Trl Ste 300
Pittsford NY 14534
585 598-0030

(G-13020)
MAGNUM SHIELDING CORPORATION
3800 Monroe Ave Ste 14f (14534-1330)
P.O. Box 827 (14534-0827)
PHONE..................585 381-9957
Scott Hurwitz, *President*
Kara Ray, *Buyer*
Chad Conklin, *Purchasing*
Sheri Anderson, *Office Mgr*
Tom Vierthaler, *Manager*
▲ EMP: 50
SQ FT: 15,000
SALES (est): 9.1MM **Privately Held**
WEB: www.magnumshielding.com
SIC: 3694 Ignition apparatus & distributors

(G-13021)
MARDEK LLC
73 N Wilmarth Rd (14534-9775)
P.O. Box 134, North Hero VT (05474-0134)
PHONE..................585 735-9333
Charles Dekar, *President*
Nick Dekar, *President*
▲ EMP: 5
SALES: 2MM **Privately Held**
SIC: 3312 Rods, iron & steel: made in steel mills

(G-13022)
MILLERCOORS LLC
1000 Pittsford Victor Rd (14534-3822)
PHONE..................585 385-0670
Dennis Perreault, *Branch Mgr*
EMP: 25
SALES (corp-wide): 11B **Publicly Held**
SIC: 2082 Beer (alcoholic beverage)
HQ: Millercoors Llc
250 S Wacker Dr Ste 800
Chicago IL 60606
312 496-2700

(G-13023)
OPTICS TECHNOLOGY INC
3800 Monroe Ave Ste 3 (14534-1330)
PHONE..................585 586-0950
John Warda, *President*
Ben Piatt, *Prdtn Mgr*
EMP: 4
SQ FT: 6,000
SALES (est): 1.1MM **Privately Held**
WEB: www.opticstechnology.com
SIC: 3827 3599 Lenses, optical: all types except ophthalmic; lens mounts; optical elements & assemblies, except ophthalmic; machine & other job shop work; machine shop, jobbing & repair

(G-13024)
PA PELLETS LLC (HQ)
1 Fischers Rd Ste 160 (14534)
PHONE..................814 848-9970
Dan Wetzel, *Principal*
Jeremy Watson, *Plant Mgr*
▼ EMP: 13 EST: 2010
SALES (est): 2.7MM
SALES (corp-wide): 22.1MM **Privately Held**
SIC: 2421 Fuelwood, from mill waste
PA: Biomaxx, Inc.
1160 Pittsford Victor Rd F
Pittsford NY 14534
585 596-8324

(G-13025)
PACTIV LLC
1169 Pittsford Victor Rd (14534-3809)
P.O. Box 5032, Lake Forest IL (60045-5032)
PHONE..................585 248-1213
EMP: 50 **Publicly Held**
WEB: www.pactiv.com
SIC: 2653 2631 Corrugated & solid fiber boxes; container board
HQ: Pactiv Llc
1900 W Field Ct
Lake Forest IL 60045
847 482-2000

(G-13026)
ROCKWELL AUTOMATION INC
1000 Pittsford Victor Rd # 17 (14534-3822)
PHONE..................585 487-2700
Brian Blaisdell, *Area Mgr*
Scott Turling, *Manager*
Carol Caranddo, *Receptionist*
EMP: 27 **Publicly Held**
SIC: 3625 Relays & industrial controls
PA: Rockwell Automation, Inc.
1201 S 2nd St
Milwaukee WI 53204

(G-13027)
UNITED TECHNOLOGIES CORP
Lenel
1212 Pittsford Victor Rd (14534-3820)
PHONE..................866 788-5095
John Merlino, *Director*
EMP: 500
SALES (corp-wide): 59.8B **Publicly Held**
SIC: 3699 Electrical equipment & supplies
PA: United Technologies Corporation
10 Farm Springs Rd
Farmington CT 06032
860 728-7000

(G-13028)
WELDRITE CLOSURES INC
11 Sutton Pt (14534-4616)
PHONE..................585 429-8790
Jason C Nelson, *President*
Jason Nelson, *President*
Greg Scace, *Vice Pres*
EMP: 40
SALES (est): 8.6MM **Privately Held**
SIC: 3731 Offshore supply boats, building & repairing

(G-13029)
XELIC INCORPORATED
1250 Pittsford Victor Rd # 370 (14534-9541)
PHONE..................585 415-2764
Mark Gibson, *President*
Doug Bush, *Vice Pres*
David Spaniol, *Engineer*
Kenny Chung, *Design Engr*
Jamie Howard, *Design Engr*
EMP: 18
SQ FT: 2,400
SALES: 3MM **Privately Held**
WEB: www.xelic.com
SIC: 3825 Integrated circuit testers

Plainview
Nassau County

(G-13030)
ADART POLYETHYLENE BAG MFG
Also Called: Adart Poly Bag Mfg
1 W Ames Ct Ste 201 (11803-2328)
P.O. Box 615 (11803-0019)
PHONE..................516 932-1001
Robert Wolk, *President*
EMP: 6 EST: 1968
SQ FT: 13,500
SALES (est): 1.1MM **Privately Held**
SIC: 2673 Bags: plastic, laminated & coated

(G-13031)
AEROFLEX HOLDING CORP
35 S Service Rd (11803-4117)
P.O. Box 6022 (11803-0622)
PHONE..................516 694-6700
Hugh Evans, *Ch of Bd*
Leonard Borow, *President*
John Buyko, *Exec VP*
Andrew F Kaminsky, *Senior VP*
Edward Wactlar, *Senior VP*
▼ EMP: 2700
SQ FT: 90,000
SALES (est): 203MM
SALES (corp-wide): 2.7B **Privately Held**
SIC: 3674 Semiconductors & related devices
HQ: Cobham Holdings Inc.
10 Cobham Dr
Orchard Park NY 14127
716 662-0006

Plainview - Nassau County (G-13032)

(G-13032)
AEROFLEX INCORPORATED (HQ)
Also Called: Cobham Semiconductor Solutions
35 S Service Rd (11803-4117)
P.O. Box 6022 (11803-0622)
PHONE..................516 694-6700
Robert B McKeon, *Ch of Bd*
Leonard J Borow, *President*
Bill Burrows, *General Mgr*
John Buyko, *Exec VP*
Tom Noonan, *Exec VP*
▲ **EMP:** 450
SQ FT: 69,000
SALES (est): 456.4MM
SALES (corp-wide): 2.7B **Privately Held**
WEB: www.aeroflex.com
SIC: 3812 3621 3677 3674 Acceleration indicators & systems components, aerospace; torque motors, electric; electronic coils, transformers & other inductors; microcircuits, integrated (semiconductor); mesh, made from purchased wire; optical instruments & apparatus
PA: Cobham Plc
Brook Road
Wimborne BH21
120 288-2020

(G-13033)
AEROFLEX PLAINVIEW INC (DH)
Also Called: Cobham
35 S Service Rd (11803-4117)
P.O. Box 6022 (11803-0622)
PHONE..................516 694-6700
Jill Kale, *CEO*
Leonard Borow, *Ch of Bd*
Carl Caruso, *Senior VP*
Kevin J Finnegan, *Vice Pres*
Rob Sichenzia, *Vice Pres*
EMP: 422
SQ FT: 69,000
SALES (est): 192.7MM
SALES (corp-wide): 2.7B **Privately Held**
SIC: 3679 3621 3674 3827 Electronic circuits; motors, electric; microcircuits, integrated (semiconductor); microprocessors; optical instruments & lenses

(G-13034)
ALCATEL-LUCENT USA INC
1 Fairchild Ct Ste 340 (11803-1720)
PHONE..................516 349-4900
EMP: 58
SALES (corp-wide): 27.3B **Privately Held**
SIC: 3661 Telephone & telegraph apparatus
HQ: Nokia Of America Corporation
600 Mountain Ave Ste 700
New Providence NJ 07974

(G-13035)
AMERICAN CASTING AND MFG CORP (PA)
51 Commercial St (11803-2490)
PHONE..................800 342-0333
Norman Wenk III, *President*
H L Christian Wenk IV, *Corp Secy*
Don Wenk, *Vice Pres*
Joseph Wenk, *Vice Pres*
Marco Castro, *Manager*
◆ **EMP:** 70 **EST:** 1916
SQ FT: 40,000
SALES: 16.1MM **Privately Held**
WEB: www.americancasting.com
SIC: 3089 3364 2759 5085 Injection molding of plastics; lead die-castings; labels & seals: printing; seals, industrial

(G-13036)
AMERICAN CASTING AND MFG CORP
65 S Terminal Dr (11803-2310)
PHONE..................516 349-7010
Norman Wenk, *Branch Mgr*
EMP: 5
SALES (corp-wide): 16.1MM **Privately Held**
WEB: www.americancasting.com
SIC: 3089 3364 3429 Injection molding of plastics; lead die-castings; manufactured hardware (general)

PA: American Casting And Manufacturing Corporation
51 Commercial St
Plainview NY 11803
800 342-0333

(G-13037)
AUDIO VIDEO INVASION INC
Also Called: AVI
53 Werman Ct (11803-4507)
PHONE..................516 345-2636
Panos Anassis, *Principal*
Mary Antonacci, *Office Mgr*
Christina Anassis, *Manager*
Jerome Oleary, *Prgrmr*
EMP: 15
SALES (est): 1.9MM **Privately Held**
SIC: 3651 5999 Household audio & video equipment; audio-visual equipment & supplies

(G-13038)
AUFHAUSER CORPORATION (PA)
39 West Mall (11803-4209)
PHONE..................516 694-8696
Keith Aufhauser, *President*
Peter Wan, *Vice Pres*
PI Tsang Wu, *Vice Pres*
Fred Wu, *Treasurer*
▲ **EMP:** 19
SQ FT: 28,000
SALES: 50MM **Privately Held**
WEB: www.aufhauser.net
SIC: 3356 5051 2899 Welding rods; solder: wire, bar, acid core, & rosin core; metals service centers & offices; fluxes: brazing, soldering, galvanizing & welding

(G-13039)
AUFHAUSER MANUFACTURING CORP
Also Called: Aufhauser Corp Canada
39 West Mall (11803-4209)
PHONE..................516 694-8696
R Keith Aufhauser, *President*
Wu PI Tsang, *Vice Pres*
Fred Wu, *Treasurer*
EMP: 20
SQ FT: 25,000
SALES: 25MM **Privately Held**
WEB: www.brazing.com
SIC: 3356 Welding rods

(G-13040)
CENTROID INC
111 E Ames Ct Unit 1 (11803-2311)
PHONE..................516 349-0070
Gerald I Starr, *Ch of Bd*
Marc A Starr, *President*
Nancy Budd, *Purch Agent*
Peggy Carey, *Office Mgr*
EMP: 23 **EST:** 1965
SQ FT: 8,000
SALES (est): 4.5MM **Privately Held**
WEB: www.centroidinc.com
SIC: 3679 Oscillators

(G-13041)
CHERRY LANE LITHOGRAPHING CORP
15 E Bethpage Rd Unit A (11803-4217)
PHONE..................516 293-9294
William Citterbart Jr, *President*
Joann Citterbart, *Corp Secy*
William Citterbart III, *Vice Pres*
Janet Frisch, *Technology*
Jo-Ann Citterbart, *Legal Staff*
EMP: 48 **EST:** 1962
SQ FT: 54,000
SALES (est): 10.1MM **Privately Held**
WEB: www.cherrylanelitho.com
SIC: 2752 Lithographing on metal

(G-13042)
COINMACH SERVICE CORP
303 Sunnyside Blvd # 70 (11803-1598)
PHONE..................516 349-8555
Robert M Doyle, *Ch of Bd*
Carol A Siebuhr, *President*
Adrian Verquer, *President*
Joe McCarley, *Database Admin*
EMP: 805
SQ FT: 11,600

SALES (est): 104.9MM
SALES (corp-wide): 356.6MM **Privately Held**
SIC: 3633 5087 Household laundry equipment; laundry equipment & supplies
HQ: Spin Holdco Inc.
303 Sunnyside Blvd # 70
Plainview NY 11803

(G-13043)
COLONIAL GROUP LLC
150 Express St Ste 2 (11803-2421)
PHONE..................516 349-8010
Pierre Lavi,
EMP: 25
SALES (est): 1.9MM **Privately Held**
SIC: 3724 Aircraft engines & engine parts

(G-13044)
CONRAD BLASIUS EQUIPMENT CO
Also Called: Cbe/New York
199 Newtown Rd (11803-4308)
PHONE..................516 753-1200
Richard Fiordelisi Sr, *President*
Richard C Fiordelisi Jr, *President*
EMP: 6
SQ FT: 10,000
SALES (est): 630K **Privately Held**
SIC: 3599 3291 2842 5084 Tubing, flexible metallic; coated abrasive products; metal polish; industrial machinery & equipment

(G-13045)
CONTROLLED CASTINGS CORP
31 Commercial Ct (11803-2403)
PHONE..................516 349-1718
Carmella Fratello, *Ch of Bd*
Peter Fratello Jr, *President*
Clifford Fratello, *Vice Pres*
EMP: 30 **EST:** 1961
SQ FT: 32,500
SALES (est): 3.8MM **Privately Held**
SIC: 3369 Nonferrous Metal Foundry

(G-13046)
CORAL CAST LLC
31 Commercial Ct (11803-2403)
PHONE..................516 349-1300
Joseph Marden,
EMP: 21
SALES (est): 3.5MM **Privately Held**
SIC: 3272 Precast terrazo or concrete products

(G-13047)
CORE SWX LLC
91b Commercial St (11803-2401)
PHONE..................516 595-7488
Jenson Seepersad, *Finance*
Ross Kanarek, *Mng Member*
EMP: 12
SALES: 5MM **Privately Held**
SIC: 3861 Cameras & related equipment

(G-13048)
COX & COMPANY INC
1664 Old Country Rd (11803-5013)
PHONE..................212 366-0200
John Smith, *Ch of Bd*
Jared Gilbert, *Business Mgr*
Thomas Ferguson, *Senior VP*
Michael Fields, *Mfg Spvr*
Jessica Lopez, *Buyer*
▲ **EMP:** 185 **EST:** 1944
SQ FT: 90,000
SALES (est): 52.3MM **Privately Held**
SIC: 3625 3743 3822 3812 Relays & industrial controls; railroad equipment; auto controls regulating residntl & coml environmt & applncs; search & navigation equipment; current-carrying wiring devices; aircraft parts & equipment; deicing equipment, aircraft

(G-13049)
CSC SW HOLDCO INC (HQ)
Also Called: CSC Serviceworks, Inc.
303 Sunnyside Blvd # 70 (11803-1597)
PHONE..................516 349-8555
Mark Hjelle, *CEO*
Stacy Weaver, *President*
Tim Gillotti, *General Mgr*
Tim Guido, *Regional Mgr*
Hector Acosta, *Area Mgr*

EMP: 92
SALES (est): 264.5MM
SALES (corp-wide): 356.6MM **Privately Held**
SIC: 3633 5087 Household laundry equipment; laundry equipment & supplies
PA: Csc Serviceworks Holdings, Inc.
303 Sunnyside Blvd # 70
Plainview NY 11803
516 349-8555

(G-13050)
DERM-BURO INC (PA)
Also Called: G-Forces
229 Newtown Rd (11803-4309)
PHONE..................516 694-8300
Frank Guthart, *President*
Mark Guthart, *Exec VP*
EMP: 46
SQ FT: 1,100
SALES (est): 4.3MM **Privately Held**
WEB: www.gforces.com
SIC: 3841 5122 5047 3842 Surgical & medical instruments; pharmaceuticals; instruments, surgical & medical; surgical appliances & supplies

(G-13051)
DIE-MATIC PRODUCTS LLC
130 Express St (11803-2477)
PHONE..................516 433-7900
Arnold Klein, *President*
Barry Blazer, *Vice Pres*
Bill Oehrlein, *Opers Mgr*
Evelyn Martinez, *Controller*
Dan Farber, *Info Tech Mgr*
EMP: 30 **EST:** 1944
SQ FT: 30,000
SALES (est): 5.2MM **Privately Held**
WEB: www.diematicproducts.com
SIC: 3469 Stamping metal for the trade

(G-13052)
EASTERNCCTV (USA) LLC (PA)
50 Commercial St (11803-2426)
PHONE..................516 870-3779
Xianjie Xiong, *President*
Charles Kanu, *Engineer*
Jimmy Theblitz, *Accounts Mgr*
Sarah Wang, *Marketing Staff*
Peter Qian, *Manager*
EMP: 15
SALES (est): 10.7MM **Privately Held**
SIC: 3861 Cameras & related equipment

(G-13053)
EBY ELECTRO INC
210 Express St (11803-2423)
PHONE..................516 576-7777
Mitchell Solomon, *President*
John Mancini, *COO*
Jim Fennell, *Opers Staff*
Margo Schein, *Purch Mgr*
Beverly Scheinberg, *Purch Mgr*
▲ **EMP:** 28
SQ FT: 20,000
SALES (est): 5.7MM **Privately Held**
WEB: www.ebyelectro.com
SIC: 3678 Electronic connectors

(G-13054)
ECONOMETRIC SOFTWARE INC
15 Gloria Pl (11803-6314)
PHONE..................516 938-5254
William H Greene, *Owner*
EMP: 5
SALES (est): 380.9K **Privately Held**
WEB: www.limdep.com
SIC: 7372 Prepackaged software

(G-13055)
EMDA INC
81 Westbury Ave (11803-3627)
PHONE..................631 243-6363
Alan Steinbok, *President*
EMP: 10
SALES: 1MM **Privately Held**
WEB: www.emdainc.com
SIC: 3861 Photographic equipment & supplies

(G-13056)
EVANS & PAUL LLC
140 Dupont St (11803-1603)
PHONE..................516 576-0800
Jeffrey Evans, *Mng Member*

Suzanne Ray,
EMP: 50
SQ FT: 30,000
SALES: 5.1MM Privately Held
SIC: 2599 2542 1799 Hospital furniture, except beds; fixtures, office: except wood; office furniture installation

(G-13057)
FACTORY WHEEL WAREHOUSE INC
30 W Ames Ct (11803-2319)
PHONE..................516 605-2131
EMP: 9 EST: 2012
SALES (est): 914.3K Privately Held
SIC: 3714 5013 5015 5085 Motor vehicle wheels & parts; wheel rims, motor vehicle; wheels, motor vehicle; wheels, motor vehicle; wheels, used: motor vehicle; bearings, bushings, wheels & gears

(G-13058)
FIBRE MATERIALS CORP
40 Dupont St (11803-1679)
PHONE..................516 349-1660
Glenn Fellows, CEO
Brian Grossberg, President
▲ **EMP:** 27 EST: 1963
SQ FT: 34,000
SALES (est): 4.7MM Privately Held
WEB: www.fibrematerials.com
SIC: 3089 5162 Washers, plastic; plastics materials & basic shapes

(G-13059)
FULL MOTION BEVERAGE INC (PA)
998 Old Country Rd (11803-4928)
PHONE..................631 585-1100
Peter Frazzetto, CEO
Vincent Butta, President
Chris Mollica, President
Paul Dua, Vice Pres
Tim Mayette, CFO
EMP: 6
SALES: 396.4K Publicly Held
WEB: www.web2corp.com
SIC: 2869 Alcohols, non-beverage

(G-13060)
HOSHIZAKI NRTHEASTERN DIST CTR
150 Dupont St Ste 100 (11803-1603)
PHONE..................516 605-1411
Toshio Mase, President
Mitsuhiro Nomura, CFO
Artic Rade, Admin Sec
▲ **EMP:** 6
SALES (est): 1.1MM
SALES (corp-wide): 2.5B Privately Held
WEB: www.hoshizaki.com
SIC: 3585 Ice making machinery
HQ: Hoshizaki America, Inc.
618 Highway 74 S
Peachtree City GA 30269
770 487-2331

(G-13061)
HOT LINE INDUSTRIES INC (PA)
Also Called: Casttle Harbor
28 South Mall (11803-4208)
PHONE..................516 764-0400
Howard Negrin, President
Jeff Negrin, Corp Secy
Elliot Negrin, Vice Pres
▲ **EMP:** 16
SQ FT: 9,000
SALES (est): 1.3MM Privately Held
WEB: www.hotlineindustries.com
SIC: 2339 Women's & misses' outerwear

(G-13062)
HOWARD J MOORE COMPANY INC
Also Called: Morco
210 Terminal Dr Ste B (11803-2322)
PHONE..................631 351-8467
Eric Moore, President
Harris Moore, Plant Mgr
Spencer Moore, Sales Mgr
EMP: 28 EST: 1945
SQ FT: 17,000
SALES (est): 5.5MM Privately Held
WEB: www.morcofab.com
SIC: 3082 2679 Unsupported plastics profile shapes; building, insulating & packaging paper

(G-13063)
INDUSTRIAL RAW MATERIALS LLC
Also Called: Industrial Wax
39 West Mall (11803-4209)
PHONE..................212 688-8080
Keith Aufhauser, Mng Member
▲ **EMP:** 19
SQ FT: 6,000
SALES (est): 4.6MM
SALES (corp-wide): 50MM Privately Held
WEB: www.industrialwax.com
SIC: 2911 5172 Paraffin wax; petroleum products
PA: Aufhauser Corporation
39 West Mall
Plainview NY 11803
516 694-8696

(G-13064)
INTELLIDYNE LLC
303 Sunnyside Blvd # 75 (11803-1597)
PHONE..................516 676-0777
Jack Hammer,
EMP: 17
SQ FT: 4,500
SALES (est): 3.5MM Privately Held
WEB: www.intellidynellc.com
SIC: 3822 Temperature controls, automatic

(G-13065)
INTERPARTS INTERNATIONAL INC (PA)
190 Express St (11803-2405)
P.O. Box 855 (11803-0855)
PHONE..................516 576-2000
Hung Da Yang, President
▲ **EMP:** 20
SQ FT: 40,000
SALES (est): 2.3MM Privately Held
SIC: 3714 5013 3566 Motor vehicle brake systems & parts; automotive brakes; speed changers, drives & gears

(G-13066)
JEM CONTAINER CORP
151 Fairchild Ave Ste 1 (11803-1716)
P.O. Box 456, Farmingdale (11735-0456)
PHONE..................800 521-0145
Ohn C Mc Laughlin, Ch of Bd
EMP: 10
SALES (est): 1.4MM Privately Held
SIC: 3086 Packaging & shipping materials, foamed plastic

(G-13067)
KAREY KASSL CORP
Also Called: Karey Products
180 Terminal Dr (11803-2324)
PHONE..................516 349-8484
Gary J Kassl, CEO
Ronald Kassl, President
▲ **EMP:** 30
SQ FT: 40,000
SALES (est): 2.5MM Privately Held
SIC: 3442 Storm doors or windows, metal

(G-13068)
KENSTAN LOCK & HARDWARE CO INC
Also Called: Kenstan Lock Co.
101 Commercial St Ste 100 (11803-2408)
PHONE..................631 423-1977
Hans E R Bosch, President
▲ **EMP:** 38 EST: 1964
SQ FT: 10,000
SALES (est): 8.4MM Privately Held
WEB: www.kenstan.com
SIC: 3429 Cabinet hardware

(G-13069)
LIFETIME CHIMNEY SUPPLY LLC
171 E Ames Ct (11803-2332)
PHONE..................516 576-8144
Abraham J Finkler, President
Deborah Grandison, General Mgr
Dennis Martinez, Vice Pres
Joshua Lang, Director
▲ **EMP:** 5
SQ FT: 6,000
SALES (est): 1.2MM Privately Held
WEB: www.lifetimechimneysupply.com
SIC: 3443 5023 Liners, industrial: metal plate; kitchenware

(G-13070)
LITTLE BIRD CHOCOLATES INC
Also Called: Little Bird Kitchen
25 Fairchild Ave Ste 200 (11803-1724)
PHONE..................646 620-6395
Sara Meyer, President
Corey Meyer, Owner
EMP: 9
SALES (est): 696.5K Privately Held
SIC: 2064 Candy & other confectionery products

(G-13071)
MACHINE COMPONENTS CORP
70 Newtown Rd (11803-4382)
PHONE..................516 694-7222
Joseph Kaplan, President
Miriam Kaplan, President
Jay Kaplan, Corp Secy
EMP: 25 EST: 1959
SQ FT: 10,000
SALES (est): 5MM Privately Held
WEB: www.machinecomp.com
SIC: 3568 3625 Clutches, except vehicular; switches, electronic applications

(G-13072)
MARCEL FINISHING CORP
4 David Ct (11803-6009)
PHONE..................718 381-2889
Marcel Brenka, President
Floarea Brenka, Admin Sec
EMP: 30
SQ FT: 7,000
SALES (est): 1.9MM Privately Held
SIC: 2269 2261 2262 Finishing plants; finishing plants, cotton; finishing plants, manmade fiber & silk fabrics

(G-13073)
METAL TEK PRODUCTS
100 Express St (11803-2405)
PHONE..................516 586-4514
Chris Loften, Principal
EMP: 8
SALES (est): 347.6K Privately Held
SIC: 3444 Sheet metal specialties, not stamped

(G-13074)
METROFAB PIPE INCORPORATED
15 Fairchild Ct (11803-1701)
PHONE..................516 349-7373
Elizabeth Ficken, President
Joe Magliato, Vice Pres
EMP: 10
SALES (est): 2.6MM Privately Held
SIC: 3462 3443 Flange, valve & pipe fitting forgings, ferrous; pipe, standpipe & culverts

(G-13075)
MGD BRANDS INC
Also Called: Finesse Accessories
30 Commercial Ct (11803-2415)
PHONE..................516 545-0150
Arthur Damast, CEO
Scott Damast, Vice Pres
Sarah Karwoski, Production
Stephen Hernandez, Director
▲ **EMP:** 50
SALES (est): 25MM Privately Held
WEB: www.finessenovelty.com
SIC: 3911 3999 5094 5131 Jewelry, precious metal; hair & hair-based products; jewelry; hair accessories; ribbons; novelties

(G-13076)
N & G OF AMERICA INC
28 W Lane Dr (11803-5436)
PHONE..................516 428-3414
Najmi Hussain, President
EMP: 12
SALES: 500K Privately Held
SIC: 3571 Electronic computers

(G-13077)
NASH PRINTING INC
Also Called: Sir Speedy
101 Dupont St Ste 2 (11803-1612)
PHONE..................516 935-4567
Noor Baqueri, President
Hussain Baqueri, CFO
Ali Baqueri, Manager
Marc Saltzman, Manager
EMP: 10
SQ FT: 4,500
SALES (est): 1.9MM Privately Held
SIC: 2752 Commercial printing, lithographic

(G-13078)
NASTEL TECHNOLOGIES INC (PA)
88 Sunnyside Blvd Ste 101 (11803-1507)
PHONE..................631 761-9100
David Mavashev, CEO
Richard Nikula, Vice Pres
Bill Norberg, Vice Pres
Michael Ragusa, Vice Pres
Oleg Ustoyev, Engineer
EMP: 48
SQ FT: 7,500
SALES (est): 20.5MM Privately Held
WEB: www.nastel.com
SIC: 7372 Prepackaged software

(G-13079)
NUCLEAR DIAGNOSTIC PDTS NY INC
130 Commercial St (11803-2414)
PHONE..................516 575-4201
Wayne Wong, Ch of Bd
Tom Poland, Manager
EMP: 7
SALES (est): 986.7K Privately Held
SIC: 3829 Medical diagnostic systems, nuclear

(G-13080)
P D R INC
Also Called: Sir Speedy
101 Dupont St (11803-1608)
PHONE..................516 829-5300
Pat Riccardi, President
EMP: 8
SQ FT: 4,500
SALES (est): 1.2MM Privately Held
SIC: 2752 2791 Commercial printing, offset; typesetting

(G-13081)
PETER DIGIOIA
Also Called: Medsurg Direct
7 Sherwood Dr (11803-3218)
PHONE..................516 644-5517
Peter Digioia, Owner
EMP: 5
SALES (est): 424.1K Privately Held
SIC: 3841 5047 Surgical & medical instruments; medical equipment & supplies

(G-13082)
PETRO INC
3 Fairchild Ct (11803-1701)
PHONE..................516 686-1717
Brian Boschert, Branch Mgr
EMP: 9 Publicly Held
SIC: 1389 Gas field services
HQ: Petro, Inc.
9 W Broad St Ste 430
Stamford CT 06902
203 325-5400

(G-13083)
PORT EVERGLADES MACHINE WORKS
Also Called: P E Machine Works
57 Colgate Dr (11803-1803)
PHONE..................516 367-2280
Steven Bellask, President
John Schaefer, Vice Pres
EMP: 10
SQ FT: 10,000
SALES (est): 966K Privately Held
SIC: 3599 3731 Machine shop, jobbing & repair; shipbuilding & repairing

Plainview - Nassau County (G-13084)

(G-13084)
PURITY PRODUCTS INC
200 Terminal Dr (11803-2312)
PHONE.................516 767-1967
Jahn Levin, *President*
Aruna Sood, *VP Opers*
Dorothy Brown, *Purch Mgr*
Michael Iwanciw, *Engineer*
Leah O'Connor, *Human Resources*
▲ **EMP:** 61
SALES (est): 14.2MM **Privately Held**
SIC: 2834 Vitamin, nutrient & hematinic preparations for human use

(G-13085)
ROMAC ELECTRONICS INC
155 E Ames Ct Unit 1 (11803-2383)
PHONE.................516 349-7900
Jerome Bloomberg, *President*
Lee Bloomberg, *Vice Pres*
Michael Bloomberg, *Vice Pres*
Ronald Bloomberg, *Vice Pres*
William Becker, *CFO*
EMP: 49 **EST:** 1952
SQ FT: 42,000
SALES (est): 9.9MM **Privately Held**
WEB: www.romacelectronics.com
SIC: 3499 Shims, metal

(G-13086)
S E A SUPPLIES LTD
Also Called: S E A Supls
1670 Old Country Rd # 104 (11803-5000)
PHONE.................516 694-6677
Martin Reynolds, *Vice Pres*
EMP: 15
SQ FT: 1,400
SALES (est): 1.5MM **Privately Held**
WEB: www.seasupplies.com
SIC: 2819 3646 Industrial inorganic chemicals; commercial indusl & institutional electric lighting fixtures

(G-13087)
SAFE SEAT USA INC
1670 Old Country Rd # 116 (11803-5000)
PHONE.................516 586-8240
Erez Barak, *President*
EMP: 10
SALES (est): 462.1K **Privately Held**
SIC: 2842 Disinfectants, household or industrial plant

(G-13088)
SMC DIODE SOLUTIONS LLC
101 Sunnyside Blvd (11803-1538)
PHONE.................631 965-0869
Yunji Corcoran, *Mng Member*
EMP: 5
SQ FT: 5,000
SALES (est): 270.2K **Privately Held**
SIC: 3674 Diodes, solid state (germanium, silicon, etc.)

(G-13089)
SPIN HOLDCO INC (DH)
303 Sunnyside Blvd # 70 (11803-1597)
PHONE.................516 349-8555
Bob Doyl, *Principal*
EMP: 1
SALES (est): 136.6MM
SALES (corp-wide): 356.6MM **Privately Held**
SIC: 3633 5087 Household laundry equipment; laundry equipment & supplies
HQ: Csc Sw Holdco, Inc.
303 Sunnyside Blvd # 70
Plainview NY 11803
516 349-8555

(G-13090)
STEVAL GRAPHICS CONCEPTS INC
Also Called: Graphic Concepts
7 Fairchild Ct Ste 200 (11803-1701)
PHONE.................516 576-0220
Stephen Trigg, *President*
EMP: 12
SQ FT: 5,000
SALES (est): 760K **Privately Held**
SIC: 2752 Commercial printing, offset

(G-13091)
SUPREME SCREW PRODUCTS INC
10 Skyline Dr Unit B (11803-2517)
PHONE.................718 293-6600
Misha Migdal, *President*
Reinaldo Lopez, *Manager*
EMP: 65 **EST:** 1963
SQ FT: 11,000
SALES (est): 5.2MM **Privately Held**
SIC: 3451 Screw machine products

(G-13092)
TECHNIC INC
Also Called: Advanced Technology Division
111 E Ames Ct Unit 2 (11803-2311)
PHONE.................516 349-0700
Tom Horigome, *Research*
Rob Sheddy, *Branch Mgr*
EMP: 15
SALES (corp-wide): 140.9MM **Privately Held**
WEB: www.technic.com
SIC: 2899 3559 Metal treating compounds; electroplating machinery & equipment
PA: Technic, Inc.
47 Molter St
Cranston RI 02910
401 781-6100

(G-13093)
TRANE US INC
245 Newtown Rd Ste 500 (11803-4300)
PHONE.................631 952-9477
Steve Wey, *District Mgr*
Brian Daigle, *Manager*
Gary Anderson, *Senior Mgr*
EMP: 20 **Privately Held**
SIC: 3585 Refrigeration & heating equipment
HQ: Trane U.S. Inc.
3600 Pammel Creek Rd
La Crosse WI 54601
608 787-2000

(G-13094)
U2O USA LLC
206 Terminal Dr (11803-2312)
PHONE.................516 813-9500
Sam Lamba, *Chairman*
Dennis Dantes, *Vice Pres*
EMP: 3
SALES (est): 6MM
SALES (corp-wide): 6.7MM **Privately Held**
SIC: 3661 5065 Headsets, telephone; mobile telephone equipment
PA: U2o Global Co.,Ltd.
4f U2o Building, No.385, Huanzhu Rd.,
Jimei District
Xiamen 36102
592 574-3713

(G-13095)
ULTRA FINE JEWELRY MFG
180 Dupont St Unit C (11803-1616)
PHONE.................516 349-2848
Benjamin Matalon, *President*
Sandra Matalon, *Vice Pres*
▲ **EMP:** 20 **EST:** 1978
SALES (est): 2.3MM **Privately Held**
SIC: 3911 Jewelry, precious metal

(G-13096)
VASOMEDICAL INC (PA)
137 Commercial St Ste 200 (11803-2410)
PHONE.................516 997-4600
Joshua Markowitz, *Ch of Bd*
David Lieberman, *Vice Ch Bd*
Jun MA, *President*
Peter C Castle, *COO*
Michael J Beecher, *CFO*
▲ **EMP:** 23
SQ FT: 8,700
SALES (est): 72.7MM **Publicly Held**
WEB: www.vasomedical.com
SIC: 3845 3841 Electromedical equipment; surgical & medical instruments; data processing & preparation

(G-13097)
VASOMEDICAL SOLUTIONS INC
137 Commercial St Ste 200 (11803-2410)
PHONE.................516 997-4600
David Nierle, *Vice Pres*

Hong Chen, *Senior Engr*
Jai Daodat, *Accountant*
Larry Liebman, *VP Sales*
Ellyn Ohara, *Manager*
EMP: 99
SALES (est): 25.6MM
SALES (corp-wide): 72.7MM **Publicly Held**
SIC: 3841 Diagnostic apparatus, medical
PA: Vasomedical, Inc.
137 Commercial St Ste 200
Plainview NY 11803
516 997-4600

(G-13098)
VEECO INSTRUMENTS INC
Also Called: Veeco Process Equipment
1 Terminal Dr (11803-2313)
PHONE.................516 349-8300
Brett Klein, *Financial Analy*
Emmanuel Lakios, *Branch Mgr*
EMP: 150
SALES (corp-wide): 484.7MM **Publicly Held**
WEB: www.veeco.com
SIC: 3612 5932 Transformers, except electric; building materials, secondhand
PA: Veeco Instruments Inc.
1 Terminal Dr
Plainview NY 11803
516 677-0200

(G-13099)
VEECO INSTRUMENTS INC (PA)
1 Terminal Dr (11803-2313)
PHONE.................516 677-0200
John R Peeler, *Ch of Bd*
William J Miller, *President*
John Trahan, *COO*
Robert Oates, *Exec VP*
John P Kiernan, *Senior VP*
▲ **EMP:** 277
SQ FT: 80,000
SALES: 484.7MM **Publicly Held**
WEB: www.veeco.com
SIC: 3559 Semiconductor manufacturing machinery

(G-13100)
VEECO PROCESS EQUIPMENT INC (HQ)
1 Terminal Dr (11803-2313)
PHONE.................516 677-0200
John R Peeler, *CEO*
Russell Low, *President*
Derek Derosia, *Regional Mgr*
David Glass, *Exec VP*
Bill Miller, *Exec VP*
▲ **EMP:** 122
SQ FT: 18,000
SALES (est): 149.1MM
SALES (corp-wide): 484.7MM **Publicly Held**
SIC: 3569 Assembly machines, non-metalworking
PA: Veeco Instruments Inc.
1 Terminal Dr
Plainview NY 11803
516 677-0200

(G-13101)
VERTIV CORPORATION
79 Express St Fl 14 (11803-2419)
PHONE.................516 349-8500
Tammy Burns, *Branch Mgr*
EMP: 8
SALES (corp-wide): 322.9MM **Privately Held**
SIC: 3823 Industrial instrmnts msrmnt display/control process variable
HQ: Vertiv Corporation
1050 Dearborn Dr
Columbus OH 43085
614 888-0246

(G-13102)
WILLIAM CHARLES PRTG CO INC
7 Fairchild Ct Ste 100 (11803-1701)
PHONE.................516 349-0900
Chris Pellegrini, *President*
Joseph Pelligrini, *President*
Charles Pelligrini, *Principal*
EMP: 35 **EST:** 1935
SQ FT: 17,000

SALES (est): 6.3MM **Privately Held**
WEB: www.williamcharlesprinting.com
SIC: 2752 2759 2789 Commercial printing, offset; letterpress printing; bookbinding & related work

(G-13103)
XPRESS PRINTING INC
Also Called: T L X
7 Fairchild Ct Ste 100 (11803-1701)
PHONE.................516 605-1000
Chris Moscatl, *President*
EMP: 8
SQ FT: 60,000
SALES (est): 885K **Privately Held**
SIC: 2759 Promotional printing

(G-13104)
Y & Z PRECISION INC
Also Called: Y & Z Precision Machine Shop
155 E Ames Ct Unit 4 (11803-2300)
PHONE.................516 349-8243
Zoltan Vays, *President*
Ryszard Dobrogowski, *Admin Sec*
EMP: 15
SQ FT: 7,400
SALES (est): 2.5MM **Privately Held**
SIC: 3671 Electron tubes

Plattsburgh
Clinton County

(G-13105)
ADIRONDACK PENNYSAVER INC
177 Margaret St (12901-1837)
PHONE.................518 563-0100
Corinne Rigby, *President*
Mark Rigby, *Corp Secy*
EMP: 25
SQ FT: 5,000
SALES (est): 2.5MM **Privately Held**
WEB: www.adkpennysaver.com
SIC: 2741 2759 Shopping news: publishing & printing; commercial printing

(G-13106)
APGN INC
Also Called: Apg Neuros
160 Banker Rd (12901-7309)
PHONE.................518 324-4150
Omar Hammoud, *President*
EMP: 30 **Privately Held**
SIC: 3564 Blowing fans: industrial or commercial
HQ: Apgn Inc
1270 Boul Michele-Bohec
Blainville QC J7C 5
450 939-0799

(G-13107)
AWR ENERGY INC
35 Melody Ln (12901-6414)
P.O. Box 3027 (12901-0298)
PHONE.................585 469-7750
Steve Baiocchi, *President*
George Klemann, *Treasurer*
EMP: 10
SALES (est): 911.9K **Privately Held**
SIC: 3511 Turbines & turbine generator sets

(G-13108)
B3CG INTERCONNECT USA INC
18 Northern Ave 100 (12903-3905)
PHONE.................450 491-4040
Stefan Baumans, *President*
Marc Brosseau, *Vice Pres*
EMP: 18 **EST:** 2008
SALES (est): 3.4MM
SALES (corp-wide): 476.3MM **Privately Held**
SIC: 3679 Harness assemblies for electronic use: wire or cable
HQ: B3cg Interconnect Inc
310 Boul Industriel
Saint-Eustache QC J7R 5
450 491-4040

▲ = Import ▼ = Export
◆ = Import/Export

GEOGRAPHIC SECTION

Plattsburgh - Clinton County (G-13135)

(G-13109)
BESTWALL LLC
Also Called: Georgia-Pacific
327 Margaret St (12901-1719)
PHONE..................518 561-3500
Kirk Stallsmith, *Vice Pres*
Michael Penfield, *Facilities Mgr*
Judy Tallada, *Manager*
Phil Racine, *Info Tech Mgr*
EMP: 540
SQ FT: 14,464
SALES (corp-wide): 42.9B **Privately Held**
WEB: www.gp.com
SIC: 2621 2676 Paper mills; sanitary paper products
HQ: Georgia-Pacific Llc
   133 Peachtree St Nw
   Atlanta GA 30303
   404 652-4000

(G-13110)
BIMBO BAKERIES USA INC
67 S Peru St (12901-3834)
PHONE..................518 563-1320
Saith Haris, *Manager*
EMP: 17 **Privately Held**
SIC: 2051 Bread, cake & related products
HQ: Bimbo Bakeries Usa, Inc
   255 Business Center Dr # 200
   Horsham PA 19044
   215 347-5500

(G-13111)
BIOTECH ENERGY INC
Also Called: Biotech Energy Systems
100 Clinton Point Dr (12901-6002)
PHONE..................800 340-1387
Stan Kinsman, *CEO*
EMP: 6 **EST:** 2015
SALES (est): 316.4K **Privately Held**
SIC: 3433 Burners, furnaces, boilers & stokers

(G-13112)
BOMBARDIER MASS TRANSIT CORP
71 Wall St (12901-3755)
PHONE..................518 566-0150
William Spurr, *President*
Rene Lalande, *Vice Pres*
James Tooley, *Vice Pres*
▲ **EMP:** 380
SALES (est): 62.2MM
SALES (corp-wide): 3.4B **Privately Held**
SIC: 3743 Railroad equipment
HQ: Brp Us Inc
   10101 Science Dr
   Sturtevant WI 53177
   715 842-8886

(G-13113)
BOMBARDIER TRNSP HOLDINGS USA
Also Called: Bombardier Corp Track
71 Wall St (12901-3755)
PHONE..................518 566-5067
George Psycharis, *General Mgr*
Charles Roush, *Buyer*
EMP: 21
SALES (corp-wide): 16.2B **Privately Held**
SIC: 3721 Aircraft
HQ: Bombardier Transportation (Holdings) Usa Inc
   1501 Lebanon Church Rd
   Pittsburgh PA 15236
   412 655-5700

(G-13114)
BRUSHTECH (DISC) INC
4 Matt Ave (12901-3736)
P.O. Box 1130 (12901-0068)
PHONE..................518 563-8420
Nora Gunjian, *President*
Zaven Gunjian, *Vice Pres*
▲ **EMP:** 18
SQ FT: 34,000
SALES (est): 3.3MM **Privately Held**
WEB: www.brushtech.com
SIC: 3991 Brushes, household or industrial

(G-13115)
CAMSO MANUFACTURING USA LTD (HQ)
1 Martina Cir (12901-7421)
PHONE..................518 561-7528
Ivan Warmuth, *Ch of Bd*
John Robare, *Prdtn Mgr*
Udaya Pathirage, *Buyer*
Mario Bouchard, *Treasurer*
▲ **EMP:** 70
SALES (est): 16.6MM **Privately Held**
SIC: 3061 Oil & gas field machinery rubber goods (mechanical)
PA: Camso Inc
   2633 Rue Macpherson
   Magog QC J1X 0
   819 868-1500

(G-13116)
CEIT CORP
625 State Route 3 Unit 2 (12901-6530)
PHONE..................518 825-0649
Fax: 518 825-0651
▲ **EMP:** 10
SQ FT: 15,000
SALES (est): 950K **Privately Held**
SIC: 3648 Mfg Lighting Equipment

(G-13117)
CINTUBE LTD
139 Distribution Way (12901-3734)
PHONE..................518 324-3333
EMP: 11
SALES (est): 1.4MM **Privately Held**
SIC: 3399 Primary metal products

(G-13118)
COMMUNITY NEWSPAPER GROUP LLC
Also Called: Plattsburgh Press-Republican
170 Margaret St (12901-1838)
P.O. Box 459 (12901-0459)
PHONE..................518 565-4114
Kevin Richard, *President*
Bob Parks, *Branch Mgr*
EMP: 19 **Privately Held**
WEB: www.clintonnc.com
SIC: 2711 Newspapers: publishing only, not printed on site
HQ: Community Newspaper Group, Llc
   3500 Colonnade Pkwy # 600
   Birmingham AL 35243

(G-13119)
DENTON PUBLICATIONS INC
Also Called: Free Trader
21 Mckinley Ave Ste 3 (12901-3800)
PHONE..................518 561-9680
Cindy Tucker, *General Mgr*
EMP: 20
SALES (corp-wide): 6MM **Privately Held**
WEB: www.denpubs.com
SIC: 2711 2721 Commercial printing & newspaper publishing combined; periodicals
PA: Denton Publications, Inc.
   14 Hand Ave
   Elizabethtown NY 12932
   518 873-6368

(G-13120)
EURO GEAR (USA) INC
1 Cumberland Ave (12901-1833)
PHONE..................518 578-1775
Eloise Beauche, *Branch Mgr*
EMP: 8
SALES (corp-wide): 5.4MM **Privately Held**
SIC: 3241 3599 Natural cement; machine & other job shop work
PA: Euro Gear (Usa), Inc.
   1395 Brickell Ave Ste 800
   Miami FL 33131
   518 578-1775

(G-13121)
FEDEX GROUND PACKAGE SYS INC
82 Gateway Dr (12901-5371)
PHONE..................800 463-3339
William Battle, *General Mgr*
EMP: 5
SALES (corp-wide): 65.4B **Publicly Held**
SIC: 3086 Packaging & shipping materials, foamed plastic
HQ: Fedex Ground Package System, Inc.
   1000 Fed Ex Dr
   Coraopolis PA 15108
   412 269-1000

(G-13122)
GRAYMONT MATERIALS INC
Also Called: Plattsburgh Quarry
111 Quarry Rd (12901-6215)
PHONE..................518 561-5200
Todd Kempainen, *President*
William Trudo, *Manager*
Lawrence Diorio, *Info Tech Mgr*
Charlie Mitchell, *Maintence Staff*
EMP: 28
SALES (est): 922.1K **Privately Held**
SIC: 3281 2951 Stone, quarrying & processing of own stone products; asphalt paving mixtures & blocks

(G-13123)
HANET PLASTICS USA INC
139 Distribution Way (12901-3734)
PHONE..................518 324-5850
EMP: 5
SALES (est): 370K **Privately Held**
SIC: 2821 Mfg Plastic Materials/Resins

(G-13124)
HERITAGE PRINTING CENTER
94 Margaret St (12901-2925)
PHONE..................518 563-8240
Roger A Conant, *Partner*
Roger W Conant, *Partner*
EMP: 7 **EST:** 1976
SQ FT: 2,200
SALES (est): 730.2K **Privately Held**
WEB: www.heritageprint.com
SIC: 2752 Commercial printing, offset

(G-13125)
IEC HOLDEN CORPORATION
51 Distribution Way (12901-3731)
PHONE..................518 213-3991
Robert Briscoe, *Ch of Bd*
▲ **EMP:** 17
SALES (est): 3.5MM **Privately Held**
SIC: 3621 Inverters, rotating: electrical

(G-13126)
INTRAPAC INTERNATIONAL CORP
4 Plant St (12901-3771)
PHONE..................518 561-2030
Robert Thiessen, *Plant Mgr*
Rick Van Engelenhove, *Plant Mgr*
Anthony Staring, *Manager*
EMP: 150
SALES (corp-wide): 120MM **Privately Held**
SIC: 3085 3221 Plastics bottles; glass containers
PA: Intrapac International Corporation
   136 Fairview Rd Ste 320
   Mooresville NC 28117
   704 360-8910

(G-13127)
ISLAND MACHINE INC
86 Boynton Ave (12901-1236)
PHONE..................518 562-1232
Marvin C Benton, *President*
Marvin Benton, *President*
Bonnie Benton, *Vice Pres*
EMP: 9
SQ FT: 2,100
SALES: 600K **Privately Held**
SIC: 3599 Machine & other job shop work

(G-13128)
JOHNS MANVILLE CORPORATION
1 Kaycee Loop Rd (12901-2010)
PHONE..................518 565-3000
Tim Barnewall, *Safety Dir*
Jim Kopaska, *Plant Mgr*
David Hardway, *Production*
Ryan Creswell, *Plant Engr*
Steve Kuhn, *Manager*
EMP: 28
SALES (corp-wide): 242.1B **Publicly Held**
WEB: www.jm.com
SIC: 2952 Roofing materials
HQ: Johns Manville Corporation
   717 17th St Ste 800
   Denver CO 80202
   303 978-2000

(G-13129)
KNORR BRAKE COMPANY LLC
613 State Route 3 Unit 1 (12901-6530)
PHONE..................518 561-1387
Phil Rockwell, *Site Mgr*
EMP: 6 **Privately Held**
WEB: www.knorrbrakecorp.com
SIC: 3743 Brakes, air & vacuum: railway; rapid transit cars & equipment
HQ: Knorr Brake Company Llc
   1 Arthur Peck Dr
   Westminster MD 21157
   410 875-0900

(G-13130)
LAKESIDE CONTAINER CORP (PA)
299 Arizona Ave (12903-4429)
P.O. Box 845 (12901-0845)
PHONE..................518 561-6150
George Bouyea, *President*
Paige Raville, *Vice Pres*
Ron Charette, *Opers Mgr*
Darrin Campbell, *Design Engr*
Carol Hollenbeck, *Marketing Staff*
EMP: 19 **EST:** 1958
SQ FT: 65,000
SALES (est): 2.2MM **Privately Held**
WEB: www.lakesidecontainer.com
SIC: 2653 Boxes, corrugated: made from purchased materials

(G-13131)
LEROUX FUELS
994 Military Tpke (12901-5926)
PHONE..................518 563-3653
Nicholas Leroux, *Principal*
EMP: 10
SALES (est): 1.5MM **Privately Held**
SIC: 2869 Fuels

(G-13132)
MATROX GRAPHICS INC
625 State Route 3 1/2 (12901-6530)
PHONE..................518 561-4417
Robert Lasalle Jr, *Manager*
EMP: 8 **Privately Held**
SIC: 3572 Computer tape drives & components
PA: Graphiques Matrox Inc
   1055 Boul Saint-Regis
   Dorval QC H9P 2
   514 822-6000

(G-13133)
MEDISCA INC (DH)
661 State Route 3 Unit C (12901-6531)
P.O. Box 2592 (12901-0229)
PHONE..................514 333-7811
Antonio Dos Santos, *Ch of Bd*
Joseph Antonecchia, *General Mgr*
Phil Blouch, *Business Mgr*
Serina Konomos, *Vice Pres*
Maria Zaccardo, *Vice Pres*
▲ **EMP:** 50
SQ FT: 6,000
SALES (est): 16.5MM **Privately Held**
SIC: 2843 Surface active agents
HQ: Medisca Pharmaceutique Inc
   6090 Boul Henri-Bourassa O
   Saint-Laurent QC H4R 3
   800 932-1039

(G-13134)
MOLD-RITE PLASTICS LLC
1 Plant St (12901-3788)
PHONE..................518 561-1812
Dennis Houpt, *Senior VP*
Barry Daggett, *Vice Pres*
Keith Kelble, *Vice Pres*
Bhojraj Naveen, *Vice Pres*
Dawn Nowicki, *Vice Pres*
EMP: 8 **Privately Held**
SIC: 3089 Injection molding of plastics
HQ: Mold-Rite Plastics, Llc
   30 N La Salle St Ste 2425
   Chicago IL 60602
   518 561-1812

(G-13135)
MONAGHAN MEDICAL CORPORATION (PA)
5 Latour Ave Ste 1600 (12901-7271)
PHONE..................518 561-7330
Gerald Slemko, *President*

Plattsburgh - Clinton County (G-13136)

Corey Lodico, *Division Mgr*
Janet Smith, *Division Mgr*
Dominic Coppolo, *Vice Pres*
William Seitz, *Vice Pres*
▲ **EMP:** 52
SALES (est): 9.9MM **Privately Held**
WEB: www.monaghanmed.com
SIC: 3842 Surgical appliances & supplies

(G-13136)
NORSK TITANIUM US INC (DH)
44 Martina Cir (12901-7420)
PHONE..........................949 735-9463
Warren Boley, *Ch of Bd*
Tamara Morytko, *COO*
Bart V Aalst, *CFO*
Gunnar Aasbo-Skinderhaug,
EMP: 9
SQ FT: 5,000
SALES (est): 3.5MM
SALES (corp-wide): 18MM **Privately Held**
SIC: 3728 Aircraft assemblies, subassemblies & parts
HQ: Norsk Titanium Equipment As
Flyplassveien 20
Honefoss 3514
321 413-52

(G-13137)
NORTH AMERICAN DOOR CORP
Also Called: Nadcor
1471 Military Tpke (12901-7453)
PHONE..........................518 566-0161
Antonio Gervasi, *President*
Anna Montesano, *Corp Secy*
Bruno Gervasi, *Vice Pres*
Patrick McCall, *Manager*
▼ **EMP:** 12
SQ FT: 20,000
SALES (est): 3.6MM **Privately Held**
WEB: www.nadcor.com
SIC: 3442 Metal doors, sash & trim

(G-13138)
NORTHEAST CONCRETE PDTS INC
1024 Military Tpke (12901-5959)
PHONE..........................518 563-0700
Arthur Spiegel, *President*
James L Neverett, *Senior VP*
Darren C Babbie, *Vice Pres*
EMP: 15 **EST:** 1938
SQ FT: 31,500
SALES (est): 1.4MM **Privately Held**
WEB: www.concretebuildingsupply.com
SIC: 3272 Precast terrazzo or concrete products

(G-13139)
NORTHEAST GROUP
Also Called: Strictly Business
12 Nepco Way (12903-3961)
PHONE..........................518 563-8214
Herb Carpenter, *Partner*
Mary Carpenter, *Partner*
Mike Carpenter, *Partner*
Elizabeth Vicencio, *CFO*
▲ **EMP:** 55
SALES (est): 6.6MM **Privately Held**
WEB: www.sbmonthly.com
SIC: 2721 Periodicals

(G-13140)
NORTHEAST PRTG & DIST CO INC
163 Idaho Ave (12903-3987)
PHONE..........................514 577-3545
EMP: 7
SALES (corp-wide): 5.6MM **Privately Held**
SIC: 2721 Periodicals
PA: Northeast Printing & Distribution Company, Inc.
12 Nepco Way
Plattsburgh NY 12903
518 563-8214

(G-13141)
NORTHEAST PRTG & DIST CO INC (PA)
Also Called: Northeast Group, The
12 Nepco Way (12903-3961)
PHONE..........................518 563-8214
Herb Carpenter, *President*

Marcia Vicencio, *Editor*
Mary E Carpenter, *Vice Pres*
Michael Carpenter, *Vice Pres*
Kelly Miller, *Facilities Mgr*
▲ **EMP:** 36
SQ FT: 115,000
SALES (est): 5.6MM **Privately Held**
WEB: www.thenortheastgroup.com
SIC: 2752 Commercial printing, offset

(G-13142)
PACTIV LLC
74 Weed St (12901-1260)
PHONE..........................518 562-6101
James Morris, *Vice Pres*
Michael Petit, *Plant Mgr*
Mark Cooley, *Safety Mgr*
Jim Armstrong, *Maint Spvr*
Cynthia Maynard, *Buyer*
EMP: 200
SQ FT: 64,904 **Privately Held**
WEB: www.pactiv.com
SIC: 2656 2657 2671 Plates, paper: made from purchased material; food containers, folding: made from purchased material; packaging paper & plastics film, coated & laminated
HQ: Pactiv Llc
1900 W Field Ct
Lake Forest IL 60045
847 482-2000

(G-13143)
PACTIV LLC
74 Weed St (12901-1260)
PHONE..........................518 562-6120
Anthony Searing, *Manager*
EMP: 120 **Privately Held**
WEB: www.pactiv.com
SIC: 3089 Plastic containers, except foam
HQ: Pactiv Llc
1900 W Field Ct
Lake Forest IL 60045
847 482-2000

(G-13144)
PERFORMANCE DIESEL SERVICE LLC
24 Latour Ave (12901-7206)
PHONE..........................315 854-5269
Scott Roketenetz,
EMP: 12
SALES (est): 1.9MM **Privately Held**
SIC: 2911 Diesel fuels

(G-13145)
PLATTCO CORPORATION (PA)
7 White St (12901-3471)
PHONE..........................518 563-4640
Douglas J Crozierm, *Ch of Bd*
Stacie Chapman, *Purch Mgr*
Logan Miller, *Design Engr*
Danielle Ross, *Sales Mgr*
John O'Brien, *Regl Sales Mgr*
◆ **EMP:** 50 **EST:** 1897
SQ FT: 60,000
SALES (est): 12.6MM **Privately Held**
WEB: www.plattco.com
SIC: 3369 3491 3322 Machinery castings, nonferrous: ex. alum., copper, die, etc.; industrial valves; malleable iron foundries

(G-13146)
PLATTCO CORPORATION
18 White St (12901-3438)
PHONE..........................518 563-4640
Craig De Boos, *QC Mgr*
Tim Boshart, *Regl Sales Mgr*
Alex Menard, *Sales Engr*
Roxanne Coleman, *Sales Staff*
Justin Soule, *Sales Staff*
EMP: 11
SALES (est): 1.4MM
SALES (corp-wide): 12.6MM **Privately Held**
WEB: www.plattco.com
SIC: 3369 Nonferrous foundries
PA: Plattco Corporation
7 White St
Plattsburgh NY 12901
518 563-4640

(G-13147)
PLATTSBURGH SHEET METAL INC
95 Sailly Ave (12901-1726)
PHONE..........................518 561-4930
Sandra Carlo, *President*
EMP: 5
SALES (est): 1MM **Privately Held**
SIC: 3444 Sheet metalwork

(G-13148)
PREVOST CAR (US) INC
260 Banker Rd (12901-7310)
PHONE..........................518 957-2052
Jason McHael, *Branch Mgr*
EMP: 150
SALES (corp-wide): 39.6B **Privately Held**
SIC: 3711 Buses, all types, assembly of
HQ: Prevost Car (Us) Inc.
7900 National Service Rd
Greensboro NC 27409
908 222-7211

(G-13149)
PRICE CHOPPER OPERATING CO
19 Centre Dr (12901-6553)
PHONE..........................518 562-3565
Tom Tsounis, *Manager*
EMP: 10
SALES (corp-wide): 3.3B **Privately Held**
SIC: 3751 Motorcycles & related parts
HQ: Price Chopper Operating Co., Inc
501 Duanesburg Rd
Schenectady NY 12306
518 379-1600

(G-13150)
PRIM HALL ENTERPRISES INC
11 Spellman Rd (12901-5326)
PHONE..........................518 561-7408
John Prim, *President*
David Hall, *Vice Pres*
EMP: 12
SQ FT: 43,000
SALES (est): 1.4MM **Privately Held**
WEB: www.primhall.com
SIC: 3555 7699 3542 7389 Printing trades machinery; industrial machinery & equipment repair; machine tools, metal forming type; design, commercial & industrial

(G-13151)
R & S MACHINE CENTER INC
Also Called: R&S Machine
4398 Route 22 (12901-5851)
P.O. Box 40 (12901-0040)
PHONE..........................518 563-4016
Robert Davenport, *President*
EMP: 10
SQ FT: 7,000
SALES (est): 1.9MM **Privately Held**
SIC: 3599 5051 Machine shop, jobbing & repair; steel

(G-13152)
RAMBACHS INTERNATIONAL BAKERY
65 S Peru St (12901-3834)
PHONE..........................518 563-1721
Gerard Rambach, *President*
Joan Rambach, *Treasurer*
EMP: 18
SQ FT: 3,500
SALES (est): 830K **Privately Held**
SIC: 2051 Bakery: wholesale or wholesale/retail combined

(G-13153)
RAPA INDEPENDENT NORTH AMERICA
Also Called: Rina
124 Connecticut Rd (12903-4955)
PHONE..........................518 561-0513
Manil Whig, *President*
▲ **EMP:** 6
SQ FT: 5,000
SALES: 200K **Privately Held**
SIC: 2013 Sausage casings, natural

(G-13154)
SALERNO PACKAGING INC (HQ)
Also Called: Salerno Plastic Film and Bags
14 Gus Lapham Ln (12901-6534)
PHONE..........................518 563-3636
Kurt Strater, *President*
Roger Sullivan, *Senior VP*
Mac Elgin, *Vice Pres*
Matt Ramsey, *Marketing Staff*
Greg Crites, *Manager*
EMP: 13
SALES (est): 37.6MM **Privately Held**
SIC: 2673 Plastic bags: made from purchased materials

(G-13155)
SEMEC CORP
20 Gateway Dr (12901-5371)
PHONE..........................518 825-0160
Mario Babin, *Manager*
Deborah Wells, *Admin Mgr*
▲ **EMP:** 15
SALES (est): 2.1MM **Privately Held**
SIC: 3743 Railroad equipment

(G-13156)
SSF PRODUCTION LLC
194 Pleasant Ridge Rd (12901-5841)
PHONE..........................518 324-3407
Tilo Hildebrand, *Plant Mgr*
Frank Filbir, *Mng Member*
Tilo Hildebrand,
▲ **EMP:** 10
SQ FT: 17,000
SALES (est): 1.8MM **Privately Held**
SIC: 3296 Acoustical board & tile, mineral wool

(G-13157)
STEELE TRUSS AND PANEL LLC
112 Trade Rd (12901-6259)
P.O. Box 1023, Peru (12972-1023)
PHONE..........................518 562-4663
Loretta Steele, *Mng Member*
Leslie Baker,
EMP: 9 **EST:** 2015
SQ FT: 12,000
SALES: 488K **Privately Held**
SIC: 3443 Truss plates, metal

(G-13158)
STEELE TRUSS COMPANY INC
118 Trade Rd (12901-6259)
PHONE..........................518 562-4663
Robert Steele, *CEO*
Joel C Steele, *President*
Thomas E Steele Sr, *President*
Loretta Steele, *Corp Secy*
Marvin Hooper, *VP Engrg*
EMP: 25
SQ FT: 80,000
SALES (est): 2MM **Privately Held**
WEB: www.steeltrusses.net
SIC: 2439 1541 Trusses, wooden roof; steel building construction

(G-13159)
STERRX LLC
141 Idaho Ave (12903-3987)
PHONE..........................518 324-7879
Terry Wiley, *VP Mfg*
Gary Hanley,
EMP: 32
SALES (est): 8.5MM **Privately Held**
SIC: 2834 Solutions, pharmaceutical

(G-13160)
STUDLEY PRINTING & PUBLISHING
Also Called: Lake Champlain Weekly
4701 State Route 9 (12901-6036)
PHONE..........................518 563-1414
William Studley, *President*
Caroline Kehne, *Editor*
Kim Mousseau, *Publications*
EMP: 18
SALES (est): 3.2MM **Privately Held**
WEB: www.studleyprinting.com
SIC: 2752 8743 Commercial printing, offset; public relations & publicity

GEOGRAPHIC SECTION

(G-13161)
SWAROVSKI LIGHTING LTD (PA)
Also Called: Schonbek
61 Industrial Blvd (12901-1908)
PHONE...................................518 563-7500
John Simms, *CEO*
Andrew Schonbek, *President*
Brock Trombley, *Opers Mgr*
Roxanne Trombly, *Production*
Deborah Buskey, *Engineer*
◆ **EMP:** 267
SQ FT: 200,000
SALES (est): 59.4MM **Privately Held**
SIC: 3645 Residential lighting fixtures

(G-13162)
SWAROVSKI LIGHTING LTD
Also Called: Schonbek Shipping Bldg
1483 Military Tpke Ste B (12901-7453)
PHONE...................................518 324-6378
PR Llier, *Principal*
EMP: 400
SALES (corp-wide): 59.4MM **Privately Held**
SIC: 3645 Chandeliers, residential
PA: Swarovski Lighting, Ltd.
61 Industrial Blvd
Plattsburgh NY 12901
518 563-7500

(G-13163)
TITHERINGTON DESIGN & MFG
102 Sharron Ave Unit 1 (12901-3828)
PHONE...................................518 324-2205
Philip D Titherington, *CEO*
EMP: 11
SALES (est): 1.9MM **Privately Held**
SIC: 3089 7336 Injection molding of plastics; package design

(G-13164)
UMS MANUFACTURING LLC
194 Pleasant Ridge Rd (12901-5841)
PHONE...................................518 562-2410
Mark Schulter, *Mng Member*
Udo Schulter,
EMP: 10
SQ FT: 57,000
SALES (est): 1.2MM **Privately Held**
SIC: 2675 Waterproof cardboard: made from purchased materials

(G-13165)
UPSTONE MATERIALS INC (DH)
111 Quarry Rd (12901-6215)
PHONE...................................518 561-5321
Sylvan Gross, *President*
EMP: 52 **EST:** 2017
SQ FT: 5,000
SALES: 40MM
SALES (corp-wide): 95.5MM **Privately Held**
SIC: 1429 3273 2951 Grits mining (crushed stone); ready-mixed concrete; asphalt & asphaltic paving mixtures (not from refineries)
HQ: Barrett Industries Corporation
73 Headquarters Plz
Morristown NJ 07960
973 533-1001

(G-13166)
UPSTONE MATERIALS INC
Also Called: Potsdam Stone Concrete
111 Quarry Rd (12901-6215)
PHONE...................................315 265-8036
Judy Fuhr, *Superintendent*
Dave Gordon, *Plant Mgr*
Donny Smith, *Manager*
EMP: 17
SQ FT: 3,769
SALES (corp-wide): 95.5MM **Privately Held**
WEB: www.graymont-ab.com
SIC: 3273 5083 Ready-mixed concrete; landscaping equipment
HQ: Upstone Materials Inc.
111 Quarry Rd
Plattsburgh NY 12901
518 561-5321

(G-13167)
VALCOUR BREWING COMPANY LLC
49 Ohio Rd (12903-4409)
PHONE...................................518 324-2337

Mary Pearl, *Mng Member*
Margaret Weicher, *Mng Member*
EMP: 27
SALES: 1.2MM **Privately Held**
SIC: 2082 5921 Malt beverages; beer (packaged)

(G-13168)
WEBER INTL PACKG CO LLC
318 Cornelia St (12901-2300)
PHONE...................................518 561-8282
K Heinz Weber, *CEO*
Tihamer Monostori,
Kateri Rock,
EMP: 54
SQ FT: 44,000
SALES (est): 10.2MM **Privately Held**
WEB: www.weberintl.com
SIC: 3089 Plastic containers, except foam

(G-13169)
WESTINGHOUSE A BRAKE TECH CORP
72 Arizona Ave (12903-4427)
PHONE...................................518 561-0044
Bob Brassee, *Manager*
EMP: 70
SALES (corp-wide): 3.8B **Publicly Held**
WEB: www.wabtecglobalservices.com
SIC: 3743 Brakes, air & vacuum: railway; locomotives & parts; freight cars & equipment; rapid transit cars & equipment
PA: Westinghouse Air Brake Technologies Corporation
1001 Airbrake Ave
Wilmerding PA 15148
412 825-1000

(G-13170)
WOODFALLS INDUSTRIES
434 Burke Rd (12901-5214)
PHONE...................................518 236-7201
Tammy Deyo, *Owner*
EMP: 10 **EST:** 2010
SALES (est): 450K **Privately Held**
SIC: 3999 Manufacturing industries

(G-13171)
XBORDER ENTERTAINMENT LLC
568 State Route 3 (12901-6526)
PHONE...................................518 726-7036
Casey Spiegel, *Mng Member*
EMP: 7
SQ FT: 35,000
SALES (est): 193.4K **Privately Held**
SIC: 7372 Application computer software

Pleasant Valley
Dutchess County

(G-13172)
SIMMONS FABRICATING SVC INC
1558 Main St (12569)
PHONE...................................845 635-3755
Robert Lalonde, *President*
Colleen Lalonde, *President*
EMP: 5
SQ FT: 5,000
SALES: 250K **Privately Held**
SIC: 3444 Sheet metalwork

Pleasantville
Westchester County

(G-13173)
CARLARA GROUP LTD
Also Called: Sir Speedy
467 Bedford Rd (10570-2928)
PHONE...................................914 769-2020
Carlos Bernard, *President*
Susana Lara, *Vice Pres*
EMP: 5
SQ FT: 3,000
SALES (est): 1MM **Privately Held**
SIC: 2752 2791 2789 Commercial printing, offset; typesetting; bookbinding & related work

(G-13174)
COUNTY FABRICATORS
175 Marble Ave (10570-3421)
PHONE...................................914 741-0219
Kevin Marino, *Engineer*
Michael Gomes, *Bookkeeper*
Kristina Benza, *Mng Member*
Mike Husband, *Director*
Laura Zapata, *Admin Dir*
EMP: 18
SQ FT: 13,200
SALES: 1.5MM **Privately Held**
WEB: www.countyfabricators.com
SIC: 3441 Fabricated structural metal

(G-13175)
OPTIMIZED DEVICES INC
220 Marble Ave (10570-3465)
PHONE...................................914 769-6100
Arthur Zuch, *President*
Robert Zuch, *Vice Pres*
EMP: 13
SQ FT: 6,000
SALES (est): 2.1MM **Privately Held**
WEB: www.optdev.com
SIC: 3825 Test equipment for electronic & electric measurement

(G-13176)
READERS DGEST YUNG FMILIES INC
Readers Digest Rd (10570)
PHONE...................................914 238-1000
Thomas O Ryder, *Ch of Bd*
EMP: 25
SALES (est): 868.4K **Privately Held**
WEB: www.rd.com
SIC: 2731 Book publishing
HQ: Trusted Media Brands, Inc.
750 3rd Ave Fl 3
New York NY 10017
914 238-1000

(G-13177)
READERS DIGEST SLS & SVCS INC
Readers Digest Rd (10570)
PHONE...................................914 238-1000
Daniel Lagani, *Ch of Bd*
Gregory Coleman, *President*
Howard Halligan, *Business Mgr*
George Scimone, *Vice Pres*
Bonnie Monahan, *Treasurer*
EMP: 156 **EST:** 1961
SALES (est): 20.9MM **Privately Held**
WEB: www.changeone.com
SIC: 2721 Periodicals
HQ: Trusted Media Brands, Inc.
750 3rd Ave Fl 3
New York NY 10017
914 238-1000

(G-13178)
SAW MILL PEDIATRICS PLLC
95 Locust Rd (10570-3333)
PHONE...................................914 449-6064
Maryann Hammel, *Principal*
EMP: 9
SALES (est): 996.9K **Privately Held**
SIC: 2421 Sawmills & planing mills, general

Poestenkill
Rensselaer County

(G-13179)
CANTON BIO-MEDICAL INC (PA)
Also Called: Saint-Gobain Performance Plas
11 Sicho Rd (12140-3102)
PHONE...................................518 283-5963
John Bedell, *Principal*
Bob Pellerin, *Controller*
EMP: 36
SQ FT: 36,000
SALES (est): 2.4MM **Privately Held**
SIC: 2822 Silicone rubbers

(G-13180)
DYNAMIC SYSTEMS INC (PA)
Also Called: D S I
323 Rte 355 (12140)
P.O. Box 1234 (12140-1234)
PHONE...................................518 283-5350

David Ferguson, *President*
Peggy Jacobsen, *General Mgr*
Brian Allen, *Vice Pres*
Jean Jacon, *Vice Pres*
Emily Warren, *Materials Mgr*
▲ **EMP:** 38 **EST:** 1957
SQ FT: 29,000
SALES (est): 6.4MM **Privately Held**
WEB: www.gleeble.com
SIC: 3829 Measuring & controlling devices

(G-13181)
INTER STATE LAMINATES INC
44 Main St (12140-3201)
P.O. Box 270 (12140-0270)
PHONE...................................518 283-8355
Harold Crandall, *President*
Debbie Crandall, *Admin Sec*
EMP: 46
SALES (est): 6.1MM **Privately Held**
WEB: www.isltops.com
SIC: 3083 2541 Plastic finished products, laminated; wood partitions & fixtures

(G-13182)
SAINT-GOBAIN PRFMCE PLAS CORP
11 Sicho Rd (12140-3102)
PHONE...................................518 283-5963
Lynn Monrow, *General Mgr*
EMP: 16
SALES (corp-wide): 213.5MM **Privately Held**
SIC: 3089 Spouting, plastic & glass fiber reinforced
HQ: Saint-Gobain Performance Plastics Corporation
31500 Solon Rd
Solon OH 44139
440 836-6900

(G-13183)
VAN SLYKE BELTING LLC
606 Snyders Corners Rd (12140-2914)
PHONE...................................518 283-5479
H Van, *Principal*
EMP: 6 **EST:** 2001
SALES (est): 652.2K **Privately Held**
SIC: 3052 Rubber belting

Poland
Herkimer County

(G-13184)
PERFEX CORPORATION
32 Case St (13431)
PHONE...................................315 826-3600
Michael E Kubick, *President*
Mike Dougherty, *Marketing Staff*
▲ **EMP:** 13 **EST:** 1924
SQ FT: 24,000
SALES (est): 2.3MM **Privately Held**
WEB: www.perfexonline.com
SIC: 3991 2392 Brooms & brushes; mops, floor & dust

Pomona
Rockland County

(G-13185)
CAMBRIDGE SECURITY SEALS LLC
1 Cambridge Plz (10970-2676)
PHONE...................................845 520-4111
Shannon McElroy, *Vice Pres*
Jill Nilsson, *Sales Staff*
Elisha Tropper, *Mng Member*
Paul Scheidegger, *Manager*
▲ **EMP:** 20
SQ FT: 25,000
SALES (est): 5.2MM **Privately Held**
SIC: 3089 Injection molding of plastics

(G-13186)
NUTRA-SCIENTIFICS LLC
108 Overlook Rd (10970-2115)
PHONE...................................917 238-8510
Patrice Mouehla,
EMP: 9 **EST:** 2012

Pomona - Rockland County (G-13187)

SALES (est): 575K Privately Held
SIC: 2834 5122 Pharmaceutical preparations; pharmaceuticals

(G-13187)
SAN JAE EDUCATIONAL RESOU
9 Chamberlain Ct (10970-2837)
PHONE............................845 364-5458
EMP: 4
SALES (est): 1MM Privately Held
SIC: 7372 Prepackaged Software Services

Port Byron
Cayuga County

(G-13188)
MARTENS COUNTRY KIT PDTS LLC
1323 Towpath Rd (13140)
P.O. Box 428 (13140-0428)
PHONE............................315 776-8821
Jill Skrupa, Sales Staff
Timothy Martens,
▲ EMP: 10
SALES (est): 859.8K Privately Held
SIC: 2099 Potatoes, dried: packaged with other ingredients

(G-13189)
MAX 200 PERFORMANCE DOG EQP
2113 State Route 31 (13140-9423)
PHONE............................315 776-9588
Irene Lamphere, President
Alfred Lamphere, Vice Pres
Joyce Scott, Director
EMP: 22
SQ FT: 18,000
SALES: 1.5MM Privately Held
WEB: www.max200.com
SIC: 3199 Dog furnishings: collars, leashes, muzzles, etc.: leather

(G-13190)
PRECISION DIECUTTING INC
1381 Spring Lake Rd (13140-3375)
PHONE............................315 776-8465
Norma Compson, President
Jamie Compson, Vice Pres
EMP: 6
SALES: 300K Privately Held
SIC: 2675 Stencil board, die-cut: made from purchased materials

Port Chester
Westchester County

(G-13191)
AIR STRUCTURES AMERCN TECH INC
211 S Ridge St Ste 3 (10573-3445)
PHONE............................914 937-4500
Donato A Fraioli, CEO
Rosemarie Fraioli, Admin Sec
▼ EMP: 50
SQ FT: 2,500
SALES (est): 10MM Privately Held
WEB: www.asati.com
SIC: 2394 Tents: made from purchased materials

(G-13192)
ALBUMX CORP
Also Called: Renanssance The Book
21 Grace Church St (10573-4911)
PHONE............................914 939-6878
Terry Huang, President
Albert Huang, Prdtn Mgr
Victor Huang, Human Resources
Pam Segovia, Supervisor
Jay Chun, Director
▲ EMP: 80
SQ FT: 27,000
SALES (est): 7.9MM Privately Held
WEB: www.renansancealbums.com
SIC: 2782 Albums

(G-13193)
ALWAYS PRINTING
149 Highland St (10573-3301)
PHONE............................914 481-5209
Jodi McCredo, Owner
EMP: 5
SALES (est): 483.6K Privately Held
SIC: 2759 Commercial printing

(G-13194)
COMPOSITE FORMS INC
7 Merritt St (10573-3502)
PHONE............................914 937-1808
Frank J Madonia, CEO
Frank Madonia Jr, President
Frank Madonia Sr, Director
EMP: 10
SQ FT: 6,500
SALES (est): 930K Privately Held
WEB: www.sidingsolutions.com
SIC: 2752 5112 Commercial printing, offset; business forms

(G-13195)
D & M ENTERPRISES INCORPORATED
Also Called: A W S
1 Mill St Ste 2 (10573-6301)
PHONE............................914 937-6430
Dino Alampi, President
Mary Alampi, Vice Pres
EMP: 8
SQ FT: 5,000
SALES: 327K Privately Held
SIC: 3088 3999 Hot tubs, plastic or fiberglass; hot tubs

(G-13196)
DESIGNS BY NOVELLO INC
505 N Main St (10573-3360)
PHONE............................914 934-7711
George Bulger, Owner
▲ EMP: 5 EST: 1997
SALES (est): 654.3K Privately Held
SIC: 3449 Bars, concrete reinforcing: fabricated steel

(G-13197)
EAGLE INSTRUMENTS INC
35 Grove St (10573-4501)
PHONE............................914 939-6843
Robert Schneider, President
EMP: 7
SQ FT: 4,000
SALES (est): 1MM Privately Held
SIC: 3599 Machine shop, jobbing & repair

(G-13198)
EHS GROUP LLC
69 Townsend St (10573-4311)
PHONE............................914 937-6162
Steven Kennedy, President
Lisa Cartolano, Corp Secy
EMP: 8
SQ FT: 6,000
SALES (est): 1.6MM Privately Held
SIC: 2759 Envelopes: printing

(G-13199)
EMPIRE COFFEE COMPANY INC
106 Purdy Ave (10573-4624)
PHONE............................914 934-1100
Steven Dunefsky, President
Michael Riger, Vice Pres
Robert Richter, Admin Sec
▲ EMP: 35
SQ FT: 30,000
SALES (est): 6.5MM Privately Held
WEB: www.empire-coffee.com
SIC: 2095 Coffee roasting (except by wholesale grocers)

(G-13200)
GMP LLC
Also Called: Graphic Management Partners
47 Purdy Ave (10573-5028)
PHONE............................914 939-0571
Paul Cherico, Vice Pres
Anthony Corrado, Vice Pres
Mike Geraghty, Vice Pres
Leah Karosos, Credit Mgr
Jim Berger, VP Human Res
EMP: 86
SQ FT: 20,000
SALES: 12.6MM Privately Held
SIC: 2752 Promotional printing, lithographic

(G-13201)
GOOD BREAD BAKERY
Also Called: Best Bread
33 New Broad St Ste 1 (10573-4651)
PHONE............................914 939-3900
Michael Beldotti, Owner
Chris Beldotti, Owner
EMP: 15
SALES (est): 1.4MM Privately Held
SIC: 2051 Bakery: wholesale or wholesale/retail combined

(G-13202)
INTEGRATED SOLAR TECH LLC
181 Westchester Ave # 409 (10573-4534)
PHONE............................914 249-9364
Oliver Koehler, CEO
▲ EMP: 5
SQ FT: 500
SALES (est): 350.4K Privately Held
SIC: 3433 Solar heaters & collectors

(G-13203)
JJ CASSONE BAKERY INC
202 S Regent St (10573-4791)
PHONE............................914 939-1568
Mary Lou Cassone, President
Dominic Ambrose, Vice Pres
Tony Crusco, Vice Pres
Jack Guarcello, Vice Pres
Greg Mancuso, Vice Pres
▲ EMP: 280
SQ FT: 180,000
SALES (est): 51MM Privately Held
WEB: www.jjcassone.com
SIC: 2051 5461 Bakery: wholesale or wholesale/retail combined; bread, all types (white, wheat, rye, etc): fresh or frozen; bakeries

(G-13204)
LANZA CORP
Also Called: Sign Design
404 Willett Ave (10573-3132)
PHONE............................914 937-6360
Joseph Lanza, President
Nick Contrata, Project Mgr
Josh Hauge, Project Mgr
Nicholas Pagnozzi, Technical Mgr
Phil Pinto, Sales Mgr
EMP: 9
SQ FT: 4,000
SALES (est): 1.4MM Privately Held
WEB: www.clicksignage.com
SIC: 2394 7389 5999 2499 Canvas awnings & canopies; sign painting & lettering shop; awnings; carved & turned wood; sign installation & maintenance; electric signs

(G-13205)
MATTHEW SHIVELY LLC
40 Merritt St (10573-3539)
PHONE............................914 937-3531
Matthew Shively,
EMP: 7
SQ FT: 5,000
SALES (est): 439.9K Privately Held
SIC: 2519 Household furniture

(G-13206)
PALETERIA FERNANDEZ INC (PA)
33 N Main St (10573-4208)
PHONE............................914 939-3694
Fernandez Paleteria, Principal
EMP: 9
SALES (est): 1.1MM Privately Held
SIC: 2024 Ice cream, bulk

(G-13207)
PARSONS & WHITTEMORE INC
4 International Dr # 300 (10573-1064)
PHONE............................914 937-9009
Arthur L Schwartz, President
George F Landegger, Chairman
Robert H Masson, Vice Pres
Jose Alvelo, Treasurer
Frank Grasso, Treasurer
EMP: 367 EST: 1853
SQ FT: 16,650
SALES (est): 83.5MM Privately Held
SIC: 2611 Pulp mills
PA: Parsons & Whittemore Enterprises Corp.
4 International Dr # 300
Port Chester NY 10573
914 937-9009

(G-13208)
PARSONS WHITTEMORE ENTPS CORP (PA)
4 International Dr # 300 (10573-1064)
PHONE............................914 937-9009
George F Landegger, Ch of Bd
Carl C Landegger, Vice Ch Bd
Steven Sweeney, CFO
Frank Grasso, Treasurer
EMP: 25
SQ FT: 16,650
SALES (est): 83.5MM Privately Held
SIC: 2611 Pulp mills

(G-13209)
SWISSBIT NA INC
18 Willett Ave 202 (10573-4326)
PHONE............................914 935-1400
Anthony Cerreta, President
Vincenzo Esposito, Managing Dir
Grady Lambert, Business Mgr
Tony Cerreta, Sales Staff
Theresa Gaudreau, Sales Staff
EMP: 3
SQ FT: 2,050
SALES: 20MM Privately Held
WEB: www.swissbitna.com
SIC: 3674 Semiconductors & related devices
HQ: Swissbit Ag
Industriestrasse 4-8
Bronschhofen SG 9552
719 130-303

(G-13210)
ULMER SALES LLC
Also Called: U K Sailmakers
10 Midland Ave Ste 1 (10573-4927)
PHONE............................718 885-1700
Charles Ulmer, President
Kerry Klinier, Vice Pres
Rob Roy, Representative
EMP: 12
SQ FT: 6,500
SALES (est): 1.6MM Privately Held
SIC: 2394 Sails: made from purchased materials

(G-13211)
ZYLOWARE CORPORATION (PA)
Also Called: Zyloware Eyewear
8 Slater St Ste 1 (10573-4984)
PHONE............................914 708-1200
Christopher Shyer, President
Robert Shyer, Principal
Jennifer Derryberry, Vice Pres
James Shyer, Vice Pres
Lisa Mulqueen, Opers Mgr
▲ EMP: 70
SQ FT: 21,000
SALES (est): 13.3MM Privately Held
WEB: www.zyloware.com
SIC: 3851 Frames & parts, eyeglass & spectacle

Port Jeff STA
Suffolk County

(G-13212)
BILTRON AUTOMOTIVE PRODUCTS
509 Bicycle Path Unit Q (11776-3491)
PHONE............................631 928-8613
Ron Stoll, President
▲ EMP: 30
SQ FT: 21,000
SALES (est): 4.7MM Privately Held
WEB: www.biltronauto.com
SIC: 3714 3566 3462 Steering mechanisms, motor vehicle; speed changers, drives & gears; iron & steel forgings

GEOGRAPHIC SECTION
Port Washington - Nassau County (G-13240)

(G-13213)
DESIGN/OL INC
200 Wilson St Unit D2 (11776-1150)
PHONE..................................631 474-5536
William Delongis, *President*
August Oetting, *Vice Pres*
Chris Siemes, *Finance Mgr*
EMP: 16
SQ FT: 12,500
SALES: 2.5MM **Privately Held**
WEB: www.design-ol.com
SIC: 3728 Aircraft assemblies, subassemblies & parts

(G-13214)
NORTH SHORE HOME IMPROVER
200 Wilson St (11776-1100)
PHONE..................................631 474-2824
David Kielhurn, *CEO*
EMP: 16
SALES (est): 910K **Privately Held**
WEB: www.lihomeshows.com
SIC: 2731 Books: publishing only

(G-13215)
NORTH SHORE ORTHTICS PRSTHTICS
591 Bicycle Path Ste D (11776-3421)
PHONE..................................631 928-3040
Robert Biaggi, *President*
EMP: 7
SQ FT: 1,000
SALES (est): 895K **Privately Held**
WEB: www.nsop.com
SIC: 3842 5999 Limbs, artificial; artificial lin.bs

(G-13216)
OCCUNOMIX INTERNATIONAL LLC
585 Bicycle Path Ste 52 (11776-3431)
PHONE..................................631 741-1940
Richard Hauser, *Mng Member*
▲ **EMP:** 45
SQ FT: 48,500
SALES (est): 9MM **Privately Held**
WEB: www.occunomix.com
SIC: 3842 2311 2326 5047 Personal safety equipment; men's & boys' uniforms; men's & boys' work clothing; medical & hospital equipment

(G-13217)
STARGATE COMPUTER CORP
24 Harmony Dr (11776-3168)
P.O. Box 11161, Hauppauge (11788-0702)
PHONE..................................516 474-4799
EMP: 5
SALES (est): 400K **Privately Held**
SIC: 3571 Mfg Electronic Computers

(G-13218)
T EASON LAND SURVEYOR
27 Poplar St (11776-1415)
PHONE..................................631 474-2200
Treimane Eason, *Owner*
EMP: 6
SALES (est): 414.8K **Privately Held**
WEB: www.teasonlandsurveyor.com
SIC: 2499 Surveyors' stakes, wood

(G-13219)
TKM TECHNOLOGIES INC
623 Bicycle Path Ste 5 (11776-3444)
P.O. Box 665, Mount Sinai (11766-0665)
PHONE..................................631 474-4700
Mike Moroff, *President*
Monika Moroff, *Vice Pres*
EMP: 6
SQ FT: 1,200
SALES: 950K **Privately Held**
WEB: www.tkmtechnologies.com
SIC: 3651 8711 Household audio & video equipment; electrical or electronic engineering

Port Jefferson
Suffolk County

(G-13220)
CHIP IT ALL LTD
366 Sheep Pasture Rd (11777-2059)
P.O. Box 959, Port Jeff STA (11776-0812)
PHONE..................................631 473-2040
Richard Edgar, *President*
Linda Edgar, *Admin Sec*
EMP: 7
SQ FT: 720
SALES (est): 885.9K **Privately Held**
SIC: 2411 Wood chips, produced in the field

(G-13221)
LONG ISLAND GEOTECH
6 Berkshire Ci (11777-1906)
PHONE..................................631 473-1044
Micheal Verruto, *President*
EMP: 5
SALES (est): 308.6K **Privately Held**
SIC: 3272 Concrete products

(G-13222)
M H MANDELBAUM ORTHOTIC
116 Oakland Ave (11777-2172)
PHONE..................................631 473-8668
Martin H Mandelbaum, *President*
Marc Werner, *Vice Pres*
EMP: 10
SQ FT: 5,300
SALES (est): 1.3MM **Privately Held**
WEB: www.mhmoandp.com
SIC: 3842 5999 8011 Orthopedic appliances; prosthetic appliances; artificial limbs; offices & clinics of medical doctors

(G-13223)
PACE WALKERS OF AMERICA INC
Also Called: Thomas Jefferson Press
105 Washington Ave (11777-2003)
P.O. Box 843, East Setauket (11733-0653)
PHONE..................................631 444-2147
Steven Jonas, *President*
EMP: 12
SALES (est): 958.5K **Privately Held**
SIC: 2731 Book publishing

(G-13224)
WHITFORD DEVELOPMENT INC
646 Main St Ste 301 (11777-2230)
PHONE..................................631 471-7711
Fax: 631 471-0332
EMP: 11
SALES (est): 1.1MM **Privately Held**
SIC: 2789 Bookbinding/Related Work

Port Jervis
Orange County

(G-13225)
CHOCOLATE LADY LLC
14 Blue Heron Ln (12771-3377)
PHONE..................................516 532-0551
Lee Perrotta-Fityo, *President*
EMP: 5
SALES (est): 226.9K **Privately Held**
SIC: 2066 Chocolate

(G-13226)
CONIC SYSTEMS INC
11 Rebel Ln (12771-3547)
PHONE..................................845 856-4053
Vincent Genovese, *President*
◆ **EMP:** 10 **EST:** 1990
SQ FT: 12,000
SALES (est): 1.6MM **Privately Held**
WEB: www.conicsystems.com
SIC: 3625 Control equipment, electric

(G-13227)
DATATRAN LABS INC
Also Called: Nireco America
11 Rebel Ln (12771-3547)
PHONE..................................845 856-4313
Vincent Genovesse, *President*
EMP: 7 **EST:** 1969
SQ FT: 11,000
SALES (est): 1MM **Privately Held**
WEB: www.datatranlabs.com
SIC: 3625 3577 Industrial controls: push button, selector switches, pilot; computer peripheral equipment

(G-13228)
FLANAGANS CREATIVE DISP INC
55 Jersey Ave (12771-2514)
P.O. Box 98 (12771-0098)
PHONE..................................845 858-2542
Michael Flanagan, *President*
EMP: 35 **EST:** 1998
SQ FT: 30,000
SALES (est): 6.9MM **Privately Held**
SIC: 3496 Miscellaneous fabricated wire products

(G-13229)
GILLINDER BROTHERS INC
Also Called: Gillinder Glass
39 Erie St 55 (12771-2809)
P.O. Box 1007 (12771-0187)
PHONE..................................845 856-5375
Charles E Gillinder, *Ch of Bd*
Dave Fox, *General Mgr*
Susan Gillinder, *Corp Secy*
Christopher Michael, *Engineer*
Roberta Gervasi, *Sales Staff*
▲ **EMP:** 70 **EST:** 1912
SQ FT: 120,000
SALES: 7MM **Privately Held**
WEB: www.gillinderglass.com
SIC: 3229 Pressed & blown glass

(G-13230)
HORNET GROUP INC
Also Called: Hgi Skydyne
100 River Rd (12771-2931)
PHONE..................................845 858-6400
Jay Benson, *CEO*
EMP: 70
SALES (est): 8.8MM **Privately Held**
WEB: www.hornetgroup.com
SIC: 3089 3449 7336 3412 Boxes, plastic; miscellaneous metalwork; package design; metal barrels, drums & pails; metal cans; luggage

(G-13231)
KALTEC FOOD PACKAGING INC
36 Center St 40 (12771)
PHONE..................................845 856-9888
Nick Mascara, *CEO*
Ed Mascara, *President*
Harriet L Mascara, *Shareholder*
▲ **EMP:** 30
SQ FT: 20,000
SALES (est): 5MM **Privately Held**
SIC: 2052 Cookies

(G-13232)
KALTECH FOOD PACKAGING INC
3640 Center St (12771)
PHONE..................................845 856-1210
Harriet L Mascara, *CEO*
Frank Mascara, *Exec VP*
Edward Mascara, *Vice Pres*
EMP: 26
SQ FT: 70,000
SALES: 2.2MM **Privately Held**
SIC: 2033 Spaghetti & other pasta sauce: packaged in cans, jars, etc.

(G-13233)
KLG USA LLC
20 W King St (12771-3061)
P.O. Box 1111 (12771-0154)
PHONE..................................845 856-5311
Joseph Healey, *Ch of Bd*
Rob Edmonds, *President*
▲ **EMP:** 1000
SQ FT: 4,210
SALES (est): 164.9MM **Privately Held**
WEB: www.kolmar.com
SIC: 2844 7389 2834 Cosmetic preparations; packaging & labeling services; pharmaceutical preparations

(G-13234)
PARAMOUNT GRAPHIX
26 Hill St (12771-2024)
PHONE..................................845 367-5003
Daniel King, *Principal*
EMP: 5
SALES (est): 310.2K **Privately Held**
SIC: 2499 Signboards, wood

(G-13235)
PORT JERVIS MACHINE CORP
176 1/2 Jersey Ave (12771-2612)
PHONE..................................845 856-6210
Sal Spiezio, *Manager*
EMP: 8
SALES (corp-wide): 737K **Privately Held**
SIC: 3599 Machine shop, jobbing & repair
PA: Port Jervis Machine Corporation
180 Jersey Ave
Port Jervis NY
845 856-3333

(G-13236)
SAMAKI INC
62 Jersey Ave (12771-2513)
P.O. Box 554, Westbrookville (12785-0554)
PHONE..................................845 858-1012
Simon Marrian, *President*
Laura Marrian, *Treasurer*
EMP: 7
SQ FT: 2,800
SALES (est): 880.8K **Privately Held**
WEB: www.samaki.com
SIC: 2091 Fish, smoked; fish, cured

(G-13237)
SKYDYNE COMPANY
100 River Rd (12771-2997)
PHONE..................................845 858-6400
Peter A Keay, *President*
Peter A Siebert, *Corp Secy*
▲ **EMP:** 70
SALES (est): 18.8MM **Privately Held**
WEB: www.skydyne.com
SIC: 2655 Containers, laminated phenolic & vulcanized fiber

(G-13238)
SWIMWEAR ANYWHERE INC
Also Called: Finals, The
21 Minisink Ave (12771-2320)
PHONE..................................845 858-4141
Brenda Blackman, *VP Sales*
Theresa Coviello, *Cust Mgr*
Nancy Piccolo, *Manager*
EMP: 40
SALES (corp-wide): 52MM **Privately Held**
SIC: 2329 2339 Bathing suits & swimwear: men's & boys'; athletic (warmup, sweat & jogging) suits: men's & boys'; bathing suits: women's, misses' & juniors'; athletic clothing: women's, misses' & juniors'
PA: Swimwear Anywhere, Inc.
85 Sherwood Ave
Farmingdale NY 11735
631 420-1400

Port Washington
Nassau County

(G-13239)
ACTIONCRAFT PRODUCTS INC
2 Manhasset Ave (11050-2008)
PHONE..................................516 883-6423
Nina Straus, *President*
EMP: 8 **EST:** 1951
SQ FT: 4,000
SALES (est): 381.6K **Privately Held**
WEB: www.industrialtest.com
SIC: 2759 Tags: printing

(G-13240)
ADVANCED POLYMER SOLUTIONS LLC
99 Seaview Blvd Ste 1a (11050-4632)
PHONE..................................516 621-5800
Rita Ryan, *Senior VP*
Purushoth Kesavan, *Production*
John M Ryan,
John Ryan,
Rita M Ryan,
EMP: 9
SQ FT: 10,000

Port Washington - Nassau County (G-13241)
GEOGRAPHIC SECTION

SALES (est): 1.7MM **Privately Held**
WEB: www.advancedpolymersolutions.com
SIC: 2891 8731 Adhesives & sealants; chemical laboratory, except testing

(G-13241)
ALAN F BOURGUET
63 Essex Ct (11050-4222)
PHONE..................................516 883-4315
Alan F Bourguet, *President*
EMP: 15 **EST:** 2001
SALES (est): 842.1K **Privately Held**
SIC: 2844 Perfumes & colognes

(G-13242)
ALMOND JEWELERS INC
Also Called: Almond Group
16 S Maryland Ave (11050-2913)
P.O. Box 471 (11050-0135)
PHONE..................................516 933-6000
Jonathan Mandelbaum, *President*
Maurice Mandelbaum, *Vice Pres*
▲ **EMP:** 15
SQ FT: 3,500
SALES: 100MM **Privately Held**
SIC: 3911 Jewelry, precious metal

(G-13243)
APPLE & EVE LLC (DH)
2 Seaview Blvd Ste 100 (11050-4634)
PHONE..................................516 621-1122
Gordon Crane, *President*
John Emerson, *President*
Chris McFadden, *Regional Mgr*
Eric Gemme, *COO*
Robert Mortati, *Vice Pres*
◆ **EMP:** 65
SQ FT: 14,000
SALES (est): 44.1MM **Privately Held**
WEB: www.appleandeve.com
SIC: 2033 Fruit juices: packaged in cans, jars, etc.
HQ: Us Juice Partners, Llc
2 Seaview Blvd
Port Washington NY 11050
516 621-1122

(G-13244)
ARENA GRAPHICS INC
Also Called: Arena Sports Center
52 Main St Frnt (11050-2952)
PHONE..................................516 767-5108
Christopher J Avazis, *President*
Steven Avazis, *Vice Pres*
EMP: 9
SQ FT: 4,700
SALES (est): 1.2MM **Privately Held**
WEB: www.arenagraphics.com
SIC: 2759 5941 2395 Screen printing; sporting goods & bicycle shops; embroidery products, except schiffli machine

(G-13245)
BEVILACQUE GROUP LLC
Also Called: Bevilacque Group LLC By Profor
19 Norwood Rd (11050-1423)
PHONE..................................212 414-8858
Mark Bevilacque,
EMP: 11
SQ FT: 2,750
SALES (est): 1.5MM **Privately Held**
WEB: www.bevilacque.com
SIC: 2752 7389 Commercial printing, lithographic; advertising, promotional & trade show services

(G-13246)
BOMBAY KITCHEN FOODS INC
76 S Bayles Ave (11050-3729)
PHONE..................................516 767-7401
Sanjiv Mody, *President*
Ajit Mody, *Treasurer*
Sachin Mody, *Admin Sec*
▲ **EMP:** 15
SQ FT: 18,000
SALES: 2.5MM **Privately Held**
SIC: 2099 Food preparations

(G-13247)
CHANNEL MANUFACTURING INC (PA)
55 Channel Dr (11050-2216)
PHONE..................................516 944-6271
Jordan Klein, *President*
▲ **EMP:** 25 **EST:** 2000
SALES (est): 2.9MM **Privately Held**
WEB: www.channelmfg.com
SIC: 2499 3537 Food handling & processing products, wood; industrial trucks & tractors

(G-13248)
CHATEAU IMPORTS LTD
8 Maple St Ste 10 (11050-2964)
PHONE..................................516 841-6343
James Millevew, *CEO*
EMP: 5 **EST:** 2011
SQ FT: 500
SALES (est): 254.8K **Privately Held**
SIC: 2086 Carbonated beverages, nonalcoholic: bottled & canned

(G-13249)
CHOICE MAGAZINE LISTENING INC
85 Channel Dr Ste 3 (11050-2278)
PHONE..................................516 883-8280
William O'Conner, *Chairman*
Lois Miller, *Manager*
Sondra Mochson, *Director*
EMP: 7
SALES (est): 799.7K **Privately Held**
WEB: www.choicemagazinelistening.org
SIC: 2721 8322 Periodicals; social services for the handicapped

(G-13250)
COMPOZ A PUZZLE INC
2 Secatoag Ave (11050-2107)
PHONE..................................516 883-2311
Robert F Krisch, *Chairman*
Richard Hinchey, *Vice Pres*
EMP: 5
SQ FT: 4,000
SALES: 500K **Privately Held**
WEB: www.compozapuzzle.com
SIC: 3944 5945 Mfg Games/Toys Ret Hobbies/Toys/Games

(G-13251)
DATA PALETTE INFO SVCS LLC
35 Marino Ave (11050-4207)
PHONE..................................718 433-1060
Joel Ronis,
Joseph Aronne,
▲ **EMP:** 75
SQ FT: 35,000
SALES (est): 10.3MM **Privately Held**
SIC: 2759 7331 7374 7389 Laser printing; mailing service; data processing & preparation;

(G-13252)
DIAMOND BOUTIQUE
77 Main St (11050-2929)
PHONE..................................516 444-3373
Joseph Daniel, *Owner*
EMP: 6
SALES: 2.5MM **Privately Held**
SIC: 3915 5944 Jewel cutting, drilling, polishing, recutting or setting; jewelry stores

(G-13253)
DJ PUBLISHING INC
25 Willowdale Ave (11050-3716)
PHONE..................................516 767-2500
Vincent P Testa, *President*
Jeannemarie Graziano, *Opers Mgr*
Chris Caruso, *Assoc Editor*
EMP: 50
SALES (est): 2.8MM **Privately Held**
WEB: www.testabags.com
SIC: 2721 Magazines: publishing only, not printed on site

(G-13254)
DOMA MARKETING INC
28 Haven Ave Ste 226 (11050-3646)
PHONE..................................516 684-1111
Doron Katz, *Owner*
EMP: 5 **EST:** 2012
SQ FT: 2,000
SALES: 100K **Privately Held**
SIC: 2066 Chocolate

(G-13255)
DRIVE MEDICAL SPV LLC
99 Seaview Blvd (11050-4606)
PHONE..................................516 998-4600
Bill Cerniglia, *President*
David Pugh, *President*
Brian Sharpe, *President*
Edward Link, *General Mgr*
Derek Lampert, *Vice Pres*
EMP: 5
SALES (est): 250.3K **Privately Held**
SIC: 3841 Medical instruments & equipment, blood & bone work
PA: Medical Depot, Inc.
99 Seaview Blvd Ste 210
Port Washington NY 11050

(G-13256)
E GLOBAL SOLUTIONS INC
Also Called: E G S
8 Haven Ave Ste 221 (11050-3636)
P.O. Box 771 (11050-0771)
PHONE..................................516 767-5138
Anthony Straggi, *Ch of Bd*
EMP: 6
SQ FT: 9,000
SALES: 690K **Privately Held**
SIC: 3822 Auto controls regulating residntl & coml environmt & applncs

(G-13257)
ELCO MANUFACTURING CO INC (PA)
26 Ivy Way (11050-3802)
P.O. Box 1759 (11050-7759)
PHONE..................................516 767-3577
Eric Weintraub, *President*
Stanley Weintraub, *Vice Pres*
E Nash, *Admin Sec*
EMP: 19 **EST:** 1904
SQ FT: 10,000
SALES: 1.5MM **Privately Held**
WEB: www.elcomfg.com
SIC: 3172 5199 Personal leather goods; advertising specialties

(G-13258)
EQUINE IMAGING LLC (PA)
20 Tibbits Ln (11050-1135)
PHONE..................................414 326-0665
Geoge Papaioannou, *Mng Member*
EMP: 32
SQ FT: 20,000
SALES: 16MM **Privately Held**
SIC: 3826 Analytical instruments

(G-13259)
FINER TOUCH PRINTING CORP
4 Yennicock Ave (11050-2131)
PHONE..................................516 944-8000
Kenny Cummings, *President*
EMP: 10
SQ FT: 2,500
SALES: 1.1MM **Privately Held**
WEB: www.comiccastle.com
SIC: 2752 Commercial printing, offset

(G-13260)
FRANKLIN-DOUGLAS INC
Also Called: Omnimusic
52 Main St Side (11050-2965)
PHONE..................................516 883-0121
Douglas Wood, *President*
Dave Hab, *Vice Pres*
Patricia Wood, *Vice Pres*
David McAllister, *Sales Executive*
EMP: 12 **EST:** 1975
SQ FT: 4,000
SALES (est): 1.1MM **Privately Held**
WEB: www.omnimusic.com
SIC: 2741 Music book & sheet music publishing

(G-13261)
G & C WELDING CO INC
39 Annette Dr (11050-2803)
PHONE..................................516 883-3228
Carmine Meluzio, *President*
EMP: 5
SALES (est): 179.5K **Privately Held**
SIC: 7692 1799 Welding repair; welding on site

(G-13262)
GE HEALTHCARE INC
Also Called: Medi-Physics
80 Seaview Blvd Ste E (11050-4618)
PHONE..................................516 626-2799
Franklyn Robinson, *Manager*
EMP: 14
SALES (corp-wide): 122B **Publicly Held**
SIC: 2833 Medicinals & botanicals
HQ: Ge Healthcare Inc.
100 Results Way
Marlborough MA 01752
800 292-8514

(G-13263)
HAWTHORNE GARDEN COMPANY (HQ)
Also Called: Hawthorne Gardening Co.
800 Port Washington Blvd (11050-3720)
PHONE..................................516 883-6550
James Hagedorn, *CEO*
Michael C Lukemire, *COO*
Randy Coleman, *CFO*
Ivan C Smith, *Ch Credit Ofcr*
Denise S Stump, *Officer*
EMP: 12
SALES (est): 85.9MM
SALES (corp-wide): 2.6B **Publicly Held**
SIC: 3542 0782 7342 Machine tools, metal forming type; lawn & garden services; pest control services
PA: The Scotts Miracle-Gro Company
14111 Scottslawn Rd
Marysville OH 43040
937 644-0011

(G-13264)
HERCULES GROUP INC
27 Seaview Blvd (11050-4610)
PHONE..................................212 813-8000
Sara Amani, *President*
▲ **EMP:** 20
SQ FT: 2,000
SALES (est): 4.2MM **Privately Held**
WEB: www.herculesgroup.com
SIC: 2385 Diaper covers, waterproof: made from purchased materials

(G-13265)
HOWMEDICA OSTEONICS CORP
95 Seaview Blvd Ste 201 (11050-4633)
PHONE..................................516 484-0897
Rich Hadrain, *Manager*
EMP: 6
SALES (corp-wide): 12.4B **Publicly Held**
SIC: 3842 Surgical appliances & supplies
HQ: Howmedica Osteonics Corp.
325 Corporate Dr
Mahwah NJ 07430
201 831-5000

(G-13266)
HURRYWORKS LLC
990 Seaview Blvd (11050)
PHONE..................................516 998-4600
Richard Kolodny, *CEO*
EMP: 99
SQ FT: 10,000
SALES (est): 2.5MM **Privately Held**
SIC: 3841 Surgical & medical instruments

(G-13267)
IDENTFICATION DATA IMAGING LLC
Also Called: IDI
26 Harbor Park Dr (11050-4602)
PHONE..................................516 484-6500
Pat Screnzel,
Jeffrey Brodsky,
▼ **EMP:** 6
SQ FT: 1,300
SALES (est): 590.7K **Privately Held**
WEB: www.idius.com
SIC: 3999 Identification badges & insignia

(G-13268)
IDEOLI GROUP INC
938 Port Washington Blvd # 1 (11050-2932)
PHONE..................................212 705-8769
George Stroumboulis, *CEO*
Chris Hartswick,
EMP: 10
SQ FT: 2,000
SALES: 213K **Privately Held**
SIC: 2599 3646 Bar, restaurant & cafeteria furniture; commercial indusl & institutional electric lighting fixtures

(G-13269)
INDUSTRIAL TEST EQP CO INC
2 Manhasset Ave (11050-2008)
PHONE..................................516 883-6423
Jay Monroe, *President*
Barbara Monroe, *Admin Sec*

▲ = Import ▼ = Export
◆ = Import/Export

GEOGRAPHIC SECTION **Port Washington - Nassau County (G-13295)**

EMP: 20
SQ FT: 8,000
SALES: 1MM Privately Held
WEB: www.rf-pwr-amps.com
SIC: 3621 3829 2759 Generating apparatus & parts, electrical; gas detectors; tags: printing

(G-13270)
INTECH 21 INC
21 Harbor Park Dr (11050-4658)
PHONE................516 626-7221
George Y Bilenko, *President*
Victor Zelmanovich, *Exec VP*
Aleksandr Baranov, *Software Engr*
Jules Leibman, *Shareholder*
▲ EMP: 12
SQ FT: 8,000
SALES (est): 1.8MM Privately Held
WEB: www.intech21.com
SIC: 3674 Computer logic modules

(G-13271)
IVY ENTERPRISES INC (HQ)
25 Harbor Park Dr (11050-4605)
PHONE................516 621-9779
Hee J Chang, *President*
Peter Kim, *Controller*
David Kim, *Finance*
Sara Chang, *Asst Mgr*
Dave Andersen, *Director*
◆ EMP: 500
SALES (est): 24.5MM
SALES (corp-wide): 35.6MM Privately Held
SIC: 3999 5087 Fingernails, artificial; beauty parlor equipment & supplies
PA: Kiss Nail Products, Inc.
    57 Seaview Blvd
    Port Washington NY 11050
    516 625-9292

(G-13272)
JAIDAN INDUSTRIES INC
Also Called: Absolute Business Products
16 Capi Ln (11050-3410)
PHONE................516 944-3650
Richard Sussman, *President*
Rhonda Sussman, *Human Res Mgr*
▲ EMP: 16
SALES (est): 3.5MM Privately Held
WEB: www.jaidan.com
SIC: 3442 Window & door frames; moldings & trim, except automobile: metal

(G-13273)
JESCO LIGHTING INC
15 Harbor Park Dr (11050-4604)
PHONE................718 366-3211
Richard Kurtz, *Chairman*
Edward MA, *Chairman*
Joan Miller, *Accounts Exec*
Paulin Tham, *VP Mktg*
▲ EMP: 50
SQ FT: 70,000
SALES (est): 11.7MM Privately Held
SIC: 3646 Commercial indusl & institutional electric lighting fixtures

(G-13274)
JESCO LIGHTING GROUP LLC (PA)
15 Harbor Park Dr (11050-4604)
PHONE................718 366-3211
Richard Kurtz, *President*
Dennis Bolton, *Sales Staff*
Shelley Leiter, *Office Mgr*
Vic Nasrudin, *Manager*
Dmitriy Ostrovskiy, *Art Dir*
▲ EMP: 50
SQ FT: 70,000
SALES (est): 8.6MM Privately Held
SIC: 3646 Commercial indusl & institutional electric lighting fixtures

(G-13275)
JWIN ELECTRONICS CORP (PA)
Also Called: Iluv
2 Harbor Park Dr (11050-4602)
PHONE................516 626-7188
Justin Kim, *Ch of Bd*
Kevin Lim, *CFO*
Jennifer Leung, *Director*
Joanne Xu, *Associate*
▲ EMP: 110
SQ FT: 132,000
SALES (est): 21.9MM Privately Held
WEB: www.jwin.com
SIC: 3651 Television receiving sets; radio receiving sets; home entertainment equipment, electronic

(G-13276)
KITTYWALK SYSTEMS INC
10 Farmview Rd (11050-4511)
PHONE................516 627-8418
Jeff King, *CEO*
Lise King, *President*
▲ EMP: 2
SALES: 1MM Privately Held
SIC: 3999 Pet supplies

(G-13277)
KLEARBAR INC
8 Graywood Rd (11050-1516)
PHONE................516 684-9892
Mark Klein, *President*
Scott Bercu, *Admin Sec*
▲ EMP: 5
SALES (est): 381.2K Privately Held
SIC: 3585 Soda fountain & beverage dispensing equipment & parts

(G-13278)
KRAUS USA INC
12 Harbor Park Dr (11050-4649)
PHONE................800 775-0703
Russel Levi, *President*
Russell Levi, *President*
Michael Rukhlin, *Principal*
Dmitry Rukhlin, *COO*
Mike Rukhlin, *Vice Pres*
▲ EMP: 10
SQ FT: 37,500
SALES (est): 2.5MM Privately Held
SIC: 3431 3261 Bathroom fixtures, including sinks; sinks: enameled iron, cast iron or pressed metal; sinks, vitreous china

(G-13279)
KRUG PRECISION INC
7 Carey Pl (11050-2421)
PHONE................516 944-9350
Michael Krug, *President*
Rosemarie Krug, *Corp Secy*
EMP: 9
SQ FT: 6,500
SALES (est): 1.3MM Privately Held
SIC: 3599 Machine shop, jobbing & repair

(G-13280)
KURTSKRAFT INC
Also Called: Minuteman Press
437 Port Washington Blvd (11050-4225)
PHONE................516 944-4449
Joel Ronis, *President*
EMP: 5
SQ FT: 1,700
SALES: 1MM Privately Held
SIC: 2752 2759 Commercial printing, offset; invitation & stationery printing & engraving

(G-13281)
LIF INDUSTRIES INC (PA)
Also Called: Long Island Fireproof Door
5 Harbor Park Dr Ste 1 (11050-4698)
PHONE................516 390-6800
Vincent Gallo, *Ch of Bd*
Joseph Gallo Jr, *President*
Anthony Gallo, *Vice Pres*
Bill Curto, *Project Mgr*
Mark Farina, *Project Mgr*
EMP: 76
SQ FT: 85,000
SALES (est): 22.9MM Privately Held
WEB: www.lifi.net
SIC: 3442 5031 Metal doors; window & door frames; door frames, all materials

(G-13282)
LIFC CORP
101 Haven Ave (11050-3936)
PHONE................516 426-5737
Brian Kenny, *President*
EMP: 5
SALES (est): 410K Privately Held
SIC: 3569 5812 Firefighting apparatus & related equipment; caterers

(G-13283)
M R C INDUSTRIES INC
Also Called: Mason Medical Products
99 Seaview Blvd Ste 210 (11050-4632)
P.O. Box 609 (11050-0609)
PHONE................516 328-6900
Leonard Horowitz, *CEO*
Bernice Wien, *Treasurer*
◆ EMP: 200
SQ FT: 60,000
SALES (est): 22.2MM Privately Held
WEB: www.masonmedical.com
SIC: 2515 Mattresses & foundations

(G-13284)
MEDER TEXTILE CO INC
20 Lynn Rd (11050-4437)
PHONE................516 883-0409
Bruce T Lindemann, *President*
EMP: 4 EST: 1936
SQ FT: 500
SALES: 1MM Privately Held
SIC: 2211 Upholstery fabrics, cotton

(G-13285)
MEDICAL DEPOT INC (PA)
Also Called: Drive / Devilbiss Healthcare
99 Seaview Blvd Ste 210 (11050-4632)
P.O. Box 842450, Boston MA (02284-2450)
PHONE................516 998-4600
Robert J Gilligan, *CEO*
Kelly Devine, *President*
Barry Fink, *President*
Thomas Reynolds, *President*
Jeff Schwartz, *Exec VP*
◆ EMP: 250
SQ FT: 43,159
SALES (est): 315.6MM Privately Held
WEB: www.drivemedical.com
SIC: 3841 Surgical & medical instruments

(G-13286)
MEDICAL INFORMATION SYSTEMS
2 Seaview Blvd Ste 104 (11050-4634)
PHONE................516 621-7200
Irving Silverberg, *President*
Roy Silverberg, *Exec VP*
Hazel Silverberg, *Admin Sec*
EMP: 5
SQ FT: 5,000
SALES: 2.3MM Privately Held
WEB: www.medinfosystems.com
SIC: 2741 Miscellaneous publishing

(G-13287)
MEDSAFE SYSTEMS INC
46 Orchard Farm Rd (11050-3338)
PHONE................516 883-8222
Bernard Shore, *President*
EMP: 6
SQ FT: 1,000
SALES: 1.2MM Privately Held
SIC: 3823 Telemetering instruments, industrial process type

(G-13288)
MEKATRONICS INCORPORATED
85 Channel Dr Ste 2 (11050-2248)
PHONE................516 883-6805
Jack Bendror, *President*
Kenneth Lines, *Engineer*
▲ EMP: 24
SQ FT: 30,000
SALES (est): 4MM Privately Held
SIC: 3679 3555 3861 Electronic circuits; printing trades machinery; microfilm equipment: cameras, projectors, readers, etc.

(G-13289)
MUSIC & SOUND RETAILER INC
Also Called: Retailer, The
25 Willowdale Ave (11050-3716)
PHONE................516 767-2500
Vincent Testa, *President*
EMP: 28
SQ FT: 1,500
SALES (est): 1.7MM Privately Held
SIC: 2721 Magazines: publishing only, not printed on site

(G-13290)
N Y BIJOUX CORP
33 Sands Point Rd (11050-1625)
PHONE................212 244-9585
Hylong Kim, *President*
▲ EMP: 5
SALES (est): 687.9K Privately Held
WEB: www.nybijouxcorp.com
SIC: 3911 Jewelry, precious metal

(G-13291)
NOVARTIS AG
18 Driftwood Dr (11050-1717)
PHONE................617 435-0469
Anthony Lancellotti, *Principal*
Lauren Monovich, *Project Mgr*
EMP: 111
SALES (est): 5.5MM Privately Held
SIC: 2834 Pharmaceutical preparations

(G-13292)
OSWALD MANUFACTURING CO INC
65 Channel Dr (11050-2216)
PHONE................516 883-8850
Fred Oswald, *President*
Angella Oswald, *Vice Pres*
▲ EMP: 30 EST: 1954
SQ FT: 22,000
SALES (est): 3.9MM Privately Held
SIC: 3531 Construction machinery

(G-13293)
OZTECK INDUSTRIES INC
65 Channel Dr (11050-2216)
PHONE................516 883-8857
Fred Oswald, *President*
Angella Oswald, *Vice Pres*
Tiffany Shackatano, *Vice Pres*
◆ EMP: 40
SQ FT: 22,000
SALES (est): 10MM Privately Held
WEB: www.oztec.com
SIC: 3531 Vibrators for concrete construction; surfacers, concrete grinding

(G-13294)
PALL BIOMEDICAL INC
Also Called: Pall Medical
25 Harbor Park Dr (11050-4605)
PHONE................516 484-3600
Eric Kransnoff, *Principal*
Stella Rivera, *Human Res Mgr*
Tim Lynch, *Manager*
John Monteiro, *Manager*
▲ EMP: 200
SALES (est): 31.5MM
SALES (corp-wide): 18.3B Publicly Held
WEB: www.pall.com
SIC: 3842 Surgical appliances & supplies
HQ: Pall Corporation
    25 Harbor Park Dr
    Port Washington NY 11050
    516 484-5400

(G-13295)
PALL CORPORATION (HQ)
25 Harbor Park Dr (11050-4664)
PHONE................516 484-5400
Rainer Blair, *President*
Yves Baratelli, *President*
Michael Egholm, *President*
Naresh Narasimhan, *President*
Wayne Miller, *Business Mgr*
▲ EMP: 1200 EST: 1946
SQ FT: 25,000
SALES (est): 2.5B
SALES (corp-wide): 18.3B Publicly Held
WEB: www.pall.com
SIC: 3714 3841 3569 2834 Filters: oil, fuel & air, motor vehicle; surgical & medical instruments; IV transfusion apparatus; filters; filters, general line: industrial; filter elements, fluid, hydraulic line; separators for steam, gas, vapor or air (machinery); solutions, pharmaceutical; air intake filters, internal combustion engine, except auto; gasoline filters, internal combustion engine, except auto; oil filters, internal combustion engine, except automotive
PA: Danaher Corporation
    2200 Penn Ave Nw Ste 800w
    Washington DC 20037
    202 828-0850

Port Washington - Nassau County (G-13296)

(G-13296)
PALL CORPORATION
Also Called: Pall Life Sciences
25 Harbor Park Dr (11050-4664)
PHONE..................516 484-2818
Noelle Britton, *Vice Pres*
Doreen Stillman, *Senior Buyer*
Alla Krivosheyeva, *Research*
Eric Janson, *Engineer*
Tore Lindstrom, *Engineer*
EMP: 750
SALES (corp-wide): 18.3B **Publicly Held**
WEB: www.pall.com
SIC: 3842 Surgical appliances & supplies
HQ: Pall Corporation
   25 Harbor Park Dr
   Port Washington NY 11050
   516 484-5400

(G-13297)
PLAY-IT PRODUCTIONS INC
735 Port Washington Blvd (11050-3735)
PHONE..................212 695-6530
Terri Tyler, *Vice Pres*
EMP: 10
SQ FT: 3,000
SALES (est): 1.2MM **Privately Held**
WEB: www.play-itproductions.net
SIC: 2752 7336 7812 7819 Commercial printing, lithographic; graphic arts & related design; audio-visual program production; video tape or disk reproduction

(G-13298)
PREMIER HEART LLC
110 Main St (11050-2860)
PHONE..................516 883-3383
Joseph T Shen, *Med Doctor*
Joseph Shen MD, *Mng Member*
Richard Hayden,
EMP: 5
SQ FT: 3,000
SALES: 1.2MM **Privately Held**
SIC: 7372 Business oriented computer software

(G-13299)
PROFICIENT SURGICAL EQP INC
99 Seaview Blvd Ste 1c (11050-4632)
PHONE..................516 487-1175
Steven Baum, *President*
Harold Mondschein, *Sales Mgr*
Chris Fiengo, *Sales Staff*
Michael Albano, *Sales Executive*
Alicia Mamarella, *Office Mgr*
▲ EMP: 6 EST: 1996
SALES (est): 710K **Privately Held**
WEB: www.proficientsurgical.com
SIC: 3842 Surgical appliances & supplies

(G-13300)
RADNOR-WALLACE (PA)
921 Port Washington Blvd # 1 (11050-2976)
PHONE..................516 767-2131
Michael O'Beirne, *Director*
EMP: 5
SQ FT: 600
SALES: 500K **Privately Held**
WEB: www.radnorwallace.com
SIC: 7372 Prepackaged software

(G-13301)
ROBERT BARTHOLOMEW LTD
Also Called: Magnus Sands Point Shop
15 Main St (11050-2916)
PHONE..................516 767-2970
Robert C Mazza, *President*
Robert S Mazza, *President*
Donal Keogh, *Vice Pres*
Laura Mazza, *Vice Pres*
Julia Matuozzi, *Marketing Mgr*
EMP: 32
SQ FT: 12,000
SALES (est): 5.1MM **Privately Held**
WEB: www.robertbartholomew.com
SIC: 3911 Jewelry, precious metal

(G-13302)
SAFAVIEH INC
40 Harbor Park Dr (11050-4602)
PHONE..................516 945-1900
Mohsen Yaraghi, *Ch of Bd*
EMP: 525
SALES: 350MM **Privately Held**
SIC: 2273 5712 Rugs, hand & machine made; furniture stores

(G-13303)
SAINT HONORE PASTRY SHOP INC
993 Port Washington Blvd (11050-2910)
PHONE..................516 767-2555
Jacques Leguelaf, *President*
EMP: 5
SQ FT: 1,500
SALES (est): 270K **Privately Held**
SIC: 2051 5461 Bread, cake & related products; bakeries

(G-13304)
SANREX CORPORATION
50 Seaview Blvd Ste 2 (11050-4615)
PHONE..................516 625-1313
Ryoji Fujimoto, *President*
▲ EMP: 15
SQ FT: 13,000
SALES: 14.9MM
SALES (corp-wide): 176.5MM **Privately Held**
WEB: www.sanrex.com
SIC: 3674 Semiconductors & related devices
PA: Sansha Electric Manufacturing Co.,Ltd.
   3-1-56, Nishiawaji, Higashiyodogawa-Ku
   Osaka OSK 533-0
   663 210-321

(G-13305)
SCHOLIUM INTERNATIONAL INC
151 Cow Neck Rd (11050-1143)
PHONE..................516 883-8032
Arthur A Candido, *President*
Elena M Candido, *Vice Pres*
EMP: 5 EST: 1970
SQ FT: 1,800
SALES (est): 319.2K **Privately Held**
WEB: www.scholium.com
SIC: 2731 5192 Book publishing; books

(G-13306)
SHAKE-N-GO FASHION INC
83 Harbor Rd (11050-2535)
PHONE..................516 944-7777
EMP: 47
SALES (corp-wide): 315.2MM **Privately Held**
SIC: 3999 Hairpin mountings
PA: Shake-N-Go Fashion, Inc.
   85 Harbor Rd
   Port Washington NY 11050
   516 944-7777

(G-13307)
SHAKE-N-GO FASHION INC (PA)
85 Harbor Rd (11050-2535)
PHONE..................516 944-7777
James K Kim, *Ch of Bd*
Mike Kim, *Vice Pres*
Betty Kim, *Treasurer*
Jessica Cho, *Controller*
Young Ryoo, *Manager*
◆ EMP: 200
SQ FT: 75,000
SALES: 315.2MM **Privately Held**
WEB: www.shake-n-gofashions.com
SIC: 3999 Hairpin mountings; wigs, including doll wigs, toupees or wiglets

(G-13308)
SHARODINE INC
18 Haven Ave Frnt 2 (11050-3642)
PHONE..................516 767-3548
Ron Sharoni, *President*
EMP: 9
SALES (est): 1.3MM **Privately Held**
SIC: 3911 Jewelry, precious metal

(G-13309)
SOUND COMMUNICATIONS INC
25 Willowdale Ave (11050-3716)
PHONE..................516 767-2500
Vincent Testa, *President*
John Carr, *Publisher*
Dan Ferrisi, *Editor*
EMP: 40
SALES (est): 2.2MM **Privately Held**
SIC: 2721 Magazines: publishing only, not printed on site

(G-13310)
SWITCH BEVERAGE COMPANY LLC
2 Seaview Blvd Fl 3 (11050-4634)
PHONE..................203 202-7383
Brian Boyd, *CEO*
Maura Mottolese, *President*
EMP: 11
SQ FT: 1,200
SALES (est): 767.3K **Privately Held**
WEB: www.switchbev.com
SIC: 2096 2086 Potato chips & similar snacks; carbonated beverages, nonalcoholic: bottled & canned
HQ: Apple & Eve, Llc
   2 Seaview Blvd Ste 100
   Port Washington NY 11050
   516 621-1122

(G-13311)
TESTA COMMUNICATIONS INC
Also Called: Sound & Communication
25 Willowdale Ave (11050-3716)
PHONE..................516 767-2500
Vincent Testa, *President*
Fred Gumm, *Software Dev*
EMP: 40
SQ FT: 1,500
SALES (est): 4.6MM **Privately Held**
WEB: www.testa.com
SIC: 2721 Magazines: publishing only, not printed on site

(G-13312)
US JUICE PARTNERS LLC (DH)
Also Called: Apple
2 Seaview Blvd (11050-4614)
PHONE..................516 621-1122
Pierre-Paul Lassonde, *Ch of Bd*
EMP: 5
SALES (est): 44.1MM **Privately Held**
SIC: 2033 Fruit juices: packaged in cans, jars, etc.
HQ: Industries Lassonde Inc
   755 Rue Principale
   Rougemont QC J0L 1
   450 469-4926

(G-13313)
WELL-MADE TOY MFG CORPORATION
146 Soundview Dr (11050-1751)
PHONE..................718 381-4225
Fred F Catapano, *President*
▲ EMP: 20
SALES (est): 2.8MM **Privately Held**
WEB: www.wellmadetoy.com
SIC: 3942 Stuffed toys, including animals

Portageville
Wyoming County

(G-13314)
FILLMORE GREENHOUSES INC
11589 State Route 19a (14536-9611)
PHONE..................585 567-2678
Mario Van Logten, *Chairman*
▲ EMP: 45
SALES (est): 6.6MM **Privately Held**
SIC: 3448 Greenhouses: prefabricated metal

Portland
Chautauqua County

(G-13315)
OLDE CHTQUA VNEYARDS LTD LBLTY
Also Called: Twentyone Brix Winery
6654 W Main Rd (14769-9621)
PHONE..................716 792-2749
Kris Kane, *General Mgr*
Marion Jordan, *General Mgr*
Bryan Jordan,
Michael Jordan,
EMP: 12
SQ FT: 10,000
SALES (est): 1.3MM **Privately Held**
SIC: 2084 5921 Wines; wine

Portville
Cattaraugus County

(G-13316)
IA CONSTRUCTION CORPORATION
Also Called: Portville Sand & Gravel Div
Rr 305 Box S (14770)
PHONE..................716 933-8787
John Taylor, *Sales/Mktg Mgr*
EMP: 5
SQ FT: 1,800
SALES (corp-wide): 95.5MM **Privately Held**
WEB: www.iaconstruction.com
SIC: 1442 Gravel mining
HQ: Ia Construction Corporation
   24 Gibb Rd
   Franklin PA 16323
   814 432-3184

Potsdam
St. Lawrence County

(G-13317)
ATLANTIS SOLAR INC
Also Called: Atlantis Solar and Wind
2302 River Rd (13676-3491)
PHONE..................916 226-9183
Lance Thomas, *President*
EMP: 12
SQ FT: 47,000
SALES (est): 926.7K
SALES (corp-wide): 3.9MM **Publicly Held**
SIC: 3433 Solar heaters & collectors
PA: Solar Thin Films, Inc.
   445 Central Ave Unit 366
   Cedarhurst NY 11516
   212 629-8260

(G-13318)
DONALD SNYDER JR
Also Called: Donald Snyder Jr Logging
528 Allen Falls Rd (13676-4032)
PHONE..................315 265-4485
EMP: 15
SALES (est): 1.1MM **Privately Held**
SIC: 2411 Logging

(G-13319)
LCDRIVES CORP
65 Main St Pytn Hl 3204 Rm 3204 Peyton Hall (13676)
PHONE..................860 712-8926
Russel Marvin, *CEO*
EMP: 13 EST: 2012
SALES (est): 2.1MM **Privately Held**
SIC: 3621 Motors & generators

(G-13320)
NORTH COUNTRY THIS WEEK
19 Depot St Ste 1 (13676-1143)
P.O. Box 975 (13676-0975)
PHONE..................315 265-1000
William C Shumway, *President*
EMP: 9
SQ FT: 2,000
SALES: 850K **Privately Held**
WEB: www.northcountrynow.com
SIC: 2711 Newspapers: publishing only, not printed on site

(G-13321)
POTSDAM SPECIALTY PAPER INC
Also Called: Pspi
547a Sissonville Rd (13676-3549)
PHONE..................315 265-4000
Mike Huth, *CEO*
WEI Qun Zhang, *President*
Ronald Charette, *General Mgr*
Roxanne Kilgore, *Senior Buyer*
Joel Behm, *Technical Mgr*
◆ EMP: 70
SQ FT: 18,400
SALES (est): 13.2MM
SALES (corp-wide): 12.8MM **Privately Held**
SIC: 2621 Paper mills

PA: Seafront (Hong Kong) Company Limited
Rm B 9/F Sun Hing Steel Furniture Coml Bldg
Mongkok KLN

(G-13322)
RANDY SIXBERRY
Also Called: Great Northern Printing Co
6 Main St Ste 101 (13676-2066)
P.O. Box 270 (13676-0270)
PHONE.................315 265-6211
Randy Sixberry, *Owner*
Ranah Matott, *Corp Secy*
EMP: 7
SQ FT: 3,800
SALES: 700K **Privately Held**
SIC: 2396 5699 Screen printing on fabric articles; T-shirts, custom printed

(G-13323)
SNYDER LOGGING
528 Allen Falls Rd (13676-4032)
PHONE.................315 265-1462
Donald Snyder, *Owner*
EMP: 12
SALES (est): 605.6K **Privately Held**
SIC: 2411 Logging camps & contractors

(G-13324)
SUNFEATHER NATURAL SOAP CO INC
Also Called: Sunfeather Herbal Soap
1551 State Highway 72 (13676-4031)
PHONE.................315 265-1776
Sandra Maine, *CEO*
EMP: 8
SQ FT: 6,000
SALES (est): 930K **Privately Held**
WEB: www.sunsoap.com
SIC: 2841 Soap & other detergents

Poughkeepsie
Dutchess County

(G-13325)
AMERICAN HORMONES INC
69 W Cedar St Ste 2 (12601-1351)
PHONE.................845 471-7272
Salvatore J Rubino, *Principal*
Ashok Kadambi, *Principal*
EMP: 12
SALES (est): 2.6MM **Privately Held**
WEB: www.americanhormones.com
SIC: 2834 Hormone preparations

(G-13326)
APPARATUS MFG INC
13 Commerce St (12603-2608)
PHONE.................845 471-5116
Norman Murley, *President*
Chris Murley, *Manager*
Nick Murley, *Manager*
EMP: 6
SQ FT: 7,500
SALES: 600K **Privately Held**
WEB: www.apparatusmfg.com
SIC: 3444 Sheet metal specialties, not stamped

(G-13327)
ARCHITECTURAL DCTG CO LLC
Also Called: Hyde Park
130 Salt Point Tpke (12601-1016)
PHONE.................845 483-1340
Eli Nassim, *President*
EMP: 20
SALES (est): 1.6MM **Privately Held**
SIC: 2499 Carved & turned wood

(G-13328)
ATLANTIS ENERGY SYSTEMS INC (PA)
7 Industry St (12603-2617)
PHONE.................845 486-4052
Frank Pao, *Principal*
Joe Morrissey, *Vice Pres*
Anmol Shah, *Research*
Keith Mack, *Manager*
Dohn Paditsone, *Manager*
▲ **EMP:** 30
SALES (est): 3.9MM **Privately Held**
SIC: 3674 Solar cells

(G-13329)
ATLANTIS ENERGY SYSTEMS INC (PA)
7 Industry St (12603-2617)
PHONE.................916 438-2930
Frank Pao, *President*
Eleanor Pao, *Director*
EMP: 3
SQ FT: 10,000
SALES (est): 1.4MM **Privately Held**
SIC: 3674 3433 Semiconductors & related devices; solar heaters & collectors

(G-13330)
AW MACK MANUFACTURING CO INC
1098 Dutchess Tpke (12603-1150)
PHONE.................845 452-4050
Albert Mack, *CEO*
John Mack, *Vice Pres*
EMP: 16
SQ FT: 19,000
SALES (est): 1.6MM **Privately Held**
SIC: 3599 Machine shop, jobbing & repair

(G-13331)
CETEK INC
19 Commerce St (12603-2608)
PHONE.................845 452-3510
Fayiz Hilal, *President*
John Hilal, *Vice Pres*
▲ **EMP:** 37
SQ FT: 20,000
SALES (est): 3.9MM **Privately Held**
SIC: 3299 3599 3444 3825 Ceramic fiber; machine shop, jobbing & repair; forming machine work, sheet metal; instruments to measure electricity; porcelain electrical supplies

(G-13332)
CHOCOVISION CORPORATION
331 Main St (12601-3145)
PHONE.................845 473-4970
Babu Mandava, *CEO*
Ian Lazarus, *VP Sales*
Abubaker Shagan, *Manager*
◆ **EMP:** 10
SALES (est): 1.8MM **Privately Held**
WEB: www.chocovision.com
SIC: 3599 Custom machinery

(G-13333)
CREATIVE COUNTER TOPS INC
17 Van Kleeck Dr (12601-2163)
PHONE.................845 471-6480
Andrew Schor, *President*
EMP: 12
SALES: 600K **Privately Held**
SIC: 2541 Counters or counter display cases, wood; cabinets, except refrigerated: show, display, etc.: wood

(G-13334)
DORSEY METROLOGY INTL INC
53 Oakley St (12601-2004)
PHONE.................845 229-2929
Devon Luty, *President*
Peter Klepp, *President*
Brigid Gisolfi, *Vice Pres*
Mark Swenson, *Vice Pres*
Ronald Moore, *Mfg Staff*
EMP: 40
SQ FT: 18,000
SALES: 6MM **Privately Held**
WEB: www.dorseymetrology.com
SIC: 3545 5084 3827 3699 Gauges (machine tool accessories); precision tools, machinists'; industrial machinery & equipment; optical instruments & lenses; optical comparators; electrical equipment & supplies

(G-13335)
DYSON-KISSNER-MORAN CORP (PA)
2515 South Rd Ste 5 (12601-5474)
PHONE.................212 661-4600
Robert R Dyson, *Ch of Bd*
Michael J Harris, *President*
Mark Chamberlin, *Vice Pres*
Lynn J McCluskey, *Treasurer*
Linda Portner, *Manager*
◆ **EMP:** 30
SALES (est): 465.2MM **Privately Held**
SIC: 3433 3625 3699 Gas burners, industrial; motor controls, electric; security devices

(G-13336)
EAW ELECTRONIC SYSTEMS INC
900 Dutchess Tpke Ste 3 (12603-1554)
PHONE.................845 471-5290
Victoria Winiarski, *President*
Edward Winiarski, *Vice Pres*
Adam Secovnie, *Design Engr*
Ana Castro, *Admin Asst*
EMP: 7
SALES (est): 1.3MM **Privately Held**
WEB: www.eawelectro.com
SIC: 3568 Power transmission equipment

(G-13337)
FACES MAGAZINE INC (PA)
46 Violet Ave (12601-1521)
PHONE.................201 843-4004
Scott Figman, *President*
Adrianne Moore, *Editor*
▲ **EMP:** 18
SALES (est): 3.3MM **Privately Held**
SIC: 2721 Teen Magazine Publisher

(G-13338)
FACES MAGAZINE INC
40 Violet Ave (12601-1521)
PHONE.................845 454-7420
Timothy Perretta, *Manager*
EMP: 100
SALES (corp-wide): 3.3MM **Privately Held**
SIC: 2731 Books-Publishing/Printing
PA: Faces Magazine Inc
46 Violet Ave
Poughkeepsie NY 12601
201 843-4004

(G-13339)
GANNETT STLLITE INFO NTWRK LLC
Also Called: Poughkeepsie Journal
85 Civic Center Plz (12604-2498)
P.O. Box 1231 (12602-1231)
PHONE.................845 454-2000
Nora Pietrafesa, *Human. Res Mgr*
Ellen Smith, *Adv Dir*
Barry Rothfeld, *Branch Mgr*
Jane Howard-Martin,
Barbara Farrell, *Assistant*
EMP: 250
SALES (corp-wide): 3.1B **Publicly Held**
WEB: www.usatoday.com
SIC: 2711 Newspapers, publishing & printing
HQ: Gannett Satellite Information Network, Llc
7950 Jones Branch Dr
Mc Lean VA 22102
703 854-6000

(G-13340)
GET REAL SURFACES INC (PA)
121 Washington St (12601-1806)
PHONE.................845 337-4483
George Bishop, *President*
Avis Bishop, *Vice Pres*
▼ **EMP:** 33
SQ FT: 19,800
SALES (est): 6.4MM **Privately Held**
WEB: www.getrealsurfaces.com
SIC: 3271 3272 Architectural concrete: block, split, fluted, screen, etc.; concrete products

(G-13341)
GLOEDE NEON SIGNS LTD INC
97 N Clinton St (12601-2032)
PHONE.................845 471-4366
Barbara Fitzgerald, *President*
Todd Lanthier, *Opers Mgr*
EMP: 12 **EST:** 1922
SQ FT: 9,500
SALES (est): 1.7MM **Privately Held**
WEB: www.gloedesigns.com
SIC: 3993 1799 Electric signs; neon signs; sign installation & maintenance

(G-13342)
GREAT EASTERN COLOR LITH (PA)
46 Violet Ave (12601-1599)
PHONE.................845 454-7420
Lawrence Perretta, *President*
Louis Perretta Jr, *Vice Pres*
EMP: 150 **EST:** 1949
SQ FT: 115,000
SALES (est): 15.5MM **Privately Held**
WEB: www.magnapublishing.com
SIC: 2752 Commercial printing, lithographic

(G-13343)
GREY HOUSE PUBLISHING INC
Also Called: Greyhouse Publshng
84 Patrick Ln Stop 3 (12603-2950)
PHONE.................845 483-3535
Jennifer Patrick, *Manager*
EMP: 25
SALES (corp-wide): 5.4MM **Privately Held**
WEB: www.greyhouse.com
SIC: 2731 2741 Books: publishing only; miscellaneous publishing
PA: Grey House Publishing, Inc.
4919 Route 22
Amenia NY 12501
518 789-8700

(G-13344)
HARMON AND CASTELLA PRINTING
164 Garden St (12601-1934)
PHONE.................845 471-9163
Frank Castella, *President*
Karen Casteila, *Vice Pres*
EMP: 13
SQ FT: 4,500
SALES (est): 2.3MM **Privately Held**
WEB: www.hcprinting.com
SIC: 2752 2759 Commercial printing, offset; letterpress printing

(G-13345)
HATFIELD METAL FAB INC
16 Hatfield Ln (12603-6250)
PHONE.................845 454-9078
Ann Hatfield, *Ch of Bd*
Christopher Hatfield, *Vice Pres*
Henry Hatfield, *Vice Pres*
EMP: 45
SQ FT: 60,000
SALES (est): 10.6MM **Privately Held**
WEB: www.hatfieldmetal.com
SIC: 3444 5051 3479 3499 Sheet metal specialties, not stamped; sheets, metal; painting, coating & hot dipping; metal household articles

(G-13346)
HVR MSO LLC
Also Called: Radloop
2678 South Rd Ste 202 (12601-5254)
PHONE.................833 345-6974
Richard Friedland, *Mng Member*
Justin Wadsworth,
EMP: 5
SALES: 350K **Privately Held**
SIC: 7372 Application computer software

(G-13347)
JABIL CIRCUIT INC
2455 South Rd (12601-5463)
PHONE.................845 471-9237
Daniel Whalen, *Manager*
EMP: 421
SALES (corp-wide): 22.1B **Publicly Held**
SIC: 3672 Printed circuit boards
PA: Jabil Inc.
10560 Dr Martin Luther
Saint Petersburg FL 33716
727 577-9749

(G-13348)
JAMES L TAYLOR MFG CO (PA)
Also Called: James L. Taylor Mfg.
130 Salt Point Tpke (12603-1016)
PHONE.................845 452-3780
Michael Burdis, *CEO*
Joseph Burdis, *Editor*
Bradley Quick, *Vice Pres*
Jacob Greenfield, *Manager*
◆ **EMP:** 21 **EST:** 1911

Poughkeepsie - Dutchess County (G-13349)

SALES (est): 4MM **Privately Held**
WEB: www.jltclamps.com
SIC: 3553 Woodworking machinery

(G-13349)
JAMES L TAYLOR MFG CO
Also Called: Jlt Lancaster Clamps Div
130 Salt Point Tpke (12603-1016)
PHONE..................................845 452-3780
Michael Burdis, *President*
Emily Burdis, *Marketing Staff*
EMP: 9
SALES (corp-wide): 4MM **Privately Held**
WEB: www.jltclamps.com
SIC: 3553 Woodworking machinery
PA: James L. Taylor Manufacturing Co.
130 Salt Point Tpke
Poughkeepsie NY 12603
845 452-3780

(G-13350)
KOSHII MAXELUM AMERICA INC
12 Van Kleeck Dr (12601-2164)
P.O. Box 352 (12602-0352)
PHONE..................................845 471-0500
Mick Morita, *Ch of Bd*
Michelle Niles, *Controller*
Linda Wheatley, *Controller*
James Ojio, *Sales Mgr*
▲ EMP: 34
SQ FT: 60,000
SALES (est): 6.8MM
SALES (corp-wide): 104.5MM **Privately Held**
WEB: www.kmamax.com
SIC: 3743 Railway maintenance cars
PA: Koshii & Co., Ltd.
1-2-158, Hirabayashikita, Suminoe-Ku
Osaka OSK 559-0
666 852-061

(G-13351)
LJMM INC
Also Called: Nilda Desserts
188 Washington St (12601-1357)
PHONE..................................845 454-5876
Linda Tritto, *President*
Jason Tritto, *Vice Pres*
EMP: 20
SQ FT: 4,000
SALES: 1.2MM **Privately Held**
SIC: 2051 Bakery: wholesale or wholesale/retail combined

(G-13352)
MACHINE TECHNOLOGY INC
104 Bushwick Rd (12603-3813)
PHONE..................................845 454-4030
Klaus Greinacher, *President*
EMP: 5
SQ FT: 3,500
SALES (est): 430K **Privately Held**
SIC: 3829 Measuring & controlling devices

(G-13353)
MARCO MANUFACTURING INC
55 Page Park Dr (12603-2583)
P.O. Box 3733 (12603-0733)
PHONE..................................845 485-1571
Michael Ratliff, *President*
Brian Lowe, *Opers Mgr*
Jim Burger, *Materials Mgr*
Jolanta Skrok, *Buyer*
Patty Jessup, *QC Mgr*
EMP: 40
SQ FT: 10,000
SALES (est): 10.8MM **Privately Held**
WEB: www.marcomanf.com
SIC: 3577 Computer peripheral equipment

(G-13354)
MID HDSON WKSHP FOR THE DSBLED
188 Washington St (12601-1357)
PHONE..................................845 471-3820
Robert Nellis, *President*
Richard Stark, *Vice Pres*
▲ EMP: 25
SQ FT: 52,000
SALES: 633.2K **Privately Held**
WEB: www.midhudsonworkshop.com
SIC: 3679 Electronic circuits

(G-13355)
MODERN CABINET COMPANY INC
Also Called: Kitchen Cabinet Co
17 Van Kleeck Dr (12601-2163)
PHONE..................................845 473-4900
Andrew Schor, *President*
Lisa Turner, *Vice Pres*
Maxine Schor, *Treasurer*
EMP: 45
SQ FT: 21,000
SALES (est): 6.2MM **Privately Held**
SIC: 2434 Wood kitchen cabinets

(G-13356)
MPI INCORPORATED
165 Smith St Stop 3 (12601-2108)
PHONE..................................845 471-7630
Bruce S Phipps, *Ch of Bd*
Jeffrey Rich, *Vice Pres*
Chris Chmura, *Project Mgr*
Fabio Alvarez, *CFO*
Terry Justyna, *Controller*
▼ EMP: 109 EST: 1951
SQ FT: 30,000
SALES (est): 18.2MM **Privately Held**
WEB: www.mpi-systems.com
SIC: 3542 Pressing machines

(G-13357)
MR SMOOTHIE
207 South Ave Ste F102 (12601)
PHONE..................................845 296-1686
Robert Botllieri, *Branch Mgr*
EMP: 5
SALES (corp-wide): 765K **Privately Held**
SIC: 2087 Concentrates, drink
PA: Mr Smoothie
1000 Ross Park Mall Dr Vc13
Pittsburgh PA 15237
412 630-9065

(G-13358)
NEW BGNNNGS WIN DOOR DSTRS LLC
28 Willowbrook Hts (12603-5708)
PHONE..................................845 214-0698
Domenica Haines, *Mng Member*
EMP: 10 EST: 2009
SALES (est): 1.2MM **Privately Held**
SIC: 3442 5031 Window & door frames; windows

(G-13359)
NILDAS DESSERTS LIMITED
188 Washington St (12601-1357)
PHONE..................................845 454-5876
James Milano, *President*
EMP: 10
SQ FT: 5,000
SALES: 500K **Privately Held**
SIC: 2051 Bakery: wholesale or wholesale/retail combined

(G-13360)
NUTRA-VET RESEARCH CORP
201 Smith St (12601-2198)
PHONE..................................845 473-1900
Robert Abady, *President*
EMP: 10 EST: 1971
SQ FT: 14,000
SALES (est): 822.8K **Privately Held**
SIC: 2048 Mineral feed supplements

(G-13361)
OPTIMUM APPLIED SYSTEMS INC
16 Victory Ln Ste 5 (12601-1563)
P.O. Box 3572 (12601-0572)
PHONE..................................845 471-3333
Edward Awiniarski, *President*
Jonathan Walters, *Cust Mgr*
EMP: 19
SALES: 950K **Privately Held**
SIC: 3699 Electrical equipment & supplies

(G-13362)
PERRETTA GRAPHICS CORP
46 Violet Ave (12601-1521)
PHONE..................................845 473-0550
Lawrence Perretta, *President*
Neil Rockwell, *Publisher*
Christopher Perretta, *Vice Pres*
Louis Perretta Jr, *Vice Pres*
James Conte, *Purch Mgr*

▲ EMP: 40
SQ FT: 115,000
SALES (est): 8.7MM **Privately Held**
SIC: 3555 Printing trades machinery

(G-13363)
ROBERT ABADY DOG FOOD CO LTD
201 Smith St (12601-2198)
PHONE..................................845 473-1900
Robert Abady, *President*
EMP: 12
SALES (est): 1.5MM **Privately Held**
SIC: 2047 Dog food; cat food

(G-13364)
ROYAL COPENHAGEN INC (PA)
63 Page Park Dr (12603-2583)
P.O. Box 610, Belmar NJ (07719-0610)
PHONE..................................845 454-4442
Nicolai Lindhardt, *President*
Karin Skipper-Ulstrup, *Marketing Mgr*
Niels Bastrup, *Creative Dir*
▲ EMP: 10
SQ FT: 6,000
SALES (est): 722.9K **Privately Held**
SIC: 2392 Tablecloths & table settings

(G-13365)
SCHATZ BEARING CORPORATION
10 Fairview Ave (12601-1312)
PHONE..................................845 452-6000
Dr Stephen D E Pomeroy, *CEO*
Bob Lanser, *Plant Mgr*
John Forbes, *Buyer*
Brad Euker CPA, *Controller*
Peggie Hyatt, *Human Res Mgr*
▲ EMP: 75
SQ FT: 50,000
SALES (est): 21.2MM **Privately Held**
WEB: www.schatzbearing.com
SIC: 3562 Ball bearings & parts

(G-13366)
SCIANE ENTERPRISES INC
Also Called: Emdroidme
2600 South Rd Ste 37 (12601-7004)
PHONE..................................845 452-2400
Diane Pawenski, *Ch of Bd*
EMP: 7
SALES (est): 149.8K **Privately Held**
SIC: 2395 2261 Embroidery products, except schiffli machine; screen printing of cotton broadwoven fabrics

(G-13367)
SPECTRA VISTA CORPORATION
29 Firemens Way Stop 3 (12603-6523)
PHONE..................................845 471-7007
William G Goffe, *Ch of Bd*
Tom Corl, *President*
Larry Slomer, *Senior Engr*
Ward Duffield, *Manager*
Sue Ohearn, *Info Tech Mgr*
EMP: 6
SQ FT: 2,000
SALES (est): 1MM **Privately Held**
SIC: 3826 Spectrometers

(G-13368)
STANFORDVILLE MCH & MFG CO INC (PA)
Also Called: Kent Gage & Tool Company
29 Victory Ln (12603-1562)
P.O. Box B, Stanfordville (12581-0152)
PHONE..................................845 868-2266
Neal Johnsen, *Ch of Bd*
Peter Johnsen, *Vice Pres*
Joe La Falce, *CFO*
Ann Marie Johnsen, *Treasurer*
Mike Bell, *Accounts Exec*
EMP: 57
SALES (est): 9MM **Privately Held**
WEB: www.stanfordville.com
SIC: 3599 Machine shop, jobbing & repair

(G-13369)
STEBE SHCJHJFF
18 Lynbrook Rd (12603-4608)
PHONE..................................839 383-9833
EMP: 10
SALES (est): 480K **Privately Held**
SIC: 2051 Mfg Bread/Related Products

(G-13370)
SUPERIOR WLLS OF HDSON VLY INC
Also Called: Superior Walls of Hudson Vly
68 Violet Ave (12601-1521)
PHONE..................................845 485-4033
Karen Ackert, *President*
Arthur Ackert Sr, *General Mgr*
Tammi Ackert, *Treasurer*
EMP: 50
SALES (est): 5.8MM **Privately Held**
WEB: www.superiorwallshv.com
SIC: 3272 Precast terrazo or concrete products; concrete products, precast

(G-13371)
VANTAGE MFG & ASSEMBLY LLC
Also Called: Vma
900 Dutchess Tpke (12603-1554)
P.O. Box 3623 (12603-0623)
PHONE..................................845 471-5290
Edward Winiarski, *President*
Greg Devine, *Production*
Bill Reagan, *Engineer*
Mike Sterbenz, *Finance Mgr*
Ana Castro, *Manager*
EMP: 48
SALES: 19.6MM **Privately Held**
SIC: 3824 Electromechanical counters

(G-13372)
VETERINARY BIOCHEMICAL LTD
201 Smith St (12601-2110)
PHONE..................................845 473-1900
Robert Abady, *President*
EMP: 5
SQ FT: 14,000
SALES (est): 650K **Privately Held**
SIC: 2048 Feed supplements

(G-13373)
VIKING IRON WORKS INC
37 Hatfield Ln (12603-6249)
PHONE..................................845 471-5010
Richard J Kunkel, *Ch of Bd*
Richard J Kunke, *President*
Jim Kunkel, *Vice Pres*
Paul Kunkel, *Vice Pres*
Laurie Lunden, *Office Mgr*
EMP: 14
SQ FT: 6,000
SALES (est): 3.3MM **Privately Held**
WEB: www.vikingironworks.com
SIC: 3462 Iron & steel forgings

Poughquag
Dutchess County

(G-13374)
FRED SCHULZ INC
Also Called: Schulz Interiors
4 Jordan Ct (12570-5039)
PHONE..................................845 724-3409
Fred Schulz, *President*
Mary Schulz, *Corp Secy*
EMP: 6
SALES (est): 549.6K **Privately Held**
WEB: www.fredschulz.com
SIC: 2511 Wood household furniture

Pound Ridge
Westchester County

(G-13375)
BIORESEARCH INC (PA)
4 Sunset Ln (10576-2318)
PHONE..................................212 734-5315
Leonard Kirth, *President*
Preston Keller, *President*
EMP: 9
SQ FT: 7,000
SALES (est): 928.8K **Privately Held**
WEB: www.bioresearch.com
SIC: 3841 Surgical & medical instruments

(G-13376)
DYNAX CORPORATION
79 Westchester Ave (10576-1702)
P.O. Box 285 (10576-0285)
PHONE..................914 764-0202
Eduard K Kleiner PHD, *President*
Louis McAdams, *Prdtn Mgr*
Bryan Rambo, *VP Sales*
▲ **EMP:** 6
SQ FT: 3,600
SALES (est): 1.3MM **Privately Held**
WEB: www.dynaxcorp.com
SIC: 2822 2824 Fluoro rubbers; fluorocarbon fibers

(G-13377)
LLOYD PRICE ICON FOOD BRANDS
Also Called: Lawdy Miss Clawdy
95 Horseshoe Hill Rd (10576-1636)
PHONE..................914 764-8624
Lloyd Price, *Ch of Bd*
EMP: 15
SQ FT: 2,500
SALES (est): 950K **Privately Held**
WEB: www.lawdymissclawdy.com
SIC: 2052 Cookies

Prattsville
Greene County

(G-13378)
COBLESKILL STONE PRODUCTS INC
Also Called: Falke's Quarry
395 Falke Rd (12468-5811)
P.O. Box 268 (12468-0268)
PHONE..................518 299-3066
Richard Mahar, *Branch Mgr*
EMP: 10
SALES (corp-wide): 115.2MM **Privately Held**
WEB: www.cobleskillstone.com
SIC: 1422 Crushed & broken limestone
PA: Cobleskill Stone Products, Inc.
  112 Rock Rd
  Cobleskill NY 12043
  518 234-0221

Pulaski
Oswego County

(G-13379)
FELIX SCHOELLER NORTH AMER INC
179 County Route 2a (13142-2546)
P.O. Box 250 (13142-0250)
PHONE..................315 298-8425
Michael Szidat, *Ch of Bd*
Thomas Scheck, *Vice Pres*
EMP: 75 **EST:** 1961
SQ FT: 150,000
SALES (est): 1.5MM
SALES (corp-wide): 482.3MM **Privately Held**
WEB: www.felix-schoeller.com
SIC: 2672 5113 Coated & laminated paper; industrial & personal service paper
HQ: Schoeller Beteiligungen Gmbh
  Burg Gretesch 1
  Osnabruck
  541 380-00

(G-13380)
FULTON BOILER WORKS INC (PA)
3981 Port St (13142-4604)
P.O. Box 257 (13142-0257)
PHONE..................315 298-5121
Ronald B Palm, *Ch of Bd*
Scott Redden, *Info Tech Dir*
▲ **EMP:** 60
SQ FT: 120,000
SALES (est): 87.2MM **Privately Held**
WEB: www.fulton.com
SIC: 3443 Boilers: industrial, power, or marine

(G-13381)
FULTON BOILER WORKS INC
972 Centerville Rd (13142-2595)
PHONE..................315 298-5121
Ronald Palm, *Manager*
EMP: 250
SALES (corp-wide): 82.1MM **Privately Held**
SIC: 3443 Fabricated plate work (boiler shop)
PA: Fulton Boiler Works, Inc.
  3981 Port St
  Pulaski NY 13142
  315 298-5121

(G-13382)
FULTON CHINA LLC
3981 Port St (13142-4604)
P.O. Box 257 (13142-0257)
PHONE..................315 298-0112
Shane Peabody, *Principal*
Ken Shanahan, *Sales Staff*
EMP: 6
SALES (est): 613.5K **Privately Held**
SIC: 3443 Fabricated plate work (boiler shop)

(G-13383)
FULTON HEATING SOLUTIONS INC
972 Centerville Rd (13142-2595)
P.O. Box 257 (13142-0257)
PHONE..................315 298-5121
Ronald B Palm Jr, *Ch of Bd*
Karen Currier, *Credit Mgr*
▲ **EMP:** 55
SQ FT: 200,000
SALES (est): 5.7MM
SALES (corp-wide): 19.1MM **Privately Held**
SIC: 3433 Burners, furnaces, boilers & stokers
PA: Hangzhou Fulton Thermal Equipment Co., Ltd.
  No.09,Street 18, Xiasha Economic And Technological Development Z
  Hangzhou 31001
  571 867-2589

(G-13384)
FULTON VOLCANIC INC (PA)
Also Called: Fulton Companies
3981 Port St (13142-4604)
P.O. Box 257 (13142-0257)
PHONE..................315 298-5121
Ronald B Palm, *President*
Jian Chen, *General Mgr*
Kathy Sega, *Exec VP*
Mark Hilton, *VP Mfg*
Julie Hemingway, *Production*
▼ **EMP:** 70
SQ FT: 20,000
SALES (est): 31.1MM **Privately Held**
WEB: www.volcanic-heater.com
SIC: 3433 Heating equipment, except electric; heating units & devices, industrial: electric; electric housewares & fans

(G-13385)
HEALTHWAY HOME PRODUCTS INC
3420 Maple Ave (13142-4502)
P.O. Box 485 (13142-0485)
PHONE..................315 298-2904
Vincent G Lobdell Sr, *Ch of Bd*
Jeffrey Herberger, *Vice Pres*
Vince Lobdell Jr, *Vice Pres*
Yinyin C Blodgett, *Opers Mgr*
Yinyin Blodgett, *Opers Mgr*
▲ **EMP:** 30
SQ FT: 20,000
SALES (est): 8.5MM **Privately Held**
WEB: www.healthway.com
SIC: 3564 Filters, air: furnaces, air conditioning equipment, etc.

Purchase
Westchester County

(G-13386)
APOLLO MANAGEMENT V LP
1 Manhattanville Rd # 201 (10577-2100)
PHONE..................914 467-6510
Lourenco Goncalves, *Ch of Bd*
Leon Black, *Mng Member*
Joshua Harris, *Mng Member*
Marc Rowan, *Mng Member*
EMP: 25
SALES (est): 6MM **Publicly Held**
SIC: 3272 3354 5051 Building materials, except block or brick: concrete; aluminum extruded products; iron & steel (ferrous) products
PA: Apollo Global Management, Llc
  9 W 57th St Fl 43
  New York NY 10019

(G-13387)
CENTRAL NAT PULP & PPR SLS INC
3 Manhattanville Rd (10577-2116)
PHONE..................914 696-9000
Kenneth L Wallach, *Chairman*
EMP: 2500
SALES (est): 76.1MM
SALES (corp-wide): 4.1B **Privately Held**
SIC: 2611 Pulp mills, mechanical & recycling processing
PA: Central National Gottesman Inc.
  3 Manhattanville Rd # 301
  Purchase NY 10577
  914 696-9000

(G-13388)
HITACHI CABLE AMERICA INC (DH)
2 Manhattanville Rd # 301 (10577-2118)
PHONE..................914 694-9200
Toro Aoki, *CEO*
Michael Ressl, *President*
Kenny Crecelius, *General Mgr*
Wes Hanson, *General Mgr*
Steve Kacines, *General Mgr*
▲ **EMP:** 13
SQ FT: 6,000
SALES (est): 167.7MM
SALES (corp-wide): 87.9B **Privately Held**
WEB: www.hitachi-cable.com
SIC: 3052 Rubber & plastics hose & beltings
HQ: Hitachi Metals America, Ltd.
  2 Manhattanville Rd # 301
  Purchase NY 10577
  914 694-9200

(G-13389)
HITACHI METALS AMERICA LTD
HI Specialties America Div
2 Manhattanville Rd # 301 (10577-2103)
PHONE..................914 694-9200
Ernie Stricsck, *President*
EMP: 24
SALES (corp-wide): 87.9B **Privately Held**
SIC: 3312 3496 3316 3315 Rods, iron & steel: made in steel mills; miscellaneous fabricated wire products; cold finishing of steel shapes; steel wire & related products
HQ: Hitachi Metals America, Ltd.
  2 Manhattanville Rd # 301
  Purchase NY 10577
  914 694-9200

(G-13390)
HITACHI METALS AMERICA LTD (DH)
2 Manhattanville Rd # 301 (10577-2103)
PHONE..................914 694-9200
Hideaki Takahashi, *CEO*
Tomoyasu Kubota, *Ch of Bd*
Tomoyuki Hatano, *President*
Hiroaki Nakanishi, *President*
Toshiki Aoki, *CFO*
▲ **EMP:** 45 **EST:** 1965
SQ FT: 25,000
SALES (est): 1.4B
SALES (corp-wide): 87.9B **Privately Held**
SIC: 3264 3577 3365 5051 Magnets, permanent: ceramic or ferrite; computer peripheral equipment; aluminum & aluminum-based alloy castings; steel; castings, rough: iron or steel; ductile iron castings; gray iron castings; automotive related machinery
HQ: Hitachi Metals, Ltd.
  1-2-70, Konan
  Minato-Ku TKY 108-0
  367 743-001

(G-13391)
LIGHTING HOLDINGS INTL LLC (PA)
4 Manhattanville Rd (10577-2139)
PHONE..................845 306-1850
Dionne Gadsden, *CEO*
Steve Imgham, *CEO*
Gregory Barry, *Vice Pres*
William Drexles, *CFO*
◆ **EMP:** 1400
SQ FT: 1,700
SALES (est): 141.7MM **Privately Held**
WEB: www.sli-lighting.com
SIC: 3641 5719 5063 4225 Electric lamps & parts for generalized applications; lamps & lamp shades; lighting fixtures; general warehousing; current-carrying wiring devices; lamp sockets & receptacles (electric wiring devices); pressed & blown glass

(G-13392)
MAM USA CORPORATION
2700 Westchester Ave # 315 (10577-2554)
PHONE..................914 269-2500
Jennifer Mitchell, *CEO*
Fritz Hirsch, *CEO*
Niklaus Schertenlieb, *President*
Bernd Deussen, *Vice Pres*
Stefan Roehrig, *Vice Pres*
▲ **EMP:** 10
SALES (est): 2.1MM **Privately Held**
SIC: 3069 5999 Baby pacifiers, rubber; infant furnishings & equipment
HQ: Mam Babyartikel Gesellschaft M.B.H.
  Lorenz Mandl-Gasse 50
  Wien 1160
  149 141-0

(G-13393)
PEPSI-COLA METRO BTLG CO INC
700 Anderson Hill Rd (10577-1444)
PHONE..................914 253-2000
Robert K Biggart, *President*
Richard Robinson, *District Mgr*
Timothy Redden, *Business Mgr*
Keith Marcom, *Project Mgr*
Ruchi Modi, *Opers Mgr*
EMP: 34
SALES (est): 2.8MM **Privately Held**
SIC: 2086 Soft drinks: packaged in cans, bottles, etc.

(G-13394)
PEPSI-COLA SALES AND DIST INC (HQ)
700 Anderson Hill Rd (10577-1444)
PHONE..................914 253-2000
Kirk Tanner, *CEO*
EMP: 8
SALES (est): 952.5K
SALES (corp-wide): 63.5B **Publicly Held**
SIC: 2086 5149 Soft drinks: packaged in cans, bottles, etc.; beverages, except coffee & tea
PA: Pepsico, Inc.
  700 Anderson Hill Rd
  Purchase NY 10577
  914 253-2000

(G-13395)
PEPSICO INC (PA)
700 Anderson Hill Rd (10577-1444)
PHONE..................914 253-2000
Albert P Carey, *CEO*
Laxman Narasimhan, *CEO*
Mike Spanos, *CEO*
Indra K Nooyi, *Ch of Bd*
Ramon Laguarta, *President*
◆ **EMP:** 1500 **EST:** 1919

Purchase - Westchester County (G-13396)

SALES: 63.5B **Publicly Held**
WEB: www.pepsico.com
SIC: **2096** 2087 2086 2037 Potato chips & similar snacks; corn chips & other corn-based snacks; potato chips & other potato-based snacks; cheese curls & puffs; flavoring extracts & syrups; syrups, drink; fruit juices: concentrated for fountain use; concentrates, drink; bottled & canned soft drinks; iced tea & fruit drinks, bottled & canned; soft drinks: packaged in cans, bottles, etc.; carbonated beverages, non-alcoholic: bottled & canned; fruit juices: cookies & crackers; cereal breakfast foods; oatmeal: prepared as cereal breakfast food

(G-13396)
PEPSICO INC
Anderson Hill Rd (10577)
PHONE..................914 253-2000
D Wayne Calloway, *Ch of Bd*
Tricia Lynch, *Supervisor*
EMP: 700
SALES (corp-wide): 63.5B **Publicly Held**
SIC: **2086** Carbonated soft drinks, bottled & canned
PA: Pepsico, Inc.
  700 Anderson Hill Rd
  Purchase NY 10577
  914 253-2000

(G-13397)
PEPSICO INC
700 Anderson Hill Rd (10577-1444)
PHONE..................914 253-2713
Denise Passarella, *Branch Mgr*
EMP: 10
SALES (corp-wide): 63.5B **Publicly Held**
SIC: **2086** Carbonated soft drinks, bottled & canned
PA: Pepsico, Inc.
  700 Anderson Hill Rd
  Purchase NY 10577
  914 253-2000

(G-13398)
PEPSICO CAPITAL RESOURCES INC
700 Anderson Hill Rd (10577-1444)
PHONE..................914 253-2000
Judy Germano, *Principal*
Marcie Escalante, *Sales Staff*
EMP: 6
SALES (est): 395.2K **Privately Held**
SIC: **2086** Bottled & canned soft drinks

(G-13399)
PEPSICO SALES INC
700 Anderson Hill Rd (10577-1444)
PHONE..................914 253-2000
Charles F Mueller, *Principal*
EMP: 6 EST: 2003
SALES (est): 91.3K
SALES (corp-wide): 63.5B **Publicly Held**
SIC: **2086** 5149 Soft drinks: packaged in cans, bottles, etc.; beverages, except coffee & tea
PA: Pepsico, Inc.
  700 Anderson Hill Rd
  Purchase NY 10577
  914 253-2000

(G-13400)
REGAL TRADING INC
Also Called: Regal Commodities
2975 Westchester Ave # 210 (10577-2500)
PHONE..................914 694-6100
Joseph Apuzzo Jr, *CEO*
Sid Abramowitz, *Vice Pres*
▲ EMP: 35
SALES (est): 5.9MM **Privately Held**
SIC: **2095** Coffee roasting (except by wholesale grocers)

Putnam Valley
Putnam County

(G-13401)
ARGOS INC
58 Seifert Ln (10579-1707)
PHONE..................845 528-0576
Steven A Roy, *President*
Roger Eriksen, *Vice Pres*
Dennis Klubnick, *Admin Sec*
EMP: 24
SQ FT: 10,000
SALES (est): 3.7MM **Privately Held**
WEB: www.argos.net
SIC: **3366** 3369 Bronze foundry; nonferrous foundries

Queens Village
Queens County

(G-13402)
ALL TIME PRODUCTS INC
21167 Jamaica Ave (11428-1621)
PHONE..................718 464-1400
Junior Lindo, *President*
Vinton Lindo, *Admin Sec*
EMP: 6
SALES (est): 726K **Privately Held**
SIC: **2752** Commercial printing, offset

(G-13403)
ALLSTAR GRAPHICS LTD
22034 Jamaica Ave (11428-2141)
PHONE..................718 740-2240
Barry Kessler, *President*
Charles Kessler, *Vice Pres*
Jeff Kessler, *Treasurer*
Al Epstein, *Admin Sec*
EMP: 20
SQ FT: 2,000
SALES (est): 1.2MM **Privately Held**
WEB: www.allstargraphics.com
SIC: **3993** Signs & advertising specialties

(G-13404)
COLGATE-PALMOLIVE COMPANY
21818 100th Ave (11429-1209)
PHONE..................718 506-3961
EMP: 279
SALES (corp-wide): 15.4B **Publicly Held**
SIC: **2844** Toothpastes or powders, dentifrices
PA: Colgate-Palmolive Company
  300 Park Ave Fl 3
  New York NY 10022
  212 310-2000

(G-13405)
EAST END VINEYARDS LLC
Also Called: Clovis Point
21548 Jamaica Ave (11428-1716)
P.O. Box 669, Jamesport (11947-0669)
PHONE..................718 468-0500
Hal R Ginsburg, *Mng Member*
▲ EMP: 7
SQ FT: 5,000
SALES: 300K **Privately Held**
SIC: **2084** Wines

(G-13406)
GRAY GLASS INC
21744 98th Ave Ste C (11429-1252)
PHONE..................718 217-2943
Christopher A Viggiano, *Ch of Bd*
William O Bryan, *Vice Pres*
Bill O'Bryan, *Vice Pres*
Dave Costa, *Plant Mgr*
Kenneth Rutowicz, *Site Mgr*
▲ EMP: 49 EST: 1946
SQ FT: 50,000
SALES: 7.8MM **Privately Held**
WEB: www.grayglass.net
SIC: **3229** 3231 Glass tubes & tubing; products of purchased glass

(G-13407)
IGNELZI INTERIORS INC
9805 217th St (11429-1234)
PHONE..................718 464-0279
Paul Ignelzi, *President*
Hugo Pomies, *Vice Pres*
EMP: 20
SQ FT: 16,000
SALES (est): 3.1MM **Privately Held**
WEB: www.ignelziinteriors.com
SIC: **2431** 2434 Woodwork, interior & ornamental; wood kitchen cabinets

(G-13408)
J3 PRINTING INC
11214 Colfax St (11429-2221)
PHONE..................516 304-6103
Robet Nelson, *Principal*
EMP: 5 EST: 2015
SALES (est): 122.8K **Privately Held**
SIC: **2752** Commercial printing, lithographic

(G-13409)
JAMAICA LAMP CORP
21220 Jamaica Ave (11428-1618)
PHONE..................718 776-5039
Irving Shernock, *President*
▲ EMP: 30 EST: 1955
SQ FT: 20,000
SALES (est): 2.8MM **Privately Held**
SIC: **3999** 3645 Shades, lamp or candle; residential lighting fixtures

(G-13410)
LAMS FOODS INC
9723 218th St (11429-1251)
PHONE..................718 217-0476
Sherlock Lam, *President*
Cleveland Lam, *Vice Pres*
Shervin Lam, *Vice Pres*
Trevor Lam, *Vice Pres*
▲ EMP: 17
SQ FT: 20,000
SALES (est): 3.3MM **Privately Held**
WEB: www.lamsnacks.com
SIC: **2099** Noodles, fried (Chinese)

(G-13411)
MSQ CORPORATION
21504 Hempstead Ave (11429-1222)
PHONE..................718 465-0900
Craig Zoly, *President*
EMP: 8
SALES (est): 295.6K **Privately Held**
SIC: **2024** Ice cream & ice milk

(G-13412)
VOLKERT PRECISION TECH INC
22240 96th Ave Ste 3 (11429-1330)
PHONE..................718 464-9500
Kenneth J Heim, *Ch of Bd*
Jerome Bloomberg, *Vice Pres*
EMP: 47
SQ FT: 50,000
SALES (est): 9.1MM **Privately Held**
WEB: www.volkertprecision.com
SIC: **3469** Stamping metal for the trade; machine parts, stamped or pressed metal

(G-13413)
XEDIT CORP
Also Called: Servo Reeler System
21831 97th Ave (11429-1232)
PHONE..................718 380-1592
Claude Karczmer, *President*
EMP: 7
SQ FT: 1,800
SALES (est): 660K **Privately Held**
WEB: www.servoreelers.com
SIC: **3679** Electronic circuits

Queensbury
Warren County

(G-13414)
ADIRONDACK PRECISION CUT STONE (PA)
536 Queensbury Ave (12804-7612)
PHONE..................518 681-3060
Kris Johnston, *Owner*
EMP: 12
SALES (est): 1.7MM **Privately Held**
SIC: **3281** Granite, cut & shaped

(G-13415)
AMSTERDAM PRINTING & LITHO INC
Resource One
428 Corinth Rd (12804-7816)
P.O. Box 267, Hagaman (12086-0267)
PHONE..................518 792-6501
Kevin Kirbey, *Manager*
EMP: 10
SQ FT: 24,000
SALES (corp-wide): 3.4B **Privately Held**
WEB: www.amsterdamprinting.com
SIC: **2752** Commercial printing, offset
HQ: Amsterdam Printing & Litho, Inc.
  166 Wallins Corners Rd
  Amsterdam NY 12010
  518 842-6000

(G-13416)
AMSTERDAM PRINTING & LITHO INC
Also Called: Web Graphics
428 Corinth Rd (12804-7816)
PHONE..................518 792-6501
Tim Taylor, *Branch Mgr*
EMP: 12
SALES (corp-wide): 3.4B **Privately Held**
WEB: www.amsterdamprinting.com
SIC: **2759** Laser printing
HQ: Amsterdam Printing & Litho, Inc.
  166 Wallins Corners Rd
  Amsterdam NY 12010
  518 842-6000

(G-13417)
ANGIODYNAMICS INC
603 Queensbury Ave (12804-7619)
PHONE..................518 761-6867
EMP: 34
SALES (corp-wide): 344.2MM **Publicly Held**
SIC: **3841** Mfg Surgical/Medical Instruments
PA: Angiodynamics, Inc.
  14 Plaza Dr
  Latham NY 12110
  518 795-1400

(G-13418)
ANGIODYNAMICS INC
603 Queensbury Ave (12804-7619)
PHONE..................518 975-1400
EMP: 400
SALES (corp-wide): 344.2MM **Publicly Held**
SIC: **3841** Surgical & medical instruments
PA: Angiodynamics, Inc.
  14 Plaza Dr
  Latham NY 12110
  518 795-1400

(G-13419)
ANGIODYNAMICS INC
543 Queensbury Ave (12804-7629)
PHONE..................518 742-4430
EMP: 275
SALES (corp-wide): 344.2MM **Publicly Held**
SIC: **3841** Surgical & medical instruments
PA: Angiodynamics, Inc.
  14 Plaza Dr
  Latham NY 12110
  518 795-1400

(G-13420)
B Q P INC
6 Collins Dr (12804-1493)
PHONE..................518 793-4999
Tom Brennen, *President*
Susan Brennen, *Vice Pres*
EMP: 8
SALES (est): 743.3K **Privately Held**
SIC: **2752** Commercial printing, offset

(G-13421)
C R BARD INC
289 Bay Rd (12804-2015)
PHONE..................518 793-2531
David Freeman, *President*
Chris Melton, *President*
Vincent Cafiso, *Vice Pres*
Ronald Greene, *Vice Pres*
Michele Weller, *Vice Pres*
EMP: 485
SALES (corp-wide): 12B **Publicly Held**
SIC: **3841** Surgical & medical instruments
HQ: C. R. Bard, Inc.
  730 Central Ave
  New Providence NJ 07974
  908 277-8000

(G-13422)
DUKE CONCRETE PRODUCTS INC
50 Duke Dr (12804-2048)
PHONE..................518 793-7743

GEOGRAPHIC SECTION

Randolph - Cattaraugus County (G-13448)

O E S Hedbring, *Ch of Bd*
John Hedbring, *President*
Gary Hukey, *Vice Pres*
Richard Schumaker, *Admin Sec*
EMP: 25
SQ FT: 9,000
SALES (est): 4.9MM **Privately Held**
WEB: www.dukeconcrete.com
SIC: 3271 5211 5082 Blocks, concrete or cinder: standard; concrete & cinder block; masonry materials & supplies; masonry equipment & supplies
PA: The Fort Miller Service Corp
688 Wilbur Ave
Greenwich NY 12834

(G-13423)
FLOWMEDICA INC
603 Queensbury Ave (12804-7619)
PHONE 800 772-6446
Jeff Elkins, *President*
EMP: 14
SQ FT: 6,614
SALES (est): 966.4K **Privately Held**
WEB: www.flowmedica.com
SIC: 3841 Surgical & medical instruments

(G-13424)
G F LABELS LLC
10 Ferguson Ln (12804-7641)
PHONE 518 798-6643
Jacob Vanness, *Vice Pres*
Robert Gray, *Mng Member*
Betsy Carney, *Admin Sec*
EMP: 14
SQ FT: 12,000
SALES (est): 2.9MM **Privately Held**
WEB: www.gflabels.com
SIC: 2752 5113 Commercial printing, lithographic; paperboard & products

(G-13425)
GEORGE LAKE DISTILLING COMPANY
2 Pinecroft Dr (12804-9350)
PHONE 518 639-1025
Robin McDougall,
John McDougall,
EMP: 5
SALES (est): 344.1K **Privately Held**
SIC: 2085 Distilled & blended liquors

(G-13426)
GLENS FALLS READY MIX INC
Also Called: Crainville Block Co
112 Big Boom Rd (12804-7861)
PHONE 518 793-1695
John Tesiero, *President*
EMP: 12
SQ FT: 195
SALES (est): 770K **Privately Held**
SIC: 3272 3273 Concrete products, precast; ready-mixed concrete

(G-13427)
HARRIS LOGGING INC
39 Mud Pond Rd (12804-7313)
PHONE 518 792-1083
Keith L Harris, *President*
Pamela Harris, *Corp Secy*
EMP: 30
SALES (est): 2.2MM **Privately Held**
SIC: 2411 Logging

(G-13428)
HJE COMPANY INC
820 Quaker Rd (12804-3811)
PHONE 518 792-8733
Joseph Tunick Strauss, *President*
EMP: 5
SQ FT: 4,500
SALES (est): 605K **Privately Held**
SIC: 3549 3399 Metalworking machinery; powder, metal

(G-13429)
JAMES KING WOODWORKING INC
656 County Line Rd (12804-7621)
PHONE 518 761-6091
Scott Kingsley, *President*
James Morris, *Vice Pres*
EMP: 6
SQ FT: 76,230
SALES (est): 660.4K **Privately Held**
SIC: 2431 Millwork

(G-13430)
JE MONAHAN FABRICATIONS LLC
559 Queensbury Ave 1/2 (12804-7613)
PHONE 518 761-0414
Harold A Smith,
Joe E Monahan,
Walter R Smith,
EMP: 11
SQ FT: 25,000
SALES: 1.2MM **Privately Held**
SIC: 3499 Welding tips, heat resistant: metal

(G-13431)
KINGSBURY PRINTING CO INC
813 Bay Rd (12804-5906)
PHONE 518 747-6606
Robert Bombard, *President*
Robert L Bombard, *Vice Pres*
Victoria Bombard-Bushey, *Director*
EMP: 6
SALES: 600K **Privately Held**
WEB: www.kingsburyprinting.com
SIC: 2752 Commercial printing, offset

(G-13432)
KOKE INC
582 Queensbury Ave (12804-7612)
PHONE 800 535-5303
Richard Koke, *President*
Michael Nelson, *CFO*
Tom Miksch, *Mktg Dir*
◆ **EMP:** 20 EST: 1972
SQ FT: 36,000
SALES (est): 5.3MM **Privately Held**
SIC: 3537 5084 Trucks, tractors, loaders, carriers & similar equipment; materials handling machinery

(G-13433)
M & S PRECISION MACHINE CO LLC
27 Casey Rd (12804-7627)
PHONE 518 747-1193
Dave Mc Donald, *Mng Member*
Michael Spirowski,
▲ **EMP:** 10
SALES: 1.2MM **Privately Held**
SIC: 3545 3599 Machine tool accessories; machine & other job shop work

(G-13434)
MORRIS PRODUCTS INC
53 Carey Rd (12804-7880)
PHONE 518 743-0523
Jeff Schwartz, *President*
Yani Cruz, *General Mgr*
Greg Sherer, *Accounts Mgr*
Mike Mensler, *Manager*
▲ **EMP:** 10
SQ FT: 20,000
SALES: 1.9MM **Privately Held**
WEB: www.morrisproducts.com
SIC: 3625 5063 Electric controls & control accessories, industrial; electrical construction materials

(G-13435)
NORTHERN DESIGN & BLDG ASSOC
Also Called: Hamilton Design Kit Homes
100 Park Rd (12804-7616)
P.O. Box 47, Hudson Falls (12839-0047)
PHONE 518 747-2200
Richard Kent McNairy, *CEO*
Douglas Thayer, *Exec VP*
Bob Niedermeyer, *Vice Pres*
EMP: 21
SQ FT: 20,000
SALES (est): 3.1MM **Privately Held**
SIC: 2452 7389 Log cabins, prefabricated, wood; design services

(G-13436)
PECKHAM ROAD CORP
375 Bay Rd Ste 101 (12804-3013)
PHONE 518 792-3157
John R Peckham, *President*
Harold Stanley, *Clerk*
EMP: 30
SALES: 14MM **Privately Held**
SIC: 2951 Asphalt paving mixtures & blocks

(G-13437)
PRAXIS POWDER TECHNOLOGY INC
604 Queensbury Ave (12804-7618)
PHONE 518 812-0112
Joseph A Grohowski, *President*
Piemme Jobe, *President*
Tracy Macneal, *Vice Pres*
Jobe Piemme, *CTO*
Kathryn Lecours, *Info Tech Mgr*
EMP: 24
SQ FT: 8,400
SALES (est): 5.4MM **Privately Held**
SIC: 3841 Diagnostic apparatus, medical

(G-13438)
PRIME WOOD PRODUCTS
1288 Vaughn Rd (12804-7356)
PHONE 518 792-1407
Richard Caravaggio, *Owner*
EMP: 6
SALES (est): 369K **Privately Held**
SIC: 2499 Decorative wood & woodwork

(G-13439)
RWS MANUFACTURING INC
22 Ferguson Ln (12804-7641)
PHONE 518 361-1657
Eric Fortin, *President*
Yvin Fortin, *Vice Pres*
EMP: 5
SALES (est): 839.2K **Privately Held**
SIC: 2429 Shavings & packaging, excelsior
PA: Litiere Royal Inc
2327 Boul Du Versant-Nord Bureau 250
Quebec QC G1N 4
418 780-3373

(G-13440)
S & H ENTERPRISES INC
Also Called: Nationwide Lifts
10b Holden Ave (12804-3316)
PHONE 888 323-8755
Andrew Darnley, *President*
EMP: 5
SALES (est): 465.9K **Privately Held**
SIC: 3534 3999 Stair elevators, motor powered; wheelchair lifts

(G-13441)
SEELEY MACHINE INC
Also Called: Seeley Machine & Fabrication
75 Big Boom Rd (12804-7858)
PHONE 518 798-9510
Daryl W Pechtel, *Ch of Bd*
Craig Seeley, *President*
Barbara Seeley, *Corp Secy*
Charles Seeley, *Vice Pres*
Ed Leonard, *Supervisor*
EMP: 25
SQ FT: 14,000
SALES (est): 5.1MM **Privately Held**
WEB: www.seeleymachine.com
SIC: 3599 Machine shop, jobbing & repair

(G-13442)
SINCLAIR INTERNATIONAL COMPANY (PA)
85 Boulevard (12804-3903)
PHONE 518 798-2361
David H Sinclair Jr, *President*
Brian Phelps, *General Mgr*
Don Bolton, *Sales Staff*
Jason Viele, *Manager*
EMP: 73
SQ FT: 28,000
SALES (est): 11.3MM **Privately Held**
SIC: 3496 3554 3569 Wire cloth & woven wire products; paper industries machinery; filters

(G-13443)
THE KINGSBURY PRINTING CO INC
632 County Line Rd (12804-7621)
PHONE 518 747-6606
Robert Bombard Jr, *Ch of Bd*
Robert L Bombard Jr, *Ch of Bd*
Janette Bombard, *Vice Pres*
EMP: 8
SQ FT: 2,070
SALES (est): 1.1MM **Privately Held**
SIC: 2752 Commercial printing, offset

(G-13444)
TRIBUNE MEDIA SERVICES INC (HQ)
Also Called: TV Data
40 Media Dr (12804-4086)
PHONE 518 792-9914
Daniel Kazan, *CEO*
John B Kelleher, *President*
Kathleen Daly, *General Mgr*
Suanne Yasko, *Asst Mgr*
Kevin Godfrey, *Software Engr*
EMP: 300
SQ FT: 38,000
SALES (est): 42.7MM
SALES (corp-wide): 1.8B **Publicly Held**
WEB: www.tvdata.com
SIC: 2741 Miscellaneous publishing
PA: Tribune Media Company
515 N State St Ste 2400
Chicago IL 60654
312 222-3394

(G-13445)
WF LAKE CORP
65 Park Rd (12804-7615)
P.O. Box 4214 (12804-0214)
PHONE 518 798-9934
Jim Meyer, *President*
John L Hodgkins III, *Corp Secy*
Sam Hodgkins, *Mfg Staff*
Kate Henderson, *Sales Staff*
▲ **EMP:** 25
SQ FT: 33,000
SALES (est): 5.5MM **Privately Held**
WEB: www.wflake.com
SIC: 3052 Rubber & plastics hose & beltings

Quogue
Suffolk County

(G-13446)
PECONIC PLASTICS INC
6062 Old Country Rd (11959)
P.O. Box 1425 (11959-1425)
PHONE 631 653-3676
Ralph Ponto, *President*
Gerhart Ponto, *Vice Pres*
EMP: 10
SALES (est): 865.4K **Privately Held**
WEB: www.peconicplastics.com
SIC: 3089 Molding primary plastic; injection molding of plastics

Randolph
Cattaraugus County

(G-13447)
FENTON MOBILITY PRODUCTS INC
26 Center St (14772-1024)
PHONE 716 484-7014
Richard I Fenton, *President*
Sean Fenton, *Vice Pres*
Scott Fenton, *CFO*
Mary Gabalski, *Consultant*
EMP: 6
SQ FT: 8,500
SALES (est): 1.4MM **Privately Held**
SIC: 3444 Coal chutes, prefabricated sheet metal

(G-13448)
METALLIC LADDER MFG CORP
Also Called: Alumidock
41 S Washington St (14772-1326)
PHONE 716 358-6201
William Wadsworth, *President*
Christian Monroe, *Sls & Mktg Exec*
Daryl Wadsworth, *Admin Sec*
▼ **EMP:** 15
SQ FT: 12,000
SALES (est): 3.2MM **Privately Held**
WEB: www.alumidock.com
SIC: 3448 3499 Docks: prefabricated metal; ladders, portable: metal

(G-13449)
RANDOLPH DIMENSION CORPORATION
216 Main St Ste 216 (14772)
PHONE..................................716 358-6901
EMP: 10 EST: 1965
SQ FT: 72,000
SALES (est): 130.2K Privately Held
SIC: 2426 2431 Hardwood Dimension/Floor Mill Mfg Millwork

(G-13450)
REGISTER GRAPHICS INC
220 Main St (14772-1213)
P.O. Box 98 (14772-0098)
PHONE..................................716 358-2921
Robert G Beach, *President*
Tim Beach, *President*
Mark Hinman, *Corp Secy*
Jean D Beach, *Vice Pres*
EMP: 23 EST: 1865
SQ FT: 13,000
SALES (est): 3.4MM Privately Held
WEB: www.registergraphics.com
SIC: 2759 Commercial printing

Ransomville
Niagara County

(G-13451)
J F MACHINING COMPANY INC
2382 Balmer Rd (14131-9787)
P.O. Box 249 (14131-0249)
PHONE..................................716 791-3910
Joseph Fleckenstein, *President*
Kelly Fleckenstein, *Vice Pres*
EMP: 10
SQ FT: 2,000
SALES (est): 800K Privately Held
SIC: 3599 Machine shop, jobbing & repair

Ravena
Albany County

(G-13452)
BLEEZARDE PUBLISHING INC
Also Called: Greenville Local
164 Main St (12143-1112)
PHONE..................................518 756-2030
Richard G Bleezarde, *President*
Keith Shoemaker, *Advt Staff*
Melanie Lekocevic, *Manager*
EMP: 8 EST: 1880
SQ FT: 5,400
SALES: 305K Privately Held
SIC: 2711 Commercial printing & newspaper publishing combined

(G-13453)
LAFARGE BUILDING MATERIALS INC
Rr (12143)
PHONE..................................518 756-5000
Martin Turecky, *Manager*
EMP: 14
SALES (corp-wide): 26.4B Privately Held
SIC: 3241 Masonry cement
HQ: Lafarge Building Materials Inc.
  8700 W Bryn Mawr Ave 300n
  Chicago IL 60631
  678 746-2000

(G-13454)
LAFARGE NORTH AMERICA INC
1916 Route 9 W (12143)
PHONE..................................518 756-5000
Bernie Dushane, *Maint Spvr*
Martin Turecky, *Branch Mgr*
Morgan Huffman, *Supervisor*
Peter Cahill, *Technician*
EMP: 27

SALES (corp-wide): 26.4B Privately Held
WEB: www.lafargenorthamerica.com
SIC: 3241 3273 3272 3271 Ready-mixed concrete; concrete products; precast terrazo or concrete products; prestressed concrete products; cylinder pipe, prestressed or pretensioned concrete; blocks, concrete or cinder: standard; construction sand & gravel; construction sand mining; gravel mining; asphalt paving mixtures & blocks; paving mixtures; asphalt & asphaltic paving mixtures (not from refineries); portland cement
HQ: Lafarge North America Inc.
  8700 W Bryn Mawr Ave
  Chicago IL 60631
  773 372-1000

Red Creek
Wayne County

(G-13455)
SMOOTHBORE INTERNATIONAL INC
13881 Westbury Cutoff Rd (13143)
PHONE..................................315 754-8124
Jason Smith, *President*
EMP: 7
SALES (est): 782.6K Privately Held
SIC: 2411 Logging camps & contractors

(G-13456)
WAYUGA COMMUNITY NEWSPAPERS (PA)
Also Called: Wayuga News
6784 Main St (13143)
PHONE..................................315 754-6229
Angelo Palermo, *President*
Carol Palermo, *Vice Pres*
Chuck Palermo, *Sales Executive*
EMP: 20
SQ FT: 9,520
SALES (est): 2.5MM Privately Held
WEB: www.wayuga.com
SIC: 2711 2741 Newspapers, publishing & printing; miscellaneous publishing

Red Hook
Dutchess County

(G-13457)
CHICKEN HAWK RACING INC
54 Elizabeth St Ste 10 (12571-1722)
PHONE..................................845 758-0700
David Podolsky, *President*
▲ EMP: 6
SALES: 850K Privately Held
WEB: www.chickenhawkracing.com
SIC: 3433 3751 Unit heaters, domestic; motorcycle accessories

(G-13458)
CORT CONTRACTING
188 W Market St (12571-2710)
PHONE..................................845 758-1190
Ralph Cort, *Owner*
EMP: 10
SALES (est): 680K Privately Held
WEB: www.cortcontracting.com
SIC: 2452 Prefabricated wood buildings

(G-13459)
UNIVERSAL BUILDERS SUPPLY INC
45 Ocallaghan Ln (12571-1776)
PHONE..................................845 758-8801
Dave Rice, *CFO*
EMP: 16
SALES (corp-wide): 20MM Privately Held
WEB: www.ubs1.com
SIC: 3357 Nonferrous wiredrawing & insulating
PA: Universal Builders Supply Inc
  27 Horton Ave Ste 5
  New Rochelle NY 10801
  914 699-2400

(G-13460)
WITH YOU DESIGNS LLC
Also Called: With You Lockets
54 Elizabeth St Ste 2 (12571-1722)
PHONE..................................800 413-0670
Troy Haley, *CEO*
EMP: 8
SALES: 1.5MM Privately Held
SIC: 3479 Engraving jewelry silverware, or metal

Rego Park
Queens County

(G-13461)
DIDCO INC
8570 67th Ave (11375-5225)
PHONE..................................212 997-5022
Malcolm Doyle, *President*
EMP: 12 EST: 2012
SALES (est): 831.8K Privately Held
SIC: 1499 Gemstone & industrial diamond mining

(G-13462)
J I INTRNTNAL CONTACT LENS LAB
6352 Saunders St Ste A (11374-2000)
PHONE..................................718 997-1212
Joseph Itzkowitz, *President*
EMP: 7 EST: 1964
SQ FT: 2,000
SALES: 750K Privately Held
SIC: 3851 Contact lenses

(G-13463)
KEFA INDUSTRIES GROUP INC
9219 63rd Dr (11374-2926)
PHONE..................................718 568-9297
Keyan Xing, *Principal*
Huicong Cong, *Manager*
▲ EMP: 7
SALES (est): 461K Privately Held
SIC: 3499 Machine bases, metal

(G-13464)
LIFEWAY NETWORK INC
8510 61st Rd (11374-2734)
PHONE..................................718 779-8075
Pat Oettinger, *Principal*
EMP: 3
SALES: 1.1MM Privately Held
SIC: 3669 Pedestrian traffic control equipment

(G-13465)
METRO LUBE (PA)
9110 Metropolitan Ave (11374-5328)
PHONE..................................718 947-1167
Fernando Magalhaes, *Principal*
EMP: 5
SALES (est): 1.4MM Privately Held
SIC: 3589 Car washing machinery

(G-13466)
MILESTONE CONSTRUCTION CORP
9229 Queens Blvd Ste C2 (11374-1099)
PHONE..................................718 459-8500
Mike S Lee, *Ch of Bd*
EMP: 6
SALES (est): 570K Privately Held
SIC: 1442 Construction sand & gravel

(G-13467)
PCB COACH BUILDERS CORP
Also Called: Picasso Coach Builders
6334 Austin St (11374-2923)
PHONE..................................718 897-7606
Gualberto Diaz, *President*
Laura Diaz, *Treasurer*
EMP: 6
SQ FT: 20,000
SALES (est): 1.6MM Privately Held
WEB: www.picassocoachbuilders.com
SIC: 3711 Automobile assembly, including specialty automobiles

(G-13468)
PROFESSIONAL PAVERS CORP
6605 Woodhaven Blvd Bsmt (11374-5235)
P.O. Box 790186, Middle Village (11379-0186)
PHONE..................................718 784-7853
Duarte N Lopes, *Ch of Bd*
Nunu Lopes, *President*
Joseph Foley, *Vice Pres*
▲ EMP: 30
SALES (est): 6.6MM Privately Held
SIC: 3531 Road construction & maintenance machinery

(G-13469)
SPECTACLE OPTICAL INC
9801 67th Ave Apt 7f (11374-4903)
PHONE..................................646 706-1015
Elizabeth Geheran, *CEO*
EMP: 5
SALES (est): 283.3K Privately Held
SIC: 3851 Spectacles

Rensselaer
Rensselaer County

(G-13470)
ALBANY INTERNATIONAL CORP
Press Fabrics Division
253 Troy Rd (12144-9473)
P.O. Box 1907, Albany (12201-1907)
PHONE..................................518 445-2200
Steve Sassaman, *General Mgr*
EMP: 180
SALES (corp-wide): 863.7MM Publicly Held
WEB: www.albint.com
SIC: 2221 2297 2241 Paper broadwoven fabrics; nonwoven fabrics; narrow fabric mills
PA: Albany International Corp.
  216 Airport Dr
  Rochester NH 03867
  603 330-5850

(G-13471)
ALBANY MOLECULAR RESEARCH INC
Also Called: Amri Rensselaer
81 Columbia Tpke (12144-3411)
PHONE..................................518 433-7700
Thomas E D'Ambra, *Ch of Bd*
EMP: 10
SALES (corp-wide): 124.9MM Privately Held
SIC: 2833 Medicinals & botanicals
HQ: Albany Molecular Research, Inc.
  26 Corporate Cir
  Albany NY 12203

(G-13472)
ALBANY MOLECULAR RESEARCH INC
Also Called: Amri
33 Riverside Ave (12144-2951)
PHONE..................................518 512-2000
Norberto Cintron, *Facilities Mgr*
Kathryn Saybe, *Purch Mgr*
Jaclyn Hernigle, *Purchasing*
Daniel Asta, *Research*
Sarya ABI-Habib, *Research*
EMP: 10
SALES (corp-wide): 124.9MM Privately Held
SIC: 2833 Medicinals & botanicals
HQ: Albany Molecular Research, Inc.
  26 Corporate Cir
  Albany NY 12203

(G-13473)
BASF CORPORATION
Chemicals Division
70 Riverside Ave (12144-2938)
PHONE..................................518 465-6534
Wayne Sinclair, *Manager*
EMP: 280
SALES (corp-wide): 76B Privately Held
WEB: www.basf.com
SIC: 2869 Industrial organic chemicals
HQ: Basf Corporation
  100 Park Ave
  Florham Park NJ 07932
  973 245-6000

GEOGRAPHIC SECTION

Richmond Hill - Queens County (G-13500)

(G-13474)
GREAT 4 IMAGE INC
Also Called: G4i
5 Forest Hills Blvd (12144-5831)
PHONE.................518 424-2058
Daren Arakelian, *President*
▲ EMP: 29
SALES: 1MM Privately Held
WEB: www.g4i.com
SIC: 2311 Men's & boys' suits & coats

(G-13475)
INTEGRATED LINER TECH INC (PA)
45 Discovery Dr (12144-3466)
PHONE.................518 621-7422
Paul Petrosino, *Ch of Bd*
Corey Hagedorn, *Production*
Ken Greene, *Project Engr*
Dee Vandyke, *Accountant*
Michele Slade, *Sales Mgr*
▲ EMP: 48
SQ FT: 30,000
SALES (est): 9.7MM Privately Held
WEB: www.integratedliner.com
SIC: 3821 2822 Chemical laboratory apparatus; synthetic rubber

(G-13476)
R J VALENTE GRAVEL INC
315 Partition St Ext (12144-2041)
PHONE.................518 432-4470
Tim Banks, *Manager*
EMP: 15
SALES (est): 768.4K
SALES (corp-wide): 17.7MM Privately Held
SIC: 1442 Construction sand & gravel
PA: R. J. Valente Gravel, Inc.
1 Madison St
Troy NY 12180
518 432-4470

(G-13477)
REGENERON PHARMACEUTICALS INC
81 Columbia Tpke (12144-3423)
PHONE.................518 488-6000
Dr Randall Rupp, *General Mgr*
Anita Berg, *Buyer*
Halit Akgun, *Manager*
Paul Chao, *Senior Mgr*
Kristyn Greco, *Senior Mgr*
EMP: 40
SALES (corp-wide): 5.8B Publicly Held
WEB: www.regeneron.com
SIC: 2834 Pharmaceutical preparations
PA: Regeneron Pharmaceuticals Inc
777 Old Saw Mill River Rd # 10
Tarrytown NY 10591
914 847-7000

(G-13478)
STEMCULTURES LLC
1 Discovery Dr (12144-3448)
PHONE.................518 621-0848
Jeffrey Stern, *CEO*
William Price, *COO*
Christopher Fasano, *Bd of Directors*
EMP: 7
SALES (est): 445.3K Privately Held
SIC: 2836 Culture media

(G-13479)
ULTRADIAN DIAGNOSTICS LLC
5 University Pl A324 (12144-3461)
PHONE.................518 618-0046
John P Willis,
EMP: 5
SQ FT: 2,000
SALES (est): 579.3K Privately Held
SIC: 3845 Electromedical equipment

Retsof
Livingston County

(G-13480)
AMERICAN ROCK SALT COMPANY LLC (PA)
3846 Retsof Rd (14539)
P.O. Box 190, Mount Morris (14510-0190)
PHONE.................585 991-6878
Gunther Buerman, *Ch of Bd*
Justin Curley, *General Mgr*
Joseph G Bucci, *Principal*
Lee McKinney, *Safety Dir*
Jim Hathaway, *Transptn Dir*
▲ EMP: 20
SALES (est): 787.2MM Privately Held
WEB: www.americanrocksalt.com
SIC: 1479 5169 Rock salt mining; salts, industrial

Rexford
Saratoga County

(G-13481)
MOBIUS LABS INC
37 Vischer Ferry Rd (12148-1617)
PHONE.................518 961-2600
Frank Lipowitz, *Principal*
EMP: 5
SALES (est): 263.7K Privately Held
SIC: 3829 Hydrometers, except industrial process type

(G-13482)
PARRINGTON INSTRUMENTS
12 Droms Rd (12148-1401)
PHONE.................518 373-8420
Josef Parrington, *Principal*
EMP: 5
SALES (est): 681.2K Privately Held
SIC: 3823 Industrial instrmnts msrmnt display/control process variable

(G-13483)
PRESTACYCLE LLC
689 Riverview Rd (12148-1427)
PHONE.................518 588-5546
David Finlayson, *Mng Member*
▲ EMP: 5
SQ FT: 2,000
SALES (est): 1.4MM Privately Held
SIC: 3751 Bicycles & related parts

(G-13484)
WERNER BROTHERS ELECTRIC INC
677 Riverview Rd (12148-1427)
PHONE.................518 377-3056
Craig Werner, *Owner*
EMP: 8
SALES (est): 1.1MM Privately Held
SIC: 3699 Electrical equipment & supplies

Rhinebeck
Dutchess County

(G-13485)
CORE GROUP DISPLAYS INC
41 Pitcher Rd (12572-1035)
PHONE.................845 876-5109
Dan Riso, *President*
Kurt Haldin, *Director*
◆ EMP: 21 EST: 2007
SALES (est): 1.2MM Privately Held
SIC: 2542 Partitions & fixtures, except wood

(G-13486)
DUTCHESS WINES LLC
Also Called: Alison Wine & Vineyard
39 Lorraine Dr (12572-1203)
P.O. Box 619 (12572-0619)
PHONE.................845 876-1319
Richard Lewit, *President*
EMP: 5
SALES: 280K Privately Held
WEB: www.alisonwine.com
SIC: 2084 Wines

(G-13487)
PDQ MANUFACTURING CO INC
29 Hilee Rd (12572-2349)
PHONE.................845 889-3123
Scott Hutchins, *Ch of Bd*
Kristin Hutchins, *President*
EMP: 45 EST: 1975
SQ FT: 40,000
SALES (est): 8.3MM Privately Held
WEB: www.pdqmfg.com
SIC: 3444 Sheet metalwork

(G-13488)
SMITHERS TOOLS & MCH PDTS INC
Also Called: Stamp
3718 Route 9g (12572-1139)
P.O. Box 391 (12572-0391)
PHONE.................845 876-3063
Roland Jennings, *Ch of Bd*
Gary L Hosey, *President*
Robert Nevins, *Vice Pres*
Joann Russell, *Vice Pres*
EMP: 63 EST: 1947
SQ FT: 35,000
SALES (est): 10MM Privately Held
WEB: www.stampinc.com
SIC: 3699 3469 7692 3599 Electrical equipment & supplies; stamping metal for the trade; welding repair; machine shop, jobbing & repair

(G-13489)
UMBRO MACHINE & TOOL CO INC
3811 Route 9g (12572-1042)
PHONE.................845 876-4669
Gerald Umbro, *President*
Claire Umbro, *Vice Pres*
Rosemary Kavanaugh, *Admin Sec*
EMP: 12 EST: 1959
SQ FT: 1,800
SALES: 1MM Privately Held
SIC: 3451 Screw machine products

(G-13490)
WARREN CUTLERY CORP
3584 Route 9g (12572-3309)
P.O. Box 289 (12572-0289)
PHONE.................845 876-3444
James Zitz, *President*
Richard Von Husen, *Vice Pres*
EMP: 10
SQ FT: 3,500
SALES (est): 1.6MM Privately Held
WEB: www.warrencutlery.com
SIC: 3421 3291 5072 5085 Cutlery; abrasive products; cutlery; abrasives

(G-13491)
WATER ORACLE
41 E Market St (12572-1634)
PHONE.................845 876-8327
Stacey Held, *Principal*
EMP: 5
SALES (est): 82.7K Privately Held
SIC: 7372 Prepackaged software

Richfield Springs
Otsego County

(G-13492)
ANDELA TOOL & MACHINE INC
Also Called: Andela Products
493 State Route 28 (13439-3739)
PHONE.................315 858-0055
Cynthia Andela, *President*
Michelle Proctor, *General Mgr*
James Andela, *Vice Pres*
▼ EMP: 8
SQ FT: 10,000
SALES (est): 1.9MM Privately Held
WEB: www.andelaproducts.ccm
SIC: 3559 Recycling machinery

(G-13493)
WELDING AND BRAZING SVCS INC
2761 County Highway 26 (13439-3049)
PHONE.................607 397-1009
David R Parker, *President*
Kay Parker, *Vice Pres*
Carter Cook, *Manager*
EMP: 5
SALES (est): 418.8K Privately Held
SIC: 7692 Brazing

Richmond Hill
Queens County

(G-13494)
131-11 ATLANTIC RE INC
Also Called: Premier
13111 Atlantic Ave Ste 1 (11418-3305)
PHONE.................718 441-7700
Kevin Leichter, *CEO*
Harry Leichter, *President*
Charles Dawson, *General Mgr*
Sari Nathan, *COO*
◆ EMP: 75
SQ FT: 250,000
SALES (est): 12.5MM Privately Held
WEB: www.premierpaintroller.com
SIC: 3991 Paint rollers

(G-13495)
ALL AMERICAN STAIRS & RAILING
13023 91st Ave (11418-3320)
PHONE.................718 441-8400
Marie Bottari, *President*
EMP: 12
SALES (est): 2.4MM Privately Held
SIC: 3446 Stairs, fire escapes, balconies, railings & ladders

(G-13496)
ATLANTIC FARM & FOOD INC
11415 Atlantic Ave (11418-3139)
PHONE.................718 441-3152
Gurcharn Singh, *Principal*
EMP: 13
SALES (est): 1.7MM Privately Held
SIC: 2037 8611 Frozen fruits & vegetables; growers' marketing advisory service

(G-13497)
BARALAN USA INC (DH)
Also Called: Arrowpak
12019 89th Ave (11418-3235)
PHONE.................718 849-5768
Roland Baranes, *President*
Ellis Rudman, *Corp Secy*
Luisa Kamelhar, *Human Res Dir*
Chris Llamas, *Manager*
Carol Carbone, *Executive Asst*
◆ EMP: 35 EST: 1980
SQ FT: 70,000
SALES (est): 4.9MM
SALES (corp-wide): 1.1MM Privately Held
WEB: www.arrowpak.com
SIC: 3221 3089 Cosmetic jars, glass; plastic containers, except foam
HQ: Baralan International Spa
Via Nicolo' Copernico 34
Trezzano Sul Naviglio MI 20090
024 844-961

(G-13498)
BELLE MAISON USA LTD
Also Called: Stylemaster
8950 127th St (11418-3323)
PHONE.................718 805-0200
Elizabeth Romano, *Ch of Bd*
Ethel Romano, *Vice Pres*
◆ EMP: 30
SALES (est): 3.2MM Privately Held
WEB: www.stylemasterusa.com
SIC: 2392 2391 Bedspreads & bed sets: made from purchased materials; curtains, window: made from purchased materials

(G-13499)
BEST TIME PROCESSOR LLC
8746 Van Wyck Expy (11418-1958)
PHONE.................917 455-4126
Charlie Bachu,
Somdat Bachu,
EMP: 5
SALES (est): 384.5K Privately Held
SIC: 2679 Paper products, converted

(G-13500)
CARLOS & ALEX ATELIER INC
Also Called: C & A Atelier
10010 91st Ave Fl 2 (11418-2118)
PHONE.................718 441-8911
Carlos Queiroz, *CEO*
EMP: 24

Richmond Hill - Queens County (G-13501)

SQ FT: 22,000
SALES (est): 2MM **Privately Held**
SIC: 2434 2511 Wood kitchen cabinets; wood household furniture

(G-13501)
ELECTRON TOP MFG CO INC
12615 89th Ave (11418-3337)
PHONE.................................718 846-7400
Craig Strauss, *President*
Frederick W Strauss III, *Vice Pres*
Kimberly S Hess, *Treasurer*
EMP: 41 **EST:** 1947
SQ FT: 20,000
SALES (est): 6.4MM **Privately Held**
WEB: www.electrontop.com
SIC: 3714 Tops, motor vehicle

(G-13502)
EMPIRE STATE METAL PDTS INC
10110 Jamaica Ave (11418-2007)
PHONE.................................718 847-1617
David Millshauser, *President*
▲ **EMP:** 20 **EST:** 1946
SQ FT: 20,475
SALES: 2MM **Privately Held**
SIC: 3965 Buttons & parts; buckles & buckle parts

(G-13503)
GAUGHAN CONSTRUCTION CORP
13034 90th Ave (11418-3309)
PHONE.................................718 850-9577
Anthony Gaughan, *President*
EMP: 5
SQ FT: 6,000
SALES (est): 731.1K **Privately Held**
SIC: 2541 Wood partitions & fixtures

(G-13504)
HILL KNITTING MILLS INC
10005 92nd Ave Ste Mgmt (11418-2910)
PHONE.................................718 846-5000
Jeff Rosen, *President*
Peter Cruciata, *Corp Secy*
EMP: 23
SQ FT: 30,000
SALES (est): 2.1MM **Privately Held**
SIC: 2257 Pile fabrics, circular knit

(G-13505)
J & E TALIT INC
13011 Atlantic Ave Fl 2 (11418-3304)
PHONE.................................718 850-1333
Eitan Talit, *President*
EMP: 8
SQ FT: 6,000
SALES (est): 1MM **Privately Held**
WEB: www.jandetalit.com
SIC: 2253 2339 T-shirts & tops, knit; sportswear, women's

(G-13506)
J & S LICATA BROS INC
Also Called: Monteforte Bakery
8931 129th St (11418-3326)
PHONE.................................718 805-6924
Salvatore Licata, *President*
Joseph Licata, *Vice Pres*
EMP: 15
SQ FT: 8,000
SALES (est): 2.2MM **Privately Held**
SIC: 2051 Bread, cake & related products

(G-13507)
OLYMPIC ICE CREAM CO INC
Also Called: Marinos Italian Ices
12910 91st Ave (11418-3317)
PHONE.................................718 849-6200
Michael Barone Sr, *President*
Frank Barone, *Vice Pres*
▼ **EMP:** 35
SQ FT: 50,000
SALES: 5MM **Privately Held**
WEB: www.marinositalianices.com
SIC: 2024 Ices, flavored (frozen dessert)

(G-13508)
PREMIER PAINT ROLLER CO LLC
13111 Atlantic Ave (11418-3397)
PHONE.................................718 441-7700
Kevin Leichter, *CEO*
EMP: 11 **EST:** 2004

SALES (est): 532.3K **Privately Held**
SIC: 3991 5198 Paint rollers; paint brushes, rollers, sprayers

(G-13509)
RESEARCH CENTRE OF KABBALAH
Also Called: Kabbalah Centre
8384 115th St (11418-1303)
PHONE.................................718 805-0380
Philip Berg, *President*
Beatrice Cohen, *Treasurer*
Karen Berg, *Admin Sec*
EMP: 6
SQ FT: 40,000
SALES (est): 536.6K **Privately Held**
WEB: www.kabbalahcentre.com
SIC: 2731 Books: publishing only; pamphlets: publishing only, not printed on site

(G-13510)
RUBIES COSTUME COMPANY INC (PA)
12008 Jamaica Ave (11418-2521)
PHONE.................................718 846-1008
Marc P Beige, *Ch of Bd*
Joanne Rudis, *Division Mgr*
Howard Beige, *Vice Pres*
Jeffrey Cohen, *Controller*
Frank Deluca, *Controller*
◆ **EMP:** 400
SQ FT: 55,000
SALES (est): 364.6MM **Privately Held**
SIC: 2389 7299 Costumes; costume rental

(G-13511)
RUBIES COSTUME COMPANY INC
12017 Jamaica Ave (11418-2522)
PHONE.................................718 441-0834
Arthur Savarese, *Branch Mgr*
EMP: 148
SALES (corp-wide): 364.6MM **Privately Held**
SIC: 2389 Costumes
PA: Rubie's Costume Company, Inc.
12008 Jamaica Ave
Richmond Hill NY 11418
718 846-1008

(G-13512)
RUBIES COSTUME COMPANY INC
1 Rubie Plz (11418)
PHONE.................................718 846-1008
Catherine Zubrovich, *Prdtn Mgr*
Maryann Depaola, *Purchasing*
Charlie Flohr, *Credit Staff*
Ellen DOE, *Human Res Dir*
Ellen Gelb, *Human Res Dir*
EMP: 148
SALES (corp-wide): 364.6MM **Privately Held**
SIC: 2389 7299 Costumes; costume rental
PA: Rubie's Costume Company, Inc.
12008 Jamaica Ave
Richmond Hill NY 11418
718 846-1008

(G-13513)
RUBIES MASQUERADE COMPANY LLC (PA)
1 Rubie Plz (11418)
PHONE.................................718 846-1008
Dave Defina, *Controller*
Dick Roche,
EMP: 3
SALES (est): 10.3MM **Privately Held**
SIC: 2389 Masquerade costumes

(G-13514)
STAIRWORLD INC
10114 Jamaica Ave (11418-2007)
PHONE.................................718 441-9722
John Franklin, *President*
Kenneth Franklin, *President*
EMP: 5
SQ FT: 3,000
SALES (est): 390K **Privately Held**
WEB: www.stairworld.com
SIC: 2431 Stair railings, wood; staircases & stairs, wood

(G-13515)
SUPER EXPRESS USA PUBG CORP
8410 101st St Apt 4l (11418-1150)
PHONE.................................212 227-5800
Ana Gierzphall, *President*
Kazimierz Szosler, *Sales Mgr*
EMP: 12
SALES (est): 801.2K **Privately Held**
SIC: 2741 Miscellaneous publishing

(G-13516)
TERBO LTD
Also Called: Interiors By Robert
8905 130th St (11418-3328)
PHONE.................................718 847-2860
Robert Boccard, *President*
EMP: 9
SQ FT: 3,400
SALES (est): 910.1K **Privately Held**
SIC: 2391 2392 7641 Curtains & draperies; household furnishings; upholstery work

(G-13517)
WOMENS HEALTH CARE PC (PA)
Also Called: Park Avenue Nutrition
11311 Jamaica Ave Ste C (11418-2476)
PHONE.................................718 850-0009
Rehana Sajjad, *CEO*
EMP: 4
SALES (est): 1.1MM **Privately Held**
SIC: 3842 7991 7299 Gynecological supplies & appliances; physical fitness facilities; personal appearance services

Richmondville
Schoharie County

(G-13518)
CHENANGO CONCRETE CORP (PA)
145 Podpadic Rd (12149-2205)
PHONE.................................518 294-9964
Martin Galasso, *President*
Timothy Gaffney Sr, *CFO*
Emil Galasso, *Treasurer*
Cathy Manchester, *Executive Asst*
EMP: 12
SALES (est): 5.9MM **Privately Held**
SIC: 3273 Ready-mixed concrete

(G-13519)
TRI-CITY HIGHWAY PRODUCTS INC
145 Podpadic Rd (12149-2205)
PHONE.................................518 294-9964
Martin Galasso, *CEO*
David Black, *Chairman*
Martin A Galasso Jr, *Chairman*
Christina Brizzee, *Controller*
EMP: 23
SALES (est): 5.3MM **Privately Held**
SIC: 2951 1442 Asphalt paving mixtures & blocks; construction sand & gravel

Ridge
Suffolk County

(G-13520)
AIRWELD INC
1740 Middle Country Rd (11961-2407)
PHONE.................................631 924-6366
John Zak, *Branch Mgr*
EMP: 5
SALES (corp-wide): 26.7MM **Privately Held**
SIC: 7692 Welding repair
PA: Airweld, Inc.
94 Marine St
Farmingdale NY 11735
631 694-4343

(G-13521)
AMERICAN PHYSICAL SOCIETY
Also Called: Physical Review
1 Research Rd (11961-2701)
PHONE.................................631 591-4025

Charles Muller, *Director*
Harvey Yau, *Executive*
EMP: 95
SALES (corp-wide): 56.6MM **Privately Held**
WEB: www.phystec.net
SIC: 2721 Trade journals: publishing only, not printed on site
PA: American Physical Society
1 Physics Ellipse
College Park MD 20740
301 209-3200

(G-13522)
OCEANS CUISINE LTD
367 Sheffield Ct (11961-2028)
PHONE.................................631 209-9200
Philip Melfi, *President*
Linda Melfi, *Admin Sec*
EMP: 15
SQ FT: 1,000
SALES (est): 1.7MM **Privately Held**
WEB: www.oceanscuisine.com
SIC: 2092 Seafoods, frozen: prepared

(G-13523)
QUALITY AND ASRN TECH CORP
Also Called: Qna Tech
18 Marginwood Dr (11961-2902)
PHONE.................................646 450-6762
Marcos Merced, *CEO*
Antonio Cefalo, *Engineer*
Daniel Corozza, *Engineer*
Jean Machado, *Engineer*
EMP: 7
SALES: 500K **Privately Held**
SIC: 7372 7379 Business oriented computer software; computer hardware requirements analysis

(G-13524)
RESIDENTIAL FENCES CORP
1760 Middle Country Rd (11961-2415)
PHONE.................................631 205-9758
John Gulino, *Branch Mgr*
EMP: 30
SALES (corp-wide): 13.4MM **Privately Held**
SIC: 3273 Ready-mixed concrete
PA: Residential Fences Corp.
1775 Middle Country Rd
Ridge NY 11961
631 924-3011

(G-13525)
WEATHER TIGHT EXTERIORS
8 Woodbrook Dr (11961-2132)
PHONE.................................631 375-5108
Rick Dandria, *Owner*
EMP: 8
SALES (est): 550K **Privately Held**
SIC: 2421 Siding (dressed lumber)

Ridgewood
Queens County

(G-13526)
333 J & M FOOD CORP
Also Called: Allsupermarkets
333 Seneca Ave (11385-1338)
PHONE.................................718 381-1493
Jose Espinal, *Ch of Bd*
EMP: 12 **EST:** 2011
SALES (est): 2.4MM **Privately Held**
SIC: 2674 Grocers' bags: made from purchased materials

(G-13527)
AABCO SHEET METAL CO INC (PA)
Also Called: Asm Mechanical Systems
47 40 Metropolitan Ave (11385)
PHONE.................................718 821-1166
Ronald J Palmerick, *President*
Richard Minieri, *President*
Edmund MEI, *President*
Phil Blackmon, *Project Mgr*
Bob Fabozzi, *Project Mgr*
EMP: 75
SQ FT: 85,000

SALES (est): 51.2MM Privately Held
SIC: 3444 1711 1761 Ducts, sheet metal; metal housings, enclosures, casings & other containers; ventilation & duct work contractor; sheet metalwork

(G-13528)
ABR MOLDING ANDY LLC
1624 Centre St (11385-5336)
PHONE..................212 576-1821
Andy Skoczek, Owner
▲ EMP: 15
SALES (est): 2.5MM Privately Held
SIC: 3089 Molding primary plastic

(G-13529)
ALPINE BUILDING SUPPLY INC
4626 Metropolitan Ave (11385-1045)
PHONE..................718 456-2522
Marcangelo Cotoia, President
EMP: 7
SALES (est): 94.9K Privately Held
SIC: 3272 Concrete products

(G-13530)
BARKER BROTHERS INCORPORATED
1666 Summerfield St Ste 1 (11385-5748)
PHONE..................718 456-6400
Kenneth A Doyle, Ch of Bd
Edwin Doyle, Ch of Bd
Walter Doyle, Vice Pres
David Thomas, Vice Pres
Thomas Vissichelli, Vice Pres
▲ EMP: 100 EST: 1911
SQ FT: 50,000
SALES (est): 16.8MM Privately Held
WEB: www.bardoabrasives.com
SIC: 3291 Buffing or polishing wheels, abrasive or nonabrasive

(G-13531)
BEST ADHESIVES COMPANY INC
4702 Metropolitan Ave (11385-1047)
PHONE..................718 417-3800
Sholm Singer, President
EMP: 6
SQ FT: 10,000
SALES (est): 670K Privately Held
SIC: 2891 Adhesives

(G-13532)
BRICK & BALLERSTEIN INC
1085 Irving Ave (11385-5745)
P.O. Box 1158, Yorktown Heights (10598-8158)
PHONE..................718 497-1400
Robert Levinson, Ch of Bd
Gary Levinson, President
Bruce Levinson, Vice Pres
▲ EMP: 82
SQ FT: 54,000
SALES (est): 15.1MM Privately Held
WEB: www.brickandballerstein.com
SIC: 2652 Setup paperboard boxes

(G-13533)
COSCO ENTERPRISES INC
Also Called: Cosco Soap & Detergent
1930 Troutman St (11385-1020)
PHONE..................718 383-4488
Andrew Cook, President
Lawrence McGreevy, Vice Pres
EMP: 7 EST: 1966
SQ FT: 10,000
SALES (est): 1.4MM Privately Held
SIC: 2841 Soap & other detergents

(G-13534)
COSCO INTERPRISES INC
Also Called: Cosco Soap and Detergent
1930 Troutman St Ste 1 (11385-1020)
PHONE..................718 417-8995
Andrew Cook, President
EMP: 35
SALES (est): 7.6MM Privately Held
SIC: 2841 Soap & other detergents

(G-13535)
ELECTRO-OPTICAL PRODUCTS CORP
6240 Forest Ave Fl 2 (11385-1929)
P.O. Box 650441, Fresh Meadows (11365-0441)
PHONE..................718 456-6000
Ziva Tuchman, President
EMP: 6
SQ FT: 1,600
SALES (est): 1MM Privately Held
WEB: www.eopc.com
SIC: 3829 Measuring & controlling devices

(G-13536)
FIVE STAR AWNINGS INC
5923 Decatur St (11385-5942)
PHONE..................718 860-6070
Christopher Rice, Principal
EMP: 13
SALES (est): 1.6MM Privately Held
SIC: 3444 Awnings & canopies

(G-13537)
GENERAL COATINGS TECH INC (PA)
24 Woodward Ave (11385-1022)
PHONE..................718 821-1232
Michael Ghitelman, President
Robert Ghitelman, Vice Pres
EMP: 25
SQ FT: 160,000
SALES (est): 8.3MM Privately Held
SIC: 2851 Paints & paint additives; varnishes

(G-13538)
GW MANUFACTURING
Also Called: G W Manufacturing
24a Woodward Ave (11385-1175)
PHONE..................718 386-8078
George Stavilla, President
▲ EMP: 32
SALES (est): 5.4MM Privately Held
SIC: 2431 Millwork

(G-13539)
J & C FINISHING
1067 Wyckoff Ave (11385-5751)
PHONE..................718 456-1087
Jose Hernandez, President
EMP: 20
SALES (est): 1.2MM Privately Held
SIC: 2389 Apparel & accessories

(G-13540)
JULIAN A MCDERMOTT CORPORATION
Also Called: McDermott Light & Signal
1639 Stephen St (11385-5345)
PHONE..................718 456-3606
Vernon McDermott, Ch of Bd
Andrea McDermott, Vice Pres
▲ EMP: 45 EST: 1943
SQ FT: 25,000
SALES (est): 6MM Privately Held
WEB: www.mcdermottlight.com
SIC: 3648 Lighting equipment

(G-13541)
L S SIGN CO INC
1030 Wyckoff Ave (11385-5355)
PHONE..................718 469-8600
Anthony Fodera, President
Joseph Fodera, Vice Pres
Christian Tomas, Treasurer
EMP: 19
SQ FT: 10,000
SALES (est): 1.6MM Privately Held
SIC: 3993 Signs, not made in custom sign painting shops

(G-13542)
LONG ISLAND STAMP & SEAL CO
Also Called: L I Stamp
5431 Myrtle Ave Ste 2 (11385-3403)
P.O. Box 863990 (11386-3990)
PHONE..................718 628-8550
Harriet Pollak, President
Harry Pollak, Vice Pres
EMP: 15
SQ FT: 4,000
SALES (est): 980K Privately Held
SIC: 3953 Date stamps, hand: rubber or metal

(G-13543)
N Y ELLI DESIGN CORP
5001 Metropolitan Ave 1 (11385-1052)
PHONE..................718 228-0014
Dimitra Ligas, CEO
▲ EMP: 15
SQ FT: 30,000
SALES (est): 5.1MM Privately Held
WEB: www.ellicorp.com
SIC: 2434 2521 2531 Wood kitchen cabinets; cabinets, office: wood; public building & related furniture; library furniture

(G-13544)
NULUX INC
1717 Troutman St (11385-1034)
PHONE..................718 383-1112
Delia Price, President
Frank Conti, Vice Pres
EMP: 33
SQ FT: 4,500
SALES (est): 6.5MM Privately Held
WEB: www.nulux.com
SIC: 3645 3646 Residential lighting fixtures; commercial indusl & institutional electric lighting fixtures

(G-13545)
ON THE SPOT BINDING INC
4805 Metropolitan Ave (11385-1007)
P.O. Box 863104 (11386-3104)
PHONE..................718 497-2200
Isaac Mutzen, President
Nathan Hirsch, Corp Secy
Jerry Josefson, Vice Pres
EMP: 26
SQ FT: 10,000
SALES (est): 2MM Privately Held
SIC: 2789 Binding & repair of books, magazines & pamphlets

(G-13546)
PLANET EMBROIDERY
6695 Forest Ave (11385-3839)
PHONE..................718 381-4827
Edwin Sotto, Owner
EMP: 12
SALES (est): 134.8K Privately Held
SIC: 2395 Embroidery products, except schiffli machine; embroidery & art needlework

(G-13547)
PRINT BETTER INC
5939 Myrtle Ave (11385-5657)
PHONE..................347 348-1841
Ayman Naguib, Ch of Bd
▲ EMP: 7
SALES (est): 587.9K Privately Held
SIC: 2752 Commercial printing, lithographic

(G-13548)
PUBLIMAX PRINTING CORP
6615 Traffic Ave (11385-3307)
PHONE..................718 366-7133
Patricia Flores, President
Taniya Flores, Office Mgr
▲ EMP: 6
SALES (est): 1MM Privately Held
WEB: www.publimaxprinting.com
SIC: 2759 Screen printing

(G-13549)
RIDGEWOOD TIMES PRTG & PUBG
Also Called: Times News Weekly
6071 Woodbine St Fl 1 (11385-3242)
PHONE..................718 821-7500
Maureen E Walthers, President
EMP: 30
SQ FT: 3,500
SALES (est): 1.7MM Privately Held
WEB: www.timesnewsweekly.com
SIC: 2711 Commercial printing & newspaper publishing combined

(G-13550)
SCHNEIDER M SOAP & CHEMICAL CO
1930 Troutman St (11385-1020)
PHONE..................718 389-1000
Andrew Cook, President
EMP: 8 EST: 1969
SQ FT: 10,000
SALES (est): 740K Privately Held
SIC: 2841 Soap: granulated, liquid, cake, flaked or chip

(G-13551)
SPARCLEAN MBL REFINISHING INC
6915 64th Pl (11385-5251)
PHONE..................718 445-2351
Rafa Colman, President
EMP: 5
SALES (est): 305.5K Privately Held
SIC: 1429 Marble, crushed & broken-quarrying

(G-13552)
SPECIALISTS LTD
Also Called: Wapons Specialists
4740 Metropolitan Ave (11385-1195)
PHONE..................212 941-7696
EMP: 12 EST: 2015
SALES (est): 1.7MM Privately Held
SIC: 3999 Manufacturing industries

(G-13553)
STUDIO SILVERSMITHS INC
6315 Traffic Ave (11385-2629)
PHONE..................718 418-6785
Arnold Godinger, Ch of Bd
Issac Godinger, President
Larry Lack, Vice Pres
▲ EMP: 40
SQ FT: 300,000
SALES (est): 3.8MM Privately Held
SIC: 3914 5199 Silverware; gifts & novelties

(G-13554)
TEC - CRETE TRANSIT MIX CORP
4673 Metropolitan Ave (11385-1044)
PHONE..................718 657-6880
Linda Gisond, Ch of Bd
EMP: 25
SQ FT: 20,000
SALES (est): 3.3MM Privately Held
SIC: 3273 Ready-mixed concrete

(G-13555)
TIBANA FINISHING INC
1630 Cody Ave (11385-5734)
PHONE..................718 417-5375
Tiberija Miksa, President
◆ EMP: 20
SQ FT: 21,000
SALES (est): 2.5MM Privately Held
WEB: www.tibana.com
SIC: 2329 2331 Men's & boys' sportswear & athletic clothing; women's & misses' blouses & shirts

(G-13556)
TRADING EDGE LTD
1923 Bleecker St Apt 1r (11385-9200)
PHONE..................347 699-7079
Michael Oniszczuk, Purch Mgr
EMP: 5
SALES (est): 130.5K Privately Held
SIC: 2741

(G-13557)
TRI-BORO SHELVING INC
1940 Flushing Ave (11385-1043)
PHONE..................718 782-8527
Fred Demaio, President
Stan Covington, Plant Mgr
John De Maio, Sales/Mktg Mgr
EMP: 15
SQ FT: 11,950
SALES (est): 2MM
SALES (corp-wide): 10.5MM Privately Held
WEB: www.triboroshelving.com
SIC: 2542 5046 5084 Shelving, office & store: except wood; shelving, commercial & industrial; materials handling machinery

Ridgewood - Queens County (G-13558)

PA: Tri-Boro Shelving, Inc.
300 Dominion Dr
Farmville VA 23901
434 315-5600

(G-13558)
VIP FOODS INC
1080 Wyckoff Ave (11385-5757)
PHONE..................718 821-5330
Edward Fruend, *President*
Mendel Fruend, *Vice Pres*
Tobias Fruend, *Treasurer*
▲ **EMP:** 25 **EST:** 1983
SQ FT: 13,000
SALES (est): 4MM **Privately Held**
WEB: www.vipfoodsinc.com
SIC: 2099 Dessert mixes & fillings; gelatin dessert preparations

Rifton
Ulster County

(G-13559)
COMMUNITY PRODUCTS LLC (PA)
Also Called: COMMUNITY PLAYTHINGS AND RIFTO
101 Woodcrest Dr (12471-7200)
P.O. Box 260 (12471-0260)
PHONE..................845 658-8799
John Rhodes, *CEO*
Jean Clement, *Sales Mgr*
Eric Nelson, *Manager*
Dorothea Maendel, *Admin Sec*
▲ **EMP:** 250
SQ FT: 5,000
SALES: 93.4MM **Privately Held**
WEB: www.communityplaythings.com
SIC: 3842 2511 3844 Orthopedic appliances; children's wood furniture; therapeutic X-ray apparatus & tubes

(G-13560)
COMMUNITY PRODUCTS LLC
2032 Route 213 St (12471-7700)
P.O. Box 903 (12471-0903)
PHONE..................845 658-8351
Christoph Meier,
EMP: 30
SALES (corp-wide): 93.4MM **Privately Held**
SIC: 3993 Signs & advertising specialties
PA: Community Products, Llc
101 Woodcrest Dr
Rifton NY 12471
845 658-8799

(G-13561)
KEITH LEWIS STUDIO INC
35 Rifton Ter (12471)
P.O. Box 357 (12471-0357)
PHONE..................845 339-5629
EMP: 9
SQ FT: 2,000
SALES: 375K **Privately Held**
SIC: 3911 5094 Jewelry, precious metal; jewelry

Ripley
Chautauqua County

(G-13562)
CHROMA LOGIC
6651 Wiley Rd (14775-9527)
PHONE..................716 736-2458
Jason W Peterson, *President*
Jhon Mara, *Vice Pres*
EMP: 2
SQ FT: 5,000
SALES: 1.5MM **Privately Held**
SIC: 3552 Dyeing, drying & finishing machinery & equipment

(G-13563)
RIPLEY MACHINE & TOOL CO INC
9825 E Main Rd (14775-9504)
PHONE..................716 736-3205
Andrew Reinwald, *President*
Quenti Besink, *Vice Pres*
EMP: 17 **EST:** 1944
SQ FT: 15,000
SALES (est): 2.6MM **Privately Held**
SIC: 3599 Machine shop, jobbing & repair

Riverhead
Suffolk County

(G-13564)
AUTO-MATE TECHNOLOGIES LLC
34 Hinda Blvd (11901-4804)
PHONE..................631 727-8886
Kenneth Herzog,
▼ **EMP:** 12
SALES (est): 1.9MM **Privately Held**
WEB: www.automatetech.com
SIC: 3365 Machinery castings, aluminum

(G-13565)
BERRY SPECIALTY TAPES LLC
1852 Old Country Rd (11901-3144)
PHONE..................631 727-6000
John Pufahl, *Vice Pres*
Robert Pufahl, *Vice Pres*
Joseph M Pufahl,
EMP: 110 **EST:** 2002
SALES (est): 14.2MM **Publicly Held**
SIC: 2672 Tape, pressure sensitive: made from purchased materials; coated paper, except photographic, carbon or abrasive
HQ: Berry Global, Inc.
101 Oakley St
Evansville IN 47710
812 424-2904

(G-13566)
CUSTOM WOODWORK LTD
Also Called: Heritage Wide Plank Flooring
205 Marcy Ave (11901-3029)
PHONE..................631 727-5260
Cathaleen Lanieri, *President*
EMP: 16
SQ FT: 3,500
SALES (est): 2.9MM **Privately Held**
WEB: www.heritagewideplankflooring.com
SIC: 2426 Flooring, hardwood

(G-13567)
DYNASTY METAL WORKS INC
787 Raynor Ave (11901-2949)
PHONE..................631 284-3719
John Harold Jr, *President*
John Harold Sr, *Treasurer*
▲ **EMP:** 7
SALES (est): 1.2MM **Privately Held**
SIC: 3272 3441 Concrete products, precast; fabricated structural metal

(G-13568)
EASTERN WELDING INC
274 Mill Rd (11901-3145)
PHONE..................631 727-0306
William Stubelek, *President*
Brian Stubelek, *Vice Pres*
EMP: 6
SQ FT: 10,000
SALES (est): 228.4K **Privately Held**
SIC: 3713 3523 3732 4226 Truck bodies (motor vehicles); farm machinery & equipment; boat building & repairing; special warehousing & storage; fabricated structural metal

(G-13569)
HALLOCK FABRICATING CORP
324 Doctors Path (11901-1509)
PHONE..................631 727-2441
Corey Hallock, *President*
Doreen Hallock, *Admin Sec*
EMP: 6 **EST:** 1953
SQ FT: 10,000
SALES (est): 973.7K **Privately Held**
SIC: 3312 3599 3441 1799 Stainless steel; machine shop, jobbing & repair; fabricated structural metal; welding on site

(G-13570)
KAPS-ALL PACKAGING SYSTEMS
200 Mill Rd (11901-3125)
PHONE..................631 574-8778
Kenneth Herzog, *Ch of Bd*
Michael Herzog, *Info Tech Mgr*
◆ **EMP:** 61
SQ FT: 60,000
SALES (est): 16.2MM **Privately Held**
WEB: www.kapsall.com
SIC: 3565 Bottling machinery: filling, capping, labeling

(G-13571)
KOPPERT CRESS USA LLC
2975 Sound Ave (11901-1114)
PHONE..................631 779-3640
Eddie Creces, *Branch Mgr*
EMP: 20 **Privately Held**
SIC: 2099 Salads, fresh or refrigerated
PA: Koppert Cress Usa Llc
23423 County Road 48
Cutchogue NY 11935

(G-13572)
LA FORGE FRANCAISE LTD INC
100 Kroemer Ave (11901-3117)
P.O. Box 1322, Boulder UT (84716-1322)
PHONE..................631 591-0572
Patrice Humbert, *President*
Marlyse Humbert, *Vice Pres*
EMP: 6
SQ FT: 1,000
SALES (est): 579.6K **Privately Held**
SIC: 2514 Metal household furniture

(G-13573)
LEHNEIS ORTHOTICS PROSTHETIC
518 E Main St (11901-2529)
PHONE..................631 369-3115
EMP: 7
SALES (corp-wide): 5MM **Privately Held**
SIC: 3842 5047 5999 Mfg Surgical Appliances/Supplies Whol Medical/Hospital Equipment Ret Misc Merchandise
PA: Lehneis Orthotics & Prosthetic Associates Ltd
13 Bedells Landing Rd
Roslyn NY
516 621-7277

(G-13574)
LONG IRELAND BREWING LLC
723 Pulaski St (11901-3039)
PHONE..................631 403-4303
Gregory Martin, *President*
EMP: 5
SALES: 668K **Privately Held**
SIC: 2082 Beer (alcoholic beverage)

(G-13575)
LONG ISLAND GREEN GUYS
26 Silverbrook Dr (11901-4269)
PHONE..................631 664-4306
Martin Hand, *Principal*
EMP: 5
SALES (est): 473.9K **Privately Held**
SIC: 3272 Grease traps, concrete

(G-13576)
LUXFER MAGTECH INC
680 Elton St (11901-2555)
PHONE..................631 727-8600
Brian Purves, *CEO*
Marc Lamensdorf, *President*
Deepak Madan, *Vice Pres*
Deborah Simsen, *Treasurer*
James Gardella, *Exec Dir*
EMP: 80
SALES (est): 14MM
SALES (corp-wide): 441.3MM **Privately Held**
SIC: 2899 5149 Desalter kits, sea water; oxidizers, inorganic; groceries & related products
PA: Luxfer Holdings Plc
Ancorage Gateway
Salford LANCS M50 3
161 300-0611

(G-13577)
MAHIN IMPRESSIONS INC
30 W Main St Ste 301 (11901-2806)
PHONE..................212 871-9777
Sharon Mahin, *President*
Brian Mahin, *Treasurer*
Anthony Goodwin, *Admin Sec*
EMP: 3
SALES: 1MM **Privately Held**
WEB: www.mahinimpressions.com
SIC: 2752 Commercial printing, offset

(G-13578)
NORTH COAST OUTFITTERS LTD
1015 E Main St Ste 1 (11901-2678)
PHONE..................631 727-5580
Charles Darling III, *President*
Maria Lafrance, *Office Mgr*
▼ **EMP:** 20 **EST:** 1996
SQ FT: 30,000
SALES (est): 2.2MM **Privately Held**
WEB: www.charlieshorse.com
SIC: 3949 3444 3354 Sporting & athletic goods; sheet metalwork; aluminum extruded products

(G-13579)
PHOENIX WOOD WRIGHTS LTD
132 Kroemer Ave 3 (11901-3117)
PHONE..................631 727-9691
James Gleason, *President*
EMP: 14 **EST:** 2007
SALES (est): 2.3MM **Privately Held**
SIC: 3553 Bandsaws, woodworking

(G-13580)
QUANTUM KNOWLEDGE LLC
356 Reeves Ave (11901-1109)
PHONE..................631 727-6111
Alexander Pozamantir,
EMP: 6
SALES (est): 848.5K **Privately Held**
SIC: 3572 Computer storage devices

(G-13581)
RAILEX WINE SERVICES LLC (PA)
Also Called: Northwest Wine Services
889 Harrison Ave (11901-2090)
PHONE..................631 369-7000
James Kleist, *Vice Pres*
Joseph Leuci, *CFO*
EMP: 45
SALES (est): 13.1MM **Privately Held**
SIC: 2084 Wines

(G-13582)
ROBERT & WILLIAM INC (PA)
224 Griffing Ave (11901-3214)
PHONE..................631 727-5780
Wil S Field, *President*
William Schofield Sr, *CEO*
Robert Frankel, *President*
▼ **EMP:** 5 **EST:** 1997
SQ FT: 3,200
SALES: 30.1MM **Privately Held**
WEB: www.randw.com
SIC: 2011 Meat by-products from meat slaughtered on site

(G-13583)
SCHILLER STORES INC (PA)
Also Called: Le Creuset
509 Tanger Mall Dr (11901-6405)
PHONE..................631 208-9400
Michael Kryivski, *Executive*
EMP: 5
SALES (est): 491K **Privately Held**
SIC: 3469 Cooking ware, porcelain enameled

(G-13584)
SENTRY AUTOMATIC SPRINKLER
735 Flanders Rd (11901-3828)
PHONE..................631 723-3095
Thomas Andracchi, *President*
EMP: 10
SALES (est): 980K **Privately Held**
SIC: 3569 Sprinkler systems, fire: automatic

(G-13585)
SPIRENT INC (HQ)
303 Griffing Ave (11901-3010)
PHONE..................631 208-0680
L John Knox, *President*
Frank V Pizzi, *Treasurer*
▲ **EMP:** 7
SQ FT: 51,000

SALES (est): 85.7MM
SALES (corp-wide): 454.8MM Privately Held
SIC: 3699 High-energy particle physics equipment
PA: Spirent Communications Plc
Northwood Park
Crawley W SUSSEX RH10
129 376-7676

(G-13586)
TIKI INDUSTPIES INC
8 Tree Haven Ln (11901-4908)
PHONE 516 779-3629
Kalani Aiwohi, *President*
EMP: 5
SALES (est): 261.3K Privately Held
SIC: 3999 1611 1622 1741 Manufacturing industries; general contractor, highway & street construction; sidewalk construction; bridge construction; masonry & other stonework; waterproofing

(G-13587)
TUTHILL CORPORATION
75 Kings Dr (11901-6202)
PHONE 631 727-1097
EMP: 467
SALES (corp-wide): 469.3MM Privately Held
SIC: 3511 Mfg Steel Turbines
PA: Tuthill Corporation
8500 S Madison St
Burr Ridge IL 60527
630 382-4900

(G-13588)
WEDEL SIGN COMPANY INC
705 W Main St (11901-2843)
PHONE 631 727-4577
Barry Wedel, *President*
EMP: 5
SQ FT: 2,000
SALES: 276.8K Privately Held
SIC: 3993 Electric signs

(G-13589)
WINE SERVICES INC
1129 Cross River Dr Ste A (11901-1703)
PHONE 631 722-3800
John White, *President*
John Flock, *Director*
EMP: 5
SQ FT: 21,000
SALES (est): 420.1K Privately Held
WEB: www.wineservices.com
SIC: 2084 Wine cellars, bonded: engaged in blenuing wines

Rochester
Monroe County

(G-13590)
A Q P INC
Also Called: Advanced Quickprinting
2975 Brighton Henrietta T (14623-2787)
PHONE 585 256-1690
James L Roach, *President*
EMP: 7
SQ FT: 3,700
SALES (est): 1MM Privately Held
SIC: 2752 7334 Commercial printing, offset; photocopying & duplicating services

(G-13591)
A R ARENA PRODUCTS INC
2101 Mount Read Blvd (14615-3708)
PHONE 585 277-1680
Anthony R Arena, *CEO*
Charles Arena, *Vice Pres*
Jeff Reeves, *Mfg Mgr*
Chris Mabry, *Engineer*
Joseph Vaccarella, *Engineer*
▲ **EMP:** 20
SQ FT: 30,000
SALES (est): 7MM Privately Held
WEB: www.arenaproducts.com
SIC: 3089 7359 Plastic containers, except foam; shipping container leasing

(G-13592)
AAA WELDING AND FABRICATION OF
1085 Lyell Ave (14606-1935)
PHONE 585 254-2830
Sam Dinch, *President*
Steven Stadtmiller, *Corp Secy*
EMP: 9
SQ FT: 16,000
SALES (est): 2MM Privately Held
WEB: www.aaawelding.com
SIC: 3441 1623 7692 Fabricated structural metal; pipe laying construction; welding repair

(G-13593)
AARON TOOL & MOLD INC
620 Trolley Blvd (14606-4215)
PHONE 585 426-5100
Daniel Morgan, *President*
Ellen Morgan, *Vice Pres*
EMP: 8
SQ FT: 6,000
SALES (est): 1.1MM Privately Held
WEB: www.aaronmold.com
SIC: 3089 Injection molding of plastics

(G-13594)
ACAD DESIGN CORP
975 Mount Read Blvd (14606-2829)
PHONE 585 254-6960
Thomas Sheen, *President*
Karen Sheen, *Vice Pres*
EMP: 13
SQ FT: 20,000
SALES: 2MM Privately Held
WEB: www.acaddesigncorp.com
SIC: 3599 7389 8711 Machine & other job shop work; design services; engineering services

(G-13595)
ACCEDE MOLD & TOOL CO INC
1125 Lexington Ave (14606-2995)
PHONE 585 254-6490
Roger Fox, *CEO*
Alton L Fox, *President*
Nancy Fox, *Vice Pres*
Brett Lindenmuth, *Vice Pres*
Mark Bernhardt, *Project Mgr*
▲ **EMP:** 58
SQ FT: 38,000
SALES (est): 12.4MM Privately Held
WEB: www.accedemold.com
SIC: 3544 3599 Forms (molds), for foundry & plastics working machinery; custom machinery

(G-13596)
ACCU COAT INC
111 Humboldt St Ste 8 (14609-7415)
PHONE 585 288-2330
Paul Meier-Wang, *President*
Patrick Iuliamello, *Vice Pres*
EMP: 7
SQ FT: 4,500
SALES (est): 1.2MM Privately Held
WEB: www.accucoatinc.com
SIC: 3827 Optical instruments & lenses

(G-13597)
ACCURATE PNT POWDR COATING INC
606 Hague St (14606-1214)
PHONE 585 235-1650
Christopher Ralph, *President*
Jeremy Seaver, *General Mgr*
EMP: 17
SQ FT: 40,000
SALES (est): 1.2MM Privately Held
SIC: 3479 Etching & engraving; coating of metals & formed products; barber & beauty shop equipment

(G-13598)
ACCURATE TOOL & DIE LLC
1085 Lyell Ave (14606-1935)
PHONE 585 254-2830
Sam Dinch,
Mark Drewiega,
Steve Drewiega,
Gene Lippa,
EMP: 15
SQ FT: 15,000
SALES: 1.1MM Privately Held
SIC: 3599 Machine shop, jobbing & repair

(G-13599)
ACME PRECISION SCREW PDTS INC
623 Glide St (14606-1345)
P.O. Box 60649 (14606-0649)
PHONE 585 328-2028
Rodney Czudak, *President*
EMP: 18
SQ FT: 10,000
SALES (est): 3.5MM Privately Held
SIC: 3451 Screw machine products

(G-13600)
ACRO INDUSTRIES INC
554 Colfax St (14606-3112)
PHONE 585 254-3661
Joseph A Noto, *President*
Robert Coyne, *CCO*
John H Gefell, *Exec VP*
James Francisco, *Opers Mgr*
Brian Gefell, *Production*
▲ **EMP:** 148
SQ FT: 150,000
SALES (est): 56.2MM Privately Held
WEB: www.acroind.com
SIC: 3444 3599 3443 3469 Culverts, flumes & pipes; amusement park equipment; fabricated plate work (boiler shop); metal stampings

(G-13601)
ACUITY POLYMERS INC
1667 Lake Ave Ste 303 (14615-3047)
PHONE 585 458-8409
James Bonafini, *President*
EMP: 8
SALES (est): 743.1K Privately Held
SIC: 3851 Contact lenses

(G-13602)
ADDISON PRECISION MFG CORP
500 Avis St (14613-3308)
P.O. Box 15393 (14615-0393)
PHONE 585 254-1386
Robert E Champagne, *CEO*
Rodney C Champagne, *President*
Roger C Champagne, *Vice Pres*
Eric Caudill, *Manager*
EMP: 72 EST: 1950
SQ FT: 40,000
SALES (est): 15.6MM Privately Held
WEB: www.addisonprec.com
SIC: 3599 Machine shop, jobbing & repair

(G-13603)
ADRIAN JULES LTD
Also Called: Adrian-Jules Custom Tailor
1392 E Ridge Rd (14621-2005)
PHONE 585 342-5886
Adriano P Roberti, *Ch of Bd*
Arnald J Roberti, *President*
Peter E Roberti, *President*
Scotti Gaylor, *Manager*
Jean Roberti, *Admin Sec*
▲ **EMP:** 80 EST: 1964
SQ FT: 14,000
SALES (est): 7.7MM Privately Held
WEB: www.adrianjules.com
SIC: 2311 5699 2325 Men's & boys' suits & coats; custom tailor; men's & boys' trousers & slacks

(G-13604)
ADVANCE CIRCUIT TECHNOLOGY INC
19 Jetview Dr (14624-4903)
PHONE 585 328-2000
James Morrison, *Ch of Bd*
Robert Drozdowski, *Business Mgr*
Bob Kajfasz, *Vice Pres*
Robert Kajfasz, *Vice Pres*
Kalman Zsamboky, *Vice Pres*
▲ **EMP:** 42 EST: 1998
SQ FT: 35,000
SALES (est): 10.5MM Privately Held
WEB: www.advcircuit.com
SIC: 3679 3672 Electronic circuits; printed circuit boards

(G-13605)
ADVANCED COATING SERVICE LLC
15 Hytec Cir (14606-4255)
P.O. Box 60387 (14606-0387)
PHONE 585 247-3970
Donald Titus, *Mng Member*
Donald E Titus Jr, *Mng Member*
EMP: 7
SALES (est): 1MM Privately Held
WEB: www.acscoating.com
SIC: 3479 Etching & engraving; coating of metals & formed products

(G-13606)
ADVANCED GLASS INDUSTRIES INC
Also Called: A G I
1335 Emerson St (14606-3006)
P.O. Box 60467 (14606-0467)
PHONE 585 458-8040
Anthony Marino, *President*
H John Fischer, *Vice Pres*
▲ **EMP:** 51
SQ FT: 42,000
SALES (est): 19.1MM Privately Held
WEB: www.agi.com
SIC: 3827 Lenses, optical: all types except ophthalmic

(G-13607)
ADVANCED MACHINE INC
439 Central Ave Ste 108 (14605-3016)
PHONE 585 423-8255
John Bauman, *President*
Jacqueline De Mario, *Treasurer*
Dana Byron, *Admin Sec*
EMP: 10
SQ FT: 5,600
SALES (est): 1.3MM Privately Held
SIC: 3599 Machine shop, jobbing & repair

(G-13608)
ADVANTAGE METALWORK FINSHG LLC
1000 University Ave # 700 (14607-1286)
PHONE 585 454-0160
Chet Wester, *CEO*
Arthur Carroll, *Exec VP*
Dale Campbell, *Vice Pres*
Gary Vogt, *VP Sales*
Kenneth Koester, *Director*
EMP: 86
SALES (est): 19.5MM Privately Held
SIC: 3542 Machine tools, metal forming type

(G-13609)
ADVANTECH INDUSTRIES INC
3850 Buffalo Rd (14624-1104)
PHONE 585 247-0701
James Gizzi, *Ch of Bd*
EMP: 115
SALES (est): 26.4MM Privately Held
WEB: www.advantechindustries.com
SIC: 3399 3444 Laminating steel; sheet metalwork

(G-13610)
AIRGAS USA LLC
77 Deep Rock Rd (14624-3519)
PHONE 585 436-7781
Bob Hewitt, *Branch Mgr*
EMP: 15
SQ FT: 12,330
SALES (corp-wide): 164.2MM Privately Held
WEB: www.airgas.com
SIC: 2813 Industrial gases
HQ: Airgas Usa, Llc
259 N Radnor Chester Rd # 100
Radnor PA 19087
610 687-5253

(G-13611)
AJL MANUFACTURING INC
100 Holleder Pkwy (14615-3800)
PHONE 585 254-1128
Albert F Porter, *Chairman*
Devin Pogue, *Business Mgr*
Joe Frillici, *Plant Mgr*
Ken Fowler, *QC Mgr*
Lyle Lynch, *Engineer*
▲ **EMP:** 112
SQ FT: 165,000

Rochester - Monroe County (G-13612)

SALES (est): 31.1MM **Privately Held**
WEB: www.ajlmfg.com
SIC: 3444 Sheet metalwork

(G-13612)
ALCOA FASTENING SYSTEMS
181 Mckee Rd (14611-2011)
PHONE..................585 368-5049
Vitaliy Rusakov, *CEO*
EMP: 8 **EST:** 2015
SALES (est): 672.1K **Privately Held**
SIC: 3353 Aluminum sheet & strip

(G-13613)
ALKEMY MACHINE LLC
Also Called: Aurora Machine
1600 Lexington Ave 103c (14606-3000)
PHONE..................585 436-8730
Kelsey Hall, *Manager*
Jonathan Amoia,
Jordan Kowalczyk,
EMP: 8
SALES (est): 1.5MM **Privately Held**
SIC: 3444 3599 Sheet metalwork; machine shop, jobbing & repair

(G-13614)
ALLESON OF ROCHESTER INC (DH)
Also Called: Alleson Athletic
2921 Brighton Henrietta (14623-2798)
PHONE..................585 272-0606
Todd Levine, *CEO*
Pete Palermo III, *COO*
Bob Baker, *CFO*
▲ **EMP:** 100 **EST:** 1966
SQ FT: 128,000
SALES: 77.9MM
SALES (corp-wide): 552.1MM **Privately Held**
SIC: 2339 2329 Women's & misses' athletic clothing & sportswear; athletic (warmup, sweat & jogging) suits: men's & boys'
HQ: Badger Sportswear, Llc
111 Badger Ln
Statesville NC 28625
704 871-0990

(G-13615)
ALLIANCE AUTOMATION SYSTEMS
400 Trabold Rd (14624-2529)
PHONE..................585 426-2700
Arthur Anderson, *CEO*
Stewart H Rodman, *Ch of Bd*
Jeffrey Hoffman, *CFO*
Robert Huener, *Director*
Robert T Isherwood, *Director*
▲ **EMP:** 125
SQ FT: 120,000
SALES: 15MM **Privately Held**
SIC: 3549 3569 Assembly machines, including robotic; assembly machines, nonmetalworking

(G-13616)
ALLIANCE PRECISION PLAS CORP (PA)
1220 Lee Rd (14606-4252)
PHONE..................585 426-5310
Walter C Butler Jr, *CEO*
Bradley C Scott, *President*
Clay Kearns, *Purchasing*
Diana Smalley, *Purchasing*
Tim Clement, *QC Mgr*
▲ **EMP:** 200 **EST:** 1998
SQ FT: 80,000
SALES (est): 64.7MM **Privately Held**
WEB: www.allianceppc.com
SIC: 3089 3544 Injection molded finished plastic products; dies, plastics forming

(G-13617)
ALLIANCE PRECISION PLAS CORP
105 Elmore Dr (14606-3429)
PHONE..................585 426-5310
Sara Bruzda, *Human Resources*
Brad Scott, *Branch Mgr*
Robert Levesque, *Maintence Staff*
EMP: 41

SALES (corp-wide): 64.7MM **Privately Held**
SIC: 3089 3544 Injection molded finished plastic products; dies, plastics forming
PA: Alliance Precision Plastics Corporation
1220 Lee Rd
Rochester NY 14606
585 426-5310

(G-13618)
ALLSTATE TOOL AND DIE INC
Also Called: Atd Precision Machining
15 Coldwater Cres (14624-2590)
PHONE..................585 426-0400
Paul Held Sr, *President*
Paul Held Jr, *President*
Elizabeth Held, *Vice Pres*
▲ **EMP:** 68
SQ FT: 37,000
SALES (est): 9.7MM **Privately Held**
WEB: www.atdprecision.com
SIC: 3544 Special dies & tools

(G-13619)
ALOI SOLUTIONS LLC (PA)
Also Called: Aloi Materials Handling
140 Commerce Dr (14623-3504)
PHONE..................585 292-0920
Jeff Gambrill, *President*
Robert Manion, *Vice Pres*
Michael Rhault, *Project Engr*
▲ **EMP:** 30 **EST:** 1987
SQ FT: 16,500
SALES (est): 7.9MM **Privately Held**
WEB: www.aloi.com
SIC: 3599 3999 Custom machinery; atomizers, toiletry

(G-13620)
ALPHA IRON WORKS LLC
65 Goodway Dr S (14623-3018)
PHONE..................585 424-7260
Evangelos Economides, *Mng Member*
Maria Economides,
EMP: 16 **EST:** 1978
SQ FT: 13,000
SALES (est): 3.3MM **Privately Held**
WEB: www.alphairon.com
SIC: 3441 Fabricated structural metal

(G-13621)
ALTON MANUFACTURING INC
825 Lee Rd (14606-4290)
PHONE..................585 458-2600
George Chornobil, *Ch of Bd*
Andrew Chornobil, *President*
Bohdan Chornobil, *Shareholder*
Christine Sykes, *Shareholder*
EMP: 90
SQ FT: 150,000
SALES (est): 16.4MM **Privately Held**
WEB: www.altonmfg.com
SIC: 3469 3544 3541 Stamping metal for the trade; special dies, tools, jigs & fixtures; machine tools, metal cutting type

(G-13622)
AMARR COMPANY
Also Called: Amarr Garage Doors
550 Mile Crssing Blvd 1 (14624)
PHONE..................585 426-8290
Demetrius Scott, *Site Mgr*
Philip Bordelen, *Manager*
Mark Fiorella, *Manager*
EMP: 10
SALES (corp-wide): 9B **Privately Held**
WEB: www.amarr.com
SIC: 3442 5211 Garage doors, overhead: metal; garage doors, sale & installation
HQ: Amarr Company
165 Carriage Ct
Winston Salem NC 27105
336 744-5100

(G-13623)
AMBRELL CORPORATION (HQ)
1655 Lyell Ave (14606-2311)
PHONE..................585 889-0236
Tony Mazzullo, *President*
Girish Dahake, *Vice Pres*
Dan King, *Project Mgr*
Steve Enes, *Opers Staff*
Evaristo Montiel, *Engineer*
▲ **EMP:** 13
SQ FT: 25,000

SALES: 21.4MM
SALES (corp-wide): 66.8MM **Publicly Held**
WEB: www.ameritherm.com
SIC: 3567 Induction heating equipment
PA: Intest Corporation
804 E Gate Dr Ste 200
Mount Laurel NJ 08054
856 505-8800

(G-13624)
AMERICAN AEROGEL CORPORATION
460 Buffalo Rd Ste 200a (14611-2026)
PHONE..................585 328-2140
Michael Hone, *CEO*
Jay McHarg, *President*
David Abruzzese, *Vice Pres*
Nick Fusilli, *Opers Mgr*
Jeff Sullivan, *Director*
EMP: 34
SQ FT: 40,000
SALES (est): 12.1MM **Privately Held**
WEB: www.americanaerogel.com
SIC: 3441 Fabricated structural metal

(G-13625)
AMERICAN PACKAGING CORPORATION
1555 Lyell Ave (14606-2145)
PHONE..................585 254-2002
Peter Scottland, *President*
Dave Hebberecht, *General Mgr*
Clarence Mitchell, *Technician*
EMP: 7
SALES (corp-wide): 231.8MM **Privately Held**
SIC: 2673 3497 2671 Bags: plastic, laminated & coated; metal foil & leaf; paper coated or laminated for packaging
PA: American Packaging Corporation
100 Apc Way
Columbus WI 53925
920 623-2291

(G-13626)
AMERICAN PACKAGING CORPORATION
777 Driving Park Ave (14613-1591)
PHONE..................585 254-9500
EMP: 113
SALES (corp-wide): 231.8MM **Privately Held**
SIC: 2673 3497 2671 2754 Bags: plastic, laminated & coated; metal foil & leaf; paper coated or laminated for packaging; rotogravure printing; bags: uncoated paper & multiwall
PA: American Packaging Corporation
100 Apc Way
Columbus WI 53925
920 623-2291

(G-13627)
AMERICAN SPECIALTY MFG CO
Also Called: Boss Sauce
272 Hudson Ave (14605-2124)
P.O. Box 31344 (14603-1344)
PHONE..................585 544-5600
Eddie Harris, *President*
Loreta Pope, *Vice Pres*
Regina Harris, *Treasurer*
EMP: 11
SQ FT: 6,500
SALES (est): 400K **Privately Held**
SIC: 2035 Seasonings, meat sauces (except tomato & dry)

(G-13628)
AMERICAN SPORTS MEDIA LLC (PA)
2604 Elmwood Ave Ste 343 (14618-2213)
PHONE..................585 377-9636
David Jones,
David Aultman,
Brian Spindler,
EMP: 1
SQ FT: 3,000
SALES (est): 1.2MM **Privately Held**
WEB: www.americansportsmedia.com
SIC: 2711 Newspapers: publishing only, not printed on site

(G-13629)
AMERICAN TIME MFG LTD
Also Called: American Products
1600 N Clinton Ave Ste 1 (14621-2200)
PHONE..................585 266-5120
Clifford Charlson, *President*
▲ **EMP:** 18
SQ FT: 7,000
SALES (est): 1.8MM **Privately Held**
WEB: www.americanproducts-ny.com
SIC: 3873 Watchcases

(G-13630)
AMETEK INC
Also Called: Ametek Power Instruments
255 Union St N (14605-2699)
P.O. Box 1764, Paoli PA (19301-0801)
PHONE..................585 263-7700
Ken McGillivray, *President*
Bo Bojczuk, *Exec VP*
Michael Botzenmayer, *Vice Pres*
Ron Oscher, *Vice Pres*
Jared Riddle, *Vice Pres*
EMP: 68
SALES (corp-wide): 4.3B **Publicly Held**
SIC: 3621 3823 3825 3812 Motors & generators; industrial instrmnts msrmnt display/control process variable; instruments to measure electricity; search & navigation equipment; electrical equipment & supplies
PA: Ametek, Inc.
1100 Cassatt Rd
Berwyn PA 19312
610 647-2121

(G-13631)
ANALOG DIGITAL TECHNOLOGY LLC
Also Called: Adtech
95 Mount Read Blvd # 149 (14611-1923)
PHONE..................585 698-1845
Tom Crumlish, *President*
Eric Hauptmann, *Vice Pres*
EMP: 9
SQ FT: 6,500
SALES (est): 1.1MM **Privately Held**
WEB: www.adtech-inst.com
SIC: 3699 5084 Chimes, electric; industrial machinery & equipment

(G-13632)
ANDEX CORP
69 Deep Rock Rd (14624-3575)
PHONE..................585 328-3790
Andrew J Cherre, *President*
EMP: 30 **EST:** 1962
SQ FT: 17,000
SALES (est): 6.6MM **Privately Held**
SIC: 2621 Filter paper

(G-13633)
ANDROS MANUFACTURING CORP
30 Hojack Park (14612-1994)
PHONE..................585 663-5700
Russell Steenhoff, *President*
Nancy Commanda, *Vice Pres*
Fred Steenhoff, *Marketing Staff*
EMP: 10
SQ FT: 12,000
SALES: 700K **Privately Held**
WEB: www.androsmfg.com
SIC: 3451 3643 Screw machine products; solderless connectors (electric wiring devices)

(G-13634)
ANMAR ACQUISITION LLC (HQ)
35 Vantage Point Dr (14624-1142)
PHONE..................585 352-7777
Lee Rudow, *CEO*
John Zimmer, *CFO*
EMP: 5
SALES (est): 2.5MM
SALES (corp-wide): 155.1MM **Publicly Held**
SIC: 3825 Radar testing instruments, electric
PA: Transcat, Inc.
35 Vantage Point Dr
Rochester NY 14624
585 352-7777

GEOGRAPHIC SECTION

Rochester - Monroe County (G-13660)

(G-13635)
ANTAB MCH SPRFINISHING LAB INC
46 Latta Rd (14612-4708)
PHONE.................................585 865-8290
Araxie Aintablian, *President*
▲ EMP: 7
SALES (est): 470K **Privately Held**
SIC: 3599 Machine shop, jobbing & repair

(G-13636)
APPLIED COATINGS HOLDING CORP (PA)
1653 E Main St Ste 1 (14609-7000)
PHONE.................................585 482-0300
Bruno Glavich, *President*
◆ EMP: 8 EST: 1998
SQ FT: 5,000
SALES (est): 5MM **Privately Held**
SIC: 3827 Optical elements & assemblies, except ophthalmic

(G-13637)
APPLIED IMAGE INC
1653 E Main St Ste 1 (14609-7090)
PHONE.................................585 482-0300
Dave Doubledee, *President*
Katie Caccamise, *General Mgr*
Glenn Jackling, *General Mgr*
Luke Hobson, *Vice Pres*
Greg Peck, *VP Opers*
EMP: 20
SQ FT: 20,000
SALES (est): 4.7MM
SALES (corp-wide): 5MM **Privately Held**
WEB: www.appliedimage.net
SIC: 3826 3827 7335 Analytical optical instruments; optical instruments & apparatus; color separation, photographic & movie film
PA: Applied Coatings Holding Corp.
1653 E Main St Ste 1
Rochester NY 14609
585 482-0300

(G-13638)
ARCH GLOBL PRCSION RCHSTER LLC
Also Called: Jasco Tools
1390 Mount Read Blvd (14606-2820)
PHONE.................................585 254-7000
Kelli Micoli, *Mng Member*
EMP: 64
SALES (est): 2.3MM **Privately Held**
SIC: 3545 Precision tools, machinists'

(G-13639)
ARM ROCHESTER INC
138 Joseph Ave (14605-1938)
PHONE.................................585 354-5077
Armando Santiago, *President*
James Jacus, *Director*
Robert Vavrina, *Director*
EMP: 15
SQ FT: 15,000
SALES (est): 1.8MM **Privately Held**
SIC: 3086 7389 Padding, foamed plastic;

(G-13640)
ARNOLD MAGNETIC TECH CORP (HQ)
Also Called: Magnetic Technology
770 Linden Ave (14625-2716)
PHONE.................................585 385-9010
Gordon H McNeil, *President*
Ted Baker, *General Mgr*
Roy Hollon, *General Mgr*
Michael Stachura, *General Mgr*
Aaron Williams, *Engineer*
▲ EMP: 193
SQ FT: 70,000
SALES (est): 234.1MM **Publicly Held**
WEB: www.arnoldmagnetics.com
SIC: 3264 3499 Magnets, permanent: ceramic or ferrite; magnets, permanent: metallic

(G-13641)
ARNPRIOR RPID MFG SLUTIONS INC (PA)
2400 Mount Read Blvd # 112 (14615-2744)
PHONE.................................585 617-6301
Leonard M Levie, *Ch of Bd*
John Wilbur, *President*

Pamela Barnard, *Principal*
Thomas Palumbo, *Principal*
Carol Rath, *Principal*
EMP: 152
SALES (est): 24.9MM **Privately Held**
SIC: 3999 Advertising display products

(G-13642)
ARNPRIOR RPID MFG SLUTIONS INC
2400 Mount Read Blvd # 1124 (14615-2744)
PHONE.................................585 617-6301
Thomas Palumbo, *Manager*
EMP: 9 **Privately Held**
SIC: 3999 Advertising display products
PA: Arnprior Rapid Manufacturing Solutions, Inc.
2400 Mount Read Blvd # 112
Rochester NY 14615

(G-13643)
ART-CRAFT OPTICAL COMPANY INC
57 Goodway Dr S (14623-3018)
PHONE.................................585 546-6640
C Thomas Eagle, *President*
Martin Gullen, *Exec VP*
Christopher Eagle, *VP Opers*
Donald Bennett, *Finance Dir*
Charles Thomas Eagle Jr, *VP Mktg*
EMP: 49
SQ FT: 90,000
SALES (est): 9.1MM **Privately Held**
WEB: www.artcraftoptical.com
SIC: 3851 Frames & parts, eyeglass & spectacle

(G-13644)
ARYZTA LLC
Rochester Div
64 Chester St (14611-2110)
PHONE.................................310 417-4700
John Menne, *Branch Mgr*
EMP: 87
SALES (corp-wide): 4.4B **Privately Held**
WEB: www.pennantfoods.com
SIC: 2045 2099 2051 Prepared flour mixes & doughs; food preparations; bread, cake & related products
HQ: Aryzta Llc
6080 Center Dr Ste 900
Los Angeles CA 90045
310 417-4700

(G-13645)
ARYZTA LLC
Also Called: Pennant Foods
235 Buffalo Rd (14611-1905)
PHONE.................................585 235-8160
Steven Smith, *Branch Mgr*
EMP: 218
SALES (corp-wide): 4.4B **Privately Held**
WEB: www.pennantfoods.com
SIC: 2051 2052 Bread, cake & related products; bakery products, dry
HQ: Aryzta Llc
6080 Center Dr Ste 900
Los Angeles CA 90045
310 417-4700

(G-13646)
ASCRIBE INC
383 Buell Rd (14624-3123)
PHONE.................................585 413-0298
Mark Shaw, *Ch of Bd*
Dean Saklis, *President*
EMP: 50
SALES (est): 3.6MM **Privately Held**
SIC: 3999 7389 3479 Atomizers, toiletry; grinding, precision: commercial or industrial; etching & engraving

(G-13647)
ASP INDUSTRIES INC
9 Evelyn St (14606-5533)
PHONE.................................585 254-9130
Suzanne M Phillips, *President*
Susan Allen, *Controller*
EMP: 20
SQ FT: 23,000
SALES: 2.8MM **Privately Held**
WEB: www.aspindustries.com
SIC: 3444 3441 Sheet metal specialties, not stamped; fabricated structural metal

(G-13648)
AVRO INC
Also Called: Avr Optics
3635 Buffalo Rd Ste 2 (14624-1120)
PHONE.................................585 445-7588
Peter Brunt, *Vice Pres*
Lane Manning, *Engineer*
EMP: 7
SALES (est): 199.3K **Privately Held**
SIC: 3821 Laboratory equipment: fume hoods, distillation racks, etc.

(G-13649)
AYCAN MEDICAL SYSTEMS LLC
693 East Ave Ste 102 (14607-2160)
PHONE.................................585 271-3078
Frank Burkhardt, *Mng Member*
EMP: 15 EST: 2003
SQ FT: 4,000
SALES (est): 1.8MM **Privately Held**
SIC: 7372 Business oriented computer software

(G-13650)
BAGEL LAND
1896 Monroe Ave (14618-1918)
PHONE.................................585 442-3080
Robert Juliano, *Owner*
EMP: 20
SALES (est): 1.1MM **Privately Held**
SIC: 2051 5461 Bagels, fresh or frozen; bakeries

(G-13651)
BAGS UNLIMITED INC
7 Canal St (14608-1910)
PHONE.................................585 436-6282
Michael Macaluso, *President*
Marion Oyer, *General Mgr*
Cheryl Ellis, *Sales Staff*
Valerie Macaluso, *Manager*
Kris Schofield, *Manager*
▲ EMP: 20
SQ FT: 90,000
SALES (est): 5MM **Privately Held**
WEB: www.bagsunlimited.com
SIC: 2673 2759 Plastic bags: made from purchased materials; bags, plastic: printing

(G-13652)
BAKER COMMODITIES INC
Rochester Division
2268 Browncroft Blvd (14625-1000)
PHONE.................................585 482-1880
William Schmieder, *Manager*
EMP: 40
SALES (corp-wide): 161.3MM **Privately Held**
WEB: www.bakercommodities.com
SIC: 2077 2048 Tallow rendering, inedible; prepared feeds
PA: Baker Commodities, Inc.
4020 Bandini Blvd
Vernon CA 90058
323 268-2801

(G-13653)
BALIVA CONCRETE PRODUCTS INC
245 Paul Rd (14624-4923)
P.O. Box 24581 (14624-0581)
PHONE.................................585 328-8442
Richard Baliva, *President*
EMP: 6 EST: 1943
SQ FT: 3,000
SALES: 1MM **Privately Held**
SIC: 3272 Concrete products

(G-13654)
BAUM CHRISTINE AND JOHN CORP
Also Called: Minuteman Press
1577 W Ridge Rd (14615-2520)
PHONE.................................585 621-8910
John Baum, *President*
Christine Baum, *Vice Pres*
EMP: 9
SQ FT: 2,500
SALES (est): 1.5MM **Privately Held**
SIC: 2752 2791 2789 Commercial printing, offset; typesetting; bookbinding & related work

(G-13655)
BAUSCH & LOMB INCORPORATED (DH)
1400 N Goodman St (14609-3596)
P.O. Box 25169, Lehigh Valley PA (18002-5169)
PHONE.................................585 338-6000
Fred Hassan, *Ch of Bd*
Brenton L Saunders, *Ch of Bd*
Robert Bertolini, *President*
Joseph Gordon, *President*
Alan H Farnsworth, *Exec VP*
◆ EMP: 400
SALES (est): 2.4B
SALES (corp-wide): 8.7B **Privately Held**
WEB: www.bausch.com
SIC: 3851 2834 3841 Ophthalmic goods; contact lenses; magnifiers (readers & simple magnifiers); pharmaceutical preparations; solutions, pharmaceutical; druggists' preparations (pharmaceuticals); vitamin preparations; ophthalmic instruments & apparatus
HQ: Bausch & Lomb Holdings Incorporated
450 Lexington Ave
New York NY 10017
585 338-6000

(G-13656)
BAUSCH & LOMB INCORPORATED
1 Bausch And Lomb Pl (14604-2799)
P.O. Box 25169, Lehigh Valley PA (18002-5169)
PHONE.................................585 338-6000
Matt Sleeman, *Business Mgr*
Denis Polyn, *Vice Pres*
Tracy Valorie, *Vice Pres*
Carlos Cabrer, *Project Mgr*
William McClain, *Project Mgr*
EMP: 53
SALES (corp-wide): 8.7B **Privately Held**
SIC: 3851 Ophthalmic goods
HQ: Bausch & Lomb Incorporated
1400 N Goodman St
Rochester NY 14609
585 338-6000

(G-13657)
BAUSCH & LOMB INCORPORATED
1400 N Goodman St (14609-3596)
PHONE.................................585 338-6000
Noel Bateman, *Project Mgr*
Charles E Conway, *Manager*
Bruce Cantie, *Manager*
Kathy Mendick, *Manager*
Robert Miers, *Manager*
EMP: 400
SQ FT: 2,336
SALES (corp-wide): 8.7B **Privately Held**
WEB: www.bausch.com
SIC: 3851 Ophthalmic goods
HQ: Bausch & Lomb Incorporated
1400 N Goodman St
Rochester NY 14609
585 338-6000

(G-13658)
BEASTONS BUDGET PRINTING
Also Called: Sir Speedy
1260 Scttsvlle Rd Ste 300 (14624)
PHONE.................................585 244-2721
Nancy Beaston, *President*
Shel Beaston, *Vice Pres*
EMP: 9
SALES (est): 1.1MM **Privately Held**
SIC: 2752 2791 2789 Commercial printing, lithographic; typesetting; bookbinding & related work

(G-13659)
BEETS LOVE PRODUCTION LLC
1150 Lee Rd (14606-4251)
PHONE.................................585 270-2471
Dave Stocklosa, *Finance Dir*
EMP: 35
SQ FT: 98,500
SALES: 1.5MM **Privately Held**
SIC: 2063 Beet sugar

(G-13660)
BEREZA IRON WORKS INC
87 Dewey Ave (14608-1289)
PHONE.................................585 254-6311

Rochester - Monroe County (G-13661)

William Goy, *President*
Irene E Gratton, *Vice Pres*
Terry Baumbarger, *Accounts Mgr*
EMP: 18
SQ FT: 15,000
SALES: 4.4MM **Privately Held**
SIC: 3441 Fabricated structural metal

(G-13661)
BETTER POWER INC
508 White Spruce Blvd (14623-1613)
PHONE.................585 475-1321
Catherine Henn, *Owner*
EMP: 6
SQ FT: 4,000
SALES (est): 1.5MM **Privately Held**
WEB: www.betterlighting.com
SIC: 3569 Gas generators

(G-13662)
BFGG INVESTORS GROUP LLC
1900 University Ave (14610-2621)
PHONE.................585 424-3456
Chris Guider, *Mng Member*
EMP: 5
SALES (est): 530K **Privately Held**
SIC: 3081 Film base, cellulose acetate or nitrocellulose plastic

(G-13663)
BIGSKY TECHNOLOGIES LLC
1600 N Clinton Ave Ste 11 (14621-2200)
PHONE.................585 270-5282
Cathy A Fleischer, *Mng Member*
EMP: 7
SQ FT: 2,000
SALES (est): 1.4MM **Privately Held**
SIC: 2843 Surface active agents

(G-13664)
BITTNER COMPANY LLC
Also Called: AlphaGraphics
75 Goodway Dr Ste 3 (14623-3000)
PHONE.................585 214-1790
EMP: 13
SALES (est): 1.5MM **Privately Held**
SIC: 2752 Comm Prtg Litho

(G-13665)
BLACKBOX BIOMETRICS INC
125 Tech Park Dr Ste 1131 (14623-2438)
PHONE.................585 329-3399
Joseph V Bridgeford, *Ch of Bd*
Scott Featherman, *Business Mgr*
Vincent Baier, *Engineer*
Ryan Ramplin, *Engineer*
Stephen Cool, *Electrical Engi*
EMP: 22
SALES (est): 2.5MM **Privately Held**
SIC: 3999 Barber & beauty shop equipment

(G-13666)
BLOCH INDUSTRIES LLC
140 Commerce Dr (14623-3504)
P.O. Box 25806 (14625-0806)
PHONE.................585 334-9600
Diane Miller, *Office Mgr*
Brian Geary, *Mng Member*
EMP: 60
SQ FT: 54,000
SALES (est): 5.7MM **Privately Held**
WEB: www.blochindustries.com
SIC: 2434 2541 2431 2521 Wood kitchen cabinets; counters or counter display cases, wood; millwork; wood office furniture

(G-13667)
BLUE CHIP MOLD INC
95 Lagrange Ave (14613-1509)
PHONE.................585 647-1790
Paul A Engert, *President*
EMP: 13
SQ FT: 10,250
SALES (est): 1.3MM **Privately Held**
SIC: 3544 Industrial molds

(G-13668)
BLUE TOAD HARD CIDER
120 Mushroom Blvd (14623-3263)
PHONE.................585 424-5508
Todd Rath, *Co-Owner*
Sarah Cunningham, *Manager*
EMP: 20

SALES: 2.1MM **Privately Held**
SIC: 3556 Presses, food: cheese, beet, cider & sugarcane

(G-13669)
BMA MEDIA SERVICES INC
Also Called: Spinergy
1655 Lyell Ave (14606-2311)
PHONE.................585 385-2060
EMP: 29 **EST:** 2013
SQ FT: 79,000
SALES (est): 1.7MM **Privately Held**
SIC: 3695 Mfg Magnetic/Optical Recording Media

(G-13670)
BODYCOTE THERMAL PROC INC
620 Buffalo Rd (14611-2006)
PHONE.................585 436-7876
Tony Schaut, *Branch Mgr*
EMP: 24
SQ FT: 10,000
SALES (corp-wide): 911.9MM **Privately Held**
SIC: 3398 Metal heat treating
HQ: Bodycote Thermal Processing, Inc.
12700 Park Central Dr # 700
Dallas TX 75251
214 904-2420

(G-13671)
BOEHM SURGICAL INSTRUMENT CORP
966 Chili Ave Ste 3 (14611-2896)
PHONE.................585 436-6584
Paul Boehm, *President*
Mary L Cooper, *Corp Secy*
EMP: 11 **EST:** 1915
SQ FT: 13,000
SALES: 1MM **Privately Held**
SIC: 3841 3843 3429 3641 Surgical & medical instruments; dental equipment; keys, locks & related hardware; electric lamps & parts for specialized applications; medical & hospital equipment

(G-13672)
BONDUELLE USA INC
100 Corporate Woods # 210 (14623-1467)
PHONE.................585 434-0399
EMP: 5 **EST:** 2017
SALES (est): 553K **Privately Held**
SIC: 2037 Frozen fruits & vegetables

(G-13673)
BOOK1ONE LLC
655 Driving Park Ave (14613-1566)
PHONE.................585 458-2101
Peter Pape, *CEO*
Marc Bardeen,
EMP: 7
SALES (est): 1MM **Privately Held**
WEB: www.book1one.com
SIC: 2732 Books: printing & binding

(G-13674)
BOYDELL & BREWER INC
Also Called: Camden House
668 Mount Hope Ave (14620-2731)
PHONE.................585 275-0419
Sue Smit, *President*
Sue Smith, *Managing Dir*
Sue Miller, *Marketing Staff*
Richard Barber, *Director*
Eloise Puls, *Director*
EMP: 12
SQ FT: 1,500
SALES (est): 1.3MM
SALES (corp-wide): 1.6MM **Privately Held**
SIC: 2731 Book music: publishing only, not printed on site
PA: Boydell & Brewer Group Limited
Unit 4 Bridge Farm Business Park
Woodbridge IP12
139 461-0600

(G-13675)
BRAYLEY TOOL & MACHINE INC
1685 Lyell Ave (14606-2311)
PHONE.................585 342-7190
Stephen Roeger, *President*
Rena Roeger, *Vice Pres*
EMP: 8
SQ FT: 6,500

SALES: 700K **Privately Held**
WEB: www.brayleytool.com
SIC: 3544 Special dies & tools

(G-13676)
BRINKMAN INTL GROUP INC (PA)
167 Ames St (14611-1701)
PHONE.................585 429-5000
Andrew J Laniak, *CEO*
Robert Brinkman, *Ch of Bd*
Daniel Bavineau, *Mfg Staff*
Doug Larson, *Engineer*
Dan Robinson, *Engineer*
EMP: 1
SQ FT: 12,000
SALES (est): 106.6MM **Privately Held**
WEB: www.brinkmanig.com
SIC: 3545 3451 3325 3542 Thread cutting dies; screw machine products; steel foundries; machine tools, metal forming type

(G-13677)
BRINKMAN PRODUCTS INC
Also Called: Davenport
167 Ames St (14611-1701)
PHONE.................585 235-4545
Andrew Laniak, *Ch of Bd*
Andrew J Laniak, *President*
Robert J Brinkman, *Principal*
Dick Huber, *Mfg Staff*
Paul Francia, *Engineer*
▲ **EMP:** 290
SQ FT: 118,000
SALES (est): 55.8MM
SALES (corp-wide): 106.6MM **Privately Held**
WEB: www.davenportmachine.com
SIC: 3541 5084 Machine tools, metal cutting type; industrial machinery & equipment
PA: Brinkman International Group, Inc.
167 Ames St
Rochester NY 14611
585 429-5000

(G-13678)
BRIO USA
85 Mushroom Blvd (14623-3201)
PHONE.................585 319-5599
Brad Hogan, *Principal*
▲ **EMP:** 7
SALES (est): 907.8K **Privately Held**
SIC: 3429 Manufactured hardware (general)

(G-13679)
BRISTOL BOARDING INC
1149 Highland Ave (14620-1869)
PHONE.................585 271-7860
Bille McDonald, *President*
Mary McDonald, *Vice Pres*
EMP: 6 **EST:** 1974
SALES (est): 1.1MM **Privately Held**
WEB: www.bristolcase.com
SIC: 2441 5099 Mfg Shipping Cases & Whol Carrying Cases

(G-13680)
BSV METAL FINISHERS INC
Also Called: Bsv Enterprises
750 Saint Paul St (14605-1737)
PHONE.................585 747-7070
Benjamin S Vasquez, *President*
EMP: 26
SQ FT: 13,000
SALES (est): 6.5MM **Privately Held**
SIC: 3398 Metal heat treating

(G-13681)
BURKE & BANNAYAN
2465 W Ridge Rd Ste 2 (14626-3046)
PHONE.................585 723-1010
Vic Bannayan, *President*
EMP: 5
SQ FT: 2,480
SALES (est): 370K **Privately Held**
SIC: 3911 7631 5944 Jewelry, precious metal; jewelry repair services; jewelry stores

(G-13682)
BURKE FRGING HEAT TREATING INC
30 Sherer St (14611-1618)
PHONE.................585 235-6060
Ronald Thompson, *Ch of Bd*
James Granville, *Vice Pres*
Martha Vanderhoof, *Treasurer*
EMP: 24
SQ FT: 58,000
SALES (est): 5.4MM **Privately Held**
SIC: 3462 3398 Iron & steel forgings; metal heat treating

(G-13683)
BURNETT PROCESS INC (HQ)
545 Colfax St (14606-3111)
PHONE.................585 254-8080
Jack Cannon, *Ch of Bd*
Scott Peters, *Design Engr*
Ronald Salayda, *Manager*
▲ **EMP:** 1
SQ FT: 60,000
SALES (est): 5.4MM
SALES (corp-wide): 38.7MM **Privately Held**
WEB: www.burnettprocessinc.com
SIC: 3296 3086 7699 Fiberglass insulation; plastics foam products; industrial equipment services
PA: Cannon Industries, Inc.
525 Lee Rd
Rochester NY 14606
585 254-8080

(G-13684)
BURNETT PROCESS INC
545 Colfax St (14606-3111)
PHONE.................585 277-1623
Ronald Salayda, *Manager*
EMP: 30
SALES (corp-wide): 38.7MM **Privately Held**
WEB: www.burnettprocessinc.com
SIC: 3569 Filters
HQ: Burnett Process, Inc.
545 Colfax St
Rochester NY 14606
585 254-8080

(G-13685)
C J WINTER MACHINE TECH (HQ)
167 Ames St (14611-1701)
PHONE.................585 429-5000
Robert Brinkman, *President*
Joe Palma, *Senior Buyer*
Paul Allart, *Engineer*
Philip Daggar, *Treasurer*
EMP: 20 **EST:** 1933
SQ FT: 118,000
SALES (est): 4MM
SALES (corp-wide): 106.6MM **Privately Held**
WEB: www.cjwinter.com
SIC: 3545 3542 3325 Thread cutting dies; machine tools, metal forming type; steel foundries
PA: Brinkman International Group, Inc.
167 Ames St
Rochester NY 14611
585 429-5000

(G-13686)
C R C MANUFACTURING INC
37 Curlew St (14606-2535)
PHONE.................585 254-8820
Todd Chapman, *CEO*
Brian Van Ocker, *Admin Sec*
EMP: 10
SQ FT: 7,000
SALES (est): 1.1MM **Privately Held**
SIC: 3599 3451 Mfg Industrial Machinery Mfg Machine Products

(G-13687)
CALIBER IMGING DIAGNOSTICS INC (PA)
50 Methodist Hill Dr (14623-4267)
PHONE.................585 239-9800
L Michael Hone, *CEO*
William J Shea, *Ch of Bd*
William J Fox, *Vice Pres*
Joseph R Williams, *Vice Pres*
Karen Howe, *CFO*

GEOGRAPHIC SECTION

Rochester - Monroe County (G-13715)

EMP: 35
SQ FT: 20,000
SALES (est): 3.3MM **Publicly Held**
WEB: www.lucid-tech.com
SIC: 3827 3845 3841 Optical instruments & lenses; electromedical equipment; surgical & medical instruments

(G-13688)
CAMPUS CRAFTS INC
160 Murray St (14606-1151)
P.O. Box 60650 (14606-0650)
PHONE..................585 328-6780
Greg Weinrieb, *President*
Kathleen Weinrieb, *Corp Secy*
▲ EMP: 6 EST: 1970
SQ FT: 7,000
SALES (est): 744.1K **Privately Held**
WEB: www.campuscrafts.com
SIC: 3231 Strengthened or reinforced glass; mirrored glass

(G-13689)
CANFIELD & TACK INC
Also Called: Dellas Graphics
925 Exchange St (14608-2802)
PHONE..................585 235-7710
Michael Guche, *CEO*
Ray Brown, *President*
Gary Cvejic, *COO*
EMP: 85 EST: 1926
SQ FT: 45,000
SALES (est): 25.9MM **Privately Held**
WEB: www.canfieldtack.com
SIC: 2752 4225 Commercial printing, offset; general warehousing & storage

(G-13690)
CANNON INDUSTRIES INC (PA)
525 Lee Rd (14606-4236)
PHONE..................585 254-8080
Jack Cannon, *CEO*
Reggie Cannon, *President*
Kiet Tran, *Plant Mgr*
Dean Rudy, *CFO*
Eric Flood, *Human Res Mgr*
▲ EMP: 97
SQ FT: 100,000
SALES (est): 38.7MM **Privately Held**
WEB: www.cannonind.com
SIC: 3444 3469 5051 3861 Sheet metalwork; metal stampings; metals service centers & offices; photocopy machines

(G-13691)
CAPS TEAMWEAR INC
65 Milburn St (14607-2914)
PHONE..................585 663-1750
Roy Brewer Jr, *Manager*
EMP: 5
SALES (est): 353K **Privately Held**
SIC: 2329 Men's & boys' sportswear & athletic clothing

(G-13692)
CARESTREAM HEALTH INC
1669 Lake Ave (14652-0001)
PHONE..................585 627-1800
EMP: 300
SALES (corp-wide): 24.5B **Privately Held**
SIC: 3861 Photographic equipment & supplies
HQ: Carestream Health, Inc.
150 Verona St
Rochester NY 14608

(G-13693)
CARTA USA LLC
1600 Lexington Ave # 116 (14606-3061)
PHONE..................585 436-3012
Mike Welch, *General Mgr*
Jake Carey, *Vice Pres*
▲ EMP: 20 EST: 1992
SALES (est): 511.6K
SALES (corp-wide): 149.1MM **Privately Held**
SIC: 2621 Paper mills
PA: Flower City Printing, Inc.
1725 Mount Read Blvd
Rochester NY 14606
585 663-9000

(G-13694)
CARTER STREET BAKERY INC
580 Child St (14606)
PHONE..................585 749-7104
Takele Delnesa, *President*
EMP: 8 EST: 2015
SALES (est): 408.2K **Privately Held**
SIC: 2051 Bakery: wholesale or wholesale/retail combined

(G-13695)
CASUAL FRIDAY INC
1561 Lyell Ave (14606-2123)
PHONE..................585 544-9470
Anthony Germano, *President*
Renee Yell, *Art Dir*
EMP: 12
SQ FT: 6,000
SALES (est): 1.6MM **Privately Held**
SIC: 2396 2395 Fabric printing & stamping; embroidery products, except schiffli machine

(G-13696)
CDJ STAMPING INC
146 Halstead St Ste 123 (14610-1954)
PHONE..................585 224-8120
Timothy Merklinger, *President*
Tim Merklinger, *Vice Pres*
Jason Schulmerich, *Vice Pres*
EMP: 5
SQ FT: 4,000
SALES (est): 442.8K **Privately Held**
WEB: www.cdjstamping.com
SIC: 3089 Injection molding of plastics; plastic processing

(G-13697)
CEIPAL LLC
722 Weiland Rd (14626-3957)
PHONE..................585 351-2934
EMP: 5 EST: 2014
SQ FT: 3,000
SALES (est): 300K **Privately Held**
SIC: 7372 Prepackaged Software Services

(G-13698)
CEIPAL LLC
687 Lee Rd Ste 208a (14606-4257)
PHONE..................585 584-1316
Deepika Nampally, *Sales Staff*
Sameer Penakalapati, *Mng Member*
Mitch Meller,
EMP: 5
SALES (est): 234.5K **Privately Held**
SIC: 7372 Application computer software

(G-13699)
CELLEC TECHNOLOGIES INC
125 Tech Park Dr Ste 2111 (14623-2448)
PHONE..................585 454-9166
Christopher Schauerman, *President*
Brian Landi, *Vice Pres*
Ryne Raffaelle, *Vice Pres*
Matthew Ganter, *Treasurer*
EMP: 5
SALES (est): 252.9K **Privately Held**
SIC: 3691 Storage batteries

(G-13700)
CENTERLESS TECHNOLOGY INC
45 Wells St (14611-2821)
PHONE..................585 436-2240
Daniel Burns, *President*
Jim Ozminskowski, *Corp Secy*
Les Malovics, *Vice Pres*
EMP: 10
SQ FT: 11,000
SALES (est): 1.6MM **Privately Held**
WEB: www.centerlesstech.com
SIC: 3599 Machine & other job shop work

(G-13701)
CENTURY MOLD COMPANY INC (PA)
25 Vantage Point Dr (14624-1142)
PHONE..................585 352-8600
Ron Ricotta, *CEO*
Jacob Vinocour, *President*
David Dick, *Exec VP*
Meg Collins, *Vice Pres*
Jeff Ricotta, *Plant Mgr*
▲ EMP: 100 EST: 1978
SQ FT: 80,000
SALES (est): 203.7MM **Privately Held**
WEB: www.centurymold.com
SIC: 3089 3544 Injection molding of plastics; industrial molds

(G-13702)
CENTURY MOLD MEXICO LLC (HQ)
25 Vantage Point Dr (14624-1142)
PHONE..................585 352-8600
Ronald Ricotta,
▲ EMP: 7
SALES (est): 49.2MM
SALES (corp-wide): 203.7MM **Privately Held**
SIC: 3089 Injection molding of plastics
PA: Century Mold Company, Inc.
25 Vantage Point Dr
Rochester NY 14624
585 352-8600

(G-13703)
CERION ENERGY INC
1 Blossom Rd (14610-1009)
PHONE..................585 271-5630
George M Stadler, *CEO*
Landon Mertz, *Ch of Bd*
Zach Lockhart, *Software Dev*
▼ EMP: 25
SALES (est): 4.5MM **Privately Held**
SIC: 2819 Industrial inorganic chemicals

(G-13704)
CERION LLC
1 Blossom Rd (14610-1009)
PHONE..................585 271-5630
George M Stadler,
EMP: 15
SALES (est): 2.8MM **Privately Held**
SIC: 2819 Industrial inorganic chemicals

(G-13705)
CHAMBERLIN RUBBER COMPANY INC
3333 Brighton Henrietta (14623-2842)
P.O. Box 22700 (14692-2700)
PHONE..................585 427-7780
Philip Collins, *President*
Stephen Anderson, *Vice Pres*
Stephen M Hayes, *Treasurer*
Andrew Chase, *Sales Mgr*
Sam Pennacchio, *Sales Staff*
▲ EMP: 31 EST: 1865
SQ FT: 30,000
SALES: 10MM **Privately Held**
WEB: www.crubber.com
SIC: 3069 Bags, rubber or rubberized fabric

(G-13706)
CHAMPION PHOTOCHEMISTRY INC
1669 Lake Ave (14615)
PHONE..................585 760-6444
R Fraser Mason, *Ch of Bd*
Peter Newton, *President*
◆ EMP: 65
SQ FT: 375,000
SALES (est): 10.4MM **Privately Held**
WEB: www.championphotochemistry.com
SIC: 3861 Photographic processing chemicals
HQ: Champion Photochemistry Limited
1760 Meyerside Dr
Mississauga ON L5T 1
905 670-7900

(G-13707)
CHAMTEK MFG INC
123 Louise St (14606-1321)
PHONE..................585 328-4900
Donald Zenkel, *President*
Thomas Williams, *Vice Pres*
Franklin Chamberlain, *Admin Sec*
EMP: 15
SQ FT: 18,000
SALES (est): 1.6MM **Privately Held**
WEB: www.chamtek.com
SIC: 3544 3444 Special dies & tools; sheet metalwork

(G-13708)
CHECKLIST BOARDS CORPORATION
763 Linden Ave Ste 2 (14625-2725)
PHONE..................585 586-0152
Rick Taylor, *President*
Jim Wemett, *Vice Pres*
EMP: 5
SALES: 500K **Privately Held**
SIC: 3993 Signs, not made in custom sign painting shops

(G-13709)
CHINA IMPRINT LLC
750 Saint Paul St (14605-1737)
PHONE..................585 563-3391
William A Dolan II,
▲ EMP: 5
SQ FT: 20,000
SALES: 2MM **Privately Held**
SIC: 2752 Promotional printing, lithographic

(G-13710)
CHRISTI PLASTICS INC
215 Tremont St (14608-2393)
PHONE..................585 436-8510
Earl Martin, *President*
Deborah Scally, *Treasurer*
EMP: 4
SQ FT: 10,500
SALES (est): 1.1MM **Privately Held**
SIC: 3089 Extruded finished plastic products

(G-13711)
CITY NEWSPAPER
250 N Goodman St Ste 1 (14607-1199)
PHONE..................585 244-3329
Mary Towler, *Publisher*
Jake Clapp, *Editor*
Eric Rezsnyak, *Editor*
Betsy Matthews, *Sales Mgr*
Christine Kubarycz, *Accounts Exec*
EMP: 8
SALES (est): 414.3K **Privately Held**
SIC: 2711 Commercial printing & newspaper publishing combined; newspapers, publishing & printing

(G-13712)
CJK MANUFACTURING LLC
160 Commerce Dr (14623-3504)
PHONE..................585 663-6370
Keith Woodward,
Charles Tutty,
EMP: 14
SQ FT: 20,000
SALES (est): 3.1MM **Privately Held**
WEB: www.cjkmanufacturing.com
SIC: 3089 Thermoformed finished plastic products

(G-13713)
CLARSONS CORP
Also Called: Express Press
215 Tremont St Ste 8 (14608-2366)
PHONE..................585 235-8775
David Clar, *President*
Robert M Clar, *President*
Joan Clar, *Admin Sec*
EMP: 11 EST: 1978
SQ FT: 4,000
SALES (est): 1MM **Privately Held**
WEB: www.expresspress.com
SIC: 2752 2791 7334 Commercial printing, offset; typesetting; photocopying & duplicating services

(G-13714)
CLERIO VISION INC
312 Susquehanna Rd (14618-2940)
PHONE..................617 216-7881
Mikael Totterman, *President*
EMP: 12
SQ FT: 2,000
SALES (est): 860K **Privately Held**
SIC: 3841 Surgical lasers

(G-13715)
COAST TO COAST CIRCUITS INC
Metro Circuits
205 Lagrange Ave (14613-1562)
PHONE..................585 254-2980
Walter Stender, *CEO*
Walt Stender, *CEO*
Cheryl Covert, *Principal*
Marry R McDonough, *Marketing Staff*
EMP: 45
SALES (corp-wide): 21.3MM **Privately Held**
WEB: www.speedycircuits.com
SIC: 3672 Wiring boards

Rochester - Monroe County (G-13716)

PA: Coast To Coast Circuits, Inc.
5331 Mcfadden Ave
Huntington Beach CA 92649
585 254-2980

(G-13716)
COATING TECHNOLOGY INC
800 Saint Paul St (14605-1032)
PHONE..........................585 546-7170
Stanley Dahle, *Ch of Bd*
Ronald L Feeley, *President*
EMP: 30
SQ FT: 40,000
SALES (est): 3.5MM
SALES (corp-wide): 17.1MM **Privately Held**
WEB: www.coatingtechnologyinc.com
SIC: 3471 Plating of metals or formed products
PA: The Metal Arts Company Inc
800 Saint Paul St
Rochester NY

(G-13717)
CONDOR ELECTRONICS CORP
295 Mount Read Blvd (14611-1931)
P.O. Box 60590 (14606-0590)
PHONE..........................585 235-1500
Wayne S Corso, *President*
Lisa Corso, *Corp Secy*
▲ **EMP:** 30
SQ FT: 18,000
SALES (est): 4.7MM **Privately Held**
WEB: www.condorelectronics.com
SIC: 3679 Harness assemblies for electronic use; wire or cable

(G-13718)
CONE BUDDY SYSTEM INC
3495 Winton Pl Ste E290 (14623-2819)
PHONE..........................585 427-9940
Robert Sotile, *President*
EMP: 15 **EST:** 1994
SALES (est): 1.4MM **Privately Held**
WEB: www.buddysystemusa.com
SIC: 2052 Cones, ice cream

(G-13719)
CONNECTION MOLD INC
585 Ling Rd (14612-1936)
PHONE..........................585 458-6463
Thomas Strecker, *President*
David Schwenger, *Design Engr*
EMP: 7
SQ FT: 6,800
SALES (est): 1MM **Privately Held**
WEB: www.connectionmold.com
SIC: 3965 Button blanks & molds

(G-13720)
CONOPCO INC
28 Mansfield St (14606-2327)
PHONE..........................585 647-8322
John Frank, *Branch Mgr*
EMP: 35
SALES (corp-wide): 63B **Privately Held**
SIC: 2844 Toilet preparations
HQ: Conopco, Inc.
700 Sylvan Ave
Englewood Cliffs NJ 07632
201 894-2727

(G-13721)
CONSOLIDATED CONTAINER CO LLC
Also Called: Liquitane
18 Champeney Ter (14605-2711)
PHONE..........................585 262-6470
Jerry Zaklick, *Plant Mgr*
EMP: 150
SALES (corp-wide): 13.7B **Publicly Held**
WEB: www.ccellc.com
SIC: 2655 2656 Fiber cans, drums & containers; sanitary food containers
HQ: Consolidated Container Company, Llc
2500 Windy Ridge Pkwy Se
Atlanta GA 30339
678 742-4600

(G-13722)
CORBETT STVES PTTERN WORKS INC
80 Lowell St (14605-1831)
PHONE..........................585 546-7109
John K Steeves Jr, *President*
Kevin Steeves, *Vice Pres*
Jorge Williams, *Engineer*
EMP: 20 **EST:** 1914
SQ FT: 20,000
SALES (est): 3.3MM **Privately Held**
WEB: www.corbett-steeves.com
SIC: 3365 3599 3553 3469 Machinery castings, aluminum; machine shop, jobbing & repair; pattern makers' machinery, woodworking; patterns on metal

(G-13723)
CRAFTSMAN MANUFACTURING CO IN
1279 Mount Read Blvd (14606-2817)
PHONE..........................585 426-5780
Kevin Contestabile, *President*
EMP: 5
SQ FT: 3,000
SALES: 320K **Privately Held**
SIC: 3599 Machine shop, jobbing & repair

(G-13724)
CRATER SERVICE GROUP INC
111 Humboldt St (14609-7463)
PHONE..........................585 482-7770
Craig Schinsing, *President*
EMP: 9
SQ FT: 8,000
SALES (est): 1.5MM **Privately Held**
WEB: www.rygan.com
SIC: 2752 Commercial printing, offset

(G-13725)
CRYOVAC INC
1525 Brooks Ave (14624-3545)
PHONE..........................585 436-3211
Mark Davis, *Manager*
EMP: 150
SALES (corp-wide): 4.4B **Publicly Held**
WEB: www.cryovac.com
SIC: 3087 Custom compound purchased resins
HQ: Cryovac, Inc.
2415 Cascade Pointe Blvd
Charlotte NC 28208
980 430-7000

(G-13726)
CRYSTAL LINTON TECHNOLOGIES
2180 Brigh Henri Town Lin (14623)
PHONE..........................585 444-8784
Rick Webb, *COO*
Melissa Logan, *Manager*
EMP: 11 **EST:** 2013
SQ FT: 15,713
SALES (est): 2.6MM **Privately Held**
SIC: 3821 Furnaces, laboratory

(G-13727)
CSW INC
Also Called: Diegraphics Group
70 Pixley Industrial Pkwy (14624-2377)
PHONE..........................585 247-4010
Jim Mootz, *Finance*
Wray Richardson, *Cust Mgr*
Joe Marciano, *Sales Staff*
Ed Reynolds, *Branch Mgr*
Charles Myers, *Info Tech Mgr*
EMP: 15
SALES (est): 3MM
SALES (corp-wide): 15.8MM **Privately Held**
WEB: www.citystamp.com
SIC: 3555 2796 2791 Printing plates; platemaking services; typesetting
PA: Csw, Inc.
45 Tyburski Rd
Ludlow MA 01056
413 589-1311

(G-13728)
CUMMINS-WAGNER-SIEWERT LLC (HQ)
Also Called: Kineflow Division
175 Akron St (14609-7209)
PHONE..........................585 482-9640
Doug Ardimger, *President*
Bruce Collins, *Manager*
Vera Rusco,
EMP: 43
SQ FT: 15,000
SALES (est): 11.7MM
SALES (corp-wide): 83.3MM **Privately Held**
WEB: www.siewertequipment.com
SIC: 3519 5084 Internal combustion engines; pumps & pumping equipment
PA: Cummins-Wagner Company, Inc.
10901 Pump House Rd
Annapolis Junction MD 20701
410 792-4230

(G-13729)
CURAEGIS TECHNOLOGIES INC (PA)
1999 Mount Read Blvd # 3 (14615-3700)
PHONE..........................585 254-1100
Richard A Kaplan, *CEO*
Gary A Siconolfi, *Ch of Bd*
Keith E Gleasman, *President*
Kathleen A Browne, *CFO*
EMP: 24
SQ FT: 13,650
SALES: 39K **Publicly Held**
WEB: www.torvec.com
SIC: 7372 3561 Business oriented computer software; pumps & pumping equipment

(G-13730)
CUSTOM SOUND AND VIDEO
Also Called: Casco Security
40 Rutter St (14606-1806)
PHONE..........................585 424-5000
Casimer S Plonczynski, *President*
Rosa F Ladelfa, *Business Mgr*
EMP: 20
SQ FT: 6,500
SALES (est): 2.2MM **Privately Held**
SIC: 3699 5731 7629 Security devices; radio, television & electronic stores; electronic equipment repair

(G-13731)
DAGOSTINO IRON WORKS INC
10 Deep Rock Rd (14624-3520)
PHONE..........................585 235-8850
Kenneth D'Agostino Jr, *President*
Kenneth J D'Agostino Jr, *President*
EMP: 9
SQ FT: 4,000
SALES (est): 1.3MM **Privately Held**
SIC: 3449 5051 5999 Bars, concrete reinforcing: fabricated steel; steel; alcoholic beverage making equipment & supplies

(G-13732)
DAILY RECORD (PA)
Also Called: Daily Media
16 W Main St Ste G9 (14614-1604)
PHONE..........................585 232-2035
Jim Dolan, *President*
EMP: 10
SQ FT: 36,000
SALES (est): 654K **Privately Held**
WEB: www.dailyrecord.com
SIC: 2752 2711 Commercial printing, lithographic; newspapers, publishing & printing

(G-13733)
DANISCO US INC
Also Called: Genencor Division Danisco US
3490 Winton Pl (14623-2829)
PHONE..........................585 256-5200
Zhong Ren, *Opers Dir*
Robert Villas, *Manager*
EMP: 75
SALES (corp-wide): 62.4B **Publicly Held**
SIC: 2835 8731 2899 2869 In vitro & in vivo diagnostic substances; commercial physical research; chemical preparations; industrial organic chemicals
HQ: Danisco Us Inc.
925 Page Mill Rd
Palo Alto CA 94304
650 846-7500

(G-13734)
DANISCO US INC
Also Called: Genencor International
1700 Lexington Ave (14606-3140)
PHONE..........................585 277-4300
Thomas Mitchell, *Branch Mgr*
Edward Di Di Cesare, *Director*
EMP: 100
SALES (corp-wide): 62.4B **Publicly Held**
SIC: 2819 2087 Industrial inorganic chemicals; flavoring extracts & syrups
HQ: Danisco Us Inc.
925 Page Mill Rd
Palo Alto CA 94304
650 846-7500

(G-13735)
DAYTON ROGERS NEW YORK LLC
150 Fedex Way (14624-1174)
PHONE..........................585 349-4040
Ron Lowry, *CEO*
Rich Vanaernum, *General Mgr*
Thomas A Pilon, *Vice Pres*
Mark D Spiczka, *Treasurer*
Jerome Mattern, *Human Res Dir*
EMP: 60
SQ FT: 38,000
SALES (est): 8.6MM
SALES (corp-wide): 78.5MM **Privately Held**
SIC: 3469 Stamping metal for the trade
PA: Dayton Rogers Manufacturing Co.
8401 W 35w Service Dr Ne
Minneapolis MN 55449
763 717-6450

(G-13736)
DEAD RINGER LLC
2100 Brghton Hnrtta St375 (14623)
PHONE..........................585 355-4685
Kristian Meyer, *Vice Pres*
Jesse Erdle,
▲ **EMP:** 2 **EST:** 2011
SALES (est): 2.6MM **Privately Held**
SIC: 3423 5091 Hand & edge tools; sharpeners, sporting goods

(G-13737)
DEAL INTERNATIONAL INC
110 Halstead St Ste 1 (14610-1952)
P.O. Box 10088 (14610-0088)
PHONE..........................585 288-4444
Menish Damani, *President*
Alice Barbarito, *Manager*
Manish Damani, *Prgrmr*
▲ **EMP:** 26
SQ FT: 6,000
SALES (est): 5.1MM **Privately Held**
WEB: www.diihq.com
SIC: 2891 Sealants

(G-13738)
DEES AUDIO & VISION
347 Seneca Pkwy (14613-1416)
PHONE..........................585 719-9256
EMP: 5
SALES (est): 150K **Privately Held**
SIC: 3571 Electronics/Audio/Sales

(G-13739)
DIAMOND PACKAGING HOLDINGS LLC
111 Commerce Dr (14623-3503)
PHONE..........................585 334-8030
Dave Rydell, *Vice Pres*
Keith Robinson,
EMP: 8
SALES (est): 1MM **Privately Held**
SIC: 2657 3089 Food containers, folding: made from purchased material; air mattresses, plastic

(G-13740)
DIEMAX OF ROCHESTER INC
1555 Lyell Ave Ste 141 (14606-2147)
PHONE..........................585 288-3912
Richard J Oliver, *President*
Wayne Rotella, *Vice Pres*
Ryan Prue, *Treasurer*
▲ **EMP:** 7
SQ FT: 900
SALES (est): 998.2K **Privately Held**
WEB: www.diemax.com
SIC: 3544 Special dies & tools

(G-13741)
DIGITRONIK LABS INC
181 Saint Paul St Apt 6d (14604-1127)
PHONE..........................585 360-0043
Shawn Mott, *President*
Chris Coon, *Vice Pres*
Stephen Mokey, *Treasurer*
Michael Brundige, *Manager*

David Coon, *Admin Sec*
EMP: 12
SQ FT: 3,000
SALES: 1.2MM **Privately Held**
SIC: 3823 8731 8711 7371 Controllers for process variables, all types; computer (hardware) development; engineering services; custom computer programming services

(G-13742)
DIMENSION TECHNOLOGIES INC
Also Called: D T I
315 Mount Read Blvd Ste 5 (14611-1900)
PHONE..............................585 436-3530
Arnold Lagergren, *CEO*
Arnold D Lagergren, *President*
Michael Casciano, *President*
Jesse B Eichenlaub, *Vice Pres*
EMP: 5
SQ FT: 3,400
SALES (est): 1.1MM **Privately Held**
WEB: www.dti3d.com
SIC: 3679 Liquid crystal displays (LCD)

(G-13743)
DIPAOLO BAKING CO INC
598 Plymouth Ave N (14608-1691)
PHONE..............................585 303-5013
Dominick P Massa, *President*
Stephen Woerner, *Vice Pres*
Jim Acquilano, *Manager*
EMP: 80 **EST:** 1910
SQ FT: 30,000
SALES (est): 12.7MM **Privately Held**
WEB: www.dipaolobread.com
SIC: 2051 5461 Bread, all types (white, wheat, rye, etc); fresh or frozen; rolls, bread type: fresh or frozen; bakeries; bread

(G-13744)
DISTECH SYSTEMS INC (HQ)
1000 University Ave # 400 (14607-1286)
PHONE..............................585 254-7020
John J Perrotti, *CEO*
Dan Schwab, *President*
▲ **EMP:** 3
SQ FT: 12,900
SALES (est): 7.3MM
SALES (corp-wide): 1B **Privately Held**
WEB: www.distechsystems.com
SIC: 3569 Assembly machines, non-metal-working
PA: Gleason Corporation
1000 University Ave
Rochester NY 14607
585 473-1000

(G-13745)
DIVERSIFIED ENVELOPE LTD
95 Mount Read Blvd # 103 (14611-1923)
PHONE..............................585 615-4697
Fax: 585 527-8106
EMP: 10
SQ FT: 13,000
SALES: 1MM **Privately Held**
SIC: 2759 2752 5112 Commercial Printing Lithographic/Offset Commerrical Printing Whol Stationery/Office Supplies

(G-13746)
DIXON TOOL AND MANUFACTURING
240 Burrows St (14606-2637)
PHONE..............................585 235-1352
Rober Hyder, *President*
EMP: 10
SQ FT: 5,224
SALES (est): 1.4MM **Privately Held**
SIC: 3544 Dies, steel rule

(G-13747)
DOCK HARDWARE INCORPORATED
Also Called: Rogers Enterprises
24 Seneca Ave Ste 4 (14621-2502)
P.O. Box 17266 (14617-0266)
PHONE..............................585 266-7920
Garry Rogers, *President*
Mike Chiumento, *Director*
EMP: 10

SALES (est): 960K **Privately Held**
WEB: www.dockhardware.com
SIC: 3545 Machine tool accessories

(G-13748)
DOCUMENT STRATEGIES LLC
185 Gibbs St (14605-2907)
P.O. Box 16065 (14616-0065)
PHONE..............................585 506-9000
James Bowen, *Principal*
Jeremy Hutchinson, *Software Dev*
EMP: 12
SALES (est): 590.5K **Privately Held**
SIC: 7372 Application computer software

(G-13749)
DOLOMITE PRODUCTS COMPANY INC (DH)
Also Called: Shadow Lake Golf & Racquet CLB
1150 Penfield Rd (14625-2202)
PHONE..............................315 524-1998
John M Odenbach Jr, *President*
John Siel, *Chairman*
Gardner Odenbach, *Treasurer*
Russ Larocca, *Manager*
John Swierkos, *Manager*
EMP: 25 **EST:** 1920
SQ FT: 5,000
SALES (est): 26.2MM
SALES (corp-wide): 29.7B **Privately Held**
WEB: www.dolomitegroup.com
SIC: 2951 1422 5031 8741 Paving mixtures; dolomite, crushed & broken-quarrying; building materials, exterior; building materials, interior; circuit management for motion picture theaters; golf club, membership; golf, tennis & ski shops

(G-13750)
DRAPERY INDUSTRIES INC
175 Humboldt St Ste 222 (14610-1060)
PHONE..............................585 232-2992
Mark Kosinski, *President*
David Geen, *Vice Pres*
EMP: 14
SQ FT: 8,000
SALES (est): 1.6MM **Privately Held**
WEB: www.draperyindustries.com
SIC: 2391 2591 1799 Curtains, window: made from purchased materials; draperies, plastic & textile: from purchased materials; window blinds; home/office interiors finishing, furnishing & remodeling; drapery track installation

(G-13751)
DRT POWER SYSTEMS LLC
500 Mile Crossing Blvd (14624-6205)
PHONE..............................585 247-5940
EMP: 5 **Privately Held**
SIC: 3545 3761 3728 Precision tools, machinists'; guided missiles & space vehicles; aircraft parts & equipment
HQ: Drt Power Systems, Llc
8694 Rite Track Way
West Chester OH 45069
513 714-4488

(G-13752)
DYNA-TECH QUALITY INC
1570 Emerson St (14606-3118)
PHONE..............................585 458-9970
Andy Masters, *President*
EMP: 5 **EST:** 1998
SALES (est): 362.4K **Privately Held**
SIC: 3599 Machine shop, jobbing & repair

(G-13753)
DYNAMASTERS INC
1570 Emerson St (14606-3118)
PHONE..............................585 458-9970
Andy Mastrodonato Sr, *President*
EMP: 5 **EST:** 2008
SALES (est): 440K **Privately Held**
SIC: 3569 Assembly machines, non-metal-working

(G-13754)
DYNAMIC DIES INC
70 Pixley Industrial Pkwy (14624-2377)
PHONE..............................585 247-4010
Fax: 585 247-7203
EMP: 14

SALES (corp-wide): 22.2MM **Privately Held**
SIC: 3544 Mfg Dies/Tools/Jigs/Fixtures
PA: Dynamic Dies, Inc.
1705 Commerce Rd
Holland OH 43528
419 865-0249

(G-13755)
EAGLE GRAPHICS INC
149 Anderson Ave (14607-1106)
PHONE..............................585 244-5006
Nancy Powell, *President*
Michael W Powell, *Vice Pres*
EMP: 9 **EST:** 1977
SQ FT: 10,000
SALES (est): 1.6MM **Privately Held**
WEB: www.eaglegraphicsinc.com
SIC: 2752 Commercial printing, lithographic

(G-13756)
EAST PATTERN & MODEL CORP (PA)
769 Trabold Rd (14624-2547)
PHONE..............................585 461-3240
Warren H Kellogg, *President*
Mark Landers, *General Mgr*
Lisa Smyder, *Opers Mgr*
Michelle E Kellogg, *Treasurer*
Paul Dalba, *Prgrmr*
EMP: 26
SQ FT: 15,000
SALES: 3MM **Privately Held**
SIC: 3544 3089 3365 3275 Industrial molds; injection molding of plastics; aluminum foundries; gypsum products

(G-13757)
EAST PATTERN & MODEL CORP
80 Saginaw Dr (14623-3132)
PHONE..............................585 461-3240
Warren Kellogg, *President*
Carl Sudore, *Sales Staff*
EMP: 10
SALES (corp-wide): 3MM **Privately Held**
SIC: 3089 3544 3442 3365 Injection molding of plastics; special dies, tools, jigs & fixtures; metal doors, sash & trim; aluminum foundries
PA: East Pattern & Model Corp.
769 Trabold Rd
Rochester NY 14624
585 461-3240

(G-13758)
EAST RIDGE QUICK PRINT
1249 Ridgeway Ave Ste Y (14615-3761)
PHONE..............................585 266-4911
Richard San Angelo, *President*
Janice San Angelo, *Vice Pres*
EMP: 10
SQ FT: 6,000
SALES (est): 1.5MM **Privately Held**
WEB: www.eastridgequickprint.com
SIC: 2752 Commercial printing, offset

(G-13759)
EASTMAN CHEMICAL COMPANY
2255 Mount Read Blvd (14615)
PHONE..............................585 722-2905
Brian Bennett, *Research*
Anthony Debboli, *Manager*
EMP: 60 **Publicly Held**
WEB: www.eastman.com
SIC: 2821 Plastics materials & resins
PA: Eastman Chemical Company
200 S Wilcox Dr
Kirigsport TN 37660

(G-13760)
EASTMAN KODAK COMPANY
233 Olde Harbour Trl (14612-2936)
PHONE..............................585 722-2187
Gus Gleichauf, *Principal*
EMP: 65
SALES (corp-wide): 1.5B **Publicly Held**
SIC: 3861 Film, sensitized motion picture, X-ray, still camera, etc.
PA: Eastman Kodak Company
343 State St
Rochester NY 14650
585 724-4000

(G-13761)
EASTMAN KODAK COMPANY (PA)
343 State St (14650-0001)
PHONE..............................585 724-4000
Jeffrey J Clarke, *CEO*
James V Continenza, *Ch of Bd*
Eric-Yves Mahe, *President*
John O'Grady, *Senior VP*
Steven Overman, *Senior VP*
EMP: 277
SALES: 1.5B **Publicly Held**
SIC: 3861 3577 7384 Film, sensitized motion picture, X-ray, still camera, etc.; cameras, still & motion picture (all types); photographic paper & cloth, all types; computer peripheral equipment; graphic displays, except graphic terminals; optical scanning devices; photofinish laboratories

(G-13762)
EASTMAN KODAK COMPANY
1669 Lake Ave Bldg 31-4 (14652-0001)
PHONE..............................585 724-5600
Tim Kiehle, *Branch Mgr*
EMP: 60
SALES (corp-wide): 1.5B **Publicly Held**
SIC: 3861 Film, sensitized motion picture, X-ray, still camera, etc.
PA: Eastman Kodak Company
343 State St
Rochester NY 14650
585 724-4000

(G-13763)
EASTMAN KODAK COMPANY
39 Kaywood Dr (14626-3753)
PHONE..............................585 726-6261
Raul Santiago, *Branch Mgr*
EMP: 65
SALES (corp-wide): 1.5B **Publicly Held**
SIC: 3861 Film, sensitized motion picture, X-ray, still camera, etc.
PA: Eastman Kodak Company
343 State St
Rochester NY 14650
585 724-4000

(G-13764)
EASTMAN KODAK COMPANY
2600 Manitou Rd (14650-0001)
PHONE..............................585 724-4000
EMP: 74
SALES (corp-wide): 1.5B **Publicly Held**
SIC: 3861 Film, sensitized motion picture, X-ray, still camera, etc.
PA: Eastman Kodak Company
343 State St
Rochester NY 14650
585 724-4000

(G-13765)
EASTMAN KODAK COMPANY
343 State St (14650-0001)
PHONE..............................800 698-3324
Lori Perez, *Branch Mgr*
EMP: 15
SALES (corp-wide): 1.5B **Publicly Held**
SIC: 3861 Film, sensitized motion picture, X-ray, still camera, etc.
PA: Eastman Kodak Company
343 State St
Rochester NY 14650
585 724-4000

(G-13766)
EASTMAN KODAK COMPANY
1999 Lake Ave 6/83/RI (14650-0001)
PHONE..............................585 722-4385
Mary J Hellyar, *Branch Mgr*
EMP: 99
SALES (corp-wide): 1.5B **Publicly Held**
SIC: 3861 Film, sensitized motion picture, X-ray, still camera, etc.
PA: Eastman Kodak Company
343 State St
Rochester NY 14650
585 724-4000

(G-13767)
EASTMAN KODAK COMPANY
300 Weiland Road (14650-0001)
PHONE..............................585 588-5598
EMP: 78

Rochester - Monroe County (G-13768) GEOGRAPHIC SECTION

SALES (corp-wide): 1.5B **Publicly Held**
SIC: 3861 Film, sensitized motion picture, X-ray, still camera, etc.
PA: Eastman Kodak Company
343 State St
Rochester NY 14650
585 724-4000

(G-13768)
EASTMAN KODAK COMPANY
343 State St (14650-0001)
PHONE.....................585 726-7000
Alan Priebe, *Technology*
EMP: 130
SALES (corp-wide): 1.5B **Publicly Held**
SIC: 3861 Film, sensitized motion picture, X-ray, still camera, etc.
PA: Eastman Kodak Company
343 State St
Rochester NY 14650
585 724-4000

(G-13769)
EASTMAN KODAK COMPANY
336 Initiative Dr (14624-6217)
PHONE.....................585 722-4007
Daniel Percey, *District Mgr*
Susan Shattuck, *Purch Agent*
Roger Lowry, *Director*
Rita Amin, *Executive Asst*
EMP: 5
SQ FT: 14,909
SALES (corp-wide): 1.5B **Publicly Held**
SIC: 3861 Film, sensitized motion picture, X-ray, still camera, etc.
PA: Eastman Kodak Company
343 State St
Rochester NY 14650
585 724-4000

(G-13770)
EASTMAN KODAK COMPANY
100 Latona Rd Gate 340 (14652-0001)
PHONE.....................585 588-3896
Jack Kosoff, *Branch Mgr*
EMP: 78
SALES (corp-wide): 1.5B **Publicly Held**
SIC: 3861 Film, sensitized motion picture, X-ray, still camera, etc.
PA: Eastman Kodak Company
343 State St
Rochester NY 14650
585 724-4000

(G-13771)
EASTMAN KODAK COMPANY
343 State St (14650-0001)
P.O. Box 15399 (14615-0399)
PHONE.....................585 724-4000
EMP: 39
SALES (corp-wide): 1.5B **Publicly Held**
SIC: 3861 Photographic equipment & supplies
PA: Eastman Kodak Company
343 State St
Rochester NY 14650
585 724-4000

(G-13772)
EASTMAN PARK MICROGRAPHICS INC
100 Latona Rd Bldg 318 (14652-0001)
PHONE.....................866 934-4376
William D Oates, *President*
Robert Breslawski, *Manager*
Susanna Records, *Info Tech Mgr*
EMP: 8
SALES (est): 889.5K **Privately Held**
SIC: 3861 Film, sensitized motion picture, X-ray, still camera, etc.
PA: Eastman Park Micrographics Inc
6300 Cedar Springs Rd
Dallas TX 75235

(G-13773)
EBERHARDT ENTERPRISES INC
1325 Mount Read Blvd (14606-2819)
PHONE.....................585 458-7681
Peter Eberhardt, *President*
▲ EMP: 10 EST: 1979
SQ FT: 18,000
SALES (est): 1.4MM **Privately Held**
SIC: 3544 Special dies, tools, jigs & fixtures

(G-13774)
EIS INC
Also Called: Light Fabrications
40 Hytec Cir (14606-4255)
PHONE.....................585 426-5330
Jim Cucinelli, *Principal*
EMP: 48
SALES (corp-wide): 16.3B **Publicly Held**
SIC: 2672 3842 7699 Adhesive backed films, foams & foils; adhesive papers, labels or tapes: from purchased material; adhesive tape & plasters, medicated or non-medicated; industrial equipment services
HQ: Eis, Inc.
2018 Powers Ferry Rd Se # 500
Atlanta GA 30339
678 255-3600

(G-13775)
ELAB SMOKERS BOUTIQUE
4373 Lake Ave (14612-4864)
PHONE.....................585 865-4513
Steve J Glover, *Partner*
Steve Glover, *Partner*
Mark Landon, *Partner*
EMP: 5
SALES (est): 621.1K **Privately Held**
SIC: 2131 5621 Chewing & smoking tobacco; boutiques

(G-13776)
ELECTRONICS & INNOVATION LTD
150 Research Blvd (14623-3436)
PHONE.....................585 214-0598
Tony Harris, *President*
John Andrews, *Vice Pres*
▼ EMP: 10
SALES (est): 2MM **Privately Held**
WEB: www.electronicsandinnovation.com
SIC: 3679 Parametric amplifiers; electronic circuits

(G-13777)
ELO TOUCH SOLUTIONS INC
2245 Brdgtn Hnrtta Twn Ln (14623)
PHONE.....................585 427-2802
Craig Witsoe, *CEO*
Jim Melton, *Vice Pres*
Sean Miller, *Vice Pres*
Dave Renner, *Vice Pres*
Bruno Thuillier, *Vice Pres*
▲ EMP: 21 EST: 2012
SALES (est): 4.6MM **Privately Held**
SIC: 3571 Computers, digital, analog or hybrid

(G-13778)
EMERSON & OLIVER LLC
44 Elton St (14607-1216)
PHONE.....................585 775-9929
Laura Bascomb-Werth, *Principal*
EMP: 5
SALES (est): 412.5K **Privately Held**
SIC: 2339 Women's & misses' outerwear

(G-13779)
EMPIRE FABRICATORS INC
Also Called: Cusimano, Michael
95 Saginaw Dr (14623-3131)
PHONE.....................585 235-3050
Michael Cusimano, *President*
Chad Cusimano, *Vice Pres*
Marty Elliott, *Production*
EMP: 7
SQ FT: 10,000
SALES (est): 1.1MM **Privately Held**
WEB: www.empirefabricators.com
SIC: 2541 5084 Counter & sink tops; countersinks

(G-13780)
EMPIRE METAL FABRICATORS INC
1385 Empire Blvd Ste 3 (14609-5915)
PHONE.....................585 288-2140
John Singer, *President*
EMP: 7
SQ FT: 4,000
SALES: 520K **Privately Held**
SIC: 3441 Fabricated structural metal

(G-13781)
EMPIRE OPTICAL INC
1249 Ridgeway Ave Ste P (14615-3761)
P.O. Box 40320 (14604-0820)
PHONE.....................585 454-4470
James Willoth, *President*
Barbara Willoth, *Treasurer*
EMP: 12
SQ FT: 2,400
SALES (est): 1MM **Privately Held**
SIC: 3851 Lens grinding, except prescription: ophthalmic

(G-13782)
ENBI INDIANA INC
1661 Lyell Ave (14606-2311)
PHONE.....................585 647-1627
Tuan Doan, *Opers Staff*
Darren Kraft, *Engineer*
Mike McMindes, *Branch Mgr*
Kim Cina, *Manager*
EMP: 25
SALES (est): 6.3MM
SALES (corp-wide): 44.9MM **Privately Held**
SIC: 3069 Printers' rolls & blankets: rubber or rubberized fabric
PA: Indiana Enbi Inc
1703 Mccall Dr
Shelbyville IN 46176
317 398-3267

(G-13783)
ENERGY HARVESTERS LLC
Also Called: Walking Charger, The
63 Garden Dr (14609-4342)
PHONE.....................617 325-9852
Lawrence Grumer, *CEO*
Sherry Handel, *COO*
EMP: 5
SALES (est): 46.6K **Privately Held**
SIC: 3629 Electrical industrial apparatus

(G-13784)
ENERGY MATERIALS CORPORATION
1999 Lake Ave (14650-0001)
PHONE.....................315 247-0880
Stephan Deluca, *CEO*
Leslie Fritzemeier, *Exec VP*
Scott Stewart, *Treasurer*
Les Fritzemeier, *Exec Dir*
EMP: 5
SALES (est): 257.6K **Privately Held**
SIC: 3674 Semiconductors & related devices

(G-13785)
ENGRAV-O-TYPE PRESS INC
Also Called: Epi Printing & Finishing
30 Bermar Park Ste 2 (14624-1541)
PHONE.....................585 262-7590
Rick Speciale, *President*
Richard Porreca, *Prdtn Mgr*
Emile L Speciale Jr, *Treasurer*
Mandy Paige, *Office Mgr*
EMP: 17
SQ FT: 12,000
SALES (est): 3.5MM **Privately Held**
WEB: www.epiprinting.com
SIC: 2752 Commercial printing, offset

(G-13786)
ENI MKS PRODUCTS GROUP
100 Highpower Rd (14623-3498)
PHONE.....................585 427-8300
Paul Eyerman, *Principal*
▲ EMP: 11
SALES (est): 1.6MM
SALES (corp-wide): 1.9B **Publicly Held**
SIC: 3663 Airborne radio communications equipment
PA: Mks Instruments, Inc.
2 Tech Dr Ste 201
Andover MA 01810
978 645-5500

(G-13787)
ENI TECHNOLOGY INC (HQ)
100 Highpower Rd (14623-3498)
PHONE.....................585 427-8300
John R Bertucci, *CEO*
Edward Maier, *General Mgr*
Michael Laska, *Engineer*
Jon Smyka, *Engineer*
Dan Barnes, *Finance*

▲ EMP: 500
SQ FT: 160,000
SALES (est): 24.9MM
SALES (corp-wide): 1.9B **Publicly Held**
WEB: www.enipower.com
SIC: 3679 3677 3663 3621 Electronic loads & power supplies; electronic coils, transformers & other inductors; radio & TV communications equipment; motors & generators
PA: Mks Instruments, Inc.
2 Tech Dr Ste 201
Andover MA 01810
978 645-5500

(G-13788)
EPP TEAM INC
Also Called: Empire Precision Plastics
500 Lee Rd Ste 400 (14606-4260)
PHONE.....................585 454-4995
Neal P Elli, *Ch of Bd*
Bob Zygulski, *COO*
Rick Wilson, *Vice Pres*
Eric Canaday, *Opers Spvr*
Hilton Ridley, *Production*
▲ EMP: 82
SQ FT: 45,000
SALES (est): 17.2MM **Privately Held**
WEB: www.empireprecision.com
SIC: 3089 Injection molded finished plastic products; injection molding of plastics

(G-13789)
ERDLE PERFORATING HOLDINGS INC (PA)
100 Pixley Indus Pkwy (14624-2325)
PHONE.....................585 247-4700
Frank Pfau, *President*
Thomas J Pariso, *Exec VP*
Clint Stevens, *Safety Mgr*
Ginny Randisi, *Accounts Exec*
EMP: 100 EST: 1870
SQ FT: 92,000
SALES (est): 25.3MM **Privately Held**
SIC: 3469 Perforated metal, stamped

(G-13790)
ERNIE GREEN INDUSTRIES INC
Also Called: Eg Industries
85 Pixley Industrial Pkwy (14624-2322)
PHONE.....................585 295-8951
EMP: 100
SALES (corp-wide): 580.4MM **Privately Held**
SIC: 3089 Injection molding of plastics
PA: Ernie Green Industries, Inc.
2030 Dividend Dr
Columbus OH 43228
614 219-1423

(G-13791)
ERNIE GREEN INDUSTRIES INC
Also Called: Eg Industries
1667 Emerson St (14606-3119)
PHONE.....................585 647-2300
Aaron Leighton, *Controller*
Nartign Vanmanen, *Manager*
EMP: 240
SALES (corp-wide): 582.7MM **Privately Held**
SIC: 3089 Injection molding of plastics; blow molded finished plastic products
PA: Ernie Green Industries, Inc.
2030 Dividend Dr
Columbus OH 43228
614 219-1423

(G-13792)
ERNIE GREEN INDUSTRIES INC
Also Called: Eg Indsturies
460 Buffalo Rd Ste 220 (14611-2022)
PHONE.....................585 647-2300
EMP: 100
SALES (corp-wide): 582.7MM **Privately Held**
SIC: 3089 Injection molding of plastics; blow molded finished plastic products
PA: Ernie Green Industries, Inc.
2030 Dividend Dr
Columbus OH 43228
614 219-1423

GEOGRAPHIC SECTION

Rochester - Monroe County (G-13820)

(G-13793)
ESTEBANIA ENTERPRISES INC
Also Called: Aries Precision Products
15 Mcardle St Ste A (14611-1513)
PHONE..................585 529-9330
Jose L Suro, *President*
EMP: 7
SQ FT: 9,600
SALES (est): 1.1MM **Privately Held**
WEB: www.connectorindustry.com
SIC: 3599 Mfg Industrial Machinery

(G-13794)
ET PRECISION OPTICS INC
33 Curlew St (14606-2535)
PHONE..................585 254-2560
Thomas R Eckler, *President*
EMP: 71
SQ FT: 3,000
SALES (est): 12.6MM **Privately Held**
WEB: www.etprecision.com
SIC: 3599 Machine shop, jobbing & repair

(G-13795)
EVOLUTION IMPRESSIONS INC
160 Commerce Dr (14623-3504)
P.O. Box 12788 (14612-0788)
PHONE..................585 473-6600
Thomas A Gruber, *President*
Craig Miller, *Principal*
Mike Buell, *Vice Pres*
Thomas Kelly, *Vice Pres*
EMP: 60
SQ FT: 28,000
SALES (est): 6.8MM **Privately Held**
WEB: www.evolutionimpressions.com
SIC: 2752 7334 Commercial printing, lithographic; photocopying & duplicating services

(G-13796)
EXACT MACHINING & MFG
305 Commerce Dr Ste 7 (14623-3538)
PHONE..................585 334-7090
Dan Bleier, *President*
Tim Bleier, *Corp Secy*
Jay Pryor, *Vice Pres*
EMP: 5
SQ FT: 3,600
SALES (est): 638.2K **Privately Held**
SIC: 3599 Machine shop, jobbing & repair

(G-13797)
EXCELSUS SOLUTIONS LLC
12 Pixley Industrial Pkwy # 40 (14624-2364)
PHONE..................585 533-0003
Mark Laniak, *CEO*
David Laniak, *General Mgr*
Chris Laniak, *Production*
Gene Snyder, *Purchasing*
John Bennett, *CFO*
EMP: 24
SQ FT: 18,000
SALES (est): 5.2MM **Privately Held**
WEB: www.excelsussolutions.com
SIC: 2752 Commercial printing, lithographic

(G-13798)
EXIGO PRECISION INC
190 Murray St (14611-1126)
P.O. Box 60917 (14606-0917)
PHONE..................585 254-5818
EMP: 7
SALES (est): 499.5K **Privately Held**
SIC: 3599 Mfg Industrial Machinery

(G-13799)
EXPOSITOR NEWSPAPERS INC
Also Called: Rochester Golf Week
2535 Brighton Henrietta (14623-2711)
PHONE..................585 427-2468
Barbara Morgenstern, *President*
Dave Eaton, *Editor*
George Morgenstern, *Editor*
EMP: 6
SALES (est): 270K **Privately Held**
SIC: 2711 Newspapers: publishing only, not printed on site

(G-13800)
EYEWORKS INC
1249 Ridgeway Ave Ste M (14615-3761)
PHONE..................585 454-4770
Mark Keehammer, *President*
Elaine Kleehammer, *Vice Pres*
▲ EMP: 7
SALES: 950K **Privately Held**
SIC: 3851 Ophthalmic goods

(G-13801)
F OLIVERS LLC
747 Park Ave (14607-3020)
PHONE..................585 244-2585
Leah Wolanski, *Branch Mgr*
EMP: 5
SALES (corp-wide): 377.3K **Privately Held**
SIC: 2079 Olive oil
PA: F. Oliver's Llc
129 S Main St
Canandaigua NY 14424
585 396-2585

(G-13802)
FARO INDUSTRIES INC
340 Lyell Ave (14606-1697)
PHONE..................585 647-6000
Matthew Mc Conville, *President*
Lisa Abbott, *Admin Sec*
EMP: 17
SQ FT: 26,000
SALES (est): 3.3MM **Privately Held**
WEB: www.faroindustries.com
SIC: 3089 Injection molding of plastics; plastic processing

(G-13803)
FIELDTEX PRODUCTS INC
3055 Brighton Henrietta (14623-2749)
PHONE..................585 427-2940
Sanford R Abbey, *President*
Jonathan Abbey, *General Mgr*
Cynthia Helander, *Plant Mgr*
Jacqueline Dunn, *Purch Agent*
Julie Miller, *Sales Staff*
▲ EMP: 130
SQ FT: 40,000
SALES (est): 27.1MM **Privately Held**
WEB: www.e-firstaidsupplies.com
SIC: 3151 3161 Leather gloves & mittens; cases, carrying

(G-13804)
FINGER LAKES CHEMICALS INC (PA)
Also Called: Finger Lakes/Castle
420 Saint Paul St (14605-1734)
PHONE..................585 454-4760
Ewald Blatter, *President*
Hans Blatter, *Vice Pres*
EMP: 50
SQ FT: 100,000
SALES: 10MM **Privately Held**
WEB: www.castlepackspower.com
SIC: 2842 5169 Specialty cleaning preparations; chemicals & allied products

(G-13805)
FIRTH RIXSON INC (DH)
Also Called: Firth Rixson Monroe
181 Mckee Rd (14611-2011)
PHONE..................585 328-1383
David C Mortimer, *CEO*
Bob Lang, *Principal*
Sharma RAO, *Purchasing*
Andrew Maskery, *Controller*
Michelle Price, *Sales Associate*
◆ EMP: 80
SQ FT: 23,821
SALES (est): 111.7MM
SALES (corp-wide): 12.9B **Publicly Held**
WEB: www.firthrixson.com
SIC: 3462 Aircraft forgings, ferrous
HQ: Firth Rixson Limited
Centre Court Building
Sheffield S4 7Q
114 219-3000

(G-13806)
FIVE STAR TOOL CO INC
125 Elmgrove Park (14624-1359)
PHONE..................585 328-9580
Kenneth Klalonde, *President*
Brian Gallo, *Opers Staff*
Joanne Rizzitano, *Purchasing*
Mark Schaefer, *Design Engr*
Stan Yates, *Sales Executive*
EMP: 23 **EST:** 1965
SQ FT: 9,200

SALES (est): 4MM **Privately Held**
SIC: 3451 3541 Screw machine products; milling machines

(G-13807)
FLINT GROUP INCORPORATED
Also Called: Flint Ink North America Div
1128 Lexington Ave Bldg 3 (14606-2909)
PHONE..................585 458-1223
Harry Reeves, *Manager*
Michael Schirching, *Senior Mgr*
Rory Pelliccia, *Technician*
EMP: 26
SALES (corp-wide): 3.5B **Privately Held**
WEB: www.flintink.com
SIC: 2893 Printing ink
PA: Flint Group Us Llc
14909 N Beck Rd
Plymouth MI 48170
734 781-4600

(G-13808)
FLOWER CITY PRINTING INC (PA)
1725 Mount Read Blvd (14606-2827)
P.O. Box 60680 (14606-0680)
PHONE..................585 663-9000
George Scharr, *CEO*
Carin Laniak, *Vice Pres*
Patty Kuhn, *Human Res Dir*
Kathy Achter, *Accounts Mgr*
Dana Jenkins, *Accounts Exec*
EMP: 197
SQ FT: 135,000
SALES (est): 149.1MM **Privately Held**
WEB: www.flowercityprinting.com
SIC: 2657 2752 Folding paperboard boxes; commercial printing, offset

(G-13809)
FLOWER CITY PRINTING INC
1001 Lee Rd (14606-4243)
PHONE..................585 512-1235
Matt Bryant, *Principal*
EMP: 5
SALES (corp-wide): 149.1MM **Privately Held**
SIC: 2752 Commercial printing, lithographic
PA: Flower City Printing, Inc.
1725 Mount Read Blvd
Rochester NY 14606
585 663-9000

(G-13810)
FLOWER CY TISSUE MILLS CO INC (PA)
700 Driving Park Ave (14613-1506)
P.O. Box 13497 (14613-0497)
PHONE..................585 458-9200
William F Shafer, *Ch of Bd*
William F Shafer IV, *Vice Pres*
Thomas Myers, *Treasurer*
Don Macdonald, *Sales Dir*
Kathy Brooks, *Office Mgr*
▲ EMP: 50
SQ FT: 46,000
SALES (est): 8.7MM **Privately Held**
WEB: www.flowercitytissue.com
SIC: 2621 Wrapping paper

(G-13811)
FLUXDATA INCORPORATED
176 Anderson Ave Ste F304 (14607-1169)
PHONE..................800 425-0176
Pano Spiliotis, *President*
Lawrence Taplin, *CTO*
Tracie Spiliotis, *Officer*
EMP: 6
SQ FT: 4,665
SALES (est): 1.3MM
SALES (co, p-wide): 1.5B **Privately Held**
SIC: 3861 Aerial cameras
PA: Halma Public Limited Company
Misbourne Court
Amersham BUCKS HP7 0
149 472-1111

(G-13812)
FORBES PRECISION INC
100 Boxart St Ste 105 (14612-5658)
PHONE..................585 865-7069
Michael Forbes, *Ch of Bd*
EMP: 11
SQ FT: 3,000

SALES: 1MM **Privately Held**
SIC: 3599 Machine shop, jobbing & repair

(G-13813)
FORGE METAL FINISHING INC
383 Buell Rd (14624-3123)
PHONE..................585 730-7340
Mark Shaw, *President*
EMP: 6 **EST:** 2012
SQ FT: 10,000
SALES (est): 540.4K **Privately Held**
SIC: 3471 Anodizing (plating) of metals or formed products

(G-13814)
FORWARD ENTERPRISES INC
Also Called: Brewer & Newell Printing
250 Cumberland St Ste 100 (14605-2847)
PHONE..................585 235-7670
Gerald Ward, *President*
Lisa Fairchild, *General Mgr*
Melinda Ward, *Vice Pres*
EMP: 10 **EST:** 1921
SQ FT: 4,000
SALES (est): 1.2MM **Privately Held**
SIC: 2759 2752 Letterpress printing; commercial printing, offset

(G-13815)
FRAMING TECHNOLOGY INC
137 Syke St (14611-1738)
PHONE..................585 464-8470
Chris Hill, *President*
Jim Hartke, *Vice Pres*
John Bryce, *Engineer*
Daniel Johnstone, *Manager*
Angela Webb, *Manager*
▲ EMP: 20
SALES: 2.2MM **Privately Held**
WEB: www.framingtech.com
SIC: 3441 Fabricated structural metal

(G-13816)
FRANK J MARTELLO
Also Called: Countertop Creations
1227 Maple St (14611-1545)
PHONE..................585 235-2780
Frank J Martello, *Owner*
EMP: 6 **EST:** 1996
SQ FT: 6,000
SALES (est): 620.9K **Privately Held**
WEB: www.countertop-creations.com
SIC: 2541 Counter & sink tops

(G-13817)
FREETIME MAGAZINE INC
1255 University Ave # 270 (14607-1643)
PHONE..................585 473-2266
Thomas Cannon, *President*
EMP: 8 **EST:** 1977
SQ FT: 1,000
SALES (est): 430K **Privately Held**
WEB: www.freetime.com
SIC: 2711 Newspapers: publishing only, not printed on site

(G-13818)
FRESHOP INC
3246 Monroe Ave Ste 1 (14618-4628)
PHONE..................585 738-6035
Brian Moyer, *CEO*
Karthik Balasubramanian, *President*
EMP: 35
SQ FT: 20,000
SALES (est): 446.9K **Privately Held**
SIC: 7372 Application computer software

(G-13819)
FTT MEDICAL INC
Also Called: Electrosurgical Instrument Co
275 Commerce Dr (14623-3505)
PHONE..................585 444-0980
John Longuil, *CEO*
Karlee Schramm, *Executive Asst*
EMP: 8
SQ FT: 9,000
SALES (est): 1.3MM **Privately Held**
WEB: www.electrosurgicalinstrument.com
SIC: 3841 Surgical & medical instruments

(G-13820)
FULCRUM ACOUSTIC LLC
25 Circle St Ste 104 (14607-1072)
PHONE..................866 234-0678
Stephen Siegel, *President*
Rich Frembes,

Rochester - Monroe County (G-13821) — GEOGRAPHIC SECTION

EMP: 5
SALES (est): 1MM **Privately Held**
SIC: 3651 Household audio & video equipment

(G-13821)
GADABOUT USA WHEELCHAIRS INC
892 E Ridge Rd (14621-1718)
P.O. Box 17890 (14617-0890)
PHONE..................................585 338-2110
Michael Fonte, *President*
EMP: 15
SALES (est): 853.6K **Privately Held**
SIC: 3842 Wheelchairs

(G-13822)
GANNETT CO INC
Also Called: Democrat & Chronicle
245 E Main St (14604-2103)
PHONE..................................585 232-7100
Eric Gustavs, *Opers Mgr*
Linda Baird, *VP Human Res*
Brian Ambor, *Branch Mgr*
Dominic Chapman, *Manager*
Pam Dailey, *Manager*
EMP: 76
SALES (corp-wide): 3.1B **Publicly Held**
SIC: 2711 Newspapers, publishing & printing
PA: Gannett Co., Inc.
7950 Jones Branch Dr
Mc Lean VA 22102
703 854-6000

(G-13823)
GATTI TOOL & MOLD INC
997 Beahan Rd (14624-3548)
PHONE..................................585 328-1350
Gino Gatti, *President*
EMP: 12
SALES (est): 1.2MM **Privately Held**
WEB: www.gattitool.com
SIC: 3544 Manufactures Molds

(G-13824)
GE MDS LLC (HQ)
Also Called: Aferge Mds
175 Science Pkwy (14620-4260)
PHONE..................................585 242-9600
Henry Garcia, *Opers Mgr*
Stephen Cyran, *Engineer*
Anthony Tatta, *Engineer*
Thomas Hodge, *Senior Engr*
Jamal Hamdani,
◆ **EMP:** 200
SALES (est): 57.3MM
SALES (corp-wide): 122B **Publicly Held**
WEB: www.microwavedata.com
SIC: 3663 Radio & TV communications equipment
PA: General Electric Company
41 Farnsworth St
Boston MA 02210
617 443-3000

(G-13825)
GEM MANUFACTURING INC
853 West Ave Bldg 17a (14611-2413)
PHONE..................................585 235-1670
Scott Keller, *President*
EMP: 5
SQ FT: 7,000
SALES (est): 773.6K **Privately Held**
WEB: www.gemmachine.com
SIC: 3599 Machine shop, jobbing & repair

(G-13826)
GENENCOR INTERNATIONAL INC
3490 Winton Pl (14623-2829)
PHONE..................................585 256-5200
Walt Golembeski, *Manager*
EMP: 9
SALES (est): 928.3K **Privately Held**
SIC: 2869 Industrial organic chemicals

(G-13827)
GENERAL PLATING LLC
850 Saint Paul St Ste 10 (14605-1065)
PHONE..................................585 423-0830
Tom Schenkel, *Partner*
Don Schenkel, *Partner*
John Schenkel, *Partner*
Richard Schenkel, *Partner*
Roger Schenkel, *Partner*
EMP: 20 **EST:** 1890
SQ FT: 35,000
SALES: 658.8K **Privately Held**
SIC: 3471 Electroplating of metals or formed products

(G-13828)
GENERAL WELDING & FABG INC
60 Saginaw Dr Ste 4 (14623-3159)
PHONE..................................585 697-7660
Cheryl Lis, *Vice Pres*
EMP: 14
SALES (corp-wide): 5.7MM **Privately Held**
WEB: www.gwfab.com
SIC: 3713 5531 7539 Truck bodies & parts; trailer hitches, automotive; trailer repair
PA: General Welding & Fabricating, Inc.
991 Maple Rd
Elma NY 14059
716 652-0033

(G-13829)
GENESEE MANUFACTURING CO INC
566 Hollenbeck St (14621-2288)
PHONE..................................585 266-3201
Kevin Hite, *President*
Donald A Kohler Jr, *Vice Pres*
EMP: 9 **EST:** 1905
SQ FT: 8,000
SALES: 558.3K **Privately Held**
WEB: www.geneseemfg.com
SIC: 3545 5084 Cutting tools for machine tools; industrial machinery & equipment

(G-13830)
GENESIS DIGITAL IMAGING INC
150 Verona St (14608-1733)
PHONE..................................310 305-7358
Joseph Eliafan, *President*
EMP: 9
SALES (est): 1MM
SALES (corp-wide): 24.5B **Privately Held**
WEB: www.genesisdigitalimaging.com
SIC: 3844 Radiographic X-ray apparatus & tubes
HQ: Carestream Health, Inc.
150 Verona St
Rochester NY 14608

(G-13831)
GERMAN MACHINE & ASSEMBLY INC
226 Jay St (14608-1623)
PHONE..................................585 546-4200
Kim Beasley, *Ch of Bd*
Scott Boheen, *President*
EMP: 25
SALES (est): 3.5MM **Privately Held**
WEB: www.germanmach.com
SIC: 3469 Machine parts, stamped or pressed metal

(G-13832)
GERMANOW-SIMON CORPORATION
Also Called: G-S Plastic Optics
408 Saint Paul St (14605-1788)
PHONE..................................585 232-1440
Andrew Germanow, *Ch of Bd*
John Hultz, *Engineer*
Ken Saunders, *Engineer*
Kati Chenot, *Mktg Dir*
Bill Chiesi, *Manager*
◆ **EMP:** 40 **EST:** 1916
SQ FT: 125,000
SALES (est): 9MM **Privately Held**
WEB: www.gsoptics.com
SIC: 3089 3559 3829 3545 Plastic processing; plastics working machinery; thermometers, liquid-in-glass & bimetal type; machine tool accessories; pressed & blown glass

(G-13833)
GETINGE GROUP LOGISTICS AMERI
1777 E Henrietta Rd (14623-3133)
PHONE..................................585 475-1400
John Aymong, *President*
Steve Nesburg, *Area Mgr*
Michael Dupont, *Vice Pres*
Shen Lu, *Vice Pres*
Darren Pavitt, *Vice Pres*
▲ **EMP:** 174
SALES (est): 25.9MM
SALES (corp-wide): 2.6B **Privately Held**
SIC: 3842 Sterilizers, hospital & surgical
PA: Getinge Ab
Lindholmspiren 7a
Goteborg 417 5
103 350-000

(G-13834)
GETINGE USA INC (HQ)
1777 E Henrietta Rd (14623-3133)
PHONE..................................800 475-9040
Andrew Ray, *Ch of Bd*
Charles Carrier, *President*
Chad Carlton, *Managing Dir*
Jeff Carrig, *Area Mgr*
Charles Dacey, *Area Mgr*
▲ **EMP:** 150 **EST:** 1971
SQ FT: 250,000
SALES (est): 186.4MM
SALES (corp-wide): 2.6B **Privately Held**
SIC: 3842 3841 Sterilizers, hospital & surgical; surgical & medical instruments
PA: Getinge Ab
Lindholmspiren 7a
Goteborg 417 5
103 350-000

(G-13835)
GH INDUCTION ATMOSPHERES LLC
35 Industrial Park Cir (14624-2403)
PHONE..................................585 368-2120
Steven Skewes,
Dale Wilcox,
▲ **EMP:** 35
SQ FT: 19,000
SALES (est): 8.2MM
SALES (corp-wide): 1.4B **Publicly Held**
WEB: www.inductionatmospheres.com
SIC: 3542 Machine tools, metal forming type
PA: Park-Ohio Holdings Corp.
6065 Parkland Blvd Ste 1
Cleveland OH 44124
440 947-2000

(G-13836)
GLASSFAB INC
257 Ormond St (14605-3024)
P.O. Box 31880 (14603-1880)
PHONE..................................585 262-4000
Robert Saltzman, *Ch of Bd*
Daniel Saltzman, *President*
Tom Kirk, *COO*
Timothy Guenther, *QC Mgr*
George Dean, *Sales Staff*
▲ **EMP:** 30
SQ FT: 30,000
SALES (est): 6.1MM **Privately Held**
WEB: www.glassfab.com
SIC: 3231 Products of purchased glass

(G-13837)
GLASTEEL PARTS & SERVICES INC (DH)
1000 West Ave (14611-2442)
P.O. Box 23600 (14692-3600)
PHONE..................................585 235-1010
Gary Brewer, *President*
EMP: 50
SQ FT: 18,000
SALES (est): 9.2MM
SALES (corp-wide): 352.2K **Privately Held**
SIC: 3229 Pressed & blown glass
HQ: Pfaudler, Inc.
1000 West Ave
Rochester NY 14611
585 235-1000

(G-13838)
GLAXOSMITHKLINE LLC
1177 Winton Rd S (14618-2240)
PHONE..................................585 738-9025
EMP: 26
SALES (corp-wide): 39.8B **Privately Held**
SIC: 2834 Pharmaceutical preparations
HQ: Glaxosmithkline Llc
5 Crescent Dr
Philadelphia PA 19112
215 751-4000

(G-13839)
GLEASON CORPORATION (PA)
1000 University Ave (14607-1286)
P.O. Box 22970 (14692-2970)
PHONE..................................585 473-1000
Maria Austria, *President*
John J Perrotti, *President*
Satish Naik, *General Mgr*
Karl-Heinz K Bler, *Managing Dir*
Masa Tomizawa, *Managing Dir*
◆ **EMP:** 800
SQ FT: 721,400
SALES (est): 1B **Privately Held**
SIC: 3541 3829 Machine tools, metal cutting type; gear cutting & finishing machines; numerically controlled machine tools; machine tool replacement & repair parts, metal cutting types; physical property testing equipment

(G-13840)
GLEASON WORKS (HQ)
1000 University Ave (14607-1286)
P.O. Box 22970 (14692-2970)
PHONE..................................585 473-1000
James S Gleason, *Ch of Bd*
John J Perrotti, *President*
Nanci Malin Peck, *Vice Pres*
Edward J Pelta, *Vice Pres*
John W Pysnack, *Vice Pres*
◆ **EMP:** 925 **EST:** 1865
SQ FT: 721,000
SALES: 279.8MM
SALES (corp-wide): 1B **Privately Held**
WEB: www.gleason.com
SIC: 3714 3728 3566 3541 Gears, motor vehicle; gears, aircraft power transmission; gears, power transmission, except automotive; gear cutting & finishing machines; numerically controlled metal cutting machine tools; machine tool replacement & repair parts, metal cutting types; physical property testing equipment; metal stampings
PA: Gleason Corporation
1000 University Ave
Rochester NY 14607
585 473-1000

(G-13841)
GLOBAL PRECISION INDS INC
955 Millstead Way (14624-5107)
PHONE..................................585 254-0010
Mark Wheeler, *CEO*
Bob Nuccitelli, *President*
Ryan Moyer, *Opers Mgr*
EMP: 15
SALES (est): 3.2MM **Privately Held**
WEB: www.global-precision.com
SIC: 3599 Machine shop, jobbing & repair

(G-13842)
GM COMPONENTS HOLDINGS LLC
Also Called: Gmch Rochester
1000 Lexington Ave (14606-2810)
P.O. Box 92700 (14692-8800)
PHONE..................................585 647-7000
Chuck Gifford, *Principal*
Chris Kiellach, *Manager*
EMP: 350
SQ FT: 2,250 **Publicly Held**
SIC: 3714 Motor vehicle parts & accessories
HQ: Gm Components Holdings, Llc
300 Renaissance Ctr
Detroit MI 48243

(G-13843)
GOLD PRIDE PRESS INC
12 Pixley Industrial Pkwy # 40 (14624-2364)
PHONE..................................585 224-8800
Ted Rhodes, *Vice Pres*
EMP: 20
SQ FT: 30,000
SALES (est): 4.4MM **Privately Held**
WEB: www.goldpride.com
SIC: 2789 Trade binding services

▲ = Import ▼ = Export
◆ = Import/Export

GEOGRAPHIC SECTION
Rochester - Monroe County (G-13868)

(G-13844)
GRADIENT LENS CORPORATION
207 Tremont St Ste 1 (14608-2398)
PHONE 585 235-2620
Douglas Kindred, *President*
Linda Plate, *Business Mgr*
Leland Atkinson, *Vice Pres*
Duncan Moore, *Director*
EMP: 35
SQ FT: 9,500
SALES (est): 4.8MM **Privately Held**
WEB: www.gradientlens.com
SIC: 3827 Optical instruments & apparatus; interferometers

(G-13845)
GRAYWOOD COMPANIES INC (PA)
Also Called: Jasco Cutting Tools
1390 Mount Read Blvd (14606-2820)
P.O. Box 60497 (14606-0497)
PHONE 585 254-7000
John M Summers, *Ch of Bd*
Eugene Baldino, *President*
Dave Krigeer, *Vice Pres*
Sam Eberhard, *Purch Mgr*
Diane Simon, *CFO*
▲ **EMP:** 40 **EST:** 2005
SQ FT: 36,000
SALES (est): 89MM **Privately Held**
SIC: 3545 3544 3398 3541 Machine tool accessories; drill bits, metalworking; taps, machine tool; reamers, machine tool; special dies, tools, jigs & fixtures; metal heat treating; boring mills

(G-13846)
GSP COMPONENTS INC
1190 Brooks Ave (14624-3112)
PHONE 585 436-3377
Ronald J Motsay, *CEO*
Tim Lynn, *QC Mgr*
Debra Bennett, *Human Res Dir*
Eric Aldridge, *Manager*
Rick Palmer, *Director*
EMP: 62 **EST:** 1951
SQ FT: 34,000
SALES (est): 17.1MM **Privately Held**
WEB: www.gspcomponents.com
SIC: 3451 Screw machine products

(G-13847)
GUPP SIGNS INC
340 Lake Ave (14608-1077)
PHONE 585 244-5070
Larry Melrose, *President*
Nancy Melrose, *Vice Pres*
EMP: 5
SALES (est): 532.2K **Privately Held**
WEB: www.guppsigns.com
SIC: 3993 Signs & advertising specialties

(G-13848)
H RISCH INC
44 Saginaw Dr (14623-3132)
PHONE 585 442-0110
Sara Tartaglia, *CEO*
Michael Pauly, *President*
Tammy Omay, *Sales Staff*
Annie Pauly, *Executive*
EMP: 60 **EST:** 1935
SQ FT: 15,000
SALES (est): 9.1MM **Privately Held**
WEB: www.hrisch.com
SIC: 3089 Floor coverings, plastic

(G-13849)
H S ASSEMBLY INC
570 Hollandback (14605)
PHONE 585 266-4287
David Marcellus, *President*
Jeff Fregoe, *Design Engr*
EMP: 5
SALES (est): 605K **Privately Held**
WEB: www.hsassembly.com
SIC: 3541 8711 Machine tools, metal cutting type; engineering services

(G-13850)
H T SPECIALTY INC
70 Bermar Park (14624-1541)
PHONE 585 458-4060
Russel W Thiel, *President*
Donna Thiel, *Vice Pres*
Susan Thomas, *Office Mgr*
EMP: 18
SQ FT: 8,400
SALES: 2.2MM **Privately Held**
SIC: 3599 Machine shop, jobbing & repair

(G-13851)
HAMTRONICS INC
39 Willnick Cir (14626-4748)
PHONE 585 392-9430
G Francis Vogt, *President*
EMP: 7
SALES: 500K **Privately Held**
SIC: 3663 5961 Radio broadcasting & communications equipment; mail order house

(G-13852)
HANSON AGGREGATES PA LLC
1535 Scottsville Rd (14623-1934)
PHONE 585 436-3250
Jeff Kramarz, *Branch Mgr*
EMP: 15
SALES (corp-wide): 20.3B **Privately Held**
SIC: 2899 1442 Concrete curing & hardening compounds; gravel mining
HQ: Hanson Aggregates Pennsylvania, Llc
7660 Imperial Way
Allentown PA 18195
610 366-4626

(G-13853)
HARRIS CORPORATION
Harris Long Range Radio
1680 University Ave (14610-1887)
PHONE 585 244-5830
Madjid Abdi, *Principal*
Bob Griffith, *Opers Staff*
Dana Mehnert, *Branch Mgr*
Tony Dal Santo, *Sr Software Eng*
James Stoffel, *Bd of Directors*
EMP: 2600
SALES (corp-wide): 6.1B **Publicly Held**
SIC: 3663 Radio & TV communications equipment
PA: Harris Corporation
1025 W Nasa Blvd
Melbourne FL 32919
321 727-9100

(G-13854)
HARRIS CORPORATION
400 Initiative Dr (14624-6219)
P.O. Box 60488 (14606-0488)
PHONE 585 269-6600
Christopher Young, *CEO*
William Brown, *President*
William Gattle, *President*
David Melcher, *President*
Heather Fernandez, *Accounts Mgr*
EMP: 800
SALES (corp-wide): 6.1B **Publicly Held**
SIC: 3812 Space vehicle guidance systems & equipment
PA: Harris Corporation
1025 W Nasa Blvd
Melbourne FL 32919
321 727-9100

(G-13855)
HARRIS CORPORATION
800 Lee Rd Bldg 601 (14606-4248)
P.O. Box 60488 (14606-0488)
PHONE 585 269-5001
William Brown, *CEO*
William Gattle, *President*
David Melcher, *President*
Richard W Wambach, *Branch Mgr*
EMP: 400
SALES (corp-wide): 6.1B **Publicly Held**
SIC: 3812 Space vehicle guidance systems & equipment
PA: Harris Corporation
1025 W Nasa Blvd
Melbourne FL 32919
321 727-9100

(G-13856)
HARRIS CORPORATION
800 Lee Rd (14606-4248)
P.O. Box 60488 (14606-0488)
PHONE 413 263-6200
Christopher Young, *CEO*
William Gattle, *President*
David McCaffrey, *Branch Mgr*
EMP: 509
SALES (corp-wide): 6.1B **Publicly Held**
SIC: 3669 Burglar alarm apparatus, electric
PA: Harris Corporation
1025 W Nasa Blvd
Melbourne FL 32919
321 727-9100

(G-13857)
HARRIS CORPORATION
2696 Manitou Rd Bldg 101 (14624-1173)
PHONE 585 269-5000
Heather Fernandez, *Accounts Mgr*
James R Kulp, *Branch Mgr*
EMP: 163
SALES (corp-wide): 6.1B **Publicly Held**
SIC: 3812 Space vehicle guidance systems & equipment
PA: Harris Corporation
1025 W Nasa Blvd
Melbourne FL 32919
321 727-9100

(G-13858)
HARRIS CORPORATION
Also Called: Rf Communications
570 Culver Rd (14609-7442)
PHONE 585 244-5830
Dana Mehnert, *Manager*
EMP: 20
SALES (corp-wide): 6.1B **Publicly Held**
SIC: 3661 3671 Telephone & telegraph apparatus; electron tubes
PA: Harris Corporation
1025 W Nasa Blvd
Melbourne FL 32919
321 727-9100

(G-13859)
HARRIS CORPORATION
50 Carlson Rd (14610-1021)
PHONE 585 244-5830
EMP: 441
SALES (corp-wide): 6.1B **Publicly Held**
SIC: 3663 Radio & TV communications equipment
PA: Harris Corporation
1025 W Nasa Blvd
Melbourne FL 32919
321 727-9100

(G-13860)
HARRIS CORPORATION
Also Called: Harris Rf Communications
1350 Jefferson Rd (14623-3106)
PHONE 585 244-5830
EMP: 441
SALES (corp-wide): 6.1B **Publicly Held**
SIC: 3663 Radio & TV communications equipment
PA: Harris Corporation
1025 W Nasa Blvd
Melbourne FL 32919
321 727-9100

(G-13861)
HARRIS GLOBL CMMUNICATIONS INC
1350 Jefferson Rd (14623-3106)
PHONE 585 244-5830
Chris Young, *President*
EMP: 1200
SALES: 1.1B
SALES (corp-wide): 6.1B **Publicly Held**
SIC: 3663 Receivers, radio communications
PA: Harris Corporation
1025 W Nasa Blvd
Melbourne FL 32919
321 727-9100

(G-13862)
HAWVER DISPLAY INC (PA)
140 Carter St (14621-5136)
PHONE 585 544-2290
Timothy Culver, *President*
EMP: 29
SQ FT: 44,000
SALES (est): 3.7MM **Privately Held**
WEB: www.hawver.com
SIC: 2542 Fixtures: display, office or store; except wood

(G-13863)
HAZLOW ELECTRONICS INC
49 Saint Bridgets Dr (14605-1899)
PHONE 585 325-5323
Alma Publow, *President*
Andrew Publow, *Vice Pres*
James Bunce, *Project Dir*
EMP: 25 **EST:** 1971
SQ FT: 40,000
SALES (est): 5.7MM **Privately Held**
WEB: www.hazlow.com
SIC: 3679 3672 Harness assemblies for electronic use: wire or cable; printed circuit boards

(G-13864)
HEALTH CARE ORIGINALS INC
1 Pleasant St Ste 442 (14604-1455)
PHONE 585 471-8215
Jared Dwarika, *Owner*
EMP: 8
SALES (est): 363.5K **Privately Held**
SIC: 3845 8731 Electromedical apparatus; medical research, commercial

(G-13865)
HICKEY FREEMAN TAILORED CL INC (DH)
1155 N Clinton Ave (14621-4454)
PHONE 585 467-7240
Stephen Granovsky, *CEO*
Alan Abramowicz, *President*
Mark Donovan, *CFO*
Ines Hyun, *Sales Staff*
Bob Galarza, *Sales Associate*
EMP: 50
SQ FT: 224,874
SALES: 45MM **Privately Held**
SIC: 2311 Jackets, tailored suit-type: men's & boys'
HQ: Luxury Men's Apparel Group Ltd
6930 Av Du Parc
Montreal QC H3N 1
514 273-7741

(G-13866)
HIGH END PRINT SOLUTIONS INC
250 Cumberland St Ste 100 (14605-2847)
PHONE 585 325-5320
Gerald Ward, *President*
EMP: 15
SQ FT: 18,000
SALES (est): 3MM **Privately Held**
WEB: www.stvincentpress.com
SIC: 2752 Commercial printing, offset

(G-13867)
HIGH FALLS BREWING COMPANY LLC (DH)
Also Called: North Americas Breweries
445 Saint Paul St (14605-1726)
P.O. Box 30762 (14603-0762)
PHONE 585 546-1030
Samuel T Hubbard Jr,
Michael C Atseff,
John Henderson,
William A Neilson,
Norman E Snyder,
▲ **EMP:** 115
SQ FT: 900,000
SALES (est): 62.3MM **Privately Held**
WEB: www.highfalls.com
SIC: 2082 Beer (alcoholic beverage); ale (alcoholic beverage)

(G-13868)
HIGH FALLS OPERATING CO LLC
445 Saint Paul St (14605-1726)
PHONE 585 546-1030
Kenneth Yartz, *Mng Member*
EMP: 800
SALES (est): 101.2MM **Privately Held**
SIC: 2082 Malt beverage products
HQ: North American Breweries, Inc.
445 Saint Paul St
Rochester NY 14605

Rochester - Monroe County (G-13869) GEOGRAPHIC SECTION

(G-13869)
HIGH SPEED HAMMER COMPANY INC
Also Called: Assembly Equipment Division
313 Norton St (14621-3331)
PHONE..................585 266-4287
David Marcellus, *President*
Richard Marcellus, *Corp Secy*
EMP: 15 **EST:** 1917
SQ FT: 12,000
SALES: 1MM **Privately Held**
SIC: 3542 3541 Riveting machines; machine tools, metal cutting: exotic (explosive, etc.); machine tool replacement & repair parts, metal cutting types

(G-13870)
HIS VISION INC
1260 Lyell Ave (14606-2040)
PHONE..................585 254-0022
Patrick Ho, *President*
Wayne Ohl, *Admin Sec*
▲ **EMP:** 48 **EST:** 1941
SQ FT: 21,000
SALES: 3.5MM **Privately Held**
WEB: www.rochesteroptical.com
SIC: 3851 Frames & parts, eyeglass & spectacle

(G-13871)
HOBART CORPORATION
3495 Winton Pl (14623-2824)
PHONE..................585 427-9000
Pat Allen, *Manager*
EMP: 50
SALES (corp-wide): 14.3B **Publicly Held**
SIC: 3589 Dishwashing machines, commercial
HQ: Hobart Llc
   701 S Ridge Ave
   Troy OH 45374
   937 332-3000

(G-13872)
HOVER-DAVIS INC (DH)
100 Paragon Dr (14624-1129)
PHONE..................585 352-9590
John Hover, *President*
Peter Davis, *Vice Pres*
▲ **EMP:** 125
SQ FT: 66,000
SALES (est): 16.1MM **Privately Held**
WEB: www.hoverdavis.com
SIC: 3549 Assembly machines, including robotic

(G-13873)
HY-TECH MOLD INC
60 Elmgrove Park (14624-1363)
PHONE..................585 247-2450
Donald Philipp, *President*
Patricia Philipp, *Vice Pres*
Stuart Norris, *Treasurer*
EMP: 30
SQ FT: 10,000
SALES: 800K **Privately Held**
WEB: www.hy-techmold.com
SIC: 3544 Industrial molds

(G-13874)
ID SIGNSYSTEMS INC
410 Atlantic Ave (14609-7356)
PHONE..................585 266-5750
Katrina Beatty, *CEO*
Paul Dudley, *President*
Jeff Ureles, *COO*
◆ **EMP:** 48
SQ FT: 15,000
SALES (est): 5.7MM **Privately Held**
WEB: www.idsignsystems.com
SIC: 3993 Electric signs

(G-13875)
IDEX HEALTH & SCIENCE LLC
55 Science Pkwy (14620-4258)
PHONE..................585 244-7220
David Durfee, *President*
David Steinchen, *Engineer*
Stanley Stephenson, *Engineer*
Mike Ransford, *Branch Mgr*
EMP: 100
SALES (corp-wide): 2.2B **Publicly Held**
SIC: 3827 3699 Optical instruments & apparatus; laser systems & equipment

HQ: Idex Health & Science Llc
   600 Park Ct
   Rohnert Park CA 94928
   707 588-2000

(G-13876)
IEC ELECTRONICS CORP
Celmet
1365 Emerson St (14606-3006)
PHONE..................585 647-1760
Tom Guiliani, *Director*
EMP: 80
SALES (corp-wide): 96.4MM **Publicly Held**
SIC: 3444 Sheet metalwork
PA: Iec Electronics Corp.
   105 Norton St
   Newark NY 14513
   315 331-7742

(G-13877)
IHEARTCOMMUNICATIONS INC
Also Called: Wham 1180 AM
100 Chestnut St Ste 1700 (14604-2418)
PHONE..................585 454-4884
Karen Carey, *President*
EMP: 120 **Publicly Held**
SIC: 3663 4832 Radio receiver networks; radio broadcasting stations
HQ: Iheartcommunications, Inc.
   20880 Stone Oak Pkwy
   San Antonio TX 78258
   210 822-2828

(G-13878)
IMAGE360
Also Called: Signs Now
275 Marketplace Dr (14623-6001)
PHONE..................585 272-1234
Julie St Germaine, *President*
Jackie Ciresi, *Treasurer*
EMP: 5
SALES (est): 712.9K **Privately Held**
WEB: www.signsnow405.com
SIC: 3993 Signs & advertising specialties

(G-13879)
IMPRESSIONS INTERNATIONAL INC
410 Alexander St Ste 2 (14607-1038)
PHONE..................585 442-5240
Terry Gersey, *President*
Harry Gersey, *Vice Pres*
▲ **EMP:** 7
SQ FT: 2,500
SALES (est): 872.7K **Privately Held**
WEB: www.checkfraud.com
SIC: 3555 Printing plates

(G-13880)
INNEX INDUSTRIES INC
6 Marway Dr (14624-2349)
PHONE..................585 247-3575
Tom Blaszczykiewicz, *President*
▼ **EMP:** 28
SQ FT: 20,000
SALES (est): 6.2MM **Privately Held**
WEB: www.innexind.com
SIC: 3545 Milling machine attachments (machine tool accessories)

(G-13881)
INSTANT AGAIN LLC
1277 Mount Read Blvd # 2 (14606-2850)
PHONE..................585 436-8003
Jim Webster, *Sales Staff*
Kathy Pfeffer, *Office Mgr*
Andrew Gross III,
EMP: 20
SALES (est): 3MM **Privately Held**
WEB: www.instantagain.com
SIC: 2752 Commercial printing, lithographic

(G-13882)
INSTANT MONOGRAMMING INC
1150 University Ave Ste 5 (14607-1647)
PHONE..................585 654-5550
Daniel Bloom, *President*
Deborah Bloom, *Corp Secy*
EMP: 7
SALES (est): 724.8K **Privately Held**
SIC: 2395 Embroidery products, except schiffli machine; emblems, embroidered

(G-13883)
INTELLIMETAL INC
2025 Brighton Henrietta (14623-2509)
PHONE..................585 424-3260
Kim Lazzara Zapiach, *President*
Scott Lazzara, *General Mgr*
Tony Delvecchio, *Opers Mgr*
EMP: 57
SALES (est): 12.8MM **Privately Held**
SIC: 3444 Sheet metalwork

(G-13884)
INTERNATIONAL PAPER COMPANY
200 Boxart St (14612-5646)
PHONE..................585 663-1000
Donna Teed, *Human Res Mgr*
Les Senft, *Manager*
John Lew, *Manager*
EMP: 150
SALES (corp-wide): 21.7B **Publicly Held**
WEB: www.internationalpaper.com
SIC: 2653 2671 Boxes, corrugated: made from purchased materials; packaging paper & plastics film, coated & laminated
PA: International Paper Company
   6400 Poplar Ave
   Memphis TN 38197
   901 419-9000

(G-13885)
INTERNATIONAL TOOL & MCH INC
121 Lincoln Ave (14611-2444)
PHONE..................585 654-6955
Eric Moore, *President*
▲ **EMP:** 10
SQ FT: 8,000
SALES: 800K **Privately Held**
SIC: 3599 Machine shop, jobbing & repair

(G-13886)
INTRINSIQ MATERIALS INC
1200 Ridgeway Ave Ste 110 (14615-3758)
PHONE..................585 301-4432
Robert Cournoyer, *President*
EMP: 7 **EST:** 2011
SALES (est): 1.1MM **Privately Held**
WEB: www.intrinsiqmaterials.com
SIC: 2893 8731 Printing ink; electronic research

(G-13887)
IROQUOIS ROCK PRODUCTS INC (DH)
1150 Penfield Rd (14625-2202)
PHONE..................585 381-7010
John Odenbach Jr, *President*
Richard E Williams, *President*
David Fingar, *Vice Pres*
Frederick J Odenbach, *Vice Pres*
Gerard Odenbach, *Vice Pres*
EMP: 10
SQ FT: 5,000
SALES (est): 2.6MM
SALES (corp-wide): 29.7B **Privately Held**
SIC: 3281 2951 3273 Stone, quarrying & processing of own stone products; paving mixtures; asphalt & asphaltic paving mixtures (not from refineries); road materials, bituminous (not from refineries); ready-mixed concrete
HQ: Dolomite Products Company Inc.
   1150 Penfield Rd
   Rochester NY 14625
   315 524-1998

(G-13888)
J MACKENZIE LTD
234 Wallace Way (14624-6216)
P.O. Box 22678 (14692-2678)
PHONE..................585 321-1770
James E Hammer, *President*
Christopher F Wieser, *Admin Sec*
▲ **EMP:** 39
SQ FT: 56,000
SALES: 3.5MM
SALES (corp-wide): 119.2MM **Privately Held**
WEB: www.jmackenzie.com
SIC: 2789 Paper cutting
PA: Hammer Packaging Corp.
   200 Lucius Gordon Dr
   West Henrietta NY 14586
   585 424-3880

(G-13889)
J VOGLER ENTERPRISE LLC
15 Evelyn St (14606-5533)
P.O. Box 24361 (14624-0361)
PHONE..................585 247-1625
Jonathan Vogler, *Engineer*
James Vogler,
EMP: 10
SQ FT: 6,000
SALES (est): 1.8MM **Privately Held**
WEB: www.jvogler.com
SIC: 3541 Machine tools, metal cutting type

(G-13890)
JAM INDUSTRIES INC
Also Called: Ace Manufacturing
9 Marway Cir (14624-2320)
PHONE..................585 458-9830
Eric L Johnson, *Ch of Bd*
Martha Moriarty, *Vice Pres*
Jeff Johnson, *Foreman/Supr*
Bill Farrell, *Purchasing*
▲ **EMP:** 45
SQ FT: 25,000
SALES (est): 8.9MM **Privately Held**
WEB: www.jamindustries.com
SIC: 3599 Machine shop, jobbing & repair; machine & other job shop work

(G-13891)
JAMES CONOLLY PRINTING CO
72 Marway Cir (14624-2380)
PHONE..................585 426-4150
Robert Conolly, *President*
Beth Calkins, *Manager*
EMP: 21 **EST:** 1968
SQ FT: 13,000
SALES (est): 3.2MM **Privately Held**
SIC: 2752 2791 2789 Commercial printing, offset; typesetting; bookbinding & related work

(G-13892)
JAMESTOWN CONT OF ROCHESTER
82 Edwards Deming Dr (14606-2842)
PHONE..................585 254-9190
Bruce Janowsky, *Ch of Bd*
Dick P Weimer, *Corp Secy*
Joseph R Palmeri, *Vice Pres*
EMP: 70
SALES (est): 22.9MM
SALES (corp-wide): 148.3MM **Privately Held**
WEB: www.jamestowncontainer.com
SIC: 2653 Boxes, corrugated: made from purchased materials
PA: Jamestown Container Corp
   14 Deming Dr
   Falconer NY 14733
   716 665-4623

(G-13893)
JAVLYN PROCESS SYSTEMS LLC
3136 Winton Rd S Ste 102 (14623-2928)
PHONE..................585 424-5580
Victor Tifone, *President*
EMP: 23
SQ FT: 8,000
SALES (est): 1.4MM
SALES (corp-wide): 225.8K **Privately Held**
SIC: 3569 8742 Liquid automation machinery & equipment; automation & robotics consultant; food & beverage consultant
HQ: Krones, Inc.
   9600 S 58th St
   Franklin WI 53132
   414 409-4000

(G-13894)
JML OPTICAL INDUSTRIES LLC
Also Called: Gregg Sadwick
820 Linden Ave (14625-2710)
PHONE..................585 248-8900
Bob Bicksler, *CEO*
Joseph Lobozzo II, *President*
Trett Sadwick, *COO*
Gradline Lynch, *Vice Pres*
Michael McCusker, *Vice Pres*
▲ **EMP:** 86
SQ FT: 72,000

SALES: 14.1MM **Privately Held**
SIC: 3827 Lenses, optical: all types except ophthalmic; mirrors, optical; prisms, optica.

(G-13895)
JOHNSON CONTROLS
90 Goodway Dr Ste 1 (14623-3039)
PHONE.................................585 288-6200
Gary Gokey, *Branch Mgr*
EMP: 74 **Privately Held**
WEB: www.simplexgrinnell.com
SIC: 3669 Emergency alarms
HQ: Johnson Controls Fire Protection Lp
  4700 Exchange Ct Ste 300
  Boca Raton FL 33431
  561 988-7200

(G-13896)
JOHNSON CONTROLS INC
90 Goodway Dr Ste 1 (14623-3039)
PHONE.................................585 924-9346
Joe Knight, *Manager*
EMP: 37 **Privately Held**
SIC: 3822 Temperature controls, automatic
HQ: Johnson Controls, Inc.
  5757 N Green Bay Ave
  Milwaukee WI 53209
  414 524-1200

(G-13897)
JOHNSON CONTROLS INC
1669 Lake Ave Bldg 333 (14652-0001)
PHONE.................................585 724-2232
Lee Arbagast, *Branch Mgr*
EMP: 120 **Privately Held**
SIC: 2531 3714 3822 Seats, automobile; motor vehicle body components & frame; instrument board assemblies, motor vehicle; lead acid batteries (storage batteries); building services monitoring controls, automatic; facilities support services
HQ: Johnson Controls, Inc.
  5757 N Green Bay Ave
  Milwaukee WI 53209
  414 524-1200

(G-13898)
JORDAN MACHINE INC
1241 Ridgeway Ave Ste I (14615-3757)
PHONE.................................585 647-3585
Thomas Lacey, *President*
Jordan Kesselring, *Vice Pres*
Christine Lacey, *CFO*
EMP: 5 EST: 2016
SALES (est): 202.8K **Privately Held**
SIC: 3599 Machine & other job shop work

(G-13899)
JTEKT TORSEN NORTH AMERICA
2 Jetview Dr (14624-4904)
PHONE.................................585 464-5000
Hiroyuki Kaijima, *President*
Joseph Parisi, *Admin Sec*
▲ EMP: 10
SQ FT: 30,000
SALES (est): 2.1MM
SALES (corp-wide): 13.5B **Privately Held**
SIC: 3714 3711 Motor vehicle parts & accessories; motor vehicles & car bodies
HQ: Jtekt North America Corporation
  7 Research Dr Ste A
  Greenville SC 29607
  440 835-1000

(G-13900)
JUST IN TIME CNC MACHININ
13 Marway Dr (14624-2351)
PHONE.................................585 247-3850
Jim Alexander, *Principal*
EMP: 5
SALES (est): 867.4K **Privately Held**
SIC: 3599 Machine shop, jobbing & repair

(G-13901)
JUST PRESS PRINT LLC
304 Whitney St (14606-1110)
PHONE.................................585 783-1300
Raphael Coccia, *President*
EMP: 7
SALES (est): 450.4K **Privately Held**
SIC: 2752 Commercial printing, offset

(G-13902)
K BARTHELMES MFG CO INC
61 Brooklea Dr (14624-2701)
PHONE.................................585 328-8140
John Wischmeyer, *President*
Janet Wischmeyer, *Admin Sec*
EMP: 15
SQ FT: 55,000
SALES (est): 1.9MM **Privately Held**
WEB: www.barthelmes.com
SIC: 3444 Mfg Sheet Metalwork

(G-13903)
KAMAN AUTOMATION INC
1000 University Ave (14607-1286)
PHONE.................................585 254-8840
Garrett Stofer, *Administration*
EMP: 66
SALES (corp-wide): 1.8B **Publicly Held**
SIC: 3625 Motor controls & accessories
HQ: Kaman Automation, Inc.
  1 Vision Way
  Bloomfield CT 06002
  860 687-5000

(G-13904)
KEVIN J KASSMAN
Also Called: Uniform Express
1408 Buffalo Rd (14624-1827)
PHONE.................................585 529-4245
Kevin J Kassman, *Owner*
EMP: 6
SQ FT: 4,500
SALES: 600K **Privately Held**
SIC: 2395 2396 Embroidery products, except schiffli machine; screen printing on fabric articles

(G-13905)
KLEE CORP
Also Called: Klees Car Wash and Detailing
340 Jefferson Rd (14623-2644)
PHONE.................................585 272-0320
Daniel Edelman, *Manager*
EMP: 7
SQ FT: 5,625
SALES (corp-wide): 21.7MM **Privately Held**
SIC: 3589 Car washing machinery
PA: Klee Corp
  38 Boulder Creek Dr
  Rush NY 14543
  585 321-1510

(G-13906)
KODAK ALARIS INC (DH)
336 Initiative Dr (14624-6217)
PHONE.................................585 290-2891
Marc Jourlait, *CEO*
Rick Costanzo, *President*
Rick Costanzom, *President*
Dennis Olbrich, *President*
Nicki Zongrone, *President*
◆ EMP: 277
SALES (est): 281.3MM **Privately Held**
SIC: 3861 Photographic equipment & supplies
HQ: Kodak Alaris Holdings Limited
  Hemel One Boundary Way
  Hemel Hempstead HERTS HP2 7
  845 757-3175

(G-13907)
KODAK GRAPHIC COMMUNICATIONS
343 State St (14650-0002)
P.O. Box 982138, El Paso TX (79998-2138)
PHONE.................................585 724-4000
Jeffrey Jacobson, *President*
EMP: 14
SALES (est): 4MM **Privately Held**
SIC: 3861 Photographic equipment & supplies

(G-13908)
KURZ AND ZOBEL INC
688 Colfax St (14606-3193)
PHONE.................................585 254-9060
Michael Zobel Jr, *President*
EMP: 8
SQ FT: 15,000
SALES (est): 867.9K **Privately Held**
SIC: 3599 3462 Machine shop, jobbing & repair; gear & chain forgings

(G-13909)
LASERMAX INC
Also Called: Lasermaxdefense
3495 Winton Pl Ste A37 (14623-2898)
PHONE.................................585 272-5420
Susan H Walter, *President*
Will H Walter, *Exec VP*
Daniel J Maier, *CFO*
EMP: 54
SQ FT: 10,250
SALES (est): 11MM **Privately Held**
WEB: www.lasermax.com
SIC: 3699 3674 Laser systems & equipment; semiconductors & related devices

(G-13910)
LAZER INCORPORATED (PA)
Also Called: Lazer Photo Engraving
1465 Jefferson Rd Ste 110 (14623-3149)
PHONE.................................336 744-8047
Gary Staford, *President*
EMP: 50
SQ FT: 10,000
SALES (est): 3.5MM **Privately Held**
WEB: www.lazerinc.com
SIC: 2796 Color separations for printing

(G-13911)
LENS TRIPTAR CO INC
439 Monroe Ave Ste 1 (14607-3787)
PHONE.................................585 473-4470
Allen Krisiloff, *President*
EMP: 5
SQ FT: 3,300
SALES (est): 821.4K **Privately Held**
WEB: www.triptar.com
SIC: 3827 Lenses, optical: all types except ophthalmic

(G-13912)
LEXINGTON MACHINING LLC
677 Buffalo Rd (14611-2014)
PHONE.................................585 235-0880
Ken Vivlamore, *Vice Pres*
Rick Donofrio, *Controller*
Kathi Horch, *Systems Staff*
EMP: 100 **Privately Held**
SIC: 3451 Screw machine products
PA: Lexington Machining Llc
  677 Buffalo Rd
  Rochester NY 14611

(G-13913)
LEXINGTON MACHINING LLC (PA)
677 Buffalo Rd (14611-2014)
PHONE.................................585 235-0880
Michael Lubin, *Ch of Bd*
Warren Delano, *President*
Timothy Duemmel, *General Mgr*
William Conner, *Director*
William Shulevitz, *Director*
EMP: 174
SALES: 22.7MM **Privately Held**
WEB: www.lexingtonmachining.com
SIC: 3451 Screw machine products

(G-13914)
LMT TECHNOLOGY SOLUTIONS
4 Commercial St Ste 400 (14614-1000)
PHONE.................................585 784-7470
Lillian Sandvik,
EMP: 10 EST: 2017
SALES (est): 391.8K **Privately Held**
SIC: 7372 Prepackaged software

(G-13915)
LOAD/N/GO BEVERAGE CORP (PA)
Also Called: Fiz Beverages
355 Portland Ave (14605-1565)
PHONE.................................585 218-4019
Paul Johnson, *President*
EMP: 10 EST: 1964
SQ FT: 11,000
SALES (est): 1.6MM **Privately Held**
SIC: 2086 5181 5149 5921 Soft drinks: packaged in cans, bottles, etc.; beer & other fermented malt liquors; soft drinks; beer (packaged)

(G-13916)
LOGICAL OPERATIONS INC
3535 Winton Pl (14623-2803)
PHONE.................................585 350-7000
Bill Rosenthal, *President*
Michelle Mattick, *CFO*
▲ EMP: 110
SALES (est): 20.6MM **Privately Held**
SIC: 2732 Books: printing & binding

(G-13917)
LOUIS HEINDL & SON INC
Also Called: Heindl Printers
306 Central Ave (14605-3007)
P.O. Box 31121 (14603-1121)
PHONE.................................585 454-5080
P J Heindl, *President*
Debra Heindl, *Vice Pres*
EMP: 6 EST: 1873
SQ FT: 3,500
SALES: 540K **Privately Held**
SIC: 2752 2759 2791 2789 Commercial printing, offset; letterpress printing; typesetting; bookbinding & related work

(G-13918)
LUMETRICS INC
1565 Jefferson Rd Ste 420 (14623-3190)
PHONE.................................585 214-2455
John Hart, *President*
Susan Baier, *Vice Pres*
Todd Blalock, *Vice Pres*
Steve Heveron-Smith, *Vice Pres*
Steve Kelly, *Vice Pres*
▼ EMP: 17
SQ FT: 4,416
SALES (est): 4.4MM **Privately Held**
WEB: www.lumetrics.com
SIC: 3827 Optical instruments & apparatus

(G-13919)
MACAUTO USA INC
80 Excel Dr (14621-3470)
PHONE.................................585 342-2060
J J Liao, *President*
Jerry Hsu, *QC Mgr*
Douglas Chang, *Treasurer*
▲ EMP: 30
SQ FT: 15,000
SALES (est): 5MM
SALES (corp-wide): 181.6MM **Privately Held**
SIC: 3089 Automotive parts, plastic
PA: Macauto Industrial Co., Ltd.
  No. 6, Yongke 5th Rd.,
  Tainan City 71041
  623 310-88

(G-13920)
MACHINECRAFT INC
1645 Lyell Ave Ste 125 (14606-2331)
PHONE.................................585 436-1070
Alan D Lintz, *Ch of Bd*
EMP: 25
SQ FT: 8,750
SALES (est): 2.4MM **Privately Held**
SIC: 3544 Special dies & tools

(G-13921)
MACINNES TOOL CORPORATION
1700 Hudson Ave Ste 3 (14617-5155)
PHONE.................................585 467-1920
Gary Haines, *President*
Sherry Haines, *Treasurer*
EMP: 20 EST: 1953
SQ FT: 6,000
SALES (est): 2.5MM **Privately Held**
WEB: www.macto.com
SIC: 3545 5085 Cutting tools for machine tools; industrial supplies

(G-13922)
MADISON & DUNN
850 Saint Paul St Ste 29 (14605-1065)
PHONE.................................585 563-7760
Christine Baliva, *Owner*
EMP: 6
SALES (est): 750.6K **Privately Held**
SIC: 2426 Flooring, hardwood

(G-13923)
MAGNA PRODUCTS CORP
777 Mount Read Blvd (14606-2129)
PHONE.................................585 647-2280
Kenneth Morrow, *President*
Pat Morrow, *Vice Pres*
Norene Bauer, *Financial Exec*
Andrew Bolton, *Sales Staff*
Genevieve Morrow, *Sales Staff*

Rochester - Monroe County (G-13924)   GEOGRAPHIC SECTION

EMP: 20
SALES (est): 4.2MM **Privately Held**
WEB: www.magnaproducts.com
SIC: 3621 3566 Servomotors, electric; drives, high speed industrial, except hydrostatic

(G-13924)
MAGNETIC TECHNOLOGIES CORP (DH)
770 Linden Ave (14625-2764)
PHONE..................585 385-9010
Gordon H McNeil, *Ch of Bd*
Dale Gulick, *Engineer*
Kathleen Palia, *Controller*
Greg Daly, *Accounting Mgr*
Debbie Deitloff, *Sales Associate*
▲ EMP: 60
SQ FT: 70,000
SALES (est): 10.2MM **Publicly Held**
WEB: www.arnoldmagnetics.com
SIC: 3677 Electronic coils, transformers & other inductors
HQ: Arnold Magnetic Technologies Corporation
    770 Linden Ave
    Rochester NY 14625
    585 385-9010

(G-13925)
MANITOU CONCRETE
1260 Jefferson Rd (14623-3104)
PHONE..................585 424-6040
John Topping, *Sales Engr*
John Pelrier, *Manager*
Jim Wagner, *Director*
EMP: 65
SQ FT: 2,536
SALES (est): 6.4MM **Privately Held**
SIC: 3273 Ready-mixed concrete

(G-13926)
MANUFACTURING RESOURCES INC
2392 Innovation Way # 4 (14624-6225)
PHONE..................631 481-0041
James Wildman, *Ch of Bd*
James Widman, *Ch of Bd*
EMP: 40 EST: 2002
SQ FT: 30,000
SALES (est): 805.7K **Privately Held**
WEB: www.mfgresource.com
SIC: 3444 3549 Sheet metalwork; assembly machines, including robotic

(G-13927)
MANUFACTURING SOLUTIONS INC
850 Saint Paul St Ste 11 (14605-1065)
PHONE..................585 235-3320
Oscar Wilson, *President*
EMP: 25
SQ FT: 5,000
SALES (est): 3.4MM **Privately Held**
WEB: www.mfgsolonline.com
SIC: 3699 Electrical equipment & supplies

(G-13928)
MARACLE INDUSTRIAL FINSHG CO
93 Kilbourn Rd (14618-3607)
PHONE..................585 387-9077
Thomas Maracle, *President*
Nelson Maracle, *Vice Pres*
EMP: 30 EST: 1960
SQ FT: 30,000
SALES (est): 3MM **Privately Held**
SIC: 3471 Finishing, metals or formed products

(G-13929)
MARDON TOOL & DIE CO INC
19 Lois St (14606-1801)
PHONE..................585 254-4545
Donald Fox, *President*
EMP: 13 EST: 1981
SQ FT: 4,000
SALES (est): 1.8MM **Privately Held**
SIC: 3599 Machine shop, jobbing & repair

(G-13930)
MAREX AQUISITION CORP
1385 Emerson St (14606-3027)
PHONE..................585 458-3940
Gary Baxter, *Ch of Bd*
John Olivieri Sr, *Ch of Bd*
Leonard Olivieri, *Vice Pres*
▲ EMP: 115
SQ FT: 55,000
SALES (est): 9.6MM
SALES (corp-wide): 51MM **Privately Held**
WEB: www.martecindustries.com
SIC: 3469 3444 3443 3441 Metal stampings; sheet metalwork; fabricated plate work (boiler shop); fabricated structural metal
PA: Peko Precision Products, Inc.
    1400 Emerson St
    Rochester NY 14606
    585 647-3010

(G-13931)
MASTRO GRAPHIC ARTS INC
67 Deep Rock Rd (14624-3519)
PHONE..................585 436-7570
Rae Mastrofilippo, *Ch of Bd*
Ms Rae Mastrofilippo, *Ch of Bd*
William Betteridge, *President*
Thomas Tortora, *CFO*
Nick Mastro, *Treasurer*
EMP: 34
SQ FT: 23,000
SALES (est): 8.1MM **Privately Held**
WEB: www.mastrographics.com
SIC: 2759 2754 Screen printing; rotary photogravure printing

(G-13932)
MCALPIN INDUSTRIES INC (PA)
255 Hollenbeck St (14621-3294)
PHONE..................585 266-3060
Kenneth McAlpin, *CEO*
John Rowe, *General Mgr*
Mike McAlpin, *Exec VP*
Dave Krieger, *Plant Mgr*
Mark Stella, *Buyer*
▲ EMP: 150 EST: 1964
SQ FT: 140,000
SALES (est): 29.5MM **Privately Held**
WEB: www.mcalpin-ind.com
SIC: 3444 Sheet metal specialties, not stamped

(G-13933)
MCALPIN INDUSTRIES INC
Also Called: Monroe Plating Div
265 Hollenbeck St (14621-3294)
PHONE..................585 544-5335
Evelin Martinez, *Cust Mgr*
Mike Mumm, *Branch Mgr*
EMP: 45
SQ FT: 8,000
SALES (corp-wide): 29.5MM **Privately Held**
WEB: www.mcalpin-ind.com
SIC: 3471 Finishing, metals or formed products
PA: Mcalpin Industries, Inc.
    255 Hollenbeck St
    Rochester NY 14621
    585 266-3060

(G-13934)
MCM NATURAL STONE INC
860 Linden Ave Ste 1 (14625-2718)
PHONE..................585 586-6510
Marilyn Valle, *President*
EMP: 12
SALES (est): 1.7MM **Privately Held**
WEB: www.mcmstone.com
SIC: 3281 5032 1423 Granite, cut & shaped; limestone, cut & shaped; granite building stone; limestone; crushed & broken granite

(G-13935)
MELIORUM TECHNOLOGIES INC
620 Park Ave 145 (14607-2943)
PHONE..................585 313-0616
Jason Rama, *President*
▼ EMP: 5
SALES (est): 487.3K **Privately Held**
SIC: 2821 2819 Silicone resins; aluminum oxide

(G-13936)
MERCURY PRINT PRODUCTIONS INC (PA)
2332 Innovation Way 4 (14624-6225)
PHONE..................585 458-7900
John Place, *CEO*
Joe Del Vecchio, *President*
Christian Schamberger, *President*
Steve Adolf, *Vice Pres*
Basil Newton, *Plant Mgr*
▲ EMP: 200
SQ FT: 80,000
SALES (est): 76.8MM **Privately Held**
WEB: www.mercuryprint.com
SIC: 2752 7334 2791 2789 Commercial printing, offset; photocopying & duplicating services; typesetting; bookbinding & related work

(G-13937)
METROPOLITAN GRANITE & MBL INC
860 Maple St Ste 100 (14611-1612)
PHONE..................585 342-7020
Helmettin Cakir, *President*
EMP: 5
SALES: 450K **Privately Held**
SIC: 2541 Counter & sink tops

(G-13938)
MICHAEL TODD STEVENS
Also Called: Rochester Screen Printing
95 Mount Read Blvd # 125 (14611-1923)
PHONE..................585 436-9957
Michael Stevens, *Owner*
EMP: 5
SALES (est): 317K **Privately Held**
SIC: 3953 Screens, textile printing

(G-13939)
MICRO INSTRUMENT CORP
Also Called: Automated Systems Group
1199 Emerson St (14606-3038)
P.O. Box 60619 (14606-0619)
PHONE..................585 458-3150
William Gunther, *President*
Anthony De Salvo, *President*
Jens Pfeffer, *Exec VP*
Chris Lindstrom, *Project Mgr*
Greg Rossetti, *Project Mgr*
EMP: 100 EST: 1944
SQ FT: 56,000
SALES (est): 25.2MM **Privately Held**
WEB: www.microinst.com
SIC: 3599 3613 7389 6552 Machine shop, jobbing & repair; control panels, electric; grinding, precision: commercial or industrial; land subdividers & developers, commercial; special dies, tools, jigs & fixtures; aluminum foundries

(G-13940)
MICRO THREADED PRODUCTS INC
325 Mount Read Blvd Ste 4 (14611-1928)
PHONE..................585 288-0080
Robert Osipovitch, *President*
EMP: 5
SALES (est): 568.8K **Privately Held**
SIC: 3451 Screw machine products

(G-13941)
MICROERA PRINTERS INC
304 Whitney St (14606-1110)
PHONE..................585 783-1300
Bruno Coccia, *Ch of Bd*
Raphael Coccia, *Vice Pres*
EMP: 22
SQ FT: 20,000
SALES (est): 3.9MM **Privately Held**
WEB: www.microera.com
SIC: 2752 Commercial printing, offset

(G-13942)
MICROMOD AUTOMATION INC
3 Townline Cir Ste 4 (14623-2537)
PHONE..................585 321-9200
Richard Keane, *President*
Wayne France, *General Mgr*
Carol McNelly, *Vice Pres*
Pat Carpenter, *Purch Mgr*
Bill Costner, *Project Engr*
EMP: 20
SALES (est): 4.2MM **Privately Held**
WEB: www.micmod.com
SIC: 3625 Industrial controls: push button, selector switches, pilot

(G-13943)
MICROMOD AUTOMTN & CONTRLS INC
3 Townline Cir Ste 4 (14623-2537)
PHONE..................585 321-9209
Wayne France, *General Mgr*
Nancy Gilbride, *CFO*
EMP: 13
SALES (est): 2.2MM **Privately Held**
SIC: 3823 Industrial process control instruments

(G-13944)
MICRON INDS ROCHESTER INC
31 Industrial Park Cir (14624-2403)
PHONE..................585 247-6130
Stephen K Schmidt, *President*
Kirk Schmidt, *Vice Pres*
Eric Schmidt, *Admin Sec*
EMP: 9
SQ FT: 20,000
SALES (est): 1.3MM **Privately Held**
WEB: www.micronindustries.com
SIC: 3544 Special dies & tools; industrial molds

(G-13945)
MILLER METAL FABRICATING INC
315 Commerce Dr (14623-3507)
PHONE..................585 359-3400
Steven Mertz, *President*
EMP: 9 EST: 1978
SQ FT: 10,500
SALES (est): 1.4MM **Privately Held**
SIC: 3443 3441 3545 7692 Weldments; fabricated structural metal for bridges; precision tools, machinists'; welding repair; sandblasting of building exteriors

(G-13946)
MINORITY REPORTER INC (PA)
19 Borrowdale Dr (14626-1751)
P.O. Box 26352 (14626-0352)
PHONE..................585 225-3628
Dave McCleary, *Principal*
EMP: 8
SALES (est): 568.2K **Privately Held**
SIC: 2711 Newspapers, publishing & printing

(G-13947)
MITCHELL MACHINE TOOL LLC
190 Murray St (14606-1126)
PHONE..................585 254-7520
Michael Mitchell,
Maryland Mitchell,
EMP: 5
SALES (est): 363K **Privately Held**
WEB: www.mitchellmachinetool.com
SIC: 3599 Machine shop, jobbing & repair

(G-13948)
MITEL NETWORKS INC
300 State St Ste 100 (14614-1047)
PHONE..................877 654-3573
Don Joos, *Branch Mgr*
EMP: 9
SALES (corp-wide): 987.6MM **Privately Held**
SIC: 3661 3663 7372 Telephone & telegraph apparatus; radio & TV communications equipment; prepackaged software
HQ: Mitel Networks, Inc.
    960 Stewart Dr
    Sunnyvale CA 94085

(G-13949)
MKS INSTRUMENTS INC
100 Highpower Rd (14623-3498)
PHONE..................585 292-7472
Bill Schumacher, *Opers Mgr*
Mary Hoopes, *Senior Buyer*
Jim Elwert, *Buyer*
Ana Espinoza, *Buyer*
David Silva, *Buyer*
EMP: 20
SALES (corp-wide): 1.9B **Publicly Held**
WEB: www.mksinst.com
SIC: 3823 Industrial instrmnts msrmnt display/control process variable

▲ = Import ▼ = Export
◆ = Import/Export

GEOGRAPHIC SECTION

Rochester - Monroe County (G-13973)

PA: Mks Instruments, Inc.
2 Tech Dr Ste 201
Andover MA 01810
978 645-5500

(G-13950)
MKS MEDICAL ELECTRONICS
Also Called: M K S
100 Highpower Rd (14623-3498)
PHONE..................585 292-7400
Paul M Eyerman, *General Mgr*
Yogi Chawla, *Design Engr*
EMP: 112
SQ FT: 20,000
SALES (est): 10.3MM
SALES (corp-wide): 1.9B Publicly Held
WEB: www.mksinst.com
SIC: 3621 3663 Generating apparatus & parts, electrical; amplifiers, RF power & IF
PA: Mks Instruments, Inc.
2 Tech Dr Ste 201
Andover MA 01810
978 645-5500

(G-13951)
MOLECULAR GLASSES INC
1667 Lake Ave Ste 278b (14615-3047)
PHONE..................585 210-2861
Michel Molaire, *CEO*
Mark Juba, *COO*
EMP: 9 EST: 2015
SQ FT: 1,000
SALES (est): 307.6K Privately Held
SIC: 2869 High purity grade chemicals, organic

(G-13952)
MONROE CNTY CHAPTER NYSARC INC
Also Called: Arcworks
1651 Lyell Ave (14606-2309)
PHONE..................585 698-1320
Daryl Bleau, *Business Mgr*
Trish Nenni, *Opers Mgr*
Micheal Czora, *Branch Mgr*
EMP: 5
SALES (corp-wide): 70.6MM Privately Held
SIC: 3085 Plastics bottles
HQ: Monroe County Chapter, Nysarc, Inc.
2060 Brighton Henrietta
Rochester NY 14623
585 271-0660

(G-13953)
MONROE COUNTY AUTO SVCS INC (PA)
Also Called: Ziebart
1505 Lyell Ave (14606-2109)
PHONE..................585 764-3741
Anthony Mattiacio, *President*
Zachary Mattiacio, *Vice Pres*
Craig Thomas, *Opers Staff*
Laron Fulmore, *Sales Mgr*
EMP: 40
SALES (est): 7MM Privately Held
SIC: 3479 5012 Coating, rust preventive; automotive brokers

(G-13954)
MONROE PIPING & SHTMTL LLC (PA)
Also Called: MP&sm
68 Humboldt St (14609-7496)
P.O. Box 90600 (14609-0600)
PHONE..................585 482-0200
Dan Englert, *CEO*
Curtis Peterson, *CEO*
Mark Lohrmann, *Division Mgr*
Jeffrey Turner, *General Mgr*
Troy Peterson, *VP Admin*
EMP: 75 EST: 1967
SQ FT: 25,000
SALES (est): 31.3MM Privately Held
WEB: www.monroepiping.com
SIC: 3444 Sheet metalwork

(G-13955)
MOONEY-KEEHLEY INC
38 Saginaw Dr (14623-3132)
PHONE..................585 271-1573
David Hedges, *President*
Kenneth Hempson, *Owner*
Elihu Hedges Jr, *Vice Pres*
Judith Gessner, *Treasurer*
Elizabeth Hedges, *Admin Sec*
EMP: 6 EST: 1944
SQ FT: 12,000
SALES (est): 910.3K Privately Held
WEB: www.mooneykeehley.com
SIC: 2752 7389 Cards, lithographed; engraving service
PA: 22 Winston, Inc.
22 Winston Pl
Rochester NY 14607
585 271-1573

(G-13956)
MORGOOD TOOLS INC
940 Millstead Way (14624-5108)
P.O. Box 24997 (14624-0997)
PHONE..................585 436-8828
Virginia L Marshall, *CEO*
Doug Meier, *President*
David Pedeville, *Vice Pres*
James Faas, *Engineer*
Diane Soper, *CFO*
EMP: 60 EST: 1945
SQ FT: 30,000
SALES (est): 9MM Privately Held
WEB: www.morgood.com
SIC: 3545 Cutting tools for machine tools; cams (machine tool accessories)

(G-13957)
MORRIS MACHINING SERVICE INC
95 Mount Read Blvd (14611-1923)
PHONE..................585 527-8100
James Morris, *President*
EMP: 5
SQ FT: 4,000
SALES (est): 220K Privately Held
SIC: 3599 Machine shop, jobbing & repair

(G-13958)
MOSAIC MICROSYSTEMS LLC
500 Lee Rd Ste 200 (14606-4261)
PHONE..................585 314-7441
Christine Whitman, *CEO*
Paul Ballentine, *President*
Andrew Pescoe, *Director*
EMP: 5
SQ FT: 10,000
SALES: 50K Privately Held
SIC: 3674 Semiconductors & related devices

(G-13959)
MULLERS CIDER HOUSE LLC
1344 University Ave # 180 (14607-1656)
PHONE..................585 287-5875
Samuel Conjerti, *Mng Member*
EMP: 5
SALES (est): 339.8K Privately Held
SIC: 2099 Cider, nonalcoholic

(G-13960)
MULTIPLE IMPRSSONS OF RCHESTER (PA)
Also Called: Minuteman Press
41 Chestnut St (14604-2303)
PHONE..................585 546-1160
William Malone Sr, *President*
Jay Malone, *Corp Secy*
Brad Amedeo, *Prdtn Mgr*
EMP: 8
SQ FT: 3,600
SALES (est): 870.9K Privately Held
WEB: www.dtmmp.com
SIC: 2752 7334 2791 2789 Commercial printing, offset; photocopying & duplicating services; typesetting; bookbinding & related work

(G-13961)
MWI INC (PA)
1269 Brighton Henrietta T (14623-2485)
PHONE..................585 424-4200
David Mc Mahon, *Ch of Bd*
Kevin Mc Mahon, *President*
Brian Mc Mahon, *COO*
Ryan Mc Mahon, *Vice Pres*
Ryan McMahon, *Vice Pres*
▲ EMP: 100
SQ FT: 28,000
SALES (est): 22.9MM Privately Held
WEB: www.mwiedm.com
SIC: 3624 Carbon & graphite products

(G-13962)
NALGE NUNC INTERNATIONAL CORP (DH)
1600 Lexington Ave # 107 (14606-3000)
PHONE..................585 498-2661
Michaeline Reed, *Principal*
L Johansen, *Manager*
▲ EMP: 903
SQ FT: 275,000
SALES (est): 233.4MM
SALES (corp-wide): 20.9B Publicly Held
WEB: www.nuncbrand.com
SIC: 3089 3949 3821 3085 Plastic processing; plastic & fiberglass tanks; sporting & athletic goods; laboratory apparatus & furniture; plastics bottles; laminated plastics plate & sheet
HQ: Fisher Scientific International Llc
81 Wyman St
Waltham MA 02451
781 622-1000

(G-13963)
NATIONWIDE CIRCUITS INC
1444 Emerson St (14606-3009)
PHONE..................585 328-0791
Alan Austin, *President*
Judith Austin, *Vice Pres*
Elaine Weber, *Sales Staff*
EMP: 28 EST: 1971
SQ FT: 20,000
SALES (est): 3.9MM Privately Held
WEB: www.nciproto.com
SIC: 3672 Wiring boards

(G-13964)
NATIONWIDE PRECISION PDTS CORP
Also Called: Hn Precision-Ny
200 Tech Park Dr (14623-2445)
PHONE..................585 272-7100
Dan Nash, *CEO*
Dan Brooks, *Vice Pres*
Rick Menaldino, *Vice Pres*
Sharon Pierce, *Vice Pres*
Paul Ainsworth, *CFO*
▲ EMP: 425 EST: 1999
SQ FT: 160,000
SALES (est): 109.9MM Privately Held
WEB: www.nationwideprecision.com
SIC: 3356 Nonferrous rolling & drawing

(G-13965)
NAVITAR INC
200 Commerce Dr (14623-3589)
PHONE..................585 359-4000
Julian Goldstein, *Ch of Bd*
Robert Prato, *General Mgr*
Tom McCune, *COO*
Craig Fitzgerald, *Vice Pres*
Jeremy Goldstein, *Vice Pres*
▼ EMP: 71
SQ FT: 19,000
SALES (est): 16.4MM Privately Held
WEB: www.navitar.com
SIC: 3699 3651 3827 3674 Laser systems & equipment; household audio & video equipment; optical instruments & lenses; semiconductors & related devices; radio & TV communications equipment; pressed & blown glass

(G-13966)
NBN TECHNOLOGIES LLC
136 Wilshire Rd (14618-1221)
PHONE..................585 355-5556
Shimon Miamon PHD,
Joseph Wodenscheck,
EMP: 6
SALES (est): 698.4K Privately Held
SIC: 3699 Electrical equipment & supplies

(G-13967)
NEW YORK MANUFACTURED PRODUCTS
6 Cairn St (14611-2416)
PHONE..................585 254-9353
Salvatore Anselmo, *Partner*
Boubane Aselmo, *Partner*
EMP: 10
SALES: 2MM Privately Held
SIC: 3441 3499 3089 Fabricated structural metal; metal household articles; injection molding of plastics

(G-13968)
NEW YORK MANUFACTURING CORP
6 Cairn St (14611-2416)
PHONE..................585 254-9353
Salvatore Anselmo,
Bouabane Anselmo,
EMP: 6
SQ FT: 20,000
SALES (est): 975K Privately Held
WEB: www.newyorkmanufacturing.com
SIC: 3599 Machine shop, jobbing & repair

(G-13969)
NEW YORK MARKING DEVICES CORP
C H Morse Stamp Co
700 Clinton Ave S Ste 2 (14620-1383)
PHONE..................585 454-5188
Joseph Stummer, *President*
Peter J Stummer, *Branch Mgr*
EMP: 6
SALES (est): 541.2K
SALES (corp-wide): 1.7MM Privately Held
WEB: www.nymarking.com
SIC: 3953 Embossing seals & hand stamps
PA: New York Marking Devices Corp
2207 Teall Ave
Syracuse NY 13206
315 463-8641

(G-13970)
NEWPORT CORPORATION
705 Saint Paul St (14605-1730)
PHONE..................585 248-4246
Linda Nittolo, *Purchasing*
Jeff Olson, *Engineer*
Ann M Brennan, *Human Resources*
Christophe Palmer, *Manager*
Brian Grove, *Technology*
EMP: 20
SALES (corp-wide): 1.9B Publicly Held
WEB: www.newport.com
SIC: 3821 Laboratory apparatus & furniture
HQ: Newport Corporation
1791 Deere Ave
Irvine CA 92606
949 863-3144

(G-13971)
NEWPORT ROCHESTER INC
705 Saint Paul St (14605-1730)
PHONE..................585 262-1325
Chris Palmer, *General Mgr*
▲ EMP: 60
SALES (est): 19.3MM
SALES (corp-wide): 1.9B Publicly Held
WEB: www.newport.com
SIC: 3827 Gratings, diffraction
HQ: Newport Corporation
1791 Deere Ave
Irvine CA 92606
949 863-3144

(G-13972)
NEXIS 3 LLC
1681 Lyell Ave (14606-2311)
PHONE..................585 285-4120
Steve Schoenacker,
EMP: 20
SQ FT: 65,000
SALES: 3.5MM Privately Held
SIC: 2434 Wood kitchen cabinets

(G-13973)
NICOFORM INC
72 Cascade Dr Ste 12 (14614-1109)
PHONE..................585 454-5530
Berl Stein, *President*
Richard Kraynik, *Vice Pres*
John Contino, *Mfg Staff*
Chris Reynolds, *QC Mgr*
Joe Jachlewski, *Engineer*
▼ EMP: 20
SQ FT: 12,000
SALES: 2.4MM Privately Held
WEB: www.nicoform.com
SIC: 3544 3599 Industrial molds; bellows, industrial: metal

(PA)=Parent Co (HQ)=Headquarters (DH)=Div Headquarters
✪ = New Business established in last 2 years

2019 Harris
New York Manufacturers Directory

Rochester - Monroe County (G-13974) — GEOGRAPHIC SECTION

(G-13974)
NORDON INC (PA)
691 Exchange St (14608-2714)
PHONE..................585 546-6200
Terry J Donovan, *CEO*
John Buck, *Project Mgr*
Gabriel Campa, *Project Mgr*
David Marianetti, *Project Mgr*
Richard Sullivan, *Sales Engr*
◆ **EMP:** 100
SQ FT: 64,000
SALES (est): 26.7MM **Privately Held**
WEB: www.nordon.org
SIC: 3089 3544 Injection molding of plastics; industrial molds

(G-13975)
NORDON INC
1600 Lexington Ave 235a (14606-3000)
PHONE..................585 546-6200
James Dickerson, *Manager*
EMP: 42
SALES (corp-wide): 26.7MM **Privately Held**
SIC: 3089 3544 Injection molding of plastics; industrial molds
PA: Nordon, Inc.
691 Exchange St
Rochester NY 14608
585 546-6200

(G-13976)
NORDON INC
711 Exchange St (14608)
PHONE..................585 546-6200
Paul Reed, *Manager*
EMP: 24
SALES (corp-wide): 26.7MM **Privately Held**
WEB: www.nordon.org
SIC: 3089 3544 Injection molding of plastics; industrial molds
PA: Nordon, Inc.
691 Exchange St
Rochester NY 14608
585 546-6200

(G-13977)
NORTH AMERICAN BREWERIES INC (DH)
Also Called: Northamerican Breweries
445 Saint Paul St (14605-1726)
PHONE..................585 546-1030
Kris Sirchio, *CEO*
Richard Lozyniak, *Ch of Bd*
Raquel Vargas, *President*
Dan Harrington, *VP Finance*
◆ **EMP:** 10
SALES (est): 354.2MM **Privately Held**
SIC: 2082 Beer (alcoholic beverage)

(G-13978)
NORTH AMRCN BRWRIES HLDNGS LLC (PA)
445 Saint Paul St (14605-1726)
PHONE..................585 546-1030
Rich Lozyniak, *CEO*
EMP: 26
SALES (est): 76.7MM **Privately Held**
SIC: 2082 Beer (alcoholic beverage)

(G-13979)
NORTHEASTERN SEALCOAT INC
470 Hollenbeck St Bldg 3 (14621-2213)
PHONE..................585 544-4372
Shawn Grimes, *President*
EMP: 10
SQ FT: 4,000
SALES (est): 1.9MM **Privately Held**
SIC: 2951 2952 4959 Asphalt paving mixtures & blocks; asphalt felts & coatings; snowplowing

(G-13980)
NORTHERN AIR SYSTEMS INC (PA)
3605 Buffalo Rd (14624-1120)
PHONE..................585 594-5050
Timothy Confer, *President*
Garland Beasley, *Vice Pres*
Joseph Denninger, *Vice Pres*
Dave Thomann, *Sales Mgr*
EMP: 46
SQ FT: 45,000
SALES (est): 11.2MM **Privately Held**
SIC: 3585 Heating & air conditioning combination units

(G-13981)
NORTHERN AIR TECHNOLOGY INC (PA)
3605 Buffalo Rd (14624-1120)
PHONE..................585 594-5050
Timothy J Confer, *President*
EMP: 1 **EST:** 2000
SQ FT: 1,000
SALES (est): 1.1MM **Privately Held**
SIC: 3648 Outdoor lighting equipment

(G-13982)
NORTHERN KING LURES INC (PA)
167 Armstrong Rd (14616-2703)
P.O. Box 12482 (14612-0482)
PHONE..................585 865-3373
Patsy Distaffen, *President*
EMP: 5
SALES (est): 733K **Privately Held**
WEB: www.northernkinglures.com
SIC: 3949 Lures, fishing; artificial

(G-13983)
NU WAYS INC
655 Pullman Ave (14615-3334)
PHONE..................585 254-7510
Edward A Coleman, *President*
Richard Albert, *Treasurer*
Michael Bater, *Finance*
EMP: 6 **EST:** 1996
SALES: 1.2MM **Privately Held**
SIC: 2591 Window blinds

(G-13984)
OLDCASTLE MATERIALS INC
1260 Jefferson Rd (14623-3104)
PHONE..................585 424-6410
John Peltier, *Manager*
Daniel Coe, *Manager*
EMP: 5
SALES (corp-wide): 29.7B **Privately Held**
WEB: www.oldcastlematerials.com
SIC: 3273 Ready-mixed concrete
HQ: Oldcastle Materials, Inc.
900 Ashwood Pkwy Ste 700
Atlanta GA 30338

(G-13985)
OLEDWORKS LLC (PA)
1645 Lyell Ave Ste 140 (14606-2331)
PHONE..................585 287-6802
David Dejoy, *CEO*
Joh Hamer, *COO*
Michael Boroson, *CTO*
Giana Phelan,
EMP: 28
SALES (est): 4MM **Privately Held**
SIC: 3641 3646 3999 3674 Electric lamps; commercial indusl & institutional electric lighting fixtures; barber & beauty shop equipment; light emitting diodes

(G-13986)
OMG DESSERTS INC
1227 Ridgeway Ave Ste J (14615-3759)
PHONE..................585 698-1561
Mary E Graham, *President*
Mary Graham, *President*
EMP: 10
SALES (est): 1MM **Privately Held**
SIC: 2099 Desserts, ready-to-mix

(G-13987)
OMNI-ID USA INC
1200 Ridgeway Ave Ste 106 (14615-3758)
PHONE..................585 697-9913
George E Daddis Jr, *President*
Tony Kington, *COO*
Ed Nabrotzky, *Exec VP*
Andre Cote, *Senior VP*
Tracy Gay, *Vice Pres*
EMP: 37
SALES (est): 6.2MM **Privately Held**
WEB: www.omni-id.com
SIC: 3825 Radio frequency measuring equipment

(G-13988)
ON SEMICONDUCTOR CORPORATION
1964 Lake Ave (14615-2316)
PHONE..................585 784-5770
Brett Nicholson, *Business Mgr*
David Sackett, *Technology*
Wilson Weir, *Network Tech*
Cindy Van Buren, *Director*
Tomas Hernandez, *Technician*
EMP: 9
SALES (est): 1.3MM **Privately Held**
SIC: 3674 Semiconductors & related devices

(G-13989)
ONTARIO PLASTICS INC
2503 Dewey Ave (14616-4728)
PHONE..................585 663-2644
Gerard Reynolds, *President*
Jim Beifus, *Principal*
Ralph E Barnes, *Vice Pres*
Dorraine Coughlin, *Asst Controller*
▲ **EMP:** 35 **EST:** 1945
SQ FT: 40,000
SALES (est): 7.8MM **Privately Held**
WEB: www.ontario-plastics.com
SIC: 3082 3089 Unsupported plastics profile shapes; plastic containers, except foam; boxes, plastic

(G-13990)
OPEN TEXT INC
1225 Jefferson Rd Ste A30 (14623-3186)
PHONE..................585 424-1950
Bob Stiner, *Software Engr*
EMP: 25
SALES (corp-wide): 2.2B **Privately Held**
SIC: 7372 Prepackaged software
HQ: Open Text Inc.
2950 S Delaware St
San Mateo CA 94403
650 645-3000

(G-13991)
ORMEC SYSTEMS CORP (PA)
19 Linden Park (14625-2776)
PHONE..................585 385-3520
Edward J Krasnicki, *CEO*
EMP: 35
SQ FT: 15,600
SALES (est): 5.7MM **Privately Held**
WEB: www.ormec.com
SIC: 3823 3672 Controllers for process variables, all types; printed circuit boards

(G-13992)
OROLIA USA INC (DH)
1565 Jefferson Rd Ste 460 (14623-3190)
PHONE..................585 321-5800
Elizabeth Withers, *President*
John Fischer, *Vice Pres*
Darrell Johanneman, *Admin Sec*
EMP: 55 **EST:** 1972
SQ FT: 26,000
SALES (est): 13.4MM **Privately Held**
WEB: www.spectracomcorp.com
SIC: 3829 Measuring & controlling devices
HQ: Orolia Holding Sas
Drakkar Batiment D
Valbonne
492 907-040

(G-13993)
ORTHO-CLINICAL DIAGNOSTICS INC
100 Latona Rd Bldg 313 (14626)
PHONE..................585 453-4771
EMP: 400
SALES (corp-wide): 696.9MM **Privately Held**
SIC: 3841 Diagnostic apparatus, medical
PA: Ortho-Clinical Diagnostics, Inc.
1001 Us Highway 202
Raritan NJ 08869
908 218-8000

(G-13994)
ORTHO-CLINICAL DIAGNOSTICS INC
Also Called: Ortho/Rochester Tech
2402 Innovation Way # 3 (14624-6226)
PHONE..................585 453-5200
EMP: 14

SALES (corp-wide): 696.9MM **Privately Held**
SIC: 3841 Diagnostic apparatus, medical
PA: Ortho-Clinical Diagnostics, Inc.
1001 Us Highway 202
Raritan NJ 08869
908 218-8000

(G-13995)
ORTHO-CLINICAL DIAGNOSTICS INC
1000 Lee Rd (14626)
PHONE..................585 453-3000
EMP: 33
SALES (corp-wide): 696.9MM **Privately Held**
WEB: www.orthoclinical.com
SIC: 2835 Blood derivative diagnostic agents
PA: Ortho-Clinical Diagnostics, Inc.
1001 Us Highway 202
Raritan NJ 08869
908 218-8000

(G-13996)
ORTHOGONAL
1999 Lake Ave (14650-0001)
PHONE..................585 254-2775
John Defranco, *CEO*
Fox Holt, *Principal*
Douglas Robello, *Research*
EMP: 5
SALES (est): 684.6K **Privately Held**
SIC: 3679 Liquid crystal displays (LCD)

(G-13997)
ORTHOTICS & PROSTHETICS DEPT
Also Called: Strong Hospital
4901 Lac De Ville Blvd (14618-5647)
PHONE..................585 341-9299
Rob Brown, *Manager*
EMP: 15
SALES (est): 1MM **Privately Held**
SIC: 3842 Orthopedic appliances

(G-13998)
OTEX PROTECTIVE INC
2180 Brighton Henrietta (14623-2704)
PHONE..................585 232-7160
Jacob Weidert, *CEO*
EMP: 6
SALES (est): 735.7K **Privately Held**
SIC: 2311 Men's & boys' uniforms

(G-13999)
OZIPKO ENTERPRISES INC
Also Called: Printing Plus
125 White Spruce Blvd (14623-1607)
PHONE..................585 424-6740
Rita Ozipko, *President*
Carl Ozipko, *Vice Pres*
Jim Ozipko, *Admin Sec*
EMP: 8
SQ FT: 3,000
SALES (est): 890K **Privately Held**
SIC: 2752 Commercial printing, offset

(G-14000)
P & H MACHINE SHOP INC
40 Industrial Park Cir (14624-2404)
PHONE..................585 247-5500
Fax: 585 247-5572
EMP: 5
SQ FT: 3,000
SALES (est): 360K **Privately Held**
SIC: 3544 Mfg Dies/Tools/Jigs/Fixtures

(G-14001)
P & R INDUSTRIES INC (PA)
1524 N Clinton Ave (14621-2206)
PHONE..................585 266-6725
Lawrence F Coyle, *President*
Janet Okane, *COO*
Charles Sheelar, *Vice Pres*
Robert Brawn, *Project Mgr*
Donna Stein, *Purch Agent*
EMP: 50
SQ FT: 22,000
SALES (est): 15MM **Privately Held**
SIC: 3544 3541 Special dies & tools; machine tools, metal cutting type

GEOGRAPHIC SECTION

Rochester - Monroe County (G-14027)

(G-14002)
P & R INDUSTRIES INC
1524 N Clinton Ave (14621-2206)
PHONE..................................585 544-1811
Nick Natali, *Branch Mgr*
EMP: 10
SALES (corp-wide): 15MM **Privately Held**
SIC: 3544 Special dies & tools
PA: P & R Industries, Inc.
1524 N Clinton Ave
Rochester NY 14621
585 266-6725

(G-14003)
P K G EQUIPMENT INCORPORATED
367 Paul Rd (14624-4925)
PHONE..................................585 436-4650
Stephen Pontarelli, *CEO*
Stephen T Pontarelli, *Ch of Bd*
Carla Pontarelli, *Vice Pres*
Maria Parker, *Treasurer*
Kathi Horch, *Manager*
EMP: 30
SQ FT: 35,000
SALES (est): 8.3MM **Privately Held**
WEB: www.pkgequipment.com
SIC: 3559 3441 Metal finishing equipment for plating, etc.; fabricated structural metal

(G-14004)
PALLET DIVISION INC
40 Silver St (14611-2208)
PHONE..................................585 328-3780
Bernie Mangold, *President*
EMP: 7
SALES (est): 1MM **Privately Held**
SIC: 2448 Pallets, wood & metal combination

(G-14005)
PALLET SERVICES INC
1681 Lyell Ave (14606-2311)
PHONE..................................585 647-4020
Donald Matre, *Branch Mgr*
EMP: 40
SALES (est): 3.3MM
SALES (corp-wide): 23MM **Privately Held**
SIC: 2448 Pallets, wood
PA: Pallet Services, Inc.
4055 Casillio Pkwy
Clarence NY 14031
716 873-7700

(G-14006)
PANTHER GRAPHICS INC (PA)
465 Central Ave (14605-3012)
PHONE..................................585 546-7163
Daryll A Jackson Sr, *President*
Josh Cummings, *General Mgr*
Daromell Jackson, *Human Res Mgr*
Henry Ehindero, *Sales Staff*
Rachael Hudson-Rodvik, *Office Mgr*
▲ EMP: 38
SQ FT: 12,000
SALES (est): 55.3MM **Privately Held**
WEB: www.panthergraphics.net
SIC: 2752 Commercial printing, offset

(G-14007)
PARADISO CNSLD ENTPS LLC
Also Called: Sailorbags
1115 E Main St Unit 58 (14609-6156)
PHONE..................................585 924-3937
Kaitlin Giardina, *Sales Mgr*
Tina Paradiso, *Mng Member*
EMP: 5 EST: 2011
SALES (est): 202.4K **Privately Held**
SIC: 3171 Handbags, women's

(G-14008)
PARAGON STEEL RULE DIES INC
979 Mount Read Blvd (14606-2829)
PHONE..................................585 254-3395
Michael McDeid, *President*
Parker Corts, *Prdtn Mgr*
Teresa McDeid, *Manager*
Jon Rector, *Manager*
EMP: 13
SQ FT: 13,000
SALES (est): 2.2MM **Privately Held**
WEB: www.paragonsrd.com
SIC: 3544 Dies, steel rule

(G-14009)
PARK ENTERPRISES ROCHESTER INC
226 Jay St (14608-1623)
PHONE..................................585 546-4200
Sook Cha Park, *President*
Hyo-Sang Park, *General Mgr*
Rob Brunskill, *Principal*
Hyo Sang Park, *Principal*
Tom Sydeski, *Principal*
▲ EMP: 200
SQ FT: 60,000
SALES (est): 33.1MM **Privately Held**
WEB: www.parkent.com
SIC: 3545 Precision tools, machinists'

(G-14010)
PEKO PRECISION PRODUCTS INC
70 Holworthy St (14606-1313)
PHONE..................................585 301-1386
Sonny Sok, *Manager*
EMP: 12
SALES (corp-wide): 51MM **Privately Held**
WEB: www.pekoprecision.com
SIC: 3599 Crankshafts & camshafts, machining; machine shop, jobbing & repair
PA: Peko Precision Products, Inc.
1400 Emerson St
Rochester NY 14606
585 647-3010

(G-14011)
PENNANT INGREDIENTS INC (DH)
64 Chester St (14611-2110)
PHONE..................................585 235-8160
Simon Teel, *President*
Karel Zimmermann, *President*
EMP: 90 EST: 2015
SALES (est): 57.1MM **Privately Held**
SIC: 2099 Seasonings & spices

(G-14012)
PERFORMANCE TECHNOLOGIES INC (DH)
3500 Winton Pl Ste 4 (14623-2860)
PHONE..................................585 256-0200
John M Slusser, *Ch of Bd*
John J Peters, *Senior VP*
J Patrick Rice, *Senior VP*
Dorrance W Lamb, *CFO*
EMP: 32
SQ FT: 32,000
SALES (est): 13.7MM
SALES (corp-wide): 612.7MM **Publicly Held**
WEB: www.pt.com
SIC: 3672 3661 3577 7373 Printed circuit boards; telephone & telegraph apparatus; computer peripheral equipment; computer integrated systems design
HQ: Sonus Networks, Inc.
4 Technology Park Dr
Westford MA 01886
978 614-8100

(G-14013)
PERI-FACTS ACADEMY
601 Elmwood Ave (14642-0001)
PHONE..................................585 275-6037
Dr James Woods, *Senior Editor*
EMP: 5
SALES (est): 273.1K **Privately Held**
SIC: 2731 Textbooks: publishing & printing

(G-14014)
PFAUDLER INC (DH)
1000 West Ave (14611-2442)
P.O. Box 23500 (14692-3600)
PHONE..................................585 235-1000
Keith Quintana, *General Mgr*
Micheal F Powers, *Principal*
Phil Hahn, *Vice Pres*
Tom Calzolaio, *Senior Buyer*
Jonathan Pond, *Engineer*
◆ EMP: 300
SQ FT: 500,000
SALES (est): 121.8MM
SALES (corp-wide): 352.2K **Privately Held**
SIC: 3559 Refinery, chemical processing & similar machinery; pharmaceutical machinery
HQ: Pfaudler Gmbh
Pfaudlerstr.
Schwetzingen 68723
620 285-0

(G-14015)
PFAUDLER US INC
1000 West Ave (14611-2442)
PHONE..................................585 235-1000
Bob Waddell, *CEO*
EMP: 200 EST: 2014
SALES (est): 29.9K
SALES (corp-wide): 352.2K **Privately Held**
SIC: 3443 Fabricated plate work (boiler shop)
HQ: Pfaudler International Sarl
Rue Edward Steichen 2
Luxembourg

(G-14016)
PH DAVID J ROSSI
50 Celtic Ln (14626-4362)
PHONE..................................585 455-1160
David Rossi, *Principal*
EMP: 5
SALES (est): 615.1K **Privately Held**
SIC: 2834 Pharmaceutical preparations

(G-14017)
PHARMA-SMART INTERNATIONAL INC
Also Called: Pharmasmart
Rochester Tech Park 773 E (14624)
PHONE..................................585 427-0730
Frederick W Sarkis II, *CEO*
Ashton S Maaraba, *COO*
Lisa M Goodwin, *Exec VP*
Lisa Goodwin, *Exec VP*
Joseph O Sarkis, *Senior VP*
▼ EMP: 39
SQ FT: 52,000
SALES (est): 7MM **Privately Held**
SIC: 3841 5047 8099 Diagnostic apparatus, medical; diagnostic equipment, medical; health screening service

(G-14018)
PHARMADVA LLC
36 King St (14608-1922)
PHONE..................................585 469-1410
Joshua Eddy, *Finance Mgr*
Jonathan Sacks, *Mng Member*
Duane Girdner,
EMP: 6
SALES: 80K **Privately Held**
SIC: 3845 Electromedical equipment

(G-14019)
PHOENIX GRAPHICS INC
464 State St 470 (14608-1739)
PHONE..................................585 232-4040
Sal De Biase III, *President*
EMP: 20
SALES (est): 5.4MM **Privately Held**
WEB: www.phoenix-graphics.com
SIC: 2752 Commercial printing, offset

(G-14020)
PHOTONAMICS INC
Also Called: Elmgrove Technologies Div
558 Elmgrove Rd (14606-3348)
PHONE..................................585 247-8990
Ross Cooley, *President*
Eric Johengen, *Vice Pres*
EMP: 10
SQ FT: 4,000
SALES (est): 2MM **Privately Held**
WEB: www.elmgrovetechnologies.com
SIC: 3672 Printed circuit boards

(G-14021)
PIERCE INDUSTRIES LLC
465 Paul Rd Ste A (14624-4779)
PHONE..................................585 458-0888
Dick Webb, *CEO*
Rick Schopinsky, *President*
Pat Sennett, *Opers Staff*
Elaine Deacon, *Engineer*
Craig Neubauer, *Engineer*
▲ EMP: 40
SQ FT: 60,000
SALES (est): 15.2MM **Privately Held**
WEB: www.pierceindustries.com
SIC: 3441 Fabricated structural metal

(G-14022)
PIERREPONT VISUAL GRAPHICS
15 Elser Ter (14611-1607)
PHONE..................................585 305-9672
Scott Zappia, *President*
Terence Zappia, *Vice Pres*
Mark Matyjakowski, *Info Tech Mgr*
EMP: 2 EST: 1958
SQ FT: 15,000
SALES: 1MM **Privately Held**
WEB: www.pierrepont.com
SIC: 2759 Screen printing

(G-14023)
PIXOS PRINT
75 Goodway Dr (14623-3000)
PHONE..................................585 500-4600
Ron Bittner, *Owner*
Mike Bittner, *Co-Owner*
Steve Patrick, *Marketing Staff*
John Green, *Manager*
Lance Eddinger, *Graphic Designe*
EMP: 6
SALES (est): 122.8K **Privately Held**
SIC: 2752 Commercial printing, offset

(G-14024)
PLUG POWER INC
1200 Ridgeway Ave Ste 123 (14615-3758)
PHONE..................................585 474-3993
EMP: 6
SALES (corp-wide): 103.2MM **Publicly Held**
SIC: 3629 3674 Electrochemical generators (fuel cells); fuel cells, solid state
PA: Plug Power Inc.
968 Albany Shaker Rd
Latham NY 12110
518 782-7700

(G-14025)
PMI INDUSTRIES LLC
350 Buell Rd (14624-3124)
PHONE..................................585 464-8050
V Sheldon Alfiero, *President*
◆ EMP: 30
SQ FT: 48,500
SALES (est): 8.9MM
SALES (corp-wide): 43.3MM **Privately Held**
WEB: www.pro-moldinc.com
SIC: 3544 3089 Industrial molds; injection molded finished plastic products
PA: Bam Enterprises, Inc.
2937 Alt Blvd
Grand Island NY 14072
716 773-7634

(G-14026)
POLYMAG TEK INC
215 Tremont St Ste 2 (14608-2371)
PHONE..................................585 235-8390
Pete Byam, *President*
Brian Giardino, *Engineer*
Jennifer Sweet, *Treasurer*
Ronald W Sweet, *Treasurer*
Joseph Rodibaugh, *Technical Staff*
EMP: 12
SALES: 2MM **Privately Held**
WEB: www.polymagtek.com
SIC: 3547 7389 5085 Rolling mill machinery; design services; mill supplies

(G-14027)
POLYMER ENGINEERED PDTS INC
23 Moonlanding Rd (14624-2505)
PHONE..................................585 426-1811
George Peroutka, *President*
Stephanie Mesiti, *Purchasing*
Tim Morgan, *Marketing Staff*
EMP: 100
SQ FT: 55,000
SALES (corp-wide): 13.6MM **Privately Held**
SIC: 3089 Injection molding of plastics

Rochester - Monroe County (G-14028)   GEOGRAPHIC SECTION

PA: Polymer Engineered Products, Inc.
595 Summer St Ste 2
Stamford CT 06901
203 324-3737

(G-14028)
POSEIDON SYSTEMS LLC
200 Canal View Blvd # 300 (14623-2851)
PHONE 585 239-6025
Ryan Brewer, *President*
Graham Martin, *Engineer*
Mike Roemer, *Engineer*
Joe Murray, *Sales Mgr*
Judd Williams, *Sales Mgr*
EMP: 11
SQ FT: 6,000
SALES (est): 2.2MM **Privately Held**
SIC: 3829 3823 Measuring & controlling devices; industrial instrmnts msrmnt display/control process variable; flow instruments, industrial process type; data loggers, industrial process type

(G-14029)
POWER-FLO TECHNOLOGIES INC
Also Called: Auburn Armature
62 Marway Cir (14624-2321)
PHONE 585 426-4607
Joe Santasia, *Manager*
EMP: 36
SALES (corp-wide): 51.8MM **Privately Held**
SIC: 7694 Electric motor repair
PA: Power-Flo Technologies, Inc.
270 Park Ave
New Hyde Park NY 11040
516 812-6800

(G-14030)
PPG ARCHITECTURAL FINISHES INC
Also Called: Glidden Professional Paint Ctr
566 Clinton Ave S (14620-1135)
PHONE 585 271-1363
Rochard Puzzolo, *Branch Mgr*
EMP: 5
SALES (corp-wide): 14.7B **Publicly Held**
WEB: www.gliddenpaint.com
SIC: 2891 Adhesives
HQ: Ppg Architectural Finishes, Inc.
1 Ppg Pl
Pittsburgh PA 15272
412 434-3131

(G-14031)
PPI CORP
Also Called: Ftt Manufacturing
275 Commerce Dr (14623-3505)
PHONE 585 880-7277
John Longuil, *President*
Darrell Gibson, *Mfg Mgr*
Mike Cianciola, *Purch Mgr*
Paul Opela, *Controller*
Janet Oliviari, *Human Resources*
EMP: 42
SALES (est): 361.2K **Privately Held**
SIC: 3541 3449 3599 3544 Numerically controlled metal cutting machine tools; miscellaneous metalwork; machine shop, jobbing & repair; special dies, tools, jigs & fixtures

(G-14032)
PPI CORP
Also Called: Ftt Mfg
275 Commerce Dr (14623-3505)
PHONE 585 243-0300
John Longuil, *CEO*
Paul Opela, *Vice Pres*
Darrel Gibson, *Mfg Mgr*
John Gunn, *QC Mgr*
Lou Giglia, *Engineer*
▲ **EMP:** 60
SQ FT: 57,000
SALES (est): 13.5MM **Privately Held**
WEB: www.fttmfg.com
SIC: 3545 3451 5047 3541 Precision tools, machinists'; screw machine products; instruments, surgical & medical; numerically controlled metal cutting machine tools; electrical discharge machining (EDM); machinery castings, aluminum

(G-14033)
PRECISE TOOL & MFG INC
9 Coldwater Cres (14624-2512)
PHONE 585 247-0700
John S Gizzi, *President*
John P Gizzi, *President*
Rose A Poirier, *Corp Secy*
Gary Mastro, *Vice Pres*
▲ **EMP:** 100
SQ FT: 150,000
SALES (est): 22.2MM **Privately Held**
WEB: www.precisetool.com
SIC: 3541 Numerically controlled metal cutting machine tools; milling machines; boring mills

(G-14034)
PRECISION DESIGN SYSTEMS INC
1645 Lyell Ave Ste 136 (14606-2386)
PHONE 585 426-4500
William J West, *President*
Jeff Sutton, *Vice Pres*
EMP: 20
SQ FT: 18,000
SALES (est): 3MM **Privately Held**
SIC: 3829 3479 Measuring & controlling devices; name plates: engraved, etched, etc.

(G-14035)
PRECISION GRINDING & MFG CORP (PA)
Also Called: P G M
1305 Emerson St (14606-3098)
PHONE 585 458-4300
Michael Hockenberger, *CEO*
William C Hockenberger, *Ch of Bd*
Todd Hockenberger, *Vice Pres*
Wendy Baker, *Prdtn Mgr*
Dan Doyle, *Purch Mgr*
▲ **EMP:** 126
SQ FT: 62,000
SALES (est): 19.3MM **Privately Held**
WEB: www.pgmcorp.com
SIC: 3545 3544 Precision tools, machinists'; special dies & tools

(G-14036)
PRECISION LASER TECHNOLOGY LLC
Also Called: Plt
1001 Lexington Ave Ste 4 (14606-2847)
PHONE 585 458-6208
Ron Natale Jr, *Mng Member*
James Garcia,
EMP: 10
SQ FT: 7,000
SALES (est): 864.5K **Privately Held**
SIC: 7692 7699 Welding repair; cash register repair

(G-14037)
PRECISION MACHINE TECH LLC
Also Called: Spex
85 Excel Dr (14621-3471)
PHONE 585 467-1840
Michael Nolan, *President*
Becky Isenberg, *Purch Mgr*
Lisa Fess, *Manager*
▲ **EMP:** 60
SQ FT: 16,000
SALES (est): 14.3MM **Privately Held**
WEB: www.spex1.com
SIC: 3599 Machine shop, jobbing & repair

(G-14038)
PRECISION MAGNETICS LLC
770 Linden Ave (14625-2716)
PHONE 585 385-9010
Andrew Albers,
Terence R Loughrey,
▲ **EMP:** 50
SQ FT: 12,000
SALES (est): 5.9MM **Privately Held**
WEB: www.precisionmagnets.com
SIC: 3499 Magnets, permanent: metallic

(G-14039)
PREMIER METALS GROUP
11 Cairn St (14611-2415)
PHONE 585 436-4020
Marc Olgin, *CEO*
Mike Diamond, *Principal*
Steve Olgin, *Exec VP*
Ed Czemeryck, *CFO*
EMP: 32
SALES (est): 5MM **Privately Held**
SIC: 3469 Metal stampings
HQ: Scholz Holding Gmbh
Berndt-Ulrich-Scholz-Str. 1
Essingen 73457
736 584-0

(G-14040)
PREMIER SIGN SYSTEMS LLC
10 Excel Dr (14621-3470)
PHONE 585 235-0390
Jeff Sherwood, *Owner*
James Peacock, *Principal*
EMP: 29
SALES (est): 4.5MM **Privately Held**
SIC: 3993 Electric signs

(G-14041)
PRESSTEK PRINTING
20 Balfour Dr (14621-3202)
PHONE 585 266-2770
Stanley E Freimuth, *CEO*
Ronald T Cardone, *Vice Pres*
Cathleen V Cavanna, *Vice Pres*
Joseph Demharter, *Vice Pres*
Arnon Dror, *Vice Pres*
EMP: 6
SALES (est): 470.1K **Privately Held**
SIC: 2752 Commercial printing, offset

(G-14042)
PRESSTEK PRINTING LLC
521 E Ridge Rd (14621-1203)
PHONE 585 467-8140
Dennis Collins, *President*
EMP: 10
SQ FT: 1,400
SALES (est): 459.7K **Privately Held**
SIC: 2752 2791 Commercial printing, offset; typesetting

(G-14043)
PRESSTEK PRINTING LLC
Also Called: Washburn Litho Envirgo Prtg
20 Balfour Dr (14621-3202)
P.O. Box 67211 (14617-7211)
PHONE 585 266-2770
Antony Disalvo, *President*
Dennis Collins, *Vice Pres*
EMP: 14
SQ FT: 6,600
SALES (est): 1.7MM **Privately Held**
SIC: 2759 2752 Commercial printing; commercial printing, lithographic

(G-14044)
PRINT ON DEMAND INITIATIVE INC
1240 Jefferson Rd (14623-3104)
PHONE 585 239-6044
Gaurav Govil, *President*
EMP: 19
SQ FT: 900
SALES (est): 118.2K **Privately Held**
SIC: 2752 Commercial printing, lithographic

(G-14045)
PRINTROC INC
620 South Ave (14620-1316)
PHONE 585 461-2556
Ronald Schutt, *President*
Daniel McCarthy, *Vice Pres*
Jesse McCarthy, *Director*
EMP: 12
SQ FT: 6,000
SALES (est): 1.2MM **Privately Held**
WEB: www.pinnacleprinters.com
SIC: 2752 Commercial printing, offset

(G-14046)
PRIVATE LBEL FODS RCHESTER INC
1686 Lyell Ave (14606-2312)
P.O. Box 60805 (14606-0805)
PHONE 585 254-9205
Bonnie Lavorato, *Ch of Bd*
Frank Lavorato III, *Vice Pres*
Russ Eliason, *CFO*
EMP: 30
SQ FT: 125,000
SALES (est): 9.3MM **Privately Held**
WEB: www.privatelabelfoods.com
SIC: 2099 Food preparations

(G-14047)
PRO-TECH WLDG FABRICATION INC
Also Called: Pro-Tech Sno Pusher
711 West Ave (14611-2412)
PHONE 585 436-9855
Michael P Weagley, *President*
EMP: 35
SQ FT: 30,000
SALES (est): 8.3MM **Privately Held**
SIC: 3531 7692 Snow plow attachments; welding repair

(G-14048)
PRO-VALUE DISTRIBUTION INC
1547 Lyell Ave Ste 3 (14606-2123)
PHONE 585 783-1461
Thomas W Mayberry, *President*
EMP: 6
SQ FT: 4,000
SALES (est): 804.4K **Privately Held**
SIC: 3714 Motor vehicle parts & accessories

(G-14049)
PRODUCT INTEGRATION & MFG INC
55 Fessenden St (14611-2815)
PHONE 585 436-6260
Tyrone Reaves, *Ch of Bd*
Long Nguyen, *Manager*
John Breedy, *Consultant*
EMP: 22
SQ FT: 25,000
SALES (est): 4.5MM **Privately Held**
SIC: 3444 Forming machine work, sheet metal

(G-14050)
PRODUCTION METAL CUTTING INC
1 Curlew St (14606-2535)
P.O. Box 60535 (14606-0535)
PHONE 585 458-7136
Leo T Glogowski, *President*
▲ **EMP:** 12
SQ FT: 34,000
SALES (est): 2.1MM
SALES (corp-wide): 2.4MM **Privately Held**
WEB: www.zedcomachinery.com
SIC: 3545 Machine tool accessories
PA: Zedco Machinery Inc
1 Curlew St
Rochester NY 14606
585 458-6920

(G-14051)
PROFESSIONAL MACHINE LLC
Also Called: PM
1390 Mount Read Blvd (14606-2820)
PHONE 508 966-5171
Joseph Kauker, *President*
▲ **EMP:** 18
SQ FT: 10,000
SALES (est): 2.9MM
SALES (corp-wide): 89.4MM **Privately Held**
SIC: 3599 Machine shop, jobbing & repair
PA: Arch Global Precision Llc
12955 Inkster Rd
Livonia MI 48150
734 266-6900

(G-14052)
PSB LTD
543 Atlantic Ave Ste 2 (14609-7396)
PHONE 585 654-7078
Robert Armitage, *President*
EMP: 13
SQ FT: 30,000
SALES (est): 2.5MM **Privately Held**
WEB: www.psb.net
SIC: 3471 Electroplating & plating

(G-14053)
PULLMAN MFG CORPORATION
77 Commerce Dr (14623-3501)
PHONE 585 334-1350
Chris Biegel, *CEO*
William A Palmer, *Shareholder*
▼ **EMP:** 6 **EST:** 1886
SQ FT: 36,000

GEOGRAPHIC SECTION

Rochester - Monroe County (G-14078)

SALES (est): 1.2MM **Privately Held**
WEB: www.pullmanmfg.com
SIC: 3495 Sash balances, spring

(G-14054)
PULSAFEEDER INC (HQ)
Also Called: Engineered Products Oper Epo
2883 Brghton Hnrietta Twn (14623-2790)
PHONE................................585 292-8000
Richard C Morgan, *Ch of Bd*
John Carter, *Ch of Bd*
Dieter Sauer, *President*
Todd Hanson, *Prdtn Dir*
Joe Patarino, *Prdtn Mgr*
◆ **EMP:** 122
SQ FT: 45,000
SALES (est): 25.3MM
SALES (corp-wide): 2.2B **Publicly Held**
WEB: www.pulsa.com
SIC: 3561 3825 3823 3822 Industrial pumps & parts; measuring instruments & meters, electric; industrial instrmnts msrmnt display/control process variable; auto controls regulating residntl & coml environmt & applncs; relays & industrial controls; measuring & dispensing pumps
PA: Idex Corporation
1925 W Field Ct Ste 200
Lake Forest IL 60045
847 498-7070

(G-14055)
PYRAGON INC
95 Mount Read Blvd Ste 14 (14611-1936)
PHONE................................585 697-0444
Thomas Crumlish, *President*
◆ **EMP:** 9
SQ FT: 3,000
SALES (est): 1.7MM **Privately Held**
WEB: www.pyragon.com
SIC: 3679 Antennas, receiving

(G-14056)
QED TECHNOLOGIES INTL INC
Also Called: Q.E.d
1040 University Ave (14607-1282)
PHONE................................585 256-6540
Andrew Kulawiec, *CEO*
Chris Hoyng, *QC Mgr*
Michael Natkin, *Research*
Chris Bond, *Engineer*
Jerry Carapella, *Engineer*
▲ **EMP:** 45
SALES (est): 15.8MM
SALES (corp-wide): 590.1MM **Publicly Held**
WEB: www.qedmrf.com
SIC: 3577 Computer peripheral equipment
PA: Cabot Microelectronics Corporation
870 N Commons Dr
Aurora IL 60504
630 375-6631

(G-14057)
QES SOLUTIONS INC (PA)
1547 Lyell Ave (14606-2123)
PHONE................................585 783-1455
Thomas W Mayberry, *Ch of Bd*
Beb Mayberry, *President*
◆ **EMP:** 100
SQ FT: 15,000
SALES (est): 18.8MM **Privately Held**
SIC: 3559 Metal finishing equipment for plating, etc.

(G-14058)
QOS ENTERPRISES LLC
282 Hollenbeck St (14621-3235)
PHONE................................585 454-0550
Edward McGrattan,
EMP: 7
SALES (est): 855.1K **Privately Held**
WEB: www.qosllc.com
SIC: 3471 Plating & polishing

(G-14059)
QUADRISTI LLC
275 Mount Read Blvd (14611-1924)
PHONE................................585 279-3318
Marc Iacona,
▲ **EMP:** 11
SQ FT: 10,000
SALES: 500K
SALES (corp-wide): 47.3MM **Privately Held**
SIC: 3644 Electric conduits & fittings

PA: Simcona Electronics Corp
275 Mount Read Blvd
Rochester NY 14611
585 328-3230

(G-14060)
QUALITY CONTRACT ASSEMBLIES
Also Called: Qca
100 Boxart St Ste 251 (14612-5656)
P.O. Box 12868 (14612-0868)
PHONE................................585 663-9030
Richard Frank, *President*
▲ **EMP:** 12
SQ FT: 5,500
SALES (est): 1.9MM **Privately Held**
WEB: www.qcacorp.com
SIC: 3679 Electronic circuits; harness assemblies for electronic use: wire or cable

(G-14061)
QUALITY VISION INTL INC (PA)
Also Called: Optical Gaging Products Div
850 Hudson Ave (14621-4839)
PHONE................................585 544-0450
Edward T Polidor, *CEO*
Keith Polidor, *COO*
Douglas Green, *Vice Pres*
Lars Avery, *Engineer*
David Lopez, *Engineer*
▲ **EMP:** 337 **EST:** 1954
SALES (est): 101.6MM **Privately Held**
SIC: 3827 Optical test & inspection equipment

(G-14062)
QUALITY VISION SERVICES INC
Also Called: Quality Vision International
1175 North St (14621-4942)
PHONE................................585 544-0450
Timothy Moriarty, *President*
George Guarino, *CFO*
▲ **EMP:** 56 **EST:** 2000
SALES (est): 11MM
SALES (corp-wide): 101.6MM **Privately Held**
SIC: 3827 8734 Optical comparators; optical test & inspection equipment; calibration & certification
PA: Quality Vision International Inc.
850 Hudson Ave
Rochester NY 14621
585 544-0450

(G-14063)
QUANTUM MEDICAL IMAGING LLC
150 Verona St (14608-1733)
PHONE................................631 567-5800
Scott Matovich, *President*
Shalom Cohen, *President*
Keith Matovich, *Vice Pres*
Anthony Coker, *Mfg Staff*
Eileen Sanchez, *Buyer*
▲ **EMP:** 100
SQ FT: 55,000
SALES (est): 26.9MM
SALES (corp-wide): 24.5B **Privately Held**
WEB: www.qmiteam.com
SIC: 3844 5047 Radiographic X-ray apparatus & tubes; medical equipment & supplies
HQ: Carestream Health, Inc.
150 Verona St
Rochester NY 14608

(G-14064)
QUANTUM SAILS ROCHESTER LLC
1461 Hudson Ave (14621-1716)
PHONE................................585 342-5200
Kristofer Werner, *President*
EMP: 5 **EST:** 2015
SALES (est): 325K **Privately Held**
SIC: 2394 7532 Convertible tops, canvas or boat: from purchased materials; sails: made from purchased materials; canvas boat seats; liners & covers, fabric: made from purchased materials; tops (canvas or plastic), installation or repair: automotive

(G-14065)
QUINTEL USA INC
1200 Ridgeway Ave Ste 132 (14615-3758)
PHONE................................585 420-8364
Robert Fishback, *CFO*
▲ **EMP:** 50
SALES (est): 10.7MM **Privately Held**
SIC: 3663 Radio & TV communications equipment

(G-14066)
R P FEDDER CORP (PA)
740 Driving Park Ave B (14613-1596)
PHONE................................585 288-1600
Stephen Quinn, *Ch of Bd*
Joseph Vancura, *President*
Joseph Pennise, *Vice Pres*
Gordon Leonard, *Engineer*
Dawn Jenkins, *Accountant*
▲ **EMP:** 28 **EST:** 1958
SQ FT: 65,000
SALES (est): 15MM **Privately Held**
WEB: www.rpfedder.com
SIC: 3564 5075 2674 Filters, air: furnaces, air conditioning equipment, etc.; air filters; bags: uncoated paper & multiwall

(G-14067)
R V DOW ENTERPRISES INC
Also Called: B J Long Co
466 Central Ave (14605-3011)
PHONE................................585 454-5862
Richard V Dow, *President*
▲ **EMP:** 17 **EST:** 1953
SQ FT: 9,000
SALES (est): 700K **Privately Held**
WEB: www.bjlong.com
SIC: 3999 Pipe cleaners

(G-14068)
RAM MACHINING LLC
1645 Lyell Ave Ste 158 (14606-2386)
P.O. Box 24685 (14624-0685)
PHONE................................585 426-1007
Daniel L Pixley,
EMP: 5
SALES (est): 400K **Privately Held**
SIC: 3599 Machine shop, jobbing & repair

(G-14069)
RAPID PRECISION MACHINING INC
Also Called: Quality Plus
50 Lafayette Rd (14609-3119)
PHONE................................585 467-0780
John Nolan, *President*
EMP: 70
SQ FT: 51,000
SALES (est): 6.6MM **Privately Held**
SIC: 3541 Machine tools, metal cutting type

(G-14070)
RED OAK SOFTWARE INC
3349 Monroe Ave Ste 175 (14618-5513)
PHONE................................585 454-3170
Greg Waffen, *Branch Mgr*
EMP: 5
SALES (corp-wide): 1.3MM **Privately Held**
WEB: www.redoaksw.com
SIC: 7372 Prepackaged software
PA: Red Oak Software Inc
115 Us Highway 46 F1000
Mountain Lakes NJ 07046
973 316-6064

(G-14071)
RHINO TRUNK & CASE INC
Also Called: Trunk Outlet
565 Blossom Rd Ste J (14610-1859)
PHONE................................585 244-4553
Gregory Hurwitz, *President*
Bob Eastwood, *Manager*
Greg Hurwitz, *Director*
EMP: 15
SALES: 5MM **Privately Held**
WEB: www.trunkoutlet.com
SIC: 3161 Luggage

(G-14072)
RID LOM PRECISION MFG
50 Regency Oaks Blvd (14624-5901)
P.O. Box 64473 (14624-6873)
PHONE................................585 594-8600
John D Rider, *President*
EMP: 20
SQ FT: 7,100
SALES (est): 2.9MM **Privately Held**
WEB: www.ridlom.com
SIC: 3544 Special dies & tools

(G-14073)
RIDGE CABINET & SHOWCASE INC
1545 Mount Read Blvd # 2 (14606-2848)
PHONE................................585 663-0560
Steve Lader, *Ch of Bd*
EMP: 20
SQ FT: 6,200
SALES (est): 3.6MM **Privately Held**
SIC: 2541 Counter & sink tops

(G-14074)
RIVERVIEW ASSOCIATES INC
Also Called: Riverside Automation
1040 Jay St (14611-1110)
PHONE................................585 235-5980
John A Christopher, *Ch of Bd*
EMP: 13
SQ FT: 20,000
SALES: 2.5MM **Privately Held**
WEB: www.riversideautomation.com
SIC: 3559 Automotive related machinery

(G-14075)
RMB EMBROIDERY SERVICE
176 Anderson Ave Ste F110 (14607-1169)
PHONE................................585 271-5560
Ruta Szabo, *Partner*
Birute Collier, *Partner*
Maria Stankus, *Partner*
EMP: 7 **EST:** 1995
SQ FT: 850
SALES: 140K **Privately Held**
SIC: 2397 Schiffli machine embroideries

(G-14076)
ROBERT J FARAONE
Also Called: O Tex
1600 N Clinton Ave (14621-2200)
PHONE................................585 232-7160
Robert J Faraone, *Owner*
EMP: 7
SALES: 500K **Privately Held**
WEB: www.otex.com
SIC: 3545 Tool holders

(G-14077)
ROCCERA LLC
771 Elmgrove Rd Bldg No2 (14624-6200)
PHONE................................585 426-0887
Syamal Ghosh, *President*
Frank Kaduc, *Vice Pres*
Peter Wojtowicz, *Opers Mgr*
EMP: 18
SQ FT: 10,000
SALES (est): 2.2MM **Privately Held**
SIC: 3297 3432 3599 Heat resistant mixtures; alumina fused refractories; plumbing fixture fittings & trim; machine & other job shop work; custom machinery

(G-14078)
ROCHESTER 100 INC
40 Jefferson Rd (14623-2132)
P.O. Box 92801 (14692-8901)
PHONE................................585 475-0200
Nicholas Sfikas, *President*
Catherine Sfikas, *Principal*
Geraldine E Warner, *Corp Secy*
William Fish, *Vice Pres*
Carleen Fien, *Admin Sec*
▲ **EMP:** 129 **EST:** 1962
SQ FT: 100,000
SALES (est): 19.6MM **Privately Held**
WEB: www.rochester100.com
SIC: 2672 2677 Adhesive papers, labels or tapes: from purchased material; envelopes

Rochester - Monroe County (G-14079)

(G-14079)
ROCHESTER ASPHALT MATERIALS (DH)
1150 Penfield Rd (14625-2202)
PHONE........................585 381-7010
John M Odenbach Jr, *President*
Gardner Odenbach, *Treasurer*
Mary Swierkos, *Admin Sec*
EMP: 8
SQ FT: 5,000
SALES (est): 12.9MM
SALES (corp-wide): 29.7B **Privately Held**
SIC: 2951 3273 Road materials, bituminous (not from refineries); ready-mixed concrete

(G-14080)
ROCHESTER ATOMATED SYSTEMS INC
40 Regency Oaks Blvd (14624-5901)
PHONE........................585 594-3222
Jerrold Potter, *President*
Frank Denaro, *Vice Pres*
George Gamer, *Vice Pres*
EMP: 20
SQ FT: 12,000
SALES (est): 3.9MM **Privately Held**
WEB: www.rochauto.com
SIC: 3599 Machine shop, jobbing & repair; custom machinery

(G-14081)
ROCHESTER BUSINESS JOURNAL
16 W Main St Ste 341 (14614-1604)
PHONE........................585 546-8303
Susan Holliday, *President*
Cynthia Belzl, *Vice Pres*
Debbie Coons, *Financial Exec*
Marilyn Meyer, *Sales Staff*
Hilda Avila, *Manager*
EMP: 35
SALES (est): 2.6MM **Privately Held**
WEB: www.rbj.net
SIC: 2711 Newspapers: publishing only, not printed on site; newspapers, publishing & printing

(G-14082)
ROCHESTER CATHOLIC PRESS (PA)
Also Called: Catholic Courier
1150 Buffalo Rd (14624-1823)
P.O. Box 24379 (14624-0379)
PHONE........................585 529-9530
Bishop S R Matano, *President*
Bishop Salvatore R Matano, *President*
Karen M Franz, *General Mgr*
William H Kedley, *Treasurer*
Rev Daniel Condon, *Admin Sec*
EMP: 16
SQ FT: 3,188
SALES: 1.3MM **Privately Held**
WEB: www.catholiccourier.com
SIC: 2711 Newspapers: publishing only, not printed on site

(G-14083)
ROCHESTER COCA COLA BOTTLING
Also Called: Coca-Cola
123 Upper Falls Blvd (14605-2156)
PHONE........................585 546-3900
George Keim, *Manager*
EMP: 65
SALES (corp-wide): 35.4B **Publicly Held**
SIC: 2086 5149 Soft drinks: packaged in cans, bottles, etc.; groceries & related products
HQ: Rochester Coca Cola Bottling Corp
300 Oak St
Pittston PA 18640
570 655-2874

(G-14084)
ROCHESTER COLONIAL MFG CORP (PA)
1794 Lyell Ave (14606-2316)
PHONE........................585 254-8191
Mark S Gionta, *CEO*
Norm Dix, *President*
Steve Trotta, *Vice Pres*
Paul Gionta, *Plant Mgr*
Carolyn Weil, *Controller*
EMP: 100
SQ FT: 100,000
SALES (est): 14.1MM **Privately Held**
WEB: www.rochestercolonial.com
SIC: 2431 3442 3231 3444 Windows & window parts & trim, wood; metal doors, sash & trim; strengthened or reinforced glass; sheet metalwork

(G-14085)
ROCHESTER COUNTERTOP INC (PA)
Also Called: Premier Cabinet Wholesalers
3300 Monroe Ave Ste 212 (14618-4621)
PHONE........................585 338-2260
Dean Pelletier, *President*
EMP: 10
SQ FT: 5,000
SALES (est): 861.6K **Privately Held**
WEB: www.premiercabinetwholesalers.com
SIC: 2541 1799 5031 Counter & sink tops; counter top installation; kitchen cabinets

(G-14086)
ROCHESTER DEMOCRAT & CHRONICLE
55 Exchange Blvd (14614-2001)
PHONE........................585 232-7100
Fax: 585 258-2734
EMP: 26
SALES (est): 2.1MM **Privately Held**
SIC: 2711 Newspapers-Publishing/Printing

(G-14087)
ROCHESTER GEAR INC
213 Norman St (14613-1875)
PHONE........................585 254-5442
Anthony J Fedor, *President*
Scott Caccamise, *Exec VP*
EMP: 37
SQ FT: 25,000
SALES (est): 6.5MM **Privately Held**
WEB: www.rochestergear.com
SIC: 3566 Gears, power transmission, except automotive

(G-14088)
ROCHESTER MIDLAND CORPORATION (PA)
155 Paragon Dr (14624-1167)
P.O. Box 64462 (14624-6862)
PHONE........................585 336-2200
H Bradley Calkins, *CEO*
Harlan D Calkins, *Ch of Bd*
Kevin McCormick, *President*
Glenn A Paynter, *President*
Cathy Lindahl, *Co-CEO*
◆ EMP: 170
SQ FT: 190,000
SALES (est): 125.6MM **Privately Held**
WEB: www.rochestermidland.com
SIC: 2842 2676 2899 Specialty cleaning, polishes & sanitation goods; floor waxes; cleaning or polishing preparations; disinfectants, household or industrial plant; feminine hygiene paper products; chemical preparations

(G-14089)
ROCHESTER ORTHOPEDIC LABS (PA)
300 Airpark Dr Ste 100 (14624-5723)
PHONE........................585 272-1060
David Forbes, *President*
Gerald Tendall, *Vice Pres*
Eric Ober, *Admin Sec*
EMP: 8 EST: 1962
SQ FT: 12,000
SALES (est): 1.9MM **Privately Held**
WEB: www.rochesterorthopediclabs.com
SIC: 3842 Limbs, artificial; braces, elastic; braces, orthopedic

(G-14090)
ROCHESTER OVERNIGHT PLTG LLC
2 Cairn St (14611-2416)
PHONE........................585 328-4590
Catherine Hurd, *President*
Kathy Hurd, *COO*
Shirley Tallman, *Office Mgr*
EMP: 60
SQ FT: 40,000
SALES (est): 5.9MM **Privately Held**
WEB: www.rochesterplatingworks.com
SIC: 3471 Plating of metals or formed products

(G-14091)
ROCHESTER PHOTONICS CORP
115 Canal Landing Blvd (14626-5105)
PHONE........................585 387-0674
Michael Morris, *CEO*
Paul Marx, *President*
EMP: 60
SQ FT: 52,000
SALES (est): 4.5MM
SALES (corp-wide): 10.1B **Publicly Held**
WEB: www.corning.com
SIC: 3827 Optical instruments & lenses
PA: Corning Incorporated
1 Riverfront Plz
Corning NY 14831
607 974-9000

(G-14092)
ROCHESTER SEAL PRO LLC
53 Northwind Way (14624-2473)
PHONE........................585 594-3818
Joshua Piron, *President*
EMP: 5
SALES: 500K **Privately Held**
SIC: 2951 0781 Asphalt paving mixtures & blocks; landscape services

(G-14093)
ROCHESTER SILVER WORKS LLC
100 Latona Rd Bldg 110 (14652-0001)
P.O. Box 15397 (14615-0397)
PHONE........................585 477-9501
David Dix, *Opers Mgr*
Bob Surash, *Technical Mgr*
Chuck Hirbour, *Regl Sales Mgr*
▲ EMP: 50
SALES (est): 13.2MM **Privately Held**
SIC: 1044 Silver ores processing

(G-14094)
ROCHESTER SILVER WORKS LLC
240 Aster St (14615)
P.O. Box 15397 (14615-0397)
PHONE........................585 743-1610
Ralph Holmes, *Purch Mgr*
Tammy Wilmier, *Accounting Mgr*
▲ EMP: 9
SALES (est): 1MM **Privately Held**
SIC: 3339 Silver refining (primary)

(G-14095)
ROCHESTER STAMPINGS INC
400 Trade Ct (14624-4773)
PHONE........................585 467-5241
L Charles Hicks, *President*
EMP: 16 EST: 1958
SQ FT: 15,000
SALES (est): 2.9MM **Privately Held**
WEB: www.rochstamp.com
SIC: 3544 3469 3452 Special dies & tools; metal stampings; bolts, nuts, rivets & washers

(G-14096)
ROCHESTER STEEL TREATING WORKS
962 E Main St (14605-2780)
PHONE........................585 546-3348
Eugene Miller, *President*
Bryan Miller, *Production*
EMP: 18
SQ FT: 13,000
SALES (est): 2MM **Privately Held**
WEB: www.rstwinc.com
SIC: 3398 Metal heat treating

(G-14097)
ROCHESTER STRUCTURAL LLC
961 Lyell Ave Bldg 5 (14606-1956)
PHONE........................585 436-1250
David Yelle, *President*
Justin Yelle, *Project Mgr*
Brian Carmer,
EMP: 25
SQ FT: 15,000
SALES (est): 7.1MM **Privately Held**
SIC: 3312 1791 Structural shapes & pilings, steel; structural steel erection

(G-14098)
ROCHESTER TOOL AND MOLD INC
515 Lee Rd (14606-4236)
PHONE........................585 464-9336
Al Kapoor, *President*
Paul Tolley, *Vice Pres*
EMP: 11
SQ FT: 5,600
SALES (est): 1.8MM **Privately Held**
WEB: www.rochestertoolandmold.com
SIC: 3544 3599 Industrial molds; machine shop, jobbing & repair

(G-14099)
ROCHESTER TUBE FABRICATORS
1128 Lexington Ave 5d (14606-2909)
PHONE........................585 254-0290
James R Bunting, *Principal*
EMP: 10
SALES (est): 1.3MM **Privately Held**
SIC: 3498 Fabricated pipe & fittings

(G-14100)
ROCHLING ADVENT TOOL & MOLD LP
999 Ridgeway Ave (14615-3819)
PHONE........................585 254-2000
Ken Desrosiers, *General Ptnr*
Paul Klingler, *Engineer*
James Andolina, *Sales Mgr*
EMP: 63
SALES (est): 21.3MM
SALES (corp-wide): 1.7B **Privately Held**
SIC: 3089 3544 3545 Injection molding of plastics; industrial molds; tools & accessories for machine tools
HQ: Rochling Engineering Plastics Se & Co. Kg
Rochlingstr. 1
Haren (Ems) 49733
593 470-10

(G-14101)
ROESSEL & CO INC
199 Lagrange Ave (14613-1593)
PHONE........................585 458-5560
William R Laitenberger, *President*
Kathy Laitenberger, *President*
Alfred P Laitenberger, *Treasurer*
David Feavearyear, *Accounts Mgr*
Glenn Zwetsch, *Sales Staff*
EMP: 8 EST: 1952
SQ FT: 6,000
SALES: 2MM **Privately Held**
WEB: www.roessel.com
SIC: 3823 Water quality monitoring & control systems

(G-14102)
ROHRBACH BREWING COMPANY INC
3859 Buffalo Rd (14624-1103)
PHONE........................585 594-9800
John Urlaub, *President*
Patricia Yahn-Urlaub, *Vice Pres*
EMP: 60
SQ FT: 6,000
SALES (est): 5.9MM **Privately Held**
WEB: www.rohrbachs.com
SIC: 2082 Beer (alcoholic beverage)

(G-14103)
ROMOLD INC
5 Moonlanding Rd (14624-2505)
PHONE........................585 529-4440
Louis Romano, *President*
Diane Romano, *Corp Secy*
Cheryl Kuhn, *Admin Asst*
▲ EMP: 16
SQ FT: 11,500
SALES (est): 1.3MM **Privately Held**
WEB: www.romold.net
SIC: 3544 Industrial molds

(G-14104)
ROTORK CONTROLS INC
Also Called: Jordon Controls
675 Mile Crossing Blvd (14624-6212)
PHONE........................585 328-1550
Brian Hennig, *Info Tech Dir*
EMP: 12

GEOGRAPHIC SECTION

Rochester - Monroe County (G-14131)

SALES (corp-wide): 848.5MM **Privately Held**
SIC: 3625 Actuators, industrial
HQ: Rotork Controls Inc.
675 Mile Crossing Blvd
Rochester NY 14624
585 247-2304

(G-14105)
ROTORK CONTROLS INC (DH)
675 Mile Crossing Blvd (14624-6212)
PHONE...................................585 247-2304
Robert H Arnold, *Ch of Bd*
William H Whiteley, *President*
Fred Dowdeswell, *Vice Pres*
▲ EMP: 160 EST: 1967
SALES (est): 48.2MM
SALES (corp-wide): 848.5MM **Privately Held**
SIC: 3625 Actuators, industrial
HQ: Rotork Overseas Limited
Rotork House
Bath
122 573-3200

(G-14106)
RPC PHOTONICS INC
330 Clay Rd (14623-3227)
PHONE...................................585 272-2840
Dr G Michael Morris, *CEO*
Mark A Hirschler, *Facilities Mgr*
Sam Ward, *Engineer*
Jeffrey Shaw, *Design Engr*
Lisa Kingsley, *Controller*
EMP: 19
SALES (est): 5MM **Privately Held**
SIC: 3827 Optical instruments & apparatus

(G-14107)
RT SOLUTIONS LLC
Also Called: Worm Power
80 Linden Oaks Ste 210 (14625-2809)
PHONE...................................585 245-3456
Thomas Herlihy, *President*
Shawn Ferro, *Manager*
EMP: 8
SQ FT: 80,000
SALES (est): 1.3MM **Privately Held**
SIC: 2873 8711 Nitrogenous fertilizers; engineering services

(G-14108)
SAFE PASSAGE INTERNATIONAL INC
333 Metro Park Ste F204 (14623-2632)
PHONE...................................585 292-4910
Andrew Figiel, *Owner*
Michael Rooksby, *COO*
Lew Pulvino, *Sales Executive*
Gregory Wahl, *Sales Executive*
Vicki Tran, *Mktg Coord*
EMP: 14
SQ FT: 3,500
SALES: 1.2MM **Privately Held**
WEB: www.safe-passage.com
SIC: 7372 7371 Prepackaged software; custom computer programming services

(G-14109)
SAMCO SCIENTIFIC LLC
Also Called: Samco Scientific Corporation
75 Panorama Creek Dr (14625-2303)
PHONE...................................800 522-3359
Tuyen Nguyen, *Principal*
◆ EMP: 167
SQ FT: 80,000
SALES (est): 15MM
SALES (corp-wide): 20.9B **Publicly Held**
WEB: www.samcosci.com
SIC: 3085 Plastics bottles
HQ: Fisher Scientific International Llc
81 Wyman St
Waltham MA 02451
781 622-1000

(G-14110)
SANDSTONE TECHNOLOGIES CORP (PA)
2117 Buffalo Rd 245 (14624-1507)
PHONE...................................585 785-5537
Timothy Williams, *President*
◆ EMP: 1
SALES: 1MM **Privately Held**
SIC: 3661 Fiber optics communications equipment

(G-14111)
SANDSTONE TECHNOLOGIES CORP
2117 Buffalo Rd Unit 245 (14624-1507)
PHONE...................................585 785-5537
Matthew Brodie, *Branch Mgr*
EMP: 7
SALES (corp-wide): 1MM **Privately Held**
SIC: 3661 Fiber optics communications equipment
PA: Sandstone Technologies Corp.
2117 Buffalo Rd 245
Rochester NY 14624
585 785-5537

(G-14112)
SATISPIE LLC
155 Balta Dr (14623-3142)
PHONE...................................716 982-4600
Mike Pinkowski,
▲ EMP: 20
SALES (est): 5.5MM **Privately Held**
WEB: www.satispie.com
SIC: 2051 Cakes, pies & pastries

(G-14113)
SAVAGE & SON INSTALLATIONS LLC
676 Pullman Ave (14615-3335)
P.O. Box 12647 (14612-0647)
PHONE...................................585 342-7533
Gerald Champman,
EMP: 30 EST: 2008
SALES (est): 4.1MM **Privately Held**
SIC: 2952 Mastic roofing composition

(G-14114)
SCHLEGEL ELECTRONIC MTLS INC (PA)
1600 Lexington Ave # 236 (14606-3068)
PHONE...................................585 295-2030
Johnny C C Lo, *President*
EMP: 15
SQ FT: 25,000
SALES (est): 2.3MM **Privately Held**
SIC: 3053 Gaskets & sealing devices

(G-14115)
SCHLEGEL SYSTEMS INC (DH)
Also Called: S S I
1555 Jefferson Rd (14623-3109)
PHONE...................................585 427-7200
Jeff Grady, *CEO*
Jonathan Petromelis, *Ch of Bd*
Santiago Garcia, *Sales Staff*
Brian Olson, *Manager*
Robert Welch, *Manager*
▲ EMP: 200 EST: 1885
SQ FT: 150,000
SALES (est): 282.3MM
SALES (corp-wide): 690.6MM **Privately Held**
WEB: www.schlegel.com
SIC: 3053 3089 3069 Gaskets, packing & sealing devices; plastic hardware & building products; pillows, sponge rubber

(G-14116)
SCHWAB CORP (DH)
900 Linden Ave (14625-2700)
PHONE...................................585 381-4900
James Brush, *President*
Denise Booream, *Partner*
Mark Lockerby, *Vice Pres*
Jerry Ronjue, *CFO*
Doug Brush, *Director*
▼ EMP: 30 EST: 1872
SQ FT: 10,000
SALES (est): 12.2MM
SALES (corp-wide): 5.2B **Publicly Held**
WEB: www.schwabcorp.com
SIC: 3499 3442 2522 Safes & vaults, metal; fire doors, metal; file drawer frames; except wood
HQ: Sentry Safe, Inc.
137 W Forest Hill Ave
Oak Creek WI 53154
585 381-4900

(G-14117)
SCJ ASSOCIATES INC
60 Commerce Dr (14623-3502)
PHONE...................................585 359-0600
Scott Sutherland, *Ch of Bd*
Laurie Rosekrans, *Project Mgr*
Mike Pieramico, *Mfg Staff*
Mark Sweers, *Mfg Staff*
Bruce Heacock, *Buyer*
EMP: 40
SQ FT: 15,000
SALES (est): 11.4MM **Privately Held**
WEB: www.scjassociates.com
SIC: 3825 Test equipment for electronic & electric measurement

(G-14118)
SDJ MACHINE SHOP INC
1215 Mount Read Blvd # 1 (14606-2895)
PHONE...................................585 458-1236
Don Celestino, *President*
EMP: 11
SQ FT: 20,000
SALES (est): 1.8MM **Privately Held**
WEB: www.sdjmachine.com
SIC: 3599 Machine shop, jobbing & repair

(G-14119)
SEISENBACHER INC
175 Humboldt St Ste 250 (14610-1058)
PHONE...................................585 730-4960
Ken Biggins, *CEO*
Werner Pumhosel, *Director*
Lisa Testa, *Admin Sec*
EMP: 10 EST: 2016
SALES (est): 137.5K **Privately Held**
SIC: 3743 Rapid transit cars & equipment

(G-14120)
SELBY MARKETING ASSOCIATES INC (PA)
Also Called: Direct 2 Market Solutions
1001 Lexington Aveste 800 (14606)
PHONE...................................585 377-0750
Richard L Selby, *President*
EMP: 15
SQ FT: 6,000
SALES: 3MM **Privately Held**
SIC: 2741 7319 Miscellaneous publishing; media buying service

(G-14121)
SEMROK INC
Also Called: Semrock
3625 Buffalo Rd Ste 6 (14624-1179)
PHONE...................................585 594-7050
Victor Mizrahi, *President*
Craig Hodgson, *Engineer*
Michael Hogan, *Engineer*
Jeremy Grace, *Design Engr*
James Kircher, *Design Engr*
EMP: 99
SQ FT: 22,000
SALES (est): 834.6K
SALES (corp-wide): 2.2B **Publicly Held**
WEB: www.semrock.com
SIC: 3229 Optical glass
PA: Idex Corporation
1925 W Field Ct Ste 200
Lake Forest IL 60045
847 498-7070

(G-14122)
SERI SYSTEMS INC
172 Metro Park (14623-2610)
PHONE...................................585 272-5515
Ron Lablanc, *Vice Pres*
Martin Sondervan, *Vice Pres*
Dan Wagner, *Vice Pres*
Robert McJury, *VP Sales*
EMP: 20
SQ FT: 6,000
SALES: 2MM **Privately Held**
SIC: 2759 Decals: printing; labels & seals: printing; screen printing

(G-14123)
SHADE TREE GREETINGS INC
704 Clinton Ave S (14620-1454)
PHONE...................................585 442-4580
Richard Cancilla, *President*
EMP: 12
SALES (est): 122.9K **Privately Held**
SIC: 2771 2759 Greeting cards; invitation & stationery printing & engraving

(G-14124)
SHAMROCK PLASTIC CORPORATION
95 Mount Read Blvd (14611-1923)
PHONE...................................585 328-6040
Timothy Kelly, *President*
EMP: 5
SALES: 1.2MM **Privately Held**
SIC: 3089 Plastic processing

(G-14125)
SHAMROCK PLASTICS & TOOL INC
95 Mount Read Blvd # 149 (14611-1933)
PHONE...................................585 328-6040
Timothy Kelly, *President*
EMP: 5
SQ FT: 10,000
SALES: 1.2MM **Privately Held**
SIC: 3089 Plastic processing

(G-14126)
SIEMENS INDUSTRY INC
50 Methodist Hill Dr # 1500 (14623-4269)
PHONE...................................585 797-2300
Greg Aiken, *Branch Mgr*
EMP: 40
SALES (corp-wide): 97.7B **Privately Held**
WEB: www.sibt.com
SIC: 3822 7629 1731 5075 Temperature controls, automatic; electrical equipment repair services; electrical work; warm air heating & air conditioning; plumbing & hydronic heating supplies
HQ: Siemens Industry, Inc.
100 Technology Dr
Alpharetta GA 30005
770 740-3000

(G-14127)
SIGN IMPRESSIONS INC
2590 W Ridge Rd Ste 6 (14626-3041)
PHONE...................................585 723-0420
Gerald Mallaber, *President*
EMP: 8
SQ FT: 3,000
SALES (est): 1MM **Privately Held**
WEB: www.signimpressions.com
SIC: 3993 Signs, not made in custom sign painting shops

(G-14128)
SIGNATURE NAME PLATE CO INC
292 Commerce Dr (14623-3506)
PHONE...................................585 321-9960
William Monell, *President*
Harry T Bain Jr, *Vice Pres*
EMP: 7
SQ FT: 9,000
SALES (est): 784.9K **Privately Held**
WEB: www.signaturenp.com
SIC: 3993 Name plates: except engraved, etched, etc.: metal

(G-14129)
SIKORSKY AIRCRAFT CORPORATION
Also Called: Impact Tech A Skrsky Innvtions
300 Canal View Blvd (14623-2811)
PHONE...................................585 424-1990
James Cycon, *General Mgr*
EMP: 68 **Publicly Held**
SIC: 3721 Aircraft
HQ: Sikorsky Aircraft Corporation
6900 Main St
Stratford CT 06614

(G-14130)
SKILLSOFT CORPORATION
Also Called: Element K
500 Canal View Blvd (14623-2800)
PHONE...................................585 240-7500
Bruce Barnes, *Chairman*
Christopher Harte, *Vice Pres*
Conrad Taylor, *Accounts Mgr*
Prabhakaran Nagarajan, *Director*
EMP: 10
SALES (corp-wide): 352.2K **Privately Held**
SIC: 7372 Educational computer software
HQ: Skillsoft Corporation
300 Innovative Way # 201
Nashua NH 03062
603 324-3000

(G-14131)
SLIM LINE CASE CO INC
64 Spencer St (14608-1423)
PHONE...................................585 546-3639
Bette Thomas, *CEO*

Rochester - Monroe County (G-14132)

Andrea Coulter, *President*
EMP: 15
SQ FT: 14,000
SALES: 560K **Privately Held**
WEB: www.slimlinecase.com
SIC: 3172 Leather cases

(G-14132)
SOCIAL SCIENCE ELECTRONIC PUBG
1239 University Ave (14607-1636)
PHONE..................585 442-8170
Greg Gordon, *President*
EMP: 16 **EST:** 1996
SALES (est): 1.2MM **Privately Held**
WEB: www.ssrn.com
SIC: 2741 8299 Miscellaneous publishing; educational services

(G-14133)
SOLID CELL INC
771 Elmgrove Rd (14624-6200)
PHONE..................585 426-5000
Sergey Somov, *Research*
Zachary Rosen, *CFO*
EMP: 10
SALES (est): 1.9MM **Privately Held**
SIC: 3674 Semiconductors & related devices

(G-14134)
SOLID SURFACES INC
1 Townline Cir (14623-2513)
PHONE..................585 292-5340
Gregg Sadwick, *President*
EMP: 100
SQ FT: 7,800
SALES (est): 4.5MM
SALES (corp-wide): 113.8MM **Privately Held**
WEB: www.solidsurfacesinc.net
SIC: 2541 2821 Counter & sink tops; table or counter tops, plastic laminated; plastics materials & resins
PA: Clio Holdings Llc
300 Park St Ste 380
Birmingham MI

(G-14135)
SOUND SOURCE INC
161 Norris Dr (14610-2422)
PHONE..................585 271-5370
John Castronova, *President*
Robert Storms, *Vice Pres*
EMP: 7
SQ FT: 7,500
SALES (est): 982.4K **Privately Held**
SIC: 3931 5731 Musical instruments; consumer electronic equipment

(G-14136)
SPECTRACOM CORPORATION (DH)
1565 Jefferson Rd Ste 460 (14623-3190)
PHONE..................585 321-5800
Jan-Yves Courtois, *President*
EMP: 39
SALES (est): 11MM **Privately Held**
SIC: 3663 Radio & TV communications equipment
HQ: Orolia Holding Sas
Drakkar Batiment D
Valbonne
492 907-040

(G-14137)
SPECTRUM CABLE CORPORATION
295 Mount Read Blvd Ste 2 (14611-1967)
PHONE..................585 235-7714
Marc Iacona, *CEO*
Mark Philip, *President*
Simon Braitman, *Corp Secy*
EMP: 6 **EST:** 1973
SQ FT: 17,000
SALES: 1.3MM **Privately Held**
WEB: www.spectrumcablecorp.com
SIC: 3315 1731 Wire & fabricated wire products; electrical work

(G-14138)
SPIN-RITE CORPORATION
30 Dubelbeiss Ln (14622-2402)
P.O. Box 67184 (14617-7184)
PHONE..................585 266-5200

Gary Bohrer, *President*
EMP: 16
SQ FT: 1,400
SALES (est): 3.5MM **Privately Held**
SIC: 3312 Tool & die steel & alloys

(G-14139)
SPX CORPORATION
SPX Flow Technology
135 Mount Read Blvd (14611-1921)
P.O. Box 31370 (14603-1370)
PHONE..................585 436-5550
Laura Dwyer, *Vice Pres*
Jim Mayers, *Branch Mgr*
EMP: 480
SALES (corp-wide): 1.4B **Publicly Held**
WEB: www.spx.com
SIC: 3443 Cooling towers, metal plate
PA: Spx Corporation
13320a Balntyn Corp Pl
Charlotte NC 28277
980 474-3700

(G-14140)
SPX FLOW US LLC (HQ)
Also Called: SPX Flow Technology
135 Mount Read Blvd (14611-1921)
PHONE..................585 436-5550
Paul Ipolito, *QC Mgr*
Christopher J Kearney,
EMP: 94
SALES (est): 281.5MM
SALES (corp-wide): 1.9B **Publicly Held**
SIC: 3824 7699 Impeller & counter driven flow meters; cash register repair
PA: Spx Flow, Inc.
13320 Balntyn Corp Pl
Charlotte NC 28277
704 752-4400

(G-14141)
STAMPER TECHNOLOGY INC
232 Wallace Way (14624-6216)
PHONE..................585 247-8370
Bruce Ha, *President*
▲ **EMP:** 7
SQ FT: 5,000
SALES (est): 1.2MM **Privately Held**
SIC: 3695 Magnetic & optical recording media

(G-14142)
STEEL WORK INC
340 Oak St (14608-1727)
PHONE..................585 232-1555
Tim Grove, *President*
EMP: 9
SQ FT: 7,000
SALES (est): 1.4MM **Privately Held**
WEB: www.steelwork.com
SIC: 3446 3444 Architectural metalwork; sheet metalwork

(G-14143)
STEFAN SYDOR OPTICS INC
31 Jetview Dr (14624-4903)
P.O. Box 20001 (14602-0001)
PHONE..................585 271-7300
James Sydor, *President*
Michael Naselaris, *General Mgr*
Jonathan Sydor, *Production*
Zachary Hobbs, *Engineer*
Michael Vergo, *Sales Engr*
▼ **EMP:** 43
SQ FT: 40,000
SALES (est): 11.1MM **Privately Held**
WEB: www.sydor.com
SIC: 3827 3229 3211 Optical instruments & apparatus; pressed & blown glass; flat glass

(G-14144)
STERILIZ LLC
150 Linden Oaks Ste B (14625-2824)
PHONE..................585 415-5411
James T Townsend,
Samuel R Trapani,
EMP: 5
SALES (est): 691.9K **Privately Held**
SIC: 3821 3842 Sterilizers; sterilizers, hospital & surgical

(G-14145)
STEVEN COFFEY PALLET S INC
3376 Edgemere Dr (14612-1128)
PHONE..................585 261-6783

Steven Coffey, *Principal*
EMP: 8
SALES (est): 960.1K **Privately Held**
SIC: 2448 Pallets, wood & wood with metal

(G-14146)
STRAUSS EYE PROSTHETICS INC
360 White Spruce Blvd (14623-1604)
PHONE..................585 424-1350
James V Strauss, *President*
Josie Strauss, *Admin Sec*
EMP: 5 **EST:** 1978
SQ FT: 2,024
SALES (est): 310K **Privately Held**
WEB: www.strausseye.com
SIC: 3851 Eyes, glass & plastic

(G-14147)
STRIKER ORTHOPEDICS
7 Linden Park (14625-2712)
PHONE..................585 381-1773
Thomas B Housler, *President*
Harold J Housler, *Corp Secy*
Robert A Housler, *Vice Pres*
EMP: 20
SQ FT: 7,800
SALES (est): 2.6MM **Privately Held**
SIC: 3841 Surgical & medical instruments

(G-14148)
SUPERIOR TECHNOLOGY INC
200 Paragon Dr (14624-1159)
PHONE..................585 352-6556
John P Shortino, *President*
Anthony J Shortino, *Vice Pres*
Joseph Shortino, *Vice Pres*
Aaron Mandarano, *Manager*
▲ **EMP:** 50 **EST:** 1987
SQ FT: 36,500
SALES (est): 10.3MM **Privately Held**
WEB: www.superiortech.org
SIC: 3599 Machine shop, jobbing & repair

(G-14149)
SWEETWATER ENERGY INC
500 Lee Rd Ste 200 (14606-4261)
PHONE..................585 647-5760
Jack Baron, *CEO*
Ron Boillat, *Exec VP*
Jonathan Sherwood, *Vice Pres*
Sharon Samjitsingh, *Project Mgr*
Rodney Smithback, *Project Mgr*
▲ **EMP:** 7
SALES (est): 1.3MM **Privately Held**
SIC: 2046 Corn sugar

(G-14150)
SWIFT MULTIGRAPHICS LLC
55 Southwood Ln (14618-4019)
PHONE..................585 442-8000
Kenneth Stahl, *Principal*
EMP: 2
SQ FT: 200
SALES: 1MM **Privately Held**
SIC: 2759 3999 Promotional printing; advertising display products

(G-14151)
SYNERGY FLAVORS NY COMPANY LLC
Also Called: Vanlab
86 White St (14608-1435)
PHONE..................585 232-6648
Bob Strassner, *Branch Mgr*
EMP: 9 **Privately Held**
SIC: 2087 Flavoring extracts & syrups
HQ: Synergy Flavors (Ny) Company Llc
1500 Synergy Dr
Wauconda IL 60084
585 232-6648

(G-14152)
SYNTEC TECHNOLOGIES INC (PA)
Also Called: Syntec Optics
515 Lee Rd (14606-4236)
PHONE..................585 768-2513
Alok Kapoor, *President*
Terry Phelix, *President*
Richard Arndt, *Vice Pres*
Steve Polvinen, *Vice Pres*
Douglas Axtell, *VP Opers*
EMP: 50
SQ FT: 25,000

SALES (est): 16.1MM **Privately Held**
WEB: www.syntecoptics.com
SIC: 3089 Injection molding of plastics

(G-14153)
SYNTEC TECHNOLOGIES INC
Also Called: Syntec Optics
515 Lee Rd (14606-4236)
PHONE..................585 464-9336
Phil Race, *Branch Mgr*
EMP: 11
SALES (corp-wide): 16.1MM **Privately Held**
WEB: www.syntecoptics.com
SIC: 3544 3599 Industrial molds; machine shop, jobbing & repair
PA: Syntec Technologies, Inc.
515 Lee Rd
Rochester NY 14606
585 768-2513

(G-14154)
T & C POWER CONVERSION INC
132 Humboldt St (14610-1046)
PHONE..................585 482-5551
Tomasz Mokrzan, *President*
EMP: 13
SQ FT: 3,000
SALES (est): 2.5MM **Privately Held**
WEB: www.tcpowerconversion.com
SIC: 3825 Radio frequency measuring equipment

(G-14155)
T & L AUTOMATICS INC
770 Emerson St (14613-1895)
PHONE..................585 647-3717
Thomas W Hassett, *President*
Vincent Buzzelli, *Senior VP*
David Murphy, *Vice Pres*
EMP: 120
SQ FT: 120,000
SALES (est): 23.3MM **Privately Held**
WEB: www.tandlautomatics.com
SIC: 3451 Screw machine products

(G-14156)
T L F GRAPHICS INC (PA)
Also Called: Tlf Graphics
235 Metro Park (14623-2618)
PHONE..................585 272-5500
Ronald Leblanc, *Ch of Bd*
Aaron Burton, *President*
Dan Wagner, *Vice Pres*
Tom Crowley, *Materials Mgr*
Ray McHargue, *Safety Mgr*
EMP: 59
SQ FT: 12,000
SALES (est): 14.4MM **Privately Held**
SIC: 2672 2759 Tape, pressure sensitive: made from purchased materials; labels (unprinted), gummed: made from purchased materials; screen printing

(G-14157)
TAC SCREW PRODUCTS INC
170 Bennington Dr (14616-4754)
PHONE..................585 663-5840
Julius Papp, *President*
Mark Laisure, *Vice Pres*
EMP: 10
SQ FT: 4,000
SALES (est): 1.4MM **Privately Held**
SIC: 3451 Screw machine products

(G-14158)
TCS INDUSTRIES INC
400 Trabold Rd (14624-2529)
PHONE..................585 426-1160
Manoj Shekar, *President*
▲ **EMP:** 80
SQ FT: 110,000
SALES: 17MM **Privately Held**
WEB: www.tcsindustries.com
SIC: 3444 Sheet metalwork

(G-14159)
TE CONNECTIVITY CORPORATION
2245 Brighton Henrta Twn (14623-2705)
PHONE..................585 785-2500
John Rowe, *Manager*
EMP: 50
SALES (corp-wide): 13.1B **Privately Held**
WEB: www.raychem.com
SIC: 3679 Electronic circuits

GEOGRAPHIC SECTION
Rochester - Monroe County (G-14184)

HQ: Te Connectivity Corporation
1050 Westlakes Dr
Berwyn PA 19312
610 893-9800

(G-14160)
TEALE MACHINE COMPANY INC
1425 University Ave (14607-1617)
P.O. Box 10340 (14610-0340)
PHONE 585 244-6700
Ronald E Larock, *Ch of Bd*
Aimee Ciulla, *Vice Pres*
Michael E Larock, *Vice Pres*
Charlie Jackson, *Maint Spvr*
Ward Earley, *Purch Mgr*
EMP: 70
SQ FT: 22,000
SALES (est): 18.1MM **Privately Held**
WEB: www.tealemachine.com
SIC: 3451 3625 Screw machine products; numerical controls

(G-14161)
TECH PARK FOOD SERVICES LLC
Also Called: Rochester Technology Park
789 Elmgrove Rd (14624-6200)
PHONE 585 295-1250
Naresh Ramarathnan, *CFO*
EMP: 5
SALES (est): 310.9K **Privately Held**
SIC: 3721 1541 Research & development on aircraft by the manufacturer; warehouse construction

(G-14162)
TEL-TRU INC
392 Saint Paul St (14605-1733)
PHONE 585 232-1440
Jay Scott, *Branch Mgr*
EMP: 6
SALES (est): 701.2K **Privately Held**
SIC: 3823 Industrial instrmnts msrmnt display/control process variable
PA: Tel-Tru, Inc.
408 Saint Paul St
Rochester NY 14605

(G-14163)
TEL-TRU INC (PA)
Also Called: Tel-Tru Manufacturing Company
408 Saint Paul St (14605-1734)
PHONE 585 295-0225
Andrew Germanow, *President*
Paul Marchand, *Engineer*
Rebecca Blitzkie, *Sales Staff*
Brian Watson, *Manager*
Suzanne Mayer, *Consultant*
EMP: 56
SALES (est): 11.1MM **Privately Held**
SIC: 3823 Temperature measurement instruments, industrial; resistance thermometers & bulbs, industrial process type

(G-14164)
TELEDYNE OPTECH INC
1046 University Ave # 149 (14607-1672)
PHONE 585 427-8310
Maxime Elbaz, *President*
EMP: 13
SALES (est): 2.3MM
SALES (corp-wide): 2.6B **Publicly Held**
SIC: 3699 3845 Laser systems & equipment; laser systems & equipment, medical
HQ: Teledyne Optech Incorporated
300 Interchange Way
Vaughan ON L4K 5
905 660-0808

(G-14165)
THE CALDWELL MANUFACTURING CO (PA)
2605 Manitou Rd Ste 100 (14624-1199)
P.O. Box 92891 (14692-8991)
PHONE 585 352-3790
Edward A Boucher, *CEO*
Eric W Mertz, *Ch of Bd*
James Boucher, *Ch of Bd*
Tom Fening, *Vice Pres*
Kevin Novak, *VP Mfg*
◆ EMP: 100 EST: 1888
SQ FT: 126,000
SALES (est): 50MM **Privately Held**
WEB: www.caldwellmfgco.com
SIC: 3495 Wire springs

(G-14166)
THERMO FISHER SCIENTIFIC INC
1999 Mnt Rd Blvd 1-3 (14615)
PHONE 585 458-8008
Helene Diederich, *Branch Mgr*
EMP: 307
SALES (corp-wide): 20.9B **Publicly Held**
WEB: www.thermo.com
SIC: 3826 Analytical instruments
PA: Thermo Fisher Scientific Inc.
168 3rd Ave
Waltham MA 02451
781 622-1000

(G-14167)
THERMO FISHER SCIENTIFIC INC
75 Panorama Creek Dr (14625-2385)
PHONE 585 899-7610
Rajat Mehta, *General Mgr*
Steve Silverman, *Vice Pres*
Jeff Cloutier, *VP Opers*
Verne Larose, *Technology*
Dave Eddy, *Director*
EMP: 900
SALES (corp-wide): 20.9B **Publicly Held**
SIC: 3826 Analytical instruments
PA: Thermo Fisher Scientific Inc.
168 3rd Ave
Waltham MA 02451
781 622-1000

(G-14168)
THREE POINT VENTURES LLC
Also Called: Skooba Design
3495 Winton Pl Ste E120 (14623-2838)
PHONE 585 697-3444
Michael J Hess,
▲ EMP: 10
SQ FT: 20,000
SALES (est): 640K **Privately Held**
WEB: www.roadwired.com
SIC: 3161 Cases, carrying

(G-14169)
THREE R ENTERPRISES INC
Also Called: Jason Manufacturing Company
447 Adirondack St (14606-2213)
PHONE 585 254-5050
Richard Wallenhorst II, *President*
EMP: 30 EST: 1981
SQ FT: 10,000
SALES (est): 4MM **Privately Held**
SIC: 2431 2541 2521 Millwork; store fixtures, wood; office fixtures, wood; cabinets, office: wood

(G-14170)
THYSSENKRUPP MATERIALS NA INC
Copper & Brass Sales
1673 Lyell Ave (14606-2311)
PHONE 585 279-0000
Dick Blake, *Branch Mgr*
EMP: 5
SALES (corp-wide): 48.7B **Privately Held**
SIC: 3317 3465 Tubes, wrought: welded or lock joint; automotive stampings
HQ: Thyssenkrupp Materials Na, Inc.
22355 W 11 Mile Rd
Southfield MI 48033
248 233-5600

(G-14171)
TODD WALBRIDGE
Also Called: T M Design Screen Printing
1916 Lyell Ave (14606-2306)
PHONE 585 254-3018
Todd Walbridge, *Owner*
EMP: 7
SQ FT: 3,500
SALES (est): 732.8K **Privately Held**
WEB: www.tmdesigncorp.com
SIC: 2759 3993 2396 2395 Screen printing; signs & advertising specialties; automotive & apparel trimmings; pleating & stitching

(G-14172)
TOKENIZE INC
125 Tech Park Dr 2137b (14623-2446)
PHONE 585 981-9919
Melanie Shapiro, *CEO*
EMP: 11 EST: 2014

SALES (est): 1.1MM **Privately Held**
SIC: 3669 8731 Intercommunication systems, electric; computer (hardware) development

(G-14173)
TOUCHSTONE TECHNOLOGY INC
350 Mile Crossing Blvd (14624-6207)
PHONE 585 458-2690
Eric B Snavely, *Ch of Bd*
Alan Robertson, *Engineer*
Todd Sheehan, *Design Engr*
David J Meisenzahl, *CFO*
Kelly Fairchild, *Controller*
▲ EMP: 16
SQ FT: 13,000
SALES (est): 5.5MM **Privately Held**
WEB: www.touchstn.com
SIC: 3575 Computer terminals, monitors & components; keyboards, computer, office machine

(G-14174)
TRANE US INC
75 Town Centre Dr Ste I (14623-4259)
PHONE 585 256-2500
Dan Wendo, *Branch Mgr*
EMP: 47 **Privately Held**
SIC: 3585 Refrigeration & heating equipment
HQ: Trane U.S. Inc.
3600 Pammel Creek Rd
La Crosse WI 54601
608 787-2000

(G-14175)
TRANSCAT INC (PA)
35 Vantage Point Dr (14624-1175)
PHONE 585 352-7777
Charles P Hadeed, *Ch of Bd*
Lee D Rudow, *President*
Peter Hadeed, *Business Mgr*
Amber Weber, *Business Mgr*
Robert A Flack, *Vice Pres*
◆ EMP: 277
SQ FT: 37,300
SALES (est): 155.1MM **Publicly Held**
WEB: www.transmationcorp.com
SIC: 3825 7699 Instruments to measure electricity; scientific equipment repair service

(G-14176)
TRIPLEX INDUSTRIES INC
100 Boxart St Ste 27 (14612-5659)
PHONE 585 621-6920
Christa Roesner, *President*
Patrick Moran, *Opers Staff*
Scott Patrick, *QC Mgr*
Jeff Jones, *Regl Sales Mgr*
EMP: 10
SQ FT: 8,500
SALES (est): 1.6MM **Privately Held**
SIC: 3544 Special dies, tools, jigs & fixtures

(G-14177)
TROYER INC
4555 Lyell Rd (14606-4316)
PHONE 585 352-5590
William Colton, *President*
EMP: 15
SQ FT: 18,000
SALES (est): 2.2MM **Privately Held**
SIC: 3711 3714 5531 Automobile assembly, including specialty automobiles; motor vehicle parts & accessories; speed shops, including race car supplies

(G-14178)
TRUESENSE IMAGING INC
1964 Lake Ave (14615-2316)
PHONE 585 784-5500
Chris McNiffe, *CEO*
Rachel Kielon, *CFO*
Stephanie Newman, *Info Tech Mgr*
Wilson Weir, *Analyst*
EMP: 207 EST: 2011
SQ FT: 260,000
SALES (est): 26.2MM
SALES (corp-wide): 5.5B **Publicly Held**
SIC: 3861 Film, sensitized motion picture, X-ray, still camera, etc.

HQ: Semiconductor Components Industries, Llc
5005 E Mcdowell Rd
Phoenix AZ 85008
800 282-9855

(G-14179)
TRUFORM MANUFACTURING CORP
1500 N Clinton Ave (14621-2206)
PHONE 585 458-1090
Tyrone Reaves, *Ch of Bd*
Rick Caesar, *Engineer*
Stuart Kristensen, *Engineer*
EMP: 70
SQ FT: 45,000
SALES (est): 14.3MM **Privately Held**
WEB: www.truformmfg.com
SIC: 3444 Sheet metalwork

(G-14180)
TRUTH HARDWARE CORPORATION
Also Called: Amesburytruth
1555 Jefferson Rd (14623-3109)
PHONE 585 627-5964
Ken Rhodam, *Manager*
EMP: 6
SALES (corp-wide): 690.6MM **Privately Held**
SIC: 2431 3442 3429 Windows & window parts & trim, wood; metal doors, sash & trim; manufactured hardware (general)
HQ: Truth Hardware Corporation
3600 Minnesota Dr Ste 800
Minneapolis MN 55435

(G-14181)
TURNER BELLOWS INC
Also Called: Tb
526 Child St Ste 1 (14606-1187)
PHONE 585 235-4456
Marilyn Yeager, *CEO*
Amanda Pontaella, *Ch of Bd*
▲ EMP: 45
SQ FT: 85,000
SALES (est): 8.3MM **Privately Held**
WEB: www.turnerbellows.com
SIC: 3081 3069 3861 Unsupported plastics film & sheet; foam rubber; photographic sensitized goods

(G-14182)
TURNING POINT TOOL LLC
135 Dodge St (14606-1503)
PHONE 585 288-7380
Rob Kirby, *Opers Mgr*
Frank Pezzulo,
Robert Kirby,
EMP: 6
SALES (est): 778.5K **Privately Held**
WEB: www.turningpointtool.com
SIC: 3544 Special dies, tools, jigs & fixtures

(G-14183)
UCB PHARMA INC (PA)
755 Jefferson Rd (14623-3270)
PHONE 919 767-2555
Roch Doliveux, *CEO*
Chad Deegan, *District Mgr*
Aimee Ennis, *District Mgr*
Lindsay Wills, *Counsel*
Fabrice Enderlin, *Exec VP*
▲ EMP: 450
SQ FT: 556,000
SALES (est): 58.9MM **Privately Held**
SIC: 2833 2834 5122 Anesthetics, in bulk form; drugs & herbs: grading, grinding & milling; pharmaceutical preparations; pharmaceuticals

(G-14184)
ULTRA TOOL AND MANUFACTURING
159 Lagrange Ave (14613-1511)
P.O. Box 17860 (14617-0860)
PHONE 585 467-3700
Daniel E Herzog, *President*
James M Schmeer, *Vice Pres*
EMP: 13
SQ FT: 4,000
SALES: 1.3MM **Privately Held**
SIC: 3599 Machine shop, jobbing & repair

Rochester - Monroe County (G-14185) GEOGRAPHIC SECTION

(G-14185)
UNICELL BODY COMPANY INC
1319 Brighton Henrietta (14623-2408)
PHONE..............................585 424-2660
Dale Wunsch, *Purch Mgr*
Steven Bones, *Manager*
Steve Bones, *Manager*
EMP: 14
SQ FT: 7,200
SALES (corp-wide): 20MM **Privately Held**
WEB: www.unicell.com
SIC: 3713 Truck bodies (motor vehicles)
PA: Unicell Body Company, Inc
 571 Howard St
 Buffalo NY 14206
 716 853-8628

(G-14186)
UNIFAB INC
215 Tremont St Ste 31 (14608-2370)
PHONE..............................585 235-1760
Brian Malark, *President*
Bill Martin, *Vice Pres*
William S Martin, *Vice Pres*
EMP: 7
SQ FT: 2,500
SALES: 1MM **Privately Held**
SIC: 3089 Injection molding of plastics; plastic processing

(G-14187)
UNITHER MANUFACTURING LLC
755 Jefferson Rd (14623-3270)
PHONE..............................585 475-9000
Kevin Haehl, *General Mgr*
▲ **EMP:** 250
SALES (est): 63.7MM
SALES (corp-wide): 6.8MM **Privately Held**
SIC: 2834 Pharmaceutical preparations
HQ: Unither Pharmaceuticals
 Espace Industriel Nord
 Amiens 80080
 322 547-300

(G-14188)
UNITHER MANUFACTURING LLC
331 Clay Rd (14623-3226)
PHONE..............................585 274-5430
EMP: 11
SALES (est): 1.1MM **Privately Held**
SIC: 2834 Pharmaceutical preparations

(G-14189)
UNIVERSAL PRECISION CORP
40 Commerce Dr (14623-3502)
PHONE..............................585 321-9760
Michael J Schmitt, *President*
Michael Domenico, *Vice Pres*
Dana Goodman, *Opers Mgr*
Sonya Dotson, *QA Dir*
Jeff Hooper, *Treasurer*
EMP: 24
SQ FT: 12,000
SALES (est): 4.3MM **Privately Held**
WEB: www.universalprecision.com
SIC: 3444 Sheet metal specialties, not stamped

(G-14190)
UNIVERSITY OF ROCHESTER
Also Called: Labortory For Laser Energetics
250 E River Rd (14623-1212)
PHONE..............................585 275-3483
Michael Bock, *Engineer*
Robert Jungquist, *Engineer*
Alex Maltsev, *Engineer*
David Weiner, *Engineer*
Rebecca Wadsworth, *Manager*
EMP: 400
SALES (corp-wide): 3.6B **Privately Held**
WEB: www.rochester.edu
SIC: 3845 8221 Laser systems & equipment, medical; university
PA: University Of Rochester
 500 Joseph C Wilson Blvd
 Rochester NY 14627
 585 275-2121

(G-14191)
UPSTATE CABINET COMPANY INC
32 Marway Cir (14624-2321)
PHONE..............................585 429-5090
Todd Whelehan, *President*
Vincenzo Delucia, *Vice Pres*
Annette Whelehan, *Manager*
Donna Demanchick, *Admin Asst*
EMP: 14
SQ FT: 30,000
SALES (est): 1.8MM **Privately Held**
WEB: www.upstatecabinet.com
SIC: 2434 5712 Wood kitchen cabinets; furniture stores

(G-14192)
UPSTATE INCRETE INCORPORATED
49 Adelaide St (14606-2205)
PHONE..............................585 254-2010
Jeff Barlette, *Principal*
EMP: 9
SALES (est): 1.1MM **Privately Held**
SIC: 2421 Building & structural materials, wood

(G-14193)
UPSTATE NIAGARA COOP INC
Also Called: Sealtest Dairy Products
45 Fulton Ave (14608-1032)
PHONE..............................585 458-1880
John Gould, *Vice Pres*
Terry Wihlen, *Maint Spvr*
Rick Holz, *Manager*
Cindy Glaser, *Administration*
Oleg Stezherinskiy, *Maintence Staff*
EMP: 150
SQ FT: 40,000
SALES (corp-wide): 893.9MM **Privately Held**
SIC: 2026 Milk processing (pasteurizing, homogenizing, bottling)
PA: Upstate Niagara Cooperative, Inc.
 25 Anderson Rd
 Buffalo NY 14225
 716 892-3156

(G-14194)
USAIRPORTS SERVICES INC
Also Called: US Airports Flight Support Svc
1295 Scottsville Rd (14624-5125)
PHONE..............................585 527-6835
Anthony Castillo, *President*
EMP: 22
SQ FT: 29,800 **Privately Held**
WEB: www.usairportsflight.com
SIC: 3728 Refueling equipment for use in flight, airplane
PA: Usairports Services, Inc
 1 Airport Way Ste 300
 Rochester NY 14624

(G-14195)
VA INC
Also Called: Vincent Associates
803 Linden Ave Ste 1 (14625-2723)
PHONE..............................585 385-5930
Kevin Farrell, *Ch of Bd*
Stephen Pasquarella, *Vice Pres*
EMP: 25
SQ FT: 6,500
SALES (est): 4.3MM **Privately Held**
WEB: www.uniblitz.com
SIC: 3861 3827 Shutters, camera; optical instruments & lenses

(G-14196)
VACCINEX INC
1895 Mount Hope Ave (14620-4540)
PHONE..............................585 271-2700
Albert D Friedberg, *Ch of Bd*
Maurice Zauderer, *President*
Raymond E Watkins, *COO*
John E Leonard, *Senior VP*
Ernest S Smith, *Senior VP*
EMP: 44
SQ FT: 31,180
SALES: 90K **Privately Held**
WEB: www.vaccinex.com
SIC: 2834 Pharmaceutical preparations

(G-14197)
VALASSIS COMMUNICATIONS INC
Also Called: Printed Deals
5 Marway Cir Ste 8 (14624-2362)
PHONE..............................585 627-4138
EMP: 5 **Privately Held**
SIC: 2721 Magazines: publishing & printing
HQ: Valassis Communications, Inc.
 19975 Victor Pkwy
 Livonia MI 48152
 734 591-3000

(G-14198)
VAN REENEN TOOL & DIE INC
350 Commerce Dr 4 (14623-3508)
PHONE..............................585 288-6000
Richard Van Reenen, *President*
Richard V Reenen, *President*
Zack V Reenen, *Managing Dir*
Amy V Reenen, *Vice Pres*
EMP: 12 **EST:** 1977
SQ FT: 35,000
SALES (est): 1.8MM **Privately Held**
WEB: www.vanreenentoolanddieinc.com
SIC: 3469 3544 3599 Stamping metal for the trade; special dies, tools, jigs & fixtures; machine shop, jobbing & repair

(G-14199)
VAN THOMAS INC
Also Called: Ruggeri Manufacturing
740 Driving Park Ave G1 (14613-1594)
PHONE..............................585 426-1414
Charles E Thomas, *President*
Gary Vander Mallie, *Vice Pres*
▲ **EMP:** 35
SQ FT: 37,000
SALES: 850K **Privately Held**
SIC: 3599 3544 Machine & other job shop work; special dies, tools, jigs & fixtures

(G-14200)
VETERANS OFFSET PRINTING INC
Also Called: Veteran Offset Printing
500 N Goodman St (14609-6136)
PHONE..............................585 288-2900
Louie Difillippo, *President*
John Duque, *Vice Pres*
EMP: 3 **EST:** 1940
SALES: 2MM **Privately Held**
SIC: 2752 2759 Commercial printing, offset; commercial printing

(G-14201)
VIGNERI CHOCOLATE INC
810 Emerson St (14613-1804)
PHONE..............................585 254-6160
Alex Vigneri, *CEO*
◆ **EMP:** 7
SQ FT: 10,000
SALES: 500K **Privately Held**
SIC: 2064 Candy bars, including chocolate covered bars; chocolate candy, except solid chocolate

(G-14202)
W M T PUBLICATIONS INC
250 N Goodman St Ste 1 (14607-1150)
PHONE..............................585 244-3329
Mary Anna Towler, *President*
William J Towler, *Treasurer*
EMP: 16
SALES (est): 879.5K **Privately Held**
SIC: 2711 Newspapers, publishing & printing

(G-14203)
WATER WISE OF AMERICA INC
75 Bermar Park Ste 5 (14624-1500)
PHONE..............................585 232-1210
Michael Bromley, *President*
Anne Jefferson, *Corp Secy*
EMP: 10
SQ FT: 2,500
SALES (est): 1.6MM **Privately Held**
WEB: www.waterwiseofamerica.com
SIC: 2899 5169 Water treating compounds; chemicals & allied products

(G-14204)
WEB SEAL INC (PA)
15 Oregon St (14605-3094)
PHONE..............................585 546-1320
John F Hurley, *President*
Betty A Hurley, *Treasurer*
Bonnie Kaufman, *Accounting Mgr*
Julia Magone, *Manager*
Craig Covel, *Technology*
EMP: 20 **EST:** 1960
SQ FT: 13,000
SALES (est): 4.7MM **Privately Held**
WEB: www.websealinc.com
SIC: 3053 5085 Gaskets & sealing devices; seals, industrial

(G-14205)
WELCH MACHINE INC
961 Lyell Ave Bldg 1-6 (14606-1956)
PHONE..............................585 647-3578
Martin Welch, *President*
EMP: 5
SQ FT: 5,000
SALES (est): 633.4K **Privately Held**
SIC: 3541 Machine tool replacement & repair parts, metal cutting types

(G-14206)
WERE FORMS INC
500 Helendale Rd Ste 190 (14609-3125)
PHONE..............................585 482-4400
Kim Hostutler, *President*
Julie Mandalero, *Info Tech Mgr*
Julie Mandelaro, *Director*
EMP: 6
SQ FT: 2,000
SALES (est): 480K **Privately Held**
WEB: www.wereforms.com
SIC: 2759 Commercial printing

(G-14207)
WHIRLWIND MUSIC DISTRS INC
99 Ling Rd (14612-1965)
PHONE..............................800 733-9473
Michael Laiacona, *Principal*
Debbie Noble, *Prdtn Mgr*
Andrew Akins, *Production*
Holly Bryan, *Purch Agent*
Carl Cornell, *Chief Engr*
▲ **EMP:** 100
SQ FT: 28,000
SALES (est): 21.3MM **Privately Held**
WEB: www.whirlwindusa.com
SIC: 3651 3678 3663 3643 Audio electronic systems; amplifiers: radio, public address or musical instrument; public address systems; electronic connectors; radio & TV communications equipment; current-carrying wiring devices; nonferrous wiredrawing & insulating

(G-14208)
WHITESTONE DEV GROUP LLC
Also Called: Ry-Gan Printing
111 Humboldt St (14609-7463)
PHONE..............................585 482-7770
Scott Wihlen, *Mng Member*
Kathleen Wihlen, *Mng Member*
EMP: 8
SALES (est): 679.2K **Privately Held**
SIC: 2752 Commercial printing, lithographic

(G-14209)
WIKOFF COLOR CORPORATION
686 Pullman Ave (14615-3335)
PHONE..............................585 458-0653
EMP: 16
SALES (corp-wide): 150MM **Privately Held**
SIC: 2893 Printing ink
PA: Wikoff Color Corporation
 1886 Merritt Rd
 Fort Mill SC 29715
 803 548-2210

(G-14210)
WINDSOR TECHNOLOGY LLC
1527 Lyell Ave (14606-2121)
PHONE..............................585 461-2500
Grant Randall, *President*
Julie Sullivan, *General Mgr*
Chad Notebaert, *Engineer*
Eric Wright, *Engineer*
Mary Carlson, *Design Engr*
EMP: 10
SQ FT: 40,000
SALES (est): 10MM **Privately Held**
WEB: www.windsortec.com
SIC: 3672 Printed circuit boards

(G-14211)
WOERNER INDUSTRIES INC
Also Called: Wizer Equipment
485 Hague St (14606-1296)
PHONE..............................585 436-1934
Philip Collins, *President*

EMP: 40
SALES (corp-wide): 4MM **Privately Held**
WEB: www.lasscowizer.com
SIC: 3555 Printing trades machinery
PA: Woerner Industries, Llc
 485 Hague St
 Rochester NY
 585 235-1991

(G-14212)
WORDINGHAM MACHINE CO INC
Also Called: Wordingham Technologies
515 Lee Rd (14606-4236)
PHONE..................585 924-2294
Alok Kapoor, *CEO*
Todd Close, *QC Mgr*
Mark Hurlbut, *CFO*
Tim Bechtold, *Accounts Mgr*
Tony Phillips, *Sales Staff*
EMP: 45
SQ FT: 26,000
SALES (est): 9MM **Privately Held**
SIC: 3599 Machine shop, jobbing & repair

(G-14213)
XACTRA TECHNOLOGIES INC
105 Mclaughlin Rd Ste F (14615-3762)
PHONE..................585 426-2030
David W Binn, *President*
Michael Binn, *Manager*
EMP: 55
SQ FT: 33,000
SALES (est): 7.7MM **Privately Held**
WEB: www.prestigeprecision.com
SIC: 3545 Precision tools, machinists'

(G-14214)
XEROX CORPORATION
225 Tech Park Dr (14623-2444)
PHONE..................585 427-4500
Dave Kreienberg, *Project Mgr*
Bob Naccarella, *Systems Staff*
EMP: 125
SALES (corp-wide): 10.2B **Publicly Held**
WEB: www.xerox.com
SIC: 3861 3577 7629 7378 Photocopy machines; computer peripheral equipment; business machine repair, electric; computer peripheral equipment repair & maintenance; fine paper; property damage insurance; fire, marine & casualty insurance: mutual
PA: Xerox Corporation
 201 Merritt 7
 Norwalk CT 06851
 203 968-3000

(G-14215)
XEROX CORPORATION
80 Linden Oaks (14625-2809)
PHONE..................585 264-5584
EMP: 200
SALES (corp-wide): 21.4B **Publicly Held**
SIC: 3861 Mfg Photographic Equipment/Supplies
PA: Xerox Corporation
 45 Glover Ave Ste 700
 Norwalk CT 06851
 203 968-3000

(G-14216)
XLI CORPORATION
55 Vanguard Pkwy (14606-3101)
PHONE..................585 436-2250
Peter Schott, *Ch of Bd*
Curt Hampton, *Safety Mgr*
Vlade Kordovich, *Engineer*
Mary Tasciotti, *Human Res Dir*
Samuel Marchiando, *Sales Staff*
EMP: 60 EST: 1967
SQ FT: 35,000
SALES (est): 10.6MM **Privately Held**
WEB: www.xlionline.com
SIC: 3544 Special dies & tools

(G-14217)
YELLOWPAGECITYCOM
280 Kenneth Dr Ste 300 (14623-5263)
PHONE..................585 410-6688
Jamie Boyd, *Opers Mgr*
Ashley Poulton, *Production*
Michelle Quilitzsch, *Accounts Exec*
Bill Waite, *Sales Associate*
Janet Nelson, *Mktg Coord*
EMP: 15

SALES (est): 2MM **Privately Held**
SIC: 3993 Signs & advertising specialties

(G-14218)
ZELLER WOODWORKS LLC
35 Norman St (14613-1809)
PHONE..................585 254-7607
Fritz Zeller, *Mng Member*
Jason Cudzilo,
Daniel Fallon,
EMP: 10 EST: 2012
SQ FT: 10,000
SALES: 1MM **Privately Held**
SIC: 2431 Woodwork, interior & ornamental

(G-14219)
ZEROVALENT NANOMETALS INC
693 East Ave Ste 103 (14607-2160)
PHONE..................585 298-8592
Joseph Fargnoli, *Principal*
EMP: 7
SALES (est): 295.4K **Privately Held**
SIC: 3339 Antimony refining (primary); cobalt refining (primary); babbitt metal (primary); beryllium metal

(G-14220)
ZIP PRODUCTS INC
565 Blossom Rd Ste E (14610-1873)
PHONE..................585 482-0044
Nikolay Petukhov, *President*
EMP: 14 EST: 1998
SQ FT: 9,500
SALES: 800K **Privately Held**
SIC: 3599 3452 3429 Machine shop, jobbing & repair; bolts, nuts, rivets & washers; dowel pins, metal; motor vehicle hardware; aircraft & marine hardware, inc. pulleys & similar items

(G-14221)
ZWEIGLES INC
651 Plymouth Ave N (14608-1689)
PHONE..................585 546-1740
Julie E Camardo-Steron, *Ch of Bd*
Roberta Camardo, *President*
Tina Steinmetz, *Purch Mgr*
Dominic Lippa, *CFO*
Michael Keller, *Treasurer*
EMP: 55 EST: 1880
SQ FT: 37,000
SALES (est): 12.1MM **Privately Held**
WEB: www.zweigles.com
SIC: 2013 Sausages from purchased meat

Rock City Falls
Saratoga County

(G-14222)
COTTRELL PAPER COMPANY INC
1135 Rock City Rd (12863-1208)
P.O. Box 35 (12863-0035)
PHONE..................518 885-1702
Jack L Cottrell, *Ch of Bd*
Ben Cottrell, *Vice Pres*
▲ EMP: 36 EST: 1926
SQ FT: 40,000
SALES (est): 9.2MM **Privately Held**
WEB: www.cottrellpaper.com
SIC: 2621 Specialty papers; insulation siding, paper

Rock Stream
Schuyler County

(G-14223)
ROCK STREAM VINEYARDS
162 Fir Tree Point Rd (14878-9700)
PHONE..................607 243-8322
Mark Karasz, *Owner*
EMP: 7
SALES (est): 682.6K **Privately Held**
SIC: 2084 Wines

Rock Tavern
Orange County

(G-14224)
CREATIVE DESIGN AND MCH INC
197 Stone Castle Rd (12575-5000)
PHONE..................845 778-9001
Clifford Broderick, *CEO*
◆ EMP: 25
SQ FT: 24,000
SALES (est): 5.3MM **Privately Held**
SIC: 3469 Machine parts, stamped or pressed metal

Rockaway Beach
Queens County

(G-14225)
EXCEL CONVEYOR LLC
350 Beach 79th St Ste 1 (11693-2068)
PHONE..................718 474-0001
Mitch Popescu, *Opers Mgr*
Hilda Masih, *Mng Member*
EMP: 10
SALES: 2.5MM **Privately Held**
SIC: 3535 7699 Conveyors & conveying equipment; industrial machinery & equipment repair

(G-14226)
WAVE PUBLISHING CO INC
Also Called: Wave of Long Island, The
8808 Rockaway Beach Blvd (11693-1608)
PHONE..................718 634-4000
Susan Locke, *President*
Carol Keenan, *Publisher*
Howie Schwach, *Editor*
Sanford Bernstein, *Treasurer*
Felicia Edwards, *Advt Staff*
EMP: 15
SQ FT: 4,500
SALES: 850K **Privately Held**
SIC: 2711 8111 Newspapers: publishing only, not printed on site; legal services

Rockaway Park
Queens County

(G-14227)
A-1 STAMPING & SPINNING CORP
225 Beach 143rd St (11694-1106)
PHONE..................718 388-2626
Ira Zapolsky, *President*
▲ EMP: 15 EST: 1947
SQ FT: 14,000
SALES (est): 2MM **Privately Held**
SIC: 3469 3646 3645 Stamping metal for the trade; spinning metal for the trade; commercial indusl & institutional electric lighting fixtures; residential lighting fixtures

(G-14228)
EVELO INC
327 Beach 101st St (11694-2831)
PHONE..................917 251-8743
Yevgeniy Morekovic, *President*
Boris Mordkovich, *Vice Pres*
Boris Morekovic, *Vice Pres*
▲ EMP: 2
SALES: 1MM **Privately Held**
SIC: 3751 Bicycles & related parts

(G-14229)
RELIANCE MICA CO INC
336 Beach 149th St (11694-1027)
PHONE..................718 788-0282
Peter Yanello Jr, *President*
Michael Parrella, *Div Sub Head*
Frank Callahan, *Vice Pres*
◆ EMP: 6 EST: 1924
SQ FT: 10,000
SALES (est): 635.4K **Privately Held**
SIC: 3299 Mica products

Rockville Centre
Nassau County

(G-14230)
CHAMPION CUTTING TOOL CORP
11-15 Saint Marks Ave (11570-4244)
P.O. Box 368 (11571-0368)
PHONE..................516 536-8200
Lowell Frey, *President*
Mike Chad, *Vice Pres*
Diane Ruggiero, *Controller*
Tom Benkowski, *Sales Staff*
Tim Buck, *Sales Staff*
▲ EMP: 50
SQ FT: 15,000
SALES (est): 6.8MM
SALES (corp-wide): 8.1MM **Privately Held**
WEB: www.championcuttingtool.com
SIC: 3545 Cutting tools for machine tools
PA: The Frey Company Inc
 190 Madison Ave
 Oceanside NY 11572
 516 536-8200

(G-14231)
CREATION BAUMANN USA INC
114 N Centre Ave (11570-3948)
PHONE..................516 764-7431
George Baumann, *President*
Gloria Mastranni, *Human Res Mgr*
Harry Persaus, *Executive*
EMP: 30
SALES (est): 1.9MM **Privately Held**
SIC: 2211 2221 5949 5131 Apparel & outerwear fabrics, cotton; broadwoven fabric mills, manmade; fabric stores piece goods; piece goods & other fabrics

(G-14232)
GRAPHIC FABRICATIONS INC
Also Called: Minuteman Press
488a Sunrise Hwy (11570-5037)
PHONE..................516 763-3222
George Dormani, *President*
EMP: 6
SQ FT: 4,000
SALES (est): 787.2K **Privately Held**
SIC: 2752 7334 2791 Commercial printing, offset; photocopying & duplicating services; typesetting

(G-14233)
HANGER INC
556 Merrick Rd Ste 101 (11570-5545)
PHONE..................516 678-3650
EMP: 16
SALES (corp-wide): 1B **Publicly Held**
SIC: 3842 Surgical appliances & supplies
PA: Hanger, Inc.
 10910 Domain Dr Ste 300
 Austin TX 78758
 512 777-3800

(G-14234)
INDUSTRIAL MCH GEAR WORKS LLC
77 Woodland Ave (11570-6015)
PHONE..................516 695-4442
Susan Lehrman, *Mng Member*
Richard C Lehrman,
EMP: 5 EST: 1944
SQ FT: 4,000
SALES: 250K **Privately Held**
SIC: 3462 Gears, forged steel

(G-14235)
LONG ISLAND CATHOLIC NEWSPAPER
50 N Park Ave (11570-4129)
PHONE..................516 594-1212
Liz O'Conner, *Principal*
Cathy Casanova, *Purchasing*
Carla Padalino,
EMP: 30
SALES (est): 1.9MM **Privately Held**
SIC: 2721 2711 Magazines: publishing only, not printed on site; newspapers

Rockville Centre - Nassau County (G-14236)

(G-14236)
MERCURY ENVELOPE CO INC
Also Called: Mercury Envelope Printing
100 Merrick Rd Ste 204e (11570-4801)
P.O. Box 200 (11571-0200)
PHONE.................516 678-6744
Scott Deutsch, *President*
Maurice Deutsch, *Vice Pres*
Maury Dautsch, *Vice Pres*
Colleen Cunningham, *CFO*
EMP: 75
SQ FT: 2,500
SALES (est): 18.8MM **Privately Held**
SIC: 2677 Envelopes

(G-14237)
PRIME GARMENTS INC
66 Randall Ave (11570-3922)
PHONE.................212 354-7294
Joseph Hamdar, *President*
▲ EMP: 14
SALES (est): 2.3MM **Privately Held**
SIC: 2342 Bras, girdles & allied garments

(G-14238)
PROGRESSUS COMPANY INC
100 Merrick Rd Ste 510w (11570-4825)
PHONE.................516 255-0245
Lawrence Hutzler, *President*
Lillian Ehrenhaus, *Vice Pres*
▲ EMP: 10
SQ FT: 60,000
SALES (est): 1.2MM **Privately Held**
WEB: www.progressus.com
SIC: 3469 Household cooking & kitchen utensils, metal

(G-14239)
QUALITY METAL STAMPING LLC (PA)
100 Merrick Rd Ste 310w (11570-4884)
PHONE.................516 255-9000
Robert Serling, *Owner*
EMP: 3
SQ FT: 2,000
SALES (est): 8.7MM **Privately Held**
SIC: 3469 Stamping metal for the trade

(G-14240)
SLEEP IMPROVEMENT CENTER INC
178 Sunrise Hwy Fl 2 (11570-4704)
PHONE.................516 536-5799
Reza Naghavi, *President*
EMP: 12
SALES (est): 1MM **Privately Held**
SIC: 2515 Sleep furniture

(G-14241)
SOLVE ADVISORS INC
265 Sunrise Hwy Ste 22 (11570-4912)
PHONE.................646 699-5041
Yevgeniy Grinberg, *President*
Gerard Nealon, *President*
EMP: 8 EST: 2011
SQ FT: 2,000
SALES (est): 687.2K **Privately Held**
SIC: 7372 Business oriented computer software

(G-14242)
SOUTHBAY FUEL INJECTORS
566 Merrick Rd Ste 3 (11570-5547)
PHONE.................516 442-4707
EMP: 7
SALES (est): 721.3K **Privately Held**
SIC: 2869 Fuels

(G-14243)
TRUEFORGE GLOBAL MCHY CORP
100 Merrick Rd Ste 208e (11570-4817)
PHONE.................516 825-7040
Ronald E Jaggie, *President*
◆ EMP: 3
SQ FT: 2,500
SALES (est): 9MM **Privately Held**
WEB: www.trueforge.com
SIC: 3542 Forging machinery & hammers

(G-14244)
VENDING TIMES INC
55 Maple Ave Ste 304 (11570-4267)
PHONE.................516 442-1850
Alicia Lavay, *President*
Nicolas Montano, *Vice Pres*
Frances Lavay, *Treasurer*
EMP: 11
SQ FT: 4,000
SALES (est): 1.1MM **Privately Held**
SIC: 2721 2741 Magazines: publishing only, not printed on site; miscellaneous publishing

---

Rome
Oneida County

(G-14245)
ALLIANCE PAVING MATERIALS INC
846 Lawrence St (13440-8102)
PHONE.................315 337-0795
Kimberly Ocuto, *President*
Roger Krol, *Manager*
EMP: 6
SQ FT: 4,000
SALES (est): 820K **Privately Held**
SIC: 2951 1771 Road materials, bituminous (not from refineries); driveway, parking lot & blacktop contractors

(G-14246)
BARTELL MACHINERY SYSTEMS LLC (DH)
6321 Elmer Hill Rd (13440-9325)
PHONE.................315 336-7600
Pat Morocco, *President*
Christopher Fatata, *Materials Mgr*
Paul Gatley, *Engineer*
Michael Gluck, *Engineer*
Devinne Jalowiec, *Engineer*
▲ EMP: 150
SQ FT: 115,000
SALES (est): 33.2MM
SALES (corp-wide): 1.2B **Privately Held**
WEB: www.bartellmachinery.com
SIC: 3549 Metalworking machinery
HQ: Pettibone L.L.C.
27501 Bella Vista Pkwy
Warrenville IL 60555
630 353-5000

(G-14247)
BAUMS CASTORINE COMPANY INC
200 Matthew St (13440)
PHONE.................315 336-8154
Charles F Mowry, *President*
Paul H Berger Jr, *Chairman*
Theodore Mowry, *Vice Pres*
▼ EMP: 7 EST: 1879
SQ FT: 22,000
SALES (est): 1.4MM **Privately Held**
WEB: www.baumscastorine.com
SIC: 2992 2841 Lubricating oils & greases; soap & other detergents

(G-14248)
BECK VAULT COMPANY
6648 Shank Ave (13440-9357)
PHONE.................315 337-7590
EMP: 5 EST: 1946
SQ FT: 4,500
SALES (est): 500K **Privately Held**
SIC: 3272 7359 Mfg Concrete Burial Vaults & Rents Burial Equipment

(G-14249)
CATHEDRAL CORPORATION (PA)
632 Ellsworth Rd (13441-4808)
PHONE.................315 338-0021
Marianne W Gaige, *President*
Lucie Shoen, *President*
Carl Falletta, *COO*
Paul Harrington, *Vice Pres*
Laurie Mitchell, *Vice Pres*
EMP: 138
SQ FT: 58,000
SALES (est): 36.2MM **Privately Held**
WEB: www.cathedralcorporation.com
SIC: 2752 Commercial printing, offset

(G-14250)
ENVIROMASTER INTERNATIONAL LLC
Also Called: E M I
5780 Success Dr (13440-1769)
P.O. Box 4729, Utica (13504-4729)
PHONE.................315 336-3716
Earl C Reed,
Timothy Reed,
▲ EMP: 100
SQ FT: 52,000
SALES (est): 11.5MM
SALES (corp-wide): 107.2MM **Privately Held**
WEB: www.ecrinternational.com
SIC: 3585 Heating & air conditioning combination units
PA: Ecr International, Inc.
2201 Dwyer Ave
Utica NY 13501
315 797-1310

(G-14251)
GOODRICH CORPORATION
104 Otis St (13441-4714)
PHONE.................315 838-1200
Jeff Meredith, *Managing Prtnr*
Steve Croke, *Vice Pres*
Rich Butler, *Opers Mgr*
Justin Hawthorne, *Purch Mgr*
John Peters, *QC Mgr*
EMP: 200
SALES (corp-wide): 59.8B **Publicly Held**
WEB: www.bfgoodrich.com
SIC: 3728 Aircraft assemblies, subassemblies & parts
HQ: Goodrich Corporation
2730 W Tyvola Rd
Charlotte NC 28217
704 423-7000

(G-14252)
HCI ENGINEERING
5880 Bartlett Rd (13440-1111)
PHONE.................315 336-3450
Jim Carrol, *General Mgr*
James Carroll, *Engineer*
Staurt Hatzinder, *Manager*
EMP: 3
SALES (est): 1MM **Privately Held**
SIC: 3829 Measuring & controlling devices

(G-14253)
HUBBARD TOOL AND DIE CORP
Rome Indus Ctr Bldg 5 (13440)
PHONE.................315 337-7840
Eric Hubbard, *President*
Randall Hubbard, *Treasurer*
EMP: 22 EST: 1957
SQ FT: 12,000
SALES: 3MM **Privately Held**
SIC: 3599 3545 Machine shop, jobbing & repair; precision tools, machinists'

(G-14254)
J DAVIS MANUFACTURING CO INC
Also Called: R-Tronics
222 Erie Blvd E (13440-6814)
PHONE.................315 337-7574
Lucille Kroeger, *CEO*
Rocco Garro, *Principal*
EMP: 20
SQ FT: 8,000
SALES (est): 4.5MM **Privately Held**
WEB: www.r-tronics.com
SIC: 3496 Cable, uninsulated wire: made from purchased wire

(G-14255)
KRIS-TECH WIRE COMPANY INC (PA)
80 Otis St (13441-4712)
P.O. Box 4377 (13442-4377)
PHONE.................315 339-5268
Jon C Brodock, *CEO*
Cheryl Ingersoll, *COO*
EMP: 37
SQ FT: 50,000
SALES (est): 17.3MM **Privately Held**
WEB: www.kristechwire.com
SIC: 3357 Appliance fixture wire, nonferrous

(G-14256)
LEONARD BUS SALES INC
730 Ellsworth Rd (13441-4309)
PHONE.................607 467-3100
Mike Leonard, *President*
EMP: 6
SALES (corp-wide): 40.5MM **Privately Held**
SIC: 3711 5012 Buses, all types, assembly of; buses
PA: Leonard Bus Sales, Inc.
4 Leonard Way
Deposit NY 13754
607 467-3100

(G-14257)
MCINTOSH BOX & PALLET CO INC
200 6th St (13440-6069)
PHONE.................315 446-9350
Dan Balitz, *Manager*
EMP: 26
SALES (corp-wide): 35.3MM **Privately Held**
WEB: www.mcintoshbox.com
SIC: 2499 2448 2441 5085 Spools, wood; wood pallets & skids; nailed wood boxes & shook; bins & containers, storage
PA: Mcintosh Box & Pallet Co., Inc.
5864 Pyle Dr
East Syracuse NY 13057
315 446-9350

(G-14258)
MGS MANUFACTURING INC (PA)
Also Called: Mgs Group, The
122 Otis St (13441-4714)
P.O. Box 4259 (13442-4259)
PHONE.................315 337-3350
Robert Johnson, *Ch of Bd*
William Gurecki, *Vice Pres*
Gordon Merrey, *Engineer*
Thomas Beland, *Electrical Engi*
Arnold Zumbrun, *Electrical Engi*
▲ EMP: 50 EST: 1957
SQ FT: 20,000
SALES (est): 18MM **Privately Held**
SIC: 3549 Wiredrawing & fabricating machinery & equipment, ex. die

(G-14259)
MSI-MOLDING SOLUTIONS INC
6247 State Route 233 (13440-1037)
PHONE.................315 736-2412
Frank Giotto, *Ch of Bd*
Thomas Bashant, *President*
▲ EMP: 20
SALES: 2.8MM
SALES (corp-wide): 108.6MM **Privately Held**
SIC: 3089 Molding primary plastic
PA: Fiber Instrument Sales, Inc.
161 Clear Rd
Oriskany NY 13424
315 736-2206

(G-14260)
NASH METALWARE CO INC
Also Called: American Metal
200 Railroad St (13440-6951)
PHONE.................315 339-5794
Donald Beebe, *Manager*
EMP: 11
SALES (corp-wide): 11.4MM **Privately Held**
SIC: 3469 5719 Household cooking & kitchen utensils, metal; kitchenware
PA: Nash Metalware Co Inc
72 N 15th St
Brooklyn NY 11222
718 384-1500

(G-14261)
NCI GROUP INC
Metal Building Components Mbci
6168 State Route 233 (13440-1033)
P.O. Box 4141 (13442-4141)
PHONE.................315 339-1245
Chuck Glady, *Branch Mgr*
EMP: 100
SALES (corp-wide): 1.7B **Publicly Held**
SIC: 3448 3444 3441 Buildings, portable: prefabricated metal; prefabricated metal components; sheet metalwork; fabricated structural metal

▲ = Import ▼ = Export
◆ = Import/Export

HQ: Nci Group, Inc.
10943 N Sam Huston Pkwy W
Houston TX 77064
281 897-7788

(G-14262)
NORAS CANDY SHOP
Also Called: Candy Land
321 N Doxtator St (13440-3121)
PHONE..................................315 337-4530
Spiro Haritatos, *Owner*
EMP: 14
SALES (est): 1.2MM **Privately Held**
SIC: 2064 5441 2066 Candy & other confectionery products; candy; chocolate & cocoa products

(G-14263)
NORTEK POWDER COATING LLC
5900 Success Dr (13440-1743)
PHONE..................................315 337-2339
Borin Chea, *Mng Member*
Borin Keith,
◆ **EMP:** 16
SALES (est): 3.2MM **Privately Held**
SIC: 2851 Paints & allied products

(G-14264)
NORTHROP GRUMMAN SYSTEMS CORP
Rr 26 Box N (13440)
PHONE..................................315 336-0500
Steve Maiser, *Manager*
EMP: 25 **Publicly Held**
WEB: www.logicon.com
SIC: 7372 Operating systems computer software
HQ: Northrop Grumman Systems Corporation
2980 Fairview Park Dr
Falls Church VA 22042
703 280-2900

(G-14265)
OMEGA WIRE INC
900 Railroad St (13440-6900)
PHONE..................................315 337-4300
James A Spargo IV, *Manager*
EMP: 50
SQ FT: 50,980
SALES (corp-wide): 455.4MM **Privately Held**
WEB: www.omegawire.com
SIC: 3366 Copper foundries
HQ: Omega Wire, Inc.
12 Masonic Ave
Camden NY 13316
315 245-3800

(G-14266)
PERATON INC
Also Called: Harris
474 Phoenix Dr (13441-4911)
PHONE..................................315 838-7000
Vic Choo, *Branch Mgr*
EMP: 40
SALES (corp-wide): 1B **Privately Held**
WEB: www.ittind.com
SIC: 3625 Control equipment, electric
HQ: Peraton Inc.
12975 Worldgate Dr # 100
Herndon VA 20170
703 668-6000

(G-14267)
PROFESSIONAL TECHNOLOGY INC
Also Called: Professional Technologies
5433 Lowell Rd (13440-7815)
PHONE..................................315 337-4156
John Puleo, *President*
EMP: 6
SALES (est): 540K **Privately Held**
SIC: 3651 1731 Speaker systems; communications specialization

(G-14268)
R&S STEEL LLC
412 Canal St (13440-6835)
PHONE..................................315 281-0123
Paul Raulli, *Mng Member*
Richie T Raulli,
Thomas Raulli,
EMP: 21
SQ FT: 5,600
SALES (est): 4.3MM **Privately Held**
SIC: 3441 Building components, structural steel

(G-14269)
RAULLI IRON WORKS INC
133 Mill St (13440-6945)
PHONE..................................315 337-8070
Agostino Raulli, *President*
Mark Raulli, *Vice Pres*
EMP: 10 **EST:** 1938
SQ FT: 3,600
SALES (est): 900K **Privately Held**
WEB: www.raulliandsonsincornamental.com
SIC: 3446 Ornamental metalwork

(G-14270)
ROME MAIN STREET ALLIANCE INC
506 N James St (13440-4216)
PHONE..................................315 271-8356
EMP: 6
SALES (est): 48.4K **Privately Held**
SIC: 2711 Newspapers, publishing & printing

(G-14271)
ROME SIGN & DISPLAY CO
510 Erie Blvd W (13440-4806)
PHONE..................................315 336-0550
Randall Denton, *President*
Terrance Denton, *Vice Pres*
EMP: 7
SQ FT: 1,000
SALES (est): 917.3K **Privately Held**
SIC: 3993 Signs, not made in custom sign painting shops

(G-14272)
ROME SPECIALTY COMPANY INC
Also Called: Rosco Div
501 W Embargo St (13440-4061)
P.O. Box 109 (13442-0109)
PHONE..................................315 337-8200
Judith Kiernan, *President*
◆ **EMP:** 20 **EST:** 1926
SQ FT: 35,000
SALES (est): 2.2MM **Privately Held**
WEB: www.roscoinc.com
SIC: 3949 Fishing equipment; fishing tackle, general

(G-14273)
RTD MANUFACTURING INC
6273 State Route 233 (13440-1037)
PHONE..................................315 337-3151
Brian P Getbehead, *President*
Robert Getbehead, *Vice Pres*
Sandra Vanslyke, *Manager*
Iva S Getbehead, *Admin Sec*
EMP: 7
SQ FT: 3,500
SALES (est): 700K **Privately Held**
WEB: www.rtdmfg.com
SIC: 3599 3541 3531 Machine shop, jobbing & repair; boring mills; crushers, grinders & similar equipment

(G-14274)
SERWAY BROS INC (PA)
Also Called: Serway Cabinet Trends
Plant 2 Rome Indus Ctr (13440)
PHONE..................................315 337-0601
Christine N Serway, *Ch of Bd*
James Pacific, *Director*
Sophia Pelose, *Admin Sec*
EMP: 30
SQ FT: 20,800
SALES (est): 2.9MM **Privately Held**
WEB: www.serway.com
SIC: 2541 5211 3648 5719 Counters or counter display cases, wood; cabinets, kitchen; lighting fixtures, except electric; residential; lighting fixtures; wood kitchen cabinets

(G-14275)
TIPS & DIES INC
505 Rome Industrial Park (13440-6948)
PHONE..................................315 337-4161
Randall Hubbard, *President*
Gary Johnson, *Sales Staff*
Peter Scribner, *Sales Staff*
Larry Derrick, *Technical Staff*
EMP: 12
SALES (est): 2.3MM **Privately Held**
WEB: www.tipsanddies.com
SIC: 3544 Special dies & tools

(G-14276)
TONYS ORNAMENTAL IR WORKS INC
6757 Martin St (13440-7106)
P.O. Box 4425 (13442-4425)
PHONE..................................315 337-3730
Anthony J Pettinelli Jr, *President*
Toni Olejarczyk, *Corp Secy*
EMP: 20
SQ FT: 13,800
SALES (est): 3.4MM **Privately Held**
SIC: 3449 3446 Mfg Misc Structural Metalwork Mfg Architectural Metalwork

(G-14277)
UTC AEROSPACE SYSTEMS
104 Otis St (13441-4714)
PHONE..................................315 838-1200
Frank Kucerak, *Principal*
Daniel Sweet, *Materials Mgr*
Paul Delorenzo, *Engineer*
Kyle Johnson, *Engineer*
David O'Hern, *Engineer*
EMP: 24
SALES (est): 3.8MM **Privately Held**
SIC: 3728 Aircraft parts & equipment

(G-14278)
VARFLEX CORPORATION
512 W Court St (13440-4000)
P.O. Box 551 (13442-0551)
PHONE..................................315 336-4400
Daniel J Burgdorf, *President*
William L Griffin, *Vice Pres*
Charles J Schoff, *Treasurer*
Charles Schoff, *Human Res Mgr*
Lisa Dombrowski, *Sales Associate*
▲ **EMP:** 150 **EST:** 1924
SQ FT: 144,000
SALES (est): 12.1MM **Privately Held**
WEB: www.varflex.com
SIC: 3644 Insulators & insulation materials, electrical

(G-14279)
WORTHINGTON INDUSTRIES INC
530 Henry St (13440-5639)
PHONE..................................315 336-5500
Roger Pratt, *Plant Mgr*
Jerry Tomassi, *Safety Mgr*
David Bovi, *Manager*
EMP: 72
SALES (corp-wide): 3.5B **Publicly Held**
SIC: 3316 Strip steel, cold-rolled: from purchased hot-rolled
PA: Worthington Industries, Inc.
200 W Wlson Bridge Rd
Worthington OH 43085
614 438-3210

Romulus
Seneca County

(G-14280)
COBBLESTONE FRM WINERY VINYRD
5102 State Route 89 (14541-9779)
PHONE..................................315 549-1004
Jennifer Clark, *Principal*
EMP: 10
SALES (est): 822K **Privately Held**
SIC: 2084 Wines

(G-14281)
SCHRADER MEAT MARKET
1937 Summerville Rd (14541-9800)
PHONE..................................607 869-6328
Keith Schrader, *Owner*
EMP: 19 **EST:** 2012
SALES (est): 600K **Privately Held**
SIC: 3421 2013 Table & food cutlery, including butchers'; sausages & other prepared meats

(G-14282)
SOUTH SENECA VINYL LLC
1585 Yale Farm Rd (14541-9761)
PHONE..................................315 585-6050
Nelson Sensenig,
EMP: 9
SQ FT: 5,000
SALES (est): 1.2MM **Privately Held**
SIC: 3211 Window glass, clear & colored

(G-14283)
SWEDISH HILL VINEYARD INC
Also Called: Swedish Hill Winery
4565 State Route 414 (14541-9769)
PHONE..................................607 403-0029
David Peterson, *CEO*
Richard Peterson, *President*
Cynthia Peterson, *Vice Pres*
Tracy Harris, *Safety Mgr*
Amanda Fitzgerald, *Finance Mgr*
EMP: 70
SALES (est): 6MM **Privately Held**
SIC: 2084 0721 Wines; vines, cultivation of

Ronkonkoma
Suffolk County

(G-14284)
A A TECHNOLOGY INC
101 Trade Zone Dr (11779-7363)
PHONE..................................631 913-0400
Henry Tang, *CEO*
Frank Rosselli, *Vice Pres*
James Stapleton, *Vice Pres*
Michael Pilson, *Engineer*
Chris Leone, *Info Tech Mgr*
◆ **EMP:** 85
SQ FT: 15,700
SALES (est): 8.6MM **Privately Held**
SIC: 3672 Printed circuit boards

(G-14285)
A FIRE INC
23 Parr Dr (11779-3019)
PHONE..................................631 897-9449
EMP: 8
SALES (est): 708.2K **Privately Held**
SIC: 3999 Manufacturing industries

(G-14286)
ACCELA INC
100 Comac St Ste 2 (11779-6928)
PHONE..................................631 563-5005
Daryl Blowes, *General Mgr*
EMP: 10 **Privately Held**
SIC: 7372 Prepackaged software
PA: Accela, Inc.
2633 Camino Ramon Ste 500
San Ramon CA 94583

(G-14287)
ACCENT LABEL & TAG CO INC (PA)
348 Woodlawn Ave (11779-5055)
PHONE..................................631 244-7066
Larry Gutman, *President*
EMP: 6
SALES (est): 592.2K **Privately Held**
WEB: www.accentlabelandtag.com
SIC: 2679 7336 Labels, paper: made from purchased material; graphic arts & related design

(G-14288)
ACE CANVAS & TENT CORP
155 Raynor Ave (11779-6666)
PHONE..................................631 648-0614
Vincent Cardillo, *Vice Pres*
▲ **EMP:** 10
SQ FT: 5,500
SALES (est): 1.5MM **Privately Held**
SIC: 3081 2394 7359 Vinyl film & sheet; canvas & related products; tent & tarpaulin rental

(G-14289)
ACME INDUSTRIES OF W BABYLON
125 Gary Way Ste 2 (11779-6576)
PHONE..................................631 737-5231
John Landrio, *President*

Ronkonkoma - Suffolk County (G-14290) — GEOGRAPHIC SECTION

EMP: 10
SQ FT: 3,000
SALES (est): 1.8MM Privately Held
SIC: 3599 7389 Machine shop, jobbing & repair; grinding, precision: commercial or industrial

(G-14290)
ADAPTIVE MFG TECH INC
181 Remington Blvd (11779-6911)
PHONE.................................631 580-5400
Terence Larocca, Ch of Bd
Kim Pecoraro, Manager
EMP: 32
SQ FT: 18,000
▲ EMP: 5
SALES (est): 7.9MM Privately Held
WEB: www.amtautomation.com
SIC: 3542 3599 Machine tools, metal forming type; custom machinery

(G-14291)
ADVANCE MICRO POWER CORP
2190 Smithtown Ave (11779-7355)
PHONE.................................631 471-6157
Jasbir Mahajan, President
▲ EMP: 15
SQ FT: 14,000
SALES (est): 1.6MM Privately Held
SIC: 3672 Printed circuit boards

(G-14292)
ADVANCED MANUFACTURING SVC INC
100 13th Ave Ste 2 (11779-6820)
PHONE.................................631 676-5210
John Nucatola, President
EMP: 28
SALES (est): 6.5MM Privately Held
SIC: 3672 Printed circuit boards

(G-14293)
ADVANCED PHOTONICS INC
151 Trade Zone Dr (11779-7384)
PHONE.................................631 471-3693
Robert Turner, President
Richard Turner, Vice Pres
Jack Raybin, CFO
EMP: 14
SQ FT: 5,000
SALES (est): 1.4MM Privately Held
WEB: www.advancedphotonicsusa.com
SIC: 3699 5084 Laser systems & equipment; industrial machinery & equipment

(G-14294)
AERO-DATA METAL CRAFTERS INC
2085 5th Ave (11779-6903)
PHONE.................................631 471-7733
Robert De Luca, President
Eric Arditti, Project Mgr
Chris Behr, Purch Agent
Andrea Savino, Human Res Mgr
Ed Fiance, Sales Executive
▼ EMP: 110
SQ FT: 100,000
SALES (est): 23.1MM Privately Held
WEB: www.metal-crafters.com
SIC: 3444 3446 3443 3441 Sheet metal specialties, not stamped; architectural metalwork; fabricated plate work (boiler shop); fabricated structural metal; cold finishing of steel shapes

(G-14295)
AIR CRAFTERS INC
2085 5th Ave (11779-6903)
PHONE.................................631 471-7788
Robert Deluca, President
Michael Hennessey, Vice Pres
Brittany Savino, Human Resources
William Mabanta, Admin Sec
EMP: 105
SQ FT: 40,000
SALES: 12MM Privately Held
WEB: www.air-crafters.com
SIC: 2542 5085 3625 3564 Fixtures, office: except wood; clean room supplies; relays & industrial controls; blowers & fans

(G-14296)
AIRGLE CORPORATION
711 Koehler Ave Ste 3 (11779-7410)
PHONE.................................866 501-7750
Yang Lo, President

Mike Anderson, Vice Pres
▲ EMP: 20 EST: 2006
SQ FT: 7,300
SALES (est): 202.9K Privately Held
SIC: 3589 3564 Water purification equipment, household type; air purification equipment

(G-14297)
AKSHAR EXTRACTS INC
59 Remington Blvd (11779-6954)
PHONE.................................631 588-9727
Jay Patel, President
Nat Patel, Vice Pres
Dee Patel, Treasurer
▲ EMP: 5
SQ FT: 3,000
SALES: 500K Privately Held
WEB: www.pureextracts.com
SIC: 2836 Mfg Biological Products

(G-14298)
ALKEN INDUSTRIES INC
2175 5th Ave (11779-6217)
PHONE.................................631 467-2000
Tami Senior, President
Anthony Landisi, President
Bridgette Senior, Vice Pres
Tom Tivenan, VP Opers
Elliot Sanabia, Facilities Mgr
EMP: 40
SQ FT: 33,000
SALES (est): 20.6MM Privately Held
WEB: www.alkenind.com
SIC: 3728 3441 Aircraft parts & equipment; fabricated structural metal

(G-14299)
ALL AROUND SPIRAL INC
10 Fleetwood Ct (11779-6907)
PHONE.................................631 588-0220
Richard Kern, Ch of Bd
EMP: 9
SALES (est): 1.2MM Privately Held
SIC: 3444 Sheet metalwork

(G-14300)
ALL PACKAGING MCHY & SUPS CORP
90 13th Ave Unit 11 (11779-6818)
PHONE.................................631 588-7310
Albert Bolla, President
Joel Busel, Vice Pres
Samul Posner, Vice Pres
Lynn Miranda, Executive
EMP: 10
SQ FT: 10,000
SALES: 2.7MM
SALES (corp-wide): 2.5MM Privately Held
WEB: www.triopackaging.com
SIC: 3565 Packaging machinery
PA: Trio Packaging Corp.
    90 13th Ave Unit 11
    Ronkonkoma NY 11779
    631 588-0800

(G-14301)
ALLIANT TCHSYSTEMS OPRTONS LLC
77 Raynor Ave (11779-6649)
PHONE.................................631 737-6100
Robert Bakos, Vice Pres
EMP: 20 Publicly Held
WEB: www.mrcwdc.com
SIC: 3721 Research & development on aircraft by the manufacturer
HQ: Alliant Techsystems Operations Llc
    4700 Nathan Ln N
    Plymouth MN 55442

(G-14302)
ALLURE METAL WORKS INC
71 Hoffman Ln (11749-5007)
PHONE.................................631 588-0220
Jillian Guido, Principal
EMP: 10
SALES (est): 1.5MM Privately Held
SIC: 3444 1711 Sheet metalwork; plumbing, heating, air-conditioning contractors

(G-14303)
ALROD ASSOCIATES INC
710 Union Pkwy Ste 9 (11779-7428)
PHONE.................................631 981-2193
Evan Alrod, President

EMP: 10
SQ FT: 6,000
SALES (est): 1.2MM Privately Held
SIC: 2541 2542 5046 Store fixtures, wood; fixtures, store; except wood; store fixtures

(G-14304)
ALTAQUIP LLC
200 13th Ave Unit 6 (11779-6815)
PHONE.................................631 580-4740
EMP: 8
SALES (corp-wide): 194.6B Publicly Held
SIC: 3699 Mfg Electrical Equipment/Supplies
HQ: Altaquip Llc
    100 Production Dr
    Harrison OH 45030
    513 674-6464

(G-14305)
AMERICAN BOTTLING COMPANY
Also Called: Snapple Distributors
2004 Orville Dr N (11779-7645)
PHONE.................................516 714-0002
Ray Russo, Manager
EMP: 19 Publicly Held
SIC: 2086 Bottled & canned soft drinks
HQ: The American Bottling Company
    5301 Legacy Dr
    Plano TX 75024

(G-14306)
AMERICAN QUALITY EMBROIDERY (PA)
740 Koehler Ave (11779-7406)
PHONE.................................631 467-3200
Robert Kalinowski, President
EMP: 1
SQ FT: 1,600
SALES (est): 17.8MM Privately Held
SIC: 2284 2395 Embroidery thread; embroidery products, except schiffli machine

(G-14307)
AMETEK INC
903 S 2nd St (11779-7201)
PHONE.................................631 467-8400
Jessica Durante, Export Mgr
EMP: 6
SALES (corp-wide): 4.3B Publicly Held
SIC: 3621 Motors & generators
PA: Ametek, Inc.
    1100 Cassatt Rd
    Berwyn PA 19312
    610 647-2121

(G-14308)
AMETEK CTS US INC (PA)
903 S 2nd St (11779-7201)
PHONE.................................631 467-8400
Mark Swanson, President
Leon Benatar, Vice Pres
Richard Janiec, Sales Dir
EMP: 25 EST: 1953
SQ FT: 10,600
SALES (est): 5.5MM Privately Held
WEB: www.ifi.com
SIC: 3663 Amplifiers, RF power & IF

(G-14309)
AMRON ELECTRONICS INC
160 Gary Way (11779-6509)
PHONE.................................631 737-1234
Rick Foora, CEO
EMP: 50
SALES (est): 2.7MM Privately Held
SIC: 3679 Commutators, electronic

(G-14310)
APOLLO DISPLAY TECH CORP (PA)
87 Raynor Ave Ste 1 (11779-6667)
PHONE.................................631 580-4360
Bernhard Staller, President
Joanne Sottile, Senior VP
Matthew Evko, Marketing Mgr
Vito Evko, CTO
Scott Makboulia, Technology
▲ EMP: 35
SQ FT: 15,000

SALES (est): 7.9MM Privately Held
WEB: www.apollodisplays.com
SIC: 3679 5065 Liquid crystal displays (LCD); electronic parts & equipment

(G-14311)
ARTISAN MACHINING INC
49 Remington Blvd (11779-6909)
PHONE.................................631 589-1416
John Caccavale, President
EMP: 7
SALES (est): 800K Privately Held
WEB: www.artisanmachining.com
SIC: 3599 Machine shop, jobbing & repair

(G-14312)
ATK GASL INC
77 Raynor Ave (11779-6649)
PHONE.................................631 737-6100
John Tilleli, Principal
EMP: 18
SALES (est): 3.1MM Privately Held
SIC: 3721 Research & development on aircraft by the manufacturer

(G-14313)
AZTEC INDUSTRIES INC
200 13th Ave Unit 5 (11779-6815)
PHONE.................................631 585-1331
Phil Del Giudice, President
Randyll Brooks, Financial Analy
EMP: 6
SQ FT: 2,500
SALES (est): 500K Privately Held
SIC: 2522 Panel systems & partitions, office: except wood

(G-14314)
B & B PRECISION COMPONENTS INC
301 Christopher St # 303 (11779-6922)
PHONE.................................631 273-3321
Lucille Bricker, President
EMP: 5
SQ FT: 12,000
SALES (est): 1.6MM Privately Held
WEB: www.bbprecisioncomponents.com
SIC: 3728 Aircraft parts & equipment

(G-14315)
B H AIRCRAFT COMPANY INC (PA)
2230 Smithtown Ave (11779-7329)
PHONE.................................631 580-9747
Vincent E Kearns, Ch of Bd
Daniel Kearns, President
Sebastian F Digiacomo, Principal
Dan Fugua, Principal
Paul Goggi, Principal
EMP: 90 EST: 1933
SQ FT: 100,000
SALES (est): 14.7MM Privately Held
WEB: www.bhaircraft.com
SIC: 3724 Aircraft engines & engine parts

(G-14316)
BANNER METALCRAFT INC
300 Trade Zone Dr (11779-7345)
PHONE.................................631 563-7303
Kenneth R Bednar, President
Nancy E Bednar, Corp Secy
Richard Martin, Foreman/Supr
Gene Crawford, QC Mgr
Kurt Butcher, Engineer
EMP: 70
SQ FT: 32,000
SALES: 12.1MM Privately Held
WEB: www.bannermetalcraft.com
SIC: 3444 Sheet metal specialties, not stamped

(G-14317)
BCM ELECTRONICS MANUF SERVICES
3279 Veterans Memorial (11779-7673)
PHONE.................................631 580-9516
K Linden, Principal
EMP: 7
SALES (est): 1MM Privately Held
SIC: 3672 Printed circuit boards

(G-14318)
BECKER ELECTRONICS INC
50 Alexander Ct Ste 2 (11779-6568)
PHONE.................................631 619-9100

Ronkonkoma - Suffolk County (G-14345)

David M Sosnow, *CEO*
Sharon Becker, *Vice Pres*
Patrick Spagnuolo, *Treasurer*
EMP: 80
SQ FT: 14,000
SALES (est): 12MM **Privately Held**
WEB: www.beckerelectronicsinc.com
SIC: 3679 5065 Harness assemblies for electronic use; wire or cable; electronic parts & equipment

(G-14319)
BETATRONIX INC
125 Comac St (11779-6931)
PHONE...................631 582-6740
Wayne Demmons, *Vice Pres*
▼ **EMP:** 30
SALES (est): 5.4MM **Privately Held**
SIC: 3823 Industrial instrmnts msrmnt display/control process variable

(G-14320)
BOBLEY-HARMANN CORPORATION
Also Called: Gift Valleys.com
200 Trade Zone Dr Unit 2 (11779-7359)
PHONE...................516 433-3800
Mark Bobley, *President*
▲ **EMP:** 8
SQ FT: 500
SALES (est): 912.1K **Privately Held**
WEB: www.bobley.com
SIC: 2731 2759 Book publishing; promotional printing

(G-14321)
BROADWAY NATIONAL GROUP LLC
Also Called: Broadway National Sign & Ltg
1900 Ocean Ave (11779-6520)
PHONE...................800 797-4467
Michael Rennie, *Opers Staff*
Diane Belkin, *Controller*
Deborah Conlon, *Accounts Mgr*
Ashley Darch, *Accounts Mgr*
Gabby Mastroeni, *Accounts Mgr*
EMP: 80
SALES (est): 14.2MM **Privately Held**
SIC: 3993 1711 7349 3648 Signs & advertising specialties; plumbing, heating, air-conditioning contractors; building maintenance services; lighting equipment

(G-14322)
BROADWAY NEON SIGN CORP
Also Called: Broadway National
1900 Ocean Ave (11779-6520)
PHONE...................908 241-4177
William Paparella, *President*
EMP: 18
SQ FT: 50,000
SALES (est): 3MM **Privately Held**
WEB: www.broadwaynational.com
SIC: 3993 3444 2431 2394 Neon signs; sheet metalwork; millwork; canvas & related products

(G-14323)
C TO C DESIGN & PRINT INC
1850 Pond Rd Unit B (11779-7210)
PHONE...................631 885-4020
Anthony Aceto, *Ch of Bd*
EMP: 10
SALES (est): 1.3MM **Privately Held**
SIC: 2752 Commercial printing, lithographic

(G-14324)
CALCHEM CORPORATION (PA)
2001 Ocean Ave (11779-6500)
P.O. Box 4258, Huntington (11743-0371)
PHONE...................631 423-5696
John H Chen, *President*
Molly Chen, *Exec VP*
▲ **EMP:** 7
SQ FT: 12,000
SALES (est): 1.9MM **Privately Held**
WEB: www.calchemcorp.com
SIC: 2893 Printing ink

(G-14325)
CANFIELD AEROSPACE & MAR INC
90 Remington Blvd (11779-6910)
PHONE...................631 648-1050
Lynn Zaun, *President*
EMP: 20 **EST:** 2000
SALES (est): 1.2MM **Privately Held**
WEB: www.canfieldam.com
SIC: 3728 Mfg Aircraft Parts/Equipment

(G-14326)
CAROLINA PRECISION PLAS LLC
Also Called: Cpp Global
115 Comac St (11779-6931)
PHONE...................631 981-0743
EMP: 94
SALES (corp-wide): 60.9MM **Privately Held**
SIC: 3089 Injection molding of plastics
PA: Carolina Precision Plastics Llc
405 Commerce Pl
Asheboro NC 27203
336 498-2654

(G-14327)
CEDAR WEST INC (PA)
1700 Ocean Ave Ste 1 (11779-6570)
PHONE...................631 467-1444
Joanne D Herman, *President*
Michael Clark, *Vice Pres*
Robert Herman, *Vice Pres*
Gloria J Smalley, *CFO*
EMP: 56
SALES (est): 6.3MM **Privately Held**
WEB: www.cedarwest.com
SIC: 2752 Commercial printing, offset

(G-14328)
COPY X/PRESS LTD
Also Called: Ocean Printing
700 Union Pkwy Ste 5 (11779-7427)
PHONE...................631 585-2200
John Harkins, *President*
David Milano, *Vice Pres*
John Berhalter, *Plant Mgr*
Terri Bligh, *Bookkeeper*
Kristyn Hovanec, *Marketing Mgr*
EMP: 63
SQ FT: 30,000
SALES (est): 8.8MM **Privately Held**
WEB: www.oceanprinting.com
SIC: 2759 Commercial printing

(G-14329)
CORNING RUBBER COMPANY INC
Also Called: Corning Wax
1744 Julia Goldbach Ave (11779-6413)
PHONE...................631 738-0041
Robert Schiemel, *President*
Claudio Acquafredda, *Vice Pres*
▲ **EMP:** 14 **EST:** 1946
SQ FT: 10,000
SALES (est): 1.2MM **Privately Held**
WEB: www.corningwax.com
SIC: 3843 Wax, dental

(G-14330)
CRYSTALONICS INC
2805 Veterans Mem Hwy 14 (11779-7680)
PHONE...................631 981-6140
Paul Weinstein, *President*
Brian Gomes, *Treasurer*
Joseph Plescia, *Treasurer*
EMP: 12
SQ FT: 14,000
SALES (est): 1.6MM **Privately Held**
WEB: www.crystalonics.com
SIC: 3674 Hybrid integrated circuits

(G-14331)
CRYSTALONICS OF NEW YORK INC
2805 Vets Memorial (11779)
PHONE...................631 981-6140
Paul Weinstein, *President*
David Weinstein, *Vice Pres*
EMP: 12
SQ FT: 3,000
SALES (est): 948.3K **Privately Held**
SIC: 3674 Semiconductors & related devices

(G-14332)
DAK MICA AND WOOD PRODUCTS
Also Called: Coronet Kitchen & Bath
2147 5th Ave (11779-6908)
PHONE...................631 467-0749
David Kaplan, *President*
EMP: 5
SQ FT: 5,800
SALES (est): 1MM **Privately Held**
SIC: 2434 5031 1751 Wood kitchen cabinets; kitchen cabinets; cabinet & finish carpentry

(G-14333)
DELLA SYSTEMS INC
951 S 2nd St (11779-7203)
PHONE...................631 580-0010
John Della Croce, *President*
EMP: 14
SQ FT: 3,000
SALES (est): 2.5MM **Privately Held**
WEB: www.dellasystems.com
SIC: 3672 8711 Printed circuit boards; engineering services

(G-14334)
DYNAMIC LABORATORIES INC
Also Called: Dynamic Labs
30 Haynes Ct (11779-7220)
PHONE...................631 231-7474
David Beauchamp, *President*
Steven Zwerman, *Vice Pres*
▲ **EMP:** 38
SQ FT: 18,000
SALES (est): 8.7MM **Privately Held**
SIC: 3827 5049 Optical instruments & lenses; optical goods

(G-14335)
EAST/WEST INDUSTRIES INC
2002 Orville Dr N (11779-7661)
PHONE...................631 981-5900
Teresa Ferraro, *President*
Mary Spinosa, *Corp Secy*
Joseph Spinosa, *Vice Pres*
Jeff Walsh, *Engineer*
EMP: 45
SQ FT: 38,000
SALES (est): 11.2MM **Privately Held**
WEB: www.eastwestindustries.com
SIC: 3728 2531 Seat ejector devices, aircraft; oxygen systems, aircraft; seats, aircraft

(G-14336)
EASTERN STOREFRONTS & MTLS INC
1739 Julia Goldbach Ave (11779-6412)
P.O. Box 431, Bohemia (11716-0431)
PHONE...................631 471-7065
Timothy Dittmeier, *Ch of Bd*
EMP: 14
SALES (est): 2.3MM **Privately Held**
SIC: 3442 Store fronts, prefabricated, metal

(G-14337)
EASTLAND ELECTRONICS CO INC
700 Union Pkwy Ste 9 (11779-7427)
PHONE...................631 580-3800
William Mercurio, *President*
Marc Mercurio, *Vice Pres*
Bill Androp, *Office Mgr*
▲ **EMP:** 7
SQ FT: 2,000
SALES (est): 1.3MM **Privately Held**
WEB: www.eastlandny.com
SIC: 3679 Electronic circuits

(G-14338)
ELEMENTAR AMERICAS INC
119 Comac St (11779-6931)
PHONE...................856 787-0022
Georg Schick, *President*
Ken Slight, *Vice Pres*
EMP: 9
SQ FT: 2,100
SALES (est): 2.3MM **Privately Held**
WEB: www.elementar-inc.com
SIC: 3826 Protein analyzers, laboratory type

(G-14339)
ES BETA INC
125 Comac St (11779-6931)
PHONE...................631 582-6740
John Karcher, *Principal*
Wayne Demmons, *Vice Pres*
EMP: 36 **EST:** 1966
SALES (est): 2.3MM
SALES (corp-wide): 88.3MM **Privately Held**
SIC: 3677 Electronic coils, transformers & other inductors
PA: Electro Switch Business Trust
775 Pleasant St Ste 1
Weymouth MA 02189
781 335-1195

(G-14340)
EXECUTIVE MIRROR DOORS INC
1 Comac Loop Unit 7 (11779-6816)
PHONE...................631 234-1090
Robert Cozzie, *President*
Carol Cozzie, *Vice Pres*
EMP: 7
SQ FT: 5,400
SALES (est): 720K **Privately Held**
WEB: www.executivemirror.com
SIC: 3231 5211 5085 Doors, glass; made from purchased glass; door & window products; industrial supplies

(G-14341)
FIRST IMPRESSIONS FINISHING
132 Remington Blvd (11779-6912)
PHONE...................631 467-2244
Scott Shapiro, *President*
Laura Shapiro, *Vice Pres*
EMP: 6
SQ FT: 4,000
SALES (est): 351.9K **Privately Held**
SIC: 3471 Finishing, metals or formed products

(G-14342)
FORMATIX CORP
9 Colt Ct (11779-6949)
PHONE...................631 467-3399
Radjesh Guptar, *CEO*
EMP: 20
SALES (est): 3.7MM **Privately Held**
SIC: 3089 Blister or bubble formed packaging, plastic

(G-14343)
FOUR PAWS PRODUCTS LTD
3125 Vtrans Mem Hwy Ste 1 (11779-7644)
PHONE...................631 436-7421
Allen Simon, *President*
Barry Askin, *Vice Pres*
Ray Gallagher, *CFO*
Tina Fabiano, *Executive*
▲ **EMP:** 85 **EST:** 1970
SQ FT: 50,000
SALES (est): 8.5MM
SALES (corp-wide): 2B **Publicly Held**
WEB: www.fourpaws.com
SIC: 3999 2844 Pet supplies; toilet preparations
PA: Central Garden & Pet Company
1340 Treat Blvd Ste 600
Walnut Creek CA 94597
925 948-4000

(G-14344)
GENERAL CUTTING INC
90 13th Ave Unit 10 (11779-6818)
PHONE...................631 580-5011
Ralph Viteritti, *President*
EMP: 12
SQ FT: 8,000
SALES (est): 946K **Privately Held**
SIC: 3599 Machine shop, jobbing & repair

(G-14345)
GLIPTONE MANUFACTURING INC
Also Called: Camco
1740 Julia Goldbach Ave (11779-6409)
PHONE...................631 285-7250
Rocco Caporaso Jr, *President*
▲ **EMP:** 10
SQ FT: 6,500

Ronkonkoma - Suffolk County (G-14346)

SALES: (est) 1.9MM **Privately Held**
WEB: www.gliptone.com
SIC: 2842 Specialty cleaning preparations; automobile polish

(G-14346)
GLOBAL ENTITY MEDIA INC
2090 5th Ave Ste 2 (11779-6958)
PHONE..................631 580-7772
Michael J Cutino, *Principal*
Michael Cutino, *Principal*
EMP: 5
SALES: (est) 600.5K **Privately Held**
SIC: 2721 Periodicals: publishing only

(G-14347)
GOT POWER INC
5 Campus Ln (11779-1924)
PHONE..................631 767-9493
Luis Duarte, *Owner*
EMP: 5
SALES: 100K **Privately Held**
SIC: 3621 Motors & generators

(G-14348)
H & H TECHNOLOGIES INC
10 Colt Ct (11779-6948)
PHONE..................631 567-3526
Henry J Kleitsch, *President*
David Puckett, *Manager*
EMP: 40
SQ FT: 14,000
SALES: (est) 7.3MM **Privately Held**
WEB: www.hhtech.com
SIC: 3599 Machine shop, jobbing & repair

(G-14349)
H A GUDEN COMPANY INC
99 Raynor Ave (11779-6634)
PHONE..................631 737-2900
Paul A Guden, *Ch of Bd*
Kirby D Moyers, *Vice Pres*
Carol Gumbrecht, *Manager*
Kirby Moyers, *Executive*
Mary L Schwarz, *Admin Sec*
▲ EMP: 25
SQ FT: 20,000
SALES: 8.5MM **Privately Held**
SIC: 3429 5072 Manufactured hardware (general); hardware

(G-14350)
HADFIELD INC
840 S 2nd St (11779-7202)
PHONE..................631 981-4314
Charles Hadfield, *President*
EMP: 10
SALES: (est) 1.2MM **Privately Held**
SIC: 7692 1799 Welding repair; welding on site

(G-14351)
HASTINGS TILE & BATH INC (PA)
711 Koehler Ave Ste 8 (11779-7410)
PHONE..................631 285-3330
Lee Kohrman, *President*
Michael Homola, *President*
Richard Kucera, *Corp Secy*
John Kamuda, *Technical Mgr*
Ryan Homola, *Sales Staff*
▲ EMP: 20
SQ FT: 36,000
SALES: (est) 5.4MM **Privately Held**
WEB: www.hastingstilebath.com
SIC: 3253 Ceramic wall & floor tile

(G-14352)
IMPALA PRESS LTD
931 S 2nd St (11779-7203)
PHONE..................631 588-4262
Peter Wolf, *President*
EMP: 8
SQ FT: 6,000
SALES: (est) 1.2MM **Privately Held**
WEB: www.impalapress.com
SIC: 2752 Commercial printing, offset

(G-14353)
INGENIOUS DESIGNS LLC
Also Called: Idl
2060 9th Ave (11779-6253)
PHONE..................631 254-3376
Joy Mangano, *Ch of Bd*
Ronni Fauci, *Vice Pres*
◆ EMP: 110

SQ FT: 63,000
SALES: (est) 32.9MM **Publicly Held**
WEB: www.ingeniousdesigns.com
SIC: 2392 5199 3089 5099 Mops, floor & dust; broom, mop & paint handles; plastic containers, except foam; containers: glass, metal or plastic
HQ: Hsn, Inc.
1 Hsn Dr
Saint Petersburg FL 33729

(G-14354)
ISLAND RESEARCH AND DEV CORP
Also Called: Island Technology
200 13th Ave Unit 12 (11779-6815)
PHONE..................631 471-7100
Robert Guy Ward, *President*
EMP: 75
SQ FT: 10,000
SALES: (est) 9.8MM **Privately Held**
WEB: www.islandresearch.net
SIC: 3679 Electronic circuits

(G-14355)
J F M SHEET METAL INC
2090 Pond Rd (11779-7216)
PHONE..................631 737-8494
Joseph Magri, *President*
Jeff Stern, *Manager*
EMP: 5
SALES: 450K **Privately Held**
SIC: 3441 Fabricated structural metal

(G-14356)
J R S PRECISION MACHINING
40 Raynor Ave Ste 2 (11779-6623)
PHONE..................631 737-1330
Scott Sopko, *President*
EMP: 8
SQ FT: 2,000
SALES: (est) 891.7K **Privately Held**
SIC: 3599 Machine shop, jobbing & repair

(G-14357)
JAAB PRECISION INC
180 Gary Way (11779-6509)
PHONE..................631 218-3725
Joseph W Aloi, *President*
Josephine Blasso, *Office Mgr*
EMP: 9
SALES: (est) 2.3MM **Privately Held**
SIC: 3441 Fabricated structural metal

(G-14358)
JET REDI MIX CONCRETE INC
Also Called: J E T
2101 Pond Rd Ste 1 (11779-7213)
PHONE..................631 580-3640
Steve Jensen, *President*
Harold Jensen, *President*
EMP: 14
SQ FT: 15,000
SALES: (est) 2.2MM **Privately Held**
WEB: www.jetredimixconcrete.com
SIC: 3273 Ready-mixed concrete

(G-14359)
JMG FUEL INC
3 Fowler Ave (11779-4105)
PHONE..................631 579-4319
Brian Gauci, *Principal*
EMP: 6 EST: 2010
SALES: (est) 681.1K **Privately Held**
SIC: 2869 Fuels

(G-14360)
KELTRON ELECTRONICS (DE CORP)
Also Called: Keltron Connector Co.
3385 Vtrans Mem Hwy Ste E (11779-7660)
PHONE..................631 567-6300
David Levison, *President*
▲ EMP: 15
SALES: (est) 2.1MM **Privately Held**
WEB: www.keltronconnectors.com
SIC: 3679 Electronic circuits

(G-14361)
KETCHAM MEDICINE CABINETS
3505 Vtrans Mem Hwy Ste L (11779-7613)
PHONE..................631 615-6151
Tracey Bonham, *General Mgr*
Gina Lacarrubba, *Vice Pres*
EMP: 25

SALES: 10MM **Privately Held**
SIC: 3431 Bathroom fixtures, including sinks

(G-14362)
KNF CLEAN ROOM PRODUCTS CORP
1800 Ocean Ave (11779-6532)
PHONE..................631 588-7000
Philip J Carcara, *Ch of Bd*
Al Shouga, *Plant Mgr*
Chris Marx, *Manager*
Randy Ferdinand, *Director*
Chuck McAteer, *Executive*
EMP: 50
SQ FT: 22,000
SALES: (est) 9.1MM **Privately Held**
SIC: 3699 1541 3081 5085 Electrical equipment & supplies; pharmaceutical manufacturing plant construction; unsupported plastics film & sheet; clean room supplies

(G-14363)
KONDOR TECHNOLOGIES INC
206 Christopher St (11779-6921)
PHONE..................631 471-8832
Nils Youngwall, *President*
▲ EMP: 10
SQ FT: 3,500
SALES: (est) 1.8MM **Privately Held**
SIC: 3599 Machine shop, jobbing & repair

(G-14364)
L W S INC
125 Gary Way Ste 1 (11779-6576)
PHONE..................631 580-0472
Leon Shapiro, *President*
EMP: 15
SQ FT: 3,000
SALES: (est) 1.4MM **Privately Held**
SIC: 3471 Finishing, metals or formed products; polishing, metals or formed products

(G-14365)
LAB CRAFTERS INC
2085 5th Ave (11779-6903)
PHONE..................631 471-7755
Bob Deluca Sr, *President*
Robert Deluca, *Principal*
Edward Fiance, *Principal*
David Rubinstein, *Project Mgr*
Chris Behr, *Manager*
EMP: 25
SQ FT: 90,000
SALES: (est) 6.7MM **Privately Held**
SIC: 3821 5049 Laboratory equipment: fume hoods, distillation racks, etc.; laboratory equipment, except medical or dental

(G-14366)
LAB-AIDS INC
17 Colt Ct (11779-6949)
PHONE..................631 737-1133
Morton Frank, *President*
David M Frank, *President*
Artie Gunston, *Vice Pres*
Rachel Porter, *Marketing Staff*
▲ EMP: 49 EST: 1963
SQ FT: 41,000
SALES: (est) 9MM **Privately Held**
WEB: www.lab-aid.com
SIC: 3999 Education aids, devices & supplies

(G-14367)
LAKELAND INDUSTRIES INC (PA)
3555 Vtrans Mem Hwy Ste C (11779-7636)
PHONE..................631 981-9700
A John Kreft, *Ch of Bd*
Christopher J Ryan, *President*
Charles D Roberson, *COO*
Daniel L Edwards, *Senior VP*
Teri W Hunt, *CFO*
▼ EMP: 208
SALES: 95.9MM **Publicly Held**
WEB: www.lakeland-ind.com
SIC: 3842 2389 Personal safety equipment; clothing, fire resistant & protective; gloves, safety; disposable garments & accessories

(G-14368)
LANCO CORPORATION
Also Called: Brijon
2905 Vtrans Mem Hwy Ste 3 (11779-7655)
PHONE..................631 231-2300
Brian Landow, *President*
Tom Kronberger, *Regional Mgr*
Irwin Landow, *Vice Pres*
Dan Ventola, *Vice Pres*
Joe Barone, *Opers Mgr*
◆ EMP: 250
SQ FT: 40,000
SALES: (est) 48.5MM **Privately Held**
WEB: www.lancopromo.com
SIC: 3993 2066 5149 2064 Signs & advertising specialties; chocolate & cocoa products; chocolate; candy & other confectionery products

(G-14369)
LANGER BIOMECHANICS INC
2905 Vtrans Mem Hwy Ste 2 (11779-7655)
PHONE..................800 645-5520
Bruce Marrison, *CEO*
Jason Kraus, *President*
EMP: 71
SALES: (est) 9.3MM
SALES: (corp-wide): 11MM **Privately Held**
SIC: 3842 Braces, orthopedic
PA: Orthotic Holdings, Inc.
2905 Veterans Mem Hwy
Ronkonkoma NY 11779
416 479-8609

(G-14370)
LINK CONTROL SYSTEMS INC
16 Colt Ct (11779-6948)
P.O. Box 1177 (11779-0588)
PHONE..................631 471-3950
William F Bowden, *President*
Francine Abramowitz, *Manager*
Clive Dillon, *Info Tech Mgr*
EMP: 15
SQ FT: 12,000
SALES: (est) 3MM **Privately Held**
WEB: www.linkconsys.com
SIC: 3613 Control panels, electric

(G-14371)
LONG ISLAND BUSINESS NEWS
2150 Smithtown Ave Ste 7 (11779-7348)
PHONE..................631 737-1700
Jordan Zeigler, *Partner*
Scott Schoen, *Vice Pres*
EMP: 22 EST: 1953
SQ FT: 6,000
SALES: (est) 1.5MM
SALES: (corp-wide): 445.1MM **Privately Held**
WEB: www.libn.com
SIC: 2711 Newspapers, publishing & printing
HQ: Dolan Llc
222 S 9th St Ste 2300
Minneapolis MN 55402

(G-14372)
LUX MUNDI CORP
10 Colt Ct (11779-6948)
PHONE..................631 244-4596
Henry Kleitsch, *President*
EMP: 8
SALES: (est) 803.8K **Privately Held**
SIC: 3999 Candles

(G-14373)
MAHARLIKA HOLDINGS LLC
Also Called: Atis Colojet
111 Trade Zone Ct Unit A (11779-7367)
PHONE..................631 319-6203
Erez Shoshoni, *General Mgr*
▲ EMP: 14
SALES: 3MM **Privately Held**
SIC: 3559 Chemical machinery & equipment

(G-14374)
MANTEL & MANTEL STAMPING CORP
802 S 4th St (11779-7200)
PHONE..................631 467-1916
Edward Mantel, *President*
EMP: 8 EST: 1977
SQ FT: 7,500

GEOGRAPHIC SECTION

Ronkonkoma - Suffolk County (G-14402)

SALES: 1MM **Privately Held**
SIC: 3544 3469 Special dies & tools; metal stampings

(G-14375)
MARCOVICCI-WENZ ENGINEERING
33 Comac Loop Unit 10 (11779-6856)
PHONE..............................631 467-9040
Ted Wenz, *President*
Peter Marcovicci, *Vice Pres*
EMP: 6
SQ FT: 4,000
SALES (est): 490K **Privately Held**
SIC: 3714 5531 3711 Motor vehicle engines & parts; speed shops, including race car supplies; automobile assembly, including specialty automobiles

(G-14376)
MAYFAIR MACHINE COMPANY INC
128 Remington Blvd (11779-6912)
PHONE..............................631 981-6644
EMP: 6
SQ FT: 1,500
SALES (est): 610K **Privately Held**
SIC: 3599 Machine Shop

(G-14377)
MICRO PHOTO ACOUSTICS INC
105 Comac St (11779-6931)
PHONE..............................631 750-6035
Xiaojie Zhao, *President*
EMP: 5
SALES (est): 754.7K **Privately Held**
SIC: 3826 Laser scientific & engineering instruments
PA: Advanced Optowave Corporation
105 Comac St
Ronkonkoma NY 11779

(G-14378)
MIN-MAX MACHINE LTD
1971 Pond Rd (11779-7244)
PHONE..............................631 585-4378
Randy Neubauer, *Ch of Bd*
Rodney Neubauer, *Corp Secy*
Ralph Neubauer, *Vice Pres*
EMP: 18
SQ FT: 18,000
SALES: 4MM **Privately Held**
SIC: 3728 Aircraft assemblies, subassemblies & parts

(G-14379)
MINUTEMEN PRECSN MCHNING TOOL
Also Called: Minutemen Precision Mch & Tl
135 Raynor Ave (11779-6666)
PHONE..............................631 467-4900
Michael Castoro, *Ch of Bd*
Carlo J Castoro, *Treasurer*
Michael Lane, *Manager*
EMP: 37
SQ FT: 14,900
SALES (est): 8.1MM **Privately Held**
SIC: 3728 3599 Aircraft parts & equipment; machine shop, jobbing & repair

(G-14380)
MNS FUEL CORP
2154 Pond Rd (11779-7216)
P.O. Box 344, East Islip (11730-0344)
PHONE..............................516 735-3835
Irene F Walsh, *Principal*
EMP: 12
SALES (est): 2.5MM **Privately Held**
SIC: 2869 Fuels

(G-14381)
MULTIMATIC PRODUCTS INC
900 Marconi Ave (11779-7212)
PHONE..............................800 767-7633
Hyman Jack Kipnes, *President*
Rohit C Chodha, *Managing Dir*
Irving Kipnes, *Corp Secy*
Bart Kipnes, *Manager*
EMP: 74 EST: 1962
SQ FT: 20,000
SALES: 3MM **Privately Held**
WEB: www.multimaticproducts.com
SIC: 3451 3541 Screw machine products; machine tools, metal cutting type

(G-14382)
N & L INSTRUMENTS INC
90 13th Ave Unit 1 (11779-6818)
PHONE..............................631 471-4000
John Walz, *President*
Anthony Kearney, *Treasurer*
EMP: 17
SQ FT: 20,000
SALES (est): 2MM **Privately Held**
WEB: www.namf.com
SIC: 3571 3444 Electronic computers; sheet metalwork

(G-14383)
NATECH PLASTICS INC
85 Remington Blvd (11779-6923)
PHONE..............................631 580-3506
Gerd Nagler, *Ch of Bd*
Thomas Nagler, *President*
Carol Nagler, *Vice Pres*
EMP: 45 EST: 1998
SQ FT: 10,000
SALES (est): 10.5MM **Privately Held**
WEB: www.natechplastics.com
SIC: 3089 Injection molding of plastics

(G-14384)
NATURES BOUNTY (NY) INC (DH)
2100 Smithtown Ave (11779-7347)
PHONE..............................631 200-2000
Dipak Golechha, *Ch of Bd*
Paul L Sturman, *President*
Steve Conboy, *CFO*
▲ EMP: 800
SQ FT: 15,000
SALES (est): 304.9MM **Publicly Held**
WEB: www.nbty.com
SIC: 2834 Vitamin preparations
HQ: The Nature's Bounty Co
2100 Smithtown Ave
Ronkonkoma NY 11779
631 200-2000

(G-14385)
NATURES BOUNTY CO
2100 Smithtown Ave (11779-7347)
PHONE..............................631 244-2021
Dorie Greenblatt, *Principal*
EMP: 90 **Publicly Held**
SIC: 2833 5122 5499 5961 Vitamins, natural or synthetic: bulk, uncompounded; vitamins & minerals; health & dietetic food stores; vitamin food stores; health foods; pharmaceuticals, mail order
HQ: The Nature's Bounty Co
2100 Smithtown Ave
Ronkonkoma NY 11779
631 200-2000

(G-14386)
NBTY MANUFACTURING LLC (DH)
2100 Smithtown Ave (11779-7347)
PHONE..............................631 567-9500
Marc Rodieck, *General Mgr*
Marilyn Figueroa, *Senior VP*
Michael Messina, *Project Mgr*
Evelyn Martinez, *Purch Mgr*
Jon Fotheringill, *Buyer*
◆ EMP: 47
SQ FT: 6,000,000
SALES (est): 106.5MM **Publicly Held**
SIC: 2833 5122 Vitamins, natural or synthetic: bulk, uncompounded; vitamins & minerals
HQ: The Nature's Bounty Co
2100 Smithtown Ave
Ronkonkoma NY 11779
631 200-2000

(G-14387)
NEW AGE PRECISION TECH INC
151 Remington Blvd (11779-6911)
PHONE..............................631 471-4000
Mario Costa, *President*
EMP: 20
SQ FT: 25,000
SALES: 1MM **Privately Held**
SIC: 3599 Machine shop, jobbing & repair

(G-14388)
OAKDALE INDUSTRIAL ELEC CORP
1995 Pond Rd (11779-7259)
PHONE..............................631 737-4090
Abraham Mamoor, *President*
Allen Mamoor, *Vice Pres*
▼ EMP: 15
SQ FT: 5,000
SALES (est): 4MM **Privately Held**
SIC: 3679 3672 5065 Electronic circuits; printed circuit boards; electronic parts

(G-14389)
OAKLEE INTERNATIONAL INC
Also Called: Pro-Tek Packaging Group
125 Raynor Ave (11779-6666)
PHONE..............................631 436-7900
Leo Lee, *President*
Alice Zebrowski, *Exec VP*
Donna Neumann, *Exec Dir*
EMP: 75
SALES (est): 11MM **Privately Held**
WEB: www.oaklee.com
SIC: 2672 3081 Adhesive papers, labels or tapes: from purchased material; unsupported plastics film & sheet

(G-14390)
OMEGA HEATER COMPANY INC
2059 9th Ave (11779-6233)
PHONE..............................631 588-8820
Alfred Gaudio, *President*
▲ EMP: 60 EST: 1970
SQ FT: 30,000
SALES: 3MM **Privately Held**
WEB: www.omegaheater.com
SIC: 3433 Heating equipment, except electric

(G-14391)
OMNTEC MFG INC
1993 Pond Rd (11779-7259)
P.O. Box 30 (11779-0030)
PHONE..............................631 981-2001
Lee J Nicholson, *President*
Tom Dalessandro, *Exec VP*
Kurt Gibson, *Sales Mgr*
▲ EMP: 34
SQ FT: 13,600
SALES (est): 6.7MM **Privately Held**
WEB: www.omntec.com
SIC: 3625 5065 Relays & industrial controls; electronic parts & equipment

(G-14392)
OPERATEIT INC
2805 Vtrans Mem Hwy Ste 2 (11779-7680)
PHONE..............................631 259-4777
Keith Tobias, *President*
EMP: 9
SALES (est): 511.9K **Privately Held**
SIC: 7372 Prepackaged software

(G-14393)
P R B METAL PRODUCTS INC
200 Christopher St (11779-6921)
PHONE..............................631 467-1800
Ronald Breunig, *President*
Peter Breunig, *Vice Pres*
EMP: 10
SQ FT: 10,000
SALES: 1MM **Privately Held**
SIC: 3444 3465 3469 Sheet metal specialties, not stamped; automotive stampings; metal stampings

(G-14394)
PAAL TECHNOLOGIES INC
152 Remington Blvd Ste 1 (11779-6964)
PHONE..............................631 319-6262
Latha Chandran, *Ch of Bd*
Prem Chandran, *Vice Pres*
EMP: 5
SALES: 300K **Privately Held**
WEB: www.paaltech.com
SIC: 3679 Harness assemblies for electronic use: wire or cable

(G-14395)
PARAMOUNT EQUIPMENT INC
Also Called: O P I Industries
201 Christopher St (11779-6956)
PHONE..............................631 981-4422
▲ EMP: 20

SQ FT: 10,000
SALES (est): 4.7MM **Privately Held**
SIC: 2673 5113 Mfg Bags-Plastic/Coated Paper Whol Industrial/Service Paper

(G-14396)
PARSLEY APPAREL CORP
2153 Pond Rd (11779-7214)
PHONE..............................631 981-7181
Ronald Colnick, *President*
EMP: 50
SQ FT: 5,000
SALES (est): 3MM **Privately Held**
SIC: 2335 Wedding gowns & dresses

(G-14397)
PAUL MICHAEL GROUP INC
Also Called: PMG
460 Hawkins Ave (11779-4248)
P.O. Box 1493 (11779-0426)
PHONE..............................631 585-5700
Vincent Gennaro, *President*
▲ EMP: 7
SQ FT: 1,500
SALES (est): 974.9K **Privately Held**
SIC: 2752 7389 Commercial printing, offset; packaging & labeling services

(G-14398)
PHOTONICS INDUSTRIES INTL INC (PA)
1800 Ocean Ave Unit A (11779-6532)
PHONE..............................631 218-2240
Yusong Yin, *President*
▲ EMP: 95
SQ FT: 184,000
SALES: 3.5MM **Privately Held**
WEB: www.photonix.com
SIC: 3826 Analytical instruments

(G-14399)
PIC A POC ENTERPRISES INC
53 Union Ave (11779-5814)
P.O. Box 338, Holbrook (11741-0338)
PHONE..............................631 981-2094
Nicholas J Ullrich II, *President*
Marilyn Ullrich, *Principal*
EMP: 5
SQ FT: 2,000
SALES: 500K **Privately Held**
SIC: 2752 7336 Commercial printing, offset; graphic arts & related design

(G-14400)
PRINTCORP INC
2050 Ocean Ave (11779-6536)
PHONE..............................631 696-0641
Joseph C Fazzingo Jr, *CEO*
Arthur Foti, *Marketing Staff*
EMP: 22 EST: 1994
SALES (est): 3.2MM **Privately Held**
SIC: 2752 Commercial printing, offset

(G-14401)
PRONTO TOOL & DIE CO INC
50 Remington Blvd (11779-6910)
PHONE..............................631 981-8920
Michael Silvestri, *President*
Donna Schecker, *Corp Secy*
Marion Silvestri, *Vice Pres*
EMP: 30 EST: 1980
SQ FT: 10,000
SALES (est): 4.5MM **Privately Held**
SIC: 3544 3599 3469 Special dies & tools; machine & other job shop work; metal stampings

(G-14402)
QUALITY KING DISTRIBUTORS INC
201 Comac St (11779-6950)
PHONE..............................631 439-2027
Glenn H Nussdorf, *CEO*
EMP: 141
SALES (corp-wide): 570.6MM **Privately Held**
SIC: 2844 5122 Toilet preparations; toilet preparations
PA: Quality King Distributors, Inc.
35 Sawgrass Dr Ste 3
Bellport NY 11713
631 439-2000

Ronkonkoma - Suffolk County (G-14403)

(G-14403)
QUALITY ONE WIRELESS LLC
2127 Lakeland Ave Unit 2 (11779-7431)
PHONE..................631 233-3337
John Chiorando, *CEO*
EMP: 250
SALES (corp-wide): 173.2MM **Privately Held**
SIC: 3661 Headsets, telephone
PA: Quality One Wireless, Llc
1500 Tradeport Dr Ste B
Orlando FL 32824
407 857-3737

(G-14404)
R S T CABLE AND TAPE INC
2130 Pond Rd Ste B (11779-7239)
PHONE..................631 981-0096
David M Rothert, *President*
William Hilder, *Vice Pres*
EMP: 8
SQ FT: 6,500
SALES (est): 2MM **Privately Held**
SIC: 3479 Painting, coating & hot dipping; coating of metals with plastic or resins

(G-14405)
RATAN RONKONKOMA
3055 Veterans Mem Hwy (11779-7612)
PHONE..................631 588-6800
Mahesh Ratanji, *Administration*
EMP: 8 **EST:** 2011
SALES (est): 1MM **Privately Held**
SIC: 3421 Table & food cutlery, including butchers'

(G-14406)
RESONANCE TECHNOLOGIES INC
109 Comac St (11779-6931)
PHONE..................631 237-4901
George Szenczy, *President*
Mark Anatov, *Director*
EMP: 35
SALES: 5MM **Privately Held**
WEB: www.res-tek.com
SIC: 3678 Electronic connectors

(G-14407)
RICK-MIC INDUSTRIES INC
1951 Ocean Ave Ste 6 (11779-6564)
PHONE..................631 563-8389
Rod Dimiano, *President*
EMP: 6
SALES (est): 420K **Privately Held**
SIC: 3599 Machine shop, jobbing & repair

(G-14408)
ROGER LATARI
Also Called: Island Precision
30 Raynor Ave Ste 1 (11779-6628)
PHONE..................631 580-2422
Roger Licari, *Owner*
EMP: 5
SALES (est): 330K **Privately Held**
WEB: www.rogerblench.info
SIC: 3599 Machine shop, jobbing & repair

(G-14409)
RONA PRECISION INC
Also Called: Rona Precision Mfg
142 Remington Blvd Ste 2 (11779-6960)
PHONE..................631 737-4034
Ronald Alber, *President*
EMP: 6
SQ FT: 3,500
SALES (est): 752.4K **Privately Held**
SIC: 3599 Machine shop, jobbing & repair

(G-14410)
SENTRY TECHNOLOGY CORPORATION
Also Called: Knogo
1881 Lakeland Ave (11779-7416)
PHONE..................631 739-2000
Peter Murdoch, *CEO*
Joane Miller, *CFO*
Elizabeth Heyder, *Admin Sec*
▲ **EMP:** 30
SQ FT: 20,000
SALES (est): 3.4MM **Publicly Held**
SIC: 3812 7359 Detection apparatus: electronic/magnetic field, light/heat; electronic equipment rental, except computers

PA: Sentry Technology Corporation
1881 Lakeland Ave
Ronkonkoma NY 11779

(G-14411)
SENTRY TECHNOLOGY CORPORATION (PA)
Also Called: Sentry Funding Partnership
1881 Lakeland Ave (11779-7416)
PHONE..................800 645-4224
Peter L Murdoch, *Ch of Bd*
Maryanne Owens, *General Mgr*
Joseph Ryan, *Vice Pres*
Matt Eckert, *Senior Engr*
Joan E Miller, *CFO*
▲ **EMP:** 13
SQ FT: 20,000
SALES (est): 9.6MM **Publicly Held**
SIC: 3812 3663 Detection apparatus: electronic/magnetic field, light/heat; television closed circuit equipment

(G-14412)
SETAUKET MANUFACTURING CO
202 Christopher St (11779-6921)
PHONE..................631 231-7272
Michael Horrigan, *President*
Linda Horrigan, *Vice Pres*
EMP: 5
SQ FT: 4,000
SALES: 500K **Privately Held**
SIC: 2833 5499 Medicinals & botanicals; health & dietetic food stores

(G-14413)
SIMON DEFENSE INC
1 Trade Zone Dr Unit 15 (11779-7343)
PHONE..................516 217-6000
CJ Calleson, *Director*
EMP: 7 **EST:** 2014
SQ FT: 2,000
SALES (est): 409.2K **Privately Held**
SIC: 3452 Bolts, metal

(G-14414)
SOC AMERICA INC
3505 Veterans Memorial Hw (11779-7613)
PHONE..................631 472-6666
Neil Sato, *President*
Karl Lindquist, *Vice Pres*
Yuichi Sato, *Vice Pres*
Sharon Terry, *Electrical Engi*
Dawn Minichello, *Executive Asst*
EMP: 15
SQ FT: 3,200
SALES (est): 2.4MM
SALES (corp-wide): 47.8MM **Privately Held**
WEB: www.san-o.com
SIC: 3613 Fuses, electric
PA: Soc Corporation
3-16-17, Takanawa
Minato-Ku TKY 108-0
354 201-011

(G-14415)
SPECIALTY MICROWAVE CORP
120 Raynor Ave (11779-6655)
PHONE..................631 737-2175
Stephen Faber, *President*
EMP: 18
SQ FT: 7,500
SALES (est): 3.4MM **Privately Held**
WEB: www.specialtymicrowave.com
SIC: 3663 Microwave communication equipment

(G-14416)
SPECIALTY MODEL & MOLD INC
2231 5th Ave Ste 22 (11779-6284)
PHONE..................631 475-0840
Nicholas Ziroli, *President*
EMP: 5
SALES (est): 743.9K **Privately Held**
SIC: 3544 3089 Industrial molds; thermoformed finished plastic products

(G-14417)
SPX CORPORATION
Also Called: SPX Precision Components
70 Raynor Ave (11779-6650)
PHONE..................631 467-2632
EMP: 50
SALES (corp-wide): 1.4B **Publicly Held**
SIC: 3443 Mfg Fabricated Plate Work

PA: Spx Corporation
13320a Balntyn Corp Pl
Charlotte NC 28277
980 474-3700

(G-14418)
ST JAMES PRINTING INC
656 Rosevale Ave (11779-3098)
PHONE..................631 981-2095
Gert Kuehnel, *President*
EMP: 5
SQ FT: 5,000
SALES (est): 300K **Privately Held**
SIC: 2759 2752 Commercial printing; commercial printing, lithographic

(G-14419)
SURF-TECH MANUFACTURING CORP
28 Colt Ct (11779-6948)
PHONE..................631 589-1194
Richard Eggert, *President*
Stephen Eggart, *Mfg Mgr*
Diana Small, *Purch Mgr*
EMP: 12
SQ FT: 8,000
SALES (est): 2.5MM **Privately Held**
WEB: www.surftechmfg.com
SIC: 3672 5045 Printed circuit boards; computers, peripherals & software

(G-14420)
SWITCHING POWER INC
3601 Veterans Mem Hwy (11779-7691)
PHONE..................631 981-7231
Melvin Kravitz, *President*
Carmen Midiri, *Purch Mgr*
Mark Herringer, *Engineer*
David Kravitz, *Engineer*
Ronald Goldstein, *CFO*
▲ **EMP:** 65
SQ FT: 30,000
SALES (est): 14.2MM **Privately Held**
WEB: www.switchpwr.com
SIC: 3613 5065 3643 3612 Power switching equipment; electronic parts & equipment; current-carrying wiring devices; transformers, except electric

(G-14421)
TRANSISTOR DEVICES INC
125 Comac St (11779-6931)
PHONE..................631 471-7492
Ron Deluca, *Manager*
EMP: 27
SALES (corp-wide): 216.8MM **Privately Held**
WEB: www.transdev.com
SIC: 3625 3612 3672 3812 Switches, electric power; power transformers, electric; printed circuit boards; search & navigation equipment
PA: Transistor Devices, Inc.
36 Newburgh Rd
Hackettstown NJ 07840
908 850-5088

(G-14422)
TRUEMADE PRODUCTS INC
910 Marconi Ave (11779-7212)
PHONE..................631 981-4755
Carmen Yvonne Mender, *President*
EMP: 5
SQ FT: 4,000
SALES: 400K **Privately Held**
SIC: 3541 Machine tools, metal cutting type

(G-14423)
U S AIR TOOL CO INC (PA)
Also Called: U S Air Tool International
60 Fleetwood Ct (11779-6907)
PHONE..................631 471-3300
Geoffrey J Percz, *Ch of Bd*
Laurence Percz, *Vice Pres*
▲ **EMP:** 14 **EST:** 1951
SQ FT: 14,000
SALES (est): 4.6MM **Privately Held**
SIC: 3423 5084 3542 Hand & edge tools; pneumatic tools & equipment; sheet metalworking machines; riveting machines

(G-14424)
UCR STEEL GROUP LLC (PA)
90 Trade Zone Ct (11779-7369)
PHONE..................718 764-3414

Charlie Starce, *Mng Member*
EMP: 15
SQ FT: 33,000
SALES (est): 4.5MM **Privately Held**
SIC: 3444 Sheet metalwork

(G-14425)
ULTRAFLEX POWER TECHNOLOGIES
158 Remington Blvd Ste 2 (11779-6966)
PHONE..................631 467-6814
Mario Metodiev, *President*
Marne Kwiatkowski, *Opers Mgr*
Marian Popov, *Engineer*
Nedelina Metodieva, *Treasurer*
Kira Schmitt, *Consultant*
EMP: 5
SQ FT: 3,000
SALES (est): 571.1K **Privately Held**
SIC: 3567 Induction heating equipment

(G-14426)
ULTRAVOLT INC
1800 Ocean Ave Unit A (11779-6532)
PHONE..................631 471-4444
James Morrison, *CEO*
EMP: 100
SQ FT: 20,000
SALES (est): 21.3MM
SALES (corp-wide): 671MM **Publicly Held**
WEB: www.ultravolt.com
SIC: 3679 5065 5084 Power supplies, all types: static; electronic parts & equipment; power plant machinery
PA: Advanced Energy Industries, Inc.
1625 Sharp Point Dr
Fort Collins CO 80525
970 221-4670

(G-14427)
VACUUM INSTRUMENT CORPORATION (PA)
Also Called: Vic Leak Detection
2101 9th Ave Ste A (11779-6276)
PHONE..................631 737-0900
Frederick Ewing II, *CEO*
John Schreiner, *Vice Pres*
Phyllis Smith, *Manager*
EMP: 100 **EST:** 1958
SQ FT: 48,000
SALES (est): 27.9MM **Privately Held**
WEB: www.vacuuminst.com
SIC: 3823 3829 3812 Industrial instrmnts msrmnt display/control process variable; measuring & controlling devices; search & navigation equipment

(G-14428)
VORMITTAG ASSOCIATES INC (PA)
Also Called: V A I
120 Comac St Ste 1 (11779-6941)
PHONE..................800 824-7776
Robert Vormittag, *President*
Russ Cereola, *Vice Pres*
Todd Peterson, *Vice Pres*
Luke Heaton, *Project Dir*
Michael Morano, *Project Dir*
EMP: 6
SQ FT: 15,000
SALES (est): 36.6MM **Privately Held**
WEB: www.vaihome.com
SIC: 7372 7371 5045 Prepackaged software; computer software systems analysis & design, custom; computers, peripherals & software

(G-14429)
VOSKY PRECISION MACHINING CORP
70 Air Park Dr (11779-7360)
PHONE..................631 737-3200
Mourad Voskinarian, *President*
Krista Philips, *Technology*
EMP: 18
SQ FT: 11,000
SALES (est): 4.1MM **Privately Held**
WEB: www.voskyprecision.com
SIC: 3728 3469 3599 Aircraft parts & equipment; machine parts, stamped or pressed metal; machine shop, jobbing & repair

▲ = Import ▼=Export
◆ =Import/Export

GEOGRAPHIC SECTION

Roslyn Heights - Nassau County (G-14455)

(G-14430)
WENNER BREAD PRODUCTS INC (PA)
2001 Orville Dr N (11779-7661)
PHONE 800 869-6262
Richard R Wenner, *CEO*
Lawrence L Wenner, *Senior VP*
Nelly Margolin, *Vice Pres*
Daniel Wenner, *Vice Pres*
John J Wenner, *Vice Pres*
▲ **EMP:** 277 **EST:** 1975
SQ FT: 140,000
SALES (est): 114.9MM **Privately Held**
WEB: www.wenner-bread.com
SIC: 2051 2053 5461 Bread, all types (white, wheat, rye, etc): fresh or frozen; frozen bakery products, except bread; bakeries

(G-14431)
WENNER BREAD PRODUCTS INC
Also Called: Wenner Bakery
2001 Orville Dr N (11779-7661)
PHONE 800 869-6262
EMP: 35
SALES (corp-wide): 114.9MM **Privately Held**
SIC: 2051 2053 5461 5149 Mfg Bread/Related Prdts Mfg Frozen Bakery Prdts Retail Bakery Whol Groceries
PA: Wenner Bread Products, Inc.
2001 Orville Dr N
Ronkonkoma NY 11779
800 869-6262

(G-14432)
WILCO INDUSTRIES INC
788 Marconi Ave (11779-7230)
P.O. Box 277 (11779-0277)
PHONE 631 676-2593
Otto Wildmann, *President*
EMP: 9
SQ FT: 8,000
SALES (est): 970K **Privately Held**
WEB: www.wilcoindustries.com
SIC: 3728 Aircraft assemblies, subassemblies & parts

(G-14433)
ZETA MACHINE CORP
206 Christopher St (11779-6921)
PHONE 631 471-8832
Frank Castelli, *President*
Carol Castelli, *Vice Pres*
EMP: 8 **EST:** 1975
SQ FT: 8,000
SALES (est): 660K **Privately Held**
SIC: 3469 Machine parts, stamped or pressed metal

Roosevelt
Nassau County

(G-14434)
AUTOSTAT CORPORATION
209 Nassau Rd 11 (11575-1756)
P.O. Box 170 (11575-0170)
PHONE 516 379-9447
Arthur Baer, *President*
▲ **EMP:** 10 **EST:** 1955
SQ FT: 9,000
SALES (est): 1.2MM **Privately Held**
SIC: 3549 Marking machines, metalworking

(G-14435)
INTRIGUE CONCEPTS INC
8 Gilbert Pl Ste 8 # 8 (11575-1718)
PHONE 800 424-8170
Dennis Barclift, *President*
EMP: 6
SALES (est): 429.2K **Privately Held**
SIC: 2326 Work shirts: men's, youths' & boys'

(G-14436)
K F I INC
33 Debevoise Ave (11575-1711)
PHONE 516 546-2904
Sion Elalouf, *President*
Jeff Denecke, *Opers Staff*
▲ **EMP:** 8

SALES (est): 491.7K **Privately Held**
WEB: www.euroyarns.com
SIC: 2299 Yarns, specialty & novelty

(G-14437)
SOUTH SHORE ICE CO INC
89 E Fulton Ave (11575-2212)
PHONE 516 379-2056
Al Farina, *President*
EMP: 10
SQ FT: 4,500
SALES (est): 1MM **Privately Held**
SIC: 2097 5999 5169 Manufactured ice; ice; dry ice

(G-14438)
TROPICAL DRIFTWOOD ORIGINALS
Also Called: Tdo Sandblasting
499 Nassau Rd (11575-1019)
PHONE 516 623-0980
John O'Brien Sr, *President*
EMP: 5
SQ FT: 4,000
SALES (est): 270K **Privately Held**
SIC: 3441 3446 3471 Fabricated structural metal; architectural metalwork; sand blasting of metal parts

Roscoe
Sullivan County

(G-14439)
PROHIBITION DISTILLERY LLC
10 Union St (12776-5210)
PHONE 917 685-8989
Brian Facquet, *Mng Member*
EMP: 8
SALES (est): 465.3K **Privately Held**
SIC: 2085 Distilled & blended liquors

Rosedale
Queens County

(G-14440)
LARRY KINGS CORPORATION
13708 250th St (11422-2110)
PHONE 718 481-8741
Larry Yoen, *President*
Clara Wong, *Treasurer*
Johnny Yoen, *Shareholder*
Penny Yoen, *Admin Sec*
EMP: 6
SALES (est): 729.8K **Privately Held**
SIC: 3825 Instruments to measure electricity

(G-14441)
MASTRO CONCRETE INC
15433 Brookville Blvd (11422-3163)
PHONE 718 528-6788
Tony Mastronardi, *President*
Mario Mastronardi, *Vice Pres*
EMP: 8
SQ FT: 10,000
SALES (est): 1.4MM **Privately Held**
SIC: 3273 Ready-mixed concrete

(G-14442)
WATER COOLING CORP
24520 Merrick Blvd (11422-1464)
P.O. Box 220056 (11422-0056)
PHONE 718 723-6500
Elliott Miller, *President*
EMP: 7 **EST:** 1939
SQ FT: 5,500
SALES (est): 1.3MM **Privately Held**
WEB: www.watcopumps.com
SIC: 3443 3561 Water tanks, metal plate; tanks, standard or custom fabricated: metal plate; pumps, domestic: water or sump; industrial pumps & parts

Roslyn
Nassau County

(G-14443)
BEACON SPCH LNGE PTHLGY PHYS
Also Called: Beacon Therapy Services
1441 Old Northern Blvd (11576-2256)
PHONE 516 626-1635
Barbar Lehrer, *Partner*
Barbara Lehrer, *Partner*
Jonathan Lehrer, *Human Res Mgr*
EMP: 16
SQ FT: 5,500
SALES: 7MM **Privately Held**
SIC: 3841 Inhalation therapy equipment

(G-14444)
CLOUD ROCK GROUP LLC
525 Bryant Ave (11576-1146)
PHONE 516 967-6023
Leon Hedvat, *Manager*
EMP: 5
SALES (est): 163.4K **Privately Held**
SIC: 7372 7389 Application computer software;

(G-14445)
CUSTOM ECO FRIENDLY LLC (PA)
Also Called: Custom Eco Friendly Bags
50 Spruce Dr (11576-2330)
PHONE 347 227-0229
Matthew Kesten, *CEO*
Jonathan Wollman, *President*
▲ **EMP:** 16
SQ FT: 250
SALES: 4MM **Privately Held**
SIC: 2674 Shopping bags: made from purchased materials

(G-14446)
DYNAMIC PHOTOGRAPHY INC
Also Called: Daisy Memory Products
48 Flamingo Rd N (11576-2606)
PHONE 516 381-2951
Robert M Deangelo Sr, *President*
Richard J Deangelo, *Vice Pres*
EMP: 5
SALES: 7MM **Privately Held**
SIC: 3674 7336 7221 Magnetic bubble memory device; commercial art & graphic design; photographer, still or video

(G-14447)
HAND CARE INC
42 Sugar Maple Dr (11576-3207)
P.O. Box 331, Albertson (11507-0331)
PHONE 516 747-5649
Harrison Fuller, *President*
Patricia Fuller, *Admin Sec*
▲ **EMP:** 2
SQ FT: 15,000
SALES: 2MM **Privately Held**
WEB: www.handcare.net
SIC: 3842 Gloves, safety; adhesive tape & plasters, medicated or non-medicated

(G-14448)
NEW YORK LASER & AESTHETICKS
1025 Nthrn Blvd Ste 206 (11576)
PHONE 516 627-7777
Ofra Grinbaum, *Owner*
EMP: 5
SALES (est): 445.8K **Privately Held**
SIC: 3845 Laser systems & equipment, medical

(G-14449)
NORTHWEST COMPANY LLC (PA)
Also Called: Wilmington Products USA
49 Bryant Ave (11576-1123)
P.O. Box 263 (11576-0263)
PHONE 516 484-6996
Ross Auerbach, *President*
Marc Friedman, *COO*
Glenn Auerbach, *Exec VP*
Robert Jolson, *CFO*
Mary Matthews, *Manager*
▲ **EMP:** 175

SQ FT: 15,000
SALES (est): 53.9MM **Privately Held**
WEB: www.thenorthwest.com
SIC: 2211 Blankets & blanketings, cotton

(G-14450)
PICO DIRECT LLC
70 Post Dr (11576-1122)
PHONE 212 947-8969
Marty Litt, *CEO*
Craig Litt, *COO*
Ronald Devereaux, *Treasurer*
EMP: 20
SQ FT: 8,700
SALES: 1.4MM **Privately Held**
SIC: 2326 Men's & boys' work clothing

(G-14451)
ROVEL MANUFACTURING CO INC
52 Wimbledon Dr (11576-3082)
PHONE 516 365-2752
William Levor, *President*
Andrew A Levor, *Vice Pres*
EMP: 5
SQ FT: 10,000
SALES: 400K **Privately Held**
SIC: 2299 Batts & batting: cotton mill waste & related material; batting, wadding, padding & fillings

(G-14452)
WM E MARTIN AND SONS CO INC
55 Bryant Ave Ste 300 (11576-1158)
PHONE 516 605-2444
William Martin Jr, *President*
William S Martin, *Vice Pres*
Martin Spencer, *Accounting Mgr*
Blake Martin, *Director*
▲ **EMP:** 22 **EST:** 1954
SQ FT: 60,000
SALES (est): 6.8MM **Privately Held**
SIC: 2099 2034 Spices, including grinding; vegetables, dried or dehydrated (except freeze-dried)

Roslyn Heights
Nassau County

(G-14453)
CABOT COACH BUILDERS INC
Also Called: Royale Limousine Manufacturers
77 Carriage Ln (11577-2615)
PHONE 516 625-4000
Lucy Berritto, *Manager*
EMP: 8
SALES (corp-wide): 11.1MM **Privately Held**
WEB: www.royalelimo.com
SIC: 3711 5511 Automobile assembly, including specialty automobiles; automobiles, new & used
PA: Cabot Coach Builders Inc.
99 Newark St
Haverhill MA 01832
978 374-4530

(G-14454)
ERGUN INC
10 Mineola Ave Unit B (11577-1067)
PHONE 631 721-0049
Omer Eguner, *President*
EMP: 2
SQ FT: 200
SALES: 15.9MM **Privately Held**
SIC: 2911 Oils, fuel

(G-14455)
HIGHWAY TOLL ADM LLC
66 Powerhouse Rd Ste 301 (11577-1372)
P.O. Box 30 (11577-0030)
PHONE 516 684-9584
David Centner, *CEO*
Jessica Sobierajski, *Personnel Assit*
Jonathan Schweiger,
▲ **EMP:** 15
SALES (est): 4.9MM **Privately Held**
SIC: 3829 Toll booths, automatic

Roslyn Heights - Nassau County (G-14456)

(G-14456)
IET LABS INC (PA)
1 Expressway Plz Ste 120 (11577-2031)
PHONE...................................516 334-5959
Sam Sheena, *President*
David Sheena, *Vice Pres*
Joel Goldberg, *Engineer*
Ben Sheena, *VP Sales*
▲ **EMP:** 12
SQ FT: 11,000
SALES (est): 5MM **Privately Held**
SIC: 3825 Test equipment for electronic & electrical circuits

(G-14457)
KIM JAE PRINTING CO INC
249 Parkside Dr (11577-2211)
PHONE...................................212 691-6289
Jae Kye Kim, *President*
Yun Kim, *Vice Pres*
EMP: 5 **EST:** 1974
SQ FT: 6,000
SALES (est): 500K **Privately Held**
SIC: 2759 2752 Newspapers: printing; commercial printing, lithographic

(G-14458)
KINGS READY MIX INC
703 3rd Ave Fl 2 Flr 2 (11577)
PHONE...................................718 853-4644
Robert Bruzzese, *CEO*
Vincent Falcone, *President*
Michael Falcone, *Corp Secy*
Michael Solomon, *CFO*
EMP: 50
SQ FT: 60,000
SALES: 7.6MM **Privately Held**
SIC: 3273 Ready-mixed concrete

(G-14459)
ROSLYN BREAD COMPANY INC
190 Mineola Ave (11577-2093)
PHONE...................................516 625-1470
EMP: 35
SQ FT: 3,500
SALES: 1.1MM **Privately Held**
SIC: 2051 5149 5461 5812 Mfg Whol Ret Bread & Restaurant

(G-14460)
SOMERSET MANUFACTURERS INC
36 Glen Cove Rd (11577-1703)
PHONE...................................516 626-3832
Jacob Ambalu, *President*
Esther Ambalu, *Vice Pres*
EMP: 20
SALES (est): 1.6MM **Privately Held**
SIC: 3911 Jewelry, precious metal

(G-14461)
US CONCRETE INC
Also Called: Kings Ready Mix
10 Powerhouse Rd (11577-1311)
PHONE...................................718 853-4644
EMP: 50
SALES (corp-wide): 1.3B **Publicly Held**
SIC: 3273 Ready-mixed concrete
PA: U.S. Concrete, Inc.
331 N Main St
Euless TX 76039
817 835-4105

Rotterdam Junction
Schenectady County

(G-14462)
SI GROUP INC
Also Called: Si Group Global Manufacturing
1000 Main St (12150)
PHONE...................................518 347-4200
David Dawood, *VP Opers*
EMP: 200 **Privately Held**
SIC: 2865 Phenol, alkylated & cumene
HQ: Si Group, Inc.
2750 Balltown Rd
Schenectady NY 12309
518 347-4200

(G-14463)
SI GROUP INC
Rr 5 Box South (12150)
P.O. Box 1046, Schenectady (12301-1046)
PHONE...................................518 347-4200
Andy Barrett, *General Mgr*
EMP: 150 **Privately Held**
WEB: www.schenectadyinternational.com
SIC: 2851 Varnishes
HQ: Si Group, Inc.
2750 Balltown Rd
Schenectady NY 12309
518 347-4200

Round Lake
Saratoga County

(G-14464)
USHERS MACHINE AND TOOL CO INC
180 Ushers Rd (12151-1806)
PHONE...................................518 877-5501
Don Lincoln, *President*
Joseph Hopeck, *President*
EMP: 20
SQ FT: 5,000
SALES (est): 4.3MM
SALES (corp-wide): 3.1B **Privately Held**
WEB: www.ushersm.com
SIC: 3599 Machine shop, jobbing & repair
PA: Aalberts Industries N.V.
Sandenburgerlaan 4
Langbroek
343 565-080

(G-14465)
WYRESTORM TECHNOLOGIES LLC
23 Wood Rd (12151-1708)
PHONE...................................518 289-1293
Derek Hulbert, *President*
Star Weisfeld, *Purchasing*
Michael Almasy, *Sales Staff*
Mark Shaughnessy, *Sales Staff*
Brandon Stewart, *Marketing Staff*
▲ **EMP:** 15
SQ FT: 2,500
SALES (est): 2.9MM **Privately Held**
SIC: 3651 Household audio & video equipment
HQ: Wyrestorm Technologies Europe Limited
Unit 22 Kelvin Road Ergo Business Park
Swindon WILTS
179 323-0343

Round Top
Greene County

(G-14466)
ROUND TOP KNIT & SCREENING
Rr 31 (12473)
P.O. Box 188 (12473-0188)
PHONE...................................518 622-3600
Manny Voss, *Owner*
EMP: 5
SQ FT: 6,000
SALES: 750K **Privately Held**
SIC: 2759 5651 2395 2396 Screen printing; family clothing stores; embroidery & art needlework; automotive & apparel trimmings

Rouses Point
Clinton County

(G-14467)
CHAMPLAIN PLASTICS INC
Also Called: Champlain Hanger
87 Pillsbury Rd (12979-1701)
P.O. Box 2947, Plattsburgh (12901-0269)
PHONE...................................518 297-3700
Alan L Taveroff, *Ch of Bd*
Joe Zalter, *President*
▲ **EMP:** 85
SALES (est): 14.7MM **Privately Held**
WEB: www.olympicpoolaccessories.com
SIC: 3089 Injection molding of plastics
PA: Canadian Buttons Limited
7020 Boul Newman
Lasalle QC H8N 3
514 363-0210

(G-14468)
PFIZER INC
Also Called: Wyeth
64 Maple St (12979-1424)
P.O. Box 34600, Memphis TN (38184-0600)
PHONE...................................518 297-6611
John Nichols, *Opers Mgr*
Scott Cota, *Research*
William Brooks, *Branch Mgr*
Joseph Whittemore, *Manager*
Scott Denicourt, *Director*
EMP: 440
SALES (corp-wide): 52.5B **Publicly Held**
WEB: www.wyeth.com
SIC: 2834 Pharmaceutical preparations
PA: Pfizer Inc.
235 E 42nd St
New York NY 10017
212 733-2323

(G-14469)
POWERTEX INC (PA)
Also Called: Powertex Bulk Ship Solutions
1 Lincoln Blvd Ste 101 (12979-1087)
PHONE...................................518 297-4000
Stephen D Podd, *President*
Karen M Lamberton, *Treasurer*
◆ **EMP:** 34 **EST:** 1977
SQ FT: 65,900
SALES (est): 8.8MM **Privately Held**
WEB: www.powertex.com
SIC: 3089 Plastic containers, except foam

(G-14470)
SANDYS DELI INC
Also Called: Last Resort, The
90 Montgomery St (12979-1018)
PHONE...................................518 297-6951
Carolyn Reid, *President*
EMP: 6 **EST:** 2016
SQ FT: 1,000
SALES: 145K
SALES (corp-wide): 450K **Privately Held**
SIC: 2599 Bar, restaurant & cafeteria furniture
PA: Sandy's Deli Inc
133 Lake St
Rouses Point NY 12979
518 297-6951

Rush
Monroe County

(G-14471)
CONVERGENT AUDIO TECH INC
85 High Tech Dr (14543-9746)
PHONE...................................585 359-2700
Ken Stevens, *President*
Truddy Stevens, *Vice Pres*
EMP: 5
SQ FT: 3,300
SALES (est): 832.7K **Privately Held**
SIC: 3651 Audio electronic systems

(G-14472)
EXTEK INC
7500 W Henrietta Rd (14543-9790)
PHONE...................................585 533-1672
Caroline Eastman, *Branch Mgr*
EMP: 50
SALES (corp-wide): 5.5MM **Privately Held**
WEB: www.sts.ethoxint.com
SIC: 3841 Surgical & medical instruments
PA: Extek, Inc.
370 Summit Point Dr
Henrietta NY
585 321-5000

(G-14473)
GPM ASSOCIATES LLC
Graphik Promotional Products
45 High Tech Dr Ste 100 (14543-9746)
PHONE...................................585 359-1770
Sean Fraser, *Sales Staff*
Kevin Webster, *Marketing Staff*
Jim McDermott,
EMP: 6
SALES (est): 591.1K
SALES (corp-wide): 15.8MM **Privately Held**
SIC: 2393 Textile bags
PA: Gpm Associates Llc
45 High Tech Dr
Rush NY 14543
585 334-4800

(G-14474)
GPP POST-CLOSING INC
Also Called: Global Precision Products
90 High Tech Dr (14543-9746)
PHONE...................................585 334-4640
Mark Labell, *CEO*
EMP: 22
SQ FT: 250,000
SALES (est): 4.4MM **Privately Held**
WEB: www.globalppi.com
SIC: 3599 Machine shop, jobbing & repair

(G-14475)
KEUKA STUDIOS INC
1011 Rush Henrietta Townl (14543-9763)
PHONE...................................585 624-5960
Dan White, *President*
Jeanne White, *Corp Secy*
Jason White, *Consultant*
▼ **EMP:** 8
SALES (est): 1.2MM **Privately Held**
WEB: www.keuka-studios.com
SIC: 3446 Architectural metalwork

(G-14476)
SPS MEDICAL SUPPLY CORP (DH)
6789 W Henrietta Rd (14543-9797)
PHONE...................................585 359-0130
Gary Steinberg, *President*
John Hughes, *General Mgr*
Rex Norton, *Opers Mgr*
Gavin Burke, *Mfg Mgr*
Mary Reed, *Finance Mgr*
◆ **EMP:** 73
SQ FT: 40,000
SALES (est): 19.7MM
SALES (corp-wide): 871.9MM **Publicly Held**
WEB: www.spsmedical.com
SIC: 3842 Surgical appliances & supplies
HQ: Crosstex International, Inc.
10 Ranick Rd
Hauppauge NY 11788
631 582-6777

Rushville
Yates County

(G-14477)
RUSH MACHINERY INC
4761 State Route 364 (14544-9721)
PHONE...................................585 554-3070
William P Freese, *President*
▲ **EMP:** 9
SQ FT: 7,000
SALES (est): 2.1MM **Privately Held**
SIC: 3541 Centering machines

Rye
Westchester County

(G-14478)
CONSOLIDATED EDISON CO NY INC
511 Theodore Fremd Ave (10580-1432)
PHONE...................................914 933-2936
William McGrath, *Principal*
EMP: 19
SALES (corp-wide): 12B **Publicly Held**
SIC: 2869 Fuels
HQ: Consolidated Edison Company Of New York, Inc.
4 Irving Pl
New York NY 10003
212 460-4600

GEOGRAPHIC SECTION
Sagaponack - Suffolk County (G-14504)

(G-14479)
GAZETTE PRESS INC
2 Clinton Ave (10580-1629)
PHONE..................914 963-8300
Richard Martinelli, *CEO*
Angelo R Martinelli, *President*
Angelo Martinelli, *Chairman*
Carol Martinelli, *Treasurer*
EMP: 20
SQ FT: 10,000
SALES (est): 2.8MM **Privately Held**
SIC: 2759 2796 2791 2789 Letterpress printing; platemaking services; typesetting; bookbinding & related work; commercial printing, lithographic

(G-14480)
GB AERO ENGINE LLC
555 Theodore Fremd Ave (10580-1451)
PHONE..................914 925-9600
Raynard Benvenuti,
Noah Roy,
Rob Wolf,
EMP: 390
SALES (est): 16.5MM **Privately Held**
SIC: 3724 3541 3769 Aircraft engines & engine parts; machine tools, metal cutting type; guided missile & space vehicle parts & auxiliary equipment

(G-14481)
GLOBAL GOLD CORPORATION (PA)
555 Theodore Fremd Ave C208 (10580-1451)
PHONE..................914 925-0020
Van Z Krikorian, *Ch of Bd*
W E S Urquhart, *Vice Pres*
Jan Dulman, *CFO*
Drury J Gallagher, *Treasurer*
EMP: 12
SALES (est): 3.3MM **Publicly Held**
WEB: www.globalgoldcorp.com
SIC: 1021 1041 1094 1044 Copper ores; gold ores; uranium ore mining; silver ores

(G-14482)
HIBERT PUBLISHING LLC
222 Purchase St (10580-2101)
PHONE..................914 381-7474
Gary Hibert, *Branch Mgr*
EMP: 5
SALES (est): 241.3K
SALES (corp-wide): 1.1MM **Privately Held**
SIC: 2741 Miscellaneous publishing
PA: Hibert Publishing Llc
    7555 E Hampden Ave # 405
    Denver CO 80231
    303 312-1000

(G-14483)
HYDRIVE ENERGY
350 Theodore Fremd Ave (10580-1573)
PHONE..................914 925-9100
Michael F Weinstein, *Chairman*
EMP: 6
SALES (est): 451.8K **Privately Held**
SIC: 2086 Mfg Bottled/Canned Soft Drinks

(G-14484)
JUDITH N GRAHAM INC
Also Called: Pink and Palmer
64 Halls Ln (10580-3124)
PHONE..................914 921-5446
James Graham, *Principal*
EMP: 7
SALES (est): 537.5K **Privately Held**
SIC: 2844 Toilet preparations

(G-14485)
MASON & GORE INC
Also Called: Gazette & Press
2 Clinton Ave (10580-1629)
PHONE..................914 921-1025
Angelo R Martinelli, *President*
EMP: 20 EST: 1956
SQ FT: 4,500
SALES (est): 2MM **Privately Held**
WEB: www.gazettepress.com
SIC: 2752 7331 7311 Commercial printing, offset; mailing service; advertising consultant

(G-14486)
MONEYPAPER INC
411 Theodore Fremd Ave # 132 (10580-1410)
P.O. Box 451 (10580-0451)
PHONE..................914 925-0022
Vita Nelson, *President*
EMP: 12
SALES (est): 807.6K **Privately Held**
WEB: www.giftsofstock.com
SIC: 2711 6282 Newspapers, publishing & printing; investment advice

(G-14487)
QUOIN LLC
555 Theodore Fremd Ave B302 (10580-1451)
PHONE..................914 967-9400
Martin Franklin, *CEO*
EMP: 1402
SALES (est): 709.4MM
SALES (corp-wide): 14.7B **Publicly Held**
WEB: www.jarden.com
SIC: 3089 Plastic containers, except foam
HQ: Jarden Corporation
    221 River St
    Hoboken NJ 07030

(G-14488)
RYE RECORD
14 Elm Pl Ste 200 (10580-2951)
PHONE..................914 713-3213
Dolores Eyler, *Partner*
Allen Clarck, *Partner*
Robin Jovanovich, *Partner*
Sylke Schuster, *Agent*
EMP: 8
SALES (est): 500K **Privately Held**
SIC: 2721 Periodicals

(G-14489)
WESTERN OIL AND GAS JV INC
Also Called: Michael Neuman
7 Mccullough Pl (10580-2934)
PHONE..................914 967-4758
Michael Neuman, *President*
Richard Neuman, *Vice Pres*
EMP: 3 EST: 2008
SALES (est): 2.1MM **Privately Held**
SIC: 1321 8748 1381 Natural gas liquids; energy conservation consultant; drilling oil & gas wells

Rye Brook
Westchester County

(G-14490)
CHROMOSENSE LLC
476 N Ridge St (10573-1108)
PHONE..................646 541-2302
Filip Mlekicki, *COO*
Masoud Ghandehari,
Alexey Sidyelyev,
EMP: 6
SALES (est): 95.6K **Privately Held**
SIC: 3826 Analytical instruments

(G-14491)
ELIAS FRAGRANCES INC (PA)
3 Hunter Dr (10573-1406)
PHONE..................718 693-6400
Robert Elias, *President*
Lewis Elias, *Exec VP*
Barbara Elias, *Admin Sec*
EMP: 17 EST: 1972
SQ FT: 8,000
SALES (est): 1.3MM **Privately Held**
SIC: 2844 5122 Perfumes, natural or synthetic; perfumes

(G-14492)
FLOW CONTROL LLC (HQ)
1 International Dr (10573-1058)
PHONE..................914 323-5700
Sonia Hollies, *Mng Member*
EMP: 250
SALES (est): 25MM **Publicly Held**
SIC: 3561 Pumps, domestic: water or sump

(G-14493)
MITSUI CHEMICALS AMERICA INC (HQ)
800 Westchester Ave N607 (10573-1328)
PHONE..................914 253-0777
Naoto Tani, *President*
Ken Migita, *General Mgr*
Kenji Miyachi, *General Mgr*
Greg Griffin, *Business Mgr*
Toshimitsu Narutaki, *Business Mgr*
◆ EMP: 40
SQ FT: 13,000
SALES (est): 307.3MM
SALES (corp-wide): 12.4B **Privately Held**
SIC: 2865 3082 8731 5169 Cyclic crudes & intermediates; unsupported plastics profile shapes; computer (hardware) development; chemical additives; loan institutions, general & industrial; plasticizer/additive based plastic materials
PA: Mitsui Chemicals,Inc.
    1-5-2, Higashishimbashi
    Minato-Ku TKY 105-0
    362 532-100

(G-14494)
PROGRESSIVE PRODUCTS LLC
4 International Dr # 224 (10573-1065)
PHONE..................914 417-6022
Jason Englander, *CEO*
Gabby Hunter, *Accounting Mgr*
Mark Zeitler,
▲ EMP: 8
SQ FT: 2,000
SALES: 10MM **Privately Held**
SIC: 2842 Cleaning or polishing preparations

(G-14495)
SNAPPLE BEVERAGE CORP (DEL) (HQ)
900 King St (10573-1226)
PHONE..................914 612-4000
Larry D Young, *CEO*
Ernie Cavallo, *President*
Scott Miller, *Vice Pres*
Michael Sandes, *Vice Pres*
EMP: 70
SQ FT: 55,000
SALES (est): 254.8MM **Publicly Held**
SIC: 2086 Soft drinks: packaged in cans, bottles, etc.

(G-14496)
XYLEM INC (PA)
1 International Dr (10573-1058)
PHONE..................914 323-5700
Markos I Tambakeras, *Ch of Bd*
D Randall Bays, *President*
Tomas Brannemo, *President*
Patrick K Decker, *President*
David Flinton, *President*
EMP: 277
SQ FT: 67,000
SALES: 4.7B **Publicly Held**
SIC: 3561 Pumps & pumping equipment

Sag Harbor
Suffolk County

(G-14497)
CAM TOUCHVIEW PRODUCTS INC
51 Division St (11963-3162)
P.O. Box 1980 (11963-0067)
PHONE..................631 842-3400
Emanuel Cardinale, *President*
EMP: 15 EST: 2013
SQ FT: 4,000
SALES: 1.2MM **Privately Held**
SIC: 3674 Thin film circuits

(G-14498)
COASTAL PUBLICATIONS INC
22 Division St (11963)
P.O. Box 1620 (11963-0058)
PHONE..................631 725-1700
Gavin Menu, *Principal*
EMP: 10
SALES (est): 663.1K **Privately Held**
SIC: 2741 Miscellaneous publishing

(G-14499)
DORTRONICS SYSTEMS INC
1668 Bhmpton Sag Hbr Tpke (11963-3706)
PHONE..................631 725-0505
Paul R Scheerer, *CEO*
John Fitzpaprick, *President*
John Fitzpatrick, *President*
Mary Scheerer, *Vice Pres*
Stuart Arthur, *Engineer*
EMP: 21
SQ FT: 10,000
SALES: 3.9MM
SALES (corp-wide): 16.7MM **Privately Held**
WEB: www.dortronics.com
SIC: 3429 3679 3625 3089 Locks or lock sets; electronic switches; switches, electronic applications; timing devices, electronic; plastic hardware & building products
PA: Sag Harbor Industries, Inc.
    1668 Bhmpton Sag Hbr Tpke
    Sag Harbor NY 11963
    631 725-0440

(G-14500)
LUBBU INC
20 Payne Ave (11963-1204)
PHONE..................917 693-9600
Robbie Vorhaus, *CEO*
EMP: 6
SALES: 125K **Privately Held**
SIC: 7372 Application computer software

(G-14501)
SAG HARBOR EXPRESS
35 Main St (11963-3012)
P.O. Box 1620 (11963-0058)
PHONE..................631 725-1700
Bryan Boyhan, *Manager*
EMP: 7
SALES (est): 494.1K **Privately Held**
WEB: www.sagharboronline.com
SIC: 2741 2711 Miscellaneous publishing; newspapers

(G-14502)
SAG HARBOR INDUSTRIES INC (PA)
1668 Bhmpton Sag Hbr Tpke (11963-3714)
PHONE..................631 725-0440
Paul R Scheerer Jr, *Ch of Bd*
Mary Scheerer, *President*
John Fitzpatrick, *Vice Pres*
Dave Leeney, *Vice Pres*
Wendy Fitzpatrick, *Manager*
EMP: 50 EST: 1946
SQ FT: 50,000
SALES (est): 16.7MM **Privately Held**
WEB: www.sagharborind.com
SIC: 3621 3672 3677 5065 Coils, for electric motors or generators; printed circuit boards; electronic coils, transformers & other inductors; electronic parts & equipment; transformers, except electric

(G-14503)
SECOND CHANCE PRESS INC
Also Called: Permanent Press
4170 Noyac Rd (11963-2809)
PHONE..................631 725-1101
Martin Shepard, *President*
Rania Graetz, *Editor*
Judith Shepard, *Vice Pres*
EMP: 6
SALES: 420K **Privately Held**
WEB: www.thepermanentpress.com
SIC: 2731 5942 Books: publishing only; book stores

Sagaponack
Suffolk County

(G-14504)
ARTICULATE
717 Daniels Ln 419 (11962-2033)
P.O. Box 419 (11962-0419)
PHONE..................646 706-7596
Adam Schwartz, *President*
EMP: 10 EST: 2017
SALES (est): 908.7K **Privately Held**
SIC: 7372 Prepackaged software

(G-14505)
WOLFFER ESTATE VINEYARD INC
Also Called: Wolffer Estate Winery
139 Sagg Rd (11962-2006)
P.O. Box 9002 (11962-9002)
PHONE..................................631 537-5106
Christian Wolffer, President
Judy Malone, Comms Dir
▲ EMP: 50
SALES (est): 9MM Privately Held
WEB: www.wolffer.com
SIC: 2084 5813 Wines; wine bar

Saint Albans
Queens County

(G-14506)
A LESLEY DUMMETT
10415 185th St (11412-1009)
PHONE..................................646 541-1168
Lesley A Dummett, Owner
EMP: 1
SALES: 10MM Privately Held
SIC: 2731 Book publishing

(G-14507)
HOUSE OF THE FOAMING CASE INC
110 08 Dunkirk St (11412)
PHONE..................................718 454-0101
EMP: 7
SALES (est): 1MM Privately Held
SIC: 3523 Mfg Farm Machinery/Equipment

(G-14508)
INTEGRATED TECH SUPPORT SVCS
Also Called: Itss
18616 Jordan Ave (11412-2308)
PHONE..................................718 454-2497
Gerald Cortez, President
Damon Kinebrew, Sales/Mktg Dir
Michael Greaves, Admin Mgr
EMP: 7
SQ FT: 1,000
SALES: 150K Privately Held
SIC: 2522 Office furniture, except wood

Saint James
Suffolk County

(G-14509)
2600 ENTERPRISES INC
Also Called: The Hacker Quarterly
2 Flowerfield Ste 30 (11780-1507)
P.O. Box 848, Middle Island (11953-0848)
PHONE..................................631 474-2677
Emmanuelle Goldstein, Principal
Eric Corley, Editor
▲ EMP: 10
SALES (est): 1MM Privately Held
WEB: www.2600.net
SIC: 2721 Magazines: publishing only, not printed on site

(G-14510)
CREATE-A-CARD INC
16 Brasswood Rd (11780-3410)
PHONE..................................631 584-2273
Arthur Messina, President
Kathy Messina, Vice Pres
Marian Abrilz, Marketing Staff
Messina Arthur, CTO
EMP: 5
SALES: 375K Privately Held
WEB: www.createacardinc.com
SIC: 2752 2759 Color lithography; post cards, picture: lithographed; visiting cards (including business): printing

(G-14511)
DESIGN SOLUTIONS LI INC
711 Middle Country Rd (11780-3209)
PHONE..................................631 656-8700
Mario Adragna, Owner
EMP: 1
SQ FT: 6,000
SALES: 4MM Privately Held
SIC: 3639 Major kitchen appliances, except refrigerators & stoves

(G-14512)
EAST COAST BUSINESS FORMS INC
Also Called: Accurate Business Systems
320 Lake Ave Ste 2 (11780-2255)
PHONE..................................631 231-9300
Dan Glenn, President
Roni O Trolio, Prdtn Mgr
EMP: 6
SALES (est): 1MM Privately Held
WEB: www.ecoastgraphics.com
SIC: 2752 Commercial printing, lithographic

(G-14513)
POLYMERS MERONA INC
Also Called: P M I
347 Lake Ave Ste 4 (11780-2278)
P.O. Box 515 (11780-0515)
PHONE..................................631 862-8010
Ricky E Profit, Ch of Bd
Barbara Profit, Corp Secy
Brian Montroy, Vice Pres
▼ EMP: 10
SQ FT: 4,000
SALES (est): 5.8MM Privately Held
WEB: www.polymers-merona.com
SIC: 2821 Plastics materials & resins

(G-14514)
RE HANSEN INDUSTRIES INC (PA)
Also Called: Islandaire
500 Middle Country Rd A (11780-3236)
PHONE..................................631 471-2900
Robert Hansen Jr, Ch of Bd
John Bonhurst, General Mgr
Somya Mishra, Engineer
Glenn Myhr, Engineer
Bob Bissinger, Design Engr
◆ EMP: 118
SALES (est): 27.2MM Privately Held
SIC: 3585 3822 3433 5722 Air conditioning equipment, complete; heat pumps, electric; auto controls regulating residntl & coml environmt & applncs; heating equipment, except electric; air conditioning room units, self-contained; plumbing, heating, air-conditioning contractors

(G-14515)
SMITHTOWN CONCRETE PRODUCTS
441 Middle Country Rd (11780-3201)
P.O. Box 612, Smithtown (11787-0612)
PHONE..................................631 265-1815
Neil Spevak, President
Barbara Spevak, Treasurer
EMP: 16 EST: 1940
SALES: 950K Privately Held
WEB: www.smithtownconcrete.com
SIC: 3271 Blocks, concrete or cinder: standard

(G-14516)
TRADEWINS PUBLISHING CORP
528 Route 25a Ste A (11780-1440)
PHONE..................................631 361-6916
Steve Schmidt, President
Jane Schmidt, Admin Sec
EMP: 5
SQ FT: 1,000
SALES (est): 297.2K Privately Held
WEB: www.tradewinspublishing.com
SIC: 2741 Miscellaneous publishing

Saint Johnsville
Montgomery County

(G-14517)
CELLECT PLASTICS LLC
12 New St (13452-1313)
PHONE..................................518 568-7036
Scott Smith, CEO
▲ EMP: 100
SQ FT: 197,952
SALES (est): 4.7MM Privately Held
SIC: 3086 Plastics foam products

(G-14518)
HANSON AGGREGATES PA INC
7904 St Hwy 5 (13452-3514)
PHONE..................................518 568-2444
Don Sheldon, Manager
EMP: 10
SALES (corp-wide): 20.3B Privately Held
SIC: 1442 1422 Common sand mining; limestones, ground
HQ: Hanson Aggregates Pennsylvania, Llc
7660 Imperial Way
Allentown PA 18195
610 366-4626

(G-14519)
HELMONT MILLS INC (HQ)
15 Lion Ave (13452-1398)
PHONE..................................518 568-7913
George G Gehring, CEO
John Geesler, Maintence Staff
EMP: 1 EST: 1992
SALES (est): 10.4MM
SALES (corp-wide): 64MM Privately Held
SIC: 2258 Lace & warp knit fabric mills
PA: Gehring Tricot Corporation
68 Ransom St
Dolgeville NY 13329
315 429-8551

(G-14520)
HIGHWAY GARAGE
110 State Highway 331 (13452-2818)
PHONE..................................518 568-2837
Rich Crum, Manager
EMP: 7 EST: 2011
SALES (est): 412.3K Privately Held
SIC: 3531 Drags, road (construction & road maintenance equipment)

(G-14521)
RC ENTPS BUS & TRCK INC
5895 State Highway 29 (13452-2413)
P.O. Box 193 (13452-0193)
PHONE..................................518 568-5753
Robert Crum, Ch of Bd
EMP: 6
SALES (est): 460K Privately Held
SIC: 7694 Motor repair services

(G-14522)
SENTINEL PRODUCTS CORP
12 New St (13452-1396)
PHONE..................................518 568-7036
Michael Tuza, Manager
EMP: 14
SALES (corp-wide): 1MM Privately Held
WEB: www.sentinelproducts.net
SIC: 3081 Polyethylene film
PA: Sentinel Products Corp
1550 Falmouth Rd
Centerville MA
508 775-5220

Salamanca
Cattaraugus County

(G-14523)
ALICE PERKINS
Also Called: A & F Trucking & Excavating
148 Washington St (14779-1045)
PHONE..................................716 378-5100
Alice Perkins, Co-Owner
Fred Perkins, Co-Owner
EMP: 6
SQ FT: 3,212
SALES: 1.5MM Privately Held
SIC: 1389 4212 1411 Excavating slush pits & cellars; dump truck haulage; granite dimension stone

(G-14524)
CAPSTREAM TECHNOLOGIES LLC
16 Main St (14779-1528)
PHONE..................................716 945-7100
Joseph Caruso, General Mgr
Michael Krysick,
EMP: 6
SALES (est): 900.6K Privately Held
SIC: 3669 Intercommunication systems, electric

(G-14525)
HIGHLAND INJECTION MOLDING
Also Called: Ubec
175 Rochester St (14779-1508)
PHONE..................................716 945-2424
Joseph G Collins, President
Lewis Jewel, Treasurer
Mary E Collins, Admin Sec
EMP: 100
SALES (est): 9.6MM Privately Held
WEB: www.highland-plastics.com
SIC: 3089 Injection molding of plastics; trays, plastic

(G-14526)
MCHONE INDUSTRIES INC
110 Elm St (14779-1500)
P.O. Box 69 (14779-0069)
PHONE..................................716 945-3380
Arnold McHone, President
Eva McHone, Vice Pres
EMP: 75
SQ FT: 75,000
SALES (est): 17.7MM Privately Held
WEB: www.mchoneind.com
SIC: 3469 3317 3569 3444 Metal stampings; steel pipe & tubes; robots, assembly line: industrial & commercial; sheet metalwork

(G-14527)
MERITOOL LLC
4496 Route 353 (14779-9781)
P.O. Box 148 (14779-0148)
PHONE..................................716 699-6005
Kevin Whited, Opers Mgr
Brent Findlay, Engineer
Karen Ward, Executive
Timm Herman,
Donna R Finnegan, Administration
▲ EMP: 28 EST: 1939
SQ FT: 29,000
SALES (est): 3.6MM Privately Held
WEB: www.meritool.com
SIC: 3546 Power-driven handtools

(G-14528)
MONROE TABLE COMPANY INC
255 Rochester St Ste 15 (14779-1563)
PHONE..................................716 945-7700
Douglas Kirchner, CEO
Orville Johnston, President
EMP: 10
SALES (est): 1MM Privately Held
SIC: 2599 Bar, restaurant & cafeteria furniture

(G-14529)
NORTON-SMITH HARDWOODS INC (PA)
Also Called: Arbor Valley Flooring
25 Morningside Ave (14779-1210)
PHONE..................................716 945-0346
Art Smith, Co-President
Dan Smith, Co-President
▼ EMP: 7
SQ FT: 18,000
SALES (est): 2MM Privately Held
SIC: 2426 Dimension, hardwood

(G-14530)
SALAMANCA LUMBER COMPANY INC
59 Rochester St (14779-1508)
P.O. Box 416 (14779-0416)
PHONE..................................716 945-4810
Reinier Taapken, CEO
Rinus Vollenberg, Vice Pres
Mike Gilbert, Safety Mgr
▼ EMP: 45
SQ FT: 3,000
SALES (est): 7.1MM Privately Held
WEB: www.salamancalumber.com
SIC: 2421 Kiln drying of lumber
PA: Leyenaar Taapken Lamaker Holding B.V.
Kamerlingh Onnesweg 7
Vianen Ut 4131
347 374-844

GEOGRAPHIC SECTION

(G-14531)
SALAMANCA PRESS PENNY SAVER
Also Called: Salamanca Penny Saver
36 River St (14779-1495)
PHONE..................716 945-1500
F David Radler, *President*
Kevin Burleson, *Principal*
Ernie Sage, *Sales/Mktg Mgr*
John H Satterwhite, *Treasurer*
EMP: 30
SALES (est): 1.7MM **Privately Held**
SIC: 2741 2759 2711 Shopping news; publishing & printing; commercial printing; newspapers

(G-14532)
SENECA MANUFACTURING COMPANY
175 Rochester St (14779-1508)
P.O. Box 496 (14779-0496)
PHONE..................716 945-4400
Gary Sanden, *Partner*
Travis Heron, *Partner*
▲ **EMP:** 8
SQ FT: 40,000
SALES (est): 1.7MM **Privately Held**
SIC: 2111 Cigarettes

(G-14533)
SNYDER MANUFACTURING INC
Also Called: SMI
255 Rochester St Unit 1 (14779-1563)
PHONE..................716 945-0354
James F Snyder, *President*
Cynthia Snyder, *Corp Secy*
▲ **EMP:** 25 **EST:** 2000
SQ FT: 40,000
SALES (est): 4.7MM **Privately Held**
WEB: www.snyder-mfg.com
SIC: 3423 Hand & edge tools

(G-14534)
STRATEGIES NORTH AMERICA INC
Also Called: Ellicottville Kitchen Eqp
150 Elm St (14779-2002)
P.O. Box 1549, Ellicottville (14731-1549)
PHONE..................716 945-6053
John Karassik, *President*
EMP: 5
SQ FT: 4,000
SALES (est): 885.7K **Privately Held**
SIC: 3589 Dishwashing machines, commercial

(G-14535)
SUN-TIMES MEDIA GROUP INC
Also Called: Salamanca Daily Reporter
36 River St (14779-1474)
P.O. Box 111 (14779-0111)
PHONE..................716 945-1644
Kevin Burleson, *Manager*
EMP: 32
SALES (corp-wide): 4.3MM **Privately Held**
SIC: 2711 Newspapers, publishing & printing
HQ: Sun-Times Media Group, Inc.
30 N Racine Ave Ste 300
Chicago IL 60607
312 321-3000

Salem
Washington County

(G-14536)
CARGILL INCORPORATED
Also Called: Agway
4186 State Route 29 (12865-3616)
PHONE..................518 854-7417
Jason Moore, *Manager*
EMP: 7
SALES (corp-wide): 51.2B **Privately Held**
WEB: www.cargill.com
SIC: 2048 Prepared feeds
PA: Cargill, Incorporated
15407 Mcginty Rd W
Wayzata MN 55391
952 742-7575

(G-14537)
CAROLINA EASTERN-VAIL INC
Also Called: Carol Vail
4134 State Route 22 (12865)
PHONE..................518 854-9785
Charles Tucker, *Branch Mgr*
EMP: 25
SALES (corp-wide): 61.9MM **Privately Held**
SIC: 2875 Fertilizers, mixing only
PA: Carolina Eastern-Vail, Inc.
831 County Rte 28
Niverville NY 12130
518 784-9166

(G-14538)
MAPLELAND FARMS LLC
647 Bunker Hill Rd (12865-1716)
PHONE..................518 854-7669
David Campbell, *President*
Terry Campbell, *Vice Pres*
EMP: 7
SALES (est): 254.7K **Privately Held**
SIC: 2087 0191 Syrups, flavoring (except drink); general farms, primarily crop

Salisbury Mills
Orange County

(G-14539)
CALLAHAN & NANNINI QUARRY INC
276 Clove Rd (12577-5224)
P.O. Box 164 (12577-0164)
PHONE..................845 496-4323
Robert Nannini, *President*
Bob Nannini, *Vice Pres*
Jay Nannini, *Vice Pres*
Leigh Nannini, *Pub Rel Mgr*
Leslie Nannini, *Admin Sec*
EMP: 5
SQ FT: 3,600
SALES (est): 4.8MM **Privately Held**
SIC: 1459 5032 Shale (common) quarrying; stone, crushed or broken

Sanborn
Niagara County

(G-14540)
BRIDGE COMPONENTS INC
2122 Cory Dr (14132-9338)
PHONE..................716 731-1184
Silvio G Derubeis, *Principal*
EMP: 6 **EST:** 2007
SALES (est): 628.8K **Privately Held**
SIC: 3399 Primary metal products

(G-14541)
BRIDGESTONE APM COMPANY
6350 Inducon Dr E (14132-9015)
PHONE..................419 423-9552
Duke Kawai, *Manager*
EMP: 60
SALES (corp-wide): 32.5B **Privately Held**
SIC: 3061 Automotive rubber goods (mechanical)
HQ: Bridgestone Apm Company
2030 Production Dr
Findlay OH 45840
419 423-9552

(G-14542)
BRUCE PIERCE
Also Called: Core Welding
2386 Lockport Rd (14132-9011)
P.O. Box 209 (14132-0209)
PHONE..................716 731-9310
Bruce Pierce, *Owner*
EMP: 5
SQ FT: 4,080
SALES (est): 500K **Privately Held**
WEB: www.brucepierce.com
SIC: 3443 3599 7692 1799 Fabricated plate work (boiler shop); machine shop, jobbing & repair; welding repair; sandblasting of building exteriors

(G-14543)
BUFFALO GEAR INC
3635 Lockport Rd (14132-9704)
PHONE..................716 731-2100
Daniel Szczygiel, *President*
Gail Nichols, *Vice Pres*
▲ **EMP:** 20 **EST:** 1962
SQ FT: 22,000
SALES (est): 4MM **Privately Held**
WEB: www.buffalogear.com
SIC: 3566 Gears, power transmission, except automotive

(G-14544)
EDWARDS VACUUM LLC (DH)
6416 Inducon Dr W (14132-9019)
PHONE..................800 848-9800
Matthew Taylor, *CEO*
John O'Sullivan, *Ch of Bd*
Butch Paddock, *President*
Michael Allison, *Vice Pres*
Nigel Wenden, *Vice Pres*
▲ **EMP:** 100
SALES (est): 166.5MM
SALES (corp-wide): 13.8B **Privately Held**
SIC: 3563 Vacuum (air extraction) systems, industrial
HQ: Edwards Limited
Innovation Drive
Burgess Hill W SUSSEX RH15 144 425-3000

(G-14545)
FINGER FOOD PRODUCTS INC
6400 Inducon Dr W (14132-9019)
P.O. Box 560, Niagara Falls (14304-0560)
PHONE..................716 297-4888
Jason Cordova, *CEO*
Nancy Flynn, *Finance Mgr*
Ann Henderson, *Office Mgr*
Darlene Valente, *Office Mgr*
EMP: 48
SQ FT: 34,000
SALES (est): 7MM **Privately Held**
WEB: www.fingerfoodproducts.com
SIC: 2038 Frozen specialties

(G-14546)
GAMBLE & GAMBLE INC (PA)
Also Called: Unit Step Company
5890 West St (14132-9245)
PHONE..................716 731-3239
Ronald H Gamble, *President*
EMP: 4
SQ FT: 2,500
SALES (est): 1.1MM **Privately Held**
SIC: 3272 Concrete products, precast

(G-14547)
INNOVATIVE CLEANING SOLUTIONS
2990 Carney Dr (14132-9305)
PHONE..................716 731-4408
EMP: 5
SQ FT: 1,600
SALES (est): 727.2K **Privately Held**
SIC: 3559 Mfg Misc Industry Machinery

(G-14548)
KATZ GROUP AMERICAS INC (DH)
Also Called: Katz Americas
3685 Lockport Rd (14132-9404)
PHONE..................716 995-3059
Tammy Gorzka, *President*
Michael Elbers, *COO*
Thomas Muraca, *Opers Mgr*
Dale Fischer, *Production*
Scott Townsend, *Production*
▲ **EMP:** 50
SQ FT: 70,000
SALES (est): 13.4MM
SALES (corp-wide): 783.1MM **Privately Held**
WEB: www.american-coaster.com
SIC: 2679 Paper products, converted
HQ: Katz Gmbh & Co. Kg
Hauptstr. 2
Weisenbach 76599
722 464-70

(G-14549)
KINSHOFER USA INC
6420 Inducon Dr W Ste G (14132-9025)
PHONE..................716 731-4333

Martin Francois, *General Mgr*
▲ **EMP:** 24
SALES (est): 5.2MM
SALES (corp-wide): 5.8B **Privately Held**
SIC: 3531 Excavators: cable, clamshell, crane, derrick, dragline, etc.; cranes
HQ: Kinshofer Gmbh
Hauptstr. 76
Waakirchen 83666
802 188-990

(G-14550)
MYLES TOOL COMPANY INC
6300 Inducon Corporate Dr (14132-9346)
PHONE..................716 731-1300
Myles Barraclough, *President*
Tim Barraclough, *Vice Pres*
Paul Reding, *Prdtn Mgr*
Joe Adams, *Manager*
Jeremy Bout, *Webmaster*
EMP: 42 **EST:** 1977
SQ FT: 4,500
SALES (est): 9.9MM **Privately Held**
WEB: www.mylestool.com
SIC: 3545 3541 Machine tool accessories; machine tools, metal cutting type

(G-14551)
PRECISION PLUS VACUUM PARTS
6416 Inducon Dr W (14132-9019)
PHONE..................716 297-2039
Joe Miller, *President*
Joseph Miller, *Superintendent*
▲ **EMP:** 62
SQ FT: 20,000
SALES (est): 11.4MM
SALES (corp-wide): 13.8B **Privately Held**
WEB: www.precisionplus.com
SIC: 3563 Vacuum pumps, except laboratory
HQ: Edwards Vacuum Llc
6416 Inducon Dr W
Sanborn NY 14132
800 848-9800

(G-14552)
PYROTEK INCORPORATED
Metaullics Systems Division
2040 Cory Dr (14132-9388)
PHONE..................716 731-3221
George Bitler, *Principal*
Kevin Scott, *Manager*
EMP: 50
SALES (corp-wide): 588.8MM **Privately Held**
SIC: 3624 3569 3999 Carbon & graphite products; filters; chairs, hydraulic, barber & beauty shop
PA: Pyrotek Incorporated
705 W 1st Ave
Spokane WA 99201
509 926-6212

(G-14553)
SHARP PRINTING INC
3477 Lockport Rd (14132-9491)
PHONE..................716 731-3994
Slade Sharpsteen, *President*
EMP: 7
SQ FT: 1,200
SALES (est): 951.6K **Privately Held**
WEB: www.sharpprinting.com
SIC: 2752 Commercial printing, offset

(G-14554)
SHIPMAN PRINTING INDS INC
6120 Lendell Dr (14132-9455)
PHONE..................716 504-7700
Gary E Blum, *Ch of Bd*
EMP: 7
SALES (est): 389.7K **Privately Held**
SIC: 2752 Commercial printing, offset

(G-14555)
UNITED BIOCHEMICALS LLC
6351 Inducon Dr E (14132-9016)
PHONE..................716 731-5161
Dr Duane Mazur, *Vice Pres*
Manuel Brocke-Benz, *Mng Member*
▲ **EMP:** 33
SALES (est): 10.2MM **Privately Held**
SIC: 2869 Industrial organic chemicals

Sanborn - Niagara County (G-14556)

HQ: Vwr International, Llc
100 W Matsonford Rd # 1
Radnor PA 19087
610 386-1700

(G-14556)
UNITED MATERIALS LLC
2186 Cory Dr (14132-9338)
PHONE.................................716 731-2332
Lean Guilinan, *Manager*
EMP: 22
SALES (corp-wide): 17.3MM **Privately Held**
SIC: 3273 Ready-mixed concrete
PA: United Materials, L.L.C.
3949 Frest Pk Way Ste 400
North Tonawanda NY 14120
716 683-1432

(G-14557)
VOSS MANUFACTURING INC
2345 Lockport Rd (14132-9636)
PHONE.................................716 731-5062
Rita Voss Kammerer, *President*
Thomas Kammerer, *Vice Pres*
Ursula Voss, *Admin Sec*
◆ **EMP:** 73
SQ FT: 55,000
SALES (est): 24.6MM **Privately Held**
WEB: www.vossmfg.com
SIC: 3444 3599 7389 3549 Sheet metalwork; custom machinery; design, commercial & industrial; metalworking machinery

Sandy Creek
Oswego County

(G-14558)
CASTERS CUSTOM SAWING
6323 Us Route 11 (13145-2191)
PHONE.................................315 387-5104
Edith Caster, *Principal*
EMP: 8
SALES (est): 934.1K **Privately Held**
SIC: 2421 Lumber: rough, sawed or planed

Sangerfield
Oneida County

(G-14559)
CHAMPION HOME BUILDERS INC
951 Rte 12 S (13455)
P.O. Box 177 (13455-0177)
PHONE.................................315 841-4122
John Copeletti, *General Mgr*
EMP: 150
SQ FT: 115,000
SALES (corp-wide): 1.5B **Publicly Held**
WEB: www.championaz.com
SIC: 2451 Mobile homes
HQ: Champion Home Builders, Inc.
755 W Big Beaver Rd # 1000
Troy MI 48084
248 614-8200

Saranac Lake
Franklin County

(G-14560)
ADIRONDACK PUBLISHING CO INC (DH)
Also Called: Adirondack Daily Enterprise
54 Broadway (12983-1704)
P.O. Box 318 (12983-0318)
PHONE.................................518 891-2600
George Ogden Nutting, *President*
Catherine Moore, *Publisher*
Peter Crowley, *Editor*
Morgan Ryan, *Editor*
EMP: 32 **EST:** 1904
SQ FT: 5,000
SALES (est): 2.9MM **Privately Held**
SIC: 2711 2752 Job printing & newspaper publishing combined; commercial printing, lithographic

HQ: The Ogden Newspapers Inc
1500 Main St
Wheeling WV 26003
304 233-0100

(G-14561)
COMPASS PRINTING PLUS (PA)
42 Main St (12983-1708)
PHONE.................................518 523-3308
Tom Connors, *Owner*
EMP: 9
SALES (est): 1.1MM **Privately Held**
SIC: 2752 Commercial printing, offset

(G-14562)
GETTING THE WORD OUT INC
Also Called: ADIRONDACK EXPLORER
36 Church St Apt 106 (12983-1850)
PHONE.................................518 891-9352
Dick Beamish, *President*
Tracy Ormsbee, *Publisher*
Phil Brown, *Editor*
Andreas Mowka, *Director*
EMP: 3
SALES: 905.2K **Privately Held**
SIC: 2721 Magazines: publishing only, not printed on site

(G-14563)
NORTHERN NEW YORK RURAL
Also Called: NORTH COUNTRY BEHAVIORAL HEALT
126 Kiwassa Rd (12983-2357)
P.O. Box 891 (12983-0891)
PHONE.................................518 891-9460
Robin Calkins, *Bookkeeper*
Samantha Dashnaw, *Manager*
Samantha Denshaw, *Manager*
Barry Brogan, *Director*
EMP: 5
SALES: 646.4K **Privately Held**
SIC: 3999 Education aids, devices & supplies

(G-14564)
UPSTONE MATERIALS INC
909 State Route 3 (12983-5109)
PHONE.................................518 891-0236
David Gordan, *Manager*
EMP: 22
SALES (corp-wide): 95.5MM **Privately Held**
WEB: www.graymont-ab.com
SIC: 1422 Crushed & broken limestone
HQ: Upstone Materials Inc.
111 Quarry Rd
Plattsburgh NY 12901
518 561-5321

Saratoga Springs
Saratoga County

(G-14565)
09 FLSHY BLL/DSERT SUNRISE LLC
2 Smith Bridge Rd (12866-5617)
PHONE.................................518 583-6638
Lindsey Heumann CPA, *Principal*
EMP: 5
SALES (est): 326.1K **Privately Held**
SIC: 3291 Hones

(G-14566)
ADIRONDACK SIGN COMPANY LLC
72 Ballston Ave (12866-4427)
PHONE.................................518 409-7446
Adam Wakulenko, *President*
Carl Wheeler, *Vice Pres*
Thomas Wheeler, *Vice Pres*
Wayne Wheeler, *Vice Pres*
EMP: 10
SQ FT: 3,200
SALES: 936K **Privately Held**
SIC: 3993 1799 Signs, not made in custom sign painting shops; sign installation & maintenance

(G-14567)
ADIRONDACK SIGN PERFECT INC
72 Ballston Ave (12866-4427)
PHONE.................................518 409-7446

John Natale, *Managing Prtnr*
Adam Wakulenko, *Managing Prtnr*
Adam Wakulenko, *Principal*
EMP: 8 **EST:** 2007
SQ FT: 3,500
SALES: 740K **Privately Held**
SIC: 3993 Electric signs

(G-14568)
ADVANTAGE PRESS INC
74 Warren St (12866-2534)
PHONE.................................518 584-3405
Mark Sutton, *President*
Kimberly Sutton, *Treasurer*
EMP: 12
SQ FT: 4,800
SALES (est): 990K **Privately Held**
WEB: www.myadvantagepress.com
SIC: 2752 Commercial printing, offset

(G-14569)
AGROCHEM INC
26 Freedom Way Saratoga Springs (12866-9075)
PHONE.................................518 226-4850
Robert J Demarco, *Principal*
John Demarco, *Vice Pres*
EMP: 20
SQ FT: 38,000
SALES (est): 6MM **Privately Held**
WEB: www.agrocheminc.com
SIC: 2879 Agricultural chemicals

(G-14570)
BALL METAL BEVERAGE CONT CORP
Also Called: Ball Metal Beverage Cont Div
11 Adams Rd (12866-9061)
PHONE.................................518 587-6030
Steve Di Loreto, *Plant Mgr*
Steven Di Lorto, *Plant Mgr*
Michael Franzen, *Plant Mgr*
Bob Nelson, *Engineer*
Robert Nelson, *Engineer*
EMP: 225
SALES (corp-wide): 10.9B **Publicly Held**
SIC: 3411 Metal cans
HQ: Ball Metal Beverage Container Corp.
9300 W 108th Cir
Westminster CO 80021

(G-14571)
BIG JOHNS ADIRONDACK INC
Also Called: Big John's Beef Jerky
45 N Milton Rd (12866-6137)
PHONE.................................518 587-3680
John Ponessa, *President*
EMP: 5
SALES: 60K **Privately Held**
SIC: 2013 Snack sticks, including jerky: from purchased meat

(G-14572)
C C INDUSTRIES INC
344 Burgoyne Rd (12866-5493)
PHONE.................................518 581-7633
Charles Carlstrom, *President*
EMP: 13
SQ FT: 9,500
SALES: 450K **Privately Held**
SIC: 2754 Imprinting, gravure

(G-14573)
CAPITAL STONE SARATOGA LLC
4295 Route 50 (12866-2962)
PHONE.................................518 226-8677
Paul Sicluna,
EMP: 6
SALES (est): 581.9K **Privately Held**
SIC: 3281 Granite, cut & shaped

(G-14574)
CAPITOL EQ 2 LLC
376 Broadway Ste 27 (12866-3115)
PHONE.................................518 886-8341
Daniel Grignon,
EMP: 3
SALES: 5MM **Privately Held**
SIC: 3531 Construction machinery

(G-14575)
CHEQUEDCOM INC
513 Broadway Ste 1 (12866-6730)
PHONE.................................888 412-0699

Greg Moran, *CEO*
John Tobison, *COO*
Gary Ito, *CFO*
Kevin Williams, *Security Dir*
EMP: 30
SALES (est): 3MM **Privately Held**
SIC: 7372 8742 Business oriented computer software; human resource consulting services
PA: Chequed Holdings, Llc
513 Broadway Ste 1
Saratoga Springs NY 12866
888 412-0699

(G-14576)
COLUMBIA CABINETS LLC
489 Broadway (12866-6738)
PHONE.................................518 283-1700
EMP: 11
SALES (corp-wide): 1.1MM **Privately Held**
SIC: 2434 Wood kitchen cabinets
PA: Columbia Cabinets, Llc
20 Maple Ave Ste F
Armonk NY 10504
212 972-7550

(G-14577)
ENCORE ELECTRONICS INC
4400 Route 50 (12866-2924)
PHONE.................................518 584-5354
Thomas J Barrett, *General Mgr*
Brian Crowe, *COO*
Jim Frederick, *Sales Mgr*
Rick Leonard, *Manager*
Tom Moeller, *Info Tech Mgr*
EMP: 25
SQ FT: 15,000
SALES (est): 5.8MM **Privately Held**
WEB: www.encore-elec.com
SIC: 3824 Mechanical & electromechanical counters & devices; electromechanical counters

(G-14578)
ESPEY MFG & ELECTRONICS CORP (PA)
233 Ballston Ave (12866-4767)
PHONE.................................518 584-4100
Howard Pinsley, *Ch of Bd*
Patrick T Enright Jr, *President*
David A O'Neil, *CFO*
Katrina L Sparano,
Peggy A Murphy, *Admin Sec*
EMP: 138 **EST:** 1928
SQ FT: 151,000
SALES: 22.5MM **Publicly Held**
WEB: www.espey.com
SIC: 3679 Power supplies, all types: static

(G-14579)
ESSITY PROF HYGIENE N AMER LLC
Also Called: ESSITY PROFESSIONAL HYGIENE NORTH AMERICA LLC
49 Geyser Rd (12866-9038)
PHONE.................................518 583-2785
Tim Cutler, *Manager*
EMP: 219
SALES (corp-wide): 7.6B **Privately Held**
SIC: 2621 Paper mills
HQ: Essity Professional Hygiene North America Llc
984 Winchester Rd
Neenah WI 54956
920 727-3770

(G-14580)
FREEDOM MFG LLC
3 Duplainville Rd Apt C (12866-9074)
PHONE.................................518 584-0441
Scott Mummert, *Principal*
EMP: 14
SALES (est): 1.5MM **Privately Held**
SIC: 3999 Barber & beauty shop equipment

(G-14581)
FRIENDLY FUEL INCORPORATED
54 Church St (12866-2007)
PHONE.................................518 581-7036
Manjinder Grewal, *Principal*
EMP: 5

SALES (est): 491.8K **Privately Held**
SIC: 2869 Fuels

(G-14582)
GOLUB CORPORATION
3045 Route 50 (12866-2919)
PHONE..................................518 583-3697
Paul R Flately, *Manager*
EMP: 28
SALES (corp-wide): 3.3B **Privately Held**
SIC: 3751 Motorcycles & related parts
PA: The Golub Corporation
 461 Nott St
 Schenectady NY 12308
 518 355-5000

(G-14583)
GREAT AMERICAN BICYCLE LLC
41 Geyser Rd (12866-9038)
PHONE..................................518 584-8100
Ben Serotta, *Mng Member*
EMP: 50
SQ FT: 15,000
SALES (est): 6.9MM **Privately Held**
WEB: www.serotta.com
SIC: 3751 5941 Bicycles & related parts; frames, motorcycle & bicycle; sporting goods & bicycle shops

(G-14584)
GREENFIELD MANUFACTURING INC
25 Freedom Way (12866-9076)
PHONE..................................518 581-2368
Duane R Palmateer, *President*
▲ EMP: 11 EST: 1996
SQ FT: 40,000
SALES (est): 2.2MM **Privately Held**
WEB: www.greenfieldmfg.com
SIC: 2899 Acid resist for etching

(G-14585)
GUYSON CORPORATION OF USA (DH)
13 Grande Blvd (12866-9090)
PHONE..................................518 587-7894
Steve Byrnes, *President*
◆ EMP: 46
SQ FT: 78,000
SALES (est): 10.2MM
SALES (corp-wide): 26.1MM **Privately Held**
WEB: www.guyson.com
SIC: 3569 Blast cleaning equipment, dustless

(G-14586)
HAPPY SOFTWARE LLC
11 Federal St (12866-4111)
PHONE..................................518 584-4668
Joseph Mastrianni, *CEO*
EMP: 7 EST: 1994
SQ FT: 1,500
SALES (est): 1MM
SALES (corp-wide): 146.7MM **Privately Held**
WEB: www.happysoftware.com
SIC: 7372 Business oriented computer software
PA: Mri Software Llc
 28925 Fountain Pkwy
 Solon OH 44139
 800 321-8770

(G-14587)
HUNTINGTON INGALLS INC
33 Cady Hill Blvd (12866-9047)
PHONE..................................518 884-3834
Peter Wedesky, *Branch Mgr*
EMP: 50 **Publicly Held**
SIC: 3731 Shipbuilding & repairing
HQ: Huntington Ingalls Incorporated
 4101 Washington Ave
 Newport News VA 23607
 757 380-2000

(G-14588)
INCENTIVATE HEALTH LLC
60 Railroad Pl Ste 101 (12866-3045)
PHONE..................................518 469-8491
J Lawrence Toole, *President*
Patricia Hasbrouck, *Co-Owner*
Robert Legrande II, *Co-Owner*
EMP: 5

SALES (est): 156K **Privately Held**
SIC: 7372 Application computer software

(G-14589)
JOURNAL REGISTER COMPANY
Also Called: Saratogian USA Today
20 Lake Ave (12866-2314)
PHONE..................................518 584-4242
Paul Tackett, *Editor*
Christopher Brown, *Traffic Mgr*
Sean Fagan, *Accounts Exec*
Jaclyn Grady, *Accounts Exec*
Brea Beck, *Sales Staff*
EMP: 80
SALES (corp-wide): 661.2MM **Privately Held**
SIC: 2711 Newspapers: publishing only, not printed on site
PA: Journal Register Company
 5 Hanover Sq Fl 25
 New York NY 10004
 212 257-7212

(G-14590)
NALCO COMPANY LLC
6 Butler Pl 2 (12866-2155)
PHONE..................................518 796-1985
Joseph Fitzhenry, *Manager*
EMP: 20
SALES (corp-wide): 13.8B **Publicly Held**
WEB: www.nalco.com
SIC: 2899 5169 Chemical preparations; chemicals & allied products
HQ: Nalco Company Llc
 1601 W Diehl Rd
 Naperville IL 77478
 630 305-1000

(G-14591)
NANOBIONOVUM LLC
117 Grand Ave (12866-4118)
P.O. Box 4434 (12866-8026)
PHONE..................................518 581-1171
Lance Bell, *CEO*
EMP: 10
SQ FT: 5,000
SALES (est): 708.6K **Privately Held**
SIC: 3841 Diagnostic apparatus, medical

(G-14592)
PHYTOFILTER TECHNOLOGIES INC
9 Kirby Rd Apt 19 (12866-9287)
PHONE..................................518 507-6399
Martin Mittelmark, *CEO*
EMP: 5 EST: 2010
SALES (est): 400K **Privately Held**
SIC: 3564 Air purification equipment

(G-14593)
PRIME TURBINE PARTS LLC
77 Railroad Pl (12866-2124)
PHONE..................................518 306-7306
Martin Harr,
◆ EMP: 3
SALES: 2MM **Privately Held**
SIC: 3511 Turbines & turbine generator sets

(G-14594)
QUAD/GRAPHICS INC
56 Duplainville Rd (12866-9050)
PHONE..................................518 581-4000
Dave Calmes, *General Mgr*
Dave Blais, *Vice Pres*
Mike Emery, *Engineer*
Tom Kazda, *Engineer*
Janette Spieldenner, *Accounts Mgr*
EMP: 900
SALES (corp-wide): 4.1B **Publicly Held**
WEB: www.qg.com
SIC: 2752 2791 2789 Commercial printing, offset; typesetting; bookbinding & related work
PA: Quad/Graphics Inc.
 N61w23044 Harrys Way
 Sussex WI 53089
 414 566-6000

(G-14595)
RECORD
Also Called. Sunday Record, The
20 Lake Ave (12866-2314)
PHONE..................................518 270-1200
Chad Beatty, *President*
Fred Degesco, *President*

Genette Brookshire, *Editor*
David Johnson, *Editor*
EMP: 1
SQ FT: 35,000
SALES (est): 1.1MM
SALES (corp-wide): 661.2MM **Privately Held**
WEB: www.troyrecord.com
SIC: 2711 Commercial printing & newspaper publishing combined; newspapers, publishing & printing
PA: Journal Register Company
 5 Hanover Sq Fl 25
 New York NY 10004
 212 257-7212

(G-14596)
REDSPRING COMMUNICATIONS INC
125 High Rock Ave (12866-2307)
PHONE..................................518 587-0547
James Hill, *President*
EMP: 44
SQ FT: 10,500
SALES (est): 3MM **Privately Held**
WEB: www.redspring.com
SIC: 2741 Newsletter publishing; posters: publishing only, not printed on site

(G-14597)
SARATOGA CHIPS LLC
63 Putnam St Ste 202 (12866-3285)
PHONE..................................877 901-6950
James R Schneider, *President*
Joseph Boff, *Vice Pres*
Danny Jameson, *Vice Pres*
Joel I Bobrow, *Vice Pres*
Tim Kennedy, *CFO*
EMP: 7
SQ FT: 1,500
SALES: 1MM **Privately Held**
SIC: 2096 Popcorn, already popped (except candy covered)

(G-14598)
SARATOGA SPRING WATER COMPANY
11 Geyser Rd (12866-9038)
PHONE..................................518 584-6363
Adam Madkour, *CEO*
Steve Gilbank, *Principal*
Michael Lawson, *Plant Mgr*
Shanon Green, *Human Res Mgr*
EMP: 22
SQ FT: 40,000
SALES (est): 6MM **Privately Held**
WEB: www.saratogaspringwater.com
SIC: 2086 Mineral water, carbonated: packaged in cans, bottles, etc.

(G-14599)
STRATEGIC SIGNAGE SOURCING LLC
2 Gilbert Rd (12866-9701)
PHONE..................................518 450-1093
Robert L Keyser, *President*
Kenneth W Wasson, *Vice Pres*
Carole Van Buren, *Project Mgr*
Suzanne K Nelson, *Marketing Staff*
Robert Keyser, *Info Tech Mgr*
EMP: 10
SALES (est): 1.1MM **Privately Held**
SIC: 3993 Electric signs

(G-14600)
TMC USA LLC (PA)
60 Railroad Pl Ste 501 (12866-3048)
PHONE..................................518 587-8920
John Halnan,
EMP: 9
SALES (est): 3.6MM **Privately Held**
WEB: www.tmcusallc.com
SIC: 2721 Periodicals

(G-14601)
WARD LAFRANCE TRUCK CORP
26 Congress St Ste 259f (12866-4168)
PHONE..................................518 893-1865
Daniel Olszansky, *President*
EMP: 15 EST: 1978
SALES: 12.8MM **Privately Held**
SIC: 3537 Trucks: freight, baggage, etc.: industrial, except mining

Saugerties
Ulster County

(G-14602)
ADIRONDACK STAIRS INC
990 Kings Hwy (12477-4373)
P.O. Box 419 (12477-0419)
PHONE..................................845 246-2525
Karl H Neumann, *President*
Mattie Anttila, *Vice Pres*
EMP: 12 EST: 1966
SALES (est): 1.3MM **Privately Held**
SIC: 2431 Staircases & stairs, wood

(G-14603)
ARISTA FLAG CORPORATION
157 W Saugerties Rd (12477-3532)
P.O. Box 319 (12477-0319)
PHONE..................................845 246-7700
Stephen Suma, *President*
Susan Suma, *Corp Secy*
Rita Mary Suma, *Vice Pres*
EMP: 12
SQ FT: 5,500
SALES (est): 1.1MM **Privately Held**
WEB: www.aristaflag.com
SIC: 2399 Banners, made from fabric; flags, fabric; pennants

(G-14604)
CERES TECHNOLOGIES INC
5 Tower Dr (12477-4386)
P.O. Box 209 (12477-0209)
PHONE..................................845 247-4701
Kevin Brady, *President*
Sharon Burton, *General Mgr*
Partha Buragohain, *Vice Pres*
Kali Brady, *Project Mgr*
Bryan Jones, *Project Mgr*
EMP: 70
SQ FT: 50,000
SALES (est): 21.1MM **Privately Held**
SIC: 3674 3823 3826 Semiconductors & related devices; industrial instrmnts msrmnt display/control process variable; analytical instruments

(G-14605)
CVD EQUIPMENT CORPORATION
1117 Kings Hwy (12477-4343)
PHONE..................................845 246-3631
Kevin Collions, *Manager*
EMP: 20
SALES (corp-wide): 41.1MM **Publicly Held**
WEB: www.cvdequipment.com
SIC: 3559 Sewing machines & hat & zipper making machinery
PA: Cvd Equipment Corporation
 355 S Technology Dr
 Central Islip NY 11722
 631 981-7081

(G-14606)
DE LUXE PACKAGING CORP
63 North St (12477-1039)
PHONE..................................416 754-4633
Richard Goulet, *President*
EMP: 50 EST: 2003
SALES (est): 7.8MM
SALES (corp-wide): 2.9B **Privately Held**
SIC: 2671 3497 Foil containers for bakery goods & frozen foods; paper coated or laminated for packaging
HQ: Novolex Holdings, Llc
 101 E Carolina Ave
 Hartsville SC 29550
 843 857-4800

(G-14607)
DELUXE PACKAGING CORP
63 North St (12477-1039)
P.O. Box 269 (12477-0269)
PHONE..................................845 246-6090
Richard Goulet, *Branch Mgr*
EMP: 19
SQ FT: 32,740
SALES (corp-wide): 2.9B **Privately Held**
WEB: www.deluxepack.com
SIC: 2676 Toilet paper: made from purchased paper

Saugerties - Ulster County (G-14608)

HQ: Papercon Canada Holding Corp
200 Av Marien
Montreal-Est QC H1B 4
514 645-4571

(G-14608)
INQUIRING MINDS INC (PA)
65 S Partition St (12477)
PHONE..................845 246-5775
Bryan Donahue, *President*
EMP: 11 **EST:** 2012
SALES (est): 1.1MM **Privately Held**
SIC: 3421 Table & food cutlery, including butchers'

(G-14609)
KENBENCO INC
Also Called: Benson Steel Fabricators
437 Route 212 (12477-4620)
P.O. Box 480 (12477-0480)
PHONE..................845 246-3066
Myron E Benson, *Owner*
EMP: 15
SQ FT: 12,000
SALES (est): 3.1MM **Privately Held**
WEB: www.bensonsteelfabricators.com
SIC: 3312 3431 Blast furnaces & steel mills; metal sanitary ware

(G-14610)
LODOLCE MACHINE CO INC
196 Malden Tpke (12477-5015)
PHONE..................845 246-7017
Michael Lodolce, *President*
▲ **EMP:** 38 **EST:** 1963
SQ FT: 65,000
SALES (est): 8.1MM **Privately Held**
WEB: www.lodolce.com
SIC: 3599 1761 3479 Machine shop, jobbing & repair; sheet metalwork; painting, coating & hot dipping

(G-14611)
NORTHEAST SOLITE CORPORATION (PA)
1135 Kings Hwy (12477-4343)
P.O. Box 437, Mount Marion (12456-0437)
PHONE..................845 246-2646
John W Roberts, *Ch of Bd*
Philip M Nesmith, *President*
Jessica Eng, *Senior VP*
James Gregory, *Vice Pres*
Max Kalafat, *Vice Pres*
EMP: 40
SALES (est): 16.2MM **Privately Held**
WEB: www.nesolite.com
SIC: 3295 Minerals, ground or treated

(G-14612)
PAPER HOUSE PRODUCTIONS INC
160 Malden Tpke Bldg 2 (12477-5015)
P.O. Box 259 (12477-0259)
PHONE..................845 246-7261
Donald A Guidi, *CEO*
Amy Hernandez-Metcalf, *General Mgr*
Pam Gardeski, *Vice Pres*
Jon Holter, *Vice Pres*
Linda Vansteenburg, *CFO*
▲ **EMP:** 25
SQ FT: 16,000
SALES (est): 4.1MM **Privately Held**
WEB: www.paperhouseproductions.com
SIC: 2771 2752 5112 5945 Greeting cards; decals, lithographed; greeting cards; hobby & craft supplies

(G-14613)
PESCES BAKERY INC
Also Called: Pesce Bakery
20 Pesce Ct (12477-5054)
PHONE..................845 246-4730
Richard Pesce, *President*
Rich Pesce, *President*
EMP: 6 **EST:** 1946
SQ FT: 3,000
SALES (est): 626.8K **Privately Held**
SIC: 2051 5461 Bakery: wholesale or wholesale/retail combined; bakeries

(G-14614)
PETE LEVIN MUSIC INC
598 Schoolhouse Rd (12477-3325)
PHONE..................845 247-9211
Peter Levin, *President*
Theresa Levin, *Vice Pres*
Theresa R Levin, *Vice Pres*
EMP: 5
SALES (est): 340K **Privately Held**
WEB: www.petelevin.com
SIC: 3652 Pre-recorded records & tapes

(G-14615)
ROTHE WELDING INC
1455 Route 212 (12477-3040)
PHONE..................845 246-3051
Dorothy L Fauci, *Chairman*
EMP: 8
SQ FT: 11,500
SALES (est): 1.8MM **Privately Held**
WEB: www.hvaccess.com
SIC: 3441 7692 Fabricated structural metal; welding repair

(G-14616)
SIMULAIDS INC
16 Simulaids Dr (12477-5067)
P.O. Box 1289 (12477-8289)
PHONE..................845 679-2475
Dean T Johnson, *CEO*
Jack McNeff, *Vice Pres*
Ernest Ballard, *Warehouse Mgr*
Nicole Heckler, *Buyer*
Margaret Hines, *Sales Staff*
EMP: 93 **EST:** 1963
SQ FT: 50,000
SALES (est): 18.1MM
SALES (corp-wide): 297.6MM **Privately Held**
WEB: www.simulaids.com
SIC: 3841 7841 3699 Surgical & medical instruments; video tape rental; electrical equipment & supplies
HQ: Nasco Healthcare Inc.
901 Janesville Ave
Fort Atkinson WI 53538
920 568-5600

(G-14617)
STAINLESS DESIGN CONCEPTS LTD
Also Called: SDC
1117 Kings Hwy (12477-4343)
P.O. Box 514, Smithtown (11787-0514)
PHONE..................845 246-3631
Len Rosenbaum, *Ch of Bd*
Bill Iacobellis, *Purch Mgr*
Glen Charles, *CFO*
Mary Sauer, *Human Res Mgr*
Craig Pacquette, *Manager*
EMP: 35 **EST:** 1986
SQ FT: 25,000
SALES: 6.5MM
SALES (corp-wide): 41.1MM **Publicly Held**
WEB: www.stainlessdesign.com
SIC: 3559 Chemical machinery & equipment
PA: Cvd Equipment Corporation
355 S Technology Dr
Central Islip NY 11722
631 981-7081

(G-14618)
STUART SPECTOR DESIGNS LTD
1450 Route 212 (12477-3028)
PHONE..................845 246-6124
Stuart Spector, *President*
Darryl Ford, *General Mgr*
▲ **EMP:** 9
SQ FT: 4,500
SALES: 850K **Privately Held**
WEB: www.ssdbass.com
SIC: 3931 Guitars & parts, electric & non-electric

(G-14619)
THE SMOKE HOUSE OF CATSKILLS
724 Route 212 (12477-4617)
PHONE..................845 246-8767
Charles Rothe, *President*
EMP: 7 **EST:** 1952
SQ FT: 2,400
SALES (est): 266.2K **Privately Held**
SIC: 2011 5421 Meat packing plants; meat markets, including freezer provisioners

(G-14620)
WORKING FAMILY SOLUTIONS INC
359 Washington Avenue Ext (12477-5221)
P.O. Box 88, Malden On Hudson (12453-0088)
PHONE..................845 802-6182
Danielle N Heller, *CEO*
EMP: 5
SALES (est): 360.9K **Privately Held**
SIC: 2835 Pregnancy test kits

Sauquoit
Oneida County

(G-14621)
CUSTOM STAIR & MILLWORK CO
Also Called: Kitchen Design Center
6 Gridley Pl (13456-3416)
PHONE..................315 839-5793
John Dweyer, *President*
EMP: 9
SQ FT: 10,000
SALES (est): 750K **Privately Held**
SIC: 2431 Staircases & stairs, wood

(G-14622)
LEATHERSTOCKING MOBILE HOME PA
2089 Doolittle Rd (13456-2409)
PHONE..................315 839-5691
Jane W Brennan, *Ch of Bd*
EMP: 5
SALES (est): 613.7K **Privately Held**
SIC: 2451 Mobile homes

Savannah
Wayne County

(G-14623)
PEARL TECHNOLOGIES INC
13297 Seneca St (13146-9663)
P.O. Box 196 (13146-0196)
PHONE..................315 365-3742
Laurent Cros, *CEO*
Linda Gillette, *VP Opers*
Bill Gillette, *Mfg Mgr*
Gary Stover, *Purch Agent*
Ray Wright, *Engineer*
EMP: 35
SQ FT: 35,000
SALES (est): 8.4MM **Privately Held**
SIC: 3559 Plastics working machinery
HQ: Gloucester Engineering Co., Inc.
11 Dory Rd
Gloucester MA 01930
978 281-1800

(G-14624)
PURE FUNCTIONAL FOODS INC
267 State Route 89 (13146-9711)
PHONE..................315 294-0733
EMP: 20
SALES (est): 3.6MM **Privately Held**
SIC: 2099 Food preparations

Sayville
Suffolk County

(G-14625)
AQUARIUM PUMP & PIPING SYSTEMS
528 Chester Rd (11782-1808)
PHONE..................631 567-5555
Charles Eckstein, *Owner*
EMP: 11
SQ FT: 2,500
SALES (est): 614.2K **Privately Held**
SIC: 3499 3089 Aquarium accessories, metal; aquarium accessories, plastic

(G-14626)
BUNGERS SURF SHOP
Also Called: Bunger Sayville
247 W Main St (11782-2522)
PHONE..................631 244-3646
Sammy Hito, *Principal*
EMP: 8 **EST:** 2012
SALES (est): 481.4K **Privately Held**
SIC: 3949 Surfboards; water sports equipment

(G-14627)
ESC CONTROL ELECTRONICS LLC
Also Called: Control Elec Div Fil-Coil
98 Lincoln Ave (11782-2711)
PHONE..................631 467-5328
Paul Alessandrini,
▲ **EMP:** 35
SQ FT: 2,000
SALES (est): 4.8MM **Privately Held**
SIC: 3677 3679 3841 3851 Electronic transformers; filtration devices, electronic; delay lines; surgical & medical instruments; ophthalmic goods
PA: Fil-Coil (Fc) Corp.
98 Lincoln Ave
Sayville NY 11782

(G-14628)
FIL-COIL (FC) CORP (PA)
Also Called: Custom Power System
98 Lincoln Ave (11782-2711)
PHONE..................631 467-5328
Carrol Trust, *CEO*
Paul Alessandrini Sr, *Ch of Bd*
Batt Trust, *Vice Pres*
▲ **EMP:** 25
SQ FT: 6,000
SALES (est): 4.8MM **Privately Held**
SIC: 3677 Filtration devices, electronic

(G-14629)
FIL-COIL INTERNATIONAL LLC
98 Lincoln Ave (11782-2711)
PHONE..................631 467-5328
Laura Ritter, *Vice Chairman*
EMP: 14
SQ FT: 1,500
SALES (est): 637.9K **Privately Held**
SIC: 3677 Transformers power supply, electronic type

(G-14630)
FIRE ISLAND TIDE PUBLICATION
Also Called: Fire Island Tide The
40 Main St (11782-2552)
P.O. Box 70 (11782-0070)
PHONE..................631 567-7470
Patricia E King, *President*
EMP: 12
SALES (est): 550K **Privately Held**
SIC: 2711 7313 Newspapers, publishing & printing; newspaper advertising representative

(G-14631)
KKW CORP
Also Called: Koster Keunen Waxes
90 Bourne Blvd (11782-3307)
PHONE..................631 589-5454
Richard B Koster, *Ch of Bd*
Jay Ehring, *QC Mgr*
▲ **EMP:** 40
SQ FT: 60,000
SALES (est): 6.1MM **Privately Held**
WEB: www.paramold.com
SIC: 3999 Candles

(G-14632)
KOSTER KEUNEN WAXES LTD
90 Bourne Blvd (11782-3307)
PHONE..................631 589-0400
Richard Koster, *President*
James Bullwinkle, *Plant Engr*
▲ **EMP:** 15
SQ FT: 45,000
SALES (est): 2MM **Privately Held**
SIC: 2911 Mineral waxes, natural

(G-14633)
OPTIKA EYES LTD
153 Main St Unit 1 (11782-2566)
PHONE..................631 567-8852
Nancy Pacella, *President*
EMP: 8
SQ FT: 1,000

SALES (est): 610K Privately Held
SIC: 3851 5995 Frames, lenses & parts, eyeglass & spectacle; contact lenses; optical goods stores

(G-14634)
REDDI CAR CORP
174 Greeley Ave (11782-2396)
PHONE.................................631 589-3141
Kenneth Johnson, *President*
EMP: 7 EST: 1957
SQ FT: 5,000
SALES (est): 517.1K Privately Held
SIC: 2851 2899 3085 Paints & paint additives; chemical preparations; fasteners, industrial: nuts, bolts, screws, etc.

(G-14635)
WEEKS & REICHEL PRINTING INC
131 Railroad Ave (11782-2799)
PHONE.................................631 589-1443
John A Weeks, *President*
Robert Reichel, *Corp Secy*
EMP: 5
SQ FT: 2,400
SALES (est): 537.1K Privately Held
SIC: 2759 2752 Letterpress printing; commercial printing, offset

Scarsdale
Westchester County

(G-14636)
AMERICAN EPOXY AND METAL INC
83 Cushman Rd (10583-3403)
PHONE.................................718 828-7828
Samer Daniel, *President*
Ralph Maccarino, *Vice Pres*
EMP: 8
SALES (est): 996.7K Privately Held
WEB: www.americanepoxy.com
SIC: 2821 2511 Epoxy resins; whatnot shelves: wood; tables, household: wood

(G-14637)
CRANIAL TECHNOLOGIES INC
495 Central Park Ave (10583-1068)
PHONE.................................914 472-0975
Tammy Jones, *Manager*
EMP: 8 Privately Held
SIC: 3842 Orthopedic appliances
PA: Cranial Technologies, Inc.
1395 W Auto Dr
Tempe AZ 85284

(G-14638)
GOTHAM CITY INDUSTRIES INC
372 Fort Hill Rd (10583-2411)
PHONE.................................914 713-0979
Barbara Chalton, *Ch of Bd*
Jay Chalson, *Vice Pres*
Roger Nafziger, *Director*
▲ EMP: 20
SQ FT: 17,000
SALES (est): 3.6MM Privately Held
WEB: www.gothamind.com
SIC: 2541 Display fixtures, wood

(G-14639)
JAPAN AMERICA LEARNING CTR INC (PA)
Also Called: Enjoy
81 Montgomery Ave (10583-5104)
P.O. Box 606, Hartsdale (10530-0606)
PHONE.................................914 723-7600
Kazuko Maeda, *President*
Roger Bunders, *VP Admin*
Norman Floerke, *Opers Staff*
Gretchen Gibbons, *Credit Staff*
EMP: 10
SQ FT: 2,000
SALES (est): 300K Privately Held
SIC: 2721 8299 Trade journals: publishing only, not printed on site; language school

(G-14640)
LAND PACKAGING CORP
7 Black Birch Ln (10583-7456)
PHONE.................................914 472-5976
Lawrence Rosefeld, *President*
Lawrence Rosenfeld, *President*

EMP: 10
SQ FT: 3,000
SALES: 5MM Privately Held
SIC: 2653 Corrugated boxes, partitions, display items, sheets & pad

(G-14641)
NATHAN PRINTING EXPRESS INC
740 Central Park Ave (10583-2504)
PHONE.................................914 472-0914
Nathan Wong, *President*
Alex Wong, *Vice Pres*
EMP: 7
SQ FT: 1,600
SALES (est): 779.6K Privately Held
SIC: 2759 Screen printing

(G-14642)
PERFORMANCE SOURCING GROUP INC (PA)
109 Montgomery Ave (10583-5531)
PHONE.................................914 636-2100
S Shwartz, *President*
Sanjay Tillu, *CFO*
EMP: 5
SALES: 35MM Privately Held
SIC: 2392 Household furnishings

(G-14643)
PLAIN DIGITAL INC
235 Garth Rd Apt D6a (10583-3949)
PHONE.................................914 310-0280
Stuart Pekowsky, *President*
EMP: 6 EST: 1999
SALES: 250K Privately Held
SIC: 7372 7389 Prepackaged software;

(G-14644)
S I COMMUNICATIONS INC
Also Called: Scarsdale Inquirer
8 Harwood Ct (10583-4104)
P.O. Box 418 (10583-0418)
PHONE.................................914 725-2500
Deborah White, *President*
Sandy Greene, *Editor*
Eileen Farrell, *Director*
EMP: 18
SALES (est): 1MM Privately Held
WEB: www.scarsdaleinquirer.com
SIC: 2711 Newspapers: publishing only, not printed on site

(G-14645)
SHERIDAN HOUSE INC
230 Nelson Rd (10583-5908)
PHONE.................................914 725-5431
Lothar Simon, *President*
Jeannine Simon, *Vice Pres*
▲ EMP: 5 EST: 1940
SQ FT: 4,000
SALES (est): 709.7K Privately Held
WEB: www.sheridanhouse.com
SIC: 2731 Book publishing

(G-14646)
ZANZANO WOODWORKING INC
91 Locust Ave (10583-6230)
PHONE.................................914 725-6025
Michael Zanzano, *Principal*
EMP: 13
SALES (est): 1.6MM Privately Held
SIC: 2431 Millwork

Schenectady
Schenectady County

(G-14647)
A W HAMEL STAIR MFG INC
3111 Amsterdam Rd (12302-6328)
PHONE.................................518 346-3031
Joseph Lucarelli, *President*
Donald Lucarelli, *Vice Pres*
EMP: 16
SQ FT: 30,000
SALES (est): 1.8MM Privately Held
SIC: 2431 Staircases & stairs, wood; stair railings, wood

(G-14648)
ALSTOM SIGNALING INC
1 River Rd (12345-6000)
PHONE.................................585 274-8700

Ian Desousa, *Manager*
EMP: 50
SALES (corp-wide): 67MM Privately Held
WEB: www.alstomsignalingsolutions.com
SIC: 3669 3743 3643 Railroad signaling devices, electric; signaling apparatus, electric; railroad equipment; current-carrying wiring devices
HQ: Alstom Signaling Inc.
1025 John St
West Henrietta NY 14586
585 783-2000

(G-14649)
AMERICAN HSPTALS PATIENT GUIDE
1890 Maxon Rd Ext (12308-1140)
P.O. Box 1031 (12301-1031)
PHONE.................................518 346-1099
Robert J Kosineski Sr, *President*
EMP: 10
SALES (est): 806.5K Privately Held
SIC: 2741 Miscellaneous publishing

(G-14650)
AUTERRA INC
2135 Technology Dr (12308-1143)
PHONE.................................518 382-9600
Eric Burnett, *President*
Steven T Jackson, *Vice Pres*
EMP: 9 EST: 2006
SALES (est): 2MM Privately Held
SIC: 2819 Industrial inorganic chemicals

(G-14651)
AXLE EXPRESS
729 Broadway (12305-2703)
PHONE.................................518 347-2220
Samuel Caldarazzo, *President*
EMP: 25
SALES (est): 2.2MM Privately Held
SIC: 3714 Motor vehicle parts & accessories

(G-14652)
BAKE-RITE INTERNATIONAL INC
412 Warren St (12305-1116)
PHONE.................................518 395-3340
Kathryn Donovan, *President*
Brian Donavan, *Vice Pres*
◆ EMP: 5 EST: 1995
SALES (est): 833.2K Privately Held
WEB: www.bake-rite.com
SIC: 3556 Food products machinery

(G-14653)
BENCHEMARK PRINTING INC
1890 Maxon Rd Ext (12308-1149)
P.O. Box 1031 (12301-1031)
PHONE.................................518 393-1361
Robert Kosineski, *President*
Denise Hecker, *Human Resources*
Joe Prock, *Accounts Exec*
Carl Roser, *Accounts Exec*
Betsy Saltsman, *Accounts Exec*
▲ EMP: 55
SQ FT: 75,000
SALES (est): 14MM Privately Held
SIC: 2752 2791 2789 2759 Commercial printing, offset; typesetting; bookbinding & related work; commercial printing

(G-14654)
BESTLINE INTERNATIONAL RES INC
224 State St (12305-1806)
PHONE.................................518 631-2177
John Polster, *Principal*
EMP: 8
SALES (est): 1.1MM Privately Held
SIC: 2992 Lubricating oils & greases

(G-14655)
BESTWALL LLC
Also Called: Georgia-Pacific
801 Corporation Park (12302-1061)
PHONE.................................518 346-6151
P J Hand, *Manager*
EMP: 180
SALES (corp-wide): 42.9B Privately Held
WEB: www.gp.com
SIC: 2653 Boxes, corrugated: made from purchased materials

HQ: Georgia-Pacific Llc
133 Peachtree St Nw
Atlanta GA 30303
404 652-4000

(G-14656)
CALLANAN INDUSTRIES INC
145 Cordell Rd (12303-2701)
P.O. Box 40, Selkirk (12158-0040)
PHONE.................................518 382-5354
Bryan Francett, *General Mgr*
Dan Broomhall, *Vice Pres*
Kevin D Browne, *Safety Dir*
Kaitlyn Bessey, *Accounting Mgr*
James Elacqua, *Marketing Staff*
EMP: 9
SALES (corp-wide): 29.7B Privately Held
SIC: 3999 Barber & beauty shop equipment
HQ: Callanan Industries, Inc.
8 Southwoods Blvd Ste 4
Albany NY 12211
518 374-2222

(G-14657)
CAPITAL DST PRINT & IMAGING
Also Called: Allegra Print & Imaging
2075 Central Ave (12304-4426)
PHONE.................................518 456-6773
Jim Cazavilan, *President*
Janet C Cazavilan, *Vice Pres*
EMP: 7
SQ FT: 2,500
SALES (est): 1MM Privately Held
WEB: www.allegraalbany.com
SIC: 2752 7334 Commercial printing, offset; photocopying & duplicating services

(G-14658)
CAPITAL STONE LLC
2241 Central Ave (12304-4379)
PHONE.................................518 382-7588
James Nass, *President*
Carmine Petti, *Manager*
EMP: 9
SQ FT: 5,000
SALES: 1MM Privately Held
SIC: 3281 Granite, cut & shaped

(G-14659)
CASCADE TECHNICAL SERVICES LLC
2846 Curry Rd Ste B (12303-3463)
PHONE.................................518 355-2201
Matthew Ednie, *Manager*
EMP: 5
SALES (corp-wide): 874.5MM Privately Held
WEB: www.teamzebra.com
SIC: 3822 Auto controls regulating residntl & coml environmt & applncs
HQ: Cascade Technical Services Llc
30 N Prospect Ave
Lynbrook NY 11563
516 596-6300

(G-14660)
CASCADES NEW YORK INC
801 Corporation Park (12302-1061)
PHONE.................................518 346-6151
Marc Andre Depin, *President*
EMP: 150
SALES (corp-wide): 3.3B Privately Held
SIC: 2653 Corrugated & solid fiber boxes
HQ: Cascades New York Inc.
1845 Emerson St
Rochester NY 14606
585 527-8110

(G-14661)
CDS PRODUCTIONS INC
108 Erie Blvd Ste 400 (12305-2223)
PHONE.................................518 385-8255
Anthony Casapullo, *President*
James Fuller, *Vice Pres*
EMP: 16
SQ FT: 15,000
SALES: 937.7K Privately Held
SIC: 2752 2791 7334 Commercial printing, lithographic; typesetting, computer controlled; photocopying & duplicating services

Schenectady - Schenectady County (G-14662)

(G-14662)
CHURCH & DWIGHT CO INC
Also Called: Arm & Hammer
706 Ennis Rd (12306-7420)
PHONE.................................518 887-5109
Douglas Waddell, *Branch Mgr*
EMP: 12
SALES (corp-wide): 3.7B **Publicly Held**
WEB: www.churchdwight.com
SIC: 2812 Sodium bicarbonate
PA: Church & Dwight Co., Inc.
500 Charles Ewing Blvd
Ewing NJ 08628
609 806-1200

(G-14663)
CLEMENTE LATHAM CONCRETE CORP
Also Called: Clemente Latham North Div
1245 Kings Rd (12303-2831)
P.O. Box 15097, Albany (12212-5097)
PHONE.................................518 374-2222
Frank A Clemente, *Ch of Bd*
Cori Kuehner, *Sales Staff*
EMP: 100 **EST:** 1993
SALES (est): 14.1MM
SALES (corp-wide): 29.7B **Privately Held**
SIC: 3273 5032 Ready-mixed concrete; brick, stone & related material
HQ: Oldcastle Materials, Inc.
900 Ashwood Pkwy Ste 700
Atlanta GA 30338

(G-14664)
CLEVELAND POLYMER TECH LLC (PA)
1691 Van Antwerp Rd (12309-1168)
PHONE.................................518 326-9146
Sam McLafferty, *CEO*
Jen Angelopoulos,
Panos Angelopoulos,
EMP: 8
SQ FT: 3,000
SALES (est): 1.4MM **Privately Held**
SIC: 3499 Machine bases, metal

(G-14665)
CODINOS LIMITED INC
704 Corporation Park # 5 (12302-1091)
PHONE.................................518 372-3308
Scott Devantier, *President*
Rita Vose, *Shareholder*
EMP: 33
SQ FT: 33,000
SALES: 6.1MM **Privately Held**
SIC: 2038 Frozen specialties

(G-14666)
CON REL AUTO ELECTRIC INC
3637 Carman Rd (12303-5401)
PHONE.................................518 356-1646
Kevin Relyea, *President*
Michael Relyea, *Corp Secy*
David O'Connell, *Vice Pres*
Gloria Mc Cue, *Financial Exec*
EMP: 35
SQ FT: 9,000
SALES: 3.9MM **Privately Held**
SIC: 3621 3694 3625 Starters, for motors; alternators, automotive; relays & industrial controls

(G-14667)
DAILY GAZETTE COMPANY (PA)
2345 Maxon Rd Ext (12308-1150)
P.O. Box 1090 (12301-1090)
PHONE.................................518 374-4141
John Hume, *President*
John Deaugustine, *Publisher*
Ken Kanniard, *Vice Pres*
Elizabeth Lind, *Vice Pres*
Ernest Grandy, *Treasurer*
EMP: 325 **EST:** 1894
SQ FT: 111,000
SALES (est): 76.4MM **Privately Held**
WEB: www.dailygazette.com
SIC: 2711 Commercial printing & newspaper publishing combined; newspapers, publishing & printing

(G-14668)
DAILY GAZETTE COMPANY
2345 Maxon Rd Ext (12308-1150)
P.O. Box 1090 (12301-1090)
PHONE.................................518 395-3060
Richard Dwyer, *Branch Mgr*
Steve Amedio, *Manager*
EMP: 110
SALES (corp-wide): 76.4MM **Privately Held**
SIC: 2711 Newspapers, publishing & printing
PA: Daily Gazette Company
2345 Maxon Rd Ext
Schenectady NY 12308
518 374-4141

(G-14669)
DSM NUTRITIONAL PRODUCTS LLC
2105 Technology Dr (12308-1143)
PHONE.................................518 372-5155
EMP: 152
SALES (corp-wide): 10.1B **Privately Held**
SIC: 2834 3295 2087 Vitamin, nutrient & hematinic preparations for human use; vitamin preparations; minerals, ground or treated; flavoring extracts & syrups
HQ: Dsm Nutritional Products, Llc
45 Waterview Blvd
Parsippany NJ 07054
800 526-0189

(G-14670)
ENER-G-ROTORS INC
17 Fern Ave (12306-2708)
PHONE.................................518 372-2608
Michael Newell, *Ch of Bd*
Edward Zampella, *President*
EMP: 5
SALES (est): 946K **Privately Held**
SIC: 3621 7694 5084 5063 Motors & generators; armature rewinding shops; hydraulic systems equipment & supplies; electrical apparatus & equipment

(G-14671)
ENERGY PANEL STRUCTURES INC
Also Called: Fingerlakes Construction
864 Burdeck St (12306-1218)
PHONE.................................518 355-6708
Kirt Burghdorf, *Vice Pres*
EMP: 7
SALES (corp-wide): 206.5MM **Privately Held**
SIC: 3448 2452 Prefabricated metal buildings; prefabricated wood buildings
HQ: Energy Panel Structures, Inc.
603 N Van Gordon Ave
Graettinger IA 51342
712 859-3219

(G-14672)
ENVIRONMENT-ONE CORPORATION
Also Called: E/One Utility Systems
2773 Balltown Rd (12309-1090)
PHONE.................................518 346-6161
Eric Lacoppola, *President*
Geoffrey Hawks, *Treasurer*
Dean Pierce, *Manager*
Gloria Pollack, *Exec Dir*
▲ **EMP:** 135
SQ FT: 78,000
SALES (est): 47.5MM
SALES (corp-wide): 242.1B **Publicly Held**
WEB: www.eone.com
SIC: 3589 3824 Sewage treatment equipment; mechanical & electromechanical counters & devices
HQ: Precision Castparts Corp.
4650 Sw Mcdam Ave Ste 300
Portland OR 97239
503 946-4800

(G-14673)
EPICOR SOFTWARE CORPORATION
Docstar
2165 Technology Dr (12308-1143)
PHONE.................................805 496-6789
Suren Pai, *Branch Mgr*
EMP: 45 **Publicly Held**
SIC: 3577 Computer peripheral equipment
HQ: Epicor Software Corporation
804 Las Cimas Pkwy # 200
Austin TX 78746

(G-14674)
F CAPPIELLO DAIRY PDTS INC
115 Van Guysling Ave (12305-2708)
PHONE.................................518 374-5064
Peter Cappiello, *President*
EMP: 40 **EST:** 1920
SALES (est): 5.3MM **Privately Held**
WEB: www.cappiello.com
SIC: 2022 Cheese, natural & processed

(G-14675)
GENERAL ELECTRIC COMPANY
1 River Rd Bldg 55 (12305-2551)
PHONE.................................518 385-4022
Rajni Burra, *Senior Engr*
Jeff Bush, *Program Mgr*
Jeff Shaffer, *Manager*
Michael St Jacques, *Manager*
EMP: 603
SQ FT: 23,808
SALES (corp-wide): 122B **Publicly Held**
SIC: 3511 3612 3641 3632 Steam turbines; gas turbines, mechanical drive; autotransformers, electric (power transformers); electric lamps & parts for generalized applications; electric light bulbs, complete; lamps, incandescent filament, electric; lamps, fluorescent, electric; refrigerators, mechanical & absorption: household; freezers, home & farm; television broadcasting stations; research & development on aircraft engines & parts
PA: General Electric Company
41 Farnsworth St
Boston MA 02210
617 443-3000

(G-14676)
GENERAL ELECTRIC COMPANY
1 River Rd Bldg 33 (12305-2551)
PHONE.................................518 385-2211
Anthony Fiorenza, *Opers Staff*
Chad Bucholtz, *Finance*
John G Rice, *Branch Mgr*
Richard Zeh, *Manager*
Angelica Hernandez, *Admin Asst*
EMP: 500
SALES (corp-wide): 122B **Publicly Held**
SIC: 3511 Turbines & turbine generator sets
PA: General Electric Company
41 Farnsworth St
Boston MA 02210
617 443-3000

(G-14677)
GENERAL ELECTRIC COMPANY
1 River Rd Bldg 43 (12345-6000)
PHONE.................................203 373-2756
Steve Bolze, *President*
EMP: 458
SALES (corp-wide): 122B **Publicly Held**
SIC: 3511 Turbines & turbine generator sets
PA: General Electric Company
41 Farnsworth St
Boston MA 02210
617 443-3000

(G-14678)
GENERAL ELECTRIC COMPANY
1 River Rd (12345-6000)
PHONE.................................518 385-3716
Damian D Foti, *Principal*
EMP: 491
SALES (corp-wide): 122B **Publicly Held**
SIC: 3511 Gas turbine generator set units, complete
PA: General Electric Company
41 Farnsworth St
Boston MA 02210
617 443-3000

(G-14679)
GENERAL ELECTRIC COMPANY
1 River Rd Bldg 37 (12345-6000)
PHONE.................................518 385-2211
John G Rice, *President*
Jeff Shaffer, *Branch Mgr*
Brittany Allesandro, *Software Engr*
Mike Norelli, *Director*
Daniel Jordy, *Associate*
EMP: 500
SALES (corp-wide): 122B **Publicly Held**
SIC: 3511 3621 Gas turbine generator set units, complete; steam turbine generator set units, complete; motors & generators
PA: General Electric Company
41 Farnsworth St
Boston MA 02210
617 443-3000

(G-14680)
GENERAL ELECTRIC COMPANY
1 Research Cir (12309-1027)
P.O. Box 8 (12301-0008)
PHONE.................................518 387-5000
Tom Shaginaw, *Business Mgr*
Dharmender Kumar, *Project Mgr*
Anveshi Charuvaka, *Research*
Guangliang Zhao, *Research*
Brian Barr, *Engineer*
EMP: 500
SALES (corp-wide): 122B **Publicly Held**
SIC: 3511 Turbines & turbine generator sets
PA: General Electric Company
41 Farnsworth St
Boston MA 02210
617 443-3000

(G-14681)
GENERAL ELECTRIC COMPANY
705 Corporation Park (12302-1092)
PHONE.................................518 385-3439
Robert Flag, *Branch Mgr*
EMP: 8
SALES (corp-wide): 122B **Publicly Held**
SIC: 3511 Turbines & turbine generator sets
PA: General Electric Company
41 Farnsworth St
Boston MA 02210
617 443-3000

(G-14682)
GENERAL ELECTRIC INTL INC
1 River Rd Bldg 53202j (12345-6000)
PHONE.................................518 385-2211
Ernie Frasier, *Manager*
EMP: 9
SALES (corp-wide): 122B **Publicly Held**
SIC: 3511 3621 3433 Gas turbine generator set units, complete; steam turbine generator set units, complete; motors & generators; solar heaters & collectors
HQ: General Electric International, Inc.
191 Rosa Parks St
Cincinnati OH 45202
617 443-3000

(G-14683)
GRANDVIEW BLOCK & SUPPLY CO
1705 Hamburg St (12304-4699)
PHONE.................................518 346-7981
Salvatore Salamone, *President*
Samuel Salamone, *Vice Pres*
James Salamone, *Admin Sec*
EMP: 20 **EST:** 1946
SQ FT: 22,500
SALES (est): 3.3MM **Privately Held**
SIC: 3271 5032 Blocks, concrete or cinder: standard; masons' materials

(G-14684)
GRANDVIEW CONCRETE CORP
1705 Hamburg St (12304-4673)
PHONE.................................518 346-7981
George Salamone, *President*
Sam Salamone, *Vice Pres*
Attilio A Salamone, *Shareholder*
Frank J Salamone, *Shareholder*
EMP: 24
SQ FT: 22,500
SALES (est): 3.1MM **Privately Held**
SIC: 3273 Ready-mixed concrete

(G-14685)
GREEN ENVIRO MACHINE LLC
Also Called: Gem
2366 Algonquin Rd (12309-1425)
PHONE.................................407 461-6412
Janice Lachman,
EMP: 5
SALES: 950K **Privately Held**
SIC: 3581 Automatic vending machines

GEOGRAPHIC SECTION
Schenectady - Schenectady County (G-14712)

(G-14686)
GUARDIAN CONCRETE INC
Also Called: Guardian Concrete Steps
2140 Maxon Rd Ext (12308-1102)
PHONE..................518 372-0080
W K Stanton, *President*
Glenda Jablonski, *Office Mgr*
EMP: 12
SQ FT: 13,000
SALES (est): 1.9MM **Privately Held**
SIC: 3272 5211 5039 Concrete products, precast; masonry materials & supplies; septic tanks

(G-14687)
HOHMANN & BARNARD INC
Sandell Moisture
310 Wayto Rd (12303-4538)
PHONE..................518 357-9757
EMP: 21
SALES (corp-wide): 242.1B **Publicly Held**
SIC: 3496 3462 Clips & fasteners, made from purchased wire; iron & steel forgings
HQ: Hohmann & Barnard, Inc.
30 Rasons Ct
Hauppauge NY 11788
631 234-0600

(G-14688)
HP HOOD LLC
816 Burdeck St (12306-1213)
PHONE..................518 218-9097
EMP: 299
SALES (corp-wide): 2.1B **Privately Held**
SIC: 2026 Fluid milk
PA: Hp Hood Llc
6 Kimball Ln Ste 400
Lynnfield MA 01940
617 887-8441

(G-14689)
IGT GLOBAL SOLUTIONS CORP
1 Broadway Ctr Fl 2 (12305-2554)
PHONE..................518 382-2900
Ed Bourghan, *Branch Mgr*
EMP: 70 **Privately Held**
WEB: www.gtech.com
SIC: 3575 Computer terminals
HQ: Igt Global Solutions Corporation
10 Memorial Blvd
Providence RI 02903
401 392-1000

(G-14690)
INTERSOURCE MANAGEMENT GROUP
144 Erie Blvd (12305-2203)
PHONE..................518 372-6798
EMP: 29
SALES (corp-wide): 1.9MM **Privately Held**
SIC: 3511 Turbines & turbine generator sets & parts
PA: Intersource Management Group
7 Corporate Dr Ste 3
Halfmoon NY 12065
518 372-6798

(G-14691)
JIM QUINN
Also Called: Jim Quinn and Associates
12 Morningside Dr (12303-5610)
PHONE..................518 356-0398
Jim Quinn, *Owner*
EMP: 10
SALES (est): 634.7K **Privately Held**
SIC: 2426 7641 Carvings, furniture: wood; office furniture repair & maintenance

(G-14692)
JOHN C DOLPH COMPANY INC
200 Von Roll Dr (12306-2443)
PHONE..................732 329-2333
Jack Hasson, *President*
▲ **EMP:** 26 **EST:** 1910
SQ FT: 50,000
SALES (est): 8.3MM
SALES (corp-wide): 336.1MM **Privately Held**
WEB: www.johncdolph.com
SIC: 2851 2821 Varnishes; epoxy resins
PA: Von Roll Holding Ag
Passwangstrasse 20
Breitenbach SO
442 043-000

(G-14693)
KERYAKOS INC
1080 Catalyn St Fl 2 (12303-1835)
PHONE..................518 344-7092
Charles Contompasis, *President*
Marika Contompasis, *Principal*
Laurie Ives, *Vice Pres*
EMP: 15
SALES (est): 1.8MM **Privately Held**
SIC: 2253 5137 Sweaters & sweater coats, knit; sweaters, women's & children's

(G-14694)
KING ROAD MATERIALS INC
145 Cordell Rd (12303-2701)
PHONE..................518 382-5354
Chris Hensler, *Manager*
EMP: 11
SQ FT: 500
SALES (corp-wide): 29.7B **Privately Held**
SIC: 2951 Asphalt & asphaltic paving mixtures (not from refineries)
HQ: King Road Materials, Inc.
8 Southwoods Blvd
Albany NY 12211
518 381-9995

(G-14695)
LATHAM INTERNATIONAL INC
Also Called: Latham Manufacturing
706 Corporation Park 1 (12302-1047)
PHONE..................518 346-5292
Tony Pagano, *Branch Mgr*
EMP: 12
SALES (corp-wide): 197MM **Privately Held**
WEB: www.pacificpools.com
SIC: 3081 Vinyl film & sheet
PA: Latham International, Inc.
787 Watervliet Shaker Rd
Latham NY 12110
518 783-7776

(G-14696)
LUCIDEON
2210 Technology Dr (12308-1145)
PHONE..................518 382-0082
Sean Hillman, *Business Mgr*
David Hodson, *Sales Engr*
Sean Borkowski, *Sales Staff*
Charlotte Campbell, *Sales Staff*
Brent Holloway, *Sales Staff*
EMP: 13
SALES (est): 1.6MM **Privately Held**
SIC: 3297 Nonclay refractories

(G-14697)
METAL COATED FIBERS INC
679 Mariaville Rd (12306-6806)
PHONE..................518 280-8514
Robert Duval, *President*
EMP: 22 **EST:** 2012
SALES (est): 1.2MM **Privately Held**
SIC: 3624 Fibers, carbon & graphite

(G-14698)
MILLIVAC INSTRUMENTS INC
2818 Curry Rd (12303-3463)
PHONE..................518 355-8300
Imek Metzger, *President*
Pola Metzger, *Corp Secy*
Jan Metzger, *Vice Pres*
EMP: 7
SQ FT: 12,000
SALES (est): 1.2MM **Privately Held**
WEB: www.millivacinstruments.com
SIC: 3825 Test equipment for electronic & electric measurement

(G-14699)
MISCELLNOUS IR FABRICATORS INC
1404 Dunnsville Rd (12306-5509)
PHONE..................518 355-1822
Helmut Giesselmann, *Ch of Bd*
Gunther Giesselmann, *President*
Daniel Eaton, *Financial Exec*
Thomas Giesselmann, *Manager*
Reinhart Giesselmann, *Admin Secy*
EMP: 22 **EST:** 1966
SQ FT: 22,000
SALES (est): 5.6MM **Privately Held**
SIC: 3441 1791 7699 Fabricated structural metal; iron work, structural; metal reshaping & replating services

(G-14700)
NEW MOUNT PLEASANT BAKERY
941 Crane St (12303-1140)
PHONE..................518 374-7577
Joe Riitano, *President*
EMP: 50 **EST:** 1932
SQ FT: 15,000
SALES (est): 4.8MM **Privately Held**
SIC: 2051 5461 2052 Bread, cake & related products; bakeries; cookies & crackers

(G-14701)
OLSON SIGN COMPANY INC
Also Called: Olson Signs & Graphics
1750 Valley Rd Ext (12302)
PHONE..................518 370-2118
Richard Olson, *President*
Kelly Lee Olson, *Vice Pres*
EMP: 8
SQ FT: 6,200
SALES (est): 580K **Privately Held**
SIC: 3993 Electric signs; displays & cutouts, window & lobby

(G-14702)
P1 GENERATOR WINDINGS LLC (PA)
2165 Technology Dr (12308-1143)
PHONE..................518 930-2879
Ron Pigliavento, *CFO*
David W Dussault, *Mng Member*
EMP: 4
SQ FT: 11,000
SALES (est): 1.1MM **Privately Held**
SIC: 3621 Coils, for electric motors or generators

(G-14703)
PACKAGE ONE INC (PA)
414 Union St (12305-1107)
PHONE..................518 344-5425
David W Dussault, *President*
Rick Greminger, *Plant Mgr*
Lawrence Pigliavento, *CFO*
Michael Visk, *Sales Staff*
▲ **EMP:** 75
SQ FT: 30,000
SALES (est): 17.9MM **Privately Held**
SIC: 3568 Power transmission equipment

(G-14704)
PIZZA BLENDS LLC
Western Blending
1411 Rottrdm Indstl Park (12306)
PHONE..................518 356-6650
Bob Morris, *Manager*
Butch Mitchell, *Executive*
EMP: 7
SALES (corp-wide): 389.2MM **Privately Held**
SIC: 2045 2041 Prepared flour mixes & doughs; pizza dough, prepared
HQ: Pizza Blends Llc
400 112th Ave Ne Ste 350
Bellevue WA 98004
800 826-1200

(G-14705)
PRINTZ AND PATTERNZ LLC
Also Called: Printz Pttrnz Scrn-Prnting EMB
1550 Altamont Ave (12303-2147)
PHONE..................518 944-6020
Daniel Crowley, *Mng Member*
Mike Crowley,
EMP: 6 **EST:** 2009
SALES (est): 778.1K **Privately Held**
SIC: 2752 2281 2396 Commercial printing, lithographic; embroidery yarn, spun; screen printing on fabric articles

(G-14706)
RAND PRODUCTS MANUFACTURING CO
Also Called: Rand Mfg
1602 Van Vranken Ave (12308-2239)
PHONE..................518 374-9871
Henry W Frick, *President*
Karen Frick Connlly, *Manager*
Karen Lewis, *Manager*
EMP: 5 **EST:** 1977
SQ FT: 7,000
SALES (est): 470K **Privately Held**
WEB: www.randmfg.com
SIC: 3444 Radiator shields or enclosures, sheet metal

(G-14707)
RAY SIGN INC
Also Called: Color Pro Sign
28 Colonial Ave (12304-4122)
PHONE..................518 377-1371
Russell Hazen, *President*
EMP: 13 **EST:** 1980
SQ FT: 5,000
SALES (est): 1.6MM **Privately Held**
SIC: 3993 1799 7389 Electric signs; sign installation & maintenance; sign painting & lettering shop

(G-14708)
REN TOOL & MANUFACTURING CO
1801 Chrisler Ave (12303-1517)
PHONE..................518 377-2123
Renato Belletti, *President*
Ellen Belletti, *Corp Secy*
EMP: 10 **EST:** 1949
SQ FT: 7,000
SALES (est): 1.5MM **Privately Held**
SIC: 3599 Machine shop, jobbing & repair

(G-14709)
SAMPSONS PRSTHTIC ORTHOTIC LAB
Also Called: Sampsons Prsthtic Orthotic Lab
1737 State St (12304-1832)
PHONE..................518 374-6011
William Sampson, *President*
EMP: 24
SQ FT: 3,500
SALES (est): 3MM **Privately Held**
WEB: www.sampsons.com
SIC: 3842 5999 Limbs, artificial; orthopedic & prosthesis applications

(G-14710)
SANZDRANZ LLC
388 Broadway (12305-2520)
PHONE..................518 894-8625
Sandro Gerbini, *Branch Mgr*
EMP: 6
SALES (corp-wide): 231K **Privately Held**
SIC: 2043 Cereal breakfast foods
PA: Sanzdranz Llc
83 Dumbarton Dr
Delmar NY 12054
518 894-8625

(G-14711)
SCHENECTADY STEEL CO INC
18 Mariaville Rd (12306-1398)
PHONE..................518 355-3220
Claudio Zullo, *President*
Charles Chamulak, *Vice Pres*
Jeffrey Hoffmann, *Treasurer*
Sandra Anderson, *Human Res Dir*
Robert Gennett, *Admin Sec*
EMP: 44
SQ FT: 77,700
SALES (est): 17.5MM **Privately Held**
SIC: 3441 Building components, structural steel

(G-14712)
SCOTIA BEVERAGES INC
Also Called: Adirondack Beverage Co Inc
701 Corporation Park (12302-1060)
PHONE..................518 370-3621
Ralph Crowley Jr, *President*
Angelo Mastrangelo, *Chairman*
Michael Mulrain, *Corp Secy*
Christopher Crowley, *Vice Pres*
Douglas Martin, *Vice Pres*
▲ **EMP:** 1000
SQ FT: 240,000
SALES (est): 180MM
SALES (corp-wide): 404.9MM **Privately Held**
WEB: www.adirondackbeverages.com
SIC: 2086 Soft drinks: packaged in cans, bottles, etc.; pasteurized & mineral waters, bottled & canned
PA: Polar Corp.
1001 Southbridge St
Worcester MA 01610
508 753-6383

Schenectady - Schenectady County (G-14713)

GEOGRAPHIC SECTION

(G-14713)
SI GROUP INC (DH)
2750 Balltown Rd (12309-1006)
P.O. Box 1046 (12301-1046)
PHONE..................518 347-4200
Frank Bozich, *President*
Thomas J Masterson, *Vice Pres*
William Scheffer, *Vice Pres*
Paul Tilley, *CFO*
William Purdy, *Supervisor*
◆ EMP: 150 EST: 1906
SALES (est): 1B **Privately Held**
WEB: www.schenectadyinternational.com
SIC: 2865 3087 2851 Phenol, alkylated & cumene; custom compound purchased resins; enamels
HQ: Addivant Usa Holdings Corp.
4 Mountainview Ter
Danbury CT 06810
203 702-6140

(G-14714)
SIERRA PROCESSING LLC
2 Moyer Ave (12306-1308)
PHONE..................518 433-0020
William Wilczak,
Dave Fusco,
EMP: 15
SALES (est): 40.3K
SALES (corp-wide): 3.3B **Privately Held**
SIC: 2611 Pulp manufactured from waste or recycled paper
HQ: Waste Connections Us, Inc.
3 Waterway Square Pl # 110
The Woodlands TX 77380

(G-14715)
SKYTRAVEL (USA) LLC
20 Talon Dr (12309-1839)
PHONE..................518 888-2610
Hongwei Jin, *Owner*
EMP: 10 EST: 2015
SALES (est): 575.6K **Privately Held**
SIC: 3593 Fluid power cylinders, hydraulic or pneumatic

(G-14716)
SQP INC
Also Called: Speciality Quality Packaging
602 Potential Pkwy (12302-1041)
PHONE..................518 831-6800
Barbara Slaming, *President*
▲ EMP: 140
SALES (est): 27.6MM **Publicly Held**
WEB: www.usfoodservice.com
SIC: 2676 2656 Sanitary paper products; straws, drinking; made from purchased material
HQ: Us Foods, Inc.
9399 W Higgins Rd Ste 500
Rosemont IL 60018

(G-14717)
STS STEEL INC
301 Nott St Bldg 304 (12305-1039)
PHONE..................518 370-2693
James A Stori, *Ch of Bd*
Jim Stori, *President*
Geoffrey Frazier, *Vice Pres*
Glenn Tabolt, *Vice Pres*
David McDermott, *Project Mgr*
EMP: 65
SQ FT: 85,000
SALES (est): 17.4MM **Privately Held**
WEB: www.stssteel.com
SIC: 3441 Building components, structural steel; fabricated structural metal for bridges

(G-14718)
SUPERPOWER INC
450 Duane Ave Ste 1 (12304-2631)
PHONE..................518 346-1414
Toru Fukushima, *Chairman*
John Dackow, *COO*
Ross B McClure, *Opers Mgr*
Ross McClure, *Opers Mgr*
Robert Schmidt, *Mfg Staff*
▲ EMP: 29
SALES (est): 8MM
SALES (corp-wide): 9B **Privately Held**
SIC: 3643 Current-carrying wiring devices
PA: Furukawa Electric Co.,Ltd.
2-2-3, Marunouchi
Chiyoda-Ku TKY 100-0
332 863-001

(G-14719)
TABLECLOTHS FOR GRANTED LTD
510 Union St (12305-1117)
PHONE..................518 370-5481
Rudolph R Grant, *President*
David Siders, *Vice Pres*
Richard Walsh, *Admin Sec*
EMP: 11
SALES (est): 1MM **Privately Held**
SIC: 2392 Tablecloths: made from purchased materials; towels, dishcloths & dust cloths

(G-14720)
TATTERSALL INDUSTRIES LLC
Also Called: Frank Murken Products
2125 Technology Dr (12308-1143)
PHONE..................518 381-4270
Derek Sutherland, *Plant Mgr*
James Dominelli, *Sales Mgr*
Chuck Polge, *Sales Staff*
John Tattersall, *Mng Member*
▼ EMP: 20 EST: 1963
SQ FT: 35,000
SALES (est): 7.6MM **Privately Held**
WEB: www.fmproducts.com
SIC: 3429 5085 5169 Manufactured hardware (general); rubber goods, mechanical; chemicals & allied products

(G-14721)
THERESE THE CHILDRENS COLLECTN
301 Nott St (12305-1039)
PHONE..................518 346-2315
Marie Guidarelli, *President*
EMP: 1
SQ FT: 4,000
SALES: 1.2MM **Privately Held**
SIC: 2369 5137 2353 2335 Girls' & children's outerwear; women's & children's clothing; hats, caps & millinery; women's, juniors' & misses' dresses; men's & boys' suits & coats

(G-14722)
TRAC MEDICAL SOLUTIONS INC
2165 Technology Dr (12308-1143)
PHONE..................518 346-7799
John Botti, *Ch of Bd*
Jeff Frankel, *President*
Brad Pivar, *Vice Pres*
EMP: 7
SALES: 500K
SALES (corp-wide): 16.3MM **Publicly Held**
WEB: www.tracmed.com
SIC: 7372 Application computer software
PA: Aeon Global Health Corp.
2225 Centennial Dr
Gainesville GA 30504
888 661-0225

(G-14723)
UNICELL BODY COMPANY INC
170 Cordell Rd (12303-2702)
PHONE..................716 853-8628
James Motler, *Sales Staff*
Carmin Sperduti, *Branch Mgr*
EMP: 14
SALES (corp-wide): 20MM **Privately Held**
WEB: www.unicell.com
SIC: 3713 5084 Truck bodies & parts; industrial machinery & equipment
PA: Unicell Body Company, Inc
571 Howard St
Buffalo NY 14206
716 853-8628

(G-14724)
UNILUX ADVANCED MFG LLC
30 Commerce Park Rd (12309-3545)
PHONE..................518 344-7490
Brian Champagne, *Controller*
Kyle Mau, *Sales Associate*
Lawrence Farrelly,
EMP: 50
SQ FT: 70,000
SALES: 11MM **Privately Held**
SIC: 3433 Boilers, low-pressure heating: steam or hot water

(G-14725)
VINCYS PRINTING LTD
1832 Curry Rd (12306-4237)
PHONE..................518 355-4363
Evelyn L Vincinguerra, *President*
EMP: 10 EST: 1967
SQ FT: 3,000
SALES (est): 1.4MM **Privately Held**
WEB: www.vincysprinting.com
SIC: 2752 2741 Commercial printing, offset; miscellaneous publishing

(G-14726)
VON ROLL USA INC
200 Von Roll Dr (12306-2443)
P.O. Box 1404, New Haven CT (06505-1404)
PHONE..................203 562-2171
EMP: 50
SALES (corp-wide): 336.1MM **Privately Held**
SIC: 2899 3644 Mfg Chemical Preparations Mfg Nonconductive Wiring Devices
HQ: Von Roll Usa, Inc.
200 Von Roll Dr
Schenectady NY 12306
518 344-7100

(G-14727)
VON ROLL USA INC (HQ)
200 Von Roll Dr (12306-2443)
PHONE..................518 344-7100
Jon Roberts, *CEO*
Eran Rosenzweig, *Ch of Bd*
Andrew T Harrin, *President*
Sanjay Dave, *Area Mgr*
Jurg Brunner, *Vice Pres*
▲ EMP: 130
SQ FT: 200,000
SALES (est): 46.1MM
SALES (corp-wide): 336.1MM **Privately Held**
SIC: 3644 Insulators & insulation materials, electrical
PA: Von Roll Holding Ag
Passwangstrasse 20
Breitenbach SO
442 043-000

(G-14728)
WHITE EAGLE PACKING CO INC
922 Congress St (12303-1728)
PHONE..................518 374-4366
Gary Markiewicz, *President*
George Markiewicz, *Vice Pres*
EMP: 12 EST: 1951
SQ FT: 15,000
SALES (est): 1.6MM **Privately Held**
SIC: 2013 Frankfurters from purchased meat

Schenevus
Otsego County

(G-14729)
A AND L HOME FUEL LLC
601 Smokey Ave (12155-4012)
PHONE..................607 638-1994
Frank Competiello, *Principal*
F Competiello, *Principal*
EMP: 9
SALES (est): 1.2MM **Privately Held**
SIC: 2869 Fuels

(G-14730)
SCEHENVUS FIRE DIST
Also Called: Scehenvus Gram Hose Co
40 Main St (12155-2020)
PHONE..................607 638-9017
Chief Pete Comion, *CEO*
EMP: 65 EST: 1900
SALES (est): 3.8MM **Privately Held**
SIC: 3711 Fire department vehicles (motor vehicles), assembly of

Schoharie
Schoharie County

(G-14731)
COBLESKILL STONE PRODUCTS INC
Also Called: Schoharie Quarry/Asphalt
163 Eastern Ave (12157-3209)
P.O. Box 220, Cobleskill (12043-0220)
PHONE..................518 295-7121
Pete Gray, *Manager*
EMP: 12
SQ FT: 1,104
SALES (est): 115.2MM **Privately Held**
WEB: www.cobleskillstone.com
SIC: 1422 Crushed & broken limestone
PA: Cobleskill Stone Products, Inc.
112 Rock Rd
Cobleskill NY 12043
518 234-0221

(G-14732)
MASICK SOIL CONSERVATION CO
Also Called: Carver Sand & Gravel
4860 State Route 30 (12157-2906)
PHONE..................518 827-5354
Carver Laraway, *Owner*
EMP: 11
SQ FT: 800
SALES (est): 500K **Privately Held**
SIC: 3274 0711 Agricultural lime; lime spreading services

Schuylerville
Saratoga County

(G-14733)
EMPIRE BUILDING PRODUCTS INC
12 Spring St (12871-1049)
PHONE..................518 695-6094
Thomas R Harrison, *President*
Paul J Martin, *Vice Pres*
EMP: 5
SQ FT: 1,500
SALES (est): 584.8K **Privately Held**
WEB: www.vtf.com
SIC: 2439 2431 Mfg Structural Wood Members Mfg Millwork
PA: Vermont Timber Frames, Inc
458 Morse Rd
Bennington VT 05201

(G-14734)
GASSHO BODY & MIND INC
76 Broad St (12871-1301)
P.O. Box 910, Saratoga Springs (12866-0836)
PHONE..................518 695-9991
Louis Hotchkiss, *President*
Junko Kobori, *Vice Pres*
◆ EMP: 5
SALES (est): 897.4K **Privately Held**
SIC: 2844 2044 5122 Face creams or lotions; bran, rice; toiletries

Scio
Allegany County

(G-14735)
HYDRAMEC INC
4393 River St (14880-9702)
P.O. Box 69 (14880-0069)
PHONE..................585 593-5190
Gregg D Shear, *President*
James Vossler, *Vice Pres*
Karen Jandrew, *Finance Mgr*
Karen Torrence, *Info Tech Dir*
▲ EMP: 23 EST: 1924
SQ FT: 23,000
SALES (est): 4.6MM **Privately Held**
WEB: www.hydrameconline.com
SIC: 3423 3542 Hand & edge tools; machine tools, metal forming type

▲ = Import ▼ = Export
◆ = Import/Export

Scipio Center
Cayuga County

(G-14736)
CUSTOM CONTROLS
2804 Skillett Rd (13147-3127)
PHONE.....................................315 253-4785
Jay Horst, *Owner*
EMP: 6
SALES (est): 702.2K **Privately Held**
SIC: 3613 Mfg Switchgear/Switchboards

(G-14737)
VANSRIDGE DAIRY LLC
2831 Black St (13147-3173)
PHONE.....................................315 364-8569
Sharon Vannostrand, *Partner*
EMP: 30
SALES (est): 1.5MM **Privately Held**
SIC: 3523 Barn, silo, poultry, dairy & livestock machinery

Scotia
Schenectady County

(G-14738)
ARCHITCTRAL SHETMETAL PDTS INC
1329 Amsterdam Rd (12302-6306)
P.O. Box 2150 (12302-0150)
PHONE.....................................518 381-6144
Toll Free:..888 -
Gary Curcio, *President*
William Donnan, *Vice Pres*
Jim Bleau, *Sales Staff*
EMP: 6
SQ FT: 8,000
SALES (est): 1.1MM **Privately Held**
SIC: 3444 Sheet metal specialties, not stamped; metal roofing & roof drainage equipment

(G-14739)
DIMENSION FABRICATORS INC
2000 7th St (12302-1051)
PHONE.....................................518 374-1936
Scott Stevens, *President*
Joel C Patrie, *Principal*
Coleen Stevens, *Corp Secy*
Scott A Mushaw, *Vice Pres*
Valerie M Borst, *Manager*
▲ **EMP:** 50
SQ FT: 46,000
SALES (est): 18.8MM **Privately Held**
WEB: www.dimensionfab.com
SIC: 3449 Bars, concrete reinforcing: fabricated steel

(G-14740)
GRENO INDUSTRIES INC
2820 Amsterdam Rd (12302-6323)
P.O. Box 542, Schenectady (12301-0542)
PHONE.....................................518 393-4195
Robert W Golden, *CEO*
Eileen Guarino, *President*
Vincent Guarino, *Treasurer*
Pauline Caldarone, *Accounting Mgr*
Patrisia Sheremeta, *Human Resources*
▲ **EMP:** 6
SQ FT: 70,000
SALES: 8.4MM **Privately Held**
WEB: www.greno.com
SIC: 3599 Machine shop, jobbing & repair

(G-14741)
HADP LLC
602 Potential Pkwy (12302-1041)
PHONE.....................................518 831-6824
Paul Epstein,
Adam Epstein,
David Epstein,
EMP: 11
SALES (est): 1.2MM **Privately Held**
SIC: 2656 Plates, paper: made from purchased material

(G-14742)
INTERACTIVE INSTRUMENTS INC
704 Corporation Park # 1 (12302-1078)
PHONE.....................................518 347-0955
Robert Skala, *President*
James Hutchison, *Vice Pres*
EMP: 6
SQ FT: 9,000
SALES (est): 920.3K **Privately Held**
WEB: www.interactiveinstruments.com
SIC: 3599 Custom machinery; machine shop, jobbing & repair

(G-14743)
JBS LLC
Also Called: J B S
6 Maple Ave (12302-4612)
PHONE.....................................518 346-0001
Tommy Bouck, *Engineer*
John Busino, *Mng Member*
EMP: 20
SQ FT: 18,000
SALES (est): 3.7MM **Privately Held**
SIC: 3441 Fabricated structural metal

(G-14744)
NEFAB PACKAGING NORTH EAST LLC
203 Glenville Indus Park (12302-1072)
PHONE.....................................518 346-9105
Brad Lawyer, *Manager*
EMP: 37
SALES (corp-wide): 454.3MM **Privately Held**
SIC: 2448 Wood pallets & skids
HQ: Nefab Packaging, Inc.
204 Airline Dr Ste 100
Coppell TX 75019
469 444-5264

(G-14745)
OAK-BARK CORPORATION
Also Called: Silar Laboratories Division
37 Maple Ave (12302-4613)
PHONE.....................................518 372-5691
Bob Ruskino, *Manager*
EMP: 8
SQ FT: 256
SALES (corp-wide): 11.2MM **Privately Held**
WEB: www.wrightcorp.com
SIC: 2869 Formaldehyde (formalin)
PA: Oak-Bark Corporation
1224 Old Nc Highway 87
Riegelwood NC 28456
910 655-9225

(G-14746)
SHIPMTES/PRINTMATES HOLDG CORP (PA)
Also Called: Velocity Print Solutions
705 Corporation Park # 2 (12302-1092)
PHONE.....................................518 370-1158
James Stiles, *CEO*
Michael Mello, *CFO*
Mike Mello, *CFO*
Gail Jeste, *Persnl Mgr*
David Benny, *Manager*
EMP: 85
SQ FT: 60,000
SALES (est): 34.3MM **Privately Held**
WEB: www.sm-pm.com
SIC: 2752 5111 7334 7319 Commercial printing, offset; printing & writing paper; photocopying & duplicating services; distribution of advertising material or sample services; direct mail advertising services

(G-14747)
SPECIALTY QUALITY PACKG LLC
Also Called: Sqp
602 Potential Pkwy (12302-1041)
PHONE.....................................914 580-3200
Paul Epstein, *Mng Member*
▲ **EMP:** 81
SQ FT: 267,000
SALES (est): 30.2MM **Privately Held**
SIC: 2679 Papier mache articles, except statuary & art goods

Scottsville
Monroe County

(G-14748)
ADRIA MACHINE & TOOL INC
966 North Rd (14546-9770)
P.O. Box 208 (14546-0208)
PHONE.....................................585 889-3360
Janos Poloznik, *President*
John Hehnen, *Opers Mgr*
David Dildy, *Accounts Mgr*
John Hartman, *Department Mgr*
EMP: 4
SQ FT: 7,000
SALES: 1MM **Privately Held**
WEB: www.adriamachine.com
SIC: 3599 Machine shop, jobbing & repair

(G-14749)
COOPERVISION INC
711 North Rd (14546-1238)
PHONE.....................................585 889-3301
Dennis Snyder, *Plant Mgr*
Joanne Roeder, *Senior Buyer*
Alicia Witter, *Engineer*
James Gardner, *Chief Mktg Ofcr*
Al Rodriguez, *Program Dir*
EMP: 594
SALES (corp-wide): 2.1B **Publicly Held**
SIC: 3851 Contact lenses
HQ: Coopervision, Inc.
209 High Point Dr Ste 100
Victor NY 14564

(G-14750)
HEANY INDUSTRIES INC
249 Briarwood Ln (14546-1244)
P.O. Box 38 (14546-0038)
PHONE.....................................585 889-2700
S Scott Zolnier, *Ch of Bd*
Charles Aldridge, *Vice Pres*
Theresa Dunn, *Purchasing*
Brian Hill, *MIS Dir*
▲ **EMP:** 58 **EST:** 1937
SQ FT: 18,000
SALES (est): 10MM **Privately Held**
WEB: www.heany.com
SIC: 3299 3479 2851 2816 Ceramic fiber; coating of metals with plastic or resins; paints & allied products; inorganic pigments

(G-14751)
JACK W MILLER
Also Called: Miller Truck Rental
2339 North Rd (14546-9737)
PHONE.....................................585 538-2399
Jack W Miller, *Owner*
EMP: 9
SQ FT: 13,000
SALES (est): 1.5MM **Privately Held**
SIC: 3519 7538 Diesel engine rebuilding; diesel engine repair: automotive

(G-14752)
POWER AND CNSTR GROUP INC
Also Called: Livingston Lighting and Power
86 River Rd (14546-9503)
PHONE.....................................585 889-6020
Philip Brooks, *Branch Mgr*
EMP: 26
SALES (corp-wide): 60MM **Privately Held**
WEB: www.valleysandandgravel.com
SIC: 3648 3647 Street lighting fixtures; streetcar lighting fixtures
PA: Power & Construction Group, Inc.
119 River Rd
Scottsville NY 14546
585 889-8500

(G-14753)
SABIN METAL CORPORATION
1647 Wheatland Center Rd (14546-9709)
P.O. Box 905 (14546-0905)
PHONE.....................................585 538-2194
George Heath, *Foreman/Supr*
John Waldon, *Maint Spvr*
Mike Nichols, *Research*
David Petishnok, *Engineer*
Vicki Strong, *Accounting Dir*
EMP: 125
SALES (corp-wide): 43.2MM **Privately Held**
WEB: www.sabinmetal.com
SIC: 3341 3339 Secondary precious metals; primary nonferrous metals
PA: Sabin Metal Corporation
300 Pantigo Pl Ste 102
East Hampton NY 11937
631 329-1695

(G-14754)
SWAIN TECHNOLOGY INC
963 North Rd (14546-1228)
PHONE.....................................585 889-2786
Daniel Swain, *President*
Richard Tucker, *General Mgr*
Linda Swain, *Vice Pres*
EMP: 15
SQ FT: 11,000
SALES (est): 1.8MM **Privately Held**
WEB: www.swaintech.com
SIC: 3479 Coating of metals & formed products

Sea Cliff
Nassau County

(G-14755)
GOTHAM T-SHIRT CORP
211 Glen Cove Ave Unit 5 (11579-1432)
PHONE.....................................516 676-0900
Howard Zwang, *Ch of Bd*
EMP: 5
SALES (est): 504.6K **Privately Held**
SIC: 2211 Shirting fabrics, cotton

(G-14756)
ROBS REALLY GOOD LLC
100 Roslyn Ave (11579-1274)
P.O. Box 355 (11579-0355)
PHONE.....................................516 671-4411
Carey Johnston, *Sales Staff*
Robert Ehrlich, *Mng Member*
EMP: 10
SALES (est): 1.5MM **Privately Held**
SIC: 2096 Potato chips & similar snacks

Seaford
Nassau County

(G-14757)
A & A GRAPHICS INC II
615 Arlington Dr (11783-1135)
PHONE.....................................516 735-0078
Eli P Pandolfi, *President*
EMP: 3 **EST:** 1999
SQ FT: 5,000
SALES (est): 1.2MM **Privately Held**
SIC: 2759 Commercial printing

(G-14758)
KYRA COMMUNICATIONS CORP
3864 Bayberry Ln (11783-1503)
PHONE.....................................516 783-6244
Richard Doherty, *President*
Carol Doherty, *Vice Pres*
EMP: 14
SALES (est): 928.6K **Privately Held**
SIC: 2741 8734 Miscellaneous publishing; testing laboratories

(G-14759)
LUCAS ELECTRIC
3524 Merrick Rd (11783-2824)
PHONE.....................................516 809-8619
EMP: 7
SALES (est): 146.9K **Privately Held**
SIC: 3699 Electrical equipment & supplies

Selden
Suffolk County

(G-14760)
BLUE TORTILLA LLC
1070 Middle Country Rd # 4 (11784-2529)
PHONE.....................................631 451-0100
Eric Gorber, *Owner*
EMP: 6

Selden - Suffolk County (G-14761)

SALES (est): 492.4K **Privately Held**
SIC: 2099 Tortillas, fresh or refrigerated

(G-14761)
CENTRAL GARDEN & PET COMPANY
1100 Middle Country Rd (11784-2513)
PHONE 631 451-8021
Stacey Rossi, *Manager*
EMP: 9
SALES (corp-wide): 2B **Publicly Held**
WEB: www.centralgardenandpet.com
SIC: 2048 Prepared feeds
PA: Central Garden & Pet Company
  1340 Treat Blvd Ste 600
  Walnut Creek CA 94597
  925 948-4000

(G-14762)
CREATIVE STONE & CABINETS
448 Middle Country Rd # 1 (11784-2657)
PHONE 631 772-6548
Juan Cuzco, *President*
EMP: 6
SALES (est): 988.9K **Privately Held**
SIC: 2434 Wood kitchen cabinets

(G-14763)
DATORIB INC
Also Called: Minuteman Press
974 Middle Country Rd (11784-2535)
PHONE 631 698-6222
William J Passeggio, *President*
Rita Passeggio, *Sales Mgr*
EMP: 5
SQ FT: 1,850
SALES (est): 637.8K **Privately Held**
SIC: 2752 Commercial printing, lithographic

(G-14764)
ILAB AMERICA INC
45 Hemlock St (11784-1327)
PHONE 631 615-5053
Wayne Boyle, *President*
EMP: 6
SALES: 800K **Privately Held**
WEB: www.ilabamerica.com
SIC: 3651 Amplifiers: radio, public address or musical instrument

(G-14765)
NORTHERN METALWORKS CORP
15 King Ave (11784-2314)
PHONE 646 523-1689
Shakir Qureshi, *President*
EMP: 5
SALES (est): 257.3K **Privately Held**
SIC: 3449 Miscellaneous metalwork

(G-14766)
PROGRESSIVE ORTHOTICS LTD (PA)
280 Middle Country Rd G (11784-2532)
PHONE 631 732-5556
Bruce Goodman, *President*
EMP: 9
SQ FT: 2,400
SALES (est): 905.9K **Privately Held**
WEB: www.progressiveorthotics.com
SIC: 3842 3841 5999 5047 Limbs, artificial; orthopedic appliances; surgical & medical instruments; orthopedic & prosthesis applications; medical & hospital equipment

Selkirk
Albany County

(G-14767)
CQ TRAFFIC CONTROL DEVICES LLC
Also Called: Cq Traffic Control Products
1521 Us Rte 9w (12158)
P.O. Box 192 (12158-0192)
PHONE 518 767-0057
William Quattrochi,
Frank Conrad,
Carol Quattrochi,
Douglas Robbins,
EMP: 5

SALES (est): 881K **Privately Held**
SIC: 3669 Pedestrian traffic control equipment

(G-14768)
GE PLASTICS
1 Noryl Ave (12158-9784)
PHONE 518 475-5011
Jeffery Immelt, *Principal*
◆ EMP: 5
SALES (est): 860.2K **Privately Held**
SIC: 2821 Plastics materials & resins

(G-14769)
OLDCASTLE PRECAST INC
Also Called: Oldcastle Precast Bldg Systems
123 County Route 101 (12158-2606)
PHONE 518 767-2112
Sheila Conners, *Controller*
Edward Soler, *Manager*
Christopher Mueller, *Manager*
EMP: 40
SALES (corp-wide): 29.7B **Privately Held**
WEB: www.oldcastle-precast.com
SIC: 3272 Concrete products, precast
HQ: Oldcastle Precast, Inc.
  1002 15th St Sw Ste 110
  Auburn WA 98001
  253 833-2777

(G-14770)
PALPROSS INCORPORATED
Also Called: L P Transportation
Maple Ave Rr 396 (12158)
P.O. Box 95 (12158-0095)
PHONE 845 469-2188
Andrew Palmer, *Manager*
EMP: 10
SQ FT: 2,400
SALES (corp-wide): 3.6MM **Privately Held**
SIC: 3537 Trucks, tractors, loaders, carriers & similar equipment
PA: Palpross Incorporated
  Rr Box 17m
  Chester NY 10918
  845 469-2188

(G-14771)
SABIC INNOVATIVE PLAS US LLC
1 Noryl Ave (12158-9765)
PHONE 518 475-5011
Charlie Crew, *Manager*
EMP: 258 **Privately Held**
WEB: www.sabic-ip.com
SIC: 2821 Plastics materials & resins
HQ: Sabic Innovative Plastics Us Llc
  2500 City W Blvd Ste 100
  Houston TX 77042

Seneca Castle
Ontario County

(G-14772)
CASTLE HARVESTER CO INC
Also Called: Castle Harvstr Met Fabricators
3165 Seneca Castle Rd (14547)
P.O. Box 167 (14547-0167)
PHONE 585 526-5884
Michael Kunes, *President*
EMP: 9
SQ FT: 10,000
SALES (est): 1.3MM **Privately Held**
SIC: 3441 Building components, structural steel

Seneca Falls
Seneca County

(G-14773)
GOULDS PUMPS (IPG) LLC
240 Fall St (13148-1573)
PHONE 315 568-2811
EMP: 6
SALES (est): 622.2K **Privately Held**
SIC: 3561 Pumps & pumping equipment

(G-14774)
GOULDS PUMPS LLC (HQ)
Also Called: Goulds Pumps Incorporated
240 Fall St (13148-1573)
PHONE 315 568-2811
Robert Pagano, *Ch of Bd*
Aris Chicles, *President*
Ken Napolitano, *President*
Tim Magill, *Project Mgr*
Stan Knecht, *Opers Mgr*
◆ EMP: 1100 EST: 1984
SALES (est): 3.5MM
SALES (corp-wide): 2.5B **Publicly Held**
WEB: www.gouldspumps.com
SIC: 3561 5084 Pumps & pumping equipment; industrial pumps & parts; pumps, oil well & field; pumps, domestic: water or sump; industrial machinery & equipment
PA: Itt Inc.
  1133 Westchester Ave N-100
  White Plains NY 10604
  914 641-2000

(G-14775)
GOULDS PUMPS LLC
Also Called: ITT Accounts Payable
280 Fall St (13148-1544)
P.O. Box 750 (13148-0750)
PHONE 315 568-2811
Mark Downing, *Engineer*
Daniel Fannin, *Engineer*
Corry Vancassele, *Sr Project Mgr*
Synkane Bawe, *Technical Staff*
EMP: 45
SALES (corp-wide): 2.5B **Publicly Held**
WEB: www.gouldspumps.com
SIC: 3561 Pumps & pumping equipment
HQ: Goulds Pumps Llc
  240 Fall St
  Seneca Falls NY 13148
  315 568-2811

(G-14776)
ITT CORPORATION
2881 E Bayard Street Ext (13148-8745)
PHONE 866 448-8372
Denise L Ramos, *Ch of Bd*
Vicky Creamer, *Senior VP*
James Buda, *Technology*
EMP: 94
SALES (est): 47.5MM **Privately Held**
SIC: 3625 Control equipment, electric

(G-14777)
ITT CORPORATION
A-C Pump Division
240 Fall St (13148-1590)
PHONE 315 568-2811
Pamela Greco, *Buyer*
Dave Menapace, *Buyer*
Joe Christofferson, *Engineer*
Steve Durham, *Engineer*
Daniel Parker, *Engineer*
EMP: 58
SALES (corp-wide): 2.5B **Publicly Held**
SIC: 3625 3823 3363 3812 Control equipment, electric; fluidic devices, circuits & systems for process control; aluminum die-castings; radar systems & equipment; infrared object detection equipment; fluid power pumps & motors; pumps & pumping equipment
HQ: Itt Llc
  1133 Westchester Ave N-100
  White Plains NY 10604
  914 641-2000

(G-14778)
ITT ENGINEERED VALVES LLC (DH)
240 Fall St (13148-1590)
Rural Route 750 (13148)
PHONE 662 257-6982
Randy Garman, *General Mgr*
▲ EMP: 53 EST: 1993
SALES (est): 13.5MM
SALES (corp-wide): 2.5B **Publicly Held**
SIC: 3592 Valves
HQ: Itt Llc
  1133 Westchester Ave N-100
  White Plains NY 10604
  914 641-2000

(G-14779)
ITT GOULDS PUMPS INC
240 Fall St (13148-1573)
PHONE 914 641-2129
Michael J Savinelli, *Principal*
Tim Murney, *Project Mgr*
Matthew Murray, *Manager*
Adam Merah, *Sales Engr*
EMP: 4500
SALES: 132MM
SALES (corp-wide): 2.5B **Publicly Held**
SIC: 3561 5084 Pumps & pumping equipment; industrial machinery & equipment
PA: Itt Inc.
  1133 Westchester Ave N-100
  White Plains NY 10604
  914 641-2000

(G-14780)
ITT LLC
Also Called: ITT Monitoring Control
240 Fall St (13148-1590)
PHONE 315 568-4733
Doug Brown, *Manager*
EMP: 5
SALES (corp-wide): 2.5B **Publicly Held**
SIC: 3625 Control equipment, electric
HQ: Itt Llc
  1133 Westchester Ave N-100
  White Plains NY 10604
  914 641-2000

(G-14781)
ITT LLC
2881 E Bayard Street Ext (13148-8745)
PHONE 914 641-2000
Kyle Fenter, *Project Mgr*
Don Radford, *Branch Mgr*
EMP: 58
SALES (corp-wide): 2.5B **Publicly Held**
WEB: www.ittind.com
SIC: 3625 3823 3363 3812 Control equipment, electric; fluidic devices, circuits & systems for process control; aluminum die-castings; radar systems & equipment; infrared object detection equipment
HQ: Itt Llc
  1133 Westchester Ave N-100
  White Plains NY 10604
  914 641-2000

(G-14782)
MONTEZUMA WINERY LLC
2981 Us Route 20 (13148-9423)
PHONE 315 568-8190
Bill Martin,
▲ EMP: 9
SALES (est): 766.9K **Privately Held**
WEB: www.montezumawinery.com
SIC: 2084 Wines

(G-14783)
SCEPTER INC
11 Lamb Rd (13148-8432)
PHONE 315 568-4225
Garney Scott III, *Manager*
EMP: 30 **Privately Held**
WEB: www.scepterinc.com
SIC: 3341 Secondary nonferrous metals
PA: Scepter, Inc
  1485 Scepter Ln
  Waverly TN 37185

(G-14784)
SENECA FALLS CAPITAL INC (PA)
Also Called: Seneca Falls Machine
314 Fall St (13148-1543)
PHONE 315 568-5804
Attila Libertiny, *President*
EMP: 2
SQ FT: 115,000
SALES (est): 5MM **Privately Held**
SIC: 3541 Machine tools, metal cutting type

(G-14785)
SENECA FALLS MACHINE TOOL CO
Also Called: Seneca Falls Technology Group
314 Fall St (13148-1543)
PHONE 315 568-5804
Attila Libertiny, *President*
EMP: 60

SQ FT: 115,000
SALES: 3MM **Privately Held**
WEB: www.sftg.com
SIC: 3541 3545 Machine tools, metal cutting type; machine tool accessories
PA: Seneca Falls Capital, Inc.
  314 Fall St
  Seneca Falls NY 13148

(G-14786)
SENECA FLS SPC & LOGISTICS CO (PA)
50 Johnston St (13148-1235)
PHONE.....................................315 568-4139
Stephen M Bregande, *President*
Bruce Hilton, *Vice Pres*
Christopher Woods, *Vice Pres*
Michael Schleahr, *CFO*
William Ingle, *Manager*
▲ **EMP:** 80 **EST:** 1880
SALES (est): 37.8MM **Privately Held**
SIC: 2653 2652 Boxes, corrugated: made from purchased materials; setup paperboard boxes

(G-14787)
TI GROUP AUTO SYSTEMS LLC
240 Fall St (13148-1590)
PHONE.....................................315 568-7042
Danielle Roetting, *Manager*
EMP: 5
SALES (corp-wide): 6.6B **Privately Held**
WEB: www.tiautomotive.com
SIC: 3317 3312 3599 3052 Tubes, seamless steel; tubes, steel & iron; hose, flexible metallic; plastic hose; fuel systems & parts, motor vehicle
HQ: Ti Group Automotive Systems, Llc
  2020 Taylor Rd
  Auburn Hills MI 48326
  248 296-8000

(G-14788)
WILSON PRESS LLC
56 Miller St (13148-1585)
PHONE.....................................315 568-9693
Don Johnson, *President*
Nancy Bellina, *Sales Staff*
Richard Ricci, *Manager*
Nora Ricci,
EMP: 20
SQ FT: 5,500
SALES: 2MM **Privately Held**
SIC: 2752 2791 2789 2759 Commercial printing, offset; typesetting; bookbinding & related work; commercial printing

(G-14789)
XYLEM INC
2881 E Bayard Street Ext (13148-8745)
P.O. Box 750 (13148-0750)
PHONE.....................................716 862-4123
Richard Blong, *Opers Staff*
Douglas Bingler, *Branch Mgr*
Ken Dover, *Manager*
Thomas Stephan, *Manager*
Marlene Fingar, *Technology*
EMP: 15 **Publicly Held**
SIC: 3561 Pumps & pumping equipment
PA: Xylem Inc.
  1 International Dr
  Rye Brook NY 10573

(G-14790)
XYLEM INC
Also Called: Global Financial Shared Svcs
2881 E Bayard Street Ext (13148-8745)
PHONE.....................................315 239-2499
Linda Lynch, *Branch Mgr*
EMP: 84 **Publicly Held**
SIC: 3561 Pumps & pumping equipment
PA: Xylem Inc.
  1 International Dr
  Rye Brook NY 10573

Setauket
Suffolk County

(G-14791)
ADVANCED RESEARCH MEDIA INC
60 Route 25a Ste 1 (11733-2872)
PHONE.....................................631 751-9696
Steve Blechman, *CEO*
Elyse Blechman, *President*
EMP: 17
SALES (est): 5MM **Privately Held**
SIC: 2721 Magazines: publishing only, not printed on site

(G-14792)
BC SYSTEMS INC
200 N Belle Mead Ave # 2 (11733-3463)
PHONE.....................................631 751-9370
Gus Blazek, *President*
Gustav Blazek, *President*
Dennis Carrigan, *Vice Pres*
Art Charych, *Vice Pres*
Pam Lomonaco, *Purch Mgr*
EMP: 50
SQ FT: 16,000
SALES (est): 11.7MM **Privately Held**
WEB: www.bcpowersys.com
SIC: 3679 Power supplies, all types: static

(G-14793)
CARL SAFINA CENTER INC
80 N Country Rd (11733-1345)
PHONE.....................................808 888-9440
Mayra Marino, *Principal*
EMP: 9 **EST:** 2015
SQ FT: 564
SALES: 589.9K **Privately Held**
SIC: 3545 Mandrels

(G-14794)
EATINGEVOLVED LLC
10 Technology Dr Unit 4 (11733-4063)
PHONE.....................................631 675-2440
Christine Cusano, *CEO*
Richard Gusmano, *COO*
EMP: 16
SALES (est): 742.4K **Privately Held**
SIC: 2064 Candy bars, including chocolate covered bars

(G-14795)
MAUSNER EQUIPMENT CO INC
8 Heritage Ln (11733-3018)
PHONE.....................................631 689-7358
Seymour Mausner, *President*
Dorothy Mausner, *Corp Secy*
Leonard Mausner, *Vice Pres*
EMP: 137
SQ FT: 17,000
SALES (est): 27.5MM **Privately Held**
SIC: 3545 5084 3823 Precision measuring tools: measuring & testing equipment, electrical; industrial instrmnts msrmnt display/control process variable

Sharon Springs
Schoharie County

(G-14796)
ADELPHI PAPER HANGINGS
102 Main St (13459-3136)
P.O. Box 135 (13459-0135)
PHONE.....................................518 284-9066
Chris Ohrstrom, *President*
Steve Larson, *Manager*
EMP: 5
SALES: 380K **Privately Held**
WEB: www.adelphipaperhangings.com
SIC: 2679 Wallpaper

(G-14797)
AMT INCORPORATED
883 Chestnut St (13459-2131)
P.O. Box 338 (13459-0338)
PHONE.....................................518 284-2910
Lanning Brandel, *President*
Beth Brandel, *Treasurer*
Scott Stevens, *Director*
EMP: 33
SQ FT: 22,000
SALES (est): 7.9MM **Privately Held**
WEB: www.amtcastings.com
SIC: 3366 3365 3354 3341 Bushings & bearings, copper (nonmachined); aluminum foundries; aerospace castings, aluminum; machinery castings, aluminum; aluminum extruded products; secondary nonferrous metals; steel foundries; miscellaneous nonferrous products; ferrous metals

(G-14798)
MONOLITHIC COATINGS INC
916 Highway Route 20 (13459-3108)
PHONE.....................................914 621-2765
EMP: 5
SALES (est): 566.1K **Privately Held**
SIC: 3674 Read-only memory (ROM)

(G-14799)
TIMOTHY L SIMPSON
5819 State Route 145 (13459-3205)
PHONE.....................................518 234-1401
Timothy L Simpson, *Principal*
EMP: 6
SALES (est): 492.5K **Privately Held**
SIC: 2411 Logging

Shelter Island
Suffolk County

(G-14800)
COECLES HBR MARINA & BOAT YARD
68 Cartwright Rd (11964)
PHONE.....................................631 749-0856
John Needham, *President*
EMP: 15
SALES (corp-wide): 3.3MM **Privately Held**
SIC: 3732 Boat building & repairing
PA: Coecles Harbor Marina & Boatyard, Inc
  18 Hudson Ave
  Shelter Island NY 11964
  631 749-0700

(G-14801)
GOODING & ASSOCIATES INC
15 Dinah Rock Rd (11964)
P.O. Box 1690 (11964-1690)
PHONE.....................................631 749-3313
A Gordon Gooding Jr, *President*
Denise Demattia, *Sales Staff*
Joy Strasser, *Office Mgr*
Kathleen Gooding, *Associate*
EMP: 14
SALES (est): 1.3MM **Privately Held**
SIC: 2741 Catalogs: publishing & printing

(G-14802)
SHELTER ISLAND REPORTER INC
Also Called: Shelter Island Cmnty Nwspapers
50 N Ferry Rd (11964)
P.O. Box 756 (11964-0756)
PHONE.....................................631 749-1000
Troy Gustavson, *President*
Andrew Olsen, *Vice Pres*
◆ **EMP:** 8
SALES (est): 490K **Privately Held**
SIC: 2711 Newspapers, publishing & printing

Sherburne
Chenango County

(G-14803)
CHENANGO VALLEY TECH INC
328 Route 12b (13460)
P.O. Box 1038 (13460-1038)
PHONE.....................................607 674-4115
Lloyd Baker, *CEO*
Lucille Baker, *President*
John Davis, *President*
Cole Williams, *QC Mgr*
Shawn Baker, *Sales Executive*
EMP: 35 **EST:** 1997
SQ FT: 30,000
SALES (est): 7MM **Privately Held**
WEB: www.chenangovalleytech.com
SIC: 3544 3089 Industrial molds; injection molding of plastics

(G-14804)
COLUMBUS WOODWORKING INC
164 Casey Cheese Fctry Rd (13460-5006)
PHONE.....................................607 674-4546
Michael Tomaselli, *President*
Stacy Tomaselli, *Corp Secy*
EMP: 5

SQ FT: 15,000
SALES (est): 653.2K **Privately Held**
SIC: 2431 Millwork

(G-14805)
EGG LOW FARMS INC
35 W State St (13460-9424)
PHONE.....................................607 674-4653
Helen Dunckel, *President*
David Dunckel, *Vice Pres*
EMP: 10
SQ FT: 38,000
SALES: 850K **Privately Held**
SIC: 2015 Egg substitutes made from eggs

(G-14806)
KENYON PRESS INC
1 Kenyon Press Dr (13460-5670)
P.O. Box 710 (13460-0710)
PHONE.....................................607 674-9066
Ray Kenyon, *President*
Kevin Crandall, *Sales Staff*
Karisha Gulbin, *Sales Staff*
Rick Condon, *Sales Associate*
Amanda Foster, *Office Mgr*
EMP: 50
SQ FT: 75,000
SALES (est): 10MM **Privately Held**
SIC: 2752 Commercial printing, offset

(G-14807)
MID-YORK PRESS INC
2808 State Highway 80 (13460-4549)
P.O. Box 733 (13460-0733)
PHONE.....................................607 674-4491
Robert W Tenney, *Ch of Bd*
Jane Eaton, *Principal*
Mary Mahoney, *Principal*
Cynthia Tenney, *Principal*
Patrick Dowdall, *Vice Pres*
EMP: 70 **EST:** 1946
SQ FT: 56,000
SALES (est): 27.8MM **Privately Held**
WEB: www.midyorkpress.com
SIC: 2679 2752 2711 Paperboard products, converted; commercial printing, offset; newspapers, publishing & printing
PA: Media Tenney Group
  28 Robinson Rd
  Clinton NY 13323
  315 853-5569

(G-14808)
READY EGG FARMS INC
35 W State St (13460-9424)
P.O. Box 843, Silverton OR (97381-0843)
PHONE.....................................607 674-4653
Patrick Green, *President*
EMP: 9
SQ FT: 40,000
SALES: 1.5MM **Privately Held**
WEB: www.readyeggfarms.com
SIC: 2015 Egg processing

(G-14809)
SHERBURNE METAL SALES INC (PA)
40 S Main St (13460-9804)
PHONE.....................................607 674-4441
David Harvey, *President*
Gregory Panagiotakis, *Vice Pres*
EMP: 19
SQ FT: 60,000
SALES (est): 36.6MM **Privately Held**
WEB: www.sherburnemetals.com
SIC: 3331 3351 Primary copper; rolled or drawn shapes: copper & copper alloy

(G-14810)
SMITH TOOL & DIE INC
714 Pleasant Valley Rd (13460-3101)
P.O. Box 205 (13460-0205)
PHONE.....................................607 674-4165
Kenneth Smith, *President*
EMP: 6
SQ FT: 2,000
SALES (est): 340K **Privately Held**
WEB: www.cncsurfacegrinding.com
SIC: 3599 Machine shop, jobbing & repair

(G-14811)
STEEL SALES INC
8085 New York St Hwy 12 (13460)
P.O. Box 539 (13460-0539)
PHONE.....................................607 674-6363
Brenda Westcott, *Ch of Bd*

Sherburne - Chenango County (G-14812) — GEOGRAPHIC SECTION

EMP: 20
SQ FT: 20,000
SALES (est): 6.1MM Privately Held
WEB: www.steelsalesinc.com
SIC: 3446 3444 3449 5051 Architectural metalwork; sheet metalwork; bars, concrete reinforcing; fabricated steel; metals service centers & offices; steel

(G-14812)
TECNOFIL CHENANGO SAC
40 S Main St (13460-9804)
PHONE.................607 674-4441
Jose Babadia, Principal
◆ EMP: 30
SALES (est): 10.4MM Privately Held
SIC: 3331 Primary copper

(G-14813)
WHITE HOUSE CABINET SHOP LLC
11 Knapp St (13460-9791)
P.O. Box 877 (13460-0877)
PHONE.................607 674-9358
Jeff Webster, Mng Member
Bruce Webster,
Mike Webster,
EMP: 8
SQ FT: 5,112
SALES (est): 797.9K Privately Held
SIC: 2434 Wood kitchen cabinets

Sheridan
Chautauqua County

(G-14814)
COTTON WELL DRILLING CO INC
Center Rd (14135)
P.O. Box 203 (14135-0203)
PHONE.................716 672-2788
Donald D Cotton, President
Mollie Cotton, Office Mgr
EMP: 8 EST: 1973
SQ FT: 2,400
SALES (est): 916K Privately Held
SIC: 1389 Oil & gas wells: building, repairing & dismantling

Sherman
Chautauqua County

(G-14815)
BISSEL-BABCOCK MILLWORK INC
3866 Kendrick Rd (14781-9628)
PHONE.................716 761-6976
James Babcock, President
Paula Babcock, Admin Sec
EMP: 11
SQ FT: 5,000
SALES: 1.1MM Privately Held
SIC: 2421 Sawmills & planing mills, general

(G-14816)
FIRE APPARATUS SERVICE TECH
7895 Lyons Rd (14781-9657)
PHONE.................716 753-3538
Danny Karges, Executive
EMP: 7
SALES (est): 894.4K Privately Held
SIC: 3669 Fire alarm apparatus, electric

(G-14817)
TRIPLE E MANUFACTURING
117 Osborn St (14781-9790)
P.O. Box 438 (14781-0438)
PHONE.................716 761-6996
Richard Watrous, Partner
Pamela Watrous, Partner
▲ EMP: 18
SQ FT: 12,000
SALES (est): 2MM Privately Held
SIC: 2399 Horse & pet accessories, textile

Sherrill
Oneida County

(G-14818)
BRIGGS & STRATTON CORPORATION
4245 Highbridge Rd (13461)
PHONE.................315 495-0100
Philip Wenzel, Manager
EMP: 15
SALES (corp-wide): 1.7B Publicly Held
SIC: 3519 Internal combustion engines
PA: Briggs & Stratton Corporation
12301 W Wirth St
Wauwatosa WI 53222
414 259-5333

(G-14819)
DLR ENTERPRISES LLC
Also Called: Noble Wood Shavings
104 E Seneca St (13461-1008)
PHONE.................315 813-2911
EMP: 5
SALES (est): 793.5K Privately Held
SIC: 2421 Sawmill/Planing Mill

(G-14820)
DUTCHLAND PLASTICS LLC
102 E Seneca St (13461-1008)
PHONE.................315 280-0247
Daven Claerbout, Branch Mgr
EMP: 223
SALES (corp-wide): 118.9MM Privately Held
SIC: 3089 Injection molding of plastics
PA: Dutchland Plastics, Llc
54 Enterprise St
Oostburg WI 53070
920 564-3633

(G-14821)
PATLA ENTERPRISES INC
Also Called: Joe's Jerky
190 E State St (13461-1232)
PHONE.................315 367-0237
Jodie-Lynn Patla, President
EMP: 14
SALES: 500K Privately Held
SIC: 2013 1541 5411 Beef, dried: from purchased meat; food products manufacturing or packing plant construction; convenience stores

(G-14822)
SHERRILL MANUFACTURING INC
102 E Seneca St (13461-1008)
PHONE.................315 280-0727
Gregory L Owens, CEO
Matthew A Roberts, President
EMP: 140
SQ FT: 1,000,000
SALES (est): 26.4MM Privately Held
WEB: www.sherrillmfg.com
SIC: 3421 3914 3471 Cutlery; silverware, silver plated; gold plating

(G-14823)
SILVER CITY GROUP INC
Also Called: Silver City Metals
27577 W Seneca St (13461)
PHONE.................315 363-0344
Dennis Tormey, President
Cliff Wittman, Vice Pres
EMP: 5
SQ FT: 2,500
SALES (est): 400K Privately Held
SIC: 3914 Pewter ware

(G-14824)
TIBRO WATER TECHNOLOGIES LTD
106 E Seneca St Unit 25 (13461-1008)
PHONE.................647 426-3415
Dhiren Chandaria, President
EMP: 15
SQ FT: 7,000
SALES: 1.2MM Privately Held
SIC: 2819 Sodium & potassium compounds, exc. bleaches, alkalies, alum.
PA: Tibro International Ltd
1 Scarsdale Rd Unit 300
North York ON M3B 2
647 426-3415

(G-14825)
WESTMOOR LTD
Also Called: Conde Pumps Div
906 W Hamilton Ave (13461-1366)
P.O. Box 99 (13461-0099)
PHONE.................315 363-1500
James R Hendry, Ch of Bd
EMP: 10 EST: 1939
SQ FT: 18,000
SALES (est): 2.7MM Privately Held
WEB: www.westmoorltd.com
SIC: 3561 3523 Industrial pumps & parts; milking machines

Shirley
Suffolk County

(G-14826)
AMERICAN REGENT INC
Also Called: American Regent Laboratories
5 Ramsey Rd (11967-4701)
P.O. Box 9001 (11967-9001)
PHONE.................631 924-4000
Ralf Lange, President
Bobby Kniffin, Managing Prtnr
Jacalyn Beltrani, Vice Pres
Jean Poulos, Vice Pres
Joe Puglisi, Facilities Mgr
EMP: 425
SQ FT: 95,000
SALES (est): 52.1MM
SALES (corp-wide): 9B Privately Held
WEB: www.osteohealth.com
SIC: 2834 Pharmaceutical preparations
HQ: Luitpold Pharmaceuticals, Inc.
5 Ramsey Rd
Shirley NY 11967
631 924-4000

(G-14827)
ANORAD CORPORATION
100 Precision Dr Ste 1 (11967-4716)
PHONE.................631 344-6600
Marco H Wishart, Ch of Bd
Geoffrey Storms, President
▲ EMP: 102
SALES (est): 17.9MM Publicly Held
WEB: www.anorad.com
SIC: 3577 3827 Computer peripheral equipment; optical instruments & lenses
PA: Rockwell Automation, Inc.
1201 S 2nd St
Milwaukee WI 53204

(G-14828)
ANTHONY GIGI INC
Also Called: Russo's Gluten Free Gourmet
45 Ramsey Rd Unit 28 (11967-4712)
PHONE.................860 984-1943
Neil Russo, President
EMP: 5
SQ FT: 2,000
SALES: 300K Privately Held
SIC: 2046 Gluten meal

(G-14829)
ATLANTIC COLOR CORP
14 Ramsey Rd (11967-4704)
PHONE.................631 345-3800
Richard Reina, Ch of Bd
EMP: 20
SALES (est): 3.1MM Privately Held
WEB: www.atlanticcolor.com
SIC: 2752 Commercial printing, offset

(G-14830)
ATLANTIC INDUSTRIAL TECH INC
90 Precision Dr (11967-4702)
PHONE.................631 234-3131
Robert Ferrara, Ch of Bd
Thomas Ferrara, Vice Pres
Jennifer Wines, Accounting Mgr
Jeff Goldhammer, Senior Mgr
EMP: 35
SQ FT: 20,000
SALES (est): 12.2MM Privately Held
WEB: www.aitzone.com
SIC: 3443 8711 7699 3594 Fabricated plate work (boiler shop); engineering services; industrial machinery & equipment repair; fluid power pumps & motors

(G-14831)
B V M ASSOCIATES
999-32 Montrell 414 (11967)
PHONE.................631 254-6220
Mike Lucyk, Owner
EMP: 8
SQ FT: 5,000
SALES (est): 510K Privately Held
SIC: 3577 Computer peripheral equipment

(G-14832)
BIODEX MEDICAL SYSTEMS INC (PA)
20 Ramsey Rd (11967-4704)
PHONE.................631 924-9000
James Reiss, Ch of Bd
Allyson Scerri, President
Kate Dimeglio, Vice Pres
Bob Ranieri, Vice Pres
John Bennett, Treasurer
▲ EMP: 170
SQ FT: 83,000
SALES (est): 28.9MM Privately Held
WEB: www.biodex.com
SIC: 3842 3841 3844 Radiation shielding aprons, gloves, sheeting, etc.; muscle exercise apparatus, ophthalmic; X-ray apparatus & tubes

(G-14833)
BIODEX MEDICAL SYSTEMS INC
49 Natcon Dr (11967-4700)
PHONE.................631 924-3146
John Ryan, Manager
EMP: 30
SALES (corp-wide): 28.9MM Privately Held
WEB: www.biodex.com
SIC: 3842 3841 Radiation shielding aprons, gloves, sheeting, etc.; muscle exercise apparatus, ophthalmic
PA: Biodex Medical Systems, Inc.
20 Ramsey Rd
Shirley NY 11967
631 924-9000

(G-14834)
FIRE ISLAND FUEL
106 Parkwood Dr (11967-3918)
PHONE.................631 772-1482
Joseph Intravaia, Principal
EMP: 6 EST: 2009
SALES (est): 587.3K Privately Held
SIC: 2869 Fuels

(G-14835)
FRANK LOWE RBR & GASKET CO INC
44 Ramsey Rd (11967-4704)
PHONE.................631 777-2707
Ira M Warren, Ch of Bd
Randy Cohen, Vice Pres
Azhar Chishti, Plant Mgr
Ruth Lyons, Purch Dir
Pat Edwards, Payroll Mgr
▲ EMP: 35
SQ FT: 60,000
SALES (est): 8.3MM Privately Held
WEB: www.franklowe.com
SIC: 3053 Gaskets, all materials

(G-14836)
INNOVATION MGT GROUP INC
999 Montauk Hwy (11967-2130)
PHONE.................800 889-0987
Jerry Hussong, Vice Pres
EMP: 10 Privately Held
WEB: www.imgpresents.com
SIC: 7372 Prepackaged software
PA: Innovation Management Group, Inc.
5348 Vegas Dr Ste 285
Las Vegas NV 89108

(G-14837)
L I F PUBLISHING CORP (PA)
Also Called: The Fisherman
14 Ramsey Rd (11967-4704)
 PHONE.................................631 345-5200
 Richard Reina Sr, *President*
 Richard S Reina, *Vice Pres*
 John Debona, *Adv Mgr*
 EMP: 56
 SQ FT: 14,000
 SALES (est): 5.5MM **Privately Held**
 SIC: 2721 2752 Magazines: publishing only, not printed on site; commercial printing, offset

(G-14838)
LUITPOLD PHARMACEUTICALS INC (HQ)
Also Called: Osteohealth
5 Ramsey Rd (11967-4701)
P.O. Box 9001 (11967-9001)
 PHONE.................................631 924-4000
 Joseph Kenneth Keller, *President*
 Dante Serricchio, *General Mgr*
 Joel Steckler, *Business Mgr*
 Deepti Uppala, *Business Mgr*
 Gopal Anyarambhatla, *Vice Pres*
 ▲ **EMP:** 500
 SALES (est): 213.6MM
 SALES (corp-wide): 9B **Privately Held**
 WEB: www.osteohealth.com
 SIC: 2834 Druggists' preparations (pharmaceuticals)
 PA: Daiichi Sankyo Company, Limited
  3-5-1, Nihombashihoncho
  Chuo-Ku TKY 103-0
  362 251-111

(G-14839)
LUITPOLD PHARMACEUTICALS INC
Osteohealth Company
5 Ramsey Rd (11967-4701)
 PHONE.................................631 924-4000
 Mary Jane Helenek, *President*
 Bethany Dudley, *Sales Mgr*
 Kevin Andrews, *Sales Staff*
 Jared Draper, *Sales Staff*
 Ilene A Russo, *Marketing Mgr*
 EMP: 20
 SALES (corp-wide): 9B **Privately Held**
 WEB: www.osteohealth.com
 SIC: 3843 Dental equipment & supplies
 HQ: Luitpold Pharmaceuticals, Inc.
  5 Ramsey Rd
  Shirley NY 11967
  631 924-4000

(G-14840)
MID ATLANTIC GRAPHICS CORP
14 Ramsey Rd (11967-4704)
 PHONE.................................631 345-3800
 Madaline Lechner, *CEO*
 Richard Reina Sr, *President*
 Richard S Reina, *Vice Pres*
 EMP: 20 **EST:** 1979
 SQ FT: 14,000
 SALES (est): 2.4MM
 SALES (corp-wide): 5.5MM **Privately Held**
 SIC: 2752 Commercial printing, offset
 PA: L I F Publishing Corp
  14 Ramsey Rd
  Shirley NY 11967
  631 345-5200

(G-14841)
MODULAR DEVICES INC
Also Called: M D I
1 Roned Rd (11967-4706)
 PHONE.................................631 345-3100
 Steven E Summer, *President*
 Henry Striegl, *Regional Mgr*
 Greg Mink, *COO*
 Henry F Striegl Jr, *Vice Pres*
 Barbara Hall, *Purch Mgr*
 ▲ **EMP:** 55
 SQ FT: 20,000
 SALES (est): 12.1MM **Privately Held**
 WEB: www.modev.com
 SIC: 3621 Motors & generators

(G-14842)
NJF PUBLISHING CORP
Also Called: The Fisherman
14 Ramsey Rd (11967-4704)
 PHONE.................................631 345-5200
 EMP: 6
 SQ FT: 1,800
 SALES (est): 680K **Privately Held**
 SIC: 2721 8412 Periodicals- Publishing/Printing Museum/Art Gallery

(G-14843)
POWR-UPS CORP
1 Roned Rd (11967-4707)
 PHONE.................................631 345-5700
 Steven Summer, *President*
 D Wheeler, *General Mgr*
 EMP: 25 **EST:** 1981
 SQ FT: 20,000
 SALES: 2.7MM **Privately Held**
 WEB: www.powrupscorp.com
 SIC: 3625 5063 Motor controls & accessories; electrical apparatus & equipment

(G-14844)
UNCLE WALLYS LLC
41 Natcon Dr (11967-4700)
 PHONE.................................631 205-0455
 Lou Avignone, *President*
 Jim Magorrian, *Plant Supt*
 Peter Albert, *Opers Staff*
 Frank Sivilli, *Opers Staff*
 Michael Petrucelli, *CFO*
 EMP: 35
 SQ FT: 60,000
 SALES (est): 1.5MM **Privately Held**
 WEB: www.unclewallys.com
 SIC: 2051 Bread, cake & related products
 HQ: Give And Go Prepared Foods Corp
  15 Marmac Dr Unit 200
  Etobicoke ON M9W 1
  416 675-0114

(G-14845)
UNITED BAKING CO INC (PA)
41 Natcon Dr (11967-4700)
 PHONE.................................631 205-0455
 Louis Avignone, *Ch of Bd*
 David Nemer, *Vice Pres*
 Jim Magorrian, *QC Mgr*
 Kim Massa, *Accountant*
 EMP: 140
 SQ FT: 60,000
 SALES (est): 37.8MM **Privately Held**
 SIC: 2052 Cookies

Shokan
Ulster County

(G-14846)
MACK WOOD WORKING
Also Called: General Specialties
2792 State Route 28 (12481-5002)
 PHONE.................................845 657-6625
 Ben Mack, *Owner*
 EMP: 8
 SQ FT: 8,000
 SALES (est): 500K **Privately Held**
 SIC: 2431 Millwork

Shortsville
Ontario County

(G-14847)
GLK FOODS LLC
Curtice Burns Foods
11 Clark St (14548-9755)
P.O. Box 450 (14548-0450)
 PHONE.................................585 289-4414
 Dave Flanagan, *Opers-Prdtn-Mfg*
 EMP: 40
 SALES (est): 6.9MM
 SALES (corp-wide): 52.8MM **Privately Held**
 SIC: 2035 2033 Sauerkraut, bulk; sauerkraut; packaged in cans, jars, etc.
 PA: Glk Foods, Llc
  3912 N Lightning Dr
  Appleton WI 54913
  715 752-4105

Sidney
Delaware County

(G-14848)
AMERICAN BLUESTONE LLC
760 Quarry Rd (13838)
P.O. Box 117 (13838-0117)
 PHONE.................................607 369-2235
 Robert McDuffey, *Mng Member*
 Deborah McDuffey
 EMP: 12
 SALES (est): 1.5MM **Privately Held**
 SIC: 3281 Granite, cut & shaped

(G-14849)
AMPHENOL AEROSPACE FRANCE INC
191 Delaware Ave (13838)
 PHONE.................................800 678-0141
 Gary Anderson, *CEO*
 Ryan Fisher, *General Mgr*
 Rick Olmstead, *Mfg Staff*
 Christopher Sheldon, *Purch Mgr*
 Mario Andrade, *Buyer*
 ▲ **EMP:** 111
 SALES (est): 49.4MM
 SALES (corp-wide): 7B **Publicly Held**
 SIC: 3678 Electronic connectors
 PA: Amphenol Corporation
  358 Hall Ave
  Wallingford CT 06492
  203 265-8900

(G-14850)
AMPHENOL CORPORATION
Also Called: Amphenol Aerospace Industrial
40-60 Delaware Ave (13838-1395)
 PHONE.................................607 563-5364
 Brad Lepoudre, *Business Mgr*
 Harvey Waltersdorf, *Business Mgr*
 Sean Barrows, *Opers Mgr*
 Steven Degraeve, *Opers Mgr*
 Tom Czernecki, *Opers Staff*
 EMP: 345
 SQ FT: 675,000
 SALES (corp-wide): 7B **Publicly Held**
 SIC: 3678 Electronic connectors
 PA: Amphenol Corporation
  358 Hall Ave
  Wallingford CT 06492
  203 265-8900

(G-14851)
AMPHENOL CORPORATION
Amphenol Aerospace Operations
40-60 Delaware Ave (13838-1395)
 PHONE.................................607 563-5011
 Brendan Harder, *Opers Mgr*
 Mark Philpott, *Opers Mgr*
 Paul Moran, *Opers Staff*
 Steve Soldinger, *Opers Staff*
 Richard Barnes, *Engineer*
 EMP: 1500
 SALES (corp-wide): 7B **Publicly Held**
 SIC: 3678 Electronic connectors
 PA: Amphenol Corporation
  358 Hall Ave
  Wallingford CT 06492
  203 265-8900

(G-14852)
DECKER FOREST PRODUCTS INC
New York State Rte 8 (13838)
P.O. Box 205 (13838-0205)
 PHONE.................................607 563-2345
 Floyd Decker, *President*
 Mark Decker, *Vice Pres*
 Carol Decker, *Admin Sec*
 EMP: 5
 SQ FT: 15,000
 SALES (est): 330K **Privately Held**
 SIC: 2411 Logging camps & contractors

(G-14853)
EGLI MACHINE COMPANY INC
240 State Highway 7 (13838-2716)
 PHONE.................................607 563-3663
 Denis Egli, *President*
 Ellen Egli, *Treasurer*
 EMP: 28
 SQ FT: 18,000
 SALES (est): 3.5MM **Privately Held**
 WEB: www.eglimachine.com
 SIC: 3545 3544 Precision tools, machinists'; special dies, tools, jigs & fixtures; molding primary plastic

(G-14854)
REFILL SERVICES LLC
16 Winkler Rd (13838-1056)
 PHONE.................................607 369-5864
 Austin Wilson, *Mng Member*
 EMP: 5
 SALES (est): 487.2K **Privately Held**
 SIC: 2621 Stationery, envelope & tablet papers

(G-14855)
TRI-TOWN NEWS INC (PA)
Also Called: Sidney Favorite Printing Div
74 Main St (13838-1134)
 PHONE.................................607 561-3515
 Paul Hamilton Sr, *President*
 Wiley Vincent, *Vice Pres*
 EMP: 25 **EST:** 1925
 SQ FT: 10,080
 SALES (est): 1.7MM **Privately Held**
 WEB: www.powerofprint.com
 SIC: 2752 2711 Commercial printing, offset; newspapers, publishing & printing

(G-14856)
UFP NEW YORK LLC
13 Winkler Rd (13838-1057)
 PHONE.................................607 563-1556
 James Brennan, *Manager*
 EMP: 45
 SQ FT: 14,988
 SALES (corp-wide): 3.9B **Publicly Held**
 WEB: www.ufpinc.com
 SIC: 2439 Structural wood members
 HQ: Ufp New York, Llc
  11 Allen St
  Auburn NY 13021
  315 253-2758

(G-14857)
UNADILLA SILO COMPANY INC
Also Called: Unadilla Laminated Products
100 West Rd (13838)
 PHONE.................................607 369-9341
 Floyd Spencer, *Manager*
 EMP: 62
 SALES (corp-wide): 8.5MM **Privately Held**
 SIC: 2431 3444 2439 Silo staves, wood; sheet metalwork; structural wood members
 PA: Unadilla Silo Company, Inc.
  18 Clifton St
  Unadilla NY 13849
  607 369-9341

(G-14858)
USA CUSTOM PAD CORP (PA)
16 Winkler Rd (13838-1056)
 PHONE.................................607 563-9550
 Eric T Wilson, *Chairman*
 Marcia Wilson, *Admin Sec*
 ◆ **EMP:** 29
 SQ FT: 20,000
 SALES (est): 7MM **Privately Held**
 WEB: www.memopads.com
 SIC: 2678 2759 2741 Tablets & pads, book & writing: from purchased materials; commercial printing; miscellaneous publishing

Silver Bay
Warren County

(G-14859)
HACKER BOAT COMPANY INC (PA)
8 Delaware Ave (12874-1815)
 PHONE.................................518 543-6731
 Ernest George Badcock III, *Ch of Bd*
 Lynn R Wagemann, *President*
 ▲ **EMP:** 20
 SALES (est): 3.8MM **Privately Held**
 WEB: www.hackerboatco.com
 SIC: 3732 Boat building & repairing

Silver Creek
Chautauqua County

(G-14860)
CHAUTAUQUA WINE COMPANY INC
Also Called: Willow Creek Winery
2627 Chapin Rd (14136-9760)
PHONE.................................716 934-9463
Holly Metzler, *President*
Holly Metzler, *President*
Dawn Ellis, *General Mgr*
EMP: 5 **EST:** 2000
SALES (est): 459K **Privately Held**
WEB: www.willowcreekwinery.com
SIC: 2084 Wines

(G-14861)
EXCELCO DEVELOPMENTS INC
65 Main St (14136-1467)
P.O. Box 230 (14136-0230)
PHONE.................................716 934-2651
Christopher J Lanski, *President*
Douglas A Newman, *Exec VP*
Andy Bouquin, *Senior Engr*
Philip J Azzarella, *CFO*
Paul Rozewicz, *Finance Mgr*
EMP: 37
SQ FT: 40,000
SALES (est): 6.3MM **Privately Held**
SIC: 3728 3731 3429 Aircraft assemblies, subassemblies & parts; shipbuilding & repairing; manufactured hardware (general)

(G-14862)
EXCELCO/NEWBROOK INC
16 Mechanic St (14136-1202)
P.O. Box 231 (14136-0231)
PHONE.................................716 934-2644
Christopher J Lanski, *CEO*
Geoff Rondeau, *General Mgr*
Paul Narraway, *Engineer*
P J Azzarella, *CFO*
Dan Uszacki, *Technology*
EMP: 85 **EST:** 1952
SQ FT: 93,000
SALES (est): 13.4MM **Privately Held**
WEB: www.excelco.net
SIC: 3728 3731 7692 Aircraft assemblies, subassemblies & parts; shipbuilding & repairing; welding repair

Silver Springs
Wyoming County

(G-14863)
MORTON SALT INC
45 Ribaud Ave (14550-9805)
P.O. Box 342 (14550-0342)
PHONE.................................585 493-2511
Matt Ashley, *Project Engr*
Steve Hull, *Human Res Mgr*
Daniel Border, *Branch Mgr*
Marlene Bassett, *Manager*
Josh Tanski, *Info Tech Mgr*
EMP: 12
SALES (corp-wide): 4.2B **Privately Held**
SIC: 1479 Salt & sulfur mining
HQ: Morton Salt, Inc.
   444 W Lake St Ste 3000
   Chicago IL 60606

Sinclairville
Chautauqua County

(G-14864)
CARLSON WOOD PRODUCTS INC (PA)
1705 Bates Rd (14782-9726)
PHONE.................................716 287-2923
William Carlson, *President*
Ivetta Carlson, *Vice Pres*
EMP: 6
SQ FT: 4,000
SALES (est): 1.3MM **Privately Held**
SIC: 2426 2421 Lumber, hardwood dimension; kiln drying of lumber

(G-14865)
CONTAINER TSTG SOLUTIONS LLC (PA)
17 Lester St (14782)
PHONE.................................716 487-3300
Brian Johnson, *Ch of Bd*
EMP: 10
SALES (est): 1.7MM **Privately Held**
SIC: 2834 Solutions, pharmaceutical

Skaneateles
Onondaga County

(G-14866)
ANYELAS VINEYARDS LLC
2433 W Lake Rd (13152-9471)
PHONE.................................315 685-3797
Patti Noceck, *Manager*
James Nocek,
EMP: 13
SQ FT: 5,000
SALES (est): 200K **Privately Held**
SIC: 2084 Wines

(G-14867)
BURDICK PUBLICATIONS INC
Also Called: EB&I Marketing
2352 E Lake Rd (13152-8924)
P.O. Box 977 (13152-0977)
PHONE.................................315 685-9500
Elaina K Burdick, *CEO*
Mary Mahoney, *Vice Pres*
EMP: 6
SQ FT: 1,200
SALES (est): 1MM **Privately Held**
WEB: www.burdickpubs.com
SIC: 2741 Miscellaneous publishing

(G-14868)
CHOHEHCO LLC
78 State St (13152-1218)
PHONE.................................315 420-4624
Vedran Psenicnik,
EMP: 7 **EST:** 2014
SALES (est): 355.4K **Privately Held**
SIC: 2086 Carbonated beverages, nonalcoholic; bottled & canned

(G-14869)
DIGITAL ANALYSIS CORPORATION
716 Visions Dr (13152-6475)
P.O. Box 95 (13152-0095)
PHONE.................................315 685-0760
Richard Pinkowski, *President*
Joseph Pinkowski, *Project Mgr*
Michael Johnson, *Manager*
EMP: 19
SQ FT: 12,000
SALES (est): 4.4MM **Privately Held**
WEB: www.digital-analysis.com
SIC: 3823 Industrial instrmnts msrmnt display/control process variable

(G-14870)
DIVINE PHOENIX LLC
Also Called: Divine Phoenix Books
2985 Benson Rd (13152-9638)
P.O. Box 1001 (13152-5001)
PHONE.................................585 737-1482
Laura Ponticello, *Principal*
EMP: 585
SQ FT: 850
SALES (est): 30K **Privately Held**
SIC: 2731 Book publishing

(G-14871)
G E INSPECTION TECHNOLOGIES LP
721 Visions Dr (13152-6475)
PHONE.................................315 554-2000
Todd Brugger, *Branch Mgr*
EMP: 175 **Privately Held**
SIC: 3829 8734 7359 3651 Physical property testing equipment; testing laboratories; equipment rental & leasing; household audio & video equipment
HQ: G E Inspection Technologies, Lp
   721 Visions Dr
   Skaneateles NY 13152
   315 554-2000

(G-14872)
GENERAL ELECTRIC COMPANY
721 Visions Dr (13152-6475)
PHONE.................................315 554-2000
Melissa Lainhart, *General Mgr*
John Barenys, *Buyer*
Sandra Gonzalez, *Buyer*
Lisa Hryckowian, *Buyer*
Ted Chilek, *Engineer*
EMP: 8
SALES (corp-wide): 122B **Publicly Held**
WEB: www.gecommercialfinance.com
SIC: 3699 3651 3634 Electrical equipment & supplies; household audio & video equipment; electric housewares & fans
PA: General Electric Company
   41 Farnsworth St
   Boston MA 02210
   617 443-3000

(G-14873)
HABA USA
4407 Jordan Rd (13152-9371)
PHONE.................................800 468-6873
Hugh Reed, *Vice Pres*
Alison Barron, *Sales Staff*
Ashley Ware, *Sales Staff*
▲ **EMP:** 6
SALES (est): 66K **Privately Held**
SIC: 3944 Games, toys & children's vehicles

(G-14874)
HABERMAASS CORPORATION
Also Called: T C Timber
4407 Jordan Rd (13152-8300)
P.O. Box 42 (13152-0042)
PHONE.................................315 685-8919
Klaus Habermaass, *President*
Rolf Sievers, *Vice Pres*
Peter Reynolds, *Natl Sales Mgr*
Ashley Ware, *Sales Staff*
Hugh Reed, *Manager*
▲ **EMP:** 12
SQ FT: 150,000
SALES (est): 2MM
SALES (corp-wide): 379.4MM **Privately Held**
SIC: 3944 5092 Mfg Games/Toys Whol Toys/Hobby Goods
PA: Habermaass Gmbh
   August-Grosch-Str. 28-38
   Bad Rodach 96476
   956 492-9601

(G-14875)
HANSON AGGREGATES PA LLC
Rr 321 (13152)
PHONE.................................315 685-3321
Ken Slater, *Plant Mgr*
Phil Wheeler, *Manager*
EMP: 25
SQ FT: 2,160
SALES (corp-wide): 20.3B **Privately Held**
SIC: 1442 1422 Common sand mining; crushed & broken limestone
HQ: Hanson Aggregates Pennsylvania, Llc
   7660 Imperial Way
   Allentown PA 18195
   610 366-4626

(G-14876)
PATIENCE BREWSTER INC
3872 Jordan Rd (13152-9317)
P.O. Box 689 (13152-0689)
PHONE.................................315 685-8336
Patience Brewster Gregg, *CEO*
Holland Gregg, *President*
▲ **EMP:** 10
SALES (est): 5MM
SALES (corp-wide): 37.3MM **Privately Held**
SIC: 3999 Christmas tree ornaments, except electrical & glass
PA: Mackenzie-Childs Llc
   3260 State Route 90
   Aurora NY 13026
   315 364-6118

(G-14877)
SCALE-TRONIX INC
4341 State Street Rd (13152-9338)
PHONE.................................914 948-8117
Carolyn Lepler, *President*
David C Hale, *Principal*
EMP: 38
SQ FT: 5,000
SALES (est): 7.4MM **Privately Held**
SIC: 3596 Baby scales; bathroom scales; weighing machines & apparatus

(G-14878)
TESSY PLASTICS CORP (PA)
700 Visions Dr (13152-6475)
PHONE.................................315 689-3924
Roland Beck, *President*
Greg Levengood, *COO*
Kate Haggard, *Vice Pres*
Michael Adrian, *Materials Mgr*
Colin Goodale, *Opers Staff*
◆ **EMP:** 260
SQ FT: 240,000
SALES (est): 301.6MM **Privately Held**
WEB: www.tessy.com
SIC: 3089 3549 Injection molding of plastics; assembly machines, including robotic

Skaneateles Falls
Onondaga County

(G-14879)
HAND HELD PRODUCTS INC (HQ)
Also Called: Honeywell Imaging and Mobility
700 Visions Dr (13153-5312)
P.O. Box 208 (13153-0208)
PHONE.................................315 554-6000
Kevin Jost, *CEO*
John F Waldron, *Ch of Bd*
Darius Adamczyk, *Chairman*
David Guido, *Vice Pres*
Joseph Hennigan, *CFO*
▲ **EMP:** 500
SQ FT: 120,000
SALES (est): 148.6MM
SALES (corp-wide): 40.5B **Publicly Held**
WEB: www.handheld.com
SIC: 3577 3571 3663 3578 Magnetic ink & optical scanning devices; electronic computers; radio & TV communications equipment; calculating & accounting equipment
PA: Honeywell International Inc.
   115 Tabor Rd
   Morris Plains NJ 07950
   973 455-2000

(G-14880)
HAND HELD PRODUCTS INC
Also Called: Honeywell Scanning & Mobility
700 Visions Dr (13153-5312)
PHONE.................................315 554-6000
EMP: 8
SALES (corp-wide): 40.5B **Publicly Held**
SIC: 3577 Magnetic ink & optical scanning devices
HQ: Hand Held Products, Inc.
   700 Visions Dr
   Skaneateles Falls NY 13153
   315 554-6000

(G-14881)
HONEYWELL INTERNATIONAL INC
700 Visions Dr (13153-5311)
PHONE.................................315 554-6643
Kevin Jost, *President*
EMP: 657
SALES (corp-wide): 40.5B **Publicly Held**
SIC: 3724 Aircraft engines & engine parts
PA: Honeywell International Inc.
   115 Tabor Rd
   Morris Plains NJ 07950
   973 455-2000

(G-14882)
WELCH ALLYN INC
Data Collection Division
4341 State Street Rd (13153-5301)
P.O. Box 220 (13153-0220)
PHONE.................................315 685-4100
Dewey Shimer, *Branch Mgr*
EMP: 1000
SALES (corp-wide): 2.7B **Publicly Held**
SIC: 3841 3577 Diagnostic apparatus, medical; computer peripheral equipment

GEOGRAPHIC SECTION

HQ: Welch Allyn Inc
4341 State Street Rd
Skaneateles Falls NY 13153
315 685-4100

(G-14883)
WELCH ALLYN INC (HQ)
4341 State Street Rd (13153-5301)
P.O. Box 220 (13153-0220)
PHONE..................315 685-4100
Stephen Meyer, *President*
Mike Ehrhart, *Exec VP*
Dan Fisher, *Exec VP*
Janie Goddard, *Exec VP*
Joseph Hennigan, *Exec VP*
◆ **EMP:** 1400
SALES (est): 793.3MM
SALES (corp-wide): 2.7B **Publicly Held**
SIC: 3841 2835 3827 Diagnostic apparatus, medical; otoscopes, except electromedical; ophthalmic instruments & apparatus; blood pressure apparatus; in vitro & in vivo diagnostic substances; optical instruments & lenses
PA: Hill-Rom Holdings, Inc.
130 E Randolph St # 1000
Chicago IL 60601
312 819-7200

(G-14884)
WELCH ALLYN INC
Also Called: Lighting Products Division
4619 Jordan Rd (13153-5313)
P.O. Box 187 (13153-0187)
PHONE..................315 685-4347
William Bolton, *Branch Mgr*
EMP: 1000
SALES (corp-wide): 2.7B **Publicly Held**
SIC: 3841 3641 Diagnostic apparatus, medical; electric lamps
HQ: Welch Allyn Inc
4341 State Street Rd
Skaneateles Falls NY 13153
315 685-4100

Slate Hill
Orange County

(G-14885)
RICHARD ROTHBARD INC
1866 Route 284 (10973-4208)
P.O. Box 480 (10973-0480)
PHONE..................845 355-2300
Richard Rothbard, *President*
Joanna Rothbard, *Admin Sec*
EMP: 9
SQ FT: 1,500
SALES (est): 675.2K **Privately Held**
SIC: 2499 Decorative wood & woodwork

Sleepy Hollow
Westchester County

(G-14886)
MOLECLAR INSGHT PHRMCTCALS INC (HQ)
Also Called: (A DEVELOPMENT STAGE COMPANY)
777 N Broadway Ste 101 (10591-1019)
PHONE..................914 789-2800
Nelson K Stacks, *CEO*
Paul A Looney, *COO*
Norman Lafrance MD, *Senior VP*
John W Babich PHD, *Officer*
EMP: 7 EST: 1997
SQ FT: 35,305
SALES (est): 6.7MM
SALES (corp-wide): 11.7MM **Publicly Held**
WEB: www.molecularinsight.com
SIC: 2834 Pharmaceutical preparations
PA: Progenics Pharmaceuticals Inc
1 World Trade Ctr Fl 47s
New York NY 10007
646 975-2500

(G-14887)
TRADER INTERNTNAL PUBLICATIONS
50 Fremont Rd (10591-1118)
P.O. Box 687, Tarrytown (10591-0687)
PHONE..................914 631-6856
Jean Sudol, *President*
Edward R Sudol, *Corp Secy*
EMP: 6
SALES: 500K **Privately Held**
SIC: 2741 2721 Miscellaneous publishing; periodicals: publishing only; trade journals: publishing only, not printed on site

(G-14888)
VALERIE BOHIGIAN
Also Called: Valian Associates
225 Hunter Ave (10591-1316)
PHONE..................914 631-8866
Valerie Bohigian, *Owner*
EMP: 6
SALES (est): 230K **Privately Held**
WEB: www.valianassociates.com
SIC: 3914 Trophies, pewter

Slingerlands
Albany County

(G-14889)
LONG LUMBER AND SUPPLY CORP
2100 New Scotland Rd (12159-3419)
PHONE..................518 439-1661
Richard L Long Jr, *President*
Robert P Long, *Vice Pres*
EMP: 10 EST: 1945
SQ FT: 10,000
SALES (est): 1MM **Privately Held**
SIC: 2511 2499 5712 5211 Wood lawn & garden furniture; fencing, wood; furniture stores; fencing

(G-14890)
SABRE ENERGY SERVICES LLC
1891 New Scotland Rd (12159-3628)
PHONE..................518 514-1572
Steven D Oesterle, *CEO*
John Y Mason, *Ch of Bd*
Michael Cecchini, *Info Tech Mgr*
Gillian Webster, *Administration*
EMP: 13
SALES (est): 3.6MM **Privately Held**
SIC: 2819 1389 Sulfur chloride; cementing oil & gas well casings

Sloansville
Schoharie County

(G-14891)
FLORIDA NORTH INC
134 Vanderwerken Rd (12160-2211)
PHONE..................518 868-2888
Daniel Nelson, *President*
EMP: 15
SQ FT: 85,000
SALES: 650K **Privately Held**
WEB: www.makarioscondos.com
SIC: 3949 Swimming pools, plastic

Sloatsburg
Rockland County

(G-14892)
CUSTOM EUROPEAN IMPORTS INC
Also Called: Tri State Awnings
100 Sterling Mine Rd (10974-2502)
PHONE..................845 357-5718
Martin Lichtman, *President*
▲ **EMP:** 20
SALES (est): 1.8MM **Privately Held**
SIC: 2394 Canvas & related products

Smithtown
Suffolk County

(G-14893)
A & G HEAT SEALING
1 Albatross Ln (11787-3301)
PHONE..................631 724-7764
George Ciunga, *President*
EMP: 8
SQ FT: 12,000
SALES (est): 790.8K **Privately Held**
WEB: www.agheatsealing.com
SIC: 3089 3565 Plastic processing; packaging machinery

(G-14894)
ANCHOR CANVAS LLC
556 W Jericho Tpke (11787-2601)
PHONE..................631 265-5602
Jon Hansen,
EMP: 6
SQ FT: 8,000
SALES (est): 675.7K **Privately Held**
SIC: 2394 Canvas & related products

(G-14895)
CERTIFIED FLAMEPROOFING CORP
17 N Ingelore Ct (11787-1544)
PHONE..................631 265-4824
Edwards Fallom, *President*
EMP: 6
SALES (est): 436.1K **Privately Held**
SIC: 3251 Fireproofing tile, clay

(G-14896)
DIGITAL ASSOCIATES LLC
50 Karl Ave Ste 303 (11787-2744)
PHONE..................631 983-6075
Vincent RE,
EMP: 8
SALES (est): 247.7K **Privately Held**
SIC: 7372 Publishers' computer software

(G-14897)
DUKE OF IRON INC
1039 W Jericho Tpke (11787-3205)
PHONE..................631 543-3600
Paul Montelbano, *President*
EMP: 6
SQ FT: 8,000
SALES: 1MM **Privately Held**
WEB: www.dukeofiron.com
SIC: 3446 Ornamental metalwork

(G-14898)
EASTEND ENFORCEMENT PRODUCTS
50 Dillmont Dr (11787-1602)
P.O. Box 309, Center Moriches (11934-0309)
PHONE..................631 878-8424
John Koenig, *Owner*
Edityh Koenig, *Manager*
EMP: 5
SALES (est): 339.3K **Privately Held**
SIC: 3559 Ammunition & explosives, loading machinery

(G-14899)
G N R PLASTICS INC
Also Called: G N R Co
11 Wandering Way (11787-1147)
PHONE..................631 724-8758
EMP: 9
SQ FT: 10,000
SALES (est): 760K **Privately Held**
SIC: 3544 3089 Mfg Dies/Tools/Jigs/Fixtures Mfg Plastic Products

(G-14900)
IGAMBIT INC (PA)
1050 W Jericho Tpke Ste A (11787-3242)
PHONE..................631 670-6777
John Salerno, *Ch of Bd*
Elisa Luqman, *Exec VP*
Elisa Lugman, *CFO*
EMP: 6
SQ FT: 1,000
SALES: 23.1K **Publicly Held**
SIC: 7372 Business oriented computer software

(G-14901)
JERIC KNIT WEAR
61 Hofstra Dr (11787-2053)
PHONE..................631 979-8827
Jerry Lobel, *Owner*
EMP: 5
SALES (est): 452.3K **Privately Held**
SIC: 2253 Sweaters & sweater coats, knit

(G-14902)
KANTIAN SKINCARE LLC
496 Smithtown Byp (11787-5005)
PHONE..................631 780-4711
Jonathan Klein,
Richard Klein,
EMP: 5 EST: 2012
SALES (est): 492.4K **Privately Held**
SIC: 2844 Cosmetic preparations

(G-14903)
NATURALLY FREE FOOD INC
35 Roundabout Rd (11787-1822)
P.O. Box 1365 (11787-0896)
PHONE..................631 361-9710
Christine Mitchell, *Principal*
EMP: 6
SALES (est): 429.1K **Privately Held**
SIC: 2099 Food preparations

(G-14904)
PBL INDUSTRIES CORP
49 Dillmont Dr (11787-1635)
PHONE..................631 979-4266
William Loffman, *President*
EMP: 10
SALES: 950K **Privately Held**
SIC: 3499 Fabricated metal products

(G-14905)
PERFECT FORMS AND SYSTEMS INC
35 Riverview Ter (11787-1155)
PHONE..................631 462-1100
Joseph Messana, *President*
Jacquelyn Cully, *Business Dir*
EMP: 15
SALES (est): 1.6MM **Privately Held**
SIC: 2752 Business form & card printing, lithographic

(G-14906)
PRECISION DENTAL CABINETS INC (PA)
900 W Jericho Tpke (11787-3206)
PHONE..................631 543-3870
Peter Loscialpo, *President*
Joseph Pisk, *Vice Pres*
EMP: 13 EST: 1965
SQ FT: 12,000
SALES (est): 2.3MM **Privately Held**
SIC: 3843 2434 1751 Cabinets, dental; wood kitchen cabinets; cabinet building & installation

(G-14907)
PSI TRANSIT MIX CORP
34 E Main St (11787-2804)
P.O. Box 178 (11787-0178)
PHONE..................631 382-7930
Albino Almeida, *President*
EMP: 5
SALES (est): 478K **Privately Held**
SIC: 2951 Concrete, asphaltic (not from refineries); concrete, bituminous

(G-14908)
QUALTRONIC DEVICES INC
130 Oakside Dr (11787-1132)
PHONE..................631 360-0859
Peter A Ferentinos, *CEO*
Steven Ferentinos, *President*
EMP: 18
SQ FT: 3,000
SALES (est): 2.2MM **Privately Held**
SIC: 3571 Electronic computers

(G-14909)
SMITHTOWN NEWS INC
Also Called: North Shore News Group
1 Brookside Dr (11787-3493)
P.O. Box 805 (11787-0805)
PHONE..................631 265-2100
Bernard Paley, *President*
EMP: 32
SQ FT: 7,000

Smithtown - Suffolk County (G-14910)

SALES (est): 1.9MM **Privately Held**
WEB: www.thesmithtownnews.com
SIC: 2711 Newspapers

(G-14910)
T-COMPANY LLC
16 Monitor Rd (11787-1867)
PHONE.................646 290-6365
Mark Grottano, *Mng Member*
Lisa Frizol,
Agatha Grottano,
EMP: 5
SQ FT: 2,100
SALES (est): 400K **Privately Held**
SIC: 2599 Factory furniture & fixtures

(G-14911)
VITAKEM NUTRACEUTICAL INC
811 W Jericho Tpke (11787-3232)
PHONE.................631 956-8343
EMP: 250
SQ FT: 35,000
SALES: 15MM **Privately Held**
SIC: 2023 Mfg Dietary Supplements Products

Smyrna
Chenango County

(G-14912)
JD GRANARY LLC
7 Railroad St (13464)
P.O. Box 12 (13464-0012)
PHONE.................607 627-6294
Mark Justh,
EMP: 5
SALES (est): 139.9K **Privately Held**
SIC: 2048 Livestock feeds

Sodus
Wayne County

(G-14913)
MIZKAN AMERICAS INC
7673 Sodus Center Rd (14551-9539)
PHONE.................315 483-6944
Carlos Mansinho, *Plant Mgr*
Ted Pouley, *Manager*
EMP: 10 **Privately Held**
SIC: 2099 Vinegar
HQ: Mizkan America, Inc.
1661 Feehanville Dr # 200
Mount Prospect IL 60056
847 590-0059

(G-14914)
NYKON INC
Also Called: Ramco Arts
8175 Stell Rd (14551-9530)
PHONE.................315 483-0504
Alice Cuvelier, *Principal*
EMP: 9
SQ FT: 5,000
SALES (est): 867.3K **Privately Held**
WEB: www.nykon.net
SIC: 3651 Music distribution apparatus

(G-14915)
TERMATEC MOLDING INC
28 Foley Dr (14551-1044)
P.O. Box 96 (14551-0096)
PHONE.................315 483-4150
Brad Cuvelier, *President*
EMP: 15
SQ FT: 6,500
SALES (est): 2.5MM **Privately Held**
SIC: 3089 Molding primary plastic

Solvay
Onondaga County

(G-14916)
BERRY GLOBAL INC
1500 Milton Ave (13209-1622)
PHONE.................315 484-0397
David Heigel, *Manager*
Peter Miller, *Manager*
EMP: 178 **Publicly Held**

SIC: 3089 3081 Bottle caps, molded plastic; unsupported plastics film & sheet
HQ: Berry Global, Inc.
101 Oakley St
Evansville IN 47710
812 424-2904

(G-14917)
EASTERN COMPANY
Also Called: Frazer & Jones Division
3000 Milton Ave (13209)
P.O. Box 4955, Syracuse (13221-4955)
PHONE.................315 468-6251
Jeffrey Getman, *Persnl Mgr*
Leonard F Leganza, *Branch Mgr*
EMP: 100
SALES (corp-wide): 204.2MM **Publicly Held**
WEB: www.easterncompany.com
SIC: 3322 Malleable iron foundries
PA: The Eastern Company
112 Bridge St
Naugatuck CT 06770
203 729-2255

(G-14918)
EVENT SERVICES CORPORATION
6171 Airport Rd (13209-9754)
P.O. Box 587 (13209-0587)
PHONE.................315 488-9357
Kevin Jankiewicz, *President*
EMP: 6
SALES (est): 440K **Privately Held**
SIC: 2099 Food preparations

Somers
Westchester County

(G-14919)
GENERAL CINEMA BEVS OF OHIO
Also Called: Pepsi Bottle and Group
1 Pepsi Way Ste 1 # 1 (10589-2212)
PHONE.................914 767-6000
Craig Weatherup, *President*
Jackie Roney, *Finance*
Bobbi Mrazek, *Sales Staff*
Tammy Wilkinson, *Sales Staff*
Kristen Jones, *Manager*
EMP: 1200
SALES (est): 63.4MM
SALES (corp-wide): 63.5B **Publicly Held**
WEB: www.joy-of-cola.com
SIC: 2086 Soft drinks: packaged in cans, bottles, etc.
HQ: Pepsi-Cola Metropolitan Bottling Company, Inc.
1111 Westchester Ave
White Plains NY 10604
914 767-6000

(G-14920)
GRAYHAWK LEASING LLC (HQ)
1 Pepsi Way (10589-2212)
PHONE.................914 767-6000
Saad Abdul-Latif, *CEO*
EMP: 7
SALES (est): 2.1MM
SALES (corp-wide): 63.5B **Publicly Held**
SIC: 2086 7359 Bottled & canned soft drinks; rental store, general
PA: Pepsico, Inc.
700 Anderson Hill Rd
Purchase NY 10577
914 253-2000

(G-14921)
PEPSI BTLG GROUP GLOBL FIN LLC (DH)
1 Pepsi Way Ste 1 # 1 (10589-2212)
PHONE.................914 767-6000
Eric J Ross, *President*
EMP: 6
SALES (est): 2.5MM
SALES (corp-wide): 63.5B **Publicly Held**
SIC: 2086 Carbonated soft drinks, bottled & canned
HQ: Pepsi-Cola Metropolitan Bottling Company, Inc.
1111 Westchester Ave
White Plains NY 10604
914 767-6000

(G-14922)
RICHARD C OWEN PUBLISHERS INC
243 Route 100 (10589-3203)
P.O. Box 585, Katonah (10536-0585)
PHONE.................914 232-3903
Richard C Owen, *President*
Phyllis Morrison, *Office Mgr*
▲ EMP: 11
SQ FT: 5,000
SALES (est): 1.5MM **Privately Held**
WEB: www.rcowen.com
SIC: 2731 Books: publishing only

(G-14923)
SIMPLE BREWER
346 Route 202 (10589-3207)
PHONE.................845 490-0182
Gregory Gates, *Principal*
EMP: 20 EST: 2012
SALES (est): 2.8MM **Privately Held**
SIC: 2082 Malt beverages

South Bethlehem
Albany County

(G-14924)
OLDCASTLE PRECAST INC
100 S County Rte 101 (12161)
PHONE.................518 767-2116
Sheila Connor, *Manager*
EMP: 10
SALES (corp-wide): 29.7B **Privately Held**
WEB: www.oldcastle-precast.com
SIC: 3272 3446 3273 Concrete products, precast; pipe, concrete or lined with concrete; open flooring & grating for construction; ready-mixed concrete
HQ: Oldcastle Precast, Inc.
1002 15th St Sw Ste 110
Auburn WA 98001
253 833-2777

South Colton
St. Lawrence County

(G-14925)
J & S LOGGING INC
3860 State Highway 56 (13687)
PHONE.................315 262-2112
Stephen Poste, *President*
Patricia Poste, *Vice Pres*
Teresa Fisher, *Director*
Jerry Poste, *Director*
EMP: 20
SALES (est): 2.1MM **Privately Held**
SIC: 2411 4212 Logging camps & contractors; local trucking, without storage

(G-14926)
NORTHEASTERN SIGN CORP
102 Cold Brook Dr (13687)
P.O. Box 340 (13687-0340)
PHONE.................315 265-6657
Anne Clarkson, *President*
EMP: 8 EST: 1991
SQ FT: 1,600
SALES (est): 983.3K **Privately Held**
SIC: 3993 Signs & advertising specialties

South Dayton
Cattaraugus County

(G-14927)
BIRDS EYE FOODS INC
Also Called: Comstock Foods Division
Mechanic St (14138)
PHONE.................716 988-3218
Sam Chiavetta, *Branch Mgr*
EMP: 6
SALES (corp-wide): 7.9B **Publicly Held**
SIC: 2037 Vegetables, quick frozen & cold pack, excl. potato products
HQ: Birds Eye Foods, Inc.
121 Woodcrest Rd
Cherry Hill NJ 08003
585 383-1850

(G-14928)
CHERRY CREEK WOODCRAFT INC (PA)
Also Called: Great Impressions
1 Cherry St (14138-9736)
P.O. Box 267 (14138-0267)
PHONE.................716 988-3211
Michael Lord, *Ch of Bd*
Martin Goldman, *President*
Michael Goldman, *Purch Mgr*
EMP: 34
SQ FT: 60,000
SALES (est): 4.4MM **Privately Held**
SIC: 2499 Trophy bases, wood

(G-14929)
COUNTRY SIDE SAND & GRAVEL
8458 Route 62 (14138-9756)
PHONE.................716 988-3271
Jason Rosier, *Manager*
EMP: 10
SALES (corp-wide): 37.6MM **Privately Held**
SIC: 1442 Construction sand mining; gravel mining
HQ: Country Side Sand & Gravel Inc
Taylor Hollow Rd
Collins NY 14034
716 988-3271

South Fallsburg
Sullivan County

(G-14930)
ALLIED WINE CORP
Also Called: Rosedub
121 Main St (12779)
PHONE.................845 796-4160
Moshe Schwartz, *President*
Abe Schwartz, *Vice Pres*
EMP: 10 EST: 1992
SQ FT: 18,000
SALES (est): 291.6K **Privately Held**
SIC: 2084 Wines; brandy & brandy spirits

(G-14931)
MB FOOD PROCESSING INC
5190 S Fallsburg Main St (12779)
P.O. Box 13 (12779-0013)
PHONE.................845 436-5001
Dean Koplik, *President*
EMP: 350
SALES (est): 1.8MM
SALES (corp-wide): 815.7K **Privately Held**
WEB: www.murraychicken.com
SIC: 2015 Poultry slaughtering & processing
PA: M.B. Consulting Group, Ltd.
5190 S Fallsburg Main
South Fallsburg NY 12779
845 434-5050

(G-14932)
MURRAY BRESKY CONSULTANTS LTD (PA)
Also Called: Murray's Chicken
5190 Main St (12779)
P.O. Box P (12779-2015)
PHONE.................845 436-5001
Murray Bresky, *President*
Ellen Gold, *Corp Secy*
Dean Koplik, *Vice Pres*
Ben Levine, *Technician*
EMP: 299
SQ FT: 40,000
SALES (est): 42.7MM **Privately Held**
SIC: 2015 Poultry slaughtering & processing

South Glens Falls
Saratoga County

(G-14933)
AMES ADVANCED MATERIALS CORP (HQ)
50 Harrison Ave (12803-4912)
PHONE.................518 792-5808
Frank Barber, *President*

▲ EMP: 57
SALES (est): 24.9MM
SALES (corp-wide): 32.8MM Privately Held
SIC: 3399 Silver powder; flakes, metal
PA: Ames Goldsmith Corp.
50 Harrison Ave
South Glens Falls NY 12803
518 792-5808

(G-14934)
ARCA INK LLC
30 Bluebird Rd (12803-5707)
PHONE..................................518 798-0100
Robert Chadwick, Mng Member
Wendy Lafountain-Chadwick, Mng Member
EMP: 6
SQ FT: 9,000
SALES (est): 971.5K Privately Held
SIC: 2759 Screen printing

(G-14935)
CASTLE POWER SOLUTIONS LLC
22 Hudson Falls Rd Ste D (12803-5067)
PHONE..................................518 743-1000
Maureen Losito, President
▲ EMP: 14
SQ FT: 3,200
SALES (est): 3MM Privately Held
SIC: 3699 Electrical equipment & supplies

(G-14936)
HEXION INC
64 Fernan Rd (12803-5047)
P.O. Box B (12803)
PHONE..................................518 792-8040
Kathleen Ervine, Manager
Adam Taylor, Maintence Staff
EMP: 20 Privately Held
SIC: 2821 2869 2891 Melamine resins, melamine-formaldehyde; formaldehyde (formalin); adhesives & sealants
HQ: Hexion Inc.
180 E Broad St Fl 26
Columbus OH 43215
614 225-4000

(G-14937)
MDI EAST INC
Also Called: Bates Industries
22 Hudson Falls Rd Ste 6 (12803-5069)
PHONE..................................518 747-8730
Tom Pendergrass, Plant Mgr
Dale Jenks, Engineer
Michael Siano, Engineer
EMP: 50
SALES (corp-wide): 17.3MM Privately Held
SIC: 3089 Injection molding of plastics
HQ: Mdi East, Inc.
6918 Ed Perkic St
Riverside CA 92504
951 509-6918

(G-14938)
NORTHEAST PROMOTIONAL GROUP IN
75 Main St (12803-4706)
PHONE..................................518 793-1024
Deana Endieveri, President
Jim Chamberlin, Vice Pres
Mike Endieveri, Vice Pres
Kindra Chamberlin, Treasurer
Kate Cochran, Representative
EMP: 5
SALES (est): 628.4K Privately Held
WEB: www.nepromo.com
SIC: 3993 7389 Advertising novelties; embroidering of advertising on shirts, etc.

(G-14939)
NORTHEAST STITCHES & INK INC
Also Called: Sperry Advertising
95 Main St (12803-4706)
PHONE..................................518 798-5549
Deana Endieveri, President
Kindra Chamberlin, Corp Secy
James Chamberlin, Vice Pres
Michael Endieveri, Vice Pres
EMP: 34
SQ FT: 20,000
SALES (est): 2.9MM Privately Held
WEB: www.nestitchesink.com
SIC: 2395 2396 Embroidery products, except schiffli machine; automotive & apparel trimmings

(G-14940)
O RAMA LIGHT INC
22 Hudson Falls Rd Ste 52 (12803-5067)
PHONE..................................518 539-9000
John N Potochnak, CEO
Dan Baldwin, Co-Owner
▲ EMP: 20 EST: 2009
SALES (est): 2.6MM Privately Held
SIC: 3577 Computer peripheral equipment

South Hempstead
Nassau County

(G-14941)
ACCESSORIES FOR ELECTRONICS
Also Called: Afe
620 Mead Ter (11550-8011)
PHONE..................................631 847-0158
William J Epstein, President
Peter Wright, Treasurer
EMP: 26
SQ FT: 3,000
SALES (est): 5.4MM Privately Held
WEB: www.afeaccess.com
SIC: 3678 3679 Electronic connectors; electronic circuits

(G-14942)
MIRANDY PRODUCTS LTD
1078 Grand Ave (11550-7902)
PHONE..................................516 489-6800
Ira Breiter, President
Mike Glassman, Treasurer
EMP: 28
SQ FT: 5,000
SALES (est): 3.5MM Privately Held
WEB: www.mirandy.com
SIC: 2842 5087 Industrial plant disinfectants or deodorants; service establishment equipment

South Otselic
Chenango County

(G-14943)
GLADDING BRAIDED PRODUCTS LLC
110 County Road 13a (13155)
P.O. Box 164 (13155-0164)
PHONE..................................315 653-7211
Sparky Christakos, President
Mike Radziwon, Vice Pres
Charles Bishop, VP Prdtn
Rick Burt, Opers Staff
▲ EMP: 40
SQ FT: 85,000
SALES: 11MM Privately Held
WEB: www.gladdingbraid.com
SIC: 2298 Rope, except asbestos & wire; cordage: abaca, sisal, henequen, hemp, jute or other fiber; cord, braided

South Ozone Park
Queens County

(G-14944)
CONTINENTAL LIFT TRUCK INC
12718 Foch Blvd (11420-2824)
PHONE..................................718 738-4738
Giuseppe Donofrio, CEO
▲ EMP: 16
SALES (est): 4.4MM Privately Held
SIC: 3537 Forklift trucks

South Richmond Hill
Queens County

(G-14945)
BUSINESS NEVER STOPS LLC
13404 97th Ave Ste 2 (11419-1616)
PHONE..................................888 479-3111
Sean Burgess, Mng Member
EMP: 8
SALES: 68K Privately Held
SIC: 2741 7334 7313 ; photocopying & duplicating services; electronic media advertising representatives

(G-14946)
MAIZTECA FOODS INC
13005 Liberty Ave (11419-3121)
PHONE..................................718 641-3933
Sixto Reyes, CEO
Carlos Reyes, President
EMP: 40
SQ FT: 10,000
SALES: 3.5MM Privately Held
SIC: 2099 Tortillas, fresh or refrigerated

(G-14947)
SHOP SKY INC
10471 128th St (11419-3011)
PHONE..................................347 686-4616
Andrei Omar, CEO
Faiza Nasroor, Executive Asst
◆ EMP: 13
SALES: 200K Privately Held
SIC: 2844 Depilatories (cosmetic); face creams or lotions; lipsticks

South Salem
Westchester County

(G-14948)
THE CENTRO COMPANY INC
215 Silver Spring Rd (10590-2525)
PHONE..................................914 533-2200
Alan Greene, Ch of Bd
Susan Green, President
EMP: 5
SALES (est): 556.7K Privately Held
SIC: 3061 Mechanical rubber goods

Southampton
Suffolk County

(G-14949)
AMERICAN COUNTRY QUILTS & LIN
Also Called: Judi Boisson American Country
134 Mariner Dr Unit C (11968-3482)
PHONE..................................631 283-5466
Judi Boisson, President
Erin Boisson, Vice Pres
EMP: 8
SQ FT: 4,000
SALES (est): 567.9K Privately Held
SIC: 2395 2269 3269 5023 Quilted fabrics or cloth; linen fabrics: dyeing, finishing & printing; art & ornamental ware, pottery; linens & towels; linens, table; decorative home furnishings & supplies; mail order house; antiques

(G-14950)
BEST MDLR HMS AFRBE P Q& S IN
495 County Road 39 (11968-5236)
PHONE..................................631 204-0049
John Distefano, Ch of Bd
Laureiann Distefano, Vice Pres
EMP: 14
SALES (est): 1.6MM Privately Held
SIC: 2452 Modular homes, prefabricated, wood

(G-14951)
CENTRAL KITCHEN CORP
871 County Road 39 (11968-5227)
PHONE..................................631 283-1029
Robert Grigo, President
Doreen Grigo, Corp Secy
EMP: 10
SQ FT: 4,000
SALES (est): 1.4MM Privately Held
WEB: www.centralkitchenscorp.com
SIC: 2434 5712 1751 5031 Wood kitchen cabinets; cabinet work, custom; cabinets, except custom made: kitchen; cabinet & finish carpentry; cabinet building & installation; kitchen cabinets

(G-14952)
DANS PAPER INC
Also Called: South of The Highway
158 County Road 39 (11968-5252)
PHONE..................................631 537-0500
Jean Lynch, Publisher
Tom Ratcliffe, Publisher
Roy E Brown, Chairman
Jason Deronde, Controller
Allison Bourquin, Sales Staff
EMP: 68
SQ FT: 2,500
SALES: 5.3MM
SALES (corp-wide): 8.9MM Privately Held
WEB: www.danspapers.com
SIC: 2711 Newspapers: publishing only, not printed on site
PA: News Communications Inc
501 Madison Ave Fl 23
New York NY 10022
212 689-2500

(G-14953)
FRONTIERS UNLIMITED INC
Also Called: Homes Land Eastrn Long Island
52 Jagger Ln (11968-4822)
PHONE..................................631 283-4663
James Miller, President
EMP: 8
SQ FT: 1,300
SALES: 1.5MM Privately Held
WEB: www.hamptonshomes.com
SIC: 2721 Periodicals-Publishing/Printing

(G-14954)
GABANI INC
81 Lee Ave (11968-4518)
PHONE..................................631 283-4930
Gabrielle Sampietro, President
Miguel Sampietro, Treasurer
EMP: 6 EST: 1978
SQ FT: 900
SALES (est): 42.6K Privately Held
SIC: 2253 Knit outerwear mills

(G-14955)
HAMPTONS MAGAZINE
67 Hampton Rd Unit 5 (11968-4962)
PHONE..................................631 283-7125
Randy Schindler, President
EMP: 50
SQ FT: 2,400
SALES: 3.5MM Privately Held
SIC: 2721 2791 2752 Magazines: publishing only, not printed on site; typesetting; commercial printing, lithographic

(G-14956)
HAMPTONS MEDIA LLC
Also Called: Hamptons Magazine
67 Hampton Rd Unit 5 (11968-4962)
PHONE..................................631 283-6900
Samantha Yanks, Publisher
Jason Binn,
EMP: 5
SALES: 149.3K
SALES (corp-wide): 41MM Privately Held
SIC: 2721 Magazines: publishing only, not printed on site
HQ: Niche Media Holdings, Llc
257 Park Ave S Fl 5
New York NY 10010
702 990-2500

(G-14957)
MORRIS GOLF VENTURES
Sebonac Inlet Rd (11968)
PHONE..................................631 283-0559
James Morris, Owner
EMP: 25
SALES (est): 1.7MM Privately Held
SIC: 3949 Golf equipment

Southampton - Suffolk County (G-14958)

(G-14958)
PAULPAC LLC
104 Foster Xing (11968-4955)
PHONE..................................631 283-7610
Michela Keszlies,
EMP: 6
SALES: 500K **Privately Held**
WEB: www.paulpac.com
SIC: 2393 Textile bags

(G-14959)
PECONIC IRONWORKS LTD
33 Flying Point Rd # 108 (11968-5280)
PHONE..................................631 204-0323
Patrick Grace, *President*
Thomas Berglin, *Vice Pres*
EMP: 13 **EST:** 1997
SALES (est): 2.4MM **Privately Held**
SIC: 3446 Architectural metalwork

(G-14960)
ROCKWELL VIDEO SOLUTIONS LLC
10 Koral Dr (11968-4307)
PHONE..................................631 745-0582
Adam Cusack,
EMP: 15
SALES: 950K **Privately Held**
SIC: 3999 Manufacturing industries

(G-14961)
SHADE & SHUTTER SYSTEMS OF NY
260 Hampton Rd (11968-5028)
PHONE..................................631 208-0275
EMP: 6
SALES (est): 630K **Privately Held**
SIC: 3442 Louvers, shutters, jalousies & similar items

(G-14962)
SOUTHAMPTON TOWN NEWSPAPERS (PA)
Also Called: Press of Manorville & Moriches
135 Windmill Ln (11968-4840)
PHONE..................................631 283-4100
Joseph Louchheim, *President*
Nick Thomas, *Business Mgr*
Todd Richter, *Opers Mgr*
Paul Conroy, *Sales Mgr*
Angela Velasquez, *Manager*
EMP: 50
SQ FT: 1,500
SALES (est): 2.9MM **Privately Held**
WEB: www.southamptonpress.com
SIC: 2711 2741 Newspapers: publishing only, not printed on site; miscellaneous publishing

(G-14963)
THEORY LLC
98 Main St (11968-4834)
PHONE..................................631 204-0231
EMP: 5
SALES (corp-wide): 19.1B **Privately Held**
SIC: 2337 Suits: women's, misses' & juniors'
HQ: Theory Llc
38 Gansevoort St
New York NY 10014
212 300-0800

(G-14964)
THOMAS MATTHEWS WDWKG LTD
15 Powell Ave (11968-3425)
PHONE..................................631 287-3657
Thomas Matthews, *Branch Mgr*
EMP: 14 **Privately Held**
SIC: 2499 Woodenware, kitchen & household
PA: Thomas Matthews Woodworking Ltd.
225 Ocean View Pkwy
Southampton NY 11968

(G-14965)
THOMAS MATTHEWS WDWKG LTD (PA)
225 Ocean View Pkwy (11968-5523)
P.O. Box 520, Bridgehampton (11932-0520)
PHONE..................................631 287-2023
Thomas Matthew, *President*
EMP: 6
SALES (est): 1.1MM **Privately Held**
SIC: 2499 Woodenware, kitchen & household

Southfields
Orange County

(G-14966)
KARLYN INDUSTRIES INC
16 Spring St (10975)
P.O. Box 310 (10975-0310)
PHONE..................................845 351-2249
Hans Bierdumpfel, *President*
Margaret Bierdumpfel, *Vice Pres*
Joyce Lasalle, *Treasurer*
▲ **EMP:** 15
SQ FT: 10,000
SALES (est): 2.4MM **Privately Held**
WEB: www.karlynsti.com
SIC: 3714 3694 Motor vehicle parts & accessories; spark plugs for internal combustion engines

Southold
Suffolk County

(G-14967)
ACADEMY PRINTING SERVICES INC
Also Called: Peconic B Shopper
42 Hortons Ln (11971)
P.O. Box 848 (11971-0848)
PHONE..................................631 765-3346
Michael Hagerman, *President*
Rita Hagerman, *Vice Pres*
EMP: 6
SQ FT: 4,000
SALES (est): 926.2K **Privately Held**
SIC: 2752 2759 Photo-offset printing; commercial printing

(G-14968)
FUTURE SCREW MACHINE PDTS INC
41155 County Road 48 (11971-5041)
PHONE..................................631 765-1610
Ellen Hufe, *President*
EMP: 10
SQ FT: 2,700
SALES (est): 1.8MM **Privately Held**
SIC: 3599 Machine shop, jobbing & repair

(G-14969)
INTERNODAL INTERNATIONAL INC
54800 Route 25 (11971-4648)
P.O. Box 606 (11971-0606)
PHONE..................................631 765-0037
Rosemary Verrecchio, *President*
Joe Stadler, *Vice Pres*
EMP: 25
SALES (est): 1.4MM **Privately Held**
WEB: www.internodalinternational.com
SIC: 7372 7389 Prepackaged software; design services

(G-14970)
NEW ENGLAND BARNS INC
45805 Route 25 (11971-4670)
P.O. Box 1447, Mattituck (11952-0925)
PHONE..................................631 445-1461
William Gorman, *Owner*
EMP: 22
SALES (est): 1.5MM **Privately Held**
SIC: 2439 Timbers, structural: laminated lumber

(G-14971)
WALLACE HOME DESIGN CTR
44500 County Road 48 (11971-5034)
P.O. Box 181, Peconic (11958-0181)
PHONE..................................631 765-3890
George Wallace, *President*
Rene Lisowy, *Owner*
EMP: 6
SQ FT: 2,400
SALES (est): 839.5K **Privately Held**
SIC: 2211 2511 2512 5713 Draperies & drapery fabrics, cotton; wood household furniture; upholstered household furniture; carpets; window furnishings

Sparrow Bush
Orange County

(G-14972)
ETERNAL LINE
1237 State Route 42 (12780-5042)
PHONE..................................845 856-1999
Marius Winograd, *Owner*
Agnes Winograd, *Co-Owner*
EMP: 2
SALES: 1.2MM **Privately Held**
SIC: 3911 Jewelry, precious metal

Speculator
Hamilton County

(G-14973)
STEPHENSON LUMBER COMPANY INC
Rr 8 (12164)
PHONE..................................518 548-7521
John Shaw, *Manager*
EMP: 5
SALES (corp-wide): 5.9MM **Privately Held**
WEB: www.riversidetruss.com
SIC: 2439 5211 Arches, laminated lumber; millwork & lumber
PA: Stephenson Lumber Company, Inc.
Riverside Station Rd
Riparius NY 12862
518 494-4733

Spencer
Tioga County

(G-14974)
STARFIRE SWORDS LTD INC
74 Railroad Ave (14883-9543)
PHONE..................................607 589-7244
Maciej Zakrzewski, *President*
Sandy Russell, *Vice Pres*
Alexandra White, *Vice Pres*
EMP: 20
SALES (est): 2.5MM **Privately Held**
WEB: www.starfireswords.com
SIC: 3421 Swords

Spencerport
Monroe County

(G-14975)
AZTEC MFG OF ROCHESTER
19 Hickory Ln (14559-2511)
PHONE..................................585 352-8152
James Monsees, *Ch of Bd*
EMP: 7
SQ FT: 5,382
SALES (est): 903.8K **Privately Held**
SIC: 3541 Machine tools, metal cutting type

(G-14976)
BOSS PRECISION LTD
2440 S Union St (14559-2230)
PHONE..................................585 352-7070
Gerd Herrman, *Ch of Bd*
Paul Dugan, *Vice Pres*
Alec Ollies, *Treasurer*
EMP: 60
SQ FT: 45,000
SALES (est): 10.9MM **Privately Held**
SIC: 3444 Sheet metal specialties, not stamped

(G-14977)
BULLET INDUSTRIES INC
Also Called: Coyote Motorsports
7 Turner Dr (14559-1930)
PHONE..................................585 352-0836
Mark Lipari, *CEO*
EMP: 6 **EST:** 2007
SALES (est): 451.8K **Privately Held**
SIC: 3799 7539 Recreational vehicles; machine shop, automotive

(G-14978)
DOLOMITE PRODUCTS COMPANY INC
2540 S Union St (14559-2232)
PHONE..................................585 352-0460
Wally Przybcien, *Principal*
EMP: 16
SALES (corp-wide): 29.7B **Privately Held**
SIC: 2951 Asphalt paving mixtures & blocks
HQ: Dolomite Products Company Inc.
1150 Penfield Rd
Rochester NY 14625
315 524-1998

(G-14979)
IMCO INC
15 Turner Dr (14559-1930)
PHONE..................................585 352-7810
David Demallie, *COO*
Audrey Mair, *Director*
EMP: 47
SQ FT: 25,000
SALES (est): 9.1MM **Privately Held**
SIC: 3089 Injection molding of plastics

(G-14980)
KLEIN REINFORCING SERVICES INC
11 Turner Dr (14559-1930)
PHONE..................................585 352-9433
Mark Kulzer, *President*
EMP: 15
SQ FT: 15,000
SALES (est): 3.7MM **Privately Held**
SIC: 3449 Bars, concrete reinforcing: fabricated steel

(G-14981)
MANUFACTURERS TOOL & DIE CO
3 Turner Dr (14559-1930)
P.O. Box 139 (14559-0139)
PHONE..................................585 352-1080
Douglas Sullivan, *President*
Dan Sullivan, *Vice Pres*
Gail Sullivan, *Office Mgr*
EMP: 5
SQ FT: 10,000
SALES: 300K **Privately Held**
SIC: 3544 Special dies & tools

(G-14982)
ROTATION DYNAMICS CORPORATION
Rotadyne
3581 Big Ridge Rd (14559-1709)
PHONE..................................585 352-9023
Scott Bleier, *COO*
Dave Baldwin, *Plant Mgr*
EMP: 36
SALES (corp-wide): 164.4MM **Privately Held**
SIC: 3069 2796 Rolls, solid or covered rubber; platemaking services
PA: Rotation Dynamics Corporation
1101 Windham Pkwy
Romeoville IL 60446
630 769-9255

(G-14983)
WESTSIDE NEWS INC
Also Called: Suburban News
1835 N Union St (14559-1153)
P.O. Box 106 (14559-0106)
PHONE..................................585 352-3411
Keith Ryan, *Ch of Bd*
EMP: 18
SQ FT: 1,000
SALES (est): 1.4MM **Privately Held**
SIC: 2711 Newspapers: publishing only, not printed on site

GEOGRAPHIC SECTION

Speonk
Suffolk County

(G-14984)
BUNCEE LLC
170 Montauk Hwy Speonk (11972)
PHONE.................................631 591-1390
Claire Cucchi, *COO*
Jared Weintraub, *Sales Dir*
Christopher Del Basso, *Marketing Staff*
Arvind Agarwal, *Manager*
Shafique Arnab, *Prgrmr*
EMP: 10
SALES (est): 969.3K **Privately Held**
SIC: 7372 Prepackaged software

(G-14985)
HENPECKED HUSBAND FARMS CORP
1212 Speonk Riverhead Rd (11972)
PHONE.................................631 728-2800
Raayah Churgin, *Principal*
Jennifer Roberts, *Administration*
EMP: 6
SQ FT: 12,000
SALES (est): 379.5K **Privately Held**
SIC: 2869 Industrial organic chemicals

(G-14986)
JOHN T MONTECALVO INC
1233 Speonk River Head Rd (11972)
P.O. Box 460 (11972-0460)
PHONE.................................631 325-1492
Debbie Timpone, *Branch Mgr*
EMP: 7
SALES (est): 625.3K
SALES (corp-wide): 4.2MM **Privately Held**
SIC: 2951 1611 Asphalt paving mixtures & blocks; surfacing & paving
PA: John T. Montecalvo, Inc.
48 Railroad Ave
Center Moriches NY
631 325-1492

Sprakers
Montgomery County

(G-14987)
BILL LAKE HOMES CONSTRUCTION
188 Flanders Rd (12166-4519)
P.O. Box 105 (12166-0105)
PHONE.................................518 673-2424
William Lake, *President*
Rick Leto, *Marketing Mgr*
Greg Erhardt, *Office Mgr*
EMP: 56
SALES (est): 8MM **Privately Held**
WEB: www.billlakehomes.com
SIC: 2452 Modular homes, prefabricated, wood

Spring Valley
Rockland County

(G-14988)
DELUXE CORPORATION
9 Lincoln Ave (10977-8938)
PHONE.................................845 362-4054
Yakov Breuer, *Branch Mgr*
EMP: 267
SALES (corp-wide): 1.9B **Publicly Held**
SIC: 2782 Checkbooks
PA: Deluxe Corporation
3680 Victoria St N
Shoreview MN 55126
651 483-7111

(G-14989)
EAGLE REGALIA CO INC
Also Called: Abbot Flag Co Div
747 Chestnut Ridge Rd # 101 (10977-6224)
PHONE.................................845 425-2245
Michael Kartzmer, *President*
Norma Kartzmer, *Vice Pres*
▲ **EMP:** 10 **EST:** 1910
SQ FT: 4,000
SALES (est): 730K **Privately Held**
SIC: 2399 3999 2395 3911 Flags, fabric; banners, made from fabric; badges, metal: policemen, firemen, etc.; plaques, picture, laminated; emblems, embroidered; medals, precious or semiprecious metal

(G-14990)
EZ LIFT OPERATOR CORP
Also Called: EZ Lift Garage Door Service
111 S Main St (10977-5617)
PHONE.................................845 356-1676
EMP: 10
SALES (est): 870K **Privately Held**
SIC: 3699 5084 5211 1751 Mfg Elec Mach/Equip/Supp Whol Industrial Equip Ret Lumber/Building Mtrl Carpentry Contractor

(G-14991)
FINAL TOUCH PRINTING INC
29 Decatur Ave Unit 1 (10977-4782)
PHONE.................................845 352-2677
Shmiel Elger, *Chairman*
EMP: 13
SALES (est): 1.3MM **Privately Held**
SIC: 2752 Commercial printing, lithographic

(G-14992)
FROZEN PASTRY PRODUCTS CORP
41 Lincoln Ave (10977-1918)
PHONE.................................845 364-9833
Dov Sandburg, *President*
EMP: 33
SQ FT: 8,000
SALES (est): 3.1MM **Privately Held**
SIC: 2041 Doughs, frozen or refrigerated

(G-14993)
GOLDEN TASTE INC
318 Roosevelt Ave (10977-5824)
PHONE.................................845 356-4133
Rachel Perlmutter, *President*
Rafiel Perlmutter, *Vice Pres*
EMP: 32
SQ FT: 20,000
SALES: 6MM **Privately Held**
SIC: 2099 Salads, fresh or refrigerated

(G-14994)
GUARDIAN BOOTH LLC
29 Roosevelt Ave Ste 301 (10977-7844)
PHONE.................................844 992-6684
Abraham Taub, *Owner*
▲ **EMP:** 10
SQ FT: 15,000
SALES (est): 770.3K **Privately Held**
SIC: 3448 Docks: prefabricated metal

(G-14995)
HOLY COW KOSHER LLC
750 Chestnut Ridge Rd (10977-6438)
PHONE.................................347 788-8620
Gilead Mooseek,
Gabi Harkham,
EMP: 5 **EST:** 2010
SALES: 400K **Privately Held**
SIC: 2013 Snack sticks, including jerky: from purchased meat

(G-14996)
ION-TOF USA INC
100 Red Schoolhouse Rd A-1 (10977-7049)
PHONE.................................845 352-8082
Ewald Niehuis, *President*
Marianne Leotta, *General Mgr*
Alfred Benninghoven, *Treasurer*
EMP: 7
SQ FT: 2,200
SALES (est): 1MM
SALES (corp-wide): 8.2MM **Privately Held**
WEB: www.ion-tof.com
SIC: 3826 Analytical instruments
PA: Iontof Technologies Gmbh
Heisenbergstr. 15
Munster 48149
251 162-2100

(G-14997)
JAY BAGS INC
55 Union Rd Ste 107 (10977-3900)
PHONE.................................845 459-6500
Gitty Rubin, *Principal*
▲ **EMP:** 3
SQ FT: 20,000
SALES: 2MM **Privately Held**
SIC: 2673 Bags: plastic, laminated & coated

(G-14998)
LECHLER LABORATORIES INC
Also Called: Lechler Labs
100 Red Schoolhse Rd C2 (10977-7049)
PHONE.................................845 426-6800
Martin Melik, *President*
Jimmy Varghese, *Research*
EMP: 25 **EST:** 1957
SALES (est): 4.1MM **Privately Held**
WEB: www.lechlerlabs.com
SIC: 2844 5961 Cosmetic preparations; colognes; catalog & mail-order houses

(G-14999)
LIPTIS PHARMACEUTICALS USA INC
110 Red Schoolhouse Rd (10977-7032)
PHONE.................................845 627-0260
Sherin Awad, *CEO*
Dick Klaus, *President*
Jenny Avalos, *Vice Pres*
Luis Vazquez, *Opers Staff*
Maria Belliard, *Purchasing*
▲ **EMP:** 1022
SALES (est): 115.6MM **Privately Held**
WEB: www.liptis.com
SIC: 2834 Pharmaceutical preparations

(G-15000)
LOUIS SCHWARTZ
Also Called: Supreme Leather Products
28 Lawrence St (10977-5038)
PHONE.................................845 356-6624
Louis Schwartz, *Owner*
EMP: 6 **EST:** 1949
SQ FT: 7,500
SALES (est): 220K **Privately Held**
SIC: 2386 Garments, leather

(G-15001)
MASTER ART CORP
131 Clinton Ln Ste E (10977-8918)
PHONE.................................845 362-6430
Tzipprah Austerlitz, *Principal*
▲ **EMP:** 8
SALES (est): 1.1MM **Privately Held**
SIC: 3944 Craft & hobby kits & sets

(G-15002)
MBH FURNITURE INNOVATIONS INC
28 Lincoln Ave (10977-1915)
PHONE.................................845 354-8202
Simcha Greenberg, *Ch of Bd*
EMP: 6
SALES (est): 620.1K **Privately Held**
SIC: 2519 Household furniture, except wood or metal: upholstered

(G-15003)
MEASUPRO INC (PA)
Also Called: Smart Weigh
1 Alpine Ct (10977-5647)
PHONE.................................845 425-8777
EMP: 14
SALES (est): 3.9MM **Privately Held**
SIC: 3596 Weighing machines & apparatus

(G-15004)
PALISADES PAPER INC
13 Jackson Ave (10977-1910)
PHONE.................................845 354-0333
Jochanan Schwaite, *President*
EMP: 6
SALES: 2MM **Privately Held**
SIC: 2621 Parchment paper

(G-15005)
REGAL SCREEN PRINTING INTL
Also Called: Shirt Shack
42 Grove St (10977-4852)
PHONE.................................845 356-8181
Stan Mesnick, *President*
Barbara Mesnick, *Vice Pres*

EMP: 6
SQ FT: 2,200
SALES (est): 789.6K **Privately Held**
SIC: 2759 Screen printing

(G-15006)
REGAL WINDOWS & DOORS LLC
Also Called: Black Millwork
254 Old Nyack Tpke (10977-5741)
PHONE.................................201 934-0100
Michael Rottenberg, *President*
Manny Rosenberg, *Controller*
Charlie Erlewein, *Sales Staff*
EMP: 13
SALES: 2.5MM **Privately Held**
SIC: 2499 2431 Carved & turned wood; moldings, wood: unfinished & prefinished

(G-15007)
RESERVE CONFECTIONS INC
Also Called: Reserve Confections Chocolate
3 Perlman Dr Ste 105 (10977-5281)
P.O. Box 186, Monsey (10952-0186)
PHONE.................................845 371-7744
Juda Fisch, *President*
▲ **EMP:** 11 **EST:** 2014
SALES (est): 1MM **Privately Held**
SIC: 2066 Chocolate

(G-15008)
STRATIVA PHARMACEUTICALS
1 Ram Ridge Rd (10977-6714)
PHONE.................................201 802-4000
Paul V Campanelli, *CEO*
Terrance J Coughlin, *COO*
Michael A Tropiano, *Exec VP*
Mark Jacob, *Manager*
Frances Amendola, *Admin Asst*
EMP: 12
SALES (est): 1MM **Privately Held**
SIC: 2834 Druggists' preparations (pharmaceuticals)

(G-15009)
TRAFFIC LOGIX CORPORATION
3 Harriet Ln (10977-1302)
PHONE.................................866 915-6449
Louis Newman, *CEO*
James Weatherall, *General Mgr*
Ben Cohen, *Treasurer*
Brett Ferrin, *Sales Staff*
▼ **EMP:** 7
SQ FT: 100
SALES (est): 1.2MM **Privately Held**
SIC: 3812 3069 5084 Radar systems & equipment; molded rubber products; safety equipment

(G-15010)
ULTRA CLARITY CORP
3101 Parkview Dr (10977-4979)
PHONE.................................719 470-1010
Goldie Halpert, *CEO*
Samuel Halpert, *Principal*
EMP: 5 **EST:** 2014
SALES (est): 289.2K **Privately Held**
SIC: 3496 5051 Cable, uninsulated wire: made from purchased wire; cable, wire

(G-15011)
UNEEDA ENTERPRIZES INC
640 Chestnut Ridge Rd (10977-5653)
P.O. Box 209 (10977-0209)
PHONE.................................800 431-2494
Bruce Fuchs, *President*
Herman Fuchs, *President*
Richard Caporusso, *Vice Pres*
Mina Fuchs, *Treasurer*
Chris Delia, *Asst Controller*
▲ **EMP:** 110 **EST:** 1967
SQ FT: 58,000
SALES (est): 22MM **Privately Held**
WEB: www.uneeda.com
SIC: 3291 5084 5085 Abrasive products; industrial machinery & equipment; abrasives

(G-15012)
UNIVERSITY TABLE CLOTH COMPANY
10 Centre St (10977)
PHONE.................................845 371-3876
Debra Timco, *President*
▲ **EMP:** 11 **EST:** 1998
SQ FT: 5,000

Spring Valley - Rockland County (G-15013)

SALES (est): 949.1K **Privately Held**
SIC: 2392 Tablecloths: made from purchased materials

(G-15013)
US POLYCHEMICAL HOLDING CORP
584 Chestnut Ridge Rd (10977-5648)
PHONE 845 356-5530
David Cherry, *CEO*
EMP: 22 **EST:** 2012
SALES (est): 4.4MM **Privately Held**
SIC: 2899 Chemical preparations

Springfield Gardens
Queens County

(G-15014)
DUNDY GLASS & MIRROR CORP
12252 Montauk St (11413-1034)
PHONE 718 723-5800
Eric Latin, *President*
Florence Latin, *Treasurer*
Ellen Latin, *Admin Sec*
▲ **EMP:** 25
SQ FT: 17,000
SALES (est): 4.2MM **Privately Held**
WEB: www.dundyglass.com
SIC: 3231 Mirrored glass; furniture tops, glass: cut, beveled or polished

Springville
Erie County

(G-15015)
DELOCON WHOLESALE INC
270 W Main St (14141-1070)
P.O. Box 4 (14141-0004)
PHONE 716 592-2711
Sherwin Lape, *President*
Ryan Beebe, *Sales Staff*
Theresa Chase, *Consultant*
EMP: 15
SALES (est): 2.2MM **Privately Held**
WEB: www.delocon.com
SIC: 2541 5211 Counter & sink tops; lumber & other building materials

(G-15016)
GERNATT ASPHALT PRODUCTS INC
Benz Dr (14141)
PHONE 716 496-5111
Mark Smith, *Vice Pres*
EMP: 7
SALES (corp-wide): 37.6MM **Privately Held**
WEB: www.gernatt.com
SIC: 2951 Asphalt paving mixtures & blocks
PA: Gernatt Asphalt Products, Inc.
13870 Taylor Hollow Rd
Collins NY 14034
716 532-3371

(G-15017)
GRAMCO INC (PA)
299 Waverly St (14141-1055)
P.O. Box 68 (14141-0068)
PHONE 716 592-2845
Robert D Mattison, *President*
Nancy J Human, *Vice Pres*
Torrance H Brooks, *Admin Sec*
EMP: 3
SQ FT: 800
SALES (est): 5.2MM **Privately Held**
WEB: www.gramcoonline.com
SIC: 2048 5999 Feed concentrates; feed & farm supply

(G-15018)
HEARY BROS LGHTNING PROTECTION
11291 Moore Rd (14141-9614)
PHONE 716 941-6141
Kenneth Heary, *President*
EMP: 40
SQ FT: 22,800
SALES (est): 3MM **Privately Held**
WEB: www.hearybros.com
SIC: 3643 Lightning protection equipment

(G-15019)
PEERLESS-WINSMITH INC
172 Eaton St (14141-1197)
PHONE 716 592-9311
Tim Mayerat, *Opers Mgr*
Phil Gott, *Mfg Mgr*
Tom Stahley, *Buyer*
Karen Thrasher, *Buyer*
Cathy Keller, *Purchasing*
EMP: 225
SALES (corp-wide): 223.8MM **Privately Held**
WEB: www.peerlesswinsmith.com
SIC: 3566 5063 Gears, power transmission, except automotive; power transmission equipment, electric
HQ: Peerless-Winsmith, Inc.
5200 Upper Metro Pl # 110
Dublin OH 43017
614 526-7000

(G-15020)
PERFECTION GEAR INC
172 Eaton St (14141-1165)
PHONE 716 592-9310
Kim Neyrett, *Manager*
EMP: 150
SALES (corp-wide): 223.8MM **Privately Held**
SIC: 3566 Reduction gears & gear units for turbines, except automotive
HQ: Perfection Gear, Inc.
9 N Bear Creek Rd
Asheville NC 28806
828 253-0000

(G-15021)
SPRINGVILLE MFG CO INC
8798 North St (14141-9648)
P.O. Box 367 (14141-0367)
PHONE 716 592-4957
Daniel J Schmauss, *President*
Joseph Schmauss, *Shareholder*
Michael Schmauss, *Shareholder*
EMP: 31 **EST:** 1958
SQ FT: 28,000
SALES (est): 7MM **Privately Held**
WEB: www.springvillemfg.com
SIC: 3593 3599 Fluid power cylinders, hydraulic or pneumatic; machine shop, jobbing & repair

Staatsburg
Dutchess County

(G-15022)
CURRANT COMPANY LLC
Also Called: Currantc
59 Walnut Ln (12580-6346)
PHONE 845 266-8999
Greg Quinn,
▲ **EMP:** 5
SALES (est): 540.1K **Privately Held**
WEB: www.currantc.com
SIC: 2026 Yogurt

(G-15023)
DUTCHESS PLUMBING & HEATING
28 Reservoir Rd (12580-5317)
PHONE 845 889-8255
Steven Eckelman, *President*
Maryanne Eckelman, *Vice Pres*
EMP: 5
SALES (est): 420K **Privately Held**
SIC: 2759 Commercial printing

(G-15024)
PROTECTIVE POWER SYSTMS & CNTR
Also Called: AC DC Power Systems & Contrls
2092 Rt 9 G Staatsburg (12580)
P.O. Box 119 (12580-0119)
PHONE 845 721-1875
Andrea Patierno, *CEO*
John Patierno, *Vice Pres*
EMP: 11
SALES (est): 2.7MM **Privately Held**
WEB: www.protectivepowersystems.com
SIC: 3621 Motors & generators

(G-15025)
UNIFUSE LLC
2092 Route 9g (12580-5426)
PHONE 845 889-4000
Jeff Bookstein, *Managing Dir*
Dan Aiello, *Principal*
EMP: 15
SQ FT: 50,000
SALES (est): 2.9MM **Privately Held**
WEB: www.unifuse.com
SIC: 3089 Injection molding of plastics

Stafford
Genesee County

(G-15026)
GENESEE BUILDING PRODUCTS LLC
7982 Byron Stafford Rd (14143)
P.O. Box 747 (14143-0747)
PHONE 585 548-2726
Ronald Wheeler, *Mng Member*
EMP: 11
SQ FT: 20,000
SALES: 4.7MM **Privately Held**
SIC: 3444 Gutters, sheet metal

(G-15027)
HANSON AGGREGATES EAST LLC
5870 Main Rd (14143-9519)
PHONE 585 343-1787
Kelly Kinney, *Office Mgr*
Jeff Curry, *Manager*
EMP: 22
SALES (corp-wide): 20.3B **Privately Held**
SIC: 2951 Asphalt paving mixtures & blocks
HQ: Hanson Aggregates East Llc
3131 Rdu Center Dr
Morrisville NC 27560
919 380-2500

(G-15028)
RJ PRECISION LLC
6662 Main Rd (14143-9554)
PHONE 585 768-8030
Kathleen Johns, *Partner*
Robert Johns,
EMP: 5
SQ FT: 5,300
SALES: 820K **Privately Held**
SIC: 3441 Fabricated structural metal

Stamford
Delaware County

(G-15029)
AUDIO-SEARS CORP
2 South St (12167-1211)
PHONE 607 652-7305
David Hartwell, *President*
Shawn Hartwell, *Vice Pres*
Vincent Pricolo, *Sales Dir*
Erik Kjellquist, *Manager*
David Fox, *Director*
▲ **EMP:** 81 **EST:** 1956
SQ FT: 25,000
SALES (est): 13.1MM **Privately Held**
WEB: www.audiosears.com
SIC: 3661 Telephones & telephone apparatus

(G-15030)
CATSKILL CRAFTSMEN INC
15 W End Ave (12167-1296)
PHONE 607 652-7321
Duncan Axtell, *Ch of Bd*
Gary Hurtibuse, *Safety Mgr*
Henry Cioccari, *Purchasing*
Ken Smith, *CFO*
Cathy Axtell, *Manager*
▲ **EMP:** 55
SQ FT: 94,000
SALES (est): 7.7MM **Privately Held**
WEB: www.catskillcraftsmen.com
SIC: 2434 2499 2511 Wood kitchen cabinets; woodenware, kitchen & household; kitchen & dining room furniture

(G-15031)
MACADOODLES
26 River St (12167-1014)
PHONE 607 652-9019
Michelle Caiazza, *Owner*
EMP: 6
SALES (est): 524.6K **Privately Held**
WEB: www.macadoodles.com
SIC: 2024 Ice cream & frozen desserts

(G-15032)
STONE CREST INDUSTRIES INC
Also Called: Generic Compositors
152 Starheim Rd (12167-1757)
PHONE 607 652-2665
Gerald Stoner, *President*
Ellen Thorn, *CFO*
EMP: 5
SALES (est): 332.7K **Privately Held**
WEB: www.genericcomp.com
SIC: 2791 Typesetting

Stanfordville
Dutchess County

(G-15033)
GALLANT GRAPHICS LTD
242 Attlebury Hill Rd (12581-5635)
PHONE 845 868-1166
Melvin Eiger, *President*
Ralph Brunks, *Vice Pres*
Julian Thorn, *Vice Pres*
Eli Raftis, *Director*
▲ **EMP:** 26
SALES (est): 4.7MM **Privately Held**
WEB: www.gallantgraphics.com
SIC: 2752 2796 2791 2759 Commercial printing, offset; platemaking services; typesetting; commercial printing

Stanley
Ontario County

(G-15034)
GIZMO PRODUCTS INC
2257 County Road 4 Bldg 3 (14561-9528)
PHONE 585 301-0970
Peter Blokhuis, *President*
Lisa Blokhuis, *Info Tech Mgr*
EMP: 8
SALES: 900K **Privately Held**
SIC: 3823 Level & bulk measuring instruments, industrial process

Star Lake
St. Lawrence County

(G-15035)
CLEARLAKE LAND CO INC
Hanks Rd (13690)
PHONE 315 848-2427
Gordon Gardner, *President*
Lynn Gardner, *Treasurer*
EMP: 10
SALES: 900K **Privately Held**
SIC: 2411 Logging

Staten Island
Richmond County

(G-15036)
828 EXPRESS INC
619 Elbe Ave (10304-3412)
PHONE 917 577-9019
Nelson Liu, *President*
EMP: 9
SALES (est): 1.1MM **Privately Held**
SIC: 3443 Containers, shipping (bombs, etc.): metal plate

GEOGRAPHIC SECTION

Staten Island - Richmond County (G-15066)

(G-15037)
A K A COMPUTER CONSULTING INC
1412 Richmond Rd (10304-2312)
PHONE..................................718 351-5200
Alex Kleyff, *Founder*
Eva Kleyff, *Vice Pres*
Leonardo Vasquez, *Prgrmr*
EMP: 5
SQ FT: 1,200
SALES (est): 812.6K **Privately Held**
WEB: www.akaconsulting.com
SIC: 7372 Prepackaged software

(G-15038)
A&B MCKEON GLASS INC
69 Roff St (10304-1856)
PHONE..................................718 525-2152
Charles Bell, *President*
EMP: 5 EST: 1976
SQ FT: 750
SALES (est): 560K **Privately Held**
SIC: 3449 1542 1793 1761 Curtain wall, metal; store front construction; glass & glazing work; architectural sheet metal work

(G-15039)
A/C DESIGN & FABRICATION CORP
638 Sharrotts Rd (10309-1992)
PHONE..................................718 227-8100
Jeff Arcello, *President*
▲ EMP: 5
SALES (est): 828.6K **Privately Held**
SIC: 3441 Fabricated structural metal

(G-15040)
ADVANCE PUBLICATIONS INC (PA)
Also Called: Staten Island Advance
950 W Fingerboard Rd (10305-1453)
PHONE..................................718 981-1234
Samuel I Newhouse III, *President*
Michael A Newhouse, *President*
Steven O Newhouse, *President*
Anthony Deprimo, *Editor*
James Yates, *Editor*
▲ EMP: 100 EST: 1924
SQ FT: 40,000
SALES (est): 5.6B **Privately Held**
WEB: www.advance.net
SIC: 2711 2731 2721 2791 Newspapers, publishing & printing; book publishing; magazines; publishing & printing; typesetting; commercial printing, lithographic

(G-15041)
ALBA HOUSE PUBLISHERS
2187 Victory Blvd (10314-6603)
PHONE..................................718 698-2759
Ignatius Staniszewski, *CEO*
▲ EMP: 25
SALES (est): 1.1MM **Privately Held**
SIC: 2731 Books: publishing only

(G-15042)
ALL SHORE INDUSTRIES INC
1 Edgewater St Ste 215 (10305-4900)
PHONE..................................718 720-0018
Sandor Goldner, *CEO*
Norman Goldner, *President*
Jean Steinmetz, *Manager*
▲ EMP: 10
SQ FT: 5,000
SALES (est): 1.8MM **Privately Held**
SIC: 3679 3677 3699 Electronic circuits; electronic coils, transformers & other inductors; appliance cords for household electrical equipment

(G-15043)
ALL SIGNS
Also Called: Woodside Decorator
63 Bridgetown St (10314-6211)
PHONE..................................973 736-2113
Vincent Iannuzzelli, *Owner*
EMP: 7
SALES: 600K **Privately Held**
SIC: 3993 Electric signs

(G-15044)
ARC TEC WLDG & FABRICATION INC
15 Harrison Ave (10302-1328)
PHONE..................................718 982-9274
Kim R Genduso, *President*
EMP: 5
SALES (est): 673.3K **Privately Held**
SIC: 7692 Welding repair

(G-15045)
ATHLETIC CAP CO INC
123 Fields Ave (10314-5066)
PHONE..................................718 398-1300
Arthur Farkas, *Ch of Bd*
Ira Farkas, *Vice Pres*
EMP: 40
SQ FT: 9,000
SALES (est): 1.2MM **Privately Held**
SIC: 2353 2396 2395 Hats & caps; automotive & apparel trimmings; pleating & stitching

(G-15046)
B & R TOOL INC
955 Rensselaer Ave (10309-2227)
PHONE..................................718 948-2729
William Nobile, *President*
EMP: 6
SALES (est): 567K **Privately Held**
SIC: 3469 Metal stampings

(G-15047)
BANDS N BOWS
34 Fieldway Ave (10308-2930)
PHONE..................................718 984-4316
Ted Mazola, *Principal*
EMP: 5
SALES (est): 296.7K **Privately Held**
SIC: 2339 Scarves, hoods, headbands, etc.: women's

(G-15048)
BARBERA TRANSDUSER SYSTEMS
21 Louis St (10304-2111)
PHONE..................................718 816-3025
Richard Barbera, *Partner*
Katherine Sanfilippo, *Partner*
EMP: 10
SALES (est): 983K **Privately Held**
SIC: 3931 5736 Guitars & parts, electric & nonelectric; musical instrument stores

(G-15049)
BEETINS WHOLESALE INC
125 Ravenhurst Ave (10310-2633)
PHONE..................................718 524-0899
Gamade Perera, *CEO*
EMP: 13
SALES (est): 1.8MM **Privately Held**
SIC: 2679 Paper products, converted

(G-15050)
BILLING BLOCKS INC
147 North Ave (10314-2653)
PHONE..................................718 442-5006
Dan Kuper, *President*
EMP: 10
SALES (est): 338.2K **Privately Held**
WEB: www.billingblocks.com
SIC: 7372 7371 Prepackaged software; custom computer programming services

(G-15051)
BLINDS TO GO (US) INC
2845 Richmond Ave (10314-5883)
PHONE..................................718 477-9523
Bill Forte, *Manager*
EMP: 30 **Privately Held**
SIC: 2591 5719 Window blinds; window furnishings
HQ: Blinds To Go (U.S.) Inc.
101 W State Rt 4
Paramus NJ 07652
201 441-9260

(G-15052)
BLOOD MOON PRODUCTIONS LTD
75 Saint Marks Pl (10301-1606)
PHONE..................................718 556-9410
Danforth Prince, *CEO*
EMP: 7
SALES (est): 494.9K **Privately Held**
WEB: www.bloodmoonproductions.com
SIC: 2741 Miscellaneous publishing

(G-15053)
BORO PARK CUTTING TOOL CORP
106b Wakefield Ave (10314-3624)
PHONE..................................718 720-0610
Vito Rubino, *President*
Steven Bruzese, *General Mgr*
Vincent Bruzese, *Treasurer*
EMP: 21
SQ FT: 10,000
SALES: 1MM **Privately Held**
SIC: 3545 5251 Cutting tools for machine tools; tools

(G-15054)
BRAZE ALLOY INC
3075 Richmond Ter (10303-1303)
PHONE..................................718 815-5757
Princie Sevaratnam, *President*
EMP: 5
SALES (est): 554.8K **Privately Held**
SIC: 3356 Solder: wire, bar, acid core, & rosin core

(G-15055)
BRITISH SCIENCE CORPORATION (PA)
100 Wheeler Ave (10314-4018)
PHONE..................................212 980-8700
David H Kingsley, *President*
Yvonne Kingsley, *Corp Secy*
EMP: 8
SALES (est): 744K **Privately Held**
SIC: 2844 7299 Shampoos, rinses, conditioners: hair; scalp treatment service

(G-15056)
BUD RAVIOLI CENTER INC
Also Called: Pastosa Ravioli
3817 Richmond Ave (10312-3828)
PHONE..................................718 356-4600
Benito Di Rosa, *President*
Lucy Di Rosa, *Vice Pres*
EMP: 6
SQ FT: 3,000
SALES (est): 818.8K **Privately Held**
WEB: www.pastosa.com
SIC: 2099 Food preparations

(G-15057)
C & R DE SANTIS INC
Also Called: Royal Press
2645 Forest Ave Ste 2 (10303-1503)
PHONE..................................718 447-5076
Robert De Santis, *President*
Lucille Chazanoff, *COO*
EMP: 22
SQ FT: 5,000
SALES (est): 83.9K **Privately Held**
WEB: www.royalpress.com
SIC: 2672 2752 Coated & laminated paper; commercial printing, offset

(G-15058)
CABINET FACTORY INC
2333 Highland Blvd (10306)
PHONE..................................718 351-8922
Michael Dellamonica, *President*
EMP: 12
SALES (est): 1.4MM **Privately Held**
SIC: 2434 Wood kitchen cabinets

(G-15059)
CADDELL DRY DOCK & REPR CO INC
Also Called: Caddell Ship Yards
1515 Richmond Ter (10310-1114)
P.O. Box 100327 (10310-0327)
PHONE..................................718 442-2112
John B Caddell, *CEO*
Steven P Kalil, *President*
Cynthia Patelli, *Corp Secy*
Luc Vaval, *Sr Corp Ofcr*
Maritza Castillo, *Human Res Mgr*
EMP: 180 EST: 1903
SQ FT: 100,000
SALES (est): 34MM **Privately Held**
WEB: www.caddelldrydock.com
SIC: 3731 Shipbuilding & repairing

(G-15060)
CALIA TECHNICAL INC
Also Called: Calia Consultants
420 Jefferson Blvd (10312-2334)
PHONE..................................718 447-3928
Anthony Calia, *President*
Robert Santagata, *Vice Pres*
EMP: 6
SALES (est): 650K **Privately Held**
SIC: 3625 8742 Control equipment, electric; training & development consultant

(G-15061)
CARMINE STREET BAGELS INC
Also Called: Bagels On The Square
107 Park Dr N (10314-5702)
PHONE..................................212 691-3041
Joseph Turchiano, *Ch of Bd*
Neil Guy, *President*
EMP: 10
SQ FT: 2,000
SALES (est): 870.7K **Privately Held**
SIC: 2051 Bakery: wholesale or wholesale/retail combined

(G-15062)
CHUTES AND COMPACTORS OF NY
1011 Westwood Ave (10314-4243)
PHONE..................................718 494-2247
EMP: 14
SALES (est): 2.5MM **Privately Held**
SIC: 3444 Sheet metalwork

(G-15063)
COCA-COLA BTLG CO OF NY INC
400 Western Ave (10303-1199)
PHONE..................................718 420-6800
Susan Stavan, *Branch Mgr*
EMP: 12
SALES (corp-wide): 35.4B **Publicly Held**
SIC: 2086 Bottled & canned soft drinks
HQ: The Coca-Cola Bottling Company Of New York Inc
2500 Windy Ridge Pkwy Se
Atlanta GA 30339
770 989-3000

(G-15064)
COFFEE HOLDING CO INC (PA)
3475 Victory Blvd Ste 4 (10314-6785)
PHONE..................................718 832-0800
Andrew Gordon, *President*
David Gordon, *Exec VP*
Erik Hansen, *Exec VP*
Erica Chavez, *Human Res Mgr*
Dorothy Roche, *Director*
◆ EMP: 74
SALES: 77.1MM **Publicly Held**
WEB: www.coffeeholding.com
SIC: 2095 5149 Roasted coffee; coffee, green or roasted

(G-15065)
CONTEMPRA DESIGN INC
20 Grille Ct (10309-1400)
PHONE..................................718 984-8586
James Pelligrino, *President*
Dominique Bifiory, *Corp Secy*
EMP: 6
SQ FT: 4,000
SALES: 800K **Privately Held**
SIC: 2541 1799 Table or counter tops, plastic laminated: showcases, except refrigerated: wood; counter top installation

(G-15066)
CORMAN USA INC
1140 Bay St Ste 2c (10305-4910)
PHONE..................................718 727-7455
Giorgio Mantovani, *Ch of Bd*
▲ EMP: 9
SALES (est): 1.2MM
SALES (corp-wide): 90.4MM **Privately Held**
SIC: 2676 Feminine hygiene paper products
PA: Corman Spa
Via Liguria 3
Lacchiarella MI 20084
029 008-097

Staten Island - Richmond County (G-15067)

(G-15067)
CYCLONE AIR POWER INC
Also Called: Four Wheel Drive
12 Van St (10310-1311)
PHONE..................718 447-3038
Robert J Meeker, *President*
▲ EMP: 9
SALES (est): 1MM **Privately Held**
WEB: www.cycloneair.com
SIC: 3599 3563 7539 Machine shop, jobbing & repair; air & gas compressors; automotive repair shops

(G-15068)
DI DOMENICO PACKAGING CO INC
304 Bertram Ave (10312-5200)
PHONE..................718 727-5454
Vincent A Di Domenico, *President*
Michael A Di Domenico, *President*
Steven M Di Domenico, *Vice Pres*
EMP: 6
SQ FT: 21,000
SALES (est): 1.2MM **Privately Held**
SIC: 2631 3089 Folding boxboard; setup boxboard; blister or bubble formed packaging, plastic

(G-15069)
DIMARZIO INC
1388 Richmond Ter (10310-1115)
P.O. Box 100387 (10310-0387)
PHONE..................718 442-6655
Lawrence Dimarzio, *President*
Steven Blucher II, *Vice Pres*
Marina Levit, *Export Mgr*
Louis Butera, *Engineer*
Marie Reagan, *Sales Staff*
▲ EMP: 30
SQ FT: 2,000
SALES (est): 4.9MM **Privately Held**
WEB: www.dimarzio.com
SIC: 3931 Guitars & parts, electric & non-electric

(G-15070)
DOUG LAMBERTSON OD
2555 Richmond Ave Ste 4 (10314-5848)
PHONE..................718 698-9300
Doug Lambertson, *Principal*
EMP: 5
SALES (est): 132.3K **Privately Held**
SIC: 3851 Ophthalmic goods

(G-15071)
E I DU PONT DE NEMOURS & CO
10 Teleport Dr (10311-1001)
PHONE..................718 761-0043
Jennifer Dupont, *Branch Mgr*
EMP: 182
SALES (corp-wide): 62.4B **Publicly Held**
SIC: 2879 Agricultural chemicals
HQ: E. I. Du Pont De Nemours And Company
974 Centre Rd
Wilmington DE 19805
302 774-1000

(G-15072)
EAG ELECTRIC INC
496 Mosel Ave (10304-1621)
PHONE..................201 376-5103
Christopher Todd, *Vice Pres*
EMP: 6
SALES: 500K **Privately Held**
SIC: 3534 Elevators & moving stairways

(G-15073)
EASTERN ENTERPRISE CORP
Also Called: Vinyl Tech Window
465 Bay St Ste 2 (10304-3842)
PHONE..................718 727-8600
Al Gargiulo Jr, *President*
Mary Waller, *Manager*
EMP: 15
SALES (est): 1.6MM **Privately Held**
SIC: 3089 Windows, plastic

(G-15074)
ENVIRO SERVICE & SUPPLY CORP
45b Marble Loop (10309-1326)
PHONE..................347 838-6500
Dom Guercio, *President*
Christopher Lorippo, *Vice Pres*
EMP: 10
SALES (est): 1.1MM **Privately Held**
SIC: 2842 2869 2841 Specialty cleaning preparations; sanitation preparations, disinfectants & deodorants; disinfectants; household or industrial plant; industrial organic chemicals; soap & other detergents

(G-15075)
F & D SERVICES INC
Also Called: F & D Printing
34 E Augusta Ave (10308-1323)
PHONE..................718 984-1635
Frank Sisino, *President*
Donald Marcus, *Vice Pres*
EMP: 14
SQ FT: 2,400
SALES (est): 1.2MM **Privately Held**
SIC: 2752 Letters, circular or form: lithographed; commercial printing, offset

(G-15076)
FEDEX OFFICE & PRINT SVCS INC
2456 Richmond Ave Ste C (10314-5804)
PHONE..................718 982-5223
Sandy Sneiderman, *Manager*
Julee Cruz, *Manager*
EMP: 6
SALES (corp-wide): 65.4B **Publicly Held**
WEB: www.kinkos.com
SIC: 2759 5099 7334 Commercial printing; signs, except electric; photocopying & duplicating services
HQ: Fedex Office And Print Services, Inc.
7900 Legacy Dr
Plano TX 75024
469 980-3000

(G-15077)
GANGI DISTRIBUTORS INC
Also Called: Snapple Distributors
135 Mcclean Ave (10305-4655)
PHONE..................718 442-5745
Santo Spallina, *President*
EMP: 12
SQ FT: 5,000
SALES (est): 890K **Privately Held**
SIC: 2086 Bottled & canned soft drinks

(G-15078)
GENERAL TRADE MARK LA
31 Hylan Blvd Apt 14c (10305-2079)
PHONE..................718 979-7261
Richard Capuozzo, *President*
Virginia Kruse, *Corp Secy*
EMP: 30 EST: 1924
SQ FT: 20,000
SALES (est): 3.3MM **Privately Held**
WEB: www.incrediblelabels.com
SIC: 2759 2671 Commercial Printing Mfg Packaging Paper/Film

(G-15079)
GLENDA INC
Also Called: Victory Sports
1732 Victory Blvd (10314-3510)
PHONE..................718 442-8981
George Siller, *President*
Glenda Siller, *Corp Secy*
EMP: 5
SQ FT: 2,500
SALES: 500K **Privately Held**
SIC: 2395 5941 Emblems, embroidered; sporting goods & bicycle shops

(G-15080)
GOTTLIEB SCHWARTZ FAMILY
724 Collfield Ave (10314-4253)
PHONE..................718 761-2010
Michael Gottlieb, *Owner*
EMP: 50 EST: 1973
SALES: 203.3K **Privately Held**
SIC: 3444 Mfg Sheet Metalwork

(G-15081)
GRADO GROUP INC
66 Willow Ave (10305-1829)
PHONE..................718 556-4200
Richard Grado, *President*
EMP: 7 EST: 2000
SQ FT: 2,900
SALES (est): 810.9K **Privately Held**
SIC: 2759 Advertising literature: printing

(G-15082)
GRAPHIC SIGNS & AWNINGS LTD
165 Industrial Loop Ste 1 (10309-1109)
PHONE..................718 227-6000
Mike Demarco, *Vice Pres*
EMP: 5
SALES: 355K **Privately Held**
SIC: 3993 5999 Signs, not made in custom sign painting shops; awnings

(G-15083)
GREAT ATL PR-CAST CON STATUARY
225 Ellis St (10307-1128)
PHONE..................718 948-5677
Frank Fresca, *President*
EMP: 4
SQ FT: 5,000
SALES: 4MM **Privately Held**
SIC: 3272 Concrete products

(G-15084)
HEINZ MR
146 Melvin Ave (10314-4748)
PHONE..................718 761-3997
Jaclyn Heinz, *Principal*
EMP: 6
SALES (est): 275.5K **Privately Held**
SIC: 2099 Food preparations

(G-15085)
HENRY MORGAN
Also Called: Pensrus
433 Tennyson Dr (10312-6545)
P.O. Box 90219 (10309-0219)
PHONE..................718 317-5013
Henry Morgan, *Owner*
Christine Voltaggio, *Sls & Mktg Exec*
Sandy Aubry, *Sales Staff*
Amanda Carbone, *Technology*
Jamie Scianna, *Graphic Designe*
EMP: 11
SALES: 5MM **Privately Held**
WEB: www.pensrus.com
SIC: 3951 Pens & mechanical pencils

(G-15086)
HOMESELL INC
4010 Hylan Blvd (10308-3331)
PHONE..................718 514-0346
Frank Lopa, *CEO*
Paul Lopa, *General Mgr*
Tracy Hardyal, *Admin Sec*
EMP: 10
SQ FT: 1,200
SALES (est): 620K **Privately Held**
WEB: www.homesell.com
SIC: 2721 Magazines: publishing & printing

(G-15087)
I D TEL CORP
Also Called: Metro Tel Communications
55 Canal St (10304-3809)
PHONE..................718 876-6000
Anthony Giammanco, *President*
Edward Pavia, *Vice Pres*
Steven Giammanco, *Technical Mgr*
Barbara Syracuse, *Sales Staff*
▲ EMP: 12
SQ FT: 4,000
SALES: 1MM **Privately Held**
SIC: 3661 Telephones & telephone apparatus

(G-15088)
IADC INC
845 Father Capodanno Blvd (10305-4039)
PHONE..................718 238-0623
EMP: 10
SALES (est): 690K **Privately Held**
SIC: 3089 Mfg Plastic Products

(G-15089)
IMAGES SI INC
Also Called: Images Scientific Instruments
109 Woods Of Arden Rd (10312-5049)
PHONE..................718 966-3694
John Iovine, *President*
Melissa Serao, *Office Mgr*
◆ SALES: 1MM **Privately Held**
WEB: www.imagesco.com
SIC: 3829 Measuring & controlling devices

(G-15090)
INFINITE SOFTWARE SOLUTIONS
Also Called: Md-Reports
1110 South Ave Ste 303 (10314-3411)
PHONE..................718 982-1315
Srikanth Gosike, *President*
Hari Gandham, *Vice Pres*
Sagarika Ramanan, *Sales Executive*
EMP: 12
SALES (est): 1.6MM **Privately Held**
WEB: www.infinitesoftsol.com
SIC: 3695 5045 Computer software tape & disks: blank, rigid & floppy; computer software

(G-15091)
ISLAND STAIRS CORP
178 Industrial Loop (10309-1145)
PHONE..................347 645-0560
Vassili Lijnev, *President*
EMP: 6
SQ FT: 5,000
SALES (est): 484.5K **Privately Held**
WEB: www.islandstairs.com
SIC: 2431 Staircases & stairs, wood

(G-15092)
ITTS INDUSTRIAL INC
165 Industrial Loop Ste C (10309-1109)
PHONE..................718 605-6934
Harvey Itts, *CEO*
Felix Tricoche, *Vice Pres*
▲ EMP: 8
SQ FT: 8,000
SALES (est): 1.4MM **Privately Held**
SIC: 3354 Aluminum extruded products

(G-15093)
J T PRINTING 21
165 Industrial Loop Ste E (10309-1109)
PHONE..................718 484-3939
EMP: 7
SALES (est): 140.1K **Privately Held**
SIC: 2759 Publication printing

(G-15094)
J V HARING & SON
Also Called: Haring, J V & Son
1277 Clove Rd Ste 2 (10301-4339)
PHONE..................718 720-1947
Connie Mauro, *President*
EMP: 10
SQ FT: 1,000
SALES (est): 760K **Privately Held**
SIC: 2752 Commercial printing, lithographic

(G-15095)
JMS ICES INC
Also Called: Ralph's Ices
501 Port Richmond Ave (10302-1720)
PHONE..................718 448-0853
Michael Scolaro, *President*
Larry Silvestro, *Corp Secy*
John Scolaro, *Vice Pres*
EMP: 15
SQ FT: 5,000
SALES (est): 3.6MM **Privately Held**
SIC: 2024 Ices, flavored (frozen dessert)

(G-15096)
JOSEPH A FILIPPAZZO SOFTWARE
106 Lovell Ave (10314-4905)
PHONE..................718 987-1626
EMP: 5 EST: 2010
SALES (est): 230K **Privately Held**
SIC: 7372 Prepackaged Software Services

(G-15097)
JOSEPH FEDELE
Also Called: Rainbow Custom Counter Tops
1950b Richmond Ter (10302-1206)
PHONE..................718 448-3658
Joseph Fedele, *Owner*
Rachel Fedele, *Office Mgr*
EMP: 6
SQ FT: 5,000
SALES (est): 580K **Privately Held**
SIC: 2541 5211 5031 1799 Counter & sink tops; cabinets, lockers & shelving; cabinets, kitchen; kitchen cabinets; counter top installation

GEOGRAPHIC SECTION

Staten Island - Richmond County (G-15129)

(G-15098)
KLEEN STIK INDUSTRIES INC
44 Lenzie St (10312-6118)
PHONE.....................718 984-5031
Edwin Wallace, President
Rosalie Wallace, Admin Sec
▲ EMP: 17
SQ FT: 20,000
SALES (est): 1.8MM Privately Held
WEB: www.kleenstik.net
SIC: 2672 Tape, pressure sensitive: made from purchased materials

(G-15099)
LAROSA CUPCAKES
314 Lake Ave (10303-2610)
PHONE.....................347 866-3920
EMP: 8
SALES (est): 437.2K Privately Held
SIC: 2051 Bread, cake & related products

(G-15100)
LASER AND VARICOSE VEIN TRTMNT
500 Seaview Ave Ste 240 (10305-3403)
PHONE.....................718 667-1777
Inam Haq, Principal
EMP: 8
SALES (est): 975K Privately Held
SIC: 3845 Laser systems & equipment, medical

(G-15101)
LOOBRICA INTERNATIONAL CORP
41 Darnell Ln (10309-1933)
PHONE.....................347 997-0296
Marshall Weinberg, Principal
▲ EMP: 8 EST: 2012
SALES (est): 960K Privately Held
SIC: 2992 8733 Lubricating oils & greases; scientific research agency

(G-15102)
M & L STEEL & ORNAMENTAL IRON
27 Housman Ave (10303-2701)
PHONE.....................718 816-8660
Lubomir P Svoboda, President
▲ EMP: 14
SALES (est): 3.1MM Privately Held
SIC: 3441 1791 Fabricated structural metal; iron work, structural

(G-15103)
MAXINE DENKER INC (PA)
Also Called: Tokens
212 Manhattan St (10307-1805)
PHONE.....................212 689-1440
Maxine Denker, President
Carla Elson, Vice Pres
EMP: 1
SALES (est): 1.2MM Privately Held
SIC: 3911 3965 Jewelry, precious metal; buckles & buckle parts; hair curlers

(G-15104)
MAY SHIP REPAIR CONTG CORP
3075 Richmond Ter Ste 3 (10303-1300)
PHONE.....................718 442-9700
Mohamed M Adam, President
Joseph Adam, Foreman/Supr
Sajira Premabandu, Accountant
Angel Heredia, Supervisor
▲ EMP: 45
SQ FT: 1,800
SALES (est): 9.9MM Privately Held
WEB: www.mayship.com
SIC: 3731 3732 Shipbuilding & repairing; boat building & repairing

(G-15105)
MILANO GRANITE AND MARBLE CORP
3521 Victory Blvd (10314-6763)
PHONE.....................718 477-7200
Joseph Moreale, President
EMP: 12
SALES (est): 1.7MM Privately Held
SIC: 3272 Art marble, concrete

(G-15106)
MORAN SHIPYARD CORPORATION (DH)
2015 Richmond Ter (10302-1298)
PHONE.....................718 981-5600
Malcolm W McLeod, President
Peter Keyes, Vice Pres
Brian Burtner, Purchasing
Lee Christensen, Treasurer
Joseph De'angelo, Treasurer
▲ EMP: 187
SQ FT: 26,400
SALES (est): 10.5MM Privately Held
SIC: 3731 Shipbuilding & repairing
HQ: Moran Towing Corporation
50 Locust Ave Ste 10
New Canaan CT 06840
203 442-2800

(G-15107)
NEWSPAPER DELIVERY SOLUTIONS
309 Bradley Ave (10314-5154)
PHONE.....................718 370-1111
Peter Priolo, CEO
EMP: 5 EST: 2011
SALES (est): 235.2K Privately Held
SIC: 2711 Newspapers

(G-15108)
NORTH AMERICAN DF INC (PA)
4591 Hylan Blvd (10312-6405)
PHONE.....................718 698-2500
Chrissy Mazzola, President
EMP: 8
SQ FT: 5,000
SALES (est): 2MM Privately Held
SIC: 2759 Advertising literature: printing

(G-15109)
NORTH AMERICAN MFG ENTPS INC (PA)
Also Called: Mht Lighting
1961 Richmond Ter (10302-1201)
PHONE.....................718 524-4370
Thomas Spinelli, Ch of Bd
▲ EMP: 32 EST: 2009
SQ FT: 56,000
SALES (est): 3.9MM Privately Held
SIC: 3646 Commercial indusl & institutional electric lighting fixtures

(G-15110)
NORTH AMERICAN MFG ENTPS INC
1961 Richmond Ter (10302-1201)
PHONE.....................718 524-4370
Joe Scalice, Director
EMP: 15
SALES (corp-wide): 3.9MM Privately Held
SIC: 3646 Commercial indusl & institutional electric lighting fixtures
PA: North American Manufacturing Enterprises, Inc.
1961 Richmond Ter
Staten Island NY 10302
718 524-4370

(G-15111)
NORTH EAST FUEL GROUP INC
51 Stuyvesant Ave (10312-3721)
PHONE.....................718 984-6774
Richard D Auria, Principal
EMP: 6
SALES (est): 670.9K Privately Held
SIC: 2869 Fuels

(G-15112)
NORTHEASTERN FUEL CORP
51 Stuyvesant Ave (10312-3721)
PHONE.....................917 560-6241
Richard Dauria, Principal
EMP: 6
SALES (est): 832.9K Privately Held
SIC: 2869 Fuels

(G-15113)
OH HOW CUTE INC
38 Androvette St (10309-1302)
PHONE.....................347 838-6031
Margaret Delia, President
EMP: 6
SQ FT: 800
SALES: 80K Privately Held
SIC: 2064 5199 5092 5145 Cake ornaments, confectionery; gifts & novelties; balloons, novelty; candy

(G-15114)
PHOTOGRAVE CORPORATION
Also Called: Www.picturesongold.com
1140 S Railroad Ave (10306-3371)
PHONE.....................718 667-4825
Bernard Schifter, CEO
Daniel Schifter, President
Frank Mongelluzzo, Graphic Designe
▲ EMP: 23
SQ FT: 3,000
SALES (est): 10.5MM Privately Held
WEB: www.photograve.com
SIC: 3911 Jewelry, precious metal

(G-15115)
PIAZZAS ICE CREAM ICE HSE INC
41 Housman Ave (10303-2701)
PHONE.....................718 818-8811
Salvatore J Piazz, Ch of Bd
Sam Conte, Manager
EMP: 16 EST: 2010
SALES (est): 2.5MM Privately Held
SIC: 2024 Ice cream, bulk

(G-15116)
PLAYFITNESS CORP
27 Palisade St (10305-4711)
PHONE.....................917 497-5443
Pavel Asanov, CEO
EMP: 5
SALES (est): 366.4K Privately Held
SIC: 7372 7999 7389 Educational computer software; physical fitness instruction;

(G-15117)
PORT AUTHORITY OF NY & NJ
2777 Goethals Rd N Fl 2 (10303-1107)
PHONE.....................718 390-2534
Jerry Deltufo, Manager
EMP: 90
SALES (corp-wide): 4.8B Privately Held
WEB: www.portnynj.com
SIC: 3441 Bridge sections, prefabricated highway
PA: The Port Authority Of New York & New Jersey
4 World Trade Ctr 150
New York NY 10007
212 435-7000

(G-15118)
POWER METRICS INTL INC
1961 Richmond Ter (10302-1201)
PHONE.....................718 524-4370
Thomas Spinelli, President
EMP: 15
SALES (est): 1.5MM Privately Held
SIC: 3699 Electrical equipment & supplies

(G-15119)
PREPARATORY MAGAZINE GROUP
1200 South Ave Ste 202 (10314-3424)
PHONE.....................718 761-4800
Luciano Rammairone, President
Gina Biancardi, President
EMP: 55
SQ FT: 9,000
SALES (est): 2.5MM Privately Held
SIC: 2721 Magazines: publishing only, not printed on site

(G-15120)
QPS DIE CUTTERS FINISHERS CORP
140 Alverson Ave (10309-1776)
PHONE.....................718 966-1811
Eva Choina, President
Semion Goldsman, Vice Pres
EMP: 42
SQ FT: 35,000
SALES (est): 3.5MM Privately Held
SIC: 3999 Advertising display products

(G-15121)
R & L PRESS INC
896 Forest Ave (10310-2413)
PHONE.....................718 447-8557
Ron Patterson, President
EMP: 5
SQ FT: 4,000
SALES (est): 776.8K Privately Held
SIC: 2752 Promotional printing, lithographic; commercial printing, offset

(G-15122)
R & L PRESS OF SI INC
Also Called: Luke's Copy Shop
2461 Hylan Blvd (10306-3146)
PHONE.....................718 667-3258
Luke Callas, President
Kim Catanese, Manager
EMP: 3
SQ FT: 1,200
SALES: 2.3MM Privately Held
SIC: 2752 7334 Commercial printing, offset; photocopying & duplicating services

(G-15123)
RALPHS FAMOUS ITALIAN ICES
4212c Hylan Blvd (10308-3314)
PHONE.....................718 605-5052
Ray Longo, Owner
EMP: 5
SALES (est): 161.4K Privately Held
SIC: 2024 5143 Ice cream & frozen desserts; ice cream & ices

(G-15124)
RAMHOLTZ PUBLISHING INC
Also Called: Collegebound Teen Magazine
1200 South Ave Ste 202 (10314-3424)
PHONE.....................718 761-4800
Luciano Rammairone, CEO
Gina Biancardi, Vice Pres
EMP: 60
SQ FT: 10,000
SALES (est): 5.5MM Privately Held
SIC: 2721 Magazines: publishing only, not printed on site

(G-15125)
RD2 CONSTRUCTION & DEM LLC
63 Trossach Rd (10304-2131)
PHONE.....................718 980-1650
Peter Dagostino,
EMP: 15
SALES (est): 2.2MM Privately Held
SIC: 1442 Construction sand & gravel

(G-15126)
REEBOK INTERNATIONAL LTD
2655 Richmond Ave (10314-5821)
PHONE.....................718 370-0471
EMP: 205
SALES (corp-wide): 25B Privately Held
SIC: 3149 Athletic shoes, except rubber or plastic
HQ: Reebok International Ltd.
25 Drydock Ave Ste 110e
Boston MA 02210
781 401-5000

(G-15127)
REMSEN FUEL INC
4668 Amboy Rd (10312-4150)
PHONE.....................718 984-9551
Natha Singh, President
EMP: 6 EST: 2012
SALES (est): 595.4K Privately Held
SIC: 2869 Fuels

(G-15128)
REYNOLDS SHIPYARD CORPORATION
200 Edgewater St (10305-4996)
P.O. Box 50010 (10305-0010)
PHONE.....................718 981-2800
Michael Reynolds, President
▲ EMP: 10
SQ FT: 30,000
SALES (est): 1.3MM Privately Held
SIC: 3731 Cargo vessels, building & repairing; tugboats, building & repairing; barges, building & repairing; scows, building & repairing

(G-15129)
RGM SIGNS INC
Also Called: Blue Boy
1234 Castleton Ave (10310-1717)
PHONE.....................718 442-0598

Staten Island - Richmond County (G-15130)

Ron Malanga, *President*
EMP: 6
SQ FT: 684
SALES (est): 646.8K **Privately Held**
WEB: www.rgmsigns.com
SIC: 3993 2752 5999 1799 Signs, not made in custom sign painting shops; offset & photolithographic printing; awnings; sign installation & maintenance

(G-15130)
RICHMOND READY MIX CORP
328 Park St (10306-1859)
PHONE 917 731-8400
EMP: 8 EST: 2015
SALES (est): 814.7K **Privately Held**
SIC: 3273 Ready-mixed concrete

(G-15131)
RICHMOND READY MIX CORP II
291 Chelsea Rd (10314-7112)
PHONE 917 731-8400
Joe Garry, *President*
Scot D'Arco, *Vice Pres*
EMP: 28 EST: 2015
SALES: 15MM **Privately Held**
SIC: 3273 Ready-mixed concrete

(G-15132)
SCARA-MIX INC
2537 Richmond Ter (10303-2390)
P.O. Box 30313 (10303-0313)
PHONE 718 442-7357
Philip Castellano, *President*
EMP: 45 EST: 1981
SQ FT: 17,000
SALES (est): 5.2MM **Privately Held**
SIC: 3273 Mfg Ready-Mixed Concrete

(G-15133)
SEA BREEZE FISH & SEAFOOD OF S (PA)
240 Page Ave (10307-1170)
PHONE 718 984-0447
Paula Dimino, *Ch of Bd*
EMP: 15
SALES (est): 3MM **Privately Held**
SIC: 2092 5421 Seafoods, frozen: prepared; fish markets

(G-15134)
SECOND GENERATION WOOD STAIRS
2581 Richmond Ter Ste 3 (10303-2323)
PHONE 718 370-0085
EMP: 10
SALES (est): 740K **Privately Held**
SIC: 2431 Staircases, stairs & railings

(G-15135)
SIGN MEN
389 Wild Ave Ste G (10314-4758)
PHONE 718 227-7446
Ricki D Amato, *Owner*
EMP: 7
SALES (est): 162.8K **Privately Held**
SIC: 3993 Advertising novelties

(G-15136)
SPECIAL TEES
250 Buel Ave (10305-1204)
PHONE 718 980-0987
Joanne Homsey, *Prgrmr*
Vicent Bonomi, *Program Dir*
EMP: 24 EST: 1995
SALES (est): 1.4MM **Privately Held**
WEB: www.specialtees-si.com
SIC: 2396 Screen printing on fabric articles

(G-15137)
ST JOHN
229 Morrison Ave (10310-2836)
PHONE 718 720-8367
Barbara A Logan, *Principal*
EMP: 5
SALES (est): 241.5K **Privately Held**
SIC: 2339 Sportswear, women's

(G-15138)
STATEN ISLAND PARENT MAGAZINE
16 Shenandoah Ave Ste 2 (10314-3652)
PHONE 718 761-4800
Orlando Frank, *Owner*
EMP: 6

SALES (est): 410.5K **Privately Held**
SIC: 2721 Magazines: publishing only, not printed on site

(G-15139)
STATEN ISLAND STAIR INC
439 Sharrotts Rd (10309-1414)
PHONE 718 317-9276
Fran Imber, *President*
EMP: 5
SALES: 500K **Privately Held**
SIC: 2431 Staircases & stairs, wood

(G-15140)
STONEY CROFT CONVERTERS INC
Also Called: Alltek Labeling Systems
364 Sharrotts Rd (10309-1990)
PHONE 718 608-9800
John Conti, *President*
Ann Conti, *Vice Pres*
Alan Sherman, *Accounts Mgr*
EMP: 16
SQ FT: 7,000
SALES (est): 4MM **Privately Held**
WEB: www.allteklabeling.com
SIC: 2672 2679 Labels (unprinted), gummed: made from purchased materials; labels, paper: made from purchased material

(G-15141)
STRADA SOFT INC
20 Clifton Ave (10305-4912)
PHONE 718 556-6940
Lou Esposito, *Principal*
EMP: 8
SALES: 300K **Privately Held**
WEB: www.stradasoft.com
SIC: 7372 Prepackaged software

(G-15142)
SUPERIOR CONFECTIONS INC
1150 South Ave (10314-3404)
PHONE 718 698-3300
George Kaye, *President*
Michael K Katsoris, *Exec VP*
Peter Kaye, *Vice Pres*
▲ EMP: 100 EST: 1951
SQ FT: 40,000
SALES (est): 10.1MM **Privately Held**
SIC: 2066 Chocolate candy, solid

(G-15143)
SUPREME CHOCOLATIER LLC
1150 South Ave Fl 1 (10314-3404)
PHONE 718 761-9600
Michael Kaye, *Marketing Staff*
George Kaye, *Info Tech Dir*
▲ EMP: 50 EST: 1999
SALES (est): 10.1MM **Privately Held**
WEB: www.supremechocolatier.com
SIC: 2061 Raw cane sugar

(G-15144)
TDS WOODWORKING INC
Also Called: TDS Woodcraft
104 Port Richmond Ave (10302-1334)
PHONE 718 442-5298
Salvatore Piscicelli, *President*
EMP: 10
SALES (est): 1.2MM **Privately Held**
SIC: 2431 Millwork

(G-15145)
TEAM BUILDERS INC
Also Called: Team Builders Management
88 New Dorp Plz S Ste 303 (10306-2902)
PHONE 718 979-1005
Christine B Fasier, *President*
EMP: 11
SQ FT: 1,100
SALES: 2MM **Privately Held**
SIC: 7372 Business oriented computer software

(G-15146)
TECH PRODUCTS INC
105 Willow Ave (10305-1896)
PHONE 718 442-4900
Kenneth Nelson Sr, *President*
Carey Nelson, *Corp Secy*
Resat Karagozler, *Plant Mgr*
Robert Rosenbaum, *CFO*
Daniel Oconnor, *VP Sales*
▼ EMP: 44 EST: 1948

SQ FT: 1,600
SALES (est): 7.7MM **Privately Held**
WEB: www.techproducts.com
SIC: 3953 3993 Marking devices; signs & advertising specialties

(G-15147)
TODT HILL AUDIOLOGICAL SVCS
78 Todt Hill Rd Ste 202 (10314-4528)
PHONE 718 816-1952
Theresa Cannon, *President*
EMP: 5
SALES (est): 587K **Privately Held**
SIC: 3842 8049 Hearing aids; audiologist

(G-15148)
TORTILLERIA OAXACA
121 Port Richmond Ave (10302-1307)
PHONE 347 355-7336
EMP: 5
SALES (est): 182.9K **Privately Held**
SIC: 2099 Tortillas, fresh or refrigerated

(G-15149)
ULTIMATE PAVERS CORP
659 Quincy Ave (10305-4100)
PHONE 917 417-2652
EMP: 27
SALES (est): 4.9MM **Privately Held**
SIC: 2951 Asphalt paving mixtures & blocks

(G-15150)
VCP MOBILITY INC
4131 Richmond Ave (10312-5633)
PHONE 718 356-7827
EMP: 400
SALES (corp-wide): 396.7MM **Privately Held**
SIC: 3842 Wheelchairs
HQ: Vcp Mobility, Inc.
6899 Winchester Cir # 200
Boulder CO 80301
303 218-4500

(G-15151)
VEZ INC
Also Called: Fastsigns
3801 Victory Blvd Ste 5 (10314-6759)
PHONE 718 273-7002
Rich Vezzuto, *President*
Kurt Kracsun, *Vice Pres*
EMP: 6
SQ FT: 2,500
SALES: 900K **Privately Held**
WEB: www.veztek.com
SIC: 3993 2759 Signs & advertising specialties; business forms: printing

(G-15152)
VF OUTDOOR INC
2655 Richmond Ave # 1570 (10314-5821)
PHONE 718 698-6215
EMP: 46
SALES (corp-wide): 11.8B **Publicly Held**
SIC: 2329 Men's & boys' leather, wool & down-filled outerwear
HQ: Vf Outdoor, Llc
2701 Harbor Bay Pkwy
Alameda CA 94502
510 618-3500

(G-15153)
YPIS OF STATEN ISLAND INC
130 Stuyvesant Pl Ste 5 (10301-1900)
PHONE 718 815-4557
Dominick Brancato, *Exec Dir*
EMP: 2
SALES: 5.5MM **Privately Held**
SIC: 7372 Business oriented computer software

Stephentown
Rensselaer County

(G-15154)
ATLANTIS EQUIPMENT CORPORATION
16941 Ny 22 (12168)
PHONE 518 733-5910
Louis Schroeter, *President*
Richard W Keeler Jr, *Vice Pres*

Nelson Furlano, *Accountant*
Catherine Beach, *Technology*
EMP: 20
SQ FT: 40,000
SALES: 5MM **Privately Held**
SIC: 3599 3441 7692 3444 Machine shop, jobbing & repair; fabricated structural metal; welding repair; sheet metalwork

(G-15155)
FOUR FAT FOWL INC
324 State Route 43 Stop B (12168-2933)
PHONE 518 733-5230
Willard Bridgham IV, *President*
Josie Madison, *Opers Mgr*
Shaleena Bridgham, *Sales Mgr*
EMP: 5
SALES: 325K **Privately Held**
SIC: 2022 Natural cheese

(G-15156)
ZWACK INCORPORATED
15875 Ny 22 (12168)
P.O. Box 100 (12168-0100)
PHONE 518 733-5135
Frank J Zwack, *President*
Maria Zwack, *Admin Sec*
EMP: 50 EST: 1971
SQ FT: 30,000
SALES (est): 9.2MM **Privately Held**
WEB: www.zwackinc.com
SIC: 3541 3714 5082 Machine tools, metal cutting type; sanders, motor vehicle safety; general construction machinery & equipment

Stillwater
Saratoga County

(G-15157)
DAMN GOOD FOODS INC
Also Called: Damn Good Jerkey
1002 Hudson Ave (12170-3431)
PHONE 518 664-1414
Greg Strope, *President*
Katherine Baldwin, *Manager*
EMP: 12
SQ FT: 7,500
SALES (est): 2.2MM **Privately Held**
WEB: www.damngoodfoods.com
SIC: 2099 Food preparations

(G-15158)
H2O SOLUTIONS INC
61 Major Dickinson Ave (12170-7729)
P.O. Box 721 (12170-0721)
PHONE 518 527-0915
Daniel Reilly, *Principal*
EMP: 15
SALES (est): 953.8K **Privately Held**
SIC: 3589 Water filters & softeners, household type

(G-15159)
STILLWATER WOOD & IRON
114 N Hudson Ave (12170)
P.O. Box 736 (12170-0736)
PHONE 518 664-4501
Charles Robert Hallum, *Owner*
C Robert Hallum, *Owner*
Bob Hallum, *Partner*
EMP: 5
SQ FT: 13,000
SALES: 650K **Privately Held**
WEB: www.stillwaterfdny.com
SIC: 2511 Unassembled or unfinished furniture, household: wood

Stittville
Oneida County

(G-15160)
DYNA-VAC EQUIPMENT INC
8963 State Route 365 (13469-1021)
PHONE 315 865-8084
Hal Reigi, *President*
Laurie Reigi, *Vice Pres*
EMP: 11
SQ FT: 6,000

SALES: 1.8MM **Privately Held**
WEB: www.dynavacequipment.com
SIC: 3589 Sewer cleaning equipment, power

Stone Ridge
Ulster County

(G-15161)
FTS SYSTEMS INC (DH)
3538 Main St (12484-5601)
PHONE..................845 687-5300
Claus Kinder, *Principal*
Denny Beals, *Parts Mgr*
Patty Dern, *Administration*
EMP: 85 EST: 1971
SQ FT: 34,000
SALES (est): 7.6MM
SALES (corp-wide): 1.4B **Privately Held**
WEB: www.ftssystems.com
SIC: 3821 3823 3585 Laboratory equipment: fume hoods, distillation racks, etc.; industrial instrmnts msrmnt display/control process variable; refrigeration & heating equipment
HQ: S P Industries, Inc.
935 Mearns Rd
Warminster PA 18974
215 672-7800

(G-15162)
PK30 SYSTEM LLC
3607 Atwood Rd (12484-5446)
P.O. Box 656 (12484-0656)
PHONE..................212 473-8050
Philip Kerzner, *Owner*
EMP: 13
SALES (est): 2MM **Privately Held**
SIC: 3442 3446 3429 Store fronts, prefabricated, metal; architectural metalwork; builders' hardware

Stony Brook
Suffolk County

(G-15163)
BABY UV/KIDS UV INC (PA)
11 Hawks Nest Rd (11790-1103)
PHONE..................917 301-9020
Francesann Dipietro, *President*
Chris Zanaty, *Principal*
EMP: 12
SALES (est): 619.3K **Privately Held**
SIC: 2369 Bathing suits & swimwear: girls', children's & infants'

(G-15164)
COGNITIVEFLOW SENSOR TECH
9 Melville Ct (11790-1851)
PHONE..................631 513-9369
EMP: 9 EST: 2011
SALES (est): 775K **Privately Held**
SIC: 3841 Mfg Surgical/Medical Instruments

(G-15165)
ELIMA-DRAFT INCORPORATED
20 Hopewell Dr (11790-2324)
PHONE..................631 375-2830
Robert W Viggers, *Ch of Bd*
EMP: 5
SQ FT: 2,100
SALES: 125K **Privately Held**
SIC: 3585 5075 Air conditioning equipment, complete; air conditioning & ventilation equipment & supplies

(G-15166)
HANGER PRSTHETCS & ORTHO INC
2500 Route 347 3 (11790-2555)
PHONE..................631 751-6966
Bill Blum, *Branch Mgr*
EMP: 5
SALES (corp-wide): 1B **Publicly Held**
SIC: 3842 Surgical appliances & supplies

HQ: Hanger Prosthetics & Orthotics, Inc.
10910 Domain Dr Ste 300
Austin TX 78758
512 777-3800

(G-15167)
INTELIBS INC
1500 Stony Brook Rd Ste 3 (11794-4600)
PHONE..................877 213-2640
Seyong Park, *President*
Dorene Weiland, *Executive*
EMP: 5
SALES (est): 929K **Privately Held**
SIC: 3663

(G-15168)
MT FUEL CORP
9 Bayles Ave (11790-2121)
PHONE..................631 445-2047
Robert Trivigno, *Principal*
EMP: 6
SALES (est): 455.2K **Privately Held**
SIC: 2869 Fuels

(G-15169)
STONY BROOK UNIVERSITY
Also Called: University Advertising Agency
310 Administration Bldg (11794-0001)
PHONE..................631 632-6434
Erin Giuliano, *Ch of Bd*
Jennifer Acosta, *Dean*
Sacha Kopp, *Dean*
Heath Martin, *Dean*
Suzanne Shane, *Counsel*
EMP: 40 **Privately Held**
WEB: www.sunysb.edu
SIC: 2752 8221 9411 Commercial printing, lithographic; colleges universities & professional schools; administration of educational programs;
HQ: Stony Brook University
100 Nicolls Rd
Stony Brook NY 11794
631 632-6000

(G-15170)
TRANSISTOR POWER TECH INC (PA)
Also Called: Tpti
38 Robert Cres (11790-3204)
PHONE..................631 491-0265
Yehuda Fogel, *President*
EMP: 5
SQ FT: 1,000
SALES: 467K **Privately Held**
SIC: 3679 Microwave components

Stony Point
Rockland County

(G-15171)
FANTASY GLASS COMPAN
61 Beach Rd (10980-2035)
PHONE..................845 786-5818
Greggory Barbutl, *Owner*
EMP: 5
SALES (est): 339.5K **Privately Held**
SIC: 3732 Boats, fiberglass: building & repairing

(G-15172)
GOTHAM INK & COLOR CO INC
19 Holt Dr (10980-1919)
PHONE..................845 947-4000
William Olson, *General Mgr*
Joseph Simons, *Vice Pres*
EMP: 5
SQ FT: 25,000
SALES (est): 3.7MM **Privately Held**
SIC: 2893 Printing ink

(G-15173)
KEON OPTICS INC
30 John F Kennedy Dr (10980-3207)
PHONE..................845 429-7103
Kevin McKeon, *President*
EMP: 10
SQ FT: 1,300
SALES (est): 815.2K **Privately Held**
SIC: 3827 Optical instruments & lenses

(G-15174)
LIGHTING SERVICES INC (PA)
2 Holt Dr (10980-1920)
PHONE..................845 942-2800
Daniel Gelman, *President*
Ken Kane, *Exec VP*
Rose Miller, *Purch Agent*
Frank Reidmiller, *Engineer*
Alexander Gonzales, *Accountant*
▲ EMP: 100 EST: 1958
SQ FT: 50,000
SALES (est): 17.9MM **Privately Held**
WEB: www.lightingservicesinc.com
SIC: 3646 Commercial indusl & institutional electric lighting fixtures

(G-15175)
PRECISION TECHNIQUES INC
25 Holt Dr (10980-1919)
PHONE..................718 991-1440
Paul Mangione, *President*
Joseph De Savage, *Corp Secy*
▲ EMP: 85
SQ FT: 70,000
SALES (est): 11.4MM **Privately Held**
WEB: www.precisiontechniquesinc.com
SIC: 3089 4783 Injection molding of plastics; packing & crating

(G-15176)
STONY POINT GRAPHICS LTD
Also Called: Shell Ann Printing
79 S Liberty Dr (10980-2321)
PHONE..................845 786-3322
Phillip Laquidara, *President*
Felix Laquidara, *Vice Pres*
Loraine Laquidara, *Admin Sec*
EMP: 5
SQ FT: 4,000
SALES: 300K **Privately Held**
SIC: 2752 2759 Commercial printing, offset; letterpress printing

(G-15177)
TIMES SQUARE STAGE LTG CO INC
Also Called: Time Square Lighting
5 Holt Dr (10980-1919)
PHONE..................845 947-3034
Robert Riccadelli, *President*
Dan Riccardelli, *Regional Mgr*
Thomas Tyler, *Engineer*
Felicia Wiiliams, *Office Mgr*
Rob Riccardelli, *Director*
▲ EMP: 50 EST: 1938
SQ FT: 32,000
SALES (est): 11MM **Privately Held**
WEB: www.tslight.com
SIC: 3648 Lighting equipment

(G-15178)
US GLOBAL LUBRICANTS INC
22 Hudson Dr (10980-1406)
PHONE..................845 271-4277
Robert Gonnelli, *Manager*
EMP: 15 EST: 2013
SALES (est): 3.7MM **Privately Held**
SIC: 2992 Lubricating oils & greases

Stormville
Dutchess County

(G-15179)
GALLI SHIRTS AND SPORTS AP
246 Judith Dr (12582-5262)
PHONE..................845 226-7305
Vincent Gallipani, *President*
Erika Gallipani, *Vice Pres*
EMP: 5
SALES: 300K **Privately Held**
WEB: www.gallishirts.com
SIC: 2396 7311 Screen printing on fabric articles; advertising consultant

(G-15180)
PACKAGE PAVEMENT COMPANY INC
3530 Route 52 (12582-5651)
P.O. Box 408 (12582-0408)
PHONE..................845 221-2224
Darren Doherty, *Ch of Bd*
Frank J Doherty, *President*
Paul Doherty, *General Mgr*

Gary Lancour, *General Mgr*
Eileen Doherty, *Vice Pres*
▲ EMP: 95 EST: 1951
SQ FT: 5,000
SALES (est): 27.3MM **Privately Held**
SIC: 2951 Asphalt & asphaltic paving mixtures (not from refineries)

Stottville
Columbia County

(G-15181)
IRV SCHRODER & SONS INC
2906 Atlantic Ave (12172-7700)
P.O. Box 300 (12172-0300)
PHONE..................518 828-0194
Jim Schroder, *President*
EMP: 20
SQ FT: 6,000
SALES (est): 3.5MM **Privately Held**
SIC: 3441 1791 Fabricated structural metal; structural steel erection

Stuyvesant
Columbia County

(G-15182)
MAPLE HILL CREAMERY LLC (PA)
285 Allendale Rd W (12173-2611)
P.O. Box 323, Kinderhook (12106-0323)
PHONE..................518 758-7777
Peter Meck, *Vice Pres*
Charles Zentay, *CFO*
Peter T Joseph, *Mng Member*
EMP: 20
SQ FT: 6,000
SALES: 8MM **Privately Held**
SIC: 2026 Yogurt

Stuyvesant Falls
Columbia County

(G-15183)
BETHS FARM KITCHEN
504 Rte 46 (12174)
P.O. Box 113 (12174-0113)
PHONE..................518 799-3414
Beth Linskey, *Owner*
EMP: 8
SALES (est): 591.2K **Privately Held**
WEB: www.bethsfarmkitchen.com
SIC: 2099 Food preparations

Suffern
Rockland County

(G-15184)
ADVANCED MEDICAL MFG CORP
Also Called: Crown Medical Products
7-11 Suffern Pl Ste 2 (10901-5501)
PHONE..................845 369-7535
Ron Resnick, *Owner*
Carol Wynne, *Controller*
EMP: 20
SALES (est): 1.4MM **Privately Held**
SIC: 2393 Cushions, except spring & carpet: purchased materials

(G-15185)
AMERICAN BEST CABINETS INC
Also Called: Malibu Cabinets
397 Spook Rock Rd (10901-5319)
PHONE..................845 369-6666
Sam Blum, *President*
Aron Feldman, *Vice Pres*
▲ EMP: 39
SQ FT: 26,000
SALES (est): 3.9MM **Privately Held**
WEB: www.malibucabinets.com
SIC: 2514 Mfg Metal Household Furniture

Suffern - Rockland County

(G-15186)
BEER MARKETERS INSIGHTS INC
49 E Maple Ave (10901-5507)
PHONE..................845 507-0040
Benj Steinman, *President*
Irene Steinman, *Treasurer*
Robin Steinman, *Treasurer*
Christopher Shepard, *Assoc Editor*
EMP: 8
SALES (est): 969.1K **Privately Held**
WEB: www.beerinsights.com
SIC: 2721 8742 Trade journals: publishing & printing; management consulting services

(G-15187)
CLASSIC CABINETS
375 Spook Rock Rd (10901-5314)
PHONE..................845 357-4331
John Cheman, *Owner*
EMP: 10
SALES (est): 767.5K **Privately Held**
WEB: www.classcabs.com
SIC: 2434 Wood kitchen cabinets

(G-15188)
DYNAMIC INTL MFRS & DISTRS INC
78 Lafayette Ave Ste 201 (10901-5551)
PHONE..................347 993-1914
Avery Engel, *President*
▲ **EMP:** 10
SALES (est): 745.6K **Privately Held**
SIC: 2678 Stationery products

(G-15189)
E-FFINERGY GROUP LLC
Also Called: Day One Lighting
355 Spook Rock Rd (10901-5314)
PHONE..................845 547-2424
Mendel Hecht, *Mng Member*
EMP: 5
SQ FT: 1,000
SALES: 1.3MM **Privately Held**
SIC: 3646 Commercial indusl & institutional electric lighting fixtures

(G-15190)
EMPIRE COACHWORKS INTL LLC
475 Haverstraw Rd (10901-3135)
PHONE..................732 257-7981
Edward Vergopia, *Mng Member*
Micheal Misseri,
EMP: 70
SQ FT: 88,000
SALES (est): 5.3MM **Privately Held**
SIC: 3711 Automobile bodies, passenger car, not including engine, etc.

(G-15191)
I TRADE TECHNOLOGY LTD
400 Rella Blvd Ste 165 (10901-8114)
PHONE..................615 348-7233
Andy Gordon, *Branch Mgr*
EMP: 6
SALES (corp-wide): 1.5MM **Privately Held**
SIC: 3678 5999 5065 Electronic connectors; electronic parts & equipment; connectors, electronic
PA: I Trade Technology, Ltd.
115 Franklin Tpke Ste 144
Mahwah NJ 07430
615 348-7233

(G-15192)
LE CHOCOLATE OF ROCKLAND LLC
1 Ramapo Ave (10901-5805)
PHONE..................845 533-4125
Simon Rottenburg,
▲ **EMP:** 25
SALES (est): 4.6MM **Privately Held**
SIC: 2066 Chocolate

(G-15193)
MEDFORCE TECHNOLOGIES INC
2 Executive Blvd Ste 410 (10901-8220)
PHONE..................845 426-0459
Esther Apter, *CEO*
Steve Bainnson, *Vice Pres*
Mark Traverson, *Sales Staff*
Benjamin Llamzon, *Business Anlyst*
Medgine Sergile, *Office Mgr*
EMP: 13
SQ FT: 4,000
SALES: 120K
SALES (corp-wide): 50.7MM **Privately Held**
SIC: 7372 Prepackaged software
PA: Ideagen Plc
Ergo House
Nottingham NOTTS NG11
162 969-9100

(G-15194)
NY CUTTING INC
Also Called: Uppercut
3 Chestnut St Ste 1 (10901-5476)
PHONE..................646 434-1355
Solomon Katz, *CEO*
▲ **EMP:** 6
SALES: 1MM **Privately Held**
SIC: 2392 2621 Placemats, plastic or textile; towels, tissues & napkins: paper & stock

(G-15195)
QUALITEA IMPORTS INC
74 Lafayette Ave (10901-5557)
PHONE..................917 624-6750
Pinchas Nussenzweig, *President*
EMP: 5
SALES (est): 139.9K **Privately Held**
SIC: 2099 Food preparations

(G-15196)
RADIATION SHIELDING SYSTEMS
415 Spook Rock Rd (10901-5308)
PHONE..................888 631-2278
Ed Delia, *CEO*
Seth Warnock, *Vice Pres*
Gary Novick, *Executive*
EMP: 11 **EST:** 2000
SALES (est): 1.7MM **Privately Held**
WEB: www.radiationshieldingsystems.com
SIC: 3444 3271 Radiator shields or enclosures, sheet metal; blocks, concrete: radiation-proof

(G-15197)
ROYAL TEES INC
29 Lafayette Ave (10901-5405)
PHONE..................845 357-9448
Al Rosenblatt, *President*
EMP: 5
SQ FT: 8,000
SALES: 750K **Privately Held**
WEB: www.royaltees.com
SIC: 2759 2395 2752 5611 Screen printing; embroidery & art needlework; transfers, decalcomania or dry: lithographed; clothing, sportswear, men's & boys'; women's sportswear

(G-15198)
SUPER CONDUCTOR MATERIALS INC
Also Called: SCM
391 Spook Rock Rd (10901-5319)
P.O. Box 701, Tallman (10982-0701)
PHONE..................845 368-0240
Aftab Dar, *President*
Neelam Dar, *Corp Secy*
▼ **EMP:** 14
SQ FT: 10,000
SALES (est): 2.3MM **Privately Held**
WEB: www.scm-inc.com
SIC: 3674 Semiconductors & related devices

(G-15199)
UNITED ROCKLAND HOLDING CO INC
9 N Airmont Rd (10901-5101)
P.O. Box 68, Tallman (10982-0068)
PHONE..................845 357-1900
Paul Wishnoff, *President*
Stanley Wishnoff, *Chairman*
Mitchell Kolata, *Treasurer*
Linda Olivo, *Manager*
EMP: 20 **EST:** 1961
SQ FT: 20,000
SALES (est): 1.6MM **Privately Held**
WEB: www.unitedrockandstairs.com
SIC: 2431 Staircases & stairs, wood; stair railings, wood

Sugar Loaf
Orange County

(G-15200)
IRINIRI DESIGNS LTD
1358 Kings Hwy (10981)
P.O. Box 378 (10981-0378)
PHONE..................845 469-7934
Rit Goldman, *Ch of Bd*
Nirit Rechtman, *President*
EMP: 12
SQ FT: 1,653
SALES (est): 1.4MM **Privately Held**
SIC: 3911 5944 Jewelry, precious metal; jewelry stores

Sunnyside
Queens County

(G-15201)
ANOTHER 99 CENT PARADISE
4206 Greenpoint Ave (11104-3004)
PHONE..................718 786-4578
Ali Gohar, *Principal*
EMP: 5
SALES (est): 452.5K **Privately Held**
SIC: 3643 Outlets, electric: convenience

(G-15202)
DEANCO DIGITAL PRINTING LLC
Also Called: NY Print Partners
4545 39th St (11104-4401)
PHONE..................212 371-2025
Joe Aziz, *Mng Member*
Pete Lamba,
EMP: 10
SQ FT: 2,500
SALES: 1.2MM **Privately Held**
SIC: 2752 Commercial printing, offset

(G-15203)
EASTERN CONCEPTS LTD
Also Called: Green Mountain Graphics
4125 39th St (11104-4201)
P.O. Box 1417, Long Island City (11101-0417)
PHONE..................718 472-3377
Eric Greenberg, *President*
Rhonda Greenberg, *Admin Sec*
EMP: 11
SQ FT: 6,000
SALES: 1.5MM **Privately Held**
WEB: www.gm-graphics.com
SIC: 3993 Signs, not made in custom sign painting shops

(G-15204)
NODUS NOODLE CORPORATION
4504 Queens Blvd (11104-2304)
PHONE..................718 309-3725
Thomas SAE Tang, *CEO*
EMP: 8
SALES (est): 335.2K **Privately Held**
SIC: 2098 Noodles (e.g. egg, plain & water), dry

(G-15205)
S DONADIC INC
Also Called: Sdi
4525 39th St (11104-4401)
PHONE..................718 361-9888
Steven Donadic, *President*
EMP: 60
SQ FT: 7,000
SALES: 2MM **Privately Held**
SIC: 2434 2431 2426 2421 Wood kitchen cabinets; millwork; hardwood dimension & flooring mills; sawmills & planing mills, general

(G-15206)
T S B A GROUP INC (PA)
3830 Woodside Ave (11104-1004)
PHONE..................718 565-6000
Samuel Brown, *Chairman*
Anthony Difiglia, *Marketing Mgr*
EMP: 30
SQ FT: 70,000
SALES (est): 19.4MM **Privately Held**
SIC: 3822 1731 Temperature controls, automatic; energy management controls

Surprise
Greene County

(G-15207)
ROYAL METAL PRODUCTS INC
463 West Rd (12176-1709)
PHONE..................518 966-4442
David M Johannesen, *President*
Steven Johannesen, *Vice Pres*
Robert Johannesen, *Treasurer*
EMP: 40 **EST:** 1956
SQ FT: 49,600
SALES (est): 4.8MM **Privately Held**
WEB: www.royalmetalproducts.com
SIC: 2514 3446 2522 3444 Metal household furniture; architectural metalwork: office furniture, except wood; sheet metalwork; products of purchased glass

Syosset
Nassau County

(G-15208)
ANDOR DESIGN CORP
20 Pond View Dr (11791-4409)
PHONE..................516 364-1619
Ralph Silvera, *President*
EMP: 7
SALES: 800K **Privately Held**
WEB: www.andordesign.com
SIC: 3829 Tensile strength testing equipment; testing equipment: abrasion, shearing strength, etc.

(G-15209)
BEKTROM FOODS INC (PA)
Also Called: Lots O' Luv
6800 Jericho Tpke 207w (11791-4445)
PHONE..................516 802-3800
Thomas Barbella, *President*
▲ **EMP:** 7
SALES (est): 12.5MM **Privately Held**
SIC: 2045 2099 Prepared flour mixes & doughs; packaged combination products: pasta, rice & potato

(G-15210)
BUFFALO DENTAL MFG CO INC
Also Called: Bdm
159 Lafayette Dr (11791-3933)
P.O. Box 678 (11791-0678)
PHONE..................516 496-7200
Donald Nevin, *President*
Marshall Nevin, *Chairman*
Doris Nevin, *Admin Sec*
▲ **EMP:** 50 **EST:** 1869
SQ FT: 25,000
SALES (est): 7.9MM **Privately Held**
SIC: 3843 Dental equipment

(G-15211)
CONTI AUTO BODY CORP
44 Jericho Tpke (11791)
PHONE..................516 921-6435
Liam Martin, *Principal*
EMP: 7
SALES (est): 775.7K **Privately Held**
SIC: 3711 3713 7532 Automobile bodies, passenger car, not including engine, etc.; truck & bus bodies; top & body repair & paint shops

(G-15212)
COSENSE INC
125 Coachman Pl W (11791-3059)
PHONE..................516 364-9161
Naim Dam, *President*
Sal Stiperi, *Vice Pres*
EMP: 35
SQ FT: 10,000

▲ = Import ▼ = Export
◆ = Import/Export

GEOGRAPHIC SECTION

Syracuse - Onondaga County (G-15239)

SALES (est): 6.6MM
SALES (corp-wide): 13.1B **Privately Held**
WEB: www.cosense.com
SIC: 3829 Measuring & controlling devices
HQ: Measurement Specialties, Inc.
1000 Lucas Way
Hampton VA 23666
757 766-1500

(G-15213)
CROSLEY MEDICAL PRODUCTS INC
Also Called: Cmp Adaptive Equipment Supply
19 Kathleen Dr (11791-5808)
PHONE.................631 595-2547
Gary Kornberg, *President*
Anthony Potenzone, *Mfg Staff*
EMP: 10
SQ FT: 4,000
SALES: 1.5MM **Privately Held**
SIC: 3842 Wheelchairs

(G-15214)
DANDREA INC
115 Eileen Way Ste 106 (11791-5302)
P.O. Box 391, Port Washington (11050-0392)
PHONE.................516 496-2200
Anthony D'Andrea, *President*
Rosemary D'Andrea, *Corp Secy*
▲ EMP: 40 EST: 1922
SQ FT: 12,000
SALES (est): 5MM **Privately Held**
SIC: 3931 5736 Musical instruments; musical instrument stores

(G-15215)
DELANEY BOOKS INC
212 Michael Dr (11791-5379)
PHONE.................516 921-8888
Michael Rudman, *President*
Frances Rudman, *Vice Pres*
EMP: 15 EST: 1968
SQ FT: 5,000
SALES (est): 1.5MM **Privately Held**
WEB: www.passbooks.com
SIC: 2731 Books: publishing only
PA: National Learning Corp
212 Michael Dr
Syosset NY 11791
516 921-8888

(G-15216)
ETERNAL LOVE PARFUMS CORP
Also Called: Eternal Love Perfumes
485 Underhill Blvd # 207 (11791-3434)
PHONE.................516 921-6100
Mahender Sabhnani, *President*
◆ EMP: 4
SALES: 4.2MM **Privately Held**
WEB: www.eternalloveparfums.com
SIC: 2844 5122 Toilet preparations; perfumes

(G-15217)
FLUID METERING INC (HQ)
5 Aerial Way Ste 500 (11791-5593)
PHONE.................516 922-6050
Harry E Pinkerton III, *President*
Robert A Warren Jr, *Vice Pres*
EMP: 50 EST: 1959
SALES (est): 15.2MM
SALES (corp-wide): 4.6B **Publicly Held**
WEB: www.fmipump.com
SIC: 3825 Meters: electric, pocket, portable, panelboard, etc.
PA: Roper Technologies, Inc
6901 Prof Pkwy E Ste 200
Sarasota FL 34240
941 556-2601

(G-15218)
FRANK MERRIWELL INC
212 Michael Dr (11791-5305)
PHONE.................516 921-8888
Jack Rudman, *President*
Frances Rudman, *Vice Pres*
EMP: 15
SQ FT: 5,000
SALES (est): 1.5MM **Privately Held**
WEB: www.frankmerriwell.com
SIC: 2731 Books: publishing only

PA: National Learning Corp
212 Michael Dr
Syosset NY 11791
516 921-8888

(G-15219)
GENERAL MICROWAVE CORPORATION (HQ)
227a Michael Dr (11791-5306)
PHONE.................516 802-0900
Deanna Lund, *CEO*
Eric Demarco, *President*
Nola Hess, *General Mgr*
Michael Fink, *Vice Pres*
Marie Mendoza, *Admin Sec*
EMP: 11 EST: 1960
SQ FT: 3,000
SALES: 10MM **Publicly Held**
SIC: 3674 5065 3825 6794 Hybrid integrated circuits; electronic parts & equipment; electronic parts; test equipment for electronic & electrical circuits; patent owners & lessors; microwave components; analytical instruments

(G-15220)
KNOLL PRINTING & PACKAGING INC
Also Called: Knoll Worldwide
149 Eileen Way (11791-5302)
PHONE.................516 621-0100
Jeremy Cohen, *Ch of Bd*
Linda Drew, *Vice Pres*
▲ EMP: 24
SALES (est): 5MM **Privately Held**
WEB: www.knollpack.com
SIC: 2657 3081 3086 Folding paperboard boxes; packing materials, plastic sheet; packaging & shipping materials, foamed plastic

(G-15221)
KUSH OASIS ENTERPRISES LLC
228 Martin Dr (11791-5406)
PHONE.................516 513-1316
Jyoti Jaiswal,
▲ EMP: 5
SALES (est): 210K **Privately Held**
SIC: 2393 Textile bags

(G-15222)
MESTEL BROTHERS STAIRS & RAILS
11 Gary Rd Ste 102 (11791-6211)
PHONE.................516 496-4127
Barry Mestel, *President*
EMP: 236
SALES (est): 13.1MM **Privately Held**
WEB: www.mestelbrothersstairs.com
SIC: 2431 3446 1751 Staircases & stairs, wood; architectural metalwork; carpentry work

(G-15223)
NASCO ENTERPRISES INC
95 Woodcrest Dr (11791-3037)
PHONE.................516 921-9696
Naimish P Shah, *President*
▲ EMP: 1
SALES: 1MM **Privately Held**
SIC: 3841 Catheters

(G-15224)
NATIONAL LEARNING CORP (PA)
212 Michael Dr (11791-5379)
PHONE.................516 921-8888
Michael Rudman, *President*
Frances Rudman, *Vice Pres*
EMP: 15
SQ FT: 15,000
SALES: 1.5MM **Privately Held**
WEB: www.delaneybooks.com
SIC: 2731 Book clubs: publishing & printing

(G-15225)
NATIONAL RDING STYLES INST INC
Also Called: N R S I
179 Lafayette Dr (11791-3933)
P.O. Box 737 (11791-0737)
PHONE.................516 921-5500

Marie Carbo, *President*
Juliet Ditroia, *Corp Secy*
EMP: 12
SQ FT: 6,400
SALES: 1.5MM **Privately Held**
WEB: www.nrsi.com
SIC: 2741 8748 Miscellaneous publishing; educational consultant

(G-15226)
NEW JERSEY PULVERIZING CO INC (PA)
4 Rita St (11791-5918)
PHONE.................516 921-9595
Martin Tanzer, *President*
Barbara Tanzer, *Vice Pres*
Barbara Deegan, *Treasurer*
EMP: 3 EST: 1915
SQ FT: 2,500
SALES (est): 2.8MM **Privately Held**
SIC: 1446 Industrial sand

(G-15227)
PARADIGM MKTG CONSORTIUM INC
Also Called: United Supply Systems
350 Michael Dr (11791-5307)
PHONE.................516 496-0000
Ralph Bianculli Jr, *CEO*
Pamela Bianculli, *President*
Thomas Bathe, *VP Sales*
Jaclyn McDuffey, *Manager*
▲ EMP: 50
SQ FT: 100,000
SALES (est): 13.8MM **Privately Held**
SIC: 2679 5087 Paper products, converted; cleaning & maintenance equipment & supplies

(G-15228)
QUALBUYS LLC
6800 Jericho Tpke 120w (11791-4436)
PHONE.................855 884-3274
Amy Kajiya, *COO*
EMP: 5 EST: 2011
SALES (est): 177.7K **Privately Held**
SIC: 3999 Barber & beauty shop equipment

(G-15229)
RAMLER INTERNATIONAL LTD
485 Underhill Blvd # 100 (11791-3434)
PHONE.................516 353-3106
Garry Ramler, *President*
Gail Gordon, *Director*
▲ EMP: 24 EST: 2010
SALES (est): 12MM **Privately Held**
SIC: 2599 Hotel furniture

(G-15230)
REAL EST BOOK OF LONG ISLAND
575 Underhill Blvd # 110 (11791-3426)
PHONE.................516 364-5000
Bryan Flynn, *President*
EMP: 10
SQ FT: 1,600
SALES: 2MM **Privately Held**
SIC: 2721 7319 Periodicals: publishing only; magazines: publishing not, not printed on site; distribution of advertising material or sample services

(G-15231)
ROTA FILE CORPORATION
Also Called: Rota Tool
159 Lafayette Dr (11791-3933)
P.O. Box 678 (11791-0678)
PHONE.................516 496-7200
Don Nevin, *President*
Richard Byalick, *General Mgr*
EMP: 20
SALES (est): 2.2MM **Privately Held**
WEB: www.rotafile.com
SIC: 3545 Cutting tools for machine tools

(G-15232)
VIDEO TECHNOLOGY SERVICES INC
5 Aerial Way Ste 300 (11791-5594)
PHONE.................516 937-9700
Andres Sierra, *President*
Philip L Pierre, *VP Engrg*
Richard Rouse, *Engineer*
Terrence Ferguson, *Manager*

EMP: 12
SQ FT: 7,200
SALES (est): 2.1MM **Privately Held**
WEB: www.videotechnologyservices.com
SIC: 3651 7622 5099 Household video equipment; video repair; video & audio equipment

(G-15233)
VIVONA BUSINESS PRINTERS INC
Also Called: PIP Printing
343 Jackson Ave (11791-4123)
PHONE.................516 496-3453
Joseph Vivonia, *CEO*
Joe Vivona, *President*
Anne Marie Bono, *Vice Pres*
EMP: 8
SALES (est): 1.3MM **Privately Held**
SIC: 2752 Commercial printing, offset

(G-15234)
ZASTECH INC
15 Ryan St (11791-2129)
PHONE.................516 496-4777
Raymond Zhou, *CEO*
▲ EMP: 20
SALES (est): 1.5MM **Privately Held**
SIC: 3674 Semiconductors & related devices

Syracuse
Onondaga County

(G-15235)
219 SOUTH WEST
219 S West St (13202-1874)
PHONE.................315 474-2065
EMP: 8
SALES (est): 560K **Privately Held**
SIC: 2448 Mfg Wood Pallets/Skids

(G-15236)
A NUCLIMATE QULTY SYSTEMS INC
1 General Motors Dr Ste 5 (13206-1122)
PHONE.................315 431-0226
Edward Campagna Sr, *President*
John Dimillo, *Vice Pres*
James Miller, *VP Engrg*
EMP: 19
SALES (est): 2.6MM **Privately Held**
SIC: 3585 3433 Heating equipment, complete; heating & air conditioning combination units; heating equipment, except electric

(G-15237)
A ZIMMER LTD
Also Called: Syracuse New Times
W Tenesee St (13204)
PHONE.................315 422-7011
Arthur Zimmer, *President*
Bill Brod, *Publisher*
Gregg Gambell, *General Mgr*
Shirley Zimmer, *CFO*
Lesli Mitchell, *Marketing Staff*
EMP: 84
SQ FT: 24,000
SALES (est): 5.5MM **Privately Held**
WEB: www.syracusenewtimes.com
SIC: 2711 5521 Newspapers, publishing & printing; used car dealers

(G-15238)
ALL TIMES PUBLISHING LLC
Also Called: Syracuse New Times
1415 W Genesee St (13204-2119)
PHONE.................315 422-7011
William Brod, *CEO*
Christopher Malone, *Editor*
James Coleman, *Vice Pres*
Bill Brod, *Officer*
EMP: 24
SALES: 2MM **Privately Held**
SIC: 2711 Newspapers

(G-15239)
ALL-STATE DIVERSIFIED PDTS INC
8 Dwight Park Dr (13209-1034)
PHONE.................315 472-4728
EMP: 50

Syracuse - Onondaga County (G-15240)   GEOGRAPHIC SECTION

SALES (est): 5.3MM **Privately Held**
SIC: **3443** Mfg Fabricated Plate Work

(G-15240)
ALLIED DECORATIONS CO INC
Also Called: Allied Sign Co
720 Erie Blvd W (13204-2226)
PHONE................................315 637-0273
Michael E Pfohl, *President*
Ken Colton, *Natl Sales Mgr*
Kim Charette, *Office Mgr*
EMP: 15
SQ FT: 45,000
SALES (est): 2MM **Privately Held**
WEB: www.alliedsigncompany.com
SIC: **3993** **7389** Electric signs; decoration service for special events; trade show arrangement

(G-15241)
ALPHA PRINTING CORP
131 Falso Dr (13211-2106)
P.O. Box 26 (13211-0026)
PHONE................................315 454-5507
Stephen Larose, *President*
Sally Godkin, *Manager*
EMP: 12
SQ FT: 5,000
SALES (est): 1.5MM **Privately Held**
SIC: **2752** Commercial printing, offset

(G-15242)
ALTIUS AVIATION LLC
113 Tuskegee Rd Ste 2 (13211-1332)
PHONE................................315 455-7555
Vaughn J Crawford, *Mng Member*
EMP: 6
SALES (est): 860.2K **Privately Held**
SIC: **3721** **6722** **8742** Aircraft; management investment, open-end; management consulting services

(G-15243)
ANSUN GRAPHICS INC
6392 Deere Rd Ste 4 (13206-1317)
PHONE................................315 437-6869
Jeff Schoenfeld, *President*
Joe Marrinan, *Shareholder*
Todd Thomas, *Admin Sec*
EMP: 12
SALES (est): 1.7MM **Privately Held**
WEB: www.ansun.biz
SIC: **2759** Commercial printing

(G-15244)
ANTHONY RIVER INC
116 Granger St (13202-2388)
PHONE................................315 475-1315
Ken Abramson, *President*
EMP: 15
SQ FT: 21,500
SALES (est): 2MM **Privately Held**
SIC: **3471** **3083** **2851** Finishing, metals or formed products; plastic finished products, laminated; paints & allied products

(G-15245)
ARCOM AUTOMATICS LLC
185 Ainsley Dr (13210-4202)
P.O. Box 6729 (13217-6729)
PHONE................................315 422-1230
Gregory A Tresness, *President*
EMP: 8
SALES (est): 1.5MM **Privately Held**
WEB: www.arcomlabs.com
SIC: **3663** Cable television equipment

(G-15246)
ARO-GRAPH CORPORATION
Also Called: Aro-Graph Displays
847 North Ave (13206-1630)
PHONE................................315 463-8693
Neal Burrei, *President*
Carol Burrei, *Vice Pres*
EMP: 5 **EST:** 1946
SQ FT: 7,000
SALES (est): 828.5K **Privately Held**
WEB: www.arograph.com
SIC: **2752** **2396** Decals, lithographed; screen printing on fabric articles

(G-15247)
ARROW-COMMUNICATION LABS INC
Also Called: Arcom Labs
185 Ainsley Dr (13210-4202)
P.O. Box 6729 (13217-6729)
PHONE................................315 422-1230
Andrew Tresness, *President*
▲ **EMP:** 300
SQ FT: 30,000
SALES (est): 52.6MM
SALES (corp-wide): 52.8MM **Privately Held**
SIC: **3663** Cable television equipment
PA: Northern Catv Sales Inc
185 Ainsley Dr
Syracuse NY
315 422-1230

(G-15248)
ATLAS BITUMINOUS CO INC
173 Farrell Rd (13209-1823)
PHONE................................315 457-2394
Charmaine Jones, *President*
Robert Shattel, *Treasurer*
James Shattel, *Admin Sec*
EMP: 11 **EST:** 1963
SQ FT: 2,500
SALES (est): 1.9MM **Privately Held**
SIC: **2951** **6513** Asphalt & asphaltic paving mixtures (not from refineries); apartment hotel operation

(G-15249)
AUTOMATION CORRECT LLC
Also Called: Automationcorrect.com
405 Parrish Ln (13205-3323)
PHONE................................315 299-3589
Neil Waelder, *President*
EMP: 5
SALES (est): 696.1K **Privately Held**
WEB: www.automationcorrect.com
SIC: **3825** Test equipment for electronic & electrical circuits

(G-15250)
AUTOMATION PAPERS INC
Also Called: National Pad & Paper
6361 Thompson Rd Stop 1 (13206-1412)
P.O. Box 572, Fayetteville (13066-0572)
PHONE................................315 432-0565
David T Carroll, *President*
Donald T Carroll, *Vice Pres*
Jean Carroll, *Admin Sec*
▼ **EMP:** 7
SQ FT: 17,000
SALES (est): 1.1MM **Privately Held**
SIC: **2621** Writing paper

(G-15251)
AVALON COPY CENTERS AMER INC (PA)
Also Called: Avalon Document Services
901 N State St (13208-2515)
PHONE................................315 471-3333
John P Midgley, *CEO*
Shawn Thrall, *President*
Andrew Guffey, *Managing Prtnr*
Chris Haag, *Managing Prtnr*
Jon Willette, *COO*
EMP: 65
SQ FT: 13,000
SALES (est): 19.6MM **Privately Held**
SIC: **2741** **7375** **7336** **7334** Art copy: publishing & printing; information retrieval services; commercial art & graphic design; photocopying & duplicating services

(G-15252)
BABBITT BEARINGS INC (PA)
Also Called: Babbit Bearings
734 Burnet Ave (13203-2999)
PHONE................................315 479-6603
Tracy S Stevenson, *CEO*
H Thomas Wart, *Vice Pres*
John Cerrone, *Treasurer*
Marian Wart, *Admin Sec*
EMP: 90
SQ FT: 34,000
SALES (est): 14.3MM **Privately Held**
SIC: **3599** Machine shop, jobbing & repair

(G-15253)
BABBITT BEARINGS INCORPORATED
734 Burnet Ave (13203-2999)
PHONE................................315 479-6603
Charles R Wart Jr, *President*
John Cerrone, *Treasurer*
Marian Wart, *Admin Sec*
EMP: 75 **EST:** 1970
SQ FT: 60,000
SALES (est): 5.2MM
SALES (corp-wide): 14.3MM **Privately Held**
WEB: www.babbitt-inc.com
SIC: **3599** **3568** Machine shop, jobbing & repair; power transmission equipment
PA: Babbitt Bearings, Inc.
734 Burnet Ave
Syracuse NY 13203
315 479-6603

(G-15254)
BARNES GROUP INC
Associated Spring
1225 State Fair Blvd (13209-1011)
PHONE................................315 457-9200
Fax: 315 457-9228
EMP: 8
SQ FT: 22,448
SALES (corp-wide): 1.4B **Publicly Held**
SIC: **3495** **3469** Mfg Wire Springs And Metal Stampings
PA: Barnes Group Inc.
123 Main St
Bristol CT 06010
860 583-7070

(G-15255)
BELLA FIGURA LETTERPRESS
509 W Fayette St (13204-2986)
PHONE................................866 699-6040
Virginia Hart, *Principal*
Sherri Mackey, *Bookkeeper*
Andrea Streeter, *Graphic Designe*
EMP: 5
SALES (est): 257.3K **Privately Held**
SIC: **2759** Letterpress printing

(G-15256)
BENCHMARK MEDIA SYSTEMS INC
203 E Hampton Pl Ste 2 (13206-1676)
PHONE................................315 437-6300
Ruth S Burdick, *CEO*
Allen H Burdick, *President*
Peter Depuy, *Prdtn Mgr*
David Siau, *Prdtn Mgr*
John Siau, *Info Tech Mgr*
EMP: 14
SQ FT: 5,500
SALES (est): 2.6MM **Privately Held**
WEB: www.benchmarkmedia.com
SIC: **3663** Radio & TV communications equipment

(G-15257)
BILLY BEEZ USA LLC
9090 Destiy Usa Dr L301 (13204)
PHONE................................315 741-5099
EMP: 16
SALES (corp-wide): 15.6MM **Privately Held**
SIC: **3949** **5137** **7999** Playground equipment; women's & children's dresses, suits, skirts & blouses; amusement ride
PA: Billy Beez Usa, Llc
3 W 35th St Fl 3 # 3
New York NY 10001
646 606-2249

(G-15258)
BITZER SCROLL INC
6055 Court Street Rd (13206-1749)
PHONE................................315 463-2101
Peter P Narreau, *CEO*
Richard Kobor, *President*
Peter Schaufler, *Principal*
Dolores Cotroneo, *Purch Mgr*
Tom O'Donnell, *Engineer*
▲ **EMP:** 97
SALES (est): 42.6MM
SALES (corp-wide): 195.3K **Privately Held**
SIC: **3822** Air conditioning & refrigeration controls
HQ: Bitzer Se
Eschenbrunnlestr. 15
Sindelfingen 71065
703 193-20

(G-15259)
BLACKBURN TRUCK BODIES LLC
6216 Thompson Rd Ste 3 (13206-1418)
PHONE................................315 448-3236
Jeff Blackburn, *Mng Member*
Ryan Blackburn, *Mng Member*
EMP: 5
SALES (est): 241.6K **Privately Held**
SIC: **3713** **5531** Truck & bus bodies; automotive accessories

(G-15260)
BOMAC INC
6477 Ridings Rd (13206-1110)
PHONE................................315 433-9181
Kevin T Knecht, *President*
Mark Pauls, *Vice Pres*
William Decoursey, *Foreman/Supr*
Karen Fear, *Purchasing*
Michael Rudd, *VP Engrg*
EMP: 18 **EST:** 1959
SQ FT: 22,000
SALES (est): 4.7MM **Privately Held**
WEB: www.bomacinc.com
SIC: **3625** Electric controls & control accessories, industrial

(G-15261)
BOXCAR PRESS INCORPORATED
509 W Fayette St Ste 135 (13204-2987)
PHONE................................315 473-0930
Harold Kyle, *Ch of Bd*
Debbi Urbanski, *Vice Pres*
Alison Cotsonas, *Project Mgr*
Adriana Sosnowski, *Opers Mgr*
Dorothy Dexter, *Buyer*
EMP: 30
SALES (est): 5.5MM **Privately Held**
WEB: www.boxcarpress.com
SIC: **2752** **5084** Commercial printing, offset; printing trades machinery, equipment & supplies

(G-15262)
BROADNET TECHNOLOGIES INC
2-212 Center For Science (13244-0001)
PHONE................................315 443-3694
Michael Sun, *CEO*
EMP: 15 **EST:** 2000
SQ FT: 2,000
SALES (est): 1.3MM **Privately Held**
SIC: **3577** Optical scanning devices

(G-15263)
BURR & SON INC
Also Called: Dover Enterprises
119 Seeley Rd (13224-1113)
PHONE................................315 446-1550
J Peter Burr, *President*
EMP: 5 **EST:** 1973
SQ FT: 3,000
SALES (est): 360K **Privately Held**
WEB: www.doverent.com
SIC: **2759** Imprinting; engraving

(G-15264)
BUSCH PRODUCTS INC
110 Baker St (13206-1701)
PHONE................................315 474-8422
Robert Brown Sr, *President*
Darlene Brown, *Vice Pres*
Paul Conley, *Engineer*
Lisa Verrillo, *Cust Mgr*
EMP: 50
SALES (est): 6.4MM **Privately Held**
WEB: www.buschproducts.com
SIC: **3281** Cut stone & stone products

(G-15265)
C & M PRODUCTS INC
1209 N Salina St Ste 1 (13208-1581)
PHONE................................315 471-3303
Charles Mott, *President*
EMP: 6 **EST:** 1965
SQ FT: 5,600

SALES (est): 579.5K *Privately Held*
SIC: 3479 3499 3089 Name plates: engraved, etched, etc.; trophies, metal, except silver; laminating of plastic

(G-15266)
C M E CORP
Also Called: Central Marking Equipment
1005 W Fayette St Ste 3c (13204-2840)
PHONE.....................................315 451-7101
Leedom Kettell, *President*
EMP: 11
SQ FT: 12,000
SALES: 1MM *Privately Held*
SIC: 3555 3953 Printing plates; marking devices

(G-15267)
CAFE KUBAL
202 Lockwood Rd (13214-2035)
PHONE.....................................315 278-2812
Matthew Godard, *Branch Mgr*
EMP: 9
SALES (corp-wide): 1.1MM *Privately Held*
SIC: 2095 Roasted coffee
PA: Cafe Kubal
3501 James St Ste 2
Syracuse NY 13206
315 278-2812

(G-15268)
CALTEX INTERNATIONAL LTD
60 Presidential Plz # 1405 (13202-2444)
PHONE.....................................315 425-1040
Kapil Kevin Sodhi, *President*
Jennifer Hetherington, *Vice Pres*
EMP: 39
SQ FT: 26,000
SALES: 6.4MM *Privately Held*
WEB: www.iscbiostrat.com
SIC: 2869 2842 3826 Industrial organic chemicals; specialty cleaning preparations; environmental testing equipment

(G-15269)
CAMFIL USA INC
Also Called: Edco Sales
6060 Tarbell Rd (13206)
PHONE.....................................315 468-3849
EMP: 12
SALES (corp-wide): 864.2MM *Privately Held*
SIC: 3564 Blowers & fans
HQ: Camfil Usa, Inc.
1 N Corporate Dr
Riverdale NJ 07457
973 616-7300

(G-15270)
CAROLS POLAR PARLOR
3800 W Genesee St (13219-1928)
PHONE.....................................315 468-3404
Carol Franceschetti, *Owner*
EMP: 5
SALES (est): 358.5K *Privately Held*
SIC: 2024 Ice cream & frozen desserts

(G-15271)
CARPENTER INDUSTRIES INC
1 General Motors Dr # 10 (13206-1129)
P.O. Box 888 (13206-0888)
PHONE.....................................315 463-4284
Edward Tibbits, *President*
EMP: 11
SQ FT: 25,000
SALES (est): 1.3MM *Privately Held*
WEB: www.carpenterindustries.com
SIC: 3471 3441 Sand blasting of metal parts; fabricated structural metal

(G-15272)
CARRIER CORPORATION
Carrier Pkwy Tr 20 (13221)
P.O. Box 4808 (13221-4808)
PHONE.....................................315 432-6000
Randall J Hogan, *President*
EMP: 400
SALES (corp-wide): 59.8B *Publicly Held*
WEB: www.carrier.com
SIC: 3822 3585 3433 Refrigeration/air-conditioning defrost controls; refrigeration & heating equipment; heating equipment, except electric

HQ: Carrier Corporation
13995 Pasteur Blvd
Palm Beach Gardens FL 33418
800 379-6484

(G-15273)
CARRIER CORPORATION
Carrier Global Account (13221)
P.O. Box 4808 (13221-4808)
PHONE.....................................315 432-6000
Geraud Darnis, *Branch Mgr*
EMP: 1200
SALES (corp-wide): 59.8B *Publicly Held*
WEB: www.carrier.com
SIC: 3585 Refrigeration & heating equipment
HQ: Carrier Corporation
13995 Pasteur Blvd
Palm Beach Gardens FL 33418
800 379-6484

(G-15274)
CATHEDRAL CANDLE CO
510 Kirkpatrick St (13208-2100)
PHONE.....................................315 422-9119
Louis J Steigerwald III, *Ch of Bd*
Mark Steigerwald, *Vice Pres*
John Hogan, *Treasurer*
Linda D Rohde, *Admin Sec*
▲ **EMP:** 52 **EST:** 1897
SQ FT: 17,000
SALES (est): 7.2MM *Privately Held*
WEB: www.cathedralcandle.com
SIC: 3999 5049 Candles; religious supplies

(G-15275)
CHAMPION MILLWORK INC
140 Hiawatha Pl (13208-1268)
PHONE.....................................315 463-0711
Micheal Duffy, *President*
EMP: 25
SALES (est): 4.6MM *Privately Held*
SIC: 2431 Millwork

(G-15276)
CHEMTRADE CHEMICALS US LLC
Also Called: General Chemical
1421 Willis Ave (13204-1051)
P.O. Box 16 (13209-0016)
PHONE.....................................315 430-7650
Biagio Vavala, *Plant Mgr*
Biagio Bavala, *Opers-Prdtn-Mfg*
EMP: 40
SALES (corp-wide): 1.1B *Privately Held*
SIC: 2819 Industrial inorganic chemicals
HQ: Chemtrade Chemicals Us Llc
90 E Halsey Rd
Parsippany NJ 07054

(G-15277)
CHEMTRADE CHEMICALS US LLC
Also Called: Syracuse Technical Center
344 W Genesee St Ste 100 (13202-1010)
PHONE.....................................315 478-2323
Joseph Hurd, *Manager*
EMP: 5
SALES (corp-wide): 1.1B *Privately Held*
SIC: 2819 Sodium compounds or salts, inorg., ex. refined sod. chloride
HQ: Chemtrade Chemicals Us Llc
90 E Halsey Rd
Parsippany NJ 07054

(G-15278)
CITY PATTERN SHOP INC
4052 New Court Ave (13206-1639)
P.O. Box 6 (13206-0006)
PHONE.....................................315 463-5239
Paul M Clisson, *President*
Robert Leonard, *Vice Pres*
EMP: 10 **EST:** 1961
SQ FT: 7,500
SALES (est): 1.2MM *Privately Held*
WEB: www.citypatternshop.com
SIC: 3543 Industrial patterns

(G-15279)
CLARK CONCRETE CO INC (PA)
Also Called: Clark Trucking Co Div
434 E Brighton Ave (13210-4144)
PHONE.....................................315 478-4101
Donald W Clark, *President*
Lyndon S Clark, *Vice Pres*

Stephen Clark, *Vice Pres*
EMP: 6 **EST:** 1920
SQ FT: 8,000
SALES (est): 1.8MM *Privately Held*
SIC: 3273 4212 Ready-mixed concrete; local trucking, without storage

(G-15280)
CLEAN ALL OF SYRACUSE LLC
838 Erie Blvd W (13204-2228)
PHONE.....................................315 472-9189
Severino Gonnella, *President*
Angela Gonnella, *Vice Pres*
EMP: 9
SQ FT: 40,000
SALES (est): 980K *Privately Held*
SIC: 2842 5999 Cleaning or polishing preparations; swimming pool chemicals, equipment & supplies

(G-15281)
CNY BUSINESS REVIEW INC
Also Called: Business Journal
269 W Jefferson St (13202-2334)
PHONE.....................................315 472-3104
Norman Poltenson, *President*
Vance Marriner, *Engineer*
Dony Kuriakose, *Consultant*
Erin Zehr, *Creative Dir*
EMP: 14
SQ FT: 3,000
SALES (est): 953.5K *Privately Held*
WEB: www.cnybj.com
SIC: 2711 2721 Newspapers: publishing only, not printed on site; periodicals

(G-15282)
CNYSHIRTS
6392 Deere Rd Ste 1 (13206-1323)
PHONE.....................................315 432-1789
Jeremy Hibbert, *Mng Member*
EMP: 7 **EST:** 2012
SALES: 350K *Privately Held*
SIC: 2759 Screen printing

(G-15283)
COASTEL CABLE TOOLS INC
Also Called: Coastel Cable Tools Intl
344 E Brighton Ave (13210-4142)
PHONE.....................................315 471-5361
Edward Dale, *President*
Mary Shaver, *Vice Pres*
John Lumia, *Manager*
EMP: 21
SQ FT: 42,000
SALES (est): 2MM *Privately Held*
WEB: www.coasteltools.com
SIC: 3541 3423 Machine tools, metal cutting type; hand & edge tools

(G-15284)
COCA-COLA BTLG CO OF NY INC
298 Farrell Rd (13209-1876)
PHONE.....................................315 457-9221
Lucky Wyrick, *Sales/Mktg Mgr*
Heaven Donner, *Manager*
EMP: 10
SQ FT: 117,740
SALES (corp-wide): 35.4B *Publicly Held*
SIC: 2086 Bottled & canned soft drinks
HQ: The Coca-Cola Bottling Company Of New York Inc
2500 Windy Ridge Pkwy Se
Atlanta GA 30339
770 989-3000

(G-15285)
COLD SPRINGS R & D INC
1207 Van Vleck Rd Ste A (13209-1017)
PHONE.....................................315 413-1237
Scott Grimshaw, *President*
Valerie Grimshaw, *Vice Pres*
EMP: 10
SQ FT: 10,000
SALES (est): 1.3MM *Privately Held*
WEB: www.csrdinc.com
SIC: 3674 Semiconductors & related devices

(G-15286)
CONCEPTS IN WOOD OF CNY
4021 New Court Ave (13206-1640)
PHONE.....................................315 463-8084
David Fuleihan, *President*
EMP: 25

SQ FT: 16,000
SALES (est): 3.4MM *Privately Held*
SIC: 2521 2511 2431 Cabinets, office: wood; filing cabinets (boxes), office: wood; wood household furniture; millwork

(G-15287)
CONSTAS PRINTING CORPORATION
Also Called: Taylor Copy Services
1120 Burnet Ave (13203-3210)
PHONE.....................................315 474-2176
Diane M Brindak, *Ch of Bd*
Diane Constas, *President*
Claudia Constas, *Vice Pres*
EMP: 7
SQ FT: 2,400
SALES (est): 798.5K *Privately Held*
SIC: 2752 7334 Commercial printing, offset; photocopying & duplicating services

(G-15288)
COOKIE CONNECTION INC
705 Park Ave (13204-2223)
PHONE.....................................315 422-2253
Kathleen Sniezak, *President*
Elizabeth Johnson, *Vice Pres*
EMP: 5
SQ FT: 1,500
SALES (est): 305.8K *Privately Held*
SIC: 2051 Bakery: wholesale or wholesale/retail combined

(G-15289)
COOPER & CLEMENT INC
1840 Lemoyne Ave (13208-1367)
PHONE.....................................315 454-8135
John Clement, *President*
Inga Clement, *Vice Pres*
Ole Westergaard, *Vice Pres*
EMP: 29
SQ FT: 35,000
SALES (est): 4.4MM *Privately Held*
SIC: 2759 2396 Promotional printing; automotive & apparel trimmings

(G-15290)
COOPER CROUSE-HINDS LLC (DH)
Also Called: Cooper Crouse Hinds Elec Pdts
1201 Wolf St (13208-1376)
P.O. Box 4999 (13221-4999)
PHONE.....................................315 477-7000
Alexander M Cutler, *CEO*
Grant L Gawronski, *President*
Tania Wells, *Materials Mgr*
Don Gilbert, *Sales Staff*
Patrick Kane, *Sales Staff*
▲ **EMP:** 500
SQ FT: 1,000,000
SALES (est): 374.5MM *Privately Held*
WEB: www.coopercrouse-hinds.com
SIC: 3699 Fire control or bombing equipment, electronic

(G-15291)
COOPER INDUSTRIES LLC
Also Called: Cooper Molded Products
Wolf & 7th North St (13208)
PHONE.....................................315 477-7000
Nancy Gianni, *Project Mgr*
Everett Miles, *Maint Spvr*
Graig Decarr, *Project Engr*
Darren Rutland, *Sales Mgr*
Curt J Anderssonn, *Branch Mgr*
EMP: 20 *Privately Held*
SIC: 3646 3648 3613 5063 Commercial indusl & institutional electric lighting fixtures; lighting equipment; switchgear & switchgear accessories; electrical supplies; electrical equipment & supplies; construction machinery
HQ: Cooper Industries, Llc
600 Travis St Ste 5400
Houston TX 77002
713 209-8400

(G-15292)
COUNTERTOPS & CABINETS INC
4073 New Court Ave (13206-1646)
PHONE.....................................315 433-1038
Emil Henry, *President*
Nick Henry, *Admin Sec*
EMP: 5

Syracuse - Onondaga County (G-15293)

SQ FT: 3,200
SALES (est): 752K **Privately Held**
WEB: www.cnytops.com
SIC: 2541 1799 Counter & sink tops; counter top installation

(G-15293)
CREATIVE LAMINATES INC
4003 Eastbourne Dr (13206-1631)
PHONE..................315 463-7580
Dennis N Brackly, *President*
EMP: 19
SQ FT: 12,000
SALES (est): 146.4K **Privately Held**
WEB: www.creativelaminates.com
SIC: 2431 Doors & door parts & trim, wood

(G-15294)
CRITICAL LINK LLC
6712 Brooklawn Pkwy # 203 (13211-2110)
PHONE..................315 425-4045
Neha Chopra, *Project Mgr*
Alex Block, *Engineer*
Tom Catalino, *Engineer*
Bill Halpin, *Engineer*
Michael Williamson, *Senior Engr*
EMP: 20
SQ FT: 8,000
SALES (est): 6MM **Privately Held**
SIC: 3571 8711 Electronic computers; engineering services

(G-15295)
CRUCIBLE INDUSTRIES LLC
575 State Fair Blvd (13209-1560)
PHONE..................800 365-1180
Jim Beckman, *President*
Lorna Carpenter, *Vice Pres*
Eric Francisco, *Project Engr*
William Lester, *CFO*
Amy Virginia, *Accounting Mgr*
◆ **EMP:** 290
SALES (est): 99.9MM **Privately Held**
SIC: 3312 Bars, iron: made in steel mills

(G-15296)
CRYOMECH INC
113 Falso Dr (13211-2106)
PHONE..................315 455-2555
Peter Gifford, *President*
Rich Dausman, *COO*
Chao Wang, *Director*
Brent Zerkle, *Director*
▲ **EMP:** 100
SQ FT: 24,000
SALES (est): 29.5MM **Privately Held**
WEB: www.cryomech.com
SIC: 3559 Cryogenic machinery, industrial

(G-15297)
CUMMINS NORTHEAST LLC
6193 Eastern Ave (13211-2208)
PHONE..................315 437-2296
Kevin N Benson, *Principal*
Robin Riewaldt, *Opers-Prdtn-Mfg*
Janet Liedka, *Administration*
EMP: 36
SQ FT: 13,760
SALES (corp-wide): 20.4B **Publicly Held**
SIC: 3519 5063 Internal combustion engines; electrical apparatus & equipment
HQ: Cummins Northeast, Llc
30 Braintree Hill Park # 101
Braintree MA 02184

(G-15298)
CUSTOM SHEET METAL CORP
1 General Motors Dr Ste 5 (13206-1122)
PHONE..................315 463-9105
Wilson C Brown, *President*
Shaun Mills, *Manager*
EMP: 8
SQ FT: 5,000
SALES (est): 1.1MM **Privately Held**
SIC: 3444 Sheet metal specialties, not stamped

(G-15299)
D & D MOTOR SYSTEMS INC
215 Park Ave (13204-2459)
PHONE..................315 701-0861
Mike Dearoff, *President*
Eric Dearoff, *Vice Pres*
Eric Dieroff, *Vice Pres*
Vic Dejohn, *Engineer*
◆ **EMP:** 20

SALES (est): 4.8MM **Privately Held**
WEB: www.ddmotorsystems.com
SIC: 3621 Motors & generators

(G-15300)
D N GANNON FABRICATING INC
404 Wavel St (13206-1728)
P.O. Box 6572 (13217-6572)
PHONE..................315 463-7466
Frank Deuel, *President*
John Noel, *Vice Pres*
EMP: 5
SQ FT: 15,000
SALES (est): 550K **Privately Held**
SIC: 3441 Building components, structural steel

(G-15301)
DAILY ORANGE CORPORATION
744 Ostrom Ave (13244-2977)
PHONE..................315 443-2314
Mike Dooling, *General Mgr*
Christopher Russo, *General Mgr*
Dave Seal, *Editor*
Nancy Peck, *Adv Dir*
Lucy Sutphin, *Adv Mgr*
EMP: 50
SALES (est): 300.2K **Privately Held**
WEB: www.dailyorange.com
SIC: 2711 Newspapers: publishing only, not printed on site

(G-15302)
DARCO MANUFACTURING INC
6756 Thompson Rd (13211-2122)
P.O. Box 6304 (13217-6304)
PHONE..................315 432-8905
David A Redding, *President*
Laura Miller, *General Mgr*
EMP: 42
SQ FT: 22,000
SALES (est): 10.5MM **Privately Held**
SIC: 3599 Machine shop, jobbing & repair

(G-15303)
DAVID FEHLMAN
Also Called: Rollers Unlimited
6729 Pickard Dr (13211-2123)
P.O. Box 5059 (13220-5059)
PHONE..................315 455-8888
David Fehlman, *Owner*
EMP: 5
SQ FT: 3,200
SALES (est): 341.9K **Privately Held**
SIC: 3599 3562 3366 3312 Machine & other job shop work; ball & roller bearings; copper foundries; blast furnaces & steel mills; synthetic rubber; platemaking services

(G-15304)
DECORATED COOKIE COMPANY LLC
314 Lakeside Rd (13209-9729)
PHONE..................315 487-2111
Peter Hess, *Mng Member*
EMP: 30
SQ FT: 13,000
SALES (est): 4.7MM **Privately Held**
SIC: 2052 Cookies

(G-15305)
DEPENDABLE TOOL & DIE CO INC
129 Dwight Park Cir # 2 (13209-1010)
PHONE..................315 453-5696
Anthony D Dantuono, *President*
Andrea Tarolli, *Admin Sec*
EMP: 8
SQ FT: 20,000
SALES (est): 1.2MM **Privately Held**
SIC: 3544 Special dies & tools

(G-15306)
DUPLI GRAPHICS CORPORATION (HQ)
Also Called: Dupli Envelope & Graphics
6761 Thompson Rd (13211-2119)
P.O. Box 11500 (13218-1500)
PHONE..................315 234-7286
J Kemper Matt, *Ch of Bd*
J Kemper Matt Jr, *President*
Todd Luchsinger, *CFO*
Jody Chastain, *Accounts Mgr*
Lisa Wysowski, *Manager*

EMP: 117
SQ FT: 150,000
SALES (est): 29.6MM
SALES (corp-wide): 28.4MM **Privately Held**
WEB: www.duplionline.com
SIC: 2752 2759 Commercial printing, lithographic; envelopes: printing
PA: Matt Industries Inc.
6761 Thompson Rd
Syracuse NY 13211
315 472-1316

(G-15307)
DUPLI GRAPHICS CORPORATION
Grafek Direct
Dupli Park Dr (13218)
P.O. Box 11500 (13218-1500)
PHONE..................315 422-4732
Kemper J Matt, *President*
Robert Cuthill, *Sales Executive*
EMP: 8
SALES (corp-wide): 28.4MM **Privately Held**
WEB: www.duplionline.com
SIC: 2759 2752 Envelopes: printing; commercial printing, offset
HQ: Dupli Graphics Corporation
6761 Thompson Rd
Syracuse NY 13211
315 234-7286

(G-15308)
DYNAMIC HYBIRDS INC
1201 E Fayette St Ste 11 (13210-1933)
PHONE..................315 426-8110
Don Hazelmyer, *President*
EMP: 7
SQ FT: 2,500
SALES (est): 1MM **Privately Held**
WEB: www.hybridcircuit.com
SIC: 3679 Electronic circuits

(G-15309)
EAGLE MEDIA PARTNERS LP (PA)
Also Called: Eagle Newspapers
2501 James St Ste 100 (13206-2996)
PHONE..................315 434-8889
H Douglas Barclay, *Partner*
Edward S Green, *Partner*
Stewart Hancock, *Partner*
David Northrup, *Partner*
EMP: 33
SQ FT: 7,000
SALES (est): 3.6MM **Privately Held**
WEB: www.cnylink.com
SIC: 2711 Commercial printing & newspaper publishing combined; newspapers, publishing & printing

(G-15310)
EASTWOOD LITHO INC
4020 New Court Ave (13206-1663)
P.O. Box 131 (13206-0131)
PHONE..................315 437-2626
Mark J Mohr, *President*
Betty E Mohr, *Vice Pres*
Betty Mohr, *Vice Pres*
Patrick H Mohr, *Treasurer*
Patrick Mohr, *Treasurer*
EMP: 30
SQ FT: 15,000
SALES (est): 4.6MM **Privately Held**
WEB: www.eastwoodlitho.com
SIC: 2759 2752 2791 2789 Letterpress printing; commercial printing, lithographic; typesetting; bookbinding & related work

(G-15311)
EATON CORPORATION
Also Called: Ephesus Lighting
125 E Jefferson St (13202-2020)
PHONE..................315 579-2872
EMP: 30 **Privately Held**
SIC: 3645 Fluorescent lighting fixtures, residential
HQ: Eaton Corporation
1000 Eaton Blvd
Cleveland OH 44122
440 523-5000

(G-15312)
EATON CROUSE-HINDS
1201 Wolf St (13208-1375)
PHONE..................315 477-7000
Scott Hearn, *Principal*
Walter Fedor, *Production*
Asiri Jayawardena, *Engineer*
Kathleen Mills, *Manager*
Kristen McDevitt, *Planning*
EMP: 200
SALES (est): 16.6MM **Privately Held**
SIC: 3648 Airport lighting fixtures: runway approach, taxi or ramp

(G-15313)
EATONS CROUSE HINDS BUSINESS
1201 Wolf St (13208-1375)
PHONE..................315 477-7000
EMP: 17
SALES (est): 2.9MM **Privately Held**
SIC: 3625 Mfg Relays/Industrial Controls

(G-15314)
ELEVATOR INTERIORS INC
1116 S Salina St (13202-3517)
PHONE..................315 218-7186
Joe Piepho, *President*
Christopher J Duke, *President*
James E Cosbey, *Vice Pres*
EMP: 20
SQ FT: 5,000
SALES (est): 6MM **Privately Held**
SIC: 3534 Elevators & equipment

(G-15315)
ELIZABETH WOOD
Also Called: Endoscopic Procedure Center
4900 Broad Rd (13215-2265)
PHONE..................315 492-5470
Elizabeth Wood, *President*
EMP: 5
SALES (est): 905.2K **Privately Held**
SIC: 3845 Endoscopic equipment, electromedical

(G-15316)
ELTON EL MANTLE INC
6072 Court Street Rd (13206-1711)
P.O. Box 3166 (13220-3166)
PHONE..................315 432-9067
Elton Mantle, *President*
EMP: 5 **EST:** 2000
SALES (est): 356.3K **Privately Held**
SIC: 3621 Motors, electric

(G-15317)
EMPIRE BREWING COMPANY INC
120 Walton St (13202-1571)
PHONE..................315 925-8308
David Katleski, *President*
Tim Butler, *Opers Staff*
Lisa Shoen, *Human Res Dir*
Karen Katleski, *Supervisor*
Monica Palmer, *Director*
EMP: 64
SALES: 3MM **Privately Held**
SIC: 2082 5812 Ale (alcoholic beverage); American restaurant

(G-15318)
EMPIRE DIVISION INC
201 Kirkpatrick St # 207 (13208-2075)
PHONE..................315 476-6273
Vincent Williams, *President*
EMP: 72
SQ FT: 9,000
SALES (est): 5MM **Privately Held**
SIC: 3589 3621 5063 5064 Vacuum cleaners & sweepers, electric: industrial; water purification equipment, household type; motors, electric; motors, electric; vacuum cleaners, household; water purification equipment; cleaning equipment & supplies; motors, electric; water purification equipment

(G-15319)
ERHARD & GILCHER INC
235 Cortland Ave (13202-3825)
P.O. Box 84 (13209-0084)
PHONE..................315 474-1072
Peter Coyne, *President*
Rosemary Coyne, *Corp Secy*

▲ = Import ▼ = Export
◆ = Import/Export

GEOGRAPHIC SECTION

Syracuse - Onondaga County (G-15346)

Lance McGee, *Vice Pres*
EMP: 35 EST: 1913
SQ FT: 25,000
SALES (est): 3.6MM **Privately Held**
SIC: 2789 Bookbinding & related work

(G-15320)
EVERGREEN CORP CENTRAL NY
Also Called: Evergreen Manufacturing
235 Cortland Ave (13202-3825)
PHONE..................315 454-4175
Rene Musso, *President*
EMP: 18
SQ FT: 4,500
SALES (est): 2.9MM **Privately Held**
SIC: 3544 2759 Paper cutting dies; commercial printing

(G-15321)
EXCEL ALUMINUM PRODUCTS INC
563 N Salina St (13208-2530)
PHONE..................315 471-0925
Frank Tafel Jr, *President*
Raymond Tafel, *Admin Sec*
EMP: 5
SQ FT: 2,000
SALES: 250K **Privately Held**
SIC: 3442 5031 Storm doors or windows, metal; windows; doors

(G-15322)
FALSO INDUSTRIES INC
Also Called: Falso Metal Fabricating
4100 New Court Ave (13206-1698)
PHONE..................315 463-0266
Raymond Falso, *President*
Dean Sharron, *General Mgr*
Richard Iorio, *Corp Secy*
Norb Kieffer, *Plant Mgr*
Heidi Dieroff, *Info Tech Mgr*
EMP: 20
SQ FT: 19,000
SALES (est): 4.2MM **Privately Held**
WEB: www.falsoindustries.com
SIC: 3469 Stamping metal for the trade

(G-15323)
FELDMEIER EQUIPMENT INC (PA)
6800 Townline Rd (13211-1325)
P.O. Box 474 (13211-0474)
PHONE..................315 823-2000
Robert E Feldmeier, *CEO*
Jean Jackson, *Vice Pres*
David Pollock, *Vice Pres*
Denny Davis, *Plant Mgr*
Ken Osborne, *Plant Mgr*
EMP: 100 EST: 1953
SQ FT: 60,000
SALES (est): 94.1MM **Privately Held**
WEB: www.feldmeier.com
SIC: 3443 Tanks, standard or custom fabricated; metal plate

(G-15324)
FORTECH INC
Also Called: Fortech Div
223 4th North St (13208-1299)
PHONE..................315 478-2048
Adrian E Ferraris, *President*
Betty Ferraris, *Vice Pres*
Larae Melfi, *Manager*
EMP: 7
SQ FT: 26,000
SALES: 650K **Privately Held**
WEB: www.fortechfab.com
SIC: 3599 Machine & other job shop work

(G-15325)
FRAZER & JONES CO
Also Called: Frasier and Jones
3000 Milton Ave (13209)
P.O. Box 4955 (13221-4955)
PHONE..................315 468-6251
Angelo Labbadia, *Managing Dir*
Mark Novakowski, *Principal*
Deborah Kinville, *Human Res Mgr*
Eric Schmidt, *Supervisor*
Damir Klapan, *Info Tech Mgr*
EMP: 90
SQ FT: 182,784
SALES (est): 9.7MM **Privately Held**
WEB: www.frazerandjones.com
SIC: 3325 Steel foundries

(G-15326)
FUTON CITY DISCOUNTERS INC
Also Called: Sleep Master
6361 Thompson Rd (13206-1448)
PHONE..................315 437-1328
Charles Vanpatten, *President*
EMP: 18
SALES (est): 3.4MM **Privately Held**
SIC: 2599 5712 Factory furniture & fixtures; furniture stores

(G-15327)
G A BRAUN INC
461 E Brighton Ave (13210-4143)
P.O. Box 3029 (13220-3029)
PHONE..................315 475-3123
Steve Bregande, *Principal*
Jim Corrigan, *Vice Pres*
Jeffrey Hohman, *Project Mgr*
Mehidin Omerovic, *Buyer*
Ed Bidwell, *Purchasing*
EMP: 25
SALES (corp-wide): 45.1MM **Privately Held**
SIC: 3582 Commercial laundry equipment
PA: G. A. Braun, Inc.
 79 General Irwin Blvd
 North Syracuse NY 13212
 315 475-3123

(G-15328)
G C HANFORD MANUFACTURING CO (PA)
Also Called: Hanford Pharmaceuticals
304 Oneida St (13202-3433)
P.O. Box 1017 (13201-1017)
PHONE..................315 476-7418
George R Hanford, *Principal*
Joseph J Heath, *Principal*
Peter Ward, *Principal*
Ronald Lauback, *Vice Pres*
Gail Goson, *Safety Mgr*
EMP: 186 EST: 1846
SQ FT: 80,000
SALES (est): 48.4MM **Privately Held**
WEB: www.hanford.com
SIC: 2834 2833 5122 Penicillin preparations; antibiotics; pharmaceuticals

(G-15329)
GARDALL SAFE CORPORATION
219 Lamson St Ste 1 (13206-2879)
P.O. Box 240 (13206-0240)
PHONE..................315 432-9115
Edward Baroody, *Ch of Bd*
David A Patton, *Treasurer*
Kris Ruffos, *Marketing Staff*
◆ EMP: 25 EST: 1950
SQ FT: 35,000
SALES (est): 4.9MM **Privately Held**
WEB: www.gardall.com
SIC: 3499 Safes & vaults, metal

(G-15330)
GARDNER DNVER OBERDORFER PUMPS
5900 Firestone Dr (13206-1103)
PHONE..................315 437-0361
Robin Watkins, *Principal*
▲ EMP: 30
SQ FT: 50,000
SALES (est): 5.1MM
SALES (corp-wide): 2.3B **Publicly Held**
SIC: 3561 Industrial pumps & parts
HQ: Gardner Denver, Inc.
 222 E Erie St Ste 500
 Milwaukee WI 53202

(G-15331)
GEAR MOTIONS INCORPORATED (PA)
Also Called: Nixon Gear
1750 Milton Ave (13209-1626)
PHONE..................315 488-0100
Samuel R Haines, *President*
Dean Burroes, *President*
EMP: 50
SQ FT: 45,000
SALES (est): 18MM **Privately Held**
WEB: www.gearmotions.com
SIC: 3462 Gears, forged steel

(G-15332)
GENERAL ELECTRIC COMPANY
5990 E Molloy Rd (13211)
PHONE..................315 456-3304
Matthew J Battle, *Branch Mgr*
EMP: 20
SQ FT: 8,000
SALES (corp-wide): 122B **Publicly Held**
SIC: 7694 Electric motor repair
PA: General Electric Company
 41 Farnsworth St
 Boston MA 02210
 617 443-3000

(G-15333)
GENERATION POWER LLC
238 W Division St (13204-1412)
PHONE..................315 234-2451
Steve Starrantino, *Vice Pres*
Bob Zywicki,
Jay Bernhardt,
EMP: 9
SALES (est): 1.8MM **Privately Held**
SIC: 3621 Motors & generators

(G-15334)
GEORGE RETZOS
Also Called: Columbus Baking Co
502 Pearl St (13203-1702)
PHONE..................315 422-2913
James Retzos, *Owner*
EMP: 5 EST: 1934
SALES (est): 485.6K **Privately Held**
SIC: 2051 Bread, all types (white, wheat, rye, etc); fresh or frozen

(G-15335)
GREENLEAF CABINET MAKERS LLC
6691 Pickard Dr (13211-2114)
PHONE..................315 432-4600
Gerard Davis, *Mng Member*
Dave Morrison, *Manager*
EMP: 10 EST: 2001
SQ FT: 3,000
SALES (est): 1.5MM **Privately Held**
SIC: 2541 Wood partitions & fixtures

(G-15336)
H C YOUNG TOOL & MACHINE CO
3700 New Court Ave (13206-1674)
PHONE..................315 463-0663
Gordon K Young, *President*
EMP: 5 EST: 1935
SQ FT: 1,000
SALES (est): 553K **Privately Held**
WEB: www.hcyoung.com
SIC: 3599 Machine shop, jobbing & repair

(G-15337)
HANGER PRSTHETCS & ORTHO INC
910 Erie Blvd E Ste 3 (13210-1060)
PHONE..................315 472-5200
Roy Ostrander, *Manager*
EMP: 5
SALES (corp-wide): 1B **Publicly Held**
SIC: 3842 Surgical appliances & supplies
HQ: Hanger Prosthetics & Orthotics, Inc.
 10910 Domain Dr Ste 300
 Austin TX 78758
 512 777-3800

(G-15338)
HARRISON BAKERY WEST
1306 W Genesee St (13204-2184)
PHONE..................315 422-1468
James Rothfeld, *President*
EMP: 30
SQ FT: 15,000
SALES (est): 5.2MM **Privately Held**
SIC: 2051 5461 Bread, all types (white, wheat, rye, etc); fresh or frozen; cakes; bakery; except frozen; doughnuts, except frozen; bread; cakes; doughnuts

(G-15339)
HART RIFLE BARREL INC
1680 Jamesville Ave (13210-4236)
P.O. Box 182, La Fayette (13084-0182)
PHONE..................315 677-9841
Jack Sutton, *Partner*
James Hart, *Partner*
EMP: 7 EST: 1955
SQ FT: 2,000
SALES: 750K **Privately Held**
WEB: www.hartbarrels.com
SIC: 3484 Rifles or rifle parts, 30 mm. & below

(G-15340)
HERALD NEWSPAPERS COMPANY INC (HQ)
Also Called: Post Standard, The
220 S Warren St (13202-1676)
PHONE..................315 470-0011
Tim Kennedy, *President*
Stephen A Rogers, *Chairman*
Donald E Newhouse, *Treasurer*
Jim Bliss, *Train & Dev Mgr*
Patrice David, *Sales Staff*
EMP: 612
SQ FT: 50,000
SALES (est): 390.5MM
SALES (corp-wide): 5.6B **Privately Held**
WEB: www.post-standard.com
SIC: 2711 Commercial printing & newspaper publishing combined
PA: Advance Publications, Inc.
 950 W Fingerboard Rd
 Staten Island NY 10305
 718 981-1234

(G-15341)
HY-GRADE METAL PRODUCTS CORP
906 Burnet Ave (13203-3206)
PHONE..................315 475-4221
Michael Donegan, *President*
EMP: 7
SQ FT: 10,000
SALES (est): 544.5K **Privately Held**
WEB: www.hy-grademetal.com
SIC: 3469 Spinning metal for the trade

(G-15342)
INDEPENDENT FIELD SVC LLC (PA)
6744 Pickard Dr (13211-2115)
PHONE..................315 559-9243
Aaron Barbaro, *Owner*
EMP: 6
SQ FT: 8,000
SALES (est): 1.2MM **Privately Held**
SIC: 3621 Power generators

(G-15343)
INGLIS CO INC
116 Granger St (13202-2315)
P.O. Box 401, Manlius (13104-0401)
PHONE..................315 475-1315
Kenneth Abramson, *President*
Anthony River, *Vice Pres*
EMP: 7
SQ FT: 5,000
SALES (est): 812.2K **Privately Held**
SIC: 2893 2851 5084 Printing ink; paints & paint additives; lacquers, varnishes, enamels & other coatings; removers & cleaners; paint spray equipment, industrial

(G-15344)
J & J PRINTING INC (PA)
500 Cambridge Ave (13208-1415)
PHONE..................315 458-7411
Matthew Joseph Farr, *President*
Betty Farr, *Vice Pres*
EMP: 8 EST: 1969
SQ FT: 3,000
SALES (est): 719.8K **Privately Held**
SIC: 2752 Commercial printing, offset

(G-15345)
JACOBS WOODWORKING LLC
801 W Fayette St (13204-2805)
PHONE..................315 427-8999
Jacob Gerros, *Mng Member*
EMP: 7
SALES (est): 632.5K **Privately Held**
SIC: 2431 Millwork

(G-15346)
JAQUITH INDUSTRIES INC
600 E Brighton Ave (13210-4248)
PHONE..................315 478-5700
D Scott Jaquith, *President*
Adam Antczak, *Buyer*
◆ EMP: 50

SQ FT: 120,000
SALES: 10.1MM Privately Held
WEB: www.jaquith.com
SIC: 3312 3648 3728 3444 Blast furnaces & steel mills; lighting equipment; aircraft parts & equipment; sheet metalwork; fabricated plate work (boiler shop); manufactured hardware (general)

(G-15347)
JOHN A EBERLY INC
136 Beattie St (13224-1102)
P.O. Box 149, Pompey (13138-0149)
PHONE....................315 449-3034
John Lee, *President*
EMP: 7 EST: 1912
SQ FT: 6,000
SALES (est): 1.3MM Privately Held
WEB: www.jaeberly.com
SIC: 3421 5084 Scissors, shears, clippers, snips & similar tools; textile machinery & equipment

(G-15348)
JOHN F KRELL JR
Also Called: Syracuse Hvac
4046 W Seneca Trpk (13215)
PHONE....................315 492-3201
John F Krell, *Partner*
Andrew Krell, *Partner*
EMP: 5
SALES (est): 609.8K Privately Held
SIC: 3585 Heating & air conditioning combination units

(G-15349)
JOHNSTON DANDY COMPANY
Cook, E F Co
100 Dippold Ave (13208-1320)
PHONE....................315 455-5773
Michael Myers, *General Mgr*
Don Wilson, *Store Mgr*
Kimberly Pinkham, *Controller*
EMP: 7
SQ FT: 12,540
SALES (est): 1.1MM
SALES (corp-wide): 10.4MM Privately Held
WEB: www.johnstondandy.com
SIC: 3547 3554 Rolling mill machinery; paper industries machinery
PA: Johnston Dandy Company
  148 Main St
  Lincoln ME 04457
  207 794-6571

(G-15350)
JORDON BOX COMPANY INC
Also Called: Jordan Box Co
140 Dickerson St (13202-2309)
P.O. Box 1054 (13201-1054)
PHONE....................315 422-3419
Rick Casper, *President*
EMP: 20
SQ FT: 30,000
SALES: 700K Privately Held
WEB: www.jordanboxco.com
SIC: 2652 Setup paperboard boxes

(G-15351)
JOY EDWARD COMPANY
Also Called: Joy Process Mechanical
105 Enderberry Cir (13224-2003)
PHONE....................315 474-3360
Leonard P Markert III, *CEO*
Gerald Carhart, *Vice Pres*
Jim Condon, *Project Mgr*
Lyn Markert Hathaway, *Admin Sec*
Lyn Hathaway, *Admin Sec*
EMP: 40 EST: 1875
SQ FT: 40,000
SALES: 15.8MM Privately Held
SIC: 3441 1711 Fabricated structural metal; mechanical contractor

(G-15352)
JPW STRUCTURAL CONTRACTING INC
Also Called: Jpw Riggers & Erectors
6376 Thompson Rd (13206-1406)
PHONE....................315 432-1111
John P Wozniczka III, *Ch of Bd*
Jeffery Exner, *Vice Pres*
Jody Wozniczka, *Vice Pres*
Patricia Wozniczka, *Treasurer*
Amy Barrett, *Controller*
EMP: 25
SQ FT: 70,000
SALES: 8.1MM Privately Held
SIC: 3441 Fabricated structural metal

(G-15353)
K&G OF SYRACUSE INC
2500 Erie Blvd E (13224-1110)
PHONE....................315 446-1921
Karamjit Grewal, *Principal*
EMP: 5
SALES (est): 526.1K Privately Held
SIC: 3578 Automatic teller machines (ATM)

(G-15354)
KASSIS SUPERIOR SIGN CO INC
6699 Old Thompson Rd (13211-2118)
PHONE....................315 463-7446
Joseph Kassis, *CEO*
Anthony Sklaney, *CFO*
Edda Kassis, *Admin Sec*
EMP: 19
SALES (est): 4.5MM Privately Held
WEB: www.kassissigns.com
SIC: 3444 5039 Sheet metalwork; awnings

(G-15355)
KILIAN MANUFACTURING CORP (HQ)
1728 Burnet Ave (13206-3340)
P.O. Box 6974 (13217-6974)
PHONE....................315 432-0700
Don Wierbinski, *President*
David Sheridan, *Controller*
Keith Flynn, *Human Res Mgr*
Dominic Leo, *Manager*
David McCaskey, *Manager*
▲ EMP: 73 EST: 1921
SQ FT: 100,000
SALES (est): 70.2MM
SALES (corp-wide): 876.7MM Publicly Held
SIC: 3562 3429 Ball bearings & parts; manufactured hardware (general)
PA: Altra Industrial Motion Corp.
  300 Granite St Ste 201
  Braintree MA 02184
  781 917-0600

(G-15356)
KINANECO INC (PA)
Also Called: Kinaneco Printing Systems
2925 Milton Ave (13209-2519)
PHONE....................315 468-6201
Greg Kinane, *Chairman*
Peter T Kinane, *Chairman*
Sue Sgarlata, *Production*
Gail Foster, *Accounting Mgr*
Gregory Kinane, *Human Res Dir*
EMP: 20 EST: 1973
SQ FT: 6,000
SALES (est): 3.6MM Privately Held
WEB: www.kinaneco.com
SIC: 2759 2752 7311 2754 Business forms; printing; commercial printing, offset; advertising agencies; color printing, gravure

(G-15357)
KNISE & KRICK INC
324 Pearl St (13203-1998)
PHONE....................315 422-3516
John P Extrom, *President*
Beth Moore, *Admin Sec*
EMP: 20 EST: 1926
SQ FT: 30,000
SALES (est): 3.7MM Privately Held
WEB: www.knisekrick.com
SIC: 3544 7389 3599 Jigs & fixtures; metal cutting services; machine & other job shop work

(G-15358)
KODIAK CUTTING TOOLS LLC
2700 Bellevue Ave (13219-3238)
PHONE....................800 892-1006
Edward Nolan, *Mng Member*
EMP: 5
SQ FT: 2,000
SALES (est): 244.3K Privately Held
SIC: 3541 Machine tools, metal cutting type

(G-15359)
LEMOYNE MACHINE PRODUCTS CORP
106 Evelyn Ter (13208-1321)
PHONE....................315 454-0708
Marvin Kisselstein, *President*
Robert Grandinetti, *Vice Pres*
EMP: 5
SQ FT: 5,000
SALES (est): 643.1K Privately Held
SIC: 3562 Ball & roller bearings

(G-15360)
LIBERTY FOOD AND FUEL
1131 N Salina St (13208-2027)
PHONE....................315 299-4039
Anwa Nagnaji, *Manager*
EMP: 6
SALES (est): 766.4K Privately Held
SIC: 2869 Fuels

(G-15361)
LIFT SAFE - FUEL SAFE INC
212 W Seneca Tpke (13205-2709)
PHONE....................315 423-7702
Daniel Sorber, *CEO*
EMP: 5
SALES (est): 1.3MM Privately Held
SIC: 2869 Fuels

(G-15362)
LINDE GAS NORTH AMERICA LLC
Also Called: Lifegas
147 Midler Park Dr (13206-1817)
PHONE....................315 431-4081
Richard Kelley, *Branch Mgr*
EMP: 19
SALES (corp-wide): 20.1B Privately Held
SIC: 2813 Nitrogen; oxygen, compressed or liquefied
HQ: Linde Gas North America Llc
  200 Somerset Corp Blvd # 7000
  Bridgewater NJ 08807

(G-15363)
LOCKHEED MARTIN CORPORATION
6060 Tarbell Rd (13206-1301)
PHONE....................315 456-6604
Mark Schmidt, *Branch Mgr*
EMP: 45 Publicly Held
WEB: www.lockheedmartin.com
SIC: 3812 Sonar systems & equipment; radar systems & equipment
PA: Lockheed Martin Corporation
  6801 Rockledge Dr
  Bethesda MD 20817

(G-15364)
LOCKHEED MARTIN INTEGRTD SYSTM
497 Electronics Pkwy (13221)
P.O. Box 4840 (13221-4840)
PHONE....................315 456-3333
EMP: 26 Publicly Held
SIC: 3812 Search & navigation equipment
HQ: Lockheed Martin Integrated Systems, Llc
  6801 Rockledge Dr
  Bethesda MD 20817

(G-15365)
LOUIS IANNETTONI
1841 Lemoyne Ave (13208-1328)
PHONE....................315 454-3231
Louis Iannettoni, *Owner*
EMP: 65
SALES (est): 4.5MM Privately Held
SIC: 3363 Aluminum die-castings

(G-15366)
M & W ALUMINUM PRODUCTS INC
321 Wavel St (13206-1726)
PHONE....................315 414-0005
Uriah P Montclair, *President*
EMP: 16
SQ FT: 12,330
SALES (est): 2.7MM Privately Held
WEB: www.mwalum.com
SIC: 3465 Body parts, automobile: stamped metal

(G-15367)
MARZULLO ELECTRIC LLC
103 Oliva Dr (13211-1902)
PHONE....................315 455-1050
Joseph Marzullo, *Owner*
EMP: 6
SALES (est): 714.8K Privately Held
SIC: 3699 Electrical equipment & supplies

(G-15368)
MATT INDUSTRIES INC (PA)
Also Called: Grphics Grafek
6761 Thompson Rd (13211-2119)
P.O. Box 11500 (13218-1500)
PHONE....................315 472-1316
J Kemper Matt, *President*
Thomas Booth, *Vice Pres*
Tom Booth, *Vice Pres*
John Mather, *Vice Pres*
J Kemper Matt Jr, *Vice Pres*
EMP: 120
SQ FT: 150,000
SALES (est): 28.4MM Privately Held
SIC: 2759 5112 Envelopes: printing; envelopes

(G-15369)
MELOON FOUNDRIES LLC
1841 Lemoyne Ave (13208-1389)
PHONE....................315 454-3231
Robert Evans, *President*
EMP: 42
SQ FT: 90,000
SALES (est): 9.6MM
SALES (corp-wide): 30MM Privately Held
SIC: 3365 3366 3291 Aluminum foundries; copper foundries; brass foundry; bronze foundry; abrasive products
HQ: Evans Industries, Inc.
  249 Boston St
  Detroit MI 48243
  313 259-2266

(G-15370)
METALICO ALUMINUM RECOVERY INC
6223 Thompson Rd (13206-1405)
P.O. Box 88, East Syracuse (13057-0088)
PHONE....................315 463-9500
Carlos E Aguero, *President*
Michael J Drury, *COO*
Arnold S Graber, *Exec VP*
David Delbianco, *Vice Pres*
Mike Drury, *Vice Pres*
▲ EMP: 40
SALES (est): 12MM
SALES (corp-wide): 476MM Privately Held
SIC: 3341 5093 Aluminum smelting & refining (secondary); scrap & waste materials
PA: Metalico, Inc.
  135 Dermody St
  Cranford NJ 07016
  908 497-9610

(G-15371)
MIDDLE AGES BREWING COMPANY
120 Wilkinson St Ste 3 (13204-2490)
PHONE....................315 476-4250
Mary Rubenstein, *President*
Isaac Rubenstein, *Vice Pres*
Marc Rubenstein, *Treasurer*
Jason Allen, *Sales Mgr*
Matt Vogelsang, *Manager*
▲ EMP: 6
SQ FT: 10,000
SALES (est): 658K Privately Held
SIC: 2082 Beer (alcoholic beverage)

(G-15372)
MIDGLEY PRINTING CORP
433 W Onondaga St Ste B (13202-3277)
PHONE....................315 475-1864
Lena Midgley, *President*
David Midgley, *Vice Pres*
Bruce Midgley, *Admin Sec*
EMP: 9 EST: 1955
SQ FT: 10,000

SALES (est): 830K Privately Held
SIC: 2752 2759 2791 2789 Commercial printing, lithographic; letterpress printing; typesetting; bookbinding & related work

(G-15373)
MIDSTATE SPRING INC
Also Called: Syracuse Midstate Spring
4054 New Court Ave (13206-1639)
P.O. Box 850 (13206-0850)
PHONE..................315 437-2623
Walter Melnikow, *President*
Mike Komurek, *COO*
Paul S Bernet, *Vice Pres*
Keith Miller, *Production*
Krystal Alger, *Engineer*
▲ EMP: 41
SQ FT: 13,000
SALES (est): 10.2MM Privately Held
WEB: www.midstatespring.com
SIC: 3493 3495 Steel springs, except wire; wire springs

(G-15374)
MINIMILL TECHNOLOGIES INC
5792 Widewaters Pkwy # 1 (13214-1847)
PHONE..................315 692-4557
Kamala G Rajan, *President*
Joseph Gasperetti, *Senior VP*
Srinivasan Balaji, *Vice Pres*
Donnie Parks, *Vice Pres*
George Rice, *Vice Pres*
EMP: 14
SALES: 6MM Privately Held
SIC: 2621 Paper mills

(G-15375)
MITTEN MANUFACTURING INC
5960 Court Street Rd (13206-1706)
PHONE..................315 437-7564
John P Mitten Jr, *CEO*
Jack Mitten, *Principal*
David Bennett, *Sales Mgr*
Gene Waggoner, *Manager*
EMP: 40
SALES (est): 5.2MM Privately Held
SIC: 3999 Atomizers, toiletry

(G-15376)
MONAGHAN MEDICAL CORPORATION
Also Called: Sales & Marketing Office
327 W Fayette St Ste 214 (13202-1516)
PHONE..................315 472-2136
Michael Amato, *Vice Pres*
EMP: 8
SALES (corp-wide): 9.9MM Privately Held
WEB: www.monaghanmed.com
SIC: 3842 Respiratory protection equipment, personal
PA: Monaghan Medical Corporation
  5 Latour Ave Ste 1600
  Plattsburgh NY 12901
  518 561-7330

(G-15377)
MUENCH-KREUZER CANDLE COMPANY (PA)
Also Called: Emkay Candle Company
617 Hiawatha Blvd E (13208-1228)
PHONE..................315 471-4515
John P Brogan, *Ch of Bd*
▲ EMP: 80
SQ FT: 100,000
SALES (est): 9.9MM Privately Held
WEB: www.emkaycandle.com
SIC: 3999 Candles

(G-15378)
MUZET INC
104 S Main St (13212-3104)
PHONE..................315 452-0050
Frank Crawford, *Manager*
EMP: 10
SALES (corp-wide): 2.2MM Privately Held
SIC: 3931 Musical instruments
PA: Muzet Inc
  219 W Commercial St
  East Rochester NY 14445
  585 586-5320

(G-15379)
N E CONTROLS LLC
7048 Interstate Island Rd (13209-9712)
PHONE..................315 626-2480
Evan Weaver, *Engineer*
Michael Majewski, *Project Engr*
Brad Stone, *Sales Staff*
Al Weaver,
Herb Smith,
EMP: 12
SQ FT: 6,000
SALES: 950K Privately Held
WEB: www.necontrols.com
SIC: 3625 5084 Control equipment, electric; industrial machinery & equipment

(G-15380)
NEPTUNE SOFT WATER INC
1201 E Fayette St Ste 6 (13210-1896)
PHONE..................315 446-5151
William Olivieri, *President*
EMP: 15 EST: 1963
SQ FT: 4,500
SALES (est): 2.4MM Privately Held
SIC: 3589 5999 5074 Water treatment equipment, industrial; water purification equipment, household type; water purification equipment; water purification equipment

(G-15381)
NEW YORK MARKING DEVICES CORP (PA)
Also Called: Jessel Marking Equipment
2207 Teall Ave (13206-1544)
P.O. Box 234 (13206-0234)
PHONE..................315 463-8641
Joseph L Stummer Jr, *President*
Amy Stummer, *Vice Pres*
Ellen Stummer, *Vice Pres*
Peter J Stummer, *Vice Pres*
Kathy Stummer, *Office Mgr*
EMP: 14
SQ FT: 7,800
SALES: 1.7MM Privately Held
WEB: www.nymarking.com
SIC: 3953 Embossing seals & hand stamps

(G-15382)
NORTH EASTERN RESCUE VEHICLES
10 Dwight Park Dr Ste 1 (13209-1091)
PHONE..................315 414-9999
Robert A Barnes, *President*
Bob Reilley, *President*
EMP: 8
SALES (est): 1.6MM Privately Held
WEB: www.nervinc.com
SIC: 3711 Motor vehicles & car bodies

(G-15383)
OBERDORFER PUMPS INC
5900 Firestone Dr (13206-1103)
PHONE..................315 437-0361
Kevin Digney, *CEO*
Timothy C Brown, *President*
Phillip J Stuecker, *Vice Pres*
Gary Young, *Technology*
EMP: 43
SQ FT: 46,000
SALES (est): 9.4MM
SALES (corp-wide): 2.3B Publicly Held
WEB: www.oberdorfer-pumps.com
SIC: 3561 Industrial pumps & parts
HQ: Gardner Denver, Inc.
  222 E Erie St Ste 500
  Milwaukee WI 53202

(G-15384)
OESTREICH METAL WORKS INC
6131 Court Street Rd (13206-1302)
PHONE..................315 463-4268
Steve Tallman, *President*
EMP: 5
SQ FT: 4,000
SALES (est): 588.2K Privately Held
SIC: 3564 Blowing fans: industrial or commercial; ventilating fans: industrial or commercial; exhaust fans: industrial or commercial

(G-15385)
OMEGA FURNITURE MANUFACTURING
102 Wavel St (13206-1303)
PHONE..................315 463-7428
George Sakellariou, *President*
EMP: 12
SQ FT: 10,000
SALES (est): 600K Privately Held
WEB: www.omegafmi.com
SIC: 2521 5712 Wood office furniture; furniture stores

(G-15386)
ONE TREE DIST
200 Midler Park Dr (13206-1819)
P.O. Box 373 (13206-0373)
PHONE..................315 701-2924
EMP: 6
SALES (est): 690.9K Privately Held
SIC: 2421 Building & structural materials, wood

(G-15387)
ONEIDA AIR SYSTEMS INC
1001 W Fayette St Ste 2a (13204-2873)
PHONE..................315 476-5151
Robert Witter, *President*
Jen McManus, *Controller*
◆ EMP: 50
SQ FT: 60,000
SALES (est): 13.5MM Privately Held
WEB: www.oneida-air.com
SIC: 3553 3564 Woodworking machinery; purification & dust collection equipment

(G-15388)
OPTOGENICS OF SYRACUSE INC
2840 Erie Blvd E (13224-1304)
P.O. Box 4894 (13221-4894)
PHONE..................315 446-3000
Kurt Schrantz, *President*
James Bradshaw, *Supervisor*
Todd Button, *Lab Dir*
EMP: 100
SQ FT: 7,000
SALES (est): 13.2MM Privately Held
WEB: www.optogenics.com
SIC: 3851 Eyeglasses, lenses & frames
HQ: Essilor Laboratories Of America, Inc.
  13515 N Stemmons Fwy
  Dallas TX 75234
  972 241-4141

(G-15389)
P C I PAPER CONVERSIONS INC (PA)
3584 Walters Rd (13209-9700)
PHONE..................315 437-1641
Lloyd M Withers, *President*
Matthew Withers, *Vice Pres*
George Callahan, *Engineer*
Raymond Ryan, *Treasurer*
Cynthia Callahan, *Controller*
▲ EMP: 120 EST: 1973
SQ FT: 121,300
SALES (est): 22MM Privately Held
WEB: www.riverleaf.com
SIC: 2679 2678 2672 Paper products, converted; stationery products; coated & laminated paper

(G-15390)
P C I PAPER CONVERSIONS INC
Stik-Withit Printworks
6761 Thompson Rd (13211-2119)
PHONE..................315 703-8300
Howard Kaye, *Managing Dir*
EMP: 100
SALES (corp-wide): 22MM Privately Held
SIC: 2891 Adhesives & sealants
PA: P. C. I. Paper Conversions, Inc.
  3584 Walters Rd
  Syracuse NY 13209
  315 437-1641

(G-15391)
P C I PAPER CONVERSIONS INC
Coated Products Division
6761 Thompson Rd (13211-2119)
PHONE..................315 634-3317
Howard Kaye, *Managing Dir*
Theresa Brown, *Mfg Mgr*
Tim Byrne, *Natl Sales Mgr*
Helen Chase, *Cust Mgr*
Jill Ladd, *Manager*
EMP: 25
SALES (corp-wide): 22MM Privately Held
SIC: 2891 Adhesives & sealants
PA: P. C. I. Paper Conversions, Inc.
  3584 Walters Rd
  Syracuse NY 13209
  315 437-1641

(G-15392)
P C I PAPER CONVERSIONS INC
Notes
6761 Thompson Rd (13211-2119)
PHONE..................315 437-1641
Peter McDermott, *Manager*
EMP: 10
SALES (corp-wide): 22MM Privately Held
SIC: 2679 Novelties, paper: made from purchased material
PA: P. C. I. Paper Conversions, Inc.
  3584 Walters Rd
  Syracuse NY 13209
  315 437-1641

(G-15393)
PARATORE SIGNS INC
1551 Brewerton Rd (13208-1403)
PHONE..................315 455-5551
John Paratore, *President*
Ian Vincent, *Prdtn Mgr*
Valoree Paratore, *VP Sls/Mktg*
Paige J Paratore, *Treasurer*
EMP: 6 EST: 1950
SQ FT: 13,000
SALES (est): 783.9K Privately Held
WEB: www.paratoresigns.com
SIC: 2759 7389 Screen printing; sign painting & lettering shop

(G-15394)
PASS & SEYMOUR INC (DH)
50 Boyd Ave (13209-2313)
P.O. Box 4822 (13221-4822)
PHONE..................315 468-6211
Halsey Cook, *CEO*
Greg Janes, *President*
Steve Schoffstall, *Principal*
Mark Sapyta, *District Mgr*
Jim Humphries, *Business Mgr*
▼ EMP: 353
SQ FT: 300,000
SALES (est): 379.2MM
SALES (corp-wide): 20.7MM Privately Held
WEB: www.passandseymour.com
SIC: 3643 5731 Current-carrying wiring devices; consumer electronic equipment
HQ: Legrand Holding, Inc.
  60 Woodlawn St
  West Hartford CT 06110
  860 233-6251

(G-15395)
PILKINGTON NORTH AMERICA INC
6412 Deere Rd Ste 1 (13206-1133)
PHONE..................315 438-3341
EMP: 225
SALES (corp-wide): 5.6B Privately Held
SIC: 3211 Flat glass
HQ: Pilkington North America, Inc.
  811 Madison Ave Fl 3
  Toledo OH 43604
  614 802-7027

(G-15396)
PINOS PRESS INC
201 E Jefferson St (13202-2644)
PHONE..................315 935-0110
Maria Marzocchi, *President*
Michael Marzocchi, *Vice Pres*
EMP: 6
SQ FT: 15,000
SALES: 467K Privately Held
SIC: 2079 Olive oil

(G-15397)
PRINTING PRMTNAL SOLUTIONS LLC
Also Called: Printing Promotional Solutions
2320 Milton Ave Ste 5 (13209-2197)
PHONE..................315 474-1110

Syracuse - Onondaga County (G-15398)

Todd Ruetsch,
EMP: 17
SALES (est): 2.8MM **Privately Held**
SIC: 2752 Commercial printing, lithographic

(G-15398)
PRINTWORKS PRINTING & DESIGN
5982 E Molloy Rd (13211-2130)
PHONE.................315 433-8587
Michael Kinsella, *President*
EMP: 5
SALES (est): 475K **Privately Held**
SIC: 2759 Commercial printing

(G-15399)
QUADRANT BIOSCIENCES INC
505 Irving Ave Ste 3100ab (13210-1718)
PHONE.................315 614-2325
Richard Uhlig, *CEO*
Bryan Greene, *VP Opers*
David Maclean, *Exec Dir*
EMP: 18
SQ FT: 2,600
SALES (est): 619.3K **Privately Held**
SIC: 3845 Patient monitoring apparatus

(G-15400)
R K B OPTO-ELECTRONICS INC (PA)
6677 Moore Rd (13211-2112)
PHONE.................315 455-6636
Bruce Dobbie, *President*
William Dobbie, *Chairman*
Fay Colvin, *Plant Mgr*
Alex Fern Ndez, *Sales Dir*
Son Hui Yo, *Admin Sec*
EMP: 10
SQ FT: 12,500
SALES (est): 1.6MM **Privately Held**
WEB: www.rkbopto.com
SIC: 3823 3825 Industrial instrmnts msrmnt display/control process variable; instruments to measure electricity

(G-15401)
RAM FABRICATING LLC
412 Wavel St (13206-1728)
PHONE.................315 437-6654
Charlie Meakin, *Vice Pres*
Tim Atkinson, *Engineer*
Rob Bullard, *Engineer*
Mike Skowron, *Engineer*
Sam Tallarino, *VP Sales*
EMP: 30
SQ FT: 15,000
SALES (est): 7.2MM **Privately Held**
SIC: 3498 Tube fabricating (contract bending & shaping)

(G-15402)
RAULLI AND SONS INC (PA)
213 Teall Ave (13210-1291)
PHONE.................315 479-6693
Richie Raulli, *President*
Thomas Raulli, *Vice Pres*
Paul Raulli, *Treasurer*
EMP: 60
SQ FT: 40,000
SALES (est): 17.9MM **Privately Held**
WEB: www.raulliandsons.com
SIC: 3441 3446 Fabricated structural metal; architectural metalwork; gates, ornamental metal; railings, prefabricated metal; stairs, staircases, stair treads: prefabricated metal

(G-15403)
RAULLI AND SONS INC
660 Burnet Ave (13203-2404)
PHONE.................315 474-1370
Dennis Raulli, *Manager*
EMP: 15
SQ FT: 9,276
SALES (corp-wide): 17.9MM **Privately Held**
WEB: www.raulliandsons.com
SIC: 3446 Stairs, staircases, stair treads: prefabricated metal
PA: Raulli And Sons, Inc.
 213 Teall Ave
 Syracuse NY 13210
 315 479-6693

(G-15404)
RAULLI AND SONS INC
920 Canal St (13210-1204)
PHONE.................315 479-2515
Joseph Ruscitto, *Branch Mgr*
EMP: 7
SALES (est): 670.6K
SALES (corp-wide): 17.9MM **Privately Held**
SIC: 3291 Abrasive metal & steel products
PA: Raulli And Sons, Inc.
 213 Teall Ave
 Syracuse NY 13210
 315 479-6693

(G-15405)
RB WOODCRAFT INC
1860 Erie Blvd E Ste 1 (13210-1255)
PHONE.................315 474-2429
Raymond A Brooks, *President*
Bill Arkerson, *Project Dir*
Gary Fritz, *Project Mgr*
Ed Vancott, *Purch Mgr*
Dave Nicoll, *Engineer*
EMP: 50
SQ FT: 40,000
SALES (est): 9.3MM **Privately Held**
WEB: www.rbwoodcraft.com
SIC: 2431 Interior & ornamental woodwork & trim

(G-15406)
REHABILTATION TECH OF SYRACUSE
Also Called: Rehab Tech
1101 Erie Blvd E Ste 209 (13210-1144)
PHONE.................315 426-9920
Michael T Hall, *President*
Theresa Hall, *Vice Pres*
EMP: 5
SQ FT: 3,000
SALES (est): 747.1K **Privately Held**
SIC: 3842 Orthopedic appliances; prosthetic appliances

(G-15407)
RIVER VALLEY PAPER COMPANY
2801 Court St (13208-3238)
P.O. Box 1911, Akron OH (44309-1911)
PHONE.................330 631-8320
EMP: 14
SALES (corp-wide): 106.8MM **Privately Held**
SIC: 2711 Newspapers
PA: River Valley Paper Company
 120 E Mill St Ste 337
 Akron OH 44308
 330 535-1001

(G-15408)
ROBOSHOP INC
226 Midler Park Dr (13206-1819)
PHONE.................315 437-6454
Frank Giovinazzo, *President*
Matthew Eddy, *Vice Pres*
Mike Carno, *Sales Engr*
EMP: 7 **EST:** 1997
SQ FT: 4,500
SALES (est): 500K **Privately Held**
SIC: 3599 Custom machinery

(G-15409)
ROBS CYCLE SUPPLY
613 Wolf St (13208-1141)
PHONE.................315 292-6878
Robert Woodward, *President*
EMP: 9
SALES (est): 1MM **Privately Held**
SIC: 3751 Motorcycles & related parts

(G-15410)
ROTH GLOBAL PLASTICS INC
Also Called: Fralo
1 General Motors Dr (13206-1117)
P.O. Box 245 (13211-0245)
PHONE.................315 475-0100
Jochen Drewniok, *Ch of Bd*
Joseph Brown, *Senior VP*
Theresa Lauer, *Senior VP*
John Pezzi, *Vice Pres*
▲ **EMP:** 20
SQ FT: 100,000
SALES (est): 5.5MM **Privately Held**
WEB: www.fralo.net
SIC: 3089 Septic tanks, plastic

(G-15411)
ROYAL ADHESIVES & SEALANTS LLC
Also Called: Advanced Polymers Intl
3584 Walters Rd Rsd (13209-9700)
PHONE.................315 451-1755
Ted Clark, *CEO*
EMP: 15
SALES (corp-wide): 2.3B **Publicly Held**
SIC: 2891 Adhesives & sealants
HQ: Royal Adhesives And Sealants Llc
 2001 W Washington St
 South Bend IN 46628
 574 246-5000

(G-15412)
SAAKSHI INC
Also Called: North Salina Cigar Store
851 N Salina St (13208-2512)
PHONE.................315 475-3988
Jay Vave, *Principal*
EMP: 6
SALES (est): 903K **Privately Held**
SIC: 3999 Cigarette & cigar products & accessories

(G-15413)
SABRE ENTERPRISES INC
6799 Townline Rd (13211-1904)
P.O. Box 68 (13211-0068)
PHONE.................315 430-3127
Bob Dumas, *President*
Gerald Vecchiarelli, *Vice Pres*
Scott Wilkinson, *Treasurer*
John White, *Admin Sec*
EMP: 7 **EST:** 2009
SQ FT: 10,000
SALES (est): 648.2K **Privately Held**
SIC: 3711 Snow plows (motor vehicles), assembly of

(G-15414)
SAGELIFE PARENTING LLC
Also Called: Sagemylife
235 Harrison St Ste 2 (13202-3119)
PHONE.................315 299-5713
EMP: 5 **EST:** 2014
SQ FT: 34,000
SALES (est): 188.5K **Privately Held**
SIC: 2741 Internet Publishing And Broadcasting

(G-15415)
SANDYS BUMPER MART INC
120 Wall St (13204-2182)
PHONE.................315 472-8149
Sandor Bozo, *President*
Romana Bozo, *Vice Pres*
Alex Bozo, *Sales Executive*
EMP: 7 **EST:** 1970
SQ FT: 10,500
SALES (est): 870.4K **Privately Held**
SIC: 3471 Electroplating of metals or formed products

(G-15416)
SCANCORP INC
1840 Lemoyne Ave (13208-1329)
PHONE.................315 454-5596
John Clement, *President*
Ole Westergaard, *Vice Pres*
EMP: 16
SQ FT: 35,000
SALES (est): 1.2MM **Privately Held**
WEB: www.scancorp.com
SIC: 2759 Promotional printing; screen printing

(G-15417)
SCHILLING FORGE INC
606 Factory Ave (13208-1437)
PHONE.................315 454-4421
Brent A Driscoll, *CEO*
James E Stitt, *Ch of Bd*
Douglas S Pelsue, *President*
John W Whelpley, *Corp Secy*
▲ **EMP:** 26 **EST:** 1975
SQ FT: 30,000
SALES (est): 3.2MM
SALES (corp-wide): 144.6MM **Privately Held**
WEB: www.schillingforge.com
SIC: 3841 3843 3462 3423 Surgical instruments & apparatus; dental equipment & supplies; iron & steel forgings; hand & edge tools; cutlery
PA: Cutco Corporation
 1116 E State St
 Olean NY 14760
 716 372-3111

(G-15418)
SCHNEIDER BROTHERS CORPORATION
7371 Eastman Rd (13212-2504)
PHONE.................315 458-8369
William D Schneider, *President*
Chris C Schneider, *Corp Secy*
Robert Schneider, *Vice Pres*
EMP: 35
SQ FT: 11,000
SALES (est): 7.2MM **Privately Held**
SIC: 3441 Fabricated structural metal

(G-15419)
SCIENTIFIC TOOL CO INC (PA)
101 Arterial Rd (13206-1585)
PHONE.................315 431-4243
Duane Krull, *President*
Chuck Gorman, *President*
Dave Spies, *Vice Pres*
▲ **EMP:** 18
SQ FT: 16,000
SALES (est): 3.2MM **Privately Held**
SIC: 3599 Machine shop, jobbing & repair

(G-15420)
SEAL & DESIGN INC
Higbee Division
6741 Thompson Rd (13211-2119)
PHONE.................315 432-8021
Larry Higbee, *President*
EMP: 40
SALES (corp-wide): 49.8MM **Privately Held**
SIC: 3053 Gaskets, all materials
PA: Seal & Design Inc.
 4015 Casillio Pkwy
 Clarence NY 14031
 716 759-2222

(G-15421)
SECUREIT TACTICAL INC (PA)
6691 Commerce Blvd (13211-2211)
PHONE.................800 651-8835
Thomas Kubiniec, *President*
EMP: 15
SALES (est): 1.6MM **Privately Held**
SIC: 3499 Locks, safe & vault: metal

(G-15422)
SELFLOCK SCREW PRODUCTS CO INC
Also Called: SSP
461 E Brighton Ave (13210-4143)
PHONE.................315 541-4464
David M Freund, *President*
Daniel H Kuhns, *Vice Pres*
EMP: 30 **EST:** 1920
SQ FT: 50,000
SALES: 4.5MM **Privately Held**
WEB: www.selflockscrew.com
SIC: 3451 3541 Screw machine products; machine tools, metal cutting type

(G-15423)
SENECA SIGNS LLC
102 Headson Dr (13214-1102)
PHONE.................315 446-9420
Steve Warner, *Mng Member*
EMP: 7
SALES (est): 55.6K **Privately Held**
WEB: www.signartwork.com
SIC: 3993 Signs & advertising specialties

(G-15424)
SHENFIELD STUDIO LLC
Also Called: Shenfield Studio Tile
6361 Thompson Rd Stop 12 (13206-1412)
PHONE.................315 436-8869
Robert C Shenfeld, *Mng Member*
EMP: 10
SALES: 930K **Privately Held**
SIC: 3292 Floor tile, asphalt

GEOGRAPHIC SECTION

Syracuse - Onondaga County (G-15450)

(G-15425)
SIGN A RAMA OF SYRACUSE
Also Called: Sign-A-Rama
3060 Erie Blvd E Ste 1 (13224-1404)
PHONE.............................315 446-9420
Steve Werner, *Partner*
EMP: 9
SALES (est): 740.9K **Privately Held**
SIC: 3993 Signs & advertising specialties

(G-15426)
SMOOTHIES STRAWBERRY NYSF
581 State Fair Blvd (13209-1551)
PHONE.............................315 406-4250
EMP: 5
SALES (est): 183.9K **Privately Held**
SIC: 2037 Frozen fruits & vegetables

(G-15427)
SPAULDING LAW PRINTING INC
231 Walton St Ste 103 (13202-1230)
PHONE.............................315 422-4805
Alexander Douglas, *President*
EMP: 3
SQ FT: 1,000
SALES: 1MM **Privately Held**
SIC: 2759 Commercial printing

(G-15428)
SPECIALTY WLDG & FABG NY INC (PA)
1025 Hiawatha Blvd E (13208-1359)
P.O. Box 145 (13211-0145)
PHONE.............................315 426-1807
Michael P Murphy, *Ch of Bd*
Randal Stier, *President*
Jack Griffiths, *Vice Pres*
Joseph Karaszewski, *QC Mgr*
Bill Colclough, *Engineer*
EMP: 61
SQ FT: 135,000
SALES (est): 27.8MM **Privately Held**
WEB: www.specweld.com
SIC: 3441 Fabricated structural metal

(G-15429)
SRCTEC LLC
5801 E Taft Rd Ste 6 (13212-3275)
PHONE.............................315 452-8700
Drew James, *President*
Tom Chappini, *Engineer*
Deborah Sabella, *Treasurer*
Mary Pat Hartnett, *Admin Sec*
EMP: 150
SALES (est): 31.6MM
SALES (corp-wide): 141.4MM **Privately Held**
WEB: www.srctecinc.com
SIC: 3812 Antennas, radar or communications
PA: Src, Inc.
7502 Round Pond Rd
North Syracuse NY 13212
315 452-8000

(G-15430)
STEPS PLUS INC
6375 Thompson Rd (13206-1495)
PHONE.............................315 432-0885
Richard R Kopp, *Ch of Bd*
Judy Taylor, *Vice Pres*
Robert H Kopp, *Treasurer*
Bert Kopp, *Admin Sec*
EMP: 100
SQ FT: 18,000
SALES (est): 14.7MM **Privately Held**
WEB: www.steps-plus.com
SIC: 3446 Architectural metalwork

(G-15431)
STERI-PHARMA LLC
429 S West St (13202-2326)
PHONE.............................315 473-7180
Lisa Bukowski, *Office Mgr*
Nick Walip, *Branch Mgr*
Yasser Alejo, *Manager*
John Connelly, *Senior Mgr*
Mark Sweeney, *Director*
EMP: 34
SQ FT: 775
SALES (est): 7.9MM **Privately Held**
WEB: www.hanford.com
SIC: 2834 Pharmaceutical preparations
PA: Steri-Pharma, Llc
120 N State Rt 17
Paramus NJ 07652

(G-15432)
SULLIVAN BAZINET BONGIO INC
Also Called: S B B
1 General Motors Dr Ste 5 (13206-1122)
PHONE.............................315 437-6500
John Bazinet, *Partner*
Vincent Bongio, *Partner*
Mike Sullivan, *Partner*
EMP: 30
SQ FT: 9,000
SALES (est): 7.4MM **Privately Held**
WEB: www.sbbinc.com
SIC: 3564 Air purification equipment

(G-15433)
SYRACO PRODUCTS INC
Also Called: Syracuse Stamping Company
1054 S Clinton St (13202-3409)
PHONE.............................315 476-5306
Fred V Honnold, *Ch of Bd*
Elizabeth Hartnett, *Treasurer*
EMP: 14
SQ FT: 103,000
SALES (est): 7.7MM **Privately Held**
WEB: www.syraco.com
SIC: 3429 3491 2655 Manufactured hardware (general); industrial valves; spools, fiber: made from purchased material

(G-15434)
SYRACUSE CASING CO INC
528 Erie Blvd W (13204-2423)
PHONE.............................315 475-0309
Peter Frey Jr, *President*
Christine Frey, *Treasurer*
▲ **EMP:** 16 **EST:** 1975
SQ FT: 150,000
SALES (est): 2.1MM **Privately Held**
SIC: 2013 Prepared pork products from purchased pork

(G-15435)
SYRACUSE CATHOLIC PRESS ASSN
Also Called: Catholic Sun, The
421 S Warren St Fl 2 (13202-2640)
P.O. Box 511 (13201-0511)
PHONE.............................315 422-8153
Rev Donald Bourgeois, *Principal*
Doug Ross, *Manager*
L D Costanza, *Associate*
EMP: 6
SALES: 850K **Privately Held**
SIC: 2711 Newspapers

(G-15436)
SYRACUSE COMPUTER FORMS INC
Also Called: Hansen & Hansen Qulty Prtg Div
216 Burnet Ave (13203-2335)
P.O. Box 6761 (13217-6761)
PHONE.............................315 478-0108
Ted Hansen, *CEO*
Michael Hansen, *President*
Toni Hansen, *CFO*
Mary Hansen, *Admin Sec*
EMP: 20
SQ FT: 38,172
SALES (est): 3.3MM **Privately Held**
WEB: www.hansenqp.com
SIC: 2761 2752 2796 2791 Computer forms, manifold or continuous; commercial printing, lithographic; commercial printing, offset; platemaking services; typesetting

(G-15437)
SYRACUSE CULTURAL WORKERS PRJ
400 Lodi St (13203-2069)
P.O. Box 6367 (13217-6367)
PHONE.............................315 474-1132
Teresa Florack, *Principal*
John Faley, *Business Mgr*
Andy Mager, *Sales Mgr*
Marie Summerwood, *Mktg Coord*
Christopher Stewart, *Office Mgr*
▲ **EMP:** 10
SQ FT: 1,800
SALES (est): 1.4MM **Privately Held**
WEB: www.syracuseculturalworkers.com
SIC: 2732 5961 Books: printing & binding; pamphlets: printing & binding, not published on site; books, mail order (except book clubs); mail order house

(G-15438)
SYRACUSE INDUSTRIAL SLS CO LTD
1850 Lemoyne Ave (13208-1282)
PHONE.............................315 478-5751
Fax: 315 472-0855
EMP: 11
SQ FT: 4,500
SALES (est): 1.8MM **Privately Held**
SIC: 2431 5251 Mfg Millwork Ret Hardware

(G-15439)
SYRACUSE LABEL CO INC
Also Called: Syracuse Label & Surround Prtg
200 Stewart Dr (13212-3426)
PHONE.............................315 422-1037
Peter Rhodes, *Ch of Bd*
Kathy Alaimo, *President*
Mark Howard, *Vice Pres*
Kevin Ekbom, *VP Mfg*
Kevin Gagnon, *VP Prdtn*
EMP: 86 **EST:** 1974
SQ FT: 35,000
SALES (est): 23.7MM **Privately Held**
WEB: www.syrlabel.com
SIC: 2672 2759 Labels (unprinted), gummed: made from purchased materials; commercial printing

(G-15440)
SYRACUSE PROSTHETIC CENTER INC
1124 E Fayette St (13210-1922)
PHONE.............................315 476-9697
John Tyo, *President*
Sheila Harrington, *Vice Pres*
EMP: 5
SQ FT: 2,000
SALES (est): 682.8K **Privately Held**
WEB: www.cnyprocenter.com
SIC: 3842 Prosthetic appliances

(G-15441)
SYRACUSE UNIVERSITY PRESS INC
621 Skytop Rd Ste 110 (13244-0001)
PHONE.............................315 443-5534
William Billy, *Manager*
Enid Darby, *Supervisor*
Alice Pfeiffer, *Director*
Pamela Socker, *Director*
Donna Adams, *Associate Dir*
▲ **EMP:** 21
SALES (est): 2.4MM
SALES (corp-wide): 994.8MM **Privately Held**
SIC: 2731 Books: publishing only
PA: Syracuse University
900 S Crouse Ave Ste 620
Syracuse NY 13244
315 443-1870

(G-15442)
TERRELLS POTATO CHIP CO INC
218 Midler Park Dr (13206-1819)
PHONE.............................315 437-2786
Jack Terrell, *President*
Brenda Terrell, *Admin Sec*
EMP: 70 **EST:** 1946
SQ FT: 30,000
SALES (est): 11.6MM **Privately Held**
SIC: 2096 5145 Potato chips & other potato-based snacks; popcorn & supplies; pretzels; potato chips

(G-15443)
THERMOPATCH CORPORATION (PA)
2204 Erie Blvd E (13224-1100)
P.O. Box 8007 (13217-8007)
PHONE.............................315 446-8110
Tom Depuit, *Ch of Bd*
Mark Matteson, *Production*
Richard Hawley, *VP Finance*
Elizabeth Bessey, *Human Res Mgr*
Bob Fudge, *VP Sales*
EMP: 100
SQ FT: 52,000
SALES (est): 37.9MM **Privately Held**
WEB: www.thermopatch.com
SIC: 3953 3582 7359 Figures (marking devices), metal; labeling machines, industrial

(G-15444)
TOMPKINS SRM LLC
Also Called: Tomkins USA
623 Oneida St (13202-3414)
PHONE.............................315 422-8763
Mike Mosher, *General Mgr*
Tracy Politis, *Office Mgr*
William Savage, *Bd of Directors*
EMP: 6
SQ FT: 31,705
SALES (est): 1MM **Privately Held**
SIC: 3559 Sewing machines & attachments, industrial

(G-15445)
TONY BAIRD ELECTRONICS INC
461 E Brighton Ave (13210-4143)
PHONE.............................315 422-4430
Tony Jeffrey Baird, *CEO*
Khaliph A Bey, *Manager*
EMP: 4
SQ FT: 1,060
SALES (est): 1.4MM **Privately Held**
WEB: tonybairdelectronics.com
SIC: 3679 5999 Harness assemblies for electronic use: wire or cable; liquid crystal displays (LCD); audio-visual equipment & supplies

(G-15446)
TRI KOLOR PRINTING & STY
1035 Montgomery St (13202-3507)
P.O. Box 669 (13201-0669)
PHONE.............................315 474-6753
Charles De Wolf, *Owner*
Mike Albanese, *Representative*
EMP: 10
SQ FT: 12,000
SALES: 580K **Privately Held**
SIC: 2752 2759 2791 7336 Commercial printing, offset; letterpress printing; typesetting; graphic arts & related design

(G-15447)
TV GUILFOIL & ASSOCIATES INC (PA)
121 Dwight Park Cir (13209-1005)
P.O. Box 187, Solvay (13209-0187)
PHONE.............................315 453-0920
Phillip H Allen III, *President*
Tim Allen, *Admin Sec*
▲ **EMP:** 7
SQ FT: 10,000
SALES (est): 816.6K **Privately Held**
WEB: www.tvguilfoil.com
SIC: 3999 Candles

(G-15448)
UNIMAR INC
3195 Vickery Rd (13212-4574)
PHONE.............................315 699-4400
Michael Marley, *President*
Beth Andrews, *General Mgr*
Thad Fink, *General Mgr*
Robert Morris, *Engineer*
Michelle Bovee, *Accountant*
◆ **EMP:** 14
SQ FT: 21,000
SALES (est): 4.8MM **Privately Held**
SIC: 3625 5084 5063 Relays & industrial controls; controlling instruments & accessories; lighting fixtures, commercial & industrial

(G-15449)
UPSTATE PRINTING INC
433 W Onondaga St (13202-3209)
PHONE.............................315 475-6140
Jack Rotondo, *President*
EMP: 14
SALES (est): 2.1MM **Privately Held**
SIC: 2752 Commercial printing, offset

(G-15450)
US BEVERAGE NET INC
225 W Jefferson St (13202-2457)
PHONE.............................315 579-2025

Syracuse - Onondaga County (G-15451)

Mark Young, *President*
EMP: 12
SALES (est): 1.2MM **Privately Held**
SIC: 3556 7371 Beverage machinery; custom computer programming services

(G-15451)
VEHICLE SAFETY DEPT
5801 E Taft Rd Ste 4 (13212-3273)
PHONE.................................315 458-6683
James Donnery, *Manager*
EMP: 18
SALES (est): 1.2MM **Privately Held**
SIC: 3714 Sanders, motor vehicle safety

(G-15452)
VERTEX INNOVATIVE SOLUTIONS
6671 Commerce Blvd (13211-2211)
PHONE.................................315 437-6711
Paul Snow, *Chairman*
EMP: 18
SALES (est): 3.1MM **Privately Held**
SIC: 3648 Lighting equipment

(G-15453)
VETERAN AIR LLC
Also Called: Veteran Air Filtration
7174 State Fair Blvd (13209-1835)
PHONE.................................315 720-1101
Christopher Clark, *Vice Pres*
David Clark, *Vice Pres*
Lawrence Clark, *Vice Pres*
Steven Clark, *Vice Pres*
Alexandra Johnsin,
EMP: 5 **Privately Held**
SIC: 3564 Air cleaning systems

(G-15454)
WARD SALES CO INC
1117 W Fayette St Ste 1 (13204-2733)
PHONE.................................315 476-5276
Richard Hayko, *President*
Joseph Hayko, *Vice Pres*
EMP: 6
SQ FT: 30,000
SALES (est): 648.6K **Privately Held**
WEB: www.wardsalescompany.com
SIC: 2261 3953 3942 5199 Screen printing of cotton broadwoven fabrics; screens, textile printing; stuffed toys, including animals; advertising specialties

(G-15455)
WEATHER PRODUCTS CORPORATION
Also Called: Dynamic Pak
102 W Division St Fl 1 (13204-1470)
PHONE.................................315 474-8593
W Davies Birchenough Jr, *Ch of Bd*
Herman Garcia, *Vice Pres*
EMP: 8
SQ FT: 30,000
SALES (est): 1.4MM **Privately Held**
SIC: 3089 7389 Thermoformed finished plastic products; packaging & labeling services; labeling bottles, cans, cartons, etc.

(G-15456)
WESTROCK - SOLVAY LLC (DH)
53 Indl Dr (13204)
PHONE.................................315 484-9050
Peter Tantalo, *General Mgr*
Peter Buck,
David H Chrismer,
▲ **EMP:** 150
SQ FT: 300,000
SALES (est): 72.2MM
SALES (corp-wide): 14.8B **Publicly Held**
WEB: www.solvaypaperboard.com
SIC: 2631 Container board
HQ: Westrock Rkt, Llc
1000 Abernathy Rd Ste 125
Atlanta GA 30328
770 448-2193

(G-15457)
WESTROCK CP LLC
53 Industrial Dr (13204-1035)
PHONE.................................315 484-9050
EMP: 86
SALES (corp-wide): 14.8B **Publicly Held**
SIC: 2631 Container board

HQ: Westrock Cp, Llc
504 Thrasher St
Norcross GA 30071

(G-15458)
WESTROCK RKT COMPANY
53 Indl Dr (13204)
PHONE.................................770 448-2193
EMP: 162
SALES (corp-wide): 14.8B **Publicly Held**
WEB: www.rocktenn.com
SIC: 2631 Folding boxboard
HQ: Westrock Rkt, Llc
1000 Abernathy Rd Ste 125
Atlanta GA 30328
770 448-2193

(G-15459)
WIZARD EQUIPMENT INC
Also Called: Bob's Signs
10 Dwight Park Dr Ste 3 (13209-1098)
PHONE.................................315 414-9999
Bob Reilly, *President*
Robert Barnes, *Vice Pres*
EMP: 5
SALES (est): 200K **Privately Held**
SIC: 3993 Signs, not made in custom sign painting shops

(G-15460)
WOLFF & DUNGEY INC
325 Temple St (13202-3417)
P.O. Box 3673 (13220-3673)
PHONE.................................315 475-2105
Maurice Birchmeyer, *CEO*
Charles M Reschke, *Vice Pres*
John Birchmeyer, *Admin Sec*
EMP: 30
SQ FT: 20,000
SALES (est): 4.5MM **Privately Held**
SIC: 3365 3543 Aluminum foundries; industrial patterns

(G-15461)
WOOD ETC INC
1175 State Fair Blvd # 2 (13209-1082)
PHONE.................................315 484-9663
Kathleen Schmidt, *President*
Arnold Schmidt, *Vice Pres*
Jesse Schmidt, *Vice Pres*
EMP: 18
SQ FT: 30,000
SALES (est): 2.6MM **Privately Held**
SIC: 2521 2599 2434 Cabinets, office: wood; cabinets, factory; wood kitchen cabinets

Tallman
Rockland County

(G-15462)
KRAMARTRON PRECISION INC
2 Spook Rock Rd Unit 107 (10982)
PHONE.................................845 368-3668
Brian Kramer, *President*
EMP: 5 **EST:** 1974
SQ FT: 3,000
SALES: 500K **Privately Held**
SIC: 3599 Machine shop, jobbing & repair

(G-15463)
LUCIDA USA LLC
Also Called: Lucida Surfaces USA
321 Route 59 Unit 327 (10982-7518)
PHONE.................................845 877-7008
Yanky Bennish,
EMP: 5 **EST:** 2015
SALES: 5MM **Privately Held**
SIC: 3253 Ceramic wall & floor tile

(G-15464)
OLD WILLIAMSBURGH CANDLE CORP
321 Route 59 (10982-7500)
P.O. Box 6, Suffern (10901-0006)
PHONE.................................718 566-1500
Merav Gold, *CEO*
Niv Zikdershtein, *Principal*
S H Fischer, *Vice Pres*
Yaniv Nazor, *CFO*
▲ **EMP:** 150
SQ FT: 120,000

SALES (est): 23MM **Privately Held**
WEB: www.palacecandlesusa.com
SIC: 3999 Candles

Tappan
Rockland County

(G-15465)
AG TECH WELDING CORP
238 Oak Tree Rd (10983-2812)
PHONE.................................845 398-0005
Martin De Joia, *President*
Agnes De Joia, *Corp Secy*
EMP: 6
SQ FT: 5,000
SALES (est): 69.3K **Privately Held**
SIC: 3599 1799 Machine shop, jobbing & repair; welding on site

(G-15466)
CARIBBEAN FOODS DELIGHT INC
117 Route 303 Ste B (10983-2136)
PHONE.................................845 398-3000
Vincent Hosang, *President*
Jeanette Hosang, *Vice Pres*
◆ **EMP:** 80
SQ FT: 100,000
SALES (est): 17.5MM **Privately Held**
WEB: www.caribbeanfooddelights.com
SIC: 2013 2011 Frozen meats from purchased meat; meat packing plants

(G-15467)
CITADEL ELECTRICAL SUP CO INC
21 Rockland Park Ave (10983-2617)
PHONE.................................646 705-0333
Jordan Lender, *CEO*
EMP: 1
SALES: 3MM **Privately Held**
SIC: 3699 5063 3613 Electrical equipment & supplies; electrical construction materials; time switches, electrical switchgear apparatus

(G-15468)
EN TECH CORP
375 Western Hwy (10983-1317)
PHONE.................................845 398-0776
EMP: 15
SALES (corp-wide): 7.8MM **Privately Held**
SIC: 3321 Gray & ductile iron foundries
PA: En Tech Corp
91 Ruckman Rd
Closter NJ 07624
718 389-2058

(G-15469)
NATIONWIDE CUSTOM SERVICES
Also Called: Custom Studio Division
77 Main St (10983-2400)
PHONE.................................845 365-0414
Norman Shaifer, *President*
Helen Newman, *Vice Pres*
EMP: 8 **EST:** 1961
SQ FT: 2,000
SALES (est): 590K **Privately Held**
SIC: 2731 8661 Books: publishing & printing; religious organizations

(G-15470)
PULMUONE FOODS USA INC
30 Rockland Park Ave (10983-2629)
PHONE.................................845 365-3300
Chang Hwang, *Branch Mgr*
EMP: 25
SALES (corp-wide): 66.9MM **Privately Held**
SIC: 2024 Tofu desserts, frozen
HQ: Pulmuone Foods Usa, Inc.
2315 Moore Ave
Fullerton CA 92833

(G-15471)
RJ HARVEY INSTRUMENT CORP
Also Called: Romark Diagnostics
11 Jane St (10983-2503)
PHONE.................................845 359-3943
Robert Maines, *President*
Angelo D'Imperio, *Vice Pres*

EMP: 10
SQ FT: 3,600
SALES (est): 1.1MM **Privately Held**
WEB: www.rjharveyinst.com
SIC: 3841 3829 Diagnostic apparatus, medical; measuring & controlling devices

Tarrytown
Westchester County

(G-15472)
AEROLASE CORPORATION
777 Old Saw Mill River Rd # 2 (10591-6717)
PHONE.................................914 345-8300
Pavel Efremkin, *CEO*
Joseph Hurley, *COO*
Yuri Vladagin, *Project Mgr*
Jennifer Edson, *Sales Mgr*
James Papavasilakis, *Sales Mgr*
EMP: 100
SQ FT: 3,000
SALES (est): 14.5MM **Privately Held**
WEB: www.friendlylight.com
SIC: 3841 Surgical lasers

(G-15473)
ALTARO CORP
Also Called: Kaffeto Gourmet
116 Tappan Landing Rd (10591-4813)
PHONE.................................855 674-2455
Rafael Arturo Almanzar, *Officer*
EMP: 18 **EST:** 2015
SALES (est): 865K **Privately Held**
SIC: 2095 Instant coffee

(G-15474)
AMPACET CORPORATION (PA)
660 White Plains Rd # 360 (10591-5171)
PHONE.................................914 631-6600
Robert A Defalco, *Ch of Bd*
Robert Felding, *Senior VP*
Sam Bhoumik, *Vice Pres*
Joel Slutsky, *CFO*
Bennett Schwartz, *Treasurer*
◆ **EMP:** 948
SQ FT: 36,000
SALES (est): 617.1MM **Privately Held**
WEB: www.ampacet.com
SIC: 2821 Plastics materials & resins

(G-15475)
BASF CORPORATION
500 White Plains Rd (10591-5102)
PHONE.................................914 785-2000
Michael Heinz, *CEO*
EMP: 15
SALES (corp-wide): 76B **Privately Held**
SIC: 2869 Industrial organic chemicals
HQ: Basf Corporation
100 Park Ave
Florham Park NJ 07932
973 245-6000

(G-15476)
CROSS BORDER TRANSACTIONS LLC (PA)
580 White Plains Rd # 660 (10591-5198)
PHONE.................................646 767-7342
David Bukovac, *CEO*
Donald Scherer, *Ch of Bd*
Mimi Song, *Vice Pres*
Lisa Zimbalist, *Vice Pres*
Alyssa Dorfman, *CFO*
EMP: 14 **EST:** 2015
SALES (est): 7.9MM **Privately Held**
SIC: 7372 Business oriented computer software

(G-15477)
DENTEK ORAL CARE INC (HQ)
660 White Plains Rd # 250 (10591-5171)
PHONE.................................865 983-1300
John M Janasheski, *CEO*
David Fox, *President*
Danielle Griffiths, *Manager*
◆ **EMP:** 63
SQ FT: 64,000
SALES (est): 9.6MM
SALES (corp-wide): 1B **Publicly Held**
WEB: www.usdentek.com
SIC: 3843 Dental equipment & supplies

▲ = Import ▼ = Export
◆ = Import/Export

GEOGRAPHIC SECTION

Thornwood - Westchester County (G-15501)

PA: Prestige Consumer Healthcare Inc.
660 White Plains Rd
Tarrytown NY 10591
914 524-6800

(G-15478)
FOSECO INC
777 Old Saw Mill River Rd (10591-6717)
PHONE..................914 345-4760
EMP: 10
SALES (corp-wide): 2.3B **Privately Held**
SIC: 2899 3569 Mfg Exorterneic Compunds Fluxes And Ceramic Filters
HQ: Foseco, Inc.
20200 Sheldon Rd
Cleveland OH 44142
440 826-4548

(G-15479)
INTERNATIONAL SOCIETY FOR MEDL
520 White Plains Rd (10591-5102)
PHONE..................520 820-8594
Terry Pena, *Ch of Bd*
EMP: 1
SALES: 1.6MM **Privately Held**
SIC: 2741 Miscellaneous publishing

(G-15480)
MAIN STREET SWEETS
35 Main St (10591-3627)
PHONE..................914 332-5757
Merlina Bertolacci, *Partner*
EMP: 10 EST: 2008
SALES (est): 738.4K **Privately Held**
SIC: 2024 Ice cream & frozen desserts

(G-15481)
MARSHALL CAVENDISH CORP
Also Called: Benchmark Books
99 White Plains Rd (10591-5502)
PHONE..................914 332-8888
Richard Farley, *President*
Hoover Herrera, *Business Mgr*
Vivian Cheng, *Director*
Anvis They, *Executive*
Ellen Lauterbach, *Education*
▲ EMP: 40
SQ FT: 30,000
SALES: 3.5MM
SALES (corp-wide): 1.3B **Privately Held**
WEB: www.marshallcavendish.com
SIC: 2731 Books: publishing only
HQ: Marshall Cavendish Limited
32-38 Saffron Hill
London EC1N

(G-15482)
MEDTECH PRODUCTS INC (HQ)
Also Called: New Skin
660 White Plains Rd (10591-5139)
PHONE..................914 524-6810
Matthew Mannelly, *President*
Timothy J Connors, *Exec VP*
Jean A Boyko PHD, *Senior VP*
John Parkinson, *Senior VP*
Jean Boyko, *Vice Pres*
▲ EMP: 16
SQ FT: 7,000
SALES (est): 15.6MM
SALES (corp-wide): 1B **Publicly Held**
SIC: 2841 2834 Soap & other detergents; pharmaceutical preparations
PA: Prestige Consumer Healthcare Inc.
660 White Plains Rd
Tarrytown NY 10591
914 524-6800

(G-15483)
MICRO POWDERS INC (PA)
Also Called: M P I
580 White Plains Rd # 400 (10591-5198)
PHONE..................914 332-6400
James Strauss, *President*
Gary Strauss, *General Mgr*
Phyllis Strauss, *Admin Sec*
Jayne Solomon, *Representative*
◆ EMP: 26
SQ FT: 2,500
SALES (est): 11.1MM **Privately Held**
WEB: www.micropowders.com
SIC: 3952 3555 2899 2893 Wax, artists'; printing trades machinery; chemical preparations; printing ink; cyclic crudes & intermediates; specialty cleaning, polishes & sanitation goods

(G-15484)
MOMENTIVE PERFORMANCE MTLS INC
Also Called: OSI Specialties
769 Old Saw Mill River Rd (10591-6732)
PHONE..................914 784-4807
Michael Pigeon, *Manager*
Susan Sperring, *Manager*
EMP: 80
SALES (corp-wide): 2.3B **Publicly Held**
WEB: www.gewaterford.com
SIC: 2843 2099 2821 8731 Surface active agents; emulsifiers, food; plastics materials & resins; commercial physical research; chemical preparations
HQ: Momentive Performance Materials Inc.
260 Hudson River Rd
Waterford NY 12188

(G-15485)
OPEN-XCHANGE INC
303 S Broadway Ste 224 (10591-5410)
P.O. Box 143, Ardsley On Hudson (10503-0143)
PHONE..................914 332-5720
Richard Seibt, *Ch of Bd*
Rafael Laguna, *President*
Carsten Dirks, *COO*
Vittorio Bertola, *Research*
Monika Schroeder, *CFO*
EMP: 10
SALES (est): 866K **Privately Held**
SIC: 2741 Guides: publishing & printing

(G-15486)
POLICY ADM SOLUTIONS INC
505 White Plains Rd (10591-5101)
PHONE..................914 332-4320
Peter Pantelides, *President*
EMP: 45
SALES: 7.5MM **Privately Held**
SIC: 3571 Mainframe computers

(G-15487)
PRESTIGE BRANDS INTL LLC
660 White Plains Rd (10591-5139)
PHONE..................914 524-6800
Timothy J Connors, *Exec VP*
Jean A Boyko PHD, *Senior VP*
Samuel C Cowley, *Vice Pres*
Ronald M Lombardi, *CFO*
Matthew M Mannelly,
◆ EMP: 14
SALES (est): 186.4K
SALES (corp-wide): 1B **Publicly Held**
SIC: 2834 Pharmaceutical preparations
PA: Prestige Consumer Healthcare Inc.
660 White Plains Rd
Tarrytown NY 10591
914 524-6800

(G-15488)
PRESTIGE CONSMR HEALTHCARE INC (PA)
Also Called: PRESTIGE BRANDS
660 White Plains Rd (10591-5139)
PHONE..................914 524-6800
Ronald M Lombardi, *Ch of Bd*
Timothy J Connors, *Exec VP*
Christopher Heye, *Senior VP*
William C P'Pool, *Senior VP*
Christine Sacco, *CFO*
EMP: 75
SALES: 1B **Publicly Held**
SIC: 2834 5122 5169 Pharmaceutical preparations; pharmaceuticals; specialty cleaning & sanitation preparations

(G-15489)
RAUCH INDUSTRIES INC
828 S Broadway (10591-6600)
PHONE..................704 867-5333
Bruce Charbeck, *Branch Mgr*
EMP: 27
SALES (corp-wide): 165.4MM **Privately Held**
SIC: 3231 Christmas tree ornaments: made from purchased glass
PA: Rauch Industries, Inc.
3800a Little Mountain Rd
Gastonia NC 28056
704 867-5333

(G-15490)
REGENERON PHARMACEUTICALS INC (PA)
777 Old Saw Mill River Rd # 10 (10591-6707)
PHONE..................914 847-7000
P Roy Vagelos, *Ch of Bd*
Leonard S Schleifer, *President*
Wrechelle Nantes, *Chairman*
Michael Pignatiell, *Counsel*
Joseph J Larosa, *Senior VP*
EMP: 277
SQ FT: 1,108,000
SALES: 5.8B **Publicly Held**
WEB: www.regeneron.com
SIC: 2834 Pharmaceutical preparations

(G-15491)
REGENRON HLTHCARE SLUTIONS INC
745 Old Saw Mill River Rd (10591-6701)
PHONE..................914 847-7000
Robert Terifay, *General Mgr*
David Robinson, *Vice Pres*
Joseph Larosa, *Admin Sec*
EMP: 603
SALES (est): 15.9MM
SALES (corp-wide): 5.8B **Publicly Held**
SIC: 2834 Pharmaceutical preparations
PA: Regeneron Pharmaceuticals Inc
777 Old Saw Mill River Rd # 10
Tarrytown NY 10591
914 847-7000

(G-15492)
SIEMENS HLTHCARE DGNOSTICS INC
511 Benedict Ave (10591-5005)
PHONE..................914 631-0475
EMP: 39
SALES (corp-wide): 89.6B **Privately Held**
SIC: 2835 8734 Mfg Diagnostic Substances Testing Laboratory
HQ: Siemens Healthcare Diagnostics Inc.
511 Benedict Ave
Tarrytown NY 10591
914 631-8000

(G-15493)
SNEAKY CHEF FOODS LLC
520 White Plains Rd (10591-5102)
PHONE..................914 301-3277
Missy Chase Lapine, *CEO*
Helen Spanjer, *COO*
Laurence Chase, *Vice Pres*
▲ EMP: 10 EST: 2012
SALES (est): 1.1MM **Privately Held**
SIC: 2033 2099 Spaghetti & other pasta sauce: packaged in cans, jars, etc.; peanut butter

(G-15494)
SPIC AND SPAN COMPANY
660 White Plains Rd # 250 (10591-5171)
PHONE..................914 524-6823
Matthew M Mannelly, *CEO*
Mark Pettie, *Ch of Bd*
Peter Anderson, *CFO*
EMP: 12 EST: 2000
SQ FT: 6,000
SALES (est): 2MM
SALES (corp-wide): 1B **Publicly Held**
SIC: 2842 Cleaning or polishing preparations
PA: Prestige Consumer Healthcare Inc.
660 White Plains Rd
Tarrytown NY 10591
914 524-6800

(G-15495)
SPX CORPORATION
220 White Plains Rd (10591-5837)
PHONE..................914 366-7402
EMP: 5
SALES (corp-wide): 1.4B **Publicly Held**
SIC: 3443 Heat exchangers, condensers & components
PA: Spx Corporation
13320a Balntyn Corp Pl
Charlotte NC 28277
980 474-3700

(G-15496)
TARRYTOWN BAKERY INC
150 Wildey St (10591-2910)
PHONE..................914 631-0209
Michael J Birrittella, *President*
EMP: 10
SQ FT: 5,000
SALES (est): 1MM **Privately Held**
WEB: www.plazaview.com
SIC: 2051 5461 Bread, all types (white, wheat, rye, etc): fresh or frozen; bakeries

(G-15497)
TRADEPAQ CORPORATION
220 White Plains Rd # 360 (10591-7800)
PHONE..................914 332-9174
Elena Serova, *Technical Mgr*
Donald Gross, *Branch Mgr*
EMP: 11 **Privately Held**
WEB: www.tradepaq.com
SIC: 7372 Prepackaged software
PA: Tradepaq Corporation
33 Maiden Ln Fl 8
New York NY

(G-15498)
ZIP-JACK INDUSTRIES LTD
Also Called: Zip Jack Custom Umbrellas
73 Carrollwood Dr (10591-5210)
PHONE..................914 592-2000
Emanuel Dubinsky, *President*
Charlotte L Dubinsky, *Treasurer*
▲ EMP: 25 EST: 1950
SQ FT: 20,000
SALES (est): 2.3MM **Privately Held**
WEB: www.zipjack.com
SIC: 3999 5699 Garden umbrellas; umbrellas

Thiells
Rockland County

(G-15499)
STEEL TECH SA LLC
7 Hillside Dr (10984-1431)
P.O. Box 361 (10984-0361)
PHONE..................845 786-3691
Allen Klein,
EMP: 5
SALES: 430K **Privately Held**
SIC: 3441 Fabricated structural metal

Thompsonville
Sullivan County

(G-15500)
MONTICELLO BLACK TOP CORP
80 Patio Dr (12784)
P.O. Box 95 (12784-0095)
PHONE..................845 434-7280
Joseph Gottlieb, *President*
EMP: 5
SQ FT: 4,000
SALES (est): 729.9K **Privately Held**
SIC: 2951 5032 Concrete, asphaltic (not from refineries); sand, construction; gravel

Thornwood
Westchester County

(G-15501)
AUTOMATED CONTROL LOGIC INC
Also Called: Acl
578 Commerce St (10594-1327)
PHONE..................914 769-8880
Preston Bruenn, *President*
Joe Escaravage, *Info Tech Mgr*
EMP: 12
SALES (est): 3.4MM **Privately Held**
WEB: www.automatedcontrollogic.com
SIC: 3674 3825 1711 Solid state electronic devices; test equipment for electrical & electrical circuits; heating & air conditioning contractors

Thornwood - Westchester County (G-15502)

(G-15502)
CARL ZEISS INC (DH)
1 Zeiss Dr (10594-1996)
P.O. Box 5943, New York (10087-5943)
PHONE..................(914) 747-1800
Cheryl Sarli, *President*
Dr Michael Kaschke, *Principal*
James Olivo, *Exec VP*
Meg Donohue, *Vice Pres*
Scott Margolin, *Vice Pres*
▲ **EMP:** 120 **EST:** 1925
SQ FT: 124,000
SALES (est): 229.4MM **Privately Held**
SIC: 3827 5049 3829 5084 Optical instruments & apparatus; optical goods; measuring & controlling devices; instruments & control equipment; analytical instruments
HQ: Carl Zeiss Ag
Carl-Zeiss-Str. 22
Oberkochen 73447
736 420-0

(G-15503)
CARL ZEISS MICROSCOPY LLC
1 Zeiss Dr (10594-1996)
P.O. Box 5943, New York (10087-5943)
PHONE..................914 747-1800
James Sharp, *President*
Lon Ensler, *VP Finance*
EMP: 300 **EST:** 2001
SQ FT: 18,000
SALES (est): 71.5MM **Privately Held**
WEB: www.zeiss.com/micro
SIC: 3827 Optical instruments & lenses
HQ: Carl Zeiss, Inc.
1 Zeiss Dr
Thornwood NY 10594
914 747-1800

(G-15504)
CARL ZEISS SBE LLC
1 Zeiss Dr (10594-1996)
PHONE..................914 747-1132
Kenner Eric, *Business Mgr*
Sven Hermann, *Exec VP*
Guadalupe Sandoval, *Finance Dir*
Nicole Balle, *Marketing Mgr*
Joan Scheppelmann, *Marketing Staff*
▲ **EMP:** 24
SQ FT: 40,000
SALES (est): 5.8MM **Privately Held**
SIC: 3827 Optical instruments & lenses
HQ: Carl Zeiss, Inc.
1 Zeiss Dr
Thornwood NY 10594
914 747-1800

(G-15505)
COMMERCE OFFSET LTD
657 Commerce St (10594-1399)
PHONE..................914 769-6671
Fax: 914 769-7845
EMP: 5
SQ FT: 8,400
SALES (est): 540K **Privately Held**
SIC: 2752 Lithographic Commercial Printing

(G-15506)
FENBAR PRCISION MACHINISTS INC
633 Commerce St (10594-1302)
PHONE..................914 769-5506
Leonard Vallender, *President*
Gloria Vallender, *Corp Secy*
Michael Allen, *Plant Mgr*
Louanne Gambino, *Manager*
EMP: 18
SQ FT: 6,500
SALES (est): 3.3MM **Privately Held**
WEB: www.fenbar.com
SIC: 3599 Machine shop, jobbing & repair

(G-15507)
HOUGHTON MIFFLIN HARCOURT PUBG
28 Claremont Ave (10594-1042)
PHONE..................914 747-2709
Glenn Polin, *Owner*
EMP: 124
SALES (corp-wide): 1.4B **Publicly Held**
WEB: www.hmco.com
SIC: 2731 Textbooks: publishing only, not printed on site

HQ: Houghton Mifflin Harcourt Publishing Company
125 High St Ste 900
Boston MA 02110
617 351-5000

(G-15508)
THORNWOOD PRODUCTS LTD
Also Called: All Star Fabricators
401 Claremont Ave Ste 7 (10594-1038)
PHONE..................914 769-9161
Peter Cuneo, *President*
EMP: 30
SALES (est): 3.7MM **Privately Held**
SIC: 2599 1799 Cabinets, factory; counter top installation

Three Mile Bay
Jefferson County

(G-15509)
ST LAWRENCE LUMBER INC
27140 County Route 57 (13693-7205)
PHONE..................315 649-2990
Gregory L Hoppel, *President*
Julie Hoppel, *Vice Pres*
EMP: 7
SALES: 1MM **Privately Held**
WEB: www.stlawrencelumber.com
SIC: 2421 Sawmills & planing mills, general

Ticonderoga
Essex County

(G-15510)
ADIRONDACK WASTE MGT INC
Also Called: Adirondack Sanitary Service
963 New York State 9n (12883)
PHONE..................518 585-2224
R D Seargent Condit, *President*
Cindy Condit, *Vice Pres*
Doran Rockhill, *Treasurer*
EMP: 7
SQ FT: 1,000
SALES: 300K **Privately Held**
SIC: 2842 Sanitation preparations

(G-15511)
INTERNATIONAL PAPER COMPANY
568 Shore Airport Rd (12883-2890)
PHONE..................518 585-6761
Bob Ballard, *Buyer*
Eugene Fox, *Engineer*
Stephen Treat, *Controller*
Chris Mallon, *Branch Mgr*
Matthew Bush, *Supervisor*
EMP: 650
SQ FT: 1,920
SALES (corp-wide): 21.7B **Publicly Held**
WEB: www.internationalpaper.com
SIC: 2621 Paper mills
PA: International Paper Company
6400 Poplar Ave
Memphis TN 38197
901 419-9000

(G-15512)
LIBBYS BAKERY CAFE LLC
92 Montcalm St (12883-1352)
P.O. Box 61 (12883-0061)
PHONE..................603 918-8825
Andrew Rasmus, *Principal*
Claire Brown, *Principal*
Katherine Lewis, *Principal*
EMP: 5
SALES (est): 407.8K **Privately Held**
SIC: 2051 Cakes, pies & pastries

(G-15513)
SPECIALTY MINERALS INC
35 Highland St (12883-1520)
PHONE..................518 585-7982
Elaine Bertrand, *General Mgr*
EMP: 6 **Publicly Held**
WEB: www.specialtyminerals.com
SIC: 2819 Industrial inorganic chemicals

HQ: Specialty Minerals Inc.
622 3rd Ave Fl 38
New York NY 10017
212 878-1800

(G-15514)
TICONDEROGA MCH & WLDG CORP
55 Race Track Rd (12883-4003)
PHONE..................518 585-7444
EMP: 5 **EST:** 1954
SQ FT: 980
SALES (est): 36.3K **Privately Held**
SIC: 3599 Machine Shop

Tillson
Ulster County

(G-15515)
WINERACKSCOM INC
819 Route 32 (12486-1724)
PHONE..................845 658-7181
Michael Babcock, *President*
Howard Babcock, *Vice Pres*
Jennifer Cristaldi, *Admin Asst*
EMP: 26 **EST:** 1990
SQ FT: 20,000
SALES (est): 4.2MM **Privately Held**
SIC: 2541 Wood partitions & fixtures

Tomkins Cove
Rockland County

(G-15516)
TILCON NEW YORK INC
Fort Of Elm (10986)
P.O. Box 217 (10986-0217)
PHONE..................845 942-0602
Rich Moon, *Superintendent*
Nathalie Boboshko, *Credit Mgr*
EMP: 22
SQ FT: 2,184
SALES (corp-wide): 29.7B **Privately Held**
WEB: www.tilconny.com
SIC: 1442 Sand mining; gravel & pebble mining
HQ: Tilcon New York Inc.
9 Entin Rd
Parsippany NJ 07054
800 789-7625

Tonawanda
Erie County

(G-15517)
3M COMPANY
305 Sawyer Ave (14150-7718)
PHONE..................716 876-1596
Mike Mazur, *Manager*
EMP: 400
SALES (corp-wide): 31.6B **Publicly Held**
WEB: www.mmm.com
SIC: 3089 2823 Sponges, plastic; cellulosic manmade fibers
PA: 3m Company
3m Center
Saint Paul MN 55144
651 733-1110

(G-15518)
ACE SPECIALTY CO INC
695 Ensminger Rd (14150-6698)
PHONE..................716 874-3670
Patrick J Allen, *President*
EMP: 9
SQ FT: 25,000
SALES (est): 1.1MM **Privately Held**
WEB: www.acespecialtycompany.com
SIC: 3544 Special dies & tools

(G-15519)
ADAMS SFC INC (HQ)
225 E Park Dr (14150-7813)
P.O. Box 963, Buffalo (14240-0963)
PHONE..................716 877-2608
Jack H Berg, *President*
Carole L Berg, *Admin Sec*
▲ **EMP:** 40

SQ FT: 65,000
SALES (est): 6.9MM
SALES (corp-wide): 62.5MM **Privately Held**
WEB: www.pacerpumps.com
SIC: 3569 3563 Filters, general line: industrial; vacuum (air extraction) systems, industrial
PA: Service Filtration Corp.
2900 Macarthur Blvd
Northbrook IL 60062
847 509-2900

(G-15520)
ALFA LAVAL KATHABAR INC
91 Sawyer Ave (14150-7716)
PHONE..................716 875-2000
EMP: 103
SALES (est): 141.6K
SALES (corp-wide): 4.1B **Privately Held**
SIC: 3585 Humidifiers & dehumidifiers
HQ: Alfa Laval U.S. Holding Inc.
5400 Intl Trade Dr
Richmond VA 23231

(G-15521)
ALRY TOOL AND DIE CO INC
386 Fillmore Ave (14150-2417)
P.O. Box 43 (14151-0043)
PHONE..................716 693-2419
Michael J Allen, *President*
Daniel T Allen, *Corp Secy*
Francis D Allen Jr, *Vice Pres*
Thomas Allen, *Vice Pres*
EMP: 20 **EST:** 1944
SQ FT: 23,500
SALES (est): 2.8MM **Privately Held**
WEB: www.alry.com
SIC: 3462 3544 Machinery forgings, ferrous; dies & die holders for metal cutting, forming, die casting

(G-15522)
ANDERSON EQUIPMENT COMPANY
2140 Military Rd (14150-6002)
PHONE..................716 877-1992
David McDermott, *Inv Control Mgr*
John Park, *Manager*
John Zappia, *Info Tech Dir*
EMP: 70
SALES (corp-wide): 98MM **Privately Held**
SIC: 3531 Construction machinery
PA: Anderson Equipment Company
1000 Washington Pike
Bridgeville PA 15017
412 343-2300

(G-15523)
ARROW GRINDING INC
525 Vicke St Tonaw Ctr (14150)
PHONE..................716 693-3333
John C Goller, *President*
Kathy Goller, *Corp Secy*
Doug Deschamps, *Mfg Staff*
Jim Whistler, *Sales Executive*
EMP: 25
SQ FT: 25,000
SALES (est): 4.1MM **Privately Held**
SIC: 3599 Machine shop, jobbing & repair

(G-15524)
AVANTI U S A LTD
412 Young St (14150-4037)
PHONE..................716 695-5800
G J Caruso, *Principal*
Gregory J Van Norman, *Vice Pres*
EMP: 15
SQ FT: 4,863
SALES (est): 1.7MM **Privately Held**
SIC: 3842 2386 3089 Surgical appliances & supplies; general warehousing; injection molding of plastics

(G-15525)
B & W HEAT TREATING COMPANY
2780 Kenmore Ave (14150-7775)
PHONE..................716 876-8184
Clifford Calvello, *Owner*
EMP: 8
SQ FT: 14,000
SALES (est): 1.2MM **Privately Held**
SIC: 3398 3471 Metal heat treating; cleaning, polishing & finishing

▲ = Import ▼ = Export
◆ = Import/Export

(G-15526)
BCO INDUSTRIES WESTERN NY INC
77 Oriskany Dr (14150-6722)
P.O. Box 100 (14151-0100)
PHONE.................................716 877-2800
Janet Soltzman, *President*
Douglas Saltzman, *President*
EMP: 31
SALES (est): 4.5MM **Privately Held**
WEB: www.bcoworld.com
SIC: 2759 2791 Thermography; visiting cards (including business): printing; facsimile letters: printing; stationery: printing; typesetting

(G-15527)
BIMBO BAKERIES USA INC
Also Called: Best Foods Baking Group
1960 Niagara Falls Blvd (14150-5542)
PHONE.................................716 692-9140
Catherine E Irish, *Branch Mgr*
EMP: 5 **Privately Held**
WEB: www.gwbakeries.com
SIC: 2051 Bakery: wholesale or wholesale/retail combined
HQ: Bimbo Bakeries Usa, Inc
255 Business Center Dr # 200
Horsham PA 19044
215 347-5500

(G-15528)
BONCRAFT INC
777 E Park Dr (14150-6708)
PHONE.................................716 662-9720
Timothy Bubar, *CEO*
James Bubar Jr, *President*
Jason Braungart, *Manager*
EMP: 75 **EST:** 1952
SQ FT: 20,400
SALES (est): 10.5MM **Privately Held**
WEB: www.boncraft.com
SIC: 2752 2791 2789 Commercial printing, offset; typesetting; bookbinding & related work

(G-15529)
BOULEVARD PRINTING
1330 Niagara Falls Blvd # 2 (14150-8900)
PHONE.................................716 837-3800
John Battistella, *Owner*
EMP: 6
SALES (est): 644.9K **Privately Held**
SIC: 2752 Commercial printing, offset

(G-15530)
BRIGHTON TOOL & DIE DESIGNERS (PA)
Also Called: Brighton Design
463 Brighton Rd (14150-6966)
PHONE.................................716 876-0879
Chris Banas, *President*
Chris Eanas, *President*
EMP: 15
SQ FT: 2,000
SALES (est): 1.7MM **Privately Held**
SIC: 3544 Special dies & tools

(G-15531)
BROTHERS-IN-LAWN PROPERTY
176 Vulcan (14150)
PHONE.................................716 279-6191
Rodney Koeppen, *President*
EMP: 9
SALES (est): 783.8K **Privately Held**
SIC: 3711 0781 Snow plows (motor vehicles), assembly of; landscape services

(G-15532)
CENTRAL REDE SIGN CO INC
317 Wheeler St (14150-3828)
PHONE.................................716 213-0797
Neal Wilcox, *Principal*
EMP: 5
SALES (est): 698.5K **Privately Held**
SIC: 3993 Signs & advertising specialties

(G-15533)
CENTRISOURCE INC
777 E Park Dr (14150-6708)
PHONE.................................716 871-1105
David Zenger, *President*
Joseph Zenger, *Treasurer*
EMP: 5
SALES (est): 440K **Privately Held**
SIC: 2732 Book printing

(G-15534)
CLIFFORD H JONES INC
608 Young St (14150-4195)
PHONE.................................716 693-2444
Phillip Jones, *President*
EMP: 15
SQ FT: 18,000
SALES (est): 4MM **Privately Held**
WEB: www.chjones.com
SIC: 3544 3089 Forms (molds), for foundry & plastics working machinery; injection molding of plastics

(G-15535)
COCA-COLA BTLG CO BUFFALO INC
200 Milens Rd (14150-6795)
PHONE.................................716 874-4610
John F Bitzer III, *President*
Rick Horn Jr, *General Mgr*
Mike U Nagorski, *Executive*
▲ **EMP:** 170
SQ FT: 75,000
SALES (est): 999.7K
SALES (corp-wide): 361.4MM **Privately Held**
SIC: 2086 Bottled & canned soft drinks
PA: Abarta, Inc.
200 Alpha Dr
Pittsburgh PA 15238
412 963-6226

(G-15536)
DIGITAL INSTRUMENTS INC
580 Ensminger Rd (14150-6668)
PHONE.................................716 874-5848
John Swanson, *President*
▲ **EMP:** 10
SQ FT: 6,000
SALES (est): 2.1MM **Privately Held**
WEB: www.digitalinstruments.com
SIC: 3625 Industrial controls: push button, selector switches, pilot

(G-15537)
E-ZOIL PRODUCTS INC
234 Fillmore Ave (14150-2340)
PHONE.................................716 213-0106
Glenn Miller, *President*
Christopher Miller, *Vice Pres*
Bill Morgan, *Natl Sales Mgr*
▲ **EMP:** 25
SQ FT: 10,000
SALES (est): 6.2MM **Privately Held**
WEB: www.ezoil.com
SIC: 2911 Fuel additives

(G-15538)
EMULSO CORP
2750 Kenmore Ave (14150-7707)
PHONE.................................716 854-2889
William Breeser, *President*
EMP: 6
SQ FT: 30,000
SALES (est): 550K **Privately Held**
WEB: www.emulso.com
SIC: 2842 2841 5087 Soap: granulated, liquid, cake, flaked or chip; waxes for wood, leather & other materials; furniture polish or wax; janitors' supplies

(G-15539)
FCMP INC
230 Fire Tower Dr (14150-5832)
PHONE.................................716 692-4623
David Callendrier, *President*
▲ **EMP:** 17 **EST:** 2000
SQ FT: 20,000
SALES (est): 3.7MM **Privately Held**
WEB: www.fcmp.com
SIC: 3714 3592 Bearings, motor vehicle; pistons & piston rings

(G-15540)
FIBER LAMINATIONS LIMITED
Also Called: C/O M&M Fowarding
600 Main St (14150-3723)
PHONE.................................716 692-1825
William Neal, *Branch Mgr*
EMP: 13 **Privately Held**
SIC: 3089 Automotive parts, plastic
PA: Fibre Laminations Ltd
651 Burlington St E
Hamilton ON L8L 4
905 312-9152

(G-15541)
FMC CORPORATION
Also Called: F M C Peroxygen Chemicals Div
78 Sawyer Ave Ste 1 (14150-7751)
PHONE.................................716 879-0400
Colm McCormack, *Business Mgr*
Robert Service, *Manager*
Rusatin Sherrill, *Director*
Wayne Troutman, *Maintence Staff*
EMP: 200
SALES (corp-wide): 2.8B **Publicly Held**
WEB: www.fmc.com
SIC: 2812 Alkalies & chlorine
PA: Fmc Corporation
2929 Walnut St
Philadelphia PA 19104
215 299-6000

(G-15542)
GREAT LAKES GEAR CO INC
126 E Niagara St Ste 2 (14150-1215)
PHONE.................................716 694-0715
Donald Eggleston, *President*
Robert Rees, *President*
Timothy Rees, *Vice Pres*
EMP: 8
SQ FT: 4,500
SALES: 900K **Privately Held**
SIC: 3462 Gears, forged steel

(G-15543)
GREAT LAKES METAL TREATING
300 E Niagara St (14150-1218)
P.O. Box 118 (14151-0118)
PHONE.................................716 694-1240
Thomas Snyder, *President*
EMP: 10
SQ FT: 18,000
SALES (est): 966.9K **Privately Held**
SIC: 3398 Metal heat treating

(G-15544)
GREEN BUFFALO FUEL LLC
Also Called: Gbf
720 Riverview Blvd (14150-7824)
PHONE.................................716 768-0600
Peter Coleman, *CEO*
EMP: 10 **EST:** 2012
SALES (est): 1.2MM **Privately Held**
SIC: 1311 1321 Natural gas production; butane (natural) production

(G-15545)
GREIF INC
2122 Colvin Blvd (14150-6908)
PHONE.................................716 836-4200
Clinton Gathins, *Opers-Prdtn-Mfg*
Brian Ellis, *Purch Mgr*
Robert Holubec, *Engineer*
Karen Muranyi, *Financial Exec*
David Pettigrew, *Manager*
EMP: 70
SALES (corp-wide): 3.6B **Publicly Held**
WEB: www.greif.com
SIC: 2655 Drums, fiber: made from purchased material
PA: Greif, Inc.
425 Winter Rd
Delaware OH 43015
740 549-6000

(G-15546)
HDM HYDRAULICS LLC
125 Fire Tower Dr (14150-5880)
PHONE.................................716 694-8004
William Anderson, *President*
▲ **EMP:** 100
SQ FT: 46,560
SALES (est): 24.9MM
SALES (corp-wide): 501.5MM **Privately Held**
WEB: www.ligonindustries.com
SIC: 3511 Hydraulic turbine generator set units, complete
PA: Ligon Industries, Llc
1927 1st Ave N Ste 500
Birmingham AL 35203
205 322-3302

(G-15547)
HEBELER LLC (PA)
2000 Military Rd (14150-6704)
PHONE.................................716 873-9300
Kenneth Snyder, *President*
Ahmed Lahrache, *COO*
Jonathan Nelson, *Project Mgr*
Eric Waters, *Project Mgr*
Rich Sanly, *Facilities Mgr*
▲ **EMP:** 140 **EST:** 1929
SQ FT: 100,000
SALES (est): 31.8MM **Privately Held**
WEB: www.hebeler.com
SIC: 3441 Fabricated structural metal

(G-15548)
HEBELER PROCESS SOLUTIONS LLC
2000 Military Rd (14150-6704)
PHONE.................................716 873-9300
Kenneth Snyder, *President*
Kenneth Snyder, *President*
EMP: 20 **EST:** 2016
SALES (est): 1.7MM **Privately Held**
SIC: 3599 Custom machinery

(G-15549)
HERR MANUFACTURING CO INC
17 Pearce Ave (14150-6711)
PHONE.................................716 754-4341
Bruce Mc Lean, *President*
EMP: 25 **EST:** 1913
SALES (est): 3.1MM **Privately Held**
SIC: 3552 Textile machinery

(G-15550)
IMA LIFE NORTH AMERICA INC
2175 Military Rd (14150-6001)
PHONE.................................716 695-6354
Giovanni Pecchioli, *President*
Sergio Marzo, *Corp Secy*
Jose Ruiz, *Exec VP*
Ernesto Renzi, *Vice Pres*
Andrew Fromm, *Engineer*
◆ **EMP:** 150
SQ FT: 43,000
SALES: 70MM **Privately Held**
SIC: 2834 Druggists' preparations (pharmaceuticals)
HQ: I.M.A. Industria Macchine Automatiche Spa
Via Bruno Tosarelli 182/184
Castenaso BO 40055
051 651-4111

(G-15551)
INPRO CORPORATION
Fireline 520
250 Cooper Ave Ste 102 (14150-6633)
PHONE.................................716 332-4699
Aj Shaw, *Manager*
EMP: 8
SALES (corp-wide): 141.3MM **Privately Held**
SIC: 3499 Barricades, metal
PA: Inpro Corporation
S80w18766 Apollo Dr
Muskego WI 53150
262 679-9010

(G-15552)
INTEGUMENT TECHNOLOGIES INC
72 Pearce Ave (14150-6711)
PHONE.................................716 873-1199
Terrence G Vargo, *President*
Terrence Vargo, *Vice Pres*
Steve Doherty, *Opers Mgr*
Jeffrey Gruszka, *Accountant*
Jennifer Smyth, *Manager*
EMP: 16
SALES (est): 2.4MM **Privately Held**
WEB: www.integument.com
SIC: 3081 Plastic film & sheet

(G-15553)
KELLER TECHNOLOGY CORPORATION (PA)
2320 Military Rd (14150-6005)
P.O. Box 103, Buffalo (14217-0103)
PHONE.................................716 693-3840
Michael A Keller, *Ch of Bd*
Arthur Keller Jr, *Ch of Bd*
Barnaby Keller, *President*
Peter Keller, *Vice Pres*

Tonawanda - Erie County (G-15554) GEOGRAPHIC SECTION

Mark Belter, *Project Mgr*
▲ **EMP:** 250 **EST:** 1947
SQ FT: 200,000
SALES (est): 63.1MM **Privately Held**
WEB: www.kellertechnology.com
SIC: 3599 Custom machinery

(G-15554)
LAFARGE NORTH AMERICA INC
4001 River Rd (14150-6513)
PHONE.................................716 876-8788
Mark Joslin, *Branch Mgr*
EMP: 13
SALES (corp-wide): 26.4B **Privately Held**
SIC: 3241 Cement, hydraulic
HQ: Lafarge North America Inc.
   8700 W Bryn Mawr Ave
   Chicago IL 60631
   773 372-1000

(G-15555)
LORNAMEAD INC
175 Cooper Ave (14150-6656)
PHONE.................................646 745-3643
Sherly Brantley, *Buyer*
Philip Nardell, *Controller*
Julie Griffiths, *Manager*
Thomas Meyers, *Director*
EMP: 76
SALES (est): 11.6MM **Privately Held**
SIC: 2844 Cosmetic preparations
HQ: Lornamead, Inc
   1359 Broadway Fl 17
   New York NY 10018
   716 874-7190

(G-15556)
MANTH MFG INC
131 Fillmore Ave (14150-2337)
P.O. Box 866 (14151-0866)
PHONE.................................716 693-6525
Duane Manth, *President*
Ron McCarthy, *Plant Mgr*
David Warchocki, *QC Mgr*
EMP: 35
SQ FT: 14,000
SALES: 1.9MM **Privately Held**
SIC: 3599 Machine shop, jobbing & repair

(G-15557)
MAY TOOL & DIE INC
9 Hackett Dr (14150-3797)
PHONE.................................716 695-1033
Martin J May, *President*
Frederick J May, *Vice Pres*
Joseph O May, *Vice Pres*
Mary Kreher, *Admin Sec*
EMP: 5 **EST:** 1970
SQ FT: 8,000
SALES: 500K **Privately Held**
SIC: 3544 Special dies & tools

(G-15558)
MIDLAND MACHINERY CO INC
101 Cranbrook Road Ext Exd (14150-4110)
PHONE.................................716 692-1200
Barre W Banks, *President*
Joseph Wechter, *Prdtn Mgr*
Lalit Kumar, *Design Engr*
Dave Rinard, *Design Engr*
Darrell Banks, *Sls & Mktg Exec*
▲ **EMP:** 59 **EST:** 1969
SQ FT: 15,000
SALES (est): 14.8MM **Privately Held**
WEB: www.midlandmachinery.com
SIC: 3531 Asphalt plant, including gravel-mix type; mixers, concrete; pavers

(G-15559)
MODU-CRAFT INC (PA)
276 Creekside Dr (14150-1435)
PHONE.................................716 694-0709
Kenneth Babka, *President*
EMP: 5
SQ FT: 30,000
SALES: 1MM **Privately Held**
SIC: 3821 2599 2542 Laboratory furniture; factory furniture & fixtures; partitions & fixtures, except wood

(G-15560)
MORNINGSTAR CONCRETE PRODUCTS
528 Young St (14150-4107)
PHONE.................................716 693-4020
Juanita Morningstar, *President*
Ray D Morningstar, *Vice Pres*
EMP: 14 **EST:** 1913
SQ FT: 120,000
SALES (est): 1.7MM **Privately Held**
WEB: www.morningstarturf.com
SIC: 3271 Blocks, concrete or cinder: standard

(G-15561)
NEW YORK IMAGING SERVICE INC
255 Cooper Ave (14150-6641)
PHONE.................................716 834-8022
Rob Muzzio, *Branch Mgr*
EMP: 11
SALES (corp-wide): 15.6MM **Privately Held**
SIC: 3844 X-ray apparatus & tubes
PA: New York Imaging Service Inc.
   1 Dalfonso Rd
   Newburgh NY 12550
   845 561-6947

(G-15562)
NIABRAZE LLC
675 Ensminger Rd (14150-6609)
PHONE.................................716 447-1082
Albert Bluemle Sr, *President*
Thomas Bluemle, *Treasurer*
EMP: 14
SALES (est): 2.3MM **Privately Held**
SIC: 3291 3425 Abrasive products; saw blades for hand or power saws

(G-15563)
NIAGARA BLOWER COMPANY (DH)
91 Sawyer Ave (14150-7716)
PHONE.................................800 426-5169
Peter G Demakos, *President*
Craig D Boyce, *Vice Pres*
▼ **EMP:** 87 **EST:** 1904
SQ FT: 60,000
SALES (est): 33.4MM
SALES (corp-wide): 4.1B **Privately Held**
WEB: www.niagarablower.com
SIC: 3585 Air conditioning units, complete: domestic or industrial

(G-15564)
NIGHTINGALE CORP ◉
750 Ensminger Rd Ste 108 (14150-6640)
PHONE.................................905 896-3434
Wiliam Breen, *CEO*
Edward Breen, *President*
EMP: 5 **EST:** 2018
SQ FT: 2,696
SALES: 1MM **Privately Held**
SIC: 2522 Office chairs, benches & stools, except wood
PA: Nightingale Corp
   2301 Dixie Rd
   Mississauga ON L4Y 1
   905 896-3434

(G-15565)
NOCO INCORPORATED (PA)
2440 Sheridan Dr Ste 202 (14150-9416)
PHONE.................................716 833-6626
James D Newman, *Ch of Bd*
R J Stapell, *Ch of Bd*
Michael Newman, *Exec VP*
Michael L Bradley, *CFO*
EMP: 5
SQ FT: 15,000
SALES (est): 417.5MM **Privately Held**
SIC: 2992 6719 5172 4924 Lubricating oils & greases; investment holding companies, except banks; petroleum products; natural gas distribution

(G-15566)
NORTH DELAWARE PRINTING INC
645 Delaware St Ste 1 (14150-5390)
PHONE.................................716 692-0576
Michael J Brown, *President*
Steven Brown, *Vice Pres*
EMP: 9
SQ FT: 3,200
SALES (est): 1.5MM **Privately Held**
WEB: www.northdelawareprinting.com
SIC: 2752 7334 Commercial printing, offset; photocopying & duplicating services

(G-15567)
ODEN MACHINERY INC (PA)
600 Ensminger Rd (14150-6637)
PHONE.................................716 874-3000
Ronald Sarto, *CEO*
Tony Fwedersky, *President*
Gregory E Simsa, *CFO*
Dave Carroll, *Sales Mgr*
Nick Bird, *Sales Staff*
EMP: 20
SQ FT: 25,000
SALES (est): 4.5MM **Privately Held**
SIC: 3823 Thermometers, filled system: industrial process type

(G-15568)
PADDOCK CHEVROLET GOLF DOME
175 Brompton Rd (14150-4534)
PHONE.................................716 504-4059
Jeff Rainey, *Director*
EMP: 25
SALES (est): 1.2MM **Privately Held**
WEB: www.tonawanda.ny.us
SIC: 3949 7999 Driving ranges, golf, electronic; tennis services & professionals

(G-15569)
PDM STUDIOS INC
510 Main St (14150-3853)
PHONE.................................716 694-8337
Paul Michalski, *President*
Samantha Crocker, *Admin Asst*
EMP: 6
SALES (est): 533.4K **Privately Held**
SIC: 2759 Screen printing

(G-15570)
PRAXAIR INC
175 E Park Dr (14150-7891)
P.O. Box 44 (14151-0044)
PHONE.................................716 879-2000
Joel Emmet, *Principal*
Tim Howley, *Senior VP*
Chuck E Terbot, *Project Mgr*
Christopher Nelson, *Opers Mgr*
John Billingham, *Research*
EMP: 15
SALES (corp-wide): 11.4B **Privately Held**
SIC: 2813 Industrial gases
PA: Praxair, Inc.
   10 Riverview Dr
   Danbury CT 06810
   203 837-2000

(G-15571)
PRAXAIR INC
135 E Park Dr (14150)
PHONE.................................716 879-4000
John Lewendowski, *Principal*
EMP: 50
SALES (corp-wide): 11.4B **Privately Held**
SIC: 2813 Industrial gases
PA: Praxair, Inc.
   10 Riverview Dr
   Danbury CT 06810
   203 837-2000

(G-15572)
R J REYNOLDS TOBACCO COMPANY
275 Cooper Ave Ste 116 (14150-6643)
PHONE.................................716 871-1553
Tracy Wozniak, *Principal*
EMP: 226
SALES (corp-wide): 26.8B **Privately Held**
SIC: 2111 Cigarettes
HQ: R. J. Reynolds Tobacco Company
   401 N Main St
   Winston Salem NC 27101
   336 741-5000

(G-15573)
S R INSTRUMENTS INC (PA)
600 Young St (14150-4188)
PHONE.................................716 693-5977
John Siegel, *President*
Todd Drachenberg, *General Mgr*
John Phillips, *Engineer*
Vernon Siegel, *Admin Sec*
Douglas Recore, *Administration*
EMP: 48 **EST:** 1971
SQ FT: 25,000
SALES (est): 6.2MM **Privately Held**
WEB: www.srinstruments.com
SIC: 3825 3596 Measuring instruments & meters, electric; weighing machines & apparatus

(G-15574)
SAFESPAN PLATFORM SYSTEMS INC
237 Fillmore Ave (14150-2339)
PHONE.................................716 694-1100
Lambros Apostolopoulos, *President*
EMP: 40 **Privately Held**
SIC: 3312 Slabs, steel; structural shapes & pilings, steel
PA: Safespan Platform Systems, Inc.
   252 Fillmore Ave
   Tonawanda NY 14150

(G-15575)
SCHWABEL FABRICATING CO INC (PA)
349 Sawyer Ave (14150-7796)
PHONE.................................716 876-2086
Gerald Schwabel, *President*
Paul Schwabel, *Vice Pres*
William Schwabel, *Admin Sec*
EMP: 23
SQ FT: 30,000
SALES (est): 3.1MM **Privately Held**
WEB: www.schwabelfab.com
SIC: 3443 3599 3552 Heat exchangers, plate type; vessels, process or storage (from boiler shops): metal plate; tanks, standard or custom fabricated: metal plate; machine shop, jobbing & repair; textile machinery

(G-15576)
SCIENTIFICS DIRECT INC
532 Main St (14150-3853)
PHONE.................................716 773-7500
Paul Gerspach, *Ch of Bd*
Tim Burns, *Director*
▲ **EMP:** 17 **EST:** 2012
SALES (est): 2.3MM **Privately Held**
SIC: 3229 5049 5961 Scientific glassware; scientific & engineering equipment & supplies; scientific instruments;

(G-15577)
SERVICE FILTRATION CORP
225 E Park Dr (14150-7813)
P.O. Box 963, Buffalo (14240-0963)
PHONE.................................716 877-2608
EMP: 30
SALES (corp-wide): 62.5MM **Privately Held**
WEB: www.pacerpumps.com
SIC: 3569 3677 Filters, general line: industrial; filtration devices, electronic
PA: Service Filtration Corp.
   2900 Macarthur Blvd
   Northbrook IL 60062
   847 509-2900

(G-15578)
SNYDER INDUSTRIES INC (PA)
340 Wales Ave (14150-2513)
PHONE.................................716 694-1240
Thomas W Snyder, *Ch of Bd*
Thomas Dunch, *Vice Pres*
Charlie Rudolph, *Vice Pres*
Marie Snyder, *Vice Pres*
Bill Snyder, *Plant Mgr*
EMP: 101 **EST:** 1971
SQ FT: 24,000
SALES (est): 23.4MM **Privately Held**
WEB: www.snyderindustriesinc.com
SIC: 3599 Machine shop, jobbing & repair

(G-15579)
SUPERIOR PRINTING INK CO INC
777 E Park Dr (14150-6708)
PHONE.................................716 877-0250
EMP: 5
SALES (corp-wide): 125.3MM **Privately Held**
SIC: 2893 Printing ink
PA: Superior Printing Ink Co Inc
   100 North St
   Teterboro NJ 07608
   201 478-5600

GEOGRAPHIC SECTION

(G-15580)
SURE FLOW EQUIPMENT INC
250 Cooper Ave Ste 102 (14150-6633)
P.O. Box 321 (14151-0321)
PHONE...................................800 263-8251
John Wordsworth, *President*
Danny Miles, *Sales Staff*
EMP: 50
SALES (est): 14MM **Privately Held**
SIC: 3494 5072 Valves & pipe fittings; hardware

(G-15581)
SWIFT RIVER ASSOCIATES INC
4051 River Rd (14150-6513)
PHONE...................................716 875-0902
Kenneth Rawe Sr, *President*
Tony Pariso, *Corp Secy*
Carmen Pariso, *Vice Pres*
Kenneth Rawe Jr, *Vice Pres*
EMP: 7
SALES (est): 1.1MM **Privately Held**
SIC: 2951 Concrete, asphaltic (not from refineries)

(G-15582)
TONAWANDA COKE CORPORATION
3875 River Rd (14150-6591)
P.O. Box 5007 (14151-5007)
PHONE...................................716 876-6222
J D Crane, *CEO*
Michael K Durkin, *President*
Ron Hostler, *Engineer*
Ken Thrun, *Project Engr*
Michael Durkin, *CFO*
▲ **EMP:** 130
SQ FT: 150,000
SALES (est): 46.3MM **Privately Held**
WEB: www.tonawandacoke.com
SIC: 3312 Coke produced in chemical recovery coke ovens

(G-15583)
TONAWANDA LIMB & BRACE INC
545 Delaware St (14150-5301)
PHONE...................................716 695-1131
Robert Catipovic, *President*
Richard C Catipovic, *Vice Pres*
Nancy Sardina, *Manager*
EMP: 5
SQ FT: 14,000
SALES (est): 728.4K **Privately Held**
SIC: 3842 Limbs, artificial; prosthetic appliances

(G-15584)
TREEHOUSE PRIVATE BRANDS INC
570 Fillmore Ave (14150-2509)
PHONE...................................716 693-4715
EMP: 175
SALES (corp-wide): 6.3B **Publicly Held**
SIC: 2052 Cookies
HQ: Treehouse Private Brands, Inc.
800 Market St Ste 2600
Saint Louis MO 63101

(G-15585)
TREYCO PRODUCTS CORP
131 Fillmore Ave (14150-2396)
P.O. Box 866 (14151-0866)
PHONE...................................716 693-6525
Duane Manth, *President*
▲ **EMP:** 5 **EST:** 1961
SQ FT: 10,000
SALES (est): 520.8K **Privately Held**
WEB: www.treyco.com
SIC: 3421 Scissors, shears, clippers, snips & similar tools; shears, hand; clippers, fingernail & toenail; snips, tinners'

(G-15586)
UNIFRAX I LLC
Fiberfrax Manufacturing
360 Fire Tower Dr (14150-5893)
PHONE...................................716 696-3000
Scott Penman, *Production*
John Di Matteo, *Engineer*
Mark Travers, *Data Proc Staff*
EMP: 165 **Publicly Held**
WEB: www.insulfrax.com
SIC: 3297 3299 3296 Nonclay refractories; ceramic fiber; mineral wool

HQ: Unifrax I Llc
600 Rverwalk Pkwy Ste 120
Tonawanda NY 14150

(G-15587)
UNIFRAX I LLC (HQ)
600 Rverwalk Pkwy Ste 120 (14150)
PHONE...................................716 768-6500
David E Brooks, *President*
Michele Wierzbicki, *Regional Mgr*
Stephen Juda, *Vice Pres*
Brian Walker, *Vice Pres*
Jack Flick, *Project Mgr*
▲ **EMP:** 110
SALES (est): 389.2MM **Publicly Held**
WEB: www.insulfrax.com
SIC: 3299 Ceramic fiber

(G-15588)
UOP LLC
175 E Park Dr (14150-7844)
P.O. Box 986 (14151-0986)
PHONE...................................716 879-7600
Charles J Schorr, *General Mgr*
EMP: 21
SALES (corp-wide): 40.5B **Publicly Held**
WEB: www.uop.com
SIC: 2819 Catalysts, chemical
HQ: Uop Llc
25 E Algonquin Rd
Des Plaines IL 60016
847 391-2000

(G-15589)
VIATRAN CORPORATION (DH)
199 Fire Tower Dr (14150-5813)
PHONE...................................716 564-7813
George A Fraas, *CEO*
Kenneth H Brown, *Ch of Bd*
Carol Starck, *Opers Mgr*
Bill Blazejewski, *Engineer*
Bill Wilson, *Engineer*
EMP: 50 **EST:** 1965
SQ FT: 18,000
SALES (est): 7.3MM
SALES (corp-wide): 4.6B **Publicly Held**
WEB: www.viatran.com
SIC: 3823 3825 5084 Pressure measurement instruments, industrial; instruments to measure electricity; industrial machinery & equipment

(G-15590)
WASHINGTON MILLS TONAWANDA INC (HQ)
1000 E Niagara St (14150-1306)
PHONE...................................716 693-4550
Ronald Campbell, *Chairman*
Kersi Dordi, *Vice Pres*
Armand Ladage, *Vice Pres*
John Redshaw, *VP Sales*
Nancy Gates, *Admin Sec*
▲ **EMP:** 30
SQ FT: 273,000
SALES (est): 48.8MM
SALES (corp-wide): 171.9MM **Privately Held**
WEB: www.exolon.com
SIC: 3291 Aluminum oxide (fused) abrasives
PA: Washington Mills Group, Inc.
20 N Main St
North Grafton MA 01536
508 839-6511

(G-15591)
WOODWARD INDUSTRIES INC
233 Fillmore Ave Ste 1 (14150-2316)
P.O. Box 410 (14151-0410)
PHONE...................................716 692-2242
Daniel Woodward, *President*
Deke Lemieux, *Project Mgr*
Jeanette Woodward, *Office Mgr*
EMP: 16 **EST:** 1953
SQ FT: 18,845
SALES (est): 1.4MM **Privately Held**
WEB: www.woodwardind.com
SIC: 3543 Industrial patterns

(G-15592)
WSF INDUSTRIES INC
7 Hackett Dr (14150-3798)
P.O. Box 400, Buffalo (14217-0400)
PHONE...................................716 692-4930
John Hettrick Jr, *CEO*
Gary Fornasiero, *President*
Pat Barrett, *Plant Mgr*
Nancy Warner, *Buyer*
Curtis Smith, *QC Mgr*
▼ **EMP:** 25 **EST:** 1941
SQ FT: 66,000
SALES (est): 2.8MM **Privately Held**
WEB: www.wsf-inc.com
SIC: 3443 Autoclaves, industrial

(G-15593)
ZENGER GROUP INC
777 E Park Dr (14150-6708)
PHONE...................................716 871-1058
Stephen Zenger, *Ch of Bd*
Norman Lawkowski, *Sales Staff*
EMP: 44
SALES (est): 4.1MM
SALES (corp-wide): 18.6MM **Privately Held**
SIC: 2752 Commercial printing, lithographic
PA: Zenger Group Inc.
777 E Park Dr
Tonawanda NY 14150
716 871-1058

Troy
Albany County

(G-15594)
ALBANY NIPPLE AND PIPE MFG
60 Cohoes Ave Ste 100a (12183-1518)
PHONE...................................518 270-2162
Robert Moss, *President*
EMP: 20
SALES (est): 2.4MM **Privately Held**
SIC: 3498 Tube fabricating (contract bending & shaping)

(G-15595)
HONEYWELL INTERNATIONAL INC
3 Tibbits Ave (12183-1433)
PHONE...................................518 270-0200
Steve Kratz, *Branch Mgr*
EMP: 80
SALES (corp-wide): 40.5B **Publicly Held**
WEB: www.honeywell.com
SIC: 3724 Aircraft engines & engine parts
PA: Honeywell International Inc.
115 Tabor Rd
Morris Plains NJ 07950
973 455-2000

(G-15596)
KAYS CAPS INC (PA)
65 Arch St (12183-1599)
PHONE...................................518 273-6079
Roberta Fine, *Ch of Bd*
EMP: 8
SQ FT: 1,000
SALES (est): 637.3K **Privately Held**
WEB: www.kayscaps.com
SIC: 2353 Uniform hats & caps

(G-15597)
LONG ISLAND PIPE SUPPLY INC
75 Cohoes Ave (12183-1506)
PHONE...................................518 270-2159
Bob Moss, *President*
Kathy Fields, *CFO*
EMP: 6
SALES (est): 1MM
SALES (corp-wide): 59.6MM **Privately Held**
SIC: 3498 Fabricated pipe & fittings
PA: Long Island Pipe Supply Inc
586 Commercial Ave
Garden City NY 11530
516 222-8008

(G-15598)
SEALY MATTRESS CO ALBANY INC
30 Veterans Memorial Dr (12183-1517)
PHONE...................................518 880-1600
David J McIlquham, *President*
EMP: 300
SQ FT: 265,000
SALES (est): 44.5MM
SALES (corp-wide): 2.7B **Publicly Held**
SIC: 2515 Mattresses, innerspring or box spring

HQ: Sealy Mattress Company
1 Office Parkway Rd
Trinity NC 27370
336 861-3500

Troy
Rensselaer County

(G-15599)
A I T COMPUTERS INC
157 Hoosick St (12180-2375)
PHONE...................................518 266-9010
Ahmed Ali, *President*
EMP: 3
SQ FT: 2,000
SALES: 1MM **Privately Held**
WEB: www.aitcomputers.com
SIC: 3577 5734 Computer peripheral equipment; computer & software stores

(G-15600)
APPRENDA INC
433 River St Ste 4001 (12180-2357)
PHONE...................................518 383-2130
Sinclair Schuller, *CEO*
Rene Hermes, *General Mgr*
Matthew Ammerman, *Vice Pres*
Wayne Boomer, *Vice Pres*
Rakesh Malhotra, *Vice Pres*
EMP: 73 **EST:** 2007
SALES (est): 9.2MM **Privately Held**
SIC: 7372 Prepackaged Software Services

(G-15601)
ARDEX COSMETICS OF AMERICA
744 Pawling Ave (12180-6212)
PHONE...................................518 283-6700
Nubar Sukljian, *President*
▲ **EMP:** 20
SQ FT: 250,000
SALES (est): 2.1MM **Privately Held**
SIC: 2844 Cosmetic preparations

(G-15602)
BATTERY ENERGY STORAGE SYSTEMS
Also Called: Besstech
291 River St Ste 318 (12180-3218)
PHONE...................................518 256-7029
Bruce Toyama, *Vice Pres*
Brian Butcher,
Benjamin Backes,
Fernando Gomez-Baquero,
Jae Ho Lee,
EMP: 6
SALES (est): 553.5K **Privately Held**
SIC: 3691 Storage batteries

(G-15603)
DEAKON HOMES AND INTERIORS
Also Called: Troy Cabinet Manufacturing Div
16 Industrial Park Rd (12180-6197)
PHONE...................................518 271-0342
Diane F Decurtis, *President*
John De Curtis, *General Mgr*
EMP: 15
SQ FT: 7,000
SALES (est): 1.4MM **Privately Held**
WEB: www.troycabinet.com
SIC: 2434 1521 2541 2522 Wood kitchen cabinets; general remodeling, single-family houses; wood partitions & fixtures; office furniture, except wood; wood office furniture; wood household furniture

(G-15604)
DOWD - WITBECK PRINTING CORP
Also Called: SCHENECTADY HERALD PRINTING CO
599 Pawling Ave (12180-5823)
PHONE...................................518 274-2421
Toll Free...................................877 -
Denise Padula, *President*
John E Hupe, *Vice Pres*
Steve Bowes, *Production*
Colleen Mooney, *Marketing Staff*
Laura Erano, *Manager*
EMP: 18
SQ FT: 10,200

Troy - Rensselaer County (G-15605)

SALES: 2.3MM **Privately Held**
WEB: www.alchar.com
SIC: **2752** 2796 2791 2789 Commercial printing, offset; platemaking services; typesetting; bookbinding & related work; commercial art & graphic design

(G-15605)
FLOAT TECH INC
216 River St Ste 1 (12180-3848)
PHONE..................................518 266-0964
Cecilia Domingos, *President*
EMP: 6
SALES (est): 480K **Privately Held**
SIC: **2385** Waterproof outerwear

(G-15606)
GEORGE M DUJACK
Also Called: Du Serv Development Co
80 Town Office Rd (12180-8817)
PHONE..................................518 279-1303
George M Dujack, *Owner*
EMP: 5 EST: 1973
SALES: 400K **Privately Held**
SIC: **2821** Silicone resins

(G-15607)
GURLEY PRECISION INSTRS INC
514 Fulton St (12180-3315)
PHONE..................................518 272-6300
O Patrick Brady, *Ch of Bd*
Yuriy Benderskiy, *Mfg Dir*
Evan Defilippo, *Engineer*
Boris Mintseris, *Engineer*
Michael Ford, *Electrical Engi*
EMP: 105
SQ FT: 78,000
SALES (est): 24.3MM **Privately Held**
WEB: www.gurley.com
SIC: **3827** 3824 3829 3823 Optical instruments & lenses; water meters; physical property testing equipment; industrial instrmnts msrmnt display/control process variable; semiconductors & related devices; radio & TV communications equipment

(G-15608)
HAMILTON PRINTING COMPANY INC
22 Hamilton Ave (12180)
PHONE..................................518 732-2161
John Paeglow, *CEO*
William Greenawalt, *Vice Pres*
Brian F Payne, *Vice Pres*
▲ EMP: 140 EST: 1912
SQ FT: 100,000
SALES (est): 16.9MM **Privately Held**
WEB: www.hamprint.com
SIC: **2732** 2789 Books: printing & binding; binding only: books, pamphlets, magazines, etc.

(G-15609)
INDUSTRIAL TOOL & DIE CO INC
14 Industrial Park Rd (12180-6197)
PHONE..................................518 273-7383
Paul V Cacciotti, *President*
▲ EMP: 14
SQ FT: 17,000
SALES (est): 2.4MM **Privately Held**
SIC: **3599** Machine shop, jobbing & repair

(G-15610)
INTERNTNAL ELCTRONIC MCHS CORP
Also Called: I E M
850 River St (12180-1239)
PHONE..................................518 268-1636
Zack Mian, *President*
Peter Hayes, *Engineer*
Bill Peabody, *Design Engr*
James Skaggs, *Sales Dir*
Robert Foss, *Manager*
◆ EMP: 29
SQ FT: 35,000
SALES: 5MM **Privately Held**
WEB: www.iem.net
SIC: **3825** 8711 Instruments to measure electricity; engineering services

(G-15611)
NEXT ADVANCE INC (PA)
2113 Ny 7 Ste 1 (12180-9188)
PHONE..................................518 674-3510
Ian Glasgow, *President*
EMP: 15
SALES (est): 212.3K **Privately Held**
WEB: www.nextadvance.com
SIC: **3821** Clinical laboratory instruments, except medical & dental

(G-15612)
NIBBLE INC BAKING CO
451 Broadway Apt 5 (12180-3355)
PHONE..................................518 334-3950
EMP: 8
SALES (est): 475K **Privately Held**
SIC: **2051** Bread, cake & related products

(G-15613)
NORTHEAST PALLET & CONT CO INC
1 Mann Ave Bldg 300 (12180)
PHONE..................................518 271-0535
James F Price, *President*
EMP: 16
SQ FT: 18,000
SALES (est): 1.4MM **Privately Held**
SIC: **2449** 2448 Rectangular boxes & crates, wood; pallets, wood

(G-15614)
PB MAPINFO CORPORATION
1 Global Vw (12180-8371)
PHONE..................................518 285-6000
Murray Martin, *CEO*
John E O'Hara, *Ch of Bd*
David Woroboff, *President*
Barret Johnson, *Vice Pres*
Andrew Naden, *Vice Pres*
EMP: 903
SQ FT: 150,000
SALES (est): 668.1K
SALES (corp-wide): 3.5B **Publicly Held**
WEB: www.mapinfo.com
SIC: **7372** Business oriented computer software
PA: Pitney Bowes Inc.
   3001 Summer St Ste 3
   Stamford CT 06905
   203 356-5000

(G-15615)
PERROTTAS BAKERY INC
766 Pawling Ave (12180-6294)
PHONE..................................518 283-4711
Charles A Perrotta, *President*
Louis Perrotta, *Corp Secy*
EMP: 9 EST: 1962
SQ FT: 5,000
SALES (est): 925.9K **Privately Held**
SIC: **2051** 5461 Bakery: wholesale or wholesale/retail combined; bakeries

(G-15616)
PITNEY BOWES INC
350 Jordan Rd Ste 1 (12180-8358)
PHONE..................................518 283-0345
Jim Gully, *Branch Mgr*
EMP: 130
SALES (corp-wide): 3.5B **Publicly Held**
SIC: **3579** Mailing machines
PA: Pitney Bowes Inc.
   3001 Summer St Ste 3
   Stamford CT 06905
   203 356-5000

(G-15617)
PLACID BAKER
250 Broadway (12180-3235)
PHONE..................................518 326-2657
Margaret Obert, *Principal*
EMP: 8 EST: 2009
SALES (est): 637.9K **Privately Held**
SIC: **2051** Cakes, bakery: except frozen

(G-15618)
R J VALENTE GRAVEL INC (PA)
1 Madison St (12180-5145)
PHONE..................................518 432-4470
Roderick J Valente, *Ch of Bd*
Joseph Panza, *Controller*
EMP: 60
SQ FT: 5,000
SALES (est): 17.7MM **Privately Held**
SIC: **1442** Construction sand & gravel

(G-15619)
RAITH AMERICA INC
Also Called: Vistec Lithography
300 Jordan Rd (12180-8346)
PHONE..................................518 874-3000
Rainer Schmid, *Branch Mgr*
EMP: 33
SALES (corp-wide): 25MM **Privately Held**
SIC: **2752** Color lithography
PA: Raith America, Inc.
   1377 Long Iisland Motor P
   Islandia NY 11749
   518 874-3020

(G-15620)
RARE FORM BREWING COMPANY
90 Congress St (12180-4123)
PHONE..................................518 313-9256
Jennifer Kemp, *President*
EMP: 7
SALES (est): 268.2K **Privately Held**
SIC: **2082** Beer (alcoholic beverage)

(G-15621)
ROSS VALVE MFG
75 102nd St (12180-1125)
PHONE..................................518 274-0961
EMP: 7
SALES (est): 672.9K **Privately Held**
SIC: **3494** Valves & pipe fittings

(G-15622)
RW GATE COMPANY (PA)
79 102nd St (12180-1125)
PHONE..................................518 874-4750
Andy Ross, *Principal*
Bill Ross, *Principal*
Evan Whipps, *Principal*
EMP: 10
SALES: 6.3MM **Privately Held**
SIC: **3441** Dam gates, metal plate

(G-15623)
RW GATE COMPANY
75 102nd St (12180-1125)
PHONE..................................518 874-4750
EMP: 60 **Privately Held**
SIC: **3441** Dam gates, metal plate

(G-15624)
SCRIVEN DUPLICATING SERVICE
Also Called: Scriven Press
100 Eastover Rd (12182-1108)
PHONE..................................518 233-8180
Kevin Rafferty, *President*
Brian Rafferty, *Vice Pres*
EMP: 6
SQ FT: 4,800
SALES (est): 750K **Privately Held**
SIC: **2752** Photo-offset printing

(G-15625)
SHAMRON MILLS LTD
484 River St (12180-2215)
PHONE..................................212 354-0430
Ronnye Shamron, *President*
▲ EMP: 3
SQ FT: 3,000
SALES: 3MM **Privately Held**
WEB: www.shamron.com
SIC: **2389** Hospital gowns

(G-15626)
SIGN STUDIO INC
1 Ingalls Ave (12180-1220)
PHONE..................................518 266-0877
Ronald Levesque, *CEO*
EMP: 12
SQ FT: 2,500
SALES (est): 1.3MM **Privately Held**
SIC: **3993** Signs, not made in custom sign painting shops

(G-15627)
SILVER GRIFFIN INC
691 Hoosick Rd (12180-8818)
PHONE..................................518 272-7771
Paul Noonan, *President*
Geoff Scarchilli, *Graphic Designe*
EMP: 15
SALES (est): 1.2MM **Privately Held**
SIC: **2759** 7299 7334 Commercial printing; wedding chapel, privately operated; ; photocopying & duplicating services

(G-15628)
STANDARD MANUFACTURING CO INC (PA)
Also Called: Sportsmaster Apparel
750 2nd Ave (12182-2290)
P.O. Box 380 (12182-0380)
PHONE..................................518 235-2200
George Arakelian, *CEO*
Dorothy King, *Corp Secy*
Christian Arakelian, *Vice Pres*
Alison Arakelian, *Manager*
▲ EMP: 65
SQ FT: 250,000
SALES (est): 8.9MM **Privately Held**
SIC: **2337** 2339 2329 Jackets & vests, except fur & leather: women's; women's & misses' outerwear; jackets (suede, leatherette, etc.), sport: men's & boys'; men's & boys' leather, wool & down-filled outerwear

(G-15629)
SUNWARD ELECTRONICS INC
Also Called: Dog Guard
258 Broadway Ste 2a (12180)
PHONE..................................518 687-0030
Rose Watkins, *President*
William Drew, *General Mgr*
James Dwiggins, *Principal*
Tricia Coward, *Controller*
Richard Dawson, *Mktg Dir*
EMP: 11
SQ FT: 5,000
SALES (est): 1.8MM **Privately Held**
WEB: www.teacherspetproducts.com
SIC: **3496** 3612 Fencing, made from purchased wire; transformers, except electric

(G-15630)
TROY BOILER WORKS INC
2800 7th Ave (12180-1587)
PHONE..................................518 274-2650
Louis E Okonski, *President*
John E Okonski Sr, *President*
Richard Okonski, *Corp Secy*
Kenneth Erskin, *Manager*
Jack Okonski, *Manager*
EMP: 50
SQ FT: 25,000
SALES (est): 14.6MM **Privately Held**
WEB: www.troyboilerworks.com
SIC: **3443** 7699 Vessels, process or storage (from boiler shops); metal plate; tanks, standard or custom fabricated: metal plate; boiler & boiler shop work; boiler repair shop

(G-15631)
VITA RARA INC
Also Called: Enable Labs
415 River St Ste 4 (12180-2834)
PHONE..................................518 369-7356
Mark Menard, *President*
John Fitzpatrick, *Opers Staff*
James Wilson, *Human Res Dir*
Patrick McConnell, *Software Engr*
Jonathan Chapman, *Software Dev*
EMP: 5
SALES: 750K **Privately Held**
WEB: www.vitarara.net
SIC: **7372** Business oriented computer software

(G-15632)
VITAL VIO INC
185 Jordan Rd Ste 1 (12180-7611)
PHONE..................................914 245-6048
Colleen Costello, *CEO*
EMP: 10
SALES (est): 245.6K **Privately Held**
SIC: **3646** 7342 Commercial indusl & institutional electric lighting fixtures; disinfecting services

(G-15633)
VM CHOPPY & SONS LLC
4 Van Buren St (12180-5596)
PHONE..................................518 266-1444
Vincent J Choppy, *Purchasing*
Anne F Choppy, *Mng Member*

GEOGRAPHIC SECTION
Ulster Park - Ulster County (G-15659)

Vincent M Choppy,
EMP: 30
SQ FT: 35,000
SALES (est): 5.7MM **Privately Held**
WEB: www.vmchoppyandsons.com
SIC: 3444 Sheet metal specialties, not stamped

(G-15634)
WANT-AD DIGEST INC
Also Called: Classified Advertising
870 Hoosick Rd Ste 1 (12180-6622)
PHONE.................................518 279-1181
William Engelke, *President*
Rose Engelke, *Vice Pres*
Rose Hastings, *Director*
EMP: 18
SQ FT: 2,000
SALES (est): 192.9K **Privately Held**
WEB: www.wantaddigest.com
SIC: 2741 5521 Directories: publishing & printing; used car dealers

(G-15635)
WEIGHING & SYSTEMS TECH INC
274 2nd St (12180-4616)
PHONE.................................518 274-2797
EMP: 7
SALES (corp-wide): 695K **Privately Held**
SIC: 3596 Mfg Scales/Balances-Nonlaboratory
PA: Weighing & Systems Technology, Inc.
4558 Morgan Pl
Liverpool NY 13090
315 451-7940

(G-15636)
WELDCOMPUTER CORPORATION
105 Jordan Rd Ste 1 (12180-7612)
PHONE.................................518 283-2897
Robert Cohen, *President*
Dr Keith Strain, *Vice Pres*
EMP: 13
SQ FT: 4,000
SALES: 1.5MM **Privately Held**
WEB: www.weldcomputer.com
SIC: 3625 Control equipment, electric

Trumansburg
Tompkins County

(G-15637)
BELLWETHE HARD CIDER
9070 State Route 89 (14886-9234)
PHONE.................................607 387-9464
William Barton, *Owner*
EMP: 10
SALES (est): 837.6K **Privately Held**
SIC: 2084 Wines

(G-15638)
EAGLE ENVELOPE COMPANY (DH)
8091 Trumansburg Rd (14886)
P.O. Box 236, Ithaca (14851-0236)
PHONE.................................607 387-3195
J Kemper Matt Sr, *CEO*
Richard Spingarn, *President*
EMP: 9
SQ FT: 3,000
SALES (est): 1MM
SALES (corp-wide): 28.4MM **Privately Held**
WEB: www.eagleprint.com
SIC: 2759 Envelopes: printing
HQ: Dupli Graphics Corporation
6761 Thompson Rd
Syracuse NY 13211
315 234-7286

(G-15639)
FLO-TECH ORTHOTIC & PROSTHETIC
7325 Halseyville Rd (14886)
P.O. Box 462 (14886-0462)
PHONE.................................607 387-3070
Robert N Brown Sr, *CEO*
Kathleen Brown, *President*
EMP: 8
SALES: 900K **Privately Held**
WEB: www.1800flo-tech.com
SIC: 3842 Prosthetic appliances

(G-15640)
FORCE DYNAMICS INC
4995 Voorheis Rd (14886-9435)
PHONE.................................607 546-5023
Micheal D Wiernicki, *Principal*
EMP: 19
SALES (est): 2.4MM **Privately Held**
WEB: www.force-dynamics.com
SIC: 3559 Special industry machinery

(G-15641)
WASHBURN MANUFACTURING TECH
9828 State Route 96 (14886-9327)
PHONE.................................607 387-3991
Thomas Washburn, *President*
EMP: 8
SQ FT: 2,000
SALES: 1MM **Privately Held**
SIC: 3599 Custom machinery

Tuckahoe
Westchester County

(G-15642)
AUTOMTIVE UPHL CNVERTIBLE TOPS
170 Marbledale Rd (10707-3118)
PHONE.................................914 961-4242
Frank Ackermann, *President*
Ron Ackermann, *Vice Pres*
EMP: 5
SQ FT: 5,000
SALES (est): 370K **Privately Held**
SIC: 2394 2399 Convertible tops, canvas or boat: from purchased materials; automotive covers, except seat & tire covers

(G-15643)
GLOBAL FOOD SOURCE & CO INC
114 Carpenter Ave (10707-2104)
PHONE.................................914 320-9615
Albert J Savarese, *President*
▲ **EMP:** 4
SALES (est): 5MM **Privately Held**
SIC: 2032 Canned specialties

(G-15644)
MEDI-RAY INC
150 Marbledale Rd (10707-3197)
PHONE.................................877 898-3003
Ralph F Farella, *President*
Barry N Dansky, *Treasurer*
Barry Dansky, *Executive*
▲ **EMP:** 63
SQ FT: 23,000
SALES (est): 11.5MM **Privately Held**
WEB: www.mediray.com
SIC: 3412 3842 5063 7623 Metal barrels, drums & pails; orthopedic appliances; electrical apparatus & equipment; refrigeration service & repair; nonferrous foundries; nonferrous rolling & drawing

(G-15645)
PACKAGING TECH & INSPTN LLC
Also Called: P T I
145 Main St (10707-2906)
PHONE.................................914 337-2005
Eddie Mancini, *Sales Staff*
Michelle Wolf, *Marketing Staff*
Oliver Stauffer, *Mng Member*
Pamela Gionta, *Administration*
Anton Stauffer,
▲ **EMP:** 35
SQ FT: 10,600
SALES: 8.5MM **Privately Held**
WEB: www.ptiusa.net
SIC: 3823 Industrial process measurement equipment; pressure measurement instruments, industrial

(G-15646)
STOFFEL POLYGON SYSTEMS INC
199 Marbledale Rd (10707-3117)
PHONE.................................914 961-2000
John F Stoffel, *President*
Michael Kambouris, *QC Mgr*
Arlene M Gruber, *Admin Sec*
Reda Riad, *Administration*
EMP: 10
SQ FT: 22,180
SALES (est): 1.2MM **Privately Held**
WEB: www.stoffelpolygon.com
SIC: 3462 Iron & steel forgings

Tully
Onondaga County

(G-15647)
APPLIED CONCEPTS INC
397 State Route 281 (13159-2486)
PHONE.................................315 696-6676
Kurt Shaffer, *CEO*
Stephen C Soos, *President*
Brian Poole, *Purch Mgr*
John Dickson, *Design Engr*
Lucas Zimmerman, *Design Engr*
EMP: 28 **EST:** 1998
SQ FT: 16,000
SALES: 4MM **Privately Held**
WEB: www.acipower.com
SIC: 3679 Power supplies, all types: static

(G-15648)
BARBER & DELINE ENRGY SVCS LLC
10 Community Dr (13159)
PHONE.................................315 696-8961
Eva Deline, *Mng Member*
EMP: 10
SALES (est): 643.7K **Privately Held**
SIC: 1389 1381 Construction, repair & dismantling services; drilling water intake wells

(G-15649)
BARBER & DELINE LLC
995 State Route 11a (13159-2426)
PHONE.................................607 749-2619
Eva Deline,
EMP: 10
SQ FT: 3,000
SALES (est): 2.7MM **Privately Held**
WEB: www.barber-deline.com
SIC: 1381 1781 Service well drilling; water well drilling

Tupper Lake
Franklin County

(G-15650)
LIZOTTE LOGGING INC
50 Haymeadow Rd (12986-1069)
PHONE.................................518 359-2200
Jeannel Lizotte, *President*
Cynthia Lizotte, *Admin Sec*
EMP: 15
SALES (est): 1.8MM **Privately Held**
SIC: 2411 Logging camps & contractors

(G-15651)
MITCHELL STONE PRODUCTS LLC
161 Main St (12986-1023)
PHONE.................................518 359-7029
Paul Mitchell, *Principal*
EMP: 6 **EST:** 2016
SALES (est): 184.7K **Privately Held**
SIC: 1442 Construction sand & gravel

(G-15652)
PAUL J MITCHELL LOGGING INC
15 Mitchell Ln (12986-1056)
PHONE.................................518 359-7029
Paul J Mitchell, *President*
Mary Michell, *Admin Sec*
EMP: 26
SQ FT: 7,000
SALES (est): 3.6MM **Privately Held**
SIC: 2411 Logging camps & contractors

(G-15653)
RICHARDS LOGGING LLC
201 State Route 3 (12986-7705)
PHONE.................................518 359-2775
Bruce Richards, *Mng Member*
Lawrence Richards,
EMP: 15
SALES (est): 2.3MM **Privately Held**
SIC: 2411 Logging camps & contractors

(G-15654)
TRILAKE THREE PRESS CORP
136 Park St (12986-1818)
PHONE.................................518 359-2462
Dan McClelland, *President*
Judy McClelland, *Vice Pres*
John Morris, *Director*
EMP: 6
SQ FT: 3,500
SALES (est): 340K **Privately Held**
SIC: 2711 Newspapers, publishing & printing

(G-15655)
TUPPER LAKE HARDWOODS INC
167 Pitchfork Pond Rd (12986-1047)
P.O. Box 748 (12986-0748)
PHONE.................................518 359-8248
Greg Paneaudeau, *President*
Robert Gibeault, *General Mgr*
EMP: 32 **EST:** 1994
SQ FT: 21,356
SALES (est): 3.6MM **Privately Held**
SIC: 2421 2426 Sawmills & planing mills, general; hardwood dimension & flooring mills

Tuxedo Park
Orange County

(G-15656)
I & I SYSTEMS
66 Table Rock Rd (10987-4720)
PHONE.................................845 753-9126
Shan Custello, *President*
EMP: 6
SALES (est): 634.5K **Privately Held**
SIC: 3953 Letters (marking devices), metal

(G-15657)
INTERNATIONAL PAPER COMPANY
1422 Long Meadow Rd (10987-3500)
PHONE.................................845 986-6409
Virginia Rizzo, *Manager*
EMP: 140
SALES (corp-wide): 21.7B **Publicly Held**
WEB: www.internationalpaper.com
SIC: 2621 8731 Paper mills; commercial physical research
PA: International Paper Company
6400 Poplar Ave
Memphis TN 38197
901 419-9000

Ulster Park
Ulster County

(G-15658)
DYNO NOBEL INC
161 Ulster Ave (12487-5019)
PHONE.................................845 338-2144
Margaret Seeger, *Opers-Prdtn-Mfg*
EMP: 55 **Privately Held**
SIC: 2892 3489 Explosives; ordnance & accessories
HQ: Dyno Nobel Inc.
2795 E Cottonwood Pkwy # 500
Salt Lake City UT 84121
801 364-4800

(G-15659)
MORESCA CLOTHING AND COSTUME
361 Union Center Rd (12487-5232)
PHONE.................................845 331-6012

Unadilla - Otsego County (G-15660)

GEOGRAPHIC SECTION

Lena Dun, *President*
EMP: 10
SQ FT: 11,000
SALES (est): 1.4MM Privately Held
WEB: www.moresca.com
SIC: 2389 5699 5136 5137 Costumes; costumes, masquerade or theatrical; men's & boys' clothing; women's & children's clothing

Unadilla
Otsego County

(G-15660)
AMES COMPANIES INC
196 Clifton St (13849-2418)
P.O. Box 644 (13849-0644)
PHONE.....................607 369-9595
Jay Gerber, *Controller*
Alexander Miller, *Branch Mgr*
EMP: 61
SQ FT: 25,000
SALES (corp-wide): 1.5B Publicly Held
WEB: www.ames.com
SIC: 3423 Garden & farm tools, including shovels
HQ: The Ames Companies Inc
465 Railroad Ave
Camp Hill PA 17011
717 737-1500

(G-15661)
ATOMIC INFORMATION SYSTEMS
Also Called: Atomicdbonline.com
1580 State Highway 357 (13849-2399)
PHONE.....................716 713-5402
Jean Le Tennier, *President*
EMP: 50
SALES (corp-wide): 10MM Privately Held
SIC: 7372 7371 Prepackaged software; custom computer programming services
PA: Atomic Information Systems Corp
5500 N Bailey Ave Unit 36
Amherst NY
716 713-5402

Uniondale
Nassau County

(G-15662)
AITHACA CHEMICAL CORP
50 Charles Lindbergh Blvd # 400 (11553-3626)
PHONE.....................516 229-2330
Eric Kastens, *President*
EMP: 10
SQ FT: 300
SALES: 1.3MM Privately Held
WEB: www.aithaca.com
SIC: 2819 5169 Chemicals, high purity: refined from technical grade; chemicals & allied products

(G-15663)
CAMBRIDGE WHOS WHO PUBG INC (PA)
498 Rxr Plz Fl 4 (11556-0400)
PHONE.....................516 833-8440
Mitchel Robbins, *CEO*
Randy Narod, *President*
Eric Lee, *COO*
EMP: 45
SALES (est): 20.3MM Privately Held
SIC: 2741 8748 Miscellaneous publishing; business consulting

(G-15664)
COTY US LLC
726 Eab Plz (11556-0726)
PHONE.....................212 389-7000
Rich Garzon, *Branch Mgr*
EMP: 284 Publicly Held
SIC: 2844 Perfumes & colognes; cosmetic preparations
HQ: Coty Us Llc
350 5th Ave
New York NY 10118

(G-15665)
ELIZABETH WILSON
Also Called: Elizabeth's
579 Edgemere Ave (11553-2517)
PHONE.....................516 486-2157
Elizabeth Wilson, *Owner*
EMP: 4
SQ FT: 1,200
SALES (est): 2.2MM Privately Held
WEB: www.elizabethwilson.com
SIC: 2339 Aprons, except rubber or plastic: women's, misses', juniors'

(G-15666)
FEI COMMUNICATIONS INC
55 Charles Lindbergh Blvd (11553-3689)
PHONE.....................516 794-4500
Harry Newman, *VP Finance*
EMP: 180
SALES (est): 23.6MM
SALES (corp-wide): 39.4MM Publicly Held
WEB: www.freqelec.com
SIC: 3679 Electronic circuits
PA: Frequency Electronics, Inc.
55 Charles Lindbergh Blvd # 2
Uniondale NY 11553
516 794-4500

(G-15667)
FEI-ZYFER INC
55 Charles Lindbergh Blvd (11553-3689)
PHONE.....................714 933-4045
EMP: 9
SALES (corp-wide): 39.4MM Publicly Held
SIC: 3663 Antennas, transmitting & communications
HQ: Fei-Zyfer, Inc.
7321 Lincoln Way
Garden Grove CA 92841

(G-15668)
FREQUENCY ELECTRONICS INC (PA)
55 Charles Lindbergh Blvd # 2 (11553-3699)
PHONE.....................516 794-4500
Martin B Bloch, *Ch of Bd*
Stanton D Sloane, *President*
James Davis, *President*
Steven Strang, *President*
Oleandro Mancini, *Senior VP*
EMP: 189 EST: 1961
SALES: 39.4MM Publicly Held
WEB: www.freqelec.com
SIC: 3825 3812 3669 3679 Elapsed time meters, electronic; frequency meters: electrical, mechanical & electronic; search & detection systems & instruments; detection apparatus: electronic/magnetic field, light/heat; intercommunication systems, electric; microwave components

(G-15669)
HEARST BUSINESS MEDIA (HQ)
Also Called: F C W Division
50 Charles Lindbergh Blvd # 103 (11553-3654)
PHONE.....................516 227-1300
Rich Malloch, *CEO*
Kathy Chacana, *VP Human Res*
EMP: 63
SALES (est): 10.1MM
SALES (corp-wide): 6.6B Publicly Held
SIC: 2721 2741 Magazines: publishing only, not printed on site; directories: publishing only, not printed on site
PA: The Hearst Corporation
300 W 57th St Fl 42
New York NY 10019
212 649-2000

(G-15670)
LOCKHEED MARTIN CORPORATION
55 Charles Lindbergh Blvd # 1 (11553-3682)
PHONE.....................516 228-2000
Michael Stein, *General Mgr*
John Piccirillo, *Managing Dir*
Joseph Cappiello, *Engineer*
Michael Chen, *Engineer*
Vincent Benischek, *Senior Engr*
EMP: 225 Publicly Held
WEB: www.lockheedmartin.com
SIC: 3812 Search & navigation equipment
PA: Lockheed Martin Corporation
6801 Rockledge Dr
Bethesda MD 20817

(G-15671)
MERCHANT SERVICE PYMNT ACCESS
626 Rxr Plz (11556-0626)
PHONE.....................212 561-5516
Sean Ellis, *President*
EMP: 5 EST: 2017
SALES: 10MM Privately Held
SIC: 3578 Calculating & accounting equipment

(G-15672)
TDK USA CORPORATION (HQ)
455 Rxr Plz (11556-3811)
PHONE.....................516 535-2600
Francis J Sweeney Jr, *Ch of Bd*
◆ **EMP:** 68
SQ FT: 60,000
SALES (est): 214.4MM
SALES (corp-wide): 11.9B Privately Held
SIC: 3679 8741 Recording & playback apparatus, including phonograph; administrative management; financial management for business
PA: Tdk Corporation
3-9-1, Shibaura
Minato-Ku TKY 108-0
368 527-300

Unionville
Orange County

(G-15673)
ROYAL FIREWORKS PRINTING CO
First Ave (10988)
PHONE.....................845 726-3333
Thomas Kemnitz, *President*
EMP: 13
SQ FT: 66,000
SALES (est): 1.8MM Privately Held
SIC: 2732 5942 Book printing; book stores

Upper Jay
Essex County

(G-15674)
AMSTUTZE WOODWORKING (PA)
246 Springfield Rd (12987-3200)
PHONE.....................518 946-8206
Steve Amstutz, *Principal*
EMP: 5
SALES (est): 456.5K Privately Held
SIC: 2431 Millwork

Utica
Oneida County

(G-15675)
ADIRONDACK DISTILLING COMPANY
601 Varick St (13502-4025)
PHONE.....................315 316-0387
Jordan Karp, *Principal*
Joseph Hoffman, *Manager*
EMP: 8 EST: 2014
SALES (est): 901.9K Privately Held
SIC: 2085 Distilled & blended liquors

(G-15676)
ADVANCE ENERGY SYSTEMS NY LLC
17 Tilton Rd (13501-6411)
PHONE.....................315 735-5125
Duane Farr, *President*
EMP: 5
SALES (est): 649.2K Privately Held
SIC: 3699 Mfg Electrical Equipment/Supplies

(G-15677)
AEROMED INC
1821 Broad St Ste 1 (13501-1115)
P.O. Box 768, Amsterdam (12010-0768)
PHONE.....................518 843-9144
William E Palmer, *President*
EMP: 5
SALES (est): 721.5K Privately Held
WEB: www.aeromed.com
SIC: 3564 Air purification equipment

(G-15678)
AUSTIN MOHAWK AND COMPANY LLC
2175 Beechgrove Pl (13501-1705)
PHONE.....................315 793-3000
John B Millet, *Plant Mgr*
Jim Bialek, *Project Mgr*
Tracy Roberts, *Project Mgr*
Richard Davies, *Controller*
▲ **EMP:** 29
SQ FT: 20,000
SALES (est): 5.5MM Privately Held
WEB: www.austinmohawk.com
SIC: 3444 3448 Canopies, sheet metal; prefabricated metal buildings

(G-15679)
BAGEL GROVE INC
7 Burrstone Rd (13502)
PHONE.....................315 724-8015
Anne Wadsworth, *President*
EMP: 25
SQ FT: 2,600
SALES: 450K Privately Held
WEB: www.bagelgrove.com
SIC: 2051 5149 5461 Bagels, fresh or frozen; crackers, cookies & bakery products; bagels

(G-15680)
BICK & HEINTZ INC
1101 Stark St (13502-4417)
P.O. Box 395 (13503-0395)
PHONE.....................315 733-7577
Thomas Bick, *President*
Robert J Bick, *Treasurer*
EMP: 18
SQ FT: 8,500
SALES (est): 2.7MM Privately Held
SIC: 3599 5531 7538 Machine shop, jobbing & repair; truck equipment & parts; general truck repair

(G-15681)
BRODOCK PRESS INC (PA)
502 Court St Ste G (13502-4233)
PHONE.....................315 735-9577
Craig S Brodock, *Chairman*
Paul Besig, *Traffic Mgr*
Brandon Brodock, *Executive*
EMP: 74 EST: 1960
SQ FT: 80,000
SALES: 12MM Privately Held
WEB: www.brodock.com
SIC: 2759 2752 2791 2789 Letterpress printing; commercial printing, lithographic; typesetting; bookbinding & related work

(G-15682)
CLARA PAPA
Also Called: Kennel Klub
1323 Blandina St 1 (13501-1915)
PHONE.....................315 733-2660
Clara Papa, *Owner*
EMP: 5
SQ FT: 15,000
SALES (est): 227.6K Privately Held
SIC: 3999 5199 Pet supplies; pet supplies

(G-15683)
CNY BUSINESS SOLUTIONS
502 Court St Ste 206 (13502-0001)
PHONE.....................315 733-5031
Jennifer Racquet, *President*
Wendy Aiello, *Principal*
EMP: 5 EST: 2010
SALES (est): 472.6K Privately Held
SIC: 3577 Printers & plotters

(G-15684)
COLLINITE CORPORATION
Also Called: Collinite Wax
1520 Lincoln Ave (13502-5200)
PHONE.....................315 732-2282

GEOGRAPHIC SECTION

Utica - Oneida County (G-15709)

Patrick Taylor, *President*
Mark Taylor, *President*
Michael Taylor, *President*
Christine Taylor, *Admin Sec*
EMP: 8 **EST:** 1912
SQ FT: 6,000
SALES (est): 914.7K **Privately Held**
WEB: www.collinite.com
SIC: 2842 5169 5999 5961 Cleaning or polishing preparations; polishing preparations & related products; waxes, except petroleum; cleaning equipment & supplies; mail order house

(G-15685)
CONMED ANDOVER MEDICAL INC (HQ)
525 French Rd Ste 3 (13502-5994)
PHONE.................................315 797-8375
Joseph J Corasanti, *CEO*
EMP: 14
SALES (est): 8.4MM
SALES (corp-wide): 796.3MM **Publicly Held**
SIC: 3845 Electromedical apparatus
PA: Conmed Corporation
   525 French Rd
   Utica NY 13502
   315 797-8375

(G-15686)
CONMED CORPORATION
Endoscopic Technologies Div
525 French Rd (13502-5994)
PHONE.................................315 797-8375
Dennis Werger, *Manager*
EMP: 83
SALES (corp-wide): 796.3MM **Publicly Held**
SIC: 3845 8731 3841 Electromedical equipment; commercial physical research; surgical & medical instruments
PA: Conmed Corporation
   525 French Rd
   Utica NY 13502
   315 797-8375

(G-15687)
CONMED CORPORATION (PA)
525 French Rd (13502-5994)
PHONE.................................315 797-8375
Mark E Tryniski, *Ch of Bd*
Curt R Hartman, *President*
Patrick J Beyer, *President*
Heather L Cohen, *Exec VP*
Daniel S Jonas, *Exec VP*
◆ **EMP:** 277
SQ FT: 500,000
SALES: 796.3MM **Publicly Held**
SIC: 3845 3841 Electromedical apparatus; electrocardiographs; patient monitoring apparatus; surgical instruments & apparatus; trocars; suction therapy apparatus; probes, surgical

(G-15688)
CRANESVILLE BLOCK CO INC
Also Called: Cranesville Concrete Co
895 Catherine St (13501-1409)
PHONE.................................315 732-2135
Mark Smith, *Branch Mgr*
EMP: 25
SQ FT: 3,462
SALES (corp-wide): 45.6MM **Privately Held**
SIC: 3273 Ready-mixed concrete
PA: Cranesville Block Co., Inc.
   1250 Riverfront Ctr
   Amsterdam NY 12010
   518 684-6154

(G-15689)
CRITICAL IMAGING LLC
2428 Chenango Rd (13502-5909)
PHONE.................................315 732-5020
Harold Wood, *Electrical Engi*
Donna Palmieri, *Finance*
Richard Evans,
EMP: 23
SALES (est): 3.6MM **Privately Held**
WEB: www.infraredcomponents.com
SIC: 3861 Cameras, still & motion picture (all types)

(G-15690)
CYBERSPORTS INC (PA)
11 Avery Pl (13502-5401)
PHONE.................................315 737-7150
Todd Hobin, *President*
Candice Hobin, *Vice Pres*
EMP: 7
SALES (est): 698.3K **Privately Held**
WEB: www.cybersportsinc.com
SIC: 7372 Prepackaged software

(G-15691)
DACOBE ENTERPRISES LLC
325 Lafayette St (13502-4228)
PHONE.................................315 368-0093
Geoff Thorp, *President*
EMP: 10
SQ FT: 20,000
SALES: 5MM **Privately Held**
SIC: 3089 Plastic processing

(G-15692)
DARMAN MANUFACTURING CO INC
1410 Lincoln Ave (13502-5019)
PHONE.................................315 724-9632
Pamela Darman, *CEO*
Cynthia J Lane, *Controller*
Gail Yakuboski, *Office Mgr*
▼ **EMP:** 16 **EST:** 1936
SQ FT: 20,800
SALES: 2MM **Privately Held**
WEB: www.darmanco.com
SIC: 3429 Cabinet hardware

(G-15693)
DEIORIO FOODS INC (PA)
Also Called: De Iorio's Bakery
2200 Bleecker St (13501-1739)
PHONE.................................315 732-7612
George Lampros, *CEO*
Michelle Burnett, *General Mgr*
Robert Horth, *Vice Pres*
Scott Hoke, *Facilities Mgr*
John Lafever, *Maint Spvr*
EMP: 200 **EST:** 1924
SALES (est): 57MM **Privately Held**
WEB: www.deiorios.com
SIC: 2053 Frozen bakery products, except bread

(G-15694)
DICO PRODUCTS CORPORATION
200 Seward Ave (13502-5750)
PHONE.................................315 797-0470
Bradford Lees Divine, *President*
▲ **EMP:** 15
SALES (est): 1.2MM **Privately Held**
WEB: www.dicoproducts.com
SIC: 3496 3429 3291 2392 Hardware cloth, woven wire; manufactured hardware (general); abrasive products; household furnishings

(G-15695)
DIMANCO INC (PA)
Also Called: Divine Bros
200 Seward Ave (13502-5750)
PHONE.................................315 797-0470
B Lees Divine, *President*
Eric Smith, *Regional Mgr*
Thomas B Dalton, *COO*
George Weaver, *Vice Pres*
Brian Carpenter, *Plant Mgr*
◆ **EMP:** 3
SQ FT: 170,000
SALES (est): 28.4MM **Privately Held**
WEB: www.dimanco.com
SIC: 3291 3562 Buffing or polishing wheels, abrasive or nonabrasive; casters

(G-15696)
DINOS SAUSAGE & MEAT CO INC
722 Catherine St (13501-1304)
PHONE.................................315 732-2661
Anthony Ferrucci, *President*
EMP: 11
SQ FT: 6,300
SALES (est): 1.7MM **Privately Held**
SIC: 2013 Sausages & related products, from purchased meat

(G-15697)
DIVA FARMS LTD
1301 Broad St (13501-1605)
PHONE.................................315 735-4397
Margherita Schuller, *President*
EMP: 7
SQ FT: 2,000
SALES (est): 550K **Privately Held**
SIC: 2099 Seasonings & spices

(G-15698)
DIVINE BROTHERS COMPANY
Also Called: Dico Products
200 Seward Ave (13502-5750)
PHONE.................................315 797-0470
Bradford W Divine, *President*
Charles H Divine, *Vice Pres*
Thomas Banks, *CFO*
◆ **EMP:** 112 **EST:** 1892
SQ FT: 112,000
SALES (est): 9.8MM
SALES (corp-wide): 28.4MM **Privately Held**
WEB: www.divinebrothers.com
SIC: 3291 Buffing or polishing wheels, abrasive or nonabrasive
PA: Dimanco Inc.
   200 Seward Ave
   Utica NY 13502
   315 797-0470

(G-15699)
ECR INTERNATIONAL INC (PA)
Also Called: Utica Boilers
2201 Dwyer Ave (13501-1101)
P.O. Box 4729 (13504-4729)
PHONE.................................315 797-1310
Ronald J Passafaro, *President*
Timothy R Reed, *President*
Eric Dorozynski, *Plant Mgr*
John Reed, *Production*
Michael Cariseo, *Purch Mgr*
◆ **EMP:** 100 **EST:** 1928
SQ FT: 190,000
SALES (est): 107.2MM **Privately Held**
WEB: www.ecrinternational.com
SIC: 3433 3443 Boilers, low-pressure heating: steam or hot water; fabricated plate work (boiler shop)

(G-15700)
FALVO MANUFACTURING CO INC
20 Harbor Point Rd (13502-2502)
PHONE.................................315 724-7925
Eugene T Falvo, *President*
EMP: 15
SQ FT: 26,000
SALES (est): 2.5MM **Privately Held**
SIC: 2441 2512 2522 2541 Packing cases, wood: nailed or lock corner; upholstered household furniture; office cabinets & filing drawers: except wood; store fixtures, wood

(G-15701)
FARRINGTON PACKAGING CORP
2007 Beechgrove Pl (13501-1703)
PHONE.................................315 733-4600
Raymond Mele, *President*
Brendan Jenkins, *Vice Pres*
Gerard Morrissey, *Controller*
Elizabeth Crawford, *Sales Executive*
Bill Richardson, *Manager*
EMP: 40
SALES (est): 5MM **Privately Held**
SIC: 2631 2541 Packaging board; wood partitions & fixtures

(G-15702)
FEDERAL SHEET METAL WORKS INC
1416 Dudley Ave (13501-4611)
P.O. Box 273 (13503-0273)
PHONE.................................315 735-4730
Leonard A Capuana, *President*
Michael Capuana, *Treasurer*
EMP: 12
SQ FT: 7,500
SALES: 1.5MM **Privately Held**
SIC: 3444 Sheet metalwork

(G-15703)
FOURTEEN ARNOLD AVE CORP
Also Called: PROGRESS INDUSTRIES SALES
14 Arnold Ave (13502-5602)
PHONE.................................315 272-1700
Angela Van Derhoof, *President*
Russell Bell, *Information Mgr*
EMP: 13
SALES: 312.3K **Privately Held**
SIC: 3565 Packing & wrapping machinery

(G-15704)
G W CANFIELD & SON INC
600 Plant St (13502-4712)
PHONE.................................315 735-5522
Mark W Canfield, *President*
Anne C Kuhn, *Vice Pres*
EMP: 6
SQ FT: 5,000
SALES (est): 868.7K **Privately Held**
WEB: www.gwcanfield.com
SIC: 2752 Commercial printing, offset

(G-15705)
GAMETIME SPORTSWEAR PLUS LLC
1206 Belle Ave (13501-2614)
PHONE.................................315 724-5893
Michael Macchione,
EMP: 6
SQ FT: 3,200
SALES (est): 460K **Privately Held**
SIC: 2329 5699 Men's & boys' sportswear & athletic clothing; sports apparel

(G-15706)
GATEHOUSE MEDIA LLC
Also Called: Observer Dispatch
350 Willowbrook Office Pa (13501)
PHONE.................................315 792-5000
Terry Cascioli, *Publisher*
Donna Donnovan, *Principal*
Ben Birnell, *Editor*
Rob Booth, *Editor*
Barbara Laible, *Editor*
EMP: 31
SALES (corp-wide): 1.3B **Publicly Held**
WEB: www.gatehousemedia.com
SIC: 2711 Newspapers, publishing & printing
HQ: Gatehouse Media, Llc
   175 Sullys Trl Ste 300
   Pittsford NY 14534
   585 598-0030

(G-15707)
H F BROWN MACHINE CO INC
708 State St (13502-3458)
PHONE.................................315 732-6129
James F Chubbuck, *President*
Joseph Chubbuck, *Vice Pres*
George Chubbuck, *Treasurer*
EMP: 10 **EST:** 1946
SQ FT: 26,000
SALES (est): 1.3MM **Privately Held**
SIC: 3599 Machine shop, jobbing & repair

(G-15708)
HARBOR POINT MINERAL PDTS INC
71 Wurz Ave (13502-2533)
PHONE.................................315 797-1300
Raymond P Villeneuve, *Ch of Bd*
Kevin Crane, *President*
Jeff Matuszczak, *Opers Mgr*
Nicholas Stacy, *Sales Mgr*
Mary Beth Dempster, *Manager*
▲ **EMP:** 10
SQ FT: 14,800
SALES (est): 1.7MM **Privately Held**
SIC: 2048 Prepared feeds

(G-15709)
HPK INDUSTRIES LLC
1208 Broad St (13501-1604)
P.O. Box 4682 (13504-4682)
PHONE.................................315 724-0196
Michael A Liberatore,
▲ **EMP:** 15
SQ FT: 11,000
SALES (est): 1.6MM **Privately Held**
WEB: www.hpkindustries.com
SIC: 2389 5131 Disposable garments & accessories; piece goods & notions

Utica - Oneida County (G-15710)　　　　　　　　　　　　　　　　　　　　　　　　　　　　　　GEOGRAPHIC SECTION

(G-15710)
HUMAN ELECTRONICS INC
155 Genesee St (13501)
PHONE..................315 724-9850
Philip Szeliga, *President*
EMP: 5 EST: 1999
SQ FT: 16,000
SALES (est): 568K **Privately Held**
WEB: www.humanelectronics.com
SIC: 3571 4813 Electronic computers; telephone communication, except radio

(G-15711)
HUMAN TECHNOLOGIES CORPORATION
Also Called: Graphtex A Div of Htc
2260 Dwyer Ave (13501-1193)
PHONE..................315 735-3532
Tom Keller, *Manager*
EMP: 10
SQ FT: 7,600
SALES (corp-wide): 16.4MM **Privately Held**
WEB: www.htcorp.net
SIC: 2396 2759 2395 Screen printing on fabric articles; screen printing; embroidery products, except schiffli machine
PA: Human Technologies Corporation
　　2260 Dwyer Ave
　　Utica NY 13501
　　315 724-9891

(G-15712)
IDG LLC
Also Called: Microfoam
31 Faass Ave (13502-3350)
PHONE..................315 797-1000
Kevin Sharrow, *Manager*
EMP: 49
SALES (corp-wide): 259.3MM **Privately Held**
SIC: 3069 Rolls, solid or covered rubber
HQ: Idg, Llc
　　1480 Gould Dr
　　Cookeville TN 38506
　　931 432-4000

(G-15713)
INDIUM CORPORATION OF AMERICA
1676 Lincoln Ave (13502-5398)
PHONE..................315 793-8200
Ning Lee, *Vice Pres*
John Sovinsky, *Opers Staff*
David Hu, *Technical Mgr*
Geoff Beckwith, *Engineer*
Marlene Natale, *Engineer*
EMP: 30
SQ FT: 31,210
SALES (corp-wide): 245.7MM **Privately Held**
WEB: www.indium.com
SIC: 3356 2899 Solder: wire, bar, acid core, & rosin core; chemical preparations
PA: Indium Corporation Of America
　　34 Robinson Rd
　　Clinton NY 13323
　　800 446-3486

(G-15714)
INDIUM CORPORATION OF AMERICA
111 Business Park Dr (13502-6303)
PHONE..................315 381-2330
Anthony Lanza, *Engineer*
EMP: 38
SALES (corp-wide): 245.7MM **Privately Held**
SIC: 3356 Solder: wire, bar, acid core, & rosin core
PA: Indium Corporation Of America
　　34 Robinson Rd
　　Clinton NY 13323
　　800 446-3486

(G-15715)
INFRARED COMPONENTS CORP
2306 Bleecker St (13501-1746)
PHONE..................315 732-1544
Thomas Clynne, *President*
EMP: 20
SQ FT: 17,000
SALES (est): 3.1MM **Privately Held**
SIC: 3812 Infrared object detection equipment; detection apparatus: electronic/magnetic field, light/heat

(G-15716)
INTERNATIONAL PAPER COMPANY
50 Harbor Point Rd (13502-2502)
PHONE..................315 797-5120
Earl Cochron, *General Mgr*
Dale Seaton, *Info Tech Mgr*
EMP: 160
SALES (corp-wide): 21.7B **Publicly Held**
SIC: 2621 Paper mills
PA: International Paper Company
　　6400 Poplar Ave
　　Memphis TN 38197
　　901 419-9000

(G-15717)
KELLY FOUNDRY & MACHINE CO
300 Hubbell St Ste 308 (13501-1404)
PHONE..................315 732-8313
Geogia M Kelley, *President*
Marsha J Kelly, *Corp Secy*
James S Kelly III, *Vice Pres*
Mark James Kelly, *Vice Pres*
Mark Kelly, *Vice Pres*
EMP: 48 EST: 1892
SQ FT: 14,632
SALES (est): 7.5MM **Privately Held**
WEB: www.kellyfoundry.com
SIC: 3369 3999 3953 Nonferrous foundries; plaques, picture, laminated; marking devices

(G-15718)
MANNYS CHEESECAKE INC
1221 Pleasant St (13501-4893)
PHONE..................315 732-0639
Richard Alpert, *President*
EMP: 5 EST: 1975
SQ FT: 3,500
SALES: 200K **Privately Held**
SIC: 2052 2051 5461 Cookies; cakes, pies & pastries; cookies; cakes

(G-15719)
METAL SOLUTIONS INC
1821 Broad St Ste 5 (13501-1115)
PHONE..................315 732-6271
Joseph Cattadoris Jr, *President*
Cathy Cattadoris, *Vice Pres*
John Kulis, *Shareholder*
EMP: 50 EST: 1954
SQ FT: 110,000
SALES (est): 13.7MM **Privately Held**
WEB: www.nhsmetal.com
SIC: 3444 Sheet metalwork

(G-15720)
METALLOGIX DESIGN FABRICATION
1305 Conkling Ave (13501-4618)
PHONE..................315 738-4554
Joel Grimaldi, *Owner*
EMP: 20
SALES (est): 2.9MM **Privately Held**
SIC: 3444 Sheet metalwork

(G-15721)
MID YORK WEEKLY & PENNYSAVER
221 Oriskany St E (13501-1201)
PHONE..................315 792-4990
Donna Donnovan, *Principal*
EMP: 5
SALES (est): 155.2K **Privately Held**
WEB: www.utica.gannett.com
SIC: 2711 Commercial printing & newspaper publishing combined; newspapers, publishing & printing

(G-15722)
MILLENNIUM ANTENNA CORP
1001 Broad St Ste 401 (13501-1545)
PHONE..................315 798-9374
David Schroeter, *President*
EMP: 10
SQ FT: 2,000
SALES (est): 950K **Privately Held**
WEB: www.millenniumantenna.com
SIC: 3663 8711 8731 Antennas, transmitting & communications; engineering services; electronic research

(G-15723)
MOBILE MINI INC
2222 Oriskany St W Ste 3 (13502-2925)
PHONE..................315 732-4555
Marc Allen, *Branch Mgr*
EMP: 10
SALES (corp-wide): 533.5MM **Publicly Held**
WEB: www.mobilemini.com
SIC: 3448 3441 3412 7359 Buildings, portable: prefabricated metal; fabricated structural metal; metal barrels, drums & pails; equipment rental & leasing
PA: Mobile Mini, Inc.
　　4646 E Van Buren St # 400
　　Phoenix AZ 85008
　　480 894-6311

(G-15724)
MUNSON MACHINERY COMPANY INC
210 Seward Ave (13502-5750)
PHONE..................315 797-0090
Charles H Divine, *CEO*
Josh Kelly, *Production*
Jackie Miller, *Purch Agent*
Robert Batson, *Engineer*
Dier Vinnie, *Engineer*
▲ EMP: 40 EST: 1828
SQ FT: 45,000
SALES (est): 11.3MM
SALES (corp-wide): 28.4MM **Privately Held**
WEB: www.munsonmachinery.com
SIC: 3532 3531 3559 3541 Crushing, pulverizing & screening equipment; mixers: ore, plaster, slag, sand, mortar, etc.; refinery, chemical processing & similar machinery; machine tools, metal cutting type; buffing & polishing machines; grinding machines, metalworking; metalworking machinery
PA: Dimanco Inc.
　　200 Seward Ave
　　Utica NY 13502
　　315 797-0470

(G-15725)
NATHAN STEEL CORP
36 Wurz Ave (13502-2534)
P.O. Box 299 (13503-0299)
PHONE..................315 797-1335
Edward Kowalsky, *President*
EMP: 15
SQ FT: 12,000
SALES (est): 4.1MM **Privately Held**
SIC: 3441 5051 Fabricated structural metal; steel

(G-15726)
NORTH COUNTRY BOOKS INC
220 Lafayette St (13502-4312)
PHONE..................315 735-4877
Robert Igoe, *President*
▲ EMP: 5 EST: 1965
SQ FT: 5,000
SALES: 1.1MM **Privately Held**
WEB: www.northcountrybooks.com
SIC: 2732 5192 Books: printing only; books

(G-15727)
NOVA HEALTH SYSTEMS INC
1001 Broad St Ste 3 (13501-1546)
P.O. Box 212, Forestport (13338-0212)
PHONE..................315 798-9018
Wade Abraham, *President*
▲ EMP: 6
SQ FT: 4,000
SALES (est): 847.1K **Privately Held**
WEB: www.novahealthsystems.com
SIC: 3842 5047 Surgical appliances & supplies; medical & hospital equipment

(G-15728)
OHIO BAKING COMPANY INC
Also Called: Spano's Bread
10585 Cosby Manor Rd (13502-1207)
PHONE..................315 724-2033
Joseph A Spano, *President*
EMP: 20 EST: 1930
SQ FT: 4,000
SALES (est): 3.5MM **Privately Held**
SIC: 2041 2051 5149 5461 Pizza dough, prepared; pizza mixes; bread, all types (white, wheat, rye, etc); fresh or frozen; bakery products; bakeries

(G-15729)
ORBCOMM INC
125 Business Park Dr (13502-6304)
PHONE..................703 433-6396
EMP: 11
SALES (corp-wide): 254.2MM **Publicly Held**
SIC: 3663 Satellites, communications
PA: Orbcomm Inc.
　　395 W Passaic St Ste 325
　　Rochelle Park NJ 07662
　　703 433-6361

(G-15730)
PRINT SHOPPE
311 Turner St Ste 310 (13501-1766)
PHONE..................315 792-9585
Steven Finch, *Partner*
Thomas Stewart, *Partner*
EMP: 7
SALES (est): 725.4K **Privately Held**
SIC: 2759 Screen printing

(G-15731)
ROBERT BOSCH LLC
2118 Beechgrove Pl (13501-1706)
PHONE..................315 733-3312
EMP: 25
SALES (corp-wide): 268.9MM **Privately Held**
SIC: 3841 Mfg Surgical/Medical Instruments
HQ: Robert Bosch Llc
　　2800 S 25th Ave
　　Broadview IL 60155
　　708 865-5200

(G-15732)
SCOOBY RENDERING & INC
Also Called: Scooby Dog Food
1930 Oriskany St W (13502-2920)
PHONE..................315 793-1014
Michael P Dote, *President*
EMP: 5
SQ FT: 3,000
SALES (est): 719.8K **Privately Held**
SIC: 2047 Dog food

(G-15733)
SHIPRITE SOFTWARE INC
1312 Genesee St (13502-4700)
PHONE..................315 733-6191
J Mark Ford, *President*
EMP: 9
SQ FT: 8,400
SALES (est): 1.1MM **Privately Held**
SIC: 7372 7359 7334 Prepackaged software; shipping container leasing; photocopying & duplicating services

(G-15734)
STURGES MANUFACTURING CO INC
2030 Sunset Ave (13502-5500)
P.O. Box 59 (13503-0059)
PHONE..................315 732-6159
Richard R Griffith, *Principal*
Tyler Griffith, *Vice Pres*
Norma Jean Rice, *Vice Pres*
Mylissa J Deetz, *Admin Sec*
▲ EMP: 75 EST: 1909
SQ FT: 58,000
SALES (est): 15.7MM **Privately Held**
WEB: www.sturgesmfg.com
SIC: 2241 Strapping webs; webbing, woven

(G-15735)
T C PETERS PRINTING CO INC
2336 W Whitesboro St (13502-3235)
PHONE..................315 724-4149
Richard Peters, *CEO*
Douglas Peters, *President*
EMP: 9
SQ FT: 13,200
SALES (est): 1.4MM **Privately Held**
SIC: 2752 Commercial printing, offset

(G-15736)
USA SEWING INC
901 Broad St Ste 2 (13501-1500)
PHONE................................315 792-8017
John D Inserra, *President*
Linda Taglimonte, *Manager*
EMP: 49
SALES (est): 4MM **Privately Held**
SIC: 3151 Leather gloves & mittens

(G-15737)
UTICA CUTLERY COMPANY
Also Called: Walco Stainless
820 Noyes St (13502-5053)
P.O. Box 10527 (13503-1527)
PHONE................................315 733-4663
A Edward Allen Jr, *Ch of Bd*
David S Allen, *Ch of Bd*
David Allen, *COO*
Phil Benbenek, *Exec VP*
Mark Carter, *Vice Pres*
▲ **EMP:** 60 **EST:** 1910
SQ FT: 100,000
SALES (est): 12.2MM **Privately Held**
WEB: www.kutmaster.com
SIC: 3914 3421 5023 5072 Flatware, stainless steel; cutlery, stainless steel; knives: butchers', hunting, pocket, etc.; stainless steel flatware; cutlery

(G-15738)
UTICA METAL PRODUCTS INC
1526 Lincoln Ave (13502-5298)
PHONE................................315 732-6163
Charles J Fields, *Ch of Bd*
Monte L Craig, *Vice Ch Bd*
Robert Moore, *COO*
Archie Omeragic, *Marketing Staff*
Hilary Walton, *Office Mgr*
EMP: 73 **EST:** 1956
SQ FT: 30,000
SALES (est): 13.8MM **Privately Held**
WEB: www.uticametals.com
SIC: 3465 3471 Body parts, automobile: stamped metal; hub caps, automobile: stamped metal; anodizing (plating) of metals or formed products

(G-15739)
WHERE IS UTICA COF RASTING INC
92 Cenesee St (13502-3519)
PHONE................................315 269-8898
Frank Ilias, *President*
EMP: 15 **EST:** 2005
SQ FT: 1,000
SALES: 300K **Privately Held**
SIC: 2095 0161 Coffee roasting (except by wholesale grocers); green lima bean farm

Valatie
Columbia County

(G-15740)
WEISS INDUSTRIES INC
Also Called: Precision Machine Parts
27 Blossom Ln (12184-9201)
PHONE................................518 784-9643
Michael Weiss, *President*
EMP: 7
SALES (est): 778.3K **Privately Held**
SIC: 3599 Machine shop, jobbing & repair

Valhalla
Westchester County

(G-15741)
EPOCH MICROELECTRONICS INC
420 Columbus Ave Ste 204 (10595-1382)
PHONE................................914 332-8570
Ken Suyama, *President*
Aleksander Dec, *Vice Pres*
EMP: 9
SALES (est): 1.1MM **Privately Held**
WEB: www.epochmicro.com
SIC: 3825 Integrated circuit testers

(G-15742)
LEGACY VALVE LLC
14 Railroad Ave (10595-1609)
P.O. Box 107 (10595-0107)
PHONE................................914 403-5075
Charles Cassidy, *President*
EMP: 14
SALES (est): 2.9MM **Privately Held**
SIC: 3494 Pipe fittings

(G-15743)
PEPSICO
100 Summit Lake Dr # 103 (10595-2318)
PHONE................................914 801-1500
▲ **EMP:** 34
SALES (est): 4.3MM **Privately Held**
SIC: 2086 Carb Sft Drnkbtlcn

(G-15744)
PEPSICO INC
100 E Stevens Ave (10595-1299)
PHONE................................914 742-4500
Noel E Anderson, *Vice Pres*
David Beneway, *Research*
Cathy Culver, *Research*
Raymond McGarvey, *Research*
Kyle Shandix, *Research*
EMP: 380
SALES (corp-wide): 63.5B **Publicly Held**
WEB: www.pepsico.com
SIC: 2086 Carbonated soft drinks, bottled & canned
PA: Pepsico, Inc.
  700 Anderson Hill Rd
  Purchase NY 10577
  914 253-2000

(G-15745)
PRESBREY-LELAND INC
Also Called: Presbrey- Leland Memorials
250 Lakeview Ave (10595-1618)
PHONE................................914 949-2264
Nancy Dylan, *President*
EMP: 5 **EST:** 1982
SALES (est): 634.2K **Privately Held**
SIC: 3272 5999 Monuments, concrete; monuments, finished to custom order; monuments & tombstones

(G-15746)
RETIA MEDICAL LLC (PA)
7 Dana Rd Ste 121 (10595-1554)
PHONE................................914 594-1986
Marc Zemel,
EMP: 5
SALES (est): 679.8K **Privately Held**
SIC: 3841 Surgical & medical instruments

(G-15747)
RUHLE COMPANIES INC
Also Called: Farrand Controls Division
99 Wall St (10595-1462)
PHONE................................914 287-4000
Frank S Ruhle, *Ch of Bd*
Robert F. Ruhle, *Exec VP*
Robert Ruhle, *Exec VP*
Richard Babcock, *Production*
Dara Gandhi, *Manager*
EMP: 50
SQ FT: 33,000
SALES (est): 8.3MM **Privately Held**
WEB: www.ruhle.com
SIC: 3679 3625 3577 3674 Transducers, electrical; control equipment, electric; computer peripheral equipment; semiconductors & related devices; radio & TV communications equipment; motors & generators

(G-15748)
SPELLMAN HIGH VLTAGE ELEC CORP
1 Commerce Park (10595-1455)
PHONE................................914 686-3600
David Burgess, *General Mgr*
Graham Chick, *Prdtn Mgr*
Loren Skeist, *Branch Mgr*
EMP: 86
SALES (corp-wide): 290.9MM **Privately Held**
SIC: 3674 Semiconductors & related devices

PA: Spellman High-Voltage Electronics Corporation
  475 Wireless Blvd
  Hauppauge NY 11788
  631 630-3000

(G-15749)
VTB HOLDINGS INC (HQ)
100 Summit Lake Dr (10595-1339)
PHONE................................914 345-2255
Juergen Stark, *CEO*
John Hanson, *CFO*
EMP: 6 **EST:** 2010
SALES: 207.1MM **Publicly Held**
SIC: 3651 Sound reproducing equipment

Valley Cottage
Rockland County

(G-15750)
ACCESS 24
570 Kings Hwy Fl 4 (10989-1231)
PHONE................................845 358-5397
John Sindelar, *Owner*
EMP: 6
SALES (est): 600K **Privately Held**
SIC: 3661 Telephones & telephone apparatus

(G-15751)
AERO HEALTHCARE (US) LLC
616 Corporate Way Ste 6 (10989-2047)
PHONE................................855 225-2376
Brian Parker, *General Mgr*
▲ **EMP:** 5 **EST:** 2012
SALES (est): 912.5K **Privately Held**
SIC: 3842 5099 Bandages & dressings; tape, adhesive: medicated or non-medicated; lifesaving & survival equipment (non-medical)
PA: Aero Healthcare Partnership
  63 Seaton St
  Armidale NSW 2350

(G-15752)
AREMCO PRODUCTS INC
707 Executive Blvd Ste B (10989-2025)
P.O. Box 517 (10989-0517)
PHONE................................845 268-0039
Peter Schwartz, *President*
Esther Schwartz, *Admin Sec*
▲ **EMP:** 15
SQ FT: 15,500
SALES (est): 3.9MM **Privately Held**
WEB: www.aremco.com
SIC: 3559 2891 2952 3253 Refinery, chemical processing & similar machinery; adhesives; cement, except linoleum & tile; coating compounds, tar; ceramic wall & floor tile

(G-15753)
CEROVENE INC (PA)
612 Corporate Way Ste 10 (10989-2027)
PHONE................................845 267-2055
Manish Shah, *President*
Ray Difalco, *Vice Pres*
Mike Papst, *QC Dir*
Matt Mennella, *Research*
Nikhil Patel, *Research*
EMP: 10
SQ FT: 40,000
SALES: 8MM **Privately Held**
WEB: www.cerovene.com
SIC: 2834 Pharmaceutical preparations

(G-15754)
FIRST SBF HOLDING INC (PA)
Also Called: Gevril
9 Pinecrest Rd Ste 101 (10989-1443)
PHONE................................845 425-9882
Samuel Friedmann, *CEO*
Keith Burns, *COO*
David Yurowitz, *Vice Pres*
Perla Hershkowitz, *Buyer*
Rachel Itzkowitz, *Bookkeeper*
▼ **EMP:** 49
SALES (est): 16.1MM **Privately Held**
WEB: www.gevril.com
SIC: 3873 Watches & parts, except crystals & jewels

(G-15755)
INNOTECH GRAPHIC EQP CORP
614 Corporate Way Ste 5 (10989-2026)
PHONE................................845 268-6900
EMP: 8
SQ FT: 7,500
SALES (est): 800K **Privately Held**
SIC: 3555 5084 Mfg Printing Trades Machinery Whol Industrial Equipment

(G-15756)
INNOVATIVE JEWELRY INC (PA)
Also Called: Fiora Italy
707 Executive Blvd Ste D (10989-2025)
PHONE................................718 408-8950
Abraham Rowe, *Vice Pres*
▲ **EMP:** 4
SQ FT: 3,000
SALES (est): 4MM **Privately Held**
SIC: 3911 Bracelets, precious metal

(G-15757)
LANDMARK GROUP INC
Also Called: National Ramp
709 Executive Blvd Ste A (10989-2024)
PHONE................................845 358-0350
Garth Walker, *Ch of Bd*
EMP: 40
SALES (est): 9.2MM **Privately Held**
SIC: 3448 Ramps: prefabricated metal

(G-15758)
LEXAR GLOBAL LLC
711 Executive Blvd Ste K (10989-2006)
PHONE................................845 352-9700
Guy Jacobs, *President*
Wanda Wallace, *Administration*
▲ **EMP:** 9
SQ FT: 18,000
SALES: 4.9MM **Privately Held**
SIC: 3555 Printing trade parts & attachments

(G-15759)
MOUNT VERNON MACHINE INC
614 Corporate Way Ste 8 (10989-2026)
PHONE................................845 268-9400
Karl Wallburg, *President*
EMP: 20
SQ FT: 16,000
SALES (est): 2.2MM **Privately Held**
WEB: www.mountvernonmachine.com
SIC: 3599 3555 Machine & other job shop work; printing trades machinery

(G-15760)
MP DISPLAYS LLC
704 Executive Blvd Ste 1 (10989-2010)
PHONE................................845 268-4113
Michael Parkes, *Mng Member*
▲ **EMP:** 9
SQ FT: 5,300
SALES (est): 1.7MM **Privately Held**
WEB: www.mpdisplays.com
SIC: 2653 3577 Display items, corrugated: made from purchased materials; display items, solid fiber: made from purchased materials; graphic displays, except graphic terminals

(G-15761)
NORTH SUNSHINE LLC
616 Corporate Way Ste 2-3 (10989-2044)
PHONE................................307 027-1634
EMP: 15 **EST:** 2016
SALES: 800K **Privately Held**
SIC: 2273 5713 Mfg Carpets/Rugs Ret Floor Covering

(G-15762)
REAL CO INC
616 Corporate Way (10989-2044)
PHONE................................347 433-8549
Raphaele Chartrand, *Principal*
Muhammad Elkateb, *COO*
▲ **EMP:** 8 **EST:** 2014
SALES (est): 258.8K **Privately Held**
SIC: 2044 2099 2899 Rice milling; sugar; salt

(G-15763)
ROSSI TOOL & DIES INC
161 Route 303 (10989-1922)
PHONE................................845 267-8246
James Veltidi, *President*
EMP: 6 **EST:** 1952

Valley Cottage - Rockland County (G-15764)

SQ FT: 4,000
SALES (est): 699.7K **Privately Held**
SIC: 3544 3599 Dies & die holders for metal cutting, forming, die casting; machine shop, jobbing & repair

(G-15764)
SCIENTA PHARMACEUTICALS LLC
612 Corporate Way Ste 9 (10989-2027)
PHONE..................................845 589-0774
EMP: 5
SQ FT: 2,000
SALES (est): 320K **Privately Held**
SIC: 2834 Mfg Pharmaceutical Preparations

(G-15765)
STAR PRESS PEARL RIVER INC
614 Corporate Way Ste 8 (10989-2026)
PHONE..................................845 268-2294
Marino Nicolich, *President*
EMP: 6 EST: 1969
SALES (est): 1MM **Privately Held**
SIC: 2752 2759 Commercial printing, lithographic; letterpress printing

(G-15766)
STATEWIDE FIREPROOF DOOR CO
178 Charles Blvd (10989-2437)
PHONE..................................845 268-6043
Joseph Caneiro, *President*
EMP: 11 EST: 1965
SQ FT: 11,000
SALES (est): 1.1MM **Privately Held**
SIC: 3442 Fire doors, metal

(G-15767)
STROMBERG BRAND CORPORATION
Also Called: Stormberg Brand
12 Ford Products Rd (10989-1238)
PHONE..................................914 739-7410
Richard Stromberg, *CEO*
Helen Stromberg, *President*
EMP: 10
SQ FT: 9,000
SALES (est): 600K **Privately Held**
WEB: www.strombergbrand.com
SIC: 2759 Screen printing

(G-15768)
SUPPLYNET INC (PA)
706 Executive Blvd Ste B (10989-2039)
PHONE..................................800 826-0279
Robert Berkey, *President*
Beverly Lewis, *CFO*
Margie Valle, *Technology*
EMP: 6
SQ FT: 7,500
SALES: 7.3MM **Privately Held**
WEB: www.thesupplynet.com
SIC: 3678 Electronic connectors

(G-15769)
ZEO HEALTH LTD
159 Route 303 (10989-1922)
PHONE..................................845 353-5185
Micah Portney, *President*
EMP: 16
SQ FT: 5,000
SALES: 500K **Privately Held**
SIC: 2834 Vitamin, nutrient & hematinic preparations for human use

Valley Falls
Rensselaer County

(G-15770)
STEPHEN BADER COMPANY INC
10 Charles St (12185-3437)
P.O. Box 297 (12185-0297)
PHONE..................................518 753-4456
Daniel W Johnson, *President*
Rosemarie Johnson, *Vice Pres*
Carrie Johnson, *Admin Sec*
▼ EMP: 10 EST: 1951
SQ FT: 14,000
SALES (est): 1.5MM **Privately Held**
WEB: www.stephenbader.com
SIC: 3541 Grinding machines, metalworking

Valley Stream
Nassau County

(G-15771)
ADC INDUSTRIES INC (PA)
181a E Jamaica Ave (11580-6069)
PHONE..................................516 596-1304
Joseph Mannino, *President*
EMP: 25
SQ FT: 2,000
SALES: 4.5MM **Privately Held**
WEB: www.airlockdoor.com
SIC: 3491 Valves, automatic control

(G-15772)
ANSA SYSTEMS OF USA INC
145 Hook Creek Blvd B6a1 (11581-2293)
PHONE..................................718 835-3743
John Olusoga, *President*
EMP: 5
SALES: 500K **Privately Held**
SIC: 7372 Application computer software

(G-15773)
AUTOMATED OFFICE SYSTEMS INC
Also Called: Aos
71 S Central Ave (11580-5495)
PHONE..................................516 396-5555
Larry Sachs, *President*
EMP: 10
SQ FT: 5,000
SALES (est): 483.5K **Privately Held**
WEB: www.aosdata.com
SIC: 7372 Business oriented computer software

(G-15774)
BLACK BEAR COMPANY INC
90 E Hawthorne Ave (11580-6302)
PHONE..................................718 784-7330
Barret T Schleicher, *President*
Jennifer Trubia, *Corp Secy*
Derek Chou, *Controller*
▲ EMP: 20
SQ FT: 25,000
SALES (est): 3.8MM **Privately Held**
WEB: www.blackbearoil.com
SIC: 2992 Lubricating oils

(G-15775)
BRAUN BROS BRUSHES INC
35 4th St (11581-1231)
P.O. Box 2822, Babylon (11703-0822)
PHONE..................................631 667-2179
James Braun, *President*
Pamela Sue Gagas, *Purch Mgr*
EMP: 5 EST: 1946
SQ FT: 1,400
SALES (est): 554.8K **Privately Held**
WEB: www.braunbrosbrushes.com
SIC: 3991 5085 Brushes, household or industrial; brushes, industrial

(G-15776)
CITY REAL ESTATE BOOK INC
9831 S Franklin Ave (11580)
PHONE..................................516 593-2949
Charles Danas, *President*
EMP: 8
SALES: 500K **Privately Held**
SIC: 2721 Magazines: publishing & printing

(G-15777)
CNI MEAT & PRODUCE INC
Also Called: Key Foods
500 W Merrick Rd (11580-5233)
PHONE..................................516 599-5929
▲ EMP: 5
SALES (est): 225K **Privately Held**
SIC: 2011 2013 Meat by-products from meat slaughtered on site; canned meats (except baby food), meat slaughtered on site; sausages & other prepared meats

(G-15778)
ELLIS PRODUCTS CORP (PA)
Also Called: Style Plus Hosiery Mills
628 Golf Dr (11581-3550)
PHONE..................................516 791-3732
Seymour Ellis, *President*
EMP: 4 EST: 1954
SALES (est): 5.9MM **Privately Held**
SIC: 2251 3944 Electronic game machines, except coin-operated; panty hose

(G-15779)
FACILAMATIC INSTRUMENT CORP
39 Clinton Ave (11580-6024)
PHONE..................................516 825-6300
Dennis West, *President*
John E Bergquist, *Vice Pres*
EMP: 15
SQ FT: 15,000
SALES: 1.8MM **Privately Held**
SIC: 3812 Aircraft/aerospace flight instruments & guidance systems; gyro gimbals, gyrocompasses, gyropilots

(G-15780)
FREQUENCY SELECTIVE NETWORKS
12 N Cottage St (11580-4647)
PHONE..................................718 424-7500
Julius Tischkewitsch, *President*
Michael Izzolo, *Vice Pres*
EMP: 10
SQ FT: 10,000
SALES (est): 1.5MM **Privately Held**
SIC: 3677 Filtration devices, electronic

(G-15781)
GLOBAL PAYMENT TECH INC
20 E Sunrise Hwy (11581-1260)
PHONE..................................516 887-0700
Stephen Katz, *Branch Mgr*
EMP: 10
SALES (corp-wide): 11.8MM **Publicly Held**
WEB: www.gptx.com
SIC: 3581 Mechanisms & parts for automatic vending machines
PA: Global Payment Technologies, Inc.
170 Wilbur Pl Ste 600
Bohemia NY 11716
631 563-2500

(G-15782)
HIGH PERFORMANCE SFTWR USA INC
Also Called: Zuant
145 Hook Creek Blvd (11581-2299)
PHONE..................................866 616-4958
Leanne Spratt, *Accounts Mgr*
Pete Gillett, *Director*
EMP: 30
SALES (est): 159.2K **Privately Held**
SIC: 7372 Application computer software

(G-15783)
JERRYS BAGELS
Also Called: Jerry's Bagels & Bakery
951 Rosedale Rd (11581-2318)
PHONE..................................516 791-0063
Jerry Jacobs, *Owner*
EMP: 8
SALES (est): 586.6K **Privately Held**
SIC: 2051 Bakery: wholesale or wholesale/retail combined

(G-15784)
L M N PRINTING COMPANY INC
23 W Merrick Rd Ste A (11580-5757)
P.O. Box 696 (11582-0696)
PHONE..................................516 285-8526
Nora Aly, *President*
Noreen Carro, *Vice Pres*
EMP: 25
SQ FT: 5,200
SALES (est): 3.8MM **Privately Held**
WEB: www.lmnprinting.com
SIC: 2752 2791 Commercial printing, offset; typesetting

(G-15785)
LELAB DENTAL LABORATORY INC
Also Called: Le Lab
550 W Merrick Rd Ste 8 (11580-5101)
PHONE..................................516 561-5050
Edmond Mardirossia, *President*
Maronlyn Mardirossian, *Vice Pres*
EMP: 5
SQ FT: 1,000
SALES (est): 669.1K **Privately Held**
SIC: 3843 Dental equipment & supplies

(G-15786)
MICHAEL FIORE LTD
126 E Fairview Ave (11580-5930)
PHONE..................................516 561-8238
Michael Fiore, *President*
EMP: 6
SQ FT: 6,000
SALES: 2MM **Privately Held**
SIC: 3545 Machine tool accessories

(G-15787)
NEW YORK RHBILITATIVE SVCS LLC
214 E Sunrise Hwy (11581-1315)
PHONE..................................516 239-0990
Michael Nadata,
EMP: 14
SALES (est): 1.9MM **Privately Held**
SIC: 3842 Prosthetic appliances

(G-15788)
ONE IN A MILLION INC
51 Franklin Ave (11580-2847)
P.O. Box 234111, Great Neck (11023-4111)
PHONE..................................516 829-1111
Sasan Shavanson, *President*
Yaso Soleimani, *Admin Sec*
EMP: 6
SQ FT: 2,000
SALES (est): 800K **Privately Held**
SIC: 2759 5112 2284 Screen printing; stationery; embroidery thread

(G-15789)
PARNASA INTERNATIONAL INC
Also Called: C-Air International
181 S Franklin Ave # 400 (11581-1138)
PHONE..................................516 394-0400
Glenn Schacher, *President*
Lucille Schacher, *Admin Sec*
▲ EMP: 8
SALES (est): 520K **Privately Held**
SIC: 2099 Food preparations

(G-15790)
PRECISELED INC
52 Railroad Ave (11580-6031)
PHONE..................................516 418-5337
Daniel Machlis, *President*
David Schachner, *Project Mgr*
Waqar Iqbal, *Engineer*
▲ EMP: 10 EST: 2015
SQ FT: 13,000
SALES (est): 608.1K **Privately Held**
SIC: 3646 3645 Commercial indusl & institutional electric lighting fixtures; residential lighting fixtures

(G-15791)
PRO METAL OF NY CORP
814 W Merrick Rd (11580-4829)
PHONE..................................516 285-0440
Michael Marin, *President*
EMP: 5
SALES (est): 701.3K **Privately Held**
SIC: 3585 1761 Heating & air conditioning combination units; sheet metalwork

(G-15792)
PSG INNOVATIONS INC
924 Kilmer Ln (11581-3130)
PHONE..................................917 299-8986
Philip Green, *CEO*
EMP: 15 EST: 2010
SQ FT: 2,500
SALES: 16MM **Privately Held**
SIC: 3648 Flashlights

(G-15793)
RAYS ITALIAN BAKERY INC
Also Called: Roma Ray Bakery
45 Railroad Ave (11580-6030)
PHONE..................................516 825-9170
Robert Degiovanni, *President*
Vincent Giovanni, *Vice Pres*
Dario Degiovanni, *Admin Sec*
EMP: 12
SQ FT: 10,000
SALES (est): 1.2MM **Privately Held**
SIC: 2051 Bread, cake & related products

(G-15794)
READY TO ASSEMBLE COMPANY INC
Also Called: Debra Fisher
115 S Corona Ave (11580-6217)
PHONE..................................516 825-4397
Bruce Wulwick, *CEO*
Phyllis Wulwick, *Treasurer*
EMP: 20
SALES (est): 2.1MM **Privately Held**
SIC: 2519 7389 Household furniture, except wood or metal: upholstered;

(G-15795)
ROMA BAKERY INC
45 Railroad Ave (11580-6030)
PHONE..................................516 825-9170
Jacoui Digiovanni, *President*
EMP: 17
SQ FT: 10,000
SALES (est): 1.8MM **Privately Held**
SIC: 2051 Bread, cake & related products

(G-15796)
SENERA CO INC
834 Glenridge Ave (11581-3019)
PHONE..................................516 639-3774
Seema Gupta, *President*
EMP: 10
SALES: 100K **Privately Held**
SIC: 3674 Switches, silicon control

(G-15797)
SHEPHERDS PI LLC
31 Keller St (11580-2641)
PHONE..................................516 647-8151
Imani Shepherd,
EMP: 5
SALES: 250K **Privately Held**
SIC: 2741

(G-15798)
SOUTH SHORE READY MIX INC
116 E Hawthorne Ave (11580-6331)
PHONE..................................516 872-3049
Joseph Dilemme, *President*
EMP: 5
SQ FT: 10,000
SALES (est): 712.7K **Privately Held**
SIC: 3273 Ready-mixed concrete

(G-15799)
TASTE AND SEE ENTRMT INC
Also Called: Taqa Entertainment
255 Dogwood Rd (11580-4039)
P.O. Box 367 (11582-0367)
PHONE..................................516 285-3010
Barry Whipple, *CEO*
EMP: 5
SALES (est): 863.1K **Privately Held**
SIC: 3652 7812 5734 7832 Pre-recorded records & tapes; motion picture & video production; computer & software stores; motion picture theaters, except drive-in; record & prerecorded tape stores

(G-15800)
TOTAL DNTL IMPLANT SLTIONS LLC
Also Called: Tag Dental Implant Solutions
260 W Sunrise Hwy (11581-1011)
PHONE..................................212 877-3777
Ariel Goldschlag,
EMP: 5
SALES: 750K **Privately Held**
SIC: 3843 Dental equipment & supplies

(G-15801)
UNIVERSAL 3D INNOVATION INC
1085 Rockaway Ave (11581-2137)
PHONE..................................516 837-9423
Tomer Yariz, *President*
EMP: 10
SQ FT: 5,000
SALES: 2.5MM **Privately Held**
SIC: 3993 Signs, not made in custom sign painting shops

Van Hornesville
Herkimer County

(G-15802)
OGD V-HVAC INC
174 Pumkinhook Rd (13475)
PHONE..................................315 858-1002
Ormonde G Drham III, *President*
Linda Bowers, *Administration*
EMP: 20
SALES: 400K **Privately Held**
SIC: 3999 Manufacturing industries

Vernon
Oneida County

(G-15803)
CHEPAUME INDUSTRIES LLC
6201 Cooper St (13476-4022)
PHONE..................................315 829-6400
Chester Poplaski,
Melissa Foppes,
EMP: 6
SQ FT: 17,114
SALES (est): 569.1K **Privately Held**
WEB: www.chepaume.com
SIC: 3479 Coating electrodes

(G-15804)
FOUR DIRECTIONS INC
4677 State Route 5 (13476-3525)
PHONE..................................315 829-8388
Peter Wiezalis, *Director*
Kelli Bradley, *Administration*
EMP: 20
SALES (est): 760.1K **Privately Held**
WEB: www.fourdirectionsmedia.com
SIC: 2711 Newspapers: publishing only, not printed on site
HQ: Oneida Nation Enterprises
5218 Patrick Rd
Verona NY 13478

(G-15805)
HP HOOD LLC
19 Ward St (13476-4415)
P.O. Box 930 (13476-0930)
PHONE..................................315 829-3339
Phil Campbell, *Plant Mgr*
Howard Holdridge, *QC Dir*
EMP: 100
SQ FT: 800
SALES (corp-wide): 2.1B **Privately Held**
WEB: www.hphood.com
SIC: 2024 2022 2026 Ice cream & frozen desserts; processed cheese; cream, sweet
PA: Hp Hood Llc
6 Kimball Ln Ste 400
Lynnfield MA 01940
617 887-8441

(G-15806)
J H RHODES COMPANY INC
10 Ward St (13476-4416)
PHONE..................................315 829-3600
J Rhodes, *Principal*
EMP: 12
SALES (corp-wide): 58MM **Privately Held**
SIC: 3674 Semiconductors & related devices
HQ: J H Rhodes Company Inc.
2800 N 44th St Ste 675
Phoenix AZ 85008
602 449-8689

Vernon Center
Oneida County

(G-15807)
MCDONOUGH HARDWOODS LTD
6426 Skinner Rd (13477-3840)
PHONE..................................315 829-3449
Daniel McDonough, *CEO*
James McDonough, *Treasurer*
EMP: 25
SALES (est): 1.1MM **Privately Held**
SIC: 2421 Sawmills & planing mills, general

Vestal
Broome County

(G-15808)
ADVANCED MTL ANALYTICS LLC
85 Murray Hl Rd Ste 2115 (13850)
PHONE..................................321 684-0528
Swastisharan Dey,
EMP: 5
SQ FT: 500
SALES: 350K **Privately Held**
SIC: 3826 Analytical instruments

(G-15809)
BARNEY & DICKENSON INC (PA)
520 Prentice Rd (13850-2197)
PHONE..................................607 729-1536
Robert S Murphy Jr, *President*
Mary M Harrison, *Vice Pres*
EMP: 49
SQ FT: 100,000
SALES (est): 8.4MM **Privately Held**
SIC: 3273 5032 1771 Ready-mixed concrete; concrete mixtures; sand, construction; gravel; concrete pumping

(G-15810)
BIMBO BAKERIES USA INC
Also Called: Stroehmann Bakeries 90
1624 Castle Gardens Rd (13850-1102)
PHONE..................................800 856-8544
Michael Hicks, *Area Mgr*
Bruce Gross, *Manager*
EMP: 20 **Privately Held**
SIC: 2051 5149 Breads, rolls & buns; groceries & related products
HQ: Bimbo Bakeries Usa, Inc
255 Business Center Dr # 200
Horsham PA 19044
215 347-5500

(G-15811)
BOB MURPHY INC
3127 Vestal Rd (13850)
PHONE..................................607 729-3553
Robert S Murphy Jr, *President*
Mary Murphy Harrison, *Vice Pres*
EMP: 17
SQ FT: 130,000
SALES: 2MM **Privately Held**
SIC: 3441 5031 Fabricated structural metal; building materials, exterior; building materials, interior

(G-15812)
C & C READY-MIX CORPORATION (PA)
3112 Vestal Rd (13850-2110)
P.O. Box 157 (13851-0157)
PHONE..................................607 797-5108
Nicholas D Cerretani Jr, *President*
Nichols Cerretani Jr, *President*
Anthony Cerretani, *Vice Pres*
EMP: 25
SQ FT: 1,500
SALES: 5.3MM **Privately Held**
WEB: www.ccreadymix.com
SIC: 3273 2951 Ready-mixed concrete; asphalt & asphaltic paving mixtures (not from refineries)

(G-15813)
CARR COMMUNICATIONS GROUP LLC
Also Called: Carr Printing
513 Prentice Rd (13850-2105)
PHONE..................................607 748-0481
Kris Osborn, *Purchasing*
James Petritz,
Anthony Defilio,
David Gannon,
Donald Kahen,
EMP: 18
SQ FT: 11,000
SALES: 1.5MM **Privately Held**
SIC: 2752 Commercial printing, offset

(G-15814)
DEAN MANUFACTURING INC
413 Commerce Rd (13850-2238)
PHONE..................................607 770-1300
Karl E Hughes Jr, *President*
EMP: 10
SALES (est): 921.8K **Privately Held**
WEB: www.centerlessgrinder.com
SIC: 3546 7389 Grinders, portable: electric or pneumatic; grinding, precision: commercial or industrial

(G-15815)
DETEKION SECURITY SYSTEMS INC
200 Plaza Dr Ste 1 (13850-3680)
PHONE..................................607 729-7179
James Walsh, *President*
Alexander Haker, *Vice Pres*
Kevin Kelly, *Engineer*
Karen Walter, *Accountant*
Bill Walsh, *Accounts Mgr*
EMP: 18
SQ FT: 7,200
SALES (est): 3.7MM **Privately Held**
SIC: 3699 5063 1731 Security control equipment & systems; burglar alarm systems; fire detection & burglar alarm systems specialization

(G-15816)
GANNETT CO INC
Also Called: Binghamton Press
4421 Vestal Pkwy E (13850-3556)
P.O. Box 1270, Binghamton (13902-1270)
PHONE..................................607 798-1234
Sherman Bodner, *President*
EMP: 77
SQ FT: 100,498
SALES (corp-wide): 3.1B **Publicly Held**
WEB: www.gannett.com
SIC: 2711 Newspapers
PA: Gannett Co., Inc.
7950 Jones Branch Dr
Mc Lean VA 22102
703 854-6000

(G-15817)
GEOWEB3D INC
4104 Vestal Rd Ste 202 (13850-3554)
P.O. Box 2019, Binghamton (13902-2019)
PHONE..................................607 323-1114
Robert Holicky, *CEO*
Vincent Autieri, *COO*
Christian Maire, *Vice Pres*
Ethan Paoletti, *Software Engr*
EMP: 15
SQ FT: 3,300
SALES (est): 458.7K **Privately Held**
WEB: www.geoweb3d.com
SIC: 7372 7371 Application computer software; computer software development

(G-15818)
GREAT AMERICAN INDUSTRIES INC (DH)
300 Plaza Dr (13850-3647)
PHONE..................................607 729-9331
Burton I Koffman, *Ch of Bd*
Richard E Koffman, *Senior VP*
Burton Koffman, *Manager*
◆ **EMP:** 1 **EST:** 1928
SQ FT: 2,000

Vestal - Broome County (G-15819)   **GEOGRAPHIC SECTION**

SALES (est): 80.7MM
SALES (corp-wide): 4MM **Privately Held**
SIC: 3086 5031 5074 3442 Plastics foam products; building materials, interior; plumbing fittings & supplies; metal doors, sash & trim; metal doors; wet suits, rubber; watersports equipment & supplies; diving equipment & supplies
HQ: Public Loan Company Inc
    300 Plaza Dr
    Vestal NY 13850
    607 584-5274

(G-15819)
K HEIN MACHINES INC
341 Vestal Pkwy E (13850-1631)
PHONE.................................607 748-1546
Walter C Hein Sr, *CEO*
W Charles Hein Jr, *President*
Steven W Hein, *Vice Pres*
EMP: 9
SQ FT: 15,000
SALES (est): 650.2K **Privately Held**
WEB: www.kheinmachines.com
SIC: 3599 Machine shop, jobbing & repair

(G-15820)
NATIONAL PIPE & PLASTICS INC (PA)
Also Called: Nppi
3421 Vestal Rd (13850-2188)
PHONE.................................607 729-9381
David J Culbertson, *CEO*
Charles E Miller, *Vice Pres*
Michael Westover, *Plant Mgr*
Victoria Schoelier, *Purch Mgr*
Amy Bebla, *Buyer*
◆ **EMP:** 170
SQ FT: 157,000
SALES (est): 92.9MM **Privately Held**
WEB: www.nationalpipe.com
SIC: 3084 Plastics pipe

(G-15821)
SCORPION SECURITY PRODUCTS INC
330 N Jensen Rd (13850-2132)
PHONE.................................607 724-9999
Pete Gulick, *President*
▲ **EMP:** 25 **EST:** 2008
SQ FT: 4,700
SALES (est): 200K **Privately Held**
SIC: 3699 Security devices

(G-15822)
SPST INC
Also Called: Embroidery Screen Prtg Netwrk
119b Rano Blvd (13850-2729)
PHONE.................................607 798-6952
James Porter, *President*
EMP: 5
SALES (est): 450K **Privately Held**
SIC: 2759 Screen printing

(G-15823)
SUPERIOR PRINT ON DEMAND
165 Charles St (13850-2431)
PHONE.................................607 240-5231
Jeff Valent, *Principal*
EMP: 8 **EST:** 2011
SALES (est): 596.1K **Privately Held**
SIC: 2752 2759 7389 Offset & photolithographic printing; financial note & certificate printing & engraving; personal service agents, brokers & bureaus

(G-15824)
TRUEBITE INC
Also Called: Fotofiles
2590 Glenwood Rd (13850-6115)
PHONE.................................607 785-7664
Edward J Calafut, *President*
◆ **EMP:** 23
SQ FT: 6,000
SALES (est): 4.5MM **Privately Held**
WEB: www.truebite.com
SIC: 3499 3674 Magnets, permanent: metallic; photoelectric magnetic devices

(G-15825)
VESTAL ASPHALT INC (PA)
201 Stage Rd (13850-1608)
PHONE.................................607 785-3393
Neil I Guiles, *President*
Justin Guiles, *Vice Pres*
Kim Hickok, *Controller*
Timothy Howell, *Manager*
Joann Juliussen, *Manager*
EMP: 14
SQ FT: 3,000
SALES (est): 3.7MM **Privately Held**
WEB: www.vestalasphalt.com
SIC: 2951 Asphalt & asphaltic paving mixtures (not from refineries)

(G-15826)
XEKU CORPORATION
2520 Vestal Pkwy E222 (13850-2078)
PHONE.................................607 761-1447
Charles S Jakaitis, *Principal*
EMP: 12
SALES (est): 830K **Privately Held**
SIC: 3829 Measuring & controlling devices

Victor
Ontario County

(G-15827)
331 HOLDING INC
Also Called: U S TEC
100 Rawson Rd Ste 205 (14564-1100)
PHONE.................................585 924-1740
William H Thompson, *President*
Dominic Piazza, *Treasurer*
EMP: 32
SALES (est): 4MM **Privately Held**
WEB: www.ustecnet.com
SIC: 3699 7373 1731 Mfg Electrical Equipment/Supplies Computer Systems Design Electrical Contractor

(G-15828)
ADVANCED INTERCONNECT MFG INC (HQ)
Also Called: A I M
780 Canning Pkwy (14564-8983)
PHONE.................................585 742-2220
John Durst, *President*
Steve Yost, *Engineer*
Diane Pepe, *Treasurer*
Gretchen Dunfey, *Human Res Mgr*
▲ **EMP:** 62
SQ FT: 50,000
SALES (est): 14.9MM
SALES (corp-wide): 61MM **Privately Held**
SIC: 3679 Harness assemblies for electronic use: wire or cable
PA: Floturn, Inc.
    4236 Thunderbird Ln
    West Chester OH 45014
    513 860-8040

(G-15829)
AMERICAN SPORTS MEDIA
106 Cobblestone Court Dr # 323 (14564-1045)
PHONE.................................585 924-4250
David Aultman, *Principal*
EMP: 6
SALES (est): 403K **Privately Held**
SIC: 2711 Newspapers, publishing & printing

(G-15830)
AVCOM OF VIRGINIA INC
Also Called: Ramsey Electronics
590 Fishers Station Dr (14564-9744)
PHONE.................................585 924-4560
Jay Evans, *Ch of Bd*
John G Ramsey, *President*
Dick Pache, *Engineer*
Rick Oddo, *Technology*
EMP: 53
SQ FT: 10,000
SALES (est): 7.8MM
SALES (corp-wide): 30MM **Privately Held**
WEB: www.brynavon.com
SIC: 3825 5961 8331 3651 Test equipment for electronic & electrical circuits; catalog & mail-order houses; job training & vocational rehabilitation services; household audio & video equipment
PA: Brynavon Group, Inc
    2000 Montgomery Ave
    Villanova PA 19085
    610 525-2102

(G-15831)
BIOREM ENVIRONMENTAL INC
100 Rawson Rd Ste 230 (14564-1177)
PHONE.................................585 924-2220
Peter Bruijns, *CEO*
Derek Webb, *Exec VP*
Douglas Newman, *CFO*
▲ **EMP:** 40
SALES (est): 7.9MM
SALES (corp-wide): 17.6MM **Privately Held**
SIC: 3822 Electric air cleaner controls, automatic
HQ: Biorem Technologies Inc
    7496 Wellington Road 34
    Puslinch ON N0B 2
    519 767-9100

(G-15832)
BIOWORKS INC (PA)
100 Rawson Rd Ste 205 (14564-1100)
PHONE.................................585 924-4362
Bill Foster, *President*
Michael Arnold, *Project Mgr*
Peter Eppeira, *Opers Staff*
Chris Hayes, *Engineer*
Joe Gionta, *Finance Dir*
▲ **EMP:** 3
SQ FT: 1,380
SALES (est): 4.5MM **Privately Held**
WEB: www.bioworksinc.com
SIC: 2879 Fungicides, herbicides

(G-15833)
BRISTOL INSTRUMENTS INC
770 Canning Pkwy (14564-8983)
P.O. Box I, Fishers (14453-0759)
PHONE.................................585 924-2620
Brian Samoriski, *President*
Michael Houk, *Vice Pres*
John Theodorsen, *Vice Pres*
Zachary Houk, *Project Mgr*
Peter Battisti, *CFO*
EMP: 6
SQ FT: 2,000
SALES (est): 1.4MM **Privately Held**
WEB: www.bristol-inst.com
SIC: 3826 Analytical instruments

(G-15834)
BUCKEYE CORRUGATED INC
Koch Container Div
797 Old Dutch Rd (14564-8972)
PHONE.................................585 924-1600
Robert Harris, *President*
Rob Bailey, *Prdtn Mgr*
Philip Trautman, *Prdtn Mgr*
Michael Fay, *Design Engr*
Norbert Wolf, *Controller*
EMP: 80
SALES (corp-wide): 188.4MM **Privately Held**
WEB: www.buckeyecorrugated.com
SIC: 2653 3993 Boxes, corrugated: made from purchased materials; signs & advertising specialties
PA: Buckeye Corrugated, Inc
    822 Kumho Dr Ste 400
    Fairlawn OH 44333
    330 576-0590

(G-15835)
CHARLES A ROGERS ENTPS INC
Also Called: Car Engineering and Mfg
51 Victor Heights Pkwy (14564-8926)
P.O. Box 627 (14564-0627)
PHONE.................................585 924-6400
Charles A Rogers, *CEO*
Yvette Rogers Pagano, *President*
Yvette Pagano, *Vice Pres*
Brian Rumsey, *Vice Pres*
Stephen Weilert, *Project Mgr*
EMP: 45
SQ FT: 40,000
SALES (est): 16.3MM **Privately Held**
WEB: www.car-eng.com
SIC: 3469 3549 3544 Stamping metal for the trade; metalworking machinery; special dies & tools

(G-15836)
CLEARCOVE SYSTEMS INC
7910 Rae Blvd (14564-8820)
PHONE.................................585 734-3012
Gregory Westbrook, *CEO*
Gary Miller, *President*
Terry Wright, *Chief Engr*
EMP: 10 **EST:** 2014
SQ FT: 750
SALES (est): 2.3MM **Privately Held**
SIC: 3589 Water treatment equipment, industrial

(G-15837)
CONSTELLATION BRANDS INC (PA)
207 High Point Dr # 100 (14564-1061)
PHONE.................................585 678-7100
Robert Sands, *CEO*
Richard Sands, *Ch of Bd*
F Paul Hetterich, *President*
William A Newlands, *President*
Christopher Stenzel, *President*
EMP: 95
SALES: 7.5B **Publicly Held**
WEB: www.cbrands.com
SIC: 2084 5182 5181 2082 Wines, brandy & brandy spirits; wine & distilled beverages; wine; neutral spirits; beer & other fermented malt liquors; beer (alcoholic beverage); distilled & blended liquors; concentrates, drink

(G-15838)
COOPERVISION INC
209 High Point Dr (14564-1061)
PHONE.................................585 385-6810
▲ **EMP:** 250
SQ FT: 35,000
SALES (est): 31.2MM
SALES (corp-wide): 1.8B **Publicly Held**
SIC: 3851 Mfg Ophthalmic Goods
HQ: Coopervision, Inc.
    209 High Point Dr
    Victor NY 14564
    585 385-6810

(G-15839)
COOPERVISION INC (HQ)
209 High Point Dr Ste 100 (14564-1061)
PHONE.................................585 385-6810
Thomas Bender, *Ch of Bd*
Andrew Sedweg, *President*
Jerry Warner, *President*
Mary Rothermel, *Vice Pres*
Charles Derringer, *Research*
▲ **EMP:** 65
SQ FT: 20,000
SALES: 329.5MM
SALES (corp-wide): 2.1B **Publicly Held**
SIC: 3851 Contact lenses
PA: The Cooper Companies Inc
    6140 Stoneridge Mall Rd # 590
    Pleasanton CA 94588
    925 460-3600

(G-15840)
DAKOTA SOFTWARE CORPORATION
7641 Pine Tree Dr (14564-8984)
PHONE.................................216 765-7100
Reginald C Shiverick, *President*
Darrin Fleming, *Partner*
Chuck Schmermund, *Business Mgr*
Dorothy Hunt, *QA Dir*
Ray Planisek, *QA Dir*
EMP: 9
SALES (corp-wide): 7.7MM **Privately Held**
WEB: www.dakotasoft.com
SIC: 7372 Prepackaged software
PA: Dakota Software Corporation
    1375 Euclid Ave Ste 500
    Cleveland OH 44115
    216 765-7100

(G-15841)
DAY AUTOMATION SYSTEMS INC (PA)
7931 Rae Blvd (14564-9017)
PHONE.................................585 924-4630
Eric J Orban, *CEO*
Bob Ormsby, *Business Mgr*
Robert Ormsby, *Vice Pres*
Donald Benwitz, *Project Mgr*
David Dunn, *Project Mgr*
EMP: 74
SALES (est): 29.6MM **Privately Held**
WEB: www.dayasi.com
SIC: 3822 Temperature controls, automatic

GEOGRAPHIC SECTION
Victor - Ontario County (G-15868)

(G-15842)
DICE AMERICA INC
7676 Netlink Dr (14564-9419)
P.O. Box 360 (14564-0360)
PHONE.................585 869-6200
Jeff Shufelt, *President*
EMP: 8
SALES: 650K **Privately Held**
WEB: www.diceamerica.com
SIC: 2821 Plastics materials & resins

(G-15843)
ELECTRICAL CONTROLS LINK
100 Rawson Rd Ste 220 (14564-1100)
PHONE.................585 924-7010
Jim Flynn, *Controller*
EMP: 42
SALES (est): 3.2MM **Privately Held**
WEB: www.han-tek.com
SIC: 3829 Measuring & controlling devices

(G-15844)
ENETICS INC
830 Canning Pkwy (14564-8940)
PHONE.................585 924-5010
William C Bush, *President*
Travis Downs, *Opers Mgr*
Thomas Jacobson, *Software Engr*
EMP: 6
SQ FT: 6,000
SALES (est): 1MM **Privately Held**
WEB: www.enetics.com
SIC: 3625 Relays & industrial controls

(G-15845)
EXHIBITS & MORE
7615 Omnitech Pl Ste 4a (14564-9767)
PHONE.................585 924-4040
Brian Pitre, *Principal*
EMP: 5
SALES (est): 207.4K **Privately Held**
SIC: 2711 5999 7319 Newspapers, publishing & printing; miscellaneous retail stores; display advertising service

(G-15846)
FLEX ENTERPRISES INC
820 Canning Pkwy (14564-8940)
PHONE.................585 742-1000
Linda Murphy, *CEO*
Guy Murphy, *President*
▲ EMP: 30
SQ FT: 15,000
SALES (est): 5.2MM **Privately Held**
WEB: www.flexenterprises.com
SIC: 3052 5085 Rubber & plastics hose & beltings; industrial supplies; hose, belting & packing; gaskets

(G-15847)
FLIGHTLINE ELECTRONICS INC (DH)
Also Called: Ultra Elec Flightline Systems
7625 Omnitech Pl (14564-9816)
PHONE.................585 924-4000
Paul Fardellone, *President*
Tom Cooper, *President*
Carlos Santiago, *Principal*
Anthony Diduro, *Vice Pres*
Kelly Selner, *Purch Mgr*
EMP: 100
SQ FT: 33,000
SALES (est): 38.7MM
SALES (corp-wide): 1B **Privately Held**
WEB: www.ultra-fei.com
SIC: 3812 Search & navigation equipment
HQ: Ultra Electronics Defense Inc.
4101 Smith School Rd
Austin TX 78744
512 327-6795

(G-15848)
GOOD HEALTH HEALTHCARE NEWSPPR
106 Cobblestone Court Dr (14564-1045)
PHONE.................585 421-8109
Wagner Dotto, *Owner*
EMP: 10
SALES (est): 264.3K **Privately Held**
WEB: www.cnyhealth.com
SIC: 2711 Newspapers: publishing only, not printed on site

(G-15849)
HUNTER MACHINE INC
6551 Anthony Dr (14564-1400)
P.O. Box 50 (14564-0050)
PHONE.................585 924-7480
John D Vouros, *President*
EMP: 20
SQ FT: 11,600
SALES: 5MM **Privately Held**
WEB: www.hmicncmachining.com
SIC: 3599 Machine shop, jobbing & repair

(G-15850)
INDUSTRIAL INDXING SYSTEMS INC
626 Fishers Run (14564-9732)
PHONE.................585 924-9181
William Schnaufer, *President*
Jon Cassano, *Vice Pres*
Chris Draper, *Purch Agent*
Kevin Sackett, *Engineer*
Andrew Wakefield, *Engineer*
EMP: 22 EST: 1977
SQ FT: 13,000
SALES (est): 5.2MM **Privately Held**
WEB: www.iis-servo.com
SIC: 3625 Relays & industrial controls

(G-15851)
JOHN RAMSEY ELEC SVCS LLC
Also Called: Jre Test
7940 Rae Blvd (14564-8933)
PHONE.................585 298-9596
Donna Dedes, *General Mgr*
John G Ramsey,
Bruce Sidari,
EMP: 8
SALES: 2.8MM **Privately Held**
SIC: 3825 Test equipment for electronic & electric measurement

(G-15852)
KIRTAS INC
749 Phillips Rd Ste 300 (14564-9434)
PHONE.................585 924-5999
EMP: 6 **Privately Held**
SIC: 3678 Electronic connectors
PA: Ristech Information Systems Inc
5115 Harvester Rd Unit 8
Burlington ON L7L 0
905 631-7451

(G-15853)
KIRTAS INC
7620 Omnitech Pl (14564-9428)
P.O. Box 729, Bolton MA (01740-0729)
PHONE.................585 924-2420
Robb Richardson, *CEO*
▼ EMP: 27
SQ FT: 12,000
SALES (est): 3.9MM **Privately Held**
WEB: www.kirtastech.com
SIC: 3678 Electronic connectors
PA: Ristech Information Systems Inc
5115 Harvester Rd Unit 8
Burlington ON L7L 0
905 631-7451

(G-15854)
LIFETIME STAINLESS STEEL CORP
7387 Ny 96 850 (14564)
PHONE.................585 924-9393
Stephen Foti, *President*
EMP: 6
SALES: 900K **Privately Held**
SIC: 3263 Cookware, fine earthenware

(G-15855)
LOGICAL CONTROL SOLUTIONS INC
829 Phillips Rd Ste 100 (14564-9431)
PHONE.................585 424-5340
James Urbanczyk, *President*
Susan Lampi, *General Mgr*
Neil Comstra, *Vice Pres*
Bill Schmid, *Project Mgr*
EMP: 18
SQ FT: 45,000
SALES (est): 4.2MM **Privately Held**
SIC: 3822 Temperature controls, automatic

(G-15856)
MAGNET-NDCTIVE SYSTEMS LTD USA
Also Called: Ultra Electronics Inc
7625 Omnitech Pl (14564-9816)
PHONE.................585 924-4000
Russell Greenway, *President*
Bill Gill, *Treasurer*
Nancy Como, *Admin Sec*
▲ EMP: 22
SQ FT: 10,000
SALES (est): 4.6MM
SALES (corp-wide): 1B **Privately Held**
SIC: 3663 Receiver-transmitter units (transceiver)
HQ: Ultra Electronics Inc
107 Church Hill Rd
Sandy Hook CT 06482
203 270-3695

(G-15857)
NEW SCALE TECHNOLOGIES INC
121 Victor Heights Pkwy (14564-8938)
PHONE.................585 924-4450
David Henderson, *CEO*
Allison Leet, *Vice Pres*
EMP: 25
SQ FT: 10,000
SALES: 4MM **Privately Held**
WEB: www.newscaletech.com
SIC: 3823 Controllers for process variables, all types

(G-15858)
NEWTEX INDUSTRIES INC (PA)
Also Called: Trident Partners III
8050 Victor Mendon Rd (14564-9109)
PHONE.................585 924-9135
Jerome Joliet, *CEO*
Douglas Bailey, *President*
Matthew Krempl, *VP Opers*
Kelly Goforth, *Controller*
Kathie Laduca, *Accounting Mgr*
▲ EMP: 45 EST: 1978
SQ FT: 103,000
SALES (est): 9MM **Privately Held**
WEB: www.newtex.com
SIC: 2221 2295 2241 Fiberglass fabrics; coated fabrics, not rubberized; narrow fabric mills

(G-15859)
NEXT STEP PUBLISHING INC
Also Called: Next Step Magazine, The
2 W Main St Ste 200 (14564-1153)
PHONE.................585 742-1260
David Mammano, *President*
EMP: 15
SQ FT: 1,500
SALES (est): 2.1MM **Privately Held**
SIC: 2721 8748 Magazines: publishing only, not printed on site; business consulting

(G-15860)
PACE WINDOW AND DOOR CORP (PA)
Also Called: Pace Window & Door
7224 State Route 96 (14564-9754)
PHONE.................585 924-8350
Robert Mehalso, *Ch of Bd*
Steven Abramson, *President*
Sara Colunio, *Purch Mgr*
Kelly Beer, *Purchasing*
Jody Taubenfeld, *Finance*
EMP: 50
SQ FT: 21,000
SALES (est): 8.7MM **Privately Held**
WEB: www.pacewindows.com
SIC: 3089 1751 Plastic hardware & building products; window & door (prefabricated) installation

(G-15861)
PREMIER PACKAGING CORPORATION
6 Framark Dr (14564-1136)
P.O. Box 352 (14564-0352)
PHONE.................585 924-8460
Robert B Bzdick, *Principal*
Joe Plummer, *Prdtn Mgr*
Joan T Bzdick, *Treasurer*
EMP: 32
SQ FT: 40,000
SALES (est): 6MM
SALES (corp-wide): 18.6MM **Publicly Held**
WEB: www.premiercustompkg.com
SIC: 2657 2675 2677 Folding paperboard boxes; die-cut paper & board; envelopes
PA: Document Security Systems Inc
200 Canal View Blvd # 300
Rochester NY 14623
585 325-3610

(G-15862)
PROGRESSIVE MCH & DESIGN LLC (PA)
Also Called: Pmd
727 Rowley Rd (14564-9728)
PHONE.................585 924-5250
Ron Richards, *Project Mgr*
Tony Silipini, *Project Mgr*
Joseph Costello, *Opers Mgr*
Bruce Allison, *Safety Mgr*
Mike Castro, *Engineer*
EMP: 225
SQ FT: 26,000
SALES (est): 39MM **Privately Held**
WEB: www.pmdautomation.com
SIC: 3599 Machine shop, jobbing & repair; custom machinery

(G-15863)
RAMSEY ELECTRONICS LLC
590 Fishers Station Dr (14564-9744)
PHONE.................585 924-4560
Richard Oddo, *CFO*
EMP: 20
SALES (est): 5.5MM **Privately Held**
SIC: 3825 5065 Test equipment for electronic & electric measurement; electronic parts & equipment

(G-15864)
RAPID PRINT AND MARKETING INC
8 High St (14564-1105)
PHONE.................585 924-1520
David Gaudieri, *Owner*
EMP: 5
SQ FT: 3,000
SALES (est): 987K **Privately Held**
SIC: 2752 7334 Commercial printing, offset; photocopying & duplicating services

(G-15865)
REDCOM LABORATORIES INC
1 Redcom Ctr (14564-9785)
PHONE.................585 924-6567
Dinah Weisberg, *CEO*
Charles Breidenstein, *President*
Klaus Gueldenpfennig, *President*
Lorraine Withey, *Buyer*
Thomas Laman, *Engineer*
▲ EMP: 200 EST: 1978
SQ FT: 140,000
SALES (est): 48.2MM **Privately Held**
WEB: www.redcom.com
SIC: 3661 8748 Switching equipment, telephone; communications consulting

(G-15866)
SENSOR FILMS INCORPORATED
687 Rowley Rd (14564-9728)
PHONE.................585 738-3500
Peter Hessney, *Principal*
EMP: 25 EST: 2013
SALES: 1.6MM **Privately Held**
SIC: 3699 Sound signaling devices, electrical

(G-15867)
SERVICE EDUCATION INCORPORATED
790 Canning Pkwy Ste 1 (14564-9019)
PHONE.................585 264-9240
Terence Wolfe, *President*
EMP: 6
SQ FT: 2,100
SALES (est): 300K **Privately Held**
WEB: www.serviceed.com
SIC: 2741 Technical manuals: publishing & printing

(G-15868)
SURMOTECH LLC
7676 Netlink Dr (14564-9419)
PHONE.................585 742-1220

Victor - Ontario County (G-15869)

GEOGRAPHIC SECTION

Jerry F Valentine, *CEO*
Arthur Kaempffe, *Vice Pres*
▲ **EMP:** 100
SQ FT: 20,000
SALES (est): 33.7MM **Privately Held**
WEB: www.surmotech.com
SIC: 3679 Electronic circuits

(G-15869)
SYCAMORE HILL DESIGNS INC
7585 Modock Rd (14564-9104)
PHONE 585 820-7322
Frank Vallone, *President*
EMP: 5
SALES (est): 300K **Privately Held**
SIC: 3484 Small arms

(G-15870)
SYRACUSA SAND AND GRAVEL INC
1389 Malone Rd (14564-9147)
P.O. Box 2 (14564-0002)
PHONE 585 924-7146
Scott Syracusa, *President*
Mark Syracusa, *Vice Pres*
EMP: 10
SQ FT: 1,000
SALES (est): 1.8MM **Privately Held**
SIC: 1442 Construction sand mining; gravel mining

(G-15871)
TEKNIC INC
115 Victor Heights Pkwy (14564-8938)
PHONE 585 784-7454
Thomas Bucella, *Ch of Bd*
David Sewhuk, *President*
Warren God, *Exec VP*
Abe Amirana, *Buyer*
Andrea Sevio, *Buyer*
▲ **EMP:** 35
SQ FT: 10,000
SALES (est): 7.7MM **Privately Held**
WEB: www.teknic.com
SIC: 3625 Motor controls & accessories

(G-15872)
TELOG INSTRUMENTS INC
830 Canning Pkwy (14564-8940)
PHONE 585 742-3000
Barry L Ceci, *President*
Charlene Donofrio, *Buyer*
Everett Lago, *Engineer*
David Baker, *Sales Staff*
Kerry Hoffman, *Sales Staff*
EMP: 30
SQ FT: 20,000
SALES: 5.7MM
SALES (corp-wide): 2.6B **Publicly Held**
WEB: www.telog.com
SIC: 3829 3823 Measuring & controlling devices; industrial instrmnts msrmnt display/control process variable
PA: Trimble Inc.
935 Stewart Dr
Sunnyvale CA 94085
408 481-8000

(G-15873)
THE CALDWELL MANUFACTURING CO
Advantage Mfg
Holland Industrial Park (14564)
PHONE 585 352-2803
Michelle McCorry, *Manager*
EMP: 18
SALES (corp-wide): 50MM **Privately Held**
SIC: 3495 Wire springs
PA: The Caldwell Manufacturing Company
2605 Manitou Rd Ste 100
Rochester NY 14624
585 352-3790

(G-15874)
TRIAD NETWORK TECHNOLOGIES
75b Victor Heights Pkwy (14564-8926)
PHONE 585 924-8505
Pete Sweltz, *President*
Paul Rheude, *General Mgr*
Frank Carusone, *Vice Pres*
Don Munn, *Accounts Exec*
Jeff Pulli, *Accounts Exec*
EMP: 20

SQ FT: 3,500
SALES (est): 3.3MM **Privately Held**
WEB: www.triadnt.com
SIC: 2298 Cable, fiber

(G-15875)
VICTOR INSULATORS INC
280 Maple Ave (14564-1385)
PHONE 585 924-2127
Ira Knickerbocker, *Ch of Bd*
Andrew E Schwalm, *President*
Nelson McKee, *Sales Mgr*
Andrew Schwalm, *Marketing Mgr*
Robert Dowdle, *Manager*
▲ **EMP:** 105
SQ FT: 327,000
SALES: 17MM **Privately Held**
WEB: www.victorinsulatorsinc.com
SIC: 3264 Insulators, electrical: porcelain

(G-15876)
W STUART SMITH INC
Also Called: Heritage Packaging
625 Fishers Run (14564-8905)
PHONE 585 742-3310
William S Smith, *Ch of Bd*
Kristin J Smith, *Vice Pres*
Randy Demkowicz, *Engineer*
Evan Smith, *Controller*
Scott Floyd, *Sales Engr*
◆ **EMP:** 40
SQ FT: 50,000
SALES (est): 8.7MM **Privately Held**
WEB: www.heritagepackaging.com
SIC: 3086 Packaging & shipping materials, foamed plastic

(G-15877)
WASHER SOLUTIONS INC
760 Canning Pkwy Ste A (14564-9018)
PHONE 585 742-6388
Mickie T Pitts, *CEO*
EMP: 10 **EST:** 2001
SQ FT: 1,200
SALES (est): 2.2MM **Privately Held**
WEB: www.washersolutions.com
SIC: 3519 Gas engine rebuilding

(G-15878)
WILLIAMSON LAW BOOK CO
790 Canning Pkwy Ste 2 (14564-9019)
PHONE 585 924-3400
Greg Chwiecko, *President*
Thomas Osborne, *Treasurer*
EMP: 12 **EST:** 1870
SQ FT: 10,800
SALES (est): 1.2MM **Privately Held**
WEB: www.wlbonline.com
SIC: 2761 7371 Manifold business forms; computer software development

Voorheesville
Albany County

(G-15879)
ATLAS COPCO COMPTEC LLC (HQ)
46 School Rd (12186-9696)
PHONE 518 765-3344
Peter Wagner, *President*
Holly Simboli, *Principal*
Paul Burdick, *Site Mgr*
Andrew Hunter, *Engineer*
John Rinaldo, *Engineer*
◆ **EMP:** 330 **EST:** 1970
SQ FT: 100,000
SALES (est): 148.5MM
SALES (corp-wide): 13.8B **Privately Held**
WEB: www.atlascopco-act.com
SIC: 3563 Air & gas compressors including vacuum pumps
PA: Atlas Copco Ab
Sickla Industriväg 3
Nacka 131 5
874 380-00

(G-15880)
SPAULDING & ROGERS MFG INC
3252 New Scotland Rd (12186)
PHONE 518 768-2070
Huck Spaulding, *Ch of Bd*
Josephine Spaulding, *President*

▲ **EMP:** 70
SALES (est): 8.3MM **Privately Held**
WEB: www.spaulding-rogers.com
SIC: 3952 Artists' equipment

Waccabuc
Westchester County

(G-15881)
MANN CONSULTANTS LLC
67 Chapel Rd (10597-1001)
PHONE 914 763-0512
Stuart Mann,
Jeffrey Mandelbaum,
EMP: 22
SALES (est): 1MM **Privately Held**
SIC: 2253 2329 T-shirts & tops, knit; men's & boys' sportswear & athletic clothing

Waddington
St. Lawrence County

(G-15882)
STRUCTURAL WOOD CORPORATION
Also Called: Roll Lock Truss
243 Lincoln Ave (13694-3203)
P.O. Box 339 (13694-0339)
PHONE 315 388-4442
Michael McGee, *CEO*
Peter Rieter, *President*
James Lyon, *General Mgr*
Bob Rochefort, *Production*
EMP: 32
SQ FT: 20,000
SALES (est): 4.4MM **Privately Held**
WEB: www.rolllocktruss.com
SIC: 2439 5031 5211 Trusses, wooden roof; doors & windows; lumber & other building materials

Wading River
Suffolk County

(G-15883)
A I P PRINTING & STATIONERS
Also Called: Airport Printing & Stationers
6198 N Country Rd (11792-1625)
PHONE 631 929-5529
George A Waldemar, *President*
EMP: 8
SALES (est): 760K **Privately Held**
SIC: 2752 Lithographing on metal

(G-15884)
FREDERICK COWAN & COMPANY INC
144 Beach Rd (11792-1305)
PHONE 631 369-0360
Thomas L Cowan, *President*
Mildred Cowan, *Corp Secy*
EMP: 14
SQ FT: 20,000
SALES (est): 2.2MM **Privately Held**
WEB: www.fcowan.com
SIC: 3612 3433 Ignition transformers, for use on domestic fuel burners; gas burners, industrial

(G-15885)
LO-CO FUEL CORP
10 Stephen Dr (11792-2126)
PHONE 631 929-5086
Michael Lopez, *Principal*
EMP: 6
SALES (est): 486.5K **Privately Held**
SIC: 2869 Fuels

(G-15886)
SAFEGUARD INC
578 Sound Ave (11792)
P.O. Box 922 (11792-0922)
PHONE 631 929-3273
Charlie Zimmerman, *President*
EMP: 15
SALES (est): 2.5MM **Privately Held**
SIC: 2899 Fire retardant chemicals

(G-15887)
SPLIT ROCK TRADING CO INC
22 Creek Rd (11792-2501)
P.O. Box 841, Shoreham (11786-0841)
PHONE 631 929-3261
Jim Loscalzo, *President*
Peggy Vonbrenewitz, *Corp Secy*
EMP: 7
SQ FT: 13,000
SALES (est): 480K **Privately Held**
WEB: www.splitrockvideo.com
SIC: 3499 5012 5013 5531 Novelties & specialties, metal; automobiles; motorcycles; automotive supplies & parts; automotive accessories; automobiles, new & used; motorcycles

(G-15888)
SWISS SPECIALTIES INC
15 Crescent Ct (11792-3004)
PHONE 631 567-8800
Daniel J George, *President*
EMP: 14
SQ FT: 5,000
SALES: 1.9MM **Privately Held**
SIC: 3541 Screw machines, automatic

Wainscott
Suffolk County

(G-15889)
MAPEASY INC
54 Industrial Rd (11975-2001)
P.O. Box 80 (11975-0080)
PHONE 631 537-6213
Gary Bradhering, *President*
Chris Harris, *Vice Pres*
▲ **EMP:** 12
SQ FT: 11,000
SALES (est): 980.4K **Privately Held**
WEB: www.mapeasy.com
SIC: 2741 4724 Maps: publishing & printing; travel agencies

Walden
Orange County

(G-15890)
AMPAC PAPER LLC (DH)
30 Coldenham Rd (12586-2036)
P.O. Box 271 (12586-0271)
PHONE 845 713-6600
John Q Baumann, *CEO*
Robert Tillis, *President*
Robert D Gregorio, *Vice Pres*
Linda Murphy, *Vice Pres*
Jon Dill, *CFO*
▲ **EMP:** 5
SQ FT: 200,000
SALES (est): 82.2MM
SALES (corp-wide): 1.3B **Privately Held**
WEB: www.ampaconline.com
SIC: 2674 2621 5162 Shopping bags: made from purchased materials; paper mills; plastics materials
HQ: Ampac Packaging, Llc
12025 Tricon Rd
Cincinnati OH 45246
513 671-1777

(G-15891)
C & C ATHLETIC INC
Also Called: Viking Jackets & Athletic Wear
11 Myrtle Ave (12586-2340)
PHONE 845 713-4670
Andrea Conklin, *President*
EMP: 5
SQ FT: 4,000
SALES (est): 318.7K **Privately Held**
WEB: www.vikingathletic.com
SIC: 2759 2339 Screen printing; athletic clothing: women's, misses' & juniors'

(G-15892)
CALFONEX COMPANY
121 Orchard St (12586-1707)
PHONE 845 778-2212
Terrance Donovan, *Owner*
EMP: 15
SALES (est): 836.8K **Privately Held**
SIC: 2899 Chemical preparations

▲ = Import ▼ = Export
◆ = Import/Export

GEOGRAPHIC SECTION

Wampsville - Madison County (G-15917)

(G-15893)
DWYER FARM LLC
40 Bowman Ln (12586-2100)
PHONE..................914 456-2742
Brian Dwyer, *Principal*
Christopher Dwyer, *Principal*
Jeannie Dwyer, *Principal*
Joseph Dwyer, *Principal*
Mel Dwyer, *Principal*
EMP: 6
SALES (est): 185.1K Privately Held
SIC: 2026 Farmers' cheese

(G-15894)
PACIFIC DIE CAST INC
Also Called: Qssi
827 Route 52 Ste 2 (12586-2747)
PHONE..................845 778-6374
Melissa Durant, *Principal*
EMP: 15
SALES (corp-wide): 11.6MM Privately Held
SIC: 3544 Special dies & tools
PA: Pacific Die Cast, Inc.
   12802 Commodity Pl
   Tampa FL 33626
   813 316-2221

(G-15895)
POLICH TALLIX INC
39 Edmunds Ln (12586-1538)
PHONE..................845 567-9464
Richard Polich, *President*
Adam Demchak, *Vice Pres*
Andrew Pharmer, *Site Mgr*
Duncan Urquhart, *CFO*
J Duncan Urquhart, *CFO*
▲ EMP: 63
SALES (est): 14.8MM Privately Held
SIC: 3369 3499 Nonferrous foundries; novelties & specialties, metal

(G-15896)
ROMAR CONTRACTING INC
630 State Route 52 (12586-2709)
P.O. Box 658 (12586-0658)
PHONE..................845 778-2737
Rod Winchell, *President*
Kyle Winchell, *Technology*
EMP: 5
SALES: 500K Privately Held
SIC: 3441 Fabricated structural metal

(G-15897)
SPENCE ENGINEERING COMPANY INC
Also Called: Nicholson Steam Trap
150 Coldenham Rd (12586-2909)
PHONE..................845 778-5566
A William Higgins, *Ch of Bd*
David A Bloss Sr, *President*
Alan R Carlsen, *Vice Pres*
Timothy Quinn, *Engineer*
Jay Deman, *Manager*
▲ EMP: 150
SQ FT: 79,000
SALES (est): 26.1MM
SALES (corp-wide): 661.7MM Publicly Held
WEB: www.spenceengineering.com
SIC: 3491 3444 3612 3494 Pressure valves & regulators, industrial; metal ventilating equipment; transformers, except electric; valves & pipe fittings
PA: Circor International, Inc.
   30 Corporate Dr Ste 200
   Burlington MA 01803
   781 270-1200

(G-15898)
TILCON NEW YORK INC
272 Berea Rd (12586-2906)
PHONE..................845 778-5591
Reinis Siplls, *Branch Mgr*
EMP: 27
SALES (corp-wide): 29.7B Privately Held
WEB: www.tilconny.com
SIC: 1429 Trap rock, crushed & broken-quarrying; dolomitic marble, crushed & broken-quarrying
HQ: Tilcon New York Inc.
   9 Entin Rd
   Parsippany NJ 07054
   800 789-7625

(G-15899)
WALLKILL LODGE NO 627 F&AM
61 Main St (12586-1824)
P.O. Box 311 (12586-0311)
PHONE..................845 778-7148
Mark Balck, *President*
EMP: 14 EST: 2001
SQ FT: 7,326
SALES (est): 514.7K Privately Held
SIC: 2711 Newspapers

Wales Center
Erie County

(G-15900)
AM BICKFORD INC
12318 Big Tree Rd (14169)
P.O. Box 201 (14169-0201)
PHONE..................716 652-1590
John Bickford, *President*
EMP: 12
SQ FT: 5,000
SALES (est): 2MM Privately Held
WEB: www.ambickford.com
SIC: 3841 Surgical & medical instruments

(G-15901)
HALE ELECTRICAL DIST SVCS INC
12088 Big Tree Rd (14169)
P.O. Box 221 (14169-0221)
PHONE..................716 818-7595
David Neveaux, *President*
EMP: 6
SALES: 1.5MM Privately Held
SIC: 3612 Distribution transformers, electric

Wallkill
Ulster County

(G-15902)
ARTCRAFT BUILDING SERVICES
85 Old Hoagerburgh Rd (12589-3419)
PHONE..................845 895-3893
Pasqual J Petrucci, *President*
Janice A Petrucci, *Vice Pres*
EMP: 5
SQ FT: 3,000
SALES (est): 660.6K Privately Held
SIC: 3537 Platforms, stands, tables, pallets & similar equipment; dollies (hand or power trucks), industrial except mining

(G-15903)
CATSMO LLC
Also Called: Solex Catsmo Fine Foods
25 Myers Rd (12589-3516)
PHONE..................845 895-2296
Markus Draxler, *CEO*
Frederic Pothier, *CFO*
◆ EMP: 12 EST: 1995
SQ FT: 15,000
SALES (est): 2.6MM Privately Held
WEB: www.catsmo.com
SIC: 2091 Salmon, smoked

(G-15904)
FAIR-RITE PRODUCTS CORP (PA)
1 Commercial Row (12589-4438)
P.O. Box 288 (12589-0288)
PHONE..................845 895-2055
Richard Parker, *Ch of Bd*
Carole U Parker, *President*
Larry Surrells, *Division Mgr*
Benjamin Friedman, *General Mgr*
Rocco Conklin, *Engineer*
▲ EMP: 125 EST: 1952
SQ FT: 80,000
SALES (est): 19.1MM Privately Held
WEB: www.fair-rite.com
SIC: 3679 Cores, magnetic

(G-15905)
JAMES B CROWELL & SONS INC
242 Lippincott Rd (12589-3643)
PHONE..................845 895-3464
James Crowell III, *President*
Wendy Sutherland, *Vice Pres*
EMP: 9 EST: 1872
SQ FT: 4,800
SALES (est): 1MM Privately Held
SIC: 3544 Industrial molds

(G-15906)
RICHTER CHARLES METAL STMP&SP
80 Cottage St (12589-3128)
P.O. Box 297 (12589-0297)
PHONE..................845 895-2025
David Richter, *President*
EMP: 40
SQ FT: 50,000
SALES (est): 3.3MM Privately Held
SIC: 3469 Metal stampings

(G-15907)
RICHTER METALCRAFT CORPORATION
Also Called: Charles Richter
80 Cottage St (12589-3128)
P.O. Box 297 (12589-0297)
PHONE..................845 895-2025
David Richter, *President*
Carol Morgan, *Vice Pres*
Carl Ulrich, *Maint Spvr*
Louise Tancriedi, *Admin Sec*
EMP: 35 EST: 1934
SQ FT: 50,000
SALES (est): 4.4MM Privately Held
WEB: www.charlesrichter.com
SIC: 3469 Stamping metal for the trade

(G-15908)
SELECT-TECH INC
3050 State Route 208 (12589-4431)
P.O. Box 259 (12589-0259)
PHONE..................845 895-8111
William Diener, *President*
Thomas Diener, *Treasurer*
▲ EMP: 5
SQ FT: 25,000
SALES: 600K Privately Held
WEB: www.select-tech.com
SIC: 3291 Abrasive products

(G-15909)
WASH QUARTERS LLC
680 Hoagerburgh Rd (12589-3424)
PHONE..................989 802-2017
Jeffrey I Maynard, *Administration*
EMP: 7 EST: 2012
SALES (est): 179K Privately Held
SIC: 3131 Quarters

Walton
Delaware County

(G-15910)
BEYOND DESIGN INC
807 Pines Brook Rd (13856-2381)
PHONE..................607 865-7487
Barbara A Salvatore, *President*
EMP: 7
SALES (est): 638.4K Privately Held
SIC: 3299 Architectural sculptures: gypsum, clay, papier mache, etc.

(G-15911)
KRAFT HEINZ FOODS COMPANY
261 Delaware St (13856-1099)
PHONE..................607 865-7131
Cynthia Waggoner, *Opers-Prdtn-Mfg*
EMP: 200
SALES (corp-wide): 26.2B Publicly Held
WEB: www.kraftfoods.com
SIC: 2026 2022 Fermented & cultured milk products; cheese, natural & processed
HQ: Kraft Heinz Foods Company
   1 Ppg Pl Ste 3200
   Pittsburgh PA 15222
   412 455-5700

(G-15912)
NORTHEAST FABRICATORS LLC
30-35 William St (13856-1497)
P.O. Box 65 (13856-0065)
PHONE..................607 865-4031
Steve Schick, *Purch Mgr*
George Sonner, *Engineer*
Judy Beardslee, *Human Res Mgr*
Peter Phraner, *Manager*
Ed Stevens, *Manager*
EMP: 70 EST: 1997
SQ FT: 80,000
SALES (est): 20.6MM Privately Held
SIC: 3444 3441 Sheet metalwork; fabricated structural metal

(G-15913)
VULTO CREAMERY LLC
3509 Dunk Hill Rd (13856-3275)
PHONE..................607 865-7059
Johannes Vulto, *Principal*
EMP: 5
SALES (est): 321K Privately Held
SIC: 2021 Creamery butter

Walworth
Wayne County

(G-15914)
MEDCO MACHINE LLC
2320 Walworth Marion Rd (14568-9501)
P.O. Box 454 (14568-0454)
PHONE..................315 986-2109
Mark Medyn,
EMP: 6
SQ FT: 4,800
SALES: 700K Privately Held
SIC: 3599 Machine shop, jobbing & repair

(G-15915)
ROCHESTER ASPHALT MATERIALS
Also Called: Dolomite Group
1200 Atlantic Ave (14568-9792)
PHONE..................315 524-4619
Harvey Smeatin, *Manager*
EMP: 7
SALES (corp-wide): 29.7B Privately Held
SIC: 3531 Asphalt plant, including gravel-mix type
HQ: Rochester Asphalt Materials Inc
   1150 Penfield Rd
   Rochester NY 14625
   585 381-7010

(G-15916)
SOFTWARE & GENERAL SERVICES CO
Also Called: S and G Imaging
1365 Fairway 5 Cir (14568-9444)
PHONE..................315 986-4184
John Larysz, *Owner*
EMP: 6
SALES (est): 480K Privately Held
WEB: www.softwareandgeneral.com
SIC: 7372 Data Management/Pim Consulting Services

Wampsville
Madison County

(G-15917)
DIEMOLDING CORPORATION (PA)
100 Donald Hicks Dew Dr (13163)
P.O. Box 26 (13163-0026)
PHONE..................315 363-4710
Donald H Dew, *CEO*
Mark Vanderveen, *Ch of Bd*
Dennis O'Brien, *President*
Carl Cook, *Plant Mgr*
Christopher Beehner, *CFO*
▲ EMP: 6 EST: 1920
SQ FT: 50,000
SALES (est): 17.2MM Privately Held
WEB: www.diemolding.com
SIC: 2655 Containers, laminated phenolic & vulcanized fiber

Wampsville - Madison County (G-15918)

(G-15918)
DIEMOLDING CORPORATION
Also Called: Dietooling
N Court St (13163)
PHONE................315 363-4710
Tom Pavente, *General Mgr*
EMP: 17
SALES (corp-wide): 17.2MM **Privately Held**
WEB: www.diemolding.com
SIC: 3544 Mfg Dies/Tools/Jigs/Fixtures
PA: Diemolding Corporation
  100 Donald Hicks Dew Dr
  Wampsville NY 13163
  315 363-4710

Wantagh
Nassau County

(G-15919)
1/2 OFF CARDS WANTAGH INC
1162 Wantagh Ave (11793-2110)
PHONE................516 809-9832
Steven Bodenstein, *CEO*
EMP: 5
SALES (est): 489.6K **Privately Held**
SIC: 2771 Greeting cards

(G-15920)
CHRISTOPHER ANTHONY PUBG CO
Also Called: Christiny
2225 Wantagh Ave (11793-3917)
PHONE................516 826-9205
Anthony Fannin, *President*
Jo Ann Fannin, *Admin Sec*
▼ **EMP:** 19 **EST:** 1978
SQ FT: 6,000
SALES: 2.5MM **Privately Held**
WEB: www.christony.com
SIC: 2741 Catalogs: publishing only, not printed on site

(G-15921)
GREENVALE BAGEL INC
3060 Merrick Rd (11793-4395)
PHONE................516 221-8221
Cesidia Facchini, *President*
Ralph Facchini, *Vice Pres*
Claudio Facchini, *Treasurer*
EMP: 30
SQ FT: 1,200
SALES (est): 3.1MM **Privately Held**
SIC: 2051 Bagels, fresh or frozen; bakery: wholesale or wholesale/retail combined

(G-15922)
HERSHEY KISS 203 INC
3536 Bunker Ave (11793-3439)
PHONE................516 503-3740
Brian Deluca, *Chairman*
EMP: 5 **EST:** 2010
SALES (est): 261.4K **Privately Held**
SIC: 2066 Chocolate & cocoa products

(G-15923)
LIFESCAN INC
15 Tardy Ln N (11793-1928)
PHONE................516 557-2693
EMP: 258
SALES (corp-wide): 343.2MM **Privately Held**
SIC: 2835 Blood derivative diagnostic agents
PA: Lifescan, Inc.
  965 Chesterbrook Blvd
  Chesterbrook PA 19087
  800 227-8862

(G-15924)
MORTGAGE PRESS LTD
1220 Wantagh Ave (11793-2202)
PHONE................516 409-1400
Russell Sickmen, *CEO*
Joel M Berman, *President*
Andrew Berman, *Exec VP*
EMP: 22
SQ FT: 4,000
SALES (est): 1.7MM **Privately Held**
WEB: www.mortgagepress.com
SIC: 2711 2741 Newspapers; miscellaneous publishing

(G-15925)
NBETS CORPORATION
Also Called: Wantagh 5 & 10
1901 Wantagh Ave (11793-3930)
PHONE................516 785-1259
John Norris, *Ch of Bd*
EMP: 8
SALES (est): 855.8K **Privately Held**
SIC: 2392 Household furnishings

(G-15926)
R M F HEALTH MANAGEMENT LLC
Also Called: Professional Health Imaging
3361 Park Ave (11793-3735)
PHONE................718 854-5400
Syndney Bemstein, *Principal*
Robyn Feldstein,
EMP: 21
SQ FT: 9,600
SALES (est): 2.9MM **Privately Held**
SIC: 3844 Nuclear irradiation equipment

(G-15927)
WANTAGH COMPUTER CENTER
10 Stanford Ct (11793-1863)
PHONE................516 826-2189
Sidney B Nudelman, *CEO*
EMP: 14
SQ FT: 4,000
SALES (est): 1.1MM **Privately Held**
SIC: 3577 3571 Computer peripheral equipment; electronic computers
PA: S B Nudelman Inc
  10 Stanford Ct
  Wantagh NY 11793

Wappingers Falls
Dutchess County

(G-15928)
CONTEMPORARY VISIONS LLC (PA)
Also Called: Sonneman-A Way of Light
151 Airport Dr (12590-6161)
PHONE................845 926-5469
Sonny Park, *Principal*
▲ **EMP:** 5
SALES (est): 1.2MM **Privately Held**
SIC: 3646 Commercial indusl & institutional electric lighting fixtures

(G-15929)
DRA IMAGING PC
169 Myers Corners Rd # 250 (12590-3868)
PHONE................845 296-1057
Richard Friedland, *CEO*
EMP: 27
SALES (est): 5.1MM **Privately Held**
SIC: 3844 X-ray apparatus & tubes

(G-15930)
FLAVORMATIC INDUSTRIES LLC
90 Brentwood Dr (12590-3344)
PHONE................845 297-9100
Jeffrey Harris, *CEO*
Rick Febles, *QC Dir*
Kathryn Reidy, *Manager*
◆ **EMP:** 20 **EST:** 1887
SQ FT: 21,000
SALES (est): 4.6MM
SALES (corp-wide): 9.2MM **Privately Held**
WEB: www.flavormatic.com
SIC: 2087 5169 Beverage bases, concentrates, syrups, powders & mixes; beverage bases; extracts, flavoring; essential oils
PA: Flavor Producers, Llc
  8521 Fllbrook Ave Ste 380
  West Hills CA 91304
  818 307-4062

(G-15931)
G BOPP USA INC
4 Bill Horton Way (12590-2018)
P.O. Box 393, Hopewell Junction (12533-0393)
PHONE................845 296-1065
George Baker, *COO*
▲ **EMP:** 7
SALES (est): 1.2MM **Privately Held**
SIC: 3496 Wire cloth & woven wire products
PA: G. Bopp & Co Ag
  Bachmannweg 21
  ZUrich ZH
  443 776-666

(G-15932)
GEM REPRODUCTION SERVICES CORP
Also Called: Signal Graphics Printing
1299 Route 9 Ste 105 (12590-4918)
PHONE................845 298-0172
Gary Mensching, *President*
Elizabeth Mensching, *Admin Sec*
EMP: 5
SQ FT: 3,300
SALES (est): 956.9K **Privately Held**
SIC: 2752 2759 Commercial printing, offset; commercial printing

(G-15933)
GLAXOSMITHKLINE LLC
6 Alpert Dr (12590-4602)
PHONE................845 797-3259
EMP: 26
SALES (corp-wide): 39.8B **Privately Held**
SIC: 2834 Pharmaceutical preparations
HQ: Glaxosmithkline Llc
  5 Crescent Dr
  Philadelphia PA 19112
  215 751-4000

(G-15934)
HIGHLAND VALLEY SUPPLY INC
30 Airport Dr (12590-6164)
PHONE................845 849-2863
Raymond Marsella, *President*
Jim Jellema, *Opers Spvr*
Jan Caparaso, *Treasurer*
EMP: 15
SQ FT: 11,000
SALES (est): 3.6MM **Privately Held**
WEB: www.highlandvalleysupply.com
SIC: 3644 Electric conduits & fittings

(G-15935)
HUDSON VALLEY LIGHTING INC
151 Airport Dr (12590-6161)
P.O. Box 393 (12590-0393)
PHONE................845 561-0300
David Littman, *President*
Brent Fields, *Vice Pres*
Kyle Jackson, *Sales Associate*
Steve Vail, *Manager*
Dottie Byrnes, *Technology*
◆ **EMP:** 75 **EST:** 1960
SQ FT: 65,000
SALES (est): 17.9MM **Privately Held**
WEB: www.hudsonvalleylighting.com
SIC: 3646 3645 Commercial indusl & institutional electric lighting fixtures; residential lighting fixtures

(G-15936)
MONEAST INC
Also Called: Sir Speedy
1708 Route 9 Ste 3 (12590-1367)
P.O. Box 1, Ford VA (23850-0001)
PHONE................845 298-8898
David Monto, *President*
Randall J Easter, *Treasurer*
Mary Alice Monto, *Admin Sec*
EMP: 6
SQ FT: 2,800
SALES (est): 907.5K **Privately Held**
SIC: 2752 2791 2789 Commercial printing, lithographic; typesetting; bookbinding & related work

(G-15937)
THINK GREEN JUNK REMOVAL INC
29 Meadow Wood Ln (12590-5937)
PHONE................845 297-7771
George Makris, *Owner*
EMP: 7
SALES (est): 842.5K **Privately Held**
SIC: 3089 Garbage containers, plastic

(G-15938)
WAPPINGERS FALLS SHOPPER INC
Also Called: Beacon Press News
84 E Main St (12590-2504)
PHONE................845 297-3723
Albert M Osten, *President*
EMP: 50 **EST:** 1959
SQ FT: 12,000
SALES (est): 3.6MM **Privately Held**
SIC: 2711 2752 Newspapers: publishing only, not printed on site; commercial printing, lithographic

Warnerville
Schoharie County

(G-15939)
ZMZ MFG INC
300 Mickle Hollow Rd (12187-2507)
PHONE................518 234-4336
Lisa Zaba Miller, *Principal*
EMP: 8
SALES (est): 697.5K **Privately Held**
SIC: 3999 Manufacturing industries

Warrensburg
Warren County

(G-15940)
LUMAZU LLC
141 Garnet Lake Rd (12885-5907)
PHONE................518 623-3372
Sheila Flanagan,
EMP: 5 **Privately Held**
SIC: 2022 2024 Cheese spreads, dips, pastes & other cheese products; sherbets, dairy based
PA: Lumazu, Llc
  484 S Johnsburg Rd
  Warrensburg NY 12885

(G-15941)
LUMAZU LLC (PA)
Also Called: Nettle Meadow Farm
484 S Johnsburg Rd (12885-5944)
PHONE................518 623-3372
Sheila Flanagan,
Lorraine Lambiase,
EMP: 15
SQ FT: 7,500
SALES: 1.4MM **Privately Held**
SIC: 2022 2024 Cheese spreads, dips, pastes & other cheese products; sherbets, dairy based

(G-15942)
NORTHEASTERN PRODUCTS CORP (PA)
Also Called: Nepco
115 Sweet Rd (12885-4754)
P.O. Box 98 (12885-0098)
PHONE................518 623-3161
Paul Schiavi, *CEO*
Gary Schiavi, *President*
Richard Morgan, *Sales Mgr*
Mark N Stauber, *Manager*
EMP: 23
SQ FT: 2,400
SALES (est): 11MM **Privately Held**
WEB: www.nep-co.com
SIC: 2493 Reconstituted wood products

(G-15943)
TUMBLEHOME BOATSHOP
684 State Route 28 (12885-5301)
PHONE................518 623-5050
Reuben Smith, *Owner*
Cynde Smith, *Managing Prtnr*
EMP: 6
SALES (est): 580.2K **Privately Held**
SIC: 3732 Boats, fiberglass: building & repairing

▲ = Import ▼ =Export ◆ =Import/Export

Warsaw
Wyoming County

(G-15944)
FAIRVIEW PAPER BOX CORP
200 Allen St (14569-1562)
PHONE..................................585 786-5230
Donald Zaas, *Ch of Bd*
Joel Zaas, *President*
Mark Cassese, *COO*
John L Asimakopoulos, *CFO*
EMP: 29
SQ FT: 55,000
SALES (est): 6.1MM
SALES (corp-wide): 59.4MM Privately Held
WEB: www.boxit.com
SIC: 2652 Setup paperboard boxes
PA: The Apex Paper Box Company
5555 Walworth Ave
Cleveland OH 44102
216 631-4000

(G-15945)
MORTON BUILDINGS INC
5616 Route 20a E (14569-9302)
PHONE..................................585 786-8191
John Edmunds, *Opers-Prdtn-Mfg*
Ed Neudeck, *Sales Mgr*
EMP: 40
SQ FT: 5,122
SALES (corp-wide): 492.6MM Privately Held
WEB: www.mortonbuildings.com
SIC: 3448 5039 Buildings, portable: prefabricated metal; prefabricated structures
PA: Morton Buildings, Inc.
252 W Adams St
Morton IL 61550
800 447-7436

(G-15946)
UNIDEX CORPORATION WESTERN NY
Also Called: Unidex Company
2416 State Route 19 N (14569-9336)
PHONE..................................585 786-3170
Arthur Crater, *President*
Susan M Gardner, *Vice Pres*
Thomas Baldwin, *Treasurer*
EMP: 16
SQ FT: 21,000
SALES (est): 3.1MM Privately Held
WEB: www.unidex-inc.com
SIC: 3549 Assembly machines, including robotic

(G-15947)
UPSTATE DOOR INC
26 Industrial St (14569-1550)
PHONE..................................585 786-3880
Robert J Fontaine, *CEO*
Brock Beckstrand, *Safety Mgr*
Jon Shisler, *Engineer*
Jason Hurley, *Sales Mgr*
David Farrell, *Sales Staff*
▲ EMP: 75
SQ FT: 55,000
SALES: 7.6MM Privately Held
WEB: www.upstatedoor.com
SIC: 2431 Interior & ornamental woodwork & trim

Warwick
Orange County

(G-15948)
AMERICAN TOWMAN NETWORK INC
Also Called: American Towman Expeditions
7 West St (10990-1447)
PHONE..................................845 986-4546
Steven L Calitri, *President*
Neila Smith, *President*
Dennis Ortiz, *Publisher*
Jimmy Santos, *General Mgr*
Brendan Dooley, *Editor*
EMP: 12
SALES (est): 1.4MM Privately Held
WEB: www.towman.com
SIC: 2721 7549 Magazines: publishing only, not printed on site; towing services; towing service, automotive

(G-15949)
DANGELO HOME COLLECTIONS INC
Also Called: Victoria Dngelo Intr Cllctions
39 Warwick Tpke (10990-3632)
P.O. Box 271 (10990-0271)
PHONE..................................917 267-8920
Victoria D'Angelo, *President*
Stuart Morrison, *Vice Pres*
▲ EMP: 7
SQ FT: 16,000
SALES: 750K Privately Held
WEB: www.dangelohome.com
SIC: 2431 Woodwork, interior & ornamental

(G-15950)
DIGITAL UNITED COLOR PRTG INC
Also Called: Warwick Press
33 South St (10990-1624)
P.O. Box 708 (10990-0708)
PHONE..................................845 986-9846
Scott J Lieberman, *Ch of Bd*
EMP: 9
SALES (est): 1.3MM Privately Held
SIC: 2752 Color lithography

(G-15951)
DREAM GREEN PRODUCTIONS
Also Called: Dream Fabric Printing
39 Warwick Tpke (10990-3632)
P.O. Box 271 (10990-0271)
PHONE..................................917 267-8920
Victoria D'Angelo, *Principal*
Victor D'Angelo, *Director*
EMP: 5
SALES (est): 220K Privately Held
SIC: 2399 Fabricated textile products

(G-15952)
GARDEN STATE SHAVINGS INC
16 Almond Tree Ln (10990-2442)
PHONE..................................845 544-2835
Kimberlee Martin, *CEO*
Barry Luyster, *Vice Pres*
▼ EMP: 15
SQ FT: 60,000
SALES (est): 1.4MM Privately Held
SIC: 2421 Sawdust, shavings & wood chips

(G-15953)
GEORGIA-PACIFIC LLC
17 Forester Ave (10990-1128)
P.O. Box 409 (10990-0409)
PHONE..................................845 986-2011
David M Root, *Manager*
EMP: 40
SALES (corp-wide): 42.9B Privately Held
WEB: www.gp.com
SIC: 3081 2759 Polyvinyl film & sheet; commercial printing
HQ: Georgia-Pacific Llc
133 Peachtree St Nw
Atlanta GA 30303
404 652-4000

(G-15954)
KECK GROUP INC (PA)
314 State Route 94 S (10990-3379)
PHONE..................................845 988-5757
Robert Koeck, *CEO*
EMP: 12
SQ FT: 20,000
SALES (est): 814.2K Privately Held
WEB: www.keckgroup.com
SIC: 2531 Pews, church

(G-15955)
KINGS QUARTET CORP
270 Kings Hwy (10990-3417)
PHONE..................................845 986-9090
Gary Bernstein, *President*
David Bernstein, *Treasurer*
Bernard Bernstein, *Admin Sec*
Kenneth Bernstein, *Admin Sec*
EMP: 5 EST: 1992

SALES (est): 309.8K Privately Held
SIC: 2435 Plywood, hardwood or hardwood faced

(G-15956)
KNG CONSTRUCTION CO INC
19 Silo Ln (10990-2872)
PHONE..................................212 595-1451
Mark V Azzopardi, *President*
Martin Azzopardi, *Opers Staff*
EMP: 10
SALES (est): 1.2MM Privately Held
SIC: 2431 1542 1521 Woodwork, interior & ornamental; commercial & office buildings, renovation & repair; general remodeling, single-family houses

(G-15957)
LABARBA-Q LLC
32 Highland Ave (10990-1819)
PHONE..................................845 806-6227
Joseph Labarbera,
EMP: 12 EST: 2015
SALES (est): 782.1K Privately Held
SIC: 2033 Barbecue sauce: packaged in cans, jars, etc.

(G-15958)
MECHANICAL RUBBER PDTS CO INC
Also Called: Minisink Rubber
77 Forester Ave Ste 1 (10990-1107)
P.O. Box 593 (10990-0593)
PHONE..................................845 986-2271
Cedric Glasper, *President*
Bill Thomas, *General Mgr*
Walter Kielb, *Sales Mgr*
Barry Moellman, *Sales Staff*
Lisa Rice, *Sales Staff*
EMP: 15
SQ FT: 53,000
SALES (est): 2.8MM Privately Held
SIC: 3061 3089 Mechanical rubber goods; molding primary plastic

(G-15959)
MEECO SULLIVAN LLC
3 Chancellor Ln (10990-3411)
PHONE..................................800 232-3625
EMP: 225
SQ FT: 50,000
SALES: 22MM Privately Held
SIC: 2499 4493 Mfg Wood Products Marina Operation

(G-15960)
TRACK 7 INC
3 Forester Ave (10990-1129)
PHONE..................................845 544-1810
Betsy Mitchell, *Principal*
EMP: 6
SALES (est): 990.8K Privately Held
SIC: 2653 Corrugated & solid fiber boxes

(G-15961)
TRANSPRTTION COLLABORATIVE INC
Also Called: Trans Tech Bus
7 Lake Station Rd (10990-3426)
PHONE..................................845 988-2333
John Phraner, *Ch of Bd*
EMP: 39
SALES (est): 9.4MM Privately Held
SIC: 3711 Motor vehicles & car bodies

(G-15962)
WARWICK VALLEY WINE CO
Also Called: Warwick Vly Winery Distillary
114 Little York Rd (10990-2231)
P.O. Box 354 (10990-0354)
PHONE..................................845 258-4858
Joseph Grizzanti, *Partner*
Jeremy Kidde, *Vice Pres*
Jason Grizzanti, *Admin Sec*
EMP: 15
SQ FT: 3,612
SALES (est): 2.8MM Privately Held
WEB: www.wvwinery.com
SIC: 2084 Wines

Washingtonville
Orange County

(G-15963)
BRISTOL GIFT CO INC
8 North St (10992-1113)
PHONE..................................845 496-2821
Matthew A Ropiecki Sr, *President*
Ellen Martarano, *Corp Secy*
Matthew J Ropiecki Jr, *Vice Pres*
EMP: 15
SQ FT: 7,000
SALES (est): 2.3MM Privately Held
WEB: www.bristolgift.net
SIC: 3499 Mfg Misc Fabricated Metal Products

(G-15964)
BROTHERHOOD AMERICAS
Also Called: Vinevrest Co
100 Brotherhood Plaza Dr (10992-2262)
P.O. Box 190 (10992-0190)
PHONE..................................845 496-3661
Hernan Donoso, *President*
Cesar Baeza, *Corp Secy*
▲ EMP: 35
SALES (est): 7.1MM Privately Held
WEB: www.brotherhoodwinery.net
SIC: 2084 Wines

Wassaic
Dutchess County

(G-15965)
PAWLING CORPORATION
Also Called: Standard Products Division
32 Nelson Hill Rd (12592-2121)
P.O. Box 200 (12592-0200)
PHONE..................................845 373-9300
Greg Holen, *Vice Pres*
Lou Musella, *Prdtn Mgr*
Ron Peck, *Purch Mgr*
Deborah Barbanti, *Purch Agent*
Tony Baruffo, *Engineer*
EMP: 65
SALES (corp-wide): 44MM Privately Held
WEB: www.pawling.com
SIC: 3061 3446 2273 Mechanical rubber goods; architectural metalwork; carpets & rugs
PA: Pawling Corporation
157 Charles Colman Blvd
Pawling NY 12564
845 855-1000

(G-15966)
PRESRAY CORPORATION
Also Called: Door Dam
32 Nelson Hill Rd (12592-2121)
P.O. Box 200 (12592-0200)
PHONE..................................845 373-9300
Theodore C Hollander, *Ch of Bd*
Jason Smith, *President*
Kevin Harris, *General Mgr*
Jered Tuberville, *Opers Mgr*
Ephraim Joseph, *Engineer*
▲ EMP: 25 EST: 1955
SQ FT: 50,000
SALES (est): 6.1MM
SALES (corp-wide): 44MM Privately Held
WEB: www.presray.com
SIC: 3442 Metal doors
PA: Pawling Corporation
157 Charles Colman Blvd
Pawling NY 12564
845 855-1000

(G-15967)
WALL PROTECTION PRODUCTS LLC
Also Called: Wallguard.com
32 Nelson Hill Rd (12592-2121)
P.O. Box 1109, Dover Plains (12522-1109)
PHONE..................................877 943-6826
Rose Davis, *General Mgr*
Ralph Skokan, *CFO*
Rose Benson, *Manager*
Sandra McKeever, *Info Tech Mgr*
EMP: 30

Water Mill - Suffolk County (G-15968) — GEOGRAPHIC SECTION

SALES (est): 3.1MM Privately Held
SIC: 3069 Rubber floor coverings, mats & wallcoverings

Water Mill
Suffolk County

(G-15968)
CAR DOCTOR MOTOR SPORTS LLC
Also Called: Car Doctor, The
610 Scuttle Hole Rd (11976-2520)
P.O. Box 1384, Amagansett (11930-1384)
PHONE...................631 537-1548
Ryan Pilla, *Owner*
EMP: 6
SALES (est): 450K Privately Held
SIC: 3949 Cartridge belts, sporting type

(G-15969)
DEERFIELD MILLWORK INC
58 Deerfield Rd Unit 2 (11976-2151)
PHONE...................631 726-9663
Keith Dutcher, *President*
EMP: 11
SQ FT: 5,000
SALES (est): 1.8MM Privately Held
WEB: www.deerfieldmillwork.com
SIC: 2431 8712 Moldings, wood: unfinished & prefinished; architectural services

(G-15970)
DUCK WALK VINYARDS
231 Montauk Hwy (11976-2639)
P.O. Box 962 (11976-0962)
PHONE...................631 726-7555
Herodotus Damianos, *President*
Alexander Damianos, *Vice Pres*
Pamela Przepiora, *Manager*
EMP: 20
SQ FT: 22,470
SALES (est): 1.9MM Privately Held
WEB: www.duckwalk.com
SIC: 2084 Wines

(G-15971)
WALPOLE WOODWORKERS INC
779 Montauk Hwy (11976-2607)
P.O. Box 1281 (11976-1281)
PHONE...................631 726-2859
Lou Maglio, *President*
EMP: 8
SALES (corp-wide): 85.2MM Privately Held
WEB: www.walpolewoodworkers.com
SIC: 2499 5211 5712 2452 Fencing, wood; fencing; outdoor & garden furniture; prefabricated wood buildings; prefabricated metal buildings; wood household furniture
PA: Walpole Woodworkers, Inc.
  767 East St
  Walpole MA 02081
  508 668-2800

(G-15972)
WONDER NATURAL FOODS CORP (PA)
670 Montauk Hwy Unit 2 (11976-3700)
PHONE...................631 726-4433
Lloyd Lasdon, *CEO*
Stuart Lasdon, *COO*
▲ EMP: 8
SALES (est): 1MM Privately Held
WEB: www.peanutwonder.com
SIC: 2099 Peanut butter

Waterford
Saratoga County

(G-15973)
CASCADES TSSUE GROUP-SALES INC
148 Hudson River Rd (12188-1908)
PHONE...................518 238-1900
Andre Lair, *Manager*
EMP: 100
SALES (corp-wide): 3.3B Privately Held
SIC: 2676 Towels, napkins & tissue paper products
HQ: Cascades Tissue Group-Sales Inc.
  148 Hudson River Rd
  Waterford NY 12188
  819 363-5100

(G-15974)
CASCADES TSSUE GROUP-SALES INC (HQ)
148 Hudson River Rd (12188-1908)
P.O. Box 369 (12188-0369)
PHONE...................819 363-5100
Daniel Morneau, *President*
Gary A Hayden, *Chairman*
Maryse Fernet, *Vice Pres*
David Pierro, *Vice Pres*
Jeffrey South, *Production*
▲ EMP: 40
SALES (est): 30.8MM
SALES (corp-wide): 3.3B Privately Held
SIC: 2621 Absorbent paper
PA: Cascades Inc
  404 Boul Marie-Victorin
  Kingsey Falls QC J0A 1
  819 363-5100

(G-15975)
EVONIK CORPORATION
7 Schoolhouse Ln (12188-1931)
P.O. Box 188 (12188-0188)
PHONE...................518 233-7090
Carlos Araujo, *Business Mgr*
Gina Pettinelli, *Counsel*
Alexander Weber, *Vice Pres*
Terri Owens, *Plant Mgr*
Jonathan Shan, *Opers Mgr*
EMP: 32
SALES (corp-wide): 2.4B Privately Held
SIC: 2869 Industrial organic chemicals
HQ: Evonik Corporation
  299 Jefferson Rd
  Parsippany NJ 07054
  973 929-8000

(G-15976)
HALFMOON TOWN WATER DEPARTMENT
8 Brookwood Rd (12188-1206)
PHONE...................518 233-7489
Frank Tironi, *Director*
EMP: 9
SALES (est): 603.6K Privately Held
SIC: 2899 Water treating compounds

(G-15977)
MAXIMUM SECURITY PRODUCTS CORP
Also Called: Hillside Iron Works
3 Schoolhouse Ln (12188-1931)
PHONE...................518 233-1800
Joseph Burch, *President*
Robert Magee, *Vice Pres*
Harold Hatfield, *Treasurer*
▲ EMP: 50
SQ FT: 100,000
SALES (est): 10.7MM Privately Held
WEB: www.maximumsecuritycorp.com
SIC: 3499 2542 2531 3446 Fire- or burglary-resistive products; partitions & fixtures, except wood; public building & related furniture; stairs, fire escapes, balconies, railings & ladders

(G-15978)
MILLWOOD INC
430 Hudson River Rd (12188-1916)
PHONE...................518 233-1475
Mike Cusack, *Branch Mgr*
EMP: 17 Privately Held
SIC: 3565 5084 Packaging machinery; packaging machinery & equipment
PA: Millwood, Inc.
  3708 International Blvd
  Vienna OH 44473

(G-15979)
MOMENTIVE PERFORMANCE LLC (DH)
260 Hudson River Rd (12188-1910)
PHONE...................281 325-3536
Douglas A Johns, *Vice Pres*
EMP: 1

SALES (est): 1.3MM
SALES (corp-wide): 2.3B Publicly Held
SIC: 2899 Chemical preparations

(G-15980)
MOMENTIVE PERFORMANCE MTLS INC
260 Hudson River Rd (12188-1910)
PHONE...................614 986-2495
Steve Delarge, *Opers Staff*
EMP: 1500
SALES (corp-wide): 2.3B Publicly Held
WEB: www.gewaterford.com
SIC: 2869 Silicones
HQ: Momentive Performance Materials Inc.
  260 Hudson River Rd
  Waterford NY 12188

(G-15981)
MOMENTIVE PERFORMANCE MTLS INC (DH)
260 Hudson River Rd (12188-1910)
PHONE...................518 237-3330
John G Boss, *President*
Nathan E Fisher, *Exec VP*
Brian Berger, *Vice Pres*
Craig R Branchfield, *Vice Pres*
Erick Asmussen, *CFO*
◆ EMP: 20
SALES: 2.3B Publicly Held
WEB: www.gewaterford.com
SIC: 2869 3479 3679 Silicones; coating of metals with silicon; electronic crystals; quartz crystals, for electronic application
HQ: Mpm Intermediate Holdings Inc.
  260 Hudson River Rd
  Waterford NY 12188
  518 237-3330

(G-15982)
MOMENTIVE PRFMCE MTLS HOLDINGS
Also Called: Momentive Prfmce Mtls Holdings
260 Hudson River Rd (12188-1910)
PHONE...................518 237-3330
Bradley J Bell, *Ch of Bd*
Douglas Johns, *Exec VP*
Gennaro Sposito, *Production*
Bill Carter, *CFO*
Geroge Knight, *Treasurer*
EMP: 9270
SALES (est): 990.1K Privately Held
SIC: 2869 3479 Silicones; coating of metals with silicon
PA: Hexion Holdings Llc
  180 E Broad St Fl 30
  Columbus OH 43215

(G-15983)
MPM HOLDINGS INC
260 Hudson River Rd (12188-1910)
PHONE...................518 237-3330
Douglas A Johns, *Branch Mgr*
EMP: 293
SALES (corp-wide): 2.3B Publicly Held
SIC: 2869 Silicones
PA: Mpm Holdings Inc.
  260 Hudson River Rd
  Waterford NY 12188
  518 237-3330

(G-15984)
MPM HOLDINGS INC (PA)
Also Called: MOMENTIVE
260 Hudson River Rd (12188-1910)
PHONE...................518 237-3330
Bradley J Bell, *Ch of Bd*
John G Boss, *President*
John D Moran, *Senior VP*
Rick Schumacher, *Vice Pres*
Bart Bills, *Project Mgr*
EMP: 5
SALES: 2.3B Publicly Held
SIC: 2869 3479 3679 Silicones; silicone resins; coating of metals with silicon; electronic crystals; quartz crystals, for electronic application

(G-15985)
MPM INTERMEDIATE HOLDINGS INC (HQ)
260 Hudson River Rd (12188-1910)
PHONE...................518 237-3330
John G Boss, *President*
Brian D Berger, *CFO*

EMP: 2 EST: 2014
SALES (est): 2.3B Publicly Held
SIC: 2869 3479 3679 Silicones; coating of metals with silicon; electronic crystals; quartz crystals, for electronic application
PA: Mpm Holdings Inc.
  260 Hudson River Rd
  Waterford NY 12188
  518 237-3330

(G-15986)
MPM SILICONES LLC
Also Called: Momentive
260 Hudson River Rd (12188-1910)
PHONE...................518 233-3330
Jack Boss, *CEO*
Erick Asnussen, *CFO*
Brian Berger, *Treasurer*
Jeffrey Stelling, *Finance*
Louise Watson, *Manager*
EMP: 4600
SALES (est): 228.8MM
SALES (corp-wide): 2.3B Publicly Held
SIC: 2869 Silicones
HQ: Momentive Performance Materials Inc.
  260 Hudson River Rd
  Waterford NY 12188

(G-15987)
SOFT-TEX INTERNATIONAL INC
Also Called: Soft-Tex Manufacturing Co
428 Hudson River Rd (12188-1916)
P.O. Box 278 (12188-0278)
PHONE...................800 366-2324
Jeff Chilton, *CEO*
Michael Wilker, *Senior VP*
Keith Bolton, *Vice Pres*
Erik Sanchez, *Vice Pres*
John Timmerman, *Vice Pres*
▲ EMP: 90
SQ FT: 120,000
SALES (est): 18.2MM Privately Held
WEB: www.bedpillows.com
SIC: 2392 Cushions & pillows

(G-15988)
STEPPING STONES ONE DAY SIGNS
105 Broad St (12188-2313)
P.O. Box 128 (12188-0128)
PHONE...................518 237-5774
John Matson, *President*
Paul Matson, *Vice Pres*
EMP: 5
SQ FT: 3,000
SALES (est): 517.4K Privately Held
SIC: 3993 Signs & advertising specialties

(G-15989)
UPSTATE PIPING PRODUCTS INC
95 Hudson River Rd (12188-1937)
P.O. Box 321 (12188-0321)
PHONE...................518 238-3457
Bob Lafountain, *President*
EMP: 3
SQ FT: 7,500
SALES (est): 2MM Privately Held
SIC: 3462 Flange, valve & pipe fitting forgings, ferrous

(G-15990)
URSULA OF SWITZERLAND INC (PA)
Also Called: Ursula Company Store
31 Mohawk Ave (12188-2290)
PHONE...................518 237-2580
Ursula G Rickenbacher, *President*
Meinrad Rickenbacher, *Treasurer*
EMP: 22
SQ FT: 35,000
SALES (est): 2.5MM Privately Held
WEB: www.ursula.com
SIC: 2335 2337 2331 Gowns, formal; ensemble dresses: women's, misses' & juniors'; women's & misses' suits & coats; women's & misses' blouses & shirts

GEOGRAPHIC SECTION

Waterloo
Seneca County

(G-15991)
EVANS CHEMETICS LP
228 E Main St (13165-1534)
PHONE 315 539-9221
Chris Jansen, *Maint Spvr*
Kenneth Weber, *Production*
Jeff Mooneyhan, *Engineer*
Pat Wrobel, *Engineer*
Bernie Souza, *Sales Mgr*
EMP: 55
SALES (est): 10.7MM
SALES (corp-wide): 29.7MM **Privately Held**
WEB: www.evanschemetics.com
SIC: 2899 Acids
PA: Evans Chemetics Lp
   Glenpointe Center West 4
   Teaneck NJ 07666
   201 992-3100

(G-15992)
FINGER LAKES CONVEYORS INC
2359 State Route 414 E (13165-9633)
PHONE 315 539-9246
Michael J Gelder, *Ch of Bd*
EMP: 9
SQ FT: 37,000
SALES: 806.5K **Privately Held**
WEB: www.flconveyors.com
SIC: 3499 1796 Fire- or burglary-resistive products; machinery installation

(G-15993)
FRAZIER INDUSTRIAL COMPANY
1291 Waterloo Geneva Rd (13165-1201)
PHONE 315 539-9256
Staci Predicho, *Human Resources*
EMP: 55
SQ FT: 62,116
SALES (corp-wide): 288MM **Privately Held**
WEB: www.ecologic.com
SIC: 2542 3441 Pallet racks: except wood; fabricated structural metal
PA: Frazier Industrial Company
   91 Fairview Ave
   Long Valley NJ 07853
   908 876-3001

(G-15994)
GHARANA INDUSTRIES LLC
Also Called: Ganesh Foods
61 Swift St (13165-1124)
PHONE 315 651-4004
◆ **EMP:** 6
SQ FT: 122,000
SALES (est): 420K **Privately Held**
SIC: 2022 Mfg Cheese

(G-15995)
HAMPSHIRE CHEMICAL CORP
228 E Main St (13165-1529)
P.O. Box 700 (13165-0700)
PHONE 315 539-9221
Richard Babiarz, *Partner*
EMP: 100
SALES (corp-wide): 62.4B **Publicly Held**
SIC: 2869 2899 2819 Industrial organic chemicals; chemical preparations; industrial inorganic chemicals
HQ: Hampshire Chemical Corp
   2 E Spit Brook Rd
   Nashua NH 03060

(G-15996)
MARROS EQUIPMENT & TRUCKS
2354 State Route 414 (13165-8473)
PHONE 315 539-8702
John Marro Jr, *President*
EMP: 14 **EST:** 1946
SQ FT: 14,400
SALES (est): 1.4MM **Privately Held**
SIC: 3713 3536 Truck bodies (motor vehicles); hoists

(G-15997)
PETER PRODUCTIONS DEVIVI INC
2494 Kingdom Rd (13165-9400)
PHONE 315 568-8484
Peter Devivi, *President*
EMP: 10
SQ FT: 9,000
SALES (est): 1.5MM **Privately Held**
WEB: www.tapertite.com
SIC: 2431 Millwork

(G-15998)
ZYP PRECISION LLC
1098 Birdsey Rd (13165-9404)
PHONE 315 539-3667
Edward Huff,
EMP: 5
SALES (est): 365.2K **Privately Held**
SIC: 3541 Lathes, metal cutting & polishing

Watertown
Jefferson County

(G-15999)
A & K EQUIPMENT INCORPORATED
407 Sherman St (13601-3958)
PHONE 705 428-3573
Jim Lowe, *President*
Kevin Lowe, *Principal*
Cathy Lowe, *Corp Secy*
Andrew Lowe, *Vice Pres*
EMP: 5
SALES (est): 425.8K **Privately Held**
SIC: 3596 5046 Scales & balances, except laboratory; scales, except laboratory

(G-16000)
ALLIED MOTION TECHNOLOGIES INC
Also Called: Stature Electric
22543 Fisher Rd (13601-1090)
P.O. Box 6660 (13601-6660)
PHONE 315 782-5910
Bill Stout, *General Mgr*
Lenissa Chenoweth, *Materials Mgr*
Ron Wenzen, *Branch Mgr*
Jeff Shearer, *Technology*
EMP: 200
SALES (corp-wide): 252MM **Publicly Held**
WEB: www.alliedmotion.com
SIC: 3621 3546 Electric motor & generator parts; motors, electric; power-driven handtools
PA: Allied Motion Technologies Inc.
   495 Commerce Dr Ste 3
   Amherst NY 14228
   716 242-8634

(G-16001)
BARRETT PAVING MATERIALS INC
26572 State Route 37 (13601-5789)
PHONE 315 788-2037
Sylvain Gross, *General Mgr*
Scott Lockerbie, *Site Mgr*
Frank Simmons, *Branch Mgr*
EMP: 12
SQ FT: 820
SALES (corp-wide): 95.5MM **Privately Held**
WEB: www.barrettpaving.com
SIC: 3273 2951 1611 Ready-mixed concrete; asphalt paving mixtures & blocks; highway & street construction
HQ: Barrett Paving Materials Inc.
   3 Becker Farm Rd Ste 307
   Roseland NJ 07068
   973 533-1001

(G-16002)
BIMBO BAKERIES USA INC
1100 Water St (13601-2146)
PHONE 315 782-4189
Rick Kimbell, *Manager*
EMP: 165 **Privately Held**
SIC: 2051 Bakery: wholesale or wholesale/retail combined
HQ: Bimbo Bakeries Usa, Inc
   255 Business Center Dr # 200
   Horsham PA 19044
   215 347-5500

(G-16003)
BLACK RIVER BREWING CO INC
500 Newell St (13601-2428)
PHONE 315 755-2739
Michael Niezabytoski, *Owner*
EMP: 5
SALES (est): 330.7K **Privately Held**
SIC: 2082 Malt beverages

(G-16004)
BOTTLING GROUP LLC
Also Called: Pepsi Beverages Company
1035 Bradley St (13601-1248)
PHONE 315 788-6751
Eric Foss, *CEO*
Dan Wiseman, *General Mgr*
Darel Jones, *Info Tech Dir*
Winnie Parker, *Administration*
EMP: 39 **EST:** 1999
SALES (est): 4MM **Privately Held**
SIC: 2086 Soft drinks: packaged in cans, bottles, etc.; carbonated soft drinks, bottled & canned

(G-16005)
CAR-FRESHNER CORPORATION (HQ)
Also Called: Little Trees
21205 Little Tree Dr (13601-5861)
P.O. Box 719 (13601-0719)
PHONE 315 788-6250
Richard O Flechtner, *Chairman*
Nichole Phillips, *Human Res Mgr*
Kathy Cheney, *Sales Mgr*
Matthew Socha, *Sales Mgr*
Elizabeth Perry, *VP Mktg*
◆ **EMP:** 250 **EST:** 1952
SQ FT: 30,000
SALES (est): 75.5MM **Privately Held**
WEB: www.little-trees.com
SIC: 2842 Deodorants, nonpersonal

(G-16006)
CAR-FRESHNER CORPORATION
22569 Fisher Cir (13601-1058)
P.O. Box 719 (13601-0719)
PHONE 315 788-6250
Robert Swank, *Principal*
Mary Crooker, *Asst Director*
EMP: 59 **Privately Held**
SIC: 2842 Cleaning or polishing preparations
HQ: Car-Freshner Corporation
   21205 Little Tree Dr
   Watertown NY 13601
   315 788-6250

(G-16007)
CHRISTIAN BUS ENDEAVORS INC (PA)
Also Called: Coughlin Printing Group
210 Court St Ste 10 (13601-4546)
PHONE 315 788-8560
Michael A Biolsi, *President*
Gary Ingram, *Treasurer*
Laura Biolsi, *Accounts Mgr*
EMP: 10
SQ FT: 5,000
SALES (est): 1.6MM **Privately Held**
WEB: www.amfcoughlin.com
SIC: 2759 7374 Commercial printing; computer graphics service

(G-16008)
CLEMENTS BURRVILLE SAWMILL
18181 Van Allen Rd N (13601-5711)
PHONE 315 782-4549
Philip Clement, *President*
Betty Clement, *Vice Pres*
EMP: 9
SQ FT: 8,820
SALES (est): 700K **Privately Held**
SIC: 2448 2426 2421 Pallets, wood; hardwood dimension & flooring mills; sawmills & planing mills, general

(G-16009)
COCA-COLA REFRESHMENTS USA INC
22614 County Route 51 (13601-5064)
PHONE 315 785-8907
Jess Duck, *Manager*
EMP: 33
SALES (corp-wide): 35.4B **Publicly Held**
WEB: www.cokecce.com
SIC: 2086 Bottled & canned soft drinks
HQ: Coca-Cola Refreshments Usa, Inc.
   2500 Windy Ridge Pkwy Se
   Atlanta GA 30339
   770 989-3000

(G-16010)
CURRENT APPLICATIONS INC
275 Bellew Ave S (13601-2381)
P.O. Box 321 (13601-0321)
PHONE 315 788-4689
George M Anderson, *President*
Roger Snyder, *Corp Secy*
Christopher Gilbert, *Vice Pres*
Robert Olin, *Vice Pres*
◆ **EMP:** 49
SQ FT: 20,000
SALES (est): 10.6MM **Privately Held**
WEB: www.currentapps.com
SIC: 3621 Motors, electric

(G-16011)
CYCLOTHERM OF WATERTOWN INC
787 Pearl St (13601-9111)
PHONE 315 782-1100
Charles E Stafford, *President*
EMP: 25
SQ FT: 20,000
SALES (est): 885.7K **Privately Held**
SIC: 3443 3554 Boiler shop products: boilers, smokestacks, steel tanks; paper industries machinery

(G-16012)
DOCO QUICK PRINT INC
808 Huntington St (13601-2864)
P.O. Box 6370 (13601-6370)
PHONE 315 782-6623
Carolyn Osborne, *President*
Daniel Osborne, *Treasurer*
EMP: 6
SQ FT: 3,000
SALES (est): 770.2K **Privately Held**
SIC: 2752 Commercial printing, offset

(G-16013)
E AND V ENERGY CORPORATION
22925 State Route 12 (13601-5034)
PHONE 315 786-2067
Bill Austin, *Branch Mgr*
EMP: 18
SALES (corp-wide): 23.8MM **Privately Held**
SIC: 2911 Still oil
PA: E. And V Energy Corporation
   2737 Erie Dr
   Weedsport NY 13166
   315 594-8076

(G-16014)
GERTRUDE HAWK CHOCOLATES INC
21182 Salmon Run Mall Loo (13601-2248)
EMP: 20
SALES (corp-wide): 240.6MM **Privately Held**
SIC: 2064 Mfg Candy/Confectionery
PA: Gertrude Hawk Chocolates, Inc.
   9 Keystone Industrial Par
   Dunmore PA 18512
   570 342-7556

(G-16015)
HANSON AGGREGATES PA LLC
25133 Nys Rt 3 (13601-1718)
P.O. Box 130 (13601-0130)
PHONE 315 782-2300
Dan O'Connor, *Manager*
EMP: 10
SALES (corp-wide): 20.3B **Privately Held**
SIC: 1442 5032 Gravel mining; stone, crushed or broken

Watertown - Jefferson County (G-16016)

HQ: Hanson Aggregates Pennsylvania, Llc
7660 Imperial Way
Allentown PA 18195
610 366-4626

(G-16016)
HENDERSON PRODUCTS INC
Also Called: Henderson Truck Equipment
22686 Fisher Rd Ste A (13601-1088)
PHONE...................315 785-0994
Dave O'Brien, *Manager*
EMP: 22 **Publicly Held**
WEB: www.henderson-mfg.com
SIC: 3822 Ice maker controls
HQ: Henderson Products, Inc.
1085 S 3rd St
Manchester IA 52057
563 927-2828

(G-16017)
JAIN IRRIGATION INC
740 Water St (13601-2114)
PHONE...................315 755-4400
Aric Olson, *President*
EMP: 70
SALES (corp-wide): 64.8MM **Privately Held**
SIC: 3052 3523 Plastic hose; fertilizing, spraying, dusting & irrigation machinery
PA: Jain Irrigation, Inc.
6975 S Union Park Ctr # 600
Midvale UT 84047
909 395-5200

(G-16018)
JEFFERSON CONCRETE CORP
22850 County Route 51 (13601-5081)
PHONE...................315 788-4171
Mark Thompson, *CEO*
EMP: 55
SQ FT: 37,000
SALES (est): 8.9MM **Privately Held**
WEB: www.jeffconcrete.com
SIC: 3272 Manhole covers or frames, concrete; septic tanks, concrete; tanks, concrete; burial vaults, concrete or precast terrazzo

(G-16019)
JOHN VESPA INC (PA)
Also Called: Vespa Sand & Stone
19626 Overlook Dr (13601-5443)
PHONE...................315 788-6330
John Vespa Jr, *President*
Dorothy Vespa, *Admin Sec*
EMP: 13 **EST:** 1941
SQ FT: 2,400
SALES: 1.5MM **Privately Held**
SIC: 1422 1442 Crushed & broken limestone; construction sand mining; gravel mining

(G-16020)
KENAL SERVICES CORP
Also Called: Metal Man Services
1109 Water St (13601-2147)
PHONE...................315 788-9226
Kenneth Moseley, *President*
Michael Vecchio, *CFO*
EMP: 7
SQ FT: 15,272
SALES (est): 600K **Privately Held**
WEB: www.metalmanservices.com
SIC: 3446 Architectural metalwork

(G-16021)
KENT NUTRITION GROUP INC
810 Waterman Dr (13601-2371)
PHONE...................315 788-0032
Brad Coolidge, *Opers-Prdtn-Mfg*
EMP: 10
SQ FT: 13,608
SALES (corp-wide): 700.7MM **Privately Held**
WEB: www.blueseal.com
SIC: 2048 Livestock feeds
HQ: Kent Nutrition Group, Inc.
1600 Oregon St
Muscatine IA 52761
866 647-1212

(G-16022)
KNORR BRAKE HOLDING CORP (DH)
748 Starbuck Ave (13601-1620)
PHONE...................315 786-5356
Heinz Hermann Thiele, *President*
Dawn Wetzel, *Admin Asst*
▲ **EMP:** 1
SALES (est): 1.2B **Privately Held**
SIC: 3743 5013 Railroad equipment; motor vehicle supplies & new parts
HQ: Knorr-Bremse Ag
Moosacher Str. 80
Munchen 80809
893 547-0

(G-16023)
KNORR BRAKE TRUCK SYSTEMS CO (DH)
Also Called: New York Air Brake
748 Starbuck Ave (13601-1620)
P.O. Box 6760 (13601-6760)
PHONE...................315 786-5200
Peter Riedlinger, *Vice Ch Bd*
Heinz Hermann Thiele, *President*
Mike Hawthorne, *President*
Jamie Perkins, *Editor*
Jason Connell, *Senior VP*
▲ **EMP:** 445
SQ FT: 250,000
SALES (est): 1B **Privately Held**
SIC: 3743 Brakes, air & vacuum: railway

(G-16024)
KNOWLTON TECHNOLOGIES LLC
213 Factory St (13601-2748)
PHONE...................315 782-0600
Frederick G Rudmann, *CEO*
James Ganter, *Exec VP*
James Lee, *Vice Pres*
Nick Cassoni, *Plant Mgr*
Marty Crossman, *Safety Mgr*
▲ **EMP:** 130
SQ FT: 287,000
SALES (est): 59.9MM **Publicly Held**
SIC: 2621 Filter paper; specialty papers
PA: Eastman Chemical Company
200 S Wilcox Dr
Kingsport TN 37660

(G-16025)
LCO DESTINY LLC
Also Called: Timeless Frames
1 Fisher Cir (13601)
P.O. Box 28 (13601-0028)
PHONE...................315 782-3302
John Pope, *Vice Pres*
Sandy Durgan, *Opers Staff*
Kevin Davis, *Production*
Liana Newton, *Buyer*
Greg Gaston, *CFO*
◆ **EMP:** 300
SQ FT: 90,000
SALES (est): 60.5MM **Privately Held**
WEB: www.timelessframes.com
SIC: 2499 Picture frame molding, finished; picture & mirror frames, wood

(G-16026)
MARTINS DENTAL STUDIO
Also Called: Martin Dental Studio
162 Sterling St (13601-3311)
P.O. Box 228 (13601-0228)
PHONE...................315 788-0800
Richard Martin Jr, *President*
EMP: 7
SQ FT: 1,400
SALES (est): 951.7K **Privately Held**
SIC: 3843 8072 Teeth, artificial (not made in dental laboratories); dental laboratories

(G-16027)
MEXICO INDEPENDENT INC (PA)
Also Called: Salmon River News
260 Washington St (13601-4669)
PHONE...................315 963-3763
Mark Backus, *President*
R Charles Backus, *Vice Pres*
Horace Backus, *Treasurer*
EMP: 20 **EST:** 1924
SQ FT: 6,139
SALES (est): 1.9MM **Privately Held**
SIC: 2711 2741 Job printing & newspaper publishing combined; catalogs: publishing & printing

(G-16028)
NEW YORK AIR BRAKE LLC
781 Pearl St (13601)
PHONE...................315 786-5576
Michael Hawthorne, *President*
EMP: 35 **Privately Held**
SIC: 3743 4783 Brakes, air & vacuum: railway; railway motor cars; containerization of goods for shipping; crating goods for shipping; packing goods for shipping
HQ: New York Air Brake Llc
748 Starbuck Ave
Watertown NY 13601

(G-16029)
NEW YORK AIR BRAKE LLC (DH)
748 Starbuck Ave (13601-1620)
P.O. Box 6760 (13601-6760)
PHONE...................315 786-5219
Heinz Thiele, *Ch of Bd*
Frank Henderson, *President*
J Paul Morgan, *President*
Marshall G Beck, *Senior VP*
Taylor Boggs, *Engineer*
▲ **EMP:** 169
SALES (est): 22.5MM **Privately Held**
SIC: 3743 Brakes, air & vacuum: railway

(G-16030)
NORTHERN AWNING & SIGN COMPANY
Also Called: N A S C O
22891 County Route 51 (13601-5005)
PHONE...................315 782-8515
Michael Fitzgerald, *President*
EMP: 5
SQ FT: 4,000
SALES (est): 581.4K **Privately Held**
WEB: www.nascosigns.com
SIC: 3993 3444 2394 Signs & advertising specialties; sheet metalwork; awnings, fabric: made from purchased materials

(G-16031)
NORTHERN NY NEWSPAPERS CORP
Also Called: Watertown Daily Times
260 Washington St (13601-4669)
PHONE...................315 782-1000
John B Johnson Jr, *CEO*
Harold B Johnson II, *President*
Rich Fyle, *Editor*
Debbie Groom, *Editor*
Jerry Moore, *Editor*
EMP: 210
SQ FT: 30,000
SALES (est): 13.2MM
SALES (corp-wide): 32MM **Privately Held**
WEB: www.lowville.com
SIC: 2711 2752 Newspapers: publishing only, not printed on site; commercial printing, lithographic
PA: Johnson Newspaper Corporation
260 Washington St
Watertown NY
315 782-1000

(G-16032)
PETRE ALII PETROLEUM
Also Called: Express Mart
1268 Arsenal St (13601-2214)
PHONE...................315 785-1037
EMP: 6
SALES (est): 200K **Privately Held**
SIC: 2911 Petroleum Refiner

(G-16033)
SEMCO CERAMICS INC
363 Eastern Blvd (13601-3140)
PHONE...................315 782-3000
Alfred E Calligaris, *President*
Tony Marra, *Vice Pres*
Douglas Millr, *Asst Controller*
Joe Branch, *Officer*
EMP: 3
SQ FT: 30,000
SALES (est): 4MM
SALES (corp-wide): 178.3MM **Privately Held**
SIC: 3253 3251 Ceramic wall & floor tile; structural brick & blocks
PA: The Stebbins Engineering And Manufacturing Company
363 Eastern Blvd
Watertown NY 13601
315 782-3000

(G-16034)
TAYLOR CONCRETE PRODUCTS INC
20475 Old Rome Rd (13601-5509)
PHONE...................315 788-2191
Thomas O'Connor, *President*
Scott Kitto, *Vice Pres*
Ellen O'Connor, *Vice Pres*
Richard O'Connor, *Vice Pres*
Carmen Eisenhauer, *Sales Mgr*
EMP: 21 **EST:** 1932
SQ FT: 2,500
SALES: 4.1MM **Privately Held**
WEB: www.taylorconcrete.com
SIC: 3271 5032 5211 3272 Blocks, concrete or cinder: standard; concrete & cinder block; concrete & cinder block; concrete products

(G-16035)
TIMELESS DECOR LLC
22419 Fisher Rd (13601-1090)
P.O. Box 28 (13601-0028)
PHONE...................315 782-5759
Kathy Watson, *Human Res Dir*
Sandra Cesario, *Product Mgr*
Lisa Weber,
EMP: 118
SALES (est): 13MM **Privately Held**
SIC: 2599 3231 3952 7699 Hotel furniture; framed mirrors; frames for artists' canvases; picture framing, custom; art, picture frames & decorations

(G-16036)
WATERTOWN CONCRETE INC
24471 State Route 12 (13601-5784)
PHONE...................315 788-1040
Joseph Belcher, *President*
Jason Belcher, *Vice Pres*
Chris Gregory, *Finance Mgr*
EMP: 16
SQ FT: 10,000
SALES (est): 2MM **Privately Held**
SIC: 3273 Ready-mixed concrete

(G-16037)
ZIEGLER TRUCK & DIESL REPR INC
22249 Fabco Rd (13601-1775)
PHONE...................315 782-7278
Charles E Ziegler, *President*
Helen Ziegler, *Admin Sec*
EMP: 5
SALES: 425K **Privately Held**
SIC: 3531 Construction machinery

Waterville
Oneida County

(G-16038)
CENTER STATE PROPANE LLC (PA)
1130 Mason Rd (13480-2139)
PHONE...................315 841-4044
James Wratten,
Mike Buell,
EMP: 4
SALES (est): 1.1MM **Privately Held**
SIC: 1321 Butane (natural) production

(G-16039)
F & R ENTERPRISES INC (PA)
Also Called: Pumilia's Pizza Shell
1594 State Route 315 (13480-1516)
P.O. Box 345 (13480-0345)
PHONE...................315 841-8189
John Pumilia, *President*
EMP: 7
SALES (est): 1.1MM **Privately Held**
SIC: 2038 Pizza, frozen

Watervliet
Albany County

(G-16040)
ACTASYS INC (PA)
805 25th St (12189)
PHONE...................914 432-2336
Miles Flamenbaum, *CEO*

▲ = Import ▼=Export
◆ =Import/Export

GEOGRAPHIC SECTION

Michael Amitay, *President*
Daniele Gallardo, *President*
David Menicovich, *President*
◆ **EMP:** 6
SQ FT: 230,000
SALES: 360K **Privately Held**
SIC: 3714 Motor vehicle parts & accessories

(G-16041)
BIGBEE STEEL AND TANK COMPANY
Also Called: New York Tank Co
958 19th St (12189-1752)
PHONE 518 273-0801
Dwight McCombs, *Credit Mgr*
Brett Hemminger, *Sales Staff*
Elizabeth Mohler, *Sales Staff*
Brett Ziegler, *Sales Staff*
Tim Silvi, *Manager*
EMP: 25
SALES (corp-wide): 42.1MM **Privately Held**
WEB: www.highlandtank.com
SIC: 3443 3714 Farm storage tanks, metal plate; motor vehicle parts & accessories
PA: Bigbee Steel And Tank Company Inc
4535 Elizabethtown Rd
Manheim PA 17545
814 893-5701

(G-16042)
BONDED CONCRETE INC (PA)
303 Watervliet Shaker Rd (12189-3424)
P.O. Box 189 (12189-0189)
PHONE 518 273-5800
Salvatore O Clemente, *Ch of Bd*
Thomas A Clemente, *President*
Philip Clemente, *Vice Pres*
Scott Face, *Safety Dir*
Jude Clemente, *Treasurer*
EMP: 25 **EST:** 1964
SQ FT: 10,000
SALES: 10.8MM **Privately Held**
WEB: www.bondedconcrete.com
SIC: 3273 Ready-mixed concrete

(G-16043)
CARDISH MACHINE WORKS INC
7 Elm St (12189-1826)
PHONE 518 273-2329
Eugene J Cardish Jr, *President*
Charles Cardish, *Vice Pres*
EMP: 33 **EST:** 1933
SALES: 6.3MM **Privately Held**
WEB: www.cardishmachineworks.com
SIC: 3599 Machine shop, jobbing & repair

(G-16044)
COMFORTEX CORPORATION (DH)
Also Called: Comfortex Window Fashions
21 Elm St (12189-1770)
PHONE 518 273-3333
Thomas Marusak, *President*
Suk-Joung Kahng, *Principal*
Jim Barss, *VP Opers*
Jack Dooley, *Facilities Mgr*
Pat Harris, *Warehouse Mgr*
◆ **EMP:** 168
SQ FT: 100,000
SALES (est): 42.6MM **Privately Held**
WEB: www.comfortex.com
SIC: 2591 Window blinds; window shades
HQ: Hunter Douglas Inc.
1 Blue Hill Plz Ste 1569
Pearl River NY 10965
845 664-7000

(G-16045)
EXTREME MOLDING LLC
25 Gibson St Ste 2 (12189-3375)
PHONE 518 326-9319
Lynn Momrow,
Joanne Moon,
▲ **EMP:** 50
SQ FT: 13,500
SALES (est): 4MM **Privately Held**
WEB: www.extrememolding.com
SIC: 3089 Injection molding of plastics

(G-16046)
GENERAL BUSINESS SUPPLY INC
Also Called: Tech Valley Printing
2550 9th Ave (12189-1962)
PHONE 518 720-3939
John Smith, *President*
Dominick Dragone, *Accounts Mgr*
EMP: 55
SALES (est): 5.3MM **Privately Held**
SIC: 2759 2752 Business forms: printing; commercial printing, offset

(G-16047)
HARTCHROM INC
25 Gibson St Ste 1 (12189-3342)
PHONE 518 880-0411
Edgar Oehler, *CEO*
Bob Smith, *Technical Staff*
▲ **EMP:** 18
SQ FT: 33,000
SALES: 4.9MM
SALES (corp-wide): 1.2B **Privately Held**
WEB: www.hartchrom.com
SIC: 3471 3541 Plating of metals or formed products; anodizing (plating) of metals or formed products; grinding, polishing, buffing, lapping & honing machines
PA: Arbonia Ag
Amriswilerstrasse 50
Arbon TG
714 474-141

(G-16048)
LWA WORKS INC
2622 7th Ave Ste 50s (12189-1963)
PHONE 518 271-8360
Lance Weinheimer, *President*
▲ **EMP:** 5
SALES (est): 500K **Privately Held**
WEB: www.lanartworks.com
SIC: 3599 Machine shop, jobbing & repair

(G-16049)
SAINT-GOBAIN ABRASIVES INC
Also Called: Coated Abrasive Division
2600 10th Ave (12189-1766)
PHONE 518 266-2200
Judy Alison, *Manager*
John Snyder, *MIS Mgr*
EMP: 400
SQ FT: 1,880
SALES (corp-wide): 213.5MM **Privately Held**
WEB: www.sgabrasives.com
SIC: 3291 Abrasive products
HQ: Saint-Gobain Abrasives, Inc.
1 New Bond St
Worcester MA 01606
508 795-5000

(G-16050)
SOLID SEALING TECHNOLOGY INC
44 Dalliba Ave Ste 240 (12189-4017)
PHONE 518 874-3600
Gary L Balfour, *Ch of Bd*
Alan Fuierer, *COO*
Thomas Forbes, *Mfg Mgr*
Jennifer Salamack, *Design Engr*
Denise Balfour, *Human Res Mgr*
EMP: 25
SQ FT: 10,000
SALES (est): 5.5MM **Privately Held**
WEB: www.solidsealing.com
SIC: 3629 Rectifiers (electrical apparatus)

(G-16051)
STRECKS INC
Also Called: Streck's Machinery
800 1st St (12189-3501)
PHONE 518 273-4410
Lloyd Demaranville, *President*
Christine Demaranville, *Vice Pres*
Emmy O'Brien, *Treasurer*
▲ **EMP:** 20 **EST:** 1952
SQ FT: 50,000
SALES (est): 3.3MM **Privately Held**
SIC: 3599 7692 7629 Machine shop, jobbing & repair; welding repair; electrical repair shops

(G-16052)
TIS ANSONIA LLC
70 Cohoes Rd (12189-1829)
PHONE 518 272-4920
Mary Matwa, *Principal*
Mike Moran, *Opers Mgr*
Doug Gerrity, *Sales Mgr*
Ron Sievert, *Asst Office Mgr*
▲ **EMP:** 11
SALES (est): 1MM **Privately Held**
SIC: 7694 Electric motor repair

(G-16053)
TROY BELTING AND SUPPLY CO (PA)
70 Cohoes Rd (12189-1895)
PHONE 518 272-4920
Jason W Smith, *Ch of Bd*
Jason Smith, *Vice Pres*
Doug Gerrity, *Sales Mgr*
Fred O'Donnell, *Sales Mgr*
Joshua Trombley, *Sales Mgr*
EMP: 67
SQ FT: 55,000
SALES (est): 16.5MM **Privately Held**
WEB: www.troybelting.com
SIC: 7694 3052 5084 5085 Electric motor repair; rubber & plastics hose & beltings; industrial machinery & equipment; industrial supplies; conveyors & conveying equipment; motors & generators

(G-16054)
TROY INDUSTRIAL SOLUTIONS
70 Cohoes Rd (12189-1829)
PHONE 518 272-4920
Dennis Pierce, *Business Mgr*
David Barcomb, *Vice Pres*
Matt Lapoint, *Project Mgr*
Mike Moran, *Opers Mgr*
Doug Rogers, *Warehouse Mgr*
EMP: 13
SALES (est): 1.3MM **Privately Held**
SIC: 7694 Electric motor repair

(G-16055)
UTILITY SYSTEMS TECH INC
70 Cohoes Rd (12189-1829)
P.O. Box 110, Latham (12110-0110)
PHONE 518 326-4142
Robert Degeneff, *President*
Doug Marble, *President*
Mark Degeneffe, *General Mgr*
David Wightman, *General Mgr*
Jeff Foran, *Engineer*
EMP: 13
SALES (est): 2.8MM **Privately Held**
WEB: www.ustpower.com
SIC: 3643 Current-carrying wiring devices

(G-16056)
VISTEC LITHOGRAPHY, INC.
125 Monroe St (12189-4019)
PHONE 518 874-3000
EMP: 45
SQ FT: 29,000 **Privately Held**
SIC: 3559 Semiconductor manufacturing machinery

(G-16057)
WICKED SMART LLC
700 5th Ave (12189-3610)
PHONE 518 459-2855
Nicole Martyn, *Sales Staff*
Sarah Brewer, *Marketing Mgr*
Todd Van Epps, *Mng Member*
Marcie Van Epps,
EMP: 15
SALES (est): 1.1MM **Privately Held**
SIC: 2396 2395 Screen printing on fabric articles; embroidery & art needlework

---

Watkins Glen
Schuyler County

(G-16058)
BMS MANUFACTURING CO INC
2857 County Line Rd (14891-9615)
PHONE 607 535-2426
William C Meehan Jr, *CEO*
Beth Meehan, *Manager*
Norm Macwilliams, *Maintence Staff*
EMP: 45
SQ FT: 50,000
SALES (est): 7.2MM **Privately Held**
WEB: www.bmsmanufacturing.com
SIC: 7692 3599 3441 Welding repair; machine & other job shop work; fabricated structural metal

(G-16059)
LAKEWOOD VINEYARDS INC
4024 State Route 14 (14891-9630)
PHONE 607 535-9252
Christopher Lamont Stamp, *President*
David A Stamp, *Vice Pres*
Beverly Stamp, *Treasurer*
Teresa Knapp, *Shareholder*
Michael E Stamp, *Shareholder*
▲ **EMP:** 12
SQ FT: 7,500
SALES (est): 930K **Privately Held**
WEB: www.lakewoodvineyards.com
SIC: 2084 Wines

(G-16060)
SKYLARK PUBLICATIONS LTD
Also Called: Hi-Lites
217 N Franklin St (14891-1201)
PHONE 607 535-9866
Damir Lazaric, *Managing Prtnr*
Flyod Vlajic, *Partner*
Millie Gernold, *Sales Mgr*
EMP: 5
SQ FT: 3,184
SALES (est): 423.5K **Privately Held**
SIC: 2741 Shopping news: publishing only, not printed on site

(G-16061)
SUIT-KOTE CORPORATION
Also Called: Central Asphalt
20 Fairgrounds Ln (14891-1632)
PHONE 607 535-2743
Kevin Suits, *Branch Mgr*
EMP: 30
SQ FT: 11,524
SALES (corp-wide): 234.8MM **Privately Held**
WEB: www.suit-kote.com
SIC: 2951 1611 2952 Asphalt paving mixtures & blocks; highway & street construction; asphalt felts & coatings
PA: Suit-Kote Corporation
1911 Lorings Crossing Rd
Cortland NY 13045
607 753-1100

(G-16062)
US SALT LLC
Salt Point Rd (14891)
PHONE 607 535-2721
Jerry Murphy, *Chief Mktg Ofcr*
Alan Parry, *Manager*
Bill Clark, *Manager*
EMP: 100 **Privately Held**
SIC: 2899 Salt
HQ: Us Salt, Llc
10955 Lowell Ave Ste 500
Overland Park KS 66210

Waverly
Tioga County

(G-16063)
CHARM MFG CO INC
Also Called: Charm Pools
251 State Route 17c (14892-9507)
P.O. Box 294 (14892-0294)
PHONE 607 565-8161
Jane Spicer, *President*
Linda Spicer, *Corp Secy*
Kay Onofre, *Vice Pres*
Richard Spicer, *Vice Pres*
EMP: 50
SQ FT: 50,000
SALES: 2.1MM **Privately Held**
WEB: www.charmpools.com
SIC: 3949 5091 5999 Swimming pools, except plastic; hot tubs; spa equipment & supplies; hot tub & spa chemicals, equipment & supplies; sauna equipment & supplies

Waverly - Tioga County (G-16064) — GEOGRAPHIC SECTION

(G-16064)
DORY ENTERPRISES INC
184 Sr 17c (14892)
PHONE..................607 565-7079
Robert Rynone, *President*
EMP: 10
SQ FT: 3,000
SALES (est): 1.3MM **Privately Held**
SIC: 2653 5113 Corrugated boxes, partitions, display items, sheets & pad; bags, paper & disposable plastic

(G-16065)
GRANITE WORKS LLC
133 William Donnelly (14892-1547)
PHONE..................607 565-7012
Fred Elias, *Admin Mgr*
Jason Vandyk,
▲ **EMP:** 20
SALES (est): 3.3MM **Privately Held**
SIC: 3281 Curbing, granite or stone

(G-16066)
HANCOR INC
1 Wm Donnelly Ind Pkwy (14892-1599)
PHONE..................607 565-3033
Dave Markie, *Manager*
EMP: 80
SALES (corp-wide): 1.3B **Publicly Held**
SIC: 3082 3084 Tubes, unsupported plastic; plastics pipe
HQ: Hancor, Inc.
4640 Trueman Blvd
Hilliard OH 43026
614 658-0050

(G-16067)
LEPRINO FOODS COMPANY
400 Leprino Ave (14892-1351)
PHONE..................570 888-9658
Kate Blanchard, *Human Res Mgr*
Neil Brown, *Manager*
Charles Cannavino, *Supervisor*
EMP: 230
SALES (corp-wide): 1.8B **Privately Held**
WEB: www.leprinofoods.com
SIC: 2022 Natural cheese
PA: Leprino Foods Company
1830 W 38th Ave
Denver CO 80211
303 480-2600

(G-16068)
NEWS NOW WAVERLY
446 Broad St Apt 2 (14892-1471)
PHONE..................607 296-6769
Michael Palmer, *President*
EMP: 15
SALES (est): 273.6K **Privately Held**
SIC: 2711 2741 Newspapers, publishing & printing;

Wawarsing
Ulster County

(G-16069)
PRECISION MACHINING AND MFG
190 Port Ben Rd (12489)
P.O. Box 104 (12489-0104)
PHONE..................845 647-5380
Nick Gajdcz, *President*
Wasyl Gajdycz, *President*
Lisia Gajdycz, *Admin Sec*
EMP: 5
SQ FT: 6,500
SALES: 270K **Privately Held**
SIC: 3544 Special dies & tools

Wayland
Steuben County

(G-16070)
BELANGERS GRAVEL & STONE INC
10184 State Route 21 (14572-9544)
PHONE..................585 728-3906
Norb Belanger, *Ch of Bd*
EMP: 7
SALES (est): 665.9K **Privately Held**
SIC: 1442 Construction sand & gravel

(G-16071)
GUNLOCKE COMPANY LLC (HQ)
1 Gunlocke Dr (14572-9515)
PHONE..................585 728-5111
Don Wharton,
▲ **EMP:** 147
SQ FT: 720,000
SALES (est): 176.5MM
SALES (corp-wide): 2.1B **Publicly Held**
WEB: www.gunlocke.com
SIC: 2521 Wood office furniture
PA: Hni Corporation
600 E 2nd St
Muscatine IA 52761
563 272-7400

(G-16072)
SPECIALTY SERVICES
Also Called: Accent Printing &GRaphics
2631e Naples St (14572)
P.O. Box 397 (14572-0397)
PHONE..................585 728-5650
Randall Bergvall, *Owner*
EMP: 5
SQ FT: 12,000
SALES (est): 432.4K **Privately Held**
SIC: 2541 2431 Display fixtures, wood; millwork

Wayne
Schuyler County

(G-16073)
NEW MARKET PRODUCTS LLC
9671 Back St (14893)
P.O. Box 135 (14893-0135)
PHONE..................607 292-6226
Aaron Hoover,
Samuel Hoover,
EMP: 9
SQ FT: 7,500
SALES: 500K **Privately Held**
SIC: 3545 Tool holders

Webster
Monroe County

(G-16074)
ASHLY AUDIO INC
847 Holt Rd Ste 1 (14580-9193)
PHONE..................585 872-0010
David Parse, *CEO*
William Thompson, *Chairman*
John Sexton, *Vice Pres*
Rich Direnzo, *Purch Mgr*
Jim Franks, *Engineer*
▲ **EMP:** 42
SQ FT: 25,000
SALES (est): 10.8MM **Privately Held**
WEB: www.ashly.com
SIC: 3651 3663 Household audio equipment; radio & TV communications equipment

(G-16075)
AUTOMATION EVOLUTION LLC
800 Salt Rd (14580-9666)
PHONE..................585 241-6010
Fritz P Ruebeck, *Mng Member*
Margaret Nichols, *Manager*
Travis Schurman,
EMP: 7
SQ FT: 41,000
SALES: 400K **Privately Held**
SIC: 3823 Industrial process control instruments

(G-16076)
CALVARY DESIGN TEAM INC (PA)
Also Called: Calvary Robotics
855 Publishers Pkwy (14580-2587)
PHONE..................585 347-6127
Mark Chaney, *President*
Jim Diederich, *Business Mgr*
Steve Hakes, *Mfg Dir*
Mark Klino, *Project Mgr*
Thomas Lawrence, *Project Mgr*
▲ **EMP:** 200
SQ FT: 375,000
SALES: 65.4MM **Privately Held**
WEB: www.calvauto.com
SIC: 3599 8711 Custom machinery; mechanical engineering; industrial engineers

(G-16077)
CDA MACHINE INC
514 Vosburg Rd (14580-1043)
PHONE..................585 671-5959
William Crosby, *President*
EMP: 9
SQ FT: 13,400
SALES (est): 1MM **Privately Held**
WEB: www.cdamachine.com
SIC: 3599 Machine shop, jobbing & repair

(G-16078)
CGS FABRICATION LLC
855 Publishers Pkwy (14580-2587)
PHONE..................585 347-6127
Mark Chaney, *Owner*
EMP: 15 EST: 2012
SALES (est): 21.6MM **Privately Held**
SIC: 3469 Machine parts, stamped or pressed metal

(G-16079)
CLASSIC AUTOMATION LLC (PA)
800 Salt Rd (14580-9666)
PHONE..................585 241-6010
Margaret Nichols, *Vice Pres*
Fritz Ruebeck, *Mng Member*
▲ **EMP:** 40
SQ FT: 17,000
SALES: 10MM **Privately Held**
SIC: 3823 Controllers for process variables, all types; boiler controls: industrial, power & marine type

(G-16080)
CLINTON SIGNS INC
1407 Empire Blvd (14580-2101)
PHONE..................585 482-1620
Michael S Mammano III, *President*
EMP: 6 EST: 1938
SQ FT: 5,700
SALES: 400K **Privately Held**
WEB: www.clintonsigns.com
SIC: 3993 7389 1799 7336 Electric signs; sign painting & lettering shop; sign installation & maintenance; commercial art & graphic design

(G-16081)
DATA-PAC MAILING SYSTEMS CORP
1217 Bay Rd Ste 12 (14580-1958)
PHONE..................585 671-0210
Richard A Yankloski, *President*
Ana Yankloski, *Vice Pres*
EMP: 10
SQ FT: 3,000
SALES (est): 2.4MM **Privately Held**
WEB: www.data-pac.com
SIC: 3571 Electronic computers

(G-16082)
DIGITAL HOME CREATIONS INC
350 Shadowbrook Dr (14580-9108)
PHONE..................585 576-7070
Ryan J Hills, *CEO*
EMP: 5
SALES: 1.4MM **Privately Held**
SIC: 3491 3651 Automatic regulating & control valves; household audio & video equipment

(G-16083)
EAST SIDE MACHINE INC
625 Phillips Rd (14580-9786)
PHONE..................585 265-4560
Paul Derleth, *President*
Patrick Derleth, *Vice Pres*
Lou Rossetti, *Vice Pres*
EMP: 26
SQ FT: 16,000
SALES (est): 5.4MM **Privately Held**
WEB: www.esm1.com
SIC: 3599 Machine shop, jobbing & repair

(G-16084)
EMPIRE STATE WEEKLIES INC
Also Called: Wayne County Mail
46 North Ave (14580-3008)
PHONE..................585 671-1533
David Young, *President*
EMP: 20 EST: 1945
SQ FT: 5,100
SALES (est): 1.5MM **Privately Held**
WEB: www.empirestateweeklies.com
SIC: 2711 Job printing & newspaper publishing combined

(G-16085)
GRIFFIN MANUFACTURING COMPANY
1656 Ridge Rd (14580-3697)
P.O. Box 308 (14580-0308)
PHONE..................585 265-1991
Angelo Papia, *President*
Kristin P Papia, *Managing Dir*
Darryl Papia, *Vice Pres*
Gary Papia, *Vice Pres*
Terry Papia, *Vice Pres*
▲ **EMP:** 20 EST: 1946
SQ FT: 6,000
SALES (est): 3.7MM **Privately Held**
WEB: www.grifhold.com
SIC: 3545 Cutting tools for machine tools

(G-16086)
HEARING SPECH CTR OF ROCHESTER
Also Called: Sonus-USA
1170 Ridge Rd Ste 2 (14580-2977)
PHONE..................585 286-9373
EMP: 31
SALES (corp-wide): 5MM **Privately Held**
SIC: 3842 Hearing aids
PA: Hearing And Speech Center Of Rochester Inc
1000 Elmwood Ave Ste 400
Rochester NY 14620
585 271-0680

(G-16087)
JOHNSON CONTROLS INC
237 Birch Ln (14580-1301)
PHONE..................585 671-1930
Peter Baranello, *Manager*
EMP: 25 **Privately Held**
SIC: 2531 Seats, automobile
HQ: Johnson Controls, Inc.
5757 N Green Bay Ave
Milwaukee WI 53209
414 524-1200

(G-16088)
KAL MANUFACTURING CORPORATION
657 Basket Rd (14580-9764)
PHONE..................585 265-4310
Alan Liwush, *CEO*
Richard Liwush, *Ch of Bd*
Tim Lindsay, *Sales Mgr*
Erika Muscato, *Manager*
Sam Sudore, *Supervisor*
EMP: 37 EST: 1943
SQ FT: 50,000
SALES (est): 9.5MM **Privately Held**
WEB: www.kal-mfg.com
SIC: 3444 3845 3599 3441 Sheet metalwork; electromedical equipment; machine & other job shop work; fabricated structural metal

(G-16089)
KATHLEEN B MEAD
Also Called: Automatic Bar Machining Co
393 Coastal View Dr (14580-9037)
PHONE..................585 247-0146
Kathleen B Mead, *Owner*
EMP: 5 EST: 1957
SQ FT: 16,800
SALES (est): 284.3K **Privately Held**
SIC: 3451 Screw machine products

(G-16090)
OPTICOOL SOLUTIONS LLC
Also Called: Opticool Technologies
855 Publishers Pkwy (14580-2587)
PHONE..................585 347-6127
Barb Patrick, *QC Mgr*
EMP: 17

▲ = Import ▼=Export
◆ =Import/Export

SALES (est): 4.6MM Privately Held
SIC: 3585 Parts for heating, cooling & refrigerating equipment

(G-16091)
PLANAR OPTICS INC
858 Hard Rd (14580-8950)
PHONE..........................585 671-0100
Horst Koch, *President*
EMP: 7
SQ FT: 5,400
SALES (est): 1MM Privately Held
SIC: 3827 Optical instruments & lenses

(G-16092)
PRACTICAL INSTRUMENT ELEC INC
Also Called: Pie
34 May St Ste 3 (14580-3055)
PHONE..........................585 872-9350
Ronald P Clarridge, *CEO*
John Siccardi, *General Mgr*
Bogdan Habovskyy, *Technician*
EMP: 10
SALES (est): 2.2MM Privately Held
WEB: www.piecal.com
SIC: 3825 Engine electrical test equipment

(G-16093)
R D SPECIALTIES INC
560 Salt Rd (14580-9718)
PHONE..........................585 265-0220
Douglas R Krasucki, *President*
Grace Krasucki, *Treasurer*
EMP: 15
SQ FT: 8,000
SALES (est): 1.1MM Privately Held
WEB: www.rdspecialties.com
SIC: 3312 Bar, rod & wire products

(G-16094)
R P M MACHINE CO
755 Gravel Rd (14580-1715)
PHONE..........................585 671-3744
Timothy Mangus, *Partner*
Richard P Mangus, *Partner*
EMP: 5 **EST:** 1976
SALES (est): 160K Privately Held
SIC: 3451 Screw machine products

(G-16095)
RADAX INDUSTRIES INC
700 Basket Rd Ste A (14580-9757)
PHONE..........................585 265-2055
Rocco Sacco, *Ch of Bd*
Richard Sacco, *President*
Amy Years Formicola, *Admin Sec*
EMP: 27
SQ FT: 55,000
SALES (est): 6.3MM Privately Held
WEB: www.radax.com
SIC: 3452 Screws, metal

(G-16096)
RESPONSE CARE INC
38 Commercial St (14580-3106)
PHONE..........................585 671-4144
Myron Kowal, *President*
Richard Moore, *Co-Owner*
EMP: 7
SQ FT: 6,500
SALES (est): 1MM Privately Held
SIC: 3669 Intercommunication systems, electric

(G-16097)
SCHUTT CIDER MILL
1063 Plank Rd (14580-9399)
PHONE..........................585 872-2924
Martin Schutt, *Owner*
EMP: 10
SQ FT: 3,308
SALES (est): 765.8K Privately Held
WEB: www.schuttsapplemill.com
SIC: 2099 5499 5149 Cider, nonalcoholic; juices, fruit or vegetable; juices

(G-16098)
SICK INC
Lazerdata Division
855 Publishers Pkwy (14580-2587)
P.O. Box 448 (14580-0448)
PHONE..........................585 347-2000
EMP: 50 Privately Held
SIC: 3599 Mfg General Industrial Machinery

HQ: Sick, Inc
6900 W 110th St
Minneapolis MN 55438
952 941-6780

(G-16099)
SKANDACOR DIRECT INC
545 Basket Rd (14580-9610)
PHONE..........................585 265-9020
Johnathan Congdon, *President*
Brad Drever, *Managing Dir*
▲ **EMP:** 7
SQ FT: 6,000
SALES (est): 2.5MM Privately Held
SIC: 3555 Printing trades machinery

(G-16100)
STUDCO BUILDING SYSTEMS US LLC
1700 Boulter Indus Park (14580-9763)
PHONE..........................585 545-3000
Samantha Ellis, *Finance Mgr*
Allan Parr, *Mng Member*
▲ **EMP:** 30
SQ FT: 65,000
SALES (est): 13.6MM Privately Held
WEB: www.studcosystems.com
SIC: 3444 Studs & joists, sheet metal

(G-16101)
TG POLYMERS INC
667 Hills Pond Rd (14580-4034)
PHONE..........................585 670-9427
Thomas G Seidewand, *President*
EMP: 1
SALES (est): 7MM Privately Held
SIC: 2673 7389 Bags: plastic, laminated & coated;

(G-16102)
TRICON MACHINE LLC
820 Coventry Dr (14580-8422)
PHONE..........................585 671-0679
Gary German, *President*
EMP: 7 **EST:** 1979
SQ FT: 10,000
SALES (est): 1MM Privately Held
WEB: www.triconmachine.com
SIC: 3599 Custom machinery

(G-16103)
TRIDENT PRECISION MFG INC
734 Salt Rd (14580-9718)
PHONE..........................585 265-2010
Nicholas Juskiw, *President*
Brent Housel, *Vice Pres*
Andrew Juskiw, *VP Opers*
Dan Nuijens, *Plant Mgr*
Giriwar Sookram, *Opers Mgr*
▲ **EMP:** 95 **EST:** 1979
SQ FT: 60,000
SALES (est): 31.6MM Privately Held
WEB: www.tridentprecision.com
SIC: 3469 3545 3569 7373 Stamping metal for the trade; machine tool accessories; assembly machines, non-metalworking; computer-aided design (CAD) systems service; computer-aided manufacturing (CAM) systems service; laser welding, drilling & cutting equipment; sheet metalwork

(G-16104)
UNISEND LLC
249 Gallant Fox Ln (14580-9034)
PHONE..........................585 414-9575
Sheikh Wasim Khaled, *Principal*
Steve Muratore, *Principal*
EMP: 5 **EST:** 2012
SALES (est): 375.6K Privately Held
SIC: 3822 Building services monitoring controls, automatic

(G-16105)
UNISTEL LLC
860 Hard Rd (14580-8825)
PHONE..........................585 341-4600
Ana Nikolovska, *Principal*
Sankar Sewnauth,
▲ **EMP:** 99
SALES (est): 8.2MM Privately Held
SIC: 3999 Manufacturing industries

(G-16106)
WEBSTER ONTRIO WLWRTH PNNYSVER
164 E Main St (14580-3230)
P.O. Box 1135 (14580-7835)
PHONE..........................585 265-3620
Geoffrey Mohr, *Partner*
Mary Jill Mohr, *Partner*
EMP: 12
SQ FT: 1,000
SALES (est): 770.7K Privately Held
WEB: www.websterpennysaver.com
SIC: 2711 Newspapers

(G-16107)
WEBSTER PRINTING CORPORATION
46 North Ave (14580-3008)
PHONE..........................585 671-1533
W David Young, *President*
Leslie Young, *Admin Sec*
EMP: 18
SQ FT: 2,500
SALES (est): 1.5MM Privately Held
SIC: 2759 2791 2789 2752 Newspapers: printing; typesetting; bookbinding & related work; commercial printing, lithographic

(G-16108)
XEROX CORPORATION
800 Phillips Rd Ste 20599 (14580-9791)
PHONE..........................585 422-4564
Fax: 585 422-8576
EMP: 700
SALES (corp-wide): 10.2B Publicly Held
SIC: 3861 Mfg Photographic Equipment/Supplies
PA: Xerox Corporation
201 Merritt 7
Norwalk CT 06851
203 968-3000

(G-16109)
ZOMEGA TERAHERTZ CORPORATION
806 Admiralty Way (14580-3912)
PHONE..........................585 347-4337
Thomas Tongue, *CEO*
Wendy Zhang, *CFO*
EMP: 15
SALES (est): 3MM Privately Held
SIC: 3829 Measuring & controlling devices

Weedsport
Cayuga County

(G-16110)
BARBER WELDING INC
Also Called: Alpha Boats Unlimited
2517 Rte 31 W (13166)
P.O. Box 690 (13166-0690)
PHONE..........................315 834-6645
Stephen L Walczyk, *President*
Dave Dunham, *Plant Mgr*
▲ **EMP:** 20
SQ FT: 18,000
SALES (est): 2.5MM Privately Held
WEB: www.barberweldinginc.com
SIC: 7692 3441 Welding repair; fabricated structural metal

Wellsville
Allegany County

(G-16111)
ANNIES ICE
35 Herman Ave (14895-9513)
PHONE..........................585 593-5605
Laurie Hennessey, *Partner*
Joseph Hennessey, *Partner*
EMP: 5 **EST:** 1993
SALES (est): 210.9K Privately Held
SIC: 2097 Manufactured ice

(G-16112)
ARVOS INC
3020 Truax Rd (14895-9531)
PHONE..........................785 243-3300
Jay T Reynolds, *Branch Mgr*

EMP: 225 Privately Held
WEB: www.boilerperformance.com
SIC: 3443 Fabricated plate work (boiler shop); air preheaters, nonrotating: plate type
HQ: Arvos Inc.
3020 Truax Rd
Wellsville NY 14895
585 593-2700

(G-16113)
ARVOS INC (DH)
Also Called: Air Preheater
3020 Truax Rd (14895-9531)
P.O. Box 372 (14895-0372)
PHONE..........................585 593-2700
David Breckinridge, *President*
Brent Beachy, *President*
Karsten Stckrath, *President*
Ludger Heuberg, *CFO*
Guillaume Boutillot, *Marketing Staff*
EMP: 2
SALES (est): 249.8MM Privately Held
SIC: 3443 Air preheaters, nonrotating: plate type
HQ: Raymond Bartlett Snow Holding Llc
850 New Burton Rd Ste 201
Dover DE 19904
630 393-1000

(G-16114)
CURRENT CONTROLS INC
353 S Brooklyn Ave (14895-1446)
PHONE..........................585 593-1544
Robert Landon, *President*
Carl Baxter, *Engineer*
Jeremy McNaughton, *Engineer*
Jason Hamer, *Sales Mgr*
Bruce McNaughton, *Manager*
EMP: 150 **EST:** 1982
SQ FT: 25,000
SALES (est): 30.6MM Privately Held
WEB: www.currentcontrols.com
SIC: 3612 Control transformers

(G-16115)
CURTISS-WRIGHT ELECTRO-
37 Coats St Ste 200 (14895-1003)
PHONE..........................585 596-3482
David Schurra, *General Mgr*
EMP: 47
SALES (corp-wide): 2.2B Publicly Held
SIC: 3491 Automatic regulating & control valves; process control regulator valves; valves, automatic control
HQ: Curtiss-Wright Electro-Mechanical Corporation
1000 Wright Way
Cheswick PA 15024
724 275-5000

(G-16116)
DRESSER-RAND COMPANY
37 Coats St (14895-1003)
P.O. Box 592 (14895-0592)
PHONE..........................585 596-3100
Jason Mattison, *Project Mgr*
Aaron Palmatier, *Mfg Mgr*
Emily Arnold, *Buyer*
James Chalker, *Engineer*
James Smith, *Engineer*
EMP: 650
SALES (corp-wide): 97.7B Privately Held
WEB: www.dresser-rand.com
SIC: 3491 3511 Industrial valves; turbines & turbine generator sets; turbines & turbine generator sets & parts
HQ: Dresser-Rand Company
500 Paul Clark Dr
Olean NY 14760
716 375-3000

(G-16117)
GENESEE METAL PRODUCTS INC
106 Railroad Ave (14895-1143)
PHONE..........................585 968-6000
Michael P Oleksiak, *President*
EMP: 20
SQ FT: 28,000
SALES (est): 2.9MM Privately Held
SIC: 3441 Fabricated structural metal

Wellsville - Allegany County (G-16118)

(G-16118)
MATTESON LOGGING INC
2808 Beech Hill Rd (14895-9779)
PHONE.................................585 593-3037
Brian Matteson, *President*
Pammy Matteson, *Vice Pres*
EMP: 5
SALES (est): 411.3K **Privately Held**
SIC: 2411 Logging camps & contractors

(G-16119)
NORTHERN LIGHTS ENTPS INC
Also Called: Northern Lights Candles
3474 Andover Rd (14895-9525)
PHONE.................................585 593-1200
Andrew Glanzman, *President*
Jeannie Skiffington, *Principal*
Christina Glanzman, *Vice Pres*
Leslie Belsito, *Buyer*
Teri Shaughnessy, *Research*
◆ EMP: 120 EST: 1977
SQ FT: 20,000
SALES (est): 14.3MM **Privately Held**
WEB: www.northernlightscandles.com
SIC: 3999 5999 Candles; candle shops

(G-16120)
RELEASE COATINGS NEW YORK INC
125 S Brooklyn Ave (14895-1453)
PHONE.................................585 593-2335
Ralph Naples, *President*
Ralph A Naples, *President*
EMP: 5
SQ FT: 7,200
SALES (est): 1MM **Privately Held**
SIC: 2822 Synthetic rubber

(G-16121)
SANDLE CUSTOM BEARING CORP
1110 State Route 19 (14895-9120)
PHONE.................................585 593-7000
Eric Sandle, *President*
Diana Sandle, *Admin Sec*
▼ EMP: 9
SQ FT: 4,000
SALES (est): 1.6MM **Privately Held**
SIC: 3562 Ball & roller bearings

(G-16122)
SENECA MEDIA INC
Also Called: Wellsville Daily Reporter
159 N Main St (14895-1149)
PHONE.................................585 593-5300
Oak Duke, *Branch Mgr*
EMP: 12
SALES (corp-wide): 8.5MM **Privately Held**
WEB: www.eveningtribune.com
SIC: 2711 Newspapers: publishing only, not printed on site
PA: Seneca Media Inc
    32 Broadway Mall
    Hornell NY 14843
    607 324-1425

(G-16123)
SIEMENS GOVERNMENT TECH INC
Also Called: Sgt Dresser-Rand
37 Coats St (14895-1003)
P.O. Box 592 (14895-0592)
PHONE.................................585 593-1234
EMP: 405
SALES (corp-wide): 97.8B **Privately Held**
WEB: www.dresser-rand.com
SIC: 3511 Turbines & turbine generator sets & parts
HQ: Siemens Government Technologies, Inc.
    2231 Crystal Dr Ste 700
    Arlington VA 22202
    703 480-8901

```
┌─────────────────────┐
│   West Babylon      │
│   Suffolk County    │
└─────────────────────┘
```

(G-16124)
110 SAND COMPANY
170 Cabot St (11704-1102)
PHONE.................................631 694-2822
Tom Murphy, *Manager*
EMP: 17
SALES (corp-wide): 5.8MM **Privately Held**
SIC: 1442 Construction sand & gravel
PA: 110 Sand Company
    136 Spagnoli Rd
    Melville NY 11747
    631 694-2822

(G-16125)
A-MARK MACHINERY CORP
101 Lamar St (11704-1301)
PHONE.................................631 643-6300
Marcel Edelstein, *President*
Shelly Edelstein, *Corp Secy*
Paul Schwartz, *Vice Pres*
▲ EMP: 15
SQ FT: 24,000
SALES (est): 5.3MM **Privately Held**
SIC: 3555 Printing trades machinery

(G-16126)
A-QUICK BINDERY LLC
30 Gleam St Unit C (11704-1207)
PHONE.................................631 491-1110
Nick Koutsoliontos, *Owner*
John Liontos,
EMP: 5
SALES (est): 778.1K **Privately Held**
SIC: 2789 Bookbinding & related work

(G-16127)
ABERDEEN BLOWER & SHTMTL WORKS
401 Columbus Ave (11704-5541)
P.O. Box 1134 (11704-0134)
PHONE.................................631 661-6100
Peter Levine, *President*
John Rolleri, *Partner*
EMP: 7 EST: 1950
SALES (est): 1.5MM **Privately Held**
SIC: 3444 Sheet metal specialties, not stamped

(G-16128)
ADCOMM GRAPHICS INC
21 Lamar St (11704-1301)
PHONE.................................212 645-1298
EMP: 25
SQ FT: 5,000
SALES (est): 2.1MM **Privately Held**
SIC: 2741 7336 Misc Publishing Commercial Art/Graphic Design

(G-16129)
ADVANCE PRECISION INDUSTRIES
9 Mahan St Unit A (11704-1319)
PHONE.................................631 491-0910
Anton Korconkiewicz, *President*
EMP: 6 EST: 1963
SQ FT: 4,000
SALES (est): 479.1K **Privately Held**
SIC: 3599 Machine shop, jobbing & repair

(G-16130)
AIRCRAFT FINISHING CORP (PA)
100 Field St Unit A (11704-5550)
PHONE.................................631 422-5000
Sam Serigano, *President*
John Serigano, *Vice Pres*
Kathleen Serigano, *Treasurer*
Ann Serigano, *Admin Sec*
EMP: 16
SQ FT: 18,000
SALES (est): 2MM **Privately Held**
SIC: 3471 3479 Plating of metals or formed products; painting of metal products

(G-16131)
ALLMETAL CHOCOLATE MOLD CO INC
135 Dale St (11704-1103)
PHONE.................................631 752-2888
Joseph Micelli, *President*
John Micelli, *Admin Sec*
EMP: 10
SQ FT: 10,000
SALES (est): 1.3MM **Privately Held**
WEB: www.micelli.com
SIC: 3544 Industrial molds

(G-16132)
AMACON CORPORATION
49 Alder St Unit A (11704-1093)
PHONE.................................631 293-1888
Costas Antoniou, *President*
Ted Antoniou, *Vice Pres*
Henry Mancura, *Vice Pres*
Donald O'Day, *Vice Pres*
EMP: 11 EST: 1969
SALES (est): 1.2MM **Privately Held**
WEB: www.amacon.com
SIC: 3599 Machine shop, jobbing & repair

(G-16133)
AMERICAN ACRYLIC CORPORATION
400 Sheffield Ave (11704-5333)
PHONE.................................631 422-2200
Mandell Ziegler, *CEO*
Thomas C Ziegler, *President*
Marjorie Klyne, *Admin Sec*
◆ EMP: 20
SQ FT: 20,000
SALES (est): 1.8MM **Privately Held**
WEB: www.americanacrylic.com
SIC: 3083 3081 2821 Laminated plastics plate & sheet; unsupported plastics film & sheet; plastics materials & resins

(G-16134)
AMERICAN METAL SPINNING PDTS
21 Eads St (11704-1125)
PHONE.................................631 454-6276
Clark Morse, *President*
Michelle Morse, *Office Mgr*
EMP: 9
SQ FT: 8,000
SALES (est): 726K **Privately Held**
WEB: www.amermetalspinning.com
SIC: 3469 Spinning metal for the trade

(G-16135)
AMSCOR INC
119 Lamar St (11704-1301)
PHONE.................................800 825-9800
Scott Silberglied, *President*
Michael Silberglied, *Vice Pres*
EMP: 15
SQ FT: 10,000
SALES (est): 2.5MM **Privately Held**
WEB: www.amscorinc.com
SIC: 2542 Shelving, office & store: except wood

(G-16136)
AUTOMATION SOURCE TECHNOLOGIES (PA)
21 Otis St Unit B (11704-1440)
PHONE.................................631 643-1678
Peter Dougherty,
▲ EMP: 12 EST: 2012
SALES (est): 2MM **Privately Held**
SIC: 3621 Phase or rotary converters (electrical equipment)

(G-16137)
BABYLON IRON WORKS INC
205 Edison Ave (11704-1030)
PHONE.................................631 643-3311
Raymond Zahralban, *President*
EMP: 16
SQ FT: 14,000
SALES (est): 3.4MM **Privately Held**
SIC: 3446 Architectural metalwork

(G-16138)
BARTOLOMEO PUBLISHING INC
Also Called: Northport Printing
100 Cabot St Unit A (11704-1133)
PHONE.................................631 420-4949
Dan Bartolomeo, *President*
Patricia Bartolomeo, *Vice Pres*
EMP: 5
SQ FT: 17,200
SALES (est): 1.3MM **Privately Held**
SIC: 2759 2752 Screen printing; letterpress printing; flexographic printing; commercial printing, offset

(G-16139)
BEAM MANUFACTURING CORP
Also Called: Sigro Precision
107 Otis St Unit A (11704-1444)
PHONE.................................631 253-2724
Ernie Lampeter, *President*
EMP: 6 EST: 1966
SQ FT: 4,000
SALES (est): 856K **Privately Held**
SIC: 3599 Machine shop, jobbing & repair

(G-16140)
BROOKVALE RECORDS INC
Also Called: Looney Tunes CD Store
31 Brookvale Ave (11704-7901)
PHONE.................................631 587-7722
Kral Groger, *President*
EMP: 11
SALES (est): 950K **Privately Held**
SIC: 2782 Record albums

(G-16141)
BSD TOP DIRECT INC
68 Route 109 (11704-6208)
PHONE.................................646 468-0156
Elisha Mishael, *CEO*
EMP: 5
SALES (est): 330K **Privately Held**
SIC: 2096 Potato chips & similar snacks

(G-16142)
BURTON INDUSTRIES INC
243 Wyandanch Ave Ste A (11704-1593)
PHONE.................................631 643-6660
Charles Seelinger, *CEO*
Richard Santos, *President*
Dariusz Siniakowicz, *Exec VP*
Warren Hartman, *Vice Pres*
Thomas Seelinger, *Vice Pres*
EMP: 35 EST: 1971
SQ FT: 38,000
SALES (est): 7.8MM **Privately Held**
WEB: www.burtonheat.com
SIC: 3398 Metal heat treating

(G-16143)
BUSINESS CARD EXPRESS INC
300 Farmingdale Rd (11704)
PHONE.................................631 669-3400
William Richards, *President*
Robert Whitfield, *General Mgr*
Jerry Peirano, *Treasurer*
EMP: 40
SQ FT: 11,000
SALES (est): 5.4MM **Privately Held**
SIC: 2759 2752 Thermography; commercial printing, lithographic

(G-16144)
C J & C SHEET METAL CORP
433 Falmouth Rd (11704-5654)
PHONE.................................631 376-9425
James Thurau, *President*
EMP: 12
SALES (est): 970K **Privately Held**
SIC: 3444 Sheet metalwork

(G-16145)
CENTURY READY MIX INC
615 Cord Ave (11704)
P.O. Box 1065 (11704-0065)
PHONE.................................631 888-2200
Nicolina Nicolia, *President*
EMP: 6
SALES (est): 426K **Privately Held**
SIC: 3273 5039 Ready-mixed concrete; mobile homes

(G-16146)
CHECK-MATE INDUSTRIES INC
370 Wyandanch Ave (11704-1524)
PHONE.................................631 491-1777
Regina M Vieweg, *CEO*
Edward Tracy, *CFO*
Jacquilene Santaro, *Legal Staff*
EMP: 45
SQ FT: 23,000
SALES (est): 11.7MM **Privately Held**
SIC: 3469 Metal stampings

West Babylon - Suffolk County (G-16175)

(G-16147)
CHEM-TAINER INDUSTRIES INC (PA)
Also Called: Todd Enterprises
361 Neptune Ave (11704-5800)
PHONE..................................631 422-8300
Stuart Pivar, *Ch of Bd*
James Glen, *President*
Anthony Lamb, *Vice Pres*
Joe Maiello, *Vice Pres*
Vincent Amalfitano, *Sales Staff*
◆ EMP: 50
SQ FT: 20,000
SALES (est): 46.5MM **Privately Held**
WEB: www.chemtainer.com
SIC: 3089 Plastic containers, except foam

(G-16148)
CHURCH BULLETIN INC
200 Dale St (11704-1124)
P.O. Box 1659, Massapequa (11758-0911)
PHONE..................................631 249-4994
George Keenan Jr, *President*
EMP: 15
SALES (est): 1.6MM **Privately Held**
WEB: www.thechurchbulletininc.com
SIC: 2741 Business service newsletters: publishing & printing

(G-16149)
COMPUTERIZED METAL BENDING SER
91 Cabot St Unit A (11704-1132)
PHONE..................................631 249-1177
Kenneth Rosner, *President*
EMP: 16 EST: 2010
SALES (est): 980.2K **Privately Held**
SIC: 3441 Fabricated structural metal

(G-16150)
CUSTOM FRAME & MOLDING CO
97 Lamar St 101 (11704-1308)
PHONE..................................631 491-9091
Nick Maminakis, *President*
Dr Steven Lewen, *Vice Pres*
Michelle Lewen, *Admin Sec*
EMP: 12
SQ FT: 15,000
SALES (est): 1.5MM **Privately Held**
SIC: 3499 Picture frames, metal

(G-16151)
CUSTOM METAL INCORPORATED
Also Called: Custom Metal Fabrication
72 Otis St (11704-1406)
PHONE..................................631 643-4075
Stephen Pratt, *President*
Nancy Pratt, *Corp Secy*
EMP: 11
SQ FT: 11,300
SALES: 1.4MM **Privately Held**
WEB: www.custommetalfabrication.com
SIC: 3469 Machine parts, stamped or pressed metal

(G-16152)
DBS INTERIORS CORP
Also Called: Island Interiors
81 Otis St (11704-1405)
P.O. Box 1780 (11704-0780)
PHONE..................................631 491-3013
Robert Laurie, *President*
Ed Bundock, *Vice Pres*
EMP: 12
SQ FT: 7,000
SALES: 2MM **Privately Held**
SIC: 2519 2541 2517 2511 Mfg Household Furniture Mfg Wood Partitions/Fixt Mfg Wd Tv/Radio Cabinets Mfg Wood Household Furn Mfg Wood Kitchen Cabinet

(G-16153)
DISPLAY COMPONENTS MFG INC
Also Called: D C M
267 Edison Ave (11704-1020)
PHONE..................................631 420-0600
James P Devine III, *President*
Julie Braga, *Controller*
Barbara Jones, *Manager*
Donna Devine, *Admin Sec*
EMP: 30
SQ FT: 25,000
SALES (est): 5.1MM **Privately Held**
WEB: www.displaycomponents.com
SIC: 2542 Fixtures: display, office or store: except wood

(G-16154)
EAST CAST CLOR COMPOUNDING INC
Also Called: Linli Color
15 Kean St (11704-1208)
PHONE..................................631 491-9000
George Benz, *CEO*
Tony Arra, *President*
Jon Shuman, *Vice Pres*
EMP: 9
SQ FT: 10,000
SALES (est): 1.6MM **Privately Held**
WEB: www.linlicolor.com
SIC: 2865 3089 Dyes & pigments; extruded finished plastic products

(G-16155)
FAMOUS BOX SCOOTER CO
75 Rogers Ct (11704-6540)
PHONE..................................631 943-2013
Charles Rubino, *Owner*
EMP: 5
SALES (est): 217.8K **Privately Held**
SIC: 3944 Scooters, children's

(G-16156)
GAMMA ENTERPRISES LLC
Also Called: Gamma Lab
113 Alder St (11704-1001)
PHONE..................................631 755-1080
Clifford Morgan, *CEO*
Matthew Alvarez, *Controller*
▼ EMP: 30
SQ FT: 19,000
SALES: 7.9MM **Privately Held**
SIC: 2834 Vitamin, nutrient & hematinic preparations for human use

(G-16157)
GREAT EASTERN PASTA WORKS LLC
Also Called: Pasta People
335 Sheffield Ave (11704-5326)
PHONE..................................631 956-0889
Kambiz Morakkabi,
EMP: 20
SQ FT: 1,500
SALES (est): 2.1MM **Privately Held**
SIC: 2099 5149 Pasta, uncooked: packaged with other ingredients; pasta & rice

(G-16158)
ISOLATION DYNAMICS CORP
Also Called: Idc
66 Otis St Unit A (11704-1427)
P.O. Box 361, Merrick (11566-0361)
PHONE..................................631 491-5670
Max Borrasso, *President*
EMP: 20
SQ FT: 4,000
SALES (est): 3.6MM **Privately Held**
WEB: www.isolator.com
SIC: 3493 Steel springs, except wire

(G-16159)
ISOLATION TECHNOLOGY INC
73 Nancy St Unit A (11704-1428)
P.O. Box 460, Massapequa (11758-0460)
PHONE..................................631 253-3314
Bob Grefe, *President*
Robert Joyner, *Corp Secy*
▲ EMP: 6
SQ FT: 4,000
SALES (est): 1.1MM **Privately Held**
WEB: www.isolationtech.com
SIC: 3699 Electric sound equipment

(G-16160)
J & T METAL PRODUCTS CO INC
89 Eads St (11704-1105)
PHONE..................................631 226-7400
Thomas Lander, *President*
EMP: 20 EST: 1964
SQ FT: 18,000
SALES (est): 1.9MM **Privately Held**
SIC: 3443 Industrial vessels, tanks & containers; tanks, standard or custom fabricated: metal plate

(G-16161)
J C INDUSTRIES INC
89 Eads St (11704-1186)
PHONE..................................631 420-1920
Joseph V Celano, *Ch of Bd*
James Celano, *Vice Pres*
EMP: 30
SQ FT: 14,000
SALES (est): 5.4MM **Privately Held**
WEB: www.jcindustries.com
SIC: 3411 Metal cans

(G-16162)
J T D STAMPING CO INC
403 Wyandanch Ave (11704-1599)
PHONE..................................631 643-4144
Giovanni Bianco, *President*
Aldo D'Adamo, *Vice Pres*
Claudia Mina, *Technology*
EMP: 39
SQ FT: 20,000
SALES: 3.5MM **Privately Held**
WEB: www.jtdstamping.com
SIC: 3469 Metal stampings

(G-16163)
JALEX INDUSTRIES LTD
86 Nancy St (11704-1404)
PHONE..................................631 491-5072
Alexander Jedynski, *President*
EMP: 15
SQ FT: 7,000
SALES (est): 1.9MM **Privately Held**
SIC: 3541 Machine tools, metal cutting type

(G-16164)
JAVIN MACHINE CORP
31 Otis St (11704-1405)
PHONE..................................631 643-3322
Geri Spiezio, *CEO*
Sal Spiezio, *President*
Vincent Spiezio, *President*
John Zielinski, *QC Mgr*
Regina Heinz, *Office Mgr*
EMP: 15
SQ FT: 16,000
SALES (est): 3MM **Privately Held**
WEB: www.javinmachine.net
SIC: 3599 Machine shop, jobbing & repair

(G-16165)
JF MACHINE SHOP INC
89 Otis St Unit A (11704-1442)
PHONE..................................631 491-7273
Anthony Schiavone, *President*
EMP: 7 EST: 1978
SQ FT: 9,000
SALES (est): 1.5MM **Privately Held**
WEB: www.jfmachine.com
SIC: 3599 Machine shop, jobbing & repair

(G-16166)
JOHNNYS MACHINE SHOP
81 Mahan St (11704-1303)
PHONE..................................631 338-9733
Juan Campos, *Owner*
EMP: 5
SALES: 200K **Privately Held**
SIC: 3599 Machine & other job shop work; machine shop, jobbing & repair

(G-16167)
KESSLER THERMOMETER CORP
40 Gleam St (11704-1205)
PHONE..................................631 841-5500
Robert Peyser, *President*
▲ EMP: 9
SALES (est): 1.1MM **Privately Held**
SIC: 3823 Thermometers, filled system: industrial process type

(G-16168)
KING ALBUM INC
20 Kean St (11704-1209)
PHONE..................................631 253-9500
Warren King, *President*
EMP: 20
SQ FT: 7,700
SALES: 2.2MM **Privately Held**
SIC: 2782 Albums

(G-16169)
L K MANUFACTURING CORP
56 Eads St (11704-1106)
P.O. Box 167, Huntington Station (11746-0137)
PHONE..................................631 243-6910
Robert Lutzker, *President*
Kay Kelly, *Vice Pres*
Samuel Martin, *Vice Pres*
EMP: 22
SQ FT: 15,000
SALES (est): 1.9MM **Privately Held**
WEB: www.lkmfg.com
SIC: 3089 5065 Kitchenware, plastic; electronic parts & equipment

(G-16170)
LETTERAMA INC (PA)
111 Cabot St (11704-1100)
PHONE..................................516 349-0800
Mark Costa, *President*
▼ EMP: 6 EST: 1959
SQ FT: 30,000
SALES: 3MM **Privately Held**
SIC: 3993 Signs & advertising specialties

(G-16171)
LINZER PRODUCTS CORP (DH)
248 Wyandanch Ave (11704-1506)
PHONE..................................631 253-3333
Brent Swenson, *President*
Tony Hazantonis, *General Mgr*
Ted Robinson, *Vice Pres*
Mark Saji, *Treasurer*
Rosemary Mailinger, *Asst Controller*
▲ EMP: 200 EST: 1892
SQ FT: 166,000
SALES: 120MM
SALES (corp-wide): 13.8MM **Privately Held**
SIC: 3991 5198 Paint & varnish brushes; paint brushes, rollers, sprayers

(G-16172)
M T D CORPORATION
41 Otis St (11704-1405)
PHONE..................................631 491-3905
Matthew Turnbull, *President*
Michael Deletto, *Vice Pres*
EMP: 10
SQ FT: 6,500
SALES (est): 1.2MM **Privately Held**
WEB: www.makeupart.net
SIC: 2521 2511 Wood office furniture; wood household furniture

(G-16173)
MAGELLAN AEROSPACE PROCESSING
Also Called: Ripak Aerospace Processing
165 Field St (11704-1210)
PHONE..................................631 694-1818
Phillip Underwood, *President*
Karen Yoshiki-Gravelsins, *Vice Pres*
John Dekker, *CFO*
EMP: 8
SQ FT: 72,000
SALES (est): 217.6K
SALES (corp-wide): 759.1MM **Privately Held**
SIC: 3724 3429 Aircraft engines & engine parts; aircraft hardware
PA: Magellan Aerospace Corporation
3160 Derry Rd E
Mississauga ON L4T 1
905 677-1889

(G-16174)
MATRIX MACHINING CORP
69 B Nancy St Unitb (11704)
PHONE..................................631 643-6690
Joseph Abdale, *President*
Ray Abdale, *Corp Secy*
EMP: 6
SQ FT: 4,700
SALES (est): 997.1K **Privately Held**
SIC: 3599 Machine shop, jobbing & repair

(G-16175)
MATRIX RAILWAY CORP
69 Nancy St Unit A (11704-1425)
PHONE..................................631 643-1483
Nelson Rivas, *Ch of Bd*
▲ EMP: 9
SQ FT: 4,000

West Babylon - Suffolk County (G-16176)

SALES (est): 1.9MM **Privately Held**
WEB: www.matrixrailway.com
SIC: 3743 Railroad equipment

(G-16176)
METRO DYNAMICS SCIE
20 Nancy St Unit A (11704-1448)
PHONE..............................631 842-4300
Steve Plaener, *President*
EMP: 15
SQ FT: 6,000
SALES (est): 1.6MM **Privately Held**
SIC: 3812 Search & navigation equipment

(G-16177)
MILLWRIGHT WDWRK INSTALLETION
991 Peconic Ave (11704-5629)
PHONE..............................631 587-2635
Martin Sherlock, *President*
EMP: 20
SQ FT: 16,000
SALES (est): 2.1MM **Privately Held**
SIC: 2431 1751 Millwork; finish & trim carpentry

(G-16178)
MPI CONSULTING INCORPORATED
Also Called: Wal Machine
87 Jersey St (11704-1206)
PHONE..............................631 253-2377
William A Toscano, *CEO*
Jennifer Luizzi, *Vice Pres*
Gary Sporing, *Manager*
EMP: 13 EST: 1966
SQ FT: 8,000
SALES: 7MM **Privately Held**
SIC: 3429 Aircraft hardware

(G-16179)
NEWMAT NORTHEAST CORP
81b Mahan St (11704-1303)
PHONE..............................631 253-9277
Timothy T Greco, *President*
EMP: 11
SQ FT: 8,000
SALES (est): 2.7MM **Privately Held**
SIC: 2821 1742 Polyvinyl chloride resins (PVC); acoustical & ceiling work

(G-16180)
OUR TERMS FABRICATORS INC
48 Cabot St (11704-1109)
PHONE..............................631 752-1517
John Friese, *President*
Greg D'Arrigo, *Vice Pres*
EMP: 32
SQ FT: 18,000
SALES (est): 4.5MM **Privately Held**
WEB: www.ourtermsfabricators.com
SIC: 3231 Furniture tops, glass: cut, beveled or polished

(G-16181)
PEYSER INSTRUMENT CORPORATION
Also Called: Chase Instrument Co
40 Gleam St (11704-1205)
PHONE..............................631 841-3600
Robert Peyser, *President*
Leonard Peyser, *Vice Pres*
▲ EMP: 20
SQ FT: 1,500
SALES (est): 2.8MM **Privately Held**
SIC: 3829 5049 Hydrometers, except industrial process type; analytical instruments

(G-16182)
PMB PRECISION PRODUCTS INC
Also Called: Spartan Instruments
725 Mount Ave (11704-1700)
PHONE..............................631 491-6753
Michael Belesis, *President*
Jan Craw, *Principal*
Richard Jackson, *Sales Mgr*
EMP: 16
SALES (est): 3MM **Privately Held**
SIC: 3399 Metal fasteners

(G-16183)
PREMIUM WOODWORKING LLC
108 Lamar St (11704-1312)
PHONE..............................631 485-3133
Bhevendra Persaud,
EMP: 5
SQ FT: 5,000
SALES: 2MM **Privately Held**
SIC: 2434 Wood kitchen cabinets

(G-16184)
QUALITY SAW & KNIFE INC
115 Otis St (11704-1429)
PHONE..............................631 491-4747
Fredrick Luberto, *President*
Paul Siegfried, *Vice Pres*
EMP: 10
SQ FT: 3,000
SALES (est): 800K **Privately Held**
SIC: 3425 7699 Saw blades, chain type; saw blades for hand or power saws; knife, saw & tool sharpening & repair

(G-16185)
R & J DISPLAYS INC
96 Otis St (11704-1430)
PHONE..............................631 491-3500
Lance Landau, *President*
EMP: 30
SQ FT: 20,000
SALES (est): 3.2MM **Privately Held**
SIC: 3993 Displays & cutouts, window & lobby

(G-16186)
RGH ASSOCIATES INC
Also Called: Richards Screw Machine
86 Nancy St (11704-1404)
PHONE..............................631 643-1111
Richard Honan, *President*
Richard Goldsmith, *Corp Secy*
EMP: 19
SQ FT: 7,200
SALES (est): 6.5MM **Privately Held**
SIC: 3599 Machine shop, jobbing & repair

(G-16187)
RICHARD MANNO & COMPANY INC
42 Lamar St (11704-1302)
PHONE..............................631 643-2200
Vincent Manno, *President*
Ilian Dimitrov, *General Mgr*
Vincent Chiappone, *Exec VP*
Jason Wagner, *Exec VP*
Christine Burns, *Vice Pres*
▲ EMP: 54
SQ FT: 18,000
SALES (est): 10.4MM **Privately Held**
WEB: www.richardmanno.com
SIC: 3599 Machine shop, jobbing & repair

(G-16188)
ROSE GRAPHICS LLC
109 Kean St (11704-1208)
PHONE..............................516 547-6142
Anthony F Severino,
EMP: 10
SQ FT: 8,000
SALES: 2MM **Privately Held**
SIC: 2759 Commercial printing

(G-16189)
S & D WELDING CORP
Also Called: S&D Welding
229 Edison Ave Ste A (11704-1042)
PHONE..............................631 454-0383
Mark Dubicki, *President*
Lucia Dubicki, *Treasurer*
EMP: 5
SALES: 275K **Privately Held**
SIC: 7692 1799 5046 Welding repair; welding on site; commercial cooking & food service equipment

(G-16190)
SAGE KNITWEAR INC
103 Jersey St Unit D (11704-1219)
P.O. Box 748231, Rego Park (11374-8231)
PHONE..............................718 628-7902
Payam Ebrani, *President*
EMP: 5
SQ FT: 3,500

SALES (est): 604.1K **Privately Held**
SIC: 2253 Sweaters & sweater coats, knit; dresses, knit; skirts, knit

(G-16191)
SAV THERMO INC
133 Cabot St (11704-1101)
PHONE..............................631 249-9444
Vincent Caputi, *President*
Anthony Bangaroo, *Vice Pres*
EMP: 10
SQ FT: 10,000
SALES (est): 1.6MM **Privately Held**
SIC: 3089 Trays, plastic

(G-16192)
SINN-TECH INDUSTRIES INC
48 Gleam St (11704-1205)
PHONE..............................631 643-1171
Daniel Tierney, *Owner*
Robert Becker, *Director*
EMP: 10
SQ FT: 7,000
SALES: 1MM **Privately Held**
WEB: www.sinn-tech.com
SIC: 3545 Machine tool accessories

(G-16193)
SONAER INC
68 Lamar St Unit D (11704-1316)
PHONE..............................631 756-4780
Donald Cierco, *Ch of Bd*
Donald Cierco, *Ch of Bd*
EMP: 8
SQ FT: 3,000
SALES (est): 1.1MM **Privately Held**
WEB: www.sonozap.com
SIC: 3679 Electronic circuits

(G-16194)
SONICOR INC
82 Otis St (11704-1406)
PHONE..............................631 920-6555
Michael J Parker, *President*
Augusto D' Agostino, *Manager*
▲ EMP: 12 EST: 1966
SQ FT: 3,500
SALES (est): 2.4MM **Privately Held**
WEB: www.sonicor.com
SIC: 3569 3559 3554 3699 Separators for steam, gas, vapor or air (machinery); electroplating machinery & equipment; paper mill machinery: plating, slitting, waxing, etc.; welding machines & equipment, ultrasonic; cleaning equipment, ultrasonic, except medical & dental; medical cleaning equipment, ultrasonic

(G-16195)
SPECIALTY BLDG SOLUTIONS INC
Eads St Ste 165a (11704)
PHONE..............................631 393-6918
John Pearson, *Owner*
Jeanne Demaio, *Office Mgr*
EMP: 8 EST: 2009
SALES (est): 535K **Privately Held**
SIC: 3479 Coating or wrapping steel pipe

(G-16196)
STERLING TOGGLE INC
99 Mahan St (11704-1303)
PHONE..............................631 491-0500
William Horne Jr, *President*
Susan Horne, *Vice Pres*
Debra Irving, *Vice Pres*
Debbie Irving, *Manager*
EMP: 12
SALES (est): 2.3MM **Privately Held**
WEB: www.sterlingtoggle.com
SIC: 3555 Printing trades machinery

(G-16197)
STRAHL & PITSCH INC
230 Great East Neck Rd (11704-7602)
P.O. Box 1098 (11704-0098)
PHONE..............................631 669-0175
William France, *Ch of Bd*
William Deluca, *President*
Hans Kestler, *Vice Pres*
Roger McKenna, *Vice Pres*
Carl Bonewald, *Warehouse Mgr*
◆ EMP: 40 EST: 1904

SALES (est): 16.5MM **Privately Held**
WEB: www.spwax.com
SIC: 2842 Waxes for wood, leather & other materials

(G-16198)
SUPER WEB INC
97 Lamar St (11704-1308)
PHONE..............................631 643-9100
Marcel Edelstein, *Ch of Bd*
Paul Schwartz, *Vice Pres*
Shelly Edelstein, *Admin Sec*
▲ EMP: 30
SQ FT: 27,000
SALES (est): 7.6MM **Privately Held**
WEB: www.superwebusa.com
SIC: 3555 5084 Printing trades machinery; printing trades machinery, equipment & supplies

(G-16199)
SWEET TOOTH ENTERPRISES LLC
Also Called: Micelli Chocalate Mold Co
135 Dale St (11704-1103)
PHONE..............................631 752-2888
Paul Hamilton,
EMP: 20
SALES (est): 4.2MM **Privately Held**
SIC: 3089 Injection molding of plastics

(G-16200)
TRIANGLE GRINDING MACHINE CORP
66 Nancy St Unit A (11704-1436)
PHONE..............................631 643-3636
Santo Turano, *President*
Domingo Turano, *Vice Pres*
George Turano, *Vice Pres*
EMP: 5
SQ FT: 800
SALES (est): 636.6K **Privately Held**
SIC: 3599 Machine shop, jobbing & repair

(G-16201)
US ELECTROPLATING CORP
100 Field St Unit A (11704-1294)
PHONE..............................631 293-1998
Robert Birmbaum, *President*
EMP: 6 EST: 1971
SQ FT: 3,000
SALES (est): 526K **Privately Held**
SIC: 3471 Plating of metals or formed products; polishing, metals or formed products

(G-16202)
VANDILAY INDUSTRIES INC
Also Called: Dualtron Manufacturing
60 Bell St Unit A (11704-1038)
PHONE..............................631 226-3064
Don Ehrlich, *President*
Chris Schleimer, *Vice Pres*
EMP: 22 EST: 1997
SQ FT: 22,000
SALES (est): 4.1MM **Privately Held**
WEB: www.dualtron.com
SIC: 3545 Machine tool accessories

(G-16203)
VILLAGE VIDEO PRODUCTIONS INC
Also Called: Village Video News
107 Alder St (11704-1001)
PHONE..............................631 752-9311
Robert Wolf, *President*
Doreen Wolf, *Manager*
EMP: 6
SQ FT: 2,000
SALES (est): 876.3K **Privately Held**
WEB: www.vvn.com
SIC: 3663 Satellites, communications

(G-16204)
WEICRO GRAPHICS INC
Also Called: Able Printing
95 Mahan St (11704-1303)
PHONE..............................631 253-3360
Sanford Weiss, *President*
Lucyna Mleczko, *Vice Pres*
EMP: 22
SQ FT: 5,500

GEOGRAPHIC SECTION

West Henrietta - Monroe County (G-16231)

SALES (est): 3.5MM **Privately Held**
WEB: www.lemontreestationery.com
SIC: 2752 2759 Commercial printing, offset; commercial printing

(G-16205)
YANKEE FUEL INC
780 Sunrise Hwy (11704-6105)
PHONE.....................................631 880-8810
Ibrahim Sergi, *Principal*
EMP: 5
SALES (est): 387.2K **Privately Held**
SIC: 2869 Fuels

West Burlington
Otsego County

(G-16206)
CONTROL LOGIC CORPORATION
2533 State Highway 80 (13482-9717)
PHONE.....................................607 965-6423
Randy Holdredge, *President*
Joanne Holdredge, *Admin Sec*
EMP: 6
SALES (est): 460K **Privately Held**
WEB: www.controllogic.com
SIC: 3577 Printers, computer

West Edmeston
Madison County

(G-16207)
SCULLY SANITATION
11146 Skaneateles Tpke (13485-3060)
PHONE.....................................315 899-8996
Timothy Scully, *Partner*
Kevin Scully, *Partner*
EMP: 8
SALES: 300K **Privately Held**
SIC: 2842 Sanitation preparations, disinfectants & deodorants

West Falls
Erie County

(G-16208)
BUTTERWOOD DESSERTS INC
Also Called: Swamp Island Dessert Co
1863 Davis Rd (14170-9701)
PHONE.....................................716 652-0131
Fax: 585 652-1759
EMP: 40
SQ FT: 15,000
SALES (est): 3.4MM **Privately Held**
SIC: 2099 2053 2052 Mfg Food Preparations Mfg Frozen Bakery Prdts Mfg Cookies/Crackers

(G-16209)
TEAM FABRICATION INC
1055 Davis Rd (14170-9734)
P.O. Box 32 (14170-0032)
PHONE.....................................716 655-4038
Robert Hopkins, *President*
EMP: 8
SQ FT: 2,376
SALES (est): 1.5MM **Privately Held**
WEB: www.teamfabrication.com
SIC: 3441 Fabricated structural metal

West Haverstraw
Rockland County

(G-16210)
VIN-CLAIR INC
Also Called: Vin-Clair Bindery
132 E Railroad Ave (10993-1418)
PHONE.....................................845 429-4998
Lou Maiello, *President*
Florence Maiello, *Vice Pres*
EMP: 10
SQ FT: 17,000
SALES (est): 77.3K **Privately Held**
SIC: 2789 Bookbinding & related work

(G-16211)
YOUR FURNITURE DESIGNERS INC
Also Called: Yfd Cabinetry
118 E Railroad Ave (10993-1416)
PHONE.....................................845 947-3046
Jose A Mata, *President*
EMP: 5
SALES (est): 654.4K **Privately Held**
SIC: 2521 2434 2542 2511 Wood office furniture; wood kitchen cabinets; vanities, bathroom: wood; shelving, office & store: except wood; wood bedroom furniture

West Hempstead
Nassau County

(G-16212)
ARTISAN WOODWORKING LTD
Also Called: Artisan Custom Interiors
163 Hempstead Tpke (11552-1622)
PHONE.....................................516 486-0818
Michael Aiello, *President*
Janet Aiello, *Corp Secy*
EMP: 6
SQ FT: 6,500
SALES (est): 834.8K **Privately Held**
WEB: www.artisancustominteriors.com
SIC: 2511 Wood household furniture

(G-16213)
AUTOMOTION PARKING SYSTEMS LLC
411 Hempstead Tpke # 200 (11552-1350)
PHONE.....................................516 565-5600
Perry Finkelman, *Managing Dir*
Daniel McCrossin, *Opers Mgr*
ARI Milstein, *Exec Dir*
Jeffrey M Hyde, *Director*
EMP: 2
SQ FT: 1,000
SALES (est): 2.1MM **Privately Held**
SIC: 3559 Parking facility equipment & supplies

(G-16214)
CENTAR FUEL CO INC
700 Nassau Blvd (11552-3531)
PHONE.....................................516 538-2424
John Skei, *Principal*
EMP: 5 EST: 2007
SALES (est): 563.8K **Privately Held**
SIC: 2869 Fuels

(G-16215)
D-BEST EQUIPMENT CORP
77 Hempstead Gardens Dr (11552-2643)
PHONE.....................................516 358-0965
Marc Cali, *CEO*
EMP: 24 EST: 1999
SALES (est): 5MM **Privately Held**
SIC: 2869 Enzymes

(G-16216)
INDEPENDENT HOME PRODUCTS LLC
59 Hempstead Gardens Dr (11552-2641)
PHONE.....................................718 541-1256
Abbie Spetner, *Principal*
Yale Lipschik, *CFO*
▲ EMP: 20
SALES (est): 3.1MM **Privately Held**
SIC: 3088 3431 Hot tubs, plastic or fiberglass; bathtubs: enameled iron, cast iron or pressed metal

(G-16217)
INTERNTONAL CONSMR CONNECTIONS
Also Called: Wilson Picture Frames
5 Terminal Rd Unit A (11552-1151)
PHONE.....................................516 481-3438
Mark Sternberg, *President*
Alan Kohn, *Shareholder*
EMP: 12
SQ FT: 5,000
SALES (est): 750K **Privately Held**
SIC: 2499 7699 Picture & mirror frames, wood; picture framing, custom

(G-16218)
J GIMBEL INC
275 Hempstead Tpke Ste A (11552-1540)
PHONE.....................................718 296-5200
Jackie Sherman, *President*
Leonard Gimbel, *Vice Pres*
Lorie Gimbel, *Treasurer*
EMP: 20
SQ FT: 17,000
SALES (est): 2.5MM **Privately Held**
WEB: www.rollershades.com
SIC: 2591 Blinds vertical; window shades

(G-16219)
KONRAD PROSTHETICS & ORTHOTICS (PA)
596 Jennings Ave (11552-3706)
PHONE.....................................516 485-9164
Kurt Konrad, *President*
Elsbeth Konrad, *Corp Secy*
EMP: 10
SQ FT: 200
SALES (est): 1.2MM **Privately Held**
SIC: 3842 7352 5999 Surgical appliances & supplies; invalid supplies rental; artificial limbs

(G-16220)
LANCO MANUFACTURING CO
384 Hempstead Tpke (11552-1304)
PHONE.....................................516 292-8953
Joseph Lancer, *Partner*
Irwin Lamcer, *Partner*
Irwin Lancer, *Partner*
EMP: 5
SQ FT: 10,000
SALES (est): 39.3K **Privately Held**
SIC: 3561 Pumps & pumping equipment

(G-16221)
MAGIC TECH CO LTD
401 Hempstead Tpke (11552-1311)
PHONE.....................................516 539-7944
EMP: 5
SALES (est): 440K **Privately Held**
SIC: 3699 5065 Mfg And Dist Karoke Machines

(G-16222)
MULTITONE FINISHING CO INC
56 Hempstead Gardens Dr (11552-2642)
PHONE.....................................516 485-1043
Edward Mc Carthy, *President*
Harvey Pollack, *Vice Pres*
EMP: 8 EST: 1963
SQ FT: 4,700
SALES (est): 726K **Privately Held**
SIC: 3471 Finishing, metals or formed products

(G-16223)
MUTUAL ENGRAVING COMPANY INC
497 Hempstead Ave (11552-2738)
P.O. Box 129 (11552-0129)
PHONE.....................................516 489-0534
Salvatore Forelli, *President*
Robert Forelli, *Vice Pres*
Lou Ewanitsko, *Treasurer*
EMP: 65 EST: 1939
SQ FT: 15,000
SALES (est): 7.8MM **Privately Held**
WEB: www.mutualengraving.com
SIC: 2754 2796 2791 2752 Stationery: gravure printing; platemaking services; typesetting; commercial printing, lithographic

(G-16224)
PROFESSIONAL REMODELERS INC
340 Hempstead Ave Unit A (11552-2061)
PHONE.....................................516 565-9300
Thomas Stallone, *President*
EMP: 5
SALES (est): 486.2K **Privately Held**
SIC: 1389 Construction, repair & dismantling services

(G-16225)
STONE EXPO & CABINETRY LLC
7 Terminal Rd (11552-1105)
PHONE.....................................516 292-2988
Annie Liu, *Mng Member*
▲ EMP: 14

SALES (est): 1.8MM **Privately Held**
SIC: 2434 2542 Wood kitchen cabinets; counters or counter display cases: except wood

(G-16226)
US PUMP CORP
707 Woodfield Rd (11552-3826)
PHONE.....................................516 303-7799
Nissim Isaacson, *Ch of Bd*
Kevan Woodworth, *Officer*
▲ EMP: 5
SALES (est): 727.2K **Privately Held**
SIC: 1381 1241 Drilling water intake wells; redrilling oil & gas wells; mining services: lignite

West Henrietta
Monroe County

(G-16227)
ALSTOM SIGNALING INC (DH)
Also Called: Alstrom Trnspt Info Solutions
1025 John St (14586-9781)
PHONE.....................................585 783-2000
Ulisses Camillo, *CEO*
Ellen O'Neill, *Vice Pres*
Michele Viale, *Vice Pres*
Craig Daniels, *Project Dir*
Chris Picard, *Opers Mgr*
▲ EMP: 261
SALES (est): 81.6MM
SALES (corp-wide): 67MM **Privately Held**
WEB: www.alstomsignalingsolutions.com
SIC: 3669 Railroad signaling devices, electric; signaling apparatus, electric
HQ: Alstom Transportation Inc.
641 Lexington Ave Fl 28
New York NY 10022
212 692-5353

(G-16228)
AMERICAN FILTRATION TECH INC
100 Thruway Park Dr (14586-9798)
PHONE.....................................585 359-4130
Richard Felber, *President*
EMP: 13
SQ FT: 36,000
SALES (est): 2.9MM **Privately Held**
SIC: 3569 3564 Filters, general line: industrial; blowers & fans

(G-16229)
APOLLO OPTICAL SYSTEMS INC
925 John St (14586-9780)
PHONE.....................................585 272-6170
G Michael Morris, *CEO*
Daniel McGarry, *President*
Claude Tribastone, *President*
Brian Markovitz, *Prdtn Mgr*
Gwen Murphy, *QC Mgr*
EMP: 38
SALES (est): 7.7MM **Privately Held**
WEB: www.apollooptical.com
SIC: 3827 Optical instruments & lenses

(G-16230)
APPAIRENT TECHNOLOGIES INC (PA)
150 Lucius Gordon Dr (14586-9687)
PHONE.....................................585 214-2460
Chris O'Donnell, *CEO*
Jim Allen, *President*
Preston Keller, *President*
EMP: 5
SQ FT: 2,500
SALES (est): 1.2MM **Privately Held**
WEB: www.appairent.com
SIC: 3663 Radio broadcasting & communications equipment

(G-16231)
B C MANUFACTURING INC
100 Thruway Park Dr (14586-9798)
PHONE.....................................585 482-1080
Bob Collins, *President*
EMP: 5
SQ FT: 5,500
SALES (est): 800.5K **Privately Held**
SIC: 3599 Machine shop, jobbing & repair

West Henrietta - Monroe County (G-16232)

(G-16232)
BRANDYS MOLD AND TOOL CTR LTD (PA)
10 Riverton Way (14586-9754)
PHONE...................585 334-8333
Michaela Perkins, *President*
Dan Morse, *General Mgr*
Franz Brandstetter, *Vice Pres*
EMP: 15
SALES (est): 1.4MM Privately Held
SIC: 3089 Injection molding of plastics

(G-16233)
BRINKMAN PRECISION INC
Also Called: B P I
100 Park Centre Dr (14586-9688)
PHONE...................585 429-5001
Andrew J Laniak, *CEO*
Robert J Brinkman, *Ch of Bd*
Bob Coffey, *QC Mgr*
Joe Morlino, *QC Mgr*
Brian Fonda, *Engineer*
EMP: 85
SALES (est): 18.3MM
SALES (corp-wide): 106.6MM Privately Held
WEB: www.brinkmanprecision.com
SIC: 3324 5047 Aerospace investment castings, ferrous; medical equipment & supplies
PA: Brinkman International Group, Inc.
    167 Ames St
    Rochester NY 14611
    585 429-5000

(G-16234)
COHBER PRESS INC (PA)
Also Called: Kodak Gallery - Cohber
1000 John St (14586-9757)
P.O. Box 93100, Rochester (14692-7300)
PHONE...................585 475-9100
Eric C Webber, *Ch of Bd*
Howard Buzz, *Chairman*
Daniel Mahany, *COO*
Chris Bowen, *Vice Pres*
Jim Laforce, *Manager*
EMP: 90 EST: 1925
SQ FT: 49,000
SALES (est): 15.8MM Privately Held
WEB: www.cohber.com
SIC: 2752 2791 2789 Commercial printing, offset; photo-offset printing; typesetting; bookbinding & related work

(G-16235)
COOPERVISION INC
180 Thruway Park Dr (14586-9798)
PHONE...................585 385-6810
Tracy Johnson, *Purchasing*
Michelle McDonagh, *Director*
EMP: 594
SALES (corp-wide): 2.1B Publicly Held
SIC: 3851 Contact lenses
HQ: Coopervision, Inc.
    209 High Point Dr Ste 100
    Victor NY 14564

(G-16236)
DELPHI POWERTRAIN SYSTEMS LLC
5500 W Henrietta Rd (14586-9701)
PHONE...................585 359-6000
Bruce Gardephe, *Engineer*
Amanda Reid, *Engineer*
Randy Welch, *Engineer*
Jim Zizzleman, *Manager*
EMP: 209
SALES (corp-wide): 1.5MM Privately Held
WEB: www.delphiauto.com
SIC: 3714 Motor vehicle parts & accessories
HQ: Delphi Powertrain Systems, Llc
    5825 Innovation Dr
    Troy MI 48098
    248 813-2000

(G-16237)
DELPHI POWERTRAIN SYSTEMS LLC
5500 W Henrietta Rd (14586-9701)
PHONE...................585 359-6000
Jim Zizleman, *Manager*
EMP: 486
SALES (corp-wide): 1.5MM Privately Held
WEB: www.delphiauto.com
SIC: 3714 8731 3694 3564 Motor vehicle parts & accessories; commercial physical research; engine electrical equipment; blowers & fans
HQ: Delphi Powertrain Systems, Llc
    5825 Innovation Dr
    Troy MI 48098
    248 813-2000

(G-16238)
DELPHI POWERTRAIN SYSTEMS LLC
5500 W Henrietta Rd (14586-9701)
PHONE...................585 359-6000
Walter Piock, *Branch Mgr*
EMP: 31
SALES (corp-wide): 1.5MM Privately Held
SIC: 3714 Motor vehicle parts & accessories
HQ: Delphi Powertrain Systems, Llc
    5825 Innovation Dr
    Troy MI 48098
    248 813-2000

(G-16239)
FORTEQ NORTH AMERICA INC
150 Park Centre Dr (14586-9688)
PHONE...................585 427-9410
Martin Van Manen, *CEO*
Rune Bakke, *Principal*
Joseph Buonocure, *Principal*
Luc Widmer, *CFO*
James Carboni, *Controller*
▲ EMP: 70
SQ FT: 29,000
SALES (est): 25.2MM Privately Held
SIC: 3089 Plastic containers, except foam
PA: Transmission Technology Holding Ag
    C/O Bar & Karrer
    Zug ZG
    582 615-900

(G-16240)
GENESEE METAL STAMPINGS INC
975 John St (14586-9780)
PHONE...................585 475-0450
Gerard Caschette, *Principal*
EMP: 5
SALES (est): 574.8K Privately Held
SIC: 3469 Stamping metal for the trade

(G-16241)
GEOSPATIAL SYSTEMS INC (DH)
150 Lucius Gordon Dr # 211 (14586-9687)
PHONE...................585 427-8310
Maxime Elbaz, *President*
Steven Randy Olson, *Vice Pres*
Robert Delach, *CFO*
EMP: 11
SQ FT: 3,000
SALES (est): 1.3MM
SALES (corp-wide): 2.6B Publicly Held
SIC: 3861 Aerial cameras
HQ: Teledyne Optech Incorporated
    300 Interchange Way
    Vaughan ON L4K 5
    905 660-0808

(G-16242)
HAMMER PACKAGING CORP (PA)
200 Lucius Gordon Dr (14586-9685)
P.O. Box 22678, Rochester (14692-2678)
PHONE...................585 424-3880
James E Hammer, *President*
Jason Hammer, *Vice Pres*
Marty Karpie, *Vice Pres*
Louis Lovoli, *Vice Pres*
Tom Mason, *Vice Pres*
▲ EMP: 350 EST: 1912
SQ FT: 92,000
SALES (est): 119.2MM Privately Held
WEB: www.hammerpackaging.com
SIC: 2759 Labels & seals: printing

(G-16243)
KATIKATI INC
150 Lucius Gordon Dr (14586-9687)
PHONE...................585 678-1764
Prathap James Ambaichelvan, *CEO*
Sanjay Hiranandani, *COO*
Allyson Hiranandani, *Vice Pres*
EMP: 5
SALES (est): 276.1K Privately Held
SIC: 3714 5013 8733 Motor vehicle electrical equipment; testing equipment, electrical: automotive; research institute

(G-16244)
ORAFOL AMERICAS INC
200 Park Centre Dr (14586-9674)
PHONE...................585 272-0290
Keith Steadman, *Engng Exec*
Bryan K Parks, *Branch Mgr*
EMP: 11
SALES (corp-wide): 561.4MM Privately Held
SIC: 3827 5048 Optical instruments & lenses; optometric equipment & supplies
HQ: Orafol Americas Inc.
    1100 Oracal Pkwy
    Black Creek GA 31308
    912 851-5000

(G-16245)
OUTDOOR GROUP LLC
1325 John St (14586-9121)
PHONE...................877 503-5483
Ricky Hayes, *Production*
Corey Risden, *Production*
Chuck Hathaway, *VP Mktg*
Greg Steil,
EMP: 150 EST: 2012
SALES (est): 18.7MM Privately Held
SIC: 3949 Archery equipment, general

(G-16246)
OVITZ CORPORATION
150 Lucius Gordon Dr # 123 (14586-9687)
PHONE...................585 474-4695
Joseph Rosenshein, *Principal*
Joung Yoon Kim, *Principal*
Walter Rusnak, *Principal*
Nader Anvari, *Director*
EMP: 9
SQ FT: 1,000
SALES (est): 529.8K Privately Held
SIC: 3841 Diagnostic apparatus, medical

(G-16247)
PERFECT FORM MANUFACTURING LLC
1325 John St (14586-9121)
PHONE...................585 500-5923
Greg Steil,
Dylan Bates,
Peter Crawford,
Matthew Kruger,
EMP: 5
SQ FT: 3,200
SALES (est): 76.9K Privately Held
SIC: 3949 Bows, archery

(G-16248)
POLYSHOT CORPORATION
75 Lucius Gordon Dr (14586-9682)
PHONE...................585 292-5010
Douglas C Hepler, *CEO*
Lou Borrelli, *President*
▲ EMP: 40
SQ FT: 13,000
SALES (est): 5.3MM Privately Held
WEB: www.polyshot.com
SIC: 3544 Industrial molds

(G-16249)
ROCHESTER PRECISION OPTICS LLC
Also Called: R P O
850 John St (14586-9748)
PHONE...................585 292-5450
William Hurley, *CEO*
Sue McDonald, *Mfg Staff*
Helen Bilak, *Purch Mgr*
Stacey Faugh, *Senior Buyer*
Jennifer Smith, *Buyer*
◆ EMP: 190
SQ FT: 104,500
SALES (est): 51.3MM Privately Held
WEB: www.rpoptics.com
SIC: 3827 Lenses, optical: all types except ophthalmic; lens mounts; lens grinding equipment, except ophthalmic; optical elements & assemblies, except ophthalmic

(G-16250)
SEMANS ENTERPRISES INC
Also Called: New Cov Manufacturing
25 Hendrix Rd Ste E (14586-9205)
PHONE...................585 444-0097
William A Semans II, *Ch of Bd*
Carol Maue- Semans, *Vice Pres*
EMP: 19
SQ FT: 10,000
SALES: 1.8MM Privately Held
SIC: 3449 Miscellaneous metalwork

(G-16251)
SIMPORE INC
150 Lucius Gordon Dr # 110 (14586-9687)
PHONE...................585 748-5980
Richard D Richmond, *Ch of Bd*
Thomas Gaborski, *President*
James Roussie, *VP Sales*
Barbara Geiss, *Administration*
EMP: 7
SQ FT: 400
SALES (est): 852K Privately Held
WEB: www.simpore.com
SIC: 3821 Laboratory equipment: fume hoods, distillation racks, etc.

(G-16252)
SWAGELOK WESTERN NY
10 Thruway Park Dr (14586-9702)
PHONE...................585 359-8470
EMP: 5
SALES (est): 569.2K Privately Held
SIC: 3823 Mfg Process Control Instruments

(G-16253)
VUZIX CORPORATION (PA)
25 Hendrix Rd Ste A (14586-9205)
PHONE...................585 359-5900
Paul J Travers, *President*
Grant Russell, *CFO*
EMP: 24 EST: 1997
SQ FT: 29,000
SALES: 5.5MM Publicly Held
WEB: www.icuiti.com
SIC: 3577 Computer peripheral equipment

(G-16254)
VWR EDUCATION LLC
Ward's Natural Science
5100 W Henrietta Rd (14586-9729)
PHONE...................585 359-2502
Susan Bernholdt, *Human Res Dir*
Michael Forney, *Cust Mgr*
Cindy Kent, *Executive*
EMP: 250 Privately Held
SIC: 2741 3821 5049 5192 Miscellaneous publishing; laboratory apparatus & furniture; scientific & engineering equipment & supplies; books, periodicals & newspapers
HQ: Vwr Education, Llc
    777 E Park Dr
    Tonawanda NY 14150
    800 242-2042

(G-16255)
WAVODYNE THERAPEUTICS INC
150 Lucius Gordon Dr (14586-9687)
PHONE...................954 632-6630
James New, *CEO*
EMP: 2 EST: 2015
SQ FT: 200
SALES: 500MM Privately Held
SIC: 2834 Druggists' preparations (pharmaceuticals)

West Hurley
Ulster County

(G-16256)
ANATOLI INC
43 Basin Rd Ste 11 (12491-5201)
PHONE...................845 334-9000
Kostas Michalopoulos, *President*
Joan Ramos, *Admin Sec*
EMP: 16
SQ FT: 4,300
SALES (est): 1.4MM Privately Held
SIC: 3911 3961 5094 Jewelry, precious metal; costume jewelry; jewelry

West Islip
Suffolk County

(G-16257)
ACT COMMUNICATIONS GROUP INC
170 Higbie Ln (11795-3238)
PHONE 631 669-2403
Richard Carpenter, *President*
Robert Carpenter, *Vice Pres*
EMP: 18
SQ FT: 1,000
SALES (est): 1.5MM **Privately Held**
WEB: www.actcommgroup.com
SIC: 2791 2752 7311 Typesetting; commercial printing, offset; advertising agencies

(G-16258)
ACTION BULLET RESISTANT
263 Union Blvd (11795-3007)
PHONE 631 422-0888
Leonard J Simonetti, *President*
Jeff Farinacci, *Project Mgr*
Brien Sweeney, *Controller*
Trish Simonetti, *Manager*
Laura Muench, *Office Admin*
EMP: 12
SQ FT: 14,000
SALES (est): 2.3MM **Privately Held**
WEB: www.actionbullet.com
SIC: 3442 Window & door frames

(G-16259)
JEM TOOL & DIE CORP
81 Paris Ct (11795-2815)
PHONE 631 539-8734
Roy Stevens, *President*
Bill Jimenez, *Vice Pres*
EMP: 10 EST: 1961
SQ FT: 8,000
SALES (est): 1.2MM **Privately Held**
SIC: 3545 Machine tool attachments & accessories

(G-16260)
V A P TOOL & DYE
436 W 4th St (11795-2414)
PHONE 631 587-5262
Victor Pons, *Owner*
EMP: 7
SQ FT: 4,700
SALES (est): 400K **Privately Held**
SIC: 3599 Machine shop, jobbing & repair

(G-16261)
W & W MANUFACTURING CO
239 Higbie Ln (11795-2825)
P.O. Box 817, Deer Park (11729-0981)
PHONE 516 942-0011
Jeffrey Weitzman, *President*
Saundrice Lucas, *Administration*
▲ EMP: 15
SALES (est): 2.2MM **Privately Held**
WEB: www.ww-manufacturing.com
SIC: 3691 3825 3663 Storage batteries; instruments to measure electricity; radio & TV communications equipment

West Monroe
Oswego County

(G-16262)
ROBINSON CONCRETE INC
Also Called: Cemento,
2735 State Route 49 (13167-3249)
PHONE 315 676-4333
Vinnie Vitale, *Branch Mgr*
EMP: 128
SALES (corp-wide): 24MM **Privately Held**
PA: Robinson Concrete, Inc.
   3486 Franklin Street Rd
   Auburn NY 13021
   315 253-6666

West Nyack
Rockland County

(G-16263)
AMP-LINE CORP
3 Amethyst Ct (10994-1142)
PHONE 845 623-3288
Guosen Luo, *President*
EMP: 10
SALES (est): 1.3MM **Privately Held**
SIC: 3699 Pulse amplifiers

(G-16264)
ANGEL MEDIA AND PUBLISHING
Also Called: Rockland Review Publishing
26 Snake Hill Rd (10994-1625)
PHONE 845 727-4949
Joseph Miele, *President*
EMP: 6
SALES (est): 407.4K **Privately Held**
WEB: www.rocklandreviewnews.com
SIC: 2711 Newspapers: publishing only, not printed on site

(G-16265)
BEL-BEE PRODUCTS INCORPORATED
100 Snake Hill Rd Ste 1 (10994-1627)
PHONE 845 353-0300
Vincent Belmont, *Ch of Bd*
Patricia Musumeci, *Purch Mgr*
Herbert Giller, *Manager*
Antone Selinger, *Manager*
EMP: 15
SQ FT: 25,000
SALES (est): 3MM **Privately Held**
WEB: www.bel-bee.com
SIC: 3544 Special dies & tools

(G-16266)
BILLY BEEZ USA LLC
1282 Palisades Center Dr (10994-6202)
PHONE 845 915-4709
EMP: 23
SALES (corp-wide): 15.6MM **Privately Held**
SIC: 3949 5137 7999 Playground equipment; women's & children's dresses, suits, skirts & blouses; amusement ride
PA: Billy Beez Usa, Llc
   3 W 35th St Fl 3 # 3
   New York NY 10001
   646 606-2249

(G-16267)
BYLADA FOODS LLC
250 W Nyack Rd Ste 110 (10994-1745)
PHONE 845 623-1300
Meade Bradshaw, *Branch Mgr*
EMP: 42
SALES (corp-wide): 9.4MM **Privately Held**
SIC: 2099 Food preparations
PA: Bylada Foods Llc
   140 W Commercial Ave
   Moonachie NJ 07074
   201 933-7474

(G-16268)
CROTON WATCH CO INC
250 W Nyack Rd Ste 114 (10994-1745)
PHONE 800 443-7639
David Mermelstein, *Ch of Bd*
▲ EMP: 26
SQ FT: 18,000
SALES (est): 4.8MM **Privately Held**
WEB: www.crotonwatch.com
SIC: 3873 Watches & parts, except crystals & jewels

(G-16269)
GANNETT STLLITE INFO NTWRK LLC
1 Crosfield Ave (10994-2222)
PHONE 845 578-2300
Tony Davenport, *Branch Mgr*
EMP: 30
SALES (corp-wide): 3.1B **Publicly Held**
WEB: www.usatoday.com
SIC: 2711 2752 Newspapers: publishing only, not printed on site; commercial printing, lithographic
HQ: Gannett Satellite Information Network, Llc
   7950 Jones Branch Dr
   Mc Lean VA 22102
   703 854-6000

(G-16270)
GENERAL BEARING CORPORATION (DH)
44 High St (10994-2702)
PHONE 845 358-6000
David L Gussack, *CEO*
Thomas J Uhlig, *President*
Corby W Self, *Vice Pres*
Corby Self, *Vice Pres*
Ed Lynch, *Plant Mgr*
◆ EMP: 120 EST: 1958
SQ FT: 190,000
SALES (est): 131.7MM
SALES (corp-wide): 9.2B **Privately Held**
WEB: www.generalbearing.com
SIC: 3562 Ball bearings & parts
HQ: Skf Usa Inc.
   890 Forty Foot Rd
   Lansdale PA 19446
   267 436-6000

(G-16271)
INTERCOS AMERICA INC
11 Centerock Rd (10994)
PHONE 845 732-3900
EMP: 5
SALES (corp-wide): 52.5MM **Privately Held**
SIC: 2844 Cosmetic preparations
HQ: Intercos America, Inc.
   200 N Route 303
   Congers NY 10920

(G-16272)
INTERCOS AMERICA INC
120 Brookhill Dr (10994-2127)
PHONE 845 732-3910
EMP: 6 EST: 2016
SALES (est): 119.8K **Privately Held**
SIC: 2844 Toilet preparations

(G-16273)
JOURNAL NEWS
200 N Route 303 (10994-1619)
PHONE 845 578-2324
EMP: 5
SALES (est): 216.8K **Privately Held**
SIC: 2711 Newspapers, publishing & printing

(G-16274)
MACABEE FOODS LLC
250 W Nyack Rd Ste 110 (10994-1745)
PHONE 845 623-1300
Laurence Silverman, *CFO*
Robert Silverman,
EMP: 5
SALES (est): 553K **Privately Held**
SIC: 2038 Frozen specialties

(G-16275)
MAINLY MONOGRAMS INC
Also Called: Mercury Apparel
260 W Nyack Rd Ste 1 (10994-1750)
PHONE 845 624-4923
Dan Alexander Sr, *CEO*
Dan Alexander Jr, *CFO*
Frank Goldrick, *CFO*
Zaharo Ula Alexander, *Treasurer*
EMP: 45
SQ FT: 19,000
SALES (est): 5.1MM **Privately Held**
SIC: 2395 7336 5611 5621 Embroidery products, except schiffli machine; silk screen design; clothing, sportswear, men's & boys'; women's sportswear; gifts & novelties

(G-16276)
NICE-PAK PRODUCTS INC
100 Brookhill Dr (10994)
PHONE 845 353-6090
Jennifer Thriston, *Manager*
EMP: 25
SALES (corp-wide): 428.1MM **Privately Held**
SIC: 2621 Towels, tissues & napkins: paper & stock; sanitary tissue paper
PA: Nice-Pak Products, Inc.
   2 Nice Pak Park
   Orangeburg NY 10962
   845 365-2772

(G-16277)
PEARL RIVER PASTRIES LLC
Also Called: Pearl River Pastry Chocolates
389 W Nyack Rd (10994-1723)
PHONE 845 735-5100
Justin Benson, *General Mgr*
Robert Serchuk, *Controller*
Steve Pierson, *VP Sales*
Renae Goyette, *Branch Mgr*
Joseph Koffman, *Mng Member*
EMP: 50
SQ FT: 10,000
SALES (est): 7.7MM **Privately Held**
SIC: 2053 Pastries (danish): frozen

(G-16278)
PEARSON EDUCATION INC
59 Brookhill Dr (10994-2122)
PHONE 201 236-7000
Michael Schuering, *Exec VP*
Cheryl Gayser, *Human Res Mgr*
EMP: 14
SALES (corp-wide): 5.9B **Privately Held**
WEB: www.phgenit.com
SIC: 2721 2731 Periodicals; book publishing
HQ: Pearson Education, Inc.
   221 River St
   Hoboken NJ 07030
   201 236-7000

(G-16279)
PICCINI MNM INC
35 Highland Ave (10994-1719)
PHONE 845 741-6770
Richard Piccininni, *President*
EMP: 7
SALES: 700K **Privately Held**
SIC: 2499 Decorative wood & woodwork

(G-16280)
PLASTIC-CRAFT PRODUCTS CORP
744 W Nyack Rd (10994-1998)
P.O. Box K (10994-0713)
PHONE 845 358-3010
Mark Brecher, *President*
Yung Nguyen, *Vice Pres*
Marge Garrieson, *Treasurer*
Marge Garrison, *Financial Exec*
Clare Archer, *Marketing Staff*
EMP: 33
SQ FT: 30,000
SALES: 4.5MM **Privately Held**
SIC: 3089 5162 Injection molding of plastics; plastics materials & basic shapes

(G-16281)
ROCKLAND MANUFACTURING CO
44 High St (10994-2702)
PHONE 845 358-6000
Seymour Gussack, *CEO*
Bruce Pope, *Manager*
Rocky Cambrea, *Executive*
EMP: 5
SALES (est): 297.2K **Privately Held**
SIC: 3531 Construction machinery

(G-16282)
TILCON NEW YORK INC
1 Crusher Rd (10994-1601)
PHONE 845 358-3100
Miranda Robinson, *Plant Engr*
Bernardo Culnes, *Systems Staff*
EMP: 65
SALES (corp-wide): 29.7B **Privately Held**
WEB: www.tilconny.com
SIC: 1429 1442 1423 Trap rock, crushed & broken-quarrying; dolomitic marble, crushed & broken-quarrying; construction sand & gravel; crushed & broken granite
HQ: Tilcon New York Inc.
   9 Entin Rd
   Parsippany NJ 07054
   800 789-7625

West Point
Orange County

(G-16283)
PENN ENTERPRISES INC
845 Washington Rd (10996-1111)
PHONE..............................845 446-0765
Joseph Fotovich, *Principal*
EMP: 13 Privately Held
WEB: www.pennenterprises.com
SIC: 3633 Household laundry equipment
PA: Penn Enterprises, Inc
5260 S Stonehaven Dr
Springfield MO 65809

West Sand Lake
Rensselaer County

(G-16284)
BONDED CONCRETE INC
Rr 43 (12196)
PHONE..............................518 674-2854
Tom Coemente, *President*
EMP: 10
SALES (corp-wide): 10.8MM Privately Held
WEB: www.bondedconcrete.com
SIC: 3273 Ready-mixed concrete
PA: Bonded Concrete, Inc.
303 Watervliet Shaker Rd
Watervliet NY 12189
518 273-5800

(G-16285)
TROY SAND & GRAVEL CO INC (PA)
34 Grange Rd (12196-2051)
P.O. Box 171, Watervliet (12189-0171)
PHONE..............................518 203-5115
Jude Clemente, *President*
Thomas Clemente, *Vice Pres*
Philip Clemente, *Treasurer*
Carl Clemente, *Sales Mgr*
Salvatore Clemente, *Admin Sec*
EMP: 6 EST: 1958
SQ FT: 1,000
SALES (est): 16.2MM Privately Held
WEB: www.troysg.com
SIC: 1442 Sand mining

(G-16286)
TROY SAND & GRAVEL CO INC
Rr 43 (12196)
P.O. Box 489 (12196-0489)
PHONE..............................518 674-2854
Jude Clemente, *President*
EMP: 15
SALES (corp-wide): 16.2MM Privately Held
SIC: 1442 5032 Construction sand & gravel; stone, crushed or broken
PA: Troy Sand & Gravel Co., Inc.
34 Grange Rd
West Sand Lake NY 12196
518 203-5115

West Sayville
Suffolk County

(G-16287)
ACCUCUT INC
120 Easy St (11796-1238)
PHONE..............................631 567-2868
Dan Carbone, *CEO*
Joanne Caruso, *Administration*
EMP: 5
SALES: 370K Privately Held
SIC: 3441 Fabricated structural metal

(G-16288)
DOR-A-MAR CANVAS PRODUCTS CO
182 Cherry Ave (11796-1200)
PHONE..............................631 750-9202
Thomas Degirolamo, *President*
EMP: 18 EST: 1959
SQ FT: 6,000
SALES: 1.5MM Privately Held
WEB: www.doramar.com
SIC: 2394 Awnings, fabric: made from purchased materials

(G-16289)
FIRE ISLAND SEA CLAM CO INC
132 Atlantic Ave (11796-1904)
P.O. Box 2124, Montauk (11954-0905)
PHONE..............................631 589-2199
John Kingston, *President*
Jean Kingston, *Admin Sec*
EMP: 3
SQ FT: 3,500
SALES: 10MM Privately Held
WEB: www.fireislandassn.org
SIC: 2431 5812 Moldings, wood: unfinished & prefinished; seafood restaurants

(G-16290)
KUSSMAUL ELECTRONICS CO INC
170 Cherry Ave (11796-1200)
P.O. Box 147, Lynnfield MA (01940-0147)
PHONE..............................631 218-0298
Thomas H Nugent, *Ch of Bd*
Marilyn Kussmaul, *Vice Pres*
Phil Sgroi, *Engineer*
Colin Chambless, *VP Sales*
Ralph Lindgren, *Sales Mgr*
◆ **EMP: 50 EST: 1970**
SQ FT: 30,000
SALES (est): 10.7MM
SALES (corp-wide): 4.9MM Privately Held
WEB: www.maul.com
SIC: 3629 3625 Battery chargers, rectifying or nonrotating; control equipment, electric
HQ: Mission Critical Electronics, Llc
2200 Ross Ave Ste 4050
Dallas TX 75201

(G-16291)
PECK & HALE LLC
180 Division Ave (11796-1303)
PHONE..............................631 589-2510
John Szeglin, *President*
Jose Diaz Bujan, *Opers Staff*
David Mazzara, *Purch Agent*
Richard Belkin, *Engineer*
Christos Efstathiou, *Engineer*
▲ **EMP: 40 EST: 1946**
SQ FT: 27,000
SALES (est): 8.8MM Privately Held
WEB: www.peckhale.com
SIC: 3743 3462 3496 Railroad equipment; iron & steel forgings; miscellaneous fabricated wire products

West Seneca
Erie County

(G-16292)
ABI PACKAGING INC
1703 Union Rd (14224-2060)
PHONE..............................716 677-2900
Roger Severson, *CEO*
EMP: 20
SALES (est): 1.5MM Privately Held
SIC: 3086 Packaging & shipping materials, foamed plastic

(G-16293)
ACI CONTROLS INC (PA)
295 Main St (14224-2818)
PHONE..............................800 333-7519
Robert D Wischerath Jr, *President*
Bob Wischerath, *Principal*
John Wischerath, *Vice Pres*
Paul Wischerath, *Vice Pres*
Tom Wischerath, *Vice Pres*
EMP: 19 EST: 1945
SQ FT: 15,000
SALES (est): 12.7MM Privately Held
WEB: www.aci-controls.com
SIC: 3569 Gas producers, generators & other gas related equipment

(G-16294)
BIG DATA BIZVIZ LLC
1075 East And West Rd (14224-3669)
PHONE..............................716 803-2367
Avin Jain, *CEO*
Rajesh Thanki, *CEO*
EMP: 2
SALES (est): 1.5MM Privately Held
SIC: 7372 Business oriented computer software

(G-16295)
BUFFALO HEARG & SPEECH
1026 Union Rd (14224-3445)
PHONE..............................716 558-1105
Joe Cozzo, *CEO*
Amy Hensley, *Manager*
EMP: 45
SALES (corp-wide): 443.2K Privately Held
SIC: 3842 Hearing aids
PA: Buffalo Hearing And Speech Center Foundation, Inc.
50 E North St
Buffalo NY 14203
716 885-8318

(G-16296)
EBENEZER RAILCAR SERVICES INC
1005 Indian Church Rd (14224-1305)
P.O. Box 363, Buffalo (14224-0363)
PHONE..............................716 674-5650
Jeffrey F Schmarje, *President*
Robert Wingels, *Vice Pres*
EMP: 80 EST: 1981
SQ FT: 30,000
SALES (est): 20.1MM
SALES (corp-wide): 28.8MM Privately Held
WEB: www.ersindustries.com
SIC: 3743 4789 Railroad equipment; railroad car repair
PA: Ers Industries, Inc.
1005 Indian Church Rd
West Seneca NY 14224
716 675-2040

(G-16297)
FIVE STAR INDUSTRIES INC
114 Willowdale Dr (14224-3571)
PHONE..............................716 674-2589
Greg Vastola, *President*
Joel Long, *Vice Pres*
EMP: 27
SQ FT: 10,000
SALES (est): 4.4MM Privately Held
SIC: 3444 3599 Sheet metalwork; machine shop, jobbing & repair

(G-16298)
GEMCOR AUTOMATION LLC
100 Gemcor Dr (14224-2055)
PHONE..............................716 674-9300
Michael Mahfet, *President*
Gary Szymkowiak, *Opers Mgr*
Al Roper, *Foreman/Supr*
Mark Alessi, *Electrical Engi*
Art Deabold, *Manager*
EMP: 87
SQ FT: 90,000
SALES (est): 16.9MM
SALES (corp-wide): 385.4MM Privately Held
SIC: 3542 Spinning, spline rolling & winding machines
HQ: Ascent Aerospace, Llc
16445 23 Mile Rd
Macomb MI 48042
586 726-0500

(G-16299)
GORDEN AUTOMOTIVE EQUIPMENT
60 N America Dr (14224-2225)
PHONE..............................716 674-2700
Richard Deney, *President*
Thomas Gormley, *Exec VP*
Herman Deney, *Vice Pres*
Michael Russo, *Treasurer*
EMP: 10
SALES (est): 978K Privately Held
SIC: 3599 Machine shop, jobbing & repair

(G-16300)
KATHERINE BLIZNIAK (PA)
525 Bullis Rd (14224-2511)
PHONE..............................716 674-8545
Katherine Blizniak, *President*
EMP: 6
SALES (est): 619.1K Privately Held
SIC: 3732 5091 Boat building & repairing; boat accessories & parts

(G-16301)
MAYER BROS APPLE PRODUCTS INC (PA)
3300 Transit Rd (14224-2525)
PHONE..............................716 668-1787
John A Mayer, *Ch of Bd*
Samantha Burris, *Manager*
Russell Wright, *Manager*
▲ **EMP: 95 EST: 1852**
SQ FT: 2,800
SALES (est): 31.7MM Privately Held
WEB: www.mayerbros.com
SIC: 2033 2086 5499 5963 Fruit juices: fresh; pasteurized & mineral waters, bottled & canned; juices, fruit or vegetable; bottled water delivery

(G-16302)
SE-MAR ELECTRIC CO INC
101 South Ave (14224-2090)
PHONE..............................716 674-7404
Robert Haungs, *President*
John Simson, *Principal*
Stephen Graham, *Mfg Staff*
Nancy J Haungs, *Treasurer*
▲ **EMP: 20**
SQ FT: 30,000
SALES: 4.9MM Privately Held
SIC: 3613 5571 Control panels, electric; motorcycles

(G-16303)
SENECA WEST PRINTING INC
860 Center Rd (14224-2207)
PHONE..............................716 675-8010
Charles Pohlman, *President*
Charles Pohlman Jr, *Vice Pres*
EMP: 6 EST: 1965
SQ FT: 4,000
SALES (est): 703.3K Privately Held
SIC: 2752 2759 Lithographing on metal; letterpress printing

(G-16304)
YOST NEON DISPLAYS INC
20 Ransier Dr (14224-2230)
PHONE..............................716 674-6780
Michael Yost, *President*
Deborah Yost, *Vice Pres*
EMP: 5
SALES (est): 475.4K Privately Held
WEB: www.yostneon.com
SIC: 3993 1751 Neon signs; cabinet building & installation

West Winfield
Herkimer County

(G-16305)
CHRISTIAN FABRICATION LLC
122 South St (13491-2827)
PHONE..............................315 822-0135
Jamie Christian, *Mng Member*
EMP: 3
SQ FT: 1,296
SALES: 1.5MM Privately Held
SIC: 3441 7353 Fabricated structural metal; heavy construction equipment rental

(G-16306)
PRECISIONMATICS CO INC
Also Called: Helmer Avenue
1 Helmer Ave (13491)
P.O. Box 250 (13491-0250)
PHONE..............................315 822-6324
Laslo Pustay, *Ch of Bd*
John Macintosh, *Engineer*
Peter McClave, *Engineer*
John Pustay, *Treasurer*
Amanda Gehrke, *Sales Staff*
EMP: 50
SQ FT: 22,000
SALES (est): 9.1MM Privately Held
WEB: www.precisionmatics.com
SIC: 3599 Machine shop, jobbing & repair; custom machinery

Westbrookville
Sullivan County

(G-16307)
GLASS MENAGERIE INC
1756 Rte 209 (12785)
PHONE..........................845 754-8344
Dumitru Costea, *President*
Barbara REA, *Vice Pres*
EMP: 5 **EST:** 1977
SQ FT: 6,000
SALES (est): 37K **Privately Held**
SIC: 3229 Novelty glassware

Westbury
Nassau County

(G-16308)
ACCURATE WELDING SERVICE INC
Also Called: Accurate Welding Svce
615 Main St (11590-4903)
PHONE..........................516 333-1730
Joseph Titone, *President*
Charles Titone Jr, *Vice Pres*
EMP: 5
SQ FT: 5,800
SALES (est): 300K **Privately Held**
SIC: 3599 7692 3446 Machine shop, jobbing & repair; welding repair; architectural metalwork

(G-16309)
ADVANCED FROZEN FOODS INC
28 Urban Ave (11590-4822)
P.O. Box 887 (11590-0887)
PHONE..........................516 333-6344
Roy Tuccillo, *President*
▲ **EMP:** 50
SALES (est): 8.4MM **Privately Held**
SIC: 2015 Poultry slaughtering & processing

(G-16310)
ADVANCED SURFACE FINISHING
111 Magnolia Ave (11590-4719)
PHONE..........................516 876-9710
Peter Tobias, *President*
Dennis Kelvey, *Prdtn Mgr*
EMP: 25
SQ FT: 15,000
SALES: 1.8MM **Privately Held**
WEB: www.advancedsurfacefinishing.com
SIC: 3479 Coating of metals & formed products; painting, coating & hot dipping

(G-16311)
AERO STRCTURES LONG ISLAND INC (PA)
717 Main St (11590-5021)
PHONE..........................516 997-5757
William Gross, *CEO*
Leonard Gross, *President*
Alex Voda, *Controller*
EMP: 80
SQ FT: 91,000
SALES: 30MM **Privately Held**
SIC: 3728 Aircraft body & wing assemblies & parts

(G-16312)
AIRNET COMMUNICATIONS CORP
Also Called: Airnet North Division
609 Cantiague Rock Rd # 5 (11590-1721)
PHONE..........................516 338-0008
Louis Pryce, *Manager*
EMP: 15 **Privately Held**
WEB: www.airnetcom.com
SIC: 3663 Radio & TV communications equipment
HQ: Airnet Communications Corporation
295 North Dr Ste G
Melbourne FL 32934

(G-16313)
ALL TYPE SCREW MACHINE PDTS
Also Called: Skelton Screw Products Co
100 New York Ave (11590-4909)
PHONE..........................516 334-5100
Eileen Sinn, *President*
EMP: 6
SQ FT: 5,000
SALES: 300K **Privately Held**
SIC: 3451 Screw machine products

(G-16314)
AMERICAN LINEAR MANUFACTURERS (PA)
629 Main St (11590-4923)
PHONE..........................516 333-1351
Frank Tabone, *President*
EMP: 10
SQ FT: 2,000
SALES: 4.3MM **Privately Held**
SIC: 3545 3599 Machine tool accessories; custom machinery

(G-16315)
AMERICAN OFFICE SUPPLY INC
400 Post Ave Ste 105 (11590-2226)
PHONE..........................516 294-9444
Joseph Caldwell, *President*
Jospeh Caldwell, *President*
EMP: 11
SALES (est): 1.6MM **Privately Held**
WEB: www.aoslink.com
SIC: 2759 5943 Commercial printing; stationery stores

(G-16316)
AN EXCELSIOR ELEVATOR CORP
640 Main St Unit 2 (11590-4937)
PHONE..........................516 408-3070
Eric Petzold, *CEO*
Nancy Snyder, *Manager*
EMP: 16
SALES (est): 3.4MM **Privately Held**
SIC: 3534 5084 7699 Elevators & equipment; elevators; elevators: inspection, service & repair

(G-16317)
ARKWIN INDUSTRIES INC (HQ)
686 Main St (11590-5093)
PHONE..........................516 333-2640
William Maglio, *Ch of Bd*
Daniel Berlin, *President*
Richard Vonsalzen, *General Mgr*
Frank Robilotto, *Chairman*
Robert Hultmark, *Vice Pres*
EMP: 242 **EST:** 1951
SQ FT: 110,000
SALES: 71.2MM
SALES (corp-wide): 3.5B **Publicly Held**
WEB: www.arkwin.com
SIC: 3728 Aircraft assemblies, subassemblies & parts
PA: Transdigm Group Incorporated
1301 E 9th St Ste 3000
Cleveland OH 44114
216 706-2960

(G-16318)
AVANEL INDUSTRIES INC
121 Hopper St (11590-4803)
PHONE..........................516 333-0990
Ingo Kurth, *President*
Chris Kurth, *Vice Pres*
EMP: 12 **EST:** 1965
SQ FT: 8,500
SALES (est): 1.5MM **Privately Held**
WEB: www.avanelindustries.com
SIC: 3825 5049 Test equipment for electronic & electric measurement; scientific & engineering equipment & supplies

(G-16319)
BIOIVT LLC (PA)
123 Frost St Ste 115 (11590-5034)
PHONE..........................516 483-1196
Jeff Gatz, *CEO*
EMP: 73
SALES (est): 25.2MM **Privately Held**
SIC: 2836 Veterinary biological products

(G-16320)
CAB-NETWORK INC
Also Called: Four Quarter
1500 Shames Dr Unit B (11590-1772)
PHONE..........................516 334-8666
Martin Chin, *President*
Patrick Chin, *Treasurer*
EMP: 6
SQ FT: 11,000
SALES: 975K **Privately Held**
SIC: 2511 Kitchen & dining room furniture

(G-16321)
COMPUTER INSTRUMENTS CORP
963a Brush Hollow Rd (11590-1710)
PHONE..........................516 876-8400
Elsa Markovits Wilen, *President*
Don Wilen, *Vice Pres*
Detta Donoghue, *Marketing Staff*
EMP: 40 **EST:** 1950
SQ FT: 20,000
SALES (est): 5.6MM **Privately Held**
WEB: www.computerinstruments.com
SIC: 3812 3823 3824 3829 Search & navigation equipment; industrial flow & liquid measuring instruments; fluid meters & counting devices; integrating & totalizing meters for gas & liquids; measuring & controlling devices; aircraft & motor vehicle measurement equipment

(G-16322)
DEPENDABLE ACME THREADED PDTS
167 School St (11590-3371)
PHONE..........................516 338-4700
Annette Farragher, *President*
Magdalene Vogric, *Corp Secy*
EMP: 6 **EST:** 1958
SQ FT: 3,000
SALES: 500K **Privately Held**
WEB: www.dependableacme.com
SIC: 3452 Nuts, metal

(G-16323)
DIONICS-USA INC
96b Urban Ave (11590-4823)
PHONE..........................516 997-7474
Bernard Kravitz, *President*
Kenneth Davis, *Director*
EMP: 7
SALES (est): 877.1K **Privately Held**
SIC: 3674 Integrated circuits, semiconductor networks, etc.

(G-16324)
E B B GRAPHICS INC
Also Called: Sir Speedy
75 State St (11590-5004)
PHONE..........................516 750-5510
Jack Bloom, *President*
Brandon Bloom, *Principal*
Adrienne Bloom, *Vice Pres*
EMP: 10
SQ FT: 1,000
SALES (est): 1.4MM **Privately Held**
WEB: www.sirspeedyny.net
SIC: 2791 2789 2752 Typesetting; bookbinding & related work; commercial printing, lithographic; commercial printing, offset

(G-16325)
EAST HILLS INSTRUMENT INC
60 Shames Dr (11590-1767)
PHONE..........................516 621-8686
Cary Ratner, *CEO*
EMP: 19
SQ FT: 10,000
SALES (est): 4.2MM **Privately Held**
SIC: 3821 3823 3824 3825 Laboratory measuring apparatus; industrial instrmnts msrmnt display/control process variable; fluid meters & counting devices; instruments to measure electricity; analytical instruments; measuring & controlling devices

(G-16326)
EI ELECTRONICS INC
Also Called: Electro Industries
1800 Shames Dr (11590-1730)
PHONE..........................516 334-0870
Erran Kagan, *Ch of Bd*
Mohammad Taher, *Opers Staff*
Sherwin Tan, *Engineer*
Elaine Landrio, *CFO*
Tom David, *Sales Mgr*
EMP: 11
SALES (est): 1.4MM **Privately Held**
SIC: 3825 Meters: electric, pocket, portable, panelboard, etc.

(G-16327)
ELM TRANSIT MIX CORPORATION
Also Called: Elm Ready Mix
482 Grand Blvd (11590-4602)
PHONE..........................516 333-6144
Sandy Nicolia, *President*
Antonio Nicolia, *Vice Pres*
Liliana Legarreta, *Accountant*
EMP: 12
SALES (est): 2.5MM **Privately Held**
SIC: 3273 Ready-mixed concrete

(G-16328)
EMITLED INC
Also Called: Led Next
2300 Shames Dr (11590-1748)
PHONE..........................516 531-3533
Asi Levy, *President*
EMP: 5
SALES (est): 649.3K **Privately Held**
SIC: 3641 Electric light bulbs, complete

(G-16329)
EXECUTIVE BUSINESS MEDIA INC
Also Called: EBM
825 Old Country Rd (11590-5589)
PHONE..........................516 334-3030
Helen Scheller, *Chairman*
Fred Schane, *Vice Pres*
EMP: 50
SQ FT: 4,100
SALES (est): 28.9MM **Privately Held**
WEB: www.ebmpubs.com
SIC: 2721 Magazines: publishing only, not printed on site

(G-16330)
FABRIC QUILTERS UNLIMITED INC
1400 Shames Dr (11590-1780)
PHONE..........................516 333-2866
John Brunning, *President*
EMP: 25
SQ FT: 7,500
SALES: 1.7MM **Privately Held**
SIC: 2392 2391 2591 Bedspreads & bed sets: made from purchased materials; comforters & quilts: made from purchased materials; draperies, plastic & textile: from purchased materials; window blinds; window shades

(G-16331)
FEINSTEIN IRON WORKS INC
990 Brush Hollow Rd (11590-1783)
PHONE..........................516 997-8300
Daniel Feinstein, *CEO*
Howard Feinstein, *President*
Murray Gold, *Vice Pres*
Howard Morris, *Technology*
Iris Echevarria, *Administration*
EMP: 32 **EST:** 1931
SQ FT: 45,000
SALES (est): 8.4MM **Privately Held**
WEB: www.feinsteinironworks.com
SIC: 3441 Fabricated structural metal

(G-16332)
FOUR K MACHINE SHOP INC
54 Brooklyn Ave (11590-4902)
PHONE..........................516 997-0752
Aaron Feder, *President*
Steven Braverman, *Corp Secy*
Joe Roysman, *Vice Pres*
EMP: 6
SQ FT: 5,000
SALES: 700K **Privately Held**
SIC: 3599 Machine shop, jobbing & repair

(G-16333)
G & G C MACHINE & TOOL CO INC
18 Sylvester St (11590-4911)
PHONE..........................516 873-0999

Westbury - Nassau County (G-16334)

George Christoforou, *President*
Georgia Christoforou, *Vice Pres*
EMP: 7
SQ FT: 8,200
SALES (est) 887.6K **Privately Held**
SIC: 3599 Machine shop, jobbing & repair

(G-16334)
G A RICHARDS & CO INC
18 Sylvester St (11590-4791)
PHONE 516 334-5412
Benjamin Jankowski, *President*
Edward Kaider, *Vice Pres*
EMP: 12
SQ FT: 5,500
SALES (est): 2.1MM **Privately Held**
SIC: 3469 Machine parts, stamped or pressed metal

(G-16335)
GARY ROTH & ASSOCIATES LTD
1400 Old Country Rd # 305 (11590-5119)
PHONE 516 333-1000
Gary Roth, *Partner*
EMP: 30
SALES (est): 4MM **Privately Held**
SIC: 3578 8742 Billing machines; management consulting services

(G-16336)
GENERAL CRYOGENIC TECH LLC
400 Shames Dr (11590-1753)
PHONE 516 334-8200
J Hanny Ruddy,
Ralph Cohan,
Peter Dahal,
Peter Dalal,
EMP: 10
SALES: 1.7MM **Privately Held**
SIC: 3559 Cryogenic machinery, industrial

(G-16337)
H FREUND WOODWORKING CO INC
589 Main St (11590-4900)
PHONE 516 334-3774
Frank Freund, *President*
Hubert Freund Jr, *Vice Pres*
EMP: 15
SQ FT: 13,000
SALES: 1.2MM **Privately Held**
SIC: 2521 Wood office furniture

(G-16338)
HALCYON BUSINESS PUBLICATIONS
Also Called: Area Development Magazine
400 Post Ave Ste 304 (11590-2226)
PHONE 800 735-2732
Dennis Shea, *President*
Dennis J Shea, *President*
Richard Bodo, *Vice Pres*
EMP: 16
SQ FT: 3,700
SALES (est): 2.4MM **Privately Held**
WEB: www.locationusa.com
SIC: 2721 Magazines: publishing only, not printed on site

(G-16339)
HANGER PRSTHETCS & ORTHO INC
5502 Brush Hollow Rd (11590-1719)
PHONE 516 338-4466
Bradford Deudne, *Principal*
Roseann Amato, *Office Mgr*
EMP: 5
SALES (corp-wide): 1B **Publicly Held**
SIC: 3842 Surgical appliances & supplies
HQ: Hanger Prosthetics & Orthotics, Inc.
10910 Domain Dr Ste 300
Austin TX 78758
512 777-3800

(G-16340)
HARPER PRODUCTS LTD
Also Called: Pencoa
117 State St (11590-5022)
PHONE 516 997-2330
Robert Perlmutter, *CEO*
Rick Perlmutter, *President*
Karen Miller, *Vice Pres*
Helen Perlmutter, *Vice Pres*
Larry Sitten, *Vice Pres*

▲ **EMP:** 106
SQ FT: 30,000
SALES (est): 13.4MM **Privately Held**
SIC: 3951 Pens & mechanical pencils

(G-16341)
IMPERIAL INSTRUMENT CORP
Also Called: Imperial Instrmnt & Mach
18 Sylvester St (11590-4911)
PHONE 516 739-6644
Andre Cassata, *President*
EMP: 7 **EST:** 1956
SQ FT: 5,000
SALES (est): 400K **Privately Held**
SIC: 3599 Machine shop, jobbing & repair

(G-16342)
IMPRESS GRAPHIC TECHNOLOGIES
141 Linden Ave (11590-3227)
P.O. Box 13187, Hauppauge (11788-0577)
PHONE 516 781-0845
Darlene Bifone, *President*
John P Bifone, *Vice Pres*
▲ **EMP:** 12
SQ FT: 7,500
SALES (est): 1.4MM **Privately Held**
SIC: 2759 Commercial printing

(G-16343)
J B TOOL & DIE CO INC
629 Main St (11590-4923)
PHONE 516 333-1480
Frank Tabone, *President*
Joseph Tabone, *Vice Pres*
EMP: 28 **EST:** 1946
SQ FT: 14,000
SALES (est): 2MM **Privately Held**
WEB: www.jbtool-die.com
SIC: 3599 3544 Machine shop, jobbing & repair; special dies, tools, jigs & fixtures

(G-16344)
JOHN HASSALL LLC (HQ)
609 Cantiague Rock Rd # 1 (11590-1721)
PHONE 516 334-6200
Monty Gillespie, *President*
▲ **EMP:** 78
SQ FT: 65,000
SALES (est): 17.1MM
SALES (corp-wide): 163.1MM **Privately Held**
SIC: 3452 3399 Rivets, metal; metal fasteners
PA: Novaria Group, L.L.C.
6300 Ridglea Pl Ste 800
Fort Worth TX 76116
817 381-3810

(G-16345)
JOHN HASSALL LLC
Also Called: Sky Aerospace Products
609 Cantiague Rock Rd # 1 (11590-1721)
PHONE 323 869-0150
Monty Gillespie, *President*
▼ **EMP:** 75
SQ FT: 17,000
SALES (est): 7.1MM
SALES (corp-wide): 163.1MM **Privately Held**
WEB: www.skymfg.net
SIC: 3452 Bolts, nuts, rivets & washers
HQ: John Hassall, Llc
609 Cantiague Rock Rd # 1
Westbury NY 11590
516 334-6200

(G-16346)
JUDITH LEWIS PRINTER INC
1915 Ladenburg Dr (11590-5917)
PHONE 516 997-7777
Judith Lewis, *President*
EMP: 6
SQ FT: 2,000
SALES (est): 460K **Privately Held**
SIC: 2752 2759 Commercial printing, offset; letterpress printing

(G-16347)
KAS DIRECT LLC
Also Called: Babyganics
1600 Stewart Ave Ste 411 (11590-6654)
PHONE 516 934-0541
Kevin Schwartz, *CEO*
Mark Ellis, *CFO*
EMP: 50 **EST:** 2008

SQ FT: 15,000
SALES (est): 16.1MM
SALES (corp-wide): 3.5B **Privately Held**
SIC: 2676 Infant & baby paper products
PA: S. C. Johnson & Son, Inc.
1525 Howe St
Racine WI 53403
262 260-2000

(G-16348)
KEMP METAL PRODUCTS INC
2300 Shames Dr (11590-1748)
PHONE 516 997-8860
Mark Raskin, *President*
Richard Raskin, *Corp Secy*
EMP: 30 **EST:** 1946
SQ FT: 10,000
SALES (est): 8.9MM **Privately Held**
WEB: www.kempmetalproducts.com
SIC: 3915 Jewelry parts, unassembled

(G-16349)
LENNY & BILL LLC
717 Main St (11590-5021)
PHONE 516 997-5757
William Gross, *CEO*
Leonard Gross, *President*
Jolis Rodriguez, *COO*
Fanis Estevez, *Engineer*
Nicholas Lamanna, *Design Engr*
EMP: 99
SALES (est): 21.1MM
SALES (corp-wide): 30MM **Privately Held**
SIC: 3728 Aircraft parts & equipment
PA: Aero Structures Long Island, Inc.
717 Main St
Westbury NY 11590
516 997-5757

(G-16350)
LIBERTY BRASS TURNING CO INC
1200 Shames Dr Unit C (11590-1766)
PHONE 718 784-2911
David Zuckerwise, *CEO*
Peter Zuckerwise, *President*
Marshall Johnson, *Safety Mgr*
Barry Bogel, *CFO*
▲ **EMP:** 45
SQ FT: 20,000
SALES (est): 12.9MM **Privately Held**
WEB: www.libertybrass.com
SIC: 3451 3429 3432 Screw machine products; manufactured hardware (general); plumbing fixture fittings & trim

(G-16351)
LONG ISLAND COMPOST CORP
100 Urban Ave (11590-4823)
PHONE 516 334-6600
Charles Vigliotti, *CEO*
Arnold Vigliotti, *Shareholder*
Dominic Vigliotti, *Shareholder*
EMP: 120
SALES (est): 29.3MM **Privately Held**
WEB: www.licompost.com
SIC: 2875 Compost

(G-16352)
LOTUS APPAREL DESIGNS INC
Also Called: Courbee
661 Oakwood Ct (11590-5926)
PHONE 646 236-9363
Fang Mercedes, *President*
Rey Mercedes, *Vice Pres*
▲ **EMP:** 2
SALES (est): 1.3MM **Privately Held**
SIC: 2339 Service apparel, washable: women's

(G-16353)
LOVE UNLIMITED NY INC
762 Summa Ave (11590-5011)
PHONE 718 359-8500
Tom Terrino, *CEO*
Carmela Triolo, *Project Mgr*
EMP: 45 **EST:** 1953
SQ FT: 25,000
SALES (est): 7.1MM **Privately Held**
WEB: www.mbslove.com
SIC: 2759 2752 Decals: printing; commercial printing, lithographic

(G-16354)
MATCH EYEWEAR LLC
1600 Shames Dr (11590-1761)
PHONE 516 877-0170
Sam Herskowitz, *COO*
Helen Junda, *VP Finance*
Shawn Chesanek, *Regl Sales Mgr*
Mike Giangrande, *Manager*
Jonathan Pratt,
▲ **EMP:** 35
SQ FT: 17,000
SALES (est): 4MM **Privately Held**
WEB: www.floateyewear.com
SIC: 3229 3827 5995 Optical glass; optical instruments & lenses; optical goods stores

(G-16355)
MATERIAL MEASURING CORPORATION
121 Hopper St (11590-4803)
PHONE 516 334-6167
Ingo O Kurth, *President*
EMP: 5
SALES: 340K **Privately Held**
SIC: 3821 Laboratory equipment: fume hoods, distillation racks, etc.

(G-16356)
METPAR CORP
95 State St (11590-5006)
P.O. Box 1873 (11590-9065)
PHONE 516 333-2600
Ronald S Mondolino, *President*
Jimmy Fallarino, *Mfg Mgr*
Vincent Salierno, *Site Mgr*
Howard Young, *Purch Mgr*
Dave Vera, *Purchasing*
◆ **EMP:** 80 **EST:** 1952
SQ FT: 65,000
SALES (est): 24.2MM **Privately Held**
WEB: www.metpar.com
SIC: 3431 3088 Metal sanitary ware; toilet fixtures, plastic

(G-16357)
MINERALBIOUS CORP
Also Called: Dr Mineral
28 Northcote Rd (11590-1504)
PHONE 516 498-9715
Dong Young Kim, *CEO*
▲ **EMP:** 12
SALES (est): 877.8K **Privately Held**
SIC: 3295 Minerals, ground or treated

(G-16358)
MONTERO INTERNATIONAL INC
Also Called: Pardazzio Uomo
149 Sullivan Ln Unit 1 (11590-3387)
PHONE 212 695-1787
Raymond Hagigi, *President*
▲ **EMP:** 6
SQ FT: 7,500
SALES (est): 750.3K **Privately Held**
SIC: 2329 2325 Shirt & slack suits: men's, youths' & boys'; men's & boys' dress slacks & shorts

(G-16359)
NEW YORK READY MIX INC
Also Called: Commercial Concrete
120 Rushmore St (11590-4816)
PHONE 516 338-6969
Rick Cerrone, *President*
Ron Notaroantonio, *Vice Pres*
EMP: 5
SQ FT: 4,000
SALES (est): 615.7K **Privately Held**
SIC: 3271 Blocks, concrete or cinder: standard

(G-16360)
P & L DEVELOPMENT LLC
200 Hicks St (11590-3323)
PHONE 516 986-1700
Mitchell Singer, *Branch Mgr*
EMP: 88 **Privately Held**
SIC: 2834 Pharmaceutical preparations
PA: P & L Development, Llc
200 Hicks St
Westbury NY 11590

GEOGRAPHIC SECTION

Westbury - Nassau County (G-16388)

(G-16361)
P & L DEVELOPMENT LLC
Also Called: Pl Developments New York
275 Grand Blvd Unit 1 (11590-3570)
PHONE..................516 986-1700
EMP: 88 Privately Held
SIC: 2834 Pharmaceutical preparations
PA: P & L Development, Llc
200 Hicks St
Westbury NY 11590

(G-16362)
P & L DEVELOPMENT LLC (PA)
Also Called: Pl Developments
200 Hicks St (11590-3323)
PHONE..................516 986-1700
Mitchell Singer, Ch of Bd
Evan Singer, President
John Francis, Senior VP
Dana S Toops, Senior VP
Linda Singer, Vice Pres
◆ EMP: 58
SALES (est): 307MM Privately Held
WEB: www.pldevelopments.com
SIC: 2834 Pharmaceutical preparations

(G-16363)
PARFUSE CORP
65 Kinkel St (11590-4914)
PHONE..................516 997-8888
Angelina J Paris, President
Amy Kuna, Corp Secy
Donald A Paris, Vice Pres
EMP: 35
SQ FT: 10,000
SALES (est): 4.1MM Privately Held
SIC: 7692 3398 3341 Brazing; metal heat treating; secondary nonferrous metals

(G-16364)
PNI CAPITAL PARTNERS
1400 Old Country Rd # 103 (11590-5119)
PHONE..................516 466-7120
Michael Packman, Ch of Bd
EMP: 7
SALES (est): 698.6K Privately Held
SIC: 3452 Pins

(G-16365)
POWER SCRUB IT INC
Also Called: Alltec Products
75 Urban Ave (11590-4829)
PHONE..................516 997-2500
Louis Mangione, President
EMP: 13
SALES (est): 1.9MM Privately Held
SIC: 3589 High pressure cleaning equipment

(G-16366)
PRECISION MECHANISMS CORP
50 Bond St (11590-5002)
PHONE..................516 333-5955
Daniel Z Petrasek, President
Emilia Petrasek, Vice Pres
Lou Libassi, Opers Staff
EMP: 30 EST: 1957
SQ FT: 5,000
SALES (est): 5.9MM Privately Held
WEB: www.precisionmechanisms.com
SIC: 3566 3625 3593 3545 Gears, power transmission, except automotive; relays & industrial controls; fluid power cylinders & actuators; machine tool accessories

(G-16367)
PRINT EARLY LLC
821 Prospect Ave Apt 1a (11590-3779)
PHONE..................718 915-7368
Autumn Zawadzki, Owner
▲ EMP: 20 EST: 2010
SALES (est): 214.3K Privately Held
SIC: 2752 Commercial printing, offset

(G-16368)
PROCOMPONENTS INC (PA)
Also Called: P C I Manufacturing Div
900 Merchants Concourse (11590-5142)
PHONE..................516 683-0909
Barry Reed Lubman, President
Alan Lubman, Corp Secy
Mitchel Lubman, Vice Pres
EMP: 25 EST: 1984
SALES (est): 3.4MM Privately Held
SIC: 3672 3674 8711 Printed circuit boards; semiconductors & related devices; consulting engineer

(G-16369)
R C HENDERSON STAIR BUILDERS
100 Summa Ave (11590-5000)
PHONE..................516 876-9898
Richard Henderson, President
Jason Henderson, Vice Pres
Julie Henderson, Treasurer
EMP: 10
SQ FT: 8,000
SALES: 1MM Privately Held
SIC: 2431 Staircases & stairs, wood; stair railings, wood

(G-16370)
RUBIES COSTUME COMPANY INC
601 Cantiague Rock Rd (11590-1708)
PHONE..................516 333-3473
Marck Bege, Branch Mgr
Salim Aziz, Manager
EMP: 40
SALES (corp-wide): 364.6MM Privately Held
SIC: 2389 Costumes
PA: Rubie's Costume Company, Inc.
12008 Jamaica Ave
Richmond Hill NY 11418
718 846-1008

(G-16371)
S & B MACHINE WORKS INC
111 New York Ave (11590-4924)
PHONE..................516 997-2666
Eileen Sinn, CEO
Frederick Sinn Jr, President
EMP: 23
SQ FT: 10,000
SALES (est): 4.7MM Privately Held
WEB: www.sbmachineworks.com
SIC: 3444 3599 Sheet metal specialties, not stamped; machine shop, jobbing & repair

(G-16372)
SENTINE PRINTING INC
Also Called: Sir Speedy
75 State St (11590-5004)
PHONE..................516 334-7400
Brandon Bloom, President
Steve Ross, President
EMP: 5
SQ FT: 2,200
SALES (est): 509.4K Privately Held
SIC: 2759 2791 2789 2752 Envelopes: printing; stationery: printing; business forms: printing; typesetting; bookbinding & related work; commercial printing, lithographic; signboards, wood

(G-16373)
SPECTRONICS CORPORATION
956 Brush Hollow Rd (11590-1714)
PHONE..................516 333-4840
William B Cooper, Ch of Bd
Jonathan D Cooper, President
Richard Cooper, Vice Pres
John Duerr, Vice Pres
Elvis Quinteros, Maint Spvr
▲ EMP: 190 EST: 1950
SQ FT: 98,000
SALES (est): 58.8MM Privately Held
WEB: www.spectroline.com
SIC: 3646 3544 Fluorescent lighting fixtures, commercial; special dies, tools, jigs & fixtures

(G-16374)
STRATHMORE DIRECTORIES LTD
Also Called: Strathmore Publications
26 Bond St (11590-5002)
PHONE..................516 997-2525
Jack Pizzo, President
EMP: 25
SALES (est): 2.6MM Privately Held
WEB: www.strathmore-ltd.com
SIC: 2721 2741 Trade journals: publishing & printing; miscellaneous publishing

(G-16375)
TAYLOR COMMUNICATIONS INC
1600 Stewart Ave Ste 301 (11590-6611)
PHONE..................718 352-0220
Chris Petro, Branch Mgr
EMP: 10
SALES (corp-wide): 3.4B Privately Held
WEB: www.stdreg.com
SIC: 2761 Manifold business forms
HQ: Taylor Communications, Inc.
4205 S 96th St
Omaha NE 68127
402 898-6422

(G-16376)
TEE PEE AUTO SALES CORP
Also Called: Tri-State Towing Equipment NY
52 Swan St (11590)
PHONE..................516 338-9333
Tom Decillis, President
Peter Pizzo, Vice Pres
EMP: 10
SALES (est): 1.1MM Privately Held
SIC: 3711 Truck & tractor truck assembly

(G-16377)
TEMPO INDUSTRIES INC
90 Hopper St (11590-4802)
PHONE..................516 334-6900
Stuart Braunstein, President
Jade Beetle, Principal
▲ EMP: 1
SALES: 1MM Privately Held
SIC: 3993 7389 Advertising novelties; telephone services

(G-16378)
TISHCON CORP (PA)
30 New York Ave (11590-4907)
P.O. Box 331 (11590-0300)
PHONE..................516 333-3056
Raj K Chopra, Ch of Bd
Vipin Patel, President
Kamal Chopra, Senior VP
Abdul Siddiqui, Manager
▲ EMP: 125 EST: 1977
SALES (est): 63.6MM Privately Held
WEB: www.qgel.com
SIC: 2834 Vitamin preparations; pills, pharmaceutical

(G-16379)
TISHCON CORP
Also Called: Geotec
37 Brooklyn Ave (11590-4901)
P.O. Box 331 (11590-0300)
PHONE..................516 333-3056
Raj Chopra, Manager
EMP: 150
SALES (corp-wide): 63.6MM Privately Held
WEB: www.qgel.com
SIC: 2834 Vitamin preparations
PA: Tishcon Corp.
30 New York Ave
Westbury NY 11590
516 333-3056

(G-16380)
TISHCON CORP
41 New York Ave (11590-4908)
PHONE..................516 333-3050
Raj Chopra, Branch Mgr
EMP: 150
SALES (corp-wide): 63.6MM Privately Held
SIC: 2834 Vitamin preparations
PA: Tishcon Corp.
30 New York Ave
Westbury NY 11590
516 333-3056

(G-16381)
TISHCON CORP
36 New York Ave (11590-4907)
PHONE..................516 333-3050
Hemant Pandit, Branch Mgr
EMP: 150
SALES (corp-wide): 63.6MM Privately Held
WEB: www.qgel.com
SIC: 2834 Vitamin preparations; pills, pharmaceutical

(G-16382)
PA: Tishcon Corp.
30 New York Ave
Westbury NY 11590
516 333-3056

TRIUMPH GROUP INC
Also Called: Triumph Structures-Long Island
717 Main St (11590-5021)
PHONE..................516 997-5757
EMP: 62
SALES (corp-wide): 3.8B Publicly Held
SIC: 3724 Mfg Aircraft Engines/Parts
PA: Triumph Group, Inc.
899 Cassatt Rd Ste 210
Berwyn PA 19312
610 251-1000

(G-16383)
TWIN COUNTY RECYCLING CORP (PA)
113 Magnolia Ave (11590-4719)
PHONE..................516 827-6900
Carlos Lizza, President
EMP: 13
SQ FT: 2,000
SALES (est): 1.2MM Privately Held
WEB: www.twincountyunitedway.com
SIC: 2951 4953 5032 Asphalt paving mixtures & blocks; recycling, waste materials; aggregate

(G-16384)
UTILITY MANUFACTURING CO INC
700 Main St (11590-5020)
PHONE..................516 997-6300
Wilbur Kranz, CEO
Audie Kranz, President
EMP: 30
SQ FT: 44,000
SALES (est): 7MM Privately Held
WEB: www.utilitychemicals.com
SIC: 2899 2891 Chemical preparations; adhesives & sealants

(G-16385)
VALPLAST INTERNATIONAL CORP
200 Shames Dr (11590-1784)
PHONE..................516 442-3923
Peter S Nagy, President
Shabab Rahman, Business Mgr
Peter Nagy, Vice Pres
Ninfa Molina, Admin Asst
▲ EMP: 11
SQ FT: 10,500
SALES: 2.5MM Privately Held
WEB: www.valplast.com
SIC: 3559 3843 Plastics working machinery; dental equipment & supplies

(G-16386)
VESCOM STRUCTURAL SYSTEMS INC
Also Called: Tms Development
100 Shames Dr Unit 1 (11590-1741)
PHONE..................516 876-8100
Joel Person, President
EMP: 10
SALES (est): 53.3K Privately Held
WEB: www.vescomstructures.com
SIC: 3299 Floor composition, magnesite

(G-16387)
WD CERTIFIED CONTRACTING LLC
112 Magnolia Ave 101-A (11590-4720)
PHONE..................516 493-9319
Pierre Desrosiers, Vice Pres
Walter Desrosiers,
EMP: 10
SALES (est): 896.4K Privately Held
SIC: 2521 1522 Wood office furniture; residential construction

(G-16388)
WORLD BEST SPORTING GOODS INC
225 Post Ave (11590-3021)
PHONE..................800 489-0908
Jay Lee, CEO
Jerry Choe, Director
EMP: 13

Westerlo
Albany County

(G-16389)
HANNAY REELS INC
553 State Route 143 (12193-7700)
PHONE..................518 797-3791
Eric A Hannay, *CEO*
Roger A Hannay, *Ch of Bd*
Elaine Hannay Gruener, *Vice Pres*
David G Hannay, *Vice Pres*
Jennifer Wing, *Vice Pres*
◆ **EMP:** 147 **EST:** 1933
SQ FT: 205,000
SALES: 55.9MM **Privately Held**
WEB: www.hannay.com
SIC: 3569 3499 Firehose equipment: driers, rack & reels; reels, cable: metal

Westfield
Chautauqua County

(G-16390)
20 BLISS ST INC
61 E Main St (14787-1305)
PHONE..................716 326-2790
Ralph Wilson, *President*
Janice Wilson, *Vice Pres*
EMP: 5
SALES: 200K **Privately Held**
SIC: 1321 Natural gasoline production

(G-16391)
A TRUSTED NAME INC
Also Called: Proforma
35 Franklin St (14787-1039)
PHONE..................716 326-7400
Jeff Gerdy, *President*
EMP: 12
SQ FT: 4,000
SALES (est): 894.9K **Privately Held**
WEB: www.atrustedname.com
SIC: 2395 5199 5941 Decorative & novelty stitching, for the trade; advertising specialties; sporting goods & bicycle shops

(G-16392)
BETTER BAKED FOODS LLC
25 Jefferson St (14787-1010)
P.O. Box D (14787)
PHONE..................716 326-4651
Greg Leone, *Facilities Mgr*
Gregory Leone, *Manager*
EMP: 100
SQ FT: 66,400
SALES (corp-wide): 4.6B **Privately Held**
WEB: www.betterbaked.com
SIC: 2051 Bread, cake & related products
HQ: Better Baked Foods, Llc
56 Smedley St
North East PA 16428
814 725-8778

(G-16393)
CROWN HILL STONE INC
59 Franklin St (14787-1037)
P.O. Box 76, Stow (14785-0076)
PHONE..................716 326-4601
Geoffrey Turner, *President*
Jeannette Turner, *Corp Secy*
EMP: 32
SQ FT: 1,296
SALES (est): 3.3MM **Privately Held**
SIC: 3272 3281 Building stone, artificial: concrete; fireplace & chimney material: concrete; cut stone & stone products

(G-16394)
NATIONAL GRAPE COOP ASSN INC (PA)
80 State St (14787)
PHONE..................716 326-5200
Randolph Graham, *President*
Joseph C Falcone, *Vice Pres*
Harold Smith, *Vice Pres*
Jerry A Czebotar, *Director*
Jon Hinkleman, *Director*
◆ **EMP:** 20
SQ FT: 50,000
SALES: 608.4MM **Privately Held**
SIC: 2033 2037 Fruit juices: packaged in cans, jars, etc.; juices: concentrated, hot pack; tomato juice: packaged in cans, jars, etc.; jams, jellies & preserves: packaged in cans, jars, etc.; frozen fruits & vegetables; fruit juices, frozen; fruit juice concentrates, frozen

(G-16395)
QUALITY GUIDES
Also Called: Westfield Publication
39 E Main St (14787-1303)
P.O. Box 38 (14787-0038)
PHONE..................716 326-3163
Ogden Newspapers, *Owner*
EMP: 7
SALES (est): 311.4K **Privately Held**
SIC: 2711 Newspapers: publishing only, not printed on site

(G-16396)
RENOLD INC
100 Bourne St (14787-9706)
PHONE..................716 326-3121
Mike Conley, *Ch of Bd*
David Odonnell, *District Mgr*
Rob Gizzi, *Mfg Spvr*
Cathy Meleen, *Purch Mgr*
Ben Dill, *Engineer*
◆ **EMP:** 100 **EST:** 1920
SQ FT: 100,000
SALES (est): 24.7MM
SALES (corp-wide): 268.4MM **Privately Held**
WEB: www.renoldajax.com
SIC: 3535 3566 3568 Conveyors & conveying equipment; belt conveyor systems, general industrial use; speed changers, drives & gears; couplings, shaft: rigid, flexible, universal joint, etc.
HQ: Renold Holdings Inc.
100 Bourne St
Westfield NY 14787
716 326-3121

(G-16397)
WAFFENBAUCH USA
165 Academy St (14787-1308)
PHONE..................716 326-4508
Sam Villafrank, *CEO*
EMP: 48
SALES: 250K **Privately Held**
SIC: 1382 Oil & gas exploration services

(G-16398)
WELCH FOODS INC A COOPERATIVE
2 S Portage St (14787-1492)
PHONE..................716 326-5252
David Moore, *General Mgr*
Robert W McMillin, *Principal*
Thomas M Curtin, *Manager*
EMP: 175
SALES (corp-wide): 608.4MM **Privately Held**
WEB: www.welchs.com
SIC: 2033 Fruit juices: packaged in cans, jars, etc.
HQ: Welch Foods Inc., A Cooperative
300 Baker Ave Ste 101
Concord MA 01742
978 371-1000

(G-16399)
WELCH FOODS INC A COOPERATIVE
100 N Portage St (14787-1092)
PHONE..................716 326-3131
Andrew Mullen, *Buyer*
Dean Kirschner, *Senior Engr*
Wilson Haller, *Branch Mgr*
EMP: 26
SALES (corp-wide): 608.4MM **Privately Held**
WEB: www.welchs.com
SIC: 2033 Canned fruits & specialties
HQ: Welch Foods Inc., A Cooperative
300 Baker Ave Ste 101
Concord MA 01742
978 371-1000

(G-16400)
WINE GROUP INC
Also Called: Mogen David Winegroup
85 Bourne St (14787-9706)
PHONE..................716 326-3151
Jean Schwartz, *Manager*
EMP: 60
SQ FT: 83,120
SALES (corp-wide): 151.9MM **Privately Held**
SIC: 2084 Wines
HQ: The Wine Group Inc
17000 E State Highway 120
Ripon CA 95366
209 599-4111

Westhampton
Suffolk County

(G-16401)
DAVE SANDEL CRANES INC
56 S Country Rd (11977-1314)
PHONE..................631 325-5588
David Sandel, *President*
EMP: 7
SALES: 1MM **Privately Held**
SIC: 3531 Cranes

(G-16402)
HAMPTON SAND CORP
1 High St (11977)
P.O. Box 601, Speonk (11972-0601)
PHONE..................631 325-5533
Barbara Dawson, *President*
EMP: 8
SQ FT: 1,000
SALES (est): 1.2MM **Privately Held**
SIC: 1442 5261 5032 4953 Sand mining; gravel mining; top soil; brick, stone & related material; recycling, waste materials

Westhampton Beach
Suffolk County

(G-16403)
FRAME WORKS AMERICA INC
Also Called: Spectaculars
146 Mill Rd (11978-2345)
PHONE..................631 288-1300
William Vetri, *President*
EMP: 40
SQ FT: 1,500
SALES: 3MM **Privately Held**
SIC: 3851 Eyeglasses, lenses & frames

(G-16404)
MICHAEL K LENNON INC
Also Called: Pine Barrens Printing
851 Riverhead Rd (11978-1210)
P.O. Box 704, Westhampton (11977-0704)
PHONE..................631 288-5200
Michael K Lennon, *President*
EMP: 30
SQ FT: 11,000
SALES (est): 4.6MM **Privately Held**
WEB: www.pinebarrensprinting.com
SIC: 2752 Commercial printing, offset

(G-16405)
SHUGAR PUBLISHING
Also Called: Qsr Medical Communications
99b Main St (11978-2607)
PHONE..................631 288-4404
Vivian Mahl, *President*
C S Pithumoni, *Editor*
Dorine Kitay, *Manager*
EMP: 8
SQ FT: 250
SALES: 1.5MM **Privately Held**
WEB: www.practicalgastro.com
SIC: 2721 Periodicals: publishing only

(G-16406)
SOUTHAMPTON TOWN NEWSPAPERS
Also Called: Western Edition
12 Mitchell Rd (11978-2609)
P.O. Box 1071 (11978-7071)
PHONE..................631 288-1100
Cailin Brophy, *Editor*
Frank Costanca, *Manager*
EMP: 10
SALES (corp-wide): 2.9MM **Privately Held**
WEB: www.southamptonpress.com
SIC: 2711 Newspapers: publishing only, not printed on site
PA: Southampton Town Newspapers Inc
135 Windmill Ln
Southampton NY 11968
631 283-4100

Westmoreland
Oneida County

(G-16407)
MOHAWK METAL MFG & SLS
4901 State Route 233 (13490-1309)
PHONE..................315 853-7663
William F Schrock, *President*
EMP: 5
SQ FT: 20,000
SALES (est): 2.5MM **Privately Held**
SIC: 2421 Building & structural materials, wood

(G-16408)
PERSONAL GRAPHICS CORPORATION
5123 State Route 233 (13490-1311)
PHONE..................315 853-3421
Paul Hillman, *President*
EMP: 7
SQ FT: 7,000
SALES: 380K **Privately Held**
SIC: 2759 Screen printing

(G-16409)
RISING STARS SOCCER CLUB CNY
4980 State Route 233 (13490-1308)
P.O. Box 423, Rome (13442-0423)
PHONE..................315 381-3096
Frank Conestabile, *Owner*
EMP: 10
SALES (est): 494.4K **Privately Held**
SIC: 3949 Sporting & athletic goods

(G-16410)
SHAFER & SONS
Also Called: Storage Sheds
4932 State Route 233 (13490-1308)
PHONE..................315 853-5285
John H Shafer, *Partner*
Jason Shafer, *Partner*
Joe Shafer, *Partner*
Kathleen Shafer, *Partner*
EMP: 5
SQ FT: 8,000
SALES (est): 709.8K **Privately Held**
WEB: www.ssheds.com
SIC: 2452 5039 Prefabricated buildings, wood; prefabricated buildings

(G-16411)
SIERSON CRANE INC
4822 State Route 233 (13490-1306)
P.O. Box 358 (13490-0358)
PHONE..................315 723-6914
Mitchell R Sierson, *President*
EMP: 13
SALES (est): 1.6MM **Privately Held**
SIC: 7692 Welding repair

(G-16412)
SIERSON WELDING INC
12 Partyka Rd (13490)
P.O. Box 358 (13490-0358)
PHONE..................315 724-3903
Mitchell Sierson, *CEO*
EMP: 7
SALES (est): 29K **Privately Held**
SIC: 7692 Welding repair

GEOGRAPHIC SECTION

White Plains - Westchester County (G-16439)

Westtown
Orange County

(G-16413)
FROST PUBLICATIONS INC
55 Laurel Hill Dr (10998-3921)
P.O. Box 178 (10998-0178)
PHONE..................................845 726-3232
Don Frost, *Owner*
EMP: 5
SALES (est): 417.9K **Privately Held**
SIC: 2721 1521 Periodicals: publishing & printing; single-family housing construction

(G-16414)
GRANT-NOREN
83 Ridge Rd (10998-2602)
PHONE..................................845 726-4281
Daniel Grant, *Partner*
Ingela Noren, *Partner*
EMP: 5
SALES: 180K **Privately Held**
SIC: 2499 Picture & mirror frames, wood

White Plains
Westchester County

(G-16415)
1KTGOLD INC
Also Called: 3 Barker Ave Ste 290
3 Barker Ave Ste 290 (10601-1545)
PHONE..................................212 302-8200
Enrique Verdeguer, *CEO*
EMP: 16
SALES (est): 546.6K **Privately Held**
SIC: 3911 Jewelry, precious metal

(G-16416)
A & C/FURIA ELECTRIC MOTORS
75 Lafayette Ave (10603-1613)
PHONE..................................914 949-0585
Andrew Cerone, *President*
Carol Cerone, *Office Mgr*
EMP: 11
SQ FT: 5,000
SALES (est): 2.1MM **Privately Held**
SIC: 7694 7699 5999 5251 Electric motor repair; pumps & pumping equipment repair; compressor repair; motors, electric; pumps & pumping equipment; fans, electric

(G-16417)
ALAMAR PRINTING INC
Also Called: PIP Printing
190 E Post Rd Frnt 1 (10601-4918)
PHONE..................................914 993-9007
Mary Jane Goldman, *President*
EMP: 10
SQ FT: 6,500
SALES (est): 1.5MM **Privately Held**
SIC: 2752 2754 Commercial printing, offset; business form & card printing, gravure; promotional printing, gravure; stationery & invitation printing, gravure

(G-16418)
ALCONOX INC
30 Glenn St Ste 309 (10603-3252)
PHONE..................................914 948-4040
Rhoda Schemin, *President*
Elliot Lebowitz, *COO*
Jill Zisnan, *Vice Pres*
Michael Moussourakis, *Senior Mgr*
Jeff Phillips, *Systems Dir*
EMP: 6 **EST**: 1946
SQ FT: 4,000
SALES (est): 1.3MM **Privately Held**
WEB: www.alconox.com
SIC: 3841 Surgical & medical instruments

(G-16419)
AMENDOLA MBL & STONE CTR INC
560 Tarrytown Rd (10607-1316)
PHONE..................................914 997-7968
Sergio Amendola, *President*
Joseph Amendola, *Vice Pres*
Shauna Dibuono, *Sales Staff*
Maria Amendola, *Admin Sec*
▲ **EMP**: 62
SQ FT: 3,500
SALES (est): 7.3MM **Privately Held**
SIC: 3281 2493 5999 5211 Granite, cut & shaped; marbleboard (stone face hard board); stones, crystalline: rough; tile, ceramic

(G-16420)
AMERICAN INTL MEDIA LLC
Also Called: Rugby Magazine
11 Martine Ave Ste 870 (10606-4025)
PHONE..................................845 359-4225
Ajon Prusmack, *Principal*
EMP: 10
SQ FT: 3,000
SALES (est): 890K **Privately Held**
SIC: 2721 Periodicals-Publishing/Printing

(G-16421)
APPLE PRESS
23 Harrison Blvd Ste 2 (10604)
PHONE..................................914 723-6660
Jody Majthenyi, *Owner*
EMP: 7
SQ FT: 4,800
SALES (est): 559.3K **Privately Held**
SIC: 2752 7334 Commercial printing, offset; photocopying & duplicating services

(G-16422)
ARLON VISCOR LTD
1133 Westchester Ave (10604-3516)
PHONE..................................914 461-1300
Arlon, *Principal*
EMP: 608
SALES (est): 26.3MM
SALES (corp-wide): 1.3B **Publicly Held**
SIC: 3356 Nonferrous rolling & drawing
HQ: Bairnco Corporation
1133 Westchester Ave N-222
White Plains NY 10604
914 461-1300

(G-16423)
ARTYARNS
70 Westmoreland Ave (10606-2315)
PHONE..................................914 428-0333
Elliot Schreier, *President*
Iris Schreier, *Vice Pres*
EMP: 8
SALES (est): 994.9K **Privately Held**
WEB: www.artyarns.com
SIC: 2269 Dyeing: raw stock yarn & narrow fabrics

(G-16424)
BAIRNCO CORPORATION (DH)
1133 Westchester Ave N-222 (10604-3516)
PHONE..................................914 461-1300
Glen M Kassan, *Ch of Bd*
John J Quicke, *President*
Lawrence C Maingot, *CFO*
◆ **EMP**: 20
SQ FT: 11,000
SALES (est): 91.6MM
SALES (corp-wide): 1.3B **Publicly Held**
WEB: www.bairnco.com
SIC: 2821 3556 Plastics materials & resins; meat, poultry & seafood processing machinery; slicers, commercial, food

(G-16425)
BAKER PRODUCTS INC
5 Oakley Rd (10606-3701)
PHONE..................................212 459-2323
Jeff Brown, *President*
▲ **EMP**: 6
SQ FT: 1,500
SALES (est): 1.2MM **Privately Held**
SIC: 3111 3172 Case leather; cosmetic bags

(G-16426)
BALLANTRAE LITHOGRAPHERS INC
96 Wayside Dr (10607-2726)
PHONE..................................914 592-3275
Steve Quagliano, *President*
Ralph Bocchimuzzo, *Vice Pres*
Rocco Quagliano, *Treasurer*
EMP: 6
SQ FT: 5,000
SALES (est): 380K **Privately Held**
SIC: 2752 Commercial printing, offset

(G-16427)
BEACON PRESS INC
32 Cushman Rd (10606-3706)
PHONE..................................212 691-5050
Kenneth B Weiner, *President*
EMP: 4 **EST**: 1913
SQ FT: 3,000
SALES (est): 2MM **Privately Held**
WEB: www.beaconpress.com
SIC: 2752 Commercial printing, offset

(G-16428)
BENFIELD CONTROL SYSTEMS INC
25 Lafayette Ave (10603-1613)
PHONE..................................914 948-6660
Daniel J McLaughlin, *President*
Dominic Devito, *Managing Dir*
Roy C Kohli, *Chairman*
Miguel Guerrero, *Project Engr*
William Roloff, *CFO*
EMP: 10
SALES (est): 5.4MM
SALES (corp-wide): 196.7MM **Privately Held**
WEB: www.benfieldcontrolsystems.com
SIC: 3613 8711 Control panels, electric; engineering services
PA: H.H. Benfield Electric Supply Company, Inc.
25 Lafayette Ave
White Plains NY 10603
914 948-6660

(G-16429)
BOTTLING GROUP LLC
Also Called: Pepsi Beverages Company
1111 Westchester Ave (10604-3525)
PHONE..................................800 789-2626
James B Lindsey Jr, *President*
Marjorie Lindsey, *Corp Secy*
Dick Graeber, *Vice Pres*
Gean Anne Asturp, *Admin Sec*
EMP: 400 **EST**: 1932
SQ FT: 1,000,000
SALES (est): 102.9MM
SALES (corp-wide): 63.5B **Publicly Held**
SIC: 2086 Carbonated beverages, nonalcoholic: bottled & canned; soft drinks: packaged in cans, bottles, etc.
HQ: Pepsi-Cola Bottling Group
1111 Westchester Ave
White Plains NY 10604
914 767-6000

(G-16430)
BOTTLING GROUP LLC (HQ)
Also Called: Pepsi Beverages Company
1111 Westchester Ave (10604-3525)
PHONE..................................914 767-6000
Albert P Carey, *CEO*
Zein Abdalla, *President*
Joe Moreno, *Production*
James Hart, *Technical Mgr*
Robert Housley, *VP Finance*
◆ **EMP**: 10
SALES (est): 10B
SALES (corp-wide): 63.5B **Publicly Held**
WEB: www.bottlinggroup.com
SIC: 2086 Bottled & canned soft drinks; carbonated soft drinks, bottled & canned; carbonated beverages, nonalcoholic: bottled & canned
PA: Pepsico, Inc.
700 Anderson Hill Rd
Purchase NY 10577
914 253-2000

(G-16431)
BRISTOL/WHITE PLAINS
305 North St (10605-2208)
PHONE..................................914 681-1800
Diane Mandracchia, *Principal*
EMP: 8
SALES (est): 985.7K **Privately Held**
SIC: 2621 Bristols

(G-16432)
BUNGE LIMITED FINANCE CORP
50 Main St (10606-1901)
PHONE..................................914 684-2800
Brian Zachman, *Principal*
Chris Nikkel, *Vice Pres*
Andrew Schneider, *Project Mgr*
Daryl Curry, *Maint Spvr*
Gregory Elkin, *Opers Staff*
EMP: 53
SALES (est): 40MM **Privately Held**
SIC: 2079 Edible fats & oils
PA: Bunge Limited
C/O Conyers, Dill & Pearman
Hamilton

(G-16433)
BYRAM CONCRETE & SUPPLY LLC
145 Virginia Rd (10603-2232)
PHONE..................................914 682-4477
John R Percham, *Principal*
Charlie Smallen, *Accounts Mgr*
EMP: 11
SALES (est): 1.2MM **Privately Held**
SIC: 3273 Ready-mixed concrete

(G-16434)
C P CHEMICAL CO INC
25 Home St (10606-2306)
PHONE..................................914 428-2517
Walter Hasselman Jr, *President*
Daryl Reich, *CTO*
EMP: 5
SQ FT: 20,000
SALES (est): 900K **Privately Held**
WEB: www.tripolymer.com
SIC: 3086 2899 2873 Insulation or cushioning material, foamed plastic; foam charge mixtures; fertilizers: natural (organic), except compost

(G-16435)
CAMEO PROCESS CORP
15 Stewart Pl Apt 7g (10603-3808)
PHONE..................................914 948-0082
Edwin Goldstein, *President*
S G Goldstein, *Treasurer*
EMP: 2
SALES: 6MM **Privately Held**
SIC: 2671 Resinous impregnated paper for packaging

(G-16436)
CARBONFREE CHEMICALS SPE I LLC
1 N Lexington Ave (10601-1712)
PHONE..................................914 421-4900
Nadeem S Nisar, *President*
Nadeem Nisar, *Managing Dir*
Heather Taormina, *Admin Asst*
EMP: 40
SALES (est): 1.6MM **Privately Held**
SIC: 3624 Carbon & graphite products

(G-16437)
CLASSIC COLLECTIONS FINE ART
20 Haarlem Ave Ste 408 (10603-2233)
PHONE..................................914 591-4500
Larry Tolchin, *President*
EMP: 6
SQ FT: 5,000
SALES (est): 596K **Privately Held**
SIC: 2741 Art copy: publishing only, not printed on site

(G-16438)
CN GROUP INCORPORATED
76 Mamaroneck Ave (10601-4217)
PHONE..................................914 358-5690
EMP: 910
SALES (est): 43.7MM **Privately Held**
SIC: 3089 3841 2821 Mfg Plastic Products Mfg Surgical/Medical Instruments Mfg Plastic Materials/Resins

(G-16439)
COMBE INCORPORATED (PA)
1101 Westchester Ave (10604-3503)
PHONE..................................914 694-5454
Richard G Powers, *President*
Jason Friedlander, *General Mgr*
Christopher B Combe, *Principal*
Jessica Eichel, *Counsel*
Jerome S Darby, *Senior VP*
◆ **EMP**: 240 **EST**: 1949
SQ FT: 68,000

White Plains - Westchester County (G-16440)

SALES (est): 170.9MM **Privately Held**
WEB: www.combe.com
SIC: **2834** 2841 Pharmaceutical preparations; soap: granulated, liquid, cake, flaked or chip

(G-16440)
COPY STOP INC
Also Called: L K Printing
50 Main St Ste 32 (10606-1920)
PHONE..................914 428-5188
Richard Koh, *President*
EMP: 5
SQ FT: 800
SALES (est): 744.3K **Privately Held**
SIC: **2752** Commercial printing, offset

(G-16441)
DANONE NUTRICIA EARLY
100 Hillside Ave (10603-2861)
PHONE..................914 872-8556
Luciana Nunez, *General Mgr*
EMP: 20 **EST**: 2014
SQ FT: 30,000
SALES (est): 1.5MM **Privately Held**
SIC: **2023** Canned baby formula

(G-16442)
DANONE US LLC (HQ)
Also Called: Dannon Company, LLC
1 Maple Ave (10605-1476)
PHONE..................914 872-8400
Geno Finan, *General Mgr*
Steve Holmes, *General Mgr*
Vanessa Vlahakis, *General Mgr*
Sergio Fuster, *Vice Pres*
Thomas Rondot, *Vice Pres*
▲ EMP: 100
SQ FT: 35,000
SALES (est): 1.1B
SALES (corp-wide): 718.1MM **Privately Held**
WEB: www.dannon.com
SIC: **2026** Yogurt
PA: Danone
  17 Boulevard Haussmann
  Paris 75009
  149 485-000

(G-16443)
DAVID YURMAN ENTERPRISES LLC
125 Westchester Ave # 1060 (10601-4546)
PHONE..................914 539-4444
David Yurman, *CEO*
Liz Candela, *Sales Staff*
EMP: 9
SALES (corp-wide): 268.5MM **Privately Held**
SIC: **3911** Jewelry, precious metal
PA: David Yurman Enterprises Llc
  24 Vestry St
  New York NY 10013
  212 896-1550

(G-16444)
EFFICIENCY PRINTING CO INC
126 S Lexington Ave (10606-2510)
P.O. Box 157, Valhalla (10595-0157)
PHONE..................914 949-8611
Fax: 914 949-8516
EMP: 13 **EST**: 1944
SQ FT: 5,000
SALES (est): 1.4MM **Privately Held**
SIC: **2752** 2759 Commercial Printer

(G-16445)
ELECTRO PLATING SERVICE INC
127 Oakley Ave (10601-3903)
PHONE..................914 948-3777
Julian Galperin, *President*
EMP: 12 **EST**: 1930
SQ FT: 27,000
SALES: 353.8K **Privately Held**
WEB: www.smithwarren.com
SIC: **3471** Electroplating of metals or formed products

(G-16446)
ESCHOLAR LLC
222 Bloomingdale Rd # 107 (10605-1517)
PHONE..................914 989-2900
Shawn Bay, *CEO*
Wolf Boehme, *President*
Marc Hoffmeister, *Director*

EMP: 11
SQ FT: 2,500
SALES (est): 2.5MM **Privately Held**
WEB: www.escholar.com
SIC: **3695** 5045 Computer software tape & disks: blank, rigid & floppy; computer software

(G-16447)
ETHIS COMMUNICATIONS INC
44 Church St Ste 200 (10601-1919)
PHONE..................212 791-1440
David Kellner, *Owner*
Jennifer Zweibel, *Editor*
Adam Gundaker, *COO*
Lindsay Hermanson, *Prdtn Mgr*
Mike Smolinsky, *Manager*
EMP: 7
SALES (est): 737.4K **Privately Held**
SIC: **2741** Miscellaneous publishing

(G-16448)
EXCELL PRINT & PROMOTIONS INC
50 Main St Ste 100 (10606-1901)
PHONE..................914 437-8668
David Quas, *President*
EMP: 8
SALES (est): 586.6K **Privately Held**
SIC: **2759** 7389 Promotional printing;

(G-16449)
F-O-R SOFTWARE LLC (PA)
Also Called: Two-Four Software
10 Bank St Ste 880 (10606-1933)
PHONE..................914 220-8800
Paul Radding, *Director*
Kevin Ouderkirk,
John Flowers,
EMP: 21
SQ FT: 2,100
SALES (est): 3.1MM **Privately Held**
WEB: www.twofour.com
SIC: **7372** Business oriented computer software

(G-16450)
FARMERS HUB LLC (HQ)
Also Called: House of Serengeti
8 Francine Ct (10607-1201)
PHONE..................914 380-2945
Oseovbie Imoukhuede, *Mng Member*
EMP: 6
SALES (est): 227.3K **Privately Held**
SIC: **2099** Tea blending
PA: Heureka Llc
  8 Francine Ct
  White Plains NY 10607
  914 380-2945

(G-16451)
FORDHAM MARBLE CO INC
45 Crane Ave (10603-3702)
PHONE..................914 682-6699
Mario Serdo, *President*
EMP: 5
SALES (est): 1.2MM **Privately Held**
SIC: **3272** 3281 Art marble, concrete; cut stone & stone products

(G-16452)
GARRETT J CRONIN
Also Called: Minute Man Printing Company
1 Stuart Way (10607-1805)
PHONE..................914 761-9299
Garrett J Cronin, *Principal*
EMP: 5
SALES (est): 171.7K **Privately Held**
SIC: **2759** 7389 Commercial printing;

(G-16453)
GAS RECOVERY SYSTEMS LLC (HQ)
Also Called: Gas Recovery Systems Illinois
1 N Lexington Ave Ste 620 (10601-1721)
PHONE..................914 421-4903
Thomas Gesicki, *President*
Anthony Albao, *Vice Pres*
EMP: 12
SQ FT: 2,500
SALES (est): 40.8MM
SALES (corp-wide): 198.7MM **Privately Held**
SIC: **1389** Removal of condensate gasoline from field (gathering) lines

PA: Fortistar Llc
  1 N Lexington Ave Ste 620
  White Plains NY 10601
  914 421-4900

(G-16454)
GREAT BRANDS OF EUROPE INC
Also Called: Lu Biscuits
100 Hillside Ave Fl 3 (10603-2862)
PHONE..................914 872-8804
Elio Pacheco, *Vice Pres*
▲ EMP: 6
SALES (est): 400K **Privately Held**
WEB: www.danone.com
SIC: **2052** Cookies & crackers

(G-16455)
GREENKISSNY INC
75 S Broadway (10601-4413)
PHONE..................914 304-4323
Ann Anderson, *CEO*
EMP: 6
SALES (est): 150.9K **Privately Held**
SIC: **2834** Pharmaceutical preparations

(G-16456)
GROWTH PRODUCTS LTD
80 Lafayette Ave (10603-1603)
PHONE..................914 428-1316
Clare Reinbergen, *Ch of Bd*
Joanne Elaslaoui, *Human Res Mgr*
Matthew Grassi, *Marketing Staff*
Melissa Mancini, *Admin Asst*
▼ EMP: 50
SALES (est): 11.9MM **Privately Held**
SIC: **2873** Nitrogenous fertilizers

(G-16457)
HAIGHTS CROSS OPERATING CO (HQ)
10 New King St Ste 102 (10604-1208)
PHONE..................914 289-9400
Peter J Quandt, *Ch of Bd*
Linda Koons, *Exec VP*
Kevin M Mc Aliley, *Exec VP*
Mark Kurtz, *Vice Pres*
Paul J Crecca, *CFO*
EMP: 26
SALES (est): 32.6MM
SALES (corp-wide): 83.8MM **Privately Held**
SIC: **2731** Book publishing
PA: Haights Cross Communications, Inc.
  295 Prncton Hightstown Rd
  Princeton Junction NJ 08550
  212 209-0500

(G-16458)
HANDCRAFT CABINETRY INC
230 Ferris Ave Ste 1 (10603-3461)
PHONE..................914 681-9437
Michael Ford, *President*
EMP: 9
SQ FT: 4,000
SALES (est): 1.3MM **Privately Held**
WEB: www.handcraftcabinetry.com
SIC: **2517** Home entertainment unit cabinets, wood

(G-16459)
HIGH LINE LUBE LLC
Also Called: Valvoline Instant Oil Change
374 Central Ave (10606-1210)
PHONE..................914 684-0170
Pat Demosthene, *Branch Mgr*
EMP: 9
SALES (corp-wide): 12.6MM **Privately Held**
SIC: **2992** Oils & greases, blending & compounding
PA: High Line Lube, Llc
  25 Main St
  Hartford CT 06106
  860 244-9310

(G-16460)
HOGIL PHARMACEUTICAL CORP
237 Mmaroneck Ave Ste 207 (10605)
PHONE..................914 681-1800
David Trager, *President*
Howard Wendy, *Chairman*
▲ EMP: 10
SQ FT: 3,500

SALES (est): 2.1MM **Privately Held**
WEB: www.hogil.com
SIC: **2834** 3841 5047 5122 Pharmaceutical preparations; surgical & medical instruments; medical & hospital equipment; drugs, proprietaries & sundries

(G-16461)
HTF COMPONENTS INC
134 Bowbell Rd (10607-1141)
PHONE..................914 703-6795
Fred Silva, *President*
Michael C Silva, *Vice Pres*
EMP: 9
SQ FT: 1,545
SALES (est): 1.5MM **Privately Held**
WEB: www.htfcomponents.com
SIC: **3699** 5065 Electrical equipment & supplies; electronic parts & equipment

(G-16462)
INFORMA BUSINESS MEDIA INC
Fleet Owner Magazine
707 Westchester Ave # 101 (10604-3102)
PHONE..................914 949-8500
Paul Kisseberth, *Branch Mgr*
EMP: 14 **Privately Held**
SIC: **2731** Book publishing
HQ: Informa Business Media, Inc.
  605 3rd Ave
  New York NY 10158
  212 204-4200

(G-16463)
ITT AEROSPACE CONTROLS LLC
4 W Red Oak Ln (10604-3603)
PHONE..................914 641-2000
Marcy Barberio, *Marketing Mgr*
Menotti Lombardi, *Mng Member*
Ken I Bianchi, *Program Mgr*
Ed Kupp, *Manager*
Kathleen Tolar, *Admin Sec*
EMP: 7
SALES (est): 1.1MM
SALES (corp-wide): 2.5B **Publicly Held**
SIC: **3625** Motor controls & accessories
HQ: Itt Llc
  1133 Westchester Ave N-100
  White Plains NY 10604
  914 641-2000

(G-16464)
ITT INC (PA)
1133 Westchester Ave N-100 (10604-3543)
PHONE..................914 641-2000
Frank T Macinnis, *Ch of Bd*
Denise L Ramos, *President*
Farrokh Batliwala, *President*
Aris C Chicles, *President*
Carlo Ghirardo, *President*
EMP: 45 **EST**: 1920
SALES: 2.5B **Publicly Held**
SIC: **3594** 3625 3823 3812 Fluid power pumps & motors; control equipment, electric; fluidic devices, circuits & systems for process control; radar systems & equipment

(G-16465)
ITT INDUSTRIES HOLDINGS INC (DH)
1133 Westchester Ave N-100 (10604-3543)
PHONE..................914 641-2000
Mary Beth Gustafsson, *President*
Steve Giuliano, *Senior VP*
Daryl Bowker, *Vice Pres*
Michael Savinelli, *Vice Pres*
Thomas Scalera, *CFO*
EMP: 8 **EST**: 2004
SALES (est): 2MM
SALES (corp-wide): 2.5B **Publicly Held**
SIC: **2611** 4731 Pulp mills; freight consolidation
HQ: International Standard Electric Corporation
  1105 N Market St Ste 1217
  Wilmington DE 19801
  302 427-3769

(G-16466)
ITT INTERNATIONAL HOLDINGS INC (DH)
1133 Westchester Ave (10604-3516)
PHONE..................914 641-2000

Michael Savinelli, *Asst Treas*
EMP: 5
SALES (est): 424.2K
SALES (corp-wide): 2.5B **Publicly Held**
SIC: 3625 Control equipment, electric
HQ: Itt Llc
1133 Westchester Ave N-100
White Plains NY 10604
914 641-2000

(G-16467)
ITT LLC (HQ)
1133 Westchester Ave N-100 (10604-3543)
PHONE.................................914 641-2000
Denise L Ramos, *President*
Farrokh Batliwala, *President*
Aris C Chicles, *President*
Neil W Yeargin, *President*
Steven C Giuliano, *Vice Pres*
◆ **EMP:** 450 **EST:** 1920
SALES: 2.5B **Publicly Held**
WEB: www.ittind.com
SIC: 3594 3625 3823 3812 Fluid power pumps & motors; control equipment, electric; fluidic devices, circuits & systems for process control; radar systems & equipment
PA: Itt Inc.
1133 Westchester Ave N-100
White Plains NY 10604
914 641-2000

(G-16468)
JOURNAL NEWS
1133 Westchester Ave N-110 (10604-3511)
PHONE.................................914 694-5000
EMP: 6
SALES (est): 180.7K **Privately Held**
SIC: 2711 Newspapers-Publishing/Printing

(G-16469)
KINRO MANUFACTURING INC (DH)
200 Mmaroneck Ave Ste 301 (10601)
PHONE.................................817 483-7791
Jason Lippert, *President*
Scott Mereness, *Vice Pres*
Gary McPhail, *CFO*
▲ **EMP:** 1 **EST:** 1997
SALES (est): 130.8MM
SALES (corp-wide): 2.1B **Publicly Held**
SIC: 3442 Metal doors, sash & trim
HQ: Kinro Manufacturing, Inc.
3501 County Road 6 E
Elkhart IN 46514
574 535-1125

(G-16470)
L K PRINTING CORP
Also Called: Royal Press
50 Main St Ste 32 (10606-1920)
PHONE.................................914 761-1944
Richard Koh, *President*
Joshua Greene, *Vice Pres*
EMP: 6
SQ FT: 1,200
SALES: 700K **Privately Held**
SIC: 2752 Commercial printing, offset

(G-16471)
L S Z INC
Also Called: Alconox
30 Glenn St Ste 309 (10603-3252)
PHONE.................................914 948-4040
Elliot Lebowitz, *CEO*
EMP: 8
SALES (est): 680.9K **Privately Held**
WEB: www.ledizolv.com
SIC: 2841 Detergents, synthetic organic or inorganic alkaline

(G-16472)
LIFE PILL LABORATORIES LLC
50 Main St Ste 100 (10606-1901)
PHONE.................................914 682-2146
Alfred Sparman,
Lena Wills, *Admin Sec*
EMP: 6
SALES (est): 267.4K **Privately Held**
SIC: 2834 Pharmaceutical preparations

(G-16473)
LSIL & CO INC
Also Called: Lori Silverman Shoes
2 Greene Ln (10605-5111)
PHONE.................................914 761-0998
Lori Silverman, *President*
EMP: 6
SALES (est): 510.3K **Privately Held**
SIC: 3144 5661 Boots, canvas or leather: women's; women's shoes

(G-16474)
MAIO FUEL COMPANY LP
46 Fairview Ave (10603-3403)
PHONE.................................914 683-1154
Mario Cafagno, *Principal*
EMP: 5
SALES (est): 252.2K **Privately Held**
SIC: 2869 Fuels

(G-16475)
MEASUREMENT INCORPORATED
7-11 S Broadway Ste 402 (10601-3546)
PHONE.................................914 682-1969
Jacob Feinberg, *Research*
EMP: 18
SALES (corp-wide): 83MM **Privately Held**
SIC: 2759 Commercial printing
PA: Measurement Incorporated
423 Morris St
Durham NC 27701
919 683-2413

(G-16476)
META-THERM CORP
Also Called: Bio-Nutritional Products
70 W Red Oak Ln (10604-3602)
PHONE.................................914 697-4840
Murray Flashner, *President*
▲ **EMP:** 15
SQ FT: 15,000
SALES: 4MM **Privately Held**
SIC: 2099 Food preparations

(G-16477)
MICROSOFT CORPORATION
125 Westchester Ave (10601-4522)
PHONE.................................914 323-2150
EMP: 599
SALES (corp-wide): 110.3B **Publicly Held**
SIC: 7372 Application computer software
PA: Microsoft Corporation
1 Microsoft Way
Redmond WA 98052
425 882-8080

(G-16478)
NATIONAL HEALTH PROM ASSOC
711 Westchester Ave # 301 (10604-3539)
PHONE.................................914 421-2525
Gilbert J Botvin, *President*
Monica Mitchell, *Accounting Mgr*
Stephanie Phillips, *Director*
EMP: 22
SQ FT: 120,000
SALES (est): 1.9MM **Privately Held**
SIC: 2741 Miscellaneous publishing

(G-16479)
NESTLE USA INC
1311 Mmroneck Ave Ste 350 (10605)
PHONE.................................914 272-4021
David Rosenbluth, *Principal*
EMP: 139
SALES (corp-wide): 90.8B **Privately Held**
SIC: 2023 Evaporated milk
HQ: Nestle Usa, Inc.
1812 N Moore St
Rosslyn VA 22209
818 549-6000

(G-16480)
NEW ENGLAND RECLAMATION INC
20 Haarlem Ave (10603-2223)
PHONE.................................914 949-2000
Janet Peckham, *Ch of Bd*
John Peckham, *President*
James V De Forest, *Exec VP*
Thomas Vitti, *Treasurer*
EMP: 15
SALES (est): 1.4MM
SALES (corp-wide): 200.6MM **Privately Held**
WEB: www.peckham.com
SIC: 3399 Metal powders, pastes & flakes

PA: Peckham Industries, Inc.
20 Haarlem Ave Ste 200
White Plains NY 10603
914 949-2000

(G-16481)
NU2 SYSTEMS LLC
155 Lafayette Ave (10603-1602)
PHONE.................................914 719-7272
Isac Tabib,
Mehdi Daryadel,
Elias Wexler,
EMP: 10
SQ FT: 15,000
SALES (est): 419K **Privately Held**
SIC: 3669 Communications Equipment, Nec, Nsk

(G-16482)
ORENOVA GROUP LLC
10 New King St Ste 106 (10604-1208)
PHONE.................................914 517-3000
Barrie Levitt MD, *Mng Member*
EMP: 5
SALES (est): 206.2K **Privately Held**
SIC: 2834 Pharmaceutical preparations

(G-16483)
OSAKA GAS ENERGY AMERICA CORP
1 N Lexington Ave Ste 504 (10601-1724)
PHONE.................................914 253-5500
Shojiro Oka, *Principal*
Tatsuro Tsukamoto, *Business Mgr*
Tomohiro Katayama, *Senior VP*
John Drake, *VP Bus Dvlpt*
▲ **EMP:** 15
SALES (est): 771.5K
SALES (corp-wide): 12.1B **Privately Held**
SIC: 2911 Gases & liquefied petroleum gases
PA: Osaka Gas Co., Ltd.
4-1-2, Hiranomachi, Chuo-Ku
Osaka OSK 541-0
662 054-537

(G-16484)
PARAMOUNT CORD & BRACKETS
6 Tournament Dr (10605-5121)
PHONE.................................212 325-9100
Gary Rosenkranz, *President*
EMP: 8
SQ FT: 8,000
SALES (est): 640K **Privately Held**
WEB: www.pccords.com
SIC: 2211 Corduroys, cotton; basket weave fabrics, cotton

(G-16485)
PATTERSON BLACKTOP CORP (HQ)
20 Haarlem Ave (10603-2223)
PHONE.................................914 949-2000
John Peckham, *President*
Janet G Peckham, *President*
John R Peckham, *President*
James V De Forest, *Exec VP*
Thomas Vitti, *Treasurer*
EMP: 30
SALES (est): 2.7MM
SALES (corp-wide): 200.6MM **Privately Held**
SIC: 2951 Asphalt paving mixtures & blocks
PA: Peckham Industries, Inc.
20 Haarlem Ave Ste 200
White Plains NY 10603
914 949-2000

(G-16486)
PATTERSON MATERIALS CORP (HQ)
20 Haarlem Ave (10603-2223)
PHONE.................................914 949-2000
Janet G Peckham, *Co-President*
John R Peckham, *Co-President*
James V De Forest, *Exec VP*
EMP: 17
SQ FT: 15,000
SALES (est): 2.8MM
SALES (corp-wide): 200.6MM **Privately Held**
SIC: 2951 Asphalt paving mixtures & blocks

PA: Peckham Industries, Inc.
20 Haarlem Ave Ste 200
White Plains NY 10603
914 949-2000

(G-16487)
PEARSON LONGMAN LLC (DH)
10 Bank St Ste 1030 (10606-1952)
PHONE.................................212 641-2400
Jeff Taylor, *President*
Roger A Brown, *Vice Pres*
John Stallon, *Vice Pres*
Herbert Yeates, *Treasurer*
Bernadette Clarke, *Credit Mgr*
EMP: 40
SALES (est): 102.5MM
SALES (corp-wide): 5.9B **Privately Held**
SIC: 2731 2711 Books: publishing & printing; newspapers, publishing & printing
HQ: Pearson Inc.
1330 Hudson St
New York NY 10013
212 641-2400

(G-16488)
PECKHAM INDUSTRIES INC (PA)
20 Haarlem Ave Ste 200 (10603-2223)
PHONE.................................914 949-2000
John R Peckham, *President*
Neil Lewis, *Superintendent*
Jack Reynaud, *Assistant VP*
Gary W Metcalf, *Vice Pres*
Joseph Wildermuth, *Vice Pres*
▲ **EMP:** 30 **EST:** 1924
SQ FT: 15,000
SALES (est): 200.6MM **Privately Held**
WEB: www.peckham.com
SIC: 2951 Concrete, asphaltic (not from refineries)

(G-16489)
PECKHAM MATERIALS CORP (HQ)
20 Haarlem Ave Ste 200 (10603-2223)
PHONE.................................914 686-2045
John R Peckham, *President*
Gary Metcalf, *Vice Pres*
Peter Simoneau, *Vice Pres*
Joe Wildermuth, *Vice Pres*
Chris Carter, *Plant Mgr*
EMP: 100
SQ FT: 5,000
SALES (est): 24.5MM
SALES (corp-wide): 200.6MM **Privately Held**
SIC: 2951 1611 5032 Asphalt & asphaltic paving mixtures (not from refineries); concrete, asphaltic (not from refineries); highway & street paving contractor; paving mixtures
PA: Peckham Industries, Inc.
20 Haarlem Ave Ste 200
White Plains NY 10603
914 949-2000

(G-16490)
PEPSI-COLA BOTTLING GROUP (DH)
Also Called: Pepsico
1111 Westchester Ave (10604-4000)
PHONE.................................914 767-6000
Sean Bishop, *President*
Micheal Matney, *Vice Pres*
Marc Fantone, *Manager*
◆ **EMP:** 2
SALES (est): 185.3MM
SALES (corp-wide): 63.5B **Publicly Held**
SIC: 2086 Carbonated soft drinks, bottled & canned
HQ: Pepsi-Cola Metropolitan Bottling Company, Inc.
1111 Westchester Ave
White Plains NY 10604
914 767-6000

(G-16491)
PEPSI-COLA METRO BTLG CO INC (HQ)
Also Called: Pepsico
1111 Westchester Ave (10604-4000)
PHONE.................................914 767-6000
Philip A Marineau, *President*
Robert Carl Biggart, *Chairman*
Dick W Boyce, *Senior VP*

White Plains - Westchester County (G-16492)

Brian Swette, *Senior VP*
Mark L Wheless, *Vice Pres*
◆ **EMP:** 5
SQ FT: 100,000
SALES (est): 22.2B
SALES (corp-wide): 63.5B **Publicly Held**
WEB: www.joy-of-cola.com
SIC: 2086 2087 Soft drinks: packaged in cans, bottles, etc.; syrups, drink
PA: Pepsico, Inc.
700 Anderson Hill Rd
Purchase NY 10577
914 253-2000

(G-16492)
PEPSI-COLA OPERATING COMPANY (HQ)
1111 Westchester Ave (10604-4000)
PHONE 914 767-6000
John Kayhill, *President*
Todd Eveland, *Senior VP*
Alex Baxter, *Vice Pres*
Tom Connolly, *Vice Pres*
Mike M Luzzi, *Project Mgr*
EMP: 43
SALES (est): 23.7MM
SALES (corp-wide): 63.5B **Publicly Held**
SIC: 2086 Bottled & canned soft drinks
PA: Pepsico, Inc.
700 Anderson Hill Rd
Purchase NY 10577
914 253-2000

(G-16493)
PEPSICO INC
1111 Westchester Ave (10604-4000)
PHONE 914 253-2000
Vincent Costa, *Sr Project Mgr*
EMP: 309
SALES (corp-wide): 63.5B **Publicly Held**
SIC: 2096 Potato chips & similar snacks
PA: Pepsico, Inc.
700 Anderson Hill Rd
Purchase NY 10577
914 253-2000

(G-16494)
PEPSICO INC
150 Airport Rd Hngr V (10604-1219)
PHONE 914 253-3474
Archie Walker, *Branch Mgr*
Robert A Baldwin, *Manager*
EMP: 28
SALES (corp-wide): 63.5B **Publicly Held**
WEB: www.pepsico.com
SIC: 2086 Carbonated soft drinks, bottled & canned
PA: Pepsico, Inc.
700 Anderson Hill Rd
Purchase NY 10577
914 253-2000

(G-16495)
PEPSICO INC
1111 Westchester Ave (10604-4000)
PHONE 914 767-6976
Jim Dohr, *Principal*
EMP: 58
SALES (corp-wide): 63.5B **Publicly Held**
SIC: 2096 Potato chips & similar snacks
PA: Pepsico, Inc.
700 Anderson Hill Rd
Purchase NY 10577
914 253-2000

(G-16496)
PETER PAUPER PRESS INC
202 Mmaroneck Ave Ste 400 (10601)
PHONE 914 681-0144
Laurence Beilenson, *President*
Evelyn Beilenson, *Principal*
Nick Beilenson, *Principal*
Esther Beilenson, *Sales Dir*
Scott Levenson, *Manager*
▲ **EMP:** 25 EST: 1982
SQ FT: 4,004
SALES (est): 3.2MM **Privately Held**
WEB: www.peterpauper.com
SIC: 2731 Books: publishing only

(G-16497)
PFIZER INC
4 Martine Ave (10606-4016)
PHONE 914 437-5868
EMP: 146

SALES (corp-wide): 49.6B **Publicly Held**
SIC: 2834 Mfg Pharmaceutical Medicinal Preparations
PA: Pfizer Inc.
235 E 42nd St
New York NY 10017
212 733-2323

(G-16498)
PLASTICYCLE CORPORATION (PA)
245 Main St Ste 430 (10601-2425)
PHONE 914 997-6882
Anthony R Corso, *Ch of Bd*
Joseph Cirillo, *Principal*
Mike Tolkov, *Manager*
EMP: 40 EST: 1998
SQ FT: 40,000
SALES (est): 9.3MM **Privately Held**
SIC: 3089 Plastic processing

(G-16499)
PREMIER WOODCRAFT LTD
277 Martine Ave 214 (10601-3401)
PHONE 610 383-6624
EMP: 40
SQ FT: 30,000
SALES (est): 3.7MM **Privately Held**
SIC: 2511 2522 2521 2434 Mfg Wood Household Furn Mfg Nonwood Office Furn Mfg Wood Office Furn Mfg Wood Kitchen Cabinet

(G-16500)
S & H UNIFORM CORP
1 Aqueduct Rd (10606-1003)
PHONE 914 937-6800
Rhoda Ross, *CEO*
Glen Ross, *President*
Rosa Greco, *Cust Mgr*
Carol Schiffman, *Accounts Exec*
▼ **EMP:** 65
SQ FT: 50,000
SALES (est): 11.4MM **Privately Held**
WEB: www.sandhuniforms.com
SIC: 2326 7389 Men's & boys' work clothing; telemarketing services

(G-16501)
SABRA DIPPING COMPANY LLC (PA)
777 Westchester Ave Fl 3 (10604-3520)
PHONE 914 372-3900
Tomer Harpaz, *CEO*
Jose Gonzalez, *Production*
Grant Hedges, *Research*
Willie Johnson, *Engineer*
Paula Fitzgerald, *CFO*
▲ **EMP:** 75
SALES (est): 290MM **Privately Held**
SIC: 2035 Spreads, sandwich: salad dressing base

(G-16502)
SAFE FLIGHT INSTRUMENT CORP
20 New King St (10604-1204)
PHONE 914 946-9500
Randall Greene, *President*
Joe Wilson, *Vice Pres*
Joseph Tiseo, *Project Dir*
Pete Barna, *Facilities Mgr*
Victor Falcaro, *Purch Mgr*
▲ **EMP:** 150 EST: 1946
SQ FT: 42,600
SALES (est): 29.9MM **Privately Held**
WEB: www.safeflight.com
SIC: 3812 7699 Aircraft flight instruments; aircraft control systems, electronic; aircraft flight instrument repair

(G-16503)
SAPPI NORTH AMERICA INC
925 Westchester Ave # 115 (10604-3562)
PHONE 914 696-5544
Katherine Haynes, *Regl Sales Mgr*
Bradley McLain, *Marketing Staff*
Brent Demichael, *Branch Mgr*
EMP: 60
SALES (corp-wide): 5.3B **Privately Held**
SIC: 2679 Paper products, converted
HQ: Sappi North America, Inc.
255 State St Fl 4
Boston MA 02109
617 423-7300

(G-16504)
SOFTLINK INTERNATIONAL
297 Knollwood Rd Ste 301 (10607-1849)
PHONE 914 574-8197
Prakash S Kamat, *CEO*
Sunil Nikhar, *President*
Praveen Lobo, *Vice Pres*
EMP: 45
SQ FT: 1,200
SALES (est): 1.5MM **Privately Held**
WEB: www.softlinkinternational.com
SIC: 7372 Prepackaged software

(G-16505)
SPX COOLING TECHNOLOGIES INC
30 Glenn St Ste 403 (10603-3245)
PHONE 914 697-5030
Bart Petterson, *Manager*
EMP: 8
SALES (corp-wide): 1.4B **Publicly Held**
WEB: www.cts.spx.com
SIC: 3443 Fabricated plate work (boiler shop)
HQ: Spx Cooling Technologies, Inc.
7401 W 129th St
Overland Park KS 66213
913 664-7400

(G-16506)
STAR BRANDS NORTH AMERICA INC (DH)
Also Called: Pladis Limited
10 Bank St Ste 1011 (10606-1933)
PHONE 914 355-9750
Brian Blanchard, *CEO*
James Ricciardi, *CFO*
EMP: 40
SALES (est): 110.9MM **Privately Held**
WEB: www.demetscandy.com
SIC: 2064 Candy & other confectionery products
HQ: Yildiz Holding Anonim Sirketi
No.6/1 Kisikli Mahallesi
Istanbul (Anatolia) 34692
216 524-2900

(G-16507)
STARFUELS INC (HQ)
50 Main St (10606-1901)
PHONE 914 289-4800
Robert Ryneveld, *Managing Dir*
EMP: 3 EST: 2012
SALES: 21.5MM
SALES (corp-wide): 1MM **Privately Held**
SIC: 3339 2911 1241 Precious metals; oils, fuel; coal mining services
PA: Starcommodities, Inc.
285 Grand Ave Bldg 3
Englewood NJ 07631
201 685-0400

(G-16508)
STEEL EXCEL INC (HQ)
1133 Westchester Ave (10604-3516)
PHONE 914 461-1300
Jack L Howard, *CEO*
Douglas Woodworth, *CFO*
▲ **EMP:** 6
SALES (est): 132.6MM
SALES (corp-wide): 1.3B **Publicly Held**
WEB: www.adaptec.com
SIC: 1389 7032 Oil & gas wells: building, repairing & dismantling; sporting & recreational camps
PA: Steel Partners Holdings L.P.
590 Madison Ave Rm 3202
New York NY 10022
212 520-2300

(G-16509)
STUDIO FUN INTERNATIONAL INC
44 S Broadway Fl 7 (10601-4417)
PHONE 914 238-1000
Harold Clark, *President*
William Magill, *Vice Pres*
Clifford Dupree, *Admin Sec*
▲ **EMP:** 30
SALES (est): 8.2MM **Privately Held**
WEB: www.rd.com
SIC: 2731 Book publishing

HQ: Trusted Media Brands, Inc.
750 3rd Ave Fl 3
New York NY 10017
914 238-1000

(G-16510)
SYMBIO TECHNOLOGIES LLC
333 Mamaroneck Ave (10605-1440)
PHONE 914 576-1205
Boyoung Kwon, *Opers Mgr*
Diane Romm, *Marketing Staff*
Gideon Romm, *CTO*
Roger Del Russo,
EMP: 7
SALES (est): 1MM **Privately Held**
WEB: www.symbio-technologies.com
SIC: 3575 Computer terminals

(G-16511)
TELEMERGENCY LTD
3 Quincy Ln (10605-5431)
PHONE 914 629-4222
Elliot I Baum, *President*
▲ **EMP:** 5
SQ FT: 1,400
SALES (est): 530K **Privately Held**
WEB: www.telemergency300.com
SIC: 3669 Emergency alarms

(G-16512)
TENSA SOFTWARE
66 Greenvale Cir (10607-1602)
PHONE 914 686-5376
Dilib Kha, *Owner*
EMP: 10
SALES (est): 600K **Privately Held**
SIC: 7372 Prepackaged software

(G-16513)
TRUSTED MEDIA BRANDS INC
44 S Broadway Fl 7 (10601-4417)
PHONE 914 244-5244
Bill Jankowski, *Info Tech Dir*
EMP: 12 **Privately Held**
SIC: 2721 2731 5961 2741 Magazines: publishing only, not printed on site; books: publishing only; books, mail order (except book clubs); record &/or tape (music or video) club, mail order; miscellaneous publishing
HQ: Trusted Media Brands, Inc.
750 3rd Ave Fl 3
New York NY 10017
914 238-1000

(G-16514)
VERONA PHARMA INC
50 Main St Ste 1000 (10606-1900)
PHONE 914 797-5007
Jan-Anders Karlsson, *CEO*
Kenneth Newman, *Vice Pres*
EMP: 11 EST: 2017
SALES (est): 531K **Privately Held**
SIC: 2834 Pharmaceutical preparations

(G-16515)
VIBRA TECH INDUSTRIES INC
126 Oakley Ave (10601-3904)
PHONE 914 946-1916
Kenneth Strati, *President*
EMP: 11 EST: 1962
SQ FT: 12,000
SALES: 730K **Privately Held**
SIC: 3471 Finishing, metals or formed products

(G-16516)
WATKINS WELDING AND MCH SP INC
87 Westmoreland Ave (10606-2316)
PHONE 914 949-6168
Charles G Watkins, *President*
Inge Watkins, *Treasurer*
EMP: 7
SQ FT: 1,850
SALES: 300K **Privately Held**
SIC: 7692 3599 Welding repair; machine shop, jobbing & repair

(G-16517)
WAYNE PRINTING INC
Also Called: Wayne Printing & Lithographic
70 W Red Oak Ln Fl 4 (10604-3602)
PHONE 914 761-2400
Jeffrey Wayne, *President*
EMP: 10 EST: 1946

SQ FT: 1,000
SALES (est): 1.5MM **Privately Held**
WEB: www.wayneprinting.com
SIC: 2752 Commercial printing, offset

(G-16518)
WESTCHESTER LAW JOURNAL INC
Also Called: Wlj Printers
199 Main St Ste 301 (10601-3206)
PHONE..................914 948-0715
Lyle Salmon, *President*
Richard L Salmon, *Vice Pres*
Marjorie Salmon, *Director*
▲ EMP: 5
SQ FT: 1,350
SALES (est): 457.9K **Privately Held**
WEB: www.westchesterlawjournal.com
SIC: 2721 7389 Trade journals: publishing only, not printed on site; legal & tax services

(G-16519)
WESTCHESTER MAILING SERVICE
Also Called: Westmail Press
39 Westmoreland Ave Fl 2 (10606-1937)
PHONE..................914 948-1116
George Lusk, *President*
EMP: 30
SQ FT: 15,000
SALES (est): 3.2MM **Privately Held**
SIC: 2752 7331 2791 2789 Commercial printing, offset; mailing service; typesetting; bookbinding & related work

(G-16520)
WESTCHESTER WINE WAREHOUSE LLC
53 Tarrytown Rd Ste 1 (10607-1655)
PHONE..................914 824-1400
Sunil Khurana, *Manager*
Ken Irving, *Director*
Ben Khurana,
Rude Seleimi,
EMP: 15
SALES (est): 2.4MM **Privately Held**
WEB: www.westchesterwine.com
SIC: 2084 2389 Wines; cummerbunds

(G-16521)
WESTFAIR COMMUNICATIONS INC
Also Called: Westchester County Bus Jurnl
3 Westchester Park Dr G7 (10604-3420)
PHONE..................914 694-3600
Dolores Delbello, *CEO*
John Mack Carter, *Shareholder*
EMP: 35
SALES (est): 2.3MM **Privately Held**
SIC: 2711 2721 Newspapers: publishing only, not printed on site; periodicals

(G-16522)
WRKBOOK LLC
19 Brookdale Ave (10603-3201)
PHONE..................914 355-1293
William De Andrade, *CEO*
Eric Wiener, *CTO*
EMP: 10 EST: 2017
SALES: 50K **Privately Held**
SIC: 7372 7389 Prepackaged software;

Whitehall
Washington County

(G-16523)
MAPLEWOOD ICE CO INC
9785 State Route 4 (12887-2317)
P.O. Box 62 (12887-0062)
PHONE..................518 499-2345
David O Wood, *President*
Donna Wood, *Corp Secy*
Douglas Wood, *Vice Pres*
EMP: 30
SQ FT: 6,000
SALES (est): 5.9MM **Privately Held**
SIC: 2097 5078 Manufactured ice; refrigeration equipment & supplies

(G-16524)
STEWARTS SHOPS CORP
60 Poultney St (12887-1516)
PHONE..................518 499-9376
James Kelley, *Branch Mgr*
EMP: 12
SALES (corp-wide): 1.5B **Privately Held**
WEB: www.stewartsshops.com
SIC: 2024 5411 Ice cream & ice milk; convenience stores
PA: Stewart's Shops Corp.
2907 State Route 9
Ballston Spa NY 12020
518 581-1201

(G-16525)
VERMONT STRUCTURAL SLATE CO
Buckley Rd (12887)
PHONE..................518 499-1912
Robert Tucker, *Manager*
EMP: 12
SALES (corp-wide): 10.3MM **Privately Held**
WEB: www.vermontstructuralslate.com
SIC: 3281 Cut stone & stone products
PA: Vermont Structural Slate Co Inc
3 Prospect St
Fair Haven VT 05743
802 265-4933

Whitesboro
Oneida County

(G-16526)
COLLEGE CALENDAR COMPANY
148 Clinton St (13492-2501)
PHONE..................315 768-8242
Carter Reul, *Owner*
Steve Tibits, *Manager*
EMP: 10
SALES: 850K **Privately Held**
SIC: 2721 Magazines: publishing only, not printed on site

(G-16527)
EVERSAN INC
34 Main St Ste 3 (13492-1039)
PHONE..................315 736-3967
Mustafa Evke, *CEO*
Allan R Roberts, *Vice Pres*
Nick Wilson, *Sales Dir*
John Liberty, *Sales Staff*
▲ EMP: 14
SALES (est): 2.6MM **Privately Held**
WEB: www.eversan.com
SIC: 3625 3674 3993 Timing devices, electronic; microprocessors; scoreboards, electric

(G-16528)
QUALITY COMPONENTS FRAMING SYS
44 Mohawk St Bldg 10 (13492-1232)
PHONE..................315 768-1167
Daniel R Webb, *President*
EMP: 13
SQ FT: 30,000
SALES (est): 1.5MM **Privately Held**
WEB: www.qcwallpanels.com
SIC: 3253 Clay wall & floor tile

(G-16529)
S R SLOAN INC (PA)
8111 Halsey Rd (13492-3707)
P.O. Box 560, New Hartford (13413-0560)
PHONE..................315 736-7730
Sheldon R Sloan, *CEO*
Stephen R Sloan, *President*
Will Compton, *Opers Mgr*
Melissa Cummings, *CFO*
Pat Passalacqua, *Sales Staff*
EMP: 77 EST: 1960
SQ FT: 60,000
SALES (est): 16.9MM **Privately Held**
WEB: www.srsloan.com
SIC: 2431 2439 Staircases & stairs, wood; trusses, wooden roof

(G-16530)
TELECOMMUNICATION CONCEPTS
Also Called: T C I
329 Oriskany Blvd (13492-1424)
PHONE..................315 736-8523
Don Ryan, *President*
EMP: 5
SALES (est): 760.5K **Privately Held**
WEB: www.telecommunicationconcepts.com
SIC: 3661 1731 Telephones & telephone apparatus; telephone & telephone equipment installation

(G-16531)
TURBINE ENGINE COMP UTICA
8273 Halsey Rd (13492-3803)
PHONE..................315 768-8070
Rob Cohen, *President*
Mike Finley, *Plant Mgr*
Travis Brisack, *Engineer*
Walter Burdick, *Engineer*
Jerry Cammer, *Engineer*
EMP: 1300
SQ FT: 250,000
SALES (est): 191.5MM **Privately Held**
SIC: 3724 3511 3429 3842 Aircraft engines & engine parts; turbines & turbine generator sets & parts; clamps, couplings, nozzles & other metal hose fittings; surgical appliances & supplies; guided missile & space vehicle parts & auxiliary equipment
PA: U C A Holdings, Inc.
1 W Pack Sq Ste 305
Asheville NC 28801

(G-16532)
WHITESBORO SPRING & ALIGNMENT (PA)
Also Called: Whitesboro Spring Svce
247 Oriskany Blvd (13492-1596)
PHONE..................315 736-4441
Stewart Wattenbe Jr, *President*
Melanie Wattenbe, *CFO*
EMP: 11
SQ FT: 2,500
SALES (est): 1.1MM **Privately Held**
SIC: 3493 7539 7538 Leaf springs: automobile, locomotive, etc.; brake repair, automotive; general automotive repair shops

Whitestone
Queens County

(G-16533)
ANTICO CASALE USA LLC
1244 Clintonville St 2c (11357-1849)
PHONE..................914 760-1100
Gerard Ambrosio, *Managing Dir*
Gaetano De Luca, *Prdtn Mgr*
Fiori Franzese,
Gianluca Nastro,
▲ EMP: 4
SQ FT: 800
SALES: 2.6MM **Privately Held**
SIC: 2032 Italian foods: packaged in cans, jars, etc.

(G-16534)
APHRODITIES
2007 Francis Lewis Blvd (11357-3930)
PHONE..................718 224-1774
John Milonas, *Owner*
EMP: 8
SALES (est): 784.5K **Privately Held**
SIC: 2051 5812 Bread, cake & related products; coffee shop; cafe

(G-16535)
ATLAS FENCE & RAILING CO INC
Also Called: Atlas Fence Co
15149 7th Ave (11357-1236)
PHONE..................718 767-2200
Toll Free:..................866
Tom Pappas, *President*
EMP: 20
SQ FT: 12,000
SALES (est): 3.7MM **Privately Held**
SIC: 3446 2499 3089 Fences, gates, posts & flagpoles; fences or posts, ornamental iron or steel; fencing, docks & other outdoor wood structural products; fences, gates & accessories: plastic

(G-16536)
BA SPORTS NUTRITION LLC
Also Called: Bodyarmor
1720 Whitestone Expy # 101 (11357-3000)
PHONE..................718 357-7402
Phil Chao, *Opers Staff*
Thomas Hadley, *CFO*
Kevin Talbot, *Controller*
Blaise Ffrench, *Marketing Staff*
Mike Repole, *Mng Member*
EMP: 106
SALES: 125MM **Privately Held**
SIC: 2086 Fruit drinks (less than 100% juice): packaged in cans, etc.

(G-16537)
CARAVELLA FOOD CORP
16611 Cryders Ln (11357-2832)
PHONE..................646 552-0455
Tatiana Odato, *President*
Danny Odato, *Vice Pres*
◆ EMP: 12
SQ FT: 3,500
SALES (est): 590.1K **Privately Held**
SIC: 3556 Oilseed crushing & extracting machinery

(G-16538)
CROWN AIRCRAFT LIGHTING INC
1021 Clintonville St # 4 (11357-1845)
P.O. Box 570432 (11357-0432)
PHONE..................718 767-3410
Michelle Virgilio, *President*
Linda Virgilio, *Vice Pres*
EMP: 9
SQ FT: 4,000
SALES (est): 990.8K **Privately Held**
SIC: 3728 Aircraft parts & equipment

(G-16539)
CT PUBLICATIONS CO
Also Called: Queens Times
1120 154th St (11357-1955)
PHONE..................718 592-2196
James Lisa, *President*
EMP: 7
SALES: 240K **Privately Held**
WEB: www.queenstimes.com
SIC: 2711 Newspapers: publishing only, not printed on site

(G-16540)
FINANCIAL TECHNOLOGIES 360 INC
Also Called: Fin-Tech360
15436 24th Ave (11357-3727)
PHONE..................862 200-1164
Remo Bidnali, *CEO*
John Marshall, *COO*
Murali Saravu, *CIO*
EMP: 7
SALES: 500K **Privately Held**
SIC: 7372 Application computer software

(G-16541)
HARRIS CORPORATION
1902 Whitestone Expy # 204 (11357-3059)
PHONE..................718 767-1100
Dominic Catinella, *Manager*
EMP: 18
SALES (corp-wide): 6.1B **Publicly Held**
SIC: 3663 5065 Radio & TV communications equipment; telephone equipment
PA: Harris Corporation
1025 W Nasa Blvd
Melbourne FL 32919
321 727-9100

(G-16542)
HENGYUAN COPPER USA INC
14107 20th Ave Ste 506 (11357-3045)
PHONE..................718 357-6666
Zhifu Yan, *President*
▲ EMP: 8
SALES (est): 823.6K **Privately Held**
SIC: 3331 Refined primary copper products

Whitestone - Queens County

PA: Shandong Hengyuan Copper Industry Co., Ltd.
Shuixidong, East Fifth Road, North Of Huaihe Rd., Dongying Distr
Dongying
546 810-9555

(G-16543)
HUDSON EASTERN INDUSTRIES INC
1118 143rd Pl (11357-2355)
P.O. Box 570085 (11357-0085)
PHONE..................................917 295-5818
Theresa Marino, *Principal*
EMP: 5
SALES (est): 202.7K **Privately Held**
SIC: 3999 Manufacturing industries

(G-16544)
JENMAR DOOR & GLASS INC
15038 12th Ave (11357-1808)
PHONE..................................718 767-7900
Millie Risi, *CEO*
Alan Risi, *Principal*
EMP: 5 **EST:** 2015
SQ FT: 12,000
SALES (est): 294.3K **Privately Held**
SIC: 3442 Metal doors

(G-16545)
LIF INDUSTRIES INC
Also Called: LI Fireproof Door
1105 Clintonville St (11357-1813)
P.O. Box 570171 (11357-0171)
PHONE..................................718 767-8800
Nick Parise, *Branch Mgr*
EMP: 50
SQ FT: 23,136
SALES (corp-wide): 22.9MM **Privately Held**
SIC: 3442 3429 7699 5211 Fire doors, metal; manufactured hardware (general); door & window repair; door & window products; door frames, all materials
PA: Lif Industries, Inc.
5 Harbor Park Dr Ste 1
Port Washington NY 11050
516 390-6800

(G-16546)
NEW YORK DIGITAL PRINT CENTER
15050 14th Rd Ste 1 (11357-2607)
PHONE..................................718 767-1953
Joann Derasmo, *President*
EMP: 6
SALES (est): 852.5K **Privately Held**
SIC: 2752 Commercial printing, offset

(G-16547)
PEPPERMINTS SALON INC
15722 Powells Cove Blvd (11357-1332)
PHONE..................................718 357-6304
Evangelia Parlionas, *President*
Margarita Parlionas, *Admin Sec*
EMP: 10
SALES (est): 1.1MM **Privately Held**
SIC: 2844 Cosmetic preparations

(G-16548)
SECURITY DEFENSE SYSTEM
15038 12th Ave (11357-1808)
PHONE..................................718 769-7900
Millie Risi, *President*
EMP: 8
SQ FT: 8,000
SALES: 11.5MM **Privately Held**
SIC: 3699 7382 Security devices; protective devices, security

(G-16549)
TOCARE LLC
Also Called: Whitestone Pharmacy
15043b 14th Ave Fl 1 (11357-1864)
PHONE..................................718 767-0618
Roberto Viola,
Nella Viola,
EMP: 10
SALES (est): 1.1MM **Privately Held**
SIC: 2834 5122 Pharmaceutical preparations; pharmaceuticals

(G-16550)
TRIBCO LLC
Also Called: Queens Tribune
15050 14th Rd Ste 2 (11357-2607)
PHONE..................................718 357-7400
Michael Schenkler,
Gary Ackerman,
EMP: 44
SQ FT: 2,000
SALES (est): 3.2MM **Privately Held**
WEB: www.queenstribune.com
SIC: 2711 Newspapers: publishing only, not printed on site

(G-16551)
TRIBOROUGH ELECTRIC
15044 11th Ave (11357-1806)
PHONE..................................718 321-2144
Peter Gargiulo, *Principal*
Lisa Narson, *Office Mgr*
EMP: 7
SALES (est): 1MM **Privately Held**
SIC: 3699 Electrical equipment & supplies

(G-16552)
WHITESTONE PANETTERIA LLC
15045 12th Rd (11357-1809)
PHONE..................................516 543-9788
EMP: 8
SALES (est): 583.5K **Privately Held**
SIC: 2051 Bread, cake & related products

(G-16553)
WORLD JOURNAL LLC (HQ)
14107 20th Ave Fl 2 (11357-6093)
PHONE..................................718 746-8889
Jacob MA, *Ch of Bd*
Pily Wang, *Vice Ch Bd*
Johnson Sung, *General Mgr*
Tina Lee, *Managing Dir*
James Yang, *Vice Pres*
▲ **EMP:** 150
SQ FT: 50,000
SALES (est): 49.7MM
SALES (corp-wide): 53.3MM **Privately Held**
WEB: www.wjnews.net
SIC: 2711 Newspapers, publishing & printing
PA: Cooper Investors Inc.
14107 20th Ave Ste 602
Flushing NY 11357
718 767-8895

Whitney Point
Broome County

(G-16554)
ADVANCED GRAPHICS COMPANY
2607 Main St (13862-2223)
P.O. Box 311 (13862-0311)
PHONE..................................607 692-7875
Rosemarie Fralick, *Owner*
▼ **EMP:** 10 **EST:** 1957
SQ FT: 5,000
SALES (est): 729.9K **Privately Held**
SIC: 3479 2759 Name plates: engraved, etched, etc.; screen printing

(G-16555)
GREEN CONVEYOR & MCH GROUP LLC
8308 Rte 79 (13862)
P.O. Box 301 (13862-0301)
PHONE..................................607 692-7050
Thomas Taylor,
EMP: 7 **EST:** 2006
SALES (est): 1MM **Privately Held**
SIC: 3535 Conveyors & conveying equipment

(G-16556)
POINT CANVAS COMPANY INC
5952 State Route 26 (13862-1211)
PHONE..................................607 692-4381
Lori Warfield, *President*
Sharon Dahulich, *Vice Pres*
Wayne Dahulich, *Treasurer*
Danny Warfield, *Admin Sec*
EMP: 5
SALES (est): 75K **Privately Held**
SIC: 2394 2395 5199 Canvas & related products; embroidery & art needlework; canvas products

Wht Sphr Spgs
Sullivan County

(G-16557)
KLEIN & SONS LOGGING INC
3114 State Route 52 (12787-5802)
PHONE..................................845 292-6682
Ronald Klein, *President*
Dale Klein, *Admin Sec*
EMP: 18
SQ FT: 3,900
SALES (est): 2.3MM **Privately Held**
SIC: 2411 Logging camps & contractors

Williamson
Wayne County

(G-16558)
FINGER LAKES TRELLIS SUPPLY
4041a Railroad Ave (14589-9391)
PHONE..................................315 904-4007
Todd Smith, *Owner*
Susana Catlin, *Principal*
▲ **EMP:** 5
SALES (est): 722.6K **Privately Held**
SIC: 2431 5211 Trellises, wood; doors, storm: wood or metal

(G-16559)
KEURIG DR PEPPER INC
Also Called: Mott's
4363 State Route 104 (14589-9332)
PHONE..................................315 589-4911
John Adam, *Facilities Dir*
Stephen Brisson, *Production*
Rick Park, *Sales Staff*
Jim Fischette, *Manager*
Tom Freeman, *Technology*
EMP: 250 **Publicly Held**
WEB: www.maunalai.com
SIC: 2086 2087 2084 Soft drinks: packaged in cans, bottles, etc.; flavoring extracts & syrups; wines, brandy & brandy spirits
PA: Keurig Dr Pepper Inc.
53 South Ave
Burlington MA 01803

(G-16560)
LAGONER FARMS INC
6895 Lake Ave (14589-9570)
PHONE..................................315 904-4109
Mark Lagoner, *President*
Dianna Lagoner, *Admin Sec*
EMP: 52
SQ FT: 8,000
SALES (est): 1.5MM **Privately Held**
SIC: 2033 0191 5431 Fruits: packaged in cans, jars, etc.; general farms, primarily crop; fruit & vegetable markets

(G-16561)
SALMON CREEK CABINETRY INC
6687 Salmon Creek Rd (14589-9557)
PHONE..................................315 589-5419
Charles Ciurca, *President*
EMP: 21
SALES (est): 1.5MM **Privately Held**
SIC: 2434 Wood kitchen cabinets

(G-16562)
THATCHER COMPANY NEW YORK INC
4135 Rte 104 (14589)
P.O. Box 118 (14589-0118)
PHONE..................................315 589-9330
Craig N Thatcher, *President*
J Christopher Pavlick, *Vice Pres*
Diane T Barlow, *Admin Sec*
▲ **EMP:** 45
SALES (est): 15.7MM
SALES (corp-wide): 177.6MM **Privately Held**
SIC: 2819 5169 Industrial inorganic chemicals; chemicals & allied products
PA: Thatcher Group, Inc
1905 W Fortune Rd
Salt Lake City UT 84104
801 972-4587

(G-16563)
TRIHEX MANUFACTURING INC
6708 Pound Rd (14589-9751)
PHONE..................................315 589-9331
Roger Lester, *President*
Dina Lester, *Manager*
EMP: 6 **EST:** 1979
SQ FT: 12,000
SALES: 600K **Privately Held**
SIC: 3451 3452 Screw machine products; bolts, nuts, rivets & washers

Williamstown
Oswego County

(G-16564)
C G & SON MACHINING INC
87 Nichols Rd (13493-2415)
PHONE..................................315 964-2430
Brian Gardner, *CEO*
EMP: 5
SALES: 703.6K **Privately Held**
SIC: 7692 Welding repair

Williamsville
Erie County

(G-16565)
17 BAKERS LLC
8 Los Robles St (14221-6719)
PHONE..................................844 687-6836
Anthony Habib, *CEO*
Anthony Habibm, *CEO*
Ashley Battaglia, *Principal*
EMP: 10 **EST:** 2015
SALES (est): 342.9K **Privately Held**
SIC: 2052 Bakery products, dry

(G-16566)
ABBOTT LABORATORIES
Also Called: Abbott Diagnostics Division
6255 Sheridan Dr Ste 406 (14221-4825)
PHONE..................................716 633-1904
Richard Stark, *Manager*
EMP: 11
SALES (corp-wide): 27.3B **Publicly Held**
WEB: www.abbott.com
SIC: 2834 Pharmaceutical preparations
PA: Abbott Laboratories
100 Abbott Park Rd
Abbott Park IL 60064
224 667-6100

(G-16567)
ALEXANDRIA PROFESSIONAL LLC
5500 Main St Ste 103 (14221-6737)
PHONE..................................716 242-8514
Lina Kennedy, *Branch Mgr*
EMP: 10 **Privately Held**
SIC: 2844 Toilet preparations
PA: 938023 Ontario Inc
85 Lakeshore Rd Unit A
St Catharines ON L2N 2
800 957-8427

(G-16568)
ASHTON-POTTER USA LTD
Also Called: Hig Capital
10 Curtwright Dr (14221-7072)
PHONE..................................716 633-2000
Miles S Nadal, *Ch of Bd*
Barry Switzer,
Joe Sheeran, *Senior VP*
Kelly Smith, *Senior VP*
Bob Morreale, *Vice Pres*
▲ **EMP:** 170
SQ FT: 104,000

GEOGRAPHIC SECTION

Williston Park - Nassau County (G-16596)

SALES (est): 27.8MM Privately Held
WEB: www.ashtonpotter.com
SIC: 2754 2759 Trading stamps: gravure printing; trading stamps: printing
HQ: H.I.G. Capital, L.L.C.
1450 Brickell Ave Fl 31
Miami FL 33131
305 379-2322

(G-16569)
BEE PUBLICATIONS INC
Also Called: Amherst Bee
5564 Main St (14221-5410)
PHONE.................................716 632-4700
Trey Measer, *President*
Bryan Jackson, *Editor*
Justin Smith, *Sales Staff*
Brenda Denk, *Advt Staff*
Teresa Eastman, *Advt Staff*
EMP: 55
SQ FT: 3,000
SALES (est): 3.1MM Privately Held
WEB: www.beenews.com
SIC: 2711 Newspapers: publishing only, not printed on site

(G-16570)
BELTONE CORPORATION
7474 Transit Rd (14221-6010)
PHONE.................................716 565-1015
EMP: 5
SALES (corp-wide): 1.5B Privately Held
SIC: 3842 Hearing aids
HQ: Beltone Corporation
2601 Patriot Blvd
Glenview IL 60026
847 832-3300

(G-16571)
BLUEBIRD TRANSPORTATION LLC
Also Called: Bluebird Mobility
5477 Main St (14221-6701)
PHONE.................................716 395-0000
Andrew J Shaevel, *CEO*
EMP: 10
SALES: 250K Privately Held
SIC: 7372 Prepackaged software

(G-16572)
BROETJE AUTOMATION-USA INC
165 Lawrence Bell Dr # 116 (14221-7900)
PHONE.................................716 204-8640
Ken Benczkowski, *President*
Jeremy Harris, *General Mgr*
Steve Silva, *Project Engr*
Brian Orourke, *Train & Dev Mgr*
EMP: 120
SQ FT: 200,000
SALES (est): 21.6MM
SALES (corp-wide): 14.1B Privately Held
SIC: 3365 Aerospace castings, aluminum
HQ: Broetje-Automation Gmbh
Am Autobahnkreuz 14
Rastede 26180
440 296-60

(G-16573)
CABOODLE PRINTING INC
1975 Wehrle Dr Ste 120 (14221-7022)
PHONE.................................716 693-6000
John Doyle, *President*
Scott Lepir, *Partner*
Gary Wodarczak, *Vice Pres*
Jack Jaeger, *Accounts Mgr*
Alexander Pawlicki, *Creative Dir*
EMP: 6
SALES (est): 887.3K Privately Held
WEB: www.caboodleprinting.com
SIC: 2752 Commercial printing, offset

(G-16574)
CANADA GOOSE US INC (DH)
300 International Dr (14221-5781)
PHONE.................................888 276-6297
Dani Reiss, *President*
EMP: 8
SALES (est): 1.6MM
SALES (corp-wide): 6.6B Privately Held
SIC: 2339 2337 Women's & misses' outerwear; women's & misses' suits & coats
HQ: Canada Goose Holdings Inc
250 Bowie Ave
Toronto ON M6E 4
416 780-9850

(G-16575)
CHAMPION AMERICA INC
2491 Wehrle Dr (14221-7141)
P.O. Box 157, Northford CT (06472-0157)
PHONE.................................716 626-1616
Tim Smith, *President*
EMP: 647
SALES (est): 22.7MM
SALES (corp-wide): 1.1B Publicly Held
SIC: 3479 Name plates: engraved, etched, etc.
PA: Brady Corporation
6555 W Good Hope Rd
Milwaukee WI 53223
414 358-6600

(G-16576)
CLOUD TORONTO INC
1967 Wehrle Dr Ste 1 (14221-8452)
PHONE.................................408 569-4542
Adam Noop, *Owner*
EMP: 10
SALES: 2.5MM Privately Held
SIC: 3679 Electronic circuits

(G-16577)
DAWN FOOD PRODUCTS INC
160 Lawrence Bell Dr # 120 (14221-7897)
PHONE.................................716 830-8214
EMP: 107
SALES (corp-wide): 1.6B Privately Held
SIC: 2045 Doughnut mixes, prepared: from purchased flour
HQ: Dawn Food Products, Inc.
3333 Sargent Rd
Jackson MI 49201

(G-16578)
ELASTOMERS INC
2095 Wehrle Dr (14221-7097)
PHONE.................................716 633-4883
Robert J Kunkel Sr, *President*
Robert J Kunkel Jr, *Vice Pres*
EMP: 8
SQ FT: 12,250
SALES: 700K Privately Held
SIC: 2821 Elastomers, nonvulcanizable (plastics)

(G-16579)
ENGINEERED PLASTICS INC
300 International Dr # 100 (14221-5783)
PHONE.................................800 682-2525
Ken Szekely, *President*
Ken Lawrence, *Vice Pres*
▲ EMP: 20
SQ FT: 2,000
SALES (est): 3.8MM Privately Held
SIC: 3996 Tile, floor: supported plastic

(G-16580)
GOODWILL INDS WSTN NY INC
4311 Transit Rd (14221-7231)
PHONE.................................716 633-3305
Tammy Smith, *General Mgr*
EMP: 15
SALES (corp-wide): 8.8MM Privately Held
SIC: 3999 Barber & beauty shop equipment
PA: Goodwill Industries Of Western New York, Inc.
1119 William St
Buffalo NY 14206
716 854-3494

(G-16581)
LEGAL SERVICING LLC
2801 Wehrle Dr Ste 5 (14221-7381)
PHONE.................................716 565-9300
EMP: 6
SALES (est): 584.3K Privately Held
SIC: 1389 Roustabout service

(G-16582)
ORTHO-CLINICAL DIAGNOSTICS INC
15 Limestone Dr (14221-7051)
PHONE.................................716 631-1281
Sue Riester, *Branch Mgr*
EMP: 37
SQ FT: 5,600
SALES (corp-wide): 696.9MM Privately Held
WEB: www.orthoclinical.com
SIC: 2835 Blood derivative diagnostic agents
PA: Ortho-Clinical Diagnostics, Inc.
1001 Us Highway 202
Raritan NJ 08869
908 218-8000

(G-16583)
PATUGA LLC
7954 Transit Rd 316 (14221-4117)
PHONE.................................716 204-7220
Joseph Pandolfino,
EMP: 5 EST: 2015
SALES (est): 270.4K Privately Held
SIC: 3911 7389 Jewelry, precious metal;

(G-16584)
RTT NEWS
1325 N Forest Rd Ste 240 (14221-2143)
PHONE.................................716 632-3400
Andrew Mariathasan,
Ravi Mariathasan,
EMP: 20
SALES (est): 608.3K Privately Held
SIC: 2711 Newspapers, publishing & printing

(G-16585)
SCHMITT SALES INC
Also Called: Robo Self Serve
5095 Main St (14221-5203)
PHONE.................................716 632-8595
Joe Betts, *Manager*
EMP: 8
SQ FT: 2,347
SALES (est): 480.8K
SALES (corp-wide): 99.9MM Privately Held
WEB: www.schmittsales.com
SIC: 1389 Gas field services
PA: Schmitt Sales, Inc.
2101 Saint Ritas Ln
Buffalo NY 14221
716 639-1500

(G-16586)
SENECA RESOURCES COMPANY LLC
165 Lawrence Bell Dr (14221-7900)
PHONE.................................716 630-6750
Scott Brown, *Principal*
EMP: 18
SALES (corp-wide): 1.5B Publicly Held
WEB: www.srcx.com
SIC: 1382 Oil & gas exploration services
HQ: Seneca Resources Company, Llc
1201 La St Ste 2600
Houston TX 77002
713 654-2600

(G-16587)
SOLMAC INC
1975 Wehrle Dr Ste 130 (14221-7022)
PHONE.................................716 630-7061
Borris Soldo, *President*
John Barrett, *General Mgr*
EMP: 9
SALES (est): 1.7MM Privately Held
SIC: 3599 Machine shop, jobbing & repair

(G-16588)
SRC LIQUIDATION COMPANY
435 Lawrence Bell Dr # 4 (14221-8440)
PHONE.................................716 631-3900
EMP: 5 Publicly Held
SIC: 2754 Printing
PA: Src Liquidation Company
600 Albany St
Dayton OH 45417
937 221-1000

(G-16589)
SUCCESSWARE INC
8860 Main St 102 (14221-7640)
PHONE.................................716 565-2338
Phil Di RE, *President*
Roy Powell, *Treasurer*
Gerri Di RE, *Admin Asst*
EMP: 15
SQ FT: 1,600
SALES (est): 926.1K Privately Held
WEB: www.successware21.com
SIC: 7372 Prepackaged software
HQ: Clockwork Home Services, Inc.
12 Greenway Plz Ste 250
Houston TX 77046
941 366-9692

(G-16590)
TEALEAFS
5416 Main St (14221-5362)
PHONE.................................716 688-8022
Sydney Hoffman, *Owner*
EMP: 5
SALES (est): 397.4K Privately Held
SIC: 2087 Beverage bases

(G-16591)
TOWN OF AMHERST
Also Called: Park's Department
450 Maple Rd (14221-3162)
PHONE.................................716 631-7113
Dan Raily, *Manager*
EMP: 40
SQ FT: 15,600 Privately Held
WEB: www.apdny.org
SIC: 2531 9111 Picnic tables or benches, park; mayors' offices
PA: Town Of Amherst
5583 Main St Ste 1
Williamsville NY 14221
716 631-7082

(G-16592)
TRICOR DIRECT INC (HQ)
Also Called: Seton Identification Products
2491 Wehrle Dr (14221-7141)
PHONE.................................716 626-1616
Tim Smith, *President*
Greg Melotto, *Engineer*
Sam Iverson, *Sales Staff*
Donna Lebert, *Manager*
▼ EMP: 4 EST: 1981
SQ FT: 150,000
SALES (est): 120.5MM
SALES (corp-wide): 1.1B Publicly Held
WEB: www.seton.com
SIC: 3479 Name plates: engraved, etched, etc.
PA: Brady Corporation
6555 W Good Hope Rd
Milwaukee WI 53223
414 358-6600

(G-16593)
WEST SENECA BEE INC
5564 Main St (14221-5410)
PHONE.................................716 632-4700
EMP: 60
SQ FT: 4,500
SALES (est): 1.5MM Privately Held
SIC: 2711 Newspapers-Publishing/Printing

Williston Park
Nassau County

(G-16594)
GREENWAY CABINETRY INC
485 Willis Ave (11596-1725)
PHONE.................................516 877-0009
Frank Tommasini, *President*
EMP: 10
SALES (est): 630K Privately Held
SIC: 2434 Wood kitchen cabinets

(G-16595)
SCHARF AND BREIT INC
2 Hillside Ave Ste F (11596-2335)
PHONE.................................516 282-0287
Christopher Aives, *President*
EMP: 50 EST: 1939
SQ FT: 22,000
SALES (est): 3.5MM Privately Held
SIC: 2329 Sweaters & sweater jackets: men's & boys'

(G-16596)
T RS GREAT AMERICAN REST
17 Hillside Ave (11596-2303)
PHONE.................................516 294-1680
Patrick Miele, *President*
EMP: 10
SALES (est): 918.8K Privately Held
SIC: 2035 Seasonings & sauces, except tomato & dry

Willsboro
Essex County

(G-16597)
CHAMPLAIN VALLEY MIL CORP INC
19 Myers Way (12996)
PHONE..................518 963-7650
Samuel M Sherman, *President*
Ayra Pettit, *Corp Secy*
Derinda Sherman, *Vice Pres*
EMP: 8
SQ FT: 9,500
SALES: 4.1MM **Privately Held**
SIC: 2041 Flour & other grain mill products

(G-16598)
COMMONWEALTH HOME FASHION INC
31 Station Rd (12996)
P.O. Box 339 (12996-0339)
PHONE..................514 384-8290
Harvey Levenson, *President*
Barb Wilson, *Manager*
▲ **EMP:** 90
SQ FT: 151,000
SALES (est): 11.4MM **Privately Held**
WEB: www.comhomfash.com
SIC: 2259 Curtains & bedding, knit
PA: Decors De Maison Commonwealth Inc
8800 Boul Pie-Ix
Montreal QC H1Z 3
514 384-8290

(G-16599)
GENERAL COMPOSITES INC
39 Myers Way (12996-4539)
PHONE..................518 963-7333
Joseph M Callahan Jr, *CEO*
Jeffrey G Allott, *Ch of Bd*
Mimi Lane, *Plant Mgr*
Ed Marvin, *Engineer*
Allison Whalen, *Office Mgr*
▲ **EMP:** 41
SQ FT: 40,000
SALES (est): 7.7MM **Privately Held**
WEB: www.generalcomposites.com
SIC: 3089 8711 Synthetic resin finished products; consulting engineer

Wilmington
Essex County

(G-16600)
ADIRONDACK CHOCOLATE CO LTD (PA)
Also Called: Candy Man
5680 Ny State Rte 86 (12997)
PHONE..................518 946-7270
Joe Dougherty, *President*
EMP: 10 **EST:** 1962
SQ FT: 800
SALES (est): 1MM **Privately Held**
WEB: www.candymanonline.com
SIC: 2066 5441 Chocolate candy, solid; candy

Wilson
Niagara County

(G-16601)
LYNX PRODUCT GROUP LLC
650 Lake St (14172-9600)
PHONE..................716 751-3100
Dawn Coe, *Purchasing*
James Scime, *Engineer*
Shawn Smith, *Engineer*
Bob Urtel, *Engineer*
Stu Monteith, *Manager*
EMP: 38
SQ FT: 28,000
SALES (est): 9.2MM **Privately Held**
WEB: www.lynxpg.com
SIC: 3582 Washing machines, laundry; commercial, incl. coin-operated

(G-16602)
VALAIR INC
87 Harbor St (14172-9749)
P.O. Box 27 (14172-0027)
PHONE..................716 751-9480
Donald E Sinclair Jr, *Ch of Bd*
John Sinclair, *President*
Linda J Sinclair, *Treasurer*
Pete Lepsch, *Planning*
EMP: 12 **EST:** 1971
SQ FT: 4,000
SALES (est): 1.9MM **Privately Held**
SIC: 3599 Machine shop, jobbing & repair

(G-16603)
WOODCOCK BROTHERS BREWING COMP
638 Lake St (14172-9600)
P.O. Box 66 (14172-0066)
PHONE..................716 333-4000
Tim Woodcock, *President*
EMP: 11
SALES (est): 1MM **Privately Held**
SIC: 2082 Beer (alcoholic beverage)

Windsor
Broome County

(G-16604)
DEVONIAN STONE NEW YORK INC
463 Atwell Hill Rd (13865-3623)
PHONE..................607 655-2600
Robert Bellospirito, *President*
Peggy Rosenthal, *Sales Mgr*
▲ **EMP:** 28
SQ FT: 7,000
SALES (est): 2.1MM **Privately Held**
WEB: www.devonianstone.com
SIC: 3281 1459 Cut stone & stone products; stoneware clay mining

(G-16605)
WINDSOR UNITED INDUSTRIES LLC
10 Park St (13865)
PHONE..................607 655-3300
Dennis Garges,
EMP: 40
SALES (est): 3.4MM **Privately Held**
SIC: 2499 Decorative wood & woodwork

Wingdale
Dutchess County

(G-16606)
HUNT COUNTRY FURNITURE INC (PA)
19 Dog Tail Corners Rd (12594-1218)
P.O. Box 396, Dover Plains (12522-0396)
PHONE..................845 832-6601
Todd Gazzoli, *General Mgr*
Randy Williams, *Chairman*
▲ **EMP:** 80
SQ FT: 60,000
SALES (est): 9.6MM **Privately Held**
WEB: www.huntcountryfurniture.com
SIC: 2511 2599 Chairs, household, except upholstered: wood; restaurant furniture, wood or metal

(G-16607)
WESTCHESTER MODULAR HOMES INC
30 Reagans Mill Rd (12594-1101)
PHONE..................845 832-9400
Charles W Hatcher, *President*
John Colucci, *Vice Pres*
Steve Sokol, *Opers Mgr*
Dave Wrocklage, *Regl Sales Mgr*
Lisa Napolitano, *Sales Staff*
EMP: 125
SQ FT: 104,000
SALES (est): 20.9MM **Privately Held**
WEB: www.westchestermodular.com
SIC: 2452 Modular homes, prefabricated, wood

Wolcott
Wayne County

(G-16608)
CAHOON FARMS INC
10951 Lummisville Rd (14590-9549)
P.O. Box 190 (14590-0190)
PHONE..................315 594-8081
Donald D Cahoon Jr, *President*
Renee Lanclos, *General Mgr*
William Cahoon, *Vice Pres*
Sheila Rigerman, *QC Mgr*
Carol Wray, *Human Res Mgr*
EMP: 35
SQ FT: 44,000
SALES (est): 10.2MM **Privately Held**
SIC: 2033 0723 2037 0175 Fruit juices: fresh; fruit (fresh) packing services; frozen fruits & vegetables; deciduous tree fruits

(G-16609)
CARBALLO CONTRACT MACHINING
Also Called: C C M
6205 Lake Ave (14590-1040)
PHONE..................315 594-2511
Jeannie Brockmyer, *Owner*
Bryan Brockmyre, *Manager*
EMP: 5
SQ FT: 3,000
SALES (est): 360K **Privately Held**
WEB: www.ccmprecision.biz
SIC: 3599 Machine & other job shop work

(G-16610)
EAGLE WELDING MACHINE
13458 Ridge Rd (14590-9602)
PHONE..................315 594-1845
Gary Buckalew, *Principal*
EMP: 9
SALES (est): 1MM **Privately Held**
SIC: 7692 Welding repair

(G-16611)
MARSHALL INGREDIENTS LLC
5786 Limekiln Rd (14590-9354)
PHONE..................800 796-9353
EMP: 6
SALES (corp-wide): 866.5K **Privately Held**
SIC: 2034 Fruits, dried or dehydrated, except freeze-dried
PA: Marshall Ingredients Llc
5740 Limekiln Rd
Wolcott NY

(G-16612)
WAYUGA COMMUNITY NEWSPAPERS
Also Called: Waguya News
12039 E Main St (14590-1021)
PHONE..................315 594-2506
Bill Bender, *Accounts Exec*
Chuck Palermo, *Manager*
EMP: 6
SQ FT: 5,004
SALES (est): 278.3K
SALES (corp-wide): 2.5MM **Privately Held**
WEB: www.wayuga.com
SIC: 2711 4225 Newspapers, publishing & printing; general warehousing
PA: Wayuga Community Newspapers Inc
6784 Main St
Red Creek NY 13143
315 754-6229

Woodbury
Nassau County

(G-16613)
ARIZONA BEVERAGE COMPANY LLC (HQ)
Also Called: Arizona Beverages USA
60 Crossways Park Dr W # 400 (11797-2018)
PHONE..................516 812-0300
Paul Negri, *Division Mgr*
Jim Dar, *Vice Pres*
Brian Williams, *Facilities Mgr*
Nicholas Panagos, *Production*
John Odonnell, *Mng Member*
▼ **EMP:** 3
SALES: 2.4MM
SALES (corp-wide): 74.6MM **Privately Held**
SIC: 2086 Iced tea & fruit drinks, bottled & canned
PA: Hornell Brewing Co., Inc.
60 Crossways Park Dr W # 400
Woodbury NY 11797
516 812-0300

(G-16614)
CLEVER DEVICES LTD (PA)
300 Crossways Park Dr (11797-2035)
PHONE..................516 433-6100
Frank Ingrassia, *CEO*
Andrew Stanton, *COO*
Buddy Coleman, *Exec VP*
Steve Bennett, *Senior VP*
Dean Soucy, *Senior VP*
EMP: 43
SQ FT: 10,000
SALES (est): 18.6MM **Privately Held**
WEB: www.cleverdevices.net
SIC: 3679 3663 Recording & playback apparatus, including phonograph; radio & TV communications equipment

(G-16615)
COMPOSITECH LTD
4 Fairbanks Blvd (11797-2604)
PHONE..................516 835-1458
Jonas Medney, *Ch of Bd*
Christopher F Johnson, *President*
Richard Depoto, *Vice Pres*
Ralph W Segalowitz, *Vice Pres*
Samuel S Gross, *Treasurer*
EMP: 110
SQ FT: 33,000
SALES (est): 11.5MM **Privately Held**
WEB: www.compositech.com
SIC: 3674 6794 Semiconductors & related devices; patent owners & lessors

(G-16616)
CRAZY COWBOY BREWING CO LLC
60 Crossways Park Dr W # 400 (11797-2018)
PHONE..................516 812-0576
David Menashi, *CEO*
EMP: 25
SALES (est): 948.7K **Privately Held**
SIC: 2082 Malt beverage products

(G-16617)
D & V ENTERPRISES INC
Also Called: Daily Jeans
119 Woodlake Dr W (11797-2307)
PHONE..................917 983-9250
Dovid Ben Yehuda, *President*
EMP: 40
SALES: 6MM **Privately Held**
SIC: 2339 7389 Jeans: women's, misses' & juniors';

(G-16618)
E & W MANUFACTURING CO INC
15 Pine Dr (11797-1509)
PHONE..................516 367-8571
Elliot Wald, *President*
EMP: 21
SQ FT: 15,000
SALES (est): 1.7MM **Privately Held**
SIC: 3991 Paint brushes

(G-16619)
F & V DISTRIBUTION COMPANY LLC
1 Arizona Plz (11797-1125)
PHONE..................516 812-0393
Don Vultaggio, *Principal*
EMP: 5 **Privately Held**
SIC: 2086 Iced tea & fruit drinks, bottled & canned
PA: F & V Distribution Company, Llc
60 Crossways Park Dr W # 400
Woodbury NY 11797

(G-16620)
GLOBAL VIDEO LLC (HQ)
Also Called: Guidance Channel
1000 Woodbury Rd Ste 1 (11797-2530)
PHONE..................516 222-2600

GEOGRAPHIC SECTION

David Rust, *President*
EMP: 60
SALES (est): 20.8MM
SALES (corp-wide): 658.3MM **Publicly Held**
WEB: www.sunburstvm.com
SIC: 2741 5961 5092 6719 Catalogs: publishing & printing; book club, mail order; educational toys; investment holding companies, except banks
PA: School Specialty, Inc.
W6316 Design Dr
Greenville WI 54942
920 734-5712

(G-16621)
HOWARD CHARLES INC
180 Froehlich Farm Blvd (11797-2923)
P.O. Box 854, Nanuet (10954-0854)
PHONE..................917 902-6934
Charles Breslin, *Principal*
EMP: 7
SALES (est): 685.4K **Privately Held**
SIC: 3089 Plastic kitchenware, tableware & houseware

(G-16622)
INLAND PRINTING COMPANY INC
36 Orchard Dr (11797-2830)
P.O. Box 414, Syosset (11791-0414)
PHONE..................516 367-4700
Steven E Spaeth, *President*
Susan Spaeth, *Vice Pres*
EMP: 3
SALES (est): 7.5MM **Privately Held**
SIC: 2752 Commercial printing, lithographic

(G-16623)
LENCORE ACOUSTICS CORP (PA)
1 Crossways Park Dr W (11797-2014)
PHONE..................516 682-9292
Jack D Leonard, *Ch of Bd*
Mark Christensen, *Regional Mgr*
Jonathan Leonard, *Vice Pres*
Lori Jewell, *Project Mgr*
Alison Friedson, *Purch Mgr*
EMP: 10
SQ FT: 2,200
SALES (est): 5.6MM **Privately Held**
WEB: www.lencore.com
SIC: 3446 Partitions & supports/studs, including accoustical systems; acoustical suspension systems, metal

(G-16624)
LI SCRIPT LLC
333 Crossways Park Dr (11797-2066)
PHONE..................631 321-3850
Michael Shamalov, *Owner*
Pietro Scardino, *Pharmacist*
EMP: 30
SALES (est): 6.7MM **Privately Held**
SIC: 2752 Commercial printing, lithographic

(G-16625)
MANHATTAN MILLING & DRYING CO
78 Pond Rd (11797-1616)
PHONE..................516 496-1041
John Mc Auley, *President*
Robert Mc Auley, *Treasurer*
EMP: 20
SQ FT: 37,500
SALES (est): 1.2MM **Privately Held**
SIC: 2099 Spice Reconditioning

(G-16626)
NEW YORK COMPUTER CONSULTING
14 Pheasant Ln (11797-1900)
PHONE..................516 921-1932
Sandra M Biondi, *President*
Bruce Biondi, *Vice Pres*
EMP: 6
SQ FT: 1,500
SALES (est): 664.4K **Privately Held**
WEB: www.nycomputer.net
SIC: 7372 7371 Prepackaged software; computer software systems analysis & design, custom

(G-16627)
PERMIT FASHION GROUP INC
27 Chauncey Pl (11797-1232)
PHONE..................212 912-0988
Zhouping Zheng, *CEO*
▲ **EMP:** 8 **EST:** 2012
SALES (est): 1.1MM **Privately Held**
SIC: 2331 2337 2339 Blouses, women's & juniors': made from purchased material; skirts, separate: women's, misses' & juniors'; jackets & vests, except fur & leather: women's; slacks: women's, misses' & juniors'

(G-16628)
PHOTO INDUSTRY INC
Also Called: Pemystifying Diital
7600 Jericho Tpke Ste 301 (11797-1705)
PHONE..................516 364-0016
Allan Lavine, *President*
Jerry Grossman, *Vice Pres*
EMP: 10
SQ FT: 1,200
SALES (est): 980K **Privately Held**
SIC: 2721 Magazines: publishing only, not printed on site

(G-16629)
PROVIDENT FUEL INC
4 Stillwell Ln (11797-1104)
PHONE..................516 224-4427
Douglas Robalino, *Principal*
EMP: 8
SALES (est): 1.1MM **Privately Held**
SIC: 2869 Fuels

(G-16630)
RESEARCH FRONTIERS INC (PA)
240 Crossways Park Dr (11797-2033)
PHONE..................516 364-1902
Joseph M Harary, *President*
Michael R Lapointe, *Vice Pres*
Steven M Slovak, *Vice Pres*
Seth L Van Voorhees, *CFO*
EMP: 7 **EST:** 1930
SQ FT: 9,500
SALES (est): 1.5MM **Publicly Held**
WEB: www.refr-spd.com
SIC: 3829 Measuring & controlling devices

(G-16631)
ROYAL PAINT ROLLER CORP
Also Called: Royal Paint Roller Mfg
1 Harvard Dr (11797-3302)
PHONE..................516 367-4370
Randy Boritz, *President*
Gloria Boritz, *Admin Sec*
EMP: 25 **EST:** 1968
SQ FT: 23,000
SALES (est): 2MM **Privately Held**
SIC: 3991 Paint rollers

(G-16632)
SORFIN YOSHIMURA LTD
100 Crossways Park Dr W # 215 (11797-2012)
PHONE..................516 802-4600
Scott Fink, *President*
◆ **EMP:** 9
SALES (est): 203.2K **Privately Held**
SIC: 3825 Battery testers, electrical

(G-16633)
VEECO INSTRUMENTS INC
100 Sunnyside Blvd Ste B (11797-2925)
PHONE..................516 677-0200
Edward Braun, *President*
Keith Johnson, *President*
Alan Kass, *Business Mgr*
Scott Priddy, *Engineer*
Dror Stevenson, *Engineer*
EMP: 230
SALES (corp-wide): 484.7MM **Publicly Held**
WEB: www.veeco.com
SIC: 3826 3823 Analytical instruments; industrial instrmnts msrmnt display/control process variable
PA: Veeco Instruments Inc.
1 Terminal Dr
Plainview NY 11803
516 677-0200

(G-16634)
WIN-HOLT EQUIPMENT CORP (PA)
Also Called: Win-Holt Equipment Group
20 Crossways Park Dr N # 205 (11797-2007)
PHONE..................516 222-0335
Jonathan J Holtz, *CEO*
Dominick Scarfogliero, *President*
Jason Womack, *President*
Courtney Guerrero, *General Mgr*
Jose Ponce, *COO*
▲ **EMP:** 45 **EST:** 1946
SQ FT: 10,000
SALES (est): 83.1MM **Privately Held**
WEB: www.winholt.com
SIC: 2099 Food preparations

(G-16635)
WOODBURY SYSTEMS GROUP INC
30 Glenn Dr (11797-2104)
P.O. Box 346, Plainview (11803-0346)
PHONE..................516 364-2653
William L Fitzgerald, *President*
Deirdre Volpe, *Vice Pres*
EMP: 6
SALES (est): 792.5K **Privately Held**
WEB: www.woodsysgrp.com
SIC: 7372 Prepackaged software

Woodhaven
Queens County

(G-16636)
JO-VIN DECORATORS INC
9423 Jamaica Ave (11421-2287)
PHONE..................718 441-9350
Vincent Pappalando, *Ch of Bd*
Leo Pappalardo, *Admin Sec*
EMP: 40 **EST:** 1956
SQ FT: 20,000
SALES (est): 4.8MM **Privately Held**
WEB: www.jo-vin.com
SIC: 2391 2299 2392 2394 Curtains & draperies; tops & top processing, man-made or other fiber; bedspreads & bed sets: made from purchased materials; shades, canvas: made from purchased materials

(G-16637)
STEINDL CAST STONE CO INC
9107 76th St (11421-2817)
PHONE..................718 296-8530
John Steindl Jr, *President*
James Steindl, *Vice Pres*
EMP: 6 **EST:** 1928
SQ FT: 2,800
SALES: 500K **Privately Held**
WEB: www.steindlcaststone.com
SIC: 3272 Cast stone, concrete

Woodhull
Steuben County

(G-16638)
OWLETTS SAW MILLS
4214 Cook Rd (14898-9630)
PHONE..................607 525-6340
Walt Owlett, *Owner*
EMP: 5
SALES (est): 324.4K **Privately Held**
SIC: 2421 Sawmills & planing mills, general

Woodmere
Nassau County

(G-16639)
ALLIED PHARMACY PRODUCTS INC
544 Green Pl (11598-1923)
PHONE..................516 374-8862
Stuart Meadow, *Principal*
Alexander Meadow, *Sales Mgr*
EMP: 5
SALES (est): 617.8K **Privately Held**
SIC: 2834 5047 Pharmaceutical preparations; medical & hospital equipment

(G-16640)
BENISHTY BROTHERS CORP
233 Mosher Ave (11598-1655)
PHONE..................646 339-9991
EMP: 5
SALES (est): 342.5K **Privately Held**
SIC: 3524 Lawn & garden mowers & accessories

(G-16641)
GLASGOW PRODUCTS INC
886 Lakeside Dr (11598-1916)
PHONE..................516 374-5937
Paul J Glasgow, *President*
Dorothy Glasgow, *Treasurer*
EMP: 25 **EST:** 1969
SQ FT: 3,000
SALES (est): 3.1MM **Privately Held**
WEB: www.glasgowproducts.com
SIC: 3535 8711 Conveyors & conveying equipment; consulting engineer

(G-16642)
SHANE TEX INC
Also Called: Henry Segal Co
717 Longacre Ave (11598-2338)
PHONE..................516 486-7522
Martin Segal, *Ch of Bd*
Robert Segal, *President*
▲ **EMP:** 18 **EST:** 1926
SQ FT: 30,000
SALES (est): 4MM **Privately Held**
WEB: www.henrysegal.com
SIC: 2311 2337 2335 Tailored suits & formal jackets; men's & boys' uniforms; uniforms, except athletic: women's, misses' & juniors'; women's & misses' suits & skirts; bridal & formal gowns

Woodridge
Sullivan County

(G-16643)
PROFESSIONAL CAB DETAILING CO
Also Called: Procab
Navograrsky Rd (12789)
P.O. Box 727 (12789-0727)
PHONE..................845 436-7282
Keith Bahr-Tioson, *Owner*
EMP: 10
SQ FT: 15,000
SALES (est): 600K **Privately Held**
WEB: www.procab.com
SIC: 2511 2431 Kitchen & dining room furniture; millwork

Woodside
Queens County

(G-16644)
A SUNSHINE GLASS & ALUMINUM
2610 Brooklyn Queens Expy (11377-7822)
PHONE..................718 932-8080
Scong Lee, *Principal*
Chris Glass, *Buyer*
Justin Lee, *Manager*
Julie Kim, *Admin Sec*
▲ **EMP:** 20
SALES (est): 1.6MM **Privately Held**
SIC: 3211 5023 Flat glass; glassware

(G-16645)
BALDWIN RIBBON & STAMPING CORP
3956 63rd St (11377-3649)
PHONE..................718 335-6700
Ronald Steinberg, *President*
EMP: 15 **EST:** 1946
SQ FT: 5,000
SALES (est): 2MM **Privately Held**
SIC: 2399 3999 Emblems, badges & insignia; military insignia

Woodside - Queens County (G-16646)

(G-16646)
BIELECKY BROS INC (PA)
5022 72nd St (11377-6084)
PHONE..................718 424-4764
Edwood Bielecky, *President*
EMP: 22
SQ FT: 24,000
SALES: 3.3MM **Privately Held**
WEB: www.bieleckybrothers.com
SIC: 2519 Rattan furniture: padded or plain; wicker & rattan furniture

(G-16647)
BLACK & DECKER CORPORATION
5615 Queens Blvd (11377-4741)
PHONE..................718 335-1042
Michael Domdrowski, *Manager*
EMP: 9
SQ FT: 6,525
SALES (corp-wide): 12.7B **Publicly Held**
WEB: www.blackanddecker.com
SIC: 3546 Power-driven handtools
HQ: The Black & Decker Corporation
701 E Joppa Rd
Towson MD 21286
410 716-3900

(G-16648)
C & T TOOL & INSTRUMENT CO
Also Called: C&T Tool & Instrmnt
4125 58th St (11377-4748)
PHONE..................718 429-1253
EMP: 24
SQ FT: 1,690
SALES (est): 2.2MM **Privately Held**
SIC: 3599 3542 3444 3441 Mfg Industrial Machinery Mfg Machine Tool-Forming Mfg Sheet Metalwork Structural Metal Fabrctn

(G-16649)
C L PRECISION MACHINE & TL CO
5015 70th St (11377-6020)
PHONE..................718 651-8475
George Lolis, *President*
EMP: 5 **EST:** 1967
SQ FT: 1,200
SALES: 250K **Privately Held**
SIC: 3599 Machine shop, jobbing & repair

(G-16650)
CAR-GO INDUSTRIES INC (PA)
5007 49th St (11377-7335)
PHONE..................718 472-1443
Drori Benman, *President*
EMP: 8
SQ FT: 5,000
SALES (est): 9.3MM **Privately Held**
SIC: 3714 Motor vehicle parts & accessories

(G-16651)
CODY PRINTING CORP
3728 56th St (11377-2438)
PHONE..................718 651-8854
Kyu Hwang, *CEO*
Kyung Shin, *President*
EMP: 9
SQ FT: 3,000
SALES (est): 1.5MM **Privately Held**
WEB: www.codyprinting.com
SIC: 2752 Commercial printing, offset

(G-16652)
DAMIANOU SPORTSWEAR INC
6001 31st Ave Ste 2 (11377-1205)
P.O. Box 463, Roslyn Heights (11577-0463)
PHONE..................718 204-5600
Paul Damianou, *President*
Pat Damianou, *Corp Secy*
Elenitsa Damianou, *Vice Pres*
EMP: 62
SQ FT: 24,000
SALES (est): 5.5MM **Privately Held**
SIC: 2335 Women's, juniors' & misses' dresses

(G-16653)
DOMOTECK INTERIORS INC
2430 Brooklyn Queens Expy # 1 (11377-7825)
PHONE..................718 433-4300
Raja Mustafa, *President*
Konstantinos Mabrikos, *Vice Pres*
EMP: 5
SQ FT: 5,000
SALES: 500K **Privately Held**
SIC: 1411 Limestone & marble dimension stone; argillite, dimension-quarrying

(G-16654)
ECUADOR NEWS INC
6403 Roosevelt Ave Fl 2 (11377-3643)
PHONE..................718 205-7014
Edgar Arboleda, *President*
EMP: 15
SALES (est): 875.1K **Privately Held**
WEB: www.ecuadornews.net
SIC: 2711 Newspapers: publishing only, not printed on site

(G-16655)
FIRECOM INC (PA)
Also Called: Bio Service
3927 59th St (11377-3435)
PHONE..................718 899-6100
Paul Mendez, *Ch of Bd*
Howard Kogan, *COO*
Howard L Kogen, *COO*
Antoine J Sayour, *Senior VP*
Patrick Adamo, *Vice Pres*
EMP: 130 **EST:** 1978
SQ FT: 16,000
SALES (est): 51.6MM **Privately Held**
SIC: 3669 1799 Fire detection systems, electric; fire escape installation

(G-16656)
FIRST LINE PRINTING INC
3728 56th St (11377-2438)
PHONE..................718 606-0860
Sergio Torres, *President*
EMP: 10
SQ FT: 10,000
SALES (est): 2.2MM **Privately Held**
SIC: 2752 Commercial printing, offset

(G-16657)
FURNITURE DSIGN BY KNOSSOS INC
2430 Bklyn Qns Expy Ste 3 (11377-7825)
PHONE..................718 729-0404
Steve Tepelidis, *Ch of Bd*
George Despo, *President*
EMP: 24
SQ FT: 23,185
SALES: 2.5MM **Privately Held**
SIC: 2499 Decorative wood & woodwork

(G-16658)
GENESIS ELECTRICAL MOTORS
Also Called: Genesis Electl Motor
6010 32nd Ave (11377-2019)
PHONE..................718 274-7030
Hercules Minnelli, *President*
Beatrice Minnelli, *Corp Secy*
EMP: 5
SQ FT: 4,000
SALES (est): 864.9K **Privately Held**
SIC: 7694 Electric motor repair

(G-16659)
GLOBE ELECTRONIC HARDWARE INC
3424 56th St (11377-2122)
P.O. Box 770727 (11377-0727)
PHONE..................718 457-0303
Caroline Dennehy, *President*
Paul Murphy, *COO*
Patrick M Dennehy, *Vice Pres*
EMP: 14 **EST:** 1976
SQ FT: 8,800
SALES (est): 2.5MM **Privately Held**
WEB: www.globelectronics.com
SIC: 3451 5072 Screw machine products; hardware

(G-16660)
KETCHAM PUMP CO INC
3420 64th St (11377-2398)
PHONE..................718 457-0800
Stuart Hruska, *President*
EMP: 15 **EST:** 1903
SQ FT: 10,000
SALES (est): 3.7MM **Privately Held**
SIC: 3561 Pumps & pumping equipment

(G-16661)
KOKOROKO CORPORATION
Also Called: Kokoroko Bakery
4755 47th St (11377-6546)
PHONE..................718 433-4321
Ivonne D Penaherrera, *President*
EMP: 7
SALES (est): 611.8K **Privately Held**
SIC: 2051 Bakery: wholesale or wholesale/retail combined

(G-16662)
MC COY TOPS AND INTERIORS INC
Also Called: Mc Coy Tops and Covers
6914 49th Ave (11377-6002)
PHONE..................718 458-5800
John Proimos, *President*
EMP: 8
SQ FT: 6,000
SALES (est): 740K **Privately Held**
SIC: 2399 2394 Seat covers, automobile; convertible tops, canvas or boat: from purchased materials

(G-16663)
METALOCKE INDUSTRIES INC
3202 57th St (11377-1919)
PHONE..................718 267-9200
Susanna Hollnsteiner, *President*
Tom Sadi, *President*
Tanveer Sadiq, *Vice Pres*
EMP: 6 **EST:** 1936
SQ FT: 10,000
SALES: 1MM **Privately Held**
SIC: 3429 5031 2431 5211 Manufactured hardware (general); millwork; millwork; millwork & lumber

(G-16664)
METRO MACHINING & FABRICATING
3234 61st St (11377-2030)
PHONE..................718 545-0104
Nicholas Dorazio, *President*
EMP: 7
SALES (est): 570K **Privately Held**
SIC: 3599 Machine shop, jobbing & repair

(G-16665)
MULTI TECH ELECTRIC
2526 50th St (11377-7823)
PHONE..................718 606-2695
Mario Torres, *Vice Pres*
EMP: 10
SALES (est): 921.7K **Privately Held**
SIC: 3699 Electrical equipment & supplies

(G-16666)
NATIONAL ELEV CAB & DOOR CORP
Also Called: Necd
5315 37th Ave (11377-2474)
PHONE..................718 478-5900
Harold Friedman, *CEO*
John Ferella, *President*
Jeffrey Friedman, *Exec VP*
George Karazim, *Plant Mgr*
Jimmy Betancourt, *Accounting Mgr*
▲ **EMP:** 50 **EST:** 1930
SQ FT: 30,000
SALES (est): 16.8MM **Privately Held**
WEB: www.necd.com
SIC: 3534 Elevators & equipment

(G-16667)
NORTH AMERICAN MBL SYSTEMS INC
3354 62nd St (11377-2236)
PHONE..................718 898-8700
Thomas Crowley, *President*
Connor Crowley, *Owner*
EMP: 33
SALES (est): 5.9MM **Privately Held**
SIC: 3663 Radio broadcasting & communications equipment

(G-16668)
NYC TRADE PRINTERS CORP
3245 62nd St (11377-2031)
PHONE..................718 606-0610
Ely Toledo, *President*
EMP: 12
SQ FT: 5,000
SALES (est): 1.6MM **Privately Held**
SIC: 2711 Commercial printing & newspaper publishing combined

(G-16669)
ORTHOPEDIC TREATMENT FACILITY
4906 Queens Blvd (11377-4462)
PHONE..................718 898-7326
Gary Marano, *President*
Anthony Marano, *Vice Pres*
EMP: 8
SQ FT: 2,800
SALES: 700K **Privately Held**
SIC: 3842 Limbs, artificial; braces, orthopedic

(G-16670)
PACEMAKER PACKAGING CORP
7200 51st Rd (11377-7631)
PHONE..................718 458-1188
Emil Romotzki, *President*
Helga Romotzki, *Admin Sec*
EMP: 10 **EST:** 1964
SQ FT: 7,000
SALES (est): 1.8MM **Privately Held**
SIC: 3565 Packaging machinery

(G-16671)
PFEIL & HOLING INC
5815 Northern Blvd (11377-2297)
PHONE..................718 545-4600
Sy Stricker, *President*
Margo Stricker, *Corp Secy*
Rosa Thompson, *Manager*
◆ **EMP:** 75 **EST:** 1923
SQ FT: 50,000
SALES (est): 14.6MM **Privately Held**
WEB: www.cakedeco.com
SIC: 2064 5046 5999 Cake ornaments, confectionery; bakery equipment & supplies; cake decorating supplies

(G-16672)
PIEMONTE HOME MADE RAVIOLI CO (PA)
Also Called: Piemonte Company
3436 65th St (11377-2329)
PHONE..................718 429-1972
Mario Bertorelli, *President*
Flavio Bertorelli, *Vice Pres*
▲ **EMP:** 16 **EST:** 1945
SQ FT: 14,000
SALES (est): 1.7MM **Privately Held**
WEB: www.piemonteravioli.com
SIC: 2098 5812 Macaroni products (e.g. alphabets, rings & shells), dry; noodles (e.g. egg, plain & water), dry; spaghetti, dry; eating places

(G-16673)
PLAYBILL INCORPORATED
3715 61st St (11377-2593)
PHONE..................718 335-4033
Lewis Cole, *Branch Mgr*
EMP: 20
SALES (corp-wide): 18.5MM **Privately Held**
SIC: 2789 Bookbinding & repairing: trade, edition, library, etc.
PA: Playbill Incorporated
729 7th Ave Fl 4
New York NY 10019
212 557-5757

(G-16674)
RE 99 CENTS INC
4905 Roosevelt Ave (11377-4457)
PHONE..................718 639-2325
EMP: 6 **EST:** 2009
SALES (est): 492.6K **Privately Held**
SIC: 3643 Mfg Conductive Wiring Devices

(G-16675)
RED WHITE & BLUE ENTPS CORP
3443 56th St (11377-2121)
PHONE..................718 565-8080
Vasilios Katranis, *President*
EMP: 5
SALES (est): 634.2K **Privately Held**
SIC: 2521 5712 2541 2434 Wood office filing cabinets & bookcases; customized furniture & cabinets; table or counter tops, plastic laminated; wood kitchen cabinets

GEOGRAPHIC SECTION — Wyoming - Wyoming County

(G-16676)
ROBERT-MASTERS CORP
3217 61st St (11377-2029)
PHONE.................................718 545-1030
Roberto C Orellana, *President*
▲ EMP: 7
SQ FT: 10,000
SALES (est): 1MM **Privately Held**
SIC: 3442 Rolling doors for industrial buildings or warehouses, metal

(G-16677)
SPAETH DESIGN INC
6006 37th Ave (11377-2541)
PHONE.................................718 606-9685
Sandra L Spaeth, *President*
David Spaeth, *Chairman*
Dorothy Spaeth, *Corp Secy*
▲ EMP: 35 EST: 1945
SQ FT: 27,000
SALES (est): 7.6MM **Privately Held**
WEB: www.spaethdesign.com
SIC: 2653 Display items, corrugated: made from purchased materials

(G-16678)
SPECTRUM ON BROADWAY
6106 34th Ave (11377-2228)
PHONE.................................718 932-5388
Harvey Brooks, *President*
Michael Gyscek, *Vice Pres*
Joseph Morra, *Vice Pres*
EMP: 12
SALES (est): 1.8MM **Privately Held**
WEB: www.spectrumsignsinc.com
SIC: 3993 Electric signs

(G-16679)
SPECTRUM SIGNS INC
6106 34th Ave (11377-2228)
PHONE.................................631 756-1010
Harvey Brooks, *President*
Michael Gyscek, *Vice Pres*
Joseph Morra, *Vice Pres*
Joseph Dimaggio, *VP Human Res*
EMP: 45
SQ FT: 20,000
SALES (est): 5.5MM **Privately Held**
SIC: 3993 Electric signs; signs, not made in custom sign painting shops

(G-16680)
STAINLESS METALS INC
6001 31st Ave Ste 1 (11377-1205)
PHONE.................................718 784-1454
Fred Meier, *President*
Dan Meier, *Vice Pres*
EMP: 11 EST: 1927
SQ FT: 14,000
SALES (est): 2.3MM **Privately Held**
WEB: www.stainlessmetals.com
SIC: 3443 3431 Tanks, standard or custom fabricated: metal plate; sinks: enameled iron, cast iron or pressed metal

(G-16681)
SYNERGX SYSTEMS INC (HQ)
3927 59th St (11377-3435)
PHONE.................................516 433-4700
Paul Mendez, *President*
Denise Hajek, *Purch Agent*
John A Poserina, *CFO*
EMP: 89
SQ FT: 16,400
SALES (est): 18.8MM **Privately Held**
SALES (corp-wide): 53.7MM **Privately Held**
WEB: www.synergxsystems.com
SIC: 3669 7382 Emergency alarms; fire alarm apparatus, electric; fire detection systems, electric; transportation signaling devices; security systems services; burglar alarm maintenance & monitoring
PA: Firecom, Inc.
3927 59th St
Woodside NY 11377
718 899-6100

(G-16682)
UTLEYS INCORPORATED
3123 61st St (11377-1222)
PHONE.................................718 956-1661
George Utley III, *President*
John Utley, *Vice Pres*
EMP: 45
SQ FT: 6,500
SALES: 7MM **Privately Held**
WEB: www.utleys.com
SIC: 3565 Packaging machinery

(G-16683)
VERNON PLATING WORKS INC
3318 57th St (11377-2298)
PHONE.................................718 639-1124
Kenneth Abrahami, *CEO*
Alan Hyman, *President*
EMP: 15
SQ FT: 20,000
SALES (est): 1.3MM **Privately Held**
SIC: 3471 Plating of metals or formed products

Woodstock
Ulster County

(G-16684)
BIG INDIE - BEAUTIFUL BOY LLC (PA)
41 Plochmann Ln (12498-1615)
PHONE.................................917 464-5599
Karl Hartman, *Executive*
Declan Baldwin,
EMP: 5 EST: 2017
SQ FT: 300
SALES (est): 733K **Privately Held**
SIC: 3861 Motion picture film

(G-16685)
CUSTOM PATCHES INC
1760 Glasco Tpke (12498-2120)
P.O. Box 22, Mount Marion (12456-0022)
PHONE.................................845 679-6320
Sophia Preza, *President*
Kari Gilbert, *Manager*
EMP: 35
SALES: 500K **Privately Held**
SIC: 2395 Embroidery & art needlework

(G-16686)
MARSHA FLEISHER
Also Called: Loominus Handwoven
18 Tinker St (12498-1233)
PHONE.................................845 679-6500
Marsha Fleisher, *Owner*
Andrea Rose, *General Mgr*
EMP: 10
SALES (est): 786.4K **Privately Held**
SIC: 2282 5632 2211 Weaving yarn: throwing & twisting; women's accessory & specialty stores; broadwoven fabric mills, cotton

(G-16687)
ROTRON INCORPORATED (HQ)
Also Called: Ametek Rotron
55 Hasbrouck Ln (12498-1894)
PHONE.................................845 679-2401
Robert J Vogel, *President*
Michael Ryan, *General Mgr*
Michael Denicola, *Vice Pres*
Telly Kassimis, *Facilities Mgr*
Kenneth Berryann, *Mfg Staff*
▲ EMP: 300
SQ FT: 110,000
SALES (est): 215.8MM
SALES (corp-wide): 4.3B **Publicly Held**
WEB: www.rotronmilaero.com
SIC: 3564 Blowers & fans
PA: Ametek, Inc.
1100 Cassatt Rd
Berwyn PA 19312
610 647-2121

(G-16688)
ROTRON INCORPORATED
Also Called: Ametek Rotron
9 Hasbrouck Ln (12498)
PHONE.................................845 679-2401
Charles Lohwasser, *Principal*
EMP: 44
SALES (corp-wide): 4.3B **Publicly Held**
SIC: 3564 Blowers & fans
HQ: Rotron Incorporated
55 Hasbrouck Ln
Woodstock NY 12498
845 679-2401

Woodville
Jefferson County

(G-16689)
RURAL HILL SAND AND GRAV CORP
10262 County Route 79 (13650-2028)
P.O. Box 128, Belleville (13611-0128)
PHONE.................................315 846-5212
David Staie, *President*
EMP: 12 EST: 1956
SQ FT: 1,000
SALES (est): 1.8MM **Privately Held**
SIC: 1442 3273 Construction sand mining; gravel mining; ready-mixed concrete

Wyandanch
Suffolk County

(G-16690)
A & D ENTRANCES LLC
105 Wyandanch Ave (11798-4441)
PHONE.................................718 989-2441
David L Viteri, *President*
Kimberly Viteri, *Vice Pres*
Alejandro Rodriguez, *Project Mgr*
Kimberly Matos, *Manager*
◆ EMP: 15
SALES (est): 4.3MM **Privately Held**
SIC: 3534 Elevators & equipment

(G-16691)
ACCRA SHEETMETAL LLC
1359 Straight Path (11798-4336)
P.O. Box 1219 (11798-0219)
PHONE.................................631 643-2100
Orlando Stokes,
EMP: 7
SQ FT: 4,000
SALES: 500K **Privately Held**
SIC: 3444 Sheet metalwork

(G-16692)
ADVANCE GRAFIX EQUIPMENT INC
150 Wyandanch Ave (11798-4436)
PHONE.................................917 202-4593
Bally Mohan, *President*
EMP: 4
SALES: 1.2MM **Privately Held**
SIC: 3555 Printing presses

(G-16693)
CANNOLI FACTORY INC
75 Wyandanch Ave (11798-4441)
PHONE.................................631 643-2700
Michael Zucaro, *President*
Geri Muller, *Clerk*
▲ EMP: 50
SQ FT: 30,000
SALES (est): 9.5MM **Privately Held**
SIC: 2051 5149 Pastries, e.g. danish: except frozen; bakery products

(G-16694)
CORINTHIAN CAST STONE INC
115 Wyandanch Ave (11798-4441)
PHONE.................................631 920-2340
Jason Hirschhorn, *Ch of Bd*
Jay Duran, *Finance*
Jim McMahon, *Sales Staff*
David Richter, *Sales Staff*
John Foy, *Marketing Staff*
▲ EMP: 47 EST: 1998
SQ FT: 20,000
SALES (est): 15.4MM **Privately Held**
WEB: www.corinthiancaststone.com
SIC: 3272 Stone, cast concrete

(G-16695)
EHRLICH ENTERPRISES INC
Also Called: Floymar Manufacturing
82 Wyandanch Ave Unit C (11798-4457)
PHONE.................................631 956-0690
Don Ehrlich, *President*
Al Schneider, *General Mgr*
EMP: 16
SQ FT: 18,000
SALES (est): 1.6MM **Privately Held**
SIC: 3599 Machine shop, jobbing & repair

(G-16696)
T G M PRODUCTS INC
90 Wyandanch Ave Unit E (11798-4458)
PHONE.................................631 491-0515
Thomas G Miller, *President*
EMP: 6
SALES (est): 610K **Privately Held**
SIC: 3841 Surgical instruments & apparatus

(G-16697)
WELD-BUILT BODY CO INC
276 Long Island Ave (11798-3199)
PHONE.................................631 643-9700
Joseph Milan, *President*
Diana Nelson, *Vice Pres*
EMP: 30 EST: 1949
SQ FT: 55,000
SALES (est): 2.1MM **Privately Held**
WEB: www.weldbuilt.com
SIC: 3713 Truck bodies (motor vehicles); car carrier bodies

Wyoming
Wyoming County

(G-16698)
AKA ENTERPRISES
164 Main St (14591-9703)
P.O. Box 58 (14591-0058)
PHONE.................................716 474-4579
Andy Kreutter, *Owner*
EMP: 20
SALES: 4MM **Privately Held**
SIC: 2434 Wood kitchen cabinets

(G-16699)
MARKIN TUBING LP (PA)
1 Markin Ln (14591)
P.O. Box 242 (14591-0242)
PHONE.................................585 495-6211
Maurice J Cunniffe, *Partner*
Allen I Skott, *Partner*
William Carter, *Partner*
John W Dyke, *Partner*
Dan Cunniffe, *COO*
▲ EMP: 107
SQ FT: 250,000
SALES (est): 30.1MM **Privately Held**
SIC: 3317 Tubes, wrought: welded or lock joint

(G-16700)
MARKIN TUBING INC
Pearl Creek Rd (14591)
PHONE.................................585 495-6211
Barton P Dambra, *President*
Maurice Cunniffe, *Chairman*
Arthur A Smith, *Vice Pres*
Matt Mess, *Production*
Deb Mistal, *Purch Agent*
EMP: 150
SALES (est): 20.7MM **Privately Held**
WEB: www.markintubing.com
SIC: 3317 3312 Tubes, wrought: welded or lock joint; structural shapes & pilings, steel

(G-16701)
TEXAS BRINE COMPANY LLC
Also Called: Plant Office
1346 Saltvale Rd (14591-9511)
PHONE.................................585 495-6228
Ted Grabowski, *President*
Bruce Martin, *Vice Pres*
Chad Morales, *Plant Mgr*
Brian Stacy, *Plant Mgr*
Scott Borne, *Opers Spvr*
EMP: 8
SALES (corp-wide): 274.6MM **Privately Held**
SIC: 2819 Brine
HQ: Texas Brine Company, Llc
4800 San Felipe St
Houston TX 77056
713 877-2700

(G-16702)
TMP TECHNOLOGIES INC
Also Called: Advanced Rubber Products
6110 Lamb Rd (14591-9754)
PHONE.................................585 495-6231
Eric Snyder, *Prdtn Mgr*

Yaphank - Suffolk County

Robert Flowers, *Manager*
Sally Scully, *Receptionist*
EMP: 60
SALES (corp-wide): 19.7MM **Privately Held**
WEB: www.tmptech.com
SIC: 3069 Medical & laboratory rubber sundries & related products
PA: Tmp Technologies, Inc.
1200 Northland Ave
Buffalo NY 14215
716 895-6100

Yaphank
Suffolk County

(G-16703)
AARCO PRODUCTS INC
21 Old Dock Rd (11980-9734)
PHONE......................631 924-5461
George M Demartino, *Ch of Bd*
Joel Goldberg, *Engineer*
Deanna Freeman, *Marketing Staff*
David Ciancio, *Administration*
▲ **EMP:** 15 **EST:** 1975
SQ FT: 10,000
SALES (est): 3.8MM **Privately Held**
WEB: www.aarcoproducts.com
SIC: 2493 2542 Bulletin boards, wood; office & store showcases & display fixtures

(G-16704)
AMERICAN ELECTRONIC PRODUCTS
Also Called: A E P
86 Horseblock Rd Unit F (11980-9743)
PHONE......................631 924-1299
Robert Gazza, *President*
Warren Azzinaro, *Vice Pres*
EMP: 15
SQ FT: 6,000
SALES (est): 2.2MM **Privately Held**
SIC: 2899 Ink or writing fluids

(G-16705)
CABLES UNLIMITED INC
3 Old Dock Rd (11980-9702)
PHONE......................631 563-6363
Darren Clark, *President*
EMP: 40
SQ FT: 12,000
SALES: 7.5MM
SALES (corp-wide): 30.9MM **Publicly Held**
WEB: www.cables-unlimited.com
SIC: 3679 5063 Harness assemblies for electronic use: wire or cable; electronic wire & cable
PA: Rf Industries, Ltd.
7610 Miramar Rd Ste 6000
San Diego CA 92126
858 549-6340

(G-16706)
CHIPLOGIC INC
14a Old Dock Rd (11980-9701)
PHONE......................631 617-6317
Harry Perry, *President*
Carmen Ramos, *QC Mgr*
EMP: 10
SQ FT: 3,500
SALES (est): 1.5MM **Privately Held**
SIC: 3679 Electronic circuits

(G-16707)
COSA XENTAUR CORPORATION (PA)
84 Horseblock Rd Unit G (11980-9742)
PHONE......................631 345-3434
Christoph Mueller, *CEO*
W Craig Allshouse, *President*
Charles Hunt, *Regional Mgr*
Kortney Cocchiaro, *Export Mgr*
Joe Burton, *Purch Mgr*
◆ **EMP:** 30 **EST:** 1969
SQ FT: 4,500
SALES (est): 12.5MM **Privately Held**
WEB: www.cosa-instrument.com
SIC: 3823 Computer interface equipment for industrial process control

(G-16708)
EMS DEVELOPMENT CORPORATION (DH)
Also Called: Ultra Electronics, Ems
95 Horseblock Rd Unit 2 (11980-2301)
PHONE......................631 924-4736
Peter A Crawford, *President*
Peter Crawford, *VP Opers*
Charles Coakley, *Plant Mgr*
Ellen Kren, *Buyer*
Carol Haunstein, *QC Mgr*
▲ **EMP:** 60
SQ FT: 60,000
SALES (est): 22.1MM
SALES (corp-wide): 1B **Privately Held**
WEB: www.ultra-ems.com
SIC: 3825 3613 3677 3621 Instruments to measure electricity; time switches, electrical switchgear apparatus; switchgear & switchgear accessories; electronic coils, transformers & other inductors; electric motor & generator parts; rectifiers (electrical apparatus)
HQ: Ultra Electronics Defense Inc.
4101 Smith School Rd
Austin TX 78744
512 327-6795

(G-16709)
EMS DEVELOPMENT CORPORATION
95 Horseblock Rd Unit 2a (11980-2301)
PHONE......................631 345-6200
Peter Crawford, *President*
EMP: 90
SALES (corp-wide): 1B **Privately Held**
SIC: 3675 3677 3577 3612 Electronic capacitors; electronic coils, transformers & other inductors; computer peripheral equipment; power & distribution transformers
HQ: Ems Development Corporation
95 Horseblock Rd Unit 2
Yaphank NY 11980
631 924-4736

(G-16710)
EMTRON HYBRIDS INC
86 Horseblock Rd Unit G (11980-9743)
PHONE......................631 924-9668
Damian Emery, *President*
EMP: 15
SQ FT: 6,000
SALES (est): 2.5MM **Privately Held**
WEB: www.emtronhybrids.com
SIC: 3674 2396 Hybrid integrated circuits; automotive & apparel trimmings

(G-16711)
FRAMERICA CORPORATION
2 Todd Ct (11980-2101)
P.O. Box 699 (11980-0699)
PHONE......................631 650-1000
Eugene Eichner, *President*
Gordon Van Vechten, *Corp Secy*
Catherine Michael, *Credit Mgr*
John Wayman, *Sales Staff*
Al Santos, *Manager*
◆ **EMP:** 100
SQ FT: 100,000
SALES (est): 32.9MM **Privately Held**
WEB: www.framerica.com
SIC: 2499 5023 Picture frame molding, finished; frames & framing, picture & mirror

(G-16712)
GEORGIA-PACIFIC LLC
319 Yaphank Ave (11980-9644)
PHONE......................631 924-7401
Craig Bigliotta, *General Mgr*
EMP: 20
SALES (corp-wide): 42.9B **Privately Held**
WEB: www.gp.com
SIC: 2611 5211 5031 Pulp mills; lumber products; lumber: rough, dressed & finished
HQ: Georgia-Pacific Llc
133 Peachtree St Nw
Atlanta GA 30303
404 652-4000

(G-16713)
H B MILLWORK INC
9 Old Dock Rd (11980-9702)
PHONE......................631 924-4195
Timothy Hollowell, *Principal*
EMP: 6
SALES (corp-wide): 2.8MM **Privately Held**
WEB: www.hbmillwork.com
SIC: 2431 Millwork
PA: H B Millwork Inc
500 Long Island Ave
Medford NY 11763
631 289-8086

(G-16714)
L D FLECKEN INC
11 Old Dock Rd Unit 11 # 11 (11980-9622)
PHONE......................631 777-4881
Leo D Flecken, *President*
EMP: 13
SQ FT: 8,000
SALES (est): 1.5MM **Privately Held**
WEB: www.ldflecken.com
SIC: 3499 Metal household articles

(G-16715)
LYNTRONICS INC
7 Old Dock Rd Unit 1 (11980-9637)
PHONE......................631 205-1061
Anthony Vigliotti, *President*
EMP: 20
SQ FT: 12,000
SALES (est): 3.1MM **Privately Held**
SIC: 3679 5063 Harness assemblies for electronic use: wire or cable; batteries, dry cell

(G-16716)
MAHARAM FABRIC CORPORATION
74 Horseblock Rd (11980-9757)
PHONE......................631 582-3434
EMP: 6
SALES (corp-wide): 2.2B **Publicly Held**
WEB: www.maharam.com
SIC: 2221 Automotive fabrics, manmade fiber
HQ: Maharam Fabric Corporation
74 Horseblock Rd
Yaphank NY 11980
631 582-3434

(G-16717)
MASTER-HALCO INC
19 Zorn Blvd (11980-2102)
PHONE......................631 585-8150
Bob Locurto, *Manager*
EMP: 14
SALES (corp-wide): 51.7B **Privately Held**
WEB: www.fenceonline.com
SIC: 3315 5039 5031 1799 Chain link fencing; wire fence, gates & accessories; fencing, wood; fence construction
HQ: Master-Halco, Inc.
3010 Lbj Fwy Ste 800
Dallas TX 75234
972 714-7300

(G-16718)
NANOPROBES INC
95 Horseblock Rd Unit 1 (11980-2301)
PHONE......................631 205-9490
James Hainfeld, *President*
Wenqiu Liu, *General Mgr*
Fred Furuya, *Vice Pres*
Frederic R Furuya, *Vice Pres*
Victoria Kowalski, *Admin Asst*
EMP: 14
SALES: 250K **Privately Held**
WEB: www.nanoprobes.com
SIC: 2836 Biological products, except diagnostic

(G-16719)
RUGA GRINDING & MFG CORP
84 Horseblock Rd Unit A (11980-9742)
PHONE......................631 924-5067
Harry Gaenzle, *President*
Ronnie Ganzle, *Treasurer*
Joie Cascillo, *Admin Sec*
EMP: 8
SQ FT: 5,000
SALES (est): 881.1K **Privately Held**
SIC: 3599 Machine shop, jobbing & repair

(G-16720)
SEARLES GRAPHICS INC (PA)
56 Old Dock Rd (11980-9701)
PHONE......................631 345-2202
Kenneth Searles, *President*
Christine Searles, *Vice Pres*
Richard Searles, *Vice Pres*
Gary Lorandini, *Prdtn Mgr*
Leigh Searles, *CFO*
EMP: 35
SALES (est): 4.5MM **Privately Held**
WEB: www.searlesgraphics.com
SIC: 2752 Commercial printing, offset

(G-16721)
SHAD INDUSTRIES INC
7 Old Dock Rd Unit 1 (11980-9637)
PHONE......................631 504-6028
Lenore A Veltry, *President*
EMP: 5
SALES (est): 457.1K **Privately Held**
SIC: 3692 Primary batteries, dry & wet

(G-16722)
SOKOLIN LLC (PA)
Also Called: Sokolin Wine
445 Sills Rd Unit K (11980)
PHONE......................631 537-4434
David Smydo, *Mng Member*
Aaron Diodato, *Consultant*
Sherri Sulkowski, *Consultant*
Dave Sokolin,
EMP: 26 **EST:** 1934
SQ FT: 15,000
SALES (est): 2.2MM **Privately Held**
SIC: 2084 Wines

(G-16723)
SWITCHES AND SENSORS INC
86 Horseblock Rd Unit J (11980-9743)
PHONE......................631 924-2167
Joe Calvitto, *President*
EMP: 10
SQ FT: 6,200
SALES (est): 1.6MM **Privately Held**
SIC: 3625 Switches, electronic applications

(G-16724)
TRIBOLOGY INC
Also Called: Tech Lube
35 Old Dock Rd (11980-9702)
PHONE......................631 345-3000
William Krause, *President*
Bruce Stebbins, *President*
Lee Day, *Sales Mgr*
Paul Anderson, *Mktg Dir*
Lori Nardello, *Director*
▲ **EMP:** 25
SQ FT: 21,000
SALES (est): 5.6MM **Privately Held**
WEB: www.techlube.com
SIC: 2992 2842 Oils & greases, blending & compounding; specialty cleaning, polishes & sanitation goods

(G-16725)
TWIN PANE INSULATED GL CO INC
86 Horseblock Rd Unit D (11980-9743)
P.O. Box 279 (11980-0279)
PHONE......................631 924-1060
William F Willett, *President*
Rachel Willett, *Treasurer*
EMP: 15
SQ FT: 11,000
SALES (est): 2.8MM **Privately Held**
SIC: 3211 5039 Construction glass; glass construction materials

(G-16726)
US EPOXY INC
11 Old Dock Rd Unit 7 (11980-9622)
PHONE......................800 332-3883
Edward Beller, *President*
EMP: 5
SQ FT: 3,000
SALES (est): 371.1K **Privately Held**
SIC: 2891 Epoxy adhesives

(G-16727)
USA FOIL INC
445 Sills Rd (11980)
PHONE......................631 234-5252
Akhtar Gadi, *Ch of Bd*
Joseph Phami, *President*

Kami Youssi, *Vice Pres*
▲ **EMP**: 20
SALES (est): 3.9MM **Privately Held**
SIC: 3353 Aluminum sheet, plate & foil

(G-16728)
W J ALBRO MACHINE WORKS INC
Also Called: Albro Gear & Instrument
86 Horseblock Rd Unit L (11980-9743)
PHONE..............................631 345-0657
Kevin Albro, *President*
William Albro, *Vice Pres*
William Ambro Jr, *Treasurer*
EMP: 6
SQ FT: 2,000
SALES: 775K **Privately Held**
SIC: 3599 3728 3621 3566 Custom machinery; gears, aircraft power transmission; aircraft propellers & associated equipment; motors & generators; speed changers, drives & gears; iron & steel forgings

(G-16729)
XENTAUR CORPORATION
84 Horseblock Rd Unit G (11980-9742)
PHONE..............................631 345-3434
Christopher Mueller, *CEO*
Craig Allshouse, *President*
Michael Schlitz, *Mfg Staff*
Brian Flanagan, *Engineer*
Betty Kenyon, *Controller*
EMP: 23
SALES (est): 5.4MM **Privately Held**
WEB: www.xentaur.com
SIC: 3823 Industrial instrmnts msrmnt display/control process variable

Yonkers
Westchester County

(G-16730)
ALETEIA USA INC
86 Main St Ste 303 (10701-8805)
PHONE..............................914 502-1855
Axel D'Epinay, *CFO*
EMP: 5
SQ FT: 900
SALES (est): 157.9K **Privately Held**
SIC: 2741

(G-16731)
ALLCOM ELECTRIC CORP
104 Crescent Pl (10704-2519)
PHONE..............................914 803-0433
Anna Protosanousis, *Principal*
EMP: 7 **EST**: 2009
SALES (est): 1MM **Privately Held**
SIC: 3699 Electrical equipment & supplies

(G-16732)
ALPHA-EN CORPORATION (PA)
28 Wells Ave Ste 2 (10701-7045)
PHONE..............................914 418-2000
Sam Pitroda, *CEO*
Jerry I Feldman, *Ch of Bd*
Steven M Payne, *President*
Michael Feldman, *Managing Dir*
George McKeegan, *Exec VP*
EMP: 15 **EST**: 1997
SQ FT: 4,000
SALES (est): 2MM **Publicly Held**
SIC: 2819 6794 Lithium compounds, inorganic; patent buying, licensing, leasing

(G-16733)
ALTMAN STAGE LIGHTING CO INC
Also Called: Altman Lighting
57 Alexander St (10701-2714)
PHONE..............................914 476-7987
Robert Altman, *Ch of Bd*
Russell Altman, *Business Mgr*
Dwarak Parvatam, *COO*
Dwarak Parvatum, *COO*
Nicolas Champion, *Vice Pres*
▲ **EMP**: 125 **EST**: 1953
SQ FT: 75,000

SALES (est): 42.9MM **Privately Held**
WEB: www.altmanlighting.com
SIC: 3648 3646 Stage lighting equipment; commercial indusl & institutional electric lighting fixtures

(G-16734)
AMERICAN CANVAS BINDERS CORP
430 Nepperhan Ave (10701-6601)
PHONE..............................914 969-0300
Richard Maslowski, *President*
EMP: 6
SQ FT: 10,000
SALES (est): 412K **Privately Held**
SIC: 2241 Narrow fabric mills

(G-16735)
AMERICAN SUGAR REFINING INC
1 Federal St (10705-1079)
PHONE..............................914 376-3386
Alan Henderson, *Vice Pres*
Mark Olson, *Vice Pres*
Greg Smith, *Vice Pres*
Becky Serafini, *Marketing Staff*
Michael Mahoney, *Manager*
EMP: 18
SALES (est): 2.7MM **Privately Held**
SIC: 2062 Cane Sugar Refining

(G-16736)
APF MANAGEMENT COMPANY LLC
60 Fullerton Ave (10704-1097)
PHONE..............................914 665-5400
Max Munn, *CEO*
EMP: 110
SALES (est): 8.7MM **Privately Held**
SIC: 3231 Framed mirrors

(G-16737)
APF MANUFACTURING COMPANY LLC (PA)
Also Called: Apf Munn Master Frame Makers
60 Fullerton Ave (10704-1097)
PHONE..............................914 963-6300
Oudit Harbhajan,
EMP: 33 **EST**: 2014
SQ FT: 52,000
SALES (est): 4.2MM **Privately Held**
SIC: 2499 3231 Picture & mirror frames, wood; framed mirrors

(G-16738)
BARRON METAL PRODUCTS INC
286 Nepperhan Ave (10701-3403)
PHONE..............................914 965-1232
Richard Cleary, *President*
Robert Cleary, *Vice Pres*
Rich Cleary, *Plant Mgr*
EMP: 20
SQ FT: 15,000
SALES (est): 1.9MM **Privately Held**
SIC: 3544 3469 Special dies & tools; metal stampings

(G-16739)
BARTIZAN DATA SYSTEMS LLC
217 Riverdale Ave (10705-1131)
PHONE..............................914 965-7977
Lewis C Hoff,
Elizabeth Mazei,
EMP: 25
SQ FT: 43,000
SALES (est): 1.9MM **Privately Held**
WEB: www.bartizan.com
SIC: 3555 Engraving machinery & equipment, except plates

(G-16740)
BELMAY HOLDING CORPORATION
Also Called: Scent 2 Market
1 Odell Plz Ste 123 (10701-6800)
PHONE..............................914 376-1515
Theodore Kesten, *CEO*
Greg Banwer, *Vice Pres*
Alan Kesten, *Treasurer*
▲ **EMP**: 25 **EST**: 1967
SQ FT: 26,000

SALES (est): 9.5MM **Privately Held**
WEB: www.belmay.com
SIC: 2844 Hair preparations, including shampoos

(G-16741)
BRUCCI LTD
861 Nepperhan Ave (10703-2013)
PHONE..............................914 965-0707
Murray Bober, *Ch of Bd*
Howard Marcus, *Vice Pres*
Allan Shapiro, *Treasurer*
EMP: 25
SQ FT: 10,800
SALES (est): 3.8MM **Privately Held**
SIC: 2844 5399 Cosmetic preparations; warehouse club stores

(G-16742)
CAROLINAS DESSERTS INC
1562 Central Park Ave (10710-6001)
PHONE..............................914 779-4000
EMP: 8
SALES (est): 587.4K **Privately Held**
SIC: 2051 Bakery: wholesale or wholesale/retail combined

(G-16743)
CAROLYN RAY INC
578 Nepperhan Ave Ste C10 (10701-6670)
PHONE..............................914 476-0619
Carolyn Ray, *President*
EMP: 6
SALES (est): 695.4K **Privately Held**
WEB: www.carolynray.com
SIC: 2261 Finishing plants, cotton

(G-16744)
CEP TECHNOLOGIES CORPORATION (PA)
763 Saw Mill River Rd (10710-4001)
PHONE..............................914 968-4100
Kenneth W Kaufman, *President*
Francine Kaufman, *Vice Pres*
▲ **EMP**: 48 **EST**: 1960
SQ FT: 22,000
SALES (est): 10.4MM **Privately Held**
SIC: 3469 Stamping metal for the trade

(G-16745)
CLOVER WIRE FORMING CO INC
1021 Saw Mill River Rd (10710-3292)
PHONE..............................914 375-0400
George Margareten, *President*
▲ **EMP**: 30 **EST**: 1957
SQ FT: 35,000
SALES (est): 5.8MM **Privately Held**
WEB: www.cloverwire.com
SIC: 3496 3316 Miscellaneous fabricated wire products; cold finishing of steel shapes

(G-16746)
CONSUMER REPORTS INC (PA)
Also Called: CONSUMERS UNION
101 Truman Ave (10703-1044)
PHONE..............................914 378-2000
Walter D Bristol, *Ch of Bd*
James Guest, *President*
Marta Tellado, *President*
Jeff Bartlett, *Editor*
Marvin Lipman, *Editor*
EMP: 400 **EST**: 1936
SQ FT: 180,000
SALES: 238.9MM **Privately Held**
SIC: 2741 2721 7389 Miscellaneous publishing; magazines: publishing only, not printed on site; fund raising organizations

(G-16747)
COSTELLO BROS PETROLEUM CORP (PA)
990 Mclean Ave Ste 3 (10704-4101)
PHONE..............................914 237-3189
Frank Costello, *President*
Kristopher Costello, *Vice Pres*
EMP: 6
SQ FT: 1,200
SALES (est): 737.7K **Privately Held**
SIC: 2999 5983 Fuel briquettes & waxes; fuel oil dealers

(G-16748)
CREATIVE SOLUTIONS GROUP INC (PA)
Also Called: Diam International
555 Tuckahoe Rd (10710-5709)
PHONE..............................914 771-4200
Edward Winder, *CEO*
Williaml Ecker, *Ch of Bd*
Robert Fodera, *Purch Agent*
▲ **EMP**: 500
SALES (est): 84.5MM **Privately Held**
WEB: www.diam-int.com
SIC: 3993 Displays & cutouts, window & lobby

(G-16749)
DAYLEEN INTIMATES INC
Also Called: Dominique Intimate Apparel
540 Nepperhan Ave (10701-6630)
PHONE..............................914 969-5900
Mike Chernoff, *President*
▲ **EMP**: 24
SQ FT: 20,000
SALES (est): 6MM **Privately Held**
SIC: 2341 4225 Women's & children's undergarments; general warehousing & storage

(G-16750)
DIMAIO MILLWORK CORPORATION
12 Bright Pl (10705-1342)
PHONE..............................914 476-1937
Ralph Dimaio Jr, *President*
Sal Fino, *Project Mgr*
Oren McDermid, *Project Mgr*
Rosemary Perrone, *Office Mgr*
Peter Chomiak, *Manager*
EMP: 35
SQ FT: 20,000
SALES (est): 5.4MM **Privately Held**
WEB: www.dimaiomillwork.com
SIC: 2431 Millwork

(G-16751)
DOLLAR POPULAR INC
473 S Broadway (10705-3249)
P.O. Box 312150, Jamaica (11431-2150)
PHONE..............................914 375-0361
Muhammad Irfan, *Ch of Bd*
EMP: 9 **EST**: 2008
SALES (est): 713.4K **Privately Held**
SIC: 3643 Outlets, electric: convenience

(G-16752)
DOMINO FOODS INC
Also Called: Domino Sugar
1 Federal St (10705-1079)
PHONE..............................800 729-4840
Dominick Tursi, *Engineer*
Gaston Cantenes, *Manager*
EMP: 13
SALES (corp-wide): 1.8B **Privately Held**
SIC: 2062 Granulated cane sugar from purchased raw sugar or syrup
HQ: Domino Foods Inc.
99 Wood Ave S Ste 901
Iselin NJ 08830
732 590-1173

(G-16753)
ECKER WINDOW CORP
1 Odell Plz (10701-1402)
PHONE..............................914 776-0000
Robert Ecker, *CEO*
Jim De Koch, *Vice Pres*
Jim Dekoch, *Vice Pres*
David Ecker, *Vice Pres*
Howard Ecker, *Vice Pres*
EMP: 100
SQ FT: 5,000
SALES (est): 22.3MM **Privately Held**
SIC: 2431 1751 Windows & window parts & trim, wood; window & door installation & erection

(G-16754)
ECONOCRAFT WORLDWIDE MFG INC
56 Worth St Frnt Unit (10701-5508)
PHONE..............................914 966-2280
Shlomo Malki, *President*
Eran Malki, *Vice Pres*
Amir Malki, *Admin Sec*
▼ **EMP**: 5

Yonkers - Westchester County (G-16755)

GEOGRAPHIC SECTION

SQ FT: 27,000
SALES (est): 907.3K **Privately Held**
WEB: www.econocraft.com
SIC: 3589 Car washing machinery

(G-16755)
ELECTRONIC DEVICES INC (HQ)
Also Called: E D I
21 Gray Oaks Ave (10710-3205)
PHONE.................................914 965-4400
Jimmy Huang, *President*
Nancy Alcantara, *General Mgr*
John Dittrich, *COO*
Zhi Huang, *Exec VP*
Steven Huang, *Vice Pres*
▲ EMP: 30
SQ FT: 45,000
SALES (est): 1.2MM **Privately Held**
WEB: www.edidiodes.com
SIC: 3674 5065 Rectifiers, solid state; diodes, solid state (germanium, silicon, etc.); solid state electronic devices; electronic parts & equipment
PA: North Technology Inc
 161 Tices Ln
 East Brunswick NJ 08816
 732 390-2828

(G-16756)
EMPIRE OPEN MRI
1915 Central Park Ave # 25 (10710-2949)
PHONE.................................914 961-1777
Michael Singer, *Owner*
EMP: 6
SALES (est): 541.9K **Privately Held**
SIC: 3845 Ultrasonic scanning devices, medical

(G-16757)
FABRIC CONCEPTS FOR INDUSTRY
Also Called: Awning Man, The
354 Ashburton Ave (10701-6014)
PHONE.................................914 375-2565
Daniel Burke, *President*
EMP: 17
SALES (est): 1.5MM **Privately Held**
SIC: 2394 Awnings, fabric: made from purchased materials

(G-16758)
FITZGERALD PUBLISHING CO INC
Also Called: Golden Legacy Ilstrd Histry
1853 Central Park Ave # 8 (10710-2948)
PHONE.................................914 793-5016
Bertram Fitzgerald, *President*
Jeanette Fitzgerald, *Vice Pres*
EMP: 5
SALES: 300K **Privately Held**
SIC: 2741 Miscellaneous publishing

(G-16759)
FLEETCOM INC
1081 Yonkers Ave (10704-3123)
PHONE.................................914 776-5582
Mike Rosenzweig, *President*
EMP: 15 EST: 1984
SALES (est): 1MM **Privately Held**
SIC: 3663 Radio broadcasting & communications equipment

(G-16760)
FOWLER ROUTE CO INC
25 Sunnyside Dr (10705-1763)
PHONE.................................917 653-4640
EMP: 56
SALES (corp-wide): 14MM **Privately Held**
SIC: 3582 Commercial laundry equipment
PA: Fowler Route Co., Inc.
 565 Rahway Ave
 Union NJ 07083
 908 686-3400

(G-16761)
GANNETT STLLITE INFO NTWRK INC
Also Called: Herald Statesman
1 Odell Plz (10701-1402)
PHONE.................................914 965-5000
John Gambrill, *Branch Mgr*
EMP: 50

SALES (corp-wide): 3.1B **Publicly Held**
WEB: www.usatoday.com
SIC: 2711 Newspapers: publishing only, not printed on site
HQ: Gannett Satellite Information Network, Llc
 7950 Jones Branch Dr
 Mc Lean VA 22102
 703 854-6000

(G-16762)
GLOBAL LIGHTING INC
201 Saw Mill River Rd 3 (10701-5711)
PHONE.................................914 591-4095
Nadeem Razi, *CEO*
EMP: 7
SALES (est): 206.8K **Privately Held**
SIC: 3646 5063 Chandeliers, commercial; lighting fixtures

(G-16763)
GOLDEN RENEWABLE ENERGY LLC
700 Nepperhan Ave (10703-2312)
PHONE.................................914 920-9800
Franklin Canosa, *CFO*
Christina Vlassis, *Human Res Mgr*
Nicholas Canosa,
Jason Provost,
EMP: 5
SALES: 950K **Privately Held**
SIC: 2869 Fuels

(G-16764)
GRAPHITE METALLIZING CORP (PA)
Also Called: Graphalloy
1050 Nepperhan Ave (10703-1432)
PHONE.................................914 968-8400
Eben T Walker, *Ch of Bd*
Viridiana Bermejo, *Business Mgr*
Giovanni Loconte, *Plant Mgr*
Michael Haynes, *Mfg Spvr*
Rohit Masih, *Engineer*
◆ EMP: 190 EST: 1913
SQ FT: 95,000
SALES (est): 36MM **Privately Held**
WEB: www.graphalloy.com
SIC: 3624 Brushes & brush stock contacts, electric

(G-16765)
GREYSTON BAKERY INC
104 Alexander St (10701-2535)
PHONE.................................914 375-1510
Michael Brady, *Ch of Bd*
Julius Walls, *President*
Joan Cotter, *Vice Pres*
◆ EMP: 130
SQ FT: 10,000
SALES (est): 1.5MM
SALES (corp-wide): 1.8MM **Privately Held**
WEB: www.greystonbakery.com
SIC: 2051 Cakes, pies & pastries
PA: Greyston Foundation Inc.
 21 Park Ave
 Yonkers NY 10703
 914 376-3900

(G-16766)
HANA SHEET METAL INC
9 Celli Pl 11 (10701-4805)
P.O. Box 156, Atlantic Beach (11509-0156)
PHONE.................................914 377-0773
Awni A Hana, *Ch of Bd*
EMP: 8
SALES (est): 1.4MM **Privately Held**
SIC: 3444 Sheet metalwork

(G-16767)
HEMISPHERE NOVELTIES INC
167 Saw Mill River Rd 3c (10701-6621)
P.O. Box 1240 (10703-8240)
PHONE.................................914 378-4100
Max Wolfeln, *President*
Jeffrey Wolfeln, *Corp Secy*
◆ EMP: 25
SQ FT: 12,000
SALES (est): 3.6MM **Privately Held**
WEB: www.hemispherenovelties.com
SIC: 3172 3965 5091 5131 Personal leather goods; fasteners, buttons, needles & pins; fishing tackle; buttons; belt & buckle assembly kits

(G-16768)
HIGHER POWER INDUSTRIES INC
11 Sunny Slope Ter (10703-1714)
PHONE.................................914 709-9800
Warren J Azzara, *President*
Anna Dibello Battista, *Vice Pres*
Victor Alonso, *Manager*
EMP: 9
SQ FT: 5,500
SALES (est): 8MM **Privately Held**
SIC: 3743 Locomotives & parts

(G-16769)
HORNE ORGANIZATION INC (PA)
15 Arthur Pl (10701-1702)
PHONE.................................914 572-1330
Leon H Horne Jr, *President*
Jackie Arce, *Office Mgr*
EMP: 10
SQ FT: 1,500
SALES (est): 2.6MM **Privately Held**
SIC: 2752 7336 Commercial printing, lithographic; graphic arts & related design

(G-16770)
HUDSON SCENIC STUDIO INC (PA)
130 Fernbrook St (10705-1764)
PHONE.................................914 375-0900
Neil Mazzella, *CEO*
John C Boyd, *Vice Pres*
▲ EMP: 130
SQ FT: 56,000
SALES (est): 17.6MM **Privately Held**
WEB: www.hudsonscenic.com
SIC: 3999 Theatrical scenery

(G-16771)
ITR INDUSTRIES INC (PA)
441 Saw Mill River Rd (10701-4913)
PHONE.................................914 964-7063
Mario F Rolla, *Ch of Bd*
Adrienne Rola, *President*
Peter M Rolla, *President*
▲ EMP: 21
SALES (est): 201.6MM **Privately Held**
SIC: 3431 3429 3446 3088 Shower stalls, metal; manufactured hardware (general); architectural metalwork; shower stalls, fiberglass & plastic

(G-16772)
J KENDALL LLC
Also Called: J K Fertility
71 Belvedere Dr (10705-2813)
PHONE.................................646 739-4956
Julius K Smalls, *CEO*
EMP: 5
SALES (est): 370K **Privately Held**
SIC: 2759 Screen printing

(G-16773)
JENRAY PRODUCTS INC
252 Lake Ave Fl 2a (10701-5706)
PHONE.................................914 375-5596
Raymond D'Urso, *President*
▲ EMP: 26 EST: 1999
SQ FT: 22,000
SALES (est): 3.3MM **Privately Held**
SIC: 3999 Sprays, artificial & preserved

(G-16774)
KAWASAKI RAIL CAR INC (DH)
29 Wells Ave Bldg 4 (10701-8815)
PHONE.................................914 376-4700
Hiroji Iwasaki, *CEO*
Yuichi Yamamoto, *President*
Steven Vangellow, *General Mgr*
Yoshinori Kanehana, *Exec VP*
Tameka Beckford-Young, *Legal Staff*
▲ EMP: 199
SQ FT: 150,000
SALES (est): 84.3MM
SALES (corp-wide): 14.7B **Privately Held**
SIC: 3743 Railroad equipment, except locomotives; railway motor cars; train cars & equipment, freight or passenger
HQ: Kawasaki Motors Manufacturing Corp., U.S.A.
 6600 Nw 27th St
 Lincoln NE 68524
 402 476-6600

(G-16775)
KIMBER MFG INC
16 Harrison Ave (10705-2606)
PHONE.................................914 965-0753
Leslie Edelman, *Owner*
EMP: 7
SALES (corp-wide): 86MM **Privately Held**
SIC: 3599 Machine shop, jobbing & repair
PA: Kimber Mfg., Inc.
 1 Lawton St
 Yonkers NY 10705
 914 964-0771

(G-16776)
KIMBER MFG INC (PA)
1 Lawton St (10705-2617)
PHONE.................................914 964-0771
Leslie Edelmen, *Ch of Bd*
Abdool Jamal, *Managing Dir*
Doron Segal, *Vice Pres*
Frank Casal, *Plant Mgr*
Kieran Kelly, *Mfg Mgr*
◆ EMP: 220
SQ FT: 50,000
SALES (est): 86MM **Privately Held**
WEB: www.kimbermfg.com
SIC: 3599 Machine shop, jobbing & repair

(G-16777)
KIMBER MFG INC
1120 Saw Mill River Rd (10701-3229)
PHONE.................................406 758-2222
Greg Grogan, *Vice Pres*
Adrian Owsianski, *Mfg Staff*
Chris Dennis, *Production*
Denis Morland, *Production*
Barry Volaski, *Purchasing*
EMP: 83
SALES (corp-wide): 86MM **Privately Held**
WEB: www.kimbermfg.com
SIC: 3599 Machine shop, jobbing & repair
PA: Kimber Mfg., Inc.
 1 Lawton St
 Yonkers NY 10705
 914 964-0771

(G-16778)
LESER ENTERPRISES LTD
Also Called: Color Story
1767 Central Park Ave (10710-2828)
PHONE.................................212 644-8921
Robert Leser, *President*
Hilary Leser, *Manager*
EMP: 11
SALES (est): 1.5MM **Privately Held**
WEB: www.colorstory.com
SIC: 3911 Jewelry, precious metal

(G-16779)
LIGHTING BY DOM YONKERS INC
Also Called: Sparkle Light Manufacturing
253 S Broadway (10705-1351)
PHONE.................................914 968-8700
Dominick Di Gennaro Jr, *President*
EMP: 5 EST: 1979
SQ FT: 5,000
SALES (est): 640K **Privately Held**
SIC: 3646 Commercial indusl & institutional electric lighting fixtures

(G-16780)
M SANTOLIQUIDO CORP
Also Called: San Signs & Awnings
925 Saw Mill River Rd (10710-3238)
PHONE.................................914 375-6674
Michael Santoliquido, *President*
Lucille Santoliquido, *Vice Pres*
EMP: 11 EST: 1995
SQ FT: 10,000
SALES (est): 1.3MM **Privately Held**
WEB: www.sansigns.com
SIC: 3993 Electric signs

(G-16781)
MAGNIFICAT INC
86 Main St Ste 303 (10701-8805)
P.O. Box 822 (10702-0822)
PHONE.................................914 502-1820
Fleurus Mame, *CEO*
Romain Lize, *Exec VP*
Axel D'Epinay, *CFO*
Francois Piebo, *Accountant*
Axel Depinay, *Info Tech Mgr*

▲ = Import ▼=Export
◆ =Import/Export

GEOGRAPHIC SECTION

Yonkers - Westchester County (G-16812)

▲ **EMP:** 18
SALES (est): 2.5MM
SALES (corp-wide): 1.6K **Privately Held**
SIC: 2721 Periodicals
PA: Magnificat Films
10 Rue De Penthievre
Paris
954 464-343

(G-16782)
MARBLE WORKS INC
681 Saw Mill River Rd (10710-4004)
PHONE.................914 376-3653
Sabo Barmaksiz, *President*
Sezen Barmaksiz, *Opers Dir*
▲ **EMP:** 30
SALES (est): 3.5MM **Privately Held**
SIC: 3281 Granite, cut & shaped; marble, building: cut & shaped

(G-16783)
MARPLEX FURNITURE CORPORATION
167 Saw Mill Rver Rd Fl 1 Flr 1 (10701)
PHONE.................914 969-7755
Peter Bizzarro, *President*
EMP: 5
SQ FT: 13,000
SALES (est): 527.4K **Privately Held**
SIC: 2541 Display fixtures, wood

(G-16784)
MICROMOLD PRODUCTS INC
7 Odell Plz 133 (10701-1407)
PHONE.................914 969-2850
Arthur Lukach, *Ch of Bd*
Justin Lukach, *President*
David Scimia, *Mfg Mgr*
Frank Pino, *Human Resources*
Tricia Lombardo, *Sales Staff*
EMP: 25 **EST:** 1954
SQ FT: 13,000
SALES (est): 5.3MM **Privately Held**
WEB: www.micromold.com
SIC: 3089 3494 3053 3084 Plastic containers, except foam; valves & pipe fittings; gaskets, packing & sealing devices; plastics pipe; steel pipe & tubes; fabricated pipe & fittings

(G-16785)
MIRROR-TECH MANUFACTURING CO
286 Nepperhan Ave (10701-3403)
PHONE.................914 965-1232
Richard Cleary, *President*
EMP: 16 **EST:** 1961
SQ FT: 7,000
SALES: 750K **Privately Held**
SIC: 3231 Mirrored glass; mirrors, truck & automobile: made from purchased glass

(G-16786)
OCTOPUS ADVANCED SYSTEMS INC
27 Covington Rd (10710-3515)
PHONE.................914 771-6110
Nikolai Prokhorenkov, *Ch of Bd*
EMP: 1
SALES (est): 2MM **Privately Held**
SIC: 3669 Emergency alarms

(G-16787)
ON LINE POWER TECHNOLOGIES
113 Sunnyside Dr (10705-2830)
PHONE.................914 968-4440
Linda Hack, *President*
Bruce Hack, *Vice Pres*
EMP: 2
SALES (est): 10MM **Privately Held**
SIC: 3568 5063 7389 Power transmission equipment; electrical apparatus & equipment;

(G-16788)
ORZA BAKERY INC
261 New Main St Ste 263 (10701-4103)
PHONE.................914 965-5736
Vital Tovar, *President*
Ubaldo Tovar, *Vice Pres*
EMP: 17
SQ FT: 8,000
SALES (est): 2.4MM **Privately Held**
SIC: 2051 Breads, rolls & buns

(G-16789)
OUREM IRON WORKS INC
498 Nepperhan Ave Ste 5 (10701-6604)
PHONE.................914 476-4856
Arthur Viera, *President*
EMP: 12 **EST:** 1977
SQ FT: 25,000
SALES (est): 2.9MM **Privately Held**
SIC: 3446 1799 Fences or posts, ornamental iron or steel; fence construction

(G-16790)
P PASCAL INC
Also Called: P Pascal Coffee Roasters
960 Nepperhan Ave (10703-1726)
P.O. Box 347 (10703-0347)
PHONE.................914 969-7933
Dean Pialtos, *President*
James Ranni, *Corp Secy*
Barbara Pialtos, *Vice Pres*
Charles Pialtos, *Vice Pres*
EMP: 27
SQ FT: 15,000
SALES (est): 4.4MM **Privately Held**
SIC: 2095 Roasted coffee

(G-16791)
PENNYSAVER GROUP INC
80 Alexander St (10701-2715)
PHONE.................914 966-1400
Ed Levitt, *Manager*
EMP: 10
SALES (corp-wide): 7.8MM **Privately Held**
WEB: www.nysaver.com
SIC: 2711 Newspapers, publishing & printing
PA: Pennysaver Group Inc.
510 Fifth Ave
Pelham NY
914 592-5222

(G-16792)
PIETRO DEMARCO IMPORTERS INC
1185 Saw Mill River Rd (10710-3240)
PHONE.................914 969-3201
Pietro Demarco, *President*
Anthony Demarco, *Vice Pres*
▲ **EMP:** 10
SALES (est): 1.2MM **Privately Held**
SIC: 2079 Olive oil

(G-16793)
POMPIAN MANUFACTURING CO INC
280 Nepperhan Ave (10701-3403)
PHONE.................914 476-7076
Fax: 914 476-7095
EMP: 8
SQ FT: 10,000
SALES: 900K **Privately Held**
SIC: 3645 5063 Mfg & Whol Electrical Equipment & Electronic Ballast

(G-16794)
PREPAC DESIGNS INC
25 Abner Pl (10704-3015)
PHONE.................914 524-7800
Manuel Mendez, *President*
Patti Miranda, *Officer*
Noemi Pabon, *Relations*
▲ **EMP:** 5
SQ FT: 1,500
SALES (est): 2.5MM **Privately Held**
WEB: www.designerschoiceline.com
SIC: 3161 Luggage

(G-16795)
REFINED SUGARS INC
1 Federal St (10705-1079)
PHONE.................914 963-2400
Jack Lay, *Principal*
EMP: 6 **EST:** 2009
SALES (est): 630.9K **Privately Held**
SIC: 2062 Cane sugar refining

(G-16796)
ROBERT VIGGIANI
Also Called: Irv & Vic Sportswear Co
37 Vredenburgh Ave Ste B (10704-2150)
PHONE.................914 423-4046
Robert Viggiani, *Owner*
EMP: 5
SQ FT: 975

SALES (est): 510.6K **Privately Held**
SIC: 2329 5699 Riding clothes:, men's, youths' & boys'; riding apparel

(G-16797)
RUMSEY CORP
Also Called: B2b Cleaning Services
15 Rumsey Rd (10705-1623)
PHONE.................914 751-3640
Anna Negron, *President*
EMP: 6
SALES (est): 300K **Privately Held**
SIC: 3672 7349 Printed circuit boards; building & office cleaning services; office cleaning or charring; cleaning service, industrial or commercial; window cleaning

(G-16798)
SKIL-CARE CORPORATION
29 Wells Ave Bldg 4 (10701-8815)
PHONE.................914 963-2040
Martin Prenskean, *Ch of Bd*
Arnold Silverman, *President*
Stephen Warhaftig, *Vice Pres*
▲ **EMP:** 135
SQ FT: 55,000
SALES (est): 17.7MM **Privately Held**
WEB: www.skilcare.com
SIC: 3842 2392 2241 Wheelchairs; household furnishings; narrow fabric mills

(G-16799)
STANSON AUTOMATED LLC
145 Saw Mill River Rd # 2 (10701-6615)
PHONE.................866 505-7826
Stewart Iskowitz, *Mng Member*
Joel Iskowitz, *Mng Member*
EMP: 10
SALES (est): 910K **Privately Held**
SIC: 3578 Automatic teller machines (ATM)

(G-16800)
STAR DESK PAD CO INC
60 Mclean Ave (10705-2317)
PHONE.................914 963-9400
Sidney Newman, *President*
▲ **EMP:** 45 **EST:** 1946
SQ FT: 60,000
SALES (est): 2.4MM **Privately Held**
WEB: www.stardesk.com
SIC: 3199 3999 Desk sets, leather; desk pads, except paper

(G-16801)
T C DUNHAM PAINT COMPANY INC
761 Nepperhan Ave (10703-2313)
PHONE.................914 969-4202
Isaac Schwartz, *Ch of Bd*
Ely Fisch, *Vice Pres*
Eoy Fisch, *Vice Pres*
EMP: 25
SQ FT: 5,000
SALES (est): 11MM **Privately Held**
WEB: www.dunhampaint.com
SIC: 2851 Paints & paint additives

(G-16802)
TODD SYSTEMS INC
50 Ash St (10701-3900)
PHONE.................914 963-3400
Kenneth Todd, *President*
K H Todd, *Chairman*
Ruthann Todd, *Vice Pres*
◆ **EMP:** 60 **EST:** 1964
SQ FT: 25,000
SALES (est): 9.4MM **Privately Held**
WEB: www.toddsystems.com
SIC: 3677 Electronic transformers

(G-16803)
TOPPS-ALL PRODUCTS OF YONKERS
148 Ludlow St Ste 2 (10705-7014)
PHONE.................914 968-4226
Edward J Bolwell Jr, *President*
EMP: 15 **EST:** 1939
SALES (est): 2.5MM **Privately Held**
SIC: 2842 Cleaning or polishing preparations; automobile polish

(G-16804)
TOY ADMIRATION CO INC
60 Mclean Ave (10705-2317)
PHONE.................914 963-9400

Sidney Newman, *President*
Alice Newman, *Treasurer*
EMP: 30 **EST:** 1945
SQ FT: 60,000
SALES: 2MM **Privately Held**
SIC: 3942 5945 Dolls, except stuffed toy animals; hobby, toy & game shops

(G-16805)
VALENTI NECKWEAR CO INC
540 Nepperhan Ave Ste 564 (10701-6611)
PHONE.................914 969-0700
Albert Valentine, *President*
EMP: 8
SALES: 250K **Privately Held**
WEB: www.valentineckwear.com
SIC: 2323 2339 Men's & boys' neckwear; neckwear & ties: women's, misses' & juniors'

(G-16806)
VINYLINE WINDOW AND DOOR INC
636 Saw Mill River Rd (10710-4009)
PHONE.................914 476-3500
Carmen Cangialosi, *President*
Henry Nagani, *Owner*
Robert Gramagila, *Vice Pres*
EMP: 10
SQ FT: 10,000
SALES: 600K **Privately Held**
SIC: 3089 Windows, plastic

(G-16807)
WHITNEY BOIN STUDIO INC
42 Warburton Ave Ste 1 (10701-2786)
PHONE.................914 377-4385
Whitney Boin, *President*
Theresa Boin, *Vice Pres*
EMP: 6
SALES (est): 820.9K **Privately Held**
WEB: www.whitneyboinstudio.com
SIC: 3911 Jewelry apparel

(G-16808)
WINESOFT INTERNATIONAL CORP
503 S Broadway Ste 220 (10705-6202)
PHONE.................914 400-6247
Marco Vicens, *Manager*
EMP: 6
SALES (est): 253.2K **Privately Held**
WEB: www.winesoftusa.com
SIC: 7372 Application computer software

(G-16809)
YEWTREE MILLWORKS CORP
372 Ashburton Ave (10701-6015)
PHONE.................914 320-5851
Keith Murphy, *President*
EMP: 5
SALES (est): 266.2K **Privately Held**
SIC: 2851 Paints & allied products

(G-16810)
YONKERS CABINET INC
1179 Yonkers Ave (10704-3210)
PHONE.................914 668-2133
Wai Hing Yip, *Ch of Bd*
EMP: 7
SALES (est): 755.1K **Privately Held**
SIC: 2434 Wood kitchen cabinets

(G-16811)
YONKERS TIME PUBLISHING CO
Also Called: Martinelli Publications
40 Larkin Plz (10701-2748)
PHONE.................914 965-4000
Franchesca Martinelli, *Owner*
EMP: 15
SQ FT: 6,000
SALES (est): 520K **Privately Held**
WEB: www.martinellipublications.com
SIC: 2711 Newspapers: publishing only, not printed on site

(G-16812)
YONKERS WHL BEER DISTRS INC
424 Riverdale Ave (10705-2908)
PHONE.................914 963-8600
Richard McDine, *Owner*
EMP: 5
SALES (est): 347.5K **Privately Held**
SIC: 2082 Beer (alcoholic beverage)

York
Livingston County

(G-16813)
DAVIS TRAILER WORLD LLC
Also Called: Davis Trlr World & Cntry Mall
1640 Main St (14592)
P.O. Box 260 (14592-0260)
PHONE.....................585 538-6640
Dean Davis,
Susan Davis,
EMP: 10 **EST:** 1987
SALES: 3MM **Privately Held**
WEB: www.davistrailerworld.com
SIC: 3715 Truck trailers

Yorktown Heights
Westchester County

(G-16814)
CHASE MEDIA GROUP
1520 Front St (10598-4638)
PHONE.....................914 962-3871
Diane Bello, *Sales Staff*
Chris Longo, *Sales Staff*
Dave Fitzmorris, *Manager*
Tania Gaffney, *Graphic Designe*
EMP: 15
SALES (est): 738.8K **Privately Held**
SIC: 2711 Newspapers: publishing only, not printed on site

(G-16815)
CROWN DELTA CORPORATION
1550 Front St (10598-4638)
PHONE.....................914 245-8910
Anthony Konopka, *CEO*
Anthony J Konopka, *CFO*
Maureen Barone, *Human Resources*
▲ **EMP:** 35
SQ FT: 30,000
SALES (est): 9.6MM **Privately Held**
WEB: www.crowndelta.com
SIC: 2869 Silicones

(G-16816)
FOLEYS GRAPHIC CENTER INC
Also Called: Foley Graphics
1661 Front St Ste 3 (10598-4650)
PHONE.....................914 245-3625
Joseph Foley III, *President*
Brenda Piekutowski, *Production*
Katy Foley, *Manager*
EMP: 25
SQ FT: 7,000
SALES (est): 2.7MM **Privately Held**
WEB: www.foleygraphics.com
SIC: 2754 2791 2789 2752 Commercial printing, gravure; typesetting; bookbinding & related work; commercial printing, lithographic; blueprinting service

(G-16817)
GAME SPORTSWEAR LTD (PA)
1401 Front St (10598-4639)
PHONE.....................914 962-1701
Enrico Genovese, *President*
Leslie Tandler, *Vice Pres*
Andrea Cancellieri, *VP Sls/Mktg*
Gina M Furano, *Treasurer*
Mario Flores, *Manager*
▲ **EMP:** 25
SQ FT: 76,000
SALES (est): 18.2MM **Privately Held**
SIC: 2253 2339 Knit outerwear mills; women's & misses' outerwear

(G-16818)
MAKARENKO STUDIOS INC
2984 Saddle Ridge Dr (10598-2327)
PHONE.....................914 968-7673
Boris Makarenko, *President*
Sviatoslaw Makarenko, *Treasurer*
EMP: 5 **EST:** 1976
SALES (est): 290K **Privately Held**
SIC: 3231 1542 Stained glass: made from purchased glass; religious building construction

(G-16819)
MEGA GRAPHICS INC
1725 Front St Ste 1 (10598-4651)
PHONE.....................914 962-1402
Robert Pierro, *Principal*
EMP: 5
SALES (est): 418.2K **Privately Held**
SIC: 2759 Commercial printing

(G-16820)
NORTHERN TIER PUBLISHING CORP
Also Called: North County News
1520 Front St (10598-4638)
PHONE.....................914 962-4748
John Chase, *President*
Jean Secor, *Vice Pres*
Rick Pezzullo, *Advt Staff*
Carla Chase, *Admin Sec*
EMP: 11
SQ FT: 2,000
SALES (est): 710.7K **Privately Held**
SIC: 2711 Newspapers-Publishing/Printing

(G-16821)
Q OMNI INC
1994 Commerce St (10598-4412)
PHONE.....................914 962-2726
Kwan Lee, *Owner*
EMP: 6
SALES (est): 542.4K **Privately Held**
SIC: 3582 Drycleaning equipment & machinery, commercial

(G-16822)
RICHARD ANTHONY CORP
Also Called: Richard Anthony Custom Mllwk
1500 Front St Ste 12 (10598-4648)
P.O. Box 240 (10598-0240)
PHONE.....................914 922-7141
Richard Scavelli, *CEO*
Angela Desiena, *Vice Pres*
EMP: 28
SALES (est): 2.8MM **Privately Held**
SIC: 2431 Millwork

(G-16823)
SHOP SMART CENTRAL INC
Also Called: Chase Press
1520 Front St (10598-4638)
PHONE.....................914 962-3871
Carla Chase, *President*
EMP: 7
SALES (est): 599.5K **Privately Held**
SIC: 2741 Business service newsletters: publishing & printing

(G-16824)
SIGNS INK LTD
3255 Crompond Rd (10598-3605)
PHONE.....................914 739-9059
Dick Hederson, *President*
Matthew Beachak, *Vice Pres*
Steve Chester, *Sales Mgr*
Timothy Beachak, *Sales Staff*
Esteban Baquero, *Department Mgr*
EMP: 10
SQ FT: 1,000
SALES (est): 1.6MM **Privately Held**
SIC: 3993 Electric signs

(G-16825)
WOODTRONICS INC
1661 Front St Ste 3 (10598-4650)
PHONE.....................914 962-5205
Jan Efraimsen, *President*
EMP: 5
SQ FT: 4,500
SALES (est): 510K **Privately Held**
SIC: 2499 Decorative wood & woodwork

(G-16826)
YORKTOWN PRINTING CORP
1520 Front St (10598-4697)
PHONE.....................914 962-2526
John W Chase, *President*
EMP: 150
SQ FT: 80,000
SALES (est): 16.6MM **Privately Held**
WEB: www.yzipmail.com
SIC: 2752 Commercial printing, offset

Yorkville
Oneida County

(G-16827)
HUBBELL GALVANIZING INC
5124 Commercial Dr (13495-1109)
P.O. Box 37, New York Mills (13417-0037)
PHONE.....................315 736-8311
Daniel Merritt Hubbell, *President*
EMP: 7
SALES (est): 112.7K **Privately Held**
SIC: 3479 Coating, rust preventive; coating electrodes

(G-16828)
O W HUBBELL & SONS INC
Also Called: Hubbell Galvanising
5124 Commercial Dr (13495-1109)
P.O. Box 37, New York Mills (13417-0037)
PHONE.....................315 736-8311
Allen W Hubbell, *Ch of Bd*
Jock Hubbell, *President*
Vinnie Pham, *Accountant*
Emmite White, *Human Resources*
Pete Hubbell, *VP Mktg*
▲ **EMP:** 35 **EST:** 1925
SQ FT: 8,000
SALES (est): 5.1MM
SALES (corp-wide): 3.7MM **Privately Held**
WEB: www.hubbellgalvanizing.com
SIC: 3479 Galvanizing of iron, steel or end-formed products
PA: W Hubbell & Sons Inc
5124 Commercial Dr
Yorkville NY 13495
315 736-8311

(G-16829)
ORISKANY MANUFACTURING LLC
2 Wurz Ave (13495-1118)
PHONE.....................315 732-4962
Michael Fitzgerald, *CEO*
EMP: 13 **EST:** 2009
SALES (est): 2.3MM **Privately Held**
SIC: 3999 Manufacturing industries

(G-16830)
ORISKANY MFG TECH LLC
Also Called: Omt
2 Wurz Ave (13495-1118)
PHONE.....................315 732-4962
Dave Pelligrini, *Vice Pres*
Clayton McKeon, *Opers Mgr*
Stephen Palmieri, *Production*
Thomas Dutcher, *Purch Mgr*
James Caraco, *Engineer*
▲ **EMP:** 30
SQ FT: 30,000
SALES (est): 7.4MM **Privately Held**
WEB: www.oriskanymfg.com
SIC: 3441 3317 Fabricated structural metal; welded pipe & tubes

(G-16831)
OTIS ELEVATOR COMPANY
5172 Commercial Dr (13495-1110)
PHONE.....................315 736-0167
Brian Craig, *General Mgr*
Lucas Jinks, *Superintendent*
Russell Morrison, *Superintendent*
Tom Stewart, *Superintendent*
Whitney Craig, *Project Mgr*
EMP: 12
SALES (corp-wide): 59.8B **Publicly Held**
WEB: www.otis.com
SIC: 3534 7699 Elevators & equipment; elevators: inspection, service & repair
HQ: Otis Elevator Company
1 Carrier Pl
Farmington CT 06032
860 674-3000

(G-16832)
VICKS LITHOGRAPH & PRTG CORP (PA)
5166 Commercial Dr (13495-1173)
P.O. Box 270 (13495-0270)
PHONE.....................315 272-2401
Dwight E Vicks III, *Ch of Bd*
Dwight E Vicks III, *Ch of Bd*
Dwight E Vicks Jr, *Chairman*
Dwight Vicks, *CIO*
EMP: 110
SQ FT: 130,000
SALES (est): 22MM **Privately Held**
SIC: 2732 2789 2752 Books: printing only; bookbinding & related work; commercial printing, lithographic

(G-16833)
VICKS LITHOGRAPH & PRTG CORP
5210 Commercial Dr (13495-1111)
P.O. Box 270 (13495-0270)
PHONE.....................315 736-9344
Frank Driscoll, *Manager*
EMP: 130
SALES (est): 3.2MM
SALES (corp-wide): 22MM **Privately Held**
SIC: 2732 2752 Book printing; commercial printing, lithographic
PA: Vicks Lithograph & Printing Corp.
5166 Commercial Dr
Yorkville NY 13495
315 272-2401

(G-16834)
W HUBBELL & SONS INC (PA)
5124 Commercial Dr (13495-1109)
P.O. Box 37, New York Mills (13417-0037)
PHONE.....................315 736-8311
Allen W Hubbell, *Principal*
Allen W Hubbel, *Principal*
Steve Mulvihill, *Principal*
EMP: 40
SQ FT: 8,000
SALES (est): 3.7MM **Privately Held**
SIC: 3479 Galvanizing of iron, steel or end-formed products

(G-16835)
WAYNES WELDING INC
66 Calder Ave (13495-1601)
PHONE.....................315 768-6146
Wayne A Ramsey, *President*
EMP: 20
SQ FT: 9,000
SALES (est): 2.7MM **Privately Held**
SIC: 7692 3599 Automotive welding; machine shop, jobbing & repair

Youngstown
Niagara County

(G-16836)
KINETIC FUEL TECHNOLOGY INC
Also Called: Kinetic Laboratories
1205 Balmer Rd (14174-9797)
PHONE.....................716 745-1461
Timothy M Booth, *Ch of Bd*
Eric Fragale, *President*
EMP: 5
SQ FT: 4,500
SALES (est): 1.2MM **Privately Held**
SIC: 2911 Fuel additives

SIC INDEX

Standard Industrial Classification Alphabetical Index

SIC NO	PRODUCT

A

3291 Abrasive Prdts
2891 Adhesives & Sealants
3563 Air & Gas Compressors
3585 Air Conditioning & Heating Eqpt
3721 Aircraft
3724 Aircraft Engines & Engine Parts
3728 Aircraft Parts & Eqpt, NEC
2812 Alkalies & Chlorine
3363 Aluminum Die Castings
3354 Aluminum Extruded Prdts
3365 Aluminum Foundries
3355 Aluminum Rolling & Drawing, NEC
3353 Aluminum Sheet, Plate & Foil
3483 Ammunition, Large
3826 Analytical Instruments
2077 Animal, Marine Fats & Oils
2389 Apparel & Accessories, NEC
2387 Apparel Belts
3446 Architectural & Ornamental Metal Work
7694 Armature Rewinding Shops
3292 Asbestos products
2952 Asphalt Felts & Coatings
3822 Automatic Temperature Controls
3581 Automatic Vending Machines
3465 Automotive Stampings
2396 Automotive Trimmings, Apparel Findings, Related Prdts

B

2673 Bags: Plastics, Laminated & Coated
2674 Bags: Uncoated Paper & Multiwall
3562 Ball & Roller Bearings
2836 Biological Prdts, Exc Diagnostic Substances
2782 Blankbooks & Looseleaf Binders
3312 Blast Furnaces, Coke Ovens, Steel & Rolling Mills
3564 Blowers & Fans
3732 Boat Building & Repairing
3452 Bolts, Nuts, Screws, Rivets & Washers
2732 Book Printing, Not Publishing
2789 Bookbinding
2731 Books: Publishing & Printing
3131 Boot & Shoe Cut Stock & Findings
2342 Brassieres, Girdles & Garments
2051 Bread, Bakery Prdts Exc Cookies & Crackers
3251 Brick & Structural Clay Tile
3991 Brooms & Brushes
3995 Burial Caskets
2021 Butter

C

3578 Calculating & Accounting Eqpt
2064 Candy & Confectionery Prdts
2033 Canned Fruits, Vegetables & Preserves
2032 Canned Specialties
2394 Canvas Prdts
3624 Carbon & Graphite Prdts
3955 Carbon Paper & Inked Ribbons
3592 Carburetors, Pistons, Rings & Valves
2273 Carpets & Rugs
2823 Cellulosic Man-Made Fibers
3241 Cement, Hydraulic
3253 Ceramic Tile
2043 Cereal Breakfast Foods
2022 Cheese
1479 Chemical & Fertilizer Mining
2899 Chemical Preparations, NEC
2067 Chewing Gum
2361 Children's & Infants' Dresses & Blouses
3261 China Plumbing Fixtures & Fittings
3262 China, Table & Kitchen Articles
2066 Chocolate & Cocoa Prdts
2111 Cigarettes
2121 Cigars
2257 Circular Knit Fabric Mills
3255 Clay Refractories
1459 Clay, Ceramic & Refractory Minerals, NEC
1241 Coal Mining Svcs
3479 Coating & Engraving, NEC
2095 Coffee
3316 Cold Rolled Steel Sheet, Strip & Bars
3582 Commercial Laundry, Dry Clean & Pressing Mchs
2759 Commercial Printing
2754 Commercial Printing: Gravure
2752 Commercial Printing: Lithographic
3646 Commercial, Indl & Institutional Lighting Fixtures
3669 Communications Eqpt, NEC
3577 Computer Peripheral Eqpt, NEC
3572 Computer Storage Devices
3575 Computer Terminals
3271 Concrete Block & Brick
3272 Concrete Prdts
3531 Construction Machinery & Eqpt
1442 Construction Sand & Gravel
2679 Converted Paper Prdts, NEC
3535 Conveyors & Eqpt
2052 Cookies & Crackers
3366 Copper Foundries
1021 Copper Ores
2298 Cordage & Twine
2653 Corrugated & Solid Fiber Boxes
3961 Costume Jewelry & Novelties
2261 Cotton Fabric Finishers
2211 Cotton, Woven Fabric
2074 Cottonseed Oil Mills
3466 Crowns & Closures
1311 Crude Petroleum & Natural Gas
1423 Crushed & Broken Granite
1422 Crushed & Broken Limestone
1429 Crushed & Broken Stone, NEC
3643 Current-Carrying Wiring Devices
2391 Curtains & Draperies
3087 Custom Compounding Of Purchased Plastic Resins
3281 Cut Stone Prdts
3421 Cutlery
2865 Cyclic-Crudes, Intermediates, Dyes & Org Pigments

D

3843 Dental Eqpt & Splys
2835 Diagnostic Substances
2675 Die-Cut Paper & Board
3544 Dies, Tools, Jigs, Fixtures & Indl Molds
1411 Dimension Stone
2047 Dog & Cat Food
3942 Dolls & Stuffed Toys
2591 Drapery Hardware, Window Blinds & Shades
2381 Dress & Work Gloves
2034 Dried Fruits, Vegetables & Soup
1381 Drilling Oil & Gas Wells

E

3263 Earthenware, Whiteware, Table & Kitchen Articles
3634 Electric Household Appliances
3641 Electric Lamps
3694 Electrical Eqpt For Internal Combustion Engines
3629 Electrical Indl Apparatus, NEC
3699 Electrical Machinery, Eqpt & Splys, NEC
3845 Electromedical & Electrotherapeutic Apparatus
3313 Electrometallurgical Prdts
3675 Electronic Capacitors
3677 Electronic Coils & Transformers
3679 Electronic Components, NEC
3571 Electronic Computers
3678 Electronic Connectors
3676 Electronic Resistors
3471 Electroplating, Plating, Polishing, Anodizing & Coloring
3534 Elevators & Moving Stairways
3431 Enameled Iron & Metal Sanitary Ware
2677 Envelopes
2892 Explosives

F

2241 Fabric Mills, Cotton, Wool, Silk & Man-Made
3499 Fabricated Metal Prdts, NEC
3498 Fabricated Pipe & Pipe Fittings
3443 Fabricated Plate Work
3069 Fabricated Rubber Prdts, NEC
3441 Fabricated Structural Steel
2399 Fabricated Textile Prdts, NEC
2295 Fabrics Coated Not Rubberized
2297 Fabrics, Nonwoven
3523 Farm Machinery & Eqpt
3965 Fasteners, Buttons, Needles & Pins
2875 Fertilizers, Mixing Only
2655 Fiber Cans, Tubes & Drums
2091 Fish & Seafoods, Canned & Cured
2092 Fish & Seafoods, Fresh & Frozen
3211 Flat Glass
2087 Flavoring Extracts & Syrups
2045 Flour, Blended & Prepared
2041 Flour, Grain Milling
3824 Fluid Meters & Counters
3593 Fluid Power Cylinders & Actuators
3594 Fluid Power Pumps & Motors
3492 Fluid Power Valves & Hose Fittings
2657 Folding Paperboard Boxes
3556 Food Prdts Machinery
2099 Food Preparations, NEC
3149 Footwear, NEC
2053 Frozen Bakery Prdts
2037 Frozen Fruits, Juices & Vegetables
2038 Frozen Specialties
2371 Fur Goods
2599 Furniture & Fixtures, NEC

G

3944 Games, Toys & Children's Vehicles
3524 Garden, Lawn Tractors & Eqpt
3053 Gaskets, Packing & Sealing Devices
2369 Girls' & Infants' Outerwear, NEC
3221 Glass Containers
3231 Glass Prdts Made Of Purchased Glass
1041 Gold Ores
3321 Gray Iron Foundries
2771 Greeting Card Publishing
3769 Guided Missile/Space Vehicle Parts & Eqpt, NEC
3761 Guided Missiles & Space Vehicles
2861 Gum & Wood Chemicals
3275 Gypsum Prdts

H

3423 Hand & Edge Tools
3425 Hand Saws & Saw Blades
3171 Handbags & Purses
3429 Hardware, NEC
3426 Hardwood Dimension & Flooring Mills
2435 Hardwood Veneer & Plywood
2353 Hats, Caps & Millinery
3433 Heating Eqpt
3536 Hoists, Cranes & Monorails
2252 Hosiery, Except Women's
2251 Hosiery, Women's Full & Knee Length
2392 House furnishings: Textile
3142 House Slippers
3639 Household Appliances, NEC
3651 Household Audio & Video Eqpt
3631 Household Cooking Eqpt
2519 Household Furniture, NEC
3633 Household Laundry Eqpt
3632 Household Refrigerators & Freezers
3635 Household Vacuum Cleaners

I

2097 Ice
2024 Ice Cream
2819 Indl Inorganic Chemicals, NEC
3823 Indl Instruments For Meas, Display & Control
3569 Indl Machinery & Eqpt, NEC
3567 Indl Process Furnaces & Ovens
3537 Indl Trucks, Tractors, Trailers & Stackers
2813 Industrial Gases
2869 Industrial Organic Chemicals, NEC
3543 Industrial Patterns
1446 Industrial Sand
3491 Industrial Valves
2816 Inorganic Pigments
3825 Instrs For Measuring & Testing Electricity
3519 Internal Combustion Engines, NEC
3462 Iron & Steel Forgings
1011 Iron Ores

J

3915 Jewelers Findings & Lapidary Work
3911 Jewelry: Precious Metal

K

2253 Knit Outerwear Mills
2254 Knit Underwear Mills
2259 Knitting Mills, NEC

L

3821 Laboratory Apparatus & Furniture
2258 Lace & Warp Knit Fabric Mills
3952 Lead Pencils, Crayons & Artist's Mtrls
2386 Leather & Sheep Lined Clothing
3151 Leather Gloves & Mittens
3199 Leather Goods, NEC
3111 Leather Tanning & Finishing
3648 Lighting Eqpt, NEC
3274 Lime

SIC INDEX

SIC NO	PRODUCT
3996	Linoleum & Hard Surface Floor Coverings, NEC
2085	Liquors, Distilled, Rectified & Blended
2411	Logging
2992	Lubricating Oils & Greases
3161	Luggage

M

SIC NO	PRODUCT
2098	Macaroni, Spaghetti & Noodles
3545	Machine Tool Access
3541	Machine Tools: Cutting
3542	Machine Tools: Forming
3599	Machinery & Eqpt, Indl & Commercial, NEC
3322	Malleable Iron Foundries
2083	Malt
2082	Malt Beverages
2761	Manifold Business Forms
3999	Manufacturing Industries, NEC
3953	Marking Devices
2515	Mattresses & Bedsprings
3829	Measuring & Controlling Devices, NEC
3586	Measuring & Dispensing Pumps
2011	Meat Packing Plants
3568	Mechanical Power Transmission Eqpt, NEC
2833	Medicinal Chemicals & Botanical Prdts
2329	Men's & Boys' Clothing, NEC
2323	Men's & Boys' Neckwear
2325	Men's & Boys' Separate Trousers & Casual Slacks
2321	Men's & Boys' Shirts
2311	Men's & Boys' Suits, Coats & Overcoats
2322	Men's & Boys' Underwear & Nightwear
2326	Men's & Boys' Work Clothing
3143	Men's Footwear, Exc Athletic
3412	Metal Barrels, Drums, Kegs & Pails
3411	Metal Cans
3442	Metal Doors, Sash, Frames, Molding & Trim
3497	Metal Foil & Leaf
3398	Metal Heat Treating
2514	Metal Household Furniture
1081	Metal Mining Svcs
1099	Metal Ores, NEC
3469	Metal Stampings, NEC
3549	Metalworking Machinery, NEC
2026	Milk
2023	Milk, Condensed & Evaporated
2431	Millwork
3296	Mineral Wool
3295	Minerals & Earths: Ground Or Treated
3532	Mining Machinery & Eqpt
3496	Misc Fabricated Wire Prdts
2741	Misc Publishing
3449	Misc Structural Metal Work
1499	Miscellaneous Nonmetallic Mining
2451	Mobile Homes
3061	Molded, Extruded & Lathe-Cut Rubber Mechanical Goods
3716	Motor Homes
3714	Motor Vehicle Parts & Access
3711	Motor Vehicles & Car Bodies
3751	Motorcycles, Bicycles & Parts
3621	Motors & Generators
3931	Musical Instruments

N

SIC NO	PRODUCT
1321	Natural Gas Liquids
2711	Newspapers: Publishing & Printing
2873	Nitrogenous Fertilizers
3297	Nonclay Refractories
3644	Noncurrent-Carrying Wiring Devices
3364	Nonferrous Die Castings, Exc Aluminum
3463	Nonferrous Forgings
3369	Nonferrous Foundries: Castings, NEC
3357	Nonferrous Wire Drawing
3299	Nonmetallic Mineral Prdts, NEC
1481	Nonmetallic Minerals Svcs, Except Fuels

O

SIC NO	PRODUCT
2522	Office Furniture, Except Wood
3579	Office Machines, NEC
1382	Oil & Gas Field Exploration Svcs
1389	Oil & Gas Field Svcs, NEC
3533	Oil Field Machinery & Eqpt
3851	Ophthalmic Goods
3827	Optical Instruments
3489	Ordnance & Access, NEC
3842	Orthopedic, Prosthetic & Surgical Appliances/Splys

P

SIC NO	PRODUCT
3565	Packaging Machinery
2851	Paints, Varnishes, Lacquers, Enamels
2671	Paper Coating & Laminating for Packaging
2672	Paper Coating & Laminating, Exc for Packaging
3554	Paper Inds Machinery
2621	Paper Mills
2631	Paperboard Mills
2542	Partitions & Fixtures, Except Wood
2951	Paving Mixtures & Blocks
3951	Pens & Mechanical Pencils
2844	Perfumes, Cosmetics & Toilet Preparations
2721	Periodicals: Publishing & Printing
3172	Personal Leather Goods
2879	Pesticides & Agricultural Chemicals, NEC
2911	Petroleum Refining
2834	Pharmaceuticals
3652	Phonograph Records & Magnetic Tape
2874	Phosphatic Fertilizers
3861	Photographic Eqpt & Splys
2035	Pickled Fruits, Vegetables, Sauces & Dressings
3085	Plastic Bottles
3086	Plastic Foam Prdts
3083	Plastic Laminated Plate & Sheet
3084	Plastic Pipe
3088	Plastic Plumbing Fixtures
3089	Plastic Prdts
3082	Plastic Unsupported Profile Shapes
3081	Plastic Unsupported Sheet & Film
2821	Plastics, Mtrls & Nonvulcanizable Elastomers
2796	Platemaking & Related Svcs
2395	Pleating & Stitching For The Trade
3432	Plumbing Fixture Fittings & Trim, Brass
3264	Porcelain Electrical Splys
2096	Potato Chips & Similar Prdts
3269	Pottery Prdts, NEC
2015	Poultry Slaughtering, Dressing & Processing
3546	Power Hand Tools
3612	Power, Distribution & Specialty Transformers
3448	Prefabricated Metal Buildings & Cmpnts
2452	Prefabricated Wood Buildings & Cmpnts
7372	Prepackaged Software
2048	Prepared Feeds For Animals & Fowls
3229	Pressed & Blown Glassware, NEC
3692	Primary Batteries: Dry & Wet
3399	Primary Metal Prdts, NEC
3339	Primary Nonferrous Metals, NEC
3334	Primary Production Of Aluminum
3331	Primary Smelting & Refining Of Copper
3672	Printed Circuit Boards
2893	Printing Ink
3555	Printing Trades Machinery & Eqpt
2999	Products Of Petroleum & Coal, NEC
2531	Public Building & Related Furniture
2611	Pulp Mills
3561	Pumps & Pumping Eqpt

R

SIC NO	PRODUCT
3663	Radio & T V Communications, Systs & Eqpt, Broadcast/Studio
3671	Radio & T V Receiving Electron Tubes
3743	Railroad Eqpt
3273	Ready-Mixed Concrete
2493	Reconstituted Wood Prdts
3695	Recording Media
3625	Relays & Indl Controls
3645	Residential Lighting Fixtures
2044	Rice Milling
2384	Robes & Dressing Gowns
3547	Rolling Mill Machinery & Eqpt
3351	Rolling, Drawing & Extruding Of Copper
3356	Rolling, Drawing-Extruding Of Nonferrous Metals
3021	Rubber & Plastic Footwear
3052	Rubber & Plastic Hose & Belting

S

SIC NO	PRODUCT
2068	Salted & Roasted Nuts & Seeds
2656	Sanitary Food Containers
2676	Sanitary Paper Prdts
2013	Sausages & Meat Prdts
2421	Saw & Planing Mills
3596	Scales & Balances, Exc Laboratory
2397	Schiffli Machine Embroideries
3451	Screw Machine Prdts
3812	Search, Detection, Navigation & Guidance Systs & Instrs
3341	Secondary Smelting & Refining Of Nonferrous Metals
3674	Semiconductors
3589	Service Ind Machines, NEC
2652	Set-Up Paperboard Boxes
3444	Sheet Metal Work
3731	Shipbuilding & Repairing
2079	Shortening, Oils & Margarine
3993	Signs & Advertising Displays
2262	Silk & Man-Made Fabric Finishers
2221	Silk & Man-Made Fiber
1044	Silver Ores
3914	Silverware, Plated & Stainless Steel Ware
3484	Small Arms
3482	Small Arms Ammunition
2841	Soap & Detergents
2086	Soft Drinks
2436	Softwood Veneer & Plywood
2842	Spec Cleaning, Polishing & Sanitation Preparations
3559	Special Ind Machinery, NEC
2429	Special Prdt Sawmills, NEC
3566	Speed Changers, Drives & Gears
3949	Sporting & Athletic Goods, NEC
2678	Stationery Prdts
3511	Steam, Gas & Hydraulic Turbines & Engines
3325	Steel Foundries, NEC
3324	Steel Investment Foundries
3317	Steel Pipe & Tubes
3493	Steel Springs, Except Wire
3315	Steel Wire Drawing & Nails & Spikes
3691	Storage Batteries
3259	Structural Clay Prdts, NEC
2439	Structural Wood Members, NEC
2063	Sugar, Beet
2061	Sugar, Cane
2062	Sugar, Cane Refining
2843	Surface Active & Finishing Agents, Sulfonated Oils
3841	Surgical & Medical Instrs & Apparatus
3613	Switchgear & Switchboard Apparatus
2824	Synthetic Organic Fibers, Exc Cellulosic
2822	Synthetic Rubber (Vulcanizable Elastomers)

T

SIC NO	PRODUCT
3795	Tanks & Tank Components
3661	Telephone & Telegraph Apparatus
2393	Textile Bags
2269	Textile Finishers, NEC
2299	Textile Goods, NEC
3552	Textile Machinery
2284	Thread Mills
2296	Tire Cord & Fabric
3011	Tires & Inner Tubes
2141	Tobacco Stemming & Redrying
2131	Tobacco, Chewing & Snuff
3799	Transportation Eqpt, NEC
3792	Travel Trailers & Campers
3713	Truck & Bus Bodies
3715	Truck Trailers
2791	Typesetting

U

SIC NO	PRODUCT
1094	Uranium, Radium & Vanadium Ores

V

SIC NO	PRODUCT
3494	Valves & Pipe Fittings, NEC
2076	Vegetable Oil Mills
3647	Vehicular Lighting Eqpt

W

SIC NO	PRODUCT
3873	Watch & Clock Devices & Parts
2385	Waterproof Outerwear
3548	Welding Apparatus
7692	Welding Repair
2046	Wet Corn Milling
2084	Wine & Brandy
3495	Wire Springs
2331	Women's & Misses' Blouses
2335	Women's & Misses' Dresses
2339	Women's & Misses' Outerwear, NEC
2337	Women's & Misses' Suits, Coats & Skirts
3144	Women's Footwear, Exc Athletic
2341	Women's, Misses' & Children's Underwear & Nightwear
2441	Wood Boxes
2449	Wood Containers, NEC
2511	Wood Household Furniture
2512	Wood Household Furniture, Upholstered
2434	Wood Kitchen Cabinets
2521	Wood Office Furniture
2448	Wood Pallets & Skids
2499	Wood Prdts, NEC
2491	Wood Preserving
2517	Wood T V, Radio, Phono & Sewing Cabinets
2541	Wood, Office & Store Fixtures
3553	Woodworking Machinery
2231	Wool, Woven Fabric

X

SIC NO	PRODUCT
3844	X-ray Apparatus & Tubes

Y

SIC NO	PRODUCT
2281	Yarn Spinning Mills
2282	Yarn Texturizing, Throwing, Twisting & Winding Mills

SIC INDEX

Standard Industrial Classification Numerical Index

SIC NO	PRODUCT

10 METAL MINING
1011 Iron Ores
1021 Copper Ores
1041 Gold Ores
1044 Silver Ores
1081 Metal Mining Svcs
1094 Uranium, Radium & Vanadium Ores
1099 Metal Ores, NEC

12 COAL MINING
1241 Coal Mining Svcs

13 OIL AND GAS EXTRACTION
1311 Crude Petroleum & Natural Gas
1321 Natural Gas Liquids
1381 Drilling Oil & Gas Wells
1382 Oil & Gas Field Exploration Svcs
1389 Oil & Gas Field Svcs, NEC

14 MINING AND QUARRYING OF NONMETALLIC MINERALS, EXCEPT FUELS
1411 Dimension Stone
1422 Crushed & Broken Limestone
1423 Crushed & Broken Granite
1429 Crushed & Broken Stone, NEC
1442 Construction Sand & Gravel
1446 Industrial Sand
1459 Clay, Ceramic & Refractory Minerals, NEC
1479 Chemical & Fertilizer Mining
1481 Nonmetallic Minerals Svcs, Except Fuels
1499 Miscellaneous Nonmetallic Mining

20 FOOD AND KINDRED PRODUCTS
2011 Meat Packing Plants
2013 Sausages & Meat Prdts
2015 Poultry Slaughtering, Dressing & Processing
2021 Butter
2022 Cheese
2023 Milk, Condensed & Evaporated
2024 Ice Cream
2026 Milk
2032 Canned Specialties
2033 Canned Fruits, Vegetables & Preserves
2034 Dried Fruits, Vegetables & Soup
2035 Pickled Fruits, Vegetables, Sauces & Dressings
2037 Frozen Fruits, Juices & Vegetables
2038 Frozen Specialties
2041 Flour, Grain Milling
2043 Cereal Breakfast Foods
2044 Rice Milling
2045 Flour, Blended & Prepared
2046 Wet Corn Milling
2047 Dog & Cat Food
2048 Prepared Feeds For Animals & Fowls
2051 Bread, Bakery Prdts Exc Cookies & Crackers
2052 Cookies & Crackers
2053 Frozen Bakery Prdts
2061 Sugar, Cane
2062 Sugar, Cane Refining
2063 Sugar, Beet
2064 Candy & Confectionery Prdts
2066 Chocolate & Cocoa Prdts
2067 Chewing Gum
2068 Salted & Roasted Nuts & Seeds
2074 Cottonseed Oil Mills
2076 Vegetable Oil Mills
2077 Animal, Marine Fats & Oils
2079 Shortening, Oils & Margarine
2082 Malt Beverages
2083 Malt
2084 Wine & Brandy
2085 Liquors, Distilled, Rectified & Blended
2086 Soft Drinks
2087 Flavoring Extracts & Syrups
2091 Fish & Seafoods, Canned & Cured
2092 Fish & Seafoods, Fresh & Frozen
2095 Coffee
2096 Potato Chips & Similar Prdts
2097 Ice
2098 Macaroni, Spaghetti & Noodles
2099 Food Preparations, NEC

21 TOBACCO PRODUCTS
2111 Cigarettes
2121 Cigars
2131 Tobacco, Chewing & Snuff
2141 Tobacco Stemming & Redrying

22 TEXTILE MILL PRODUCTS
2211 Cotton, Woven Fabric
2221 Silk & Man-Made Fiber
2231 Wool, Woven Fabric
2241 Fabric Mills, Cotton, Wool, Silk & Man-Made
2251 Hosiery, Women's Full & Knee Length
2252 Hosiery, Except Women's
2253 Knit Outerwear Mills
2254 Knit Underwear Mills
2257 Circular Knit Fabric Mills
2258 Lace & Warp Knit Fabric Mills
2259 Knitting Mills, NEC
2261 Cotton Fabric Finishers
2262 Silk & Man-Made Fabric Finishers
2269 Textile Finishers, NEC
2273 Carpets & Rugs
2281 Yarn Spinning Mills
2282 Yarn Texturizing, Throwing, Twisting & Winding Mills
2284 Thread Mills
2295 Fabrics Coated Not Rubberized
2296 Tire Cord & Fabric
2297 Fabrics, Nonwoven
2298 Cordage & Twine
2299 Textile Goods, NEC

23 APPAREL AND OTHER FINISHED PRODUCTS MADE FROM FABRICS AND SIMILAR MATERIAL
2311 Men's & Boys' Suits, Coats & Overcoats
2321 Men's & Boys' Shirts
2322 Men's & Boys' Underwear & Nightwear
2323 Men's & Boys' Neckwear
2325 Men's & Boys' Separate Trousers & Casual Slacks
2326 Men's & Boys' Work Clothing
2329 Men's & Boys' Clothing, NEC
2331 Women's & Misses' Blouses
2335 Women's & Misses' Dresses
2337 Women's & Misses' Suits, Coats & Skirts
2339 Women's & Misses' Outerwear, NEC
2341 Women's, Misses' & Children's Underwear & Nightwear
2342 Brassieres, Girdles & Garments
2353 Hats, Caps & Millinery
2361 Children's & Infants' Dresses & Blouses
2369 Girls' & Infants' Outerwear, NEC
2371 Fur Goods
2381 Dress & Work Gloves
2384 Robes & Dressing Gowns
2385 Waterproof Outerwear
2386 Leather & Sheep Lined Clothing
2387 Apparel Belts
2389 Apparel & Accessories, NEC
2391 Curtains & Draperies
2392 House furnishings: Textile
2393 Textile Bags
2394 Canvas Prdts
2395 Pleating & Stitching For The Trade
2396 Automotive Trimmings, Apparel Findings, Related Prdts
2397 Schiffli Machine Embroideries
2399 Fabricated Textile Prdts, NEC

24 LUMBER AND WOOD PRODUCTS, EXCEPT FURNITURE
2411 Logging
2421 Saw & Planing Mills
2426 Hardwood Dimension & Flooring Mills
2429 Special Prdt Sawmills, NEC
2431 Millwork
2434 Wood Kitchen Cabinets
2435 Hardwood Veneer & Plywood
2436 Softwood Veneer & Plywood
2439 Structural Wood Members, NEC
2441 Wood Boxes
2448 Wood Pallets & Skids
2449 Wood Containers, NEC
2451 Mobile Homes
2452 Prefabricated Wood Buildings & Cmpnts
2491 Wood Preserving
2493 Reconstituted Wood Prdts
2499 Wood Prdts, NEC

25 FURNITURE AND FIXTURES
2511 Wood Household Furniture
2512 Wood Household Furniture, Upholstered
2514 Metal Household Furniture
2515 Mattresses & Bedsprings
2517 Wood T V, Radio, Phono & Sewing Cabinets
2519 Household Furniture, NEC
2521 Wood Office Furniture
2522 Office Furniture, Except Wood
2531 Public Building & Related Furniture
2541 Wood, Office & Store Fixtures
2542 Partitions & Fixtures, Except Wood
2591 Drapery Hardware, Window Blinds & Shades
2599 Furniture & Fixtures, NEC

26 PAPER AND ALLIED PRODUCTS
2611 Pulp Mills
2621 Paper Mills
2631 Paperboard Mills
2652 Set-Up Paperboard Boxes
2653 Corrugated & Solid Fiber Boxes
2655 Fiber Cans, Tubes & Drums
2656 Sanitary Food Containers
2657 Folding Paperboard Boxes
2671 Paper Coating & Laminating for Packaging
2672 Paper Coating & Laminating, Exc for Packaging
2673 Bags: Plastics, Laminated & Coated
2674 Bags: Uncoated Paper & Multiwall
2675 Die-Cut Paper & Board
2676 Sanitary Paper Prdts
2677 Envelopes
2678 Stationery Prdts
2679 Converted Paper Prdts, NEC

27 PRINTING, PUBLISHING, AND ALLIED INDUSTRIES
2711 Newspapers: Publishing & Printing
2721 Periodicals: Publishing & Printing
2731 Books: Publishing & Printing
2732 Book Printing, Not Publishing
2741 Misc Publishing
2752 Commercial Printing: Lithographic
2754 Commercial Printing: Gravure
2759 Commercial Printing
2761 Manifold Business Forms
2771 Greeting Card Publishing
2782 Blankbooks & Looseleaf Binders
2789 Bookbinding
2791 Typesetting
2796 Platemaking & Related Svcs

28 CHEMICALS AND ALLIED PRODUCTS
2812 Alkalies & Chlorine
2813 Industrial Gases
2816 Inorganic Pigments
2819 Indl Inorganic Chemicals, NEC
2821 Plastics, Mtrls & Nonvulcanizable Elastomers
2822 Synthetic Rubber (Vulcanizable Elastomers)
2823 Cellulosic Man-Made Fibers
2824 Synthetic Organic Fibers, Exc Cellulosic
2833 Medicinal Chemicals & Botanical Prdts
2834 Pharmaceuticals
2835 Diagnostic Substances
2836 Biological Prdts, Exc Diagnostic Substances
2841 Soap & Detergents
2842 Spec Cleaning, Polishing & Sanitation Preparations
2843 Surface Active & Finishing Agents, Sulfonated Oils
2844 Perfumes, Cosmetics & Toilet Preparations
2851 Paints, Varnishes, Lacquers, Enamels
2861 Gum & Wood Chemicals
2865 Cyclic-Crudes, Intermediates, Dyes & Org Pigments
2869 Industrial Organic Chemicals, NEC
2873 Nitrogenous Fertilizers
2874 Phosphatic Fertilizers
2875 Fertilizers, Mixing Only
2879 Pesticides & Agricultural Chemicals, NEC
2891 Adhesives & Sealants
2892 Explosives
2893 Printing Ink
2899 Chemical Preparations, NEC

29 PETROLEUM REFINING AND RELATED INDUSTRIES
2911 Petroleum Refining
2951 Paving Mixtures & Blocks
2952 Asphalt Felts & Coatings
2992 Lubricating Oils & Greases
2999 Products Of Petroleum & Coal, NEC

30 RUBBER AND MISCELLANEOUS PLASTICS PRODUCTS
3011 Tires & Inner Tubes
3021 Rubber & Plastic Footwear
3052 Rubber & Plastic Hose & Belting
3053 Gaskets, Packing & Sealing Devices
3061 Molded, Extruded & Lathe-Cut Rubber Mechanical Goods
3069 Fabricated Rubber Prdts, NEC
3081 Plastic Unsupported Sheet & Film
3082 Plastic Unsupported Profile Shapes

SIC INDEX

SIC NO	PRODUCT
3083	Plastic Laminated Plate & Sheet
3084	Plastic Pipe
3085	Plastic Bottles
3086	Plastic Foam Prdts
3087	Custom Compounding Of Purchased Plastic Resins
3088	Plastic Plumbing Fixtures
3089	Plastic Prdts

31 LEATHER AND LEATHER PRODUCTS

3111	Leather Tanning & Finishing
3131	Boot & Shoe Cut Stock & Findings
3142	House Slippers
3143	Men's Footwear, Exc Athletic
3144	Women's Footwear, Exc Athletic
3149	Footwear, NEC
3151	Leather Gloves & Mittens
3161	Luggage
3171	Handbags & Purses
3172	Personal Leather Goods
3199	Leather Goods, NEC

32 STONE, CLAY, GLASS, AND CONCRETE PRODUCTS

3211	Flat Glass
3221	Glass Containers
3229	Pressed & Blown Glassware, NEC
3231	Glass Prdts Made Of Purchased Glass
3241	Cement, Hydraulic
3251	Brick & Structural Clay Tile
3253	Ceramic Tile
3255	Clay Refractories
3259	Structural Clay Prdts, NEC
3261	China Plumbing Fixtures & Fittings
3262	China, Table & Kitchen Articles
3263	Earthenware, Whiteware, Table & Kitchen Articles
3264	Porcelain Electrical Splys
3269	Pottery Prdts, NEC
3271	Concrete Block & Brick
3272	Concrete Prdts
3273	Ready-Mixed Concrete
3274	Lime
3275	Gypsum Prdts
3281	Cut Stone Prdts
3291	Abrasive Prdts
3292	Asbestos products
3295	Minerals & Earths: Ground Or Treated
3296	Mineral Wool
3297	Nonclay Refractories
3299	Nonmetallic Mineral Prdts, NEC

33 PRIMARY METAL INDUSTRIES

3312	Blast Furnaces, Coke Ovens, Steel & Rolling Mills
3313	Electrometallurgical Prdts
3315	Steel Wire Drawing & Nails & Spikes
3316	Cold Rolled Steel Sheet, Strip & Bars
3317	Steel Pipe & Tubes
3321	Gray Iron Foundries
3322	Malleable Iron Foundries
3324	Steel Investment Foundries
3325	Steel Foundries, NEC
3331	Primary Smelting & Refining Of Copper
3334	Primary Production Of Aluminum
3339	Primary Nonferrous Metals, NEC
3341	Secondary Smelting & Refining Of Nonferrous Metals
3351	Rolling, Drawing & Extruding Of Copper
3353	Aluminum Sheet, Plate & Foil
3354	Aluminum Extruded Prdts
3355	Aluminum Rolling & Drawing, NEC
3356	Rolling, Drawing-Extruding Of Nonferrous Metals
3357	Nonferrous Wire Drawing
3363	Aluminum Die Castings
3364	Nonferrous Die Castings, Exc Aluminum
3365	Aluminum Foundries
3366	Copper Foundries
3369	Nonferrous Foundries: Castings, NEC
3398	Metal Heat Treating
3399	Primary Metal Prdts, NEC

34 FABRICATED METAL PRODUCTS, EXCEPT MACHINERY AND TRANSPORTATION EQUIPMENT

3411	Metal Cans
3412	Metal Barrels, Drums, Kegs & Pails
3421	Cutlery
3423	Hand & Edge Tools
3425	Hand Saws & Saw Blades
3429	Hardware, NEC
3431	Enameled Iron & Metal Sanitary Ware
3432	Plumbing Fixture Fittings & Trim, Brass
3433	Heating Eqpt
3441	Fabricated Structural Steel
3442	Metal Doors, Sash, Frames, Molding & Trim
3443	Fabricated Plate Work
3444	Sheet Metal Work
3446	Architectural & Ornamental Metal Work
3448	Prefabricated Metal Buildings & Cmpnts
3449	Misc Structural Metal Work
3451	Screw Machine Prdts
3452	Bolts, Nuts, Screws, Rivets & Washers
3462	Iron & Steel Forgings
3463	Nonferrous Forgings
3465	Automotive Stampings
3466	Crowns & Closures
3469	Metal Stampings, NEC
3471	Electroplating, Plating, Polishing, Anodizing & Coloring
3479	Coating & Engraving, NEC
3482	Small Arms Ammunition
3483	Ammunition, Large
3484	Small Arms
3489	Ordnance & Access, NEC
3491	Industrial Valves
3492	Fluid Power Valves & Hose Fittings
3493	Steel Springs, Except Wire
3494	Valves & Pipe Fittings, NEC
3495	Wire Springs
3496	Misc Fabricated Wire Prdts
3497	Metal Foil & Leaf
3498	Fabricated Pipe & Pipe Fittings
3499	Fabricated Metal Prdts, NEC

35 INDUSTRIAL AND COMMERCIAL MACHINERY AND COMPUTER EQUIPMENT

3511	Steam, Gas & Hydraulic Turbines & Engines
3519	Internal Combustion Engines, NEC
3523	Farm Machinery & Eqpt
3524	Garden, Lawn Tractors & Eqpt
3531	Construction Machinery & Eqpt
3532	Mining Machinery & Eqpt
3533	Oil Field Machinery & Eqpt
3534	Elevators & Moving Stairways
3535	Conveyors & Eqpt
3536	Hoists, Cranes & Monorails
3537	Indl Trucks, Tractors, Trailers & Stackers
3541	Machine Tools: Cutting
3542	Machine Tools: Forming
3543	Industrial Patterns
3544	Dies, Tools, Jigs, Fixtures & Indl Molds
3545	Machine Tool Access
3546	Power Hand Tools
3547	Rolling Mill Machinery & Eqpt
3548	Welding Apparatus
3549	Metalworking Machinery, NEC
3552	Textile Machinery
3553	Woodworking Machinery
3554	Paper Inds Machinery
3555	Printing Trades Machinery & Eqpt
3556	Food Prdts Machinery
3559	Special Ind Machinery, NEC
3561	Pumps & Pumping Eqpt
3562	Ball & Roller Bearings
3563	Air & Gas Compressors
3564	Blowers & Fans
3565	Packaging Machinery
3566	Speed Changers, Drives & Gears
3567	Indl Process Furnaces & Ovens
3568	Mechanical Power Transmission Eqpt, NEC
3569	Indl Machinery & Eqpt, NEC
3571	Electronic Computers
3572	Computer Storage Devices
3575	Computer Terminals
3577	Computer Peripheral Eqpt, NEC
3578	Calculating & Accounting Eqpt
3579	Office Machines, NEC
3581	Automatic Vending Machines
3582	Commercial Laundry, Dry Clean & Pressing Mchs
3585	Air Conditioning & Heating Eqpt
3586	Measuring & Dispensing Pumps
3589	Service Ind Machines, NEC
3592	Carburetors, Pistons, Rings & Valves
3593	Fluid Power Cylinders & Actuators
3594	Fluid Power Pumps & Motors
3596	Scales & Balances, Exc Laboratory
3599	Machinery & Eqpt, Indl & Commercial, NEC

36 ELECTRONIC AND OTHER ELECTRICAL EQUIPMENT AND COMPONENTS, EXCEPT COMPUTER

3612	Power, Distribution & Specialty Transformers
3613	Switchgear & Switchboard Apparatus
3621	Motors & Generators
3624	Carbon & Graphite Prdts
3625	Relays & Indl Controls
3629	Electrical Indl Apparatus, NEC
3631	Household Cooking Eqpt
3632	Household Refrigerators & Freezers
3633	Household Laundry Eqpt
3634	Electric Household Appliances
3635	Household Vacuum Cleaners
3639	Household Appliances, NEC
3641	Electric Lamps
3643	Current-Carrying Wiring Devices
3644	Noncurrent-Carrying Wiring Devices
3645	Residential Lighting Fixtures
3646	Commercial, Indl & Institutional Lighting Fixtures
3647	Vehicular Lighting Eqpt
3648	Lighting Eqpt, NEC
3651	Household Audio & Video Eqpt
3652	Phonograph Records & Magnetic Tape
3661	Telephone & Telegraph Apparatus
3663	Radio & T V Communications, Systs & Eqpt, Broadcast/Studio
3669	Communications Eqpt, NEC
3671	Radio & T V Receiving Electron Tubes
3672	Printed Circuit Boards
3674	Semiconductors
3675	Electronic Capacitors
3676	Electronic Resistors
3677	Electronic Coils & Transformers
3678	Electronic Connectors
3679	Electronic Components, NEC
3691	Storage Batteries
3692	Primary Batteries: Dry & Wet
3694	Electrical Eqpt For Internal Combustion Engines
3695	Recording Media
3699	Electrical Machinery, Eqpt & Splys, NEC

37 TRANSPORTATION EQUIPMENT

3711	Motor Vehicles & Car Bodies
3713	Truck & Bus Bodies
3714	Motor Vehicle Parts & Access
3715	Truck Trailers
3716	Motor Homes
3721	Aircraft
3724	Aircraft Engines & Engine Parts
3728	Aircraft Parts & Eqpt, NEC
3731	Shipbuilding & Repairing
3732	Boat Building & Repairing
3743	Railroad Eqpt
3751	Motorcycles, Bicycles & Parts
3761	Guided Missiles & Space Vehicles
3769	Guided Missile/Space Vehicle Parts & Eqpt, NEC
3792	Travel Trailers & Campers
3795	Tanks & Tank Components
3799	Transportation Eqpt, NEC

38 MEASURING, ANALYZING AND CONTROLLING INSTRUMENTS; PHOTOGRAPHIC, MEDICAL AN

3812	Search, Detection, Navigation & Guidance Systs & Instrs
3821	Laboratory Apparatus & Furniture
3822	Automatic Temperature Controls
3823	Indl Instruments For Meas, Display & Control
3824	Fluid Meters & Counters
3825	Instrs For Measuring & Testing Electricity
3826	Analytical Instruments
3827	Optical Instruments
3829	Measuring & Controlling Devices, NEC
3841	Surgical & Medical Instrs & Apparatus
3842	Orthopedic, Prosthetic & Surgical Appliances/Splys
3843	Dental Eqpt & Splys
3844	X-ray Apparatus & Tubes
3845	Electromedical & Electrotherapeutic Apparatus
3851	Ophthalmic Goods
3861	Photographic Eqpt & Splys
3873	Watch & Clock Devices & Parts

39 MISCELLANEOUS MANUFACTURING INDUSTRIES

3911	Jewelry: Precious Metal
3914	Silverware, Plated & Stainless Steel Ware
3915	Jewelers Findings & Lapidary Work
3931	Musical Instruments
3942	Dolls & Stuffed Toys
3944	Games, Toys & Children's Vehicles
3949	Sporting & Athletic Goods, NEC
3951	Pens & Mechanical Pencils
3952	Lead Pencils, Crayons & Artist's Mtrls
3953	Marking Devices
3955	Carbon Paper & Inked Ribbons
3961	Costume Jewelry & Novelties
3965	Fasteners, Buttons, Needles & Pins
3991	Brooms & Brushes
3993	Signs & Advertising Displays
3995	Burial Caskets
3996	Linoleum & Hard Surface Floor Coverings, NEC
3999	Manufacturing Industries, NEC

73 BUSINESS SERVICES

7372	Prepackaged Software

76 MISCELLANEOUS REPAIR SERVICES

7692	Welding Repair
7694	Armature Rewinding Shops

SIC SECTION

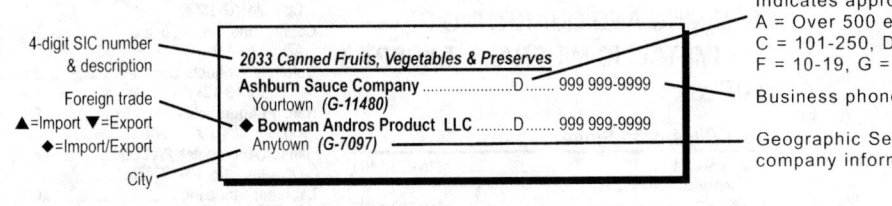

- 4-digit SIC number & description
- Foreign trade
  - ▲=Import ▼=Export
  - ◆=Import/Export
- City

2033 Canned Fruits, Vegetables & Preserves
Ashburn Sauce Company ....D....... 999 999-9999
  Yourtown *(G-11480)*
◆ Bowman Andros Product LLC ....D....... 999 999-9999
  Anytown *(G-7097)*

- Indicates approximate employment figure
  - A = Over 500 employees, B = 251-500
  - C = 101-250, D = 51-100, E = 20-50
  - F = 10-19, G = 5-9
- Business phone
- Geographic Section entry number where full company information appears.

See footnotes for symbols and codes identification.
- The SIC codes in this section are from the latest Standard Industrial Classification manual published by the U.S. Government's Office of Management and Budget. For more information regarding SICs, see the Explanatory Notes.
- Companies may be listed under multiple classifications.

10 METAL MINING

1011 Iron Ores
▲ Essar Steel Minnesota LLC ....F 212 292-2600
  New York *(G-9707)*

1021 Copper Ores
Global Gold Corporation ....F 914 925-0020
  Rye *(G-14481)*

1041 Gold Ores
Andes Gold Corporation ....D....... 212 541-2495
  New York *(G-8856)*
▲ Capital Gold Corporation ....G....... 212 668-0842
  New York *(G-9203)*
Fuda Group (usa) Corporation ....G....... 646 751-7488
  New York *(G-9858)*
Global Gold Corporation ....F 914 925-0020
  Rye *(G-14481)*
Gncc Capital Inc ....G....... 702 951-9793
  New York *(G-9949)*
Surtic Mining Company LLC ....F 718 434-0477
  Brooklyn *(G-2544)*

1044 Silver Ores
Global Gold Corporation ....F 914 925-0020
  Rye *(G-14481)*
▲ Rochester Silver Works LLC ....E 585 477-9501
  Rochester *(G-14093)*

1081 Metal Mining Svcs
Advanced Biomedical Tech Inc ....G....... 718 766-7898
  New York *(G-8752)*
◆ Coremet Trading Inc ....G....... 212 964-3600
  New York *(G-9400)*

1094 Uranium, Radium & Vanadium Ores
Global Gold Corporation ....F 914 925-0020
  Rye *(G-14481)*

1099 Metal Ores, NEC
American Douglas Metals Inc ....F 716 856-3170
  Buffalo *(G-2695)*

12 COAL MINING

1241 Coal Mining Svcs
Desku Group Inc ....G....... 646 436-1464
  Brooklyn *(G-1771)*
Dowa International Corp ....F 212 697-3217
  New York *(G-9566)*
Lessoilcom ....G....... 516 319-5052
  Franklin Square *(G-5118)*
Starfuels Inc ....G....... 914 289-4800
  White Plains *(G-16507)*
Trimet Coal LLC ....E 718 951-3654
  Brooklyn *(G-2585)*
▲ US Pump Corp ....G....... 516 303-7799
  West Hempstead *(G-16226)*

13 OIL AND GAS EXTRACTION

1311 Crude Petroleum & Natural Gas
Chanse Petroleum Corporation ....G....... 212 682-3789
  New York *(G-9259)*

China N E Petro Holdings Ltd ....A....... 212 307-3568
  New York *(G-9281)*
County Energy Corp ....G....... 718 626-7000
  Brooklyn *(G-1723)*
Dlh Energy Service LLC ....G....... 716 410-0028
  Lakewood *(G-6994)*
Flownet LLC ....G....... 716 685-4036
  Lancaster *(G-7020)*
Green Buffalo Fuel LLC ....F 716 768-0600
  Tonawanda *(G-15544)*
Hess Corporation ....B....... 212 997-8500
  New York *(G-10085)*
Hess Energy Exploration Ltd ....G....... 732 750-6500
  New York *(G-10086)*
Hess Explrtion Prod Hldngs Ltd ....G....... 732 750-6000
  New York *(G-10087)*
Hess Pipeline Corporation ....G....... 212 997-8500
  New York *(G-10089)*
Lukoil Americas Corporation ....C....... 212 421-4141
  New York *(G-10628)*
MRC Global (us) Inc ....F 607 739-8575
  Horseheads *(G-6322)*
Repsol Oil & Gas Usa LLC ....G....... 607 562-4000
  Horseheads *(G-6325)*
Reserve Gas Company Inc ....G....... 716 937-9484
  Alden *(G-175)*
Resource PTRlm&ptrochmcl Intl ....E 212 537-3856
  New York *(G-11370)*
Rocket Tech Fuel Corp ....F 516 810-8947
  Bay Shore *(G-716)*
Speedway LLC ....F 631 738-2536
  Lake Grove *(G-6969)*
Stedman Energy Inc ....G....... 716 789-3018
  Mayville *(G-7924)*
Zenith Energy US Logistics ....G....... 212 993-1280
  New York *(G-12173)*

1321 Natural Gas Liquids
20 Bliss St Inc ....G....... 716 326-2790
  Westfield *(G-16390)*
Center State Propane LLC ....G....... 315 841-4044
  Waterville *(G-16038)*
Green Buffalo Fuel LLC ....F 716 768-0600
  Tonawanda *(G-15544)*
Nfe Management LLC ....F 212 798-6100
  New York *(G-10960)*
Okra Energy LLC ....G....... 206 495-7574
  New York *(G-11035)*
Western Oil and Gas JV Inc ....G....... 914 967-4758
  Rye *(G-14489)*

1381 Drilling Oil & Gas Wells
Alden Aurora Gas Company Inc ....G....... 716 937-9484
  Alden *(G-167)*
Barber & Deline Enrgy Svcs LLC ....F 315 696-8961
  Tully *(G-15648)*
Barber & Deline LLC ....F 607 749-2619
  Tully *(G-15649)*
Copper Ridge Oil Inc ....G....... 716 372-4021
  Jamestown *(G-6710)*
Geotechnical Drilling Inc ....D....... 516 616-6055
  Mineola *(G-8224)*
Lenape Energy Inc ....G....... 585 344-1200
  Alexander *(G-179)*
Lukoil North America LLC ....E 212 421-4141
  New York *(G-10629)*
Schneider Amalco Inc ....F 917 470-9674
  New York *(G-11507)*
Steel Partners Holdings LP ....D....... 212 520-2300
  New York *(G-11699)*

Turner Undgrd Instllations Inc ....F 585 739-0238
  Henrietta *(G-6038)*
U S Energy Development Corp ....D....... 716 636-0401
  Getzville *(G-5354)*
▲ US Pump Corp ....G....... 516 303-7799
  West Hempstead *(G-16226)*
Western Oil and Gas JV Inc ....G....... 914 967-4758
  Rye *(G-14489)*

1382 Oil & Gas Field Exploration Svcs
Able Environmental Services ....G....... 631 567-6585
  Bohemia *(G-968)*
Aegis Oil Limited Ventures LLC ....F 646 233-4900
  New York *(G-8762)*
America Capital Energy Corp ....G....... 212 983-8316
  New York *(G-8820)*
▲ Aquifer Drilling & Testing Inc ....D....... 516 616-6026
  Mineola *(G-8204)*
▲ Aterra Exploration LLC ....E 212 315-0030
  New York *(G-8947)*
Bistate Oil Management Corp ....F 212 935-4110
  New York *(G-9092)*
FT Seismic Support Inc ....C....... 607 527-8595
  Campbell *(G-3203)*
Hess Energy Exploration Ltd ....G....... 732 750-6500
  New York *(G-10086)*
Hess Explrtion Prod Hldngs Ltd ....G....... 732 750-6000
  New York *(G-10087)*
KKR Ntral Rsources Fund I-A LP ....G....... 212 750-8300
  New York *(G-10455)*
Lenape Energy Inc ....G....... 585 344-1200
  Alexander *(G-179)*
Lenape Resources Inc ....F 585 344-1200
  Alexander *(G-180)*
Madoff Energy III LLC ....G....... 212 744-1918
  New York *(G-10658)*
Native Amercn Enrgy Group Inc ....G....... 718 408-2323
  Forest Hills *(G-5077)*
Norse Energy Corp USA ....G....... 716 568-2048
  Buffalo *(G-2974)*
Occidental Energy Mktg Inc ....G....... 212 632-4950
  New York *(G-11026)*
Range Rsurces - Appalachia LLC ....E 716 753-3385
  Mayville *(G-7923)*
Sanguine Gas Exploration LLC ....E 212 582-8555
  New York *(G-11483)*
Schlumberger Technology Corp ....C....... 607 378-0105
  Horseheads *(G-6328)*
Seneca Resources Company LLC ......F 716 630-6750
  Williamsville *(G-16586)*
Smith International Inc ....D....... 212 350-9400
  New York *(G-11625)*
Somerset Production Co LLC ....G....... 716 932-6480
  Buffalo *(G-3068)*
▲ Springfield Oil Services Inc ....F 914 315-6812
  Harrison *(G-5734)*
U S Energy Development Corp ....D....... 716 636-0401
  Getzville *(G-5354)*
Waffenbauch USA ....E 716 326-4508
  Westfield *(G-16397)*
Warren Energy Services LLC ....F 212 697-9660
  New York *(G-12075)*
Wellspring Omni Holdings Corp ....A....... 212 318-9800
  New York *(G-12093)*

1389 Oil & Gas Field Svcs, NEC
A & Mt Realty Group LLC ....F 718 974-5871
  Brooklyn *(G-1451)*
Ah Elctronic Test Eqp Repr Ctr ....F 631 234-8979
  Central Islip *(G-3354)*

Alba Fuel Corp ....G.... 718 931-1700
Bronx *(G-1214)*
Alice Perkins ....G.... 716 378-5100
Salamanca *(G-14523)*
Archrock Inc ....F.... 716 763-1553
Lakewood *(G-6988)*
Arm Construction Company Inc ....G.... 646 235-6520
East Elmhurst *(G-4217)*
Babula Construction Inc ....G.... 716 681-0886
Lancaster *(G-7009)*
Barber & Deline Enrgy Svcs LLC ....F.... 315 696-8961
Tully *(G-15648)*
Bass Oil & Chemical Llc ....F.... 718 628-4444
Brooklyn *(G-1587)*
Bluebar Oil Co Inc ....F.... 315 245-4328
Blossvale *(G-963)*
Case Brothers Inc ....G.... 716 925-7172
Limestone *(G-7157)*
Cotton Well Drilling Co Inc ....G.... 716 672-2788
Sheridan *(G-14814)*
Darrell Mitchell ....G.... 646 659-7075
Arverne *(G-414)*
Dimension Development Corp ....G.... 718 361-8825
Long Island City *(G-7426)*
Essar Americas ....G.... 212 292-2600
New York *(G-9706)*
Fame Construction Inc ....E.... 718 626-1000
Astoria *(G-429)*
Fuel Energy Services USA Ltd ....E.... 607 846-2650
Horseheads *(G-6316)*
Gas Field Specialists Inc ....D.... 716 378-6422
Horseheads *(G-6317)*
Gas Recovery Systems LLC ....F.... 914 421-4903
White Plains *(G-16453)*
Gotham Energy 360 LLC ....F.... 917 338-1023
New York *(G-9960)*
Grit Energy Services Inc ....G.... 212 701-4500
New York *(G-9992)*
I & S of NY Inc ....F.... 716 373-7001
Allegany *(G-191)*
Jay Little Oil Well Servi ....G.... 716 925-8905
Limestone *(G-7158)*
Jemcap Servicing LLC ....G.... 212 213-9353
New York *(G-10325)*
Legal Servicing LLC ....G.... 716 565-9300
Williamsville *(G-16581)*
Lenape Energy Inc ....G.... 585 344-1200
Alexander *(G-179)*
Marcellus Energy Services LLC ....E.... 607 236-0038
Candor *(G-3253)*
Metro Group Inc ....D.... 718 729-7200
Long Island City *(G-7523)*
Northeastern Air Quality Inc ....F.... 518 857-3641
Albany *(G-107)*
P & C Gas Measurements Service ....F.... 716 257-3412
Cattaraugus *(G-3313)*
Petro Inc ....G.... 516 686-1717
Plainview *(G-13082)*
Petro Inc ....G.... 516 686-1900
Hicksville *(G-6126)*
Professional Remodelers Inc ....G.... 516 565-9300
West Hempstead *(G-16224)*
Rpc Inc ....E.... 347 873-3935
Elmont *(G-4524)*
Sabre Energy Services LLC ....F.... 518 514-1572
Slingerlands *(G-14890)*
Schlumberger Foundation Inc ....G.... 212 350-9400
New York *(G-11505)*
Schlumberger Technology Corp ....C.... 607 378-0105
Horseheads *(G-6328)*
Schmitt Sales Inc ....G.... 716 632-8595
Williamsville *(G-16585)*
Schneider Amalco Inc ....F.... 917 470-9674
New York *(G-11507)*
Smith International Inc ....D.... 212 350-9400
New York *(G-11625)*
Sovereign Servicing System LLC ....F.... 914 779-1400
Bronxville *(G-1426)*
▲ **Steel Excel Inc** ....G.... 914 461-1300
White Plains *(G-16508)*
Superior Energy Services Inc ....G.... 716 483-0100
Jamestown *(G-6754)*
T A S Sales Service LLC ....G.... 518 234-4919
Cobleskill *(G-3604)*
Terra Enrgy Resource Tech Inc ....F.... 212 286-9197
New York *(G-11801)*
U S Energy Development Corp ....D.... 716 636-0401
Getzville *(G-5354)*
Uniformed Fire Officer Assoiat ....F.... 212 293-9300
New York *(G-11942)*
Wellspring Omni Holdings Corp ....A.... 212 318-9800
New York *(G-12093)*

14 MINING AND QUARRYING OF NONMETALLIC MINERALS, EXCEPT FUELS

1411 Dimension Stone

Alice Perkins ....G.... 716 378-5100
Salamanca *(G-14523)*
Dominic De Nigris Inc ....E.... 718 597-4460
Bronx *(G-1258)*
Domoteck Interiors Inc ....G.... 718 433-4300
Woodside *(G-16653)*
Euro Marmol Gran ....G.... 631 940-9165
Deer Park *(G-3975)*
Hillburn Granite Company Inc ....G.... 845 357-8900
Hillburn *(G-6153)*
Imerys Usa Inc ....F.... 315 287-0780
Gouverneur *(G-5491)*
▲ **Minerals Technologies Inc** ....E.... 212 878-1800
New York *(G-10817)*
▲ **New York Quarries Inc** ....F.... 518 756-3138
Alcove *(G-165)*
Suffolk Granite Manufacturing ....E.... 631 226-4774
Lindenhurst *(G-7197)*
Vermont Multicolor Slate ....G.... 518 642-2400
Middle Granville *(G-8113)*

1422 Crushed & Broken Limestone

Barrett Paving Materials Inc ....F.... 315 737-9471
Clayville *(G-3554)*
Buffalo Crushed Stone Inc ....E.... 716 632-6963
Clarence *(G-3526)*
Cayuga Crushed Stone Inc ....E.... 607 533-4273
Lansing *(G-7055)*
Cobleskill Stone Products Inc ....F.... 518 299-3066
Prattsville *(G-13378)*
Cobleskill Stone Products Inc ....F.... 518 295-7121
Schoharie *(G-14731)*
Cobleskill Stone Products Inc ....F.... 518 234-0221
Cobleskill *(G-3601)*
Cobleskill Stone Products Inc ....F.... 607 637-4271
Hancock *(G-5710)*
Dolomite Products Company Inc ....E.... 315 524-1998
Rochester *(G-13749)*
Hanson Aggregates PA Inc ....E.... 315 858-1100
Jordanville *(G-6844)*
Hanson Aggregates PA Inc ....F.... 518 568-2444
Saint Johnsville *(G-14518)*
Hanson Aggregates PA LLC ....E.... 315 469-5501
Jamesville *(G-6768)*
Hanson Aggregates PA LLC ....E.... 315 685-3321
Skaneateles *(G-14875)*
Hanson Aggregates PA LLC ....F.... 315 393-3743
Ogdensburg *(G-12574)*
Hanson Aggregates PA LLC ....E.... 585 624-1220
Honeoye Falls *(G-6267)*
Hanson Aggregates PA LLC ....F.... 315 821-7222
Oriskany Falls *(G-12767)*
Hanson Aggregates PA LLC ....E.... 315 789-6202
Oaks Corners *(G-12528)*
Jml Quarries Inc ....E.... 845 932-8206
Cochecton *(G-3606)*
John Vespa Inc ....F.... 315 788-6330
Watertown *(G-16019)*
Lilac Quarries LLC ....G.... 607 867-4016
Mount Upton *(G-8371)*
Patterson Materials Corp ....E.... 845 832-6000
New Windsor *(G-8654)*
Schaefer Entps Deposit Inc ....E.... 607 467-4990
Deposit *(G-4110)*
Shelby Crushed Stone Inc ....E.... 585 798-4501
Medina *(G-7989)*
◆ **Specialty Minerals Inc** ....E.... 212 878-1800
New York *(G-11661)*
Upstone Materials Inc ....E.... 518 891-0236
Saranac Lake *(G-14564)*

1423 Crushed & Broken Granite

MCM Natural Stone Inc ....F.... 585 586-6510
Rochester *(G-13934)*
Suffolk Granite Manufacturing ....E.... 631 226-4774
Lindenhurst *(G-7197)*
Tilcon New York Inc ....D.... 845 358-3100
West Nyack *(G-16282)*

1429 Crushed & Broken Stone, NEC

Barrett Paving Materials Inc ....F.... 315 737-9471
Clayville *(G-3554)*
County Line Stone Co Inc ....E.... 716 542-5435
Akron *(G-17)*
Dolomite Products Company Inc ....E.... 585 586-2568
Penfield *(G-12940)*
Hanson Aggregates PA LLC ....F.... 315 393-3743
Ogdensburg *(G-12574)*
Hanson Aggregates PA LLC ....F.... 315 821-7222
Oriskany Falls *(G-12767)*
Labrador Stone Inc ....G.... 570 465-2120
Binghamton *(G-901)*
Masten Enterprises LLC ....C.... 845 932-8206
Cochecton *(G-3607)*
Peckham Materials Corp ....E.... 518 747-3353
Hudson Falls *(G-6384)*
Rock Iroquois Products Inc ....E.... 585 637-6834
Brockport *(G-1194)*
Shelby Crushed Stone Inc ....E.... 585 798-4501
Medina *(G-7989)*
Sparclean MBL Refinishing Inc ....G.... 718 445-2351
Ridgewood *(G-13551)*
Tilcon New York Inc ....E.... 845 778-5591
Walden *(G-15898)*
Tilcon New York Inc ....D.... 845 480-3249
Flushing *(G-5053)*
Tilcon New York Inc ....D.... 845 615-0216
Goshen *(G-5484)*
Tilcon New York Inc ....D.... 845 457-3158
Montgomery *(G-8318)*
Tilcon New York Inc ....D.... 845 358-3100
West Nyack *(G-16282)*
Upstone Materials Inc ....D.... 518 561-5321
Plattsburgh *(G-13165)*

1442 Construction Sand & Gravel

110 Sand Company ....E.... 631 694-2822
Melville *(G-7994)*
110 Sand Company ....F.... 631 694-2822
West Babylon *(G-16124)*
A Colarusso and Son Inc ....E.... 518 828-3218
Hudson *(G-6336)*
Barrett Paving Materials Inc ....G.... 607 723-5367
Binghamton *(G-864)*
Belangers Gravel & Stone Inc ....G.... 585 728-3906
Wayland *(G-16070)*
Buffalo Crushed Stone Inc ....F.... 716 566-9636
Franklinville *(G-5122)*
Buffalo Crushed Stone Inc ....G.... 607 587-8102
Alfred Station *(G-186)*
Callanan Industries Inc ....E.... 845 331-6868
Kingston *(G-6892)*
Carver Sand & Gravel LLC ....E.... 518 355-6034
Altamont *(G-196)*
Central Dover Development ....G.... 917 709-3266
Dover Plains *(G-4143)*
Country Side Sand & Gravel ....G.... 716 988-3271
Collins *(G-3672)*
Country Side Sand & Gravel ....F.... 716 988-3271
South Dayton *(G-14929)*
Dalrymple Grav & Contg Co Inc ....F.... 607 739-0391
Pine City *(G-12999)*
Dalrymple Grav & Contg Co Inc ....E.... 607 529-3235
Chemung *(G-3463)*
Dalrymple Holding Corp ....E.... 607 737-6200
Pine City *(G-13000)*
Dicks Concrete Co Inc ....E.... 845 374-5966
New Hampton *(G-8499)*
Diehl Development Inc ....G.... 585 494-2920
Bergen *(G-819)*
E F Lippert Co Inc ....F.... 716 373-1100
Allegany *(G-189)*
E Tetz & Sons Inc ....D.... 845 692-4486
Middletown *(G-8148)*
East Coast Mines Ltd ....E.... 631 653-5445
East Quogue *(G-4277)*
Elam Sand & Gravel Corp ....E.... 585 657-8000
Bloomfield *(G-953)*
Frew Run Gravel Products Inc ....G.... 716 569-4712
Frewsburg *(G-5208)*
Genoa Sand & Gravel Lnsg ....G.... 607 533-4551
Freeville *(G-5192)*
Gernatt Asphalt Products Inc ....E.... 716 532-3371
Collins *(G-3674)*
Greenebuild LLC ....F.... 917 562-0556
Brooklyn *(G-1951)*
H L Robinson Sand & Gravel ....F.... 607 659-5153
Candor *(G-3252)*

Hampton Sand Corp .... G 631 325-5533
Westhampton *(G-16402)*

Hanson Aggregates East LLC .... G 315 536-9391
Penn Yan *(G-12957)*

Hanson Aggregates PA Inc .... E 315 858-1100
Jordanville *(G-6844)*

Hanson Aggregates PA Inc .... F 518 568-2444
Saint Johnsville *(G-14518)*

Hanson Aggregates PA LLC .... E 585 624-1220
Honeoye Falls *(G-6267)*

Hanson Aggregates PA LLC .... E 315 469-5501
Jamesville *(G-6768)*

Hanson Aggregates PA LLC .... E 315 685-3321
Skaneateles *(G-14875)*

Hanson Aggregates PA LLC .... F 315 782-2300
Watertown *(G-16015)*

Hanson Aggregates PA LLC .... F 315 821-7222
Oriskany Falls *(G-12767)*

Hanson Aggregates PA LLC .... E 315 789-6202
Oaks Corners *(G-12528)*

Hanson Aggregates PA LLC .... E 585 624-3800
Honeoye Falls *(G-6266)*

Hanson Aggregates PA LLC .... F 585 436-3250
Rochester *(G-13852)*

IA Construction Corporation .... G 716 933-8787
Portville *(G-13316)*

John Vespa Inc .... F 315 788-6330
Watertown *(G-16019)*

Johnson S Sand Gravel Inc .... G 315 771-1450
La Fargeville *(G-6943)*

Lafarge North America Inc .... E 716 651-9235
Lancaster *(G-7027)*

Lafarge North America Inc .... E 518 756-5000
Ravena *(G-13454)*

Lazarek Inc .... G 315 343-1242
Oswego *(G-12780)*

Little Valley Sand & Gravel .... G 716 938-6676
Little Valley *(G-7221)*

McEwan Trucking & Grav Produc .... G 716 609-1828
East Concord *(G-4214)*

Milestone Construction Corp .... G 718 459-8500
Rego Park *(G-13466)*

Mitchell Stone Products LLC .... G 518 359-7029
Tupper Lake *(G-15651)*

Northeast Solite Corporation .... E 845 246-2177
Mount Marion *(G-8365)*

R G King General Construction .... G 315 583-3560
Adams Center *(G-4)*

R J Valente Gravel Inc .... D 518 432-4470
Troy *(G-15618)*

R J Valente Gravel Inc .... E 518 279-1001
Cropseyville *(G-3909)*

R J Valente Gravel Inc .... F 518 432-4470
Rensselaer *(G-13476)*

Rd2 Construction & Dem LLC .... F 718 980-1650
Staten Island *(G-15125)*

Republic Construction Co Inc .... G 914 235-3654
New Rochelle *(G-8626)*

Robinson Concrete Inc .... E 315 253-6666
Auburn *(G-498)*

Rock Mountain Farms Inc .... G 845 647-9084
Ellenville *(G-4443)*

Ruby Engineering LLC .... G 646 391-4600
Brooklyn *(G-2426)*

Rural Hill Sand and Grav Corp .... F 315 846-5212
Woodville *(G-16689)*

Rush Gravel Corp .... G 585 533-1740
Honeoye Falls *(G-6272)*

Seneca Stone Corporation .... G 607 737-6200
Pine City *(G-13001)*

Seven Springs Gravel Pdts LLC .... G 585 343-4336
Batavia *(G-634)*

Shelby Crushed Stone Inc .... E 585 798-4501
Medina *(G-7989)*

Smith Sand & Gravel Inc .... G 315 673-4124
Marcellus *(G-7795)*

Sparrow Mining Co .... G 718 519-6600
Bronx *(G-1389)*

Speyside Holdings LLC .... E 845 928-2221
Highland Mills *(G-6152)*

Syracusa Sand and Gravel Inc .... F 585 924-7146
Victor *(G-15870)*

Tilcon New York Inc .... E 845 942-0602
Tomkins Cove *(G-15516)*

Tilcon New York Inc .... D 845 358-3100
West Nyack *(G-16282)*

Titus Mountain Sand & Grav LLC .... G 518 483-3740
Malone *(G-7728)*

Tri City Highway Products Inc .... E 607 722-2967
Binghamton *(G-921)*

Tri-City Highway Products Inc .... E 518 294-9964
Richmondville *(G-13519)*

Troy Sand & Gravel Co Inc .... G 518 203-5115
West Sand Lake *(G-16285)*

Troy Sand & Gravel Co Inc .... F 518 674-2854
West Sand Lake *(G-16286)*

United Materials LLC .... G 716 662-0564
Orchard Park *(G-12748)*

US Allegro Inc .... E 347 408-6601
Maspeth *(G-7874)*

1446 Industrial Sand

◆ American Minerals Inc .... F 646 747-4222
New York *(G-8834)*

New Jersey Pulverizing Co Inc .... G 516 921-9595
Syosset *(G-15226)*

Precision Elctro Mnrl Pmco Inc .... E 716 284-2484
Niagara Falls *(G-12326)*

St Silicones Inc .... G 518 664-0745
Mechanicville *(G-7934)*

1459 Clay, Ceramic & Refractory Minerals, NEC

Applied Minerals Inc .... F 212 226-4265
Brooklyn *(G-1543)*

Callahan & Nannini Quarry Inc .... G 845 496-4323
Salisbury Mills *(G-14539)*

▲ Devonian Stone New York Inc .... E 607 655-2600
Windsor *(G-16604)*

Grosso Materials Inc .... F 845 361-5211
Montgomery *(G-8312)*

1479 Chemical & Fertilizer Mining

▲ American Rock Salt Company LLC .... E 585 991-6878
Retsof *(G-13480)*

Morton Salt Inc .... F 585 493-2511
Silver Springs *(G-14863)*

Steel City Salt LLC .... G 716 532-0000
Collins *(G-3675)*

1481 Nonmetallic Minerals Svcs, Except Fuels

▲ Crystal Ceres Industries Inc .... D 716 283-0445
Niagara Falls *(G-12275)*

Resource Capital Funds LP .... G 631 692-9111
Jericho *(G-6799)*

1499 Miscellaneous Nonmetallic Mining

Avs Gem Stone Corp .... G 212 944-6380
New York *(G-8981)*

◆ Barton Mines Company LLC .... C 518 798-5462
Glens Falls *(G-5418)*

▲ Capital Gold Corporation .... G 212 668-0842
New York *(G-9203)*

Didco Inc .... F 212 997-5022
Rego Park *(G-13461)*

Hargrave Development .... F 716 877-7880
Kenmore *(G-6859)*

Herkimer Diamond Mines Inc .... E 315 891-7355
Herkimer *(G-6041)*

Kotel Importers Inc .... F 212 245-6200
New York *(G-10473)*

Ray Griffiths Inc .... G 212 689-7209
New York *(G-11330)*

Romance & Co Inc .... G 212 382-0337
New York *(G-11427)*

Signature Diamond Entps LLC .... E 212 869-5115
New York *(G-11587)*

20 FOOD AND KINDRED PRODUCTS

2011 Meat Packing Plants

A To Z Kosher Meat Products Co .... E 718 384-7400
Brooklyn *(G-1458)*

Bliss-Poston The Second Wind .... G 212 481-1055
New York *(G-9102)*

◆ Caribbean Foods Delight Inc .... D 845 398-3000
Tappan *(G-15466)*

Chefs Delight Packing Co .... F 718 388-8581
Brooklyn *(G-1691)*

▲ Cni Meat & Produce Inc .... G 516 599-5929
Valley Stream *(G-15777)*

▼ Crescent Duck Farm Inc .... E 631 722-8700
Aquebogue *(G-374)*

▲ Domestic Casing Co .... G 718 522-1902
Brooklyn *(G-1787)*

◆ DRG New York Holdings Corp .... C 914 668-9000
Mount Vernon *(G-8395)*

Frank Wardynski & Sons Inc .... E 716 854-6083
Buffalo *(G-2833)*

Gold Medal Packing Inc .... D 315 337-1911
Oriskany *(G-12758)*

Hilltown Pork Inc .... E 518 781-4050
Canaan *(G-3206)*

Ives Farm Market .... G 315 592-4880
Fulton *(G-5222)*

Joel Kiryas Meat Market Corp .... F 845 782-9194
Monroe *(G-8273)*

Kamerys Wholesale Meats Inc .... G 716 372-6756
Olean *(G-12603)*

Orleans Custom Packing Inc .... G 585 314-8227
Holley *(G-6227)*

▼ Robert & William Inc .... G 631 727-5780
Riverhead *(G-13582)*

▲ Sahlen Packing Company Inc .... D 716 852-8677
Buffalo *(G-3056)*

Sam A Lupo & Sons Inc .... G 800 388-5352
Endicott *(G-4609)*

Side Hill Farmers Coop Inc .... G 315 447-4693
Canastota *(G-3248)*

The Smoke House of Catskills .... G 845 246-8767
Saugerties *(G-14619)*

Tri-Town Packing Corp .... F 315 389-5101
Brasher Falls *(G-1125)*

USA Halal Foods Inc .... G 718 291-9111
Long Island City *(G-7626)*

We Work .... G 877 673-6628
New York *(G-12083)*

2013 Sausages & Meat Prdts

◆ Alle Processing Corp .... C 718 894-2000
Maspeth *(G-7818)*

Alps Provision Co Inc .... E 718 721-4477
Astoria *(G-421)*

Arnolds Meat Food Products .... E 718 384-8071
Brooklyn *(G-1554)*

Atlantic Pork & Provisions Inc .... E 718 272-9550
Jamaica *(G-6626)*

Big Johns Adirondack Inc .... G 518 587-3680
Saratoga Springs *(G-14571)*

Brooklyn Bangers LLC .... F 718 875-3535
Brooklyn *(G-1637)*

Brooklyn Casing Co Inc .... G 718 522-0866
Brooklyn *(G-1639)*

Buffalo Provisions Co Inc .... F 718 292-4300
Elmhurst *(G-4462)*

Camellia General Provision Co .... E 716 893-5352
Buffalo *(G-2760)*

◆ Caribbean Foods Delight Inc .... D 845 398-3000
Tappan *(G-15466)*

▲ Cni Meat & Produce Inc .... G 516 599-5929
Valley Stream *(G-15777)*

De Ans Pork Products Inc .... E 718 788-2464
Brooklyn *(G-1762)*

Dinos Sausage & Meat Co Inc .... F 315 732-2661
Utica *(G-15696)*

▲ Domestic Casing Co .... G 718 522-1902
Brooklyn *(G-1787)*

Elmgang Enterprises I Inc .... F 212 868-4142
New York *(G-9657)*

Frank Wardynski & Sons Inc .... E 716 854-6083
Buffalo *(G-2833)*

Grossglockner Inc .... G 585 266-4960
Canandaigua *(G-3223)*

Hilltown Pork Inc .... E 518 781-4050
Canaan *(G-3206)*

Holy Cow Kosher LLC .... G 347 788-8620
Spring Valley *(G-14995)*

Jacks Gourmet LLC .... F 718 954-4681
Brooklyn *(G-2028)*

Julian Freirich Company Inc .... E 718 361-9111
Long Island City *(G-7482)*

Lancaster Quality Pork Inc .... F 718 439-8822
Brooklyn *(G-2093)*

Life Earth Company .... G 310 751-0627
New York *(G-10562)*

Marathon Enterprises Inc .... D 718 665-2560
Bronx *(G-1321)*

Milan Provision Co Inc .... E 718 899-7678
Corona *(G-3850)*

Mineo & Sapio Meats Inc .... G 716 884-2398
Buffalo *(G-2947)*

Mr Pierogi LLC .... F 718 499-7821
Brooklyn *(G-2233)*

▲ Niagara Tying Service Inc .... E 716 825-0066
Buffalo *(G-2971)*

Orchard Sausages Inc .... F 718 381-9388
Brooklyn *(G-2290)*

SIC

Employee Codes: A=Over 500 employees, B=251-500
C=101-250, D=51-100, E=20-50, F=10-19, G=5-9

2019 Harris
New York Manufacturers Directory

647

20 FOOD AND KINDRED PRODUCTS

Original Crunch Roll Fctry LLC .... G 716 402-5030
  Amherst *(G-247)*
Patla Enterprises Inc .... F 315 367-0237
  Sherrill *(G-14821)*
Picone Meat Specialties Ltd .... G 914 381-3002
  Mamaroneck *(G-7753)*
Pork King Sausage Inc .... E 718 542-2810
  Bronx *(G-1362)*
▲ Prime Food Processing Corp .... D 718 963-2323
  Brooklyn *(G-2342)*
Provisionaire & Co LLC .... E 646 681-8600
  Brooklyn *(G-2360)*
▲ Rapa Independent North America .... G 518 561-0513
  Plattsburgh *(G-13153)*
Reliable Brothers Inc .... E 518 273-6732
  Green Island *(G-5611)*
Rosina Food Products Inc .... C 716 668-0123
  Buffalo *(G-3045)*
Rosina Holding Inc .... G 716 668-0123
  Buffalo *(G-3046)*
Salarinos Italian Foods Inc .... F 315 697-9766
  Canastota *(G-3247)*
Schaller Manufacturing Corp .... D 718 721-5480
  New York *(G-11501)*
Schaller Manufacturing Corp .... F 212 879-3047
  New York *(G-11502)*
Schonwetter Enterprises Inc .... E 518 237-0171
  Cohoes *(G-3620)*
Schrader Meat Market .... F 607 869-6328
  Romulus *(G-14281)*
▲ Sun Ming Jan Inc .... F 718 418-8221
  Brooklyn *(G-2531)*
▲ Syracuse Casing Co Inc .... F 315 475-0309
  Syracuse *(G-15434)*
Tower Isles Frozen Foods Ltd .... D 718 495-2626
  Brooklyn *(G-2577)*
White Eagle Packing Co Inc .... F 518 374-4366
  Schenectady *(G-14728)*
Wilson Beef Farms LLC .... F 607 545-8308
  Canaseraga *(G-3239)*
Zweigles Inc .... D 585 546-1740
  Rochester *(G-14221)*

2015 Poultry Slaughtering, Dressing & Processing

▲ Advanced Frozen Foods Inc .... E 516 333-6344
  Westbury *(G-16309)*
◆ Alle Processing Corp .... C 718 894-2000
  Maspeth *(G-7818)*
Campanellis Poultry Farm Inc .... G 845 482-2222
  Bethel *(G-835)*
▼ Crescent Duck Farm Inc .... E 631 722-8700
  Aquebogue *(G-374)*
Egg Low Farms Inc .... F 607 674-4653
  Sherburne *(G-14805)*
Goya Foods Inc .... D 716 549-0076
  Angola *(G-369)*
Hlw Acres LLC .... G 585 591-0795
  Attica *(G-460)*
◆ Hoskie Co Inc .... D 718 628-8672
  Brooklyn *(G-1985)*
Hudson Valley Foie Gras LLC .... F 845 292-2500
  Ferndale *(G-4934)*
JW Consulting Inc .... G 845 325-7070
  Monroe *(G-8274)*
▲ K&Ns Foods Usa LLC .... E 315 598-8080
  Fulton *(G-5224)*
MB Food Processing Inc .... B 845 436-5001
  South Fallsburg *(G-14931)*
Murray Bresky Consultants Ltd .... B 845 436-5001
  South Fallsburg *(G-14932)*
Ready Egg Farms Inc .... F 607 674-4653
  Sherburne *(G-14808)*
Sing Ah Poultry .... G 718 625-7253
  Brooklyn *(G-2479)*
Vineland Kosher Poultry Inc .... F 718 921-1347
  Brooklyn *(G-2625)*
Wendels Poultry Farm .... G 716 592-2299
  East Concord *(G-4215)*

2021 Butter

◆ O-At-Ka Milk Products Coop Inc .... B 585 343-0536
  Batavia *(G-632)*
Pure Ghee Inc .... G 718 224-7399
  Flushing *(G-5041)*
Vulto Creamery LLC .... G 607 865-7059
  Walton *(G-15913)*

2022 Cheese

Agri-Mark Inc .... D 518 497-6644
  Chateaugay *(G-3426)*
Artisanal Brands Inc .... E 914 441-3591
  Bronxville *(G-1423)*
Castelli America LLC .... D 716 782-2101
  Ashville *(G-415)*
Cemac Foods Corp .... F 914 835-0526
  Harrison *(G-5724)*
Crosswinds Farm & Creamery .... G 607 327-0363
  Ovid *(G-12790)*
East Hill Creamery LLC .... G 585 237-3622
  Perry *(G-12968)*
Emkay Trading Corp .... G 914 592-9000
  Elmsford *(G-4541)*
Emkay Trading Corp .... E 585 492-3800
  Arcade *(G-382)*
Empire Cheese Inc .... C 585 968-1552
  Cuba *(G-3919)*
▲ Euphrates Inc .... D 518 762-3488
  Johnstown *(G-6827)*
F Cappiello Dairy Pdts Inc .... E 518 374-5064
  Schenectady *(G-14674)*
Fly Creek Cder Mill Orchrd Inc .... G 607 547-9692
  Fly Creek *(G-5064)*
Four Fat Fowl Inc .... G 518 733-5230
  Stephentown *(G-15155)*
Friendship Dairies LLC .... C 585 973-3031
  Friendship *(G-5210)*
◆ Gharana Industries LLC .... G 315 651-4004
  Waterloo *(G-15994)*
Great Lakes Cheese NY Inc .... D 315 232-4511
  Adams *(G-3)*
▲ Habco Corp .... E 631 789-1400
  Amityville *(G-279)*
HP Hood LLC .... D 315 829-3339
  Vernon *(G-15805)*
HP Hood LLC .... E 607 295-8134
  Arkport *(G-399)*
▲ Hudson Valley Creamery LLC .... F 518 851-2570
  Hudson *(G-6356)*
Instantwhip of Buffalo Inc .... E 716 892-7031
  Buffalo *(G-2885)*
Kraft Heinz Foods Company .... B 315 376-6575
  Lowville *(G-7651)*
Kraft Heinz Foods Company .... B 607 527-4584
  Campbell *(G-3204)*
Kraft Heinz Foods Company .... C 607 865-7131
  Walton *(G-15911)*
Lactalis American Group Inc .... D 716 827-2622
  Buffalo *(G-2916)*
◆ Lactalis American Group Inc .... G 716 823-6262
  Buffalo *(G-2917)*
Leprino Foods Company .... C 570 888-9658
  Waverly *(G-16067)*
Losurdo Foods Inc .... C 315 344-2444
  Heuvelton *(G-6044)*
Lumazu LLC .... G 518 623-3372
  Warrensburg *(G-15940)*
Lumazu LLC .... F 518 623-3372
  Warrensburg *(G-15941)*
Mondelez Global LLC .... G 845 567-4701
  Newburgh *(G-12234)*
▼ Mongiello Sales Inc .... E 845 436-4200
  Hurleyville *(G-6466)*
Mozzarella Fresca Incorporated .... G 559 752-4823
  Buffalo *(G-2954)*
▲ Noga Dairies Inc .... F 516 293-5448
  Farmingdale *(G-4837)*
Original Hrkmer Cnty Chese Inc .... D 315 895-7428
  Ilion *(G-6477)*
Pecoraro Dairy Products Inc .... G 718 388-2379
  Brooklyn *(G-2308)*
Rainbeau Ridge Farm .... G 914 234-2197
  Bedford Hills *(G-779)*
Sandvoss Farms LLC .... G 585 297-7044
  East Bethany *(G-4213)*
Sargento Foods Inc .... C 920 893-8484
  New York *(G-11489)*
Sorrento Lactalis Inc .... G 716 823-6262
  Buffalo *(G-3072)*
▲ Taam Tov Foods Inc .... F 718 788-8880
  Brooklyn *(G-2551)*
Upstate Farms Cheese LLC .... B 607 527-4584
  Campbell *(G-3205)*
Wny Cheese Enterprise LLC .... E 585 243-6516
  Pavilion *(G-12890)*
◆ World Cheese Co Inc .... F 718 965-1700
  Brooklyn *(G-2657)*

2023 Milk, Condensed & Evaporated

Alpina Foods Inc .... F 855 886-1914
  Batavia *(G-609)*
America Health Corp .... G 800 860-1868
  New York *(G-8821)*
Baby Central LLC .... G 718 372-2229
  Brooklyn *(G-1581)*
Century Tom Inc .... G 347 654-3179
  Jamaica *(G-6632)*
Danone Nutricia Early .... E 914 872-8556
  White Plains *(G-16441)*
Dynatabs LLC .... F 718 376-6084
  Brooklyn *(G-1801)*
El-Gen LLC .... G 631 218-3400
  Bohemia *(G-1021)*
Friendship Dairies LLC .... C 585 973-3031
  Friendship *(G-5210)*
FriesIndcmpina Ingrdnts N Amer .... E 607 746-0196
  Delhi *(G-4074)*
▼ GNI Commerce Inc .... G 347 275-1155
  Brooklyn *(G-1935)*
◆ Hain Celestial Group Inc .... C 516 587-5000
  New Hyde Park *(G-8538)*
Infant Formula Laboratory Svc .... F 718 257-3000
  Brooklyn *(G-2001)*
◆ Kerry Bfnctnal Ingredients Inc .... D 608 363-1200
  Norwich *(G-12488)*
◆ Nationwide Dairy Inc .... G 347 689-8148
  Brooklyn *(G-2247)*
Nestle Usa Inc .... E 914 272-4021
  White Plains *(G-16479)*
Nestle Usa Inc .... C 212 688-2490
  New York *(G-10910)*
◆ O-At-Ka Milk Products Coop Inc .... B 585 343-0536
  Batavia *(G-632)*
◆ Rich Products Corporation .... A 716 878-8000
  Buffalo *(G-3037)*
Solivaira Specialties Inc .... D 716 693-4009
  North Tonawanda *(G-12452)*
◆ Sugar Foods Corporation .... E 212 753-6900
  New York *(G-11734)*
Upstate Niagara Coop Inc .... G 716 892-2121
  Buffalo *(G-3114)*
Vitakem Nutraceutical Inc .... C 631 956-8343
  Smithtown *(G-14911)*

2024 Ice Cream

▲ Allied Food Products Inc .... F 718 230-4227
  Brooklyn *(G-1510)*
Ample Hills Creamery Inc .... E 347 725-4061
  Brooklyn *(G-1531)*
Ample Hills Creamery Inc .... E 718 809-1678
  Brooklyn *(G-1532)*
Ample Hills Holdings Inc .... G 347 725-4061
  Brooklyn *(G-1533)*
Beyond Better Foods LLC .... G 212 888-1120
  Bronx *(G-1228)*
Bleecker Pastry Tartufo Inc .... G 718 937-9830
  Long Island City *(G-7402)*
Blue Marble Ice Cream LLC .... G 718 858-5551
  Brooklyn *(G-1619)*
Blue Pig Ice Cream Factory .... G 914 271-3850
  Croton On Hudson *(G-3912)*
Byrne Dairy Inc .... B 315 475-2121
  La Fayette *(G-6946)*
Carols Polar Parlor .... G 315 468-3404
  Syracuse *(G-15270)*
Chobani Idaho LLC .... G 208 432-2248
  Norwich *(G-12482)*
▲ Crepini LLC .... E 347 422-0829
  Brooklyn *(G-1730)*
▼ Crowley Foods Inc .... E 800 637-0019
  Binghamton *(G-877)*
Delicioso Coco Helado Inc .... F 718 292-1930
  Bronx *(G-1257)*
Df Mavens Inc .... E 347 813-4705
  Astoria *(G-424)*
Elegant Desserts By Metro Inc .... F 718 388-1323
  Brooklyn *(G-1822)*
Ffc Holding Corp Subsidiaries .... F 716 366-5400
  Dunkirk *(G-4170)*
◆ Fieldbrook Foods Corporation .... B 716 366-5400
  Dunkirk *(G-4171)*
Four Brothers Italian Bakery .... G 914 741-5434
  Hawthorne *(G-5986)*
Fresh Ice Cream Company LLC .... F 347 603-6021
  Brooklyn *(G-1908)*
G Pesso & Sons Inc .... G 718 224-9130
  Bayside *(G-746)*

▲ Grom Columbus LLC G 212 974-3444
New York (G-9995)
HP Hood LLC D 315 829-3339
Vernon (G-15805)
HP Hood LLC A 607 772-6580
Binghamton (G-890)
Ice Cream Man Inc E 518 692-8382
Greenwich (G-5642)
Indulge Desserts Holdings LLC G 212 231-8600
New York (G-10201)
JMS Ices Inc F 718 448-0853
Staten Island (G-15095)
Jones Humdinger F 607 771-6501
Binghamton (G-900)
Kan Pak LLC G 620 440-2319
Penn Yan (G-12961)
Kozy Shack Enterprises LLC C 516 870-3000
Hicksville (G-6100)
La Cremeria G 212 226-6758
New York (G-10500)
▲ LArte Del Gelato Gruppo Inc F 718 383-6600
Long Island City (G-7496)
Lickity Splits G 585 345-6091
Batavia (G-629)
Lumazu LLC G 518 623-3372
Warrensburg (G-15940)
Lumazu LLC F 518 623-3372
Warrensburg (G-15941)
Macadoodles G 607 652-9019
Stamford (G-15031)
▲ Macedonia Ltd F 718 462-3596
Brooklyn (G-2149)
Main Street Sweets F 914 332-5757
Tarrytown (G-15480)
Marina Ice Cream G 718 235-3000
Brooklyn (G-2168)
Marvel Dairy Whip Inc G 516 889-4232
Lido Beach (G-7148)
MSQ Corporation G 718 465-0900
Queens Village (G-13411)
My Most Favorite Food G 212 580-5130
New York (G-10864)
Ninas Custard E 716 636-0345
Getzville (G-5350)
Nutrifast LLC F 347 671-3181
New York (G-11010)
NY Froyo LLC G 516 312-4588
Deer Park (G-4020)
▼ Olympic Ice Cream Co Inc E 718 849-6200
Richmond Hill (G-13507)
Paleteria Fernandez Inc F 914 315-1598
Mamaroneck (G-7752)
Paleteria Fernandez Inc G 914 939-3694
Port Chester (G-13206)
▲ Perrys Ice Cream Company Inc B 716 542-5492
Akron (G-21)
Phyljohn Distributors Inc F 518 459-2775
Albany (G-115)
Piazzas Ice Cream Ice Hse Inc F 718 818-8811
Staten Island (G-15115)
Primo Frozen Desserts Inc G 718 252-2312
Brooklyn (G-2343)
Pulmuone Foods Usa Inc E 845 365-3300
Tappan (G-15470)
Purity Ice Cream Co Inc F 607 272-1545
Ithaca (G-6607)
Quaker Bonnet Inc G 716 885-7208
Buffalo (G-3024)
▼ Quality Dairy Farms Inc E 315 942-2611
Boonville (G-1120)
Ralphs Famous Italian Ices G 718 605-5052
Staten Island (G-15123)
Ralphs Ices of Levittown F 516 520-0618
Oceanside (G-12553)
Scoops R US Incorporated G 212 730-7959
New York (G-11521)
Smartys Corner G 607 239-5276
Endicott (G-4610)
Stewarts Processing Corp D 518 581-1200
Ballston Spa (G-597)
Stewarts Shops Corp F 518 499-9376
Whitehall (G-16524)
▲ Sweet Melodys LLC E 716 580-3227
East Amherst (G-4192)
Swirl Bliss LLC G 516 867-9475
North Baldwin (G-12368)
Tia Lattrell G 845 373-9494
Amenia (G-207)
▲ TLC-Lc Inc E 212 756-8900
New York (G-11852)
Unilever United States Inc G 212 546-0200
New York (G-11944)
Unilever United States Inc C 212 546-0200
New York (G-11945)
▲ Van Leeuwen Artisan Ice Cream G 718 701-1630
Brooklyn (G-2616)
Vanilla Sky LLC G 347 738-4195
Long Island City (G-7628)
Victory Garden G 212 206-7273
New York (G-12029)
Washburns Dairy Inc E 518 725-0629
Gloversville (G-5472)
Wicked Spoon Inc F 646 335-2890
New York (G-12107)
Zings Company LLC G 631 454-0339
Farmingdale (G-4908)

2026 Milk

Bliss Foods Inc G 212 732-8888
New York (G-9100)
Bliss Foods Inc F 212 732-8888
New York (G-9101)
Byrne Dairy Inc B 315 475-2121
La Fayette (G-6946)
◆ Chobani LLC C 607 337-1246
Norwich (G-12481)
Chobani LLC G 607 847-6181
New Berlin (G-8487)
▼ Crowley Foods Inc E 800 637-0019
Binghamton (G-877)
▲ Currant Company LLC G 845 266-8999
Staatsburg (G-15022)
Dairy Farmers America Inc E 816 801-6440
East Syracuse (G-4333)
Dairy Farmers America Inc D 585 409-2200
Batavia (G-622)
▲ Danone Us LLC D 914 872-8400
White Plains (G-16442)
Dean Foods Company D 315 452-5001
East Syracuse (G-4335)
Dwyer Farm LLC G 914 456-2742
Walden (G-15893)
Emkay Trading Corp E 585 492-3800
Arcade (G-382)
▲ Fage USA Dairy Industry Inc B 518 762-5912
Johnstown (G-6828)
◆ Fage USA Holdings G 518 762-5912
Johnstown (G-6829)
Finger Lakes Cheese Trail F 607 857-5726
Odessa (G-12567)
Garelick Farms LLC C 518 283-0820
East Greenbush (G-4229)
▼ Hanan Products Company Inc E 516 938-1000
Hicksville (G-6094)
HP Hood LLC D 607 295-8134
Arkport (G-399)
HP Hood LLC C 315 363-3870
Oneida (G-12611)
HP Hood LLC B 315 658-2132
La Fargeville (G-6942)
HP Hood LLC B 518 218-9097
Schenectady (G-14688)
HP Hood LLC A 607 772-6580
Binghamton (G-890)
HP Hood LLC D 315 829-3339
Vernon (G-15805)
Instantwhip of Buffalo Inc E 716 892-7031
Buffalo (G-2885)
Kesso Foods Inc G 718 777-5303
East Elmhurst (G-4222)
▲ Kong Kee Food Corp E 718 937-2746
Long Island City (G-7490)
Kraft Heinz Foods Company C 607 865-7131
Walton (G-15911)
Kraft Heinz Foods Company B 607 527-4584
Campbell (G-3204)
Maple Hill Creamery LLC E 518 758-7777
Stuyvesant (G-15182)
Maple Hill Creamery LLC G 518 758-7777
Kinderhook (G-6880)
Midland Farms Inc D 518 436-7038
Menands (G-8089)
Mountain Side Farms Inc E 718 526-3442
Jamaica (G-6664)
▲ Noga Dairies Inc F 516 293-5448
Farmingdale (G-4837)
◆ O-At-Ka Milk Products Coop Inc B 585 343-0536
Batavia (G-632)
P & F Bakers Inc G 516 931-6821
Hicksville (G-6120)
Purity Ice Cream Co Inc F 607 272-1545
Ithaca (G-6607)
Saputo Dairy Foods Usa LLC D 607 746-2141
Delhi (G-4075)
Steuben Foods Incorporated C 716 655-4000
Elma (G-4460)
Steuben Foods Incorporated F 718 291-3333
Elma (G-4459)
Stewarts Processing Corp D 518 581-1200
Ballston Spa (G-597)
Swirls Twirls Incorporated G 516 541-9400
Massapequa (G-7887)
Twist It Top It F 718 793-8947
Forest Hills (G-5081)
Upstate Niagara Coop Inc D 716 892-3156
Buffalo (G-3113)
Upstate Niagara Coop Inc C 585 458-1880
Rochester (G-14193)
Upstate Niagara Coop Inc E 716 484-7178
Jamestown (G-6759)
Upstate Niagara Coop Inc D 315 389-5111
North Lawrence (G-12393)
Upstate Niagara Coop Inc C 716 892-2121
Buffalo (G-3114)
Whitney Foods Inc F 718 291-3333
Jamaica (G-6691)
Wny Enterprise LLC E 585 243-6514
Pavilion (G-12891)
Yogolicious Inc G 914 236-3455
Briarcliff Manor (G-1178)

2032 Canned Specialties

▲ A & G Food Distributors LLC G 917 939-3457
Bayside (G-740)
▲ Antico Casale Usa LLC G 914 760-1100
Whitestone (G-16533)
◆ Beech-Nut Nutrition Company B 518 839-0300
Amsterdam (G-328)
Borgattis Ravioli Egg Noodles G 718 367-3799
Bronx (G-1231)
Delicious Foods Inc F 718 446-9352
Corona (G-3843)
Edesia World Wide LLC G 646 705-3505
New York (G-9626)
◆ Eve Sales Corp F 718 589-6800
Bronx (G-1269)
▲ Global Food Source & Co Inc G 914 320-9615
Tuckahoe (G-15643)
Goya Foods Inc D 716 549-0076
Angola (G-369)
Grandma Browns Beans Inc F 315 963-7221
Mexico (G-8108)
Indira Foods Inc F 718 343-1500
Floral Park (G-4966)
Kawasho Foods USA Inc F 212 841-7400
New York (G-10420)
Marketplace Slutions Group LLC E 631 868-0111
Holbrook (G-6198)
Morris Kitchen Inc F 646 413-5186
Brooklyn (G-2227)
◆ Sahadi Fine Foods Inc E 718 369-0100
Brooklyn (G-2445)
Sangster Foods Inc F 212 993-9129
Brooklyn (G-2447)
Steuben Foods Incorporated F 718 291-3333
Elma (G-4459)

2033 Canned Fruits, Vegetables & Preserves

Amiram Dror Inc F 212 979-9505
Brooklyn (G-1529)
Andros Bowman Products LLC G 540 217-4100
Lyndonville (G-7679)
◆ Apple & Eve LLC D 516 621-1122
Port Washington (G-13243)
Brooklyns Best Pasta Co Inc G 917 881-3007
Brooklyn (G-1651)
Cahoon Farms Inc E 315 594-8081
Wolcott (G-16608)
Cheribundi Inc E 800 699-0460
Geneva (G-5320)
◆ Cliffstar LLC A 716 366-6100
Dunkirk (G-4165)
Dells Cherries LLC E 718 624-4380
Brooklyn (G-1765)
Dells Cherries LLC E 718 624-4380
Brooklyn (G-1766)
Eleanors Best F 845 809-5621
Garrison (G-5303)
Fly Creek Cder Mill Orchrd Inc G 607 547-9692
Fly Creek (G-5064)

20 FOOD AND KINDRED PRODUCTS

Fresh Fanatic Inc .... G 516 521-6574
  Brooklyn *(G-1907)*
▼ Fruitcrown Products Corp .... E 631 694-5800
  Farmingdale *(G-4767)*
◆ Giovanni Food Co Inc .... D 315 457-2373
  Baldwinsville *(G-555)*
Glk Foods LLC .... E 585 289-4414
  Shortsville *(G-14847)*
Goya Foods Inc .... D 716 549-0076
  Angola *(G-369)*
Green Valley Foods LLC .... G 315 926-4280
  Marion *(G-7801)*
Hc Brill Co Inc .... G 716 685-4000
  Lancaster *(G-7023)*
Jets Lefrois Corp .... G 585 637-5003
  Brockport *(G-1193)*
Jus By Julie LLC .... G 718 266-3906
  Brooklyn *(G-2060)*
Kaltech Food Packaging Inc .... E 845 856-1210
  Port Jervis *(G-13232)*
Kensington & Sons LLC .... E 646 430-8298
  New York *(G-10433)*
▲ L and S Packing Co .... D 631 845-1717
  Farmingdale *(G-4804)*
Labarba-Q LLC .... F 845 806-6227
  Warwick *(G-15957)*
Lagoner Farms Inc .... D 315 904-4109
  Williamson *(G-16560)*
◆ Lidestri Foods Inc .... B 585 377-7700
  Fairport *(G-4639)*
Life Juice Brands LLC .... G 585 944-7982
  Pittsford *(G-13018)*
Lollipop Tree Inc .... E 845 471-8733
  Auburn *(G-488)*
▲ Mayer Bros Apple Products Inc ...... D 716 668-1787
  West Seneca *(G-16301)*
Mizkan America Inc .... D 585 765-9171
  Lyndonville *(G-7680)*
Morris Kitchen Inc .... F 646 413-5186
  Brooklyn *(G-2227)*
◆ Motts LLP .... C 972 673-8088
  Elmsford *(G-4552)*
◆ National Grape Coop Assn Inc .... E 716 326-5200
  Westfield *(G-16394)*
New York Pasta Authority Inc .... F 347 787-2130
  Brooklyn *(G-2263)*
▼ Old Dutch Mustard Co Inc .... G 516 466-0522
  Great Neck *(G-5576)*
Olive Branch Foods LLC .... G 631 343-7070
  Islandia *(G-6536)*
Pressed Juice LLC .... G 646 573-9157
  Brooklyn *(G-2339)*
Sarabeths Kitchen LLC .... E 718 589-2900
  Bronx *(G-1380)*
▲ Sbk Preserves Inc .... E 800 773-7378
  Bronx *(G-1381)*
Seneca Foods Corporation .... E 315 926-8100
  Marion *(G-7806)*
Seneca Foods Corporation .... C 315 781-8733
  Geneva *(G-5332)*
Seneca Foods Corporation .... F 315 926-4277
  Marion *(G-7808)*
Seneca Foods Corporation .... E 585 658-2211
  Leicester *(G-7129)*
▲ Sneaky Chef Foods LLC .... F 914 301-3277
  Tarrytown *(G-15493)*
Spf Holdings II LLC .... G 212 750-8300
  New York *(G-11668)*
US Juice Partners LLC .... G 516 621-1122
  Port Washington *(G-13312)*
◆ Victoria Fine Foods LLC .... D 718 649-1635
  Brooklyn *(G-2621)*
Victoria Fine Foods Holding Co .... G 718 649-1635
  Brooklyn *(G-2622)*
Vincents Food Corp .... F 516 481-3544
  Carle Place *(G-3273)*
Welch Foods Inc A Cooperative .... C 716 326-5252
  Westfield *(G-16398)*
Welch Foods Inc A Cooperative .... E 716 326-3131
  Westfield *(G-16399)*
Wolfgang B Gourmet Foods Inc .... F 518 719-1727
  Catskill *(G-3310)*

2034 Dried Fruits, Vegetables & Soup

▲ Allied Food Products Inc .... F 718 230-4227
  Brooklyn *(G-1510)*
◆ Associated Brands Inc .... B 585 798-3475
  Medina *(G-7970)*
Goya Foods Inc .... D 716 549-0076
  Angola *(G-369)*

◆ Hain Celestial Group Inc .... C 516 587-5000
  New Hyde Park *(G-8538)*
Marshall Ingredients LLC .... G 800 796-9353
  Wolcott *(G-16611)*
▲ Settons Intl Foods Inc .... D 631 543-8090
  Commack *(G-3702)*
Shoreline Fruit LLC .... D 585 765-2639
  Lyndonville *(G-7681)*
▲ Wm E Martin and Sons Co Inc .... E 516 605-2444
  Roslyn *(G-14452)*

2035 Pickled Fruits, Vegetables, Sauces & Dressings

Allen Pickle Works Inc .... F 516 676-0640
  Glen Cove *(G-5359)*
American Specialty Mfg Co .... F 585 544-5600
  Rochester *(G-13627)*
Baldwin Richardson Foods Co .... C 315 986-2727
  Macedon *(G-7695)*
Batampte Pickle Products Inc .... D 718 251-2100
  Brooklyn *(G-1589)*
Bushwick Kitchen LLC .... G 917 297-1045
  Brooklyn *(G-1659)*
Conway Import Co Inc .... G 914 592-1312
  Elmsford *(G-4537)*
Elwood International Inc .... F 631 842-6600
  Copiague *(G-3757)*
French Associates Inc .... E 718 387-9880
  Fresh Meadows *(G-5198)*
Glk Foods LLC .... E 585 289-4414
  Shortsville *(G-14847)*
Goya Foods Inc .... D 716 549-0076
  Angola *(G-369)*
Gravymaster Inc .... C 203 453-1893
  Canajoharie *(G-3207)*
Heintz & Weber Co Inc .... G 716 852-7171
  Buffalo *(G-2870)*
Instantwhip of Buffalo Inc .... G 716 892-7031
  Buffalo *(G-2885)*
Jets Lefrois Corp .... G 585 637-5003
  Brockport *(G-1193)*
Kensington & Sons LLC .... E 646 430-8298
  New York *(G-10433)*
▲ L and S Packing Co .... D 631 845-1717
  Farmingdale *(G-4804)*
Lollipop Tree Inc .... E 845 471-8733
  Auburn *(G-488)*
Lucinas Gourmet Food Inc .... G 646 835-9784
  Long Island City *(G-7505)*
▲ Mandarin Soy Sauce Inc .... E 845 343-1505
  Middletown *(G-8162)*
◆ Materne North America Corp ...... B 212 675-7881
  New York *(G-10727)*
Mizkan America Inc .... F 585 798-5720
  Medina *(G-7985)*
Mizkan America Inc .... D 585 765-9171
  Lyndonville *(G-7680)*
▲ Moldova Pickles & Salads Inc .... G 718 284-2220
  Brooklyn *(G-2223)*
▼ Old Dutch Mustard Co Inc .... G 516 466-0522
  Great Neck *(G-5576)*
◆ Pure Golds Family Corp .... D 516 483-5600
  Hempstead *(G-6024)*
▲ Rob Salamida Company Inc .... F 607 729-4868
  Johnson City *(G-6821)*
▲ Sabra Dipping Company LLC .... D 914 372-3900
  White Plains *(G-16501)*
T RS Great American Rest .... F 516 294-1680
  Williston Park *(G-16596)*
▲ Twin Marquis Inc .... D 718 386-6868
  Brooklyn *(G-2596)*
Unilever United States Inc .... G 212 546-0200
  New York *(G-11944)*
Unilever United States Inc .... C 212 546-0200
  New York *(G-11945)*
United Farm Processing Corp .... C 718 933-6060
  Bronx *(G-1411)*
United Pickle Products Corp .... E 718 933-6060
  Bronx *(G-1412)*
◆ Victoria Fine Foods LLC .... D 718 649-1635
  Brooklyn *(G-2621)*
Victoria Fine Foods Holding Co .... G 718 649-1635
  Brooklyn *(G-2622)*
▲ Wanjashan International LLC ...... F 845 343-1505
  Middletown *(G-8183)*
Whalens Horseradish Products ...... E 518 587-6404
  Galway *(G-5241)*

2037 Frozen Fruits, Juices & Vegetables

Atlantic Farm & Food Inc .... F 718 441-3152
  Richmond Hill *(G-13496)*
Birds Eye Foods Inc .... G 716 988-3218
  South Dayton *(G-14927)*
Blend Smoothie Bar .... G 845 568-7366
  New Windsor *(G-8637)*
Bonduelle USA Inc .... G 585 434-0399
  Rochester *(G-13672)*
C O P R A Inc .... G 917 224-1727
  New York *(G-9170)*
Cahoon Farms Inc .... E 315 594-8081
  Wolcott *(G-16608)*
Cheribundi Inc .... E 800 699-0460
  Geneva *(G-5320)*
▲ Dynamic Health Labs Inc .... E 718 858-0100
  Brooklyn *(G-1799)*
Fly Creek Cder Mill Orchrd Inc .... G 607 547-9692
  Fly Creek *(G-5064)*
H&F Products Inc .... G 845 651-6100
  Monroe *(G-8271)*
Hain Blueprint Inc .... F 212 414-5741
  New Hyde Park *(G-8537)*
Kj Astoria Gourmet Inc .... G 718 545-6900
  Astoria *(G-432)*
◆ National Grape Coop Assn Inc ..... E 716 326-5200
  Westfield *(G-16394)*
◆ Pepsico Inc .... A 914 253-2000
  Purchase *(G-13395)*
▲ Prime Food Processing Corp .... D 718 963-2323
  Brooklyn *(G-2342)*
Pura Fruta LLC .... F 415 279-5727
  Long Island City *(G-7563)*
Seneca Foods Corporation .... E 315 926-8100
  Marion *(G-7806)*
Smoothies Strawberry Nysf .... G 315 406-4250
  Syracuse *(G-15426)*
T & Smoothie Inc .... G 631 804-6653
  Patchogue *(G-12878)*
Tami Great Food Corp .... G 845 352-7901
  Monsey *(G-8301)*
Zoe Sakoutis LLC .... F 212 414-5741
  New York *(G-12181)*

2038 Frozen Specialties

◆ Alle Processing Corp .... C 718 894-2000
  Maspeth *(G-7818)*
▲ America NY RI Wang Fd Group Co ... E 718 628-8999
  Maspeth *(G-7820)*
Beetnpath LLC .... G 607 319-5585
  Ithaca *(G-6558)*
Codinos Limited Inc .... E 518 372-3308
  Schenectady *(G-14665)*
D R M Management Inc .... E 716 668-0333
  Depew *(G-4086)*
Delicious Foods Inc .... F 718 446-9352
  Corona *(G-3843)*
Dufour Pastry Kitchens Inc .... E 718 402-8800
  Bronx *(G-1260)*
▲ Dvash Foods Inc .... F 845 578-1959
  Monsey *(G-8288)*
F & R Enterprises Inc .... G 315 841-8189
  Waterville *(G-16039)*
Finger Food Products Inc .... E 716 297-4888
  Sanborn *(G-14545)*
Food Basket USA Company Ltd ...... E 631 231-8999
  Bay Shore *(G-687)*
▲ Freeze-Dry Foods Inc .... E 585 589-6399
  Albion *(G-157)*
Hain Refrigerated Foods Inc .... F 425 485-2476
  New Hyde Park *(G-8539)*
▲ Julians Recipe LLC .... G 888 640-8880
  Brooklyn *(G-2057)*
Juno Chefs .... D 845 294-5400
  Goshen *(G-5480)*
Kraft Heinz Foods Company .... B 585 226-4400
  Avon *(G-519)*
Les Chateaux De France Inc .... E 516 239-6795
  Inwood *(G-6494)*
Macabee Foods LLC .... G 845 623-1300
  West Nyack *(G-16274)*
▲ Milmar Food Group II LLC .... C 845 294-5400
  Goshen *(G-5482)*
Rhosey LLC .... G 718 382-1226
  Brooklyn *(G-2400)*
Salarinos Italian Foods Inc .... F 315 697-9766
  Canastota *(G-3247)*
▲ Seviroli Foods Inc .... C 516 222-6220
  Garden City *(G-5281)*

SIC SECTION

20 FOOD AND KINDRED PRODUCTS

Tami Great Food Corp ....G....... 845 352-7901
Monsey *(G-8301)*

▲ Tuv Taam Corp ....E....... 718 855-2207
Brooklyn *(G-2594)*

Unilever United States Inc....................G....... 212 546-0200
New York *(G-11944)*

Unilever United States Inc...................C....... 212 546-0200
New York *(G-11945)*

▲ Wlf Founders Corporation ....D....... 718 777-8899
Astoria *(G-450)*

2041 Flour, Grain Milling

ADM Milling Co.......................................D....... 716 849-7333
Buffalo *(G-2686)*

Archer-Daniels-Midland Company ....D....... 716 849-7333
Buffalo *(G-2708)*

Archer-Daniels-Midland Company ....E....... 518 828-4691
Hudson *(G-6339)*

Archer-Daniels-Midland Company ....D....... 518 828-4691
Hudson *(G-6340)*

Archer-Daniels-Midland Company ....G....... 585 346-2311
Lakeville *(G-6984)*

Ardent Mills LLC ....D....... 518 447-1700
Albany *(G-43)*

◆ Birkett Mills ....G....... 315 536-3311
Penn Yan *(G-12949)*

Birkett Mills...E....... 315 536-4112
Penn Yan *(G-12950)*

Champlain Valley Mil Corp Inc..............G....... 518 963-7650
Willsboro *(G-16597)*

Cochecton Mills Inc ....E....... 845 932-8282
Cochecton *(G-3605)*

Frozen Pastry Products Corp ....E....... 845 364-9833
Spring Valley *(G-14992)*

General Mills Inc ....E....... 716 856-6060
Buffalo *(G-2845)*

Losurdo Foods Inc..................................E....... 518 842-1500
Amsterdam *(G-345)*

Ohio Baking Company Inc ....E....... 315 724-2033
Utica *(G-15728)*

Pizza Blends LLC ....G....... 518 356-6650
Schenectady *(G-14704)*

◆ Sheppard Grain Enterprises LLC.....E....... 315 548-9271
Phelps *(G-12981)*

2043 Cereal Breakfast Foods

◆ Associated Brands Inc......................B....... 585 798-3475
Medina *(G-7970)*

Chia Usa LLC...G....... 212 226-7512
New York *(G-9274)*

Gabila Food Products Inc ....E....... 631 789-2220
Copiague *(G-3760)*

General Mills Inc ....D....... 716 856-6060
Buffalo *(G-2846)*

Group International LLC........................G....... 718 475-8805
Flushing *(G-5003)*

◆ Pepsico Inc ....A....... 914 253-2000
Purchase *(G-13395)*

Sangster Foods Inc................................F 212 993-9129
Brooklyn *(G-2447)*

Sanzdranz LLC.......................................G....... 518 894-8625
Delmar *(G-4078)*

Sanzdranz LLC.......................................G....... 518 894-8625
Schenectady *(G-14710)*

2044 Rice Milling

◆ Gassho Body & Mind Inc..................C....... 518 695-9991
Schuylerville *(G-14734)*

▲ Real Co Inc ....G....... 347 433-8549
Valley Cottage *(G-15762)*

2045 Flour, Blended & Prepared

Aryzta LLC ....D....... 310 417-4700
Rochester *(G-13644)*

▲ Bektrom Foods Inc ....G....... 516 802-3800
Syosset *(G-15209)*

Cohens Bakery Inc.................................E....... 716 892-8149
Buffalo *(G-2771)*

Dawn Food Products Inc.......................C....... 716 830-8214
Williamsville *(G-16577)*

Elis Bread (eli Zabar) Inc ....F....... 212 772-2011
New York *(G-9649)*

Lollipop Tree Inc ....E....... 845 471-8733
Auburn *(G-488)*

New Hope Mills Inc ....F 315 252-2676
Auburn *(G-491)*

Pizza Blends LLC...................................G....... 518 356-6650
Schenectady *(G-14704)*

Rhosey LLC ....G....... 718 382-1226
Brooklyn *(G-2400)*

2046 Wet Corn Milling

Anthony Gigi Inc ....G....... 860 984-1943
Shirley *(G-14828)*

Machoonjdgroup.....................................G....... 856 345-4689
Medford *(G-7959)*

Sunoco Inc..G....... 315 593-0500
Fulton *(G-5232)*

▲ Sweetwater Energy Inc.....................G....... 585 647-5760
Rochester *(G-14149)*

2047 Dog & Cat Food

Colgate-Palmolive Company ....A....... 212 310-2000
New York *(G-9349)*

Dog Good Products LLC........................G....... 212 789-7000
New York *(G-9545)*

Hills Pet Products Inc............................G....... 212 310-2000
New York *(G-10100)*

Hound & Gatos Pet Foods Corp............G....... 212 618-1917
New York *(G-10133)*

Nestle Purina Petcare Company............B....... 716 366-8080
Dunkirk *(G-4174)*

◆ Pet Proteins LLC ....G....... 888 293-1029
New York *(G-11166)*

Robert Abady Dog Food Co Ltd ....F 845 473-1900
Poughkeepsie *(G-13363)*

Scooby Rendering & Inc ....G....... 315 793-1014
Utica *(G-15732)*

2048 Prepared Feeds For Animals & Fowls

Bailey Boonville Mills Inc.......................G....... 315 942-2131
Boonville *(G-1114)*

Baker Commodities Inc..........................E....... 585 482-1880
Rochester *(G-13652)*

Cargill Incorporated...............................D....... 585 345-1160
Batavia *(G-616)*

Cargill Incorporated...............................G....... 716 665-6570
Kennedy *(G-6866)*

Cargill Incorporated...............................E....... 315 287-0241
Gouverneur *(G-5487)*

Cargill Incorporated...............................G....... 518 854-7417
Salem *(G-14536)*

Cargill Incorporated...............................E....... 315 622-3533
Liverpool *(G-7228)*

Central Garden & Pet Company ....G....... 631 451-8021
Selden *(G-14761)*

Cochecton Mills Inc ....E....... 845 932-8282
Cochecton *(G-3605)*

Commodity Resource Corporation ....F 585 538-9500
Caledonia *(G-3154)*

Eastport Feeds Inc.................................G....... 631 325-0077
Eastport *(G-4384)*

Gramco Inc ....G....... 716 592-2845
Springville *(G-15017)*

Grandma Maes Cntry Nturals LLC ....G....... 212 348-8171
New York *(G-9973)*

▲ Harbor Point Mineral Pdts Inc...........F 315 797-1300
Utica *(G-15708)*

Heath Manufacturing Company.............G....... 800 444-3140
Batavia *(G-627)*

JD Granary LLC......................................G....... 607 627-6294
Smyrna *(G-14912)*

Kent Nutrition Group Inc........................F 315 788-0032
Watertown *(G-16021)*

Lowville Farmers Coop Inc ....E....... 315 376-6587
Lowville *(G-7652)*

Narrowsburg Feed & Grain Co ....F 845 252-3936
Narrowsburg *(G-8474)*

Nutra-Vet Research Corp ....F 845 473-1900
Poughkeepsie *(G-13360)*

Pine Tree Farms Inc...............................E....... 607 532-4312
Interlaken *(G-6483)*

Scotts Feed Inc ....E....... 518 483-3110
Malone *(G-7725)*

Veterinary Biochemical Ltd....................G....... 845 473-1900
Poughkeepsie *(G-13372)*

Wagners LLC..G....... 516 933-6580
Jericho *(G-6807)*

2051 Bread, Bakery Prdts Exc Cookies & Crackers

3rd Avenue Doughnut Inc ....F 718 748-3294
Brooklyn *(G-1439)*

40 Street Baking Inc...............................G....... 212 683-4700
Brooklyn *(G-1441)*

527 Franco Bakery Corporation ....G....... 718 993-4200
Bronx *(G-1197)*

999 Bagels Inc..G....... 718 915-0742
Brooklyn *(G-1448)*

A & M Appel Distributing Inc..................G....... 516 735-1172
Massapequa *(G-7876)*

A Angonoa Inc..C....... 718 762-4466
College Point *(G-3634)*

A T A Bagel Shoppe Inc.........................G....... 718 352-4948
Bayside *(G-741)*

Above The Rest Baking Corp ....D....... 718 313-9222
Bronx *(G-1205)*

Addeo Bakers Inc...................................F 718 367-8316
Bronx *(G-1212)*

Aladdin Bakers Inc.................................C....... 718 499-1818
Brooklyn *(G-1498)*

Alicias Bakery Inc ....G....... 914 235-4689
New Rochelle *(G-8588)*

▲ Alrajs Inc ....E....... 631 225-0300
Lindenhurst *(G-7159)*

Always Baked Fresh ....G....... 631 648-0811
Holbrook *(G-6171)*

American Vintage Wine Biscuit ....G....... 718 361-1003
New York *(G-8839)*

Amiram Dror Inc......................................F 212 979-9505
Brooklyn *(G-1529)*

Andreas Protein Cakery Inc ....G....... 646 801-9826
New York *(G-8859)*

Aphrodities ....G....... 718 224-1774
Whitestone *(G-16534)*

Aryzta LLC ....C....... 585 235-8160
Rochester *(G-13645)*

Aryzta LLC...D....... 310 417-4700
Rochester *(G-13644)*

B & D Enterprises of Utica ....D....... 315 735-3311
New Hartford *(G-8501)*

Bagel Club Inc...F 718 423-6106
Bayside *(G-743)*

Bagel Grove Inc......................................E....... 315 724-8015
Utica *(G-15679)*

Bagel Land...E....... 585 442-3080
Rochester *(G-13650)*

Bagelovers Inc ....F 607 844-3683
Dryden *(G-4149)*

Bakery & Coffee Shop ....G....... 315 287-1829
Gouverneur *(G-5486)*

Better Baked Foods LLC.........................D....... 716 326-4651
Westfield *(G-16392)*

Bien Cuit LLC...E....... 718 852-0200
Brooklyn *(G-1609)*

Bimbo Bakeries.......................................G....... 631 274-4906
Deer Park *(G-3951)*

Bimbo Bakeries.......................................F 518 463-2221
Albany *(G-48)*

Bimbo Bakeries Usa Inc.........................G....... 716 692-9140
Tonawanda *(G-15527)*

Bimbo Bakeries Usa Inc.........................E....... 518 993-3300
Nelliston *(G-8481)*

Bimbo Bakeries Usa Inc.........................G....... 718 601-1561
Bronx *(G-1229)*

Bimbo Bakeries Usa Inc.........................F 845 255-4345
New Paltz *(G-8575)*

Bimbo Bakeries Usa Inc.........................E....... 516 877-2850
Mineola *(G-8207)*

Bimbo Bakeries Usa Inc.........................C....... 716 372-8444
Olean *(G-12593)*

Bimbo Bakeries Usa Inc.........................E....... 631 951-5183
Bay Shore *(G-663)*

Bimbo Bakeries Usa Inc.........................F 516 887-1024
Lynbrook *(G-7661)*

Bimbo Bakeries Usa Inc.........................F 315 379-9069
Canton *(G-3254)*

Bimbo Bakeries Usa Inc.........................F 518 563-1320
Plattsburgh *(G-13110)*

Bimbo Bakeries Usa Inc.........................C....... 718 463-6300
Maspeth *(G-7828)*

Bimbo Bakeries Usa Inc.........................F 518 489-4053
Albany *(G-49)*

Bimbo Bakeries Usa Inc.........................E....... 203 531-2311
Bay Shore *(G-664)*

Bimbo Bakeries Usa Inc.........................F 716 706-0450
Lancaster *(G-7010)*

Bimbo Bakeries Usa Inc.........................D....... 845 568-0943
Newburgh *(G-12217)*

Bimbo Bakeries Usa Inc.........................E....... 800 856-8544
Vestal *(G-15810)*

Bimbo Bakeries Usa Inc.........................C....... 315 782-4189
Watertown *(G-16002)*

Bimbo Bakeries Usa Inc.........................F 845 294-5282
Goshen *(G-5476)*

▲ Bimbo Foods Bakeries Inc.................C....... 631 273-6000
Bay Shore *(G-665)*

Employee Codes: A=Over 500 employees, B=251-500
C=101-250, D=51-100, E=20-50, F=10-19, G=5-9

2019 Harris
New York Manufacturers Directory

651

Blackbirds Brooklyn LLC....................E....... 917 362-4080
Brooklyn *(G-1618)*
Blondie S Bakeshop Inc....................G....... 631 424-4545
Centerport *(G-3347)*
Bread Factory LLC....................E....... 914 637-8150
New Rochelle *(G-8593)*
Brooklyn Sweet Spot Inc....................G....... 718 522-2577
Brooklyn *(G-1649)*
Bushwick Bakery Corp....................G....... 917 460-5994
Brooklyn *(G-1657)*
▲ Cannoli Factory Inc....................E....... 631 643-2700
Wyandanch *(G-16693)*
Caputo Bakery Inc....................G....... 718 875-6871
Brooklyn *(G-1675)*
Carmine Street Bagels Inc....................F....... 212 691-3041
Staten Island *(G-15061)*
Carolinas Desserts Inc....................G....... 914 779-4000
Yonkers *(G-16742)*
Carter Street Bakery Inc....................G....... 585 749-7104
Rochester *(G-13694)*
Chambord LLC....................E....... 718 859-1110
Brooklyn *(G-1687)*
Charlotte Neuville Design LLC....................G....... 646 530-4570
Brooklyn *(G-1690)*
Chocnyc LLC....................G....... 917 804-4848
New York *(G-9286)*
Circle 5 Deli Corp....................G....... 718 525-5687
Jamaica *(G-6634)*
City Bakery Inc....................E....... 212 366-1414
New York *(G-9310)*
Coccadotts Inc....................F....... 518 438-4937
Albany *(G-65)*
Cohens Bakery Inc....................E....... 716 892-8149
Buffalo *(G-2771)*
Commitment 2000 Inc....................E....... 716 439-1206
Buffalo *(G-2775)*
Cookie Connection Inc....................G....... 315 422-2253
Syracuse *(G-15288)*
Costanzos Bakery Inc....................C....... 716 656-9093
Buffalo *(G-2782)*
Cupcake Contessas Corporation....................G....... 516 307-1222
North Bellmore *(G-12376)*
Cuzins Duzin Corp....................G....... 347 724-6200
Kew Gardens *(G-6872)*
D-Lite Donuts....................G....... 718 626-5953
Astoria *(G-423)*
Daly Meghan....................F....... 347 699-3259
Brooklyn *(G-1752)*
Damascus Bakery Inc....................D....... 718 855-1456
Brooklyn *(G-1753)*
Delicias Andinas Food Corp....................E....... 718 416-2922
Flushing *(G-4995)*
Dipaolo Baking Co Inc....................D....... 585 303-5013
Rochester *(G-13743)*
Eileens Special Cheesecake....................G....... 212 966-5585
New York *(G-9637)*
Enterprise Bagels Inc....................F....... 845 896-3823
Fishkill *(G-4945)*
Ericeira Inc....................G....... 516 294-4034
Mineola *(G-8220)*
Famous Doughnuts Inc....................G....... 716 834-6356
Buffalo *(G-2824)*
FB Sale LLC....................G....... 315 986-9999
Macedon *(G-7699)*
Felix Roma & Sons Inc....................D....... 607 748-3336
Endicott *(G-4593)*
▲ Ferrara Bakery & Cafe Inc....................D....... 212 226-6150
New York *(G-9795)*
Flour Power Bakery Cafe....................G....... 917 747-6895
Livingston Manor *(G-7276)*
Food Gems Ltd....................E....... 718 296-7788
Ozone Park *(G-12826)*
Fotis Oneonta Italian Bakery....................G....... 607 432-3871
Oneonta *(G-12638)*
Fratellis LLC....................E....... 607 722-5663
Binghamton *(G-885)*
Fritters & Buns Inc....................G....... 845 227-6609
Hopewell Junction *(G-6285)*
Fung Wong Bakery Inc....................E....... 212 267-4037
New York *(G-9862)*
Gabila & Sons Mfg Inc....................E....... 631 789-2220
Copiague *(G-3759)*
Geddes Bakery Co Inc....................E....... 315 437-8084
North Syracuse *(G-12403)*
Gennaris Itln French Bky Inc....................G....... 516 997-8968
Carle Place *(G-3265)*
George Retzos....................G....... 315 422-2913
Syracuse *(G-15334)*
Giovanni Bakery Corp....................F....... 212 695-4296
New York *(G-9924)*
Glenn Wayne Wholesale Bky Inc....................D....... 631 289-9200
Bohemia *(G-1029)*
▼ Gluten Free Bake Shop Inc....................E....... 845 782-5307
Mountainville *(G-8455)*
Golden Glow Cookie Co Inc....................E....... 718 379-6223
Bronx *(G-1283)*
Good Bread Bakery....................F....... 914 939-3900
Port Chester *(G-13201)*
Gourmet Toast Corp....................G....... 718 852-4536
Brooklyn *(G-1944)*
Great American Dessert Co LLC....................D....... 718 894-3494
Maspeth *(G-7849)*
Greenvale Bagel Inc....................E....... 516 221-8221
Wantagh *(G-15921)*
◆ Greyston Bakery Inc....................C....... 914 375-1510
Yonkers *(G-16765)*
H & S Edible Products Corp....................E....... 914 413-3489
Mount Vernon *(G-8404)*
H H B Bakery of Little Neck....................G....... 718 631-7004
Flushing *(G-5004)*
Hagadah Passover Bakery....................G....... 718 638-1589
Brooklyn *(G-1960)*
Hahns Old Fashioned Cake Co....................F....... 631 249-3456
Farmingdale *(G-4779)*
Hana Pastries Inc....................G....... 718 369-7593
Brooklyn *(G-1964)*
Harrison Bakery West....................E....... 315 422-1468
Syracuse *(G-15338)*
Have Your Cake Kitchen LLC....................G....... 646 820-8074
Brooklyn *(G-1968)*
▲ Heidelberg Group Inc....................E....... 315 866-0999
Herkimer *(G-6040)*
Herris Gourmet Inc....................G....... 917 578-2308
Brooklyn *(G-1976)*
Hum Limited Liability Corp....................G....... 631 525-2174
Nesconset *(G-8484)*
Indulge Desserts Holdings LLC....................G....... 212 231-8600
New York *(G-10201)*
J & S Licata Bros Inc....................F....... 718 805-6924
Richmond Hill *(G-13506)*
Jane Bakes Inc....................G....... 845 920-1100
Pearl River *(G-12903)*
Jarets Stuffed Cupcakes....................G....... 607 658-9096
Endicott *(G-4597)*
Jerrys Bagels....................G....... 516 791-0063
Valley Stream *(G-15783)*
JGM Wholesale Bakery Inc....................G....... 631 396-0131
Farmingdale *(G-4793)*
Jim Romas Bakery Inc....................E....... 607 748-7425
Endicott *(G-4600)*
▲ JJ Cassone Bakery Inc....................B....... 914 939-1568
Port Chester *(G-13203)*
Jonathan Lord Corp....................F....... 631 563-4445
Bohemia *(G-1043)*
Juniors Cheesecake Inc....................G....... 718 852-5257
Brooklyn *(G-2059)*
King Cracker Corp....................F....... 516 539-9251
Hempstead *(G-6017)*
Kokoroko Corporation....................G....... 718 433-4321
Woodside *(G-16661)*
Kossars On Grand LLC....................F....... 212 473-4810
New York *(G-10472)*
L American Ltd....................F....... 716 372-9480
Olean *(G-12604)*
La Calenita Bakery & Cafeteria....................G....... 718 205-8273
Elmhurst *(G-4468)*
La Prima Bakery Inc....................F....... 718 584-4442
Bronx *(G-1313)*
Ladybird Bakery Inc....................G....... 718 499-8108
Brooklyn *(G-2089)*
Larosa Cupcakes....................G....... 347 866-3920
Staten Island *(G-15099)*
Libbys Bakery Cafe LLC....................G....... 603 918-8825
Ticonderoga *(G-15512)*
Lillys Homestyle Bakeshop Inc....................D....... 718 491-2904
Brooklyn *(G-2123)*
Ljmm Inc....................E....... 845 454-5876
Poughkeepsie *(G-13351)*
M & M Bagel Corp....................F....... 516 295-1222
Cedarhurst *(G-3333)*
Mac Crete Corporation....................F....... 718 932-1803
Long Island City *(G-7509)*
Made Close LLC....................G....... 917 837-1357
Brooklyn *(G-2151)*
Mannys Cheesecake Inc....................G....... 315 732-0639
Utica *(G-15718)*
Maplehurst Bakeries LLC....................B....... 315 735-5000
Frankfort *(G-5109)*
Maxwell Bakery Inc....................E....... 718 498-2200
Brooklyn *(G-2182)*
McKee Foods Corporation....................A....... 631 979-9364
Hauppauge *(G-5883)*
Mds Hot Bagels Deli Inc....................G....... 718 438-5650
Brooklyn *(G-2184)*
Melita Corp....................C....... 718 392-7280
Astoria *(G-435)*
Millers Bulk Food and Bakery....................G....... 585 798-9700
Medina *(G-7984)*
Miss Grimble Associates Inc....................F....... 718 665-2253
Bronx *(G-1333)*
Modern Itln Bky of W Babylon....................C....... 631 589-7300
Oakdale *(G-12518)*
New Hope Mills Mfg Inc....................E....... 315 252-2676
Auburn *(G-492)*
New Mount Pleasant Bakery....................E....... 518 374-7577
Schenectady *(G-14700)*
New Star Bakery....................E....... 718 961-8868
Flushing *(G-5027)*
Nibble Inc Baking Co....................G....... 518 334-3950
Troy *(G-15612)*
Niebylski Bakery Inc....................G....... 718 721-5152
Astoria *(G-437)*
▼ Nightingale Food Entps Inc....................G....... 347 577-1630
New York *(G-10966)*
Nildas Desserts Limited....................F....... 845 454-5876
Poughkeepsie *(G-13359)*
Ohio Baking Company Inc....................E....... 315 724-2033
Utica *(G-15728)*
Operative Cake Corp....................E....... 718 278-5600
Bronx *(G-1348)*
Orza Bakery Inc....................F....... 914 965-5736
Yonkers *(G-16788)*
Ossining Bakery Lmp Inc....................G....... 914 941-2654
Ossining *(G-12772)*
OWayne Enterprises Inc....................E....... 718 326-2200
Maspeth *(G-7865)*
Oz Baking Company Ltd....................G....... 516 466-5114
Great Neck *(G-5578)*
▲ Palagonia Bakery Co Inc....................D....... 718 272-5400
Brooklyn *(G-2299)*
▼ Peking Food LLC....................E....... 718 628-8080
Brooklyn *(G-2309)*
Perrottas Bakery Inc....................G....... 518 283-4711
Troy *(G-15615)*
Pesces Bakery Inc....................G....... 845 246-4730
Saugerties *(G-14613)*
Placid Baker....................G....... 518 326-2657
Troy *(G-15617)*
Presser Kosher Baking Corp....................E....... 718 375-5088
Brooklyn *(G-2340)*
Quaker Bonnet Inc....................G....... 716 885-7208
Buffalo *(G-3024)*
R & H Baking Co Inc....................E....... 718 852-1768
Brooklyn *(G-2375)*
Rambachs International Bakery....................F....... 518 563-1721
Plattsburgh *(G-13152)*
Rays Italian Bakery Inc....................F....... 516 825-9170
Valley Stream *(G-15793)*
▲ Rays Restaurant & Bakery Inc....................G....... 718 441-7707
Jamaica *(G-6673)*
Reisman Bros Bakery Inc....................F....... 718 331-1975
Brooklyn *(G-2394)*
Richard Engdal Baking Corp....................F....... 914 777-9600
Mamaroneck *(G-7755)*
Rm Bakery LLC....................E....... 718 472-3036
Bronx *(G-1372)*
Rock Hill Bakehouse Ltd....................E....... 518 743-1627
Gansevoort *(G-5246)*
Roma Bakery Inc....................F....... 516 825-9170
Valley Stream *(G-15795)*
Roslyn Bread Company Inc....................E....... 516 625-1470
Roslyn Heights *(G-14459)*
◆ Royal Sweet Bakery Inc....................F....... 718 567-7770
Brooklyn *(G-2424)*
Saint Honore Pastry Shop Inc....................G....... 516 767-2555
Port Washington *(G-13303)*
▼ Saj of Freeport Corp....................C....... 516 623-8800
Freeport *(G-5180)*
Sapienza Pastry Inc....................E....... 516 352-5232
Elmont *(G-4525)*
▲ Satispie LLC....................E....... 716 982-4600
Rochester *(G-14112)*
Scaife Enterprises Inc....................F....... 585 454-5231
Fairport *(G-4656)*
◆ Secure International....................G....... 716 206-2500
Lancaster *(G-7048)*
Settepani Inc....................E....... 718 349-6524
Brooklyn *(G-2458)*
Silver Bell Baking Co....................G....... 718 335-9539
Middle Village *(G-8127)*

Slims Bagels Unlimited Inc .... E 718 229-1140
  Oakland Gardens *(G-12526)*
Smith Street Bread Co LLC .... F 718 797-9712
  Brooklyn *(G-2489)*
Soutine Inc .... G 212 496-1450
  New York *(G-11655)*
Stebe Shcjʰjff 839 383-9833
  Poughkeepsie *(G-13369)*
Sugarbear Cupcakes .... G 917 698-9005
  Jamaica *(G-6680)*
▲ Sullivan St Bky - Hlls Kit Inc .... E 212 265-5580
  New York *(G-11735)*
T&B Bakery Corp .... G 646 642-4300
  Maspeth *(G-7872)*
Tarrytown Bakery Inc .... F 914 631-0209
  Tarrytown *(G-15496)*
Tates Wholesale LLC .... C 631 780-6511
  East Moriches *(G-4258)*
Tilaros Bakery Inc .... G 716 488-3209
  Jamestown *(G-6757)*
▲ Tphg 419 Ltd .... F 212 683-0444
  New York *(G-11879)*
Triboro Bagel Co Inc 718 359-9245
  Flushing *(G-5055)*
Uncle Wallys LLC .... E 631 205-0455
  Shirley *(G-14844)*
Village Lantern Baking Corp .... G 631 225-1690
  Lindenhurst *(G-7205)*
Vito & Sons Bakery .... F 201 617-8501
  Brooklyn *(G-2631)*
Waldorf Bakers Inc .... F 718 665-2253
  Bronx *(G-1417)*
▲ Wenner Bread Products Inc .... B 800 869-6262
  Ronkonkoma *(G-14430)*
Wenner Bread Products Inc .... E 800 869-6262
  Ronkonkoma *(G-14431)*
Whitestone Panetteria LLC .... E 516 543-9788
  Whitestone *(G-16552)*
Zaro Bake Shop Inc .... C 718 993-7327
  Bronx *(G-1422)*

2052 Cookies & Crackers

17 Bakers LLC .... F 844 687-6836
  Williamsville *(G-16565)*
212kiddish Inc 718 705-7227
  Brooklyn *(G-1434)*
AAA Noodle Products Mfg .... G 212 431-4090
  New York *(G-8703)*
▲ Alrajs Inc .... E 631 225-0300
  Lindenhurst *(G-7159)*
▲ Aron Streit Inc .... E 212 475-7000
  Orangeburg *(G-12670)*
Aryzta LLC .... C 585 235-8160
  Rochester *(G-13645)*
Butterwood Desserts Inc .... E 716 652-0131
  West Falls *(G-16208)*
Chipita America Inc .... E 845 292-2540
  Ferndale *(G-4931)*
Cone Buddy System Inc .... F 585 427-9940
  Rochester *(G-13718)*
▲ Cookies United LLC .... C 631 581-4000
  Islip *(G-6545)*
Cooking With Chef Michelle LLC .... E 516 662-2324
  Calverton *(G-3164)*
◆ Creative Food Ingredients Inc .... C 585 237-2213
  Perry *(G-12967)*
D F Stauffer Biscuit Co Inc .... E 585 968-2700
  Cuba *(G-3917)*
Danny Macaroons Inc 260 622-8463
  New York *(G-9469)*
Decorated Cookie Company LLC ...... E 315 487-2111
  Syracuse *(G-15304)*
▲ Elenis Nyc Inc .... E 718 361-8136
  Long Island City *(G-7437)*
Falcones Cookie Land Ltd .... E 718 236-4200
  Brooklyn *(G-1866)*
Golden Glow Cookie Co Inc .... F 718 379-6223
  Bronx *(G-1283)*
▲ Great Brands of Europe Inc .... G 914 872-8804
  White Plains *(G-16454)*
Jonathan Lord Corp .... F 631 563-4445
  Bohemia *(G-1043)*
▲ Kaltec Food Packaging Inc .... E 845 856-9888
  Port Jervis *(G-13231)*
Keebler Company .... F 585 948-8010
  Oakfield *(G-12524)*
Ladybird Bakery Inc .... G 718 499-8108
  Brooklyn *(G-2089)*
▲ Larte Del Gelato Inc .... G 212 366-0570
  New York *(G-10519)*

Linden Cookies Inc .... E 845 268-5050
  Congers *(G-3719)*
Lloyd Price Icon Food Brands .... F 914 764-8624
  Pound Ridge *(G-13377)*
Mannys Cheesecake Inc 315 732-0639
  Utica *(G-15718)*
My Most Favorite Food .... G 212 580-5130
  New York *(G-10864)*
New Mount Pleasant Bakery 518 374-7577
  Schenectady *(G-14700)*
Pdi Cone Co Inc .... D 716 825-8750
  Buffalo *(G-2994)*
◆ Pepsico Inc .... A 914 253-2000
  Purchase *(G-13395)*
Quaker Bonnet Inc 716 885-7208
  Buffalo *(G-3024)*
Sapienza Pastry Inc .... E 516 352-5232
  Elmont *(G-4525)*
Treehouse Private Brands Inc .... C 716 693-4715
  Tonawanda *(G-15584)*
U Serve Brands Inc .... F 877 632-6654
  New York *(G-11927)*
United Baking Co Inc .... F 631 413-5116
  Central Islip *(G-3387)*
United Baking Co Inc .... E 631 205-0455
  Shirley *(G-14845)*
Wonton Food Inc .... E 718 784-8178
  Long Island City *(G-7642)*
▲ Wonton Food Inc 718 628-6868
  Brooklyn *(G-2655)*
Zaro Bake Shop Inc .... C 718 993-7327
  Bronx *(G-1422)*

2053 Frozen Bakery Prdts

Bello LLC .... C 516 623-8800
  Freeport *(G-5145)*
Butterwood Desserts Inc .... E 716 652-0131
  West Falls *(G-16208)*
▲ Circle Peak Capital MGT LLC .... E 646 230-8812
  New York *(G-9302)*
Culinary Arts Specialties Inc .... G 716 656-8943
  Cheektowaga *(G-3439)*
Deiorio Foods Inc .... C 315 732-7612
  Utica *(G-15693)*
Dufour Pastry Kitchens Inc .... E 718 402-8800
  Bronx *(G-1260)*
Fratellis LLC .... E 607 722-5663
  Binghamton *(G-885)*
Ko Fro Foods Inc .... E 718 972-6480
  Brooklyn *(G-2079)*
▲ LArte Del Gelato Gruppo Inc .... F 718 383-6600
  Long Island City *(G-7496)*
Liddabit Sweets 917 912-1370
  Brooklyn *(G-2117)*
Maplehurst Bakeries LLC .... B 315 735-5000
  Frankfort *(G-5109)*
Micosta Enterprises Inc .... G 518 822-9708
  Hudson *(G-6364)*
Pearl River Pastries LLC .... E 845 735-5100
  West Nyack *(G-16277)*
◆ Rich Holdings Inc 716 878-8000
  Buffalo *(G-3036)*
◆ Rich Products Corporation .... A 716 878-8000
  Buffalo *(G-3037)*
▲ Wenner Bread Products Inc .... B 800 869-6262
  Ronkonkoma *(G-14430)*
Wenner Bread Products Inc .... E 800 869-6262
  Ronkonkoma *(G-14431)*

2061 Sugar, Cane

▲ Supreme Chocolatier LLC .... E 718 761-9600
  Staten Island *(G-15143)*
US Sweeteners Corp .... E 718 854-8714
  Brooklyn *(G-2613)*

2062 Sugar, Cane Refining

American Sugar Refining Inc .... F 914 376-3386
  Yonkers *(G-16735)*
Cane Sugar LLC .... G 212 329-2695
  New York *(G-9195)*
Domino Foods Inc .... F 800 729-4840
  Yonkers *(G-16752)*
Refined Sugars Inc .... F 914 963-2400
  Yonkers *(G-16795)*
▲ Sweeteners Plus Inc .... D 585 728-3770
  Lakeville *(G-6987)*

2063 Sugar, Beet

Beets Love Production LLC .... E 585 270-2471
  Rochester *(G-13659)*

2064 Candy & Confectionery Prdts

▲ 5th Avenue Chocolatiere Ltd .... G 212 935-5454
  Freeport *(G-5134)*
Aigner Chocolates .... F 718 544-1850
  Forest Hills *(G-5070)*
▲ Alrajs Inc 631 225-0300
  Lindenhurst *(G-7159)*
Amiram Dror Inc .... F 212 979-9505
  Brooklyn *(G-1529)*
Anyas Licorice Inc 917 935-1916
  Brooklyn *(G-1538)*
Bader Enterprise Inc .... G 718 965-9434
  Brooklyn *(G-1583)*
C Howard Company Inc 631 286-7940
  Bellport *(G-800)*
▼ Calico Cottage Inc .... C 631 841-2100
  Amityville *(G-266)*
▲ Chocolat Moderne LLC .... G 212 229-4797
  New York *(G-9287)*
▲ Chocolate Delivery Systems Inc ..... E 716 877-3146
  Buffalo *(G-2765)*
Chocolate Pizza Company Inc .... F 315 673-4098
  Marcellus *(G-7793)*
Chocolations LLC .... G 914 777-3600
  Mamaroneck *(G-7738)*
Dilese International Inc .... F 716 855-3500
  Buffalo *(G-2801)*
Eatingevolved LLC .... F 631 675-2440
  Setauket *(G-14794)*
◆ Fairbanks Mfg LLC .... C 845 341-0002
  Middletown *(G-8152)*
Fine and Raw Chocolate .... F 718 366-3633
  Brooklyn *(G-1881)*
Gertrude Hawk Chocolates Inc .... E ....
  Watertown *(G-16014)*
▲ Godiva Chocolatier Inc .... E 212 984-5900
  New York *(G-9950)*
▲ Gourmet Nut Inc .... F 877 830-9030
  Brooklyn *(G-1943)*
Gravymaster Inc .... E 203 453-1893
  Canajoharie *(G-3207)*
Handsome Dans LLC .... F 917 965-2499
  New York *(G-10030)*
Hercules Candy Co .... G 315 463-4339
  East Syracuse *(G-4346)*
Hudson Valley Chocolatier Inc .... F 845 831-8240
  Beacon *(G-759)*
▼ In Room Plus Inc .... E 716 838-9433
  Buffalo *(G-2882)*
Jo-Mart Candies Corp .... F 718 375-1277
  Brooklyn *(G-2041)*
Joseph Shalhoub & Son Inc .... F 718 871-6300
  Brooklyn *(G-2048)*
◆ Joyva Corp .... D 718 497-0170
  Brooklyn *(G-2052)*
Keep Healthy Inc .... F 631 651-9090
  Northport *(G-12469)*
Koppers Choclat Specialty Inc .... G 917 834-2290
  New York *(G-10469)*
L A Burdick Chocolates .... E 212 796-0143
  New York *(G-10492)*
Lady-N-Th-window Chocolates Inc .... F 631 549-1059
  Huntington *(G-6403)*
◆ Lanco Corporation .... C 631 231-2300
  Ronkonkoma *(G-14368)*
▲ Landies Candies Co Inc .... F 716 834-8212
  Buffalo *(G-2920)*
Little Bird Chocolates Inc .... G 646 620-6395
  Plainview *(G-13070)*
Momn Pops Inc .... E 845 567-0640
  Cornwall *(G-3834)*
▲ Mrchocolatecom LLC .... F 718 875-9772
  Brooklyn *(G-2235)*
▲ N Make Mold Inc .... E 716 877-3146
  Buffalo *(G-2960)*
▼ Naples Vly Mrgers Acqstns LLC ..... G 585 490-1339
  Naples *(G-8473)*
▲ Nassau Candy Distributors Inc .... C 516 433-7100
  Hicksville *(G-6113)*
Noras Candy Shop .... F 315 337-4530
  Rome *(G-14262)*
OH How Cute Inc 347 888-6031
  Staten Island *(G-15113)*
Pachanga Inc .... F 212 832-0022
  New York *(G-11087)*

Employee Codes: A=Over 500 employees, B=251-500
C=101-250, D=51-100, E=20-50, F=10-19, G=5-9

2019 Harris
New York Manufacturers Directory

20 FOOD AND KINDRED PRODUCTS SIC SECTION

Papa Bubble ....G.... 212 966-2599
New York *(G-11100)*
◆ **Pfeil & Holing Inc** ....D.... 718 545-4600
Woodside *(G-16671)*
Premium Sweets USA Inc ....G.... 718 739-6000
Jamaica *(G-6669)*
▲ **Rajbhog Foods Inc** ....E.... 718 358-5105
Flushing *(G-5042)*
▲ **Richardson Brands Company** ....C.... 800 839-8938
Canajoharie *(G-3208)*
Robert Pikcilingis ....F.... 518 355-1860
Altamont *(G-201)*
Roger L Urban Inc ....E.... 716 693-5391
North Tonawanda *(G-12449)*
Salty Road Inc ....G.... 347 673-3925
Brooklyn *(G-2446)*
◆ **Satin Fine Foods Inc** ....D.... 845 469-1034
Chester *(G-3483)*
▲ **Scaccianoce Inc** ....F.... 718 991-4462
Bronx *(G-1382)*
Seaward Candies ....G.... 585 638-6761
Holley *(G-6229)*
◆ **Settons Intl Foods Inc** ....D.... 631 543-8090
Commack *(G-3702)*
▲ **Simply Natural Foods LLC** ....C.... 631 543-9600
Commack *(G-3703)*
Star Brands North America Inc ....E.... 914 355-9750
White Plains *(G-16506)*
Steve & Andys Organics Inc ....G.... 718 499-7933
Brooklyn *(G-2521)*
Stones Homemade Candies Inc ....G.... 315 343-8401
Oswego *(G-12789)*
◆ **Sweetworks Inc** ....C.... 716 634-4545
Buffalo *(G-3082)*
◆ **Tomric Systems Inc** ....F.... 716 854-6050
Buffalo *(G-3098)*
Valenti Distributing ....G.... 716 824-2304
Blasdell *(G-932)*
▲ **Vidal Candies USA Inc** ....G.... 609 781-8169
New York *(G-12030)*
◆ **Vigneri Chocolate Inc** ....G.... 585 254-6160
Rochester *(G-14201)*
Wellspring Corp ....G.... 212 529-5454
New York *(G-12092)*

2066 Chocolate & Cocoa Prdts

5th Avenue Chocolatiere LLC ....E.... 516 868-8070
Freeport *(G-5133)*
▲ **5th Avenue Chocolatiere Ltd** ....G.... 212 935-5454
Freeport *(G-5134)*
Adirondack Chocolate Co Ltd ....F.... 518 946-7270
Wilmington *(G-16600)*
Aigner Chocolates ....F.... 718 544-1850
Forest Hills *(G-5070)*
Amiram Dror Inc ....F.... 212 979-9505
Brooklyn *(G-1529)*
◆ **Associated Brands Inc** ....B.... 585 798-3475
Medina *(G-7970)*
Big Heart Pet Brands ....E.... 716 891-6566
Buffalo *(G-2733)*
▲ **Cemoi Inc** ....G.... 212 583-4920
New York *(G-9238)*
Chocolate Lady LLC ....G.... 516 532-0551
Port Jervis *(G-13225)*
Chocolate Pizza Company Inc ....F.... 315 673-4098
Marcellus *(G-7793)*
▲ **Chocomize Inc** ....F.... 631 506-6085
Long Island City *(G-7408)*
Commodore Chocolatier USA Inc ....F.... 845 561-3960
Newburgh *(G-12218)*
Ctac Holdings LLC ....E.... 212 924-2280
Brooklyn *(G-1738)*
Dilese International Inc ....F.... 716 855-3500
Buffalo *(G-2801)*
Dolce Vite International LLC ....G.... 713 962-5767
Brooklyn *(G-1785)*
Doma Marketing Inc ....G.... 516 684-1111
Port Washington *(G-13254)*
Eating Evolved Inc ....G.... 516 510-2601
East Setauket *(G-4300)*
Emvi Inc ....G.... 518 883-5111
Broadalbin *(G-1188)*
Fox 416 Corp ....E.... 718 385-4600
Brooklyn *(G-1903)*
Gnosis Chocolate Inc ....G.... 646 688-5549
Long Island City *(G-7458)*
▲ **Godiva Chocolatier Inc** ....E.... 212 984-5900
New York *(G-9950)*
Godiva Chocolatier Inc ....E.... 718 271-3603
Elmhurst *(G-4466)*
Greenwood Winery LLC ....E.... 315 432-8132
East Syracuse *(G-4343)*
Hershey Kiss 203 Inc ....G.... 516 503-3740
Wantagh *(G-15922)*
Jo-Mart Candies Corp ....F.... 718 375-1277
Brooklyn *(G-2041)*
◆ **Joyva Corp** ....D.... 718 497-0170
Brooklyn *(G-2052)*
Lady-N-Th-wndow Chocolates Inc ....F.... 631 549-1059
Huntington *(G-6403)*
◆ **Lanco Corporation** ....C.... 631 231-2300
Ronkonkoma *(G-14368)*
▲ **Le Chocolate of Rockland LLC** ....E.... 845 533-4125
Suffern *(G-15192)*
▲ **Max Brenner Union Square LLC** ....G.... 646 467-8803
New York *(G-10733)*
Mbny LLC ....F.... 646 467-8810
New York *(G-10737)*
Menrose USA LLC ....G.... 718 221-5540
Brooklyn *(G-2191)*
Micosta Enterprises Inc ....G.... 518 822-9708
Hudson *(G-6364)*
Momn Pops Inc ....E.... 845 567-0640
Cornwall *(G-3834)*
Nibmor Project LLC ....F.... 718 374-5091
Great Neck *(G-5573)*
Noras Candy Shop ....F.... 315 337-4530
Rome *(G-14262)*
Parkside Candy Co Inc ....F.... 716 833-7540
Buffalo *(G-2992)*
▲ **Reserve Confections Inc** ....F.... 845 371-7744
Spring Valley *(G-15007)*
Rip Van Wafels Inc ....E.... 415 529-5403
Brooklyn *(G-2404)*
Robert Pikcilingis ....F.... 518 355-1860
Altamont *(G-201)*
Roger L Urban Inc ....E.... 716 693-5391
North Tonawanda *(G-12449)*
◆ **Settons Intl Foods Inc** ....D.... 631 543-8090
Commack *(G-3702)*
▲ **Simply Natural Foods LLC** ....C.... 631 543-9600
Commack *(G-3703)*
▲ **Superior Confections Inc** ....D.... 718 698-3300
Staten Island *(G-15142)*
◆ **Sweetworks Inc** ....C.... 716 634-4545
Buffalo *(G-3082)*
The Chocolate Shop ....G.... 716 882-5055
Buffalo *(G-3092)*
Yes Were Nuts Ltd ....G.... 516 374-1940
Hewlett *(G-6055)*

2067 Chewing Gum

▲ **Ford Gum & Machine Company Inc** ....D.... 716 542-4561
Akron *(G-18)*
◆ **Sweetworks Inc** ....C.... 716 634-4545
Buffalo *(G-3082)*

2068 Salted & Roasted Nuts & Seeds

▲ **American Almond Pdts Co Inc** ....D.... 718 875-8310
Brooklyn *(G-1519)*
Our Daily Eats LLC ....F.... 518 810-8412
Albany *(G-109)*
◆ **Sahadi Fine Foods Inc** ....E.... 718 369-0100
Brooklyn *(G-2445)*
▲ **Scaccianoce Inc** ....F.... 718 991-4462
Bronx *(G-1382)*
◆ **Settons Intl Foods Inc** ....D.... 631 543-8090
Commack *(G-3702)*
◆ **Sugar Foods Corporation** ....E.... 212 753-6900
New York *(G-11734)*
Whitsons Food Svc Bronx Corp ....B.... 631 424-2700
Islandia *(G-6540)*

2074 Cottonseed Oil Mills

▲ **Perimondo LLC** ....G.... 212 749-0721
New York *(G-11157)*

2076 Vegetable Oil Mills

▲ **Jax Coco USA LLC** ....G.... 347 688-8198
New York *(G-10311)*

2077 Animal, Marine Fats & Oils

Baker Commodities Inc ....E.... 585 482-1880
Rochester *(G-13652)*
Darling Ingredients Inc ....F.... 716 895-0655
Buffalo *(G-2793)*
Ellenburg Recyclers ....F.... 518 594-3900
Ellenburg Depot *(G-4436)*

2079 Shortening, Oils & Margarine

▲ **Bonelli Foods LLC** ....G.... 212 346-0942
New York *(G-9119)*
Bunge Limited Finance Corp ....D.... 914 684-2800
White Plains *(G-16432)*
C B S Food Products Corp ....F.... 718 452-2500
Brooklyn *(G-1663)*
Consumer Flavoring Extract Co ....F.... 718 435-0201
Brooklyn *(G-1712)*
F Olivers LLC ....G.... 585 244-2585
Rochester *(G-13801)*
Gourmet Factory Inc ....G.... 631 231-4548
Hauppauge *(G-5836)*
▲ **Healthy Brand Oil Corp** ....E.... 718 937-0806
Long Island City *(G-7467)*
◆ **Kerry Bfnctnal Ingredients Inc** ....D.... 608 363-1200
Norwich *(G-12488)*
L LLC ....E.... 716 885-3918
Buffalo *(G-2914)*
Lesieur Cristal Inc ....G.... 646 604-4314
Long Island City *(G-7497)*
▲ **Pietro Demarco Importers Inc** ....F.... 914 969-3201
Yonkers *(G-16792)*
Pinos Press Inc ....G.... 315 935-0110
Syracuse *(G-15396)*

2082 Malt Beverages

Anheuser-Busch LLC ....G.... 315 638-0365
Baldwinsville *(G-549)*
Anheuser-Busch LLC ....C.... 315 638-0365
Baldwinsville *(G-550)*
Anheuser-Busch LLC ....C.... 212 573-8800
New York *(G-8865)*
Anheuser-Busch Companies LLC ....G.... 718 589-2610
Bronx *(G-1221)*
Anheuser-Busch Inbev Fin Inc ....F.... 212 573-8800
New York *(G-8866)*
Anheuser-Busch Inbev Svcs LLC ....G.... 314 765-4729
New York *(G-8867)*
Barrier Brewing Company LLC ....G.... 516 316-4429
Long Beach *(G-7357)*
Black River Brewing Co Inc ....G.... 315 755-2739
Watertown *(G-16003)*
Brazen Street LLC ....E.... 516 305-7951
Brooklyn *(G-1632)*
▲ **Brewery Ommegang Ltd** ....E.... 607 286-4144
Cooperstown *(G-3742)*
Butternuts Beer and Ale LLC ....G.... 607 263-5070
Garrattsville *(G-5302)*
C H Evans Brewing Co ....F.... 518 447-9000
Albany *(G-53)*
▲ **Castle Brands Inc** ....E.... 646 356-0200
New York *(G-9223)*
Constellation Brands Inc ....D.... 585 678-7100
Victor *(G-15837)*
Coopers Cave Ale Co S-Corp ....F.... 518 792-0007
Glens Falls *(G-5422)*
Cooperstown Brewing Co LLC ....G.... 607 286-9330
Oneonta *(G-12634)*
Crazy Cowboy Brewing Co LLC ....E.... 516 812-0576
Woodbury *(G-16616)*
Custom Brewcrafters Inc ....F.... 585 624-4386
Honeoye Falls *(G-6263)*
Duvel Mortgage USA Inc ....G.... 607 267-6121
Cooperstown *(G-3744)*
Empire Brewing Company Inc ....D.... 315 925-8308
Syracuse *(G-15317)*
Equilibrium Brewery LLC ....G.... 201 245-0292
Middletown *(G-8151)*
Five Burroughs Brewing Co ....G.... 718 355-8575
Brooklyn *(G-1886)*
Gilded Otter Brewing Co ....D.... 845 256-1700
New Paltz *(G-8577)*
▲ **High Falls Brewing Company LLC** ....C.... 585 546-1030
Rochester *(G-13867)*
High Falls Operating Co LLC ....A.... 585 546-1030
Rochester *(G-13868)*
Hoptron Brewtique ....G.... 631 438-0296
Patchogue *(G-12866)*
Horns & Halos Cft Brewing LLC ....E.... 585 507-7248
Caledonia *(G-3156)*
Hyde Park Brewing Co Inc ....E.... 845 229-8277
Hyde Park *(G-6469)*
Indian Ladder Farmstead Brewer ....G.... 518 577-1484
Altamont *(G-197)*
Ithaca Beer Company Inc ....E.... 607 272-1305
Ithaca *(G-6587)*
Keegan Ales LLC ....F.... 845 331-2739
Kingston *(G-6903)*

SIC SECTION

20 FOOD AND KINDRED PRODUCTS

Keuka Brewing Co LLC G 607 868-4648
Hammondsport *(G-5706)*

Kings Cnty Brwers Cllctive LLC F 917 207-2739
Brooklyn *(G-2075)*

▲ Labatt USA LLC D 716 604-1050
Buffalo *(G-2915)*

Lock 1 Distilling Company LLC G 315 934-4376
Phoenix *(G-12989)*

Long Ireland Brewing LLC G 631 403-4303
Riverhead *(G-13574)*

▲ Mad Scntsts Brwing Prtners LLC E 347 766-2739
Brooklyn *(G-2150)*

▲ Marnier-Lapostolle Inc D 212 207-4350
New York *(G-10715)*

▲ Middle Ages Brewing Company G 315 476-4250
Syracuse *(G-15371)*

Millercoors LLC E 585 385-0670
Pittsford *(G-13022)*

Montauk Brewing Company Inc F 631 668-8471
Montauk *(G-8305)*

Newburgh Brewing Company LLC F 845 569-2337
Newburgh *(G-12235)*

◆ North American Breweries Inc F 585 546-1030
Rochester *(G-13977)*

North Amrcn Brwries Hldngs LLC E 585 546-1030
Rochester *(G-13978)*

Other Half Brewing Co G 347 987-3527
Brooklyn *(G-2295)*

Oyster Bay Brewing Company F 516 802-5546
Oyster Bay *(G-12817)*

Rare Form Brewing Company G 518 313-9256
Troy *(G-15620)*

Remarkable Liquids LLC D 518 861-5351
Altamont *(G-200)*

Rising Sons 6 Brewing Coinc G 607 368-4836
Corning *(G-3824)*

Rohrbach Brewing Company Inc D 585 594-9800
Rochester *(G-14102)*

Simple Brewer E 845 490-0182
Somers *(G-14923)*

Spectacle Brewing LLC F 845 942-8776
Garnerville *(G-5301)*

Valcour Brewing Company LLC E 518 324-2337
Plattsburgh *(G-13167)*

▲ Vanberg & Dewulf Co Inc G 607 547-8184
Cooperstown *(G-3745)*

Vernon Wine & Liquor Inc G 718 784-5096
Long Island City *(G-7630)*

Wagner Vineyards & Brewing Co E 607 582-6574
Lodi *(G-7355)*

Woodcock Brothers Brewing Comp F 716 333-4000
Wilson *(G-16603)*

Yonkers Whl Beer Distrs Inc G 914 963-8600
Yonkers *(G-16812)*

2083 Malt

▲ Great Western Malting Co G 800 496-7732
Champlain *(G-3409)*

Queen City Malting LLC G 716 481-1313
Buffalo *(G-3027)*

2084 Wine & Brandy

Allied Wine Corp F 845 796-4160
South Fallsburg *(G-14930)*

Americana Vineyards & Winery F 607 387-6801
Interlaken *(G-6480)*

Anthony Road Wine Co Inc F 315 536-2182
Penn Yan *(G-12948)*

Anyelas Vineyards LLC F 315 685-3797
Skaneateles *(G-14866)*

Arrowhead Spring Vineyards LLC G 716 434-8030
Lockport *(G-7285)*

Atwater Estate Vineyards LLC E 607 546-8463
Burdett *(G-3140)*

Austin Nichols & Co Inc E 519 561-5225
New York *(G-8965)*

Bellwethe Hard Cider F 607 387-9464
Trumansburg *(G-15637)*

Bibo International LLC F 617 304-2242
New York *(G-9071)*

Billsboro Winery G 315 789-9538
Geneva *(G-5317)*

Brooklyn Winery LLC F 347 763-1506
Brooklyn *(G-1650)*

▲ Brotherhood Americas E 845 496-3661
Washingtonville *(G-15964)*

Casa Larga Vineyards E 585 223-4210
Fairport *(G-4627)*

Casa Larga Vineyards G 585 223-4210
Fairport *(G-4628)*

Cascade Mountain Winery & Rest F 845 373-9021
Amenia *(G-205)*

▲ Cava Spiliadis USA E 212 247-8214
New York *(G-9232)*

Chautauqua Wine Company Inc G 716 934-9463
Silver Creek *(G-14860)*

Clinton Vineyards Inc G 845 266-5372
Clinton Corners *(G-3590)*

Cobblestone Frm Winery Vinyrd F 315 549-1004
Romulus *(G-14280)*

Constellation Brands Inc D 585 678-7100
Victor *(G-15837)*

Constellation Brands Inc E 585 393-4880
Canandaigua *(G-3215)*

Constellation Brands Smo LLC G 585 396-7161
New York *(G-9385)*

Constellation Brands US Oprs A 585 396-7600
Canandaigua *(G-3216)*

▲ Constellation Brands US Oprs B 585 396-7600
Canandaigua *(G-3217)*

Coyote Moon LLC F 315 686-5600
Clayton *(G-3553)*

▼ Cruzin Management Inc E 212 641-8700
New York *(G-9428)*

David F De Marco G 315 536-0882
Penn Yan *(G-12952)*

◆ Davos Brands LLC F 212 779-1911
New York *(G-9491)*

Deer Run Enterprises Inc G 585 346-0850
Geneseo *(G-5314)*

Di Borghese Castello LLC F 631 734-5111
Cutchogue *(G-3921)*

▲ Dorset Farms Inc F 631 734-6010
Peconic *(G-12914)*

▲ Dreyfus Ashby Inc E 212 818-0770
New York *(G-9578)*

Duck Walk Vinyards E 631 726-7555
Water Mill *(G-15970)*

▲ Dutch Spirits LLC F 518 398-1022
Pine Plains *(G-13005)*

Dutchess Wines LLC G 845 876-1319
Rhinebeck *(G-13486)*

▲ Eagle Crest Vineyard LLC G 585 346-5760
Conesus *(G-3708)*

East Branch Winery Inc G 607 292-3999
Dundee *(G-4156)*

▲ East End Vineyards LLC G 718 468-0500
Queens Village *(G-13405)*

Edrington Group Usa LLC E 212 352-6000
New York *(G-9629)*

Fly Creek Cder Mill Orchrd Inc G 607 547-9692
Fly Creek *(G-5064)*

Fox Run Vineyards Inc F 315 536-4616
Penn Yan *(G-12956)*

Frank Wines Inc G 646 765-6637
New York *(G-9842)*

Freedom Run Winery Inc G 716 433-4136
Lockport *(G-7302)*

Gabriella Importers Inc F 212 579-3945
New York *(G-9874)*

Glenora Farm Inc G 607 243-8383
Dundee *(G-4158)*

Glenora Wine Cellars Inc E 607 243-9500
Dundee *(G-4159)*

Greenwood Winery LLC E 315 432-8132
East Syracuse *(G-4343)*

Hazlitts 1852 Vineyards Inc E 607 546-9463
Hector *(G-5999)*

▲ Hermann J Wiemer Vineyard G 607 243-7971
Dundee *(G-4160)*

Heron Hill Vineyards Inc E 607 868-4241
Hammondsport *(G-5705)*

Hickory Road Land Co LLC G 607 243-9114
Dundee *(G-4161)*

Hoffman & Hoffman G 315 536-4773
Penn Yan *(G-12958)*

Hosmer Inc F 888 467-9463
Ovid *(G-12791)*

Hunt Country Vineyards E 315 595-2812
Branchport *(G-1123)*

▲ J Petrocelli Wine Cellars LLC E 631 765-1100
Peconic *(G-12915)*

Joseph Zakon Winery Ltd G 718 604-1430
Brooklyn *(G-2049)*

Keurig Dr Pepper Inc C 315 589-4911
Williamson *(G-16559)*

▲ Konstantin D FRAnk& Sons Vini E 607 868-4884
Hammondsport *(G-5707)*

L & D Acquisition LLC F 585 531-9000
Naples *(G-8471)*

Lafayette Chateau E 607 546-2062
Hector *(G-6000)*

▲ Lakewood Vineyards Inc F 607 535-9252
Watkins Glen *(G-16059)*

Lamoreaux Landing WI D 607 582-6162
Lodi *(G-7353)*

Leonard Oakes Estate Winery G 585 318-4418
Medina *(G-7982)*

Lieb Cellars LLC E 631 298-1942
Mattituck *(G-7914)*

Lucas Vineyards Inc F 607 532-4825
Interlaken *(G-6482)*

Malina Management Company Inc E 607 535-9614
Montour Falls *(G-8326)*

Merritt Estate Winery Inc F 716 965-4800
Forestville *(G-5086)*

▲ Millbrook Winery Inc F 845 677-8383
Millbrook *(G-8190)*

▲ Montezuma Winery LLC G 315 568-8190
Seneca Falls *(G-14782)*

Negys New Land Vinyrd Winery G 315 585-4432
Geneva *(G-5330)*

▲ North House Vineyards Inc G 631 779-2817
Jamesport *(G-6693)*

Olde Chtqua Vneyards Ltd Lblty F 716 792-2749
Portland *(G-13315)*

▲ Paumanok Vineyards Ltd E 631 722-8800
Aquebogue *(G-375)*

Pellegrini Vineyards LLC G 631 734-4111
Cutchogue *(G-3922)*

Pindar Vineyards LLC E 631 734-6200
Peconic *(G-12916)*

Prejean Winery Inc F 315 536-7524
Penn Yan *(G-12962)*

▲ Premium Wine Group LLC E 631 298-1900
Mattituck *(G-7916)*

Pugliese Vineyards Inc G 631 734-4057
Cutchogue *(G-3923)*

Quinn and Co of NY Ltd D 212 868-1900
New York *(G-11303)*

Railex Wine Services LLC E 631 369-7000
Riverhead *(G-13581)*

Red Newt Cellars Inc F 607 546-4100
Hector *(G-6001)*

Red Tail Ridge Inc F 315 536-4580
Penn Yan *(G-12963)*

Rock Stream Vineyards G 607 243-8322
Rock Stream *(G-14223)*

Royal Wine Corporation F 845 236-4000
Marlboro *(G-7813)*

Schulze Vineyards & Winery LLC F 716 778-8090
Burt *(G-3144)*

Sheldrake Point Vineyard LLC F 607 532-8967
Ovid *(G-12793)*

▲ Shinn Winery LLC G 631 804-0367
Mattituck *(G-7917)*

Sokolin LLC E 631 537-4434
Yaphank *(G-16722)*

▲ Solstars Inc G 212 605-0430
New York *(G-11640)*

Spanish Artisan Wine Group LLC G 914 414-6982
Patterson *(G-12885)*

Standing Stone Vineyards G 607 582-6051
Hector *(G-6002)*

Swedish Hill Vineyard Inc D 607 403-0029
Romulus *(G-14283)*

Thirsty Owl Wine Company G 607 869-5805
Ovid *(G-12794)*

Thousand Islands Winery LLC E 315 482-9306
Alexandria Bay *(G-183)*

Tickle Hill Winery G 607 546-7740
Hector *(G-6003)*

Trader Joes Company E 212 529-6326
New York *(G-11883)*

Tug Hill Vineyards G 315 376-4336
Lowville *(G-7657)*

Vedell North Fork LLC G 631 323-3526
Cutchogue *(G-3924)*

Ventosa Vineyards LLC G 315 719-0000
Geneva *(G-5336)*

Wagner Vineyards LLC G 607 582-6976
Lodi *(G-7354)*

Wagner Vineyards & Brewing Co E 607 582-6574
Lodi *(G-7355)*

Warwick Valley Wine Co F 845 258-4858
Warwick *(G-15962)*

Westchester Wine Warehouse LLC F 914 824-1400
White Plains *(G-16520)*

Wine Group Inc D 716 326-3151
Westfield *(G-16400)*

S I C

Employee Codes: A=Over 500 employees, B=251-500
C=101-250, D=51-100, E=20-50, F=10-19, G=5-9

2019 Harris
New York Manufacturers Directory

655

20 FOOD AND KINDRED PRODUCTS SIC SECTION

Wine Services Inc ..... G 631 722-3800
Riverhead *(G-13589)*
▲ **Wolffer Estate Vineyard Inc** ..... E 631 537-5106
Sagaponack *(G-14505)*
Woodbury Vineyards Inc ..... G 716 679-9463
Fredonia *(G-5130)*

2085 Liquors, Distilled, Rectified & Blended

21st Century Spirits Corp ..... G 718 499-0606
Brooklyn *(G-1435)*
Adirondack Distilling Company ..... G 315 316-0387
Utica *(G-15675)*
Austin Nichols & Co Inc ..... E 519 561-5225
New York *(G-8965)*
Braided Oak Spirits LLC ..... F 845 381-1525
Middletown *(G-8140)*
▲ **Castle Brands Inc** ..... E 646 356-0200
New York *(G-9223)*
Constellation Brands Inc ..... D 585 678-7100
Victor *(G-15837)*
▼ **Cruzin Management Inc** ..... E 212 641-8700
New York *(G-9428)*
▲ **Dutch Spirits LLC** ..... F 518 398-1022
Pine Plains *(G-13005)*
Ellicottville Distillery LLC ..... G 716 597-6121
Ellicottville *(G-4445)*
Evolution Spirits Inc ..... G 917 543-7880
New York *(G-9742)*
Finger Lakes Distilling ..... F 607 546-5510
Burdett *(G-3141)*
George Lake Distilling Company ..... G 518 639-1025
Queensbury *(G-13425)*
Honeoye Falls Distillery LLC ..... F 201 780-4618
Honeoye Falls *(G-6268)*
Infirmary Nyc ..... G 504 606-6280
New York *(G-10205)*
Iron Smoke Whiskey LLC ..... G 585 388-7584
Fairport *(G-4635)*
▲ **Leblon Holdings LLC** ..... E 212 741-2675
New York *(G-10533)*
▲ **Leblon LLC** ..... F 954 649-0148
New York *(G-10534)*
▲ **Leblon LLC** ..... E 786 281-5672
New York *(G-10535)*
Lockhouse Distillery ..... G 716 768-4898
Buffalo *(G-2927)*
Madison County Distillery LLC ..... G 315 391-6070
Cazenovia *(G-3321)*
▲ **Marnier-Lapostolle Inc** ..... D 212 207-4350
New York *(G-10715)*
Prohibition Distillery LLC ..... G 917 685-8989
Roscoe *(G-14439)*
◆ **Russian Standard Vodka USA Inc** ..... G 212 679-1894
New York *(G-11450)*
▲ **Sovereign Brands LLC** ..... G 212 343-8366
New York *(G-11656)*
Stilltheone Distillery LLC ..... G 914 217-0347
Harrison *(G-5736)*
Tirado Distillery Inc ..... G 718 620-2244
Bronx *(G-1403)*
▲ **Tuthilltown Spirits LLC** ..... F 845 255-1527
Gardiner *(G-5296)*

2086 Soft Drinks

3v Company Inc ..... E 718 858-7333
Brooklyn *(G-1440)*
A Health Obsession LLC ..... E 347 850-4587
Brooklyn *(G-1457)*
Alpha Wolf LLC ..... G 516 778-5812
Carle Place *(G-3260)*
American Bottling Company ..... F 516 714-0002
Ronkonkoma *(G-14305)*
Ariesun Inc ..... E 866 274-3049
Mount Vernon *(G-8378)*
▼ **Arizona Beverage Company LLC** ..... G 516 812-0300
Woodbury *(G-16613)*
Austin Nichols & Co Inc ..... E 519 561-5225
New York *(G-8965)*
Ba Sports Nutrition LLC ..... C 718 357-7402
Whitestone *(G-16536)*
Beverage Works Incorporated ..... G 718 834-0500
Brooklyn *(G-1607)*
Beverage Works Nj Inc ..... E 631 293-3501
Farmingdale *(G-4728)*
Beverage Works Ny Inc ..... E 718 812-2034
Brooklyn *(G-1608)*
▲ **Big Geyser Inc** ..... C 718 821-2200
Maspeth *(G-7827)*
▲ **Blue Star Beverages Corp** ..... G 718 381-3535
Brooklyn *(G-1622)*
Borabora Fruit Juices Inc ..... G 914 438-8744
Highland *(G-6142)*
Bottling Group LLC ..... E 315 788-6751
Watertown *(G-16004)*
Bottling Group LLC ..... B 800 789-2626
White Plains *(G-16429)*
◆ **Bottling Group LLC** ..... F 914 767-6000
White Plains *(G-16430)*
▲ **Boylan Bottling Co Inc** ..... E 800 289-7978
New York *(G-9130)*
▲ **Brands Within Reach LLC** ..... E 847 720-9090
Mamaroneck *(G-7735)*
▲ **Cell-Nique Corporation** ..... G 203 856-8550
Castleton On Hudson *(G-3295)*
Cham Cold Brew LLC ..... G 646 926-0206
New York *(G-9257)*
Chateau Imports Ltd ..... G 516 841-6343
Port Washington *(G-13248)*
Cheribundi Inc ..... E 800 699-0460
Geneva *(G-5320)*
Chohehco LLC ..... G 315 420-4624
Skaneateles *(G-14868)*
◆ **Cliffstar LLC** ..... A 716 366-6100
Dunkirk *(G-4165)*
Clintons Ditch Coop Co Inc ..... C 315 699-2695
Cicero *(G-3515)*
Coca-Cola Bottling Company ..... E 518 483-0422
Malone *(G-7720)*
▲ **Coca-Cola Btlg Co Buffalo Inc** ..... C 716 874-4610
Tonawanda *(G-15535)*
Coca-Cola Btlg Co of NY Inc ..... F 845 562-3037
New Windsor *(G-8642)*
Coca-Cola Btlg Co of NY Inc ..... F 518 459-2010
Albany *(G-64)*
Coca-Cola Btlg Co of NY Inc ..... E 718 416-7575
Maspeth *(G-7830)*
Coca-Cola Btlg Co of NY Inc ..... F 315 457-9221
Syracuse *(G-15284)*
Coca-Cola Btlg Co of NY Inc ..... E 631 434-3535
Hauppauge *(G-5792)*
Coca-Cola Btlg Co of NY Inc ..... F 718 420-6800
Staten Island *(G-15063)*
Coca-Cola Btlg Co of NY Inc ..... F 914 789-1580
Elmsford *(G-4536)*
Coca-Cola Refreshments USA Inc ..... E 718 401-5200
Bronx *(G-1242)*
Coca-Cola Refreshments USA Inc ..... E 315 785-8907
Watertown *(G-16009)*
Coca-Cola Refreshments USA Inc ..... G 914 592-0806
Hawthorne *(G-5985)*
Cornell Beverages Inc ..... F 718 381-3000
Brooklyn *(G-1718)*
Crystal Rock LLC ..... E 716 626-7460
Buffalo *(G-2785)*
Dirty Lemon Beverages LLC ..... G 877 897-7784
New York *(G-9533)*
Doheny Nice and Easy ..... G 518 793-1733
Glens Falls *(G-5423)*
East Coast Cultures LLC ..... F 917 261-3010
Kingston *(G-6899)*
▼ **Energy Brands Inc** ..... E 212 545-6000
New York *(G-9680)*
F & V Distribution Company LLC ..... G 516 812-0393
Woodbury *(G-16619)*
Fancy Flamingo LLC ..... G 516 209-7306
New York *(G-9779)*
Fevertree USA Inc ..... F 718 852-5577
Brooklyn *(G-1876)*
Gangi Distributors Inc ..... F 718 442-5745
Staten Island *(G-15077)*
General Cinema Bevs of Ohio ..... A 914 767-6000
Somers *(G-14919)*
Global Brands Inc ..... G 845 358-1212
Nyack *(G-12508)*
▲ **Good-O-Beverage Inc** ..... F 718 328-6400
Bronx *(G-1284)*
Grayhawk Leasing LLC ..... G 914 767-6000
Somers *(G-14920)*
Green Zone Food Service Inc ..... G 917 709-1728
Corona *(G-3844)*
◆ **Hain Celestial Group Inc** ..... C 516 587-5000
New Hyde Park *(G-8538)*
Heart of Tea ..... F 917 725-3164
New York *(G-10073)*
Hmo Beverage Corporation ..... G 917 371-6100
Brooklyn *(G-1978)*
Hydrive Energy ..... G 914 925-9100
Rye *(G-14483)*
Johnnie Ryan Co Inc ..... F 716 282-1606
Niagara Falls *(G-12301)*
Juices Enterprises Inc ..... G 718 953-1860
Brooklyn *(G-2056)*
Just Beverages LLC ..... F 480 388-1133
Glens Falls *(G-5428)*
Just Goods Inc ..... F 917 294-0043
New York *(G-10385)*
Keurig Dr Pepper Inc ..... C 315 589-4911
Williamson *(G-16559)*
Keurig Dr Pepper Inc ..... D 914 846-2300
Elmsford *(G-4548)*
Keurig Dr Pepper Inc ..... G 718 246-6200
Brooklyn *(G-2069)*
La Cola 1 Inc ..... G 917 509-6669
New York *(G-10499)*
Life Earth Company ..... G 310 751-0627
New York *(G-10562)*
▲ **Liquid Management Partners LLC** ..... F 516 775-5050
New Hyde Park *(G-8548)*
Load/N/Go Beverage Corp ..... F 585 218-4019
Rochester *(G-13915)*
Long Blockchain Corp ..... F 855 542-2832
Farmingdale *(G-4810)*
Long Island Brand Bevs LLC ..... D 855 542-2832
Long Island City *(G-7504)*
Manhattan Special Bottling ..... F 718 388-4144
Brooklyn *(G-2159)*
▲ **Mayer Bros Apple Products Inc** ..... D 716 668-1787
West Seneca *(G-16301)*
Monfefo LLC ..... G 347 779-2600
Brooklyn *(G-2224)*
N Y Winstons Inc ..... G 212 665-3166
New York *(G-10870)*
Nantucket Allserve Inc ..... B 914 612-4000
Elmsford *(G-4555)*
New York Bottling Co Inc ..... F 718 963-3232
Bronx *(G-1340)*
▲ **New York Spring Water Inc** ..... E 212 777-4649
New York *(G-10942)*
Nexbev Industries LLC ..... F 646 648-1255
Blauvelt *(G-938)*
▲ **Nirvana Inc** ..... C 315 942-4900
Forestport *(G-5083)*
Owens Table Mixers LLC ..... G 650 303-7342
New York *(G-11073)*
Pepsi Beverages Co ..... G 518 782-2150
Latham *(G-7088)*
Pepsi Bottling Ventures LLC ..... D 631 772-6144
Patchogue *(G-12874)*
Pepsi Bottling Ventures LLC ..... E 631 226-9000
Amityville *(G-312)*
Pepsi Btlg Group Globl Fin LLC ..... G 914 767-6000
Somers *(G-14921)*
Pepsi-Cola Bottling Co NY Inc ..... C 914 699-2600
Mount Vernon *(G-8429)*
Pepsi-Cola Bottling Co NY Inc ..... A 718 392-1000
College Point *(G-3660)*
Pepsi-Cola Bottling Co NY Inc ..... D 718 892-1570
Bronx *(G-1355)*
◆ **Pepsi-Cola Bottling Group** ..... G 914 767-6000
White Plains *(G-16490)*
◆ **Pepsi-Cola Metro Btlg Co Inc** ..... G 914 767-6000
White Plains *(G-16491)*
Pepsi-Cola Metro Btlg Co Inc ..... E 914 253-2000
Purchase *(G-13393)*
Pepsi-Cola Metro Btlg Co Inc ..... B 518 834-7811
Keeseville *(G-6854)*
Pepsi-Cola Newburgh Btlg Inc ..... C 845 562-5400
Newburgh *(G-12241)*
Pepsi-Cola Operating Company ..... E 914 767-6000
White Plains *(G-16492)*
Pepsi-Cola Sales and Dist Inc ..... G 914 253-2000
Purchase *(G-13394)*
Pepsico ..... F 419 252-0247
Hawthorne *(G-5995)*
▲ **Pepsico** ..... E 914 801-1500
Valhalla *(G-15743)*
Pepsico Inc ..... B 914 742-4500
Valhalla *(G-15744)*
Pepsico Inc ..... A 914 253-2000
Purchase *(G-13396)*
Pepsico Inc ..... E 914 253-3474
White Plains *(G-16494)*
Pepsico Inc ..... F 914 253-2713
Purchase *(G-13397)*
◆ **Pepsico Inc** ..... A 914 253-2000
Purchase *(G-13395)*
Pepsico Capital Resources Inc ..... G 914 253-2000
Purchase *(G-13398)*
Pepsico Sales Inc ..... G 914 253-2000
Purchase *(G-13399)*

Purely Maple LLC .... F 203 997-9309
New York *(G-11278)*
Rochester Coca Cola Bottling .... E 607 739-5678
Horseheads *(G-6327)*
Rochester Coca Cola Bottling .... D 585 546-3900
Rochester *(G-14083)*
Royal Crown Financial .... G 718 234-7237
Brooklyn *(G-2419)*
Saratoga Spring Water Company .... E 518 584-6363
Saratoga Springs *(G-14598)*
Save More Beverage Corp .... G 518 371-2520
Halfmoon *(G-5669)*
▲ Scotia Beverages Inc .... A 518 370-3621
Schenectady *(G-14712)*
Shopping Center Wine & Liquor .... G 914 528-1600
Mohegan Lake *(G-8259)*
Snapp Too Enterprise .... G 718 224-5252
Flushing *(G-5046)*
Snapple Beverage Corp (del) .... D 914 612-4000
Rye Brook *(G-14495)*
Stewarts Processing Corp .... D 518 581-1200
Ballston Spa *(G-597)*
Street King LLC .... G 212 400-2200
New York *(G-11719)*
Superleaf LLC .... G 888 887-4318
Brooklyn *(G-2539)*
Switch Beverage Company LLC .... F 203 202-7383
Port Washington *(G-13310)*
Treo Brands LLC .... G 914 341-1850
Harrison *(G-5737)*
Unilever United States Inc .... G 212 546-0200
New York *(G-11944)*
Unilever United States Inc .... C 212 546-0200
New York *(G-11945)*

2087 Flavoring Extracts & Syrups

3v Company Inc .... E 718 858-7333
Brooklyn *(G-1440)*
Agua Enerviva LLC .... F 516 597-5440
Bethpage *(G-839)*
▲ American Almond Pdts Co Inc .... D 718 875-8310
Brooklyn *(G-1519)*
American Juice Company LLC .... G 347 620-0252
New York *(G-8833)*
Baldwin Richardson Foods Co .... C 315 986-2727
Macedon *(G-7695)*
Better Fresh Corp .... G 718 628-3682
Brooklyn *(G-1606)*
▲ Boylan Bottling Co Inc .... E 800 289-7978
New York *(G-9130)*
▲ Buffalo Blends Inc .... E 716 825-4422
Buffalo *(G-2741)*
◆ Citrus and Allied Essences Ltd .... C 516 354-1200
Floral Park *(G-4960)*
◆ Comax Manufacturing Corp .... D 631 249-0505
Melville *(G-8010)*
Constellation Brands Inc .... D 585 678-7100
Victor *(G-15837)*
Consumer Flavoring Extract Co .... F 718 435-0201
Brooklyn *(G-1712)*
Craftmaster Flavor Technology .... F 631 789-8607
Amityville *(G-270)*
Danisco US Inc .... D 585 277-4300
Rochester *(G-13734)*
▲ Delbia Do Company Inc .... E 718 585-2226
Bronx *(G-1255)*
Delbia Do Company Inc .... F 718 585-2226
Bronx *(G-1256)*
DSM Nutritional Products LLC .... C 518 372-5155
Schenectady *(G-14669)*
DSM Nutritional Products LLC .... C 518 372-5155
Glenville *(G-5445)*
▲ Esense LLC .... F 718 887-9779
Long Island City *(G-7439)*
◆ Flavormatic Industries LLC .... E 845 297-9100
Wappingers Falls *(G-15930)*
Fox 416 Corp .... E 718 385-4600
Brooklyn *(G-1903)*
Interntnal Flvors Frgrnces Inc .... C 212 765-5500
New York *(G-10251)*
Keurig Dr Pepper Inc .... C 315 589-4911
Williamson *(G-16559)*
Life On Earth Inc .... F 866 928-5070
New York *(G-10563)*
Mapleland Farms LLC .... G 518 854-7669
Salem *(G-14538)*
◆ Motts LLP .... C 972 673-8088
Elmsford *(G-4552)*
Mr Smoothie .... G 845 296-1686
Poughkeepsie *(G-13357)*
Natural Organics Labs Inc .... B 631 957-5600
Amityville *(G-305)*
◆ Pepsi-Cola Metro Btlg Co Inc .... G 914 767-6000
White Plains *(G-16491)*
◆ Pepsico Inc .... A 914 253-2000
Purchase *(G-13395)*
▼ Roar Beverages LLC .... E 631 683-5565
Huntington *(G-6410)*
Sabila Corp .... G 845 981-7128
Pine Island *(G-13003)*
◆ Star Kay White Inc .... D 845 268-2600
Congers *(G-3720)*
Synergy Flavors NY Company LLC .... G 585 232-6648
Rochester *(G-14151)*
Tealeafs .... G 716 688-8022
Williamsville *(G-16590)*
Terre Products Co Inc .... G 212 925-8989
New York *(G-11870)*
◆ Virginia Dare Extract Co Inc .... C 718 788-6320
Brooklyn *(G-2626)*
Wynn Starr Flavors Inc .... D 845 584-3080
Congers *(G-3723)*

2091 Fish & Seafoods, Canned & Cured

◆ Acme Smoked Fish Corp .... D 954 942-5598
Brooklyn *(G-1479)*
▲ Banner Smoked Fish Inc .... D 718 449-1992
Brooklyn *(G-1584)*
Blue Ocean Food Trading LLC .... G 718 689-4291
Brooklyn *(G-1620)*
◆ Catsmo LLC .... F 845 895-2296
Wallkill *(G-15903)*
Harbors Maine Lobster LLC .... E 516 775-2400
New Hyde Park *(G-8540)*
Incro Marketing USA Corp .... G 917 365-5552
New York *(G-10194)*
▲ Premium Ocean LLC .... F 917 231-1061
Bronx *(G-1365)*
Samaki Inc .... G 845 858-1012
Port Jervis *(G-13236)*
Sangster Foods Inc .... F 212 993-9129
Brooklyn *(G-2447)*

2092 Fish & Seafoods, Fresh & Frozen

6th Ave Gourmet Inc .... G 845 782-9067
Monroe *(G-8262)*
AB Seafood Trading Inc .... G 718 353-8848
Flushing *(G-4978)*
▲ Foo Yuan Food Products Co Inc .... G 212 925-2840
Long Island City *(G-7451)*
Montauk Inlet Seafood Inc .... G 631 668-3419
Montauk *(G-8306)*
Oceans Cuisine Ltd .... F 631 209-9200
Ridge *(G-13522)*
◆ Rich Products Corporation .... A 716 878-8000
Buffalo *(G-3037)*
Sea Breeze Fish & Seafood of S .... F 718 984-0447
Staten Island *(G-15133)*
▲ Shine Foods USA Inc .... G 516 784-9674
Glen Oaks *(G-5387)*

2095 Coffee

Altaro Corp .... F 855 674-2455
Tarrytown *(G-15473)*
Arista Coffee Inc .... F 347 531-0813
Maspeth *(G-7823)*
▲ Bh Coffee Company LLC .... D 914 377-2500
Elmsford *(G-4532)*
Birch Guys LLC .... G 917 763-0751
Long Island City *(G-7400)*
BK Associates Intl Inc .... F 607 432-1499
Oneonta *(G-12626)*
Brooklyn Roasting Works LLC .... G 718 855-1000
Brooklyn *(G-1647)*
Cafe Kubal .... G 315 278-2812
Syracuse *(G-15267)*
◆ Coffee Holding Co Inc .... D 718 832-0800
Staten Island *(G-15064)*
▼ Coffee Holding Company Inc .... G 718 832-0800
Brooklyn *(G-1704)*
Death Wish Coffee Company LLC .... F 518 400-1050
Ballston Spa *(G-579)*
▲ Eldorado Coffee Roasters Ltd .... D 718 418-4100
Maspeth *(G-7842)*
Elite Roasters Inc .... F 716 626-0307
East Amherst *(G-4189)*
▲ Empire Coffee Company Inc .... E 914 934-1100
Port Chester *(G-13199)*
Gillies Coffee Company .... E 718 499-7766
Brooklyn *(G-1927)*
Irving Farm Coffee Co Inc .... G 212 206-0707
New York *(G-10274)*
John A Vassilaros & Son Inc .... E 718 886-4140
Flushing *(G-5014)*
Jonathan Brose .... G 716 417-8978
Lockport *(G-7312)*
List & Beisler GMBH .... E 646 866-6960
New York *(G-10577)*
▲ Orens Daily Roast Inc .... G 212 348-5400
New York *(G-11061)*
P Pascal Inc .... E 914 969-7933
Yonkers *(G-16790)*
▲ Paul De Lima Company Inc .... D 315 457-3725
Liverpool *(G-7253)*
Paul De Lima Company Inc .... E 315 457-3725
Cicero *(G-3520)*
▲ Paul Delima Coffee Company .... G 315 457-3725
Cicero *(G-3521)*
Peaks Coffee Company .... G 315 565-1900
Cazenovia *(G-3325)*
Pintail Coffee Inc .... G 631 396-0808
Farmingdale *(G-4849)*
▲ Regal Trading Inc .... E 914 694-6100
Purchase *(G-13400)*
▲ S J McCullagh Inc .... E 716 856-3473
Buffalo *(G-3053)*
Sangster Foods Inc .... F 212 993-9129
Brooklyn *(G-2447)*
Star Mountain JFK Inc .... G 718 553-6787
Jamaica *(G-6679)*
Vega Coffee Inc .... G 415 881-7969
New York *(G-12003)*
Where Is Utica Cof Rasting Inc .... F 315 269-8898
Utica *(G-15739)*
▲ White Coffee Corp .... D 718 204-7900
Astoria *(G-449)*

SIC

2096 Potato Chips & Similar Prdts

BSD Top Direct Inc .... G 646 468-0156
West Babylon *(G-16141)*
▲ Emmi USA Inc .... F 845 268-9990
Orangeburg *(G-12675)*
Frito-Lay North America Inc .... D 607 775-7000
Binghamton *(G-886)*
◆ Hain Celestial Group Inc .... C 516 587-5000
New Hyde Park *(G-8538)*
◆ Ideal Snacks Corporation .... C 845 292-7000
Liberty *(G-7144)*
◆ Pepsico Inc .... A 914 253-2000
Purchase *(G-13395)*
Pepsico Inc .... B 914 253-2000
White Plains *(G-16493)*
Pepsico Inc .... D 914 767-6976
White Plains *(G-16495)*
Proformance Foods Inc .... G 703 869-3413
Brooklyn *(G-2355)*
Robs Really Good LLC .... F 516 671-4411
Sea Cliff *(G-14756)*
Saratoga Chips LLC .... G 877 901-6950
Saratoga Springs *(G-14597)*
Switch Beverage Company LLC .... F 203 202-7383
Port Washington *(G-13310)*
Terrells Potato Chip Co Inc .... D 315 437-2786
Syracuse *(G-15442)*
▲ TLC-Lc Inc .... E 212 756-8900
New York *(G-11852)*
Tortilleria Chinantla Inc .... G 718 302-0101
Brooklyn *(G-2574)*

2097 Ice

Adirondack Ice & Air Inc .... F 518 483-4340
Malone *(G-7717)*
Annies Ice .... G 585 593-5605
Wellsville *(G-16111)*
Arctic Glacier Newburgh Inc .... G 718 456-2013
Brooklyn *(G-1548)*
Arctic Glacier Newburgh Inc .... F 845 561-0549
Newburgh *(G-12215)*
Clayville Ice Co Inc .... G 315 839-5405
Clayville *(G-3556)*
Henry Newman LLC .... F 607 273-8512
Ithaca *(G-6581)*
Huntington Ice & Cube Corp .... F 718 456-2013
Brooklyn *(G-1988)*
Ice Cube Inc .... G 613 254-0071
Deer Park *(G-3986)*
◆ Mamitas Ices Ltd .... F 718 738-3238
Ozone Park *(G-12830)*
Maplewood Ice Co Inc .... E 518 499-2345
Whitehall *(G-16523)*

Employee Codes: A=Over 500 employees, B=251-500
C=101-250, D=51-100, E=20-50, F=10-19, G=5-9
2019 Harris
New York Manufacturers Directory
657

20 FOOD AND KINDRED PRODUCTS SIC SECTION

South Shore Ice Co Inc..........F....... 516 379-2056
Roosevelt *(G-14437)*

2098 Macaroni, Spaghetti & Noodles

AAA Noodle Products Mfg..........G....... 212 431-4090
New York *(G-8703)*
Bedessee Imports Ltd..........E....... 718 272-1300
Brooklyn *(G-1592)*
Borgattis Ravioli Egg Noodles..........G....... 718 367-3799
Bronx *(G-1231)*
Canton Noodle Corporation..........G....... 212 226-3276
New York *(G-9198)*
Cassinelli Food Products Inc..........G....... 718 274-4881
Long Island City *(G-7406)*
Deer Park Macaroni Co Inc..........F....... 631 667-4600
Deer Park *(G-3964)*
Deer Park Macaroni Co Inc..........F....... 631 667-4600
Deer Park *(G-3965)*
Momofuku 171 First Avenue LLC..........D....... 212 777-7773
New York *(G-10835)*
Nodus Noodle Corporation..........G....... 718 309-3725
Sunnyside *(G-15204)*
Noodle Education Inc..........E....... 646 289-7800
New York *(G-10987)*
▲ Piemonte Home Made Ravioli Co..........F....... 718 429-1972
Woodside *(G-16672)*
Piemonte Home Made Ravioli Co..........G....... 212 226-0475
New York *(G-11192)*
Queen Ann Macaroni Mfg Co Inc..........G....... 718 256-1061
Brooklyn *(G-2371)*
Ravioli Store Inc..........G....... 718 729-9300
Long Island City *(G-7572)*
▲ Twin Marquis Inc..........D....... 718 386-6868
Brooklyn *(G-2596)*
Wing Heung Noodle Inc..........F....... 212 966-7496
New York *(G-12119)*
Wing Kei Noodle Inc..........F....... 212 226-1644
New York *(G-12120)*
Wonton Food Inc..........F....... 212 677-8865
New York *(G-12131)*
Yum Yum Noodle Bar..........G....... 845 679-7992
Kingston *(G-6933)*

2099 Food Preparations, NEC

212kiddish Inc..........G....... 718 705-7227
Brooklyn *(G-1434)*
3v Company Inc..........E....... 718 858-7333
Brooklyn *(G-1440)*
ABC Peanut Butter LLC..........B....... 212 661-6886
New York *(G-8707)*
Ahhmigo LLC..........F....... 212 315-1818
New York *(G-8772)*
▲ American Almond Pdts Co Inc..........D....... 718 875-8310
Brooklyn *(G-1519)*
Andros Bowman Products LLC..........G....... 540 217-4100
Lyndonville *(G-7679)*
Armour Bearer Group Inc..........G....... 646 812-4487
Arverne *(G-413)*
Aromasong Usa Inc..........F....... 718 838-9669
Brooklyn *(G-1555)*
Aryzta LLC..........D....... 310 417-4700
Rochester *(G-13644)*
◆ Associated Brands Inc..........B....... 585 798-3475
Medina *(G-7970)*
Bainbridge & Knight LLC..........E....... 212 986-5100
New York *(G-9005)*
Baldwin Richardson Foods Co..........C....... 315 986-2727
Macedon *(G-7695)*
▲ Barilla America Ny Inc..........C....... 585 226-5600
Avon *(G-518)*
▲ Bektrom Foods Inc..........G....... 516 802-3800
Syosset *(G-15209)*
Beths Farm Kitchen..........G....... 518 799-3414
Stuyvesant Falls *(G-15183)*
Blue Tortilla LLC..........G....... 631 451-0100
Selden *(G-14760)*
▲ Bombay Kitchen Foods Inc..........F....... 516 767-7401
Port Washington *(G-13246)*
Brightline Ventures I LLC..........E....... 212 626-6829
New York *(G-9141)*
Brooklyns Best Pasta Co Inc..........G....... 917 881-3007
Brooklyn *(G-1651)*
Brooklynwrap Inc..........G....... 718 258-8088
Brooklyn *(G-1652)*
Bud Ravioli Center Inc..........G....... 718 356-4600
Staten Island *(G-15056)*
Buna Besta Tortillas..........G....... 347 987-3995
Brooklyn *(G-1655)*
Butterwood Desserts Inc..........E....... 716 652-0131
West Falls *(G-16208)*
Bylada Foods LLC..........E....... 845 623-1300
West Nyack *(G-16267)*
Cafe Spice Gct Inc..........C....... 845 863-0910
New Windsor *(G-8638)*
Capitol City Specialties Co..........G....... 518 486-8935
Albany *(G-56)*
Casablanca Foods LLC..........G....... 212 317-1111
New York *(G-9221)*
◆ Castella Imports Inc..........C....... 631 231-5500
Edgewood *(G-4398)*
Chan & Chan (usa) Corp..........G....... 718 388-9633
Brooklyn *(G-1688)*
Chan Kee Dried Bean Curd Inc..........G....... 718 622-0820
Brooklyn *(G-1689)*
▲ Chemicolloid Laboratories Inc..........F....... 516 747-2666
New Hyde Park *(G-8522)*
Child Nutrition Prog Dept Ed..........D....... 212 371-1000
New York *(G-9275)*
▲ China Huaren Organic Pdts Inc..........G....... 212 232-0120
New York *(G-9278)*
Chopt Creative Salad Co LLC..........F....... 646 233-2923
New York *(G-9288)*
Cookiebaker LLC..........G....... 716 878-8000
Buffalo *(G-2780)*
D R M Management Inc..........E....... 716 668-0333
Depew *(G-4086)*
Damn Good Foods Inc..........F....... 518 664-1414
Stillwater *(G-15157)*
Deedee Desserts LLC..........G....... 716 627-2330
Lake View *(G-6982)*
Diva Farms Ltd..........G....... 315 735-4397
Utica *(G-15697)*
▲ Dundee Foods LLC..........F....... 585 377-7700
Fairport *(G-4632)*
Event Services Corporation..........G....... 315 488-9357
Solvay *(G-14918)*
▲ Extreme Spices Inc..........G....... 917 496-4081
Maspeth *(G-7843)*
Fanshawe Foods LLC..........F....... 212 757-3130
New York *(G-9780)*
▲ Far Eastern Coconut Company..........F....... 631 851-8800
Central Islip *(G-3369)*
Farmers Hub LLC..........G....... 914 380-2945
White Plains *(G-16450)*
Fleischmanns Vinegar Co Inc..........E....... 315 587-4414
North Rose *(G-12394)*
Flik International/Compass..........E....... 212 450-4750
New York *(G-9817)*
Freshly Inc..........E....... 844 373-7459
New York *(G-9849)*
Frito-Lay North America Inc..........D....... 607 775-7000
Binghamton *(G-886)*
Gillies Coffee Company..........E....... 718 499-7766
Brooklyn *(G-1927)*
▼ Glenn Foods Inc..........F....... 516 377-1400
Freeport *(G-5158)*
Golden Taste Inc..........E....... 845 356-4133
Spring Valley *(G-14993)*
▲ Gourmet Boutique LLC..........C....... 718 977-1200
Jamaica *(G-6647)*
Gourmet Crafts Inc..........F....... 718 372-0505
Brooklyn *(G-1942)*
Gourmet Toast Corp..........G....... 718 852-4536
Brooklyn *(G-1944)*
Gravymaster Inc..........E....... 203 453-1893
Canajoharie *(G-3207)*
Great Eastern Pasta Works LLC..........E....... 631 956-0889
West Babylon *(G-16157)*
H & S Edible Products Corp..........E....... 914 413-3489
Mount Vernon *(G-8404)*
◆ Harney & Sons Tea Corp..........C....... 518 789-2100
Millerton *(G-8193)*
Heinz Mr..........G....... 718 761-3997
Staten Island *(G-15084)*
HP Hood LLC..........D....... 607 295-8134
Arkport *(G-399)*
Instantwhip of Buffalo Inc..........E....... 716 892-7031
Buffalo *(G-2885)*
▲ Johns Ravioli Company Inc..........F....... 914 576-7030
New Rochelle *(G-8618)*
◆ Joyva Corp..........D....... 718 497-0170
Brooklyn *(G-2052)*
Kale Factory Inc..........G....... 917 363-6361
Brooklyn *(G-2066)*
Kaneka America LLC..........D....... 212 705-4340
New York *(G-10404)*
◆ Kerry Bfnctnal Ingredients Inc..........D....... 608 363-1200
Norwich *(G-12488)*
Koppert Cress USA LLC..........E....... 631 779-3640
Riverhead *(G-13571)*
◆ Kozy Shack Enterprises LLC..........C....... 516 870-3000
Hicksville *(G-6099)*
Kozy Shack Enterprises LLC..........C....... 516 870-3000
Hicksville *(G-6100)*
Kraft Heinz Foods Company..........B....... 585 226-4400
Avon *(G-519)*
La Escondida Inc..........G....... 845 562-1387
Newburgh *(G-12230)*
▲ La Flor Products Company Inc..........E....... 631 851-9601
Hauppauge *(G-5863)*
Labella Pasta Inc..........G....... 845 331-9130
Kingston *(G-6906)*
Lakeside Cider Mill Farm Inc..........G....... 518 399-8359
Ballston Lake *(G-568)*
▲ Lams Foods Inc..........F....... 718 217-0476
Queens Village *(G-13410)*
Land OLakes Inc..........G....... 516 681-2980
Hicksville *(G-6102)*
▲ Larte Del Gelato Inc..........G....... 212 366-0570
New York *(G-10519)*
Lollipop Tree Inc..........E....... 845 471-8733
Auburn *(G-488)*
Lucky Lous Inc..........G....... 631 672-1932
Lake Grove *(G-6967)*
Lugo Nutrition Inc..........G....... 302 573-2503
Nyack *(G-12509)*
M & M Food Products Inc..........F....... 718 821-1970
Brooklyn *(G-2142)*
Maizteca Foods Inc..........E....... 718 641-3933
South Richmond Hill *(G-14946)*
Mandalay Food Products Inc..........G....... 718 230-3370
Brooklyn *(G-2155)*
Manhattan Milling & Drying Co..........E....... 516 496-1041
Woodbury *(G-16625)*
▲ Maramont Corporation..........B....... 718 439-8900
Brooklyn *(G-2163)*
▲ Martens Country Kit Pdts LLC..........F....... 315 776-8821
Port Byron *(G-13188)*
▲ Mediterrean Dyro Company..........E....... 718 786-4888
Long Island City *(G-7521)*
Merb LLC..........F....... 631 393-3621
Farmingdale *(G-4820)*
▲ Meta-Therm Corp..........F....... 914 697-4840
White Plains *(G-16476)*
Mighty Quinns Barbeque LLC..........C....... 973 777-8340
New York *(G-10802)*
Milnot Holding Corporation..........G....... 518 839-0300
Amsterdam *(G-349)*
Mizkan America Inc..........F....... 585 798-5720
Medina *(G-7985)*
Mizkan America Inc..........D....... 585 765-9171
Lyndonville *(G-7680)*
Mizkan Americas Inc..........F....... 315 483-6944
Sodus *(G-14913)*
Moira New Hope Food Pantry..........E....... 518 529-6524
Moira *(G-8261)*
Momentive Performance Mtls Inc..........D....... 914 784-4807
Tarrytown *(G-15484)*
Mondelez Global LLC..........G....... 585 345-3300
Batavia *(G-630)*
Morris Kitchen Inc..........F....... 646 413-5186
Brooklyn *(G-2227)*
Mullers Cider House LLC..........G....... 585 287-5875
Rochester *(G-13959)*
▲ Natural Lab Inc..........G....... 718 321-8848
Flushing *(G-5026)*
Natural Matters Inc..........G....... 212 337-3077
New York *(G-10892)*
Naturally Free Food Inc..........G....... 631 361-9710
Smithtown *(G-14903)*
Nestle Healthcare Ntrtn Inc..........G....... 516 249-5085
Farmingdale *(G-4835)*
New York Ravioli Pasta Co Inc..........E....... 516 270-2852
New Hyde Park *(G-8553)*
Nine Pin Ciderworks LLC..........F....... 518 449-9999
Albany *(G-105)*
Noaspence Inc..........G....... 516 433-7848
Hicksville *(G-6114)*
North Shore Farms Two Ltd..........G....... 516 280-6880
Mineola *(G-8239)*
▼ Old Dutch Mustard Co Inc..........G....... 516 466-0522
Great Neck *(G-5576)*
Omg Desserts Inc..........F....... 585 698-1561
Rochester *(G-13986)*
▲ Once Again Nut Butter Collectv..........D....... 585 468-2535
Nunda *(G-12497)*
Original Hrkmer Cnty Chese Inc..........D....... 315 895-7428
Ilion *(G-6477)*
▲ Parnasa International Inc..........G....... 516 394-0400
Valley Stream *(G-15789)*

Peaceful Valley Maple Farm ....G 518 762-0491
Johnstown *(G-6835)*

▲ **Peanut Butter & Co Inc** ....E 212 757-3130
New York *(G-11128)*

Pelican Bay Ltd ....F 718 729-9300
Long Island City *(G-7552)*

Pellicano Specialty Foods Inc ....F 716 822-2366
Buffalo *(G-2995)*

Pennant Ingredients Inc ....D 585 235-8160
Rochester *(G-14011)*

Ponti Rossi Inc ....G 347 506-9616
Brooklyn *(G-2327)*

Pride Pak Inc ....D 905 828-2149
Medina *(G-7986)*

Private Lbel Fods Rchester Inc ....E 585 254-9205
Rochester *(G-14046)*

Pure Functional Foods Inc ....E 315 294-0733
Savannah *(G-14624)*

▲ **Pure Golds Family Corp** ....D 516 483-5600
Hempstead *(G-6024)*

Qualitea Imports Inc ....G 917 624-6750
Suffern *(G-15195)*

Radicle Farm LLC ....G 315 226-3294
New York *(G-11315)*

▲ **Raw Indulgence Ltd** ....F 866 498-4671
Elmsford *(G-4561)*

Rawpothecary Inc ....G 917 783-7770
Brooklyn *(G-2385)*

▲ **Real Co Inc** ....G 347 433-8549
Valley Cottage *(G-15762)*

▲ **Redland Foods Corp** ....F 716 288-9061
Cheektowaga *(G-3457)*

◆ **Rich Products Corporation** ....A 716 878-8000
Buffalo *(G-3037)*

▲ **Rob Salamida Company Inc** ....F 607 729-4868
Johnson City *(G-6821)*

Royal Kosher Foods LLC ....G 347 221-1867
Brooklyn *(G-2421)*

Salvador Colletti Blank ....G 718 217-6725
Douglaston *(G-4139)*

Sapienza Pastry Inc ....E 516 352-5232
Elmont *(G-4525)*

Schutt Cider Mill ....F 585 872-2924
Webster *(G-16097)*

▲ **Seasons Soyfood Inc** ....G 718 797-9896
Brooklyn *(G-2454)*

◆ **Settons Intl Foods Inc** ....D 631 543-8090
Commack *(G-3702)*

Sfoglini LLC ....F 646 872-1035
Brooklyn *(G-2459)*

▲ **Sneaky Chef Foods LLC** ....F 914 301-3277
Tarrytown *(G-15493)*

Spf Holdings II LLC ....G 212 750-8300
New York *(G-11668)*

Spread-Mmms LLC ....G 917 727-8116
Brooklyn *(G-2504)*

▲ **Steinway Pasta & Gelati Inc** ....F 718 246-5414
Lindenhurst *(G-7194)*

◆ **Sugar Foods Corporation** ....E 212 753-6900
New York *(G-11734)*

Sugar Shack Desert Company Inc ....G 518 523-7540
Lake Placid *(G-6978)*

Sunrise Snacks Rockland Inc ....F 845 352-2676
Monsey *(G-8298)*

Tea Life LLC ....G 516 365-7711
Manhasset *(G-7773)*

Tortilla Heaven Inc ....E 845 339-1550
Kingston *(G-6924)*

Tortilleria Oaxaca ....G 347 355-7336
Staten Island *(G-15148)*

▲ **Tuv Taam Corp** ....E 718 855-2207
Brooklyn *(G-2594)*

▲ **Twin Marquis Inc** ....D 718 386-6868
Brooklyn *(G-2596)*

◆ **U S Sugar Co Inc** ....E 716 828-1170
Buffalo *(G-3107)*

UFS Industries Inc ....D 718 822-1100
Mount Vernon *(G-8452)*

Ultra Thin Ready To Bake Pizza ....E 516 679-6655
Deer Park *(G-4053)*

◆ **Victoria Fine Foods LLC** ....D 718 649-1635
Brooklyn *(G-2621)*

Victoria Fine Foods Holding Co ....G 718 649-1635
Brooklyn *(G-2622)*

Vinegar Hill Asset LLC ....G 718 469-0342
Brooklyn *(G-2624)*

▲ **VIP Foods Inc** ....E 718 821-5330
Ridgewood *(G-13558)*

Whitsons Food Svc Bronx Corp ....B 631 424-2700
Islandia *(G-6540)*

▲ **Win-Holt Equipment Corp** ....E 516 222-0335
Woodbury *(G-16634)*

▲ **Wm E Martin and Sons Co Inc** ....E 516 605-2444
Roslyn *(G-14452)*

▲ **Wonder Natural Foods Corp** ....G 631 726-4433
Water Mill *(G-15972)*

Wonton Food Inc ....E 718 784-8178
Long Island City *(G-7642)*

▲ **Wonton Food Inc** ....C 718 628-6868
Brooklyn *(G-2655)*

Wonton Food Inc ....F 212 677-8865
New York *(G-12131)*

21 TOBACCO PRODUCTS

2111 Cigarettes

East End ....F 716 532-2622
Collins *(G-3673)*

Epuffer Inc ....G 718 374-6030
Brooklyn *(G-1844)*

Jacobs Tobacco Company ....E 518 358-4948
Hogansburg *(G-6165)*

Onondaga Nation ....G 315 469-3230
Nedrow *(G-8479)*

Philip Morris Intl Inc ....D 917 663-2000
New York *(G-11181)*

PMI Global Services Inc ....E 917 663-2000
New York *(G-11213)*

R J Reynolds Tobacco Company ....C 716 871-1553
Tonawanda *(G-15572)*

Schweitzer-Mauduit Intl Inc ....C 518 329-4222
Ancram *(G-365)*

▲ **Seneca Manufacturing Company** ....G 716 945-4400
Salamanca *(G-14532)*

Seneca Nation Enterprise ....F 716 934-7430
Irving *(G-6501)*

Vector Group Ltd ....B 212 409-2800
New York *(G-12002)*

2121 Cigars

American Cigar ....G 718 969-0008
Fresh Meadows *(G-5194)*

Mafco Consolidated Group Inc ....F 212 572-8600
New York *(G-10659)*

2131 Tobacco, Chewing & Snuff

Elab Smokers Boutique ....G 585 865-4513
Rochester *(G-13775)*

Mafco Consolidated Group Inc ....F 212 572-8600
New York *(G-10659)*

National Tobacco Company LP ....F 212 253-8185
New York *(G-10888)*

Standard Diversified Inc ....G 302 824-7062
Mineola *(G-8250)*

2141 Tobacco Stemming & Redrying

Schweitzer-Mauduit Intl Inc ....C 518 329-4222
Ancram *(G-365)*

22 TEXTILE MILL PRODUCTS

2211 Cotton, Woven Fabric

1510 Associates LLC ....G 212 828-8720
New York *(G-8665)*

A and J Apparel Corp ....G 212 398-8899
New York *(G-8690)*

A3 Apparel LLC ....G 888 403-9669
New York *(G-8701)*

Accolade USA Inc ....C 866 423-5071
Cheektowaga *(G-3434)*

Advanced Fashions Technology ....G 212 221-0606
New York *(G-8755)*

▲ **Ann Gish Inc** ....G 212 969-9200
New York *(G-8871)*

▲ **Apollo Apparel Group LLC** ....F 212 398-6585
New York *(G-8885)*

Avitto Leather Goods Inc ....G 212 219-7501
New York *(G-8979)*

▲ **Axis Na LLC** ....F 212 840-4005
New York *(G-8984)*

Bandier Corp ....G 212 242-5400
New York *(G-9011)*

◆ **Basileus Company LLC** ....F 315 963-3516
Manlius *(G-7774)*

▲ **Benartex LLC** ....E 212 840-3250
New York *(G-9043)*

▲ **Beyond Loom Inc** ....G 212 575-3100
New York *(G-9064)*

▲ **Blu Sand LLC** ....G 212 564-1147
New York *(G-9105)*

Brooklyn Denim Co ....F 718 782-2600
Brooklyn *(G-1642)*

▲ **Brunschwig & Fils LLC** ....F 800 538-1880
Bethpage *(G-840)*

◆ **Cai Inc** ....E 212 819-0008
New York *(G-9176)*

Charming Fashion Inc ....G 212 730-2872
New York *(G-9266)*

Comet Intl Trdg Co Inc ....F 731 599-2430
Brooklyn *(G-1708)*

Creation Baumann USA Inc ....E 516 764-7431
Rockville Centre *(G-14231)*

Cy Fashion Corp ....G 212 730-8600
New York *(G-9440)*

Designway Ltd ....G 212 254-2220
New York *(G-9509)*

▲ **Equipment Apparel LLC** ....D 212 502-1890
New York *(G-9697)*

▲ **Erin Snow Ltd** ....G 212 675-7762
New York *(G-9703)*

Fab Industries Corp ....B 516 498-3200
Great Neck *(G-5553)*

▲ **French Accnt Rugs & Tapestries** ....G 212 686-6097
New York *(G-9845)*

Geordie Magee Uphl & Canvas ....G 315 676-7679
Brewerton *(G-1150)*

◆ **Gerli & Co Inc** ....B 212 213-1919
New York *(G-9913)*

Gotham T-Shirt Corp ....G 516 676-0900
Sea Cliff *(G-14755)*

H Group LLC ....F 212 719-5500
New York *(G-10015)*

Haleys Comet Seafood Corp ....E 212 571-1828
New York *(G-10022)*

Hanesbrands Inc ....G 212 576-9300
New York *(G-10032)*

▲ **Horizon Apparel Mfg Inc** ....G 516 361-4878
Atlantic Beach *(G-456)*

In2green LLC ....G 914 693-5054
Hastings On Hudson *(G-5749)*

Internationl Studios Inc ....G 212 819-1616
New York *(G-10250)*

Joy of Learning ....G 718 443-6463
Brooklyn *(G-2050)*

▲ **Jrg Apparel Group Company Ltd** ....E 212 997-0900
New York *(G-10372)*

Knightly Endeavors ....F 845 340-0949
Kingston *(G-6905)*

▲ **La Lame Inc** ....G 212 921-9770
New York *(G-10502)*

◆ **Lydall Performance Mtl Inc** ....C 518 273-6320
Green Island *(G-5609)*

▲ **Magic Brands International LLC** ....F 212 563-4999
New York *(G-10666)*

Marsha Fleisher ....F 845 679-6500
Woodstock *(G-16686)*

▼ **Mason Contract Products LLC** ....D 516 328-6900
New Hyde Park *(G-8550)*

Meder Textile Co Inc ....G 516 883-0409
Port Washington *(G-13284)*

Medline Industries Inc ....B 845 344-3301
Middletown *(G-8163)*

Melwood Partners Inc ....F 631 923-0134
Melville *(G-8045)*

Mgk Group Inc ....E 212 989-2732
New York *(G-10788)*

Michael Stuart Inc ....E 718 821-0704
Brooklyn *(G-2204)*

N Y Contract Seating Inc ....G 718 417-9298
Maspeth *(G-7860)*

Navas Designs Inc ....E 818 988-9050
New York *(G-10898)*

▲ **Neilson International Inc** ....G 631 454-0400
Farmingdale *(G-4834)*

Nochairs Inc ....G 917 748-8731
New York *(G-10983)*

◆ **Northpoint Trading Inc** ....F 212 481-8001
New York *(G-10997)*

▲ **Northwest Company LLC** ....C 516 484-6996
Roslyn *(G-14449)*

▲ **Ortex Home Textile Inc** ....G 718 241-7298
Brooklyn *(G-2291)*

Pacific City International ....F 646 309-1250
New York *(G-11090)*

Paramount Cord & Brackets ....G 212 325-9100
White Plains *(G-16484)*

Perfect Print Inc ....E 718 832-5280
Brooklyn *(G-2313)*

Employee Codes: A=Over 500 employees, B=251-500
C=101-250, D=51-100, E=20-50, F=10-19, G=5-9

2019 Harris
New York Manufacturers Directory

659

▲ **Phoenix Usa LLC** ....G.... 646 351-6598
New York *(G-11184)*
Premium 5 Kids LLC ....F.... 212 563-4999
New York *(G-11231)*
▲ **Renaissnce Crpt Tapestries Inc** ....F.... 212 696-0080
New York *(G-11360)*
▲ **Scalamandre Wallpaper Inc** ....B.... 631 467-8800
Hauppauge *(G-5934)*
Schneider Mills Inc ....C.... 828 632-0801
New York *(G-11511)*
SD Eagle Global Inc ....G.... 516 822-1778
Jericho *(G-6803)*
Shahin Designs Ltd ....G.... 212 737-7225
New York *(G-11554)*
Shindo Usa Inc ....G.... 212 868-9311
New York *(G-11567)*
▲ **Sita Finishing Inc** ....F.... 718 417-5295
Brooklyn *(G-2482)*
Sky Laundromat Inc ....E.... 718 639-7070
Jamaica *(G-6677)*
Ssjjj Manufacturing LLC ....B.... 516 498-3200
Great Neck *(G-5590)*
Success Apparel LLC ....G.... 212 502-1890
New York *(G-11733)*
▲ **US Design Group Ltd** ....F.... 212 354-4070
New York *(G-11974)*
Versailles Drapery Upholstery ....F.... 212 533-2059
Long Island City *(G-7631)*
Vf Services LLC ....G.... 212 575-7820
New York *(G-12022)*
Wallace Home Design Ctr ....G.... 631 765-3890
Southold *(G-14971)*
◆ **Westpoint Home LLC** ....A.... 212 930-2000
New York *(G-12096)*
▲ **Xing Lin USA Intl Corp** ....G.... 212 947-4846
New York *(G-12151)*

2221 Silk & Man-Made Fiber

A B C Elastic Corp ....G.... 718 388-2953
Brooklyn *(G-1453)*
Albany International Corp ....C.... 518 445-2200
Rensselaer *(G-13470)*
Apex Texicon Inc ....E.... 516 239-4400
New York *(G-8883)*
Art People Inc ....G.... 212 431-4865
New York *(G-8915)*
▲ **Beyond Loom Inc** ....G.... 212 575-3100
New York *(G-9064)*
▲ **Chf Industries Inc** ....E.... 212 951-7800
New York *(G-9273)*
▲ **Concepts Nyc Inc** ....E.... 212 244-1033
New York *(G-9372)*
Creation Baumann USA Inc ....E.... 516 764-7431
Rockville Centre *(G-14231)*
Eastern Silk Mills Inc ....G.... 212 730-1300
New York *(G-9611)*
Ess Bee Industries Inc ....E.... 718 894-5202
Brooklyn *(G-1850)*
◆ **Fabric Resources Intl Ltd** ....F.... 516 829-4550
Great Neck *(G-5554)*
◆ **Fiber Glass Industries Inc** ....D.... 518 842-4000
Amsterdam *(G-337)*
Fibrix LLC ....E.... 716 683-4100
Depew *(G-4089)*
▲ **Frp Apparel Group LLC** ....G.... 212 695-8000
New York *(G-9853)*
◆ **Gerli & Co Inc** ....B.... 212 213-1919
New York *(G-9913)*
Himatsingka America Inc ....E.... 212 252-0802
New York *(G-10102)*
Intertex USA Inc ....F.... 212 279-3601
New York *(G-10253)*
◆ **Ivi Services Inc** ....D.... 607 729-5111
Binghamton *(G-897)*
▲ **Jag Manufacturing Inc** ....E.... 518 762-9558
Johnstown *(G-6832)*
Jakob Schlaepfer Inc ....G.... 212 221-2323
New York *(G-10302)*
JM Manufacturer Inc ....G.... 212 869-0626
New York *(G-10344)*
Kragel Co Inc ....G.... 716 648-1344
Hamburg *(G-5685)*
▲ **La Lame Inc** ....G.... 212 921-9770
New York *(G-10502)*
▼ **Laregence Inc** ....E.... 212 736-2548
New York *(G-10517)*
Maharam Fabric Corporation ....G.... 631 582-3434
Yaphank *(G-16716)*
Marly Home Industries USA Inc ....G.... 718 388-3030
Brooklyn *(G-2172)*
Mgk Group Inc ....E.... 212 989-2732
New York *(G-10788)*
National Contract Industries ....G.... 212 249-0045
New York *(G-10881)*
▲ **New York Poplin LLC** ....G.... 718 768-3296
Brooklyn *(G-2264)*
▲ **Newtex Industries Inc** ....E.... 585 924-9135
Victor *(G-15858)*
Pierce Arrow Drapery Mfg ....G.... 716 876-3023
Buffalo *(G-3003)*
▲ **Polytex Inc** ....D.... 716 549-5100
Angola *(G-370)*
▲ **Scalamandre Silks Inc** ....D.... 212 980-3888
New York *(G-11499)*
▲ **Scalamandre Wallpaper Inc** ....B.... 631 467-8800
Hauppauge *(G-5934)*
Schneider Mills Inc ....C.... 828 632-0801
New York *(G-11511)*
Shengkun North America Inc ....F.... 212 217-2460
New York *(G-11563)*
Stern & Stern Industries Inc ....D.... 607 324-4485
Hornell *(G-6303)*
Superior Fiber Mills Inc ....E.... 718 782-7500
Brooklyn *(G-2538)*
Tli Import Inc ....G.... 917 578-4568
Brooklyn *(G-2568)*
Toltec Fabrics Inc ....C.... 212 706-9310
New York *(G-11857)*
Toray Industries Inc ....G.... 212 697-8150
New York *(G-11869)*
◆ **Unique Quality Fabrics Inc** ....G.... 845 343-3070
Middletown *(G-8182)*
▲ **US Home Textiles Group LLC** ....G.... 212 768-3030
New York *(G-11977)*
◆ **Westpoint Home LLC** ....A.... 212 930-2000
New York *(G-12096)*
▲ **Zorlu USA Inc** ....D.... 212 689-4622
New York *(G-12184)*

2231 Wool, Woven Fabric

▲ **Acker & Ll Mills Corporation** ....G.... 212 307-7247
New York *(G-8727)*
Alicia Adams Alpaca Inc ....G.... 845 868-3366
Millbrook *(G-8187)*
▲ **Beyond Loom Inc** ....G.... 212 575-3100
New York *(G-9064)*
◆ **Citisource Industries Inc** ....E.... 212 683-1033
New York *(G-9307)*
◆ **Fabric Resources Intl Ltd** ....F.... 516 829-4550
Great Neck *(G-5554)*
▲ **Hawkins Fabrics Inc** ....E.... 518 773-9550
Johnstown *(G-6830)*
▲ **Interaxissourcingcom Inc** ....E.... 212 905-6001
New York *(G-10236)*
▲ **Light House Hill Marketing** ....F.... 212 354-1338
New York *(G-10567)*
▲ **Loomstate LLC** ....E.... 212 219-2300
New York *(G-10602)*
Nazim Izzak Inc ....G.... 212 920-5546
Long Island City *(G-7534)*
▲ **Oakhurst Partners LLC** ....G.... 212 502-3220
New York *(G-11024)*
▲ **Pinder International Inc** ....G.... 631 273-0324
Hauppauge *(G-5915)*
▲ **Scalamandre Wallpaper Inc** ....B.... 631 467-8800
Hauppauge *(G-5934)*
◆ **Warren Corporation** ....C.... 917 379-3434
New York *(G-12074)*
Woolmark Americas Inc ....G.... 347 767-3160
New York *(G-12133)*
▲ **Yarnz International Inc** ....G.... 212 868-5883
New York *(G-12160)*

2241 Fabric Mills, Cotton, Wool, Silk & Man-Made

Albany International Corp ....C.... 518 445-2200
Rensselaer *(G-13470)*
Ambind Corp ....G.... 716 836-4365
Buffalo *(G-2693)*
American Canvas Binders Corp ....G.... 914 969-0300
Yonkers *(G-16734)*
▲ **American Trim Mfg Inc** ....E.... 518 239-8151
Durham *(G-4183)*
▲ **Bardwil Industries Inc** ....C.... 212 944-1870
New York *(G-9014)*
Breton Industries Inc ....C.... 518 842-3030
Amsterdam *(G-329)*
Champion Zipper Corp ....G.... 212 239-0414
New York *(G-9258)*
▲ **Colonial Tag & Label Co Inc** ....F.... 516 482-0508
Great Neck *(G-5546)*
▲ **Danray Textiles Corp** ....F.... 212 354-5213
New York *(G-9470)*
Depot Label Company Inc ....G.... 631 467-2952
Patchogue *(G-12864)*
Eiseman-Ludmar Co Inc ....F.... 516 932-6990
Hicksville *(G-6083)*
▲ **Essential Ribbons Inc** ....G.... 212 967-4173
New York *(G-9710)*
▲ **Fashion Ribbon Co Inc** ....E.... 718 482-0100
Long Island City *(G-7445)*
Imperial-Harvard Label Co ....F.... 212 736-8420
New York *(G-10186)*
Itc Mfg Group Inc ....F.... 212 684-3696
New York *(G-10278)*
▲ **J & M Textile Co Inc** ....F.... 212 268-8000
New York *(G-10282)*
Jakob Schlaepfer Inc ....G.... 212 221-2323
New York *(G-10302)*
▲ **La Lame Inc** ....G.... 212 921-9770
New York *(G-10502)*
Label Source Inc ....G.... 212 244-1403
New York *(G-10503)*
▲ **Labels Inter-Global Inc** ....F.... 212 398-0006
New York *(G-10504)*
Labeltex Mills Inc ....G.... 212 279-6165
New York *(G-10505)*
Marketing Action Xecutives Inc ....G.... 212 971-9155
New York *(G-10712)*
▲ **Mergence Studios Ltd** ....F.... 212 288-5616
Hauppauge *(G-5887)*
New York Binding Co Inc ....E.... 718 729-2454
Long Island City *(G-7539)*
▲ **Newtex Industries Inc** ....E.... 585 924-9135
Victor *(G-15858)*
▲ **R-Pac International Corp** ....E.... 212 465-1818
New York *(G-11313)*
▲ **Scalamandre Silks Inc** ....D.... 212 980-3888
New York *(G-11499)*
▲ **Schoen Trimming & Cord Co Inc** ....F.... 212 255-3949
New York *(G-11512)*
▲ **Skil-Care Corporation** ....C.... 914 963-2040
Yonkers *(G-16798)*
▲ **Sml USA Inc** ....E.... 212 736-8800
New York *(G-11626)*
Solstiss Inc ....G.... 212 719-9194
New York *(G-11641)*
▲ **Sturges Manufacturing Co Inc** ....D.... 315 732-6159
Utica *(G-15734)*
Triangle Label Tag Inc ....G.... 718 875-3030
Brooklyn *(G-2583)*
Valley Industrial Products Inc ....E.... 631 385-9300
Huntington *(G-6424)*

2251 Hosiery, Women's Full & Knee Length

Brach Knitting Mills Inc ....F.... 845 651-4450
Florida *(G-4968)*
▲ **Classic Hosiery Inc** ....E.... 845 342-6661
Middletown *(G-8142)*
Ellis Products Corp ....G.... 516 791-3732
Valley Stream *(G-15778)*
▲ **Fine Sheer Industries Inc** ....F.... 212 594-4224
New York *(G-9804)*
◆ **Gina Group LLC** ....E.... 212 947-2445
New York *(G-9922)*
▼ **Hot Sox Company Incorporated** ....E.... 212 957-2000
New York *(G-10130)*
▲ **Trimfit Inc** ....E.... 215 245-1122
New York *(G-11900)*

2252 Hosiery, Except Women's

▲ **Ace Drop Cloth Canvas Pdts Inc** ....E.... 718 731-1550
Bronx *(G-1208)*
▲ **Ashko Group LLC** ....F.... 212 594-6050
New York *(G-8931)*
Customize Elite Socks LLC ....G.... 212 533-8551
New York *(G-9437)*
▲ **Fine Sheer Industries Inc** ....F.... 212 594-4224
New York *(G-9804)*
Galiva Inc ....G.... 903 600-5755
Brooklyn *(G-1916)*
Gbg Socks LLC ....E.... 646 839-7000
New York *(G-9887)*
◆ **Gina Group LLC** ....E.... 212 947-2445
New York *(G-9922)*
▲ **Haddad Hosiery LLC** ....G.... 212 251-0022
New York *(G-10019)*
▲ **High Point Design LLC** ....F.... 212 354-2400
New York *(G-10094)*

▼ Hot Sox Company Incorporated ..... E 212 957-2000
New York (G-10130)
La Strada Dance Footwear Inc ..... G 631 242-1401
Deer Park (G-3999)
▲ Leadertex Intl Inc ..... E 212 563-2242
New York (G-10531)
▲ Look By M Inc ..... G 212 213-4019
New York (G-10599)
Lr Acquisition LLC ..... F 212 301-8765
New York (G-10620)
▲ Majesty Brands LLC ..... G 212 283-3400
New York (G-10676)
New Hampton Creations Inc ..... G 212 244-7474
New York (G-10925)
◆ Palmbay Ltd ..... G 718 424-3388
Flushing (G-5034)
Sockbin ..... G 917 519-1119
Brooklyn (G-2491)
Socks and More of NY Inc ..... G 718 769-1785
Brooklyn (G-2492)
Sticky Socks LLC ..... S 212 541-5927
New York (G-11712)
Strassburg Medical LLC ..... G 716 433-9368
North Tonawanda (G-12456)
▲ Trimfit Inc ..... E 215 245-1122
New York (G-11900)
United Retail II ..... G 212 966-9692
New York (G-11954)
▲ You and ME Legwear LLC ..... F 212 279-9292
New York (G-12165)

2253 Knit Outerwear Mills

▲ 180s LLC ..... E 410 534-6320
New York (G-8666)
79 Metro Ltd ..... E 212 944-4030
New York (G-8685)
A & B Finishing Inc ..... E 718 522-4702
Brooklyn (G-1449)
Accurate Knitting Corp ..... G 646 552-2216
Brooklyn (G-1472)
Alpha Knitting Mills Inc ..... F 718 628-6300
Brooklyn (G-1513)
American T Shirts Inc ..... G 212 563-7125
New York (G-8838)
Andrea Strongwater ..... G 212 873-0905
New York (G-8858)
▲ Asian Global Trading Corp ..... F 718 786-0998
Long Island City (G-7390)
▲ B & E Sweater Mills Inc ..... F 718 456-8693
Brooklyn (G-1578)
▲ Betsy & Adam Ltd ..... E 212 302-3750
New York (G-9061)
▲ Binghamton Knitting Co Inc ..... E 607 722-6941
Binghamton (G-866)
Blueberry Knitting Inc ..... F 718 599-6520
Brooklyn (G-1623)
▲ Bock Family Holdings Inc ..... E 212 921-5688
New York (G-9116)
Central Mills Inc ..... C 212 764-9011
New York (G-9244)
▲ Charter Ventures LLC ..... F 212 868-0222
New York (G-9267)
▲ Domani Fashions Corp ..... G 718 797-0505
Brooklyn (G-1786)
▲ Dressy Tessy Inc ..... G 212 869-0750
New York (G-9576)
E I Du Pont De Nemours & Co ..... E 716 876-4420
Buffalo (G-2807)
Elegant Headwear Co Inc ..... G 212 695-8520
New York (G-9642)
▲ Emerald Holdings Inc ..... G 718 797-4404
Brooklyn (G-1829)
Fashion Avenue Knits Inc ..... F 718 456-9000
New York (G-9786)
▲ Freedom Rains Inc ..... G 646 710-4512
New York (G-9844)
Gabani Inc ..... G 631 283-4930
Southampton (G-14954)
▲ GAME Sportswear Ltd ..... E 914 962-1701
Yorktown Heights (G-16817)
▲ Gce International Inc ..... D 212 704-4800
New York (G-9890)
▲ Gildan Apparel USA Inc ..... D 212 476-0341
New York (G-9919)
▲ Golden Leaves Knitwear Inc ..... F 718 875-8235
Brooklyn (G-1938)
Grand Processing Inc ..... E 718 388-0600
Brooklyn (G-1948)
Great Adirondack Yarn Company ..... F 518 843-3381
Amsterdam (G-339)

▲ Hamil America Inc ..... F 212 244-2645
New York (G-10025)
Hania By Anya Cole LLC ..... G 212 302-3550
New York (G-10033)
▲ Hertling Trousers Inc ..... F 718 784-6100
Brooklyn (G-1977)
IaMmaliamills LLC ..... G 805 845-2137
Brooklyn (G-1992)
▲ J & D Walter Distributors Inc ..... F 518 449-1606
Glenmont (G-5413)
J & E Talit Inc ..... G 718 850-1333
Richmond Hill (G-13505)
Jeric Knit Wear ..... G 631 979-8827
Smithtown (G-14901)
Jfs Inc ..... G 646 264-1200
New York (G-10335)
▲ Jj Basics LLC ..... E 212 768-4779
New York (G-10342)
▲ Julia Knit Inc ..... G 718 848-1900
Ozone Park (G-12828)
K & S Childrens Wear Inc ..... G 718 624-0006
Brooklyn (G-2062)
KD Dids Inc ..... G 718 402-2012
Bronx (G-1305)
Keryakos Inc ..... F 518 344-7092
Schenectady (G-14693)
Knit Resource Center Ltd ..... G 212 221-1990
New York (G-10459)
Lids Corporation ..... E 518 459-7060
Albany (G-95)
▲ Lloyds Fashions Inc ..... D 631 435-3353
Brentwood (G-1141)
Lynch Knitting Mills Inc ..... G 718 821-3436
Brooklyn (G-2139)
▲ M A M Knitting Mills Corp ..... E 800 570-0C93
Brooklyn (G-2144)
▲ M B M Manufacturing Inc ..... F 718 769-4148
Brooklyn (G-2146)
Machinit Inc ..... G 631 454-9297
Farmingdale (G-4813)
Mann Consultants LLC ..... E 914 763-0512
Waccabuc (G-15881)
Manrico Usa Inc ..... G 212 794-4200
New York (G-10693)
Marble Knits Inc ..... E 718 237-7990
New York (G-2164)
Mars Fashions Inc ..... E 718 402-2200
Bronx (G-1323)
Matchables Inc ..... F 718 389-9318
Brooklyn (G-2178)
Mdj Sales Associates Inc ..... G 914 420-5897
Mamaroneck (G-7749)
Mongru Neckwear Inc ..... E 718 706-0406
Long Island City (G-7529)
Native Textiles Inc ..... G 212 951-5100
New York (G-10889)
New York Sweater Company Inc ..... E 845 629-9533
New York (G-10943)
North Star Knitting Mills Inc ..... G 718 894-4848
Glendale (G-5405)
NY Denim Inc ..... E 212 764-6668
New York (G-11011)
Phillips-Van Heusen Europe ..... F 212 381-3500
New York (G-11183)
Premier Knits Ltd ..... F 718 323-8264
Ozone Park (G-12831)
◆ Pvh Corp ..... D 212 381-3500
New York (G-11281)
Pvh Corp ..... G 212 549-6000
New York (G-11282)
Rags Knitwear Ltd ..... F 718 782-8417
Brooklyn (G-2378)
Ralph Lauren Corporation ..... B 212 318-7000
New York (G-11321)
S & T Knitting Co Inc ..... E 607 722-7558
Conklin (G-3732)
S & V Knits Inc ..... E 631 752-1595
Farmingdale (G-4872)
S & W Knitting Mills Inc ..... E 718 237-2416
Brooklyn (G-2436)
Sage Knitwear Inc ..... G 718 628-7902
West Babylon (G-16190)
Sarug Inc ..... D 718 339-2791
Brooklyn (G-2448)
▲ Summit Apparel Inc ..... E 631 213-8299
Hauppauge (G-5951)
Sweater Brand Inc ..... G 718 797-0505
Brooklyn (G-2545)
▲ T & R Knitting Mills Inc ..... F 718 497-4017
Glendale (G-5409)

T & R Knitting Mills Inc ..... F 212 840-8665
New York (G-11767)
Tomas Maier ..... G 212 988-8686
New York (G-11861)
▲ United Knitwear International ..... G 212 354-2920
New York (G-11953)
Vilebrequin ..... G 212 546-9220
New York (G-12034)
Warm ..... F 212 925-1200
New York (G-12069)
Warnaco Inc ..... F 718 722-3000
Brooklyn (G-2639)
Winter Water Factory ..... G 646 387-3247
Brooklyn (G-2654)
WR Design Corp ..... E 212 354-9000
New York (G-12144)

2254 Knit Underwear Mills

▲ Balanced Tech Corp ..... E 212 768-8330
New York (G-9007)
In Toon Amkor Fashions Inc ..... E 718 937-4546
Long Island City (G-7474)
Jockey International Inc ..... E 212 840-4900
New York (G-10348)
Maidenform LLC ..... F 201 436-9200
New York (G-10672)
Native Textiles Inc ..... G 212 951-5100
New York (G-10889)

2257 Circular Knit Fabric Mills

A-One Moving & Storage Inc ..... E 718 266-6002
Brooklyn (G-1465)
Apex Aridyne Corp ..... E 516 239-4400
Inwood (G-6484)
Apex Texicon Inc ..... E 516 239-4400
New York (G-8883)
Cap USA Jerseyman Harlem Inc ..... G 212 222-7942
New York (G-9200)
Gehring Tricot Corporation ..... C 315 429-8551
Dolgeville (G-4134)
Hill Knitting Mills Inc ..... E 718 846-5000
Richmond Hill (G-13504)
Lemral Knitwear Inc ..... D 718 210-0175
Brooklyn (G-2109)
▲ Lifestyle Design Usa Ltd ..... E 212 279-9400
New York (G-10565)
S & W Knitting Mills Inc ..... E 718 237-2416
Brooklyn (G-2436)

2258 Lace & Warp Knit Fabric Mills

Apex Aridyne Corp ..... G 516 239-4400
Inwood (G-6484)
Apex Texicon Inc ..... E 516 239-4400
New York (G-8883)
Eagle Lace Dyeing Corp ..... F 212 947-2712
New York (G-9603)
Fab Industries Corp ..... B 516 498-3200
Great Neck (G-5553)
▲ Gehring Tricot Corporation ..... D 315 429-8551
Dolgeville (G-4133)
Gehring Tricot Corporation ..... C 315 429-8551
Dolgeville (G-4134)
George Knitting Mills Corp ..... E 212 242-3300
New York (G-9910)
Helmont Mills Inc ..... G 518 568-7913
Saint Johnsville (G-14519)
Hosel & Ackerson Inc ..... G 212 575-1490
New York (G-10125)
Hudson Fabrics LLC ..... F 518 671-6100
Hudson (G-6355)
▲ Klauber Brothers Inc ..... E 212 686-2531
New York (G-10457)
Litchfield Fabrics of NC ..... G 518 773-9500
Gloversville (G-5461)
Mary Bright Inc ..... G 212 677-1970
New York (G-10721)
Mohawk Fabric Company Inc ..... F 518 842-3090
Amsterdam (G-350)
Orbit Industries LLC ..... F 914 244-1500
Mount Kisco (G-8353)
Solstiss Inc ..... G 212 719-9194
New York (G-11641)
Somerset Dyeing & Finishing ..... E 518 773-7383
Gloversville (G-5465)
▲ Somerset Industries Inc ..... E 518 773-7383
Gloversville (G-5466)
Ssjjj Manufacturing LLC ..... B 516 498-3200
Great Neck (G-5590)
Sunwin Global Industry Inc ..... G 646 370-6196
New York (G-11745)

22 TEXTILE MILL PRODUCTS SIC SECTION

Super-Trim Inc .... E 212 255-2370
New York (G-11747)
▲ Veratex Inc .... F 212 683-9300
New York (G-12009)

2259 Knitting Mills, NEC

▲ Bank-Miller Co Inc .... E 914 227-9357
Pelham (G-12933)
▲ Commonwealth Home Fashion Inc .. D 514 384-8290
Willsboro (G-16598)
▲ Hawkins Fabrics Inc .... E 518 773-9550
Johnstown (G-6830)
Maidenform LLC .... F 201 436-9200
New York (G-10672)
Nochairs Inc .... G 917 748-8731
New York (G-10983)
▲ Sextet Fabrics Inc .... F 516 593-0608
East Rockaway (G-4295)

2261 Cotton Fabric Finishers

All About Art Inc .... F 718 321-0755
Flushing (G-4983)
B & K Dye Cutting Inc .... G 718 497-5216
Brooklyn (G-1579)
Basiloff LLC .... G 646 671-0353
New York (G-9025)
Carolyn Ray Inc .... G 914 476-0619
Yonkers (G-16743)
Central Textiles Inc .... F 212 213-8740
New York (G-9245)
D & R Silk Screening Ltd .... F 631 234-7464
Central Islip (G-3367)
Dyenamix Inc .... G 212 941-6642
New York (G-9593)
Dynamic Screenprinting .... G 518 487-4256
Albany (G-69)
Lee Dyeing Company NC Inc .... F 518 736-5232
Johnstown (G-6834)
Loremanss Embroidery Engrav .... F 518 834-9205
Keeseville (G-6852)
Marcel Finishing Corp .... E 718 381-2889
Plainview (G-13072)
Mountain T-Shirts Inc .... G 518 943-4533
Catskill (G-3307)
Printery .... G 315 253-7403
Auburn (G-496)
Prismatic Dyeing & Finshg Inc .... D 845 561-1800
Newburgh (G-12242)
Reynolds Drapery Service Inc .... F 315 845-8632
Newport (G-12256)
▲ Santee Print Works .... B 212 997-1570
New York (G-11485)
Sciane Enterprises Inc .... G 845 452-2400
Poughkeepsie (G-13366)
Steve Poli Sales .... G 315 487-0394
Camillus (G-3197)
Tramwell Inc .... G 315 789-2762
Geneva (G-5334)
Ward Sales Co Inc .... G 315 476-5276
Syracuse (G-15454)

2262 Silk & Man-Made Fabric Finishers

American Spray-On Corp .... E 212 929-2100
New York (G-8837)
▲ Ann Gish Inc .... G 212 969-9200
New York (G-8871)
▲ Beckmann Converting Inc .... E 518 842-0073
Amsterdam (G-327)
Central Textiles Inc .... F 212 213-8740
New York (G-9245)
Dyenamix Inc .... G 212 941-6642
New York (G-9593)
Eastern Silk Mills Inc .... G 212 730-1300
New York (G-9611)
Efs Designs LLC .... G 718 852-9511
Brooklyn (G-1816)
◆ Fabric Resources Intl Ltd .... F 516 829-4550
Great Neck (G-5554)
▲ Gehring Tricot Corporation .... D 315 429-8551
Dolgeville (G-4133)
Intertex USA Inc .... F 212 279-3601
New York (G-10253)
Knucklehead Embroidery Inc .... G 607 797-2725
Johnson City (G-6814)
Marcel Finishing Corp .... E 718 381-2889
Plainview (G-13072)
▲ Mv Corp Inc .... C 631 273-8020
Bay Shore (G-703)
Prismatic Dyeing & Finshg Inc .... D 845 561-1800
Newburgh (G-12242)
▲ Raxon Fabrics Corp .... F 212 532-6816
New York (G-11329)
Rescuestuff Inc .... G 718 318-7570
Peekskill (G-12923)
Screen Gems Inc .... G 845 561-0036
New Windsor (G-8659)
Toltec Fabrics Inc .... C 212 706-9310
New York (G-11857)
Valley Stream Sporting Gds Inc .... E 516 593-7800
Lynbrook (G-7677)

2269 Textile Finishers, NEC

American Country Quilts & Lin .... G 631 283-5466
Southampton (G-14949)
Artyarns .... G 914 428-0333
White Plains (G-16423)
Ben-Sak Textile Inc .... G 212 279-5122
New York (G-9042)
▲ China Ting Fashion Group (usa) ...... G 212 716-1600
New York (G-9283)
▲ Duck River Textiles Inc .... F 212 679-2980
New York (G-9583)
Hosel & Ackerson Inc .... G 212 575-1490
New York (G-10125)
▲ Majestic Rayon Corporation .... E 212 929-6443
New York (G-10675)
Marcel Finishing Corp .... E 718 381-2889
Plainview (G-13072)
National Spinning Co Inc .... E 212 382-6400
New York (G-10886)
Newcastle Fabrics Corp .... G 718 388-6600
Brooklyn (G-2266)
Prismatic Dyeing & Finshg Inc .... D 845 561-1800
Newburgh (G-12242)
Skin Prints Inc .... G 845 920-8756
Pearl River (G-12911)
▲ Sml USA Inc .... E 212 736-8800
New York (G-11626)

2273 Carpets & Rugs

Aladdin Manufacturing Corp .... C 212 561-8715
New York (G-8781)
Auto-Mat Company Inc .... E 516 938-7373
Hicksville (G-6062)
Bentley Mills Inc .... G 212 463-0606
New York (G-9048)
Bloomsburg Carpet Inds Inc .... G 212 688-7447
New York (G-9103)
▲ Carpet Fabrications Intl .... E 914 381-6060
Mamaroneck (G-7736)
▲ Elizabeth Eakins Inc .... F 212 628-1950
New York (G-9653)
Eskayel Inc .... G 347 703-8084
Brooklyn (G-1848)
▲ Excellent Art Mfg Corp .... F 718 388-7075
Inwood (G-6489)
Interfaceflor LLC .... E 212 686-8284
New York (G-10240)
Jbl Trading LLC .... G 347 394-5592
New York (G-10316)
Kalati Company Inc .... G 516 423-9132
Great Neck (G-5565)
Lanes Flr Cvrngs Intriors Inc .... E 212 532-5200
New York (G-10515)
▲ Loom Concepts LLC .... G 212 813-9586
New York (G-10601)
▲ Lorena Canals USA Inc .... G 844 567-3622
Hastings On Hudson (G-5751)
▲ Mark Nelson Designs LLC .... F 646 422-7020
New York (G-10707)
Mgk Group Inc .... E 212 989-2732
New York (G-10788)
Michaelian & Kohlberg Inc .... G 212 431-9009
New York (G-10793)
North Sunshine LLC .... F 307 027-1634
Valley Cottage (G-15761)
◆ Northpoint Trading Inc .... F 212 481-8001
New York (G-10997)
Odegard Inc .... F 212 545-0069
Long Island City (G-7542)
Pawling Corporation .... D 845 373-9300
Wassaic (G-15965)
Quality Carpet One Floor & HM .... G 718 941-4200
Brooklyn (G-2365)
▲ Renaissnce Crpt Tapestries Inc .... F 212 696-0080
New York (G-11360)
Rosecore Division .... F 516 504-4530
Great Neck (G-5585)
Safavieh Inc .... A 516 945-1900
Port Washington (G-13302)
▲ Scalamandre Silks Inc .... D 212 980-3888
New York (G-11499)
Shyam Ahuja Limited .... G 212 644-5910
New York (G-11573)
▲ Sunrise Tile Inc .... G 718 939-0538
Flushing (G-5050)
Tdg Operations LLC .... G 212 779-4300
New York (G-11789)
Tiger 21 LLC .... G 212 360-1700
New York (G-11832)
▲ Tsar USA LLC .... F 646 415-7968
New York (G-11909)
Wells Rugs Inc .... G 516 676-2056
Glen Cove (G-5378)

2281 Yarn Spinning Mills

Advanced Yarn Technologies Inc .... E 518 239-6600
Durham (G-4182)
▲ Colortex Inc .... G 212 564-2000
New York (G-9355)
Great Adirondack Yarn Company .... F 518 843-3381
Amsterdam (G-339)
▲ Missiontex Inc .... G 718 532-9053
Brooklyn (G-2215)
National Spinning Co Inc .... E 212 382-6400
New York (G-10886)
Printz and Patternz LLC .... G 518 944-6020
Schenectady (G-14705)
▼ United Thread Mills Corp .... G 516 536-3900
Oceanside (G-12562)

2282 Yarn Texturizing, Throwing, Twisting & Winding Mills

Janes Designer Yrn Pttrns Inc .... G 347 260-3071
New York (G-10306)
▲ La Lame Inc .... G 212 921-9770
New York (G-10502)
▲ Majestic Rayon Corporation .... E 212 929-6443
New York (G-10675)
Marsha Fleisher .... F 845 679-6500
Woodstock (G-16686)

2284 Thread Mills

Albany International Corp .... C 607 749-7226
Homer (G-6252)
American Quality Embroidery .... G 631 467-3200
Ronkonkoma (G-14306)
One In A Million Inc .... G 516 829-1111
Valley Stream (G-15788)
▼ United Thread Mills Corp .... G 516 536-3900
Oceanside (G-12562)

2295 Fabrics Coated Not Rubberized

▲ A-One Laminating Corp .... G 718 266-6002
Brooklyn (G-1464)
A-One Moving & Storage Inc .... E 718 266-6002
Brooklyn (G-1465)
Architectural Fiberglass Corp .... E 631 842-4772
Copiague (G-3750)
▲ Beckmann Converting Inc .... E 518 842-0073
Amsterdam (G-327)
Breton Industries Inc .... C 518 842-3030
Amsterdam (G-329)
▲ Chemprene Inc .... C 845 831-2800
Beacon (G-755)
▲ Chemprene Holding Inc .... C 845 831-2800
Beacon (G-756)
▲ Comfort Care Textiles Inc .... E 631 543-0531
Commack (G-3687)
▲ Eurotex Inc .... F 716 205-8861
Niagara Falls (G-12282)
◆ Fabric Resources Intl Ltd .... F 516 829-4550
Great Neck (G-5554)
◆ GE Polymershapes .... F 516 433-4092
Hicksville (G-6089)
GM Insulation Corp .... F 516 354-6000
Elmont (G-4519)
Kaneka America LLC .... D 212 705-4340
New York (G-10404)
Kiltronx Enviro Systems LLC .... E 917 971-7177
Hauppauge (G-5855)
New York Cutting & Gumming Co .... E 212 563-4146
Middletown (G-8168)
▲ Newtex Industries Inc .... E 585 924-9135
Victor (G-15858)
▼ Perry Plastics Inc .... F 718 747-5600
Flushing (G-5037)
Precision Custom Coatings LLC .... C 212 868-5770
New York (G-11228)

◆ Tonoga Inc....C.... 518 658-3202
Petersburg (G-12973)
▲ Tpi Industries LLC....E.... 845 692-2820
Middletown (G-8179)

2296 Tire Cord & Fabric

Albany International Corp....C.... 518 445-2230
Menands (G-8079)
Designatronics Incorporated....B.... 516 328-3300
Hicksville (G-6080)
Haines Equipment Inc....E.... 607 566-8531
Avoca (G-516)
York Industries Inc....E.... 516 746-3736
Garden City Park (G-5290)

2297 Fabrics, Nonwoven

Albany International Corp....C.... 518 445-2200
Rensselaer (G-13470)
◆ Fabrication Enterprises Inc....E.... 914 591-9300
Elmsford (G-4543)
▲ Legendary Auto Interiors Ltd....E.... 315 331-1212
Newark (G-12198)
Mgk Group Inc....E.... 212 989-2732
New York (G-10788)
◆ Saint-Gobain Adfors Amer Inc....D.... 716 775-3900
Grand Island (G-5512)
Saint-Gobain Adfors Amer Inc....D.... 585 589-4401
Albion (G-163)

2298 Cordage & Twine

Albany International Corp....C.... 607 749-7226
Homer (G-6252)
All-Lifts Incorporated....E.... 518 465-3461
Albany (G-38)
Cables and Chips Inc....E.... 212 619-3132
New York (G-9173)
▲ Continental Cordage Corp....D.... 315 655-9800
Cazenovia (G-3317)
Cortland Company Inc....D.... 607 753-8276
Cortland (G-3866)
◆ Fiber Instrument Sales Inc....C.... 315 736-2206
Oriskany (G-12757)
Fiberone LLC....F.... 315 434-8877
East Syracuse (G-4339)
▲ Gladding Braided Products LLC....E.... 315 653-7211
South Otselic (G-14943)
Laseoptics Corp....F.... 716 462-5078
Buffalo (G-2921)
T M International LLC....G.... 718 842-0949
Bronx (G-1399)
Triad Network Technologies....E.... 585 924-8505
Victor (G-15874)

2299 Textile Goods, NEC

A Thousand Cranes Inc....F.... 212 724-9596
New York (G-8698)
▲ Ace Drop Cloth Canvas Pdts Inc....E.... 718 731-1550
Bronx (G-1208)
◆ American Home Mfg LLC....G.... 212 643-0680
New York (G-8829)
▲ Arabella Textiles LLC....G.... 212 679-0611
New York (G-8897)
Architectural Textiles USA Inc....E.... 212 213-6972
New York (G-8901)
◆ Benson Mills Inc....E.... 718 236-6743
Brooklyn (G-1600)
Blc Textiles Inc....E.... 844 500-7900
Mineola (G-8208)
Buperiod PBC....G.... 917 406-9804
Brooklyn (G-1656)
◆ Copen United LLC....G.... 212 819-0008
New York (G-9395)
Courtaulds Textiles Ltd....F.... 212 946-8000
New York (G-9410)
◆ David King Linen Inc....F.... 718 241-7298
New York (G-9482)
Dean Trading Corp....F.... 718 485-0600
Brooklyn (G-1763)
Eskayel Inc....G.... 347 703-8084
Brooklyn (G-1848)
▲ Feldman Company Inc....F.... 212 966-1303
New York (G-9792)
Fibrix LLC....E.... 716 683-4100
Depew (G-4089)
Fil Doux Inc....F.... 212 202-1459
Brooklyn (G-1879)
▲ Ghani Textiles Inc....G.... 718 859-4561
Brooklyn (G-1925)
▲ Global Resources Sg Inc....F.... 212 686-1411
New York (G-9945)
Ino-Tex LLC....G.... 212 400-2205
New York (G-10221)
◆ Ivi Services Inc....D.... 607 729-5111
Binghamton (G-897)
▲ James Thompson & Company Inc....E.... 212 686-4242
New York (G-10304)
Jo-Vin Decorators Inc....E.... 718 441-9350
Woodhaven (G-16636)
Jonice Industires....G.... 516 640-4283
Hempstead (G-6016)
▲ K F I Inc....G.... 516 546-2904
Roosevelt (G-14436)
▲ La Lame Inc....G.... 212 921-9770
New York (G-10502)
▲ Lintex Linens Inc....B.... 212 679-8046
New York (G-10574)
▲ Lr Paris LLC....F.... 212 634-9372
New York (G-10621)
▲ Manrico Usa Inc....G.... 212 794-4200
New York (G-10694)
▲ Navy Plum LLC....G.... 845 641-7441
Monsey (G-8291)
Novita Fabrics Furnishing Corp....F.... 516 299-4500
Mineola (G-8242)
Rovel Manufacturing Co Inc....G.... 516 365-2752
Roslyn (G-14451)
S Hellerman Inc....F.... 718 622-2995
Brooklyn (G-2440)
◆ Sabbsons International Inc....F.... 718 360-1947
Brooklyn (G-2442)
▲ Sam Salem & Son LLC....F.... 212 695-6020
New York (G-11475)
▼ Shannon Entps Wstn NY Inc....D.... 716 693-7954
North Tonawanda (G-12450)
▲ Simple Elegance New York Inc....F.... 718 360-1947
Brooklyn (G-2477)
Sk Capital Partners II LP....F.... 212 826-2700
New York (G-11604)
Sk Titan Holdings LLC....G.... 212 826-2700
New York (G-11605)
Solivaira Specialties Inc....D.... 716 693-4009
North Tonawanda (G-12452)
◆ Solvaira Specialties Inc....C.... 716 693-4040
North Tonawanda (G-12453)
Solvaira Specialty LP....E.... 716 693-4040
North Tonawanda (G-12454)
Solvaira Specialty LP....D.... 716 693-4040
North Tonawanda (G-12455)
◆ Soundcoat Company Inc....D.... 631 242-2200
Deer Park (G-4047)
Southern Adrndck Fbr Prdcrs CP....G.... 518 692-2700
Greenwich (G-5645)
Superior Fiber Mills Inc....E.... 718 782-7500
Brooklyn (G-2538)
Thistle Hill Weavers....G.... 518 284-2729
Cherry Valley (G-3466)
▼ TRM Linen Inc....G.... 718 686-6075
Brooklyn (G-2588)
Vincent Manufacturing Co Inc....F.... 315 823-0280
Little Falls (G-7216)
▲ Yankee Corp....F.... 718 589-1377
Bronx (G-1420)

23 APPAREL AND OTHER FINISHED PRODUCTS MADE FROM FABRICS AND SIMILAR MATERIAL

2311 Men's & Boys' Suits, Coats & Overcoats

▲ Adrian Jules Ltd....D.... 585 342-5886
Rochester (G-13603)
▲ Advance Apparel Intl Inc....G.... 212 944-0984
New York (G-8745)
Allytex LLC....G.... 518 376-7539
Ballston Spa (G-576)
Bestec Concept Inc....G.... 718 937-5848
Brooklyn (G-1604)
Bindle and Keep....G.... 917 740-5002
Brooklyn (G-1615)
▲ Blue Duck Trading Ltd....G.... 212 268-3122
New York (G-9107)
▲ Canali USA Inc....E.... 212 767-0205
New York (G-9191)
Centric Brands Inc....D.... 323 890-1800
New York (G-9246)
▲ Check Group LLC....D.... 212 221-4700
New York (G-9268)
▲ Christian Casey LLC....E.... 212 500-2200
New York (G-9289)
Christian Casey LLC....E.... 212 500-2200
New York (G-9290)
▲ Concorde Apparel Company LLC....G.... 212 307-7848
New York (G-9374)
Crisada Inc....G.... 718 729-9730
Long Island City (G-7417)
▲ Crye Precision LLC....C.... 718 246-3838
Brooklyn (G-1736)
Donna Karan Company LLC....C.... 212 789-1500
New York (G-9550)
◆ Donna Karan Company LLC....B.... 212 789-1500
New York (G-9551)
▲ Excelled Sheepskin & Lea Coat....F.... 212 594-5843
New York (G-9750)
▲ G-III Apparel Group Ltd....B.... 212 403-0500
New York (G-9869)
G-III Apparel Group Ltd....F.... 212 840-7272
New York (G-9871)
Giliberto Designs Inc....E.... 212 695-0216
New York (G-9920)
▲ Great 4 Image Inc....E.... 518 424-2058
Rensselaer (G-13474)
▲ Hana Sportswear Inc....E.... 315 639-6332
Dexter (G-4115)
Hickey Freeman Tailored CL Inc....E.... 585 467-7240
Rochester (G-13865)
◆ Hugo Boss Usa Inc....D.... 212 940-0600
New York (G-10146)
J & X Production Inc....F.... 718 200-1228
New York (G-10283)
John Kochis Custom Designs....G.... 212 244-6046
New York (G-10351)
▲ Kozinn+sons Merchant Tailors....E.... 212 643-1916
New York (G-10475)
▲ L F Fashion Orient Intl Co Ltd....G.... 917 667-3398
New York (G-10494)
Lvl Xiii Brands Inc....F.... 646 530-2795
New York (G-10633)
▲ M Hidary & Co Inc....D.... 212 736-6540
New York (G-10639)
▲ Manchu New York Inc....G.... 212 921-5050
New York (G-10682)
▲ Martin Greenfield Clothiers....C.... 718 497-5480
Brooklyn (G-2174)
Med-Eng LLC....E.... 315 713-0103
Ogdensburg (G-12577)
▲ Michael Andrews LLC....F.... 212 677-1755
New York (G-10790)
▲ Mv Corp Inc....C.... 631 273-8020
Bay Shore (G-703)
▲ Occunomix International LLC....E.... 631 741-1940
Port Jeff STA (G-13216)
Opposuits USA Inc....E.... 917 438-8878
New York (G-11052)
Otex Protective Inc....G.... 585 232-7160
Rochester (G-13998)
Pat & Rose Dress Inc....D.... 212 279-1357
New York (G-11121)
Primo Coat Corp....E.... 718 349-2070
Long Island City (G-7560)
Proper Cloth LLC....G.... 646 964-4221
New York (G-11265)
Ps38 LLC....G.... 212 302-1108
New York (G-11268)
Ralph Lauren Corporation....B.... 212 318-7000
New York (G-11321)
▲ Roth Clothing Co Inc....G.... 718 384-4927
Brooklyn (G-2416)
Royal Clothing Corp....G.... 718 436-5841
Brooklyn (G-2418)
▲ Shane Tex Inc....F.... 516 486-7522
Woodmere (G-16642)
Strong Group Inc....G.... 516 766-6300
Oceanside (G-12558)
Therese The Childrens Collectn....G.... 518 346-2315
Schenectady (G-14721)
Tom James Company....F.... 212 593-0204
New York (G-11860)
Uniforms By Park Coats Inc....E.... 718 499-1182
Brooklyn (G-2600)
▲ Urban Textiles Inc....F.... 212 777-1900
New York (G-11970)
Vf Imagewear Inc....E.... 718 352-2363
Bayside (G-751)
▲ Wp Lavori USA Inc....G.... 212 244-6074
New York (G-12143)
Yong Ji Productions Inc....E.... 917 559-4616
Corona (G-3857)

Employee Codes: A=Over 500 employees, B=251-500
C=101-250, D=51-100, E=20-50, F=10-19, G=5-9
2019 Harris
New York Manufacturers Directory
663

23 APPAREL AND OTHER FINISHED PRODUCTS MADE FROM FABRICS AND SIMILAR MATERIAL SIC SECTION

2321 Men's & Boys' Shirts

Americo Group Inc....E.... 212 563-2700
New York (G-8840)
▲ Americo Group Inc....E.... 212 563-2700
New York (G-8841)
▲ Andy & Evan Industries Inc....G.... 212 967-7908
New York (G-8861)
Arthur Gluck Shirtmakers Inc....F.... 212 755-8165
Brooklyn (G-1559)
▲ August Silk Inc....E.... 212 643-2400
New York (G-8961)
August Silk Inc....G.... 212 643-2400
New York (G-8962)
◆ Bowe Industries Inc....D.... 718 441-6464
Glendale (G-5392)
Bowe Industries Inc....D.... 718 441-6464
Glendale (G-5393)
▲ Check Group LLC....D.... 212 221-4700
New York (G-9268)
▲ Christian Casey LLC....E.... 212 500-2200
New York (G-9289)
Christian Casey LLC....E.... 212 500-2200
New York (G-9290)
Colony Holdings Intl LLC....F.... 212 868-2800
New York (G-9352)
Cyberlimit Inc....F.... 212 840-9597
New York (G-9441)
◆ Donna Karan International Inc....F.... 212 789-1500
New York (G-9552)
Donna Karan International Inc....G.... 212 768-5800
New York (G-9553)
◆ Garan Incorporated....C.... 212 563-1292
New York (G-9882)
▼ Garan Manufacturing Corp....G.... 212 563-2000
New York (G-9883)
Gbg National Brands Group LLC....G.... 646 839-7000
New York (G-9886)
Gce International Inc....D.... 773 263-1210
New York (G-9892)
Grayers America Inc....G.... 310 953-2742
New York (G-9980)
◆ Great Universal Corp....E.... 917 302-0065
New York (G-9982)
Groupe 16sur20 LLC....F.... 212 625-1620
New York (G-9998)
▲ Grunt Apparel Inc....G.... 646 878-6171
New York (G-10002)
▲ Haddad Bros Inc....F.... 212 563-2117
New York (G-10018)
Ibrands International LLC....F.... 212 354-1330
New York (G-10166)
Interbrand LLC....G.... 212 840-9595
New York (G-10237)
Jacks and Jokers 52 LLC....G.... 917 740-2595
New York (G-10292)
Jordache Enterprises Inc....D.... 212 944-1330
New York (G-10360)
▲ Jordache Enterprises Inc....C.... 212 643-8400
New York (G-10361)
Just Brass Inc....G.... 212 724-5447
New York (G-10384)
▲ Kt Group Inc....G.... 212 760-2500
New York (G-10485)
Lt2 LLC....E.... 212 684-1510
New York (G-10623)
▲ M S B International Ltd....F.... 212 302-5551
New York (G-10642)
▲ Mega Sourcing Inc....G.... 646 682-0304
Merrick (G-8103)
Miltons of New York Inc....G.... 212 997-3359
New York (G-10813)
▲ Mulitex Usa Inc....G.... 212 398-0440
New York (G-10857)
▲ Nat Nast Company Inc....E.... 212 575-1186
New York (G-10876)
Oved Mens LLC....E.... 212 563-4999
New York (G-11070)
Oxford Industries Inc....F.... 212 840-2288
New York (G-11077)
Perry Ellis International Inc....F.... 212 536-5400
New York (G-11160)
Perry Ellis International Inc....G.... 212 536-5499
New York (G-11161)
◆ Perry Ellis Menswear LLC....C.... 212 221-7500
New York (G-11162)
Phillips-Van Heusen Europe....F.... 212 381-3500
New York (G-11183)
◆ Pvh Corp....D.... 212 381-3500
New York (G-11281)
Pvh Corp....G.... 845 561-0233
New Windsor (G-8656)
Pvh Corp....G.... 631 254-8200
Deer Park (G-4031)
Pvh Corp....G.... 212 549-6000
New York (G-11282)
Pvh Corp....G.... 212 719-2600
New York (G-11285)
Ralph Lauren Corporation....B.... 212 318-7000
New York (G-11321)
▲ Roffe Accessories Inc....E.... 212 213-1440
New York (G-11419)
Saad Collection Inc....G.... 212 937-0341
New York (G-11461)
▲ Schwartz Textile LLC....E.... 718 499-8243
Brooklyn (G-2451)
Sifonya Inc....G.... 212 620-4512
New York (G-11581)
▲ Sue & Sam Co Inc....E.... 718 436-1672
Brooklyn (G-2530)
◆ Warnaco Inc....B.... 212 287-8000
New York (G-12071)
Warnaco Inc....F.... 718 722-3000
Brooklyn (G-2639)
Whittall & Shon....G.... 212 594-2626
New York (G-12106)
Yale Trouser Corporation....F.... 516 255-0700
Oceanside (G-12566)

2322 Men's & Boys' Underwear & Nightwear

▲ Apparel Partnership Group LLC....G.... 212 302-7722
New York (G-8889)
Becks Classic Mfg Inc....D.... 631 435-3800
Brentwood (G-1128)
▲ Candlesticks Inc....F.... 212 947-8900
New York (G-9194)
▲ Check Group LLC....D.... 212 221-4700
New York (G-9268)
▲ Christian Casey LLC....E.... 212 500-2200
New York (G-9289)
Christian Casey LLC....E.... 212 500-2200
New York (G-9290)
▲ Comme-Ci Comme-CA AP Group....E.... 631 300-1035
Hauppauge (G-5795)
▲ Revolutionwear Inc....G.... 617 669-9191
New York (G-11379)
▲ Sleepwear Holdings Inc....C.... 516 466-4738
New York (G-11618)
▲ Tommy John Inc....E.... 800 708-3490
New York (G-11864)
◆ Twist Intimate Group LLC....G.... 212 695-5990
New York (G-11918)
◆ Warnaco Group Inc....E.... 212 287-8000
New York (G-12070)
◆ Warnaco Inc....B.... 212 287-8000
New York (G-12071)
Warnaco Inc....F.... 718 722-3000
Brooklyn (G-2639)
▲ Waterbury Garment LLC....E.... 212 725-1500
New York (G-12080)
▲ Wickers Sportswear Inc....G.... 631 543-1700
Commack (G-3707)

2323 Men's & Boys' Neckwear

Countess Mara Inc....G.... 212 768-7300
New York (G-9409)
Emunas Sales Inc....F.... 718 621-3138
Brooklyn (G-1835)
JS Blank & Co Inc....E.... 212 689-4835
New York (G-10373)
Mallory & Church LLC....G.... 212 868-7888
New York (G-10679)
▲ MANe Enterprises Inc....D.... 718 472-4955
Long Island City (G-7512)
Mongru Neckwear Inc....E.... 718 706-0406
Long Island City (G-7529)
◆ Perry Ellis Menswear LLC....C.... 212 221-7500
New York (G-11162)
Ralph Lauren Corporation....B.... 212 318-7000
New York (G-11321)
Randa Accessories Lea Gds LLC....D.... 212 354-5100
New York (G-11325)
▲ Roffe Accessories Inc....E.... 212 213-1440
New York (G-11419)
▲ S Broome and Co Inc....D.... 718 663-6800
Long Island City (G-7583)
▲ Tie King Inc....E.... 718 768-8484
Brooklyn (G-2567)
Tie King Inc....G.... 212 714-9611
New York (G-11831)
Valenti Neckwear Co Inc....G.... 914 969-0700
Yonkers (G-16805)
W B Bow Tie Corp....F.... 212 683-6130
New York (G-12060)
◆ Warnaco Inc....B.... 212 287-8000
New York (G-12071)
Wetherall Contracting NY Inc....G.... 718 894-7011
Middle Village (G-8128)

2325 Men's & Boys' Separate Trousers & Casual Slacks

▲ Adrian Jules Ltd....D.... 585 342-5886
Rochester (G-13603)
Bruno & Canio Ltd....E.... 845 624-3060
Nanuet (G-8460)
Centric Brands Inc....D.... 323 890-1800
New York (G-9246)
Centric Denim Usa LLC....F.... 646 839-7000
New York (G-9247)
▲ Check Group LLC....D.... 212 221-4700
New York (G-9268)
▲ Christian Casey LLC....E.... 212 500-2200
New York (G-9289)
Christian Casey LLC....E.... 212 500-2200
New York (G-9290)
Donna Karan Company LLC....C.... 212 789-1500
New York (G-9550)
◆ Donna Karan Company LLC....B.... 212 789-1500
New York (G-9551)
◆ Donna Karan International Inc....F.... 212 789-1500
New York (G-9552)
Donna Karan International Inc....G.... 212 768-5800
New York (G-9553)
Groupe 16sur20 LLC....F.... 212 625-1620
New York (G-9998)
Guess Inc....E.... 716 298-3561
Niagara Falls (G-12292)
▲ Hertling Trousers Inc....E.... 718 784-6100
Brooklyn (G-1977)
Hot Kiss Inc....G.... 212 730-0404
New York (G-10129)
◆ Hugo Boss Usa Inc....D.... 212 940-0600
New York (G-10146)
▲ Int Trading USA LLC....C.... 212 760-2338
New York (G-10229)
Jordache Enterprises Inc....D.... 212 944-1330
New York (G-10360)
▲ Jordache Enterprises Inc....C.... 212 643-8400
New York (G-10361)
Kalikow Brothers LP....E.... 212 643-0315
New York (G-10398)
Kaltex America Inc....F.... 212 971-0575
New York (G-10400)
Leng Universal Inc....F.... 212 398-6800
New York (G-10545)
Levi Strauss & Co....F.... 917 213-6263
Flushing (G-5022)
▲ M Hidary & Co Inc....D.... 212 736-6540
New York (G-10639)
▲ M S B International Ltd....F.... 212 302-5551
New York (G-10642)
▲ Martin Greenfield Clothiers....C.... 718 497-5480
Brooklyn (G-2174)
Messex Group Inc....G.... 646 229-2582
New York (G-10782)
Miltons of New York Inc....G.... 212 997-3359
New York (G-10813)
▲ Montero International Inc....G.... 212 695-1787
Westbury (G-16358)
▲ Mulitex Usa Inc....G.... 212 398-0440
New York (G-10857)
▲ One Jeanswear Group Inc....B.... 212 575-2571
New York (G-11042)
◆ Passport Brands Inc....E.... 646 459-2625
New York (G-11120)
Pat & Rose Dress Inc....D.... 212 279-1357
New York (G-11121)
Perry Ellis International Inc....F.... 212 536-5400
New York (G-11160)
◆ Perry Ellis Menswear LLC....C.... 212 221-7500
New York (G-11162)
Primo Coat Corp....E.... 718 349-2070
Long Island City (G-7560)
Ralph Lauren Corporation....B.... 212 318-7000
New York (G-11321)
◆ Ryba General Merchandise Inc....G.... 718 522-2028
Brooklyn (G-2430)
Sean John Clothing Inc....E.... 212 500-2200
New York (G-11526)

Sean John Clothing Inc ... E ... 212 500-2200
New York (G-11527)
Yale Trouser Corporation ... F ... 516 255-0700
Oceanside (G-12566)

2326 Men's & Boys' Work Clothing

5 Star Apparel LLC ... G ... 212 563-1233
New York (G-8681)
▲ Ace Drop Cloth Canvas Pdts Inc ... E ... 718 731-1550
Bronx (G-1208)
▲ Adar Medical Uniform LLC ... F ... 718 935-1197
Brooklyn (G-1481)
American Apparel Ltd ... G ... 516 504-4559
Great Neck (G-5533)
Badgley Mischka Licensing LLC ... E ... 212 921-1585
New York (G-8999)
Beardslee Realty ... G ... 516 747-5557
Mineola (G-8206)
▲ Best Medical Wear Ltd ... G ... 718 858-5544
Brooklyn (G-1603)
Bestec Concept Inc ... G ... 718 937-5848
Brooklyn (G-1604)
▲ Billion Tower Intl LLC ... F ... 212 220-0608
New York (G-9082)
Broadway Knitting Mills Inc ... G ... 716 692-4421
North Tonawanda (G-12418)
Classic Designer Workshop Inc ... G ... 212 730-8480
New York (G-9319)
Dalcom USA Ltd ... F ... 516 466-7733
Great Neck (G-5549)
Doral Apparel Group Inc ... G ... 917 208-5652
New York (G-9558)
▲ Du Monde Trading Inc ... E ... 212 944-1306
New York (G-9581)
▲ E J Manufacturing Inc ... G ... 516 313-9380
Merrick (G-8097)
Enzo Manzoni LLC ... G ... 212 464-7000
Brooklyn (G-1839)
Far East Industries Inc ... G ... 718 687-2482
New Hyde Park (G-8534)
Ferris USA LLC ... G ... 617 895-8102
New York (G-9796)
◆ HC Contracting Inc ... D ... 212 643-9292
New York (G-10054)
Hillary Merchant Inc ... G ... 646 575-9242
New York (G-10099)
Intrigue Concepts Inc ... G ... 800 424-8170
Roosevelt (G-14435)
Kollage Work Too Ltd ... G ... 212 695-1821
New York (G-10466)
Kse Sportsman Media Inc ... D ... 212 852-6600
New York (G-10483)
Lady Brass Co Inc ... G ... 516 887-8040
Hewlett (G-6047)
LLC Major Major ... E ... 212 354-8550
New York (G-10586)
Medline Industries Inc ... B ... 845 344-3301
Middletown (G-8163)
▲ Mesh LLC ... E ... 646 839-7000
New York (G-10780)
New York Hospital Disposable ... E ... 718 384-1620
Brooklyn (G-2262)
Norcorp Inc ... E ... 914 666-1310
Mount Kisco (G-8352)
▲ Occunomix International LLC ... E ... 631 741-1940
Port Jeff STA (G-13216)
▲ Penfli Industries Inc ... F ... 212 947-6080
Great Neck (G-5581)
Pico Direct LLC ... E ... 212 947-8969
Roslyn (G-14450)
▲ Rag & Bone Industries LLC ... D ... 212 278-8214
New York (G-11316)
Richard Manufacturing Co Inc ... G ... 718 254-0958
Brooklyn (G-2401)
▼ S & H Uniform Corp ... D ... 914 937-6800
White Plains (G-16500)
Shanghai Harmony AP Intl LLC ... E ... 646 569-5680
New Rochelle (G-8628)
Stealth Inc ... F ... 718 252-7900
Brooklyn (G-2515)
▲ Untuckit LLC ... E ... 201 214-9054
New York (G-11965)
Untuckit LLC ... C ... 646 724-1857
New York (G-11966)
▲ Ventura Enterprise Co Inc ... E ... 212 391-0170
New York (G-12006)
Vf Imagewear Inc ... E ... 718 352-2363
Bayside (G-751)

2329 Men's & Boys' Clothing, NEC

Adpro Sports LLC ... D ... 716 854-5116
Buffalo (G-2687)
▲ Alexander Wang Incorporated ... D ... 212 532-3103
New York (G-8794)
All Net Ltd ... F ... 516 504-4559
Great Neck (G-5531)
Alleson of Rochester Inc ... E ... 315 548-3635
Geneva (G-5316)
▲ Alleson of Rochester Inc ... D ... 585 272-0606
Rochester (G-13614)
▲ Alpha 6 Distributions LLC ... F ... 516 801-8290
Locust Valley (G-7345)
▲ American Challenge Enterprises ... G ... 631 595-7171
New Hyde Park (G-8515)
Apogee Retail NY ... G ... 516 731-1727
Levittown (G-7130)
Bandit International Ltd ... F ... 718 402-2100
Bronx (G-1225)
▲ Beluga Inc ... E ... 212 594-5511
New York (G-9041)
◆ Benetton Trading Usa Inc ... G ... 212 593-0290
New York (G-9045)
Bernette Apparel LLC ... F ... 212 279-5526
New York (G-9053)
▲ Big Idea Brands LLC ... F ... 212 938-0270
New York (G-9078)
Bilco Industries Inc ... F ... 917 783-5008
New York (G-9081)
Billion Tower USA LLC ... G ... 212 220-0608
New York (G-9083)
Brigantine Inc ... G ... 212 354-8550
New York (G-9139)
Broadway Knitting Mills Inc ... G ... 716 692-4421
North Tonawanda (G-12418)
▲ Broken Threads Inc ... G ... 212 730-4351
New York (G-9147)
▲ Brunschwig & Fils LLC ... F ... 800 538-1880
Bethpage (G-840)
By Robert James ... G ... 212 253-2121
New York (G-9165)
Caps Teamwear Inc ... G ... 585 663-1750
Rochester (G-13691)
▲ Caribbean Fashion Group Inc ... G ... 212 706-8851
New York (G-9207)
Caroda Inc ... E ... 212 630-9986
New York (G-9210)
Central Mills Inc ... C ... 212 764-9011
New York (G-9244)
City Jeans Inc ... G ... 718 239-5353
Bronx (G-1241)
▲ Comme-Ci Comme-CA AP Group ... E ... 631 300-1035
Hauppauge (G-5795)
Continental Knitting Mills ... G ... 631 242-5330
Deer Park (G-3958)
▲ Cotton Emporium Inc ... G ... 718 894-3365
Glendale (G-5397)
Craftatlantic LLC ... F ... 646 726-4205
New York (G-9417)
▲ David Peyser Sportswear Inc ... C ... 631 231-7788
Bay Shore (G-678)
David Peyser Sportswear Inc ... E ... 212 695-7716
New York (G-9483)
▲ Eb Couture Ltd ... E ... 212 912-0190
New York (G-9615)
▲ Endurance LLC ... E ... 212 719-2500
New York (G-9678)
Eon Collections ... E ... 212 695-1263
New York (G-9692)
◆ Eternal Fortune Fashion LLC ... G ... 212 965-5322
New York (G-9721)
Ferris USA LLC ... G ... 617 895-8102
New York (G-9796)
Feyem USA Inc ... G ... 845 363-6253
Brewster (G-1165)
▲ G-III Apparel Group Ltd ... B ... 212 403-0500
New York (G-9869)
Gametime Sportswear Plus LLC ... G ... 315 724-5893
Utica (G-15705)
◆ General Sportwear Company Inc ... C ... 212 764-5820
New York (G-9902)
Groupe 16sur20 LLC ... F ... 212 625-1620
New York (G-9998)
Haculla Nyc Inc ... F ... 718 886-3163
Fresh Meadows (G-5199)
Hansae Co Ltd ... G ... 212 354-6690
New York (G-10035)
▼ Herman Kay Company Ltd ... C ... 212 239-2025
New York (G-10083)
◆ Hf Mfg Corp ... D ... 212 594-9142
New York (G-10090)
Hockey Facility ... G ... 518 452-7396
Albany (G-83)
House Pearl Fashions (us) Ltd ... F ... 212 840-3183
New York (G-10138)
▲ I Spiewak & Sons Inc ... E ... 212 695-1620
New York (G-10162)
Icer Sports LLC ... F ... 212 221-4700
New York (G-10169)
Ifg Corp ... C ... 212 629-9600
New York (G-10176)
Ifg Corp ... G ... 212 239-8615
New York (G-10177)
Jacob Hidary Foundation Inc ... F ... 212 736-6540
New York (G-10297)
Joseph (uk) Inc ... G ... 212 570-0077
New York (G-10363)
Just Bottoms & Tops Inc ... F ... 212 564-3202
New York (G-10383)
Kicks Closet Sportswear Inc ... G ... 347 577-0857
Bronx (G-1308)
▲ Kidz World Inc ... F ... 212 563-4949
New York (G-10442)
▲ King Sales Inc ... F ... 718 301-9862
Brooklyn (G-2073)
▲ Komar Luxury Brands ... G ... 646 472-0060
New York (G-10468)
Linder New York LLC ... F ... 646 678-5819
New York (G-10572)
▲ London Paris Ltd ... G ... 718 564-4793
Brooklyn (G-2133)
Luxe Imagine Consulting LLC ... G ... 212 273-9770
New York (G-10632)
▲ M A M Knitting Mills Corp ... E ... 800 570-0093
Brooklyn (G-2144)
▲ M Hidary & Co Inc ... D ... 212 736-6540
New York (G-10639)
Maiyet Inc ... G ... 212 343-9999
New York (G-10674)
Mann Consultants LLC ... E ... 914 763-0512
Waccabuc (G-15881)
Mayberry Shoe Company Inc ... G ... 315 692-4086
Manlius (G-7780)
▲ Mee Accessories LLC ... B ... 917 262-1000
New York (G-10762)
▲ Miss Group ... G ... 212 391-2535
New York (G-10822)
▲ Montero International Inc ... G ... 212 695-1787
Westbury (G-16358)
▲ Nautica International Inc ... D ... 212 541-5757
New York (G-10895)
◆ Nautica Opco LLC ... B ... 212 541-5757
New York (G-10896)
▲ Nepenthes America Inc ... G ... 212 343-4262
Long Island City (G-7536)
Nine West Holdings Inc ... G ... 212 575-2571
New York (G-10975)
▲ North American Mills Inc ... F ... 212 695-6146
New York (G-10992)
▲ Nyc Idol Apparel Inc ... G ... 212 997-9797
New York (G-11013)
On The Double Inc ... G ... 518 431-3571
Germantown (G-5339)
▲ One Step Up Ltd ... D ... 212 398-1110
New York (G-11043)
Oxford Industries Inc ... E ... 212 247-7712
New York (G-11076)
P & I Sportswear Inc ... G ... 718 934-4587
New York (G-11082)
Predator Mountainwear Inc ... G ... 315 727-3241
Auburn (G-495)
Prestige Global NY Sls Corp ... G ... 212 776-4322
New York (G-11237)
Pride & Joys Inc ... F ... 212 594-9820
New York (G-11239)
Ps38 LLC ... F ... 212 819-1123
New York (G-11269)
▲ Pti-Pacific Inc ... G ... 212 414-8495
New York (G-11271)
Pvh Corp ... G ... 212 381-3800
New York (G-11283)
R J Liebe Athletic Company ... D ... 585 237-6111
Perry (G-12970)
▲ Rainforest Inc ... F ... 212 575-7620
New York (G-11319)
Ralph Lauren Corporation ... B ... 212 318-7000
New York (G-11321)
▲ Ramsbury Property Us Inc ... F ... 212 223-6250
New York (G-11322)

23 APPAREL AND OTHER FINISHED PRODUCTS MADE FROM FABRICS AND SIMILAR MATERIAL SIC SECTION

Robert Viggiani ....G....... 914 423-4046
Yonkers *(G-16796)*
Rp55 Inc ....G....... 212 840-4035
New York *(G-11442)*
▲ S & S Fashions Inc ....G....... 718 328-0001
Bronx *(G-1375)*
S & W Knitting Mills Inc ....E....... 718 237-2416
Brooklyn *(G-2436)*
Sanctuary Brands LLC ....G....... 212 704-4014
New York *(G-11479)*
Sandy Dalal Ltd ....G....... 212 532-5822
New York *(G-11482)*
▼ Sb Corporation ....G....... 212 822-3166
New York *(G-11495)*
Scharf and Breit Inc ....E....... 516 282-0287
Williston Park *(G-16595)*
▲ Schwartz Textile LLC ....E....... 718 499-8243
Brooklyn *(G-2451)*
Siskind Group Inc ....F....... 212 840-0880
New York *(G-11601)*
▲ Sister Sister Inc ....G....... 212 629-9600
New York *(G-11602)*
Sport Athleisure Ltd ....F....... 212 868-6505
New York *(G-11673)*
▲ Standard Manufacturing Co Inc ....D....... 518 235-2200
Troy *(G-15628)*
▲ Sterling Possessions Ltd ....G....... 212 594-0418
New York *(G-11707)*
Swimwear Anywhere Inc ....E....... 845 858-4141
Port Jervis *(G-13238)*
Tamka Sport LLC ....G....... 718 224-7820
Douglaston *(G-4142)*
Tbhl International LLC ....F....... 212 799-2007
New York *(G-11787)*
◆ Tibana Finishing Inc ....E....... 718 417-5375
Ridgewood *(G-13555)*
▲ Tillsonburg Company USA Inc ....E....... 267 994-8096
New York *(G-11835)*
Under Armour Inc ....E....... 518 761-6787
Lake George *(G-6966)*
▲ Uniqlo USA LLC ....F....... 877 486-4756
New York *(G-11948)*
Valley Stream Sporting Gds Inc ....E....... 516 593-7800
Lynbrook *(G-7677)*
▲ Versailles Industries LLC ....G....... 212 792-9615
New York *(G-12013)*
Vf Outdoor Inc ....E....... 718 698-6215
Staten Island *(G-15152)*
Vf Outdoor LLC ....E....... 845 928-4900
Central Valley *(G-3398)*
◆ Warnaco Group Inc ....E....... 212 287-8000
New York *(G-12070)*
◆ Warnaco Inc ....B....... 212 287-8000
New York *(G-12071)*
Warnaco Inc ....F....... 718 722-3000
Brooklyn *(G-2639)*

2331 Women's & Misses' Blouses

18 Rocks LLC ....E....... 631 465-9990
Melville *(G-7995)*
79 Metro Ltd ....G....... 212 944-4030
New York *(G-8685)*
▲ Accessries Direct Intl USA Inc ....E....... 646 448-8200
New York *(G-8722)*
Agi Brooks Production Co Inc ....F....... 212 268-1533
New York *(G-8768)*
▲ Alexander Wang Incorporated ....D....... 212 532-3103
New York *(G-8794)*
▲ Alfred Dunner Inc ....B....... 212 478-4300
New York *(G-8795)*
Amerex Corporation ....G....... 212 221-3151
New York *(G-8819)*
▲ Anna Sui Corp ....E....... 212 941-8406
New York *(G-8873)*
Apparel Group Ltd ....E....... 212 328-1200
New York *(G-8888)*
▲ August Silk Inc ....E....... 212 643-2400
New York *(G-8961)*
August Silk Inc ....G....... 212 643-2400
New York *(G-8962)*
▲ Bernard Chaus Inc ....D....... 212 354-1280
New York *(G-9051)*
Bernard Chaus Inc ....C....... 646 562-4700
New York *(G-9052)*
◆ Bowe Industries Inc ....D....... 718 441-6464
Glendale *(G-5392)*
Brach Knitting Mills Inc ....F....... 845 651-4450
Florida *(G-4968)*
Cyberlimit Inc ....F....... 212 840-9597
New York *(G-9441)*
▲ Cynthia Rowley Inc ....F....... 212 242-3803
New York *(G-9443)*
Donna Karan Company LLC ....C....... 212 789-1500
New York *(G-9550)*
◆ Donna Karan Company LLC ....B....... 212 789-1500
New York *(G-9551)*
◆ Donna Karan International Inc ....F....... 212 789-1500
New York *(G-9552)*
Donna Karan International Inc ....G....... 212 768-5800
New York *(G-9553)*
Elie Tahari Ltd ....G....... 212 398-2622
New York *(G-9645)*
Elie Tahari Ltd ....D....... 212 763-2000
New York *(G-9647)*
Embassy Apparel Inc ....F....... 212 768-8330
New York *(G-9663)*
Feyem USA Inc ....G....... 845 363-6253
Brewster *(G-1165)*
Fourtys Ny Inc ....F....... 212 382-0301
New York *(G-9833)*
Fuller Sportswear Co Inc ....G....... 516 773-3353
Great Neck *(G-5559)*
Gabrielle Andra ....G....... 212 366-9624
New York *(G-9875)*
◆ Garan Incorporated ....C....... 212 563-1292
New York *(G-9882)*
▼ Garan Manufacturing Corp ....G....... 212 563-2000
New York *(G-9883)*
▲ Gce International Inc ....D....... 212 704-4800
New York *(G-9890)*
Geoffrey Beene Inc ....E....... 212 371-5570
New York *(G-9908)*
▲ Gildan Apparel USA Inc ....D....... 212 476-0341
New York *(G-9919)*
Glamourpuss Nyc LLC ....G....... 212 722-1370
New York *(G-9929)*
Grey State Apparel LLC ....E....... 212 255-4216
New York *(G-9986)*
Hansae Co Ltd ....G....... 212 354-6690
New York *(G-10035)*
Icer Sports LLC ....F....... 212 221-4700
New York *(G-10169)*
▲ International Direct Group Inc ....E....... 212 921-9036
New York *(G-10246)*
▲ Jeanjer LLC ....A....... 212 944-1330
New York *(G-10323)*
Jordache Enterprises Inc ....D....... 212 944-1330
New York *(G-10360)*
▲ Jordache Enterprises Inc ....C....... 212 643-8400
New York *(G-10361)*
◆ Kate Spade & Company LLC ....B....... 212 354-4900
New York *(G-10415)*
▼ Krasner Group Inc ....G....... 212 268-4100
New York *(G-10479)*
Ksk International Inc ....E....... 212 354-7770
New York *(G-10484)*
◆ Land n Sea Inc ....D....... 212 444-6000
New York *(G-10513)*
Lea & Viola Inc ....G....... 646 918-6866
New York *(G-10529)*
▲ Liberty Apparel Company Inc ....E....... 718 625-4000
New York *(G-10560)*
Lt2 LLC ....E....... 212 684-1510
New York *(G-10623)*
▲ M S B International Ltd ....F....... 212 302-5551
New York *(G-10642)*
▲ Maggy London International Ltd ....C....... 212 944-7199
New York *(G-10665)*
▲ Mega Sourcing Inc ....G....... 646 682-0304
Merrick *(G-8103)*
▲ Mulitex Usa Inc ....G....... 212 398-0440
New York *(G-10857)*
▲ Necessary Objects Ltd ....E....... 212 334-9888
Long Island City *(G-7535)*
▲ Nyc Knitwear Inc ....E....... 212 840-1313
New York *(G-11014)*
Orchard Apparel Group Ltd ....G....... 212 268-8701
New York *(G-11057)*
Orchid Manufacturing Co Inc ....F....... 212 840-5700
New York *(G-11059)*
Paddy Lee Fashions Inc ....F....... 718 786-6020
Long Island City *(G-7547)*
Pat & Rose Dress Inc ....D....... 212 279-1357
New York *(G-11121)*
▲ Permit Fashion Group Inc ....G....... 212 912-0988
Woodbury *(G-16627)*
Phillips-Van Heusen Europe ....F....... 212 381-3500
New York *(G-11183)*
Plugg LLC ....F....... 212 840-6655
New York *(G-11212)*
◆ Pvh Corp ....D....... 212 381-3500
New York *(G-11281)*
Pvh Corp ....G....... 212 549-6000
New York *(G-11282)*
Pvh Corp ....G....... 212 719-2600
New York *(G-11285)*
▲ Ramy Brook LLC ....E....... 212 744-2789
New York *(G-11324)*
▲ Raven New York LLC ....G....... 212 584-9690
New York *(G-11328)*
▲ Rhoda Lee Inc ....D....... 212 840-5700
New York *(G-11384)*
Robert Danes Danes Inc ....G....... 212 226-1351
New York *(G-11406)*
▲ S & S Manufacturing Co Inc ....D....... 212 444-6000
New York *(G-11456)*
Saad Collection Inc ....G....... 212 937-0341
New York *(G-11461)*
Soho Apparel Ltd ....G....... 212 840-1109
New York *(G-11636)*
Spencer AB Inc ....G....... 646 831-3728
New York *(G-11667)*
Stitch & Couture Inc ....E....... 212 947-9204
New York *(G-11713)*
T Rj Shirts Inc ....G....... 347 642-3071
East Elmhurst *(G-4225)*
Tahari ASL LLC ....B....... 212 763-2800
New York *(G-11775)*
◆ Tibana Finishing Inc ....E....... 718 417-5375
Ridgewood *(G-13555)*
▲ Triumph Apparel Corporation ....E....... 212 302-2606
New York *(G-11901)*
Turn On Products Inc ....F....... 212 764-4545
New York *(G-11914)*
▲ Turn On Products Inc ....D....... 212 764-2121
New York *(G-11913)*
Ursula of Switzerland Inc ....E....... 518 237-2580
Waterford *(G-15990)*
Vanity Room Inc ....F....... 212 921-7154
New York *(G-11993)*
▲ Ventura Enterprise Co Inc ....E....... 212 391-0170
New York *(G-12006)*
Yeohlee Inc ....F....... 212 631-8099
New York *(G-12161)*

2335 Women's & Misses' Dresses

18 Rocks LLC ....E....... 631 465-9990
Melville *(G-7995)*
◆ A & M Rosenthal Entps Inc ....E....... 646 638-9600
New York *(G-8688)*
Ace & Jig LLC ....G....... 347 227-0318
Brooklyn *(G-1475)*
Agi Brooks Production Co Inc ....F....... 212 268-1533
New York *(G-8768)*
Allison Che Fashion Inc ....F....... 212 391-1433
New York *(G-8800)*
Alvina Vlenta Couture Collectn ....F....... 212 921-7058
New York *(G-8814)*
▲ Amj DOT LLC ....G....... 718 775-3288
Brooklyn *(G-1530)*
Anna B Inc ....G....... 516 680-6609
New York *(G-8872)*
▲ Anna Sui Corp ....E....... 212 941-8406
New York *(G-8873)*
Arcangel Inc ....G....... 347 771-0789
New York *(G-8899)*
▲ August Silk Inc ....E....... 212 643-2400
New York *(G-8961)*
August Silk Inc ....G....... 212 643-2400
New York *(G-8962)*
B S J Limited ....E....... 212 764-4600
New York *(G-8990)*
▲ B S J Limited ....E....... 212 221-8403
New York *(G-8991)*
Bari-Jay Fashions Inc ....E....... 212 921-1551
New York *(G-9018)*
Birnbaum & Bullock Ltd ....G....... 212 242-2914
New York *(G-9090)*
▲ Cachet Industries Inc ....E....... 212 944-2188
New York *(G-9175)*
Carol Peretz ....F....... 516 248-6300
Mineola *(G-8210)*
▲ China Ting Fashion Group (usa) ....G....... 212 716-1600
New York *(G-9283)*
Christian Siriano Holdings LLC ....G....... 212 695-5494
New York *(G-9292)*
▲ Christos Inc ....E....... 212 921-0025
New York *(G-9295)*
▲ Couture Inc ....G....... 212 921-1166
New York *(G-9411)*

Crisada Inc ... G ... 718 729-9730
Long Island City *(G-7417)*

▲ Csco LLC ... E ... 212 375-6180
New York *(G-9429)*

CTS LLC ... G ... 212 278-0058
New York *(G-9430)*

▲ Cynthia Rowley Inc ... F ... 212 242-3803
New York *(G-9443)*

D J Night Ltd ... E ... 212 302-9050
New York *(G-9447)*

Dalma Dress Mfg Co Inc ... E ... 212 391-8296
Greenvale *(G-5629)*

Damianou Sportswear Inc ... D ... 718 204-5600
Woodside *(G-16652)*

▲ Dave & Johnny Ltd ... E ... 212 302-9050
New York *(G-9477)*

Donna Karan Company LLC ... C ... 212 789-1500
New York *(G-9550)*

Donna Karan Company LLC ... C ... 716 297-0752
Niagara Falls *(G-12278)*

◆ Donna Karan Company LLC ... B ... 212 789-1500
New York *(G-9551)*

◆ Donna Karan International Inc ... F ... 212 789-1500
New York *(G-9552)*

Donna Karan International Inc ... G ... 212 768-5800
New York *(G-9553)*

Elana Laderos Ltd ... F ... 212 764-0840
New York *(G-9639)*

Elizabeth Fillmore LLC ... G ... 212 647-0863
New York *(G-9654)*

Everlasting Memories ... G ... 716 833-1111
Blasdell *(G-926)*

▲ Faviana International Inc ... E ... 212 594-4422
New York *(G-9789)*

Four Seasons Fashion Mfg Inc ... E ... 212 947-6820
New York *(G-9832)*

G-III Apparel Group Ltd ... E ... 212 403-0500
New York *(G-9870)*

Geoffrey Beene Inc ... E ... 212 371-5570
New York *(G-9908)*

Haddad Bros Inc ... E ... 718 377-5505
Brooklyn *(G-1959)*

▲ Halmode Apparel Inc ... A ... 212 819-9114
New York *(G-10023)*

Haute By Blair Stanley LLC ... G ... 212 557-7868
New York *(G-10049)*

▲ I S C A Corp ... F ... 212 719-5123
New York *(G-10160)*

▲ Icer Scrubs LLC ... F ... 212 221-4700
New York *(G-10168)*

Infinity Sourcing Services LLC ... G ... 212 868-2900
New York *(G-10204)*

J R Nites ... G ... 212 354-9670
New York *(G-10288)*

Jaclyn Inc ... F ... 212 736-5657
New York *(G-10295)*

▲ Jiranimo Industries Ltd ... F ... 212 921-5106
New York *(G-10341)*

▲ Jon Teri Sports Inc ... E ... 212 398-0657
New York *(G-10357)*

◆ Jovani Fashion Ltd ... E ... 212 279-0222
New York *(G-10369)*

▲ Judys Group Inc ... E ... 212 921-0515
New York *(G-10375)*

▲ Jump Design Group Inc ... C ... 212 869-3300
New York *(G-10378)*

◆ Kasper Group LLC ... C ... 212 354-4311
New York *(G-10414)*

▲ Kelly Grace Corp ... C ... 212 704-9603
New York *(G-10428)*

▼ Krasner Group Inc ... G ... 212 268-4100
New York *(G-10479)*

▲ L F Fashion Orient Intl Co Ltd ... G ... 917 667-3398
New York *(G-10494)*

◆ Lily & Taylor Inc ... F ... 212 564-5459
New York *(G-10571)*

Lmr Group Inc ... G ... 212 730-9221
New York *(G-10587)*

▲ Lou Sally Fashions Corp ... E ... 212 354-9670
New York *(G-10615)*

Lou Sally Fashions Corp ... E ... 212 354-1283
New York *(G-10616)*

▲ McCall Pattern Company ... C ... 212 465-6800
New York *(G-10739)*

▲ Millennium Productions Inc ... F ... 212 944-6203
New York *(G-10808)*

◆ Milliore Fashion Inc ... G ... 212 302-0001
New York *(G-10811)*

▲ Nasserati Inc ... G ... 212 947-8100
New York *(G-10875)*

▲ Necessary Objects Ltd ... E ... 212 334-9888
Long Island City *(G-7535)*

Nine West Holdings Inc ... G ... 212 391-5000
New York *(G-10973)*

▲ Paris Wedding Center Corp ... F ... 347 368-4085
Flushing *(G-5035)*

Paris Wedding Center Corp ... E ... 212 267-8088
New York *(G-11114)*

Parsley Apparel Corp ... E ... 631 981-7181
Ronkonkoma *(G-14396)*

Pat & Rose Dress Inc ... D ... 212 279-1357
New York *(G-11121)*

Paula Varsalona Ltd ... F ... 212 570-9100
New York *(G-11125)*

PJ Designs Inc ... E ... 212 355-3100
New York *(G-11203)*

Plugg LLC ... F ... 212 840-6655
New York *(G-11212)*

▲ Product Development Intl LLC ... G ... 212 279-6170
New York *(G-11255)*

▲ Pronovias USA Inc ... E ... 212 897-6393
New York *(G-11262)*

Quality Patterns Inc ... D ... 212 704-0355
New York *(G-11297)*

▲ R & M Richards Inc ... D ... 212 921-8820
New York *(G-11310)*

▲ Raven New York LLC ... G ... 212 584-9690
New York *(G-11328)*

Rogan LLC ... G ... 212 680-1407
New York *(G-11420)*

▲ Rogan LLC ... E ... 646 496-9339
New York *(G-11421)*

◆ Ronni Nicole Group LLC ... E ... 212 764-1000
New York *(G-11429)*

Sg Nyc LLC ... E ... 310 210-1837
New York *(G-11548)*

▲ Shane Tex Inc ... F ... 516 486-7522
Woodmere *(G-16642)*

Spencer AB Inc ... G ... 646 831-3728
New York *(G-11667)*

▲ SSG Fashions Ltd ... G ... 212 221-0933
New York *(G-11689)*

Stitch & Couture Inc ... E ... 212 947-9204
New York *(G-11713)*

Tabrisse Collections Inc ... F ... 212 921-1014
New York *(G-11773)*

Tahari ASL LLC ... B ... 212 763-2800
New York *(G-11775)*

▲ Texport Fabrics Corp ... F ... 212 226-6066
New York *(G-11805)*

Therese The Childrens Collectn ... G ... 518 346-2315
Schenectady *(G-14721)*

▲ Thread LLC ... G ... 212 414-8844
New York *(G-11827)*

Tom & Linda Platt Inc ... F ... 212 221-7208
New York *(G-11858)*

Turn On Products Inc ... F ... 212 764-4545
New York *(G-11914)*

Ursula of Switzerland Inc ... E ... 518 237-2580
Waterford *(G-15990)*

Vanity Room Inc ... F ... 212 921-7154
New York *(G-11993)*

▲ Vera Wang Group LLC ... C ... 212 575-6400
New York *(G-12007)*

▲ Wear Abouts Apparel Inc ... F ... 212 827-0888
New York *(G-12085)*

▲ Worth Collection Ltd ... E ... 212 268-0312
New York *(G-12139)*

Yeohlee Inc ... F ... 212 631-8099
New York *(G-12161)*

2337 Women's & Misses' Suits, Coats & Skirts

2h International Corp ... G ... 347 623-9380
Forest Hills *(G-5069)*

79 Metro Ltd ... G ... 212 944-4030
New York *(G-8685)*

▲ Adar Medical Uniform LLC ... F ... 718 935-1197
Brooklyn *(G-1481)*

Adrienne Landau Designs Inc ... F ... 212 695-8362
New York *(G-8742)*

▲ Age Manufacturers Inc ... D ... 718 927-0048
Brooklyn *(G-1494)*

Agi Brooks Production Co Inc ... F ... 212 268-1533
New York *(G-8768)*

▲ Alfred Dunner Inc ... B ... 212 478-4300
New York *(G-8795)*

Alicia Adams Alpaca Inc ... G ... 845 868-3366
Millbrook *(G-8187)*

▲ Anna Sui Corp ... E ... 212 941-8406
New York *(G-8873)*

Bestec Concept Inc ... G ... 718 937-5848
Brooklyn *(G-1604)*

Bindle and Keep ... G ... 917 740-5002
Brooklyn *(G-1615)*

▲ Blatt Searle & Company Ltd ... E ... 212 730-7717
Long Island City *(G-7401)*

Bruno & Canio Ltd ... E ... 845 624-3060
Nanuet *(G-8460)*

Canada Goose Us Inc ... G ... 888 276-6297
Williamsville *(G-16574)*

▼ Carolina Herrera Ltd ... E ... 212 944-5757
New York *(G-9214)*

Centric Brands Inc ... D ... 323 890-1800
New York *(G-9246)*

▲ Countess Corporation ... G ... 212 869-7070
New York *(G-9408)*

Donna Karan Company LLC ... F ... 212 372-6500
New York *(G-9549)*

Donna Karan Company LLC ... C ... 212 789-1500
New York *(G-9550)*

◆ Donna Karan Company LLC ... B ... 212 789-1500
New York *(G-9551)*

◆ Donna Karan International Inc ... F ... 212 789-1500
New York *(G-9552)*

Donna Karan International Inc ... G ... 212 768-5800
New York *(G-9553)*

Elie Tahari Ltd ... D ... 212 398-2622
New York *(G-9646)*

Elie Tahari Ltd ... D ... 631 329-8883
East Hampton *(G-4237)*

Elie Tahari Ltd ... D ... 973 671-6300
New York *(G-9648)*

Elie Tahari Ltd ... D ... 212 763-2000
New York *(G-9647)*

Elie Tahari Ltd ... G ... 212 398-2622
New York *(G-9645)*

▲ Excelled Sheepskin & Lea Coat ... F ... 212 594-5843
New York *(G-9750)*

Four Seasons Fashion Mfg Inc ... E ... 212 947-6820
New York *(G-9832)*

▲ G-III Apparel Group Ltd ... B ... 212 403-0500
New York *(G-9869)*

G-III Leather Fashions Inc ... E ... 212 403-0500
New York *(G-9872)*

G18 Corporation ... G ... 212 869-0010
New York *(G-9873)*

Geoffrey Beene Inc ... E ... 212 371-5570
New York *(G-9908)*

▲ Global Gold Inc ... F ... 212 239-4657
New York *(G-9942)*

◆ Hampshire Sub II Inc ... D ... 631 321-0923
New York *(G-10027)*

▲ Harrison Sportswear Inc ... F ... 212 391-1051
New York *(G-10041)*

▼ Herman Kay Company Ltd ... C ... 212 239-2025
New York *(G-10083)*

◆ Hugo Boss Usa Inc ... D ... 212 940-0600
New York *(G-10146)*

◆ J Percy For Mrvin Rchards Ltd ... E ... 212 944-5300
New York *(G-10286)*

▲ Jeanjer LLC ... A ... 212 944-1330
New York *(G-10323)*

▲ Jon Teri Sports Inc ... E ... 212 398-0657
New York *(G-10357)*

▲ Judys Group Inc ... E ... 212 921-0515
New York *(G-10375)*

Kayo of California ... G ... 212 354-6336
New York *(G-10423)*

▲ Kozinn+sons Merchant Tailors ... E ... 212 643-1916
New York *(G-10475)*

Lady Brass Co Inc ... G ... 516 887-8040
Hewlett *(G-6047)*

▲ Levy Group Inc ... C ... 212 398-0707
New York *(G-10557)*

▲ Lf Outerwear LLC ... D ... 212 239-2025
New York *(G-10558)*

◆ Lily & Taylor Inc ... F ... 212 564-5459
New York *(G-10571)*

Linrich Designs Inc ... G ... 212 382-2257
New York *(G-10573)*

▲ Maggy Boutique Ltd ... E ... 212 997-5222
New York *(G-10664)*

▲ Marlou Garments Inc ... F ... 516 739-7100
New Hyde Park *(G-8549)*

Miny Group Inc ... D ... 212 925-6722
New York *(G-10820)*

Mp Studio Inc ... G ... 212 302-5666
New York *(G-10849)*

Employee Codes: A=Over 500 employees, B=251-500
C=101-250, D=51-100, E=20-50, F=10-19, G=5-9

2019 Harris
New York Manufacturers Directory

667

23 APPAREL AND OTHER FINISHED PRODUCTS MADE FROM FABRICS AND SIMILAR MATERIAL SIC SECTION

Nine West Holdings Inc.......C....... 212 642-3860
New York *(G-10972)*
▲ Nyc Idol Apparel Inc.......G....... 212 997-9797
New York *(G-11013)*
Opposuits USA Inc.......E....... 917 438-8878
New York *(G-11052)*
Pat & Rose Dress Inc.......D....... 212 279-1357
New York *(G-11121)*
▲ Permit Fashion Group Inc.......G....... 212 912-0988
Woodbury *(G-16627)*
Primo Coat Corp.......E....... 718 349-2070
Long Island City *(G-7560)*
Ps38 LLC.......G....... 212 302-1108
New York *(G-11268)*
▲ R & M Richards Inc.......D....... 212 921-8820
New York *(G-11310)*
▲ Rhoda Lee Inc.......D....... 212 840-5700
New York *(G-11384)*
▲ Shane Tex Inc.......F....... 516 486-7522
Woodmere *(G-16642)*
▲ Standard Manufacturing Co Inc.......D....... 518 235-2200
Troy *(G-15628)*
Tenby LLC.......C....... 646 863-5890
New York *(G-11800)*
Terrapin Station Ltd.......F....... 716 874-6677
Buffalo *(G-3091)*
Theory LLC.......D....... 212 762-2300
New York *(G-11811)*
Theory LLC.......G....... 212 879-0265
New York *(G-11812)*
Theory LLC.......G....... 631 204-0231
Southampton *(G-14963)*
▲ Tiger J LLC.......E....... 212 465-9300
New York *(G-11833)*
Turn On Products Inc.......F....... 212 764-4545
New York *(G-11914)*
Uniforms By Park Coats Inc.......E....... 718 499-1182
Brooklyn *(G-2600)*
▲ Uniqlo USA LLC.......F....... 877 486-4756
New York *(G-11948)*
Ursula of Switzerland Inc.......E....... 518 237-2580
Waterford *(G-15990)*
View Collections Inc.......F....... 212 944-4030
New York *(G-12031)*
Yeohlee Inc.......F....... 212 631-8099
New York *(G-12161)*

2339 Women's & Misses' Outerwear, NEC

1 Atelier LLC.......G....... 917 916-2968
New York *(G-8664)*
▲ 31 Phillip Lim LLC.......E....... 212 354-6540
New York *(G-8678)*
525 America LLC.......G....... 212 921-5688
New York *(G-8682)*
◆ 5th & Ocean Clothing Inc.......C....... 716 604-9000
Buffalo *(G-2677)*
▲ 6th Avenue Showcase Inc.......G....... 212 382-0400
New York *(G-8684)*
A & B Finishing Inc.......E....... 718 522-4702
Brooklyn *(G-1449)*
▲ Accessory Street LLC.......F....... 212 686-8990
New York *(G-8721)*
▲ Accessries Direct Intl USA Inc.......E....... 646 448-8200
New York *(G-8722)*
Adpro Sports LLC.......D....... 716 854-5116
Buffalo *(G-2687)*
Aerobic Wear Inc.......G....... 631 673-1830
Huntington Station *(G-6428)*
▲ Age Manufacturers Inc.......D....... 718 927-0048
Brooklyn *(G-1494)*
▲ Alfred Dunner Inc.......B....... 212 478-4300
New York *(G-8795)*
▲ Alleson of Rochester Inc.......D....... 585 272-0606
Rochester *(G-13614)*
Alleson of Rochester Inc.......E....... 315 548-3635
Geneva *(G-5316)*
Ally Nyc Corp.......G....... 212 447-7277
New York *(G-8804)*
▲ Alpha 6 Distributions LLC.......F....... 516 801-8290
Locust Valley *(G-7345)*
▲ Amber Bever Inc.......G....... 212 391-4911
Brooklyn *(G-1516)*
American Apparel Trading Corp.......G....... 212 764-5990
New York *(G-8823)*
▲ American Challenge Enterprises.......G....... 631 595-7171
New Hyde Park *(G-8515)*
▲ Angel-Made In Heaven Inc.......F....... 212 869-5678
New York *(G-8863)*
Angel-Made In Heaven Inc.......G....... 718 832-4778
Brooklyn *(G-1534)*
▲ Anna Sui Corp.......E....... 212 941-8406
New York *(G-8873)*
▲ Argee America Inc.......G....... 212 768-9840
New York *(G-8905)*
Authentic Brands Group LLC.......C....... 212 760-2410
New York *(G-8966)*
▲ Avalin LLC.......F....... 212 842-2286
New York *(G-8971)*
AZ Yashir Bapaz Inc.......G....... 212 947-7357
New York *(G-8985)*
▲ B Tween LLC.......F....... 212 819-9040
New York *(G-8993)*
Bag Bazaar Ltd.......E....... 212 689-3508
New York *(G-9002)*
▲ Bagznyc Corp.......F....... 212 643-8202
New York *(G-9003)*
Bam Sales LLC.......G....... 212 781-3000
New York *(G-9009)*
Bandier Corp.......G....... 212 242-5400
New York *(G-9011)*
Bandit International Ltd.......F....... 718 402-2100
Bronx *(G-1225)*
Bands N Bows.......G....... 718 984-4316
Staten Island *(G-15047)*
▲ Bank-Miller Co Inc.......E....... 914 227-9357
Pelham *(G-12933)*
▲ Bernard Chaus Inc.......D....... 212 354-1280
New York *(G-9051)*
Bernard Chaus Inc.......C....... 646 562-4700
New York *(G-9052)*
Bestec Concept Inc.......G....... 718 937-5848
Brooklyn *(G-1604)*
▲ Bh Brand Inc.......E....... 212 239-1635
New York *(G-9068)*
Bilco Industries Inc.......F....... 917 783-5008
New York *(G-9081)*
▲ Blue Duck Trading Ltd.......G....... 212 268-3122
New York *(G-9107)*
▲ Bock Family Holdings Inc.......E....... 212 921-5688
New York *(G-9116)*
Botkier Ny LLC.......G....... 212 343-2782
New York *(G-9125)*
Brigantine Inc.......G....... 212 354-8550
New York *(G-9139)*
C & C Athletic Inc.......G....... 845 713-4670
Walden *(G-15891)*
▲ Cai Design Inc.......F....... 212 401-9973
New York *(G-9177)*
Canada Goose Inc.......G....... 888 276-6297
New York *(G-9189)*
Canada Goose Inc.......G....... 888 668-0625
New York *(G-9190)*
Canada Goose Us Inc.......G....... 888 276-6297
Williamsville *(G-16574)*
▲ Candlesticks Inc.......F....... 212 947-8900
New York *(G-9194)*
▲ Caribbean Fashion Group Inc.......G....... 212 706-8851
New York *(G-9207)*
▲ Carolina Amato Inc.......G....... 212 768-9095
New York *(G-9213)*
▼ Carolina Herrera Ltd.......E....... 212 944-5757
New York *(G-9214)*
Casuals Etc Inc.......D....... 212 838-1319
New York *(G-9225)*
◆ Cathy Daniels Ltd.......E....... 212 354-8000
New York *(G-9231)*
◆ Central Apparel Group Ltd.......F....... 212 868-6505
New York *(G-9242)*
Central Mills Inc.......C....... 212 764-9011
New York *(G-9244)*
Centric Brands Inc.......D....... 323 890-1800
New York *(G-9246)*
Centric Denim Usa LLC.......F....... 646 839-7000
New York *(G-9247)*
Centric West LLC.......C....... 646 839-7000
New York *(G-9248)*
▲ China Ting Fashion Group (usa).......G....... 212 716-1600
New York *(G-9283)*
▲ Chloe International Inc.......F....... 212 730-6661
New York *(G-9285)*
▲ Christina Sales Inc.......F....... 212 391-0710
New York *(G-9293)*
▲ City Sites Sportswear Inc.......E....... 718 375-2990
Brooklyn *(G-1698)*
▲ Collection Xiix Ltd.......F....... 212 686-8990
New York *(G-9351)*
▲ Comint Apparel Group LLC.......F....... 212 947-7474
New York *(G-9363)*
▲ Comme-Ci Comme-CA AP Group.......E....... 631 300-1035
Hauppauge *(G-5795)*
Consolidated Fashion Corp.......G....... 212 719-3000
New York *(G-9383)*
Continental Knitting Mills.......G....... 631 242-5330
Deer Park *(G-3958)*
▲ Cynthia Rowley Inc.......F....... 212 242-3803
New York *(G-9443)*
D & V Enterprises Inc.......E....... 917 983-9250
Woodbury *(G-16617)*
▲ Daily Wear Sportswear Corp.......G....... 718 972-0533
Brooklyn *(G-1751)*
Dalma Dress Mfg Co Inc.......E....... 212 391-8296
Greenvale *(G-5629)*
Dana Michele LLC.......G....... 917 757-7777
New York *(G-9463)*
▲ Dani II Inc.......F....... 212 869-5999
New York *(G-9466)*
Danice Stores Inc.......F....... 212 665-0389
New York *(G-9467)*
▲ DFA New York LLC.......E....... 212 523-0021
New York *(G-9517)*
Dianos Kathryn Designs.......G....... 212 267-1584
New York *(G-9524)*
Donna Karan Company LLC.......C....... 212 789-1500
New York *(G-9550)*
◆ Donna Karan Company LLC.......B....... 212 789-1500
New York *(G-9551)*
◆ Donna Karan International Inc.......F....... 212 789-1500
New York *(G-9552)*
Donna Karan International Inc.......G....... 212 768-5800
New York *(G-9553)*
Doral Apparel Group Inc.......G....... 917 208-5652
New York *(G-9558)*
Double Take Fashions Inc.......G....... 718 832-9000
New York *(G-9561)*
▼ Dr Jayscom.......G....... 888 437-5297
New York *(G-9571)*
▲ Drew Philips Corp.......G....... 212 354-0095
New York *(G-9577)*
▲ Du Monde Trading Inc.......E....... 212 944-1306
New York *(G-9581)*
El-La Design Inc.......G....... 212 382-1080
New York *(G-9638)*
Elie Tahari Ltd.......G....... 212 398-2622
New York *(G-9645)*
Elie Tahari Ltd.......D....... 212 398-2622
New York *(G-9646)*
◆ Elizabeth Gillett Ltd.......G....... 212 629-7993
New York *(G-9655)*
Elizabeth Wilson.......G....... 516 486-2157
Uniondale *(G-15665)*
Elliot Mann Nyc Inc.......G....... 212 260-0658
New York *(G-9656)*
▲ Emerald Holdings Inc.......G....... 718 797-4404
Brooklyn *(G-1829)*
Emerson & Oliver LLC.......G....... 585 775-9929
Rochester *(G-13778)*
▲ F & J Designs Inc.......G....... 212 302-8755
New York *(G-9761)*
▲ Fad Inc.......E....... 631 385-2460
Huntington *(G-6398)*
Falls Manufacturing Inc.......G....... 518 672-7189
Philmont *(G-12986)*
Fashion Ave Sweater Knits LLC.......D....... 212 302-8282
New York *(G-9785)*
▲ Feldman Manufacturing Corp.......D....... 718 433-1700
Long Island City *(G-7446)*
First Love Fashions LLC.......F....... 212 256-1089
New York *(G-9808)*
Four Seasons Fashion Mfg Inc.......E....... 212 947-6820
New York *(G-9832)*
▲ French Atmosphere Inc.......F....... 516 371-9100
New York *(G-9846)*
Fusion Pro Performance Ltd.......F....... 917 833-0761
New York *(G-9864)*
▲ G-III Apparel Group Ltd.......B....... 212 403-0500
New York *(G-9869)*
G-III Leather Fashions Inc.......E....... 212 403-0500
New York *(G-9872)*
▲ GAME Sportswear Ltd.......E....... 914 962-1701
Yorktown Heights *(G-16817)*
◆ Garan Incorporated.......C....... 212 563-1292
New York *(G-9882)*
▼ Garan Manufacturing Corp.......G....... 212 563-2000
New York *(G-9883)*
Geoffrey Beene Inc.......E....... 212 371-5570
New York *(G-9908)*
▲ Gfb Fashions Ltd.......F....... 212 239-9230
New York *(G-9915)*
Giulietta LLC.......G....... 212 334-1859
Brooklyn *(G-1928)*

SIC SECTION — 23 APPAREL AND OTHER FINISHED PRODUCTS MADE FROM FABRICS AND SIMILAR MATERIAL

◆ Gloria Apparel Inc.....F 212 947-0869
New York *(G-9946)*
▲ GMC Mercantile Corp.....F 212 498-9488
New York *(G-9948)*
▲ Golden Leaves Knitwear Inc.....E 718 875-8235
Brooklyn *(G-1938)*
▲ Great Wall Corp.....C 212 704-4372
Long Island City *(G-7463)*
▲ H2gear Fashions LLC.....G 347 787-7508
Brooklyn *(G-1958)*
▲ Halmode Apparel Inc.....A 212 819-9114
New York *(G-10023)*
◆ Hampshire Sub II Inc.....D 631 321-0923
New York *(G-10027)*
▲ Hana Sportswear Inc.....E 315 639-6332
Dexter *(G-4115)*
▲ HB Athletic Inc.....F 914 560-8422
New Rochelle *(G-8613)*
◆ HC Contracting Inc.....D 212 643-9292
New York *(G-10054)*
Hearts of Palm LLC.....E 212 944-6660
New York *(G-10074)*
Hearts of Palm LLC.....D 212 944-6660
New York *(G-10075)*
▼ Herman Kay Company Ltd.....C 212 239-2025
New York *(G-10083)*
Hoehn Inc.....F 518 463-8900
Albany *(G-84)*
▲ Hot Line Industries Inc.....F 516 764-0400
Plainview *(G-13061)*
House Pearl Fashions (us) Ltd.....F 212 840-3183
New York *(G-10138)*
I Shalom & Co Inc.....C 212 532-7911
New York *(G-10161)*
Ifg Corp.....C 212 629-9600
New York *(G-10176)*
▲ Ikeddi Enterprises Inc.....F 212 302-7644
New York *(G-10180)*
Ikeddi Enterprises Inc.....G 212 302-7644
New York *(G-10181)*
▲ Int Trading USA LLC.....C 212 760-2338
New York *(G-10229)*
▲ Intriguing Threads Apparel Inc.....F 212 768-8733
New York *(G-10260)*
J & E Talit Inc.....G 718 850-1333
Richmond Hill *(G-13505)*
◆ J Percy For Mrvin Rchards Ltd.....E 212 944-5300
New York *(G-10286)*
Jaxis Inc.....G 212 302-7611
Brooklyn *(G-2034)*
Jaya Apparel Group LLC.....E 212 764-4980
New York *(G-10313)*
▲ Jeanjer LLC.....A 212 944-1330
New York *(G-10323)*
▲ JEnvie Sport Inc.....G 212 967-2322
New York *(G-10327)*
Jesse Joeckel.....G 631 668-2772
Montauk *(G-8304)*
◆ Joe Benbasset Inc.....E 212 594-8440
New York *(G-10349)*
Jomat New York Inc.....E 718 369-7641
Brooklyn *(G-2044)*
▲ Jonathan Michael Coat Corp.....G 212 239-9230
New York *(G-10359)*
▲ Jonden Manufacturing Co Inc.....F 516 442-4895
Oceanside *(G-12542)*
Jordache Enterprises Inc.....D 212 944-1330
New York *(G-10360)*
▲ Jordache Enterprises Inc.....C 212 643-8400
New York *(G-10361)*
▲ Jsc Designs Ltd.....E 212 302-1001
New York *(G-10374)*
▲ Judys Group Inc.....E 212 921-0515
New York *(G-10375)*
Just Bottoms & Tops Inc.....F 212 564-3202
New York *(G-10383)*
▼ K T P Design Co inc.....F 212 481-6613
New York *(G-10391)*
Kaltex America Inc.....F 212 971-0575
New York *(G-10400)*
Karen Kane Inc.....F 212 827-0980
New York *(G-10408)*
Kasper Group LLC.....F 212 354-4311
New York *(G-10413)*
▲ Katz Martell Fashion Trdg Intl.....G 212 840-0070
New York *(G-10418)*
Kayo of California.....G 212 354-6336
New York *(G-10423)*
Kicks Closet Sportswear Inc.....G 347 577-0857
Bronx *(G-1308)*

▼ Krasner Group Inc.....G 212 268-4100
New York *(G-10479)*
Ksk International Inc.....E 212 354-7770
New York *(G-10484)*
▲ L D Weiss Inc.....G 212 697-3023
New York *(G-10493)*
▲ Lahoya Enterprise Inc.....E 718 886-8799
College Point *(G-3652)*
▲ Lai Apparel Design Inc.....E 212 382-1075
New York *(G-10509)*
◆ Land n Sea Inc.....D 212 444-6000
New York *(G-10513)*
Leesa Designs Ltd.....G 631 261-3991
Centerport *(G-3349)*
◆ Leggiadro International Inc.....E 212 997-8766
New York *(G-10541)*
Lemral Knitwear Inc.....D 718 210-0175
Brooklyn *(G-2109)*
Leng Universal Inc.....F 212 398-6800
New York *(G-10545)*
▲ Leslie Stuart Co Inc.....F 212 629-4551
New York *(G-10555)*
Lgb Inc.....E 212 278-8280
New York *(G-10559)*
▲ Liberty Apparel Company Inc.....E 718 625-4000
New York *(G-10560)*
Life Style Design Group.....E 212 391-8666
New York *(G-10564)*
▲ Light Inc.....G 212 629-3255
New York *(G-10568)*
◆ Lily & Taylor Inc.....F 212 564-5459
New York *(G-10571)*
Linrich Designs Inc.....G 212 382-2257
New York *(G-10573)*
▲ Liquid Knits Inc.....F 718 706-6600
Long Island City *(G-7501)*
▲ Lotus Apparel Designs Inc.....G 646 236-9363
Westbury *(G-16352)*
Luxe Imagine Consulting LLC.....G 212 273-9770
New York *(G-10632)*
▲ M A M Knitting Mills Corp.....E 800 570-0093
Brooklyn *(G-2144)*
▲ Mag Brands LLC.....D 212 629-9600
New York *(G-10660)*
▲ Maggy Boutique Ltd.....E 212 997-5222
New York *(G-10664)*
Maiyet Inc.....G 212 343-9999
New York *(G-10674)*
Malia Mills Inc.....F 212 354-4200
Brooklyn *(G-2154)*
▲ Manchu New York Inc.....G 212 921-5050
New York *(G-10682)*
▲ Manchu Times Fashion Inc.....G 212 921-5050
New York *(G-10683)*
▲ Mango Usa Inc.....E 718 998-6050
Brooklyn *(G-2156)*
Marcasiano Inc.....G 212 614-9412
New York *(G-10697)*
▲ Marconi Intl USA Co Ltd.....G 212 391-2626
New York *(G-10699)*
Marina Holding Corp.....F 718 646-9283
Brooklyn *(G-2167)*
Mars Fashions Inc.....E 718 402-2200
Bronx *(G-1323)*
Mayberry Shoe Company Inc.....G 315 692-4086
Manlius *(G-7780)*
▲ Medi-Tech International Corp.....G 800 333-0109
Brooklyn *(G-2187)*
▲ Meryl Diamond Ltd.....D 212 730-0333
New York *(G-10779)*
Michael Feldman Inc.....D 718 433-1700
Long Island City *(G-7524)*
Miguelina Inc.....F 212 925-0320
New York *(G-10803)*
◆ Mikael Aghal LLC.....F 212 596-4010
New York *(G-10804)*
▲ Millennium Productions Inc.....F 212 944-6203
New York *(G-10808)*
Miltons of New York Inc.....G 212 997-3359
New York *(G-10813)*
MISS Sportswear Inc.....G 212 391-2535
Brooklyn *(G-2212)*
▲ MISS Sportswear Inc.....G 212 391-2535
Brooklyn *(G-2213)*
MISS Sportswear Inc.....F 718 369-6012
Brooklyn *(G-2214)*
▲ Moes Wear Apparel Inc.....F 718 940-1597
Brooklyn *(G-2222)*
Morelle Products Ltd.....F 212 391-8070
New York *(G-10841)*

▲ Mv Corp Inc.....C 631 273-8020
Bay Shore *(G-703)*
▲ Mystic Inc.....C 212 239-2025
New York *(G-10869)*
▲ Necessary Objects Ltd.....E 212 334-9888
Long Island City *(G-7535)*
▲ New Concepts of New York LLC.....E 212 695-4999
Brooklyn *(G-2257)*
▲ New York Accessory Group Inc.....E 212 532-7911
New York *(G-10932)*
Nine West Holdings Inc.....G 212 642-3860
New York *(G-10971)*
Nine West Holdings Inc.....G 212 221-6376
New York *(G-10974)*
Nine West Holdings Inc.....E 212 642-3860
New York *(G-10977)*
Nine West Holdings Inc.....E 212 822-1300
New York *(G-10978)*
Nine West Holdings Inc.....E 215 785-4000
New York *(G-10979)*
Nine West Holdings Inc.....G 212 575-2571
New York *(G-10975)*
Nlhe LLC.....E 212 594-0012
Brooklyn *(G-2270)*
▲ Noah Enterprises Ltd.....E 212 736-2888
New York *(G-10982)*
▲ Ocean Waves Swim LLC.....G 212 967-4481
New York *(G-11027)*
▲ ODY Accessories Inc.....E 212 239-0580
New York *(G-11032)*
On The Double Inc.....G 518 431-3571
Germantown *(G-5339)*
▲ One Jeanswear Group Inc.....B 212 575-2571
New York *(G-11042)*
▲ One Step Up Ltd.....D 212 398-1110
New York *(G-11043)*
Only Hearts Ltd.....E 212 268-0886
New York *(G-11046)*
P & I Sportswear Inc.....G 718 934-4587
New York *(G-11082)*
Pacific Alliance Usa Inc.....G 336 500-8184
New York *(G-11088)*
▲ Pacific Alliance Usa Inc.....D 646 839-7000
New York *(G-11089)*
Paddy Lee Fashions Inc.....F 718 786-6020
Long Island City *(G-7547)*
Park Avenue Sportswear Ltd.....F 718 369-0520
Brooklyn *(G-2305)*
◆ Passport Brands Inc.....E 646 459-2625
New York *(G-11120)*
Pat & Rose Dress Inc.....D 212 279-1357
New York *(G-11121)*
▲ Penfli Industries Inc.....F 212 947-6080
Great Neck *(G-5581)*
▲ Permit Fashion Group Inc.....G 212 912-0988
Woodbury *(G-16627)*
Petrunia LLC.....G 607 277-1930
Ithaca *(G-6604)*
Plugg LLC.....F 212 840-6655
New York *(G-11212)*
▲ Popnyc 1 LLC.....G 646 684-4600
New York *(G-11218)*
Pride & Joys Inc.....F 212 594-9820
New York *(G-11239)*
Primo Coat Corp.....E 718 349-2070
Long Island City *(G-7560)*
▲ Pti-Pacific Inc.....G 212 414-8495
New York *(G-11271)*
Pvh Corp.....D 212 502-6300
New York *(G-11284)*
Pvh Corp.....G 212 381-3800
New York *(G-11283)*
RAK Finishing Corp.....E 718 416-4242
Howard Beach *(G-6331)*
▲ Ramsbury Property Us Inc.....F 212 223-6250
New York *(G-11322)*
▲ RD Intrntnl Style.....G 212 382-2360
New York *(G-11335)*
Rene Portier Inc.....G 718 853-7896
Brooklyn *(G-2398)*
▲ Republic Clothing Corporation.....E 212 719-3000
New York *(G-11365)*
Republic Clothing Group Inc.....C 212 719-3000
New York *(G-11366)*
▲ Rhoda Lee Inc.....D 212 840-5700
New York *(G-11384)*
Richard Manufacturing Co Inc.....G 718 254-0958
Brooklyn *(G-2401)*
▲ Ritchie Corp.....F 212 768-0083
New York *(G-11397)*

SIC

Employee Codes: A=Over 500 employees, B=251-500
C=101-250, D=51-100, E=20-50, F=10-19, G=5-9
2019 Harris
New York Manufacturers Directory
669

23 APPAREL AND OTHER FINISHED PRODUCTS MADE FROM FABRICS AND SIMILAR MATERIAL SIC SECTION

Robespierre Inc....G.... 212 764-8810
New York *(G-11409)*
▲ Robespierre Inc....C.... 212 594-0012
New York *(G-11410)*
Rogers Group Inc....E.... 212 643-9292
New York *(G-11423)*
▲ Rvc Enterprises LLC....E.... 212 391-4600
New York *(G-11451)*
▲ S & S Manufacturing Co Inc....D.... 212 444-6000
New York *(G-11456)*
S & V Knits Inc....E.... 631 752-1595
Farmingdale *(G-4872)*
S & W Knitting Mills Inc....E.... 718 237-2416
Brooklyn *(G-2436)*
▲ S Broome and Co Inc....D.... 718 663-6800
Long Island City *(G-7583)*
▲ S2 Sportswear Inc....F.... 347 335-0713
Brooklyn *(G-2441)*
Salisbury Sportswear Inc....E.... 516 221-9519
Bellmore *(G-794)*
▲ Sam Hee International Inc....G.... 212 594-7815
New York *(G-11474)*
▲ Sarina Accessories LLC....F.... 212 239-8106
New York *(G-11490)*
▲ Sea Waves Inc....G.... 516 766-4201
Oceanside *(G-12556)*
▲ Sensational Collection Inc....G.... 212 840-7388
New York *(G-11543)*
Shanghai Harmony AP Intl LLC....E.... 646 569-5680
New Rochelle *(G-8628)*
Shirl-Lynn of New York....F.... 315 363-5898
Oneida *(G-12621)*
Siskind Group Inc....F.... 212 840-0880
New York *(G-11601)*
▲ Smooth Industries Incorporated....E.... 212 869-1080
New York *(G-11628)*
Snowman....G.... 212 239-8818
New York *(G-11632)*
Spectrum Apparel Inc....D.... 212 239-2025
New York *(G-11664)*
Sport Athleisure Ltd....F.... 212 868-6505
New York *(G-11673)*
▲ SRP Apparel Group Inc....G.... 212 764-4810
New York *(G-11687)*
Ssa Trading Ltd....F.... 646 465-9500
New York *(G-11688)*
▲ SSG Fashions Ltd....G.... 212 221-0933
New York *(G-11689)*
St John....G.... 718 720-8367
Staten Island *(G-15137)*
St John....G.... 718 771-4541
Brooklyn *(G-2506)*
▲ Standard Manufacturing Co Inc....D.... 518 235-2200
Troy *(G-15628)*
▲ Sterling Possessions Ltd....G.... 212 594-0418
New York *(G-11707)*
Stony Apparel Corp....G.... 212 391-0022
New York *(G-11716)*
▲ Street Beat Sportswear Inc....F.... 718 302-1500
Brooklyn *(G-2524)*
▲ Sunynams Fashions Ltd....G.... 212 268-5200
New York *(G-11746)*
▲ Survival Inc....G.... 631 385-5060
Centerport *(G-3352)*
Swatfame Inc....G.... 212 944-8022
New York *(G-11756)*
◆ Swimwear Anywhere Inc....D.... 631 420-1400
Farmingdale *(G-4886)*
Swimwear Anywhere Inc....E.... 845 858-4141
Port Jervis *(G-13238)*
Tahari ASL LLC....B.... 212 763-2800
New York *(G-11775)*
▲ Tailored Sportsman LLC....F.... 646 366-8733
New York *(G-11776)*
Tamka Sport LLC....G.... 718 224-7820
Douglaston *(G-4142)*
Tbhl International LLC....F.... 212 799-2007
New York *(G-11787)*
▲ THE Design Group Inc....F.... 212 681-1548
New York *(G-11808)*
▲ Tiger J LLC....E.... 212 465-9300
New York *(G-11833)*
▲ Tillsonburg Company USA Inc....E.... 267 994-8096
New York *(G-11835)*
Toni Industries Inc....F.... 212 921-0700
Great Neck *(G-5596)*
▲ TR Designs Inc....E.... 212 398-9300
New York *(G-11882)*
▲ Turn On Products Inc....D.... 212 764-2121
New York *(G-11913)*
Turn On Products Inc....F.... 212 764-4545
New York *(G-11914)*
▲ Untuckit LLC....E.... 201 214-9054
New York *(G-11965)*
Untuckit LLC....C.... 646 724-1857
New York *(G-11966)*
▲ Urban Apparel Group Inc....E.... 212 947-7009
New York *(G-11968)*
▲ Uspa Accessories LLC....C.... 212 868-2590
New York *(G-11981)*
Valenti Neckwear Co Inc....G.... 914 969-0700
Yonkers *(G-16805)*
▲ Venus Manufacturing Co Inc....D.... 315 639-3100
Dexter *(G-4116)*
Vf Imagewear Inc....E.... 718 352-2363
Bayside *(G-751)*
Vf Outdoor LLC....E.... 845 928-4900
Central Valley *(G-3398)*
◆ Warnaco Group Inc....E.... 212 287-8000
New York *(G-12070)*
▲ White Gate Holdings Inc....E.... 212 564-3266
New York *(G-12102)*
Yigal-Azrouel Inc....E.... 212 302-1194
New York *(G-12162)*
▲ Z-Ply Corp....E.... 212 398-7011
New York *(G-12167)*
▼ Zar Group LLC....G.... 212 944-2510
New York *(G-12169)*
◆ Zg Apparel Group LLC....E.... 212 944-2510
New York *(G-12175)*
Zia Power Inc....E.... 845 661-8388
New York *(G-12176)*
▲ Zoomers Inc....E.... 718 369-2656
Brooklyn *(G-2670)*

2341 Women's, Misses' & Children's Underwear & Nightwear

Allure Fashions Inc....G.... 516 829-2470
Great Neck *(G-5532)*
▲ Ann Gish Inc....G.... 212 969-9200
New York *(G-8871)*
▲ Apparel Partnership Group LLC....G.... 212 302-7722
New York *(G-8889)*
▲ Ariela and Associates Intl LLC....C.... 212 683-4131
New York *(G-8907)*
Becks Classic Mfg Inc....D.... 631 435-3800
Brentwood *(G-1128)*
▲ Candlesticks Inc....F.... 212 947-8900
New York *(G-9194)*
Classic Designer Workshop Inc....G.... 212 730-8480
New York *(G-9319)*
▲ Comme-Ci Comme-CA AP Group....E.... 631 300-1035
Hauppauge *(G-5795)*
▲ Dayleen Intimates Inc....E.... 914 969-5900
Yonkers *(G-16749)*
Enticing Lingerie Inc....E.... 718 998-8625
Brooklyn *(G-1838)*
Faye Bernard Loungewear....G.... 718 951-7245
Brooklyn *(G-1871)*
▲ Handcraft Manufacturing Corp....C.... 212 251-0022
New York *(G-10029)*
◆ Intimateco LLC....G.... 212 239-4411
New York *(G-10256)*
▲ Kokin Inc....E.... 212 643-8225
New York *(G-10465)*
▲ Komar Layering LLC....E.... 212 725-1500
New York *(G-10467)*
▲ Komar Luxury Brands....G.... 646 472-0060
New York *(G-10468)*
Lady Ester Lingerie Corp....E.... 212 689-1729
New York *(G-10506)*
Loungehouse LLC....E.... 646 524-2965
New York *(G-10618)*
Luxerdame Co Inc....E.... 718 752-9800
Long Island City *(G-7507)*
Mrt Textile Inc....G.... 800 674-1073
New York *(G-10854)*
Natori Company Incorporated....E.... 212 532-7796
New York *(G-10891)*
▲ Natori Company Incorporated....D.... 212 532-7796
New York *(G-10890)*
Only Hearts Ltd....E.... 212 268-0886
New York *(G-11046)*
▲ Sleepwear Holdings Inc....C.... 516 466-4738
New York *(G-11618)*
Vanity Fair Brands LP....C.... 212 548-1548
New York *(G-11992)*
Wacoal International Corp....D.... 212 532-6100
New York *(G-12064)*
◆ Warnaco Group Inc....E.... 212 287-8000
New York *(G-12070)*
◆ Warnaco Inc....B.... 212 287-8000
New York *(G-12071)*
Warnaco Inc....F.... 718 722-3000
Brooklyn *(G-2639)*
▲ Waterbury Garment LLC....E.... 212 725-1500
New York *(G-12080)*
▲ Wickers Sportswear Inc....G.... 631 543-1700
Commack *(G-3707)*

2342 Brassieres, Girdles & Garments

Burlen Corp....F.... 212 684-0052
New York *(G-9159)*
▲ Cupid Foundations Inc....C.... 212 686-6224
New York *(G-9434)*
Deunall Corporation....C.... 516 667-8875
Levittown *(G-7133)*
E P Sewing Pleating Inc....E.... 212 967-2575
New York *(G-9596)*
East Coast Molders Inc....C.... 516 240-6000
Oceanside *(G-12536)*
Edith Lances Corp....E.... 212 683-1990
New York *(G-9627)*
Enticing Lingerie Inc....E.... 718 998-8625
Brooklyn *(G-1838)*
Higgins Supply Company Inc....D.... 607 836-6474
Mc Graw *(G-7927)*
Luxerdame Co Inc....E.... 718 752-9800
Long Island City *(G-7507)*
▲ New York Elegance Entps Inc....F.... 212 685-3088
New York *(G-10936)*
▲ Prime Garments Inc....F.... 212 354-7294
Rockville Centre *(G-14237)*
▼ Rago Foundations LLC....E.... 718 728-8436
Astoria *(G-441)*
Sensual Inc....E.... 212 869-1450
New York *(G-11544)*
▲ Valmont Inc....F.... 212 685-1653
New York *(G-11987)*
Wacoal America Inc....E.... 212 743-9600
New York *(G-12063)*
◆ Warnaco Group Inc....E.... 212 287-8000
New York *(G-12070)*
◆ Warnaco Inc....B.... 212 287-8000
New York *(G-12071)*
Warnaco Inc....F.... 718 722-3000
Brooklyn *(G-2639)*

2353 Hats, Caps & Millinery

▲ A-1 Skull Cap Corp....E.... 718 633-9333
Brooklyn *(G-1463)*
Albrizio Inc....G.... 212 719-5290
Brooklyn *(G-1501)*
Athletic Cap Co Inc....E.... 718 398-1300
Staten Island *(G-15045)*
Bollman Hat Company....G.... 212 981-9836
New York *(G-9118)*
Bonk Sam Unforms Civilian Cap....E.... 718 585-0665
Bronx *(G-1230)*
▲ Cookies Inc....A.... 646 452-5552
New York *(G-9393)*
Dorel Hat Co....E.... 845 831-5231
Beacon *(G-757)*
▲ Flexfit Llc....D.... 516 932-8800
Hicksville *(G-6086)*
Gce International Inc....F.... 212 868-0500
New York *(G-9891)*
Hankin Brothers Cap Co....F.... 716 892-8840
Buffalo *(G-2864)*
◆ Hat Attack Inc....E.... 718 994-1000
Bronx *(G-1288)*
Kays Caps Inc....G.... 518 273-6079
Troy *(G-15596)*
▲ Kim Eugenia Inc....G.... 212 674-1345
New York *(G-10444)*
▲ Kingform Cap Company Inc....D.... 516 822-2501
Hicksville *(G-6098)*
▲ Kokin Inc....E.... 212 643-8225
New York *(G-10465)*
▲ Kraft Hat Manufacturers Inc....D.... 845 735-6200
Pearl River *(G-12904)*
▲ Lenore Marshall Inc....G.... 212 947-5945
New York *(G-10547)*
▲ Lloyds Fashions Inc....D.... 631 435-3353
Brentwood *(G-1141)*
Matthews Hats....G.... 718 859-4683
Brooklyn *(G-2181)*
Mega Power Sports Corporation....G.... 212 627-3380
New York *(G-10764)*

New ERA Cap Co Inc .... B 716 604-9000
Buffalo (G-2964)
◆ New ERA Cap Co Inc .... B 716 604-9000
Buffalo (G-2965)
New ERA Cap Co Inc .... F 716 549-0445
Derby (G-4114)
Paletot Ltd .... F 212 268-3774
New York (G-11094)
Room At The Top Inc .... G 718 257-0766
Brooklyn (G-2414)
Therese The Childrens Collectn ..... G 518 346-2315
Schenectady (G-14721)
▲ Weinfeld Skull Cap Mfg Co Inc ... G 718 854-3864
Brooklyn (G-2641)
Whittall & Shon .... G 212 594-2626
New York (G-12106)

2361 Children's & Infants' Dresses & Blouses

▲ Andy & Evan Industries Inc .... G 212 967-7908
New York (G-8861)
◆ Bowe Industries Inc .... D 718 441-6464
Clendale (G-5392)
◆ Brooke Maya Inc .... E 212 268-2626
New York (G-9148)
▲ Cheri Mon Baby LLC .... G 212 354-5511
New York (G-9270)
▲ Consolidated Childrens AP Inc ... G 212 239-8615
New York (G-9381)
Cream Bebe .... F 917 578-2088
Brooklyn (G-1726)
E-Play Brands LLC .... G 212 563-2646
New York (G-9600)
◆ Garan Incorporated .... C 212 563-1292
New York (G-9882)
▼ Garan Manufacturing Corp .... G 212 563-2000
New York (G-9883)
Gce International Inc .... F 212 868-0500
New York (G-9891)
◆ General Sportwear Company Inc .. C ... 212 764-5820
New York (G-9902)
◆ Gerson & Gerson Inc .... C 212 244-6775
New York (G-9914)
▲ Grand Knitting Mills Inc .... E 631 226-5000
Amityville (G-278)
◆ Great Universal Corp .... E 917 302-0065
New York (G-9982)
◆ Gw Acquisition LLC .... E 212 736-4848
New York (G-10011)
Haddad Bros Inc .... E 718 377-5505
Brooklyn (G-1959)
▲ Haddad Bros Inc .... F 212 563-2117
New York (G-10018)
Hard Ten Clothing Inc .... G 212 302-1321
New York (G-10036)
◆ JM Originals Inc .... C 845 647-3003
Ellenville (G-4439)
Jordache Enterprises Inc .... D 212 944-1330
New York (G-10360)
▲ Jordache Enterprises Inc .... C 212 643-8400
New York (G-10361)
◆ Land n Sea Inc .... D 212 444-6000
New York (G-10513)
▲ Manchu New York Inc .... G 212 921-5050
New York (G-10682)
Michael Stuart Inc .... E 718 821-0704
Brooklyn (G-2204)
Rosenau Beck Inc .... F 212 279-6202
New York (G-11433)
▲ S & C Bridal LLC .... F 212 789-7000
New York (G-11454)
S & C Bridals LLC .... G 213 624-4477
New York (G-11455)
▲ Silly Phillie Creations Inc .... E 718 492-6300
Brooklyn (G-2471)
◆ Skip Hop Inc .... G 646 902-9874
New York (G-11610)
Skip Hop Holdings Inc .... G 212 868-9850
New York (G-11611)
Sports Products America LLC .... E 212 594-5511
New York (G-11676)
▲ Star Childrens Dress Co Inc ...... D 212 279-1524
New York (G-11695)
▲ Sue & Sam Co Inc .... G 718 436-1672
Brooklyn (G-2530)
Thats My Girl Inc .... G 212 695-0020
Brooklyn (G-2563)
▲ Zinnias Inc .... F 718 746-8551
Bellerose (G-783)

2369 Girls' & Infants' Outerwear, NEC

6 Shore Road LLC .... G 212 274-9666
New York (G-8683)
Aerobic Wear Inc .... G 631 673-1830
Huntington Station (G-6428)
Baby Uv/Kids Uv Inc .... F 917 301-9020
Stony Brook (G-15163)
◆ Babyfair Inc .... E 212 736-7989
New York (G-8997)
▲ Best Brands Consumer Pdts Inc .. G ... 212 684-7456
New York (G-9057)
▲ Candlesticks Inc .... F 212 947-8900
New York (G-9194)
Detour Apparel Inc .... E 212 221-3265
New York (G-9512)
▲ Devil Dog Manufacturing Co Inc .. G 845 647-4411
Ellenville (G-4438)
▲ Domani Fashions Corp .... G 718 797-0505
Brooklyn (G-1786)
E-Play Brands LLC .... G 212 563-2646
New York (G-9600)
▲ Fine Sheer Industries Inc .... F 212 594-4224
New York (G-9804)
▲ Franco Apparel Group Inc .... D 212 967-7272
New York (G-9839)
◆ Garan Incorporated .... C 212 563-1292
New York (G-9882)
▼ Garan Manufacturing Corp .... G 212 563-2000
New York (G-9883)
◆ General Sportwear Company Inc .. C ... 212 764-5820
New York (G-9902)
◆ Gerson & Gerson Inc .... C 212 244-6775
New York (G-9914)
◆ Gw Acquisition LLC .... E 212 736-4848
New York (G-10011)
Haddad Bros Inc .... E 718 377-5505
Brooklyn (G-1959)
▲ Ideal Creations Inc .... C 212 563-5928
New York (G-10171)
▲ In Mocean Group LLC .... D 212 944-0317
New York (G-10190)
▲ Isfel Co Inc .... G 212 736-6216
New York (G-10275)
▲ Jeanjer LLC .... A 212 944-1330
New York (G-10323)
Jgx LLC .... G 212 575-1244
New York (G-10336)
◆ JM Originals Inc .... C 845 647-3003
Ellenville (G-4439)
Jomat New York Inc .... G 718 369-7641
Brooklyn (G-2044)
Jordache Enterprises Inc .... D 212 944-1330
New York (G-10360)
▲ Jordache Enterprises Inc .... C 212 643-8400
New York (G-10361)
K & S Childrens Wear Inc .... G 718 624-0006
Brooklyn (G-2062)
Kahn-Lucas-Lancaster Inc .... D 212 239-2407
New York (G-10395)
◆ Land n Sea Inc .... D 212 444-6000
New York (G-10513)
Leng Universal Inc .... F 212 398-6800
New York (G-10545)
▲ Liberty Apparel Company Inc ..... E 718 625-4000
New York (G-10560)
◆ Lollytogs Ltd .... D 212 502-6000
New York (G-10595)
▲ M Hidary & Co Inc .... D 212 736-6540
New York (G-10639)
Michael Stuart Inc .... E 718 821-0704
Brooklyn (G-2204)
Miltons of New York Inc .... G 212 997-3359
New York (G-10813)
Nyc Bronx Inc .... G 917 417-0509
Bronx (G-1346)
◆ Oxygen Inc .... G 516 433-1144
Hicksville (G-6118)
Pink Crush LLC .... G 718 788-6978
New York (G-11198)
▲ Pti-Pacific Inc .... G 212 414-8495
New York (G-11271)
Rogers Group Inc .... E 212 643-9292
New York (G-11423)
◆ S Rothschild & Co Inc .... G 212 354-8550
New York (G-11459)
Sch Dpx Corporation .... G 917 405-5377
New York (G-11500)
▲ Silly Phillie Creations Inc .... E 718 492-6300
Brooklyn (G-2471)
▲ Sister Sister Inc .... G 212 629-9600
New York (G-11602)
Sleepy Head Inc .... F 718 237-9655
Brooklyn (G-2485)
Swatfame Inc .... G 212 944-8022
New York (G-11756)
Therese The Childrens Collectn ..... G 518 346-2315
Schenectady (G-14721)
◆ Warnaco Group Inc .... E 212 287-8000
New York (G-12070)
◆ Waterbury Garment LLC .... E 212 725-1500
New York (G-12080)
Yigal-Azrouel Inc .... E 212 302-1194
New York (G-12162)
▲ Z-Ply Corp .... E 212 398-7011
New York (G-12167)
▲ Zinnias Inc .... F 718 746-8551
Bellerose (G-783)

2371 Fur Goods

▲ Anage Inc .... F 212 944-6533
New York (G-8852)
Anastasia Furs International .... G 212 868-9241
New York (G-8855)
Arbeit Bros Inc .... G 212 736-9761
New York (G-8898)
▲ Avante .... G 516 782-4888
Great Neck (G-5538)
B Smith Furs Inc .... F 212 967-5290
New York (G-8992)
▲ Best Brands Consumer Pdts Inc .. G ... 212 684-7456
New York (G-9057)
▲ Blum & Fink Inc .... F 212 695-2606
New York (G-9112)
▲ CPT Usa LLC .... E 212 575-1616
New York (G-9414)
▲ Dennis Basso Couture Inc .... F 212 794-4500
New York (G-9501)
Fox Unlimited Inc .... G 212 736-3071
New York (G-9835)
Georgy Creative Fashions Inc .... G 212 279-4885
New York (G-9912)
◆ J Percy For Mrvin Rchards Ltd ... G 212 944-5300
New York (G-10286)
Jerry Sorbara Furs Inc .... F 212 594-3897
New York (G-10328)
◆ Kaitery Furs Ltd .... G 718 204-1396
Long Island City (G-7486)
Miller & Berkowitz Ltd .... F 212 244-5459
New York (G-10809)
Mink Mart Inc .... G 212 868-2785
New York (G-10819)
Mksf Inc .... G 212 563-3877
New York (G-10827)
Moschos Furs Inc .... G 212 244-0255
New York (G-10845)
Samuel Schulman Furs Inc .... F 212 736-5550
New York (G-11478)
Sekas International Ltd .... F 212 629-6095
New York (G-11536)
▲ Stallion Inc .... E 718 706-0111
Long Island City (G-7596)
Stefan Furs Inc .... G 212 594-2788
New York (G-11701)
Steves Original Furs Inc .... F 212 967-8007
New York (G-11711)
Superior Furs Inc .... F 516 365-4123
Manhasset (G-7772)
Xanadu .... G 212 465-0580
New York (G-12149)

2381 Dress & Work Gloves

Falls Manufacturing Inc .... G 518 672-7189
Philmont (G-12986)
◆ Fownes Brothers & Co Inc .... E 212 683-0150
New York (G-9834)
Fownes Brothers & Co Inc .... E 518 752-4411
Gloversville (G-5456)
Gce International Inc .... G 212 868-0500
New York (G-9891)
▲ Manzella Knitting .... G 716 825-0808
Orchard Park (G-12727)

2384 Robes & Dressing Gowns

Authentic Brands Group LLC .... C 212 760-2410
New York (G-8966)
◆ Komar Luxury Brands .... G 646 472-0060
New York (G-10468)
Lady Ester Lingerie Corp .... E 212 689-1729
New York (G-10506)

23 APPAREL AND OTHER FINISHED PRODUCTS MADE FROM FABRICS AND SIMILAR MATERIAL SIC SECTION

Mata Fashions LLC....G.... 917 716-7894
New York (G-10724)
▲ Natori Company Incorporated ....D.... 212 532-7796
New York (G-10890)
◆ Nautica Opco LLC....B.... 212 541-5757
New York (G-10896)
◆ Palmbay Ltd....G.... 718 424-3388
Flushing (G-5034)
Sketch Studio Trading Inc....G.... 212 244-2875
New York (G-11607)

2385 Waterproof Outerwear

A W R Group Inc....F.... 718 729-0412
Long Island City (G-7363)
◆ Essex Manufacturing Inc....D.... 212 239-0080
New York (G-9712)
Float Tech Inc....G.... 518 266-0964
Troy (G-15605)
▲ Hercules Group Inc....E.... 212 813-8000
Port Washington (G-13264)
▲ Levy Group Inc....C.... 212 398-0707
New York (G-10557)
▲ Mpdw Inc....G.... 925 631-6878
New York (G-10851)
▲ Top Fortune Usa Ltd....G.... 516 608-2694
Lynbrook (G-7676)

2386 Leather & Sheep Lined Clothing

▲ Andrew M Schwartz LLC....G.... 212 391-7070
New York (G-8860)
Avanti U S A Ltd....F.... 716 695-5800
Tonawanda (G-15524)
Cockpit Usa Inc....F.... 212 575-1616
New York (G-9343)
Cockpit Usa Inc....F.... 908 558-9704
New York (G-9344)
▲ Excelled Sheepskin & Lea Coat....F.... 212 594-5843
New York (G-9750)
▲ G-III Apparel Group Ltd....B.... 212 403-0500
New York (G-9869)
G-III Leather Fashions Inc....E.... 212 403-0500
New York (G-9872)
Georgy Creative Fashions Inc....G.... 212 279-4885
New York (G-9912)
▲ J Lowy Co....G.... 718 338-7324
Brooklyn (G-2024)
◆ J Percy For Mrvin Rchards Ltd....E.... 212 944-5300
New York (G-10286)
Lost Worlds Inc....G.... 212 923-3423
New York (G-10613)
Louis Schwartz....G.... 845 356-6624
Spring Valley (G-15000)
Studio One Leather Design Inc....F.... 212 760-1701
New York (G-11728)
▲ US Authentic LLC....G.... 914 767-0295
Katonah (G-6847)

2387 Apparel Belts

Barrera Jose & Maria Co Ltd....E.... 212 239-1994
New York (G-9021)
Centric Brands Inc....D.... 323 890-1800
New York (G-9246)
▲ Courtlandt Boot Jack Co Inc....E.... 718 445-6200
Flushing (G-4994)
▲ Daniel M Friedman & Assoc Inc....E.... 212 695-5545
New York (G-9468)
Dynasty Belts Inc....E.... 516 625-6280
New Hyde Park (G-8529)
Gbg USA Inc....D.... 646 839-7083
New York (G-9888)
Gbg USA Inc....E.... 212 615-3400
New York (G-9889)
Nassau Suffolk Brd of Womens....E.... 631 666-8835
Bay Shore (G-704)
▲ New Classic Inc....F.... 718 609-1100
Long Island City (G-7537)
P M Belts Usa Inc....E.... 800 762-3580
Brooklyn (G-2297)
◆ Perry Ellis Menswear LLC....C.... 212 221-7500
New York (G-11162)
Randa Accessories Lea Gds LLC....D.... 212 354-5100
New York (G-11325)
Sandy Duftler Designs Ltd....F.... 516 379-3084
North Baldwin (G-12366)
Sh Leather Novelty Company....G.... 718 387-7742
Brooklyn (G-2461)
◆ Tapestry Inc....B.... 212 594-1850
New York (G-11784)
▲ Trafalgar Company LLC....G.... 212 768-8800
New York (G-11885)

Universal Elliot Corp....G.... 212 736-8877
New York (G-11960)
Xinya International Trading Co....G.... 212 216-9681
New York (G-12152)

2389 Apparel & Accessories, NEC

▲ A Lunt Design Inc....F.... 716 662-0781
Orchard Park (G-12695)
▲ Accessries Direct Intl USA Inc....E.... 646 448-8200
New York (G-8722)
▲ Adf Accessories Inc....G.... 516 450-5755
Oceanside (G-12530)
▲ Apollo Apparel Group LLC....F.... 212 398-6585
New York (G-8885)
Barbara Matera Ltd....D.... 212 475-5006
New York (G-9012)
▲ Bh Brand Inc....E.... 212 239-1635
New York (G-9068)
Brooklyn Denim Co....F.... 718 782-2600
Brooklyn (G-1642)
▲ Carter Enterprises LLC....E.... 718 853-5052
Brooklyn (G-1679)
Costume Armour Inc....F.... 845 534-9120
Cornwall (G-3832)
▲ Costume Culture By Franco LLC....G.... 718 821-7100
Glendale (G-5396)
Craft Clerical Clothes Inc....G.... 212 764-6122
New York (G-9416)
Creative Costume Co....G.... 212 564-5552
Liverpool (G-7231)
Cygnet Studio Inc....F.... 646 450-4550
New York (G-9442)
D-C Theatricks....G.... 716 847-0180
Buffalo (G-2791)
David & Young Co Inc....G.... 212 594-6034
New York (G-9479)
Davis....G.... 716 833-4678
Buffalo (G-2794)
▲ Dreamwave LLC....E.... 212 594-4250
New York (G-9574)
▲ Dvf Studio LLC....D.... 212 741-6607
New York (G-9589)
Dvf Studio LLC....G.... 646 576-8009
New York (G-9590)
▲ Eb Couture Ltd....E.... 212 912-0190
New York (G-9615)
Eric Winterling Inc....E.... 212 629-7686
New York (G-9700)
▼ Euroco Costumes Inc....G.... 212 629-9665
New York (G-9730)
Foot Locker Retail Inc....F.... 516 827-5306
Hicksville (G-6087)
▲ Gce International Inc....D.... 212 704-4800
New York (G-9890)
▲ HB Athletic Inc....F.... 914 560-8422
New Rochelle (G-8613)
Hoehn Inc....F.... 518 463-8900
Albany (G-84)
▲ Hpk Industries LLC....F.... 315 724-0196
Utica (G-15709)
Hudson Dying & Finishing LLC....E.... 518 752-4389
Gloversville (G-5459)
I Shalom & Co Inc....C.... 212 532-7911
New York (G-10161)
Intercotton Company Inc....G.... 212 265-3809
New York (G-10239)
Izquierdo Studios Ltd....F.... 212 807-9757
New York (G-10279)
J & C Finishing....E.... 718 456-1087
Ridgewood (G-13539)
JC California Inc....G.... 212 334-4380
New York (G-10317)
Jersey Express Inc....F.... 716 834-6151
Buffalo (G-2894)
▲ Jimeale Incorporated....G.... 917 686-5383
New York (G-10339)
▲ JM Studio Inc....F.... 646 546-5514
New York (G-10345)
John Kristiansen New York Inc....F.... 212 388-1097
New York (G-10352)
Jolibe Atelier LLC....F.... 917 319-5908
New York (G-10356)
Jonathan Meizler LLC....G.... 212 213-2977
New York (G-10358)
▲ Joseph Industries Inc....E.... 212 764-0010
New York (G-10364)
▲ Kidz Concepts LLC....D.... 212 398-1110
New York (G-10441)
Kiton Building Corp....E.... 212 486-3224
New York (G-10453)

Koon Enterprises LLC....G.... 718 886-3163
Fresh Meadows (G-5200)
Kww Productions Corp....F.... 212 398-8181
New York (G-10488)
▲ L D Weiss Inc....G.... 212 697-3023
New York (G-10493)
▼ Lakeland Industries Inc....C.... 631 981-9700
Ronkonkoma (G-14367)
Linder New York LLC....F.... 646 678-5819
New York (G-10572)
▲ Lr Paris LLC....F.... 212 634-9372
New York (G-10621)
M2 Fashion Group Holdings Inc....G.... 917 208-2948
New York (G-10645)
Masquerade LLC....F.... 212 673-4546
New York (G-10723)
▲ Meryl Diamond Ltd....D.... 212 730-0333
New York (G-10779)
Moresca Clothing and Costume....F.... 845 331-6012
Ulster Park (G-15659)
Mountain and Isles LLC....F.... 212 354-1890
New York (G-10848)
My Hanky Inc....F.... 646 321-0869
Brooklyn (G-2238)
▲ New York Accessory Group Inc....E.... 212 532-7911
New York (G-10932)
New York Hospital Disposable....E.... 718 384-1620
Brooklyn (G-2262)
NY 1 Art Gallery Inc....G.... 917 698-0626
New Hyde Park (G-8554)
▲ NY Orthopedic Usa Inc....D.... 718 852-5330
Brooklyn (G-2279)
▲ Onia LLC....E.... 646 701-0008
New York (G-11045)
Parsons-Meares Ltd....D.... 212 242-3378
Long Island City (G-7549)
Patient-Wear LLC....G.... 914 740-7770
Bronx (G-1353)
◆ Perry Ellis Menswear LLC....C.... 212 221-7500
New York (G-11162)
▲ Ppr Direct Marketing LLC....G.... 718 965-8600
Brooklyn (G-2332)
▲ Prolink Industries Inc....F.... 212 354-5690
New York (G-11259)
RA Newhouse Inc....D.... 516 248-6670
Mineola (G-8244)
▲ Rainforest Apparel LLC....G.... 212 840-0880
New York (G-11318)
Randa Accessories Lea Gds LLC....D.... 212 354-5100
New York (G-11325)
Ribz LLC....G.... 212 764-9595
New York (G-11385)
▲ Rjm2 Ltd....G.... 212 944-1660
New York (G-11401)
Robert Miller Associates LLC....F.... 718 392-1640
Long Island City (G-7576)
▲ Rose Solomon Co....E.... 718 855-1788
Brooklyn (G-2415)
▲ Rosetti Handbags and ACC....E.... 646 839-7945
New York (G-11434)
▲ Roth Clothing Co Inc....G.... 718 384-4927
Brooklyn (G-2416)
◆ Rubies Costume Company Inc....B.... 718 846-1008
Richmond Hill (G-13510)
Rubies Costume Company Inc....D.... 631 777-3300
Bay Shore (G-719)
Rubies Costume Company Inc....C.... 718 441-0834
Richmond Hill (G-13511)
Rubies Costume Company Inc....C.... 631 951-3688
Bay Shore (G-720)
Rubies Costume Company Inc....E.... 516 333-3473
Westbury (G-16370)
Rubies Costume Company Inc....F.... 631 435-7912
Bay Shore (G-721)
Rubies Costume Company Inc....E.... 516 326-1500
Bay Shore (G-722)
Rubies Costume Company Inc....C.... 718 846-1008
Richmond Hill (G-13512)
Rubies Masquerade Company LLC....G.... 718 846-1008
Richmond Hill (G-13513)
▲ S & B Fashion Inc....G.... 718 482-1386
Long Island City (G-7582)
Schneeman Studio Limited....G.... 212 244-3330
New York (G-11506)
▲ Shamron Mills Ltd....G.... 212 354-0430
Troy (G-15625)
South Central Boyz....G.... 718 496-7270
Brooklyn (G-2501)
▲ Swank Inc....B.... 212 867-2600
New York (G-11753)

▲ Timeless Fashions LLC ....G....... 212 730-9328
New York *(G-11846)*
Tr Apparel LLC ....E....... 310 595-4337
New York *(G-11880)*
Tr Apparel LLC ....G....... 646 358-3888
New York *(G-11881)*
▲ Trafalgar Company LLC 212 768-8800
New York *(G-11885)*
Trash and Vaudeville Inc 212 777-1727
New York *(G-11888)*
Twcc Product and Sales ....E...... 212 614-9364
New York *(G-11917)*
▲ Ufo Contemporary Inc ....F...... 212 226-5400
New York *(G-11932)*
Unified Inc Ied ....F...... 646 370-4650
New York *(G-11939)*
Warner ....G....... 716 446-0663
Buffalo *(G-3124)*
Westchester Wine Warehouse LLC ....F...... 914 824-1400
White Plains *(G-16520)*
White Plains Coat Apron Co Inc ....G....... 914 736-2610
Peekskill *(G-12931)*

2391 Curtains & Draperies

Abalene Decorating Services ....E....... 718 782-2000
New York *(G-8705)*
Anthony Lawrence of New York ....E....... 212 206-8820
Long Island City *(G-7380)*
Associated Drapery & Equipment ....F....... 516 671-5245
Monroe *(G-8263)*
◆ Baby Signature Inc ....G....... 212 686-1700
New York *(G-8996)*
◆ Belle Maison USA Ltd ....E....... 718 805-0200
Richmond Hill *(G-13498)*
Bettertex Inc ....F....... 212 431-3373
New York *(G-9062)*
◆ Bramson House Inc ....C....... 516 764-5006
Freeport *(G-5146)*
C & G of Kingston Inc ....D....... 845 331-0148
Kingston *(G-6890)*
Cabriole Designs Inc ....E....... 212 593-4528
New York *(G-9174)*
◆ County Draperies Inc ....F....... 845 342-9009
Middletown *(G-8144)*
Deangelis Ltd ....E....... 212 348-8225
Glen Head *(G-5379)*
Drapery Industries Inc ....F....... 585 232-2992
Rochester *(G-13750)*
Fabric Quilters Unlimited Inc ....E....... 516 333-2866
Westbury *(G-16330)*
▲ J Edlin Interiors Ltd ....F....... 212 243-2111
New York *(G-10285)*
Jo-Vin Decorators Inc ....E....... 718 441-9350
Woodhaven *(G-16636)*
Laminated Window Products Inc ....F....... 631 242-6883
Bay Shore *(G-693)*
▼ Laregence Inc ....E....... 212 736-2548
New York *(G-10517)*
Majestic Curtains LLC ....G....... 718 898-0774
Elmhurst *(G-4469)*
▼ Macon Contract Products LLC ....D....... 516 328-6900
New Hyde Park *(G-8550)*
▲ Mistdoda Inc ....E....... 919 735-7111
New York *(G-10824)*
▲ Mutual Sales Corp ....E....... 718 361-8373
Long Island City *(G-7530)*
Northast Coml Win Trtments Inc ....D....... 845 331-0148
Kingston *(G-6912)*
◆ Revman International Inc ....E....... 212 894-3100
New York *(G-11378)*
Reynolds Drapery Service Inc ....F....... 315 845-8632
Newport *(G-12256)*
◆ Richloom Fabrics Corp ....F....... 212 685-5400
New York *(G-11391)*
▲ Richloom Fabrics Group Inc ....G....... 212 685-5400
New York *(G-11392)*
Seaway Mats Inc ....G....... 518 483-2560
Malone *(G-7726)*
Showeray Co ....D....... 718 965-3633
Brooklyn *(G-2466)*
Shyam Ahuja Limited ....G....... 212 644-5910
New York *(G-11573)*
Terbo Ltd ....G....... 718 847-2860
Richmond Hill *(G-13516)*
Wayne Decorators Inc ....G....... 718 529-4200
Jamaica *(G-6690)*
Wcd Window Coverings Inc ....E....... 845 336-4511
Lake Katrine *(G-6973)*
White Workroom Inc ....G....... 212 941-5910
New York *(G-12104)*

2392 House furnishings: Textile

388 Associates Inc ....G....... 267 367-0990
Brooklyn *(G-1437)*
AEP Environmental LLC ....F....... 716 446-0739
Buffalo *(G-2690)*
▲ Alen Sands York Associates Ltd .....F....... 212 563-6305
New York *(G-8790)*
Alexandra Ferguson LLC ....G....... 718 788-7768
New Rochelle *(G-8587)*
▲ Anhui Skyworth LLC ....D....... 917 940-6903
Hempstead *(G-6005)*
▲ Ann Gish Inc ....G....... 212 969-9200
New York *(G-8871)*
Apex Real Holdings Inc ....G....... 877 725-2150
Brooklyn *(G-1540)*
▲ Area Inc ....G....... 212 924-7084
New York *(G-8904)*
▲ Arlee Home Fashions Inc ....G....... 212 689-0020
New York *(G-8908)*
▲ August Silk Inc ....G....... 212 643-2400
New York *(G-8961)*
August Silk Inc ....G....... 212 643-2400
New York *(G-8962)*
◆ Baby Signature Inc ....G....... 212 686-1700
New York *(G-8996)*
▲ Bardwil Industries Inc ....C....... 212 944-1870
New York *(G-9014)*
◆ Belle Maison USA Ltd ....E....... 718 805-0200
Richmond Hill *(G-13498)*
▲ Bramson House Inc ....C....... 516 764-5006
Freeport *(G-5146)*
▲ Broder Mfg Inc ....G....... 718 366-1667
Brooklyn *(G-1636)*
C & G of Kingston Inc ....D....... 845 331-0148
Kingston *(G-6890)*
▲ Caddy Concepts Inc ....G....... 516 570-6279
Great Neck *(G-5541)*
▲ Catalina Products Corp ....F....... 718 336-8288
Brooklyn *(G-1683)*
▲ Cathay Home Inc ....E....... 212 213-0988
New York *(G-9229)*
▲ Continental Quilting Co Inc ....G....... 718 499-9100
New Hyde Park *(G-8525)*
◆ County Draperies Inc ....F....... 845 342-9009
Middletown *(G-8144)*
◆ Cpac Inc ....E....... 585 382-3223
Leicester *(G-7126)*
▲ Creative Home Furnishings ....G....... 631 582-8000
Central Islip *(G-3364)*
Creative Scents USA Inc ....G....... 718 522-5901
Brooklyn *(G-1729)*
▲ Dico Products Corporation ....F....... 315 797-0470
Utica *(G-15694)*
▲ E & F Home Fashions Inc ....G....... 718 968-9719
Brooklyn *(G-1802)*
▲ Elegant Linen Inc ....F....... 718 492-0297
Brooklyn *(G-1823)*
Ess Bee Industries Inc ....E....... 718 894-5202
Brooklyn *(G-1850)*
▲ Excellent Art Mfg Corp ....F....... 718 388-7075
Inwood *(G-6489)*
EY Industries Inc ....F....... 718 624-9122
Brooklyn *(G-1860)*
Fabric Quilters Unlimited Inc ....E....... 516 333-2866
Westbury *(G-16330)*
▲ Franks Cushions Inc ....F....... 718 848-1216
Maspeth *(G-7847)*
▲ Handy Laundry Products Corp ....G....... 845 701-1111
Airmont *(G-12)*
▲ Himatsingka America Inc ....E....... 212 824-2949
New York *(G-10101)*
Hollander HM Fshons Hldngs LLC ......F....... 212 575-0400
New York *(G-10116)*
Hollander Sleep Products LLC ....D....... 212 575-0400
New York *(G-10117)*
▲ Home Fashions Intl LLC ....E....... 212 689-3579
New York *(G-10119)*
Home Fashions Intl LLC ....G....... 212 684-0091
New York *(G-10120)*
◆ Indigo Home Inc ....G....... 212 684-4146
New York *(G-10199)*
▲ Ingenious Designs LLC ....G....... 631 254-3376
Ronkonkoma *(G-14353)*
Jdt International LLC ....G....... 212 400-7570
New York *(G-10321)*
Jo-Vin Decorators Inc ....E....... 718 441-9350
Woodhaven *(G-16636)*
▲ Josie Accessories Inc ....D....... 212 889-6376
New York *(G-10366)*

▲ Kaltex North America Inc ....F....... 212 894-3200
New York *(G-10401)*
◆ Kartell Us Inc ....G....... 212 966-6665
New York *(G-10409)*
◆ Kim Seybert Inc ....F....... 212 564-7850
New York *(G-10445)*
Medline Industries Inc ....B....... 845 344-3301
Middletown *(G-8163)*
Mgk Group Inc ....E....... 212 989-2732
New York *(G-10788)*
Michael Stuart Inc ....F....... 718 821-0704
Brooklyn *(G-2204)*
MMS H& F Inc ....G....... 718 785-6663
Jamaica *(G-6663)*
Moga Trading Company Inc ....G....... 718 760-2966
Corona *(G-3851)*
▲ National Wire & Metal Tech Inc ......E....... 716 661-9180
Jamestown *(G-6740)*
▲ Nationwide Tarps Incorporated ....D....... 518 843-1545
Amsterdam *(G-353)*
Nbets Corporation ....G....... 516 785-1259
Wantagh *(G-15925)*
◆ Northpoint Trading Inc ....F....... 212 481-8001
New York *(G-10997)*
▲ NY Cutting Inc ....G....... 646 434-1355
Suffern *(G-15194)*
Paramount Textiles Inc ....F....... 212 966-1040
New York *(G-11109)*
▲ Perfex Corporation ....F....... 315 826-3600
Poland *(G-13184)*
Performance Sourcing Group Inc .....G....... 914 636-2100
Scarsdale *(G-14642)*
◆ Place Vendome Holding Co Inc ......C....... 212 696-0765
New York *(G-11205)*
Premier Skirting Products Inc ....F....... 516 239-6581
Lawrence *(G-7107)*
▲ Q Squared Design LLC ....E....... 212 686-8860
New York *(G-11290)*
▲ R & M Industries Inc ....G....... 212 366-6414
New York *(G-11309)*
Repellem Consumer Pdts Corp ....F....... 631 273-3992
Bohemia *(G-1082)*
◆ Revman International Inc ....E....... 212 894-3100
New York *(G-11378)*
◆ Richloom Fabrics Corp ....F....... 212 685-5400
New York *(G-11391)*
▲ Richloom Fabrics Group Inc ....G....... 212 685-5400
New York *(G-11392)*
▲ Royal Copenhagen Inc ....F....... 845 454-4442
Poughkeepsie *(G-13364)*
Showeray Co ....D....... 718 965-3633
Brooklyn *(G-2466)*
▲ Silly Phillie Creations Inc ....F....... 718 492-6300
Brooklyn *(G-2471)*
▲ Skil-Care Corporation ....C....... 914 963-2040
Yonkers *(G-16798)*
Sleepable Sofas Ltd ....D....... 973 546-4502
New York *(G-11617)*
▲ Sleeping Partners Intl Inc ....F....... 212 254-1515
Brooklyn *(G-2484)*
▲ Soft-Tex International Inc ....D....... 800 366-2324
Waterford *(G-15987)*
Sterling Shelf Liners Inc ....G....... 631 676-5175
Holbrook *(G-6211)*
◆ Sunham Home Fashions LLC ....D....... 212 695-1218
New York *(G-11742)*
Superior Decorators Inc ....F....... 718 381-4793
Glendale *(G-5408)*
Sure Fit Inc ....E....... 212 395-9340
New York *(G-11749)*
Tablecloths For Granted Ltd ....F....... 518 370-5481
Schenectady *(G-14719)*
Terbo Ltd ....G....... 718 847-2860
Richmond Hill *(G-13516)*
▲ University Table Cloth Company .....F....... 845 371-3876
Spring Valley *(G-15012)*
Wayne Decorators Inc ....G....... 718 529-4200
Jamaica *(G-6690)*
William Harvey Studio Inc ....G....... 718 599-4343
Brooklyn *(G-2648)*

2393 Textile Bags

▲ Ace Drop Cloth Canvas Pdts Inc ....E....... 718 731-1550
Bronx *(G-1208)*
Advanced Medical Mfg Corp ....E....... 845 369-7535
Suffern *(G-15184)*
▲ Aka Sport Inc ....F....... 631 858-9888
Dix Hills *(G-4118)*
Carry Hot Inc ....F....... 212 279-7535
New York *(G-9216)*

23 APPAREL AND OTHER FINISHED PRODUCTS MADE FROM FABRICS AND SIMILAR MATERIAL SIC SECTION

GPM Associates LLC..........G....... 585 359-1770
Rush *(G-14473)*
GPM Associates LLC..........E....... 585 335-3940
Dansville *(G-3926)*
▲ **H G Maybeck Co Inc**..........E....... 718 297-4410
Jamaica *(G-6649)*
▲ **Health Matters America Inc**..........F....... 716 235-8772
Buffalo *(G-2869)*
◆ **Ivi Services Inc**..........D....... 607 729-5111
Binghamton *(G-897)*
▲ **Jag Manufacturing Inc**..........E....... 518 762-9558
Johnstown *(G-6832)*
Jakes Sneakers Inc..........G....... 718 233-1132
Brooklyn *(G-2033)*
Johnson Outdoors Inc..........C....... 607 779-2200
Binghamton *(G-899)*
Kragel Co Inc..........G....... 716 648-1344
Hamburg *(G-5685)*
▲ **Kush Oasis Enterprises LLC**..........G....... 516 513-1316
Syosset *(G-15221)*
Mgk Group Inc..........E....... 212 989-2732
New York *(G-10788)*
Paulpac LLC..........G....... 631 283-7610
Southampton *(G-14958)*
Prima Satchel Inc..........G....... 929 367-7770
Monroe *(G-8279)*
▼ **Select Fabricators Inc**..........F....... 585 393-0650
Canandaigua *(G-3233)*
Spray Moret LLC..........G....... 917 213-9592
New York *(G-11679)*
Wayne Decorators Inc..........G....... 718 529-4200
Jamaica *(G-6690)*

2394 Canvas Prdts

125-127 Main Street Corp..........F....... 631 477-1500
Greenport *(G-5625)*
Abble Awning Co Inc..........G....... 516 822-1200
Bethpage *(G-837)*
▲ **Ace Canvas & Tent Corp**..........F....... 631 648-0614
Ronkonkoma *(G-14288)*
▲ **Ace Drop Cloth Canvas Pdts Inc**..........E....... 718 731-1550
Bronx *(G-1208)*
Acme Awning Co Inc..........F....... 718 409-1881
Bronx *(G-1210)*
▼ **Air Structures Amercn Tech Inc**..........E....... 914 937-4500
Port Chester *(G-13191)*
Allen Boat Co Inc..........G....... 716 842-0800
Buffalo *(G-2691)*
AMS Star Structures Inc..........G....... 914 584-0898
Nyack *(G-12499)*
Anchor Canvas LLC..........G....... 631 265-5602
Smithtown *(G-14894)*
Automtive Uphl Cnvertible Tops..........G....... 914 961-4242
Tuckahoe *(G-15642)*
Awning Mart Inc..........G....... 315 699-5928
Cicero *(G-3514)*
Breton Industries Inc..........C....... 518 842-3030
Amsterdam *(G-329)*
Broadway Neon Sign Corp..........F....... 908 241-4177
Ronkonkoma *(G-14322)*
Brock Awnings Ltd..........F....... 631 765-5200
Hampton Bays *(G-5708)*
C E King & Sons Inc..........G....... 631 324-4944
East Hampton *(G-4233)*
Canvas Products Company Inc..........F....... 516 742-1058
Mineola *(G-8209)*
Capitol Awning Co Inc..........F....... 212 505-1717
Jamaica *(G-6631)*
Classic Awnings Inc..........F....... 716 649-0390
Hamburg *(G-5674)*
▲ **Covergrip Corporation**..........G....... 855 268-3747
Manorville *(G-7783)*
▲ **Custom Canvas Manufacturing Co**..........E....... 716 852-6372
Buffalo *(G-2789)*
▲ **Custom European Imports Inc**..........E....... 845 357-5718
Sloatsburg *(G-14892)*
▲ **Dhs Systems LLC**..........F....... 845 359-6066
Orangeburg *(G-12674)*
Di Sanos Creative Canvas Inc..........G....... 315 894-3137
Frankfort *(G-5105)*
Dor-A-Mar Canvas Products Co..........F....... 631 750-9202
West Sayville *(G-16288)*
◆ **Durasol Systems Inc**..........D....... 845 610-1100
Chester *(G-3473)*
Fabric Concepts For Industry..........F....... 914 375-2565
Yonkers *(G-16757)*
▲ **Jag Manufacturing Inc**..........E....... 518 762-9558
Johnstown *(G-6832)*
Jamestown Awning Inc..........G....... 716 483-1435
Jamestown *(G-6726)*
Jo-Vin Decorators Inc..........E....... 718 441-9350
Woodhaven *(G-16636)*
Johnson Outdoors Inc..........C....... 607 779-2200
Binghamton *(G-899)*
Ke Durasol Awnings Inc..........F....... 845 610-1100
Chester *(G-3477)*
Kingston Building Products LLC..........G....... 914 665-0707
Mount Vernon *(G-8415)*
Kohler Awning Inc..........E....... 716 685-3333
Buffalo *(G-2911)*
Kragel Co Inc..........G....... 716 648-1344
Hamburg *(G-5685)*
Kraus & Sons Inc..........F....... 212 620-0408
New York *(G-10480)*
Laminated Window Products Inc..........F....... 631 242-6883
Bay Shore *(G-693)*
Lanza Corp..........G....... 914 937-6360
Port Chester *(G-13204)*
▲ **Leiter Sukkahs Inc**..........G....... 718 436-0303
Brooklyn *(G-2108)*
M & M Canvas & Awnings Inc..........G....... 631 424-5370
Islandia *(G-6534)*
Mauceri Sign Inc..........F....... 718 656-7700
Jamaica *(G-6659)*
Mc Coy Tops and Interiors Inc..........G....... 718 458-5800
Woodside *(G-16662)*
▼ **Melbourne C Fisher Yacht Sails**..........G....... 631 673-5055
Huntington Station *(G-6451)*
▼ **Meyco Products Inc**..........E....... 631 421-9800
Melville *(G-8046)*
▲ **Nationwide Tarps Incorporated**..........D....... 518 843-1545
Amsterdam *(G-353)*
Northern Awning & Sign Company..........G....... 315 782-8515
Watertown *(G-16030)*
Perma Tech Inc..........E....... 716 854-0707
Buffalo *(G-3000)*
Point Canvas Company Inc..........G....... 607 692-4381
Whitney Point *(G-16556)*
Quantum Sails Rochester LLC..........G....... 585 342-5200
Rochester *(G-14064)*
Sausbiers Awning Shop Inc..........G....... 518 828-3748
Hudson *(G-6371)*
▼ **Select Fabricators Inc**..........F....... 585 393-0650
Canandaigua *(G-3233)*
Service Canvas Co Inc..........F....... 716 853-0558
Buffalo *(G-3062)*
Steinway Awning II LLC..........G....... 718 729-2965
Astoria *(G-446)*
TG Peppe Inc..........G....... 516 239-7852
Lawrence *(G-7110)*
Toptec Products LLC..........F....... 631 421-9800
Melville *(G-8072)*
Ulmer Sales LLC..........F....... 718 885-1700
Port Chester *(G-13210)*
Utility Canvas Inc..........G....... 845 255-9290
Gardiner *(G-5297)*
Vinyl Works Inc..........E....... 518 786-1200
Latham *(G-7097)*
▲ **Y & A Trading Inc**..........F....... 718 436-6333
Brooklyn *(G-2661)*

2395 Pleating & Stitching For The Trade

A Trusted Name Inc..........F....... 716 326-7400
Westfield *(G-16391)*
▲ **Active World Solutions Inc**..........G....... 718 922-9404
Brooklyn *(G-1480)*
Aditiany Inc..........G....... 212 997-8440
New York *(G-8738)*
All About Art Inc..........F....... 718 321-0755
Flushing *(G-4983)*
All American Awards Inc..........F....... 631 567-2025
Bohemia *(G-975)*
American Country Quilts & Lin..........G....... 631 283-5466
Southampton *(G-14949)*
American Quality Embroidery..........G....... 631 467-3200
Ronkonkoma *(G-14306)*
Arena Graphics Inc..........G....... 516 767-5108
Port Washington *(G-13244)*
Athletic Cap Co Inc..........E....... 718 398-1300
Staten Island *(G-15045)*
Casual Friday Inc..........F....... 585 544-9470
Rochester *(G-13695)*
Clpa Embroidery..........G....... 516 409-0002
Bellmore *(G-787)*
Control Research Inc..........G....... 631 225-1111
Amityville *(G-269)*
Custom Patches Inc..........E....... 845 679-6320
Woodstock *(G-16685)*
Design Archives Inc..........G....... 212 768-0617
New York *(G-9504)*
Dirt T Shirts Inc..........E....... 845 336-4230
Kingston *(G-6898)*
▲ **Eagle Regalia Co Inc**..........F....... 845 425-2245
Spring Valley *(G-14989)*
East Coast Embroidery Ltd..........G....... 631 254-3878
Deer Park *(G-3969)*
Eiseman-Ludmar Co Inc..........F....... 516 932-6990
Hicksville *(G-6083)*
Expressions Punching & Digitiz..........G....... 718 291-1177
Jamaica *(G-6642)*
F X Graphix Inc..........G....... 716 871-1511
Buffalo *(G-2823)*
Glenda Inc..........G....... 718 442-8981
Staten Island *(G-15079)*
▲ **Holland & Sherry Inc**..........E....... 212 542-8410
New York *(G-10115)*
Hosel & Ackerson Inc..........G....... 212 575-1490
New York *(G-10125)*
Human Technologies Corporation..........F....... 315 735-3532
Utica *(G-15711)*
Instant Monogramming Inc..........G....... 585 654-5550
Rochester *(G-13882)*
▲ **Jomar Industries Inc**..........E....... 845 357-5773
Airmont *(G-14)*
Kabrics..........G....... 607 962-6344
Corning *(G-3821)*
Karishma Fashions Inc..........G....... 718 565-5404
Jackson Heights *(G-6620)*
Kevin J Kassman..........G....... 585 529-4245
Rochester *(G-13904)*
Knucklehead Embroidery Inc..........G....... 607 797-2725
Johnson City *(G-6814)*
Loremanss Embroidery Engrav..........F....... 518 834-9205
Keeseville *(G-6852)*
Mainly Monograms Inc..........E....... 845 624-4923
West Nyack *(G-16275)*
Milaaya Inc..........G....... 212 764-6386
New York *(G-10806)*
Mrinalini Inc..........G....... 646 510-2747
New York *(G-10852)*
Northeast Stitches & Ink Inc..........E....... 518 798-5549
South Glens Falls *(G-14939)*
▲ **NY Embroidery Inc**..........E....... 516 822-6456
Hicksville *(G-6116)*
On The Job Embroidery & AP..........G....... 914 381-3556
Mamaroneck *(G-7750)*
Pass Em-Entries Inc..........F....... 718 392-0100
Long Island City *(G-7550)*
Penn & Fletcher Inc..........F....... 212 239-6868
Long Island City *(G-7553)*
Pink Inc..........E....... 212 352-8282
New York *(G-11197)*
Planet Embroidery..........F....... 718 381-4827
Ridgewood *(G-13546)*
Point Canvas Company Inc..........G....... 607 692-4381
Whitney Point *(G-16556)*
Quist Industries Ltd..........F....... 718 243-2800
Brooklyn *(G-2373)*
Rescuestuff Inc..........G....... 718 318-7570
Peekskill *(G-12923)*
Ross L Sports Screening Inc..........F....... 716 824-5350
Buffalo *(G-3047)*
Round Top Knit & Screening..........G....... 518 622-3600
Round Top *(G-14466)*
Royal Tees Inc..........G....... 845 357-9448
Suffern *(G-15197)*
Sand Hill Industries Inc..........G....... 518 885-7991
Ballston Spa *(G-595)*
Sciane Enterprises Inc..........G....... 845 452-2400
Poughkeepsie *(G-13366)*
Screen Gems Inc..........G....... 845 561-0036
New Windsor *(G-8659)*
Screen The World Inc..........F....... 631 475-0023
Holtsville *(G-6244)*
Shykat Promotions..........G....... 866 574-2757
Forestville *(G-5088)*
Stephen M Kiernan..........E....... 716 836-6300
Buffalo *(G-3076)*
Stucki Embroidery Works Inc..........F....... 845 657-2308
Boiceville *(G-1110)*
Stylist Pleating Corp..........F....... 718 384-8181
Brooklyn *(G-2529)*
Todd Walbridge..........G....... 585 254-3018
Rochester *(G-14171)*
U All Inc..........E....... 518 438-2558
Albany *(G-136)*
Uniform Namemakers Inc..........F....... 716 626-5474
Buffalo *(G-3110)*
Verdonette Inc..........G....... 212 719-2003
New York *(G-12010)*

Vogue Too Plting Stitching EMB .... F 212 354-1022
New York *(G-12052)*

Voyager Emblems Inc .... C 416 255-3421
Buffalo *(G-3121)*

Wicked Smart LLC .... F 518 459-2855
Watervliet *(G-16057)*

2396 Automotive Trimmings, Apparel Findings, Related Prdts

Acorn Products Corp .... F 315 894-4868
Ilion *(G-6473)*

Albert Siy .... G 718 359-0389
Flushing *(G-4982)*

American Spray-On Corp .... E 212 929-2100
New York *(G-8837)*

▲ Amoseastern Apparel Inc .... F 212 921-1859
New York *(G-8846)*

Angel Textiles Inc .... G 212 532-0900
New York *(G-8862)*

▲ Apple Imprints Apparel Inc .... E 716 893-1130
Buffalo *(G-2706)*

▲ Apsco Sports Enterprises Inc .... D 718 965-9500
Brooklyn *(G-1545)*

Aro-Graph Corporation .... G 315 463-8693
Syracuse *(G-15246)*

▲ Artistic Ribbon Novelty Co Inc .... E 212 255-4224
New York *(G-8922)*

Athletic Cap Co Inc .... E 718 398-1300
Staten Island *(G-15045)*

Barnaby Prints Inc .... F 845 477-2501
Greenwood Lake *(G-5648)*

Bondy Printing Corp .... G 631 242-1510
Bay Shore *(G-666)*

Bpe Studio Inc .... G 212 868-9896
New York *(G-9131)*

C H Thompson Company Inc .... D 607 724-1094
Binghamton *(G-874)*

◆ Cai Inc .... E 212 819-0008
New York *(G-9176)*

Casual Friday Inc .... F 585 544-9470
Rochester *(G-13695)*

Coe Displays Inc .... G 718 937-5658
Long Island City *(G-7412)*

Cooper & Clement Inc .... E 315 454-8135
Syracuse *(G-15289)*

D & R Silk Screening Ltd .... F 631 234-7464
Central Islip *(G-3367)*

Decal Makers Inc .... E 516 221-7200
Bellmore *(G-788)*

Dirt T Shirts Inc .... E 845 336-4230
Kingston *(G-6898)*

Eagle Finishing .... E 718 497-7875
Brooklyn *(G-1807)*

Eagle Lace Dyeing Corp .... F 212 947-2712
New York *(G-9603)*

Emtron Hybrids Inc .... F 631 924-9668
Yaphank *(G-16710)*

Flp Group LLC .... F 315 252-7583
Auburn *(G-480)*

Folder Factory Inc .... F 540 477-3852
Amityville *(G-275)*

▲ Freeport Screen & Stamping .... E 516 379-0330
Freeport *(G-5157)*

Galli Shirts and Sports AP .... G 845 226-7305
Stormville *(G-15179)*

Hollywood Advertising Banners .... E 631 842-3000
Copiague *(G-3764)*

Human Technologies Corporation .... F 315 735-3532
Utica *(G-15711)*

Ihd Motorsports LLC .... F 979 690-1669
Binghamton *(G-894)*

Irene Cerone .... G 315 668-2899
Brewerton *(G-1151)*

J M L Productions Inc .... D 718 643-1674
Brooklyn *(G-2025)*

Jack J Florio Jr .... G 716 434-9123
Lockport *(G-7311)*

Kenmar Shirts Inc .... E 718 824-3880
Bronx *(G-1307)*

Kevin J Kassman .... G 585 529-4245
Rochester *(G-13904)*

L I C Screen Printing Inc .... E 516 546-7289
Merrick *(G-8100)*

▲ Legendary Auto Interiors Ltd .... E 315 331-1212
Newark *(G-12198)*

Lending Trimming Co Inc .... D 212 242-7502
New York *(G-10544)*

Loremanss Embroidery Engrav .... F 518 834-9205
Keeseville *(G-6852)*

Mas Cutting Inc .... G 212 869-0826
New York *(G-10722)*

Master Craft Finishers Inc .... E 631 586-0540
Deer Park *(G-4007)*

Master Image Printing Inc .... G 914 347-4400
Elmsford *(G-4550)*

Mountain T-Shirts Inc .... G 518 943-4533
Catskill *(G-3307)*

New York Binding Co Inc .... E 718 729-2454
Long Island City *(G-7539)*

Northeast Stitches & Ink Inc .... E 518 798-5549
South Glens Falls *(G-14939)*

▲ Pangea Brands LLC .... F 617 638-0001
New York *(G-11098)*

Pangea Brands LLC .... G 617 638-0001
New York *(G-11099)*

Patrick Rohan .... G 718 781-2573
Monticello *(G-8323)*

Paula Varsalona Ltd .... F 212 570-9100
New York *(G-11125)*

▲ Perfect Shoulder Company Inc .... E 914 699-8100
Mount Vernon *(G-8430)*

Polkadot Usa Inc .... G 914 835-3697
Mamaroneck *(G-7754)*

Printz and Patternz LLC .... G 518 944-6020
Schenectady *(G-14705)*

Rainbow Lettering .... G 607 732-5751
Elmira *(G-4501)*

Randy Sixberry .... G 315 265-6211
Potsdam *(G-13322)*

Round Top Knit & Screening .... G 518 622-3600
Round Top *(G-14466)*

Sellco Industries Inc .... E 607 756-7594
Cortland *(G-3894)*

Solidus Industries Inc .... D 607 749-4540
Homer *(G-6259)*

Special Tees .... E 718 980-0987
Staten Island *(G-15136)*

Starline Usa Inc .... C 716 773-0100
Grand Island *(G-5514)*

Todd Walbridge .... G 585 254-3018
Rochester *(G-14171)*

U All Inc .... E 518 438-2558
Albany *(G-136)*

Viewsport International Inc .... G 585 259-1562
Penfield *(G-12947)*

Wicked Smart LLC .... F 518 459-2855
Watervliet *(G-16057)*

2397 Schiffli Machine Embroideries

American Images Inc .... F 716 825-8888
Buffalo *(G-2696)*

Rmb Embroidery Service .... G 585 271-5560
Rochester *(G-14075)*

2399 Fabricated Textile Prdts, NEC

AAa Amercn Flag Dctg Co Inc .... G 212 279-3524
New York *(G-8702)*

Ace Banner & Flag Company .... F 212 620-9111
New York *(G-8724)*

▲ American Leather Specialties .... D 800 556-6488
Brooklyn *(G-1523)*

American Puff Corp .... D 516 379-1300
Freeport *(G-5143)*

Arista Flag Corporation .... F 845 246-7700
Saugerties *(G-14603)*

Automtive Uphl Cnvertible Tops .... G 914 961-4242
Tuckahoe *(G-15642)*

Baldwin Ribbon & Stamping Corp .... F 718 335-6700
Woodside *(G-16645)*

Becks Classic Mfg Inc .... D 631 435-3800
Brentwood *(G-1128)*

▲ Big Apple Sign Corp .... D 212 629-3650
New York *(G-9076)*

Big Apple Sign Corp .... E 631 342-0303
Islandia *(G-6522)*

Breton Industries Inc .... C 518 842-3030
Amsterdam *(G-329)*

City Signs Inc .... G 718 375-5933
Brooklyn *(G-1697)*

Dkm Sales LLC .... E 716 893-7777
Buffalo *(G-2802)*

Dream Green Productions .... G 917 267-8920
Warwick *(G-15951)*

▲ Eagle Regalia Co Inc .... F 845 425-2245
Spring Valley *(G-14989)*

Hampton Transport Inc .... F 631 716-4445
Coram *(G-3798)*

HMS Productions LLC .... G 212 719-9190
Mineola *(G-8227)*

Hollywood Banners Inc .... E 631 842-3000
Copiague *(G-3765)*

Jeans Inc .... G 646 223-1122
New York *(G-10324)*

Jim Henson Company Inc .... E 212 794-2400
Long Island City *(G-7479)*

▲ Kamali Group Inc .... G 516 627-4000
Great Neck *(G-5567)*

Koring Bros Inc .... G 888 233-1292
New Rochelle *(G-8619)*

Kraus & Sons Inc .... F 212 620-0408
New York *(G-10480)*

Mc Coy Tops and Interiors Inc .... G 718 458-5800
Woodside *(G-16662)*

▲ National Flag & Display Co Inc .... E 212 228-6600
New York *(G-10882)*

National Parachute Industries .... E 908 782-1646
Palenville *(G-12844)*

Osprey Boat .... G 631 331-4153
Mount Sinai *(G-8369)*

▲ Penthouse Manufacturing Co Inc .... B 516 379-1300
Freeport *(G-5173)*

Regal Emblem Co Inc .... F 212 925-8833
New York *(G-11347)*

Saratoga Horseworks Ltd .... E 518 843-6756
Amsterdam *(G-359)*

Sellco Industries Inc .... E 607 756-7594
Cortland *(G-3894)*

▲ Skd Tactical Inc .... G 845 897-2889
Highland Falls *(G-6149)*

Stonegate Stabless .... G 518 746-7133
Fort Edward *(G-5101)*

▲ Triple E Manufacturing .... F 716 761-6996
Sherman *(G-14817)*

Tulmar Manufacturing Inc .... G 315 393-7191
Ogdensburg *(G-12580)*

Yoland Corporation .... E 718 499-4803
Brooklyn *(G-2665)*

24 LUMBER AND WOOD PRODUCTS, EXCEPT FURNITURE

2411 Logging

3b Timber Company Inc .... F 315 942-6580
Boonville *(G-1113)*

Attica Package Company Inc .... F 585 591-0510
Attica *(G-459)*

▼ B & B Forest Products Ltd .... F 518 622-0811
Cairo *(G-3146)*

Baker Logging & Firewood .... G 585 374-5733
Naples *(G-8470)*

Bart Ostrander Trckg Log Corp .... G 518 661-6535
Mayfield *(G-7919)*

▲ C J Logging Equipment Inc .... E 315 942-5431
Boonville *(G-1117)*

Central Timber Co Inc .... G 518 638-6338
Granville *(G-5518)*

Chad Pierson .... G 518 251-0186
Bakers Mills *(G-537)*

Chip It All Ltd .... G 631 473-2040
Port Jefferson *(G-13220)*

Clearlake Land Co Inc .... F 315 848-2427
Star Lake *(G-15035)*

Couture Timber Harvesting .... G 607 836-4719
Mc Graw *(G-7926)*

Daniel & Lois Lyndaker Logging .... G 315 346-6527
Castorland *(G-3299)*

Davis Logging & Lumber .... G 315 245-1040
Camden *(G-3187)*

Decker Forest Products Inc .... G 607 563-2345
Sidney *(G-14852)*

Donald Snyder Jr .... F 315 265-4485
Potsdam *(G-13318)*

Ed Beach Forest Management .... G 607 538-1745
Bloomville *(G-960)*

Finger Lakes Timber Co Inc .... G 585 346-2990
Livonia *(G-7278)*

George Chilson Logging .... G 607 732-1558
Elmira *(G-4488)*

GL & RL Logging Inc .... F 518 883-3936
Broadalbin *(G-1189)*

Got Wood LLC .... G 315 440-8857
Cleveland *(G-3561)*

Guldenschuh Logging & Lbr LLC .... G 585 538-4750
Caledonia *(G-3155)*

Harris Logging Inc .... E 518 792-1083
Queensbury *(G-13427)*

Homer Logging Contractor .... G 607 753-8553
Homer *(G-6257)*

Employee Codes: A=Over 500 employees, B=251-500
C=101-250, D=51-100, E=20-50, F=10-19, G=5-9
2019 Harris
New York Manufacturers Directory
675

24 LUMBER AND WOOD PRODUCTS, EXCEPT FURNITURE

J & S Logging Inc .... E 315 262-2112
  South Colton *(G-14925)*
Kapstone Container Corporation .... D 518 842-2450
  Amsterdam *(G-342)*
Kevin Regan Logging Ltd .... G 315 245-3890
  Camden *(G-3190)*
Klein & Sons Logging Inc .... F 845 292-6682
  Wht Sphr Spgs *(G-16557)*
Lizotte Logging Inc .... F 518 359-2200
  Tupper Lake *(G-15650)*
Lyndaker Timber Harvesting LLC .... F 315 346-1328
  Castorland *(G-3300)*
Matteson Logging Inc .... G 585 593-3037
  Wellsville *(G-16118)*
Mountain Forest Products Inc .... G 518 597-3674
  Crown Point *(G-3916)*
Murray Logging LLC .... G 518 834-7372
  Keeseville *(G-6853)*
Northern Timber Harvesting LLC .... F 585 233-7330
  Alfred Station *(G-187)*
Oak Valley Logging Inc .... G 518 622-8249
  Cairo *(G-3151)*
Paul J Mitchell Logging Inc .... E 518 359-7029
  Tupper Lake *(G-15652)*
Peters LLC .... G 607 637-5470
  Hancock *(G-5713)*
Richard Bauer Logging .... G 585 343-4149
  Alexander *(G-181)*
Richards Logging LLC .... F 518 359-2775
  Tupper Lake *(G-15653)*
Robert W Butts Logging Co .... G 518 643-2897
  Peru *(G-12972)*
Russell Bass .... F 607 637-5253
  Hancock *(G-5714)*
Schaefer Logging Inc .... F 607 467-4990
  Deposit *(G-4111)*
Seaway Timber Harvesting Inc .... D 315 769-5970
  Massena *(G-7908)*
Smoothbore International Inc .... G 315 754-8124
  Red Creek *(G-13455)*
Snyder Logging .... G 315 265-1462
  Potsdam *(G-13323)*
Tim Cretin Logging & Sawmill .... F 315 946-4476
  Lyons *(G-7688)*
Timothy L Simpson .... G 518 234-1401
  Sharon Springs *(G-14799)*
Tonche Timber LLC .... G 845 389-3489
  Amsterdam *(G-360)*
Van Cpeters Logging Inc .... G 607 637-3574
  Hancock *(G-5715)*
Wadsworth Logging Inc .... F 518 863-6870
  Gloversville *(G-5471)*
William Ward Logging .... F 518 946-7826
  Jay *(G-6775)*

2421 Saw & Planing Mills

A D Bowman & Son Lumber Co .... E 607 692-2595
  Castle Creek *(G-3294)*
Adams Lumber Co Inc .... F 716 358-2815
  Cattaraugus *(G-3311)*
Amish Structure .... F 607 257-1070
  Dryden *(G-4148)*
Angelica Forest Products Inc .... G 585 466-3205
  Angelica *(G-366)*
Axtell Bradtke Lumber Co .... G 607 265-3850
  Masonville *(G-7814)*
B & B Lumber Company Inc .... C 866 282-0582
  Jamesville *(G-6763)*
B & J Lumber Co Inc .... G 518 677-3845
  Cambridge *(G-3177)*
Bissel-Babcock Millwork Inc .... F 716 761-6976
  Sherman *(G-14815)*
Bono Sawdust Supply Co Inc .... G 718 446-1374
  Corona *(G-3839)*
Brookside Lumber Inc .... F 315 497-0937
  Moravia *(G-8332)*
Cannonsville Lumber Inc .... G 607 467-3380
  Deposit *(G-4106)*
Capital Sawmill Service .... G 518 479-0729
  Nassau *(G-8476)*
Carlson Wood Products Inc .... G 716 287-2923
  Sinclairville *(G-14864)*
Casters Custom Sawing .... G 315 387-5104
  Sandy Creek *(G-14558)*
Clements Burrville Sawmill .... G 315 782-4549
  Watertown *(G-16008)*
Cote Hardwood Products Inc .... F 607 898-5737
  Locke *(G-7281)*
▲ Curran Renewable Energy LLC ..... E 315 769-2000
  Massena *(G-7901)*

Dansville Logging & Lumber .... E 585 335-5879
  Dansville *(G-3925)*
Dlr Enterprises LLC .... G 315 813-2911
  Sherrill *(G-14819)*
Donver Incorporated .... F 716 945-1910
  Kill Buck *(G-6878)*
Embassy Millwork Inc .... F 518 839-0965
  Amsterdam *(G-336)*
Farney Lumber Corporation .... F 315 346-6013
  Lowville *(G-7650)*
▼ Garden State Shavings Inc .... F 845 544-2835
  Warwick *(G-15952)*
◆ GM Palmer Inc .... F 585 492-2990
  Arcade *(G-383)*
Great Jones Lumber Corp .... F 212 254-5560
  New York *(G-9981)*
Greater Niagara Bldg Ctr Inc .... F 716 299-0543
  Niagara Falls *(G-12290)*
Greene Lumber Co LP .... E 607 278-6101
  Davenport *(G-3928)*
Gutchess Freedom Inc .... D 716 492-2824
  Freedom *(G-5131)*
◆ Gutchess Lumber Co Inc .... C 607 753-3393
  Cortland *(G-3876)*
Gutchess Lumber Co Inc .... G 716 492-2824
  Freedom *(G-5132)*
Hennig Custom Woodwork Corp .... G 516 536-3460
  Oceanside *(G-12540)*
◆ J & J Log & Lumber Corp .... D 845 832-6535
  Dover Plains *(G-4144)*
J A Yansick Lumber Co Inc .... E 585 492-4312
  Arcade *(G-385)*
L J Valente Inc .... G 518 674-3750
  Averill Park *(G-515)*
Machina Deus Lex Inc .... G 917 577-0972
  Jamaica *(G-6657)*
Mallery Lumber LLC .... G 607 637-2236
  Hancock *(G-5712)*
McDonough Hardwoods Ltd .... E 315 829-3449
  Vernon Center *(G-15807)*
Meltz Lumber Co of Mellenville .... E 518 672-7021
  Hudson *(G-6363)*
Mettowee Lumber & Plastics Co .... C 518 642-1100
  Granville *(G-5522)*
Mohawk Metal Mfg & Sls .... G 315 853-7663
  Westmoreland *(G-16407)*
One Tree Dist .... G 315 701-2924
  Syracuse *(G-15386)*
Owletts Saw Mills .... G 607 525-6340
  Woodhull *(G-16638)*
▼ PA Pellets LLC .... F 814 848-9970
  Pittsford *(G-13024)*
Pallets Inc .... E 518 747-4177
  Fort Edward *(G-5097)*
PDJ Inc .... E 315 655-8824
  Cazenovia *(G-3324)*
Petteys Lumber .... G 518 792-5943
  Fort Ann *(G-5090)*
Piccini Industries Ltd .... G 845 365-0614
  Orangeburg *(G-12685)*
Potter Lumber Co Inc .... E 716 373-1260
  Allegany *(G-192)*
Rudy Stempel & Family Sawmill .... G 518 872-0431
  East Berne *(G-4212)*
Russell Bass .... F 607 637-5253
  Hancock *(G-5714)*
S Donadic Inc .... D 718 361-9888
  Sunnyside *(G-15205)*
▼ Salamanca Lumber Company Inc .. E 716 945-4810
  Salamanca *(G-14530)*
Saw Mill Pediatrics Pllc .... G 914 449-6064
  Pleasantville *(G-13178)*
Simplicity Bandsaw Inc .... G 716 557-8805
  Hinsdale *(G-6162)*
Sirianni Hardwoods Inc .... E 607 962-4688
  Painted Post *(G-12841)*
Spiegel Woodworks Inc .... F 845 336-8090
  Kingston *(G-6918)*
St Lawrence Lumber Inc .... G 315 649-2990
  Three Mile Bay *(G-15509)*
Swanson Lumber .... G 716 499-1726
  Gerry *(G-5341)*
▲ Tri-State Brick & Stone NY Inc ...... D 212 366-0300
  New York *(G-11895)*
Tupper Lake Hardwoods Inc .... E 518 359-8248
  Tupper Lake *(G-15655)*
Upstate Increte Incorporated .... G 585 254-2010
  Rochester *(G-14192)*
Urrey Lumber .... G 518 827-4451
  Middleburgh *(G-8130)*

Wagner Hardwoods LLC .... C 607 594-3321
  Cayuta *(G-3315)*
Wagner Hardwoods LLC .... G 607 229-8198
  Friendship *(G-5211)*
▼ Wagner Millwork Inc .... D 607 687-5362
  Owego *(G-12805)*
Wagner Nineveh Inc .... F 607 693-2689
  Afton *(G-9)*
Weather Tight Exteriors .... G 631 375-5108
  Ridge *(G-13525)*
Wolski Wood Works Inc .... F 718 577-9816
  Flushing *(G-5060)*
Wyde Lumber .... F 845 513-5571
  Monticello *(G-8324)*

2426 Hardwood Dimension & Flooring Mills

A D Bowman & Son Lumber Co .... E 607 692-2595
  Castle Creek *(G-3294)*
◆ Artistic Frame Corp .... C 212 289-2100
  New York *(G-8921)*
B & B Lumber Company Inc .... C 866 282-0582
  Jamesville *(G-6763)*
Carlson Wood Products Inc .... G 716 287-2923
  Sinclairville *(G-14864)*
Clements Burrville Sawmill .... G 315 782-4549
  Watertown *(G-16008)*
Custom Woodwork Ltd .... F 631 727-5260
  Riverhead *(G-13566)*
Donver Incorporated .... F 716 945-1910
  Kill Buck *(G-6878)*
Essequattro USA Inc .... G 917 862-0005
  New York *(G-9711)*
Fibron Products Inc .... F 716 886-2378
  Buffalo *(G-2826)*
▼ Fitzpatrick and Weller Inc .... D 716 699-2393
  Ellicottville *(G-4446)*
Fountain Tile Outlet Inc .... G 718 927-4555
  Brooklyn *(G-1901)*
Guldenschuh Logging & Lbr LLC .... G 585 538-4750
  Caledonia *(G-3155)*
◆ Gutchess Lumber Co Inc .... C 607 753-3393
  Cortland *(G-3876)*
H B Millwork Inc .... E 631 289-8086
  Medford *(G-7949)*
Horizon Floors I LLC .... G 212 509-9686
  New York *(G-10123)*
◆ J & J Log & Lumber Corp .... D 845 832-6535
  Dover Plains *(G-4144)*
J A Yansick Lumber Co Inc .... E 585 492-4312
  Arcade *(G-385)*
Jim Quinn .... F 518 356-0398
  Schenectady *(G-14691)*
▲ Legno Veneto USA .... G 716 651-9169
  Depew *(G-4094)*
Madison & Dunn .... G 585 563-7760
  Rochester *(G-13922)*
Mason Carvings Inc .... G 716 484-7884
  Jamestown *(G-6737)*
Mm of East Aurora LLC .... G 716 651-9663
  Buffalo *(G-2949)*
◆ MP Caroll Inc .... F 716 683-8520
  Cheektowaga *(G-3452)*
Mullican Flooring LP .... G 716 537-2642
  Holland *(G-6220)*
North Hudson Woodcraft Corp .... E 315 429-3105
  Dolgeville *(G-4135)*
▼ Norton-Smith Hardwoods Inc .... G 716 945-0346
  Salamanca *(G-14529)*
Petteys Lumber .... G 518 792-5943
  Fort Ann *(G-5090)*
Potter Lumber Co Inc .... E 716 373-1260
  Allegany *(G-192)*
Premier Hardwood Products Inc .... E 315 492-1786
  Jamesville *(G-6769)*
Randolph Dimension Corporation ...... F 716 358-6901
  Randolph *(G-13449)*
Revival Industries Inc .... F 315 868-1085
  Ilion *(G-6479)*
S Donadic Inc .... D 718 361-9888
  Sunnyside *(G-15205)*
▲ Tectonic Flooring USA LLC .... G 212 686-2700
  New York *(G-11795)*
Tupper Lake Hardwoods Inc .... E 518 359-8248
  Tupper Lake *(G-15655)*
Vitobob Furniture Inc .... G 516 676-1696
  Long Island City *(G-7632)*
▼ Wagner Millwork Inc .... D 607 687-5362
  Owego *(G-12805)*
Wood Floor Expo Inc .... G 212 472-0671
  New York *(G-12132)*

Wrights Hardwoods Inc .... E 716 595-2345
Cassadaga *(G-3291)*

2429 Special Prdt Sawmills, NEC

RWS Manufacturing Inc .... G 518 361-1657
Queensbury *(G-13439)*

2431 Millwork

A Losee & Sons .... G 516 676-3060
Glen Cove *(G-5358)*

A W Hamel Stair Mfg Inc .... F 518 346-3031
Schenectady *(G-14647)*

Ace Fire Door Corp .... E 718 901-0001
Bronx *(G-1209)*

Adams Interior Fabrications .... F 631 249-8282
Massapequa *(G-7878)*

Adirondack Stairs Inc .... F 845 246-2525
Saugerties *(G-14602)*

▲ Adriatic Wood Products Inc .... E 718 922-4621
Brooklyn *(G-1484)*

American Wood Column Corp .... G 718 782-3163
Brooklyn *(G-1528)*

Amstutze Woodworking .... G 518 946-8206
Upper Jay *(G-15674)*

Apollo Windows & Doors Inc .... F 718 386-3326
Brooklyn *(G-1541)*

Architctral Mllwk Installation .... E 631 499-0755
East Northport *(G-4260)*

Architactural Enhancements Inc .... F 845 343-9663
Middletown *(G-8137)*

Artistic Iron Works Inc .... G 631 665-4285
Bay Shore *(G-659)*

Atlantic Stairs Corp .... G 718 417-8818
Brooklyn *(G-1571)*

▲ Attica Millwork Inc .... F 585 591-2333
Attica *(G-458)*

Auburn Custom Millwork Inc .... G 315 253-3843
Auburn *(G-463)*

Bator Bintor Inc .... F 347 546-6503
Brooklyn *(G-1590)*

▲ Bauerschmidt & Sons Inc .... D 718 528-3500
Jamaica *(G-6630)*

Beaver Creek Industries Inc .... G 607 545-6382
Canaseraga *(G-3238)*

Bennett Stair Company Inc .... G 518 384-1554
Ballston Lake *(G-566)*

Bloch Industries LLC .... D 585 334-9600
Rochester *(G-13666)*

Blooming Grove Stair Co .... F 845 783-4245
Monroe *(G-8265)*

Blooming Grove Stair Co .... G 845 791-4016
Monticello *(G-8320)*

BNC Innovative Woodworking .... F 718 277-2800
Brooklyn *(G-1624)*

Braga Woodworks .... G 845 342-4636
Middletown *(G-8139)*

Brauen Constrution .... G 585 492-0042
Arcade *(G-380)*

Broadway Neon Sign Corp .... F 908 241-4177
Ronkonkoma *(G-14322)*

▲ Burt Millwork Corporation .... E 718 257-4601
Albertson *(G-147)*

Capital District Stairs Inc .... G 518 383-2449
Halfmoon *(G-5661)*

Capital Kit Cab & Door Mfrs .... G 718 886-0303
College Point *(G-3641)*

Carob Industries Inc .... F 631 225-0900
Lindenhurst *(G-7166)*

◆ Case Group LLC .... E 518 720-3100
Green Island *(G-5603)*

Champion Millwork Inc .... E 315 463-0711
Syracuse *(G-15275)*

Chautauqua Woods Corporation .... E 716 366-3808
Dunkirk *(G-4164)*

Christiana Millwork Inc .... E 315 492-9099
Jamesville *(G-6765)*

▲ City Store Gates Mfg Corp .... E 718 939-9700
College Point *(G-3642)*

Clearwood Custom Carpentry and .... E 315 432-8422
East Syracuse *(G-4331)*

Columbus Woodworking Inc .... G 607 674-4546
Sherburne *(G-14804)*

Concepts In Wood of CNY .... E 315 463-8084
Syracuse *(G-15286)*

Cousins Furniture & Hm Imprvs .... E 631 254-3752
Deer Park *(G-3959)*

Craftsmen Woodworkers Ltd .... E 718 326-3350
Maspeth *(G-7832)*

Creative Laminates Inc .... F 315 463-7580
Syracuse *(G-15293)*

Crown Mill Work Corp .... G 845 371-2200
Nanuet *(G-8462)*

Crown Woodworking Corp .... G 718 974-6415
Brooklyn *(G-1733)*

Cuccio-Zanetti Inc .... G 518 587-1363
Middle Grove *(G-8115)*

▲ Custom Door & Mirror Inc .... E 631 414-7725
Farmingdale *(G-4745)*

Custom Stair & Millwork Co .... G 315 839-5793
Sauquoit *(G-14621)*

Custom Wood Inc .... G 718 927-4700
Brooklyn *(G-1744)*

D K P Wood Railings & Stairs .... F 631 665-8656
Bay Shore *(G-677)*

D R Cornue Woodworks .... G 315 655-9463
Cazenovia *(G-3318)*

▲ DAngelo Home Collections Inc .... G 917 267-8920
Warwick *(G-15949)*

Dbs Interiors Corp .... F 631 491-3013
West Babylon *(G-16152)*

DC Contracting & Building Corp .... F 631 385-1117
Huntington Station *(G-6438)*

Deer Pk Stair Bldg Mllwk Inc .... E 631 363-5000
Blue Point *(G-964)*

Deerfield Millwork Inc .... F 631 726-9663
Water Mill *(G-15969)*

Dimaio Millwork Corporation .... E 914 476-1937
Yonkers *(G-16750)*

▲ Dorm Company Corporation .... G 502 551-6195
Cheektowaga *(G-3441)*

Duncan & Son Carpentry Inc .... E 914 664-4311
Mount Vernon *(G-8396)*

Ecker Window Corp .... D 914 776-0000
Yonkers *(G-16753)*

Ed Negron Fine Woodworking .... G 718 246-1016
Brooklyn *(G-1812)*

Efj Inc .... D 518 234-4799
Cobleskill *(G-3602)*

EM Pfaff & Son Inc .... F 607 739-3691
Horseheads *(G-6313)*

Empire Building Products Inc .... G 518 695-6094
Schuylerville *(G-14733)*

Excelsior Wood Products LLC .... F 845 339-6630
Kingston *(G-6900)*

▲ Fancy Windows & Doors Mfg Corp .. G 718 366-7800
Brooklyn *(G-1868)*

▲ Finger Lakes Trellis Supply .... G 315 904-4007
Williamson *(G-16558)*

Fire Island Sea Clam Co Inc .... G 631 589-2199
West Sayville *(G-16289)*

Five Star Millwork LLC .... F 845 920-0247
Pearl River *(G-12896)*

Fontrick Door Inc .... E 585 345-6032
Batavia *(G-624)*

Grace Ryan & Magnus Mllwk LLC .... D 914 665-0902
Mount Vernon *(G-8402)*

◆ Griffon Corporation .... E 212 957-5000
New York *(G-9988)*

▲ Gw Manufacturing .... E 718 386-8078
Ridgewood *(G-13538)*

H B Millwork Inc .... E 631 289-8086
Medford *(G-7949)*

H B Millwork Inc .... G 631 924-4195
Yaphank *(G-16713)*

Highland Organization Corp .... E 631 991-3240
Deer Park *(G-3984)*

Hulley Holding Company Inc .... F 716 332-3982
Kenmore *(G-6862)*

Humboldt Woodworking .... G 718 707-0022
Long Island City *(G-7471)*

I Meglio Corp .... E 631 617-6900
Brentwood *(G-1135)*

▲ Ideal Wood Products Inc .... E 315 823-1124
Little Falls *(G-7210)*

Ignelzi Interiors Inc .... E 718 464-0279
Queens Village *(G-13407)*

Inform Studio Inc .... F 718 401-6149
Bronx *(G-1297)*

Island Stairs Corp .... G 347 645-0560
Staten Island *(G-15091)*

Island Street Lumber Co Inc .... G 716 692-4127
North Tonawanda *(G-12434)*

J Percoco Industries Inc .... G 631 312-4572
Bohemia *(G-1038)*

Jacobs Woodworking LLC .... G 315 427-8999
Syracuse *(G-15345)*

James King Woodworking Inc .... G 518 761-6091
Queensbury *(G-13429)*

Jays Furniture Products Inc .... E 716 876-8854
Buffalo *(G-2890)*

John Langenbacher Co Inc .... E 718 328-0141
Bronx *(G-1304)*

KB Millwork Inc .... G 516 280-2183
Levittown *(G-7135)*

Kelly Window Systems Inc .... E 631 420-8500
Farmingdale *(G-4801)*

Kng Construction Co Inc .... F 212 595-1451
Warwick *(G-15956)*

Living Doors Inc .... F 631 924-5393
Medford *(G-7958)*

M & D Millwork LLC .... F 631 789-1439
Amityville *(G-299)*

Mack Wood Working .... G 845 657-6625
Shokan *(G-14846)*

Marretti USA Inc .... G 212 255-5565
New York *(G-10716)*

Mason Woodworks LLC .... G 917 363-7052
Brooklyn *(G-2176)*

Medina Millworks LLC .... G 585 798-2969
Medina *(G-7983)*

Mensch Mill & Lumber Corp .... E 718 359-7500
Bronx *(G-1326)*

Mestel Brothers Stairs & Rails .... C 516 496-4127
Syosset *(G-15222)*

Metalocke Industries Inc .... G 718 267-9200
Woodside *(G-16663)*

Michael Bernstein Design Assoc .... E 718 456-9277
Brooklyn *(G-2203)*

Michbi Doors Inc .... D 631 231-9050
Brentwood *(G-1142)*

Millco Woodworking LLC .... F 585 526-6844
Hall *(G-5671)*

▲ Miller Blaker Inc .... D 718 665-0500
Bronx *(G-1332)*

Millwright Wdwrk Installetion .... E 631 587-2635
West Babylon *(G-16177)*

Mind Designs Inc .... G 631 563-3644
Farmingville *(G-4924)*

Monroe Stair Products Inc .... E 845 783-4245
Monroe *(G-8278)*

Monroe Stair Products Inc .... G 845 791-4016
Monticello *(G-8322)*

Ne & Ws Inc .... G 718 326-4699
Maspeth *(G-7861)*

▲ Nordic Interior Inc .... C 718 456-7000
Brooklyn *(G-2272)*

North Fork Wood Works Inc .... G 631 255-4028
Mattituck *(G-7915)*

Northern Forest Pdts Co Inc .... G 315 942-6955
Boonville *(G-1118)*

Old World Mouldings Inc .... G 631 563-8660
Bohemia *(G-1070)*

Overhead Door Corporation .... D 518 828-7652
Hudson *(G-6366)*

P H Custom Woodworking Corp .... E 917 801-1444
Bronx *(G-1349)*

Paul David Enterprises Inc .... G 646 667-5530
New York *(G-11123)*

Pella Corporation .... B 607 223-2023
Johnson City *(G-6816)*

Pella Corporation .... B 607 231-8550
Johnson City *(G-6817)*

Pella Corporation .... B 607 238-2812
Johnson City *(G-6818)*

Pella Corporation .... B 516 385-3622
Albertson *(G-152)*

Pella Corporation .... B 607 238-2812
Johnson City *(G-6819)*

Pella Corporation .... B 516 385-3622
Albertson *(G-153)*

Pella Corporation .... B 607 231-8550
Johnson City *(G-6820)*

Pella Corporation .... C 631 208-0710
Calverton *(G-3168)*

Peter Productions Devivi Inc .... F 315 568-8484
Waterloo *(G-15997)*

▲ Pgs Millwork Inc .... D 518 828-2608
Hudson *(G-6368)*

Piccini Industries Ltd .... E 845 365-0614
Orangeburg *(G-12685)*

Professional Cab Detailing Co .... F 845 436-7282
Woodridge *(G-16643)*

Props Displays & Interiors .... F 212 620-3840
New York *(G-11266)*

Quaker Millwork & Lumber Inc .... E 716 662-3388
Orchard Park *(G-12741)*

▲ Quality Millwork Corp .... E 718 892-2250
Bronx *(G-1369)*

Quality Stair Builders Inc .... F 631 694-0711
Farmingdale *(G-4861)*

Employee Codes: A=Over 500 employees, B=251-500
C=101-250, D=51-100, E=20-50, F=10-19, G=5-9
2019 Harris
New York Manufacturers Directory
677

R C Henderson Stair Builders................F 516 876-9898
Westbury *(G-16369)*
Randolph Dimension Corporation ....F 716 358-6901
Randolph *(G-13449)*
RB Woodcraft Inc..................................E 315 474-2429
Syracuse *(G-15405)*
Red Tail Moulding & Mllwk LLC............G....... 516 852-4613
Center Moriches *(G-3340)*
Regal Windows & Doors LLC ....F 201 934-0100
Spring Valley *(G-15006)*
Richard Anthony Corp...........................E 914 922-7141
Yorktown Heights *(G-16822)*
Rj Millworkers Inc ....E 607 433-0525
Oneonta *(G-12645)*
Robert Strahan Custom Wdwkg............G....... 718 349-3570
Brooklyn *(G-2409)*
Rochester Colonial Mfg Corp ....D....... 585 254-8191
Rochester *(G-14084)*
Rochester Lumber Company.................E 585 924-7171
Farmington *(G-4919)*
Rockaway Stairs Ltd.............................G....... 718 945-0047
Far Rockaway *(G-4703)*
Roode Hoek & Co Inc ....F 718 522-5921
Brooklyn *(G-2413)*
Royal Windows Mfg Corp......................E 631 435-8888
Bay Shore *(G-718)*
Royalton Millwork & Design..................G....... 716 439-4092
Lockport *(G-7329)*
S Donadic Inc ....D....... 718 361-9888
Sunnyside *(G-15205)*
S R Sloan Inc...D....... 315 736-7730
Whitesboro *(G-16529)*
▲ Scanga Woodworking Corp ....E 845 265-9115
Cold Spring *(G-3628)*
Second Generation Wood Stairs ....F 718 370-0085
Staten Island *(G-15134)*
Select Interior Door Ltd........................E 585 535-9900
North Java *(G-12392)*
Shawmut Woodworking & Sup Inc........C....... 212 920-8900
New York *(G-11560)*
Specialty Services ....G....... 585 728-5650
Wayland *(G-16072)*
Spiegel Woodworks Inc.........................F 845 336-8090
Kingston *(G-6918)*
Stairworld Inc ....G....... 718 441-9722
Richmond Hill *(G-13514)*
Staten Island Stair Inc ....G....... 718 317-9276
Staten Island *(G-15139)*
Stealth Archtctral Windows Inc ....F 718 821-6666
Brooklyn *(G-2514)*
Syracuse Industrial Sls Co Ltd.............F 315 478-5751
Syracuse *(G-15438)*
TDS Woodworking Inc...........................F 718 442-5298
Staten Island *(G-15144)*
Three R Enterprises Inc.........................E 585 254-5050
Rochester *(G-14169)*
Tiedemann Waldemar Inc......................F 716 875-5665
Buffalo *(G-3095)*
Truth Hardware Corporation.................G....... 585 627-5964
Rochester *(G-14180)*
Unadilla Silo Company Inc...................D....... 607 369-9341
Sidney *(G-14857)*
Unicenter Millwork Inc..........................G....... 716 741-8201
Clarence Center *(G-3550)*
United Rockland Holding Co Inc ....E 845 357-1900
Suffern *(G-15199)*
Universal Custom Millwork Inc.............D....... 518 330-6622
Amsterdam *(G-362)*
▲ Upstate Door Inc ....D....... 585 786-3880
Warsaw *(G-15947)*
Urban Woodworks Ltd...........................G....... 718 827-1570
Brooklyn *(G-2611)*
Vander Heyden Woodworking ....G....... 212 242-0525
New York *(G-11990)*
▼ Wagner Millwork Inc ....D....... 607 687-5362
Owego *(G-12805)*
Wolfe Lumber Mill Inc............................G....... 716 772-7750
Gasport *(G-5309)*
Wood Innovations of Suffolk ....G....... 631 698-2345
Medford *(G-7969)*
Wood Talk..G....... 631 940-3085
Bay Shore *(G-734)*
Xylon Industries Inc...............................G....... 631 293-4717
Farmingdale *(G-4907)*
Yesteryears Vintage Doors LLC ....G....... 315 324-5250
Hammond *(G-5701)*
Zanzano Woodworking Inc ....F 914 725-6025
Scarsdale *(G-14646)*
Zeller Woodworks LLC ....F 585 254-7607
Rochester *(G-14218)*

2434 Wood Kitchen Cabinets

A-1 Manhattan Custom Furn Inc............G....... 212 750-9800
Island Park *(G-6510)*
Able Kitchen...F 877 268-1264
Cedarhurst *(G-3330)*
Acme Kitchenettes Corp ....E 518 828-4191
Hudson *(G-6337)*
Aka Enterprises......................................E 716 474-4579
Wyoming *(G-16698)*
▲ Aki Cabinets Inc ....E 718 721-2541
Astoria *(G-420)*
Andike Millwork Inc ....G....... 718 894-1796
Maspeth *(G-7821)*
▲ Artone LLC..D....... 716 664-2232
Jamestown *(G-6699)*
Atlantic States Distributing...................G....... 518 427-6364
Menands *(G-8082)*
Auburn-Watson Corp.............................F 716 876-8000
Depew *(G-4079)*
Aucapina Cabinets Inc ....G....... 718 609-9054
Maspeth *(G-7825)*
▲ Bauerschmidt & Sons Inc ....D....... 718 528-3500
Jamaica *(G-6630)*
Bloch Industries LLC.............................D....... 585 334-9600
Rochester *(G-13666)*
Cabinet Factory Inc................................F 718 351-8922
Staten Island *(G-15058)*
Cabinet Shapes Corp.............................F 718 784-6255
Long Island City *(G-7404)*
Cabinetry By Tbr Inc..............................G....... 516 365-8500
Manhasset *(G-7764)*
Cabinets By Stanley Inc ....G....... 718 222-5861
Brooklyn *(G-1668)*
Cambridge Kitchens Mfg Inc ....F 516 935-5100
Hicksville *(G-6067)*
Candlelight Cabinetry Inc......................C 716 434-2114
Lockport *(G-7289)*
Capital Kit Cab & Door Mfrs..................G....... 718 886-0303
College Point *(G-3641)*
Carefree Kitchens Inc.............................G....... 631 567-2120
Holbrook *(G-6175)*
Carlos & Alex Atelier Inc ....E 718 441-8911
Richmond Hill *(G-13500)*
Casa Collection Inc.................................G....... 718 694-0272
Brooklyn *(G-1681)*
▲ Catskill Craftsmen Inc ....D....... 607 652-7321
Stamford *(G-15030)*
Central Kitchen Corp..............................F 631 283-1029
Southampton *(G-14951)*
Chicone Builders LLC ....G....... 607 535-6540
Montour Falls *(G-8325)*
Classic Cabinets ....F 845 357-4331
Suffern *(G-15187)*
Clearwood Custom Carpentry and........E 315 432-8422
East Syracuse *(G-4331)*
Cleary Custom Cabinets Inc ....F 516 939-2475
Hicksville *(G-6070)*
Columbia Cabinets LLC ....G....... 212 972-7550
Armonk *(G-402)*
Columbia Cabinets LLC ....F 518 283-1700
Saratoga Springs *(G-14576)*
▼ Craft Custom Woodwork Co Inc.......F 718 821-2162
Maspeth *(G-7831)*
Creative Stone & Cabinets.....................G....... 631 772-6548
Selden *(G-14762)*
Custom CAS Inc......................................E 718 726-3575
Long Island City *(G-7418)*
Custom Woodcraft LLC ....F 315 843-4234
Munnsville *(G-8458)*
D & M Custom Cabinets Inc...................F 516 678-2818
Oceanside *(G-12534)*
Dak Mica and Wood Products ....G....... 631 467-0749
Ronkonkoma *(G-14332)*
Dbs Interiors Corp ....F 631 491-3013
West Babylon *(G-16152)*
Deakon Homes and Interiors ....F 518 271-0342
Troy *(G-15603)*
Di Fiore and Sons Custom Wdwkg ....G....... 718 278-1663
Long Island City *(G-7425)*
East End Country Kitchens Inc ....F 631 727-2258
Calverton *(G-3165)*
EC Wood & Company Inc.......................F 718 388-2287
Deer Park *(G-3971)*
EM Pfaff & Son Inc.................................F 607 739-3691
Horseheads *(G-6313)*
Enterprise Wood Products Inc ....F 718 853-9243
Brooklyn *(G-1837)*
Fina Cabinet Corp...................................G....... 718 409-2900
Mount Vernon *(G-8398)*
Finger Lkes Stirs Cabinets LLC.............G....... 315 638-3150
Baldwinsville *(G-554)*
Fra-Rik Formica Fabg Co Inc.................G....... 718 597-3335
Bronx *(G-1275)*
▲ Glissade New York LLC ....E 631 756-4800
Farmingdale *(G-4772)*
Greenway Cabinetry Inc.........................F 516 877-0009
Williston Park *(G-16594)*
Hearth Cabinets and More Ltd...............G....... 315 641-1197
Liverpool *(G-7234)*
Hendrickson Custom Cabinetry ....F 718 401-0137
Bronx *(G-1291)*
Home Ideal Inc...G....... 718 762-8998
Flushing *(G-5009)*
Huntington Woodworking Inc................G....... 631 271-7897
Huntington Station *(G-6446)*
Ignelzi Interiors Inc................................E 718 464-0279
Queens Village *(G-13407)*
J Percoco Industries Inc ....G....... 631 312-4572
Bohemia *(G-1038)*
JEm Wdwkg & Cabinets Inc...................F 518 828-5361
Hudson *(G-6358)*
Jordache Woodworking Corp................F 718 349-3373
Brooklyn *(G-2045)*
K-Binet Inc...G....... 845 348-1149
Blauvelt *(G-936)*
▲ Kw Distributors Group Inc ....F 718 843-3500
Ozone Park *(G-12829)*
Longo Commercial Cabinets Inc...........E 631 225-4290
Lindenhurst *(G-7176)*
Lyn Jo Kitchens Inc ....G....... 718 336-6060
Brooklyn *(G-2138)*
▲ Material Process Systems Inc ....F 718 302-3081
Brooklyn *(G-2179)*
Matteo & Antonio Bartolotta ....F 315 252-2220
Auburn *(G-490)*
McGraw Wood Products LLC ....E 607 836-6465
Mc Graw *(G-7928)*
Methods Tooling & Mfg Inc ....E 845 246-7100
Mount Marion *(G-8364)*
▲ Metro Kitchens Corp.........................F....... 718 434-1166
Brooklyn *(G-2200)*
Michael Bernstein Design Assoc ....E 718 456-9277
Brooklyn *(G-2203)*
Michael P Mmarr ....G....... 315 623-9380
Constantia *(G-3740)*
Millco Woodworking LLC ....F 585 526-6844
Hall *(G-5671)*
Modern Cabinet Company Inc ....E 845 473-4900
Poughkeepsie *(G-13355)*
▲ N Y Elli Design Corp ....F 718 228-0014
Ridgewood *(G-13543)*
Nagad Cabinets Inc.................................G....... 718 382-7200
Brooklyn *(G-2241)*
Neo Cabinetry LLC..................................F 718 403-0456
Brooklyn *(G-2252)*
▲ New York Vanity and Mfg Co............E 718 417-1010
Freeport *(G-5169)*
Nexis 3 LLC ....E 585 285-4120
Rochester *(G-13972)*
NY Cabinet Factory Inc...........................F 718 256-6541
Brooklyn *(G-2278)*
▲ Pgs Millwork Inc ....D....... 518 828-2608
Hudson *(G-6368)*
Piccini Industries Ltd..............................E 845 365-0614
Orangeburg *(G-12685)*
Precision Dental Cabinets Inc ....F 631 543-3870
Smithtown *(G-14906)*
Premier Woodcraft Ltd ....E 610 383-6624
White Plains *(G-16499)*
Premium Woodworking LLC..................G....... 631 485-3133
West Babylon *(G-16183)*
R & M Thermofoil Doors Inc...................G....... 718 206-4991
Jamaica *(G-6671)*
Ralph Payne ....G....... 718 222-4200
Brooklyn *(G-2383)*
Red White & Blue Entps Corp................G....... 718 565-8080
Woodside *(G-16675)*
Ribble Lumber Inc....................................G....... 315 536-6221
Penn Yan *(G-12964)*
Royal Custom Cabinets...........................G....... 315 376-6042
Lowville *(G-7656)*
S & V Custom Furniture Mfg ....F 516 746-8299
Mineola *(G-8248)*
S Donadic Inc ....D....... 718 361-9888
Sunnyside *(G-15205)*
▲ Salko Kitchens Inc ....F 845 565-4420
New Windsor *(G-8658)*
Salmon Crek Cabinetry Inc ....E 315 589-5419
Williamson *(G-16561)*

24 LUMBER AND WOOD PRODUCTS, EXCEPT FURNITURE

Serway Bros Inc .... E 315 337-0601
 Rome (G-14274)
Silva Cabinetry Inc .... E 914 737-7697
 Buchanan (G-2674)
Skyline Custom Cabinetry Inc .... G 631 393-2983
 Farmingdale (G-4875)
▲ Stone Expo & Cabinetry LLC .... F 516 292-2988
 West Hempstead (G-16225)
Tristate Contract Sales LLC .... G 845 782-2614
 Chester (G-3489)
Upstate Cabinet Company Inc .... F 585 429-5090
 Rochester (G-14191)
Viola Cabinet Corporation .... G 716 284-6327
 Niagara Falls (G-12347)
▲ W Designe Inc .... E 914 736-1058
 Peekskill (G-12927)
White House Cabinet Shop LLC .... G 607 674-9358
 Sherburne (G-14813)
William Brooks Woodworking .... F 718 495-9767
 Brooklyn (G-2647)
▲ Win Wood Cabinetry Inc .... G 516 304-2216
 Greenvale (G-5634)
Wood Etc Inc .... F 315 484-9663
 Syracuse (G-15461)
Yonkers Cabinet Inc .... E 914 668-2133
 Yonkers (G-16810)
Your Furniture Designers Inc .... G 845 947-3046
 West Haverstraw (G-16211)
Your Way Custom Cabinets Inc .... E 914 371-1870
 Mount Vernon (G-8454)

2435 Hardwood Veneer & Plywood

Geonex International Corp .... G 212 473-4555
 New York (G-9909)
Kings Quartet Corp .... G 845 986-9090
 Warwick (G-15955)
▲ Veneer One Inc .... E 516 536-6480
 Oceanside (G-12563)

2436 Softwood Veneer & Plywood

H B Millwork Inc .... E 631 289-8086
 Medford (G-7949)

2439 Structural Wood Members, NEC

Architctral Mllwk Installation .... E 631 499-0755
 East Northport (G-4260)
Empire Building Products Inc .... G 518 695-6094
 Schuylerville (G-14733)
Faulkner Truss Company Inc .... G 315 536-8894
 Dresden (G-4147)
Harvest Homes Inc .... E 518 895-2341
 Delanson (G-4069)
New England Barns Inc .... E 631 445-1461
 Southold (G-14970)
Pdj Components Inc .... E 845 469-9191
 Chester (G-3479)
Proof Industries Inc .... E 631 694-7663
 Farmingdale (G-4859)
Rochester Lumber Company .... E 585 924-7171
 Farmington (G-4919)
S R Sloan Inc .... D 315 736-7730
 Whitesboro (G-16529)
Steele Truss Company Inc .... E 518 562-4663
 Plattsburgh (G-13158)
Stephenson Lumber Company Inc .... G 518 548-7521
 Speculator (G-14973)
Structural Wood Corporation .... E 315 388-4442
 Waddington (G-15882)
Timber Frames Inc .... G 585 374-6405
 Canandaigua (G-3235)
Ufp New York LLC .... E 716 496-5484
 Chaffee (G-3405)
Ufp New York LLC .... E 518 828-2888
 Hudson (G-6375)
Ufp New York LLC .... E 315 253-2758
 Auburn (G-507)
Ufp New York LLC .... E 607 563-1556
 Sidney (G-14856)
Unadilla Silo Company Inc .... D 607 369-9341
 Sidney (G-14857)

2441 Wood Boxes

Abbot & Abbot Box Corp .... F 888 930-5972
 Long Island City (G-7365)
Bragley Mfg Co Inc .... E 718 622-7469
 Brooklyn (G-1631)
Bristol Boarding Inc .... G 585 271-7860
 Rochester (G-13679)

Falvo Manufacturing Co Inc .... F 315 724-7925
 Utica (G-15700)
Great Lakes Specialites .... E 716 672-4622
 Fredonia (G-5127)
M &L Industry of NY Inc .... G 845 827-6255
 Highland Mills (G-6151)
McGraw Wood Products LLC .... G 607 836-6465
 Mc Graw (G-7928)
McIntosh Box & Pallet Co Inc .... F 315 789-8750
 Geneva (G-5329)
McIntosh Box & Pallet Co Inc .... D 315 675-8511
 Bernhards Bay (G-833)
McIntosh Box & Pallet Co Inc .... E 315 446-9350
 Rome (G-14257)
Philpac Corporation .... E 716 875-8005
 Buffalo (G-3002)
Quality Woodworking Corp .... F 718 875-3437
 Brooklyn (G-2370)
Reuter Pallet Pkg Sys Inc .... G 845 457-9937
 Montgomery (G-8317)
Technical Packaging Inc .... F 516 223-2300
 Baldwin (G-545)

2448 Wood Pallets & Skids

219 South West .... G 315 474-2065
 Syracuse (G-15235)
A D Bowman & Son Lumber Co .... E 607 692-2595
 Castle Creek (G-3294)
Abbot & Abbot Box Corp .... F 888 930-5972
 Long Island City (G-7365)
▲ Airline Container Services .... G 516 371-4125
 Lido Beach (G-7147)
B & B Lumber Company Inc .... G 866 282-0582
 Jamesville (G-6763)
B&B Albany Pallet Company LLC .... E 315 492-1786
 Jamesville (G-6764)
Berry Industries Group Inc .... G 845 353-8338
 Nyack (G-12501)
Best Pallet & Crate LLC .... G 518 438-2945
 Albany (G-47)
CDF Indstrial Pckg Sltions Inc .... F 716 672-2984
 Fredonia (G-5125)
Chemung Cnty Chpter Nysarc Inc .... C 607 734-6151
 Elmira (G-4477)
Clements Burrville Sawmill .... E 315 782-4549
 Watertown (G-16008)
▼ Concord Express Cargo Inc .... G 718 276-7200
 Jamaica (G-6638)
Custom Shipping Products Inc .... F 716 355-4437
 Clymer (G-3599)
Dimensional Mills Inc .... E 518 746-1047
 Hudson Falls (G-6377)
Dwa Pallet Inc .... E 518 746-1047
 Hudson Falls (G-6378)
Essex Box & Pallet Co Inc .... E 518 834-7279
 Keeseville (G-6850)
Four-Way Pallet Corp .... E 631 351-3401
 Huntington Station (G-6442)
Great Lakes Specialites .... E 716 672-4622
 Fredonia (G-5127)
Just Wood Pallets Inc .... G 718 644-7013
 New Windsor (G-8647)
Lindley Wood Works Inc .... F 607 523-7786
 Lindley (G-7207)
McIntosh Box & Pallet Co Inc .... F 716 825-4122
 Buffalo (G-2942)
McIntosh Box & Pallet Co Inc .... D 315 675-8511
 Bernhards Bay (G-833)
McIntosh Box & Pallet Co Inc .... F 315 789-8750
 Geneva (G-5329)
McIntosh Box & Pallet Co Inc .... E 315 446-9350
 Rome (G-14257)
Nefab Packaging North East LLC .... E 518 346-9105
 Scotia (G-14744)
Neville Mfg Svc & Dist Inc .... E 716 834-3038
 Cheektowaga (G-3454)
North Shore Pallet Inc .... G 631 673-4700
 Huntington Station (G-6454)
Northeast Pallet & Cont Co Inc .... F 518 271-0535
 Troy (G-15613)
Ongweoweh Corp .... E 607 266-7070
 Ithaca (G-6602)
Orleans Pallet Company Inc .... F 585 589-0781
 Albion (G-160)
Pallet Division Inc .... G 585 328-3780
 Rochester (G-14004)
Pallet Services Inc .... C 716 873-7700
 Clarence (G-3537)
Pallet Services Inc .... E 585 647-4020
 Rochester (G-14005)

Pallets Inc .... E 518 747-4177
 Fort Edward (G-5097)
Pallets R US Inc .... E 631 758-2360
 Bellport (G-811)
Paul Bunyan Products Inc .... E 315 696-6164
 Cortland (G-3888)
Peco Pallet Inc .... E 914 376-5444
 Irvington (G-6509)
Peter C Herman Inc .... E 315 926-4100
 Marion (G-7805)
Pooran Pallet Inc .... E 718 938-7970
 Bronx (G-1361)
Reuter Pallet Pkg Sys Inc .... G 845 457-9937
 Montgomery (G-8317)
Sanjay Pallets Inc .... E 347 590-2485
 Bronx (G-1379)
▼ Sg Blocks Inc .... E 615 585-2639
 Brooklyn (G-2460)
Steven Coffey Pallet S Inc .... E 585 261-6783
 Rochester (G-14145)
Taylor Brothers Inc .... F 607 625-2828
 Apalachin (G-372)
Vansantis Development Inc .... E 315 461-0113
 Liverpool (G-7268)
Wolfe Lumber Mill Inc .... G 716 772-7750
 Gasport (G-5309)

2449 Wood Containers, NEC

Abbot & Abbot Box Corp .... F 888 930-5972
 Long Island City (G-7365)
David Isseks & Sons Inc .... E 212 966-8694
 New York (G-9481)
Essex Box & Pallet Co Inc .... E 518 834-7279
 Keeseville (G-6850)
Great Lakes Specialites .... E 716 672-4622
 Fredonia (G-5127)
Hood Industries Inc .... F 716 836-0301
 Buffalo (G-2874)
J & M Packaging Inc .... F 631 608-3069
 Hauppauge (G-5852)
Northeast Pallet & Cont Co Inc .... F 518 271-0535
 Troy (G-15613)
Pluribus Products Inc .... E 718 852-1614
 Bayville (G-753)
R D A Container Corporation .... E 585 247-2323
 Gates (G-5312)
Rosenwach Tank Co Inc .... E 212 972-4411
 Astoria (G-442)
Wolfe Lumber Mill Inc .... G 716 772-7750
 Gasport (G-5309)

2451 Mobile Homes

All Star Carts & Vehicles Inc .... D 631 666-5581
 Bay Shore (G-654)
Champion Home Builders Inc .... C 315 841-4122
 Sangerfield (G-14559)
Leatherstocking Mobile Home PA .... G 315 839-5691
 Sauquoit (G-14622)

2452 Prefabricated Wood Buildings & Cmpnts

Alta Industries Ltd .... F 845 586-3336
 Halcottsville (G-5657)
Beaver Mountain Log Homes Inc .... G 607 467-2700
 Hancock (G-5709)
Best Mdlr HMS Afrbe P Q& S In .... F 631 204-0049
 Southampton (G-14950)
Bill Lake Homes Construction .... D 518 673-2424
 Sprakers (G-14987)
Cort Contracting .... F 845 758-1190
 Red Hook (G-13458)
Duro-Shed Inc .... E 585 344-0800
 Buffalo (G-2805)
Eastern Exterior Wall .... E 631 589-3880
 Bohemia (G-1019)
Energy Panel Structures Inc .... G 315 923-7777
 Clyde (G-3592)
Energy Panel Structures Inc .... G 585 343-1777
 Clyde (G-3593)
Energy Panel Structures Inc .... G 518 355-6708
 Schenectady (G-14671)
Fishers Storage Sheds .... E 585 382-9580
 Leicester (G-7128)
Harvest Homes Inc .... E 518 895-2341
 Delanson (G-4069)
Jabo Agricultural Inc .... E 631 475-1800
 Patchogue (G-12867)
Lapp Management Corp .... G 607 243-5141
 Himrod (G-6160)

24 LUMBER AND WOOD PRODUCTS, EXCEPT FURNITURE

Northern Design & Bldg Assoc ....E 518 747-2200
  Queensbury *(G-13435)*
Roscoe Brothers Inc ....F 607 844-3750
  Dryden *(G-4151)*
Shafer & Sons ....G 315 853-5285
  Westmoreland *(G-16410)*
▲ Shelter Enterprises Inc ....D 518 237-4100
  Cohoes *(G-3621)*
Timberbuilt Inc ....F 716 337-0012
  North Collins *(G-12389)*
Walpole Woodworkers Inc ....G 631 726-2859
  Water Mill *(G-15971)*
Westchester Modular Homes Inc ....C 845 832-9400
  Wingdale *(G-16607)*
Whitley East LLC ....D 718 403-0050
  Brooklyn *(G-2644)*
Wood Tex Products LLC ....D 607 243-5141
  Himrod *(G-6161)*

2491 Wood Preserving

Bestway Enterprises Inc ....E 607 753-8261
  Cortland *(G-3860)*
Bestway of New York Inc ....G 607 753-8261
  Cortland *(G-3861)*
▲ Colorspec Coatings Intl Inc ....E 631 472-8251
  Holbrook *(G-6179)*
Donver Incorporated ....F 716 945-1910
  Kill Buck *(G-6878)*
Genesee Reserve Buffalo LLC ....E 716 824-3116
  Buffalo *(G-2848)*
Northeast Treaters Inc ....E 518 945-2660
  Athens *(G-451)*
Northeast Treaters NY LLC ....E 518 945-2660
  Athens *(G-452)*
◆ Osmose Holdings Inc ....A 716 882-5905
  Depew *(G-4099)*
Wego International Floors LLC ....F 516 487-3510
  Great Neck *(G-5600)*

2493 Reconstituted Wood Prdts

▲ Aarco Products Inc ....F 631 924-5461
  Yaphank *(G-16703)*
▲ Amendola MBL & Stone Ctr Inc ....D 914 997-7968
  White Plains *(G-16419)*
Bedford Wdwrk Instllations Inc ....G 914 764-9434
  Bedford *(G-768)*
▲ Continental Buchanan LLC ....D 703 480-3800
  Buchanan *(G-2672)*
Hi-Temp Fabrication Inc ....F 716 852-5655
  Buffalo *(G-2872)*
Niagara Fiberboard Inc ....E 716 434-8881
  Lockport *(G-7322)*
Northeastern Products Corp ....E 518 623-3161
  Warrensburg *(G-15942)*
Zircar Refr Composites Inc ....F 845 651-2200
  Florida *(G-4974)*

2499 Wood Prdts, NEC

A Van Hoek Woodworking Limited ....G 718 599-4388
  Brooklyn *(G-1459)*
◆ Aakron Rule Corp ....C 716 542-5483
  Akron *(G-16)*
▲ Abbott Industries Inc ....B 718 291-0800
  Jamaica *(G-6622)*
AC Moore Incorporated ....G 516 796-5831
  Bethpage *(G-838)*
Adams Interior Fabrications ....F 631 249-8282
  Massapequa *(G-7878)*
▲ Amci Ltd ....D 718 937-5858
  Long Island City *(G-7376)*
American Casino Equipment Mfg ....F 631 242-2440
  Deer Park *(G-3939)*
American Woods & Veneers Works .....E 718 937-2195
  Long Island City *(G-7378)*
Andike Millwork Inc ....G 718 894-1796
  Maspeth *(G-7821)*
Apf Manufacturing Company LLC ....E 914 963-6300
  Yonkers *(G-16737)*
Architectural Dctg Co LLC ....E 845 483-1340
  Poughkeepsie *(G-13327)*
Art Essentials of New York ....G 845 368-1100
  Airmont *(G-11)*
Atelier Viollet Corp ....G 718 782-1727
  Brooklyn *(G-1568)*
Atlas Fence & Railing Co Inc ....E 718 767-2200
  Whitestone *(G-16535)*
Babcock Co Inc ....E 607 776-3341
  Bath *(G-640)*
◆ Betterbee Inc ....F 518 314-0575
  Greenwich *(G-5637)*

▲ Brooks Woodworking Inc ....F 914 666-2029
  Mount Kisco *(G-8338)*
Budd Woodwork Inc ....F 718 389-1110
  Brooklyn *(G-1654)*
Cabinet Shapes Corp ....F 718 784-6255
  Long Island City *(G-7404)*
▲ Catskill Craftsmen Inc ....D 607 652-7321
  Stamford *(G-15030)*
▲ Cffco USA Inc ....G 718 747-1118
  Jericho *(G-6781)*
▼ Cfp Purchasing Inc ....G 705 806-0383
  Flushing *(G-4989)*
▲ Channel Manufacturing Inc ....E 516 944-6271
  Port Washington *(G-13247)*
Charles Freihofer Baking Co ....E 518 463-2221
  Albany *(G-58)*
Cherry Creek Woodcraft Inc ....E 716 988-3211
  South Dayton *(G-14928)*
▲ Cowee Forest Products Inc ....E 518 658-2233
  Berlin *(G-830)*
Craz Woodworking Assoc Inc ....E 631 205-1890
  Bellport *(G-801)*
Daniel Demarco and Assoc Inc ....E 631 598-7000
  Amityville *(G-271)*
Designs By Robert Scott Inc ....E 718 609-2535
  Brooklyn *(G-1770)*
Di Fiore and Sons Custom Wdwkg ....G 718 278-1663
  Long Island City *(G-7425)*
Digital Fabrication Wkshp Inc ....G 518 249-6500
  Hudson *(G-6346)*
Drummond Framing Inc ....F 212 647-1701
  New York *(G-9580)*
Ed Negron Fine Woodworking ....G 718 246-1016
  Brooklyn *(G-1812)*
Elephants Custom Furniture Inc ....D 917 509-3581
  Brooklyn *(G-1826)*
Encore Retail Systems Inc ....F 718 385-3443
  Mamaroneck *(G-7743)*
Essex Box & Pallet Co Inc ....E 518 834-7279
  Keeseville *(G-6850)*
▲ FG Galassi Moulding Co Inc ....E 845 258-2100
  Goshen *(G-5479)*
Fibron Products Inc ....E 716 886-2378
  Buffalo *(G-2826)*
Frame Shoppe & Art Gallery ....G 516 365-6014
  Manhasset *(G-7767)*
◆ Framerica Corporation ....G 631 650-1000
  Yaphank *(G-16711)*
▲ Fred M Lawrence Co Inc ....E 718 786-7227
  Bay Shore *(G-688)*
Furniture Design By Knossos Inc ....E 718 729-0404
  Woodside *(G-16657)*
Galas Framing Services ....F 718 706-0007
  Long Island City *(G-7454)*
General Art Company Inc ....F 212 255-1298
  New York *(G-9899)*
▲ Globus Cork Inc ....F 347 963-4059
  Bronx *(G-1282)*
Grant-Noren ....G 845 726-4281
  Westtown *(G-16414)*
Graphics Slution Providers Inc ....F 845 677-5088
  Lagrangeville *(G-6956)*
Green Renewable Inc ....E 518 658-2233
  Berlin *(G-831)*
Grohe America Inc ....G 212 206-8820
  New York *(G-9993)*
Hennig Custom Woodwork Corp ....G 516 536-3460
  Oceanside *(G-12540)*
House of Heydenryk Jr Inc ....F 212 206-9611
  New York *(G-10135)*
Hubray Inc ....F 800 645-2855
  North Baldwin *(G-12364)*
▲ Imperial Frames & Albums LLC ....E 718 832-9793
  Brooklyn *(G-1995)*
Innova Interiors Inc ....F 718 401-2122
  Bronx *(G-1298)*
Interntonal Consmr Connections ....F 516 481-3438
  West Hempstead *(G-16217)*
Interstate Wood Products Inc ....F 631 842-4488
  Amityville *(G-288)*
Ivan Horning ....G 315 536-3028
  Penn Yan *(G-12959)*
Jeffrey John ....G 631 842-2850
  Amityville *(G-291)*
Jordache Woodworking Corp ....F 718 349-3373
  Brooklyn *(G-2045)*
Julius Lowy Frame Restoring Co ....E 212 861-8585
  New York *(G-10377)*
K & B Woodworking Inc ....G 518 634-7253
  Cairo *(G-3150)*

Lanwood Industries Inc ....E 718 786-3000
  Bay Shore *(G-694)*
Lanza Corp ....G 914 937-6360
  Port Chester *(G-13204)*
◆ Lco Destiny LLC ....B 315 782-3302
  Watertown *(G-16025)*
Long Lumber and Supply Corp ....F 518 439-1661
  Slingerlands *(G-14889)*
M & R Woodworking & Finishing ....G 718 486-5480
  Brooklyn *(G-2143)*
▲ M A Moslow & Bros Inc ....E 716 896-2950
  Buffalo *(G-2929)*
McGraw Wood Products LLC ....E 607 836-6465
  Mc Graw *(G-7928)*
McIntosh Box & Pallet Co Inc ....E 315 446-9350
  Rome *(G-14257)*
Meeco Sullivan LLC ....C 800 232-3625
  Warwick *(G-15959)*
◆ N Sketch Build Inc ....G 800 975-0597
  Fishkill *(G-4950)*
▲ North American Enclosures Inc ....E 631 234-9500
  Central Islip *(G-3381)*
◆ Northast Ctr For Bekeeping LLC ....F 800 632-3379
  Greenwich *(G-5643)*
Northern Forest Pdts Co Inc ....G 315 942-6955
  Boonville *(G-1118)*
P B & H Moulding Corporation ....E 315 455-1756
  Fayetteville *(G-4929)*
Paramount Graphix ....E 845 367-5003
  Port Jervis *(G-13234)*
Pdj Components Inc ....E 845 469-9191
  Chester *(G-3479)*
Pella Corporation ....C 631 208-0710
  Calverton *(G-3168)*
▲ Pgs Millwork Inc ....D 518 828-2608
  Hudson *(G-6368)*
Piccini Mnm Inc ....G 845 741-6770
  West Nyack *(G-16279)*
Picture Perfect Framing ....G 718 851-1884
  Brooklyn *(G-2316)*
Premium Mulch & Materials Inc ....F 631 320-3666
  Coram *(G-3803)*
Prime Wood Products ....E 518 792-1407
  Queensbury *(G-13438)*
▲ Putnam Rolling Ladder Co Inc ....F 212 226-5147
  New York *(G-11280)*
Putnam Rolling Ladder Co Inc ....E 718 381-8219
  Brooklyn *(G-2363)*
Quattro Frameworks Inc ....F 718 361-2620
  Long Island City *(G-7569)*
▲ R P M Industries Inc ....E 315 255-1105
  Auburn *(G-497)*
Regal Windows & Doors LLC ....F 201 934-0100
  Spring Valley *(G-15006)*
Regence Picture Frames Inc ....E 718 779-0888
  Lynbrook *(G-7672)*
Revival Industries Inc ....F 315 868-1085
  Ilion *(G-6479)*
Richard Rothbard Inc ....G 845 355-2300
  Slate Hill *(G-14885)*
Rose Fence Inc ....F 516 223-0777
  Baldwin *(G-541)*
Ryers Creek Corp ....E 607 523-6617
  Corning *(G-3825)*
Sentine Printing Inc ....G 516 334-7400
  Westbury *(G-16372)*
Sky Frame & Art Inc ....E 212 925-7856
  New York *(G-11613)*
▲ Structural Industries Inc ....C 631 471-5200
  Bohemia *(G-1092)*
Superior Wood Turnings ....F 716 483-1254
  Jamestown *(G-6756)*
T Eason Land Surveyor ....G 631 474-2200
  Port Jeff STA *(G-13218)*
Thomas Matthews Wdwkg Ltd ....F 631 287-3657
  Southampton *(G-14964)*
Thomas Matthews Wdwkg Ltd ....G 631 287-2023
  Southampton *(G-14965)*
Ultimate Styles of America ....F 631 254-0219
  Bay Shore *(G-733)*
▲ Unisource Food Eqp Systems Inc .....G 516 681-0537
  Holbrook *(G-6217)*
Walpole Woodworkers Inc ....G 631 726-2859
  Water Mill *(G-15971)*
Wholesale Mulch & Sawdust Inc ....G 607 687-2637
  Owego *(G-12806)*
Windsor United Industries LLC ....E 607 655-3300
  Windsor *(G-16605)*
Wood Innovations of Suffolk ....G 631 698-2345
  Medford *(G-7969)*

Woodmotif Inc .... F 516 564-8325
 Hempstead *(G-6028)*
Woodtronics Inc .... G 914 962-5205
 Yorktown Heights *(G-16825)*
▲ York Ladder Inc .... F 718 784-6666
 Long Island City *(G-7646)*

25 FURNITURE AND FIXTURES

2511 Wood Household Furniture

A & S Woodworking Inc .... G 518 821-0832
 Hudson *(G-6335)*
A-1 Manhattan Custom Furn Inc ...... E 718 937-4780
 Island Park *(G-6511)*
American Epoxy and Metal Inc .... G 718 828-7828
 Scarsdale *(G-14636)*
Anthony Lawrence of New York ...... E 212 206-8820
 Long Island City *(G-7380)*
Arthur Brown W Mfg Co .... F 631 243-5594
 Deer Park *(G-3946)*
▲ Arthur Lauer Inc .... E 845 255-7871
 Gardiner *(G-5291)*
Artisan Woodworking Ltd .... G 516 486-0818
 West Hempstead *(G-16212)*
Atelier Viollet Corp .... G 718 782-1727
 Brooklyn *(G-1568)*
▲ Benchmark Furniture Mfg .... D 718 257-4707
 Brooklyn *(G-1597)*
Black River Woodworking LLC .... G 315 376-8405
 Castorland *(G-3298)*
Brueton Industries Inc .... D 516 379-3400
 Freeport *(G-5147)*
◆ Bush Industries Inc .... C 716 665-2000
 Jamestown *(G-6704)*
Cab-Network Inc .... G 516 334-8666
 Westbury *(G-16320)*
Carlos & Alex Atelier Inc .... E 718 441-8911
 Richmond Hill *(G-13500)*
Carver Creek Enterprises Inc .... G 585 657-7511
 Bloomfield *(G-949)*
▲ Catskill Craftsmen Inc .... D 607 652-7321
 Stamford *(G-15030)*
▲ Charles H Beckley Inc .... F 718 665-2218
 Bronx *(G-1239)*
Comerford Hennessy At Home Inc .. G 631 537-6200
 Bridgehampton *(G-1180)*
▲ Community Products LLC .... C 845 658-8799
 Rifton *(G-13559)*
Concepts In Wood of CNY .... E 315 463-8084
 Syracuse *(G-15286)*
Conesus Lake Association Inc .... E 585 346-6864
 Lakeville *(G-6985)*
Cousins Furniture & Hm Imprvs ...... E 631 254-3752
 Deer Park *(G-3959)*
Custom Display Manufacture .... G 516 783-6491
 North Bellmore *(G-12377)*
Custom Woodcraft LLC .... F 315 843-4234
 Munnsville *(G-8458)*
▲ D & W Design Inc .... E 845 343-3366
 Middletown *(G-8146)*
David Sutherland Showrooms - N ... G 212 871-9717
 New York *(G-9485)*
Dbs Interiors Corp .... F 631 491-3013
 West Babylon *(G-16152)*
Dcl Furniture Manufacturing .... E 516 248-2683
 Mineola *(G-8215)*
Deakon Homes and Interiors .... F 518 271-0342
 Troy *(G-15603)*
Designs By Robert Scott Inc .... E 718 609-2535
 Brooklyn *(G-1770)*
Dessin/Fournir Inc .... F 212 758-0844
 New York *(G-9510)*
▲ Dinette Depot Ltd .... D 516 515-9623
 Brooklyn *(G-1780)*
Ducduc LLC .... F 212 226-1868
 New York *(G-9582)*
▲ Dune Inc .... G 212 925-6171
 New York *(G-9585)*
▲ Eclectic Cntract Furn Inds Inc .... F 212 967-5504
 New York *(G-9622)*
El Greco Woodworking Inc .... G 716 483-0315
 Jamestown *(G-6713)*
Emilia Interiors Inc .... F 718 629-4202
 Brooklyn *(G-1831)*
▲ Ercole Nyc Inc .... F 212 675-2218
 Brooklyn *(G-1846)*
Eugenia Selective Living Inc .... F 631 277-1461
 Islip *(G-6546)*
Falcon Chair and Table Inc .... E 716 664-7136
 Falconer *(G-4677)*

▲ Feinkind Inc .... G 800 289-6136
 Irvington *(G-6504)*
Fenix Furniture Co .... E 631 273-3500
 Bay Shore *(G-686)*
▲ Fiber-Seal of New York Inc .... C 212 888-5580
 New York *(G-9797)*
Final Dimension Inc .... G 718 786-0100
 Maspeth *(G-7845)*
Fine Arts Furniture Inc .... G 212 744-9139
 Long Island City *(G-7447)*
◆ Forecast Consoles Inc .... E 631 253-9000
 Hauppauge *(G-5827)*
Franz Fischer Inc .... F 718 821-1300
 Brooklyn *(G-1905)*
Fred Schulz Inc .... G 845 724-3409
 Poughquag *(G-13374)*
French & Itln Furn Craftsmen .... G 718 599-5000
 Brooklyn *(G-1906)*
Furniture Doctor Inc .... F 585 657-6941
 Bloomfield *(G-954)*
Glendale Architectural WD Pdts .... E 718 326-2700
 Glendale *(G-5401)*
◆ Hard Manufacturing Co Inc .... E 716 893-1800
 Buffalo *(G-2865)*
◆ Harden Furniture LLC .... C 315 675-3600
 Mc Connellsville *(G-7925)*
Hayman-Chaffey Designs Inc .... F 212 889-7771
 New York *(G-10050)*
▲ Hunt Country Furniture Inc .... G 845 832-6601
 Wingdale *(G-16606)*
Icon Design LLC .... E 585 768-6040
 Le Roy *(G-7119)*
Innovant Inc .... G 212 929-4883
 New York *(G-10218)*
▲ Inova LLC .... E 866 528-2804
 Guilderland Center *(G-5656)*
Inter Craft Custom Furniture .... G 718 278-2573
 Astoria *(G-431)*
J Percoco Industries Inc .... G 631 312-4572
 Bohemia *(G-1038)*
K & B Woodworking Inc .... G 518 634-7253
 Cairo *(G-3150)*
Kazac Inc .... G 631 249-7299
 Farmingdale *(G-4799)*
Kittinger Company Inc .... E 716 876-1000
 Buffalo *(G-2907)*
Knoll Inc .... D 212 343-4124
 New York *(G-10460)*
▲ L& JG Stickley Incorporated ...... A 315 682-5500
 Manlius *(G-7779)*
Lanoves Inc .... E 718 384-1880
 Brooklyn *(G-2094)*
Lemode Concepts Inc .... G 631 841-0796
 Amityville *(G-297)*
Little Wolf Cabinet Shop Inc .... E 212 734-1116
 New York *(G-10581)*
Long Lumber and Supply Corp .... F 518 439-1661
 Slingerlands *(G-14889)*
▲ M & C Furniture .... G 718 422-2136
 Brooklyn *(G-2140)*
M T D Corporation .... F 631 491-3905
 West Babylon *(G-16172)*
Machias Furniture Factory Inc .... G 716 353-8687
 Machias *(G-7706)*
◆ Mackenzie-Childs LLC .... C 315 364-6118
 Aurora *(G-511)*
Manchester Wood Inc .... C 518 642-9518
 Granville *(G-5521)*
McGraw Wood Products LLC .... F 607 836-6465
 Mc Graw *(G-7928)*
Mica International Ltd .... F 516 378-3400
 Freeport *(G-5167)*
New Day Woodwork Inc .... F 718 275-1721
 Glendale *(G-5404)*
Nicholas Dfine Furn Decorators ..... F 914 245-8982
 Bronx *(G-1343)*
▲ Patrick Mackin Custom Furn .... G 718 237-2592
 Brooklyn *(G-2307)*
Piccini Industries Inc .... E 845 365-0614
 Orangeburg *(G-12685)*
▼ Pillow Perfections Ltd Inc .... G 718 383-2259
 Brooklyn *(G-2318)*
Plexi Craft Quality Products .... F 212 924-3244
 New York *(G-11211)*
Premier Woodcraft Ltd .... E 610 383-6624
 White Plains *(G-16499)*
◆ Premiere Living Products LLC .... G 631 873-4337
 Dix Hills *(G-4123)*
Professional Cab Detailing Co .... F 845 436-7282
 Woodridge *(G-16643)*

Raff Enterprises .... G 518 218-7883
 Albany *(G-122)*
Recycled Brooklyn Group LLC .... F 917 902-0662
 Brooklyn *(G-2391)*
▼ Reis D Furniture Mfg .... E 516 248-5676
 Mineola *(G-8246)*
◆ Renco Group Inc .... G 212 541-6000
 New York *(G-11361)*
Sitecraft Inc .... G 718 729-4900
 Astoria *(G-444)*
Stillwater Wood & Iron .... G 518 664-4501
 Stillwater *(G-15159)*
▲ Sundown Ski & Sport Shop Inc ... E 631 737-8600
 Lake Grove *(G-6970)*
▲ Triple J Bedding LLC .... G 718 643-8005
 Brooklyn *(G-2587)*
Universal Designs Inc .... G 718 721-1111
 Long Island City *(G-7625)*
Wallace Home Design Ctr .... G 631 765-3890
 Southold *(G-14971)*
Walpole Woodworkers Inc .... G 631 726-2859
 Water Mill *(G-15971)*
Walter P Sauer LLC .... E 718 937-0600
 Brooklyn *(G-2638)*
William Somerville Maintenance .... D 212 534-4600
 New York *(G-12113)*
Woodmotif Inc .... F 516 564-8325
 Hempstead *(G-6028)*
◆ World Trading Center Inc .... G 631 273-3330
 Hauppauge *(G-5978)*
Your Furniture Designers Inc .... G 845 947-3046
 West Haverstraw *(G-16211)*

2512 Wood Household Furniture, Upholstered

▲ Arthur Lauer Inc .... E 845 255-7871
 Gardiner *(G-5291)*
▲ Artone LLC .... D 716 664-2232
 Jamestown *(G-6699)*
August Studios .... G 718 706-6487
 Long Island City *(G-7395)*
▲ Avanti Furniture Corp .... F 516 293-8220
 Farmingdale *(G-4725)*
▲ Classic Sofa Ltd .... D 212 620-0485
 New York *(G-9321)*
Deangelis Ltd .... E 212 348-8225
 Glen Head *(G-5379)*
Doreen Interiors Ltd .... E 212 255-9008
 New Hyde Park *(G-8528)*
Elan Upholstery Inc .... F 631 563-0650
 Bohemia *(G-1022)*
Falvo Manufacturing Co Inc .... F 315 724-7925
 Utica *(G-15700)*
▲ Fiber-Seal of New York Inc .... C 212 888-5580
 New York *(G-9797)*
Furniture By Craftmaster Ltd .... F 631 750-0658
 Bohemia *(G-1025)*
H & H Furniture Co .... G 718 850-5252
 Jamaica *(G-6648)*
Hallagan Manufacturing Co Inc ..... D 315 331-4640
 Newark *(G-12195)*
◆ Harden Furniture LLC .... C 315 675-3600
 Mc Connellsville *(G-7925)*
Jackson Dakota Inc .... F 718 786-8600
 New York *(G-10293)*
▲ Jackson Dakota Inc .... G 212 838-9444
 New York *(G-10294)*
Jays Furniture Products Inc .... E 716 876-8854
 Buffalo *(G-2890)*
Kittinger Company Inc .... E 716 876-1000
 Buffalo *(G-2907)*
◆ Mackenzie-Childs LLC .... C 315 364-6118
 Aurora *(G-511)*
Matteo & Antonio Bartolotta .... F 315 252-2220
 Auburn *(G-490)*
Mazza Classics Incorporated .... G 631 390-9060
 Farmingdale *(G-4818)*
Nicholas Dfine Furn Decorators ..... F 914 245-8982
 Bronx *(G-1343)*
Pheonix Custom Furniture Ltd .... E 212 727-2648
 Long Island City *(G-7555)*
◆ Princeton Upholstery Co Inc .... D 845 343-2196
 Middletown *(G-8172)*
Rob Herschenfeld Design Inc .... F 718 456-6801
 Brooklyn *(G-2408)*
Simon S Decorating Inc .... G 718 339-2931
 Brooklyn *(G-2476)*
▲ Slava Industries Incorporated .... G 718 499-4850
 Brooklyn *(G-2483)*

Sleepable Sofas Ltd.....D.....973 546-4502
New York (G-11617)
▲ Smith & Watson.....E.....212 686-6444
New York (G-11624)
Two Worlds Arts Ltd.....G.....212 929-2210
Brooklyn (G-2597)
Versailles Drapery Upholstery.....F.....212 533-2059
Long Island City (G-7631)
Wallace Home Design Ctr.....G.....631 765-3890
Southold (G-14971)
Yepes Fine Furniture.....E.....718 383-0221
Brooklyn (G-2663)

2514 Metal Household Furniture

▲ American Best Cabinets Inc.....E.....845 369-6666
Suffern (G-15185)
Brueton Industries Inc.....D.....516 379-3400
Freeport (G-5147)
◆ Charles P Rogers Brass Beds.....F.....212 675-4400
New York (G-9264)
▲ CIDC Corp.....F.....718 342-5820
Glendale (G-5395)
▲ D & W Design Inc.....E.....845 343-3366
Middletown (G-8146)
◆ Embassy Dinettes Inc.....G.....631 253-2292
Deer Park (G-3973)
F&M Ornamental Designs LLC.....G.....212 353-2600
New York (G-9763)
▲ F&M Ornamental Designs LLC.....F.....908 241-7776
New York (G-9764)
Furniture Doctor Inc.....G.....585 657-6941
Bloomfield (G-954)
▲ Glissade New York LLC.....E.....631 756-4800
Farmingdale (G-4772)
◆ Hard Manufacturing Co Inc.....E.....716 893-1800
Buffalo (G-2865)
▲ Hellas Stone Inc.....G.....718 545-4716
Astoria (G-430)
La Forge Francaise Ltd Inc.....G.....631 591-0572
Riverhead (G-13572)
▲ Majestic Home Imprvs Distr.....G.....718 853-5079
Brooklyn (G-2152)
Manhattan Cabinets Inc.....G.....212 548-2436
New York (G-10684)
Meeker Sales Corp.....G.....718 384-5400
Brooklyn (G-2188)
Methods Tooling & Mfg Inc.....E.....845 246-7100
Mount Marion (G-8364)
▲ NK Medical Products Inc.....G.....716 759-7200
Amherst (G-241)
▲ Novum Medical Products Inc.....F.....716 759-7200
Amherst (G-242)
Precision Orna Ir Works Inc.....G.....718 379-5200
Bronx (G-1363)
◆ Renco Group Inc.....G.....212 541-6000
New York (G-11361)
Royal Metal Products Inc.....E.....518 966-4442
Surprise (G-15207)
▲ Slava Industries Incorporated.....G.....718 499-4850
Brooklyn (G-2483)
Steelcraft Manufacturing Co.....F.....718 277-2404
Brooklyn (G-2516)

2515 Mattresses & Bedsprings

Acworth Foundation.....G.....631 784-7802
Huntington (G-6389)
▲ Brook North Farms Inc.....F.....315 834-9390
Auburn (G-472)
▲ Charles H Beckley Inc.....F.....718 665-2218
Bronx (G-1239)
Duxiana Dux Bed.....G.....212 755-2600
New York (G-9588)
◆ Hard Manufacturing Co Inc.....E.....716 893-1800
Buffalo (G-2865)
▼ Ideal Manufacturing Inc.....E.....585 872-7190
East Rochester (G-4287)
KKR Millennium GP LLC.....A.....212 750-8300
New York (G-10454)
◆ M R C Industries Inc.....C.....516 328-6900
Port Washington (G-13283)
Metro Mattress Corp.....E.....716 205-2300
Niagara Falls (G-12310)
Natural Dreams LLC.....G.....718 760-4202
Corona (G-3852)
▲ Otis Bedding Mfg Co Inc.....E.....716 825-2599
Buffalo (G-2983)
◆ Quality Foam Inc.....F.....718 381-3644
Brooklyn (G-2366)
Rollers Inc.....G.....716 837-0700
Buffalo (G-3044)
▲ Royal Bedding Co Buffalo Inc.....E.....716 895-1414
Buffalo (G-3049)
Sealy Mattress Co Albany Inc.....B.....518 880-1600
Troy (G-15598)
Sleep Improvement Center Inc.....F.....516 536-5799
Rockville Centre (G-14240)
Sleepable Sofas Ltd.....D.....973 546-4502
New York (G-11617)
▲ Steinbock-Braff Inc.....E.....718 972-6500
Brooklyn (G-2520)
◆ VSM Investors LLC.....G.....212 351-1600
New York (G-12057)

2517 Wood T V, Radio, Phono & Sewing Cabinets

Dbs Interiors Corp.....F.....631 491-3013
West Babylon (G-16152)
Handcraft Cabinetry Inc.....G.....914 681-9437
White Plains (G-16458)
Time Base Corporation.....E.....631 293-4068
Edgewood (G-4420)
▲ W Designe Inc.....E.....914 736-1058
Peekskill (G-12927)

2519 Household Furniture, NEC

3phase Industries LLC.....G.....347 763-2942
Brooklyn (G-1438)
Albert Menin Interiors Ltd.....F.....212 876-3041
Bronx (G-1215)
Anandamali Inc.....F.....212 343-8964
New York (G-8854)
Bielecky Bros Inc.....E.....718 424-4764
Woodside (G-16646)
▲ Comely International Trdg Inc.....G.....212 683-1240
New York (G-9362)
Culin/Colella Inc.....G.....914 698-7727
Mamaroneck (G-7741)
Dbs Interiors Corp.....F.....631 491-3013
West Babylon (G-16152)
Eugenia Selective Living Inc.....F.....631 277-1461
Islip (G-6546)
Harome Designs LLC.....E.....631 864-1900
Commack (G-3694)
▲ Holland & Sherry Inc.....E.....212 542-8410
New York (G-10115)
▲ L& JG Stickley Incorporated.....A.....315 682-5500
Manlius (G-7779)
Matthew Shively LLC.....G.....914 937-3531
Port Chester (G-13205)
Mbh Furniture Innovations Inc.....G.....845 354-8202
Spring Valley (G-15002)
▲ Olollo Inc.....G.....877 701-0110
Brooklyn (G-2287)
Ready To Assemble Company Inc.....E.....516 825-4397
Valley Stream (G-15794)
Safcore LLC.....F.....917 627-5263
Brooklyn (G-2443)
Two Worlds Arts Ltd.....G.....212 929-2210
New York (G-11920)
Universal Interiors LLC.....F.....518 298-4400
Champlain (G-3417)
▲ Vondom LLC.....G.....212 207-3252
New York (G-12055)
Yogibo LLC.....F.....518 456-1762
Albany (G-144)

2521 Wood Office Furniture

▲ A G Master Crafts Ltd.....F.....516 745-6262
Garden City (G-5249)
▲ Artone LLC.....D.....716 664-2232
Jamestown (G-6699)
B D B Typewriter Supply Works.....E.....718 232-4800
Brooklyn (G-1580)
▲ Bauerschmidt & Sons Inc.....D.....718 528-3500
Jamaica (G-6630)
Bloch Industries LLC.....D.....585 334-9600
Rochester (G-13666)
Brueton Industries Inc.....D.....516 379-3400
Freeport (G-5147)
◆ Bush Industries Inc.....C.....716 665-2000
Jamestown (G-6704)
▼ Ccn International Inc.....D.....315 789-4400
Geneva (G-5319)
Centre Interiors Wdwkg Co Inc.....E.....718 323-1343
Ozone Park (G-12822)
Chicone Builders LLC.....G.....607 535-6540
Montour Falls (G-8325)
Commercial Display Design LLC.....F.....607 336-7353
Norwich (G-12483)
Concepts In Wood of CNY.....E.....315 463-8084
Syracuse (G-15286)
▼ Craft Custom Woodwork Co Inc.....F.....718 821-2162
Maspeth (G-7831)
Culin/Colella Inc.....G.....914 698-7727
Mamaroneck (G-7741)
DAF Office Networks Inc.....G.....315 699-7070
Cicero (G-3516)
Davinci Designs Inc.....F.....631 595-1095
Deer Park (G-3962)
Dcl Furniture Manufacturing.....E.....516 248-2683
Mineola (G-8215)
Deakon Homes and Interiors.....F.....518 271-0342
Troy (G-15603)
Designs By Robert Scott Inc.....E.....718 609-2535
Brooklyn (G-1770)
Divine Art Furniture Inc.....G.....718 834-0111
Brooklyn (G-1782)
▲ E-Systems Group LLC.....E.....607 775-1100
Conklin (G-3727)
Eugenia Selective Living Inc.....F.....631 277-1461
Islip (G-6546)
Exhibit Corporation America.....E.....718 937-2600
Long Island City (G-7441)
F E Hale Mfg Co.....D.....315 894-5490
Frankfort (G-5106)
Fina Cabinet Corp.....G.....718 409-2900
Mount Vernon (G-8398)
▲ Forecast Consoles Inc.....E.....631 253-9000
Hauppauge (G-5827)
Furniture By Craftmaster Ltd.....G.....631 750-0658
Bohemia (G-1025)
Glendale Architectural WD Pdts.....E.....718 326-2700
Glendale (G-5401)
Gothic Cabinet Craft Inc.....D.....347 881-1420
Maspeth (G-7848)
▲ Gunlocke Company LLC.....C.....585 728-5111
Wayland (G-16071)
H Freund Woodworking Co Inc.....F.....516 334-3774
Westbury (G-16337)
◆ Harden Furniture LLC.....C.....315 675-3600
Mc Connellsville (G-7925)
Heartwood Specialties Inc.....G.....607 654-0102
Hammondsport (G-5704)
Hni Corporation.....C.....212 683-2232
New York (G-10110)
◆ Humanscale Corporation.....E.....212 725-4749
New York (G-10150)
▲ Innovant Inc.....G.....631 348-1900
Islandia (G-6531)
Interior Solutions of Wny LLC.....G.....716 332-0372
Buffalo (G-2887)
Kazac Inc.....G.....631 249-7299
Farmingdale (G-4799)
Kimball Office Inc.....E.....212 753-6161
New York (G-10446)
Kittinger Company Inc.....E.....716 876-1000
Buffalo (G-2907)
Knoll Inc.....D.....716 891-1700
Buffalo (G-2908)
Knoll Inc.....D.....212 343-4124
New York (G-10460)
▲ Lake Country Woodworkers Ltd.....E.....585 374-6353
Naples (G-8472)
Longo Commercial Cabinets Inc.....E.....631 225-4290
Lindenhurst (G-7176)
M T D Corporation.....F.....631 491-3905
West Babylon (G-16172)
▲ Manhattan Comfort Inc.....G.....908 888-0818
Brooklyn (G-2157)
Materials Design Workshop.....F.....718 893-1954
Bronx (G-1325)
Matteo & Antonio Bartolotta.....F.....315 252-2220
Auburn (G-490)
▲ Miller Blaker Inc.....D.....718 665-0500
Bronx (G-1332)
Millers Millworks Inc.....E.....585 494-1420
Bergen (G-825)
▲ N Y Elli Design Corp.....F.....718 228-0014
Ridgewood (G-13543)
New Dimensions Office Group.....D.....718 387-0995
Brooklyn (G-2259)
Nicholas Dfine Furn Decorators.....F.....914 245-8982
Bronx (G-1343)
Omega Furniture Manufacturing.....F.....315 463-7428
Syracuse (G-15385)
Pheonix Custom Furniture Ltd.....E.....212 727-2648
Long Island City (G-7555)
Piccini Industries Ltd.....E.....845 365-0614
Orangeburg (G-12685)

◆ Poppin Inc .... D 212 391-7200
New York *(G-11219)*
Premier Woodcraft Ltd .... E 610 383-6624
White Plains *(G-16499)*
▲ Prince Seating Corp .... E 718 363-2300
Brooklyn *(G-2345)*
◆ Princeton Upholstery Co Inc .... D 845 343-2196
Middletown *(G-8172)*
Red White & Blue Entps Corp .... G 718 565-8080
Woodside *(G-16675)*
Riverfront Costume Design .... G 716 693-2501
North Tonawanda *(G-12447)*
Saraval Industries .... G 516 768-9033
Nyack *(G-12510)*
Stylecraft Interiors Inc .... F 516 487-2133
Great Neck *(G-5594)*
▲ Technology Desking Inc .... E 212 257-6998
New York *(G-11794)*
Three R Enterprises Inc .... E 585 254-5050
Rochester *(G-14169)*
Universal Designs Inc .... G 718 721-1111
Long Island City *(G-7625)*
▲ Upstate Office Liquidators Inc .... F 607 722-9234
Johnson City *(G-6822)*
WD Certified Contracting LLC .... F 516 493-9319
Westbury *(G-16387)*
Wood Etc Inc .... F 315 484-9663
Syracuse *(G-15461)*
Woodmotif Inc .... F 516 564-8325
Hempstead *(G-6028)*
Your Furniture Designers Inc .... G 845 947-3046
West Haverstraw *(G-16211)*
Zographos Designs Ltd .... G 212 545-0227
New York *(G-12182)*

2522 Office Furniture, Except Wood

3phase Industries LLC .... G 347 763-2942
Brooklyn *(G-1438)*
Able Steel Equipment Co Inc .... F 718 361-9240
Long Island City *(G-7366)*
Afco Systems Inc .... C 631 249-9441
Farmingdale *(G-4708)*
Allcraft Fabricators Inc .... D 631 951-4100
Hauppauge *(G-5760)*
Aronowitz Metal Works .... G 845 356-1660
Monsey *(G-8285)*
▲ Artistic Products LLC .... E 631 435-0200
Hauppauge *(G-5771)*
▲ Artone LLC .... D 716 664-2232
Jamestown *(G-6699)*
Aztec Industries Inc .... G 631 585-1331
Ronkonkoma *(G-14313)*
▲ Bisley Inc .... G 212 675-3055
New York *(G-9091)*
Brueton Industries Inc .... D 516 379-3400
Freeport *(G-5147)*
▲ Davies Office Refurbishing Inc .... C 518 426-7188
Albany *(G-67)*
Davinci Designs Inc .... F 631 595-1095
Deer Park *(G-3962)*
Dcl Furniture Manufacturing .... E 516 248-2683
Mineola *(G-8215)*
Deakon Homes and Interiors .... F 518 271-0342
Troy *(G-15603)*
▲ E-Systems Group LLC .... E 607 775-1100
Conklin *(G-3727)*
Eugenia Selective Living Inc .... F 631 277-1461
Islip *(G-6546)*
Exhibit Corporation America .... E 718 937-2600
Long Island City *(G-7441)*
Falvo Manufacturing Co Inc .... F 315 724-7925
Utica *(G-15700)*
▲ Forecast Consoles Inc .... E 631 253-9000
Hauppauge *(G-5827)*
FX INC .... F 212 244-2240
New York *(G-9865)*
Gothic Cabinet Craft Inc .... D 347 881-1420
Maspeth *(G-7848)*
◆ Hergo Ergonomic Support .... E 718 894-0639
Maspeth *(G-7851)*
Hudson Valley Office Furn Inc .... G 845 565-6673
Newburgh *(G-12227)*
Inscape Inc .... E 716 665-6210
Falconer *(G-4682)*
Integrated Tech Support Svcs .... G 718 454-2497
Saint Albans *(G-14508)*
▲ International Office .... G 212 334-4617
New York *(G-10249)*
Knoll Inc .... D 212 343-4124
New York *(G-10460)*
Larson Metal Manufacturing Co .... G 716 665-6807
Jamestown *(G-6736)*
▲ Lucia Group Inc .... G 631 392-4900
Deer Park *(G-4004)*
Modern Metal Fabricators Inc .... G 518 966-4142
Hannacroix *(G-5716)*
▲ Natural Stone & Cabinet Inc .... G 718 388-2988
Brooklyn *(G-2248)*
New Dimensions Office Group .... D 718 387-0995
Brooklyn *(G-2259)*
Nightingale Corp .... G 905 896-3434
Tonawanda *(G-15564)*
Piccini Industries Ltd .... E 845 365-0614
Orangeburg *(G-12685)*
◆ Poppin Inc .... D 212 391-7200
New York *(G-11219)*
Premier Woodcraft Ltd .... E 610 383-6624
White Plains *(G-16499)*
Riverfront Costume Design .... G 716 693-2501
North Tonawanda *(G-12447)*
Roberts Office Furn Cncpts Inc .... E 315 451-9185
Liverpool *(G-7260)*
Royal Metal Products Inc .... E 518 966-4442
Surprise *(G-15207)*
▼ Schwab Corp .... E 585 381-4900
Rochester *(G-14116)*
Seating Inc .... E 800 468-2475
Nunda *(G-12498)*
▼ Ulrich Planfiling Eqp Corp .... E 716 763-1815
Lakewood *(G-6998)*
◆ Vitra Inc .... F 212 463-5700
New York *(G-12047)*
Workplace Interiors LLC .... E 585 425-7420
Fairport *(G-4667)*
Zographos Designs Ltd .... G 212 545-0227
New York *(G-12182)*

2531 Public Building & Related Furniture

Able Steel Equipment Co Inc .... F 718 361-9240
Long Island City *(G-7366)*
American Bptst Chrches Mtro NY .... G 212 870-3195
New York *(G-8824)*
Artistry In Wood of Syracuse .... F 315 431-4022
East Syracuse *(G-4322)*
▲ Artone LLC .... D 716 664-2232
Jamestown *(G-6699)*
B/E Aerospace Inc .... E 631 563-6400
Bohemia *(G-985)*
E & D Specialty Stands Inc .... E 716 337-0161
North Collins *(G-12385)*
East/West Industries Inc .... E 631 981-5900
Ronkonkoma *(G-14335)*
▲ Forecast Consoles Inc .... E 631 253-9000
Hauppauge *(G-5827)*
Hartford Hwy Dept .... G 315 724-0654
New Hartford *(G-8506)*
▲ Inova LLC .... E 866 528-2804
Guilderland Center *(G-5656)*
Jays Furniture Products Inc .... E 716 876-8854
Buffalo *(G-2890)*
Jcdecaux Mallscape LLC .... F 646 834-1200
New York *(G-10319)*
Johnson Controls Inc .... D 518 884-8313
Ballston Spa *(G-586)*
Johnson Controls Inc .... G 518 694-4822
Albany *(G-89)*
Johnson Controls Inc .... E 585 671-1930
Webster *(G-16087)*
Johnson Controls Inc .... C 585 724-2232
Rochester *(G-13897)*
Keck Group Inc .... F 845 988-5757
Warwick *(G-15954)*
▲ Maximum Security Products Corp .... E 518 233-1800
Waterford *(G-15977)*
Maxsecure Systems Inc .... G 800 657-4336
Buffalo *(G-2940)*
▲ N Y Elli Design Corp .... F 718 228-0014
Ridgewood *(G-13543)*
Pluribus Products Inc .... E 718 852-1614
Bayville *(G-753)*
Rosenwach Tank Co Inc .... E 212 972-4411
Astoria *(G-442)*
Seating Inc .... E 800 468-2475
Nunda *(G-12498)*
▲ Steeldeck Ny Inc .... F 718 599-3700
Brooklyn *(G-2517)*
▼ Stidd Systems Inc .... E 631 477-2400
Greenport *(G-5626)*
▲ Studio 21 LA Inc .... E 718 965-6579
Brooklyn *(G-2525)*
◆ Testori Interiors Inc .... E 518 298-4400
Champlain *(G-3414)*
Town of Amherst .... E 716 631-7113
Williamsville *(G-16591)*
Tymor Park .... G 845 724-5691
Lagrangeville *(G-6963)*
▲ Unifor Inc .... F 212 673-3434
New York *(G-11941)*
Universal Interiors LLC .... F 518 298-4400
Champlain *(G-3417)*

2541 Wood, Office & Store Fixtures

Abaco Steel Products Inc .... G 631 589-1800
Bohemia *(G-967)*
▲ Abbott Industries Inc .... B 718 291-0800
Jamaica *(G-6622)*
All Merchandise Display Corp .... G 718 257-2221
Highland Mills *(G-6150)*
Allegany Laminating and Supply .... G 716 372-2424
Allegany *(G-188)*
Alrod Associates Inc .... F 631 981-2193
Ronkonkoma *(G-14303)*
Arcy Plastic Laminates Inc .... E 518 235-0753
Albany *(G-42)*
▲ Array Marketing Group Inc .... E 212 750-3367
New York *(G-8911)*
▲ Artone LLC .... D 716 664-2232
Jamestown *(G-6699)*
Auburn Custom Millwork Inc .... G 315 253-3843
Auburn *(G-463)*
▲ Auratic Inc .... G 914 413-8154
New York *(G-8964)*
Bator Bintor Inc .... F 347 546-6503
Brooklyn *(G-1590)*
▲ Bauerschmidt & Sons Inc .... D 718 528-3500
Jamaica *(G-6630)*
Bloch Industries LLC .... D 585 334-9600
Rochester *(G-13666)*
Contempra Design Inc .... G 718 984-8586
Staten Island *(G-15065)*
Countertops & Cabinets Inc .... G 315 433-1038
Syracuse *(G-15292)*
Creative Counter Tops Inc .... F 845 471-6480
Poughkeepsie *(G-13333)*
Custom Countertops Inc .... G 716 685-2871
Depew *(G-4085)*
Custom Design Kitchens Inc .... F 518 355-4446
Duanesburg *(G-4155)*
Custom Wood Inc .... G 718 927-4700
Brooklyn *(G-1744)*
▲ David Flatt Furniture Ltd .... F 718 937-7944
Long Island City *(G-7421)*
Dbs Interiors Corp .... F 631 491-3013
West Babylon *(G-16152)*
Deakon Homes and Interiors .... F 518 271-0342
Troy *(G-15603)*
Delocon Wholesale Inc .... F 716 592-2711
Springville *(G-15015)*
E F Thresh Inc .... G 315 437-7301
East Syracuse *(G-4336)*
Empire Archtctural Systems Inc .... E 518 773-5109
Johnstown *(G-6826)*
Empire Fabricators Inc .... G 585 235-3050
Rochester *(G-13779)*
Encore Retail Systems Inc .... F 718 385-3443
Mamaroneck *(G-7743)*
Falvo Manufacturing Co Inc .... F 315 724-7925
Utica *(G-15700)*
Farrington Packaging Corp .... E 315 733-4600
Utica *(G-15701)*
▲ Fifty Door Partners LLC .... E 845 562-3332
New Windsor *(G-8644)*
Fina Cabinet Corp .... G 718 409-2900
Mount Vernon *(G-8398)*
Fleetwood Cabinet Co Inc .... G 516 379-2139
Brooklyn *(G-1891)*
▲ Forecast Consoles Inc .... E 631 253-9000
Hauppauge *(G-5827)*
Frank J Martello .... G 585 235-2780
Rochester *(G-13816)*
Gaughan Construction Corp .... G 718 850-9577
Richmond Hill *(G-13503)*
▲ Gotham City Industries Inc .... E 914 713-0979
Scarsdale *(G-14638)*
Greenleaf Cabinet Makers LLC .... F 315 432-4600
Syracuse *(G-15335)*
▲ Hamlet Products Inc .... F 914 665-0307
Mount Vernon *(G-8405)*
Heartwood Specialties Inc .... G 607 654-0102
Hammondsport *(G-5704)*

S
I
C

25 FURNITURE AND FIXTURES

Home Ideal Inc ....G 718 762-8998
  Flushing (G-5009)
▲ Home4u Inc ....G 347 262-7214
  Brooklyn (G-1983)
Hunter Metal Industries Inc ....D 631 475-5900
  East Patchogue (G-4275)
▲ Icestone LLC ....E 718 624-4900
  Brooklyn (G-1993)
▲ Industrial Support Inc ....D 716 662-2954
  Buffalo (G-2883)
Integrated Wood Components Inc .....E 607 467-1739
  Deposit (G-4108)
Inter State Laminates Inc ....E 518 283-8355
  Poestenkill (G-13181)
J M P Display Fixture Co Inc ....G 718 649-0333
  Brooklyn (G-2026)
Johnny Mica Inc ....G 631 225-5213
  Lindenhurst (G-7173)
Joseph Fedele ....G 718 448-3658
  Staten Island (G-15097)
▲ Karp Associates Inc ....D 631 768-8300
  Melville (G-8041)
Kitchen Specialty Craftsmen ....G 607 739-0833
  Elmira (G-4496)
Koeppels Kustom Kitchens Inc ....G 518 489-0092
  Albany (G-93)
L & J Interiors Inc ....G 631 218-0838
  Bohemia (G-1044)
▲ Leo D Bernstein & Sons Inc ....E 212 337-9578
  New York (G-10548)
Lif Distributing Inc ....F 631 630-6900
  Islandia (G-6533)
▲ Lifestyle-Trimco ....E 718 257-9101
  Brooklyn (G-2118)
Longo Commercial Cabinets Inc ....E 631 225-4290
  Lindenhurst (G-7176)
▲ Madjek Inc ....D 631 842-4475
  Amityville (G-300)
◆ Marietta Corporation ....B 607 753-6746
  Cortland (G-3881)
Marplex Furniture Corporation ....G 914 969-7755
  Yonkers (G-16783)
Metropolitan Granite & MBL Inc ....E 585 342-7020
  Rochester (G-13937)
Michael P Mmarr ....G 315 623-9380
  Constantia (G-3740)
▲ Mrp Supports LLC ....F 716 332-7673
  Orchard Park (G-12731)
▲ New Business Solutions Inc ....E 631 789-1500
  Amityville (G-306)
New Dimensions Office Group ....D 718 387-0995
  Brooklyn (G-2259)
Nlr Counter Tops LLC ....G 347 295-0410
  New York (G-10980)
P & B Woodworking Inc ....F 845 744-2508
  Pine Bush (G-12998)
Pine Hill Fabricators ....G 716 823-2474
  Buffalo (G-3005)
Precision Built Tops LLC ....E 607 336-5417
  Norwich (G-12491)
▲ Premier Woodworking Inc ....E 631 236-4100
  Hauppauge (G-5922)
R H Guest Incorporated ....G 718 675-7600
  Brooklyn (G-2376)
Red White & Blue Entps Corp ....E 718 565-8080
  Woodside (G-16675)
Ridge Cabinet & Showcase Inc ....E 585 663-0560
  Rochester (G-14073)
Rochester Countertop Inc ....F 585 338-2260
  Rochester (G-14085)
Serway Bros Inc ....E 315 337-0601
  Rome (G-14274)
Sharonana Enterprises Inc ....E 631 875-5619
  Coram (G-3804)
Solid Surfaces Inc ....D 585 292-5340
  Rochester (G-14134)
▲ Space-Craft Worldwide Inc ....E 631 603-3000
  Hauppauge (G-5942)
Specialty Services ....G 585 728-5650
  Wayland (G-16072)
Steelcraft Manufacturing Co ....F 718 277-2404
  Brooklyn (G-2516)
▲ Steeldeck Ny Inc ....F 718 599-3700
  Brooklyn (G-2517)
Stein Industries Inc ....E 631 789-2222
  Amityville (G-316)
Stereo Advantage Inc ....F 716 656-7161
  Cheektowaga (G-3459)
Telesca-Heyman Inc ....F 212 534-3442
  New York (G-11797)

Three R Enterprises Inc ....E 585 254-5050
  Rochester (G-14169)
Triad Counter Corp ....E 631 750-0615
  Bohemia (G-1098)
Universal Designs Inc ....G 718 721-1111
  Long Island City (G-7625)
Vitarose Corp of America ....G 718 951-9700
  Brooklyn (G-2630)
Wilbedone Inc ....E 607 756-8813
  Cortland (G-3897)
Wilsonart Intl Holdings LLC ....E 516 935-6980
  Bethpage (G-854)
Winerackscom Inc ....G 845 658-7181
  Tillson (G-15515)
Wolak Inc ....G 315 839-5366
  Clayville (G-3560)

2542 Partitions & Fixtures, Except Wood

260 Oak Street Inc ....G 877 852-4676
  Buffalo (G-2676)
▲ Aarco Products Inc ....F 631 924-5461
  Yaphank (G-16703)
Abaco Steel Products Inc ....E 631 589-1800
  Bohemia (G-967)
▲ Abbott Industries Inc ....B 718 291-0800
  Jamaica (G-6622)
Able Steel Equipment Co Inc ....E 718 361-9240
  Long Island City (G-7366)
Air Crafters Inc ....C 631 471-7788
  Ronkonkoma (G-14295)
▲ All American Metal Corporation ...G 516 223-1760
  Freeport (G-5139)
All American Metal Corporation ....E 516 623-0222
  Freeport (G-5140)
Alrod Associates Inc ....F 631 981-2193
  Ronkonkoma (G-14303)
American Standard Mfg Inc ....E 518 868-2512
  Central Bridge (G-3353)
Amscor Inc ....F 800 825-9800
  West Babylon (G-16135)
ASAP Rack Rental Inc ....G 718 499-4495
  Brooklyn (G-1561)
▲ Avf Group Inc ....F 951 360-7111
  Cheektowaga (G-3435)
Bobrick Washroom Equipment Inc ....D 518 877-7444
  Clifton Park (G-3565)
▲ Bridge Metal Industries LLC ....C 914 663-9200
  Mount Vernon (G-8382)
Clark Specialty Co Inc ....E 607 776-3193
  Bath (G-642)
◆ Core Group Displays Inc ....E 845 876-5109
  Rhinebeck (G-13485)
Custom Fixtures Inc ....G 718 965-1141
  Brooklyn (G-1741)
Dakota Systems Mfg Corp ....E 631 249-5811
  Farmingdale (G-4748)
Data Control Inc ....G 585 265-2980
  Ontario (G-12651)
Display Components Mfg Inc ....E 631 420-0600
  West Babylon (G-16153)
Display Shop Inc ....F 646 202-9494
  New York (G-9537)
▲ Display Technologies LLC ....E 718 321-3100
  New Hyde Park (G-8527)
▲ E-Systems Group LLC ....E 607 775-1100
  Conklin (G-3727)
Evans & Paul LLC ....E 516 576-0800
  Plainview (G-13056)
▲ Fifty Door Partners LLC ....E 845 562-3332
  New Windsor (G-8644)
◆ Fixtures 2000 Inc ....B 631 236-4100
  Hauppauge (G-5825)
Four S Showcase Manufacturing ......G 718 649-4900
  Brooklyn (G-1902)
Frazier Industrial Company ....D 315 539-9256
  Waterloo (G-15993)
◆ Gaylord Bros Inc ....G 315 457-5070
  North Syracuse (G-12402)
▲ GF Packaging LLC ....G 716 692-2705
  Cheektowaga (G-3447)
▲ Glaro Inc ....E 631 234-1717
  Hauppauge (G-5835)
▲ Glasbau Hahn America LLC ....G 845 566-3331
  Newburgh (G-12224)
◆ Global Steel Products Corp ....C 631 586-3455
  Deer Park (G-3981)
▲ Hamlet Products Inc ....E 914 665-0307
  Mount Vernon (G-8405)
Hawver Display Inc ....E 585 544-2290
  Rochester (G-13862)

◆ Hergo Ergonomic Support ....E 718 894-0639
  Maspeth (G-7851)
Hunter Metal Industries Inc ....D 631 475-5900
  East Patchogue (G-4275)
◆ Inscape (new York) Inc ....D 716 665-6210
  Falconer (G-4681)
Inscape Inc ....E 716 665-6210
  Falconer (G-4682)
Jack Luckner Steel Shelving Co ....D 718 363-0500
  Maspeth (G-7854)
Joldeson One Aerospace Inds ....D 718 848-7396
  Ozone Park (G-12827)
▲ Knickerbocker Partition Corp ......C 516 546-0550
  Melville (G-8042)
Ledan Inc ....E 631 239-1226
  Northport (G-12470)
▲ Lifestyle-Trimco ....E 718 257-9101
  Brooklyn (G-2118)
Locker Masters Inc ....E 518 288-3203
  Granville (G-5519)
▲ Lucia Group Inc ....E 631 392-4900
  Deer Park (G-4004)
Manhattan Display Inc ....G 718 392-1365
  Long Island City (G-7514)
▲ Mass Mdsg Self Selection Eqp ...E 631 234-3300
  Bohemia (G-1056)
▲ Maximum Security Products Corp ...E 518 233-1800
  Waterford (G-15977)
▲ Millennium Stl Rack Rntals Inc ....G 718 965-4736
  Brooklyn (G-2208)
▲ Milton Merl & Associates Inc ......G 212 634-9292
  New York (G-10812)
▲ Mobile Media Inc ....E 845 744-8080
  Pine Bush (G-12997)
Modern Craft Bar Rest Equip ....G 631 226-5647
  Lindenhurst (G-7181)
Modu-Craft Inc ....E 716 694-0709
  Tonawanda (G-15559)
Nationwide Exhibitor Svcs Inc ....F 631 467-2034
  Central Islip (G-3379)
▲ New Business Solutions Inc ....E 631 789-1500
  Amityville (G-306)
▲ Parabit Systems Inc ....E 516 378-4800
  Bellmore (G-791)
R H Guest Incorporated ....G 718 675-7600
  Brooklyn (G-2376)
S & K Counter Tops Inc ....G 716 662-7986
  Orchard Park (G-12743)
Sterling Shelf Liners Inc ....G 631 676-5175
  Holbrook (G-6211)
Steven Kraus Associates Inc ....E 631 923-2033
  Huntington (G-6417)
▲ Stone Expo & Cabinetry LLC ....F 516 292-2988
  West Hempstead (G-16225)
Storflex Holdings Inc ....C 607 962-2137
  Corning (G-3826)
▲ Sturdy Store Displays Inc ....E 718 389-9919
  Brooklyn (G-2528)
Traco Manufacturing Inc ....G 585 343-2434
  Batavia (G-638)
Tri-Boro Shelving Inc ....F 718 782-8527
  Ridgewood (G-13557)
Trylon Wire & Metal Works Inc ....E 718 542-4472
  Bronx (G-1409)
Visual Millwork & Fix Mfg Inc ....E 718 267-7800
  Deer Park (G-4061)
Yaloz Mould & Die Co Inc ....E 718 389-1131
  Brooklyn (G-2662)
Your Furniture Designers Inc ....E 845 947-3046
  West Haverstraw (G-16211)

2591 Drapery Hardware, Window Blinds & Shades

Abalene Decorating Services ....E 718 782-2000
  New York (G-8705)
Blinds To Go (us) Inc ....E 718 477-9523
  Staten Island (G-15051)
▲ Blindtek Designer Systems Inc ...F 914 347-7100
  Elmsford (G-4533)
◆ Comfortex Corporation ....C 518 273-3333
  Watervliet (G-16044)
D & D Window Tech Inc ....G 212 308-2822
  New York (G-9446)
Drapery Industries Inc ....F 585 232-2992
  Rochester (G-13750)
Fabric Quilters Unlimited Inc ....E 516 333-2866
  Westbury (G-16330)
▲ Hunter Douglas Inc ....D 845 664-7000
  Pearl River (G-12901)

Hunter Douglas Inc ....C 212 588-0564
New York (G-10152)
Instant Verticals Inc ....F 631 501-0001
Farmingdale (G-4786)
J Gimbel Inc ....E 718 296-5200
West Hempstead (G-16218)
KPP Ltd ....G 516 338-5201
Jericho (G-6793)
▲ Levolor Inc ....B 845 664-7000
Pearl River (G-12905)
▼ Manhattan Shade & Glass Co Inc ....E 212 288-5616
Great Neck (G-5570)
Manhattan Shade & Glass Co Inc ....E 212 288-5616
Hauppauge (G-5880)
◆ Mechoshade Systems Inc ....C 718 729-2020
Long Island City (G-7520)
Nu Ways Inc ....G 585 254-7510
Rochester (G-13983)
◆ P E Guerin ....D 212 243-5270
New York (G-11084)
Pj Decorators Inc ....E 516 735-9693
East Meadow (G-4255)
Solar Screen Co Inc ....G 718 592-8222
Corona (G-3855)
Tentina Window Fashions Inc ....C 631 957-9585
Lindenhurst (G-7201)
TLC Vision (usa) Corporation ....G 914 395-3949
Hartsdale (G-5746)
Vertical Research Partners LLC ....F 212 257-6499
New York (G-12018)
Wcd Window Coverings Inc ....E 845 336-4511
Lake Katrine (G-6973)
▲ Windowcraft Inc ....F 516 294-3580
Garden City Park (G-5289)
Windowtex Inc ....F 877 294-3580
New Hyde Park (G-8573)

2599 Furniture & Fixtures, NEC

▼ A-Plus Restaurant Equipment ....G 718 522-2656
Brooklyn (G-1466)
▲ Adirondack Scenic Inc ....D 518 638-8000
Argyle (G-398)
▲ AFC Industries Inc ....D 718 747-0237
College Point (G-3638)
All Star Carts & Vehicles Inc ....D 631 666-5581
Bay Shore (G-654)
▲ Arper USA Inc ....G 212 647-8900
New York (G-8910)
Artistry In Wood of Syracuse ....F 315 431-4022
East Syracuse (G-4322)
Brandt Equipment LLC ....G 718 994-0800
Bronx (G-1232)
Bullock Boys LLC ....F 518 783-6161
Latham (G-7066)
Carts Mobile Food Eqp Corp ....E 718 788-5540
Brooklyn (G-1680)
Dellet Industries Inc ....F 718 965-0101
Brooklyn (G-1764)
Dine Rite Seating Products Inc ....E 631 226-8899
Lindenhurst (G-7170)
Durall Dolly LLC ....F 802 728-7122
Brooklyn (G-1796)
Evans & Paul LLC ....E 516 576-0800
Plainview (G-13056)
Futon City Discounters Inc ....F 315 437-1328
Syracuse (G-15326)
G Z G Rest & Kit Met Works ....F 718 788-8621
Brooklyn (G-1914)
Halfway House LLC ....G 518 873-2198
Elizabethtown (G-4432)
◆ Hard Manufacturing Co Inc ....E 716 893-1800
Buffalo (G-2865)
▲ Hunt Country Furniture Inc ....D 845 832-6601
Wingdale (G-16606)
Ideoli Group Inc ....F 212 705-8769
Port Washington (G-13268)
Inova LLC ....F 518 861-3400
Altamont (G-198)
▲ Inova LLC ....E 866 528-2804
Guilderland Center (G-5656)
Interiors-Pft Inc ....E 212 244-9600
Long Island City (G-7476)
J P Installations Warehouse ....F 914 576-3188
New Rochelle (G-8617)
Kedco Inc ....F 516 454-7800
Farmingdale (G-4800)
Kinfolk Studios Inc ....F 770 617-5592
Brooklyn (G-2070)
Kinfolk Studios Inc ....F 347 799-2946
Brooklyn (G-2071)
Kinplex Corp ....E 631 242-4800
Edgewood (G-4408)
L & D Manufacturing Corp ....G 718 665-5226
Bronx (G-1311)
Lafayette Pub Inc ....E 212 925-4242
New York (G-10507)
▲ Lb Furniture Industries LLC ....C 518 828-1501
Hudson (G-6362)
▲ Maxsun Corporation ....F 718 418-6800
Maspeth (G-7859)
Modern Craft Bar Rest Equip ....G 631 226-5647
Lindenhurst (G-7181)
Modu-Craft Inc ....G 716 694-0709
North Tonawanda (G-12438)
Modu-Craft Inc ....G 716 694-0709
Tonawanda (G-15559)
Monroe Table Company Inc ....F 716 945-7700
Salamanca (G-14528)
▲ N3a Corporation ....D 516 284-6799
Inwood (G-6496)
▲ NK Medical Products Inc ....G 716 759-7200
Amherst (G-241)
▲ Novum Medical Products Inc ....F 716 759-7200
Amherst (G-242)
R V H Estates Inc ....G 914 664-9888
Mount Vernon (G-8438)
▲ Ramler International Ltd ....E 516 353-3106
Syosset (G-15229)
Restaurant 570 8th Avenue LLC ....F 646 722-8191
New York (G-11371)
Rollhaus Seating Products Inc ....F 718 729-9111
Long Island City (G-7577)
Sandys Deli Inc ....G 518 297-6951
Rouses Point (G-14470)
Smart Space Products LLC ....G 877 777-2441
New York (G-11622)
▼ Starliner Shipping & Travel ....G 718 385-1515
Brooklyn (G-2513)
T O Gronlund Company Inc ....F 212 679-3535
New York (G-11771)
T-Company LLC ....G 646 290-6365
Smithtown (G-14910)
Tao Group LLC ....G 646 625-4818
New York (G-11781)
Thornwood Products Ltd ....E 914 769-9161
Thornwood (G-15508)
Timeless Decor LLC ....C 315 782-5759
Watertown (G-16035)
◆ VSM Investors LLC ....G 212 351-1600
New York (G-12057)
Wood Etc Inc ....F 315 484-9663
Syracuse (G-15461)

26 PAPER AND ALLIED PRODUCTS

2611 Pulp Mills

Advanced Recovery & Recycl LLC ....F 315 450-3301
Baldwinsville (G-548)
Andritz Inc ....E 518 745-2988
Glens Falls (G-5415)
APC Paper Company Inc ....D 315 384-4225
Norfolk (G-12356)
▲ Cenibra Inc ....G 212 818-8242
New York (G-9239)
Central Nat Pulp & Ppr Sls Inc ....A 914 696-9000
Purchase (G-13387)
Fcr LLC ....G 845 926-1071
Beacon (G-758)
Georgia-Pacific Corrugated LLC ....D 585 343-3800
Batavia (G-625)
Georgia-Pacific LLC ....E 631 924-7401
Yaphank (G-16712)
Hamlin Bottle & Can Return Inc ....G 585 259-1301
Brockport (G-1192)
Harvest Technologies Inc ....G 518 899-7124
Ballston Spa (G-585)
International Paper Company ....C 607 775-1550
Conklin (G-3728)
ITT Industries Holdings Inc ....G 914 641-2000
White Plains (G-16465)
Norton Pulpstones Incorporated ....G 716 433-9400
Lockport (G-7324)
Parsons & Whittemore Inc ....B 914 937-9009
Port Chester (G-13207)
Parsons Whittemore Entps Corp ....E 914 937-9009
Port Chester (G-13208)
R D S Mountain View Trucking ....G 315 823-4265
Little Falls (G-7213)
◆ Repapers Corporation ....F 305 691-1635
Hicksville (G-6128)
Sierra Processing LLC ....F 518 433-0020
Schenectady (G-14714)
Suffolk Indus Recovery Corp ....D 631 732-6403
Coram (G-3805)

2621 Paper Mills

▲ A-One Laminating Corp ....G 718 266-6002
Brooklyn (G-1464)
Albany International Corp ....C 518 445-2230
Menands (G-8079)
▲ Ampac Paper LLC ....G 845 713-6600
Walden (G-15890)
Andex Corp ....E 585 328-3790
Rochester (G-13632)
APC Paper Company Inc ....D 315 384-4225
Norfolk (G-12356)
Atlas Recycling LLC ....G 212 925-3280
New York (G-8956)
▼ Automation Papers Inc ....G 315 432-0565
Syracuse (G-15250)
Bestwall LLC ....A 518 561-3500
Plattsburgh (G-13109)
▲ Bigrow Paper Mfg Corp ....F 718 624-4439
Brooklyn (G-1611)
Bristol Core Inc ....F 585 919-0302
Canandaigua (G-3212)
Bristol/White Plains ....G 914 681-1800
White Plains (G-16431)
BSD Aluminum Foil LLC ....E 347 689-3875
Brooklyn (G-1653)
Burrows Paper Corporation ....D 315 823-2300
Little Falls (G-7208)
Burrows Paper Corporation ....D 315 823-2300
Little Falls (G-7209)
▲ Carta Usa LLC ....E 585 436-3012
Rochester (G-13693)
▲ Cascades Tssue Group-Sales Inc ....E 819 363-5100
Waterford (G-15974)
Citigroup Inc ....D 212 816-6000
New York (G-9306)
Clearwater Paper Corporation ....D 315 287-1200
Gouverneur (G-5489)
▲ Cottrell Paper Company Inc ....E 518 885-1702
Rock City Falls (G-14222)
◆ Crosstex International Inc ....D 631 582-6777
Hauppauge (G-5805)
▲ Daniel O Reich Incorporated ....F 718 748-6000
Brooklyn (G-1756)
Datagraphic Business Systems ....G 516 485-9069
Brentwood (G-1130)
Donne Dieu Paper Mill Inc ....G 212 226-0573
Brooklyn (G-1788)
Dunmore Corporation ....D 845 279-5061
Brewster (G-1163)
Dunn Paper - Natural Dam Inc ....D 315 287-1200
Gouverneur (G-5490)
Essity Prof Hygiene N Amer LLC ....E 518 692-8434
Greenwich (G-5638)
Essity Prof Hygiene N Amer LLC ....C 518 583-2785
Saratoga Springs (G-14579)
Euro Fine Paper Inc ....G 516 238-5253
Garden City (G-5258)
▲ Flower Cy Tissue Mills Co Inc ....E 585 458-9200
Rochester (G-13810)
◆ Freeport Paper Industries Inc ....D 631 851-1555
Central Islip (G-3370)
◆ Global Tissue Group Inc ....E 631 924-3019
Medford (G-7948)
▼ Gooding Co Inc ....E 716 266-6252
Lockport (G-7308)
Gratitude & Company Inc ....G 607 277-3188
Ithaca (G-6579)
Hollingsworth & Vose Company ....C 518 695-8000
Greenwich (G-5641)
Huhtamaki Inc ....A 315 593-5311
Fulton (G-5220)
International Paper Company ....A 518 585-6761
Ticonderoga (G-15511)
International Paper Company ....C 845 986-6409
Tuxedo Park (G-15657)
International Paper Company ....C 315 797-5120
Utica (G-15716)
International Paper Company ....C 607 775-1550
Conklin (G-3728)
▲ Irving Consumer Products Inc ....B 518 747-4151
Fort Edward (G-5096)
Kapstone Container Corporation ....D 518 842-2450
Amsterdam (G-342)
Kimberly-Clark Corporation ....D 212 554-4252
New York (G-10447)

SIC

Employee Codes: A=Over 500 employees, B=251-500
C=101-250, D=51-100, E=20-50, F=10-19, G=5-9
2019 Harris
New York Manufacturers Directory
685

▲ **Knowlton Technologies LLC** ... C ... 315 782-0600
Watertown *(G-16024)*
◆ **Lenaro Paper Co Inc** ... F ... 631 439-8800
Central Islip *(G-3376)*
▲ **Linden Meyr Munroe Inc** ... F ... 518 471-5111
Latham *(G-7086)*
Lion Die-Cutting Co Inc ... E ... 718 383-8841
Brooklyn *(G-2127)*
Minimill Technologies Inc ... F ... 315 692-4557
Syracuse *(G-15374)*
Mohawk Fine Papers Inc ... E ... 518 237-1741
Cohoes *(G-3615)*
▲ **Mohawk Fine Papers Inc** ... B ... 518 237-1740
Cohoes *(G-3614)*
Morcon Inc ... D ... 518 677-8511
Cambridge *(G-3182)*
National Paper Converting Inc ... G ... 607 687-6049
Owego *(G-12800)*
◆ **Nice-Pak Products Inc** ... B ... 845 365-2772
Orangeburg *(G-12684)*
Nice-Pak Products Inc ... E ... 845 353-6090
West Nyack *(G-16276)*
North End Paper Co Inc ... G ... 315 593-8100
Fulton *(G-5229)*
▲ **NY Cutting Inc** ... G ... 646 434-1355
Suffern *(G-15194)*
◆ **Omniafiltra LLC** ... E ... 315 346-7300
Beaver Falls *(G-767)*
Palisades Paper Inc ... G ... 845 354-0333
Spring Valley *(G-15004)*
◆ **Plastirun Corporation** ... E ... 631 273-2626
Brentwood *(G-1143)*
◆ **Potsdam Specialty Paper Inc** ... D ... 315 265-4000
Potsdam *(G-13321)*
▲ **Precare Corp** ... G ... 631 667-1055
Hauppauge *(G-5920)*
◆ **Precision Charts Inc** ... E ... 631 244-8295
Bohemia *(G-1077)*
◆ **Professional Disposables Inc** ... A ... 845 365-1700
Orangeburg *(G-12689)*
Refill Services LLC ... G ... 607 369-5864
Sidney *(G-14854)*
Sabin Robbins Paper Company ... E ... 513 874-5270
New York *(G-11462)*
▲ **Scalamandre Wallpaper Inc** ... B ... 631 467-8800
Hauppauge *(G-5934)*
Schweitzer-Mauduit Intl Inc ... C ... 518 329-4222
Ancram *(G-365)*
Stephen Singer Pattern Co Inc ... F ... 212 947-2902
New York *(G-11706)*
Summit Fincl Disclosure LLC ... E ... 212 913-0510
New York *(G-11739)*
▲ **T & L Trading Co** ... G ... 718 782-5550
Brooklyn *(G-2547)*
Tag Envelope Co Inc ... E ... 718 389-6844
College Point *(G-3669)*
Twin Rivers Paper Company LLC ... E ... 315 348-8491
Lyons Falls *(G-7690)*
Twin Rivers Paper Company LLC ... B ... 315 823-2300
Little Falls *(G-7215)*
▲ **US Alliance Paper Inc** ... C ... 631 254-3030
Edgewood *(G-4422)*
Verso Corporation ... B ... 212 599-2700
New York *(G-12014)*
Verso Paper Management LP ... A ... 781 320-8660
New York *(G-12015)*
Verso Paper Management LP ... G ... 212 599-2700
New York *(G-12016)*

2631 Paperboard Mills

Alpine Paper Box Co Inc ... E ... 718 345-4040
Brooklyn *(G-1514)*
▲ **American Wire Tie Inc** ... E ... 716 337-2412
North Collins *(G-12383)*
▲ **Burt Rigid Box Inc** ... F ... 607 433-2510
Oneonta *(G-12629)*
Carthage Specialty Pprbd Inc ... G ... 315 493-2120
Carthage *(G-3287)*
Cascades New York Inc ... C ... 716 285-3681
Niagara Falls *(G-12268)*
▼ **Continental Kraft Corp** ... G ... 516 681-9090
Jericho *(G-6783)*
Di Domenico Packaging Co Inc ... G ... 718 727-5454
Staten Island *(G-15068)*
Enterprise Folding Box Co Inc ... E ... 716 876-6421
Buffalo *(G-2821)*
Farrington Packaging Corp ... E ... 315 733-4600
Utica *(G-15701)*
▲ **Greenpac Mill LLC** ... C ... 716 299-0560
Niagara Falls *(G-12291)*
Interface Performance Mtls Inc ... D ... 518 686-3400
Hoosick Falls *(G-6276)*
International Paper Company ... C ... 607 775-1550
Conklin *(G-3728)*
Kapstone Container Corporation ... D ... 518 842-2450
Amsterdam *(G-342)*
M&F Stringing LLC ... E ... 914 664-1600
Mount Vernon *(G-8420)*
Ms Paper Products Co Inc ... G ... 718 624-0248
Brooklyn *(G-2236)*
Niagara Fiberboard Inc ... E ... 716 434-8881
Lockport *(G-7322)*
Pactiv LLC ... E ... 585 248-1213
Pittsford *(G-13025)*
Paper Box Corp ... D ... 212 226-7490
New York *(G-11101)*
Pdf Seal Incorporated ... E ... 631 595-7035
Deer Park *(G-4024)*
Pkg Group ... G ... 212 965-0112
New York *(G-11204)*
Prestige Box Corporation ... E ... 516 773-3115
Great Neck *(G-5583)*
Professional Packg Svcs Inc ... E ... 518 677-5100
Eagle Bridge *(G-4185)*
Sonoco Products Company ... D ... 518 392-2000
Chatham *(G-3430)*
▲ **Tin Box Company of America Inc** ... E ... 631 845-1600
Farmingdale *(G-4897)*
▲ **Westrock - Solvay Llc** ... C ... 315 484-9050
Syracuse *(G-15456)*
Westrock CP LLC ... D ... 315 484-9050
Syracuse *(G-15457)*
Westrock Mwv LLC ... C ... 212 688-5000
New York *(G-12097)*
Westrock Rkt Company ... C ... 770 448-2193
Syracuse *(G-15458)*

2652 Set-Up Paperboard Boxes

A Fleisig Paper Box Corp ... F ... 212 226-7490
New York *(G-8693)*
American Package Company Inc ... E ... 718 389-4444
Brooklyn *(G-1525)*
▲ **Brick & Ballerstein Inc** ... D ... 718 497-1400
Ridgewood *(G-13532)*
Burt Rigid Box Inc ... D ... 607 433-2510
Oneonta *(G-12628)*
Cascades New York Inc ... D ... 718 340-2100
Maspeth *(G-7829)*
Drescher Paper Box Inc ... F ... 716 854-0288
Clarence *(G-3528)*
Earlville Paper Box Co Inc ... E ... 315 691-2131
Earlville *(G-4188)*
▲ **F M Howell & Company** ... D ... 607 734-6291
Elmira *(G-4486)*
Fairview Paper Box Corp ... E ... 585 786-5230
Warsaw *(G-15944)*
Jordon Box Company Inc ... E ... 315 422-3419
Syracuse *(G-15350)*
Lionel Habas Associates Inc ... F ... 212 860-8454
New York *(G-10575)*
Parlor City Paper Box Co Inc ... D ... 607 772-0600
Binghamton *(G-909)*
▲ **Paul T Freund Corporation** ... D ... 315 597-4873
Palmyra *(G-12859)*
Prestige Box Corporation ... E ... 516 773-3115
Great Neck *(G-5583)*
Propak Inc ... G ... 518 677-5100
Eagle Bridge *(G-4186)*
▲ **Pure Trade Us Inc** ... E ... 212 256-1600
New York *(G-11276)*
▲ **Seneca FLS Spc & Logistics Co** ... D ... 315 568-4139
Seneca Falls *(G-14786)*

2653 Corrugated & Solid Fiber Boxes

Action Paper Co Inc ... G ... 718 665-1652
Bronx *(G-1211)*
Ares Printing and Packg Corp ... C ... 718 858-8760
Brooklyn *(G-1550)*
▼ **Arma Container Corp** ... E ... 631 254-1200
Deer Park *(G-3945)*
Bellotti Packaging Inc ... F ... 315 433-0131
Liverpool *(G-7223)*
Bestwall LLC ... C ... 518 346-6151
Schenectady *(G-14655)*
Brand Box USA LLC ... G ... 607 584-7682
Binghamton *(G-871)*
Buckeye Corrugated Inc ... D ... 585 924-1600
Victor *(G-15834)*
Burt Rigid Box Inc ... D ... 607 433-2510
Oneonta *(G-12628)*
Calpac Incorporated ... F ... 631 789-0502
Amityville *(G-267)*
Cascades New York Inc ... C ... 518 346-6151
Schenectady *(G-14660)*
Cattaraugus Containers Inc ... E ... 716 676-2000
Franklinville *(G-5123)*
▲ **Color Carton Corp** ... D ... 718 665-0840
Bronx *(G-1243)*
Displays & Beyond Inc ... F ... 718 805-7786
Glendale *(G-5398)*
Dory Enterprises Inc ... F ... 607 565-7079
Waverly *(G-16064)*
Fennell Industries LLC ... E ... 607 733-6693
Elmira *(G-4487)*
Fiber USA Corp ... G ... 718 888-1512
Flushing *(G-5000)*
Gavin Mfg Corp ... E ... 631 467-0040
Farmingdale *(G-4770)*
▲ **General Die and Die Cutng Inc** ... D ... 516 665-3584
Massapequa Park *(G-7890)*
◆ **General Fibre Products Corp** ... D ... 516 358-7500
New Hyde Park *(G-8536)*
International Paper Company ... C ... 585 663-1000
Rochester *(G-13884)*
International Paper Company ... C ... 607 775-1550
Conklin *(G-3728)*
International Paper Company ... F ... 716 852-2144
Buffalo *(G-2888)*
International Paper Company ... D ... 518 372-6461
Glenville *(G-5446)*
J & M Packaging Inc ... F ... 631 608-3069
Hauppauge *(G-5852)*
Jamestown Cont of Rochester ... D ... 585 254-9190
Rochester *(G-13892)*
▼ **Jamestown Container Corp** ... C ... 716 665-4623
Falconer *(G-4684)*
Kapstone Container Corporation ... D ... 518 842-2450
Amsterdam *(G-342)*
Key Container Corp ... G ... 631 582-3847
East Islip *(G-4244)*
Lakeside Container Corp ... F ... 518 561-6150
Plattsburgh *(G-13130)*
Land Packaging Corp ... F ... 914 472-5976
Scarsdale *(G-14640)*
M C Packaging Corporation ... E ... 631 643-3763
Babylon *(G-529)*
▲ **Mkt329 Inc** ... E ... 631 249-5500
Farmingdale *(G-4829)*
▲ **Mp Displays LLC** ... G ... 845 268-4113
Valley Cottage *(G-15760)*
▲ **Niagara Sheets LLC** ... D ... 716 692-1129
North Tonawanda *(G-12439)*
Norampac New York City Inc ... C ... 718 340-2100
Maspeth *(G-7863)*
▲ **Orange Die Cutting Corp** ... C ... 845 562-0900
Newburgh *(G-12238)*
Packaging Corporation America ... C ... 315 457-6780
Liverpool *(G-7251)*
Pactiv LLC ... C ... 315 457-6780
Liverpool *(G-7252)*
Pactiv LLC ... E ... 585 248-1213
Pittsford *(G-13025)*
Parlor City Paper Box Co Inc ... D ... 607 772-0600
Binghamton *(G-909)*
Philpac Corporation ... E ... 716 875-8005
Buffalo *(G-3002)*
President Cont Group II LLC ... E ... 845 516-1600
Middletown *(G-8171)*
Prestige Box Corporation ... E ... 516 773-3115
Great Neck *(G-5583)*
Professional Packg Svcs Inc ... E ... 518 677-5100
Eagle Bridge *(G-4185)*
R D A Container Corporation ... E ... 585 247-2323
Gates *(G-5312)*
▲ **Seneca FLS Spc & Logistics Co** ... D ... 315 568-4139
Seneca Falls *(G-14786)*
▲ **Spaeth Design Inc** ... E ... 718 606-9685
Woodside *(G-16677)*
▲ **Specialized Packg Group Inc** ... G ... 315 638-4355
Baldwinsville *(G-561)*
Specialized Packg Radisson LLC ... C ... 315 638-4355
Baldwinsville *(G-562)*
Syracuse Corrugated Box Corp ... F ... 315 437-9901
East Syracuse *(G-4372)*
Technical Library Service Inc ... F ... 212 219-0770
Brooklyn *(G-2558)*
Technical Packaging Inc ... F ... 516 223-2300
Baldwin *(G-545)*
Tin Inc ... D ... 607 775-1550
Conklin *(G-3734)*

SIC SECTION
26 PAPER AND ALLIED PRODUCTS

Track 7 Inc .... G 845 544-1810
Warwick *(G-15960)*
Valentine Packaging Corp .... F 718 418-6000
Maspeth *(G-7875)*
Westrock - Southern Cont LLC .... C 315 487-6111
Camillus *(G-3200)*
Westrock Cp LLC .... C 770 448-2193
New Hartford *(G-8513)*
Westrock Cp LLC .... C 716 692-6510
North Tonawanda *(G-12462)*
Westrock CP LLC .... C 716 694-1000
North Tonawanda *(G-12463)*
Westrock Rkt LLC .... C 631 586-6000
Deer Park *(G-4062)*
Westrock Rkt LLC .... F 315 487-6111
Camillus *(G-3201)*
Westrock Rkt Company .... C 770 448-2193
Camillus *(G-3202)*

2655 Fiber Cans, Tubes & Drums

Acran Spill Containment Inc .... F 631 841-2300
Massapequa *(G-7877)*
American Intrmdal Cont Mfg LLC .... G 631 774-6790
Hauppauge *(G-5767)*
Caraustar Industries Inc .... G 716 874-0393
Buffalo *(G-2761)*
Carthage Fibre Drum Inc .... E 315 493-2730
Carthage *(G-3286)*
Consolidated Container Co LLC .... C 585 262-6470
Rochester *(G-13721)*
▲ Custom Manufacturing Inc .... G 607 569-2738
Hammondsport *(G-5703)*
▲ Diemolding Corporation .... G 315 363-4710
Wampsville *(G-15917)*
Greif Inc .... D 716 836-4200
Tonawanda *(G-15545)*
Industrial Paper Tube Inc .... F 718 893-5000
Bronx *(G-1296)*
Philpac Corporation .... E 716 875-8005
Buffalo *(G-3002)*
▲ Skydyne Company .... D 845 858-6400
Port Jervis *(G-13237)*
Syraco Products Inc .... F 315 476-5306
Syracuse *(G-15433)*

2656 Sanitary Food Containers

Amscan Inc .... F 845 469-9116
Chester *(G-3468)*
Amscan Inc .... E 845 782-0490
Newburgh *(G-12214)*
Apexx Omni-Graphics Inc .... D 718 326-3330
Maspeth *(G-7822)*
Consolidated Container Co LLC .... C 585 262-6470
Rochester *(G-13721)*
Hadp LLC .... F 518 831-6824
Scotia *(G-14741)*
International Paper Company .... C 607 775-1550
Conklin *(G-3728)*
▲ Last Straw Inc .... E 516 371-2727
Lawrence *(G-7104)*
Pactiv LLC .... C 518 562-6101
Plattsburgh *(G-13142)*
◆ Plastirun Corporation .... E 631 273-2626
Brentwood *(G-1143)*
▲ Sqp Inc .... C 518 831-6800
Schenectady *(G-14716)*

2657 Folding Paperboard Boxes

Abbot & Abbot Box Corp .... F 888 930-5972
Long Island City *(G-7365)*
Alpha Packaging Industries Inc .... E 718 267-4115
Long Island City *(G-7374)*
▲ Arkay Packaging Corporation .... E 631 273-2000
Hauppauge *(G-5769)*
Burt Rigid Box Inc .... D 607 433-2510
Oneonta *(G-12628)*
Cattaraugus Containers Inc .... E 716 676-2000
Franklinville *(G-5123)*
Climax Packaging Inc .... C 315 376-8000
Lowville *(G-7649)*
▲ Color Carton Corp .... D 718 665-0840
Bronx *(G-1243)*
Designers Folding Box Corp .... E 716 853-5141
Buffalo *(G-2800)*
Diamond Packaging Holdings LLC .... G 585 334-8030
Rochester *(G-13739)*
Disc Graphics Inc .... C 631 300-1129
Hauppauge *(G-5811)*
▲ Disc Graphics Inc .... C 631 234-1400
Hauppauge *(G-5812)*

▲ F M Howell & Company .... D 607 734-6291
Elmira *(G-4486)*
Flower City Printing Inc .... C 585 663-9000
Rochester *(G-13808)*
Gavin Mfg Corp .... E 631 467-0040
Farmingdale *(G-4770)*
◆ Gaylord Bros Inc .... D 315 457-5070
North Syracuse *(G-12402)*
Genpak Industries Inc .... E 518 798-9511
Middletown *(G-8154)*
▲ HSM Packaging Corporation .... D 315 476-7996
Liverpool *(G-7235)*
▲ Knoll Printing & Packaging Inc .... E 516 621-0100
Syosset *(G-15220)*
M C Packaging Corporation .... E 631 643-3763
Babylon *(G-529)*
◆ Mod-Pac Corp .... C 716 898-8480
Buffalo *(G-2951)*
Multi Packg Solutions Intl Ltd .... F 646 885-0005
New York *(G-10859)*
▲ Novel Box Company Ltd .... E 718 965-2222
Brooklyn *(G-2275)*
Pactiv LLC .... C 518 562-6101
Plattsburgh *(G-13142)*
Paper Box Corp .... D 212 226-7490
New York *(G-11101)*
Premier Packaging Corporation .... E 585 924-8460
Victor *(G-15861)*
Prestige Box Corporation .... E 516 773-3115
Great Neck *(G-5583)*
▲ Specialized Packg Group Inc .... G 315 638-4355
Baldwinsville *(G-561)*
Specialized Packg Radisson LLC .... C 315 638-4355
Baldwinsville *(G-562)*
▲ Standard Group .... E 718 335-5500
Great Neck *(G-5591)*
▲ Standard Group LLC .... C 718 507-6430
Great Neck *(G-5592)*
Viking Industries Inc .... D 845 883-6325
New Paltz *(G-8584)*
Visitainer Corp .... E 718 636-0300
Brooklyn *(G-2629)*

2671 Paper Coating & Laminating for Packaging

▲ Allied Converters Inc .... E 914 235-1585
New Rochelle *(G-8589)*
American Packaging Corporation .... C 585 537-4650
Churchville *(G-3506)*
American Packaging Corporation .... G 585 254-2002
Rochester *(G-13625)*
American Packaging Corporation .... C 585 254-9500
Rochester *(G-13626)*
Anasia Inc .... G 718 588-1407
Bronx *(G-1220)*
Apexx Omni-Graphics Inc .... D 718 326-3330
Maspeth *(G-7822)*
Ares Box LLC .... D 718 858-8760
Brooklyn *(G-1549)*
Berry Plastics Corporation .... B 315 986-6270
Macedon *(G-7697)*
Brook & Whittle Limited .... E 716 691-4348
Amherst *(G-219)*
Brook & Whittle Limited .... C 716 853-1688
Buffalo *(G-2736)*
Cameo Process Corp .... G 914 948-0082
White Plains *(G-16435)*
CCL Label Inc .... C 716 852-2155
Buffalo *(G-2762)*
Classic Labels Inc .... E 631 467-2300
Patchogue *(G-12863)*
Colad Group LLC .... D 716 961-1776
Buffalo *(G-2772)*
Cove Point Holdings LLC .... E 212 599-3388
New York *(G-9413)*
Craft Packaging Inc .... G 718 633-4045
Brooklyn *(G-1725)*
De Luxe Packaging Corp .... E 416 754-4633
Saugerties *(G-14606)*
Depot Label Company Inc .... G 631 467-2952
Patchogue *(G-12864)*
▲ Dolco LLC .... E 585 657-7777
Bloomfield *(G-952)*
Ecoplast & Packaging LLC .... G 718 996-0800
Brooklyn *(G-1811)*
▲ F M Howell & Company .... D 607 734-6291
Elmira *(G-4486)*
▲ Folene Packaging LLC .... G 917 626-6740
Brooklyn *(G-1895)*

◆ General Fibre Products Corp .... D 516 358-7500
New Hyde Park *(G-8536)*
General Trade Mark La .... E 718 979-7261
Staten Island *(G-15078)*
Idesco Corp .... F 212 889-2530
New York *(G-10174)*
International Paper Company .... C 585 663-1000
Rochester *(G-13884)*
▲ K Sidrane Inc .... E 631 393-6974
Farmingdale *(G-4796)*
Mason Transparent Package Inc .... E 718 792-6000
Bronx *(G-1324)*
Multi Packaging Solutions Inc .... C 516 488-2000
Hicksville *(G-6112)*
◆ Multi Packaging Solutions Inc .... E 646 885-0005
New York *(G-10858)*
Nameplate Mfrs of Amer .... E 631 752-0055
Farmingdale *(G-4831)*
Nova Packaging Ltd Inc .... E 914 232-8406
Katonah *(G-6845)*
Pactiv LLC .... C 518 562-6101
Plattsburgh *(G-13142)*
Paperworks Industries Inc .... F 913 621-0922
Baldwinsville *(G-559)*
Patco Tapes Inc .... G 718 497-1527
Maspeth *(G-7867)*
Penta-Tech Coated Products LLC .... F 315 986-4098
Macedon *(G-7702)*
Pliant LLC .... B 315 986-6286
Macedon *(G-7703)*
▲ Printex Packaging Corporation .... D 631 234-4300
Islandia *(G-6537)*
▲ Quality Circle Products Inc .... D 914 736-6600
Montrose *(G-8329)*
▲ RMS Packaging Inc .... F 914 205-2070
Peekskill *(G-12924)*
Saint-Gobain Prfmce Plas Corp .... C 518 642-2200
Granville *(G-5524)*
▲ Shaant Industries Inc .... E 716 366-3654
Dunkirk *(G-4179)*
Smart USA Inc .... F 631 969-1111
Bay Shore *(G-724)*
▲ Time Release Sciences Inc .... E 716 823-4580
Buffalo *(G-3096)*
◆ Transcntinental Ultra Flex Inc .... B 718 272-9100
Brooklyn *(G-2579)*
▲ Tri-Plex Packaging Corporation .... E 212 481-6070
New York *(G-11894)*
▲ Universal Packg Systems Inc .... A 631 543-2277
Hauppauge *(G-5966)*
Valley Industrial Products Inc .... E 631 385-9300
Huntington *(G-6424)*
W E W Container Corporation .... E 718 827-8150
Brooklyn *(G-2637)*
Westrock Mwv LLC .... C 212 688-5000
New York *(G-12097)*

2672 Paper Coating & Laminating, Exc for Packaging

▲ A-One Laminating Corp .... G 718 266-6002
Brooklyn *(G-1464)*
Albany International Corp .... D 518 447-6400
Menands *(G-8080)*
Avery Dennison Corporation .... C 626 304-2000
New York *(G-8976)*
Berry Specialty Tapes LLC .... C 631 727-6000
Riverhead *(G-13565)*
C & R De Santis Inc .... E 718 447-5076
Staten Island *(G-15057)*
CCL Label Inc .... C 716 852-2155
Buffalo *(G-2762)*
Classic Labels Inc .... E 631 467-2300
Patchogue *(G-12863)*
Clp Holdings LLC .... G 917 846-5094
New York *(G-9334)*
Cove Point Holdings LLC .... E 212 599-3388
New York *(G-9413)*
Cytec Industries Inc .... D 716 372-9650
Olean *(G-12598)*
Dunmore Corporation .... D 845 279-5061
Brewster *(G-1163)*
Eis Inc .... E 585 426-5330
Rochester *(G-13774)*
Felix Schoeller North Amer Inc .... D 315 298-8425
Pulaski *(G-13379)*
Greenbush Tape & Label Inc .... E 518 465-2389
Albany *(G-79)*
Itac Label & Tag Corp .... G 718 625-2148
Brooklyn *(G-2018)*

Employee Codes: A=Over 500 employees, B=251-500
C=101-250, D=51-100, E=20-50, F=10-19, G=5-9
2019 Harris
New York Manufacturers Directory
687

26 PAPER AND ALLIED PRODUCTS

Janice Moses Represents .... G 212 898-4898
  New York *(G-10307)*
▲ K Sidrane Inc .... E 631 393-6974
  Farmingdale *(G-4796)*
▲ Kleen Stik Industries Inc .... F 718 984-5031
  Staten Island *(G-15098)*
Label Gallery Inc .... E 607 334-3244
  Norwich *(G-12489)*
Liberty Label Mfg Inc .... F 631 737-2365
  Holbrook *(G-6195)*
◆ Merco Hackensack Inc .... G 845 357-3699
  Hillburn *(G-6154)*
Micro Essential Laboratory .... E 718 338-3618
  Brooklyn *(G-2205)*
Miken Companies Inc .... D 716 668-6311
  Buffalo *(G-2946)*
▲ Mohawk Fine Papers Inc .... B 518 237-1740
  Cohoes *(G-3614)*
Neenah Northeast LLC .... C 315 376-3571
  Lowville *(G-7654)*
New York Cutting & Gumming Co ..... E 212 563-4146
  Middletown *(G-8168)*
Oaklee International Inc .... D 631 436-7900
  Ronkonkoma *(G-14389)*
▲ Overnight Labels Inc .... E 631 242-4240
  Deer Park *(G-4022)*
▲ P C I Paper Conversions Inc .... C 315 437-1641
  Syracuse *(G-15389)*
Patco Tapes Inc .... G 718 497-1527
  Maspeth *(G-7867)*
Princeton Label & Packaging .... E 609 490-0800
  Patchogue *(G-12875)*
▲ Rochester 100 Inc .... C 585 475-0200
  Rochester *(G-14078)*
▲ S & S Prtg Die-Cutting Co Inc .... F 718 388-8990
  Brooklyn *(G-2434)*
Stoney Croft Converters Inc .... F 718 608-9800
  Staten Island *(G-15140)*
Syracuse Label Co Inc .... D 315 422-1037
  Syracuse *(G-15439)*
T L F Graphics Inc .... D 585 272-5500
  Rochester *(G-14156)*
◆ Tape-It Inc .... E 631 243-4100
  Bay Shore *(G-730)*
▲ Tri-Flex Label Corp .... E 631 293-0411
  Farmingdale *(G-4898)*
Triangle Label Tag Inc .... G 718 875-3030
  Brooklyn *(G-2583)*
▲ Uniflex Holdings LLC .... F 516 932-2000
  Hauppauge *(G-5964)*
Valley Industrial Products Inc .... E 631 385-9300
  Huntington *(G-6424)*

2673 Bags: Plastics, Laminated & Coated

Adart Polyethylene Bag Mfg .... G 516 932-1001
  Plainview *(G-13030)*
▲ Aladdin Packaging LLC .... D 631 273-4747
  Hauppauge *(G-5759)*
Alco Plastics Inc .... B 716 683-3020
  Lancaster *(G-7005)*
▲ Allied Converters Inc .... E 914 235-1585
  New Rochelle *(G-8589)*
▲ Amby International Inc .... F 718 645-0964
  Brooklyn *(G-1517)*
American Packaging Corporation ..... G 585 254-2002
  Rochester *(G-13625)*
American Packaging Corporation ..... C 585 254-9500
  Rochester *(G-13626)*
▲ API Industries Inc .... B 845 365-2200
  Orangeburg *(G-12668)*
API Industries Inc .... C 845 365-2200
  Orangeburg *(G-12669)*
▲ Bag Arts The Art Packaging LLC ... G 212 684-7020
  New York *(G-9001)*
▲ Bags Unlimited Inc .... E 585 436-6282
  Rochester *(G-13651)*
Berry Global Inc .... C 315 986-2161
  Macedon *(G-7696)*
▲ Bison Bag Co Inc .... D 716 434-4380
  Lockport *(G-7287)*
Capitol Poly Corp .... E 718 855-6000
  Brooklyn *(G-1674)*
Centre De Conformite ICC Inc .... E 716 283-0002
  Niagara Falls *(G-12270)*
Clear View Bag Company Inc .... E 518 458-7153
  Albany *(G-59)*
Colden Closet LLC .... G 716 713-6125
  East Aurora *(G-4196)*
Connover Packaging Inc .... G 585 377-2510
  East Rochester *(G-4282)*

D Bag Lady Inc .... G 585 425-8095
  Fairport *(G-4630)*
Ecoplast & Packaging LLC .... G 718 996-0800
  Brooklyn *(G-1811)*
Edco Supply Corporation .... D 718 788-8108
  Brooklyn *(G-1813)*
Excellent Poly Inc .... F 718 768-6555
  Brooklyn *(G-1856)*
Filmpak Extrusion LLC .... D 631 293-6767
  Melville *(G-8024)*
▲ Fortune Poly Products Inc .... F 718 361-0767
  Jamaica *(G-6643)*
▼ Franklin Poly Film Inc .... E 718 492-3523
  Brooklyn *(G-1904)*
Garb-O-Liner Inc .... G 914 235-1585
  New Rochelle *(G-8607)*
Golden Group International Ltd .... G 845 440-1025
  Patterson *(G-12882)*
▲ H G Maybeck Co Inc .... E 718 297-4410
  Jamaica *(G-6649)*
◆ Ivi Services Inc .... D 607 729-5111
  Binghamton *(G-897)*
Jad Corp of America .... E 718 762-8900
  College Point *(G-3650)*
▲ Jay Bags Inc .... G 845 459-6500
  Spring Valley *(G-14997)*
▲ JM Murray Center Inc .... F 607 756-9913
  Cortland *(G-3879)*
JM Murray Center Inc .... F 607 756-0246
  Cortland *(G-3880)*
▲ Josh Packaging Inc .... E 631 822-1660
  Hauppauge *(G-5854)*
Kemco Sales LLC .... F 203 762-1902
  East Rochester *(G-4288)*
▲ Maco Bag Corporation .... C 315 226-1000
  Newark *(G-12199)*
▲ Magcrest Packaging Inc .... G 845 425-0451
  Monsey *(G-8289)*
Manhattan Poly Bag Corporation ..... E 917 689-7549
  Brooklyn *(G-2158)*
Mason Transparent Package Inc ...... F 718 792-6000
  Bronx *(G-1324)*
▲ Metropolitan Packg Mfg Corp ...... E 718 383-2700
  Brooklyn *(G-2202)*
Mint-X Products Corporation .... F 877 646-8224
  College Point *(G-3656)*
Modern Plastic Bags Mfg Inc .... G 718 237-2985
  Brooklyn *(G-2221)*
▲ Nap Industries Inc .... F 718 625-4948
  Brooklyn *(G-2243)*
▲ New York Packaging Corp .... E 516 746-0600
  New Hyde Park *(G-8552)*
▲ New York Packaging II LLC .... E 516 746-0600
  Garden City Park *(G-5286)*
▲ Noteworthy Industries Inc .... E 518 842-2662
  Amsterdam *(G-356)*
Nova Packaging Ltd Inc .... E 914 232-8406
  Katonah *(G-6845)*
▲ Pacific Poly Product Corp .... F 718 786-7129
  Long Island City *(G-7546)*
▲ Pack America Corp .... G 212 508-6666
  New York *(G-11092)*
Pactiv LLC .... C 585 394-5125
  Canandaigua *(G-3228)*
Pactiv LLC .... C 518 793-2524
  Glens Falls *(G-5439)*
Paradise Plastics LLC .... E 718 788-3733
  Brooklyn *(G-2302)*
▲ Paramount Equipment Inc .... E 631 981-4422
  Ronkonkoma *(G-14395)*
◆ Poly Craft Industries Corp .... E 631 630-6731
  Hauppauge *(G-5918)*
◆ Poly-Pak Industries Inc .... E 631 293-6767
  Melville *(G-8057)*
Polyseal Packaging Corp .... E 718 792-5530
  Bronx *(G-1359)*
▲ Primo Plastics Inc .... E 718 349-1000
  Brooklyn *(G-2344)*
Rainbow Poly Bag Co Inc .... E 718 386-3500
  Brooklyn *(G-2382)*
▲ Rege Inc .... F 845 565-7772
  New Windsor *(G-8657)*
Repellem Consumer Pdts Corp .... F 631 273-3992
  Bohemia *(G-1082)*
▲ Rtr Bag & Co Ltd .... G 212 620-0011
  New York *(G-11444)*
Salerno Packaging Inc .... F 518 563-3636
  Plattsburgh *(G-13154)*
▼ Select Fabricators Inc .... F 585 393-0650
  Canandaigua *(G-3233)*

Star Poly Bag Inc .... F 718 384-3130
  Brooklyn *(G-2510)*
Star Poly Bag Inc .... G 718 384-5342
  Brooklyn *(G-2511)*
Supreme Poly Plastics Inc .... E 718 456-9300
  Brooklyn *(G-2541)*
▲ T M I Plastics Industries Inc .... F 718 383-0363
  Brooklyn *(G-2548)*
▲ Tai Seng .... G 718 399-6311
  Brooklyn *(G-2554)*
Technipoly Manufacturing Inc .... E 718 383-0363
  Brooklyn *(G-2559)*
Tg Polymers Inc .... G 585 670-9427
  Webster *(G-16101)*
▲ Trinity Packaging Corporation ...... E 914 273-4111
  Armonk *(G-411)*
Trinity Packaging Corporation .... E 716 668-3111
  Buffalo *(G-3103)*
▲ Uniflex Holdings LLC .... F 516 932-2000
  Hauppauge *(G-5964)*
United Plastics Inc .... F 718 389-2255
  Brooklyn *(G-2603)*
W E W Container Corporation .... E 718 827-8150
  Brooklyn *(G-2637)*

2674 Bags: Uncoated Paper & Multiwall

333 J & M Food Corp .... F 718 381-1493
  Ridgewood *(G-13526)*
American Packaging Corporation ..... C 585 254-9500
  Rochester *(G-13626)*
▲ Ampac Paper LLC .... G 845 713-6600
  Walden *(G-15890)*
APC Paper Company Inc .... D 315 384-4225
  Norfolk *(G-12356)*
▲ Bag Arts The Art Packaging LLC ... G 212 684-7020
  New York *(G-9001)*
▲ Custom Eco Friendly LLC .... F 347 227-0229
  Roslyn *(G-14445)*
Kapstone Container Corporation ..... D 518 842-2450
  Amsterdam *(G-342)*
Lin Jin Feng .... G 718 232-3039
  Brooklyn *(G-2124)*
Polyseal Packaging Corp .... E 718 792-5530
  Bronx *(G-1359)*
▲ R P Fedder Corp .... E 585 288-1600
  Rochester *(G-14066)*
▲ Rtr Bag & Co Ltd .... G 212 620-0011
  New York *(G-11444)*
◆ Shalam Imports Inc .... F 718 686-6271
  Brooklyn *(G-2463)*
▲ Uniflex Holdings LLC .... F 516 932-2000
  Hauppauge *(G-5964)*

2675 Die-Cut Paper & Board

Able National Corp .... E 718 386-8801
  Brooklyn *(G-1471)*
All Out Die Cutting Inc .... E 718 346-6666
  Brooklyn *(G-1508)*
Allied Sample Card Co Inc .... E 718 238-0523
  Brooklyn *(G-1508)*
American Dsplay Die Ctters Inc .... E 212 645-1274
  New York *(G-8826)*
Art Industries of New York .... E 212 633-9200
  New York *(G-8914)*
▲ Borden & Riley Paper Co Inc .... E 718 454-9494
  Hollis *(G-6231)*
Dia .... G 212 675-4097
  New York *(G-9518)*
▲ General Die and Die Cutng Inc .... D 516 665-3584
  Massapequa Park *(G-7890)*
◆ General Fibre Products Corp .... D 516 358-7500
  New Hyde Park *(G-8536)*
Hubray Inc .... F 800 645-2855
  North Baldwin *(G-12364)*
◆ Kleer-Fax Inc .... D 631 225-1100
  Amityville *(G-295)*
Leather Indexes Corp .... D 516 827-1900
  Hicksville *(G-6103)*
Lion Die-Cutting Co Inc .... E 718 383-8841
  Brooklyn *(G-2127)*
Manufacturers Indexing Pdts .... G 631 271-0956
  Halesite *(G-5658)*
Mid Island Die Cutting Corp .... C 631 293-0180
  Farmingdale *(G-4823)*
Miken Companies Inc .... D 716 668-6311
  Buffalo *(G-2946)*
New Horizon Graphics Inc .... E 631 231-8055
  Hauppauge *(G-5901)*
New York Cutting & Gumming Co ..... E 212 563-4146
  Middletown *(G-8168)*

SIC SECTION
26 PAPER AND ALLIED PRODUCTS

Norampac New York City Inc ..... C 718 340-2100
Maspeth *(G-7863)*
▲ Paperworld Inc ..... E 516 221-2702
Bellmore *(G-790)*
Precision Diecutting Inc ..... G 315 776-8465
Port Byron *(G-13190)*
Premier Packaging Corporation ..... E 585 924-8460
Victor *(G-15861)*
▲ S & S Prtg Die-Cutting Co Inc ..... F 718 388-8990
Brooklyn *(G-2434)*
Spectrum Prtg Lithography Inc ..... E 212 255-3131
New York *(G-11665)*
Ums Manufacturing LLC ..... F 518 562-2410
Plattsburgh *(G-13164)*

2676 Sanitary Paper Prdts

▲ Alyk Inc ..... F 917 968-2552
New York *(G-8815)*
Attends Healthcare Inc ..... A 212 338-5100
New York *(G-8958)*
Becks Classic Mfg Inc ..... D 631 435-3800
Brentwood *(G-1128)*
◆ Bentley Manufacturing Inc ..... G 212 714-1800
New York *(G-9047)*
Bestwall LLC ..... A 518 561-3500
Plattsburgh *(G-13109)*
Cascades Tssue Group-Sales Inc ..... D 518 238-1900
Waterford *(G-15973)*
▲ Cellu Tissue - Long Island LLC ..... C 631 232-2626
Central Islip *(G-3361)*
▲ Corman USA Inc ..... G 718 727-7455
Staten Island *(G-15066)*
◆ Crosstex International Inc ..... D 631 582-6777
Hauppauge *(G-5805)*
Deluxe Packaging Corp ..... F 845 246-6090
Saugerties *(G-14607)*
First Quality Hygienic Inc ..... G 516 829-3030
Great Neck *(G-5556)*
◆ First Quality Products Inc ..... F 516 829-4949
Great Neck *(G-5557)*
▲ Florelle Tissue Corporation ..... E 647 997-7405
Brownville *(G-2671)*
HFC Prestige Intl US LLC ..... A 212 389-7800
New York *(G-10091)*
Kas Direct LLC ..... E 516 934-0541
Westbury *(G-16347)*
Kimberly-Clark Corporation ..... D 212 554-4252
New York *(G-10447)*
L VII Resilient LLC ..... F 631 987-5819
Medford *(G-7957)*
▲ Maxim Hygiene Products Inc ..... F 516 621-3323
Mineola *(G-8236)*
Monthly Gift Inc ..... G 888 444-9661
New York *(G-10840)*
▲ Mr Disposable Inc ..... F 718 388-8574
Brooklyn *(G-2231)*
▲ N3a Corporation ..... D 516 284-6799
Inwood *(G-6496)*
◆ Nice-Pak Products Inc ..... B 845 365-2772
Orangeburg *(G-12684)*
Nutek Disposables Inc ..... G 516 829-3030
Great Neck *(G-5574)*
Precare Corp ..... G 631 524-5171
Hauppauge *(G-5919)*
▲ Precare Corp ..... G 631 667-1055
Hauppauge *(G-5920)*
◆ Professional Disposables Inc ..... A 845 365-1700
Orangeburg *(G-12689)*
◆ Rochester Midland Corporation ..... C 585 336-2200
Rochester *(G-14088)*
▲ Select Products Holdings LLC ..... E 631 421-6000
Huntington *(G-6416)*
◆ Skip Hop Inc ..... E 646 902-9874
New York *(G-11610)*
Skip Hop Holdings Inc ..... G 212 868-9850
New York *(G-11611)*
▲ Sqp Inc ..... C 518 831-6800
Schenectady *(G-14716)*
Waymor1 Inc ..... E 518 677-8511
Cambridge *(G-3184)*

2677 Envelopes

3dflam Inc ..... F 631 647-2694
Bay Shore *(G-650)*
Apec Paper Industries Ltd ..... G 212 730-0088
New York *(G-8882)*
Buffalo Envelope Inc ..... F 716 686-0100
Depew *(G-4082)*
▲ Cambridge-Pacific Inc ..... E 518 677-5988
Cambridge *(G-3178)*
Conformer Products Inc ..... F 516 504-6300
Great Neck *(G-5547)*
East Cast Envlope Graphics LLC ..... E 718 326-2424
Maspeth *(G-7840)*
Jacmax Industries LLC ..... G 718 439-3743
Brooklyn *(G-2029)*
◆ Kleer-Fax Inc ..... D 631 225-1100
Amityville *(G-295)*
Mercury Envelope Co Inc ..... D 516 678-6744
Rockville Centre *(G-14236)*
◆ Poly-Pak Industries Inc ..... B 631 293-6767
Melville *(G-8057)*
Premier Packaging Corporation ..... E 585 924-8460
Victor *(G-15861)*
▲ Rochester 100 Inc ..... C 585 475-0200
Rochester *(G-14078)*
Westrock Mwv LLC ..... C 212 688-5000
New York *(G-12097)*
X-L Envelope and Printing Inc ..... F 716 852-2135
Buffalo *(G-3134)*

2678 Stationery Prdts

Allen William & Company Inc ..... C 212 675-6461
Glendale *(G-5391)*
▲ Anne Taintor Inc ..... G 718 483-9312
Brooklyn *(G-1536)*
▲ Cos TEC Manufacturing Corp ..... G 631 589-7170
Bohemia *(G-999)*
Drimark ..... F 516 484-6200
Bethpage *(G-841)*
Duck Flats Pharma ..... G 315 689-3407
Elbridge *(G-4428)*
▲ Dynamic Intl Mfrs & Distrs Inc ..... F 347 993-1914
Suffern *(G-15188)*
▲ General Diaries Corporation ..... F 516 371-2244
Inwood *(G-6491)*
▲ Innovative Designs LLC ..... E 212 695-0892
New York *(G-10219)*
▲ International Design Assoc Ltd ..... G 212 687-0333
New York *(G-10245)*
◆ Kleer-Fax Inc ..... D 631 225-1100
Amityville *(G-295)*
Leather Indexes Corp ..... D 516 827-1900
Hicksville *(G-6103)*
▲ P C I Paper Conversions Inc ..... C 315 437-1641
Syracuse *(G-15389)*
Paper Magic Group Inc ..... B 631 521-3682
New York *(G-11102)*
▲ Princton Archtctural Press LLC ..... F 518 671-6100
Hudson *(G-6369)*
◆ USA Custom Pad Corp ..... E 607 563-9550
Sidney *(G-14858)*
Westrock Mwv LLC ..... C 212 688-5000
New York *(G-12097)*

2679 Converted Paper Prdts, NEC

Accent Label & Tag Co Inc ..... G 631 244-7066
Ronkonkoma *(G-14287)*
Adelphi Paper Hangings ..... G 518 284-9066
Sharon Springs *(G-14796)*
▲ Aigner Label Holder Corp ..... F 845 562-4510
New Windsor *(G-8634)*
▲ Allied Converters Inc ..... E 914 235-1585
New Rochelle *(G-8589)*
Aniiwe Inc ..... G 347 683-1891
Brooklyn *(G-1535)*
Apexx Omni-Graphics Inc ..... D 718 326-3330
Maspeth *(G-7822)*
▼ Auto Data Systems Inc ..... E 631 667-2382
Deer Park *(G-3948)*
▼ Avco Industries Inc ..... F 631 851-1555
Central Islip *(G-3358)*
Beetins Wholesale Inc ..... F 718 524-0899
Staten Island *(G-15049)*
Best Time Processor LLC ..... G 917 455-4126
Richmond Hill *(G-13499)*
Bigname Commerce LLC ..... D 631 693-1070
Amityville *(G-265)*
▲ CCT (us) Inc ..... F 716 297-7509
Niagara Falls *(G-12269)*
Depot Label Company Inc ..... G 631 467-2952
Patchogue *(G-12864)*
Eagles Nest Holdings LLC ..... E 513 874-5270
New York *(G-9604)*
Emergent Power Inc ..... G 201 441-3590
Latham *(G-7072)*
Eskayel Inc ..... G 347 703-8084
Brooklyn *(G-1848)*
Flavor Paper Ltd ..... F 718 422-0230
Brooklyn *(G-1889)*
Folia Water Inc ..... G 412 802-5083
New York *(G-9821)*
▲ Gardei Industries LLC ..... F 716 693-7100
North Tonawanda *(G-12429)*
Gavin Mfg Corp ..... E 631 467-0040
Farmingdale *(G-4770)*
◆ Gaylord Bros Inc ..... D 315 457-5070
North Syracuse *(G-12402)*
◆ General Fibre Products Corp ..... D 516 358-7500
New Hyde Park *(G-8536)*
Gerald McGlone ..... G 518 482-2613
Colonie *(G-3678)*
▼ Gooding Co Inc ..... E 716 266-6252
Lockport *(G-7308)*
▲ Graphic Cntrls Acqisition Corp ..... B 716 853-7500
Buffalo *(G-2853)*
Graphic Controls Holdings Inc ..... F 716 853-7500
Buffalo *(G-2854)*
Howard J Moore Company Inc ..... E 631 351-8467
Plainview *(G-13062)*
Interface Performance Mtls ..... F 315 346-3100
Beaver Falls *(G-766)*
▲ Interntnal Bus Cmmncations Inc ..... E 516 352-4505
New Hyde Park *(G-8542)*
Jerry Tomaselli ..... F 718 965-1400
Brooklyn *(G-2036)*
▲ K Sidrane Inc ..... E 631 393-6974
Farmingdale *(G-4796)*
▲ Katz Group Americas Inc ..... E 716 995-3059
Sanborn *(G-14548)*
Larkin Anya Ltd ..... G 718 361-1827
Long Island City *(G-7495)*
▲ M C Packaging Corporation ..... C 631 694-3012
Farmingdale *(G-4812)*
M C Packaging Corporation ..... E 631 643-3763
Babylon *(G-529)*
▲ Marketing Group International ..... G 631 754-8095
Northport *(G-12472)*
Master Image Printing Inc ..... G 914 347-4400
Elmsford *(G-4550)*
Mid-York Press Inc ..... D 607 674-4491
Sherburne *(G-14807)*
National Advertising & Prtg ..... G 212 629-7650
New York *(G-10880)*
▲ Noteworthy Industries Inc ..... C 518 842-2662
Amsterdam *(G-356)*
▲ P C I Paper Conversions Inc ..... C 315 437-1641
Syracuse *(G-15389)*
P C I Paper Conversions Inc ..... F 315 437-1641
Syracuse *(G-15392)*
▲ Pack America Corp ..... G 212 508-6666
New York *(G-11092)*
▲ Paperworld Inc ..... E 516 221-2702
Bellmore *(G-790)*
▲ Paradigm Mktg Consortium Inc ..... E 516 496-0000
Syosset *(G-15227)*
▲ Plug Power Inc ..... B 518 782-7700
Latham *(G-7091)*
Precision Label Corporation ..... F 631 270-4490
Farmingdale *(G-4857)*
Quadra Flex Corp ..... G 607 758-7066
Cortland *(G-3891)*
▲ Quality Circle Products Inc ..... D 914 736-6600
Montrose *(G-8329)*
RB Converting Inc ..... G 607 777-1325
Binghamton *(G-911)*
Sappi North America Inc ..... D 914 696-5544
White Plains *(G-16503)*
Setterstix Inc ..... E 716 257-3451
Cattaraugus *(G-3314)*
▲ Shell Containers Inc (ny) ..... E 516 352-4505
New Hyde Park *(G-8562)*
▲ Sml USA Inc ..... E 212 736-8800
New York *(G-11626)*
▲ Specialty Quality Packg LLC ..... D 914 580-3200
Scotia *(G-14747)*
Stanley Paper Co Inc ..... F 518 489-1131
Albany *(G-129)*
Stickershopcom Inc ..... G 631 563-4323
Bayport *(G-739)*
Stoney Croft Converters Inc ..... F 718 608-9800
Staten Island *(G-15140)*
Sunnyside Decorative Prints Co ..... G 516 671-1935
Glen Cove *(G-5377)*
Tag Envelope Co Inc ..... E 718 389-6844
College Point *(G-3669)*
▲ Tri-Flex Label Corp ..... E 631 293-0411
Farmingdale *(G-4898)*
▲ Tri-Seal International Inc ..... G 845 353-3300
Blauvelt *(G-944)*

S
I
C

26 PAPER AND ALLIED PRODUCTS

▲ Trinity Packaging Corporation.........F...... 914 273-4111
  Armonk *(G-411)*
Waymor1 Inc...........................E...... 518 677-8511
  Cambridge *(G-3184)*
Web-Tech Packaging Inc..............F...... 716 684-4520
  Lancaster *(G-7054)*

27 PRINTING, PUBLISHING, AND ALLIED INDUSTRIES

2711 Newspapers: Publishing & Printing

21st Century Fox America Inc............G...... 212 782-8000
  New York *(G-8672)*
50+ Lifestyle...........................G...... 631 286-0058
  Bellport *(G-796)*
◆ A C J Communications Inc............F...... 631 587-5612
  Babylon *(G-523)*
A Zimmer Ltd..........................D...... 315 422-7011
  Syracuse *(G-15237)*
Adirondack Publishing Co Inc.........E...... 518 891-2600
  Saranac Lake *(G-14560)*
Advance Magazine Publs Inc...........C...... 212 450-7000
  New York *(G-8750)*
▲ Advance Publications Inc...........D...... 718 981-1234
  Staten Island *(G-15040)*
Advertiser Perceptions Inc............G...... 212 626-6683
  New York *(G-8761)*
Advertiser Publications Inc............F...... 845 783-1111
  Chester *(G-3467)*
▲ Afro Times Newspaper..............G...... 718 636-9500
  Brooklyn *(G-1493)*
After 50 Inc............................G...... 716 832-9300
  Lancaster *(G-7003)*
Albany Catholic Press Assoc...........G...... 518 453-6688
  Albany *(G-32)*
Albany Student Press Inc..............G...... 518 442-5665
  Albany *(G-37)*
Albion-Holley Pennysaver Inc.........E...... 585 589-5641
  Albion *(G-154)*
Algemeiner Journal Inc................G...... 718 771-0400
  Brooklyn *(G-1505)*
All Island Media Inc...................C...... 631 698-8400
  Edgewood *(G-4395)*
All Island Media Inc...................E...... 516 942-8400
  Hicksville *(G-6057)*
All Times Publishing LLC.............E...... 315 422-7011
  Syracuse *(G-15238)*
Alm Media LLC.......................B...... 212 457-9400
  New York *(G-8805)*
Alm Media Holdings Inc..............B...... 212 457-9400
  New York *(G-8806)*
American City Bus Journals Inc.......E...... 716 541-1654
  Buffalo *(G-2694)*
American Sports Media................G...... 585 924-4250
  Victor *(G-15829)*
American Sports Media LLC..........G...... 585 377-9636
  Rochester *(G-13628)*
Amnews Corporation..................G...... 212 932-7400
  New York *(G-8844)*
Amnewyork.............................D...... 212 239-5555
  New York *(G-8845)*
Angel Media and Publishing..........G...... 845 727-4949
  West Nyack *(G-16264)*
Angola Penny Saver Inc..............F...... 716 549-1164
  Angola *(G-368)*
AR Publishing Company Inc.........F...... 212 482-0303
  New York *(G-8896)*
Architects Newspaper LLC.............G...... 212 966-0630
  New York *(G-8900)*
Asahi Shimbun America Inc.........F...... 212 398-0257
  New York *(G-8929)*
Aspect Printing Inc....................E...... 347 789-4284
  Brooklyn *(G-1564)*
Auburn Publishing Co.................D...... 315 253-5311
  Auburn *(G-465)*
Bangla Patrika Inc.....................G...... 718 482-9923
  Long Island City *(G-7397)*
Bee Publications Inc...................D...... 716 632-4700
  Williamsville *(G-16569)*
Belsito Communications Inc..........F...... 845 534-9700
  New Windsor *(G-8636)*
Beth Kobliner Company LLC........G...... 212 501-8407
  New York *(G-9059)*
Bleezarde Publishing Inc..............F...... 518 756-2030
  Ravena *(G-13452)*
Blue and White Publishing Inc.......F...... 215 431-3339
  New York *(G-9106)*
BNH Lead Examiner Corp............G...... 718 807-1365
  Brooklyn *(G-1626)*

Boonville Herald Inc....................G...... 315 942-4449
  Boonville *(G-1115)*
Bornomala USA Inc...................G...... 347 753-2355
  Jackson Heights *(G-6618)*
Bradford Publications Inc.............F...... 716 373-2500
  Olean *(G-12594)*
Brasilans Press Pblcations Inc........E...... 212 764-6161
  New York *(G-9136)*
Brooklyn Journal Publications........F...... 718 422-7400
  Brooklyn *(G-1644)*
Brooklyn Rail Inc......................F...... 718 349-8427
  Brooklyn *(G-1645)*
Buffalo Law Journal...................G...... 716 541-1600
  Buffalo *(G-2745)*
▲ Buffalo News Inc..................F...... 716 849-4401
  Buffalo *(G-2750)*
Buffalo Standard Printing Corp......F...... 716 835-9454
  Buffalo *(G-2753)*
Bureau of National Affairs Inc.......E...... 212 687-4530
  New York *(G-9158)*
Business First of New York..........F...... 716 854-5822
  Buffalo *(G-2756)*
Business First of New York..........E...... 518 640-6800
  Latham *(G-7067)*
Business Journals......................F...... 212 790-5100
  New York *(G-9163)*
Camden News Inc.....................G...... 315 245-1849
  Camden *(G-3185)*
Canandaigua Msgnr Incorported....C...... 585 394-0770
  Canandaigua *(G-3213)*
Canarsie Courier Inc..................F...... 718 257-0600
  Brooklyn *(G-1671)*
Capital Region Wkly Newspapers....F...... 518 877-7160
  Albany *(G-55)*
Catskill Delaware Publications........F...... 845 887-5200
  Callicoon *(G-3160)*
Catskill Mountain Publishing..........F...... 845 586-2601
  Arkville *(G-400)*
Chase Media Group...................F...... 914 962-3871
  Yorktown Heights *(G-16814)*
Chester West County Press..........G...... 914 684-0006
  Mount Vernon *(G-8386)*
China Daily Distribution Corp........E...... 212 537-8888
  New York *(G-9277)*
China Newsweek Corporation.......F...... 212 481-2510
  New York *(G-9282)*
▲ Chinese Medical Report Inc.......G...... 718 359-5676
  Flushing *(G-4990)*
Christian Press Inc....................G...... 718 886-4400
  Flushing *(G-4991)*
Chronicle Express......................F...... 315 536-4422
  Penn Yan *(G-12951)*
Citizen Publishing Corp...............F...... 845 627-1414
  Nanuet *(G-8461)*
City Newspaper........................G...... 585 244-3329
  Rochester *(G-13711)*
Citywire LLC...........................F...... 646 503-2216
  New York *(G-9315)*
Clarion Publications Inc..............F...... 585 243-3530
  Geneseo *(G-5313)*
Cnhi LLC..............................E...... 585 798-1400
  Medina *(G-7975)*
Cnhi LLC..............................D...... 716 693-1000
  Niagara Falls *(G-12272)*
Cnhi LLC..............................D...... 716 282-2311
  Niagara Falls *(G-12273)*
Cnhi LLC..............................F...... 716 439-9222
  Lockport *(G-7291)*
CNY Business Review Inc............F...... 315 472-3104
  Syracuse *(G-15281)*
Columbia Daily Spectator............F...... 212 854-9550
  New York *(G-9356)*
Community Media Group Inc.......D...... 315 789-3333
  Geneva *(G-5321)*
Community Media Group LLC......F...... 518 439-4949
  Delmar *(G-4077)*
Community Media LLC..............E...... 212 229-1890
  New York *(G-9368)*
Community News Group LLC......C...... 718 260-2500
  Brooklyn *(G-1710)*
Community Newspaper Group LLC...F...... 607 432-1000
  Oneonta *(G-12633)*
Community Newspaper Group LLC....F...... 518 565-4114
  Plattsburgh *(G-13118)*
Copia Interactive LLC................F...... 212 481-0520
  New York *(G-9396)*
Cortland Standard Printing Co......D...... 607 756-5665
  Cortland *(G-3871)*
Country Folks.........................G...... 585 343-9721
  Batavia *(G-621)*

Courier-Life Inc........................C...... 718 260-2500
  Brooklyn *(G-1724)*
CT Publications Co....................G...... 718 592-2196
  Whitestone *(G-16539)*
Daily Cornell Sun......................E...... 607 273-0746
  Ithaca *(G-6574)*
Daily Freeman.........................F...... 845 331-5000
  Kingston *(G-6897)*
Daily Gazette Company..............B...... 518 374-4141
  Schenectady *(G-14667)*
Daily Gazette Company..............C...... 518 395-3060
  Schenectady *(G-14668)*
Daily Mail & Greene Cnty News....F...... 518 943-2100
  Hudson *(G-6345)*
▲ Daily News LP...................A...... 212 210-2100
  New York *(G-9455)*
Daily Orange Corporation............E...... 315 443-2314
  Syracuse *(G-15301)*
▼ Daily Racing Form Inc............C...... 212 366-7600
  New York *(G-9456)*
Daily Racing Form LLC..............F...... 212 514-2180
  New York *(G-9457)*
Daily Record...........................F...... 585 232-2035
  Rochester *(G-13732)*
Daily World Press Inc................F...... 212 922-9201
  New York *(G-9458)*
Dale Press Inc.........................F...... 718 543-6200
  Bronx *(G-1253)*
Danet Inc..............................F...... 718 266-4444
  Brooklyn *(G-1755)*
Dans Paper Inc........................F...... 631 537-0500
  Southampton *(G-14952)*
Das Yidishe Licht Inc.................F...... 718 387-3166
  Brooklyn *(G-1758)*
Dbg Media.............................G...... 718 599-6828
  Brooklyn *(G-1761)*
Delaware County Times Inc.........F...... 607 746-2176
  Delhi *(G-4072)*
Denton Publications Inc..............D...... 518 873-6368
  Elizabethtown *(G-4430)*
Denton Publications Inc..............E...... 518 561-9680
  Plattsburgh *(G-13119)*
Der Blatt..............................F...... 845 783-1148
  Monroe *(G-8268)*
Digital One USA Inc..................F...... 718 396-4890
  Flushing *(G-4996)*
▲ Document Journal Inc............G...... 646 586-3099
  New York *(G-9544)*
DOT Publishing.......................F...... 315 593-2510
  Fulton *(G-5215)*
▲ Dow Jones & Company Inc.....B...... 609 627-2999
  New York *(G-9563)*
Dow Jones & Company Inc........E...... 212 597-5983
  New York *(G-9564)*
Dray Enterprises Inc..................F...... 585 768-2201
  Le Roy *(G-7116)*
E W Smith Publishing Co.............F...... 845 562-1218
  New Windsor *(G-8643)*
Eagle Media Partners LP.............G...... 315 434-8889
  Syracuse *(G-15309)*
East Hampton Ind News Inc........F...... 631 324-2500
  East Hampton *(G-4235)*
East Hampton Star Inc...............F...... 631 324-0002
  East Hampton *(G-4236)*
Ecclesiastical Communications......F...... 212 688-2399
  New York *(G-9620)*
Economist Newspaper NA Inc......E...... 212 554-0676
  New York *(G-9625)*
Ecuador News Inc....................F...... 718 205-7014
  Woodside *(G-16654)*
El Diario LLC.........................C...... 212 807-4600
  Brooklyn *(G-1818)*
Empire Publishing Inc................F...... 516 829-4000
  Far Rockaway *(G-4700)*
Empire State Weeklies Inc..........F...... 585 671-1533
  Webster *(G-16084)*
Event Journal Inc....................F...... 516 470-1811
  Jericho *(G-6787)*
Evercore Partners Svcs E LLC......A...... 212 857-3100
  New York *(G-9735)*
Exhibits & More......................G...... 585 924-4040
  Victor *(G-15845)*
Expositor Newspapers Inc...........G...... 585 427-2468
  Rochester *(G-13799)*
▲ Fairchild Publications Inc........A...... 212 630-4000
  New York *(G-9773)*
Finger Lakes Media Inc..............F...... 607 243-7600
  Dundee *(G-4157)*
Fire Island Tide Publication..........F...... 631 567-7470
  Sayville *(G-14630)*

27 PRINTING, PUBLISHING, AND ALLIED INDUSTRIES

Company	Code	Phone
Firefighters Journal	E	718 391-0283
Long Island City (G-7448)		
First Choice News Inc	G	212 477-2044
New York (G-9806)		
Five Islands Publishing Inc	F	631 583-5345
Bronx (G-1271)		
Four Directions Inc	E	315 829-8388
Vernon (G-15804)		
▲ Francepress LLC	G	646 202-9828
New York (G-9837)		
Fredonia Pennysaver Inc	G	716 679-1509
Fredonia (G-5126)		
Freetime Magazine Inc	G	585 473-2266
Rochester (G-13817)		
French Morning LLC	G	646 290-7463
New York (G-9847)		
▲ FT Publications Inc	D	212 641-6500
New York (G-9856)		
FT Publications Inc	E	212 641-2420
New York (G-9857)		
Fulton Newspapers Inc	E	315 598-6397
Fulton (G-5216)		
Gallagher Printing Inc	F	716 873-2434
Buffalo (G-2838)		
Gannett Co Inc	D	585 232-7100
Rochester (G-13822)		
Gannett Co Inc	D	585 924-3406
Farmington (G-4914)		
Gannett Co inc	G	914 278-9315
New Rochelle (G-8606)		
Gannett Co Inc	D	607 798-1234
Vestal (G-15816)		
Gannett Stllite Info Ntwrk Inc	E	914 965-5000
Yonkers (G-16761)		
Gannett Stllite Info Ntwrk Inc	D	585 798-1400
Medina (G-7978)		
Gannett Stllite Info Ntwrk LLC	E	845 578-2300
West Nyack (G-16269)		
Gannett Stllite Info Ntwrk LLC	C	845 454-2000
Poughkeepsie (G-13339)		
Gannett Stllite Info Ntwrk LLC	F	914 381-3400
Mamaroneck (G-7745)		
▲ Gatehouse Media LLC	B	585 598-0030
Pittsford (G-13013)		
Gatehouse Media LLC	E	315 792-5000
Utica (G-15706)		
Gatehouse Media LLC	G	607 776-2121
Bath (G-343)		
Gatehouse Media LLC	F	315 866-2220
Herkimer (G-6039)		
Gatehouse Media LLC	D	607 936-4651
Corning (G-3819)		
Gatehouse Media LLC	D	585 394-0770
Canandaigua (G-3222)		
Gatehouse Media LLC	C	607 324-1425
Hornell (G-6299)		
Gatehouse Media PA Holdings Inc	E	585 598-0030
Pittsford (G-13014)		
General Media Strategies Inc	E	212 586-4141
New York (G-9901)		
Gleaner Company Ltd	G	718 657-0788
Jamaica (G-6646)		
Glens Falls Newspapers Inc	G	518 792-3131
Glens Falls (G-5426)		
Good Health Healthcare Newspr	F	585 421-8109
Victor (G-15848)		
Guardian News & Media LLC	E	917 900-4663
New York (G-10004)		
Guest of A Guest Inc	G	212 206-0397
New York (G-10006)		
Guidance Group Inc	G	631 619-2600
Bohemia (G-1031)		
Guidance Group Inc	F	631 756-4618
Melville (G-8029)		
▲ Hagedorn Communications Inc	D	914 636-7400
New Rochelle (G-8609)		
Hagedorn Communications Inc	G	914 636-7400
New York (G-10020)		
Haitian Times Inc	G	718 230-8700
New Rochelle (G-8610)		
Hamodia Corp	G	718 338-5637
Brooklyn (G-1962)		
Hamodia Corp	F	718 853-9094
Brooklyn (G-1963)		
Hearst Business Media Corp	F	631 650-4441
New York (G-10056)		
▲ Hearst Communications Inc	A	212 649-2000
New York (G-10058)		
▲ Hearst Corporation	A	212 649-2000
New York (G-10061)		
Hearst Corporation	A	518 454-5694
Albany (G-82)		
Hearst Corporation	E	212 649-2275
New York (G-10070)		
Herald Newspapers Company Inc	A	315 470-0011
Syracuse (G-15340)		
Herald Publishing Company LLC	G	315 470-2022
New York (G-10082)		
High Ridge News LLC	G	718 548-7412
Bronx (G-1292)		
Highline Media LLC	E	859 692-2100
New York (G-10097)		
Holdens Screen Supply Corp	G	212 627-2727
New York (G-10114)		
Home Reporter Inc	E	718 238-6600
Brooklyn (G-1982)		
Hudson News Inc	G	212 971-6800
New York (G-10143)		
Hudson Valley Black Press	G	845 562-1313
Newburgh (G-12226)		
Huersch Marketing Group LLC	F	518 874-1045
Green Island (G-5607)		
IMG The Daily	G	212 541-5640
New York (G-10185)		
▲ Impremedia LLC	D	212 807-4600
Brooklyn (G-1997)		
India Abroad Publications Inc	D	212 929-1727
New York (G-10198)		
Informa Uk Ltd	G	646 957-8966
New York (G-10213)		
Investment News	E	212 210-0100
New York (G-10263)		
Investors Business Daily Inc	F	212 626-7676
New York (G-10264)		
Irish Echo Newspaper Corp	F	212 482-4818
New York (G-10271)		
Irish Tribune Inc	F	212 684-3366
New York (G-10272)		
Ithaca Journal News Co Inc	E	607 272-2321
Ithaca (G-6588)		
Jewish Journal	G	718 630-9350
Brooklyn (G-2039)		
Jewish Press Inc	C	718 330-1100
Brooklyn (G-2040)		
Jewish Week Inc	E	212 921-7822
New York (G-10332)		
Jobs Weekly Inc	F	716 648-5627
Hamburg (G-5682)		
John Lor Publishing Ltd	E	631 475-1000
Patchogue (G-12868)		
Johnson Acquisition Corp	F	518 828-1616
Hudson (G-6360)		
Johnson Newspaper Corporation	E	518 483-4700
Malone (G-7722)		
Journal News	G	914 694-5000
White Plains (G-16468)		
Journal News	G	845 578-2324
West Nyack (G-16273)		
Journal Register Company	D	518 584-4242
Saratoga Springs (G-14589)		
Journal Register Company	F	212 257-7212
New York (G-10368)		
Kch Publications Inc	E	516 671-2360
Glen Cove (G-5369)		
▲ Korea Central Daily News Inc	D	718 361-7700
Long Island City (G-7491)		
▲ Korea Times New York Inc	D	718 784-4526
Long Island City (G-7492)		
Korea Times New York Inc	G	718 729-5555
Long Island City (G-7493)		
Korea Times New York Inc	G	718 961-7979
Flushing (G-5019)		
L & M Publications Inc	E	516 378-3133
Garden City (G-5264)		
Lee Enterprises Incorporated	C	518 792-3131
Glens Falls (G-5431)		
Lee Newspapers Inc	F	518 673-3237
Palatine Bridge (G-12842)		
Lee Publications Inc	D	518 673-3237
Palatine Bridge (G-12843)		
LI Community Newspapers Inc	G	516 747-8282
Mineola (G-8233)		
Litmor Publishing Inc	F	516 931-0012
Garden City (G-5266)		
Livingston County News	G	585 243-1234
Geneseo (G-5315)		
Lmg National Publishing Inc	E	585 598-6874
Fairport (G-4640)		
Local Media Group Inc	B	845 341-1100
Middletown (G-8159)		
Local Media Group Inc	E	845 341-1100
Middletown (G-8160)		
Local Media Group Inc	D	845 341-1100
Middletown (G-8161)		
Local Media Group Inc	F	845 794-3712
Monticello (G-8321)		
Local Media Group Inc	E	845 340-4910
Kingston (G-6908)		
Local Media Group Holdings LLC	G	585 598-0030
Pittsford (G-13019)		
Long Island Business News	E	631 737-1700
Ronkonkoma (G-14371)		
Long Island Catholic Newspaper	E	516 594-1212
Rockville Centre (G-14235)		
Long Island Cmnty Nwsppers Inc	D	516 482-4490
Mineola (G-8235)		
Long Island Cmnty Nwsppers Inc	F	631 427-7000
Huntington (G-6404)		
Long Islander Newspapers LLC	G	631 427-7000
Huntington (G-6405)		
Los Angles Tmes Cmmnctions LLC	E	212 418-9600
New York (G-10612)		
Louis Vuitton North Amer Inc	G	212 644-2574
New York (G-10617)		
Lowville Newspaper Corporation	G	315 376-3525
Lowville (G-7653)		
Made Fresh Daily	G	212 285-2253
New York (G-10655)		
Main Street Connect LLC	F	203 803-4110
Armonk (G-407)		
Manchester Newspaper Inc	E	518 642-1234
Granville (G-5520)		
Manhattan Media LLC	F	212 268-8600
New York (G-10686)		
Manhattan Times Inc	F	212 569-5800
New York (G-10689)		
Mark I Publications Inc	E	718 205-8000
Glendale (G-5403)		
Market Place Publications	E	516 997-7909
Carle Place (G-3270)		
Massapequa Post	E	516 798-5100
Massapequa Park (G-7893)		
McClary Media Inc	G	800 453-6397
Amsterdam (G-346)		
Melmont Fine Pringng/Graphics	G	516 939-2253
Bethpage (G-847)		
Merchandiser Inc	G	315 462-6411
Clifton Springs (G-3582)		
Mexico Independent Inc	E	315 963-3763
Watertown (G-16027)		
Miami Media LLC	F	212 268-8600
New York (G-10789)		
Mid York Weekly & Pennysaver	G	315 792-4990
Utica (G-15721)		
Mid-York Press Inc	D	607 674-4491
Sherburne (G-14807)		
Ming Pao (new York) Inc	E	718 786-2888
Long Island City (G-7525)		
Ming Pao (new York) Inc	F	212 334-2220
New York (G-10818)		
Ming Pao (new York) Inc	D	718 786-2888
Long Island City (G-7526)		
Minority Reporter Inc	G	585 225-3628
Rochester (G-13946)		
Moneypaper Inc	F	914 925-0022
Rye (G-14486)		
Mortgage Press Ltd	E	516 409-1400
Wantagh (G-15924)		
Nassau County Publications	G	516 481-5400
Hempstead (G-6022)		
▲ National Herald Inc	E	718 784-5255
Long Island City (G-7533)		
NC Audience Exchange LLC	F	212 416-3400
New York (G-10901)		
Neighbor Newspapers	G	631 226-2636
Farmingdale (G-4833)		
Neighbor To Neighbor News Inc	G	585 492-2525
Arcade (G-387)		
New Living Inc	G	631 751-8819
Patchogue (G-12871)		
New Media Investment Group Inc	B	212 479-3160
New York (G-10927)		
New Republic	G	212 989-8200
New York (G-10929)		
New Ski Inc	E	607 277-7000
Ithaca (G-6600)		
New York Cvl Srvc Emplys Pblsh	F	212 962-2690
New York (G-10934)		
New York Daily Challenge Inc	E	718 636-9500
Brooklyn (G-2261)		

Employee Codes: A=Over 500 employees, B=251-500
C=101-250, D=51-100, E=20-50, F=10-19, G=5-9

27 PRINTING, PUBLISHING, AND ALLIED INDUSTRIES SIC SECTION

New York Daily News G 212 248-2100
New York *(G-10935)*

▲ **New York IL Bo Inc** F 718 961-1538
Flushing *(G-5028)*

New York Press Inc E 212 268-8600
New York *(G-10941)*

New York Times Company B 212 556-1234
New York *(G-10944)*

New York Times Company F 718 281-7000
Flushing *(G-5029)*

New York Times Company F 212 556-4300
New York *(G-10946)*

New York University E 212 998-4300
New York *(G-10947)*

New York1 News Operations F 212 379-3311
New York *(G-10948)*

News Communications Inc F 212 689-2500
New York *(G-10951)*

News Corporation C 212 416-3400
New York *(G-10952)*

News India Usa LLC G 212 675-7515
New York *(G-10953)*

News India USA Inc F 212 675-7515
New York *(G-10954)*

News Now Waverly F 607 296-6769
Waverly *(G-16068)*

News of The Highlands Inc F 845 534-7771
Cornwall *(G-3836)*

News Report Inc E 718 851-6607
Brooklyn *(G-2267)*

Newsday LLC B 631 843-4050
Melville *(G-8050)*

Newsday LLC C 631 843-3135
Melville *(G-8051)*

Newspaper Delivery Solutions G 718 370-1111
Staten Island *(G-15107)*

Newspaper Publisher LLC F 607 775-0472
Conklin *(G-3730)*

Newspaper Times Union F 518 454-5676
Albany *(G-104)*

Newsweek LLC G 646 867-7100
New York *(G-10956)*

Nick Lugo Inc F 212 348-2100
New York *(G-10963)*

Nikkei America Inc E 212 261-6200
New York *(G-10968)*

Nikkei America Holdings Inc D 212 261-6200
New York *(G-10969)*

Nordic Press Inc G 212 686-3356
New York *(G-10988)*

North Country This Week G 315 265-1000
Potsdam *(G-13320)*

Northern NY Newspapers Corp C 315 782-1000
Watertown *(G-16031)*

Northern Tier Publishing Corp F 914 962-4748
Yorktown Heights *(G-16820)*

▲ **Noticia Hispanoamericana Inc** E 516 223-5678
North Baldwin *(G-12365)*

Novoye Rsskoye Slovo Pubg Corp D 646 460-4566
Brooklyn *(G-2276)*

Nyc Community Media LLC F 212 229-1890
Brooklyn *(G-2281)*

Nyc Trade Printers Corp F 718 606-0610
Woodside *(G-16668)*

Nyp Holdings Inc D 718 260-2500
Brooklyn *(G-2282)*

▲ **Nyp Holdings Inc** A 212 997-9272
New York *(G-11018)*

Nyt Capital LLC F 212 556-1234
New York *(G-11021)*

Nytimes Corporate G 212 556-1234
New York *(G-11022)*

Oak Lone Publishing Co Inc E 518 792-1126
Glens Falls *(G-5437)*

Observer Daily Sunday Newsppr D 716 366-3000
Dunkirk *(G-4175)*

Observer Media LLC E 212 755-2400
New York *(G-11025)*

Ogden Newspapers Inc C 716 487-1111
Jamestown *(G-6741)*

Oneida Publications Inc E 315 363-5100
Oneida *(G-12618)*

Ottaway Newspapers Inc G 845 343-2181
Middletown *(G-8169)*

Owego Pennysaver Press Inc F 607 687-2434
Owego *(G-12802)*

Page Front Group Inc G 716 823-8222
Lackawanna *(G-6950)*

Panagraphics Inc G 716 312-8088
Orchard Park *(G-12734)*

Patchogue Advance Inc E 631 475-1000
Patchogue *(G-12873)*

▲ **Peace Times Weekly Inc** G 718 762-6500
Flushing *(G-5036)*

◆ **Pearson Inc** D 212 641-2400
New York *(G-11133)*

Pearson Longman LLC E 212 641-2400
White Plains *(G-16487)*

Pennysaver Group Inc F 914 966-1400
Yonkers *(G-16791)*

Permanent Observer Mission G 212 883-0140
New York *(G-11159)*

Post Journal F 716 487-1111
Jamestown *(G-6742)*

Prometheus International Inc F 718 472-0700
Long Island City *(G-7561)*

Prospect News Inc F 212 374-2800
New York *(G-11267)*

Publishing Group America Inc F 646 658-0550
New York *(G-11274)*

Putnam Cnty News Recorder LLC F 845 265-2468
Cold Spring *(G-3626)*

Quality Guides G 716 326-3163
Westfield *(G-16395)*

Queens Ldgr/Grenpoint Star Inc F 718 639-7000
Maspeth *(G-7869)*

R W Publications Div of Wtrhs E 716 714-5620
Elma *(G-4456)*

R W Publications Div of Wtrhs E 716 714-5620
Elma *(G-4457)*

Realtimetraderscom E 716 632-6600
Buffalo *(G-3033)*

Record G 518 270-1200
Saratoga Springs *(G-14595)*

Record Advertiser E 716 693-1000
North Tonawanda *(G-12445)*

Record Review LLC F 914 244-0533
Katonah *(G-6846)*

Richner Communications Inc C 516 569-4000
Garden City *(G-5278)*

Richner Communications Inc G 516 569-4000
Lawrence *(G-7108)*

Ridgewood Times Prtg & Pubg E 718 821-7500
Ridgewood *(G-13549)*

River Valley Paper Company F 330 631-8320
Syracuse *(G-15407)*

Rizzoli Intl Publications Inc F 212 308-2000
New York *(G-11400)*

Rochester Business Journal E 585 546-8303
Rochester *(G-14081)*

Rochester Catholic Press F 585 529-9530
Rochester *(G-14082)*

Rochester Democrat & Chronicle E 585 232-7100
Rochester *(G-14086)*

Rocket Communications Inc F 716 873-2594
Buffalo *(G-3042)*

Rome Main Street Alliance Inc G 315 271-8356
Rome *(G-14270)*

Royal News Corp F 212 564-8972
New York *(G-11439)*

Rtt News E 716 632-3400
Williamsville *(G-16584)*

Ruby Newco LLC G 212 852-7000
New York *(G-11445)*

Russkaya Reklama Inc E 718 769-3000
Brooklyn *(G-2429)*

S G New York LLC F 631 698-8400
Edgewood *(G-4414)*

S G New York LLC E 631 665-4000
Bohemia *(G-1084)*

S I Communications Inc F 914 725-2500
Scarsdale *(G-14644)*

Sag Harbor Express G 631 725-1700
Sag Harbor *(G-14501)*

Salamanca Press Penny Saver E 716 945-1500
Salamanca *(G-14531)*

Sample News Group LLC D 315 343-3800
Oswego *(G-12787)*

Sb New York Inc D 212 457-7790
New York *(G-11496)*

Schneps Publications Inc E 718 224-5863
Bayside *(G-749)*

Seabay Media Holdings LLC G 212 457-7790
New York *(G-11525)*

Second Amendment Foundation G 716 885-6408
Buffalo *(G-3061)*

Seneca County Area Shopper G 607 532-4333
Ovid *(G-12792)*

Seneca Media Inc C 607 324-1425
Hornell *(G-6302)*

Seneca Media Inc F 585 593-5300
Wellsville *(G-16122)*

Service Advertising Group Inc F 718 361-6161
Long Island City *(G-7588)*

◆ **Shelter Island Reporter Inc** G 631 749-1000
Shelter Island *(G-14802)*

Sing Tao Newspapers NY Ltd F 212 431-9030
Brooklyn *(G-2480)*

Sing Tao Newspapers NY Ltd E 718 821-0123
Brooklyn *(G-2481)*

▲ **Sing Tao Newspapers NY Ltd** E 212 699-3800
New York *(G-11598)*

SM News Plus Incorporated G 212 888-0153
New York *(G-11620)*

Smithtown News Inc E 631 265-2100
Smithtown *(G-14909)*

South Shore Tribune Inc G 516 431-5628
Island Park *(G-6518)*

Southampton Town Newspapers E 631 283-4100
Southampton *(G-14962)*

Southampton Town Newspapers F 631 288-1100
Westhampton Beach *(G-16406)*

Spartacist Publishing Co E 212 732-7860
New York *(G-11659)*

Spartan Publishing Inc F 716 664-7373
Jamestown *(G-6748)*

Sports Pblications Prod NY LLC D 212 366-7700
New York *(G-11675)*

Sports Reporter Inc G 212 737-2750
New York *(G-11677)*

Spring Publishing Corporation G 718 782-0881
Brooklyn *(G-2505)*

Ssrja LLC F 718 725-7020
Jamaica *(G-6678)*

▲ **St Lawrence County Newspapers** D 315 393-1003
Canton *(G-3258)*

Star Community Publishing C 631 843-4050
Melville *(G-8065)*

Star Sports Corp E 516 773-4075
Great Neck *(G-5593)*

Star-Gazette Fund Inc C 607 734-5151
Elmira *(G-4503)*

Steffen Publishing Inc D 315 865-4100
Holland Patent *(G-6225)*

Stratconglobal Inc G 212 989-2355
New York *(G-11718)*

Straus Communications F 845 782-4000
Chester *(G-3485)*

Straus Newspapers Inc E 845 782-4000
Chester *(G-3486)*

Stuart Communications Inc F 845 252-7414
Narrowsburg *(G-8475)*

Sun-Times Media Group Inc E 716 945-1644
Salamanca *(G-14535)*

Syracuse Catholic Press Assn G 315 422-8153
Syracuse *(G-15435)*

Tablet Publishing Company Inc E 718 965-7333
Brooklyn *(G-2553)*

Tegna Inc C 716 849-2222
Buffalo *(G-3089)*

Tenney Media Group D 315 853-5569
Clinton *(G-3589)*

The Earth Times Foundation G 718 297-0488
Brooklyn *(G-2564)*

The Sandhar Corp G 718 523-0819
Jamaica *(G-6684)*

Thestreet Inc D 212 321-5000
New York *(G-11814)*

Thousand Islands Printing Co G 315 482-2581
Alexandria Bay *(G-182)*

Times Beacon Record Newspapers F 631 331-1154
East Setauket *(G-4312)*

Times Review Newspaper Corp E 631 354-8031
Mattituck *(G-7918)*

Tioga County Courier G 607 687-0108
Owego *(G-12804)*

Tompkins Weekly Inc G 607 539-7100
Ithaca *(G-6612)*

Tri-Town News Inc E 607 561-3515
Sidney *(G-14855)*

Tri-Village Publishers Inc D 518 843-1100
Amsterdam *(G-361)*

Tribco LLC E 718 357-7400
Whitestone *(G-16550)*

Tribune Entertainment Co Del E 203 866-2204
New York *(G-11897)*

Tricycle Foundation Inc G 800 873-9871
New York *(G-11898)*

Trilake Three Press Corp G 518 359-2462
Tupper Lake *(G-15654)*

Tryp Times Square ....G 212 246-8800
New York *(G-11908)*

Ubm Inc ....A 212 600-3000
New York *(G-11929)*

Ubm LLC ....F 516 562-5000
New York *(G-11930)*

Ubm LLC ....D 516 562-7800
New Hyde Park *(G-8568)*

Ulster County Press Office ....G 845 687-4480
High Falls *(G-6141)*

Ulster Publishing Co Inc ....E 845 334-8205
Kingston *(G-6926)*

Ulster Publishing Co Inc ....F 845 255-7005
New Paltz *(G-8583)*

Unified Media Inc ....F 917 595-2710
New York *(G-11940)*

Urdu Times ....G 718 297-8700
Jamaica *(G-6688)*

USA Today International Corp ....G 703 854-3400
New York *(G-11980)*

Village Herald ....G 516 569-4403
Lawrence *(G-7111)*

Vnovom Svete ....G 212 302-9480
New York *(G-12050)*

Vpj Publication Inc ....E 718 845-3221
Howard Beach *(G-6333)*

W H White Publications Inc ....G 914 725-2500
Dobbs Ferry *(G-4132)*

W M T Publications Inc ....F 585 244-3329
Rochester *(G-14202)*

Wallkill Lodge No 627 F&Am ....F 845 778-7148
Walden *(G-15899)*

Wallkill Valley Publications ....E 845 561-0170
Newburgh *(G-12251)*

Wappingers Falls Shopper Inc ....E 845 297-3723
Wappingers Falls *(G-15938)*

Wave Publishing Co Inc ....F 718 634-4000
Rockaway Beach *(G-14226)*

Wayuga Community Newspapers ....E 315 754-6229
Red Creek *(G-13456)*

Wayuga Community Newspapers ....G 315 594-2506
Wolcott *(G-16612)*

Webster Ontrio Wlwrth Pnnysver ....F 585 265-3620
Webster *(G-16106)*

Weekly Ajkal ....F 718 565-2100
Jackson Heights *(G-6621)*

Weekly Business News Corp ....G 212 689-5888
New York *(G-12086)*

Weisbeck Publishing Printing ....G 716 937-9226
Alden *(G-178)*

West Seneca Bee Inc ....D 716 632-4700
Williamsville *(G-16593)*

Westbury Times ....D 516 747-8282
Mineola *(G-8252)*

Westfair Communications Inc ....E 914 694-3600
White Plains *(G-16521)*

Westside News Inc ....F 585 352-3411
Spencerport *(G-14983)*

William B Collins Company ....D 518 773-8272
Gloversville *(G-5473)*

William Boyd Printing Co Inc ....C 518 339-5832
Latham *(G-7098)*

William J Kline & Son Inc ....D 518 843-1100
Amsterdam *(G-364)*

Williamsburg Bulletin ....G 718 387-0123
Brooklyn *(G-2650)*

Wolfe Publications Inc ....C 585 394-0770
Canandaigua *(G-3236)*

▲ World Journal LLC ....C 718 746-8889
Whitestone *(G-16553)*

World Journal LLC ....F 718 871-5000
Brooklyn *(G-2658)*

Wp Company LLC ....G 212 445-5050
New York *(G-12142)*

▲ Yated Neeman Inc ....F 845 369-1600
Monsey *(G-8303)*

Yonkers Time Publishing Co ....F 914 965-4000
Yonkers *(G-16811)*

Zenith Color Comm Group Inc ....E 212 989-4400
Long Island City *(G-7648)*

2721 Periodicals: Publishing & Printing

21st Century Fox America Inc ....D 212 447-4600
New York *(G-8674)*

21st Century Fox America Inc ....D 212 852-7000
New York *(G-8673)*

▲ 2600 Enterprises Inc ....F 631 474-2677
Saint James *(G-14509)*

A Guideposts Church Corp ....C 212 251-8100
New York *(G-8695)*

Abp International Inc ....E 212 490-3999
New York *(G-8712)*

Academy of Political Science ....G 212 870-2500
New York *(G-8716)*

Access Intelligence LLC ....A 212 204-4269
New York *(G-8719)*

Adirondack Life Inc ....F 518 946-2191
Jay *(G-6773)*

Adirondack Life Inc ....G 518 946-2191
Jay *(G-6774)*

▲ Advance Magazine Publs Inc ....A 212 286-2860
New York *(G-8747)*

Advance Magazine Publs Inc ....D 212 790-4422
New York *(G-8748)*

Advance Magazine Publs Inc ....D 212 286-2860
New York *(G-8749)*

Advance Magazine Publs Inc ....C 212 450-7000
New York *(G-8750)*

Advance Magazine Publs Inc ....D 212 697-0126
New York *(G-8751)*

▲ Advance Publications Inc ....D 718 981-1234
Staten Island *(G-15040)*

Advanced Research Media Inc ....F 631 751-9696
Setauket *(G-14791)*

Adventure Publishing Group ....E 212 575-4510
New York *(G-8760)*

Aeon America Inc ....G 914 584-0275
Brooklyn *(G-1491)*

▲ Alcoholics Anonymous Grapevine ....F 212 870-3400
New York *(G-8787)*

Alm Media LLC ....B 212 457-9400
New York *(G-8805)*

Alm Media Holdings Inc ....B 212 457-9400
New York *(G-8806)*

▲ Alpha Media Group Inc ....B 212 302-2626
New York *(G-8808)*

America Press Inc ....E 212 581-4640
New York *(G-8822)*

American Graphic Design Awards ....G 212 696-4380
New York *(G-8827)*

▲ American Inst Chem Engineers ....D 646 495-1355
New York *(G-8830)*

American Institute Physics Inc ....C 516 576-2410
Melville *(G-8002)*

American Intl Media LLC ....F 845 359-4225
White Plains *(G-16420)*

American Jewish Committee ....G 212 891-1400
New York *(G-8831)*

American Jewish Congress Inc ....E 212 879-4500
New York *(G-8832)*

American Physical Society ....D 631 591-4025
Ridge *(G-13521)*

American Towman Network Inc ....F 845 986-4546
Warwick *(G-15948)*

Analysts In Media (aim) Inc ....E 212 488-1777
New York *(G-8853)*

Animal Fair Media Inc ....F 212 629-0392
New York *(G-8869)*

Annointed Buty Ministries LLC ....G 646 867-3796
Brooklyn *(G-1537)*

Archaelogy Magazine ....E 718 472-3050
Long Island City *(G-7385)*

Archie Comic Publications Inc ....D 914 381-5155
Pelham *(G-12932)*

Artifex Press LLC ....F 212 414-1482
New York *(G-8920)*

▲ Artnews Ltd ....F 212 398-1690
New York *(G-8925)*

Aspire One Communications LLC ....F 201 281-2998
Cornwall *(G-3830)*

Aspire One Communications Inc ....G 845 534-6110
Cornwall *(G-3831)*

Association For Cmpt McHy Inc ....D 212 869-7440
New York *(G-8938)*

Athlon Spt Communications Inc ....E 212 478-1910
New York *(G-8949)*

Atlantic Monthly Group Inc ....E 202 266-7000
New York *(G-8950)*

Backstage LLC ....E 212 493-4243
Brooklyn *(G-1582)*

▲ Bazaar ....G 212 903-5497
New York *(G-9029)*

Beauty Fashion Inc ....E 212 840-8800
New York *(G-9032)*

Bedford Freeman & Worth ....C 212 576-9400
New York *(G-9034)*

Bedford Communications Inc ....E 212 807-8220
New York *(G-9036)*

Beer Marketers Insights Inc ....G 845 507-0040
Suffern *(G-15186)*

Bellerophon Publications Inc ....E 212 627-9977
New York *(G-9040)*

▲ Berger & Wild LLC ....G 646 415-8459
New York *(G-9050)*

Bernhard Arnold & Company Inc ....G 212 907-1500
New York *(G-9054)*

▲ Bertelsmann Inc ....E 212 782-1000
New York *(G-9055)*

Bertelsmann Pubg Group Inc ....A 212 782-1000
New York *(G-9056)*

▲ Beverage Media Group Inc ....F 212 571-3232
New York *(G-9063)*

Binah Magazines Corp ....E 718 305-5200
Brooklyn *(G-1614)*

Bizbash Media Inc ....D 646 638-3602
New York *(G-9093)*

BJ Magazines Inc ....G 212 367-9705
New York *(G-9094)*

Blackbook Media Corp ....E 212 334-1800
New York *(G-9097)*

Blue Horizon Media Inc ....F 212 661-7878
New York *(G-9108)*

Bnei Aram Soba Inc ....F 718 645-4460
Brooklyn *(G-1625)*

Boardman Simons Publishing ....E 212 620-7200
New York *(G-9115)*

Brownstone Publishers Inc ....E 212 473-8200
New York *(G-9151)*

Buffalo Spree Publishing Inc ....E 716 783-9119
Buffalo *(G-2752)*

Bullett Media LLC ....F 212 242-2123
New York *(G-9157)*

Bust Inc ....G 212 675-1707
Brooklyn *(G-1662)*

Bz Media LLC ....F 631 421-4158
Melville *(G-8005)*

C Q Communications Inc ....E 516 681-2922
Hicksville *(G-6066)*

Cambridge University Press ....D 212 337-5000
New York *(G-9186)*

Canopy Canopy Canopy Inc ....G 347 529-5182
New York *(G-9196)*

Capco Marketing ....F 315 699-1687
Baldwinsville *(G-552)*

Capital Reg Wkly Newsppr Group ....F 518 674-2841
Averill Park *(G-513)*

Carol Group Ltd ....G 212 505-2030
New York *(G-9212)*

▼ Centennial Media LLC ....F 646 527-7320
New York *(G-9240)*

Center For Inquiry Inc ....F 716 636-4869
Amherst *(G-221)*

Cfo Publishing LLC ....E 212 459-3004
New York *(G-9253)*

Choice Magazine Listening Inc ....G 516 883-8280
Port Washington *(G-13249)*

City and State Ny LLC ....E 212 268-0442
New York *(G-9309)*

City Real Estate Book Inc ....G 516 593-2949
Valley Stream *(G-15776)*

Civil Svc Rtred Employees Assn ....F 718 937-0290
Long Island City *(G-7409)*

Clarion Publications Inc ....F 585 243-3530
Geneseo *(G-5313)*

▲ Clp Pb LLC ....E 212 340-8100
New York *(G-9335)*

▲ CMX Media LLC ....E 917 793-5831
New York *(G-9338)*

CNY Business Review Inc ....F 315 472-3104
Syracuse *(G-15281)*

Coda Media Inc ....G 917 478-2565
New York *(G-9345)*

College Calendar Company ....F 315 768-8242
Whitesboro *(G-16526)*

Commentary Inc ....F 212 891-1400
New York *(G-9364)*

Commonweal Foundation Inc ....F 212 662-4200
New York *(G-9366)*

Complex Media Inc ....E 917 793-5831
New York *(G-9371)*

Conde Nast Entertainment LLC ....A 212 286-2860
New York *(G-9375)*

Conference Board Inc ....C 212 759-0900
New York *(G-9377)*

Congress For Jewish Culture ....G 212 505-8040
New York *(G-9379)*

Consumer Reports Inc ....B 914 378-2000
Yonkers *(G-16746)*

Continuity Publishing Inc ....F 212 869-4170
New York *(G-9388)*

SIC

27 PRINTING, PUBLISHING, AND ALLIED INDUSTRIES

Convenience Store News .... G 214 217-7800
  New York *(G-9391)*
Cornell University .... E 607 254-2473
  Ithaca *(G-6573)*
Cosmopolitan Magazine .... G 212 649-2000
  New York *(G-9403)*
Crain Communications Inc .... C 212 210-0100
  New York *(G-9418)*
Crains New York Business .... E 212 210-0250
  New York *(G-9419)*
Creative Magazine Inc .... G 516 378-0800
  Merrick *(G-8095)*
Credit Union Journal Inc .... G 212 803-8200
  New York *(G-9423)*
▲ Daily Beast Company LLC .... E 212 445-4600
  New York *(G-9454)*
Data Key Communication LLC .... F 315 445-2347
  Fayetteville *(G-4927)*
Davler Media Group LLC .... G 212 315-0800
  New York *(G-9490)*
Delaware County Times Inc .... G 607 746-2176
  Delhi *(G-4072)*
Demos Medical Publishing LLC .... F 516 889-1791
  New York *(G-9499)*
Dennis Publishing Inc .... D 646 717-9500
  New York *(G-9502)*
Denton Publications Inc .... E 518 561-9680
  Plattsburgh *(G-13119)*
Direct Mktg Edctl Fndation Inc .... G 212 790-1512
  New York *(G-9531)*
Discover Media LLC .... E 212 624-4800
  New York *(G-9535)*
Dissent Magazine .... F 212 316-3120
  New York *(G-9538)*
Distinction Magazine Inc .... E 631 843-3522
  Melville *(G-8016)*
Dj Publishing Inc .... E 516 767-2500
  Port Washington *(G-13253)*
Doctorow Communications Inc .... F 845 708-5166
  New City *(G-8491)*
Dotto Wagner .... G 315 342-8020
  Oswego *(G-12776)*
▲ Dow Jones & Company Inc .... B 609 627-2999
  New York *(G-9563)*
Dow Jones & Company Inc .... E 212 597-5983
  New York *(G-9564)*
Dow Jones Aer Company Inc .... A 212 416-2000
  New York *(G-9565)*
Downtown Media Group LLC .... F 646 723-4510
  New York *(G-9568)*
E W Williams Publications .... G 212 661-1516
  New York *(G-9598)*
Earl G Graves Pubg Co Inc .... D 212 242-8000
  New York *(G-9605)*
Ebner Publishing International .... G 646 742-0740
  New York *(G-9617)*
Economist Intelligence Unit NA .... D 212 554-0600
  New York *(G-9624)*
Eidosmedia Inc .... E 646 795-2100
  New York *(G-9636)*
Elite Traveler LLC .... F 646 430-7900
  New York *(G-9652)*
Elmont North Little League .... G 516 775-8210
  Elmont *(G-4518)*
Envy Publishing Group Inc .... G 212 253-9874
  New York *(G-9691)*
Equal Opprtnity Pblcations Inc .... F 631 421-9421
  Melville *(G-8019)*
▲ Essence Communications Inc ..... C 212 522-1212
  Brooklyn *(G-1851)*
Essence Ventures LLC .... C 212 522-1212
  New York *(G-9708)*
Essential Publications US LLC .... G 646 707-0898
  New York *(G-9709)*
Excelsior Publications .... G 607 746-7600
  Delhi *(G-4073)*
Executive Business Media Inc .... E 516 334-3030
  Westbury *(G-16329)*
▲ Faces Magazine Inc .... F 201 843-4004
  Poughkeepsie *(G-13337)*
Fader Inc .... F 212 741-7100
  New York *(G-9771)*
Fahy-Williams Publishing Inc .... F 315 781-6820
  Geneva *(G-5323)*
▲ Fairchild Publications Inc .... A 212 630-4000
  New York *(G-9773)*
Fairchild Publishing LLC .... G 212 286-3897
  New York *(G-9774)*
Family Publishing Group Inc .... E 914 381-7474
  Mamaroneck *(G-7744)*

Fashion Calendar International .... G 212 289-0420
  New York *(G-9787)*
Forum Publishing Co .... G 631 754-5000
  Centerport *(G-3348)*
Foundtion For A Mndful Soc Inc ...... G 902 431-8062
  New York *(G-9827)*
Four M Studios .... C 212 557-6600
  New York *(G-9828)*
Four M Studios .... D 212 557-6600
  New York *(G-9829)*
Four M Studios .... F 212 499-2000
  New York *(G-9830)*
Four M Studios .... D 515 284-2157
  New York *(G-9831)*
Francis Emory Fitch Inc .... E 212 619-3800
  New York *(G-9838)*
Fridge Magazine Inc .... G 212 997-7673
  New York *(G-9850)*
Frontiers Unlimited Inc .... G 631 283-4663
  Southampton *(G-14953)*
Frost Publications Inc .... G 845 726-3232
  Westtown *(G-16413)*
▲ Frozen Food Digest Inc .... G 212 557-8600
  New York *(G-9852)*
Fun Media Inc .... G 646 472-0135
  New York *(G-9861)*
Genomeweb LLC .... F 212 651-5636
  New York *(G-9906)*
Getting The Word Out Inc .... G 518 891-9352
  Saranac Lake *(G-14562)*
Glamour Magazine .... G 212 286-2860
  New York *(G-9928)*
Global Entity Media Inc .... G 631 580-7772
  Ronkonkoma *(G-14346)*
Global Finance Magazine .... G 212 524-3223
  New York *(G-9938)*
Global Finance Media Inc .... F 212 447-7900
  New York *(G-9939)*
▲ Golfing Magazine .... G 516 822-5446
  Hicksville *(G-6093)*
Government Data Publication .... E 347 789-8719
  Brooklyn *(G-1945)*
Grants Financial Publishing .... F 212 809-7994
  New York *(G-9975)*
▲ Graphis Inc .... F 212 532-9387
  New York *(G-9978)*
Green Apple Courage Inc .... G 716 614-4673
  Buffalo *(G-2858)*
Gruner + Jahr Prtg & Pubg Co .... C 212 463-1000
  New York *(G-10000)*
◆ Gruner + Jahr USA Group Inc ..... B 866 323-9336
  New York *(G-10001)*
Guernica .... F 914 414-7318
  Brooklyn *(G-1954)*
Guilford Publications Inc .... D 212 431-9800
  New York *(G-10008)*
H F W Communications Inc .... F 315 703-7979
  East Syracuse *(G-4344)*
H W Wilson Company Inc .... B 718 588-8635
  Bronx *(G-1287)*
Halcyon Business Publications .... F 800 735-2732
  Westbury *(G-16338)*
Hamptons Magazine .... E 631 283-7125
  Southampton *(G-14955)*
Hamptons Media LLC .... G 631 283-6900
  Southampton *(G-14956)*
Harpers Magazine Foundation .... E 212 420-5720
  New York *(G-10040)*
Hart Energy Publishing Lllp .... G 212 621-4621
  New York *(G-10045)*
Hatherleigh Company Ltd .... G 607 538-1092
  Hobart *(G-6163)*
Haymarket Group Ltd .... F 212 239-0855
  New York *(G-10051)*
▲ Haymarket Media Inc .... C 646 638-6000
  New York *(G-10052)*
Healthy Way of Life Magazine .... G 718 616-1681
  Brooklyn *(G-1970)*
Hearst Bus Communications Inc .... G 212 649-2000
  New York *(G-10055)*
Hearst Business Media .... D 516 227-1300
  Uniondale *(G-15669)*
Hearst Business Media Corp .... G 631 650-6151
  Great River *(G-5601)*
Hearst Business Media Corp .... F 631 650-4441
  New York *(G-10056)*
Hearst Business Publishing Inc ...... F 212 969-7500
  New York *(G-10057)*
Hearst Communications Inc .... C 212 649-2000
  New York *(G-10060)*

▲ Hearst Corporation .... A 212 649-2000
  New York *(G-10061)*
Hearst Corporation .... E 212 649-3100
  New York *(G-10062)*
Hearst Corporation .... E 212 903-5366
  New York *(G-10063)*
Hearst Corporation .... B 212 767-5800
  New York *(G-10064)*
Hearst Corporation .... D 516 382-4580
  New York *(G-10065)*
Hearst Corporation .... A 518 454-5694
  Albany *(G-82)*
Hearst Corporation .... D 212 649-4271
  New York *(G-10066)*
Hearst Corporation .... D 212 204-4300
  New York *(G-10067)*
Hearst Corporation .... D 212 903-5000
  New York *(G-10068)*
Hearst Corporation .... D 212 649-3204
  New York *(G-10069)*
Hearst Corporation .... D 212 649-2275
  New York *(G-10070)*
▲ Hearst Holdings Inc .... F 212 649-2000
  New York *(G-10072)*
Herman Hall Communications .... F 718 941-1879
  Brooklyn *(G-1975)*
Highline Media LLC .... C 859 692-2100
  New York *(G-10097)*
▲ Historic TW Inc .... G 212 484-8000
  New York *(G-10106)*
Homesell Inc .... F 718 514-0346
  Staten Island *(G-15086)*
Human Life Foundation Inc .... G 212 685-5210
  New York *(G-10148)*
▲ Humana Press Inc .... E 212 460-1500
  New York *(G-10149)*
I On Youth .... G 716 832-6509
  Buffalo *(G-2878)*
Icarus Enterprises Inc .... G 917 969-4461
  New York *(G-10167)*
Icd Publications Inc .... E 631 246-9300
  Islandia *(G-6530)*
Imek Media LLC .... E 212 422-9000
  New York *(G-10183)*
Impact Journals LLC .... G 800 922-0957
  Orchard Park *(G-12718)*
Impressions Inc .... E 212 594-5954
  New York *(G-10188)*
Index Magazine .... G 212 243-1428
  New York *(G-10197)*
Informa Business Media Inc .... C 212 204-4200
  New York *(G-10209)*
▲ Informa Media Inc .... B 212 204-4200
  New York *(G-10210)*
Informa Media Inc .... G 212 204-4200
  New York *(G-10211)*
Ink Publishing Corporation .... G 347 294-1220
  Brooklyn *(G-2003)*
Institute of Electrical and El .... E 212 705-8900
  New York *(G-10228)*
Intellignc The Ftr Cmptng Nwsl .... F 212 222-1123
  New York *(G-10232)*
Intellitravel Media Inc .... G 646 695-6700
  New York *(G-10233)*
Intercultural Alliance Artists .... G 917 406-1202
  Flushing *(G-5011)*
Interhellenic Publishing Inc .... G 212 967-5016
  New York *(G-10241)*
International Center For Postg .... G 607 257-5860
  Ithaca *(G-6585)*
International Data Group Inc .... E 212 331-7883
  New York *(G-10244)*
Interntnl Publcatns Media Grup ...... G 917 604-9602
  New York *(G-10252)*
Interview New York .... G 857 928-4120
  New York *(G-10254)*
Irish America Inc .... E 212 725-2993
  New York *(G-10270)*
Japan America Learning Ctr Inc ..... F 914 723-7600
  Scarsdale *(G-14639)*
Jerome Levy Forecasting Center ..... G 914 244-8617
  Mount Kisco *(G-8345)*
▲ Jobson Medical Information LLC . C 212 274-7000
  New York *(G-10347)*
JSD Communications Inc .... F 914 588-1841
  Bedford *(G-769)*
Kbs Communications LLC .... F 212 765-7124
  New York *(G-10425)*
Kids Discover LLC .... G 212 677-4457
  New York *(G-10439)*

SIC SECTION
27 PRINTING, PUBLISHING, AND ALLIED INDUSTRIES

▼ **L F International Inc**........D...... 212 756-5000
New York *(G-10495)*
L I F Publishing Corp........D...... 631 345-5200
Shirley *(G-14837)*
Lagardere North America Inc........E...... 212 477-7373
New York *(G-10508)*
▲ **Latina Media Ventures LLC**........E...... 212 642-0200
New York *(G-10522)*
Laurtom Inc........E...... 914 273-2233
Mount Kisco *(G-8349)*
Leadership Directories Inc........D...... 212 627-4140
New York *(G-10530)*
Livid Magazine........F...... 929 340-7123
Brooklyn *(G-2130)*
Locations Magazine........G...... 212 288-4745
New York *(G-10589)*
▲ **Lockwood Trade Journal Co Inc**........E...... 212 391-2060
Long Island City *(G-7503)*
Long Island Catholic Newspaper........E...... 516 594-1212
Rockville Centre *(G-14235)*
Ltb Media (usa) Inc........D...... 212 447-9555
New York *(G-10624)*
Lucky Magazine........F...... 212 286-6220
New York *(G-10625)*
Luminary Publishing Inc........F...... 845 334-8600
Kingston *(G-6909)*
Luria Communications Inc........G...... 631 329-4922
East Hampton *(G-4240)*
M Shanken Communications Inc........C...... 212 684-4224
New York *(G-10644)*
▲ **Macfadden Cmmnctions Group LLC**........C...... 212 979-4800
New York *(G-10647)*
Macmillan Holdings LLC........F...... 212 576-9428
New York *(G-10650)*
Mag Inc........E...... 607 257-6970
Ithaca *(G-6593)*
Magazine I Spectrum E........E...... 212 419-7555
New York *(G-10661)*
▲ **Magnificat Inc**........F...... 914 502-1820
Yonkers *(G-16781)*
Manhattan Media LLC........F...... 212 268-8600
New York *(G-10686)*
Mann Publications Inc........E...... 212 840-6266
New York *(G-10690)*
Mansueto Ventures LLC........C...... 212 389-5300
New York *(G-10696)*
▲ **Marie Claire USA**........D...... 212 841-8493
New York *(G-10702)*
Maritime Activity Reports........E...... 212 477-6700
New York *(G-10704)*
▲ **Mark Levine**........F...... 212 677-4457
New York *(G-10706)*
▲ **Martha Stewart Living**........C...... 212 827-8000
New York *(G-10717)*
▲ **Martha Stewart Living Omni LLC**........B...... 212 827-8000
New York *(G-10718)*
Martinelli Holdings LLC........E...... 302 504-1361
Harrison *(G-5730)*
▲ **Marvel Entertainment LLC**........C...... 212 576-4000
New York *(G-10719)*
Mary Ann Liebert Inc........D...... 914 740-2100
New Rochelle *(G-8620)*
Mass Appeal Magazine........G...... 718 858-0979
Brooklyn *(G-2177)*
Mathisen Ventures Inc........G...... 212 986-1025
New York *(G-10728)*
McCarthy LLC........F...... 646 862-5354
New York *(G-10740)*
McMahon Group LLC........D...... 212 957-5300
New York *(G-10745)*
Med Reviews LLC........E...... 212 239-5860
New York *(G-10750)*
Media Press Corp........E...... 212 791-6347
New York *(G-10752)*
Medikidz Usa Inc........G...... 646 895-9319
New York *(G-10759)*
Medizine Operating LLC........D...... 212 695-2223
New York *(G-10761)*
Mergent Inc........B...... 212 413-7700
New York *(G-10773)*
Metrosource Publishing Inc........F...... 212 691-5127
New York *(G-10786)*
Miami Media LLC........F...... 212 268-8600
New York *(G-10789)*
Mishpacha Magazine Inc........G...... 718 686-9339
Brooklyn *(G-2211)*
Modern Farmer Media Inc........F...... 518 828-7447
Hudson *(G-6365)*
Music & Sound Retailer Inc........E...... 516 767-2500
Port Washington *(G-13289)*
Nation Company LLC........E...... 212 209-5400
New York *(G-10878)*
Nation Magazine........E...... 212 209-5400
New York *(G-10879)*
National Ggraphic Partners LLC........G...... 212 656-0726
New York *(G-10883)*
National Review Inc........E...... 212 679-7330
New York *(G-10885)*
▼ **Nature America Inc**........B...... 212 726-9200
New York *(G-10893)*
Nautilusthink Inc........G...... 646 239-6858
New York *(G-10897)*
NCM Publishers Inc........G...... 212 691-9100
New York *(G-10902)*
Nervecom Inc........F...... 212 625-9914
New York *(G-10906)*
New Art Publications Inc........F...... 718 636-9100
Brooklyn *(G-2256)*
New Hope Media LLC........G...... 646 366-0830
New York *(G-10926)*
New York Fshion Week Guide LLC........F...... 646 757-9119
New York *(G-10939)*
New York Media LLC........C...... 212 508-0700
New York *(G-10940)*
Next Step Publishing Inc........F...... 585 742-1260
Victor *(G-15859)*
Niche Media Holdings LLC........E...... 702 990-2500
New York *(G-10961)*
Nickelodeon Magazines Inc........G...... 212 541-1949
New York *(G-10964)*
Njf Publishing Corp........G...... 631 345-5200
Shirley *(G-14842)*
▲ **Northeast Group**........D...... 518 563-8214
Plattsburgh *(G-13139)*
Northeast Prtg & Dist Co Inc........G...... 514 577-3545
Plattsburgh *(G-13140)*
Northside Media Group LLC........F...... 917 318-6513
Brooklyn *(G-2273)*
Northside Media Group LLC........E...... 917 318-6513
Brooklyn *(G-2274)*
Nova Science Publishers Inc........F...... 631 231-7269
Hauppauge *(G-5902)*
Nsgv Inc........E...... 212 367-3167
New York *(G-11003)*
Nsgv Inc........E...... 212 367-3100
New York *(G-11004)*
Nyemac Inc........G...... 631 668-1303
Montauk *(G-8307)*
Nylon LLc........E...... 212 226-6454
New York *(G-11015)*
Nylon Media Inc........F...... 212 226-6454
New York *(G-11016)*
Nyrev Inc........E...... 212 757-8070
New York *(G-11019)*
Odyssey Mag Pubg Group Inc........G...... 212 545-4800
New York *(G-11033)*
Optionline LLC........E...... 516 218-3225
Garden City *(G-5273)*
Pageant Media US Limited........E...... 646 891-2110
New York *(G-11093)*
Paper Publishing Company Inc........E...... 212 226-4405
New York *(G-11103)*
Parade Publications Inc........E...... 212 450-7000
New York *(G-11107)*
Parents Guide Network Corp........E...... 212 213-8840
New York *(G-11110)*
Paris Review Foundation Inc........G...... 212 343-1333
New York *(G-11113)*
Pati Inc........F...... 718 244-6788
Jamaica *(G-6667)*
Pearson Education Inc........F...... 201 236-7000
West Nyack *(G-16278)*
▲ **Penhouse Media Group Inc**........C...... 212 702-6000
New York *(G-11149)*
Pensions & Investments........E...... 212 210-0763
New York *(G-11150)*
Periodical Services Co Inc........F...... 518 822-9300
Hudson *(G-6367)*
Photo Industry Inc........F...... 516 364-0016
Woodbury *(G-16628)*
Playbill Incorporated........C...... 212 557-5757
New York *(G-11207)*
Pointwise Information Service........F...... 315 457-4111
Liverpool *(G-7255)*
Preparatory Magazine Group........D...... 718 761-4800
Staten Island *(G-15119)*
Prescribing Reference Inc........D...... 646 638-6000
New York *(G-11233)*
Professnal Spt Pblications Inc........D...... 212 697-1460
New York *(G-11256)*
Professnal Spt Pblications Inc........D...... 516 327-9500
Elmont *(G-4523)*
Psychonomic Society Inc........E...... 512 381-1494
New York *(G-11270)*
Public Relations Soc Amer Inc........E...... 212 460-1400
New York *(G-11273)*
Q Communications Inc........G...... 212 594-6520
New York *(G-11288)*
Quest Media Llc........F...... 646 840-3404
New York *(G-11301)*
Ragozin Data........E...... 212 674-3123
Long Island City *(G-7570)*
Raharney Capital LLC........G...... 212 220-9084
Brooklyn *(G-2379)*
Ralph Martinelli........E...... 914 345-3055
Elmsford *(G-4560)*
Ramholtz Publishing Inc........D...... 718 761-4800
Staten Island *(G-15124)*
Rda Holding Co........E...... 914 238-1000
New York *(G-11336)*
Readers Digest Assn Incthe........F...... 414 423-0100
New York *(G-11338)*
Readers Digest Sls & Svcs Inc........C...... 914 238-1000
Pleasantville *(G-13177)*
Real Est Book of Long Island........F...... 516 364-5000
Syosset *(G-15230)*
Real Estate Media Inc........E...... 212 929-6976
New York *(G-11339)*
Redbook Magazine........F...... 212 649-3331
New York *(G-11342)*
◆ **Relx Inc**........E...... 212 309-8100
New York *(G-11355)*
Relx Inc........E...... 212 463-6644
New York *(G-11356)*
Relx Inc........B...... 212 633-3900
New York *(G-11357)*
Rfp LLC........E...... 212 838-7733
New York *(G-11381)*
Risk Society Management Pubg........E...... 212 286-9364
New York *(G-11396)*
Rnd Enterprises Inc........G...... 212 627-0165
New York *(G-11403)*
Rodale Inc........B...... 212 697-2040
New York *(G-11417)*
Rolling Stone Magazine........G...... 212 484-1616
New York *(G-11425)*
Romantic Times Inc........F...... 718 237-1097
Brooklyn *(G-2412)*
Ross Communications Associates........F...... 631 393-5089
Melville *(G-8062)*
Rough Draft Publishing LLC........F...... 212 741-4773
New York *(G-11436)*
Rsl Media LLC........G...... 212 307-6760
New York *(G-11443)*
Ruby Newco LLC........G...... 212 852-7000
New York *(G-11445)*
Rye Record........G...... 914 713-3213
Rye *(G-14488)*
Sandow Media LLC........F...... 646 805-0200
New York *(G-11481)*
Saveur Magazine........E...... 212 219-7400
New York *(G-11493)*
▲ **Scholastic Corporation**........G...... 212 343-6100
New York *(G-11513)*
◆ **Scholastic Inc**........A...... 800 724-6527
New York *(G-11514)*
▲ **Securities Data Publishing Inc**........G...... 212 631-1411
New York *(G-11530)*
Security Letter........G...... 212 348-1553
New York *(G-11531)*
Shoreline Publishing Inc........G...... 914 738-7869
Pelham *(G-12938)*
Shugar Publishing........G...... 631 288-4404
Westhampton Beach *(G-16405)*
Simmons-Boardman Pubg Corp........E...... 212 620-7200
New York *(G-11594)*
Sky Art Media Inc........G...... 917 355-9022
New York *(G-11612)*
Small Business Advisors Inc........F...... 516 374-1387
Atlantic Beach *(G-457)*
Smart & Strong LLC........E...... 212 938-2051
New York *(G-11621)*
Smooth Magazine........F...... 212 925-1150
New York *(G-11629)*
Society For The Study........G...... 212 822-8806
New York *(G-11634)*
Sound Communications Inc........E...... 516 767-2500
Port Washington *(G-13309)*
▲ **Source Media LLC**........C...... 212 803-8200
New York *(G-11653)*

Employee Codes: A=Over 500 employees, B=251-500
C=101-250, D=51-100, E=20-50, F=10-19, G=5-9
2019 Harris
New York Manufacturers Directory
695

27 PRINTING, PUBLISHING, AND ALLIED INDUSTRIES SIC SECTION

Spin Magazine Media	E	212 231-7400	New York *(G-11670)*
▲ Sports Illustrated For Kids	E	212 522-1212	New York *(G-11674)*
Spotlight Publications LLC	G	914 345-9473	Elmsford *(G-4571)*
Springer Adis Us LLC	F	212 460-1500	New York *(G-11681)*
Springer Healthcare LLC	E	212 460-1500	New York *(G-11683)*
Springer Publishing Co LLC	E	212 431-4370	New York *(G-11684)*
◆ Springer Scnce + Bus Media LLC	D	212 460-1500	New York *(G-11685)*
Standard Analytics Io Inc	G	917 882-5422	New York *(G-11691)*
Staten Island Parent Magazine	G	718 761-4800	Staten Island *(G-15138)*
Steffen Publishing Inc	D	315 865-4100	Holland Patent *(G-6225)*
Strathmore Directories Ltd	E	516 997-2525	Westbury *(G-16374)*
Stuff Magazine	G	212 302-2626	New York *(G-11729)*
Suburban Publishing Inc	F	845 463-0542	Fishkill *(G-4952)*
Suburban Publishing Inc	G	914 345-0601	Elmsford *(G-4572)*
Suffolk Community Council Inc	G	631 434-9277	Deer Park *(G-4049)*
Summit Professional Networks	D	212 557-7480	New York *(G-11740)*
Surface Magazine	E	646 805-0200	New York *(G-11751)*
Sussex Publishers LLC	E	212 260-7210	New York *(G-11752)*
Swaps Monitor Publications Inc	F	212 742-8550	New York *(G-11754)*
Swift Fulfillment Services	G	516 593-1198	Lynbrook *(G-7675)*
T V Trade Media Inc	F	212 288-3933	New York *(G-11772)*
Testa Communications Inc	E	516 767-2500	Port Washington *(G-13311)*
The PRS Group Inc	F	315 431-0511	East Syracuse *(G-4373)*
Thestreet Inc	D	212 321-5000	New York *(G-11814)*
Thomas Publishing Company LLC	G	212 695-0500	New York *(G-11820)*
Thomas Publishing Company LLC	G	212 695-0500	New York *(G-11821)*
Thomas Publishing Company LLC	B	212 695-0500	New York *(G-11818)*
Time Inc	E	212 522-1212	New York *(G-11837)*
◆ Time Inc	A	212 522-1212	New York *(G-11838)*
Time Inc	E	212 522-0361	New York *(G-11839)*
▲ Time Inc Affluent Media Group	B	212 382-5600	New York *(G-11840)*
Time Inc Affluent Media Group	G	212 382-5600	New York *(G-11841)*
Time Out America LLC	C	646 432-3000	New York *(G-11842)*
▲ Time Out New York Partners LP	D	646 432-3000	New York *(G-11843)*
Time Warner Companies Inc	D	212 484-8000	New York *(G-11845)*
TMC Usa LLC	G	518 587-8920	Saratoga Springs *(G-14600)*
Towse Publishing Co	F	914 235-3095	New Rochelle *(G-8629)*
Trader Interntnal Publications	G	914 631-6856	Sleepy Hollow *(G-14887)*
Trans-High Corporation	E	212 387-0500	New York *(G-11886)*
▲ Trend Pot Inc	E	212 431-9970	New York *(G-11890)*
◆ Trusted Media Brands Inc	A	914 238-1000	New York *(G-11907)*
Trusted Media Brands Inc	F	914 244-5244	White Plains *(G-16513)*
TV Guide Magazine LLC	G	800 866-1400	New York *(G-11915)*
▲ TV Guide Magazine Group Inc	D	212 852-7500	New York *(G-11916)*
▲ U S Japan Publication NY Inc	G	212 252-8833	New York *(G-11926)*
Ubm Inc	A	212 600-3000	New York *(G-11929)*
Ubm LLC	D	516 562-7800	New Hyde Park *(G-8568)*
Ubm LLC	F	516 562-5000	New York *(G-11930)*
Ulster Publishing Co Inc	E	845 334-8205	Kingston *(G-6926)*
Universal Cmmncations of Miami	C	212 986-5100	New York *(G-11958)*
Untitled Media	E	212 780-0960	New York *(G-11964)*
Uptown Media Group LLC	E	212 360-5073	New York *(G-11967)*
Urbandaddy Inc	F	212 929-7905	New York *(G-11971)*
US China Magazine	E	212 663-4333	New York *(G-11973)*
US Frontline News Inc	E	212 922-9090	New York *(G-11976)*
▲ US News & World Report Inc	C	212 716-6800	New York *(G-11978)*
US Weekly LLC	D	212 484-1616	New York *(G-11979)*
Valassis Communications Inc	G	585 627-4138	Rochester *(G-14197)*
Valiant Entertainment LLC	E	212 972-0361	New York *(G-11986)*
Value Line Inc	D	212 907-1500	New York *(G-11988)*
Value Line Publishing LLC	C	201 842-8054	New York *(G-11989)*
◆ Vanity Fair	F	212 286-6052	New York *(G-11991)*
Vending Times Inc	F	516 442-1850	Rockville Centre *(G-14244)*
Veranda Publications Inc	G	212 903-5206	New York *(G-12008)*
Vibe Media Group LLC	D	212 448-7300	New York *(G-12026)*
Vickers Stock Research Corp	E	212 425-7500	New York *(G-12027)*
▲ Visionaire Publishing LLC	E	646 434-6091	New York *(G-12043)*
Wall Street Reporter Magazine	D	212 363-2600	New York *(G-12067)*
Wallkill Valley Publications	E	845 561-0170	Newburgh *(G-12251)*
Watch Journal LLC	G	212 229-1500	New York *(G-12077)*
Weider Publications LLC	C	212 545-4800	New York *(G-12087)*
Welcome Magazine Inc	F	716 839-3121	Amherst *(G-261)*
▲ Wenner Media LLC	C	212 484-1616	New York *(G-12094)*
▲ Westchester Law Journal Inc	G	914 948-0715	White Plains *(G-16518)*
Western New York Family Mag	G	716 836-3486	Buffalo *(G-3129)*
Westfair Communications Inc	E	914 694-3600	White Plains *(G-16521)*
Wine & Spirits Magazine Inc	G	212 695-4660	New York *(G-12118)*
Winsight LLC	G	646 708-7309	New York *(G-12123)*
Womens E News Inc	G	212 244-1720	New York *(G-12130)*
Working Mother Media Inc	D	212 351-6400	New York *(G-12134)*
World Business Media LLC	F	212 344-0759	Massapequa Park *(G-7896)*
World Guide Publishing	E	800 331-7840	New York *(G-12137)*
Wsn Inc	G	212 924-7620	New York *(G-12145)*
Yale Robbins Inc	D	212 683-5700	New York *(G-12158)*
▲ Ziff Davis Publishing LLC	D	212 503-3500	New York *(G-12177)*

2731 Books: Publishing & Printing

450 Ridge St Inc	G	716 754-2789	Lewiston *(G-7138)*
A Lesley Dummett	G	646 541-1168	Saint Albans *(G-14506)*
▲ Abbeville Press Inc	E	212 366-5585	New York *(G-8706)*
Adir Publishing Co	F	718 633-9437	Brooklyn *(G-1483)*
▲ Advance Publications Inc	D	718 981-1234	Staten Island *(G-15040)*
Ai Entertainment Holdings LLC	F	212 247-6400	New York *(G-8774)*
Aip Publishing LLC	C	516 576-2200	Melville *(G-7999)*
▲ Alba House Publishers	E	718 698-2759	Staten Island *(G-15041)*
Alfred Publishing Co Inc	D	315 736-1572	Oriskany *(G-12750)*
▲ Allworth Communications Inc	F	212 777-8395	New York *(G-8803)*
Alm Media LLC	B	212 457-9400	New York *(G-8805)*
Alm Media Holdings Inc	B	212 457-9400	New York *(G-8806)*
Amereon Ltd	G	631 298-5100	Mattituck *(G-7913)*
▲ American Inst Chem Engineers	D	646 495-1355	New York *(G-8830)*
American Institute Physics Inc	C	516 576-2410	Melville *(G-8002)*
Amherst Media Inc	G	716 874-4450	Buffalo *(G-2698)*
▼ Amsco School Publications Inc	D	212 886-6500	New York *(G-8849)*
Annuals Publishing Co Inc	G	212 505-0950	New York *(G-8874)*
▲ Anthroposophic Press Inc	G	518 851-2054	Clifton Park *(G-3563)*
Apollo Investment Fund VII LP	G	212 515-3200	New York *(G-8886)*
▲ Assouline Publishing Inc	F	212 989-6769	New York *(G-8939)*
▲ Ateres Publishing & Bk Bindery	F	718 935-9355	Brooklyn *(G-1569)*
Atlas & Company LLC	G	212 234-3100	New York *(G-8953)*
◆ Barrons Educational Series Inc	C	631 434-3311	Hauppauge *(G-5778)*
Beauty Fashion Inc	E	212 840-8800	New York *(G-9032)*
Bedford Freeman & Worth	D	212 375-7000	New York *(G-9035)*
Bedford Freeman & Worth	C	212 576-9400	New York *(G-9034)*
Bedrock Communications	G	212 532-4150	New York *(G-9037)*
▲ Benchmark Education Co LLC	D	914 637-7200	New Rochelle *(G-8592)*
▲ Bertelsmann Inc	E	212 782-1000	New York *(G-9055)*
Bertelsmann Pubg Group Inc	A	212 782-1000	New York *(G-9056)*
▲ Bicker Inc	F	212 688-0085	New York *(G-9072)*
▲ Bloomsbury Publishing Inc	D	212 419-5300	New York *(G-9104)*
Bmg Rights Management (us) LLC	E	212 561-3000	New York *(G-9113)*
Boardman Simons Publishing	E	212 620-7200	New York *(G-9115)*
▲ Bobley-Harmann Corporation	G	516 433-3800	Ronkonkoma *(G-14320)*
Bonnier Publishing Usa Inc	E	212 321-0237	New York *(G-9120)*
Booklinks Publishing Svcs LLC	G	718 852-2116	Brooklyn *(G-1628)*
Booklyn Artists Alliance Inc	G	718 383-9621	Brooklyn *(G-1629)*
Boydell & Brewer Inc	F	585 275-0419	Rochester *(G-13674)*
▲ Bright Kids Nyc Inc	E	917 539-4575	New York *(G-9140)*
British American Publishing	D	518 786-6000	Latham *(G-7065)*
Brown Publishing Network Inc	G	212 682-3330	New York *(G-9150)*
▼ Burns Archive Photographic Dis	G	212 889-1938	New York *(G-9160)*
Byliner Inc	E	415 680-3608	New York *(G-9168)*
Callaway Arts & Entrmt Inc	F	646 465-4667	New York *(G-9181)*
Cambridge University Press	D	212 337-5000	New York *(G-9186)*
Campus Course Paks Inc	G	516 877-3967	Garden City *(G-5254)*
Canopy Books LLC	G	516 354-4888	Massapequa *(G-7879)*

27 PRINTING, PUBLISHING, AND ALLIED INDUSTRIES

Castle Connolly Medical Ltd .... E 212 367-8400
New York (G-9224)
CB Publishing LLC .... G 516 354-4888
Floral Park (G-4959)
CCC Publications Inc .... F 718 306-1008
Brooklyn (G-1684)
▲ Central Cnfrnce of Amrcn Rbbis ..... F 212 972-3636
New York (G-9243)
Chain Store Age Magazine .... G 212 756-5000
New York (G-9255)
Changdu Technology (usa) Co .... F 917 340-1976
North Bellmore (G-12374)
▼ Church Publishing Incorporated ...... G 212 592-1800
New York (G-9296)
Cinderella Press Ltd .... G 212 431-3130
New York (G-9298)
▲ Clarkson N Potter Inc .... E 212 782-9000
New York (G-9317)
Codesters Inc .... E 646 232-1025
New York (G-9346)
▲ Columbia University Press .... E 212 459-0600
New York (G-9358)
Columbia University Press .... E 212 459-0600
New York (G-9359)
Columbia University Press .... E 212 459-0600
New York (G-9360)
Confrtrnity of Prescious Blood .... G 718 436-1120
Brooklyn (G-1711)
Congress For Jewish Culture .... E 212 505-8040
New York (G-9379)
Continuum Intl Pubg Group Inc .... F 646 649-4215
New York (G-9390)
Cornell University .... D 607 277-2338
Ithaca (G-6572)
Crabtree Publishing Inc .... E 212 496-5040
New York (G-9415)
Curriculum Associates LLC .... E 978 313-1355
Brooklyn (G-1740)
D C I Technical Inc .... F 516 355-0464
Franklin Square (G-5116)
Daheshist Publishing Co Ltd .... G 212 581-8360
New York (G-9453)
Definition Press Inc .... F 212 777-4490
New York (G-9495)
Delaney Books Inc .... F 516 921-8888
Syosset (G-15215)
Demos Medical Publishing LLC .... F 516 889-1791
New York (G-9499)
Der Yid Inc .... E 718 797-3900
Brooklyn (G-1769)
Divine Phoenix LLC .... A 585 737-1482
Skaneateles (G-14870)
▲ Dorling Kindersley Publishing .... D 212 213-4800
New York (G-9560)
Dreams To Print .... G 718 483-8020
Brooklyn (G-1793)
E W Williams Publications .... G 212 661-1516
New York (G-9598)
Eagle Art Publishing Inc .... G 212 685-7411
New York (G-9602)
Edwin Mellen Press Inc .... E 716 754-2796
Lewiston (G-7140)
▲ Egmont US Inc .... G 212 685-0102
New York (G-9635)
▲ Entertainment Weekly Inc .... C 212 522-5600
New York (G-9688)
F P H Communications .... G 212 528-1728
New York (G-9762)
Faces Magazine Inc .... D 845 454-7420
Poughkeepsie (G-13338)
▲ Fairchild Publications Inc .... A 212 630-4000
New York (G-9773)
Family Publishing Group Inc .... E 914 381-7474
Mamaroneck (G-7744)
Feminist Press Inc .... G 212 817-7915
New York (G-9794)
Folio Graphics Co Inc .... F 718 763-2076
Brooklyn (G-1896)
Four M Studios .... D 515 284-2157
New York (G-9831)
▲ Foxhill Press Inc .... E 212 995-9620
New York (G-9836)
Frank Merriwell Inc .... F 516 921-8888
Syosset (G-15218)
Franklin Report LLC .... G 212 639-9100
New York (G-9843)
Ggp Publishing Inc .... F 914 834-8896
Harrison (G-5728)
Government Data Publication .... E 347 789-8719
Brooklyn (G-1945)

Gq Magazine .... G 212 286-2860
New York (G-9966)
Grand Central Publishing .... C 212 364-1200
New York (G-9970)
▲ Graphis Inc .... F 212 532-9387
New York (G-9978)
Grey House Publishing Inc .... E 845 483-3535
Poughkeepsie (G-13343)
Grey House Publishing Inc .... E 518 789-8700
Amenia (G-206)
Grolier International Inc .... F 212 343-6100
New York (G-9994)
Guilford Publications Inc .... D 212 431-9800
New York (G-10008)
Guilford Publications Inc 800 365-7006
New York (G-10009)
H W Wilson Company Inc .... B 718 588-8635
Bronx (G-1287)
◆ Hachette Book Group Inc 800 759-0190
New York (G-10016)
Hachette Book Group USA .... E 212 364-1200
New York (G-10017)
Haights Cross Operating Co 914 289-9400
White Plains (G-16457)
Harpercollins 212 207-7000
New York (G-10037)
▲ Harpercollins Publishers LLC .... A 212 207-7000
New York (G-10038)
Harpercollins Publishers LLC 212 553-4200
New York (G-10039)
▲ Harry N Abrams Incorporated .... D 212 206-7715
New York (G-10042)
Harvard University Press 212 337-0280
New York (G-10047)
Hearst Business Media Corp .... F 631 650-4441
New York (G-10056)
▲ Hearst Corporation .... A 212 649-2000
New York (G-10061)
Hearst Corporation 212 649-2275
New York (G-10070)
▲ Henry Holt and Company LLC .... D 646 307-5095
New York (G-10081)
Highline Media LLC .... C 859 692-2100
New York (G-10097)
▲ Hippocrene Books Inc 212 685-4371
New York (G-10104)
Houghton Mifflin Harcourt Pubg .... E 212 420-5800
New York (G-10131)
Houghton Mifflin Harcourt Pubg 914 747-2709
Thornwood (G-15507)
▲ Hudson Park Press Inc .... G 212 929-8898
New York (G-10144)
▲ Humana Press Inc 212 460-1500
New York (G-10149)
Iat Interactive LLC 914 273-2233
Mount Kisco (G-8343)
▲ Infobase Holdings Inc .... D 212 967-8800
New York (G-10206)
Infobase Publishing Company .... G 212 967-8800
New York (G-10207)
Informa Business Media Inc 914 949-8500
White Plains (G-16462)
Interntnl Publcatns Media Grup 917 604-9602
New York (G-10252)
Ir Media Group (usa) Inc .... E 212 425-9649
New York (G-10267)
James Morgan Publishing .... G 212 655-5470
New York (G-10303)
John Wiley & Sons Inc 845 457-6250
Montgomery (G-8313)
▲ Jonathan David Publishers Inc ...... F 718 456-8611
Middle Village (G-8123)
▲ Judaica Press Inc 718 972-6202
Brooklyn (G-2054)
▲ Juris Publishing Inc .... F 631 351-5430
Huntington (G-6402)
▲ K T A V Publishing House Inc .... F 201 963-9524
Brooklyn (G-2065)
Kaplan Inc .... E 212 752-1840
New York (G-10405)
Kensington Publishing Corp .... D 212 407-1500
New York (G-10434)
▲ Klutz .... E 650 687-2600
New York (G-10458)
Kobalt Music Pubg Amer Inc .... D 212 247-6204
New York (G-10461)
▲ Kodansha USA Inc 917 322-6200
New York (G-10464)
Kwesi Legesse LLC 347 581-9872
Brooklyn (G-2084)

▲ Le Book Publishing Inc .... G 212 334-5252
New York (G-10526)
Learningexpress LLC .... E 646 274-6454
New York (G-10532)
▲ Lee & Low Books Incorporated ..... F 212 779-4400
New York (G-10537)
Legal Strategies Inc 516 377-3940
Merrick (G-8102)
Lexis Publishing .... C 518 487-3000
Menands (G-8086)
Lippincott Massie McQuilkin L .... F 212 352-2055
New York (G-10576)
▲ Literary Classics of US .... F 212 308-3360
New York (G-10578)
Liveright Publishing Corp 212 354-5500
New York (G-10584)
Living Well Innovations Inc .... G 646 517-3200
Hauppauge (G-5866)
Looseleaf Law Publications Inc .... F 718 359-5559
Flushing (G-5025)
Macmillan Audio .... G 646 600-7856
New York (G-10648)
Macmillan College Pubg Co Inc .... F 212 702-2000
New York (G-10649)
▲ Macmillan Publishers Inc .... A 646 307-5151
New York (G-10651)
◆ Macmillan Publishing Group LLC ... B 212 674-5145
New York (G-10652)
▲ Malhame Publs & Importers Inc 631 694-8600
Bohemia (G-1055)
▲ Marshall Cavendish Corp .... E 914 332-8888
Tarrytown (G-15481)
▲ Martha Stewart Living .... C 212 827-8000
New York (G-10717)
Mary Ann Liebert Inc .... D 914 740-2100
New Rochelle (G-8620)
Mathisen Ventures Inc .... G 212 986-1025
New York (G-10728)
▲ McBooks Press Inc .... G 607 272-2114
Ithaca (G-6594)
McGraw-Hill Education Inc .... D 646 766-2000
New York (G-10741)
McGraw-Hill School Education H .... B 646 766-2000
New York (G-10742)
McGraw-Hill School Educatn LLC ..... A 646 766-2060
New York (G-10743)
Mediaplanet Publishing Hse Inc 646 922-1400
New York (G-10755)
Medikidz Usa Inc .... G 646 895-9319
New York (G-10759)
Meegenius Inc 212 283-7285
New York (G-10763)
▲ Melcher Media Inc .... F 212 727-2322
New York (G-10769)
Merkos LInyonei Chinuch Inc .... E 718 778-0226
Brooklyn (G-2196)
▲ Mesorah Publications Ltd .... E 718 921-9000
Brooklyn (G-2198)
Metro Creative Graphics Inc .... E 212 947-5100
New York (G-10784)
Micro Publishing Inc 212 533-9180
New York (G-10795)
Modern Language Assn Amer Inc .... C 646 576-5000
New York (G-10829)
▲ Monacelli Press LLC 212 229-9925
New York (G-10836)
▲ Mondo Publishing Inc .... E 212 268-3560
New York (G-10837)
▲ Moznaim Publishing Co Inc .... G 718 853-0525
Brooklyn (G-2229)
▲ Mud Puddle Books Inc .... G 212 647-9168
New York (G-10856)
◆ Multi Packaging Solutions Inc .... E 646 885-0005
New York (G-10858)
N A R Associates Inc .... G 845 557-8713
Barryville (G-607)
National Learning Corp .... F 516 921-8888
Syosset (G-15224)
Nationwide Custom Services .... G 845 365-0414
Tappan (G-15469)
Natural E Creative LLC .... F 516 488-1143
New Hyde Park (G-8551)
▲ NBM Publishing Inc 646 559-4681
New York (G-10900)
NC Audience Exchange LLC .... F 212 416-3400
New York (G-10901)
New City Press Inc 845 229-0335
Hyde Park (G-6470)
New Directions Publishing .... F 212 255-0230
New York (G-10920)

Employee Codes: A=Over 500 employees, B=251-500
C=101-250, D=51-100, E=20-50, F=10-19, G=5-9

New Press E 212 629-8802
New York *(G-10928)*
New York Legal Publishing G 518 459-1100
Menands *(G-8090)*
New York Qrtrly Foundation Inc F 917 843-8825
Brooklyn *(G-2265)*
Newkirk Products Inc C 518 862-3200
Albany *(G-103)*
News Corporation C 212 416-3400
New York *(G-10952)*
News India USA Inc F 212 675-7515
New York *(G-10954)*
North Shore Home Improver F 631 474-2824
Port Jeff STA *(G-13214)*
▲ **North-South Books Inc** E 212 706-4545
New York *(G-10995)*
Nova Science Publishers Inc F 631 231-7269
Hauppauge *(G-5902)*
Origin Press Inc G 516 746-2262
Mineola *(G-8243)*
Other Press LLC G 212 414-0054
New York *(G-11068)*
Oxford Book Company Inc C 212 227-2120
New York *(G-11074)*
◆ **Oxford University Press LLC** B 212 726-6000
New York *(G-11078)*
Oxford University Press LLC G 212 726-6000
New York *(G-11079)*
Ozmodyl Ltd G 212 226-0622
New York *(G-11081)*
P J D Publications Ltd G 516 626-0650
New Hyde Park *(G-8557)*
Pace Walkers of America Inc F 631 444-2147
Port Jefferson *(G-13223)*
▲ **Palgrave Macmillan Ltd** G 646 307-5028
New York *(G-11095)*
▲ **Papercutz Inc** G 646 559-4681
New York *(G-11104)*
▲ **Parachute Publishing LLC** E 212 337-6743
New York *(G-11106)*
Pearson Education Inc E 845 340-8700
Kingston *(G-6914)*
Pearson Education Inc F 212 782-3337
New York *(G-11130)*
Pearson Education Inc E 212 366-2000
New York *(G-11131)*
Pearson Education Inc F 201 236-7000
West Nyack *(G-16278)*
▲ **Pearson Education Holdings Inc** A 201 236-6716
New York *(G-11132)*
◆ **Pearson Inc** D 212 641-2400
New York *(G-11133)*
Pearson Longman LLC C 917 981-2200
New York *(G-11134)*
Pearson Longman LLC E 212 641-2400
White Plains *(G-16487)*
Pegasus Books NY Ltd G 646 343-9502
New York *(G-11140)*
▲ **Penguin Putnam Inc** G 212 366-2000
New York *(G-11144)*
Penguin Random House LLC E 212 782-1000
New York *(G-11145)*
▲ **Penguin Random House LLC** B 212 782-9000
New York *(G-11146)*
Penguin Random House LLC A 212 572-6162
New York *(G-11147)*
Penguin Random House LLC A 212 782-9000
New York *(G-11148)*
Penguin Random House LLC C 212 366-2377
Albany *(G-113)*
Peri-Facts Academy G 585 275-6037
Rochester *(G-14013)*
Peter Lang Publishing Inc F 212 647-7700
New York *(G-11168)*
▲ **Peter Mayer Publishers Inc** F 212 673-2210
New York *(G-11169)*
▲ **Peter Pauper Press Inc** E 914 681-0144
White Plains *(G-16496)*
▲ **Phaidon Press Inc** E 212 652-5400
New York *(G-11179)*
▲ **Philipp Feldheim Inc** G 845 356-2282
Nanuet *(G-8467)*
Picador USA F 646 307-5629
New York *(G-11189)*
Poetry Mailing List Marsh Hawk G 516 766-1891
Oceanside *(G-12551)*
Poets House Inc F 212 431-7920
New York *(G-11215)*
▲ **Powerhouse Cultural Entrmt Inc** F 212 604-9074
Brooklyn *(G-2330)*

Preserving Chrstn Publications G 315 942-6617
Boonville *(G-1119)*
▲ **Prestel Publishing LLC** G 212 995-2720
New York *(G-11236)*
▲ **Princton Archtctural Press LLC** F 518 671-6100
Hudson *(G-6369)*
Project Energy Savers LLC F 718 596-4231
Brooklyn *(G-2356)*
▲ **Prometheus Books Inc** E 716 691-2158
Amherst *(G-248)*
PSR Press Ltd F 716 754-2266
Lewiston *(G-7142)*
▲ **Quarto Group Inc** E 212 779-0700
New York *(G-11299)*
Rapid Intellect Group Inc F 518 929-3210
Chatham *(G-3429)*
Rda Holding Co E 914 238-1000
New York *(G-11336)*
Readers Dgest Yung Fmilies Inc E 914 238-1000
Pleasantville *(G-13176)*
◆ **Relx Inc** E 212 309-8100
New York *(G-11355)*
Repertoire International De Ll E 212 817-1990
New York *(G-11364)*
Research Centre of Kabbalah G 718 805-0380
Richmond Hill *(G-13509)*
▲ **Richard C Owen Publishers Inc** F 914 232-3903
Somers *(G-14922)*
◆ **Rizzoli Intl Publications Inc** E 212 387-3400
New York *(G-11398)*
Rizzoli Intl Publications Inc F 212 387-3572
New York *(G-11399)*
▲ **Rosen Publishing Group Inc** C 212 777-3017
New York *(G-11432)*
▲ **Ryland Peters & Small Inc** G 646 791-5410
New York *(G-11453)*
S P Books Inc G 212 431-5011
New York *(G-11458)*
Samuel French Inc E 212 206-8990
New York *(G-11477)*
▲ **Scholastic Corporation** G 212 343-6100
New York *(G-11513)*
◆ **Scholastic Inc** A 800 724-6527
New York *(G-11514)*
Scholastic Inc E 212 343-6100
New York *(G-11515)*
Scholium International Inc G 516 883-8032
Port Washington *(G-13305)*
Second Chance Press Inc G 631 725-1101
Sag Harbor *(G-14503)*
▲ **Seven Stories Press Inc** G 212 226-8760
New York *(G-11547)*
▲ **Sheridan House Inc** G 914 725-5431
Scarsdale *(G-14645)*
Simmons-Boardman Pubg Corp E 212 620-7200
New York *(G-11594)*
Simon & Schuster Inc D 212 698-7000
New York *(G-11595)*
Simon Schuster Digital Sls Inc D 212 698-4391
New York *(G-11597)*
▲ **Skyhorse Publishing Inc** E 212 643-6816
New York *(G-11614)*
Social Register Association F 646 612-7314
New York *(G-11633)*
Soho Press Inc G 212 260-1900
New York *(G-11637)*
Spartacist Publishing Co E 212 732-7860
New York *(G-11659)*
Springer Adis Us LLC F 212 460-1500
New York *(G-11681)*
Springer Customer Svc Ctr LLC B 212 460-1500
New York *(G-11682)*
Springer Publishing Co LLC E 212 431-4370
New York *(G-11684)*
◆ **Springer Scnce + Bus Media LLC** D 212 460-1500
New York *(G-11685)*
▲ **Square One Publishers Inc** F 516 535-2010
Garden City Park *(G-5288)*
Station Hill of Barrytown G 845 758-5293
Barrytown *(G-606)*
Steffen Publishing Inc D 315 865-4100
Holland Patent *(G-6225)*
STf Services Inc E 315 463-8506
East Syracuse *(G-4371)*
Stonesong Press LLC G 212 929-4600
New York *(G-11715)*
Storybooks Forever F 716 822-7845
Buffalo *(G-3078)*
▲ **Studio Fun International Inc** E 914 238-1000
White Plains *(G-16509)*

Suny At Binghamton D 607 777-2316
Binghamton *(G-916)*
Sweet Mouth Inc E 800 433-7758
New York *(G-11757)*
▲ **Syracuse University Press Inc** E 315 443-5534
Syracuse *(G-15441)*
T G S Inc G 516 629-6905
Locust Valley *(G-7352)*
Targum Press USA Inc G 248 355-2266
Brooklyn *(G-2556)*
Taylor & Francis Group LLC C 212 216-7800
New York *(G-11786)*
Thornwillow Press Ltd G 212 980-0738
New York *(G-11826)*
Time Home Entertainment Inc E 212 522-1212
New York *(G-11836)*
Time Inc E 212 522-1212
New York *(G-11837)*
Tom Doherty Associates Inc E 212 388-0100
New York *(G-11859)*
◆ **Trusted Media Brands Inc** A 914 238-1000
New York *(G-11907)*
Trusted Media Brands Inc F 914 244-5244
White Plains *(G-16513)*
▲ **Unisystems Inc** E 212 826-0850
New York *(G-11951)*
▲ **United Synggue Cnsrvtive Jdism** E 212 533-7800
New York *(G-11956)*
▲ **Vaad LHafotzas Sichoes** F 718 778-5436
Brooklyn *(G-2614)*
▲ **Vandam Inc** F 212 929-0416
Long Island City *(G-7627)*
Vaultcom Inc E 212 366-4212
New York *(G-12001)*
Verso Inc G 718 246-8160
Brooklyn *(G-2619)*
▲ **W W Norton & Company Inc** C 212 354-5500
New York *(G-12061)*
W W Norton & Company Inc G 212 354-5500
New York *(G-12062)*
▲ **Waldman Publishing Corporation** F 212 730-9590
New York *(G-12066)*
Warodean Corporation G 718 359-5559
Flushing *(G-5059)*
◆ **William H Sadlier Inc** C 212 233-3646
New York *(G-12111)*
William S Hein & Co Inc C 716 882-2600
Getzville *(G-5356)*
William S Hein & Co Inc D 716 882-2600
Buffalo *(G-3132)*
Windows Media Publishing LLC E 917 732-7892
Brooklyn *(G-2653)*
Wolters Kluwer US Inc F 212 894-8920
New York *(G-12129)*
Woodward/White Inc F 718 509-6082
Brooklyn *(G-2656)*
Wordwise Inc G 914 232-5366
Katonah *(G-6848)*
◆ **Workman Publishing Co Inc** C 212 254-5900
New York *(G-12135)*
Workman Publishing Co Inc C 212 254-5900
New York *(G-12136)*
Worth Publishers Inc C 212 475-6000
New York *(G-12140)*
▲ **YS Publishing Co Inc** G 212 682-9360
New York *(G-12166)*
▲ **Ziff Davis Publishing LLC** D 212 503-3500
New York *(G-12177)*
Zinepak LLC F 212 706-8621
New York *(G-12178)*

2732 Book Printing, Not Publishing

450 Ridge St Inc G 716 754-2789
Lewiston *(G-7138)*
Bedford Freeman & Worth C 212 576-9400
New York *(G-9034)*
Bmg Printing and Promotion LLC G 631 231-9200
Bohemia *(G-989)*
Book1one LLC G 585 458-2101
Rochester *(G-13673)*
Bridge Enterprises Inc G 718 625-6622
Brooklyn *(G-1633)*
Cct Inc G 212 532-3355
New York *(G-9233)*
Centrisource Inc G 716 871-1105
Tonawanda *(G-15533)*
E Graphics Corporation G 718 486-9767
Brooklyn *(G-1804)*
▲ **Experiment LLC** G 212 889-1659
New York *(G-9754)*

SIC SECTION
27 PRINTING, PUBLISHING, AND ALLIED INDUSTRIES

Flare Multicopy Corp ....E 718 258-8860
Brooklyn *(G-1887)*
▲ Hamilton Printing Company Inc ....C 518 732-2161
Troy *(G-15608)*
▲ Hudson Valley Paper Works Inc ....F 845 569-8883
Newburgh *(G-12228)*
Hys LLC ....F 212 716-6600
New York *(G-10157)*
In-House Inc ....F 718 445-9007
College Point *(G-3646)*
▲ Kravitz Design Inc ....G 212 625-1644
New York *(G-10482)*
▲ Literary Classics of US ....F 212 308-3360
New York *(G-10578)*
▲ Logical Operations Inc ....C 585 350-7000
Rochester *(G-13916)*
▲ North Country Books Inc ....G 315 735-4877
Utica *(G-15726)*
Printing Factory LLC ....F 718 451-0500
Brooklyn *(G-2349)*
Promotional Sales Books LLC ....G 212 675-0364
New York *(G-11260)*
Royal Fireworks Printing Co ....F 845 726-3333
Unionville *(G-15673)*
Steffen Publishing Inc ....D 315 865-4100
Holland Patent *(G-6225)*
▼ Sterling Pierce Company Inc ....E 516 593-1170
East Rockaway *(G-4296)*
Stop Entertainment Inc ....F 212 242-7867
Monroe *(G-8281)*
▲ Syracuse Cultural Workers Prj ....F 315 474-1132
Syracuse *(G-15437)*
The Nugent Organization Inc ....F 212 645-6600
Oceanside *(G-12561)*
Tobay Printing Co Inc ....E 631 842-3300
Copiague *(G-3788)*
◆ Twp America Inc ....G 212 274-8090
New York *(G-11921)*
Vicks Lithograph & Prtg Corp ....C 315 272-2401
Yorkville *(G-16832)*
Vicks Lithograph & Prtg Corp ....C 315 736-9344
Yorkville *(G-16833)*
Willis Mc Donald Co Inc ....F 212 366-1526
New York *(G-12115)*
Worzalla Publishing Company ....C 212 967-7909
New York *(G-12141)*

2741 Misc Publishing

▲ 212 Media LLC ....E 212 710-3092
New York *(G-8671)*
Abkco Music & Records Inc ....E 212 399-0300
New York *(G-8710)*
ABRA Media Inc ....G 518 398-1010
Pine Plains *(G-13004)*
Absolute Color Corporation ....G 212 868-0404
New York *(G-8715)*
Adcomm Graphics Inc ....E 212 645-1298
West Babylon *(G-16128)*
Add Associates Inc ....G 315 449-3474
Cicero *(G-3513)*
Adirondack Pennysaver Inc ....E 518 563-0100
Plattsburgh *(G-13105)*
Adsmain LLC ....G 347 560-5060
Brooklyn *(G-1486)*
Ai Media Group Inc ....F 212 660-2400
New York *(G-8775)*
Albany Student Press Inc ....E 518 442-5665
Albany *(G-37)*
Albion-Holley Pennysaver Inc ....E 585 589-5641
Albion *(G-154)*
Aleteia Usa Inc ....G 914 502-1855
Yonkers *(G-16730)*
▼ Alfred Mainzer Inc ....E 718 392-4200
Long Island City *(G-7370)*
Alley Music Corp ....E 212 779-7977
New York *(G-8797)*
Alm Media LLC ....B 212 457-9400
New York *(G-8805)*
Alm Media Holdings Inc ....B 212 457-9400
New York *(G-8806)*
Alphonse Lduc - Rbert King Inc ....G 508 238-8118
New York *(G-8809)*
American Hsptals Patient Guide ....F 518 346-1099
Schenectady *(G-14649)*
Amy Pak Publishing Inc ....G 585 964-8188
Holley *(G-6226)*
An Group Inc ....G 631 549-4090
Melville *(G-8003)*
Answer Printing Inc ....F 212 922-2922
New York *(G-8875)*
Art Asiapacific Publishing LLC ....G 212 255-6003
New York *(G-8913)*
Associated Publishing Company ....E 325 676-4032
Buffalo *(G-2710)*
Atlas Music Publishing LLC ....G 646 502-5170
New York *(G-8954)*
Auto Market Publications Inc ....G 631 667-0500
Deer Park *(G-3949)*
Avalon Copy Centers Amer Inc ....D 315 471-3333
Syracuse *(G-15251)*
Avalon Copy Centers Amer Inc ....E 716 995-7777
Buffalo *(G-2717)*
Award Publishing Limited ....G 212 246-0405
New York *(G-8982)*
Bdg Media Inc ....C 917 551-6510
New York *(G-9030)*
Bear Port Publishing Company ....F 877 337-8577
New York *(G-9031)*
▲ Black Book Photography Inc ....F 212 979-6700
New York *(G-9096)*
Blood Moon Productions Ltd ....G 718 556-9410
Staten Island *(G-15052)*
▲ Boosey and Hawkes Inc ....E 212 358-5300
New York *(G-9122)*
Bourne Music Publishers ....F 212 391-4300
New York *(G-9129)*
Bright Line Eting Slutions LLC ....E 585 245-2956
Pittsford *(G-13009)*
Brownstone Publishers Inc ....E 212 473-8200
New York *(G-9151)*
Bucksense Inc ....E 877 710-2825
New York *(G-9154)*
Bulkley Dunton ....E 212 863-1800
New York *(G-9155)*
Burdick Publications Inc ....G 315 685-9500
Skaneateles *(G-14867)*
Business Directory Inc ....F 718 486-8099
Brooklyn *(G-1660)*
Business Expert Press LLC ....F 212 661-8810
New York *(G-9161)*
Business Never Stops LLC ....G 888 479-3111
South Richmond Hill *(G-14945)*
Byliner Inc ....E 415 680-3608
New York *(G-9168)*
◆ Bys Publishing LLC ....G 315 655-9431
Cazenovia *(G-3316)*
▲ C F Peters Corp ....E 718 416-7800
Glendale *(G-5394)*
Cambridge Info Group Inc ....F 301 961-6700
New York *(G-9185)*
Cambridge Whos Who Pubg Inc ....E 516 833-8440
Uniondale *(G-15663)*
Carbert Music Inc ....E 212 725-9277
New York *(G-9206)*
Carl Fischer LLC ....E 212 777-0900
New York *(G-9208)*
Castle Connolly Medical Ltd ....E 212 367-8400
New York *(G-9224)*
Catholic News Publishing Co ....F 914 632-7771
Mamaroneck *(G-7737)*
Cayuga Press Cortland Inc ....E 888 229-8421
Liverpool *(G-7230)*
Ceo Cast Inc ....F 212 732-4300
New York *(G-9251)*
Charing Cross Music Inc ....G 212 541-7571
New York *(G-9260)*
Cherry Lane Magazine LLC ....D 212 561-3000
New York *(G-9271)*
▼ Christopher Anthony Pubg Co ....F 516 826-9205
Wantagh *(G-15920)*
Church Bulletin Inc ....F 631 249-4994
West Babylon *(G-16148)*
City of New York ....E 718 965-8787
Brooklyn *(G-1695)*
▲ City Post Express Inc ....G 718 995-8690
Jamaica *(G-6636)*
Classic Collections Fine Art ....G 914 591-4500
White Plains *(G-16437)*
Classpass Inc ....E 888 493-5953
New York *(G-9322)*
Clearstep Technologies LLC ....G 315 952-3628
Camillus *(G-3195)*
Cnhi LLC ....D 716 282-2311
Niagara Falls *(G-12273)*
Coastal Publications Inc ....F 631 725-1700
Sag Harbor *(G-14498)*
Color Unlimited Inc ....G 212 802-7547
New York *(G-9353)*
Community Cpons Frnchising Inc ....E 516 277-1968
Glen Cove *(G-5363)*
Complete Publishing Solutions ....G 212 242-7321
New York *(G-9370)*
Comps Inc ....F 516 676-0400
Glen Cove *(G-5364)*
Consumer Reports Inc ....B 914 378-2000
Yonkers *(G-16746)*
Couture Press ....F 310 734-4831
New York *(G-9412)*
D C I Technical Inc ....F 516 355-0464
Franklin Square *(G-5116)*
Dailycandy Inc ....E 646 230-8719
New York *(G-9459)*
Dapper Dads Inc ....G 917 903-8045
Brooklyn *(G-1757)*
Dayton T Brown Inc ....B 631 589-6300
Bohemia *(G-1011)*
Dezawy LLC ....G 917 436-8820
New York *(G-9516)*
Directory Major Malls Inc ....G 845 348-7000
Nyack *(G-12505)*
▲ DK Publishing ....F 212 366-2000
New York *(G-9541)*
Dlc Comprehensive Medical PC ....F 718 857-1200
Brooklyn *(G-1783)*
Dohnsco Inc ....G 516 773-4800
Manhasset *(G-7766)*
Downtown Music LLC ....G 212 625-2980
New York *(G-9569)*
Draper Associates Incorporated ....F 212 255-2727
New York *(G-9573)*
Dryve LLC ....G 646 279-3648
Bronx *(G-1259)*
Dwell Life Inc ....E 212 382-2010
New York *(G-9591)*
East Meet East Inc ....G 646 481-0033
New York *(G-9609)*
Easy Book Publishing Inc ....G 518 459-6281
Albany *(G-70)*
Elite Daily Inc ....F 212 402-9097
New York *(G-9650)*
◆ Elsevier Inc ....B 212 989-5800
New York *(G-9659)*
Energy Intelligence Group Inc ....D 212 532-1112
New York *(G-9681)*
Enhance A Colour Corp ....E 212 490-3620
New York *(G-9684)*
Enjoy City North Inc ....D 607 584-5061
Binghamton *(G-883)*
Entrainant Inc ....G 212 946-4724
New York *(G-9689)*
Epost International Inc ....G 212 352-9390
New York *(G-9694)*
Equityarcade LLC ....G 678 232-1301
Brooklyn *(G-1845)*
Ethis Communications Inc ....G 212 791-1440
White Plains *(G-16447)*
Euphorbia Productions Ltd ....G 212 533-1700
New York *(G-9727)*
▲ Experiment Publishing LLC ....G 212 889-1273
New York *(G-9755)*
F+w Media Inc ....G 212 447-1400
New York *(G-9765)*
Family Publications Ltd ....F 212 947-2177
New York *(G-9778)*
Fantasy Sports Media Group Inc ....E 416 917-6002
New York *(G-9782)*
▲ Fashiondex Inc ....G 914 271-6121
New York *(G-9788)*
First Games Publr Netwrk Inc ....D 212 983-0501
New York *(G-9807)*
Fischler Hockey Service ....F 212 749-4152
New York *(G-9812)*
Fitzgerald Publishing Co Inc ....G 914 793-5016
Yonkers *(G-16758)*
▲ Foundation Center Inc ....C 212 620-4230
New York *(G-9826)*
Franklin-Douglas Inc ....F 516 883-0121
Port Washington *(G-13260)*
Fredonia Pennysaver Inc ....G 716 679-1509
Fredonia *(G-5126)*
Freeville Publishing Co Inc ....F 607 844-9119
Freeville *(G-5191)*
Froebe Group LLC ....G 646 649-2150
New York *(G-9851)*
▲ G Schirmer Inc ....G 212 254-2100
New York *(G-9868)*
G Schirmer Inc ....E 845 469-4699
Chester *(G-3475)*
▲ Galison Publishing LLC ....E 212 354-8840
New York *(G-9876)*

S I C

Employee Codes: A=Over 500 employees, B=251-500
C=101-250, D=51-100, E=20-50, F=10-19, G=5-9
2019 Harris
New York Manufacturers Directory
699

27 PRINTING, PUBLISHING, AND ALLIED INDUSTRIES SIC SECTION

Gannett Co Inc ....D 607 352-2702
Johnson City *(G-6809)*
Gds Publishing Inc ....F 212 796-2000
New York *(G-9893)*
Gen Publishing Inc ....D 914 834-3880
New Rochelle *(G-8608)*
Genius Media Group Inc ....F 509 670-7502
Brooklyn *(G-1922)*
Glassview LLC ....E 646 844-4922
New York *(G-9933)*
Global Grind Digital ....E 212 840-9399
New York *(G-9943)*
Global Video LLC ....D 516 222-2600
Woodbury *(G-16620)*
Golden Eagle Marketing LLC ....G 212 726-1242
New York *(G-9954)*
Golf Directories USA Inc ....G 516 365-5351
Manhasset *(G-7768)*
Gooding & Associates Inc ....F 631 749-3313
Shelter Island *(G-14801)*
Government Data Publication ....E 347 789-8719
Brooklyn *(G-1945)*
Grant Hamilton ....F 716 652-0320
East Aurora *(G-4201)*
Grey House Publishing Inc ....E 518 789-8700
Amenia *(G-206)*
Grey House Publishing Inc ....E 845 483-3535
Poughkeepsie *(G-13343)*
Guest Informat LLC ....F 212 557-3010
New York *(G-10005)*
Guilford Publications Inc ....D 212 431-9800
New York *(G-10008)*
Guilford Publications Inc ....G 800 365-7006
New York *(G-10009)*
Hagedorn Communications Inc ....G 914 636-7400
New York *(G-10020)*
Hampton Press Incorporated ....G 646 638-3800
New York *(G-10028)*
Harborside Press ....G 631 470-4967
Huntington *(G-6399)*
Hart Energy Publishing Lllp ....G 212 621-4621
New York *(G-10045)*
Hearst Business Media ....D 516 227-1300
Uniondale *(G-15669)*
Hearst Communications Inc ....G 212 247-1014
New York *(G-10059)*
Hearst Digital Studios Inc ....E 212 969-7552
New York *(G-10071)*
Heed LLC ....E 646 708-7111
New York *(G-10077)*
Helium Media Inc ....G 917 596-4081
New York *(G-10078)*
▲ Helvetica Press Incorporated ....G 212 737-1857
New York *(G-10079)*
Herff Jones LLC ....E 607 936-2366
Corning *(G-3820)*
Hibert Publishing LLC ....G 914 381-7474
Rye *(G-14482)*
◆ Hibu Inc ....C 516 730-1900
East Meadow *(G-4253)*
Highline Media LLC ....C 859 692-2100
New York *(G-10097)*
▲ Historic TW Inc ....E 212 484-8000
New York *(G-10106)*
History Publishing Company LLC ....G 845 398-8161
Palisades *(G-12846)*
Hola Publishing Co ....G 718 424-3129
Long Island City *(G-7470)*
Holmes Group The Inc ....G 212 333-2300
New York *(G-10118)*
▲ Humana Press Inc ....E 212 460-1500
New York *(G-10149)*
Humor Rainbow Inc ....E 646 402-9113
New York *(G-10151)*
Infoservices International ....F 631 549-1805
Cold Spring Harbor *(G-3631)*
Integrated Copyright Group ....E 615 329-3999
New York *(G-10230)*
International Society For Medl ....G 520 820-8594
Tarrytown *(G-15479)*
Intuition Publishing Limited ....G 212 838-7115
New York *(G-10262)*
Israeli Yellow Pages ....E 718 520-1000
Kew Gardens *(G-6874)*
Jewish Heritage For Blind ....G 718 338-4999
Brooklyn *(G-2038)*
▲ Jobson Medical Information LLC ....C 212 274-7000
New York *(G-10347)*
▲ John Szoke Graphics Inc ....G 212 219-8300
New York *(G-10354)*
Johnny Bienstock Music ....E 212 779-7977
New York *(G-10355)*
Kalel Partners LLC ....F 347 561-7804
Flushing *(G-5015)*
Kendor Music Inc ....F 716 492-1254
Delevan *(G-4071)*
Kjckd Inc ....G 518 435-9696
Latham *(G-7078)*
Korangy Publishing Inc ....C 212 260-1332
New York *(G-10470)*
▲ Korean Yellow Pages ....F 718 461-0073
Flushing *(G-5020)*
Kraus Organization Limited ....D 212 686-5411
New York *(G-10481)*
Kyra Communications Corp ....F 516 783-6244
Seaford *(G-14758)*
Lagunatic Music & Filmworks ....F 212 353-9600
Brooklyn *(G-2091)*
Language and Graphics Inc ....G 212 315-5266
New York *(G-10516)*
Largo Music Inc ....G 212 756-5080
New York *(G-10518)*
Leadership Directories Inc ....D 212 627-4140
New York *(G-10530)*
Ledes Group Inc ....F 212 840-8800
New York *(G-10536)*
Lefrak Entertainment Co Ltd ....G 212 586-3600
New York *(G-10540)*
Lightbulb Press Inc ....E 212 485-8800
New York *(G-10569)*
Lino Press Inc ....E 718 665-2625
Bronx *(G-1319)*
Llcs Publishing Corp ....F 718 569-2703
Brooklyn *(G-2131)*
London Theater News Ltd ....F 212 517-8608
New York *(G-10596)*
Long Islands Best Inc ....G 855 542-3785
Bohemia *(G-1049)*
Lucky Peach LLC ....G 212 228-0031
New York *(G-10626)*
Ludlow Music Inc ....F 212 594-9795
New York *(G-10627)*
Luminary Publishing Inc ....F 845 334-8600
Kingston *(G-6909)*
Mac Innes Enterprises Inc ....E 325 676-4032
Buffalo *(G-2931)*
Mailers-Pblsher Wlfare Tr Fund ....G 212 869-5986
New York *(G-10673)*
▲ Mapeasy Inc ....F 631 537-6213
Wainscott *(G-15889)*
Market Partners International ....G 212 447-0855
New York *(G-10711)*
Marketresearchcom Inc ....F 212 807-2600
New York *(G-10713)*
Mary Ann Liebert Inc ....D 914 740-2100
New Rochelle *(G-8620)*
Mathisen Ventures Inc ....G 212 986-1025
New York *(G-10728)*
▲ Media Transcripts Inc ....E 212 362-1481
New York *(G-10753)*
Media Trust LLC ....G 212 802-1162
New York *(G-10754)*
Medical Daily Inc ....E 646 867-7100
New York *(G-10757)*
Medical Information Systems ....G 516 621-7200
Port Washington *(G-13286)*
Mens Journal LLC ....G 212 484-1616
New York *(G-10771)*
▲ Menucha Publishers Inc ....F 718 232-0856
Brooklyn *(G-2192)*
Merrill Corporation ....D 212 620-5600
New York *(G-10777)*
Metro Group Inc ....G 716 434-4055
Lockport *(G-7317)*
Mexico Independent Inc ....E 315 963-3763
Watertown *(G-16027)*
Michael Karp Music Inc ....G 212 840-3285
New York *(G-10792)*
Millennium Medical Publishing ....F 212 995-2211
New York *(G-10807)*
Mindbodygreen LLC ....E 347 529-6952
Brooklyn *(G-2209)*
Minyanville Media Inc ....E 212 991-6200
New York *(G-10821)*
Mom Dad Publishing Inc ....E 646 476-9170
New York *(G-10834)*
Morey Publishing ....E 516 284-3300
Farmingdale *(G-4830)*
Mortgage Press Ltd ....E 516 409-1400
Wantagh *(G-15924)*
Mosby Holdings Corp ....G 212 309-8100
New York *(G-10844)*
Mt Morris Shopper Inc ....G 585 658-3520
Mount Morris *(G-8367)*
Mtm Publishing Inc ....G 212 242-6930
New York *(G-10855)*
Multi-Health Systems Inc ....D 800 456-3003
Cheektowaga *(G-3453)*
▲ Music Sales Corporation ....G 212 254-2100
New York *(G-10861)*
My Publisher Inc ....G 212 935-5215
New York *(G-10865)*
Napean LLC ....G 917 968-6757
New York *(G-10874)*
Narratively Inc ....E 203 536-0332
Brooklyn *(G-2244)*
National Health Prom Assoc ....E 914 421-2525
White Plains *(G-16478)*
National Rding Styles Inst Inc ....F 516 921-5500
Syosset *(G-15225)*
Nature Publishing Co ....G 212 726-9200
New York *(G-10894)*
New York Legal Publishing ....G 518 459-1100
Menands *(G-8090)*
New York Times Company ....G 212 556-1200
New York *(G-10945)*
Newbay Media LLC ....D 212 378-0400
New York *(G-10949)*
News Now Waverly ....F 607 296-6769
Waverly *(G-16068)*
Newsweek Media Group Inc ....E 646 867-7100
New York *(G-10957)*
Nimbletv Inc ....F 646 502-7010
New York *(G-10970)*
O Val Nick Music Co Inc ....G 212 873-2179
New York *(G-11023)*
Oakwood Publishing Co ....G 516 482-7720
Great Neck *(G-5575)*
One Story Inc ....G 917 816-3659
Brooklyn *(G-2289)*
Open-Xchange Inc ....F 914 332-5720
Tarrytown *(G-15485)*
Openroad Integrated Media Inc ....E 212 691-0900
New York *(G-11049)*
▲ Osprey Publishing Inc ....G 212 419-5300
New York *(G-11067)*
Outreach Publishing Corp ....G 718 773-0525
Brooklyn *(G-2296)*
Pace Editions Inc ....E 212 421-3237
New York *(G-11085)*
Pace Editions Inc ....G 212 675-7431
New York *(G-11086)*
Panoply Media LLC ....E 646 382-5423
Brooklyn *(G-2300)*
Paragon Publishing Inc ....G 718 302-2093
Brooklyn *(G-2303)*
▲ Peer International Corp ....E 212 265-3910
New York *(G-11136)*
Peermusic III Ltd ....F 212 265-3910
New York *(G-11138)*
Peermusic Ltd ....F 212 265-3910
New York *(G-11139)*
▲ Per Annum Inc ....E 212 647-8700
New York *(G-11152)*
Pictoure Inc ....G 212 641-0098
New York *(G-11190)*
Playlife LLC ....G 646 207-9082
New York *(G-11208)*
Portfolio Media Inc ....C 646 783-7100
New York *(G-11221)*
Press Express ....G 914 592-3790
Elmsford *(G-4558)*
Primary Wave Publishing LLC ....G 212 661-6990
New York *(G-11240)*
Princess Music Publishing Co ....E 212 586-0240
New York *(G-11243)*
Pro Publica Inc ....D 212 514-5250
New York *(G-11253)*
Professnal Spt Pblications Inc ....E 516 327-9500
Elmont *(G-4522)*
Publishers Clearing House LLC ....E 516 249-4063
Melville *(G-8059)*
Pwxyz LLC ....E 212 377-5500
New York *(G-11287)*
Qtalk Publishing LLC ....G 877 549-1841
New York *(G-11293)*
Quality Patterns Inc ....D 212 704-0355
New York *(G-11297)*
Qworldstar Inc ....G 212 768-4500
New York *(G-11307)*

SIC SECTION

27 PRINTING, PUBLISHING, AND ALLIED INDUSTRIES

R W Publications Div of Wtrhs ....E 716 714-5620
Elma (G-4456)
Rda Holding Co ....E 914 238-1000
New York (G-11336)
Redspring Communications Inc ....E 518 587-0547
Saratoga Springs (G-14596)
Refinery 29 Inc ....D 212 966-3112
New York (G-11346)
Regan Arts LLC ....F 646 488-6610
New York (G-11349)
▲ Reliable Press II Inc ....F 718 840-5812
Hempstead (G-6025)
Renegade Nation Online LLC ....G 212 868-9000
New York (G-11363)
Repertoire International De Ll ....E 212 817-1990
New York (G-11364)
Reservoir Media Management Inc ....F 212 675-0541
New York (G-11367)
Reuters Loan Pricing Corp ....D 212 833-9200
New York (G-11374)
Riot New Media Group Inc ....G 604 700-4896
Brooklyn (G-2403)
Rolling Stone Magazine ....G 212 484-1616
New York (G-11425)
Rosemont Press Incorporated ....G 212 239-4770
Deer Park (G-4037)
▲ Rough Guides US Ltd ....D 212 414-3635
New York (G-11437)
Royalty Network Inc ....G 212 967-4300
New York (G-11441)
Rsl Media LLC ....G 212 307-6760
New York (G-11443)
S G New York LLC ....E 631 665-4000
Bohemia (G-1084)
Sacks and Company New York ....G 212 741-1000
New York (G-11463)
Sag Harbor Express ....G 631 725-1700
Sag Harbor (G-14501)
Sagelife Parenting LLC ....G 315 299-5713
Syracuse (G-15414)
Salamanca Press Penny Saver ....E 716 945-1500
Salamanca (G-14531)
◆ Scepter Publishers Inc ....G 212 354-0670
New Rochelle (G-8627)
Scholastic Inc ....D 212 343-7100
New York (G-11516)
Screen Gems-EMI Music Inc ....D 212 786-8000
New York (G-11523)
Seabay Media Holdings LLC ....G 212 457-7790
New York (G-11525)
Selby Marketing Associates Inc ....F 585 377-0750
Rochester (G-14120)
Select Information Exchange ....F 212 496-6435
New York (G-11538)
Sentinel Printing Services Inc ....D 845 562-1218
New Windsor (G-8660)
Sephardic Yellow Pages ....E 718 998-0299
Brooklyn (G-2456)
Service Advertising Group Inc ....F 718 361-6161
Long Island City (G-7588)
Service Education Incorporated ....G 585 264-9240
Victor (G-15867)
▲ Shapiro Bernstein & Co Inc ....F 212 588-0878
New York (G-11558)
Sharedbook Inc ....E 646 442-8840
New York (G-11559)
Shepherds Pl LLC ....G 516 647-8151
Valley Stream (G-15797)
Shop Smart Central Inc ....G 914 962-3871
Yorktown Heights (G-16823)
▲ Sing Tao Newspapers NY Ltd ....E 212 699-3800
New York (G-11598)
Skylark Publications Ltd ....G 607 535-9866
Watkins Glen (G-16060)
Slosson Eductl Publications ....F 716 652-0930
East Aurora (G-4210)
Sneaker News Inc ....G 347 687-1588
New York (G-11630)
Social Science Electronic Pubg ....F 585 442-8170
Rochester (G-14132)
Soho Editions Inc ....E 914 591-5100
Mohegan Lake (G-8260)
◆ Sony Music Holdings Inc ....A 212 833-8000
New York (G-11649)
▲ Sony/Atv Music Publishing LLC ....E 212 833-7730
New York (G-11650)
Southampton Town Newspapers ....E 631 283-4100
Southampton (G-14962)
Space 150 ....C 612 332-6458
Brooklyn (G-2502)
Spirit Music Group Inc ....E 212 533-7672
New York (G-11671)
Sportsgrid Inc ....F 646 849-4085
New York (G-11678)
Standard Analytics Io Inc ....G 917 882-5422
New York (G-11691)
Statebook LLC ....G 845 383-1991
Kingston (G-6919)
Stephen Singer Pattern Co Inc ....F 212 947-2902
New York (G-11706)
STf Services Inc ....E 315 463-8506
East Syracuse (G-4371)
Straight Arrow Publishing Co ....C 212 484-1616
New York (G-11717)
Strathmore Directories Ltd ....E 516 997-2525
Westbury (G-16374)
Student Lifeline Inc ....E 516 327-0800
Franklin Square (G-5121)
Summit Communications ....G 914 273-5504
Armonk (G-409)
Super Express USA Pubg Corp ....F 212 227-5800
Richmond Hill (G-13515)
Supermedia LLC ....D 212 513-9700
New York (G-11748)
Tablet Publishing Company Inc ....E 718 965-7333
Brooklyn (G-2553)
▲ Te Neues Publishing Company ....F 212 627-9090
New York (G-11790)
Tenney Media Group ....D 315 853-5569
Clinton (G-3589)
Thehuffingtonpostcom Inc ....E 212 245-7844
New York (G-11809)
Theskimm Inc ....F 646 213-4754
New York (G-11813)
Thomas Publishing Company LLC ....B 212 695-0500
New York (G-11818)
Thomas Publishing Company LLC ....D 212 695-0500
New York (G-11819)
Thomson Reuters Corporation ....F 212 393-9461
New York (G-11824)
▲ Thomson Reuters Corporation ....A 646 223-4000
New York (G-11825)
Time Warner Companies Inc ....D 212 484-8000
New York (G-11845)
Total Webcasting Inc ....G 845 883-0909
New Paltz (G-8581)
Trader Interntnal Publications ....G 914 631-6856
Sleepy Hollow (G-14887)
Tradewins Publishing Corp ....G 631 361-6916
Saint James (G-14516)
Trading Edge Ltd ....G 347 699-7079
Ridgewood (G-13556)
Treiman Publications Corp ....G 607 657-8473
Berkshire (G-829)
Tribune Entertainment Co Del ....E 203 866-2204
New York (G-11897)
Tribune Media Services Inc ....B 518 792-9914
Queensbury (G-13444)
▲ Triumph Learning LLC ....E 212 652-0200
New York (G-11902)
◆ Trusted Media Brands Inc ....A 914 238-1000
New York (G-11907)
Trusted Media Brands Inc ....F 914 244-5244
White Plains (G-16513)
Tunecore Inc ....F 646 651-1060
Brooklyn (G-2592)
Turbo Express Inc ....G 718 723-3686
Jamaica (G-6686)
Two Palms Press Inc ....F 212 965-8598
New York (G-11919)
Ubm Inc ....A 212 600-3000
New York (G-11929)
Ucc Guide Inc ....F 518 434-0909
Albany (G-137)
Underline Communications LLC ....F 212 994-4340
New York (G-11937)
▲ Universal Edition Inc ....D 917 213-2177
New York (G-11959)
Urban Mapping Inc ....F 415 946-8170
New York (G-11969)
◆ USA Custom Pad Corp ....E 607 563-9550
Sidney (G-14858)
Value Line Inc ....D 212 907-1500
New York (G-11988)
▲ Vandam Inc ....F 212 929-0416
Long Island City (G-7627)
Vending Times Inc ....F 516 442-1850
Rockville Centre (G-14244)
Vendome Group LLC ....D 646 795-3899
New York (G-12004)
Viamedia Corporation ....G 718 485-7792
Brooklyn (G-2620)
Viewfinder Inc ....G 212 831-0939
New York (G-12032)
Vincys Printing Ltd ....F 518 355-4363
Schenectady (G-14725)
Vinous Group LLC ....G 917 275-5184
New York (G-12036)
Visant Secondary Holdings Corp ....E 914 595-8200
Armonk (G-412)
VWR Education LLC ....C 585 359-2502
West Henrietta (G-16254)
Want-Ad Digest Inc ....F 518 279-1181
Troy (G-15634)
▼ Warner Music Inc ....D 212 275-2000
New York (G-12073)
Watchanish LLC ....F 917 558-0404
New York (G-12078)
Wayuga Community Newspapers ....E 315 754-6229
Red Creek (G-13456)
Welcome Rain Publishers LLC ....G 212 686-1909
New York (G-12089)
Winterwheat Corp ....G 212 203-2064
New York (G-12124)
Wmg Acquisition Corp ....F 212 275-2000
New York (G-12126)
▲ Won & Lee Inc ....E 516 222-0712
Garden City (G-5284)
Yam TV LLC ....G 917 932-5418
New York (G-12159)
Yellow Pages Inc ....G 845 639-6060
New City (G-8496)
Zazoom LLC ....F 212 321-2100
New York (G-12170)

2752 Commercial Printing: Lithographic

12pt Printing LLC ....G 718 376-2120
Brooklyn (G-1433)
2 1 2 Postcards Inc ....E 212 767-8227
New York (G-8667)
2 X 4 Inc ....E 212 647-1170
New York (G-8668)
21st Century Fox America Inc ....D 212 852-7000
New York (G-8673)
450 Ridge St Inc ....G 716 754-2789
Lewiston (G-7138)
514 Adams Corporation ....G 516 352-6948
Franklin Square (G-5114)
518 Prints LLC ....G 518 674-5346
Averill Park (G-512)
6727 11th Ave Corp ....F 718 837-8787
Brooklyn (G-1444)
A & M Litho Inc ....E 516 342-9727
Bethpage (G-836)
▲ A Esteban & Company Inc ....E 212 989-7000
New York (G-8691)
A Esteban & Company Inc ....E 212 714-2227
New York (G-8692)
A I P Printing & Stationers ....G 631 929-5529
Wading River (G-15883)
A M & J Digital ....G 518 434-2579
Menands (G-8077)
A National Printing Co Inc ....G 631 243-3395
Farmingville (G-4922)
A Q P Inc ....G 585 256-1690
Rochester (G-13590)
Academy Printing Services Inc ....G 631 765-3346
Southold (G-14967)
Accuprint ....G 518 456-2431
Albany (G-28)
Ace Printing & Publishing Inc ....F 718 939-0040
Flushing (G-4980)
Act Communications Group Inc ....F 631 669-2403
West Islip (G-16257)
Ad-Vantage Printing Inc ....F 718 820-0688
Kew Gardens (G-6870)
Adirondack Publishing Co Inc ....E 518 891-2600
Saranac Lake (G-14560)
Ads-N-Color Inc ....E 718 797-0900
Brooklyn (G-1485)
▲ Advance Publications Inc ....D 718 981-1234
Staten Island (G-15040)
Advanced Business Group Inc ....F 212 398-1010
New York (G-8753)
Advanced Digital Printing LLC ....E 718 649-1500
New York (G-8754)
Advanced Printing New York Inc ....G 212 840-8108
New York (G-8756)
Advantage Press Inc ....F 518 584-3405
Saratoga Springs (G-14568)

Employee Codes: A=Over 500 employees, B=251-500
C=101-250, D=51-100, E=20-50, F=10-19, G=5-9

2019 Harris
New York Manufacturers Directory

701

27 PRINTING, PUBLISHING, AND ALLIED INDUSTRIES

▲ Advantage Quick Print Inc ....G..... 212 989-5644
  New York *(G-8758)*
Advertising Lithographers ....F..... 212 966-7771
  Long Island City *(G-7368)*
Agrecolor Inc ....F..... 516 741-8700
  Mineola *(G-8202)*
Ahw Printing Corp ....F..... 516 536-3600
  Oceanside *(G-12531)*
Alamar Printing Inc ....F..... 914 993-9007
  White Plains *(G-16417)*
Albany Letter Shop Inc 518 434-1172
  Albany *(G-33)*
Albert Siy ....G..... 718 359-0389
  Flushing *(G-4982)*
Aldine Inc (ny) ....D..... 212 226-2870
  New York *(G-8788)*
All Color Business Spc Ltd ....G..... 516 420-0649
  Deer Park *(G-3936)*
All Color Offset Printers Inc 516 420-0649
  Farmingdale *(G-4714)*
All Time Products Inc ....G..... 718 464-1400
  Queens Village *(G-13402)*
Allen William & Company Inc ....C..... 212 675-6461
  Glendale *(G-5391)*
Allied Reproductions Inc....................E..... 212 255-2472
  New York *(G-8799)*
Allstatebannerscom Corporation ....G..... 718 300-1256
  Long Island City *(G-7372)*
Alpha Printing Corp ....G..... 315 454-5507
  Syracuse *(G-15241)*
Alpina Color Graphics Inc ....G..... 212 285-2700
  New York *(G-8810)*
Alpina Copyworld Inc ....G..... 212 683-3511
  New York *(G-8811)*
Alpine Business Group Inc ....F..... 212 989-4198
  New York *(G-8812)*
Amax Printing Inc ....F..... 718 384-8600
  Maspeth *(G-7819)*
American Business Forms Inc ....E..... 716 836-5111
  Amherst *(G-213)*
American Icon Industries Inc ....G..... 845 561-1299
  Newburgh *(G-12213)*
American Print Solutions Inc ....G..... 718 246-7800
  Brooklyn *(G-1526)*
Amsterdam Printing & Litho Inc ....F..... 518 792-6501
  Queensbury *(G-13415)*
Amsterdam Printing & Litho Inc ....F..... 518 842-6000
  Amsterdam *(G-325)*
Amsterdam Printing & Litho Inc ....E..... 518 842-6000
  Amsterdam *(G-326)*
▲ Anne Taintor Inc ....G..... 718 483-9312
  Brooklyn *(G-1536)*
Answer Printing Inc ....F..... 212 922-2922
  New York *(G-8875)*
Apple Press ....G..... 914 723-6660
  White Plains *(G-16421)*
Ares Printing and Packg Corp ....C..... 718 858-8760
  Brooklyn *(G-1550)*
Argo Envelope Corp ....D..... 718 729-2700
  Long Island City *(G-7386)*
Argo Lithographers Inc ....E..... 718 729-2700
  Long Island City *(G-7388)*
Arista Innovations Inc ....E..... 516 746-2262
  Mineola *(G-8205)*
Arnold Printing Corp ....F..... 607 272-7800
  Ithaca *(G-6557)*
Arnold Taylor Printing Inc ....G..... 516 781-0564
  Bellmore *(G-785)*
Aro-Graph Corporation ....G..... 315 463-8693
  Syracuse *(G-15246)*
Art Digital Technologies LLC ....F..... 646 649-4820
  Brooklyn *(G-1557)*
Art Scroll Printing Corp ....F..... 212 929-2413
  New York *(G-8917)*
Artina Group Inc ....E..... 914 592-1850
  Elmsford *(G-4530)*
Artscroll Printing Corp ....E..... 212 929-2413
  New York *(G-8926)*
Asn Inc ....E..... 718 894-0800
  Maspeth *(G-7824)*
At Copy Inc ....G..... 718 624-6136
  Brooklyn *(G-1566)*
Atlantic Color Corp ....E..... 631 345-3800
  Shirley *(G-14829)*
Atlas Print Solutions Inc ....E..... 212 949-8775
  New York *(G-8955)*
Avm Printing Inc ....F..... 631 351-1331
  Hauppauge *(G-5775)*
▲ Avon Reproductions Inc ....E..... 631 273-2400
  Hauppauge *(G-5776)*

B & P Jays Inc ....G..... 716 668-8408
  Buffalo *(G-2721)*
B D B Typewriter Supply Works ....E..... 718 232-4800
  Brooklyn *(G-1580)*
B Q P Inc ....G..... 518 793-4999
  Queensbury *(G-13420)*
Bajan Group Inc ....G..... 518 464-2884
  Latham *(G-7064)*
Ballantrae Lithographers Inc ....G..... 914 592-3275
  White Plains *(G-16426)*
Barone Offset Printing Corp ....G..... 212 989-5500
  Mohegan Lake *(G-8257)*
Bartolomeo Publishing Inc ....G..... 631 420-4949
  West Babylon *(G-16138)*
Batavia Press LLC ....E..... 585 343-4429
  Batavia *(G-612)*
Bates Jackson Engraving Co Inc ....E..... 716 854-3000
  Buffalo *(G-2725)*
Baum Christine and John Corp 585 621-8910
  Rochester *(G-13654)*
Beacon Press Inc 212 691-5050
  White Plains *(G-16427)*
Beastons Budget Printing ....G..... 585 244-2721
  Rochester *(G-13658)*
Beehive Press Inc 718 654-1200
  Bronx *(G-1226)*
Bel Aire Offset Corp 718 539-8333
  College Point *(G-3640)*
▲ Benchmark Printing Inc 518 393-1361
  Schenectady *(G-14653)*
Benchmark Graphics Ltd ....F..... 212 683-1711
  New York *(G-9044)*
Benjamin Printing Inc 315 788-7922
  Adams *(G-2)*
Bennett Multimedia Inc ....F..... 718 629-1454
  Brooklyn *(G-1598)*
Bennett Printing Corporation 718 629-1454
  Brooklyn *(G-1599)*
Bernard Hall ....G..... 585 425-3340
  Fairport *(G-4625)*
Bevilacque Group LLC 212 414-8858
  Port Washington *(G-13245)*
▲ Beyer Graphics Inc ....D..... 631 543-3900
  Commack *(G-3682)*
Billing Coding and Prtg Inc ....G..... 718 827-9409
  Brooklyn *(G-1613)*
Bishop Print Shop Inc 607 965-8155
  Edmeston *(G-4425)*
Bittner Company LLC 585 214-1790
  Rochester *(G-13664)*
Bk Printing Inc 315 565-5396
  East Syracuse *(G-4326)*
Bklynfavors Party Print ....G..... 718 277-0233
  Brooklyn *(G-1617)*
Bluesoho ....F..... 646 805-2583
  New York *(G-9111)*
Bmg Printing and Promotion LLC ....G..... 631 231-9200
  Bohemia *(G-989)*
Boka Printing Inc ....G..... 607 725-3235
  Binghamton *(G-870)*
Boncraft ....D..... 716 662-9720
  Tonawanda *(G-15528)*
Bondy Printing Corp ....G..... 631 242-1510
  Bay Shore *(G-666)*
Boulevard Printing 716 837-3800
  Tonawanda *(G-15529)*
Boxcar Press Incorporated ....E..... 315 473-0930
  Syracuse *(G-15261)*
BP Beyond Printing Inc ....G..... 516 328-2700
  Hempstead *(G-6008)*
▼ BP Digital Imaging LLC ....G..... 607 753-0022
  Cortland *(G-3864)*
Brennans Quick Print Inc ....G..... 518 793-4999
  Glens Falls *(G-5419)*
Bridge Printing Inc ....G..... 212 243-5390
  Long Island City *(G-7403)*
Brigar X-Press Solutions Inc ....D..... 518 438-7817
  Albany *(G-50)*
Brodock Press Inc ....D..... 315 735-9577
  Utica *(G-15681)*
Brooklyn Circus ....F..... 718 858-0919
  Brooklyn *(G-1640)*
Brooks Litho Digital Group Inc ....G..... 631 789-4500
  Deer Park *(G-3955)*
Brown Printing Company 212 782-7800
  New York *(G-9149)*
Business Card Express Inc ....G..... 631 669-3400
  West Babylon *(G-16143)*
C & R De Santis Inc ....E..... 718 447-5076
  Staten Island *(G-15057)*

C K Printing ....G..... 718 965-0388
  Brooklyn *(G-1664)*
C To C Design & Print Inc ....F..... 631 885-4020
  Ronkonkoma *(G-14323)*
Cabba Printing Incorporated ....G..... 212 319-4747
  New York *(G-9172)*
Caboodle Printing Inc ....G..... 716 693-6000
  Williamsville *(G-16573)*
Canaan Printing Inc ....G..... 718 729-3100
  Bayside *(G-744)*
Canandaigua Msgnr Incorporated ....C..... 585 394-0770
  Canandaigua *(G-3213)*
Canastota Publishing Co Inc ....G..... 315 697-9010
  Canastota *(G-3242)*
Candid Litho Printing Ltd 212 431-3800
  Farmingdale *(G-4732)*
Canfield & Tack Inc ....D..... 585 235-7710
  Rochester *(G-13689)*
Canyon Publishing Inc ....F..... 212 334-0227
  New York *(G-9199)*
Capital Dst Print & Imaging ....G..... 518 456-6773
  Schenectady *(G-14657)*
Carges Entps of Canandaigua 585 394-2600
  Canandaigua *(G-3214)*
Carlara Group Ltd 914 769-2020
  Pleasantville *(G-13173)*
Carnels Printing Inc 516 883-3355
  Great Neck *(G-5543)*
Carr Communications Group LLC ....F..... 607 748-0481
  Vestal *(G-15813)*
Castlereagh Printcraft Inc ....D..... 516 623-1728
  Freeport *(G-5148)*
Cathedral Corporation 315 338-0021
  Rome *(G-14249)*
Catskill Delaware Publications ....F..... 845 887-5200
  Callicoon *(G-3160)*
Cayuga Press Cortland Inc ....E..... 888 229-8421
  Liverpool *(G-7230)*
▲ Cazar Printing & Advertising ....G..... 718 446-4606
  Corona *(G-3840)*
Cds Productions Inc 518 385-8255
  Schenectady *(G-14661)*
Cedar West Inc ....D..... 631 467-1444
  Ronkonkoma *(G-14327)*
Chakra Communications Inc ....E..... 607 748-7491
  Endicott *(G-4584)*
Chakra Communications Inc ....E..... 716 505-7300
  Lancaster *(G-7013)*
Challenge Graphics Svcs Inc ....E..... 631 586-0171
  Deer Park *(G-3956)*
Chenango Union Printing Inc 607 334-2112
  Norwich *(G-12479)*
Cherry Lane Lithographing Corp ....E..... 516 293-9294
  Plainview *(G-13041)*
▲ China Imprint LLC 585 563-3391
  Rochester *(G-13709)*
Chromagraphics Press Inc ....G..... 631 367-6160
  Melville *(G-8007)*
Cilyox Inc ....F..... 716 853-3809
  Buffalo *(G-2766)*
Circle Press Inc ....D..... 212 924-4277
  New York *(G-9303)*
Clarsons Corp ....F..... 585 235-8775
  Rochester *(G-13713)*
▲ Classic Business Solutions ....G..... 212 563-9100
  New York *(G-9318)*
Classic Color Graphics Inc 516 822-9090
  Hicksville *(G-6068)*
Classic Color Graphics Inc 516 822-9090
  Hicksville *(G-6069)*
Cloud Printing ....G..... 212 775-0888
  New York *(G-9331)*
Cobico Productions Inc 347 417-5883
  New York *(G-9342)*
Cody Printing Corp ....G..... 718 651-8854
  Woodside *(G-16651)*
Coe Displays Inc ....G..... 718 937-5658
  Long Island City *(G-7412)*
Cohber Press Inc ....D..... 585 475-9100
  West Henrietta *(G-16234)*
Colad Group LLC ....D..... 716 961-1776
  Buffalo *(G-2772)*
Color Card LLC ....F..... 631 232-1300
  Central Islip *(G-3363)*
▲ Color Carton Corp ....D..... 718 665-0840
  Bronx *(G-1243)*
Color-Aid Corporation 212 673-5500
  Hudson Falls *(G-6376)*
Colorfast ....F..... 212 929-2440
  New York *(G-9354)*

SIC SECTION
27 PRINTING, PUBLISHING, AND ALLIED INDUSTRIES

Colorfully Yours Inc .... F 631 242-8600
Bay Shore *(G-674)*
Combine Graphics Corp .... G 212 695-4044
Forest Hills *(G-5073)*
Commerce Offset Ltd .... G 914 769-6671
Thornwood *(G-15505)*
Commercial Press Inc .... G 315 274-0028
Canton *(G-3255)*
Commercial Print & Imaging .... E 716 597-0100
Buffalo *(G-2774)*
Community Media LLC .... E 212 229-1890
New York *(G-9368)*
Community Newspaper Group LLC .... F 607 432-1000
Oneonta *(G-12633)*
Compass Printing Plus .... G 518 523-3308
Saranac Lake *(G-14561)*
Complemar Print LLC .... F 716 875-7238
Buffalo *(G-2776)*
Composite Forms Inc .... F 914 937-1808
Port Chester *(G-13194)*
▲ **Compucolor Associates Inc** .... E 516 358-0000
New Hyde Park *(G-8524)*
▲ **Concept Printing Inc** .... G 845 353-4040
Nyack *(G-12503)*
Consolidated Color Press Inc .... F 212 929-8197
New York *(G-9382)*
Constas Printing Corporation .... G 315 474-2176
Syracuse *(G-15287)*
Copy Stop Inc .... G 914 428-5188
White Plains *(G-16440)*
Coral Color Process Ltd .... E 631 543-5200
Commack *(G-3688)*
▲ **Coral Graphic Services Inc** .... C 516 576-2100
Hicksville *(G-6072)*
Coral Graphic Services Inc .... C 516 576-2100
Hicksville *(G-6073)*
Cosmos Communications Inc .... C 718 482-1800
Long Island City *(G-7416)*
Courier Printing Corp .... E 607 467-2191
Deposit *(G-4107)*
Craig Envelope Corp .... E 718 786-4277
Hicksville *(G-6074)*
Crater Service Group Inc .... G 585 482-7770
Rochester *(G-13724)*
Crawford Print Shop Inc .... G 607 359-4970
Addison *(G-5)*
Create-A-Card Inc .... G 631 584-2273
Saint James *(G-14510)*
Creative Forms Inc .... G 212 431-7540
New York *(G-9420)*
Creative Printing Corp .... G 212 226-3870
New York *(G-9421)*
Cronin Enterprises Inc .... G 914 345-9600
Elmsford *(G-4540)*
D G M Graphics Inc .... F 516 223-2220
Merrick *(G-8096)*
D W S Associates Inc .... E 631 667-6666
Deer Park *(G-3961)*
Daily Record .... F 585 232-2035
Rochester *(G-13732)*
Dan Trent Company Inc .... G 716 822-1422
Buffalo *(G-2792)*
Dark Star Lithograph Corp .... G 845 634-3780
New City *(G-8490)*
Datorib Inc .... G 631 698-6222
Selden *(G-14763)*
David Helsing .... G 607 796-2681
Horseheads *(G-6311)*
Dawn Paper Co Inc .... F 516 596-9110
East Rockaway *(G-4294)*
Deanco Digital Printing LLC .... F 212 371-2025
Sunnyside *(G-15202)*
Decal Makers Inc .... E 516 221-7200
Bellmore *(G-788)*
Decal Techniques Inc .... G 631 491-1800
Bay Shore *(G-679)*
Dell Communications Inc .... G 212 989-3434
New York *(G-9498)*
Delta Press Inc .... E 212 989-3445
High Falls *(G-6140)*
Denton Advertising Inc .... F 631 586-4333
Bohemia *(G-1013)*
Denton Publications Inc .... D 518 873-6368
Elizabethtown *(G-4430)*
Dependable Lithographers Inc .... F 718 472-4200
Long Island City *(G-7423)*
▲ **Design Distributors Inc** .... D 631 242-2000
Deer Park *(G-3966)*
Design Lithographers Inc .... F 212 645-8900
New York *(G-9505)*
Designlogocom Inc .... G 212 564-0200
New York *(G-9508)*
Dick Bailey Service Inc .... F 718 522-4363
Brooklyn *(G-1775)*
Digital Color Concepts Inc .... E 212 989-4888
New York *(G-9526)*
Digital Imaging Tech LLC .... G 518 885-4400
Ballston Spa *(G-580)*
Digital United Color Prtg Inc .... G 845 986-9846
Warwick *(G-15950)*
Dispatch Graphics Inc .... F 212 307-5943
New York *(G-9536)*
Distinctive Printing Inc .... G 212 727-3000
New York *(G-9539)*
Diversified Envelope Ltd .... F 585 615-4697
Rochester *(G-13745)*
Doco Quick Print Inc .... G 315 782-6623
Watertown *(G-16012)*
Donmar Printing Co .... F 516 280-2239
Mineola *(G-8216)*
▲ **Donnelley Financial LLC** .... B 212 425-0298
New York *(G-9555)*
Donnelley Financial LLC .... D 212 351-9000
New York *(G-9556)*
Dovelin Printing Company Inc .... F 718 302-3951
Brooklyn *(G-1790)*
Dowd - Witbeck Printing Corp .... F 518 274-2421
Troy *(G-15604)*
DP Murphy Co Inc .... D 631 673-9400
Deer Park *(G-3968)*
Dual Print & Mail LLC .... D 716 775-8001
Grand Island *(G-5497)*
Dual Print & Mail LLC .... D 716 684-3825
Cheektowaga *(G-3442)*
Dupli Graphics Corporation .... C 315 234-7286
Syracuse *(G-15306)*
Dupli Graphics Corporation .... G 315 422-4732
Syracuse *(G-15307)*
Dyenamix Inc .... G 212 941-6642
New York *(G-9593)*
E B B Graphics Inc .... F 516 750-5510
Westbury *(G-16324)*
E L Smith Printing Co Inc .... E 201 373-0111
New City *(G-8492)*
E W Smith Publishing Co .... F 845 562-1218
New Windsor *(G-8643)*
Eagle Graphics Inc .... G 585 244-5006
Rochester *(G-13755)*
Earth Enterprises Inc .... E 212 741-3999
New York *(G-9607)*
East Coast Business Forms Inc .... G 631 231-9300
Saint James *(G-14512)*
East Coast Thermographers Inc .... E 718 321-3211
College Point *(G-3643)*
East Ridge Quick Print .... F 585 266-4911
Rochester *(G-13758)*
Eastern Hills Printing .... G 716 741-3300
Clarence *(G-3530)*
Eastwood Litho Inc .... E 315 437-2626
Syracuse *(G-15310)*
Echo Appellate Press Inc .... G 516 432-3601
Long Beach *(G-7358)*
Edgian Press Inc .... G 516 931-2114
Hicksville *(G-6082)*
Edwards Graphic Co Inc .... G 718 548-6858
Bronx *(G-1267)*
Efficiency Printing Co Inc .... F 914 949-8611
White Plains *(G-16444)*
Electronic Printing Inc .... G 631 218-2200
Hauppauge *(G-5819)*
Elmat Quality Printing Ltd .... F 516 569-5722
Cedarhurst *(G-3331)*
Empire Press Co .... G 718 756-9500
Brooklyn *(G-1833)*
Endeavor Printing LLC .... G 718 570-2720
Long Island City *(G-7438)*
Engrav-O-Type Press Inc .... F 585 262-7590
Rochester *(G-13785)*
Entermarket .... G 914 437-7268
Mount Kisco *(G-8342)*
Enterprise Press Inc .... C 212 741-2111
New York *(G-9687)*
Evenhouse Printing .... G 716 649-2666
Hamburg *(G-5679)*
Evolution Impressions Inc .... D 585 473-6600
Rochester *(G-13795)*
Excel Graphics Services Inc .... F 212 929-2183
New York *(G-9748)*
Excelsior Graphics Inc .... G 212 730-6200
New York *(G-9751)*
Excelsus Solutions LLC .... E 585 533-0003
Rochester *(G-13797)*
F & B Photo Offset Co Inc .... G 516 431-5433
Island Park *(G-6514)*
F & D Services Inc .... F 718 984-1635
Staten Island *(G-15075)*
F & T Graphics Inc .... F 631 643-1000
Hauppauge *(G-5822)*
F J Remey Co Inc .... E 516 741-5112
Mineola *(G-8222)*
F5 Networks Inc .... G 888 882-7535
New York *(G-9768)*
Fambus Inc .... G 607 785-3700
Endicott *(G-4592)*
Farthing Press Inc .... G 716 852-4674
Buffalo *(G-2825)*
Fasprint .... G 518 483-4631
Malone *(G-7721)*
Federal Envelope Inc .... F 212 243-8380
New York *(G-9790)*
Final Touch Printing Inc .... F 845 352-2677
Spring Valley *(G-14991)*
Finer Touch Printing Corp .... F 516 944-8000
Port Washington *(G-13259)*
▲ **First Displays Inc** .... F 347 642-5972
Long Island City *(G-7449)*
First Line Printing Inc .... F 718 606-0860
Woodside *(G-16656)*
▲ **Five Star Prtg & Mailing Svcs** .... F 212 929-0300
New York *(G-9815)*
Flare Multicopy Corp .... E 718 258-8860
Brooklyn *(G-1887)*
Flower City Printing Inc .... G 585 512-1235
Rochester *(G-13809)*
Flower City Printing Inc .... C 585 663-9000
Rochester *(G-13808)*
Flp Group LLC .... F 315 252-7583
Auburn *(G-480)*
▲ **Flynns Inc** .... E 212 339-8700
New York *(G-9819)*
Folder Factory Inc .... F 540 477-3852
Amityville *(G-275)*
Foleys Graphic Center Inc .... E 914 245-3625
Yorktown Heights *(G-16816)*
Fort Orange Press Inc .... E 518 489-3233
Albany *(G-75)*
Forward Enterprises Inc .... F 585 235-7670
Rochester *(G-13814)*
Francis Emory Fitch Inc .... E 212 619-3800
New York *(G-9838)*
Frederick Coon Inc .... E 716 683-6812
Elma *(G-4450)*
Freeville Publishing Co Inc .... F 607 844-9119
Freeville *(G-5191)*
Fulton Newspapers Inc .... E 315 598-6397
Fulton *(G-5216)*
G & P Printing Inc .... G 212 274-8092
New York *(G-9866)*
G F Labels LLC .... F 518 798-6643
Queensbury *(G-13424)*
G W Canfield & Son Inc .... G 315 735-5522
Utica *(G-15704)*
Gallagher Printing Inc .... E 716 873-2434
Buffalo *(G-2838)*
▲ **Gallant Graphics Ltd** .... E 845 868-1166
Stanfordville *(G-15033)*
Gannett Stllite Info Ntwrk LLC .... E 845 578-2300
West Nyack *(G-16269)*
Gatehouse Media LLC .... D 585 394-0770
Canandaigua *(G-3222)*
Gateway Prtg & Graphics Inc .... E 716 823-3873
Hamburg *(G-5680)*
Gazette Press Inc .... E 914 963-8300
Rye *(G-14479)*
Gem Reproduction Services Corp .... G 845 298-0172
Wappingers Falls *(G-15932)*
Gemson Graphics Inc .... G 516 873-8400
Albertson *(G-149)*
General Business Supply Inc .... D 518 720-3939
Watervliet *(G-16046)*
Geneva Printing Company Inc .... G 315 789-8191
Geneva *(G-5326)*
Genie Instant Printing Co Inc .... F 212 575-8258
New York *(G-9905)*
Glens Falls Printing LLC .... F 518 793-0555
Glens Falls *(G-5427)*
Global Graphics Inc .... F 718 939-4967
Flushing *(G-5002)*
Gmp LLC .... D 914 939-0571
Port Chester *(G-13200)*

S I C

Employee Codes: A=Over 500 employees, B=251-500
C=101-250, D=51-100, E=20-50, F=10-19, G=5-9
2019 Harris
New York Manufacturers Directory
703

Gn Printing ....E 718 784-1713
Long Island City (G-7457)
Golos Printing Inc....G 607 732-1896
Elmira Heights (G-4511)
▼ Gooding Co Inc....E 716 266-6252
Lockport (G-7308)
Government Data Publication....E 347 789-8719
Brooklyn (G-1945)
GPM Associates LLC....E 585 335-3940
Dansville (G-3926)
Grafconect Corp....G 212 714-1795
New York (G-9968)
Grand Meridian Printing Inc....E 718 937-3888
Long Island City (G-7460)
Grand Prix Litho Inc....E 631 242-4182
Holbrook (G-6187)
▲ Graphic Cntrls Acqisition Corp ....B 716 853-7500
Buffalo (G-2853)
Graphic Controls Holdings Inc....F 716 853-7500
Buffalo (G-2854)
Graphic Fabrications Inc....G 516 763-3222
Rockville Centre (G-14232)
Graphicomm Inc....G 716 283-0830
Niagara Falls (G-12289)
Graphics Plus Printing Inc....E 607 299-0500
Cortland (G-3875)
Great Eastern Color Lith....C 845 454-7420
Poughkeepsie (G-13342)
Green Girl Prtg & Msgnr Inc....G 212 575-0357
New York (G-9983)
Grover Cleveland Press Inc....F 716 564-2222
Amherst (G-230)
Guaranteed Printing Svc Co Inc....E 212 929-2410
Long Island City (G-7464)
H T L & S Ltd....F 718 435-4474
Brooklyn (G-1957)
H&E Service Corp....D 646 472-1936
Garden City (G-5261)
Haig Press Inc....E 631 582-5800
Hauppauge (G-5838)
Hamptons Magazine....E 631 283-7125
Southampton (G-14955)
Harmon and Castella Printing....F 845 471-9163
Poughkeepsie (G-13344)
Hearst Corporation....A 518 454-5694
Albany (G-82)
Hempstead Sentinel Inc....F 516 486-5000
Hempstead (G-6013)
Heritage Printing Center....G 518 563-8240
Plattsburgh (G-13124)
HI Speed Envelope Co Inc....F 718 617-1600
Mount Vernon (G-8406)
High End Print Solutions Inc....F 585 325-5320
Rochester (G-13866)
Hill Crest Press....G 518 943-0671
Catskill (G-3304)
Hillside Printing Inc....F 718 658-6719
Jamaica (G-6650)
Hks Printing Company Inc....F 212 675-2529
New York (G-10109)
▲ Hooek Produktion Inc....G 212 367-9111
New York (G-10121)
Horne Organization Inc....F 914 572-1330
Yonkers (G-16769)
Hospitality Graphics Inc....G 212 643-6700
New York (G-10127)
Huckleberry Inc....G 631 630-5450
Hauppauge (G-5847)
▲ Hudson Envelope Corporation....E 212 473-6666
New York (G-10142)
▲ Hudson Park Press Inc....G 212 929-8898
New York (G-10144)
Hudson Printing Co Inc....E 718 937-8600
New York (G-10145)
Hugh F McPherson Inc....G 716 668-6107
Cheektowaga (G-3450)
I 2 Print Inc....F 718 937-8800
Long Island City (G-7472)
Impala Press Ltd....G 631 588-4262
Ronkonkoma (G-14352)
In-House Inc....F 718 445-9007
College Point (G-3646)
In-Step Marketing Inc....F 212 797-3450
New York (G-10191)
Ink Well....G 718 253-9736
Brooklyn (G-2004)
Ink-It Printing Inc....G 718 229-5590
College Point (G-3647)
Inland Printing Company Inc....G 516 367-4700
Woodbury (G-16622)
Instant Again LLC....E 585 436-8003
Rochester (G-13881)
Instant Stream Inc....E 917 438-7182
New York (G-10227)
Insty-Prints of Buffalo Inc....G 716 853-6483
Buffalo (G-2886)
International Newsppr Prtg Co....E 516 626-6095
Glen Head (G-5381)
Interstate Litho Corp....D 631 232-6025
Brentwood (G-1136)
Iron Horse Graphics Ltd....G 631 537-3400
Bridgehampton (G-1181)
Iver Printing Inc....G 718 275-2070
New Hyde Park (G-8543)
J & J Printing Inc....G 315 458-7411
Syracuse (G-15344)
J A T Printing Inc....G 631 427-1155
Huntington (G-6401)
J F B & Sons Lithographers....D 631 467-1444
Lake Ronkonkoma (G-6981)
J P Printing Inc....G 516 293-6110
Farmingdale (G-4790)
J V Haring & Son....F 718 720-1947
Staten Island (G-15094)
J3 Printing Inc....G 516 304-6103
Queens Village (G-13408)
Jack J Florio Jr....G 716 434-9123
Lockport (G-7311)
Jacobs Press Inc....F 315 252-4861
Auburn (G-485)
Jam Printing Publishing Inc....G 914 345-8400
Elmsford (G-4547)
James Conolly Printing Co....E 585 426-4150
Rochester (G-13891)
Jane Lewis....G 607 722-0584
Binghamton (G-898)
Japan Printing & Graphics Inc....G 212 406-2905
New York (G-10308)
JDS Graphics Inc....F 973 330-3300
New York (G-10320)
Johnnys Ideal Printing Co....G 518 828-6666
Hudson (G-6359)
Jon Lyn Ink Inc....G 516 546-2312
Merrick (G-8099)
◆ Joseph Paul....G 718 693-4269
Brooklyn (G-2047)
Judith Lewis Printer Inc....G 516 997-7777
Westbury (G-16346)
Jurist Company Inc....G 212 243-8008
Long Island City (G-7483)
Just Press Print LLC....G 585 783-1300
Rochester (G-13901)
Kaleidoscope Imaging Inc....E 212 631-9947
New York (G-10396)
Karr Graphics Corp....E 212 645-6000
Long Island City (G-7487)
Kas-Ray Industries Inc....F 212 620-3144
New York (G-10410)
Kaufman Brothers Printing....G 212 563-1854
New York (G-10419)
Kaymil Printing Company Inc....G 212 594-3718
New York (G-10422)
Keeners East End Litho Inc....G 631 324-8565
East Hampton (G-4239)
Keller Bros & Miller Inc....G 716 854-2374
Buffalo (G-2903)
Kent Associates Inc....G 212 675-0722
New York (G-10435)
Kenyon Press Inc....E 607 674-9066
Sherburne (G-14806)
Key Brand Entertainment Inc....C 212 966-5400
New York (G-10437)
Kim Jae Printing Co Inc....G 212 691-6289
Roslyn Heights (G-14457)
Kinaneco Inc....E 315 468-6201
Syracuse (G-15356)
King Lithographers Inc....E 914 667-4200
Mount Vernon (G-8414)
Kingsbury Printing Co Inc....G 518 747-6606
Queensbury (G-13431)
Kjckd Inc....G 518 435-9696
Latham (G-7078)
▲ Kling Magnetics Inc....E 518 392-4000
Chatham (G-3428)
Kurtskraft Inc....G 516 944-4449
Port Washington (G-13280)
◆ Kwik Ticket Inc....F 718 421-3800
Brooklyn (G-2085)
L & K Graphics Inc....G 631 667-2269
Deer Park (G-3997)
L I F Publishing Corp....D 631 345-5200
Shirley (G-14837)
L K Printing Corp....G 914 761-1944
White Plains (G-16470)
L M N Printing Company Inc....E 516 285-8526
Valley Stream (G-15784)
Label Gallery Inc....E 607 334-3244
Norwich (G-12489)
Lake Placid Advertisers Wkshp....E 518 523-3359
Lake Placid (G-6976)
▼ Laser Printer Checks Corp....G 845 782-5837
Monroe (G-8275)
Leader Printing Inc....F 516 546-1544
Merrick (G-8101)
Lee Printing Inc....G 718 237-1651
Brooklyn (G-2104)
Lehmann Printing Company Inc....G 212 929-2395
New York (G-10542)
Leigh Scott Enterprises Inc....G 718 343-5440
Bellerose (G-781)
Lennons Litho Inc....F 315 866-3156
Herkimer (G-6043)
Levon Graphics Corp....D 631 753-2022
Deer Park (G-4001)
LI Script LLC....E 631 321-3850
Woodbury (G-16624)
Liberty Label Mfg Inc....F 631 737-2365
Holbrook (G-6195)
Litho Dynamics Inc....G 914 769-1759
Hawthorne (G-5991)
Lithomatic Business Forms Inc....G 212 255-6700
New York (G-10579)
Litmor Publishing Corp....F 516 931-0012
Garden City (G-5266)
Lmg National Publishing Inc....E 585 598-6874
Fairport (G-4640)
Logo Print Company....G 607 324-5403
Hornell (G-6301)
Loudon Ltd....G 631 757-4447
East Northport (G-4267)
Louis Heindl & Son Inc....G 585 454-5080
Rochester (G-13917)
Love Unlimited NY Inc....E 718 359-8500
Westbury (G-16353)
Loy L Press Inc....G 716 634-5966
Buffalo (G-2928)
Lynmar Printing Corp....G 631 957-8500
Amityville (G-298)
▲ M L Design Inc....F 212 233-0213
New York (G-10641)
M T M Printing Co Inc....F 718 353-3297
College Point (G-3654)
M&M Printing Inc....F 516 796-3020
Carle Place (G-3269)
Madison Printing Corp....G 607 273-3535
Ithaca (G-6592)
Magazines & Brochures Inc....G 716 875-9699
Buffalo (G-2933)
Mahin Impressions Inc....G 212 871-9777
Riverhead (G-13577)
Malone Industrial Press Inc....G 518 483-5880
Malone (G-7724)
Manifestation-Glow Press Inc....G 718 380-5259
Fresh Meadows (G-5202)
Mansfield Press Inc....F 212 265-5411
New York (G-10695)
Marcal Printing Inc....G 516 942-9500
Hicksville (G-6105)
Marcy Printing Inc....G 718 935-9100
Brooklyn (G-2166)
Mark T Westinghouse....G 518 678-3262
Catskill (G-3306)
Marks Corpex Banknote Co....G 631 968-0277
Bay Shore (G-698)
Marlow Printing Co Inc....E 718 625-4948
Brooklyn (G-2171)
▼ Marsid Group Ltd....G 516 334-1603
Carle Place (G-3271)
Mason & Gore Inc....E 914 921-1025
Rye (G-14485)
Master Image Printing Inc....G 914 347-4400
Elmsford (G-4550)
Mc Squared Nyc Inc....F 212 947-2260
New York (G-10738)
McG Graphics Inc....G 631 499-0730
Dix Hills (G-4122)
McPc Inc....D 212 583-6000
New York (G-10746)
Mdi Holdings LLC....A 212 559-1127
New York (G-10747)

Mdr Printing Corp .... G 516 627-3221
Manhasset *(G-7769)*

▲ Medallion Associates Inc .... E 212 929-9130
New York *(G-10751)*

▲ Mercury Print Productions Inc .... C 585 458-7900
Rochester *(G-13936)*

Merrill New York Company Inc .... C 212 229-6500
New York *(G-10778)*

Messenger Press .... G 518 885-9231
Ballston Spa *(G-591)*

Michael K Lennon Inc .... E 631 288-5200
Westhampton Beach *(G-16404)*

Mickelberry Communications Inc .... G 212 832-0303
New York *(G-10794)*

Microera Printers Inc .... E 585 783-1300
Rochester *(G-13941)*

Mid Atlantic Graphics Corp .... E 631 345-3800
Shirley *(G-14840)*

Mid-York Press Inc .... D 607 674-4491
Sherburne *(G-14807)*

Middletown Press .... G 845 343-1895
Middletown *(G-8164)*

Midgley Printing Corp .... G 315 475-1864
Syracuse *(G-15372)*

Midstate Printing Corp .... E 315 475-4101
Liverpool *(G-7247)*

Mikam Graphics LLC .... D 212 684-9393
New York *(G-10805)*

Miken Companies Inc .... D 716 668-6311
Buffalo *(G-2946)*

Miller Place Printing Inc .... G 631 473-1158
Miller Place *(G-8191)*

Miller Printing & Litho Inc .... G 518 842-0001
Amsterdam *(G-348)*

▲ Mines Press Inc .... C 914 788-1800
Cortlandt Manor *(G-3903)*

Minuteman Press Inc .... G 845 623-2277
Nanuet *(G-8466)*

Minuteman Press Intl Inc .... G 718 343-5440
Jamaica *(G-6662)*

Mitchell Prtg & Mailing Inc .... F 315 343-3531
Oswego *(G-12781)*

MJB Printing Corp .... G 631 581-0177
Islip *(G-6549)*

Mod-Pac Corp .... D 716 447-9013
Buffalo *(G-2952)*

Monarch Graphics Inc .... F 631 232-1300
Central Islip *(G-3378)*

Moneast Inc .... G 845 298-8898
Wappingers Falls *(G-15936)*

Monte Press Inc .... G 718 325-4999
Bronx *(G-1336)*

Mooney-Keehley Inc .... G 585 271-1573
Rochester *(G-13955)*

Moore Printing Company Inc .... G 585 394-1533
Canandaigua *(G-3225)*

Multimedia Services Inc .... E 607 936-3186
Corning *(G-3822)*

Multiple Imprssons of Rchester .... G 585 546-1160
Rochester *(G-13960)*

Mutual Engraving Company Inc .... D 516 489-0534
West Hempstead *(G-16223)*

Nameplate Mfrs of Amer .... E 631 752-0055
Farmingdale *(G-4831)*

Nash Printing Inc .... F 516 935-4567
Plainview *(G-13077)*

National Reproductions Inc .... E 212 619-3800
New York *(G-10884)*

NCR Corporation .... C 607 273-5310
Ithaca *(G-6599)*

Nesher Printing Inc .... G 212 760-2521
New York *(G-10909)*

New Goldstar 1 Printing Corp .... G 212 343-3909
New York *(G-10924)*

New Horizon Graphics Inc .... E 631 231-8055
Hauppauge *(G-5901)*

New York Digital Print Center .... G 718 767-1953
Whitestone *(G-16546)*

New York Typing & Printing Co .... G 718 268-7900
Forest Hills *(G-5079)*

Newburgh Envelope Corp .... G 845 566-4211
Newburgh *(G-12236)*

Newport Graphics Inc .... E 212 924-2600
New York *(G-10950)*

North Delaware Printing Inc .... G 716 692-0576
Tonawanda *(G-15566)*

Northeast Commercial Prtg Inc .... G 518 459-5047
Albany *(G-106)*

▲ Northeast Prtg & Dist Co Inc .... E 518 563-8214
Plattsburgh *(G-13141)*

Northern NY Newspapers Corp .... C 315 782-1000
Watertown *(G-16031)*

▲ Nova Inc .... G 212 967-1139
New York *(G-10999)*

Observer Daily Sunday Newsppr .... D 716 366-3000
Dunkirk *(G-4175)*

Office Grabs NY Inc .... G 212 444-1331
Brooklyn *(G-2285)*

▼ Official Offset Corporation .... E 631 957-8500
Amityville *(G-307)*

Olympic Press Inc .... F 212 242-4934
New York *(G-11038)*

Orbis Brynmore Lithographics .... G 212 987-2100
New York *(G-11055)*

Orffeo Printing & Imaging Inc .... G 716 681-5757
Lancaster *(G-7034)*

▲ Orlandi Inc .... D 631 756-0110
Farmingdale *(G-4840)*

Orlandi Inc .... E 631 756-0110
Farmingdale *(G-4841)*

Ozipko Enterprises Inc .... G 585 424-6740
Rochester *(G-13999)*

P & W Press Inc .... E 646 486-3417
New York *(G-11083)*

P D R Inc .... G 516 829-5300
Plainview *(G-13080)*

Pace Editions Inc .... G 212 675-7431
New York *(G-11086)*

Paladino Prtg & Graphics Inc .... G 718 279-6000
Flushing *(G-5033)*

Pama Enterprises Inc .... G 516 504-6300
Great Neck *(G-5579)*

▲ Panther Graphics Inc .... E 585 546-7163
Rochester *(G-14006)*

▲ Paper House Productions Inc .... E 845 246-7261
Saugerties *(G-14612)*

Park Slope Copy Center .... F 718 783-0268
Brooklyn *(G-2306)*

Parkside Printing Co Inc .... F 516 933-5423
Jericho *(G-6796)*

Parrinello Printing Inc .... F 716 633-7780
Buffalo *(G-2993)*

Patrick Ryans Modern Press .... F 518 434-2921
Albany *(G-111)*

▲ Paul Michael Group Inc .... G 631 585-5700
Ronkonkoma *(G-14397)*

Paya Printing of NY Inc .... G 516 625-8346
Albertson *(G-151)*

PBR Graphics Inc .... G 518 458-2909
Albany *(G-112)*

Peachtree Enterprises Inc .... E 212 989-3445
Long Island City *(G-7551)*

Perfect Forms and Systems Inc .... F 631 462-1100
Smithtown *(G-14905)*

Persch Service Print Inc .... G 716 366-2677
Dunkirk *(G-4176)*

Petcap Press Corporation .... F 718 609-0910
Long Island City *(G-7554)*

Petit Printing Corp .... G 716 871-9490
Getzville *(G-5352)*

Phillip Tissicher .... F 718 282-3310
Brooklyn *(G-2314)*

Phoenix Graphics Inc .... E 585 232-4040
Rochester *(G-14019)*

Pic A Poc Enterprises Inc .... G 631 981-2094
Ronkonkoma *(G-14399)*

Pine Bush Printing Co Inc .... G 518 456-2431
Albany *(G-116)*

Pioneer Printers Inc .... F 716 693-7100
North Tonawanda *(G-12442)*

PIP Inc .... G 518 861-0133
Latham *(G-7090)*

Pixos Print .... G 585 500-4600
Rochester *(G-14023)*

Platinum Printing & Graphics .... G 631 249-3325
Farmingdale *(G-4852)*

Play-It Productions Inc .... F 212 695-6530
Port Washington *(G-13297)*

Pollack Graphics Inc .... G 212 727-8400
New York *(G-11216)*

Pop Printing Incorporated .... F 212 808-7800
Brooklyn *(G-2328)*

Positive Print Litho Offset .... G 212 431-4850
New York *(G-11223)*

Post Road .... F 203 545-2122
New York *(G-11224)*

Pre Cycled Inc .... G 845 278-7611
Brewster *(G-1174)*

Precision Envelope Co Inc .... G 631 694-3990
Farmingdale *(G-4856)*

Preebro Printing .... G 718 633-7300
Brooklyn *(G-2337)*

Presstek Printing .... G 585 266-2770
Rochester *(G-14041)*

Presstek Printing LLC .... F 585 467-8140
Rochester *(G-14042)*

Presstek Printing LLC .... F 585 266-2770
Rochester *(G-14043)*

Prestige Envelope & Lithograph .... F 631 521-7043
Merrick *(G-8105)*

Prestone Press LLC .... C 347 468-7900
Long Island City *(G-7558)*

Pricet Printing .... G 315 655-0369
Cazenovia *(G-3326)*

Print & Graphics Group .... G 518 371-4649
Clifton Park *(G-3573)*

▲ Print Better Inc .... G 347 348-1841
Ridgewood *(G-13547)*

Print By Premier LLC .... G 212 947-1365
New York *(G-11245)*

Print Center Inc .... G 718 643-9559
Cold Spring Harbor *(G-3632)*

Print Cottage LLC .... F 516 369-1749
Massapequa Park *(G-7894)*

▲ Print Early LLC .... E 718 915-7368
Westbury *(G-16367)*

▲ Print House Inc .... D 718 443-7500
Brooklyn *(G-2346)*

Print It Here .... G 516 308-7785
Massapequa *(G-7883)*

Print It Inc .... G 845 371-2227
Monsey *(G-8294)*

Print Management Group Inc .... G 212 213-1555
New York *(G-11247)*

Print Market Inc .... G 631 940-8181
Deer Park *(G-4029)*

▲ Print Media Inc .... D 212 563-4040
New York *(G-11248)*

Print On Demand Initiative Inc .... F 585 239-6044
Rochester *(G-14044)*

Print Seforim Bzul Inc .... G 718 679-1011
Brooklyn *(G-2348)*

Print Solutions Plus Inc .... G 315 234-3801
Liverpool *(G-7258)*

Printcorp Inc .... E 631 696-0641
Ronkonkoma *(G-14400)*

Printech Business Systems Inc .... F 212 290-2542
New York *(G-11249)*

Printers 3 Inc .... F 631 351-1331
Hauppauge *(G-5923)*

Printing Prmtnal Solutions LLC .... F 315 474-1110
Syracuse *(G-15397)*

Printing Resources Inc .... E 518 482-2470
Albany *(G-119)*

Printing Sales Group Limited .... E 718 258-8860
Brooklyn *(G-2351)*

Printing Spectrum Inc .... F 631 689-1010
East Setauket *(G-4308)*

Printing X Press Ions .... G 631 242-1992
Dix Hills *(G-4124)*

Printinghouse Press Ltd .... G 212 719-0990
New York *(G-11251)*

Printroc Inc .... F 585 461-2556
Rochester *(G-14045)*

Printutopia .... F 718 788-1545
Brooklyn *(G-2352)*

Printz and Patternz LLC .... G 518 944-6020
Schenectady *(G-14705)*

Pro Printing .... G 516 561-9700
Lynbrook *(G-7670)*

Professional Solutions Print .... G 631 231-9300
Hauppauge *(G-5925)*

Profile Printing & Graphics .... G 631 273-2727
Hauppauge *(G-5926)*

Progressive Color Graphics .... E 212 292-8787
Great Neck *(G-5584)*

Progressive Graphics & Prtg .... G 315 331-3635
Newark *(G-12205)*

Prompt Printing Inc .... G 631 454-6524
Farmingdale *(G-4858)*

Pronto Printer .... G 914 737-0800
Cortlandt Manor *(G-3904)*

Psychonomic Society Inc .... E 512 381-1494
New York *(G-11270)*

Quad/Graphics Inc .... A 518 581-4000
Saratoga Springs *(G-14594)*

Quad/Graphics Inc .... C 212 672-1300
New York *(G-11294)*

Quad/Graphics Inc .... A 212 206-5535
New York *(G-11295)*

SIC

Employee Codes: A=Over 500 employees, B=251-500
C=101-250, D=51-100, E=20-50, F=10-19, G=5-9

2019 Harris
New York Manufacturers Directory

705

Quad/Graphics Inc ....A.... 212 741-1001
New York *(G-11296)*
Quadrangle Quickprints Ltd ....G.... 631 694-4464
Melville *(G-8060)*
Quality Graphics Tri State ....G.... 845 735-2523
Pearl River *(G-12909)*
Quicker Printer Inc ....G.... 607 734-8622
Elmira *(G-4500)*
Quickprint ....G.... 585 394-2600
Canandaigua *(G-3232)*
R & J Graphics Inc ....F.... 631 293-6611
Farmingdale *(G-4863)*
R & L Press Inc ....G.... 718 447-8557
Staten Island *(G-15121)*
R & L Press of SI Inc ....G.... 718 667-3258
Staten Island *(G-15122)*
R D Printing Associates Inc ....F.... 631 390-5964
Farmingdale *(G-4864)*
▲ **R Hochman Papers Incorporated** ....F.... 516 466-6414
Brooklyn *(G-2377)*
Raith America Inc ....E.... 518 874-3000
Troy *(G-15619)*
Rapid Print and Marketing Inc ....G.... 585 924-1520
Victor *(G-15864)*
Rapid Rays Printing & Copying ....G.... 716 852-0550
Buffalo *(G-3031)*
Rapid Reproductions LLC ....G.... 607 843-2221
Oxford *(G-12808)*
Rapid Service Engraving Co ....G.... 716 896-4555
Buffalo *(G-3032)*
Rasco Graphics Inc ....G.... 212 206-0447
New York *(G-11327)*
Ready Check Glo Inc ....G.... 516 547-1849
East Northport *(G-4270)*
Redi Records Payroll ....F.... 718 854-6990
Brooklyn *(G-2392)*
Reflex Offset Inc ....G.... 516 746-4142
Deer Park *(G-4035)*
REM Printing Inc ....G.... 518 438-7338
Albany *(G-125)*
Remsen Graphics Corp ....G.... 718 643-7500
Brooklyn *(G-2397)*
Resonant Legal Media LLC ....E.... 212 687-7100
New York *(G-11368)*
Resonant Legal Media LLC ....D.... 800 781-3591
New York *(G-11369)*
Rgm Signs Inc ....G.... 718 442-0598
Staten Island *(G-15129)*
Richard Ruffner ....F.... 631 234-4600
Central Islip *(G-3383)*
RIT Printing Corp ....F.... 631 586-6220
Bay Shore *(G-715)*
Rmd Holding Inc ....G.... 845 628-0030
Mahopac *(G-7712)*
Rmf Print Management Group ....F.... 716 683-4351
Depew *(G-4105)*
▲ **Rmf Printing Technologies Inc** ....E.... 716 683-7500
Lancaster *(G-7045)*
Robert Tabatznik Assoc Inc ....F.... 845 336-4555
Kingston *(G-6916)*
▲ **Rosemont Press Incorporated** ....E.... 212 239-4770
New York *(G-11430)*
Rosen Mandell & Immerman Inc ....E.... 212 691-2277
New York *(G-11431)*
Royal Tees Inc ....G.... 845 357-9448
Suffern *(G-15197)*
Rv Printing ....G.... 631 567-8658
Holbrook *(G-6207)*
Ryan Printing Inc ....E.... 845 535-3235
Blauvelt *(G-940)*
Sample News Group LLC ....D.... 315 343-3800
Oswego *(G-12787)*
Sand Hill Industries Inc ....G.... 518 885-7991
Ballston Spa *(G-595)*
▲ **Sanford Printing Inc** ....G.... 718 461-1202
Flushing *(G-5044)*
Scotti Graphics Inc ....E.... 212 367-9602
Long Island City *(G-7585)*
Scriven Duplicating Service ....G.... 518 233-8180
Troy *(G-15624)*
Seaboard Graphic Services LLC ....E.... 315 652-4200
East Syracuse *(G-4369)*
Searles Graphics Inc ....E.... 631 345-2202
Yaphank *(G-16720)*
Security Offset Services Inc ....G.... 631 944-6031
Huntington *(G-6415)*
Seifert Graphics Inc ....F.... 315 736-2744
Oriskany *(G-12761)*
Select-A-Form Inc ....D.... 631 981-3076
Holbrook *(G-6208)*

Seneca West Printing Inc ....G.... 716 675-8010
West Seneca *(G-16303)*
Sentine Printing Inc ....G.... 516 334-7400
Westbury *(G-16372)*
Sharp Printing Inc ....G.... 716 731-3994
Sanborn *(G-14553)*
Shield Press Inc ....G.... 212 431-7489
New York *(G-11565)*
Shipman Printing Inds Inc ....E.... 716 504-7700
Niagara Falls *(G-12336)*
Shipman Printing Inds Inc ....G.... 716 504-7700
Sanborn *(G-14554)*
Shipmtes/Printmates Holdg Corp ....D.... 518 370-1158
Scotia *(G-14746)*
Shoreline Publishing Inc ....G.... 914 738-7869
Pelham *(G-12938)*
Sign Shop Inc ....G.... 631 226-4145
Copiague *(G-3782)*
Sign World Inc ....E.... 212 619-9000
Brooklyn *(G-2469)*
Sizzal LLC ....E.... 212 354-6123
Long Island City *(G-7593)*
Sloane Design Inc ....G.... 212 539-0184
Brooklyn *(G-2487)*
Source Envelope Inc ....G.... 866 284-0707
Farmingdale *(G-4877)*
South Bridge Press Inc ....G.... 212 233-4047
New York *(G-11654)*
Spectrum Prtg Lithography Inc ....E.... 212 255-3131
New York *(G-11665)*
Speedcard Inc ....G.... 631 472-1904
Holbrook *(G-6210)*
Speedway Press Inc ....G.... 315 343-3531
Oswego *(G-12788)*
Speedy Enterprise of USA Corp ....G.... 718 463-3000
Flushing *(G-5047)*
Sputnick 84 LLC ....G.... 844 667-7468
New York *(G-11686)*
St James Printing Inc ....G.... 631 981-2095
Ronkonkoma *(G-14418)*
▲ **St Lawrence County Newspapers** ....D.... 315 393-1003
Canton *(G-3258)*
▲ **Standwill Packaging Inc** ....E.... 631 752-1236
Farmingdale *(G-4879)*
Star Press Pearl River Inc ....G.... 845 268-2294
Valley Cottage *(G-15765)*
▲ **Star Quality Printing Inc** ....F.... 631 273-1900
Hauppauge *(G-5949)*
Steffen Publishing Inc ....D.... 315 865-4100
Holland Patent *(G-6225)*
Sterling North America Inc ....E.... 631 243-6933
Hauppauge *(G-5950)*
▼ **Sterling Pierce Company Inc** ....E.... 516 593-1170
East Rockaway *(G-4296)*
Steval Graphics Concepts Inc ....F.... 516 576-0220
Plainview *(G-13090)*
Stevens Bandes Graphics Corp ....F.... 212 675-1128
New York *(G-11710)*
Stevenson Printing Co Inc ....G.... 516 676-1233
Glen Cove *(G-5376)*
Stony Brook University ....E.... 631 632-6434
Stony Brook *(G-15169)*
Stony Point Graphics Ltd ....G.... 845 786-3322
Stony Point *(G-15176)*
Stubbs Printing Inc ....G.... 315 769-8641
Massena *(G-7909)*
Studio 22 Print ....G.... 212 679-2656
New York *(G-11726)*
Studley Printing & Publishing ....F.... 518 563-1414
Plattsburgh *(G-13160)*
Stylistic Press Inc ....F.... 212 675-0797
New York *(G-11731)*
Suffolk Copy Center Inc ....G.... 631 665-0570
Bay Shore *(G-727)*
Summit MSP LLC ....G.... 716 433-1014
Lockport *(G-7332)*
Summit Print & Mail LLC ....G.... 716 433-1014
Lockport *(G-7333)*
Sun Printing Incorporated ....E.... 607 337-3034
Norwich *(G-12493)*
Superior Print On Demand ....G.... 607 240-5231
Vestal *(G-15823)*
Syracuse Computer Forms Inc ....E.... 315 478-0108
Syracuse *(G-15436)*
Sz - Design & Print Inc ....F.... 845 659-2273
Monsey *(G-8299)*
T C Peters Printing Co Inc ....G.... 315 724-4149
Utica *(G-15735)*
Taylor Communications Inc ....G.... 718 361-1000
Long Island City *(G-7612)*

Technipoly Manufacturing Inc ....E.... 718 383-0363
Brooklyn *(G-2559)*
◆ **Tele-Pak Inc** ....E.... 845 426-2300
Monsey *(G-8302)*
Teller Printing Corp ....G.... 718 486-3662
Brooklyn *(G-2562)*
The Kingsbury Printing Co Inc ....G.... 518 747-6606
Queensbury *(G-13443)*
The Nugent Organization Inc ....F.... 212 645-6600
Oceanside *(G-12561)*
Thomas Group Inc ....F.... 212 947-6400
New York *(G-11817)*
Three Star Offset Printing ....F.... 516 867-8223
Freeport *(G-5187)*
Tobay Printing Co Inc ....E.... 631 842-3300
Copiague *(G-3788)*
Tom & Jerry Printcraft Forms ....E.... 914 777-7468
Mamaroneck *(G-7758)*
Torsaf Printers Inc ....G.... 516 569-5577
Hewlett *(G-6051)*
Total Concept Graphic Inc ....G.... 212 229-2626
New York *(G-11873)*
Tovie Asarese Royal Prtg Co ....G.... 716 885-7692
Buffalo *(G-3100)*
Trade Mark Graphics Inc ....G.... 718 306-0001
Brooklyn *(G-2578)*
Transaction Printer Group ....G.... 607 274-2500
Ithaca *(G-6614)*
◆ **Transcntinental Ultra Flex Inc** ....B.... 718 272-9100
Brooklyn *(G-2579)*
Transcontinental Printing GP ....G.... 716 626-3078
Amherst *(G-256)*
Tremont Offset Inc ....G.... 718 892-7333
Bronx *(G-1404)*
Tri Kolor Printing & Sty ....F.... 315 474-6753
Syracuse *(G-15446)*
Tri-Lon Clor Lithographers Ltd ....E.... 212 255-6140
New York *(G-11893)*
Tri-Star Offset Corp ....E.... 718 894-5555
Maspeth *(G-7873)*
Tri-Town News Inc ....E.... 607 561-3515
Sidney *(G-14855)*
Triad Printing Inc ....G.... 845 343-2722
Middletown *(G-8180)*
Tripi Engraving Co Inc ....E.... 718 383-6500
Brooklyn *(G-2586)*
Tropp Printing Corp ....G.... 212 233-4519
New York *(G-11903)*
Troy Sign & Printing ....G.... 718 994-4482
Bronx *(G-1407)*
True Type Printing Co Inc ....G.... 718 706-6900
Amityville *(G-324)*
Tucker Printers Inc ....D.... 585 359-3030
Henrietta *(G-6037)*
▲ **Twenty-First Century Press Inc** ....F.... 716 837-0800
Buffalo *(G-3106)*
Twin Counties Pro Printers Inc ....F.... 518 828-3278
Hudson *(G-6374)*
Upstate Printing Inc ....F.... 315 475-6140
Syracuse *(G-15449)*
V & J Graphics Inc ....G.... 315 363-1933
Oneida *(G-12622)*
V C N Group Ltd Inc ....G.... 516 223-4812
North Baldwin *(G-12369)*
Vanguard Graphics LLC ....C.... 607 272-1212
Ithaca *(G-6615)*
▲ **Variable Graphics LLC** ....G.... 212 691-2323
New York *(G-11994)*
Veterans Offset Printing Inc ....G.... 585 288-2900
Rochester *(G-14200)*
Vic-Gina Printing Company Inc ....G.... 914 636-0200
New Rochelle *(G-8631)*
Vicks Lithograph & Prtg Corp ....C.... 315 736-9344
Yorkville *(G-16833)*
Vicks Lithograph & Prtg Corp ....C.... 315 272-2401
Yorkville *(G-16832)*
Vincys Printing Ltd ....F.... 518 355-4363
Schenectady *(G-14725)*
VIP Printing ....G.... 718 641-9361
Howard Beach *(G-6332)*
▲ **Virgil Mountain Inc** ....G.... 212 378-0007
New York *(G-12037)*
Vivona Business Printers Inc ....G.... 516 496-3453
Syosset *(G-15233)*
Wallkill Valley Publications ....E.... 845 561-0170
Newburgh *(G-12251)*
Walnut Printing Inc ....G.... 718 707-0100
Long Island City *(G-7633)*
Wappingers Falls Shopper Inc ....E.... 845 297-3723
Wappingers Falls *(G-15938)*

Warren Printing Inc .... F 212 627-5000
 Long Island City (G-7634)
Wayne Printing Inc .... F 914 761-2400
 White Plains (G-16517)
Webb-Mason Inc .... E 716 276-8792
 Buffalo (G-3126)
Webster Printing Corporation ...... F 585 671-1533
 Webster (G-16107)
Weeks & Reichel Printing Inc ...... G 631 589-1443
 Sayville (G-14635)
Weicro Graphics Inc .... E 631 253-3360
 West Babylon (G-16204)
Westchester Mailing Service .... E 914 948-1116
 White Plains (G-16519)
Westmore Litho Inc .... G 718 361-9403
 Long Island City (G-7636)
Westypo Printers Inc .... G 914 737-7394
 Peekskill (G-12930)
Whitestone Dev Group LLC .... E 585 482-7770
 Rochester (G-14208)
William Boyd Printing Co Inc ...... C 518 339-5832
 Latham (G-7098)
William Charles Prtg Co Inc .... F 516 349-0900
 Plainview (G-13102)
William J Kline & Son Inc .... D 518 843-1100
 Amsterdam (G-364)
William J Ryan .... G 585 392-6200
 Hilton (G-6159)
Wilson Press LLC .... E 315 568-9693
 Seneca Falls (G-14788)
Winner Press Inc .... E 718 937-7715
 Long Island City (G-7640)
Winson Surnamer Inc .... G 718 729-8787
 Long Island City (G-7641)
▲ Won & Lee Inc .... E 516 222-0712
 Garden City (G-5284)
Woodbury Printing Plus + Inc ..... G 845 928-6610
 Central Valley (G-3399)
Worldwide Ticket Craft .... D 516 538-6200
 Merrick (G-8107)
Wynco Press One Inc .... G 516 354-6145
 Glen Oaks (G-5388)
X Myles Mar Inc .... E 212 683-2015
 New York (G-12148)
X-L Envelope and Printing Inc .... F 716 852-2135
 Buffalo (G-3134)
Yorktown Printing Corp .... C 914 962-2526
 Yorktown Heights (G-16826)
Zacmel Graphics LLC .... G 631 944-6031
 Deer Park (G-4066)
Zenger Group Inc .... E 716 871-1058
 Tonawanda (G-15593)
Zenger Partners LLC .... E 716 876-2284
 Kenmore (G-6865)

2754 Commercial Printing: Gravure

Alamar Printing Inc .... F 914 993-9007
 White Plains (G-16417)
Alfa Card Inc .... G 718 326-7107
 Glendale (G-5390)
American Packaging Corporation . C 585 254-9500
 Rochester (G-13626)
American Print Solutions Inc ...... G 718 208-2309
 Brooklyn (G-1527)
▲ Ashton-Potter USA Ltd .... C 716 633-2000
 Williamsville (G-16568)
C C Industries Inc .... F 518 581-7633
 Saratoga Springs (G-14572)
Clarion Publications Inc .... F 585 243-3530
 Geneseo (G-5310)
▲ Clintrak Clinical Labeling S ..... D 888 479-3900
 Bohemia (G-995)
Color Industries LLC .... G 718 392-8301
 Long Island City (G-7413)
Copy Corner Inc .... G 718 388-4545
 Brooklyn (G-1717)
Dijifi LLC .... F 646 519-2447
 Brooklyn (G-1778)
Ecoplast & Packaging LLC .... G 718 996-0800
 Brooklyn (G-1811)
Foleys Graphic Center Inc .... E 914 245-3625
 Yorktown Heights (G-16816)
◆ Gruner + Jahr USA Group Inc . B 866 323-9336
 New York (G-10001)
Image Sales & Marketing Inc .... G 516 238-7023
 Massapequa Park (G-7891)
Jack J Florio Jr .... G 716 434-9123
 Lockport (G-7311)
Janco Press Inc .... F 631 563-3003
 Bohemia (G-1040)

Karr Graphics Corp .... E 212 645-6000
 Long Island City (G-7487)
Kinaneco Inc .... E 315 468-6201
 Syracuse (G-15356)
Krepe Kraft Inc .... B 716 826-7086
 Buffalo (G-2912)
Leonardo Printing Corp .... G 914 664-7890
 Mount Vernon (G-8417)
Liberty Label Mfg Inc .... F 631 737-2365
 Holbrook (G-6195)
Mastro Graphic Arts Inc .... E 585 436-7570
 Rochester (G-13931)
McG Graphics Inc .... G 631 499-0730
 Dix Hills (G-4122)
Mod-Pac Corp .... D 716 447-9013
 Buffalo (G-2952)
Mrs John L Strong & Co LLC .... F 212 838-3775
 New York (G-10853)
Mutual Engraving Company Inc . D 516 489-0534
 West Hempstead (G-16223)
▲ Niagara Label Company Inc ... F 716 542-3000
 Akron (G-20)
Paya Printing of NY Inc .... G 516 625-8346
 Albertson (G-151)
Sommer and Sons Printing Inc .. F 716 822-4311
 Buffalo (G-3069)
SRC Liquidation Company .... F 716 631-3900
 Williamsville (G-16588)
◆ Tele-Pak Inc .... E 845 426-2300
 Monsey (G-8302)
Trust of Colum Unive In The Ci .. F 212 854-2793
 New York (G-11906)

2759 Commercial Printing

2 1 2 Postcards Inc .... E 212 767-8227
 New York (G-8667)
4 Over 4com Inc .... E 718 932-2700
 Astoria (G-419)
461 New Lots Avenue LLC .... G 347 303-9305
 Brooklyn (G-1442)
5 Stars Printing Corp .... F 718 461-4612
 Flushing (G-4977)
6727 11th Ave Corp .... F 718 837-8787
 Brooklyn (G-1444)
A & A Graphics Inc II .... G 516 735-0078
 Seaford (G-14757)
▲ A Graphic Printing Inc .... G 212 233-9696
 New York (G-8694)
A Promos USA Inc .... F 516 377-0186
 Freeport (G-5135)
A Tradition of Excellence Inc ..... G 845 638-4595
 New City (G-8489)
◆ Abigal Press Inc .... D 718 641-5350
 Ozone Park (G-12821)
Academy Printing Services Inc .. G 631 765-3346
 Southold (G-14967)
Accel Printing & Graphics .... G 914 241-3369
 Mount Kisco (G-8337)
Acme Screenprinting LLC .... G 716 565-1052
 Buffalo (G-2684)
Action Envelope & Prtg Co Inc .. F 631 225-3900
 Amityville (G-263)
Actioncraft Products Inc .... G 516 883-6423
 Port Washington (G-13239)
▲ Active World Solutions Inc ..... G 718 922-9404
 Brooklyn (G-1480)
Ad Publications Inc .... F 585 248-2888
 Pittsford (G-13007)
Adirondack Pennysaver Inc .... F 518 563-0100
 Plattsburgh (G-13105)
Advance Finance Group LLC .... D 212 630-5900
 New York (G-8746)
▼ Advanced Graphics Company . F 607 692-7875
 Whitney Point (G-16554)
Albert Siy .... G 718 359-0389
 Flushing (G-4982)
Aldine Inc (ny) .... D 212 226-2870
 New York (G-8788)
Alicia F Herdlein .... G 585 344-4411
 Batavia (G-608)
▲ Allsafe Technologies Inc .... F 716 691-0400
 Amherst (G-212)
Alpina Copyworld Inc .... F 212 683-3511
 New York (G-8811)
Alpine Business Group Inc .... F 212 989-4198
 New York (G-8812)
Always Printing .... G 914 481-5209
 Port Chester (G-13193)
AMA Precision Screening Inc ... F 585 293-0820
 Churchville (G-3505)

Amax Printing Inc .... F 718 384-8600
 Maspeth (G-7819)
◆ American Casting and Mfg Corp . D .. 800 342-0333
 Plainview (G-13035)
American Office Supply Inc .... F 516 294-9444
 Westbury (G-16315)
Amerikom Group Inc .... D 212 675-1329
 New York (G-8842)
Amstead Press Corp .... G 347 416-2373
 New York (G-8850)
Amsterdam Printing & Litho Inc . F 518 792-6501
 Queensbury (G-13416)
Andrew J George .... G 518 462-4662
 Albany (G-41)
Ansun Graphics Inc .... G 315 437-6869
 Syracuse (G-15243)
Apple Enterprises Inc .... E 718 361-2200
 Long Island City (G-7381)
April Printing Co Inc .... F 212 685-7455
 New York (G-8893)
Arca Ink LLC .... G 518 798-0100
 South Glens Falls (G-14934)
Arena Graphics Inc .... E 516 767-5108
 Port Washington (G-13244)
Argo Envelope Corp .... D 718 729-2700
 Long Island City (G-7386)
Argo Lithographers Inc .... E 718 729-2700
 Long Island City (G-7388)
Arista Innovations Inc .... E 516 746-2262
 Mineola (G-8205)
▲ Artistic Typography Corp .... F 212 463-8880
 New York (G-8923)
Artscroll Printing Corp .... E 212 929-2413
 New York (G-8926)
▲ Ashton-Potter USA Ltd .... C 716 633-2000
 Williamsville (G-16568)
Asn Inc .... E 718 894-0800
 Maspeth (G-7824)
Aspect Printing Inc .... E 347 789-4284
 Brooklyn (G-1564)
Astro Label & Tag Ltd .... G 718 435-4474
 Brooklyn (G-1565)
▲ Bags Unlimited Inc .... E 585 436-6282
 Rochester (G-13651)
Balajee Enterprises Inc .... G 212 629-6150
 New York (G-9006)
Barnaby Prints Inc .... G 845 477-2501
 Greenwood Lake (G-5648)
Bartolomeo Publishing Inc .... G 631 420-4949
 West Babylon (G-16138)
Batavia Legal Printing Inc .... F 585 768-2100
 Le Roy (G-7113)
Batavia Press LLC .... E 585 343-4429
 Batavia (G-612)
Bates Jackson Engraving Co Inc . E 716 854-3000
 Buffalo (G-2725)
Bco Industries Western NY Inc . E 716 877-2800
 Tonawanda (G-15526)
BDR Creative Concepts Inc ...... F 516 942-7768
 Farmingdale (G-4726)
Bedford Freeman & Worth .... C 212 576-9400
 New York (G-263)
Beebie Printing & Art Agcy Inc .. G 518 725-4528
 Gloversville (G-5453)
Beis Moshiach Inc .... E 718 778-8000
 Brooklyn (G-1594)
Bella Figura Letterpress .... G 866 699-6040
 Syracuse (G-15255)
▲ Benchemark Printing Inc .... D 518 393-1361
 Schenectady (G-14653)
Berkshire Business Forms Inc . F 518 828-2600
 Hudson (G-6343)
Bestmade Printing LLC .... G 718 384-0719
 Brooklyn (G-1605)
Bestype Digital Imaging LLC .... F 212 966-6886
 New York (G-9058)
Bfc Print Network Inc .... G 716 838-4532
 Amherst (G-217)
Bidpress LLC .... G 267 973-8876
 New York (G-9073)
▲ Big Apple Sign Corp .... D 212 629-3650
 New York (G-9076)
Bizbash Media Inc .... D 646 638-3602
 New York (G-9093)
▲ Bobley-Harmann Corporation . G 516 433-3800
 Ronkonkoma (G-14320)
Body Builders Inc .... F 718 492-7997
 Brooklyn (G-1627)
Bondy Printing Corp .... G 631 242-1510
 Bay Shore (G-666)

BP Beyond Printing Inc ....G.... 516 328-2700
Hempstead *(G-6008)*
Bradley Marketing Group Inc ....G.... 212 967-6100
New York *(G-9132)*
Bridge Fulfillment Inc ....G.... 718 625-6622
Brooklyn *(G-1634)*
Brodock Press Inc ....D.... 315 735-9577
Utica *(G-15681)*
Brooks Litho Digital Group Inc ....G.... 631 789-4500
Deer Park *(G-3955)*
Buffalo Newspress Inc ....C.... 716 852-1600
Buffalo *(G-2751)*
Burr & Son Inc ....G.... 315 446-1550
Syracuse *(G-15263)*
Business Card Express Inc ....E.... 631 669-3400
West Babylon *(G-16143)*
C & C Athletic Inc ....G.... 845 713-4670
Walden *(G-15891)*
Cama Graphics Inc ....F.... 718 707-9747
Long Island City *(G-7405)*
Candid Worldwide LLC ....G.... 212 799-5300
Farmingdale *(G-4733)*
▲ Century Direct LLC ....C.... 212 763-0600
Islandia *(G-6524)*
Chakra Communications Inc ....E.... 607 748-7491
Endicott *(G-4584)*
Check-O-Matic Inc ....G.... 845 781-7675
Monroe *(G-8267)*
Chenango Union Printing Inc ....G.... 607 334-2112
Norwich *(G-12479)*
Christian Bus Endeavors Inc ....F.... 315 788-8560
Watertown *(G-16007)*
Chroma Communications Inc ....G.... 631 289-8871
Medford *(G-7943)*
CHv Printed Company ....F.... 516 997-1101
East Meadow *(G-4247)*
Citation Healthcare Labels LLC ....G.... 631 293-4646
Hauppauge *(G-5790)*
Classic Album ....E.... 718 388-2818
Brooklyn *(G-1699)*
Classic Labels Inc ....E.... 631 467-2300
Patchogue *(G-12863)*
Cnyshirts ....G.... 315 432-1789
Syracuse *(G-15282)*
Colad Group LLC ....D.... 716 961-1776
Buffalo *(G-2772)*
Colonial Label Systems Inc ....E.... 631 254-0111
Bay Shore *(G-672)*
▲ Colonial Tag & Label Co Inc ....F.... 516 482-0508
Great Neck *(G-5546)*
Color Card LLC ....F.... 631 232-1300
Central Islip *(G-3363)*
Comgraph Sales Service ....G.... 716 601-7243
Elma *(G-4449)*
Commercial Press Inc ....G.... 315 274-0028
Canton *(G-3255)*
Con-Tees Custom Printing Ltd ....G.... 914 664-0251
Mount Vernon *(G-8390)*
Control Research Inc ....G.... 631 225-1111
Amityville *(G-269)*
Cooper & Clement Inc ....E.... 315 454-8135
Syracuse *(G-15289)*
Copy Room Inc ....F.... 212 371-8600
New York *(G-9397)*
Copy X/Press Ltd ....D.... 631 585-2200
Ronkonkoma *(G-14328)*
Craig Envelope Corp ....E.... 718 786-4277
Hicksville *(G-6074)*
Create-A-Card Inc ....G.... 631 584-2273
Saint James *(G-14510)*
Crisray Printing Corp ....E.... 631 293-3770
Farmingdale *(G-4741)*
Curtis Prtg Co The Del Press ....G.... 518 477-4820
East Greenbush *(G-4228)*
Custom 101 Prints Inc ....F.... 718 708-4425
Bronx *(G-1249)*
Custom Prtrs Guilderland Inc ....F.... 518 456-2811
Guilderland *(G-5654)*
Custom Sportswear Corp ....G.... 914 666-9200
Bedford Hills *(G-773)*
D B F Associates ....G.... 718 328-0005
Bronx *(G-1250)*
D G M Graphics Inc ....F.... 516 223-2220
Merrick *(G-8096)*
D3 Repro Group ....G.... 347 507-1075
Long Island City *(G-7420)*
DArcy Printing and Lithog ....G.... 212 924-1554
New York *(G-9471)*
Dash Printing Inc ....G.... 212 643-8534
New York *(G-9472)*
Data Flow Inc ....G.... 631 436-9200
Medford *(G-7945)*
▲ Data Palette Info Svcs LLC ....D.... 718 433-1060
Port Washington *(G-13251)*
Delft Printing Inc ....G.... 716 683-1100
Lancaster *(G-7015)*
Dental Tribune America LLC ....F.... 212 244-7181
New York *(G-9503)*
▲ Design Distributors Inc ....D.... 631 242-2000
Deer Park *(G-3966)*
DEW Graphics Inc ....E.... 212 727-8820
New York *(G-9515)*
Diamond Inscription Tech ....F.... 646 366-7944
New York *(G-9523)*
Digital Evolution Inc ....E.... 212 732-2722
New York *(G-9527)*
Direct Print Inc ....F.... 212 987-6003
New York *(G-9532)*
Dit Prints Incorporated ....G.... 518 885-4400
Ballston Spa *(G-581)*
Diversified Envelope Ltd ....F.... 585 615-4697
Rochester *(G-13745)*
Division Den-Bar Enterprises ....G.... 914 381-2220
Mamaroneck *(G-7742)*
Dkm Sales LLC ....E.... 716 893-7777
Buffalo *(G-2802)*
Doctor Print Inc ....E.... 631 873-4560
Hauppauge *(G-5814)*
Donald Bruhnke ....F.... 212 600-1260
New York *(G-9547)*
Doremus FP LLC ....E.... 212 366-3800
New York *(G-9559)*
▲ Drns Corp ....F.... 718 369-4530
Brooklyn *(G-1795)*
Dupli Graphics Corporation ....G.... 315 422-4732
Syracuse *(G-15307)*
Dupli Graphics Corporation ....C.... 315 234-7286
Syracuse *(G-15306)*
Dutchess Plumbing & Heating ....G.... 845 889-8255
Staatsburg *(G-15023)*
Dynamic Packaging Inc ....F.... 718 388-0800
Brooklyn *(G-1800)*
E&I Printing ....F.... 212 206-0506
New York *(G-9599)*
Eagle Envelope Company ....G.... 607 387-3195
Trumansburg *(G-15638)*
East Coast Thermographers Inc ....E.... 718 321-3211
College Point *(G-3643)*
Eastwood Litho Inc ....E.... 315 437-2626
Syracuse *(G-15310)*
Edgian Press Inc ....G.... 516 931-2114
Hicksville *(G-6082)*
Effective Slling Solutions LLC ....G.... 716 771-8503
Lake View *(G-6983)*
Efficiency Printing Co Inc ....F.... 914 949-8611
White Plains *(G-16444)*
Efs Designs LLC ....G.... 718 852-9511
Brooklyn *(G-1816)*
Ehs Group LLC ....G.... 914 937-6162
Port Chester *(G-13198)*
Elm Graphics Inc ....G.... 315 737-5984
New Hartford *(G-8503)*
Empire Business Forms Inc ....F.... 845 562-7780
Newburgh *(G-12221)*
Enterprise Press Inc ....C.... 212 741-2111
New York *(G-9687)*
Evergreen Corp Central NY ....F.... 315 454-4175
Syracuse *(G-15320)*
Excell Print & Promotions Inc ....G.... 914 437-8668
White Plains *(G-16448)*
Excellent Printing Inc ....G.... 718 384-7272
Brooklyn *(G-1857)*
Exotic Print and Paper Inc ....F.... 212 807-0465
New York *(G-9753)*
▲ Expedi-Printing Inc ....C.... 516 513-0919
Great Neck *(G-5551)*
F & B Photo Offset Co Inc ....G.... 516 431-5433
Island Park *(G-6514)*
Fairmount Press ....G.... 212 255-2300
New York *(G-9775)*
Farthing Press Inc ....G.... 716 852-4674
Buffalo *(G-2825)*
Federal Envelope Inc ....F.... 212 243-8380
New York *(G-9790)*
Fedex Office & Print Svcs Inc ....G.... 718 982-5223
Staten Island *(G-15076)*
Fineline Thermographers Inc ....G.... 718 643-1100
Brooklyn *(G-1882)*
First2print Inc ....G.... 212 868-6886
New York *(G-9809)*
Fleaheart Inc ....F.... 718 521-4958
Brooklyn *(G-1890)*
Flp Group LLC ....F.... 315 252-7583
Auburn *(G-480)*
Folder Factory Inc ....F.... 540 477-3852
Amityville *(G-275)*
Force Digital Media Inc ....G.... 631 243-0243
Deer Park *(G-3977)*
Forward Enterprises Inc ....F.... 585 235-7670
Rochester *(G-13814)*
Franklin Packaging Inc ....G.... 631 582-8900
Northport *(G-12468)*
Frederick Coon Inc ....E.... 716 683-6812
Elma *(G-4450)*
▲ Freeport Screen & Stamping ....E.... 516 379-0330
Freeport *(G-5157)*
Freeville Publishing Co Inc ....F.... 607 844-9119
Freeville *(G-5191)*
Fresh Prints LLC ....E.... 917 826-2752
New York *(G-9848)*
Fulcrum Promotions & Prtg LLC ....G.... 203 909-6362
New York *(G-9859)*
G&J Graphics Inc ....G.... 718 409-9874
Bronx *(G-1277)*
Gailer Stamping Diecutting LLC ....F.... 212 243-5662
Long Island City *(G-7453)*
▲ Gallant Graphics Ltd ....E.... 845 868-1166
Stanfordville *(G-15033)*
Garrett J Cronin ....G.... 914 761-9299
White Plains *(G-16452)*
Gary Stock Corporation ....G.... 914 276-2700
Croton Falls *(G-3911)*
▲ Gatehouse Media LLC ....B.... 585 598-0030
Pittsford *(G-13013)*
Gazette Press Inc ....E.... 914 963-8300
Rye *(G-14479)*
GE Healthcare Fincl Svcs Inc ....G.... 212 713-2000
New York *(G-9894)*
Gem Reproduction Services Corp ....G.... 845 298-0172
Wappingers Falls *(G-15932)*
Gemson Graphics Inc ....G.... 516 873-8400
Albertson *(G-149)*
General Business Supply Inc ....D.... 518 720-3939
Watervliet *(G-16046)*
General Trade Mark La ....E.... 718 979-7261
Staten Island *(G-15078)*
Genie Instant Printing Co Inc ....F.... 212 575-8258
New York *(G-9905)*
Georgia-Pacific LLC ....E.... 845 986-2011
Warwick *(G-15953)*
Glenn Horowitz Bookseller Inc ....G.... 212 691-9100
New York *(G-9934)*
Golos Printing Inc ....G.... 607 732-1896
Elmira Heights *(G-4511)*
Grado Group Inc ....G.... 718 556-4200
Staten Island *(G-15081)*
Grand Meridian Printing Inc ....E.... 718 937-3888
Long Island City *(G-7460)*
Graph-Tex Inc ....F.... 607 756-7791
Cortland *(G-3873)*
Graph-Tex Inc ....G.... 607 756-1875
Cortland *(G-3874)*
Graphic Lab Inc ....E.... 212 682-1815
New York *(G-9976)*
Graphic Printing ....G.... 718 701-4433
Bronx *(G-1285)*
Graphics 247 Corp ....G.... 718 729-2470
Long Island City *(G-7461)*
Graphics For Industry Inc ....F.... 212 889-6202
New York *(G-9977)*
Graphics Plus Printing Inc ....E.... 607 299-0500
Cortland *(G-3875)*
Graphics Service Bureau Inc ....F.... 212 684-3600
Long Island City *(G-7462)*
Greenbush Tape & Label Inc ....E.... 518 465-2389
Albany *(G-79)*
Grover Cleveland Press Inc ....F.... 716 564-2222
Amherst *(G-230)*
Gruber Display Co Inc ....F.... 718 882-8220
Bronx *(G-1286)*
H T L & S Ltd ....F.... 718 435-4474
Brooklyn *(G-1957)*
Haig Press Inc ....E.... 631 582-5800
Hauppauge *(G-5838)*
▲ Hammer Packaging Corp ....B.... 585 424-3880
West Henrietta *(G-16242)*
Handone Studios Inc ....G.... 585 421-8175
Fairport *(G-4634)*
Harmon and Castella Printing ....F.... 845 471-9163
Poughkeepsie *(G-13344)*

27 PRINTING, PUBLISHING, AND ALLIED INDUSTRIES

Hart Reproduction Services............G...... 212 704-0556
New York *(G-10046)*

Herrmann Group LLC ....G...... 716 876-9798
Kenmore *(G-6860)*

HI Speed Envelope Co Inc ....F...... 718 617-1600
Mount Vernon *(G-8406)*

Hi-Tech Packg World-Wide LLC........G...... 845 947-1912
New Windsor *(G-8646)*

Hill Crest Press ....G...... 518 943-0671
Catskill *(G-3304)*

Horace J Metz ....G...... 716 873-9103
Kenmore *(G-6861)*

Hospitality Inc ....E...... 212 268-1930
New York *(G-10128)*

▲ Hudson Envelope Corporation.........E...... 212 473-6666
New York *(G-10142)*

Human Technologies Corporation ....F...... 315 735-3532
Utica *(G-15711)*

▲ I N K T Inc ....F...... 212 957-2700
New York *(G-10159)*

Image Typography Inc ....G...... 631 218-6932
Holbrook *(G-6188)*

▲ Impress Graphic Technologies.........F...... 516 781-0845
Westbury *(G-16342)*

Impressive Imprints ....F...... 716 692-0905
North Tonawanda *(G-12432)*

Imprint Branded Content LLC...........G...... 212 888-8073
New York *(G-10189)*

Incodema3d LLC..............................F...... 607 269-4390
Ithaca *(G-6583)*

Industrial Test Eqp Co Inc ....E...... 516 883-6423
Port Washington *(G-13269)*

Info Label Inc ....F...... 518 664-0791
Halfmoon *(G-5663)*

Integrated Graphics Inc....................G...... 212 592-5600
New York *(G-10231)*

Iron Horse Graphics Ltd...................G...... 631 537-3400
Bridgehampton *(G-1181)*

Island Silkscreen Inc ....G...... 631 757-4567
East Northport *(G-4265)*

Issacs Yisroel ....G...... 718 851-7430
Brooklyn *(G-2016)*

Itc Mfg Group Inc ....F...... 212 684-3696
New York *(G-10278)*

J Kendall LLC ....G...... 646 739-4956
Yonkers *(G-16772)*

J M L Productions Inc ....D...... 718 643-1674
Brooklyn *(G-2025)*

J N White Associates Inc ....D...... 585 237-5191
Perry *(G-12969)*

J T Printing 21 ....G...... 718 481-3939
Staten Island *(G-15093)*

Jack J Florio Jr ....G...... 716 434-9123
Lockport *(G-7311)*

Janco Press Inc................................F...... 631 563-3003
Bohemia *(G-1040)*

Japan Printing & Graphics Inc.........G...... 212 406-2905
New York *(G-10308)*

Joed Press ....G...... 212 243-3620
New York *(G-10350)*

John Auguliaro Printing Co ....G...... 718 382-5283
Brooklyn *(G-2043)*

Johnnys Ideal Printing Co ....G...... 518 828-6666
Hudson *(G-6359)*

▲ Jomar Industries Inc ....E...... 845 357-5773
Airmont *(G-14)*

Jomart Associates Inc.....................E...... 212 627-2153
Islandia *(G-6532)*

Jon Lyn Ink Inc ....G...... 516 546-2312
Merrick *(G-8099)*

Judith Lewis Printer Inc ....G...... 516 997-7777
Westbury *(G-16346)*

K & B Stamping Co Inc....................G...... 914 664-8555
Mount Vernon *(G-8412)*

Kallen Corp ....G...... 212 242-1470
New York *(G-10399)*

Karr Graphics Corp..........................G...... 212 645-6000
Long Island City *(G-7487)*

▲ Kates Paperie Ltd ....G...... 212 966-3304
New York *(G-10416)*

Kaufman Brothers Printing..............G...... 212 563-1854
New York *(G-10419)*

Kaymil Printing Company Inc ....G...... 212 594-3718
New York *(G-10422)*

▲ Kenan International Trading ....G...... 718 672-4922
Corona *(G-3847)*

Kenmar Shirts Inc ....E...... 718 824-3880
Bronx *(G-1307)*

Key Computer Svcs of Chelsea ....D...... 212 206-8060
New York *(G-10438)*

Kim Jae Printing Co Inc...................G...... 212 691-6289
Roslyn Heights *(G-14457)*

Kinaneco Inc....................................E...... 315 468-6201
Syracuse *(G-15356)*

Knucklehead Embroidery Inc ....G...... 607 797-2725
Johnson City *(G-6814)*

Kurrier Inc ....G...... 718 389-3018
Brooklyn *(G-2082)*

Kurtskraft Inc ....G...... 516 944-4449
Port Washington *(G-13280)*

L & M Uniserv Corp.........................G...... 718 854-3700
Brooklyn *(G-2087)*

L I C Screen Printing Inc ....E...... 516 546-7289
Merrick *(G-8100)*

▲ Labels Inter-Global Inc ....F...... 212 398-0006
New York *(G-10504)*

Lake Placid Advertisers Wkshp.......E...... 518 523-3359
Lake Placid *(G-6976)*

Landlord Guard Inc..........................F...... 212 695-6505
New York *(G-10514)*

Lauricella Press Inc ....E...... 516 931-5906
Brentwood *(G-1140)*

Lennons Litho Inc............................F...... 315 866-3156
Herkimer *(G-6043)*

Leo Paper Inc...................................G...... 917 305-0708
New York *(G-10550)*

Levon Graphics Corp ....D...... 631 753-2022
Deer Park *(G-4001)*

Linco Printing Inc............................G...... 718 937-5141
Long Island City *(G-7499)*

Linda Campbell ....G...... 718 994-4026
Bronx *(G-1318)*

Linden Forms & Systems Inc ....E...... 212 219-1100
Brooklyn *(G-2126)*

Lion In The Sun Park Slope Ltd ......G...... 718 369-4006
Brooklyn *(G-2128)*

Logomax Inc....................................G...... 631 420-0484
Farmingdale *(G-4809)*

Loremanss Embroidery Engrav........F...... 518 834-9205
Keeseville *(G-6852)*

Louis Heindl & Son Inc ....G...... 585 454-5080
Rochester *(G-13917)*

Love Unlimited NY Inc ....F...... 718 359-8500
Westbury *(G-16353)*

Loy L Press Inc................................G...... 716 634-5966
Buffalo *(G-2928)*

M C Packaging Corporation ....G...... 631 643-3763
Babylon *(G-529)*

M T M Printing Co Inc ....F...... 718 353-3297
College Point *(G-3654)*

Magazines & Brochures Inc ....G...... 716 875-9699
Buffalo *(G-2933)*

Malone Industrial Press Inc ....G...... 518 483-5880
Malone *(G-7724)*

Mark T Westinghouse ....G...... 518 678-3262
Catskill *(G-3306)*

Marlow Printing Co Inc....................E...... 718 625-4948
Brooklyn *(G-2171)*

Mart-Tex Athletics Inc ....E...... 631 454-9583
Farmingdale *(G-4817)*

Mason Transparent Package Inc .....E...... 718 792-6000
Bronx *(G-1324)*

Maspeth Press Inc...........................G...... 718 429-2363
Maspeth *(G-7857)*

Master Image Printing Inc ....G...... 914 347-4400
Elmsford *(G-4550)*

◆ Mastercraft Decorators Inc ....E...... 585 223-5150
Fairport *(G-4641)*

Mastro Graphic Arts Inc ....E...... 585 436-7570
Rochester *(G-13931)*

Matt Industries Inc..........................C...... 315 472-1316
Syracuse *(G-15368)*

Matthew-Lee Corporation ....F...... 631 226-0100
Lindenhurst *(G-7179)*

McAuliffe Paper Inc.........................E...... 315 453-2222
Liverpool *(G-7245)*

Measurement Incorporated..............F...... 914 682-1969
White Plains *(G-16475)*

▲ Medallion Associates Inc ....E...... 212 929-9130
New York *(G-10751)*

Mega Graphics Inc...........................G...... 914 962-1402
Yorktown Heights *(G-16819)*

Merchandiser Inc.............................G...... 315 462-6411
Clifton Springs *(G-3582)*

Merrill Communications LLC...........G...... 212 620-5600
New York *(G-10775)*

Merrill Corporation ....D...... 917 934-7300
New York *(G-10776)*

Merrill New York Company Inc ....C...... 212 229-6500
New York *(G-10778)*

Metro Creative Graphics Inc ....E...... 212 947-5100
New York *(G-10784)*

Middletown Press ....G...... 845 343-1895
Middletown *(G-8164)*

Midgley Printing Corp......................G...... 315 475-1864
Syracuse *(G-15372)*

Miken Companies Inc ....D...... 716 668-6311
Buffalo *(G-2946)*

Miller Place Printing Inc ....G...... 631 473-1158
Miller Place *(G-8191)*

Mimeocom Inc ....B...... 212 847-3000
New York *(G-10814)*

▲ Mines Press Inc..............................C...... 914 788-1800
Cortlandt Manor *(G-3903)*

Mini Graphics Inc............................D...... 516 223-6464
Hauppauge *(G-5893)*

Mixture Screen Printing ....G...... 845 561-2857
Newburgh *(G-12232)*

Modern Decal Co ....G...... 315 622-2778
Liverpool *(G-7248)*

Moore Printing Company Inc ....G...... 585 394-1533
Canandaigua *(G-3225)*

Mpe Graphics Inc ....F...... 631 582-8900
Bohemia *(G-1060)*

◆ Multi Packaging Solutions Inc ....E...... 646 885-0005
New York *(G-10858)*

▲ Mv Corp Inc ....C...... 631 273-8020
Bay Shore *(G-703)*

Nathan Printing Express Inc ....G...... 914 472-0914
Scarsdale *(G-14641)*

New Art Signs Co Inc ....G...... 718 443-0900
Glen Head *(G-5383)*

New Buffalo Shirt Factory Inc ....F...... 716 436-5839
Buffalo *(G-2963)*

▲ New Deal Printing Corp ....G...... 718 729-5800
New York *(G-10919)*

New York Christan Times Inc..........G...... 718 638-6397
Brooklyn *(G-2260)*

New York Legal Publishing ....G...... 518 459-1100
Menands *(G-8090)*

Newport Business Solutions Inc .....F...... 631 319-6129
Bohemia *(G-1064)*

▲ Niagara Label Company Inc ....F...... 716 542-3000
Akron *(G-20)*

Niagara Sample Book Co Inc ....F...... 716 284-6151
Niagara Falls *(G-12313)*

Noble Checks Inc ....G...... 212 537-6241
Brooklyn *(G-2271)*

Nomad Editions LLC ....F...... 212 918-0992
Bronxville *(G-1425)*

North American DF Inc ....G...... 718 698-2500
Staten Island *(G-15108)*

North American Graphics Inc ....F...... 212 725-2200
New York *(G-10991)*

North Six Inc ....F...... 212 463-7227
New York *(G-10994)*

Northwind Graphics.........................G...... 518 899-9651
Ballston Spa *(G-593)*

Nys Nyu-Cntr Intl Cooperation ....E...... 212 998-3680
New York *(G-11020)*

Okey Enterprises Inc.......................G...... 212 213-2640
New York *(G-11034)*

One In A Million Inc ....G...... 516 829-1111
Valley Stream *(G-15788)*

Ontario Label Graphics Inc ....F...... 716 434-8505
Lockport *(G-7325)*

P & W Press Inc...............................E...... 646 486-3417
New York *(G-11083)*

Pace Editions Inc ....G...... 212 675-7431
New York *(G-11086)*

Paratore Signs Inc ....G...... 315 455-5551
Syracuse *(G-15393)*

▲ Paris Art Label Co Inc ....D...... 631 467-2300
Patchogue *(G-12872)*

Park Avenue Imprints LLC ....G...... 716 822-5737
Buffalo *(G-2991)*

Patrick Rohan ....G...... 718 781-2573
Monticello *(G-8323)*

Patrick Kraft ....G...... 315 343-9376
Oswego *(G-12786)*

Patrick Ryans Modern Press ....F...... 518 434-2921
Albany *(G-111)*

Paulin Investment Company ....E...... 631 957-8500
Amityville *(G-311)*

PDM Studios Inc..............................G...... 716 694-8337
Tonawanda *(G-15569)*

PDQ Shipping Services ....G...... 845 255-5500
New Paltz *(G-8580)*

Penny Lane Printing Inc ....D...... 585 226-8111
Avon *(G-521)*

Employee Codes: A=Over 500 employees, B=251-500
C=101-250, D=51-100, E=20-50, F=10-19, G=5-9

27 PRINTING, PUBLISHING, AND ALLIED INDUSTRIES

Company	Code	Phone
Personal Graphics Corporation	G	315 853-3421
Westmoreland (G-16408)		
Peter Papastrat	G	607 723-8112
Binghamton (G-910)		
Pierrepont Visual Graphics	G	585 305-9672
Rochester (G-14022)		
▲ Poly-Flex Corp	F	631 586-9500
Edgewood (G-4410)		
Pony Farm Press & Graphics	G	607 432-9020
Oneonta (G-12644)		
Precision Envelope Co Inc	G	631 694-3990
Farmingdale (G-4856)		
Precision Label Corporation	F	631 270-4490
Farmingdale (G-4857)		
Premier Ink Systems Inc	E	845 782-5802
Harriman (G-5721)		
Presstek Printing LLC	G	585 266-2770
Rochester (G-14043)		
Print City Corp	F	212 487-9778
New York (G-11246)		
Print Mall	G	718 437-7700
Brooklyn (G-2347)		
Print Shoppe	G	315 792-9585
Utica (G-15730)		
Printech Business Systems Inc	F	212 290-2542
New York (G-11249)		
Printed Image	G	716 821-1880
Buffalo (G-3015)		
Printery	G	516 922-3250
Oyster Bay (G-12818)		
Printfacility Inc	G	212 349-4009
New York (G-11250)		
Printing Max New York Inc	G	718 692-1400
Brooklyn (G-2350)		
Printing Resources Inc	E	518 482-2470
Albany (G-119)		
Printworks Printing & Design	G	315 433-8587
Syracuse (G-15398)		
Proof 7 Ltd	F	212 680-1843
New York (G-11264)		
▲ Publimax Printing Corp	G	718 366-7133
Ridgewood (G-13548)		
Quadra Flex Corp	G	607 758-7066
Cortland (G-3891)		
Quality Impressions Inc	G	646 613-0002
Long Island City (G-7567)		
Quality Offset LLC	G	347 342-4660
Long Island City (G-7568)		
Quist Industries Ltd	F	718 243-2800
Brooklyn (G-2373)		
R & M Graphics of New York	F	212 929-0294
New York (G-11308)		
R R Donnelley & Sons Company	F	716 763-2613
Lakewood (G-6996)		
R R Donnelley & Sons Company	D	716 773-0647
Grand Island (G-5510)		
R R Donnelley & Sons Company	D	518 438-9722
Albany (G-121)		
R R Donnelley & Sons Company	G	646 755-8125
New York (G-11312)		
Rainbow Lettering	G	607 732-5751
Elmira (G-4501)		
Regal Screen Printing Intl	G	845 356-8181
Spring Valley (G-15005)		
Register Graphics Inc	E	716 358-2921
Randolph (G-13450)		
Republican Registrar Inc	G	315 497-1551
Moravia (G-8334)		
Rfn Inc	F	516 764-5100
Bay Shore (G-714)		
Richard Ruffner	F	631 234-4600
Central Islip (G-3383)		
Richs Sttches EMB Screenprint	G	845 621-1561
Mahopac (G-7711)		
▲ Rike Enterprises Inc	F	631 277-8338
Islip (G-6550)		
RIT Printing Corp	G	631 586-6220
Bay Shore (G-715)		
Rose Graphics LLC	F	516 547-6142
West Babylon (G-16188)		
Round Top Knit & Screening	G	518 622-3600
Round Top (G-14466)		
Royal Tees Inc	G	845 357-9448
Suffern (G-15197)		
▲ S & S Prtg Die-Cutting Co Inc	F	718 388-8990
Brooklyn (G-2434)		
S L C Industries Incorporated	G	607 775-2299
Binghamton (G-913)		
Salamanca Press Penny Saver	E	716 945-1500
Salamanca (G-14531)		
Sand Hill Industries Inc	G	518 885-7991
Ballston Spa (G-595)		
Scan-A-Chrome Color Inc	G	631 532-6146
Copiague (G-3779)		
Scancorp Inc	F	315 454-5596
Syracuse (G-15416)		
Scotti Graphics Inc	E	212 367-9602
Long Island City (G-7585)		
Screen The World Inc	G	631 475-0023
Holtsville (G-6244)		
Select-A-Form Inc	D	631 981-3076
Holbrook (G-6208)		
Seneca West Printing Inc	G	716 675-8010
West Seneca (G-16303)		
Sentine Printing Inc	G	516 334-7400
Westbury (G-16372)		
Sephardic Yellow Pages	E	718 998-0299
Brooklyn (G-2456)		
Seri Systems Inc	E	585 272-5515
Rochester (G-14122)		
Shade Tree Greetings Inc	F	585 442-4580
Rochester (G-14123)		
Shapeways Inc	C	914 356-5816
New York (G-11557)		
Shapeways Inc	G	646 470-3576
Long Island City (G-7589)		
Shipman Printing Inds Inc	E	716 504-7700
Niagara Falls (G-12336)		
Shore Line Monogramming Inc	F	914 698-8000
Mamaroneck (G-7757)		
Short Run Forms Inc	D	631 567-7171
Bohemia (G-1089)		
Shykat Promotions	G	866 574-2757
Forestville (G-5088)		
Sign Shop Inc	G	631 226-4145
Copiague (G-3782)		
Silk Screen Art Inc	F	518 762-8423
Johnstown (G-6839)		
Silver Griffin Co	F	518 272-7771
Troy (G-15627)		
◆ Sino Printing Inc	F	212 334-6896
New York (G-11600)		
Soho Letterpress Inc	F	718 788-2518
Brooklyn (G-2493)		
Solarz Bros Printing Corp	G	718 383-1330
Brooklyn (G-2497)		
Source Envelope Inc	G	866 284-0707
Farmingdale (G-4877)		
Spaulding Law Printing Inc	G	315 422-4805
Syracuse (G-15427)		
Spectrum Prtg Lithography Inc	E	212 255-3131
New York (G-11665)		
Spst Inc	G	607 798-6952
Vestal (G-15822)		
St James Printing Inc	G	631 981-2095
Ronkonkoma (G-14418)		
▲ Standwill Packaging Inc	E	631 752-1236
Farmingdale (G-4879)		
Star Press Pearl River Inc	G	845 268-2294
Valley Cottage (G-15765)		
Starbrook Incorporated	G	212 514-5212
Brooklyn (G-2512)		
Starcraft Press Inc	G	718 383-6700
Long Island City (G-7600)		
Starfire Printing Inc	G	631 736-1495
Holtsville (G-6245)		
Stellar Printing Inc	D	718 361-1600
Long Island City (G-7603)		
Stickershopcom Inc	G	631 563-4323
Bayport (G-739)		
Stony Point Graphics Ltd	G	845 786-3322
Stony Point (G-15176)		
Stromberg Brand Corporation	F	914 739-7410
Valley Cottage (G-15767)		
Structured 3d Inc	G	346 704-2614
Amityville (G-317)		
Superior Print On Demand	G	607 240-5231
Vestal (G-15823)		
Swift Multigraphics LLC	G	585 442-8000
Rochester (G-14150)		
Syracuse Label Co Inc	D	315 422-1037
Syracuse (G-15439)		
▲ Syracuse Letter Company Inc	F	315 476-8328
Bridgeport (G-1184)		
T L F Graphics Inc	D	585 272-5500
Rochester (G-14156)		
T S O General Corp	E	631 952-5320
Brentwood (G-1144)		
T&K Printing Inc	F	718 439-9454
Brooklyn (G-2550)		
T-Base Communications USA Inc	E	315 713-0013
Ogdensburg (G-12579)		
Table Tops Paper Corp	G	718 831-6440
Brooklyn (G-2552)		
Tannens	G	718 292-4646
Bronx (G-1400)		
▲ Tape Printers Inc	F	631 249-5585
Farmingdale (G-4890)		
Tapemaker Supply Company LLC	G	914 693-3407
Hartsdale (G-5745)		
Tara Rific Screen Printing Inc	G	718 583-6864
Bronx (G-1401)		
Tc Transcontinental USA Inc	G	818 993-4767
New York (G-11788)		
Tcmf Inc	D	607 724-1094
Binghamton (G-918)		
◆ Tele-Pak Inc	E	845 426-2300
Monsey (G-8302)		
The Gramecy Group	G	518 348-1325
Clifton Park (G-3579)		
Thomson Press (india) Limited	G	646 318-0369
Long Island City (G-7616)		
Todd Walbridge	G	585 254-3018
Rochester (G-14171)		
Toppan Vintage Inc	D	212 596-7747
New York (G-11867)		
Toprint Ltd	G	718 439-0469
Brooklyn (G-2573)		
Total Solution Graphics Inc	G	718 706-1540
Long Island City (G-7617)		
Tovie Asarese Royal Prtg Co	G	716 885-7692
Buffalo (G-3100)		
◆ Transcntinental Ultra Flex Inc	B	718 272-9100
Brooklyn (G-2579)		
Tri Kolor Printing & Sty	F	315 474-6753
Syracuse (G-15446)		
▲ Tri Star Label Inc	G	914 237-4800
Mount Vernon (G-8448)		
Tri-Lon Clor Lithographers Ltd	E	212 255-6140
New York (G-11893)		
Triangle Label Tag Inc	G	718 875-3030
Brooklyn (G-2583)		
Tripi Engraving Co Inc	E	718 383-6500
Brooklyn (G-2586)		
U All Inc	E	518 438-2558
Albany (G-136)		
United Print Group Inc	F	718 392-4242
Long Island City (G-7623)		
▲ Universal Screening Associates	F	718 232-2744
Brooklyn (G-2609)		
Unlimited Ink Inc	E	631 582-0696
Hauppauge (G-5967)		
◆ USA Custom Pad Corp	E	607 563-9550
Sidney (G-14858)		
Varick Street Litho Inc	G	646 843-0800
New York (G-11995)		
Venus Printing Company	F	212 967-8900
Hewlett (G-6053)		
Veterans Offset Printing Inc	G	585 288-2900
Rochester (G-14200)		
Vez Inc	G	718 273-7002
Staten Island (G-15151)		
▲ Viking Athletics Ltd	E	631 957-8000
Lindenhurst (G-7203)		
Voss Signs LLC	E	315 682-6418
Manlius (G-7781)		
W N Vanalstine & Sons Inc	D	518 237-1436
Cohoes (G-3624)		
Webster Printing Corporation	F	585 671-1533
Webster (G-16107)		
Weeks & Reichel Printing Inc	G	631 589-1443
Sayville (G-14635)		
Weicro Graphics Inc	F	631 253-3360
West Babylon (G-16204)		
Were Forms Inc	G	585 482-4400
Rochester (G-14206)		
Westypo Printers Inc	G	914 737-7394
Peekskill (G-12930)		
Willco Fine Art Ltd	F	718 935-9567
New York (G-12109)		
William Charles Prtg Co Inc	E	516 349-0900
Plainview (G-13102)		
William J Ryan	G	585 392-6200
Hilton (G-6159)		
Willis Mc Donald Co Inc	E	212 366-1526
New York (G-12115)		
Wilson Press LLC	G	315 568-9693
Seneca Falls (G-14788)		
▲ Won & Lee Inc	E	516 222-0712
Garden City (G-5284)		

27 PRINTING, PUBLISHING, AND ALLIED INDUSTRIES

Worldwide Ticket Craft .... D 516 538-6200
  Merrick *(G-8107)*
X Myles Mar Inc .... E 212 683-2015
  New York *(G-12148)*
X Press Screen Printing .... G 716 679-7788
  Dunkirk *(G-4181)*
XI Graphics Inc .... E 212 929-8700
  New York *(G-12153)*
Xpress Printing Inc .... G 516 605-1000
  Plainview *(G-13103)*
Yoman Madeo Fano .... G 631 438-0246
  Patchogue *(G-12879)*
▲ Zacks Enterprises Inc .... E 800 366-4924
  Orangeburg *(G-12693)*

2761 Manifold Business Forms

▲ Abra-Ka-Data Systems Ltd .... E 631 667-5550
  Deer Park *(G-3932)*
Amsterdam Printing & Litho Inc .... F 518 842-6000
  Amsterdam *(G-325)*
Amsterdam Printing & Litho Inc .... E 518 842-6000
  Amsterdam *(G-326)*
Bmg Printing and Promotion LLC ..... G 631 231-9200
  Bohemia *(G-989)*
Boces Business Office .... F 607 763-3300
  Binghamton *(G-869)*
Five Boro Holding LLC .... G 718 431-9500
  Brooklyn *(G-1885)*
Gateway Prtg & Graphics Inc .... G 716 823-3873
  Hamburg *(G-5680)*
Linden Forms & Systems Inc .... E 212 219-1100
  Brooklyn *(G-2126)*
Maggio Data Forms .... C 631 348-0343
  Hauppauge *(G-5877)*
Marcy Business Forms Inc .... G 718 935-9100
  Brooklyn *(G-2165)*
◆ Multi Packaging Solutions Inc ...... E 646 885-0005
  New York *(G-10858)*
P P I Business Forms Inc .... F 716 825-1241
  Buffalo *(G-2985)*
Resonant Legal Media LLC .... D 800 781-3591
  New York *(G-11369)*
Richard Ruffner .... F 631 234-4600
  Central Islip *(G-3383)*
RR Donnelley & Sons Company ...... D 716 773-0300
  Grand Island *(G-5511)*
Select-A-Form Inc .... D 631 981-3076
  Holbrook *(G-6208)*
▲ Specialized Printed Forms Inc ...... E 585 538-2381
  Caledonia *(G-3158)*
Syracuse Computer Forms Inc .... E 315 478-0108
  Syracuse *(G-15436)*
Taylor Communications Inc .... F 937 221-1303
  Melville *(G-8069)*
Taylor Communications Inc .... F 718 352-0220
  Westbury *(G-16375)*
Williamson Law Book Co .... F 585 924-3400
  Victor *(G-15878)*

2771 Greeting Card Publishing

1/2 Off Cards Wantagh Inc .... G 516 839-9832
  Wantagh *(G-15919)*
▲ Anne Taintor Inc .... G 718 483-9312
  Brooklyn *(G-1536)*
Avanti Press Inc .... E 212 414-1025
  New York *(G-8972)*
Massimo Friedman Inc .... E 716 836-0408
  Buffalo *(G-2938)*
▲ Paper House Productions Inc .... E 845 246-7261
  Saugerties *(G-14612)*
Paper Magic Group Inc .... B 631 521-3682
  New York *(G-11102)*
▲ Quotable Cards Inc .... G 212 420-7552
  New York *(G-11305)*
Shade Tree Greetings Inc .... F 585 442-4580
  Rochester *(G-14123)*

2782 Blankbooks & Looseleaf Binders

Acco Brands USA LLC .... C 847 541-9500
  Ogdensburg *(G-12568)*
▲ Albumx Corp .... D 914 939-6878
  Port Chester *(G-13192)*
Brewer-Cantelmo Co Inc .... E 212 244-4600
  New York *(G-9138)*
Brookvale Records Inc .... F 631 587-7422
  West Babylon *(G-16140)*
Classic Album .... E 718 388-2818
  Brooklyn *(G-1699)*
▲ Classic Album LLC .... D 718 388-2818
  Brooklyn *(G-1700)*

Colad Group LLC .... D 716 961-1776
  Buffalo *(G-2772)*
Consolidated Loose Leaf Inc .... E 212 924-5800
  New York *(G-9384)*
Dalee Bookbinding Co Inc .... F 914 965-1660
  Croton On Hudson *(G-3913)*
▲ Datamax International Inc .... E 212 693-0933
  New York *(G-9476)*
Deluxe Corporation .... B 845 362-4054
  Spring Valley *(G-14988)*
Dorose Novelty Co Inc .... F 718 451-3088
  East Elmhurst *(G-4220)*
Federal Sample Card Corp .... D 718 458-1344
  Elmhurst *(G-4464)*
Folder Factory Inc .... F 540 477-3852
  Amityville *(G-275)*
Foster - Gordon Manufacturing .... G 631 589-6776
  Bohemia *(G-1024)*
▲ General Diaries Corporation .... F 516 371-2244
  Inwood *(G-6491)*
GPM Associates LLC .... E 585 335-3940
  Dansville *(G-3926)*
King Album Inc .... E 631 253-9500
  West Babylon *(G-16168)*
Lanwood Industries Inc .... E 718 786-3000
  Bay Shore *(G-694)*
Leather Craftsmen Inc .... D 631 752-9000
  Farmingdale *(G-4808)*
Leather Indexes Corp .... E 516 827-1900
  Hicksville *(G-6103)*
Motema Music LLC .... G 212 860-6969
  New York *(G-10847)*
▲ Mypublisher Inc .... F 914 773-4312
  Elmsford *(G-4553)*
Niagara Sample Book Co Inc .... F 716 284-6151
  Niagara Falls *(G-12313)*
▲ Quotable Cards Inc .... G 212 420-7552
  New York *(G-11305)*
Renegade Nation Ltd .... G 212 868-9000
  New York *(G-11362)*
▲ Roger Michael Press Inc .... G 732 752-0800
  Brooklyn *(G-2411)*
Sellco Industries Inc .... F 607 756-7594
  Cortland *(G-3894)*
Simon & Simon LLC .... G 202 419-0490
  New York *(G-11596)*
Tm Music Inc .... F 212 471-4000
  New York *(G-11853)*
Tommy Boy Entertainment LLC ...... F 212 388-8300
  New York *(G-11863)*
Wmg Acquisition Corp .... F 212 275-2000
  New York *(G-12126)*
Wood Designs Deluxe Corp .... G 917 414-4640
  Island Park *(G-6519)*

2789 Bookbinding

514 Adams Corporation .... G 516 352-6948
  Franklin Square *(G-5114)*
A-1 Products Inc .... G 718 789-1818
  Brooklyn *(G-1462)*
A-Quick Bindery LLC .... G 631 491-1110
  West Babylon *(G-16126)*
Agrecolor Inc .... F 516 741-8700
  Mineola *(G-8202)*
Argo Lithographers Inc .... F 718 729-2700
  Long Island City *(G-7388)*
Arista Innovations Inc .... E 516 746-2262
  Mineola *(G-8205)*
▲ Ateres Publishing & Bk Bindery .... F 718 935-9355
  Brooklyn *(G-1569)*
Baum Christine and John Corp ...... G 585 621-8910
  Rochester *(G-13654)*
Beastons Budget Printing .... G 585 244-2721
  Rochester *(G-13658)*
▲ Benchemark Printing Inc .... D 518 393-1361
  Schenectady *(G-14653)*
Bernard Hall .... G 585 425-3340
  Fairport *(G-4625)*
▲ Beyer Graphics Inc .... D 631 543-3900
  Commack *(G-3682)*
Bg Bindery Inc .... G 631 767-4242
  Maspeth *(G-7826)*
Boncraft Inc .... D 716 662-9720
  Tonawanda *(G-15528)*
Bondy Printing Corp .... G 631 242-1510
  Bay Shore *(G-666)*
Brodock Press Inc .... D 315 735-9577
  Utica *(G-15681)*
Brooks Litho Digital Group Inc .... G 631 789-4500
  Deer Park *(G-3955)*

C & C Bindery Co Inc .... E 631 752-7078
  Farmingdale *(G-4730)*
Carlara Group Ltd .... G 914 769-2020
  Pleasantville *(G-13173)*
Carnels Printing Inc .... E 516 883-3355
  Great Neck *(G-5543)*
Castlereagh Printcraft Inc .... D 516 623-1728
  Freeport *(G-5148)*
Chakra Communications Inc .... E 607 748-7491
  Endicott *(G-4584)*
Challenge Graphics Svcs Inc .... E 631 586-0171
  Deer Park *(G-3956)*
Classic Album .... E 718 388-2818
  Brooklyn *(G-1699)*
Cohber Press Inc .... D 585 475-9100
  West Henrietta *(G-16234)*
Copy Corner Inc .... G 718 388-4545
  Brooklyn *(G-1717)*
Copy Room Inc .... F 212 371-8600
  New York *(G-9397)*
Cosmos Communications Inc .... C 718 482-1800
  Long Island City *(G-7416)*
D G M Graphics Inc .... F 516 223-2220
  Merrick *(G-8096)*
Dalee Bookbinding Co Inc .... F 914 965-1660
  Croton On Hudson *(G-3913)*
David Helsing .... G 607 796-2681
  Horseheads *(G-6311)*
Dependable Lithographers Inc .... F 718 472-4200
  Long Island City *(G-7423)*
▲ Dime Trading Inc .... G 718 797-0303
  Brooklyn *(G-1779)*
Dispatch Graphics Inc .... F 212 307-5943
  New York *(G-9536)*
Division Den-Bar Enterprises .... G 914 381-2220
  Mamaroneck *(G-7742)*
Dowd - Witbeck Printing Corp .... F 518 274-2421
  Troy *(G-15604)*
DP Murphy Co Inc .... D 631 673-9400
  Deer Park *(G-3968)*
E B B Graphics Inc .... F 516 750-5510
  Westbury *(G-16324)*
E L Smith Printing Co Inc .... D 201 373-0111
  New City *(G-8492)*
Eastwood Litho Inc .... E 315 437-2626
  Syracuse *(G-15310)*
Erhard & Gilcher Inc .... E 315 474-1072
  Syracuse *(G-15319)*
Flare Multicopy Corp .... E 718 258-8860
  Brooklyn *(G-1887)*
Flp Group LLC .... F 315 252-7583
  Auburn *(G-480)*
Foleys Graphic Center Inc .... E 914 245-3625
  Yorktown Heights *(G-16816)*
Foster - Gordon Manufacturing .... G 631 589-6776
  Bohemia *(G-1024)*
Fulton Newspapers Inc .... E 315 598-6397
  Fulton *(G-5216)*
Gateway Prtg & Graphics Inc .... G 716 823-3873
  Hamburg *(G-5680)*
Gazette Press Inc .... E 914 963-8300
  Rye *(G-14479)*
Gild-Rite Inc .... G 631 752-9000
  Farmingdale *(G-4771)*
Gold Pride Press Inc .... E 585 224-8800
  Rochester *(G-13843)*
Graphicomm Inc .... G 716 283-0830
  Niagara Falls *(G-12289)*
Haig Press Inc .... E 631 582-5800
  Hauppauge *(G-5838)*
▲ Hamilton Printing Company Inc .... C 518 732-2161
  Troy *(G-15608)*
Hudson Printing Co Inc .... E 718 937-8600
  New York *(G-10145)*
In-House Inc .... F 718 445-9007
  College Point *(G-3646)*
Interstate Litho Corp .... D 631 232-6025
  Brentwood *(G-1136)*
▲ J Mackenzie Ltd .... E 585 321-1770
  Rochester *(G-13888)*
Jack J Florio Jr .... G 716 434-9123
  Lockport *(G-7311)*
James Conolly Printing Co .... E 585 426-4150
  Rochester *(G-13891)*
Jane Lewis .... G 607 722-0584
  Binghamton *(G-898)*
Johnnys Ideal Printing Co .... G 518 828-6666
  Hudson *(G-6359)*
Jon Lyn Ink Inc .... G 516 546-2312
  Merrick *(G-8099)*

Employee Codes: A=Over 500 employees, B=251-500
C=101-250, D=51-100, E=20-50, F=10-19, G=5-9

2019 Harris
New York Manufacturers Directory

Kaufman Brothers Printing ... G ... 212 563-1854
New York *(G-10419)*
King Lithographers Inc ... E ... 914 667-4200
Mount Vernon *(G-8414)*
Louis Heindl & Son Inc ... G ... 585 454-5080
Rochester *(G-13917)*
Loy L Press Inc ... G ... 716 634-5966
Buffalo *(G-2928)*
▲ **Melcher Media Inc** ... F ... 212 727-2322
New York *(G-10769)*
▲ **Mercury Print Productions Inc** ... C ... 585 458-7900
Rochester *(G-13936)*
Mid Island Group ... E ... 631 293-0180
Farmingdale *(G-4824)*
Mid-Island Bindery Inc ... E ... 631 293-0180
Farmingdale *(G-4825)*
Midgley Printing Corp ... G ... 315 475-1864
Syracuse *(G-15372)*
▲ **Mines Press Inc** ... C ... 914 788-1800
Cortlandt Manor *(G-3903)*
Moneast Inc ... G ... 845 298-8898
Wappingers Falls *(G-15936)*
Multiple Imprssons of Rchester ... G ... 585 546-1160
Rochester *(G-13960)*
Mutual Library Bindery Inc ... E ... 315 455-6638
East Syracuse *(G-4359)*
Newport Graphics Inc ... E ... 212 924-2600
New York *(G-10950)*
On The Spot Binding Inc ... E ... 718 497-2200
Ridgewood *(G-13545)*
Piroke Trade Inc ... G ... 646 515-1537
Brooklyn *(G-2321)*
Playbill Incorporated ... E ... 718 335-4033
Woodside *(G-16673)*
Prestige Envelope & Lithograph ... F ... 631 521-7043
Merrick *(G-8105)*
Printech Business Systems Inc ... F ... 212 290-2542
New York *(G-11249)*
Printing Resources Inc ... E ... 518 482-2470
Albany *(G-119)*
Pro Printing ... G ... 516 561-9700
Lynbrook *(G-7670)*
Progressive Graphics & Prtg ... G ... 315 331-3635
Newark *(G-12205)*
Prompt Bindery Co Inc ... F ... 212 675-5181
New York *(G-11261)*
Psychonomic Society Inc ... E ... 512 381-1494
New York *(G-11270)*
Quad/Graphics Inc ... A ... 518 581-4000
Saratoga Springs *(G-14594)*
Quality Bindery Service Inc ... E ... 716 883-5185
Buffalo *(G-3025)*
Reynolds Book Bindery LLC ... F ... 607 772-8937
Binghamton *(G-912)*
Richard Ruffner ... F ... 631 234-4600
Central Islip *(G-3383)*
Rmd Holding Inc ... G ... 845 628-0030
Mahopac *(G-7712)*
▲ **Roger Michael Press Inc** ... D ... 732 752-0800
Brooklyn *(G-2411)*
▲ **Rosemont Press Incorporated** ... E ... 212 239-4770
New York *(G-11430)*
Rosen Mandell & Immerman Inc ... E ... 212 691-2277
New York *(G-11431)*
S L C Industries Incorporated ... F ... 607 775-2299
Binghamton *(G-913)*
Sentine Printing Inc ... G ... 516 334-7400
Westbury *(G-16372)*
Shipman Printing Inds Inc ... E ... 716 504-7700
Niagara Falls *(G-12336)*
Spectrum Prtg Lithography Inc ... E ... 212 255-3131
New York *(G-11665)*
▼ **Sterling Pierce Company Inc** ... E ... 516 593-1170
East Rockaway *(G-4296)*
Thomas Group Inc ... F ... 212 947-6400
New York *(G-11817)*
Tobay Printing Co Inc ... E ... 631 842-3300
Copiague *(G-3788)*
Tom & Jerry Printcraft Forms ... E ... 914 777-7468
Mamaroneck *(G-7758)*
Tri-Lon Clor Lithographers Ltd ... E ... 212 255-6140
New York *(G-11893)*
▲ **Twenty-First Century Press Inc** ... F ... 716 837-0800
Buffalo *(G-3106)*
Vicks Lithograph & Prtg Corp ... C ... 315 272-2401
Yorkville *(G-16832)*
Vin-Clair Inc ... F ... 845 429-4998
West Haverstraw *(G-16210)*
Webster Printing Corporation ... F ... 585 671-1533
Webster *(G-16107)*
Westchester Mailing Service ... E ... 914 948-1116
White Plains *(G-16519)*
Whitford Development Inc ... F ... 631 471-7711
Port Jefferson *(G-13224)*
William Charles Prtg Co Inc ... E ... 516 349-0900
Plainview *(G-13102)*
Wilson Press LLC ... E ... 315 568-9693
Seneca Falls *(G-14788)*
▲ **Won & Lee Inc** ... E ... 516 222-0712
Garden City *(G-5284)*
Wynco Press One Inc ... G ... 516 354-6145
Glen Oaks *(G-5388)*
X Myles Mar Inc ... E ... 212 683-2015
New York *(G-12148)*
Zenger Partners LLC ... E ... 716 876-2284
Kenmore *(G-6865)*

2791 Typesetting

514 Adams Corporation ... G ... 516 352-6948
Franklin Square *(G-5114)*
Act Communications Group Inc ... F ... 631 669-2403
West Islip *(G-16257)*
▲ **Advance Publications Inc** ... D ... 718 981-1234
Staten Island *(G-15040)*
Agrecolor Inc ... F ... 516 741-8700
Mineola *(G-8202)*
Alabaster Group Inc ... G ... 516 867-8223
Freeport *(G-5138)*
Albion-Holley Pennysaver Inc ... E ... 585 589-5641
Albion *(G-154)*
Arista Innovations Inc ... E ... 516 746-2262
Mineola *(G-8205)*
▲ **Art Resources Transfer Inc** ... G ... 212 255-2919
New York *(G-8916)*
▲ **Artistic Typography Corp** ... F ... 212 463-8880
New York *(G-8923)*
Artscroll Printing Corp ... E ... 212 929-2413
New York *(G-8926)*
Bates Jackson Engraving Co Inc ... E ... 716 854-3000
Buffalo *(G-2725)*
Baum Christine and John Corp ... G ... 585 621-8910
Rochester *(G-13654)*
Bco Industries Western NY Inc ... E ... 716 877-2800
Tonawanda *(G-15526)*
Beastons Budget Printing ... G ... 585 244-2721
Rochester *(G-13658)*
Beehive Press Inc ... G ... 718 654-1200
Bronx *(G-1226)*
▲ **Benchemark Printing Inc** ... D ... 518 393-1361
Schenectady *(G-14653)*
Bernard Hall ... G ... 585 425-3340
Fairport *(G-4625)*
▲ **Beyer Graphics Inc** ... D ... 631 543-3900
Commack *(G-3682)*
Boncraft Inc ... D ... 716 662-9720
Tonawanda *(G-15528)*
Bondy Printing Corp ... G ... 631 242-1510
Bay Shore *(G-666)*
Brodock Press Inc ... D ... 315 735-9577
Utica *(G-15681)*
Brooks Litho Digital Group Inc ... G ... 631 789-4500
Deer Park *(G-3955)*
Bytheway Publishing Services ... F ... 607 334-8365
Norwich *(G-12477)*
Carlara Group Ltd ... G ... 914 769-2020
Pleasantville *(G-13173)*
Carnels Printing Inc ... G ... 516 883-3355
Great Neck *(G-5543)*
Castlereagh Printcraft Inc ... D ... 516 623-1728
Freeport *(G-5148)*
Cds Productions Inc ... F ... 518 385-8255
Schenectady *(G-14661)*
Chakra Communications Inc ... E ... 716 505-7300
Lancaster *(G-7013)*
Chakra Communications Inc ... E ... 607 748-7491
Endicott *(G-4584)*
Challenge Graphics Svcs Inc ... E ... 631 586-0171
Deer Park *(G-3956)*
Clarsons Corp ... F ... 585 235-8775
Rochester *(G-13713)*
Cohber Press Inc ... D ... 585 475-9100
West Henrietta *(G-16234)*
Consolidated Color Press Inc ... F ... 212 929-8197
New York *(G-9382)*
Cortland Standard Printing Co ... D ... 607 756-5665
Cortland *(G-3871)*
Cosmos Communications Inc ... C ... 718 482-1800
Long Island City *(G-7416)*
Csw Inc ... F ... 585 247-4010
Rochester *(G-13727)*
D G M Graphics Inc ... F ... 516 223-2220
Merrick *(G-8096)*
Desktop Publishing Concepts ... F ... 631 752-1934
Farmingdale *(G-4750)*
Digital Color Concepts Inc ... E ... 212 989-4888
New York *(G-9526)*
Digital Page LLC ... F ... 518 446-9129
Albany *(G-68)*
Dispatch Graphics Inc ... F ... 212 307-5943
New York *(G-9536)*
Dowd - Witbeck Printing Corp ... F ... 518 274-2421
Troy *(G-15604)*
DP Murphy Co Inc ... D ... 631 673-9400
Deer Park *(G-3968)*
Draper Associates Incorporated ... F ... 212 255-2727
New York *(G-9573)*
E B B Graphics Inc ... F ... 516 750-5510
Westbury *(G-16324)*
Eastwood Litho Inc ... E ... 315 437-2626
Syracuse *(G-15310)*
Empire Press Co ... G ... 718 756-9500
Brooklyn *(G-1833)*
Flare Multicopy Corp ... E ... 718 258-8860
Brooklyn *(G-1887)*
Flp Group LLC ... F ... 315 252-7583
Auburn *(G-480)*
Foleys Graphic Center Inc ... E ... 914 245-3625
Yorktown Heights *(G-16816)*
Fort Orange Press Inc ... E ... 518 489-3233
Albany *(G-75)*
Fulton Newspapers Inc ... E ... 315 598-6397
Fulton *(G-5216)*
▲ **Gallant Graphics Ltd** ... E ... 845 868-1166
Stanfordville *(G-15033)*
Gateway Prtg & Graphics Inc ... E ... 716 823-3873
Hamburg *(G-5680)*
Gazette Press Inc ... E ... 914 963-8300
Rye *(G-14479)*
▲ **Gg Design and Printing** ... G ... 718 321-3220
New York *(G-9916)*
Graphic Fabrications Inc ... G ... 516 763-3222
Rockville Centre *(G-14232)*
Graphicomm Inc ... G ... 716 283-0830
Niagara Falls *(G-12289)*
Grid Typographic Services Inc ... F ... 212 627-0303
New York *(G-9987)*
Hamptons Magazine ... E ... 631 283-7125
Southampton *(G-14955)*
Hks Printing Company Inc ... F ... 212 675-2529
New York *(G-10109)*
Hugh F McPherson Inc ... G ... 716 668-6107
Cheektowaga *(G-3450)*
In-House Inc ... F ... 718 445-9007
College Point *(G-3646)*
Interstate Litho Corp ... D ... 631 232-6025
Brentwood *(G-1136)*
Jack J Florio Jr ... G ... 716 434-9123
Lockport *(G-7311)*
James Conolly Printing Co ... E ... 585 426-4150
Rochester *(G-13891)*
Jane Lewis ... G ... 607 722-0584
Binghamton *(G-898)*
Johnnys Ideal Printing Co ... G ... 518 828-6666
Hudson *(G-6359)*
Jon Lyn Ink Inc ... G ... 516 546-2312
Merrick *(G-8099)*
L M N Printing Company Inc ... E ... 516 285-8526
Valley Stream *(G-15784)*
Lake Placid Advertisers Wkshp ... E ... 518 523-3359
Lake Placid *(G-6976)*
Leigh Scott Enterprises Inc ... G ... 718 343-5440
Bellerose *(G-781)*
Litmor Publishing Corp ... F ... 516 931-0012
Garden City *(G-5266)*
Loudon Ltd ... G ... 631 757-4447
East Northport *(G-4267)*
Louis Heindl & Son Inc ... G ... 585 454-5080
Rochester *(G-13917)*
Loy L Press Inc ... G ... 716 634-5966
Buffalo *(G-2928)*
Mechon Beiss Uvas ... G ... 718 436-1489
Brooklyn *(G-2186)*
▲ **Medallion Associates Inc** ... E ... 212 929-9130
New York *(G-10751)*
▲ **Mercury Print Productions Inc** ... C ... 585 458-7900
Rochester *(G-13936)*
Midgley Printing Corp ... G ... 315 475-1864
Syracuse *(G-15372)*
▲ **Mines Press Inc** ... C ... 914 788-1800
Cortlandt Manor *(G-3903)*

Moneast Inc ... G ... 845 298-8898
Wappingers Falls (G-15936)
Multiple Imprssons of Rchester ... G ... 585 546-1160
Rochester (G-13960)
Mutual Engraving Company Inc ... D ... 516 489-0534
West Hempstead (G-16223)
News India USA Inc ... F ... 212 675-7515
New York (G-10954)
Newspaper Publisher LLC ... F ... 607 775-0472
Conklin (G-3730)
▼ Official Offset Corporation ... E ... 631 957-8500
Amityville (G-307)
P D R Inc ... G ... 516 829-5300
Plainview (G-13080)
Panagraphics Inc ... G ... 716 312-8088
Orchard Park (G-12734)
Patrick Ryans Modern Press ... F ... 518 434-2921
Albany (G-111)
Presstek Printing LLC ... F ... 585 467-8140
Rochester (G-14042)
Prestige Envelope & Lithograph ... F ... 631 521-7043
Merrick (G-8105)
Printery ... G ... 516 922-3250
Oyster Bay (G-12818)
Printing Resources Inc ... E ... 518 482-2470
Albany (G-119)
Pro Printing ... G ... 516 561-9700
Lynbrook (G-7670)
Progressive Graphics & Prtg ... G ... 315 331-3635
Newark (G-12205)
Publishing Synthesis Ltd ... G ... 212 219-0135
New York (G-11275)
Quad/Graphics Inc ... A ... 518 581-4000
Saratoga Springs (G-14594)
Quicker Printer Inc ... G ... 607 734-8622
Elmira (G-4500)
Rmd Holding Inc ... G ... 845 628-0030
Mahopac (G-7712)
Rubber Stamps Inc ... E ... 212 675-1180
Mineola (G-8247)
Scotti Graphics Inc ... E ... 212 367-9602
Long Island City (G-7585)
Sentine Printing Inc ... G ... 516 334-7400
Westbury (G-16372)
▲ Star Composition Services Inc ... G ... 212 684-4001
Brooklyn (G-2509)
Stone Crest Industries Inc ... G ... 607 652-2665
Stamford (G-15032)
Syracuse Computer Forms Inc ... E ... 315 478-0108
Syracuse (G-15436)
Thomas Group Inc ... F ... 212 947-6400
New York (G-11817)
Times Review Newspaper Corp ... E ... 631 354-8031
Mattituck (G-7918)
Tobay Printing Co Inc ... E ... 631 842-3300
Copiague (G-3788)
Tom & Jerry Printcraft Forms ... E ... 914 777-7468
Mamaroneck (G-7758)
Torsaf Printers Inc ... G ... 516 569-5577
Hewlett (G-6051)
Tri Kolor Printing & Sty ... F ... 315 474-6753
Syracuse (G-15446)
Tri-Lon Clor Lithographers Ltd ... E ... 212 255-6140
New York (G-11893)
Tripi Engraving Co Inc ... E ... 718 383-6500
Brooklyn (G-2586)
Voss Signs LLC ... E ... 315 682-6418
Manlius (G-7781)
Wallkill Valley Publications ... E ... 845 561-0170
Newburgh (G-12251)
Webster Printing Corporation ... F ... 585 671-1533
Webster (G-16107)
Westchester Mailing Service ... E ... 914 948-1116
White Plains (G-16519)
Wilson Press LLC ... E ... 315 568-9693
Seneca Falls (G-14788)
Woodbury Printing Plus + Inc ... G ... 845 928-6610
Central Valley (G-3399)
Worldwide Ticket Craft ... D ... 516 538-6200
Merrick (G-8107)
Wynco Press One Inc ... G ... 516 354-6145
Glen Oaks (G-5388)
X Myles Mar Inc ... E ... 212 683-2015
New York (G-12148)
Zenger Partners LLC ... E ... 716 876-2284
Kenmore (G-6865)

2796 Platemaking & Related Svcs

Absolute Color Corporation ... G ... 212 868-0404
New York (G-8715)
Aldine Inc (ny) ... D ... 212 226-2870
New York (G-8788)
Allstate Sign & Plaque Corp ... F ... 631 242-2828
Deer Park (G-3938)
Chakra Communications Inc ... E ... 716 505-7300
Lancaster (G-7013)
Charles Henricks Inc ... F ... 212 243-5800
New York (G-9262)
Circle Press Inc ... D ... 212 924-4277
New York (G-9303)
Csw Inc ... F ... 585 247-4010
Rochester (G-13727)
▲ Custom House Engravers Inc ... G ... 631 567-3004
Bohemia (G-1004)
D & A Offset Services Inc ... F ... 212 924-0612
New York (G-9445)
David Fehlman ... G ... 315 455-8888
Syracuse (G-15303)
Dowd - Witbeck Printing Corp ... F ... 518 274-2421
Troy (G-15604)
Eastern Color Stripping Inc ... F ... 631 563-3700
Bohemia (G-1018)
▲ Gallant Graphics Ltd ... E ... 845 868-1166
Stanfordville (G-15033)
Gazette Press Inc ... E ... 914 963-8300
Rye (G-14479)
Karr Graphics Corp ... E ... 212 645-6000
Long Island City (G-7487)
Koehlr-Gibson Mkg Graphics Inc ... E ... 716 838-5960
Buffalo (G-2910)
Lazer Incorporated ... E ... 336 744-8047
Rochester (G-13910)
Leo P Callahan Inc ... F ... 607 797-7314
Binghamton (G-902)
Lgn Materials & Solutions ... F ... 888 414-0005
Mount Vernon (G-8418)
Micro Publishing Inc ... G ... 212 533-9180
New York (G-10795)
Miroddi Imaging Inc ... G ... 516 624-6898
Oyster Bay (G-12816)
Mutual Engraving Company Inc ... D ... 516 489-0534
West Hempstead (G-16223)
P & H Thermotech Inc ... G ... 585 624-1310
Lima (G-7154)
Rapid Service Engraving Co ... G ... 716 896-4555
Buffalo (G-3032)
▲ Rigidized Metals Corporation ... E ... 716 849-4703
Buffalo (G-3038)
Rotation Dynamics Corporation ... E ... 585 352-9023
Spencerport (G-14982)
Syracuse Computer Forms Inc ... E ... 315 478-0108
Syracuse (G-15436)
Tobay Printing Co Inc ... E ... 631 842-3300
Copiague (G-3788)
Tripi Engraving Co Inc ... E ... 718 383-6500
Brooklyn (G-2586)
Wilcro Inc ... G ... 716 632-4204
Buffalo (G-3130)

28 CHEMICALS AND ALLIED PRODUCTS

2812 Alkalies & Chlorine

Chemours Company Fc LLC ... E ... 716 278-5100
Niagara Falls (G-12271)
Church & Dwight Co Inc ... F ... 518 887-5109
Schenectady (G-14662)
FMC Corporation ... C ... 716 879-0400
Tonawanda (G-15541)
Indian Springs Mfg Co Inc ... F ... 315 635-6101
Baldwinsville (G-556)
Occidental Chemical Corp ... E ... 716 278-7795
Niagara Falls (G-12318)
Occidental Chemical Corp ... E ... 716 773-8100
Grand Island (G-5509)
Occidental Chemical Corp ... C ... 716 278-7794
Niagara Falls (G-12319)
Occidental Chemical Corp ... G ... 716 694-3827
North Tonawanda (G-12440)
Olin Chlor Alkali Logistics ... C ... 716 278-6411
Niagara Falls (G-12320)

2813 Industrial Gases

Air Products and Chemicals Inc ... D ... 518 463-4273
Glenmont (G-5410)
Airgas Inc ... F ... 518 690-0068
Albany (G-30)
Airgas Usa LLC ... F ... 585 436-7781
Rochester (G-13610)
Fountainhead Group Inc ... C ... 708 598-7100
New York Mills (G-12187)
Linde Gas North America LLC ... E ... 518 713-2015
Cohoes (G-3612)
Linde Gas North America LLC ... F ... 315 431-4081
Syracuse (G-15362)
Linde LLC ... E ... 716 847-0748
Buffalo (G-2924)
Linde LLC ... D ... 518 439-8187
Feura Bush (G-4935)
Linde Merchant Production Inc ... G ... 315 593-1360
Fulton (G-5227)
Matheson Tri-Gas Inc ... G ... 518 203-5003
Cohoes (G-3613)
Neon ... F ... 212 727-5628
New York (G-10905)
◆ Oxair Ltd ... G ... 716 298-8288
Niagara Falls (G-12321)
Praxair Inc ... F ... 716 879-2000
Tonawanda (G-15570)
Praxair Inc ... E ... 716 649-1600
Hamburg (G-5690)
Praxair Inc ... E ... 518 482-4360
Albany (G-117)
Praxair Inc ... E ... 716 286-4600
Niagara Falls (G-12324)
Praxair Inc ... C ... 845 359-4200
Orangeburg (G-12686)
Praxair Inc ... E ... 716 879-4000
Tonawanda (G-15571)
Praxair Distribution Inc ... G ... 315 457-5821
Liverpool (G-7256)
Praxair Distribution Inc ... F ... 315 735-6153
Marcy (G-7797)

2816 Inorganic Pigments

Applied Minerals Inc ... F ... 212 226-4265
Brooklyn (G-1543)
▲ Heany Industries Inc ... D ... 585 889-2700
Scottsville (G-14750)

2819 Indl Inorganic Chemicals, NEC

Aithaca Chemical Corp ... F ... 516 229-2330
Uniondale (G-15662)
Akzo Nobel Chemicals LLC ... C ... 914 674-5008
Dobbs Ferry (G-4129)
Alpha-En Corporation ... F ... 914 418-2000
Yonkers (G-16732)
Ames Goldsmith Corp ... F ... 518 792-7435
Glens Falls (G-5414)
Amtek Research LLC ... E ... 416 400-2906
Niagara Falls (G-12261)
Amtek Research LLC ... E ... 212 537-6462
Niagara Falls (G-12262)
Anchor Commerce Trading Corp ... G ... 516 881-3485
Atlantic Beach (G-455)
Arkema Inc ... C ... 585 243-6359
Piffard (G-12995)
Auterra Inc ... G ... 518 382-9600
Schenectady (G-14650)
Benzsay & Harrison Inc ... G ... 518 895-2311
Delanson (G-4067)
◆ Buffalo Tungsten Inc ... D ... 716 683-9170
Depew (G-4084)
Byk USA Inc ... E ... 845 469-5800
Chester (G-3470)
Calgon Carbon Corporation ... G ... 716 531-9113
North Tonawanda (G-12421)
Carbide-Usa LLC ... G ... 607 331-9353
Elmira (G-4476)
Carbon Activated Corporation ... G ... 716 662-2005
Orchard Park (G-12705)
Carbon Activated Corporation ... E ... 716 677-6661
Blasdell (G-925)
▼ Cerion Energy Inc ... E ... 585 271-5630
Rochester (G-13703)
Cerion LLC ... F ... 585 271-5630
Rochester (G-13704)
Chemours Company Fc LLC ... E ... 716 278-5100
Niagara Falls (G-12271)
Chemtrade Chemicals US LLC ... E ... 315 430-7650
Syracuse (G-15276)
Chemtrade Chemicals US LLC ... G ... 315 478-2323
Syracuse (G-15277)
Danisco US Inc ... D ... 585 277-4300
Rochester (G-13734)
▲ Dynasty Chemical Corp ... E ... 518 463-1146
Menands (G-8084)
Element St Johns Corp ... G ... 917 349-2139
Brooklyn (G-1824)

S
I
C

Employee Codes: A=Over 500 employees, B=251-500
C=101-250, D=51-100, E=20-50, F=10-19, G=5-9
2019 Harris
New York Manufacturers Directory
713

Elementis Srl Inc....C....845 692-3914
Huguenot *(G-6385)*
Emco Chemical (usa) Corp....E....718 797-3652
Brooklyn *(G-1828)*
◆ Esm Group Inc....F....716 446-8914
Amherst *(G-226)*
Esm Group Inc....G....724 265-1766
Buffalo *(G-2822)*
Esm Special Metals & Tech Inc....E....716 446-8914
Amherst *(G-228)*
Ferro Corporation....E....585 586-8770
East Rochester *(G-4284)*
Ferro Corporation....C....315 536-3357
Penn Yan *(G-12953)*
Ferro Electronics Materials....C....716 278-9400
Niagara Falls *(G-12285)*
FMC Corporation....E....716 735-3761
Middleport *(G-8132)*
▲ Germanium Corp America Inc....F....315 853-4900
Clinton *(G-3585)*
Hampshire Chemical Corp....D....315 539-9221
Waterloo *(G-15995)*
Incitec Pivot Limited....G....212 238-3010
New York *(G-10192)*
▲ Innovative Municipal Pdts US....E....800 387-5777
Glenmont *(G-5412)*
Isonics Corporation....G....212 356-7400
New York *(G-10277)*
◆ Kowa American Corporation....E....212 303-7800
New York *(G-10474)*
Lakeshore Carbide Inc....G....716 462-4349
Buffalo *(G-2919)*
Lawn Elements Inc....F....631 656-9711
Holbrook *(G-6194)*
▼ Meliorum Technologies Inc....G....585 313-0616
Rochester *(G-13935)*
▲ Minerals Technologies Inc....E....212 878-1800
New York *(G-10817)*
Moog Inc....D....716 731-6300
Niagara Falls *(G-12311)*
Multisorb Tech Intl LLC....G....716 824-8900
Buffalo *(G-2957)*
Multisorb Technologies Inc....E....716 656-1402
Buffalo *(G-2958)*
Next Potential LLC....G....401 742-5190
New York *(G-10959)*
▲ Niagara Refining LLC....E....716 706-1400
Depew *(G-4097)*
◆ Norfalco LLC....F....416 775-1431
New York *(G-10989)*
◆ North American Hoganas Inc....E....716 285-3451
Niagara Falls *(G-12315)*
Poly Scientific R&D Corp....E....631 586-0400
Bay Shore *(G-707)*
◆ Polyset Company Inc....E....518 664-6000
Mechanicville *(G-7932)*
Precision Elctro Mnrl Pmco Inc....E....716 284-2484
Niagara Falls *(G-12326)*
PVS Chemical Solutions Inc....D....716 825-5762
Buffalo *(G-3020)*
PVS Technologies Inc....E....716 825-5762
Buffalo *(G-3021)*
S E A Supplies Ltd....F....516 694-6677
Plainview *(G-13086)*
Sabre Energy Services LLC....F....518 514-1572
Slingerlands *(G-14890)*
Scientific Polymer Products....G....585 265-0413
Ontario *(G-12665)*
Signa Chemistry Inc....F....212 933-4101
New York *(G-11586)*
Somerville Acquisitions Co Inc....F....845 856-5261
Huguenot *(G-6386)*
Somerville Tech Group Inc....D....908 782-9500
Huguenot *(G-6387)*
Specialty Minerals Inc....G....518 585-7982
Ticonderoga *(G-15513)*
◆ Specialty Minerals Inc....E....212 878-1800
New York *(G-11661)*
Srlh Holdings Inc....C....929 529-7951
Huguenot *(G-6388)*
▼ Tangram Company LLC....E....631 758-0460
Holtsville *(G-6247)*
Texas Brine Company LLC....G....585 495-6228
Wyoming *(G-16701)*
▲ Thatcher Company New York Inc....E....315 589-9330
Williamson *(G-16562)*
Tibro Water Technologies Ltd....F....647 426-3415
Sherrill *(G-14824)*
Transport National Dev Inc....E....716 662-0270
Orchard Park *(G-12747)*
UOP LLC....E....716 879-7600
Tonawanda *(G-15588)*
US Peroxide....G....716 775-5585
Grand Island *(G-5517)*
◆ Vanchlor Company Inc....F....716 434-2624
Lockport *(G-7341)*
Vanchlor Company Inc....F....716 434-2624
Lockport *(G-7342)*
◆ Vandemark Chemical Inc....D....716 433-6764
Lockport *(G-7343)*
◆ Washingtom Mills Elec Mnrls....D....716 278-6600
Niagara Falls *(G-12349)*

2821 Plastics, Mtrls & Nonvulcanizable Elastomers

▲ Adam Scott Designs Inc....E....212 420-8866
New York *(G-8732)*
◆ American Acrylic Corporation....E....631 422-2200
West Babylon *(G-16133)*
American Epoxy and Metal Inc....G....718 828-7828
Scarsdale *(G-14636)*
◆ Ampacet Corporation....A....914 631-6600
Tarrytown *(G-15474)*
◆ APS American Polymers Svcs Inc....G....212 362-7711
New York *(G-8894)*
▼ Ashley Resin Corp....G....718 851-8111
Brooklyn *(G-1563)*
Atc Plastics LLC....E....212 375-2515
New York *(G-8943)*
◆ Bairnco Corporation....E....914 461-1300
White Plains *(G-16424)*
◆ Bamberger Polymers Intl Corp....F....516 622-3600
Jericho *(G-6780)*
▲ Barrett Bronze Inc....E....914 699-6060
Mount Vernon *(G-8380)*
Bso Energy Corp....F....212 520-1827
New York *(G-9153)*
Ccmi Inc....G....315 781-3270
Geneva *(G-5318)*
Clarence Resins and Chemicals....G....716 406-9804
Clarence Center *(G-3543)*
CN Group Incorporated....A....914 358-5690
White Plains *(G-16438)*
▲ Coda Resources Ltd....D....718 649-1666
Brooklyn *(G-1703)*
Craftech....D....518 828-5011
Chatham *(G-3427)*
Creations In Lucite Inc....G....718 871-2000
Brooklyn *(G-1727)*
Cytec Industries Inc....D....716 372-9650
Olean *(G-12598)*
De Originals Ltd....G....516 474-6544
Old Westbury *(G-12590)*
▲ Dewitt Plastics Inc....F....315 255-1209
Auburn *(G-476)*
Dice America Inc....G....585 869-6200
Victor *(G-15842)*
Durez Corporation....F....716 286-0100
Niagara Falls *(G-12279)*
E I Du Pont De Nemours & Co....E....716 876-4420
Buffalo *(G-2807)*
Eastman Chemical Company....D....585 722-2905
Rochester *(G-13759)*
Elastomers Inc....G....716 633-4883
Williamsville *(G-16578)*
Empire Plastics Inc....E....607 754-9132
Endwell *(G-4616)*
Endurart Inc....E....212 473-7000
New York *(G-9679)*
Everfab Inc....D....716 655-1550
East Aurora *(G-4198)*
▲ Fougera Pharmaceuticals Inc....C....631 454-7677
Melville *(G-8026)*
◆ GE Plastics....G....518 475-5011
Selkirk *(G-14768)*
▲ General Vy-Coat LLC....E....718 266-6002
Brooklyn *(G-1921)*
George M Dujack....G....518 279-1303
Troy *(G-15606)*
Global Plastics LP....E....800 417-4605
New York *(G-9944)*
Hanet Plastics Usa Inc....G....518 324-5850
Plattsburgh *(G-13123)*
Hexion Inc....E....518 792-8040
South Glens Falls *(G-14936)*
Imbibitive Tech Amer Corp....G....888 843-2323
Niagara Falls *(G-12294)*
Imbibitive Technologies Corp....G....888 843-2323
Niagara Falls *(G-12295)*
Imperial Polymers Inc....G....718 387-4741
Brooklyn *(G-1996)*
International Casein Corp Cal....G....516 466-4363
Great Neck *(G-5562)*
▲ John C Dolph Company Inc....E....732 329-2333
Schenectady *(G-14692)*
▲ Jrlon Inc....D....315 597-4067
Palmyra *(G-12855)*
◆ Kent Chemical Corporation....E....212 521-1700
New York *(G-10436)*
Kuraray America Inc....F....212 986-2230
New York *(G-10486)*
Macneil Polymers Inc....F....716 681-7755
Buffalo *(G-2932)*
Majestic Mold & Tool Inc....F....315 695-2079
Phoenix *(G-12990)*
Manufacturers Indexing Pdts....G....631 271-0956
Halesite *(G-5658)*
Maviano Corp....G....845 494-2598
Monsey *(G-8290)*
▲ MB Plastics Inc....F....718 523-1180
Greenlawn *(G-5623)*
▼ Meliorum Technologies Inc....G....585 313-0616
Rochester *(G-13935)*
◆ Mitsui Chemicals America Inc....E....914 253-0777
Rye Brook *(G-14493)*
Momentive Performance Mtls Inc....D....914 784-4807
Tarrytown *(G-15484)*
▲ Nationwide Tarps Incorporated....D....518 843-1545
Amsterdam *(G-353)*
Newmat Northeast Corp....F....631 253-9277
West Babylon *(G-16179)*
Parker-Hannifin Corporation....E....315 926-4211
Marion *(G-7804)*
▼ Pawling Corporation....C....845 855-1000
Pawling *(G-12893)*
Perfect Poly Inc....E....631 265-0539
Nesconset *(G-8486)*
Plaslok Corp....E....716 681-7755
Buffalo *(G-3006)*
Polycast Industries Inc....G....631 595-2530
Bay Shore *(G-708)*
▼ Polymers Merona Inc....F....631 862-8010
Saint James *(G-14513)*
▲ Queen City Manufacturing Inc....G....716 877-1102
Buffalo *(G-3028)*
Rodgard Corporation....E....716 852-1435
Buffalo *(G-3043)*
Sabic Innovative Plas US LLC....B....518 475-5011
Selkirk *(G-14771)*
Sabic Innovative Plastics....E....713 448-7474
East Greenbush *(G-4231)*
▲ Saga International Recycl LLC....G....718 621-5900
Brooklyn *(G-2444)*
Saint-Gobain Prfmce Plas Corp....C....518 686-7301
Hoosick Falls *(G-6280)*
Saint-Gobain Prfmce Plas Corp....C....518 686-7301
Hoosick Falls *(G-6281)*
Saint-Gobain Prfmce Plas Corp....C....518 642-2200
Granville *(G-5524)*
▲ SC Medical Overseas Inc....G....516 935-8500
Jericho *(G-6802)*
Sk Capital Partners II LP....F....212 826-2700
New York *(G-11604)*
Sk Titan Holdings LLC....G....212 826-2700
New York *(G-11605)*
◆ Solepoxy Inc....D....716 372-6300
Olean *(G-12607)*
Solid Surfaces Inc....D....585 292-5340
Rochester *(G-14134)*
Telechemische Inc....G....845 561-3237
Newburgh *(G-12247)*
▼ Terphane Holdings LLC....G....585 657-5800
Bloomfield *(G-956)*
◆ Terphane LLC....D....585 657-5800
Bloomfield *(G-957)*
▼ Tmp Technologies Inc....D....716 895-6100
Buffalo *(G-3097)*
◆ Toray Holding (usa) Inc....E....212 697-8150
New York *(G-11868)*
Toray Industries Inc....G....212 697-8150
New York *(G-11869)*
▲ Transpo Industries Inc....E....914 636-1000
New Rochelle *(G-8630)*
Tri-Seal Holdings Inc....D....845 353-3300
Blauvelt *(G-943)*
Wilsonart Intl Holdings LLC....E....516 935-6980
Bethpage *(G-854)*
WR Smith & Sons Inc....G....845 620-9400
Nanuet *(G-8469)*

SIC SECTION
28 CHEMICALS AND ALLIED PRODUCTS

2822 Synthetic Rubber (Vulcanizable Elastomers)

Company	Code	Phone
Canton Bio-Medical Inc	E	518 283-5963
Poestenkill *(G-13179)*		
David Fehlman	G	315 455-8888
Syracuse *(G-15303)*		
▲ Depco Inc	F	631 582-1995
Hauppauge *(G-5809)*		
▲ Dynax Corporation	G	914 764-0202
Pound Ridge *(G-13376)*		
▲ Formosa Polymer Corporation	G	718 326-1769
Maspeth *(G-7846)*		
▲ Hilord Chemical Corporation	E	631 234-7373
Hauppauge *(G-5845)*		
▲ Integrated Liner Tech Inc	E	518 621-7422
Rensselaer *(G-13475)*		
Release Coatings New York Inc	G	585 593-2335
Wellsville *(G-16120)*		
Silicone Products & Technology	C	716 684-1155
Lancaster *(G-7050)*		
▲ Specialty Silicone Pdts Inc	D	518 885-8826
Ballston Spa *(G-596)*		
Vasquez Tito	F	212 944-0441
New York *(G-11999)*		

2823 Cellulosic Man-Made Fibers

Company	Code	Phone
3M Company	B	716 876-1596
Tonawanda *(G-15517)*		
◆ Cortland Cable Company Inc	E	607 753-8276
Cortland *(G-3865)*		
Cytec Industries Inc	D	716 372-9650
Olean *(G-12598)*		
E I Du Pont De Nemours & Co	B	716 876-4420
Buffalo *(G-2807)*		
International Fiber Corp	E	716 693-4040
North Tonawanda *(G-12433)*		
Solivaira Specialties Inc	D	716 693-4009
North Tonawanda *(G-12452)*		
◆ Solvaira Specialties Inc	C	716 693-4040
North Tonawanda *(G-12453)*		
Solvaira Specialty LP	E	716 693-4040
North Tonawanda *(G-12454)*		
Solvaira Specialty LP	D	716 693-4040
North Tonawanda *(G-12455)*		

2824 Synthetic Organic Fibers, Exc Cellulosic

Company	Code	Phone
Dal-Tile Corporation	G	718 894-9574
Maspeth *(G-7834)*		
▲ Dynax Corporation	G	914 764-0202
Pound Ridge *(G-13376)*		
Fibrix LLC	E	716 683-4100
Depew *(G-4089)*		
Marly Home Industries USA Inc	G	718 388-3030
Brooklyn *(G-2172)*		
Solid Surface Acrylics LLC	F	716 743-1870
North Tonawanda *(G-12451)*		
Solutia Business Entps Inc	F	314 674-1000
New York *(G-11643)*		
◆ Stein Fibers Ltd	F	518 489-5700
Albany *(G-130)*		

2833 Medicinal Chemicals & Botanical Prdts

Company	Code	Phone
Abh Natures Products Inc	E	631 249-5783
Edgewood *(G-4391)*		
Accredo Health Incorporated	G	718 353-3012
Flushing *(G-4979)*		
▼ Ajes Pharmaceuticals LLC	E	631 608-1728
Copiague *(G-3749)*		
Albany Molecular Research Inc	F	518 433-7700
Rensselaer *(G-13471)*		
Albany Molecular Research Inc	F	518 512-2000
Rensselaer *(G-13472)*		
Alo Acquisition LLC	G	518 464-0279
Albany *(G-39)*		
Asept Pak Inc	E	518 651-2026
Malone *(G-7719)*		
◆ Bio-Botanica Inc	D	631 231-0987
Hauppauge *(G-5780)*		
Biobat Inc	G	718 270-1011
Brooklyn *(G-1616)*		
Biotemper	G	516 302-7985
Carle Place *(G-3263)*		
Conversion Labs Inc	F	866 351-5907
New York *(G-9392)*		
Cosmic Enterprise	G	718 342-6257
Brooklyn *(G-1722)*		
Country Life LLC	C	631 231-1031
Hauppauge *(G-5804)*		
Custom Nutraceuticals LLC	E	631 755-1388
Bohemia *(G-1005)*		
G C Hanford Manufacturing Co	C	315 476-7418
Syracuse *(G-15328)*		
GE Healthcare Inc	F	516 626-2799
Port Washington *(G-13262)*		
▲ Gemini Pharmaceuticals Inc	B	631 543-3334
Commack *(G-3693)*		
Good Earth Inc	G	716 684-8111
Lancaster *(G-7021)*		
Healthee Endeavors Inc	G	718 653-5499
Bronx *(G-1289)*		
Healthy N Fit Intl Inc	F	800 338-5200
Brewster *(G-1166)*		
Kamwo Meridian Herbs LLC	E	212 966-6370
New York *(G-10402)*		
Kannalife Sciences Inc	G	516 669-3219
Lloyd Harbor *(G-7280)*		
Lee Yuen Fung Trading Co Inc	F	212 594-9595
New York *(G-10539)*		
▲ Mercer Milling Co	E	315 701-1334
Liverpool *(G-7246)*		
Natures Bounty Co	D	631 244-2021
Ronkonkoma *(G-14385)*		
Natures Bounty Co	G	631 588-3492
Holbrook *(G-6202)*		
Nbty Inc	G	631 200-2062
Holbrook *(G-6203)*		
◆ Nbty Manufacturing LLC	G	631 567-9500
Ronkonkoma *(G-14386)*		
Nutra Solutions USA Inc	G	631 392-1900
Deer Park *(G-4019)*		
Nutraqueen LLC	F	347 368-6568
New York *(G-11009)*		
Nutrascience Labs Inc	E	631 247-0660
Farmingdale *(G-4838)*		
◆ Only Natural Inc	F	516 897-7001
Oceanside *(G-12549)*		
Pfizer Inc	A	212 733-2323
New York *(G-11174)*		
Pfizer Overseas LLC	G	212 733-2323
New York *(G-11178)*		
Proper Chemical Ltd	G	631 420-8000
Farmingdale *(G-4860)*		
Setauket Manufacturing Co	G	631 231-7272
Ronkonkoma *(G-14412)*		
▲ Ucb Pharma Inc	B	919 767-2555
Rochester *(G-14183)*		
Vitalize Labs LLC	G	212 966-6130
New York *(G-12046)*		
Wacf Enterprise Inc	E	631 745-5841
Northport *(G-12474)*		
▲ Wellquest International Inc	F	212 689-9094
New York *(G-12091)*		

2834 Pharmaceuticals

Company	Code	Phone
3v Company Inc	E	718 858-7333
Brooklyn *(G-1440)*		
5th Avenue Pharmacy Inc	G	718 439-8585
Brooklyn *(G-1443)*		
872 Hunts Point Pharmacy Inc	G	718 991-3519
Bronx *(G-1198)*		
888 Pharmacy Inc	F	718 871-8833
Brooklyn *(G-1447)*		
A & Z Pharmaceutical Inc	D	631 952-3802
Hauppauge *(G-5752)*		
◆ A & Z Pharmaceutical Inc	B	631 952-3800
Hauppauge *(G-5753)*		
Abbott Laboratories	F	716 633-1904
Williamsville *(G-16566)*		
Abeona Therapeutics Inc	F	646 813-4712
New York *(G-8709)*		
Abh Pharma Inc	D	866 922-4669
Edgewood *(G-4392)*		
Abraxis Bioscience LLC	G	716 773-0800
Grand Island *(G-5494)*		
▲ Acorda Therapeutics Inc	C	914 347-4300
Ardsley *(G-392)*		
Actavis Laboratories Ny Inc	D	631 693-8000
Copiague *(G-3747)*		
Actinium Pharmaceuticals Inc	E	646 677-3870
New York *(G-8730)*		
Advance Pharmaceutical Inc	D	631 981-4600
Holtsville *(G-6236)*		
▲ Affymax Inc	F	650 812-8700
New York *(G-8766)*		
Aiping Pharmaceutical Inc	G	631 952-3802
Hauppauge *(G-5757)*		
Akari Therapeutics PLC	F	646 350-0702
New York *(G-8779)*		
▲ Alfred Khalily Inc	F	516 504-0059
Great Neck *(G-5530)*		
Allied Pharmacy Products Inc	G	516 374-8862
Woodmere *(G-16639)*		
▲ Altaire Pharmaceuticals Inc	C	631 722-5988
Aquebogue *(G-373)*		
Amarantus Bscence Holdings Inc	F	917 686-5317
New York *(G-8816)*		
American Bio Medica Corp	D	518 758-8158
Kinderhook *(G-6879)*		
American Hlth Formulations Inc	G	631 392-1756
Hauppauge *(G-5766)*		
American Hormones Inc	G	845 471-7272
Poughkeepsie *(G-13325)*		
American Regent Inc	B	631 924-4000
Shirley *(G-14826)*		
Amneal Pharmaceuticals LLC	G	908 231-1911
Brookhaven *(G-1427)*		
Amneal Pharmaceuticals LLC	E	631 952-0214
Brookhaven *(G-1428)*		
▲ Amneal Pharmaceuticals NY LLC	G	908 947-3120
Brookhaven *(G-1429)*		
Anacor Pharmaceuticals Inc	G	212 733-2323
New York *(G-8851)*		
Angiogenex Inc	G	347 468-6799
New York *(G-8864)*		
Anima Mundi Herbals LLC	G	415 279-5727
Long Island City *(G-7379)*		
Anterios Inc	G	212 303-1683
New York *(G-8876)*		
Apothecus Pharmaceutical Corp	F	516 624-8200
Oyster Bay *(G-12810)*		
Ark Sciences Inc	G	646 943-1520
Islandia *(G-6521)*		
▲ Ascent Pharmaceuticals Inc	D	631 851-0550
Central Islip *(G-3356)*		
Asence Inc	E	347 335-2606
New York *(G-8930)*		
Athenex Inc	D	716 427-2950
Buffalo *(G-2712)*		
Athenex Pharma Solutions LLC	G	877 463-7823
Clarence *(G-3525)*		
Athenex Pharmaceutical Div LLC	F	877 463-7823
Buffalo *(G-2713)*		
Atlantic Essential Pdts Inc	D	631 434-8333
Hauppauge *(G-5772)*		
Auven Therapeutics MGT LP	F	212 616-4000
New York *(G-8968)*		
Avenue Therapeutics Inc	F	781 652-4500
New York *(G-8975)*		
Axim Biotechnologies Inc	F	212 751-0001
New York *(G-8983)*		
Azurrx Biopharma Inc	F	646 699-7855
Brooklyn *(G-1577)*		
▲ Bactolac Pharmaceutical Inc	B	631 951-4908
Hauppauge *(G-5777)*		
▲ Barc Usa Inc	E	516 719-1052
New Hyde Park *(G-8519)*		
Bausch & Lomb Holdings Inc	G	585 338-6000
New York *(G-9028)*		
◆ Bausch & Lomb Incorporated	B	585 338-6000
Rochester *(G-13655)*		
Baxter Healthcare Corporation	G	800 356-3454
Medina *(G-7972)*		
Baxter International Inc	G	845 457-9370
Montgomery *(G-8308)*		
Beyondspring Inc	F	646 305-6387
New York *(G-9066)*		
Beyondspring Phrmceuticals Inc	F	646 305-6387
New York *(G-9067)*		
Bi Nutraceuticals Inc	D	631 232-1105
Central Islip *(G-3360)*		
◆ Bio-Botanica Inc	D	631 231-0987
Hauppauge *(G-5780)*		
Biomed Pharmaceuticals Inc	G	914 592-0525
Hawthorne *(G-5984)*		
▲ Biospecifics Technologies Corp	G	516 593-7000
Lynbrook *(G-7662)*		
Biotie Therapies Inc	F	650 244-4850
Ardsley *(G-394)*		
Bli International Inc	F	631 940-9000
Deer Park *(G-3952)*		
Bristol-Myers Squibb Company	A	212 546-4000
New York *(G-9144)*		
Bristol-Myers Squibb Company	E	315 432-2000
East Syracuse *(G-4327)*		
Bristol-Myers Squibb Company	C	516 832-2191
Garden City *(G-5253)*		

Employee Codes: A=Over 500 employees, B=251-500
C=101-250, D=51-100, E=20-50, F=10-19, G=5-9

Campbell Alliance Group Inc ....E 212 377-2740
New York (G-9188)
Cas Biosciences LLC ....C 844 227-2467
New York (G-9220)
Cellectis Inc ....F 347 809-5980
New York (G-9235)
Central Islip Pharmacy Inc ....G 631 234-6039
Central Islip (G-3362)
Century Grand Inc ....F 212 925-3838
New York (G-9250)
Cerovene Inc ....F 845 359-1101
Orangeburg (G-12671)
Cerovene Inc ....F 845 267-2055
Valley Cottage (G-15753)
Chartwell Pharma Nda B2 Holdin ....G 845 268-5000
Congers (G-3713)
Chartwell Pharmaceuticals LLC ....D 845 268-5000
Congers (G-3714)
Chartwell Rx LLC ....E 845 268-5000
Congers (G-3715)
Citypharma Inc ....G 917 832-6035
Jackson Heights (G-6619)
Cleveland Biolabs Inc ....E 716 849-6810
Buffalo (G-2768)
Cognigen Corporation ....D 716 633-3463
Buffalo (G-2770)
◆ Combe Incorporated ....C 914 694-5454
White Plains (G-16439)
Container Tstg Solutions LLC ....F 716 487-3300
Jamestown (G-6709)
Container Tstg Solutions LLC ....F 716 487-3300
Sinclairville (G-14865)
Contract Pharmacal Corp ....E 631 231-4610
Hauppauge (G-5798)
Contract Pharmacal Corp ....C 631 231-4610
Hauppauge (G-5799)
Contract Pharmacal Corp ....E 631 231-4610
Hauppauge (G-5800)
Contract Pharmacal Corp ....D 631 231-4610
Hauppauge (G-5801)
Contract Pharmacal Corp ....C 631 231-4610
Hauppauge (G-5802)
Contract Pharmacal Corp ....F 631 231-4610
Hauppauge (G-5803)
Contract Phrmctcals Ltd Nagara ....C 716 887-3400
Buffalo (G-2779)
Coopersurgical Inc ....F 716 693-6230
North Tonawanda (G-12424)
▲ CRS Nuclear Services LLC ....F 716 810-0688
Cheektowaga (G-3438)
▲ Danbury Pharma LLC ....E 631 393-6333
Farmingdale (G-4749)
Delcath Systems Inc ....E 212 489-2100
New York (G-9497)
Dr Reddys Laboratories NY Inc ....E 518 827-7702
Middleburgh (G-8129)
DSM Nutritional Products LLC ....C 518 372-5155
Schenectady (G-14669)
DSM Nutritional Products LLC ....C 518 372-5155
Glenville (G-5445)
Durata Therapeutics Inc ....G 646 871-6400
New York (G-9587)
Easton Pharmaceuticals Inc ....G 347 284-0192
Lewiston (G-7139)
▼ Edlaw Pharmaceuticals Inc ....E 631 454-6888
Farmingdale (G-4758)
Eli Lilly and Company ....F 516 622-2244
New Hyde Park (G-8532)
Emilior Phrm Compounding Inc ....E 855 426-6768
Bronx (G-1268)
Emphascience ....G 585 348-9415
Pittsford (G-13011)
▲ Encysive Pharmaceuticals Inc ....E 212 733-2323
New York (G-9674)
Enumeral Biomedical Corp ....G 347 227-4787
New York (G-9690)
Enzo Life Sciences Inc ....E 631 694-7070
Farmingdale (G-4760)
◆ Enzo Life Sciences Intl Inc ....E 610 941-0430
Farmingdale (G-4761)
Eon Labs Inc ....F 516 478-9700
New Hyde Park (G-8533)
▲ Epic Pharma LLC ....C 718 276-8600
Laurelton (G-7099)
Equinox Aegis LLC ....G 212 316-9078
New York (G-9696)
Erika T Schwartz MD PC ....G 212 873-3420
New York (G-9702)
Eyenovia Inc ....G 917 289-1117
New York (G-9760)
▲ FB Laboratories Inc ....E 631 750-0000
Hauppauge (G-5823)
Fera Pharmaceuticals LLC ....F 516 277-1449
Locust Valley (G-7346)
Flushing Pharmacy Inc ....C 718 260-8999
Brooklyn (G-1894)
▲ Forest Laboratories LLC ....C 212 421-7850
New York (G-9822)
Forest Laboratories LLC ....D 212 421-7850
Hauppauge (G-5828)
Forest Laboratories LLC ....C 631 858-6010
Commack (G-3690)
Forest Labs ....G 631 755-1185
Farmingdale (G-4766)
Forest Research Institute Inc ....F 631 858-5200
Commack (G-3691)
Fortress Biotech Inc ....E 781 652-4500
New York (G-9825)
▲ Fougera Pharmaceuticals Inc ....C 631 454-7677
Melville (G-8026)
Fougera Pharmaceuticals Inc ....C 631 454-7677
Hicksville (G-6088)
Freeda Vitamins Inc ....E 718 433-4337
Long Island City (G-7452)
Fresenius Kabi Usa LLC ....B 716 773-0053
Grand Island (G-5500)
Fresenius Kabi USA LLC ....E 716 773-0800
Grand Island (G-5501)
▲ Futurebiotics LLC ....E 631 273-6300
Hauppauge (G-5830)
G C Hanford Manufacturing Co ....C 315 476-7418
Syracuse (G-15328)
▼ Gamma Enterprises LLC ....E 631 755-1080
West Babylon (G-16156)
▲ Gemini Pharmaceuticals Inc ....B 631 543-3334
Commack (G-3693)
▲ Generic Pharmaceutical Svcs ....E 631 348-6900
Hauppauge (G-5832)
▲ Generics Bidco I LLC ....G 256 859-4011
Chestnut Ridge (G-3492)
Genzyme Corporation ....D 212 698-0300
New York (G-9907)
▲ Geritrex LLC ....E 914 668-4003
Middletown (G-8156)
Geritrex Holdings Inc ....G 914 668-4003
Mount Vernon (G-8399)
Ges Ges ....G 631 291-9624
Hauppauge (G-5834)
Glaxosmithkline LLC ....E 845 341-7590
Montgomery (G-8311)
Glaxosmithkline LLC ....E 845 797-3259
Wappingers Falls (G-15933)
Glaxosmithkline LLC ....E 585 738-9025
Rochester (G-13838)
Glaxosmithkline LLC ....E 716 913-5679
Buffalo (G-2850)
Glaxosmithkline LLC ....E 518 852-9637
Mechanicville (G-7931)
Glaxosmithkline LLC ....D 518 239-6901
East Durham (G-4216)
Global Alliance For Tb ....E 212 227-7540
New York (G-9935)
Glycobia Inc ....G 607 339-0051
Ithaca (G-6578)
Greenkissny Inc ....G 914 304-4323
White Plains (G-16455)
Greentree Pharmacy Inc ....F 718 768-2700
Brooklyn (G-1952)
Guosa Life Sciences Inc ....F 718 813-7806
New York (G-10010)
▲ H W Naylor Co Inc ....F 607 263-5145
Morris (G-8335)
Health Care Products ....G 631 789-8228
Amityville (G-282)
Healthone Pharmacy Inc ....F 718 495-9015
Brooklyn (G-1969)
HHS Pharmaceuticals Inc ....F 347 674-1670
New York (G-10093)
▲ Hi-Tech Pharmacal Co Inc ....C 631 789-8228
Amityville (G-284)
Hi-Tech Pharmacal Co Inc ....F 631 789-8228
Amityville (G-285)
Hoffmann-La Roche Inc ....G 973 890-2291
New York (G-10111)
▲ Hogil Pharmaceutical Corp ....F 914 681-1800
White Plains (G-16460)
Hospira Inc ....C 716 684-9400
Buffalo (G-2875)
Ibio Inc ....E 302 355-0650
New York (G-10165)
◆ Ima Life North America Inc ....C 716 695-6354
Tonawanda (G-15550)
Innogenix Inc ....F 631 450-4704
Amityville (G-287)
Innovative Labs LLC ....D 631 231-5522
Hauppauge (G-5849)
Inolife Tchnlgies Oprtions Inc ....G 212 386-5575
New York (G-10222)
Intercept Pharmaceuticals Inc ....D 646 747-1000
New York (G-10238)
▲ Intra-Cellular Therapies Inc ....E 646 440-9333
New York (G-10257)
Intstrux LLC ....E 646 688-2782
New York (G-10261)
Invagen Pharmaceuticals Inc ....C 631 949-6367
Central Islip (G-3372)
▲ Invagen Pharmaceuticals Inc ....B 631 231-3233
Hauppauge (G-5851)
Ip Med Inc ....G 516 766-3800
Oceanside (G-12541)
Irx Therapeutics Inc ....G 347 442-0640
Brooklyn (G-2015)
Izun Pharmaceuticals Corp ....F 212 618-6357
New York (G-10280)
Jerome Stvens Phrmcuticals Inc ....F 631 567-1113
Bohemia (G-1041)
◆ JRS Pharma LP ....E 845 878-8300
Patterson (G-12883)
▲ Kabco Pharmaceuticals Inc ....G 631 842-3600
Amityville (G-292)
Kadmon Corporation LLC ....F 212 308-6000
New York (G-10393)
Kadmon Holdings Inc ....D 212 308-6000
New York (G-10394)
Kaneka America LLC ....D 212 705-4340
New York (G-10404)
Kannalife Sciences Inc ....G 516 669-3219
Lloyd Harbor (G-7280)
Kbl Healthcare LP ....G 212 319-5555
New York (G-10424)
◆ Kent Chemical Corporation ....E 212 521-1700
New York (G-10436)
Kingston Pharma LLC ....D 315 705-4019
Massena (G-7904)
▲ Klg Usa LLC ....A 845 856-5311
Port Jervis (G-13233)
Life Pill Laboratories LLC ....G 914 682-2146
White Plains (G-16472)
▲ Liptis Pharmaceuticals USA Inc ....A 845 627-0260
Spring Valley (G-14999)
LNK International Inc ....D 631 435-3500
Hauppauge (G-5867)
LNK International Inc ....D 631 435-3500
Hauppauge (G-5868)
LNK International Inc ....D 631 435-3500
Hauppauge (G-5869)
LNK International Inc ....D 631 543-3787
Hauppauge (G-5870)
LNK International Inc ....D 631 435-3500
Hauppauge (G-5871)
LNK International Inc ....D 631 231-4020
Hauppauge (G-5872)
▲ Lotta Luv Beauty LLC ....F 646 786-2847
New York (G-10614)
▲ Luitpold Pharmaceuticals Inc ....B 631 924-4000
Shirley (G-14838)
Makers Nutrition LLC ....E 631 456-5397
Hauppauge (G-5879)
Maks Pharma & Diagnostics Inc ....G 631 270-1528
Baldwin (G-540)
▲ Marco Hi-Tech JV LLC ....G 212 798-8100
New York (G-10698)
◆ Marietta Corporation ....B 607 753-6746
Cortland (G-3881)
Marken LLP ....G 631 396-7454
Farmingdale (G-4815)
Medek Laboratories Inc ....E 845 943-4988
Monroe (G-8277)
▲ Medtech Products Inc ....F 914 524-6810
Tarrytown (G-15482)
◆ Mentholatum Company ....E 716 677-2500
Orchard Park (G-12730)
▲ Mercer Milling Co ....E 315 701-1334
Liverpool (G-7246)
Mesoblast Inc ....G 212 880-2060
New York (G-10781)
Moleclar Insght Phrmctcals Inc ....G 914 789-2800
Sleepy Hollow (G-14886)
Mustang Bio Inc ....G 781 652-4500
New York (G-10862)

Mylan Health Management LLC ..... G 917 262-2950
New York *(G-10867)*

Nanorx Inc ..... G 914 671-0224
Chappaqua *(G-3423)*

Natural Organics Labs Inc ..... B 631 957-5600
Amityville *(G-305)*

Natures Bounty (ny) Inc ..... G 631 567-9500
Bohemia *(G-1062)*

▲ Natures Bounty (ny) Inc ..... A 631 200-2000
Ronkonkoma *(G-14384)*

▲ Natures Value Inc ..... B 631 846-2500
Coram *(G-3800)*

ND Labs Inc ..... F 516 612-4900
Lynbrook *(G-7669)*

Neurotrope Inc ..... G 973 242-0005
New York *(G-10915)*

Noho Health Inc ..... E 877 227-3631
New York *(G-10985)*

▲ Norwich Pharmaceuticals Inc ..... B 607 335-3000
Norwich *(G-12490)*

Novartis AG ..... C 617 435-0469
Port Washington *(G-13291)*

Novartis Corporation ..... D 718 276-8600
Laurelton *(G-7100)*

Novartis Pharmaceuticals Corp ..... G 888 669-6682
New York *(G-11000)*

Novartis Pharmaceuticals Corp ..... G 718 276-8600
Laurelton *(G-7101)*

Noven Pharmaceuticals Inc ..... E 212 682-4420
New York *(G-11001)*

Nutra-Scientifics LLC ..... G 917 238-8510
Pomona *(G-13186)*

Nutraceutical Wellness LLC ..... G 888 454-3320
New York *(G-11008)*

Nutrascience Labs Inc ..... E 631 247-0660
Farmingdale *(G-4938)*

Nutratech Labs Inc ..... G 315 695-2256
Phoenix *(G-12991)*

NY Phrmacy Compounding Ctr Inc ..... G 201 403-5151
Astoria *(G-438)*

Ony Biotech Inc ..... E 716 636-9096
Amherst *(G-246)*

Ony Inc Baird Researchpark ..... E 716 636-9096
Buffalo *(G-2981)*

Ophthotech Corporation ..... C 212 845-8200
New York *(G-11051)*

Orenova Group LLC ..... G 914 517-3000
White Plains *(G-16482)*

OSI Pharmaceuticals LLC ..... D 631 847-0175
Farmingdale *(G-4842)*

▼ OSI Pharmaceuticals LLC ..... G 631 962-2000
Farmingdale *(G-4843)*

Ovid Therapeutics Inc ..... E 646 661-7661
New York *(G-11072)*

P & L Development LLC ..... D 516 986-1700
Westbury *(G-16360)*

P & L Development LLC ..... D 516 986-1700
Westbury *(G-16361)*

◆ P & L Development LLC ..... D 516 986-1700
Westbury *(G-16362)*

Pace Up Pharmaceuticals LLC ..... G 631 450-4495
Lindenhurst *(G-7189)*

▲ Pall Corporation ..... A 516 484-5400
Port Washington *(G-13295)*

▲ Par Pharmaceutical Inc ..... B 845 573-5500
Chestnut Ridge *(G-3494)*

Par Phrmceutical Companies Inc ..... E 845 573-5500
Chestnut Ridge *(G-3495)*

Par Sterile Products LLC ..... E 845 573-5500
Chestnut Ridge *(G-3496)*

Pdk Labs Inc ..... D 631 273-2630
Hauppauge *(G-5910)*

Perrigo Company ..... E 718 960-9900
Bronx *(G-1356)*

Perrigo New York Inc ..... F 718 901-2800
Bronx *(G-1357)*

◆ Perrigo New York Inc ..... B 718 960-9900
Bronx *(G-1358)*

▲ Pfizer HCP Corporation ..... F 212 733-2323
New York *(G-11173)*

Pfizer Inc ..... B 518 297-6611
Rouses Point *(G-14468)*

Pfizer Inc ..... C 914 437-5868
White Plains *(G-16497)*

Pfizer Inc ..... C 937 746-3603
New York *(G-11175)*

Pfizer Inc ..... D 212 733-6276
New York *(G-11176)*

Pfizer Inc ..... C 212 733-2323
New York *(G-11177)*

Pfizer Inc ..... A 212 733-2323
New York *(G-11174)*

Pfizer Overseas LLC ..... G 212 733-2323
New York *(G-11178)*

PH David J Rossi ..... G 585 455-1160
Rochester *(G-14016)*

▲ Pharbest Pharmaceuticals Inc ..... E 631 249-5130
Farmingdale *(G-4846)*

▲ Pharmaceutic Labs LLC ..... F 518 608-1060
Albany *(G-114)*

Pharmalife Inc ..... G 631 249-4040
Farmingdale *(G-4847)*

▲ Pharmavantage LLC ..... G 631 321-8171
Babylon *(G-531)*

Phoenix Laboratories Inc ..... C 516 822-1230
Farmingdale *(G-4848)*

Polygen Pharmaceuticals Inc ..... E 631 392-4044
Edgewood *(G-4411)*

Precision Pharma Services Inc ..... C 631 752-7314
Melville *(G-8058)*

Premium Processing Corp ..... D 631 232-1105
Babylon *(G-533)*

◆ Prestige Brands Intl LLC ..... F 914 524-6800
Tarrytown *(G-15487)*

Prestige Consmr Healthcare Inc ..... D 914 524-6800
Tarrytown *(G-15488)*

▲ Prime Pack LLC ..... F 732 253-7734
New York *(G-11241)*

Progenics Pharmaceuticals Inc ..... D 646 975-2500
New York *(G-11257)*

Protein Sciences Corporation ..... E 203 686-0800
Pearl River *(G-12908)*

Purine Pharma LLC ..... E 315 705-4030
Mount Vernon *(G-8436)*

Purinepharma LLC ..... G 732 485-1400
Massena *(G-7907)*

▲ Purity Products Inc ..... D 516 767-1967
Plainview *(G-13084)*

Quality Nature Inc ..... G 718 484-4666
Brooklyn *(G-2367)*

Quogue Capital LLC ..... G 212 554-4475
New York *(G-11304)*

Quva Pharma Inc ..... G 973 224-7795
New York *(G-11306)*

R J S Direct Marketing Inc ..... F 631 667-5768
Deer Park *(G-4033)*

Randob Labs Ltd ..... G 845 534-2197
Cornwall *(G-3837)*

Regeneron Pharmaceuticals Inc ..... B 914 847-7000
Tarrytown *(G-15490)*

Regeneron Pharmaceuticals Inc ..... E 518 488-6000
Rensselaer *(G-13477)*

Regenlab USA LLC ..... G 800 220-9082
New York *(G-11350)*

Regenron Hlthcare Slutions Inc ..... A 914 847-7000
Tarrytown *(G-15491)*

Relmada Therapeutics Inc ..... F 646 677-3853
New York *(G-11354)*

Retrophin LLC ..... G 646 564-3680
New York *(G-11373)*

Rij Pharmaceutical Corporation ..... E 845 692-5799
Middletown *(G-8173)*

Rk Pharma Inc ..... G 646 884-3765
Pearl River *(G-12910)*

Rls Holdings Inc ..... G 716 418-7274
Clarence *(G-3540)*

Roche Tcrc Inc ..... G 800 626-3553
New York *(G-11414)*

Ropack USA Inc ..... F 631 482-7777
Commack *(G-3700)*

S1 Biopharma Inc ..... G 201 839-0941
New York *(G-11460)*

▲ Safetec of America Inc ..... D 716 895-1822
Buffalo *(G-3054)*

Salutem Group LLC ..... G 347 620-2640
New York *(G-11473)*

Saptalis Pharmaceuticals LLC ..... E 631 231-2751
Hauppauge *(G-5933)*

Satnam Distributors LLC ..... G 516 802-0600
Jericho *(G-6801)*

Scarguard Labs LLC ..... F 516 482-8050
Great Neck *(G-5589)*

Sciarra Laboratories Inc ..... G 516 933-7853
Hicksville *(G-6131)*

▲ Sciegen Pharmaceuticals Inc ..... D 631 434-2723
Hauppauge *(G-5936)*

Scienta Pharmaceuticals LLC ..... G 845 589-0774
Valley Cottage *(G-15764)*

Seidlin Consulting ..... G 212 496-2043
New York *(G-11535)*

Sellas Life Sciences Group Inc ..... F 917 438-4353
New York *(G-11540)*

Shennong Pharmaceuticals Inc ..... E 347 422-2200
New York *(G-11564)*

Shrineeta Pharmacy ..... G 212 234-7959
New York *(G-11571)*

Shrineeta Pharmacy Inc ..... E 212 234-7959
New York *(G-11572)*

Siga Technologies Inc ..... E 212 672-9100
New York *(G-11582)*

▲ Silarx Pharmaceuticals Inc ..... D 845 352-4020
Carmel *(G-3281)*

Silver Oak Pharmacy Inc ..... G 718 922-3400
Brooklyn *(G-2472)*

Sincerus LLC ..... G 800 419-2804
Brooklyn *(G-2478)*

Skills Alliance Inc ..... G 646 492-5300
New York *(G-11608)*

Skincare Products Inc ..... G 917 837-5255
New York *(G-11609)*

Specgx LLC ..... A 607 538-9124
Hobart *(G-6164)*

Stemline Therapeutics Inc ..... E 646 502-2311
New York *(G-11703)*

Steri-Pharma LLC ..... E 315 473-7180
Syracuse *(G-15431)*

Sterrx LLC ..... E 518 324-7879
Plattsburgh *(G-13159)*

Strativa Pharmaceuticals ..... F 201 802-4000
Spring Valley *(G-15008)*

Sunquest Pharmaceuticals Inc ..... F 855 478-6779
Hicksville *(G-6135)*

Synergy Pharmaceuticals Inc ..... B 212 297-0020
New York *(G-11764)*

Syntho Pharmaceuticals Inc ..... G 631 755-9898
Farmingdale *(G-4887)*

Teva Pharmaceuticals Usa Inc ..... G 212 259-2030
New York *(G-11804)*

Tg Therapeutics Inc ..... D 212 554-4484
New York *(G-11806)*

▲ Time-Cap Laboratories Inc ..... C 631 753-9090
Farmingdale *(G-4896)*

▲ Tishcon Corp ..... C 516 333-3056
Westbury *(G-16378)*

Tishcon Corp ..... C 516 333-3056
Westbury *(G-16379)*

Tishcon Corp ..... C 516 333-3050
Westbury *(G-16380)*

Tishcon Corp ..... C 516 333-3050
Westbury *(G-16381)*

▼ Tmp Technologies Inc ..... D 716 895-6100
Buffalo *(G-3097)*

Tocare LLC ..... F 718 767-0618
Whitestone *(G-16549)*

Tongli Pharmaceuticals USA Inc ..... F 212 842-8837
Flushing *(G-5054)*

Tonix Pharmaceuticals Inc ..... G 212 980-9155
New York *(G-11865)*

Tonix Phrmceuticals Holdg Corp ..... F 212 980-9155
New York *(G-11866)*

▲ Topiderm Inc ..... C 631 226-7979
Amityville *(G-321)*

▲ Topix Pharmaceuticals Inc ..... C 631 226-7979
Amityville *(G-322)*

Triceutical Inc ..... F 631 249-0003
Bronx *(G-1406)*

Tyme Inc ..... G 646 205-1603
New York *(G-11924)*

Tyme Technologies Inc ..... F 212 461-2315
New York *(G-11925)*

▲ Ucb Pharma Inc ..... B 919 767-2555
Rochester *(G-14183)*

▼ Unipharm Inc ..... D 212 594-3260
New York *(G-11947)*

United-Guardian Inc ..... E 631 273-0900
Hauppauge *(G-5965)*

▲ Unither Manufacturing LLC ..... C 585 475-9000
Rochester *(G-14187)*

Unither Manufacturing LLC ..... F 585 274-5430
Rochester *(G-14188)*

Vaccinex Inc ..... E 585 271-2700
Rochester *(G-14196)*

▲ Velocity Pharma LLC ..... G 631 393-2905
Farmingdale *(G-4902)*

Ventrus Biosciences Inc ..... G 646 706-5208
New York *(G-12005)*

Verona Pharma Inc ..... F 914 797-5007
White Plains *(G-16514)*

Vida-Blend LLC ..... E 518 627-4138
Amsterdam *(G-363)*

Employee Codes: A=Over 500 employees, B=251-500
C=101-250, D=51-100, E=20-50, F=10-19, G=5-9
2019 Harris
New York Manufacturers Directory
717

Viropro Inc ....E 650 300-5190
New York (G-12039)
Vita-Gen Laboratories LLC ....G 631 450-4357
Commack (G-3705)
▲ Vita-Nat Inc ....G 631 293-6000
Farmingdale (G-4903)
Vitalis LLC ....G 646 831-7338
New York (G-12045)
◆ Vitane Pharmaceuticals Inc ....E 845 267-6700
Congers (G-3722)
Vvs International Inc ....G 212 302-5410
New York (G-12058)
Watson Laboratories Inc ....F 951 493-5300
Carmel (G-3284)
Wavodyne Therapeutics Inc ....G 954 632-6630
West Henrietta (G-16255)
Wellmill LLC ....E 631 465-9245
Commack (G-3706)
Wyeth Holdings LLC ....D 845 602-5000
Pearl River (G-12913)
◆ Wyeth LLC ....A 973 660-5000
New York (G-12146)
▲ X-Gen Pharmaceuticals Inc ....G 607 562-2700
Big Flats (G-857)
X-Gen Pharmaceuticals Inc ....E 631 261-8188
Northport (G-12475)
Xstelos Holdings Inc ....G 212 729-4962
New York (G-12155)
Y-Mabs Therapeutics Inc ....F 917 817-2992
New York (G-12156)
You First Services Inc ....F 716 204-7215
Buffalo (G-3135)
Ys Marketing Inc ....E 718 778-6080
Brooklyn (G-2667)
Zenith Solutions ....G 718 575-8570
Flushing (G-5062)
Zeo Health Ltd ....F 845 353-5185
Valley Cottage (G-15769)
▲ Zitomer LLC ....G 212 737-5560
New York (G-12180)

2835 Diagnostic Substances

Bella International Inc ....G 716 484-0102
Jamestown (G-6700)
Biochemical Diagnostics Inc ....E 631 595-9200
Edgewood (G-4397)
▲ Biopool Us Inc ....E 716 483-3851
Jamestown (G-6701)
▲ Chembio Diagnostic Systems Inc ....C 631 924-1135
Medford (G-7941)
▲ Chembio Diagnostics Inc ....C 631 924-1135
Medford (G-7942)
▲ Clark Laboratories Inc ....F 716 483-3851
Jamestown (G-6706)
Danisco US Inc ....D 585 256-5200
Rochester (G-13733)
◆ E-Z-Em Inc ....E 609 524-2864
Melville (G-8018)
Enzo Life Sciences Inc ....E 631 694-7070
Farmingdale (G-4760)
Gotham Veterinary Center PC ....E 212 222-1900
New York (G-9961)
Immco Diagnostics Inc ....G 716 691-0091
Buffalo (G-2881)
Inolife Tchnlgies Oprtions Inc ....G 212 386-5575
New York (G-10222)
Ithaca Pregancy Center ....G 607 753-3909
Cortland (G-3877)
Kannalife Sciences Inc ....G 516 669-3219
Lloyd Harbor (G-7280)
Ken-Ton Open Mri PC ....G 716 876-7000
Kenmore (G-6863)
Lesanne Life Sciences LLC ....G 914 234-0860
Bedford (G-770)
Lifelink Monitoring Corp ....F 845 336-2098
Bearsville (G-764)
Lifescan Inc ....B 516 557-2693
Wantagh (G-15923)
Northeast Doulas ....G 845 621-0654
Mahopac (G-7710)
Ortho-Clinical Diagnostics Inc ....E 716 631-1281
Williamsville (G-16582)
Ortho-Clinical Diagnostics Inc ....E 585 453-3000
Rochester (G-13995)
Petnet Solutions Inc ....G 865 218-2000
New York (G-11171)
Siemens Hlthcare Dgnostics Inc ....E 914 631-0475
Tarrytown (G-15492)
Tiziana Therapeutics Inc ....G 646 396-4970
New York (G-11851)
Ufc Biotechnology ....G 716 777-3776
Amherst (G-258)
▲ US Diagnostics Inc ....E 866 216-5308
New York (G-11975)
◆ Welch Allyn Inc ....A 315 685-4100
Skaneateles Falls (G-14883)
Working Family Solutions Inc ....G 845 802-6182
Saugerties (G-14620)

2836 Biological Prdts, Exc Diagnostic Substances

▲ Acorda Therapeutics Inc ....C 914 347-4300
Ardsley (G-392)
Advance Biofactures Corp ....E 516 593-7000
Lynbrook (G-7658)
◆ AG Biotech Inc ....G 585 346-0020
Livonia (G-7277)
▲ Akshar Extracts Inc ....G 631 588-9727
Ronkonkoma (G-14297)
Albany Molecular Research Inc ....G 518 512-2234
Albany (G-34)
▲ Albany Molecular Research Inc ....B 518 512-2000
Albany (G-35)
Angus Chemical Company ....E 716 283-1434
Niagara Falls (G-12263)
AV Therapeutics Inc ....E 917 497-5523
New York (G-8969)
Bioivt LLC ....D 516 483-1196
Westbury (G-16319)
Coral Blood Service ....F 800 483-4888
Elmsford (G-4538)
Cypress Bioscience Inc ....F 858 452-2323
New York (G-9444)
D C I Plasma Center Inc ....G 914 241-1646
Mount Kisco (G-8340)
Debmar-Mercury ....G 212 669-5025
New York (G-9494)
▲ Ecological Laboratories Inc ....D 516 823-3441
Island Park (G-6513)
Instrumentation Laboratory Co ....C 845 680-0028
Orangeburg (G-12681)
International Aids Vaccine Ini ....D 646 381-8066
Brooklyn (G-2009)
International Aids Vccne Inttv ....D 212 847-1111
New York (G-10242)
Ip Med Inc ....G 516 766-3800
Oceanside (G-12541)
Kadmon Holdings Inc ....D 212 308-6000
New York (G-10394)
Lake Immunogenics Inc ....F 585 265-1973
Ontario (G-12656)
Man of World ....G 212 915-0017
New York (G-10681)
Meiragtx Holdings PLC ....E 646 490-2965
New York (G-10765)
Nanoprobes Inc ....F 631 205-9490
Yaphank (G-16718)
Nelco Laboratories Inc ....E 631 242-0082
Deer Park (G-4014)
Omrix Biopharmaceuticals Inc ....C 908 218-0707
New York (G-11039)
Rentschler Biotechnologie GMBH ....G 631 656-7137
Hauppauge (G-5928)
Roar Biomedical Inc ....G 631 591-2749
Calverton (G-3170)
Siga Technologies Inc ....E 212 672-9100
New York (G-11582)
Stemcultures LLC ....G 518 621-0848
Rensselaer (G-13478)
Synergy Pharmaceuticals Inc ....G 212 227-8611
New York (G-11763)
Vyera Pharmaceuticals LLC ....E 646 356-5577
New York (G-12059)
Wyeth Holdings LLC ....D 845 602-5000
Pearl River (G-12913)
◆ Wyeth LLC ....A 973 660-5000
New York (G-12146)
▼ Zeptometrix Corporation ....D 716 882-0920
Buffalo (G-3138)

2841 Soap & Detergents

Aura Detergent LLC ....G 718 824-2162
Bronx (G-1223)
▼ Baums Castorine Company Inc ....G 315 336-8154
Rome (G-14247)
Bfma Holding Corporation ....G 607 753-6746
Cortland (G-3862)
Cleanse TEC ....E 718 346-9111
Brooklyn (G-1701)
Colgate-Palmolive Company ....A 212 310-2000
New York (G-9349)
Colgate-Palmolive Nj Inc ....E 212 310-2000
New York (G-9350)
◆ Combe Incorporated ....C 914 694-5454
White Plains (G-16439)
Cosco Enterprises Inc ....G 718 383-4488
Ridgewood (G-13533)
Cosco Interprises Inc ....E 718 417-8995
Ridgewood (G-13534)
◆ Cpac Inc ....E 585 382-3223
Leicester (G-7126)
◆ Crosstex International Inc ....D 631 582-6777
Hauppauge (G-5805)
Dr Jacobs Naturals LLC ....E 718 265-1522
Brooklyn (G-1791)
Ecolab Inc ....F 716 683-6298
Cheektowaga (G-3443)
Emulso Corp ....G 716 854-2889
Tonawanda (G-15538)
Enviro Service & Supply Corp ....F 347 838-6500
Staten Island (G-15074)
Gfl USA Inc ....G 917 297-8701
Brooklyn (G-1924)
Glissen Chemical Co Inc ....E 718 436-4200
Brooklyn (G-1932)
Greenmaker Industries LLC ....F 866 684-7800
Farmingdale (G-4776)
▲ H & H Laboratories Inc ....F 718 624-8041
Brooklyn (G-1955)
H & H Laboratories Inc ....G 718 624-8041
Brooklyn (G-1956)
HFC Prestige Intl US LLC ....A 212 389-7800
New York (G-10091)
◆ King Research Inc ....E 718 788-0122
Brooklyn (G-2072)
L S Z Inc ....G 914 948-4040
White Plains (G-16471)
Marietta Corporation ....B 607 753-0982
Cortland (G-3882)
Marietta Corporation ....A 323 589-8181
Cortland (G-3883)
Maybelline Inc ....A 212 885-1310
New York (G-10735)
▲ Medtech Products Inc ....F 914 524-6810
Tarrytown (G-15482)
▲ Monroe Fluid Technology Inc ....E 585 392-3434
Hilton (G-6157)
Mooseberry Soap Co LLC ....G 315 332-8913
Newark (G-12202)
Natures Warehouse ....F 800 215-4372
Philadelphia (G-12985)
Pro-Line Solutions Inc ....G 914 664-0002
Mount Vernon (G-8434)
▲ Robert Racine ....E 518 677-0224
Cambridge (G-3183)
Ronbar Laboratories Inc ....F 718 937-6755
Long Island City (G-7578)
S & S Soap Co Inc ....E 718 585-2900
Bronx (G-1376)
Schneider M Soap & Chemical Co ....G 718 389-1000
Ridgewood (G-13550)
Sunfeather Natural Soap Co Inc ....G 315 265-1776
Potsdam (G-13324)
▲ T S Pink Corp ....F 607 432-1100
Oneonta (G-12646)
Unilever United States Inc ....G 212 546-0200
New York (G-11944)
Unilever United States Inc ....C 212 546-0200
New York (G-11945)

2842 Spec Cleaning, Polishing & Sanitation Preparations

Adirondack Waste MGT Inc ....G 518 585-2224
Ticonderoga (G-15510)
American Wax Company Inc ....E 718 392-8080
Long Island City (G-7377)
▲ Bennett Manufacturing Co Inc ....C 716 937-9161
Alden (G-168)
Bono Sawdust Supply Co Inc ....G 718 446-1374
Corona (G-3839)
Caltex International Ltd ....E 315 425-1040
Syracuse (G-15268)
◆ Car-Freshner Corporation ....C 315 788-6250
Watertown (G-16005)
Car-Freshner Corporation ....D 315 788-6250
Watertown (G-16006)
Castoleum Corporation ....F 914 664-5877
Mount Vernon (G-8385)

SIC SECTION
28 CHEMICALS AND ALLIED PRODUCTS

▲ Chemclean Corporation....E.... 718 525-4500
Jamaica *(G-6633)*
City of New York....C.... 718 236-2693
Brooklyn *(G-1696)*
Clean All of Syracuse LLC....G.... 315 472-9189
Syracuse *(G-15280)*
Cleanse TEC....E.... 718 346-9111
Brooklyn *(G-1701)*
Colgate-Palmolive Company....A.... 212 310-2000
New York *(G-9349)*
Collinite Corporation....G.... 315 732-2282
Utica *(G-15684)*
Connie French Cleaners Inc....G.... 516 487-1343
Great Neck *(G-5548)*
Connies Laundry....G.... 716 822-2800
Buffalo *(G-2778)*
Conrad Blasius Equipment Co....G.... 516 753-1200
Plainview *(G-13044)*
◆ Cpac Inc....E.... 585 382-3223
Leicester *(G-7126)*
▲ Crescent Marketing Inc....C.... 716 337-0145
North Collins *(G-12384)*
◆ Crosstex International Inc....D.... 631 582-6777
Hauppauge *(G-5805)*
Emulso Corp....G.... 716 854-2889
Tonawanda *(G-15538)*
Enviro Service & Supply Corp....F.... 347 838-6500
Staten Island *(G-15074)*
FBC Chemical Corporation....G.... 716 681-1581
Lancaster *(G-7019)*
Finger Lakes Chemicals Inc....E.... 585 454-4760
Rochester *(G-13804)*
Four Sasons Multi-Services Inc....G.... 347 843-6262
Bronx *(G-1274)*
George Basch Co Inc....F.... 516 378-8100
North Bellmore *(G-12378)*
▲ Gliptone Manufacturing Inc....F.... 631 285-7250
Ronkonkoma *(G-14345)*
Greenmaker Industries LLC....F.... 866 684-7800
Farmingdale *(G-4776)*
Griffin Chemical Company LLC....G.... 716 693-2465
North Tonawanda *(G-12431)*
Grillbot LLC....G.... 646 258-5639
New York *(G-9989)*
HFC Prestige Intl US LLC....A.... 212 389-7800
New York *(G-10091)*
James Richard Specialty Chem....G.... 914 478-7500
Hastings On Hudson *(G-5750)*
▲ Jescar Enterprises Inc....G.... 845 352-5850
Nanuet *(G-8465)*
◆ King Research Inc....E.... 718 788-0122
Brooklyn *(G-2072)*
▲ Laundress Inc....F.... 212 209-0074
New York *(G-10524)*
Lb Laundry Inc....G.... 347 399-8030
Flushing *(G-5021)*
Mdi Holdings LLC....A.... 212 559-1127
New York *(G-10747)*
◆ Micro Powders Inc....E.... 914 332-6400
Tarrytown *(G-15483)*
Mirandy Products Ltd....E.... 516 489-6800
South Hempstead *(G-14942)*
Noble Pine Products Co Inc....F.... 914 664-5877
Mount Vernon *(G-8425)*
Nuvite Chemical Compounds Corp....F.... 718 383-8351
Brooklyn *(G-2277)*
Olin Chlor Alkali Logistics....C.... 716 278-6411
Niagara Falls *(G-12320)*
Omg Cleaners Inc....G.... 718 282-2011
Brooklyn *(G-2288)*
P S M Group Inc....E.... 716 532-6686
Forestville *(G-5087)*
▲ Premier Brands America Inc....C.... 914 667-6200
Mount Vernon *(G-8432)*
Premier Brands of America Inc....E.... 718 325-3000
Mount Vernon *(G-8433)*
Premier Brands of America Inc....G.... 718 325-3000
Bronx *(G-1364)*
▲ Progressive Products LLC....G.... 914 417-6022
Rye Brook *(G-14494)*
Pure Green LLC....G.... 800 306-9122
Oyster Bay *(G-12819)*
◆ Rochester Midland Corporation....C.... 585 336-2200
Rochester *(G-14088)*
Royce Associates A Ltd Partnr....G.... 516 367-6298
Jericho *(G-6800)*
Safe Seat USA Inc....F.... 516 586-8240
Plainview *(G-13087)*
▲ Safetec of America Inc....D.... 716 895-1822
Buffalo *(G-3054)*

Scully Sanitation....G.... 315 899-8996
West Edmeston *(G-16207)*
Sensor & Decontamination Inc....F.... 301 526-8389
Binghamton *(G-914)*
Simply Amazing Enterprises Inc....G.... 631 503-6452
Melville *(G-8064)*
Solvents Company Inc....F.... 631 595-9300
Kingston *(G-6917)*
Spic and Span Company....F.... 914 524-6823
Tarrytown *(G-15494)*
Spongebath LLC....G.... 917 475-1347
Astoria *(G-445)*
Spray Nine Corporation....D.... 800 477-7299
Johnstown *(G-6841)*
◆ Strahl & Pitsch Inc....E.... 631 669-0175
West Babylon *(G-16197)*
Tjb Sunshine Enterprises....F.... 518 384-6483
Ballston Lake *(G-573)*
Topps-All Products of Yonkers....F.... 914 968-4226
Yonkers *(G-16803)*
▲ Tribology Inc....E.... 631 345-3000
Yaphank *(G-16724)*
TWI-Laq Industries Inc....E.... 718 638-5860
Bronx *(G-1410)*
U S Plychmical Overseas Corp....E.... 845 356-5530
Chestnut Ridge *(G-3498)*
◆ US Nonwovens Corp....A.... 631 952-0100
Brentwood *(G-1147)*
▲ Walter G Legge Company Inc....G.... 914 737-5040
Peekskill *(G-12928)*
Wedding Gown Preservation Co....D.... 607 748-7999
Endicott *(G-4615)*

2843 Surface Active & Finishing Agents, Sulfonated Oils

▲ Androme Leather Inc....F.... 518 773-7945
Gloversville *(G-5451)*
Bigsky Technologies LLC....G.... 585 270-5282
Rochester *(G-13663)*
Comander Terminals LLC....F.... 516 922-7600
Oyster Bay *(G-12812)*
Halmark Architectural Finshg....E.... 718 272-1831
Brooklyn *(G-1961)*
▲ Medisca Inc....E.... 514 333-7811
Plattsburgh *(G-13133)*
Momentive Performance Mtls Inc....D.... 914 784-4807
Tarrytown *(G-15484)*
Suit-Kote Corporation....F.... 716 683-8850
Buffalo *(G-3079)*

2844 Perfumes, Cosmetics & Toilet Preparations

Abbe Laboratories Inc....F.... 631 756-2223
Farmingdale *(G-4707)*
AEP Environmental LLC....F.... 716 446-0739
Buffalo *(G-2690)*
Alabu Inc....G.... 518 665-0411
Mechanicville *(G-7929)*
Alan F Bourguet....F.... 516 883-4315
Port Washington *(G-13241)*
▲ Albion Cosmetics America Inc....G.... 212 869-1052
New York *(G-8785)*
Alexandria Professional LLC....F.... 716 242-8514
Williamsville *(G-16567)*
◆ All Cultures Inc....E.... 631 293-3143
Greenlawn *(G-5620)*
▲ Allan John Company....F.... 212 940-2210
New York *(G-8796)*
Angel Tips Nail Salon....G.... 718 225-8300
Little Neck *(G-7217)*
Antimony New York LLC....G.... 917 232-1836
New York *(G-8878)*
▲ Ardex Cosmetics of America....E.... 518 283-6700
Troy *(G-15601)*
Aromasong Usa Inc....F.... 718 838-9669
Brooklyn *(G-1555)*
Bare Escentuals Inc....G.... 646 537-0070
New York *(G-9016)*
▲ Becca Inc....D.... 646 568-6250
New York *(G-9033)*
▲ Belmay Holding Corporation....E.... 914 376-1515
Yonkers *(G-16740)*
◆ Bio-Botanica Inc....D.... 631 231-0987
Hauppauge *(G-5780)*
▲ Borghese Inc....E.... 212 659-5318
New York *(G-9123)*
British Science Corporation....G.... 212 980-8700
Staten Island *(G-15055)*

Brucci Ltd....E.... 914 965-0707
Yonkers *(G-16741)*
▲ Bycmac Corp....E.... 845 255-0884
Gardiner *(G-5292)*
▲ California Fragrance Company....E.... 631 424-4023
Huntington Station *(G-6435)*
Cassini Parfums Ltd....G.... 212 753-7540
New York *(G-9222)*
▲ China Huaren Organic Pdts Inc....G.... 212 232-0120
New York *(G-9278)*
◆ Christian Dior Perfumes LLC....E.... 212 931-2200
New York *(G-9291)*
Clark Botanicals Inc....F.... 914 826-4319
Bronxville *(G-1424)*
Classique Perfumes Inc....G.... 718 657-8200
Jamaica *(G-6637)*
Clean Beauty Collective Inc....E.... 212 269-1387
New York *(G-9325)*
▲ Clinique Laboratories LLC....G.... 212 572-4200
New York *(G-9327)*
Clinique Services Inc....G.... 212 572-4200
New York *(G-9328)*
Colgat-Plmolive Centl Amer Inc....G.... 212 310-2000
New York *(G-9348)*
Colgate-Palmolive Company....A.... 212 310-2000
New York *(G-9349)*
Colgate-Palmolive Company....B.... 718 506-3961
Queens Village *(G-13404)*
Common Sense Natural Soap....E.... 518 677-0224
Cambridge *(G-3179)*
Conopco Inc....E.... 585 647-8322
Rochester *(G-13720)*
Coty Inc....C.... 212 389-7000
New York *(G-9404)*
◆ Coty Inc....D.... 212 389-7300
New York *(G-9405)*
▲ Coty US LLC....C.... 212 389-7000
New York *(G-9406)*
Coty US LLC....B.... 212 389-7000
Uniondale *(G-15664)*
◆ Cpac Inc....E.... 585 382-3223
Leicester *(G-7126)*
▲ D & H Amazing Deals Inc....G.... 347 318-3805
Brooklyn *(G-1745)*
Delbia Do Company Inc....F.... 718 585-2226
Bronx *(G-1256)*
▲ Delbia Do Company Inc....E.... 718 585-2226
Bronx *(G-1255)*
▲ Dermatech Labs Inc....F.... 631 225-1700
Lindenhurst *(G-7169)*
Distribio USA LLC....G.... 212 989-6077
New York *(G-9540)*
Editions De Prfums Madison LLC....F.... 646 666-0527
New York *(G-9628)*
◆ EL Erman International Ltd....G.... 212 444-9440
Brooklyn *(G-1819)*
Elias Fragrances Inc....F.... 718 693-6400
Rye Brook *(G-14491)*
▲ Elite Parfums Ltd....D.... 212 983-2640
New York *(G-9651)*
Elizabeth Arden Inc....C.... 845 810-2175
Central Valley *(G-3396)*
Epic Beauty Co LLC....G.... 212 327-3059
New York *(G-9693)*
◆ Essie Cosmetics Ltd....D.... 212 818-1500
New York *(G-9713)*
Estee Lauder Companies Inc....A.... 917 606-3240
New York *(G-9714)*
Estee Lauder Companies Inc....E.... 212 572-4200
New York *(G-9715)*
Estee Lauder Companies Inc....G.... 212 756-4800
New York *(G-9716)*
Estee Lauder Companies Inc....F.... 646 762-7718
New York *(G-9717)*
Estee Lauder Companies Inc....D.... 631 694-2601
Melville *(G-8020)*
◆ Estee Lauder Companies Inc....A.... 212 572-4200
New York *(G-9718)*
Estee Lauder Companies Inc....A.... 212 572-4200
Melville *(G-8021)*
Estee Lauder Companies Inc....A.... 646 602-7590
New York *(G-9719)*
Estee Lauder Inc....D.... 631 531-1000
Melville *(G-8022)*
▲ Estee Lauder International Inc....G.... 212 572-4200
New York *(G-9720)*
◆ Eternal Love Parfums Corp....G.... 516 921-6100
Syosset *(G-15216)*
Ex-It Medical Devices Inc....G.... 212 653-0637
New York *(G-9746)*

SIC

Employee Codes: A=Over 500 employees, B=251-500
C=101-250, D=51-100, E=20-50, F=10-19, G=5-9
2019 Harris
New York Manufacturers Directory
719

▲ F L Demeter Inc ....E 516 487-5187
Great Neck *(G-5552)*
◆ Forsythe Cosmetic Group Ltd ....E 516 239-4200
Freeport *(G-5156)*
▲ Four Paws Products Ltd ....D 631 436-7421
Ronkonkoma *(G-14343)*
▲ Fragrance Acquisitions LLC ....D 845 534-9172
Newburgh *(G-12222)*
▲ Fsr Beauty Ltd ....G 212 447-0036
New York *(G-9855)*
◆ Gassho Body & Mind Inc ....G 518 695-9991
Schuylerville *(G-14734)*
Gfl USA Inc ....G 917 297-8701
Brooklyn *(G-1924)*
Glacee Skincare LLC ....G 212 690-7632
New York *(G-9927)*
Good Home Co Inc ....G 212 352-1509
New York *(G-9957)*
▲ H & H Laboratories Inc ....F 718 624-8041
Brooklyn *(G-1955)*
H & H Laboratories Inc ....G 718 624-8041
Brooklyn *(G-1956)*
◆ Hain Celestial Group Inc ....C 516 587-5000
New Hyde Park *(G-8538)*
Hair Ventures LLC ....F 718 664-7689
Irvington *(G-6506)*
HFC Prestige Intl US LLC ....A 212 389-7800
New York *(G-10091)*
Hnc Enterprises LLC ....G 904 448-9387
Brooklyn *(G-1979)*
Hogan Flavors & Fragrances ....E 212 598-4310
New York *(G-10112)*
Iles Formula Inc ....G 315 834-2478
New York *(G-10182)*
▲ Inter Parfums Inc ....D 212 983-2640
New York *(G-10234)*
Inter Parfums Usa LLC ....G 212 983-2640
New York *(G-10235)*
Intercos America Inc ....G 845 732-3900
West Nyack *(G-16271)*
Intercos America Inc ....G 845 732-3910
West Nyack *(G-16272)*
Interntnal Flvors Frgrnces Inc ....C 212 765-5500
New York *(G-10251)*
▲ Jackel Inc ....E 908 359-2039
New York *(G-10291)*
◆ Jean Philippe Fragrances LLC ....D 212 983-2640
New York *(G-10322)*
▲ JP Filling Inc ....D 845 534-4793
Mountainville *(G-8456)*
Judith N Graham Inc ....G 914 921-5446
Rye *(G-14484)*
June Jacobs Labs LLC ....D 212 471-4830
New York *(G-10381)*
Kantian Skincare LLC ....G 631 780-4711
Smithtown *(G-14902)*
Kind Group LLC ....G 212 645-0800
New York *(G-10448)*
◆ King Research Inc ....E 718 788-0122
Brooklyn *(G-2072)*
▲ Klg Usa LLC ....A 845 856-5311
Port Jervis *(G-13233)*
▲ Lady Burd Exclusive Cosmt Inc ....C 631 454-0444
Farmingdale *(G-4807)*
▲ Le Labo Holding LLC ....E 646 490-6200
Brooklyn *(G-2100)*
Le Labo Holding LLC ....E 646 719-1740
Brooklyn *(G-2101)*
Lechler Laboratories Inc ....E 845 426-6800
Spring Valley *(G-14998)*
Liddell Corporation ....F 716 297-8557
Niagara Falls *(G-12305)*
LOreal Usa Inc ....B 212 818-1500
New York *(G-10606)*
LOreal Usa Inc ....B 917 606-9554
New York *(G-10607)*
LOreal Usa Inc ....E 212 389-4201
New York *(G-10608)*
▲ LOreal USA Products Inc ....G 212 818-1500
New York *(G-10609)*
Lornamead Inc ....D 646 745-3643
Tonawanda *(G-15555)*
◆ Lornamead Inc ....D 716 874-7190
New York *(G-10611)*
Malin + Goetz Inc ....F 212 244-7771
New York *(G-10678)*
◆ Mana Products Inc ....B 718 361-2550
Long Island City *(G-7510)*
Mana Products Inc ....B 718 361-5204
Long Island City *(G-7511)*
◆ Marietta Corporation ....B 607 753-6746
Cortland *(G-3881)*
Marvellissima Intl Ltd ....G 212 682-7306
New York *(G-10720)*
Maybelline Inc ....A 212 885-1310
New York *(G-10735)*
Medisonic Inc ....F 516 653-2345
Great Neck *(G-5572)*
▲ Mehron Inc ....E 845 426-1700
Chestnut Ridge *(G-3493)*
◆ Mentholatum Company ....E 716 677-2500
Orchard Park *(G-12730)*
▲ MZB Accessories LLC ....D 718 472-7500
Long Island City *(G-7531)*
Nature Only Inc ....G 917 922-6539
Forest Hills *(G-5078)*
Naturpathica Holistic Hlth Inc ....D 631 329-8792
East Hampton *(G-4241)*
New Avon LLC ....F 716 572-4842
Buffalo *(G-2962)*
▲ New Avon LLC ....B 212 282-6000
New York *(G-10918)*
▲ Newburgh Distribution Corp ....G 845 561-6330
New Windsor *(G-8652)*
Nr Fragrances & Cosmetics Inc ....G 212 686-4006
New York *(G-11002)*
Oasis Cosmetic Labs Inc ....F 631 758-0038
Holtsville *(G-6241)*
Olan Laboratories Inc ....G 631 582-2082
Hauppauge *(G-5904)*
◆ P S Pibbs Inc ....D 718 445-8046
Flushing *(G-5032)*
▲ Paula Dorf Cosmetics Inc ....E 212 582-0073
New York *(G-11124)*
Pdk Labs Inc ....D 631 273-2630
Hauppauge *(G-5910)*
Peppermints Salon Inc ....F 718 357-6304
Whitestone *(G-16547)*
▼ Perfume Amrcana Whlesalers Inc ....F 212 683-8029
New York *(G-11155)*
▲ Perfumers Workshop Intl Ltd ....G 212 644-8950
New York *(G-11156)*
▲ Peter Thomas Roth Labs LLC ....E 212 581-5800
New York *(G-11170)*
Plastic & Reconstructive Svcs ....G 914 584-5605
Mount Kisco *(G-8355)*
Precision Cosmetics Mfg Co ....G 914 667-1200
Mount Vernon *(G-8431)*
Prescriptives Inc ....G 212 572-4400
New York *(G-11234)*
Procter & Gamble Company ....C 646 885-4201
New York *(G-11254)*
Professional Buty Holdings Inc ....F 631 787-8576
Hauppauge *(G-5924)*
Provisions 5 Corp ....G 718 809-5292
New Hyde Park *(G-8558)*
Pureology Research LLC ....F 212 984-4360
New York *(G-11279)*
Quality King Distributors Inc ....C 631 439-2027
Ronkonkoma *(G-14402)*
Quip Nyc Inc ....G 917 331-3993
Brooklyn *(G-2372)*
REB Lybss Inc ....G 845 238-5633
Monroe *(G-8280)*
▼ Redken 5th Avenue NYC LLC ....C 212 818-1500
New York *(G-11343)*
Redken 5th Avenue Nyc LLC ....G 212 984-5113
New York *(G-11344)*
Restorsea LLC ....G 212 828-8878
New York *(G-11372)*
▲ Revlon Inc ....B 212 527-4000
New York *(G-11376)*
▲ Revlon Consumer Products Corp ....B 212 527-4000
New York *(G-11377)*
▲ Robell Research Inc ....G 212 755-6577
New York *(G-11405)*
▲ Robert Racine ....E 518 677-0224
Cambridge *(G-3183)*
Salonclick LLC ....F 718 643-6793
New York *(G-11472)*
Scent-A-Vision Inc ....E 631 424-4905
Huntington Station *(G-6457)*
Scientific Solutions Globl LLC ....F 516 543-3376
Carle Place *(G-3272)*
Selective Beauty Corporation ....F 585 336-7600
New York *(G-11539)*
◆ Shiseido Americas Corporation ....G 212 805-2300
New York *(G-11570)*
◆ Shop Sky Inc ....F 347 686-4616
South Richmond Hill *(G-14947)*
Sixthscents Paper Products Ltd ....G 212 627-5066
Long Island City *(G-7592)*
▼ Skin Atelier Inc ....F 845 294-1202
Goshen *(G-5483)*
Sml Acquisition LLC ....C 914 592-3130
Elmsford *(G-4570)*
▼ Soft Sheen Products Inc ....G 212 818-1500
New York *(G-11635)*
▲ Solabia USA Inc ....G 212 847-2397
New York *(G-11638)*
St Tropez Inc ....G 800 366-6383
New York *(G-11690)*
Sundial Brands ....G 631 842-8800
Farmingdale *(G-4883)*
▲ Sundial Brands LLC ....C 631 842-8800
Amityville *(G-318)*
Sundial Group LLC ....E 631 842-8800
Amityville *(G-320)*
Temptu Inc ....G 718 937-9503
Long Island City *(G-7613)*
▲ Thompson Ferrier LLC ....G 212 244-2212
New York *(G-11823)*
▲ Tomia Beauty Brands LLC ....G 917 301-0125
New York *(G-11862)*
▲ Topiderm Inc ....C 631 226-7979
Amityville *(G-321)*
▼ Unike Products Inc ....G 347 686-4616
Jamaica *(G-6687)*
Unilever United States Inc ....G 212 546-0200
New York *(G-11944)*
Unilever United States Inc ....C 212 546-0200
New York *(G-11945)*
United-Guardian Inc ....E 631 273-0900
Hauppauge *(G-5965)*
▲ Universal Packg Systems Inc ....A 631 543-2277
Hauppauge *(G-5966)*
▲ Verla International Ltd ....B 845 561-2440
New Windsor *(G-8663)*
▲ Victoria Albi International ....F 212 689-2600
New York *(G-12028)*
Xania Labs Inc ....G 718 361-2550
Long Island City *(G-7644)*
▲ Zela International Co ....E 518 436-1833
Albany *(G-145)*
Zotos International Inc ....B 315 781-3207
Geneva *(G-5337)*

2851 Paints, Varnishes, Lacquers, Enamels

A & B Color Corp (del) ....G 718 441-5482
Kew Gardens *(G-6869)*
Absolute Coatings Inc ....E 914 636-0700
New Rochelle *(G-8586)*
▲ Angiotech Biocoatings Corp ....E 585 321-1130
Henrietta *(G-6030)*
Anthony River Inc ....F 315 475-1315
Syracuse *(G-15244)*
Atc Plastics LLC ....E 212 375-2515
New York *(G-8943)*
Atlas Coatings Group Corp ....D 718 469-8787
Brooklyn *(G-1572)*
B & F Architectural Support Gr ....E 212 279-6488
New York *(G-8987)*
Barson Composites Corporation ....E 516 752-7882
Old Bethpage *(G-12583)*
Benjamin Moore & Co ....E 518 736-1723
Johnstown *(G-6824)*
Cytec Industries Inc ....D 716 372-9650
Olean *(G-12598)*
Delta Polymers Inc ....G 631 254-6240
Bay Shore *(G-681)*
Designer Epoxy Finishes Inc ....G 646 943-6044
Melville *(G-8015)*
Elantas Pdg Inc ....G 716 372-9650
Olean *(G-12602)*
▲ Emco Finishing Products Inc ....G 716 483-1176
Jamestown *(G-6715)*
◆ Enecon Corporation ....D 516 349-0022
Medford *(G-7946)*
Eric S Turner & Company Inc ....F 914 235-7114
New Rochelle *(G-8602)*
Fayette Street Coatings Inc ....F 315 488-5401
Liverpool *(G-7233)*
▲ Fougera Pharmaceuticals Inc ....C 631 454-7677
Melville *(G-8026)*
G & M Dege Inc ....F 631 475-1450
East Patchogue *(G-4273)*
Garco Manufacturing Corp Inc ....G 718 287-3330
Brooklyn *(G-1917)*
General Coatings Tech Inc ....E 718 821-1232
Ridgewood *(G-13537)*

▲ **General Vy-Coat LLC** ... E ... 718 266-6002
Brooklyn *(G-1921)*
▲ **Heany Industries Inc** ... D ... 585 889-2700
Scottsville *(G-14750)*
Industrial Finishing Products ... F ... 718 342-4871
Brooklyn *(G-2000)*
Inglis Co Inc ... G ... 315 475-1315
Syracuse *(G-15343)*
Insulating Coatings Corp ... F ... 607 723-1727
Binghamton *(G-896)*
▲ **John C Dolph Company Inc** ... E ... 732 329-2333
Schenectady *(G-14692)*
▲ **Jrlon Inc** ... D ... 315 597-4067
Palmyra *(G-12855)*
Liberty Panel Center Inc ... F ... 718 647-2763
Brooklyn *(G-2116)*
Masterdisk Corporation ... F ... 212 541-5022
Elmsford *(G-4551)*
▲ **Mercury Paint Corporation** ... D ... 718 469-8787
Brooklyn *(G-2194)*
Nautical Marine Paint Corp ... E ... 718 462-7000
Brooklyn *(G-2249)*
◆ **Nortek Powder Coating LLC** ... F ... 315 337-2339
Rome *(G-14263)*
◆ **Paint Over Rust Products Inc** ... E ... 914 636-0700
New Rochelle *(G-8621)*
▲ **Peter Kwasny Inc** ... G ... 727 641-1462
Hauppauge *(G-5913)*
Rapid Removal LLC ... F ... 716 665-4663
Falconer *(G-4689)*
Reddi Car Corp ... G ... 631 589-3141
Sayville *(G-14634)*
Robert Greenburg ... G ... 845 586-2226
Margaretville *(G-7799)*
Royce Associates A Ltd Partnr ... G ... 516 367-6298
Jericho *(G-6800)*
Si Group Inc ... C ... 518 347-4200
Rotterdam Junction *(G-14463)*
◆ **Si Group Inc** ... C ... 518 347-4200
Schenectady *(G-14713)*
▲ **Sml Brothers Holding Corp** ... D ... 718 402-2000
Bronx *(G-1387)*
Starlite Pnt & Varnish Co Inc ... G ... 718 292-6420
Bronx *(G-1393)*
T C Dunham Paint Company Inc ... E ... 914 969-4202
Yonkers *(G-16801)*
▼ **T J Ronan Paint Corp** ... E ... 718 292-1100
Bronx *(G-1398)*
▼ **Uc Coatings LLC** ... E ... 716 833-9366
Buffalo *(G-3108)*
Yewtree Millworks Corp ... G ... 914 320-5851
Yonkers *(G-16809)*

2861 Gum & Wood Chemicals

▲ **Metro Products & Services LLC** ... F ... 866 846-8486
Brooklyn *(G-2201)*
▲ **Oci USA Inc** ... G ... 646 589-6180
New York *(G-11029)*
Ocip Holding LLC ... G ... 646 589-6180
New York *(G-11030)*
Prismatic Dyeing & Finshg Inc ... D ... 845 561-1800
Newburgh *(G-12242)*
◆ **Tioga Hardwoods Inc** ... G ... 607 657-8686
Berkshire *(G-828)*
Westrock Mwv LLC ... C ... 212 688-5000
New York *(G-12097)*

2865 Cyclic-Crudes, Intermediates, Dyes & Org Pigments

Chemours Company Fc LLC ... E ... 716 278-5100
Niagara Falls *(G-12271)*
▲ **Crowley Tar Products Co Inc** ... G ... 212 682-1200
New York *(G-9425)*
Durez Corporation ... F ... 716 286-0100
Niagara Falls *(G-12279)*
East Cast Clor Compounding Inc ... G ... 631 491-9000
West Babylon *(G-16154)*
F M Group Inc ... F ... 845 589-0102
Congers *(G-3716)*
◆ **Jos H Lowenstein and Sons Inc** ... D ... 718 388-5410
Brooklyn *(G-2046)*
▲ **LTS Inc** ... F ... 845 494-2940
Orangeburg *(G-12682)*
Magic Tank LLC ... G ... 877 646-2442
New York *(G-10669)*
◆ **Micro Powders Inc** ... E ... 914 332-6400
Tarrytown *(G-15483)*
◆ **Mitsui Chemicals America Inc** ... E ... 914 253-0777
Rye Brook *(G-14493)*
Premier Brands of America Inc ... E ... 718 325-3000
Mount Vernon *(G-8433)*
◆ **Si Group Inc** ... C ... 518 347-4200
Schenectady *(G-14713)*
Si Group Inc ... C ... 518 347-4200
Rotterdam Junction *(G-14462)*
▲ **Sml Brothers Holding Corp** ... D ... 718 402-2000
Bronx *(G-1387)*

2869 Industrial Organic Chemicals, NEC

A and L Home Fuel LLC ... G ... 607 638-1994
Schenevus *(G-14729)*
Akzo Nobel Chemicals LLC ... G ... 716 778-8554
Burt *(G-3143)*
Akzo Nobel Functional Chem LLC ... D ... 845 276-8200
Brewster *(G-1155)*
American Hlth Formulations Inc ... G ... 631 392-1756
Hauppauge *(G-5766)*
Ames Goldsmith Corp ... F ... 518 792-7435
Glens Falls *(G-5414)*
Arcadia Chem Preservative LLC ... G ... 516 466-5258
Great Neck *(G-5535)*
Arkema Inc ... C ... 585 243-6359
Piffard *(G-12995)*
Avstar Fuel Systems Inc ... G ... 315 255-1955
Auburn *(G-468)*
Balchem Corporation ... B ... 845 326-5600
New Hampton *(G-8497)*
Bamboo Global Industries ... G ... 973 943-1878
New York *(G-9010)*
BASF Corporation ... B ... 914 737-2554
Peekskill *(G-12917)*
BASF Corporation ... F ... 914 785-2000
Tarrytown *(G-15475)*
BASF Corporation ... B ... 518 465-6534
Rensselaer *(G-13473)*
BASF Corporation ... C ... 631 689-0200
East Setauket *(G-4299)*
Caltex International Ltd ... E ... 315 425-1040
Syracuse *(G-15268)*
Castle Fuels Corporation ... E ... 914 381-6600
Harrison *(G-5723)*
Centar Fuel Co Inc ... G ... 516 538-2424
West Hempstead *(G-16214)*
China Ruitai Intl Holdings Ltd ... G ... 718 740-2278
Hollis *(G-6232)*
Classic Flavors Fragrances Inc ... G ... 212 777-0004
New York *(G-9320)*
Comax Aromatics Corporation ... E ... 631 249-0505
Melville *(G-8009)*
Comboland Packing Corp ... D ... 718 858-4200
Brooklyn *(G-1707)*
Consolidated Edison Co NY Inc ... F ... 914 933-2936
Rye *(G-14478)*
Craftmaster Flavor Technology ... F ... 631 789-8607
Amityville *(G-270)*
▲ **Crown Delta Corporation** ... E ... 914 245-8910
Yorktown Heights *(G-16815)*
◆ **Cumberland Packing Corp** ... B ... 718 858-4200
Brooklyn *(G-1739)*
D-Best Equipment Corp ... E ... 516 358-0965
West Hempstead *(G-16215)*
Danisco US Inc ... D ... 585 256-5200
Rochester *(G-13733)*
Degennaro Fuel Service LLC ... F ... 518 239-6350
Medusa *(G-7993)*
Dib Managmnt Inc ... F ... 718 439-8190
Brooklyn *(G-1774)*
Dulcette Technologies LLC ... G ... 631 752-8700
Lindenhurst *(G-7171)*
Enviro Service & Supply Corp ... F ... 347 838-6500
Staten Island *(G-15074)*
Evonik Corporation ... E ... 518 233-7090
Waterford *(G-15975)*
Family Fuel Co Inc ... G ... 718 232-2009
Brooklyn *(G-1867)*
Fire Island Fuel ... G ... 631 772-1482
Shirley *(G-14834)*
Flavors Holdings Inc ... F ... 212 572-8677
New York *(G-9816)*
Friendly Fuel Incorporated ... G ... 518 581-7036
Saratoga Springs *(G-14581)*
Friendly Star Fuel Inc ... G ... 718 369-8801
Brooklyn *(G-1909)*
Fuel Energy Services USA Ltd ... E ... 607 846-2650
Horseheads *(G-6316)*
Fuel Soul ... G ... 516 379-0810
Merrick *(G-8098)*
Full Motion Beverage Inc ... G ... 631 585-1100
Plainview *(G-13059)*
Genencor International Inc ... G ... 585 256-5200
Rochester *(G-13826)*
Givaudan Fragrances Corp ... C ... 212 649-8800
New York *(G-9925)*
Golden Renewable Energy LLC ... G ... 914 920-9800
Yonkers *(G-16763)*
Hampshire Chemical Corp ... D ... 315 539-9221
Waterloo *(G-15995)*
Henpecked Husband Farms Corp ... G ... 631 728-2800
Speonk *(G-14985)*
Hexion Inc ... E ... 518 792-8040
South Glens Falls *(G-14936)*
Highrange Fuels Inc ... G ... 914 930-8300
Cortlandt Manor *(G-3902)*
Hudson Technologies Company ... E ... 845 735-6000
Pearl River *(G-12900)*
Hunts Point Clean Energy LLC ... G ... 203 451-5143
Pearl River *(G-12902)*
▼ **International Mtls & Sups Inc** ... G ... 518 834-9899
Keeseville *(G-6851)*
Interntnal Flvors Frgrnces Inc ... C ... 212 765-5500
New York *(G-10251)*
▲ **Islechem LLC** ... E ... 716 773-8401
Grand Island *(G-5503)*
J&R Fuel of LI Inc ... G ... 631 234-1959
Central Islip *(G-3375)*
Jmg Fuel Inc ... G ... 631 579-4319
Ronkonkoma *(G-14359)*
◆ **Jos H Lowenstein and Sons Inc** ... D ... 718 388-5410
Brooklyn *(G-2046)*
JRs Fuels Inc ... G ... 518 622-9939
Cairo *(G-3149)*
◆ **Kent Chemical Corporation** ... E ... 212 521-1700
New York *(G-10436)*
Kore Infrastructure LLC ... G ... 646 532-9060
Glen Cove *(G-5370)*
Leroux Fuels ... F ... 518 563-3653
Plattsburgh *(G-13131)*
Liberty Food and Fuel ... G ... 315 299-4039
Syracuse *(G-15360)*
Lift Safe - Fuel Safe Inc ... G ... 315 423-7702
Syracuse *(G-15361)*
Lo-Co Fuel Corp ... G ... 631 929-5086
Wading River *(G-15885)*
Logo ... G ... 212 846-2568
New York *(G-10592)*
Mafco Consolidated Group Inc ... F ... 212 572-8600
New York *(G-10659)*
Maio Fuel Company LP ... G ... 914 683-1154
White Plains *(G-16474)*
▲ **Marval Industries Inc** ... D ... 914 381-2400
Mamaroneck *(G-7748)*
Metro Fuel LLC ... C ... 212 836-9608
New York *(G-10785)*
MNS Fuel Corp ... F ... 516 735-3835
Ronkonkoma *(G-14380)*
Molecular Glasses Inc ... G ... 585 210-2861
Rochester *(G-13951)*
Momentive Performance Mtls Inc ... A ... 614 986-2495
Waterford *(G-15980)*
◆ **Momentive Performance Mtls Inc** ... E ... 518 237-3330
Waterford *(G-15981)*
Momentive Prfmce Mtls Holdings ... A ... 518 237-3330
Waterford *(G-15982)*
Mpm Holdings Inc ... B ... 518 237-3330
Waterford *(G-15983)*
Mpm Holdings Inc ... G ... 518 237-3330
Waterford *(G-15984)*
Mpm Intermediate Holdings Inc ... G ... 518 237-3330
Waterford *(G-15985)*
Mpm Silicones LLC ... A ... 518 233-3330
Waterford *(G-15986)*
Mt Fuel Corp ... G ... 631 445-2047
Stony Brook *(G-15168)*
N & L Fuel Corp ... G ... 718 863-3538
Bronx *(G-1337)*
Nagle Fuel Corporation ... G ... 212 304-4618
New York *(G-10871)*
North East Fuel Group Inc ... G ... 718 984-6774
Staten Island *(G-15111)*
Northeastern Fuel Corp ... G ... 917 560-6241
Staten Island *(G-15112)*
Oak-Bark Corporation ... G ... 518 372-5691
Scotia *(G-14745)*
Oceanconnect Marine Inc ... G ... 203 328-3117
New York *(G-11028)*
Patdan Fuel Corporation ... G ... 718 326-3668
Middle Village *(G-8126)*
Poly Scientific R&D Corp ... E ... 631 586-0400
Bay Shore *(G-707)*

S I C

Polymer Slutions Group Fin LLC ....G....... 212 771-1717
New York *(G-11217)*
Pretty Fuel Inc ....G....... 315 823-4063
Little Falls *(G-7212)*
Provident Fuel Inc ....G....... 516 224-4427
Woodbury *(G-16629)*
Quality Fuel 1 Corporation ....G....... 631 392-4090
North Babylon *(G-12361)*
Remsen Fuel Inc ....G....... 718 984-9551
Staten Island *(G-15127)*
▲ Rose Solomon Co ....E....... 718 855-1788
Brooklyn *(G-2415)*
Royce Associates A Ltd Partnr ....G....... 516 367-6298
Jericho *(G-6800)*
S&B Alternative Fuels Inc ....G....... 631 585-6637
Lake Grove *(G-6968)*
Solvents Company Inc ....F....... 631 595-9300
Kingston *(G-6917)*
Southbay Fuel Injectors ....G....... 516 442-4707
Rockville Centre *(G-14242)*
▲ Specialty Silicone Pdts Inc ....D....... 518 885-8826
Ballston Spa *(G-596)*
◆ Sugar Foods Corporation ....E....... 212 753-6900
New York *(G-11734)*
Sundial Fragrances & Flavors ....E....... 631 842-8800
Amityville *(G-319)*
Sunoco Inc ....G....... 315 593-0500
Fulton *(G-5232)*
Symrise Inc ....E....... 646 459-5000
New York *(G-11760)*
Telechemische Inc ....G....... 845 561-3237
Newburgh *(G-12247)*
▲ Twin Lake Chemical Inc ....F....... 716 433-3824
Lockport *(G-7339)*
Unified Solutions For Clg Inc ....F....... 718 782-8800
Brooklyn *(G-2599)*
▲ United Biochemicals LLC ....E....... 716 731-5161
Sanborn *(G-14555)*
Value Fragrances & Flavors Inc ....F....... 845 294-5726
Goshen *(G-5485)*
Wecare Organics LLC ....E....... 315 689-1937
Jordan *(G-6843)*
Western New York Energy LLC ....E....... 585 798-9693
Medina *(G-7992)*
Yankee Fuel Inc ....G....... 631 880-8810
West Babylon *(G-16205)*
York Fuel Incorporated ....G....... 718 951-0202
Brooklyn *(G-2666)*
Zymtrnix Catalytic Systems Inc ....G....... 607 351-2639
Ithaca *(G-6617)*

2873 Nitrogenous Fertilizers

C P Chemical Co Inc ....G....... 914 428-2517
White Plains *(G-16434)*
▼ Growth Products Ltd ....E....... 914 428-1316
White Plains *(G-16456)*
▲ Oci USA Inc ....G....... 646 589-6180
New York *(G-11029)*
Ocip Holding LLC ....G....... 646 589-6180
New York *(G-11030)*
Rt Solutions LLC ....G....... 585 245-3456
Rochester *(G-14107)*
Scotts Company LLC ....G....... 631 478-6843
Hauppauge *(G-5937)*

2874 Phosphatic Fertilizers

◆ International Ord Tech Inc ....D....... 716 664-1100
Jamestown *(G-6724)*
Mdi Holdings LLC ....A....... 212 559-1127
New York *(G-10747)*
Occidental Chemical Corp ....C....... 716 278-7794
Niagara Falls *(G-12319)*

2875 Fertilizers, Mixing Only

Biosoil Farm Inc ....G....... 518 344-4920
Glenville *(G-5444)*
Carolina Eastern-Vail Inc ....E....... 518 854-9785
Salem *(G-14537)*
Commodity Resource Corporation ....F....... 585 538-9500
Caledonia *(G-3154)*
Long Island Compost Corp ....C....... 516 334-6600
Westbury *(G-16351)*

2879 Pesticides & Agricultural Chemicals, NEC

Agrochem Inc ....E....... 518 226-4850
Saratoga Springs *(G-14569)*
▲ Bioworks Inc ....G....... 585 924-4362
Victor *(G-15832)*

E I Du Pont De Nemours & Co ....C....... 718 761-0043
Staten Island *(G-15071)*
FMC Corporation ....E....... 716 735-3761
Middleport *(G-8132)*
Island Marketing Corp ....G....... 516 739-0500
Mineola *(G-8229)*
Noble Pine Products Co Inc ....F....... 914 664-5877
Mount Vernon *(G-8425)*

2891 Adhesives & Sealants

Able National Corp ....E....... 718 386-8801
Brooklyn *(G-1471)*
Adirondack Spclty Adhsives Inc ....F....... 518 869-5736
Albany *(G-29)*
Advanced Polymer Solutions LLC ....G....... 516 621-5800
Port Washington *(G-13240)*
All Out Die Cutting Inc ....E....... 718 346-6666
Brooklyn *(G-1508)*
▲ Angiotech Biocoatings Corp ....E....... 585 321-1130
Henrietta *(G-6030)*
▲ Aremco Products Inc ....F....... 845 268-0039
Valley Cottage *(G-15752)*
▲ Astro Chemical Company Inc ....E....... 518 399-5338
Ballston Lake *(G-565)*
◆ Beacon Adhesives Inc ....E....... 914 699-3400
Mount Vernon *(G-8381)*
Best Adhesives Company Inc ....G....... 718 417-3800
Ridgewood *(G-13531)*
Classic Labels Inc ....E....... 631 467-2300
Patchogue *(G-12863)*
▲ Continental Buchanan LLC ....D....... 703 480-3800
Buchanan *(G-2672)*
▲ Deal International Inc ....E....... 585 288-4444
Rochester *(G-13737)*
Hexion Inc ....E....... 518 792-8040
South Glens Falls *(G-14936)*
Hudson Industries Corporation ....E....... 518 762-4638
Johnstown *(G-6831)*
J M Canty Inc ....E....... 716 625-4227
Lockport *(G-7310)*
Legacy USA LLC ....F....... 718 292-5333
Bronx *(G-1315)*
Meridian Adhesives Group LLC ....G....... 212 771-1717
New York *(G-10774)*
P C I Paper Conversions Inc ....D....... 315 703-8300
Syracuse *(G-15390)*
P C I Paper Conversions Inc ....E....... 315 634-3317
Syracuse *(G-15391)*
Polycast Industries Inc ....G....... 631 595-2530
Bay Shore *(G-708)*
◆ Polyset Company Inc ....E....... 518 664-6000
Mechanicville *(G-7932)*
PPG Architectural Finishes Inc ....G....... 585 271-1363
Rochester *(G-14030)*
R-Co Products Corporation ....F....... 800 854-7657
Lakewood *(G-6997)*
Ran Mar Enterprises Ltd ....F....... 631 666-4754
Bay Shore *(G-713)*
Royal Adhesives & Sealants LLC ....F....... 315 451-1755
Syracuse *(G-15411)*
▲ Saint Gobain Grains & Powders ....A....... 716 731-8200
Niagara Falls *(G-12332)*
Saint-Gobain Prfmce Plas Corp ....C....... 518 642-2200
Granville *(G-5524)*
US Epoxy Inc ....G....... 800 332-3883
Yaphank *(G-16726)*
USA Sealing Inc ....E....... 716 288-9952
Cheektowaga *(G-3462)*
Utility Manufacturing Co Inc ....E....... 516 997-6300
Westbury *(G-16384)*
Walsh & Hughes Inc ....G....... 631 427-5904
Huntington Station *(G-6464)*
Web-Cote Industries ....E....... 914 630-1600
Larchmont *(G-7060)*
Wild Works Incorporated ....G....... 716 891-4197
Albany *(G-142)*

2892 Explosives

Dyno Nobel Inc ....D....... 845 338-2144
Ulster Park *(G-15658)*

2893 Printing Ink

Atlas Coatings Corp ....D....... 718 402-2000
Bronx *(G-1222)*
Bishop Print Shop Inc ....G....... 607 965-8155
Edmeston *(G-4425)*
▲ Calchem Corporation ....G....... 631 423-5696
Ronkonkoma *(G-14324)*
Flint Group Incorporated ....E....... 585 458-1223
Rochester *(G-13807)*

Gotham Ink & Color Co Inc ....E....... 845 947-4000
Stony Point *(G-15172)*
Inglis Co Inc ....G....... 315 475-1315
Syracuse *(G-15343)*
Intrinsiq Materials Inc ....G....... 585 301-4432
Rochester *(G-13886)*
INX International Ink Co ....E....... 716 366-6010
Dunkirk *(G-4172)*
◆ Micro Powders Inc ....E....... 914 332-6400
Tarrytown *(G-15483)*
Millennium Rmnfctred Toner Inc ....F....... 718 585-9887
Bronx *(G-1331)*
Mitsubishi Chemical Amer Inc ....E....... 212 223-3043
New York *(G-10825)*
▲ Specialty Ink Co Inc ....F....... 631 586-3666
Blue Point *(G-965)*
▼ Standard Screen Supply Corp ....F....... 212 627-2727
New York *(G-11693)*
Superior Printing Ink Co Inc ....G....... 716 877-0250
Tonawanda *(G-15579)*
Wikoff Color Corporation ....F....... 585 458-0653
Rochester *(G-14209)*

2899 Chemical Preparations, NEC

Aiping Pharmaceutical Inc ....G....... 631 952-3802
Hauppauge *(G-5757)*
Akzo Nobel Chemicals LLC ....G....... 716 778-8554
Burt *(G-3143)*
Akzo Nobel Chemicals LLC ....C....... 914 674-5008
Dobbs Ferry *(G-4129)*
▲ Alonzo Fire Works Display Inc ....G....... 518 664-9994
Mechanicville *(G-7930)*
American Electronic Products ....F....... 631 924-1299
Yaphank *(G-16704)*
Amtek Research LLC ....E....... 416 400-2906
Niagara Falls *(G-12261)*
Anabec Inc ....G....... 716 759-1674
Clarence *(G-3524)*
▲ Ask Chemicals Hi-Tech LLC ....C....... 607 587-9146
Alfred Station *(G-185)*
▲ Aufhauser Corporation ....F....... 516 694-8696
Plainview *(G-13038)*
Balchem Corporation ....B....... 845 326-5600
New Hampton *(G-8497)*
Barson Composites Corporation ....E....... 516 752-7882
Old Bethpage *(G-12583)*
Bass Oil Company Inc ....E....... 718 628-4444
Brooklyn *(G-1588)*
▼ Bcp Ingredients Inc ....D....... 845 326-5600
New Hampton *(G-8498)*
Beyond Beauty Basics LLC ....F....... 516 731-7100
Levittown *(G-7131)*
◆ Bonide Products Inc ....C....... 315 736-8231
Oriskany *(G-12751)*
◆ C & A Service Inc ....G....... 516 354-1200
Floral Park *(G-4958)*
C P Chemical Co Inc ....G....... 914 428-2517
White Plains *(G-16434)*
Calfonex Company ....F....... 845 778-2212
Walden *(G-15892)*
◆ Citrus and Allied Essences Ltd ....C....... 516 354-1200
Floral Park *(G-4960)*
Classic Flavors Fragrances Inc ....G....... 212 777-0004
New York *(G-9320)*
Concrete Designs Inc ....G....... 607 738-0309
Elmira *(G-4479)*
◆ Coventya Inc ....D....... 216 351-1500
Oriskany *(G-12753)*
Coventya Inc ....F....... 315 768-6635
Oriskany *(G-12754)*
Crystal Fusion Tech Inc ....F....... 631 253-9800
Lindenhurst *(G-7167)*
Cytec Industries Inc ....D....... 716 372-9650
Olean *(G-12598)*
Danisco US Inc ....D....... 585 256-5200
Rochester *(G-13733)*
▲ Ecological Laboratories Inc ....D....... 516 823-3441
Island Park *(G-6513)*
Engineering Maint Pdts Inc ....F....... 516 624-9774
Oyster Bay *(G-12813)*
Evans Chemetics LP ....D....... 315 539-9221
Waterloo *(G-15991)*
F M Group Inc ....F....... 845 589-0102
Congers *(G-3716)*
◆ Fireworks By Grucci Inc ....E....... 631 286-0088
Bellport *(G-804)*
▼ Fitzsimmons Systems Inc ....F....... 315 214-7010
Cazenovia *(G-3319)*
▼ Flame Control Coatings LLC ....E....... 716 282-1399
Niagara Falls *(G-12286)*

Foseco Inc ... F ... 914 345-4760
Tarrytown *(G-15478)*

Fppf Chemical Co Inc ... G ... 716 856-9607
Buffalo *(G-2832)*

▲ Geliko LLC ... E ... 212 876-5620
New York *(G-9895)*

Gordon Fire Equipment LLC ... G ... 845 691-5700
Highland *(G-6143)*

▲ Greenfield Manufacturing Inc ... F ... 518 581-2368
Saratoga Springs *(G-14584)*

Halfmoon Town Water Department ... G ... 518 233-7489
Waterford *(G-15976)*

Hampshire Chemical Corp ... D ... 315 539-9221
Waterloo *(G-15995)*

Hanson Aggregates PA LLC ... F ... 585 436-3250
Rochester *(G-13852)*

HHS Pharmaceuticals Inc ... F ... 347 674-1670
New York *(G-10093)*

▼ I A S National Inc ... E ... 631 423-6900
Huntington Station *(G-6447)*

Icynene US Acquisition Corp ... G ... 800 758-7325
Buffalo *(G-2879)*

Indium Corporation of America ... E ... 315 793-8200
Utica *(G-15713)*

Instrumentation Laboratory Co ... C ... 845 680-0028
Orangeburg *(G-12681)*

International Fire-Shield Inc ... F ... 315 255-1006
Auburn *(G-483)*

◆ Island Pyrochemical Inds Corp ... C ... 516 746-2100
Mineola *(G-8231)*

Johnson Manufacturing Company ... F ... 716 881-3030
Buffalo *(G-2897)*

Kaneka America LLC ... D ... 212 705-4340
New York *(G-10404)*

◆ Kent Chemical Corporation ... E ... 212 521-1700
New York *(G-10436)*

Luxfer Magtech Inc ... D ... 631 727-8600
Riverhead *(G-13576)*

Mdi Holdings LLC ... A ... 212 559-1127
New York *(G-10747)*

◆ Micro Powders Inc ... E ... 914 332-6400
Tarrytown *(G-15483)*

Momentive Performance LLC ... G ... 281 325-3536
Waterford *(G-15979)*

Momentive Performance Mtls Inc ... D ... 914 784-4807
Tarrytown *(G-15484)*

▲ Monroe Fluid Technology Inc ... E ... 585 392-3434
Hilton *(G-6157)*

Nalco Company LLC ... E ... 518 796-1985
Saratoga Springs *(G-14590)*

Natures Warehouse ... F ... 800 215-4372
Philadelphia *(G-12985)*

New Fine Chemicals Inc ... G ... 631 321-8151
Lindenhurst *(G-7183)*

▲ Penetron International Ltd ... F ... 631 941-9700
East Setauket *(G-4306)*

Pure Kemika LLC ... G ... 718 745-2200
Bellmore *(G-792)*

PVS Chemical Solutions Inc ... D ... 716 825-5762
Buffalo *(G-3020)*

▲ Real Co Inc ... G ... 347 433-8549
Valley Cottage *(G-15762)*

Reddi Car Corp ... G ... 631 589-3141
Sayville *(G-14634)*

Reliance Fluid Tech LLC ... E ... 716 332-0988
Niagara Falls *(G-12329)*

◆ Rochester Midland Corporation ... C ... 585 336-2200
Rochester *(G-14088)*

Roto Salt Company Inc ... E ... 315 536-3742
Penn Yan *(G-12965)*

Royce Associates A Ltd Partnr ... G ... 516 367-6298
Jericho *(G-6800)*

Safeguard Inc ... F ... 631 929-3273
Wading River *(G-15886)*

Solenis LLC ... G ... 718 383-1717
Brooklyn *(G-2498)*

Solenis LLC ... G ... 315 461-4730
Liverpool *(G-7262)*

Solvents Company Inc ... F ... 631 595-9300
Kingston *(G-6917)*

▲ Specialty Ink Co Inc ... F ... 631 586-3666
Blue Point *(G-965)*

◆ Specialty Minerals Inc ... E ... 212 878-1800
New York *(G-11661)*

▼ Supresta US LLC ... E ... 914 674-9434
Ardsley *(G-396)*

▲ Tam Ceramics LLC ... D ... 716 278-9480
Niagara Falls *(G-12341)*

▼ Tangram Company LLC ... E ... 631 758-0460
Holtsville *(G-6247)*

Technic Inc ... F ... 516 349-0700
Plainview *(G-13092)*

▲ Topaz Industries Inc ... F ... 631 207-0700
Holtsville *(G-6249)*

Torre Products Co Inc ... G ... 212 925-8989
New York *(G-11870)*

US Polychemical Holding Corp ... E ... 845 356-5530
Spring Valley *(G-15013)*

US Salt LLC ... D ... 607 535-2721
Watkins Glen *(G-16062)*

Utility Manufacturing Co Inc ... E ... 516 997-6300
Westbury *(G-16384)*

Venue Graphics Supply Inc ... F ... 718 361-1690
Long Island City *(G-7629)*

Von Roll Usa Inc ... E ... 203 562-2171
Schenectady *(G-14726)*

Water Wise of America Inc ... F ... 585 232-1210
Rochester *(G-14203)*

◆ Watson Bowman Acme Corp ... C ... 716 691-8162
Amherst *(G-260)*

Wyeth Holdings LLC ... D ... 845 602-5000
Pearl River *(G-12913)*

Yiwen Usa Inc ... F ... 212 370-0828
New York *(G-12163)*

▲ Young Explosives Corp ... D ... 585 394-1783
Canandaigua *(G-3237)*

Yr Blanc & Co LLC ... G ... 716 800-3999
Buffalo *(G-3137)*

29 PETROLEUM REFINING AND RELATED INDUSTRIES

2911 Petroleum Refining

209 Discount Oil ... E ... 845 386-2090
Middletown *(G-8135)*

Algafuel America ... G ... 516 295-2257
Hewlett *(G-6046)*

◆ C & A Service Inc ... G ... 516 354-1200
Floral Park *(G-4958)*

California Petro Trnspt Corp ... G ... 212 302-5151
New York *(G-9179)*

◆ Citrus and Allied Essences Ltd ... C ... 516 354-1200
Floral Park *(G-4960)*

E and V Energy Corporation ... F ... 315 786-2067
Watertown *(G-16013)*

▲ E-Zoil Products Inc ... E ... 716 213-0106
Tonawanda *(G-15537)*

Ergun Inc ... G ... 631 721-0049
Roslyn Heights *(G-14454)*

Fppf Chemical Co Inc ... G ... 716 856-9607
Buffalo *(G-2832)*

Fuel Energy Services USA Ltd ... E ... 607 846-2650
Horseheads *(G-6316)*

Heat USA II LLC ... E ... 212 564-4328
New York *(G-10076)*

Hess Corporation ... B ... 212 997-8500
New York *(G-10085)*

Hess Oil Virgin Island Corp ... A ... 212 997-8500
New York *(G-10088)*

Hess Pipeline Corporation ... C ... 212 997-8500
New York *(G-10089)*

Hygrade Fuel Inc ... G ... 516 741-0723
Mineola *(G-8228)*

Iep Energy Holding LLC ... A ... 212 702-4300
New York *(G-10175)*

▲ Industrial Raw Materials LLC ... F ... 212 688-8080
Plainview *(G-13063)*

◆ Kent Chemical Corporation ... E ... 212 521-1700
New York *(G-10436)*

Kinetic Fuel Technology Inc ... G ... 716 745-1461
Youngstown *(G-16836)*

Koch Supply & Trading LP ... G ... 212 319-4895
New York *(G-10463)*

▲ Koster Keunen Waxes Ltd ... F ... 631 589-0400
Sayville *(G-14632)*

Northern Biodiesel Inc ... G ... 585 545-4534
Ontario *(G-12657)*

Oil Solutions Intl Inc ... G ... 631 608-8889
Amityville *(G-309)*

▲ Osaka Gas Energy America Corp ... F ... 914 253-5500
White Plains *(G-16483)*

Performance Diesel Service LLC ... F ... 315 854-5269
Plattsburgh *(G-13144)*

Petre Alii Petroleum ... G ... 315 785-1037
Watertown *(G-16032)*

R H Crown Co Inc ... E ... 518 762-4589
Johnstown *(G-6838)*

Shell Pipe Line Corporation ... G ... 212 740-8786
New York *(G-11561)*

Solvents Company Inc ... F ... 631 595-9300
Kingston *(G-6917)*

Starfuels Inc ... G ... 914 289-4800
White Plains *(G-16507)*

Suit-Kote Corporation ... F ... 585 268-7127
Belmont *(G-817)*

2951 Paving Mixtures & Blocks

A Colarusso and Son Inc ... E ... 518 828-3218
Hudson *(G-6336)*

Advanced Pavement Group Corp ... G ... 631 277-8400
Islip *(G-6543)*

Albany Asp & Aggregates Corp ... E ... 518 436-8916
Albany *(G-31)*

Alliance Paving Materials Inc ... G ... 315 337-0795
Rome *(G-14245)*

Atlas Bituminous Co Inc ... F ... 315 457-2394
Syracuse *(G-15248)*

Barrett Paving Materials Inc ... E ... 315 353-6611
Norwood *(G-12495)*

Barrett Paving Materials Inc ... E ... 315 652-4585
Liverpool *(G-7222)*

Barrett Paving Materials Inc ... F ... 315 737-9471
Clayville *(G-3554)*

Barrett Paving Materials Inc ... F ... 315 737-8310
Clayville *(G-3555)*

Barrett Paving Materials Inc ... G ... 607 723-5367
Binghamton *(G-864)*

Barrett Paving Materials Inc ... F ... 315 788-2037
Watertown *(G-16001)*

Bross Quality Paving ... G ... 845 532-7116
Ellenville *(G-4437)*

C & C Ready-Mix Corporation ... E ... 607 797-5108
Vestal *(G-15812)*

C & C Ready-Mix Corporation ... F ... 607 687-1690
Owego *(G-12796)*

Callanan Industries Inc ... E ... 845 457-3158
Montgomery *(G-8309)*

▲ Callanan Industries Inc ... C ... 518 374-2222
Albany *(G-54)*

Callanan Industries Inc ... E ... 845 331-6868
Kingston *(G-6892)*

Canal Asphalt Inc ... F ... 914 667-8500
Mount Vernon *(G-8384)*

Cobleskill Stone Products Inc ... F ... 607 432-8321
Oneonta *(G-12632)*

Cobleskill Stone Products Inc ... F ... 607 637-4271
Hancock *(G-5710)*

Cofire Paving Corporation ... E ... 718 463-1403
Flushing *(G-4993)*

Cold Mix Manufacturing Corp ... F ... 718 463-1444
Mount Vernon *(G-8389)*

Cosmicoat of Wny Inc ... G ... 716 772-2644
Gasport *(G-5305)*

Deans Paving Inc ... G ... 315 736-7601
Marcy *(G-7796)*

Doctor Pavers ... G ... 516 342-6016
Commack *(G-3689)*

Dolomite Products Company Inc ... E ... 315 524-1998
Rochester *(G-13749)*

Dolomite Products Company Inc ... F ... 607 324-3636
Hornell *(G-6295)*

Dolomite Products Company Inc ... F ... 585 768-7295
Le Roy *(G-7115)*

Dolomite Products Company Inc ... F ... 585 352-0460
Spencerport *(G-14978)*

Gernatt Asphalt Products Inc ... G ... 716 496-5111
Springville *(G-15016)*

Grace Associates Inc ... G ... 718 767-9000
Harrison *(G-5729)*

Graymont Materials Inc ... E ... 518 561-5200
Plattsburgh *(G-13122)*

Hanson Aggregates East LLC ... E ... 585 343-1787
Stafford *(G-15027)*

Hanson Aggregates PA LLC ... E ... 585 624-3800
Honeoye Falls *(G-6266)*

Iroquois Rock Products Inc ... F ... 585 381-7010
Rochester *(G-13887)*

J Pahura Contractors ... G ... 585 589-5793
Albion *(G-158)*

Jamestown Macadam Inc ... F ... 716 664-5108
Jamestown *(G-6730)*

Jet-Black Sealers Inc ... G ... 716 891-4197
Buffalo *(G-2895)*

John T Montecalvo Inc ... G ... 631 325-1492
Speonk *(G-14986)*

Kal-Harbour Inc ... F ... 518 266-0690
Albany *(G-90)*

King Road Materials Inc ... E ... 518 381-9995
Albany *(G-91)*

29 PETROLEUM REFINING AND RELATED INDUSTRIES

King Road Materials Inc .... F 518 382-5354
　Schenectady *(G-14694)*
Kings Park Asphalt Corporation .... G 631 269-9774
　Hauppauge *(G-5856)*
Lafarge North America Inc .... E 518 756-5000
　Ravena *(G-13454)*
▲ McConnaughay Technologies .... G 607 753-1100
　Cortland *(G-3884)*
Monticello Black Top Corp .... G 845 434-7280
　Thompsonville *(G-15500)*
▲ Nicolia Concrete Products Inc .... D 631 669-0700
　Lindenhurst *(G-7185)*
Northeastern Sealcoat Inc .... F 585 544-4372
　Rochester *(G-13979)*
Northern Bituminous Mix Inc .... G 315 598-2141
　Fulton *(G-5230)*
▲ Package Pavement Company Inc ..... D 845 221-2224
　Stormville *(G-15180)*
Pallette Stone Corporation .... E 518 584-2421
　Gansevoort *(G-5244)*
Patterson Blacktop Corp .... E 914 949-2000
　White Plains *(G-16485)*
Patterson Materials Corp .... E 914 949-2000
　White Plains *(G-16486)*
Pavco Asphalt Inc .... E 631 289-3223
　Holtsville *(G-6242)*
▲ Peckham Industries Inc .... E 914 949-2000
　White Plains *(G-16488)*
Peckham Industries Inc .... G 518 943-0155
　Catskill *(G-3308)*
Peckham Industries Inc .... E 518 893-2176
　Greenfield Center *(G-5619)*
Peckham Industries Inc .... G 518 945-1120
　Athens *(G-453)*
Peckham Materials Corp .... G 845 562-5370
　Newburgh *(G-12240)*
Peckham Materials Corp .... D 914 686-2045
　White Plains *(G-16489)*
Peckham Materials Corp .... G 518 945-1120
　Athens *(G-454)*
Peckham Materials Corp .... F 518 494-2313
　Chestertown *(G-3491)*
Peckham Materials Corp .... F 518 747-3353
　Hudson Falls *(G-6384)*
Peckham Road Corp .... G 518 792-3157
　Queensbury *(G-13436)*
Posillico Materials LLC .... F 631 249-1872
　Farmingdale *(G-4854)*
Prima Asphalt and Concrete .... F 631 289-3223
　Holtsville *(G-6243)*
PSI Transit Mix Corp .... G 631 382-7930
　Smithtown *(G-14907)*
R Schleider Contracting Corp .... G 631 269-4249
　Kings Park *(G-6886)*
Rochester Asphalt Materials .... E 585 381-7010
　Rochester *(G-14079)*
Rochester Seal Pro LLC .... G 585 594-3818
　Rochester *(G-14092)*
Sheldon Slate Products Co Inc .... E 518 642-1280
　Middle Granville *(G-8112)*
◆ Suit-Kote Corporation .... C 607 753-1100
　Cortland *(G-3895)*
Suit-Kote Corporation .... F 315 735-8501
　Oriskany *(G-12763)*
Suit-Kote Corporation .... E 607 535-2743
　Watkins Glen *(G-16061)*
Suit-Kote Corporation .... E 716 664-3750
　Jamestown *(G-6752)*
Swift River Associates Inc .... G 716 875-0902
　Tonawanda *(G-15581)*
Thalle Industries Inc .... E 914 762-3415
　Briarcliff Manor *(G-1177)*
Tilcon New York Inc .... D 845 638-3594
　Haverstraw *(G-5982)*
Tri City Highway Products Inc .... E 607 722-2967
　Binghamton *(G-921)*
Tri-City Highway Products Inc .... E 518 294-9964
　Richmondville *(G-13519)*
Twin County Recycling Corp .... F 516 827-6900
　Westbury *(G-16383)*
Ultimate Pavers Corp .... E 917 417-2652
　Staten Island *(G-15149)*
▲ Unilock New York Inc .... G 845 278-6700
　Brewster *(G-1175)*
Universal Ready Mix Inc .... G 516 746-4535
　New Hyde Park *(G-8571)*
Upstate Materials Inc .... E 518 873-2275
　Lewis *(G-7137)*
Upstone Materials Inc .... D 518 561-5321
　Plattsburgh *(G-13165)*

Vestal Asphalt Inc .... F 607 785-3393
　Vestal *(G-15825)*
Zielinskis Asphalt Inc .... F 315 306-4057
　Oriskany Falls *(G-12768)*

2952 Asphalt Felts & Coatings

▲ Aremco Products Inc .... F 845 268-0039
　Valley Cottage *(G-15752)*
Barrett Paving Materials Inc .... E 315 353-6611
　Norwood *(G-12495)*
Callanan Industries Inc .... E 845 457-3158
　Montgomery *(G-8309)*
Johns Manville Corporation .... E 518 565-3000
　Plattsburgh *(G-13128)*
K-D Stone Inc .... F 518 642-2082
　Middle Granville *(G-8111)*
◆ Marathon Roofing Products Inc .... F 716 685-3340
　Orchard Park *(G-12728)*
Northeastern Sealcoat Inc .... F 585 544-4372
　Rochester *(G-13979)*
Peckham Materials Corp .... F 518 747-3353
　Hudson Falls *(G-6384)*
◆ Polyset Company Inc .... E 518 664-6000
　Mechanicville *(G-7932)*
Savage & Son Installations LLC .... E 585 342-7533
　Rochester *(G-14113)*
Sheldon Slate Products Co Inc .... E 518 642-1280
　Middle Granville *(G-8112)*
Spray-Tech Finishing Inc .... F 716 664-6317
　Jamestown *(G-6749)*
Suit-Kote Corporation .... E 607 535-2743
　Watkins Glen *(G-16061)*
Tntpaving .... F 607 372-4911
　Endicott *(G-4612)*

2992 Lubricating Oils & Greases

▲ Battenfeld Grease Oil Corp NY .... E 716 695-2100
　North Tonawanda *(G-12417)*
▼ Battenfeld-American Inc .... F 716 822-8410
　Buffalo *(G-2726)*
▲ Baums Castorine Company Inc ...... G 315 336-8154
　Rome *(G-14247)*
Beka World LP 905 821-1050
　Buffalo *(G-2728)*
Bestline International RES Inc .... F 518 631-2177
　Schenectady *(G-14654)*
▲ Black Bear Company Inc .... E 718 784-7330
　Valley Stream *(G-15774)*
▲ Blaser Production Inc .... F 845 294-3200
　Goshen *(G-5477)*
◆ Blaser Swisslube Holding Corp .... F 845 294-3200
　Goshen *(G-5478)*
Castoleum Corporation .... F 914 664-5877
　Mount Vernon *(G-8385)*
◆ Chemlube International LLC .... F 914 381-5800
　Harrison *(G-5725)*
◆ Chemlube Marketing Inc .... F 914 381-5800
　Harrison *(G-5726)*
◆ Finish Line Technologies Inc .... F 631 666-7300
　Hauppauge *(G-5824)*
High Line Lube LLC .... G 914 684-0170
　White Plains *(G-16459)*
Industrial Oil Tank Service .... F 315 736-6080
　Oriskany *(G-12759)*
▲ Inland Vacuum Industries Inc .... F 585 293-3330
　Churchville *(G-3510)*
▲ Interdynamics .... F 914 241-1423
　Mount Kisco *(G-8344)*
▲ Loobrica International Corp .... G 347 997-0296
　Staten Island *(G-15101)*
Mdi Holdings LLC .... A 212 559-1127
　New York *(G-10747)*
▲ Monroe Fluid Technology Inc .... E 585 392-3434
　Hilton *(G-6157)*
Noco Incorporated .... G 716 833-6626
　Tonawanda *(G-15565)*
Oil and Lubricant Depot LLC .... F 718 258-9220
　Amityville *(G-308)*
Polycast Industries Inc .... F 631 595-2530
　Bay Shore *(G-708)*
Safety-Kleen Systems Inc .... F 716 855-2212
　Buffalo *(G-3055)*
◆ Specialty Silicone Pdts Inc .... D 518 885-8826
　Ballston Spa *(G-596)*
◆ Summit Lubricants Inc .... E 585 815-0798
　Batavia *(G-636)*
▲ Tribology Inc .... F 631 345-3000
　Yaphank *(G-16724)*
US Global Lubricants Inc .... F 845 271-4277
　Stony Point *(G-15178)*

2999 Products Of Petroleum & Coal, NEC

◆ Cooks Intl Ltd Lblty Co .... G 212 741-4407
　New York *(G-9394)*
Costello Bros Petroleum Corp .... G 914 237-3189
　Yonkers *(G-16747)*
Hh Liquidating Corp .... A 646 282-2500
　New York *(G-10092)*
Industrial Raw Materials LLC .... G 212 688-8080
　New York *(G-10202)*
▲ Premier Ingridients Inc .... G 516 641-6763
　Great Neck *(G-5582)*

30 RUBBER AND MISCELLANEOUS PLASTICS PRODUCTS

3011 Tires & Inner Tubes

East Coast Intl Tire Inc .... F 718 386-9088
　Maspeth *(G-7841)*
▼ Handy & Harman Ltd .... A 212 520-2300
　New York *(G-10031)*
McCarthy Tire Svc Co NY Inc .... F 518 449-5185
　Menands *(G-8088)*
New York CT Loc246 Seiu Wel BF ..... G 212 233-0616
　New York *(G-10933)*
Roli Retreads Inc 631 694-7670
　Farmingdale *(G-4868)*
Sph Group Holdings LLC 212 520-2300
　New York *(G-11669)*

3021 Rubber & Plastic Footwear

▲ Anthony L & S LLC .... G 212 386-7245
　New York *(G-8877)*
Crocs Inc .... F 845 928-3002
　Central Valley *(G-3394)*
▲ Detny Footwear Inc 212 423-1040
　New York *(G-9511)*
Homegrown For Good LLC .... F 857 540-6361
　New Rochelle *(G-8615)*
Inkkas LLC 646 845-9803
　New York *(G-10216)*
Little Eric Shoes On Madison .... G 212 717-1513
　New York *(G-10580)*
Lust For Life Footwear LLC .... F 646 732-9742
　Pearl River *(G-12906)*
▲ Mango Usa Inc .... E 718 998-6050
　Brooklyn *(G-2156)*
Nike Inc 212 226-5433
　New York *(G-10967)*
Nike Inc .... F 631 242-3014
　Deer Park *(G-4017)*
Nike Inc .... E 631 960-0184
　Islip Terrace *(G-6553)*
Nike Inc .... F 716 298-5615
　Niagara Falls *(G-12314)*
Skechers USA Inc .... F 718 585-3024
　Bronx *(G-1386)*
▲ Soludos LLC .... F 212 219-1101
　New York *(G-11642)*
▲ Timing Group LLC .... F 646 878-2600
　New York *(G-11848)*
Vans Inc .... F 631 724-1011
　Lake Grove *(G-6971)*
Vans Inc .... F 718 349-2311
　Brooklyn *(G-2617)*

3052 Rubber & Plastic Hose & Belting

▲ Anchor Tech Products Corp .... E 914 592-0240
　Elmsford *(G-4529)*
Cataract Hose Co .... E 914 941-9019
　Ossining *(G-12769)*
Deer Park Driveshaft & Hose .... G 631 667-4091
　Deer Park *(G-3963)*
▲ Flex Enterprises Inc .... E 585 742-1000
　Victor *(G-15846)*
Habasit America Inc 716 824-8484
　Buffalo *(G-2860)*
▲ Hitachi Cable America Inc .... F 914 694-9200
　Purchase *(G-13388)*
Index Incorporated .... F 440 632-5400
　Bronx *(G-1295)*
Jain Irrigation Inc .... D 315 755-4400
　Watertown *(G-16017)*
Jed Lights Inc .... F 516 812-5001
　Deer Park *(G-3992)*
◆ Mason Industries Inc .... B 631 348-0282
　Hauppauge *(G-5881)*
▲ Mercer Rubber Co .... C 631 348-0282
　Hauppauge *(G-5886)*

Moreland Hose & Belting Corp .... G 631 563-7071
Oakdale *(G-12519)*

◆ Peraflex Hose Inc .... F 716 876-8806
Buffalo *(G-2998)*

▲ Sampla Belting North Amer LLC .... E 716 667-7450
Lackawanna *(G-6953)*

Standard Motor Products Inc .... B 718 392-0200
Long Island City *(G-7598)*

▲ Superflex Ltd .... E 718 768-1400
Brooklyn *(G-2535)*

TI Group Auto Systems LLC .... G 315 568-7042
Seneca Falls *(G-14787)*

Troy Belting and Supply Co .... D 518 272-4920
Watervliet *(G-16053)*

Van Slyke Belting LLC .... G 518 283-5479
Poestenkill *(G-13183)*

▲ WF Lake Corp .... E 518 798-9934
Queensbury *(G-13445)*

3053 Gaskets, Packing & Sealing Devices

A L Sealing .... G 315 699-6900
Chittenango *(G-3500)*

▲ Allstate Gasket & Packing Inc .... F 631 254-4050
Deer Park *(G-3937)*

American Sealing Technology .... F 631 254-0019
Deer Park *(G-3941)*

Apple Rubber Products Inc .... C 716 684-7649
Lancaster *(G-7008)*

▲ Bag Arts Ltd .... G 212 684-7020
New York *(G-9000)*

Boonville Manufacturing Corp .... G 315 942-4368
Boonville *(G-1116)*

Commercial Gaskets New York .... F 212 244-8130
New York *(G-9365)*

▲ Everlast Seals and Supply LLC .... F 718 388-7373
Brooklyn *(G-1855)*

▲ Frank Lowe Rbr & Gasket Co Inc .... E 631 777-2707
Shirley *(G-14835)*

Gaddis Industrial Equipment .... F 516 759-3100
Glen Cove *(G-5367)*

Garlock Sealing Tech LLC .... A 315 597-4811
Palmyra *(G-12853)*

GM Components Holdings LLC .... D 716 439-2402
Lockport *(G-7307)*

Hollingsworth & Vose Company .... C 518 695-8000
Greenwich *(G-5641)*

Interface Performance Mtls Inc .... C 315 592-8100
Fulton *(G-5221)*

Interface Performance Mtls Inc .... D 518 686-3400
Hoosick Falls *(G-6276)*

Jed Lights Inc .... F 516 812-5001
Deer Park *(G-3992)*

John Crane Inc .... D 315 593-6237
Fulton *(G-5223)*

▲ Loomis Root Inc .... F 716 564-7668
Amherst *(G-236)*

▲ Make-Waves Instrument Corp .... E 716 681-7524
Buffalo *(G-2936)*

Micromold Products Inc .... E 914 969-2850
Yonkers *(G-16784)*

◆ Noroc Enterprises Inc .... C 718 585-3230
Bronx *(G-1344)*

▲ Prince Rubber & Plas Co Inc .... E 225 272-1653
Buffalo *(G-3014)*

▲ SAS Industries Inc .... F 631 727-1441
Manorville *(G-7785)*

Schlegel Electronic Mtls Inc .... F 585 295-2030
Rochester *(G-14114)*

▲ Schlegel Systems Inc .... C 585 427-7200
Rochester *(G-14115)*

Seal & Design Inc .... E 315 432-8021
Syracuse *(G-15420)*

SKF USA Inc .... D 716 661-2600
Jamestown *(G-6747)*

Technical Packaging Inc .... F 516 223-2300
Baldwin *(G-545)*

Temper Corporation .... E 518 853-3467
Fonda *(G-5067)*

Unique Packaging Corporation .... G 514 341-5872
Champlain *(G-3416)*

USA Sealing Inc .... E 716 288-9952
Cheektowaga *(G-3462)*

Web Seal Inc .... E 585 546-1320
Rochester *(G-14204)*

▲ Xto Incorporated .... D 315 451-7807
Liverpool *(G-7273)*

3061 Molded, Extruded & Lathe-Cut Rubber Mechanical Goods

Apple Rubber Products Inc .... C 716 684-7649
Lancaster *(G-7008)*

Bridgestone APM Company .... D 419 423-9552
Sanborn *(G-14541)*

▲ Camso Manufacturing Usa Ltd .... D 518 561-7528
Plattsburgh *(G-13115)*

Delford Industries Inc .... D 845 342-3901
Middletown *(G-8147)*

Finzer Holding LLC .... E 315 597-1147
Palmyra *(G-12852)*

Mechanical Rubber Pdts Co Inc .... F 845 986-2271
Warwick *(G-15958)*

▲ Moldtech Inc .... E 716 685-3344
Lancaster *(G-7033)*

Ms Spares LLC .... G 607 223-3024
Clay *(G-3551)*

▼ Pawling Corporation .... C 845 855-1000
Pawling *(G-12893)*

Pawling Corporation .... D 845 373-9300
Wassaic *(G-15965)*

Pawling Engineered Pdts Inc .... C 845 855-1000
Pawling *(G-12894)*

Pilot Products Inc .... F 718 728-2141
Long Island City *(G-7556)*

R & A Industrial Products .... G 716 823-4300
Buffalo *(G-3029)*

The Centro Company Inc .... G 914 533-2200
South Salem *(G-14948)*

▲ Triangle Rubber Co Inc .... E 631 589-9400
Bohemia *(G-1099)*

3069 Fabricated Rubber Prdts, NEC

▲ Adam Scott Designs Inc .... E 212 420-8866
New York *(G-8732)*

Advanced Back Technologies .... G 631 231-0076
Hauppauge *(G-5754)*

▲ Apple Rubber Products Inc .... C 716 684-6560
Lancaster *(G-7007)*

Apple Rubber Products Inc .... C 716 684-7649
Lancaster *(G-7008)*

Buffalo Lining & Fabricating .... G 716 883-6500
Buffalo *(G-2746)*

▼ Cementex Latex Corp .... F 212 741-1770
New York *(G-9236)*

Certified Health Products Inc .... E 718 339-7498
Brooklyn *(G-1686)*

▲ Chamberlin Rubber Company Inc .... E 585 427-7780
Rochester *(G-13705)*

▲ Chemprene Inc .... C 845 831-2800
Beacon *(G-755)*

▲ Chemprene Holding Inc .... C 845 831-2800
Beacon *(G-756)*

Continental Latex Corp .... F 718 783-7883
Brooklyn *(G-1713)*

Enbi Indiana Inc .... E 585 647-1627
Rochester *(G-13782)*

Enviroform Recycled Pdts Inc .... G 315 789-1810
Geneva *(G-5322)*

Finzer Holding LLC .... E 315 597-1147
Palmyra *(G-12852)*

Foam Products Inc .... E 718 292-4830
Bronx *(G-1273)*

▲ Geri-Gentle Corporation .... G 917 804-7807
Brooklyn *(G-1923)*

◆ Great American Industries Inc .... G 607 729-9331
Vestal *(G-15818)*

▲ Hampton Art LLC .... E 631 924-1335
Medford *(G-7950)*

Hti Recycling LLC .... E 716 433-9294
Lockport *(G-7309)*

Hutchinson Industries Inc .... E 716 852-1435
Buffalo *(G-2876)*

Idg LLC .... E 315 797-1000
Utica *(G-15712)*

Impladent Ltd .... E 718 465-1810
Jamaica *(G-6651)*

Inflation Systems Inc .... E 914 381-8070
Mamaroneck *(G-7746)*

Jamestown Scientific Inds LLC .... F 716 665-3224
Jamestown *(G-6732)*

Kelson Products Inc .... G 716 825-2585
Orchard Park *(G-12723)*

Life Medical Technologies LLC .... F 845 894-2121
Hopewell Junction *(G-6291)*

◆ Magic Touch Icewares Intl .... G 212 794-2852
New York *(G-10670)*

▲ Mam USA Corporation .... F 914 269-2500
Purchase *(G-13392)*

◆ Mason Industries Inc .... B 631 348-0282
Hauppauge *(G-5881)*

▲ Mercer Rubber Co .... C 631 348-0282
Hauppauge *(G-5886)*

Mhxco Foam Company LLC .... F 518 843-8400
Amsterdam *(G-347)*

▲ Moldtech Inc .... E 716 685-3344
Lancaster *(G-7033)*

Newyork Pedorthic Associates .... G 718 236-7700
Brooklyn *(G-2268)*

▲ Package Print Technologies .... F 716 871-9905
Buffalo *(G-2988)*

Par-Foam Products Inc .... C 716 855-2066
Buffalo *(G-2990)*

▼ Pawling Corporation .... C 845 855-1000
Pawling *(G-12893)*

▲ Prince Rubber & Plas Co Inc .... E 225 272-1653
Buffalo *(G-3014)*

Remedies Surgical Supplies .... G 718 599-5301
Brooklyn *(G-2396)*

Rotation Dynamics Corporation .... E 585 352-9023
Spencerport *(G-14982)*

Rubber Stamps Inc .... E 212 675-1180
Mineola *(G-8247)*

▼ Rubberform Recycled Pdts LLC .... F 716 478-0404
Lockport *(G-7330)*

▲ Schlegel Systems Inc .... C 585 427-7200
Rochester *(G-14115)*

SD Christie Associates Inc .... G 914 734-1800
Peekskill *(G-12925)*

Seaway Mats Inc .... G 518 483-2560
Malone *(G-7726)*

Short Jj Associates Inc .... F 315 986-3511
Macedon *(G-7704)*

▲ Tire Conversion Tech Inc .... E 518 372-1600
Latham *(G-7093)*

▼ Tmp Technologies Inc .... D 716 895-6100
Buffalo *(G-3097)*

Tmp Technologies Inc .... D 585 495-6231
Wyoming *(G-16702)*

▼ Traffic Logix Corporation .... G 866 915-6449
Spring Valley *(G-15009)*

▲ Triangle Rubber Co Inc .... E 631 589-9400
Bohemia *(G-1099)*

▲ Turner Bellows Inc .... E 585 235-4456
Rochester *(G-14181)*

Vehicle Manufacturers Inc .... E 631 851-1700
Hauppauge *(G-5968)*

Wall Protection Products LLC .... E 877 943-6826
Wassaic *(G-15967)*

3081 Plastic Unsupported Sheet & Film

▲ Ace Canvas & Tent Corp .... F 631 648-0614
Ronkonkoma *(G-14288)*

Albert F Stager Inc .... G 315 434-7240
East Syracuse *(G-4316)*

◆ American Acrylic Corporation .... E 631 422-2200
West Babylon *(G-16133)*

▲ API Industries Inc .... B 845 365-2200
Orangeburg *(G-12668)*

API Industries Inc .... C 845 365-2200
Orangeburg *(G-12669)*

▲ Astra Products Inc .... G 631 464-4747
Copiague *(G-3753)*

Berry Global Inc .... C 315 986-2161
Macedon *(G-7696)*

Berry Global Inc .... C 315 484-0397
Solvay *(G-14916)*

Berry Plastics Corporation .... B 315 986-6270
Macedon *(G-7697)*

Bfgg Investors Group LLC .... G 585 424-3456
Rochester *(G-13662)*

Clear View Bag Company Inc .... C 518 458-7153
Albany *(G-59)*

▲ Comco Plastics Inc .... E 718 849-9000
Huntington Station *(G-6436)*

Dunmore Corporation .... D 845 279-5061
Brewster *(G-1163)*

Ecoplast & Packaging LLC .... G 718 996-0800
Brooklyn *(G-1811)*

Edco Supply Corporation .... D 718 788-8108
Brooklyn *(G-1813)*

Excellent Poly Inc .... F 718 768-6555
Brooklyn *(G-1856)*

Farber Plastics Inc .... E 516 378-4860
Freeport *(G-5153)*

Farber Trucking Corp .... E 516 378-4860
Freeport *(G-5154)*

▲ Favorite Plastic Corp .... C 718 253-7000
Brooklyn *(G-1870)*

Employee Codes: A=Over 500 employees, B=251-500
C=101-250, D=51-100, E=20-50, F=10-19, G=5-9

2019 Harris
New York Manufacturers Directory

725

30 RUBBER AND MISCELLANEOUS PLASTICS PRODUCTS

▼ Franklin Poly Film Inc .... E 718 492-3523
  Brooklyn *(G-1904)*
Georgia-Pacific LLC .... E 845 986-2011
  Warwick *(G-15953)*
Great Lakes Plastics Co Inc .... E 716 896-3100
  Buffalo *(G-2856)*
Integument Technologies Inc .... F 716 873-1199
  Tonawanda *(G-15552)*
◆ Island Pyrochemical Inds Corp ..... C 516 746-2100
  Mineola *(G-8231)*
▲ Kent Chemical Corporation .... E 212 521-1700
  New York *(G-10436)*
Kings Film & Sheet Inc .... E 718 624-7510
  Brooklyn *(G-2076)*
Knf Clean Room Products Corp ...... E 631 588-7000
  Ronkonkoma *(G-14362)*
▲ Knoll Printing & Packaging Inc ..... E 516 621-0100
  Syosset *(G-15220)*
Latham International Inc .... F 518 346-5292
  Schenectady *(G-14695)*
◆ Latham International Inc .... G 518 783-7776
  Latham *(G-7080)*
▲ Maco Bag Corporation .... C 315 226-1000
  Newark *(G-12199)*
Msi Inc .... F 845 639-6683
  New City *(G-8494)*
▲ Nationwide Tarps Incorporated .... D 518 843-1545
  Amsterdam *(G-353)*
Nova Packaging Ltd Inc .... E 914 232-8406
  Katonah *(G-6845)*
Oaklee International Inc .... D 631 436-7900
  Ronkonkoma *(G-14389)*
Orafol Americas Inc .... E 585 272-0309
  Henrietta *(G-6036)*
Pace Polyethylene Mfg Co Inc .... E 914 381-3000
  Harrison *(G-5732)*
Pacific Designs Intl Inc .... G 718 364-2867
  Bronx *(G-1350)*
▲ Plascal Corp .... G 516 249-2200
  Farmingdale *(G-4851)*
Pliant LLC .... B 315 986-6286
  Macedon *(G-7703)*
▲ Potential Poly Bag Inc .... E 718 258-0800
  Brooklyn *(G-2329)*
R & F Boards & Dividers Inc .... E 718 331-1529
  Brooklyn *(G-2374)*
Rainbow Poly Bag Co Inc .... E 718 386-3500
  Brooklyn *(G-2382)*
Robeco/Ascot Products Inc .... E 516 248-1521
  Garden City *(G-5279)*
Sand Hill Industries Inc .... G 518 885-7991
  Ballston Spa *(G-595)*
▲ Scapa North America .... E 315 413-1111
  Liverpool *(G-7261)*
Sentinel Products Corp .... F 518 568-7036
  Saint Johnsville *(G-14522)*
▲ Shaant Industries Inc .... E 716 366-3654
  Dunkirk *(G-4179)*
◆ Swimline Corp .... C 631 254-2155
  Edgewood *(G-4416)*
Toray Industries Inc .... G 212 697-8150
  New York *(G-11869)*
Tri-Seal Holdings Inc .... D 845 353-3300
  Blauvelt *(G-943)*
Trinity Packaging Corporation .... E 716 668-3111
  Buffalo *(G-3103)*
▲ Turner Bellows Inc .... E 585 235-4456
  Rochester *(G-14181)*
Vinyl Materials Inc .... E 631 586-9444
  Deer Park *(G-4060)*

3082 Plastic Unsupported Profile Shapes

Chelsea Plastics Inc .... F 212 924-4530
  New York *(G-9269)*
▲ Comco Plastics Inc .... E 718 849-9000
  Huntington Station *(G-6436)*
▲ Finger Lakes Extrusion Corp .... E 585 905-0632
  Canandaigua *(G-3221)*
▼ Franklin Poly Film Inc .... E 718 492-3523
  Brooklyn *(G-1904)*
Great Lakes Plastics Co Inc .... E 716 896-3100
  Buffalo *(G-2856)*
Hancor Inc .... D 607 565-3033
  Waverly *(G-16066)*
Howard J Moore Company Inc .... E 631 351-8467
  Plainview *(G-13062)*
◆ Mitsui Chemicals America Inc ..... G 914 253-0777
  Rye Brook *(G-14493)*
▲ Ontario Plastics Inc .... E 585 663-2644
  Rochester *(G-13989)*

3083 Plastic Laminated Plate & Sheet

▼ ADC Acquisition Company .... E 518 377-6471
  Niskayuna *(G-12352)*
Advanced Structures Corp .... F 631 667-5000
  Deer Park *(G-3934)*
Allred & Associates Inc .... E 315 252-2559
  Elbridge *(G-4427)*
◆ American Acrylic Corporation ...... E 631 422-2200
  West Babylon *(G-16133)*
Anthony River Inc .... F 315 475-1315
  Syracuse *(G-15244)*
Architctral Dsign Elements LLC ...... G 718 218-7800
  Brooklyn *(G-1546)*
▲ Blue Sky Plastic Production .... F 718 366-3966
  Brooklyn *(G-1621)*
▲ Clear Cast Technologies Inc .... E 914 945-0848
  Ossining *(G-12770)*
Displays By Rioux Inc .... E 315 458-3639
  North Syracuse *(G-12399)*
▲ Favorite Plastic Corp .... C 718 253-7000
  Brooklyn *(G-1870)*
◆ Griffon Corporation .... E 212 957-5000
  New York *(G-9988)*
▲ Inland Paper Products Corp .... E 718 827-8150
  Brooklyn *(G-2005)*
Inter State Laminates Inc .... E 518 283-8355
  Poestenkill *(G-13181)*
Iridium Industries Inc .... E 516 504-9700
  Great Neck *(G-5563)*
Jaguar Industries Inc .... F 845 947-1800
  Haverstraw *(G-5979)*
Jay Moulding Corporation .... F 518 237-4200
  Cohoes *(G-3611)*
▲ Nalge Nunc International Corp .... A 585 498-2661
  Rochester *(G-13962)*
On Time Plastics Inc .... G 516 442-4280
  Freeport *(G-5170)*
Strux Corp .... E 516 768-3969
  Lindenhurst *(G-7196)*
Synthetic Textiles Inc .... G 716 842-2598
  Buffalo *(G-3083)*
▲ Unico Special Products Inc .... E 845 562-9255
  Newburgh *(G-12248)*

3084 Plastic Pipe

▲ BMC LLC .... E 716 681-7755
  Buffalo *(G-2735)*
Hancor Inc .... D 607 565-3033
  Waverly *(G-16066)*
Micromold Products Inc .... E 914 969-2850
  Yonkers *(G-16784)*
◆ National Pipe & Plastics Inc .... C 607 729-9381
  Vestal *(G-15820)*
North American Pipe Corp .... F 516 338-2863
  East Williston *(G-4382)*
▲ Prince Rubber & Plas Co Inc .... E 225 272-1653
  Buffalo *(G-3014)*

3085 Plastic Bottles

▲ Alphamed Bottles Inc .... E 631 524-5577
  Central Islip *(G-3355)*
Alpla Inc .... G 607 250-8101
  Cortland *(G-3859)*
▼ Capitol Plastic Products Inc .... C 518 627-0051
  Amsterdam *(G-331)*
◆ Chapin International Inc .... C 585 343-3140
  Batavia *(G-617)*
◆ Chapin Manufacturing Inc .... C 585 343-3140
  Batavia *(G-618)*
Cortland Plastics Intl LLC .... C 607 662-0120
  Cortland *(G-3869)*
David Johnson .... F 315 493-4735
  Carthage *(G-3290)*
Intrapac International Corp .... C 518 561-2030
  Plattsburgh *(G-13126)*
Kybod Group LLC .... G 408 306-1657
  New York *(G-10489)*
Monroe Cnty Chapter Nysarc Inc .... G 585 698-1320
  Rochester *(G-13952)*
▲ Nalge Nunc International Corp .... A 585 498-2661
  Rochester *(G-13962)*
Pvc Container Corporation .... C 518 672-7721
  Philmont *(G-12987)*
◆ Samco Scientific LLC .... C 800 522-3359
  Rochester *(G-14109)*
▲ Schless Bottles Inc .... E 718 236-2790
  Brooklyn *(G-2450)*

3086 Plastic Foam Prdts

24 Seven Enterprises Inc .... G 845 563-9033
  New Windsor *(G-8632)*
ABI Packaging Inc .... E 716 677-2900
  West Seneca *(G-16292)*
Arm Rochester Inc .... F 585 354-5077
  Rochester *(G-13639)*
Barclay Brown Corp .... F 718 376-7166
  Brooklyn *(G-1586)*
Berry Plastics Corporation .... B 315 986-6270
  Macedon *(G-7697)*
▲ Burnett Process Inc .... E 585 254-8080
  Rochester *(G-13683)*
C P Chemical Co Inc .... G 914 428-2517
  White Plains *(G-16434)*
Calpac Incorporated .... F 631 789-0502
  Amityville *(G-267)*
Carlisle Construction Mtls LLC .... D 386 753-0786
  Montgomery *(G-8310)*
▲ Cellect Plastics LLC .... D 518 568-7036
  Saint Johnsville *(G-14517)*
Chesu Inc .... F 239 564-2803
  East Hampton *(G-4234)*
China Xd Plastics Company Ltd ..... G 212 747-1118
  New York *(G-9284)*
Dura Foam Inc .... E 718 894-2488
  Maspeth *(G-7838)*
Fedex Ground Package Sys Inc ...... E 800 463-3339
  Plattsburgh *(G-13121)*
First Qlty Packg Solutions LLC .... F 516 829-3030
  Great Neck *(G-5555)*
Foam Products Inc .... E 718 292-4830
  Bronx *(G-1273)*
▲ General Vy-Coat LLC .... E 718 266-6002
  Brooklyn *(G-1921)*
◆ Great American Industries Inc .... G 607 729-9331
  Vestal *(G-15818)*
▲ Interntnal Bus Cmmncations Inc . E 516 352-4505
  New Hyde Park *(G-8542)*
▲ J & M Packaging Inc .... F 631 608-3069
  Hauppauge *(G-5852)*
▼ Jamestown Container Corp .... C 716 665-4623
  Falconer *(G-4684)*
Jem Container Corp .... F 800 521-0145
  Plainview *(G-13066)*
▲ Knoll Printing & Packaging Inc ... E 516 621-0100
  Syosset *(G-15220)*
▲ Lamar Plastics Packaging Ltd ..... D 516 378-2500
  Freeport *(G-5163)*
◆ Latham International Inc .... G 518 783-7776
  Latham *(G-7080)*
Latham Pool Products Inc .... E 260 432-8731
  Latham *(G-7083)*
Lewis & Myers Inc .... F 585 494-1410
  Bergen *(G-823)*
New York State Foam Enrgy LLC ... G 845 534-4656
  Cornwall *(G-3835)*
Par-Foam Products Inc .... C 716 855-2066
  Buffalo *(G-2990)*
Philpac Corporation .... E 716 875-8005
  Buffalo *(G-3002)*
Plastpac Inc .... E 908 272-7200
  Brooklyn *(G-2323)*
Pliant LLC .... B 315 986-6286
  Macedon *(G-7703)*
▲ Printex Packaging Corporation .... D 631 234-4300
  Islandia *(G-6537)*
Professional Packg Svcs Inc .... E 518 677-5100
  Eagle Bridge *(G-4185)*
R D A Container Corporation .... E 585 247-2323
  Gates *(G-5312)*
Rimco Plastics Corp .... E 607 739-3864
  Horseheads *(G-6326)*
Saint-Gobain Prfmce Plas Corp ...... C 518 642-2200
  Granville *(G-5524)*
▲ Shell Containers Inc (ny) .... E 516 352-4505
  New Hyde Park *(G-8562)*
▲ Shelter Enterprises Inc .... D 518 237-4100
  Cohoes *(G-3621)*
▲ Skd Distribution Corp .... E 718 525-6000
  Jericho *(G-6805)*
Snow Craft Co Inc .... E 516 739-1399
  New Hyde Park *(G-8563)*
◆ Soundcoat Company Inc .... D 631 242-2200
  Deer Park *(G-4047)*
Strux Corp .... E 516 768-3969
  Lindenhurst *(G-7196)*
Technical Packaging Inc .... F 516 223-2300
  Baldwin *(G-545)*

SIC SECTION
30 RUBBER AND MISCELLANEOUS PLASTICS PRODUCTS

▲ Thermal Foams/Syracuse Inc .... G 716 874-6474
  Buffalo (G-3093)
Thermal Foams/Syracuse Inc .... E 315 699-8734
  Cicero (G-3523)
▼ Tmp Technologies Inc .... D 716 895-6100
  Buffalo (G-3097)
TSS Foam Industries Corp .... F 585 538-2321
  Caledonia (G-3159)
◆ W Stuart Smith Inc .... E 585 742-3310
  Victor (G-15876)
Walnut Packaging Inc .... E 631 293-3836
  Farmingdale (G-4905)

3087 Custom Compounding Of Purchased Plastic Resins

Advance Chemicals Usa Inc .... G 718 633-1030
  Brooklyn (G-1487)
Atc Plastics LLC .... E 212 375-2515
  New York (G-8943)
Cryovac Inc .... C 585 436-3211
  Rochester (G-13725)
Lahr Recycling & Resins Inc .... F 585 425-8608
  Fairport (G-4638)
▲ Marval Industries Inc .... D 914 381-2400
  Mamaroneck (G-7748)
◆ Polyset Company Inc .... E 518 664-6000
  Mechanicville (G-7932)
◆ Si Group Inc .... C 518 347-4200
  Schenectady (G-14713)

3088 Plastic Plumbing Fixtures

Allegany Laminating and Supply .... G 716 372-2424
  Allegany (G-188)
An-Cor Industrial Plastics Inc .... D 716 695-3141
  North Tonawanda (G-12411)
▼ Bow Industrial Corporation .... D 518 561-0190
  Champlain (G-3406)
D & M Enterprises Incorporated .... G 914 937-6430
  Port Chester (G-13195)
Gms Hicks Street Corporation .... E 718 858-1010
  Brooklyn (G-1934)
H Rindustries .... G 516 487-3825
  Mineola (G-8226)
▲ Independent Home Products LLC .... E 718 541-1256
  West Hempstead (G-16216)
▲ ITR Industries Inc .... E 914 964-7063
  Yonkers (G-16771)
◆ Metpar Corp .... D 516 333-2600
  Westbury (G-16356)
◆ Quality Enclosures Inc .... E 631 234-0115
  Central Islip (G-3382)

3089 Plastic Prdts

▲ 311 Industries Corp .... G 607 846-4520
  Endicott (G-4580)
3M Company .... B 716 876-1596
  Tonawanda (G-15517)
A & G Heat Sealing .... G 631 724-7764
  Smithtown (G-14893)
▲ A R Arena Products Inc .... E 585 277-1680
  Rochester (G-13591)
A R V Precision Mfg Inc .... G 631 293-9643
  Farmingdale (G-4705)
A-1 Products Inc .... G 718 789-1818
  Brooklyn (G-1462)
Aaron Tool & Mold Inc .... G 585 426-5100
  Rochester (G-13593)
▲ Abbott Industries Inc .... B 718 291-0800
  Jamaica (G-6622)
▲ Abr Molding Andy LLC .... F 212 576-1821
  Ridgewood (G-13528)
Ace Molding & Tool Inc .... G 631 567-2355
  Bohemia (G-972)
Acme Awning Co Inc .... F 718 409-1881
  Bronx (G-1210)
◆ Adirondack Plas & Recycl Inc .... E 518 746-9212
  Argyle (G-397)
Albany International Corp .... C 607 749-7226
  Homer (G-6252)
◆ Albea Cosmetics America Inc .... E 212 371-5100
  New York (G-8784)
▲ Albest Metal Stamping Corp .... D 718 388-6000
  Brooklyn (G-1500)
▲ Allen Field Co Inc .... F 631 665-2782
  Brightwaters (G-1185)
▲ Alliance Precision Plas Corp .... C 585 426-5310
  Rochester (G-13616)
Alliance Precision Plas Corp .... E 585 426-5310
  Rochester (G-13617)

▲ Allsafe Technologies Inc .... D 716 691-0400
  Amherst (G-212)
Alpha Incorporated .... G 718 765-1614
  Brooklyn (G-1512)
Aluminum Injection Mold Co LLC .... G 585 502-6087
  Le Roy (G-7112)
Amadeo Serrano .... G 516 608-8359
  Freeport (G-5142)
Amcor Rigid Plastics Usa LLC .... E 716 366-2440
  Dunkirk (G-4162)
◆ American Casting and Mfg Corp .... D 800 342-0333
  Plainview (G-13035)
American Casting and Mfg Corp .... G 516 349-7010
  Plainview (G-13036)
▲ American Intl Trimming .... G 718 369-9643
  Brooklyn (G-1522)
American Package Company Inc .... E 718 389-4444
  Brooklyn (G-1525)
American Spacer Technologies .... G 518 828-1339
  Hudson (G-6338)
American Visuals Inc .... G 631 694-6104
  Farmingdale (G-4720)
An-Cor Industrial Plastics Inc .... D 716 695-3141
  North Tonawanda (G-12411)
▲ Anka Tool & Die Inc .... E 845 268-4116
  Congers (G-3709)
▲ Anna Young Assoc Ltd .... G 516 546-4400
  Freeport (G-5144)
Apexx Omni-Graphics Inc .... D 718 326-3330
  Maspeth (G-7822)
Aquarium Pump & Piping Systems .... F 631 567-5555
  Sayville (G-14625)
▼ Armstrong Mold Corporation .... E 315 437-1517
  East Syracuse (G-4320)
Armstrong Mold Corporation .... D 315 437-1517
  East Syracuse (G-4321)
Atlas Fence & Railing Co Inc .... D 718 767-2200
  Whitestone (G-16535)
Auburn Vacuum Forming Co Inc .... F 315 253-2440
  Auburn (G-467)
▲ Autronic Plastics Inc .... D 516 333-7577
  Central Islip (G-3357)
▲ Avanti Advanced Mfg Corp .... F 716 791-9001
  Buffalo (G-2718)
Avanti U S A Ltd .... G 716 695-5800
  Tonawanda (G-15524)
Aztec Tool Co Inc .... E 631 243-1144
  Edgewood (G-4396)
▲ Baird Mold Making Inc .... G 631 667-0322
  Bay Shore (G-661)
◆ Baralan Usa Inc .... E 718 849-5768
  Richmond Hill (G-13497)
Barton Tool Inc .... G 716 665-2801
  Falconer (G-4672)
Berry Global Inc .... G 315 986-2161
  Macedon (G-7696)
Berry Global Inc .... C 315 484-0397
  Solvay (G-14916)
▲ Billie-Ann Plastics Pkg Corp .... F 718 497-3409
  Brooklyn (G-1612)
Bin Optics .... G 604 257-3200
  Ithaca (G-6561)
▼ Bo-Mer Plastics LLC .... E 315 252-7216
  Auburn (G-471)
Bragley Mfg Co Inc .... F 718 622-7469
  Brooklyn (G-1631)
Brandys Mold and Tool Ctr Ltd .... F 585 334-8333
  West Henrietta (G-16232)
Bst United Corp .... F 631 777-2110
  Farmingdale (G-4729)
Buffalo Polymer Processors Inc .... E 716 537-3153
  Holland (G-6218)
Burnham Polymeric Inc .... G 518 792-3040
  Fort Edward (G-5094)
Buttons & Trimcom Inc .... F 212 868-1971
  New York (G-9164)
C & M Products Inc .... G 315 471-3303
  Syracuse (G-15265)
▲ Cambridge Security Seals LLC .... E 845 520-4111
  Pomona (G-13185)
Capco Wai Shing LLC .... G 212 268-1976
  New York (G-9201)
Capitol Cups Inc .... E 518 627-0051
  Amsterdam (G-330)
Carolina Precision Plas LLC .... D 631 981-0743
  Ronkonkoma (G-14326)
Cast-All Corporation .... E 516 741-4025
  Mineola (G-8211)
Cast-All Corporation .... E 516 741-4025
  Mineola (G-8212)

Castino Corporation .... G 845 229-0341
  Hyde Park (G-6468)
Cdj Stamping Inc .... G 585 224-8120
  Rochester (G-13696)
▼ Cementex Latex Corp .... F 212 741-1770
  New York (G-9236)
Centro Inc .... B 212 791-9450
  New York (G-9249)
▲ Century Mold Company Inc .... D 585 352-8600
  Rochester (G-13701)
▲ Century Mold Mexico LLC .... E 585 352-8600
  Rochester (G-13702)
Certainteed Corporation .... B 716 827-7560
  Buffalo (G-2764)
▲ Champlain Plastics Inc .... D 518 297-3700
  Rouses Point (G-14467)
◆ Chem-Tainer Industries Inc .... E 631 422-8300
  West Babylon (G-16147)
Chem-Tek Systems Inc .... E 631 253-3010
  Bay Shore (G-670)
Chenango Valley Tech Inc .... E 607 674-4115
  Sherburne (G-14803)
Christi Plastics Inc .... G 585 436-8510
  Rochester (G-13710)
Cjk Manufacturing LLC .... F 585 663-6370
  Rochester (G-13712)
Clifford H Jones Inc .... F 716 693-2444
  Tonawanda (G-15534)
CN Group Incorporated .... A 914 358-5690
  White Plains (G-16438)
▲ Colonie Plastics Corp .... C 631 434-6969
  Bay Shore (G-673)
Color Craft Finishing Corp .... F 631 563-3230
  Bohemia (G-998)
Comet Intl Trdg Co Inc .... F 731 599-2430
  Brooklyn (G-1708)
▲ Commodore Machine Co Inc .... E 585 657-6916
  Bloomfield (G-950)
◆ Confer Plastics Inc .... C 800 635-3213
  North Tonawanda (G-12423)
Consolidated Container Co LLC .... F 585 343-9351
  Batavia (G-620)
Continental Latex Corp .... F 718 783-7883
  Brooklyn (G-1713)
CPI of Falconer Inc .... E 716 664-4444
  Falconer (G-4674)
Craftech .... D 518 828-5011
  Chatham (G-3427)
Craftech Industries Inc .... D 518 828-5001
  Hudson (G-6344)
▲ CSP Technologies Inc .... E 518 627-0051
  Amsterdam (G-334)
CT Industrial Supply Co Inc .... F 718 417-3226
  Brooklyn (G-1737)
▲ Currier Plastics Inc .... D 315 255-1779
  Auburn (G-474)
▲ Custom Door & Mirror Inc .... E 631 414-7725
  Farmingdale (G-4745)
▲ Custom House Engravers Inc .... E 631 567-3004
  Bohemia (G-1004)
Custom Lucite Creations Inc .... F 718 871-2000
  Brooklyn (G-1743)
Custom Molding Solutions Inc .... E 585 293-1702
  Churchville (G-3508)
▲ Cy Plastics Works Inc .... E 585 229-2555
  Honeoye (G-6260)
Dacobe Enterprises LLC .... F 315 368-0093
  Utica (G-15691)
Dawnex Industries Inc .... D 718 384-0199
  Brooklyn (G-1760)
Di Domenico Packaging Co Inc .... F 718 727-5454
  Staten Island (G-15068)
Diamond Packaging Holdings LLC .... E 585 334-8030
  Rochester (G-13739)
▲ Digitac Inc .... F 732 215-4020
  Brooklyn (G-1767)
Discover Casting Inc .... F 212 302-5060
  New York (G-9534)
Displays By Rioux Inc .... G 315 458-3639
  North Syracuse (G-12399)
▲ Dolco LLC .... E 585 657-7777
  Bloomfield (G-952)
Dortronics Systems Inc .... E 631 725-0505
  Sag Harbor (G-14499)
Dutchland Plastics LLC .... G 315 280-0247
  Sherrill (G-14820)
◆ E & T Plastic Mfg Co Inc .... F 718 729-6226
  Long Island City (G-7432)
East Cast Clor Compounding Inc .... G 631 491-9000
  West Babylon (G-16154)

Employee Codes: A=Over 500 employees, B=251-500
C=101-250, D=51-100, E=20-50, F=10-19, G=5-9

2019 Harris
New York Manufacturers Directory

30 RUBBER AND MISCELLANEOUS PLASTICS PRODUCTS

East Pattern & Model Corp ....F 585 461-3240
 Rochester *(G-13757)*
East Pattern & Model Corp ....E 585 461-3240
 Rochester *(G-13756)*
Eastern Enterprise Corp 718 727-8600
 Staten Island *(G-15073)*
Eastern Industrial Steel Corp ....F 845 639-9749
 New City *(G-8493)*
▲ Eck Plastic Arts Inc ....E 607 722-3227
 Binghamton *(G-880)*
Egli Machine Company Inc 607 563-3663
 Sidney *(G-14853)*
▲ Elara Fdsrvice Disposables LLC ......G 877 893-3244
 Jericho *(G-6786)*
Em-Kay Molds Inc ....G 716 895-6180
 Buffalo *(G-2816)*
▲ Engineered Composites Inc ....E 716 362-0295
 Buffalo *(G-2819)*
▲ Epp Team Inc ....D 585 454-4995
 Rochester *(G-13788)*
Erie Engineered Products Inc ....E 716 206-0204
 Lancaster *(G-7018)*
Ernie Green Industries Inc ....D 585 295-8951
 Rochester *(G-13790)*
Ernie Green Industries Inc ....C 585 647-2300
 Rochester *(G-13791)*
Ernie Green Industries Inc ....D 585 647-2300
 Rochester *(G-13792)*
▲ Etna Products Co Inc ....F 212 989-7591
 New York *(G-9722)*
▲ Eugene G Danner Mfg Inc ....E 631 234-5261
 Central Islip *(G-3368)*
Euro Woodworking Inc 718 246-9172
 Brooklyn *(G-1853)*
Everblock Systems LLC 844 422-5625
 New York *(G-9734)*
▲ Extreme Molding LLC ....E 518 326-9319
 Watervliet *(G-16045)*
Faro Industries Inc ....F 585 647-6000
 Rochester *(G-13802)*
Fbm Galaxy Inc ....F 315 463-5144
 East Syracuse *(G-4338)*
Fei Products LLC 716 693-6230
 North Tonawanda *(G-12427)*
◆ Felchar Manufacturing Corp ....A 607 723-3106
 Binghamton *(G-884)*
Fiber Laminations Limited ....F 716 692-1825
 Tonawanda *(G-15540)*
▲ Fibre Materials Corp ....E 516 349-1660
 Plainview *(G-13058)*
▲ Finger Lakes Extrusion Corp ....E 585 905-0632
 Canandaigua *(G-3221)*
Form A Rockland Plastics Inc ....G 315 848-3300
 Cranberry Lake *(G-3907)*
Form-Tec Inc ....E 516 867-0200
 Freeport *(G-5155)*
Formatix Corp ....E 631 467-3399
 Ronkonkoma *(G-14342)*
Formed Plastics Inc 516 334-2300
 Carle Place *(G-3264)*
▲ Forteq North America Inc ....D 585 427-9410
 West Henrietta *(G-16239)*
Frisch Plastics Corp ....E 973 685-5936
 Hartsdale *(G-5743)*
G and G Service ....G 518 785-9247
 Latham *(G-7073)*
G N R Plastics Inc 631 724-8758
 Smithtown *(G-14899)*
▲ Gagne Associates Inc 800 800-5954
 Johnson City *(G-6808)*
▲ Galt Industries Inc ....G 212 758-0770
 New York *(G-9878)*
◆ Gary Plastic Packaging Corp ....B 718 893-2200
 Bronx *(G-1279)*
Gen-West Associates LLC ....G 315 255-1779
 Auburn *(G-481)*
▲ General Composites Inc ....E 518 963-7333
 Willsboro *(G-16599)*
Genpak LLC ....C 845 343-7971
 Middletown *(G-8155)*
◆ Germanow-Simon Corporation ......E 585 232-1440
 Rochester *(G-13832)*
▲ Global Hanger & Display Inc ....G 631 475-5900
 East Patchogue *(G-4274)*
Global Marine Power Inc 631 208-2933
 Calverton *(G-3166)*
Global Security Tech LLC 917 838-4507
 Cedarhurst *(G-3332)*
GPM Associates LLC ....E 585 335-3940
 Dansville *(G-3926)*

GSE Composites Inc ....F 631 389-1300
 Hauppauge *(G-5837)*
H & H Hulls Inc ....G 518 828-1339
 Hudson *(G-6352)*
H Risch Inc ....D 585 442-0110
 Rochester *(G-13848)*
▲ Hamlet Products Inc ....F 914 665-0307
 Mount Vernon *(G-8405)*
▲ Hansa Plastics Inc ....F 631 269-9050
 Kings Park *(G-6883)*
Harbec Inc ....D 585 265-0010
 Ontario *(G-12654)*
Hart To Hart Industries Inc 716 492-2709
 Chaffee *(G-3404)*
Highland Injection Molding 716 945-2424
 Salamanca *(G-14525)*
Hornet Group Inc ....D 845 858-6400
 Port Jervis *(G-13230)*
Howard Charles Inc 917 902-6934
 Woodbury *(G-16621)*
Iadc Inc ....F 718 238-0623
 Staten Island *(G-15088)*
Ilion Plastics Inc ....F 315 894-4868
 Ilion *(G-6475)*
Illinois Tool Works Inc ....D 860 435-2574
 Millerton *(G-8194)*
Imco Inc 585 352-7810
 Spencerport *(G-14979)*
Imperial Polymers Inc ....G 718 387-4741
 Brooklyn *(G-1996)*
Industrial Paper Tube Inc ....F 718 893-5000
 Bronx *(G-1296)*
◆ Ingenious Designs LLC ....C 631 254-3376
 Ronkonkoma *(G-14353)*
▼ Innovative Plastics Corp ....C 845 359-7500
 Orangeburg *(G-12680)*
Inteva Products LLC ....B 248 655-8886
 New York *(G-10255)*
Iridium Industries Inc ....E 516 504-9700
 Great Neck *(G-5563)*
▲ ISO Plastics Corp ....D 914 663-8300
 Mount Vernon *(G-8410)*
J M R Plastics Corporation ....G 718 898-9825
 Middle Village *(G-8122)*
J T Systematic 607 754-0929
 Endwell *(G-4617)*
Jamestown Plastics Inc ....D 716 792-4144
 Brocton *(G-1196)*
Joe Pietryka Incorporated 845 855-1201
 Pawling *(G-12892)*
JSM Vinyl Products Inc 516 775-4520
 New Hyde Park *(G-8545)*
▲ K & H Industries Inc ....F 716 312-0088
 Hamburg *(G-5683)*
K & H Industries Inc ....F 716 312-0088
 Hamburg *(G-5684)*
K & H Precision Products Inc ....E 585 624-4894
 Honeoye Falls *(G-6269)*
K2 Plastics Inc ....G 585 494-2727
 Bergen *(G-822)*
Kaneka America LLC ....D 212 705-4340
 New York *(G-10404)*
▲ Kasson & Keller Inc ....A 518 853-3421
 Fonda *(G-5065)*
Kc Tag Co ....G 518 842-6666
 Amsterdam *(G-343)*
▲ Kelta Inc ....E 631 789-5000
 Edgewood *(G-4406)*
Kenney Manufacturing Displays ......F 631 231-5563
 Brentwood *(G-1139)*
Kernow North America ....F 585 586-3590
 Pittsford *(G-13017)*
▲ Kleer-Fax Inc ....F 631 225-1100
 Amityville *(G-295)*
▲ Kling Magnetics Inc ....E 518 392-4000
 Chatham *(G-3428)*
◆ Kobe Steel USA Holdings Inc ......G 212 751-9400
 New York *(G-10462)*
▲ Koonichi Inc ....G 718 886-8338
 Fresh Meadows *(G-5201)*
L I C Screen Printing Inc 516 546-7289
 Merrick *(G-8100)*
L K Manufacturing Corp ....E 631 243-6910
 West Babylon *(G-16169)*
Leidel Corporation 631 244-0900
 Bohemia *(G-1047)*
▲ Line By Line Design Inc ....G 716 655-4680
 East Aurora *(G-4203)*
▲ M & M Molding Corp ....C 631 582-1900
 Central Islip *(G-3377)*

M I T Poly-Cart Corp ....G 212 724-7290
 New York *(G-10640)*
▲ Macauto Usa Inc ....E 585 342-2060
 Rochester *(G-13919)*
Madison Lifestyle Ny LLC ....G 212 725-4002
 New York *(G-10657)*
▲ Major-IPC Inc ....G 845 292-2200
 Liberty *(G-7145)*
Mam Molding Inc ....E 607 433-2121
 Oneonta *(G-12639)*
Markwik Corp ....F 516 470-1990
 Hicksville *(G-6108)*
▲ Marval Industries Inc ....G 914 381-2400
 Mamaroneck *(G-7748)*
Mdi East Inc ....E 518 747-8730
 South Glens Falls *(G-14937)*
Mechanical Rubber Pdts Co Inc ......F 845 986-2271
 Warwick *(G-15958)*
Memory Protection Devices Inc ......F 631 249-0001
 Farmingdale *(G-4819)*
▲ Mercury Plastics Corp ....E 718 498-5400
 Brooklyn *(G-2195)*
▲ Metal Cladding Inc ....D 716 434-5513
 Lockport *(G-7316)*
Metropltan Data Sltons MGT Inc .....F 516 586-5520
 Farmingdale *(G-4822)*
Mettowee Lumber & Plastics Co .....C 518 642-1100
 Granville *(G-5522)*
Micromold Products Inc ....E 914 969-2850
 Yonkers *(G-16784)*
Midbury Industries Inc ....F 516 868-0600
 Freeport *(G-5168)*
Miller Technology Inc ....G 631 694-2224
 Farmingdale *(G-4826)*
Milne Mfg Inc ....F 716 772-2536
 Gasport *(G-5308)*
Minico Industries Inc ....G 631 595-1455
 Bay Shore *(G-702)*
▲ Mirage Moulding Mfg Inc ....F 631 843-6168
 Farmingdale *(G-4827)*
▲ Mold-A-Matic Corporation ....E 607 433-2121
 Oneonta *(G-12641)*
Mold-Rite Plastics LLC ....G 518 561-1812
 Plattsburgh *(G-13134)*
▲ Monarch Plastics Inc ....E 716 569-2175
 Frewsburg *(G-5209)*
▲ Msi-Molding Solutions Inc ....E 315 736-2412
 Rome *(G-14259)*
◆ Multi Packaging Solutions Inc .....E 646 885-0005
 New York *(G-10858)*
▲ Nalge Nunc International Corp ....A 585 498-2661
 Rochester *(G-13962)*
Natech Plastics Inc ....E 631 580-3506
 Ronkonkoma *(G-14383)*
Neo Plastics LLC ....F 646 542-1499
 Brooklyn *(G-2253)*
New York Cutting & Gumming Co 212 563-4146
 Middletown *(G-8168)*
New York Manufactured Products ...F 585 254-9353
 Rochester *(G-13967)*
Niagara Fiberglass Inc ....E 716 822-3921
 Buffalo *(G-2966)*
◆ Nordon Inc ....D 585 546-6200
 Rochester *(G-13974)*
Nordon Inc ....E 585 546-6200
 Rochester *(G-13975)*
Nordon Inc ....E 585 546-6200
 Rochester *(G-13976)*
▲ Northeast Windows Usa Inc ....E 516 378-6577
 Merrick *(G-8104)*
Norwesco Inc ....F 607 687-8081
 Owego *(G-12801)*
▲ Novel Box Company Ltd ....E 718 965-2222
 Brooklyn *(G-2275)*
▲ Novelty Crystal Corp ....D 718 458-6700
 Long Island City *(G-7540)*
◆ Ocala Group LLC ....F 516 233-2750
 New Hyde Park *(G-8555)*
▲ Oneida Molded Plastics LLC ....C 315 363-7980
 Oneida *(G-12616)*
Oneida Molded Plastics LLC ....D 315 363-7990
 Oneida *(G-12617)*
Oneonta Fence ....G 607 433-6707
 Oneonta *(G-12642)*
▲ Ontario Plastics Inc ....E 585 663-2644
 Rochester *(G-13989)*
P M Plastics Inc ....E 716 662-1255
 Orchard Park *(G-12733)*
P V C Molding Technologies ....F 315 331-1212
 Newark *(G-12204)*

Pace Window and Door Corp .... E 585 924-8350
Victor (G-15860)
Pactiv Corporation .... C 518 743-3100
Glens Falls (G-5438)
Pactiv LLC 847 482-2000
Canandaigua (G-3229)
Pactiv LLC .... C 518 562-6120
Plattsburgh (G-13143)
Pactiv LLC .... A 585 393-3149
Canandaigua (G-3230)
Pactiv LLC .... A 585 394-5125
Canandaigua (G-3228)
Pactiv LLC .... C 518 793-2524
Glens Falls (G-5439)
Patmian LLC .... B 212 758-0770
New York (G-11122)
▼ Pawling Corporation .... C 845 855-1000
Pawling (G-12893)
Pawling Engineered Pdts Inc .... C 845 855-1000
Pawling (G-12894)
Peconic Plastics Inc .... F 631 653-3676
Quogue (G-13146)
▲ Peek A Boo USA Inc .... G 201 533-8700
New York (G-11135)
▲ Pelican Products Co Inc .... E 718 860-3220
Bronx (G-1354)
Peninsula Plastics Ltd .... D 716 854-3050
Buffalo (G-2996)
Performance Advantage Co Inc .... F 716 683-7413
Lancaster (G-7039)
Perma Tech Inc .... E 716 854-0707
Buffalo (G-3000)
Philcom Ltd .... F 716 875-8005
Buffalo (G-3001)
Pii Holdings Inc .... G 716 876-9951
Buffalo (G-3004)
Piper Plastics Corp .... E 631 842-6889
Copiague (G-3772)
Piper Plastics Corp .... G 631 842-6889
Copiague (G-3773)
Plascoline Inc .... F 917 410-5754
New York (G-11206)
Plastic Solutions Inc .... E 631 234-9013
Bayport (G-738)
Plastic Sys/Gr Bflo Inc .... D 716 835-7555
Buffalo (G-3007)
Plastic Works .... G 914 576-2050
New Rochelle (G-8622)
Plastic-Craft Products Corp .... E 845 358-3010
West Nyack (G-16280)
Plasticware LLC .... F 845 267-0790
Monsey (G-8293)
Plasticycle Corporation .... E 914 997-6882
White Plains (G-16498)
Plastitel Usa Inc .... G 450 687-0600
Chazy (G-3433)
Pleasure Chest Sales Ltd .... F 212 242-2158
New York (G-11209)
◆ PMI Industries LLC .... E 585 464-8050
Rochester (G-14025)
Polymer Conversions Inc .... D 716 662-8550
Orchard Park (G-12737)
Polymer Engineered Pdts Inc .... D 585 426-1811
Rochester (G-14027)
◆ Powertex Inc .... E 518 297-4000
Rouses Point (G-14469)
Precision Extrusion Inc .... E 518 792-1199
Glens Falls (G-5440)
▲ Precision Packaging Pdts Inc .... C 585 638-8200
Holley (G-6228)
▲ Precision Techniques Inc .... D 718 991-1440
Stony Point (G-15175)
Prestige Hangers Str Fixs Corp .... G 718 522-6777
Brooklyn (G-2341)
Primoplast Inc .... F 631 750-0680
Bohemia (G-1078)
▲ Prince Rubber & Plas Co Inc .... E 225 272-1653
Buffalo (G-3014)
▲ Printex Packaging Corporation .... D 631 234-4300
Islandia (G-6537)
◆ Protective Industries Inc .... C 716 876-9951
Buffalo (G-3017)
Protective Industries Inc .... C 716 876-9855
Buffalo (G-3018)
▲ Protective Lining Corp .... D 718 854-3838
Brooklyn (G-2358)
Pulse Plastics Products Inc .... E 718 328-5224
Bronx (G-1367)
Pvc Container Corporation .... C 518 672-7721
Philmont (G-12987)

Pvc Industries Inc .... E 518 877-8670
Clifton Park (G-3574)
Pylantis New York LLC .... G 310 429-5911
Groton (G-5653)
▲ Q Squared Design LLC .... E 212 686-8860
New York (G-11290)
Quality Lineals Usa Inc .... D 516 378-6577
Merrick (G-8106)
Quoin LLC .... A 914 967-9400
Rye (G-14487)
▲ R P M Industries Inc .... C 315 255-1105
Auburn (G-497)
▲ Rainbow Plastics Inc .... F 718 218-7288
Brooklyn (G-2381)
Richlar Industries Inc .... F 315 463-5144
East Syracuse (G-4366)
Rimco Plastics Corp .... E 607 739-3864
Horseheads (G-6326)
Robinson Knife .... F 716 685-6300
Buffalo (G-3041)
Rochling Advent Tool & Mold LP .... D 585 254-2000
Rochester (G-14100)
▲ Poth Global Plastics Inc .... F 315 475-0100
Syracuse (G-15410)
◆ Royal Industries Inc .... E 718 369-3046
Brooklyn (G-2420)
▲ Royal Plastics Corp .... F 718 647-7500
Brooklyn (G-2423)
Royce Associates A Ltd Partnr .... G 516 367-6298
Jericho (G-6800)
▲ Rui Xing International Trdg Co .... G 516 298-2667
Hicksville (G-6129)
Rus Auto Parts Inc .... G 800 410-2669
Brooklyn (G-2427)
Russell Plastics Tech Co Inc .... C 631 963-8602
Lindenhurst (G-7191)
Saint-Gobain Prfmce Plas Corp .... E 518 283-5963
Poestenkill (G-13182)
SAV Thermo Inc .... F 631 249-9444
West Babylon (G-16191)
▲ Schlegel Systems Inc .... C 585 427-7200
Rochester (G-14115)
Seal Reinforced Fiberglass Inc .... E 631 842-2230
Copiague (G-3780)
Seal Reinforced Fiberglass Inc 631 842-2230
Copiague (G-3781)
Seaway Mats Inc 518 483-2560
Malone (G-7726)
Shamrock Plastic Corporation .... G 585 328-6040
Rochester (G-14124)
Shamrock Plastics & Tool Inc 585 328-6040
Rochester (G-14125)
Sigma Worldwide LLC 646 217-0629
New York (G-11583)
Silgan Plastics LLC .... C 315 536-5690
Penn Yan (G-12966)
Silvatrim Corp 212 675-0933
New York (G-11590)
▲ Skd Distribution Corp .... E 718 525-6000
Jericho (G-6805)
▲ Sonoco-Crellin Intl Inc .... B 518 392-2000
Chatham (G-3431)
▲ Southern Tier Plastics Inc 607 723-2601
Binghamton (G-915)
Space Age Plstic Fbrcators Inc .... F 718 324-4062
Bronx (G-1388)
Space Sign .... F 718 961-1112
College Point (G-3667)
Specialty Model & Mold Inc .... G 631 475-0840
Ronkonkoma (G-14416)
Specialty Products Inc .... E 866 869-4335
Center Moriches (G-3341)
Staroba Plastics Inc .... C 716 537-3153
Holland (G-6222)
▲ Sterling Molded Products Inc .... E 845 344-4546
Middletown (G-8177)
▲ Structural Industries Inc .... C 631 471-5200
Bohemia (G-1092)
Stuart Mold & Manufacturing .... F 716 488-9765
Falconer (G-4693)
◆ Summit Manufacturing LLC 631 952-1570
Bay Shore (G-728)
▲ Supreme Poultry Inc .... F 718 472-0300
Long Island City (G-7610)
▲ Surprise Plastics Inc .... C 718 492-6355
Brooklyn (G-2543)
Sweet Tooth Enterprises LLC .... F 631 752-2888
West Babylon (G-16199)
Syntec Technologies Inc .... E 585 768-2513
Rochester (G-14152)

▲ Syracuse Plastics LLC .... C 315 637-9881
Liverpool (G-7265)
T A Tool & Molding Inc .... F 631 293-0172
Farmingdale (G-4888)
Termatec Molding Inc .... F 315 483-4150
Sodus (G-14915)
◆ Tessy Plastics Corp .... B 315 689-3924
Skaneateles (G-14878)
Tessy Plastics Corp .... A 315 689-3924
Elbridge (G-4429)
▲ Thermold Corporation .... C 315 697-3924
Canastota (G-3249)
Think Green Junk Removal Inc .... G 845 297-7771
Wappingers Falls (G-15937)
▲ Tii Technologies Inc .... E 516 364-9300
Edgewood (G-4419)
Tint World .... G 631 458-1999
Medford (G-7967)
Titherington Design & Mfg .... F 518 324-2205
Plattsburgh (G-13163)
▲ Toolroom Express Inc .... D 607 723-5373
Conklin (G-3735)
Toray Industries Inc .... G 212 697-8150
New York (G-11869)
▲ Transpo Industries Inc .... E 914 636-1000
New Rochelle (G-8630)
Tri-State Window Factory Corp .... D 631 667-8600
Deer Park (G-4052)
Trimac Molding Services .... G 607 967-2900
Bainbridge (G-535)
Tulip Molded Plastics Corp .... D 716 282-1261
Niagara Falls (G-12344)
Tully Products Inc .... G 716 773-3166
Grand Island (G-5516)
▲ TVI Imports LLC .... F 631 793-3077
Massapequa Park (G-7895)
Unifab Inc .... G 585 235-1760
Rochester (G-14186)
Unifuse LLC .... F 845 889-4000
Staatsburg (G-15025)
United Plastics Inc .... G 718 389-2255
Brooklyn (G-2603)
Usheco Inc .... F 845 658-9200
Kingston (G-6930)
▲ Van Blarcom Closures Inc .... C 718 855-3810
Brooklyn (G-2615)
◆ Viele Manufacturing Corp .... B 718 893-2200
Bronx (G-1416)
Villeroy & Boch Usa Inc .... F 212 213-8149
New York (G-12035)
Vinyl Materials Inc .... E 631 586-9444
Deer Park (G-4060)
Vinyline Window and Door Inc ..... G 914 476-3500
Yonkers (G-16806)
Visitainer Corp .... E 718 636-0300
Brooklyn (G-2629)
Vitarose Corp of America .... G 718 951-9700
Brooklyn (G-2630)
Vpulse Inc .... G 646 729-5675
Brooklyn (G-2635)
◆ W Kintz Plastics Inc .... F 518 296-8513
Howes Cave (G-6334)
Waddington North America Inc ... F 585 638-8200
Holley (G-6230)
Weather Products Corporation ..... G 315 474-8593
Syracuse (G-15455)
Weber Intl Packg Co LLC .... D 518 561-8282
Plattsburgh (G-13168)
Window Tech Systems Inc .... E 518 899-9000
Ballston Spa (G-598)
Zone Fabricators Inc .... F 718 272-0200
Ozone Park (G-12834)

31 LEATHER AND LEATHER PRODUCTS

3111 Leather Tanning & Finishing

A-1 Products Inc .... G 718 789-1818
Brooklyn (G-1462)
▲ Adam Scott Designs Inc .... E 212 420-8866
New York (G-8732)
▲ Androme Leather Inc .... F 518 773-7945
Gloversville (G-5451)
Ariel Tian LLC .... G 212 457-1266
Forest Hills (G-5072)
▲ Arrow Leather Finishing Inc .... E 518 762-3121
Johnstown (G-6823)
▲ Aston Leather Inc .... G 212 481-2760
New York (G-8940)

31 LEATHER AND LEATHER PRODUCTS

Automotive Leather Group LLC .... F 516 627-4000
 Great Neck *(G-5537)*
▲ Baker Products Inc .... G 212 459-2323
 White Plains *(G-16425)*
Centric Brands Inc .... D 323 890-1800
 New York *(G-9246)*
▲ Colonial Tanning Corporation .... G 518 725-7171
 Gloversville *(G-5454)*
▲ Corium Corporation .... F 914 381-0100
 Mamaroneck *(G-7740)*
▲ Edsim Leather Co Inc .... E 212 695-8500
 New York *(G-9630)*
Givi Inc .... F 212 586-5029
 New York *(G-9926)*
Graphic Image Associates LLC .... D 631 249-9600
 Melville *(G-8028)*
Hastings Hide Inc .... G 516 295-2400
 Inwood *(G-6492)*
◆ Hat Attack Inc .... E 718 994-1000
 Bronx *(G-1288)*
Hohenforst Splitting Co Inc .... G 518 725-0012
 Gloversville *(G-5458)*
John Gailer Inc .... E 212 243-5662
 Long Island City *(G-7480)*
Justin Gregory Inc .... G 631 249-5187
 Deer Park *(G-3994)*
Kamali Automotive Group Inc .... F 516 627-4000
 Great Neck *(G-5566)*
▲ Kamali Group Inc .... G 516 627-4000
 Great Neck *(G-5567)*
▲ Legendary Auto Interiors Ltd .... E 315 331-1212
 Newark *(G-12198)*
Mohawk River Leather Works .... F 518 853-3900
 Fultonville *(G-5237)*
◆ Myers Group LLC .... G 973 761-6414
 New York *(G-10866)*
▲ Pacific Worldwide Inc .... F 212 502-3360
 New York *(G-11091)*
▲ Pan American Leathers Inc .... G 978 741-4150
 New York *(G-11097)*
▲ Pearl Leather Finishers Inc .... F 518 762-4543
 Johnstown *(G-6836)*
▲ Pearl Leather Group LLC .... G 516 627-4047
 Great Neck *(G-5580)*
▲ Rainbow Leather Inc .... F 718 939-8762
 College Point *(G-3663)*
Shadal LLC .... G 212 319-5946
 New York *(G-11551)*
▲ Simco Leather Corporation .... E 518 762-7100
 Johnstown *(G-6840)*
▲ Street Smart Designs Inc .... G 646 865-0056
 New York *(G-11720)*
Studio One Leather Design Inc .... F 212 760-1701
 New York *(G-11728)*
System of AME Binding .... G 631 390-8560
 Central Islip *(G-3386)*
Tandy Leather Factory Inc .... G 845 480-3588
 Nyack *(G-12511)*
Vic Demayos Inc .... G 845 626-4343
 Accord *(G-1)*
◆ Wood & Hyde Leather Co Inc .... E 518 725-7105
 Gloversville *(G-5474)*

3131 Boot & Shoe Cut Stock & Findings

▲ Age Manufacturers Inc .... D 718 927-0048
 Brooklyn *(G-1494)*
Counter Evolution .... G 212 647-7505
 New York *(G-9407)*
Custom Countertops Inc .... G 716 685-2871
 Depew *(G-4085)*
Custom Design Kitchens Inc .... F 518 355-4446
 Duanesburg *(G-4155)*
MBA Orthotics Inc .... G 631 392-4755
 Bay Shore *(G-699)*
Northwest Urgent Care .... G 646 870-6406
 New York *(G-10998)*
▲ Premier Brands America Inc .... C 914 667-6200
 Mount Vernon *(G-8432)*
Premier Brands of America Inc .... G 718 325-3000
 Bronx *(G-1364)*
Priscilla Quart Co Firts .... G 516 365-2755
 Manhasset *(G-7771)*
▲ Randall Loeffler Inc .... E 212 226-8787
 New York *(G-11326)*
Wash Quarters LLC .... G 989 802-2017
 Wallkill *(G-15909)*

3142 House Slippers

RG Barry Corporation .... F 212 244-3145
 New York *(G-11382)*

3143 Men's Footwear, Exc Athletic

Air Skate & Air Jump Corp .... G 212 967-1201
 New York *(G-8778)*
▲ Air Skate & Air Jump Corp .... F 212 967-1201
 Brooklyn *(G-1496)*
▲ Detny Footwear Inc .... G 212 423-1040
 New York *(G-9511)*
▲ GH Bass & Co .... E 646 768-4600
 New York *(G-9917)*
◆ Jerry Miller Molded Shoes Inc .... F 716 881-3920
 Buffalo *(G-2893)*
Kcp Holdco Inc .... E 212 265-1500
 New York *(G-10426)*
Kenneth Cole Productions LP .... E 212 265-1500
 New York *(G-10430)*
▲ Kenneth Cole Productions Inc .... B 212 265-1500
 New York *(G-10431)*
Lake View Manufacturing LLC .... F 315 364-7892
 King Ferry *(G-6881)*
▲ Neumann Jutta New York Inc .... F 212 982-7048
 New York *(G-10914)*
Nicholas Kirkwood LLC .... G 646 559-5239
 New York *(G-10962)*
▲ Pedifix Inc .... G 845 277-2850
 Brewster *(G-1173)*
Phillips-Van Heusen Europe .... E 212 381-3500
 New York *(G-11183)*
◆ Pvh Corp .... G 212 381-3500
 New York *(G-11281)*
Pvh Corp .... G 212 549-6000
 New York *(G-11282)*
Steven Madden Ltd .... B 718 446-1800
 Long Island City *(G-7604)*
T O Dey Service Corp .... F 212 683-6300
 New York *(G-11770)*
◆ Tapestry Inc .... B 212 594-1850
 New York *(G-11784)*
▲ Tic TAC Toes Mfg Corp .... D 518 773-8187
 Gloversville *(G-5470)*
Tru Mold Shoes Inc .... F 716 881-4484
 Buffalo *(G-3105)*

3144 Women's Footwear, Exc Athletic

▲ Adl Design Inc .... G 516 949-6658
 Huntington *(G-6390)*
Akh Group LLC .... G 646 320-8720
 New York *(G-8780)*
◆ Alpargatas Usa Inc .... E 646 277-7171
 New York *(G-8807)*
Attitudes Footwear Inc .... G 212 754-9113
 New York *(G-8959)*
▲ Detny Footwear Inc .... G 212 423-1040
 New York *(G-9511)*
Everlast Worldwide Inc .... E 212 239-0990
 New York *(G-9738)*
▲ GH Bass & Co .... E 646 768-4600
 New York *(G-9917)*
Jag Footwear ACC & Ret Corp .... A 800 999-1877
 New York *(G-10299)*
◆ Jerry Miller Molded Shoes Inc .... F 716 881-3920
 Buffalo *(G-2893)*
▲ Kenneth Cole Productions Inc .... B 212 265-1500
 New York *(G-10431)*
Lake View Manufacturing LLC .... F 315 364-7892
 King Ferry *(G-6881)*
Lsil & Co Inc .... G 914 761-0998
 White Plains *(G-16473)*
▲ Mango Usa Inc .... E 718 998-6050
 Brooklyn *(G-2156)*
▲ Neumann Jutta New York Inc .... F 212 982-7048
 New York *(G-10914)*
Nicholas Kirkwood LLC .... G 646 559-5239
 New York *(G-10962)*
Nine West Holdings Inc .... G 212 642-3860
 New York *(G-10976)*
▲ Pedifix Inc .... E 845 277-2850
 Brewster *(G-1173)*
S & W Ladies Wear .... G 718 431-2800
 Brooklyn *(G-2437)*
Scott Silverstein Llc .... G 212 781-1818
 New York *(G-11522)*
Steven Madden Ltd .... D 212 695-5545
 New York *(G-11709)*
Steven Madden Ltd .... B 718 446-1800
 Long Island City *(G-7604)*
T O Dey Service Corp .... F 212 683-6300
 New York *(G-11770)*
◆ Tapestry Inc .... B 212 594-1850
 New York *(G-11784)*
▲ Tic TAC Toes Mfg Corp .... D 518 773-8187
 Gloversville *(G-5470)*
Tru Mold Shoes Inc .... F 716 881-4484
 Buffalo *(G-3105)*

3149 Footwear, NEC

Custom Sports Lab Inc .... G 212 832-1648
 New York *(G-9436)*
Everlast Worldwide Inc .... E 212 239-0990
 New York *(G-9738)*
▲ GH Bass & Co .... E 646 768-4600
 New York *(G-9917)*
Kicks Closet Sportswear Inc .... G 347 577-0857
 Bronx *(G-1308)*
La Strada Dance Footwear Inc .... G 631 242-1401
 Deer Park *(G-3999)*
▲ Mango Usa Inc .... E 718 998-6050
 Brooklyn *(G-2156)*
Mayberry Shoe Company Inc .... G 315 692-4086
 Manlius *(G-7780)*
McM Products USA Inc .... E 646 756-4090
 New York *(G-10744)*
Reebok International Ltd .... E 718 370-0471
 Staten Island *(G-15126)*
Steven Madden Ltd .... B 718 446-1800
 Long Island City *(G-7604)*
▲ Vsg International LLC .... G 718 300-8171
 Brooklyn *(G-2636)*

3151 Leather Gloves & Mittens

American Target Marketing Inc .... E 518 725-4369
 Gloversville *(G-5450)*
▲ Fieldtex Products Inc .... C 585 427-2940
 Rochester *(G-13803)*
◆ Fownes Brothers & Co Inc .... E 212 683-0150
 New York *(G-9834)*
Fownes Brothers & Co Inc .... E 518 752-4411
 Gloversville *(G-5456)*
▲ J & D Walter Distributors Inc .... E 518 449-1606
 Glenmont *(G-5413)*
Protech (llc) .... E 518 725-7785
 Gloversville *(G-5463)*
Samco LLC .... E 518 725-4705
 Gloversville *(G-5464)*
USA Sewing Inc .... E 315 792-8017
 Utica *(G-15736)*

3161 Luggage

▲ 212 Biz LLC .... G 212 391-4444
 New York *(G-8669)*
▲ Adam Scott Designs Inc .... E 212 420-8866
 New York *(G-8732)*
▲ Aka Sport Inc .... F 631 858-9888
 Dix Hills *(G-4118)*
Atlantic Specialty Co Inc .... E 845 356-2502
 Monsey *(G-8286)*
Barclay Brown Corp .... F 718 376-7166
 Brooklyn *(G-1586)*
Bragley Mfg Co Inc .... E 718 622-7469
 Brooklyn *(G-1631)*
Calvin Klein Inc .... E 212 292-9000
 New York *(G-9184)*
▲ Carry-All Canvas Bag Co Inc .... G 718 375-4230
 Brooklyn *(G-1678)*
Deluxe Travel Store Inc .... G 718 435-8111
 Brooklyn *(G-1767)*
◆ Dlx Industries Inc .... D 718 272-9420
 Brooklyn *(G-1784)*
Donna Morgan LLC .... E 212 575-2550
 New York *(G-9554)*
Ead Cases .... F 845 343-2111
 Middletown *(G-8149)*
Fibre Case & Novelty Co Inc .... G 212 254-6060
 New York *(G-9798)*
▲ Fieldtex Products Inc .... C 585 427-2940
 Rochester *(G-13803)*
◆ Fish & Crown Ltd .... D 212 707-9603
 New York *(G-9813)*
▲ Golden Bridge Group Inc .... G 718 335-8882
 Elmhurst *(G-4467)*
Goyard Inc .... G 212 813-0005
 New York *(G-9963)*
Goyard Miami LLC .... G 212 813-0005
 New York *(G-9964)*
▲ Goyard NM Beverly Hills LLC .... G 212 355-3872
 New York *(G-9965)*
Hornet Group Inc .... D 845 858-6400
 Port Jervis *(G-13230)*
Junk In My Trunk Inc .... G 631 420-5865
 Farmingdale *(G-4795)*

▲ Lo & Sons Inc ....F 917 775-4025
Brooklyn (G-2132)
▲ Merzon Leather Co Inc ....C 718 782-6260
Brooklyn (G-2197)
▲ Prepac Designs Inc ....G 914 524-7800
Yonkers (G-16794)
Progressive Fibre Products Co ....E 212 566-2720
New York (G-11258)
Randa Accessories Lea Gds LLC ....D 212 354-5100
New York (G-11325)
Rhino Trunk & Case Inc ....F 585 244-4553
Rochester (G-14071)
▲ Roadie Products Inc ....E 631 567-8588
Holbrook (G-6206)
◆ Rose Trunk Mfg Co Inc ....F 516 766-6686
Oceanside (G-12554)
◆ Royal Industries Inc ....E 718 369-3046
Brooklyn (G-2420)
Sigma Worldwide LLC ....G 646 217-0629
New York (G-11583)
▲ Three Point Ventures LLC ....F 585 697-3444
Rochester (G-14168)
▲ Trafalgar Company LLC ....G 212 768-8800
New York (G-11885)
▲ Trunk & Trolley LLC ....G 212 947-9001
New York (G-11905)
Xstatic Pro Inc ....F 718 237-2299
Brooklyn (G-2660)

3171 Handbags & Purses

▲ Affordable Luxury Group Inc ....G 631 523-9266
New York (G-8765)
▲ Ahq LLC ....E 212 328-1560
New York (G-8773)
Akh Group LLC ....G 646 320-8720
New York (G-8780)
Atalla Handbags Inc ....G 718 965-5500
Brooklyn (G-1567)
▲ Bagznyc Corp ....F 212 643-8202
New York (G-9003)
▲ Baikal Inc ....D 212 239-4650
New York (G-9004)
Coach Inc ....F 718 760-0624
Elmhurst (G-4463)
Coach Leatherware Intl ....G 212 594-1850
New York (G-9339)
Coach Services Inc ....G 212 594-1850
New York (G-9340)
Dani Accessories Inc ....E 631 692-4505
Cold Spring Harbor (G-3630)
Deux Lux Inc ....G 212 620-0801
New York (G-9513)
◆ Essex Manufacturing Inc ....D 212 239-0080
New York (G-9712)
Formart Corp ....F 212 819-1819
New York (G-9824)
Jag Footwear ACC & Ret Corp ....A 800 999-1877
New York (G-10299)
Kcp Holdco Inc ....F 212 265-1500
New York (G-10426)
▲ Kenneth Cole Productions Inc ....B 212 265-1500
New York (G-10431)
McM Products USA Inc ....E 646 756-4090
New York (G-10744)
Paradiso Cnsld Entps LLC ....G 585 924-3937
Rochester (G-14007)
▲ Pure Trade Us Inc ....E 212 256-1600
New York (G-11276)
Quilted Koala Ltd ....F 800 223-5678
New York (G-11302)
◆ Renco Group Inc ....G 212 541-6000
New York (G-11361)
▲ Roadie Products Inc ....E 631 567-8588
Holbrook (G-6206)
▲ Rodem Incorporated ....F 212 779-7122
New York (G-11418)
Tapestry Inc ....G 212 615-2082
New York (G-11783)
◆ Tapestry Inc ....B 212 594-1850
New York (G-11784)

3172 Personal Leather Goods

▲ Ada Gems Corp ....G 212 719-0100
New York (G-8731)
American Puff Corp ....D 516 379-1300
Freeport (G-5143)
Astucci US Ltd ....F 718 752-9700
Long Island City (G-7392)
▲ Astucci US Ltd ....G 212 725-3171
New York (G-8941)
Atlantic Specialty Co Inc ....E 845 356-2502
Monsey (G-8286)
▲ Baker Products Inc ....G 212 459-2323
White Plains (G-16425)
▲ Bauble Bar Inc ....E 646 846-2044
New York (G-9027)
▲ Datamax International Inc ....E 212 693-0933
New York (G-9476)
Elco Manufacturing Co Inc ....F 516 767-3577
Port Washington (G-13257)
▲ Excelled Sheepskin & Lea Coat ....F 212 594-5843
New York (G-9750)
Fahrenheit NY Inc ....G 212 354-6554
New York (G-9772)
▲ First Manufacturing Co Inc ....E 516 763-0400
Oceanside (G-12538)
Form A Rockland Plastics Inc ....G 315 848-3300
Cranberry Lake (G-3907)
Grownbeans Inc ....G 212 989-3486
New York (G-9999)
▲ Helgen Industries Inc ....C 631 841-6300
Amityville (G-283)
◆ Hemisphere Novelties Inc ....E 914 378-4100
Yonkers (G-16767)
House of Portfolios Co Inc ....E 212 206-7323
New York (G-10136)
House of Portfolios Co Inc ....F 212 206-7323
New York (G-10137)
International Time Products ....G 516 931-0005
Jericho (G-6791)
Just Brass Inc ....G 212 724-5447
New York (G-10384)
K Displays ....F 718 854-6045
Brooklyn (G-2063)
L Y Z Creations Ltd Inc ....E 718 768-2977
Brooklyn (G-2088)
Leather Artisan ....G 518 359-3102
Childwold (G-3499)
◆ M G New York Inc ....F 212 371-5566
New York (G-10636)
▲ Merzon Leather Co Inc ....C 718 782-6260
Brooklyn (G-2197)
▲ Neumann Jutta New York Inc ....F 212 982-7048
New York (G-10914)
▲ Penthouse Manufacturing Co Inc ....B 516 379-1300
Freeport (G-5173)
Randa Accessories Lea Gds LLC ....D 212 354-5100
New York (G-11325)
Roma Industries LLC ....G 212 268-0723
New York (G-11426)
Slim Line Case Co Inc ....F 585 546-3639
Rochester (G-14131)
◆ Tapestry Inc ....B 212 594-1850
New York (G-11784)
▲ Trafalgar Company LLC ....G 212 768-8800
New York (G-11885)
Unique Packaging Corporation ....G 514 341-5872
Champlain (G-3416)

3199 Leather Goods, NEC

Adirondack Leather Pdts Inc ....F 607 547-5798
Fly Creek (G-5063)
▲ Courtlandt Boot Jack Co Inc ....E 718 445-6200
Flushing (G-4994)
Deluxe Travel Store Inc ....G 718 435-8111
Brooklyn (G-1767)
Dog Good Products LLC ....G 212 789-7000
New York (G-9545)
▲ Dvf Studio LLC ....D 212 741-6607
New York (G-9589)
Dvf Studio LLC ....G 646 576-8009
New York (G-9590)
East West Global Sourcing Inc ....G 917 887-2286
Brooklyn (G-1808)
Equicenter Inc ....E 585 742-2522
Honeoye Falls (G-6264)
Fahrenheit NY Inc ....G 212 354-6554
New York (G-9772)
▼ Finger Lakes Lea Crafters LLC ....F 315 252-4107
Auburn (G-478)
▲ First Manufacturing Co Inc ....E 516 763-0400
Oceanside (G-12538)
▲ Helgen Industries Inc ....C 631 841-6300
Amityville (G-283)
▲ Import-Export Corporation ....F 718 707-0880
Long Island City (G-7473)
Kamali Leather LLC ....G 518 762-2522
Johnstown (G-6833)
Leather Outlet ....G 518 668-0328
Lake George (G-6964)
Max 200 Performance Dog Eqp ....E 315 776-9588
Port Byron (G-13189)
McM Products USA Inc ....E 646 756-4090
New York (G-10744)
▲ Perrone Leather LLC ....D 518 853-4300
Fultonville (G-5239)
▲ Sampla Belting North Amer LLC ....E 716 667-7450
Lackawanna (G-6953)
▲ Star Desk Pad Co Inc ....E 914 963-9400
Yonkers (G-16800)
◆ Tucano Usa Inc ....G 212 966-9211
New York (G-11911)
◆ Unique Overseas Inc ....G 516 466-9792
Great Neck (G-5597)

32 STONE, CLAY, GLASS, AND CONCRETE PRODUCTS

3211 Flat Glass

▲ A Sunshine Glass & Aluminum ....E 718 932-8080
Woodside (G-16644)
Corning Incorporated ....D 315 379-3200
Canton (G-3256)
Corning Incorporated ....G 607 974-6729
Painted Post (G-12837)
Europrojects Intl Inc ....F 917 262-0795
New York (G-9731)
Express Building Supply Inc ....E 516 608-0379
Oceanside (G-12537)
Glass Apps LLC ....F 310 987-1536
New York (G-9930)
▲ Global Glass Corp ....G 516 681-2309
Hicksville (G-6091)
Guardian Industries LLC ....B 315 787-7000
Geneva (G-5327)
▲ Hecht & Sohn Glass Co Inc ....G 718 782-8295
Brooklyn (G-1971)
▲ Lafayette Mirror & Glass Co ....G 718 768-0660
New Hyde Park (G-8547)
▲ Lazer Marble & Granite Corp ....G 718 859-9644
Brooklyn (G-2096)
▼ Manhattan Shade & Glass Co Inc ....E 212 288-5616
Great Neck (G-5570)
Manhattan Shade & Glass Co Inc ....E 212 288-5616
Hauppauge (G-5880)
Mr Glass Tempering LLC ....F 718 576-3826
Brooklyn (G-2232)
◆ Munn Works LLC ....E 914 665-6100
Mount Vernon (G-8424)
Pilkington North America Inc ....C 315 438-3341
Syracuse (G-15395)
RG Glass Creations Inc ....E 212 675-0030
New York (G-11383)
Saxon Glass Technologies Inc ....F 607 587-9630
Alfred (G-184)
◆ Schott Corporation ....D 914 831-2200
Elmsford (G-4564)
Schott Gemtron Corporation ....C 423 337-3522
Elmsford (G-4565)
▲ Schott Solar Pv Inc ....G 888 457-6527
Elmsford (G-4568)
South Seneca Vinyl LLC ....G 315 585-6050
Romulus (G-14282)
▼ Stefan Sydor Optics Inc ....E 585 271-7300
Rochester (G-14143)
▲ Tempco Glass Fabrication LLC ....D 718 461-6888
Flushing (G-5052)
Twin Pane Insulated GL Co Inc ....F 631 924-1060
Yaphank (G-16725)
Window-Fix Inc ....E 718 854-3475
Brooklyn (G-2651)
▲ Zered Inc ....F 718 353-7464
College Point (G-3670)

3221 Glass Containers

Anchor Glass Container Corp ....B 607 737-1933
Elmira Heights (G-4509)
◆ Baralan Usa Inc ....E 718 849-5768
Richmond Hill (G-13497)
Certainteed Corporation ....C 716 823-3684
Lackawanna (G-6948)
▲ Glopak USA Corp ....E 844 445-6725
Hicksville (G-6092)
Intrapac International Corp ....C 518 561-2030
Plattsburgh (G-13126)
◆ Lidestri Foods Inc ....B 585 377-7700
Fairport (G-4639)
Owens-Brockway Glass Cont Inc ....C 315 258-3211
Auburn (G-494)

SIC

Employee Codes: A=Over 500 employees, B=251-500
C=101-250, D=51-100, E=20-50, F=10-19, G=5-9
2019 Harris
New York Manufacturers Directory
731

32 STONE, CLAY, GLASS, AND CONCRETE PRODUCTS

Pennsauken Packing Company LLC.....G...... 585 377-7700
  Fairport *(G-4649)*
▲ Rocco Bormioli Glass Co Inc..........E...... 212 719-0606
  New York *(G-11413)*
▲ Saint Gobain Grains & Powders.....A...... 716 731-8200
  Niagara Falls *(G-12332)*
◆ Schott Corporation.........................D...... 914 831-2200
  Elmsford *(G-4564)*
▲ SGD North America.........................E...... 212 753-4200
  New York *(G-11549)*
SGD Pharma Packaging Inc...................E...... 212 223-7100
  New York *(G-11550)*
Velvet Healing By Alma Corp................G...... 347 271-4220
  Bronx *(G-1414)*

3229 Pressed & Blown Glassware, NEC

Architectural Glass Inc......................F...... 845 831-3116
  Beacon *(G-754)*
▼ Bedford Downing Glass.....................G...... 718 418-6409
  Brooklyn *(G-1593)*
Biolitec Inc..................................E...... 413 525-0600
  New York *(G-9088)*
▲ Bronx Wstchester Tempering Inc.....E...... 914 663-9400
  Mount Vernon *(G-8383)*
Co-Optics America Lab Inc..................E...... 607 432-0557
  Oneonta *(G-12631)*
Complete Fiber Solutions Inc................G...... 718 828-8900
  Bronx *(G-1245)*
◆ Corning Incorporated......................A...... 607 974-9000
  Corning *(G-3809)*
Corning Incorporated........................D...... 607 974-9000
  Corning *(G-3810)*
Corning Incorporated........................... 607 974-1274
  Painted Post *(G-12836)*
Corning Incorporated........................... 607 974-9000
  Corning *(G-3811)*
Corning Incorporated........................D...... 315 379-3200
  Canton *(G-3256)*
Corning Incorporated........................E...... 607 433-3100
  Oneonta *(G-12635)*
Corning Incorporated........................... 607 248-1200
  Corning *(G-3812)*
Corning Incorporated........................G...... 646 521-9600
  New York *(G-9402)*
Corning Incorporated........................F...... 607 962-6036
  Painted Post *(G-12838)*
Corning Incorporated........................G...... 607 974-4488
  Corning *(G-3813)*
Corning Incorporated........................... 607 974-8496
  Corning *(G-3814)*
Corning Incorporated........................... 607 974-6729
  Painted Post *(G-12837)*
▼ Corning International Corp................. 607 974-9000
  Corning *(G-3815)*
Corning Specialty Mtls Inc................... 607 974-9000
  Corning *(G-3817)*
Corning Tropel Corporation.................C...... 585 377-3200
  Fairport *(G-4629)*
◆ Corning Vitro Corporation................A...... 607 974-8605
  Corning *(G-3818)*
▲ Daylight Technology USA Inc...........G...... 973 255-8100
  Maspeth *(G-7835)*
▲ Depp Glass Inc..............................F...... 718 784-8500
  Long Island City *(G-7424)*
Formcraft Display Products..................G...... 914 632-1410
  New Rochelle *(G-8603)*
◆ Germanow-Simon Corporation...........E...... 585 232-1440
  Rochester *(G-13832)*
▲ Gillinder Brothers Inc....................D...... 845 856-5375
  Port Jervis *(G-13229)*
Glass Menagerie Inc.......................... 845 754-8344
  Westbrookville *(G-16307)*
Glasteel Parts & Services Inc..............E...... 585 235-1010
  Rochester *(G-13837)*
▲ Gray Glass Inc..............................E...... 718 217-2943
  Queens Village *(G-13406)*
Ion Optics Inc................................F...... 518 339-6853
  Albany *(G-86)*
▲ Jay Strongwater Holdings LLC..........A...... 646 657-0558
  New York *(G-10312)*
▲ Jinglebell Inc..............................G...... 914 219-5395
  Armonk *(G-406)*
◆ King Research Inc.........................E...... 718 788-0122
  Brooklyn *(G-2072)*
▲ Led Lumina USA LLC.......................E...... 631 750-4433
  Bohemia *(G-1045)*
◆ Lighting Holdings Intl LLC...............A...... 845 306-1850
  Purchase *(G-13391)*
▲ Match Eyewear LLC........................E...... 516 877-0170
  Westbury *(G-16354)*

▼ Navitar Inc..................................D...... 585 359-4000
  Rochester *(G-13965)*
New York Energy Synthetics Inc..........G...... 212 634-4787
  New York *(G-10937)*
Niche Design Inc..............................F...... 212 777-2101
  Beacon *(G-761)*
Owens Corning Sales LLC..................B...... 518 475-3600
  Feura Bush *(G-4936)*
▲ Pasabahce USA...............................E...... 212 683-1600
  New York *(G-11119)*
Photonic Controls LLC.......................F...... 607 562-4585
  Horseheads *(G-6324)*
Schott Corporation...........................D...... 315 255-2791
  Auburn *(G-499)*
◆ Schott Corporation.........................D...... 914 831-2200
  Elmsford *(G-4564)*
▲ Schott North America Inc................ 914 831-2200
  Elmsford *(G-4567)*
▲ Scientifics Direct Inc....................F...... 716 773-7500
  Tonawanda *(G-15576)*
Semrok Inc....................................D...... 585 594-7050
  Rochester *(G-14121)*
Somers Stain Glass Inc.....................F...... 631 586-7772
  Deer Park *(G-4046)*
▼ Stefan Sydor Optics Inc..................E...... 585 271-7300
  Rochester *(G-14143)*
◆ Volpi Manufacturing USA Co Inc.......D...... 315 255-1737
  Auburn *(G-508)*

3231 Glass Prdts Made Of Purchased Glass

Adirondack Stained Glass Works..........G...... 518 725-0387
  Gloversville *(G-5449)*
Apf Management Company LLC............C...... 914 665-5400
  Yonkers *(G-16736)*
Apf Manufacturing Company LLC........F...... 914 963-6300
  Yonkers *(G-16737)*
◆ Avenue Mosaic Company..................G...... 216 245-6306
  New York *(G-8974)*
Batavia Precision Glass LLC..............G...... 585 343-6050
  Buffalo *(G-2724)*
Benson Industries Inc.......................F...... 212 779-3230
  New York *(G-9046)*
C B Management Services Inc.............F...... 845 735-2300
  Pearl River *(G-12895)*
▲ Campus Crafts Inc........................G...... 585 328-6780
  Rochester *(G-13688)*
Carvart Glass Inc............................E...... 212 675-0030
  New York *(G-9218)*
Community Glass Inc........................G...... 607 737-8860
  Elmira *(G-4478)*
▲ Depp Glass Inc..............................F...... 718 784-8500
  Long Island City *(G-7424)*
Dillmeier Enterprises Inc..................F...... 800 325-0596
  Garden City *(G-5255)*
▲ Dundy Glass & Mirror Corp.............E...... 718 723-5800
  Springfield Gardens *(G-15014)*
Dunlea Whl GL & Mirror Inc................G...... 914 664-5277
  Mount Vernon *(G-8397)*
Executive Mirror Doors Inc................. 631 234-1090
  Ronkonkoma *(G-14340)*
Exquisite Glass & Stone Inc...............G...... 718 937-9266
  Astoria *(G-428)*
Flickinger Glassworks Inc.................G...... 718 875-1531
  Brooklyn *(G-1892)*
G & M Clearview Inc........................G...... 845 781-4877
  Monroe *(G-8270)*
▲ Glassfab Inc................................E...... 585 262-4000
  Rochester *(G-13836)*
▲ Global Glass Corp..........................G...... 516 681-2309
  Hicksville *(G-6091)*
▲ Gmd Industries Inc........................G...... 718 445-8779
  College Point *(G-3645)*
Granville Glass & Granite.................. 518 812-0492
  Hudson Falls *(G-6381)*
▲ Gray Glass Inc..............................E...... 718 217-2943
  Queens Village *(G-13406)*
▲ Hecht & Sohn Glass Co Inc.............G...... 718 782-8295
  Brooklyn *(G-1971)*
Immco Diagnostics Inc....................... 716 691-0091
  Buffalo *(G-2881)*
▲ Jimmy Crystal New York Co Ltd......E...... 212 594-0858
  New York *(G-10340)*
▲ Jinglebell Inc..............................G...... 914 219-5395
  Armonk *(G-406)*
▲ Kasson & Keller Inc......................A...... 518 853-3421
  Fonda *(G-5065)*
▲ Lafayette Mirror & Glass Co...........G...... 718 768-0660
  New Hyde Park *(G-8547)*
Lalique North America Inc.................E...... 212 355-6550
  New York *(G-10512)*

Makarenko Studios Inc.....................G...... 914 968-7673
  Yorktown Heights *(G-16818)*
Manhattan Shade & Glass Co Inc.......E...... 212 288-5616
  Hauppauge *(G-5880)*
Michbi Doors Inc..............................D...... 631 231-9050
  Brentwood *(G-1142)*
Mirror-Tech Manufacturing Co...........F...... 914 965-1232
  Yonkers *(G-16785)*
Mri Northtowns Group PC.................F...... 716 836-4646
  Buffalo *(G-2955)*
◆ Munn Works LLC...........................E...... 914 665-6100
  Mount Vernon *(G-8424)*
Oldcastle Building Envelope..............F...... 212 957-5400
  New York *(G-11036)*
Oldcastle Buildingenvelope Inc..........C...... 631 234-2200
  Hauppauge *(G-5905)*
Oneida International Inc.....................E...... 315 361-3000
  Oneida *(G-12615)*
Oneida Silversmiths Inc..................... 315 361-3000
  Oneida *(G-12619)*
Our Terms Fabricators Inc................E...... 631 752-1517
  West Babylon *(G-16180)*
Pal Manufacturing Corp..................... 516 937-1990
  Hicksville *(G-6122)*
Potters Industries LLC..................... 315 265-4920
  Norwood *(G-12496)*
Press Glass Na Inc.........................G...... 212 631-3044
  New York *(G-11235)*
◆ Quality Enclosures Inc................... 631 234-0115
  Central Islip *(G-3382)*
Rauch Industries Inc........................E...... 704 867-5333
  Tarrytown *(G-15489)*
RB Wyatt Mfg Co Inc........................F...... 718 209-9682
  Brooklyn *(G-2387)*
Rochester Colonial Mfg Corp.............D...... 585 254-8191
  Rochester *(G-14084)*
◆ Rochester Insulated Glass Inc.........D...... 585 289-3611
  Manchester *(G-7761)*
Rohlfs Stined Leaded GL Studio........E...... 914 699-4848
  Mount Vernon *(G-8440)*
◆ Rosco Inc...................................C...... 718 526-2601
  Jamaica *(G-6675)*
Royal Metal Products Inc..................E...... 518 966-4442
  Surprise *(G-15207)*
Select Interior Door Ltd..................E...... 585 535-9900
  North Java *(G-12392)*
Somers Stain Glass Inc.....................F...... 631 586-7772
  Deer Park *(G-4046)*
▲ Stark Aquarium Products Co Inc......E...... 718 445-5357
  Flushing *(G-5048)*
Sunburst Studios Inc.......................G...... 718 768-6360
  Brooklyn *(G-2532)*
▲ Swift Glass Co Inc.........................D...... 607 733-7166
  Elmira Heights *(G-4515)*
▲ Taylor Made Group LLC..................E...... 518 725-0681
  Gloversville *(G-5468)*
▲ Taylor Products Inc.......................E...... 518 773-9312
  Gloversville *(G-5469)*
TEC Glass & Inst LLC.....................E...... 315 926-7639
  Marion *(G-7809)*
Timeless Decor LLC........................C...... 315 782-5759
  Watertown *(G-16035)*
Upstate Insulated Glass Inc...............E...... 315 475-4960
  Central Square *(G-3393)*
Vitarose Corp of America.................G...... 718 951-9700
  Brooklyn *(G-2630)*
Vitrix Inc....................................G...... 607 936-8707
  Corning *(G-3828)*

3241 Cement, Hydraulic

Ciment St-Laurent Inc......................C...... 518 943-4040
  Catskill *(G-3302)*
Euro Gear (usa) Inc........................G...... 518 578-1775
  Plattsburgh *(G-13120)*
Hanson Aggregates New York LLC.....F...... 716 665-4620
  Jamesville *(G-6766)*
Holcim (us) Inc...............................G...... 518 828-8478
  Hudson *(G-6353)*
Lafarge Building Materials Inc..........F...... 518 756-5000
  Ravena *(G-13453)*
Lafarge North America Inc................E...... 716 651-9235
  Lancaster *(G-7027)*
Lafarge North America Inc................. 716 854-5791
  Buffalo *(G-2918)*
Lafarge North America Inc................. 716 772-2621
  Lockport *(G-7313)*
Lafarge North America Inc................D...... 914 930-3027
  Buchanan *(G-2673)*
Lafarge North America Inc................E...... 518 756-5000
  Ravena *(G-13454)*

SIC SECTION
32 STONE, CLAY, GLASS, AND CONCRETE PRODUCTS

Lafarge North America Inc .... F 716 876-8788
  Tonawanda *(G-15554)*
▲ Lehigh Cement Company .... C 518 792-1137
  Glens Falls *(G-5432)*
Pallette Stone Corporation .... E 518 584-2421
  Gansevoort *(G-5244)*
Upstone Materials Inc .... G 518 873-2275
  Lewis *(G-7137)*

3251 Brick & Structural Clay Tile
Certified Flameproofing Corp .... G 631 265-4824
  Smithtown *(G-14895)*
Everblock Systems LLC .... G 844 422-5625
  New York *(G-9734)*
◆ Noroc Enterprises Inc .... C 718 585-3230
  Bronx *(G-1344)*
Semco Ceramics Inc .... G 315 782-3000
  Watertown *(G-16033)*
▲ Stone and Bath Gallery .... G 718 438-4500
  Brooklyn *(G-2523)*

3253 Ceramic Tile
▲ Aremco Products Inc .... F 845 268-0039
  Valley Cottage *(G-15752)*
Artsaics Studios Inc .... G 631 254-2558
  Deer Park *(G-3947)*
◆ Avenue Mosaic Company .... G 216 245-6306
  New York *(G-8974)*
Dal-Tile Corporation .... G 914 835-1801
  Harrison *(G-5727)*
▲ Ercole Nyc Inc .... F 212 675-2218
  Brooklyn *(G-1846)*
▲ Hastings Tile & Bath Inc .... E 631 285-3330
  Ronkonkoma *(G-14351)*
▲ Lazer Marble & Granite Corp .... G 718 859-9644
  Brooklyn *(G-2096)*
Lucida Usa LLC .... G 845 877-7008
  Tallman *(G-15465)*
NY Tilemakers .... G 989 278-8453
  Brooklyn *(G-2280)*
Quality Components Framing Sys ...... F 315 768-1167
  Whitesboro *(G-16528)*
Semco Ceramics Inc .... G 315 782-3000
  Watertown *(G-16033)*

3255 Clay Refractories
Filtros Ltd .... E 585 586-8770
  East Rochester *(G-4285)*
◆ Saint-Gobain Strl Ceramics .... A 716 278-6233
  Niagara Falls *(G-12335)*
Upstate Refractory Svcs Inc .... G 315 331-2955
  Newark *(G-12210)*

3259 Structural Clay Prdts, NEC
▲ American Chimney Supplies Inc ...... G 631 434-2020
  Hauppauge *(G-5764)*
Bistrian Cement Corporation .... F 631 324-1123
  East Hampton *(G-4232)*
▲ Boston Valley Pottery Inc .... D 716 649-7490
  Orchard Park *(G-12701)*
Chimney Doctors Americas Corp .... G 631 868-3586
  Bayport *(G-737)*
Jq Woodworking Inc .... G 516 766-3424
  Oceanside *(G-12543)*
Lenon Models Inc .... G 212 229-1581
  New York *(G-10546)*

3261 China Plumbing Fixtures & Fittings
◆ AMG JV LLC .... G 212 602-1818
  New York *(G-8843)*
▲ Gamma Products Inc .... D 845 562-3332
  New Windsor *(G-8645)*
▲ Kraus USA Inc .... F 800 775-0703
  Port Washington *(G-13278)*
▲ Larcent Enterprises Inc .... E 845 562-3332
  New Windsor *(G-8648)*
▲ Stone and Bath Gallery .... G 718 438-4500
  Brooklyn *(G-2523)*

3262 China, Table & Kitchen Articles
Jill Fagin Enterprises Inc .... G 212 674-9383
  New York *(G-10337)*
◆ Korin Japanese Trading Corp .... E 212 587-7021
  New York *(G-10471)*
Oneida International Inc .... G 315 361-3000
  Oneida *(G-12615)*
Oneida Silversmiths Inc .... G 315 361-3000
  Oneida *(G-12619)*

Prime Cook (wttc) Inc .... G 646 881-0068
  Flushing *(G-5039)*
Swissmar Inc .... G 905 764-1121
  Niagara Falls *(G-12339)*

3263 Earthenware, Whiteware, Table & Kitchen Articles
Ceramica Varm .... G 914 381-6215
  New Rochelle *(G-8596)*
◆ Green Wave International Inc .... G 718 499-3371
  Brooklyn *(G-1950)*
◆ Korin Japanese Trading Corp .... E 212 587-7021
  New York *(G-10471)*
Lifetime Stainless Steel Corp .... G 585 924-9393
  Victor *(G-15854)*
◆ Mackenzie-Childs LLC .... C 315 364-6118
  Aurora *(G-511)*
Williams-Sonoma Stores Inc .... F 212 633-2203
  New York *(G-12114)*

3264 Porcelain Electrical Splys
▲ Arnold Magnetic Tech Corp .... C 585 385-9010
  Rochester *(G-13640)*
◆ Cetek Inc .... E 845 452-3510
  Poughkeepsie *(G-13331)*
Corning Incorporated .... E 607 974-1274
  Painted Post *(G-12836)*
Eneflux Armtek Magnetics Inc .... G 516 576-3434
  Medford *(G-7947)*
Ferro Electronics Materials .... C 716 278-9400
  Niagara Falls *(G-12285)*
◆ Ferro Electronics Materials .... G 315 536-3357
  Penn Yan *(G-12954)*
Ferro Electronics Materials .... G 315 536-3357
  Penn Yan *(G-12955)*
Filtros Ltd .... E 585 586-8770
  East Rochester *(G-4285)*
▲ Hitachi Metals America Ltd .... G 914 694-9200
  Purchase *(G-13390)*
◆ Hoosier Magnetics Inc .... G 315 323-5832
  Ogdensburg *(G-12575)*
◆ Pfisterer Lapp LLC .... C 585 768-6221
  Le Roy *(G-7124)*
▲ Victor Insulators Inc .... C 585 924-2127
  Victor *(G-15875)*

3269 Pottery Prdts, NEC
American Country Quilts & Lin .... G 631 283-5466
  Southampton *(G-14949)*
▲ Saint Gobain Grains & Powders ...... A 716 731-8200
  Niagara Falls *(G-12332)*
▲ Saint-Gbain Advnced Crmics LLC ... C 716 278-6066
  Niagara Falls *(G-12333)*
Schiller Stores Inc .... G 845 928-4316
  Central Valley *(G-3397)*

3271 Concrete Block & Brick
Ace Cntracting Consulting Corp .... G 631 567-4752
  Bohemia *(G-971)*
All American Concrete Corp .... G 718 497-3301
  Brooklyn *(G-1506)*
Arnan Development Corp .... D 607 432-8391
  Oneonta *(G-12625)*
Barrasso & Sons Trucking Inc .... E 631 581-0360
  Islip Terrace *(G-6552)*
Brickit .... E 631 727-8977
  Hauppauge *(G-5784)*
Chenango Concrete Corp .... G 607 334-2545
  Norwich *(G-12478)*
Chimney Doctors Americas Corp .... G 631 868-3586
  Bayport *(G-737)*
Colonie Block and Supply Co .... G 518 869-8411
  Colonie *(G-3677)*
Cossitt Concrete Products Inc .... F 315 824-2700
  Hamilton *(G-5698)*
▲ Cranesville Block Co Inc .... E 518 684-6154
  Amsterdam *(G-333)*
Cranesville Block Co Inc .... E 315 773-2296
  Felts Mills *(G-4930)*
Creative Yard Designs Inc .... G 315 706-6143
  Manlius *(G-7776)*
Crest Haven Precast Inc .... E 518 483-4750
  Burke *(G-3142)*
Dicks Concrete Co Inc .... G 845 374-5966
  New Hampton *(G-8499)*
Duke Concrete Products Inc .... E 518 793-7743
  Queensbury *(G-13422)*
Edgewood Industries Inc .... G 516 227-2447
  Garden City *(G-5257)*

Everblock Systems LLC .... G 844 422-5625
  New York *(G-9734)*
Felicetti Concrete Products .... G 716 284-5740
  Niagara Falls *(G-12283)*
▼ Fort Miller Service Corp .... F 518 695-5000
  Greenwich *(G-5640)*
▼ Get Real Surfaces Inc .... G 845 337-4483
  Poughkeepsie *(G-13340)*
Gone South Concrete Block Inc .... E 315 598-2141
  Fulton *(G-5218)*
Grace Associates Inc .... G 718 767-9000
  Harrison *(G-5729)*
Grandview Block & Supply Co .... E 518 346-7981
  Schenectady *(G-14683)*
Great American Awning & Patio .... F 518 899-2300
  Ballston Spa *(G-584)*
Hanson Aggregates New York LLC ..... G 607 276-5881
  Almond *(G-193)*
▲ Imperia Masonry Supply Corp .... E 914 738-0900
  Pelham *(G-12936)*
Jenna Concrete Corporation .... E 718 842-5250
  Bronx *(G-1302)*
Jenna Harlem River Inc .... E 718 842-5997
  Bronx *(G-1303)*
Lafarge North America Inc .... G 518 756-5000
  Ravena *(G-13454)*
Modern Block LLC .... G 315 923-7443
  Clyde *(G-3596)*
Montfort Brothers Inc .... E 845 896-6694
  Fishkill *(G-4949)*
Morningstar Concrete Products .... F 716 693-4020
  Tonawanda *(G-15560)*
New York Ready Mix Inc .... G 516 338-6969
  Westbury *(G-16359)*
▲ Nicolia Concrete Products Inc .... D 631 669-0700
  Lindenhurst *(G-7185)*
Northeast Mesa LLC .... G 845 878-9344
  Carmel *(G-3278)*
Oldcastle Apg Northeast Inc .... E 585 924-2103
  Fishers *(G-4941)*
Palumbo Block Co Inc .... E 845 832-6100
  Dover Plains *(G-4145)*
Phelps Cement Products Inc .... G 315 548-9415
  Phelps *(G-12979)*
Radiation Shielding Systems .... F 888 631-2278
  Suffern *(G-15196)*
Riefler Concrete Products LLC .... C 716 649-3260
  Hamburg *(G-5693)*
Smithtown Concrete Products .... F 631 265-1815
  Saint James *(G-14515)*
Suffolk Cement Products Inc .... E 631 727-2317
  Calverton *(G-3173)*
Superior Block Corp .... F 718 421-0900
  Brooklyn *(G-2536)*
Taylor Concrete Products Inc .... E 315 788-2191
  Watertown *(G-16034)*
Troys Landscape Supply Co Inc .... E 518 785-1526
  Cohoes *(G-3622)*
Unilock Ltd .... E 716 822-6074
  Buffalo *(G-3111)*
▲ Unilock New York Inc .... G 845 278-6700
  Brewster *(G-1175)*

3272 Concrete Prdts
A & R Concrete Products LLC .... E 845 562-0640
  New Windsor *(G-8633)*
Access Products Inc .... G 800 679-4022
  Buffalo *(G-2682)*
Accurate Precast .... F 718 345-2910
  Brooklyn *(G-1473)*
▲ Afco Precast Sales Corp .... D 631 924-7114
  Middle Island *(G-8116)*
▲ Alp Stone Inc .... F 718 706-6166
  Long Island City *(G-7373)*
Alpine Building Supply Inc .... G 718 456-2522
  Ridgewood *(G-13529)*
▲ American Chimney Supplies Inc .... G 631 434-2020
  Hauppauge *(G-5764)*
Apollo Management V LP .... E 914 467-6510
  Purchase *(G-13386)*
Arnan Development Corp .... D 607 432-8391
  Oneonta *(G-12625)*
Baliva Concrete Products Inc .... E 585 328-8442
  Rochester *(G-13653)*
Barrett Paving Materials Inc .... F 315 737-9471
  Clayville *(G-3554)*
Beck Vault Company .... G 315 337-7590
  Rome *(G-14248)*
Binghamton Burial Vault Co Inc .... F 607 722-4931
  Binghamton *(G-865)*

Binghamton Precast & Sup Corp .... E 607 722-0334
Binghamton *(G-867)*
Bistrian Cement Corporation .... F 631 324-1123
East Hampton *(G-4232)*
Bonsal American Inc .... F 585 343-4741
Batavia *(G-614)*
Bonsal American Inc .... E 631 208-8073
Calverton *(G-3162)*
Buffalo Crushed Stone Inc .... E 716 826-7310
Buffalo *(G-2742)*
Callanan Industries Inc .... E 315 697-9569
Canastota *(G-3241)*
▲ **Callanan Industries Inc** .... C 518 374-2222
Albany *(G-54)*
Callanan Industries Inc .... E 845 331-6868
Kingston *(G-6892)*
Callanan Industries Inc .... G 518 785-5666
Latham *(G-7068)*
▲ **Castek Inc** .... G 914 636-1000
New Rochelle *(G-8595)*
▲ **Chim-Cap Corp** .... E 800 262-9622
Farmingdale *(G-4734)*
Chimney Doctors Americas Corp .... G 631 868-3586
Bayport *(G-737)*
City Mason Corp .... F 718 658-3796
Jamaica *(G-6635)*
▲ **Coastal Pipeline Products Corp** .... E 631 369-4000
Calverton *(G-3163)*
▲ **Copeland Coating Company Inc** .... F 518 766-2932
Nassau *(G-8477)*
Coral Cast LLC .... E 516 349-1300
Plainview *(G-13046)*
▲ **Corinthian Cast Stone Inc** .... E 631 920-2340
Wyandanch *(G-16694)*
Coronado .... G 718 386-7425
Brooklyn *(G-1719)*
Cossitt Concrete Products Inc .... F 315 824-2700
Hamilton *(G-5698)*
Crown Hill Stone Inc .... E 716 326-4601
Westfield *(G-16393)*
David Kucera Inc .... E 845 255-1044
Gardiner *(G-5293)*
Diamond Precast Products Inc .... F 631 874-3777
Center Moriches *(G-3338)*
Dillner Precast Inc .... G 631 421-9130
Lloyd Harbor *(G-7279)*
Dillner Precast Inc .... G 631 421-9130
Huntington Station *(G-6439)*
Doric Vault of Wny Inc .... F 716 828-1776
Buffalo *(G-2803)*
Duke Company .... G 607 347-4455
Ithaca *(G-6575)*
Duranm Inc .... G 914 774-3367
Cortlandt Manor *(G-3899)*
▲ **Dynasty Metal Works Inc** .... G 631 284-3719
Riverhead *(G-13567)*
East Main Associates .... D 585 624-1990
Lima *(G-7151)*
▲ **Eaton Brothers Corp** .... G 716 649-8250
Hamburg *(G-5676)*
Elderlee Incorporated .... C 315 789-6670
Oaks Corners *(G-12527)*
Express Concrete Inc .... G 631 273-4224
Brentwood *(G-1133)*
Fordham Marble Co Inc .... F 914 682-6699
White Plains *(G-16451)*
Foro Marble Co Inc .... E 718 852-2322
Brooklyn *(G-1898)*
▲ **Fort Miller Group Inc** .... B 518 695-5000
Greenwich *(G-5639)*
▼ **Fort Miller Service Corp** .... F 518 695-5000
Greenwich *(G-5640)*
Galle & Zinter Inc .... G 716 833-4212
Buffalo *(G-2839)*
Gamble & Gamble Inc .... G 716 731-3239
Sanborn *(G-14546)*
Geotech Associates Ltd .... G 631 286-0251
Brookhaven *(G-1430)*
▼ **Get Real Surfaces Inc** .... E 845 337-4483
Poughkeepsie *(G-13340)*
Glens Falls Ready Mix Inc .... F 518 793-1695
Queensbury *(G-13426)*
Glenwood Cast Stone Inc .... G 718 859-6500
Brooklyn *(G-1931)*
Grace Associates Inc .... G 718 767-9000
Harrison *(G-5729)*
Great ATL Pr-Cast Con Statuary .... G 718 948-5677
Staten Island *(G-15083)*
Guardian Concrete Inc .... F 518 372-0080
Schenectady *(G-14686)*
H F Cary & Sons .... G 607 598-2563
Lockwood *(G-7344)*
Hanson Aggregates East LLC .... G 716 372-1574
Allegany *(G-190)*
Healthy Basement Systems LLC .... F 516 650-9046
Medford *(G-7952)*
Ideal Burial Vault Company .... G 585 599-2242
Corfu *(G-3807)*
Island Ready Mix Inc .... E 631 874-3777
Center Moriches *(G-3339)*
Jab Concrete Supply Corp .... E 718 842-5250
Bronx *(G-1300)*
Jefferson Concrete Corp .... D 315 788-4171
Watertown *(G-16018)*
Jenna Concrete Corporation .... E 718 842-5250
Bronx *(G-1302)*
Jenna Harlem River Inc .... G 718 842-5997
Bronx *(G-1303)*
John E Potente & Sons Inc .... G 516 935-8585
Hicksville *(G-6097)*
▲ **Key Cast Stone Company Inc** .... E 631 789-2145
Amityville *(G-294)*
Lafarge North America Inc .... E 518 756-5000
Ravena *(G-13454)*
Lakelands Concrete Pdts Inc .... E 585 624-1990
Lima *(G-7152)*
Lhv Precast Inc .... E 845 336-8880
Kingston *(G-6907)*
Long Island Geotech .... G 631 473-1044
Port Jefferson *(G-13221)*
Long Island Green Guys .... G 631 664-4306
Riverhead *(G-13575)*
Long Island Precast Inc .... E 631 286-0240
Brookhaven *(G-1431)*
M K Ulrich Construction Inc .... F 716 893-5777
Buffalo *(G-2930)*
Meditub Incorporated .... F 866 633-4882
Lawrence *(G-7106)*
Mid-Hudson Concrete Pdts Inc .... F 845 265-3141
Cold Spring *(G-3625)*
Milano Granite and Marble Corp .... F 718 477-7200
Staten Island *(G-15105)*
Murcadom Corporation .... F 585 412-2176
Canandaigua *(G-3226)*
▲ **Nicolia Concrete Products Inc** .... D 631 669-0700
Lindenhurst *(G-7185)*
▲ **Nicolock Paving Stones LLC** .... D 631 669-0700
Lindenhurst *(G-7188)*
Northeast Concrete Pdts Inc .... F 518 563-0700
Plattsburgh *(G-13138)*
▲ **NY Tempering LLC** .... G 718 326-8989
Maspeth *(G-7864)*
Oldcastle Precast Inc .... F 518 767-2116
South Bethlehem *(G-14924)*
Oldcastle Precast Inc .... E 518 767-2112
Selkirk *(G-14769)*
P J R Industries Inc .... E 716 825-9300
Buffalo *(G-2984)*
Pelkowski Precast Corp .... F 631 269-5727
Kings Park *(G-6885)*
Preload Concrete Structures .... E 631 231-8100
Hauppauge *(G-5921)*
Presbrey-Leland Inc .... G 914 949-2264
Valhalla *(G-15745)*
Quikrete Companies LLC .... E 716 213-2027
Lackawanna *(G-6951)*
Quikrete Companies LLC .... E 315 673-2020
Marcellus *(G-7794)*
Rain Catchers Seamless Gutters .... G 516 520-1956
Bethpage *(G-852)*
Riefler Concrete Products LLC .... C 716 649-3260
Hamburg *(G-5693)*
Robert M Vault .... G 315 243-1447
Bridgeport *(G-1183)*
Robinson Concrete Inc .... E 315 253-6666
Auburn *(G-498)*
Roman Stone Construction Co .... E 631 667-0566
Bay Shore *(G-717)*
▲ **Royal Marble & Granite Inc** .... G 516 536-5900
Oceanside *(G-12555)*
St Raymond Monument Co .... G 718 824-3600
Bronx *(G-1391)*
Stag Brothers Cast Stone Co .... G 718 629-0975
Brooklyn *(G-2507)*
Standard Industries Inc .... G 212 821-1600
New York *(G-11692)*
Steindl Cast Stone Co Inc .... G 718 296-8530
Woodhaven *(G-16637)*
▲ **Suhor Industries Inc** .... F 585 377-5100
Fairport *(G-4663)*
Suhor Industries Inc .... G 716 483-6818
Jamestown *(G-6751)*
Sunnycrest Inc .... E 315 252-7214
Auburn *(G-501)*
Superior Aggragates Supply LLC .... E 516 333-2923
Lindenhurst *(G-7199)*
Superior Walls Upstate NY Inc .... D 585 624-9390
Lima *(G-7156)*
Superior Wlls of Hdson Vly Inc .... E 845 485-4033
Poughkeepsie *(G-13370)*
Taylor Concrete Products Inc .... E 315 788-2191
Watertown *(G-16034)*
Towne House Restorations Inc .... G 718 497-9200
Long Island City *(G-7619)*
▲ **Transpo Industries Inc** .... E 914 636-1000
New Rochelle *(G-8630)*
Trinic LLC .... F 607 655-1517
Kirkwood *(G-6941)*
▲ **Unilock New York Inc** .... G 845 278-6700
Brewster *(G-1175)*
Universal Step Inc .... G 315 437-7611
East Syracuse *(G-4379)*
Upstone Materials Inc .... G 518 483-2671
Malone *(G-7729)*
Upstone Materials Inc .... G 518 873-2275
Lewis *(G-7137)*
Urban Precast LLC .... E 845 331-6299
Kingston *(G-6928)*
▲ **Walter G Legge Company Inc** .... G 914 737-5040
Peekskill *(G-12928)*
Wel Made Enterprises Inc .... F 631 752-1238
Farmingdale *(G-4906)*
Woodards Concrete Products Inc .... E 845 361-3471
Bullville *(G-3139)*
▲ **Woodside Granite Industries** .... G 585 589-6500
Albion *(G-164)*

3273 Ready-Mixed Concrete

Advanced Ready Mix Corp .... F 718 497-5020
Brooklyn *(G-1488)*
Advanced Transit Mix Corp .... G 718 497-5020
Brooklyn *(G-1489)*
All American Transit Mix Corp .... G 718 417-3654
Brooklyn *(G-1507)*
Anbriella Sand & Gravel Corp .... E 631 586-2111
Bay Shore *(G-657)*
Atlas Concrete Batching Corp .... D 718 523-3000
Jamaica *(G-6627)*
Atlas Transit Mix Corp .... C 718 523-3000
Jamaica *(G-6628)*
Barney & Dickenson Inc .... E 607 729-1536
Vestal *(G-15809)*
Barrett Paving Materials Inc .... F 315 788-2037
Watertown *(G-16001)*
Best Concrete Mix Corp .... E 718 463-5500
Flushing *(G-4988)*
Bonded Concrete Inc .... E 518 273-5800
Watervliet *(G-16042)*
Bonded Concrete Inc .... F 518 674-2854
West Sand Lake *(G-16284)*
▲ **Brewster Transit Mix Corp** .... D 845 279-3738
Brewster *(G-1160)*
Brewster Transit Mix Corp .... E 845 279-3738
Brewster *(G-1161)*
Byram Concrete & Supply LLC .... F 914 682-4477
White Plains *(G-16433)*
C & C Ready-Mix Corporation .... E 607 797-5108
Vestal *(G-15812)*
C & C Ready-Mix Corporation .... F 607 687-1690
Owego *(G-12796)*
Capital Concrete Inc .... G 716 648-8001
Hamburg *(G-5673)*
Casa Redimix Concrete Corp .... F 718 589-1555
Bronx *(G-1235)*
Ccz Ready Mix Concrete Corp .... G 516 579-7352
Levittown *(G-7132)*
Cemex Cement Inc .... D 212 317-6000
New York *(G-9237)*
Century Ready Mix Inc .... G 631 888-2200
West Babylon *(G-16145)*
Champion Materials Inc .... G 315 493-2654
Carthage *(G-3289)*
Chenango Concrete Corp .... F 518 294-9964
Richmondville *(G-13518)*
Clark Concrete Co Inc .... G 315 478-4101
Syracuse *(G-15279)*
Clemente Latham Concrete Corp .... D 518 374-2222
Schenectady *(G-14663)*
Cobleskill Red E Mix & Supply .... F 518 234-2015
Amsterdam *(G-332)*

Corona Ready Mix Inc ....F 718 271-5940
Corona (G-3842)
Cortland Ready Mix Inc ....F 607 753-3063
Cortland (G-3870)
Cossitt Concrete Products Inc ....F 315 824-2700
Hamilton (G-5698)
Costanza Ready Mix Inc ....G 516 783-4444
North Bellmore (G-12375)
Cranesville Block Co Inc ....E 315 732-2135
Utica (G-15688)
Cranesville Block Co Inc ....F 845 292-1585
Liberty (G-7143)
Cranesville Block Co Inc ....E 845 896-5687
Fishkill (G-4944)
Cranesville Block Co Inc ....E 845 331-1775
Kingston (G-6896)
Cranesville Block Co Inc ....G 315 384-4000
Norfolk (G-12357)
▲ Cranesville Block Co Inc ....E 518 684-6154
Amsterdam (G-333)
Cranesville Block Co Inc ....E 315 773-2296
Felts Mills (G-4930)
Custom Mix Inc ....G 516 797-7090
Massapequa Park (G-7889)
Dalrymple Grav & Contg Co Inc ....F 607 739-0391
Pine City (G-12999)
Dalrymple Holding Corp ....E 607 737-6200
Pine City (G-13000)
Deer Park Sand & Gravel Corp ....E 631 586-2323
Bay Shore (G-680)
Dicks Concrete Co Inc ....E 845 374-5966
New Hampton (G-8499)
Dunkirk Construction Products ....G 716 366-5220
Dunkirk (G-4166)
E Tetz & Sons Inc ....D 845 692-4486
Middletown (G-8148)
East Coast Spring Mix Inc ....G 845 355-1215
New Hampton (G-8500)
Elam Materials Inc ....F 585 658-2248
Mount Morris (G-8366)
Electric City Concrete Co Inc ....E 518 887-5560
Amsterdam (G-335)
Elm Transit Mix Corporation ....F 516 333-6144
Westbury (G-16327)
Empire Transit Mix Inc ....E 718 384-3000
Brooklyn (G-1834)
F H Stickles & Son Inc ....F 518 851-9048
Livingston (G-7275)
Ferrara Bros LLC ....E 718 939-3030
Flushing (G-4999)
Frey Concrete Inc ....G 716 213-5832
North Tonawanda (G-12428)
Fulmont Ready-Mix Company Inc ....F 518 887-5560
Amsterdam (G-338)
G & J Rdymx & Masnry Sup Inc ....F 718 454-0800
Hollis (G-6234)
Glens Falls Ready Mix Inc ....F 518 793-1695
Queensbury (G-13426)
Grandview Concrete Corp ....E 518 346-7981
Schenectady (G-14684)
Haley Concrete Inc ....F 716 492-0849
Delevan (G-4070)
Hanson Aggregates East LLC ....F 585 798-0762
Medina (G-7980)
Hanson Aggregates East LLC ....F 716 372-1574
Falconer (G-4679)
Hanson Aggregates New York LLC ....F 716 665-4620
Jamestown (G-6721)
Hanson Aggregates New York LLC ....F 585 638-5841
Pavilion (G-12889)
Hanson Aggregates New York LLC ....C 315 469-5501
Jamesville (G-6767)
Inwood Material ....F 516 371-1842
Inwood (G-6493)
Iroquois Rock Products Inc ....F 585 381-7010
Rochester (G-13887)
Island Ready Mix Inc ....E 631 874-3777
Center Moriches (G-3339)
James Town Macadam Inc ....D 716 665-4504
Falconer (G-4683)
Jenna Concrete Corporation ....E 718 842-5250
Bronx (G-1302)
Jenna Harlem River Inc ....G 718 842-5997
Bronx (G-1303)
Jet Redi Mix Concrete Inc ....F 631 580-3640
Ronkonkoma (G-14358)
King Road Materials Inc ....F 518 382-5354
Albany (G-92)
Kings Park Ready Mix Corp ....F 631 269-4330
Kings Park (G-6884)
Kings Ready Mix Inc ....E 718 853-4644
Roslyn Heights (G-14458)
Knight Sttlement Sand Grav LLC ....E 607 776-2048
Bath (G-646)
Lafarge North America Inc ....E 518 756-5000
Ravena (G-13454)
Lage Industries Corporation ....F 718 342-3400
Brooklyn (G-2090)
Lakeside Concrete Services Inc ....G 716 681-7510
Lancaster (G-7028)
Lazarek Inc ....G 315 343-1242
Oswego (G-12780)
Lehigh Cement Company ....E 518 943-5940
Catskill (G-3305)
Liberty Ready Mix Inc ....F 718 526-1700
Jamaica (G-6655)
Long Island Ready Mix ....G 516 485-5260
Hempstead (G-6018)
Manitou Concrete ....D 585 424-6040
Rochester (G-13925)
Manzione Ready Mix Corp ....G 718 628-3837
Brooklyn (G-2162)
Mastro Concrete Inc ....G 718 528-6788
Rosedale (G-14441)
Mix N Mac LLC ....G 845 381-5536
Middletown (G-8165)
N Y Western Concrete Corp ....G 585 343-6850
Batavia (G-631)
New Atlantic Ready Mix Corp ....G 718 812-0739
Hollis (G-6235)
Nex-Gen Ready Mix Corp ....G 347 231-0073
Bronx (G-1342)
Nicolia Ready Mix Inc ....D 631 669-7000
Lindenhurst (G-7186)
Nicolia Ready Mix Inc ....E 631 669-7000
Lindenhurst (G-7187)
Northern Ready Mix LLC ....F 315 336-7900
North Syracuse (G-12408)
Oldcastle Materials Inc ....G 585 424-6410
Rochester (G-13984)
Oldcastle Precast Inc ....F 518 767-2116
South Bethlehem (G-14924)
Otsego Ready Mix Inc ....F 607 432-3400
Oneonta (G-12643)
Precision Ready Mix Inc ....G 718 658-5600
Jamaica (G-6668)
Presti Ready Mix Concrete Inc ....G 516 378-6006
Freeport (G-5175)
Quality Ready Mix Inc ....F 516 437-0100
New Hyde Park (G-8559)
Queens Ready Mix Inc ....G 718 526-4919
Jamaica (G-6670)
Residential Fences Corp ....E 631 205-9758
Ridge (G-13524)
Richmond Ready Mix Corp ....G 917 731-8400
Staten Island (G-15130)
Richmond Ready Mix Corp II ....E 917 731-8400
Staten Island (G-15131)
Riefler Concrete Products LLC ....C 716 649-3260
Hamburg (G-5693)
Robinson Concrete Inc ....E 315 253-6666
Auburn (G-498)
Robinson Concrete Inc ....C 315 676-4333
West Monroe (G-16262)
Robinson Concrete Inc ....F 315 492-6200
Jamesville (G-6770)
Robinson Concrete Inc ....F 315 676-4662
Brewerton (G-1152)
Rochester Asphalt Materials ....D 585 924-7360
Farmington (G-4918)
Rochester Asphalt Materials ....G 585 381-7010
Rochester (G-14079)
Rural Hill Sand and Grav Corp ....F 315 846-5212
Woodville (G-16689)
Russian Mix Inc ....G 347 385-7198
Brooklyn (G-2428)
Saunders Concrete Co Inc ....F 607 756-7905
Cortland (G-3893)
Scara-Mix Inc ....E 718 442-7357
Staten Island (G-15132)
Seville Central Mix Corp ....D 516 868-3000
Freeport (G-5183)
Seville Central Mix Corp ....D 516 293-6190
Old Bethpage (G-12587)
Seville Central Mix Corp ....E 516 239-8333
Lawrence (G-7109)
South Shore Ready Mix Inc ....G 516 872-3049
Valley Stream (G-15798)
Star Ready Mix East Inc ....F 631 289-8787
East Hampton (G-4243)
Star Ready Mix Inc ....F 631 289-8787
Medford (G-7966)
Stephen Miller Gen Contrs Inc ....E 518 661-5601
Gloversville (G-5467)
Suffolk Cement Precast Inc ....G 631 727-4432
Calverton (G-3172)
Suffolk Cement Products Inc ....E 631 727-2317
Calverton (G-3173)
Sullivan Concrete Inc ....F 845 888-2235
Cochecton (G-3608)
T Mix Inc ....G 646 379-6814
Brooklyn (G-2549)
TEC - Crete Transit Mix Corp ....E 718 657-6880
Ridgewood (G-13554)
Thousand Island Ready Mix Con ....G 315 686-3203
La Fargeville (G-6944)
Torrington Industries Inc ....G 315 676-4662
Central Square (G-3392)
United Materials LLC ....D 716 683-1432
North Tonawanda (G-12461)
United Materials LLC ....E 716 731-2332
Sanborn (G-14556)
United Materials LLC ....G 716 662-0564
Orchard Park (G-12748)
United Transit Mix Inc ....F 718 416-3400
Brooklyn (G-2604)
Upstone Materials Inc ....F 315 265-8036
Plattsburgh (G-13166)
Upstone Materials Inc ....G 315 764-0251
Massena (G-7910)
Upstone Materials Inc ....G 518 873-2275
Lewis (G-7137)
Upstone Materials Inc ....D 518 561-5321
Plattsburgh (G-13165)
US Concrete Inc ....E 718 853-4644
Roslyn Heights (G-14461)
US Concrete Inc ....E 718 438-6800
Brooklyn (G-2612)
W F Saunders & Sons Inc ....F 315 469-3217
Nedrow (G-8480)
W F Saunders & Sons Inc ....G 607 257-6930
Etna (G-4623)
Watertown Concrete Inc ....F 315 788-1040
Watertown (G-16036)

3274 Lime

Lime Energy Co ....G 704 892-4442
Buffalo (G-2923)
Masick Soil Conservation Co ....F 518 827-5354
Schoharie (G-14732)
▲ Minerals Technologies Inc ....E 212 878-1800
New York (G-10817)

3275 Gypsum Prdts

▲ Continental Buchanan LLC ....D 703 480-3800
Buchanan (G-2672)
East Pattern & Model Corp ....E 585 461-3240
Rochester (G-13756)
Lafarge North America Inc ....D 914 930-3027
Buchanan (G-2673)
United States Gypsum Company ....C 585 948-5221
Oakfield (G-12525)

3281 Cut Stone Prdts

6478 Ridge Road LLC ....G 716 625-8400
Lockport (G-7282)
6478 Ridge Road LLC ....F 716 625-8400
Lockport (G-7283)
A&A Marble & Granite ....F 347 810-9595
Bronx (G-1202)
Adirondack Precision Cut Stone ....F 518 681-3060
Queensbury (G-13414)
Alart Inc ....G 212 840-1508
New York (G-8782)
▲ Amendola MBL & Stone Ctr Inc ....D 914 997-7968
White Plains (G-16419)
American Bluestone LLC ....F 607 369-2235
Sidney (G-14848)
Aurora Stone Group LLC ....F 315 471-6869
East Syracuse (G-4324)
▲ Barra & Trumbore Inc ....G 845 626-5442
Kerhonkson (G-6867)
Busch Products Inc ....E 315 474-8422
Syracuse (G-15264)
Callanan Industries Inc ....E 845 331-6868
Kingston (G-6892)
Capital Stone LLC ....G 518 382-7588
Schenectady (G-14658)
Capital Stone Saratoga LLC ....G 518 226-8677
Saratoga Springs (G-14573)

S I C

Crown Hill Stone Inc....E....716 326-4601
Westfield (G-16393)
Dalrymple Holding Corp....E....607 737-6200
Pine City (G-13000)
Denton Stoneworks Inc....F....516 746-1500
Garden City Park (G-5285)
▲ Devonian Stone New York Inc....E....607 655-2600
Windsor (G-16604)
Dicamillo Marble and Granite....E....845 878-0078
Patterson (G-12880)
Dominic De Nigris Inc....E....718 597-4460
Bronx (G-1258)
▲ European Marble Works Co Inc....F....718 387-9778
Garden City (G-5259)
◆ Evergreen Slate Company Inc....D....518 642-2530
Middle Granville (G-8109)
First Presbyterian Church....G....315 252-3861
Auburn (G-479)
Fordham Marble Co Inc....F....914 682-6699
White Plains (G-16451)
Geneva Granite Co Inc....F....315 789-8142
Geneva (G-5325)
▲ Glen Plaza Marble & Gran Inc....G....516 671-1100
Glen Cove (G-5368)
▲ Granite & Marble Works Inc....E....518 584-2800
Gansevoort (G-5243)
Granite Tops Inc....E....914 699-2909
Mount Vernon (G-8403)
▲ Granite Works LLC....E....607 565-7012
Waverly (G-16065)
Graymont Materials Inc....E....518 561-5200
Plattsburgh (G-13122)
Hanson Aggregates East LLC....F....315 493-3721
Great Bend (G-5526)
Hanson Aggregates PA LLC....E....315 789-6202
Oaks Corners (G-12528)
▲ Hilltop Slate Inc....E....518 642-1453
Middle Granville (G-8110)
House of Stone Inc....G....845 782-7271
Monroe (G-8272)
▲ Icestone LLC....E....718 624-4900
Brooklyn (G-1993)
▲ International Stone Accessrs....G....718 522-5399
Brooklyn (G-2012)
Iroquois Rock Products Inc....F....585 381-7010
Rochester (G-13887)
▲ Italian Marble & Granite Inc....F....716 741-1800
Clarence Center (G-3545)
Jamestown Kitchen & Bath Inc....G....716 665-2299
Jamestown (G-6729)
▲ Marble Works Inc....E....914 376-3653
Yonkers (G-16782)
Masonville Stone Incorporated....G....607 265-3597
Masonville (G-7815)
MCM Natural Stone Inc....F....585 586-6510
Rochester (G-13934)
▲ Minerals Technologies Inc....E....212 878-1800
New York (G-10817)
Monroe Industries Inc....G....585 226-8230
Avon (G-520)
▲ New York Quarries Inc....F....518 756-3138
Alcove (G-165)
North American Slate Inc....G....518 642-1702
Granville (G-5523)
North Shore Monuments Inc....G....516 759-2156
Glen Head (G-5385)
Northeast Solite Corporation....E....845 246-2177
Mount Marion (G-8365)
Pallette Stone Corporation....E....518 584-2421
Gansevoort (G-5244)
PR & Stone & Tile Inc....G....718 383-1115
Brooklyn (G-2333)
Puccio Design International....F....516 248-6426
Garden City (G-5277)
Roto Salt Company Inc....E....315 536-3742
Penn Yan (G-12965)
▲ Royal Marble & Granite Inc....G....516 536-5900
Oceanside (G-12555)
Salsburg Dimensional Stone....F....631 653-6790
Brookhaven (G-1432)
Sanford Stone LLC....E....607 467-1313
Deposit (G-4109)
Seneca Stone Corporation....F....315 549-8253
Fayette (G-4926)
Seneca Stone Corporation....G....607 737-6200
Pine City (G-13001)
Sheldon Slate Products Co Inc....E....518 642-1280
Middle Granville (G-8112)
Stone & Terrazzo World Inc....G....718 361-6899
Long Island City (G-7605)
Suffolk Granite Manufacturing....E....631 226-4774
Lindenhurst (G-7197)
Thalle Industries Inc....E....914 762-3415
Briarcliff Manor (G-1177)
▲ Unilock New York Inc....G....845 278-6700
Brewster (G-1175)
▲ Unique MBL Gran Orgnztion Corp....G....718 482-0440
Long Island City (G-7622)
Vermont Natural Stoneworks....E....518 642-2460
Middle Granville (G-8114)
Vermont Structural Slate Co....F....518 499-1912
Whitehall (G-16525)
W F Saunders & Sons Inc....F....315 469-3217
Nedrow (G-8480)
White Plains Marble Inc....G....914 347-6000
Elmsford (G-4578)

3291 Abrasive Prdts

09 Flshy Bll/Dsert Sunrise LLC....G....518 583-6638
Saratoga Springs (G-14565)
American Douglas Metals Inc....F....716 856-3170
Buffalo (G-2695)
▲ Barker Brothers Incorporated....D....718 456-6400
Ridgewood (G-13530)
◆ Barton Mines Company LLC....C....518 798-5462
Glens Falls (G-5418)
Bedrock Landscaping Mtls Corp....G....631 587-4950
Babylon (G-525)
▼ Brick-It Inc....G....631 244-3993
Hauppauge (G-5783)
▲ Buffalo Abrasives Inc....E....716 693-3856
North Tonawanda (G-12419)
Conrad Blasius Equipment Co....G....516 753-1200
Plainview (G-13044)
◆ Datum Alloys Inc....G....607 239-6274
Endicott (G-4586)
▲ Dedeco International Sales Inc....E....845 887-4840
Long Eddy (G-7361)
▲ Dico Products Corporation....F....315 797-0470
Utica (G-15694)
◆ Dimanco Inc....G....315 797-0470
Utica (G-15695)
◆ Divine Brothers Company....C....315 797-0470
Utica (G-15698)
▼ EAC Holdings of NY Corp....E....716 822-2500
Buffalo (G-2808)
◆ Electro Abrasives LLC....E....716 822-2500
Buffalo (G-2814)
Global Abrasive Products Inc....E....716 438-0047
Lockport (G-7303)
Imerys Fsed Mnrl Ngara FLS Inc....G....716 286-1250
Niagara Falls (G-12296)
▲ Imerys Fsed Mnrl Ngara FLS Inc....E....716 286-1250
Niagara Falls (G-12297)
Jta USA Inc....G....718 722-0902
Brooklyn (G-2053)
Malyn Industrial Ceramics Inc....G....716 741-1510
Clarence Center (G-3548)
Meloon Foundries LLC....E....315 454-3231
Syracuse (G-15369)
Niabraze LLC....F....716 447-1082
Tonawanda (G-15562)
▲ Pellets LLC....G....716 693-1750
North Tonawanda (G-12441)
▲ Precision Abrasives Corp....E....716 826-5833
Orchard Park (G-12738)
Precision Elctro Mnrl Pmco Inc....E....716 284-2484
Niagara Falls (G-12326)
Raulli and Sons Inc....G....315 479-2515
Syracuse (G-15404)
Saint-Gbain Advnced Crmics LLC....E....716 691-2000
Amherst (G-249)
Saint-Gobain Abrasives Inc....B....518 266-2200
Watervliet (G-16049)
▲ Select-Tech Inc....G....845 895-8111
Wallkill (G-15908)
Smm - North America Trade Corp....G....212 604-0710
New York (G-11627)
Sunbelt Industries Inc....F....315 823-2947
Little Falls (G-7214)
▲ Uneeda Enterprizes Inc....C....800 431-2494
Spring Valley (G-15011)
Warren Cutlery Corp....F....845 876-3444
Rhinebeck (G-13490)
◆ Washington Mills Elec Mnrls....D....716 278-6600
Niagara Falls (G-12349)
▲ Washington Mills Tonawanda Inc....E....716 693-4550
Tonawanda (G-15590)

3292 Asbestos products

Andujar Asbestos and Lead....G....716 228-6757
Buffalo (G-2700)
Regional MGT & Consulting Inc....F....718 599-3718
Brooklyn (G-2393)
Shenfield Studio LLC....F....315 436-8869
Syracuse (G-15424)

3295 Minerals & Earths: Ground Or Treated

A&B Conservation LLC....G....845 282-7272
Monsey (G-8283)
Allied Aero Services Inc....G....631 277-9368
Brentwood (G-1126)
DSM Nutritional Products LLC....C....518 372-5155
Schenectady (G-14669)
DSM Nutritional Products LLC....C....518 372-5155
Glenville (G-5445)
Magnesium Technologies Corp....F....905 689-7361
Buffalo (G-2934)
▲ Mineralbious Corp....F....516 498-9715
Westbury (G-16357)
▲ Minerals Technologies Inc....E....212 878-1800
New York (G-10817)
Norlite LLC....B....518 235-0030
Cohoes (G-3616)
Northeast Solite Corporation....E....845 246-2646
Saugerties (G-14611)
Northeast Solite Corporation....E....845 246-2177
Mount Marion (G-8365)
Nutech Biosciences Inc....F....315 505-6500
Oneida (G-12613)
Oro Avanti Inc....G....516 487-5185
Great Neck (G-5577)
Skyline LLC....E....631 403-4131
East Setauket (G-4310)

3296 Mineral Wool

▲ Burnett Process Inc....G....585 254-8080
Rochester (G-13683)
Elliot Industries Inc....G....716 287-3100
Ellington (G-4448)
Fbm Galaxy Inc....F....315 463-5144
East Syracuse (G-4338)
Lencore Acoustics Corp....F....315 384-9114
Norfolk (G-12358)
Mecho Systems....F....718 729-8373
Long Island City (G-7519)
Owens Corning Sales LLC....B....518 475-3600
Feura Bush (G-4936)
Richlar Industries Inc....F....315 463-5144
East Syracuse (G-4366)
◆ Soundcoat Company Inc....D....631 242-2200
Deer Park (G-4047)
▲ Ssf Production LLC....F....518 324-3407
Plattsburgh (G-13156)
Unifrax Corporation....E....716 278-3800
Niagara Falls (G-12345)
Unifrax I LLC....C....716 696-3000
Tonawanda (G-15586)

3297 Nonclay Refractories

▲ Blasch Precision Ceramics Inc....D....518 436-1263
Menands (G-8083)
Capitol Restoration Corp....G....516 783-1425
North Bellmore (G-12373)
Filtros Ltd....E....585 586-8770
East Rochester (G-4285)
Global Alumina Services Co....B....212 309-8060
New York (G-9936)
Hanyan & Higgins Company Inc....G....315 769-8838
Massena (G-7903)
Lucideon....F....518 382-0082
Schenectady (G-14696)
◆ Monofrax LLC....C....716 483-7200
Falconer (G-4687)
▼ Rembar Company LLC....E....914 693-2620
Dobbs Ferry (G-4130)
Roccera LLC....F....585 426-0887
Rochester (G-14077)
Saint-Gobain Dynamics Inc....F....716 278-6007
Niagara Falls (G-12334)
▲ Silicon Carbide Products Inc....E....607 562-8599
Horseheads (G-6329)
Surmet Ceramics Corporation....F....716 875-4091
Buffalo (G-3081)
Unifrax I LLC....C....716 696-3000
Tonawanda (G-15586)
▲ Zircar Ceramics Inc....E....845 651-6600
Florida (G-4973)

▲ Zircar Refr Composites Inc ... G ... 845 651-4481
Florida *(G-4975)*
▲ Zircar Zirconia Inc ... E ... 845 651-3040
Florida *(G-4976)*

3299 Nonmetallic Mineral Prdts, NEC

American Crmic Process RES LLC ... G ... 315 828-6268
Phelps *(G-12974)*
American Wood Column Corp ... G ... 718 782-3163
Brooklyn *(G-1528)*
Argosy Composite Advanced Mate ... F ... 212 268-0003
New York *(G-8906)*
B & R Promotional Products ... G ... 212 563-0040
New York *(G-8988)*
▲ Barrett Bronze Inc ... E ... 914 699-6060
Mount Vernon *(G-8380)*
Beyond Design Inc ... G ... 607 865-7487
Walton *(G-15910)*
Brooklyn Remembers Inc ... F ... 718 491-1705
Brooklyn *(G-1646)*
▲ Cetek Inc ... E ... 845 452-3510
Poughkeepsie *(G-13331)*
▲ Design Research Ltd ... C ... 212 228-7675
New York *(G-9506)*
Dream Statuary Inc ... G ... 718 647-2024
Brooklyn *(G-1792)*
Enrg Inc ... F ... 716 873-2939
Buffalo *(G-2820)*
Essex Works Ltd ... F ... 718 495-4575
Brooklyn *(G-1852)*
Everblock Systems LLC ... G ... 844 422-5625
New York *(G-9734)*
▲ Foster Reeve & Associates Inc ... G ... 718 609-0090
Brooklyn *(G-1900)*
Fra-Rik Formica Fabg Co Inc ... G ... 718 597-3335
Bronx *(G-1275)*
Glasson Sculpture Works ... G ... 845 255-2969
Gardiner *(G-5294)*
Halo Associates ... G ... 212 691-9549
New York *(G-10024)*
▲ Heany Industries Inc ... D ... 585 889-2700
Scottsville *(G-14750)*
Jonas Louis Paul Studios Inc ... G ... 518 851-2211
Hudson *(G-6361)*
Kodiak Studios Inc ... G ... 718 769-5399
Brooklyn *(G-2080)*
▲ Reliance Mica Co Inc ... G ... 718 788-0282
Rockaway Park *(G-14229)*
▲ S & J Trading Inc ... G ... 718 347-1323
Floral Park *(G-4967)*
▲ Starfire Systems Inc ... F ... 518 899-9336
Glenville *(G-5447)*
Studio Associates of New York ... G ... 212 268-1163
New York *(G-11727)*
▲ Ufx Holding I Corporation ... G ... 212 644-5900
New York *(G-11933)*
Ufx Holding II Corporation ... G ... 212 644-5900
New York *(G-11934)*
Unifrax Holding Co ... G ... 212 644-5900
New York *(G-11943)*
▲ Unifrax I LLC ... C ... 716 768-6500
Tonawanda *(G-15587)*
Unifrax I LLC ... C ... 716 696-3000
Tonawanda *(G-15586)*
Vescom Structural Systems Inc ... F ... 516 876-8100
Westbury *(G-16386)*

33 PRIMARY METAL INDUSTRIES

3312 Blast Furnaces, Coke Ovens, Steel & Rolling Mills

A-1 Iron Works Inc ... G ... 718 927-4766
Brooklyn *(G-1461)*
Albaluz Films LLC ... G ... 347 613-2321
New York *(G-8733)*
▲ Allvac ... F ... 716 433-4411
Lockport *(G-7284)*
▲ American Chimney Supplies Inc ... G ... 631 434-2020
Hauppauge *(G-5764)*
Artistic Iron Works Inc ... G ... 631 665-4285
Bay Shore *(G-659)*
B H M Metal Products Co ... G ... 845 292-5297
Kauneonga Lake *(G-6849)*
Baker Tool & Die ... G ... 716 694-2025
North Tonawanda *(G-12415)*
Baker Tool & Die & Die ... G ... 716 694-2025
North Tonawanda *(G-12416)*
▲ Bebitz USA Inc ... G ... 516 280-8378
Hicksville *(G-6065)*
Belmet Products Inc ... E ... 718 542-8220
Bronx *(G-1227)*
Bonura and Sons Iron Works ... F ... 718 381-4100
Franklin Square *(G-5115)*
China Industrial Steel Inc ... G ... 646 328-1502
New York *(G-9279)*
Coventry Manufacturing Co Inc ... E ... 914 668-2212
Mount Vernon *(G-8391)*
◆ Crucible Industries LLC ... B ... 800 365-1180
Syracuse *(G-15295)*
Dakota Systems Mfg Corp ... G ... 631 249-5811
Farmingdale *(G-4748)*
David Fehlman ... G ... 315 455-8888
Syracuse *(G-15303)*
◆ Dunkirk Specialty Steel LLC ... C ... 716 366-1000
Dunkirk *(G-4168)*
Elderlee Incorporated ... C ... 315 789-6670
Oaks Corners *(G-12527)*
Empire Steel Works Inc ... F ... 516 561-3500
Hicksville *(G-6084)*
Fuller Tool Incorporated ... F ... 315 891-3183
Newport *(G-12255)*
Hallock Fabricating Corp ... G ... 631 727-2441
Riverhead *(G-13569)*
▼ Handy & Harman Ltd ... A ... 212 520-2300
New York *(G-10031)*
Hitachi Metals America Ltd ... E ... 914 694-9200
Purchase *(G-13389)*
Hmi Metal Powders ... C ... 315 839-5421
Clayville *(G-3557)*
▲ Homogeneous Metals Inc ... D ... 315 839-5421
Clayville *(G-3558)*
Hudson Valley Steel Products ... G ... 845 565-2270
Newburgh *(G-12229)*
Image Iron Works Inc ... G ... 718 592-8276
Corona *(G-3845)*
◆ Jaquith Industries Inc ... E ... 315 478-5700
Syracuse *(G-15346)*
Jfe Engineering Corporation ... F ... 212 310-9320
New York *(G-10333)*
Jfe Steel America Inc ... G ... 212 310-9320
New York *(G-10334)*
▲ Juniper Elbow Co Inc ... C ... 718 326-2546
Middle Village *(G-8124)*
Kenbenco Inc ... F ... 845 246-3066
Saugerties *(G-14609)*
Lino International Inc ... G ... 516 482-7100
Great Neck *(G-5569)*
▲ Mardek LLC ... G ... 585 735-9333
Pittsford *(G-13021)*
Markin Tubing LP ... F ... 585 495-6211
Buffalo *(G-2937)*
Markin Tubing Inc ... C ... 585 495-6211
Wyoming *(G-16700)*
Matrix Steel Company Inc ... G ... 718 381-6800
Brooklyn *(G-2180)*
N C Iron Works Inc ... G ... 718 633-4660
Brooklyn *(G-2240)*
Nitro Wheels Inc ... F ... 716 337-0709
North Collins *(G-12387)*
▲ Nucor Steel Auburn Inc ... B ... 315 253-4561
Auburn *(G-493)*
Qsf Inc ... G ... 585 247-6200
Gates *(G-5311)*
Quality Stainless Steel NY Inc ... F ... 718 748-1785
Brooklyn *(G-2368)*
Quest Manufacturing Inc ... E ... 716 312-8000
Hamburg *(G-5691)*
R D Specialties Inc ... F ... 585 265-0220
Webster *(G-16093)*
Recon Construction Corp ... E ... 718 939-1305
Little Neck *(G-7219)*
◆ Renco Group Inc ... G ... 212 541-6000
New York *(G-11361)*
Republic Steel Inc ... B ... 716 827-2800
Blasdell *(G-928)*
Rochester Structural LLC ... E ... 585 436-1250
Rochester *(G-14097)*
Safespan Platform Systems Inc ... E ... 716 694-1100
Tonawanda *(G-15574)*
Samuel Son & Co Inc ... G ... 716 856-6500
Blasdell *(G-929)*
Sims Group USA Holdings Corp ... D ... 718 786-6031
Long Island City *(G-7591)*
Sph Group Holdings LLC ... F ... 212 520-2300
New York *(G-11669)*
Spin-Rite Corporation ... F ... 585 266-5200
Rochester *(G-14138)*
Tdy Industries LLC ... E ... 716 433-4411
Lockport *(G-7334)*
TI Group Auto Systems LLC ... G ... 315 568-7042
Seneca Falls *(G-14787)*
Tms International LLC ... G ... 315 253-8925
Auburn *(G-504)*
▲ Tonawanda Coke Corporation ... C ... 716 876-6222
Tonawanda *(G-15582)*
Tri Valley Iron Inc ... F ... 845 365-1013
Palisades *(G-12848)*
Vell Company Inc ... G ... 845 365-1013
Palisades *(G-12849)*
◆ Viraj - USA Inc ... G ... 516 280-8380
Hicksville *(G-6138)*

3313 Electrometallurgical Prdts

◆ CCA Holding Inc ... C ... 716 446-8800
Amherst *(G-220)*
Globe Metallurgical Inc ... D ... 716 804-0862
Niagara Falls *(G-12288)*
▲ Golden Egret LLC ... G ... 516 922-2839
East Norwich *(G-4272)*
◆ Medima LLC ... C ... 716 741-0400
Clarence *(G-3535)*
Thyssenkrupp Materials NA Inc ... F ... 212 972-8800
New York *(G-11829)*

3315 Steel Wire Drawing & Nails & Spikes

A&B Iron Works Inc ... G ... 347 466-3193
Brooklyn *(G-1460)*
▲ Able Industries Inc ... F ... 914 739-5685
Cortlandt Manor *(G-3898)*
▲ Aerospace Wire & Cable Inc ... E ... 718 358-2345
College Point *(G-3637)*
▲ American Wire Tie Inc ... E ... 716 337-2412
North Collins *(G-12383)*
▲ Aruvil International Inc ... G ... 212 447-5020
New York *(G-8928)*
Bekaert Corporation ... E ... 716 830-1321
Amherst *(G-216)*
▲ Braun Horticulture Inc ... G ... 716 282-6101
Niagara Falls *(G-12265)*
CFS Enterprises Inc ... E ... 718 585-0500
Bronx *(G-1238)*
▲ Cobra Manufacturing Corp ... G ... 845 514-2505
Lake Katrine *(G-6972)*
▲ Continental Cordage Corp ... D ... 315 655-9800
Cazenovia *(G-3317)*
◆ Dragon Trading Inc ... G ... 212 717-1496
New York *(G-9572)*
▲ Dsr International Corp ... G ... 631 427-2600
Great Neck *(G-5550)*
EB Acquisitions LLC ... D ... 212 355-3310
New York *(G-9614)*
Forsyth Industries Inc ... E ... 716 652-1070
Buffalo *(G-2831)*
Hitachi Metals America Ltd ... E ... 914 694-9200
Purchase *(G-13389)*
◆ Hohmann & Barnard Inc ... E ... 631 234-0600
Hauppauge *(G-5846)*
▲ Island Industries Corp ... G ... 631 451-8825
Coram *(G-3799)*
▲ Lee Spring Company LLC ... C ... 718 362-5183
Brooklyn *(G-2105)*
Liberty Fabrication Inc ... G ... 718 495-5735
Brooklyn *(G-2115)*
Master-Halco Inc ... F ... 631 585-8150
Yaphank *(G-16717)*
▲ Nupro Technologies LLC ... F ... 412 422-5922
Canandaigua *(G-3227)*
▲ Nyi Building Products Inc ... F ... 518 458-7500
Clifton Park *(G-3572)*
Omega Wire Inc ... D ... 315 689-7115
Jordan *(G-6842)*
Oneonta Fence ... G ... 607 433-6707
Oneonta *(G-12642)*
▲ Rolling Gate Supply Corp ... G ... 718 366-5258
Glendale *(G-5407)*
Rose Fence Inc ... F ... 516 223-0777
Baldwin *(G-541)*
Sigmund Cohn Corp ... D ... 914 664-5300
Mount Vernon *(G-8443)*
Spectrum Cable Corporation ... G ... 585 235-7714
Rochester *(G-14137)*
▲ Styles Manufacturing Corp ... G ... 516 763-5303
Oceanside *(G-12559)*
▲ Tappan Wire & Cable Inc ... C ... 845 353-9000
Blauvelt *(G-942)*
Technical Wldg Fabricators LLC ... F ... 518 463-2229
Albany *(G-132)*
Web Associates Inc ... G ... 716 883-3377
Buffalo *(G-3125)*

Employee Codes: A=Over 500 employees, B=251-500
C=101-250, D=51-100, E=20-50, F=10-19, G=5-9

2019 Harris
New York Manufacturers Directory

737

33 PRIMARY METAL INDUSTRIES

3316 Cold Rolled Steel Sheet, Strip & Bars

▼ Aero-Data Metal Crafters Inc..........C ... 631 471-7733
  Ronkonkoma *(G-14294)*
▲ Clover Wire Forming Co Inc..........E ... 914 375-0400
  Yonkers *(G-16745)*
◆ Gibraltar Industries Inc..............D ... 716 826-6500
  Buffalo *(G-2849)*
Hitachi Metals America Ltd............E ... 914 694-9200
  Purchase *(G-13389)*
Niagara Lasalle Corporation..........D ... 716 827-7010
  Buffalo *(G-2968)*
Northeast Cnstr Inds Inc..............F ... 845 565-1000
  Montgomery *(G-8314)*
◆ Renco Group Inc....................G ... 212 541-6000
  New York *(G-11361)*
Rough Brothers Holding Co...........D ... 716 826-6500
  Buffalo *(G-3048)*
Worthington Industries Inc...........D ... 315 336-5500
  Rome *(G-14279)*

3317 Steel Pipe & Tubes

Coventry Manufacturing Co Inc.......E ... 914 668-2212
  Mount Vernon *(G-8391)*
Liberty Pipe Incorporated............G ... 516 747-2472
  Mineola *(G-8234)*
▲ Markin Tubing LP...................C ... 585 495-6211
  Wyoming *(G-16699)*
Markin Tubing LP....................F ... 585 495-6211
  Buffalo *(G-2937)*
Markin Tubing Inc....................C ... 585 495-6211
  Wyoming *(G-16700)*
McHone Industries Inc................D ... 716 945-3380
  Salamanca *(G-14526)*
Micromold Products Inc..............E ... 914 969-2850
  Yonkers *(G-16784)*
▲ Oriskany Mfg Tech LLC............E ... 315 732-4962
  Yorkville *(G-16830)*
Stony Brook Mfg Co Inc..............E ... 631 369-9530
  Calverton *(G-3171)*
▲ Super Steelworks Corporation.....G ... 718 386-4770
  Deer Park *(G-4050)*
Thyssenkrupp Materials NA Inc......G ... 585 279-0000
  Rochester *(G-14170)*
TI Group Auto Systems LLC..........G ... 315 568-7042
  Seneca Falls *(G-14787)*
▼ Tricon Piping Systems Inc.........F ... 315 697-8787
  Canastota *(G-3250)*
▲ Welded Tube Usa Inc...............D ... 716 828-1111
  Lackawanna *(G-6954)*

3321 Gray Iron Foundries

Acme Nipple Mfg Co Inc..............G ... 716 873-7491
  Buffalo *(G-2683)*
Auburn Foundry Inc..................F ... 315 253-4441
  Auburn *(G-464)*
Cpp - Guaymas.......................C ... 315 687-0014
  Chittenango *(G-3503)*
◆ Dragon Trading Inc.................G ... 212 717-1496
  New York *(G-9572)*
En Tech Corp.........................F ... 845 398-0776
  Tappan *(G-15468)*
Field Wares LLC......................G ... 508 380-6545
  Brooklyn *(G-1878)*
▲ Hitachi Metals America Ltd........E ... 914 694-9200
  Purchase *(G-13390)*
Jamestown Iron Works Inc...........F ... 716 665-2818
  Falconer *(G-4685)*
Matrix Steel Company Inc............G ... 718 381-6800
  Brooklyn *(G-2180)*
McWane Inc..........................B ... 607 734-2211
  Elmira *(G-4497)*
▲ Noresco Industrial Group Inc......E ... 516 759-3355
  Glen Cove *(G-5371)*
Oneida Foundries Inc.................E ... 315 363-4570
  Oneida *(G-12614)*
Penner Elbow Company Inc..........F ... 718 526-9000
  Elmhurst *(G-4470)*
S M S C Inc..........................G ... 315 942-4394
  Boonville *(G-1121)*

3322 Malleable Iron Foundries

Eastern Company.....................D ... 315 468-6251
  Solvay *(G-14917)*
Emcom Industries Inc................G ... 716 852-3711
  Buffalo *(G-2817)*
▲ Noresco Industrial Group Inc......E ... 516 759-3355
  Glen Cove *(G-5371)*
◆ Plattco Corporation.................E ... 518 563-4640
  Plattsburgh *(G-13145)*

3324 Steel Investment Foundries

Brinkman Precision Inc...............D ... 585 429-5001
  West Henrietta *(G-16233)*
Consoldted Precision Pdts Corp.....B ... 315 687-0014
  Chittenango *(G-3502)*
▲ Cpp-Syracuse Inc..................E ... 315 687-0014
  Chittenango *(G-3504)*
Jbf Stainless LLC.....................E ... 315 569-2800
  Frankfort *(G-5108)*
Quality Castings Inc..................E ... 732 409-3203
  Long Island City *(G-7566)*
Worldwide Resources Inc............F ... 718 760-5000
  Brooklyn *(G-2659)*

3325 Steel Foundries, NEC

A & V Castings Inc...................E ... 212 997-0042
  New York *(G-8689)*
Amt Incorporated.....................E ... 518 284-2910
  Sharon Springs *(G-14797)*
Brinkman Intl Group Inc..............G ... 585 429-5000
  Rochester *(G-13676)*
C J Winter Machine Tech............E ... 585 429-5000
  Rochester *(G-13685)*
Eastern Industrial Steel Corp........E ... 845 639-9749
  New City *(G-8493)*
Frazer & Jones Co....................D ... 315 468-6251
  Syracuse *(G-15325)*
Steel Craft Rolling Door..............F ... 631 608-8662
  Copiague *(G-3783)*

3331 Primary Smelting & Refining Of Copper

▲ Hengyuan Copper USA Inc........G ... 718 357-6666
  Whitestone *(G-16542)*
Sherburne Metal Sales Inc..........F ... 607 674-4441
  Sherburne *(G-14809)*
◆ Tecnofil Chenango SAC...........E ... 607 674-4441
  Sherburne *(G-14812)*

3334 Primary Production Of Aluminum

Alcoa USA Corp......................E ... 315 764-4011
  Massena *(G-7898)*
American Std Shtmtl Sup Corp......F ... 718 888-9350
  Flushing *(G-4985)*
Greene Brass & Alum Fndry LLC....G ... 607 656-4204
  Bloomville *(G-962)*

3339 Primary Nonferrous Metals, NEC

▲ AAA Catalytic Recycling Inc......F ... 631 920-7944
  Farmingdale *(G-4706)*
All American Funding & Ref LLC....G ... 516 978-7531
  Farmingdale *(G-4713)*
Ames Goldsmith Corp................F ... 518 792-7435
  Glens Falls *(G-5414)*
Billanti Casting Co Inc................E ... 516 775-4800
  New Hyde Park *(G-8520)*
Doral Refining Corp..................E ... 516 223-3684
  Freeport *(G-5151)*
Eco-Bat America LLC................E ... 845 692-4414
  Middletown *(G-8150)*
Electro Alloy Recovery Inc...........G ... 631 879-7530
  Bohemia *(G-1023)*
Euro Pacific Precious Metals........E ... 212 481-0310
  New York *(G-9729)*
General Refining & Smelting........G ... 516 538-4747
  Hempstead *(G-6011)*
General Refining Corporation.......G ... 516 538-4747
  Hempstead *(G-6012)*
Globe Metallurgical Inc...............F ... 716 804-0862
  Niagara Falls *(G-12288)*
Goldmark Products Inc..............E ... 631 777-3343
  Farmingdale *(G-4773)*
▼ Handy & Harman Ltd..............F ... 212 520-2300
  New York *(G-10031)*
Hh Liquidating Corp..................A ... 646 282-2500
  New York *(G-10092)*
Marina Jewelry Co Inc...............E ... 212 354-5027
  New York *(G-10703)*
Materion Advanced Materials.......E ... 800 327-1355
  Brewster *(G-1170)*
◆ Medima LLC........................C ... 716 741-0400
  Clarence *(G-3535)*
▲ Rochester Silver Works LLC......E ... 585 743-1610
  New Hartford *(G-14094)*
S & W Metal Trading Corp..........G ... 212 719-5070
  Brooklyn *(G-2438)*
Sabin Metal Corporation.............C ... 585 538-2194
  Scottsville *(G-14753)*
▲ Saes Smart Materials Inc.........E ... 315 266-2026
  New Hartford *(G-8511)*

Sigmund Cohn Corp..................D ... 914 664-5300
  Mount Vernon *(G-8443)*
Sph Group Holdings LLC.............F ... 212 520-2300
  New York *(G-11669)*
Starfuels Inc..........................E ... 914 289-4800
  White Plains *(G-16507)*
Tdy Industries Inc....................E ... 716 433-4411
  Lockport *(G-7334)*
▲ Umicore Technical Materials.....C ... 518 792-7700
  Glens Falls *(G-5441)*
Umicore USA Inc....................E ... 919 874-7171
  Glens Falls *(G-5442)*
Wallace Refiners Inc.................G ... 212 391-2649
  New York *(G-12068)*
Zerovalent Nanometals Inc.........G ... 585 298-8592
  Rochester *(G-14219)*

3341 Secondary Smelting & Refining Of Nonferrous Metals

Advanced Precision Technology....F ... 845 279-3540
  Brewster *(G-1154)*
Amt Incorporated.....................E ... 518 284-2910
  Sharon Springs *(G-14797)*
Ben Weitsman of Albany LLC.......E ... 518 462-4444
  Albany *(G-45)*
Cora Materials Corp..................F ... 516 488-6300
  New Hyde Park *(G-8526)*
Eco-Bat America LLC................E ... 845 692-4414
  Middletown *(G-8150)*
Encore Refining and Recycling.....G ... 631 319-1910
  Holbrook *(G-6185)*
General Refining & Smelting........G ... 516 538-4747
  Hempstead *(G-6011)*
▲ Germanium Corp America Inc...F ... 315 853-4900
  Clinton *(G-3585)*
Island Recycling Corp...............G ... 631 234-6688
  Central Islip *(G-3373)*
Karbra Company.....................C ... 212 736-9300
  New York *(G-10407)*
▲ Metalico Aluminum Recovery Inc..E ... 315 463-9500
  Syracuse *(G-15370)*
Parfuse Corp.........................E ... 516 997-8888
  Westbury *(G-16363)*
Pluribus Products Inc................F ... 718 852-1614
  Bayville *(G-753)*
S & W Metal Trading Corp..........G ... 212 719-5070
  Brooklyn *(G-2438)*
▲ Sabin Metal Corporation..........F ... 631 329-1695
  East Hampton *(G-4242)*
Sabin Metal Corporation.............C ... 585 538-2194
  Scottsville *(G-14753)*
Scepter Inc...........................G ... 315 568-4225
  Seneca Falls *(G-14783)*
Sims Group USA Holdings Corp...D ... 718 786-6031
  Long Island City *(G-7591)*
Special Metals Corporation..........F ... 716 366-5663
  Dunkirk *(G-4180)*

3351 Rolling, Drawing & Extruding Of Copper

Aurubis Buffalo Inc...................F ... 716 879-6700
  Buffalo *(G-2714)*
▲ Aurubis Buffalo Inc................B ... 716 879-6700
  Buffalo *(G-2715)*
Camden Wire Co Inc.................A ... 315 245-3800
  Camden *(G-3186)*
▲ Continental Cordage Corp........D ... 315 655-9800
  Cazenovia *(G-3317)*
International Wire Group.............F ... 315 245-3800
  Camden *(G-3188)*
Jaguar Industries Inc.................F ... 845 947-1800
  Haverstraw *(G-5979)*
◆ Milward Alloys Inc..................E ... 716 434-5536
  Lockport *(G-7318)*
Omega Wire Inc.....................D ... 315 689-7115
  Jordan *(G-6842)*
▲ Omega Wire Inc....................B ... 315 245-3800
  Camden *(G-3191)*
▲ Owi Corporation....................E ... 315 245-4305
  Camden *(G-3192)*
Sherburne Metal Sales Inc..........F ... 607 674-4441
  Sherburne *(G-14809)*

3353 Aluminum Sheet, Plate & Foil

Alcoa Fastening Systems............E ... 585 368-5049
  Rochester *(G-13612)*
Alcoa USA Corp......................E ... 315 764-4106
  Massena *(G-7899)*
◆ Alufoil Products Co Inc............F ... 631 231-4141
  Hauppauge *(G-5762)*

American Douglas Metals Inc ....F 716 856-3170
Buffalo *(G-2695)*
◆ Arconic Inc ....D 212 836-2758
New York *(G-8903)*
Arconic Inc ....G 315 764-4011
Massena *(G-7900)*
BSD Aluminum Foil LLC ....E 347 689-3875
Brooklyn *(G-1653)*
Golden Argosy LLC ....G 212 268-0003
New York *(G-9953)*
Novelis Corporation ....B 315 342-1036
Oswego *(G-12783)*
Novelis Corporation ....B 315 349-0121
Oswego *(G-12784)*
▲ USA Foil Inc ....E 631 234-5252
Yaphank *(G-16727)*

3354 Aluminum Extruded Prdts

◆ A-Fab Initiatives Inc ....F 716 877-5257
Buffalo *(G-2680)*
Alumi-Tech LLC ....G 585 663-7010
Penfield *(G-12939)*
Amt Incorporated ....E 518 284-2910
Sharon Springs *(G-14797)*
Apollo Management V LP ....E 914 467-6510
Purchase *(G-13386)*
◆ Arconic Inc ....D 212 836-2758
New York *(G-8903)*
Arconic Inc ....G 315 764-4011
Massena *(G-7900)*
Constellium ....E 212 675-5087
New York *(G-9386)*
▼ Flagpoles Incorporated ....D 631 751-5500
East Setauket *(G-4301)*
▲ Itts Industrial Inc ....G 718 605-6934
Staten Island *(G-15092)*
▼ J Sussman Inc ....E 718 297-0228
Jamaica *(G-6652)*
Jem Threading Specialties Inc ....G 718 665-3341
Bronx *(G-1301)*
▲ Keymark Corporation ....A 518 853-3421
Fonda *(G-5066)*
▲ Minitec Framing Systems LLC ....E 585 924-4690
Farmington *(G-4917)*
North American Pipe Corp ....F 516 338-2863
East Williston *(G-4382)*
▼ North Coast Outfitters Ltd ....E 631 727-5580
Riverhead *(G-13578)*
▲ Nyahb Inc ....G 845 352-5300
Monsey *(G-8292)*
Pioneer Window Holdings Inc ....E 518 762-5526
Johnstown *(G-6837)*
Super Sweep Inc ....F 631 223-8205
Huntington Station *(G-6459)*
Swiss Tool Corporation ....E 631 842-7766
Copiague *(G-3785)*

3355 Aluminum Rolling & Drawing, NEC

Alcoa Corporation ....B 412 315-2900
Massena *(G-7897)*
◆ Arconic Inc ....D 212 836-2758
New York *(G-8903)*
Arconic Inc ....G 315 764-4011
Massena *(G-7900)*
Irtronics Instruments Inc ....F 914 693-6291
Ardsley *(G-395)*
Mitsubishi Chemical Amer Inc ....E 212 223-3043
New York *(G-10825)*
▲ N A Alumil Corporation ....G 718 355-9393
Long Island City *(G-7532)*
Novelis Inc ....E 315 349-0121
Oswego *(G-12785)*
▲ SI Partners Inc ....G 516 433-1415
Hicksville *(G-6132)*

3356 Rolling, Drawing-Extruding Of Nonferrous Metals

Arlon Viscor Ltd ....A 914 461-1300
White Plains *(G-16422)*
▲ Aufhauser Corporation ....F 516 694-8696
Plainview *(G-13038)*
Aufhauser Manufacturing Corp ....E 516 694-8696
Plainview *(G-13039)*
Braze Alloy Inc ....G 718 815-5757
Staten Island *(G-15054)*
▲ Cathay Resources Inc ....G 516 922-2839
East Norwich *(G-4271)*
▲ Continental Cordage Corp ....D 315 655-9800
Cazenovia *(G-3317)*
▲ Cpp-Syracuse Inc ....E 315 687-0014
Chittenango *(G-3504)*
Eco-Bat America LLC ....C 845 692-4414
Middletown *(G-8150)*
Hh Liquidating Corp ....A 646 282-2500
New York *(G-10092)*
▲ Indium Corporation of America ....E 800 446-3486
Clinton *(G-3586)*
Indium Corporation of America ....E 315 793-8200
Utica *(G-15713)*
Indium Corporation of America ....E 315 381-2330
Utica *(G-15714)*
Jewelers Solder Supply Inc ....F 718 637-1256
Brooklyn *(G-2037)*
▲ Medi-Ray Inc ....D 877 898-3003
Tuckahoe *(G-15644)*
Mustard Tin ....G 315 769-8409
Massena *(G-7906)*
▲ Nationwide Precision Pdts Corp ....B 585 272-7100
Rochester *(G-13964)*
Nickel City Studios Photo Jour ....G 716 200-0956
Buffalo *(G-2972)*
RB Diamond Inc ....G 212 398-4560
New York *(G-11334)*
▲ Selectrode Industries Inc ....D 631 547-5470
Huntington Station *(G-6458)*
Sigmund Cohn Corp ....D 914 664-5300
Mount Vernon *(G-8443)*
Special Metals Corporation ....B 315 798-2900
New Hartford *(G-8512)*
T L Diamond & Company Inc ....G 212 249-6660
New York *(G-11768)*
Titanium Dem Remediation Group ....F 716 433-4100
Lockport *(G-7336)*
▲ Vestal Electronic Devices LLC ....F 607 773-8461
Endicott *(G-4614)*

3357 Nonferrous Wire Drawing

Caldwell Bennett Inc ....E 315 337-8540
Oriskany *(G-12752)*
Camden Wire Co Inc ....A 315 245-3800
Camden *(G-3186)*
Colonial Wire & Cable Co Inc ....D 631 234-8500
Hauppauge *(G-5793)*
Colonial Wire Cable Co NJ Inc ....G 631 234-8500
Hauppauge *(G-5794)*
Complete Fiber Solutions Inc ....G 718 828-8900
Bronx *(G-1245)*
▲ Continental Cordage Corp ....D 315 655-9800
Cazenovia *(G-3317)*
▲ Convergent Cnnctivity Tech Inc ....G 845 651-5250
Florida *(G-4969)*
Corning Incorporated ....G 607 974-6729
Painted Post *(G-12837)*
◆ Corning Incorporated ....A 607 974-9000
Corning *(G-3809)*
Corning Incorporated ....E 607 248-1200
Corning *(G-3812)*
Corning Optcal Cmmncations LLC ....F 607 974-7543
Corning *(G-3816)*
Corning Specialty Mtls Inc ....G 607 974-9000
Corning *(G-3817)*
◆ Cortland Cable Company Inc ....E 607 753-8276
Cortland *(G-3865)*
▲ CS Business Systems Inc ....E 716 886-6521
Buffalo *(G-2786)*
▲ Fiberall Corp ....E 516 371-5200
Inwood *(G-6490)*
▲ Fiberdyne Labs Inc ....D 315 895-8470
Frankfort *(G-5107)*
Global Technologies Inc ....D 631 243-7924
Deer Park *(G-3982)*
Hyperline Systems Inc ....G 613 736-8500
Brooklyn *(G-1991)*
▲ International Wire Group Inc ....B 315 245-2000
Camden *(G-3189)*
Jaguar Industries Inc ....F 845 947-1800
Haverstraw *(G-5979)*
Kris-Tech Wire Company Inc ....E 315 339-5268
Rome *(G-14255)*
◆ Leviton Manufacturing Co Inc ....B 631 812-6000
Melville *(G-8043)*
▲ Monroe Cable Company Inc ....C 845 692-2800
Middletown *(G-8166)*
Performance Wire & Cable Inc ....F 315 245-2594
Camden *(G-3193)*
▲ Rdi Inc ....F 914 773-1000
Mount Kisco *(G-8357)*
◆ Remee Products Corp ....D 845 651-4431
Florida *(G-4972)*
Rockland Insulated Wire Cable ....G 845 429-3103
Haverstraw *(G-5980)*
Siemens Corporation ....F 202 434-7800
New York *(G-11577)*
Siemens USA Holdings Inc ....B 212 258-4000
New York *(G-11580)*
Sinclair Technologies Inc ....E 716 874-3682
Hamburg *(G-5695)*
Steelflex Electro Corp ....D 516 226-4466
Lindenhurst *(G-7193)*
▲ Tappan Wire & Cable Inc ....C 845 353-9000
Blauvelt *(G-942)*
TLC-The Light Connection Inc ....D 315 736-7384
Oriskany *(G-12766)*
▲ United Wire Technologies Inc ....F 315 623-7203
Constantia *(G-3741)*
Universal Builders Supply Inc ....F 845 758-8801
Red Hook *(G-13459)*
▲ Whirlwind Music Distrs Inc ....D 800 733-9473
Rochester *(G-14207)*

3363 Aluminum Die Castings

▲ Albest Metal Stamping Corp ....D 718 388-6000
Brooklyn *(G-1500)*
Crown Die Casting Corp ....E 914 667-5400
Mount Vernon *(G-8392)*
Greene Brass & Alum Fndry LLC ....G 607 656-4204
Bloomville *(G-962)*
▲ Greenfield Industries Inc ....D 516 623-9230
Freeport *(G-5160)*
ITT Corporation ....D 315 568-2811
Seneca Falls *(G-14777)*
ITT LLC ....D 914 641-2000
Seneca Falls *(G-14781)*
Louis Iannettoni ....D 315 454-3231
Syracuse *(G-15365)*
▲ Pinnacle Manufacturing Co Inc ....E 585 343-5664
Batavia *(G-633)*
Tpi Arcade Inc ....D 585 492-0122
Arcade *(G-390)*

3364 Nonferrous Die Castings, Exc Aluminum

▲ Albest Metal Stamping Corp ....D 718 388-6000
Brooklyn *(G-1500)*
▲ AM Cast Inc ....F 631 750-1644
Bohemia *(G-977)*
◆ American Casting and Mfg Corp ....D 800 342-0333
Plainview *(G-13035)*
American Casting and Mfg Corp ....G 516 349-7010
Plainview *(G-13036)*
Cast-All Corporation ....E 516 741-4025
Mineola *(G-8212)*
Cast-All Corporation ....E 516 741-4025
Mineola *(G-8211)*
Crown Die Casting Corp ....E 914 667-5400
Mount Vernon *(G-8392)*
Crown Novelty Works Inc ....G 631 253-0949
Melville *(G-8013)*
Greenfield Die Casting Corp ....E 516 623-9230
Freeport *(G-5159)*
Mar-A-Thon Filters Inc ....G 631 957-4774
Lindenhurst *(G-7177)*
▲ Pinnacle Manufacturing Co Inc ....E 585 343-5664
Batavia *(G-633)*

3365 Aluminum Foundries

Airflex Industrial Inc ....E 631 752-1234
Farmingdale *(G-4710)*
American Blade Mfg LLC ....F 607 432-4518
Oneonta *(G-12624)*
American Blade Mfg LLC ....G 607 656-4204
Greene *(G-5612)*
Amt Incorporated ....E 518 284-2910
Sharon Springs *(G-14797)*
▼ Armstrong Mold Corporation ....E 315 437-1517
East Syracuse *(G-4320)*
Armstrong Mold Corporation ....D 315 437-1517
East Syracuse *(G-4321)*
◆ August Thomsen Corp ....E 516 676-7100
Glen Cove *(G-5361)*
▼ Auto-Mate Technologies LLC ....F 631 727-8886
Riverhead *(G-13564)*
Broetje Automation-Usa Inc ....C 716 204-8640
Williamsville *(G-16572)*
Consoldted Precision Pdts Corp ....B 315 687-0014
Chittenango *(G-3502)*
Corbett Stves Pttern Works Inc ....E 585 546-7109
Rochester *(G-13722)*

Crown Die Casting Corp.....E.....914 667-5400
Mount Vernon *(G-8392)*
E M T Manufacturing Inc.....F.....516 333-1917
East Meadow *(G-4250)*
East Pattern & Model Corp.....E.....585 461-3240
Rochester *(G-13756)*
East Pattern & Model Corp.....F.....585 461-3240
Rochester *(G-13757)*
Eastern Castings Co.....F.....518 677-5610
Cambridge *(G-3180)*
Eastern Strategic Materials.....E.....212 332-1619
New York *(G-9612)*
▲ Hitachi Metals America Ltd.....E.....914 694-9200
Purchase *(G-13390)*
J & J Bronze & Aluminum Cast.....E.....718 383-2111
Brooklyn *(G-2021)*
Massena Metals Inc.....F.....315 769-3846
Massena *(G-7905)*
Meloon Foundries LLC.....E.....315 454-3231
Syracuse *(G-15369)*
Micro Instrument Corp.....D.....585 458-3150
Rochester *(G-13939)*
◆ Milward Alloys Inc.....E.....716 434-5536
Lockport *(G-7318)*
▲ Ppi Corp.....D.....585 243-0300
Rochester *(G-14032)*
Pyrotek Incorporated.....D.....607 756-3050
Cortland *(G-3890)*
Smart USA Inc.....F.....631 969-1111
Bay Shore *(G-724)*
Taylor Metalworks Inc.....C.....716 662-3113
Orchard Park *(G-12745)*
Wolff & Dungey Inc.....E.....315 475-2105
Syracuse *(G-15460)*

3366 Copper Foundries

American Blade Mfg LLC.....G.....607 656-4204
Greene *(G-5612)*
American Blade Mfg LLC.....F.....607 432-4518
Oneonta *(G-12624)*
Amt Incorporated.....E.....518 284-2910
Sharon Springs *(G-14797)*
Argos Inc.....E.....845 528-0576
Putnam Valley *(G-13401)*
Art Bedi-Makky Foundry Corp.....G.....718 383-4191
Brooklyn *(G-1556)*
David Fehlman.....G.....315 455-8888
Syracuse *(G-15303)*
Discover Casting Inc.....F.....212 302-5060
New York *(G-9534)*
▲ Eastern Finding Corp.....F.....516 747-6640
New Hyde Park *(G-8530)*
J & J Bronze & Aluminum Cast.....E.....718 383-2111
Brooklyn *(G-2021)*
Meloon Foundries LLC.....E.....315 454-3231
Syracuse *(G-15369)*
▲ Modern Art Foundry Inc.....E.....718 728-2030
Astoria *(G-436)*
Omega Wire Inc.....E.....315 337-4300
Rome *(G-14265)*
Omega Wire Inc.....D.....315 689-7115
Jordan *(G-6842)*

3369 Nonferrous Foundries: Castings, NEC

Allstar Casting Corporation.....E.....212 563-0909
New York *(G-8801)*
Argos Inc.....E.....845 528-0576
Putnam Valley *(G-13401)*
Buffalo Metal Casting Co Inc.....E.....716 874-6211
Buffalo *(G-2747)*
▲ Cardona Industries USA Ltd.....G.....516 466-5200
Great Neck *(G-5542)*
Carrera Casting Corp.....C.....212 382-3296
New York *(G-9215)*
Cast-All Corporation.....E.....516 741-4025
Mineola *(G-8211)*
City Casting Corp.....G.....212 938-0511
New York *(G-9311)*
Controlled Castings Corp.....E.....516 349-1718
Plainview *(G-13045)*
▲ Cpp-Syracuse Inc.....E.....315 687-0014
Chittenango *(G-3504)*
Crown Die Casting Corp.....E.....914 667-5400
Mount Vernon *(G-8392)*
General Motors LLC.....B.....315 764-2000
Massena *(G-7902)*
Globalfoundries US Inc.....D.....518 305-9013
Malta *(G-7730)*
Globalfoundries US Inc.....F.....408 462-3900
Ballston Spa *(G-583)*
Greenfield Die Casting Corp.....E.....516 623-9230
Freeport *(G-5159)*
J & J Bronze & Aluminum Cast.....E.....718 383-2111
Brooklyn *(G-2021)*
▼ Jamestown Bronze Works Inc.....G.....716 665-2302
Jamestown *(G-6727)*
K & H Precision Products Inc.....E.....585 624-4894
Honeoye Falls *(G-6269)*
Karbra Company.....C.....212 736-9300
New York *(G-10407)*
Kelly Foundry & Machine Co.....E.....315 732-8313
Utica *(G-15717)*
Lamothermic Corp.....D.....845 278-6118
Brewster *(G-1169)*
▲ Medi-Ray Inc.....D.....877 898-3003
Tuckahoe *(G-15644)*
Miller Technology Inc.....G.....631 694-2224
Farmingdale *(G-4826)*
◆ Plattco Corporation.....E.....518 563-4640
Plattsburgh *(G-13145)*
Plattco Corporation.....F.....518 563-4640
Plattsburgh *(G-13146)*
▲ Polich Tallix Inc.....D.....845 567-9464
Walden *(G-15895)*
Quality Castings Inc.....E.....732 409-3203
Long Island City *(G-7566)*
Summit Aerospace Inc.....G.....718 433-1326
Long Island City *(G-7608)*
Wemco Casting LLC.....D.....631 563-8050
Bohemia *(G-1108)*
▲ Zierick Manufacturing Corp.....D.....800 882-8020
Mount Kisco *(G-8361)*

3398 Metal Heat Treating

A1 International Heat Treating.....G.....718 863-5552
Bronx *(G-1204)*
Aterian Investment Partners LP.....E.....212 547-2806
New York *(G-8946)*
B & W Heat Treating Company.....G.....716 876-8184
Tonawanda *(G-15525)*
Bodycote Syracuse Heat Treatin.....E.....315 451-0000
Liverpool *(G-7224)*
Bodycote Thermal Proc Inc.....E.....585 436-7876
Rochester *(G-13670)*
BSV Metal Finishers Inc.....E.....585 747-7070
Rochester *(G-13680)*
Buffalo Armory LLC.....G.....716 935-6346
Buffalo *(G-2740)*
Burke Frging Heat Treating Inc.....E.....585 235-6060
Rochester *(G-13682)*
Burton Industries Inc.....E.....631 643-6660
West Babylon *(G-16142)*
Cpp - Steel Treaters.....E.....315 736-3081
Oriskany *(G-12755)*
Elmira Heat Treating Inc.....E.....607 734-1577
Elmira *(G-4484)*
Expedient Heat Treating Corp.....G.....716 433-1177
North Tonawanda *(G-12426)*
◆ Gibraltar Industries Inc.....D.....716 826-6500
Buffalo *(G-2849)*
▲ Graywood Companies Inc.....E.....585 254-7000
Rochester *(G-13845)*
Great Lakes Metal Treating.....F.....716 694-1240
Tonawanda *(G-15543)*
Hercules Heat Treating Corp.....E.....718 625-1266
Brooklyn *(G-1973)*
Hi-Temp Brazing Inc.....E.....631 491-4917
Deer Park *(G-3983)*
◆ International Ord Tech Inc.....D.....716 664-1100
Jamestown *(G-6724)*
Jasco Heat Treating Inc.....E.....585 388-0071
Fairport *(G-4637)*
Kittredge & Sons Inc.....D.....978 567-0998
Niagara Falls *(G-12303)*
Metal Improvement Company LLC.....F.....631 567-2610
Bay Shore *(G-700)*
Metal Improvement Company LLC.....D.....607 533-7000
Lansing *(G-7056)*
Milgo Industrial Inc.....D.....718 388-6476
Brooklyn *(G-2206)*
Milgo Industrial Inc.....G.....718 387-0406
Brooklyn *(G-2207)*
Parfuse Corp.....E.....516 997-8888
Westbury *(G-16363)*
Rochester Steel Treating Works.....F.....585 546-3348
Rochester *(G-14096)*
Rough Brothers Holding Co.....G.....716 826-6500
Buffalo *(G-3048)*

3399 Primary Metal Prdts, NEC

Advantech Industries Inc.....C.....585 247-0701
Rochester *(G-13609)*
Aip Mc Holdings LLC.....G.....212 627-2360
New York *(G-8777)*
▲ Ames Advanced Materials Corp.....D.....518 792-5808
South Glens Falls *(G-14933)*
Ames Goldsmith Corp.....F.....518 792-7435
Glens Falls *(G-5414)*
Bridge Components Inc.....G.....716 731-1184
Sanborn *(G-14540)*
◆ Buffalo Tungsten Inc.....D.....716 683-9170
Depew *(G-4084)*
Cintube Ltd.....F.....518 324-3333
Plattsburgh *(G-13117)*
Custom Design Metals Inc.....G.....631 563-2444
Bohemia *(G-1003)*
▲ Cws Powder Coatings Company LP.....G.....845 398-2911
Blauvelt *(G-934)*
Hje Company Inc.....G.....518 792-8733
Queensbury *(G-13428)*
▼ HK Metal Trading Ltd.....G.....212 868-3333
New York *(G-10108)*
▲ Imerys Steelcasting Usa Inc.....D.....716 278-1634
Niagara Falls *(G-12298)*
▲ John Hassall LLC.....D.....516 334-6200
Westbury *(G-16344)*
New England Reclamation Inc.....F.....914 949-2000
White Plains *(G-16480)*
Oerlikon Metco (us) Inc.....G.....716 270-2228
Amherst *(G-245)*
Pmb Precision Products Inc.....F.....631 491-6753
West Babylon *(G-16182)*
Reed Systems Ltd.....F.....845 647-3660
Ellenville *(G-4442)*
▼ Rembar Company LLC.....E.....914 693-2620
Dobbs Ferry *(G-4130)*
Robert J Deluca Associates.....G.....845 357-3212
New York *(G-11408)*
Specialty Fabricators.....F.....631 256-6982
Oakdale *(G-12520)*
Tam Ceramics Group of Ny LLC.....D.....716 278-9400
Niagara Falls *(G-12340)*
◆ Universal Metals Inc.....G.....516 829-0896
Great Neck *(G-5598)*

34 FABRICATED METAL PRODUCTS, EXCEPT MACHINERY AND TRANSPORTATION EQUIPMENT

3411 Metal Cans

Anheuser-Busch Companies LLC.....G.....718 589-2610
Bronx *(G-1221)*
Ardagh Metal Packaging USA Inc.....C.....607 584-3300
Conklin *(G-3724)*
Ball Metal Beverage Cont Corp.....C.....845 692-3800
Middletown *(G-8138)*
Ball Metal Beverage Cont Corp.....C.....518 587-6030
Saratoga Springs *(G-14570)*
Brakewell Stl Fabricators Inc.....E.....845 469-9131
Chester *(G-3469)*
Cmc-Kuhnke Inc.....F.....518 694-3310
Albany *(G-60)*
Crown Cork & Seal Usa Inc.....C.....845 343-9586
Middletown *(G-8145)*
Erie Engineered Products Inc.....E.....716 206-0204
Lancaster *(G-7018)*
Hornet Group Inc.....D.....845 858-6400
Port Jervis *(G-13230)*
J C Industries Inc.....E.....631 420-1920
West Babylon *(G-16161)*
Marley Spoon Inc.....C.....646 934-6970
New York *(G-10714)*
Metal Container Corporation.....C.....845 567-1500
New Windsor *(G-8650)*
◆ Reynolds Metals Company LLC.....G.....212 518-5400
New York *(G-11380)*
Seneca Foods Corporation.....D.....315 926-0531
Marion *(G-7807)*
Silgan Containers Mfg Corp.....C.....315 946-4826
Lyons *(G-7687)*
Tio Foods LLC.....F.....917 946-1160
New York *(G-11849)*

3412 Metal Barrels, Drums, Kegs & Pails

Abbot & Abbot Box Corp.....F.....888 930-5972
Long Island City *(G-7365)*

SIC SECTION — 34 FABRICATED METAL PRODUCTS, EXCEPT MACHINERY AND TRANSPORTATION EQUIPMENT

Erie Engineered Products Inc .... E 716 206-0204
  Lancaster (G-7018)
Hornet Group Inc .... D 845 858-6400
  Port Jervis (G-13230)
J R Cooperage Co Inc .... G 718 387-1664
  Brooklyn (G-2027)
▲ Medi-Ray Inc .... D 877 898-3003
  Tuckahoe (G-15644)
Mobile Mini Inc .... F 315 732-4555
  Utica (G-15723)
Westrock - Southern Cont LLC .... C 315 487-6111
  Camillus (G-3200)
Westrock CP LLC .... C 716 694-1000
  North Tonawanda (G-12463)

3421 Cutlery

Advanced Machine Design Co Inc .... E 716 826-2000
  Buffalo (G-2689)
BSD Aluminum Foil LLC .... E 347 689-3875
  Brooklyn (G-1653)
Gibar Inc .... C 315 452-5656
  Cicero (G-3518)
▲ Great American Tool Co Inc .... G 716 646-5700
  Hamburg (G-5681)
HFC Prestige Intl US LLC .... A 212 389-7800
  New York (G-10091)
Inquiring Minds Inc .... F 845 246-5775
  Saugerties (G-14608)
John A Eberly Inc .... E 315 449-3034
  Syracuse (G-15347)
▲ Klein Cutlery LLC .... E 585 928-2500
  Bolivar (G-1111)
◆ Korin Japanese Trading Corp .... E 212 587-7021
  New York (G-10471)
◆ Lifetime Brands Inc .... B 516 683-6000
  Garden City (G-5265)
Mpdraw LLC .... E 212 228-8383
  New York (G-10850)
▲ Novelty Crystal Corp .... D 718 458-6700
  Long Island City (G-7540)
Oneida International Inc .... G 315 361-3000
  Oneida (G-12615)
Oneida Silversmiths Inc .... G 315 361-3000
  Oneida (G-12619)
◆ Ontario Knife Company .... G 716 676-5527
  Franklinville (G-5124)
Palladia Inc .... C 212 206-3669
  New York (G-11096)
Ratan Ronkonkoma .... G 631 588-6800
  Ronkonkoma (G-14405)
▲ Revlon Consumer Products Corp ...... B 212 527-4000
  New York (G-11377)
▲ Schilling Forge Inc .... E 315 454-4421
  Syracuse (G-15417)
Schrader Meat Market .... F 607 869-6328
  Romulus (G-14281)
Servotronics Inc .... C 716 655-5990
  Elma (G-4458)
Sherrill Manufacturing Inc .... C 315 280-0727
  Sherrill (G-14822)
Starfire Swords Ltd Inc .... E 607 589-7244
  Spencer (G-14974)
▲ Treyco Products Corp .... G 716 693-6525
  Tonawanda (G-15585)
▲ Utica Cutlery Company .... D 315 733-4663
  Utica (G-15737)
Warren Cutlery Corp .... F 845 876-3444
  Rhinebeck (G-13490)
Woods Knife Corporation .... E 516 798-4972
  Massapequa (G-7888)

3423 Hand & Edge Tools

Allway Tools Inc .... D 718 792-3636
  Bronx (G-1217)
Ames Companies Inc .... E 607 739-4544
  Pine Valley (G-13006)
Ames Companies Inc .... D 607 369-9595
  Unadilla (G-15660)
Best Way Tools By Anderson Inc .... G 631 586-4702
  Deer Park (G-3950)
Boucheron Joaillerie USA Inc .... E 212 715-7330
  New York (G-9126)
Classic Tool Design Inc .... E 845 562-8700
  New Windsor (G-8641)
Clopay Ames True Temper .... F 212 957-5096
  New York (G-9330)
Coastel Cable Tools Inc .... E 315 471-5361
  Syracuse (G-15283)
▲ Dead Ringer LLC .... G 585 355-4685
  Rochester (G-13736)

▲ Design Source By Lg Inc .... E 212 274-0022
  New York (G-9507)
▲ Dresser-Argus Inc .... G 718 643-1540
  Brooklyn (G-1794)
Edward C Lyons Company Inc .... F 718 515-5361
  Bronx (G-1265)
Edward C Muller Corp .... F 718 881-7270
  Bronx (G-1266)
Empire Devleopment .... G 716 789-2097
  Mayville (G-7920)
Gei International Inc .... G 315 463-9261
  East Syracuse (G-4342)
Huron TI Cutter Grinding Inc .... E 631 420-7000
  Farmingdale (G-4782)
▲ Hydramec Inc .... F 585 593-5190
  Scio (G-14735)
◆ Ivy Classic Industries Inc .... E 914 632-8200
  New Rochelle (G-8616)
▲ Lancaster Knives Inc .... E 716 683-5050
  Lancaster (G-7029)
Metro City Group Inc .... E 516 781-2500
  Bellmore (G-789)
Nyc District Council Ubcja .... G 212 366-7500
  New York (G-11012)
Robinson Tools LLC .... G 585 586-5432
  Penfield (G-12944)
Royal Molds Inc .... F 718 382-7686
  Brooklyn (G-2422)
▲ Schilling Forge Inc .... E 315 454-4421
  Syracuse (G-15417)
▲ Snyder Manufacturing Inc .... E 716 945-0354
  Salamanca (G-14533)
▲ Swimline International Corp .... G 631 254-2155
  Edgewood (G-4417)
▲ U S Air Tool Co Inc .... F 631 471-3300
  Ronkonkoma (G-14423)
Wall Tool & Tape Corp .... E 718 641-6813
  Ozone Park (G-12833)
Winters Railroad Service Inc .... G 716 337-2668
  North Collins (G-12390)
Woods Knife Corporation .... E 516 798-4972
  Massapequa (G-7888)
York Industries Inc .... G 516 746-3736
  Garden City Park (G-5290)

3425 Hand Saws & Saw Blades

Allway Tools Inc .... D 718 792-3636
  Bronx (G-1217)
◆ Amana Tool Corp .... D 631 752-1300
  Farmingdale (G-4718)
▲ Diamond Saw Works Inc .... F 716 496-7417
  Chaffee (G-3402)
Dinosaw Inc .... E 518 828-9942
  Hudson (G-6347)
Niabraze LLC .... F 716 447-1082
  Tonawanda (G-15562)
Quality Saw & Knife Inc .... F 631 491-4747
  West Babylon (G-16184)
▼ Suffolk McHy & Pwr Tl Corp .... G 631 289-7153
  Patchogue (G-12877)

3429 Hardware, NEC

A & L Doors & Hardware LLC .... F 718 585-8400
  Bronx (G-1199)
Advantage Wholesale Supply LLC .... D 718 284-5346
  Brooklyn (G-1490)
American Casting and Mfg Corp .... G 516 349-7010
  Plainview (G-13036)
Amertac Holdings Inc .... G 610 336-1330
  Monsey (G-8284)
Barry Industries Inc .... F 212 242-5200
  New York (G-9022)
Bfg Marine Inc .... F 516 586-5500
  Bay Shore (G-662)
Boa Security Technologies Corp .... G 516 576-0295
  Huntington (G-6395)
Boehm Surgical Instrument Corp .... F 585 436-6584
  Rochester (G-13671)
▲ Brio USA .... E 585 319-5599
  Rochester (G-13678)
▲ Cant Live Without It LLC .... D 844 517-9355
  New York (G-9197)
Cast-All Corporation .... E 516 741-4025
  Mineola (G-8211)
▲ City Store Gates Mfg Corp .... F 718 939-9700
  College Point (G-3642)
▲ Classic Brass Inc .... G 716 763-1400
  Lakewood (G-6991)
▲ Crest Lock Co Inc .... F 718 345-9898
  Brooklyn (G-1731)

D Best Service Co Inc .... G 718 972-6133
  Brooklyn (G-1746)
Daniel Demarco and Assoc Inc .... E 631 598-7000
  Amityville (G-271)
▼ Darman Manufacturing Coinc .... F 315 724-9632
  Utica (G-15692)
▲ Decorative Hardware .... F 914 238-5251
  Chappaqua (G-3421)
▲ Delta Lock Company LLC .... F 631 238-7035
  Bohemia (G-1012)
Designatronics Incorporated .... B 516 328-3300
  Hicksville (G-6080)
▲ Dico Products Corporation .... F 315 797-0470
  Utica (G-15694)
Dortronics Systems Inc .... E 631 725-0505
  Sag Harbor (G-14499)
Dover Marine Mfg & Sup Co Inc .... G 631 667-4300
  Deer Park (G-3967)
Eazy Locks LLC .... F 718 327-7770
  Far Rockaway (G-4699)
▲ ER Butler & Co Inc .... E 212 925-3565
  New York (G-9699)
Excelco Developments Inc .... F 716 934-2651
  Silver Creek (G-14861)
Fastener Dimensions Inc .... F 718 847-6321
  Ozone Park (G-12825)
Fuccillo Ford Nelliston Inc .... G 518 993-5555
  Nelliston (G-8482)
G Marks Hdwr Liquidating Corp .... D 631 225-5400
  Amityville (G-276)
Grow Computer Inc .... G 646 535-2037
  Brooklyn (G-1953)
▲ H A Guden Company Inc .... F 631 737-2900
  Ronkonkoma (G-14349)
Hesperus Nauticals Inc .... G 516 974-3016
  Hicksville (G-6095)
Industrial Electronic Hardware .... D 718 492-4440
  Brooklyn (G-1999)
Ingham Industries Inc .... G 631 242-2493
  Holbrook (G-6189)
International Key Supply LLC .... F 631 983-6096
  Farmingdale (G-4788)
▲ ITR Industries Inc .... E 914 964-7063
  Yonkers (G-16771)
◆ Jaquith Industries Inc .... E 315 478-5700
  Syracuse (G-15346)
▲ Kenstan Lock & Hardware Co Inc ... E 631 423-1977
  Plainview (G-13068)
▲ Key High Vacuum Products Inc ...... E 631 584-5959
  Nesconset (G-8485)
▲ Kilian Manufacturing Corp .... D 315 432-0700
  Syracuse (G-15355)
Kyntec Corporation .... G 716 810-6956
  Buffalo (G-2913)
▲ Legendary Auto Interiors Ltd .... E 315 331-1212
  Newark (G-12198)
Lewis Avenue LLC .... F 718 669-0579
  Brooklyn (G-2113)
▲ Liberty Brass Turning Co Inc .... E 718 784-2911
  Westbury (G-16350)
Lif Industries Inc .... E 718 767-8800
  Whitestone (G-16545)
Magellan Aerospace Processing .... F 631 694-1818
  West Babylon (G-16173)
Metalocke Industries Inc .... G 718 267-9200
  Woodside (G-16663)
Morgik Metal Designs .... F 212 463-0304
  New York (G-10842)
Mpi Consulting Incorporated .... F 631 253-2377
  West Babylon (G-16178)
◆ Nanz Custom Hardware Inc .... E 212 367-7000
  New York (G-10873)
Nanz Custom Hardware Inc .... C 212 367-7000
  Deer Park (G-4012)
Napco Security Tech Inc .... C 631 842-9400
  Amityville (G-304)
◆ Northknight Logistics Inc .... F 716 283-3090
  Niagara Falls (G-12316)
▲ Orbital Holdings Inc .... E 951 360-7100
  Buffalo (G-2982)
◆ P & F Industries Inc .... F 631 694-9800
  Melville (G-8055)
◆ P E Guerin .... D 212 243-5270
  New York (G-11084)
Pk30 System LLC .... F 212 473-8050
  Stone Ridge (G-15162)
▲ Progressive Hardware Co Inc .... E 631 445-1826
  East Northport (G-4269)
Real Design Inc .... F 315 429-3071
  Dolgeville (G-4137)

Employee Codes: A=Over 500 employees, B=251-500
C=101-250, D=51-100, E=20-50, F=10-19, G=5-9

2019 Harris
New York Manufacturers Directory

Rollson Inc ....E 631 423-9578
Huntington (G-6412)
◆ Rosco Inc ....C 718 526-2601
Jamaica (G-6675)
▲ Safe Skies LLC ....G 888 632-5027
New York (G-11464)
▼ Samscreen Inc ....E 607 722-3979
Conklin (G-3733)
Southco Inc ....B 585 624-2545
Honeoye Falls (G-6273)
Syraco Products Inc ....F 315 476-5306
Syracuse (G-15433)
▼ Tattersall Industries LLC ....E 518 381-4270
Schenectady (G-14720)
▲ Taylor Made Group LLC ....E 518 725-0681
Gloversville (G-5468)
Tools & Stamping Corp ....G 718 392-4040
Brooklyn (G-2570)
Trico Manufacturing Corp ....G 718 349-6565
Brooklyn (G-2584)
Truth Hardware Corporation ....G 585 627-5964
Rochester (G-14180)
Turbine Engine Comp Utica ....A 315 768-8070
Whitesboro (G-16531)
▲ United Metal Industries Inc ....G 516 354-6800
New Hyde Park (G-8569)
▲ Water Street Brass Corporation ....E 716 763-0059
Lakewood (G-6999)
▲ Weber-Knapp Company ....C 716 484-9135
Jamestown (G-6761)
William H Jackson Company ....G 718 784-4482
Long Island City (G-7639)
◆ Wolo Mfg Corp ....E 631 242-0333
Deer Park (G-4064)
Yaloz Mould & Die Co Inc ....E 718 389-1131
Brooklyn (G-2662)
York Industries Inc ....E 516 746-3736
Garden City Park (G-5290)
Zip Products Inc ....F 585 482-0044
Rochester (G-14220)

3431 Enameled Iron & Metal Sanitary Ware

◆ Advance Tabco Inc ....D 631 242-8270
Edgewood (G-4394)
▲ Independent Home Products LLC ....E 718 541-1256
West Hempstead (G-16216)
▲ ITR Industries Inc ....E 914 964-7063
Yonkers (G-16771)
Kenbenco Inc ....F 845 246-3066
Saugerties (G-14609)
Ketcham Medicine Cabinets ....E 631 615-6151
Ronkonkoma (G-14361)
▲ Kraus USA Inc ....F 800 775-0703
Port Washington (G-13278)
◆ Metpar Corp ....D 516 333-2600
Westbury (G-16356)
Porcelain Refinishing Corp ....F 516 352-4841
Flushing (G-5038)
▲ Sola Home Expo Inc ....G 718 646-3383
Brooklyn (G-2494)
Stainless Metals Inc ....F 718 784-1454
Woodside (G-16680)
Vanity Fair Bathmart Inc ....F 718 584-6700
Bronx (G-1413)
▲ Watermark Designs Holdings Ltd ....D 718 257-2800
Brooklyn (G-2640)

3432 Plumbing Fixture Fittings & Trim, Brass

A B S Brass Products Inc ....F 718 497-2115
Brooklyn (G-1454)
Acme Parts Inc ....E 718 649-1750
Brooklyn (G-1478)
Artys Sprnklr Svc Instllation ....F 516 538-4371
East Meadow (G-4246)
Corona Plumbing & Htg Sup Inc ....G 718 424-4133
Corona (G-3841)
Coronet Parts Mfg Co Inc ....E 718 649-1750
Brooklyn (G-1720)
Coronet Parts Mfg Co Inc ....E 718 649-1750
Brooklyn (G-1721)
▲ ER Butler & Co Inc ....E 212 925-3565
New York (G-9699)
Faucets and More Incorporated ....G 734 328-2387
Brooklyn (G-1869)
G Sicuranza Ltd ....G 516 759-0259
Glen Cove (G-5366)
Giagni Enterprises LLC ....G 914 699-6500
Mount Vernon (G-8400)
Giagni International Corp ....G 914 699-6500
Mount Vernon (G-8401)

Hanco Metal Products Inc ....F 212 787-5992
Brooklyn (G-1965)
▲ I W Industries Inc ....C 631 293-9494
Melville (G-8036)
L A S Replacement Parts Inc ....F 718 583-4700
Bronx (G-1312)
▲ Liberty Brass Turning Co Inc ....E 718 784-2911
Westbury (G-16350)
Malyn Industrial Ceramics Inc ....G 716 741-1510
Clarence Center (G-3548)
Mark Posner ....G 718 258-6241
Brooklyn (G-2169)
◆ P E Guerin ....D 212 243-5270
New York (G-11084)
Roccera LLC ....F 585 426-0887
Rochester (G-14077)
Toto USA Inc ....G 917 237-0665
New York (G-11874)
▲ Watermark Designs Holdings Ltd ....D 718 257-2800
Brooklyn (G-2640)

3433 Heating Eqpt

A Nuclimate Qulty Systems Inc ....F 315 431-0226
Syracuse (G-15236)
American Comfort Direct LLC ....E 201 364-8309
New York (G-8825)
Atlantis Energy Systems Inc ....G 916 438-2930
Poughkeepsie (G-13329)
Atlantis Solar Inc ....F 916 226-9183
Potsdam (G-13317)
Best Boilers Inc ....F 718 372-4210
Brooklyn (G-1602)
Biotech Energy Inc ....G 800 340-1387
Plattsburgh (G-13111)
Carrier Corporation ....B 315 432-6000
Syracuse (G-15272)
▲ Chentronics Corporation ....E 607 334-5531
Norwich (G-12480)
▲ Chicken Hawk Racing Inc ....G 845 758-0700
Red Hook (G-13457)
▲ CIDC Corp ....F 718 342-5820
Glendale (G-5395)
Dandelion Energy Inc ....F 603 781-2663
Brooklyn (G-1754)
◆ Dyson-Kissner-Moran Corp ....E 212 661-4600
Poughkeepsie (G-13335)
Economy Pump & Motor Repr Inc ....G 718 433-2600
Astoria (G-425)
◆ ECR International Inc ....D 315 797-1310
Utica (G-15699)
ECR International Inc ....C 716 366-5500
Dunkirk (G-4169)
▲ Embassy Industries Inc ....C 631 435-0209
Hauppauge (G-5820)
Empire Industrial Burner Svc ....F 631 242-4619
Deer Park (G-3974)
Fisonic Corp ....G 212 732-3777
Long Island City (G-7450)
▲ Fisonic Corp ....F 716 763-0295
New York (G-9814)
Frederick Cowan & Company Inc ....F 631 369-0360
Wading River (G-15884)
▲ Fulton Heating Solutions Inc ....D 315 298-5121
Pulaski (G-13383)
▼ Fulton Volcanic Inc ....D 315 298-5121
Pulaski (G-13384)
General Electric Intl Inc ....G 518 385-2211
Schenectady (G-14682)
Great Rock Automation Inc ....F 631 270-1508
Farmingdale (G-4774)
I-Evolve Techonology Services ....F 801 566-5268
Amherst (G-231)
▲ Integrated Solar Tech LLC ....G 914 249-9364
Port Chester (G-13202)
▲ Juniper Elbow Co Inc ....C 718 326-2546
Middle Village (G-8124)
Jus-Sar Fuel Inc ....G 845 791-8900
Harris (G-5722)
◆ Mx Solar USA LLC ....C 732 356-7300
New York (G-10863)
Nanopv Corporation ....C 609 851-3666
Liverpool (G-7249)
New Energy Systems Group ....C 917 573-0302
New York (G-10921)
▲ North Pk Innovations Group Inc ....E 716 699-2031
Ellicottville (G-4447)
▲ Omega Heater Company Inc ....D 631 588-8820
Ronkonkoma (G-14390)
▲ Prism Solar Technologies Inc ....E 845 883-4200
Highland (G-6146)

◆ RE Hansen Industries Inc ....C 631 471-2900
Saint James (G-14514)
▲ Roberts-Gordon LLC ....D 716 852-4400
Buffalo (G-3040)
Rockmills Steel Products Corp ....F 718 366-8300
Maspeth (G-7871)
▲ Slant/Fin Corporation ....B 516 484-2600
Greenvale (G-5632)
Solar Energy Systems LLC ....F 718 389-1545
Brooklyn (G-2495)
Unilux Advanced Mfg LLC ....E 518 344-7490
Schenectady (G-14724)
Vincent Genovese ....G 631 281-8170
Mastic Beach (G-7912)

3441 Fabricated Structural Steel

760 NI Holdings ....E 716 821-1391
Buffalo (G-2678)
▲ A & T Iron Works Inc ....E 914 632-8992
New Rochelle (G-8585)
◆ A-Fab Initiatives Inc ....F 716 877-5257
Buffalo (G-2680)
▲ A/C Design & Fabrication Corp ....G 718 227-8100
Staten Island (G-15039)
AAA Welding and Fabrication of ....G 585 254-2830
Rochester (G-13592)
Abalon Precision Mfg Corp ....E 914 665-7700
Mount Vernon (G-8373)
Abalon Precision Mfg Corp ....F 718 589-5682
Mount Vernon (G-8374)
▲ Acadia Stairs ....G 845 765-8600
Fishkill (G-4942)
Accucut Inc ....G 631 567-2868
West Sayville (G-16287)
Ackroyd Metal Fabricators Inc ....F 518 434-1281
Menands (G-8078)
Adsco Manufacturing Corp ....D 716 827-5450
Buffalo (G-2688)
Advanced Thermal Systems Inc ....E 716 681-1800
Lancaster (G-7002)
Advantage Machining Inc ....F 716 731-6418
Niagara Falls (G-12258)
▼ Aero-Data Metal Crafters Inc ....C 631 471-7733
Ronkonkoma (G-14294)
Aldo Frustacci Iron Works Inc ....F 718 768-0707
Brooklyn (G-1502)
Alken Industries Inc ....E 631 467-2000
Ronkonkoma (G-14298)
All-City Metal Inc ....E 718 937-3975
Maspeth (G-7817)
Alpha Iron Works LLC ....F 585 424-7260
Rochester (G-13620)
American Aerogel Corporation ....E 585 328-2140
Rochester (G-13624)
Apollo Steel Corporation ....F 716 283-8758
Niagara Falls (G-12264)
Asp Industries Inc ....E 585 254-9130
Rochester (G-13647)
Atlantis Equipment Corporation ....E 518 733-5910
Stephentown (G-15154)
B H M Metal Products Co ....G 845 292-5297
Kauneonga Lake (G-6849)
B P Nash Co Inc ....F 315 445-1310
East Syracuse (G-4325)
▲ Barber Welding Inc ....E 315 834-6645
Weedsport (G-16110)
Barker Steel LLC ....E 518 465-6221
Albany (G-44)
Barry Steel Fabrication Inc ....E 716 433-2144
Lockport (G-7286)
Bear Metal Works Inc ....F 716 824-4350
Buffalo (G-2727)
▲ Bennett Manufacturing Co Inc ....C 716 937-9161
Alden (G-168)
Bereza Iron Works Inc ....F 585 254-6311
Rochester (G-13660)
Blackstone Advanced Tech LLC ....C 716 665-5410
Jamestown (G-6702)
Bms Manufacturing Co Inc ....E 607 535-2426
Watkins Glen (G-16058)
Bob Murphy Inc ....F 607 729-3553
Vestal (G-15811)
Bombardier Transportation ....D 607 324-0216
Hornell (G-6294)
Bombardier Trnsp Holdings USA ....D 607 776-4791
Bath (G-641)
Bristol Metals Inc ....F 585 657-7665
Bloomfield (G-948)
Buffalo Metal Fabricating Corp ....F 716 892-7800
Buffalo (G-2748)

Buffalo Structural Steel Inc E 814 827-1350
Buffalo *(G-2754)*
Burnt Hills Fabricators Inc F 518 885-1115
Ballston Spa *(G-578)*
C & C Custom Metal Fabricators G 631 235-9646
Hauppauge *(G-5785)*
C & C Metal Fabrications Inc F 315 598-7607
Fulton *(G-5212)*
C & T Tool & Instrument Co E 718 429-1253
Woodside *(G-16648)*
Cameron Bridge Works LLC E 607 734-9456
Elmira *(G-4474)*
Carpenter Industries Inc F 315 463-4284
Syracuse *(G-15271)*
Castle Harvester Co Inc G 585 526-5884
Seneca Castle *(G-14772)*
CBM Fabrications Inc E 518 399-8023
Ballston Lake *(G-567)*
Chautauqua Machine Spc LLC F 716 782-3276
Ashville *(G-416)*
Christian Fabrication LLC G 315 822-0135
West Winfield *(G-16305)*
Cives Corporation C 315 287-2200
Gouverneur *(G-5488)*
Cobbe Industries Inc E 716 287-2661
Gerry *(G-5340)*
Cobra Operating Industries LLC G 607 639-1700
Afton *(G-8)*
Coco Architectureal Grilles G 631 482-9449
Farmingdale *(G-4736)*
Computerized Metal Bending Ser F 631 249-1177
West Babylon *(G-16149)*
Cottonwood Metals Inc E 646 807-8674
Bohemia *(G-1000)*
County Fabricators F 914 741-0219
Pleasantville *(G-13174)*
Cyncal Steel Fabricators Inc F 631 254-5600
Bay Shore *(G-676)*
D N Gannon Fabricating Inc G 315 463-7466
Syracuse *(G-15300)*
Dennies Manufacturing Inc E 585 393-4646
Canandaigua *(G-3218)*
Diversified Manufacturing Inc F 716 681-7670
Lancaster *(G-7016)*
Donald Stefan G 716 492-1110
Chaffee *(G-3403)*
▲ **Dynasty Metal Works Inc** G 631 284-3719
Riverhead *(G-13567)*
E B Atlas Steel Corp F 716 876-0900
Buffalo *(G-2806)*
Eastern Manufacturing Inc F 716 741-4572
Clarence *(G-3531)*
Eastern Welding Inc G 631 727-0306
Riverhead *(G-13568)*
Elevator Accessories Mfg F 914 739-7004
Peekskill *(G-12919)*
Empire Industrial Systems Corp F 631 242-4619
Bay Shore *(G-685)*
Empire Metal Fabricators Inc G 585 288-2140
Rochester *(G-13780)*
Empro Niagara Inc G 716 433-2769
Lockport *(G-7298)*
Eps Iron Works Inc G 516 294-5840
Mineola *(G-8219)*
Erie Engineered Products Inc E 716 206-0204
Lancaster *(G-7018)*
Everfab Inc D 716 655-1550
East Aurora *(G-4198)*
Excel Industries Inc E 716 542-5468
Clarence *(G-3533)*
Farmingdale Iron Works Inc G 631 249-5995
Farmingdale *(G-4763)*
Feinstein Iron Works Inc E 516 997-8300
Westbury *(G-16331)*
Fence Plaza Corp G 718 469-2200
Brooklyn *(G-1874)*
Five Corners Repair Inc F 585 322-7369
Bliss *(G-946)*
▼ **Flagpoles Incorporated** D 631 751-5500
East Setauket *(G-4301)*
▲ **Fort Miller Group Inc** B 518 695-5000
Greenwich *(G-5639)*
▲ **Framing Technology Inc** E 585 464-8470
Rochester *(G-13815)*
Frazier Industrial Company D 315 539-9256
Waterloo *(G-15993)*
Fred A Nudd Corporation D 315 524-2531
Ontario *(G-12653)*
Fred Santucci Inc F 716 483-1411
Jamestown *(G-6716)*
Gasport Welding & Fabg Inc F 716 772-7205
Gasport *(G-5306)*
Genesee Metal Products Inc E 585 968-6000
Wellsville *(G-16117)*
George Industries LLC D 607 748-3371
Endicott *(G-4595)*
◆ **Gibraltar Industries Inc** D 716 826-6500
Buffalo *(G-2849)*
Glenridge Fabricators Inc F 718 456-2297
Glendale *(G-5402)*
Hallock Fabricating Corp G 631 727-2441
Riverhead *(G-13569)*
Hansen Steel E 585 398-2020
Farmington *(G-4915)*
▲ **Hebeler LLC** C 716 873-9300
Tonawanda *(G-15547)*
Homer Iron Works LLC G 607 749-3963
Homer *(G-6256)*
Industrial Fabricating Corp E 315 437-3353
East Syracuse *(G-4348)*
▲ **Industrial Support Inc** D 716 662-2954
Buffalo *(G-2883)*
◆ **Inscape (new York) Inc** D 716 665-6210
Falconer *(G-4681)*
Inter Metal Fabricators Inc F 718 852-4000
Brooklyn *(G-2007)*
International Metals Trdg LLC G 866 923-0182
Melville *(G-8039)*
Irony Limited Inc G 631 329-4065
East Hampton *(G-4238)*
Irv Schroder & Sons Inc E 518 828-0194
Stottville *(G-15181)*
Irving Woodlands LLC E 607 723-4862
Conklin *(G-3729)*
J F M Sheet Metal Inc G 631 737-8494
Ronkonkoma *(G-14355)*
J M Haley Corp C 631 845-5200
Farmingdale *(G-4789)*
Jaab Precision Inc G 631 218-3725
Ronkonkoma *(G-14357)*
James Woerner Inc G 631 454-9330
Farmingdale *(G-4791)*
Jbs LLC E 518 346-0001
Scotia *(G-14743)*
Jentsch & Co Inc G 716 852-4111
Buffalo *(G-2892)*
Joy Edward Company E 315 474-3360
Syracuse *(G-15351)*
Jpw Structural Contracting Inc E 315 432-1111
Syracuse *(G-15352)*
K & E Fabricating Company Inc F 716 829-1829
Buffalo *(G-2899)*
Kal Manufacturing Corporation E 585 265-4310
Webster *(G-16088)*
KDO Industries Inc G 631 608-4612
Amityville *(G-293)*
King Steel Iron Work Corp F 718 384-7500
Brooklyn *(G-2074)*
Kleinfelder John G 716 753-3163
Mayville *(G-7921)*
Knj Fabricators LLC F 347 234-6985
Bronx *(G-1310)*
Koenig Iron Works Inc E 718 433-0900
Long Island City *(G-7489)*
Kryten Iron Works Inc G 914 345-0990
Hawthorne *(G-5990)*
Kuno Steel Products Corp F 516 938-8500
Hicksville *(G-6101)*
Lindenhurst Fabricators Inc G 631 226-3737
Lindenhurst *(G-7174)*
Linita Design & Mfg Corp E 716 566-7753
Lackawanna *(G-6949)*
M & E Mfg Co Inc D 845 331-7890
Kingston *(G-6910)*
▲ **M & L Steel & Ornamental Iron** F 718 816-8660
Staten Island *(G-15102)*
▲ **Mageba USA LLC** E 212 317-1991
New York *(G-10662)*
▲ **Major-IPC Inc** G 845 292-2200
Liberty *(G-7145)*
▲ **Marex Aquisition Corp** C 585 458-3940
Rochester *(G-13930)*
▲ **Marovato Industries Inc** F 718 389-0800
Brooklyn *(G-2173)*
◆ **Mason Industries Inc** B 631 348-0282
Hauppauge *(G-5881)*
Maspeth Steel Fabricators Inc G 718 361-9192
Long Island City *(G-7516)*
Maspeth Welding Inc E 718 497-5430
Maspeth *(G-7858)*
Metal Concepts G 845 592-1863
Beacon *(G-760)*
Metal Crafts Inc G 718 443-3333
Brooklyn *(G-2199)*
Metal Fab LLC G 607 775-3200
Binghamton *(G-905)*
Metal Works of NY Inc G 718 525-9440
Jamaica *(G-6660)*
Metro Iron Corp G 631 842-5929
Amityville *(G-303)*
Miller Metal Fabricating Inc G 585 359-3400
Rochester *(G-13945)*
Miscellnous Ir Fabricators Inc E 518 355-1822
Schenectady *(G-14699)*
Mobile Mini Inc F 315 732-4555
Utica *(G-15723)*
Mount Vernon Iron Works Inc G 914 668-7064
Mount Vernon *(G-8423)*
Nathan Steel Corp F 315 797-1335
Utica *(G-15725)*
Nb Elctrcal Enclsures Mfrs Inc G 718 272-8792
Brooklyn *(G-2250)*
Nci Group Inc D 315 339-1245
Rome *(G-14261)*
Neversink Steel Corp G 845 292-4611
Liberty *(G-7146)*
New Vision Industries Inc F 607 687-7700
Endicott *(G-4604)*
New York Manufactured Products F 585 254-9353
Rochester *(G-13967)*
North E Rggers Erectors NY Inc E 518 842-6377
Amsterdam *(G-354)*
▲ **North Eastern Fabricators Inc** E 718 542-0450
New York *(G-10993)*
Northeast Fabricators LLC D 607 865-4031
Walton *(G-15912)*
Oehlers Wldg & Fabrication Inc F 716 821-1800
Buffalo *(G-2977)*
Orange County Ironworks LLC E 845 769-3000
Montgomery *(G-8315)*
▲ **Oriskany Mfg Tech LLC** E 315 732-4962
Yorkville *(G-16830)*
P K G Equipment Incorporated E 585 436-4650
Rochester *(G-14003)*
Patsy Strocchia & Sons Iron Wo F 516 625-8800
Albertson *(G-150)*
Pcx Aerostructures LLC E 631 467-2632
Farmingdale *(G-4844)*
Pecker Iron Works LLC G 914 665-0100
Mount Kisco *(G-8354)*
Penasack Machine Company Inc E 585 589-7044
Albion *(G-161)*
Peralta Metal Works Inc G 718 649-8661
Brooklyn *(G-2312)*
Perma Tech Inc E 716 854-0707
Buffalo *(G-3000)*
▲ **Pierce Industries LLC** E 585 458-0888
Rochester *(G-14021)*
Pierce Steel Fabricators F 716 372-7652
Olean *(G-12606)*
Pirod Inc E 631 231-7660
Hauppauge *(G-5916)*
Port Authority of NY & NJ D 718 390-2534
Staten Island *(G-15117)*
Portfab LLC E 718 542-3600
Amityville *(G-313)*
Precision Metals Corp E 631 586-5032
Bay Shore *(G-709)*
Precision Polish LLC E 315 894-3792
Frankfort *(G-5111)*
Prime Materials Recovery Inc G 315 697-5251
Canastota *(G-3245)*
▲ **Productand Design Inc** F 718 858-2440
Brooklyn *(G-2353)*
R&S Steel LLC E 315 281-0123
Rome *(G-14268)*
Raulli and Sons Inc D 315 479-6693
Syracuse *(G-15402)*
REO Welding Inc F 518 238-1022
Cohoes *(G-3618)*
▲ **Risa Management Corp** E 718 361-2606
Maspeth *(G-7870)*
Riverside Iron LLC F 315 535-4864
Gouverneur *(G-5492)*
RJ Precision LLC G 585 768-8030
Stafford *(G-15028)*
▲ **Robert E Derecktor Inc** D 914 698-0962
Mamaroneck *(G-7756)*
Roman Iron Works Inc F 516 621-1103
Greenvale *(G-5631)*

Employee Codes: A=Over 500 employees, B=251-500
C=101-250, D=51-100, E=20-50, F=10-19, G=5-9
2019 Harris
New York Manufacturers Directory
743

34 FABRICATED METAL PRODUCTS, EXCEPT MACHINERY AND TRANSPORTATION EQUIPMENT SIC SECTION

Romar Contracting Inc ....G....... 845 778-2737
Walden ***(G-15896)***
Roth Design & Consulting Inc ....E....... 718 209-0193
Brooklyn ***(G-2417)***
Rothe Welding Inc ....G....... 845 246-3051
Saugerties ***(G-14615)***
Rough Brothers Holding Co ....G....... 716 826-6500
Buffalo ***(G-3048)***
Rs Automation ....F....... 585 589-0199
Albion ***(G-162)***
▲ Rus Industries Inc ....E....... 716 284-7828
Niagara Falls ***(G-12331)***
Rw Gate Company ....F....... 518 874-4750
Troy ***(G-15622)***
Rw Gate Company ....D....... 518 874-4750
Troy ***(G-15623)***
▼ Salit Specialty Rebar Inc ....E....... 716 299-1990
Buffalo ***(G-3057)***
Savaco Inc ....G....... 716 751-9455
Newfane ***(G-12253)***
Schenectady Steel Co Inc ....E....... 518 355-3220
Schenectady ***(G-14711)***
Schneider Brothers Corporation ....E....... 315 458-8369
Syracuse ***(G-15418)***
Schuler-Subra Inc ....G....... 716 893-3100
Buffalo ***(G-3058)***
▲ Seibel Modern Mfg & Wldg Corp ....D....... 716 683-1536
Lancaster ***(G-7049)***
Sentry Metal Blast Inc ....E....... 716 285-5241
Lockport ***(G-7331)***
Silverstone Shtmtl Fbrications ....G....... 718 422-0380
Brooklyn ***(G-2474)***
Specialty Steel Fabg Corp ....F....... 718 893-6326
Bronx ***(G-1390)***
Specialty Wldg & Fabg NY Inc ....D....... 315 426-1807
Syracuse ***(G-15428)***
Steel Tech SA LLC ....G....... 845 786-3691
Thiells ***(G-15499)***
▲ Stone Bridge Iron and Stl Inc ....D....... 518 695-3752
Gansevoort ***(G-5247)***
▼ Stone Well Bodies & Mch Inc ....E....... 315 497-3512
Genoa ***(G-5338)***
STS Steel Inc ....D....... 518 370-2693
Schenectady ***(G-14717)***
Supreme Steel Inc ....F....... 631 884-1320
Lindenhurst ***(G-7200)***
Team Fabrication Inc ....G....... 716 655-4038
West Falls ***(G-16209)***
Titan Steel Corp ....F....... 315 656-7046
Kirkville ***(G-6936)***
Tms Structures Inc ....C....... 646 740-7646
New York ***(G-11854)***
Torino Indus Fabrication Inc ....G....... 631 509-1640
Bellport ***(G-815)***
Triboro Iron Works Inc ....G....... 718 361-9600
Long Island City ***(G-7621)***
Triton Builders Inc ....E....... 631 841-2534
Amityville ***(G-323)***
Tropical Driftwood Originals ....G....... 516 623-0980
Roosevelt ***(G-14438)***
Tymetal Corp ....E....... 518 692-9930
Greenwich ***(G-5646)***
Ulster Precision Inc ....E....... 845 338-0995
Kingston ***(G-6925)***
United Iron Inc ....E....... 914 667-5700
Mount Vernon ***(G-8453)***
United Structure Solution Inc ....F....... 347 227-7526
New York ***(G-11955)***
Universal Metal Works LLC ....F....... 315 598-7607
Fulton ***(G-5233)***
▲ Vance Metal Fabricators Inc ....D....... 315 789-5626
Geneva ***(G-5335)***
Vulcan Iron Works Inc ....G....... 631 395-6846
Manorville ***(G-7787)***
Vulcraft of New York Inc ....C....... 607 529-9000
Chemung ***(G-3464)***
Ward Steel Company Inc ....E....... 315 451-4566
Liverpool ***(G-7270)***
◆ Watson Bowman Acme Corp ....C....... 716 691-8162
Amherst ***(G-260)***
Waverly Iron Corp ....E....... 631 732-2800
Medford ***(G-7968)***
Welding Metallurgy Inc ....E....... 631 253-0500
Hauppauge ***(G-5974)***
Whitacre Engineering Company ....G....... 315 622-1075
Liverpool ***(G-7272)***
Wilston Enterprises Inc ....F....... 716 483-1411
Jamestown ***(G-6762)***
Winters Railroad Service Inc ....G....... 716 337-2668
North Collins ***(G-12390)***

3442 Metal Doors, Sash, Frames, Molding & Trim

A & L Doors & Hardware LLC ....F....... 718 585-8400
Bronx ***(G-1199)***
▲ A & S Window Associates Inc ....E....... 718 275-7900
Glendale ***(G-5389)***
A G M Deco Inc ....F....... 718 624-6200
Brooklyn ***(G-1455)***
▲ A G M Deco Inc ....D....... 718 624-6200
Brooklyn ***(G-1456)***
Accurate Metal Weather Strip ....G....... 914 668-6042
Mount Vernon ***(G-8375)***
Ace Fire Door Corp ....E....... 718 901-0001
Bronx ***(G-1209)***
▲ Acme Architectural Pdts Inc ....D....... 718 384-7800
Brooklyn ***(G-1477)***
Action Bullet Resistant ....F....... 631 422-0888
West Islip ***(G-16258)***
Advanced Door Solutions Inc ....G....... 631 773-6100
Holbrook ***(G-6169)***
Air Tite Manufacturing Inc ....C....... 516 897-0295
Long Beach ***(G-7356)***
All United Window Corp ....E....... 718 624-0490
Brooklyn ***(G-1509)***
Altype Fire Door Corporation ....G....... 718 292-3500
Bronx ***(G-1218)***
▲ Alumil Fabrication Inc ....F....... 845 469-2874
Newburgh ***(G-12212)***
Amarr Company ....F....... 585 426-8290
Rochester ***(G-13622)***
American Steel Gate Corp ....G....... 718 291-4050
Jamaica ***(G-6624)***
Assa Abloy Entrance Systems US ....E....... 315 492-6600
East Syracuse ***(G-4323)***
Corkhill Manufacturing Co Inc ....G....... 718 528-7413
Jamaica ***(G-6639)***
D D & L Inc ....F....... 607 729-9131
Binghamton ***(G-878)***
Dawson Metal Company Inc ....C....... 716 664-3811
Jamestown ***(G-6711)***
▲ Dayton Industries Inc ....E....... 718 542-8144
Bronx ***(G-1254)***
Dural Door Company Inc ....F....... 718 729-1333
Long Island City ***(G-7430)***
East Pattern & Model Corp ....F....... 585 461-3240
Rochester ***(G-13757)***
Eastern Storefronts & Mtls Inc ....F....... 631 471-7065
Ronkonkoma ***(G-14336)***
◆ Ellison Bronze Inc ....D....... 716 665-6522
Falconer ***(G-4675)***
Empire Archtctural Systems Inc ....E....... 518 773-5109
Johnstown ***(G-6826)***
Excel Aluminum Products Inc ....G....... 315 471-0925
Syracuse ***(G-15321)***
▲ F A Alpine Windows Mfg ....F....... 845 469-5700
Chester ***(G-3474)***
Five Boro Doors Mouldings Inc ....G....... 718 865-9371
Oceanside ***(G-12539)***
Gamma North Corporation ....E....... 716 902-5100
Alden ***(G-171)***
General Fire-Proof Door Corp ....E....... 718 893-5500
Bronx ***(G-1280)***
◆ Global Steel Products Corp ....C....... 631 586-3455
Deer Park ***(G-3981)***
◆ Great American Industries Inc ....G....... 607 729-9331
Vestal ***(G-15818)***
◆ Griffon Corporation ....E....... 212 957-5000
New York ***(G-9988)***
Gscp Emax Acquisition LLC ....G....... 212 902-1000
New York ***(G-10003)***
▲ Hopes Windows Inc ....C....... 716 665-5124
Jamestown ***(G-6722)***
I Fix Screen ....G....... 631 421-1938
Centereach ***(G-3344)***
◆ Inscape (new York) Inc ....D....... 716 665-6210
Falconer ***(G-4681)***
Inter-Fence Co Inc ....E....... 718 939-9700
College Point ***(G-3648)***
International Fireproof Door ....F....... 718 783-1310
Brooklyn ***(G-2010)***
▲ Interstate Window Corporation ....D....... 631 231-0800
Brentwood ***(G-1137)***
▼ J Sussman Inc ....E....... 718 297-0228
Jamaica ***(G-6652)***
▲ Jaidan Industries Inc ....F....... 516 944-3650
Port Washington ***(G-13272)***
Jenmar Door & Glass Inc ....G....... 718 767-7900
Whitestone ***(G-16544)***
▲ Karey Kassl Corp ....E....... 516 349-8484
Plainview ***(G-13067)***
▲ Karp Associates Inc ....D....... 631 768-8300
Melville ***(G-8041)***
▲ Kasson & Keller Inc ....A....... 518 853-3421
Fonda ***(G-5065)***
Kelly Window Systems Inc ....E....... 631 420-8500
Farmingdale ***(G-4801)***
▲ Kinro Manufacturing Inc ....G....... 817 483-7791
White Plains ***(G-16469)***
L & L Overhead Garage Doors ....G....... 718 721-2518
Long Island City ***(G-7494)***
Lif Industries Inc ....D....... 516 390-6800
Port Washington ***(G-13281)***
Lif Industries Inc ....E....... 718 767-8800
Whitestone ***(G-16545)***
▼ M & D Installers Inc ....D....... 718 782-6978
Brooklyn ***(G-2141)***
Markar Architectural Products ....G....... 716 685-4104
Lancaster ***(G-7032)***
▲ McKeon Rolling Stl Door Co Inc ....E....... 631 803-3000
Bellport ***(G-808)***
Mercury Lock and Door Service ....E....... 718 542-7048
Bronx ***(G-1327)***
Metalline Fire Door Co Inc ....E....... 718 583-2320
Bronx ***(G-1328)***
Michbi Doors Inc ....D....... 631 231-9050
Brentwood ***(G-1142)***
Milanese Commercial Door LLC ....F....... 518 658-0398
Berlin ***(G-832)***
Milgo Industrial Inc ....D....... 718 388-6476
Brooklyn ***(G-2206)***
Milgo Industrial Inc ....G....... 718 387-0406
Brooklyn ***(G-2207)***
Munschauer Inc ....F....... 716 895-8888
Buffalo ***(G-2959)***
New Bgnnngs Win Door Dstrs LLC ....F....... 845 214-0698
Poughkeepsie ***(G-13358)***
▼ North American Door Corp ....F....... 518 566-0161
Plattsburgh ***(G-13137)***
◆ Optimum Window Mfg Corp ....E....... 845 647-1900
Ellenville ***(G-4441)***
Overhead Door Corporation ....D....... 518 828-7652
Hudson ***(G-6366)***
Pal Manufacturing Corp ....E....... 516 937-1990
Hicksville ***(G-6122)***
Pioneer Window Holdings Inc ....F....... 516 822-7000
Hicksville ***(G-6127)***
Pioneer Window Holdings Inc ....E....... 518 762-5526
Johnstown ***(G-6837)***
Pk30 System LLC ....F....... 212 473-8050
Stone Ridge ***(G-15162)***
▲ Presray Corporation ....E....... 845 373-9300
Wassaic ***(G-15966)***
Raydoor Inc ....G....... 212 421-0641
New York ***(G-11333)***
Revival Sash & Door LLC ....G....... 973 500-4242
New York ***(G-11375)***
▲ Robert-Masters Corp ....G....... 718 545-1030
Woodside ***(G-16676)***
Rochester Colonial Mfg Corp ....D....... 585 254-8191
Rochester ***(G-14084)***
Rochester Lumber Company ....E....... 585 924-7171
Farmington ***(G-4919)***
Rohlfs Stined Leaded GL Studio ....E....... 914 699-4848
Mount Vernon ***(G-8440)***
Roly Door Sales Inc ....G....... 716 877-1515
Hamburg ***(G-5694)***
▼ Schwab Corp ....E....... 585 381-4900
Rochester ***(G-14116)***
Shade & Shutter Systems of NY ....G....... 631 208-0275
Southampton ***(G-14961)***
Slanto Manufacturing Inc ....E....... 516 759-5721
Glen Cove ***(G-5375)***
Statewide Fireproof Door Co ....F....... 845 268-6043
Valley Cottage ***(G-15766)***
Steelmasters Inc ....E....... 718 498-2854
Brooklyn ***(G-2518)***
Sunrise Door Solutions ....G....... 631 464-4139
Copiague ***(G-3784)***
Superior Stl Door Trim Co Inc ....F....... 716 665-3256
Jamestown ***(G-6755)***
Supreme Fire Proof Door Co ....F....... 718 665-4224
Bronx ***(G-1396)***
Texas Home Security Inc ....E....... 516 747-2100
New Hyde Park ***(G-8566)***
Thermal Tech Doors Inc ....E....... 516 745-0100
Garden City ***(G-5283)***
Thompson Overhead Door Co Inc ....F....... 718 788-2470
Brooklyn ***(G-2566)***
Truth Hardware Corporation ....G....... 585 627-5964
Rochester ***(G-14180)***

34 FABRICATED METAL PRODUCTS, EXCEPT MACHINERY AND TRANSPORTATION EQUIPMENT

United Steel Products Inc .... D 914 968-7782
Flushing (G-5058)
▲ United Steel Products Inc .... D 718 478-5330
Corona (G-3856)
Universal Fire Proof Door .... E 718 455-8442
Brooklyn (G-2607)
Vr Containment LLC .... G 917 972-3441
Fresh Meadows (G-5205)
Window Tech Systems Inc .... E 518 899-9000
Ballston Spa (G-593)
Windowman Inc (usa) .... G 718 246-2626
Brooklyn (G-2652)

3443 Fabricated Plate Work

828 Express Inc .... G 917 577-9019
Staten Island (G-15036)
▲ A K Allen Co Inc .... C 516 747-5450
Melville (G-7996)
A L Eastmond & Sons Inc .... D 718 378-3000
Bronx (G-1201)
▲ Aavid Niagara LLC .... E 716 297-0652
Niagara Falls (G-12257)
▲ Acro Industries Inc .... C 585 254-3661
Rochester (G-13600)
▲ Aerco International Inc .... C 845 580-8000
Blauvelt (G-933)
▼ Aero-Data Metal Crafters Inc .... C 631 471-7733
Ronkonkoma (G-14294)
All-State Diversified Pdts Inc .... E 315 472-4728
Syracuse (G-15239)
▲ Allstate Gasket & Packing Inc .... F 631 254-4050
Deer Park (G-3937)
American Boiler Tank Wldg Inc .... E 518 463-5012
Albany (G-40)
◆ American Precision Inds Inc .... C 716 691-9100
Amherst (G-214)
▼ Amherst Stnless Fbrication LLC .... E 716 691-7012
Amherst (G-215)
◆ API Heat Transf Thermasys Corp .... A 716 684-6700
Buffalo (G-2704)
API Heat Transfer Company 716 684-6700
Buffalo (G-2705)
API Heat Transfer Inc .... C 585 496-5755
Arcade (G-377)
Arvos Inc 785 243-3300
Wellsville (G-16112)
Arvos Inc .... G 585 593-2700
Wellsville (G-16113)
Atlantic Industrial Tech Inc .... E 631 234-3131
Shirley (G-14830)
Aurora Indus Machining Inc 716 826-7911
Orchard Park (G-12699)
Bellmore Steel Products Corp .... F 516 785-9667
Bellmore (G-786)
Bigbee Steel and Tank Company .... E 518 273-0801
Watervliet (G-16041)
Blackstone Advanced Tech LLC .... C 716 665-5410
Jamestown (G-6702)
Bos-Hatten Inc .... F 716 662-7030
Orchard Park (G-12700)
Breton Industries Inc .... C 518 842-3030
Amsterdam (G-329)
Bridgehampton Steel & Wldg Inc .... F 631 537-2486
Bridgehampton (G-1179)
Bruce Pierce .... G 716 731-9310
Sanborn (G-14542)
◆ Buflovak LLC .... E 716 895-2100
Buffalo (G-2755)
Byelocorp Scientific Inc .... E 212 785-2580
New York (G-9166)
C & F Fabricators & Erectors .... G 607 432-3520
Colliersville (G-3671)
Cardinal Tank Corp .... E 718 625-4350
Brooklyn (G-1676)
▲ Charles Ross & Son Company .... D 631 234-0500
Hauppauge (G-5788)
Chart Industries Inc .... E 716 691-0202
Amherst (G-222)
▲ Cigar Box Studios Inc .... F 845 236-9283
Marlboro (G-7812)
CMS Heat Transfer Division Inc .... E 631 968-0084
Bohemia (G-997)
Contech Engnered Solutions LLC .... F 716 870-9091
Orchard Park (G-12710)
▼ Costanzos Welding Inc 716 282-0845
Niagara Falls (G-12274)
Crown Tank Company LLC 855 276-9682
Horseheads (G-6310)
Cyclotherm of Watertown Inc .... E 315 782-1100
Watertown (G-16011)

David Isseks & Sons Inc .... E 212 966-8694
New York (G-9481)
Direkt Force LLC .... E 716 652-3022
East Aurora (G-4197)
Doyle & Roth Mfg Co Inc .... D 212 269-7840
New York (G-9570)
Easco Boiler Corp .... E 718 378-3000
Bronx (G-1264)
◆ ECR International Inc .... D 315 797-1310
Utica (G-15699)
ECR International Inc .... E 716 366-5500
Dunkirk (G-4169)
Empire Industrial Systems Corp .... F 631 242-4619
Bay Shore (G-685)
Endicott Precision Inc .... E 607 754-7076
Endicott (G-4589)
Energy Nuclear Operations .... E 315 342-0055
Oswego (G-12777)
Erie Engineered Products Inc .... E 716 206-0204
Lancaster (G-7018)
Exergy LLC .... E 516 832-9300
Garden City (G-5260)
Expert Industries Inc .... E 718 434-6060
Brooklyn (G-1859)
Feldmeier Equipment Inc .... D 315 823-2000
Syracuse (G-15323)
Fluid Handling LLC .... C 716 897-2800
Cheektowaga (G-3444)
Fross Industries Inc .... E 716 297-0652
Niagara Falls (G-12287)
Fuel Efficiency LLC .... E 315 923-2511
Clyde (G-3594)
▲ Fulton Boiler Works Inc .... E 315 298-5121
Pulaski (G-13380)
Fulton Boiler Works Inc .... C 315 298-5121
Pulaski (G-13381)
Fulton China LLC .... E 315 298-0112
Pulaski (G-13382)
Gasport Welding & Fabg Inc .... F 716 772-7205
Gasport (G-5306)
General Oil Equipment Co Inc .... E 716 691-7012
Amherst (G-229)
Glenridge Fabricators Inc .... E 718 456-2297
Glendale (G-5402)
◆ Global Steel Products Corp .... C 631 586-3455
Deer Park (G-3981)
Graham Corporation .... B 585 343-2216
Batavia (G-626)
Hyperbaric Technologies Inc .... E 518 842-3030
Amsterdam (G-340)
Industrial Fabricating Corp .... E 315 437-8234
East Syracuse (G-4349)
Inex Inc .... E 716 537-2270
Holland (G-6219)
J & T Metal Products Co Inc .... E 631 226-7400
West Babylon (G-16160)
J M Canty Inc .... E 716 625-4227
Lockport (G-7310)
J W Stevens Co Inc .... E 315 472-6311
East Syracuse (G-4354)
◆ Jaquith Industries Inc .... E 315 478-5700
Syracuse (G-15346)
Jbren Corp .... E 716 332-5928
Buffalo (G-2891)
John R Robinson Inc .... E 718 786-6088
Long Island City (G-7481)
K Industries Inc .... G 631 897-2125
Bellport (G-806)
Kintex Inc .... E 716 297-0652
Niagara Falls (G-12302)
Lane Enterprises Inc .... E 607 776-3366
Bath (G-647)
▲ Lifetime Chimney Supply LLC .... E 516 576-8144
Plainview (G-13069)
Manhattan Cooling Towers Inc .... F 212 279-1045
Long Island City (G-7513)
▲ Marex Aquisition Corp .... C 585 458-3940
Rochester (G-13930)
Marine Boiler & Welding Inc .... E 718 378-1900
Bronx (G-1322)
Methods Tooling & Mfg Inc .... E 845 246-7100
Mount Marion (G-8364)
Metrofab Pipe Incorporated .... F 516 349-7373
Plainview (G-13074)
Miller Metal Fabricating Inc .... E 585 359-3400
Rochester (G-13945)
Mitsubishi Chemical Amer Inc .... E 212 223-3043
New York (G-10825)
Modutank Inc .... E 718 392-1112
Long Island City (G-7528)

Mono-Systems Inc .... E 716 821-1344
Buffalo (G-2953)
▲ Motivair Corporation .... E 716 691-9222
Amherst (G-239)
Mount Kisco Transfer Stn Inc .... G 914 666-6350
Mount Kisco (G-8350)
Niagara Cooler Inc .... E 716 434-1235
Lockport (G-7321)
Nitram Energy Inc .... E 716 662-6540
Orchard Park (G-12732)
North American Svcs Group LLC .... F 518 885-1820
Ballston Spa (G-592)
Perforated Screen Surfaces .... E 866 866-8690
Conklin (G-3731)
Pfaudler US Inc .... C 585 235-1000
Rochester (G-14015)
Roemac Industrial Sales Inc .... G 716 692-7332
North Tonawanda (G-12448)
Rosenwach Tank Co Inc .... E 212 972-4411
Astoria (G-442)
Ross Metal Fabricators Inc .... E 631 586-7000
Deer Park (G-4038)
Saraga Industries Corp .... G 631 842-4049
Amityville (G-315)
Sargent Manufacturing Inc .... E 212 722-7000
New York (G-11488)
Schwabel Fabricating Co Inc .... E 716 876-2086
Tonawanda (G-15575)
▲ Seibel Modern Mfg & Wldg Corp .... D 716 683-1536
Lancaster (G-7049)
▲ Slant/Fin Corporation .... B 516 484-2600
Greenvale (G-5632)
Slantco Manufacturing Inc .... E 516 484-2600
Greenvale (G-5633)
SPX Cooling Technologies Inc .... G 914 697-5030
White Plains (G-16505)
SPX Corporation .... G 914 366-2512
Tarrytown (G-15495)
SPX Corporation .... E 631 467-2632
Ronkonkoma (G-14417)
SPX Corporation .... B 585 436-5550
Rochester (G-14139)
Stainless Metals Inc .... F 718 784-1454
Woodside (G-16680)
▲ Stavo Industries Inc .... F 845 331-4552
Kingston (G-6920)
Steele Truss and Panel LLC .... G 518 562-4663
Plattsburgh (G-13157)
Steelways Inc .... E 845 562-0860
Newburgh (G-12246)
Stutzman Management Corp .... F 800 735-2013
Lancaster (G-7051)
Supreme Boilers Inc .... G 718 342-2220
Brooklyn (G-2540)
Taylor Tank Company Inc .... E 718 434-1300
Brooklyn (G-2557)
Themis Chimney Inc .... E 718 937-4716
Brooklyn (G-2565)
Thermotech Corp .... G 716 823-3311
Buffalo (G-3094)
Troy Boiler Works Inc .... E 518 274-2650
Troy (G-15630)
United Wind Inc .... F 888 313-3353
Brooklyn (G-2605)
Vertarib Inc .... G 561 683-0888
Jericho (G-6806)
◆ Vship Co .... F 718 706-8566
Astoria (G-447)
Wastequip Manufacturing Co LLC .... E 800 235-0734
New Lebanon (G-8574)
Water Cooling Corp .... G 718 723-6500
Rosedale (G-14442)
Wayne Integrated Tech Corp .... E 631 242-0213
Edgewood (G-4423)
West Metal Works Inc .... E 716 895-4900
Buffalo (G-3128)
▼ Wsf Industries Inc .... E 716 692-4930
Tonawanda (G-15592)
▲ Yula Corporation .... E 718 991-0900
Bronx (G-1421)
Zone Fabricators Inc .... F 718 272-0200
Ozone Park (G-12834)

3444 Sheet Metal Work

303 Contracting Inc .... E 716 896-2122
Orchard Park (G-12694)
A & L Shtmtl Fabrications Corp .... E 718 842-1600
Bronx (G-1200)
Aabco Sheet Metal Co Inc .... D 718 821-1166
Ridgewood (G-13527)

Employee Codes: A=Over 500 employees, B=251-500
C=101-250, D=51-100, E=20-50, F=10-19, G=5-9

34 FABRICATED METAL PRODUCTS, EXCEPT MACHINERY AND TRANSPORTATION EQUIPMENT SIC SECTION

Abdo Shtmtl & Fabrication Inc ....G ... 315 894-4664
Barneveld *(G-601)*

Aberdeen Blower & Shtmtl Works ....G ... 631 661-6100
West Babylon *(G-16127)*

Accra Sheetmetal LLC ....G ... 631 643-2100
Wyandanch *(G-16691)*

Accurate Specialty Metal Fabri ....E ... 718 418-6895
Middle Village *(G-8119)*

▲ Acme Architectural Pdts Inc ....D ... 718 384-7800
Brooklyn *(G-1477)*

▲ Acro Industries Inc ....C ... 585 254-3661
Rochester *(G-13600)*

Acro-Fab Ltd ....E ... 315 564-6688
Hannibal *(G-5717)*

Advanced Precision Technology ....F ... 845 279-3540
Brewster *(G-1154)*

Advantech Industries Inc ....C ... 585 247-0701
Rochester *(G-13609)*

Aero Trades Mfg Corp ....E ... 516 746-3360
Mineola *(G-8200)*

▼ Aero-Data Metal Crafters Inc ....C ... 631 471-7733
Ronkonkoma *(G-14294)*

Aeroduct Inc ....E ... 516 248-9550
Mineola *(G-8201)*

Afco Systems Inc ....G ... 631 249-9441
Farmingdale *(G-4708)*

Air Louver & Damper Inc ....F ... 718 392-3232
Long Island City *(G-7369)*

Aj Genco Mch Sp McHy Rdout Svc .....F ... 716 664-4925
Falconer *(G-4669)*

▲ Ajl Manufacturing Inc ....C ... 585 254-1128
Rochester *(G-13611)*

Albany Mtal Fbrcation Holdings ....G ... 518 463-5161
Albany *(G-36)*

Aldo Frustacci Iron Works Inc ....F ... 718 768-0707
Brooklyn *(G-1502)*

Aleta Industries Inc ....F ... 718 349-0040
Brooklyn *(G-1504)*

Alfred B Parella ....G ... 518 872-1238
Altamont *(G-194)*

Alkemy Machine LLC ....G ... 585 436-8730
Rochester *(G-13613)*

All Around Spiral Inc ....G ... 631 588-0220
Ronkonkoma *(G-14292)*

All Island Blower & Shtmtl ....F ... 631 567-7070
Bohemia *(G-976)*

All Metal Specialties Inc ....E ... 716 664-6009
Jamestown *(G-6696)*

All Star Carts & Vehicles Inc ....D ... 631 666-5581
Bay Shore *(G-654)*

All Star Sheet Metal Inc ....F ... 718 456-1567
Farmingdale *(G-4715)*

▲ Allen Machine Products Inc ....E ... 631 630-8800
Hauppauge *(G-5761)*

Alliance Welding & Steel Fabg ....F ... 516 775-7600
Floral Park *(G-4954)*

Allure Metal Works Inc ....F ... 631 588-0220
Ronkonkoma *(G-14302)*

Alpine Machine Inc ....F ... 607 272-1344
Ithaca *(G-6556)*

▲ Alternative Service Inc ....F ... 631 345-9500
Bellport *(G-798)*

American Std Shtmtl Sup Corp ....F ... 718 888-9350
Flushing *(G-4985)*

Amsco Inc ....F ... 716 823-4213
Buffalo *(G-2699)*

Apparatus Mfg Inc ....G ... 845 471-5116
Poughkeepsie *(G-13326)*

▲ Arcadia Mfg Group Inc ....E ... 518 434-6213
Green Island *(G-5602)*

Arcadia Mfg Group Inc ....G ... 518 434-6213
Menands *(G-8081)*

Architctral Shetmetal Pdts Inc ....G ... 518 381-6144
Scotia *(G-14738)*

Arlan Damper Corporation ....E ... 631 589-7431
Bohemia *(G-983)*

Art Precision Metal Products ....F ... 631 842-8889
Copiague *(G-3752)*

▲ Ascension Industries Inc ....C ... 716 693-9381
North Tonawanda *(G-12413)*

Asm USA Inc ....F ... 212 925-2906
New York *(G-8934)*

Asp Industries Inc ....E ... 585 254-9130
Rochester *(G-13647)*

Atech-Seh Metal Fabricator ....E ... 716 895-8888
Buffalo *(G-2711)*

Atlantis Equipment Corporation ....E ... 518 733-5910
Stephentown *(G-15154)*

Auburn Tank & Manufacturing Co ....F ... 315 255-2788
Auburn *(G-466)*

▲ Austin Mohawk and Company LLC .E ... 315 793-3000
Utica *(G-15678)*

Auto Body Services LLC ....F ... 631 431-4640
Lindenhurst *(G-7162)*

Avalanche Fabrication Inc ....F ... 585 545-4000
Ontario *(G-12648)*

◆ B & B Sheet Metal Inc ....E ... 718 433-2501
Long Island City *(G-7396)*

B & H Precision Fabricators ....F ... 631 563-9620
Bohemia *(G-984)*

B & R Sheet ....E ... 718 558-5544
Jamaica *(G-6629)*

Banner Metalcraft Inc ....D ... 631 563-7303
Ronkonkoma *(G-14316)*

Bargold Storage Systems LLC ....E ... 718 247-7000
Long Island City *(G-7398)*

Batavia Enclosures Inc ....G ... 585 344-1797
Arcade *(G-378)*

Berjen Metal Industries Ltd ....G ... 631 673-7979
Huntington *(G-6394)*

Best Tinsmith Supply Inc ....G ... 518 863-2541
Northville *(G-12476)*

Blackstone Advanced Tech LLC ....C ... 716 665-5410
Jamestown *(G-6702)*

Bmg Systems ....F ... 716 432-5160
Depew *(G-4081)*

Boss Precision Ltd ....D ... 585 352-7070
Spencerport *(G-14976)*

Broadway Neon Sign Corp ....F ... 908 241-4177
Ronkonkoma *(G-14322)*

Brothers Roofing Supplies Co ....E ... 718 779-0280
East Elmhurst *(G-4218)*

Brzozka Industries Inc ....E ... 631 588-8164
Holbrook *(G-6173)*

C & T Tool & Instrument Co ....E ... 718 429-1253
Woodside *(G-16648)*

C J & C Sheet Metal Corp ....F ... 631 376-9425
West Babylon *(G-16144)*

▲ Cameron Mfg & Design Inc ....C ... 607 739-3606
Horseheads *(G-6308)*

▲ Cannon Industries Inc ....D ... 585 254-8080
Rochester *(G-13690)*

CBM Fabrications Inc ....E ... 518 399-8023
Ballston Lake *(G-567)*

Center Sheet Metal Inc ....E ... 718 378-4476
Bronx *(G-1237)*

▲ Cetek Inc ....E ... 845 452-3510
Poughkeepsie *(G-13331)*

Chamtek Mfg Inc ....F ... 585 328-4900
Rochester *(G-13707)*

Chutes and Compactors of NY ....F ... 718 494-2247
Staten Island *(G-15062)*

Citros Building Materials Co ....E ... 718 779-0727
East Elmhurst *(G-4219)*

City Cooling Enterprises Inc ....E ... 718 331-7400
Brooklyn *(G-1694)*

Clark Specialty Co Inc ....E ... 607 776-3193
Bath *(G-642)*

Construction Parts Whse Inc ....G ... 315 445-1310
East Syracuse *(G-4332)*

CPI Industries Inc ....D ... 631 909-3434
Manorville *(G-7784)*

Craft-Tech Mfg Corp ....G ... 631 563-4949
Bohemia *(G-1001)*

Crown Die Casting Corp ....G ... 914 667-5400
Mount Vernon *(G-8392)*

Custom Sheet Metal Corp ....G ... 315 463-9105
Syracuse *(G-15298)*

Cutting Edge Metal Works ....E ... 631 981-8333
Holtsville *(G-6239)*

Cw Metals Inc ....E ... 917 416-7906
Long Island City *(G-7419)*

D & G Sheet Metal Co Inc ....F ... 718 326-9111
Maspeth *(G-7833)*

D and D Sheet Metal Corp ....F ... 718 465-7585
Jamaica *(G-6641)*

Dart Awning Inc ....G ... 516 544-2082
Freeport *(G-5150)*

Dawson Metal Company Inc ....C ... 716 664-3811
Jamestown *(G-6711)*

Dayton T Brown Inc ....E ... 631 589-6300
Bohemia *(G-1011)*

Delta Sheet Metal Corp ....E ... 718 429-5805
Long Island City *(G-7422)*

Dimar Manufacturing Corp ....C ... 716 759-0351
Clarence *(G-3527)*

▲ Dj Acquisition Management Corp ...E ... 585 265-3000
Ontario *(G-12652)*

Doortec Archtctural Met GL LLC ....E ... 718 567-2730
Brooklyn *(G-1789)*

Dundas-Jafine Inc ....E ... 716 681-9690
Alden *(G-170)*

Dynasty Stainless Steel & Meta ....E ... 718 205-6623
Maspeth *(G-7839)*

E G M Restaurant Equipment Mfg ....G ... 718 782-9800
Brooklyn *(G-1803)*

Elderlee Incorporated ....C ... 315 789-6670
Oaks Corners *(G-12527)*

Elevator Accessories Mfg ....F ... 914 739-7004
Peekskill *(G-12919)*

Elitsac Inc ....E ... 585 493-2628
Castile *(G-3293)*

Elmsford Sheet Metal Works Inc ....D ... 914 739-6300
Cortlandt Manor *(G-3900)*

Empire Air Specialties Inc ....E ... 518 689-4440
Albany *(G-72)*

Empire Ventilation Eqp Co Inc ....F ... 718 728-2143
Florida *(G-4970)*

Endicott Precision Inc ....C ... 607 754-7076
Endicott *(G-4589)*

Engineering Mfg Tech LLC ....D ... 607 754-7111
Endicott *(G-4591)*

Expert Industries Inc ....E ... 718 434-6060
Brooklyn *(G-1859)*

F M L Industries Inc ....G ... 607 749-7273
Homer *(G-6254)*

Federal Sheet Metal Works Inc ....F ... 315 735-4730
Utica *(G-15702)*

Fenton Mobility Products Inc ....F ... 716 484-7014
Randolph *(G-13447)*

Five Star Awnings Inc ....F ... 718 860-6070
Ridgewood *(G-13536)*

Five Star Industries Inc ....E ... 716 674-2589
West Seneca *(G-16297)*

Franchet Metal Craft Inc ....G ... 718 658-6400
Jamaica *(G-6644)*

Fred A Nudd Corporation ....D ... 315 524-2531
Ontario *(G-12653)*

Genesee Building Products LLC ....F ... 585 548-2726
Stafford *(G-15026)*

Goergen-Mackwirth Co Inc ....E ... 716 874-4800
Buffalo *(G-2852)*

Golden Group International Ltd ....C ... 845 440-1025
Patterson *(G-12882)*

Gottlieb Schwartz Family ....E ... 718 761-2010
Staten Island *(G-15080)*

Greene Technologies Inc ....D ... 607 656-4166
Greene *(G-5615)*

Gt Innovations LLC ....G ... 585 739-7659
Bergen *(G-820)*

H & M Leasing Corp ....G ... 631 225-5246
Copiague *(G-3761)*

H Klein & Sons Inc ....E ... 516 746-0163
Mineola *(G-8225)*

Hana Sheet Metal Inc ....G ... 914 377-0773
Yonkers *(G-16766)*

Hansen Steel ....E ... 585 398-2020
Farmington *(G-4915)*

Harbor Elc Fabrication Tls Inc ....E ... 914 636-4400
New Rochelle *(G-8612)*

Hart To Hart Industries Inc ....F ... 716 492-2709
Chaffee *(G-3404)*

Hatfield Metal Fab Inc ....E ... 845 454-9078
Poughkeepsie *(G-13345)*

◆ Hergo Ergonomic Support ....F ... 718 894-0639
Maspeth *(G-7851)*

Hermann Gerdens Inc ....E ... 631 841-3132
Copiague *(G-3763)*

Hi-Tech Industries NY Inc ....E ... 607 217-7361
Johnson City *(G-6810)*

Hrd Metal Products Inc ....G ... 631 243-6700
Deer Park *(G-3985)*

Hri Metals LLC ....E ... 518 822-1013
Hudson *(G-6354)*

▲ Hunter Douglas Inc ....D ... 845 664-7000
Pearl River *(G-12901)*

I Rauchs Sons Inc ....E ... 718 507-8844
East Elmhurst *(G-4221)*

IEC Electronics Corp ....D ... 585 647-1760
Rochester *(G-13876)*

Illinois Tool Works Inc ....E ... 607 770-4945
Binghamton *(G-895)*

Imperial Damper & Louver Co ....E ... 718 731-3800
Bronx *(G-1294)*

▼ Incodema Inc ....E ... 607 277-7070
Ithaca *(G-6582)*

Industrial Fabricating Corp ....E ... 315 437-3353
East Syracuse *(G-4348)*

Intellimetal Inc ....D ... 585 424-3260
Rochester *(G-13883)*

Interior Metals .... E 718 439-7324
Brooklyn *(G-2008)*
Jamestown Advanced Pdts Corp .... E 716 483-3406
Jamestown *(G-6725)*
◆ **Jaquith Industries Inc** .... E 315 478-5700
Syracuse *(G-15346)*
Jar Metals Inc .... F 845 425-8901
Nanuet *(G-8464)*
Joe P Industries Inc .... F 631 293-7889
Farmingdale *(G-4794)*
▲ **Juniper Elbow Co Inc** .... C 718 326-2546
Middle Village *(G-8124)*
K Barthelmes Mfg Co Inc .... F 585 328-8140
Rochester *(G-13902)*
Kal Manufacturing Corporation .... E 585 265-4310
Webster *(G-16088)*
Karo Sheet Metal Inc .... E 718 542-8420
Brooklyn *(G-2067)*
Kassis Superior Sign Co Inc .... F 315 463-7446
Syracuse *(G-15354)*
▲ **Kenan International Trading** .... G 718 672-4922
Corona *(G-3847)*
Kittredge & Sons Inc .... D 978 567-0998
Niagara Falls *(G-12303)*
Ksm Group Ltd .... G 716 751-6006
Newfane *(G-12252)*
▲ **Lambro Industries Inc** .... D 631 842-8088
Amityville *(G-296)*
Lane Enterprises Inc .... E 518 885-4385
Ballston Spa *(G-587)*
Leader Sheet Metal Inc .... F 347 271-4961
Bronx *(G-1314)*
Liffey Sheet Metal Corp .... F 347 381-1134
Long Island City *(G-7498)*
Lotus Awnings Enterprises Inc .... G 718 965-4824
Brooklyn *(G-2136)*
M&G Duravent Inc .... E 518 463-7284
Albany *(G-96)*
Maloya Laser Inc .... E 631 543-2327
Commack *(G-3697)*
Manufacturing Resources Inc .... E 631 481-0041
Rochester *(G-13926)*
▲ **Marex Aquisition Corp** .... C 585 458-3940
Rochester *(G-13930)*
Mariah Metal Products Inc .... G 516 938-9783
Hicksville *(G-6106)*
▲ **McAlpin Industries Inc** .... C 585 266-3060
Rochester *(G-13932)*
McHone Industries Inc .... D 716 945-3380
Salamanca *(G-14526)*
MD International Industries .... E 631 254-3100
Deer Park *(G-4009)*
▲ **Melto Metal Products Co Inc** .... E 516 546-8866
Freeport *(G-5166)*
Merz Metal & Machine Corp .... E 716 893-7786
Buffalo *(G-2944)*
Metal Solutions Inc .... E 315 732-6271
Utica *(G-15719)*
Metal Tek Products .... G 516 586-4514
Plainview *(G-13073)*
Metallogix Design Fabrication .... E 315 738-4554
Utica *(G-15720)*
Metalsmith Inc .... G 631 467-1500
Holbrook *(G-6200)*
Methods Tooling & Mfg Inc .... E 845 246-7100
Mount Marion *(G-8364)*
Metro Duct Systems Inc .... F 718 278-4294
Long Island City *(G-7522)*
Middleby Corporation .... E 631 226-6688
Lindenhurst *(G-7180)*
Mitsubishi Chemical Amer Inc .... E 212 223-3043
New York *(G-10825)*
▼ **Monarch Metal Fabrication Inc** .... G 631 563-8967
Bohemia *(G-1059)*
Monroe Piping & Shtmtl LLC .... D 585 482-0200
Rochester *(G-13954)*
Ms Spares LLC .... G 607 223-3024
Clay *(G-3551)*
N & L Instruments Inc .... F 631 471-4000
Ronkonkoma *(G-14382)*
Nci Group Inc .... D 315 339-1245
Rome *(G-14261)*
Nelson Air Device Corporation .... C 718 729-3801
Maspeth *(G-7862)*
▼ **North Coast Outfitters Ltd** .... E 631 727-5580
Riverhead *(G-13578)*
Northeast Fabricators LLC .... D 607 865-4031
Walton *(G-15912)*
Northern Awning & Sign Company .... G 315 782-8515
Watertown *(G-16030)*

Olympic Manufacturing Inc .... E 631 231-8900
Hauppauge *(G-5906)*
Omc Inc .... C 718 731-5001
Bronx *(G-1347)*
P R B Metal Products Inc .... F 631 467-1800
Ronkonkoma *(G-14393)*
Pal Aluminum Inc .... G 516 937-1990
Hicksville *(G-6121)*
Pal Aluminum Inc .... E 718 262-0091
Jamaica *(G-6666)*
Pathfinder Industries Inc .... E 315 593-2483
Fulton *(G-5231)*
PDQ Manufacturing Co Inc .... E 845 889-3123
Rhinebeck *(G-13487)*
Penner Elbow Company Inc .... F 718 526-9000
Elmhurst *(G-4470)*
Phoenix Envmtl Svcs Corp .... F 718 381-8100
Glendale *(G-5406)*
Pirnat Precise Metals Inc .... G 631 293-9169
Farmingdale *(G-4850)*
Plattsburgh Sheet Metal Inc .... G 518 561-4930
Plattsburgh *(G-13147)*
Precision Fabrication LLC .... G 585 591-3449
Attica *(G-461)*
Precision Metals Corp .... E 631 586-5032
Bay Shore *(G-709)*
Precision Mtal Fabricators Inc .... F 718 832-9805
Brooklyn *(G-2335)*
Precision Systems Mfg Inc .... E 315 451-3480
Liverpool *(G-7257)*
Product Integration & Mfg Inc .... E 585 436-6260
Rochester *(G-14049)*
Prokosch and Sonn Sheet Metal .... E 845 562-4211
Newburgh *(G-12243)*
Protofast Holding Corp .... G 631 753-2549
Copiague *(G-3775)*
R & J Sheet Metal Distributors .... G 518 433-1525
Albany *(G-120)*
R D R Industries Inc .... F 315 866-5020
Mohawk *(G-8256)*
Radiation Shielding Systems .... F 888 631-2278
Suffern *(G-15196)*
Rand Products Manufacturing Co .... G 518 374-9871
Schenectady *(G-14706)*
Rayco Manufacturing Co Inc .... F 516 431-2006
Jamaica *(G-6672)*
Read Manufacturing Company Inc .... E 631 567-4487
Holbrook *(G-6205)*
Reynolds Manufacturing Inc .... F 607 562-8936
Big Flats *(G-856)*
▲ **Rigidized Metals Corporation** .... E 716 849-4703
Buffalo *(G-3038)*
▲ **Robert E Derecktor Inc** .... D 914 698-0962
Mamaroneck *(G-7756)*
Rochester Colonial Mfg Corp .... D 585 254-8191
Rochester *(G-14084)*
Rollson Inc .... E 631 423-9578
Huntington *(G-6412)*
Royal Metal Products Inc .... E 518 966-4442
Surprise *(G-15207)*
S & B Machine Works Inc .... E 516 997-2666
Westbury *(G-16371)*
S & J Sheet Metal Supply .... G 718 384-0800
Brooklyn *(G-2431)*
S & T Machine Inc .... F 718 272-2484
Brooklyn *(G-2435)*
Service Mfg Group Inc .... E 716 893-1482
Buffalo *(G-3064)*
Service Mfg Group Inc .... F 716 893-1482
Buffalo *(G-3063)*
Shanghai Stove Inc .... F 718 599-4583
Brooklyn *(G-2464)*
Simmons Fabricating Svc Inc .... G 845 635-3755
Pleasant Valley *(G-13172)*
Smg Metal Products LLC .... G 716 633-6439
Cheektowaga *(G-3458)*
Solidus Industries Inc .... D 607 749-4540
Homer *(G-6259)*
Space Sign .... F 718 961-1112
College Point *(G-3667)*
▲ **Spence Engineering Company Inc** ... C 845 778-5566
Walden *(G-15897)*
Standard Industrial Works Inc .... F 631 888-0130
Bay Shore *(G-726)*
Steel Sales Inc .... E 607 674-6363
Sherburne *(G-14811)*
Steel Work Inc .... G 585 232-1555
Rochester *(G-14142)*
Steelcraft Manufacturing Co .... F 718 277-2404
Brooklyn *(G-2516)*

Sterling Industries Inc .... E 631 753-3070
Farmingdale *(G-4882)*
▲ **Studco Building Systems US LLC** .... E 585 545-3000
Webster *(G-16100)*
Superior Elec Enclosure Inc .... G 718 797-9090
Brooklyn *(G-2537)*
Superior Exteriors of Buffalo .... F 716 873-1000
East Amherst *(G-4191)*
T Lemme Mechanical Inc .... E 518 436-4136
Menands *(G-8092)*
Tatra Mfg Corporation .... F 631 691-1184
Copiague *(G-3786)*
▲ **TCS Industries Inc** .... D 585 426-1160
Rochester *(G-14158)*
Technimetal Precision Inds .... E 631 231-8900
Hauppauge *(G-5956)*
Themis Chimney Inc .... F 718 937-4716
Brooklyn *(G-2565)*
Tri-Metal Industries Inc .... E 716 691-3323
Amherst *(G-257)*
Tri-State Metals LLC .... F 914 347-8157
Elmsford *(G-4574)*
▲ **Tri-Technologies Inc** .... E 914 699-2001
Mount Vernon *(G-8449)*
▲ **Trident Precision Mfg Inc** .... D 585 265-2010
Webster *(G-16103)*
Tripar Manufacturing Co Inc .... G 631 563-0855
Bohemia *(G-1100)*
Truform Manufacturing Corp .... D 585 458-1090
Rochester *(G-14179)*
Trylon Wire & Metal Works Inc .... E 718 542-4472
Bronx *(G-1409)*
Ucr Steel Group LLC .... F 718 764-3414
Ronkonkoma *(G-14424)*
Ulster Precision Inc .... E 845 338-0995
Kingston *(G-6925)*
▼ **Ultimate Prcision Met Pdts Inc** .... C 631 249-9441
Farmingdale *(G-4901)*
Unadilla Silo Company Inc .... D 607 369-9341
Sidney *(G-14857)*
United Sheet Metal Corp .... E 718 482-1197
Long Island City *(G-7624)*
Universal Precision Corp .... E 585 321-9760
Rochester *(G-14189)*
Universal Shielding Corp .... E 631 667-7900
Deer Park *(G-4055)*
▲ **Vance Metal Fabricators Inc** .... D 315 789-5626
Geneva *(G-5335)*
Vin Mar Precision Metals Inc .... F 631 563-6608
Copiague *(G-3792)*
Vitarose Corp of America .... G 718 951-9700
Brooklyn *(G-2630)*
VM Choppy & Sons LLC .... E 518 266-1444
Troy *(G-15633)*
◆ **Voss Manufacturing Inc** .... D 716 731-5062
Sanborn *(G-14557)*
▲ **Wainland Inc** .... E 718 626-2233
Astoria *(G-448)*
Wayne Integrated Tech Corp .... E 631 242-0213
Edgewood *(G-4423)*
Wenig Corporation .... E 718 542-3600
Bronx *(G-1419)*
Wg Sheet Metal Corp .... G 718 235-3093
Brooklyn *(G-2643)*
William Kanes Mfg Corp .... G 718 346-1515
Brooklyn *(G-2649)*
▲ **Zahk Sales Inc** .... G 631 851-0851
Islandia *(G-6541)*

3446 Architectural & Ornamental Metal Work

786 Iron Works Corp .... G 718 418-4808
Brooklyn *(G-1446)*
▲ **A & T Iron Works Inc** .... E 914 632-8992
New Rochelle *(G-8585)*
A1 Ornamental Iron Works Inc .... G 718 265-3055
Brooklyn *(G-1467)*
Aca Quality Building Pdts LLC .... E 718 991-2423
Bronx *(G-1207)*
Accurate Welding Service Inc .... G 516 333-1730
Westbury *(G-16308)*
▲ **Acme Architectural Pdts Inc** .... D 718 384-7800
Brooklyn *(G-1477)*
▼ **Aero-Data Metal Crafters Inc** .... C 631 471-7733
Ronkonkoma *(G-14294)*
Airflex Corp .... D 631 752-1219
Farmingdale *(G-4709)*
Airflex Industrial Inc .... E 631 752-1234
Farmingdale *(G-4710)*
Airflex Industrial Inc .... D 631 752-1234
Farmingdale *(G-4711)*

SIC

Employee Codes: A=Over 500 employees, B=251-500
C=101-250, D=51-100, E=20-50, F=10-19, G=5-9
2019 Harris
New York Manufacturers Directory
747

Aldo Frustacci Iron Works Inc .... F 718 768-0707
Brooklyn (G-1502)
Aldos Iron Works Inc .... G 718 834-0408
Brooklyn (G-1503)
All American Metal Corporation .... E 516 623-0222
Freeport (G-5140)
All American Stairs & Railing .... F 718 441-8400
Richmond Hill (G-13495)
▲ Allied Bronze Corp (del Corp) .... E 646 421-6400
New York (G-8798)
▲ Arcadia Mfg Group Inc .... E 518 434-6213
Green Island (G-5602)
Arcadia Mfg Group Inc .... G 518 434-6213
Menands (G-8081)
Armento Incorporated .... G 716 875-2423
Kenmore (G-6857)
Artistic Iron Works Inc .... G 631 665-4285
Bay Shore (G-659)
Atlas Fence & Railing Co Inc .... E 718 767-2200
Whitestone (G-16535)
Babylon Iron Works Inc .... F 631 643-3311
West Babylon (G-16137)
Bobrick Washroom Equipment Inc .... D 518 877-7444
Clifton Park (G-3565)
Bracci Ironworks Inc .... F 718 629-2374
Brooklyn (G-1630)
C & F Iron Works Inc .... F 914 592-2450
Elmsford (G-4534)
C & F Steel Corp .... F 914 592-3928
Elmsford (G-4535)
Cabezon Design Group Inc .... G 718 488-9868
Brooklyn (G-1667)
Caliper Studio Inc .... E 718 302-2427
Brooklyn (G-1669)
▲ City Store Gates Mfg Corp .... E 718 939-9700
College Point (G-3642)
Creative Metal Fabricators .... G 631 567-2266
Bohemia (G-1002)
D V S Iron & Aluminum Works .... G 718 768-7961
Brooklyn (G-1748)
Duke of Iron Inc .... G 631 543-3600
Smithtown (G-14897)
E & J Iron Works Inc .... E 718 665-6040
Bronx (G-1262)
E F Iron Works & Construction .... G 631 242-4766
Bay Shore (G-684)
▲ E S P Metal Crafts Inc .... G 718 381-2443
Brooklyn (G-1805)
Ej Group Inc .... G 315 699-2601
Cicero (G-3517)
Elevator Accessories Mfg .... F 914 739-7004
Peekskill (G-12919)
Empire Steel Works Inc .... F 516 561-3500
Hicksville (G-6084)
Fence Plaza Corp .... G 718 469-2200
Brooklyn (G-1874)
▼ Flagpoles Incorporated .... D 631 751-5500
East Setauket (G-4301)
Flushing Iron Weld Inc .... E 718 359-2208
Flushing (G-5001)
Forest Iron Works Inc .... G 516 671-4229
Locust Valley (G-7348)
▼ Giumenta Corp .... E 718 832-1200
Brooklyn (G-1929)
Giumenta Corp .... E 718 832-1200
Brooklyn (G-1930)
◆ Global Steel Products Corp .... C 631 586-3455
Deer Park (G-3981)
Grillmaster Inc .... E 718 272-9191
Howard Beach (G-6330)
Hi-Tech Metals Inc .... E 718 894-1212
Maspeth (G-7852)
Imperial Damper & Louver Co .... E 718 731-3800
Bronx (G-1294)
Inter-Fence Co Inc .... E 718 939-9700
College Point (G-3648)
Iron Art Inc .... G 914 592-7977
Elmsford (G-4546)
Irony Limited Inc .... G 631 329-4065
East Hampton (G-4238)
▲ ITR Industries Inc .... E 914 964-7063
Yonkers (G-16771)
Jamaica Iron Works Inc .... F 718 657-4849
Jamaica (G-6653)
Jamestown Fab Stl & Sup Inc .... G 716 665-2227
Jamestown (G-6728)
▲ Jaxson Rollforming Inc .... E 631 842-7775
Amityville (G-290)
Jerry Cardullo Iron Works Inc .... F 631 242-8881
Bay Shore (G-692)
▲ Jonathan Metal & Glass Ltd .... C 718 846-8000
Jamaica (G-6654)
Kenal Services Corp .... G 315 788-9226
Watertown (G-16020)
Kendi Iron Works Inc .... G 718 821-2722
Brooklyn (G-2068)
▼ Keuka Studios Inc .... G 585 624-5960
Rush (G-14475)
Kleinfelder John .... G 716 753-3163
Mayville (G-7921)
Kms Contracting Inc .... F 718 495-6500
Brooklyn (G-2077)
Koenig Iron Works Inc .... E 718 433-0900
Long Island City (G-7489)
Kryten Iron Works Inc .... G 914 345-0990
Hawthorne (G-5990)
Lencore Acoustics Corp .... F 516 682-9292
Woodbury (G-16623)
Lopopolo Iron Works Inc .... G 718 339-0572
Brooklyn (G-2135)
M B C Metal Inc .... F 718 384-6713
Brooklyn (G-2145)
Martin Orna Ir Works II Inc .... G 516 354-3923
Elmont (G-4520)
▲ Material Process Systems Inc .... F 718 302-3081
Brooklyn (G-2179)
▲ Maximum Security Products Corp ... E 518 233-1800
Waterford (G-15977)
McAllisters Precision Wldg Inc .... F 518 221-3455
Menands (G-8087)
Mestel Brothers Stairs & Rails .... C 516 496-4127
Syosset (G-15222)
Metalworks Inc .... E 718 319-0011
Bronx (G-1329)
▼ Metro Door Inc .... D 800 669-3667
Islandia (G-6535)
Milgo Industrial Inc .... D 718 388-6476
Brooklyn (G-2206)
Milgo Industrial Inc .... G 718 387-0406
Brooklyn (G-2207)
▲ Mison Concepts Inc .... G 516 933-8000
Hicksville (G-6110)
▲ Modern Art Foundry Inc .... E 718 728-2030
Astoria (G-436)
Moon Gates Company .... G 718 426-0023
East Elmhurst (G-4224)
Morgik Metal Designs .... F 212 463-0304
New York (G-10842)
Moro Corporation .... E 607 724-4241
Binghamton (G-906)
New Dimensions Office Group .... D 718 387-0995
Brooklyn (G-2259)
▲ Old Dutchmans Wrough Iron Inc ...... G 716 688-2034
Getzville (G-5351)
Oldcastle Precast Inc .... F 518 767-2116
South Bethlehem (G-14924)
Ornametal Inc .... G 845 562-5151
Newburgh (G-12239)
Ourem Iron Works Inc .... F 914 476-4856
Yonkers (G-16789)
▲ Paragon Aquatics .... E 845 452-5500
Lagrangeville (G-6960)
Pawling Corporation .... D 845 373-9300
Wassaic (G-15965)
Peconic Ironworks Ltd .... F 631 204-0323
Southampton (G-14959)
Phoenix Metal Designs Inc .... G 516 597-4100
Brooklyn (G-2315)
Pk30 System LLC .... F 212 473-8050
Stone Ridge (G-15162)
◆ Pole-Tech Co Inc .... F 631 689-5525
East Setauket (G-4307)
Railings By New Star Brass .... E 516 358-1153
Brooklyn (G-2380)
Raulli and Sons Inc .... F 315 474-1370
Syracuse (G-15403)
Raulli and Sons Inc .... D 315 479-6693
Syracuse (G-15402)
Raulli Iron Works Inc .... F 315 337-8070
Rome (G-14269)
Riverside Iron LLC .... F 315 535-4864
Gouverneur (G-5492)
Rollson Inc .... E 631 423-9578
Huntington (G-6412)
Roman Iron Works Inc .... F 516 621-1103
Greenvale (G-5631)
Royal Metal Products Inc .... E 518 966-4442
Surprise (G-15207)
▲ S A Baxter LLC .... G 845 469-7995
Chester (G-3482)
▲ Shanker Industries Realty Inc .... G 631 940-9889
Deer Park (G-4044)
Steel Sales Inc .... E 607 674-6363
Sherburne (G-14811)
Steel Work Inc .... G 585 232-1555
Rochester (G-14142)
Steps Plus Inc .... D 315 432-0885
Syracuse (G-15430)
Studio 40 Inc .... G 212 420-8631
Brooklyn (G-2526)
Superior Metal & Woodwork Inc .... E 631 465-9004
Farmingdale (G-4884)
Tee Pee Fence and Railing .... F 718 658-8323
Jamaica (G-6683)
◆ Tensator Inc .... D 631 666-0300
Bay Shore (G-731)
Tonys Ornamental Ir Works Inc .... E 315 337-3730
Rome (G-14276)
Tri State Shearing Bending Inc .... F 718 485-2200
Brooklyn (G-2581)
Triple H Construction Inc .... E 516 280-8252
East Meadow (G-4256)
Tropical Driftwood Originals .... G 516 623-0980
Roosevelt (G-14438)
Tymetal Corp .... E 518 692-9930
Greenwich (G-5646)
United Iron Inc .... E 914 667-5700
Mount Vernon (G-8453)
United Steel Products Inc .... D 914 968-7782
Flushing (G-5058)
Universal Steel Fabricators .... F 718 342-0782
Brooklyn (G-2610)
Village Wrought Iron Inc .... F 315 683-5589
Fabius (G-4624)
Vr Containment LLC .... G 917 972-3441
Fresh Meadows (G-5205)
West End Iron Works Inc .... G 518 456-1105
Albany (G-141)
Z-Studios Dsign Fbrication LLC .... G 347 512-4210
Brooklyn (G-2668)

3448 Prefabricated Metal Buildings & Cmpnts

All American Building .... G 607 797-7123
Binghamton (G-859)
▲ Austin Mohawk and Company LLC . E 315 793-3000
Utica (G-15678)
◆ Birdair Inc .... D 716 633-9500
Amherst (G-218)
Deraffele Mfg Co Inc .... E 914 636-6850
New Rochelle (G-8598)
Energy Panel Structures Inc .... G 315 923-7777
Clyde (G-3592)
Energy Panel Structures Inc .... G 585 343-1777
Clyde (G-3593)
Energy Panel Structures Inc .... G 518 355-6708
Schenectady (G-14671)
▲ Fillmore Greenhouses Inc .... E 585 567-2678
Portageville (G-13314)
▲ Guardian Booth LLC .... F 844 992-6684
Spring Valley (G-14994)
Landmark Group Inc .... E 845 358-0350
Valley Cottage (G-15757)
Latium USA Trading LLC .... D 631 563-4000
Holbrook (G-6193)
Man Products Inc .... E 631 789-6500
Farmingdale (G-4814)
▼ Metallic Ladder Mfg Corp .... F 716 358-6201
Randolph (G-13448)
Metals Building Products .... E 844 638-2527
Holbrook (G-6199)
Mobile Mini Inc .... F 315 732-4555
Utica (G-15723)
Mobile Mini Inc .... E 631 543-4900
Commack (G-3698)
Morton Buildings Inc .... E 585 786-8191
Warsaw (G-15945)
Nci Group Inc .... D 315 339-1245
Rome (G-14261)
Overhead Door Corporation .... D 518 828-7652
Hudson (G-6366)
Precision Fabrication LLC .... G 585 591-3449
Attica (G-461)
Sunbilt Solar Pdts By Sussman .... D 718 297-0228
Jamaica (G-6681)
T Shore Products Ltd .... G 315 252-9174
Auburn (G-502)
Universal Shielding Corp .... E 631 667-7900
Deer Park (G-4055)

Walpole Woodworkers Inc .... G 631 726-2859
Water Mill (G-15971)

3449 Misc Structural Metal Work

A&B McKeon Glass Inc .... G 718 525-2152
Staten Island (G-15038)
▲ Abasco Inc .... E 716 649-4790
Hamburg (G-5672)
Accurate Metal Weather Strip .... G 914 668-6042
Mount Vernon (G-8375)
Agl Industries Inc .... E 718 326-7597
Maspeth (G-7816)
▲ AM Architectural Metal & Glass ...... E 845 942-8848
Garnerville (G-5299)
Arista Steel Designs Corp .... G 718 965-7077
Brooklyn (G-1552)
▲ Baco Enterprises Inc .... G 718 589-6225
Bronx (G-1224)
Barker Steel LLC .... G 518 465-6221
Albany (G-44)
City Evolutionary .... G 718 861-7585
Bronx (G-1240)
Coral Management Corp .... G 718 893-9286
Bronx (G-1246)
DAgostino Iron Works Inc .... G 585 235-8850
Rochester (G-13731)
▲ Designs By Novello Inc .... G 914 934-7711
Port Chester (G-13196)
▲ Dimension Fabricators Inc .... E 518 374-1936
Scotia (G-14739)
Empire Metal Finishing Inc .... G 718 545-6700
Astoria (G-427)
Ferro Fabricators Inc .... F 718 703-0007
Brooklyn (G-1875)
GCM Metal Industries Inc .... F 718 386-4059
Brooklyn (G-1919)
Halmark Architectural Finshg .... G 718 272-1831
Brooklyn (G-1961)
Harbor Wldg & Fabrication Corp .... F 631 667-1880
Copiague (G-3762)
Hornet Group Inc .... D 845 858-6400
Port Jervis (G-13230)
◆ Inscape (new York) Inc .... D 716 665-6210
Falconer (G-4681)
Janed Enterprises .... F 631 694-4494
Farmingdale (G-4792)
Jpl Designs Ltd .... G 212 689-7096
New York (G-10371)
Klein Reinforcing Services Inc .... F 585 352-9433
Spencerport (G-14980)
Kraman Iron Works Inc .... F 212 460-8400
New York (G-10478)
▲ Lakeside Capital Corporation .... E 716 664-2555
Jamestown (G-6735)
Lane Enterprises Inc .... E 518 885-4385
Ballston Spa (G-587)
▲ Longstem Organizers Inc .... G 914 777-2174
Jefferson Valley (G-6777)
▲ Metal Products Intl LLC .... F 716 215-1930
Niagara Falls (G-12309)
Metalsigma Usa Inc .... G 212 731-4346
New York (G-10783)
New York Steel Services Co .... F 718 291-7770
Jamaica (G-6665)
Northern Metalworks Corp .... G 646 523-1689
Selden (G-14765)
Orange County Ironworks LLC .... E 845 769-3000
Montgomery (G-8315)
▲ Orbital Holdings Inc .... E 951 360-7100
Buffalo (G-2982)
▲ Paragon Aquatics .... E 845 452-5500
Lagrangeville (G-6960)
Ppi Corp .... G 585 880-7277
Rochester (G-14031)
▲ Risa Management Corp .... E 718 361-2606
Maspeth (G-7870)
Riverside Iron LLC .... F 315 535-4864
Gouverneur (G-5492)
▲ Rolite Mfg Inc .... E 716 683-0259
Lancaster (G-7046)
▲ Rollform of Jamestown Inc .... F 716 665-5310
Jamestown (G-6745)
Semans Enterprises Inc .... F 585 444-0097
West Henrietta (G-16250)
Signature Metal MBL Maint LLC .... D 718 292-8280
Bronx (G-1385)
Sims Steel Corporation .... E 631 587-8670
Lindenhurst (G-7192)
▲ Siw Inc .... F 631 888-0130
Bay Shore (G-723)

Steel Sales Inc .... E 607 674-6363
Sherburne (G-14811)
Tebbens Steel LLC .... F 631 208-8330
Calverton (G-3174)
Tonys Ornamental Ir Works Inc .... F 315 337-3730
Rome (G-14276)
Torino Industrial Inc .... E 631 509-1640
Bellport (G-816)
United Iron Inc .... E 914 667-5700
Mount Vernon (G-8453)
West Metal Works Inc .... E 716 895-4900
Buffalo (G-3128)
Wide Flange Inc .... F 718 492-8705
Brooklyn (G-2645)

3451 Screw Machine Prdts

Acme Precision Screw Pdts Inc .... F 585 328-2028
Rochester (G-13599)
Action Machined Products Inc .... F 631 842-2333
Copiague (G-3748)
Albert Gates Inc .... D 585 594-9401
North Chili (G-12381)
All Type Screw Machine Pdts .... G 516 334-5100
Westbury (G-16313)
▲ Alpha Fasteners Corp .... E 516 867-6188
Freeport (G-5141)
American-Swiss Products Co Inc .... E 585 292-1720
Pittsford (G-13008)
▲ Anderson Precision Inc .... D 716 484-1148
Jamestown (G-6698)
Andros Manufacturing Corp .... E 585 663-5700
Rochester (G-13633)
Brinkman Intl Group Inc .... E 585 429-5000
Rochester (G-13676)
Broda Machine Co Inc .... F 716 297-3221
Niagara Falls (G-12266)
C R C Manufacturing Inc .... E 585 254-8820
Rochester (G-13686)
C&C Automatics Inc .... F 315 331-1436
Newark (G-12193)
Century Metal Parts Corp .... F 631 667-0800
Bay Shore (G-669)
Craftech Industries Inc .... D 518 828-5001
Hudson (G-6344)
Curtis Screw Co Inc .... E 716 898-7800
Buffalo (G-2788)
Emory Machine & Tool Co Inc .... E 585 436-9610
Farmington (G-4913)
Five Star Tool Co Inc .... E 585 328-9580
Rochester (G-13806)
Globe Electronic Hardware Inc .... F 718 457-0303
Woodside (G-16659)
Gsp Components Inc .... D 585 436-3377
Rochester (G-13846)
Hanco Metal Products Inc .... F 212 787-5992
Brooklyn (G-1965)
▲ I W Industries Inc .... C 631 293-9494
Melville (G-8036)
J & J Swiss Precision Inc .... E 631 243-5584
Deer Park (G-3988)
Kaddis Manufacturing Corp .... E 585 624-3070
Honeoye Falls (G-6270)
Kathleen B Mead .... G 585 247-0146
Webster (G-16089)
Lexington Machining LLC .... D 585 235-0880
Rochester (G-13912)
Lexington Machining LLC .... D 585 235-0880
Rochester (G-13913)
▲ Liberty Brass Turning Co Inc .... E 718 784-2911
Westbury (G-16350)
M Manastrip-M Corporation .... G 518 664-2089
Clifton Park (G-3570)
Manacraft Precision Inc .... G 914 654-0967
Pelham (G-12937)
Manth-Brownell Inc .... F 315 687-7263
Kirkville (G-6934)
Marmach Machine Inc .... E 585 768-8800
Le Roy (G-7122)
Micro Threaded Products Inc .... E 585 288-0080
Rochester (G-13940)
Miggins Screw Products Inc .... E 845 279-2307
Brewster (G-1172)
Muller Tool Inc .... E 716 895-3658
Buffalo (G-2956)
Multimatic Products Inc .... G 800 767-7633
Ronkonkoma (G-14381)
▲ Murphy Manufacturing Co Inc .... E 585 223-0100
Fairport (G-4644)
Norwood Screw Machine Parts .... F 516 481-6644
Mineola (G-8241)

▲ Park-Ohio Inds Trsry Co Inc .... F 212 966-3310
Albany (G-110)
▲ Ppi Corp .... D 585 243-0300
Rochester (G-14032)
R P M Machine Co .... G 585 671-3744
Webster (G-16094)
Ranney Precision .... F 716 731-6418
Niagara Falls (G-12328)
Selflock Screw Products Co Inc .... E 315 541-4464
Syracuse (G-15422)
Supreme Screw Products Inc .... G 718 293-6600
Plainview (G-13091)
T & L Automatics Inc .... C 585 647-3717
Rochester (G-14155)
TAC Screw Products Inc .... E 585 663-5840
Rochester (G-14157)
Taylor Metalworks Inc .... C 716 662-3113
Orchard Park (G-12745)
Teale Machine Company Inc .... G 585 244-6700
Rochester (G-14160)
▲ Thuro Metal Products Inc .... E 631 435-0444
Brentwood (G-1145)
▲ Tri-Technologies Inc .... E 914 699-2001
Mount Vernon (G-8449)
Trihex Manufacturing Inc .... G 315 589-9331
Williamson (G-16563)
Triple Point Manufacturing .... G 631 218-4988
Bohemia (G-1101)
Umbro Machine & Tool Co Inc .... F 845 876-4669
Rhinebeck (G-13489)
Vanguard Metals Inc .... F 631 234-6500
Central Islip (G-3388)
Verns Machine Co Inc .... G 315 926-4223
Marion (G-7810)

3452 Bolts, Nuts, Screws, Rivets & Washers

▲ Alcoa Fastening Systems .... C 845 334-7203
Kingston (G-6887)
Allied Bolt Products LLC .... F 516 512-7600
New Hyde Park (G-8514)
▲ American Pride Fasteners LLC ..... E 631 940-8292
Bay Shore (G-656)
Anthony Manno & Co Inc .... G 631 445-1834
Deer Park (G-3943)
▲ Baco Enterprises Inc .... D 718 589-6225
Bronx (G-1224)
Buckley Qc Fasteners Inc .... E 716 662-1490
Orchard Park (G-12702)
Craftech Industries Inc .... D 518 828-5001
Hudson (G-6344)
Dependable Acme Threaded Pdts ..... C 516 338-4700
Westbury (G-16322)
Fastener Dimensions Inc .... E 718 847-6321
Ozone Park (G-12825)
Huck International Inc .... E 845 331-7300
Kingston (G-6902)
Jem Threading Specialties Inc .... G 718 665-3341
Bronx (G-1301)
John F Rafter Inc .... E 716 992-3425
Eden (G-4389)
▲ John Hassall LLC .... D 516 334-6200
Westbury (G-16344)
▼ John Hassall LLC .... D 323 869-0150
Westbury (G-16345)
Kinemotive Corporation .... E 631 249-6440
Farmingdale (G-4803)
LD McCauley LLC .... C 716 662-6744
Orchard Park (G-12726)
◆ Marksmen Manufacturing Corp ...... E 800 305-6942
Deer Park (G-4006)
▲ Park-Ohio Inds Trsry Co Inc .... F 212 966-3310
Albany (G-110)
Pin Pharma Inc .... E 212 543-2583
New York (G-11195)
Pins N Needles .... F 212 535-6222
New York (G-11199)
Pni Capital Partners .... G 516 466-7120
Westbury (G-16364)
Radax Industries Inc .... E 585 265-2055
Webster (G-16095)
Rochester Stampings Inc .... F 585 467-5241
Rochester (G-14095)
Schaefer Machine Co Inc .... E 516 248-6880
Mineola (G-8249)
▲ Sesco Industries Inc .... F 718 939-5137
College Point (G-3665)
Simon Defense Inc .... G 516 217-6000
Ronkonkoma (G-14413)
Socket Products Mfg Corp .... G 631 232-9870
Islandia (G-6538)

Southco Inc .... B 585 624-2545
Honeoye Falls *(G-6273)*
Superior Washer & Gasket Corp .... D 631 273-8282
Hauppauge *(G-5952)*
Ta Chen International Inc .... F 845 352-5300
Monsey *(G-8300)*
▲ **Tamperproof Screw Company Inc** .... F 516 931-1616
Hicksville *(G-6136)*
Teka Precision Inc .... G 845 753-1900
Nyack *(G-12512)*
Treo Industries Inc .... G 631 737-4022
Bohemia *(G-1097)*
Trihex Manufacturing Inc .... G 315 589-9331
Williamson *(G-16563)*
▲ **Zierick Manufacturing Corp** .... D 800 882-8020
Mount Kisco *(G-8361)*
Zip Products Inc .... F 585 482-0044
Rochester *(G-14220)*

3462 Iron & Steel Forgings

Alry Tool and Die Co Inc .... E 716 693-2419
Tonawanda *(G-15521)*
▲ **Ball Chain Mfg Co Inc** .... D 914 664-7500
Mount Vernon *(G-8379)*
▲ **Biltron Automotive Products** .... E 631 928-8613
Port Jeff STA *(G-13212)*
▲ **Borgwarner Morse TEC LLC** .... C 607 257-6700
Ithaca *(G-6568)*
Burke Frging Heat Treating Inc .... E 585 235-6060
Rochester *(G-13682)*
Delaware Valley Forge Co Inc .... G 716 447-9140
Buffalo *(G-2796)*
Delaware Valley Forge Inc .... E 716 447-9140
Buffalo *(G-2797)*
▲ **Designatronics Incorporated** .... G 516 328-3300
Hicksville *(G-6079)*
◆ **Dragon Trading Inc** .... G 212 717-1496
New York *(G-9572)*
Extreme Shale Performance LLC .... G 814 688-7956
Elmira *(G-4485)*
◆ **Firth Rixson Inc** .... D 585 328-1383
Rochester *(G-13805)*
Gear Motions Incorporated .... E 716 885-1080
Buffalo *(G-2843)*
Gear Motions Incorporated .... E 315 488-0100
Syracuse *(G-15331)*
Great Lakes Gear Co Inc .... G 716 694-0715
Tonawanda *(G-15542)*
▲ **Hammond & Irving Inc** .... D 315 253-6265
Auburn *(G-482)*
◆ **Hohmann & Barnard Inc** .... E 631 234-0600
Hauppauge *(G-5846)*
Hohmann & Barnard Inc .... E 518 357-9757
Schenectady *(G-14687)*
Industrial Mch Gear Works LLC .... G 516 695-4442
Rockville Centre *(G-14234)*
▲ **Jrlon Inc** .... D 315 597-4067
Palmyra *(G-12855)*
Kurz and Zobel Inc .... G 585 254-9060
Rochester *(G-13908)*
Mattessich Iron LLC .... G 315 409-8496
Memphis *(G-8076)*
Metrofab Pipe Incorporated .... F 516 349-7373
Plainview *(G-13074)*
▲ **Peck & Hale LLC** .... E 631 589-2510
West Sayville *(G-16291)*
Perfect Gear & Instrument .... F 516 328-3330
Hicksville *(G-6125)*
Perfect Gear & Instrument .... E 516 873-6122
Garden City Park *(G-5287)*
Pro-Gear Co Inc .... G 716 684-3811
Buffalo *(G-3016)*
Riley Gear Corporation .... E 716 694-0900
North Tonawanda *(G-12446)*
S R & R Industries Inc .... G 845 692-8329
Middletown *(G-8175)*
▲ **Schilling Forge Inc** .... E 315 454-4421
Syracuse *(G-15417)*
▲ **Secs Inc** .... E 914 667-5600
Mount Vernon *(G-8441)*
Secs Inc .... E 914 667-5600
Mount Vernon *(G-8442)*
Special Metals Corporation .... D 716 366-5663
Dunkirk *(G-4180)*
Stoffel Polygon Systems Inc .... F 914 961-2000
Tuckahoe *(G-15646)*
Superior Motion Controls Inc .... E 516 420-2921
Farmingdale *(G-4885)*
Superite Gear Instr of Hppauge .... G 631 234-0100
Hauppauge *(G-5953)*
Upstate Piping Products Inc .... G 518 238-3457
Waterford *(G-15989)*
Viking Iron Works Inc .... F 845 471-5010
Poughkeepsie *(G-13373)*
▲ **Vulcan Steam Forging Co** .... E 716 875-3680
Buffalo *(G-3122)*
W J Albro Machine Works Inc .... G 631 345-0657
Yaphank *(G-16728)*
York Industries Inc .... E 516 746-3736
Garden City Park *(G-5290)*

3463 Nonferrous Forgings

◆ **Arconic Inc** .... D 212 836-2758
New York *(G-8903)*
Arconic Inc .... G 315 764-4011
Massena *(G-7900)*
▲ **Nak International Corp** .... D 516 334-6245
Jericho *(G-6794)*
Penn State Metal Fabri .... G 718 786-8814
Brooklyn *(G-2311)*
Special Metals Corporation .... D 716 366-5663
Dunkirk *(G-4180)*

3465 Automotive Stampings

Albert Kemperle Inc .... E 718 629-1084
Brooklyn *(G-1499)*
Automotive LLC .... F 248 728-8642
Batavia *(G-611)*
Kustom Korner .... F 716 646-0173
Hamburg *(G-5686)*
M & W Aluminum Products Inc .... F 315 414-0005
Syracuse *(G-15366)*
P R B Metal Products Inc .... F 631 467-1800
Ronkonkoma *(G-14393)*
Qpbc Inc .... E 718 685-1900
Long Island City *(G-7564)*
▲ **Racing Industries Inc** .... E 631 905-0100
Calverton *(G-3169)*
Thyssenkrupp Materials NA Inc .... G 585 279-0000
Rochester *(G-14170)*
Utica Metal Products Inc .... D 315 732-6163
Utica *(G-15738)*

3466 Crowns & Closures

Protocase Incorporated .... C 866 849-3911
Lewiston *(G-7141)*
Reynolds Packaging McHy Inc .... D 716 358-6451
Falconer *(G-4690)*
▲ **Van Blarcom Closures Inc** .... C 718 855-3810
Brooklyn *(G-2615)*

3469 Metal Stampings, NEC

4m Precision Industries Inc .... E 315 252-8415
Auburn *(G-462)*
▲ **A-1 Stamping & Spinning Corp** .... F 718 388-2626
Rockaway Park *(G-14227)*
Able National Corp .... E 718 386-8801
Brooklyn *(G-1471)*
Acme Architectural Products .... B 718 360-0700
Brooklyn *(G-1476)*
Acme Kitchenettes Corp .... E 518 828-4191
Hudson *(G-6337)*
▲ **Acro Industries Inc** .... C 585 254-3661
Rochester *(G-13600)*
Advanced Structures Corp .... F 631 667-5000
Deer Park *(G-3934)*
Afco Systems Inc .... C 631 249-9441
Farmingdale *(G-4708)*
▲ **Albest Metal Stamping Corp** .... D 718 388-6000
Brooklyn *(G-1500)*
All Out Die Cutting Inc .... E 718 346-6666
Brooklyn *(G-1508)*
▲ **Allen Machine Products Inc** .... E 631 630-8800
Hauppauge *(G-5761)*
▲ **Allied Metal Spinning Corp** .... D 718 893-3300
Bronx *(G-1216)*
Alton Manufacturing Inc .... D 585 458-2600
Rochester *(G-13621)*
American Metal Spinning Pdts .... G 631 454-6276
West Babylon *(G-16134)*
American Mtal Stmping Spinning .... F 718 384-1500
Brooklyn *(G-1524)*
Arnell Inc .... G 516 486-7098
Hempstead *(G-6007)*
Arro Manufacturing LLC .... F 716 763-6203
Lakewood *(G-6989)*
Arro Tool & Die Inc .... F 716 763-6203
Lakewood *(G-6990)*
Art Precision Metal Products .... F 631 842-8889
Copiague *(G-3752)*
B & R Tool Inc .... G 718 948-2729
Staten Island *(G-15046)*
B H M Metal Products Co .... G 845 292-5297
Kauneonga Lake *(G-6849)*
Bailey Manufacturing Co LLC .... E 716 965-2731
Forestville *(G-5085)*
Barnes Group Inc .... G 315 457-9200
Syracuse *(G-15254)*
Barron Metal Products Inc .... E 914 965-1232
Yonkers *(G-16738)*
Bcs Access Systems Us LLC .... B 315 258-3469
Auburn *(G-469)*
Belmet Products Inc .... E 718 542-8220
Bronx *(G-1227)*
Belrix Industries Inc .... G 716 821-5964
Buffalo *(G-2729)*
Bowen Products Corporation .... G 315 498-4481
Nedrow *(G-8478)*
▲ **Brach Machine Inc** .... F 585 343-9134
Batavia *(G-615)*
Bridgeport Metalcraft Inc .... G 315 623-9597
Constantia *(G-3739)*
C & H Precision Tools Inc .... E 631 758-3806
Holtsville *(G-6238)*
▲ **Cameo Metal Products Inc** .... E 718 788-1106
Brooklyn *(G-1670)*
▲ **Cannon Industries Inc** .... D 585 254-8080
Rochester *(G-13690)*
▲ **Cep Technologies Corporation** .... E 914 968-4100
Yonkers *(G-16744)*
Cgs Fabrication LLC .... F 585 347-6127
Webster *(G-16078)*
Charles A Rogers Entps Inc .... E 585 924-6400
Victor *(G-15835)*
Check-Mate Industries Inc .... E 631 491-1777
West Babylon *(G-16146)*
Chivvis Enterprises Inc .... F 631 842-9055
Copiague *(G-3755)*
Cobbe Industries Inc .... E 716 287-2661
Gerry *(G-5340)*
▲ **Coda Resources Ltd** .... D 718 649-1666
Brooklyn *(G-1703)*
Coil Stamping Inc .... F 631 588-3040
Holbrook *(G-6178)*
Colonial Precision Machinery .... G 631 249-0738
Farmingdale *(G-4737)*
Compac Development Corporation .... D 631 881-4903
Hauppauge *(G-5797)*
Compar Manufacturing Corp .... E 212 304-2777
New York *(G-9369)*
Corbett Stves Pttern Works Inc .... E 585 546-7109
Rochester *(G-13722)*
◆ **Corning Vitro Corporation** .... A 607 974-8605
Corning *(G-3818)*
◆ **Creative Design and Mch Inc** .... E 845 778-9001
Rock Tavern *(G-14224)*
Crosby Company .... E 716 852-3522
Buffalo *(G-2784)*
Custom Metal Incorporated .... F 631 643-4075
West Babylon *(G-16151)*
D-K Manufacturing Corp .... E 315 592-4327
Fulton *(G-5214)*
▲ **Dayton Industries Inc** .... E 718 542-8144
Bronx *(G-1254)*
Dayton Rogers New York LLC .... D 585 349-4040
Rochester *(G-13735)*
Die-Matic Products LLC .... E 516 433-7900
Plainview *(G-13051)*
▼ **Dunkirk Metal Products Wny LLC** .... E 716 366-2555
Dunkirk *(G-4167)*
Electric Motors and Pumps Inc .... G 718 935-9118
Brooklyn *(G-1820)*
Endicott Precision Inc .... C 607 754-7076
Endicott *(G-4589)*
Engineering Mfg Tech LLC .... D 607 754-7111
Endicott *(G-4591)*
Erdle Perforating Holdings Inc .... D 585 247-4700
Rochester *(G-13789)*
Falso Industries Inc .... E 315 463-0266
Syracuse *(G-15322)*
▲ **Feldware Inc** .... E 718 372-0486
Brooklyn *(G-1873)*
Forkey Construction & Fabg Inc .... E 607 849-4879
Cortland *(G-3872)*
Forsyth Industries Inc .... E 716 652-1070
Buffalo *(G-2831)*
▲ **Freeport Screen & Stamping** .... E 516 379-0330
Freeport *(G-5157)*

SIC SECTION 34 FABRICATED METAL PRODUCTS, EXCEPT MACHINERY AND TRANSPORTATION EQUIPMENT

G A Richards & Co Inc............F....... 516 334-5412
Westbury *(G-16334)*
▲ Gasser & Sons Inc............C....... 631 543-6600
Commack *(G-3692)*
Gay Sheet Metal Dies Inc............G....... 716 877-0208
Buffalo *(G-2842)*
Gem Metal Spinning & Stamping............G....... 718 729-7014
Long Island City *(G-7456)*
Genesee Metal Stampings Inc............G....... 585 475-0450
West Henrietta *(G-16240)*
German Machine & Assembly Inc............E....... 585 546-4200
Rochester *(G-13831)*
◆ Gleason Works............A....... 585 473-1000
Rochester *(G-13840)*
Great Lakes Pressed Steel Corp............E....... 716 885-4037
Buffalo *(G-2857)*
Greene Technologies Inc............D....... 607 656-4166
Greene *(G-5615)*
Hy-Grade Metal Products Corp............G....... 315 475-4221
Syracuse *(G-15341)*
▲ Hyman Podrusnick Co Inc............G....... 718 853-4502
Brooklyn *(G-1990)*
◆ International Ord Tech Inc............D....... 716 664-1100
Jamestown *(G-6724)*
J T D Stamping Co Inc............E....... 631 643-4144
West Babylon *(G-16162)*
Johnson & Hoffman LLC............D....... 516 742-3333
Carle Place *(G-3267)*
▲ Kerns Manufacturing Corp............C....... 718 784-4044
Long Island City *(G-7488)*
▼ Koch Metal Spinning Co Inc............D....... 716 835-3631
Buffalo *(G-2909)*
◆ Korin Japanese Trading Corp............E....... 212 587-7021
New York *(G-10471)*
Lamparts Co Inc............F....... 914 723-8986
Mount Vernon *(G-8416)*
▲ Lancaster Knives Inc............E....... 716 683-5050
Lancaster *(G-7029)*
▲ Lb Furniture Industries LLC............C....... 518 828-1501
Hudson *(G-6362)*
Long Island Metalform Inc............F....... 631 242-9088
Deer Park *(G-4003)*
M F Manufacturing Enterprises............G....... 516 822-5135
Hicksville *(G-6104)*
Maehr Industries Inc............G....... 631 924-1661
Bellport *(G-807)*
▲ Magic Novelty Co Inc............E....... 212 304-2777
New York *(G-10667)*
Mantel & Mantel Stamping Corp............G....... 631 467-1916
Ronkonkoma *(G-14374)*
▲ Marex Aquisition Corp............C....... 585 458-3940
Rochester *(G-13930)*
Matov Industries Inc............E....... 718 392-5060
Long Island City *(G-7518)*
McHone Industries Inc............D....... 716 945-3380
Salamanca *(G-14526)*
Mega Tool & Mfg Corp............E....... 607 734-8398
Elmira *(G-4498)*
Nash Metalware Co Inc............F....... 315 339-5794
Rome *(G-14260)*
National Computer & Electronic............G....... 631 242-7222
Deer Park *(G-4013)*
National Die & Button Mould Co............E....... 201 939-7800
Brooklyn *(G-2245)*
▲ National Wire & Metal Tech Inc............E....... 716 661-9180
Jamestown *(G-6740)*
▲ Novel Box Company Ltd............E....... 718 965-2222
Brooklyn *(G-2275)*
▲ OEM Solutions Inc............G....... 716 864-9324
Clarence *(G-3536)*
▲ Oxo International Inc............C....... 212 242-3333
New York *(G-11080)*
P R B Metal Products Inc............F....... 631 467-1800
Ronkonkoma *(G-14393)*
▲ P&G Metal Components Corp............D....... 716 896-7900
Buffalo *(G-2986)*
P&G Steel Inc............F....... 716 896-7900
Buffalo *(G-2987)*
Pall Corporation............A....... 607 753-6041
Cortland *(G-3885)*
Pervi Precision Company Inc............G....... 631 589-5557
Bohemia *(G-1074)*
◆ Phoenix Metal Products Inc............F....... 516 546-4200
Freeport *(G-5174)*
Precision Photo-Fab Inc............D....... 716 821-9393
Buffalo *(G-3011)*
Premier Metals Group............E....... 585 436-4020
Rochester *(G-14039)*
▲ Progressus Company Inc............F....... 516 255-0245
Rockville Centre *(G-14238)*
Pronto Tool & Die Co Inc............E....... 631 981-8920
Ronkonkoma *(G-14401)*
Quality Metal Stamping LLC............G....... 516 255-9000
Rockville Centre *(G-14239)*
▲ R G Flair Co Inc............E....... 631 586-7311
Bay Shore *(G-712)*
Rayco Manufacturing Co Inc............F....... 516 431-2006
Jamaica *(G-6672)*
Reynolds Manufacturing Inc............F....... 607 562-8936
Big Flats *(G-856)*
Richter Charles Metal STMp&sp............E....... 845 895-2025
Wallkill *(G-15906)*
Richter Metalcraft Corporation............E....... 845 895-2025
Wallkill *(G-15907)*
▲ Rigidized Metals Corporation............E....... 716 849-4703
Buffalo *(G-3038)*
Rochester Stampings Inc............F....... 585 467-5241
Rochester *(G-14095)*
▲ Rolite Mfg Inc............E....... 716 683-0259
Lancaster *(G-7046)*
Russco Metal Spinning Co Inc............F....... 516 872-6055
Baldwin *(G-542)*
▲ S & S Prtg Die-Cutting Co Inc............F....... 718 388-8990
Brooklyn *(G-2434)*
S D Z Metal Spinning Stamping............F....... 718 778-3600
Brooklyn *(G-2439)*
Schiller Stores Inc............G....... 631 208-9400
Riverhead *(G-13583)*
Seneca Ceramics Corp............G....... 315 781-0100
Phelps *(G-12980)*
Sharon Manufacturing Co Inc............G....... 631 242-8870
Deer Park *(G-4045)*
Simplex Manufacturing Co Inc............F....... 315 252-7524
Auburn *(G-500)*
Smithers Tools & Mch Pdts Inc............D....... 845 876-3063
Rhinebeck *(G-13488)*
Solidus Industries Inc............D....... 607 749-4540
Homer *(G-6259)*
Square Stamping Mfg Corp............E....... 315 896-2641
Barneveld *(G-605)*
▼ Stampcrete International Ltd............E....... 315 451-2837
Liverpool *(G-7264)*
▲ Stamped Fittings Inc............E....... 607 733-9988
Elmira Heights *(G-4514)*
▲ Stever-Locke Industries Inc............G....... 585 624-3450
Honeoye Falls *(G-6274)*
Surving Studios............F....... 845 355-1430
Middletown *(G-8178)*
Tooling Enterprises Inc............F....... 716 842-0445
Buffalo *(G-3099)*
Tools & Stamping Corp............G....... 718 392-4040
Brooklyn *(G-2570)*
▲ Tri-Technologies Inc............E....... 914 699-2001
Mount Vernon *(G-8449)*
▲ Trident Precision Mfg Inc............D....... 585 265-2010
Webster *(G-16103)*
TRW Automotive Inc............B....... 315 255-3311
Auburn *(G-506)*
▲ Twinco Mfg Co Inc............E....... 631 231-0022
Hauppauge *(G-5963)*
▼ Ultimate Prcision Met Pdts Inc............C....... 631 249-9441
Farmingdale *(G-4901)*
▲ Unicel Corporation............E....... 760 741-3912
Deer Park *(G-4054)*
Universal Shielding Corp............E....... 631 667-7900
Deer Park *(G-4055)*
Van Reenen Tool & Die Inc............F....... 585 288-6000
Rochester *(G-14198)*
Vanity Fair Bathmart Inc............F....... 718 584-6700
Bronx *(G-1413)*
Volkert Precision Tech Inc............E....... 718 464-9500
Queens Village *(G-13412)*
Vosky Precision Machining Corp............F....... 631 737-3200
Ronkonkoma *(G-14429)*
W & H Stampings Inc............E....... 631 234-6161
Hauppauge *(G-5972)*
Web Associates Inc............G....... 716 883-3377
Buffalo *(G-3125)*
Wessie Machine Inc............G....... 315 926-4060
Marion *(G-7811)*
Wilmax Usa LLC............F....... 917 388-2790
New York *(G-12116)*
WR Smith & Sons Inc............G....... 845 620-9400
Nanuet *(G-8469)*
Zeta Machine Corp............G....... 631 471-8832
Ronkonkoma *(G-14433)*

3471 Electroplating, Plating, Polishing, Anodizing & Coloring

21st Century Finishes Inc............F....... 516 221-7000
North Bellmore *(G-12372)*
Abetter Processing Corp............F....... 718 252-2223
Brooklyn *(G-1469)*
Able Anodizing Corp............F....... 718 252-0660
Brooklyn *(G-1470)*
ABS Metal Corp............G....... 646 302-9018
Hewlett *(G-6045)*
Aircraft Finishing Corp............F....... 631 422-5000
West Babylon *(G-16130)*
Airmarine Electroplating Corp............G....... 516 623-4406
Freeport *(G-5137)*
Anthony River Inc............F....... 315 475-1315
Syracuse *(G-15244)*
Astro Electroplating Inc............E....... 631 968-0656
Bay Shore *(G-660)*
B & W Heat Treating Company............G....... 716 876-8184
Tonawanda *(G-15525)*
Barnes Metal Finishing Inc............F....... 585 798-4817
Medina *(G-7971)*
▲ Berkman Bros Inc............E....... 718 782-1827
Brooklyn *(G-1601)*
Bfg Manufacturing Services Inc............E....... 716 362-0888
Buffalo *(G-2732)*
Buffalo Metal Finishing Co............G....... 716 883-2751
Buffalo *(G-2749)*
C H Thompson Company Inc............D....... 607 724-1094
Binghamton *(G-874)*
Carpenter Industries Inc............F....... 315 463-4284
Syracuse *(G-15271)*
▲ Cnc Systems 2000 Inc............E....... 585 265-0160
Ontario *(G-12649)*
Coating Technology Inc............E....... 585 546-7170
Rochester *(G-13716)*
Control Electropolishing Corp............F....... 718 858-6634
Brooklyn *(G-1714)*
D & I Finishing Inc............G....... 631 471-3034
Bohemia *(G-1007)*
D & W Enterprises LLC............F....... 585 590-6727
Medina *(G-7976)*
Dan Kane Plating Co Inc............F....... 212 675-4947
New York *(G-9462)*
Deming Electro-Plating Corp............G....... 585 968-2355
Cuba *(G-3918)*
Dura Spec Inc............F....... 718 526-3053
North Baldwin *(G-12362)*
Eastside Oxide Co............E....... 607 734-1253
Elmira *(G-4483)*
Electro Plating Service Inc............F....... 914 948-3777
White Plains *(G-16445)*
Empire Metal Finishing Inc............E....... 718 545-6700
Astoria *(G-427)*
Epner Technology Inc............G....... 718 782-8722
Brooklyn *(G-1840)*
▼ Epner Technology Incorporated............E....... 718 782-5948
Brooklyn *(G-1841)*
Epner Technology Incorporated............E....... 718 782-8722
Brooklyn *(G-1842)*
Eric S Turner & Company Inc............F....... 914 235-7114
New Rochelle *(G-8602)*
▲ Ever-Nu-Metal Products Inc............F....... 646 423-5833
Brooklyn *(G-1854)*
F & H Metal Finishing Co Inc............F....... 585 798-2151
Medina *(G-7977)*
Fallon Inc............E....... 718 326-7226
Maspeth *(G-7844)*
Finest Cc Corp............G....... 917 574-4525
Bronx *(G-1270)*
First Impressions Finishing............G....... 631 467-2244
Ronkonkoma *(G-14341)*
Forge Metal Finishing Inc............G....... 585 730-7340
Rochester *(G-13813)*
Galmer Ltd............G....... 718 392-4609
Long Island City *(G-7455)*
General Galvanizing Sup Co Inc............D....... 718 589-4300
Bronx *(G-1281)*
General Plating LLC............E....... 585 423-0830
Rochester *(G-13827)*
Greene Technologies Inc............D....... 607 656-4166
Greene *(G-5615)*
Halmark Architectural Finshg............E....... 718 272-1831
Brooklyn *(G-1961)*
▲ Hartchrom Inc............F....... 518 880-0411
Watervliet *(G-16047)*
▲ I W Industries Inc............C....... 631 293-9494
Melville *(G-8036)*
▲ Jay Strongwater Holdings LLC............A....... 646 657-0558
New York *(G-10312)*

S I C

Employee Codes: A=Over 500 employees, B=251-500
C=101-250, D=51-100, E=20-50, F=10-19, G=5-9
2019 Harris
New York Manufacturers Directory
751

34 FABRICATED METAL PRODUCTS, EXCEPT MACHINERY AND TRANSPORTATION EQUIPMENT — SIC SECTION

John Larocca & Son Inc .... G 631 423-5256
   Huntington Station *(G-6449)*
Key Tech Finishing .... E 716 832-1232
   Buffalo *(G-2904)*
▲ Keymark Corporation .... A 518 853-3421
   Fonda *(G-5066)*
Keystone Corporation 716 832-1232
   Buffalo *(G-2906)*
Kittredge & Sons Inc .... D 978 567-0998
   Niagara Falls *(G-12303)*
L W S Inc .... F 631 580-0472
   Ronkonkoma *(G-14364)*
Maracle Industrial Finshg Co .... E 585 387-9077
   Rochester *(G-13928)*
Master Craft Finishers Inc .... E 631 586-0540
   Deer Park *(G-4007)*
McAlpin Industries Inc .... E 585 544-5335
   Rochester *(G-13933)*
Metal Man Restoration .... F 914 662-4218
   Mount Vernon *(G-8421)*
Multitone Finishing Co Inc .... G 516 485-1043
   West Hempstead *(G-16222)*
▲ Nas CP Corp 718 961-6757
   College Point *(G-3657)*
Nassau Chromium Plating Co Inc ... E 516 746-6666
   Mineola *(G-8238)*
North East Finishing Co Inc 631 789-8000
   Copiague *(G-3771)*
Oerlikon Blzers Cating USA Inc 716 564-8557
   Buffalo *(G-2978)*
Paradigm Group LLC 718 860-1538
   Bronx *(G-1351)*
Praxair Surface Tech Inc 845 398-8322
   Orangeburg *(G-12687)*
▲ Precious Plate Inc 716 283-0690
   Niagara Falls *(G-12325)*
Premier Finishing Inc .... F 716 484-6271
   Jamestown *(G-6743)*
Psb Ltd .... F 585 654-7078
   Rochester *(G-14052)*
Qos Enterprises LLC 585 454-0550
   Rochester *(G-14058)*
Rainbow Powder Coating Corp 631 586-4019
   Deer Park *(G-4034)*
Rayco of Schenectady Inc .... F 518 212-5113
   Amsterdam *(G-358)*
Reynolds Tech Fabricators Inc 315 437-0532
   East Syracuse *(G-4365)*
Rochester Overnight Pltg LLC .... D 585 328-4590
   Rochester *(G-14090)*
Saccomize Inc 818 287-3000
   Bronx *(G-1378)*
Sandys Bumper Mart Inc 315 472-8149
   Syracuse *(G-15415)*
Sas Maintenance Services Inc .... F 718 837-2124
   Brooklyn *(G-2449)*
Sherrill Manufacturing Inc 315 280-0727
   Sherrill *(G-14822)*
Silverman & Gorf Inc 718 625-1309
   Brooklyn *(G-2473)*
Square One Coating Systems LLC .. F 315 790-5921
   Oriskany *(G-12762)*
Surface Finish Technology .... E 607 732-2909
   Elmira *(G-4504)*
T & M Plating Inc .... E 212 967-1110
   New York *(G-11766)*
Tcmf Inc 607 724-1094
   Binghamton *(G-918)*
Tompkins Metal Finishing Inc 585 344-2600
   Batavia *(G-637)*
Tripp Plating Works Inc 716 894-2424
   Buffalo *(G-3104)*
Tronic Plating Co Inc .... F 516 293-7883
   Farmingdale *(G-4900)*
Tropical Driftwood Originals .... G 516 623-0980
   Roosevelt *(G-14438)*
Tru-Tone Metal Products Inc 718 386-5960
   Brooklyn *(G-2590)*
US Electroplating Corp .... G 631 293-1998
   West Babylon *(G-16201)*
Utica Metal Products Inc 315 732-6163
   Utica *(G-15738)*
Vernon Plating Works Inc .... F 718 639-1124
   Woodside *(G-16683)*
Vibra Tech Industries Inc 914 946-1916
   White Plains *(G-16515)*
▲ Victoria Plating Co Inc 718 589-1550
   Bronx *(G-1415)*
West Falls Machine Co Inc .... F 716 655-0440
   East Aurora *(G-4211)*

3479 Coating & Engraving, NEC

72 Steel and Aluminium Work .... G 917 667-3033
   Brooklyn *(G-1445)*
Accurate Pnt Powdr Coating Inc .... F 585 235-1650
   Rochester *(G-13597)*
Advanced Coating Service LLC 585 247-3970
   Rochester *(G-13605)*
Advanced Coating Techniques .... E 631 643-4555
   Babylon *(G-524)*
▼ Advanced Graphics Company ..... F 607 692-7875
   Whitney Point *(G-16554)*
Advanced Surface Finishing 516 876-9710
   Westbury *(G-16310)*
Aircraft Finishing Corp .... F 631 422-5000
   West Babylon *(G-16130)*
All Spec Finishing Inc 607 770-9174
   Binghamton *(G-860)*
▲ Angiotech Biocoatings Corp ...... E 585 321-1130
   Henrietta *(G-6030)*
Applause Coating LLC .... F 631 231-5223
   Brentwood *(G-1127)*
Ascribe Inc 585 413-0298
   Rochester *(G-13646)*
Barson Composites Corporation 516 752-7882
   Old Bethpage *(G-12583)*
▲ Berkman Bros Inc 718 782-1827
   Brooklyn *(G-1601)*
Buffalo Finishing Works Inc .... G 716 893-5266
   Buffalo *(G-2743)*
Buffalo Metal Finishing Co 716 883-2751
   Buffalo *(G-2749)*
C & M Products Inc 315 471-3303
   Syracuse *(G-15265)*
C H Thompson Company Inc .... D 607 724-1094
   Binghamton *(G-874)*
Champion America Inc .... A 716 626-1616
   Williamsville *(G-16575)*
Chepaume Industries LLC 315 829-6400
   Vernon *(G-15803)*
Chromalloy Gas Turbine LLC 845 692-8912
   Middletown *(G-8141)*
Clad Metal Specialties Inc .... F 631 666-7750
   Bay Shore *(G-671)*
Cnv Architectural Coatings Inc 718 418-9584
   Brooklyn *(G-1702)*
Color Craft Finishing Corp .... F 631 563-3230
   Bohemia *(G-998)*
▲ Custom House Engravers Inc 631 567-3004
   Bohemia *(G-1004)*
Custom Laser Inc .... E 716 434-8600
   Lockport *(G-7292)*
D & I Finishing Inc 631 471-3034
   Bohemia *(G-1007)*
Deloka LLC .... G 315 946-6910
   Lyons *(G-7684)*
Duzmor Painting Inc 585 768-4760
   Le Roy *(G-7117)*
Dynocoat Inc 631 244-9344
   Holbrook *(G-6183)*
Eastern Silver of Boro Park .... G 718 854-5600
   Brooklyn *(G-1810)*
▲ Electronic Coating Tech Inc ...... F 518 688-2048
   Cohoes *(G-3610)*
Elegance Coating Ltd .... E 386 668-8379
   Champlain *(G-3408)*
F & H Metal Finishing Co Inc 585 798-2151
   Medina *(G-7977)*
▲ Fougera Pharmaceuticals Inc .... C 631 454-7677
   Melville *(G-8026)*
▲ Frontier Ht-Dip Glvanizing Inc .. F 716 875-2091
   Buffalo *(G-2835)*
Future Spray Finishing Co 631 242-6252
   Deer Park *(G-3980)*
Greene Technologies Inc .... D 607 656-4166
   Greene *(G-5615)*
Harold Wood Co Inc 716 873-1535
   Buffalo *(G-2867)*
Hatfield Metal Fab Inc .... E 845 454-9078
   Poughkeepsie *(G-13345)*
▲ Heany Industries Inc .... D 585 889-2700
   Scottsville *(G-14750)*
▲ Hilord Chemical Corporation ..... E 631 234-7373
   Hauppauge *(G-5845)*
Hitemco Med Applications Inc .... C 516 752-7882
   Old Bethpage *(G-12585)*
Hubbell Galvanizing Inc .... G 315 736-8311
   Yorkville *(G-16827)*
Hudson Valley Coatings LLC 845 398-1778
   Congers *(G-3717)*

Industrial Paint Services Corp .... F 607 687-0107
   Owego *(G-12797)*
▼ Jamestown Bronze Works Inc .... G 716 665-2302
   Jamestown *(G-6727)*
▲ Jrlon Inc .... D 315 597-4067
   Palmyra *(G-12855)*
▲ Keymark Corporation .... A 518 853-3421
   Fonda *(G-5066)*
Kwong CHI Metal Fabrication .... G 718 369-6429
   Brooklyn *(G-2086)*
▲ Lodolce Machine Co Inc .... E 845 246-7017
   Saugerties *(G-14610)*
Mac Artspray Finishing Corp .... F 718 649-3800
   Brooklyn *(G-2148)*
Master Craft Finishers Inc 631 586-0540
   Deer Park *(G-4007)*
▲ Metal Cladding Inc .... D 716 434-5513
   Lockport *(G-7316)*
Micromatter Tech Inc USA 631 580-2522
   Holbrook *(G-6201)*
Modern Coating and Research .... F 315 597-3517
   Palmyra *(G-12858)*
◆ Momentive Performance Mtls Inc ... E 518 237-3330
   Waterford *(G-15981)*
Momentive Prfmce Mtls Holdings ... A 518 237-3330
   Waterford *(G-15982)*
Monroe County Auto Svcs Inc .... E 585 764-3741
   Rochester *(G-13953)*
Mpm Holdings Inc 518 237-3330
   Waterford *(G-15984)*
Mpm Intermediate Holdings Inc 518 237-3330
   Waterford *(G-15985)*
Nameplate Mfrs of Amer 631 752-0055
   Farmingdale *(G-4831)*
Newchem Inc .... E 315 331-7680
   Ithaca *(G-6601)*
▲ O W Hubbell & Sons Inc .... E 315 736-8311
   Yorkville *(G-16828)*
Oerlikon Blzers Cating USA Inc 716 270-2228
   Amherst *(G-243)*
Oerlikon Blzers Cating USA Inc 716 270-2228
   Amherst *(G-244)*
Oerlikon Blzers Cating USA Inc 716 564-8557
   Buffalo *(G-2978)*
Paradigm Group LLC .... G 718 860-1538
   Bronx *(G-1351)*
Piper Plastics Corp .... E 631 842-6889
   Copiague *(G-3772)*
Precision Design Systems Inc 585 426-4500
   Rochester *(G-14034)*
Pro-Tech Catings Solutions Inc ...... G 631 707-9400
   Edgewood *(G-4412)*
Pro-Teck Coating Inc .... F 716 537-2619
   Holland *(G-6221)*
▲ Qualicoat Inc .... D 585 293-2650
   Churchville *(G-3512)*
R S T Cable and Tape Inc .... G 631 981-0096
   Ronkonkoma *(G-14404)*
Rayana Designs Inc .... E 718 786-2040
   Long Island City *(G-7573)*
Read Manufacturing Company Inc .. E 631 567-4487
   Holbrook *(G-6205)*
Rims Like New Inc .... F 845 537-0396
   Middletown *(G-8174)*
Sentry Metal Blast Inc .... E 716 285-5241
   Lockport *(G-7331)*
Sequa Corporation .... E 201 343-1122
   Orangeburg *(G-12692)*
Solidus Industries Inc .... D 607 749-4540
   Homer *(G-6259)*
Specialty Bldg Solutions Inc .... G 631 393-6918
   West Babylon *(G-16195)*
Steel Partners Holdings LP .... D 212 520-2300
   New York *(G-11699)*
Stuart-Dean Co Inc .... F 718 472-1326
   Long Island City *(G-7606)*
▲ Superior Metals & Processing .... G 718 545-7500
   Long Island City *(G-7609)*
Swain Technology Inc .... F 585 889-2786
   Scottsville *(G-14754)*
Tailored Coatings Inc 716 893-4869
   Buffalo *(G-3086)*
The Gramecy Group .... G 518 348-1325
   Clifton Park *(G-3579)*
Tj Powder Coaters LLC 607 724-4779
   Binghamton *(G-920)*
Tobeyco Manufacturing Co Inc ...... F 607 962-2446
   Corning *(G-3827)*
▼ Tricor Direct Inc .... G 716 626-1616
   Williamsville *(G-16592)*

34 FABRICATED METAL PRODUCTS, EXCEPT MACHINERY AND TRANSPORTATION EQUIPMENT

Trojan Metal Fabrication Inc ....E 631 968-5040
 Bay Shore (G-732)
▲ Turbine Arfoil Cating Repr LLC ....C 845 692-8912
 Middletown (G-8181)
W Hubbell & Sons Inc ....E 315 736-8311
 Yorkville (G-16834)
W W Custom Clad Inc ....D 518 673-3322
 Canajoharie (G-3209)
With You Designs LLC ....G 800 413-0670
 Red Hook (G-13460)

3482 Small Arms Ammunition

Benjamin Sheridan Corporation ....G 585 657-6161
 Bloomfield (G-947)
CIC International Ltd ....D 212 213-0089
 Brooklyn (G-1692)
▲ Crosman Corporation ....E 585 657-6161
 Bloomfield (G-951)
Crosman Corporation ....E 585 398-3920
 Farmington (G-4911)

3483 Ammunition, Large

CIC International Ltd ....D 212 213-0089
 Brooklyn (G-1692)
Circor Aerospace Inc ....D 631 737-1900
 Hauppauge (G-5789)

3484 Small Arms

Benjamin Sheridan Corporation ....G 585 657-6161
 Bloomfield (G-947)
▲ Crosman Corporation ....E 585 657-6161
 Bloomfield (G-951)
Crosman Corporation ....E 585 398-3920
 Farmington (G-4911)
Dan Wesson Corp ....F 607 336-1174
 Norwich (G-12484)
Hart Rifle Barrel Inc ....G 315 677-9841
 Syracuse (G-15339)
Kyntec Corporation ....G 716 810-6956
 Buffalo (G-2913)
Magpump LLC ....G 585 444-9812
 Henrietta (G-6035)
Oriskany Arms Inc ....F 315 737-2196
 Oriskany (G-12760)
▼ Redding-Hunter Inc ....E 607 753-3331
 Cortland (G-3892)
Remington Arms Company LLC ....A 315 895-3482
 Ilion (G-6478)
Sycamore Hill Designs Inc ....G 585 820-7322
 Victor (G-15869)
▲ Tri-Technologies Inc ....E 914 699-2001
 Mount Vernon (G-8449)

3489 Ordnance & Access, NEC

CIC International Ltd ....D 212 213-0089
 Brooklyn (G-1692)
Dyno Nobel Inc ....D 845 338-2144
 Ulster Park (G-15658)
◆ Island Ordnance Systems LLC ....F 516 746-2100
 Mineola (G-8230)
▲ Magellan Aerospace NY Inc ....C 718 699-4000
 Corona (G-3849)

3491 Industrial Valves

ADC Industries Inc ....E 516 596-1304
 Valley Stream (G-15771)
▲ Air System Products Inc ....F 716 683-0435
 Lancaster (G-7004)
Byelocorp Scientific Inc ....E 212 785-2580
 New York (G-9166)
Caithness Equities Corporation ....E 212 599-2112
 New York (G-9178)
Curtiss-Wright Electro- ....E 585 596-3482
 Wellsville (G-16115)
◆ Curtiss-Wright Flow Ctrl Corp ....C 631 293-3800
 Farmingdale (G-4743)
Curtiss-Wright Flow Ctrl Corp ....C 631 293-3800
 Farmingdale (G-4744)
Digital Home Creations Inc ....G 585 576-7070
 Webster (G-16082)
Doyle & Roth Mfg Co Inc ....D 212 269-7840
 New York (G-9570)
Dresser-Rand Company ....A 585 596-3100
 Wellsville (G-16116)
◆ Flomatic Corporation ....E 518 761-9797
 Glens Falls (G-5425)
▲ Flow-Safe Inc ....E 716 662-2585
 Orchard Park (G-12714)

Hy Cert Services Inc ....G 631 231-7005
 Brentwood (G-1134)
J H Buscher Inc ....G 716 667-2003
 Orchard Park (G-12721)
▲ John N Fehlinger Co Inc ....F 212 233-5656
 New York (G-10353)
McWane Inc ....B 607 734-2211
 Elmira (G-4497)
▲ Murphy Manufacturing Co Inc ....G 585 223-0100
 Fairport (G-4644)
◆ Plattco Corporation ....E 518 563-4640
 Plattsburgh (G-13145)
◆ Precision Valve & Automtn Inc ....C 518 371-2684
 Cohoes (G-3617)
▲ Spence Engineering Company Inc ....C 845 778-5566
 Walden (G-15897)
Syraco Products Inc ....F 315 476-5306
 Syracuse (G-15433)
▲ Total Energy Fabrication Corp ....E 580 363-1500
 North Salem (G-12397)
Trac Regulators Inc ....E 914 699-9352
 Mount Vernon (G-8447)
Tyco Simplexgrinnell ....E 315 437-9664
 East Syracuse (G-4376)
◆ William E Williams Valve Corp ....E 718 392-1660
 Long Island City (G-7638)

3492 Fluid Power Valves & Hose Fittings

▲ A K Allen Co Inc ....C 516 747-5450
 Melville (G-7996)
Aalborg Instrs & Contrls Inc ....D 845 398-3160
 Orangeburg (G-12667)
▲ Aerco International Inc ....C 845 580-8000
 Blauvelt (G-933)
▲ BW Elliott Mfg Co LLC ....B 607 772-0404
 Binghamton (G-873)
Direkt Force LLC ....E 716 652-3022
 East Aurora (G-4197)
Dmic Inc ....G 716 743-4360
 North Tonawanda (G-12425)
Dynamic Sealing Tech Inc ....G 716 376-0708
 Olean (G-12600)
▲ Key High Vacuum Products Inc ....E 631 584-5959
 Nesconset (G-8485)
Kinemotive Corporation ....E 631 249-6440
 Farmingdale (G-4803)
▲ KSA Manufacturing LLC ....C 315 488-0809
 Camillus (G-3196)
Lourdes Industries Inc ....D 631 234-6600
 Hauppauge (G-5873)
Moog Inc ....B 716 687-4954
 East Aurora (G-4207)
◆ Moog Inc ....A 716 652-2000
 Elma (G-4453)
Own Instrument Inc ....F 914 668-6546
 Mount Vernon (G-8427)
Servotronics Inc ....E 716 655-5990
 Elma (G-4458)
▲ Steel & Obrien Mfg Inc ....D 585 492-5800
 Arcade (G-389)
Tactair Fluid Controls Inc ....C 315 451-3928
 Liverpool (G-7266)
Upstate Tube Inc ....G 315 488-5636
 Camillus (G-3199)
Young & Franklin Inc ....D 315 457-3110
 Liverpool (G-7274)

3493 Steel Springs, Except Wire

Angelica Spring Company Inc ....F 585 466-7892
 Angelica (G-367)
Isolation Dynamics Corp ....E 631 491-5670
 West Babylon (G-16158)
▲ Lee Spring Company LLC ....C 718 362-5183
 Brooklyn (G-2105)
▲ Midstate Spring Inc ....E 315 437-2623
 Syracuse (G-15373)
▲ Red Onyx Industrial Pdts LLC ....E 516 459-6035
 Huntington (G-6409)
Temper Corporation ....E 518 853-3467
 Fonda (G-5067)
Whitesboro Spring & Alignment ....F 315 736-4441
 Whitesboro (G-16532)
Whiting Door Mfg Corp ....D 716 542-3070
 Akron (G-25)

3494 Valves & Pipe Fittings, NEC

▲ A K Allen Co Inc ....C 516 747-5450
 Melville (G-7996)
Aalborg Instrs & Contrls Inc ....D 845 398-3160
 Orangeburg (G-12667)

Advanced Thermal Systems Inc ....E 716 681-1800
 Lancaster (G-7002)
▲ Anderson Precision Inc ....D 716 484-1148
 Jamestown (G-6698)
◆ Curtiss-Wright Flow Ctrl Corp ....C 631 293-3800
 Farmingdale (G-4743)
▼ Devin Mfg Inc ....F 585 496-5770
 Arcade (G-381)
◆ Flomatic Corporation ....E 518 761-9797
 Glens Falls (G-5425)
Ford Regulator Valve Corp ....G 718 497-3255
 Brooklyn (G-1897)
Goodman Main Stopper Mfg Co ....F 718 875-5140
 Brooklyn (G-1940)
Holyoke Fittings Inc ....E 718 649-0710
 Brooklyn (G-1981)
J H Robotics Inc ....E 607 729-3758
 Johnson City (G-6812)
▲ Key High Vacuum Products Inc ....E 631 584-5959
 Nesconset (G-8485)
Kingston Hoops Summer ....G 845 401-6830
 Kingston (G-6904)
Lance Valves ....E 716 681-5825
 Lancaster (G-7030)
Legacy Valve LLC ....F 914 403-5075
 Valhalla (G-15742)
Lemode Plumbing & Heating ....E 718 545-3336
 Astoria (G-433)
M Manastrip-M Corporation ....G 518 664-2089
 Clifton Park (G-3570)
▲ Make-Waves Instrument Corp ....E 716 681-7524
 Buffalo (G-2936)
Micromold Products Inc ....E 914 969-2850
 Yonkers (G-16784)
Rand Machine Products, Inc. ....C 716 665-5219
 Falconer (G-4688)
Ross Valve Mfg ....G 518 274-0961
 Troy (G-15621)
Sigmamotor Inc ....E 716 735-3115
 Middleport (G-8134)
▲ Spence Engineering Company Inc ....C 845 778-5566
 Walden (G-15897)
▲ Steel & Obrien Mfg Inc ....D 585 492-5800
 Arcade (G-389)
Sure Flow Equipment Inc ....E 800 263-8251
 Tonawanda (G-15580)
▲ United Pipe Nipple Co Inc ....F 516 295-2468
 Hewlett (G-6052)
Venco Sales Inc ....E 631 754-0782
 Huntington (G-6426)
Westchester Valve & Fitting Co ....G 914 762-6600
 Clifton Park (G-3580)
William E Williams Valve Corp ....E 718 392-1660
 Long Island City (G-7637)
◆ William E Williams Valve Corp ....E 718 392-1660
 Long Island City (G-7638)

3495 Wire Springs

Ajax Wire Specialty Co Inc ....F 516 935-2333
 Hicksville (G-6056)
Barnes Group Inc ....G 315 457-9200
 Syracuse (G-15254)
Commerce Spring Corp ....F 631 293-4844
 Farmingdale (G-4738)
Commercial Communications LLC ....G 845 343-9078
 Middletown (G-8143)
Fennell Spring Company LLC ....D 607 739-3541
 Horseheads (G-6315)
Kinemotive Corporation ....E 631 249-6440
 Farmingdale (G-4803)
▲ Lee Spring Company LLC ....C 718 362-5183
 Brooklyn (G-2105)
Lee Spring LLC ....E 718 236-2222
 Brooklyn (G-2106)
▲ Midstate Spring Inc ....E 315 437-2623
 Syracuse (G-15373)
▼ Pullman Mfg Corporation ....E 585 334-1350
 Rochester (G-14053)
Teka Precision Inc ....E 845 753-1900
 Nyack (G-12512)
◆ The Caldwell Manufacturing Co ....E 585 352-3790
 Rochester (G-14165)
The Caldwell Manufacturing Co ....F 585 352-2803
 Victor (G-15873)
Unimex Corporation ....D 212 755-8800
 New York (G-11946)
Unimex Corporation ....C 718 236-2222
 Brooklyn (G-2601)

3496 Misc Fabricated Wire Prdts

369 River Road Inc ....E .... 716 694-5001 North Tonawanda *(G-12409)*
▲ Abbott Industries Inc ....B .... 718 291-0800 Jamaica *(G-6622)*
▲ Aeroflex Incorporated ....B .... 516 694-6700 Plainview *(G-13032)*
▲ Albest Metal Stamping Corp ....D .... 718 388-6000 Brooklyn *(G-1500)*
All-Lifts Incorporated ....E .... 518 465-3461 Albany *(G-38)*
▲ American Intl Trimming ....G .... 718 369-9643 Brooklyn *(G-1522)*
▲ American Wire Tie Inc ....E .... 716 337-2412 North Collins *(G-12383)*
Angelica Spring Company Inc ....F .... 585 466-7892 Angelica *(G-367)*
Bayshore Wire Products Corp ....F .... 631 451-8825 Coram *(G-3796)*
▲ Better Wire Products Inc ....E .... 716 883-3377 Buffalo *(G-2731)*
▲ Bison Steel Incorporated ....G .... 716 683-0900 Depew *(G-4080)*
▲ Brook North Farms Inc ....F .... 315 834-9390 Auburn *(G-472)*
▲ Cable Management Solutions Inc ....E .... 631 674-0004 Bay Shore *(G-667)*
▲ Chemprene Inc ....C .... 845 831-2800 Beacon *(G-755)*
▲ Chemprene Holding Inc ....C .... 845 831-2800 Beacon *(G-756)*
▲ Clover Wire Forming Co Inc ....E .... 914 375-0400 Yonkers *(G-16745)*
▼ Cobra Systems Inc ....F .... 845 338-6675 Bloomington *(G-959)*
Columbus McKinnon Corporation ....C .... 716 689-5400 Getzville *(G-5344)*
Columbus McKinnon Corporation ....C .... 716 689-5400 Getzville *(G-5345)*
Columbus McKinnon Corporation ....C .... 716 689-5400 Getzville *(G-5346)*
Compar Manufacturing Corp ....E .... 212 304-2777 New York *(G-9369)*
▲ Continental Cordage Corp ....D .... 315 655-9800 Cazenovia *(G-3317)*
◆ Cortland Cable Company Inc ....E .... 607 753-8276 Cortland *(G-3865)*
▲ Cuba Specialty Mfg Co Inc ....F .... 585 567-4176 Fillmore *(G-4937)*
Cuddeback Machining Inc ....G .... 585 392-5889 Hilton *(G-6156)*
▲ Dico Products Corporation ....F .... 315 797-0470 Utica *(G-15694)*
Engineering Mfg Tech LLC ....D .... 607 754-7111 Endicott *(G-4591)*
Flanagans Creative Disp Inc ....E .... 845 858-2542 Port Jervis *(G-13228)*
Flatcut LLC ....G .... 212 542-5732 Brooklyn *(G-1888)*
▲ G Bopp USA Inc ....G .... 845 296-1065 Wappingers Falls *(G-15931)*
Habasit America Inc ....D .... 716 824-8484 Buffalo *(G-2860)*
Hanes Supply Inc ....F .... 518 438-0139 Albany *(G-80)*
Hitachi Metals America Ltd ....E .... 914 694-9200 Purchase *(G-13389)*
◆ Hohmann & Barnard Inc ....E .... 631 234-0600 Hauppauge *(G-5846)*
Hohmann & Barnard Inc ....E .... 518 357-9757 Schenectady *(G-14687)*
Interstate Wood Products Inc ....E .... 631 842-4488 Amityville *(G-288)*
J Davis Manufacturing Co Inc ....E .... 315 337-7574 Rome *(G-14254)*
Joldeson One Aerospace Inds ....D .... 718 848-7396 Ozone Park *(G-12827)*
Kehr-Buffalo Wire Frame Co Inc ....E .... 716 897-2288 Buffalo *(G-2902)*
Lyn Jo Enterprises Ltd ....G .... 716 753-2776 Mayville *(G-7922)*
▲ Magic Novelty Co Inc ....E .... 212 304-2777 New York *(G-10667)*
▲ Nexans Energy USA Inc ....C .... 845 469-2141 Chester *(G-3478)*
Oneida Sales & Service Inc ....E .... 716 822-8205 Buffalo *(G-2980)*
▲ Owl Wire & Cable LLC ....C .... 315 697-2011 Canastota *(G-3244)*
▲ Peck & Hale LLC ....E .... 631 589-2510 West Sayville *(G-16291)*
Quality Industrial Services ....F .... 716 667-7703 Orchard Park *(G-12742)*
Reelcology Inc ....F .... 845 258-1880 Pine Island *(G-13002)*
◆ Renco Group Inc ....G .... 212 541-6000 New York *(G-11361)*
▲ Rose Fence Inc ....E .... 516 223-0777 Freeport *(G-5179)*
Rose Fence Inc ....D .... 516 790-2308 Halesite *(G-5659)*
Rose Fence Inc ....F .... 516 223-0777 Baldwin *(G-541)*
SCI Bore Inc ....G .... 212 674-7128 New York *(G-11518)*
▲ Selectrode Industries Inc ....D .... 631 547-5470 Huntington Station *(G-6458)*
Sigmund Cohn Corp ....D .... 914 664-5300 Mount Vernon *(G-8443)*
Sinclair International Company ....D .... 518 798-2361 Queensbury *(G-13442)*
Star Wire Mesh Fabricators ....G .... 212 831-4133 New York *(G-11696)*
Sunward Electronics Inc ....F .... 518 687-0030 Troy *(G-15629)*
Teka Precision Inc ....G .... 845 753-1900 Nyack *(G-12512)*
Trylon Wire & Metal Works Inc ....E .... 718 542-4472 Bronx *(G-1409)*
Ultra Clarity Corp ....G .... 719 470-1010 Spring Valley *(G-15010)*
Utility Engineering Co ....F .... 845 735-8900 Pearl River *(G-12912)*
▲ Weico Wire & Cable Inc ....E .... 631 254-2970 Edgewood *(G-4424)*

3497 Metal Foil & Leaf

◆ Alufoil Products Co Inc ....F .... 631 231-4141 Hauppauge *(G-5762)*
American Packaging Corporation ....G .... 585 254-2002 Rochester *(G-13625)*
American Packaging Corporation ....C .... 585 254-9500 Rochester *(G-13626)*
De Luxe Packaging Corp ....E .... 416 754-4633 Saugerties *(G-14606)*
Oak-Mitsui Inc ....D .... 518 686-8060 Hoosick Falls *(G-6278)*
▲ Oak-Mitsui Technologies LLC ....E .... 518 686-4961 Hoosick Falls *(G-6279)*
Pactiv LLC ....C .... 518 793-2524 Glens Falls *(G-5439)*
Quick Roll Leaf Mfg Co Inc ....E .... 845 457-1500 Montgomery *(G-8316)*
Steel Partners Holdings LP ....D .... 212 520-2300 New York *(G-11699)*
Thermal Process Cnstr Co ....E .... 631 293-6400 Farmingdale *(G-4894)*
Tri-State Food Jobbers Inc ....G .... 718 921-1211 Brooklyn *(G-2582)*

3498 Fabricated Pipe & Pipe Fittings

Accord Pipe Fabricators Inc ....E .... 718 657-3900 Jamaica *(G-6623)*
Advanced Thermal Systems Inc ....E .... 716 681-1800 Lancaster *(G-7002)*
Albany Nipple and Pipe Mfg ....E .... 518 270-2162 Troy *(G-15594)*
▲ Arcadia Mfg Group Inc ....E .... 518 434-6213 Green Island *(G-5602)*
Arcadia Mfg Group Inc ....G .... 518 434-6213 Menands *(G-8081)*
▲ Cobey Inc ....C .... 716 362-9550 Buffalo *(G-2769)*
Coventry Manufacturing Co Inc ....E .... 914 668-2212 Mount Vernon *(G-8391)*
D & G Welding Inc ....G .... 716 873-3088 Buffalo *(G-2790)*
Daikin Applied Americas Inc ....D .... 315 253-2771 Auburn *(G-475)*
Falcon Perspectives Inc ....G .... 718 706-9168 Long Island City *(G-7444)*
Flatcut LLC ....G .... 212 542-5732 Brooklyn *(G-1888)*
H & H Metal Specialty Inc ....E .... 716 665-2110 Jamestown *(G-6720)*
J D Steward Inc ....G .... 718 358-0169 Flushing *(G-5013)*
James Woerner Inc ....G .... 631 454-9330 Farmingdale *(G-4791)*
▲ Juniper Elbow Co Inc ....C .... 718 326-2546 Middle Village *(G-8124)*
▲ Juniper Industries Florida Inc ....G .... 718 326-2546 Middle Village *(G-8125)*
▲ Leo International Inc ....E .... 718 290-8005 Brooklyn *(G-2112)*
◆ Leroy Plastics Inc ....D .... 585 768-8158 Le Roy *(G-7121)*
Long Island Pipe Supply Inc ....E .... 516 222-8008 Garden City *(G-5267)*
Long Island Pipe Supply Inc ....G .... 718 456-7877 Flushing *(G-5024)*
Long Island Pipe Supply Inc ....G .... 518 270-2159 Troy *(G-15597)*
Long Island Pipe Supply Inc ....E .... 516 222-8008 Garden City *(G-5268)*
M Manastrip-M Corporation ....G .... 518 664-2089 Clifton Park *(G-3570)*
Met Weld International LLC ....D .... 518 765-2318 Altamont *(G-199)*
Micromold Products Inc ....E .... 914 969-2850 Yonkers *(G-16784)*
Ram Fabricating LLC ....E .... 315 437-6654 Syracuse *(G-15401)*
Rochester Tube Fabricators ....F .... 585 254-0290 Rochester *(G-14099)*
▲ Spinco Metal Products Inc ....D .... 315 331-6285 Newark *(G-12207)*
Star Tubing Corp ....G .... 716 483-1703 Jamestown *(G-6750)*
Tag Flange & Machining Inc ....G .... 516 536-1300 Oceanside *(G-12560)*
▲ Total Piping Solutions Inc ....F .... 716 372-0160 Olean *(G-12608)*
Truly Tubular Fitting Corp ....F .... 914 664-8686 Mount Vernon *(G-8450)*
Tube Fabrication Company Inc ....F .... 716 673-1871 Fredonia *(G-5128)*

3499 Fabricated Metal Prdts, NEC

▲ Access Display Group Inc ....F .... 516 678-7772 Freeport *(G-5136)*
Alpine Paper Box Co Inc ....E .... 718 345-4040 Brooklyn *(G-1514)*
American Standard Mfg Inc ....E .... 518 868-2512 Central Bridge *(G-3353)*
Aquarium Pump & Piping Systems ....F .... 631 567-5555 Sayville *(G-14625)*
▲ Arnold Magnetic Tech Corp ....C .... 585 385-9010 Rochester *(G-13640)*
Brakewell Stl Fabricators Inc ....E .... 845 469-9131 Chester *(G-3469)*
Bristol Gift Co Inc ....F .... 845 496-2821 Washingtonville *(G-15963)*
Brooklyn Cstm Met Fbrction Inc ....G .... 718 499-1573 Brooklyn *(G-1641)*
Buttons & Trimcom Inc ....F .... 212 868-1971 New York *(G-9164)*
C & M Products Inc ....G .... 315 471-3303 Syracuse *(G-15265)*
▲ Carpentier Industries LLC ....F .... 585 385-5550 East Rochester *(G-4281)*
◆ Chapin International Inc ....C .... 585 343-3140 Batavia *(G-617)*
◆ Chapin Manufacturing Inc ....C .... 585 343-3140 Batavia *(G-618)*
Clad Industries LLC ....G .... 585 413-4359 Macedon *(G-7698)*
▲ Classic Medallics Inc ....E .... 718 392-5410 Mount Vernon *(G-8388)*
Cleveland Polymer Tech LLC ....G .... 518 326-9146 Schenectady *(G-14664)*
Consolidated Barricades Inc ....G .... 518 922-7944 Fultonville *(G-5235)*
Criterion Bell & Specialty ....E .... 718 788-2600 Brooklyn *(G-1732)*
Crystalizations Systems Inc ....F .... 631 467-0090 Holbrook *(G-6180)*
Custom Frame & Molding Co ....F .... 631 491-9091 West Babylon *(G-16150)*
Di Highway Sign Structure Corp ....E .... 315 736-8312 New York Mills *(G-12185)*
Dimar Manufacturing Corp ....C .... 716 759-0351 Clarence *(G-3527)*
Dobrin Industries Inc ....G .... 800 353-2229 Lockport *(G-7295)*
Dz9 Power LLC ....G .... 877 533-5530 Olean *(G-12601)*
Elias Artmetal Inc ....F .... 516 873-7501 Mineola *(G-8217)*

SIC SECTION
35 INDUSTRIAL AND COMMERCIAL MACHINERY AND COMPUTER EQUIPMENT

Empire Metal Finishing Inc ....E 718 545-6700
  Astoria *(G-427)*
Factory East ....E 718 280-1558
  Brooklyn *(G-1864)*
Finger Lakes Conveyors Inc ....G 315 539-9246
  Waterloo *(G-15992)*
Frame Shoppe & Art Gallery ....E 516 365-6014
  Manhasset *(G-7767)*
Galmer Ltd ....E 718 392-4609
  Long Island City *(G-7455)*
◆ Gardall Safe Corporation ....E 315 432-9115
  Syracuse *(G-15329)*
▲ Garment Care Systems LLC ....G 518 674-1826
  Averill Park *(G-514)*
◆ Gibraltar Industries Inc ....D 716 826-6500
  Buffalo *(G-2849)*
◆ Hannay Reels Inc ....C 518 797-3791
  Westerlo *(G-16389)*
Hatfield Metal Fab Inc ....E 845 454-9078
  Poughkeepsie *(G-13345)*
▲ Icestone LLC ....F 718 624-4900
  Brooklyn *(G-1993)*
Inpro Corporation ....G 716 332-4699
  Tonawanda *(G-15551)*
▲ Inter Pacific Consulting Corp ....E 718 460-2787
  Flushing *(G-5010)*
James D Rubino Inc ....E 631 244-8730
  Bohemia *(G-1039)*
▲ Jay Strongwater Holdings LLC ....A 646 657-0558
  New York *(G-10312)*
JE Monahan Fabrications LLC ....F 518 761-0414
  Queensbury *(G-13430)*
▼ Jordan Panel Systems Corp ....E 631 754-4900
  East Northport *(G-4266)*
▲ Kefa Industries Group Inc ....G 718 568-9297
  Rego Park *(G-13463)*
Kwong CHI Metal Fabrication ....G 718 369-6429
  Brooklyn *(G-2086)*
L D Flecken Inc ....F 631 777-4881
  Yaphank *(G-16714)*
▲ Lr Paris LLC ....F 212 634-9372
  New York *(G-10621)*
Machinery Mountings Inc ....E 631 851-0480
  Hauppauge *(G-5876)*
Magnaworks Technology Inc ....G 631 218-3431
  Bohemia *(G-1054)*
▲ Magnetic Aids Inc ....G 845 863-1400
  Newburgh *(G-12231)*
▲ Materion Brewster LLC ....D 845 279-0900
  Brewster *(G-1171)*
▲ Maximum Security Products Corp ...E 518 233-1800
  Waterford *(G-15977)*
McD Metals LLC ....F 518 456-9694
  Albany *(G-97)*
▼ Metallic Ladder Mfg Corp ....F 716 358-6201
  Randolph *(G-13448)*
MMC Magnetics Corp ....F 631 435-9888
  Hauppauge *(G-5895)*
Mpl Metal Inc ....G 718 338-4952
  Brooklyn *(G-2230)*
National Maint Contg Corp ....D 716 285-1583
  Niagara Falls *(G-12312)*
New Dimension Awards Inc ....G 718 236-8200
  Brooklyn *(G-2258)*
New York Manufactured Products ......F 585 254-9353
  Rochester *(G-13967)*
▲ Nrd LLC ....E 716 773-7634
  Grand Island *(G-5508)*
PBL Industries Corp ....F 631 979-4266
  Smithtown *(G-14904)*
Peak Motion Inc ....G 716 534-4925
  Clarence *(G-3538)*
▲ Peelle Company ....E 631 231-6000
  Hauppauge *(G-5911)*
Picture Perfect Framing ....G 718 851-1884
  Brooklyn *(G-2316)*
▲ Polich Tallix Inc ....D 845 567-9464
  Walden *(G-15895)*
▲ Polymag Inc ....E 631 286-4111
  Bellport *(G-813)*
▲ Precision Magnetics LLC ....E 585 385-9010
  Rochester *(G-14038)*
Precision Spclty Fbrctions LLC ....E 716 824-2108
  Buffalo *(G-3012)*
Protocase Incorporated ....C 866 849-3911
  Lewiston *(G-7141)*
Range Repair Warehouse ....G 585 235-0980
  Penfield *(G-12943)*
Raytech Corp Asbestos Personal ....A 516 747-0300
  Mineola *(G-8245)*

Reelcology Inc ....F 845 258-1880
  Pine Island *(G-13002)*
Romac Electronics Inc ....E 516 349-7900
  Plainview *(G-13085)*
Rough Brothers Holding Co ....G 716 826-6500
  Buffalo *(G-3048)*
▲ Rush Gold Manufacturing Ltd ....D 516 781-3155
  Bellmore *(G-793)*
▼ Schwab Corp ....E 585 381-4900
  Rochester *(G-14116)*
Secureit Tactical Inc ....G 800 651-8835
  Syracuse *(G-15421)*
◆ Seetin Design Group Inc ....F 718 486-5610
  Brooklyn *(G-2455)*
▲ Sono-Tek Corporation ....D 845 795-2020
  Milton *(G-8197)*
Split Rock Trading Co Inc ....G 631 929-3261
  Wading River *(G-15887)*
▲ Structural Industries Inc ....C 631 471-5200
  Bohemia *(G-1092)*
▲ Stylebuilt Accessories Inc ....F 917 439-0578
  East Rockaway *(G-4297)*
▲ Technomag Inc ....G 631 246-6142
  East Setauket *(G-4311)*
Thyssenkrupp Materials NA Inc ....F 212 972-8800
  New York *(G-11829)*
Total Metal Resource ....F 718 384-7818
  Brooklyn *(G-2575)*
▲ Truebite Inc ....E 607 785-7664
  Vestal *(G-15824)*
Ulster County Iron Works LLC ....G 845 255-0003
  New Paltz *(G-8582)*

35 INDUSTRIAL AND COMMERCIAL MACHINERY AND COMPUTER EQUIPMENT

3511 Steam, Gas & Hydraulic Turbines & Engines

Atlantic Projects Company Inc ....F 518 878-2065
  Clifton Park *(G-3564)*
Awr Energy Inc ....F 585 469-7750
  Plattsburgh *(G-13107)*
Beowawe Binary LLC ....E 646 829-3900
  New York *(G-9049)*
▲ Cooper Turbocompressor Inc ....B 716 896-6600
  Buffalo *(G-2781)*
Dresser-Rand Company ....A 585 596-3100
  Wellsville *(G-16116)*
Dresser-Rand Group Inc ....D 716 375-3000
  Olean *(G-12599)*
Frontier Hydraulics Corp ....F 716 694-2070
  Buffalo *(G-2836)*
▲ Gas Turbine Controls Corp ....E 914 693-0830
  Hawthorne *(G-5987)*
GE Global Research ....G 518 387-5000
  Niskayuna *(G-12353)*
General Electric Company ....E 518 385-4022
  Schenectady *(G-14675)*
General Electric Company ....B 518 385-2211
  Schenectady *(G-14676)*
General Electric Company ....B 203 373-2756
  Schenectady *(G-14677)*
General Electric Company ....B 518 385-3716
  Schenectady *(G-14678)*
General Electric Company ....B 518 385-2211
  Schenectady *(G-14679)*
General Electric Company ....B 518 387-5000
  Schenectady *(G-14680)*
General Electric Company ....E 518 385-7620
  Niskayuna *(G-12354)*
General Electric Company ....E 518 385-3439
  Schenectady *(G-14681)*
General Electric Intl Inc ....E 518 385-2211
  Schenectady *(G-14682)*
▲ Hdm Hydraulics LLC ....F 716 694-8004
  Tonawanda *(G-15546)*
Intersource Management Group ....G 518 372-6798
  Halfmoon *(G-5664)*
Intersource Management Group ....E 518 372-6798
  Schenectady *(G-14690)*
▲ Mannesmann Corporation ....D 212 258-4000
  New York *(G-10691)*
Mission Critical Energy Inc ....G 716 276-8465
  Getzville *(G-5349)*
◆ Prime Turbine Parts LLC ....G 518 306-7306
  Saratoga Springs *(G-14593)*

Siemens Government Tech Inc ....B 585 593-1234
  Wellsville *(G-16123)*
Signa Chemistry Inc ....F 212 933-4101
  New York *(G-11586)*
▲ Stork H & E Turbo Blading Inc ....C 607 277-4968
  Ithaca *(G-6610)*
Tgp Flying Cloud Holdings LLC ....E 646 829-3900
  New York *(G-11807)*
Turbine Engine Comp Utica ....A 315 768-8070
  Whitesboro *(G-16531)*
Turbo Machined Products LLC ....E 315 895-3010
  Frankfort *(G-5113)*
Tuthill Corporation ....B 631 727-1097
  Riverhead *(G-13587)*
Weaver Wind Energy LLC ....C 607 379-9463
  Freeville *(G-5193)*
Worldwide Gas Turbine Pdts Inc ....G 518 877-7200
  Clifton Park *(G-3587)*

3519 Internal Combustion Engines, NEC

AB Engine ....G 518 557-3510
  Latham *(G-7061)*
Briggs & Stratton Corporation ....F 315 495-0100
  Sherrill *(G-14818)*
Briggs & Stratton Corporation ....C 315 495-0100
  Munnsville *(G-8457)*
Cummins - Allison Corp ....D 718 263-2482
  Kew Gardens *(G-6871)*
◆ Cummins Inc ....D 716 456-2676
  Lakewood *(G-6992)*
Cummins Inc ....G 716 456-2111
  Lakewood *(G-6993)*
Cummins Northeast LLC ....E 315 437-2296
  Syracuse *(G-15297)*
Cummins-Wagner-Siewert LLC ....E 585 482-9640
  Rochester *(G-13728)*
D & W Diesel Inc ....F 518 437-1300
  Latham *(G-7070)*
Jack W Miller ....G 585 538-2399
  Scottsville *(G-14751)*
▲ Mannesmann Corporation ....D 212 258-4000
  New York *(G-10691)*
Perkins International Inc ....C 309 675-1000
  Buffalo *(G-2999)*
Washer Solutions Inc ....F 585 742-6388
  Victor *(G-15877)*

3523 Farm Machinery & Eqpt

Bdp Industries Inc ....E 518 695-6851
  Greenwich *(G-5636)*
▲ Bean King International LLC ....E 845 268-3135
  Congers *(G-3711)*
◆ Chapin Manufacturing Inc ....C 585 343-3140
  Batavia *(G-618)*
Don Beck Inc ....G 585 493-3040
  Castile *(G-3292)*
Eastern Welding Inc ....G 631 727-0306
  Riverhead *(G-13568)*
◆ Fountainhead Group Inc ....C 315 736-0037
  New York Mills *(G-12186)*
Good Earth Organics Corp ....E 716 684-8111
  Lancaster *(G-7022)*
Haines Equipment Inc ....E 607 566-8531
  Avoca *(G-516)*
House of The Foaming Case Inc ....G 718 454-0101
  Saint Albans *(G-14507)*
Jain Irrigation Inc ....D 315 755-4400
  Watertown *(G-16017)*
L&M Specialty Fabrication ....G 585 283-4847
  Albion *(G-159)*
Landpro Equipment LLC ....E 716 665-3110
  Falconer *(G-4686)*
▲ Oxbo International Corporation ....D 585 548-2665
  Byron *(G-3145)*
Plant-Tech2o Inc ....G 516 483-7845
  Hempstead *(G-6023)*
Renaldos Sales & Service Ctr ....G 716 337-3760
  North Collins *(G-12388)*
Richard Stewart ....G 518 632-5363
  Hartford *(G-5741)*
Road Cases USA Inc ....E 631 563-0633
  Bohemia *(G-1083)*
Vansridge Dairy LLC ....E 315 364-8569
  Scipio Center *(G-14737)*
Westmoor Ltd ....F 315 363-1500
  Sherrill *(G-14825)*
Zappala Farms AG Systems Inc ....E 315 626-6293
  Cato *(G-3301)*

3524 Garden, Lawn Tractors & Eqpt

Benishty Brothers Corp ....G.... 646 339-9991
Woodmere *(G-16640)*
Briggs & Stratton Corporation ....C.... 315 495-0100
Munnsville *(G-8457)*
Capital E Financial Group ....F.... 212 319-6550
New York *(G-9202)*
◆ **Chapin International Inc** ....C.... 585 343-3140
Batavia *(G-617)*
◆ **Chapin Manufacturing Inc** ....C.... 585 343-3140
Batavia *(G-618)*
Clopay Ames True Temper ....F.... 212 957-5096
New York *(G-9330)*
▲ **Eaton Brothers Corp** ....G.... 716 649-8250
Hamburg *(G-5676)*
Fradan Manufacturing Corp ....F.... 914 632-3653
New Rochelle *(G-8605)*
Real Bark Mulch LLC ....G.... 518 747-3650
Fort Edward *(G-5099)*
Rhett M Clark Inc ....G.... 585 538-9570
Caledonia *(G-3157)*
Saxby Implement Corp ....F.... 585 624-2938
Mendon *(G-8094)*

3531 Construction Machinery & Eqpt

▲ **AAAA York Inc** ....F.... 718 784-6666
Long Island City *(G-7364)*
Air-Flo Mfg Co Inc ....D.... 607 733-8284
Elmira *(G-4473)*
Anderson Equipment Company ....D.... 716 877-1992
Tonawanda *(G-15522)*
Applied Technology Mfg Corp ....E.... 607 687-2200
Owego *(G-12795)*
▲ **BW Elliott Mfg Co LLC** ....B.... 607 772-0404
Binghamton *(G-873)*
Capitol Eq 2 LLC ....G.... 518 886-8341
Saratoga Springs *(G-14574)*
CCS Machinery Inc ....F.... 631 968-0900
Bay Shore *(G-668)*
Ceno Technologies Inc ....G.... 716 885-5050
Buffalo *(G-2763)*
City of Jamestown ....D.... 716 483-7545
Jamestown *(G-6705)*
Cives Corporation ....D.... 315 543-2321
Harrisville *(G-5740)*
Cooper Industries LLC ....E.... 315 477-7000
Syracuse *(G-15291)*
Crane Equipment & Service Inc ....G.... 716 689-5400
Amherst *(G-223)*
Dave Sandel Cranes Inc ....G.... 631 325-5588
Westhampton *(G-16401)*
Diamond Coring & Cutting Inc ....G.... 718 381-4545
Maspeth *(G-7836)*
◆ **Dover Global Holdings Inc** ....F.... 212 922-1640
New York *(G-9562)*
Drillco National Group Inc ....E.... 718 726-9801
Long Island City *(G-7428)*
ET Oakes Corporation ....E.... 631 232-0002
Hauppauge *(G-5821)*
Gei International Inc ....E.... 315 463-9261
East Syracuse *(G-4342)*
Got Wood LLC ....G.... 315 440-8857
Cleveland *(G-3561)*
Highway Garage ....G.... 518 568-2837
Saint Johnsville *(G-14520)*
Kinedyne Inc ....F.... 716 667-6833
Orchard Park *(G-12724)*
▲ **Kinshofer Usa Inc** ....E.... 716 731-4333
Sanborn *(G-14549)*
Kyntec Corporation ....G.... 716 810-6956
Buffalo *(G-2913)*
Line Ward Corporation ....G.... 716 675-7373
Buffalo *(G-2925)*
Lomin Construction Company ....G.... 516 759-5734
Glen Head *(G-5382)*
▲ **Midland Machinery Co Inc** ....D.... 716 692-1200
Tonawanda *(G-15558)*
▲ **Munson Machinery Company Inc** ....E.... 315 797-0090
Utica *(G-15724)*
New Eagle Silo Corp ....G.... 585 492-1300
Arcade *(G-388)*
▲ **Northrock Industries Inc** ....E.... 631 924-6130
Bohemia *(G-1068)*
Oneida Sales & Service Inc ....E.... 716 822-8205
Buffalo *(G-2980)*
▲ **Oswald Manufacturing Co Inc** ....E.... 516 883-8850
Port Washington *(G-13292)*
◆ **Ozteck Industries Inc** ....E.... 516 883-8857
Port Washington *(G-13293)*
Park Ave Bldg & Roofg Sups LLC ....E.... 718 403-0100
Brooklyn *(G-2304)*
Patterson Blacktop Corp ....G.... 845 628-3425
Carmel *(G-3279)*
Pauls Rods & Restos Inc ....G.... 631 665-7637
Deer Park *(G-4023)*
Peckham Materials Corp ....E.... 518 747-3353
Hudson Falls *(G-6384)*
Penn Can Equipment Corporation ....G.... 315 378-0337
Lyons *(G-7686)*
Penn State Metal Fabri ....G.... 718 786-8814
Brooklyn *(G-2311)*
Pier-Tech Inc ....E.... 516 442-5420
Oceanside *(G-12550)*
▲ **Precision Product Inc** ....G.... 718 852-7127
Brooklyn *(G-2336)*
Presti Ready Mix Concrete Inc ....G.... 516 378-6006
Freeport *(G-5175)*
Primoplast Inc ....F.... 631 750-0680
Bohemia *(G-1078)*
Pro-Tech Wldg Fabrication Inc ....E.... 585 436-9855
Rochester *(G-14047)*
▲ **Professional Pavers Corp** ....E.... 718 784-7853
Rego Park *(G-13468)*
Railworks Transit Systems Inc ....E.... 212 502-7900
New York *(G-11317)*
Rapistak Corporation ....G.... 716 822-2804
Blasdell *(G-927)*
Rochester Asphalt Materials ....G.... 315 524-4619
Walworth *(G-15915)*
Rockland Manufacturing Co ....G.... 845 358-6000
West Nyack *(G-16281)*
RTD Manufacturing Inc ....G.... 315 337-3151
Rome *(G-14273)*
S R & R Industries Inc ....G.... 845 692-8329
Middletown *(G-8175)*
▲ **Schutte-Buffalo Hammermill LLC** ....E.... 716 855-1202
Buffalo *(G-3059)*
Seville Central Mix Corp ....D.... 516 293-6190
Old Bethpage *(G-12587)*
T S P Corp ....F.... 585 768-6769
Le Roy *(G-7125)*
Technopaving New York Inc ....G.... 631 351-6472
Huntington Station *(G-6461)*
Town of Ohio ....E.... 315 392-2055
Forestport *(G-5084)*
Vanhouten Motorsports ....G.... 315 387-6312
Lacona *(G-6955)*
X-Treme Ready Mix Inc ....G.... 718 739-3384
Jamaica *(G-6692)*
Ziegler Truck & Diesl Repr Inc ....G.... 315 782-7278
Watertown *(G-16037)*

3532 Mining Machinery & Eqpt

American Material Processing ....F.... 315 318-0017
Phoenix *(G-12988)*
▲ **Drillco Equipment Co Inc** ....E.... 718 777-5986
Long Island City *(G-7427)*
Flatcut LLC ....G.... 212 542-5732
Brooklyn *(G-1888)*
Lawson M Whiting Inc ....G.... 315 986-3064
Macedon *(G-7701)*
▲ **Munson Machinery Company Inc** ....E.... 315 797-0090
Utica *(G-15724)*
Universal Metal Fabricators ....F.... 845 331-8248
Kingston *(G-6927)*

3533 Oil Field Machinery & Eqpt

Anchor Commerce Trading Corp ....G.... 516 881-3485
Atlantic Beach *(G-455)*
Basin Holdings LLC ....E.... 212 695-7376
New York *(G-9026)*
◆ **Blue Tee Corp** ....G.... 212 598-0880
New York *(G-9109)*
◆ **Derrick Corporation** ....C.... 716 683-9010
Buffalo *(G-2799)*
Derrick Corporation ....B.... 716 685-4892
Cheektowaga *(G-3440)*
▼ **Desmi-Afti Inc** ....E.... 716 662-0632
Orchard Park *(G-12713)*
Schlumberger Technology Corp ....C.... 607 378-0105
Horseheads *(G-6328)*
Smith International Inc ....F.... 585 265-2330
Ontario *(G-12666)*

3534 Elevators & Moving Stairways

◆ **A & D Entrances LLC** ....F.... 718 989-2441
Wyandanch *(G-16690)*
Access Elevator & Lift Inc ....G.... 716 483-3696
Jamestown *(G-6694)*
◆ **Allround Logistics Inc** ....G.... 718 544-8945
Forest Hills *(G-5071)*
An Excelsior Elevator Corp ....F.... 516 408-3070
Westbury *(G-16316)*
Ankom Development LLC ....G.... 315 986-1937
Macedon *(G-7692)*
Automated Elevator Systems ....E.... 845 595-1063
Greenwood Lake *(G-5647)*
Bhi Elevator Cabs Inc ....F.... 516 431-5665
Island Park *(G-6512)*
Big Apple Elevtr Srv & Consult ....G.... 212 279-0700
New York *(G-9075)*
CEC Elevator Cab Corp ....D.... 718 328-3632
Bronx *(G-1236)*
◆ **Dover Global Holdings Inc** ....F.... 212 922-1640
New York *(G-9562)*
Dural Door Company Inc ....F.... 718 729-1333
Long Island City *(G-7430)*
E Z Entry Doors Inc ....F.... 716 434-3440
Lockport *(G-7297)*
Eag Electric Inc ....G.... 201 376-5103
Staten Island *(G-15072)*
▲ **Eazylift Albany LLC** ....G.... 518 452-6929
Latham *(G-7071)*
Elevator Accessories Mfg ....F.... 914 739-7004
Peekskill *(G-12919)*
Elevator Interiors Inc ....E.... 315 218-7186
Syracuse *(G-15314)*
Elevator Ventures Corporation ....D.... 212 375-1900
Ozone Park *(G-12824)*
GAI Manufacturing Co LLC ....D.... 718 292-9000
Bronx *(G-1278)*
Interface Products Co Inc ....G.... 631 242-4605
Bay Shore *(G-690)*
Island Custom Stairs Inc ....G.... 631 205-5335
Medford *(G-7954)*
▲ **Monitor Elevator Products LLC** ....D.... 631 543-4334
Hauppauge *(G-5897)*
▲ **National Elev Cab & Door Corp** ....E.... 718 478-5900
Woodside *(G-16666)*
Northern Lifts Elevator Co LLC ....G.... 518 644-2831
Bolton Landing *(G-1112)*
Otis Elevator Company ....F.... 315 736-0167
Yorkville *(G-16831)*
Otis Elevator Company ....E.... 917 339-9600
New York *(G-11069)*
Palmer Industries Inc ....G.... 607 754-8741
Endicott *(G-4606)*
Rokon Tech LLC ....G.... 718 429-0729
Elmhurst *(G-4471)*
S & H Enterprises Inc ....G.... 888 323-8755
Queensbury *(G-13440)*
Schindler Elevator Corporation ....C.... 212 708-1000
New York *(G-11503)*
Schindler Elevator Corporation ....E.... 800 225-3123
New York *(G-11504)*
Velis Associates Inc ....G.... 631 225-4220
Lindenhurst *(G-7202)*

3535 Conveyors & Eqpt

American Material Processing ....F.... 315 318-0017
Phoenix *(G-12988)*
Automated Biomass Systems LLC ....F.... 607 849-7800
Marathon *(G-7788)*
▲ **Chemprene Inc** ....C.... 845 831-2800
Beacon *(G-755)*
▲ **Chemprene Holding Inc** ....C.... 845 831-2800
Beacon *(G-756)*
Columbus McKinnon Corporation ....C.... 716 689-5400
Getzville *(G-5344)*
Columbus McKinnon Corporation ....C.... 716 689-5400
Getzville *(G-5345)*
Columbus McKinnon Corporation ....C.... 716 689-5400
Getzville *(G-5346)*
▲ **Crownbrook ACC LLC** ....E.... 718 626-0760
Brooklyn *(G-1734)*
◆ **Dairy Conveyor Corp** ....D.... 845 278-7878
Brewster *(G-1162)*
▼ **Desmi-Afti Inc** ....E.... 716 662-0632
Orchard Park *(G-12713)*
Excel Conveyor LLC ....F.... 718 474-0001
Rockaway Beach *(G-14225)*
General Splice Corporation ....G.... 914 271-5131
Croton On Hudson *(G-3914)*
Glasgow Products Inc ....E.... 516 374-5937
Woodmere *(G-16641)*
Green Conveyor & Mch Group LLC ....G.... 607 692-7050
Whitney Point *(G-16555)*
Haines Equipment Inc ....E.... 607 566-8531
Avoca *(G-516)*

Hohl Machine & Conveyor Co Inc ....E 716 882-7210
Buffalo *(G-2873)*

▼ I J White Corporation ....D 631 293-3788
Farmingdale *(G-4783)*

International Robotics Inc ....F 914 630-1060
Larchmont *(G-7057)*

▲ J D Handling Systems Inc ....F 518 828-9676
Ghent *(G-5357)*

Joldeson One Aerospace Inds ....D 718 848-7396
Ozone Park *(G-12827)*

Kinematic Technologies Inc ....G 518 346-7686
Niskayuna *(G-12355)*

▲ Nerak Systems Inc ....F 914 763-8259
Fishkill *(G-4951)*

Northeast Conveyors Inc ....F 585 768-8912
Lima *(G-7153)*

Noto Industrial Corp ....G 631 736-7600
Coram *(G-3802)*

Pacline Conveyors Inc ....E 716 932-7858
Buffalo *(G-2989)*

◆ Raymond Corporation ....A 607 656-2311
Greene *(G-5617)*

Raymond Corporation ....E 315 643-5000
East Syracuse *(G-4364)*

Re-Al Industrial Corp ....G 716 542-4556
Akron *(G-22)*

◆ Renold Inc ....D 716 326-3121
Westfield *(G-16396)*

▲ Rlp Holdings Inc ....G 716 852-0832
Buffalo *(G-3039)*

Rota Pack Inc ....F 631 274-1037
Farmingdale *(G-4869)*

Shako Inc ....G 315 437-1294
East Syracuse *(G-4370)*

Speedways Conveyors Inc ....E 716 893-2222
Buffalo *(G-3075)*

Troy Belting and Supply Co ....D 518 272-4920
Watervliet *(G-16053)*

▲ Ward Industrial Equipment Inc ....G 716 856-6966
Buffalo *(G-3123)*

3536 Hoists, Cranes & Monorails

▼ Acme Marine Hoist Inc ....G 631 472-3030
Calverton *(G-3161)*

C M Insurance Company Inc ....G 716 689-5409
Getzville *(G-5343)*

Columbus McKinnon Corporation ....C 716 689-5400
Getzville *(G-5344)*

Columbus McKinnon Corporation ....C 716 689-5400
Getzville *(G-5345)*

Columbus McKinnon Corporation ....C 716 689-5400
Getzville *(G-5346)*

Columbus McKinnon Corporation ....D 716 689-5400
Getzville *(G-5347)*

Debrucque Cleveland Tramrail S ....G 315 697-5160
Canastota *(G-3243)*

Dun-Rite Spclized Carriers LLC ....F 718 991-1100
Bronx *(G-1261)*

◆ Gorbel Inc ....C 585 924-6262
Fishers *(G-4940)*

Kleinfelder John ....G 716 753-3163
Mayville *(G-7921)*

Konecranes Inc ....F 585 359-4450
Henrietta *(G-6033)*

▲ Mannesmann Corporation ....D 212 258-4000
New York *(G-10691)*

Marros Equipment & Trucks ....F 315 539-8702
Waterloo *(G-15996)*

▲ Mohawk Resources Ltd ....D 518 842-1431
Amsterdam *(G-351)*

▲ Reimann & Georger Corporation ....E 716 895-1156
Buffalo *(G-3034)*

T Shore Products Ltd ....G 315 252-9174
Auburn *(G-502)*

Thego Corporation ....G 631 776-2472
Bellport *(G-814)*

◆ US Hoists Corp ....G 631 472-3030
Calverton *(G-3175)*

3537 Indl Trucks, Tractors, Trailers & Stackers

Artcraft Building Services ....G 845 895-3893
Wallkill *(G-15902)*

ASAP Rack Rental Inc ....G 718 499-4495
Brooklyn *(G-1561)*

Atlantic Engineer Products LLC ....E 518 822-1800
Hudson *(G-6341)*

▲ Channel Manufacturing Inc ....E 516 944-6271
Port Washington *(G-13247)*

Columbus McKinnon Corporation ....C 716 689-5400
Getzville *(G-5344)*

Columbus McKinnon Corporation ....C 716 689-5400
Getzville *(G-5345)*

Columbus McKinnon Corporation ....C 716 689-5400
Getzville *(G-5346)*

▲ Continental Lift Truck Inc ....F 718 738-4738
South Ozone Park *(G-14944)*

Crown Equipment Corporation ....D 516 822-5100
Hicksville *(G-6076)*

▼ Devin Mfg Inc ....F 585 496-5770
Arcade *(G-381)*

DI Manufacturing Inc ....E 315 432-8977
North Syracuse *(G-12400)*

◆ Ducon Technologies Inc ....F 631 694-1700
New York *(G-9584)*

Ducon Technologies Inc ....E 631 420-4900
Farmingdale *(G-4753)*

E-One Inc ....D 716 646-6790
Hamburg *(G-5675)*

Elramida Holdings Inc ....E 646 280-0503
Brooklyn *(G-1827)*

Jasper Transport LLC ....G 315 729-5760
Penn Yan *(G-12960)*

◆ Koke Inc ....E 800 535-5303
Queensbury *(G-13432)*

Meteor Express Inc ....F 718 551-9177
Jamaica *(G-6661)*

Mil & Mir Steel Products Co ....G 718 328-7596
Bronx *(G-1330)*

Palpross Incorporated ....F 845 469-2188
Selkirk *(G-14770)*

Pb08 Inc ....G 347 866-7353
Hicksville *(G-6123)*

Raymond Corporation ....E 315 643-5000
East Syracuse *(G-4364)*

◆ Raymond Corporation ....A 607 656-2311
Greene *(G-5617)*

Raymond Sales Corporation ....G 607 656-2311
Greene *(G-5618)*

Sherco Services LLC ....F 516 676-3028
Glen Cove *(G-5374)*

Speedways Conveyors Inc ....E 716 893-2222
Buffalo *(G-3075)*

Stanley Industrial Eqp LLC ....G 315 656-8733
Kirkville *(G-6935)*

Ward Lafrance Truck Corp ....F 518 893-1865
Saratoga Springs *(G-14601)*

3541 Machine Tools: Cutting

Abtex Corporation ....E 315 536-7403
Dresden *(G-4146)*

Advanced Machine Design Co Inc ....E 716 826-2000
Buffalo *(G-2689)*

Alpine Machine Inc ....F 607 272-1344
Ithaca *(G-6556)*

▲ Alternative Service Inc ....F 631 345-9500
Bellport *(G-798)*

Alton Manufacturing Inc ....D 585 458-2600
Rochester *(G-13621)*

▲ Ascension Industries Inc ....C 716 693-9381
North Tonawanda *(G-12413)*

Aztec Mfg of Rochester ....G 585 352-8152
Spencerport *(G-14975)*

▲ Baldwin Machine Works Inc ....G 631 842-9110
Copiague *(G-3754)*

▲ Brinkman Products Inc ....B 585 235-4545
Rochester *(G-13677)*

Coastel Cable Tools Inc ....E 315 471-5361
Syracuse *(G-15283)*

Connex Grinding & Machining ....G 315 946-4340
Lyons *(G-7683)*

Dinosaw Inc ....E 518 828-9942
Hudson *(G-6347)*

Dunlap Machine LLC ....F 315 926-1013
Marion *(G-7800)*

East Coast Tool & Mfg ....G 716 826-5183
Buffalo *(G-2810)*

Five Star Tool Co Inc ....E 585 328-9580
Rochester *(G-13806)*

Gallery of Machines LLC ....G 607 849-6028
Marathon *(G-7789)*

Gb Aero Engine LLC ....B 914 925-9600
Rye *(G-14480)*

Genco John ....G 716 483-5446
Jamestown *(G-6717)*

◆ Gleason Corporation ....A 585 473-1000
Rochester *(G-13839)*

◆ Gleason Works ....A 585 473-1000
Rochester *(G-13840)*

▲ Graywood Companies Inc ....E 585 254-7000
Rochester *(G-13845)*

H S Assembly Inc ....G 585 266-4287
Rochester *(G-13849)*

Halpern Tool Corp ....F 914 633-0038
New Rochelle *(G-8611)*

▲ Hardinge Inc ....B 607 734-2281
Elmira *(G-4490)*

▲ Hartchrom Inc ....F 518 880-0411
Watervliet *(G-16047)*

High Speed Hammer Company Inc ....F 585 266-4287
Rochester *(G-13869)*

IPC/Razor LLC ....D 212 551-4500
New York *(G-10266)*

J Vogler Enterprise LLC ....F 585 247-1625
Rochester *(G-13889)*

Jalex Industries Ltd ....F 631 491-5072
West Babylon *(G-16163)*

Johnson Mch & Fibr Pdts Co Inc ....F 716 665-2003
Jamestown *(G-6734)*

Kodiak Cutting Tools LLC ....G 800 892-1006
Syracuse *(G-15358)*

◆ Kps Capital Partners LP ....E 212 338-5100
New York *(G-10476)*

Kyocera Precision Tools Inc ....F 607 687-0012
Owego *(G-12798)*

▲ Lancaster Knives Inc ....E 716 683-5050
Lancaster *(G-7029)*

Lk Industries Inc ....G 716 941-9202
Glenwood *(G-5448)*

▲ Montrose Equipment Sales Inc ....F 718 388-7446
Brooklyn *(G-2225)*

Mortech Industries Inc ....G 845 628-6138
Mahopac *(G-7709)*

Multimatic Products Inc ....D 800 767-7633
Ronkonkoma *(G-14381)*

▲ Munson Machinery Company Inc ....E 315 797-0090
Utica *(G-15724)*

Myles Tool Company Inc ....E 716 731-1300
Sanborn *(G-14550)*

Nifty Bar Grinding & Cutting ....E 585 381-0450
Penfield *(G-12942)*

▼ Omega Consolidated Corporation ....E 585 392-9262
Hilton *(G-6158)*

▲ Omega Tool Measuring Mchs Inc ....E 585 598-7800
Fairport *(G-4645)*

P & R Industries Inc ....E 585 266-6725
Rochester *(G-14001)*

Ppi Corp ....E 585 880-7277
Rochester *(G-14031)*

▲ Ppi Corp ....D 585 243-0300
Rochester *(G-14032)*

▲ Precise Tool & Mfg Inc ....D 585 247-0700
Rochester *(G-14033)*

Producto Corporation ....C 716 484-7131
Jamestown *(G-6744)*

R Steiner Technologies Inc ....E 585 425-5912
Fairport *(G-4655)*

Rapid Precision Machining Inc ....D 585 467-0780
Rochester *(G-14069)*

RTD Manufacturing Inc ....G 315 337-3151
Rome *(G-14273)*

▲ Rush Machinery Inc ....G 585 554-3070
Rushville *(G-14477)*

▲ S & S Machinery Corp ....E 718 492-7400
Brooklyn *(G-2432)*

S & S Machinery Corp ....E 718 492-7400
Brooklyn *(G-2433)*

Selflock Screw Products Co Inc ....E 315 541-4464
Syracuse *(G-15422)*

Seneca Falls Capital Inc ....G 315 568-5804
Seneca Falls *(G-14784)*

Seneca Falls Machine Tool Co ....D 315 568-5804
Seneca Falls *(G-14785)*

▲ Simmons Machine Tool Corp ....C 518 462-5431
Menands *(G-8091)*

▼ Stephen Bader Company Inc ....F 518 753-4456
Valley Falls *(G-15770)*

Swiss Specialties Inc ....F 631 567-8800
Wading River *(G-15888)*

Teka Precision Inc ....G 845 753-1900
Nyack *(G-12512)*

Transport National Dev Inc ....E 716 662-0270
Orchard Park *(G-12746)*

Truemade Products Inc ....G 631 981-4755
Ronkonkoma *(G-14422)*

Verns Machine Co Inc ....E 315 926-4223
Marion *(G-7810)*

Welch Machine Inc ....G 585 647-3578
Rochester *(G-14205)*

Employee Codes: A=Over 500 employees, B=251-500
C=101-250, D=51-100, E=20-50, F=10-19, G=5-9
2019 Harris
New York Manufacturers Directory
757

▼ World LLC F 631 940-9121
Deer Park (G-4065)
Zwack Incorporated E 518 733-5135
Stephentown (G-15156)
Zyp Precision LLC G 315 539-3667
Waterloo (G-15998)

3542 Machine Tools: Forming

Adaptive Mfg Tech Inc E 631 580-5400
Ronkonkoma (G-14290)
Advanced Machine Design Co Inc E 716 826-2000
Buffalo (G-2689)
Advantage Metalwork Finshg LLC D 585 454-0160
Rochester (G-13608)
American Racing Headers Inc E 631 608-1427
Deer Park (G-3940)
Arconic Inc G 716 358-6451
Falconer (G-4671)
Austin Industries Inc G 585 589-1353
Albion (G-155)
Bdp Industries Inc E 518 695-6851
Greenwich (G-5636)
Brinkman Intl Group Inc G 585 429-5000
Rochester (G-13676)
Buffalo Machine Tls of Niagara F 716 201-1310
Lockport (G-7288)
C & T Tool & Instrument Co E 718 429-1253
Woodside (G-16648)
C J Winter Machine Tech E 585 429-5000
Rochester (G-13685)
Commodore Manufacutring Corp E 718 788-2600
Brooklyn (G-1709)
◆ Dover Global Holdings Inc F 212 922-1640
New York (G-9562)
Dunlap Machine LLC F 315 926-1013
Marion (G-7800)
▼ Ecko Fin & Tooling Inc F 716 487-0200
Jamestown (G-6712)
Gemcor Automation LLC D 716 674-9300
West Seneca (G-16298)
▲ Gh Induction Atmospheres LLC E 585 368-2120
Rochester (G-13835)
Hawthorne Garden Company F 516 883-6550
Port Washington (G-13263)
High Speed Hammer Company Inc F 585 266-4287
Rochester (G-13869)
▲ Hydramec Inc E 585 593-5190
Scio (G-14735)
◆ Kobe Steel USA Holdings Inc G 212 751-9400
New York (G-10462)
Lourdes Systems Inc F 631 234-7077
Hauppauge (G-5874)
Manhasset Tool & Die Co Inc F 716 684-6066
Lancaster (G-7031)
Miller Mechanical Services Inc E 518 792-0430
Glens Falls (G-5434)
▼ Mpi Incorporated C 845 471-7630
Poughkeepsie (G-13356)
Precision Eforming LLC F 607 753-7730
Cortland (G-3889)
Prim Hall Enterprises Inc F 518 561-7408
Plattsburgh (G-13150)
Producto Corporation C 716 484-7131
Jamestown (G-6744)
Raloid Tool Co Inc F 518 664-4261
Mechanicville (G-7933)
Schaefer Machine Co Inc E 516 248-6880
Mineola (G-8249)
Servotec Usa LLC G 518 671-6120
Hudson (G-6372)
▼ Smart High Voltage Solutions F 631 563-6724
Bohemia (G-1090)
Special Metals Corporation D 716 366-5663
Dunkirk (G-4180)
▲ Standard Paper Box Machine Co E 718 328-3300
Bronx (G-1392)
◆ Strippit Inc C 716 542-4511
Akron (G-23)
Taumel Metalforming Corp G 845 878-3100
Patterson (G-12886)
◆ Trueforge Global McHy Corp G 516 825-7040
Rockville Centre (G-14243)
▲ U S Air Tool Co Inc F 631 471-3300
Ronkonkoma (G-14423)
Uhmac Inc F 716 537-2343
Holland (G-6223)
Vader Systems LLC F 716 688-1600
Getzville (G-5355)
▼ Win Set Technologies LLC F 631 234-7077
Centereach (G-3346)

3543 Industrial Patterns

A & T Tooling LLC G 716 601-7299
Lancaster (G-7000)
▼ Armstrong Mold Corporation E 315 437-1517
East Syracuse (G-4320)
Armstrong Mold Corporation D 315 437-1517
East Syracuse (G-4321)
Bianca Group Ltd G 212 768-3011
New York (G-9070)
City Pattern Shop Inc F 315 463-5239
Syracuse (G-15278)
G Haynes Holdings Inc G 607 538-1160
Bloomville (G-961)
K & H Precision Products Inc E 585 624-4894
Honeoye Falls (G-6269)
Studio One Leather Design Inc F 212 760-1701
New York (G-11728)
W N R Pattern & Tool Inc G 716 681-9334
Lancaster (G-7053)
Wolff & Dungey Inc E 315 475-2105
Syracuse (G-15460)
Woodward Industries Inc F 716 692-2242
Tonawanda (G-15591)

3544 Dies, Tools, Jigs, Fixtures & Indl Molds

A & D Tool Inc G 631 243-4339
Dix Hills (G-4117)
▲ Accede Mold & Tool Co Inc D 585 254-6490
Rochester (G-13595)
Ace Specialty Co Inc G 716 874-3670
Tonawanda (G-15518)
All Out Die Cutting Inc E 718 346-6666
Brooklyn (G-1508)
▲ Alliance Precision Plas Corp C 585 426-5310
Rochester (G-13616)
Alliance Precision Plas Corp E 585 426-5310
Rochester (G-13617)
Allmetal Chocolate Mold Co Inc F 631 752-2888
West Babylon (G-16131)
▲ Allstate Tool and Die Inc D 585 426-0400
Rochester (G-13618)
Alry Tool and Die Co Inc E 716 693-2419
Tonawanda (G-15521)
Alton Manufacturing Inc D 585 458-2600
Rochester (G-13621)
▲ Amada Tool America Inc D 585 344-3900
Batavia (G-610)
American Dies Inc F 718 387-1900
Brooklyn (G-1521)
American Dsplay Die Ctters Inc E 212 645-1274
New York (G-8826)
American Orthotic Lab Co Inc G 718 961-6487
College Point (G-3639)
Amsco Inc F 716 823-4213
Buffalo (G-2699)
▲ Anka Tool & Die Inc E 845 268-4116
Congers (G-3709)
Arnell Inc G 516 486-7098
Hempstead (G-6007)
Arro Manufacturing LLC F 716 763-6203
Lakewood (G-6989)
Arro Tool & Die Inc F 716 763-6203
Lakewood (G-6990)
Art Precision Metal Products F 631 842-8889
Copiague (G-3752)
Artisan Management Group Inc G 716 569-4094
Frewsburg (G-5206)
▲ Ascension Industries Inc C 716 693-9381
North Tonawanda (G-12413)
Barron Metal Products Inc E 914 965-1232
Yonkers (G-16738)
Bel-Bee Products Incorporated F 845 353-0300
West Nyack (G-16265)
Bennett Die & Tool Inc E 607 739-5629
Horseheads (G-6307)
Bennett Die & Tool Inc F 607 273-2836
Ithaca (G-6559)
Blue Chip Mold Inc F 585 647-1790
Rochester (G-13667)
Brayley Tool & Machine Inc G 585 342-7190
Rochester (G-13675)
Brighton Tool & Die Designers F 716 876-0879
Tonawanda (G-15530)
Carbaugh Tool Company Inc E 607 739-3293
Elmira (G-4475)
▲ Century Mold Company Inc D 585 352-8600
Rochester (G-13701)
Chamtek Mfg Inc F 585 328-4900
Rochester (G-13707)
Charles A Rogers Entps Inc E 585 924-6400
Victor (G-15835)
Chenango Valley Tech Inc E 607 674-4115
Sherburne (G-14803)
Clifford H Jones Inc F 716 693-2444
Tonawanda (G-15534)
Columbia Dentoform Corporation D 718 482-1569
Long Island City (G-7414)
Cosmo Electronic Machine Corp E 631 249-2535
Farmingdale (G-4739)
Cuddeback Machining Inc G 585 392-5889
Hilton (G-6156)
▲ Cy Plastics Works Inc E 585 229-2555
Honeoye (G-6260)
▲ D Maldari & Sons Inc E 718 499-3555
Brooklyn (G-1747)
Dependable Tool & Die Co Inc G 315 453-5696
Syracuse (G-15305)
▲ Diemax of Rochester Inc G 585 288-3912
Rochester (G-13740)
Diemolding Corporation F 315 363-4710
Wampsville (G-15918)
Dixon Tool and Manufacturing F 585 235-1352
Rochester (G-13746)
Dynamic Dies Inc F 585 247-4010
Rochester (G-13754)
East Pattern & Model Corp E 585 461-3240
Rochester (G-13756)
East Pattern & Model Corp F 585 461-3240
Rochester (G-13757)
▲ Eberhardt Enterprises Inc F 585 458-7681
Rochester (G-13773)
▼ Eden Tool & Die Inc G 716 992-4240
Eden (G-4388)
Egli Machine Company Inc E 607 563-3663
Sidney (G-14853)
Electronic Die Corp F 718 455-3200
Brooklyn (G-1821)
Enhanced Tool Inc E 716 691-5200
Amherst (G-225)
Etna Tool & Die Corporation F 212 475-4350
New York (G-9723)
Everfab Inc D 716 655-1550
East Aurora (G-4198)
Evergreen Corp Central NY F 315 454-4175
Syracuse (G-15320)
▲ F M EDM Inc G 716 655-1784
East Aurora (G-4200)
Fuller Tool Incorporated F 315 891-3183
Newport (G-12255)
G N R Plastics Inc G 631 724-8758
Smithtown (G-14899)
Gatti Tool & Mold Inc F 585 328-1350
Rochester (G-13823)
Gay Sheet Metal Dies Inc G 716 877-0208
Buffalo (G-2842)
▲ General Die and Die Cutng Inc D 516 665-3584
Massapequa Park (G-7890)
▲ Globmarble LLC G 347 717-4088
Brooklyn (G-1933)
▲ Graywood Companies Inc E 585 254-7000
Rochester (G-13845)
Great Lakes Pressed Steel Corp E 716 885-4037
Buffalo (G-2857)
Handy Tool & Mfg Co Inc E 718 478-9203
Brooklyn (G-1967)
HNST Mold Inspections LLC G 845 215-9258
Pearl River (G-12899)
Hy-Tech Mold Inc F 585 247-2450
Rochester (G-13873)
▲ Hytech Tool & Die Inc G 716 488-2796
Jamestown (G-6723)
Intek Precision G 585 293-0853
Churchville (G-3511)
Inter Molds Inc G 631 667-8580
Bay Shore (G-689)
Intri-Cut Inc F 716 691-5200
Amherst (G-233)
J B Tool & Die Co Inc E 516 333-1480
Westbury (G-16343)
J T Systematic G 607 754-0929
Endwell (G-4617)
James B Crowell & Sons Inc G 845 895-3464
Wallkill (G-15905)
James Wire Die Co G 315 894-3233
Ilion (G-6476)
K & H Precision Products Inc E 585 624-4894
Honeoye Falls (G-6269)
K D M Die Company Inc F 716 828-9000
Buffalo (G-2900)

35 INDUSTRIAL AND COMMERCIAL MACHINERY AND COMPUTER EQUIPMENT

Keyes Machine Works Inc .... G 585 426-5059
  Gates (G-5310)
Knise & Krick Inc .... E 315 422-3516
  Syracuse (G-15357)
▲ Light Waves Concept Inc .... F 212 677-6400
  Brooklyn (G-2121)
Long Island Tool & Die Inc .... G 631 225-0600
  Copiague (G-3767)
M J M Tooling Corp .... G 718 292-3590
  Bronx (G-1320)
Machinecraft Inc .... E 585 436-1070
  Rochester (G-13920)
Magnus Precision Mfg Inc .... D 315 548-8032
  Phelps (G-12978)
Manhasset Tool & Die Co Inc .... F 716 684-6066
  Lancaster (G-7031)
▲ Mannesmann Corporation .... D 212 258-4000
  New York (G-10691)
Mantel & Mantel Stamping Corp ...... G 631 467-1916
  Ronkonkoma (G-14374)
Manufacturers Tool & Die Co .... E 585 352-1080
  Spencerport (G-14981)
May Tool & Die Inc .... G 716 695-1033
  Tonawanda (G-15557)
Mega Tool & Mfg Corp .... E 607 734-8398
  Elmira (G-4498)
Micro Instrument Corp .... D 585 458-3150
  Rochester (G-13939)
Micron Inds Rochester Inc .... E 585 247-6130
  Rochester (G-13944)
Moldcraft Inc .... E 716 684-1126
  Depew (G-4096)
Ms Machining Inc .... G 607 723-1105
  Binghamton (G-907)
Multifold Die Cctng Finshg Corp .... G 631 232-1235
  Hauppauge (G-5898)
Mustang-Major Tool & Die Co .... G 716 992-9200
  Eden (G-4390)
▲ Nas CP Corp .... E 718 961-6757
  College Point (G-3657)
National Steel Rule Die Inc .... F 718 402-1396
  Bronx (G-1339)
Niagara Fiberglass Inc .... E 716 822-3921
  Buffalo (G-2966)
Niagara Punch & Die Corp .... G 716 896-7619
  Buffalo (G-2969)
▼ Nicoform Inc .... E 585 454-5530
  Rochester (G-13973)
Nijon Tool Co Inc .... F 631 242-3434
  Deer Park (G-4016)
◆ Nordon Inc .... D 585 546-6200
  Rochester (G-13974)
Nordon Inc .... E 585 546-6200
  Rochester (G-13975)
Nordon Inc .... E 585 546-6200
  Rochester (G-13976)
Northern Design Inc .... G 716 652-7071
  East Aurora (G-4209)
P & H Machine Shop Inc .... E 585 247-5500
  Rochester (G-14000)
P & R Industries Inc .... E 585 266-6725
  Rochester (G-14001)
P & R Industries Inc .... E 585 544-1811
  Rochester (G-14002)
P Tool & Die Co Inc .... E 585 889-1340
  North Chili (G-12382)
▲ P&G Metal Components Corp ..... D 716 896-7900
  Buffalo (G-2986)
Pacific Die Cast Inc .... F 845 778-6374
  Walden (G-15894)
Palma Tool & Die Company Inc .... E 716 681-4464
  Lancaster (G-7035)
Paragon Steel Rule Dies Inc .... F 585 254-3395
  Rochester (G-14008)
Patmian LLC .... B 212 758-0770
  New York (G-11122)
Peak Motion Inc .... G 716 534-4925
  Clarence (G-3538)
Phelinger Tool & Die Corp .... G 716 685-1780
  Alden (G-174)
Pivot Punch Corporation .... D 716 625-8000
  Lockport (G-7326)
Plastic Solutions Inc .... E 631 234-9013
  Bayport (G-738)
◆ PMI Industries LLC .... E 585 464-8050
  Rochester (G-14025)
▲ Polyshot Corporation .... E 585 292-5010
  West Henrietta (G-16248)
Ppi Corp .... E 585 880-7277
  Rochester (G-14031)

Precise Punch Corporation .... F 716 625-8000
  Lockport (G-7327)
▲ Precision Grinding & Mfg Corp .... C 585 458-4300
  Rochester (G-14035)
Precision Machining and Mfg .... G 845 647-5380
  Wawarsing (G-16069)
Precision Systems Mfg Inc .... E 315 451-3480
  Liverpool (G-7257)
Prime Tool & Die LLC .... G 607 334-5435
  Norwich (G-12492)
Producto Corporation .... C 716 484-7131
  Jamestown (G-6744)
Pronto Tool & Die Co Inc .... F 631 981-8920
  Ronkonkoma (G-14401)
Quality Lineals Usa Inc .... E 516 378-6577
  Freeport (G-5177)
Raloid Tool Co Inc .... F 518 664-4261
  Mechanicville (G-7933)
Rand Machine Products, Inc. .... C 716 665-5217
  Falconer (G-4688)
Rid Lom Precision Mfg .... F 585 594-8600
  Rochester (G-14072)
Rochester Stampings Inc .... F 585 467-5241
  Rochester (G-14095)
Rochester Tool and Mold Inc .... F 585 464-9336
  Rochester (G-14098)
Rochling Advent Tool & Mold LP 585 254-2000
  Rochester (G-14100)
▲ Romold Inc .... F 585 529-4440
  Rochester (G-14103)
Rossi Tool & Dies Inc .... G 845 267-8246
  Valley Cottage (G-15763)
Royal Molds Inc .... F 718 382-7686
  Brooklyn (G-2422)
S B Whistler & Sons Inc .... E 585 798-3000
  Medina (G-7988)
Saturn Industries Inc .... E 518 828-9956
  Hudson (G-6370)
Sb Molds LLC .... D 845 352-3700
  Monsey (G-8297)
Silicone Products & Technology ...... C 716 684-1155
  Lancaster (G-7050)
Specialty Model & Mold Inc .... G 631 475-0840
  Ronkonkoma (G-14416)
▲ Spectronics Corporation .... C 516 333-4840
  Westbury (G-16373)
Stamp Rite Tool & Die Inc .... G 718 752-0334
  Long Island City (G-7597)
Star Mold Co Inc .... G 631 694-2283
  Farmingdale (G-4880)
◆ Strippit Inc .... C 716 542-4511
  Akron (G-23)
Stuart Tool & Die Inc .... E 716 488-1975
  Falconer (G-4694)
Synergy Tooling Systems Inc .... F 716 834-4457
  Amherst (G-253)
Syntec Technologies Inc .... F 585 464-9336
  Rochester (G-14153)
T A Tool & Molding Inc .... F 631 293-0172
  Farmingdale (G-4888)
Thayer Tool & Die Inc .... F 716 782-4841
  Ashville (G-418)
Tips & Dies Inc .... F 315 337-4161
  Rome (G-14275)
Tooling Enterprises Inc .... F 716 842-0445
  Buffalo (G-3099)
Tools & Stamping Corp .... E 718 392-4040
  Brooklyn (G-2570)
Trimaster/Htech Holding LLC .... G 212 257-6772
  New York (G-11899)
Trinity Tools Inc .... E 716 694-1111
  North Tonawanda (G-12460)
Triplex Industries Inc .... F 585 621-6920
  Rochester (G-14176)
Turning Point Tool LLC .... G 585 288-7380
  Rochester (G-14182)
▼ Ultimate Prcision Met Pdts Inc ..... C 631 249-9441
  Farmingdale (G-4901)
Universal Tooling Corporation .... F 716 985-4691
  Gerry (G-5342)
Van Reenen Tool & Die Inc .... F 585 288-6000
  Rochester (G-14198)
▲ Van Thomas Inc .... E 585 426-1414
  Rochester (G-14199)
W N R Pattern & Tool Inc .... G 716 681-9334
  Lancaster (G-7053)
Xli Corporation .... D 585 436-2250
  Rochester (G-14216)
Z Works Inc .... E 631 750-0612
  Bohemia (G-1109)

3545 Machine Tool Access

◆ Acu-Rite Companies Inc .... G 716 661-1700
  Jamestown (G-6695)
Advance D Tech Inc .... F 845 534-8248
  Cornwall (G-3829)
Ale-Techniques Inc .... F 845 687-7200
  High Falls (G-6139)
Ameri-Cut Tool Grinding Inc .... G 716 692-3900
  North Tonawanda (G-12410)
American Linear Manufacturers .... F 516 333-1351
  Westbury (G-16314)
Arch Globl Prcsion Rchster LLC ...... D 585 254-7000
  Rochester (G-13638)
▲ Baldwin Machine Works Inc .... G 631 842-9110
  Copiague (G-3754)
Bdp Industries Inc .... E 518 695-6851
  Greenwich (G-5636)
Bnm Product Service .... G 631 750-1586
  Holbrook (G-6172)
Boro Park Cutting Tool Corp .... E 718 720-0610
  Staten Island (G-15053)
Brinkman Intl Group Inc .... G 585 429-5000
  Rochester (G-13676)
C J Winter Machine Tech .... E 585 429-5000
  Rochester (G-13685)
Carl Safina Center Inc .... G 808 888-9440
  Setauket (G-14793)
▲ Champion Cutting Tool Corp .... E 516 536-8200
  Rockville Centre (G-14230)
Circo File Corp .... G 516 922-1848
  Oyster Bay (G-12811)
▲ Curran Manufacturing Corp .... E 631 273-1010
  Hauppauge (G-5807)
Curran Manufacturing Corp .... E 631 273-1010
  Hauppauge (G-5808)
Custom Service Solutions Inc .... E 585 637-3760
  Brockport (G-1190)
▲ Designatronics Incorporated .... E 516 328-3300
  Hicksville (G-6079)
Dinosaw Inc .... E 518 828-9942
  Hudson (G-6347)
Dock Hardware Incorporated .... F 585 266-7920
  Rochester (G-13747)
Dorsey Metrology Intl Inc .... E 845 229-2929
  Poughkeepsie (G-13334)
Drt Power Systems LLC .... G 585 247-5940
  Rochester (G-13751)
Dura-Mill Inc .... E 518 899-2255
  Ballston Spa (G-582)
Egli Machine Company Inc .... E 607 563-3663
  Sidney (G-14853)
Everfab Inc .... D 716 655-1550
  East Aurora (G-4198)
▲ F W Roberts Mfg Co Inc .... F 716 434-3555
  Lockport (G-7300)
Flashflo Manufacturing Inc .... F 716 826-9500
  Buffalo (G-2827)
▲ Flexbar Machine Corporation ...... E 631 582-8440
  Islandia (G-6528)
Fred M Velepec Co Inc .... F 718 821-6636
  Glendale (G-5400)
▲ Gardei Industries LLC .... F 716 693-7100
  North Tonawanda (G-12429)
Genesee Manufacturing Co Inc .... E 585 266-3201
  Rochester (G-13829)
◆ Germanow-Simon Corporation .... E 585 232-1440
  Rochester (G-13832)
▲ Graywood Companies Inc .... E 585 254-7000
  Rochester (G-13845)
▲ Griffin Manufacturing Company ... E 585 265-1991
  Webster (G-16085)
▲ Hardinge Inc .... B 607 734-2281
  Elmira (G-4490)
▲ Helmel Engineering Pdts Inc .... E 716 297-8644
  Niagara Falls (G-12293)
Hubbard Tool and Die Corp .... E 315 337-7840
  Rome (G-14253)
Huron TI Cutter Grinding Inc .... E 631 420-7000
  Farmingdale (G-4782)
▼ Innex Industries Inc .... E 585 247-3575
  Rochester (G-13880)
Innovative Automation Inc .... F 631 439-3300
  Farmingdale (G-4785)
J H Robotics Inc .... E 607 729-3758
  Johnson City (G-6812)
JD Tool Inc .... G 607 786-3129
  Endicott (G-4599)
Jem Tool & Die Corp .... F 631 539-8734
  West Islip (G-16259)

◆ **Kps Capital Partners LP** ....E.... 212 338-5100
New York *(G-10476)*
▲ **Lancaster Knives Inc** ....E.... 716 683-5050
Lancaster *(G-7029)*
Linde LLC ....D.... 716 773-7552
Grand Island *(G-5506)*
▲ **M & S Precision Machine Co LLC** ....F.... 518 747-1193
Queensbury *(G-13433)*
Macinnes Tool Corporation ....E.... 585 467-1920
Rochester *(G-13921)*
▲ **Make-Waves Instrument Corp** ....E.... 716 681-7524
Buffalo *(G-2936)*
Mausner Equipment Co Inc ....C.... 631 689-7358
Setauket *(G-14795)*
Melland Gear Instr of Huppauge ....E.... 631 234-0100
Hauppauge *(G-5885)*
Methods Tooling & Mfg Inc ....E.... 845 246-7100
Mount Marion *(G-8364)*
◆ **Mibro Group** ....D.... 716 631-5713
Buffalo *(G-2945)*
Michael Fiore Ltd ....G.... 516 561-8238
Valley Stream *(G-15786)*
Miller Metal Fabricating Inc ....G.... 585 359-3400
Rochester *(G-13945)*
Morgood Tools Inc ....D.... 585 436-8828
Rochester *(G-13956)*
Myles Tool Company Inc ....E.... 716 731-1300
Sanborn *(G-14550)*
New Market Products LLC ....G.... 607 292-6226
Wayne *(G-16073)*
Northfeld Precision Instr Corp ....E.... 516 431-1112
Island Park *(G-6517)*
Novatech Inc ....E.... 716 892-6682
Cheektowaga *(G-3455)*
▲ **Omega Tool Measuring Mchs Inc** ....E.... 585 598-7800
Fairport *(G-4645)*
▲ **Park Enterprises Rochester Inc** ....C.... 585 546-4200
Rochester *(G-14009)*
Parlec LLC ....D.... 585 425-4400
Fairport *(G-4648)*
▲ **Ppi Corp** ....D.... 585 243-0300
Rochester *(G-14032)*
▲ **Precision Grinding & Mfg Corp** ....C.... 585 458-4300
Rochester *(G-14035)*
Precision Mechanisms Corp ....E.... 516 333-5955
Westbury *(G-16366)*
▲ **Production Metal Cutting Inc** ....F.... 585 458-7136
Rochester *(G-14050)*
Prz Technologies Inc ....F.... 716 683-1300
Lancaster *(G-7042)*
Ptc Precision LLC ....E.... 607 748-8294
Endwell *(G-4620)*
Robert J Faraone ....G.... 585 232-7160
Rochester *(G-14076)*
Rochling Advent Tool & Mold LP ....D.... 585 254-2000
Rochester *(G-14100)*
Ross JC Inc ....G.... 716 439-1161
Lockport *(G-7328)*
Rota File Corporation ....E.... 516 496-7200
Syosset *(G-15231)*
▲ **S & S Machinery Corp** ....E.... 718 492-7400
Brooklyn *(G-2432)*
S S Precision Gear & Instr ....G.... 718 457-7474
Corona *(G-3854)*
◆ **Schenck Corporation** ....D.... 631 242-4010
Deer Park *(G-4040)*
◆ **Schenck Trebel Corp** ....D.... 631 242-4010
Deer Park *(G-4041)*
Scomac Inc ....F.... 585 494-2200
Bergen *(G-827)*
Seneca Falls Machine Tool Co ....D.... 315 568-5804
Seneca Falls *(G-14785)*
Sinn- Tech Industries Inc ....F.... 631 643-1171
West Babylon *(G-16192)*
Socket Products Mfg Corp ....G.... 631 232-9870
Islandia *(G-6538)*
Steiner Technologies Inc ....F.... 585 425-5910
Fairport *(G-4660)*
Streamline Precision Inc ....G.... 585 421-9050
Fairport *(G-4661)*
Streamline Precision Inc ....G.... 585 421-9050
Fairport *(G-4662)*
◆ **Strippit Inc** ....C.... 716 542-4511
Akron *(G-23)*
▲ **Thuro Metal Products Inc** ....E.... 631 435-0444
Brentwood *(G-1145)*
Townline Machine Co Inc ....E.... 315 462-3413
Clifton Springs *(G-3584)*
Transport National Dev Inc ....E.... 716 662-0270
Orchard Park *(G-12747)*
▲ **Trident Precision Mfg Inc** ....D.... 585 265-2010
Webster *(G-16103)*
Trimaster/Htech Holding LLC ....G.... 212 257-6772
New York *(G-11899)*
Trinity Tools Inc ....E.... 716 694-1111
North Tonawanda *(G-12460)*
▲ **Truebite Inc** ....F.... 607 786-3184
Endicott *(G-4613)*
Universal Tooling Corporation ....F.... 716 985-4691
Gerry *(G-5342)*
Vandilay Industries Inc ....E.... 631 226-3064
West Babylon *(G-16202)*
Velmex Inc ....E.... 585 657-6151
Bloomfield *(G-958)*
Xactra Technologies Inc ....D.... 585 426-2030
Rochester *(G-14213)*

3546 Power Hand Tools

Allied Motion Technologies Inc ....C.... 315 782-5910
Watertown *(G-16000)*
▲ **Awt Supply Corp** ....G.... 516 437-9105
Elmont *(G-4517)*
Black & Decker (us) Inc ....B.... 914 235-6300
Brewster *(G-1159)*
Black & Decker (us) Inc ....G.... 716 884-6220
Buffalo *(G-2734)*
Black & Decker (us) Inc ....G.... 631 952-2008
Hauppauge *(G-5781)*
Black & Decker Corporation ....G.... 718 335-1042
Woodside *(G-16647)*
Dean Manufacturing Inc ....F.... 607 770-1300
Vestal *(G-15814)*
▲ **Dynabrade Inc** ....C.... 716 631-0100
Clarence *(G-3529)*
▲ **Great American Tool Co Inc** ....G.... 716 646-5700
Hamburg *(G-5681)*
Huck International Inc ....C.... 845 331-7300
Kingston *(G-6902)*
◆ **Ivy Classic Industries Inc** ....E.... 914 632-8200
New Rochelle *(G-8616)*
Kelley Farm & Garden Inc ....E.... 518 234-2332
Cobleskill *(G-3603)*
▲ **Meritool LLC** ....E.... 716 699-6005
Salamanca *(G-14527)*
New York Industrial Works Inc ....F.... 718 292-0615
Bronx *(G-1341)*
◆ **P & F Industries Inc** ....E.... 631 694-9800
Melville *(G-8055)*
◆ **Rbhammers Corp** ....F.... 845 353-5042
Blauvelt *(G-939)*
▲ **Reimann & Georger Corporation** ....E.... 716 895-1156
Buffalo *(G-3034)*
Stature Electric Inc ....D.... 716 242-7535
Amherst *(G-251)*
▼ **Thomas C Wilson LLC** ....E.... 718 729-3360
Long Island City *(G-7615)*

3547 Rolling Mill Machinery & Eqpt

Anthony Manufacturing Inc ....G.... 631 957-9424
Lindenhurst *(G-7161)*
◆ **Ivy Classic Industries Inc** ....E.... 914 632-8200
New Rochelle *(G-8616)*
Johnston Dandy Company ....G.... 315 455-5773
Syracuse *(G-15349)*
▲ **Mannesmann Corporation** ....D.... 212 258-4000
New York *(G-10691)*
Polymag Tek Inc ....F.... 585 235-8390
Rochester *(G-14026)*

3548 Welding Apparatus

Apogee Translite Inc ....E.... 631 254-6975
Deer Park *(G-3944)*
McAllisters Precision Wldg Inc ....F.... 518 221-3455
Menands *(G-8087)*
Riverview Industries Inc ....G.... 845 265-5284
Cold Spring *(G-3627)*
▲ **Vante Inc** ....F.... 716 778-7691
Newfane *(G-12254)*

3549 Metalworking Machinery, NEC

Advanced Machine Design Co Inc ....E.... 716 826-2000
Buffalo *(G-2689)*
▲ **Alliance Automation Systems** ....C.... 585 426-2700
Rochester *(G-13615)*
▲ **Autostat Corporation** ....F.... 516 379-9447
Roosevelt *(G-14434)*
▲ **Bartell Machinery Systems LLC** ....C.... 315 336-7600
Rome *(G-14246)*
Carpenter Manufacturing Co ....E.... 315 682-9176
Manlius *(G-7775)*
Charles A Rogers Entps Inc ....E.... 585 924-6400
Victor *(G-15835)*
Duall Finishing Inc ....G.... 716 827-1707
Buffalo *(G-2804)*
▲ **Esm II Inc** ....E.... 716 446-8888
Amherst *(G-227)*
▲ **Expert Metal Slitters Corp** ....G.... 718 361-2735
Long Island City *(G-7443)*
▲ **Hardinge Inc** ....B.... 607 734-2281
Elmira *(G-4490)*
Hje Company Inc ....G.... 518 792-8733
Queensbury *(G-13428)*
▲ **Hover-Davis Inc** ....C.... 585 352-9590
Rochester *(G-13872)*
Manufacturing Resources Inc ....E.... 631 481-0041
Rochester *(G-13926)*
▲ **MGS Manufacturing Inc** ....E.... 315 337-3350
Rome *(G-14258)*
▲ **Mold-A-Matic Corporation** ....E.... 607 433-2121
Oneonta *(G-12641)*
Mono-Systems Inc ....E.... 716 821-1344
Buffalo *(G-2953)*
Mtwli Precision Corp ....G.... 631 244-3767
Bohemia *(G-1061)*
▲ **Munson Machinery Company Inc** ....E.... 315 797-0090
Utica *(G-15724)*
Pems Tool & Machine Inc ....E.... 315 823-3595
Little Falls *(G-7211)*
Precision Systems Mfg Inc ....E.... 315 451-3480
Liverpool *(G-7257)*
▲ **Reelex Packaging Solutions Inc** ....E.... 845 878-7878
Patterson *(G-12884)*
Riverside Machinery Company ....E.... 718 492-7400
Brooklyn *(G-2407)*
▲ **S & S Machinery Corp** ....E.... 718 492-7400
Brooklyn *(G-2432)*
S & S Machinery Corp ....E.... 718 492-7400
Brooklyn *(G-2433)*
Serge Duct Designs Inc ....E.... 718 783-7799
Brooklyn *(G-2457)*
▲ **Standard Bots Company** ....G.... 646 876-2687
Locust Valley *(G-7351)*
◆ **Strippit Inc** ....C.... 716 542-4511
Akron *(G-23)*
◆ **Tessy Plastics Corp** ....B.... 315 689-3924
Skaneateles *(G-14878)*
Unidex Corporation Western NY ....F.... 585 786-3170
Warsaw *(G-15946)*
Vader Systems LLC ....F.... 716 688-1600
Getzville *(G-5355)*
▲ **Van Blarcom Closures Inc** ....C.... 718 855-3810
Brooklyn *(G-2615)*
◆ **Voss Manufacturing Inc** ....D.... 716 731-5062
Sanborn *(G-14557)*
▲ **Xto Incorporated** ....D.... 315 451-7807
Liverpool *(G-7273)*
You First Services Inc ....F.... 716 204-7215
Buffalo *(G-3135)*

3552 Textile Machinery

Aglika Trade LLC ....F.... 727 424 1944
Middle Village *(G-8120)*
Angel Textiles Inc ....G.... 212 532-0900
New York *(G-8862)*
Big Apple Sign Corp ....E.... 631 342-0303
Islandia *(G-6522)*
Chroma Logic ....G.... 716 736-2458
Ripley *(G-13562)*
Corbertex LLC ....G.... 212 971-0008
New York *(G-9399)*
◆ **Eastman Machine Company** ....C.... 716 856-2200
Buffalo *(G-2812)*
EMC Tech Inc ....F.... 716 488-9071
Falconer *(G-4676)*
Herr Manufacturing Co Inc ....E.... 716 754-4341
Tonawanda *(G-15549)*
Herrmann Group LLC ....G.... 716 876-9798
Kenmore *(G-6860)*
Mjk Cutting Inc ....F.... 718 384-7613
Brooklyn *(G-2216)*
Mohawk Valley Knt McHy Co Inc ....F.... 315 736-3038
New York Mills *(G-12189)*
Rfb Associates Inc ....F.... 518 271-0551
Fort Edward *(G-5100)*
Schwabel Fabricating Co Inc ....E.... 716 876-2086
Tonawanda *(G-15575)*
Screen Team Inc ....F.... 718 786-2424
Long Island City *(G-7586)*

3553 Woodworking Machinery

Company	Emp	Phone
Simtec Industries Corporation	G	631 293-0080
Farmingdale *(G-4874)*		
Thread Check Inc	D	631 231-1515
Hauppauge *(G-5958)*		

3553 Woodworking Machinery

Company	Emp	Phone
901 D LLC	E	845 369-1111
Airmont *(G-10)*		
Corbett Stves Pttern Works Inc	E	585 546-7109
Rochester *(G-13722)*		
Downtown Interiors Inc	F	212 337-0230
New York *(G-9567)*		
▲ Hardinge Inc	B	607 734-2281
Elmira *(G-4490)*		
Hat Factory Furniture Co	G	914 788-6288
Peekskill *(G-12921)*		
◆ James L Taylor Mfg Co	E	845 452-3780
Poughkeepsie *(G-13348)*		
James L Taylor Mfg Co	E	845 452-3780
Poughkeepsie *(G-13349)*		
◆ Merritt Machinery LLC	E	716 434-5558
Lockport *(G-7315)*		
◆ Oneida Air Systems Inc	E	315 476-5151
Syracuse *(G-15387)*		
Phoenix Wood Wrights Ltd	F	631 727-9691
Riverhead *(G-13579)*		
US Sander LLC	G	518 875-9157
Esperance *(G-4622)*		
Wood-Mizer Holdings Inc	G	315 564-5722
Hannibal *(G-5718)*		

3554 Paper Inds Machinery

Company	Emp	Phone
Automecha International Ltd	E	607 843-2235
Oxford *(G-12807)*		
Cyclotherm of Watertown Inc	E	315 782-1100
Watertown *(G-16011)*		
▲ F W Roberts Mfg Co Inc	F	716 434-3555
Lockport *(G-7300)*		
Fbm Galaxy Inc	F	315 463-5144
East Syracuse *(G-4338)*		
Gailer Stamping Diecutting LLC	F	212 243-5662
Long Island City *(G-7453)*		
GL&v USA Inc	C	518 747-2444
Hudson Falls *(G-6380)*		
Haanen Packard Machinery Inc	E	518 747-2330
Hudson Falls *(G-6382)*		
Jacob Inc	E	646 450-3067
Brooklyn *(G-2030)*		
Johnston Dandy Company	G	315 455-5773
Syracuse *(G-15349)*		
Kadant Inc	E	518 793-8801
Glens Falls *(G-5429)*		
Lake Image Systems Inc	F	585 321-3630
Henrietta *(G-6034)*		
Richlar Industries Inc	F	315 463-5144
East Syracuse *(G-4366)*		
Rsb Associates Inc	F	518 281-5067
Altamont *(G-202)*		
Sinclair International Company	D	518 798-2361
Queensbury *(G-13442)*		
▲ Sonicor Inc	F	631 920-6555
West Babylon *(G-16194)*		
▲ Standard Paper Box Machine Co	E	718 328-3300
Bronx *(G-1392)*		
Verso Corporation	B	212 599-2700
New York *(G-12014)*		

3555 Printing Trades Machinery & Eqpt

Company	Emp	Phone
▲ A-Mark Machinery Corp	F	631 643-6300
West Babylon *(G-16125)*		
Advance Grafix Equipment Inc	G	917 202-4593
Wyandanch *(G-16692)*		
Anand Printing Machinery Inc	G	631 667-3079
Deer Park *(G-3942)*		
Apexx Omni-Graphics Inc	D	718 326-3330
Maspeth *(G-7822)*		
▲ Awt Supply Corp	G	516 437-9105
Elmont *(G-4517)*		
Bartizan Data Systems LLC	E	914 965-7977
Yonkers *(G-16739)*		
▲ Bmp America Inc	C	585 798-0950
Medina *(G-7973)*		
C M E Corp	F	315 451-7101
Syracuse *(G-15266)*		
Castlereagh Printcraft Inc	D	516 623-1728
Freeport *(G-5148)*		
Copy4les Inc	F	212 487-9778
New York *(G-9398)*		
Csw Inc	F	585 247-4010
Rochester *(G-13727)*		
Daige Products Inc	F	516 621-2100
Albertson *(G-148)*		
Davis International Inc	G	585 421-8175
Fairport *(G-4631)*		
Exacta LLC	G	716 406-2303
Clarence Center *(G-3544)*		
Halm Instrument Co Inc	D	516 676-6700
Glen Head *(G-5380)*		
◆ Hodgins Engraving Co Inc	E	585 343-4444
Batavia *(G-628)*		
▲ Impressions International Inc	G	585 442-5240
Rochester *(G-13879)*		
Innotech Graphic Eqp Corp	G	845 268-6900
Valley Cottage *(G-15755)*		
▲ International Imaging Mtls Inc	B	716 691-6333
Amherst *(G-232)*		
▲ Lexar Global LLC	G	845 352-9700
Valley Cottage *(G-15758)*		
▲ Mekatronics Incorporated	E	516 883-6805
Port Washington *(G-13288)*		
◆ Micro Powders Inc	G	914 332-6400
Tarrytown *(G-15483)*		
Mount Vernon Machine Inc	G	845 268-9400
Valley Cottage *(G-15759)*		
Newport Business Solutions Inc	F	631 319-6129
Bohemia *(G-1064)*		
▲ Package Print Technologies	F	716 871-9905
Buffalo *(G-2988)*		
◆ Perretta Graphics Corp	E	845 473-0550
Poughkeepsie *(G-13362)*		
Prim Hall Enterprises Inc	F	518 561-7408
Plattsburgh *(G-13150)*		
Rollers Inc	G	716 837-0700
Buffalo *(G-3044)*		
Rubber Stamps Inc	E	212 675-1180
Mineola *(G-8247)*		
▲ Skandacor Direct Inc	E	585 265-9020
Webster *(G-16099)*		
Southern Graphic Systems LLC	E	315 695-7079
Phoenix *(G-12993)*		
Specilty Bus Mchs Holdings LLC	F	212 587-9600
New York *(G-11663)*		
Sterling Toggle Inc	F	631 491-0500
West Babylon *(G-16196)*		
▲ Super Web Inc	E	631 643-9100
West Babylon *(G-16198)*		
Universal Metal Fabricators	E	845 331-8248
Kingston *(G-6927)*		
◆ Vits International Inc	E	845 353-5000
Blauvelt *(G-945)*		
Voodoo Manufacturing Inc	E	646 893-8366
Brooklyn *(G-2634)*		
Woerner Industries Inc	E	585 436-1934
Rochester *(G-14211)*		

3556 Food Prdts Machinery

Company	Emp	Phone
Acai of America Inc	G	862 205-9334
New York *(G-8717)*		
◆ Ag-Pak Inc	F	716 772-2651
Gasport *(G-5304)*		
◆ Bairnco Corporation	E	914 461-1300
White Plains *(G-16424)*		
◆ Bake-Rite International Inc	G	518 395-3340
Schenectady *(G-14652)*		
Bakers Pride Oven Co Inc	C	914 576-0200
New Rochelle *(G-8591)*		
Bari Engineering Corp	E	212 966-2080
New York *(G-9017)*		
Blue Toad Hard Cider	F	585 424-5508
Rochester *(G-13668)*		
Bonduelle USA Inc	E	585 948-5252
Oakfield *(G-12523)*		
▲ Brooklyn Brew Shop LLC	F	718 874-0119
Brooklyn *(G-1638)*		
◆ Buflovak LLC	F	716 895-2100
Buffalo *(G-2755)*		
C-Flex Bearing Co Inc	E	315 895-7454
Frankfort *(G-5104)*		
◆ Caravella Food Corp	E	646 552-0455
Whitestone *(G-16537)*		
Carts Mobile Food Eqp Corp	E	718 788-5540
Brooklyn *(G-1680)*		
▲ Chemicolloid Laboratories Inc	F	516 747-2666
New Hyde Park *(G-8522)*		
Chester-Jensen Company	E	610 876-6276
Cattaraugus *(G-3312)*		
Delaval Inc	F	585 599-4696
Corfu *(G-3806)*		
Delsur Parts	G	631 630-1606
Brentwood *(G-1131)*		
Desu Machinery Corporation	D	716 681-5798
Depew *(G-4087)*		
Esquire Mechanical Corp	G	718 625-4006
Brooklyn *(G-1849)*		
ET Oakes Corporation	E	631 232-0002
Hauppauge *(G-5821)*		
Expert Industries Inc	F	718 434-6060
Brooklyn *(G-1859)*		
Goodnature Products Inc	E	716 855-3325
Orchard Park *(G-12716)*		
Haines Equipment Inc	E	607 566-8531
Avoca *(G-516)*		
Home Maide Inc	F	845 837-1700
Harriman *(G-5719)*		
▼ I J White Corporation	D	631 293-3788
Farmingdale *(G-4783)*		
Janel Corporation	G	516 256-8143
Lynbrook *(G-7666)*		
Kedco Inc	F	516 454-7800
Farmingdale *(G-4800)*		
Kings Cnty Brwers Cllctive LLC	F	917 207-2739
Brooklyn *(G-2075)*		
Kinplex Corp	E	631 242-4800
Edgewood *(G-4408)*		
Los Olivos Ltd	F	631 773-6439
Farmingdale *(G-4811)*		
Lyophilization Systems Inc	G	845 338-0456
New Paltz *(G-8579)*		
Mary F Morse	G	315 866-2741
Mohawk *(G-8255)*		
Mohawk Valley Manufacturing	G	315 797-0851
Frankfort *(G-5110)*		
◆ National Equipment Corporation	F	718 585-0200
Harrison *(G-5731)*		
National Equipment Corporation	E	718 585-0200
Bronx *(G-1338)*		
▲ Olmstead Products Corp	F	516 681-3700
Hicksville *(G-6117)*		
P & M LLC	E	631 842-2200
Amityville *(G-310)*		
Pic Nic LLC	G	914 245-6500
Amawalk *(G-204)*		
▲ Precision N Amer Fd McHy LLC	F	518 462-3387
Albany *(G-118)*		
▲ Purvi Enterprises Incorporated	G	347 808-9448
Maspeth *(G-7868)*		
Sidco Food Distribution Corp	F	718 733-3939
Bronx *(G-1383)*		
▲ Simply Natural Foods LLC	C	631 543-9600
Commack *(G-3703)*		
Singlecut Beersmiths LLC	F	718 606-0788
Astoria *(G-443)*		
SPX Flow Us LLC	A	716 692-3000
Getzville *(G-5353)*		
▲ Unisource Food Eqp Systems Inc	G	516 681-0537
Holbrook *(G-6217)*		
US Beverage Net Inc	E	315 579-2025
Syracuse *(G-15450)*		
▲ Vr Food Equipment Inc	F	315 531-8133
Farmington *(G-4921)*		
Wired Coffee and Bagel Inc	F	518 506-3194
Malta *(G-7733)*		

3559 Special Ind Machinery, NEC

Company	Emp	Phone
Accurate McHning Incorporation	F	315 689-1428
Elbridge *(G-4426)*		
▲ Addex Inc	G	781 344-5800
Newark *(G-12192)*		
◆ Adirondack Plas & Recycl Inc	E	518 746-9212
Argyle *(G-397)*		
▼ Andela Tool & Machine Inc	G	315 858-0055
Richfield Springs *(G-13492)*		
Applied Materials Inc	E	845 227-5000
Hopewell Junction *(G-6282)*		
◆ Arbe Machinery Inc	F	631 756-2477
Farmingdale *(G-4722)*		
▲ Aremco Products Inc	E	845 268-0039
Valley Cottage *(G-15752)*		
Automotion Parking Systems LLC	E	516 565-5600
West Hempstead *(G-16213)*		
B&K Precision Corporation	G	631 369-2665
Manorville *(G-7782)*		
Ben Weitsman of Albany LLC	E	518 462-4444
Albany *(G-45)*		
Blue Star Products Inc	F	631 952-3204
Hauppauge *(G-5782)*		
▲ Cameo Metal Products Inc	E	718 788-1106
Brooklyn *(G-1670)*		
◆ Caswell Inc	F	315 946-1213
Lyons *(G-7682)*		

Employee Codes: A=Over 500 employees, B=251-500
C=101-250, D=51-100, E=20-50, F=10-19, G=5-9

CBA Group LLC A 607 779-7522
Conklin *(G-3725)*
◆ **Century-Tech Inc** E 516 493-9800
Hempstead *(G-6010)*
▲ **Charles Ross & Son Company** D 631 234-0500
Hauppauge *(G-5788)*
Cleaning Tech Group LLC E 716 665-2340
Jamestown *(G-6707)*
Crumbrubber Technology Inc F 718 468-3988
Hollis *(G-6233)*
▲ **Cryomech Inc** D 315 455-2555
Syracuse *(G-15296)*
Curtin-Hebert Co Inc F 518 725-7157
Gloversville *(G-5455)*
Cvd Equipment Corporation E 845 246-3631
Saugerties *(G-14605)*
Cvd Equipment Corporation F 631 582-4365
Central Islip *(G-3366)*
▲ **Designatronics Incorporated** G 516 328-3300
Hicksville *(G-6079)*
Digital Matrix Corp E 516 481-7990
Farmingdale *(G-4752)*
Eastend Enforcement Products G 631 878-8424
Smithtown *(G-14898)*
Eltee Tool & Die Co F 607 748-4301
Endicott *(G-4587)*
Emhart Glass Manufacturing Inc C 607 734-3671
Horseheads *(G-6314)*
Force Dynamics Inc F 607 546-5023
Trumansburg *(G-15640)*
General Cryogenic Tech LLC F 516 334-8200
Westbury *(G-16336)*
George Ponte Inc G 914 243-4202
Jefferson Valley *(G-6776)*
◆ **Germanow-Simon Corporation** E 585 232-1440
Rochester *(G-13832)*
Globalfoundries US Inc E 512 457-3900
Hopewell Junction *(G-6287)*
Gordon S Anderson Mfg Co G 845 677-3304
Millbrook *(G-8188)*
Haanen Packard Machinery Inc G 518 747-2330
Hudson Falls *(G-6382)*
Herbert Jaffe Inc G 718 392-1956
Long Island City *(G-7468)*
▲ **High Frequency Tech Co Inc** F 631 242-3020
Bohemia *(G-1032)*
▲ **Hitachi Metals America Ltd** E 914 694-9200
Purchase *(G-13390)*
Illinois Tool Works Inc C 716 681-8222
Lancaster *(G-7024)*
▲ **Innovation Associates Inc** C 607 798-9376
Johnson City *(G-6811)*
▼ **Innovation In Motion Inc** G 407 878-7561
Long Beach *(G-7359)*
Innovative Cleaning Solutions G 716 731-4408
Sanborn *(G-14547)*
Jado Sewing Machines Inc E 718 784-2314
Long Island City *(G-7478)*
James Morris E 315 824-8519
Hamilton *(G-5699)*
Kabar Manufacturing Corp E 631 694-1036
Farmingdale *(G-4798)*
▲ **Kabar Manufacturing Corp** E 631 694-6857
Farmingdale *(G-4797)*
Lam Research Corporation E 845 896-0606
Fishkill *(G-4947)*
▲ **Maharlika Holdings LLC** F 631 319-6203
Ronkonkoma *(G-14373)*
Michael Benalt Inc E 845 628-1008
Mahopac *(G-7708)*
▲ **Munson Machinery Company Inc** E 315 797-0090
Utica *(G-15724)*
◆ **National Equipment Corporation** F 718 585-0200
Harrison *(G-5731)*
National Equipment Corporation E 718 585-0200
Bronx *(G-1338)*
Northeast Data G 845 331-5554
Kingston *(G-6913)*
Nycon Diamond & Tools Corp G 855 937-6922
Bohemia *(G-1069)*
◆ **Optipro Systems LLC** D 585 265-0160
Ontario *(G-12659)*
P K G Equipment Incorporated E 585 436-4650
Rochester *(G-14003)*
▲ **Park Assist LLC** D 646 666-7525
New York *(G-11115)*
Parkmatic Car Prkg Systems LLC G 516 224-7700
Long Island City *(G-7548)*
Parkmatic Car Prkg Systems LLC G 800 422-5438
College Point *(G-3659)*
Pearl Technologies Inc E 315 365-3742
Savannah *(G-14623)*
◆ **Pfaudler Inc** B 585 235-1000
Rochester *(G-14014)*
▲ **Precision Process Inc** D 716 731-1587
Niagara Falls *(G-12327)*
◆ **Qes Solutions Inc** D 585 783-1455
Rochester *(G-14057)*
▲ **Quality Strapping Inc** D 718 418-1111
Brooklyn *(G-2369)*
▼ **Queenaire Technologies Inc** G 315 393-5454
Ogdensburg *(G-12578)*
R & B Machinery Corp G 716 894-3332
Buffalo *(G-3030)*
Reefer Tek Llc F 347 590-1067
Bronx *(G-1371)*
Reynolds Tech Fabricators Inc E 315 437-0532
East Syracuse *(G-4365)*
Rfb Associates Inc F 518 271-0551
Fort Edward *(G-5100)*
Riverview Associates Inc F 585 235-5980
Rochester *(G-14074)*
Shred Center G 716 664-3052
Jamestown *(G-6746)*
Sj Associates Inc E 516 942-3232
Jericho *(G-6804)*
▲ **Sonicor Inc** F 631 920-6555
West Babylon *(G-16194)*
Spectrum Catalysts Inc G 631 560-3683
Central Islip *(G-3384)*
Stainless Design Concepts Ltd E 845 246-3631
Saugerties *(G-14617)*
Surepure Inc G 917 368-8480
New York *(G-11750)*
T-Rex Supply Corporation G 516 308-0505
Hempstead *(G-6026)*
Technic Inc F 516 349-0700
Plainview *(G-13092)*
Tompkins Srm LLC G 315 422-8763
Syracuse *(G-15444)*
Ui Acquisition Holding Co G 607 779-7522
Conklin *(G-3736)*
Ui Holding Company G 607 779-7522
Conklin *(G-3737)*
▲ **Ultrepet LLC** D 781 275-6400
Albany *(G-138)*
◆ **Universal Instruments Corp** C 800 842-9732
Conklin *(G-3738)*
Universal Thin Film Lab Corp G 845 562-0601
Newburgh *(G-12249)*
▲ **Valplast International Corp** F 516 442-3923
Westbury *(G-16385)*
▲ **Veeco Instruments Inc** B 516 677-0200
Plainview *(G-13099)*
Vistec Lithography, Inc E 518 874-3000
Watervliet *(G-16056)*
West Metal Works Inc E 716 895-4900
Buffalo *(G-3128)*
Wilt Industries Inc G 518 548-4961
Lake Pleasant *(G-6979)*

3561 Pumps & Pumping Eqpt

Air Flow Pump Corp G 718 241-2800
Brooklyn *(G-1495)*
▲ **Air Techniques Inc** B 516 433-7676
Melville *(G-8000)*
◆ **Armstrong Pumps Inc** D 716 693-8813
North Tonawanda *(G-12412)*
▲ **Buffalo Pumps Inc** C 716 693-1850
North Tonawanda *(G-12420)*
Century-Tech Inc F 718 326-9400
Hempstead *(G-6009)*
Curaegis Technologies Inc E 585 254-1100
Rochester *(G-13729)*
Daikin Applied Americas Inc D 315 253-2771
Auburn *(G-475)*
▲ **Federal Pump Corporation** E 718 451-2000
New York *(G-9791)*
Fisonic Corp G 212 732-3777
Long Island City *(G-7450)*
▲ **Fisonic Corp** F 716 763-0295
New York *(G-9814)*
Flow Control LLC C 914 323-5700
Rye Brook *(G-14492)*
▲ **Fluid Handling LLC** G 716 897-2800
Cheektowaga *(G-3445)*
▲ **Gardner Dnver Oberdorfer Pumps** E 315 437-0361
Syracuse *(G-15330)*
Geopump Inc G 585 798-6666
Medina *(G-7979)*
Goulds Pumps (ipg) LLC G 315 568-2811
Seneca Falls *(G-14773)*
◆ **Goulds Pumps LLC** A 315 568-2811
Seneca Falls *(G-14774)*
Goulds Pumps LLC E 315 568-2811
Seneca Falls *(G-14775)*
ITT Corporation D 315 568-2811
Seneca Falls *(G-14777)*
ITT Goulds Pumps Inc A 914 641-2129
Seneca Falls *(G-14779)*
▲ **John N Fehlinger Co Inc** F 212 233-5656
New York *(G-10353)*
Ketcham Pump Co Inc F 718 457-0800
Woodside *(G-16660)*
Lanco Manufacturing Co G 516 292-8953
West Hempstead *(G-16220)*
◆ **Liberty Pumps Inc** C 800 543-2550
Bergen *(G-824)*
Linde LLC D 716 773-7552
Grand Island *(G-5506)*
▲ **Mannesmann Corporation** D 212 258-4000
New York *(G-10691)*
McWane Inc B 607 734-2211
Elmira *(G-4497)*
Oberdorfer Pumps Inc E 315 437-0361
Syracuse *(G-15383)*
▲ **Oyster Bay Pump Works Inc** F 516 933-4500
Hicksville *(G-6119)*
Pentair Water Pool and Spa Inc E 845 452-5500
Lagrangeville *(G-6961)*
◆ **Pulsafeeder Inc** C 585 292-8000
Rochester *(G-14054)*
Pumpcrete Corporation G 716 667-7867
Orchard Park *(G-12739)*
▲ **Sihi Pumps Inc** E 716 773-6450
Grand Island *(G-5513)*
▲ **Stavo Industries Inc** F 845 331-4552
Kingston *(G-6920)*
Trench & Marine Pump Co Inc E 212 423-9098
Bronx *(G-1405)*
◆ **Voss Usa Inc** C 212 995-2255
New York *(G-12056)*
◆ **Wastecorp Pumps LLC** F 888 829-2783
New York *(G-12076)*
Water Cooling Corp G 718 723-6500
Rosedale *(G-14442)*
Westmoor Ltd F 315 363-1500
Sherrill *(G-14825)*
Xylem Inc F 716 862-4123
Seneca Falls *(G-14789)*
Xylem Inc C 315 258-4949
Auburn *(G-510)*
Xylem Inc D 315 239-2499
Seneca Falls *(G-14790)*
Xylem Inc B 914 323-5700
Rye Brook *(G-14496)*

3562 Ball & Roller Bearings

A Hyatt Ball Co Ltd G 518 747-0272
Fort Edward *(G-5093)*
American Refuse Supply Inc G 718 893-8157
Bronx *(G-1219)*
David Fehlman G 315 455-8888
Syracuse *(G-15303)*
◆ **Dimanco Inc** G 315 797-0470
Utica *(G-15695)*
◆ **General Bearing Corporation** C 845 358-6000
West Nyack *(G-16270)*
▲ **Kilian Manufacturing Corp** D 315 432-0700
Syracuse *(G-15355)*
Lemoyne Machine Products Corp G 315 454-0708
Syracuse *(G-15359)*
▲ **Mageba USA LLC** E 212 317-1991
New York *(G-10662)*
▲ **Nes Bearing Company Inc** E 716 372-6532
Olean *(G-12605)*
Raydon Precision Bearing Co G 516 887-2582
Lynbrook *(G-7671)*
▼ **Sandle Custom Bearing Corp** G 585 593-7000
Wellsville *(G-16121)*
▲ **Schatz Bearing Corporation** D 845 452-6000
Poughkeepsie *(G-13365)*
SKF USA Inc D 716 661-2869
Falconer *(G-4691)*
SKF USA Inc D 716 661-2600
Falconer *(G-4692)*
SKF USA Inc D 716 661-2600
Jamestown *(G-6747)*
Workshop Art Fabrication F 845 331-0385
Kingston *(G-6932)*

35 INDUSTRIAL AND COMMERCIAL MACHINERY AND COMPUTER EQUIPMENT

3563 Air & Gas Compressors

▲ Adams Sfc Inc .... E 716 877-2608
Tonawanda (G-15519)
▲ Air Techniques Inc .... B 516 433-7676
Melville (G-8000)
◆ Atlas Copco Comptec LLC .... B 518 765-3344
Voorheesville (G-15879)
Auto Body Services LLC .... F 631 431-4640
Lindenhurst (G-7162)
Bedford Precision Parts Corp .... E 914 241-2211
Bedford Hills (G-772)
Buffalo Compressed Air Inc .... G 716 783-8673
Cheektowaga (G-3436)
◆ Chapin International Inc .... C 585 343-3140
Batavia (G-617)
▲ Chapin Manufacturing Inc .... C 585 343-3140
Batavia (G-618)
Comairco Equipment Inc .... G 716 656-0211
Cheektowaga (G-3437)
▲ Cooper Turbocompressor Inc .... B 716 896-6600
Buffalo (G-2781)
▲ Crosman Corporation .... E 585 657-6161
Bloomfield (G-951)
Crosman Corporation .... E 585 398-3920
Farmington (G-4911)
▲ Cyclone Air Power Inc .... G 718 447-3038
Staten Island (G-15067)
Dresser-Rand (delaware) LLC .... G 607 937-2011
Painted Post (G-12839)
Dresser-Rand Group Inc .... D 716 375-3000
Olean (G-12599)
▲ Eastern Air Products LLC .... E 716 391-1866
Lancaster (G-7017)
▲ Edwards Vacuum LLC .... D 800 848-9800
Sanborn (G-14544)
◆ Fountainhead Group Inc .... C 315 736-0037
New York Mills (G-12186)
Fountainhead Group Inc .... C 708 598-7100
New York Mills (G-12187)
Gas Tchnlgy Enrgy Cncepts LLC .... G 716 831-9695
Buffalo (G-2841)
GM Components Holdings LLC .... B 716 439-2463
Lockport (G-7305)
GM Components Holdings LLC .... B 716 439-2011
Lockport (G-7306)
Graham Corporation .... B 585 343-2216
Batavia (G-626)
Ingersoll-Rand Company .... E 716 896-6600
Buffalo (G-2884)
Mahle Indstrbeteiligungen GMBH .... D 716 319-6700
Amherst (G-237)
▲ Precision Plus Vacuum Parts .... D 716 297-2039
Sanborn (G-14551)
Screw Compressor Tech Inc .... F 716 827-6600
Buffalo (G-3060)
Spfm Corp .... G 718 788-6800
Brooklyn (G-2503)
Turbopro Inc .... G 716 681-8651
Alden (G-177)
Vac Air Service Inc .... F 716 665-2206
Jamestown (G-6760)

3564 Blowers & Fans

Acme Engineering Products Inc .... E 518 236-5659
Mooers (G-8330)
Aeromed Inc .... G 518 843-9144
Utica (G-15677)
Air Crafters Inc .... C 631 471-7788
Ronkonkoma (G-14295)
Air Engineering Filters Inc .... G 914 238-5945
Chappaqua (G-3419)
Air Export Mechanical .... G 917 709-5310
Flushing (G-4981)
▲ Airgle Corporation .... E 866 501-7750
Ronkonkoma (G-14296)
American Filtration Tech Inc .... F 585 359-4130
West Henrietta (G-16228)
Apgn Inc .... E 518 324-4150
Plattsburgh (G-13106)
Applied Safety LLC .... G 718 608-6292
Long Island City (G-7383)
◆ Austin Air Systems Limited .... D 716 856-3700
Buffalo (G-2716)
Beecher Emssn Sltn Tchnlgs LLC ..... F 607 796-0149
Horseheads (G-6305)
Beltran Associates Inc .... E 718 252-2996
Brooklyn (G-1595)
▲ Beltran Technologies Inc .... E 718 338-3311
Brooklyn (G-1596)

▲ Buffalo Filter LLC .... D 716 835-7000
Lancaster (G-7011)
Camfil Usa Inc .... F 315 468-3849
Syracuse (G-15269)
▲ Canarm Ltd .... G 800 267-4427
Ogdensburg (G-12572)
Clean Gas Systems Inc .... E 631 467-1600
Commack (G-3686)
Daikin Applied Americas Inc .... D 315 253-2771
Auburn (G-475)
Delphi Powertrain Systems LLC .... B 585 359-6000
West Henrietta (G-16237)
◆ Ducon Technologies Inc .... F 631 694-1700
New York (G-9584)
Ducon Technologies Inc .... E 631 420-4900
Farmingdale (G-4753)
Dundas-Jafine Inc .... G 716 681-9690
Alden (G-170)
Filta Clean Co Inc .... G 718 495-3800
Brooklyn (G-1880)
Filtros Ltd .... E 585 586-8770
East Rochester (G-4285)
Flanders Precisionaire NY .... G 518 751-5640
Hudson (G-6349)
▲ Healthway Home Products Inc .... E 315 298-2904
Pulaski (G-13385)
Healthway Products Company .... E 315 207-1410
Oswego (G-12778)
◆ Hilliard Corporation .... B 607 733-7121
Elmira (G-4492)
Hilliard Corporation .... E 607 733-7121
Elmira (G-4493)
◆ Howden North America Inc .... D 803 741-2700
Depew (G-4092)
Howden North America Inc .... D 716 817-6900
Depew (G-4093)
Isolation Systems Inc .... F 716 694-6390
North Tonawanda (G-12435)
Jr Engineering Enterprise LLC .... G 716 909-2693
Grand Island (G-5504)
JT Systems Inc .... F 315 622-1980
Liverpool (G-7241)
▲ Low-Cost Mfg Co Inc .... E 516 627-3282
Carle Place (G-3268)
Moffitt Fan Corporation .... F 585 768-7010
Le Roy (G-7123)
Nexstar Holding Corp .... G 716 929-9000
Amherst (G-240)
▼ North American Filter Corp .... D 800 265-8943
Newark (G-12203)
◆ Northland Filter Intl LLC .... G 315 207-1410
Oswego (G-12782)
Oestreich Metal Works Inc .... G 315 463-4268
Syracuse (G-15384)
◆ Oneida Air Systems Inc .... E 315 476-5151
Syracuse (G-15387)
Parker-Hannifin Corporation .... G 716 685-4040
Lancaster (G-7037)
Phytofilter Technologies Inc .... G 518 507-6399
Saratoga Springs (G-14592)
Pliotron Company America LLC .... G 716 298-4457
Niagara Falls (G-12323)
▲ R P Fedder Corp .... E 585 288-1600
Rochester (G-14066)
Rapid Fan & Blower Inc .... F 718 786-2060
Long Island City (G-7571)
Roome Technologies Inc .... G 585 229-4437
Honeoye (G-6261)
▲ Rotron Incorporated .... B 845 679-2401
Woodstock (G-16687)
Rotron Incorporated .... E 845 679-2401
Woodstock (G-16688)
Sbb Inc .... G 315 422-2376
East Syracuse (G-4368)
Standard Motor Products Inc .... B 718 392-0200
Long Island City (G-7598)
Sullivan Bazinet Bongio Inc .... E 315 437-6500
Syracuse (G-15432)
Vent-A-Kiln Corporation .... G 716 876-2023
Buffalo (G-3116)
Veteran Air LLC .... G 315 720-1101
Syracuse (G-15453)

3565 Packaging Machinery

A & G Heat Sealing .... G 631 724-7764
Smithtown (G-14893)
All Packaging McHy & Sups Corp ..... F 631 588-7310
Ronkonkoma (G-14300)
Automecha International Ltd .... E 607 843-2235
Oxford (G-12807)

Brooks Bottling Co LLC .... F 607 432-1782
Oneonta (G-12627)
Crandall Filling Machinery Inc .... G 716 897-3486
Buffalo (G-2783)
Desu Machinery Corporation .... D 716 681-5798
Depew (G-4087)
◆ Dover Global Holdings Inc .... F 212 922-1640
New York (G-9562)
▲ Elmar Industries Inc .... D 716 681-5650
Depew (G-4088)
Filling Equipment Co Inc .... F 718 445-2111
College Point (G-3644)
Fourteen Arnold Ave Corp .... F 315 272-1700
Utica (G-15703)
Haines Equipment Inc .... F 607 566-8531
Avoca (G-516)
▲ Kabar Manufacturing Corp .... E 631 694-6857
Farmingdale (G-4797)
◆ Kaps-All Packaging Systems .... D 631 574-8778
Riverhead (G-13570)
Millwood Inc .... E 518 233-1475
Waterford (G-15978)
▲ Modern Packaging Inc .... D 631 595-2437
Deer Park (G-4011)
National Equipment Corporation .... E 718 585-0200
Bronx (G-1338)
Niagara Scientific Inc .... D 315 437-0821
East Syracuse (G-4360)
▲ Orics Industries Inc .... E 718 461-8613
Farmingdale (G-4839)
Overhead Door Corporation .... D 518 828-7652
Hudson (G-6366)
Pacemaker Packaging Corp .... F 718 458-1188
Woodside (G-16670)
◆ Packaging Dynamics Ltd .... F 631 563-4499
Bohemia (G-1071)
Reynolds Packaging McHy Inc .... D 716 358-6451
Falconer (G-4690)
Rfb Associates Inc .... E 518 271-0551
Fort Edward (G-5100)
Rota Pack Inc .... F 631 274-1037
Farmingdale (G-4869)
Save O Seal Corporation Inc .... G 914 592-3031
Elmsford (G-4563)
Sharon Manufacturing Co Inc .... G 631 242-8870
Deer Park (G-4045)
▲ Turbofil Packaging Mchs LLC .... F 914 239-3878
Mount Vernon (G-8451)
▲ Universal Packg Systems Inc .... A 631 543-2277
Hauppauge (G-5966)
Utleys Incorporated .... E 718 956-1661
Woodside (G-16682)
▲ Vetroelite Inc .... G 925 724-7900
New York (G-12019)
Volckening Inc .... E 718 748-0294
Brooklyn (G-2633)

3566 Speed Changers, Drives & Gears

American Torque Inc .... F 718 526-2433
Jamaica (G-6625)
▲ Biltron Automotive Products .... E 631 928-8613
Port Jeff STA (G-13212)
▲ Buffalo Gear Inc .... E 716 731-2100
Sanborn (G-14543)
Designatronics Incorporated .... B 516 328-3300
Hicksville (G-6080)
◆ Gleason Works .... A 585 473-1000
Rochester (G-13840)
Harmonic Drive LLC .... E 631 231-6630
Hauppauge (G-5840)
▲ Interparts International Inc .... E 516 576-2000
Plainview (G-13065)
◆ John G Rubino Inc .... E 315 253-7396
Auburn (G-486)
▲ Jrlon Inc .... D 315 597-4067
Palmyra (G-12855)
Khk Usa Inc .... E 516 248-3850
Mineola (G-8232)
Magna Products Corp .... E 585 647-2280
Rochester (G-13923)
McGuigan Inc .... E 631 750-6222
Bohemia (G-1057)
Niagara Gear Corporation .... E 716 874-3131
Buffalo (G-2967)
Nidec Indus Automtn USA LLC .... E 716 774-1193
Grand Island (G-5507)
▲ Nuttall Gear L L C .... E 716 298-4100
Niagara Falls (G-12317)
Oliver Gear Inc .... E 716 885-1080
Buffalo (G-2979)

Employee Codes: A=Over 500 employees, B=251-500
C=101-250, D=51-100, E=20-50, F=10-19, G=5-9

35 INDUSTRIAL AND COMMERCIAL MACHINERY AND COMPUTER EQUIPMENT

◆ Ondrivesus Corp .... E 516 771-6777
  Freeport *(G-5171)*
Peerless-Winsmith Inc .... C 716 592-9311
  Springville *(G-15019)*
Perfection Gear Inc .... C 716 592-9310
  Springville *(G-15020)*
Precipart Corporation .... C 631 694-3100
  Farmingdale *(G-4855)*
Precision Mechanisms Corp .... E 516 333-5955
  Westbury *(G-16366)*
◆ Renold Inc .... D 716 326-3121
  Westfield *(G-16396)*
Rochester Gear Inc .... E 585 254-5442
  Rochester *(G-14087)*
W J Albro Machine Works Inc .... G 631 345-0657
  Yaphank *(G-16728)*

3567 Indl Process Furnaces & Ovens

▲ Ambrell Corporation .... F 585 889-0236
  Rochester *(G-13623)*
◆ Buflovak LLC .... E 716 895-2100
  Buffalo *(G-2755)*
◆ Cooks Intl Ltd Lblty Co .... G 212 741-4407
  New York *(G-9394)*
Cosmos Electronic Machine Corp .... E 631 249-2535
  Farmingdale *(G-4740)*
Cvd Equipment Corporation .... F 631 582-4365
  Central Islip *(G-3366)*
▲ Embassy Industries Inc .... C 631 435-0209
  Hauppauge *(G-5820)*
▼ Fulton Volcanic Inc .... D 315 298-5121
  Pulaski *(G-13384)*
◆ Harper International Corp .... D 716 276-9900
  Buffalo *(G-2868)*
Harper International Corp .... G 716 276-9900
  Depew *(G-4091)*
▲ Hpi Co Inc .... B 718 851-2753
  Brooklyn *(G-1986)*
Igniter Systems Inc .... E 716 542-5511
  Akron *(G-19)*
J H Buhrmaster Company Inc .... C 518 843-1700
  Amsterdam *(G-341)*
Linde LLC .... D 716 773-7552
  Grand Island *(G-5506)*
Parker-Hannifin Corporation .... D 716 685-4040
  Lancaster *(G-7038)*
Radiant Pro Ltd .... G 516 763-5678
  Oceanside *(G-12552)*
Specified Air Solutions LLC .... E 716 852-4400
  Buffalo *(G-3074)*
Thermal Process Cnstr Co .... E 631 293-6400
  Farmingdale *(G-4894)*
Ultraflex Power Technologies .... G 631 467-6814
  Ronkonkoma *(G-14425)*
Vincent Genovese .... G 631 281-8170
  Mastic Beach *(G-7912)*

3568 Mechanical Power Transmission Eqpt, NEC

Advanced Thermal Systems Inc .... E 716 681-1800
  Lancaster *(G-7002)*
Babbitt Bearings Incorporated .... D 315 479-6603
  Syracuse *(G-15253)*
▲ Borgwarner Morse TEC LLC .... C 607 257-6700
  Ithaca *(G-6568)*
▲ BW Elliott Mfg Co LLC .... B 607 772-0404
  Binghamton *(G-873)*
C-Flex Bearing Co Inc .... F 315 895-7454
  Frankfort *(G-5104)*
Champlain Hudson Power Ex Inc .... G 518 465-0710
  Albany *(G-57)*
Designatronics Incorporated .... B 516 328-3300
  Hicksville *(G-6080)*
Eaw Electronic Systems Inc .... G 845 471-5290
  Poughkeepsie *(G-13336)*
▲ Fait Usa Inc .... G 215 674-5310
  New York *(G-9776)*
◆ Howden North America Inc .... D 803 741-2700
  Depew *(G-4092)*
Hudson Power Transmission Co .... G 718 622-3869
  Brooklyn *(G-1987)*
Huron TI Cutter Grinding Inc .... E 631 420-7000
  Farmingdale *(G-4782)*
Kaddis Manufacturing Corp .... G 585 624-3070
  Honeoye Falls *(G-6270)*
Kinemotive Corporation .... E 631 249-6440
  Farmingdale *(G-4803)*
Liston Manufacturing Inc .... E 716 695-2111
  North Tonawanda *(G-12437)*

Ls Power Equity Partners LP .... G 212 615-3456
  New York *(G-10622)*
Machine Components Corp .... E 516 694-7222
  Plainview *(G-13071)*
◆ Magtrol Inc .... E 716 668-5555
  Buffalo *(G-2935)*
Metallized Carbon Corporation .... C 914 941-3738
  Ossining *(G-12771)*
On Line Power Technologies .... G 914 968-4440
  Yonkers *(G-16787)*
▲ Package One Inc .... D 518 344-5425
  Schenectady *(G-14703)*
◆ Renold Inc .... D 716 326-3121
  Westfield *(G-16396)*
▲ Sepac Inc .... E 607 732-2030
  Elmira *(G-4502)*
◆ Watson Bowman Acme Corp .... C 716 691-8162
  Amherst *(G-260)*
York Industries Inc .... E 516 746-3736
  Garden City Park *(G-5290)*

3569 Indl Machinery & Eqpt, NEC

ACI Controls Inc .... F 800 333-7519
  West Seneca *(G-16293)*
Acme Engineering Products Inc .... E 518 236-5659
  Mooers *(G-8330)*
▲ Adams Sfc Inc .... E 716 877-2608
  Tonawanda *(G-15519)*
▲ Advanced Tchncal Solutions Inc .... F 914 214-8230
  Mahopac *(G-7707)*
Airsep Corporation .... D 716 691-0202
  Amherst *(G-208)*
▲ Alliance Automation Systems .... C 585 426-2700
  Rochester *(G-13615)*
Allied Inspection Services LLC .... F 716 489-3199
  Falconer *(G-4670)*
◆ American Felt & Filter Co Inc .... D 845 561-3560
  New Windsor *(G-8635)*
American Filtration Tech Inc .... F 585 359-4130
  West Henrietta *(G-16228)*
American Material Processing .... F 315 318-0017
  Phoenix *(G-12988)*
◆ Audubon Machinery Corporation .... D 716 564-5165
  North Tonawanda *(G-12414)*
Automated Cells & Eqp Inc .... E 607 936-1341
  Painted Post *(G-12835)*
Better Power Inc .... F 585 475-1321
  Rochester *(G-13661)*
Bowen Products Corporation .... G 315 498-4481
  Nedrow *(G-8478)*
◆ Bullex Inc .... F 518 689-2023
  Albany *(G-51)*
Burnett Process Inc .... F 585 277-1623
  Rochester *(G-13684)*
Cleaning Tech Group LLC .... F 716 665-2340
  Jamestown *(G-6707)*
◆ Cross Filtration Ltd Lblty Co .... G 315 412-1539
  Moravia *(G-8333)*
▲ Distech Systems Inc .... F 585 254-7020
  Rochester *(G-13744)*
Drasgow Inc .... E 585 786-3603
  Gainesville *(G-5240)*
Dynamasters Inc .... F 585 458-9970
  Rochester *(G-13753)*
Eastern Precision Mfg .... E 845 358-1951
  Nyack *(G-12506)*
▲ Filter Tech Inc .... D 315 682-8815
  Manlius *(G-7777)*
▲ Finesse Creations Inc .... F 718 692-2100
  Brooklyn *(G-1883)*
First Due Fire Equipment Inc .... F 845 222-1329
  Garnerville *(G-5300)*
Foseco Inc .... F 914 345-4760
  Tarrytown *(G-15478)*
◆ Fountainhead Group Inc .... F 315 736-0037
  New York Mills *(G-12186)*
Graver Technologies LLC .... F 585 624-1330
  Honeoye Falls *(G-6265)*
◆ Guyson Corporation of USa .... E 518 587-7894
  Saratoga Springs *(G-14585)*
◆ Hannay Reels Inc .... F 518 797-3791
  Westerlo *(G-16389)*
◆ Hilliard Corporation .... E 607 733-7121
  Elmira *(G-4492)*
Hilliard Corporation .... E 607 733-7121
  Elmira *(G-4493)*
Honeybee Robotics Ltd .... E 212 966-0661
  Brooklyn *(G-1984)*
▲ Hubco Inc .... G 716 683-5940
  Alden *(G-172)*

Island Automated Gate Co LLC .... G 631 425-0196
  Huntington Station *(G-6448)*
J H Robotics Inc .... E 607 729-3758
  Johnson City *(G-6812)*
Javlyn Process Systems LLC .... E 585 424-5580
  Rochester *(G-13893)*
Kyntec Corporation .... G 716 810-6956
  Buffalo *(G-2913)*
Lifc Corp .... G 516 426-5737
  Port Washington *(G-13282)*
Lydall Performance Mtls Inc .... F 518 273-6320
  Green Island *(G-5610)*
Markpericom .... G 516 208-6824
  Oceanside *(G-12548)*
McHone Industries Inc .... D 716 945-3380
  Salamanca *(G-14526)*
New Vision Industries Inc .... F 607 687-7700
  Endicott *(G-4604)*
▼ North American Filter Corp .... D 800 265-8943
  Newark *(G-12203)*
▲ Pall Corporation .... A 516 484-5400
  Port Washington *(G-13295)*
Pall Corporation .... A 607 753-6041
  Cortland *(G-3885)*
Parker-Hannifin Corporation .... D 716 685-4040
  Lancaster *(G-7037)*
Peerless Mfg Co .... E 716 539-7400
  Orchard Park *(G-12736)*
Peregrine Industries Inc .... G 631 838-2870
  New York *(G-11153)*
Pyrotek Incorporated .... E 716 731-3221
  Sanborn *(G-14552)*
Quality Manufacturing Sys LLC .... G 716 763-0988
  Lakewood *(G-6995)*
◆ Reliable Autmtc Sprnklr Co Inc .... B 800 431-1588
  Elmsford *(G-4562)*
Rfb Associates Inc .... F 518 271-0551
  Fort Edward *(G-5100)*
▲ SC Supply Chain Management LLC .... G 212 344-3322
  New York *(G-11498)*
Sentry Automatic Sprinkler .... F 631 723-3095
  Riverhead *(G-13584)*
Service Filtration Corp .... E 716 877-2608
  Tonawanda *(G-15577)*
Sidco Filter Corporation .... E 585 289-3100
  Manchester *(G-7762)*
Sigelock Systems LLC .... G 888 744-3562
  Oceanside *(G-12557)*
Sinclair International Company .... D 518 798-2361
  Queensbury *(G-13442)*
▲ Sonicor Inc .... F 631 920-6555
  West Babylon *(G-16194)*
▲ Stavo Industries Inc .... F 845 331-4552
  Kingston *(G-6920)*
Stavo Industries Inc .... E 845 331-5389
  Kingston *(G-6921)*
▲ Sussman-Automatic Corporation .... D 347 609-7652
  Long Island City *(G-7611)*
▲ Taylor Devices Inc .... C 716 694-0800
  North Tonawanda *(G-12459)*
▲ Trident Precision Mfg Inc .... F 585 265-2010
  Webster *(G-16103)*
Tyco Simplexgrinnell .... E 315 437-9664
  East Syracuse *(G-4376)*
Universal Metal Fabricators .... B 845 331-8248
  Kingston *(G-6927)*
▲ Veeco Process Equipment Inc .... C 516 677-0200
  Plainview *(G-13100)*
William R Shoemaker Inc .... E 716 649-0511
  Hamburg *(G-5697)*

3571 Electronic Computers

Apple Commuter Inc .... G 917 299-0066
  New Hyde Park *(G-8516)*
Apple Healing & Relaxation .... G 718 278-1089
  Long Island City *(G-7382)*
Apple Intercom and Elec Inc .... G 914 633-5101
  New Rochelle *(G-8590)*
Apple Med Urgent Care PC .... G 914 523-5965
  Mount Vernon *(G-8377)*
▲ Argon Corp .... E 516 487-5314
  Great Neck *(G-5536)*
Arnouse Digital Devices Corp .... E 516 673-4444
  New Hyde Park *(G-8517)*
B-Reel Films Inc .... E 917 388-3836
  New York *(G-8994)*
Bak USA Technologies Corp .... E 716 248-2704
  Buffalo *(G-2722)*
▲ Binghamton Simulator Co Inc .... E 607 321-2980
  Binghamton *(G-868)*

SIC SECTION
35 INDUSTRIAL AND COMMERCIAL MACHINERY AND COMPUTER EQUIPMENT

Computer Conversions Corp ... E ... 631 261-3300
East Northport *(G-4261)*
Critical Link LLC ... E ... 315 425-4045
Syracuse *(G-15294)*
Data-Pac Mailing Systems Corp ... F ... 585 671-0210
Webster *(G-16081)*
Datacom Systems Inc ... E ... 315 463-9541
East Syracuse *(G-4334)*
Dees Audio & Vision ... G ... 585 719-9256
Rochester *(G-13738)*
▲ **Digicom International Inc** ... F ... 631 249-8999
Farmingdale *(G-4751)*
Doar Inc ... G ... 516 872-8140
Lynbrook *(G-7664)*
▲ **Dynamic Decisions Inc** ... F ... 908 755-5000
Fresh Meadows *(G-5196)*
▲ **E-Systems Group LLC** ... E ... 607 775-1100
Conklin *(G-3727)*
Ebc Technologies LLC ... D ... 631 729-8182
Hauppauge *(G-5817)*
Electronic Systems Inc ... G ... 631 589-4389
Holbrook *(G-6184)*
▲ **Elo Touch Solutions Inc** ... E ... 585 427-2802
Rochester *(G-13777)*
Envent Systems Inc ... G ... 646 294-6980
Pelham *(G-12935)*
Facsimile Cmmncations Inds Inc ... D ... 212 741-6400
New York *(G-9770)*
G S Communications USA Inc ... E ... 718 389-7371
Brooklyn *(G-1913)*
Go Go Apple Inc ... G ... 646 264-8909
Elmhurst *(G-4465)*
Group Enterainment LLC ... G ... 212 868-5233
New York *(G-9997)*
H&L Computers Inc ... E ... 516 873-8088
Flushing *(G-5005)*
▲ **Hand Held Products Inc** ... B ... 315 554-6000
Skaneateles Falls *(G-14879)*
Hi-Tech Advanced Solutions Inc ... F ... 718 926-3488
Forest Hills *(G-5075)*
HP Inc ... E ... 650 857-1501
Albany *(G-85)*
HP Inc ... F ... 650 857-1501
New York *(G-10140)*
Human Electronics Inc ... G ... 315 724-9850
Utica *(G-15710)*
IBM World Trade Corporation ... G ... 914 765-1900
Armonk *(G-403)*
Irpenscom ... G ... 585 507-7997
Penfield *(G-12941)*
J & N Computer Services Inc ... F ... 585 388-8780
Fairport *(G-4636)*
▲ **Kemp Technologies Inc** ... E ... 631 345-5292
New York *(G-10429)*
M&C Associates LLC ... E ... 631 467-8760
Hauppauge *(G-5875)*
Medsim-Eagle Simulation Inc ... F ... 607 658-9354
Endicott *(G-4601)*
N & G of America Inc ... F ... 516 428-3414
Plainview *(G-13076)*
N & L Instruments Inc ... F ... 631 471-4000
Ronkonkoma *(G-14382)*
NCR Corporation ... C ... 516 876-7200
Jericho *(G-6795)*
Northpoint Digital LLC ... G ... 212 819-1700
New York *(G-10996)*
▲ **Partech Inc** ... C ... 315 738-0600
New Hartford *(G-8509)*
Photon Vision Systems Inc ... F ... 607 749-2689
Homer *(G-6258)*
Policy ADM Solutions Inc ... E ... 914 332-4320
Tarrytown *(G-15486)*
Qualtronic Devices Inc ... F ... 631 360-0859
Smithtown *(G-14908)*
Revivn Public Benefit Corp ... F ... 347 762-8193
Brooklyn *(G-2399)*
Stargate Computer Corp ... G ... 516 474-4799
Port Jeff STA *(G-13217)*
▲ **Telxon Corporation** ... E ... 631 738-2400
Holtsville *(G-6248)*
Todd Enterprises Inc ... D ... 516 773-8087
Great Neck *(G-5595)*
▲ **Toshiba Amer Info Systems Inc** ... B ... 949 583-3000
New York *(G-11871)*
◆ **Toshiba America Inc** ... E ... 212 596-0600
New York *(G-11872)*
Transland Sourcing LLC ... G ... 718 596-5704
Brooklyn *(G-2580)*
Wantagh Computer Center ... F ... 516 826-2189
Wantagh *(G-15927)*
Wilcro Inc ... G ... 716 632-4204
Buffalo *(G-3130)*
Yellow E House Inc ... G ... 718 888-2000
Flushing *(G-5061)*

3572 Computer Storage Devices

Datalink Computer Products ... F ... 914 666-2358
Mount Kisco *(G-8341)*
EMC Corporation ... C ... 212 564-6866
New York *(G-9666)*
Emcs LLC ... G ... 716 523-2002
Hamburg *(G-5678)*
Formats Unlimited Inc ... F ... 631 249-9200
Deer Park *(G-3978)*
Garland Technology LLC ... E ... 716 242-8500
Buffalo *(G-2840)*
Gim Electronics Corp ... F ... 516 942-3382
Hicksville *(G-6090)*
Globalfoundries US Inc ... D ... 518 305-9013
Malta *(G-7730)*
Matrox Graphics Inc ... G ... 518 561-4417
Plattsburgh *(G-13132)*
Quantum Asset Recovery ... G ... 716 393-2712
Buffalo *(G-3026)*
Quantum Knowledge LLC ... G ... 631 727-6111
Riverhead *(G-13580)*
Quantum Logic Corp ... G ... 516 746-1380
New Hyde Park *(G-8560)*
Quantum Mechanics Ny LLC ... G ... 917 519-7077
Huntington *(G-6408)*
Sale 121 Corp ... D ... 240 855-8988
New York *(G-11467)*
◆ **Sony Corporation of America** ... C ... 212 833-8000
New York *(G-11645)*
▲ **Technologies Application LLC** ... F ... 607 275-0345
Cortland *(G-3896)*
Todd Enterprises Inc ... D ... 516 773-8087
Great Neck *(G-5595)*
▲ **Toshiba Amer Info Systems Inc** ... B ... 949 583-3000
New York *(G-11871)*
William S Hein & Co Inc ... C ... 716 882-2600
Getzville *(G-5356)*

3575 Computer Terminals

AG Neovo Professional Inc ... F ... 212 647-9080
New York *(G-8767)*
Cine Design Group LLC ... G ... 646 747-0734
New York *(G-9299)*
▲ **Clayton Dubilier & Rice Fun** ... E ... 212 407-5200
New York *(G-9324)*
Doar Inc ... G ... 516 872-8140
Lynbrook *(G-7664)*
Igt Global Solutions Corp ... D ... 518 382-2900
Schenectady *(G-14689)*
Integra Microsystem 1988 Inc ... G ... 718 609-6099
Brooklyn *(G-2006)*
Nu - Communitek LLC ... F ... 516 433-3553
Hicksville *(G-6115)*
Orbit International Corp ... D ... 631 435-8300
Hauppauge *(G-5907)*
PC Solutions & Consulting ... G ... 607 735-0466
Elmira *(G-4499)*
Shadowtv Inc ... G ... 212 445-2540
New York *(G-11552)*
Symbio Technologies LLC ... G ... 914 576-1205
White Plains *(G-16510)*
▲ **Touchstone Technology Inc** ... F ... 585 458-2690
Rochester *(G-14173)*
Ultra-Scan Corporation ... F ... 716 832-6269
Amherst *(G-259)*
Wey Inc ... G ... 212 532-3299
New York *(G-12099)*

3577 Computer Peripheral Eqpt, NEC

A I T Computers Inc ... G ... 518 266-9010
Troy *(G-15599)*
Aalborg Instrs & Contrls Inc ... D ... 845 398-3160
Orangeburg *(G-12667)*
Advanced Barcode Tech Inc ... F ... 516 570-8100
Great Neck *(G-5527)*
Aero-Vision Technologies Inc ... G ... 631 643-8349
Melville *(G-7998)*
Aeroflex Plainview Inc ... C ... 631 231-9100
Hauppauge *(G-5756)*
◆ **Andrea Electronics Corporation** ... G ... 631 719-1800
Bohemia *(G-980)*
Annese & Associates Inc ... G ... 716 972-0076
Buffalo *(G-2701)*
▲ **Anorad Corporation** ... C ... 631 344-6600
Shirley *(G-14827)*
Aruba Networks Inc ... G ... 732 343-1305
New York *(G-8927)*
Atlaz International Ltd ... F ... 516 239-1854
Lawrence *(G-7102)*
▲ **Aventura Technologies Inc** ... E ... 631 300-4000
Commack *(G-3680)*
B V M Associates ... G ... 631 254-6220
Shirley *(G-14831)*
▲ **Binghamton Simulator Co Inc** ... E ... 607 321-2980
Binghamton *(G-868)*
Blue Skies ... G ... 631 392-1140
Deer Park *(G-3953)*
Broadnet Technologies Inc ... F ... 315 443-3694
Syracuse *(G-15262)*
Chemung Cnty Chpter Nysarc Inc ... C ... 607 734-6151
Elmira *(G-4477)*
Cisco Systems Inc ... C ... 212 714-4000
New York *(G-9304)*
▲ **Clayton Dubilier & Rice Fun** ... E ... 212 407-5200
New York *(G-9324)*
CNy Business Solutions ... G ... 315 733-5031
Utica *(G-15683)*
Control Logic Corporation ... G ... 607 965-6423
West Burlington *(G-16206)*
▲ **Data Device Corporation** ... B ... 631 567-5600
Bohemia *(G-1008)*
Datatran Labs Inc ... G ... 845 856-4313
Port Jervis *(G-13227)*
▲ **Digiorange Inc** ... G ... 718 787-1500
Brooklyn *(G-1776)*
▲ **Dynamic Decisions Inc** ... F ... 908 755-5000
Fresh Meadows *(G-5196)*
Eastman Kodak Company ... B ... 585 724-4000
Rochester *(G-13761)*
Ems Development Corporation ... D ... 631 345-6200
Yaphank *(G-16709)*
Epicor Software Corporation ... E ... 805 496-6789
Schenectady *(G-14673)*
Future Star Digatech ... F ... 718 666-0350
Brooklyn *(G-1911)*
◆ **Gasoft Equipment Inc** ... F ... 845 863-1010
Newburgh *(G-12223)*
Glowa Manufacturing Inc ... E ... 607 770-0811
Binghamton *(G-887)*
▲ **Hand Held Products Inc** ... B ... 315 554-6000
Skaneateles Falls *(G-14879)*
Hand Held Products Inc ... G ... 315 554-6000
Skaneateles Falls *(G-14880)*
▲ **Hauppauge Computer Works Inc** ... E ... 631 434-1600
Hauppauge *(G-5841)*
▲ **Hauppauge Digital Inc** ... E ... 631 434-1600
Hauppauge *(G-5842)*
◆ **Hergo Ergonomic Support** ... E ... 718 894-0639
Maspeth *(G-7851)*
Hf Technologies LLC ... E ... 585 254-5030
Hamlin *(G-5700)*
▲ **Hitachi Metals America Ltd** ... E ... 914 694-9200
Purchase *(G-13390)*
◆ **Humanscale Corporation** ... E ... 212 725-4749
New York *(G-10150)*
IBM World Trade Corporation ... G ... 914 765-1900
Armonk *(G-403)*
Innovative Systems of New York ... G ... 516 541-7410
Massapequa Park *(G-7892)*
Iweb Design Inc ... F ... 805 243-8305
Bronx *(G-1299)*
Jadak Technologies Inc ... C ... 315 701-0678
North Syracuse *(G-12407)*
▲ **Kantek Inc** ... E ... 516 594-4600
Oceanside *(G-12544)*
Lsc Peripherals Incorporated ... G ... 631 244-0707
Bohemia *(G-1051)*
Luminescent Systems Inc ... B ... 716 655-0800
East Aurora *(G-4204)*
Macrolink Inc ... E ... 631 924-8200
Medford *(G-7960)*
Maia Systems LLC ... G ... 718 206-0100
Jamaica *(G-6658)*
Marco Manufacturing Inc ... E ... 845 485-1571
Poughkeepsie *(G-13353)*
Mdi Holdings LLC ... A ... 212 559-1127
New York *(G-10747)*
Medsim-Eagle Simulation Inc ... F ... 607 658-9354
Endicott *(G-4601)*
Mg Imaging ... G ... 212 704-4073
New York *(G-10787)*
Mirion Technologies Ist Corp ... D ... 607 562-4300
Horseheads *(G-6321)*
▲ **Mp Displays LLC** ... G ... 845 268-4113
Valley Cottage *(G-15760)*

SIC

Employee Codes: A=Over 500 employees, B=251-500
C=101-250, D=51-100, E=20-50, F=10-19, G=5-9
2019 Harris
New York Manufacturers Directory
765

NCR Corporation..................C....... 607 273-5310
Ithaca *(G-6599)*
▲ **Norazza Inc**..................G....... 716 706-1160
Buffalo *(G-2973)*
▲ **O Rama Light Inc**..................E....... 518 539-9000
South Glens Falls *(G-14940)*
Office Grabs LLC..................G....... 347 678-3993
Brooklyn *(G-2284)*
Orbit International Corp..................D....... 631 435-8300
Hauppauge *(G-5907)*
P C Rfrs Radiology..................G....... 212 586-5700
Long Island City *(G-7544)*
Pda Panache Corp..................G....... 631 776-0523
Bohemia *(G-1073)*
Peak Performance Design LLC..................G....... 518 302-9198
Lake Placid *(G-6977)*
Peoples Choice M R I..................F....... 716 681-7377
Buffalo *(G-2997)*
Performance Technologies Inc..................E....... 585 256-0200
Rochester *(G-14012)*
Phoenix Venture Fund LLC..................E....... 212 759-1909
New York *(G-11185)*
▲ **QED Technologies Intl Inc**..................E....... 585 256-6540
Rochester *(G-14056)*
▲ **Rdi Inc**..................F....... 914 773-1000
Mount Kisco *(G-8357)*
Reliable Elec Mt Vernon Inc..................E....... 914 668-4440
Mount Vernon *(G-8439)*
Rodale Wireless Inc..................E....... 631 231-0044
Hauppauge *(G-5929)*
Ruhle Companies Inc..................E....... 914 287-4000
Valhalla *(G-15747)*
S G I..................G....... 917 386-0385
New York *(G-11457)*
Scroll Media Inc..................G....... 617 395-8904
New York *(G-11524)*
▲ **Sima Technologies LLC**..................G....... 412 828-9130
Hauppauge *(G-5940)*
◆ **Sony Corporation of America**..................C....... 212 833-8000
New York *(G-11645)*
▲ **Symbol Technologies LLC**..................A....... 631 737-6851
Holtsville *(G-6246)*
Symbol Technologies LLC..................F....... 631 738-2400
Bohemia *(G-1093)*
Symbol Technologies LLC..................F....... 631 218-3907
Holbrook *(G-6214)*
T&K Printing Inc..................F....... 718 439-9454
Brooklyn *(G-2550)*
▲ **Technomag Inc**..................G....... 631 246-6142
East Setauket *(G-4311)*
Todd Enterprises Inc..................D....... 516 773-8087
Great Neck *(G-5595)*
Torrent Ems LLC..................F....... 716 312-4099
Lockport *(G-7337)*
▲ **Toshiba Amer Info Systems Inc**..................B....... 949 583-3000
New York *(G-11871)*
Transact Technologies Inc..................D....... 607 257-8901
Ithaca *(G-6613)*
Vader Systems LLC..................F....... 716 688-1600
Getzville *(G-5355)*
▲ **Vishay Thin Film LLC**..................C....... 716 283-4025
Niagara Falls *(G-12348)*
Vuzix Corporation..................E....... 585 359-5900
West Henrietta *(G-16253)*
Wantagh Computer Center..................F....... 516 826-2189
Wantagh *(G-15927)*
▼ **Watson Productions LLC**..................F....... 516 334-9766
Hauppauge *(G-5973)*
Welch Allyn Inc..................A....... 315 685-4100
Skaneateles Falls *(G-14882)*
Wilson & Wilson Group..................G....... 212 729-4736
Forest Hills *(G-5082)*
X Brand Editions..................G....... 718 482-7646
Long Island City *(G-7643)*
Xerox Corporation..................C....... 585 427-4500
Rochester *(G-14214)*
▲ **Z-Axis Inc**..................D....... 315 548-5000
Phelps *(G-12984)*
Zebra Technologies Entp Corp..................E....... 800 722-6234
Holtsville *(G-6251)*

3578 Calculating & Accounting Eqpt

Gary Roth & Associates Ltd..................E....... 516 333-1000
Westbury *(G-16335)*
▲ **Hand Held Products Inc**..................B....... 315 554-6000
Skaneateles Falls *(G-14879)*
International Mdse Svcs Inc..................G....... 914 699-4000
Mount Vernon *(G-8409)*
Jpmorgan Chase Bank Nat Assn..................G....... 718 767-3592
College Point *(G-3651)*
K&G of Syracuse Inc..................G....... 315 446-1921
Syracuse *(G-15353)*
Kenney Manufacturing Displays..................F....... 631 231-5563
Brentwood *(G-1139)*
◆ **Logic Controls Inc**..................E....... 516 248-0400
Bethpage *(G-845)*
Merchant Service Pymnt Access..................G....... 212 561-5516
Uniondale *(G-15671)*
Mid Enterprise Inc..................G....... 631 924-3933
Middle Island *(G-8118)*
▲ **Parabit Systems Inc**..................E....... 516 378-4800
Bellmore *(G-791)*
Powa Technologies Inc..................E....... 347 344-7848
New York *(G-11225)*
Stanson Automated LLC..................F....... 866 505-7826
Yonkers *(G-16799)*

3579 Office Machines, NEC

Action Technologies Inc..................G....... 718 278-1000
Long Island City *(G-7367)*
Automecha International Ltd..................E....... 607 843-2235
Oxford *(G-12807)*
Central Time Clock Inc..................F....... 718 784-4900
Long Island City *(G-7407)*
Cummins - Allison Corp..................D....... 718 263-2482
Kew Gardens *(G-6871)*
Gradual LLC..................F....... 347 293-0974
Long Island City *(G-7459)*
National Time Recording Eqp Co..................F....... 212 227-3310
New York *(G-10887)*
Neopost USA Inc..................E....... 631 435-9100
Hauppauge *(G-5900)*
Pitney Bowes Inc..................E....... 212 564-7548
New York *(G-11200)*
Pitney Bowes Inc..................E....... 203 356-5000
New York *(G-11201)*
Pitney Bowes Inc..................C....... 518 283-0345
Troy *(G-15616)*
Pitney Bowes Inc..................E....... 516 822-0900
Jericho *(G-6797)*
▲ **Staplex Company Inc**..................E....... 718 768-3333
Brooklyn *(G-2508)*
Widmer Time Recorder Company..................F....... 212 227-0405
New York *(G-12108)*

3581 Automatic Vending Machines

American Lckr SEC Systems Inc..................E....... 716 699-2773
Ellicottville *(G-4444)*
Cubic Trnsp Systems Inc..................F....... 212 255-1810
New York *(G-9431)*
Global Payment Tech Inc..................F....... 516 887-0700
Valley Stream *(G-15781)*
▲ **Global Payment Tech Inc**..................E....... 631 563-2500
Bohemia *(G-1030)*
Green Enviro Machine LLC..................G....... 407 461-6412
Schenectady *(G-14685)*
Vengo Inc..................G....... 866 526-7054
Bethpage *(G-853)*

3582 Commercial Laundry, Dry Clean & Pressing Mchs

Fowler Route Co Inc..................D....... 917 653-4640
Yonkers *(G-16760)*
▲ **G A Braun Inc**..................C....... 315 475-3123
North Syracuse *(G-12401)*
G A Braun Inc..................E....... 315 475-3123
Syracuse *(G-15327)*
Lb Laundry Inc..................G....... 347 399-8030
Flushing *(G-5021)*
Lynx Product Group LLC..................E....... 716 751-3100
Wilson *(G-16601)*
▼ **Maxi Companies Inc**..................G....... 315 446-1002
De Witt *(G-3930)*
Q Omni Inc..................G....... 914 962-2726
Yorktown Heights *(G-16821)*
Thermopatch Corporation..................D....... 315 446-8110
Syracuse *(G-15443)*

3585 Air Conditioning & Heating Eqpt

A Nuclimate Qulty Systems Inc..................F....... 315 431-0226
Syracuse *(G-15236)*
A&S Refrigeration Equipment..................G....... 718 993-6030
Bronx *(G-1203)*
AC Air Cooling Co Inc..................F....... 718 933-1011
Bronx *(G-1206)*
Advance Energy Tech Inc..................E....... 518 371-2140
Halfmoon *(G-5660)*
Alfa Laval Kathabar Inc..................C....... 716 875-2000
Tonawanda *(G-15520)*
American Refrigeration Inc..................G....... 212 699-4000
New York *(G-8836)*
▲ **Atmost Refrigeration Co Inc**..................G....... 518 828-2180
Hudson *(G-6342)*
Balticare Inc..................F....... 646 380-9470
New York *(G-9008)*
Besicorp Ltd..................F....... 845 336-7700
Kingston *(G-6889)*
Bombardier Trnsp Holdings USA..................D....... 607 776-4791
Bath *(G-641)*
Carrier Corporation..................B....... 315 463-5744
East Syracuse *(G-4328)*
Carrier Corporation..................A....... 315 432-6000
Syracuse *(G-15273)*
Carrier Corporation..................B....... 315 432-6000
East Syracuse *(G-4329)*
Carrier Corporation..................B....... 315 432-3844
East Syracuse *(G-4330)*
Carrier Corporation..................B....... 315 432-6000
Syracuse *(G-15272)*
Chudnow Manufacturing Co Inc..................E....... 516 593-4222
Oceanside *(G-12533)*
Cleanroom Systems Inc..................E....... 315 452-7400
North Syracuse *(G-12398)*
Coil Craft Inc..................G....... 718 369-1210
Ozone Park *(G-12823)*
Colburns AC Rfrgn..................F....... 716 569-3695
Frewsburg *(G-5207)*
▲ **Columbia Pool Accessories Inc**..................G....... 718 993-0389
Bronx *(G-1244)*
Daikin Applied Americas Inc..................D....... 315 253-2771
Auburn *(G-475)*
Dundas-Jafine Inc..................E....... 716 681-9690
Alden *(G-170)*
▲ **Duro Dyne Corporation**..................C....... 631 249-9000
Bay Shore *(G-682)*
◆ **Duro Dyne Machinery Corp**..................E....... 631 249-9000
Bay Shore *(G-683)*
Economy Pump & Motor Repr Inc..................G....... 718 433-2600
Astoria *(G-425)*
Elima-Draft Incorporated..................G....... 631 375-2830
Stony Brook *(G-15165)*
EMC Tech Inc..................F....... 716 488-9071
Falconer *(G-4676)*
Empire Air Systems LLC..................F....... 718 377-1549
Brooklyn *(G-1832)*
▲ **Enviromaster International LLC**..................D....... 315 336-3716
Rome *(G-14250)*
Environmental Temp Systems LLC..................G....... 516 640-5818
Mineola *(G-8218)*
Foster Refrigerators Entp..................F....... 518 671-6036
Hudson *(G-6350)*
Fts Systems Inc..................D....... 845 687-5300
Stone Ridge *(G-15161)*
GM Components Holdings LLC..................B....... 716 439-2463
Lockport *(G-7305)*
GM Components Holdings LLC..................B....... 716 439-2011
Lockport *(G-7306)*
Graham Corporation..................B....... 585 343-2216
Batavia *(G-626)*
Grillmaster Inc..................E....... 718 272-9191
Howard Beach *(G-6330)*
Healthway Products Company..................E....... 315 207-1410
Oswego *(G-12778)*
▲ **Hoshizaki Nrtheastern Dist Ctr**..................G....... 516 605-1411
Plainview *(G-13060)*
▲ **Hydro-Air Components Inc**..................C....... 716 827-6510
Buffalo *(G-2877)*
▲ **Ice Air LLC**..................E....... 914 668-4700
Mount Vernon *(G-8408)*
JE Miller Inc..................F....... 315 437-6811
East Syracuse *(G-4355)*
John F Krell Jr..................G....... 315 492-3201
Syracuse *(G-15348)*
Kedco Inc..................F....... 516 454-7800
Farmingdale *(G-4800)*
Keeler Services..................G....... 607 776-5757
Bath *(G-645)*
▲ **Klearbar Inc**..................G....... 516 684-9892
Port Washington *(G-13277)*
Layton Manufacturing Corp..................E....... 718 498-6000
Brooklyn *(G-2095)*
M M Tool and Manufacturing..................G....... 845 691-4140
Highland *(G-6145)*
Manning Lewis Div Rubicon Inds..................E....... 908 687-2400
Brooklyn *(G-2160)*
▼ **Mgr Equipment Corp**..................E....... 516 239-3030
Inwood *(G-6495)*
◆ **Millrock Technology Inc**..................E....... 845 339-5700
Kingston *(G-6911)*

Mohawk Cabinet Company Inc ....F 518 725-0645
Gloversville (G-5462)
▲ Motivair Corporation ....E 716 691-9222
Amherst (G-239)
MSP Technologycom LLC ....G 631 424-7542
Centerport (G-3351)
▼ Nationwide Coils Inc ....G 914 277-7396
Mount Kisco (G-8351)
▼ Niagara Blower Company ....D 800 426-5169
Tonawanda (G-15563)
Northern Air Systems Inc ....E 585 594-5050
Rochester (G-13980)
Opticool Solutions LLC ....F 585 347-6127
Webster (G-16090)
Parker-Hannifin Corporation ....D 716 685-4040
Lancaster (G-7038)
◆ Pfannenberg Inc ....D 716 685-6866
Lancaster (G-7040)
Pfannenberg Manufacturing LLC ....D 716 685-6866
Lancaster (G-7041)
Pro Metal of NY Corp ....G 516 285-0440
Valley Stream (G-15791)
◆ RE Hansen Industries Inc ....C 631 471-2900
Saint James (G-14514)
Roemac Industrial Sales Inc ....G 716 692-7332
North Tonawanda (G-12448)
▲ Rubicon Industries Corp ....E 718 434-4700
Brooklyn (G-2425)
S & V Restaurant Eqp Mfrs Inc ....E 718 220-1140
Bronx (G-1377)
Siemens Industry Inc ....E 716 568-0983
Buffalo (G-3065)
Specified Air Solutions LLC ....E 716 852-4400
Buffalo (G-3074)
Split Systems Corp ....G 516 223-5511
North Baldwin (G-12367)
Standard Motor Products Inc ....B 718 392-0200
Long Island City (G-7598)
Supermarket Equipment Depo Inc ....G 718 665-6200
Bronx (G-1395)
Thomson Industries Inc ....F 716 691-9100
Amherst (G-255)
Trane US Inc ....D 718 721-8844
Long Island City (G-7620)
Trane US Inc ....G 914 593-0303
Elmsford (G-4573)
Trane US Inc ....E 315 234-1500
East Syracuse (G-4375)
Trane US Inc ....E 518 785-1315
Latham (G-7094)
Trane US Inc ....E 585 256-2500
Rochester (G-14174)
Trane US Inc ....E 716 626-1260
Buffalo (G-3101)
Trane US Inc ....E 631 952-9477
Plainview (G-13093)
▲ Transit Air Inc ....E 607 324-0216
Hornell (G-6304)
▲ Universal Coolers Inc ....G 718 788-8621
Brooklyn (G-2606)
Universal Parent and Youth ....F 917 754-2426
Brooklyn (G-2608)
York International Corporation ....D 718 389-4152
Long Island City (G-7645)

3586 Measuring & Dispensing Pumps

Aptargroup Inc ....C 845 639-3700
Congers (G-3710)
▲ Charles Ross & Son Company ....D 631 234-0500
Hauppauge (G-5788)
Economy Pump & Motor Repr Inc ....G 718 433-2600
Astoria (G-425)
◆ Pulsafeeder Inc ....C 585 292-8000
Rochester (G-14054)
Schlumberger Technology Corp ....C 607 378-0105
Horseheads (G-6328)
▲ Valois of America Inc ....C 845 639-3700
Congers (G-3721)

3589 Service Ind Machines, NEC

240 Michigan Street Inc ....F 716 434-6010
Buffalo (G-2675)
Abe Pool Service ....G 845 473-7730
Hyde Park (G-6467)
Advance Food Service Co Inc ....C 631 242-4800
Edgewood (G-4393)
◆ Advance Tabco Inc ....D 631 242-8270
Edgewood (G-4394)
▲ Airgle Corporation ....E 866 501-7750
Ronkonkoma (G-14296)
American Comfort Direct LLC ....E 201 364-8309
New York (G-8825)
Arista Coffee Inc ....F 347 531-0813
Maspeth (G-7823)
◆ Atlantic Ultraviolet Corp ....E 631 234-3275
Hauppauge (G-5773)
▲ Attias Oven Corp ....G 718 499-0145
Brooklyn (G-1573)
Bakers Pride Oven Co Inc ....C 914 576-0200
New Rochelle (G-8591)
◆ Blue Tee Corp ....G 212 598-0880
New York (G-9109)
Bolton Point Wtr Trtmnt Plant ....G 607 277-0660
Ithaca (G-6563)
Business Advisory Services ....G 718 337-3740
Far Rockaway (G-4698)
Carts Mobile Food Eqp Corp ....E 718 788-5540
Brooklyn (G-1680)
City of Kingston ....F 845 331-2490
Kingston (G-6895)
City of Olean ....G 716 376-5694
Olean (G-12595)
City of Oneonta ....G 607 433-3470
Oneonta (G-12630)
Clearcove Systems Inc ....F 585 734-3012
Victor (G-15836)
Custom Klean Corp ....F 315 865-8101
Holland Patent (G-6224)
Dyna-Vac Equipment Inc ....F 315 865-8084
Stittville (G-15160)
▼ Econocraft Worldwide Mfg Inc ....G 914 966-2280
Yonkers (G-16754)
Empire Division Inc ....D 315 476-6273
Syracuse (G-15318)
▲ Environment-One Corporation ....C 518 346-6161
Schenectady (G-14672)
Ewt Holdings III Corp ....F 212 644-5900
New York (G-9744)
Ferguson Enterprises Inc ....E 800 437-1146
New Hyde Park (G-8535)
H2o Solutions Inc ....F 518 527-0915
Stillwater (G-15158)
Heliojet Cleaning Tech Inc ....F 585 768-8710
Le Roy (G-7118)
Hercules International Inc ....E 631 423-6900
Huntington Station (G-6444)
Hobart Corporation ....E 585 427-9000
Rochester (G-13871)
▲ Hubco Inc ....G 716 683-5940
Alden (G-172)
▼ I A S National Inc ....E 631 423-6900
Huntington Station (G-6447)
IMC Teddy Food Service ....E 631 789-8881
Amityville (G-286)
▲ Integrated Water Management ....G 607 844-4276
Dryden (G-4150)
▲ Key High Vacuum Products Inc ....E 631 584-5959
Nesconset (G-8485)
▲ Kinplex Corp ....E 631 242-4800
Edgewood (G-4407)
Kinplex Corp ....E 631 242-4800
Edgewood (G-4408)
Klee Corp ....G 585 272-0320
Rochester (G-13905)
◆ Korin Japanese Trading Corp ....E 212 587-7021
New York (G-10471)
Liquid Industries Inc ....G 716 628-2999
Niagara Falls (G-12306)
Menpin Supply Corp ....F 718 415-4168
Brooklyn (G-2190)
Metro Group Inc ....D 718 729-7200
Long Island City (G-7523)
Metro Lube ....G 718 947-1167
Rego Park (G-13465)
National Vac Envmtl Svcs Corp ....E 518 743-0563
Glens Falls (G-5435)
Neptune Soft Water Inc ....F 315 446-5151
Syracuse (G-15380)
New Windsor Waste Water Plant ....F 845 561-2550
New Windsor (G-8651)
Ossining Village of Inc ....G 914 202-9668
Ossining (G-12773)
Oxford Cleaners ....G 212 734-0006
New York (G-11075)
▲ Oyster Bay Pump Works Inc ....F 516 933-4500
Hicksville (G-6119)
Pathfinder 103 Inc ....G 315 363-4260
Oneida (G-12620)
Pentair Water Pool and Spa Inc ....E 845 452-5500
Lagrangeville (G-6961)
▲ Pleatco LLC ....D 516 609-0200
Glen Cove (G-5372)
Power Scrub It Inc ....F 516 997-2500
Westbury (G-16365)
Pure Planet Waters LLC ....F 718 676-7900
Brooklyn (G-2362)
R C Kolstad Water Corp ....G 585 216-2230
Ontario (G-12661)
▲ R-S Restaurant Eqp Mfg Corp ....F 212 925-0335
New York (G-11314)
Roger & Sons Inc ....G 212 226-4734
New York (G-11422)
Strategies North America Inc ....G 716 945-6053
Salamanca (G-14534)
▲ Toga Manufacturing Inc ....G 631 242-4800
Edgewood (G-4421)
Water Energy Systems LLC ....G 844 822-7665
New York (G-12079)
▲ Water Technologies Inc ....G 315 986-0000
Macedon (G-7705)
Wetlook Detailing Inc ....G 212 390-8877
Brooklyn (G-2642)
Yr Blanc & Co LLC ....G 716 800-3999
Buffalo (G-3137)

3592 Carburetors, Pistons, Rings & Valves

▲ Fcmp Inc ....F 716 692-4623
Tonawanda (G-15539)
▲ ITT Engineered Valves LLC ....D 662 257-6982
Seneca Falls (G-14778)
Valvetech Inc ....E 315 548-4551
Phelps (G-12983)

3593 Fluid Power Cylinders & Actuators

▲ A K Allen Co Inc ....C 516 747-5450
Melville (G-7996)
Actuant Corporation ....E 607 753-8276
Cortland (G-3858)
▲ Ameritool Mfg Inc ....E 315 668-2172
Central Square (G-3390)
Direkt Force LLC ....E 716 652-3022
East Aurora (G-4197)
▲ ITT Enidine Inc ....B 716 662-1900
Orchard Park (G-12720)
Precision Mechanisms Corp ....E 516 333-5955
Westbury (G-16366)
Skytravel (usa) LLC ....F 518 888-2610
Schenectady (G-14715)
Springville Mfg Co Inc ....E 716 592-4957
Springville (G-15021)
Starcyl USA Corp ....F 877 782-7295
Champlain (G-3413)
Tactair Fluid Controls Inc ....C 315 451-3928
Liverpool (G-7266)
Triumph Actuation Systems LLC ....D 516 378-0162
Freeport (G-5188)
Young & Franklin Inc ....D 315 457-3110
Liverpool (G-7274)

3594 Fluid Power Pumps & Motors

Atlantic Industrial Tech Inc ....E 631 234-3131
Shirley (G-14830)
Huck International Inc ....C 845 331-7300
Kingston (G-6902)
Hydroacoustics Inc ....F 585 359-1000
Henrietta (G-6032)
ITT Corporation ....D 315 568-2811
Seneca Falls (G-14777)
ITT Inc ....E 914 641-2000
White Plains (G-16464)
◆ ITT LLC ....B 914 641-2000
White Plains (G-16467)
Parker-Hannifin Corporation ....C 716 686-6400
Lancaster (G-7036)
Parker-Hannifin Corporation ....B 631 231-3737
Hauppauge (G-5909)
Parker-Hannifin Corporation ....C 585 425-7000
Fairport (G-4647)
Trench & Marine Pump Co Inc ....E 212 423-9098
Bronx (G-1405)
Triumph Actuation Systems LLC ....D 516 378-0162
Freeport (G-5188)

3596 Scales & Balances, Exc Laboratory

A & K Equipment Incorporated ....G 705 428-3573
Watertown (G-15999)
▲ Circuits & Systems Inc ....E 516 593-4301
East Rockaway (G-4293)

SIC

35 INDUSTRIAL AND COMMERCIAL MACHINERY AND COMPUTER EQUIPMENT

◆ Itin Scale Co Inc .... E 718 336-5900
Brooklyn *(G-2019)*
Measupro Inc .... F 845 425-8777
Spring Valley *(G-15003)*
S R Instruments Inc .... E 716 693-5977
Tonawanda *(G-15573)*
Scale-Tronix Inc .... E 914 948-8117
Skaneateles *(G-14877)*
Weighing & Systems Tech Inc .... G 518 274-2797
Troy *(G-15635)*

3599 Machinery & Eqpt, Indl & Commercial, NEC

A & G Precision Corp .... F 631 957-5613
Amityville *(G-262)*
A & L Machine Company Inc .... G 631 463-3111
Islandia *(G-6520)*
A P Manufacturing .... G 909 228-3049
Bohemia *(G-966)*
A R V Precision Mfg Corp .... G 631 293-9643
Farmingdale *(G-4705)*
A-Line Technologies Inc .... F 607 772-2439
Binghamton *(G-858)*
Absolute Manufacturing Inc .... G 631 563-7466
Bohemia *(G-969)*
Acad Design Corp .... F 585 254-6960
Rochester *(G-13594)*
▲ Accede Mold & Tool Co Inc .... D 585 254-6490
Rochester *(G-13595)*
▲ Accurate Industrial Machining .... E 631 242-0566
Holbrook *(G-6168)*
Accurate Tool & Die LLC .... F 585 254-2830
Rochester *(G-13598)*
Accurate Welding Service Inc .... G 516 333-1730
Westbury *(G-16308)*
Acme Industries of W Babylon .... F 631 737-5231
Ronkonkoma *(G-14289)*
▲ Acro Industries Inc .... C 585 254-3661
Rochester *(G-13600)*
Acro-Fab Ltd .... E 315 564-6688
Hannibal *(G-5717)*
Active Manufacturing Inc .... F 607 775-3162
Kirkwood *(G-6937)*
Adaptive Mfg Tech Inc .... E 631 580-5400
Ronkonkoma *(G-14290)*
Addison Precision Mfg Corp .... D 585 254-1386
Rochester *(G-13602)*
Adria Machine & Tool Inc .... G 585 889-3360
Scottsville *(G-14748)*
Advan-Tech Manufacturing Inc .... E 716 667-1500
Orchard Park *(G-12698)*
Advance Precision Industries .... G 631 491-0910
West Babylon *(G-16129)*
Advanced Machine Inc .... F 585 423-8255
Rochester *(G-13607)*
Advanced Mfg Techniques .... G 518 877-8560
Clifton Park *(G-3562)*
Aero Specialties Manufacturing .... F 631 242-7200
Deer Park *(G-3935)*
AG Tech Welding Corp .... G 845 398-0005
Tappan *(G-15465)*
Aj Genco Mch Sp McHy Rdout Svc .... F 716 664-4925
Falconer *(G-4669)*
Akraturn Mfg Inc .... D 607 775-2802
Kirkwood *(G-6938)*
Aljo Precision Products Inc .... E 516 420-4419
Old Bethpage *(G-12581)*
Aljo-Gefa Precision Mfg LLC .... E 516 420-4419
Old Bethpage *(G-12582)*
Alkemy Machine LLC .... G 585 436-8730
Rochester *(G-13613)*
Allen Tool Phoenix Inc .... E 315 463-7533
East Syracuse *(G-4317)*
Alliance Innovative Mfg Inc .... F 716 822-1626
Lackawanna *(G-6947)*
Allied Industrial Products Co .... G 716 664-3893
Jamestown *(G-6697)*
▲ Aloi Solutions LLC .... E 585 292-0920
Rochester *(G-13619)*
Alpha Manufacturing Corp .... G 631 249-3700
Farmingdale *(G-4717)*
Alpine Machine Inc .... F 607 272-1344
Ithaca *(G-6556)*
Alro Machine Tool & Die Co Inc .... F 631 226-5020
Lindenhurst *(G-7160)*
Altamont Spray Welding Inc .... G 518 861-8870
Altamont *(G-195)*
Amacon Corporation .... F 631 293-1888
West Babylon *(G-16132)*

American Linear Manufacturers .... F 516 333-1351
Westbury *(G-16314)*
▲ American Wire Tie Inc .... E 716 337-2412
North Collins *(G-12383)*
▲ Antab Mch Sprfinishing Lab Inc ...... G 585 865-8290
Rochester *(G-13635)*
Applied Technology Mfg Corp .... E 607 687-2200
Owego *(G-12795)*
◆ Arbe Machinery Inc .... F 631 756-2477
Farmingdale *(G-4722)*
Archimedes Products Inc .... G 631 589-1215
Bohemia *(G-982)*
Architectural Coatings Inc .... F 718 418-9584
Brooklyn *(G-1547)*
Argencord Machine Corp Inc .... G 631 842-8990
Copiague *(G-3751)*
Argo General Machine Work Inc .... G 718 392-4605
Long Island City *(G-7387)*
Armstrong Mold Corporation .... D 315 437-1517
East Syracuse *(G-4321)*
Arrow Grinding Inc .... E 716 693-3333
Tonawanda *(G-15523)*
Art Precision Metal Products .... G 631 842-8889
Copiague *(G-3752)*
Artisan Machining Inc .... G 631 589-1416
Ronkonkoma *(G-14311)*
Artisan Management Group Inc .... G 716 569-4094
Frewsburg *(G-5206)*
Astra Tool & Instrument Mfg .... G 914 747-3863
Hawthorne *(G-5983)*
Atlantis Equipment Corporation .... E 518 733-5910
Stephentown *(G-15154)*
Atwood Tool & Machine Inc .... G 607 648-6543
Chenango Bridge *(G-3465)*
Auburn Bearing & Mfg Inc .... G 315 986-7600
Macedon *(G-7694)*
AW Mack Manufacturing Co Inc .... F 845 452-4050
Poughkeepsie *(G-13330)*
B & B Precision Mfg Inc .... F 585 226-6226
Avon *(G-517)*
B & R Industries Inc .... F 631 736-2275
Medford *(G-7938)*
B C Manufacturing Inc .... G 585 482-1080
West Henrietta *(G-16231)*
Babbitt Bearings Inc .... D 315 479-6603
Syracuse *(G-15252)*
Babbitt Bearings Incorporated .... D 315 479-6603
Syracuse *(G-15253)*
Badge Machine Products Inc .... E 585 394-0330
Canandaigua *(G-3211)*
Barton Tool Inc .... G 716 665-2801
Falconer *(G-4672)*
BEAM Manufacturing Corp .... G 631 253-2724
West Babylon *(G-16139)*
Belden Manufacturing Inc .... F 607 238-0998
Kirkwood *(G-6939)*
Bick & Heintz Inc .... F 315 733-7577
Utica *(G-15680)*
Bill Shea Enterprises Inc .... G 585 343-2284
Batavia *(G-613)*
Birch Machine & Tool Inc .... F 716 735-9802
Middleport *(G-8131)*
Blading Services Unlimited LLC .... E 315 875-5313
Canastota *(G-3240)*
Blair Cnstr Fabrication Sp .... G 315 253-2321
Auburn *(G-470)*
Bliss Machine Inc .... F 585 492-5128
Arcade *(G-379)*
Blue Manufacturing Co Inc .... G 607 796-2463
Millport *(G-8195)*
Bms Manufacturing Co Inc .... G 607 535-2426
Watkins Glen *(G-16058)*
Breed Enterprises Inc .... G 585 388-0126
Fairport *(G-4626)*
Broadalbin Manufacturing Corp .... E 518 883-5313
Broadalbin *(G-1187)*
Bruce Pierce .... G 716 731-9310
Sanborn *(G-14542)*
Bryant Machine & Development .... F 716 894-8282
Buffalo *(G-2737)*
Bryant Machine Co Inc .... F 716 894-8282
Buffalo *(G-2738)*
Bryant Manufacturing Wny Inc .... F 716 894-8282
Buffalo *(G-2739)*
Buxton Machine and Tool Co Inc .... F 716 876-2312
Buffalo *(G-2757)*
C & H Machining Inc .... F 631 582-6737
Bohemia *(G-991)*
C & T Tool & Instrument Co .... F 718 429-1253
Woodside *(G-16648)*

C L Precision Machine & Tl Co .... G 718 651-8475
Woodside *(G-16649)*
C R C Manufacturing Inc .... F 585 254-8820
Rochester *(G-13686)*
▲ Calvary Design Team Inc .... C 585 347-6127
Webster *(G-16076)*
Canfield Machine & Tool LLC .... E 315 593-8062
Fulton *(G-5213)*
▲ Capy Machine Shop Inc .... E 631 694-6916
Melville *(G-8006)*
Carballo Contract Machining .... G 315 594-2511
Wolcott *(G-16609)*
Carbaugh Tool Company Inc .... E 607 739-3293
Elmira *(G-4475)*
Cardish Machine Works Inc .... E 518 273-2329
Watervliet *(G-16043)*
Casey Machine Co Inc .... D 716 651-0150
Lancaster *(G-7012)*
Catapult .... G 323 839-6204
New York *(G-9227)*
Cayuga Tool and Die Inc .... E 607 533-7400
Groton *(G-5651)*
CBM Fabrications Inc .... E 518 399-8023
Ballston Lake *(G-567)*
Cda Machine Inc .... G 585 671-5959
Webster *(G-16077)*
Cdl Manufacturing Inc .... G 585 589-2533
Albion *(G-156)*
◆ Cem Machine Inc .... E 315 493-4258
Carthage *(G-3288)*
Centerless Technology Inc .... E 585 436-2240
Rochester *(G-13700)*
Certified Prcsion McHining Inc .... G 631 244-3671
Bohemia *(G-993)*
▲ Cetek Inc .... E 845 452-3510
Poughkeepsie *(G-13331)*
Charl Industries Inc .... E 631 234-0100
Hauppauge *(G-5787)*
Chassix Automotive Corp .... F 585 815-1700
Batavia *(G-619)*
Chautqua Prcsion Machining Inc .... F 716 763-3752
Ashville *(G-417)*
◆ Chocovision Corporation .... F 845 473-4970
Poughkeepsie *(G-13332)*
▼ City Gear Inc .... G 914 450-4746
Irvington *(G-6503)*
Cjn Machinery Corp .... G 631 244-8030
Holbrook *(G-6176)*
Classic Auto Crafts Inc .... E 518 966-8003
Greenville *(G-5635)*
Cnc Manufacturing Inc .... E 718 728-6800
Long Island City *(G-7411)*
Conesus Lake Association Inc .... E 585 346-6864
Lakeville *(G-6985)*
Conrad Blasius Equipment Co .... F 516 753-1200
Plainview *(G-13044)*
Converter Design Inc .... F 518 745-7138
Glens Falls *(G-5421)*
Corbett Stves Pttern Works Inc .... F 585 546-7109
Rochester *(G-13722)*
Cortland Machine and Tool Co .... F 607 756-5852
Cortland *(G-3868)*
Courser Inc .... E 607 739-3861
Elmira *(G-4480)*
Craftsman Manufacturing Co In .... G 585 426-5780
Rochester *(G-13723)*
Crowley Fabg Machining Co Inc .... E 607 484-0299
Endicott *(G-4585)*
▼ Cubitek Inc .... G 631 665-6900
Brentwood *(G-1129)*
▲ Cyclone Air Power Inc .... G 718 447-3038
Staten Island *(G-15067)*
D J Crowell Co Inc .... E 716 684-3343
Alden *(G-169)*
D K Machine Inc .... F 518 747-0626
Fort Edward *(G-5095)*
D-K Manufacturing Corp .... E 315 592-4327
Fulton *(G-5214)*
Darco Manufacturing Inc .... E 315 432-8905
Syracuse *(G-15302)*
Daves Precision Machine Shop .... F 845 626-7263
Kerhonkson *(G-6868)*
David Fehlman .... G 315 455-8888
Syracuse *(G-15303)*
Davidson Grinding Corp .... F 631 563-3982
Bohemia *(G-1009)*
Deck Bros Inc .... E 716 852-0262
Buffalo *(G-2795)*
Delaney Machine Products Ltd .... G 631 225-1032
Lindenhurst *(G-7168)*

Dennies Manufacturing Inc ....E 585 393-4646
Canandaigua *(G-3218)*
Denny Machine Co Inc ....E 716 873-6865
Buffalo *(G-2798)*
Dern Moore Machine Company Inc ....G 716 433-6243
Lockport *(G-7294)*
Derosa Fabrications Inc ....E 631 563-0640
Bohemia *(G-1014)*
▼ Devin Mfg Inc ....F 585 496-5770
Arcade *(G-381)*
Dewey Machine & Tool Inc ....G 607 749-3930
Homer *(G-6253)*
DMD Machining Technology Inc ....G 585 659-8180
Kendall *(G-6856)*
Dormitory Authority - State NY ....G 631 434-1487
Brentwood *(G-1132)*
Dougs Machine Shop Inc ....G 585 905-0004
Canandaigua *(G-3219)*
Duetto Integrated Systems Inc ....F 631 851-0102
Islandia *(G-6527)*
Dunlap Machine LLC ....F 315 926-1013
Marion *(G-7800)*
Dyna-Tech Quality Inc ....G 585 458-9970
Rochester *(G-13752)*
Dynak Inc ....F 585 271-2255
Churchville *(G-3509)*
E & R Machine Inc ....E 716 434-6639
Lockport *(G-7296)*
E B Trottnow Machine Spc ....F 716 694-0600
Eden *(G-4387)*
E J Willis Company Inc ....F 315 891-7602
Middleville *(G-8186)*
E M T Manufacturing Inc ....F 516 333-1917
East Meadow *(G-4250)*
▲ Eagle Bridge Machine & Tl Inc ....E 518 686-4541
Eagle Bridge *(G-4184)*
Eagle Instruments Inc ....G 914 939-6843
Port Chester *(G-13197)*
East Side Machine Inc ....E 585 265-4560
Webster *(G-16083)*
Eastern Machine and Electric ....G 716 284-8271
Niagara Falls *(G-12280)*
Eastern Precision Machining ....G 631 286-4758
Bellport *(G-802)*
EDM Mfg ....G 631 669-1966
Babylon *(G-527)*
Edr Industries Inc ....F 516 868-1928
Freeport *(G-5152)*
▲ Edsal Machine Products Inc ....F 718 439-9163
Brooklyn *(G-1815)*
▲ Edwin J McKenica & Sons Inc ....F 716 823-4646
Buffalo *(G-2813)*
Ehrlich Enterprises Inc ....F 631 956-0690
Wyandanch *(G-16695)*
Electro Form Corp ....F 607 722-6404
Binghamton *(G-881)*
Elite Machine Inc ....G 585 289-4733
Manchester *(G-7760)*
Elite Precise Manufacturer LLC ....G 518 993-3040
Fort Plain *(G-5102)*
Emcom Industries Inc ....G 716 852-3711
Buffalo *(G-2817)*
Emory Machine & Tool Co Inc ....E 585 436-9610
Farmington *(G-4913)*
Empire Plastics Inc ....E 607 754-9132
Endwell *(G-4616)*
Endicott Precision Inc ....C 607 754-7076
Endicott *(G-4589)*
Engineering Mfg Tech LLC ....D 607 754-7111
Endicott *(G-4591)*
Estebania Enterprises Inc ....G 585 529-9330
Rochester *(G-13793)*
ET Oakes Corporation ....E 631 232-0002
Hauppauge *(G-5821)*
ET Precision Optics Inc ....D 585 254-2560
Rochester *(G-13794)*
Etna Tool & Die Corporation ....F 212 475-4350
New York *(G-9723)*
Euro Gear (usa) Inc ....G 518 578-1775
Plattsburgh *(G-13120)*
Everfab Inc ....D 716 655-1550
East Aurora *(G-4198)*
Exact Machining & Mfg ....G 585 334-7090
Rochester *(G-13796)*
Excel Industries Inc ....E 716 542-5468
Clarence *(G-3533)*
Exigo Precision Inc ....G 585 254-5818
Rochester *(G-13798)*
Expert Machine Services Inc ....G 718 786-1200
Long Island City *(G-7442)*

F M L Industries Inc ....G 607 749-7273
Homer *(G-6254)*
Falk Precision Inc ....E 315 437-4545
East Syracuse *(G-4337)*
Farrant Screw Machine Products ....G 585 457-3213
Java Village *(G-6772)*
Felton Machine Co Inc ....E 716 215-9001
Niagara Falls *(G-12284)*
Fenbar Prcision Machinists Inc ....F 914 769-5506
Thornwood *(G-15506)*
Fermer Precision Inc ....D 315 822-6371
Ilion *(G-6474)*
Ferraro Manufacturing Company ....G 631 752-1509
Farmingdale *(G-4764)*
Ferro Machine Co Inc ....G 845 398-3641
Orangeburg *(G-12678)*
▲ Finesse Creations Inc ....F 718 692-2100
Brooklyn *(G-1883)*
Five Star Industries Inc ....E 716 674-2589
West Seneca *(G-16297)*
▲ Flex-Hose Company Inc ....E 315 437-1903
East Syracuse *(G-4340)*
Forbes Precision Inc ....F 585 865-7069
Rochester *(G-13812)*
Fortech Inc ....G 315 478-2048
Syracuse *(G-15324)*
Four K Machine Shop Inc ....G 516 997-0752
Westbury *(G-16332)*
Frederick Machine Repair Inc ....G 716 332-0104
Buffalo *(G-2834)*
Fronhofer Tool Company Inc ....E 518 692-2496
Cossayuna *(G-3905)*
Fross Industries Inc ....E 716 297-0652
Niagara Falls *(G-12287)*
Fulton Tool Co Inc ....E 315 598-2900
Fulton *(G-5217)*
Fultonville Machine & Tool Co ....F 518 853-4441
Fultonville *(G-5236)*
Future Screw Machine Pdts Inc ....F 631 765-1610
Southold *(G-14968)*
G & G C Machine & Tool Co Inc ....G 516 873-0999
Westbury *(G-16333)*
Gamma Instrument Co Inc ....G 516 486-5526
Farmingdale *(G-4769)*
Gefa Instrument Corp ....F 516 420-4419
Old Bethpage *(G-12584)*
Gem Manufacturing Inc ....G 585 235-1670
Rochester *(G-13825)*
Genco John ....G 716 483-5446
Jamestown *(G-6717)*
General Cutting Inc ....F 631 580-5011
Ronkonkoma *(G-14344)*
Genesis Machining Corp ....F 516 377-1197
North Baldwin *(G-12363)*
Gentner Precision Components ....G 315 597-5734
Palmyra *(G-12854)*
Giuliante Machine Tool Inc ....E 914 835-0008
Peekskill *(G-12920)*
Gli-Dex Sales Corp ....E 716 692-6501
North Tonawanda *(G-12430)*
Global Precision Inds Inc ....F 585 254-0010
Rochester *(G-13841)*
Gmr Manufacturing Inc ....G 631 582-2600
Central Islip *(G-3371)*
Gorden Automotive Equipment ....F 716 674-2700
West Seneca *(G-16299)*
Gpp Post-Closing Inc ....E 585 334-4640
Rush *(G-14474)*
▲ Greno Industries Inc ....G 518 393-4195
Scotia *(G-14740)*
Grind ....G 646 558-3250
New York *(G-9990)*
Gullo Machine & Tool Inc ....F 585 657-7318
Bloomfield *(G-955)*
H & H Technologies Inc ....E 631 567-3526
Ronkonkoma *(G-14348)*
H C Young Tool & Machine Co ....G 315 463-0663
Syracuse *(G-15336)*
H F Brown Machine Co Inc ....F 315 732-6129
Utica *(G-15707)*
H T Specialty Inc ....F 585 458-4060
Rochester *(G-13850)*
Hagner Industries Inc ....G 716 873-5720
Buffalo *(G-2862)*
Hallock Fabricating Corp ....G 631 727-2441
Riverhead *(G-13569)*
Hartman Enterprises Inc ....D 315 363-7300
Oneida *(G-12610)*
Harwitt Industries Inc ....F 516 623-9787
Freeport *(G-5161)*

Haskell Machine & Tool Inc ....F 607 749-2421
Homer *(G-6255)*
Hebeler Process Solutions LLC ....E 716 873-9300
Tonawanda *(G-15548)*
Herkimer Tool & Machining Corp ....F 315 866-2110
Herkimer *(G-6042)*
Hes Inc ....G 607 359-2974
Addison *(G-6)*
Hi-Tech Cnc Machining Corp ....G 914 668-5090
Mount Vernon *(G-8407)*
Hi-Tech Industries NY Inc ....E 607 217-7361
Johnson City *(G-6810)*
Hoercher Industries Inc ....G 585 398-2982
East Rochester *(G-4286)*
Hohl Machine & Conveyor Co Inc ....E 716 882-7210
Buffalo *(G-2873)*
▲ HSM Machine Works Inc ....E 631 924-6600
Medford *(G-7953)*
Hubbard Tool and Die Corp ....E 315 337-7840
Rome *(G-14253)*
Hunter Machine Inc ....E 585 924-7480
Victor *(G-15849)*
Hw Specialties Co Inc ....F 631 589-0745
Bohemia *(G-1033)*
I D Machine Inc ....G 607 796-2549
Elmira *(G-4494)*
Imperial Instrument Corp ....G 516 739-6644
Westbury *(G-16341)*
Indian Springs Mfg Co Inc ....F 315 635-6101
Baldwinsville *(G-556)*
Indus Precision Manufacturing ....F 845 268-0782
Congers *(G-3718)*
Industrial Precision Pdts Inc ....E 315 343-4421
Oswego *(G-12779)*
Industrial Services of Wny ....G 716 799-7788
Niagara Falls *(G-12299)*
▲ Industrial Tool & Die Co Inc ....F 518 273-7383
Troy *(G-15609)*
Ingleside Machine Co Inc ....D 585 924-3046
Farmington *(G-4916)*
Integrity Tool Incorporated ....F 315 524-4409
Ontario *(G-12655)*
Interactive Instruments Inc ....G 518 347-0955
Scotia *(G-14742)*
International Climbing Mchs ....G 607 288-4001
Ithaca *(G-6586)*
▲ International Tool & Mch Inc ....F 585 654-6955
Rochester *(G-13885)*
Ironshore Holdings Inc ....F 315 457-1052
Liverpool *(G-7239)*
Ish Precision Machine Corp ....F 718 436-8858
Lynbrook *(G-7665)*
Island Instrument Corp ....G 631 243-0550
Deer Park *(G-3987)*
Island Machine Inc ....G 518 562-1232
Plattsburgh *(G-13127)*
▲ ISO Plastics Corp ....D 914 663-8300
Mount Vernon *(G-8410)*
J & G Machine & Tool Co Inc ....F 315 310-7130
Marion *(G-7803)*
J & J Swiss Precision Inc ....E 631 243-5584
Deer Park *(G-3988)*
J & J Tl Die Mfg & Stampg Corp ....G 845 228-0242
Carmel *(G-3276)*
J & L Precision Co Inc ....G 585 768-6388
Le Roy *(G-7120)*
J B Tool & Die Co Inc ....E 516 333-1480
Westbury *(G-16343)*
J D Cousins Inc ....E 716 824-1098
Buffalo *(G-2889)*
J F Machining Company Inc ....F 716 791-3910
Ransomville *(G-13451)*
J R S Precision Machining ....G 631 737-1330
Ronkonkoma *(G-14356)*
J T Systematic ....G 607 754-0929
Endwell *(G-4617)*
Jack Merkel Inc ....G 631 234-2600
Hauppauge *(G-5853)*
Jacobi Tool & Die Mfg Inc ....G 631 736-5394
Medford *(G-7955)*
▲ Jam Industries Inc ....E 585 458-9830
Rochester *(G-13890)*
Jamar Precision Products Co ....F 631 254-0234
Deer Park *(G-3989)*
Jamestown Iron Works Inc ....F 716 665-2818
Falconer *(G-4685)*
Javcon Machine Inc ....G 631 586-1890
Deer Park *(G-3991)*
Javin Machine Corp ....F 631 643-3322
West Babylon *(G-16164)*

SIC

Employee Codes: A=Over 500 employees, B=251-500
C=101-250, D=51-100, E=20-50, F=10-19, G=5-9
2019 Harris
New York Manufacturers Directory
769

35 INDUSTRIAL AND COMMERCIAL MACHINERY AND COMPUTER EQUIPMENT SIC SECTION

Jet Sew Corporation F 315 896-2683
Barneveld *(G-602)*
Jewelers Machinist Co Inc G 631 661-5020
Babylon *(G-528)*
JF Machine Shop Inc G 631 491-7273
West Babylon *(G-16165)*
John J Mazur Inc F 631 242-4554
Deer Park *(G-3993)*
Johnnys Machine Shop G 631 338-9733
West Babylon *(G-16166)*
Johnson Mch & Fibr Pdts Co Inc F 716 665-2003
Jamestown *(G-6734)*
Johnston Precision Inc G 315 253-4181
Auburn *(G-487)*
Jolin Machining Corp F 631 589-1305
Bohemia *(G-1042)*
Jordan Machine Inc G 585 647-3585
Rochester *(G-13898)*
▲ **Jrb Machine-Tool Inc** G 716 206-0355
Lancaster *(G-7025)*
Jt Precision Inc E 716 795-3860
Barker *(G-600)*
Just In Time Cnc Machinin G 585 247-3850
Rochester *(G-13900)*
Just In Time Cnc Machining F 585 335-2010
Dansville *(G-3927)*
JW Burg Machine & Tool Inc G 716 434-0015
Clarence Center *(G-3547)*
▲ **K & H Industries Inc** F 716 312-0088
Hamburg *(G-5683)*
K & H Precision Products Inc E 585 624-4894
Honeoye Falls *(G-6269)*
K D M Die Company Inc F 716 828-9000
Buffalo *(G-2900)*
K Hein Machines Inc G 607 748-1546
Vestal *(G-15819)*
Kal Manufacturing Corporation E 585 265-4310
Webster *(G-16088)*
▲ **Keller Technology Corporation** C 716 693-3840
Tonawanda *(G-15553)*
Kenwell Corporation D 315 592-4263
Fulton *(G-5225)*
Keyes Machine Works Inc G 585 426-5059
Gates *(G-5310)*
Kimber Mfg Inc G 914 965-0753
Yonkers *(G-16775)*
◆ **Kimber Mfg Inc** C 914 964-0771
Yonkers *(G-16776)*
Kimber Mfg Inc D 406 758-2222
Yonkers *(G-16777)*
Kinemotive Corporation E 631 249-6440
Farmingdale *(G-4803)*
Kittredge & Sons Inc D 978 567-0998
Niagara Falls *(G-12303)*
▲ **KMA Corporation** G 518 743-1330
Glens Falls *(G-5430)*
Knise & Krick Inc E 315 422-3516
Syracuse *(G-15357)*
Konar Precision Mfg Inc G 631 242-4466
Deer Park *(G-3996)*
▲ **Kondor Technologies Inc** F 631 471-8832
Ronkonkoma *(G-14363)*
Kramartron Precision Inc G 845 368-3668
Tallman *(G-15462)*
Kronenberger Mfg Corp E 585 385-2340
East Rochester *(G-4289)*
Krug Precision Inc G 516 944-9350
Port Washington *(G-13279)*
Kurtz Truck Equipment Inc F 607 849-3468
Marathon *(G-7790)*
Kurz and Zobel Inc G 585 254-9060
Rochester *(G-13908)*
Kz Precision Inc F 716 683-3202
Lancaster *(G-7026)*
L & S Metals Inc E 716 692-6865
North Tonawanda *(G-12436)*
L P R Precision Parts & Tls Co F 631 293-7334
Farmingdale *(G-4805)*
Labco of Palmyra Inc F 315 597-5202
Palmyra *(G-12857)*
▲ **Lagasse Works Inc** G 315 946-9202
Lyons *(G-7685)*
Lakeside Industries Inc F 716 386-3031
Bemus Point *(G-818)*
Lakeside Precision Inc E 716 366-5030
Dunkirk *(G-4173)*
Laser & Electron Beam Inc G 603 626-6080
New York *(G-10520)*
Lasticks Aerospace Inc F 631 242-8484
Bay Shore *(G-695)*
Leetech Manufacturing Inc G 631 563-1442
Bohemia *(G-1046)*
Lewis Machine Co Inc G 718 625-0799
Brooklyn *(G-2114)*
Liberty Machine & Tool G 315 699-3242
Cicero *(G-3519)*
▲ **Linda Tool & Die Corporation** E 718 522-2066
Brooklyn *(G-2125)*
▲ **Lodolce Machine Co Inc** E 845 246-7017
Saugerties *(G-14610)*
Loughlin Manufacturing Corp F 631 585-4422
Bohemia *(G-1050)*
Lovejoy Chaplet Corporation E 518 686-5232
Hoosick Falls *(G-6277)*
▲ **Lwa Works Inc** G 518 271-8360
Watervliet *(G-16048)*
▲ **M & S Precision Machine Co LLC** F 518 747-1193
Queensbury *(G-13433)*
Macro Tool & Machine Company G 845 223-3824
Lagrangeville *(G-6958)*
Maehr Industries Inc G 631 924-1661
Bellport *(G-807)*
▲ **Magellan Aerospace Bethel Inc** C 203 798-9373
Corona *(G-3848)*
Magellan Aerospace NY Inc C 631 589-2440
Bohemia *(G-1053)*
▲ **Makamah Enterprises Inc** F 631 231-0200
Hauppauge *(G-5878)*
Malisa Branko Inc F 631 225-9741
Copiague *(G-3768)*
Manth Mfg Inc E 716 693-6525
Tonawanda *(G-15556)*
Mar-A-Thon Filters Inc G 631 957-4774
Lindenhurst *(G-7177)*
Mardon Tool & Die Co Inc F 585 254-4545
Rochester *(G-13929)*
◆ **Marksmen Manufacturing Corp** E 800 305-6942
Deer Park *(G-4006)*
Massapqua Prcsion McHining Ltd G 631 789-1485
Amityville *(G-302)*
▲ **Master Machine Incorporated** F 716 487-2555
Jamestown *(G-6738)*
Matic Industries Inc G 718 886-5470
College Point *(G-3655)*
Matrix Machining Corp G 631 643-6690
West Babylon *(G-16174)*
Mayfair Machine Company Inc G 631 981-6644
Ronkonkoma *(G-14376)*
Mc Ivor Manufacturing Inc G 716 825-1808
Buffalo *(G-2941)*
McGuigan Inc E 631 750-6222
Bohemia *(G-1057)*
Meade Machine Co Inc G 315 923-1703
Clyde *(G-3595)*
Medco Machine LLC G 315 986-2109
Walworth *(G-15914)*
Mega Tool & Mfg Corp E 607 734-8398
Elmira *(G-4498)*
Meridian Manufacturing Inc G 518 885-0450
Ballston Spa *(G-590)*
Metro Machining & Fabricating G 718 545-0104
Woodside *(G-16664)*
Micro Instrument Corp D 585 458-3150
Rochester *(G-13939)*
Micro-Tech Machine Inc E 315 331-6671
Newark *(G-12201)*
Miles Machine Inc F 716 484-6026
Jamestown *(G-6739)*
Milex Precision Inc F 631 595-2393
Bay Shore *(G-701)*
Miller Technology Inc G 631 694-2224
Farmingdale *(G-4826)*
Minutemen Precsn McHning Tool E 631 467-4900
Ronkonkoma *(G-14379)*
Mitchell Machine Tool LLC G 585 254-7520
Rochester *(G-13947)*
▲ **Modern Packaging Inc** D 631 595-2437
Deer Park *(G-4011)*
Modern-TEC Manufacturing Inc G 716 625-8700
Lockport *(G-7319)*
Morco Products Corp F 718 853-4005
Brooklyn *(G-2226)*
Morris Machining Service Inc G 585 527-8100
Rochester *(G-13957)*
Mount Vernon Machine Inc E 845 268-9400
Valley Cottage *(G-15759)*
Ms Machining Inc G 607 723-1105
Binghamton *(G-907)*
Ms Spares LLC G 607 223-3024
Clay *(G-3551)*
Muller Tool Inc E 716 895-3658
Buffalo *(G-2956)*
Nassau Tool Works Inc E 631 328-7031
Bay Shore *(G-705)*
Neptune Machine Inc E 718 852-4100
Brooklyn *(G-2254)*
NET & Die Inc E 315 592-4311
Fulton *(G-5228)*
New Age Precision Tech Inc E 631 471-4000
Ronkonkoma *(G-14387)*
New York Manufacturing Corp G 585 254-9353
Rochester *(G-13968)*
New York State Tool Co Inc F 315 737-8985
Chadwicks *(G-3400)*
Niagara Precision Inc E 716 439-0956
Lockport *(G-7323)*
▼ **Nicoform Inc** E 585 454-5530
Rochester *(G-13973)*
Nitro Manufacturing LLC G 716 646-9900
North Collins *(G-12386)*
North-East Machine Inc G 518 746-1837
Hudson Falls *(G-6383)*
Northeast Hardware Specialties F 516 487-6868
Mineola *(G-8240)*
Northeastern Water Jet Inc F 518 843-4988
Amsterdam *(G-355)*
Northern Machining Inc F 315 384-3189
Norfolk *(G-12359)*
Northern Tier Cnc Inc G 518 236-4702
Mooers Forks *(G-8331)*
O & S Machine & Tool Co Inc G 716 941-5542
Colden *(G-3633)*
Olmstead Machine Inc F 315 587-9864
North Rose *(G-12396)*
Optics Technology Inc G 585 586-0950
Pittsford *(G-13023)*
▲ **P & F Industries of NY Corp** G 718 894-3501
Maspeth *(G-7866)*
P T E Inc F 516 775-3839
Floral Park *(G-4964)*
Pall Corporation A 607 753-6041
Cortland *(G-3885)*
▲ **Pall Corporation** A 516 484-5400
Port Washington *(G-13295)*
▲ **Park-Ohio Inds Trsry Co Inc** F 212 966-3310
Albany *(G-110)*
Parker Machine Company Inc F 518 747-0675
Fort Edward *(G-5098)*
Peko Precision Products Inc F 585 301-1386
Rochester *(G-14010)*
Pems Tool & Machine Inc E 315 823-3595
Little Falls *(G-7211)*
Performance Mfg Inc F 716 735-3500
Middleport *(G-8133)*
Pervi Precision Company Inc G 631 589-5557
Bohemia *(G-1074)*
Phoenix Mch Pdts of Hauppauge G 631 234-0100
Hauppauge *(G-5914)*
Pol-Tek Industries Ltd F 716 823-1502
Buffalo *(G-3009)*
Port Everglades Machine Works F 516 367-2280
Plainview *(G-13083)*
Port Jervis Machine Corp G 845 856-6210
Port Jervis *(G-13235)*
▼ **Posimech Inc** E 631 924-5959
Medford *(G-7964)*
Ppi Corp E 585 880-7277
Rochester *(G-14031)*
▲ **Ppi Corp** D 585 243-0300
Rochester *(G-14032)*
Pre-Tech Plastics Inc E 518 942-5950
Mineville *(G-8254)*
Precision Arms Inc G 845 225-1130
Carmel *(G-3280)*
▲ **Precision Machine Tech LLC** D 585 467-1840
Rochester *(G-14037)*
Precision Metals Corp E 631 586-5032
Bay Shore *(G-709)*
Precision Systems Mfg Inc E 315 451-3480
Liverpool *(G-7257)*
Precision Tool and Mfg E 518 678-3130
Palenville *(G-12845)*
Precisionmatics Co Inc E 315 822-6324
West Winfield *(G-16306)*
Premier Machining Tech Inc G 716 608-1311
Buffalo *(G-3013)*
Production Milling Company G 914 666-0792
Bedford Hills *(G-778)*
▲ **Professional Machine LLC** F 508 966-5171
Rochester *(G-14051)*

SIC SECTION
35 INDUSTRIAL AND COMMERCIAL MACHINERY AND COMPUTER EQUIPMENT

Progressive Mch & Design LLC C 585 924-5250
Victor *(G-15862)*
Progressive Tool Company Inc E 607 748-8294
Endwell *(G-4619)*
Pronto Tool & Die Co Inc E 631 981-8920
Ronkonkoma *(G-14401)*
Proto Machine Inc F 631 392-1159
Bay Shore *(G-711)*
Prototype Manufacturing Corp F 716 695-1700
North Tonawanda *(G-12443)*
▲ **Qmc Technologies Inc** F 716 681-0810
Depew *(G-4103)*
Qta Machining Inc F 716 862-8108
Buffalo *(G-3023)*
Qualified Manufacturing Corp F 631 249-4440
East Islip *(G-4245)*
Quality Machining Service Inc G 315 736-5774
New York Mills *(G-12190)*
Qualtech Tool & Machine Inc F 585 223-9227
Fairport *(G-4654)*
R & S Machine Center Inc F 518 563-4016
Plattsburgh *(G-13151)*
R E F Precision Products F 631 242-4471
Deer Park *(G-4032)*
Ram Machining LLC G 585 426-1007
Rochester *(G-14068)*
Ram Precision Tool Inc G 716 759-8722
Lancaster *(G-7043)*
Rand Machine Products, Inc. C 716 665-5217
Falconer *(G-4688)*
▼ **Redding-Hunter Inc** E 607 753-3331
Cortland *(G-3892)*
Reliance Machining Inc E 718 784-0314
Long Island City *(G-7574)*
Ren Tool & Manufacturing Co F 518 377-2123
Schenectady *(G-14708)*
RGH Associates Inc F 631 643-1111
West Babylon *(G-16186)*
▲ **Richard Manno & Company Inc** D 631 643-2200
West Babylon *(G-16187)*
Richards Machine Tool Co Inc E 716 683-3380
Lancaster *(G-7044)*
Rick-Mic Industries Inc G 631 563-8389
Ronkonkoma *(G-14407)*
Rinaldi Precision Machine F 631 242-4141
Deer Park *(G-4036)*
Ripley Machine & Tool Co Inc F 716 736-3205
Ripley *(G-13563)*
Riverside Machinery Company G 718 492-7400
Brooklyn *(G-2406)*
Rjs Machine Works Inc G 716 826-1778
Lackawanna *(G-6952)*
Rmw Filtration Products Co LLC G 631 226-9412
Copiague *(G-3778)*
Roboshop Inc G 315 437-6454
Syracuse *(G-15408)*
Roccera LLC F 585 426-0887
Rochester *(G-14077)*
Rochester Atomated Systems Inc E 585 594-3222
Rochester *(G-14080)*
Rochester Tool and Mold Inc F 585 464-9336
Rochester *(G-14098)*
Roger Latari G 631 580-2422
Ronkonkoma *(G-14408)*
Rona Precision Inc G 631 737-4034
Ronkonkoma *(G-14409)*
Rossi Tool & Dies Inc G 845 267-8246
Valley Cottage *(G-15763)*
Rozal Industries Inc E 631 420-4277
Farmingdale *(G-4870)*
RS Precision Industries Inc E 631 420-0424
Farmingdale *(G-4871)*
Rt Machined Specialties G 716 731-2055
Niagara Falls *(G-12330)*
RTD Manufacturing Inc G 315 337-3151
Rome *(G-14273)*
Ruga Grinding & Mfg Corp G 631 924-5067
Yaphank *(G-16719)*
S & B Machine Works Inc E 516 997-2666
Westbury *(G-16371)*
S & H Machine Company Inc G 716 834-1194
Buffalo *(G-3051)*
S & R Tool Inc G 585 346-2029
Lakeville *(G-6986)*
S R & R Industries Inc G 845 692-8329
Middletown *(G-8175)*
Saturn Industries Inc E 518 828-9956
Hudson *(G-6370)*
Schwabel Fabricating Co Inc E 716 876-2086
Tonawanda *(G-15575)*
▲ **Scientific Tool Co Inc** F 315 431-4243
Syracuse *(G-15419)*
SDJ Machine Shop Inc F 585 458-1236
Rochester *(G-14118)*
Seanair Machine Co Inc F 631 694-2820
Farmingdale *(G-4873)*
Seeley Machine Inc E 518 798-9510
Queensbury *(G-13441)*
Semi-Linear Inc G 212 243-2108
New York *(G-11541)*
▲ **Service Machine & Tool Company** E 607 732-0413
Elmira Heights *(G-4513)*
Shar-Mar Machine Company G 631 567-8040
Bohemia *(G-1088)*
Sick Inc E 585 347-2000
Webster *(G-16098)*
Sigma Manufacturing Inds Inc F 718 842-9180
Bronx *(G-1384)*
Sigmamotor Inc E 716 735-3115
Middleport *(G-8134)*
Smidgens Inc G 585 624-1486
Lima *(G-7155)*
Smith Metal Works Newark Inc E 315 331-1651
Newark *(G-12206)*
Smith Tool & Die Inc G 607 674-4165
Sherburne *(G-14810)*
Smithers Tools & Mch Pdts Inc D 845 876-3063
Rhinebeck *(G-13488)*
Snyder Industries Inc C 716 694-1240
Tonawanda *(G-15578)*
Solmac Inc G 716 630-7061
Williamsville *(G-16587)*
▲ **Sotek Inc** D 716 821-5961
Blasdell *(G-930)*
Source Technologies F 718 708-0305
Brooklyn *(G-2500)*
Springville Mfg Co Inc E 716 592-4957
Springville *(G-15021)*
Stanfordville Mch & Mfg Co Inc D 845 868-2266
Poughkeepsie *(G-13368)*
Staub Machine Company Inc E 716 649-4211
Hamburg *(G-5696)*
Stony Manufacturing Inc G 716 652-6730
Elma *(G-4461)*
▲ **Strecks Inc** E 518 273-4410
Watervliet *(G-16051)*
Strong Forge & Fabrication E 585 343-5251
Batavia *(G-635)*
Summit Instrument Corp G 516 433-0140
Hicksville *(G-6134)*
▲ **Superior Technology Inc** E 585 352-6556
Rochester *(G-14148)*
Superior Welding G 631 676-2751
Holbrook *(G-6213)*
Swissway Inc E 631 351-5350
Huntington Station *(G-6460)*
▲ **Sylhan LLC** E 631 243-6600
Edgewood *(G-4418)*
Syntec Technologies Inc F 585 464-9336
Rochester *(G-14153)*
T M Machine Inc G 716 822-0817
Buffalo *(G-3085)*
T R P Machine Inc E 631 567-9620
Bohemia *(G-1094)*
Tangent Machine & Tool Corp F 631 249-3088
Farmingdale *(G-4889)*
Tarsia Technical Industries G 631 231-8322
Hauppauge *(G-5955)*
Taylor Precision Machining G 607 535-3101
Montour Falls *(G-8328)*
Tchnologies N MRC Ameerica LLC G 716 822-4300
Buffalo *(G-3087)*
Ted Westbrook G 716 625-4443
Lockport *(G-7335)*
Temrick Inc G 631 567-8860
Bohemia *(G-1095)*
Tennyson Machine Co Inc F 914 668-5468
Mount Vernon *(G-8445)*
Theodosiou Inc G 718 728-6800
Long Island City *(G-7614)*
TI Group Auto Systems LLC G 315 568-7042
Seneca Falls *(G-14787)*
Ticonderoga Mch & Wldg Corp G 518 585-7444
Ticonderoga *(G-15514)*
Tioga Tool Inc F 607 785-6005
Endicott *(G-4611)*
Tobeyco Manufacturing Co Inc F 607 962-2446
Corning *(G-3827)*
▲ **Toolroom Express Inc** D 607 723-5373
Conklin *(G-3735)*
Towpath Machine Corp G 315 252-0112
Auburn *(G-505)*
Trebor Instrument Corp G 631 423-7026
Dix Hills *(G-4127)*
Triangle Grinding Machine Corp G 631 643-3636
West Babylon *(G-16200)*
Tricon Machine LLC G 585 671-0679
Webster *(G-16102)*
Tripar Manufacturing Co Inc G 631 563-0855
Bohemia *(G-1100)*
Triple Point Manufacturing G 631 218-4988
Bohemia *(G-1101)*
Triplett Machine Inc D 315 548-3198
Phelps *(G-12982)*
Truarc Fabrication G 518 691-0430
Gansevoort *(G-5248)*
▲ **Twinco Mfg Co Inc** E 631 231-0022
Hauppauge *(G-5963)*
Two Bills Machine & Tool Co F 516 437-2585
Floral Park *(G-4965)*
U-Cut Enterprises Inc E 315 492-9316
Jamesville *(G-6771)*
Ultra Tool and Manufacturing F 585 467-3700
Rochester *(G-14184)*
United Machining Inc G 631 589-6751
Bohemia *(G-1103)*
Universal Metal Fabricators F 845 331-8248
Kingston *(G-6927)*
▲ **Upturn Industries Inc** E 607 967-2923
Bainbridge *(G-536)*
Ushers Machine and Tool Co Inc E 518 877-5501
Round Lake *(G-14464)*
V A P Tool & Dye G 631 587-5262
West Islip *(G-16260)*
V Lake Industries Inc G 716 885-9141
Buffalo *(G-3115)*
Vader Systems LLC F 716 688-1600
Getzville *(G-5355)*
Valair Inc F 716 751-9480
Wilson *(G-16602)*
Van Laeken Richard G 315 331-0289
Newark *(G-12211)*
Van Reenen Tool & Die Inc F 585 288-6000
Rochester *(G-14198)*
▲ **Van Thomas Inc** E 585 426-1414
Rochester *(G-14199)*
Vanguard Metals Inc F 631 234-6500
Central Islip *(G-3388)*
Verns Machine Co Inc E 315 926-4223
Marion *(G-7810)*
Victoria Precision Inc G 845 473-9309
Hyde Park *(G-6472)*
Village Decoration Ltd E 315 437-2522
East Syracuse *(G-4380)*
Visimetrics Corporation G 716 871-7070
Buffalo *(G-3120)*
Vosky Precision Machining Corp F 631 737-3200
Ronkonkoma *(G-14429)*
◆ **Voss Manufacturing Inc** D 716 731-5062
Sanborn *(G-14557)*
Vytek Inc F 631 750-1770
Bohemia *(G-1107)*
W H Jones & Son Inc F 716 875-8233
Kenmore *(G-6864)*
W J Albro Machine Works Inc G 631 345-0657
Yaphank *(G-16728)*
Walsh & Sons Machine Inc G 845 526-0301
Mahopac *(G-7716)*
Washburn Manufacturing Tech G 607 387-3991
Trumansburg *(G-15641)*
Watkins Welding and Mch Sp Inc G 914 949-6168
White Plains *(G-16516)*
Wayne Integrated Tech Corp E 631 242-0213
Edgewood *(G-4423)*
Waynes Welding Inc E 315 768-6146
Yorkville *(G-16835)*
Weaver Machine & Tool Co Inc F 315 253-4422
Auburn *(G-509)*
Weiss Industries Inc G 518 784-9643
Valatie *(G-15740)*
◆ **Wendt Corporation** D 716 391-1200
Buffalo *(G-3127)*
West Falls Machine Co Inc F 716 655-0440
East Aurora *(G-4211)*
▲ **Westchstr Crnkshft Grndng** G 718 651-3900
East Elmhurst *(G-4226)*
Wiggby Precision Machine Corp E 718 439-6900
Brooklyn *(G-2646)*
Willard Machine F 716 885-1630
Buffalo *(G-3131)*

S I C

Employee Codes: A=Over 500 employees, B=251-500
C=101-250, D=51-100, E=20-50, F=10-19, G=5-9

35 INDUSTRIAL AND COMMERCIAL MACHINERY AND COMPUTER EQUIPMENT — SIC SECTION

Company	Code	Phone
▲ Willemin-Macodel Inc, Elmsford *(G-4579)*	G	914 345-3504
William Kanes Mfg Corp, Brooklyn *(G-2649)*	G	718 346-1515
William Moon Iron Works Inc, Catskill *(G-3309)*	F	518 943-3861
Williams Tool Inc, Chadwicks *(G-3401)*	E	315 737-7226
Winn Manufacturing Inc, Granville *(G-5525)*	G	518 642-3515
Woods Machine and Tool LLC, Nichols *(G-12351)*	F	607 699-3253
Wordingham Machine Co Inc, Rochester *(G-14212)*	E	585 924-2294
Wrightcut EDM & Machine Inc, Elmira *(G-4508)*	G	607 733-5018
Zip Products Inc, Rochester *(G-14220)*	F	585 482-0044

36 ELECTRONIC AND OTHER ELECTRICAL EQUIPMENT AND COMPONENTS, EXCEPT COMPUTER

3612 Power, Distribution & Specialty Transformers

Company	Code	Phone
Arstan Products International, Hicksville *(G-6061)*	F	516 433-1313
Berkshire Transformer, Central Islip *(G-3359)*	G	631 467-5328
Buffalo Power Electronics Ctr, Depew *(G-4083)*	F	716 651-1600
Caddell Burns Manufacturing Co, Northport *(G-12465)*	E	631 757-1772
Cooper Power Systems LLC, Olean *(G-12597)*	B	716 375-7100
Current Controls Inc, Wellsville *(G-16114)*	C	585 593-1544
Dyco Electronics Inc, Hornell *(G-6296)*	D	607 324-2030
Electron Coil Inc, Norwich *(G-12485)*	D	607 336-7414
Ems Development Corporation, Yaphank *(G-16709)*	D	631 345-6200
Exxelia-Raf Tabtronics LLC, Piffard *(G-12996)*	E	585 243-4331
Frederick Cowan & Company Inc, Wading River *(G-15884)*	F	631 369-0360
General Electric Company, Schenectady *(G-14675)*	A	518 385-4022
General Electric Company, Niskayuna *(G-12354)*	E	518 385-7620
Hale Electrical Dist Svcs Inc, Wales Center *(G-15901)*	F	716 818-7595
K Road Power Management LLC, New York *(G-10390)*	D	212 351-0535
Kepco Inc, Flushing *(G-5016)*	E	718 461-7000
Kepco Inc, Flushing *(G-5017)*	D	718 461-7000
Kepco Inc, Flushing *(G-5018)*	E	718 461-7000
Marvel Equipment Corp Inc, Brooklyn *(G-2175)*	G	718 383-6597
Mitchell Electronics Corp, Mount Vernon *(G-8422)*	E	914 699-3800
▲ Niagara Transformer Corp, Buffalo *(G-2970)*	D	716 896-6500
▲ Piller Power Systems Inc, Middletown *(G-8170)*	E	845 695-6658
Precision Electronics Inc, Copiague *(G-3774)*	F	631 842-4900
Railworks Corporation, Farmingdale *(G-4865)*	G	904 296-5055
Ram Transformer Technologies, New Rochelle *(G-8624)*	F	914 632-3988
Reenergy Black River LLC, Fort Drum *(G-5092)*	E	315 773-2314
Sag Harbor Industries Inc, Sag Harbor *(G-14502)*	F	631 725-0440
Schneider Electric It Corp, New York *(G-11509)*	F	646 335-0216
Schneider Electric Usa Inc, Penfield *(G-12945)*	F	585 377-1313
Siemens Corporation, New York *(G-11577)*	F	202 434-7800
Siemens USA Holdings Inc, New York *(G-11580)*	B	212 258-4000
▲ Spence Engineering Company Inc, Walden *(G-15897)*	C	845 778-5566
Sunward Electronics Inc, Troy *(G-15629)*	F	518 687-0030
▲ Switching Power Inc, Ronkonkoma *(G-14420)*	D	631 981-7231
Telephone Sales & Service Co, New York *(G-11796)*	E	212 233-8505
Transistor Devices Inc, Ronkonkoma *(G-14421)*	E	631 471-7492
Veeco Instruments Inc, Plainview *(G-13098)*	C	516 349-8300

3613 Switchgear & Switchboard Apparatus

Company	Code	Phone
▲ Abasco Inc, Hamburg *(G-5672)*	E	716 649-4790
All City Switchboard Corp, Long Island City *(G-7371)*	E	718 956-7244
Allied Circuits LLC, Buffalo *(G-2692)*	E	716 551-0285
Atlas Switch Co Inc, Garden City *(G-5251)*	E	516 222-6280
Avanti Control Systems Inc, Gloversville *(G-5452)*	G	518 921-4368
Benfield Control Systems Inc, White Plains *(G-16428)*	F	914 948-6660
Boulay Fabrication Inc, La Fayette *(G-6945)*	F	315 677-5247
C A M Graphics Co Inc, Farmingdale *(G-4731)*	E	631 842-3400
Citadel Electrical Sup Co Inc, Tappan *(G-15467)*	E	646 705-0333
Claddagh Electronics Ltd, Long Island City *(G-7410)*	E	718 784-0571
Cooper Industries LLC, Syracuse *(G-15291)*	E	315 477-7000
Cooper Power Systems LLC, Olean *(G-12597)*	B	716 375-7100
Custom Controls, Scipio Center *(G-14736)*	G	315 253-4785
Electric Swtchbard Sltions LLC, New Hyde Park *(G-8531)*	G	718 643-1105
Electrotech Service Eqp Corp, Astoria *(G-426)*	E	718 626-7700
▲ Ems Development Corporation, Yaphank *(G-16708)*	D	631 924-4736
Inertia Switch Inc, Orangeburg *(G-12679)*	E	845 359-8300
Junior Achevement of Eastrn NY, Latham *(G-7076)*	G	518 783-4336
◆ Leviton Manufacturing Co Inc, Melville *(G-8043)*	B	631 812-6000
Link Control Systems Inc, Ronkonkoma *(G-14370)*	F	631 471-3950
▲ Marquardt Switches Inc, Cazenovia *(G-3323)*	C	315 655-8050
Micro Instrument Corp, Rochester *(G-13939)*	D	585 458-3150
Odyssey Controls Inc, Bergen *(G-826)*	G	585 548-9800
Pacs Switchgear LLC, Bethpage *(G-851)*	G	516 465-7100
Product Station Inc, Jericho *(G-6798)*	F	516 942-4220
Schneider Electric Usa Inc, New York *(G-11510)*	C	646 335-0220
▲ Se-Mar Electric Co Inc, West Seneca *(G-16302)*	E	716 674-7404
Select Controls Inc, Bohemia *(G-1087)*	E	631 567-9010
Sinclair Technologies Inc, Hamburg *(G-5695)*	E	716 874-3682
Smith Control Systems Inc, Hudson *(G-6373)*	F	518 828-7646
Soc America Inc, Ronkonkoma *(G-14414)*	E	631 472-6666
▲ Switching Power Inc, Ronkonkoma *(G-14420)*	D	631 981-7231
Trac Regulators Inc, Mount Vernon *(G-8447)*	E	914 699-9352
▲ Transit Air Inc, Hornell *(G-6304)*	E	607 324-0216

3621 Motors & Generators

Company	Code	Phone
▲ Aeroflex Incorporated, Plainview *(G-13032)*	B	516 694-6700
Aeroflex Plainview Inc, Plainview *(G-13033)*	B	516 694-6700
Aeroflex Plainview Inc, Hauppauge *(G-5756)*	C	631 231-9100
Allied Motion Control Corp, Amherst *(G-209)*	G	716 242-7535
▲ Allied Motion Technologies Inc, Amherst *(G-211)*	C	716 242-8634
Allied Motion Technologies Inc, Watertown *(G-16000)*	C	315 782-5910
◆ American Precision Inds Inc, Amherst *(G-214)*	C	716 691-9100
Ametek Inc, Ronkonkoma *(G-14307)*	C	631 467-8400
Ametek Inc, Binghamton *(G-862)*	D	607 763-4700
Ametek Inc, Rochester *(G-13630)*	D	585 263-7700
Apogee Power Usa Inc, Hartsdale *(G-5742)*	F	202 746-2890
▲ Applied Power Systems Inc, Hicksville *(G-6059)*	E	516 935-2230
▲ ARC Systems Inc, Hauppauge *(G-5768)*	E	631 582-8020
▲ Automation Source Technologies, West Babylon *(G-16136)*	E	631 643-1678
Cellgen Inc, Freeport *(G-5149)*	G	516 889-9300
Con Rel Auto Electric Inc, Schenectady *(G-14666)*	E	518 356-1646
◆ Current Applications Inc, Watertown *(G-16010)*	E	315 788-4689
◆ D & D Motor Systems Inc, Syracuse *(G-15299)*	E	315 701-0861
Designatronics Incorporated, Hicksville *(G-6080)*	B	516 328-3300
EDP Renewables North Amer LLC, Albany *(G-71)*	E	518 426-1650
Electron Coil Inc, Norwich *(G-12485)*	D	607 336-7414
Elton El Mantle Inc, Syracuse *(G-15316)*	G	315 432-9067
Emes Motor Inc, Brooklyn *(G-1830)*	G	718 387-2445
Empire Division Inc, Syracuse *(G-15318)*	D	315 476-6273
▲ Ems Development Corporation, Yaphank *(G-16708)*	D	631 924-4736
Ener-G-Rotors Inc, Schenectady *(G-14670)*	G	518 372-2608
▲ Eni Technology Inc, Rochester *(G-13787)*	B	585 427-8300
▲ Faradyne Motors LLC, Palmyra *(G-12851)*	F	315 331-5985
◆ Felchar Manufacturing Corp, Binghamton *(G-884)*	A	607 723-3106
Franklin Electric Co Inc, Jamaica *(G-6645)*	A	718 244-7744
General Electric Company, Schenectady *(G-14679)*	B	518 385-2211
General Electric Intl Inc, Schenectady *(G-14682)*	B	518 385-2211
Generation Power LLC, Syracuse *(G-15333)*	G	315 234-2451
▲ Getec Inc, Ferndale *(G-4933)*	F	845 292-0800
Got Power Inc, Ronkonkoma *(G-14347)*	G	631 767-9493
Hes Inc, Addison *(G-6)*	G	607 359-2974
▲ IEC Holden Corporation, Plattsburgh *(G-13125)*	F	518 213-3991
Independent Field Svc LLC, Syracuse *(G-15342)*	G	315 559-9243
Industrial Test Eqp Co Inc, Port Washington *(G-13269)*	E	516 883-6423
Intelligen Power Systems LLC, Old Bethpage *(G-12586)*	G	212 750-0373
Island Components Group Inc, Holbrook *(G-6191)*	F	631 563-4224
◆ John G Rubino Inc, Auburn *(G-486)*	E	315 253-7396
Kaddis Manufacturing Corp, Honeoye Falls *(G-6270)*	G	585 624-3070
Lcdrives Corp, Potsdam *(G-13319)*	F	860 712-8926
Magna Products Corp, Rochester *(G-13923)*	E	585 647-2280
▲ Makerbot Industries LLC, Brooklyn *(G-2153)*	C	347 334-6800
Mks Medical Electronics, Rochester *(G-13950)*	C	585 292-7400

SIC SECTION
36 ELECTRONIC AND OTHER ELECTRICAL EQUIPMENT AND COMPONENTS, EXCEPT COMPUTER

▲ Modular Devices Inc .... D 631 345-3100
  Shirley *(G-14841)*
▲ Moley Magnetics Inc .... F 716 434-4023
  Lockport *(G-7320)*
Nidec Motor Corporation .... F 315 434-9303
  East Syracuse *(G-4361)*
P1 Generator Windings LLC .... G 518 930-2879
  Schenectady *(G-14702)*
▲ Power and Composite Tech LLC ... D 518 843-6825
  Amsterdam *(G-357)*
Power Gneration Indus Engs Inc ... E 315 633-9389
  Bridgeport *(G-1182)*
Premco Inc .... F 914 636-7095
  New Rochelle *(G-8623)*
Princetel Inc .... F 914 579-2410
  Hawthorne *(G-5996)*
Protective Power Systms & Cntr .... F 845 721-1875
  Staatsburg *(G-15024)*
Ruhle Companies Inc .... E 914 287-4000
  Valhalla *(G-15747)*
Sag Harbor Industries Inc .... E 631 725-0440
  Sag Harbor *(G-14502)*
▲ Sima Technologies LLC .... G 412 828-9130
  Hauppauge *(G-5940)*
▲ Sopark Corp .... D 716 822-0434
  Buffalo *(G-3070)*
Stature Electric Inc .... D 716 242-7535
  Amherst *(G-251)*
Suez Energy Astoria LLC .... C 718 274-7700
  Flushing *(G-5049)*
Supergen Products LLC .... G 315 573-7887
  Newark *(G-12208)*
▲ Taro Manufacturing Company Inc ... F 315 252-9430
  Auburn *(G-503)*
Troy Belting and Supply Co .... D 518 272-4920
  Watervliet *(G-16053)*
▲ Vdc Electronics Inc .... F 631 683-5850
  Huntington *(G-6425)*
W J Albro Machine Works Inc .... G 631 345-0657
  Yaphank *(G-16728)*

3624 Carbon & Graphite Prdts

▲ Americarb Inc .... D 419 281-5800
  Niagara Falls *(G-12259)*
Americarb International Corp .... G 419 281-5800
  Niagara Falls *(G-12260)*
▲ Carbon Graphite Materials Inc .... G 716 792-7979
  Brocton *(G-1195)*
Carbonfree Chemicals Spe I LLC ... E 914 421-4900
  White Plains *(G-16436)*
Go Blue Technologies Ltd .... G 631 404-6285
  North Babylon *(G-12360)*
◆ Graphite Metallizing Corp .... C 914 968-8400
  Yonkers *(G-16764)*
Hh Liquidating Corp .... A 646 282-2500
  New York *(G-10092)*
J V Precision Inc .... G 518 851-3200
  Hudson *(G-6357)*
Metal Coated Fibers Inc .... E 518 280-8514
  Schenectady *(G-14697)*
Metallized Carbon Corporation ..... C 914 941-3738
  Ossining *(G-12771)*
▲ Mwi Inc .... D 585 424-4200
  Rochester *(G-13961)*
Pyrotek Incorporated .... E 716 731-3221
  Sanborn *(G-14552)*
Saturn Industries Inc .... E 518 828-9956
  Hudson *(G-6370)*
Xactiv Inc .... F 585 288-7220
  Fairport *(G-4668)*

3625 Relays & Indl Controls

Addex Inc .... G 315 331-7700
  Newark *(G-12191)*
Adeptronics Incorporated .... G 631 667-0659
  Bay Shore *(G-652)*
Afi Cybernetics Corporation .... E 607 732-3244
  Elmira *(G-4472)*
Air Crafters Inc .... C 631 471-7788
  Ronkonkoma *(G-14295)*
◆ Altronix Corp .... D 718 567-8181
  Brooklyn *(G-1515)*
◆ American Precision Inds Inc ...... C 716 691-9100
  Amherst *(G-214)*
▲ Anderson Instrument Co Inc ...... D 518 922-5315
  Fultonville *(G-5234)*
Baco Controls Inc .... F 315 635-2500
  Baldwinsville *(G-551)*
Bakery Innovative Tech Corp .... F 631 758-3081
  Patchogue *(G-12861)*

Bemco of Western Ny Inc .... G 716 823-8400
  Buffalo *(G-2730)*
Bomac Inc .... G 315 433-9181
  Syracuse *(G-15260)*
▲ Burgess-Manning Inc .... D 716 662-6540
  Orchard Park *(G-12704)*
▲ C D A Inc .... G 631 473-1595
  Nesconset *(G-8483)*
Calia Technical Inc .... G 718 447-3928
  Staten Island *(G-15060)*
Con Rel Auto Electric Inc .... E 518 356-1646
  Schenectady *(G-14666)*
◆ Conic Systems Inc .... F 845 856-4053
  Port Jervis *(G-13226)*
Continental Instruments LLC .... E 631 842-9400
  Amityville *(G-268)*
▲ Cox & Company Inc .... C 212 366-0200
  Plainview *(G-13048)*
Datatran Labs Inc .... G 845 856-4313
  Port Jervis *(G-13227)*
Designatronics Incorporated .... B 516 328-3300
  Hicksville *(G-6080)*
▲ Designatronics Incorporated ..... G 516 328-3300
  Hicksville *(G-6079)*
Deutsch Relays .... F 631 342-1700
  Hauppauge *(G-5810)*
▲ Digital Instruments Inc .... F 716 874-5848
  Tonawanda *(G-15536)*
Dortronics Systems Inc .... E 631 725-0505
  Sag Harbor *(G-14499)*
▲ Dri Relays Inc .... D 631 342-1700
  Hauppauge *(G-5815)*
◆ Dyson-Kissner-Moran Corp .... E 212 661-4600
  Poughkeepsie *(G-13335)*
Eaton Corporation .... C 516 353-3017
  East Meadow *(G-4251)*
Eatons Crouse Hinds Business ..... F 315 477-7000
  Syracuse *(G-15313)*
Edo LLC .... C 631 630-4000
  Amityville *(G-274)*
Electronic Machine Parts LLC ...... F 631 434-3700
  Hauppauge *(G-5818)*
Enetics Inc .... G 585 924-5010
  Victor *(G-15844)*
Entertron Industries Inc .... E 716 772-7216
  Lockport *(G-7299)*
▲ Eversan Inc .... F 315 736-3967
  Whitesboro *(G-16527)*
Exfo Burleigh Pdts Group Inc .... D 585 301-1530
  Canandaigua *(G-3220)*
Fortitude Industries Inc .... D 607 324-1500
  Hornell *(G-6298)*
G C Controls Inc .... E 607 656-4117
  Greene *(G-5614)*
Gemtrol Inc .... G 716 894-0716
  Buffalo *(G-2844)*
General Control Systems Inc .... E 518 270-8045
  Green Island *(G-5605)*
General Oil Equipment Co Inc ...... E 716 691-7012
  Amherst *(G-229)*
Goddard Design Co .... G 718 599-0170
  Brooklyn *(G-1936)*
▲ Hasco Componets .... E 516 328-9292
  New Hyde Park *(G-8541)*
▲ I D E Processes Corporation ..... F 718 544-1177
  Kew Gardens *(G-6873)*
I E D Corp .... F 631 348-0424
  Islandia *(G-6529)*
▲ ICM Controls Corp .... F 315 233-5266
  North Syracuse *(G-12405)*
Industrial Indxing Systems Inc ...... E 585 924-9181
  Victor *(G-15850)*
Inertia Switch Inc .... E 845 359-8300
  Orangeburg *(G-12679)*
▲ Infitec Inc .... D 315 433-1150
  East Syracuse *(G-4352)*
▲ Interntnal Cntrls Msrmnts Corp ... C 315 233-5266
  North Syracuse *(G-12406)*
ITT Aerospace Controls LLC .... G 914 641-2000
  White Plains *(G-16463)*
ITT Corp .... E 716 662-1900
  Orchard Park *(G-12719)*
ITT Corporation .... E 585 269-7109
  Hemlock *(G-6004)*
ITT Corporation .... D 866 448-8372
  Seneca Falls *(G-14776)*
ITT Corporation .... D 315 568-2811
  Seneca Falls *(G-14777)*
ITT Inc .... E 914 641-2000
  White Plains *(G-16464)*

ITT International Holdings Inc ...... G 914 641-2000
  White Plains *(G-16466)*
ITT LLC .... G 315 568-4733
  Seneca Falls *(G-14780)*
ITT LLC .... D 315 258-4904
  Auburn *(G-484)*
ITT LLC .... G 914 641-2000
  Seneca Falls *(G-14781)*
◆ ITT LLC .... B 914 641-2000
  White Plains *(G-16467)*
JE Miller Inc .... F 315 437-6811
  East Syracuse *(G-4355)*
Kaman Automation Inc .... E 585 254-8840
  Rochester *(G-13903)*
◆ Kearney-National Inc .... F 212 661-4600
  New York *(G-10427)*
◆ Kussmaul Electronics Co Inc ..... E 631 218-0298
  West Sayville *(G-16290)*
L-3 Cmmnctons Ntronix Holdings ... D 212 697-1111
  New York *(G-10496)*
Linde LLC .... D 716 773-7552
  Grand Island *(G-5506)*
Logitek Inc .... G 631 567-1100
  Bohemia *(G-1048)*
Machine Components Corp .... E 516 694-7222
  Plainview *(G-13071)*
Magnus Precision Mfg Inc .... D 315 548-8032
  Phelps *(G-12978)*
◆ Magtrol Inc .... E 716 668-5555
  Buffalo *(G-2935)*
▲ Makerbot Industries LLC .... C 347 334-6800
  Brooklyn *(G-2153)*
▲ Marine & Indus Hydraulics Inc ... F 914 698-2036
  Mamaroneck *(G-7747)*
▲ Marquardt Switches Inc .... C 315 655-8050
  Cazenovia *(G-3323)*
◆ Mason Industries Inc .... B 631 348-0282
  Hauppauge *(G-5881)*
Mason Industries Inc .... E 631 348-0282
  Hauppauge *(G-5882)*
Micromod Automation Inc .... E 585 321-9200
  Rochester *(G-13942)*
▼ Micropen Technologies Corp ..... D 585 624-2610
  Honeoye Falls *(G-6271)*
Moog Inc .... E 716 687-4778
  Elma *(G-4454)*
◆ Moog Inc .... A 716 652-2000
  Elma *(G-4453)*
▲ Morris Products Inc .... F 518 743-0523
  Queensbury *(G-13434)*
N E Controls LLC .... F 315 626-2480
  Syracuse *(G-15379)*
▲ Nas-Tra Automotive Inds Inc ..... C 631 225-1225
  Lindenhurst *(G-7182)*
National Time Recording Eqp Co ... F 212 227-3310
  New York *(G-10887)*
Nitram Energy Inc .... E 716 662-6540
  Orchard Park *(G-12732)*
North Point Technologies .... E 607 238-1114
  Johnson City *(G-6815)*
North Point Technology LLC .... F 866 885-3377
  Endicott *(G-4605)*
Nsi Industries LLC .... C 800 841-2505
  Mount Vernon *(G-8426)*
▲ Omntec Mfg Inc .... E 631 981-2001
  Ronkonkoma *(G-14391)*
Panelogic Inc .... E 607 962-6319
  Corning *(G-3823)*
Peerless Instrument Co Inc .... C 631 396-6500
  Farmingdale *(G-4845)*
Peraton Inc .... E 315 838-7000
  Rome *(G-14266)*
Powr-UPS Corp .... E 631 345-5700
  Shirley *(G-14843)*
Precision Electronics Inc .... F 631 842-4900
  Copiague *(G-3774)*
Precision Mechanisms Corp .... E 516 333-5955
  Westbury *(G-16366)*
◆ Pulsafeeder Inc .... C 585 292-8000
  Rochester *(G-14054)*
Rasp Incorporated .... E 518 747-8020
  Gansevoort *(G-5245)*
▲ Rochester Industrial Ctrl Inc ..... C 315 524-4555
  Ontario *(G-12663)*
Rockwell Automation Inc .... E 585 487-2700
  Pittsford *(G-13026)*
Rotork Controls Inc .... F 585 328-1550
  Rochester *(G-14104)*
▲ Rotork Controls Inc .... C 585 247-2304
  Rochester *(G-14105)*

Employee Codes: A=Over 500 employees, B=251-500
C=101-250, D=51-100, E=20-50, F=10-19, G=5-9

Ruhle Companies Inc .... E 914 287-4000
Valhalla *(G-15747)*

◆ **Schmersal Inc** .... E 914 347-4775
Hawthorne *(G-5997)*

Select Controls Inc .... E 631 567-9010
Bohemia *(G-1087)*

Service Mfg Group Inc .... F 716 893-1482
Buffalo *(G-3063)*

▲ **Soft-Noze Usa Inc** .... G 315 732-2726
Frankfort *(G-5112)*

◆ **Soundcoat Company Inc** .... D 631 242-2200
Deer Park *(G-4047)*

Ssac Inc .... E 800 843-8848
Baldwinsville *(G-563)*

▲ **Stetron International Inc** .... F 716 854-3443
Buffalo *(G-3077)*

Switches and Sensors Inc .... F 631 924-2167
Yaphank *(G-16723)*

Teale Machine Company Inc .... D 585 244-6700
Rochester *(G-14160)*

Techniflo Corporation .... G 716 741-3500
Clarence Center *(G-3549)*

▲ **Teknic Inc** .... E 585 784-7454
Victor *(G-15871)*

▲ **Tork Inc** .... D 914 664-3542
Mount Vernon *(G-8446)*

Transistor Devices Inc .... E 631 471-7492
Ronkonkoma *(G-14421)*

Trident Valve Actuator Co .... F 914 698-2650
Mamaroneck *(G-7759)*

◆ **Unimar Inc** .... F 315 699-4400
Syracuse *(G-15448)*

US Drives Inc .... D 716 731-1606
Niagara Falls *(G-12346)*

Vibration & Noise Engrg Corp .... G 716 827-4959
Orchard Park *(G-12749)*

▲ **Vibration Eliminator Co Inc** .... E 631 841-4000
Copiague *(G-3791)*

Weldcomputer Corporation .... F 518 283-2897
Troy *(G-15636)*

Young & Franklin Inc .... D 315 457-3110
Liverpool *(G-7274)*

Zeppelin Electric Company Inc .... G 631 928-9467
East Setauket *(G-4315)*

3629 Electrical Indl Apparatus, NEC

▲ **Alliance Control Systems Inc** .... G 845 279-4430
Brewster *(G-1156)*

Applied Energy Solutions LLC .... E 585 538-3270
Caledonia *(G-3153)*

▲ **Applied Power Systems Inc** .... E 516 935-2230
Hicksville *(G-6059)*

C & M Circuits Inc .... E 631 589-0208
Bohemia *(G-992)*

Calibration Technologies Inc .... G 631 676-6133
Centereach *(G-3343)*

China Lithium Technologies .... G 212 391-2688
New York *(G-9280)*

▲ **Curtis Instruments Inc** .... C 914 666-2971
Mount Kisco *(G-8339)*

Curtis/Palmer Hydroelectric LP .... F 518 654-6297
Corinth *(G-3808)*

Cygnus Automation Inc .... E 631 981-0909
Bohemia *(G-1006)*

Eluminocity US Inc .... G 651 528-1165
New York *(G-9660)*

▲ **Ems Development Corporation** .... D 631 924-4736
Yaphank *(G-16708)*

Endicott Research Group Inc .... D 607 754-9187
Endicott *(G-4590)*

Energy Harvesters LLC .... G 617 325-9852
Rochester *(G-13783)*

◆ **G B International Trdg Co Ltd** .... C 607 785-0938
Endicott *(G-4594)*

General Electric Company .... E 518 459-4110
Albany *(G-77)*

General Electric Company .... B 518 746-5750
Hudson Falls *(G-6379)*

GM Components Holdings LLC .... B 716 439-2463
Lockport *(G-7305)*

GM Components Holdings LLC .... B 716 439-2011
Lockport *(G-7306)*

GW Lisk Company Inc .... E 315 548-2165
Phelps *(G-12977)*

Key Signals .... G 631 433-2962
East Moriches *(G-4257)*

◆ **Kussmaul Electronics Co Inc** .... E 631 218-0298
West Sayville *(G-16290)*

▲ **Nrd LLC** .... E 716 773-7634
Grand Island *(G-5508)*

Plug Power Inc .... G 585 474-3993
Rochester *(G-14024)*

Solid Sealing Technology Inc .... E 518 874-3600
Watervliet *(G-16050)*

◆ **Tonoga Inc** .... C 518 658-3202
Petersburg *(G-12973)*

Viking Technologies Ltd .... E 631 957-8000
Lindenhurst *(G-7204)*

▲ **Walter R Tucker Entps Ltd** .... E 607 467-2866
Deposit *(G-4112)*

3631 Household Cooking Eqpt

Applince Installation Svc Corp .... E 716 884-7425
Buffalo *(G-2707)*

Bakers Pride Oven Co Inc .... C 914 576-0200
New Rochelle *(G-8591)*

◆ **Korin Japanese Trading Corp** .... E 212 587-7021
New York *(G-10471)*

▲ **Oxo International Inc** .... C 212 242-3333
New York *(G-11080)*

▲ **Podravka International USA** .... F 212 661-0125
New York *(G-11214)*

Steelstone Group LLC .... G 888 552-0033
Brooklyn *(G-2519)*

◆ **Toshiba America Inc** .... E 212 596-0600
New York *(G-11872)*

3632 Household Refrigerators & Freezers

Acme Kitchenettes Corp .... E 518 828-4191
Hudson *(G-6337)*

Ae Fund Inc .... E 315 698-7650
Brewerton *(G-1149)*

General Electric Company .... A 518 385-4022
Schenectady *(G-14675)*

Robin Industries Ltd .... F 718 218-9616
Brooklyn *(G-2410)*

Sure-Kol Refrigerator Co Inc .... F 718 625-0601
Brooklyn *(G-2542)*

3633 Household Laundry Eqpt

AES Electronics Inc .... G 212 371-8120
New York *(G-8763)*

Coinmach Service Corp .... A 516 349-8555
Plainview *(G-13042)*

CSC SW Holdco Inc .... D 516 349-8555
Plainview *(G-13049)*

Penn Enterprises Inc .... F 845 446-0765
West Point *(G-16283)*

Pluslux LLC .... G 516 371-4400
Inwood *(G-6499)*

Spin Holdco Inc .... G 516 349-8555
Plainview *(G-13089)*

3634 Electric Household Appliances

A & M LLC .... G 212 354-1341
New York *(G-8687)*

▲ **Abbott Industries Inc** .... B 718 291-0800
Jamaica *(G-6622)*

▲ **Advanced Response Corporation** .... G 212 459-0887
New York *(G-8757)*

Algonquin Power .... G 315 393-5595
Ogdensburg *(G-12569)*

American Comfort Direct LLC .... E 201 364-8309
New York *(G-8825)*

Bino Products LLC .... E 212 689-6008
New York *(G-9085)*

▲ **Brumis Imports Inc** .... D 646 845-6000
New York *(G-9152)*

Dampits International Inc .... G 212 581-3047
New York *(G-9461)*

▼ **Fulton Volcanic Inc** .... D 315 298-5121
Pulaski *(G-13384)*

General Electric Company .... G 315 554-2000
Skaneateles *(G-14872)*

Goodnature Products Inc .... E 716 855-3325
Orchard Park *(G-12716)*

▲ **Harrys Inc** .... D 888 212-6855
New York *(G-10044)*

▲ **Peek A Boo USA Inc** .... G 201 533-8700
New York *(G-11135)*

▲ **Quality Life Inc** .... F 718 939-5787
College Point *(G-3662)*

Quip Nyc Inc .... G 917 331-3993
Brooklyn *(G-2372)*

Remedies Surgical Supplies .... G 718 599-5301
Brooklyn *(G-2396)*

Sundance Industries Inc .... G 845 795-5809
Milton *(G-8198)*

▲ **Tactica International Inc** .... E 212 575-0500
New York *(G-11774)*

◆ **Uniware Houseware Corp** .... E 631 242-7400
Brentwood *(G-1146)*

US Health Equipment Company .... E 845 658-7576
Kingston *(G-6929)*

Valad Electric Heating Corp .... F 888 509-4927
Montgomery *(G-8319)*

Vincent Genovese .... G 631 281-8170
Mastic Beach *(G-7912)*

◆ **World Trading Center Inc** .... G 631 273-3330
Hauppauge *(G-5978)*

3635 Household Vacuum Cleaners

American Comfort Direct LLC .... E 201 364-8309
New York *(G-8825)*

D & C Cleaning Inc .... F 631 789-5659
Copiague *(G-3756)*

▲ **Global Resources Sg Inc** .... F 212 686-1411
New York *(G-9945)*

▲ **Nationwide Sales and Service** .... F 631 491-6625
Farmingdale *(G-4832)*

Tri County Custom Vacuum .... G 845 774-7595
Monroe *(G-8282)*

3639 Household Appliances, NEC

A Gatty Products Inc .... G 914 592-3903
Elmsford *(G-4527)*

◆ **Ajmadison Corp** .... D 718 532-1800
Brooklyn *(G-1497)*

Barrage .... E 212 586-9390
New York *(G-9020)*

Design Solutions Ll Inc .... G 631 656-8700
Saint James *(G-14511)*

Hobart Corporation .... E 631 864-3440
Commack *(G-3695)*

Platinum Carting Corp .... F 631 649-4322
Bay Shore *(G-706)*

Talmu NY LLC .... G 347 434-6700
Brooklyn *(G-2555)*

3641 Electric Lamps

◆ **Atlantic Ultraviolet Corp** .... E 631 234-3275
Hauppauge *(G-5773)*

Boehm Surgical Instrument Corp .... F 585 436-6584
Rochester *(G-13671)*

Emitled Inc .... G 516 531-3533
Westbury *(G-16328)*

General Electric Company .... A 518 385-4022
Schenectady *(G-14675)*

Goldstar Lighting LLC .... F 646 543-6811
New York *(G-9956)*

▲ **K & H Industries Inc** .... F 716 312-0088
Hamburg *(G-5683)*

K & H Industries Inc .... E 716 312-0088
Hamburg *(G-5684)*

▲ **Kreon Inc** .... G 516 470-9522
Bethpage *(G-844)*

▲ **La Mar Lighting Co Inc** .... E 631 777-7700
Farmingdale *(G-4806)*

▲ **Led Waves Inc** .... F 347 416-6182
Brooklyn *(G-2103)*

◆ **Lighting Holdings Intl LLC** .... A 845 306-1850
Purchase *(G-13391)*

▲ **Lowel-Light Manufacturing Inc** .... E 718 921-0600
Brooklyn *(G-2137)*

▲ **Make-Waves Instrument Corp** .... E 716 681-7524
Buffalo *(G-2936)*

Oledworks LLC .... E 585 287-6802
Rochester *(G-13985)*

Philips Elec N Amer Corp .... C 607 776-3692
Bath *(G-648)*

Preston Glass Industries Inc .... E 718 997-8888
Forest Hills *(G-5080)*

▲ **Ric-Lo Productions Ltd** .... E 845 469-2285
Chester *(G-3481)*

▲ **Saratoga Lighting Holdings LLC** .... A 212 906-7800
New York *(G-11487)*

◆ **Satco Products Inc** .... D 631 243-2022
Edgewood *(G-4415)*

Siemens Corporation .... F 202 434-7800
New York *(G-11577)*

Siemens USA Holdings Inc .... B 212 258-4000
New York *(G-11580)*

Welch Allyn Inc .... A 315 685-4347
Skaneateles Falls *(G-14884)*

▲ **Westron Corporation** .... E 516 678-2300
Oceanside *(G-12565)*

3643 Current-Carrying Wiring Devices

99cent World and Variety Corp.............G....... 212 740-0010
New York *(G-8686)*
Alstom Signaling Inc.............E....... 585 274-8700
Schenectady *(G-14648)*
Andros Manufacturing Corp.............F....... 585 663-5700
Rochester *(G-13633)*
Another 99 Cent Paradise.............G....... 718 786-4578
Sunnyside *(G-15201)*
Associated Lightning Rod Co.............F....... 845 373-8309
Millerton *(G-8192)*
Atc Plastics LLC.............E....... 212 375-2515
New York *(G-8943)*
Automatic Connector Inc.............F....... 631 543-5000
Hauppauge *(G-5774)*
Belden Inc.............B....... 607 796-5600
Horseheads *(G-6306)*
Bronx New Way Corp.............G....... 347 431-1385
Bronx *(G-1233)*
C A M Graphics Co Inc.............E....... 631 842-3400
Farmingdale *(G-4731)*
Charlton Precision Products.............G....... 845 338-2351
Kingston *(G-6894)*
Command Components Corporation.............G....... 631 666-4411
Bay Shore *(G-675)*
Cooper Power Systems LLC.............B....... 716 375-7100
Olean *(G-12597)*
▲ **Cox & Company Inc**.............C....... 212 366-0200
Plainview *(G-13048)*
Crown Die Casting Corp.............E....... 914 667-5400
Mount Vernon *(G-8392)*
▲ **Delfingen Us-New York Inc**.............E....... 716 215-0300
Niagara Falls *(G-12277)*
Dollar Popular Inc.............G....... 914 375-0361
Yonkers *(G-16751)*
EB Acquisitions LLC.............D....... 212 355-3310
New York *(G-9614)*
Exxelia-Raf Tabtronics LLC.............E....... 585 243-4331
Piffard *(G-12996)*
◆ **Fiber Instrument Sales Inc**.............C....... 315 736-2206
Oriskany *(G-12757)*
Heary Bros Lghtning Protection.............E....... 716 941-6141
Springville *(G-15018)*
Hubbell Inc.............E....... 845 586-2707
Margaretville *(G-7798)*
Inertia Switch Inc.............E....... 845 359-8300
Orangeburg *(G-12679)*
International Key Supply LLC.............F....... 631 983-6096
Farmingdale *(G-4788)*
Jaguar Industries Inc.............F....... 845 947-1800
Haverstraw *(G-5979)*
Joldeson One Aerospace Inds.............D....... 718 848-7396
Ozone Park *(G-12827)*
▲ **K & H Industries Inc**.............F....... 716 312-0088
Hamburg *(G-5683)*
▲ **Kelta Inc**.............E....... 631 789-5000
Edgewood *(G-4406)*
L3 Technologies Inc.............A....... 631 436-7400
Hauppauge *(G-5859)*
◆ **Leviton Manufacturing Co Inc**.............B....... 631 812-6000
Melville *(G-8043)*
◆ **Lighting Holdings Intl LLC**.............A....... 845 306-1850
Purchase *(G-13391)*
Lite Brite Manufacturing Inc.............F....... 718 855-9797
Brooklyn *(G-2129)*
Lourdes Industries Inc.............D....... 631 234-6600
Hauppauge *(G-5873)*
▲ **Micro Contacts Inc**.............E....... 516 433-4830
Hicksville *(G-6109)*
Mini-Circuits Fort Wayne LLC.............B....... 718 934-4500
Brooklyn *(G-2210)*
▲ **Monarch Electric Products Inc**.............G....... 718 583-7996
Bronx *(G-1335)*
Mono-Systems Inc.............E....... 716 821-1344
Buffalo *(G-2953)*
▲ **NEa Manufacturing Corp**.............E....... 516 371-4200
Inwood *(G-6497)*
Orbit International Corp.............D....... 631 435-8300
Hauppauge *(G-5907)*
▼ **Pass & Seymour Inc**.............B....... 315 468-6211
Syracuse *(G-15394)*
RE 99 Cents Inc.............G....... 718 639-2325
Woodside *(G-16674)*
Reynolds Packaging McHy Inc.............D....... 716 358-6451
Falconer *(G-4690)*
Rodale Wireless Inc.............E....... 631 231-0044
Hauppauge *(G-5929)*
Saturn Industries Inc.............E....... 518 828-9956
Hudson *(G-6370)*
▼ **Sector Microwave Inds Inc**.............D....... 631 242-2245
Deer Park *(G-4043)*
Sinclair Technologies Inc.............E....... 716 874-3682
Hamburg *(G-5695)*
▲ **Stever-Locke Industries Inc**.............G....... 585 624-3450
Honeoye Falls *(G-6274)*
▲ **Superpower Inc**.............E....... 518 346-1414
Schenectady *(G-14718)*
▲ **Switching Power Inc**.............D....... 631 981-7231
Ronkonkoma *(G-14420)*
Swivelier Company Inc.............D....... 845 353-1455
Blauvelt *(G-941)*
▲ **Tappan Wire & Cable Inc**.............C....... 845 353-9000
Blauvelt *(G-942)*
▲ **Tii Technologies Inc**.............E....... 516 364-9300
Edgewood *(G-4419)*
Utility Systems Tech Inc.............F....... 518 326-4142
Watervliet *(G-16055)*
▲ **Whirlwind Music Distrs Inc**.............D....... 800 733-9473
Rochester *(G-14207)*
▲ **Zierick Manufacturing Corp**.............D....... 800 882-8020
Mount Kisco *(G-8361)*

3644 Noncurrent-Carrying Wiring Devices

Cables and Chips Inc.............E....... 212 619-3132
New York *(G-9173)*
Chase Corporation.............F....... 631 827-0476
Northport *(G-12466)*
Complete SEC & Contrls Inc.............F....... 631 421-7200
Huntington Station *(G-6437)*
▲ **Gerome Technologies Inc**.............D....... 518 463-1324
Menands *(G-8085)*
Highland Valley Supply Inc.............F....... 845 849-2863
Wappingers Falls *(G-15934)*
▲ **J H C Fabrications Inc**.............E....... 718 649-0065
Brooklyn *(G-2022)*
◆ **Pfisterer Lapp LLC**.............C....... 585 768-6221
Le Roy *(G-7124)*
◆ **Producto Electric Corp**.............E....... 845 359-4900
Orangeburg *(G-12688)*
▲ **Quadristi LLC**.............F....... 585 279-3318
Rochester *(G-14059)*
Speedzone Inc.............G....... 631 750-1973
Oakdale *(G-12521)*
▲ **Superflex Ltd**.............E....... 718 768-1400
Brooklyn *(G-2535)*
▲ **Varflex Corporation**.............C....... 315 336-4400
Rome *(G-14278)*
▲ **Veja Electronics Inc**.............D....... 631 321-6086
Deer Park *(G-4058)*
▲ **Volt Tek Inc**.............F....... 585 377-2050
Fairport *(G-4666)*
▲ **Von Roll Usa Inc**.............C....... 518 344-7100
Schenectady *(G-14727)*
Von Roll Usa Inc.............E....... 203 562-2171
Schenectady *(G-14726)*
▲ **Zierick Manufacturing Corp**.............D....... 800 882-8020
Mount Kisco *(G-8361)*

3645 Residential Lighting Fixtures

▲ **A-1 Stamping & Spinning Corp**.............F....... 718 388-2626
Rockaway Park *(G-14227)*
◆ **Adesso Inc**.............E....... 212 736-4440
New York *(G-8735)*
▲ **Aesthonics Inc**.............D....... 646 723-2463
Brooklyn *(G-1492)*
Artemis Studios Inc.............D....... 718 788-6022
Brooklyn *(G-1558)*
Az-Light Inc.............G....... 716 837-5533
Buffalo *(G-2719)*
▲ **Canarm Ltd**.............G....... 800 267-4427
Ogdensburg *(G-12572)*
▲ **Cooper Lighting LLC**.............C....... 516 470-1000
Hicksville *(G-6071)*
Custom Lampshades Inc.............F....... 718 254-0500
Brooklyn *(G-1742)*
▲ **David Weeks Studio**.............F....... 212 966-3433
New York *(G-9486)*
▲ **Dreyfus Ashby Inc**.............E....... 212 818-0770
New York *(G-9578)*
Eaton Corporation.............E....... 315 579-2872
Syracuse *(G-15311)*
▲ **ER Butler & Co Inc**.............E....... 212 925-3565
New York *(G-9699)*
◆ **Hudson Valley Lighting Inc**.............D....... 845 561-0300
Wappingers Falls *(G-15935)*
▲ **Jamaica Lamp Corp**.............E....... 718 776-5039
Queens Village *(G-13409)*
Jimco Lamp & Manufacturing Co.............G....... 631 218-2152
Islip *(G-6547)*
Judis Lampshades Inc.............G....... 917 561-3921
Brooklyn *(G-2055)*
▲ **Litelab Corp**.............C....... 716 856-4300
Buffalo *(G-2926)*
Matov Industries Inc.............E....... 718 392-5060
Long Island City *(G-7518)*
▲ **Modulightor Inc**.............F....... 212 371-0336
New York *(G-10832)*
New Generation Lighting Inc.............F....... 212 966-0328
New York *(G-10923)*
Nulux Inc.............E....... 718 383-1112
Ridgewood *(G-13544)*
Philips Elec N Amer Corp.............C....... 607 776-3692
Bath *(G-648)*
Pompian Manufacturing Co Inc.............G....... 914 476-7076
Yonkers *(G-16793)*
▲ **Preciseled Inc**.............F....... 516 418-5337
Valley Stream *(G-15790)*
▲ **Prestigeline Inc**.............D....... 631 273-3636
Bay Shore *(G-710)*
▲ **Quality HM Brands Holdings LLC**.............G....... 718 292-2024
Bronx *(G-1368)*
Quoizel Inc.............E....... 631 436-4402
Hauppauge *(G-5927)*
Rapid-Lite Fixture Corporation.............F....... 347 599-2600
Brooklyn *(G-2384)*
Remains Lighting.............E....... 212 675-8051
New York *(G-11358)*
Sandy Littman Inc.............G....... 845 562-1112
Newburgh *(G-12245)*
▲ **Saratoga Lighting Holdings LLC**.............A....... 212 906-7800
New York *(G-11487)*
◆ **Satco Products Inc**.............D....... 631 243-2022
Edgewood *(G-4415)*
Savwatt Usa Inc.............G....... 646 478-2676
New York *(G-11494)*
▲ **Solarwaterway Inc**.............E....... 888 998-5337
Brooklyn *(G-2496)*
◆ **Swarovski Lighting Ltd**.............B....... 518 563-7500
Plattsburgh *(G-13161)*
Swarovski Lighting Ltd.............B....... 518 324-6378
Plattsburgh *(G-13162)*
Swivelier Company Inc.............D....... 845 353-1455
Blauvelt *(G-941)*
Tarsier Ltd.............C....... 646 880-8680
New York *(G-11785)*
Tudor Electrical Supply Co Inc.............G....... 212 867-7550
New York *(G-11912)*
Two Worlds Arts Ltd.............G....... 212 929-2210
New York *(G-11920)*
Ulster Precision Inc.............E....... 845 338-0995
Kingston *(G-6925)*
▲ **Vaughan Designs Inc**.............F....... 212 319-7070
New York *(G-12000)*
▲ **Vision Quest Lighting Inc**.............E....... 631 737-4800
East Setauket *(G-4314)*
▲ **Wainland Inc**.............E....... 718 626-2233
Astoria *(G-448)*

3646 Commercial, Indl & Institutional Lighting Fixtures

▲ **A-1 Stamping & Spinning Corp**.............F....... 718 388-2626
Rockaway Park *(G-14227)*
AEP Environmental LLC.............F....... 716 446-0739
Buffalo *(G-2690)*
▲ **Aesthonics Inc**.............D....... 646 723-2463
Brooklyn *(G-1492)*
▲ **Altman Stage Lighting Co Inc**.............C....... 914 476-7987
Yonkers *(G-16733)*
Apogee Translite Inc.............E....... 631 254-6975
Deer Park *(G-3944)*
▲ **Apparatus Studio**.............E....... 646 527-9732
New York *(G-8887)*
Aquarii Inc.............G....... 315 672-8807
Camillus *(G-3194)*
Aristocrat Lighting Inc.............F....... 718 522-0003
Brooklyn *(G-1553)*
▲ **Arlee Lighting Corp**.............G....... 516 595-8558
Inwood *(G-6485)*
Big Shine Worldwide Inc.............G....... 845 444-5255
Newburgh *(G-12216)*
▲ **Canarm Ltd**.............G....... 800 267-4427
Ogdensburg *(G-12572)*
▲ **Coldstream Group Inc**.............F....... 914 698-5959
Mamaroneck *(G-7739)*
▲ **Contemporary Visions LLC**.............G....... 845 926-5469
Wappingers Falls *(G-15928)*
Cooper Industries LLC.............E....... 315 477-7000
Syracuse *(G-15291)*

S I C

Employee Codes: A=Over 500 employees, B=251-500
C=101-250, D=51-100, E=20-50, F=10-19, G=5-9

2019 Harris
New York Manufacturers Directory

775

36 ELECTRONIC AND OTHER ELECTRICAL EQUIPMENT AND COMPONENTS, EXCEPT COMPUTER

▲ Cooper Lighting LLC .... C 516 470-1000
   Hicksville *(G-6071)*
▲ Dreyfus Ashby Inc .... E 212 818-0770
   New York *(G-9578)*
E-Ffinergy Group LLC .... G 845 547-2424
   Suffern *(G-15189)*
▲ Edison Price Lighting Inc .... C 718 685-0700
   Long Island City *(G-7433)*
Edison Price Lighting Inc .... D 718 685-0700
   Long Island City *(G-7434)*
Electric Lighting Agencies .... E 212 645-4580
   New York *(G-9640)*
Energy Conservation & Sup Inc .... E 718 855-5888
   Brooklyn *(G-1836)*
G&G Led LLC .... E 800 285-6780
   Clifton Park *(G-3566)*
Global Lighting Inc .... G 914 591-4095
   Yonkers *(G-16762)*
Green Beam Led Inc .... E 718 439-6262
   Brooklyn *(G-1949)*
▲ Green Energy Concepts Inc .... G 845 238-2574
   Chester *(G-3476)*
◆ Hudson Valley Lighting Inc .... D 845 561-0300
   Wappingers Falls *(G-15935)*
Ideoli Group Inc .... F 212 705-8769
   Port Washington *(G-13268)*
▲ Jesco Lighting Inc .... E 718 366-3211
   Port Washington *(G-13273)*
▲ Jesco Lighting Group LLC .... E 718 366-3211
   Port Washington *(G-13274)*
▲ La Mar Lighting Co Inc .... E 631 777-7700
   Farmingdale *(G-4806)*
LDI Lighting Inc .... G 718 384-4490
   Brooklyn *(G-2097)*
LDI Lighting Inc .... G 718 384-4490
   Brooklyn *(G-2098)*
▲ Legion Lighting Co Inc .... E 718 498-1770
   Brooklyn *(G-2107)*
▲ Light Waves Concept Inc .... F 212 677-6400
   Brooklyn *(G-2121)*
Lighting By Dom Yonkers Inc .... G 914 968-8700
   Yonkers *(G-16779)*
▲ Lighting Services Inc .... D 845 942-2800
   Stony Point *(G-15174)*
▲ Linear Lighting Corporation .... C 718 361-7552
   Long Island City *(G-7500)*
Lite Brite Manufacturing Inc .... F 718 855-9797
   Brooklyn *(G-2129)*
▲ Lite-Makers Inc .... E 718 739-9300
   Jamaica *(G-6656)*
Litelab Corp .... E 718 361-6829
   Long Island City *(G-7502)*
▲ Litelab Corp .... C 716 856-4300
   Buffalo *(G-2926)*
▲ LSI Lightron Inc .... A 845 562-5500
   New Windsor *(G-8649)*
▲ Lukas Lighting Inc .... E 800 841-4011
   Long Island City *(G-7506)*
Luminatta Inc .... G 914 664-3600
   Mount Vernon *(G-8419)*
Luminescent Systems Inc .... B 716 655-0800
   East Aurora *(G-4204)*
▲ Magniflood Inc .... E 631 226-1000
   Amityville *(G-301)*
Matov Industries Inc .... E 718 392-5060
   Long Island City *(G-7518)*
▲ Modulightor Inc .... F 212 371-0336
   New York *(G-10832)*
Mtz Enterprises Inc .... E 347 834-2716
   Brooklyn *(G-2237)*
▲ North American Mfg Entps Inc ..... E 718 524-4370
   Staten Island *(G-15109)*
North American Mfg Entps Inc .... E 718 524-4370
   Staten Island *(G-15110)*
Nulux Inc .... E 718 383-1112
   Ridgewood *(G-13544)*
Oledworks LLC .... E 585 287-6802
   Rochester *(G-13985)*
Philips Lighting N Amer Corp .... C 646 265-7170
   New York *(G-11182)*
▲ Preciseled Inc .... F 516 418-5337
   Valley Stream *(G-15790)*
Primelite Manufacturing Corp .... F 516 868-4411
   Freeport *(G-5176)*
Rapid-Lite Fixture Corporation .... F 347 599-2600
   Brooklyn *(G-2384)*
Remains Lighting .... E 212 675-8051
   New York *(G-11358)*
◆ Rle Industries LLC .... E 973 276-1444
   New York *(G-11402)*

S E A Supplies Ltd .... F 516 694-6677
   Plainview *(G-13086)*
Sandy Littman Inc .... G 845 562-1112
   Newburgh *(G-12245)*
Santucci Custom Lighting .... F 866 853-1929
   Clinton *(G-3588)*
▲ Saratoga Lighting Holdings LLC ... A 212 906-7800
   New York *(G-11487)*
▲ Savenergy Inc .... G 516 239-1958
   Garden City *(G-5280)*
Savwatt Usa Inc .... G 646 478-2676
   New York *(G-11494)*
▲ Selux Corporation .... C 845 691-7723
   Highland *(G-6147)*
Solarpath Inc .... G 201 490-4499
   New York *(G-11639)*
▲ Solarwaterway Inc .... E 888 998-5337
   Brooklyn *(G-2496)*
▲ Spectronics Corporation .... G 516 333-4840
   Westbury *(G-16373)*
Swivelier Company Inc .... D 845 353-1455
   Blauvelt *(G-941)*
Twinkle Lighting Inc .... G 718 225-0939
   Flushing *(G-5056)*
Versaponents Inc .... F 631 242-3387
   Deer Park *(G-4059)*
▲ Vision Quest Lighting Inc .... E 631 737-4800
   East Setauket *(G-4314)*
Vital Vio Inc .... G 914 245-6048
   Troy *(G-15632)*
Xeleum Lighting LLC .... G 954 617-8170
   Mount Kisco *(G-8360)*
▲ Zumtobel Lighting Inc .... C 845 691-6262
   Highland *(G-6148)*

3647 Vehicular Lighting Eqpt

Aerospace Lighting Corporation ..... D 631 563-6400
   Bohemia *(G-974)*
▲ Astronics Corporation .... C 716 805-1599
   East Aurora *(G-4194)*
B/E Aerospace Inc .... E 631 563-6400
   Bohemia *(G-985)*
Copy Cat .... G 718 934-2192
   Brooklyn *(G-1716)*
Licenders .... G 212 759-5200
   New York *(G-10561)*
Luminescent Systems Inc .... B 716 655-0800
   East Aurora *(G-4204)*
▼ Mobile Fleet Inc .... G 631 206-2920
   Hauppauge *(G-5896)*
Power and Cnstr Group Inc .... E 585 889-6020
   Scottsville *(G-14752)*
Truck-Lite Co LLC .... E 716 665-2614
   Falconer *(G-4695)*
◆ Truck-Lite Co LLC .... B 716 665-6214
   Falconer *(G-4696)*
◆ Wolo Mfg Corp .... E 631 242-0333
   Deer Park *(G-4064)*

3648 Lighting Eqpt, NEC

▲ Altman Stage Lighting Co Inc ...... C 914 476-7987
   Yonkers *(G-16733)*
Broadway National Group LLC .... D 800 797-4467
   Ronkonkoma *(G-14321)*
▲ CEIT Corp .... F 518 825-0649
   Plattsburgh *(G-13116)*
Cooper Industries LLC .... E 315 477-7000
   Syracuse *(G-15291)*
◆ Creative Stage Lighting Co Inc ... E 518 251-3302
   North Creek *(G-12391)*
Eaton Crouse-Hinds .... C 315 477-7000
   Syracuse *(G-15312)*
Edison Power & Light Co Inc .... F 718 522-0002
   Brooklyn *(G-1814)*
Eluminocity US Inc .... G 651 528-1165
   New York *(G-9660)*
▲ Enchante Lites LLC .... G 212 602-1818
   New York *(G-9673)*
▲ Expo Furniture Designs Inc .... F 516 674-1420
   Glen Cove *(G-5365)*
▲ Fabbian USA Corp .... G 973 882-3824
   New York *(G-9769)*
General Led Corp .... G 516 280-2854
   Mineola *(G-8223)*
Goddard Design Co .... G 718 599-0170
   Brooklyn *(G-1936)*
Gordon S Anderson Mfg Co .... G 845 677-3304
   Millbrook *(G-8188)*
Gti Graphic Technology Inc .... E 845 562-7066
   Newburgh *(G-12225)*

Island Lite Louvers Inc .... E 631 608-4250
   Amityville *(G-289)*
J M Canty Inc .... E 716 625-4227
   Lockport *(G-7310)*
Jag Lighting .... G 917 226-3575
   Maspeth *(G-7855)*
◆ Jaquith Industries Inc .... E 315 478-5700
   Syracuse *(G-15346)*
Jed Lights Inc .... F 516 812-5001
   Deer Park *(G-3992)*
Jt Roselle Lighting & Sup Inc .... F 914 666-3700
   Mount Kisco *(G-8346)*
▲ Julian A McDermott Corporation .. E 718 456-3606
   Ridgewood *(G-13540)*
▲ La Mar Lighting Co Inc .... E 631 777-7700
   Farmingdale *(G-4806)*
Lamparts Co Inc .... F 914 723-8986
   Mount Vernon *(G-8416)*
Light Blue USA LLC .... G 718 475-2515
   Brooklyn *(G-2119)*
Lighting Collaborative Inc .... G 212 253-7220
   Brooklyn *(G-2122)*
Lighting N Beyond LLC .... G 718 669-9142
   Blauvelt *(G-937)*
Lighting Sculptures Inc .... F 631 242-3387
   Deer Park *(G-4002)*
Luminescent Systems Inc .... B 716 655-0800
   East Aurora *(G-4204)*
Medtek Skin Care Inc .... E 518 745-7264
   Glens Falls *(G-5433)*
Methods Tooling & Mfg Inc .... E 845 246-7100
   Mount Marion *(G-8364)*
Mjk Enterprises LLC .... G 917 653-9042
   Brooklyn *(G-2217)*
Northern Air Technology Inc .... E 585 594-5050
   Rochester *(G-13981)*
◆ Olive Led Lighting Inc .... E 718 746-0830
   College Point *(G-3658)*
Power and Cnstr Group Inc .... E 585 889-6020
   Scottsville *(G-14752)*
Psg Innovations Inc .... F 917 299-8986
   Valley Stream *(G-15792)*
▲ Ric-Lo Productions Ltd .... E 845 469-2285
   Chester *(G-3481)*
Rodac USA Corp .... E 716 741-3931
   Clarence *(G-3541)*
▲ Saratoga Lighting Holdings LLC . A 212 906-7800
   New York *(G-11487)*
Secret Celebrity Licensing LLC ...... G 212 812-9277
   New York *(G-11528)*
Sensio America .... E 877 501-5337
   Clifton Park *(G-3576)*
▲ Sensio America LLC .... E 877 501-5337
   Clifton Park *(G-3577)*
Serway Bros Inc .... E 315 337-0601
   Rome *(G-14274)*
Shakuff LLC .... G 212 675-0383
   Brooklyn *(G-2462)*
Siemens Electro Industrial Sa .... A 212 258-4000
   New York *(G-11578)*
▲ Sir Industries Inc .... E 631 234-2444
   Hauppauge *(G-5941)*
◆ Star Headlight Lantern Co Inc ..... C 585 226-9500
   Avon *(G-522)*
Strider Global LLC .... F 212 726-1302
   New York *(G-11723)*
Tarsier Ltd .... C 646 880-8680
   New York *(G-11785)*
▲ Tecnolux Incorporated .... E 718 369-3900
   Brooklyn *(G-2560)*
▲ Times Square Stage Ltg Co Inc .. E 845 947-3034
   Stony Point *(G-15177)*
Truck-Lite Co LLC .... E 716 665-2614
   Falconer *(G-4695)*
▲ USA Illumination Inc .... E 845 565-8500
   New Windsor *(G-8662)*
Vertex Innovative Solutions .... F 315 437-6711
   Syracuse *(G-15452)*
Vincent Conigliaro .... F 845 340-0489
   Kingston *(G-6931)*
▲ Visual Effects Inc .... F 718 324-0011
   Jamaica *(G-6689)*
Vivid Rgb Lighting LLC .... G 718 635-0817
   Peekskill *(G-12926)*

3651 Household Audio & Video Eqpt

▲ Accent Speaker Technology Ltd .. G 631 738-2540
   Holbrook *(G-6167)*
▲ Aguilar Amplification LLC .... F 212 431-9109
   New York *(G-8771)*

36 ELECTRONIC AND OTHER ELECTRICAL EQUIPMENT AND COMPONENTS, EXCEPT COMPUTER

Amplitech Group Inc ....G....... 631 521-7831
  Bohemia *(G-979)*
◆ Andrea Electronics Corporation ...G....... 631 719-1800
  Bohemia *(G-980)*
▲ Ashly Audio Inc ....E....... 585 872-0010
  Webster *(G-16074)*
▲ Audio Technology New York inc ....F....... 718 369-7528
  Brooklyn *(G-1576)*
Audio Video Invasion Inc ....F....... 516 345-2636
  Plainview *(G-13037)*
▼ Audiosavings Inc ....F....... 888 445-1555
  Inwood *(G-6486)*
Avcom of Virginia Inc ....D....... 585 924-4560
  Victor *(G-15830)*
AVI-Spl Employee ....B....... 212 840-4801
  New York *(G-8977)*
B & H Electronics Corp ....E....... 845 782-5000
  Monroe *(G-8264)*
▲ B & K Components Ltd ....D....... 323 776-4277
  Buffalo *(G-2720)*
Bayit Home Automation Corp ....E....... 973 988-2638
  Brooklyn *(G-1591)*
Broadcast Manager Inc ....G....... 212 509-1200
  New York *(G-9145)*
▲ Communication Power Corp ....E....... 631 434-7306
  Hauppauge *(G-5796)*
Convergent Audio Tech Inc ....G....... 585 359-2700
  Rush *(G-14471)*
Covington Sound ....G....... 646 256-7486
  Bronx *(G-1247)*
▲ Digitac Inc ....F....... 732 215-4020
  Brooklyn *(G-1777)*
Digital Home Creations Inc ....G....... 585 576-7070
  Webster *(G-16082)*
Fulcrum Acoustic LLC ....G....... 866 234-0678
  Rochester *(G-13820)*
G E Inspection Technologies LP ...C....... 315 554-2000
  Skaneateles *(G-14871)*
General Electric Company ....G....... 315 554-2000
  Skaneateles *(G-14872)*
Gilmores Sound Advice Inc ....F....... 212 265-4445
  New York *(G-9921)*
▲ Global Market Development Inc ....E....... 631 667-1000
  Edgewood *(G-4402)*
Granada Electronics Inc ....F....... 718 387-1157
  Brooklyn *(G-1947)*
Hope International Productions ....F....... 212 247-3188
  New York *(G-10122)*
Ilab America Inc ....G....... 631 615-5053
  Selden *(G-14764)*
▲ Jwin Electronics Corp ....C....... 516 626-7188
  Port Washington *(G-13275)*
▲ Key Digital Systems Inc ....E....... 914 667-9700
  Mount Vernon *(G-8413)*
L A R Electronics Corp ....G....... 716 285-0555
  Niagara Falls *(G-12304)*
L3 Technologies Inc ....A....... 631 436-7400
  Hauppauge *(G-5859)*
Laird Telemedia ....C....... 845 339-9555
  Mount Marion *(G-8363)*
Lamm Industries Inc ....G....... 718 368-0181
  Brooklyn *(G-2092)*
Masterdisk Corporation ....F....... 212 541-5022
  Elmsford *(G-4551)*
▼ Navitar Inc ....D....... 585 359-4000
  Rochester *(G-13965)*
▲ NEa Manufacturing Corp ....E....... 516 371-4200
  Inwood *(G-6497)*
New Audio LLC ....E....... 212 213-6060
  New York *(G-10917)*
New Wop Records ....G....... 631 617-9732
  Deer Park *(G-4015)*
Nykon Inc ....G....... 315 483-0504
  Sodus *(G-14914)*
Octave Music Group Inc ....G....... 212 991-6540
  New York *(G-11031)*
Professional Technology Inc ....G....... 315 337-4156
  Rome *(G-14267)*
Pure Acoustics Inc ....G....... 718 788-4411
  Brooklyn *(G-2361)*
Request Inc ....E....... 518 899-1254
  Halfmoon *(G-5667)*
Request Serious Play LLC ....G....... 518 899-1254
  Halfmoon *(G-5668)*
Sage Audio Video Tech LLC ....E....... 212 213-1523
  New York *(G-11465)*
◆ Samson Technologies Corp ....D....... 631 784-2200
  Hicksville *(G-6130)*
◆ Scy Manufacturing Inc ....G....... 516 986-3083
  Inwood *(G-6500)*

Shyk International Corp ....G....... 212 663-3302
  New York *(G-11574)*
▲ Sima Technologies LLC ....G....... 412 828-9130
  Hauppauge *(G-5940)*
Sing Trix ....F....... 212 352-1500
  New York *(G-11599)*
◆ Sony Corporation of America ....C....... 212 833-8000
  New York *(G-11645)*
▲ Sound Video Systems Wny LLC ....F....... 716 684-8200
  Buffalo *(G-3073)*
Speaqua Corp ....E....... 858 334-9042
  Deer Park *(G-4048)*
Theodore A Rapp Associates ....G....... 845 469-2100
  Chester *(G-3488)*
Tkm Technologies Inc ....G....... 631 474-4700
  Port Jeff STA *(G-13219)*
◆ Toshiba America Inc ....E....... 212 596-0600
  New York *(G-11872)*
Touchtunes Music Corporation .....D....... 847 419-3300
  New York *(G-11876)*
Tunecore Inc ....E....... 646 651-1060
  Brooklyn *(G-2591)*
Video Technology Services Inc .....F....... 516 937-9700
  Syosset *(G-15232)*
Vincent Conigliaro ....F....... 845 340-0489
  Kingston *(G-6931)*
Vtb Holdings Inc ....G....... 914 345-2255
  Valhalla *(G-15749)*
▲ Whirlwind Music Distrs Inc ....D....... 800 733-9473
  Rochester *(G-14207)*
Widgetworks Unlimited LLC ....G....... 914 666-6395
  Chappaqua *(G-3424)*
▲ Wyrestorm Technologies LLC ...F....... 518 289-1293
  Round Lake *(G-14465)*
▲ Yorkville Sound Inc ....G....... 716 297-2920
  Niagara Falls *(G-12350)*

3652 Phonograph Records & Magnetic Tape

▲ A To Z Media Inc ....E....... 212 260-0237
  New York *(G-8699)*
Abkco Music & Records Inc ....E....... 212 399-0300
  New York *(G-8710)*
Atlantic Recording Corp ....B....... 212 707-2000
  New York *(G-8951)*
▲ Bertelsmann Inc ....E....... 212 782-1000
  New York *(G-9055)*
Bridge Records Inc ....G....... 914 654-9270
  New Rochelle *(G-8594)*
Chesky Records Inc ....F....... 212 586-7799
  New York *(G-9272)*
Columbia Records Inc ....B....... 212 833-8000
  New York *(G-9357)*
Cult Records LLC ....G....... 718 395-2077
  New York *(G-9432)*
▲ Dorling Kindersley Publishing ....D....... 212 213-4800
  New York *(G-9560)*
Eks Manufacturing Inc ....F....... 917 217-0784
  Brooklyn *(G-1817)*
Emusiccom Inc ....E....... 212 201-9240
  New York *(G-9672)*
Europadisk LLC ....E....... 718 407-7300
  Long Island City *(G-7440)*
▲ Extreme Group Holdings LLC ....F....... 212 833-8000
  New York *(G-9757)*
High Quality Video Inc ....F....... 212 686-9534
  New York *(G-10095)*
His Productions USA Inc ....F....... 212 594-3737
  New York *(G-10105)*
▲ Historic TW Inc ....F....... 212 484-8000
  New York *(G-10106)*
Hope International Productions ....F....... 212 247-3188
  New York *(G-10122)*
Lefrak Entertainment Co Ltd ....F....... 212 586-3600
  New York *(G-10540)*
Masterdisk Corporation ....F....... 212 541-5022
  Elmsford *(G-4551)*
Media Technologies Ltd ....F....... 631 467-7900
  Eastport *(G-4385)*
Peer-Southern Productions Inc .....E....... 212 265-3910
  New York *(G-11137)*
Pete Levin Music Inc ....G....... 845 247-9211
  Saugerties *(G-14614)*
Pivot Records LLC ....F....... 718 417-1213
  Brooklyn *(G-2322)*
▲ Recorded Anthology of Amrcn Mus ....F....... 212 290-1695
  Brooklyn *(G-2390)*
Roadrunner Records Inc ....E....... 212 274-7500
  New York *(G-11404)*
Side Hustle Music Group LLC ....F....... 800 219-4003
  New York *(G-11575)*

▲ Sony Broadband Entertainment ....F....... 212 833-6800
  New York *(G-11644)*
◆ Sony Corporation of America ....C....... 212 833-8000
  New York *(G-11645)*
Sony Music Entertainment ....A....... 212 833-8000
  New York *(G-11647)*
Sony Music Entertainment Inc ......E....... 212 833-5057
  New York *(G-11648)*
◆ Sony Music Holdings Inc ....A....... 212 833-8000
  New York *(G-11649)*
Sterling Sound Inc ....F....... 212 604-9433
  New York *(G-11708)*
Taste and See Entrmt Inc ....G....... 516 285-3010
  Valley Stream *(G-15799)*
Time Warner Companies Inc ....D....... 212 484-8000
  New York *(G-11845)*
▲ Universal Mus Group Hldngs Inc ....B....... 212 333-8000
  New York *(G-11961)*
Universal Music Group Inc ....B....... 212 333-8237
  New York *(G-11962)*
Vaire LLC ....G....... 631 271-4933
  Huntington Station *(G-6463)*
Warner Music Group Corp ....B....... 212 275-2000
  New York *(G-12072)*
▼ Warner Music Inc ....D....... 212 275-2000
  New York *(G-12073)*
Wea International Inc ....D....... 212 275-1300
  New York *(G-12084)*

3661 Telephone & Telegraph Apparatus

ABS Talkx Inc ....G....... 631 254-9100
  Bay Shore *(G-651)*
Access 24 ....G....... 845 358-5397
  Valley Cottage *(G-15750)*
▼ Aines Manufacturing Corp ....E....... 631 471-3900
  Islip *(G-6544)*
Alcatel-Lucent USA Inc ....D....... 516 349-4900
  Plainview *(G-13034)*
Alternative Technology Corp ....G....... 914 478-5900
  Hastings On Hudson *(G-5747)*
▲ Audio-Sears Corp ....D....... 607 652-7305
  Stamford *(G-15029)*
Avaya Services Inc ....G....... 866 462-8292
  New York *(G-8973)*
Call Forwarding Technologies ....G....... 516 621-3600
  Greenvale *(G-5628)*
▲ Clayton Dubilier & Rice Fun ....E....... 212 407-5200
  New York *(G-9324)*
Corning Incorporated ....E....... 607 248-1200
  Corning *(G-3812)*
Corning Incorporated ....G....... 607 974-6729
  Painted Post *(G-12837)*
◆ Corning Incorporated ....A....... 607 974-9000
  Corning *(G-3809)*
Eagle Telephonics Inc ....F....... 631 471-3600
  Bohemia *(G-1017)*
▲ ESi Cases & Accessories Inc ....E....... 212 883-8838
  New York *(G-9705)*
◆ Fiber Instrument Sales Inc ....C....... 315 736-2206
  Oriskany *(G-12757)*
▲ Fiberwave Corporation ....C....... 718 802-9011
  Brooklyn *(G-1877)*
▲ Forerunner Technologies Inc .....E....... 631 337-2100
  Edgewood *(G-4401)*
Fujitsu Ntwrk Cmmnications Inc ....F....... 845 731-2000
  Pearl River *(G-12897)*
Gac Express Inc ....G....... 718 438-2227
  Brooklyn *(G-1915)*
Harris Corporation ....E....... 585 244-5830
  Rochester *(G-13858)*
▲ I D Tel Corp ....F....... 718 876-6000
  Staten Island *(G-15087)*
Interdgital Communications LLC ...C....... 631 622-4000
  Melville *(G-8038)*
▲ Kelta Inc ....E....... 631 789-5000
  Edgewood *(G-4406)*
L3 Technologies Inc ....A....... 631 436-7400
  Hauppauge *(G-5859)*
Luxcore Networks Inc ....F....... 212 618-1724
  New York *(G-10631)*
Maia Systems LLC ....G....... 718 206-0100
  Jamaica *(G-6658)*
Mitel Networks Inc ....G....... 877 654-3573
  Rochester *(G-13948)*
▲ Parabit Systems Inc ....E....... 516 378-4800
  Bellmore *(G-791)*
Performance Technologies Inc ......E....... 585 256-0200
  Rochester *(G-14012)*
▲ Powermate Cellular ....G....... 718 833-9400
  Brooklyn *(G-2331)*

Employee Codes: A=Over 500 employees, B=251-500
C=101-250, D=51-100, E=20-50, F=10-19, G=5-9

36 ELECTRONIC AND OTHER ELECTRICAL EQUIPMENT AND COMPONENTS, EXCEPT COMPUTER SIC SECTION

Prager Metis Cpas LLC........F 212 972-7555
New York *(G-11226)*
Quality One Wireless LLC........C 631 233-3337
Ronkonkoma *(G-14403)*
R I R Communications Systems........E 718 706-9957
Mount Vernon *(G-8437)*
▲ **Redcom Laboratories Inc**........C 585 924-6567
Victor *(G-15865)*
▲ **Rus Industries Inc**........E 716 284-7828
Niagara Falls *(G-12331)*
◆ **Sandstone Technologies Corp**........G 585 785-5537
Rochester *(G-14110)*
Sandstone Technologies Corp........G 585 785-5537
Rochester *(G-14111)*
Siemens Corporation........F 202 434-7800
New York *(G-11577)*
Siemens USA Holdings Inc........B 212 258-4000
New York *(G-11580)*
▼ **Simrex Corporation**........G 716 206-0174
Buffalo *(G-3066)*
▲ **Snake Tray International LLC**........E 631 674-0004
Bay Shore *(G-725)*
▼ **Splice Technologies Inc**........G 631 924-8108
Manorville *(G-7786)*
Telecommunication Concepts........G 315 736-8523
Whitesboro *(G-16530)*
Telephonics Corporation........D 631 755-7659
Farmingdale *(G-4891)*
▲ **Telephonics Corporation**........A 631 755-7000
Farmingdale *(G-4892)*
Terahertz Technologies Inc........G 315 736-3642
Oriskany *(G-12765)*
▲ **Tii Technologies Inc**........E 516 364-9300
Edgewood *(G-4419)*
▲ **Toshiba Amer Info Systems Inc**........B 949 583-3000
New York *(G-11871)*
◆ **Toshiba America Inc**........E 212 596-0600
New York *(G-11872)*
U2o Usa LLC........G 516 813-9500
Plainview *(G-13094)*

3663 Radio & T V Communications, Systs & Eqpt, Broadcast/Studio

2p Agency Usa Inc........G 212 203-5586
Brooklyn *(G-1436)*
Advanced Comm Solutions........G 914 693-5076
Ardsley *(G-393)*
Airnet Communications Corp........F 516 338-0008
Westbury *(G-16312)*
Ametek CTS Us Inc........E 631 467-8400
Ronkonkoma *(G-14308)*
Amplitech Inc........G 631 521-7738
Bohemia *(G-978)*
Amplitech Group Inc........G 631 521-7831
Bohemia *(G-979)*
◆ **Andrea Electronics Corporation**........G 631 719-1800
Bohemia *(G-980)*
▲ **Apex Airtronics Inc**........E 718 485-8560
Brooklyn *(G-1539)*
Appairent Technologies Inc........G 585 214-2460
West Henrietta *(G-16230)*
Arcom Automatics LLC........G 315 422-1230
Syracuse *(G-15245)*
▲ **Armstrong Transmitter Corp**........F 315 673-1269
Marcellus *(G-7792)*
▲ **Arrow-Communication Labs Inc**........B 315 422-1230
Syracuse *(G-15247)*
▲ **Ashly Audio Inc**........E 585 872-0010
Webster *(G-16074)*
AVI-Spl Employee........B 212 840-4801
New York *(G-8977)*
B & H Electronics Corp........E 845 782-5000
Monroe *(G-8264)*
Basil S Kadhim........G 888 520-5192
New York *(G-9024)*
Bayside Beepers & Cellular........G 718 343-3888
Glen Oaks *(G-5386)*
Belden Inc........B 607 796-5600
Horseheads *(G-6306)*
Benchmark Media Systems Inc........F 315 437-6300
Syracuse *(G-15256)*
Big Fish Entertainment LLC........C 646 797-4955
New York *(G-9077)*
Bullitt Mobile LLC........D 631 424-1749
Bohemia *(G-990)*
Century Metal Parts Corp........E 631 667-0800
Bay Shore *(G-669)*
Chyronhego Corporation........C 631 845-2000
Melville *(G-8008)*
▼ **CJ Component Products LLC**........G 631 567-3733
Oakdale *(G-12514)*
Clever Devices Ltd........E 516 433-6100
Woodbury *(G-16614)*
Click It Inc........D 631 686-2900
Hauppauge *(G-5791)*
▲ **Cmb Wireless Group LLC**........B 631 750-4700
Bohemia *(G-996)*
Cntry Cross Communications LLC........F 386 758-9696
Jamestown *(G-6708)*
▲ **Communication Power Corp**........E 631 434-7306
Hauppauge *(G-5796)*
▲ **Comtech PST Corp**........C 631 777-8900
Melville *(G-8011)*
◆ **Comtech Telecom Corp**........C 631 962-7000
Melville *(G-8012)*
Digifab Systems Inc........G 212 944-9882
New York *(G-9525)*
▲ **Eagle Comtronics Inc**........C 315 451-3313
Liverpool *(G-7232)*
◆ **Edo LLC**........G 631 630-4000
Amityville *(G-272)*
Edo LLC........A 631 630-4200
Amityville *(G-273)*
Eeg Enterprises Inc........F 516 293-7472
Farmingdale *(G-4759)*
▼ **Electro-Metrics Corporation**........E 518 762-2600
Johnstown *(G-6825)*
Elite Cellular Accessories Inc........E 877 390-2502
Deer Park *(G-3972)*
▲ **Eni Mks Products Group**........F 585 427-8300
Rochester *(G-13786)*
▲ **Eni Technology Inc**........B 585 427-8300
Rochester *(G-13787)*
Evado Filip........F 917 774-8666
New York *(G-9733)*
Fei-Zyfer Inc........G 714 933-4045
Uniondale *(G-15667)*
Fleetcom Inc........F 914 776-5582
Yonkers *(G-16759)*
Flycell Inc........D 212 400-1212
New York *(G-9818)*
Fujitsu Ntwrk Cmmnications Inc........F 845 731-2000
Pearl River *(G-12897)*
◆ **GE Mds LLC**........C 585 242-9600
Rochester *(G-13824)*
Geosync Microwave Inc........G 631 760-5567
Hauppauge *(G-5833)*
Ghostek LLC........F 855 310-3439
Brooklyn *(G-1926)*
◆ **Griffon Corporation**........E 212 957-5000
New York *(G-9988)*
Gti America Inc........G 716 332-6151
Buffalo *(G-2859)*
Gurley Precision Instrs Inc........C 518 272-6300
Troy *(G-15607)*
Hamtronics Inc........G 585 392-9430
Rochester *(G-13851)*
▲ **Hand Held Products Inc**........B 315 554-6000
Skaneateles Falls *(G-14879)*
Harris Corporation........A 585 244-5830
Rochester *(G-13853)*
Harris Corporation........B 585 244-5830
Rochester *(G-13859)*
Harris Corporation........F 718 767-1100
Whitestone *(G-16541)*
Harris Corporation........B 585 244-5830
Rochester *(G-13860)*
Harris Globl Cmmunications Inc........A 585 244-5830
Rochester *(G-13861)*
Hopewell Precision Inc........E 845 221-2737
Hopewell Junction *(G-6288)*
Icell Inc........C 516 590-0007
Hempstead *(G-6014)*
▲ **Icon Enterprises Intl Inc**........E 718 752-9764
Mohegan Lake *(G-8258)*
Iheartcommunications Inc........C 585 454-4884
Rochester *(G-13877)*
Iheartcommunications Inc........E 212 603-4660
New York *(G-10178)*
▼ **Innovation In Motion Inc**........G 407 878-7561
Long Beach *(G-7359)*
Intelibs Inc........G 877 213-2640
Stony Brook *(G-15167)*
It Commodity Sourcing Inc........G 718 677-1577
Brooklyn *(G-2017)*
▲ **John Mezzalingua Assoc LLC**........A 315 431-7100
Liverpool *(G-7240)*
▲ **L3 Foreign Holdings Inc**........D 212 697-1111
New York *(G-10497)*
L3 Technologies Inc........B 631 231-1700
Hauppauge *(G-5858)*
L3 Technologies Inc........A 631 436-7400
Hauppauge *(G-5859)*
L3 Technologies Inc........D 631 231-1700
Hauppauge *(G-5861)*
L3 Technologies Inc........D 631 436-7400
Hauppauge *(G-5862)*
L3 Technologies Inc........B 212 697-1111
New York *(G-10498)*
Listec Video Corp........G 631 273-3029
Hauppauge *(G-5865)*
Loral Space & Commnctns Holdng........E 212 697-1105
New York *(G-10603)*
Loral Space Communications Inc........E 212 697-1105
New York *(G-10604)*
Loral Spacecom Corporation........E 212 697-1105
New York *(G-10605)*
▲ **Magnet-Ndctive Systems Ltd USA**...E 585 924-4000
Victor *(G-15856)*
▲ **Maritime Broadband Inc**........E 347 404-6041
Long Island City *(G-7515)*
Mark Peri International........F 516 208-6824
Oceanside *(G-12547)*
Millennium Antenna Corp........F 315 798-9374
Utica *(G-15722)*
Mini-Circuits Fort Wayne LLC........B 718 934-4500
Brooklyn *(G-2210)*
Mirion Tech Imaging LLC........E 607 562-4300
Horseheads *(G-6320)*
Mitel Networks Inc........G 877 654-3573
Rochester *(G-13948)*
Mks Medical Electronics........C 585 292-7400
Rochester *(G-13950)*
Motorola Solutions Inc........C 518 348-0833
Halfmoon *(G-5665)*
Motorola Solutions Inc........C 518 869-9517
Albany *(G-100)*
Movin On Sounds and SEC Inc........E 516 489-2350
Franklin Square *(G-5119)*
▼ **Navitar Inc**........D 585 359-4000
Rochester *(G-13965)*
North American MBL Systems Inc........E 718 898-8700
Woodside *(G-16667)*
Nycom Business Solutions Inc........G 516 345-6000
Franklin Square *(G-5120)*
Orbcomm Inc........F 703 433-6396
Utica *(G-15729)*
Persistent Systems LLC........E 212 561-5895
New York *(G-11164)*
▲ **Prime View USA Inc**........G 212 730-4905
New York *(G-11242)*
Quanta Electronics Inc........F 631 961-9953
Centereach *(G-3345)*
▲ **Quintel Usa Inc**........E 585 420-8364
Rochester *(G-14065)*
Rehabilitation International........G 212 420-1500
Jamaica *(G-6674)*
Rodale Wireless Inc........E 631 231-0044
Hauppauge *(G-5929)*
Ruhle Companies Inc........E 914 287-4000
Valhalla *(G-15747)*
Sartek Industries Inc........G 631 473-3555
East Setauket *(G-4309)*
Sdr Technology Inc........G 716 583-1249
Alden *(G-176)*
▲ **Sentry Technology Corporation**........F 800 645-4224
Ronkonkoma *(G-14411)*
Silverlight Digital LLC........G 646 650-5330
New York *(G-11591)*
Sinclair Technologies Inc........E 716 874-3682
Hamburg *(G-5695)*
Specialty Microwave Corp........F 631 737-2175
Ronkonkoma *(G-14415)*
Spectracom Corporation........E 585 321-5800
Rochester *(G-14136)*
Srtech Industry Corp........E 718 496-7001
College Point *(G-3668)*
STI-Co Industries Inc........E 716 662-2680
Orchard Park *(G-12744)*
Telebyte Inc........E 631 423-3232
Hauppauge *(G-5957)*
▲ **Telephonics Corporation**........A 631 755-7000
Farmingdale *(G-4892)*
▲ **Telxon Corporation**........E 631 738-2400
Holtsville *(G-6248)*
Thewave Communications LLC........G 646 973-8294
Bronx *(G-1402)*
Times Square Studios Ltd........C 212 930-7720
New York *(G-11847)*

Toura LLC ....F 646 652-8668
  Brooklyn (G-2576)
United Satcom Inc ....G 718 359-4100
  Flushing (G-5057)
Vicon Industries Inc ....C 631 952-2288
  Hauppauge (G-5970)
Village Video Productions Inc ....G 631 752-9311
  West Babylon (G-16203)
▲ W & W Manufacturing Co ....F 516 942-0011
  West Islip (G-16261)
▲ Whirlwind Music Distrs Inc ....D 800 733-9473
  Rochester (G-14207)
Wireless Communications Inc ....G 845 353-5921
  Nyack (G-12513)
Zetek Corporation ....F 212 668-1485
  New York (G-12174)

3669 Communications Eqpt, NEC

All Metro Emrgncy Response Sys ....G 516 750-9100
  Lynbrook (G-7659)
▲ Alstom Signaling Inc ....B 585 783-2000
  West Henrietta (G-16227)
Alstom Signaling Inc ....E 585 274-8700
  Schenectady (G-14648)
Andrea Systems LLC ....E 631 390-3140
  Farmingdale (G-4721)
Apex Signal Corporation ....D 631 567-1100
  Bohemia (G-981)
Apple Core Electronics Inc ....F 718 628-4068
  Brooklyn (G-1542)
AVI-Spl Employee ....B 212 840-4801
  New York (G-8977)
BNo Intl Trdg Co Inc ....G 716 487-1900
  Jamestown (G-6703)
Capstream Technologies LLC ....G 716 945-7100
  Salamanca (G-14524)
Comet Flasher Inc ....G 716 821-9595
  Buffalo (G-2773)
Cq Traffic Control Devices LLC ....G 518 767-0057
  Selkirk (G-14767)
Curbe'l Medical Products Inc ....F 716 667-2520
  Orchard Park (G-12711)
▲ Curbell Medical Products Inc ....C 716 667-2520
  Orchard Park (G-12712)
Datasonic Inc ....G 516 248-7330
  East Meadow (G-4249)
Fire Apparatus Service Tech ....G 716 753-3538
  Sherman (G-14816)
Firecom Inc ....C 718 899-6100
  Woodside (G-16655)
Firetronics Inc ....G 516 997-5151
  Jericho (G-6789)
Frequency Electronics Inc ....C 516 794-4500
  Uniondale (G-15668)
Fuel Watchman Sales & Service ....F 718 665-6100
  Bronx (G-1276)
Global Technologies Inc ....D 631 243-7924
  Deer Park (G-3982)
Goddard Design Co ....G 718 599-0170
  Brooklyn (G-1936)
Harris Corporation ....A 413 263-6200
  Rochester (G-13856)
Intelligent Traffic Systems ....G 631 567-5994
  Bohemia (G-1037)
Johnson Controls ....D 585 288-6200
  Rochester (G-13895)
Johnson Controls ....E 518 952-6040
  Clifton Park (G-3568)
Johnson Controls ....G 845 774-4120
  Harriman (G-5720)
Johnson Controls ....F 607 338-5100
  East Syracuse (G-4356)
▲ L3 Foreign Holdings Inc ....D 212 697-1111
  New York (G-10497)
L3 Technologies Inc ....B 212 697-1111
  New York (G-10498)
Lifewatch Inc ....F 800 716-1433
  Hewlett (G-6048)
Lifeway Network Inc ....G 718 779-8075
  Rego Park (G-13464)
Light Phone Inc ....G 415 595-0044
  Brooklyn (G-2120)
Lik LLC ....F 516 848-5135
  Northport (G-12471)
▲ McDowell Research Co Inc ....D 315 332-7100
  Newark (G-12200)
Napco Security Tech Inc ....C 631 842-9400
  Amityville (G-304)
▲ Nrd LLC ....E 716 773-7634
  Grand Island (G-5508)

Nu2 Systems LLC ....F 914 719-7272
  White Plains (G-16481)
Octopus Advanced Systems Inc ....G 914 771-6110
  Yonkers (G-16786)
Power Line Constructors Inc ....E 315 853-6183
  Clinton (G-3587)
Response Care Inc ....G 585 671-4144
  Webster (G-16096)
▼ Roanwell Corporation ....E 718 401-0288
  Bronx (G-1373)
Sentry Devices Corp ....G 631 491-3191
  Dix Hills (G-4126)
▼ Simrex Corporation ....G 716 206-0174
  Buffalo (G-3066)
◆ Star Headlight Lantern Co Inc ....E 585 226-9500
  Avon (G-522)
Synergx Systems Inc ....D 516 433-4700
  Woodside (G-16681)
▲ Telemergency Ltd ....E 914 629-4222
  White Plains (G-16511)
▲ Telephonics Corporation ....A 631 755-7000
  Farmingdale (G-4892)
Telephonics Corporation ....E 631 755-7000
  Huntington (G-6419)
Tokenize Inc ....E 585 981-9919
  Rochester (G-14172)
Toweriq Inc ....F 844 626-7638
  Long Island City (G-7618)
Traffic Lane Closures LLC ....G 845 228-6100
  Carmel (G-3283)
▲ Twinco Mfg Co Inc ....E 631 231-0022
  Hauppauge (G-5963)
▲ TX Rx Systems Inc ....C 716 549-4700
  Angola (G-371)
Unitone Communication Systems ....G 212 777-9090
  New York (G-11957)
UTC Fire SEC Americas Corp Inc ....D 518 456-0444
  Albany (G-139)
Vicon Industries Inc ....C 631 952-2288
  Hauppauge (G-5970)
◆ Visiontron Corp ....E 631 582-8600
  Hauppauge (G-5971)
▲ Werma (usa) Inc ....G 315 414-0200
  East Syracuse (G-4381)
Zetek Corporation ....F 212 668-1485
  New York (G-12174)

3671 Radio & T V Receiving Electron Tubes

▲ E-Beam Services Inc ....G 516 622-1422
  Hicksville (G-6081)
Harris Corporation ....E 585 244-5830
  Rochester (G-13858)
◆ New Sensor Corporation ....D 718 937-8300
  Long Island City (G-7538)
Passur Aerospace Inc ....G 631 589-6800
  Bohemia (G-1072)
▲ Thomas Electronics Inc ....C 315 923-2051
  Clyde (G-3598)
Y & Z Precision Inc ....F 516 349-8243
  Plainview (G-13104)

3672 Printed Circuit Boards

◆ A A Technology Inc ....D 631 913-0400
  Ronkonkoma (G-14284)
Adco Circuits Inc ....G 716 668-6600
  Buffalo (G-2685)
▲ Advance Circuit Technology Inc ....E 585 328-2000
  Rochester (G-13604)
▲ Advance Micro Power Corp ....F 631 471-6157
  Ronkonkoma (G-14291)
Advanced Digital Info Corp ....E 607 266-4000
  Ithaca (G-6554)
Advanced Manufacturing Svc Inc ....E 631 676-5210
  Ronkonkoma (G-14292)
American Quality Technology ....F 607 777-9488
  Binghamton (G-861)
◆ American Tchncal Ceramics Corp .....B 631 622-4700
  Huntington Station (G-6430)
▲ Ansen Corporation ....G 315 393-3573
  Ogdensburg (G-12570)
Ansen Corporation ....G 315 393-3573
  Ogdensburg (G-12571)
▲ Badger Technologies Inc ....D 585 869-7101
  Farmington (G-4910)
BCM Electronics Manuf Services ....G 631 580-9516
  Ronkonkoma (G-14317)
Bsu Inc ....E 607 272-8100
  Ithaca (G-6569)
Buffalo Circuits Inc ....G 716 662-2115
  Orchard Park (G-12703)

▲ C & D Assembly Inc ....E 607 898-4275
  Groton (G-5650)
C A M Graphics Co Inc ....E 631 842-3400
  Farmingdale (G-4731)
Chautauqua Circuits Inc ....G 716 366-5771
  Dunkirk (G-4163)
Coast To Coast Circuits Inc ....E 585 254-2980
  Rochester (G-13715)
Cygnus Automation Inc ....E 631 981-0909
  Bohemia (G-1006)
Della Systems Inc ....F 631 580-0010
  Ronkonkoma (G-14333)
▲ Electronic Coating Tech Inc ....F 518 688-2048
  Cohoes (G-3610)
Ems Technologies Inc ....E 607 723-3676
  Binghamton (G-882)
Entertron Industries Inc ....E 716 772-7216
  Lockport (G-7299)
Falconer Electronics Inc ....D 716 665-4176
  Falconer (G-4678)
Geometric Circuits Inc ....D 631 249-0230
  Holbrook (G-6186)
Global Technologies Inc ....D 631 243-7924
  Deer Park (G-3982)
Hazlow Electronics Inc ....E 585 325-5323
  Rochester (G-13863)
I 3 Manufacturing Services Inc ....E 607 238-7077
  Binghamton (G-891)
◆ I3 Electronics Inc ....C 607 238-7077
  Binghamton (G-893)
I3 Electronics Inc ....D 607 238-7077
  Endicott (G-4596)
▲ IEC Electronics Corp ....E 315 331-7742
  Newark (G-12196)
IEC Electronics Wire Cable Inc ....D 585 924-9010
  Newark (G-12197)
Irtronics Instruments Inc ....F 914 693-6291
  Ardsley (G-395)
▲ Isine Inc ....E 631 913-4400
  Melville (G-8040)
Jabil Circuit Inc ....B 845 471-9237
  Poughkeepsie (G-13347)
Kendall Circuits Inc ....E 631 473-3636
  Mount Sinai (G-8368)
Kingboard Holdings Limited ....A 705 844-1993
  New York (G-10452)
Mpl Inc ....E 607 266-0480
  Ithaca (G-6597)
Nationwide Circuits Inc ....E 585 328-0791
  Rochester (G-13963)
▲ NEa Manufacturing Corp ....E 516 371-4200
  Inwood (G-6497)
▼ Oakdale Industrial Elec Corp ....F 631 737-4090
  Ronkonkoma (G-14388)
Ormec Systems Corp ....E 585 385-3520
  Rochester (G-13991)
▲ Park Electrochemical Corp ....D 631 465-3600
  Melville (G-8056)
Performance Technologies Inc ....E 585 256-0200
  Rochester (G-14012)
Photonamics Inc ....F 585 247-8990
  Rochester (G-14020)
Procomponents Inc ....E 516 683-0909
  Westbury (G-16368)
Rce Manufacturing LLC ....G 631 856-9005
  Commack (G-3699)
▲ Rochester Industrial Ctrl Inc ....D 315 524-4555
  Ontario (G-12663)
Rumsey Corp ....G 914 751-3640
  Yonkers (G-16797)
S K Circuits Inc ....F 703 376-8718
  Canastota (G-3246)
Sag Harbor Industries Inc ....E 631 725-0440
  Sag Harbor (G-14502)
Sanmina Corporation ....B 607 689-5000
  Owego (G-12803)
▲ Sopark Corp ....D 716 822-0434
  Buffalo (G-3070)
▲ Stetron International Inc ....F 716 854-3443
  Buffalo (G-3077)
▲ Stever-Locke Industries Inc ....G 585 624-3450
  Honeoye Falls (G-6274)
Surf-Tech Manufacturing Corp ....F 631 589-1194
  Ronkonkoma (G-14419)
TCS Electronics Inc ....E 585 337-4301
  Farmington (G-4920)
Transistor Devices Inc ....E 631 471-7492
  Ronkonkoma (G-14421)
Vexos Inc ....E 855 711-3227
  New York (G-12021)

Employee Codes: A=Over 500 employees, B=251-500
C=101-250, D=51-100, E=20-50, F=10-19, G=5-9

Windsor Technology LLC ....F 585 461-2500
Rochester *(G-14210)*

3674 Semiconductors

Able Electronics Inc ....F 631 924-5386
Bellport *(G-797)*
Accumetrics Associates Inc ....F 518 393-2200
Latham *(G-7062)*
▲ **Acolyte Technologies Corp** ....F 212 629-3239
New York *(G-8728)*
Adco Circuits Inc ....G 716 668-6600
Buffalo *(G-2685)*
Advis Inc ....G 585 568-0100
Caledonia *(G-3152)*
▼ **Aeroflex Holding Corp** ....A 516 694-6700
Plainview *(G-13031)*
▲ **Aeroflex Incorporated** ....B 516 694-6700
Plainview *(G-13032)*
Aeroflex Plainview Inc ....B 516 694-6700
Plainview *(G-13033)*
Aeroflex Plainview Inc ....C 631 231-9100
Hauppauge *(G-5756)*
Akoustis Inc ....E 585 919-3073
Canandaigua *(G-3210)*
Applied Materials Inc ....G 518 245-1400
Ballston Spa *(G-577)*
▲ **Artemis Inc** ....G 631 232-2424
Hauppauge *(G-5770)*
▲ **Atlantis Energy Systems Inc** ....E 845 486-4052
Poughkeepsie *(G-13328)*
Atlantis Energy Systems Inc ....G 916 438-2930
Poughkeepsie *(G-13329)*
Autodyne Manufacturing Co Inc ....F 631 957-5858
Lindenhurst *(G-7163)*
Automated Control Logic Inc ....F 914 769-8880
Thornwood *(G-15501)*
Beech Grove Technology Inc ....G 845 223-6844
Hopewell Junction *(G-6283)*
Besicorp Ltd ....F 845 336-7700
Kingston *(G-6889)*
Bga Technology LLC ....E 631 750-4600
Bohemia *(G-988)*
Bharat Electronics Limited ....G 516 248-4021
Garden City *(G-5252)*
CAM Touchview Products Inc ....F 631 842-3400
Sag Harbor *(G-14497)*
▲ **Central Semiconductor Corp** ....D 631 435-1110
Hauppauge *(G-5786)*
Ceres Technologies Inc ....D 845 247-4701
Saugerties *(G-14604)*
Cold Springs R & D Inc ....F 315 413-1237
Syracuse *(G-15285)*
Compositech Ltd ....C 516 835-1458
Woodbury *(G-16615)*
Convergent Med MGT Svcs LLC ....G 718 921-6159
Brooklyn *(G-1715)*
Cooper Power Systems LLC ....B 716 375-7100
Olean *(G-12597)*
Corning Incorporated ....E 607 248-1200
Corning *(G-3812)*
◆ **Corning Incorporated** ....A 607 974-9000
Corning *(G-3809)*
Corning Incorporated ....G 607 974-6729
Painted Post *(G-12837)*
Corning Specialty Mtls Inc ....G 607 974-9000
Corning *(G-3817)*
Crystalonics Inc ....F 631 981-6140
Ronkonkoma *(G-14330)*
Crystalonics of New York Inc ....F 631 981-6140
Ronkonkoma *(G-14331)*
Curtiss-Wright Controls ....F 631 756-4740
Farmingdale *(G-4742)*
▲ **Cvd Equipment Corporation** ....C 631 981-7081
Central Islip *(G-3365)*
Cypress Semiconductor Corp ....F 631 261-1358
Northport *(G-12467)*
▲ **Data Device Corporation** ....B 631 567-5600
Bohemia *(G-1008)*
▲ **Data Display USA Inc** ....C 631 218-2130
Holbrook *(G-6182)*
Dionics-Usa Inc ....G 516 997-7474
Westbury *(G-16323)*
DJS Nyc Inc ....G 845 445-8618
Monsey *(G-8287)*
Dynamic Photography Inc ....G 516 381-2951
Roslyn *(G-14446)*
▲ **Electronic Devices Inc** ....E 914 965-4400
Yonkers *(G-16755)*
Elite Semi Conductor Products ....G 631 884-8400
Lindenhurst *(G-7172)*
Ely Beach Solar LLC ....G 718 796-9400
New York *(G-9661)*
Emagin Corporation ....D 845 838-7900
Hopewell Junction *(G-6284)*
Emtron Hybrids Inc ....F 631 924-9668
Yaphank *(G-16710)*
▲ **Endicott Interconnect Tech Inc** ....A 866 820-4820
Endicott *(G-4588)*
Energy Materials Corporation ....G 315 247-0880
Rochester *(G-13784)*
Enrg Inc ....F 716 873-2939
Buffalo *(G-2820)*
▲ **Eversan Inc** ....F 315 736-3967
Whitesboro *(G-16527)*
Exceltech Inc ....F 718 423-7262
Fresh Meadows *(G-5197)*
General Led Holdings LLC ....F 212 629-6830
New York *(G-9900)*
General Microwave Corporation ....F 516 802-0900
Syosset *(G-15219)*
General Semiconductor Inc ....G 631 300-3818
Hauppauge *(G-5831)*
Globalfoundries US 2 LLC ....C 512 457-3900
Hopewell Junction *(G-6286)*
Globalfoundries US Inc ....E 512 457-3900
Hopewell Junction *(G-6287)*
Globalfoundries US Inc ....F 408 462-3900
Ballston Spa *(G-583)*
Green Logic Led Elec Sup Inc ....E 516 280-2854
Farmingdale *(G-4775)*
Gurley Precision Instrs Inc ....C 518 272-6300
Troy *(G-15607)*
H K Technologies Inc ....G 718 255-1898
Long Island City *(G-7465)*
Hi-Tron Semiconductor Corp ....E 631 231-1500
Hauppauge *(G-5844)*
▲ **Hipotronics Inc** ....C 845 279-8091
Brewster *(G-1167)*
▲ **Hisun Optoelectronics Co Ltd** ....F 718 886-6966
Flushing *(G-5008)*
I E D Corp ....F 631 348-0424
Islandia *(G-6529)*
Idalia Solar Technologies LLC ....G 212 792-3913
New York *(G-10170)*
Ilc Holdings Inc ....G 631 567-5600
Bohemia *(G-1034)*
▲ **Ilc Industries LLC** ....F 631 567-5600
Bohemia *(G-1036)*
Imperium Partners Group LLC ....C 212 433-1360
New York *(G-10187)*
▲ **Intech 21 Inc** ....F 516 626-7221
Port Washington *(G-13270)*
INTEL Corporation ....D 408 765-8080
Getzville *(G-5348)*
International Bus Mchs Corp ....E 212 324-5000
New York *(G-10243)*
International Bus Mchs Corp ....C 800 426-4968
Hopewell Junction *(G-6289)*
Intex Company Inc ....D 516 223-0200
Freeport *(G-5162)*
▲ **Isine Inc** ....E 631 913-4400
Melville *(G-8040)*
Isonics Corporation ....G 212 356-7400
New York *(G-10277)*
J H Rhodes Company Inc ....F 315 829-3600
Vernon *(G-15806)*
▲ **Kionix Inc** ....C 607 257-1080
Ithaca *(G-6590)*
KLA-Tencor Corporation ....F 845 897-1723
Hopewell Junction *(G-6290)*
▲ **Lakestar Semi Inc** ....F 212 974-6254
New York *(G-10510)*
Lasermax Inc ....D 585 272-5420
Rochester *(G-13909)*
◆ **Leviton Manufacturing Co Inc** ....B 631 812-6000
Melville *(G-8043)*
Light Blue USA LLC ....G 718 475-2515
Brooklyn *(G-2119)*
Lightspin Technologies Inc ....G 301 656-7600
Endwell *(G-4618)*
Logitek Inc ....D 631 567-1100
Bohemia *(G-1048)*
▲ **LSI Computer Systems** ....E 631 271-0400
Melville *(G-8044)*
M C Products ....E 631 471-4070
Holbrook *(G-6197)*
Marcon Services ....G 516 223-8019
Freeport *(G-5165)*
▲ **Marktech International Corp** ....E 518 956-2980
Latham *(G-7087)*
▲ **Materion Advanced Materials** ....C 800 327-1355
Buffalo *(G-2939)*
▲ **Materion Brewster LLC** ....D 845 279-0900
Brewster *(G-1171)*
▼ **McG Electronics Inc** ....E 631 586-5125
Deer Park *(G-4008)*
Micro Contract Manufacturing ....D 631 738-7874
Medford *(G-7961)*
▲ **Micro Semicdtr Researches LLC** ....G 646 863-6070
New York *(G-10796)*
Microchip Technology Inc ....G 631 233-3280
Hauppauge *(G-5890)*
Microchip Technology Inc ....C 607 785-5992
Endicott *(G-4602)*
Micromem Technologies ....F 212 672-1806
New York *(G-10797)*
Mini-Circuits Fort Wayne LLC ....B 718 934-4500
Brooklyn *(G-2210)*
MMC Magnetics Corp ....F 631 435-9888
Hauppauge *(G-5895)*
Monolithic Coatings Inc ....G 914 621-2765
Sharon Springs *(G-14798)*
Mosaic Microsystems LLC ....G 585 314-7441
Rochester *(G-13958)*
Moser Baer Technologies Inc ....F 585 749-0480
Fairport *(G-4643)*
Nanomas Technologies Inc ....F 607 821-4208
Endicott *(G-4603)*
▲ **Nationwide Tarps Incorporated** ....D 518 843-1545
Amsterdam *(G-353)*
▼ **Navitar Inc** ....D 585 359-4000
Rochester *(G-13965)*
Nsi Industries LLC ....C 800 841-2505
Mount Vernon *(G-8426)*
Oledworks LLC ....E 585 287-6802
Rochester *(G-13985)*
On Semiconductor Corporation ....G 585 784-5770
Rochester *(G-13988)*
▲ **Onyx Solar Group LLC** ....G 917 951-9732
New York *(G-11047)*
Orbit International Corp ....D 631 435-8300
Hauppauge *(G-5907)*
▲ **Park Electrochemical Corp** ....D 631 465-3600
Melville *(G-8056)*
▲ **Passive-Plus Inc** ....F 631 425-0938
Huntington *(G-6407)*
◆ **Philips Medical Systems Mr** ....B 518 782-1122
Latham *(G-7089)*
Piezo Electronics Research ....F 845 735-9349
Pearl River *(G-12907)*
▲ **Plug Power Inc** ....B 518 782-7700
Latham *(G-7091)*
Plug Power Inc ....G 585 474-3993
Rochester *(G-14024)*
Plures Technologies Inc ....G 585 905-0554
Canandaigua *(G-3231)*
Procomponents Inc ....E 516 683-0909
Westbury *(G-16368)*
Pvi Solar Inc ....G 212 280-2100
New York *(G-11286)*
Renewable Energy Inc ....G 718 690-2691
Little Neck *(G-7220)*
Riverhawk Company LP ....E 315 624-7171
New Hartford *(G-8510)*
▲ **RSM Electron Power Inc** ....D 631 586-7600
Deer Park *(G-4039)*
RSM Electron Power Inc ....D 631 586-7600
Hauppauge *(G-5931)*
Ruhle Companies Inc ....E 914 287-4000
Valhalla *(G-15747)*
S3j Electronics LLC ....E 716 206-1309
Lancaster *(G-7047)*
▲ **Sanrex Corporation** ....F 516 625-1313
Port Washington *(G-13304)*
Schott Corporation ....D 315 255-2791
Auburn *(G-499)*
Schott Lithotec USA Corp ....D 845 463-5300
Elmsford *(G-4566)*
▲ **Schott Solar Pv Inc** ....G 888 457-6527
Elmsford *(G-4568)*
Semitronics Corp ....E 516 223-0200
Freeport *(G-5182)*
Sendyne Corp ....G 212 966-0663
New York *(G-11542)*
Senera Co Inc ....F 516 639-3774
Valley Stream *(G-15796)*
Sinclair Technologies Inc ....E 716 874-3682
Hamburg *(G-5695)*
SMC Diode Solutions LLC ....G 631 965-0869
Plainview *(G-13088)*

SIC SECTION 36 ELECTRONIC AND OTHER ELECTRICAL EQUIPMENT AND COMPONENTS, EXCEPT COMPUTER

▲ **Solar Thin Films Inc** ... E ... 212 629-8260
Cedarhurst *(G-3337)*
Solid Cell Inc ... F ... 585 426-5000
Rochester *(G-14133)*
Sonotec US Inc ... C ... 631 415-4758
Islandia *(G-6539)*
▲ **Spectron Glass & Electronics** ... F ... 631 582-5600
Hauppauge *(G-5943)*
Spectron Systems Technology ... F ... 631 582-5600
Hauppauge *(G-5944)*
Spellman High Vltage Elec Corp ... D ... 914 686-3600
Valhalla *(G-15748)*
▲ **Standard Microsystems Corp** ... D ... 631 435-6000
Hauppauge *(G-5948)*
▲ **Stetron International Inc** ... F ... 716 854-3443
Buffalo *(G-3077)*
▲ **Sumitomo Elc USA Holdings Inc** ... G ... 212 490-6610
New York *(G-11738)*
▼ **Super Conductor Materials Inc** ... F ... 845 368-0240
Suffern *(G-15198)*
Swissbit Na Inc ... G ... 914 935-1400
Port Chester *(G-13209)*
Symwave Inc ... G ... 949 542-4400
Hauppauge *(G-5954)*
Tarsier Ltd ... C ... 646 880-8680
New York *(G-11785)*
▲ **Tel Technology Center Amer LLC** ... E ... 512 424-4200
Albany *(G-133)*
Telephonics Corporation ... E ... 631 549-6000
Huntington *(G-6418)*
Telephonics Tlsi Corp ... C ... 631 470-8854
Huntington *(G-6421)*
Thales Laser SA ... D ... 585 223-2370
Fairport *(G-4664)*
Thermo Cidtec Inc ... E ... 315 451-9410
Liverpool *(G-7267)*
Thermoaura Inc ... F ... 518 813-4997
Albany *(G-134)*
Tlsi Incorporated ... D ... 631 470-8880
Huntington *(G-6422)*
Tokyo Electron America Inc ... G ... 518 289-3100
Malta *(G-7732)*
Tokyo Electron America Inc ... G ... 518 292-4200
Albany *(G-135)*
▲ **Tork Inc** ... D ... 914 664-3542
Mount Vernon *(G-8446)*
◆ **Truebite Inc** ... E ... 607 785-7664
Vestal *(G-15824)*
Veriled Inc ... G ... 877 521-5520
New York *(G-12011)*
Vgg Holding LLC ... G ... 212 415-6700
New York *(G-12023)*
Viking Technologies Ltd ... E ... 631 957-8000
Lindenhurst *(G-7204)*
Warner Energy LLC ... G ... 315 457-3828
Liverpool *(G-7271)*
Washington Foundries Inc ... G ... 516 374-8447
Hewlett *(G-6054)*
▲ **Zastech Inc** ... E ... 516 496-4777
Syosset *(G-15234)*

3675 Electronic Capacitors

◆ **American Tchncal Ceramics Corp** ... B ... 631 622-4700
Huntington Station *(G-6430)*
▲ **American Techical Ceramics** ... G ... 631 622-4758
Huntington Station *(G-6431)*
American Technical Ceramics ... B ... 631 622-4700
Huntington Station *(G-6432)*
AVX Corporation ... D ... 716 372-6611
Olean *(G-12592)*
▲ **Custom Electronics Inc** ... D ... 607 432-3880
Oneonta *(G-12637)*
Electron Coil Inc ... D ... 607 336-7414
Norwich *(G-12485)*
Ems Development Corporation ... D ... 631 345-6200
Yaphank *(G-16709)*
▲ **Hipotronics Inc** ... C ... 845 279-8091
Brewster *(G-1167)*
Integer Holdings Corporation ... E ... 716 937-5100
Alden *(G-173)*
Kemet Properties LLC ... G ... 718 654-8079
Bronx *(G-1306)*
▲ **Knowles Cazenovia Inc** ... C ... 315 655-8710
Cazenovia *(G-3320)*
▲ **MTK Electronics Inc** ... E ... 631 924-7666
Medford *(G-7962)*
▲ **Passive-Plus Inc** ... F ... 631 425-0938
Huntington *(G-6407)*
▲ **Roberts-Gordon LLC** ... D ... 716 852-4400
Buffalo *(G-3040)*

▲ **Russell Industries Inc** ... G ... 516 536-5000
Lynbrook *(G-7673)*
▲ **Stk Electronics Inc** ... E ... 315 655-8476
Cazenovia *(G-3327)*
Strux Corp ... E ... 516 768-3969
Lindenhurst *(G-7196)*
▲ **Tronser Inc** ... G ... 315 655-9528
Cazenovia *(G-3328)*
Viking Technologies Ltd ... E ... 631 957-8000
Lindenhurst *(G-7204)*
Voltronics LLC ... E ... 410 749-2424
Cazenovia *(G-3329)*

3676 Electronic Resistors

Betapast Holdings LLC ... D ... 631 582-6740
Hauppauge *(G-5779)*
Microgen Systems Inc ... G ... 585 214-2426
Fairport *(G-4642)*
▼ **Micropen Technologies Corp** ... D ... 585 624-2610
Honeoye Falls *(G-6271)*
▲ **Passive-Plus Inc** ... F ... 631 425-0938
Huntington *(G-6407)*
▲ **Stetron International Inc** ... F ... 716 854-3443
Buffalo *(G-3077)*
▲ **Vishay Thin Film LLC** ... C ... 716 283-4025
Niagara Falls *(G-12348)*

3677 Electronic Coils & Transformers

▲ **Aeroflex Incorporated** ... B ... 516 694-6700
Plainview *(G-13032)*
▲ **All Shore Industries Inc** ... F ... 718 720-0018
Staten Island *(G-15042)*
▲ **Allen Avionics Inc** ... E ... 516 248-8080
Mineola *(G-8203)*
◆ **American Precision Inds Inc** ... C ... 716 691-9100
Amherst *(G-214)*
American Precision Inds Inc ... D ... 716 652-3600
East Aurora *(G-4193)*
American Precision Inds Inc ... D ... 585 496-5755
Arcade *(G-376)*
American Trans-Coil Corp ... F ... 516 922-9640
Oyster Bay *(G-12809)*
▲ **Applied Power Systems Inc** ... E ... 516 935-2230
Hicksville *(G-6059)*
Atlantic Transformer Inc ... F ... 716 795-3258
Barker *(G-599)*
▲ **Bel Transformer Inc** ... D ... 516 239-5777
Inwood *(G-6487)*
Beta Transformer Tech Corp ... E ... 631 244-7393
Bohemia *(G-987)*
▲ **Bright Way Supply Inc** ... F ... 718 833-2882
Brooklyn *(G-1635)*
Caddell Burns Manufacturing Co ... E ... 631 757-1772
Northport *(G-12465)*
▲ **Data Device Corporation** ... B ... 631 567-5600
Bohemia *(G-1008)*
Electron Coil Inc ... D ... 607 336-7414
Norwich *(G-12485)*
Ems Development Corporation ... D ... 631 345-6200
Yaphank *(G-16709)*
▲ **Ems Development Corporation** ... D ... 631 924-4736
Yaphank *(G-16708)*
▲ **Eni Technology Inc** ... B ... 585 427-8300
Rochester *(G-13787)*
Es Beta Inc ... E ... 631 582-6740
Ronkonkoma *(G-14339)*
▲ **Esc Control Electronics LLC** ... E ... 631 467-5328
Sayville *(G-14627)*
Exxelia-Raf Tabtronics LLC ... E ... 585 243-4331
Piffard *(G-12996)*
▲ **Fil-Coil (fc) Corp** ... E ... 631 467-5328
Sayville *(G-14628)*
Fil-Coil International LLC ... F ... 631 467-5328
Sayville *(G-14629)*
Frequency Selective Networks ... F ... 718 424-7500
Valley Stream *(G-15780)*
Fuse Electronics Inc ... G ... 607 352-3222
Kirkwood *(G-6940)*
Gowanda - Bti LLC ... D ... 716 492-4081
Arcade *(G-384)*
▲ **Hammond Manufacturing Co Inc** ... F ... 716 630-7030
Cheektowaga *(G-3448)*
▲ **Hipotronics Inc** ... C ... 845 279-8091
Brewster *(G-1167)*
Island Audio Engineering ... G ... 631 543-2372
Commack *(G-3696)*
M F L B Inc ... F ... 631 254-8300
Bay Shore *(G-697)*
▲ **Magnetic Technologies Corp** ... D ... 585 385-9010
Rochester *(G-13924)*

Microwave Filter Company Inc ... E ... 315 438-4700
East Syracuse *(G-4358)*
Mini-Circuits Fort Wayne LLC ... B ... 718 934-4500
Brooklyn *(G-2210)*
▲ **Misonix Inc** ... D ... 631 694-9555
Farmingdale *(G-4828)*
Mitchell Electronics Corp ... E ... 914 699-3800
Mount Vernon *(G-8422)*
Mohawk Electro Techniques Inc ... D ... 315 896-2661
Barneveld *(G-603)*
▲ **MTK Electronics Inc** ... E ... 631 924-7666
Medford *(G-7962)*
▲ **NEa Manufacturing Corp** ... E ... 516 371-4200
Inwood *(G-6497)*
New York Fan Coil LLC ... G ... 646 580-1344
Coram *(G-3801)*
Precision Electronics Inc ... F ... 631 842-4900
Copiague *(G-3774)*
▲ **Rdi Inc** ... F ... 914 773-1000
Mount Kisco *(G-8357)*
Sag Harbor Industries Inc ... E ... 631 725-0440
Sag Harbor *(G-14502)*
Service Filtration Corp ... E ... 716 877-2608
Tonawanda *(G-15577)*
◆ **Todd Systems Inc** ... D ... 914 963-3400
Yonkers *(G-16802)*
Tte Filters LLC ... F ... 716 532-2234
Gowanda *(G-5493)*
Urban Technologies Inc ... G ... 716 672-2709
Fredonia *(G-5129)*

3678 Electronic Connectors

Accessories For Electronics ... E ... 631 847-0158
South Hempstead *(G-14941)*
▲ **Amphenol Aerospace France Inc** ... C ... 800 678-0141
Sidney *(G-14849)*
▲ **Amphenol Cables On Demand Corp** ... F ... 607 321-2115
Endicott *(G-4581)*
Amphenol Corporation ... B ... 607 563-5364
Sidney *(G-14850)*
Amphenol Corporation ... A ... 607 563-5011
Sidney *(G-14851)*
Automatic Connector Inc ... F ... 631 543-5000
Hauppauge *(G-5774)*
Belden Inc ... B ... 607 796-5600
Horseheads *(G-6306)*
▲ **Casa Innovations Inc** ... G ... 718 965-6600
Brooklyn *(G-1682)*
▲ **CS Business Systems Inc** ... E ... 716 886-6521
Buffalo *(G-2786)*
▲ **EBY Electro Inc** ... E ... 516 576-7777
Plainview *(G-13053)*
▲ **Executive Machines Inc** ... E ... 718 965-6600
Brooklyn *(G-1858)*
◆ **Felchar Manufacturing Corp** ... A ... 607 723-3106
Binghamton *(G-884)*
I Trade Technology Ltd ... E ... 845 357-4943
Airmont *(G-13)*
I Trade Technology Ltd ... G ... 615 348-7233
Suffern *(G-15191)*
Ieh Corporation ... C ... 718 492-4440
Brooklyn *(G-1994)*
▲ **Keystone Electronics Corp** ... C ... 516 328-7500
New Hyde Park *(G-8546)*
Kirtas Inc ... G ... 585 924-5999
Victor *(G-15852)*
▼ **Kirtas Inc** ... E ... 585 924-2420
Victor *(G-15853)*
◆ **Leviton Manufacturing Co Inc** ... B ... 631 812-6000
Melville *(G-8043)*
◆ **Mason Industries Inc** ... B ... 631 348-0282
Hauppauge *(G-5881)*
▲ **Mill-Max Mfg Corp** ... C ... 516 922-6000
Oyster Bay *(G-12815)*
Mini-Circuits Fort Wayne LLC ... B ... 718 934-4500
Brooklyn *(G-2210)*
▲ **NEa Manufacturing Corp** ... E ... 516 371-4200
Inwood *(G-6497)*
Pei/Genesis Inc ... G ... 631 256-1747
Farmingville *(G-4925)*
▲ **Power Connector Inc** ... E ... 631 563-7878
Bohemia *(G-1075)*
◆ **Ppc Broadband Inc** ... B ... 315 431-7200
East Syracuse *(G-4363)*
Princetel Inc ... F ... 914 579-2410
Hawthorne *(G-5996)*
▲ **Rdi Inc** ... F ... 914 773-1000
Mount Kisco *(G-8357)*
Resonance Technologies Inc ... E ... 631 237-4901
Ronkonkoma *(G-14406)*

SIC

Employee Codes: A=Over 500 employees, B=251-500
C=101-250, D=51-100, E=20-50, F=10-19, G=5-9
2019 Harris
New York Manufacturers Directory
781

36 ELECTRONIC AND OTHER ELECTRICAL EQUIPMENT AND COMPONENTS, EXCEPT COMPUTER — SIC SECTION

Sitewatch Technology LLC ....G..... 207 778-3246
East Quogue *(G-4279)*
Supplynet Inc ....G..... 800 826-0279
Valley Cottage *(G-15768)*
▲ Taro Manufacturing Company Inc ....F..... 315 252-9430
Auburn *(G-503)*
▲ Universal Remote Control Inc ....D..... 914 630-4343
Harrison *(G-5738)*
▲ Whirlwind Music Distrs Inc ....D..... 800 733-9473
Rochester *(G-14207)*

3679 Electronic Components, NEC

3835 Lebron Rest Eqp & Sup Inc ....E..... 212 942-8258
New York *(G-8679)*
▲ A K Allen Co Inc ....C..... 516 747-5450
Melville *(G-7996)*
A R V Precision Mfg Inc ....G..... 631 293-9643
Farmingdale *(G-4705)*
Accessories For Electronics ....E..... 631 847-0158
South Hempstead *(G-14941)*
Adco Circuits Inc ....G..... 716 668-6600
Buffalo *(G-2685)*
▲ Advance Circuit Technology Inc ......E..... 585 328-2000
Rochester *(G-13604)*
▲ Advanced Interconnect Mfg Inc ......D..... 585 742-2220
Victor *(G-15828)*
Aeroflex Plainview Inc ....B..... 516 694-6700
Plainview *(G-13033)*
Aeroflex Plainview Inc ....C..... 631 231-9100
Hauppauge *(G-5756)*
▲ Albatros North America Inc ....E..... 518 381-7100
Ballston Spa *(G-575)*
▲ All Shore Industries Inc ....F..... 718 720-0018
Staten Island *(G-15042)*
▲ Allen Avionics Inc ....E..... 516 248-8080
Mineola *(G-8203)*
Alloy Machine & Tool Co Inc ....G..... 516 593-3445
Lynbrook *(G-7660)*
Altec Datacom LLC ....G..... 631 242-2417
Bay Shore *(G-655)*
American Aerospace Contrls Inc ....E..... 631 694-5100
Farmingdale *(G-4719)*
American Quality Technology ....F..... 607 777-9488
Binghamton *(G-861)*
▲ Amphenol Intrconnect Pdts Corp ......G..... 607 754-4444
Endicott *(G-4582)*
Ampro International Inc ....G..... 845 278-4910
Brewster *(G-1157)*
Amron Electronics Inc ....E..... 631 737-1234
Ronkonkoma *(G-14309)*
▲ Anaren Inc ....B..... 315 432-8909
East Syracuse *(G-4318)*
Antenna & Radome Res Assoc ....E..... 631 231-8400
Bay Shore *(G-658)*
▲ Apollo Display Tech Corp ....E..... 631 580-4360
Ronkonkoma *(G-14310)*
Applied Concepts Inc ....E..... 315 696-6676
Tully *(G-15647)*
▲ Applied Power Systems Inc ....E..... 516 935-2230
Hicksville *(G-6059)*
▲ Apx Technologies Inc ....E..... 516 433-1313
Hicksville *(G-6060)*
▲ Arnold-Davis LLC ....C..... 607 772-1201
Binghamton *(G-863)*
Arstan Products International ....F..... 516 433-1313
Hicksville *(G-6061)*
B H M Metal Products Co ....G..... 845 292-5297
Kauneonga Lake *(G-6849)*
B3cg Interconnect Usa Inc ....F..... 450 491-4040
Plattsburgh *(G-13108)*
Badger Technologies Inc ....E..... 585 869-7101
Farmington *(G-4909)*
BC Systems Inc ....E..... 631 751-9370
Setauket *(G-14792)*
Becker Electronics Inc ....D..... 631 619-9100
Ronkonkoma *(G-14318)*
Berkshire Transformer ....G..... 631 467-5328
Central Islip *(G-3359)*
Bud Barger Assoc Inc ....E..... 631 696-6703
Farmingville *(G-4923)*
C A M Graphics Co Inc ....E..... 631 842-3400
Farmingdale *(G-4731)*
Cables Unlimited Inc ....E..... 631 563-6363
Yaphank *(G-16705)*
▲ Canfield Electronics Inc ....E..... 631 585-4100
Lindenhurst *(G-7165)*
Celmet Co ....E..... 585 647-1760
Newark *(G-12194)*
Centroid Inc ....E..... 516 349-0070
Plainview *(G-13040)*

Chiplogic Inc ....F..... 631 617-6317
Yaphank *(G-16706)*
Clever Devices Ltd ....E..... 516 433-6100
Woodbury *(G-16614)*
Cloud Toronto LLC ....F..... 408 569-4542
Williamsville *(G-16576)*
Cobham Holdings (us) Inc ....A..... 716 662-0006
Orchard Park *(G-12707)*
Cobham Holdings Inc ....F..... 716 662-0006
Orchard Park *(G-12708)*
▲ Condor Electronics Corp ....F..... 585 235-1500
Rochester *(G-13717)*
Crystal Is Inc ....E..... 518 271-7375
Green Island *(G-5604)*
D & S Supplies Inc ....F..... 718 721-5256
Astoria *(G-422)*
Dimension Technologies Inc ....F..... 585 436-3530
Rochester *(G-13742)*
Dortronics Systems Inc ....E..... 631 725-0505
Sag Harbor *(G-14499)*
Dynamic Hybirds Inc ....G..... 315 426-8110
Syracuse *(G-15308)*
▲ Eastland Electronics Co Inc ....F..... 631 580-3800
Ronkonkoma *(G-14337)*
◆ Edo LLC ....G..... 631 630-4000
Amityville *(G-272)*
▼ Electronics & Innovation Ltd ....F..... 585 214-0598
Rochester *(G-13776)*
Engagement Technology LLC ....F..... 914 591-7600
Elmsford *(G-4542)*
▲ Eni Technology Inc ....E..... 585 427-8300
Rochester *(G-13787)*
▲ Esc Control Electronics LLC ....F..... 631 467-5328
Sayville *(G-14627)*
Espey Mfg & Electronics Corp ....C..... 518 584-4100
Saratoga Springs *(G-14578)*
▲ Fair-Rite Products Corp ....C..... 845 895-2055
Wallkill *(G-15904)*
Fei Communications Inc ....C..... 516 794-4500
Uniondale *(G-15666)*
Felluss Recording ....G..... 212 727-8055
New York *(G-9793)*
Fine Sounds Group Inc ....F..... 212 364-0219
New York *(G-9805)*
Frequency Electronics Inc ....C..... 516 794-4500
Uniondale *(G-15668)*
General Microwave Corporation ....F..... 516 802-0900
Syosset *(G-15219)*
Gotenna Inc ....F..... 415 894-2616
Brooklyn *(G-1941)*
▲ Grado Laboratories Inc ....F..... 718 435-5340
Brooklyn *(G-1946)*
▲ Haynes Roberts Inc ....F..... 212 989-1901
New York *(G-10053)*
Hazlow Electronics Inc ....F..... 585 325-5323
Rochester *(G-13863)*
▲ Hipotronics Inc ....C..... 845 279-8091
Brewster *(G-1167)*
Hudson Valley Tech Dev Ctr Inc ....F..... 845 391-8214
Highland *(G-6144)*
Hypres Inc ....E..... 914 592-1190
Elmsford *(G-4545)*
I3 Assembly LLC ....D..... 607 238-7077
Binghamton *(G-892)*
▲ IEC Electronics Corp ....B..... 315 331-7742
Newark *(G-12196)*
Imrex LLC ....B..... 516 479-3675
Oyster Bay *(G-12814)*
Innovative Power Products Inc ....E..... 631 563-0088
Holbrook *(G-6190)*
Island Circuits International ....B..... 516 625-5555
College Point *(G-3649)*
Island Research and Dev Corp ....E..... 631 471-7100
Ronkonkoma *(G-14354)*
▲ Jenlor Ltd ....E..... 315 637-9080
Fayetteville *(G-4928)*
◆ Kearney-National Inc ....F..... 212 661-4600
New York *(G-10427)*
▲ Keltron Electronics (de Corp) ....F..... 631 567-6300
Ronkonkoma *(G-14360)*
▲ L3 Foreign Holdings Inc ....A..... 212 697-1111
New York *(G-10497)*
L3 Technologies Inc ....E..... 631 289-0363
Patchogue *(G-12870)*
L3 Technologies Inc ....B..... 212 697-1111
New York *(G-10498)*
Lexan Industries Inc ....F..... 631 434-7586
Bay Shore *(G-696)*
Lighthouse Components ....E..... 917 993-6820
New York *(G-10570)*

Logitek Inc ....D..... 631 567-1100
Bohemia *(G-1048)*
Lyntronics Inc ....E..... 631 205-1061
Yaphank *(G-16715)*
M W Microwave Corp ....F..... 516 295-1814
Lawrence *(G-7105)*
Marcon Electronic Systems LLC ....G..... 516 633-6396
Freeport *(G-5164)*
Mechanical Pwr Conversion LLC ....F..... 607 766-9620
Binghamton *(G-903)*
▲ Mekatronics Incorporated ....F..... 516 883-6805
Port Washington *(G-13288)*
▲ Meridian Technologies Inc ....F..... 516 285-1000
Elmont *(G-4521)*
▲ Merit Electronic Design Co Inc ....E..... 631 667-9699
Edgewood *(G-4409)*
Mezmeriz Inc ....E..... 607 216-8140
Ithaca *(G-6595)*
Microwave Filter Company Inc ....E..... 315 438-4700
East Syracuse *(G-4358)*
▲ Mid Hdson Wkshp For The Dsbled ....E..... 845 471-3820
Poughkeepsie *(G-13354)*
Mini-Circuits Fort Wayne LLC ....B..... 718 934-4500
Brooklyn *(G-2210)*
Mirion Technologies Ist Corp ....D..... 607 562-4300
Horseheads *(G-6321)*
MLS Sales ....F..... 516 681-2736
Bethpage *(G-848)*
◆ Momentive Performance Mtls Inc ....E..... 518 237-3330
Waterford *(G-15981)*
Mpm Holdings Inc ....E..... 518 237-3330
Waterford *(G-15984)*
Mpm Intermediate Holdings Inc ....E..... 518 237-3330
Waterford *(G-15985)*
▲ NEa Manufacturing Corp ....E..... 516 371-4200
Inwood *(G-6497)*
Nelson Holdings Ltd ....F..... 607 772-1794
Binghamton *(G-908)*
New York Digital Corporation ....F..... 631 630-9798
Huntington Station *(G-6453)*
▲ North Hills Signal Proc Corp ....E..... 631 244-7393
Bohemia *(G-1067)*
▼ Oakdale Industrial Elec Corp ....F..... 631 737-4090
Ronkonkoma *(G-14388)*
Opus Technology Corporation ....F..... 631 271-1883
Melville *(G-8054)*
Orbit International Corp ....D..... 631 435-8300
Hauppauge *(G-5907)*
Orbit International Corp ....D..... 631 435-8300
Hauppauge *(G-5908)*
Orthogonal ....E..... 585 254-2775
Rochester *(G-13996)*
Paal Technologies Inc ....G..... 631 319-6262
Ronkonkoma *(G-14394)*
▲ Passive-Plus Inc ....F..... 631 425-0938
Huntington *(G-6407)*
Pcb Group Inc ....E..... 716 684-0001
Depew *(G-4100)*
Pcb Piezotronics Inc ....F..... 716 684-0003
Depew *(G-4102)*
◆ Philips Medical Systems Mr ....B..... 518 782-1122
Latham *(G-7089)*
Plura Broadcast Inc ....G..... 516 997-5675
Massapequa *(G-7882)*
Polycast Industries Inc ....G..... 631 595-2530
Bay Shore *(G-708)*
▲ Precision Assembly Tech Inc ....E..... 631 699-9400
Bohemia *(G-1076)*
Premier Systems LLC ....G..... 631 587-9700
Babylon *(G-532)*
Pvi Solar Inc ....G..... 212 280-2100
New York *(G-11286)*
◆ Pyragon Inc ....E..... 585 697-0444
Rochester *(G-14055)*
▲ Quality Contract Assemblies ....F..... 585 663-9030
Rochester *(G-14060)*
R L C Electronics Inc ....D..... 914 241-1334
Mount Kisco *(G-8356)*
▲ Rdi Inc ....F..... 914 773-1000
Mount Kisco *(G-8357)*
Rem-Tronics Inc ....D..... 716 934-2697
Dunkirk *(G-4177)*
Rochester Industrial Ctrl Inc ....D..... 315 524-4555
Ontario *(G-12664)*
▲ Rochester Industrial Ctrl Inc ....E..... 315 524-4555
Ontario *(G-12663)*
Ruhle Companies Inc ....E..... 914 287-4000
Valhalla *(G-15747)*
▲ Russell Industries Inc ....G..... 516 536-5000
Lynbrook *(G-7673)*

SIC SECTION
36 ELECTRONIC AND OTHER ELECTRICAL EQUIPMENT AND COMPONENTS, EXCEPT COMPUTER

Safe Circuits Inc ....G .... 631 586-3682 Dix Hills *(G-4125)*
Sayeda Manufacturing Corp ....F .... 631 345-2525 Medford *(G-7965)*
SC Textiles Inc ....G .... 631 944-6262 Huntington *(G-6414)*
▲ **Scientific Components Corp** ....B .... 718 934-4500 Brooklyn *(G-2452)*
Scientific Components Corp ....B .... 718 368-2060 Brooklyn *(G-2453)*
Secs Inc ....E .... 914 667-5600 Mount Vernon *(G-8442)*
Sendec Corp ....E .... 585 425-5965 Fairport *(G-4657)*
Sln Group Inc ....G .... 718 677-5969 Brooklyn *(G-2486)*
Sonaer Inc ....G .... 631 756-4780 West Babylon *(G-16193)*
▲ **Sopark Corp** ....D .... 716 822-0434 Buffalo *(G-3070)*
Space Coast Semiconductor Inc ....F .... 631 414-7131 Farmingdale *(G-4878)*
▲ **Spectron Glass & Electronics** ....F .... 631 582-5600 Hauppauge *(G-5943)*
Spellman Hgh-Voltage Elec Corp ....B .... 631 630-3000 Hauppauge *(G-5947)*
▲ **Stetron International Inc** ....F .... 716 854-3443 Buffalo *(G-3077)*
Sturges Elec Pdts Co Inc ....E .... 607 844-8604 Dryden *(G-4152)*
Sturges Electronics LLC ....F .... 607 844-8604 Dryden *(G-4153)*
Superior Motion Controls Inc ....E .... 516 420-2921 Farmingdale *(G-4885)*
▲ **Surmotech LLC** ....D .... 585 742-1220 Victor *(G-15868)*
T-S-K Electronics Inc ....G .... 716 693-3916 North Tonawanda *(G-12457)*
TCS Electronics Inc ....E .... 585 337-4301 Farmington *(G-4920)*
◆ **Tdk USA Corporation** ....D .... 516 535-2600 Uniondale *(G-15672)*
Te Connectivity Corporation ....E .... 585 785-2500 Rochester *(G-14159)*
Telephonics Corporation ....E .... 631 549-6000 Huntington *(G-6418)*
▲ **Telephonics Corporation** ....A .... 631 755-7000 Farmingdale *(G-4892)*
Three Five III-V Materials Inc ....F .... 212 213-8290 New York *(G-11828)*
Tlsi Incorporated ....D .... 631 470-8880 Huntington *(G-6422)*
Tony Baird Electronics Inc ....G .... 315 422-4430 Syracuse *(G-15445)*
Torotron Corporation ....G .... 718 428-6992 Fresh Meadows *(G-5204)*
▲ **Trading Services International** ....F .... 212 501-0142 New York *(G-11884)*
Traffic Lane Closures LLC ....F .... 845 228-6100 Carmel *(G-3283)*
Transistor Power Tech Inc ....G .... 631 491-0265 Stony Brook *(G-15170)*
▲ **Ultralife Corporation** ....B .... 315 332-7100 Newark *(G-12209)*
Ultravolt Inc ....D .... 631 471-4444 Ronkonkoma *(G-14426)*
Unison Industries LLC ....B .... 607 335-5000 Norwich *(G-12494)*
▲ **Vestal Electronic Devices LLC** ....F .... 607 773-8461 Endicott *(G-4614)*
Voices For All LLC ....G .... 518 261-1664 Mechanicville *(G-7935)*
W D Technology Inc ....G .... 914 779-8738 Eastchester *(G-4383)*
▲ **Walter G Legge Company Inc** ....G .... 914 737-5040 Peekskill *(G-12928)*
Werlatone Inc ....E .... 845 278-2220 Patterson *(G-12887)*
Xedit Corp ....G .... 718 380-1592 Queens Village *(G-13413)*

3691 Storage Batteries

Amco Intl Mfg & Design Inc ....E .... 718 388-8668 Brooklyn *(G-1518)*
Battery Energy Storage Systems ....G .... 518 256-7029 Troy *(G-15602)*
Battery Research and Tstg Inc ....F .... 315 342-2373 Oswego *(G-12775)*
▲ **Battsco LLC** ....G .... 516 586-6544 Hicksville *(G-6064)*
Bren-Trnics Batteries Intl Inc ....G .... 631 499-5155 Commack *(G-3683)*
Bren-Trnics Batteries Intl LLC ....E .... 631 499-5155 Commack *(G-3684)*
◆ **Bren-Tronics Inc** ....C .... 631 499-5155 Commack *(G-3685)*
Cellec Technologies Inc ....G .... 585 454-9166 Rochester *(G-13699)*
China Lithium Technologies ....G .... 212 391-2688 New York *(G-9280)*
El-Don Battery Post Inc ....G .... 716 627-3697 Hamburg *(G-5677)*
Exide Technologies ....G .... 585 344-0656 Batavia *(G-623)*
Johnson Controls Inc ....C .... 585 724-2232 Rochester *(G-13897)*
New Energy Systems Group ....C .... 917 573-0302 New York *(G-10921)*
Synergy Digital ....F .... 718 643-2742 Brooklyn *(G-2546)*
▲ **Ultralife Corporation** ....B .... 315 332-7100 Newark *(G-12209)*
▲ **W & W Manufacturing Co** ....F .... 516 242-0011 West Islip *(G-16261)*

3692 Primary Batteries: Dry & Wet

◆ **Bren-Tronics Inc** ....C .... 631 499-5155 Commack *(G-3685)*
◆ **Electrochem Solutions Inc** ....D .... 716 759-5800 Clarence *(G-3532)*
Shad Industries Inc ....G .... 631 504-6028 Yaphank *(G-16721)*

3694 Electrical Eqpt For Internal Combustion Engines

▲ **ARC Systems Inc** ....E .... 631 582-8020 Hauppauge *(G-5768)*
▲ **Autel US Inc** ....G .... 631 923-2620 Farmingdale *(G-4724)*
Con Rel Auto Electric Inc ....E .... 518 356-1646 Schenectady *(G-14666)*
Delphi Powertrain Systems LLC ....B .... 585 359-6000 West Henrietta *(G-16237)*
Eastern Unit Exch Rmnfacturing ....F .... 718 739-7113 Floral Park *(G-4963)*
Eluminocity US Inc ....G .... 651 528-1165 New York *(G-9660)*
Ev-Box North America Inc ....G .... 646 930-6305 New York *(G-9732)*
Fairbanks Morse Engine ....G .... 608 364-8465 Palmyra *(G-12850)*
International Key Supply LLC ....F .... 631 983-6096 Farmingdale *(G-4788)*
▲ **Karlyn Industries Inc** ....F .... 845 351-2249 Southfields *(G-14966)*
◆ **Kearney-National Inc** ....F .... 212 661-4600 New York *(G-10427)*
◆ **Leviton Manufacturing Co Inc** ....B .... 631 812-6000 Melville *(G-8043)*
▲ **Magnum Shielding Corporation** ....E .... 585 381-9957 Pittsford *(G-13020)*
Martinez Specialties Inc ....G .... 607 898-3053 Groton *(G-5652)*
▲ **Nas-Tra Automotive Inds Inc** ....C .... 631 225-1225 Lindenhurst *(G-7182)*
▲ **Sopark Corp** ....D .... 716 822-0434 Buffalo *(G-3070)*
Standard Motor Products Inc ....B .... 718 392-0200 Long Island City *(G-7598)*
▲ **Taro Manufacturing Company Inc** ....F .... 315 252-9430 Auburn *(G-503)*
▲ **Zenith Autoparts Corp** ....E .... 845 344-1382 Middletown *(G-8185)*
▲ **Zierick Manufacturing Corp** ....D .... 800 882-8020 Mount Kisco *(G-8361)*

3695 Recording Media

Aarfid LLC ....G .... 716 992-3999 Eden *(G-4386)*
BMA Media Services Inc ....E .... 585 385-2060 Rochester *(G-13669)*
Connectiva Systems Inc ....F .... 646 722-8741 New York *(G-9380)*
Dm2 Media LLC ....E .... 646 419-4357 New York *(G-9542)*
Ember Media Corporation ....F .... 212 695-1919 New York *(G-9664)*
Escholar LLC ....F .... 914 989-2900 White Plains *(G-16446)*
Infinite Software Solutions ....F .... 718 982-1315 Staten Island *(G-15090)*
John J Richardson ....F .... 516 538-6339 Lawrence *(G-7103)*
▲ **L & M Optical Disc LLC** ....D .... 718 649-3500 New York *(G-10491)*
Longtail Studios Inc ....E .... 646 443-8146 New York *(G-10598)*
Medicine Rules Inc ....G .... 631 334-5395 East Setauket *(G-4303)*
Multi-Health Systems Inc ....D .... 800 456-3003 Cheektowaga *(G-3453)*
Next Big Sound Inc ....G .... 646 657-9837 New York *(G-10958)*
Orpheo USA Corp ....G .... 212 464-8255 New York *(G-11062)*
▲ **Professional Tape Corporation** ....G .... 516 656-5519 Glen Cove *(G-5373)*
◆ **Sony Corporation of America** ....C .... 212 833-8000 New York *(G-11645)*
Sony Dadc US Inc ....B .... 212 833-8800 New York *(G-11646)*
▲ **Stamper Technology Inc** ....G .... 585 247-8370 Rochester *(G-14141)*

3699 Electrical Machinery, Eqpt & Splys, NEC

303 Contracting Inc ....E .... 716 896-2122 Orchard Park *(G-12694)*
331 Holding Inc ....E .... 585 924-1740 Victor *(G-15827)*
3krf LLC ....G .... 516 208-6824 Oceanside *(G-12529)*
A & S Electric ....G .... 212 228-2030 Brooklyn *(G-1452)*
Aabacs Group Inc ....F .... 718 961-3577 College Point *(G-3635)*
Advance Energy Systems NY LLC ....G .... 315 735-5125 Utica *(G-15676)*
Advanced Mfg Techniques ....G .... 518 877-8560 Clifton Park *(G-3562)*
Advanced Photonics Inc ....F .... 631 471-3693 Ronkonkoma *(G-14293)*
▲ **Albatros North America Inc** ....E .... 518 381-7100 Ballston Spa *(G-575)*
Alexy Associates Inc ....E .... 845 482-3000 Bethel *(G-834)*
▲ **All Shore Industries Inc** ....F .... 718 720-0018 Staten Island *(G-15042)*
Allcom Electric Corp ....G .... 914 803-0433 Yonkers *(G-16731)*
Altaquip LLC ....G .... 631 580-4740 Ronkonkoma *(G-14304)*
◆ **Altronix Corp** ....D .... 718 567-8181 Brooklyn *(G-1515)*
American Avionic Tech Corp ....D .... 631 924-8200 Medford *(G-7937)*
Amertac Holdings Inc ....G .... 610 336-1330 Monsey *(G-8284)*
Ameta International Co Ltd ....G .... 416 992-8036 Buffalo *(G-2697)*
Ametek Inc ....D .... 585 263-7700 Rochester *(G-13630)*
AMP-Line Corp ....F .... 845 623-3288 West Nyack *(G-16263)*
Analog Digital Technology LLC ....G .... 585 698-1845 Rochester *(G-13631)*
Arise At Marshall Farms Inc ....G .... 315 687-6727 Chittenango *(G-3501)*
Assa Abloy Entrance Systems US ....E .... 315 492-6600 East Syracuse *(G-4323)*
▲ **Atlantic Electronic Tech LLC** ....G .... 800 296-2177 Brooklyn *(G-1570)*
Atlas Switch Co Inc ....E .... 516 222-6280 Garden City *(G-5251)*
Audible Difference Inc ....E .... 212 662-4848 Brooklyn *(G-1574)*
Audible Difference Inc ....G .... 212 662-4848 Brooklyn *(G-1575)*
Auraspace Inc ....G .... 212 905-6100 New York *(G-8963)*
B & H Electronics Corp ....E .... 845 782-5000 Monroe *(G-8264)*
Bare Beauty Laser Hair Removal ....G .... 718 278-2273 New York *(G-9015)*
▲ **Binghamton Simulator Co Inc** ....E .... 607 321-2980 Binghamton *(G-868)*
Bombardier Trnsp Holdings USA ....D .... 607 776-4791 Bath *(G-641)*
Branson Ultrasonics Corp ....E .... 585 624-8000 Honeoye Falls *(G-6262)*

S I C

Employee Codes: A=Over 500 employees, B=251-500
C=101-250, D=51-100, E=20-50, F=10-19, G=5-9
2019 Harris
New York Manufacturers Directory
783

◆ **Bren-Tronics Inc** C 631 499-5155
Commack *(G-3685)*
BSC Associates LLC F 607 321-2980
Binghamton *(G-872)*
▲ **Buffalo Filter LLC** D 716 835-7000
Lancaster *(G-7011)*
C & G Video Systems Inc G 315 452-1490
Liverpool *(G-7226)*
Canary Connect Inc C 212 390-8576
New York *(G-9192)*
▲ **Castle Power Solutions LLC** F 518 743-1000
South Glens Falls *(G-14935)*
Cathay Global Co Inc G 718 229-0920
Bayside Hills *(G-752)*
Ces Industries Inc E 631 782-7088
Islandia *(G-6525)*
Citadel Electrical Sup Co Inc G 646 705-0333
Tappan *(G-15467)*
Comsec Ventures International G 518 523-1600
Lake Placid *(G-6975)*
▲ **Cooper Crouse-Hinds LLC** B 315 477-7000
Syracuse *(G-15290)*
Cooper Industries LLC E 315 477-7000
Syracuse *(G-15291)*
Cooper Power Systems LLC B 716 375-7100
Olean *(G-12597)*
Cooperfriedman Elc Sup Co Inc G 718 269-4906
Long Island City *(G-7415)*
Custom Sound and Video E 585 424-5000
Rochester *(G-13730)*
Da Electric E 347 270-3422
Bronx *(G-1252)*
Dahill Distributors Inc G 347 371-9453
Brooklyn *(G-1750)*
Denmar Electric F 845 624-4430
Nanuet *(G-8463)*
Detekion Security Systems Inc F 607 729-7179
Vestal *(G-15815)*
Dorsey Metrology Intl Inc E 845 229-2929
Poughkeepsie *(G-13334)*
◆ **Dyson-Kissner-Moran Corp** E 212 661-4600
Poughkeepsie *(G-13335)*
Eastco Manufacturing Corp F 914 738-5667
Pelham *(G-12934)*
Edo LLC A 631 630-4200
Amityville *(G-273)*
Emco Electric Services LLC G 212 420-9766
New York *(G-9667)*
▲ **Emcom Inc** D 315 255-5300
Auburn *(G-477)*
Empire Plastics Inc E 607 754-9132
Endwell *(G-4616)*
Exfo Burleigh Pdts Group Inc D 585 301-1530
Canandaigua *(G-3220)*
Eyelock Corporation F 855 393-5625
New York *(G-9758)*
Eyelock LLC F 855 393-5625
New York *(G-9759)*
EZ Lift Operator Corp F 845 356-1676
Spring Valley *(G-14990)*
Fairview Bell and Intercom G 718 627-8621
Brooklyn *(G-1865)*
◆ **Fiber Instrument Sales Inc** C 315 736-2206
Oriskany *(G-12757)*
Fire Fox Security Corp G 917 981-9280
Brooklyn *(G-1884)*
Forte Network E 631 390-9050
East Northport *(G-4264)*
Full Circle Studios LLC G 716 875-7740
Buffalo *(G-2837)*
Gb Group Inc G 212 594-3748
New York *(G-9885)*
General Electric Company G 315 554-2000
Skaneateles *(G-14872)*
▲ **Gerome Technologies Inc** D 518 463-1324
Menands *(G-8085)*
Green Island Power Authority F 518 273-0661
Green Island *(G-5606)*
Gsa Upstate NY G 631 244-5744
Oakdale *(G-12517)*
Guardian Systems Tech Inc F 716 481-5597
East Aurora *(G-4202)*
▲ **Hampton Technologies LLC** E 631 924-1335
Medford *(G-7951)*
◆ **Hawk-I Security Inc** G 631 656-1056
Hauppauge *(G-5843)*
◆ **Hergo Ergonomic Support** E 718 894-0639
Maspeth *(G-7851)*
Highlander Realty Inc E 914 235-8073
New Rochelle *(G-8614)*
Htf Components Inc G 914 703-6795
White Plains *(G-16461)*
▲ **Iba Industrial Inc** E 631 254-6800
Edgewood *(G-4403)*
Iconix Inc F 516 513-1420
Hauppauge *(G-5848)*
Idex Health & Science LLC D 585 244-7220
Rochester *(G-13875)*
Ingham Industries Inc G 631 242-2493
Holbrook *(G-6189)*
Innovative Video Tech Inc F 631 388-5700
Hauppauge *(G-5850)*
Intellicheck Inc E 516 992-1900
Melville *(G-8037)*
Intelligent Ctrl Systems LLC G 516 340-1011
Farmingdale *(G-4787)*
▲ **Isolation Technology Inc** G 631 253-3314
West Babylon *(G-16159)*
Issco Corporation F 212 732-8748
Garden City *(G-5263)*
◆ **Itin Scale Co Inc** E 718 336-5900
Brooklyn *(G-2019)*
J H M Engineering E 718 871-1810
Brooklyn *(G-2023)*
▲ **Kinetic Marketing Inc** G 212 620-0600
New York *(G-10450)*
Knf Clean Room Products Corp E 631 588-7000
Ronkonkoma *(G-14362)*
▲ **Koregon Enterprises Inc** G 450 218-6836
Champlain *(G-3411)*
Kyle R Lawrence Electric Inc G 315 502-4181
Palmyra *(G-12856)*
L-3 Cmmnctons Ntronix Holdings D 212 697-1111
New York *(G-10496)*
Lasermax Inc D 585 272-5420
Rochester *(G-13909)*
Lucas Electric G 516 809-8619
Seaford *(G-14759)*
Lyn Jo Enterprises Ltd G 716 753-2776
Mayville *(G-7922)*
Madison Electric F 718 358-4121
Cambria Heights *(G-3176)*
Magic Tech Co Ltd G 516 539-7944
West Hempstead *(G-16221)*
Manhattan Scientifics Inc F 212 541-2405
New York *(G-10688)*
Manhole Brrier SEC Systems Inc E 516 741-1032
Kew Gardens *(G-6877)*
Manor Electric Supply Corp F 718 648-8003
Brooklyn *(G-2161)*
Manufacturing Solutions Inc E 585 235-3320
Rochester *(G-13927)*
Marzullo Electric LLC G 315 455-1050
Syracuse *(G-15367)*
Mitsubishi Elc Pwr Pdts Inc G 516 962-2813
Melville *(G-8048)*
Mkj Communications Corp F 212 206-0072
Brooklyn *(G-2219)*
Multi Tech Electric F 718 606-2695
Woodside *(G-16665)*
Napco Security Tech Inc C 631 842-9400
Amityville *(G-304)*
National Security Systems Inc E 516 627-2222
Manhasset *(G-7770)*
▼ **Navitar Inc** D 585 359-4000
Rochester *(G-13965)*
Nbn Technologies LLC G 585 355-5556
Rochester *(G-13966)*
▲ **Ncc Ny LLC** E 718 943-7000
Brooklyn *(G-2251)*
News/Sprts Microwave Rentl Inc E 619 670-0572
New York *(G-10955)*
Nk Electric LLC G 914 271-0222
Croton On Hudson *(G-3915)*
Northrop Grumman Intl Trdg Inc G 716 626-7233
Buffalo *(G-2975)*
▲ **OEM Solutions Inc** G 716 864-9324
Clarence *(G-3536)*
Optimum Applied Systems Inc F 845 471-3333
Poughkeepsie *(G-13361)*
▲ **Parabit Systems Inc** E 516 378-4800
Bellmore *(G-791)*
▲ **Piller Power Systems Inc** E 845 695-6658
Middletown *(G-8170)*
Pinpoint Systems Intl Inc D 631 775-2100
Bellport *(G-812)*
Power Metrics Intl Inc F 718 524-4370
Staten Island *(G-15118)*
▲ **Protex International Corp** D 631 563-4250
Bohemia *(G-1080)*
Rbw Studio LLC E 212 388-1621
Brooklyn *(G-2388)*
Rodale Wireless Inc E 631 231-0044
Hauppauge *(G-5929)*
▲ **Ross Electronics Ltd** E 718 569-6643
Haverstraw *(G-5981)*
Schuler-Haas Electric Corp G 607 936-3514
Painted Post *(G-12840)*
▲ **Scorpion Security Products Inc** E 607 724-9999
Vestal *(G-15821)*
Security Defense System G 718 769-7900
Whitestone *(G-16548)*
▲ **Security Dynamics Inc** F 631 392-1701
Bohemia *(G-1086)*
Sensor Films Incorporated E 585 738-3500
Victor *(G-15866)*
Shield Security Doors Ltd G 202 468-3308
Brooklyn *(G-2465)*
▲ **Sima Technologies LLC** G 412 828-9130
Hauppauge *(G-5940)*
Simulaids Inc D 845 679-2475
Saugerties *(G-14616)*
Skae Power Solutions LLC E 845 365-9103
Palisades *(G-12847)*
Smithers Tools & Mch Pdts Inc D 845 876-3063
Rhinebeck *(G-13488)*
▲ **Sonicor Inc** F 631 920-6555
West Babylon *(G-16194)*
▲ **Spirent Inc** G 631 208-0680
Riverhead *(G-13585)*
Sunwire Electric Corp G 718 456-7500
Brooklyn *(G-2533)*
T Jn Electric F 917 560-0981
Mahopac *(G-7714)*
T Jn Electric Inc G 845 628-6970
Mahopac *(G-7715)*
Tectran Inc G 800 776-5549
Cheektowaga *(G-3461)*
Teledyne Optech Inc F 585 427-8310
Rochester *(G-14164)*
Telephonics Corporation D 631 755-7000
Farmingdale *(G-4893)*
Telephonics Corporation D 631 470-8800
Huntington *(G-6420)*
Tory Electric G 914 292-5036
Bedford *(G-771)*
Triborough Electric G 718 321-2144
Whitestone *(G-16551)*
▲ **Trident Precision Mfg Inc** D 585 265-2010
Webster *(G-16103)*
U E Systems Incorporated E 914 592-1220
Elmsford *(G-4575)*
▲ **Uncharted Power Inc** E 646 675-7783
New York *(G-11936)*
United Technologies Corp B 866 788-5095
Pittsford *(G-13027)*
Uptek Solutions Corp F 631 256-5565
Bohemia *(G-1104)*
▲ **V E Power Door Co Inc** E 631 231-4500
Brentwood *(G-1148)*
Werner Brothers Electric Inc G 518 377-3056
Rexford *(G-13484)*
Windowman Inc (usa) G 718 246-2626
Brooklyn *(G-2652)*
◆ **World Trading Center Inc** G 631 273-3330
Hauppauge *(G-5978)*
▲ **Z-Axis Inc** D 315 548-5000
Phelps *(G-12984)*
Zappone Chrysler Jeep Ddge Inc F 518 982-0610
Halfmoon *(G-5670)*

37 TRANSPORTATION EQUIPMENT

3711 Motor Vehicles & Car Bodies

AB Fire Inc G 917 416-6444
Brooklyn *(G-1468)*
Antiques & Collectible Autos G 716 825-3990
Buffalo *(G-2702)*
Antonicelli Vito Race Car G 716 684-2205
Buffalo *(G-2703)*
Armor Dynamics Inc F 845 658-9200
Kingston *(G-6888)*
▲ **Auto Sport Designs Inc** F 631 425-1555
Huntington Station *(G-6433)*
Brothers-In-Lawn Property G 716 279-6191
Tonawanda *(G-15531)*
Cabot Coach Builders Inc G 516 625-4000
Roslyn Heights *(G-14453)*
CIC International Ltd D 212 213-0089
Brooklyn *(G-1692)*

SIC SECTION
37 TRANSPORTATION EQUIPMENT

Conti Auto Body Corp ....G.... 516 921-6435
Syosset *(G-15211)*
▲ Daimler Buses North Amer Inc ....A.... 315 768-8101
Oriskany *(G-12756)*
Dejana Trck Utility Eqp Co LLC ....C.... 631 544-9000
Kings Park *(G-6882)*
Dejana Trck Utility Eqp Co LLC ....E.... 631 549-0944
Huntington *(G-6397)*
Empire Coachworks Intl LLC ....D.... 732 257-7981
Suffern *(G-15190)*
◆ Global Fire Corporation ....E.... 888 320-1799
New York *(G-9940)*
▲ Jtekt Torsen North America ....F.... 585 464-5000
Rochester *(G-13899)*
Kovatch Mobile Equipment Corp ....F.... 518 785-0900
Latham *(G-7079)*
Leonard Bus Sales Inc ....G.... 607 467-3100
Rome *(G-14256)*
Marcovicci-Wenz Engineering ....G.... 631 467-9040
Ronkonkoma *(G-14375)*
◆ Medical Coaches Incorporated ....E.... 607 432-1333
Oneonta *(G-12640)*
North Eastern Rescue Vehicles ....G.... 315 414-9999
Syracuse *(G-15382)*
Pcb Coach Builders Corp ....G.... 718 897-7606
Rego Park *(G-13467)*
Prevost Car (us) Inc ....C.... 518 957-2052
Plattsburgh *(G-13148)*
▲ Ranger Design Us Inc ....E.... 800 565-5321
Ontario *(G-12662)*
Roberts Nichols Fire Apparatus ....G.... 518 431-1945
Cohoes *(G-3619)*
Sabre Enterprises Inc ....G.... 315 430-3127
Syracuse *(G-15413)*
Scehenvus Fire Dist ....D.... 607 638-9017
Schenevus *(G-14730)*
Siemens Mobility Inc ....G.... 916 717-8174
New York *(G-11579)*
Smart Systems Inc ....E.... 607 776-5380
Bath *(G-649)*
Tee Pee Auto Sales Corp ....F.... 516 338-9333
Westbury *(G-16376)*
Tesla Motors Inc ....A.... 212 206-1204
New York *(G-11803)*
Transprttion Collaborative Inc ....E.... 845 988-2333
Warwick *(G-15961)*
Troyer Inc ....F.... 585 352-5590
Rochester *(G-14177)*
Wendys Auto Express Inc ....G.... 845 624-6100
Nanuet *(G-8468)*

3713 Truck & Bus Bodies

Able Weldbuilt Industries Inc ....F.... 631 643-9700
Deer Park *(G-3931)*
Bay Horse Innovations Nyinc ....G.... 607 898-3337
Groton *(G-5649)*
Blackburn Truck Bodies LLC ....G.... 315 448-3236
Syracuse *(G-15259)*
▲ Brunner International Inc ....C.... 585 798-6000
Medina *(G-7974)*
◆ Concrete Mixer Supplycom Inc ....G.... 716 375-5565
Olean *(G-12596)*
Conti Auto Body Corp ....G.... 516 921-6435
Syosset *(G-15211)*
▲ Daimler Buses North Amer Inc ....A.... 315 768-8101
Oriskany *(G-12756)*
Demartini Oil Equipment Svc ....G.... 518 463-5752
Glenmont *(G-5411)*
Donver Incorporated ....F.... 716 945-1910
Kill Buck *(G-6878)*
Eastern Welding Inc ....G.... 631 727-0306
Riverhead *(G-13568)*
Ekostinger Inc ....F.... 585 739-0450
East Rochester *(G-4283)*
General Welding & Fabg Inc ....F.... 585 697-7660
Rochester *(G-13828)*
Jeffersonville Volunteer ....E.... 845 482-3110
Jeffersonville *(G-6779)*
Kurtz Truck Equipment Inc ....F.... 607 849-3468
Marathon *(G-7790)*
Marros Equipment & Trucks ....F.... 315 539-8702
Waterloo *(G-15996)*
Premium Bldg Components Inc ....E.... 518 885-0194
Ballston Spa *(G-594)*
Renaldos Sales & Service Ctr ....G.... 716 337-3760
North Collins *(G-12388)*
Rexford Services Inc ....G.... 716 366-6671
Dunkirk *(G-4178)*
▲ Tectran Mfg Inc ....D.... 800 776-5549
Buffalo *(G-3088)*

Unicell Body Company Inc ....E.... 716 353-8628
Buffalo *(G-3109)*
Unicell Body Company Inc ....F.... 716 853-8628
Schenectady *(G-14723)*
Unicell Body Company Inc ....F.... 585 424-2660
Rochester *(G-14185)*
USA Body Inc ....G.... 315 852-6123
De Ruyter *(G-3929)*
Weld-Built Body Co Inc ....E.... 631 643-9700
Wyandanch *(G-16697)*

3714 Motor Vehicle Parts & Access

4bumpers Llc ....F.... 212 721-9600
New York *(G-8680)*
A-Line Technologies Inc ....F.... 607 772-2439
Binghamton *(G-858)*
◆ Actasys Inc ....G.... 914 432-2336
Watervliet *(G-16040)*
Agri Services Co ....G.... 716 937-6618
Alden *(G-166)*
Allomatic Products Company ....G.... 516 775-0330
Floral Park *(G-4955)*
▲ Alloy Metal Products LLC ....F.... 315 676-2405
Central Square *(G-3389)*
American Auto ACC Incrporation ....E.... 718 886-6600
Flushing *(G-4984)*
American Refuse Supply Inc ....G.... 718 893-8157
Bronx *(G-1219)*
Anchor Commerce Trading Corp ....G.... 516 881-3485
Atlantic Beach *(G-455)*
◆ API Heat Transf Thermasys Corp ....A.... 716 684-6700
Buffalo *(G-2704)*
▲ ARC Remanufacturing Inc ....D.... 718 728-0701
Long Island City *(G-7384)*
Auburn Bearing & Mfg Inc ....G.... 315 986-7600
Macedon *(G-7694)*
Automotive Accessories Group ....B.... 212 736-8100
New York *(G-8967)*
Axle Express ....E.... 518 347-2220
Schenectady *(G-14651)*
◆ Axle Teknology LLC ....G.... 631 423-3044
Huntington *(G-6393)*
Bam Enterprises Inc ....G.... 716 773-7634
Grand Island *(G-5496)*
Banner Transmission & Eng Co ....F.... 516 221-9459
Melville *(G-8004)*
Bigbee Steel and Tank Company ....E.... 518 273-0801
Watervliet *(G-16041)*
▲ Biltron Automotive Products ....E.... 631 928-8613
Port Jeff STA *(G-13212)*
Borgwarner Inc ....F.... 607 257-6700
Ithaca *(G-6564)*
Borgwarner Inc ....E.... 607 257-1800
Ithaca *(G-6565)*
Borgwarner Ithaca LLC ....B.... 607 257-6700
Ithaca *(G-6566)*
Borgwarner Morse TEC Inc ....D.... 607 266-5111
Ithaca *(G-6567)*
▲ Borgwarner Morse TEC LLC ....C.... 607 257-6700
Ithaca *(G-6568)*
Borgwarner Morse TEC LLC ....D.... 607 257-6700
Cortland *(G-3863)*
Car-Go Industries Inc ....G.... 718 472-1443
Woodside *(G-16650)*
Classic & Performance Spc ....E.... 716 759-1800
Lancaster *(G-7014)*
▲ CRS Remanufacturing Co Inc ....F.... 718 739-1720
Jamaica *(G-6640)*
Cubic Trnsp Systems Inc ....F.... 212 255-1810
New York *(G-9431)*
Cummins Inc ....A.... 716 456-2111
Lakewood *(G-6993)*
Curtis L Maclean L C ....B.... 716 898-7800
Buffalo *(G-2787)*
▲ Custom Sitecom LLC ....F.... 631 420-4238
Farmingdale *(G-4746)*
Deer Park Driveshaft & Hose ....G.... 631 667-4091
Deer Park *(G-3963)*
Delphi Automotive LLP ....G.... 716 438-4886
Amherst *(G-224)*
Delphi Powertrain Systems LLC ....C.... 585 359-6000
West Henrietta *(G-16236)*
Delphi Powertrain Systems LLC ....B.... 585 359-6000
West Henrietta *(G-16237)*
Delphi Powertrain Systems LLC ....E.... 585 359-6000
West Henrietta *(G-16238)*
Delphi Thermal Systems ....F.... 716 439-2454
Lockport *(G-7293)*
Dennys Drive Shaft Service ....G.... 716 875-6640
Kenmore *(G-6858)*

Dmic Inc ....G.... 716 743-4360
North Tonawanda *(G-12425)*
Drive Shaft Shop Inc ....F.... 631 348-1818
Hauppauge *(G-5816)*
Electron Top Mfg Co Inc ....E.... 718 846-7400
Richmond Hill *(G-13501)*
Electronic Machine Parts LLC ....F.... 631 434-3700
Hauppauge *(G-5818)*
Enplas America Inc ....G.... 646 892-7811
New York *(G-9686)*
Exten II LLC ....F.... 716 895-2214
East Aurora *(G-4199)*
▲ Extreme Auto Accessories Corp ....F.... 718 978-6722
Mineola *(G-8221)*
Factory Wheel Warehouse Inc ....G.... 516 605-2131
Plainview *(G-13057)*
▲ Fast By Gast Inc ....G.... 716 773-1536
Grand Island *(G-5499)*
▲ Fcmp Inc ....F.... 716 692-4623
Tonawanda *(G-15539)*
General Motors LLC ....A.... 716 879-5000
Buffalo *(G-2847)*
General Motors LLC ....B.... 315 764-2000
Massena *(G-7902)*
◆ Gleason Works ....A.... 585 473-1000
Rochester *(G-13840)*
GM Components Holdings LLC ....C.... 716 439-2237
Lockport *(G-7304)*
GM Components Holdings LLC ....B.... 585 647-7000
Rochester *(G-13842)*
GM Components Holdings LLC ....B.... 716 439-2463
Lockport *(G-7305)*
GM Components Holdings LLC ....B.... 716 439-2011
Lockport *(G-7306)*
Interntnal Auto Voluntary Untd ....G.... 718 743-8732
Brooklyn *(G-2013)*
▲ Interparts International Inc ....E.... 516 576-2000
Plainview *(G-13065)*
▲ ITT Enidine Inc ....B.... 716 662-1900
Orchard Park *(G-12720)*
Johnson Controls Inc ....C.... 585 724-2232
Rochester *(G-13897)*
▲ Jtekt Torsen North America ....F.... 585 464-5000
Rochester *(G-13899)*
K M Drive Line Inc ....G.... 718 599-0628
Brooklyn *(G-2064)*
▲ Karlyn Industries Inc ....F.... 845 351-2249
Southfields *(G-14966)*
Katikati Inc ....G.... 585 678-1764
West Henrietta *(G-16243)*
◆ Kearney-National Inc ....F.... 212 661-4600
New York *(G-10427)*
▲ Kerns Manufacturing Corp ....C.... 718 784-4044
Long Island City *(G-7488)*
Kurtz Truck Equipment Inc ....F.... 607 849-3468
Marathon *(G-7790)*
▲ Lee World Industries LLC ....F.... 212 265-8866
New York *(G-10538)*
Lemans Corporation ....G.... 518 885-7500
Ballston Spa *(G-588)*
M2 Race Systems Inc ....G.... 607 882-9078
Ithaca *(G-6591)*
◆ Magtrol Inc ....E.... 716 668-5555
Buffalo *(G-2935)*
Mahle Behr USA Inc ....B.... 716 439-2011
Lockport *(G-7314)*
Mahle Industries Incorporated ....F.... 248 735-3623
Amherst *(G-238)*
Marcovicci-Wenz Engineering ....G.... 631 467-9040
Ronkonkoma *(G-14375)*
Mohawk Innovative Tech Inc ....F.... 518 862-4290
Albany *(G-99)*
▲ Motor Components LLC ....D.... 607 737-8011
Elmira Heights *(G-4512)*
▲ Nas-Tra Automotive Inds Inc ....C.... 631 225-1225
Lindenhurst *(G-7182)*
Nassau Auto Remanufacturer ....G.... 516 485-4500
North Bellmore *(G-12380)*
Northeastern Transparts Inc ....F.... 716 833-0792
Hamburg *(G-5688)*
◆ P & F Industries Inc ....E.... 631 694-9800
Melville *(G-8055)*
▲ Pall Corporation ....A.... 516 484-5400
Port Washington *(G-13295)*
Pall Corporation ....A.... 607 753-6041
Cortland *(G-3885)*
Par-Foam Products Inc ....C.... 716 855-2066
Buffalo *(G-2990)*
Parker-Hannifin Corporation ....D.... 716 685-4040
Lancaster *(G-7037)*

SIC

Employee Codes: A=Over 500 employees, B=251-500
C=101-250, D=51-100, E=20-50, F=10-19, G=5-9
2019 Harris
New York Manufacturers Directory
785

37 TRANSPORTATION EQUIPMENT

Performance Designed By Peters ....F...... 585 223-9062
  Fairport (G-4650)
Phillip J Ortiz Manufacturing ....G...... 845 226-7030
  Hopewell Junction (G-6292)
▲ Powerflow Inc ....D...... 716 892-1014
  Buffalo (G-3010)
Pro Torque ....E...... 631 218-8700
  Bohemia (G-1079)
Pro-Value Distribution Inc ....G...... 585 783-1461
  Rochester (G-14048)
◆ Rosco Inc ....C...... 718 526-2601
  Jamaica (G-6675)
▲ Rpb Distributors LLC ....G...... 914 244-3600
  Mount Kisco (G-8358)
Smith Metal Works Newark Inc ....E...... 315 331-1651
  Newark (G-12206)
▲ Specialty Silicone Pdts Inc ....D...... 518 885-8826
  Ballston Spa (G-596)
Standard Motor Products Inc ....B...... 718 392-0200
  Long Island City (G-7598)
Steering Columns Galore Inc ....G...... 845 278-5762
  Mahopac (G-7713)
Temper Corporation ....G...... 518 853-3467
  Fonda (G-5068)
Tesla Motors Inc ....A...... 212 206-1204
  New York (G-11803)
TI Group Auto Systems LLC ....G...... 315 568-7042
  Seneca Falls (G-14787)
▲ Titanx Engine Cooling Inc ....B...... 716 665-7129
  Jamestown (G-6758)
Transcedar Industries Ltd ....G...... 716 731-6442
  Niagara Falls (G-12343)
Troyer Inc ....F...... 585 352-5590
  Rochester (G-14177)
TRW Automotive Inc ....B...... 315 255-3311
  Auburn (G-506)
Vehicle Safety Dept ....F...... 315 458-6683
  Syracuse (G-15451)
▼ Whiting Door Mfg Corp ....B...... 716 542-5427
  Akron (G-24)
◆ Wolo Mfg Corp ....E...... 631 242-0333
  Deer Park (G-4064)
Yomiuri International Inc ....G...... 212 752-2196
  New York (G-12164)
Zwack Incorporated ....E...... 518 733-5135
  Stephentown (G-15156)

3715 Truck Trailers

◆ Blue Tee Corp ....G...... 212 598-0880
  New York (G-9109)
Cross Country Mfg Inc ....F...... 607 656-4103
  Greene (G-5613)
Davis Trailer World LLC ....F...... 585 538-6640
  York (G-16813)
G L 7 Sales Plus Ltd ....G...... 631 696-8290
  Coram (G-3797)
General Welding & Fabg Inc ....G...... 716 652-0033
  Elma (G-4451)
Seneca Truck & Trailer Inc ....G...... 315 781-1100
  Geneva (G-5333)
▼ Stone Well Bodies & Mch Inc ....E...... 315 497-3512
  Genoa (G-5338)

3716 Motor Homes

Authority Transportation Inc ....F...... 888 933-1268
  Dix Hills (G-4120)

3721 Aircraft

Alliant Tchsystems Oprtons LLC ......E...... 631 737-6100
  Ronkonkoma (G-14301)
Altius Aviation LLC ....G...... 315 455-7555
  Syracuse (G-15242)
Atk Gasl Inc ....E...... 631 737-6100
  Ronkonkoma (G-14312)
Barclay Tagg Racing ....E...... 631 404-8269
  Floral Park (G-4957)
Boeing Company ....A...... 201 259-9400
  New York (G-9117)
Bombardier Trnsp Holdings USA ......E...... 518 566-5067
  Plattsburgh (G-13113)
◆ Calspan Corporation ....C...... 716 631-6955
  Buffalo (G-2758)
Calspan Corporation ....F...... 716 236-1040
  Niagara Falls (G-12267)
Calspan Holdings LLC ....F...... 716 631-6955
  Buffalo (G-2759)
CIC International Ltd ....D...... 212 213-0089
  Brooklyn (G-1692)
Grumman Field Support Services ....D...... 516 575-0574
  Bethpage (G-842)

Lesly Enterprise & Associates ....G...... 631 988-1301
  Deer Park (G-4000)
Lockheed Martin Corporation ....E...... 716 297-1000
  Niagara Falls (G-12307)
Lockheed Martin Corporation ....D...... 315 793-5800
  New Hartford (G-8507)
Luminati Aerospace LLC ....F...... 631 574-2616
  Calverton (G-3167)
M & H Research and Dev Corp ....G...... 607 734-2346
  Beaver Dams (G-765)
Moog Inc ....B...... 716 687-4954
  East Aurora (G-4207)
Northrop Grumman Systems Corp ....A...... 516 575-0574
  Bethpage (G-850)
Northrop Grumman Systems Corp ....D...... 716 626-4600
  Buffalo (G-2976)
Northrop Grumman Systems Corp ....G...... 631 423-1014
  Huntington (G-6406)
Pro Drones Usa LLC ....F...... 718 530-3558
  New York (G-11252)
Sikorsky Aircraft Corporation ....D...... 585 424-1990
  Rochester (G-14129)
Tech Park Food Services LLC ....G...... 585 295-1250
  Rochester (G-14161)
Xactiv Inc ....F...... 585 288-7220
  Fairport (G-4668)

3724 Aircraft Engines & Engine Parts

Advanced Atomization Tech LLC ......B...... 315 923-2341
  Clyde (G-3591)
▲ ARC Systems Inc ....E...... 631 582-8020
  Hauppauge (G-5768)
B H Aircraft Company Inc ....D...... 631 580-9747
  Ronkonkoma (G-14315)
Chromalloy American LLC ....E...... 845 230-7355
  Orangeburg (G-12672)
Chromalloy Gas Turbine LLC ....D...... 845 359-2462
  Orangeburg (G-12673)
Chromalloy Gas Turbine LLC ....E...... 845 692-8912
  Middletown (G-8141)
Colonial Group LLC ....B...... 516 349-8010
  Plainview (G-13043)
▲ Davis Aircraft Products Co Inc ....C...... 631 563-1500
  Bohemia (G-1010)
▲ Dyna-Empire Inc ....C...... 516 222-2700
  Garden City (G-5256)
Gb Aero Engine LLC ....B...... 914 925-9600
  Rye (G-14480)
General Electric Company ....E...... 518 385-7620
  Niskayuna (G-12354)
General Electric Company ....A...... 518 385-4022
  Schenectady (G-14675)
Honeywell International Inc ....D...... 518 270-0200
  Troy (G-15595)
Honeywell International Inc ....A...... 315 554-6643
  Skaneateles Falls (G-14881)
Honeywell International Inc ....G...... 716 631-2197
  Cheektowaga (G-3449)
Honeywell International Inc ....F...... 631 577-2661
  Melville (G-8031)
Honeywell International Inc ....E...... 516 577-2000
  Melville (G-8032)
Honeywell International Inc ....F...... 516 577-2813
  Melville (G-8033)
Honeywell International Inc ....A...... 845 342-4400
  Middletown (G-8158)
Honeywell International Inc ....A...... 212 964-5111
  Melville (G-8034)
Honeywell International Inc ....B...... 516 577-2000
  Melville (G-8035)
Honeywell International Inc ....F...... 315 463-7208
  East Syracuse (G-4347)
Honeywell International Inc ....A...... 631 471-2202
  Lake Ronkonkoma (G-6980)
Howe Machine & Tool Corp ....F...... 516 931-5687
  Bethpage (G-843)
▲ ITT Enidine Inc ....B...... 716 662-1900
  Orchard Park (G-12720)
▲ Kerns Manufacturing Corp ....C...... 718 784-4044
  Long Island City (G-7488)
Lourdes Industries Inc ....D...... 631 234-6600
  Hauppauge (G-5873)
▲ Magellan Aerospace Bethel Inc ....C...... 203 798-9373
  Corona (G-3848)
Magellan Aerospace Processing ....G...... 631 694-1818
  West Babylon (G-16173)
McGuigan Inc ....E...... 631 750-6222
  Bohemia (G-1057)
Nell-Joy Industries Inc ....E...... 631 842-8989
  Copiague (G-3770)

SOS International LLC ....B...... 212 742-2410
  New York (G-11651)
▲ Therm Incorporated ....C...... 607 272-8500
  Ithaca (G-6611)
Triumph Actuation Systems LLC ......D...... 516 378-0162
  Freeport (G-5188)
Triumph Group Inc ....D...... 516 997-5757
  Westbury (G-16382)
Turbine Engine Comp Utica ....A...... 315 768-8070
  Whitesboro (G-16531)
United Technologies Corp ....G...... 315 432-7849
  East Syracuse (G-4378)

3728 Aircraft Parts & Eqpt, NEC

AAR Allen Services Inc ....E...... 516 222-9000
  Garden City (G-5250)
Aero Strctures Long Island Inc ....D...... 516 997-5757
  Westbury (G-16311)
Aero Trades Mfg Corp ....E...... 516 746-3360
  Mineola (G-8200)
Air Industries Group ....D...... 631 881-4920
  Hauppauge (G-5758)
▲ Air Industries Machining Corp ....C...... 631 328-7000
  Bay Shore (G-653)
Alken Industries Inc ....E...... 631 467-2000
  Ronkonkoma (G-14298)
Ancon Gear & Instrument Corp ....F...... 631 694-5255
  Amityville (G-264)
Arkwin Industries Inc ....C...... 516 333-2640
  Westbury (G-16317)
Armacel Armor Corporation ....E...... 805 384-1144
  New York (G-8909)
▲ Astronics Corporation ....C...... 716 805-1599
  East Aurora (G-4194)
Ausco Inc ....E...... 516 944-9882
  Farmingdale (G-4723)
B & B Precision Components Inc .....C...... 631 273-3321
  Ronkonkoma (G-14314)
B/E Aerospace Inc ....E...... 631 563-6400
  Bohemia (G-985)
▲ Blair Industries Inc ....H...... 631 924-6600
  Medford (G-7939)
Canfield Aerospace & Mar Inc ....E...... 631 648-1050
  Ronkonkoma (G-14325)
Caravan International Corp ....G...... 212 223-7190
  New York (G-9205)
Carleton Technologies Inc ....B...... 716 662-0006
  Orchard Park (G-12706)
Circor Aerospace Inc ....D...... 631 737-1900
  Hauppauge (G-5789)
▲ Cox & Company Inc ....C...... 212 366-0200
  Plainview (G-13048)
CPI Aerostructures Inc ....B...... 631 586-5200
  Edgewood (G-4399)
Crown Aircraft Lighting Inc ....C...... 718 767-3410
  Whitestone (G-16538)
▲ Davis Aircraft Products Co Inc ....C...... 631 563-1500
  Bohemia (G-1010)
Design/OI Inc ....F...... 631 474-5536
  Port Jeff STA (G-13213)
▲ Dresser-Argus Inc ....G...... 718 643-1540
  Brooklyn (G-1794)
Drt Power Systems LLC ....G...... 585 247-5940
  Rochester (G-13751)
Ducommun Aerostructures NY Inc ...B...... 518 731-2791
  Coxsackie (G-3906)
▲ Dyna-Empire Inc ....C...... 516 222-2700
  Garden City (G-5256)
East/West Industries Inc ....E...... 631 981-5900
  Ronkonkoma (G-14335)
Eastern Precision Machining ....G...... 631 286-4758
  Bellport (G-802)
◆ Edo LLC ....E...... 631 630-4000
  Amityville (G-272)
Engineered Metal Products Inc ....E...... 631 842-3780
  Copiague (G-3758)
Enlighten Air Inc ....G...... 917 656-1248
  New York (G-9685)
Ensil Technical Services Inc ....E...... 716 282-1020
  Niagara Falls (G-12281)
Excelco Developments Inc ....E...... 716 934-2651
  Silver Creek (G-14861)
Excelco/Newbrook Inc ....D...... 716 934-2644
  Silver Creek (G-14862)
Fluid Mechanisms Hauppauge Inc ...E...... 631 234-0100
  Hauppauge (G-5826)
GE Aviation Systems LLC ....C...... 631 467-5500
  Bohemia (G-1026)
▲ GKN Aerospace Monitor Inc ....B...... 562 619-8558
  Amityville (G-277)

◆ Gleason Works ....A 585 473-1000
Rochester (G-13840)
Goodrich Corporation ....C 315 838-1200
Rome (G-14251)
Handy Tool & Mfg Co Inc..................E 718 478-9203
Brooklyn (G-1967)
Hicksville Machine Works Corp..................F 516 931-1524
Hicksville (G-6096)
▲ HSM Machine Works Inc ....E 631 924-6600
Medford (G-7953)
Jac Usa Inc..................G 212 841-7430
New York (G-10290)
Jamco Aerospace Inc..................E 631 586-7900
Deer Park (G-3990)
◆ Jaquith Industries Inc ....E 315 478-5700
Syracuse (G-15346)
Joldeson One Aerospace Inds ....D 718 848-7396
Ozone Park (G-12827)
Jrsmm LLC..................G 607 331-1549
Elmira (G-4495)
Lai International Inc..................E 763 780-0060
Green Island (G-5608)
Lenny & Bill LLC..................D 516 997-5757
Westbury (G-16349)
Loar Group Inc..................C 212 210-9348
New York (G-10588)
▲ Magellan Aerospace Bethel Inc..................C 203 798-9373
Corona (G-3848)
Magellan Aerospace NY Inc ....C 631 589-2440
Bohemia (G-1053)
▲ Magellan Aerospace NY Inc ....C 718 699-4000
Corona (G-3849)
MD International Industries..................E 631 254-3100
Deer Park (G-4009)
Metadure Parts & Sales Inc..................F 631 249-2141
Farmingdale (G-4821)
◆ Metal Dynamics Intl Corp ....G 631 231-1153
Hauppauge (G-5888)
Milex Precision Inc..................F 631 595-2393
Bay Shore (G-701)
Military Parts Exchange LLC ....F 631 243-1700
Melville (G-8047)
Min-Max Machine Ltd..................F 631 585-4378
Ronkonkoma (G-14378)
Minutemen Precsn McHning Tool ....E 631 467-4900
Ronkonkoma (G-14379)
◆ Moog Inc..................A 716 652-2000
Elma (G-4453)
Nassau Tool Works Inc..................E 631 328-7031
Bay Shore (G-705)
Norsk Titanium US Inc..................G 949 735-9463
Plattsburgh (G-13136)
Parker-Hannifin Corporation..................C 631 231-3737
Clyde (G-3597)
▼ Posimech Inc..................E 631 924-5959
Medford (G-7964)
Precision Cnc..................G 631 847-3999
Deer Park (G-4028)
▲ Precision Gear Incorporated..................C 718 321-7200
College Point (G-3661)
Reese Manufacturing Inc ....G 631 842-3780
Copiague (G-3777)
Ripi Precision Co Inc..................F 631 694-2453
Farmingdale (G-4866)
S & L Aerospace Metals LLC ....D 718 326-1821
Flushing (G-5043)
Santa Fe Manufacturing Corp..................G 631 234-0100
Hauppauge (G-5932)
Servotronics Inc..................C 716 655-5990
Elma (G-4458)
▲ Styles Aviation Inc..................G 845 677-8185
Lagrangeville (G-6962)
▼ Sumner Industries Inc ....F 631 666-7290
Bay Shore (G-729)
Superior Motion Controls Inc ....E 516 420-2921
Farmingdale (G-4885)
Tangent Machine & Tool Corp ....F 631 249-3088
Farmingdale (G-4889)
Tek Precision Co Ltd ....E 631 242-0330
Deer Park (G-4051)
Tens Machine Company Inc..................E 631 981-3321
Holbrook (G-6215)
TPC Inc..................G 315 438-8605
East Syracuse (G-4374)
Triumph Actuation Systems LLC ....D 516 378-0162
Freeport (G-5188)
Universal Armor Systems Corp..................E 631 838-1836
Levittown (G-7136)
Usairports Services Inc..................E 585 527-6835
Rochester (G-14194)
UTC Aerospace Systems ....E 315 838-1200
Rome (G-14277)
Vosky Precision Machining Corp ....F 631 737-3200
Ronkonkoma (G-14429)
W J Albro Machine Works Inc..................G 631 345-0657
Yaphank (G-16728)
Wilco Industries Inc..................G 631 676-2593
Ronkonkoma (G-14432)
Young & Franklin Inc ....D 315 457-3110
Liverpool (G-7274)

3731 Shipbuilding & Repairing

Caddell Dry Dock & Repr Co Inc ....C 718 442-2112
Staten Island (G-15059)
◆ Dragon Trading Inc..................G 212 717-1496
New York (G-9572)
Excelco Developments Inc..................E 716 934-2651
Silver Creek (G-14861)
Excelco/Newbrook Inc..................D 716 934-2644
Silver Creek (G-14862)
Highland Museum & Lighthouse ....F 508 487-1121
Cairo (G-3148)
Huntington Ingalls Inc..................E 518 884-3834
Saratoga Springs (G-14587)
▲ May Ship Repair Contg Corp ....E 718 442-9700
Staten Island (G-15104)
McQuilling Partners Inc..................E 516 227-5718
Garden City (G-5270)
▼ Metalcraft Marine Us Inc..................F 315 501-4015
Cape Vincent (G-3259)
▲ Moran Shipyard Corporation ....C 718 981-5600
Staten Island (G-15106)
Port Everglades Machine Works ....F 516 367-2280
Plainview (G-13083)
▲ Reynolds Shipyard Corporation..................F 718 981-2800
Staten Island (G-15128)
▲ Robert E Derecktor Inc..................D 914 698-0962
Mamaroneck (G-7756)
Steelways Inc ....E 845 562-0860
Newburgh (G-12246)
Viking Mar Wldg Ship Repr LLC ....F 718 758-4116
Brooklyn (G-2623)
Weldrite Closures Inc ....E 585 429-8790
Pittsford (G-13028)
World Maritime News..................G 212 477-6700
New York (G-12138)

3732 Boat Building & Repairing

Allen Boat Co Inc ....G 716 842-0800
Buffalo (G-2691)
▼ American Metalcraft Marine ....G 315 686-9891
Clayton (G-3552)
Ashco Management Inc..................F 212 960-8428
Brooklyn (G-1562)
▲ AVS Laminates Inc ....E 631 286-2136
Bellport (G-799)
Cayuga Wooden Boatworks Inc ....E 315 253-7447
Ithaca (G-6570)
Coecles Hbr Marina & Boat Yard ....F 631 749-0856
Shelter Island (G-14800)
Eastern Welding Inc..................G 631 727-0306
Riverhead (G-13568)
Fantasy Glass Compan ....G 845 786-5818
Stony Point (G-15171)
Gar Wood Custom Boats ....G 518 494-2966
Brant Lake (G-1124)
Global Marine Power Inc ....E 631 208-2933
Calverton (G-3166)
▲ Hacker Boat Company Inc ....E 518 543-6731
Silver Bay (G-14859)
Hampton Shipyards Inc..................F 631 653-6777
East Quogue (G-4278)
▲ Jag Manufacturing Inc..................E 518 762-9558
Johnstown (G-6832)
Katherine Blizniak..................G 716 674-8545
West Seneca (G-16300)
▼ Marathon Boat Group Inc..................F 607 849-3211
Marathon (G-7791)
▲ May Ship Repair Contg Corp ....E 718 442-9700
Staten Island (G-15104)
▼ Metalcraft Marine Us Inc..................F 315 501-4015
Cape Vincent (G-3259)
Mokai Manufacturing Inc..................G 845 566-8287
Newburgh (G-12233)
▲ Robert E Derecktor Inc..................D 914 698-0962
Mamaroneck (G-7756)
Rocking The Boat Inc ....F 718 466-5799
Bronx (G-1374)
Scarano Boat Building Inc ....E 518 463-3401
Albany (G-126)
Scarano Boatbuilding Inc..................E 518 463-3401
Albany (G-127)
Superboats Inc..................G 631 226-1761
Lindenhurst (G-7198)
Tumblehome Boatshop ....G 518 623-5050
Warrensburg (G-15943)
Wooden Boatworks ....G 631 477-6507
Greenport (G-5627)

3743 Railroad Eqpt

Acf Industries Holding LLC..................G 212 702-4363
New York (G-8726)
Alstom Signaling Inc ....E 585 274-8700
Schenectady (G-14648)
▲ Bombardier Mass Transit Corp..................B 518 566-0150
Plattsburgh (G-13112)
Bombardier Transportation..................D 607 324-0216
Hornell (G-6294)
CAF Usa Inc..................D 607 737-3004
Elmira Heights (G-4510)
▲ Cox & Company Inc ....C 212 366-0200
Plainview (G-13048)
▲ Eagle Bridge Machine & Tl Inc..................E 518 686-4541
Eagle Bridge (G-4184)
Ebenezer Railcar Services Inc..................D 716 674-5650
West Seneca (G-16296)
▲ Gray Manufacturing Inds LLC..................F 607 281-1325
Hornell (G-6300)
Highcrest Investors LLC ....D 212 702-4323
New York (G-10096)
Higher Power Industries Inc ....G 914 709-9800
Yonkers (G-16768)
Horne Products Inc..................G 631 293-0773
Farmingdale (G-4781)
Hudson Machine Works Inc ....C 845 279-1413
Brewster (G-1168)
▲ Kawasaki Rail Car Inc..................C 914 376-4700
Yonkers (G-16774)
Knorr Brake Company LLC..................G 518 561-1387
Plattsburgh (G-13129)
▲ Knorr Brake Holding Corp ....G 315 786-5356
Watertown (G-16022)
▲ Knorr Brake Truck Systems Co ....B 315 786-5200
Watertown (G-16023)
▲ Koshii Maxelum America Inc ....E 845 471-0500
Poughkeepsie (G-13350)
▲ Matrix Railway Corp..................G 631 643-1483
West Babylon (G-16175)
New York Air Brake LLC..................E 315 786-5576
Watertown (G-16028)
▲ New York Air Brake LLC ....C 315 786-5219
Watertown (G-16029)
▲ Peck & Hale LLC ....E 631 589-2510
West Sayville (G-16291)
Rand Machine Products, Inc...................C 716 665-5217
Falconer (G-4688)
Seisenbacher Inc ....F 585 730-4960
Rochester (G-14119)
▲ Semec Corp..................F 518 825-0160
Plattsburgh (G-13155)
Siemens Mobility Inc ....G 916 717-8174
New York (G-11579)
Starfire Holding Corporation ....E 914 614-7000
New York (G-11697)
▲ Strato Transit Components LLC..................G 518 686-4541
Eagle Bridge (G-4187)
Transco Railway Products Inc..................E 716 825-1663
Buffalo (G-3102)
Transco Railway Products Inc..................E 716 824-1219
Blasdell (G-931)
▲ Twinco Mfg Co Inc ....E 631 231-0022
Hauppauge (G-5963)
Westcode Incorporated ....E 607 766-9881
Binghamton (G-923)
Westinghouse A Brake Tech Corp..................D 518 561-0044
Plattsburgh (G-13169)
Westinghouse A Brake Tech Corp..................F 914 347-8650
Elmsford (G-4577)

3751 Motorcycles, Bicycles & Parts

Bignay Inc..................G 786 346-1673
New York (G-9080)
▲ Chicken Hawk Racing Inc ....G 845 758-0700
Red Hook (G-13457)
▲ East Coast Cycle LLC..................G 631 780-5360
Farmingdale (G-4756)
▲ Evelo Inc ....G 917 251-8743
Rockaway Park (G-14228)
Golub Corporation..................E 518 943-3903
Catskill (G-3303)

SIC

Employee Codes: A=Over 500 employees, B=251-500
C=101-250, D=51-100, E=20-50, F=10-19, G=5-9
2019 Harris
New York Manufacturers Directory
787

37 TRANSPORTATION EQUIPMENT

Golub Corporation .... E 518 899-6063
  Malta *(G-7731)*
Golub Corporation .... E 315 363-0679
  Oneida *(G-12609)*
Golub Corporation .... E 607 336-2588
  Norwich *(G-12486)*
Golub Corporation .... E 518 583-3697
  Saratoga Springs *(G-14582)*
Golub Corporation .... E 518 822-0076
  Hudson *(G-6351)*
Golub Corporation .... E 607 235-7240
  Binghamton *(G-888)*
Golub Corporation .... E 845 344-0327
  Middletown *(G-8157)*
Great American Bicycle LLC .... E 518 584-8100
  Saratoga Springs *(G-14583)*
Ihd Motorsports LLC .... F 979 690-1669
  Binghamton *(G-894)*
Indian Larry Legacy .... G 718 609-9184
  Brooklyn *(G-1998)*
▲ KG Motors Inc .... E 607 562-2877
  Big Flats *(G-855)*
Orange County Choppers Inc ....G 845 522-5200
  Newburgh *(G-12237)*
◆ Piaggio Group Americas Inc .... E 212 380-4400
  New York *(G-11187)*
▲ Prestacycle Llc .... G 518 588-5546
  Rexford *(G-13483)*
Price Chopper Operating Co .... F 518 562-3565
  Plattsburgh *(G-13149)*
Price Chopper Operating Co .... F 518 456-5115
  Guilderland *(G-5655)*
Robs Cycle Supply .... G 315 292-6878
  Syracuse *(G-15409)*
▲ Social Bicycles Inc .... E 917 746-7624
  Brooklyn *(G-2490)*
Sumax Cycle Products Inc .... F 315 768-1058
  Oriskany *(G-12764)*
Super Price Chopper Inc .... F 716 893-3323
  Buffalo *(G-3080)*
Ying Ke Youth Age Group Inc .... F 929 402-8458
  Dix Hills *(G-4128)*

3761 Guided Missiles & Space Vehicles

Drt Power Systems LLC .... G 585 247-5940
  Rochester *(G-13751)*
Edo LLC .... A 631 630-4200
  Amityville *(G-273)*
Lockheed Martin Corporation ....A 315 456-0123
  Liverpool *(G-7242)*
Lockheed Martin Corporation ....A 607 751-2000
  Owego *(G-12799)*

3769 Guided Missile/Space Vehicle Parts & Eqpt, NEC

Gb Aero Engine LLC .... B 914 925-9600
  Rye *(G-14480)*
▲ GKN Aerospace Monitor Inc .... B 562 619-8558
  Amityville *(G-277)*
▲ L3 Foreign Holdings Inc .... D 212 697-1111
  New York *(G-10497)*
L3 Technologies Inc .... A 631 436-7400
  Hauppauge *(G-5859)*
L3 Technologies Inc .... B 212 697-1111
  New York *(G-10498)*
Lockheed Martin Corporation .... E 716 297-1000
  Niagara Falls *(G-12307)*
▲ Magellan Aerospace NY Inc .... C 718 699-4000
  Corona *(G-3849)*
◆ Moog Inc .... A 716 652-2000
  Elma *(G-4453)*
Saturn Industries Inc .... E 518 828-9956
  Hudson *(G-6370)*
Servotronics Inc .... F 716 655-5990
  Elma *(G-4458)*
SKF USA Inc .... D 716 661-2869
  Falconer *(G-4691)*
SKF USA Inc .... D 716 661-2600
  Falconer *(G-4692)*
Turbine Engine Comp Utica .... A 315 768-8070
  Whitesboro *(G-16531)*
Unison Industries LLC .... B 607 335-5000
  Norwich *(G-12494)*

3792 Travel Trailers & Campers

All Star Carts & Vehicles Inc .... D 631 666-5581
  Bay Shore *(G-654)*

3795 Tanks & Tank Components

Lourdes Industries Inc .... D 631 234-6600
  Hauppauge *(G-5873)*
◆ Tecmotiv (usa) Inc .... E 905 669-5911
  Niagara Falls *(G-12342)*

3799 Transportation Eqpt, NEC

Adirondack Power Sports .... G 518 481-6269
  Malone *(G-7718)*
Bombardier Trnsp Holdings USA ...... D 607 776-4791
  Bath *(G-641)*
Bullet Industries Inc .... G 585 352-0836
  Spencerport *(G-14977)*
Clopay Ames True Temper .... F 212 957-5096
  New York *(G-9330)*
Kens Service & Sales Inc .... F 716 683-1155
  Elma *(G-4452)*
Performance Custom Trailer .... G 518 504-4021
  Lake George *(G-6965)*
Rolling Star Manufacturing Inc .... E 315 896-4767
  Barneveld *(G-604)*
Tectran .... G 800 776-5549
  Cheektowaga *(G-3461)*
Truck-Lite Sub Inc .... G 800 888-7095
  Falconer *(G-4697)*
Truxton Corp .... G 718 842-6000
  Bronx *(G-1408)*

38 MEASURING, ANALYZING AND CONTROLLING INSTRUMENTS; PHOTOGRAPHIC, MEDICAL AN

3812 Search, Detection, Navigation & Guidance Systs & Instrs

Accipiter Radar Corporation .... G 716 508-4432
  Orchard Park *(G-12697)*
Accutrak Inc .... F 212 925-5330
  New York *(G-8723)*
◆ Aeroflex Incorporated .... B 516 694-6700
  Plainview *(G-13032)*
Ametek Inc .... D 585 263-7700
  Rochester *(G-13630)*
Arsenal Holdings LLC .... G 212 398-9139
  New York *(G-8912)*
▲ Artemis Inc .... G 631 232-2424
  Hauppauge *(G-5770)*
▲ Aventura Technologies Inc .... E 631 300-4000
  Commack *(G-3680)*
B & Z Technologies LLC .... G 631 675-9666
  East Setauket *(G-4298)*
B/E Aerospace Inc .... E 631 589-0877
  Bohemia *(G-986)*
▲ Bae Systems Controls Inc .... A 607 770-2000
  Endicott *(G-4583)*
Bae Systems Info & Elec Sys .... G 631 912-1525
  Greenlawn *(G-5621)*
Bae Systems PLC .... E 631 261-7000
  Greenlawn *(G-5622)*
C Speed LLC .... E 315 453-1043
  Liverpool *(G-7227)*
C-Flex Bearing Co Inc .... F 315 895-7454
  Frankfort *(G-5104)*
CIC International Ltd .... D 212 213-0089
  Brooklyn *(G-1692)*
CIT Aerospace LLC .... G 212 461-5200
  New York *(G-9305)*
▲ Clayton Dubilier & Rice Fun .... E 212 407-5200
  New York *(G-9324)*
Cobham Holdings (us) Inc .... A 716 662-0006
  Orchard Park *(G-12707)*
Cobham Holdings Inc .... E 716 662-0006
  Orchard Park *(G-12708)*
◆ Cobham Management Services Inc .. A 716 662-0006
  Orchard Park *(G-12709)*
Computer Instruments Corp .... E 516 876-8400
  Westbury *(G-16321)*
▲ Cox & Company Inc .... C 212 366-0200
  Plainview *(G-13048)*
▲ Dyna-Empire Inc .... C 516 222-2700
  Garden City *(G-5256)*
Eastern Strategic Materials .... E 212 332-1619
  New York *(G-9612)*
Edo LLC .... A 631 630-4200
  Amityville *(G-273)*
◆ Edo LLC .... A 631 630-4000
  Amityville *(G-272)*

Emergency Beacon Corp .... F 914 576-2700
  New Rochelle *(G-8600)*
Excelsior Mlt-Cltural Inst Inc .... F 706 627-4285
  Flushing *(G-4998)*
Facilamatic Instrument Corp .... F 516 825-6300
  Valley Stream *(G-15779)*
Flightline Electronics Inc .... D 585 924-4000
  Victor *(G-15847)*
Frequency Electronics Inc .... C 516 794-4500
  Uniondale *(G-15668)*
GE Aviation Systems LLC .... D 513 243-9104
  Bohemia *(G-1027)*
Gryphon Sensors LLC .... F 315 452-8882
  North Syracuse *(G-12404)*
Harris Corporation .... A 585 269-6600
  Rochester *(G-13854)*
Harris Corporation .... B 585 269-5001
  Rochester *(G-13855)*
Harris Corporation .... E 631 630-4000
  Amityville *(G-280)*
Harris Corporation .... E 585 269-5000
  Rochester *(G-13857)*
◆ Ihi Inc .... E 212 599-8100
  New York *(G-10179)*
Inertia Switch Inc .... E 845 359-8300
  Orangeburg *(G-12679)*
▲ Inficon Inc .... C 315 434-1100
  East Syracuse *(G-4350)*
Infrared Components Corp .... E 315 732-1544
  Utica *(G-15715)*
ITT Corporation .... D 315 568-2811
  Seneca Falls *(G-14777)*
ITT Inc .... E 914 641-2000
  White Plains *(G-16464)*
◆ ITT LLC .... B 914 641-2000
  White Plains *(G-16467)*
ITT LLC .... E 914 641-2000
  Seneca Falls *(G-14781)*
Joldeson One Aerospace Inds .... D 718 848-7396
  Ozone Park *(G-12827)*
▲ Kerns Manufacturing Corp .... C 718 784-4044
  Long Island City *(G-7488)*
Klx Inc .... F 845 534-0401
  Cornwall *(G-3833)*
▲ Kwadair LLC .... G 646 824-2511
  Brooklyn *(G-2083)*
▲ L3 Foreign Holdings Inc .... D 212 697-1111
  New York *(G-10497)*
L3 Technologies Inc .... B 212 697-1111
  New York *(G-10498)*
L3 Technologies Inc .... G 631 231-3994
  Hauppauge *(G-5860)*
Laufer Wind Group LLC .... F 212 792-3912
  New York *(G-10523)*
Lockheed Martin Corporation .... B 212 953-1510
  New York *(G-10590)*
Lockheed Martin Corporation .... C 516 228-2000
  Uniondale *(G-15670)*
Lockheed Martin Corporation .... A 607 751-2000
  Owego *(G-12799)*
Lockheed Martin Corporation .... E 315 456-6604
  Syracuse *(G-15363)*
Lockheed Martin Corporation .... D 212 697-1105
  New York *(G-10591)*
Lockheed Martin Corporation .... E 716 297-1000
  Niagara Falls *(G-12307)*
Lockheed Martin Corporation .... A 315 456-0123
  Liverpool *(G-7242)*
Lockheed Martin Global Inc .... E 315 456-2982
  Liverpool *(G-7243)*
Lockheed Martin Integrtd Systm .... E 315 456-3333
  Syracuse *(G-15364)*
Lockheed Martin Overseas .... F 315 456-0123
  Liverpool *(G-7244)*
Logitek Inc .... D 631 567-1100
  Bohemia *(G-1048)*
▲ Magellan Aerospace NY Inc .... C 718 699-4000
  Corona *(G-3849)*
Metro Dynamics Scie .... F 631 842-4300
  West Babylon *(G-16176)*
Mirion Technologies Ist Corp .... D 607 562-4300
  Horseheads *(G-6321)*
Mod-A-Can Inc .... D 516 931-8545
  Hicksville *(G-6111)*
◆ Moog Inc .... A 716 652-2000
  Elma *(G-4453)*
Moog Inc .... C 716 805-8100
  East Aurora *(G-4208)*
Moog Inc .... B 716 687-5486
  Elma *(G-4455)*

No Longer Empty Inc ..... G 202 413-4262
New York *(G-10981)*
Northrop Grumman Corporation ..... A 703 280-2900
Bethpage *(G-849)*
Orthstar Enterprises Inc ..... D 607 562-2100
Horseheads *(G-6323)*
Penetradar Corporation ..... F 716 731-2629
Niagara Falls *(G-12322)*
Rodale Wireless Inc ..... E 631 231-0044
Hauppauge *(G-5929)*
Saab Defense and SEC USA LLC ..... F 315 445-5009
East Syracuse *(G-4367)*
▲ Safe Flight Instrument Corp ..... C 914 946-9500
White Plains *(G-16502)*
▼ Select Fabricators Inc ..... F 585 393-0650
Canandaigua *(G-3233)*
Sensormatic Electronics LLC ..... F 845 365-3125
Orangeburg *(G-12691)*
▲ Sentry Technology Corporation ..... E 631 739-2000
Ronkonkoma *(G-14410)*
▲ Sentry Technology Corporation ..... F 800 645-4224
Ronkonkoma *(G-14411)*
Srctec LLC ..... C 315 452-8700
Syracuse *(G-15429)*
Systems Drs C3 Inc ..... B 716 631-6200
Buffalo *(G-3084)*
▲ Telephonics Corporation ..... A 631 755-7000
Farmingdale *(G-4892)*
▼ Traffic Logix Corporation ..... G 866 915-6449
Spring Valley *(G-15009)*
Transistor Devices Inc ..... E 631 471-7492
Ronkonkoma *(G-14421)*
Tusk Manufacturing Inc ..... F 631 567-3349
Bohemia *(G-1102)*
U E Systems Incorporated ..... E 914 592-1220
Elmsford *(G-4575)*
U S Tech Corporation ..... F 315 437-7207
East Syracuse *(G-4377)*
UNI Source Technology ..... F 514 748-8888
Champlain *(G-3415)*
Vacuum Instrument Corporation ..... D 631 737-0900
Ronkonkoma *(G-14427)*
Virtualapt Corp ..... F 917 293-3173
Brooklyn *(G-2627)*
◆ VJ Technologies Inc ..... E 631 589-8800
Bohemia *(G-1106)*
Woodbine Products Inc ..... E 631 586-3770
Hauppauge *(G-5977)*
▼ Worldwide Arntcal Cmpnents Inc ..... E 631 842-3780
Copiague *(G-3794)*
Worldwide Arntcal Cmpnents Inc ..... G 631 842-3780
Copiague *(G-3795)*

3821 Laboratory Apparatus & Furniture

▲ Air Techniques Inc ..... B 516 433-7676
Melville *(G-8000)*
Anaren Microwave Inc ..... G 315 432-8909
East Syracuse *(G-4319)*
Ankom Technology Corp ..... E 315 986-8090
Macedon *(G-7693)*
Avro Inc ..... G 585 445-7588
Rochester *(G-13648)*
Biodesign Inc of New York ..... F 845 454-6610
Carmel *(G-3274)*
Biospherix Ltd ..... E 315 387-3414
Parish *(G-12860)*
Crystal Linton Technologies ..... F 585 444-8784
Rochester *(G-13726)*
▲ Dynamica Inc ..... F 212 818-1900
New York *(G-9594)*
East Hills Instrument Inc ..... F 516 621-8686
Westbury *(G-16325)*
Fts Systems Inc ..... D 845 687-5300
Stone Ridge *(G-15161)*
◆ Fungilab Inc ..... G 631 750-6361
Hauppauge *(G-5829)*
Healthalliance Hospital ..... G 845 338-2500
Kingston *(G-6901)*
▲ Hyman Podrusnick Co Inc ..... G 718 853-4502
Brooklyn *(G-1990)*
Instrumentation Laboratory Co ..... C 845 680-0028
Orangeburg *(G-12681)*
▲ Integrated Liner Tech Inc ..... E 518 621-7422
Rensselaer *(G-13475)*
Integrted Work Envronments LLC ..... G 716 725-5088
East Amherst *(G-4190)*
◆ Itin Scale Co Inc ..... E 718 336-5900
Brooklyn *(G-2019)*
▲ J H C Fabrications Inc ..... E 718 649-0065
Brooklyn *(G-2022)*

▲ Jamestown Metal Products LLC ..... C 716 665-5313
Jamestown *(G-6731)*
Lab Crafters Inc ..... E 631 471-7755
Ronkonkoma *(G-14365)*
Lomir Inc ..... F 518 483-7697
Malone *(G-7723)*
Maripharm Laboratories ..... F 716 984-6520
Niagara Falls *(G-12308)*
Material Measuring Corporation ..... G 516 334-6167
Westbury *(G-16355)*
Modu-Craft Inc ..... G 716 694-0709
Tonawanda *(G-15559)*
Modu-Craft Inc ..... G 716 694-0709
North Tonawanda *(G-12438)*
▲ Nalge Nunc International Corp ..... A 585 498-2661
Rochester *(G-13962)*
Newport Corporation ..... E 585 248-4246
Rochester *(G-13970)*
Next Advance Inc ..... F 518 674-3510
Troy *(G-15611)*
Radon Testing Corp of America ..... F 914 345-3380
Elmsford *(G-4559)*
S P Industries Inc ..... D 845 255-5000
Gardiner *(G-5295)*
Scientific Industries Inc ..... E 631 567-4700
Bohemia *(G-1085)*
Simpore Inc ..... G 585 748-5980
West Henrietta *(G-16251)*
SPS Medical Supply Corp ..... F 585 968-2377
Cuba *(G-3920)*
▲ Staplex Company Inc ..... E 718 768-3333
Brooklyn *(G-2508)*
Steriliz LLC ..... G 585 415-5411
Rochester *(G-14144)*
▲ Vistalab Technologies Inc ..... E 914 244-6226
Brewster *(G-1176)*
Vivus Technologies LLC ..... G 585 798-6658
Medina *(G-7991)*
VWR Education LLC ..... C 585 359-2502
West Henrietta *(G-16254)*

3822 Automatic Temperature Controls

▲ A K Allen Co Inc ..... C 516 747-5450
Melville *(G-7996)*
Advantex Solutions Inc ..... G 718 278-2290
Bellerose *(G-780)*
Air Louver & Damper Inc ..... F 718 392-3232
Long Island City *(G-7369)*
Airflex Industrial Inc ..... E 631 752-1234
Farmingdale *(G-4710)*
▲ Anderson Instrument Co Inc ..... D 518 922-5315
Fultonville *(G-5234)*
Automated Bldg MGT Systems Inc ..... E 516 216-5603
Floral Park *(G-4956)*
Automated Building Controls ..... G 914 381-2860
Mamaroneck *(G-7734)*
Bilbee Controls Inc ..... F 518 622-3033
Cairo *(G-3147)*
▲ Biorem Environmental Inc ..... E 585 924-2220
Victor *(G-15831)*
▲ Bitzer Scroll Inc ..... D 315 463-2101
Syracuse *(G-15258)*
Black River Generations LLC ..... E 315 773-2314
Fort Drum *(G-5091)*
Building Management Assoc Inc ..... E 718 542-4779
Bronx *(G-1234)*
Care Enterprises Inc ..... G 631 472-8155
Bayport *(G-735)*
Carrier Corporation ..... B 315 432-6000
Syracuse *(G-15272)*
Cascade Technical Services LLC ..... F 516 596-6300
Lynbrook *(G-7663)*
Cascade Technical Services LLC ..... G 518 355-2201
Schenectady *(G-14659)*
Clean Room Depot Inc ..... F 631 589-3033
Holbrook *(G-6177)*
▲ Cox & Company Inc ..... C 212 366-0200
Plainview *(G-13048)*
Daikin Applied Americas Inc ..... D 315 253-2771
Auburn *(G-475)*
Day Automation Systems Inc ..... D 585 924-4630
Victor *(G-15841)*
E Global Solutions Inc ..... G 516 767-5138
Port Washington *(G-13256)*
East Hudson Watershed Corp ..... G 845 319-6349
Patterson *(G-12881)*
Eastern Strategic Materials ..... E 212 332-1619
New York *(G-9612)*
Fuel Watchman Sales & Service ..... F 718 665-6100
Bronx *(G-1276)*

Grillmaster Inc ..... E 718 272-9191
Howard Beach *(G-6330)*
Heating & Burner Supply Inc ..... G 718 665-0006
Bronx *(G-1290)*
Henderson Products Inc ..... E 315 785-0994
Watertown *(G-16016)*
▲ Infitec Inc ..... D 315 433-1150
East Syracuse *(G-4352)*
Intellidyne LLC ..... F 516 676-0777
Plainview *(G-13064)*
Intrepid Control Service Inc ..... G 718 886-8771
Flushing *(G-5012)*
Irtronics Instruments Inc ..... F 914 693-6291
Ardsley *(G-395)*
Johnson Controls Inc ..... E 585 924-9346
Rochester *(G-13896)*
Johnson Controls Inc ..... E 914 593-5200
Hawthorne *(G-5989)*
Johnson Controls Inc ..... E 716 688-7340
Buffalo *(G-2896)*
Johnson Controls Inc ..... C 585 724-2232
Rochester *(G-13897)*
Leo Schultz ..... G 716 969-0945
Cheektowaga *(G-3451)*
Logical Control Solutions Inc ..... F 585 424-5340
Victor *(G-15855)*
Long Island Analytical Labs ..... F 631 472-3400
Holbrook *(G-6196)*
Microb Phase Services ..... F 518 877-8948
Clifton Park *(G-3571)*
Pii Holdings Inc ..... G 716 876-9951
Buffalo *(G-3004)*
Protective Industries Inc ..... D 716 876-9951
Buffalo *(G-3019)*
◆ Protective Industries Inc ..... C 716 876-9951
Buffalo *(G-3017)*
◆ Pulsafeeder Inc ..... C 585 292-8000
Rochester *(G-14054)*
◆ RE Hansen Industries Inc ..... C 631 471-2900
Saint James *(G-14514)*
Reuse Action Incorporated ..... G 716 949-0900
Buffalo *(G-3035)*
Siemens Industry Inc ..... D 716 568-0983
Amherst *(G-250)*
Siemens Industry Inc ..... E 585 797-2300
Rochester *(G-14126)*
▲ Svyz Trading Corp ..... G 718 220-1140
Bronx *(G-1397)*
T S B A Group Inc ..... E 718 565-6000
Sunnyside *(G-15206)*
▲ Transit Air Inc ..... E 607 324-0216
Hornell *(G-6304)*
Unisend LLC ..... G 585 414-9575
Webster *(G-16104)*
Use Acquisition LLC ..... F 516 812-6800
New Hyde Park *(G-8572)*
Virtual Super LLC ..... G 212 685-6400
New York *(G-12041)*
Zebra Environmental Corp ..... F 516 596-6300
Lynbrook *(G-7678)*

3823 Indl Instruments For Meas, Display & Control

Aalborg Instrs & Contrls Inc ..... D 845 398-3160
Orangeburg *(G-12667)*
Ametek Inc ..... D 585 263-7700
Rochester *(G-13630)*
Anchor Commerce Trading Corp ..... G 516 881-3485
Atlantic Beach *(G-455)*
▲ Anderson Instrument Co Inc ..... D 518 922-5315
Fultonville *(G-5234)*
▲ Applied Power Systems Inc ..... E 516 935-2230
Hicksville *(G-6059)*
Aspex Incorporated ..... E 212 966-0410
New York *(G-8936)*
ATI Trading Inc ..... F 718 888-7918
Flushing *(G-4987)*
Aureonic ..... G 518 791-9331
Gansevoort *(G-5242)*
Automation Evolution LLC ..... G 585 241-6010
Webster *(G-16075)*
Beauty America LLC ..... E 917 744-1430
Great Neck *(G-5539)*
Betapast Holdings LLC ..... D 631 582-6740
Hauppauge *(G-5779)*
▼ Betatronix Inc ..... E 631 582-6740
Ronkonkoma *(G-14319)*
◆ Blue Tee Corp ..... G 212 598-0880
New York *(G-9109)*

S
I
C

Employee Codes: A=Over 500 employees, B=251-500
C=101-250, D=51-100, E=20-50, F=10-19, G=5-9

2019 Harris
New York Manufacturers Directory

789

38 MEASURING, ANALYZING AND CONTROLLING INSTRUMENTS; PHOTOGRAPHIC, MEDICAL AN

▲ Calibrated Instruments Inc .... F   914 741-5700
  Manhasset *(G-7765)*
Ceres Technologies Inc .... D   845 247-4701
  Saugerties *(G-14604)*
▲ Classic Automation LLC .... E   585 241-6010
  Webster *(G-16079)*
Computer Instruments Corp .... E   516 876-8400
  Westbury *(G-16321)*
Conax Technologies LLC C   716 684-4500
  Buffalo *(G-2777)*
▲ Cosa Xentaur Corporation .... E   631 345-3434
  Yaphank *(G-16707)*
Danaher Corporation C   516 443-9432
  New York *(G-9464)*
◆ Defelsko Corporation .... D   315 393-4450
  Ogdensburg *(G-12573)*
Digital Analysis Corporation .... F   315 685-0760
  Skaneateles *(G-14869)*
Digitronik Labs Inc .... F   585 360-0043
  Rochester *(G-13741)*
Display Logic USA Inc .... G   631 406-1922
  Hauppauge *(G-5813)*
▲ Dyna-Empire Inc C   516 222-2700
  Garden City *(G-5256)*
East Hills Instrument Inc .... F   516 621-8686
  Westbury *(G-16325)*
Electrcal Instrumentation Ctrl .... F   518 861-5789
  Delanson *(G-4068)*
Electronic Machine Parts LLC .... F   631 434-3700
  Hauppauge *(G-5818)*
Emerson Electric Co .... E   212 244-2490
  New York *(G-9668)*
Ewt Holdings III Corp .... F   212 644-5900
  New York *(G-9744)*
Fts Systems Inc .... D   845 687-5300
  Stone Ridge *(G-15161)*
Gizmo Products Inc .... G   585 301-0970
  Stanley *(G-15034)*
Gurley Precision Instrs Inc C   518 272-6300
  Troy *(G-15607)*
Hades Manufacturing Corp .... F   631 249-4244
  Farmingdale *(G-4778)*
Herman H Sticht Company Inc .... G   718 852-7602
  Brooklyn *(G-1974)*
◆ Hilliard Corporation .... B   607 733-7121
  Elmira *(G-4492)*
Hilliard Corporation .... B   607 733-7121
  Elmira *(G-4493)*
Industrial Machine Repair .... G   607 272-0717
  Ithaca *(G-6584)*
▲ Inficon Inc C   315 434-1100
  East Syracuse *(G-4350)*
Inficon Holding AG .... G   315 434-1100
  East Syracuse *(G-4351)*
▲ Integrated Control Corp .... E   631 673-5100
  Huntington *(G-6400)*
ITT Corporation .... D   315 568-2811
  Seneca Falls *(G-14777)*
ITT Inc .... E   914 641-2000
  White Plains *(G-16464)*
ITT LLC .... D   914 641-2000
  Seneca Falls *(G-14781)*
◆ ITT LLC .... B   914 641-2000
  White Plains *(G-16467)*
▲ Kessler Thermometer Corp .... G   631 841-5500
  West Babylon *(G-16167)*
▲ Koehler Instrument Company Inc ... D   631 589-3800
  Holtsville *(G-6240)*
◆ Ktk Thermal Technologies Inc .... E   585 678-9025
  Macedon *(G-7700)*
Macrolink Inc .... E   631 924-8200
  Medford *(G-7960)*
◆ Magtrol Inc .... E   716 668-5555
  Buffalo *(G-2935)*
Malcon Inc .... F   914 666-7146
  Bedford Hills *(G-777)*
Mark - 10 Corporation .... E   631 842-9200
  Copiague *(G-3769)*
Mausner Equipment Co Inc .... F   631 689-7358
  Setauket *(G-14795)*
Medsafe Systems Inc .... G   516 883-8222
  Port Washington *(G-13287)*
Micromod Automtn & Contrls Corp ... F   585 321-9209
  Rochester *(G-13943)*
Mks Instruments Inc .... E   585 292-7472
  Rochester *(G-13949)*
New Scale Technologies Inc .... F   585 924-4450
  Victor *(G-15857)*
Nidec Indus Automtn USA LLC .... E   716 774-1193
  Grand Island *(G-5507)*

Nutec Components Inc .... F   631 242-1224
  Deer Park *(G-4018)*
Oden Machinery Inc .... E   716 874-3000
  Tonawanda *(G-15567)*
Ormec Systems Corp .... E   585 385-3520
  Rochester *(G-13991)*
Orthstar Enterprises Inc .... D   607 562-2100
  Horseheads *(G-6323)*
▲ Packaging Tech & Insptn LLC .... E   914 337-2005
  Tuckahoe *(G-15645)*
Parrington Instruments .... G   518 373-8420
  Rexford *(G-13482)*
Partlow Corporation C   518 922-5315
  Fultonville *(G-5238)*
Pcb Group Inc .... E   716 684-0001
  Depew *(G-4100)*
▲ Pneumercator Company Inc .... E   631 293-8450
  Hauppauge *(G-5917)*
Poseidon Systems LLC .... F   585 239-6025
  Rochester *(G-14028)*
◆ Pulsafeeder Inc .... E   585 292-8000
  Rochester *(G-14054)*
R K B Opto-Electronics Inc .... F   315 455-6636
  Syracuse *(G-15400)*
Riverhawk Company LP .... E   315 624-7171
  New Hartford *(G-8510)*
Robat Inc .... G   518 812-6244
  Clifton Park *(G-3575)*
Roessel & Co Inc .... G   585 458-5560
  Rochester *(G-14101)*
Rotronic Instrument Corp .... G   631 427-3898
  Huntington *(G-6413)*
▲ Rotronic Instrument Corp .... F   631 348-6844
  Hauppauge *(G-5930)*
Rwb Controls Inc .... G   716 897-4341
  Buffalo *(G-3050)*
Schneider Elc Systems USA Inc .... F   214 527-3099
  New York *(G-11508)*
Select Controls Inc .... E   631 567-9010
  Bohemia *(G-1087)*
Sixnet LLC .... D   518 877-5173
  Ballston Lake *(G-571)*
▲ Sixnet Holdings LLC .... D   518 877-5173
  Ballston Lake *(G-572)*
Solar Metrology LLC .... E   845 247-4701
  Holbrook *(G-6209)*
Springfield Control Systems .... G   718 631-0870
  Douglaston *(G-4141)*
Swagelok Western NY .... G   585 359-8470
  West Henrietta *(G-16252)*
Taber Acquisition Corp .... D   716 694-4000
  North Tonawanda *(G-12458)*
Tel-Tru Inc .... E   585 232-1440
  Rochester *(G-14162)*
Tel-Tru Inc .... D   585 295-0225
  Rochester *(G-14163)*
Telog Instruments Inc .... G   585 742-3000
  Victor *(G-15872)*
Thread Check Inc .... D   631 231-1515
  Hauppauge *(G-5958)*
▼ Transtech Systems Inc .... E   518 370-5558
  Latham *(G-7095)*
Vacuum Instrument Corporation .... D   631 737-0900
  Ronkonkoma *(G-14427)*
Veeco Instruments Inc .... E   516 677-0200
  Woodbury *(G-16633)*
▲ Vermont Medical Inc C   802 463-9976
  Buffalo *(G-3118)*
Vertiv Corporation .... E   516 349-8500
  Plainview *(G-13101)*
Vetra Systems Corporation .... G   631 434-3185
  Hauppauge *(G-5969)*
Viatran Corporation .... E   716 564-7813
  Tonawanda *(G-15589)*
Vibro-Laser Instrs Corp LLC .... E   518 874-2700
  Glens Falls *(G-5443)*
Webinfinity Americas Inc .... F   516 331-5180
  Huntington *(G-6427)*
▲ Weiss Instruments Inc .... D   631 207-1200
  Holtsville *(G-6250)*
▲ Winters Instruments Inc .... E   281 880-8607
  Buffalo *(G-3133)*
Xentaur Corporation .... E   631 345-3434
  Yaphank *(G-16729)*

3824 Fluid Meters & Counters

Aalborg Instrs & Contrls Inc .... D   845 398-3160
  Orangeburg *(G-12667)*
Cmp Advnced Mech Sltons NY LLC .. C   607 352-1712
  Binghamton *(G-875)*

Computer Instruments Corp .... E   516 876-8400
  Westbury *(G-16321)*
▲ Curtis Instruments Inc C   914 666-2971
  Mount Kisco *(G-8339)*
▲ Designatronics Incorporated .... G   516 328-3300
  Hicksville *(G-6079)*
East Hills Instrument Inc .... F   516 621-8686
  Westbury *(G-16325)*
Encore Electronics Inc .... E   518 584-5354
  Saratoga Springs *(G-14577)*
▲ Environment-One Corporation ...... E   518 346-6161
  Schenectady *(G-14672)*
Flexim Americas Corporation .... F   631 492-2300
  Edgewood *(G-4400)*
Gurley Precision Instrs Inc C   518 272-6300
  Troy *(G-15607)*
K-Technologies Inc .... E   716 828-4444
  Buffalo *(G-2901)*
Melland Gear Instr of Huppauge .... E   631 234-0100
  Hauppauge *(G-5885)*
Schlumberger Technology Corp C   607 378-0105
  Horseheads *(G-6328)*
Siemens Industry Inc .... F   631 231-3600
  Hauppauge *(G-5938)*
SPX Flow Us LLC .... E   585 436-5550
  Rochester *(G-14140)*
Turbo Machined Products LLC .... E   315 895-3010
  Frankfort *(G-5113)*
Vantage Mfg & Assembly LLC .... E   845 471-5290
  Poughkeepsie *(G-13371)*
Vepo Solutions LLC .... G   914 384-2121
  Cross River *(G-3910)*
▲ Walter R Tucker Entps Ltd .... E   607 467-2866
  Deposit *(G-4112)*

3825 Instrs For Measuring & Testing Electricity

Advanced Testing Tech Inc C   631 231-8777
  Hauppauge *(G-5755)*
Agilent Technologies Inc .... A   877 424-4536
  New York *(G-8769)*
Ah Elctronic Test Eqp Repr Ctr .... F   631 234-8979
  Central Islip *(G-3354)*
Allied Motion Systems Corp .... F   716 691-5868
  Amherst *(G-210)*
▲ Allied Motion Technologies Inc C   716 242-8634
  Amherst *(G-211)*
American Quality Technology .... F   607 777-9488
  Binghamton *(G-861)*
Ametek Inc .... D   585 263-7700
  Rochester *(G-13630)*
Anmar Acquisition LLC .... G   585 352-7777
  Rochester *(G-13634)*
Apogee Power Usa Inc .... F   202 746-2890
  Hartsdale *(G-5742)*
Aurora Technical Services Ltd .... G   716 652-1463
  East Aurora *(G-4195)*
Automated Control Logic Inc .... F   914 769-8880
  Thornwood *(G-15501)*
Automation Correct LLC .... G   315 299-3589
  Syracuse *(G-15249)*
Avanel Industries Inc .... E   516 333-0990
  Westbury *(G-16318)*
Avcom of Virginia Inc .... D   585 924-4560
  Victor *(G-15830)*
C Speed LLC .... E   315 453-1043
  Liverpool *(G-7227)*
C-Flex Bearing Co Inc .... F   315 895-7454
  Frankfort *(G-5104)*
Calmetrics Inc .... G   631 580-2522
  Holbrook *(G-6174)*
▲ Cetek Inc .... E   845 452-3510
  Poughkeepsie *(G-13331)*
Cgw Corp .... E   631 472-6600
  Bayport *(G-736)*
Clarke Hess Communication RES .... G   631 698-3350
  Medford *(G-7944)*
▲ Clayton Dubilier & Rice Fun .... E   212 407-5200
  New York *(G-9324)*
▲ Comtech PST Corp C   631 777-8900
  Melville *(G-8011)*
▲ Curtis Instruments Inc C   914 666-2971
  Mount Kisco *(G-8339)*
East Hills Instrument Inc .... F   516 621-8686
  Westbury *(G-16325)*
Edo LLC .... F   631 218-1413
  Bohemia *(G-1020)*
Edo LLC .... A   631 630-4200
  Amityville *(G-273)*

El Electronics Inc....F....516 334-0870
Westbury (G-16326)
▲ Ems Development Corporation....D....631 924-4736
Yaphank (G-16708)
Enertiv Inc....G....646 350-3525
New York (G-9682)
Epoch Microelectronics Inc....G....914 332-8570
Valhalla (G-15741)
Everest Bbn Inc....F....212 268-7979
New York (G-9736)
Fluid Metering Inc....E....516 922-6050
Syosset (G-15217)
Frequency Electronics Inc....C....516 794-4500
Uniondale (G-15668)
Gcns Technology Group Inc....G....347 713-8160
Brooklyn (G-1920)
General Microwave Corporation....F....516 802-0900
Syosset (G-15219)
Hamilton Marketing Corporation....G....585 395-0678
Brockport (G-1191)
Herman H Sticht Company Inc....G....718 852-7602
Brooklyn (G-1974)
▲ Hipotronics Inc....C....845 279-8091
Brewster (G-1167)
▲ Iet Labs Inc....F....516 334-5959
Roslyn Heights (G-14456)
◆ Interntnal Elctronic Mchs Corp....E....518 268-1636
Troy (G-15610)
John Ramsey Elec Svcs LLC....G....585 298-9596
Victor (G-15851)
Larry Kings Corporation....G....718 481-8741
Rosedale (G-14440)
Lexan Industries Inc....F....631 434-7586
Bay Shore (G-696)
Linde LLC....D....716 773-7552
Grand Island (G-5506)
Logitek Inc....D....631 567-1100
Bohemia (G-1048)
▼ Ludl Electronic Products Ltd....E....914 769-6111
Hawthorne (G-5992)
▲ Magnetic Analysis Corporation....D....914 530-2000
Elmsford (G-4549)
◆ Magtrol Inc....E....716 668-5555
Buffalo (G-2935)
▲ Make-Waves Instrument Corp....E....716 681-7524
Buffalo (G-2936)
Millivac Instruments Inc....G....518 355-8300
Schenectady (G-14698)
▲ Nas CP Corp....E....718 961-6757
College Point (G-3657)
New York Enrgy Synthetics Inc....G....212 634 4787
New York (G-10937)
North Atlantic Industries Inc....E....631 567-1100
Bohemia (G-1065)
North Atlantic Industries Inc....C....631 567-1100
Bohemia (G-1066)
Northeast Metrology Corp....F....716 827-3770
Depew (G-4098)
Omni-ID Usa Inc....E....585 697-9913
Rochester (G-13987)
Optimized Devices Inc....F....914 769-6100
Pleasantville (G-13175)
Peerless Instrument Co Inc....C....631 396-6500
Farmingdale (G-4845)
Performance Systems Contg Inc....E....607 277-6240
Ithaca (G-6603)
Photonix Technologies Inc....F....607 786-4600
Endicott (G-4608)
Practical Instrument Elec Inc....F....585 872-9350
Webster (G-16092)
Pragmatics Technology Inc....G....845 795-5071
Milton (G-8196)
Precision Filters Inc....E....607 277-3550
Ithaca (G-6606)
Primesouth Inc....F....585 567-4191
Fillmore (G-4938)
◆ Pulsafeeder Inc....C....585 292-8000
Rochester (G-14054)
Pulsar Technology Systems Inc....G....718 361-9292
Long Island City (G-7562)
▲ Quadlogic Controls Corporation....D....212 930-9300
Long Island City (G-7565)
R K B Opto-Electronics Inc....F....315 455-6636
Syracuse (G-15400)
Ramsey Electronics LLC....E....585 924-4560
Victor (G-15863)
Rodale Wireless Inc....E....631 231-0044
Hauppauge (G-5929)
S R Instruments Inc....E....716 693-5977
Tonawanda (G-15573)
Schlumberger Technology Corp....C....607 378-0105
Horseheads (G-6328)
Scientific Components Corp....E....631 243-4901
Deer Park (G-4042)
Scj Associates Inc....E....585 359-0600
Rochester (G-14117)
◆ Sorfin Yoshimura Ltd....G....516 802-4600
Woodbury (G-16632)
T & C Power Conversion Inc....F....585 482-5551
Rochester (G-14154)
▲ Teledyne Lecroy Inc....C....845 425-2000
Chestnut Ridge (G-3497)
◆ Transcat Inc....B....585 352-7777
Rochester (G-14175)
Trek Inc....F....716 438-7555
Lockport (G-7338)
▲ Vermed Inc....D....800 669-6905
Buffalo (G-3117)
Viatran Corporation....E....716 564-7813
Tonawanda (G-15589)
▲ W & W Manufacturing Co....F....516 942-0011
West Islip (G-16261)
W D Technology Inc....G....914 779-8738
Eastchester (G-4383)
▲ Walter R Tucker Entps Ltd....E....607 467-2866
Deposit (G-4112)
Xelic Incorporated....F....585 415-2764
Pittsford (G-13029)
▲ Zumbach Electronics Corp....D....914 241-7080
Mount Kisco (G-8362)

3826 Analytical Instruments

A S A Precision Co Inc....G....845 482-4870
Jeffersonville (G-6778)
Advanced Mtl Analytics LLC....G....321 684-0528
Vestal (G-15808)
Advion Inc....E....607 266-9162
Ithaca (G-6555)
Applied Image Inc....E....585 482-0300
Rochester (G-13637)
Bristol Instruments Inc....G....585 924-2620
Victor (G-15833)
Brookhaven Instruments Corp....E....631 758-3200
Holtsville (G-6237)
Caltex International Ltd....E....315 425-1040
Syracuse (G-15268)
Cambridge Manufacturing LLC....G....516 326-1350
New Hyde Park (G-8521)
▲ Carl Zeiss Inc....C....914 747-1800
Thornwood (G-15502)
Ceres Technologies Inc....D....845 247-4701
Saugerties (G-14604)
Chromosense LLC....G....646 541-2302
Rye Brook (G-14490)
Corning Incorporated....G....607 974-6729
Painted Post (G-12837)
CTB Enterprise LLC....F....631 563-0088
Holbrook (G-6181)
East Coast Envmtl Group Inc....G....516 352-1946
Farmingdale (G-4757)
East Hills Instrument Inc....F....516 621-8686
Westbury (G-16325)
Elementar Americas Inc....G....856 787-0022
Ronkonkoma (G-14338)
Equine Imaging LLC....E....414 326-0665
Port Washington (G-13258)
Ewt Holdings III Corp....F....212 644-5900
New York (G-9744)
Exfo Burleigh Pdts Group Inc....D....585 301-1530
Canandaigua (G-3220)
Finger Lakes Radiology LLC....G....315 787-5399
Geneva (G-5324)
Gemprint Corporation....E....212 997-0007
New York (G-9897)
General Microwave Corporation....F....516 802-0900
Syosset (G-15219)
High Voltage Inc....E....518 329-3275
Copake (G-3746)
Industrial Municipal Equipment....F....631 665-6712
Brightwaters (G-1186)
Ion-Tof Usa Inc....G....845 352-8082
Spring Valley (G-14996)
Islandia Mri Associates PC....F....631 234-2828
Central Islip (G-3374)
Life Technologies Corporation....D....716 774-6700
Grand Island (G-5505)
Micro Photo Acoustics Inc....G....631 750-6035
Ronkonkoma (G-14377)
▲ MMC Enterprises Corp....G....800 435-1088
Hauppauge (G-5894)
▼ Multiwire Laboratories Ltd....G....607 257-3378
Ithaca (G-6598)
Nanotronics Imaging Inc....E....212 401-6209
Brooklyn (G-2242)
▲ Nexgen Enviro Systems Inc....G....631 226-2930
Lindenhurst (G-7184)
Niagara Scientific Inc....D....315 437-0821
East Syracuse (G-4360)
◆ Nikon Instruments Inc....D....631 547-4200
Melville (G-8052)
▲ Photonics Industries Intl Inc....D....631 218-2240
Ronkonkoma (G-14398)
Phymetrix Inc....G....631 627-3950
Medford (G-7963)
Porous Materials Inc....F....607 257-5544
Ithaca (G-6605)
▲ Qioptiq, Inc.....E....585 223-2370
Fairport (G-4652)
Rheonix Inc....D....607 257-1242
Ithaca (G-6608)
Smartpill Corporation....E....716 882-0701
Buffalo (G-3067)
Spectra Vista Corporation....G....845 471-7007
Poughkeepsie (G-13367)
Thermo Fisher Scientific Inc....E....585 899-7780
Penfield (G-12946)
Thermo Fisher Scientific Inc....G....716 774-6700
Grand Island (G-5515)
Thermo Fisher Scientific Inc....B....585 458-8008
Rochester (G-14166)
Thermo Fisher Scientific Inc....A....585 899-7610
Rochester (G-14167)
Uptek Solutions Corp....F....631 256-5565
Bohemia (G-1104)
Veeco Instruments Inc....C....516 677-0200
Woodbury (G-16633)
Velp Scientific Inc....G....631 573-6002
Bohemia (G-1105)

3827 Optical Instruments

21st Century Optics Inc....E....347 527-1079
Long Island City (G-7362)
Accu Coat Inc....G....585 288-2330
Rochester (G-13596)
▲ Advanced Glass Industries Inc....D....585 458-8040
Rochester (G-13606)
▲ Aeroflex Incorporated....B....516 694-6700
Plainview (G-13032)
Aeroflex Plainview Inc....B....516 694-6700
Plainview (G-13033)
▲ Anorad Corporation....C....631 344-6600
Shirley (G-14827)
Apollo Optical Systems Inc....E....585 272-6170
West Henrietta (G-16229)
◆ Applied Coatings Holding Corp....G....585 482-0300
Rochester (G-13636)
Applied Image Inc....E....585 482-0300
Rochester (G-13637)
Ariel Optics Inc....G....585 265-4820
Ontario (G-12647)
▼ Binoptics LLC....E....607 257-3200
Ithaca (G-6562)
Caliber Imging Diagnostics Inc....E....585 239-9800
Rochester (G-13687)
▲ Carl Zeiss Inc....C....914 747-1800
Thornwood (G-15502)
Carl Zeiss Microscopy LLC....B....914 747-1800
Thornwood (G-15503)
▲ Carl Zeiss Sbe LLC....E....914 747-1132
Thornwood (G-15504)
Cartiheal Inc....G....917 703-6992
New York (G-9217)
CK Coatings....G....585 502-0425
Le Roy (G-7114)
▲ Cnc Systems 2000 Inc....E....585 265-0160
Ontario (G-12649)
Corning Tropel Corporation....C....585 377-3200
Fairport (G-4629)
Cross Bronx Optical....G....917 667-6611
Bronx (G-1248)
▲ Digitac Inc....F....732 215-4020
Brooklyn (G-1777)
Dorsey Metrology Intl Inc....E....845 229-2929
Poughkeepsie (G-13334)
▲ Dynamic Laboratories Inc....E....631 231-7474
Ronkonkoma (G-14334)
Enplas America Inc....G....646 892-7811
New York (G-9686)
Exfo Burleigh Pdts Group Inc....D....585 301-1530
Canandaigua (G-3220)

S I C

Employee Codes: A=Over 500 employees, B=251-500
C=101-250, D=51-100, E=20-50, F=10-19, G=5-9
2019 Harris
New York Manufacturers Directory
791

Gradient Lens Corporation....................E....... 585 235-2620
Rochester *(G-13844)*
Gurley Precision Instrs Inc....................C....... 518 272-6300
Troy *(G-15607)*
Halo Optical Products Inc....................D....... 518 773-4256
Gloversville *(G-5457)*
◆ **Hart Specialties Inc**....................D....... 631 226-5600
Amityville *(G-281)*
Hudson Mirror LLC....................E....... 914 930-8906
Peekskill *(G-12922)*
Idex Health & Science LLC....................D....... 585 244-7220
Rochester *(G-13875)*
▲ **Isp Optics Corporation**....................D....... 914 591-3070
Irvington *(G-6507)*
▲ **Jml Optical Industries LLC**....................D....... 585 248-8900
Rochester *(G-13894)*
Keon Optics Inc....................F....... 845 429-7103
Stony Point *(G-15173)*
Kevin Freeman....................G....... 631 447-5321
Patchogue *(G-12869)*
Leica Microsystems Inc....................G....... 716 686-3000
Depew *(G-4095)*
Lens Triptar Co Inc....................G....... 585 473-4470
Rochester *(G-13911)*
▼ **Lumetrics Inc**....................F....... 585 214-2455
Rochester *(G-13918)*
Machida Incorporated....................G....... 845 365-0600
Orangeburg *(G-12683)*
▲ **Match Eyewear LLC**....................E....... 516 877-0170
Westbury *(G-16354)*
Micatu Inc....................G....... 888 705-8836
Horseheads *(G-6319)*
▼ **Navitar Inc**....................D....... 585 359-4000
Rochester *(G-13965)*
▲ **Newport Rochester Inc**....................D....... 585 262-1325
Rochester *(G-13971)*
▲ **North American Enclosures Inc**....................E....... 631 234-9500
Central Islip *(G-3381)*
Optics Technology Inc....................G....... 585 586-0950
Pittsford *(G-13023)*
Optimax Systems Inc....................C....... 585 265-1020
Ontario *(G-12658)*
◆ **Optipro Systems LLC**....................D....... 585 265-0160
Ontario *(G-12659)*
Orafol Americas Inc....................F....... 585 272-0290
West Henrietta *(G-16244)*
Photon Gear Inc....................F....... 585 265-3360
Ontario *(G-12660)*
Planar Optics Inc....................G....... 585 671-0100
Webster *(G-16091)*
Plx Inc....................E....... 631 586-4190
Deer Park *(G-4026)*
▲ **Qioptiq, Inc.**....................E....... 585 223-2370
Fairport *(G-4652)*
▲ **Quality Vision Intl Inc**....................B....... 585 544-0450
Rochester *(G-14061)*
▲ **Quality Vision Services Inc**....................D....... 585 544-0450
Rochester *(G-14062)*
Rochester Photonics Corp....................D....... 585 387-0674
Rochester *(G-14091)*
◆ **Rochester Precision Optics LLC**....................C....... 585 292-5450
West Henrietta *(G-16249)*
RPC Photonics Inc....................F....... 585 272-2840
Rochester *(G-14106)*
Santa Fe Manufacturing Corp....................G....... 631 234-0100
Hauppauge *(G-5932)*
▲ **Schneider Optics Inc**....................E....... 631 761-5000
Hauppauge *(G-5935)*
Schott Corporation....................D....... 315 255-2791
Auburn *(G-499)*
Spectral Systems LLC....................E....... 845 896-2200
Hopewell Junction *(G-6293)*
Spectrum Thin Films Inc....................E....... 631 901-1010
Hauppauge *(G-5946)*
▼ **Stefan Sydor Optics Inc**....................E....... 585 271-7300
Rochester *(G-14143)*
Steven John Opticians....................G....... 718 543-3336
Bronx *(G-1394)*
Surgical Design Corp....................F....... 914 273-2445
Armonk *(G-410)*
▲ **Tele-Vue Optics Inc**....................E....... 845 469-4551
Chester *(G-3487)*
Va Inc....................E....... 585 385-5930
Rochester *(G-14195)*
Videk Inc....................E....... 585 377-0377
Fairport *(G-4665)*
◆ **Welch Allyn Inc**....................A....... 315 685-4100
Skaneateles Falls *(G-14883)*
Westchester Technologies Inc....................E....... 914 736-1034
Peekskill *(G-12929)*

3829 Measuring & Controlling Devices, NEC

Accuvein Inc....................D....... 816 997-9400
Medford *(G-7936)*
Amarantus Bscence Holdings Inc....................F....... 917 686-5317
New York *(G-8816)*
Andor Design Corp....................G....... 516 364-1619
Syosset *(G-15208)*
Aspex Incorporated....................E....... 212 966-0410
New York *(G-8936)*
Aurora Technical Services Ltd....................G....... 716 652-1463
East Aurora *(G-4195)*
Biodesign Inc of New York....................F....... 845 454-6610
Carmel *(G-3274)*
▲ **Carl Zeiss Inc**....................C....... 914 747-1800
Thornwood *(G-15502)*
Circor Aerospace Inc....................D....... 631 737-1900
Hauppauge *(G-5789)*
Climatronics Corp....................F....... 541 471-7111
Bohemia *(G-994)*
Computer Instruments Corp....................E....... 516 876-8400
Westbury *(G-16321)*
Cosense Inc....................E....... 516 364-9161
Syosset *(G-15212)*
Cubic Trnsp Systems Inc....................F....... 212 255-1810
New York *(G-9431)*
Dayton T Brown Inc....................B....... 631 589-6300
Bohemia *(G-1011)*
◆ **Defelsko Corporation**....................D....... 315 393-4450
Ogdensburg *(G-12573)*
Dispersion Technology Inc....................G....... 914 241-4777
Bedford Hills *(G-775)*
Dylix Corporation....................E....... 719 773-2985
Grand Island *(G-5498)*
▲ **Dyna-Empire Inc**....................C....... 516 222-2700
Garden City *(G-5256)*
▲ **Dynamic Systems Inc**....................E....... 518 283-5350
Poestenkill *(G-13180)*
East Hills Instrument Inc....................F....... 516 621-8686
Westbury *(G-16325)*
Eastern Niagra Radiology....................E....... 716 882-6544
Buffalo *(G-2811)*
Electrical Controls Link....................E....... 585 924-7010
Victor *(G-15843)*
Electro-Optical Products Corp....................G....... 718 456-6000
Ridgewood *(G-13535)*
Elsag North America LLC....................G....... 877 773-5724
Brewster *(G-1164)*
Erbessd Reliability LLC....................E....... 518 874-2700
Glens Falls *(G-5424)*
▲ **Fougera Pharmaceuticals Inc**....................C....... 631 454-7677
Melville *(G-8026)*
Freeman Technology Inc....................E....... 732 829-8345
Bayside *(G-745)*
G E Inspection Technologies LP....................C....... 315 554-2000
Skaneateles *(G-14871)*
Gei International Inc....................E....... 315 463-9261
East Syracuse *(G-4342)*
◆ **Germanow-Simon Corporation**....................E....... 585 232-1440
Rochester *(G-13832)*
◆ **Gleason Corporation**....................A....... 585 473-1000
Rochester *(G-13839)*
◆ **Gleason Works**....................A....... 585 473-1000
Rochester *(G-13840)*
Gurley Precision Instrs Inc....................C....... 518 272-6300
Troy *(G-15607)*
H D M Labs Inc....................G....... 516 431-8357
Island Park *(G-6515)*
Hci Engineering....................G....... 315 336-3450
Rome *(G-14252)*
Herman H Sticht Company Inc....................G....... 718 852-7602
Brooklyn *(G-1974)*
▲ **Highway Toll ADM LLC**....................F....... 516 684-9584
Roslyn Heights *(G-14455)*
▲ **Hipotronics Inc**....................C....... 845 279-8091
Brewster *(G-1167)*
◆ **Images Si Inc**....................F....... 718 966-3694
Staten Island *(G-15089)*
Imaginant Inc....................E....... 585 264-0480
Pittsford *(G-13015)*
Industrial Test Eqp Co Inc....................E....... 516 883-6423
Port Washington *(G-13269)*
◆ **Itin Scale Co Inc**....................E....... 718 336-5900
Brooklyn *(G-2019)*
James A Staley Co Inc....................F....... 845 878-3344
Carmel *(G-3277)*
Kem Medical Products Corp....................G....... 631 454-6565
Farmingdale *(G-4802)*
Kinemotive Corporation....................E....... 631 249-6440
Farmingdale *(G-4803)*

Kistler Instrument Corporation....................D....... 716 691-5100
Amherst *(G-234)*
Kld Labs Inc....................E....... 631 549-4222
Hauppauge *(G-5857)*
L N D Incorporated....................E....... 516 678-6141
Oceanside *(G-12545)*
Liberty Controls Inc....................G....... 718 461-0600
College Point *(G-3653)*
Machine Technology Inc....................G....... 845 454-4030
Poughkeepsie *(G-13352)*
▲ **Magnetic Analysis Corporation**....................D....... 914 530-2000
Elmsford *(G-4549)*
◆ **Magtrol Inc**....................E....... 716 668-5555
Buffalo *(G-2935)*
▲ **Make-Waves Instrument Corp**....................E....... 716 681-7524
Buffalo *(G-2936)*
◆ **Mason Industries Inc**....................B....... 631 348-0282
Hauppauge *(G-5881)*
Mechanical Technology Inc....................E....... 518 218-2550
Albany *(G-98)*
Mirion Tech Conax Nuclear Inc....................E....... 716 681-1973
Buffalo *(G-2948)*
Mirion Technologies Ist Corp....................D....... 607 562-4300
Horseheads *(G-6321)*
Mobius Labs Inc....................G....... 518 961-2600
Rexford *(G-13481)*
MTI Instruments Inc....................F....... 518 218-2550
Albany *(G-101)*
Nuclear Diagnostic Pdts NY Inc....................G....... 516 575-4201
Plainview *(G-13079)*
Orolia Usa Inc....................D....... 585 321-5800
Rochester *(G-13992)*
▲ **Oyster Bay Pump Works Inc**....................F....... 516 933-4500
Hicksville *(G-6119)*
Pcb Piezotronics Inc....................F....... 716 684-0001
Depew *(G-4101)*
Peerless Instrument Co Inc....................C....... 631 396-6500
Farmingdale *(G-4845)*
▲ **Peyser Instrument Corporation**....................E....... 631 841-3600
West Babylon *(G-16181)*
Poseidon Systems LLC....................F....... 585 239-6025
Rochester *(G-14028)*
Precision Design Systems Inc....................E....... 585 426-4500
Rochester *(G-14034)*
Pronto Gas Heating Sups Inc....................G....... 718 292-0707
Bronx *(G-1366)*
Qhi Group Incorporated....................G....... 646 512-5727
New York *(G-11291)*
▲ **Qualitrol Company LLC**....................C....... 586 643-3717
Fairport *(G-4653)*
Research Frontiers Inc....................G....... 516 364-1902
Woodbury *(G-16630)*
Riverhawk Company LP....................E....... 315 624-7171
New Hartford *(G-8510)*
RJ Harvey Instrument Corp....................F....... 845 359-3943
Tappan *(G-15471)*
◆ **Schenck Corporation**....................D....... 631 242-4010
Deer Park *(G-4040)*
◆ **Schenck Trebel Corp**....................D....... 631 242-4010
Deer Park *(G-4041)*
◆ **Schott Corporation**....................D....... 914 831-2200
Elmsford *(G-4564)*
SKF USA Inc....................D....... 716 661-2600
Jamestown *(G-6747)*
▲ **Teledyne Lecroy Inc**....................C....... 845 425-2000
Chestnut Ridge *(G-3497)*
Telog Instruments Inc....................E....... 585 742-3000
Victor *(G-15872)*
Titan Controls Inc....................F....... 516 358-2407
New York *(G-11850)*
U E Systems Incorporated....................E....... 914 592-1220
Elmsford *(G-4575)*
Vacuum Instrument Corporation....................D....... 631 737-0900
Ronkonkoma *(G-14427)*
Vector Magnetics LLC....................E....... 607 273-8351
Ithaca *(G-6616)*
Videk Inc....................E....... 585 377-0377
Fairport *(G-4665)*
◆ **VJ Technologies Inc**....................E....... 631 589-8800
Bohemia *(G-1106)*
▲ **Weiss Instruments Inc**....................D....... 631 207-1200
Holtsville *(G-6250)*
Xeku Corporation....................F....... 607 761-1447
Vestal *(G-15826)*
York Industries Inc....................E....... 516 746-3736
Garden City Park *(G-5290)*
Zomega Terahertz Corporation....................F....... 585 347-4337
Webster *(G-16109)*

3841 Surgical & Medical Instrs & Apparatus

▲ **A Titan Instruments Inc** F 716 667-9211
Orchard Park *(G-12696)*

Abyrx Inc F 914 357-2600
Irvington *(G-6502)*

Advanced Placement LLC E 949 281-9086
Holbrook *(G-6170)*

Advantage Plus Diagnostics Inc G 631 393-5044
Melville *(G-7997)*

Aerolase Corporation D 914 345-8300
Tarrytown *(G-15472)*

Ala Scientific Instruments Inc F 631 393-6401
Farmingdale *(G-4712)*

Alconox Inc G 914 948-4040
White Plains *(G-16418)*

AM Bickford Inc F 716 652-1590
Wales Center *(G-15900)*

American Bio Medica Corp D 518 758-8158
Kinderhook *(G-6879)*

◆ **American Diagnostic Corp** D 631 273-6155
Hauppauge *(G-5765)*

▲ **American Healthcare Supply Inc** F 212 674-3636
New York *(G-8828)*

Angiodynamics Inc E 518 761-6867
Queensbury *(G-13417)*

Angiodynamics Inc B 518 975-1400
Queensbury *(G-13418)*

Angiodynamics Inc B 518 792-4112
Glens Falls *(G-5416)*

Angiodynamics Inc B 518 742-4430
Queensbury *(G-13419)*

Angiodynamics Inc B 518 795-1400
Latham *(G-7063)*

Angiodynamics Inc C 706 846-3126
Glens Falls *(G-5417)*

Argon Medical Devices Inc G 585 321-1130
Henrietta *(G-6031)*

Astra Tool & Instrument Mfg E 914 747-3863
Hawthorne *(G-5983)*

Avery Biomedical Devices Inc F 631 864-1600
Commack *(G-3681)*

◆ **Bausch & Lomb Incorporated** B 585 338-6000
Rochester *(G-13655)*

Beacon Spch Lnge Pthlgy Phys F 516 626-1635
Roslyn *(G-14443)*

Becton Dickinson and Company B 845 353-3371
Nyack *(G-12500)*

Biochemical Diagnostics Inc E 631 595-9200
Edgewood *(G-4397)*

▲ **Biodex Medical Systems Inc** C 631 924-9000
Shirley *(G-14832)*

Biodex Medical Systems Inc E 631 924-3146
Shirley *(G-14833)*

Bioresearch Inc G 212 734-5315
Pound Ridge *(G-13375)*

Boehm Surgical Instrument Corp F 585 436-6584
Rochester *(G-13671)*

▲ **Buffalo Filter LLC** D 716 835-7000
Lancaster *(G-7011)*

▲ **Buxton Medical Equipment Corp** E 631 957-4500
Lindenhurst *(G-7164)*

C R Bard Inc B 518 793-2531
Queensbury *(G-13421)*

C R Bard Inc A 518 793-2531
Glens Falls *(G-5420)*

Caliber Imging Diagnostics Inc E 585 239-9800
Rochester *(G-13687)*

Clerio Vision Inc F 617 216-7881
Rochester *(G-13714)*

CN Group Incorporated A 914 358-5690
White Plains *(G-16438)*

Cognitiveflow Sensor Tech G 631 513-9369
Stony Brook *(G-15164)*

Common Sense Marketing Inc G 516 282-1214
Mineola *(G-8213)*

◆ **Conmed Corporation** B 315 797-8375
Utica *(G-15687)*

Conmed Corporation D 315 797-8375
Utica *(G-15686)*

Corning Tropel Corporation C 585 377-3200
Fairport *(G-4629)*

Cynosure Inc G 516 594-3333
Hicksville *(G-6078)*

Daxor Corporation F 212 330-8500
New York *(G-9492)*

Delcath Systems Inc E 212 489-2100
New York *(G-9497)*

Derm-Buro Inc E 516 694-8300
Plainview *(G-13050)*

▲ **Designs For Vision Inc** C 631 585-3300
Bohemia *(G-1016)*

Drive Medical Spv LLC G 516 998-4600
Port Washington *(G-13255)*

◆ **E-Z-Em Inc** E 609 524-2864
Melville *(G-8018)*

▲ **Elliquence LLC** F 516 277-9000
Baldwin *(G-538)*

Endovor Inc G 214 679-7385
New York *(G-9676)*

Endovor LLC G 214 679-7385
New York *(G-9677)*

▲ **Esc Control Electronics LLC** E 631 467-5328
Sayville *(G-14627)*

Extek Inc E 585 533-1672
Rush *(G-14472)*

Eyeglass Service Industries G 914 666-3150
Bedford Hills *(G-776)*

◆ **Fabrication Enterprises Inc** E 914 591-9300
Elmsford *(G-4543)*

▲ **Flexbar Machine Corporation** E 631 582-8440
Islandia *(G-6528)*

Flowmedica Inc F 800 772-6446
Queensbury *(G-13423)*

Fluorologic Inc G 585 248-2796
Pittsford *(G-13012)*

Ftt Medical Inc G 585 444-0980
Rochester *(G-13819)*

◆ **Future Diagnostics LLC** E 347 434-6700
Brooklyn *(G-1910)*

▲ **Gaymar Industries Inc** B 800 828-7341
Orchard Park *(G-12715)*

▲ **Getinge Usa Inc** C 800 475-9040
Rochester *(G-13834)*

Gradian Health Systems Inc G 212 537-0340
New York *(G-9967)*

▲ **Harmac Medical Products Inc** B 716 897-4500
Buffalo *(G-2866)*

▲ **Hogil Pharmaceutical Corp** F 914 681-1800
White Plains *(G-16460)*

Huron Tl Cutter Grinding Inc E 631 420-7000
Farmingdale *(G-4782)*

Hurryworks LLC D 516 998-4600
Port Washington *(G-13266)*

Incredible Scents Inc G 516 656-3300
Greenvale *(G-5630)*

Integer Holdings Corporation D 716 759-5200
Clarence *(G-3534)*

Intersurgical Incorporated E 315 451-2900
East Syracuse *(G-4353)*

Ip Med Inc G 516 766-3800
Oceanside *(G-12541)*

J H M Engineering E 718 871-1810
Brooklyn *(G-2023)*

J Jamner Surgical Instrs Inc E 914 592-9051
Hawthorne *(G-5988)*

Jaracz Jr Joseph Paul G 716 533-1377
Orchard Park *(G-12722)*

Ken-Ton Open Mri PC G 716 876-7000
Kenmore *(G-6863)*

Lake Region Medical Inc C 716 662-5025
Orchard Park *(G-12725)*

Liberty Install Inc F 631 651-5655
Centerport *(G-3350)*

Manhattan Eastside Dev Corp F 212 305-3275
New York *(G-10685)*

◆ **Medical Depot Inc** C 516 998-4600
Port Washington *(G-13285)*

Medical Technology Products G 631 285-6640
Greenlawn *(G-5624)*

Medipoint Inc F 516 294-8822
Mineola *(G-8237)*

Medline Industries Inc B 845 344-3301
Middletown *(G-8163)*

Medsource Technologies LLC D 716 662-5025
Orchard Park *(G-12729)*

Memory Md Inc G 917 318-0215
New York *(G-10770)*

▲ **Misonix Inc** D 631 694-9555
Farmingdale *(G-4828)*

Modular Medical Corp E 718 829-2626
Bronx *(G-1334)*

◆ **Moog Inc** A 716 652-2000
Elma *(G-4453)*

N Y B P Inc G 585 624-2541
Mendon *(G-8093)*

Nano Vibronix Inc G 516 374-8330
Cedarhurst *(G-3335)*

Nanobionovum LLC F 518 581-1171
Saratoga Springs *(G-14591)*

▲ **Nasco Enterprises Inc** G 516 921-9696
Syosset *(G-15223)*

Nasiff Associates Inc G 315 676-2346
Central Square *(G-3391)*

▲ **Navilyst Medical Inc** A 800 833-9973
Glens Falls *(G-5436)*

Njr Medical Devices E 440 258-8204
Cedarhurst *(G-3336)*

▲ **Novamed-Usa Inc** E 914 789-2100
Elmsford *(G-4556)*

◆ **Ocala Group LLC** F 516 233-2750
New Hyde Park *(G-8555)*

Omnicare Anesthesia PC E 718 433-0044
Astoria *(G-439)*

▲ **Orics Industries Inc** E 718 461-8613
Farmingdale *(G-4839)*

Ortho Medical Products E 212 879-3700
New York *(G-11063)*

Ortho-Clinical Diagnostics Inc B 585 453-4771
Rochester *(G-13993)*

Ortho-Clinical Diagnostics Inc F 585 453-5200
Rochester *(G-13994)*

Orthocon Inc E 914 357-2600
Irvington *(G-6508)*

Ovitz Corporation G 585 474-4695
West Henrietta *(G-16246)*

▲ **P-Ryton Corp** F 718 937-7052
Long Island City *(G-7545)*

▲ **Pall Corporation** A 516 484-5400
Port Washington *(G-13295)*

Pall Corporation A 607 753-6041
Cortland *(G-3885)*

Parace Bionics LLC G 877 727-2231
New York *(G-11105)*

Parkchester Dps LLC C 718 823-4411
Bronx *(G-1352)*

Pavmed Inc G 212 401-1951
New York *(G-11127)*

Peter Digioia G 516 644-5517
Plainview *(G-13081)*

▼ **Pharma-Smart International Inc** E 585 427-0730
Rochester *(G-14017)*

Praxis Powder Technology Inc E 518 812-0112
Queensbury *(G-13437)*

Precimed Inc E 716 759-5600
Clarence *(G-3539)*

▲ **Proactive Medical Products LLC** G 845 205-6004
Mount Vernon *(G-8435)*

Professional Medical Devices F 914 835-0614
Harrison *(G-5733)*

Progressive Orthotics Ltd G 631 732-5556
Selden *(G-14766)*

Rdd Pharma Inc G 302 319-9970
New York *(G-11337)*

▲ **Reichert Inc** C 716 686-4500
Depew *(G-4104)*

Repro Med Systems Inc D 845 469-2042
Chester *(G-3480)*

Responselink Inc G 518 424-7776
Latham *(G-7092)*

Retia Medical LLC G 914 594-1986
Valhalla *(G-15746)*

RJ Harvey Instrument Corp F 845 359-3943
Tappan *(G-15471)*

Robert Bosch LLC E 315 733-3312
Utica *(G-15731)*

▲ **Schilling Forge Inc** E 315 454-4421
Syracuse *(G-15417)*

Seedlngs Lf Scnce Ventures LLC G 917 913-8511
New York *(G-11532)*

Seneca TEC Inc G 585 381-2645
Fairport *(G-4658)*

▼ **Sigma Intl Gen Med Apprtus LLC** B 585 798-3901
Medina *(G-7990)*

Simulaids Inc D 845 679-2475
Saugerties *(G-14616)*

Skyler Brand Ventures LLC G 646 979-5904
New York *(G-11615)*

Solid-Look Corporation G 917 683-1780
Douglaston *(G-4140)*

Soniquence LLC F 516 267-6400
Baldwin *(G-543)*

Sonomed Inc E 516 354-0900
New Hyde Park *(G-8564)*

St Silicones Corporation F 518 406-3208
Clifton Park *(G-3578)*

Striker Orthopedics E 585 381-1773
Rochester *(G-14147)*

Surgical Design Corp F 914 273-2445
Armonk *(G-410)*

S I C

38 MEASURING, ANALYZING AND CONTROLLING INSTRUMENTS; PHOTOGRAPHIC, MEDICAL AN SIC SECTION

Symmetry Medical Inc G 845 368-4573
Hillburn *(G-6155)*
T G M Products Inc G 631 491-0515
Wyandanch *(G-16696)*
Tril Inc G 631 645-7989
Copiague *(G-3789)*
▲ **Vante Inc** F 716 778-7691
Newfane *(G-12254)*
▲ **Vasomedical Inc** E 516 997-4600
Plainview *(G-13096)*
Vasomedical Solutions Inc D 516 997-4600
Plainview *(G-13097)*
Viterion Corporation F 914 333-6033
Elmsford *(G-4576)*
Vizio Medical Devices LLC F 646 845-7382
New York *(G-12049)*
▲ **W A Baum Co Inc** D 631 226-3940
Copiague *(G-3793)*
Welch Allyn Inc A 315 685-4100
Skaneateles Falls *(G-14882)*
◆ **Welch Allyn Inc** A 315 685-4100
Skaneateles Falls *(G-14883)*
Welch Allyn Inc A 315 685-4347
Skaneateles Falls *(G-14884)*
Wyeth Holdings LLC D 845 602-5000
Pearl River *(G-12913)*

3842 Orthopedic, Prosthetic & Surgical Appliances/Splys

Aaaaar Orthopedics Inc G 845 278-4938
Brewster *(G-1153)*
ACS Custom USA LLC G 646 559-5642
New York *(G-8729)*
▲ **Advanced Enterprises Inc** F 845 342-1009
Middletown *(G-8136)*
Advanced Prosthetics Orthotics F 516 365-7225
Manhasset *(G-7763)*
Advantage Orthotics Inc G 631 368-1754
East Northport *(G-4259)*
▲ **Aero Healthcare (us) LLC** G 855 225-2376
Valley Cottage *(G-15751)*
Agnovos Healthcare LLC F 646 502-5860
New York *(G-8770)*
Apollo Orthotics Corp G 516 333-3223
Carle Place *(G-3261)*
Argon Medical Devices Inc G 585 321-1130
Henrietta *(G-6031)*
Arimed Orthotics Prosthetics F 718 875-8754
Brooklyn *(G-1551)*
▲ **Atlantic Er Inc** E 516 294-3200
New Hyde Park *(G-8518)*
Avanti U S A Ltd F 716 695-5800
Tonawanda *(G-15524)*
Backtech Inc G 973 279-0838
New York *(G-8998)*
Beltone Corporation G 716 565-1015
Williamsville *(G-16570)*
Benway-Haworth-Lwlr-Iacosta He F 518 432-4070
Albany *(G-46)*
Bio-Chem Barrier Systems LLC G 631 261-2682
Northport *(G-12464)*
▲ **Biodex Medical Systems Inc** C 631 924-9000
Shirley *(G-14832)*
Biodex Medical Systems Inc E 631 924-3146
Shirley *(G-14833)*
Bionic Eye Technologies Inc G 845 505-5254
Fishkill *(G-4943)*
Brannock Device Co Inc E 315 475-9862
Liverpool *(G-7225)*
Buffalo Hearg & Speech E 716 558-1105
West Seneca *(G-16295)*
Byer California G 212 944-8989
New York *(G-9167)*
Center For Prosthetic G 845 336-7762
Kingston *(G-6893)*
Centinel Spine LLC G 212 583-9700
New York *(G-9241)*
Church Communities NY Inc E 518 589-5103
Elka Park *(G-4433)*
Church Communities NY Inc E 518 589-5103
Elka Park *(G-4434)*
▲ **Cirrus Healthcare Products LLC** E 631 692-7600
Cold Spring Harbor *(G-3629)*
Cityscape Ob/Gyn PLLC F 212 683-3595
New York *(G-9314)*
Columbia Dentoform Corporation D 718 482-1569
Long Island City *(G-7414)*
▲ **Community Products LLC** C 845 658-8799
Rifton *(G-13559)*
Community Products LLC E 845 658-7720
Chester *(G-3471)*
Community Products LLC E 845 572-3433
Chester *(G-3472)*
Community Products LLC G 518 589-5103
Elka Park *(G-4435)*
Complete Orthopedic Svcs Inc E 516 357-9113
East Meadow *(G-4248)*
Cranial Technologies Inc G 914 472-0975
Scarsdale *(G-14637)*
Creative Orthotics & Prosthet F 607 734-7215
Elmira *(G-4481)*
Creative Orthotics Prosthetics G 607 771-4672
Binghamton *(G-876)*
Creative Orthotics Prosthetics G 607 431-2526
Oneonta *(G-12636)*
Crosley Medical Products Inc F 631 595-2547
Syosset *(G-15213)*
▲ **Crye Precision LLC** C 718 246-3838
Brooklyn *(G-1736)*
Custom Sports Lab Inc G 212 832-1648
New York *(G-9436)*
▲ **Cy Plastics Works Inc** E 585 229-2555
Honeoye *(G-6260)*
Depuy Synthes Inc C 607 271-2500
Horseheads *(G-6312)*
Derm-Buro Inc E 516 694-8300
Plainview *(G-13050)*
East Cast Orthtics Prosthetics F 716 856-5192
Buffalo *(G-2809)*
▲ **East Coast Orthoic & Pros Cor** D 516 248-5566
Deer Park *(G-3970)*
East Coast Orthoic & Pros Cor F 212 923-2161
New York *(G-9608)*
Eis Inc E 585 426-5330
Rochester *(G-13774)*
Elwood Specialty Products Inc F 716 877-6622
Buffalo *(G-2815)*
Eschen Prosthetic & Orthotic L E 212 606-1262
New York *(G-9704)*
Eschen Prsthetic Orthotic Labs F 516 871-0029
Hicksville *(G-6085)*
◆ **Euromed Inc** D 845 359-4039
Orangeburg *(G-12677)*
Family Hearing Center G 845 897-3059
Fishkill *(G-4946)*
Far Rockaway Drugs Inc F 718 471-2500
Far Rockaway *(G-4701)*
Fiber Foot Appliances Inc F 631 465-9199
Farmingdale *(G-4765)*
Flexible Lifeline Systems Inc E 716 896-4949
Buffalo *(G-2829)*
Flo-Tech Orthotic & Prosthetic G 607 387-3070
Trumansburg *(G-15639)*
Gadabout USA Wheelchairs Inc F 585 338-2110
Rochester *(G-13821)*
▲ **Getinge Group Logistics Ameri** C 585 475-1400
Rochester *(G-13833)*
▲ **Getinge Usa Inc** C 800 475-9040
Rochester *(G-13834)*
Gfh Orthotic & Prosthetic Labs G 631 467-3725
Bohemia *(G-1028)*
Go Blue Technologies Ltd G 631 404-6285
North Babylon *(G-12360)*
Goldberg Prosthetic & Orthotic F 631 689-6606
East Setauket *(G-4302)*
Grand Slam Holdings LLC E 212 583-5000
New York *(G-9971)*
Great Lakes Orthpd Labs Inc G 716 878-7307
Buffalo *(G-2855)*
Green Prosthetics & Orthotics G 716 484-1088
Jamestown *(G-6719)*
Hakson Safety Wears Inc F 613 667-3015
Buffalo *(G-2863)*
▲ **Hand Care Inc** G 516 747-5649
Roslyn *(G-14447)*
Hanger Inc E 518 435-0840
Albany *(G-81)*
Hanger Inc E 518 438-4546
East Syracuse *(G-4345)*
Hanger Inc G 718 575-5504
Forest Hills *(G-5074)*
Hanger Inc F 516 678-3650
Rockville Centre *(G-14233)*
Hanger Prsthetcs & Ortho Inc G 631 751-6966
Stony Brook *(G-15166)*
Hanger Prsthetcs & Ortho Inc G 516 338-4466
Westbury *(G-16339)*
Hanger Prsthetcs & Ortho Inc F 607 277-6620
Ithaca *(G-6580)*
Hanger Prsthetcs & Ortho Inc G 607 776-8013
Bath *(G-644)*
Hanger Prsthetcs & Ortho Inc G 607 771-4672
Binghamton *(G-889)*
Hanger Prsthetcs & Ortho Inc G 315 472-5200
Syracuse *(G-15337)*
Hanger Prsthetcs & Ortho Inc D 607 795-1220
Elmira *(G-4489)*
Hanger Prsthetcs & Ortho Inc G 607 334-3320
Norwich *(G-12487)*
Hanger Prsthetcs & Ortho Inc G 315 789-4810
Geneva *(G-5328)*
◆ **Harvy Surgical Supply Corp** E 718 939-1122
Flushing *(G-5007)*
Hearing Spech Ctr of Rochester E 585 286-9373
Webster *(G-16086)*
Hersco-Orthotic Labs Corp E 718 391-0416
Long Island City *(G-7469)*
Higgins Supply Company Inc D 607 836-6474
Mc Graw *(G-7927)*
Howmedica Osteonics Corp G 518 783-1880
Latham *(G-7074)*
Howmedica Osteonics Corp G 516 484-0897
Port Washington *(G-13265)*
Hygrade G 718 488-9000
Brooklyn *(G-1989)*
Instrumentation Laboratory Co C 845 680-0028
Orangeburg *(G-12681)*
Integer Holdings Corporation D 716 759-5200
Clarence *(G-3534)*
J P R Pharmacy Inc F 718 327-0600
Far Rockaway *(G-4702)*
J-K Prosthetics & Orthotics E 914 699-2077
Mount Vernon *(G-8411)*
Kem Medical Products Corp G 631 454-6565
Farmingdale *(G-4802)*
Klemmt Orthotics & Prosthetics G 607 770-4400
Johnson City *(G-6813)*
Konrad Prosthetics & Orthotics F 516 485-9164
West Hempstead *(G-16219)*
▼ **Lakeland Industries Inc** C 631 981-9700
Ronkonkoma *(G-14367)*
Langer Biomechanics Inc D 800 645-5520
Ronkonkoma *(G-14369)*
Latorre Orthopedic Laboratory F 518 786-8655
Latham *(G-7085)*
Lehneis Orthotics Prosthetic G 516 790-1897
Hauppauge *(G-5864)*
Lehneis Orthotics Prosthetic G 631 369-3115
Riverhead *(G-13573)*
Lorelei Orthotics Prosthetics G 212 727-2011
New York *(G-10610)*
M H Mandelbaum Orthotic F 631 473-8668
Port Jefferson *(G-13222)*
Mayflower Splint Co E 631 549-5131
Dix Hills *(G-4121)*
▲ **Medi-Ray Inc** D 877 898-3003
Tuckahoe *(G-15644)*
▲ **Medi-Tech International Corp** G 800 333-0109
Brooklyn *(G-2187)*
Medical Acoustics LLC F 716 218-7353
Buffalo *(G-2943)*
Medical Action Industries Inc C 631 231-4600
Hauppauge *(G-5884)*
Medline Industries Inc B 845 344-3301
Middletown *(G-8163)*
▲ **Monaghan Medical Corporation** D 518 561-7330
Plattsburgh *(G-13135)*
Monaghan Medical Corporation G 315 472-2136
Syracuse *(G-15376)*
National Prosthetic Orthot G 718 767-8400
Bayside *(G-748)*
New Dynamics Corporation E 845 692-0022
Middletown *(G-8167)*
New England Orthotic & Prost G 212 682-9313
New York *(G-10922)*
New York Rhbilitative Svcs LLC F 516 239-0990
Valley Stream *(G-15787)*
North Shore Orthtics Prsthtics G 631 928-3040
Port Jeff STA *(G-13215)*
▲ **Nova Health Systems Inc** G 315 798-9018
Utica *(G-15727)*
Nucare Pharmacy Inc F 212 426-9300
New York *(G-11005)*
Nucare Pharmacy West LLC F 212 462-2525
New York *(G-11006)*
▲ **NY Orthopedic Usa Inc** D 718 852-5330
Brooklyn *(G-2279)*
▲ **Occunomix International LLC** E 631 741-1940
Port Jeff STA *(G-13216)*

Orcam Inc F 800 713-3741
New York *(G-11056)*
Ortho Medical Products E 212 879-3700
New York *(G-11063)*
Ortho Rite Inc E 914 235-9100
Mamaroneck *(G-7751)*
Orthocraft Inc G 718 951-1700
Brooklyn *(G-2292)*
Orthopedic Arts Laboratory Inc G 718 858-2400
Brooklyn *(G-2293)*
Orthopedic Treatment Facility G 718 898-7326
Woodside *(G-16669)*
Orthotics & Prosthetics Dept F 585 341-9299
Rochester *(G-13997)*
Overhead Door Corporation D 518 828-7652
Hudson *(G-6366)*
▲ **Pall Biomedical Inc** C 516 484-3600
Port Washington *(G-13294)*
Pall Corporation A 607 753-6041
Cortland *(G-3885)*
Pall Corporation A 607 753-6041
Cortland *(G-3886)*
Pall Corporation A 516 484-2818
Port Washington *(G-13296)*
Pall Corporation A 607 753-6041
Cortland *(G-3887)*
Palmer Industries Inc G 607 754-8741
Endicott *(G-4606)*
▲ **Palmer Industries Inc** E 607 754-2957
Endicott *(G-4607)*
Paradigm Spine LLC E 888 273-9897
New York *(G-11108)*
Peak Performance Design LLC G 518 302-9198
Lake Placid *(G-6977)*
▲ **Premier Brands America Inc** C 914 667-6200
Mount Vernon *(G-8432)*
Premier Brands of America Inc G 718 325-3000
Bronx *(G-1364)*
▲ **Proficient Surgical Eqp Inc** G 516 487-1175
Port Washington *(G-13299)*
▲ **Profoot Inc** E 718 965-8600
Brooklyn *(G-2354)*
Progressive Orthotics Ltd G 631 732-5556
Selden *(G-14766)*
Progressive Orthotics Ltd F 631 447-3860
East Patchogue *(G-4276)*
Prosthetic Rehabilitation Ctr G 845 565-8255
Newburgh *(G-12244)*
Prosthetics By Nelson Inc F 716 894-6666
Cheektowaga *(G-3456)*
Queue Solutions LLC F 631 750-6440
Bohemia *(G-1081)*
Rehabilitation Tech of Syracuse G 315 426-9920
Syracuse *(G-15406)*
Robert Cohen G 718 789-0996
Ozone Park *(G-12832)*
Rochester Orthopedic Labs G 585 272-1060
Rochester *(G-14089)*
▲ **Roner Inc** G 718 392-6020
Long Island City *(G-7579)*
Roner Inc C 718 392-6020
Long Island City *(G-7580)*
Sampsons Prsthtic Orthotic Lab E 518 374-6011
Schenectady *(G-14709)*
Schuster & Richard Labortories G 718 358-8607
College Point *(G-3664)*
Scientific Plastics Inc F 212 967-1199
New York *(G-11519)*
◆ **Silipos Holding LLC** G 716 283-0700
Niagara Falls *(G-12337)*
▲ **Skil-Care Corporation** C 914 963-2040
Yonkers *(G-16798)*
◆ **SPS Medical Supply Corp** D 585 359-0130
Rush *(G-14476)*
SPS Medical Supply Corp F 585 968-2377
Cuba *(G-3920)*
Stafford Labs Orthotics/Prosth F 845 692-5227
Middletown *(G-8176)*
Steriliz LLC G 585 415-5411
Rochester *(G-14144)*
Steris Corporation G 877 887-1788
Melville *(G-8066)*
Steris Corporation G 845 469-4087
Chester *(G-3484)*
Stj Orthotic Services Inc F 631 956-0181
Lindenhurst *(G-7195)*
Superior Glove Works USA Ltd E 716 626-9500
Cheektowaga *(G-3460)*
Syracuse Prosthetic Center Inc G 315 476-9697
Syracuse *(G-15440)*
▲ **Tape Systems Inc** F 914 668-3700
Mount Vernon *(G-8444)*
Thomas F Egan E 607 669-4822
Binghamton *(G-919)*
Todt Hill Audiological Svcs G 718 816-1952
Staten Island *(G-15147)*
Tonawanda Limb & Brace Inc G 716 695-1131
Tonawanda *(G-15583)*
Tumble Forms Inc E 315 429-3101
Dolgeville *(G-4138)*
Turbine Engine Comp Utica A 315 768-8070
Whitesboro *(G-16531)*
Ultrapedics Ltd G 718 748-4806
Brooklyn *(G-2598)*
Vcp Mobility Inc B 718 356-7827
Staten Island *(G-15150)*
Venture Respiratory Inc F 718 437-3633
Brooklyn *(G-2618)*
◆ **VSM Investors LLC** G 212 351-1600
New York *(G-12057)*
▲ **Widex Usa Inc** D 718 360-1000
Hauppauge *(G-5975)*
William H Shapiro G 212 263-7037
New York *(G-12112)*
Womens Health Care PC G 718 850-0009
Richmond Hill *(G-13517)*
Wyeth Holdings LLC D 845 602-5000
Pearl River *(G-12913)*
Xylon Industries Inc G 631 293-4717
Farmingdale *(G-4907)*

3843 Dental Eqpt & Splys

▲ **Air Techniques Inc** B 516 433-7676
Melville *(G-8000)*
Avalonbay Communities Inc E 516 484-7766
Glen Cove *(G-5362)*
Boehm Surgical Instrument Corp F 585 436-6584
Rochester *(G-13671)*
Brandt Equipment LLC G 718 994-0800
Bronx *(G-1232)*
▲ **Buffalo Dental Mfg Co Inc** E 516 496-7200
Syosset *(G-15210)*
Cettel Studio of New York Inc G 518 494-3622
Chestertown *(G-3490)*
▲ **Cmp Export Co Inc** E 518 434-3147
Albany *(G-61)*
◆ **Cmp Industries LLC** E 518 434-3147
Albany *(G-62)*
Cmp Industries LLC G 518 434-3147
Albany *(G-63)*
Columbia Dentoform Corporation D 718 482-1569
Long Island City *(G-7414)*
▲ **Corning Rubber Company Inc** F 631 738-0041
Ronkonkoma *(G-14329)*
Cpac Equipment Inc F 585 382-3223
Leicester *(G-7127)*
◆ **Crosstex International Inc** D 631 582-6777
Hauppauge *(G-5805)*
Crosstex International Inc F 631 582-6777
Hauppauge *(G-5806)*
Cynosure Inc G 516 594-3333
Hicksville *(G-6078)*
Darby Dental Supply G 516 688-6421
Jericho *(G-6785)*
▲ **Dedeco International Sales Inc** E 845 887-4840
Long Eddy *(G-7361)*
◆ **DenTek Oral Care Inc** D 865 983-1300
Tarrytown *(G-15477)*
Gallery 57 Dental E 212 246-8700
New York *(G-9877)*
Gan Kavod Inc G 315 797-3114
New Hartford *(G-8505)*
Glaxosmithkline LLC D 518 239-6901
East Durham *(G-4216)*
Grasers Dental Ceramics G 716 649-5100
Orchard Park *(G-12717)*
Henry Schein Fincl Svcs LLC G 631 843-5500
Melville *(G-8030)*
Impladent Ltd E 718 465-1810
Jamaica *(G-6651)*
J H M Engineering E 718 871-1810
Brooklyn *(G-2023)*
Jeffrey D Menoff G 716 665-1468
Jamestown *(G-6733)*
▲ **JM Murray Center Inc** C 607 756-9913
Cortland *(G-3879)*
JM Murray Center Inc C 607 756-0246
Cortland *(G-3880)*
Kay See Dental Mfg Co F 816 842-2817
New York *(G-10421)*
Lelab Dental Laboratory Inc G 516 561-5050
Valley Stream *(G-15785)*
Light Dental Labs Inc G 516 785-7730
Massapequa *(G-7881)*
◆ **Lornamead Inc** D 716 874-7190
New York *(G-10611)*
Lucas Dental Equipment Co Inc F 631 244-2807
Bohemia *(G-1052)*
Luitpold Pharmaceuticals Inc E 631 924-4000
Shirley *(G-14839)*
Marotta Dental Studio Inc E 631 249-7520
Farmingdale *(G-4816)*
Martins Dental Studio G 315 788-0800
Watertown *(G-16026)*
Mini-Max Dntl Repr Eqpmnts Inc G 631 242-0322
Deer Park *(G-4010)*
Nu Life Restorations of L I D 516 489-5200
Old Westbury *(G-12591)*
Oramaax Dental Products Inc F 516 771-8514
Freeport *(G-5172)*
Precision Dental Cabinets Inc F 631 543-3870
Smithtown *(G-14906)*
Precision Dental Ceramics of B F 716 681-4133
Bowmansville *(G-1122)*
Professional Manufacturers F 631 586-2440
Deer Park *(G-4030)*
Safe-Dent Enterprises LLC G 845 362-0141
Monsey *(G-8296)*
▲ **Schilling Forge Inc** E 315 454-4421
Syracuse *(G-15417)*
Smile Specialists G 877 337-6135
New York *(G-11623)*
Stylecraft Interiors Inc F 516 487-2133
Great Neck *(G-5594)*
Temrex Corporation E 516 868-6221
Freeport *(G-5186)*
Tiger Supply Inc G 631 293-2700
Farmingdale *(G-4895)*
Total Dntl Implant Sltions LLC G 212 877-3777
Valley Stream *(G-15800)*
▲ **Valplast International Corp** F 516 442-3923
Westbury *(G-16385)*
Vincent Martino Dental Lab F 716 674-7800
Buffalo *(G-3119)*

3844 X-ray Apparatus & Tubes

▲ **Air Techniques Inc** B 516 433-7676
Melville *(G-8000)*
American Access Care LLC F 631 582-9729
Hauppauge *(G-5763)*
▲ **Biodex Medical Systems Inc** C 631 924-9000
Shirley *(G-14832)*
▲ **Community Products LLC** C 845 658-8799
Rifton *(G-13559)*
Dra Imaging PC E 845 296-1057
Wappingers Falls *(G-15929)*
▲ **Flow X Ray Corporation** D 631 242-9729
Deer Park *(G-3976)*
Genesis Digital Imaging Inc G 310 305-7358
Rochester *(G-13830)*
Mitegen LLC G 607 266-8877
Ithaca *(G-6596)*
▼ **Multiwire Laboratories Ltd** G 607 257-3378
Ithaca *(G-6598)*
New York Imaging Service Inc F 716 834-8022
Tonawanda *(G-15561)*
Phantom Laboratory Inc F 518 692-1190
Greenwich *(G-5644)*
Photo Medic Equipment Inc D 631 242-6600
Deer Park *(G-4025)*
▲ **Quantum Medical Imaging LLC** D 631 567-5800
Rochester *(G-14063)*
R M F Health Management L L C E 718 854-5400
Wantagh *(G-15926)*
Siemens Corporation F 202 434-7800
New York *(G-11577)*
Siemens USA Holdings Inc B 212 258-4000
New York *(G-11580)*
Surescan Corporation E 607 321-0042
Binghamton *(G-917)*
Varex Imaging Corporation A 315 234-6853
Liverpool *(G-7269)*
◆ **VJ Technologies Inc** E 631 589-8800
Bohemia *(G-1106)*
◆ **Wolf X-Ray Corporation** D 631 242-9729
Deer Park *(G-4063)*

3845 Electromedical & Electrotherapeutic Apparatus

Advd Heart Phys & Surgs ....F 212 434-3000
New York (G-8759)
Argon Medical Devices Inc ....G 585 321-1130
Henrietta (G-6031)
▲ Biofeedback Instrument Corp ....G 212 222-5665
New York (G-9087)
▲ Buffalo Filter LLC ....D 716 835-7000
Lancaster (G-7011)
C R Bard Inc ....A 518 793-2531
Glens Falls (G-5420)
Caliber Imging Diagnostics Inc ....E 585 239-9800
Rochester (G-13687)
City Sports Imaging Inc ....E 212 481-3600
New York (G-9313)
Complex Biosystems Inc ....G 315 464-8007
Baldwinsville (G-553)
Conmed Andover Medical Inc ....F 315 797-8375
Utica (G-15685)
Conmed Corporation ....D 315 797-8375
Utica (G-15686)
◆ Conmed Corporation ....B 315 797-8375
Utica (G-15687)
Ddc Technologies Inc ....G 516 594-1533
Oceanside (G-12535)
Elizabeth Wood ....G 315 492-5470
Syracuse (G-15315)
Empire Open Mri ....G 914 961-1777
Yonkers (G-16756)
Equivital Inc ....E 646 513-4169
New York (G-9698)
Excel Technology Inc ....F 212 355-3400
New York (G-9749)
Fonar Corporation ....C 631 694-2929
Melville (G-8025)
Forest Medical LLC ....G 315 434-9000
East Syracuse (G-4341)
Gary Gelbfish MD ....G 718 258-3004
Brooklyn (G-1918)
Global Instrumentation LLC ....F 315 682-0272
Manlius (G-7778)
Gravity East Village Inc ....G 212 388-9788
New York (G-9979)
Health Care Originals Inc ....G 585 471-8215
Rochester (G-13864)
Imacor Inc ....E 516 393-0970
Garden City (G-5262)
▲ Infimed Inc ....D 315 453-4545
Liverpool (G-7236)
Infimed Inc ....G 585 383-1710
Pittsford (G-13016)
Integrated Medical Devices ....G 315 457-4200
Liverpool (G-7238)
Isimulate LLC ....G 877 947-2831
Albany (G-87)
J H M Engineering ....E 718 871-1810
Brooklyn (G-2023)
Jaracz Jr Joseph Paul ....G 716 533-1377
Orchard Park (G-12722)
Jarvik Heart Inc ....E 212 397-3911
New York (G-10309)
Juvly Aesthetics Inc ....D 614 686-3627
New York (G-10388)
Kal Manufacturing Corporation ....E 585 265-4310
Webster (G-16088)
Laser and Varicose Vein Trtmnt ....G 718 667-1777
Staten Island (G-15100)
Med Services Inc ....D 631 218-6450
Bohemia (G-1058)
▲ Misonix Inc ....D 631 694-9555
Farmingdale (G-4828)
Nanovibronix Inc ....F 914 233-3004
Elmsford (G-4554)
Natus Medical Incorporated ....G 631 457-4430
Hauppauge (G-5899)
Netech Corporation ....F 631 531-0100
Farmingdale (G-4836)
New Primecare ....G 516 822-4031
Hewlett (G-6049)
New York Laser & Aestheticks ....G 516 627-7777
Roslyn (G-14448)
Nirx Medical Technologies LLC ....F 516 676-6479
Glen Head (G-5384)
▲ Novamed-Usa Inc ....E 914 789-2100
Elmsford (G-4556)
Ocean Cardiac Monitoring ....G 631 777-3700
Deer Park (G-4021)
Pharmadva LLC ....G 585 469-1410
Rochester (G-14018)
◆ Philips Medical Systems Mr ....B 518 782-1122
Latham (G-7089)
Qrs Technologies Inc ....G 315 457-5300
Liverpool (G-7259)
Quadrant Biosciences Inc ....F 315 614-2325
Syracuse (G-15399)
▲ Radiancy Inc ....F 845 398-1647
Orangeburg (G-12690)
Ray Medica Inc ....E 952 885-0500
New York (G-11331)
▲ Sonicor Inc ....F 631 920-6555
West Babylon (G-16194)
Sonomed Inc ....E 516 354-0900
New Hyde Park (G-8564)
▲ Soterix Medical Inc ....F 888 990-8327
New York (G-11652)
Sun Scientific Inc ....G 914 479-5108
Dobbs Ferry (G-4131)
Teledyne Optech Inc ....F 585 427-8310
Rochester (G-14164)
Ultradian Diagnostics LLC ....G 518 618-0046
Rensselaer (G-13479)
University of Rochester ....B 585 275-3483
Rochester (G-14190)
▲ Vasomedical Inc ....E 516 997-4600
Plainview (G-13096)
▲ Vermed Inc ....D 800 669-6905
Buffalo (G-3117)
▲ Vermont Medical Inc ....C 802 463-9976
Buffalo (G-3118)
▲ Z-Axis Inc ....D 315 548-5000
Phelps (G-12984)

3851 Ophthalmic Goods

21st Century Optics Inc ....E 347 527-1079
Long Island City (G-7362)
Acuity Polymers Inc ....G 585 458-8409
Rochester (G-13601)
Alden Optical Laboratory Inc ....F 716 937-9181
Lancaster (G-7006)
Art-Craft Optical Company Inc ....E 585 546-6640
Rochester (G-13643)
Bausch & Lomb Holdings Inc ....G 585 338-6000
New York (G-9028)
◆ Bausch & Lomb Incorporated ....B 585 338-6000
Rochester (G-13655)
Bausch & Lomb Incorporated ....D 585 338-6000
Rochester (G-13656)
Bausch & Lomb Incorporated ....B 585 338-6000
Rochester (G-13657)
Co-Optics America Lab Inc ....E 607 432-0557
Oneonta (G-12631)
Colors In Optics Ltd ....D 718 845-0300
New Hyde Park (G-8523)
Coopervision Inc ....A 585 385-6810
West Henrietta (G-16235)
Coopervision Inc ....A 585 889-3301
Scottsville (G-14749)
▲ Coopervision Inc ....C 585 385-6810
Victor (G-15838)
▲ Coopervision Inc ....D 585 385-6810
Victor (G-15839)
▲ Corinne McCormack Inc ....F 212 868-7919
New York (G-9401)
Corneal Design Corporation ....F 301 670-7076
Lima (G-7150)
▲ Designs For Vision Inc ....C 631 585-3300
Bohemia (G-1016)
Doug Lambertson Od ....G 718 698-9300
Staten Island (G-15070)
Edroy Products Co Inc ....G 845 358-6600
Nyack (G-12507)
Empire Optical Inc ....F 585 454-4470
Rochester (G-13781)
Eponym Inc ....G 646 918-4586
Brooklyn (G-1843)
Equicheck LLC ....G 631 987-6356
Patchogue (G-12865)
▲ Esc Control Electronics LLC ....E 631 467-5328
Sayville (G-14627)
Essilor Laboratories Amer Inc ....E 845 365-6700
Orangeburg (G-12676)
▲ Eyeworks Inc ....G 585 454-4470
Rochester (G-13800)
Frame Works America Inc ....E 631 288-1300
Westhampton Beach (G-16403)
Glasses USA LLC ....F 212 784-6094
New York (G-9932)
Hirsch Optical Corp ....D 516 752-2211
Farmingdale (G-4780)
▲ His Vision Inc ....E 585 254-0022
Rochester (G-13870)
Humanware USA Inc ....E 800 722-3393
Champlain (G-3410)
J I Intrntnal Contact Lens Lab ....G 718 997-1212
Rego Park (G-13462)
Kathmando Valley Preservation ....F 212 727-0074
New York (G-10417)
Lens Lab ....G 718 379-2020
Bronx (G-1317)
Lens Lab Express ....G 718 921-5488
Brooklyn (G-2110)
Lens Lab Express of Graham Ave ....G 718 486-0117
Brooklyn (G-2111)
Lens Lab Express Southern Blvd ....G 718 626-5184
Astoria (G-434)
M Factory USA Inc ....G 917 410-7878
Brooklyn (G-2147)
Mager & Gougelman Inc ....G 212 661-3939
New York (G-10663)
Mager & Gougelman Inc ....G 212 661-3939
Hempstead (G-6019)
Mager & Gougelman Inc ....G 516 489-0202
Hempstead (G-6020)
Mark F Rosenhaft N A O ....G 516 374-1010
Cedarhurst (G-3334)
Modo Retail LLC ....E 212 965-4900
New York (G-10830)
▲ Moscot Wholesale Corp ....G 212 647-1550
New York (G-10846)
North Bronx Retinal & Ophthlmi ....G 347 535-4932
Bronx (G-1345)
Optika Eyes Ltd ....G 631 567-8852
Sayville (G-14633)
▲ Optisource International Inc ....E 631 924-8360
Bellport (G-810)
Optogenics of Syracuse Inc ....D 315 446-3000
Syracuse (G-15388)
▲ Parker Warby Retail Inc ....E 646 517-5223
New York (G-11117)
Provision Supply LLC ....F 347 623-0237
Brooklyn (G-2359)
Spectacle Optical Inc ....G 646 706-1015
Rego Park (G-13469)
Strauss Eye Prosthetics Inc ....G 585 424-1350
Rochester (G-14146)
Surgical Design Corp ....F 914 273-2445
Armonk (G-410)
▲ Tri-Supreme Optical LLC ....D 631 249-2020
Farmingdale (G-4899)
Winchester Optical Company ....E 607 734-4251
Elmira (G-4507)
Wyeth Holdings LLC ....D 845 602-5000
Pearl River (G-12913)
Xinya International Trading Co ....G 212 216-9681
New York (G-12152)
▲ Zyloware Corporation ....D 914 708-1200
Port Chester (G-13211)

3861 Photographic Eqpt & Splys

▲ Air Techniques Inc ....B 516 433-7676
Melville (G-8000)
▲ All-Pro Imaging Corp ....E 516 433-7676
Melville (G-8001)
Apexx Omni-Graphics Inc ....D 718 326-3330
Maspeth (G-7822)
Astrodyne Inc ....G 516 536-5755
Oceanside (G-12532)
AVI-Spl Employee ....B 212 840-4801
New York (G-8977)
Avid Technology Inc ....E 212 983-2424
New York (G-8978)
▲ Bescor Video Accessories Ltd ....F 631 420-1717
Farmingdale (G-4727)
Big Indie - Beautiful Boy LLC ....G 917 464-5599
Woodstock (G-16684)
▲ Cannon Industries Inc ....D 585 254-8080
Rochester (G-13690)
Carestream Health Inc ....B 585 627-1800
Rochester (G-13692)
◆ Champion Photochemistry Inc ....D 585 760-6444
Rochester (G-13706)
Chemung Cnty Chpter Nysarc Inc ....C 607 734-6151
Elmira (G-4477)
Cine Magnetics Inc ....E 914 667-6707
Mount Vernon (G-8387)
Core Swx LLC ....F 516 595-7488
Plainview (G-13047)
◆ Cpac Inc ....E 585 382-3223
Leicester (G-7126)

Creatron Services Inc .... E 516 437-5119
Floral Park *(G-4961)*
Critical Imaging LLC .... E 315 732-5020
Utica *(G-15689)*
▲ Dnp Electronics America LLC .... D 212 503-1060
New York *(G-9543)*
Dolby Laboratories Inc .... F 212 767-1700
New York *(G-9546)*
Easterncctv (usa) LLC .... F 516 870-3779
Plainview *(G-13052)*
Eastman Kodak Company .... D 585 722-2187
Rochester *(G-13760)*
Eastman Kodak Company .... B 585 724-4000
Rochester *(G-13761)*
Eastman Kodak Company .... D 585 724-5600
Rochester *(G-13762)*
Eastman Kodak Company .... D 585 722-9695
Pittsford *(G-13010)*
Eastman Kodak Company .... D 585 726-6261
Rochester *(G-13763)*
Eastman Kodak Company .... D 585 724-4000
Rochester *(G-13764)*
Eastman Kodak Company .... F 800 698-3324
Rochester *(G-13765)*
Eastman Kodak Company .... D 585 722-4385
Rochester *(G-13766)*
Eastman Kodak Company .... D 585 588-5598
Rochester *(G-13767)*
Eastman Kodak Company .... C 585 726-7000
Rochester *(G-13768)*
Eastman Kodak Company .... G 585 722-4007
Rochester *(G-13769)*
Eastman Kodak Company .... D 585 588-3896
Rochester *(G-13770)*
Eastman Kodak Company .... E 585 724-4000
Rochester *(G-13771)*
Eastman Park Micrographics Inc .... G 866 934-4376
Rochester *(G-13772)*
Ebsco Industries Inc .... G 585 398-2000
Farmington *(G-4912)*
Efam Enterprises LLC .... E 718 204-1760
Long Island City *(G-7435)*
Emda Inc .... F 631 243-6363
Plainview *(G-13055)*
Facsimile Cmmncations Inds Inc .... D 212 741-6400
New York *(G-9770)*
Fanvision Entertainment LLC .... G 917 297-7428
New York *(G-9783)*
Fluxdata Incorporated .... G 800 425-0176
Rochester *(G-13811)*
Garys Loft .... G 212 244-0970
New York *(G-9884)*
Geospatial Systems Inc .... F 585 427-8310
West Henrietta *(G-16241)*
Gpc International Inc .... C 631 752-9600
Melville *(G-8027)*
Henrys Deals Inc .... E 347 821-4685
Brooklyn *(G-1972)*
▲ Hilord Chemical Corporation .... E 631 234-7373
Hauppauge *(G-5845)*
Jack L Popkin & Co Inc .... G 718 361-6700
Kew Gardens *(G-6875)*
Just Lamps of New York Inc .... F 716 626-2240
Buffalo *(G-2898)*
Kelmar Systems Inc .... F 631 421-1230
Huntington Station *(G-6450)*
◆ Kodak Alaris Inc .... B 585 290-2891
Rochester *(G-13906)*
Kodak Graphic Communications .... F 585 724-4000
Rochester *(G-13907)*
▲ Konica Mnolta Sups Mfg USA Inc .... D 845 294-8400
Goshen *(G-5481)*
Kyle Editing LLC .... G 212 675-3464
New York *(G-10490)*
Labgrafix Printing Inc .... G 516 280-8300
Lynbrook *(G-7667)*
Lake Image Systems Inc .... F 585 321-3630
Henrietta *(G-6034)*
Lasertech Crtridge RE-Builders .... G 518 373-1246
Clifton Park *(G-3569)*
▲ Lowel-Light Manufacturing Inc .... E 718 921-0600
Brooklyn *(G-2137)*
▲ Mekatronics Incorporated .... E 516 883-6805
Port Washington *(G-13288)*
Mirion Technologies Ist Corp .... D 607 562-4300
Horseheads *(G-6321)*
▲ Norazza Inc .... G 716 706-1160
Buffalo *(G-2973)*
◆ Printer Components Inc .... G 585 924-5190
Fairport *(G-4651)*
Qls Solutions Group Inc .... E 716 852-2203
Buffalo *(G-3022)*
▲ Rear View Safety Inc .... E 855 815-3842
Brooklyn *(G-2389)*
Rockland Colloid Corp .... G 845 359-5559
Piermont *(G-12994)*
Rosco Collision Avoidance Inc .... G 718 526-2601
Jamaica *(G-6676)*
Seneca TEC Inc .... G 585 381-2645
Fairport *(G-4658)*
Shelley Promotions Inc .... G 212 924-4987
New York *(G-11562)*
▲ Sima Technologies LLC .... G 412 828-9130
Hauppauge *(G-5940)*
Stallion Technologies Inc .... G 315 622-1176
Liverpool *(G-7263)*
Thermo Cidtec Inc .... E 315 451-9410
Liverpool *(G-7267)*
Tiffen Company LLC .... G 631 273-2500
Hauppauge *(G-5959)*
▲ Tiffen Company LLC .... D 631 273-2500
Hauppauge *(G-5960)*
Toner-N-More Inc .... G 718 232-6200
Brooklyn *(G-2569)*
Truesense Imaging Inc .... C 585 784-5500
Rochester *(G-14178)*
▲ Turner Bellows Inc .... E 585 235-4456
Rochester *(G-14181)*
Va Inc .... E 585 385-5930
Rochester *(G-14195)*
▲ Vishay Thin Film LLC .... C 716 283-4025
Niagara Falls *(G-12348)*
Watec America Corporation .... E 702 434-6111
Middletown *(G-8184)*
Xerox Corporation .... A 585 422-4564
Webster *(G-16108)*
Xerox Corporation .... D 212 330-1386
New York *(G-12150)*
Xerox Corporation .... E 518 434-6543
Albany *(G-143)*
Xerox Corporation .... C 585 427-4500
Rochester *(G-14214)*
Xerox Corporation .... C 585 264-5584
Rochester *(G-14215)*

3873 Watch & Clock Devices & Parts

▲ American Time Mfg Ltd .... F 585 266-5120
Rochester *(G-13629)*
▲ Croton Watch Co Inc .... E 800 443-7639
West Nyack *(G-16268)*
▲ E Gluck Corporation .... C 718 784-0700
Little Neck *(G-7218)*
▲ Ewatchfactory Corp .... G 212 564-8318
New York *(G-9743)*
▼ First Sbf Holding Inc .... E 845 425-9882
Valley Cottage *(G-15754)*
▲ Game Time LLC .... F 914 557-9662
New York *(G-9879)*
Gelber & Mundy Jewelry Co Inc .... G 516 482-1585
Great Neck *(G-5560)*
▲ Geneva Watch Company Inc .... E 212 221-1177
New York *(G-9904)*
H Best Ltd .... F 212 354-2400
New York *(G-10013)*
Hammerman Bros Inc .... G 212 956-2800
New York *(G-10026)*
Justa Company .... G 718 932-6139
Long Island City *(G-7484)*
Life Watch Technology Inc .... D 917 669-2428
Flushing *(G-5023)*
Marco Moore Inc .... D 212 575-2090
Great Neck *(G-5571)*
National Time Recording Eqp Co .... F 212 227-3310
New York *(G-10887)*
Olympic Jewelry Inc .... G 212 768-7004
New York *(G-11037)*
◆ Pavana USA Inc .... G 646 833-8811
New York *(G-11126)*
◆ Pedre Corp .... E 212 868-2935
Hicksville *(G-6124)*
▲ Precision International Co Inc .... G 212 268-9090
New York *(G-11229)*
Richemont North America Inc .... G 212 355-7052
New York *(G-11386)*
Richemont North America Inc .... G 212 644-9500
New York *(G-11387)*
▲ Sarina Accessories LLC .... F 212 239-8106
New York *(G-11490)*
◆ Stuhrling Original LLC .... E 718 840-5760
Brooklyn *(G-2527)*
▲ TWI Watches LLC .... E 718 663-3969
Brooklyn *(G-2595)*
▲ Watchcraft Inc .... G 347 531-0382
Long Island City *(G-7635)*

39 MISCELLANEOUS MANUFACTURING INDUSTRIES

3911 Jewelry: Precious Metal

1ktgold Inc .... F 212 302-8200
White Plains *(G-16415)*
A & V Castings Inc .... G 212 997-0042
New York *(G-8689)*
A Jaffe Inc .... C 212 843-7464
New York *(G-8697)*
Aaron Group LLC .... D 718 392-5454
Mount Vernon *(G-8372)*
Abraham Jwly Designers & Mfrs .... F 212 944-1149
New York *(G-8713)*
Abrimian Bros Corp .... F 212 382-1106
New York *(G-8714)*
Adamor Inc .... G 212 688-8885
New York *(G-8733)*
AF Design Inc .... G 347 548-5273
New York *(G-8764)*
Alart Inc .... G 212 840-1508
New York *(G-8782)*
◆ Albea Cosmetics America Inc .... E 212 371-5100
New York *(G-8784)*
Alchemy Simya Inc .... E 646 230-1122
New York *(G-8786)*
◆ Ale Viola LLC .... D 212 868-3808
New York *(G-8789)*
Alex Archer Designs Ltd .... G 212 219-8664
New York *(G-8791)*
Alex Sepkus Inc .... F 212 391-8466
New York *(G-8792)*
Alexander Primak Jewelry Inc .... D 212 398-0287
New York *(G-8793)*
▲ Alfred Butler Inc .... F 516 829-7460
Great Neck *(G-5529)*
All The Rage Inc .... G 516 605-2001
Hicksville *(G-6058)*
▲ Almond Jewelers Inc .... F 516 933-6000
Port Washington *(G-13242)*
▲ Alpine Creations Ltd .... G 212 308-9353
New York *(G-8813)*
Ambras Fine Jewelry Inc .... E 718 784-5252
Long Island City *(G-7375)*
American Craft Jewelers Inc .... G 718 972-0945
Brooklyn *(G-1520)*
American Originals Corporation .... G 212 836-4155
New York *(G-8835)*
Anatoli Inc .... F 845 334-9000
West Hurley *(G-16256)*
▲ Anima Group LLC .... G 917 913-2053
New York *(G-8868)*
Apicella Jewelers Inc .... E 212 840-2024
New York *(G-8884)*
▲ AR & AR Jewelry Inc .... E 212 764-7916
New York *(G-8895)*
Arringement International Inc .... G 347 323-7974
Flushing *(G-4986)*
Art-TEC Jewelry Designs Ltd .... E 212 719-2941
New York *(G-8918)*
Ateliers Tamalet Corp .... E 929 325-7976
New York *(G-8944)*
Ateret LLC .... G 212 819-0777
New York *(G-8945)*
Atlantic Precious Metal Cast .... G 718 937-7100
Long Island City *(G-7394)*
Atr Jewelry Inc .... F 212 819-0075
New York *(G-8957)*
B K Jewelry Contractor Inc .... E 212 398-9093
New York *(G-8989)*
Barber Brothers Jewelry Mfg .... F 212 819-0666
New York *(G-9013)*
Baroka Creations Inc .... G 212 768-0527
New York *(G-9019)*
Bartholomew Mazza Ltd Inc .... E 212 935-4530
New York *(G-9023)*
Bellataire Diamonds Inc .... F 212 687-8881
New York *(G-9039)*
Benlee Enterprises LLC .... F 212 730-7330
Long Island City *(G-7399)*
▲ BH Multi Com Corp .... E 212 944-0020
New York *(G-9069)*
Bielka Inc .... G 212 980-6841
New York *(G-9074)*

SIC

Employee Codes: A=Over 500 employees, B=251-500
C=101-250, D=51-100, E=20-50, F=10-19, G=5-9

2019 Harris
New York Manufacturers Directory

797

Billanti Casting Co Inc.....E..... 516 775-4800
New Hyde Park (G-8520)
BJG Services LLC.....E..... 516 592-5692
New York (G-9095)
Bourghol Brothers Inc.....G..... 845 268-9752
Congers (G-3712)
Bral Nader Fine Jewelry Inc.....G..... 800 493-1222
New York (G-9134)
▲ Brannkey Inc.....D..... 212 371-1515
New York (G-9135)
Brilliant Jewelers/Mjj Inc.....C..... 212 353-2326
New York (G-9142)
Brilliant Stars Collection Inc.....G..... 516 365-9000
Great Neck (G-5540)
Bristol Seamless Ring Corp.....F..... 212 874-2645
New York (G-9143)
Burke & Bannayan.....G..... 585 723-1010
Rochester (G-13681)
Carlo Monte Designs Inc.....G..... 212 935-5611
New York (G-9209)
Carr Manufacturing Jewelers.....G..... 518 783-6093
Latham (G-7069)
Carvin French Jewelers Inc.....E..... 212 755-6474
New York (G-9219)
Chaindom Enterprises Inc.....G..... 212 719-4778
New York (G-9256)
Chameleon Gems Inc.....F..... 516 829-3333
Great Neck (G-5544)
Charis & Mae Inc.....G..... 212 641-0816
New York (G-9261)
Charles Krypell Inc.....E..... 212 752-3313
New York (G-9263)
Charles Perrella Inc.....E..... 845 348-4777
Nyack (G-12502)
▲ Charles Vaillant Inc.....G..... 212 752-4832
New York (G-9265)
▲ Christopher Designs Inc.....E..... 212 382-1013
New York (G-9294)
▲ Cigar Oasis LLC.....G..... 516 520-5258
Farmingdale (G-4735)
▲ CJ Jewelry Inc.....F..... 212 719-2464
New York (G-9316)
▲ Clyde Duneier Inc.....D..... 212 398-1122
New York (G-9336)
Concord Jewelry Mfg Co LLC.....E..... 212 719-4030
New York (G-9373)
▲ Creative Gold LLC.....E..... 718 686-2225
Brooklyn (G-1728)
Crown Jewelers Intl Inc.....G..... 212 420-7800
New York (G-9426)
▲ Csi International Inc.....E..... 800 441-2895
Niagara Falls (G-12276)
▲ D R S Inc.....E..... 212 819-0237
New York (G-9449)
David Friedman Chain Co Inc.....F..... 212 684-1760
New York (G-9480)
David Howell Product Design.....E..... 914 666-4080
Bedford Hills (G-774)
▲ David S Diamonds Inc.....F..... 212 921-8029
New York (G-9484)
David Weisz & Sons USA LLC.....G..... 212 840-4747
New York (G-9487)
David Yurman Enterprises LLC.....G..... 914 539-4444
White Plains (G-16443)
◆ David Yurman Enterprises LLC.....B..... 212 896-1550
New York (G-9488)
David Yurman Enterprises LLC.....G..... 845 928-8660
Central Valley (G-3395)
David Yurman Retail LLC.....G..... 877 226-1400
New York (G-9489)
Diamond Distributors Inc.....G..... 212 921-9188
New York (G-9522)
Diana Kane Incorporated.....G..... 718 638-6520
Brooklyn (G-1772)
Dimoda Designs Inc.....E..... 212 355-8166
New York (G-9530)
Donna Distefano Ltd.....G..... 212 594-3757
New York (G-9548)
Doris Panos Designs Ltd.....G..... 631 245-0580
Melville (G-8017)
▲ Duran Jewelry Inc.....G..... 212 431-1959
New York (G-9586)
Dweck Industries Inc.....G..... 718 615-1695
Brooklyn (G-1797)
▲ Eagle Regalia Co Inc.....F..... 845 425-2245
Spring Valley (G-14989)
Earring King Jewelry Mfg Inc.....G..... 718 544-7947
New York (G-9606)
Eastern Jewelry Mfg Co Inc.....E..... 212 840-0001
New York (G-9610)
Echo Group Inc.....F..... 917 608-7440
New York (G-9621)
Eclipse Collection Jewelers.....G..... 212 764-6883
New York (G-9623)
Ed Levin Inc.....E..... 518 677-8595
Cambridge (G-3181)
Efron Designs Ltd.....G..... 718 482-8440
Long Island City (G-7436)
Elegant Jewelers Mfg Co Inc.....F..... 212 869-4951
New York (G-9643)
▼ Ema Jewelry Inc.....D..... 212 575-8989
New York (G-9662)
Emsaru USA Corp.....G..... 212 459-9355
New York (G-9669)
Eternal Line.....G..... 845 856-1999
Sparrow Bush (G-14972)
Euro Bands Inc.....F..... 212 719-9777
New York (G-9728)
F M Abdulky Inc.....F..... 607 272-7373
Ithaca (G-6576)
F M Abdulky Inc.....G..... 607 272-7373
Ithaca (G-6577)
Fam Creations.....E..... 212 869-4833
New York (G-9777)
Fantasia Jewelry Inc.....E..... 212 921-9590
New York (G-9781)
Feldman Jewelry Creations Inc.....G..... 718 438-8895
Brooklyn (G-1872)
Five Star Creations Inc.....E..... 845 783-1187
Monroe (G-8269)
Frank Blancato Inc.....F..... 212 768-1495
New York (G-9841)
Fuzion Creations Intl LLC.....E..... 718 369-8800
Brooklyn (G-1912)
Gemoro Inc.....G..... 212 768-8844
New York (G-9896)
Gemveto Jewelry Company Inc.....E..... 212 755-2522
New York (G-9898)
George Lederman Inc.....G..... 212 753-4556
New York (G-9911)
Giovane Ltd.....E..... 212 332-7373
New York (G-9923)
Global Gem Corporation.....G..... 212 350-9936
New York (G-9941)
Gold & Diamonds Wholesale Outl.....G..... 718 438-7888
Brooklyn (G-1937)
Goldarama Company Inc.....G..... 212 730-7299
New York (G-9951)
Golden Integrity Inc.....E..... 212 764-6753
New York (G-9955)
Goldmark Products Inc.....E..... 631 777-3343
Farmingdale (G-4773)
Gorga Fehren Fine Jewelry LLC.....G..... 646 861-3595
New York (G-9959)
Gottlieb & Sons Inc.....E..... 212 575-1907
New York (G-9962)
▲ Gramercy Jewelry Mfg Corp.....E..... 212 268-0461
New York (G-9969)
Grandeur Creations Inc.....G..... 212 643-1277
New York (G-9972)
Grinnell Designs Ltd.....E..... 212 391-5277
New York (G-9991)
▲ Guild Diamond Products Inc.....F..... 212 871-0007
New York (G-10007)
H & T Goldman Corporation.....G..... 800 822-0272
New York (G-10012)
H C Kionka & Co Inc.....F..... 212 227-3155
New York (G-10014)
Hammerman Bros Inc.....G..... 212 956-2800
New York (G-10026)
Hanna Altinis Co Inc.....E..... 718 706-1134
Long Island City (G-7466)
▲ Hansa Usa LLC.....E..... 646 412-6407
New York (G-10034)
▲ Harry Winston Inc.....C..... 212 399-1000
New York (G-10043)
▲ Haskell Jewels Ltd.....E..... 212 764-3332
New York (G-10048)
Henry Design Studios Inc.....G..... 516 801-2760
Locust Valley (G-7349)
Henry Dunay Designs Inc.....E..... 212 768-9700
New York (G-10080)
▲ Hjn Inc.....F..... 212 398-9564
New York (G-10107)
Horo Creations LLC.....G..... 212 719-4818
New York (G-10124)
Houles USA Inc.....G..... 212 935-3900
New York (G-10132)
Hw Holdings Inc.....G..... 212 399-1000
New York (G-10153)
Ilico Jewelry Inc.....G..... 516 482-0201
Great Neck (G-5561)
Imena Jewelry Manufacturer Inc.....F..... 212 827-0073
New York (G-10184)
Incon Gems Inc.....F..... 212 221-8560
New York (G-10193)
▲ Indonesian Imports Inc.....E..... 888 800-5899
New York (G-10200)
▲ Innovative Jewelry Inc.....G..... 718 408-8950
Valley Cottage (G-15756)
Inori Jewels.....F..... 347 703-5078
New York (G-10223)
Intentions Jewelry LLC.....G..... 845 226-4650
Lagrangeville (G-6957)
Iradj Moini Couture Ltd.....F..... 212 594-9242
New York (G-10268)
Iridesse Inc.....F..... 212 230-6000
New York (G-10269)
Iriniri Designs Ltd.....F..... 845 469-7934
Sugar Loaf (G-15200)
J J Creations Inc.....E..... 718 392-2828
Long Island City (G-7477)
J R Gold Designs Ltd.....F..... 212 922-9292
New York (G-10287)
▲ Jacmel Jewelry Inc.....C..... 718 349-4300
New York (G-10296)
Jacobs & Cohen Inc.....E..... 212 714-2702
New York (G-10298)
▲ Jacoby Enterprises LLC.....G..... 718 435-0289
Brooklyn (G-2032)
Jaguar Casting Co Inc.....E..... 212 869-0197
New York (G-10300)
Jaguar Jewelry Casting NY Inc.....G..... 212 768-4848
New York (G-10301)
▲ Jane Bohan Inc.....G..... 212 529-6090
New York (G-10305)
Jasani Designs Usa Inc.....G..... 212 257-6465
New York (G-10310)
▲ Jay Strongwater Holdings LLC.....A..... 646 657-0558
New York (G-10312)
Jay-Aimee Designs Inc.....C..... 718 609-0333
Great Neck (G-5564)
Jayden Star LLC.....E..... 212 686-0400
New York (G-10314)
▲ JC Crystal Inc.....E..... 212 594-0858
New York (G-10318)
Jeff Cooper Inc.....F..... 516 333-8200
Carle Place (G-3266)
Jewelry Arts Manufacturing.....E..... 212 382-3583
New York (G-10329)
Jewelry By Sarah Belle.....G..... 518 793-1626
Fort Ann (G-5089)
Jewels By Star Ltd.....E..... 212 308-3490
New York (G-10330)
Jeweltex Mfg Corp.....F..... 212 921-8188
New York (G-10331)
▲ Jimmy Crystal New York Co Ltd.....E..... 212 594-0858
New York (G-10340)
JK Manufacturing Inc.....G..... 212 683-3535
Locust Valley (G-7350)
Joan Boyce Ltd.....G..... 212 867-7474
New York (G-10346)
Jordan Scott Designs Ltd.....E..... 212 947-4250
New York (G-10362)
▲ Jotaly Inc.....A..... 212 886-6000
New York (G-10367)
Julius Cohen Jewelers Inc.....G..... 212 371-3050
Brooklyn (G-2058)
▲ Justin Ashley Designs Inc.....G..... 718 707-0200
Long Island City (G-7485)
▲ Justperfectmsp Ltd.....E..... 877 201-0005
New York (G-10386)
▲ Justyna Kaminska NY Inc.....G..... 917 423-5527
New York (G-10387)
▲ Kaprielian Enterprises Inc.....D..... 212 645-6623
New York (G-10406)
Karbra Company.....C..... 212 736-9300
New York (G-10407)
Keith Lewis Studio Inc.....G..... 845 339-5629
Rifton (G-13561)
Krainz Creations Inc.....E..... 212 583-1555
New York (G-10477)
▼ Krasner Group Inc.....G..... 212 268-4100
New York (G-10479)
Kurt Gaum Inc.....F..... 212 719-2836
New York (G-10487)
▲ La Fina Design Inc.....G..... 212 689-6725
New York (G-10501)
Lali Jewelry Inc.....G..... 212 944-2277
New York (G-10511)

▲ Le Hook Rouge LLC .... G 212 947-6272
Brooklyn *(G-2099)*
Le Paveh Ltd .... F 212 736-6110
New York *(G-10527)*
▲ Le Vian Corp .... D 516 466-7200
Great Neck *(G-5568)*
Le Vian Corp .... E 516 466-7200
New York *(G-10528)*
Leo Ingwer Inc .... E 212 719-1342
New York *(G-10549)*
Leo Schachter & Co Inc .... D 212 688-2000
New York *(G-10551)*
Leon Mege Inc .... F 212 768-3868
New York *(G-10553)*
Leser Enterprises Ltd .... F 212 644-8921
Yonkers *(G-16778)*
▲ Lokai Holdings LLC .... F 646 979-3474
New York *(G-10594)*
Love Bright Jewelry Inc .... E 516 620-2509
Oceanside *(G-12546)*
M & S Quality Co Ltd .... F 212 302-8757
New York *(G-10634)*
M A R A Metals Ltd .... G 718 786-7868
Long Island City *(G-7508)*
M H Manufacturing Incorporated .... G 212 461-6900
New York *(G-10637)*
M Heskia Company Inc .... G 212 768-1845
New York *(G-10638)*
M S Riviera Inc .... E 212 391-0206
New York *(G-10643)*
Magnum Creation Inc .... F 212 642-0993
New York *(G-10671)*
Manny Grunberg Inc .... E 212 302-6173
New York *(G-10692)*
Marco Moore Inc .... D 212 575-2090
Great Neck *(G-5571)*
Marina Jewelry Co Inc .... G 212 354-5027
New York *(G-10703)*
Mark King Jewelry Inc .... G 212 921-0746
New York *(G-10705)*
Mark Robinson Inc .... G 212 223-3515
New York *(G-10708)*
Markowitz Jewelry Co Inc .... E 845 774-1175
Monroe *(G-8276)*
Marlborough Jewels Inc .... G 718 768-2000
Brooklyn *(G-2170)*
Master Craft Jewelry Co Inc .... D 516 599-1012
Lynbrook *(G-7668)*
Maxine Denker Inc .... G 212 689-1440
Staten Island *(G-15103)*
▲ MB Plastics Inc .... F 718 523-1180
Greenlawn *(G-5623)*
ME & Ro Inc .... G 212 431-8744
New York *(G-10748)*
▲ Mellem Corporation .... F 607 723-0001
Binghamton *(G-904)*
◆ Mer Gems Corp .... G 212 714-9129
New York *(G-10772)*
▲ Mgd Brands Inc .... E 516 545-0150
Plainview *(G-13075)*
Michael Bondanza Inc .... E 212 869-0043
New York *(G-10791)*
Midura Jewels Inc .... G 213 265-8090
New York *(G-10801)*
Mimi So International LLC .... E 212 300-8600
New York *(G-10815)*
Min Ho Designs Inc .... G 212 838-3667
New York *(G-10816)*
▲ MJM Jewelry Corp .... D 212 354-5014
New York *(G-10826)*
MJM Jewelry Corp .... D 718 596-1600
Brooklyn *(G-2218)*
Monelle Jewelry .... G 212 977-9535
New York *(G-10838)*
Mwsi Inc .... D 914 347-4200
Hawthorne *(G-5993)*
▲ N Y Bijoux Corp .... G 212 244-9585
Port Washington *(G-13290)*
Neil Savalia Inc .... F 212 869-0123
New York *(G-10903)*
▲ Nicolo Raineri .... G 212 925-6128
New York *(G-10965)*
Oscar Heyman & Bros Inc .... E 212 593-0400
New York *(G-11065)*
Osnat Gad Inc .... G 212 957-0535
New York *(G-11066)*
Overnight Mountings Inc .... D 516 865-3000
New Hyde Park *(G-8556)*
Parijat Jewels Inc .... G 212 302-2549
New York *(G-11112)*
Park West Jewelery Inc .... G 646 329-6145
New York *(G-11116)*
Patuga LLC .... G 716 204-7220
Williamsville *(G-16583)*
Pearl Erwin Inc .... E 212 889-7410
New York *(G-11129)*
Pesselnik & Cohen Inc .... G 212 925-0287
New York *(G-11165)*
Peter Atman Inc .... F 212 644-8882
New York *(G-11167)*
PHC Restoration Holdings LLC .... F 212 643-0517
New York *(G-11180)*
▲ Photograve Corporation .... E 718 667-4825
Staten Island *(G-15114)*
▲ Pink Box Accessories LLC .... G 718 435-2821
Brooklyn *(G-2319)*
▲ Premier Jewelry Designs LLC .... G 212 391-8778
New York *(G-11230)*
Pronto Jewelry Inc .... E 212 719-9455
New York *(G-11263)*
◆ Q Ed Creations .... G 212 391-1155
New York *(G-11289)*
R & R Grosbard Inc .... E 212 575-0077
New York *(G-11311)*
R Klein Jewelry Co Inc .... D 516 482-3260
Massapequa *(G-7884)*
R M Reynolds .... G 315 789-7365
Geneva *(G-5331)*
Rand & Paseka Mfg Co Inc .... E 516 867-1500
Freeport *(G-5178)*
▲ Regal Jewelry Inc .... G 212 382-1695
New York *(G-11348)*
Reinhold Brothers Inc .... E 212 867-8310
New York *(G-11351)*
Renaissance Bijou Ltd .... G 212 869-1969
New York *(G-11359)*
Richards & West Inc .... D 585 461-4088
East Rochester *(G-4291)*
Richline Group Inc .... E 212 643-2908
New York *(G-11388)*
Richline Group Inc .... C 212 764-8454
New York *(G-11389)*
Richline Group Inc .... C 914 699-0000
New York *(G-11390)*
▲ Riva Jewelry Manufacturing Inc .... C 718 361-3100
Brooklyn *(G-2405)*
Robert Bartholomew Ltd .... E 516 767-2970
Port Washington *(G-13301)*
Robin Stanley Inc .... G 212 871-0007
New York *(G-11411)*
Rosy Blue Inc .... E 212 687-8838
New York *(G-11435)*
▲ Royal Jewelry Mfg Inc .... D 212 302-2500
Great Neck *(G-5586)*
Royal Miracle Corp .... E 212 921-5797
New York *(G-11438)*
Rubinstein Jewelry Mfg Co .... F 718 784-8650
Long Island City *(G-7581)*
Rudolf Friedman Inc .... F 212 869-5070
New York *(G-11446)*
Rumson Acquisition LLC .... G 718 349-4300
New York *(G-11447)*
▲ Ryan Gems Inc .... E 212 697-0149
New York *(G-11452)*
▲ S & M Ring Corp .... F 212 382-0900
Hewlett *(G-6050)*
▲ S Kashi & Sons Inc .... F 212 869-9393
Great Neck *(G-5587)*
S Scharf Inc .... F 516 541-9552
Massapequa *(G-7885)*
▲ Samuel B Collection Inc .... G 516 466-1826
Great Neck *(G-5588)*
Sanoy Inc .... E 212 695-6384
New York *(G-11484)*
Sarkisians Jewelry Co .... G 212 869-1060
New York *(G-11491)*
Satco Castings Service Inc .... E 516 354-1500
New Hyde Park *(G-8561)*
Satellite Incorporated .... G 212 221-6687
New York *(G-11492)*
▲ Select Jewelry Inc .... D 718 784-3626
Long Island City *(G-7587)*
▲ Shah Diamonds Inc .... F 212 888-9393
New York *(G-11553)*
Shanu Gems Inc .... F 212 921-4470
New York *(G-11556)*
Sharodine Inc .... G 516 767-3548
Port Washington *(G-13308)*
Shining Creations Inc .... G 845 358-4911
New City *(G-8495)*
▲ Shiro Limited .... G 212 780-0007
New York *(G-11569)*
Simka Diamond Corp .... F 212 921-4420
New York *(G-11593)*
Somerset Manufacturers Inc .... E 516 626-3832
Roslyn Heights *(G-14460)*
▲ Spark Creations Inc .... F 212 575-8385
New York *(G-11657)*
Standard Wedding Band Co .... G 516 294-0954
Garden City *(G-5282)*
Stanley Creations Inc .... C 718 361-6100
Long Island City *(G-7599)*
Stanmark Jewelry Inc .... G 212 730-2557
New York *(G-11694)*
▲ Sterling Possessions Ltd .... G 212 594-0418
New York *(G-11707)*
Stone House Associates Inc .... G 212 221-7447
New York *(G-11714)*
◆ Sube Inc .... E 212 243-6930
New York *(G-11732)*
Sumer Gold Ltd .... G 212 354-8677
New York *(G-11737)*
Suna Bros Inc .... E 212 869-5670
New York *(G-11741)*
Sunrise Jewelers of NY Inc .... G 516 541-1302
Massapequa *(G-7886)*
Tambetti Inc .... G 212 751-9584
New York *(G-11778)*
Tamsen Z LLC .... G 212 292-6412
New York *(G-11779)*
Tanagro Jewelry Corp .... E 212 753-2817
New York *(G-11780)*
Technical Service Industries .... E 212 719-9800
Jamaica *(G-6682)*
Teena Creations Inc .... G 516 867-1500
Freeport *(G-5185)*
▲ Temple St Clair LLC .... E 212 219-8664
New York *(G-11799)*
Thomas Sasson Co Inc .... G 212 697-4998
New York *(G-11822)*
Tiga Holdings Inc .... E 845 838-3000
Beacon *(G-763)*
▲ Trianon Collection Inc .... E 212 921-9450
New York *(G-11896)*
▲ Ultra Fine Jewelry Mfg .... E 516 349-2848
Plainview *(G-13095)*
▲ UNI Jewelry Inc .... G 212 398-1818
New York *(G-11938)*
Unique Designs Inc .... F 212 575-7701
New York *(G-11949)*
United Brothers Jewelry Inc .... E 212 921-2558
New York *(G-11952)*
Valentin & Kalich Jwly Mfg Ltd .... E 212 575-9044
New York *(G-11984)*
Valentine Jewelry Mfg Co Inc .... E 212 382-0606
New York *(G-11985)*
▲ Variety Gem Co Inc .... F 212 921-1820
Great Neck *(G-5599)*
Viktor Gold Enterprise Corp .... G 212 768-8885
New York *(G-12033)*
Von Musulin Patricia .... G 212 206-8345
New York *(G-12053)*
W & B Mazza & Sons Inc .... E 516 379-4130
North Baldwin *(G-12371)*
Weisco Inc .... F 212 575-8989
New York *(G-12088)*
Whitney Boin Studio Inc .... G 914 377-4385
Yonkers *(G-16807)*
William Goldberg Diamond Corp .... E 212 980-4343
New York *(G-12110)*
Xomox Jewelry Inc .... G 212 944-8428
New York *(G-12154)*
▲ Yofah Religious Articles Inc .... F 718 435-3288
Brooklyn *(G-2664)*
Zeeba Jewelry Mfg Inc .... G 212 997-1009
New York *(G-12172)*
Zelman & Friedman Jwly Mfg Co .... E 718 349-3400
Long Island City *(G-7647)*

3914 Silverware, Plated & Stainless Steel Ware

All American Awards Inc .... F 631 567-2025
Bohemia *(G-975)*
Atlantic Trophy Co Inc .... G 212 684-6020
New York *(G-8952)*
▲ Csi International Inc .... E 800 441-2895
Niagara Falls *(G-12276)*
▲ D W Haber & Son Inc .... E 718 993-6405
Bronx *(G-1251)*

Denvin Inc......E...... 718 232-3389
Brooklyn *(G-1768)*
▲ Dwm International Inc......F...... 646 290-7448
Long Island City *(G-7431)*
Endurart Inc......E...... 212 473-7000
New York *(G-9679)*
Oneida International Inc......G...... 315 361-3000
Oneida *(G-12615)*
Oneida Silversmiths Inc......G...... 315 361-3000
Oneida *(G-12619)*
▼ Quest Bead & Cast Inc......G...... 212 354-1737
New York *(G-11300)*
R Goldsmith......F...... 718 239-1396
Bronx *(G-1370)*
Sherrill Manufacturing Inc......C...... 315 280-0727
Sherrill *(G-14822)*
Silver City Group Inc......G...... 315 363-0344
Sherrill *(G-14823)*
▲ Studio Silversmiths Inc......E...... 718 418-6785
Ridgewood *(G-13553)*
▲ Utica Cutlery Company......D...... 315 733-4663
Utica *(G-15737)*
Valerie Bohigian......G...... 914 631-8866
Sleepy Hollow *(G-14888)*

3915 Jewelers Findings & Lapidary Work

A J C Jewelry Contracting Inc......G...... 212 594-3703
New York *(G-8696)*
A J M Enterprises......F...... 716 626-7294
Buffalo *(G-2679)*
Ace Diamond Corp......G...... 212 730-8231
New York *(G-8725)*
Allstar Casting Corporation......E...... 212 563-0909
New York *(G-8801)*
Ampex Casting Corporation......F...... 212 719-1318
New York *(G-8847)*
Antwerp Diamond Distributors......F...... 212 319-3300
New York *(G-8879)*
Antwerp Sales Intl Inc......F...... 212 354-6515
New York *(G-8880)*
Asa Manufacturing Inc......E...... 718 853-3033
Brooklyn *(G-1560)*
Asco Castings Inc......G...... 212 719-9800
Long Island City *(G-7389)*
Asur Jewelry Inc......G...... 718 472-1687
Long Island City *(G-7393)*
Baroka Creations Inc......G...... 212 768-0527
New York *(G-9019)*
Boucheron Joaillerie USA Inc......G...... 212 715-7330
New York *(G-9126)*
Carrera Casting Corp......C...... 212 382-3296
New York *(G-9215)*
▲ Christopher Designs Inc......E...... 212 382-1013
New York *(G-9294)*
Classic Creations Inc......G...... 516 498-1991
Great Neck *(G-5545)*
▲ Creative Tools & Supply Inc......G...... 212 279-7077
New York *(G-9422)*
D M J Casting Inc......G...... 212 719-1951
New York *(G-9448)*
D R S Watch Materials......E...... 212 819-0470
New York *(G-9450)*
Danhier Co LLC......F...... 212 563-7683
New York *(G-9465)*
Dialase Inc......G...... 212 575-8833
New York *(G-9519)*
Diamex Inc......G...... 212 575-8145
New York *(G-9520)*
Diamond Boutique......G...... 516 444-3373
Port Washington *(G-13252)*
Diamond Constellation Corp......G...... 212 819-0324
New York *(G-9521)*
Dresdiam Inc......E...... 212 819-2217
New York *(G-9575)*
Dweck Industries Inc......E...... 718 615-1695
Brooklyn *(G-1798)*
▲ E Schreiber Inc......E...... 212 382-0280
New York *(G-9597)*
Engelack Gem Corporation......G...... 212 719-3094
New York *(G-9683)*
Eugene Biro Corp......E...... 212 997-0146
New York *(G-9726)*
Fine Cut Diamonds Corporation......G...... 212 575-8780
New York *(G-9803)*
Fischer Diamonds Inc......F...... 212 869-1990
New York *(G-9810)*
▲ Fischler Diamonds Inc......G...... 212 921-8196
New York *(G-9811)*
Forever Grown Diamonds Inc......G...... 212 354-2827
New York *(G-9823)*
Frank Billanti Casting Co Inc......F...... 212 221-0440
New York *(G-9840)*
Gemini Manufactures......F...... 716 633-0306
Cheektowaga *(G-3446)*
Goldmark Inc......E...... 718 438-0295
Brooklyn *(G-1939)*
▲ Guild Diamond Products Inc......F...... 212 871-0007
New York *(G-10007)*
Hershel Horowitz Corp......G...... 212 719-1710
New York *(G-10084)*
J A G Diamond Manufacturers......G...... 212 575-0660
New York *(G-10284)*
Jaguar Casting Co Inc......E...... 212 869-0197
New York *(G-10300)*
Jewelry Arts Manufacturing......E...... 212 382-3583
New York *(G-10329)*
Jim Wachtler Inc......G...... 212 755-4367
New York *(G-10338)*
▲ Julius Klein Group......E...... 212 719-1811
New York *(G-10376)*
Kaleko Bros......G...... 212 819-0100
New York *(G-10397)*
▲ Kaprielian Enterprises Inc......D...... 212 645-6623
New York *(G-10406)*
Karbra Company......C...... 212 736-9300
New York *(G-10407)*
Kemp Metal Products Inc......E...... 516 997-8860
Westbury *(G-16348)*
Lazare Kaplan Intl Inc......D...... 212 972-9700
New York *(G-10525)*
Leo Schachter Diamonds LLC......D...... 212 688-2000
New York *(G-10552)*
Levi Shabtai......G...... 212 302-7393
New York *(G-10556)*
▲ Magic Novelty Co Inc......E...... 212 304-2777
New York *(G-10667)*
Max Kahan Inc......F...... 212 575-4646
New York *(G-10734)*
ME & Ro Inc......G...... 212 431-8744
New York *(G-10748)*
Miller & Veit Inc......F...... 212 247-2275
New York *(G-10810)*
Nathan Berrie & Sons Inc......G...... 516 432-8500
Island Park *(G-6516)*
New York Findings Corp......F...... 212 925-5745
New York *(G-10938)*
Nyman Jewelry Inc......G...... 212 944-1976
New York *(G-11017)*
▲ Perma Glow Ltd Inc......F...... 212 575-9677
New York *(G-11158)*
Precision Diamond Cutters Inc......G...... 212 719-4438
Brooklyn *(G-2334)*
▲ R G Flair Co Inc......E...... 631 586-7311
Bay Shore *(G-712)*
Renco Manufacturing Inc......E...... 718 392-8877
Long Island City *(G-7575)*
Satco Castings Service Inc......E...... 516 354-1500
New Hyde Park *(G-8561)*
▲ Shah Diamonds Inc......F...... 212 888-9393
New York *(G-11553)*
Stephen J Lipkins Inc......G...... 631 249-8866
Farmingdale *(G-4881)*
Sunshine Diamond Cutter Inc......G...... 212 221-1028
New York *(G-11744)*
T M W Diamonds Mfg Co......G...... 212 869-8444
New York *(G-11769)*
▲ Touch Adjust Clip Co Inc......G...... 631 589-3077
Bohemia *(G-1096)*
▲ Townley Inc......E...... 212 779-0544
New York *(G-11877)*
United Gemdiam Inc......E...... 718 851-5083
Brooklyn *(G-2602)*
Via America Fine Jewelry Inc......G...... 212 302-1218
New York *(G-12025)*
Waldman Alexander M Diamond Co......E...... 212 921-8098
New York *(G-12065)*
William Goldberg Diamond Corp......E...... 212 980-4343
New York *(G-12110)*
Windiam Usa Inc......G...... 212 542-0949
New York *(G-12117)*
◆ Zak Jewelry Tools Inc......F...... 212 768-8122
New York *(G-12168)*
Zirconia Creations Intl......G...... 212 239-3730
New York *(G-12179)*

3931 Musical Instruments

Albert Augustine Ltd......D...... 718 913-9635
Mount Vernon *(G-8376)*
Barbera Transduser Systems......F...... 718 816-3025
Staten Island *(G-15048)*
DAddario & Company Inc......D...... 631 439-3300
Melville *(G-8014)*
DAddario & Company Inc......E...... 718 599-6660
Brooklyn *(G-1749)*
◆ DAddario & Company Inc......A...... 631 439-3300
Farmingdale *(G-4747)*
▲ DAndrea Inc......E...... 516 496-2200
Syosset *(G-15214)*
▲ Dimarzio Inc......E...... 718 442-6655
Staten Island *(G-15069)*
▲ E & O Mari Inc......D...... 845 562-4400
Newburgh *(G-12220)*
▲ Evans Manufacturing LLC......D...... 631 439-3300
Farmingdale *(G-4762)*
Gluck Orgelbau Inc......G...... 212 233-2684
New York *(G-9947)*
Guitar Specialist Inc......G...... 914 401-9052
Goldens Bridge *(G-5475)*
▲ Hipshot Products Inc......F...... 607 532-9404
Interlaken *(G-6481)*
J D Calato Manufacturing Co......E...... 716 285-3546
Niagara Falls *(G-12300)*
Jason Ladanye Guitar Piano & H......E...... 518 527-3973
Albany *(G-88)*
Kerner and Merchant......G...... 315 463-8023
East Syracuse *(G-4357)*
▲ Leonard Carlson......G...... 518 477-4710
East Greenbush *(G-4230)*
Magic Reed......F...... 914 630-4006
Larchmont *(G-7058)*
▲ Mari Strings Inc......F...... 212 799-6781
New York *(G-10701)*
Muzet Inc......F...... 315 452-0050
Syracuse *(G-15378)*
Nathan Love LLC......F...... 212 925-7111
New York *(G-10877)*
◆ New Sensor Corporation......D...... 718 937-8300
Long Island City *(G-7538)*
Roli USA Inc......F...... 412 600-4840
New York *(G-11424)*
▲ Sadowsky Guitars Ltd......F...... 718 433-1990
Long Island City *(G-7584)*
◆ Samson Technologies Corp......D...... 631 784-2200
Hicksville *(G-6130)*
Siegfrieds Call Inc......G...... 845 765-2275
Beacon *(G-762)*
Sound Source Inc......G...... 585 271-5370
Rochester *(G-14135)*
▲ Steinway Inc......A...... 718 721-2600
Long Island City *(G-7601)*
◆ Steinway and Sons......C...... 718 721-2600
Long Island City *(G-7602)*
◆ Steinway Musical Instrs Inc......E...... 781 894-9770
New York *(G-11702)*
▲ Stuart Spector Designs Ltd......G...... 845 246-6124
Saugerties *(G-14618)*

3942 Dolls & Stuffed Toys

◆ ADC Dolls Inc......C...... 212 244-4500
New York *(G-8734)*
Beila Group Inc......F...... 212 260-1948
New York *(G-9038)*
◆ Commonwealth Toy Novelty Inc......E...... 212 242-4070
New York *(G-9367)*
Community Products LLC......G...... 518 589-5103
Elka Park *(G-4435)*
Cosmetics Plus Ltd......G...... 516 768-7250
Amagansett *(G-203)*
Dana Michele LLC......G...... 917 757-7777
New York *(G-9463)*
Fierce Fun Toys LLC......G...... 646 322-7172
New York *(G-9801)*
▲ Goldberger Company LLC......F...... 212 924-1194
New York *(G-9952)*
◆ Jupiter Creations Inc......G...... 917 493-9393
New York *(G-10382)*
◆ Lovee Doll & Toy Co Inc......G...... 212 242-1545
New York *(G-10619)*
Madame Alexander Doll 2018 LLC......G...... 917 576-8381
New York *(G-10653)*
Madame Alexander Doll Co LLC......D...... 212 244-4500
New York *(G-10654)*
Mattel Inc......F...... 716 714-8514
East Aurora *(G-4205)*
Minted Green Inc......G...... 845 458-1845
Airmont *(G-15)*
North American Bear Co Inc......F...... 212 388-0700
New York *(G-10990)*
◆ Skip Hop Inc......E...... 646 902-9874
New York *(G-11610)*

SIC SECTION
39 MISCELLANEOUS MANUFACTURING INDUSTRIES

Skip Hop Holdings Inc ... G ... 212 868-9850
New York *(G-11611)*

▲ Tonner Doll Company Inc ... E ... 845 339-9537
Kingston *(G-6923)*

Toy Admiration Co Inc ... E ... 914 963-9400
Yonkers *(G-16804)*

Ward Sales Co Inc ... G ... 315 476-5276
Syracuse *(G-15454)*

▲ Well-Made Toy Mfg Corporation ... E ... 718 381-4225
Port Washington *(G-13313)*

3944 Games, Toys & Children's Vehicles

212 Db Corp ... E ... 212 652-5600
New York *(G-8670)*

▲ Babysafe Usa LLC ... G ... 877 367-4141
Afton *(G-7)*

◆ Barron Games Intl Co LLC ... F ... 716 630-0054
Buffalo *(G-2723)*

Buffalo Games LLC ... D ... 716 827-8393
Buffalo *(G-2744)*

C T A Digital Inc ... F ... 718 963-9845
Brooklyn *(G-1665)*

▲ C T A Digital Inc ... E ... 845 513-0433
Monroe *(G-8266)*

Church Communities NY Inc ... E ... 518 589-5103
Elka Park *(G-4433)*

Church Communities NY Inc ... E ... 518 589-5103
Elka Park *(G-4434)*

Cioccolato 7 LLC ... G ... 347 240-7115
Brooklyn *(G-1693)*

Compoz A Puzzle Inc ... G ... 516 883-2311
Port Washington *(G-13250)*

▲ Dakott LLC ... G ... 888 805-6795
New York *(G-9460)*

Dana Michele LLC ... G ... 917 757-7777
New York *(G-9463)*

▲ Design Works Craft Inc ... F ... 631 244-5749
Bohemia *(G-1015)*

Drescher Paper Box Inc ... F ... 716 854-0288
Clarence *(G-3528)*

▲ E C C Corp ... G ... 518 873-6494
Elizabethtown *(G-4431)*

▲ Eeboo Corporation ... F ... 212 222-0823
New York *(G-9632)*

Ellis Products Corp ... G ... 516 791-3732
Valley Stream *(G-15778)*

Famous Box Scooter Co ... G ... 631 943-2013
West Babylon *(G-16155)*

Gargraves Trackage Corporation ... G ... 315 483-6577
North Rose *(G-12395)*

▲ Haba USA ... G ... 800 468-6873
Skaneateles *(G-14873)*

▲ Habermaass Corporation ... F ... 315 685-8919
Skaneateles *(G-14874)*

▲ Innovative Designs LLC ... E ... 212 695-0892
New York *(G-10219)*

Joel Zelcer ... F ... 917 525-6790
Brooklyn *(G-2042)*

◆ Jupiter Creations Inc ... G ... 917 493-9393
New York *(G-10382)*

▲ Kidtellect Inc ... G ... 617 803-1456
New York *(G-10440)*

Kidz Toyz Inc ... G ... 914 261-4453
Mount Kisco *(G-8347)*

▲ Kling Magnetics Inc ... E ... 518 392-4000
Chatham *(G-3428)*

Littlebits Electronics Inc ... E ... 917 464-4577
New York *(G-10582)*

▲ Marvel Entertainment LLC ... C ... 212 576-4000
New York *(G-10719)*

▲ Master Art Corp ... G ... 845 362-6430
Spring Valley *(G-15001)*

Master Juvenile Products Inc ... F ... 845 647-8400
Ellenville *(G-4440)*

Matel LLC ... G ... 646 825-6760
New York *(G-10726)*

Mattel Inc ... F ... 716 714-8514
East Aurora *(G-4205)*

Mattel Inc ... E ... 310 252-2000
East Aurora *(G-4206)*

▲ Mechanical Displays Inc ... G ... 718 258-5588
Brooklyn *(G-2185)*

▲ Ogosport LLC ... G ... 718 554-0777
Brooklyn *(G-2286)*

Pidyon Controls Inc ... F ... 212 683-9523
New York *(G-11191)*

Pride Lines Ltd ... G ... 631 225-0033
Lindenhurst *(G-7190)*

R F Giardina Co ... F ... 516 922-1364
Oyster Bay *(G-12820)*

Sandbox Brands Inc ... G ... 212 647-8877
New York *(G-11480)*

Spectrum Crafts Inc ... E ... 631 244-5749
Bohemia *(G-1091)*

Toymax Inc ... G ... 212 633-6611
New York *(G-11878)*

Tucker Jones House Inc ... E ... 631 642-9092
East Setauket *(G-4313)*

Vogel Applied Technologies ... G ... 212 677-3136
New York *(G-12051)*

Way Out Toys Inc ... G ... 212 689-9094
New York *(G-12082)*

Whats Next Manufacturing Inc ... E ... 585 492-1014
Arcade *(G-391)*

Wobbleworks Inc ... E ... 718 618-9904
New York *(G-12127)*

3949 Sporting & Athletic Goods, NEC

A Hyatt Ball Co Ltd ... G ... 518 747-0272
Fort Edward *(G-5093)*

Absolute Fitness US Corp ... D ... 732 979-8582
Bayside *(G-742)*

Adirondack Outdoor Center LLC ... G ... 315 369-2300
Old Forge *(G-12589)*

Adpro Sports LLC ... D ... 716 854-5116
Buffalo *(G-2687)*

Alternatives For Children ... E ... 631 271-0777
Dix Hills *(G-4119)*

▲ Apparel Production Inc ... E ... 212 278-8362
New York *(G-8890)*

▲ Athalon Sportgear Inc ... G ... 212 268-8070
New York *(G-8948)*

Azibi Ltd ... F ... 212 869-6550
New York *(G-8986)*

Bears Management Group Inc ... G ... 585 624-5694
Lima *(G-7149)*

Billy Beez Usa LLC ... F ... 315 741-5099
Syracuse *(G-15257)*

Billy Beez Usa LLC ... F ... 646 606-2249
New York *(G-9084)*

Billy Beez Usa LLC ... E ... 845 915-4709
West Nyack *(G-16266)*

▼ Blades ... F ... 212 477-1059
New York *(G-9098)*

Bruynswick Sales Inc ... F ... 845 789-2049
New Paltz *(G-8576)*

Bungers Surf Shop ... G ... 631 244-3646
Sayville *(G-14626)*

Burnt Mill Smithing ... G ... 585 293-2380
Churchville *(G-3507)*

Burton Corporation ... D ... 802 862-4500
Champlain *(G-3407)*

Car Doctor Motor Sports LLC ... G ... 631 537-1548
Water Mill *(G-15968)*

Cascade Helmets Holdings Inc ... G ... 315 453-3073
Liverpool *(G-7229)*

▲ Chapman Skateboard Co Inc ... G ... 631 321-4773
Deer Park *(G-3957)*

Charm Mfg Co Inc ... E ... 607 565-8161
Waverly *(G-16063)*

City Sports Inc ... G ... 212 730-2009
New York *(G-9312)*

Cooperstown Bat Company Inc ... F ... 607 547-2415
Cooperstown *(G-3743)*

▲ Copper John Corporation ... F ... 315 258-9269
Auburn *(G-473)*

Cortland Line Mfg LLC ... E ... 607 756-2851
Cortland *(G-3867)*

▲ Cy Plastics Works Inc ... E ... 585 229-2555
Honeoye *(G-6260)*

D Squared Technologies Inc ... G ... 516 932-7319
Jericho *(G-6784)*

▼ Devin Mfg Inc ... F ... 585 496-5770
Arcade *(G-381)*

◆ Eastern Jungle Gym Inc ... E ... 845 878-9800
Carmel *(G-3275)*

▲ Everlast Sports Mfg Corp ... E ... 212 239-0990
New York *(G-9737)*

Everlast Worldwide Inc ... E ... 212 239-0990
New York *(G-9738)*

▲ Excellent Art Mfg Corp ... F ... 718 388-7075
Inwood *(G-6489)*

Fishing Valley LLC ... G ... 716 523-6158
Lockport *(G-7301)*

Fitsmo LLC ... G ... 585 519-1956
Fairport *(G-4633)*

Florida North Inc ... F ... 518 868-2888
Sloansville *(G-14891)*

Fly-Tyers Carry-All LLC ... G ... 607 821-1460
Charlotteville *(G-3425)*

◆ Fownes Brothers & Co Inc ... E ... 212 683-0150
New York *(G-9834)*

Fownes Brothers & Co Inc ... E ... 518 752-4411
Gloversville *(G-5456)*

Good Show Sportwear Inc ... F ... 212 334-8751
New York *(G-9958)*

Grace Wheeler ... G ... 716 483-1254
Jamestown *(G-6718)*

Grand Slam Safety LLC ... G ... 315 766-7008
Croghan *(G-3908)*

▼ Gym Store Inc ... G ... 718 366-7804
Maspeth *(G-7850)*

▲ Hana Sportswear Inc ... E ... 315 639-6332
Dexter *(G-4115)*

Hart Sports Inc ... G ... 631 385-1805
Huntington Station *(G-6443)*

Heads & Tails Lure Co ... G ... 607 739-7900
Horseheads *(G-6318)*

Hector Pt Sr Rehab Svc Pllc ... G ... 518 371-5554
Clifton Park *(G-3567)*

Herrmann Group LLC ... G ... 716 876-9798
Kenmore *(G-6860)*

Hinspergers Poly Industries ... E ... 585 798-6625
Medina *(G-7981)*

▲ Hypoxico Inc ... G ... 212 972-1009
New York *(G-10156)*

◆ Imperial Pools Inc ... C ... 518 786-1200
Latham *(G-7075)*

▲ International Leisure Pdts Inc ... E ... 631 254-2155
Edgewood *(G-4405)*

▲ J R Products Inc ... G ... 716 633-7565
Clarence Center *(G-3546)*

▲ Jag Manufacturing Inc ... E ... 518 762-9558
Johnstown *(G-6832)*

Joe Moro ... G ... 607 272-0591
Ithaca *(G-6589)*

Johnson Outdoors Inc ... C ... 607 779-2200
Binghamton *(G-899)*

Kohlberg Sports Group Inc ... G ... 914 241-7430
Mount Kisco *(G-8348)*

Latham International Mfg Corp ... B ... 800 833-3800
Latham *(G-7081)*

◆ Latham Pool Products Inc ... C ... 518 951-1000
Latham *(G-7082)*

▲ Mac Swed Inc ... F ... 212 684-7730
New York *(G-10646)*

Makiplastic ... G ... 716 772-2222
Gasport *(G-5307)*

Mattel Inc ... F ... 716 714-8514
East Aurora *(G-4205)*

▲ Maverik Lacrosse LLC ... A ... 516 213-3050
New York *(G-10732)*

Morris Golf Ventures ... E ... 631 283-0559
Southampton *(G-14957)*

▲ Nalge Nunc International Corp ... A ... 585 498-2661
Rochester *(G-13962)*

▼ North Coast Outfitters Ltd ... E ... 631 727-5580
Riverhead *(G-13578)*

Northern King Lures Inc ... G ... 585 865-3373
Rochester *(G-13982)*

▲ Olympia Sports Company Inc ... F ... 914 347-4737
Elmsford *(G-4557)*

▲ Otis Products Inc ... C ... 315 348-4300
Lyons Falls *(G-7689)*

Outdoor Group LLC ... C ... 877 503-5483
West Henrietta *(G-16245)*

Paddock Chevrolet Golf Dome ... E ... 716 504-4059
Tonawanda *(G-15568)*

Peloton Interactive Inc ... F ... 866 679-9129
New York *(G-11142)*

▲ Peloton Interactive Inc ... E ... 866 650-1996
New York *(G-11143)*

Perfect Form Manufacturing LLC ... G ... 585 500-5923
West Henrietta *(G-16247)*

▲ Performance Lacrosse Group Inc ... G ... 315 453-3073
Liverpool *(G-7254)*

▲ Physicalmind Institute ... F ... 212 343-2150
New York *(G-11186)*

Pilates Designs LLC ... G ... 718 721-5929
Astoria *(G-440)*

Pilgrim Surf & Supply ... G ... 718 218-7456
Brooklyn *(G-2317)*

PNC Sports ... G ... 516 665-2244
Deer Park *(G-4027)*

Polytech Pool Mfg Inc ... F ... 718 492-8991
Brooklyn *(G-2326)*

PRC Liquidating Company ... E ... 212 823-9626
New York *(G-11227)*

▲ Quaker Boy Inc ... E ... 716 662-3979
Orchard Park *(G-12740)*

S
I
C

Employee Codes: A=Over 500 employees, B=251-500
C=101-250, D=51-100, E=20-50, F=10-19, G=5-9

2019 Harris
New York Manufacturers Directory

801

39 MISCELLANEOUS MANUFACTURING INDUSTRIES

Qubicaamf Worldwide LLC ....C 315 376-6541
  Lowville *(G-7655)*
Rawlings Sporting Goods Co Inc ....D 315 429-8511
  Dolgeville *(G-4136)*
Rising Stars Soccer Club CNY ....F 315 381-3096
  Westmoreland *(G-16409)*
◆ Rome Specialty Company Inc ....E 315 337-8200
  Rome *(G-14272)*
Rottkamp Tennis Inc ....E 631 421-0040
  Huntington Station *(G-6455)*
Sea Isle Custom Rod Builders ....G 516 868-8855
  Freeport *(G-5181)*
Seaway Mats Inc ....G 518 483-2560
  Malone *(G-7726)*
Shehawken Archery Co Inc ....F 607 967-8333
  Bainbridge *(G-534)*
Sportsfield Specialties Inc ....G 607 746-8911
  Delhi *(G-4076)*
Stephenson Custom Case Company ....E 905 542-8762
  Niagara Falls *(G-12338)*
Sunny Scuba Inc ....G 212 333-4915
  New York *(G-11743)*
◆ Swimline Corp ....C 631 254-2155
  Edgewood *(G-4416)*
▲ TDS Fitness Equipment Corp ....F 607 733-6789
  Elmira *(G-4505)*
TDS Foundry Corporation 607 733-6789
  Elmira *(G-4506)*
Tosch Products Ltd ....G 315 672-3040
  Camillus *(G-3198)*
▲ Vertical Lax Inc 518 669-3699
  Albany *(G-140)*
▲ Viking Athletics Ltd ....E 631 957-8000
  Lindenhurst *(G-7203)*
Watson Adventures LLC ....G 212 564-8293
  New York *(G-12081)*
▲ Wilbar International Inc ....D 631 951-9800
  Hauppauge *(G-5976)*
World Best Sporting Goods Inc ....F 800 489-0908
  Westbury *(G-16388)*

3951 Pens & Mechanical Pencils

◆ Aakron Rule Corp ....C 716 542-5483
  Akron *(G-16)*
▲ Harper Products Ltd ....C 516 997-2330
  Westbury *(G-16340)*
Henry Morgan ....F 718 317-5013
  Staten Island *(G-15085)*
▲ Mark Dri Products Inc ....C 516 484-6200
  Bethpage *(G-846)*
▲ Mercury Pen Company Inc ....G 518 899-9653
  Ballston Lake *(G-569)*
▲ Pelican Products Co Inc ....E 718 860-3220
  Bronx *(G-1354)*
Pintrill LLC ....F 718 782-1000
  Brooklyn *(G-2320)*
▲ STS Refill America LLC ....E 516 934-8008
  Hicksville *(G-6133)*

3952 Lead Pencils, Crayons & Artist's Mtrls

◆ Aakron Rule Corp ....C 716 542-5483
  Akron *(G-16)*
Clapper Hollow Designs Inc 518 234-9561
  Cobleskill *(G-3600)*
◆ Golden Artist Colors Inc 607 847-6154
  New Berlin *(G-8488)*
Handmade Frames Inc ....F 718 782-8364
  Brooklyn *(G-1966)*
Lopez Restorations Inc 718 383-1555
  Brooklyn *(G-2134)*
◆ Micro Powders Inc ....E 914 332-6400
  Tarrytown *(G-15483)*
North America Pastel Artists ....G 718 463-4701
  Flushing *(G-5030)*
▲ R & F Handmade Paints Inc ....F 845 331-3112
  Kingston *(G-6915)*
▲ Simon Liu Inc ....F 718 567-2011
  Brooklyn *(G-2475)*
▲ Sml Brothers Holding Corp 718 402-2000
  Bronx *(G-1387)*
▲ Spaulding & Rogers Mfg Inc ....D 518 768-2070
  Voorheesville *(G-15880)*
Timeless Decor LLC ....C 315 782-5759
  Watertown *(G-16035)*

3953 Marking Devices

A & M Steel Stamps Inc 516 741-6223
  Mineola *(G-8199)*
Bianca Group Ltd ....G 212 768-3011
  New York *(G-9070)*

C M E Corp ....F 315 451-7101
  Syracuse *(G-15266)*
▲ Cannizzaro Seal & Engraving Co ....G 718 513-6125
  Brooklyn *(G-1673)*
▼ Crafters Workshop Inc 914 345-2838
  Elmsford *(G-4539)*
Dab-O-Matic Corp 914 699-7070
  Mount Vernon *(G-8394)*
East Coast Thermographers Inc ....E 718 321-3211
  College Point *(G-3643)*
◆ Hampton Art LLC ....F 631 924-1335
  Medford *(G-7950)*
◆ Hodgins Engraving Co Inc ....D 585 343-4444
  Batavia *(G-628)*
I & I Systems 845 753-9126
  Tuxedo Park *(G-15656)*
Joseph Treu Successors Inc 212 691-7026
  New York *(G-10365)*
Kelly Foundry & Machine Co ....E 315 732-8313
  Utica *(G-15717)*
Koehlr-Gibson Mkg Graphics Inc 716 838-5960
  Buffalo *(G-2910)*
Krengel Manufacturing Co Inc ....F 212 227-1901
  Fulton *(G-5226)*
Long Island Stamp & Seal Co ....F 718 628-8550
  Ridgewood *(G-13542)*
Michael Todd Stevens ....G 585 436-9957
  Rochester *(G-13938)*
Name Base Inc ....F 212 545-1400
  New York *(G-10872)*
New York Marking Devices Corp ....G 585 454-5188
  Rochester *(G-13969)*
New York Marking Devices Corp ....F 315 463-8641
  Syracuse *(G-15381)*
Rubber Stamp X Press 631 423-1322
  Huntington Station *(G-6456)*
Rubber Stamps Inc ....E 212 675-1180
  Mineola *(G-8247)*
Sales Tax Asset Rceivable Corp ....F 212 788-5874
  New York *(G-11470)*
Samoss Group Ltd 212 239-6677
  New York *(G-11476)*
▲ Specialty Ink Co Inc ....F 631 586-3666
  Blue Point *(G-965)*
▼ Tech Products Inc ....E 718 442-4900
  Staten Island *(G-15146)*
Thermopatch Corporation ....D 315 446-8110
  Syracuse *(G-15443)*
UI Corp ....G 201 203-4453
  Bayside *(G-750)*
◆ United Silicone Inc 716 681-8222
  Lancaster *(G-7052)*
United Sttes Brnze Sign of Fla ....E 516 352-5155
  New Hyde Park *(G-8570)*
Ward Sales Co Inc 315 476-5276
  Syracuse *(G-15454)*

3955 Carbon Paper & Inked Ribbons

Guttz Corporation of America ....F 914 591-9600
  Irvington *(G-6505)*
Hf Technologies LLC ....E 585 254-5030
  Hamlin *(G-5700)*
◆ International Imaging Mtls Inc ....B 716 691-6333
  Amherst *(G-232)*
Northeast Toner Inc 518 899-5545
  Ballston Lake *(G-570)*
◆ Printer Components Inc ....G 585 924-5190
  Fairport *(G-4651)*
Qls Solutions Group Inc 716 852-2203
  Buffalo *(G-3022)*
Smartoners Inc ....G 718 975-0197
  Brooklyn *(G-2488)*
▲ Summit Technologies LLC ....E 631 590-1040
  Holbrook *(G-6212)*

3961 Costume Jewelry & Novelties

Accessory Plays LLC ....E 212 564-7301
  New York *(G-8720)*
◆ Allure Jewelry and ACC LLC ....F 646 226-8057
  New York *(G-8802)*
Anatoli Inc 845 334-9000
  West Hurley *(G-16256)*
Aniiwe Inc ....G 347 683-1891
  Brooklyn *(G-1535)*
Barrera Jose & Maria Co Ltd 212 239-1994
  New York *(G-9021)*
Beth Ward Studios LLC ....F 646 922-7575
  New York *(G-9060)*
Bnns Co Inc ....G 212 302-1844
  New York *(G-9114)*

Carol For Eva Graham Inc ....F 212 889-8686
  New York *(G-9211)*
Carvin French Jewelers Inc ....E 212 755-6474
  New York *(G-9219)*
Catherine Stein Designs Inc ....E 212 840-1188
  New York *(G-9230)*
Ciner Manufacturing Co Inc 212 947-3770
  New York *(G-9301)*
▲ Columbus Trading Corp ....E 212 564-1780
  New York *(G-9361)*
Dabby-Reid Ltd ....F 212 356-0040
  New York *(G-9452)*
▼ Ema Jewelry Inc ....D 212 575-8989
  New York *(G-9662)*
Erickson Beamon Ltd ....F 212 643-4810
  New York *(G-9701)*
▲ Eu Design LLC 212 420-7788
  New York *(G-9725)*
Fantasia Jewelry Inc 212 921-9590
  New York *(G-9781)*
Fashion Accents LLC ....F 401 331-6626
  New York *(G-9784)*
Five Star Creations Inc ....E 845 783-1187
  Monroe *(G-8269)*
Formart Corp 212 819-1819
  New York *(G-9824)*
Greenbeads Llc ....G 212 327-2765
  New York *(G-9984)*
Holbrooke Inc 646 397-4674
  New York *(G-10113)*
▲ I Love Accessories Inc 212 239-1875
  New York *(G-10158)*
▲ International Inspirations Ltd ....D 212 465-8500
  New York *(G-10247)*
▲ J & H Creations Inc ....E 212 465-0962
  New York *(G-10281)*
J J Creations Inc ....E 718 392-2828
  Long Island City *(G-7477)*
Jay Turoff ....F 718 856-7300
  Brooklyn *(G-2035)*
Jaymar Jewelry Co Inc ....F 212 564-4788
  New York *(G-10315)*
Jewelry Arts Manufacturing ....E 212 382-3583
  New York *(G-10329)*
Jill Fagin Enterprises Inc ....G 212 674-9383
  New York *(G-10337)*
Jj Fantasia Inc 212 868-1198
  New York *(G-10343)*
▲ K2 International Corp 212 947-1734
  New York *(G-10392)*
Kenneth J Lane Inc ....F 212 868-1780
  New York *(G-10432)*
▲ Lesilu Productions Inc ....E 212 947-6419
  New York *(G-10554)*
▲ Magic Novelty Co Inc 212 304-2777
  New York *(G-10667)*
Marlborough Jewels Inc 718 768-2000
  Brooklyn *(G-2170)*
▲ Mataci Inc ....D 212 502-1899
  New York *(G-10725)*
Maurice Max Inc ....E 212 334-6573
  New York *(G-10730)*
Mel Bernie and Company Inc ....G 212 889-8576
  New York *(G-10768)*
Mercado Global Inc ....G 718 838-9908
  Brooklyn *(G-2193)*
Mwsi Inc ....D 914 347-4200
  Hawthorne *(G-5993)*
▲ Nes Jewelry Inc ....D 212 502-0025
  New York *(G-10908)*
Noir Jewelry LLC 212 465-8500
  New York *(G-10986)*
Pearl Erwin Inc ....E 212 889-7410
  New York *(G-11129)*
Pepe Creations Inc ....F 212 391-1514
  New York *(G-11151)*
Pincharming Inc 516 663-5115
  Garden City *(G-5274)*
Reino Manufacturing Co Inc ....F 914 636-8990
  New Rochelle *(G-8625)*
▲ Rush Gold Manufacturing Ltd ....D 516 781-3155
  Bellmore *(G-793)*
▲ Salmco Jewelry Corp ....F 212 695-8792
  New York *(G-11471)*
Sanoy Inc 212 695-6384
  New York *(G-11484)*
▲ Sarina Accessories LLC ....F 212 239-8106
  New York *(G-11490)*
Shira Accessories Ltd ....F 212 594-4455
  New York *(G-11568)*

Steezys LLC ..... G 646 276-5333
New York *(G-11700)*
▲ **Stephan & Company ACC Ltd** ..... E 212 481-3888
New York *(G-11705)*
Swarovski North America Ltd ..... G 212 695-1502
New York *(G-11755)*
▲ **Toho Shoji (new York) Inc** ..... F 212 868-7466
New York *(G-11856)*
▲ **Tycoon International Inc** ..... G 212 563-7107
New York *(G-11922)*
▲ **Vetta Jewelry Inc** ..... E 212 564-8250
New York *(G-12020)*
▲ **Vitafede** ..... F 213 488-0136
New York *(G-12044)*
Von Musulin Patricia ..... G 212 206-8345
New York *(G-12053)*
Yacoubian Jewelers Inc ..... E 212 302-6729
New York *(G-12157)*

3965 Fasteners, Buttons, Needles & Pins

▲ **American Pride Fasteners LLC** ..... E 631 940-8292
Bay Shore *(G-656)*
Buttons & Trimcom Inc ..... F 212 868-1971
New York *(G-9164)*
Champion Zipper Corp ..... G 212 239-0414
New York *(G-9258)*
▲ **Clo-Shure Intl Inc** ..... G 212 268-5029
New York *(G-9329)*
Columbia Button Nailhead Corp ..... F 718 386-3414
Brooklyn *(G-1706)*
Connection Mold Inc ..... G 585 458-6463
Rochester *(G-13719)*
CPI of Falconer Inc ..... E 716 664-4444
Falconer *(G-4674)*
Cw Fasteners & Zippers Corp ..... F 212 594-3203
New York *(G-9439)*
▲ **E-Won Industrial Co Inc** ..... E 212 750-9610
New York *(G-9601)*
▲ **Empire State Metal Pdts Inc** ..... E 718 847-1617
Richmond Hill *(G-13502)*
◆ **Emsig Manufacturing Corp** ..... F 718 784-7717
New York *(G-9670)*
Emsig Manufacturing Corp ..... F 518 828-7301
Hudson *(G-6348)*
Emsig Manufacturing Corp ..... E 718 784-7717
New York *(G-9671)*
▲ **Eu Design LLC** ..... G 212 420-7788
New York *(G-9725)*
◆ **Hemisphere Novelties Inc** ..... E 914 378-4100
Yonkers *(G-16767)*
Ideal Fastener Corporation ..... C 212 244-0260
New York *(G-10172)*
Itc Mfg Group Inc ..... F 212 684-3696
New York *(G-10278)*
Jem Threading Specialties Inc ..... G 718 665-3341
Bronx *(G-1301)*
▲ **Joyce Trimming Inc** ..... G 212 719-3110
New York *(G-10370)*
Kane-M Inc ..... G 973 777-2797
New York *(G-10403)*
Karp Overseas Corporation ..... E 718 784-2105
Maspeth *(G-7856)*
Kenwin Sales Corp ..... G 516 933-7553
Deer Park *(G-3995)*
Kraus & Sons Inc ..... F 212 620-0408
New York *(G-10480)*
M H Stryke Co Inc ..... F 631 242-2660
Deer Park *(G-4005)*
Maxine Denker Inc ..... G 212 689-1440
Staten Island *(G-15103)*
National Die & Button Mould Co ..... E 201 939-7800
Brooklyn *(G-2245)*
Rings Wire Inc ..... G 212 741-9779
New York *(G-11393)*
▲ **Riri USA Inc** ..... G 212 268-3866
New York *(G-11394)*
Rome Fastener Sales Corp ..... E 212 741-9779
New York *(G-11428)*
Shimada Shoji (hk) Limited ..... G 212 268-0465
New York *(G-11566)*

3991 Brooms & Brushes

◆ **131-11 Atlantic RE Inc** ..... D 718 441-7700
Richmond Hill *(G-13494)*
Abtex Corporation ..... E 315 536-7403
Dresden *(G-4146)*
Braun Bros Brushes Inc ..... G 631 667-2179
Valley Stream *(G-15775)*
▲ **Braun Industries Inc** ..... F 516 741-6000
Albertson *(G-146)*
▲ **Brushtech (disc) Inc** ..... F 518 563-8420
Plattsburgh *(G-13114)*
Colgate-Palmolive Company ..... A 212 310-2000
New York *(G-9349)*
◆ **Cpac Inc** ..... E 585 382-3223
Leicester *(G-7126)*
▲ **Culicover & Shapiro Inc** ..... G 516 597-4888
Hicksville *(G-6077)*
E & W Manufacturing Co Inc ..... E 516 367-8571
Woodbury *(G-16618)*
▲ **Excel Paint Applicators Inc** ..... E 347 221-1968
Inwood *(G-6488)*
▲ **FM Brush Co Inc** ..... C 718 821-5939
Glendale *(G-5399)*
▲ **Full Circle Home LLC** ..... G 212 432-0001
New York *(G-9860)*
K & R Allied Inc ..... F 718 625-6610
Brooklyn *(G-2061)*
▲ **Kirschner Brush LLC** ..... F 718 292-1809
Bronx *(G-1309)*
▲ **Linzer Products Corp** ..... C 631 253-3333
West Babylon *(G-16171)*
Pan American Roller Inc ..... F 914 762-8700
Ossining *(G-12774)*
▲ **Perfex Corporation** ..... F 315 826-3600
Poland *(G-13184)*
Premier Paint Roller Co LLC ..... F 718 441-7700
Richmond Hill *(G-13508)*
Royal Paint Roller Corp ..... E 516 367-4370
Woodbury *(G-16631)*
Teka Fine Line Brushes Inc ..... G 718 692-2928
Brooklyn *(G-2561)*
Volckening Inc ..... E 718 748-0294
Brooklyn *(G-2633)*
▲ **Walter R Tucker Entps Ltd** ..... E 607 467-2866
Deposit *(G-4112)*
Young & Swartz Inc ..... F 716 852-2171
Buffalo *(G-3136)*

3993 Signs & Advertising Displays

A B C Mc Cleary Sign Co Inc ..... F 315 493-3550
Carthage *(G-3285)*
A M S Sign Designs ..... G 631 467-7722
Centereach *(G-3342)*
◆ **Aakron Rule Corp** ..... C 716 542-5483
Akron *(G-16)*
ABC Windows and Signs Corp ..... F 718 353-6210
College Point *(G-3636)*
Accurate Signs & Awnings Inc ..... F 718 788-0302
Brooklyn *(G-1474)*
Acme Signs of Baldwinsville ..... G 315 638-4865
Baldwinsville *(G-547)*
Ad Makers Long Island Inc ..... F 631 595-9100
Deer Park *(G-3933)*
Adirondack Sign Company LLC ..... F 518 409-7446
Saratoga Springs *(G-14566)*
Adirondack Sign Perfect Inc ..... G 518 409-7446
Saratoga Springs *(G-14567)*
Adstream America LLC ..... E 212 804-8498
New York *(G-8743)*
All Signs ..... G 973 736-2113
Staten Island *(G-15043)*
Alley Cat Signs Inc ..... F 631 924-7446
Middle Island *(G-8117)*
Allied Decorations Co Inc ..... F 315 637-0273
Syracuse *(G-15240)*
Allied Maker ..... F 516 200-9145
Glen Cove *(G-5360)*
Allstar Graphics Ltd ..... E 718 740-2240
Queens Village *(G-13403)*
Allstate Sign & Plaque Corp ..... F 631 242-2828
Deer Park *(G-3938)*
American Car Signs Inc ..... G 518 227-1173
Duanesburg *(G-4154)*
American Visuals Inc ..... G 631 694-6104
Farmingdale *(G-4720)*
Amsterdam Printing & Litho Inc ..... F 518 842-6000
Amsterdam *(G-325)*
Amsterdam Printing & Litho Inc ..... E 518 842-6000
Amsterdam *(G-326)*
Architectural Sign Group Inc ..... G 516 326-1800
Elmont *(G-4516)*
Aric Signs & Awnings Inc ..... G 516 350-0409
Hempstead *(G-6006)*
Art Parts Signs Inc ..... G 585 381-2134
East Rochester *(G-4280)*
Artkraft Strauss LLC ..... E 212 265-5155
New York *(G-8924)*
Artscroll Printing Corp ..... E 212 929-2413
New York *(G-8926)*
Asi Sign Systems Inc ..... G 646 742-1320
New York *(G-8932)*
Asi Sign Systems Inc ..... G 716 775-0104
Grand Island *(G-5495)*
Bannerboy Corporation ..... G 646 691-6524
Brooklyn *(G-1585)*
BC Communications Inc ..... G 631 549-8833
Huntington Station *(G-6434)*
Bedford Precision Parts Corp ..... E 914 241-2211
Bedford Hills *(G-772)*
Big Apple Sign Corp ..... E 631 342-0303
Islandia *(G-6522)*
▲ **Big Apple Sign Corp** ..... D 212 629-3650
New York *(G-9076)*
Bmg Printing and Promotion LLC ..... G 631 231-9200
Bohemia *(G-989)*
Broadway National Group LLC ..... D 800 797-4467
Ronkonkoma *(G-14321)*
Broadway Neon Sign Corp ..... F 908 241-4177
Ronkonkoma *(G-14322)*
Brooklyn Signs LLC ..... G 718 252-7575
Brooklyn *(G-1648)*
Buckeye Corrugated Inc ..... D 585 924-1600
Victor *(G-15834)*
Cab Signs Inc ..... E 718 479-2424
Brooklyn *(G-1666)*
Central Rede Sign Co Inc ..... G 716 213-0797
Tonawanda *(G-15532)*
▲ **Chameleon Color Cards Ltd** ..... D 716 625-9452
Lockport *(G-7290)*
Chautauqua Sign Co Inc ..... G 716 665-2222
Falconer *(G-4673)*
Checklist Boards Corporation ..... G 585 586-0152
Rochester *(G-13708)*
City Signs Inc ..... G 718 375-5933
Brooklyn *(G-1697)*
Climax Packaging Inc ..... C 315 376-8000
Lowville *(G-7649)*
Clinton Signs Inc ..... G 585 482-1620
Webster *(G-16080)*
Coe Displays Inc ..... G 718 937-5658
Long Island City *(G-7412)*
Colad Group LLC ..... D 716 961-1776
Buffalo *(G-2772)*
Colonial Redi Record Corp ..... E 718 972-7433
Brooklyn *(G-1705)*
Community Products LLC ..... E 845 658-8351
Rifton *(G-13560)*
▲ **Creative Solutions Group Inc** ..... B 914 771-4200
Yonkers *(G-16748)*
▲ **Crown Sign Systems Inc** ..... F 914 375-2118
Mount Vernon *(G-8393)*
Custom Display Manufacture ..... G 516 783-6491
North Bellmore *(G-12377)*
Decal Makers Inc ..... E 516 221-7200
Bellmore *(G-788)*
Decree Signs & Graphics Inc ..... F 973 278-3603
Floral Park *(G-4962)*
Designplex LLC ..... G 845 358-6647
Nyack *(G-12504)*
Display Marketing Group Inc ..... E 631 348-4450
Islandia *(G-6526)*
Display Presentations Ltd ..... D 631 951-4050
Brooklyn *(G-1781)*
▲ **Display Producers Inc** ..... C 718 904-1200
New Rochelle *(G-8599)*
Displays & Beyond Inc ..... F 718 805-7786
Glendale *(G-5398)*
Dkm Sales LLC ..... E 716 893-7777
Buffalo *(G-2802)*
▲ **DSI Group Inc** ..... C 800 553-2202
Maspeth *(G-7837)*
Dura Engraving Corporation ..... E 718 706-6400
Long Island City *(G-7429)*
East End Sign Design Inc ..... G 631 399-2574
Mastic *(G-7911)*
Eastern Concepts Ltd ..... F 718 472-3377
Sunnyside *(G-15203)*
▼ **Eastern Metal of Elmira Inc** ..... D 607 734-2295
Elmira *(G-4482)*
▼ **Edge Display Group Entp Inc** ..... F 631 498-1373
Bellport *(G-803)*
Elderlee Incorporated ..... C 315 789-6670
Oaks Corners *(G-12527)*
▲ **Eversan Inc** ..... F 315 736-3967
Whitesboro *(G-16527)*
Executive Sign Corp ..... G 212 397-4050
Cornwall On Hudson *(G-3838)*
Executive Sign Corporation ..... G 212 397-4050
New York *(G-9752)*

S I C

Employee Codes: A=Over 500 employees, B=251-500
C=101-250, D=51-100, E=20-50, F=10-19, G=5-9
2019 Harris
New York Manufacturers Directory
803

Exhibit Corporation America ....E 718 937-2600
Long Island City *(G-7441)*
▲ **Faster-Form Corp** ....D 800 327-3676
New Hartford *(G-8504)*
Fastsigns ....F 518 456-7446
Albany *(G-73)*
▲ **Five Star Prtg & Mailing Svcs** ....F 212 929-0300
New York *(G-9815)*
Flado Enterprises Inc ....G 716 668-6400
Depew *(G-4090)*
▲ **Flair Display Inc** ....D 718 324-9330
Bronx *(G-1272)*
Fletcher Enterprises Inc ....G 716 837-7446
Buffalo *(G-2828)*
Flexlume Sign Corporation ....G 716 884-2020
Buffalo *(G-2830)*
Forrest Engraving Co Inc ....F 845 228-0200
New Rochelle *(G-8604)*
Fortune Sign ....G 646 383-8682
Brooklyn *(G-1899)*
▼ **Fossil Industries Inc** ....E 631 254-9200
Deer Park *(G-3979)*
G I Certified Inc ....G 212 397-1945
New York *(G-9867)*
Gloede Neon Signs Ltd Inc ....F 845 471-4366
Poughkeepsie *(G-13341)*
Graphic Signs & Awnings Ltd ....G 718 227-6000
Staten Island *(G-15082)*
Graphitek Inc ....F 518 686-5966
Hoosick Falls *(G-6275)*
Greyline Signs Inc ....G 716 947-4526
Derby *(G-4113)*
Gupp Signs Inc ....G 585 244-5070
Rochester *(G-13847)*
Hadley Exhibits Inc ....D 716 874-3666
Buffalo *(G-2861)*
Hanson Sign Screen Prcess Corp ....E 716 661-3900
Falconer *(G-4680)*
Hermosa Corp ....E 315 768-4320
New York Mills *(G-12188)*
HI Tech Signs of NY Inc ....G 516 794-7880
East Meadow *(G-4252)*
Hollywood Signs Inc ....G 917 577-7333
Brooklyn *(G-1980)*
Hospitality Graphic Systems ....F 212 563-9334
New York *(G-10126)*
◆ **ID Signsystems Inc** ....E 585 266-5750
Rochester *(G-13874)*
Ideal Signs Inc ....G 718 292-9196
Bronx *(G-1293)*
Image360 ....G 585 272-1234
Rochester *(G-13878)*
Impressive Imprints Inc ....G 631 293-6161
Farmingdale *(G-4784)*
Island Nameplate Inc ....G 845 651-4005
Florida *(G-4971)*
▲ **Jaf Converters Inc** ....E 631 842-3131
Copiague *(G-3766)*
Jal Signs Inc ....F 516 536-7280
Baldwin *(G-539)*
Jax Signs and Neon Inc ....G 607 727-3420
Endicott *(G-4598)*
Jay Turoff ....F 718 856-7300
Brooklyn *(G-2035)*
Jem Sign Corp ....G 516 867-4466
Hempstead *(G-6015)*
▲ **Jomar Industries Inc** ....E 845 357-5773
Airmont *(G-14)*
Joseph Struhl Co Inc ....F 516 741-3660
New Hyde Park *(G-8544)*
JP Signs ....G 518 569-3907
Chazy *(G-3432)*
K & B Stamping Co Inc ....G 914 664-8555
Mount Vernon *(G-8412)*
Keep America Beautiful Inc ....G 518 842-4388
Amsterdam *(G-344)*
▲ **Kenan International Trading** ....G 718 672-4922
Corona *(G-3847)*
Kennyetto Graphics Inc ....E 518 883-6360
Gloversville *(G-5460)*
King Displays Inc ....F 212 629-8455
New York *(G-10451)*
▲ **Kling Magnetics Inc** ....E 518 392-4000
Chatham *(G-3428)*
KP Industries Inc ....F 516 679-3161
North Bellmore *(G-12379)*
Kraus & Sons Inc ....F 212 620-0408
New York *(G-10480)*
L I C Screen Printing Inc ....E 516 546-7289
Merrick *(G-8100)*

L Miller Design Inc ....G 631 242-1163
Deer Park *(G-3998)*
L S Sign Co Inc ....F 718 469-8600
Ridgewood *(G-13541)*
L Y Z Creations Ltd Inc ....E 718 768-2977
Brooklyn *(G-2088)*
▲ **Lamar Plastics Packaging Ltd** ....D 516 378-2500
Freeport *(G-5163)*
◆ **Lanco Corporation** ....C 631 231-2300
Ronkonkoma *(G-14368)*
Lanza Corp ....G 914 937-6360
Port Chester *(G-13204)*
▼ **Letterama Inc** ....G 516 349-0800
West Babylon *(G-16170)*
Liberty Awnings & Signs Inc ....G 347 203-1470
East Elmhurst *(G-4223)*
▲ **Lifestyle-Trimco** ....E 718 257-9101
Brooklyn *(G-2118)*
Linear Signs Inc ....F 631 532-5330
Lindenhurst *(G-7175)*
M Santoliquido Corp ....F 914 375-6674
Yonkers *(G-16780)*
Manhattan Neon Sign Corp ....F 212 714-0430
New York *(G-10687)*
Marigold Signs Inc ....F 516 433-7446
Hicksville *(G-6107)*
Mastercraft Manufacturing Co ....G 718 729-5620
Long Island City *(G-7517)*
Mauceri Sign Inc ....F 718 656-7700
Jamaica *(G-6659)*
Mekanism Inc ....E 212 226-2772
New York *(G-10767)*
Metropolitan Signs Inc ....F 315 638-1448
Baldwinsville *(G-558)*
▲ **Millennium Signs & Display Inc** ....E 516 292-8000
Hempstead *(G-6021)*
Miller Mohr Display Inc ....G 631 941-2769
East Setauket *(G-4304)*
Mixture Screen Printing ....G 845 561-2857
Newburgh *(G-12232)*
Modern Decal Co ....G 315 622-2778
Liverpool *(G-7248)*
Modulex New York Inc ....G 646 742-1320
New York *(G-10831)*
Mohawk Sign Systems Inc ....E 518 842-5303
Amsterdam *(G-352)*
Monasani Signs Inc ....G 631 266-2635
East Northport *(G-4268)*
Morris Brothers Sign Svc Inc ....G 212 675-9130
New York *(G-10843)*
Motion Message Inc ....F 631 924-9500
Bellport *(G-809)*
Movinads & Signs LLC ....G 518 378-3000
Halfmoon *(G-5666)*
Mr Sign Usa Inc ....F 718 218-3321
Brooklyn *(G-2234)*
▼ **Mystic Display Co Inc** ....G 718 485-2651
Brooklyn *(G-2239)*
Nameplate Mfrs of Amer ....E 631 752-0055
Farmingdale *(G-4831)*
Nas Quick Sign Inc ....G 716 876-7599
Buffalo *(G-2961)*
National Advertising & Prtg ....G 212 629-7650
New York *(G-10880)*
National Prfmce Solutions Inc ....D 718 833-4767
Brooklyn *(G-2246)*
Nationwide Exhibitor Svcs Inc ....F 631 467-2034
Central Islip *(G-3379)*
New Art Signs Co Inc ....G 718 443-0900
Glen Head *(G-5383)*
▲ **New Dimensions Research Corp** ....C 631 694-1356
Melville *(G-8049)*
New Kit On The Block ....G 631 757-5655
Bohemia *(G-1063)*
New Style Signs Limited Inc ....F 212 242-7848
New York *(G-10930)*
▲ **Newline Products Inc** ....C 972 881-3318
New Windsor *(G-8653)*
Noel Assoc ....G 516 371-5420
Inwood *(G-6498)*
Norampac New York City Inc ....C 718 340-2100
Maspeth *(G-7863)*
North Shore Neon Sign Co Inc ....E 718 937-4848
Flushing *(G-5031)*
Northeast Promotional Group In ....G 518 793-1024
South Glens Falls *(G-14938)*
Northeastern Sign Corp ....G 315 265-6657
South Colton *(G-14926)*
Northern Awning & Sign Company ....G 315 782-8515
Watertown *(G-16030)*

▲ **Nysco Products LLC** ....D 718 792-9000
Hawthorne *(G-5994)*
Olson Sign Company Inc ....G 518 370-2118
Schenectady *(G-14701)*
On The Mark Digital Printing & ....G 716 823-3373
Hamburg *(G-5689)*
▲ **Orlandi Inc** ....D 631 756-0110
Farmingdale *(G-4840)*
Orlandi Inc ....E 631 756-0110
Farmingdale *(G-4841)*
Pama Enterprises Inc ....G 516 504-6300
Great Neck *(G-5579)*
Penn Signs Inc ....E 718 797-1112
Brooklyn *(G-2310)*
Pereira & ODell LLC ....G 212 897-1000
New York *(G-11154)*
▲ **Platinum Sales Promotion Inc** ....G 718 361-0200
Long Island City *(G-7557)*
Polyplastic Forms Inc ....E 631 249-5011
Farmingdale *(G-4853)*
Poncio Signs ....G 718 543-4851
Bronx *(G-1360)*
Precision Signscom Inc ....D 631 841-7500
Amityville *(G-314)*
Premier Sign Systems LLC ....E 585 235-0390
Rochester *(G-14040)*
▲ **Promotional Development Inc** ....D 718 485-8550
Brooklyn *(G-2357)*
Props Displays & Interiors ....F 212 620-3840
New York *(G-11266)*
Pyx Inc ....G 718 469-4253
Brooklyn *(G-2364)*
Quick Sign F X ....F 516 249-6531
Farmingdale *(G-4862)*
Quorum Group LLC ....D 585 798-8888
Medina *(G-7987)*
R & J Displays Inc ....E 631 491-3500
West Babylon *(G-16185)*
Rapp Signs Inc ....F 607 656-8167
Greene *(G-5616)*
Ray Sign Inc ....F 518 377-1371
Schenectady *(G-14707)*
Resonant Legal Media LLC ....D 800 781-3591
New York *(G-11369)*
Rgm Signs Inc ....G 718 442-0598
Staten Island *(G-15129)*
Riverwood Signs By Dandev Desi ....G 845 229-0282
Hyde Park *(G-6471)*
Rocket Fuel Inc ....F 212 594-8888
New York *(G-11415)*
Rome Sign & Display Co ....G 315 336-0550
Rome *(G-14271)*
▲ **Royal Promotion Group Inc** ....D 212 246-3780
New York *(G-11440)*
Rpf Associates Inc ....G 631 462-7446
Commack *(G-3701)*
◆ **Rsquared Ny Inc** ....D 631 521-8700
Edgewood *(G-4413)*
Saxton Corporation ....E 518 732-7705
Castleton On Hudson *(G-3297)*
Sellco Industries Inc ....E 607 756-7594
Cortland *(G-3894)*
Seneca Signs LLC ....G 315 446-9420
Syracuse *(G-15423)*
Sign & Signs ....G 718 941-6200
Brooklyn *(G-2467)*
Sign A Rama Inc ....G 631 952-3324
Hauppauge *(G-5939)*
Sign A Rama of Syracuse ....G 315 446-9420
Syracuse *(G-15425)*
Sign Center Inc ....F 212 967-2113
New York *(G-11584)*
Sign City of New York Inc ....G 718 661-1118
College Point *(G-3666)*
Sign Company ....G 212 967-2113
New York *(G-11585)*
▲ **Sign Design Group New York Inc** ....F 718 392-0779
Long Island City *(G-7590)*
Sign Group Inc ....E 718 438-7103
Brooklyn *(G-2468)*
Sign Here Enterprises LLC ....G 914 328-3111
Hartsdale *(G-5744)*
Sign Impressions Inc ....G 585 723-0420
Rochester *(G-14127)*
Sign Language Inc ....G 585 237-2620
Perry *(G-12971)*
Sign Men ....G 718 227-7446
Staten Island *(G-15135)*
Sign Studio Inc ....F 518 266-0877
Troy *(G-15626)*

Sign Works Incorporated ... E ... 914 592-0700
Elmsford *(G-4569)*
Sign World Inc ... E ... 212 619-9000
Brooklyn *(G-2469)*
Signature Industries Inc ... F ... 516 679-5177
Freeport *(G-5184)*
Signature Name Plate Co Inc ... G ... 585 321-9960
Rochester *(G-14128)*
Signexpo Enterprises Inc ... F ... 212 925-8585
New York *(G-11588)*
▲ **Signs & Decal Corp** ... E ... 718 486-6400
Brooklyn *(G-2470)*
Signs Inc ... G ... 518 483-4759
Malone *(G-7727)*
Signs Ink Ltd ... F ... 914 739-9059
Yorktown Heights *(G-16824)*
Signs of Success Ltd ... F ... 516 295-6000
Lynbrook *(G-7674)*
Smith Graphics Inc ... G ... 631 420-4180
Farmingdale *(G-4876)*
Snyders Neon Displays Inc ... G ... 518 857-4100
Colonie *(G-3679)*
Space Sign ... F ... 718 961-1112
College Point *(G-3667)*
Spanjer Corp ... G ... 347 448-8033
Long Island City *(G-7595)*
Specialty Signs Co Inc ... F ... 212 243-8521
New York *(G-11662)*
Spectrum On Broadway ... F ... 718 932-5388
Woodside *(G-16678)*
Spectrum Signs Inc ... E ... 631 756-1010
Woodside *(G-16679)*
Speedy Sign A Rama USA Inc ... G ... 516 783-1075
Bellmore *(G-795)*
Sportsdepot Inc ... G ... 516 543-5018
Baldwin *(G-544)*
Starlite Media LLC ... G ... 212 909-7700
New York *(G-11698)*
Steel-Brite Ltd ... F ... 631 589-4044
Oakdale *(G-12522)*
Stepping Stones One Day Signs ... G ... 518 237-5774
Waterford *(G-15988)*
Stickershopcom Inc ... G ... 631 563-4323
Bayport *(G-739)*
Strategic Signage Sourcing LLC ... F ... 518 450-1093
Saratoga Springs *(G-14599)*
Substrate LLC ... E ... 212 913-9600
Long Island City *(G-7607)*
Suma Industries Inc ... G ... 646 436-5202
New York *(G-11736)*
Super Neon Light Co Inc ... G ... 718 236-5667
Brooklyn *(G-2534)*
T J Signs Unlimited LLC ... E ... 631 273-4800
Islip *(G-6551)*
▼ **Tech Products Inc** ... E ... 718 442-4900
Staten Island *(G-15146)*
▲ **Tempo Industries Inc** ... G ... 516 334-6900
Westbury *(G-16377)*
Three Gems Inc ... G ... 516 248-0388
New Hyde Park *(G-8567)*
Timely Signs Inc ... G ... 516 285-5339
Elmont *(G-4526)*
Timely Signs of Kingston Inc ... F ... 845 331-8710
Kingston *(G-6922)*
Tj Signs Unlimited LLC ... C ... 631 273-4800
Hicksville *(G-6137)*
Todd Walbridge ... G ... 585 254-3018
Rochester *(G-14171)*
Trans-Lux Corporation ... D ... 800 243-5544
New York *(G-11887)*
Tru-Art Sign Co Inc ... F ... 718 658-5068
Jamaica *(G-6685)*
Turoff Tower Graphics Inc ... F ... 718 856-7300
Brooklyn *(G-2593)*
Ulrich Sign Co Inc ... E ... 716 434-0167
Lockport *(G-7340)*
Ultimate Signs & Designs Inc ... E ... 516 481-0800
Hempstead *(G-6027)*
Unique Display Mfg Corp ... G ... 516 546-3800
Freeport *(G-5189)*
United Print Group Inc ... F ... 718 392-4242
Long Island City *(G-7623)*
United Sttes Brnze Sign of Fla ... E ... 516 352-5155
New Hyde Park *(G-8570)*
Universal 3d Innovation Inc ... F ... 516 837-9423
Valley Stream *(G-15801)*
Universal Signs and Svc Inc ... E ... 631 446-1121
Deer Park *(G-4056)*
USA Signs of America Inc ... D ... 631 254-6900
Deer Park *(G-4057)*
Valle Signs and Awnings ... F ... 516 408-3440
Copiague *(G-3790)*
Valley Creek Side Inc ... G ... 315 839-5526
Clayville *(G-3559)*
Vez Inc ... G ... 718 273-7002
Staten Island *(G-15151)*
Viana Signs Corp ... F ... 516 887-2000
Oceanside *(G-12564)*
Victory Signs Inc ... G ... 315 762-0220
Canastota *(G-3251)*
▲ **Visual Citi Inc** ... C ... 631 482-3030
Lindenhurst *(G-7206)*
▲ **Visual Effects Inc** ... F ... 718 324-0011
Jamaica *(G-6689)*
Visual ID Source Inc ... F ... 516 307-9759
Mineola *(G-8251)*
Visual Impact Graphics Inc ... G ... 585 548-7118
Batavia *(G-639)*
Vital Signs & Graphics Co Inc ... G ... 518 237-8372
Cohoes *(G-3623)*
▲ **Von Pok & Chang New York Inc** ... G ... 212 599-0556
New York *(G-12054)*
Voss Signs LLC ... E ... 315 682-6418
Manlius *(G-7781)*
Wedel Sign Company Inc ... G ... 631 727-4577
Riverhead *(G-13588)*
Westchester Signs Inc ... G ... 914 666-7446
Mount Kisco *(G-8359)*
Whispr Group Inc ... F ... 212 924-3979
New York *(G-12101)*
Wizard Equipment Inc ... G ... 315 414-9999
Syracuse *(G-15459)*
▲ **WI Concepts & Production Inc** ... G ... 516 538-5300
Freeport *(G-5190)*
Woodbury Printing Plus + Inc ... G ... 845 928-6610
Central Valley *(G-3399)*
Yellowpagecitycom ... F ... 585 410-6688
Rochester *(G-14217)*
Yost Neon Displays Inc ... G ... 716 674-6780
West Seneca *(G-16304)*
Z-Car-D Corp ... E ... 631 424-2077
Huntington Station *(G-6465)*

3995 Burial Caskets

Milso Industries Inc ... F ... 631 234-1133
Hauppauge *(G-5892)*
North Hudson Woodcraft Corp ... E ... 315 429-3105
Dolgeville *(G-4135)*

3996 Linoleum & Hard Surface Floor Coverings, NEC

East To West Architectral Pdts ... G ... 631 433-9690
East Northport *(G-4262)*
▲ **Engineered Plastics Inc** ... E ... 800 682-2525
Williamsville *(G-16579)*
Heritage Contract Flooring LLC ... E ... 716 853-1555
Buffalo *(G-2871)*

3999 Manufacturing Industries, NEC

A & L Asset Management Ltd ... C ... 718 566-1500
Brooklyn *(G-1450)*
A & W Metal Works Inc ... F ... 845 352-2346
Garnerville *(G-5298)*
A Fire Inc ... G ... 631 897-9449
Ronkonkoma *(G-14285)*
A&M Model Makers LLC ... G ... 626 813-9661
Macedon *(G-7691)*
Accenta Incorporated ... G ... 716 565-6262
Buffalo *(G-2681)*
Accessible Bath Tech LLC ... F ... 518 937-1518
Albany *(G-27)*
Accurate Pnt Powdr Coating Inc ... F ... 585 235-1650
Rochester *(G-13597)*
Active Manufacturing Inc ... F ... 607 775-3162
Kirkwood *(G-6937)*
Adel Rootstein (usa) Inc ... E ... 718 499-5650
Brooklyn *(G-1482)*
Adults and Children With Learn ... E ... 516 593-8230
East Rockaway *(G-4292)*
Advanced Assembly Services Inc ... G ... 716 217-8144
Lancaster *(G-7001)*
AFP Manufacturing Corp ... F ... 516 466-6464
Great Neck *(G-5528)*
▲ **Age Manufacturers Inc** ... D ... 718 927-0048
Brooklyn *(G-1494)*
▲ **Aloi Solutions LLC** ... E ... 585 292-0920
Rochester *(G-13619)*
▲ **American Culture Hair Inc** ... E ... 631 242-3142
Huntington Station *(G-6429)*
Animal Pantry ... G ... 631 673-3666
Huntington *(G-6391)*
▲ **Arcadia Mfg Group Inc** ... E ... 518 434-6213
Green Island *(G-5602)*
Arcadia Mfg Group Inc ... G ... 518 434-6213
Menands *(G-8081)*
Arnprior Rpid Mfg Slutions Inc ... C ... 585 617-6301
Rochester *(G-13641)*
Arnprior Rpid Mfg Slutions Inc ... G ... 585 617-6301
Rochester *(G-13642)*
Artemis Studios Inc ... D ... 718 788-6022
Brooklyn *(G-1558)*
Ascribe Inc ... E ... 585 413-0298
Rochester *(G-13646)*
◆ **Astron Candle Manufacturing Co** ... G ... 718 728-3330
Long Island City *(G-7391)*
Atlas Metal Industries Inc ... G ... 607 776-2048
Hammondsport *(G-5702)*
B & R Promotional Products ... G ... 212 563-0040
New York *(G-8988)*
B F G Elcpltg and Mfg Co ... E ... 716 362-0888
Blasdell *(G-924)*
Balance Enterprises Inc ... G ... 516 822-3183
Hicksville *(G-6063)*
Baldwin Ribbon & Stamping Corp ... F ... 718 335-6700
Woodside *(G-16645)*
Bee Green Industries Inc ... G ... 516 334-3525
Carle Place *(G-3262)*
Best Priced Products Inc ... G ... 914 345-3800
Elmsford *(G-4531)*
◆ **Betterbee Inc** ... F ... 518 314-0575
Greenwich *(G-5637)*
Biocontinuum Group Inc ... G ... 212 406-1060
New York *(G-9086)*
Blackbox Biometrics Inc ... E ... 585 329-3399
Rochester *(G-13665)*
Blanche P Field LLC ... E ... 212 355-6616
New York *(G-9099)*
◆ **Boom LLC** ... E ... 646 218-0752
New York *(G-9121)*
Brooklyn Industries LLC ... G ... 718 788-5250
Brooklyn *(G-1643)*
Bullex Inc ... E ... 518 689-2023
Albany *(G-52)*
Bushwick Bottling LLC ... F ... 929 666-3618
Brooklyn *(G-1658)*
Callanan Industries Inc ... G ... 518 382-5354
Schenectady *(G-14656)*
▲ **Candle In The Window Inc** ... F ... 718 852-5743
Brooklyn *(G-1672)*
Candles By Foster ... G ... 914 739-9226
Peekskill *(G-12918)*
▲ **Cathedral Candle Co** ... D ... 315 422-9119
Syracuse *(G-15274)*
▲ **Cemecon Inc** ... E ... 607 562-2363
Horseheads *(G-6309)*
Center Line Studios Inc ... G ... 845 534-7143
New Windsor *(G-8639)*
▲ **Center Line Studios Inc** ... F ... 845 534-7143
New Windsor *(G-8640)*
Chan & Chan (usa) Corp ... G ... 718 388-9633
Brooklyn *(G-1688)*
◆ **Christian Dior Perfumes LLC** ... E ... 212 931-2200
New York *(G-9291)*
Clara Papa ... G ... 315 733-2660
Utica *(G-15682)*
Columbia Dentoform Corporation ... D ... 718 482-1569
Long Island City *(G-7414)*
Commercial Fabrics Inc ... F ... 716 694-0641
North Tonawanda *(G-12422)*
Consolidated Spring LLC ... F ... 845 391-8855
Newburgh *(G-12219)*
Copesetic Inc ... F ... 315 684-7780
Morrisville *(G-8336)*
Costume Armour Inc ... F ... 845 534-9120
Cornwall *(G-3832)*
Creative Models & Prototypes ... G ... 516 433-6828
Hicksville *(G-6075)*
Criterion Bell & Specialty ... E ... 718 788-2600
Brooklyn *(G-1732)*
◆ **Crusader Candle Co Inc** ... E ... 718 625-0005
Brooklyn *(G-1735)*
D & M Enterprises Incorporated ... G ... 914 937-6430
Port Chester *(G-13195)*
D3 Led LLC ... E ... 917 757-9671
New York *(G-9451)*
Dark Storm Industries LLC ... G ... 631 967-3170
Oakdale *(G-12515)*
▲ **De Meo Brothers Inc** ... G ... 212 268-1400
New York *(G-9493)*

Deva Concepts LLC E 212 343-0344
New York *(G-9514)*

Diane Studios Inc D 718 788-6007
Brooklyn *(G-1773)*

Dj Pirrone Industries Inc G 518 864-5496
Pattersonville *(G-12888)*

Dolmen F 912 596-1537
Conklin *(G-3726)*

Donorwall Inc F 212 766-9670
New York *(G-9557)*

Dyco Manufacturing LLC D 607 324-2030
Hornell *(G-6297)*

E-Z Global Wholesale Inc G 888 769-7888
Brooklyn *(G-1806)*

▲ **Eagle Regalia Co Inc** F 845 425-2245
Spring Valley *(G-14989)*

East Penn Manufacturing Co G 631 321-7161
Babylon *(G-526)*

▲ **Eastern Feather & Down Corp** G 718 387-4100
Brooklyn *(G-1809)*

◆ **Eser Realty Corp** E 718 383-0565
Brooklyn *(G-1847)*

Essex Industries G 518 942-6671
Mineville *(G-8253)*

◆ **Essex Manufacturing Inc** D 212 239-0080
New York *(G-9712)*

Eton Institute F 855 334-3688
New York *(G-9724)*

Everstone Industries LLC E 347 777-8150
New York *(G-9739)*

▲ **Faster-Form Corp** D 800 327-3676
New Hartford *(G-8504)*

Federal Sample Card Corp D 718 458-1344
Elmhurst *(G-4464)*

Feraco Industries G 631 547-8120
Huntington Station *(G-6440)*

Fingerprint America Inc G 518 435-1609
Albany *(G-74)*

◆ **Fish & Crown Ltd** D 212 707-9603
New York *(G-9813)*

Five Star Creations Inc E 845 783-1187
Monroe *(G-8269)*

▲ **Four Paws Products Ltd** D 631 436-7421
Ronkonkoma *(G-14343)*

Freedom Mfg LLC F 518 584-0441
Saratoga Springs *(G-14580)*

Fun Industries of NY F 631 845-3805
Farmingdale *(G-4768)*

▲ **Genesis Mannequins USA II Inc** G 212 505-6600
New York *(G-9903)*

Givi Inc F 212 586-5029
New York *(G-9926)*

Goldmont Enterprises Inc F 212 947-3633
Middle Village *(G-8121)*

Goodwill Inds of Greater NY C 914 621-0781
Baldwin Place *(G-546)*

Goodwill Inds Wstn NY Inc F 716 633-3305
Williamsville *(G-16580)*

Grand Island Animal Hospital E 716 773-7645
Grand Island *(G-5502)*

▲ **Gustbuster Ltd** G 631 391-9000
Farmingdale *(G-4777)*

Hair Color Research Group Inc E 718 445-6026
Flushing *(G-5006)*

Handmade Frames Inc F 718 782-8364
Brooklyn *(G-1966)*

◆ **Hoskie Co Inc** D 718 628-8672
Brooklyn *(G-1985)*

Hs Homeworx LLC G 646 870-0406
New York *(G-10141)*

Hudson Eastern Industries Inc G 917 295-5818
Whitestone *(G-16543)*

▲ **Hudson Scenic Studio Inc** C 914 375-0900
Yonkers *(G-16770)*

▼ **Identfication Data Imaging LLC** G 516 484-6500
Port Washington *(G-13267)*

Ilc Industries Inc E 631 567-5600
Bohemia *(G-1035)*

Image Tech F 716 635-0167
Buffalo *(G-2880)*

Impressart F 631 940-9530
Edgewood *(G-4404)*

Innovative Industries LLC G 718 784-7300
Long Island City *(G-7475)*

▲ **International Design Assoc Ltd** G 212 687-0333
New York *(G-10245)*

Iquit Cig LLC G 718 475-1422
Brooklyn *(G-2014)*

Islip Miniture Golf G 631 940-8900
Bay Shore *(G-691)*

◆ **Ivy Enterprises Inc** B 516 621-9779
Port Washington *(G-13271)*

◆ **J & A Usa Inc** G 631 243-3336
Brentwood *(G-1138)*

J & R Unique Giftware E 718 821-0398
Maspeth *(G-7853)*

J T Systematic G 607 754-0929
Endwell *(G-4617)*

Jacobs Juice Corp G 646 255-2860
Brooklyn *(G-2031)*

Jags Manufacturing Network Inc G 631 750-6367
Holbrook *(G-6192)*

▲ **Jamaica Lamp Corp** E 718 776-5039
Queens Village *(G-13409)*

Jason & Jean Products Inc F 718 271-8300
Corona *(G-3846)*

▲ **Jenalex Creative Marketing Inc** G 212 935-2266
New York *(G-10326)*

▲ **Jenray Products Inc** E 914 375-5596
Yonkers *(G-16773)*

JG Innovative Industries Inc G 718 784-7300
Kew Gardens *(G-6876)*

Jimco Lamp & Manufacturing Co G 631 218-2152
Islip *(G-6547)*

John Gailer Inc E 212 243-5662
Long Island City *(G-7480)*

John Prior G 516 520-9801
East Meadow *(G-4254)*

Joya LLC F 718 852-6979
Brooklyn *(G-2051)*

Jpm Fine Woodworking LLC G 516 236-7605
Jericho *(G-6792)*

Just Right Carbines LLC G 585 261-5331
Canandaigua *(G-3224)*

K Dymond Industries Inc F 631 828-0826
Medford *(G-7956)*

Kafko (us) Corp G 877 721-7665
Latham *(G-7077)*

Kaylon Industries LLC G 315 303-2119
Baldwinsville *(G-557)*

Kelly Foundry & Machine Co E 315 732-8313
Utica *(G-15717)*

Ketchum Manufacturing Co Inc F 518 696-3331
Lake Luzerne *(G-6974)*

Kevco Industries G 845 255-7407
New Paltz *(G-8578)*

King Displays Inc F 212 629-8455
New York *(G-10451)*

▲ **Kittywalk Systems Inc** G 516 627-8418
Port Washington *(G-13276)*

▲ **Kkw Corp** E 631 589-5454
Sayville *(G-14631)*

▲ **Lab-Aids Inc** E 631 737-1133
Ronkonkoma *(G-14366)*

Lemetric Hair Centers Inc F 212 986-5620
New York *(G-10543)*

Lemon Brothers Foundation Inc F 347 920-2749
Bronx *(G-1316)*

▲ **Leo D Bernstein & Sons Inc** E 212 337-9578
New York *(G-10548)*

Liberty Displays Inc E 716 743-1757
Amherst *(G-235)*

▲ **Lifestyle-Trimco** E 718 257-9101
Brooklyn *(G-2118)*

Lois Kitchen LLC G 216 308-9335
New York *(G-10593)*

Lux Mundi Corp G 631 244-4596
Ronkonkoma *(G-14372)*

M & S Schmalberg Inc F 212 244-2090
New York *(G-10635)*

M and J Hair Center Inc F 516 872-1010
Garden City *(G-5269)*

Mack Studios Displays Inc E 315 252-7542
Auburn *(G-489)*

Madison Mfg & Mch Inc G 315 922-4476
Erieville *(G-4621)*

Malouf Colette Inc F 212 941-9588
New York *(G-10680)*

▲ **Meisel-Peskin Co Inc** D 718 497-1840
Brooklyn *(G-2189)*

▲ **Mgd Brands Inc** E 516 545-0150
Plainview *(G-13075)*

Miss Jessies LLC G 718 643-9016
New York *(G-10823)*

Mission Crane Service Inc D 718 937-3333
Long Island City *(G-7527)*

▲ **Mitco Manufacturing** G 800 338-8908
Garden City *(G-5272)*

Mitten Manufacturing Inc E 315 437-7564
Syracuse *(G-15375)*

▲ **Moti Inc** F 718 436-4280
Brooklyn *(G-2228)*

▲ **Muench-Kreuzer Candle Company** D 315 471-4515
Syracuse *(G-15377)*

Nationwide Exhibitor Svcs Inc F 631 467-2034
Central Islip *(G-3379)*

Nitro Manufacturing LLC F 716 646-9900
Hamburg *(G-5687)*

◆ **Northast Ctr For Bekeeping LLC** F 800 632-3379
Greenwich *(G-5643)*

◆ **Northern Lights Entps Inc** C 585 593-1200
Wellsville *(G-16119)*

Northern New York Rural G 518 891-9460
Saranac Lake *(G-14563)*

Nsj Group Ltd F 631 893-9300
Babylon *(G-530)*

Nubian Heritage G 631 265-3551
Hauppauge *(G-5903)*

O Brien Gere Mfg Inc G 315 437-6100
Liverpool *(G-7250)*

Ogd V-Hvac Inc E 315 858-1002
Van Hornesville *(G-15802)*

▲ **Ohserase Manufacturing LLC** E 518 358-9309
Akwesasne *(G-26)*

▲ **Ohserase Manufacturing LLC** G 518 358-9309
Hogansburg *(G-6166)*

▲ **Old Williamsburgh Candle Corp** C 718 566-1500
Tallman *(G-15464)*

Oledworks LLC E 585 287-6802
Rochester *(G-13985)*

Omicron Technologies Inc E 631 434-7697
Holbrook *(G-6204)*

Oriskany Manufacturing LLC F 315 732-4962
Yorkville *(G-16829)*

▲ **Orlandi Inc** D 631 756-0110
Farmingdale *(G-4840)*

Orlandi Inc E 631 756-0110
Farmingdale *(G-4841)*

Oso Industries Inc G 917 709-2050
Brooklyn *(G-2294)*

◆ **Our Own Candle Company Inc** F 716 769-5000
Findley Lake *(G-4939)*

◆ **P S Pibbs Inc** D 718 445-8046
Flushing *(G-5032)*

Paperworks Industries Inc F 913 621-0922
Baldwinsville *(G-559)*

Paratus Industries Inc E 716 826-2000
Orchard Park *(G-12735)*

▲ **Patience Brewster Inc** F 315 685-8336
Skaneateles *(G-14876)*

PCI Industries Corp E 914 662-2700
Mount Vernon *(G-8428)*

Performance Precision Mfg LLC G 518 993-3033
Fort Plain *(G-5103)*

Premium Assure Inc G 605 252-9999
Brooklyn *(G-2338)*

▲ **Production Resource Group LLC** D 877 774-7088
Armonk *(G-408)*

Production Resource Group LLC E 845 567-5700
New Windsor *(G-8655)*

▲ **Promotional Development Inc** D 718 485-8550
Brooklyn *(G-2357)*

Props Displays & Interiors F 212 620-3840
New York *(G-11266)*

Pyrotek Incorporated E 716 731-3221
Sanborn *(G-14552)*

Qps Die Cutters Finishers Corp E 718 966-1811
Staten Island *(G-15120)*

Qualbuys LLC G 855 884-3274
Syosset *(G-15228)*

Quality Candle Mfg Co Inc F 631 842-8475
Copiague *(G-3776)*

Quest Manufacturing Inc E 716 312-8000
Hamburg *(G-5692)*

▲ **R V Dow Enterprises Inc** F 585 454-5862
Rochester *(G-14067)*

Rave Inc D 716 695-1110
North Tonawanda *(G-12444)*

Ray Gold Shade Inc F 718 377-8892
Brooklyn *(G-2386)*

Rockwell Video Solutions LLC F 631 745-0582
Southampton *(G-14960)*

Rutcarele Inc G 347 830-5353
Corona *(G-3853)*

Ryers Creek Corp E 607 523-6617
Corning *(G-3825)*

S & H Enterprises Inc G 888 323-8755
Queensbury *(G-13440)*

S B Manufacturing LLC F 845 352-3700
Monsey *(G-8295)*

Saakshi Inc G 315 475-3988
Syracuse *(G-15412)*
▲ Select Industries New York Inc F 800 723-5333
New York *(G-11537)*
Shake-N-Go Fashion Inc E 516 944-7777
Port Washington *(G-13306)*
◆ Shake-N-Go Fashion Inc C 516 944-7777
Port Washington *(G-13307)*
Shenzhen Xnhdingsheng Tech Ltd E 510 506-5753
Flushing *(G-5045)*
Shyam Ahuja Limited G 212 644-5910
New York *(G-11573)*
▲ Siegel & Stockman Inc G 212 633-1508
New York *(G-11576)*
▲ Simcha Candle Co Inc G 845 783-0406
New Windsor *(G-8661)*
Skaffles Group LLC F 212 944-9494
New York *(G-11606)*
▲ Soggy Doggy Productions LLC G 877 504-4811
Larchmont *(G-7059)*
Sonaal Industries Inc G 718 383-3860
Brooklyn *(G-2499)*
◆ Spartan Brands Inc F 212 340-0320
New York *(G-11660)*
Specialists Ltd F 212 941-7696
Ridgewood *(G-13552)*
Spectrum Brands Inc B 631 232-1200
Hauppauge *(G-5945)*
▲ Star Desk Pad Co Inc E 914 963-9400
Yonkers *(G-16800)*
Stasi Industries Inc G 516 334-2742
Old Bethpage *(G-12588)*
▲ Steeldeck Ny Inc F 718 599-3700
Brooklyn *(G-2517)*
Stiegelbauer Associates Inc E 718 624-0835
Brooklyn *(G-2522)*
Swift Multigraphics LLC G 585 442-8000
Rochester *(G-14150)*
▲ Tactica International Inc E 212 575-0500
New York *(G-11774)*
Talisman Industries LLC G 908 433-7116
New York *(G-11777)*
Techgrass F 646 719-2000
New York *(G-11793)*
▲ Tent and Table Com LLC F 716 570-0258
Buffalo *(G-3090)*
Thomas F Egan E 607 669-4822
Binghamton *(G-919)*
▲ Thompson Ferrier LLC G 212 244-2212
New York *(G-11823)*
Tii Industries Inc F 631 789-5000
Copiague *(G-3787)*
Tiki Industries Inc G 516 779-3629
Riverhead *(G-13586)*
Toho Company Limited G 212 391-9058
New York *(G-11855)*
▲ Topoo Industries Incorporated G 718 331-3755
Brooklyn *(G-2572)*
Trendsformers Ltd Liability Co G 888 700-2423
New York *(G-11891)*
▼ Tri-Force Sales LLC E 732 261-5507
New York *(G-11892)*
▲ Tri-Plex Packaging Corporation E 212 481-6070
New York *(G-11894)*
Trove Inc F 212 268-2046
Brooklyn *(G-2589)*
▲ TV Guilfoil & Associates Inc G 315 453-0920
Syracuse *(G-15447)*
Ubees Inc F 916 505-8470
New York *(G-11928)*
▲ Unique Petz LLC E 212 714-1800
New York *(G-11950)*
▲ Unistel LLC D 585 341-4600
Webster *(G-16105)*
▲ Water Splash Inc G 800 936-3430
Champlain *(G-3418)*
Wave Float Rooms LLC G 844 356-2876
Clarence *(G-3542)*
Woodfalls Industries F 518 236-7201
Plattsburgh *(G-13170)*
Zebrowski Industries Inc G 716 532-3911
Collins *(G-3676)*
▲ Zip-Jack Industries Ltd E 914 592-2000
Tarrytown *(G-15498)*
Zmz Mfg Inc G 518 234-4336
Warnerville *(G-15939)*

73 BUSINESS SERVICES

7372 Prepackaged Software

2k Inc G 646 536-3007
New York *(G-8675)*
30dc Inc F 212 962-4400
New York *(G-8676)*
30dc Inc F 212 962-4400
New York *(G-8677)*
A K A Computer Consulting Inc G 718 351-5200
Staten Island *(G-15037)*
A2ia Corp G 917 237-0390
New York *(G-8700)*
Aarfid LLC G 716 992-3999
Eden *(G-4386)*
Abacus Labs Inc E 917 426-6642
New York *(G-8704)*
Abel Noser Solutions LLC E 646 432-4000
New York *(G-8708)*
Ableton Inc G 646 723-4586
New York *(G-8711)*
Accela Inc F 631 563-5005
Ronkonkoma *(G-14286)*
Accelify Solutions LLC E 888 922-2354
New York *(G-8718)*
Adfin Solutions Inc F 650 464-0742
New York *(G-8736)*
Adgorithmics LLC G 646 277-8728
New York *(G-8737)*
Adl Data Systems Inc E 914 591-1800
Elmsford *(G-4528)*
Adobe Systems Inc E 212 471-0904
New York *(G-8739)*
Adobe Systems Incorporated C 212 592-1400
New York *(G-8740)*
Adobe Systems Incorporated E 212 471-0904
New York *(G-8741)*
Adtech Us Inc C 212 402-4840
New York *(G-8744)*
Advanced Cmpt Sftwr Consulting G 718 300-3577
Bronx *(G-1213)*
Advanced Comfort Systems Inc F 518 884-8444
Ballston Spa *(G-574)*
Advanced Cyber Security Corp E 866 417-9155
Bohemia *(G-973)*
Agrinetix Cmpt Systems LLC F 877 978-5477
Henrietta *(G-6029)*
Aimsun Inc G 917 267-8534
New York *(G-8776)*
Amcom Software Inc G 212 951-7600
New York *(G-8817)*
Amenity Analytics Inc E 646 786-8316
New York *(G-8818)*
Amplience Inc G 917 410-7189
New York *(G-8848)*
Andigo New Media Inc G 212 727-8445
New York *(G-8857)*
Anju Sylogent LLC F 480 326-2358
New York *(G-8870)*
Ansa Systems of USA Inc G 718 835-3743
Valley Stream *(G-15772)*
Anyvision US Inc F 606 901-4894
New York *(G-8881)*
Appfigures Inc F 212 343-7900
New York *(G-8891)*
Application Resources Inc G 516 636-6200
Great Neck *(G-5534)*
Application Security Inc D 212 912-4100
New York *(G-8892)*
Apprenda Inc D 518 383-2130
Troy *(G-15600)*
Appsbidder Inc G 917 880-4269
Brooklyn *(G-1544)*
APS Enterprise Software Inc E 631 784-7720
Huntington *(G-6392)*
Archive360 Inc E 212 731-2438
New York *(G-8902)*
Articulate F 646 706-7596
Sagaponack *(G-14504)*
Articulate Global Inc C 800 861-4880
New York *(G-8919)*
Arumai Technologies Inc F 914 217-0038
Armonk *(G-401)*
Asite LLC D 203 545-3089
New York *(G-8933)*
Aspen Research Group Ltd G 212 425-9588
New York *(G-8935)*
Assessment Technologies Inc G 646 530-8666
New York *(G-8937)*

AT&T Corp F 212 317-7048
New York *(G-8942)*
Atomic Information Systems E 716 713-5402
Unadilla *(G-15661)*
Augury Inc E 866 432-0976
New York *(G-8960)*
Automated & MGT Solutions LLC G 518 833-0315
East Greenbush *(G-4227)*
Automated Office Systems Inc F 516 396-5555
Valley Stream *(G-15773)*
Avalanche Studios New York Inc D 212 993-6447
New York *(G-8970)*
AVM Software Inc F 646 381-2468
New York *(G-8980)*
Aycan Medical Systems LLC F 585 271-3078
Rochester *(G-13649)*
B601 V2 Inc G 646 391-6431
New York *(G-8995)*
Base Systems Inc G 845 278-1991
Brewster *(G-1158)*
Beyondly Inc E 646 658-3665
New York *(G-9065)*
Big Data Bizviz LLC G 716 803-2367
West Seneca *(G-16294)*
Big White Wall Holding Inc F 917 281-2649
New York *(G-9079)*
Bigwood Systems Inc G 607 257-0915
Ithaca *(G-6560)*
Billing Blocks Inc F 718 442-5006
Staten Island *(G-15050)*
Birdsigns Inc G 201 388-7613
New York *(G-9089)*
Blue Wolf Group LLC D 866 455-9653
New York *(G-9110)*
Bluebird Transportation LLC F 716 395-0000
Williamsville *(G-16571)*
Botify Corporation G 617 576-2005
New York *(G-9124)*
Boulevard Arts Inc G 917 968-8693
New York *(G-9127)*
Boundless Spatial Inc E 646 831-5531
New York *(G-9128)*
Brainpop LLC E 212 574-6017
New York *(G-9133)*
Braze Inc E 504 327-7269
New York *(G-9137)*
Brigadoon Software Inc G 845 624-0909
Nanuet *(G-8459)*
Broadway Technology LLC E 646 912-6450
New York *(G-9146)*
Bull Street LLC G 212 495-9855
New York *(G-9156)*
Buncee LLC F 631 591-1390
Speonk *(G-14984)*
Business Integrity Inc G 718 238-2008
New York *(G-9162)*
Business Management Systems F 914 245-8558
Brooklyn *(G-1661)*
Byte Consulting Inc G 646 500-8606
New York *(G-9169)*
C S I G Inc G 845 383-3800
Kingston *(G-6891)*
Ca Inc A 800 225-5224
New York *(G-9171)*
Ca Inc G 800 225-5224
Islandia *(G-6523)*
California US Holdings Inc A 212 726-6500
New York *(G-9180)*
Callaway Digital Arts Inc E 212 675-3050
New York *(G-9182)*
Callidus Software Inc F 212 554-7300
New York *(G-9183)*
Caminus Corporation D 212 515-3600
New York *(G-9187)*
Candex Solutions Inc G 215 650-3214
New York *(G-9193)*
Capital Programs Inc G 212 842-4640
New York *(G-9204)*
Careconnector G 919 360-2987
Brooklyn *(G-1677)*
Catalyst Group Inc G 212 243-7777
New York *(G-9226)*
Catch Ventures Inc F 347 620-4351
New York *(G-9228)*
Catholic News Publishing Co F 914 632-7771
Mamaroneck *(G-7737)*
Cbord Group Inc C 607 257-2410
Ithaca *(G-6571)*
Cdml Computer Services Ltd G 718 428-9063
Fresh Meadows *(G-5195)*

S I C

73 BUSINESS SERVICES SIC SECTION

Cegid Corporation ....F 212 757-9038
New York (G-9234)
Ceipal LLC ....G....... 585 351-2934
Rochester (G-13697)
Ceipal LLC ....G....... 585 584-1316
Rochester (G-13698)
Celonis Inc ....G....... 941 615-9670
Brooklyn (G-1685)
Ceros Inc ....E 347 744-9250
New York (G-9252)
Cgi Technologies Solutions Inc ....F 212 682-7411
New York (G-9254)
Chequedcom Inc ....E 888 412-0699
Saratoga Springs (G-14575)
Childrens Progress Inc ....E 212 730-0905
New York (G-9276)
Cinch Technologies Inc ....G....... 212 266-0022
New York (G-9297)
Cinedigm Software ....G....... 212 206-9001
New York (G-9300)
Citic Intl (usa) Travel Inc ....G....... 718 888-9577
Flushing (G-4992)
Citixsys Technologies Inc ....G....... 212 745-1365
New York (G-9308)
Classroom Inc ....E 212 545-8400
New York (G-9323)
▲ Clayton Dubilier & Rice Fun ....E 212 407-5200
New York (G-9324)
Clearview Social Inc ....G....... 801 414-7675
Buffalo (G-2767)
Clever Goats Media LLC ....G....... 917 512-0340
New York (G-9326)
Cloud Rock Group LLC ....G....... 516 967-6023
Roslyn (G-14444)
Cloudparc Inc ....G....... 954 665-5962
New York (G-9332)
Cloudscale365 Inc ....G....... 888 608-6245
Jericho (G-6782)
Cloudsense Inc ....G....... 917 880-6195
New York (G-9333)
Cmnty Corporation ....G....... 646 712-9949
New York (G-9337)
Coalition On Positive Health ....F 212 633-2500
New York (G-9341)
Cognotion Inc ....G....... 347 692-0640
New York (G-9347)
Commercehub Inc ....F 518 810-0700
Albany (G-66)
Comprehensive Dental Tech ....G....... 607 467-4456
Hancock (G-5711)
Condeco Software Inc ....E 408 508-7330
New York (G-9376)
Confiant Inc ....F 646 397-4198
New York (G-9378)
Construction Technology Inc ....E 914 747-8900
Chappaqua (G-3420)
Contactive Inc ....E 646 476-9059
New York (G-9387)
Continuity Software Inc ....E 646 216-8628
New York (G-9389)
Coocoo SMS Inc ....F 646 459-4260
Huntington (G-6396)
Cross Border Transactions LLC ....F 646 767-7342
Tarrytown (G-15476)
Crowd Media Inc ....G....... 212 497-1100
New York (G-9424)
Crunched Inc ....G....... 415 484-9909
New York (G-9427)
CTI Software Inc ....F 631 253-3550
Deer Park (G-3960)
Cuffs Planning & Models Ltd ....G....... 914 632-1883
New Rochelle (G-8597)
Cultureiq Inc ....E 212 755-8633
New York (G-9433)
Curaegis Technologies Inc ....E 585 254-1100
Rochester (G-13729)
Cureatr Inc ....E 212 203-3927
New York (G-9435)
Customshow Inc ....G....... 800 255-5303
New York (G-9438)
Cybersports Inc ....G....... 315 737-7150
Utica (G-15690)
Dakota Software Corporation ....G....... 216 765-7100
Victor (G-15840)
Dartcom Incorporated ....G....... 315 790-5456
New Hartford (G-8502)
Dashlane Inc ....E 212 596-7510
New York (G-9473)
Data Implementation Inc ....G....... 212 979-2015
New York (G-9474)
Datadog Inc ....E 866 329-4466
New York (G-9475)
Davel Systems Inc ....G....... 718 382-6024
Brooklyn (G-1759)
Dbase LLC ....G....... 607 729-0234
Binghamton (G-879)
Defran Systems Inc ....E 212 727-8342
New York (G-9496)
Deniz Information Systems ....G....... 212 750-5199
New York (G-9500)
Digital Associates LLC ....G....... 631 983-6075
Smithtown (G-14896)
Diligent Board Member Svcs LLC ....E 212 741-8181
New York (G-9528)
Diligent Corporation ....C 212 741-8181
New York (G-9529)
Document Strategies LLC ....F 585 506-9000
Rochester (G-13748)
Dow Jones & Company Inc ....E 212 597-5983
New York (G-9564)
Dropcar Operating Company Inc ....G....... 646 342-1595
New York (G-9579)
Dwnld Inc ....E 484 483-6572
New York (G-9592)
Dynamo Development Inc ....G....... 212 385-1552
New York (G-9595)
E H Hurwitz & Associates ....G....... 718 884-3766
Bronx (G-1263)
Eastnets Americas Corp ....F 212 631-0666
New York (G-9613)
Easy Analytic Software Inc ....G....... 718 740-7930
Flushing (G-4997)
Ebeling Associates Inc ....F 518 688-8700
Halfmoon (G-5662)
EBM Care Inc ....G....... 212 500-5000
New York (G-9616)
Ebrevia Inc ....E 203 870-3000
New York (G-9618)
Eccella Corporation ....G....... 718 612-0451
New York (G-9619)
Econometric Software Inc ....G....... 516 938-5254
Plainview (G-13054)
Educational Networks Inc ....G....... 866 526-0200
New York (G-9631)
Efront Financial Solutions Inc ....E 212 220-0660
New York (G-9633)
Eft Analytics Inc ....G....... 212 290-2300
New York (G-9634)
Electronic Arts Inc ....G....... 212 672-0722
New York (G-9641)
Elepath Inc ....G....... 347 417-4975
Brooklyn (G-1825)
Elevondata Labs Inc ....E 470 222-5438
New York (G-9644)
Elodina Inc ....G....... 646 402-5202
New York (G-9658)
Emblaze Systems Inc ....C 212 371-1100
New York (G-9665)
Empire Innovation Group LLC ....F 716 852-5000
Buffalo (G-2818)
Endava Inc ....F 212 920-7240
New York (G-9675)
Enterprise Tech Group Inc ....F 914 588-0327
New Rochelle (G-8601)
Equilend Holdings LLC ....E 212 901-2200
New York (G-9695)
Ert Software Inc ....G....... 845 358-5721
Blauvelt (G-935)
Evidon Inc ....D 917 262-2530
New York (G-9740)
Evocate Media LLC ....F 646 361-3014
New York (G-9741)
Ex El Enterprises Ltd ....F 212 489-4500
New York (G-9745)
Exact Solutions Inc ....F 212 707-8627
New York (G-9747)
Exchange My Mail Inc ....F 516 605-1835
Jericho (G-6788)
Express Checkout LLC ....G....... 646 512-2068
New York (G-9756)
EZ Newsletter LLC ....F 412 943-7777
Brooklyn (G-1861)
EZ Systems US Inc ....C 929 295-0699
Brooklyn (G-1862)
F R A M Technologies Inc ....G....... 718 338-6230
Brooklyn (G-1863)
F-O-R Software LLC ....F 212 231-9506
New York (G-9766)
F-O-R Software LLC ....E 914 220-8800
White Plains (G-16449)
F-O-R Software LLC ....G....... 212 724-3920
New York (G-9767)
Falconstor Software Inc ....C 631 777-5188
Melville (G-8023)
Fastnet Software Intl Inc ....F 888 740-7790
East Northport (G-4263)
Femtech Women Powered Software ....D 516 328-2631
Franklin Square (G-5117)
Fidelus Technologies LLC ....D 212 616-7800
New York (G-9799)
Fidesa US Corporation ....B 212 269-9000
New York (G-9800)
Filestream Inc ....F 516 759-4100
Locust Valley (G-7347)
Financial Technologies 360 Inc ....G....... 862 200-1164
Whitestone (G-16540)
Findmine Inc ....F 925 787-6181
New York (G-9802)
Flextrade Systems Inc ....C 516 627-8993
Great Neck (G-5558)
Flogic Inc ....F 914 478-1352
Hastings On Hudson (G-5748)
Fog Creek Software Inc ....G....... 866 364-2733
New York (G-9820)
Formats Unlimited Inc ....F 631 249-9200
Deer Park (G-3978)
Frazer Computing Inc ....E 315 379-3500
Canton (G-3257)
Freshop Inc ....E 585 738-6035
Rochester (G-13818)
Fruit St Hlth Pub Beneft Corp ....G....... 347 960-6400
New York (G-9854)
Fuel Data Systems Inc ....G....... 800 447-7870
Middletown (G-8153)
Fusion Connect Inc ....C 212 201-2400
New York (G-9863)
Galaxy Software LLC ....G....... 631 244-8405
Oakdale (G-12516)
Gameclub Inc ....G....... 415 359-5742
New York (G-9880)
Games For Change Inc ....G....... 212 242-4922
New York (G-9881)
Gcom Software Inc ....E 518 869-1671
Albany (G-76)
Geoweb3d Inc ....F 607 323-1114
Vestal (G-15817)
Gifts Software Inc ....E 904 438-6000
New York (G-9918)
Glassbox US Inc ....D 917 378-2933
New York (G-9931)
Glitnir Ticketing Inc ....G....... 516 390-5168
Levittown (G-7134)
Global Applctions Solution LLC ....G....... 212 741-9595
New York (G-9937)
Globalquest Solutions Inc ....F 716 601-3524
Buffalo (G-2851)
Grantoo LLC ....G....... 646 356-0460
New York (G-9974)
Great Dane Parent LLC ....G....... 518 810-0700
Albany (G-78)
Gresham Technologies (us) Inc ....F 646 943-5955
New York (G-9985)
Group Commerce Inc ....F 646 346-0598
New York (G-9996)
Hailo Network Usa Inc ....G....... 646 561-8552
New York (G-10021)
Hallmark Hlth Care Sltions LLC ....F 516 513-0959
Hauppauge (G-5839)
Happy Software LLC ....G....... 518 584-4668
Saratoga Springs (G-14586)
Health Care Compliance ....F 516 478-4100
Jericho (G-6790)
Heartland Commerce Inc ....E 845 920-0800
Pearl River (G-12898)
Heineck Associates Inc ....G....... 631 207-2347
Bellport (G-805)
High Performance Sftwr USA Inc ....E 866 616-4958
Valley Stream (G-15782)
Highside Inc ....F 917 525-3340
New York (G-10098)
Hinge Inc ....F 502 445-3111
New York (G-10103)
Hourglass Interactive LLC ....F 954 254-2853
New York (G-10134)
Hovee Inc ....F 646 249-6200
New York (G-10139)
Hudson Software Corporation ....E 914 773-0400
Elmsford (G-4544)
Human Condition Safety Inc ....F 646 867-0644
New York (G-10147)

SIC SECTION 73 BUSINESS SERVICES

Huntington Services Inc....G....516 795-8500
Massapequa (G-7880)
Hvr Mso LLC....G....833 345-6974
Poughkeepsie (G-13346)
Hydrogen Technology Corp....E....800 315-9554
New York (G-10154)
Hyperlaw Inc....F....212 873-6982
New York (G-10155)
IAC Search LLC....E....212 314-7300
New York (G-10163)
Iac/Interactivecorp....A....212 314-7300
New York (G-10164)
Identifycom Inc....G....212 235-0000
New York (G-10173)
Igambit Inc....G....631 670-6777
Smithtown (G-14900)
Incentivate Health LLC....G....518 469-8491
Saratoga Springs (G-14588)
Incycle Software Corp....F....212 626-2608
New York (G-10195)
Indegy Inc....E....866 801-5394
New York (G-10196)
Infinity Augmented Reality Inc....G....917 677-2084
New York (G-10203)
Info Quick Solutions....E....315 463-1400
Liverpool (G-7237)
▲ Infobase Holdings Inc....D....212 967-8800
New York (G-10206)
Infobase Publishing Company....G....212 967-8800
New York (G-10207)
Infomir LLC....F....631 482-6636
Brooklyn (G-2002)
Infor Global Solutions Inc....D....646 336-1700
New York (G-10208)
Informa Solutions Inc....E....516 543-3733
New York (G-10212)
Informatica LLC....F....212 845-7650
New York (G-10214)
Informerly Inc....G....646 238-7137
New York (G-10215)
Innofun Digital Entrmt LLC....F....347 708-0078
New York (G-10217)
Innovation MGT Group Inc....F....800 889-0987
Shirley (G-14836)
Innroad Inc....E....631 458-1437
New York (G-10220)
Inprotopia Corporation....F....917 338-7501
New York (G-10224)
Insight Unlimited Inc....G....914 861-2090
Chappaqua (G-3422)
Insight Venture Partners IV....C....212 230-9200
New York (G-10225)
Inspired Entertainment Inc....F....646 565-3861
New York (G-10226)
INTEL Corporation....D....408 765-8080
Getzville (G-5348)
International Bus Mchs Corp....E....914 345-5219
Armonk (G-404)
International Bus Mchs Corp....E....914 499-2000
Armonk (G-405)
International Identity LLC....G....787 864-0379
Brooklyn (G-2011)
International MGT Netwrk....F....646 401-0032
New York (G-10248)
Internodal International Inc....E....631 765-0037
Southold (G-14969)
Intralinks Holdings Inc....E....212 543-7700
New York (G-10258)
Intraworlds Inc....G....631 602-5333
New York (G-10259)
Invision Inc....G....212 557-5554
New York (G-10265)
Ipsidy Inc....F....407 951-8640
Long Beach (G-7360)
Irv Inc....E....212 334-4507
New York (G-10273)
Isisnet LLC....G....212 239-1205
New York (G-10276)
Ivalua Inc....F....650 930-9710
Brooklyn (G-2020)
J9 Technologies Inc....E....412 586-5038
New York (G-10289)
Joseph A Filippazzo Software....G....718 987-1626
Staten Island (G-15096)
Jump Ramp Games Inc....E....212 500-1456
New York (G-10379)
Jumprope Inc....G....347 927-5867
New York (G-10380)
Jvl Ventures LLC....D....212 365-7555
New York (G-10389)

Kaseya US Sales LLC....D....415 694-5700
New York (G-10411)
Kasisto Inc....E....917 734-4750
New York (G-10412)
Kastor Consulting Inc....G....718 224-9109
Bayside (G-747)
Key Computer Svcs of Chelsea....D....212 206-8060
New York (G-10438)
Keynote Systems Corporation....G....716 564-1332
Buffalo (G-2905)
Kik Us Inc....F....519 505-7616
New York (G-10443)
Kindling Inc....F....212 400-6296
New York (G-10449)
Klara Technologies Inc....F....844 215-5272
New York (G-10456)
Knight Life Entertainment....G....646 733-8911
Brooklyn (G-2078)
Kronos Incorporated....E....518 459-5545
Albany (G-94)
Latchable Inc....E....646 833-0604
New York (G-10521)
Latham Software Sciences Inc....F....518 785-1100
Latham (G-7084)
Laurus Development Inc....F....716 823-1202
Buffalo (G-2922)
Learningateway LLC....G....212 920-7969
Brooklyn (G-2102)
Liftforward Inc....E....917 693-4993
New York (G-10566)
Lincdoc LLC....G....585 563-1669
East Rochester (G-4290)
Live Vote II Inc....G....646 343-9053
New York (G-10583)
Livetiles Corp....F....917 472-7887
New York (G-10585)
Lmt Technology Solutions....F....585 784-7470
Rochester (G-13914)
Lookbooks Media Inc....F....646 737-3360
New York (G-10600)
Lovingly LLC....E....845 977-0775
Fishkill (G-4948)
Loyaltyplant Inc....F....551 221-2701
Forest Hills (G-5076)
Lubbu Inc....G....917 693-9600
Sag Harbor (G-14500)
Luluvise Inc....E....914 309-7812
New York (G-10630)
Madhat Inc....G....518 947-0732
New York (G-10656)
Magic Numbers Inc....G....646 839-8578
New York (G-10668)
Magsoft Corporation....G....518 877-8390
Ballston Spa (G-589)
Maler Technologies Inc....G....212 391-2070
New York (G-10677)
Mall Inc....G....315 751-9490
Cazenovia (G-3322)
Marcus Goldman Inc....F....212 431-0707
New York (G-10700)
Market Factory Inc....F....212 625-9988
New York (G-10709)
Market Logic Software Inc....F....646 405-1041
New York (G-10710)
Matrixcare Inc....G....518 583-6400
New York (G-10729)
Maven Marketing LLC....G....615 510-3248
New York (G-10731)
Maz Systems Inc....F....855 629-3444
New York (G-10736)
Mdcare911 LLC....G....917 640-4869
Brooklyn (G-2183)
Mealplan Corp....G....909 706-8398
New York (G-10749)
Medforce Technologies Inc....F....845 426-0459
Suffern (G-15193)
Mediapost Communications LLC....E....212 204-2000
New York (G-10756)
Medidata Solutions Inc....B....212 918-1800
New York (G-10758)
Medius Software Inc....F....877 295-0058
New York (G-10760)
Mej Beats LLC....G....516 707-6655
New York (G-10766)
Meta Pharmacy Systems Inc....E....516 488-6189
Garden City (G-5271)
Micro Systems Specialists Inc....G....845 677-6150
Millbrook (G-8189)
Microcad Trning Consulting Inc....G....617 923-0500
Lagrangeville (G-6959)

Microcad Trning Consulting Inc....G....631 291-9484
Hauppauge (G-5889)
Microsoft Corporation....A....914 323-2150
White Plains (G-16477)
Microsoft Corporation....G....631 760-2340
Huntington Station (G-6452)
Microsoft Corporation....F....212 245-2100
New York (G-10798)
Microsoft Corporation....D....516 380-1531
Hauppauge (G-5891)
Microstrategy Incorporated....F....888 537-8135
New York (G-10799)
Midas Mdici Group Holdings Inc....G....212 792-0920
New York (G-10800)
Mitel Networks Inc....G....877 654-3573
Rochester (G-13948)
Mml Software Ltd....E....631 941-1313
East Setauket (G-4305)
Mnn Holding Company LLC....F....404 558-5251
Brooklyn (G-2220)
Mobileapp Systems LLC....G....716 667-2780
Buffalo (G-2950)
Mobo Systems Inc....D....212 260-0895
New York (G-10828)
Molabs Inc....G....310 721-6828
New York (G-10833)
Mongodb Inc....C....646 727-4092
New York (G-10839)
Multimedia Plus Inc....F....212 982-3229
New York (G-10860)
Mymee Inc....F....917 476-4122
New York (G-10868)
Nastel Technologies Inc....E....631 761-9100
Plainview (G-13078)
Navatar Group Inc....E....212 863-9655
New York (G-10899)
Nemaris Inc....E....646 794-8648
New York (G-10904)
Nervve Technologies Inc....E....716 800-2250
New York (G-10907)
Netegrity Inc....C....631 342-6000
Central Islip (G-3380)
Netologic Inc....E....212 269-3796
New York (G-10911)
Netsuite Inc....G....646 652-5700
New York (G-10912)
Network Infrstructure Tech Inc....G....212 404-7340
New York (G-10913)
Neverware Inc....F....516 302-3223
New York (G-10916)
New Triad For Collaborative....E....212 873-9610
New York (G-10931)
New York Computer Consulting....G....516 921-1932
Woodbury (G-16626)
New York State Assoc....F....518 434-2281
Albany (G-102)
Nift Group Inc....G....504 505-1144
Brooklyn (G-2269)
Nikish Software Corp....G....631 754-1618
Northport (G-12473)
Noetic Partners Inc....F....212 836-4351
New York (G-10984)
Northrop Grumman Systems Corp....E....315 336-0500
Rome (G-14264)
Numerix LLC....D....212 302-2220
New York (G-11007)
Obout Software Inc....F....212 380-3500
Brooklyn (G-2283)
Olympic Software & Consulting....G....631 351-0655
Melville (G-8053)
Omx (us) Inc....A....646 428-2800
New York (G-11040)
On Demand Books LLC....G....212 966-2222
New York (G-11041)
One-Blue LLC....G....212 223-4380
New York (G-11044)
Open Text Inc....E....585 424-1950
Rochester (G-13990)
Openfin Inc....G....917 450-8822
New York (G-11048)
Operateit Inc....G....631 259-4777
Ronkonkoma (G-14392)
Operative Media Inc....D....212 994-8930
New York (G-11050)
Oracle America Inc....D....518 427-9353
Albany (G-108)
Oracle America Inc....D....585 317-4648
Fairport (G-4646)
Oracle Corporation....C....212 508-7700
New York (G-11053)

SIC

Employee Codes: A=Over 500 employees, B=251-500
C=101-250, D=51-100, E=20-50, F=10-19, G=5-9
2019 Harris
New York Manufacturers Directory
809

73 BUSINESS SERVICES

Company	Location	Code	Phone
Orangenius Inc	New York (G-11054)	F	631 742-0648
Orchard Platform Advisors LLC	New York (G-11058)	E	888 217-2718
Ordergroove Inc	New York (G-11060)	E	866 253-1261
Orthstar Enterprises Inc	Horseheads (G-6323)	D	607 562-2100
Os33 Inc	New York (G-11064)	G	708 336-3466
Ougra Inc	Long Island City (G-7543)	G	646 342-4575
Overture Media Inc	New York (G-11071)	G	917 446-7455
P8h Inc	Brooklyn (G-2298)	E	212 343-1142
Pap Chat Inc	Brooklyn (G-2301)	G	516 350-1888
Par Technology Corporation	New Hartford (G-8508)	D	315 738-0600
Pareteum Corporation	New York (G-11111)	F	212 984-1096
Parlor Labs Inc	New York (G-11118)	G	866 801-7323
Patient Portal Tech Inc	Baldwinsville (G-560)	F	315 638-2030
Pb Mapinfo Corporation	Troy (G-15614)	A	518 285-6000
Peer Software Incorporated	Hauppauge (G-5912)	G	631 979-1770
Pegasystems Inc	New York (G-11141)	E	212 626-6550
Perry Street Software Inc	New York (G-11163)	G	415 935-1429
Pexip Inc	New York (G-11172)	E	703 338-3544
Piano Software Inc	New York (G-11188)	D	646 350-1999
Pilot Inc	New York (G-11193)	G	212 951-1133
Pilot Inc	New York (G-11194)	G	212 951-1133
Pingmd Inc	New York (G-11196)	G	212 632-2665
Piwik Pro LLC	New York (G-11202)	E	888 444-0049
Plain Digital Inc	Scarsdale (G-14643)	G	914 310-0280
Platform Experts Inc	Brooklyn (G-2324)	G	646 843-7100
Playfitness Corp	Staten Island (G-15116)	G	917 497-5443
Playground NY Inc	Brooklyn (G-2325)	F	505 920-7236
Plectica LLC	New York (G-11210)	G	917 304-7052
Pointman LLC	Buffalo (G-3008)	G	716 842-1439
Portfolio Decisionware Inc	New York (G-11220)	E	212 947-1326
Portware LLC	New York (G-11222)	D	212 425-5233
Powa Technologies Inc	New York (G-11225)	E	347 344-7848
Practicepro Software Systems	Garden City (G-5275)	G	516 222-0010
Premier Heart LLC	Port Washington (G-13298)	G	516 883-3383
Preplay Inc	New York (G-11232)	G	917 297-7428
Pricing Engine Inc	New York (G-11238)	F	917 549-3289
Prime Research Solutions LLC	Flushing (G-5040)	F	917 836-7941
Principia Partners LLC	New York (G-11244)	D	212 480-2270
Proginet Corporation	Garden City (G-5276)	E	516 535-3600
Pts Financial Technology LLC	(G-11272)	F	844 825-7634
Purebase Networks Inc	New York (G-11277)	G	646 670-8964
Qlogix Entertainment LLC	New York (G-11292)	G	215 459-6315
Quality and Asrn Tech Corp	Ridge (G-13523)	G	646 450-6762
Quartet Financial Systems Inc	New York (G-11298)	F	845 358-6071
Radnor-Wallace	Port Washington (G-13300)	G	516 767-2131
Raleigh and Drake Pbc	New York (G-11320)	F	212 625-8212
Ramsey Solutions LLC	New York (G-11323)	F	888 329-1055
Rational Retention LLC	Albany (G-123)	E	518 489-3000
Rational Retention LLC	Albany (G-124)	E	518 489-3000
Ray Theta Inc	New York (G-11332)	G	646 757-4956
Reality Analytics Inc	New York (G-11340)	F	347 363-2200
Reason Software Company Inc	New York (G-11341)	F	646 664-1038
Red Oak Software Inc	Rochester (G-14070)	G	585 454-3170
Reentry Games Inc	New York (G-11345)	G	646 421-0080
Relavis Corporation	New York (G-11352)	E	212 995-2900
Reliant Security	New York (G-11353)	F	917 338-2200
Remarkety Inc	Brooklyn (G-2395)	G	800 570-7564
Revivn Public Benefit Corp	Brooklyn (G-2399)	F	347 762-8193
Ringlead Inc	Melville (G-8061)	F	310 906-0545
Rision Inc	New York (G-11395)	F	212 987-2628
Ritnoa Inc	Bellerose (G-782)	F	212 660-2148
Robert Ehrlich	New York (G-11407)	G	516 353-4617
Robly Digital Marketing LLC	New York (G-11412)	E	917 238-0730
Robocom Us LLC	Farmingdale (G-4867)	F	631 861-2045
Robot Fruit Inc	Huntington (G-6411)	F	631 423-7250
Rockport Pa LLC	New York (G-11416)	F	212 482-8580
RPS Holdings Inc	Ithaca (G-6609)	F	607 257-7778
Runs Capital Inc	New York (G-11448)	E	212 618-1201
Runs Inc	New York (G-11449)	E	212 618-1201
Ryba Software Inc	Fresh Meadows (G-5203)	G	718 264-9352
Safe Passage International Inc	Rochester (G-14108)	F	585 292-4910
Sakonnet Technology LLC	New York (G-11466)	E	212 849-9267
Salentica Corp	New York (G-11468)	E	212 672-1777
Sales Hacker Inc	New York (G-11469)	G	516 660-2836
San Jae Educational Resou	Pomona (G-13187)	G	845 364-5458
Sapphire Systems Inc	New York (G-11486)	F	212 905-0100
SC Building Solutions LLC	New York (G-11497)	D	800 564-1152
▲ Scholastic Corporation	New York (G-11513)	F	212 343-6100
◆ Scholastic Inc	New York (G-11514)	A	800 724-6527
Schoolnet Inc	New York (G-11517)	C	646 496-9000
Sciterra LLC	New York (G-11520)	G	646 883-3724
Secured Services Inc	New York (G-11529)	G	866 419-3900
Sefaira Inc	New York (G-11533)	E	855 733-2472
Segovia Technology Co	New York (G-11534)	F	212 868-4412
Serraview America Inc	New York (G-11545)	D	800 903-3716
Servicenow Inc	New York (G-11546)	F	914 318-1168
Shake Inc	New York (G-11555)	G	650 544-5479
Shiprite Software Inc	Utica (G-15733)	G	315 733-6191
Siemens Product Life Mgmt Sftw	Fairport (G-4659)	E	585 389-8699
Siemens Product Life Mgmt Sftw	Melville (G-8063)	B	631 549-2300
Signpost Inc	New York (G-11589)	C	877 334-2837
Similarweb Inc	New York (G-11592)	F	347 685-5422
Sixteen Markets Inc	New York (G-11603)	F	347 759-1024
Skillsoft Corporation	Rochester (G-14130)	F	585 240-7500
Skyop LLC	Canandaigua (G-3234)	F	585 598-4737
Skystem LLC	New York (G-11616)	F	877 778-3320
Slidebean Incorporated	New York (G-11619)	F	866 365-0588
Slyde Inc	Long Island City (G-7594)	F	917 331-2114
Sneakers Software Inc	New York (G-11631)	F	800 877-9221
▲ Social Bicycles Inc	Brooklyn (G-2490)	E	917 746-7624
Softlink International	White Plains (G-16504)	F	914 574-8197
Software & General Services Co	Walworth (G-15916)	G	315 986-4184
Solve Advisors Inc	Rockville Centre (G-14241)	G	646 699-5041
Somml Health Inc	Albany (G-128)	G	518 880-2170
Soroc Technology Corp	Buffalo (G-3071)	F	716 849-5913
Sparta Commercial Services Inc	(G-11658)	F	212 239-2666
Special Circle Inc	New Hyde Park (G-8565)	F	516 595-9988
Spektrix Inc	New York (G-11666)	G	646 741-5110
Splacer Inc	New York (G-11672)	G	646 853-9789
Spring Inc	New York (G-11680)	G	646 732-0323
SS&c Financial Services LLC	Harrison (G-5735)	C	914 670-3600
Stensul Inc	New York (G-11704)	F	212 380-8620
Stop N Shop LLC	Albany (G-131)	G	518 512-9657
Strada Soft Inc	Staten Island (G-15141)	G	718 556-6940
Streetcred Nyc LLC	New York (G-11721)	G	646 675-0073
Striata Inc	New York (G-11722)	D	212 918-4677
Structured Retail Products	New York (G-11724)	G	212 224-3692
Structuredweb Inc	New York (G-11725)	E	201 325-3110
Styleclick Inc	New York (G-11730)	D	212 329-0300
Successware Inc	Williamsville (G-16589)	F	716 565-2338
Suite Solutions Inc	Amherst (G-252)	F	716 929-3050
Sutton Place Software Inc	Melville (G-8067)	G	631 421-1737
Symantec Corporation	New York (G-11758)	D	646 487-6000
Symphony Talent LLC	New York (G-11759)	D	212 999-9000
Synced Inc	New York (G-11761)	G	917 565-5591
Synco Technologies Inc	New York (G-11762)	G	212 255-2031
Synergy Resources Inc	Central Islip (G-3385)	D	631 665-2050
Syntel Inc	New York (G-11765)	F	212 785-9810
Syrasoft LLC	Baldwinsville (G-564)	F	315 708-0341
Systems Trading Inc	Melville (G-8068)	G	718 261-8900
Tabi Inc	Flushing (G-5051)	G	347 701-1051
Tap2play LLC	New York (G-11782)	G	914 960-6232
Targetprocess Inc	Amherst (G-254)	F	877 718-2617
Teachergaming LLC	New York (G-11791)	F	866 644-9323
Teachley LLC	New York (G-11792)	G	347 552-1272

Team Builders Inc .... F 718 979-1005
Staten Island *(G-15145)*
Tech Software LLC .... G 516 986-3050
Melville *(G-8070)*
Tel Tech International .... E 516 393-5174
Melville *(G-8071)*
Telmar Information Services .... E 212 725-3000
New York *(G-11798)*
Tensa Software .... F 914 686-5376
White Plains *(G-16512)*
Tequipment Inc .... D 516 922-3508
Huntington Station *(G-6462)*
Terranua US Corp .... F 212 852-9028
New York *(G-11802)*
Theirapp LLC .... E 212 896-1255
New York *(G-11810)*
Thing Daemon Inc .... E 917 746-9895
New York *(G-11815)*
Thinktrek Inc .... F 212 884-8399
New York *(G-11816)*
▲ **Thomson Reuters Corporation** .... A 646 223-4000
New York *(G-11825)*
Tibco Software Inc .... G 646 495-2600
New York *(G-11830)*
Tika Mobile Inc .... G 646 650-5545
New York *(G-11834)*
Time To Know Inc .... F 212 230-1210
New York *(G-11844)*
Tootter Inc .... E 212 204-7937
Brooklyn *(G-2571)*
Total Defense Inc .... D 631 257-3258
Hauppauge *(G-5961)*
Touchcare P LLC .... F 646 824-5373
New York *(G-11875)*
Tpa Computer Corp .... F 877 866-6044
Carmel *(G-3282)*
Trac Medical Solutions Inc .... G 518 346-7799
Schenectady *(G-14722)*
Tradepaq Corporation .... F 914 332-9174
Tarrytown *(G-15497)*
Transportgistics Inc .... F 631 567-4100
Mount Sinai *(G-8370)*
Treauu Inc .... G 703 731-0196
New York *(G-11889)*
Trueex LLC .... E 646 786-8526
New York *(G-11904)*
Trustfort LLC .... G 781 787-0906
Holbrook *(G-6216)*
Ttg LLC .... G 917 777-0959
New York *(G-11910)*
Tunaverse Media Inc .... G 631 778-8350
Hauppauge *(G-5962)*
Tyme Global Technologies LLC .... E 212 796-1950
New York *(G-11923)*
U X World Inc .... G 914 375-6167
Hawthorne *(G-5998)*
Udisense Inc .... F 866 696-2648
New York *(G-11931)*
Ul Information & Insights Inc .... E 518 640-9200
Latham *(G-7096)*
Ullink Inc .... F 646 565-6675
New York *(G-11935)*
▲ **United Data Systems Inc** .... G 631 549-6900
Huntington *(G-6423)*
Unqork Inc .... E 844 486-7675
New York *(G-11963)*
Upstate Records Management LLC .... G 518 834-1144
Keeseville *(G-6855)*
Urthworx Inc .... G 646 373-7535
New York *(G-11972)*
Usq Group LLC .... G 212 777-7751
New York *(G-11982)*
Uxc Eclipse (usa) Inc .... D 212 965-6400
New York *(G-11983)*
Value Spring Technology Inc .... F 917 705-4658
Harrison *(G-5739)*
Varnish Software Inc .... G 201 857-2832
New York *(G-11996)*
Varonis Systems Inc .... D 877 292-8767
New York *(G-11997)*
Varsity Monitor LLC .... G 212 691-6292
New York *(G-11998)*
Vehicle Tracking Solutions LLC .... E 631 586-7400
Commack *(G-3704)*
Verint Americas Inc .... F 631 962-9334
Melville *(G-8073)*
Verint SEC Intelligence Inc .... D 631 962-9300
Melville *(G-8074)*
Verint Systems Inc .... C 631 962-9600
Melville *(G-8075)*
Verris Inc .... G 201 565-1648
New York *(G-12012)*
Vertana Group LLC .... G 646 430-8226
New York *(G-12017)*
Vhx Corporation .... F 347 689-1446
New York *(G-12024)*
Viridis Learning Inc .... G 347 420-9181
New York *(G-12038)*
Virtual Frameworks Inc .... F 646 690-8207
New York *(G-12040)*
Virtusphere Inc .... F 607 760-2207
Binghamton *(G-922)*
Virtuvent Inc .... G 855 672-8677
Brooklyn *(G-2628)*
Visible Systems Corporation .... E 508 628-1510
Oneida *(G-12623)*
Vision Logic Inc .... G 212 729-4606
New York *(G-12042)*
Vita Rara Inc .... G 518 369-7356
Troy *(G-15631)*
Vizbee Inc .... G 650 787-1424
New York *(G-12048)*
Vline Inc .... G 512 222-5464
Brooklyn *(G-2632)*
Vormittag Associates Inc .... G 800 824-7776
Ronkonkoma *(G-14428)*
Vortex Ventures Inc .... G 516 946-8345
North Baldwin *(G-12370)*
Wagner Technical Services Inc .... F 845 566-4018
Newburgh *(G-12250)*
Water Oracle .... G 845 876-8327
Rhinebeck *(G-13491)*
West Internet Trading Company .... G 415 484-5848
New York *(G-12095)*
Wetpaintcom Inc .... E 206 859-6300
New York *(G-12098)*
Whentech LLC .... F 212 571-0042
New York *(G-12100)*
White Label Partners LLC .... G 917 445-6650
New York *(G-12103)*
Whiteboard Ventures Inc .... F 855 972-6346
New York *(G-12105)*
Winesoft International Corp .... G 914 400-6247
Yonkers *(G-16808)*
Wink Inc .... E 212 389-1382
New York *(G-12121)*
Wink Labs Inc .... E 916 717-0437
New York *(G-12122)*
Wizq Inc .... F 586 381-9048
New York *(G-12125)*
Wochit Inc .... G 212 979-8343
New York *(G-12128)*
Woodbury Systems Group Inc .... G 516 364-2653
Woodbury *(G-16635)*
Wrkbook LLC .... F 914 355-1293
White Plains *(G-16522)*
X Function Inc .... E 212 231-0092
New York *(G-12147)*
Xborder Entertainment LLC .... G 518 726-7036
Plattsburgh *(G-13171)*
Ypis of Staten Island Inc .... G 718 815-4557
Staten Island *(G-15153)*
Zedge Inc .... D 330 577-3424
New York *(G-12171)*
Zipari Inc .... E 855 558-7884
Brooklyn *(G-2669)*
Zoomifier Corporation .... D 800 255-5303
New York *(G-12183)*
Zydoc Med Transcription LLC .... F 631 273-1963
Islandia *(G-6542)*

76 MISCELLANEOUS REPAIR SERVICES

7692 Welding Repair

303 Contracting Inc .... E 716 896-2122
Orchard Park *(G-12694)*
A & J Machine & Welding Inc .... F 631 845-7586
Farmingdale *(G-4704)*
AAA Welding and Fabrication of .... G 585 254-2830
Rochester *(G-13592)*
Accurate Welding Service Inc .... G 516 333-1730
Westbury *(G-16308)*
Acro-Fab Ltd .... E 315 564-6688
Hannibal *(G-5717)*
Airweld Inc .... G 631 924-6366
Ridge *(G-13520)*
Aj Genco Mch Sp McHy Rdout Svc .... F 716 664-4925
Falconer *(G-4669)*
Allen Tool Phoenix Inc .... E 315 463-7533
East Syracuse *(G-4317)*
Alliance Services Corp .... F 516 775-7600
Floral Park *(G-4953)*
Alliance Welding & Steel Fabg .... F 516 775-7600
Floral Park *(G-4954)*
Alloy Metal Works Inc .... G 631 694-8163
Farmingdale *(G-4716)*
Alpine Machine Inc .... F 607 272-1344
Ithaca *(G-6556)*
Andersens Spring & Wldg Corp .... G 516 785-7337
Bellmore *(G-784)*
ARC TEC Wldg & Fabrication Inc .... G 718 982-9274
Staten Island *(G-15044)*
Atlantis Equipment Corporation .... E 518 733-5910
Stephentown *(G-15154)*
▲ **Barber Welding Inc** .... E 315 834-6645
Weedsport *(G-16110)*
Benemy Welding & Fabrication .... G 315 548-8500
Phelps *(G-12975)*
Big Apple Welding Supply .... G 718 439-3959
Brooklyn *(G-1610)*
Bms Manufacturing Co Inc .... E 607 535-2426
Watkins Glen *(G-16058)*
Boilermatic Welding Inds Inc .... E 631 654-1341
Medford *(G-7940)*
Bracci Ironworks Inc .... F 718 629-2374
Brooklyn *(G-1630)*
Brenseke George Wldg Ir Works .... G 631 271-4870
Deer Park *(G-3954)*
Broadalbin Manufacturing Corp .... E 518 883-5313
Broadalbin *(G-1187)*
Bruce Pierce .... G 716 731-9310
Sanborn *(G-14542)*
C G & Son Machining Inc .... G 315 964-2430
Williamstown *(G-16564)*
CBM Fabrications Inc .... E 518 399-8023
Ballston Lake *(G-567)*
Chautauqua Machine Spc LLC .... F 716 782-3276
Ashville *(G-416)*
Competicion Mower Repair .... G 516 280-6584
Mineola *(G-8214)*
Cs Automation Inc .... F 315 524-5123
Ontario *(G-12650)*
Custom Laser Inc .... E 716 434-8600
Lockport *(G-7292)*
D & G Welding Inc .... G 716 873-3088
Buffalo *(G-2790)*
DC Fabrication & Welding Inc .... G 845 295-0215
Ferndale *(G-4932)*
Deck Bros Inc .... E 716 852-0262
Buffalo *(G-2795)*
Dennies Manufacturing Inc .... E 585 393-4646
Canandaigua *(G-3218)*
Donald Stefan .... G 716 492-1110
Chaffee *(G-3403)*
Dorgan Welding Service .... G 315 462-9030
Phelps *(G-12976)*
E B Industries LLC .... E 631 293-8565
Farmingdale *(G-4754)*
E B Industries LLC .... E 631 293-8565
Farmingdale *(G-4755)*
Eagle Welding Machine .... G 315 594-1845
Wolcott *(G-16610)*
Etna Tool & Die Corporation .... F 212 475-4350
New York *(G-9723)*
Excelco/Newbrook Inc .... D 716 934-2644
Silver Creek *(G-14862)*
F M L Industries Inc .... G 607 749-7273
Homer *(G-6254)*
Flushing Boiler & Welding Co .... G 718 463-1266
Brooklyn *(G-1893)*
Formac Welding Inc .... G 631 421-5525
Huntington Station *(G-6441)*
Fred Santucci Inc .... F 716 483-1411
Jamestown *(G-6716)*
G & C Welding Co Inc .... G 516 883-3228
Port Washington *(G-13261)*
Gasport Welding & Fabg Inc .... F 716 772-7205
Gasport *(G-5306)*
Gc Mobile Services Inc .... G 914 736-9730
Cortlandt Manor *(G-3901)*
Genco John .... G 716 483-5446
Jamestown *(G-6717)*
General Welding & Fabg Inc .... G 716 652-0033
Elma *(G-4451)*
Guthrie Heli-ARC Inc .... G 585 548-5053
Bergen *(G-821)*
Hadfield Inc .... F 631 981-4314
Ronkonkoma *(G-14350)*

SIC

Employee Codes: A=Over 500 employees, B=251-500
C=101-250, D=51-100, E=20-50, F=10-19, G=5-9
2019 Harris
New York Manufacturers Directory
811

76 MISCELLANEOUS REPAIR SERVICES

Hadleys Fab-Weld Inc ....G...... 315 926-5101
 Marion (G-7802)
Hansen Steel ....E...... 585 398-2020
 Farmington (G-4915)
Hartman Enterprises Inc ....D...... 315 363-7300
 Oneida (G-12610)
Haskell Machine & Tool Inc ....F...... 607 749-2421
 Homer (G-6255)
Haun Welding Supply Inc ....G...... 607 846-2289
 Elmira (G-4491)
Haun Welding Supply Inc ....G...... 315 592-5012
 Fulton (G-5219)
Homer Iron Works LLC ....G...... 607 749-3963
 Homer (G-6256)
Huntington Welding & Iron ....G...... 631 423-3331
 Huntington Station (G-6445)
Ingleside Machine Co Inc ....D...... 585 924-3046
 Farmington (G-4916)
Jacksons Welding LLC ....G...... 607 756-2725
 Cortland (G-3878)
Kittredge & Sons Inc ....D...... 978 567-0998
 Niagara Falls (G-12303)
▼ Kon Tat Group Corporation ....G...... 718 207-5022
 Brooklyn (G-2081)
L & S Metals Inc ....E...... 716 692-6865
 North Tonawanda (G-12436)
▲ Lagasse Works Inc ....G...... 315 946-9202
 Lyons (G-7685)
Linita Design & Mfg Corp ....E...... 716 566-7753
 Lackawanna (G-6949)
M M Welding ....E...... 315 363-3980
 Oneida (G-12612)
Maple Grove Corp ....E...... 585 492-5286
 Arcade (G-386)
Maria Dionisio Welding Inc ....G...... 631 956-0815
 Lindenhurst (G-7178)
Maspeth Welding Inc ....E...... 718 497-5430
 Maspeth (G-7858)
Meades Welding and Fabricating ....G...... 631 581-1555
 Islip (G-6548)
Mega Tool & Mfg Corp ....E...... 607 734-8398
 Elmira (G-4498)
Miller Metal Fabricating Inc ....G...... 585 359-3400
 Rochester (G-13945)
▲ Modern Mechanical Fab Inc ....G...... 518 298-5177
 Champlain (G-3412)
Mooradian Hydraulics & Eqp Co ....F...... 518 766-3866
 Castleton On Hudson (G-3296)
Ms Spares LLC ....G...... 607 223-3024
 Clay (G-3551)
New Age Ironworks Inc ....F...... 718 277-1895
 Brooklyn (G-2255)

NY Iron Inc ....F...... 718 302-9000
 Long Island City (G-7541)
Parfuse Corp ....E...... 516 997-8888
 Westbury (G-16363)
Phillip J Ortiz Manufacturing ......G...... 845 226-7030
 Hopewell Junction (G-6292)
Phoenix Welding & Fabg Inc ....G...... 315 695-2223
 Phoenix (G-12992)
Precision Laser Technology LLC ....F...... 585 458-6208
 Rochester (G-14036)
Pro-Tech Wldg Fabrication Inc ....G...... 585 436-9855
 Rochester (G-14047)
Qsf Inc ....G...... 585 247-6200
 Gates (G-5311)
Quality Industrial Services ....F...... 716 667-7703
 Orchard Park (G-12742)
R & B Fabrication Inc ....F...... 315 640-9901
 Cicero (G-3522)
Reliable Welding & Fabrication ....G...... 631 758-2637
 Patchogue (G-12876)
REO Welding Inc ....F...... 518 238-1022
 Cohoes (G-3618)
Rini Tank & Truck Service ....F...... 718 384-6606
 Brooklyn (G-2402)
Rj Welding & Fabricating Inc ......G...... 315 523-1288
 Clifton Springs (G-3583)
Robert M Brown ....F...... 607 426-6250
 Montour Falls (G-8327)
Rothe Welding Inc ....G...... 845 246-3051
 Saugerties (G-14615)
S & D Welding Corp ....G...... 631 454-0383
 West Babylon (G-16189)
S J B Fabrication ....F...... 716 895-0281
 Buffalo (G-3052)
Sierson Crane Inc ....F...... 315 723-6914
 Westmoreland (G-16411)
Sierson Welding Inc ....G...... 315 724-3903
 Westmoreland (G-16412)
Smithers Tools & Mch Pdts Inc ....D...... 845 876-3063
 Rhinebeck (G-13488)
▲ Strecks Inc ....E...... 518 273-4410
 Watervliet (G-16051)
Tracey Welding Co Inc ....G...... 518 756-6309
 Coeymans (G-3609)
W R P Welding Ltd ....G...... 631 249-8859
 Farmingdale (G-4904)
Walters & Walters Inc ....G...... 347 202-8535
 Bronx (G-1418)
Watkins Welding and Mch Sp Inc ....G...... 914 949-6168
 White Plains (G-16516)
Waynes Welding Inc ....E...... 315 768-6146
 Yorkville (G-16835)

Welding and Brazing Svcs Inc ....G...... 607 397-1009
 Richfield Springs (G-13493)
Welding Chapter of New York ....G...... 212 481-1496
 New York (G-12090)
West Metal Works Inc ....E...... 716 895-4900
 Buffalo (G-3128)

7694 Armature Rewinding Shops

A & C/Furia Electric Motors ....F...... 914 949-0585
 White Plains (G-16416)
Accurate Marine Specialties ....G...... 631 589-5502
 Bohemia (G-970)
Armor Machining Services, Inc. ....E...... 716 825-0190
 Buffalo (G-2709)
Bayshore Electric Motors ....G...... 631 475-1397
 Patchogue (G-12862)
Daves Electric Motors & Pumps ....G...... 212 982-2930
 New York (G-9478)
Electric Motor Specialty Inc ....G...... 716 487-1458
 Jamestown (G-6714)
Ener-G-Rotors Inc ....G...... 518 372-2608
 Schenectady (G-14670)
General Electric Company ....E...... 315 456-3304
 Syracuse (G-15332)
General Electric Company ....E...... 518 459-4110
 Albany (G-77)
Genesis Electrical Motors ....G...... 718 274-7030
 Woodside (G-16658)
Lawtons Electric Motor Service ....G...... 315 393-2728
 Ogdensburg (G-12576)
Longo New York Inc ....F...... 212 929-7128
 New York (G-10597)
Power-Flo Technologies Inc ....D...... 315 399-5801
 East Syracuse (G-4362)
Power-Flo Technologies Inc ....E...... 585 426-4607
 Rochester (G-14029)
Premco Inc ....F...... 914 636-7095
 New Rochelle (G-8623)
Prime Electric Motors Inc ....G...... 718 784-1124
 Long Island City (G-7559)
RC Entps Bus & Trck Inc ....G...... 518 568-5753
 Saint Johnsville (G-14521)
Sunset Ridge Holdings Inc ....G...... 716 487-1458
 Jamestown (G-6753)
▲ Tis Ansonia LLC ....F...... 518 272-4920
 Watervliet (G-16052)
Troy Belting and Supply Co ....D...... 518 272-4920
 Watervliet (G-16053)
Troy Industrial Solutions ....F...... 518 272-4920
 Watervliet (G-16054)
United Richter Electrical Mtrs ....F...... 716 855-1945
 Buffalo (G-3112)

ALPHABETIC SECTION

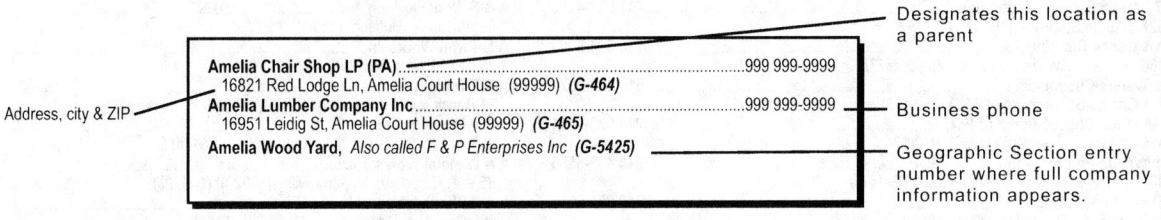

- Designates this location as a parent
- Business phone
- Geographic Section entry number where full company information appears.

Address, city & ZIP

Amelia Chair Shop LP (PA) 999 999-9999
16821 Red Lodge Ln, Amelia Court House (99999) *(G-464)*
Amelia Lumber Company Inc 999 999-9999
16951 Leidig St, Amelia Court House (99999) *(G-465)*
Amelia Wood Yard, *Also called F & P Enterprises Inc (G-5425)*

See footnotes for symbols and codes identification.
* Companies listed alphabetically.
* Complete physical or mailing address.

---

09 FIshy BII/Dsert Sunrise LLC 518 583-6638
2 Smith Bridge Rd Saratoga Springs (12866) *(G-14565)*
1 Atelier LLC 917 916-2968
347 W 36th St New York (10018) *(G-8664)*
1/2 Off Cards Wantagh Inc 516 809-9832
1162 Wantagh Ave Wantagh (11793) *(G-15919)*
110 Sand Company (PA) 631 694-2822
136 Spagnoli Rd Melville (11747) *(G-7994)*
110 Sand Company 631 694-2822
170 Cabot St West Babylon (11704) *(G-16124)*
116 26 Street, Brooklyn *Also called Angel-Made In Heaven Inc (G-1534)*
125-127 Main Street Corp 631 477-1500
125 Main St 127 Greenport (11944) *(G-5625)*
12pt Printing LLC 718 376-2120
2053 E 1st St Brooklyn (11223) *(G-1433)*
131-11 Atlantic RE Inc 718 441-7700
13111 Atlantic Ave Ste 1 Richmond Hill (11418) *(G-13494)*
1510 Associates LLC 212 828-8720
1500 Lexington Ave New York (10029) *(G-8665)*
17 Bakers LLC 844 687-6836
8 Los Robles St Williamsville (14221) *(G-16565)*
18 Rocks LLC 631 465-9990
102 Marcus Dr Melville (11747) *(G-7995)*
180s LLC (HQ) 410 534-6320
1 Liberty Plz Rm 3500 New York (10006) *(G-8666)*
1884 Collection, New York *Also called Anima Group LLC (G-8868)*
1928 Jewelry Co, New York *Also called Mel Bernie and Company Inc (G-10768)*
1gpn, New York *Also called First Games Publr Netwrk Inc (G-9807)*
1ktgold Inc 212 302-8200
3 Barker Ave Ste 290 White Plains (10601) *(G-16415)*
1st Responder Newspaper, New Windsor *Also called Belsito Communications Inc (G-8636)*
2 1 2 Postcards Inc 212 767-8227
121 Varick St Frnt B New York (10013) *(G-8667)*
2 X 4 Inc 212 647-1170
180 Varick St Rm 1610 New York (10014) *(G-8668)*
20 Bliss St Inc 716 326-2790
61 E Main St Westfield (14787) *(G-16390)*
209 Discount Oil 845 386-2090
10 Sands Station Rd Middletown (10940) *(G-8135)*
212 Biz LLC (PA) 212 391-4444
525 Fashion Ave Rm 2301 New York (10018) *(G-8669)*
212 Db Corp 212 652-5600
30 W 22nd St Fl 6 New York (10010) *(G-8670)*
212 Media LLC 212 710-3092
460 Park Ave S Fl 4 New York (10016) *(G-8671)*
212kiddish Inc 718 705-7227
168 Spencer St Brooklyn (11205) *(G-1434)*
219 South West 315 474-2065
219 S West St Syracuse (13202) *(G-15235)*
21st Century Finishes Inc 516 221-7000
1353 Newbridge Rd Unit A North Bellmore (11710) *(G-12372)*
21st Century Fox America Inc 212 782-8000
1185 Av Of The Americas New York (10036) *(G-8672)*
21st Century Fox America Inc (HQ) 212 852-7000
1211 Ave Of The Americas New York (10036) *(G-8673)*
21st Century Fox America Inc 212 447-4600
200 Madison Ave Fl 8 New York (10016) *(G-8674)*
21st Century Optics Inc (HQ) 347 527-1079
4700 33rd St Ste 1r Long Island City (11101) *(G-7362)*
21st Century Spirits Corp 718 499-0606
137 12th St Brooklyn (11215) *(G-1435)*
24 Seven Enterprises Inc 845 563-9033
1073 State Route 94 Ste 9 New Windsor (12553) *(G-8632)*
240 Michigan Street Inc. 716 434-6010
96 Darwin Dr Buffalo (14226) *(G-2675)*
260 Oak Street Inc 877 852-4676
260 Oak St Buffalo (14203) *(G-2676)*
2600 Enterprises Inc 631 474-2677
2 Flowerfield Ste 30 Saint James (11780) *(G-14509)*
2fish 5loaves Comminty Pantry, Arverne *Also called Armour Bearer Group Inc (G-413)*

2h International Corp 347 623-9380
6766 108th St Apt D1 Forest Hills (11375) *(G-5069)*
2k Inc 646 536-3007
622 Broadway Fl 6 New York (10012) *(G-8675)*
2nd Skin Armor, Levittown *Also called Universal Armor Systems Corp (G-7136)*
2p Agency Usa Inc 212 203-5586
1674 E 22nd St Apt 3a Brooklyn (11229) *(G-1436)*
3 Barker Ave Ste 290, White Plains *Also called 1ktgold Inc (G-16415)*
30 Degrees Weatherproof, New York *Also called David Peyser Sportswear Inc (G-9483)*
303 Contracting Inc (HQ) 716 896-2122
5486 Powers Rd Orchard Park (14127) *(G-12694)*
30dc Inc (PA) 212 962-4400
80 Broad St Fl 5 New York (10004) *(G-8676)*
30dc Inc 212 962-4400
80 Broad St Fl 5 New York (10004) *(G-8677)*
31 Phillip Lim LLC (PA) 212 354-6540
304 Hudson St Fl 8 New York (10013) *(G-8678)*
311 Industries Corp 607 846-4520
434 Airport Rd Endicott (13760) *(G-4580)*
3239603400 La Head Quarters, New York *Also called Peer International Corp (G-11136)*
331 Holding Inc 585 924-1740
100 Rawson Rd Ste 205 Victor (14564) *(G-15827)*
333 J & M Food Corp 718 381-1493
333 Seneca Ave Ridgewood (11385) *(G-13526)*
369 River Road Inc 716 694-5001
369 River Rd North Tonawanda (14120) *(G-12409)*
3835 Lebron Rest Eqp & Sup Inc (PA) 212 942-8258
3835 9th Ave New York (10034) *(G-8679)*
388 Associates Inc 267 367-0990
385 Harman St Brooklyn (11237) *(G-1437)*
39th Street Music-Div, New York *Also called Michael Karp Music Inc (G-10792)*
3b Timber Company Inc 315 942-6580
8745 Industrial Dr Boonville (13309) *(G-1113)*
3dflam Inc 631 647-2694
1460 N Clinton Ave Ste I9 Bay Shore (11706) *(G-650)*
3doodler, New York *Also called Wobbleworks Inc (G-12127)*
3krf LLC 516 208-6824
3516 Hargale Rd Oceanside (11572) *(G-12529)*
3M Company 716 876-1596
305 Sawyer Ave Tonawanda (14150) *(G-15517)*
3phase Industries LLC 347 763-2942
481 Van Buren St Unit 9a Brooklyn (11221) *(G-1438)*
3rd Avenue Doughnut Inc 718 748-3294
7111 3rd Ave Brooklyn (11209) *(G-1439)*
3v Company Inc 718 858-7333
110 Bridge St Ste 3 Brooklyn (11201) *(G-1440)*
4 Over 4com Inc 718 932-2700
1941 46th St Astoria (11105) *(G-419)*
40 Street Baking Inc 212 683-4700
8617 17th Ave Brooklyn (11214) *(G-1441)*
450 Ridge St Inc 716 754-2789
450 Ridge St Lewiston (14092) *(G-7138)*
461 New Lots Avenue LLC 347 303-9305
461 New Lots Ave Brooklyn (11207) *(G-1442)*
4bumpers Llc 212 721-9600
285 New Wstmnster End Ave New York (10023) *(G-8680)*
4m Precision Industries Inc 315 252-8415
4000 Technology Park Blvd Auburn (13021) *(G-462)*
5 Star Apparel LLC 212 563-1233
31 W 34th St Fl 7 New York (10001) *(G-8681)*
5 Stars Printing Corp 718 461-4612
13330 32nd Ave Flushing (11354) *(G-4977)*
50+ Lifestyle 631 286-0058
146 S Country Rd Ste 4 Bellport (11713) *(G-796)*
514 Adams Corporation 516 352-6948
781 Hempstead Tpke Franklin Square (11010) *(G-5114)*
518 Prints LLC 518 674-5346
1548 Burden Lake Rd Ste 4 Averill Park (12018) *(G-512)*
525 America, New York *Also called Bock Family Holdings Inc (G-9116)*

(PA)=Parent Co (HQ)=Headquarters (DH)=Div Headquarters

2019 Harris
New York Manufacturers Directory

813

525 America LLC (PA) ALPHABETIC SECTION

525 America LLC (PA) 212 921-5688
525 7th Ave Rm 1000 New York (10018) ***(G-8682)***
527 Franco Bakery Corporation 718 993-4200
527 E 138th St Bronx (10454) ***(G-1197)***
5th & Ocean Clothing Inc 716 604-9000
160 Delaware Ave Buffalo (14202) ***(G-2677)***
5th Avenue Chocolatiere LLC 516 868-8070
114 Church St Freeport (11520) ***(G-5133)***
5th Avenue Chocolatiere Ltd (PA) 212 935-5454
114 Church St Freeport (11520) ***(G-5134)***
5th Avenue Pharmacy Inc 718 439-8585
4818 5th Ave Ste 1 Brooklyn (11220) ***(G-1443)***
6 Shore Road LLC 212 274-9666
54 Thompson St Fl 5 New York (10012) ***(G-8683)***
6478 Ridge Road LLC (PA) 716 625-8400
6251 S Transit Rd Lockport (14094) ***(G-7282)***
6478 Ridge Road LLC 716 625-8400
6478 Ridge Rd Lockport (14094) ***(G-7283)***
6727 11th Ave Corp 718 837-8787
6727 11th Ave Brooklyn (11219) ***(G-1444)***
6th Ave Gourmet Inc 845 782-9067
51 Forest Rd Unit 116 Monroe (10950) ***(G-8262)***
6th Avenue Showcase Inc 212 382-0400
241 W 37th St Frnt 2 New York (10018) ***(G-8684)***
72 Steel and Aluminium Work 917 667-3033
220 42nd St Brooklyn (11232) ***(G-1445)***
760 NI Holdings 716 821-1391
760 Northland Ave Buffalo (14211) ***(G-2678)***
786 Iron Works Corp 718 418-4808
50 Morgan Ave Brooklyn (11237) ***(G-1446)***
79 Metro Ltd (PA) 212 944-4030
265 W 37th St Rm 205 New York (10018) ***(G-8685)***
828 Express Inc 917 577-9019
619 Elbe Ave Staten Island (10304) ***(G-15036)***
872 Hunts Point Pharmacy Inc 718 991-3519
872 Hunts Point Ave Bronx (10474) ***(G-1198)***
888 Pharmacy Inc 718 871-8833
4821 8th Ave Brooklyn (11220) ***(G-1447)***
901 D LLC 845 369-1111
360 Route 59 Ste 3 Airmont (10952) ***(G-10)***
999 Bagels Inc 718 915-0742
1410 86th St Brooklyn (11228) ***(G-1448)***
99cent World and Variety Corp 212 740-0010
4242 Broadway New York (10033) ***(G-8686)***
A & A Graphics Inc II 516 735-0078
615 Arlington Dr Seaford (11783) ***(G-14757)***
A & B Color Corp (del) (PA) 718 441-5482
8204 Lefferts Blvd # 356 Kew Gardens (11415) ***(G-6869)***
A & B Finishing Inc 718 522-4702
401 Park Ave Brooklyn (11205) ***(G-1449)***
A & C/Furia Electric Motors 914 949-0585
75 Lafayette Ave White Plains (10603) ***(G-16416)***
A & D Entrances LLC 718 989-2441
105 Wyandanch Ave Wyandanch (11798) ***(G-16690)***
A & D Tool Inc 631 243-4339
30 Pashen Pl Dix Hills (11746) ***(G-4117)***
A & F Trucking & Excavating, Salamanca *Also called Alice Perkins* ***(G-14523)***
A & G Food Distributors LLC 917 939-3457
21610 47th Ave Apt 3b Bayside (11361) ***(G-740)***
A & G Heat Sealing 631 724-7764
1 Albatross Ln Smithtown (11787) ***(G-14893)***
A & G Precision Corp 631 957-5613
680 Albany Ave Amityville (11701) ***(G-262)***
A & J Machine & Welding Inc 631 845-7586
6040 New Hwy Farmingdale (11735) ***(G-4704)***
A & J Washroom Accessories, New Windsor *Also called Gamma Products Inc* ***(G-8645)***
A & K Equipment Incorporated 705 428-3573
407 Sherman St Watertown (13601) ***(G-15999)***
A & L Asset Management Ltd 718 566-1500
143 Alabama Ave Brooklyn (11207) ***(G-1450)***
A & L Doors & Hardware LLC 718 585-8400
375 E 163rd St Frnt 2 Bronx (10451) ***(G-1199)***
A & L Machine Company Inc 631 463-3111
200 Blydenburg Rd Ste 9 Islandia (11749) ***(G-6520)***
A & L Shtmtl Fabrications Corp 718 842-1600
1243 Oakpoint Ave Bronx (10474) ***(G-1200)***
A & M LLC 212 354-1341
29 W 46th St New York (10036) ***(G-8687)***
A & M Appel Distributing Inc 516 735-1172
500 N Atlanta Ave Massapequa (11758) ***(G-7876)***
A & M Home Improvement, Maspeth *Also called Andike Millwork Inc* ***(G-7821)***
A & M Litho Inc 516 342-9727
4 Hunt Pl Bethpage (11714) ***(G-836)***
A & M Rosenthal Entps Inc (PA) 646 638-9600
8 W 38th St Fl 4 New York (10018) ***(G-8688)***
A & M Steel Stamps Inc 516 741-6223
55 Windsor Ave Mineola (11501) ***(G-8199)***
A & Mt Realty Group LLC 718 974-5871
1979 Pacific St Fl 1 Brooklyn (11233) ***(G-1451)***
A & R Concrete Products LLC 845 562-0640
7 Ruscitti Rd New Windsor (12553) ***(G-8633)***
A & S Electric 212 228-2030
952 Flushing Ave Brooklyn (11206) ***(G-1452)***
A & S Window Associates Inc 718 275-7900
8819 76th Ave Glendale (11385) ***(G-5389)***
A & S Woodworking Inc 518 821-0832
9 Partition St Hudson (12534) ***(G-6335)***
A & T Iron Works Inc 914 632-8992
25 Cliff St New Rochelle (10801) ***(G-8585)***
A & T Tooling LLC 716 601-7299
91 Beach Ave Lancaster (14086) ***(G-7000)***
A & V Castings Inc 212 997-0042
257 W 39th St Fl 16w New York (10018) ***(G-8689)***
A & W Metal Works Inc 845 352-2346
55 W Railroad Ave 5 Garnerville (10923) ***(G-5298)***
A & Z Pharmaceutical Inc 631 952-3802
180 Oser Ave Hauppauge (11788) ***(G-5752)***
A & Z Pharmaceutical Inc (PA) 631 952-3800
350 Wireless Blvd Ste 200 Hauppauge (11788) ***(G-5753)***
A A C, Farmingdale *Also called American Aerospace Contrls Inc* ***(G-4719)***
A A P C O Screen Prntng/Sprtwr, Binghamton *Also called Peter Papastrat* ***(G-910)***
A A Technology Inc 631 913-0400
101 Trade Zone Dr Ronkonkoma (11779) ***(G-14284)***
A and J Apparel Corp 212 398-8899
209 W 38th St Rm 1207 New York (10018) ***(G-8690)***
A and L Home Fuel LLC 607 638-1994
601 Smokey Ave Schenevus (12155) ***(G-14729)***
A Angonoa Inc (PA) 718 762-4466
11505 15th Ave College Point (11356) ***(G-3634)***
A B C Elastic Corp 718 388-2953
889 Metropolitan Ave Brooklyn (11211) ***(G-1453)***
A B C Mc Cleary Sign Co Inc 315 493-3550
40230 State Route 3 Carthage (13619) ***(G-3285)***
A B S Brass Products Inc 718 497-2115
185 Moore St Brooklyn (11206) ***(G-1454)***
A C J Communications Inc 631 587-5612
65 Deer Park Ave Ste 2 Babylon (11702) ***(G-523)***
A Colarusso and Son Inc (PA) 518 828-3218
91 Newman Rd Hudson (12534) ***(G-6336)***
A D Bowman & Son Lumber Co 607 692-2595
1737 Us Highway 11 Castle Creek (13744) ***(G-3294)***
A D C, Hauppauge *Also called American Diagnostic Corp* ***(G-5765)***
A D M, North Tonawanda *Also called Riverfront Costume Design* ***(G-12447)***
A D T, Mineola *Also called Aquifer Drilling & Testing Inc* ***(G-8204)***
A Division A & Liquid Systems, North Tonawanda *Also called Buffalo Pumps Inc* ***(G-12420)***
A E P, Yaphank *Also called American Electronic Products* ***(G-16704)***
A Esteban & Company Inc (PA) 212 989-7000
132 W 36th St Rm 1000 New York (10018) ***(G-8691)***
A Esteban & Company Inc 212 714-2227
132 W 36th St Rm 1000 New York (10018) ***(G-8692)***
A Fire Inc 631 897-9449
23 Parr Dr Ronkonkoma (11779) ***(G-14285)***
A Fleisig Paper Box Corp 212 226-7490
1751 2nd Ave Apt 10a New York (10128) ***(G-8693)***
A G I, Rochester *Also called Advanced Glass Industries Inc* ***(G-13606)***
A G M Deco Inc 718 624-6200
305 Wallabout St 307 Brooklyn (11206) ***(G-1455)***
A G M Deco Inc (PA) 718 624-6200
741 Myrtle Ave Brooklyn (11205) ***(G-1456)***
A G Master Crafts Ltd 516 745-6262
5 South St Ste A Garden City (11530) ***(G-5249)***
A Gatty Products Inc 914 592-3903
1 Warehouse Ln Elmsford (10523) ***(G-4527)***
A Gatty Svce, Elmsford *Also called A Gatty Products Inc* ***(G-4527)***
A Graphic Printing Inc 212 233-9696
49 Market St Frnt 2 New York (10002) ***(G-8694)***
A Guideposts Church Corp 212 251-8100
16 E 34th St Fl 21 New York (10016) ***(G-8695)***
A Health Obsession LLC 347 850-4587
2184 Mcdonald Ave Brooklyn (11223) ***(G-1457)***
A Hyatt Ball Co Ltd 518 747-0272
School St Fort Edward (12828) ***(G-5093)***
A I M, Victor *Also called Advanced Interconnect Mfg Inc* ***(G-15828)***
A I P Printing & Stationers 631 929-5529
6198 N Country Rd Wading River (11792) ***(G-15883)***
A I T Computers Inc 518 266-9010
157 Hoosick St Troy (12180) ***(G-15599)***
A J C Jewelry Contracting Inc 212 594-3703
247 W 30th St Fl 3 New York (10001) ***(G-8696)***
A J Congress, New York *Also called American Jewish Congress Inc* ***(G-8832)***
A J Gnco Mch Shp/Mchnery Rdout, Falconer *Also called Aj Genco Mch Sp McHy Rdout Svc* ***(G-4669)***
A J Hollander Enterprises, Inwood *Also called Hastings Hide Inc* ***(G-6492)***
A J M Enterprises 716 626-7294
348 Cayuga Rd Buffalo (14225) ***(G-2679)***
A Jaffe Inc 212 843-7464
592 5th Ave Fl 3 New York (10036) ***(G-8697)***
A K A Computer Consulting Inc 718 351-5200
1412 Richmond Rd Staten Island (10304) ***(G-15037)***
A K Allen Co Inc 516 747-5450
1860 Walt Whitman Rd # 900 Melville (11747) ***(G-7996)***
A L Eastmond & Sons Inc (PA) 718 378-3000
1175 Leggett Ave Bronx (10474) ***(G-1201)***

ALPHABETIC SECTION — Abbot & Abbot Box Corp

A L Sealing 315 699-6900
  2280 Osborne Rd Chittenango (13037) *(G-3500)*
A Lesley Dummett 646 541-1168
  10415 185th St Saint Albans (11412) *(G-14506)*
A Losee & Sons 516 676-3060
  68 Landing Rd Glen Cove (11542) *(G-5358)*
A Lunt Design Inc 716 662-0781
  5755 Big Tree Rd Orchard Park (14127) *(G-12695)*
A M & J Digital 518 434-2579
  800 N Pearl St Ste 5 Menands (12204) *(G-8077)*
A M I, New York Also called Weider Publications LLC *(G-12087)*
A M S Sign Designs 631 467-7722
  2360 Middle Country Rd Centereach (11720) *(G-3342)*
A National Printing Co Inc 631 243-3395
  51 Leeds Blvd Farmingville (11738) *(G-4922)*
A Nuclimate Qulty Systems Inc 315 431-0226
  1 General Motors Dr Ste 5 Syracuse (13206) *(G-15236)*
A P Manufacturing 909 228-3049
  21 Floyds Run Bohemia (11716) *(G-966)*
A P S, Hicksville Also called Applied Power Systems Inc *(G-6059)*
A Petteys Lumber, Fort Ann Also called Petteys Lumber *(G-5090)*
A Promos USA Inc 516 377-0186
  143 E Merrick Rd Freeport (11520) *(G-5135)*
A Q P Inc 585 256-1690
  2975 Brighton Henrietta T Rochester (14623) *(G-13590)*
A R Arena Products Inc 585 277-1680
  2101 Mount Read Blvd Rochester (14615) *(G-13591)*
A R V Precision Mfg Inc 631 293-9643
  60 Baiting Place Rd Ste B Farmingdale (11735) *(G-4705)*
A S A Precision Co Inc 845 482-4870
  295 Jffersonville N Br Rd Jeffersonville (12748) *(G-6778)*
A S P, Albany Also called Albany Student Press Inc *(G-37)*
A Strongwater Designs, New York Also called Andrea Strongwater *(G-8858)*
A Sunshine Glass & Aluminum 718 932-8080
  2610 Brooklyn Queens Expy Woodside (11377) *(G-16644)*
A T A Bagel Shoppe Inc 718 352-4948
  20814 Cross Island Pkwy Bayside (11360) *(G-741)*
A T C, Oyster Bay Also called American Trans-Coil Corp *(G-12809)*
A T M, Hornell Also called Fortitude Industries Inc *(G-6298)*
A T T I, Hauppauge Also called Advanced Testing Tech Inc *(G-5755)*
A Thousand Cranes Inc 212 724-9596
  208 W 79th St Apt 2 New York (10024) *(G-8698)*
A Titan Instruments Inc 716 667-9211
  10 Centere Dr Orchard Park (14127) *(G-12696)*
A To Z Kosher Meat Products Co 718 384-7400
  123 Borinquen Pl Brooklyn (11211) *(G-1458)*
A To Z Media Inc (PA) 212 260-0237
  243 W 30th St Fl 6 New York (10001) *(G-8699)*
A Tradition of Excellence Inc 845 638-4595
  85b Maple Ave New City (10956) *(G-8489)*
A Trusted Name Inc 716 326-7400
  35 Franklin St Westfield (14787) *(G-16391)*
A V T, New York Also called AV Therapeutics Inc *(G-8969)*
A Van Hoek Woodworking Limited 718 599-4388
  71 Montrose Ave Brooklyn (11206) *(G-1459)*
A W Hamel Stair Mfg Inc 518 346-3031
  3111 Amsterdam Rd Schenectady (12302) *(G-14647)*
A W R Group Inc 718 729-0412
  3715 Hunters Point Ave Long Island City (11101) *(G-7363)*
A W S, Port Chester Also called D & M Enterprises Incorporated *(G-13195)*
A Weinfeld Skull Cap Mfg, Brooklyn Also called Weinfeld Skull Cap Mfg Co Inc *(G-2641)*
A Yashir Bapa, New York Also called AZ Yashir Bapaz Inc *(G-8985)*
A Zimmer Ltd 315 422-7011
  W Tenesee St Syracuse (13204) *(G-15237)*
A&A Marble & Granite 347 810-9595
  1190 Commerce Ave Bronx (10462) *(G-1202)*
A&B Conservation LLC 845 282-7272
  12 Maple Leaf Rd Monsey (10952) *(G-8283)*
A&B Iron Works Inc 347 466-3193
  137 Conover St Brooklyn (11231) *(G-1460)*
A&B McKeon Glass Inc 718 525-2152
  69 Roff St Staten Island (10304) *(G-15038)*
A&M Model Makers LLC 626 813-9661
  1675 Wayneport Rd Ste 1 Macedon (14502) *(G-7691)*
A&S Refrigeration Equipment 718 993-6030
  557 Longfellow Ave Bronx (10474) *(G-1203)*
A-1 Iron Works Inc 718 927-4766
  2413 Atlantic Ave Brooklyn (11233) *(G-1461)*
A-1 Manhattan Custom Furn Inc 212 750-9800
  4315 Austin Blvd Island Park (11558) *(G-6510)*
A-1 Manhattan Custom Furn Inc (PA) 718 937-4780
  4315 Austin Blvd Island Park (11558) *(G-6511)*
A-1 Products Inc 718 789-1818
  165 Classon Ave Brooklyn (11205) *(G-1462)*
A-1 Skull Cap Corp 718 633-9333
  1212 36th St Brooklyn (11218) *(G-1463)*
A-1 Stamping & Spinning Corp 718 388-2626
  225 Beach 143rd St Rockaway Park (11694) *(G-14227)*
A-Fab Initiatives Inc 716 877-5257
  99 Bud Mil Dr Buffalo (14206) *(G-2680)*

A-Line Technologies Inc 607 772-2439
  197 Corporate Dr Binghamton (13904) *(G-858)*
A-Mark Machinery Corp 631 643-6300
  101 Lamar St West Babylon (11704) *(G-16125)*
A-One Laminating Corp 718 266-6002
  1636 Coney Island Ave 2b Brooklyn (11230) *(G-1464)*
A-One Moving & Storage Inc 718 266-6002
  1725 Avenue M Brooklyn (11230) *(G-1465)*
A-Plus Restaurant Equipment 718 522-2656
  623 Sackett St Brooklyn (11217) *(G-1466)*
A-Quick Bindery LLC 631 491-1110
  30 Gleam St Unit C West Babylon (11704) *(G-16126)*
A-R Payne Cabinet Comp, Brooklyn Also called Ralph Payne *(G-2383)*
A.L. Blades, Hornell Also called Dolomite Products Company Inc *(G-6295)*
A.S.I. Fancies Ltd, New York Also called Antwerp Sales Intl Inc *(G-8880)*
A/C Design & Fabrication Corp 718 227-8100
  638 Sharrotts Rd Staten Island (10309) *(G-15039)*
A1 International Heat Treating 718 863-5552
  905 Brush Ave Bronx (10465) *(G-1204)*
A1 Ornamental Iron Works Inc 718 265-3055
  61 Jefferson St Brooklyn (11206) *(G-1467)*
A1 Skullcaps, Brooklyn Also called A-1 Skull Cap Corp *(G-1463)*
A2ia Corp 917 237-0390
  24 W 40th St Fl 3 New York (10018) *(G-8700)*
A3 Apparel LLC 888 403-9669
  1407 Broadway Rm 716a New York (10018) *(G-8701)*
AAa Amercn Flag Dctg Co Inc 212 279-3524
  36 W 37th St Rm 409 New York (10018) *(G-8702)*
AAA Catalytic Recycling Inc 631 920-7944
  345 Eastern Pkwy Farmingdale (11735) *(G-4706)*
AAA Noodle Products Mfg 212 431-4090
  102 Bowery New York (10013) *(G-8703)*
AAA Welding and Fabrication of 585 254-2830
  1085 Lyell Ave Rochester (14606) *(G-13592)*
AAAA York Inc 718 784-6666
  3720 12th St Long Island City (11101) *(G-7364)*
Aaaaaa Creative Designs, New York Also called Paper Box Corp *(G-11101)*
Aaaaar Orthopedics Inc 845 278-4938
  141 Main St Brewster (10509) *(G-1153)*
Aabacs Group Inc 718 961-3577
  1509 132nd St College Point (11356) *(G-3635)*
Aabco Sheet Metal Co Inc (PA) 718 821-1166
  47 40 Metropolitan Ave Ridgewood (11385) *(G-13527)*
Aakron Rule Corp (PA) 716 542-5483
  8 Indianola Ave Akron (14001) *(G-16)*
Aalborg Instrs & Cntrls Inc 845 398-3160
  20 Corporate Dr Orangeburg (10962) *(G-12667)*
Aand D Maintenance, Bridgehampton Also called Bridgehampton Steel & Wldg Inc *(G-1179)*
AAR Allen Services Inc 516 222-9000
  747 Zeckendorf Blvd Garden City (11530) *(G-5250)*
Aarco Products Inc 631 924-5461
  21 Old Dock Rd Yaphank (11980) *(G-16703)*
Aarfid LLC (PA) 716 992-3999
  3780 Yochum Rd Eden (14057) *(G-4386)*
Aaron Group LLC 718 392-5454
  115 S Macquesten Pkwy Mount Vernon (10550) *(G-8372)*
Aaron Tool & Mold Inc 585 426-5100
  620 Trolley Blvd Rochester (14606) *(G-13593)*
Aarrow Promotions, Freeport Also called A Promos USA Inc *(G-5135)*
Aatc, Medford Also called American Avionic Tech Corp *(G-7937)*
Aatech, Clyde Also called Advanced Atomization Tech LLC *(G-3591)*
Aavid Niagara LLC (HQ) 716 297-0652
  3315 Haseley Dr Niagara Falls (14304) *(G-12257)*
AB Engine 518 557-3510
  4a Northway Ln Latham (12110) *(G-7061)*
AB Fire Inc 917 416-6444
  1554 61st St Brooklyn (11219) *(G-1468)*
AB Seafood Trading Inc 718 353-8848
  3129 Higgins St Flushing (11354) *(G-4978)*
Abaco Steel Products Inc 631 589-1800
  40 Aero Rd Ste 4 Bohemia (11716) *(G-967)*
Abacus Labs Inc 917 426-6642
  14 E 38th St Fl 9 New York (10016) *(G-8704)*
Abalene Decorating Services 718 782-2000
  315 W 39th St Rm 611 New York (10018) *(G-8705)*
Abalon Precision Mfg Corp (PA) 914 665-7700
  717 S 3rd Ave Mount Vernon (10550) *(G-8373)*
Abalon Precision Mfg Corp 718 589-5682
  717 S 3rd Ave Mount Vernon (10550) *(G-8374)*
Abasco Inc 716 649-4790
  5225 Southwestern Blvd Hamburg (14075) *(G-5672)*
Abbe Laboratories Inc 631 756-2223
  1095 Broadhollow Rd Ste E Farmingdale (11735) *(G-4707)*
Abbeville Press Inc 212 366-5585
  116 W 23rd St Fl 5 New York (10011) *(G-8706)*
Abbeville Publishing Group, New York Also called Abbeville Press Inc *(G-8706)*
Abble Awning Co Inc 516 822-1200
  313 Broadway Ste 315 Bethpage (11714) *(G-837)*
Abbot & Abbot Box Corp 888 930-5972
  3711 10th St Long Island City (11101) *(G-7365)*

(PA)=Parent Co (HQ)=Headquarters (DH)=Div Headquarters

Abbot & Abbot Packing Service, Long Island City *Also called Abbot & Abbot Box Corp* ***(G-7365)***
Abbot Flag Co Div, Spring Valley *Also called Eagle Regalia Co Inc* ***(G-14989)***
Abbott Diagnostics Division, Williamsville *Also called Abbott Laboratories* ***(G-16566)***
Abbott Industries Inc (PA)....718 291-0800
9525 149th St Jamaica (11435) ***(G-6622)***
Abbott Laboratories....716 633-1904
6255 Sheridan Dr Ste 406 Williamsville (14221) ***(G-16566)***
ABC Casting, Jamaica *Also called Technical Service Industries* ***(G-6682)***
ABC Peanut Butter LLC....212 661-6886
295 Madison Ave Ste 1618 New York (10017) ***(G-8707)***
ABC Television Network, New York *Also called Times Square Studios Ltd* ***(G-11847)***
ABC Windows and Signs Corp....718 353-6210
12606 18th Ave College Point (11356) ***(G-3636)***
Abdo Shtmtl & Fabrication Inc....315 894-4664
11470 N Gage Rd Barneveld (13304) ***(G-601)***
Abe Pool Service....845 473-7730
793 Violet Ave Hyde Park (12538) ***(G-6467)***
Abel Noser Solutions LLC....646 432-4000
1 Battery Park Plz # 601 New York (10004) ***(G-8708)***
Abeona Therapeutics Inc (PA)....646 813-4712
1330 Avenue Of Americas Flr 33 New York (10019) ***(G-8709)***
Abercrombie & Fitch, Brooklyn *Also called Apsco Sports Enterprises Inc* ***(G-1545)***
Aberdeen Blower & Shtmtl Works....631 661-6100
401 Columbus Ave West Babylon (11704) ***(G-16127)***
Abetter Processing Corp....718 252-2223
984 E 35th St Brooklyn (11210) ***(G-1469)***
ABG Accessories, New York *Also called Elegant Headwear Co Inc* ***(G-9642)***
Abh Natures Products Inc....631 249-5783
131 Heartland Blvd Edgewood (11717) ***(G-4391)***
Abh Pharma Inc....866 922-4669
131 Heartland Blvd Edgewood (11717) ***(G-4392)***
ABI Packaging Inc....716 677-2900
1703 Union Rd West Seneca (14224) ***(G-16292)***
Abigal Press Inc....718 641-5350
9735 133rd Ave Ozone Park (11417) ***(G-12821)***
Abkco Music & Records Inc (PA)....212 399-0300
85 5th Ave Fl 11 New York (10003) ***(G-8710)***
Able Anodizing Corp....718 252-0660
1767 Bay Ridge Ave Brooklyn (11204) ***(G-1470)***
Able Electronics Inc....631 924-5386
18 Sawgrass Dr Bellport (11713) ***(G-797)***
Able Environmental Services....631 567-6585
1599 Ocean Ave Bohemia (11716) ***(G-968)***
Able Industries Inc....914 739-5685
18 Brook Ln Cortlandt Manor (10567) ***(G-3898)***
Able Kitchen....877 268-1264
540 Willow Ave Unit B Cedarhurst (11516) ***(G-3330)***
Able Kitchen Supplies, Cedarhurst *Also called Able Kitchen* ***(G-3330)***
Able National Corp....718 386-8801
49 Wyckoff Ave Brooklyn (11237) ***(G-1471)***
Able Printing, West Babylon *Also called Weicro Graphics Inc* ***(G-16204)***
Able Steel Equipment Co Inc....718 361-9240
5002 23rd St Long Island City (11101) ***(G-7366)***
Able Weldbuilt Industries Inc....631 643-9700
1050 Grand Blvd Deer Park (11729) ***(G-3931)***
Able Wire Co, Cortlandt Manor *Also called Able Industries Inc* ***(G-3898)***
Ableton Inc....646 723-4586
36 W Colo Blvd Ste 300 New York (10013) ***(G-8711)***
Above The Rest Baking Corp....718 313-9222
531-533 Bryant Ave Bronx (10474) ***(G-1205)***
Abp International Inc....212 490-3999
1466 Broadway Ste 910 New York (10036) ***(G-8712)***
Abr Molding Andy LLC....212 576-1821
1624 Centre St Ridgewood (11385) ***(G-13528)***
ABRA Media Inc....518 398-1010
2773 W Church St Pine Plains (12567) ***(G-13004)***
Abra-Ka-Data Systems Ltd....631 667-5550
39 W Jefryn Blvd Ste 1 Deer Park (11729) ***(G-3932)***
Abraham Jwly Designers & Mfrs....212 944-1149
71 W 47th St Ste 905 New York (10036) ***(G-8713)***
Abraxis Bioscience LLC....716 773-0800
3159 Staley Rd Grand Island (14072) ***(G-5494)***
Abrimian Bros Corp....212 382-1106
48 W 48th St Ste 805 New York (10036) ***(G-8714)***
ABS Metal Corp....646 302-9018
58 Holly Rd Hewlett (11557) ***(G-6045)***
ABS Talkx Inc....631 254-9100
34 Cleveland Ave Bay Shore (11706) ***(G-651)***
Absolute Business Products, Port Washington *Also called Jaidan Industries Inc* ***(G-13272)***
Absolute Coatings Inc....914 636-0700
38 Portman Rd New Rochelle (10801) ***(G-8586)***
Absolute Color Corporation....212 868-0404
109 W 27th St Frnt 2 New York (10001) ***(G-8715)***
Absolute Engineering Company, Bohemia *Also called Absolute Manufacturing Inc* ***(G-969)***
Absolute Fitness US Corp....732 979-8582
21337 39th Ave Ste 322 Bayside (11361) ***(G-742)***
Absolute Manufacturing Inc....631 563-7466
210 Knickerbocker Ave Bohemia (11716) ***(G-969)***
ABT, Great Neck *Also called Advanced Barcode Tech Inc* ***(G-5527)***
Abtex Corporation....315 536-7403
89 Main St Dresden (14441) ***(G-4146)***
Abyrx Inc....914 357-2600
1 Bridge St Ste 121 Irvington (10533) ***(G-6502)***
AC Air Cooling Co Inc....718 933-1011
1637 Stillwell Ave Bronx (10461) ***(G-1206)***
AC DC Power Systems & Contrls, Staatsburg *Also called Protective Power Systms & Cntr* ***(G-15024)***
AC Moore Incorporated....516 796-5831
3988 Hempstead Tpke Bethpage (11714) ***(G-838)***
Aca Quality Building Pdts LLC....718 991-2423
1322 Garrison Ave Bronx (10474) ***(G-1207)***
Acad Design Corp....585 254-6960
975 Mount Read Blvd Rochester (14606) ***(G-13594)***
Academy of Political Science....212 870-2500
475 Riverside Dr Ste 1274 New York (10115) ***(G-8716)***
Academy Printing Services Inc....631 765-3346
42 Hortons Ln Southold (11971) ***(G-14967)***
Acadia Stairs....845 765-8600
73 Route 9 Ste 3 Fishkill (12524) ***(G-4942)***
Acai of America Inc....862 205-9334
225 W 34th St Fl 9 New York (10122) ***(G-8717)***
Accede Mold & Tool Co Inc....585 254-6490
1125 Lexington Ave Rochester (14606) ***(G-13595)***
Accel Printing & Graphics....914 241-3369
128 Radio Circle Dr Ste 2 Mount Kisco (10549) ***(G-8337)***
Accela Inc....631 563-5005
100 Comac St Ste 2 Ronkonkoma (11779) ***(G-14286)***
Accelify Solutions LLC....888 922-2354
16 W 36th St Rm 902 New York (10018) ***(G-8718)***
Accent Label & Tag Co Inc (PA)....631 244-7066
348 Woodlawn Ave Ronkonkoma (11779) ***(G-14287)***
Accent Printing &GRaphics, Wayland *Also called Specialty Services* ***(G-16072)***
Accent Speaker Technology Ltd....631 738-2540
1511 Lincoln Ave Holbrook (11741) ***(G-6167)***
Accenta Incorporated....716 565-6262
150 Lawrence Bell Dr # 108 Buffalo (14221) ***(G-2681)***
Accesory Headquarters, New York *Also called Ahq LLC* ***(G-8773)***
Access 24....845 358-5397
570 Kings Hwy Fl 4 Valley Cottage (10989) ***(G-15750)***
Access Display Group Inc....516 678-7772
151 S Main St Freeport (11520) ***(G-5136)***
Access Elevator & Lift Inc (PA)....716 483-3696
1209 E 2nd St Jamestown (14701) ***(G-6694)***
Access Intelligence LLC....212 204-4269
249 W 17th St New York (10011) ***(G-8719)***
Access Products Inc....800 679-4022
241 Main St Ste 100 Buffalo (14203) ***(G-2682)***
Accessible Bath Tech LLC....518 937-1518
6 Albright Ave Albany (12203) ***(G-27)***
Accessories For Electronics....631 847-0158
620 Mead Ter South Hempstead (11550) ***(G-14941)***
Accessory Plays LLC....212 564-7301
29 W 36th St New York (10018) ***(G-8720)***
Accessory Street LLC....212 686-8990
1370 Broadway New York (10018) ***(G-8721)***
Accessries Direct Intl USA Inc....646 448-8200
1450 Broadway Fl 22 New York (10018) ***(G-8722)***
Accipiter Radar Corporation....716 508-4432
40 Centre Dr Ste 3 Orchard Park (14127) ***(G-12697)***
Acco Brands USA LLC....847 541-9500
941 Acco Way Ogdensburg (13669) ***(G-12568)***
Acco North America, Ogdensburg *Also called Acco Brands USA LLC* ***(G-12568)***
Accolade USA Inc....866 423-5071
60 Industrial Pkwy # 397 Cheektowaga (14227) ***(G-3434)***
Accord Pipe Fabricators Inc....718 657-3900
9226 180th St Jamaica (11433) ***(G-6623)***
Accra Sheetmetal LLC....631 643-2100
1359 Straight Path Wyandanch (11798) ***(G-16691)***
Accredo Health Incorporated....718 353-3012
14330 38th Ave Apt 1f Flushing (11354) ***(G-4979)***
Accu Coat Inc....585 288-2330
111 Humboldt St Ste 8 Rochester (14609) ***(G-13596)***
Accucut Inc....631 567-2868
120 Easy St West Sayville (11796) ***(G-16287)***
Accumetrics Associates Inc....518 393-2200
6 British American Blvd # 100 Latham (12110) ***(G-7062)***
Accuprint (PA)....518 456-2431
2005 Western Ave Ste 1 Albany (12203) ***(G-28)***
Accurate Business Systems, Saint James *Also called East Coast Business Forms Inc* ***(G-14512)***
Accurate Industrial Machining....631 242-0566
1711 Church St Holbrook (11741) ***(G-6168)***
Accurate Knitting Corp....646 552-2216
1478 E 26th St Brooklyn (11210) ***(G-1472)***
Accurate Marine Specialties....631 589-5502
2200 Artic Ave Bohemia (11716) ***(G-970)***
Accurate McHning Incorporation....315 689-1428
251 State Route 5 Elbridge (13060) ***(G-4426)***
Accurate Metal Weather Strip....914 668-6042
725 S Fulton Ave Mount Vernon (10550) ***(G-8375)***

Accurate Pnt Powdr Coating Inc 585 235-1650
606 Hague St Rochester (14606) *(G-13597)*
Accurate Precast 718 345-2910
1957 Pitkin Ave Brooklyn (11207) *(G-1473)*
Accurate Signs & Awnings Inc 718 788-0302
247 Prospect Ave Ste 2 Brooklyn (11215) *(G-1474)*
Accurate Specialty Metal Fabri 718 418-6895
6420 Admiral Ave Middle Village (11379) *(G-8119)*
Accurate Tool & Die LLC 585 254-2830
1085 Lyell Ave Rochester (14606) *(G-13598)*
Accurate Welding Service Inc 516 333-1730
615 Main St Westbury (11590) *(G-16308)*
Accurate Welding Svce, Westbury *Also called Accurate Welding Service Inc (G-16308)*
Accusonic Voice Systems, Edgewood *Also called Global Market Development Inc (G-4402)*
Accutrak Inc 212 925-5330
432 Washington St Ste 113 New York (10013) *(G-8723)*
Accuvein Inc 816 997-9400
3243 Route 112 Ste 2 Medford (11763) *(G-7936)*
Ace, Brooklyn *Also called Montrose Equipment Sales Inc (G-2225)*
Ace & Jig LLC (PA) 347 227-0318
323 Dean St Ste 2 Brooklyn (11217) *(G-1475)*
Ace Banner & Flag Company 212 620-9111
107 W 27th St New York (10001) *(G-8724)*
Ace Banner Flag & Graphics, New York *Also called Ace Banner & Flag Company (G-8724)*
Ace Canvas & Tent Corp 631 648-0614
155 Raynor Ave Ronkonkoma (11779) *(G-14288)*
Ace Cntracting Consulting Corp 631 567-4752
1650 Sycamore Ave Ste 18 Bohemia (11716) *(G-971)*
Ace Diamond Corp 212 730-8231
30 W 47th St Ste 808r New York (10036) *(G-8725)*
Ace Drop Cloth Canvas Pdts Inc 718 731-1550
4216 Park Ave Bronx (10457) *(G-1208)*
Ace Drop Cloth Co, Bronx *Also called Ace Drop Cloth Canvas Pdts Inc (G-1208)*
Ace Fire Door Corp 718 901-0001
4000 Park Ave Bronx (10457) *(G-1209)*
Ace Manufacturing, Rochester *Also called Jam Industries Inc (G-13890)*
Ace Molding & Tool Inc 631 567-2355
51 Floyds Run Bohemia (11716) *(G-972)*
Ace Printing & Publishing Inc 718 939-0040
14951 Roosevelt Ave Flushing (11354) *(G-4980)*
Ace Printing Co, Flushing *Also called Ace Printing & Publishing Inc (G-4980)*
Ace Specialty Co Inc 716 874-3670
695 Ensminger Rd Tonawanda (14150) *(G-15518)*
Acec, New York *Also called America Capital Energy Corp (G-8820)*
Acem, Deer Park *Also called American Casino Equipment Mfg (G-3939)*
Acf Industries Holding LLC (HQ) 212 702-4363
767 5th Ave New York (10153) *(G-8726)*
ACI Controls Inc (PA) 800 333-7519
295 Main St West Seneca (14224) *(G-16293)*
Acj Communications, Massapequa Park *Also called Massapequa Post (G-7893)*
Acker & LI Mills Corporation 212 307-7247
44 W 62nd St Apt 3b New York (10023) *(G-8727)*
Ackroyd Metal Fabricators Inc 518 434-1281
966 Broadway Ste 2 Menands (12204) *(G-8078)*
Acl, Thornwood *Also called Automated Control Logic Inc (G-15501)*
ACM, New York *Also called Association For Cmpt McHy Inc (G-8938)*
Acme Architectural Products 718 360-0700
513 Porter Ave Brooklyn (11222) *(G-1476)*
Acme Architectural Pdts Inc (PA) 718 384-7800
251 Lombardy St Brooklyn (11222) *(G-1477)*
Acme Architectural Walls, Brooklyn *Also called Acme Architectural Pdts Inc (G-1477)*
Acme Awning Co Inc 718 409-1881
435 Van Nest Ave Bronx (10460) *(G-1210)*
Acme Engineering Products Inc 518 236-5659
2330 State Route 11 Mooers (12958) *(G-8330)*
Acme Industries of W Babylon 631 737-5231
125 Gary Way Ste 2 Ronkonkoma (11779) *(G-14289)*
Acme Kitchenettes Corp 518 828-4191
4269 Us Route 9 Hudson (12534) *(G-6337)*
Acme Marine, Calverton *Also called US Hoists Corp (G-3175)*
Acme Marine Hoist, Bellport *Also called Thego Corporation (G-814)*
Acme Marine Hoist Inc 631 472-3030
800 Burman Blvd Calverton (11933) *(G-3161)*
Acme Nipple Mfg Co Inc 716 873-7491
1930 Elmwood Ave Buffalo (14207) *(G-2683)*
Acme Office Group, Brooklyn *Also called New Dimensions Office Group (G-2259)*
Acme Parts Inc 718 649-1750
901 Elton St Brooklyn (11208) *(G-1478)*
Acme Precision Screw Pdts Inc 585 328-2028
623 Glide St Rochester (14606) *(G-13599)*
Acme Screenprinting LLC 716 565-1052
247 Cayuga Rd Ste 25e Buffalo (14225) *(G-2684)*
Acme Signs of Baldwinsville 315 638-4865
3 Marble St Baldwinsville (13027) *(G-547)*
Acme Smoked Fish Corp (PA) 954 942-5598
30 Gem St 56 Brooklyn (11222) *(G-1479)*
Acolyte Industries, New York *Also called General Led Holdings LLC (G-9900)*
Acolyte Technologies Corp 212 629-3239
44 E 32nd St Rm 901 New York (10016) *(G-8728)*
Acorda Therapeutics Inc (PA) 914 347-4300
420 Saw Mill River Rd Ardsley (10502) *(G-392)*
Acorn, New York *Also called Music Sales Corporation (G-10861)*
Acorn Products Corp 315 894-4868
27 Pleasant Ave Ilion (13357) *(G-6473)*
Acran Spill Containment Inc (PA) 631 841-2300
898 N Broadway Ste 1 Massapequa (11758) *(G-7877)*
Acro Industries Inc 585 254-3661
554 Colfax St Rochester (14606) *(G-13600)*
Acro-Fab Ltd 315 564-6688
55 Rochester St Hannibal (13074) *(G-5717)*
Acrolite, Elbridge *Also called Accurate McHning Incorporation (G-4426)*
ACS, Ballston Spa *Also called Advanced Comfort Systems Inc (G-574)*
ACS Custom USA LLC 646 559-5642
520 W 25th St New York (10001) *(G-8729)*
Act Communications Group Inc 631 669-2403
170 Higbie Ln West Islip (11795) *(G-16257)*
Actasys Inc (PA) 914 432-2336
805 25th St Watervliet (12189) *(G-16040)*
Actavis Laboratories Ny Inc 631 693-8000
33 Ralph Ave Copiague (11726) *(G-3747)*
Actinium Pharmaceuticals Inc (PA) 646 677-3870
275 Madison Ave Ste 702 New York (10016) *(G-8730)*
Action Bullet Resistant 631 422-0888
263 Union Blvd West Islip (11795) *(G-16258)*
Action Envelope & Prtg Co Inc 631 225-3900
5300 New Horizons Blvd Amityville (11701) *(G-263)*
Action Machined Products Inc 631 842-2333
1355 Bangor St Copiague (11726) *(G-3748)*
Action Paper Co Inc 718 665-1652
429 E 164th St Bronx (10456) *(G-1211)*
Action Technologies Inc 718 278-1000
3809 33rd St Apt 1 Long Island City (11101) *(G-7367)*
Actioncraft Products Inc 516 883-6423
2 Manhasset Ave Port Washington (11050) *(G-13239)*
Active Business Systems, Long Island City *Also called Action Technologies Inc (G-7367)*
Active Manufacturing Inc 607 775-3162
32 Laughlin Rd Kirkwood (13795) *(G-6937)*
Active Process Supply, New York *Also called Standard Screen Supply Corp (G-11693)*
Active World Solutions Inc 718 922-9404
609 Fountain Ave Brooklyn (11208) *(G-1480)*
Actuant Corporation 607 753-8276
44 River St Cortland (13045) *(G-3858)*
Acu-Rite Companies Inc 716 661-1700
1 Precision Way Jamestown (14701) *(G-6695)*
Acuity Polymers Inc 585 458-8409
1667 Lake Ave Ste 303 Rochester (14615) *(G-13601)*
Acworth Foundation 631 784-7802
775 Park Ave Ste 255 Huntington (11743) *(G-6389)*
Ad Makers Long Island Inc 631 595-9100
60 E Jefryn Blvd Ste 3 Deer Park (11729) *(G-3933)*
Ad Publications Inc 585 248-2888
8 Greenwood Park Pittsford (14534) *(G-13007)*
Ad-Vantage Printing Inc 718 820-0688
12034 Queens Blvd Vd Kew Gardens (11415) *(G-6870)*
Ada Gems Corp 212 719-0100
10 W 47th St Ste 707 New York (10036) *(G-8731)*
Adam Scott Designs Inc 212 420-8866
118 E 25th St Fl 11 New York (10010) *(G-8732)*
Adamor Inc 212 688-8885
17 E 48th St Rm 901 New York (10017) *(G-8733)*
Adams Interior Fabrications 631 249-8282
8 Iroquois Pl Massapequa (11758) *(G-7878)*
Adams Lumber Co Inc 716 358-2815
6052 Adams Rd Cattaraugus (14719) *(G-3311)*
Adams Press, Franklin Square *Also called 514 Adams Corporation (G-5114)*
Adams Ridge, Lancaster *Also called Markar Architectural Products (G-7032)*
Adams Sfc Inc (HQ) 716 877-2608
225 E Park Dr Tonawanda (14150) *(G-15519)*
Adaptive Mfg Tech Inc 631 580-5400
181 Remington Blvd Ronkonkoma (11779) *(G-14290)*
Adar Medical Uniform LLC 718 935-1197
307 Richardson St Brooklyn (11222) *(G-1481)*
Adart Poly Bag Mfg, Plainview *Also called Adart Polyethylene Bag Mfg (G-13030)*
Adart Polyethylene Bag Mfg 516 932-1001
1 W Ames Ct Ste 201 Plainview (11803) *(G-13030)*
ADC Acquisition Company 518 377-6471
2 Commerce Park Rd Niskayuna (12309) *(G-12352)*
ADC Dolls Inc 212 244-4500
112 W 34th St Ste 1207 New York (10120) *(G-8734)*
ADC Industries Inc (PA) 516 596-1304
181a E Jamaica Ave Valley Stream (11580) *(G-15771)*
Adco Circuits Inc 716 668-6600
160 Lawrence Bell Dr # 122 Buffalo (14221) *(G-2685)*
Adcomm Graphics Inc 212 645-1298
21 Lamar St West Babylon (11704) *(G-16128)*
Add Associates Inc 315 449-3474
6333 Daedalus Rd Cicero (13039) *(G-3513)*
Addeo Bakers Inc 718 367-8316
2372 Hughes Ave Bronx (10458) *(G-1212)*
Addex Inc 315 331-7700
251 Murray St Newark (14513) *(G-12191)*

A L P H A B E T I C

(PA)=Parent Co (HQ)=Headquarters (DH)=Div Headquarters
2019 Harris
New York Manufacturers Directory
817

Addex Inc (PA)...781 344-5800
251 Murray St Newark (14513) ***(G-12192)***
Addison Precision Mfg Corp...585 254-1386
500 Avis St Rochester (14615) ***(G-13602)***
Additude Magazine, New York *Also called New Hope Media LLC* ***(G-10926)***
Adel Rootstein (usa) Inc...718 499-5650
145 18th St Brooklyn (11215) ***(G-1482)***
Adelphi Paper Hangings...518 284-9066
102 Main St Sharon Springs (13459) ***(G-14796)***
Adeptronics Incorporated...631 667-0659
281 Skip Ln Ste C Bay Shore (11706) ***(G-652)***
Adesso Inc (PA)...212 736-4440
353 W 39th St Fl 2 New York (10018) ***(G-8735)***
Adf Accessories Inc...516 450-5755
3539 Lawson Blvd Oceanside (11572) ***(G-12530)***
Adfin Solutions Inc...650 464-0742
25 W 31st St Fl 4 New York (10001) ***(G-8736)***
Adgorithmics LLC (PA)...646 277-8728
260 Madison Ave Fl 8 New York (10016) ***(G-8737)***
ADI, Brooklyn *Also called Audible Difference Inc* ***(G-1574)***
Adir Publishing Co...718 633-9437
1212 36th St Brooklyn (11218) ***(G-1483)***
Adirondack Beverage Co Inc, Schenectady *Also called Scotia Beverages Inc* ***(G-14712)***
Adirondack Chocolate Co Ltd (PA)...518 946-7270
5680 Ny State Rte 86 Wilmington (12997) ***(G-16600)***
Adirondack Daily Enterprise, Saranac Lake *Also called Adirondack Publishing Co Inc* ***(G-14560)***
Adirondack Distilling Company...315 316-0387
601 Varick St Utica (13502) ***(G-15675)***
ADIRONDACK EXPLORER, Saranac Lake *Also called Getting The Word Out Inc* ***(G-14562)***
Adirondack Home News, Holland Patent *Also called Steffen Publishing Inc* ***(G-6225)***
Adirondack Ice & Air Inc...518 483-4340
26 Railroad St Malone (12953) ***(G-7717)***
Adirondack Leather Pdts Inc...607 547-5798
196 Cemetery Rd Fly Creek (13337) ***(G-5063)***
Adirondack Life Inc (PA)...518 946-2191
Rr 9 Box North Jay (12941) ***(G-6773)***
Adirondack Life Inc...518 946-2191
12961 Nys Route 9n Jay (12941) ***(G-6774)***
Adirondack Life Magazine, Jay *Also called Adirondack Life Inc* ***(G-6773)***
Adirondack Life Magazine, Jay *Also called Adirondack Life Inc* ***(G-6774)***
Adirondack Outdoor Center LLC (PA)...315 369-2300
2839 State Route 28 Old Forge (13420) ***(G-12589)***
Adirondack Pennysaver Inc...518 563-0100
177 Margaret St Plattsburgh (12901) ***(G-13105)***
Adirondack Plas & Recycl Inc (PA)...518 746-9212
453 County Route 45 Argyle (12809) ***(G-397)***
Adirondack Power Sports...518 481-6269
5378 State Route 37 Malone (12953) ***(G-7718)***
Adirondack Precision Cut Stone (PA)...518 681-3060
536 Queensbury Ave Queensbury (12804) ***(G-13414)***
Adirondack Publishing Co Inc (HQ)...518 891-2600
54 Broadway Saranac Lake (12983) ***(G-14560)***
Adirondack Sanitary Service, Ticonderoga *Also called Adirondack Waste MGT Inc* ***(G-15510)***
Adirondack Scenic Inc...518 638-8000
439 County Route 45 Ste 1 Argyle (12809) ***(G-398)***
Adirondack Sign Company LLC...518 409-7446
72 Ballston Ave Saratoga Springs (12866) ***(G-14566)***
Adirondack Sign Perfect Inc...518 409-7446
72 Ballston Ave Saratoga Springs (12866) ***(G-14567)***
Adirondack Spclty Adhsives Inc...518 869-5736
4258 Albany St Albany (12205) ***(G-29)***
Adirondack Stained Glass Works...518 725-0387
29 W Fulton St Ste 6 Gloversville (12078) ***(G-5449)***
Adirondack Stairs Inc...845 246-2525
990 Kings Hwy Saugerties (12477) ***(G-14602)***
Adirondack Studios, Argyle *Also called Adirondack Scenic Inc* ***(G-398)***
Adirondack Waste MGT Inc...518 585-2224
963 New York State 9n Ticonderoga (12883) ***(G-15510)***
Adirondex, Malone *Also called Adirondack Ice & Air Inc* ***(G-7717)***
Aditiany Inc...212 997-8440
37 W 39th St Rm 1100 New York (10018) ***(G-8738)***
Adjmi Apparel Group, New York *Also called Beluga Inc* ***(G-9041)***
Adjustable Shelving, Melville *Also called Karp Associates Inc* ***(G-8041)***
Adl Data Systems Inc...914 591-1800
565 Taxter Rd Ste 100 Elmsford (10523) ***(G-4528)***
Adl Design Inc...516 949-6658
4 W Mall Dr Huntington (11743) ***(G-6390)***
ADM, Buffalo *Also called Archer-Daniels-Midland Company* ***(G-2708)***
ADM, Hudson *Also called Archer-Daniels-Midland Company* ***(G-6339)***
ADM, Hudson *Also called Archer-Daniels-Midland Company* ***(G-6340)***
ADM, Lakeville *Also called Archer-Daniels-Midland Company* ***(G-6984)***
ADM Milling Co...716 849-7333
250 Ganson St Buffalo (14203) ***(G-2686)***
Admor Blinds & Window Fashion, Jericho *Also called KPP Ltd* ***(G-6793)***
Adobe Systems Inc...212 471-0904
1540 Broadway Fl 17 New York (10036) ***(G-8739)***
Adobe Systems Incorporated...212 592-1400
100 5th Ave Fl 5 New York (10011) ***(G-8740)***
Adobe Systems Incorporated...212 471-0904
8 W 40th St Fl 8 # 8 New York (10018) ***(G-8741)***
Adotta America, New York *Also called Europrojects Intl Inc* ***(G-9731)***
Adpro Sports LLC...716 854-5116
55 Amherst Villa Rd Buffalo (14225) ***(G-2687)***
Adrean Printing, New Rochelle *Also called Vic-Gina Printing Company Inc* ***(G-8631)***
Adria Machine & Tool Inc...585 889-3360
966 North Rd Scottsville (14546) ***(G-14748)***
Adrian Jules Ltd...585 342-5886
1392 E Ridge Rd Rochester (14621) ***(G-13603)***
Adrian-Jules Custom Tailor, Rochester *Also called Adrian Jules Ltd* ***(G-13603)***
Adriatic Wood Products Inc...718 922-4621
1994 Industrial Park Rd Brooklyn (11207) ***(G-1484)***
Adrienne Landau Designs Inc...212 695-8362
519 8th Ave Fl 21 New York (10018) ***(G-8742)***
Ads-N-Color Inc...718 797-0900
20 Jay St Ste 530 Brooklyn (11201) ***(G-1485)***
Adsco Manufacturing Corp...716 827-5450
4979 Lake Ave Buffalo (14219) ***(G-2688)***
Adsmain LLC...347 560-5060
1072 Bedford Ave Pmb 107 Brooklyn (11216) ***(G-1486)***
Adstream America LLC (HQ)...212 804-8498
345 7th Ave Fl 6 New York (10001) ***(G-8743)***
Adtech, Rochester *Also called Analog Digital Technology LLC* ***(G-13631)***
Adtech Us Inc...212 402-4840
770 Broadway Fl 4 New York (10003) ***(G-8744)***
Adults and Children With Learn...516 593-8230
22 Alice Ct East Rockaway (11518) ***(G-4292)***
Advan-Tech Manufacturing Inc...716 667-1500
3645 California Rd Orchard Park (14127) ***(G-12698)***
Advance Apparel Intl Inc...212 944-0984
265 W 37th St Rm 906 New York (10018) ***(G-8745)***
Advance Biofactures Corp...516 593-7000
35 Wilbur St Lynbrook (11563) ***(G-7658)***
Advance Chemicals Usa Inc...718 633-1030
1230 57th St Brooklyn (11219) ***(G-1487)***
Advance Circuit Technology Inc...585 328-2000
19 Jetview Dr Rochester (14624) ***(G-13604)***
Advance Construction Group, New York *Also called B & F Architectural Support Gr* ***(G-8987)***
Advance D Tech Inc...845 534-8248
2 Mill St Stop 19 Cornwall (12518) ***(G-3829)***
Advance Energy Systems NY LLC...315 735-5125
17 Tilton Rd Utica (13501) ***(G-15676)***
Advance Energy Tech Inc...518 371-2140
1 Solar Dr Halfmoon (12065) ***(G-5660)***
Advance Finance Group LLC...212 630-5900
101 Park Ave Frnt New York (10178) ***(G-8746)***
Advance Food Service Co Inc...631 242-4800
200 Heartland Blvd Edgewood (11717) ***(G-4393)***
Advance Grafix Equipment Inc...917 202-4593
150 Wyandanch Ave Wyandanch (11798) ***(G-16692)***
Advance Magazine Publs Inc (HQ)...212 286-2860
1 World Trade Ctr Fl 43 New York (10007) ***(G-8747)***
Advance Magazine Publs Inc...212 790-4422
1 World Trade Ctr Fl 20 New York (10007) ***(G-8748)***
Advance Magazine Publs Inc...212 286-2860
1166 Ave Of The Amrcs 1 New York (10036) ***(G-8749)***
Advance Magazine Publs Inc...212 450-7000
711 3rd Ave Rm 700 New York (10017) ***(G-8750)***
Advance Magazine Publs Inc...212 697-0126
750 3rd Ave Frnt G New York (10017) ***(G-8751)***
Advance Micro Power Corp...631 471-6157
2190 Smithtown Ave Ronkonkoma (11779) ***(G-14291)***
Advance Pharmaceutical Inc (PA)...631 981-4600
895 Waverly Ave Holtsville (11742) ***(G-6236)***
Advance Precision Industries...631 491-0910
9 Mahan St Unit A West Babylon (11704) ***(G-16129)***
Advance Pressure Products, Ithaca *Also called Porous Materials Inc* ***(G-6605)***
Advance Publications Inc (PA)...718 981-1234
950 W Fingerboard Rd Staten Island (10305) ***(G-15040)***
Advance Tabco Inc (HQ)...631 242-8270
200 Heartland Blvd Edgewood (11717) ***(G-4394)***
Advanced Assembly Services Inc...716 217-8144
44 Knollwood Dr Lancaster (14086) ***(G-7001)***
Advanced Atomization Tech LLC...315 923-2341
124 Columbia St Clyde (14433) ***(G-3591)***
Advanced Back Technologies...631 231-0076
89 Ste F Cabot Ct Hauppauge (11788) ***(G-5754)***
Advanced Barcode Tech Inc...516 570-8100
175 E Shore Rd Ste 228 Great Neck (11023) ***(G-5527)***
Advanced Biomedical Tech Inc...718 766-7898
350 5th Ave Fl 59 New York (10118) ***(G-8752)***
Advanced Business Group Inc...212 398-1010
266 W 37th St Fl 15 New York (10018) ***(G-8753)***
Advanced Cmpt Sftwr Consulting...718 300-3577
2236 Pearsall Ave Bronx (10469) ***(G-1213)***
Advanced Coating Service LLC...585 247-3970
15 Hytec Cir Rochester (14606) ***(G-13605)***
Advanced Coating Techniques...631 643-4555
313 Wyandanch Ave Babylon (11704) ***(G-524)***
Advanced Coating Technologies, Amherst *Also called Bekaert Corporation* ***(G-216)***

ALPHABETIC SECTION — AFP Industries, Lancaster

Advanced Comfort Systems Inc 518 884-8444
  12b Commerce Dr Ballston Spa (12020) *(G-574)*
Advanced Comm Solutions 914 693-5076
  38 Ridge Rd Ardsley (10502) *(G-393)*
Advanced Comm Solutions Ltd, New York Also called ACS Custom USA LLC *(G-8729)*
Advanced Cyber Security Corp 866 417-9155
  3880 Veterans Memorial Hw Bohemia (11716) *(G-973)*
Advanced Digital Info Corp 607 266-4000
  10 Brown Rd Ithaca (14850) *(G-6554)*
Advanced Digital Printing LLC 718 649-1500
  65 W 36th St Fl 11 New York (10018) *(G-8754)*
Advanced Door Solutions Inc 631 773-6100
  1363 Lincoln Ave Ste 7 Holbrook (11741) *(G-6169)*
Advanced Doors, Holbrook Also called Advanced Door Solutions Inc *(G-6169)*
Advanced Enterprises Inc 845 342-1009
  366 Highland Ave Ext Middletown (10940) *(G-8136)*
Advanced Fashions Technology 212 221-0606
  110 W 40th St Rm 1100 New York (10018) *(G-8755)*
Advanced Foam Products Div, Buffalo Also called Tmp Technologies Inc *(G-3097)*
Advanced Frozen Foods Inc 516 333-6344
  28 Urban Ave Westbury (11590) *(G-16309)*
Advanced Glass Industries Inc 585 458-8040
  1335 Emerson St Rochester (14606) *(G-13606)*
Advanced Graphics Company 607 692-7875
  2607 Main St Whitney Point (13862) *(G-16554)*
Advanced Interconnect Mfg Inc (HQ) 585 742-2220
  780 Canning Pkwy Victor (14564) *(G-15828)*
Advanced Machine Design Co Inc 716 826-2000
  45 Roberts Ave Buffalo (14206) *(G-2689)*
Advanced Machine Inc 585 423-8255
  439 Central Ave Ste 108 Rochester (14605) *(G-13607)*
Advanced Manufacturing Svc Inc 631 676-5210
  100 13th Ave Ste 2 Ronkonkoma (11779) *(G-14292)*
Advanced Medical Mfg Corp 845 369-7535
  7-11 Suffern Pl Ste 2 Suffern (10901) *(G-15184)*
Advanced Mfg Techniques 518 877-8560
  453 Kinns Rd Clifton Park (12065) *(G-3562)*
Advanced Mtl Analytics LLC 321 684-0528
  85 Murray Hl Rd Ste 2115 Vestal (13850) *(G-15808)*
Advanced Pavement Group Corp (PA) 631 277-8400
  2 W Beech St Islip (11751) *(G-6543)*
Advanced Photonics Inc 631 471-3693
  151 Trade Zone Dr Ronkonkoma (11779) *(G-14293)*
Advanced Placement LLC 949 281-9086
  60 Lorraine Ct Holbrook (11741) *(G-6170)*
Advanced Polymer Solutions LLC 516 621-5800
  99 Seaview Blvd Ste 1a Port Washington (11050) *(G-13240)*
Advanced Polymers Intl, Syracuse Also called Royal Adhesives & Sealants LLC *(G-15411)*
Advanced Precision Technology 845 279-3540
  577 N Main St Ste 7 Brewster (10509) *(G-1154)*
Advanced Printing New York Inc 212 840-8108
  263 W 38th St New York (10018) *(G-8756)*
Advanced Prosthetics Orthotics 516 365-7225
  50 Maple Pl Manhasset (11030) *(G-7763)*
Advanced Quickprinting, Rochester Also called A Q P Inc *(G-13590)*
Advanced Ready Mix Corp 718 497-5020
  239 Ingraham St Brooklyn (11237) *(G-1488)*
Advanced Recovery & Recycl LLC 315 450-3301
  3475 Linda Ln Baldwinsville (13027) *(G-548)*
Advanced Research Media Inc 631 751-9696
  60 Route 25a Ste 1 Setauket (11733) *(G-14791)*
Advanced Response Corporation 212 459-0887
  345 W 58th St Apt 11a New York (10019) *(G-8757)*
Advanced Rubber Products, Wyoming Also called Tmp Technologies Inc *(G-16702)*
Advanced Structures Corp (PA) 631 667-5000
  235 W Industry Ct Deer Park (11729) *(G-3934)*
Advanced Surface Finishing 516 876-9710
  111 Magnolia Ave Westbury (11590) *(G-16310)*
Advanced Tchncal Solutions Inc 914 214-8230
  8 Lupi Plz Mahopac (10541) *(G-7707)*
Advanced Technology Division, Plainview Also called Technic Inc *(G-13092)*
Advanced Testing Tech Inc (PA) 631 231-8777
  110 Ricefield Ln Hauppauge (11788) *(G-5755)*
Advanced Thermal Systems Inc 716 681-1800
  15 Enterprise Dr Lancaster (14086) *(G-7002)*
Advanced Transit Mix Corp 718 497-5020
  610 Johnson Ave Brooklyn (11237) *(G-1489)*
Advanced Yarn Technologies Inc 518 239-6600
  4750 State Hwy 145 Durham (12422) *(G-4182)*
Advantage Machining Inc 716 731-6418
  6421 Wendt Dr Niagara Falls (14304) *(G-12258)*
Advantage Metalwork Finshg LLC 585 454-0160
  1000 University Ave # 700 Rochester (14607) *(G-13608)*
Advantage Orthotics Inc 631 368-1754
  337 Larkfield Rd East Northport (11731) *(G-4259)*
Advantage Plus Diagnostics Inc 631 393-5044
  200 Broadhollow Rd Melville (11747) *(G-7997)*
Advantage Press Inc 518 584-3405
  74 Warren St Saratoga Springs (12866) *(G-14568)*
Advantage Quick Print Inc 212 989-5654
  30 E 33rd St Frnt B New York (10016) *(G-8758)*

Advantage Wholesale Supply LLC 718 284-5346
  172 Empire Blvd Brooklyn Brooklyn (11225) *(G-1490)*
Advantage Wood Shop, Cheektowaga Also called Stereo Advantage Inc *(G-3459)*
Advantech Industries Inc 585 247-0701
  3850 Buffalo Rd Rochester (14624) *(G-13609)*
Advantex Solutions Inc 718 278-2290
  24845 Jericho Tpke Bellerose (11426) *(G-780)*
Advd Heart Phys & Surgs 212 434-3000
  130 E 77th St Fl 4 New York (10075) *(G-8759)*
Adventure Publishing Group 212 575-4510
  307 7th Ave Rm 1601 New York (10001) *(G-8760)*
Advertiser, Albany Also called Capital Region Wkly Newspapers *(G-55)*
Advertiser Perceptions Inc 212 626-6683
  1120 Ave Of The Americas New York (10036) *(G-8761)*
Advertiser Publications Inc 845 783-1111
  148 State Route 17m Chester (10918) *(G-3467)*
Advertiser, The, Averill Park Also called Capital Reg Wkly Newsppr Group *(G-513)*
Advertising Lithographers 212 966-7771
  2812 41st Ave Long Island City (11101) *(G-7368)*
Advion Inc (PA) 607 266-9162
  61 Brown Rd Ithaca (14850) *(G-6555)*
Advis Inc 585 568-0100
  2218 River Rd Caledonia (14423) *(G-3152)*
Ae Fund Inc 315 698-7650
  5860 Mckinley Rd Brewerton (13029) *(G-1149)*
Aegis Oil Limited Ventures LLC 646 233-4900
  14 Wall St Fl 20 New York (10005) *(G-8762)*
Aeon America Inc 914 584-0275
  68 Jay St Ste 201 Brooklyn (11201) *(G-1491)*
AEP Environmental LLC 716 446-0739
  2495 Main St Ste 230 Buffalo (14214) *(G-2690)*
Aerco International Inc (HQ) 845 580-8000
  100 Oritani Dr Blauvelt (10913) *(G-933)*
Aero Brand Inks, Blue Point Also called Specialty Ink Co Inc *(G-965)*
Aero Healthcare (us) LLC 855 225-2376
  616 Corporate Way Ste 6 Valley Cottage (10989) *(G-15751)*
Aero Specialties Manufacturing 631 242-7200
  20 Burt Dr Deer Park (11729) *(G-3935)*
Aero Strctures Long Island Inc (PA) 516 997-5757
  717 Main St Westbury (11590) *(G-16311)*
Aero Trades Mfg Corp 516 746-3360
  65 Jericho Tpke Mineola (11501) *(G-8200)*
Aero-Data Metal Crafters Inc 631 471-7733
  2085 5th Ave Ronkonkoma (11779) *(G-14294)*
Aero-Vision Technologies Inc (PA) 631 643-8349
  7 Round Tree Dr Melville (11747) *(G-7998)*
Aerobic Wear Inc 631 673-1830
  16 Depot Rd Huntington Station (11746) *(G-6428)*
Aeroduct Inc 516 248-9550
  134 Herricks Rd Mineola (11501) *(G-8201)*
Aeroflex Holding Corp 516 694-6700
  35 S Service Rd Plainview (11803) *(G-13031)*
Aeroflex Incorporated (HQ) 516 694-6700
  35 S Service Rd Plainview (11803) *(G-13032)*
Aeroflex Plainview Inc (HQ) 516 694-6700
  35 S Service Rd Plainview (11803) *(G-13033)*
Aeroflex Plainview Inc 631 231-9100
  350 Kennedy Dr Hauppauge (11788) *(G-5756)*
Aerolase Corporation 914 345-8300
  777 Old Saw Mill River Rd # 2 Tarrytown (10591) *(G-15472)*
Aeromed Inc 518 843-9144
  1821 Broad St Ste 1 Utica (13501) *(G-15677)*
Aerospace Lighting Corporation (HQ) 631 563-6400
  355 Knickerbocker Ave Bohemia (11716) *(G-974)*
Aerospace Wire & Cable Inc 718 358-2345
  12909 18th Ave College Point (11356) *(G-3637)*
AES Electronics Inc 212 371-8120
  135 E 54th St Apt 10j New York (10022) *(G-8763)*
Aesthonics Inc 646 723-2463
  21 Belvidere St Fl 3 Brooklyn (11206) *(G-1492)*
AF Design Inc 347 548-5273
  1239 Broadway Ste 310 New York (10001) *(G-8764)*
Afab Initiative, Buffalo Also called American Douglas Metals Inc *(G-2695)*
AFC Industries Inc 718 747-0237
  1316 133rd Pl Ste 1 College Point (11356) *(G-3638)*
Afco Modular Enclosure Systems, Farmingdale Also called Afco Systems Inc *(G-4708)*
Afco Precast Sales Corp 631 924-7114
  114 Rocky Point Rd Middle Island (11953) *(G-8116)*
Afco Systems Inc 631 249-9441
  200 Finn Ct Ste 1 Farmingdale (11735) *(G-4708)*
Afe, South Hempstead Also called Accessories For Electronics *(G-14941)*
Aferge Mds, Rochester Also called GE Mds LLC *(G-13824)*
Affco, New Windsor Also called American Felt & Filter Co Inc *(G-8635)*
Affiliated Services Group, Huntington Also called SC Textiles Inc *(G-6414)*
Affordable Luxury Group Inc 631 523-9266
  10 W 33rd St Rm 615 New York (10001) *(G-8765)*
Affymax Inc 650 812-8700
  630 5th Ave Ste 2260 New York (10111) *(G-8766)*
Afi Cybernetics Corporation 607 732-3244
  713 Batavia St Elmira (14904) *(G-4472)*
AFP Industries, Lancaster Also called Air System Products Inc *(G-7004)*

(PA)=Parent Co (HQ)=Headquarters (DH)=Div Headquarters

AFP Manufacturing Corp 516 466-6464
9 Park Pl Great Neck (11021) **(G-5528)**
African American Observer, New York *Also called General Media Strategies Inc* **(G-9901)**
Afro Times Newspaper 718 636-9500
1195 Atlantic Ave Brooklyn (11216) **(G-1493)**
After 50 Inc 716 832-9300
5 W Main St Rear Lancaster (14086) **(G-7003)**
AG Biotech Inc 585 346-0020
3578 Shoreline Dr Livonia (14487) **(G-7277)**
AG Kids, New York *Also called Premium 5 Kids LLC* **(G-11231)**
AG Neovo Professional Inc 212 647-9080
156 5th Ave Ste 434 New York (10010) **(G-8767)**
AG Tech Welding Corp 845 398-0005
238 Oak Tree Rd Tappan (10983) **(G-15465)**
Ag-Pak Inc 716 772-2651
8416 Telegraph Rd Gasport (14067) **(G-5304)**
Age Manufacturers Inc 718 927-0048
10624 Avenue D Brooklyn (11236) **(G-1494)**
Age Timberline Mamba, Farmingdale *Also called Amana Tool Corp* **(G-4718)**
Agi Brooks Production Co Inc (PA) 212 268-1533
7 E 14th St Apt 615 New York (10003) **(G-8768)**
Agilent Technologies Inc 877 424-4536
399 Park Ave New York (10022) **(G-8769)**
Agl Industries Inc 718 326-7597
5912 57th St Maspeth (11378) **(G-7816)**
Aglika Trade LLC 727 424-1944
5905 74th St Middle Village (11379) **(G-8120)**
Agn Professional, New York *Also called AG Neovo Professional Inc* **(G-8767)**
Agnovos Healthcare LLC 646 502-5860
140 Broadway Fl 46 New York (10005) **(G-8770)**
Agrecolor Inc (PA) 516 741-8700
400 Sagamore Ave Mineola (11501) **(G-8202)**
Agri Services Co 716 937-6618
13899 North Rd Alden (14004) **(G-166)**
Agri-Mark Inc 518 497-6644
39 Mccadam Ln Chateaugay (12920) **(G-3426)**
Agrinetix Cmpt Systems LLC 877 978-5477
370 Summit Point Dr 1a Henrietta (14467) **(G-6029)**
Agrinetix, LLC, Henrietta *Also called Agrinetix Cmpt Systems LLC* **(G-6029)**
Agrochem Inc 518 226-4850
26 Freedom Way Saratoga Springs Saratoga Springs (12866) **(G-14569)**
Agua Brands, Bethpage *Also called Agua Enerviva LLC* **(G-839)**
Agua Enerviva LLC 516 597-5440
15 Grumman Rd W Ste 1300 Bethpage (11714) **(G-839)**
Aguilar Amplification LLC 212 431-9109
599 Broadway Fl 7 New York (10012) **(G-8771)**
Agway, Salem *Also called Cargill Incorporated* **(G-14536)**
Agway, Cobleskill *Also called Kelley Farm & Garden Inc* **(G-3603)**
Ah Elctronic Test Eqp Repr Ctr 631 234-8979
7 Olive St Central Islip (11722) **(G-3354)**
Ahhmigo LLC 212 315-1818
120 Cent Park S Rm 7c New York (10019) **(G-8772)**
Ahlstrom Kamyr, Glens Falls *Also called Andritz Inc* **(G-5415)**
Ahq LLC 212 328-1560
10 W 33rd St Rm 306 New York (10001) **(G-8773)**
Ahw Printing Corp 516 536-3600
2920 Long Beach Rd Oceanside (11572) **(G-12531)**
Ai Entertainment Holdings LLC (HQ) 212 247-6400
730 5th Ave Fl 20 New York (10019) **(G-8774)**
Ai Media Group Inc 212 660-2400
1359 Broadway Fl 5 New York (10018) **(G-8775)**
Aiche, New York *Also called American Inst Chem Engineers* **(G-8830)**
Aicm, Hauppauge *Also called American Intrmdal Cont Mfg LLC* **(G-5767)**
Aigner Chocolates (PA) 718 544-1850
10302 Metropolitan Ave Forest Hills (11375) **(G-5070)**
Aigner Index,, New Windsor *Also called Aigner Label Holder Corp* **(G-8634)**
Aigner Label Holder Corp 845 562-4510
218 Mac Arthur Ave New Windsor (12553) **(G-8634)**
Aimee Kestenberg, New York *Also called Affordable Luxury Group Inc* **(G-8765)**
Aimsun Inc 917 267-8534
20 W 22nd St Ste 612 New York (10010) **(G-8776)**
Aines Manufacturing Corp 631 471-3900
96 E Bayberry Rd Islip (11751) **(G-6544)**
Aip Mc Holdings LLC (PA) 212 627-2360
330 Madison Ave Fl 28 New York (10017) **(G-8777)**
Aip Publishing LLC 516 576-2200
1305 Walt Whitman Rd # 300 Melville (11747) **(G-7999)**
Aiping Pharmaceutical Inc 631 952-3802
350w Wireless Blvd Hauppauge (11788) **(G-5757)**
Air Conditioning, Bronx *Also called AC Air Cooling Co Inc* **(G-1206)**
Air Crafters Inc 631 471-7788
2085 5th Ave Ronkonkoma (11779) **(G-14295)**
Air Engineering Filters Inc 914 238-5945
17 Memorial Dr Chappaqua (10514) **(G-3419)**
Air Export Mechanical 917 709-5310
4108 Parsons Blvd Apt 4r Flushing (11355) **(G-4981)**
Air Flow Pump Corp 718 241-2800
8412 Foster Ave Brooklyn (11236) **(G-1495)**
Air Flow Pump Supply, Brooklyn *Also called Air Flow Pump Corp* **(G-1495)**
Air Industries Group (PA) 631 881-4920
360 Motor Pkwy Ste 100 Hauppauge (11788) **(G-5758)**
Air Industries Machining Corp 631 328-7000
1460 5th Ave Bay Shore (11706) **(G-653)**
Air Louver & Damper Inc (PA) 718 392-3232
2121 44th Rd Long Island City (11101) **(G-7369)**
Air Preheater, Wellsville *Also called Arvos Inc* **(G-16113)**
Air Products and Chemicals Inc 518 463-4273
461 River Rd Glenmont (12077) **(G-5410)**
Air Skate & Air Jump Corp 212 967-1201
1385 Broadway New York (10018) **(G-8778)**
Air Skate & Air Jump Corp (PA) 212 967-1201
2208 E 5th St Brooklyn (11223) **(G-1496)**
Air Structures Amercn Tech Inc 914 937-4500
211 S Ridge St Ste 3 Port Chester (10573) **(G-13191)**
Air System Products Inc 716 683-0435
51 Beach Ave Lancaster (14086) **(G-7004)**
Air Techniques Inc (HQ) 516 433-7676
1295 Walt Whitman Rd Melville (11747) **(G-8000)**
Air Tite Manufacturing Inc 516 897-0295
724 Park Pl Ste B Long Beach (11561) **(G-7356)**
Air-Flo Mfg Co Inc 607 733-8284
365 Upper Oakwood Ave Elmira (14903) **(G-4473)**
Air-O-Tronics, Cazenovia *Also called Stk Electronics Inc* **(G-3327)**
Aircraft Finishing Corp (PA) 631 422-5000
100 Field St Unit A West Babylon (11704) **(G-16130)**
Airflex Corp 631 752-1219
965 Conklin St Farmingdale (11735) **(G-4709)**
Airflex Industrial Inc (PA) 631 752-1234
965 Conklin St Farmingdale (11735) **(G-4710)**
Airflex Industrial Inc 631 752-1234
937 Conklin St Farmingdale (11735) **(G-4711)**
Airgas Inc 518 690-0068
84 Karner Rd Albany (12205) **(G-30)**
Airgas Usa LLC 585 436-7781
77 Deep Rock Rd Rochester (14624) **(G-13610)**
Airgle Corporation 866 501-7750
711 Koehler Ave Ste 3 Ronkonkoma (11779) **(G-14296)**
Airline Container Services 516 371-4125
354 Harbor Dr Lido Beach (11561) **(G-7147)**
Airline Container Svces, Lido Beach *Also called Airline Container Services* **(G-7147)**
Airmarine Electroplating Corp 516 623-4406
388 Woodcleft Ave Freeport (11520) **(G-5137)**
Airnet Communications Corp 516 338-0008
609 Cantiague Rock Rd # 5 Westbury (11590) **(G-16312)**
Airnet North Division, Westbury *Also called Airnet Communications Corp* **(G-16312)**
Airport Press, The, Jamaica *Also called Pati Inc* **(G-6667)**
Airport Printing & Stationers, Wading River *Also called A I P Printing & Stationers* **(G-15883)**
Airsep, Amherst *Also called Chart Industries Inc* **(G-222)**
Airsep Corporation 716 691-0202
260 Creekside Dr Ste 100 Amherst (14228) **(G-208)**
Airtech Lab, Brooklyn *Also called Dib Managmnt Inc* **(G-1774)**
Airweld Inc 631 924-6366
1740 Middle Country Rd Ridge (11961) **(G-13520)**
Aithaca Chemical Corp 516 229-2330
50 Charles Lindbergh Blvd # 400 Uniondale (11553) **(G-15662)**
Aj Genco Mch Sp McHy Rdout Svc 716 664-4925
235 Carter St Falconer (14733) **(G-4669)**
Ajax Wire Specialty Co Inc 516 935-2333
119 Bloomingdale Rd Hicksville (11801) **(G-6056)**
Ajes Pharmaceuticals LLC 631 608-1728
11a Lincoln St Copiague (11726) **(G-3749)**
Ajl Manufacturing Inc 585 254-1128
100 Holleder Pkwy Rochester (14615) **(G-13611)**
Ajmadison Corp 718 532-1800
3605 13th Ave Brooklyn (11218) **(G-1497)**
AJW Architectural Products, New Windsor *Also called Fifty Door Partners LLC* **(G-8644)**
Aka Enterprises 716 474-4579
164 Main St Wyoming (14591) **(G-16698)**
Aka Sport Inc 631 858-9888
16 Princeton Dr Dix Hills (11746) **(G-4118)**
Akari Therapeutics PLC 646 350-0702
24 W 40th St Fl 8 New York (10018) **(G-8779)**
Akh Group LLC 646 320-8720
601 W 26th St Rm M228 New York (10001) **(G-8780)**
Akhon Samoy Weekly, Flushing *Also called Digital One USA Inc* **(G-4996)**
Aki Cabinets Inc 718 721-2541
2636 2nd St Astoria (11102) **(G-420)**
Akoustis Inc 585 919-3073
5450 Campus Dr Ste 100 Canandaigua (14424) **(G-3210)**
Akraturn Mfg Inc 607 775-2802
1743 Us Route 11 Kirkwood (13795) **(G-6938)**
Akribos Watches, Brooklyn *Also called TWI Watches LLC* **(G-2595)**
Akron-Corfu Pennysaver, Elma *Also called R W Publications Div of Wtrhs* **(G-4456)**
Akshar Extracts Inc 631 588-9727
59 Remington Blvd Ronkonkoma (11779) **(G-14297)**
Akzo Nobel Central Research, Dobbs Ferry *Also called Akzo Nobel Chemicals LLC* **(G-4129)**
Akzo Nobel Chemicals LLC 914 674-5008
7 Livingstone Ave Dobbs Ferry (10522) **(G-4129)**
Akzo Nobel Chemicals LLC 716 778-8554
2153 Lockport Olcott Rd Burt (14028) **(G-3143)**

Akzo Nobel Functional Chem LLC...845 276-8200
281 Fields Ln Brewster (10509) **(G-1155)**
Al Cohens Famous Rye Bread Bky, Buffalo *Also called Cohens Bakery Inc* **(G-2771)**
Ala Scientific Instruments Inc...631 393-6401
60 Marine St Ste 1 Farmingdale (11735) **(G-4712)**
Alabaster Group Inc...516 867-8223
188 N Main St Freeport (11520) **(G-5138)**
Alabu Inc...518 665-0411
30 Graves Rd Mechanicville (12118) **(G-7929)**
Alabu Skin Care, Mechanicville *Also called Alabu Inc* **(G-7929)**
Aladdin Bakers Inc (PA)...718 499-1818
240 25th St Brooklyn (11232) **(G-1498)**
Aladdin Manufacturing Corp...212 561-8715
295 5th Ave Ste 1412 New York (10016) **(G-8781)**
Aladdin Packaging LLC...631 273-4747
115 Engineers Rd Ste 100 Hauppauge (11788) **(G-5759)**
Alamar Printing Inc...914 993-9007
190 E Post Rd Frnt 1 White Plains (10601) **(G-16417)**
Alan F Bourguet...516 883-4315
63 Essex Ct Port Washington (11050) **(G-13241)**
Alart Inc...212 840-1508
578 5th Ave Unit 33 New York (10036) **(G-8782)**
Alba Fuel Corp...718 931-1700
2135 Wllmsbrdge Rd Fl 2 Flr 2 Bronx (10461) **(G-1214)**
Alba House Publishers...718 698-2759
2187 Victory Blvd Staten Island (10314) **(G-15041)**
Albaluz Films LLC...347 613-2321
954 Lexington Ave New York (10021) **(G-8783)**
Albany Asp & Aggregates Corp...518 436-8916
101 Dunham Dr Albany (12202) **(G-31)**
Albany Catholic Press Assoc...518 453-6688
40 N Main Ave Ste 2 Albany (12203) **(G-32)**
Albany International Corp...518 445-2230
1373 Broadway Menands (12204) **(G-8079)**
Albany International Corp...607 749-7226
156 S Main St Homer (13077) **(G-6252)**
Albany International Corp...518 447-6400
1373 Broadway Menands (12204) **(G-8080)**
Albany International Corp...518 445-2200
253 Troy Rd Rensselaer (12144) **(G-13470)**
Albany Letter Shop Inc...518 434-1172
16 Van Zandt St Ste 20 Albany (12207) **(G-33)**
Albany Molecular Research Inc...518 512-2234
21 Corporate Cir Albany (12203) **(G-34)**
Albany Molecular Research Inc...518 433-7700
81 Columbia Tpke Rensselaer (12144) **(G-13471)**
Albany Molecular Research Inc (HQ)...518 512-2000
26 Corporate Cir Albany (12203) **(G-35)**
Albany Molecular Research Inc...518 512-2000
33 Riverside Ave Rensselaer (12144) **(G-13472)**
Albany Mtal Fbrcation Holdings...518 463-5161
67 Henry Johnson Blvd Albany (12210) **(G-36)**
Albany Nipple and Pipe Mfg...518 270-2162
60 Cohoes Ave Ste 100a Troy (12183) **(G-15594)**
Albany Pump Station, Albany *Also called C H Evans Brewing Co* **(G-53)**
Albany Student Press Inc...518 442-5665
1400 Washington Ave Cc329 Albany (12222) **(G-37)**
Albatros North America Inc...518 381-7100
6 Mccrea Hill Rd Ballston Spa (12020) **(G-575)**
Albea Cosmetics America Inc (HQ)...212 371-5100
595 Madison Ave Fl 10 New York (10022) **(G-8784)**
Albert Augustine Ltd...718 913-9635
161 S Macquesten Pkwy Mount Vernon (10550) **(G-8376)**
Albert F Stager Inc...315 434-7240
6805 Crossbow Dr East Syracuse (13057) **(G-4316)**
Albert Gates Inc...585 594-9401
3434 Union St North Chili (14514) **(G-12381)**
Albert Kemperle Inc...718 629-1084
890 E 51st St Brooklyn (11203) **(G-1499)**
Albert Menin Interiors Ltd...212 876-3041
2417 3rd Ave Fl 3 Bronx (10451) **(G-1215)**
Albert Siy...718 359-0389
13508 Booth Memorial Ave Flushing (11355) **(G-4982)**
Albest Metal Stamping Corp...718 388-6000
1 Kent Ave Brooklyn (11249) **(G-1500)**
Albion Cosmetics America Inc...212 869-1052
1350 Avenue Of The New York (10019) **(G-8785)**
Albion-Holley Pennysaver Inc...585 589-5641
170 N Main St Albion (14411) **(G-154)**
Albrizio Couture, Brooklyn *Also called Albrizio Inc* **(G-1501)**
Albrizio Inc...212 719-5290
257 Varet St Ste Mgmt Brooklyn (11206) **(G-1501)**
Albro Gear & Instrument, Yaphank *Also called W J Albro Machine Works Inc* **(G-16728)**
Albumx Corp...914 939-6878
21 Grace Church St Port Chester (10573) **(G-13192)**
Alcatel-Lucent USA Inc...516 349-4900
1 Fairchild Ct Ste 340 Plainview (11803) **(G-13034)**
Alchemy Simya Inc...646 230-1122
161 Avnue Of The Americas New York (10013) **(G-8786)**
Alco Plastics Inc...716 683-3020
35 Ward Rd Lancaster (14086) **(G-7005)**
Alco Products Div, Orchard Park *Also called Nitram Energy Inc* **(G-12732)**
Alco Products USA, Orchard Park *Also called Peerless Mfg Co* **(G-12736)**
Alcoa, Falconer *Also called Arconic Inc* **(G-4671)**
Alcoa Corporation...412 315-2900
45 County Route 42 Massena (13662) **(G-7897)**
Alcoa Fastening Systems...585 368-5049
181 Mckee Rd Rochester (14611) **(G-13612)**
Alcoa Fastening Systems...845 334-7203
1 Corporate Dr Kingston (12401) **(G-6887)**
Alcoa USA Corp...315 764-4011
45 County Route 42 Massena (13662) **(G-7898)**
Alcoa USA Corp...315 764-4106
1814 State Highway 131 Massena (13662) **(G-7899)**
Alcoholics Anonymous Grapevine (PA)...212 870-3400
475 Riverside Dr Ste 1264 New York (10115) **(G-8787)**
Alconox, White Plains *Also called L S Z Inc* **(G-16471)**
Alconox Inc...914 948-4040
30 Glenn St Ste 309 White Plains (10603) **(G-16418)**
Alden Advertiser, Alden *Also called Weisbeck Publishing Printing* **(G-178)**
Alden Aurora Gas Company Inc...716 937-9484
13441 Railroad St Alden (14004) **(G-167)**
Alden Optical Laboratory Inc...716 937-9181
6 Lancaster Pkwy Lancaster (14086) **(G-7006)**
Aldine Inc (ny)...212 226-2870
150 Varick St Fl 5 New York (10013) **(G-8788)**
Aldo Frustacci Iron Works Inc...718 768-0707
165 27th St Brooklyn (11232) **(G-1502)**
Aldos Iron Works Inc...718 834-0408
75 Van Brunt St Brooklyn (11231) **(G-1503)**
Ale Viola LLC...212 868-3808
259 W 30th St Fl 9th10th New York (10001) **(G-8789)**
Ale-Techniques Inc...845 687-7200
2452 Lucas Tpke Ste B High Falls (12440) **(G-6139)**
Alen Sands York Associates Ltd...212 563-6305
236 W 26th St Rm 801 New York (10001) **(G-8790)**
Aleta Industries Inc...718 349-0040
40 Ash St Brooklyn (11222) **(G-1504)**
Aleteia Usa Inc...914 502-1855
86 Main St Ste 303 Yonkers (10701) **(G-16730)**
Alex Archer Designs Ltd...212 219-8664
594 Broadway Rm 306 New York (10012) **(G-8791)**
Alex Sepkus Inc...212 391-8466
42 W 48th St Ste 501 New York (10036) **(G-8792)**
Alexander Primak Jewelry Inc...212 398-0287
529 5th Ave Fl 15 New York (10017) **(G-8793)**
Alexander Wang Incorporated (PA)...212 532-3103
386 Broadway Fl 3 New York (10013) **(G-8794)**
Alexandra Ferguson LLC...718 788-7768
180 Davenport Ave New Rochelle (10805) **(G-8587)**
Alexandre Furs, New York *Also called Samuel Schulman Furs Inc* **(G-11478)**
Alexandria Professional LLC...716 242-8514
5500 Main St Ste 103 Williamsville (14221) **(G-16567)**
Alexandros, New York *Also called Anastasia Furs International* **(G-8855)**
Alexy Associates Inc...845 482-3000
86 Jim Stephenson Rd Bethel (12720) **(G-834)**
Alfa Card Inc...718 326-7107
7915 Cooper Ave Glendale (11385) **(G-5390)**
Alfa Chem, Great Neck *Also called Alfred Khalily Inc* **(G-5530)**
Alfa Laval Kathabar Inc...716 875-2000
91 Sawyer Ave Tonawanda (14150) **(G-15520)**
Alfred B Parella...518 872-1238
20 Reservoir Rd Altamont (12009) **(G-194)**
Alfred Butler Inc...516 829-7460
107 Grace Ave Great Neck (11021) **(G-5529)**
Alfred Dunner Inc (PA)...212 478-4300
1333 Broadway Fl 11 New York (10018) **(G-8795)**
Alfred Khalily Inc...516 504-0059
2 Harbor Way Great Neck (11024) **(G-5530)**
Alfred Mainzer Inc (PA)...718 392-4200
2708 40th Ave Long Island City (11101) **(G-7370)**
Alfred Music, Oriskany *Also called Alfred Publishing Co Inc* **(G-12750)**
Alfred Publishing Co Inc...315 736-1572
123 Dry Rd Oriskany (13424) **(G-12750)**
Algafuel America...516 295-2257
289 Meadowview Ave Hewlett (11557) **(G-6046)**
Algemeiner Journal Inc...718 771-0400
508 Montgomery St Brooklyn (11225) **(G-1505)**
Algonquin Books Chapel Hl Div, New York *Also called Workman Publishing Co Inc* **(G-12135)**
Algonquin Power...315 393-5595
19 Mill St Ogdensburg (13669) **(G-12569)**
Ali Ro, New York *Also called Donna Morgan LLC* **(G-9554)**
Alice & Trixie, New York *Also called Millennium Productions Inc* **(G-10808)**
Alice Perkins...716 378-5100
148 Washington St Salamanca (14779) **(G-14523)**
Alicia Adams Alpaca Inc...845 868-3366
3262 Franklin Ave Millbrook (12545) **(G-8187)**
Alicia F Herdlein...585 344-4411
5450 E Main Street Rd Batavia (14020) **(G-608)**
Alicias Bakery Inc...914 235-4689
498 Main St Ste A New Rochelle (10801) **(G-8588)**
Alison Wine & Vineyard, Rhinebeck *Also called Dutchess Wines LLC* **(G-13486)**

ALPHABETIC

(PA)=Parent Co (HQ)=Headquarters (DH)=Div Headquarters

Aljo Precision Products Inc ...516 420-4419
205 Bethpge Sweet Holw Old Bethpage (11804) ***(G-12581)***
Aljo-Gefa Precision Mfg LLC ...516 420-4419
205 Bethpage Sweet Holw Old Bethpage (11804) ***(G-12582)***
Alkemy Machine LLC ...585 436-8730
1600 Lexington Ave 103c Rochester (14606) ***(G-13613)***
Alken Industries Inc ...631 467-2000
2175 5th Ave Ronkonkoma (11779) ***(G-14298)***
All About Art Inc ...718 321-0755
4128 Murray St Flushing (11355) ***(G-4983)***
All American Awards Inc ...631 567-2025
331 Knickerbocker Ave Bohemia (11716) ***(G-975)***
All American Building ...607 797-7123
109 Crestmont Rd Binghamton (13905) ***(G-859)***
All American Concrete Corp ...718 497-3301
239 Ingraham St Brooklyn (11237) ***(G-1506)***
All American Funding & Ref LLC ...516 978-7531
345 Eastern Pkwy Farmingdale (11735) ***(G-4713)***
All American Metal Corporation (PA) ...516 223-1760
200 Buffalo Ave Freeport (11520) ***(G-5139)***
All American Metal Corporation ...516 623-0222
200 Buffalo Ave Freeport (11520) ***(G-5140)***
All American Stairs & Railing ...718 441-8400
13023 91st Ave Richmond Hill (11418) ***(G-13495)***
All American Transit Mix Corp ...718 417-3654
46 Knickerbocker Ave Brooklyn (11237) ***(G-1507)***
All American Uniform, Bohemia *Also called All American Awards Inc* ***(G-975)***
All Around Spiral Inc ...631 588-0220
10 Fleetwood Ct Ronkonkoma (11779) ***(G-14299)***
All Cast Foundry, Brooklyn *Also called J & J Bronze & Aluminum Cast* ***(G-2021)***
All City Switchboard Corp ...718 956-7244
3541 11th St Long Island City (11106) ***(G-7371)***
All Color Business Spc Ltd ...516 420-0649
305 Suburban Ave Deer Park (11729) ***(G-3936)***
All Color Business Specialties, Farmingdale *Also called All Color Offset Printers Inc* ***(G-4714)***
All Color Offset Printers Inc ...516 420-0649
51 Henry St Ste A Farmingdale (11735) ***(G-4714)***
All Craft Jewelry Supply, New York *Also called Creative Tools & Supply Inc* ***(G-9422)***
All Cultures Inc ...631 293-3143
12 Gates St Greenlawn (11740) ***(G-5620)***
All Island Blower & Shtmtl ...631 567-7070
1585 Smithtown Ave Unit C Bohemia (11716) ***(G-976)***
All Island Media Inc (PA) ...631 698-8400
1 Rodeo Dr Edgewood (11717) ***(G-4395)***
All Island Media Inc ...516 942-8400
325 Duffy Ave Unit 2 Hicksville (11801) ***(G-6057)***
All Merchandise Display Corp ...718 257-2221
4 Pheasant Run Highland Mills (10930) ***(G-6150)***
All Metal Specialties Inc ...716 664-6009
300 Livingston Ave Jamestown (14701) ***(G-6696)***
All Metro Emrgncy Response Sys ...516 750-9100
50 Broadway Lynbrook (11563) ***(G-7659)***
All Net Ltd ...516 504-4559
15 Cuttermill Rd Ste 145 Great Neck (11021) ***(G-5531)***
All Out Die Cutting Inc ...718 346-6666
49 Wyckoff Ave Ste 1 Brooklyn (11237) ***(G-1508)***
All Packaging McHy & Sups Corp ...631 588-7310
90 13th Ave Unit 11 Ronkonkoma (11779) ***(G-14300)***
All Shore Industries Inc ...718 720-0018
1 Edgewater St Ste 215 Staten Island (10305) ***(G-15042)***
All Signs ...973 736-2113
63 Bridgetown St Staten Island (10314) ***(G-15043)***
All Spec Finishing Inc ...607 770-9174
219 Clinton St Binghamton (13905) ***(G-860)***
All Star Carts & Vehicles Inc ...631 666-5581
1565 5th Industrial Ct B Bay Shore (11706) ***(G-654)***
All Star Fabricators, Thornwood *Also called Thornwood Products Ltd* ***(G-15508)***
All Star Sheet Metal Inc ...718 456-1567
25 Rome St Farmingdale (11735) ***(G-4715)***
All The Rage Inc ...516 605-2001
147 W Cherry St Unit 1 Hicksville (11801) ***(G-6058)***
All Time Products Inc ...718 464-1400
21167 Jamaica Ave Queens Village (11428) ***(G-13402)***
All Times Publishing LLC ...315 422-7011
1415 W Genesee St Syracuse (13204) ***(G-15238)***
All Type Screw Machine Pdts ...516 334-5100
100 New York Ave Westbury (11590) ***(G-16313)***
All United Window Corp ...718 624-0490
97 Classon Ave Brooklyn (11205) ***(G-1509)***
All Worth Press, New York *Also called Skyhorse Publishing Inc* ***(G-11614)***
All-City Metal Inc ...718 937-3975
5435 46th St Maspeth (11378) ***(G-7817)***
All-Lifts Incorporated ...518 465-3461
27-39 Thatcher St Albany (12207) ***(G-38)***
All-Pro Imaging Corp ...516 433-7676
1295 Walt Whitman Rd Melville (11747) ***(G-8001)***
All-State Diversified Pdts Inc ...315 472-4728
8 Dwight Park Dr Syracuse (13209) ***(G-15239)***
All-Tech, Brooklyn *Also called Integra Microsystem 1988 Inc* ***(G-2006)***
Allan John Company ...212 940-2210
611 5th Ave Fl 7 New York (10022) ***(G-8796)***
Allcom Electric Corp ...914 803-0433
104 Crescent Pl Yonkers (10704) ***(G-16731)***
Allcraft Fabricators Inc ...631 951-4100
150 Wireless Blvd Hauppauge (11788) ***(G-5760)***
Alle Processing Corp ...718 894-2000
5620 59th St Maspeth (11378) ***(G-7818)***
Allegany Laminating and Supply ...716 372-2424
158 W Main St Allegany (14706) ***(G-188)***
Allegiant Health, Deer Park *Also called Bli International Inc* ***(G-3952)***
Allegra Print & Imaging, Schenectady *Also called Capital Dst Print & Imaging* ***(G-14657)***
Allegra Printing, Buffalo *Also called Loy L Press Inc* ***(G-2928)***
Allen Air, Melville *Also called A K Allen Co Inc* ***(G-7996)***
Allen Avionics Inc ...516 248-8080
255 E 2nd St Mineola (11501) ***(G-8203)***
Allen Boat Co Inc ...716 842-0800
370 Babcock St Rear Buffalo (14206) ***(G-2691)***
Allen Field Co Inc ...631 665-2782
256 Orinoco Dr Ste A Brightwaters (11718) ***(G-1185)***
Allen Machine Products Inc ...631 630-8800
120 Ricefield Ln Ste 100 Hauppauge (11788) ***(G-5761)***
Allen Pickle Works Inc ...516 676-0640
36 Garvies Point Rd Glen Cove (11542) ***(G-5359)***
Allen Tool Phoenix Inc ...315 463-7533
6821 Ellicott Dr East Syracuse (13057) ***(G-4317)***
Allen William & Company Inc ...212 675-6461
7119 80th St Ste 8315 Glendale (11385) ***(G-5391)***
Alleson Athletic, Rochester *Also called Alleson of Rochester Inc* ***(G-13614)***
Alleson of Rochester Inc (HQ) ...585 272-0606
2921 Brighton Henrietta Rochester (14623) ***(G-13614)***
Alleson of Rochester Inc ...315 548-3635
833 Canandaigua Rd Ste 40 Geneva (14456) ***(G-5316)***
Alley Cat Signs Inc ...631 924-7446
506 Middle Country Rd Middle Island (11953) ***(G-8117)***
Alley Music Corp ...212 779-7977
126 E 38th St New York (10016) ***(G-8797)***
Alliance Automation Systems ...585 426-2700
400 Trabold Rd Rochester (14624) ***(G-13615)***
Alliance Control Systems Inc ...845 279-4430
577 N Main St Ste 9 Brewster (10509) ***(G-1156)***
Alliance Innovative Mfg Inc ...716 822-1626
1 Alliance Dr Lackawanna (14218) ***(G-6947)***
Alliance Paving Materials Inc ...315 337-0795
846 Lawrence St Rome (13440) ***(G-14245)***
Alliance Precision Plas Corp (PA) ...585 426-5310
1220 Lee Rd Rochester (14606) ***(G-13616)***
Alliance Precision Plas Corp ...585 426-5310
105 Elmore Dr Rochester (14606) ***(G-13617)***
Alliance Services Corp ...516 775-7600
23 Van Siclen Ave Floral Park (11001) ***(G-4953)***
Alliance Welding & Steel Fabg ...516 775-7600
15 Van Siclen Ave Floral Park (11001) ***(G-4954)***
Alliant Tchsystems Oprtons LLC ...631 737-6100
77 Raynor Ave Ronkonkoma (11779) ***(G-14301)***
Allied, Buffalo *Also called Mibro Group* ***(G-2945)***
Allied Aero Services Inc ...631 277-9368
506 Grand Blvd Brentwood (11717) ***(G-1126)***
Allied Bolt Products LLC ...516 512-7600
3000 Marcus Ave Ste 3e09 New Hyde Park (11042) ***(G-8514)***
Allied Bronze Corp (del Corp) ...646 421-6400
32 Avenue Of The Americas New York (10013) ***(G-8798)***
Allied Circuits LLC ...716 551-0285
22 James E Casey Dr Buffalo (14206) ***(G-2692)***
Allied Converters Inc ...914 235-1585
64 Drake Ave New Rochelle (10805) ***(G-8589)***
Allied Decorations Co Inc ...315 637-0273
720 Erie Blvd W Syracuse (13204) ***(G-15240)***
Allied Food Products Inc ...718 230-4227
251 Saint Marks Ave Brooklyn (11238) ***(G-1510)***
Allied Industrial Products Co ...716 664-3893
880 E 2nd St Jamestown (14701) ***(G-6697)***
Allied Industries, Jamestown *Also called Allied Industrial Products Co* ***(G-6697)***
Allied Inspection Services LLC ...716 489-3199
4 Carter St Falconer (14733) ***(G-4670)***
Allied K & R Broom & Brush Co, Brooklyn *Also called K & R Allied Inc* ***(G-2061)***
Allied Maker ...516 200-9145
108 Glen Cove Ave Glen Cove (11542) ***(G-5360)***
Allied Metal Spinning Corp ...718 893-3300
1290 Viele Ave Bronx (10474) ***(G-1216)***
Allied Motion Control Corp ...716 242-7535
495 Commerce Dr Ste 3 Amherst (14228) ***(G-209)***
Allied Motion Systems Corp (HQ) ...716 691-5868
495 Commerce Dr Ste 3 Amherst (14228) ***(G-210)***
Allied Motion Technologies Inc (PA) ...716 242-8634
495 Commerce Dr Ste 3 Amherst (14228) ***(G-211)***
Allied Motion Technologies Inc ...315 782-5910
22543 Fisher Rd Watertown (13601) ***(G-16000)***
Allied Orthopedics, Ozone Park *Also called Robert Cohen* ***(G-12832)***
Allied Pharmacy Products Inc ...516 374-8862
544 Green Pl Woodmere (11598) ***(G-16639)***
Allied Products, New York *Also called Biofeedback Instrument Corp* ***(G-9087)***
Allied Reproductions Inc ...212 255-2472
70 W 36th St Rm 500 New York (10018) ***(G-8799)***

Allied Sample Card Co Inc 718 238-0523
140 58th St Ste 7a Brooklyn (11220) ***(G-1511)***
Allied Sign Co, Syracuse *Also called Allied Decorations Co Inc* ***(G-15240)***
Allied Wine Corp 845 796-4160
121 Main St South Fallsburg (12779) ***(G-14930)***
Allison Che Fashion Inc (PA) 212 391-1433
1400 Broadway Lbby 5 New York (10018) ***(G-8800)***
Allmetal Chocolate Mold Co Inc 631 752-2888
135 Dale St West Babylon (11704) ***(G-16131)***
Allomatic Products Company 516 775-0330
102 Jericho Tpke Ste 104 Floral Park (11001) ***(G-4955)***
Alloy Machine & Tool Co Inc 516 593-3445
169 Vincent Ave Lynbrook (11563) ***(G-7660)***
Alloy Metal Products LLC 315 676-2405
193 Us Route 11 Central Square (13036) ***(G-3389)***
Alloy Metal Works Inc 631 694-8163
146 Verdi St Farmingdale (11735) ***(G-4716)***
Allred & Associates Inc 315 252-2559
321 Rte 5 W Elbridge (13060) ***(G-4427)***
Allround Logistics Inc (PA) 718 544-8945
7240 Ingram St Forest Hills (11375) ***(G-5071)***
Allround Maritime Services, Forest Hills *Also called Allround Logistics Inc* ***(G-5071)***
Allsafe Technologies Inc 716 691-0400
290 Creekside Dr Amherst (14228) ***(G-212)***
Allstar Casting Corporation 212 563-0909
240 W 37th St Frnt 7 New York (10018) ***(G-8801)***
Allstar Graphics Ltd 718 740-2240
22034 Jamaica Ave Queens Village (11428) ***(G-13403)***
Allstate Banners, Long Island City *Also called Allstatebannerscom Corporation* ***(G-7372)***
Allstate Gasket & Packing Inc 631 254-4050
31 Prospect Pl Deer Park (11729) ***(G-3937)***
Allstate Sign & Plaque Corp 631 242-2828
70 Burt Dr Deer Park (11729) ***(G-3938)***
Allstate Tool and Die Inc 585 426-0400
15 Coldwater Cres Rochester (14624) ***(G-13618)***
Allstatebannerscom Corporation 718 300-1256
3511 9th St Long Island City (11106) ***(G-7372)***
Allstateelectronics, Brooklyn *Also called Henrys Deals Inc* ***(G-1972)***
Allsupermarkets, Ridgewood *Also called 333 J & M Food Corp* ***(G-13526)***
Alltec Products, Westbury *Also called Power Scrub It Inc* ***(G-16365)***
Alltek Labeling Systems, Staten Island *Also called Stoney Croft Converters Inc* ***(G-15140)***
Allure Fashions Inc 516 829-2470
8 Barstow Rd Apt 2e Great Neck (11021) ***(G-5532)***
Allure Jewelry and ACC LLC (PA) 646 226-8057
15 W 36th St Fl 12 New York (10018) ***(G-8802)***
Allure Metal Works Inc 631 588-0220
71 Hoffman Ln Ronkonkoma (11749) ***(G-14302)***
Allvac 716 433-4411
695 Ohio St Lockport (14094) ***(G-7284)***
Allway Tools Inc 718 792-3636
1255 Seabury Ave Bronx (10462) ***(G-1217)***
Allworth Communications Inc 212 777-8395
10 E 23rd St Ste 510 New York (10010) ***(G-8803)***
Allworth Press, New York *Also called Allworth Communications Inc* ***(G-8803)***
Ally Nyc Corp 212 447-7277
230 W 39th St Rm 525 New York (10018) ***(G-8804)***
Allytex LLC 518 376-7539
540 Acland Blvd Ballston Spa (12020) ***(G-576)***
Alm Media LLC (HQ) 212 457-9400
150 E 42nd St New York (10017) ***(G-8805)***
Alm Media Holdings Inc (PA) 212 457-9400
120 Broadway Fl 5 New York (10271) ***(G-8806)***
Almond Group, Port Washington *Also called Almond Jewelers Inc* ***(G-13242)***
Almond Jewelers Inc 516 933-6000
16 S Maryland Ave Port Washington (11050) ***(G-13242)***
Almost Famous Clothing, New York *Also called Turn On Products Inc* ***(G-11913)***
Alo Acquisition LLC (HQ) 518 464-0279
26 Corporate Cir Albany (12203) ***(G-39)***
Aloi Materials Handling, Rochester *Also called Aloi Solutions LLC* ***(G-13619)***
Aloi Solutions LLC (PA) 585 292-0920
140 Commerce Dr Rochester (14623) ***(G-13619)***
Alonzo Fire Works Display Inc (PA) 518 664-9994
12 County Route 75 Mechanicville (12118) ***(G-7930)***
Alp Stone Inc 718 706-6166
2520 50th Ave Fl 2 Long Island City (11101) ***(G-7373)***
Alpargatas Usa Inc 646 277-7171
33 E 33rd St Rm 501 New York (10016) ***(G-8807)***
Alpha 6 Distributions LLC 516 801-8290
11 Oyster Bay Rd Locust Valley (11560) ***(G-7345)***
Alpha Boats Unlimited, Weedsport *Also called Barber Welding Inc* ***(G-16110)***
Alpha Fasteners Corp 516 867-6188
154 E Merrick Rd Freeport (11520) ***(G-5141)***
Alpha Incorporated 718 765-1614
265 80th St Brooklyn (11209) ***(G-1512)***
Alpha Iron Works LLC 585 424-7260
65 Goodway Dr S Rochester (14623) ***(G-13620)***
Alpha Knitting Mills Inc 718 628-6300
41 Varick Ave Ste Mgmt Brooklyn (11237) ***(G-1513)***
Alpha Manufacturing Corp 631 249-3700
152 Verdi St Farmingdale (11735) ***(G-4717)***
Alpha Media Group Inc (PA) 212 302-2626
415 Madison Ave Fl 4 New York (10017) ***(G-8808)***
Alpha Packaging Industries Inc 718 267-4115
2004 33rd St Long Island City (11105) ***(G-7374)***
Alpha Printing Corp 315 454-5507
131 Falso Dr Syracuse (13211) ***(G-15241)***
Alpha Wolf LLC 516 778-5812
241 Rushmore Ave Carle Place (11514) ***(G-3260)***
Alpha-En Corporation (PA) 914 418-2000
28 Wells Ave Ste 2 Yonkers (10701) ***(G-16732)***
AlphaGraphics, Rochester *Also called Bittner Company LLC* ***(G-13664)***
Alphamed Bottles Inc 631 524-5577
300 S Technology Dr Central Islip (11722) ***(G-3355)***
Alphonse Lduc - Rbert King Inc 508 238-8118
180 Madison Ave 24 New York (10016) ***(G-8809)***
Alpina Color Graphics Inc 212 285-2700
27 Cliff St Rm 502 New York (10038) ***(G-8810)***
Alpina Copyworld Inc (PA) 212 683-3511
134 E 28th St New York (10016) ***(G-8811)***
Alpina Digital, New York *Also called Alpina Copyworld Inc* ***(G-8811)***
Alpina Foods Inc 855 886-1914
5011 Agpark Dr W Batavia (14020) ***(G-609)***
Alpine Building Supply Inc 718 456-2522
4626 Metropolitan Ave Ridgewood (11385) ***(G-13529)***
Alpine Business Group Inc (PA) 212 989-4198
30 E 33rd St Frnt A New York (10016) ***(G-8812)***
Alpine Creations Ltd 212 308-9353
17 E 48th St Fl 6 New York (10017) ***(G-8813)***
Alpine Creative Group, New York *Also called Alpine Business Group Inc* ***(G-8812)***
Alpine Machine Inc 607 272-1344
1616 Trumansburg Rd Ithaca (14850) ***(G-6556)***
Alpine Paper Box Co Inc 718 345-4040
2246 Fulton St Brooklyn (11233) ***(G-1514)***
Alpla Inc 607 250-8101
106 Central Ave Cortland (13045) ***(G-3859)***
Alps Provision Co Inc 718 721-4477
2270 45th St Astoria (11105) ***(G-421)***
Alps Sweet Shop, Beacon *Also called Hudson Valley Chocolatier Inc* ***(G-759)***
Alrajs Inc (PA) 631 225-0300
146 Albany Ave Lindenhurst (11757) ***(G-7159)***
Alro Machine Company, Lindenhurst *Also called Alro Machine Tool & Die Co Inc* ***(G-7160)***
Alro Machine Tool & Die Co Inc 631 226-5020
585 W Hoffman Ave Lindenhurst (11757) ***(G-7160)***
Alrod Associates Inc 631 981-2193
710 Union Pkwy Ste 9 Ronkonkoma (11779) ***(G-14303)***
Alry Tool and Die Co Inc 716 693-2419
386 Fillmore Ave Tonawanda (14150) ***(G-15521)***
Alstom Signaling Inc (HQ) 585 783-2000
1025 John St West Henrietta (14586) ***(G-16227)***
Alstom Signaling Inc 585 274-8700
1 River Rd Schenectady (12345) ***(G-14648)***
Alstrom Trnspt Info Solutions, West Henrietta *Also called Alstom Signaling Inc* ***(G-16227)***
Alta Industries Ltd 845 586-3336
46966 State Hwy 30 Halcottsville (12438) ***(G-5657)***
Alta Log Homes, Halcottsville *Also called Alta Industries Ltd* ***(G-5657)***
Altaire Pharmaceuticals Inc 631 722-5988
311 West Ln Aquebogue (11931) ***(G-373)***
Altamont Spray Welding Inc 518 861-8870
133 Lewis Rd Altamont (12009) ***(G-195)***
Altaquip LLC 631 580-4740
200 13th Ave Unit 6 Ronkonkoma (11779) ***(G-14304)***
Altaro Corp 855 674-2455
116 Tappan Landing Rd Tarrytown (10591) ***(G-15473)***
Altec Datacom LLC 631 242-2417
70 Corbin Ave Ste I Bay Shore (11706) ***(G-655)***
Alternative Parts, Bellport *Also called Alternative Service Inc* ***(G-798)***
Alternative Service Inc 631 345-9500
7 Sawgrass Dr Bellport (11713) ***(G-798)***
Alternative Technology Corp 914 478-5900
1 North St Ste 1 # 1 Hastings On Hudson (10706) ***(G-5747)***
Alternatives For Children 631 271-0777
600 S Service Rd Dix Hills (11746) ***(G-4119)***
Altius Aviation LLC 315 455-7555
113 Tuskegee Rd Ste 2 Syracuse (13211) ***(G-15242)***
Altman Lighting, Yonkers *Also called Altman Stage Lighting Co Inc* ***(G-16733)***
Altman Stage Lighting Co Inc 914 476-7987
57 Alexander St Yonkers (10701) ***(G-16733)***
Alton Manufacturing Inc 585 458-2600
825 Lee Rd Rochester (14606) ***(G-13621)***
Altro Business Forms Div, New York *Also called New Deal Printing Corp* ***(G-10919)***
Altronix Corp 718 567-8181
140 58th St Bldg A3w Brooklyn (11220) ***(G-1515)***
Altum Press, Long Island City *Also called Cama Graphics Inc* ***(G-7405)***
Altype Fire Door Corporation 718 292-3500
886 E 149th St Bronx (10455) ***(G-1218)***
Aluf Plastics Division, Orangeburg *Also called API Industries Inc* ***(G-12668)***
Alufoil Products Co Inc 631 231-4141
135 Oser Ave Ste 3 Hauppauge (11788) ***(G-5762)***
Alumi-Tech LLC 585 663-7010
1640 Harris Rd Penfield (14526) ***(G-12939)***
Alumidock, Randolph *Also called Metallic Ladder Mfg Corp* ***(G-13448)***

(PA)=Parent Co (HQ)=Headquarters (DH)=Div Headquarters

Alumil Fabrication Inc...845 469-2874
1900 Corporate Blvd Newburgh (12550) ***(G-12212)***
Alumil NA Fabrication, Long Island City *Also called N A Alumil Corporation* ***(G-7532)***
Aluminum Injection Mold Co LLC...585 502-6087
8741 Lake Street Rd Ste 4 Le Roy (14482) ***(G-7112)***
Alvin J Bart, Glendale *Also called Allen William & Company Inc* ***(G-5391)***
Alvina Vlenta Couture Collectn...212 921-7058
525 Fashion Ave Rm 1703 New York (10018) ***(G-8814)***
Always Baked Fresh...631 648-0811
331 Dante Ct Ste F Holbrook (11741) ***(G-6171)***
Always Printing...914 481-5209
149 Highland St Port Chester (10573) ***(G-13193)***
Alyk Inc...917 968-2552
440 Park Ave S Fl 14 New York (10016) ***(G-8815)***
AM Architectural Metal & Glass...845 942-8848
5 Bridge St Garnerville (10923) ***(G-5299)***
AM Bickford Inc...716 652-1590
12318 Big Tree Rd Wales Center (14169) ***(G-15900)***
AM Cast Inc (PA)...631 750-1644
34 Aero Rd Bohemia (11716) ***(G-977)***
AM Display, Highland Mills *Also called All Merchandise Display Corp* ***(G-6150)***
Am-Best Emblems, Boiceville *Also called Stucki Embroidery Works Inc* ***(G-1110)***
Am-Pol Eagle, Buffalo *Also called Buffalo Standard Printing Corp* ***(G-2753)***
AMA Precision Screening Inc...585 293-0820
456 Sanford Rd N Churchville (14428) ***(G-3505)***
Amacon Corporation...631 293-1888
49 Alder St Unit A West Babylon (11704) ***(G-16132)***
Amada Tool America Inc...585 344-3900
4 Treadeasy Ave Ste A Batavia (14020) ***(G-610)***
Amadeo Serrano...516 608-8359
36 Frankel Ave Freeport (11520) ***(G-5142)***
Amana Tool Corp...631 752-1300
120 Carolyn Blvd Farmingdale (11735) ***(G-4718)***
Amarantus Bscence Holdings Inc (PA)...917 686-5317
110 Wall St New York (10005) ***(G-8816)***
Amarr Company...585 426-8290
550 Mile Crssing Blvd 1 Rochester (14624) ***(G-13622)***
Amarr Garage Doors, Rochester *Also called Amarr Company* ***(G-13622)***
Amax Printing Inc...718 384-8600
6417 Grand Ave Maspeth (11378) ***(G-7819)***
Amazing Meals, Maspeth *Also called Alle Processing Corp* ***(G-7818)***
Amber Bever Inc...212 391-4911
8604 Avenue M 1 Brooklyn (11236) ***(G-1516)***
Ambind Corp...716 836-4365
Cheektowaga Buffalo (14225) ***(G-2693)***
Ambras Fine Jewelry Inc...718 784-5252
3100 47th Ave Unit 3 Long Island City (11101) ***(G-7375)***
Ambras Fjc, Long Island City *Also called Ambras Fine Jewelry Inc* ***(G-7375)***
Ambrell Corporation (HQ)...585 889-0236
1655 Lyell Ave Rochester (14606) ***(G-13623)***
Amby International Inc...718 645-0964
1460 E 12th St Brooklyn (11230) ***(G-1517)***
Amci Ltd...718 937-5858
3302 48th Ave Long Island City (11101) ***(G-7376)***
Amco Intl Mfg & Design Inc...718 388-8668
10 Conselyea St Brooklyn (11211) ***(G-1518)***
Amcom Software Inc...212 951-7600
256 W 38th St Fl 8 New York (10018) ***(G-8817)***
Amcor Rigid Plastics Usa LLC...716 366-2440
1 Cliffstar Ave Dunkirk (14048) ***(G-4162)***
Amendola MBL & Stone Ctr Inc...914 997-7968
560 Tarrytown Rd White Plains (10607) ***(G-16419)***
Amenity Analytics Inc...646 786-8316
387 Park Ave S Fl 9 New York (10016) ***(G-8818)***
Amereon Ltd...631 298-5100
800 Wickham Ave Mattituck (11952) ***(G-7913)***
Amerex Corporation...212 221-3151
512 7th Ave Fl 9 New York (10018) ***(G-8819)***
Ameri Serv South, Jamestown *Also called Vac Air Service Inc* ***(G-6760)***
Ameri-Cut Tool Grinding Inc...716 692-3900
1020 Oliver St North Tonawanda (14120) ***(G-12410)***
America Capital Energy Corp...212 983-8316
405 Lexington Ave Fl 65 New York (10174) ***(G-8820)***
America Health Corp...800 860-1868
708 3rd Ave Ste 600 New York (10017) ***(G-8821)***
America NY RI Wang Fd Group Co...718 628-8999
5885 58th Ave Maspeth (11378) ***(G-7820)***
America Press Inc (PA)...212 581-4640
1212 Ave Of The Americas New York (10036) ***(G-8822)***
American Access Care LLC...631 582-9729
32 Central Ave Hauppauge (11788) ***(G-5763)***
American Acrylic Corporation...631 422-2200
400 Sheffield Ave West Babylon (11704) ***(G-16133)***
American Aerogel Corporation...585 328-2140
460 Buffalo Rd Ste 200a Rochester (14611) ***(G-13624)***
American Aerospace Contrls Inc...631 694-5100
570 Smith St Farmingdale (11735) ***(G-4719)***
American Almond Pdts Co Inc (PA)...718 875-8310
103 Walworth St Brooklyn (11205) ***(G-1519)***
American Apparel Ltd...516 504-4559
15 Cuttermill Rd Ste 145 Great Neck (11021) ***(G-5533)***
American Apparel Trading Corp (PA)...212 764-5990
209 W 38th St Rm 1004 New York (10018) ***(G-8823)***
American Attitude, New York *Also called Kww Productions Corp* ***(G-10488)***
American Auto ACC Incrporation (PA)...718 886-6600
3506 Leavitt St Apt Cfc Flushing (11354) ***(G-4984)***
American Avionic Tech Corp...631 924-8200
25 Industrial Blvd Medford (11763) ***(G-7937)***
American Best Cabinets Inc...845 369-6666
397 Spook Rock Rd Suffern (10901) ***(G-15185)***
American Bio Medica Corp (PA)...518 758-8158
122 Smith Rd Kinderhook (12106) ***(G-6879)***
American Blade Mfg LLC (PA)...607 432-4518
138 Roundhouse Rd Oneonta (13820) ***(G-12624)***
American Blade Mfg LLC...607 656-4204
47 Birdsall St Greene (13778) ***(G-5612)***
American Bluestone LLC...607 369-2235
760 Quarry Rd Sidney (13838) ***(G-14848)***
American Boiler Tank Wldg Inc...518 463-5012
53 Pleasant St Albany (12207) ***(G-40)***
American Bottling Company...516 714-0002
2004 Orville Dr N Ronkonkoma (11779) ***(G-14305)***
American Bptst Chrches Mtro NY...212 870-3195
527 W 22nd St New York (10011) ***(G-8824)***
American Business Forms Inc...716 836-5111
3840 E Robinson Rd # 249 Amherst (14228) ***(G-213)***
American Canvas Binders Corp...914 969-0300
430 Nepperhan Ave Yonkers (10701) ***(G-16734)***
American Car Signs Inc...518 227-1173
1483 W Duane Lake Rd Duanesburg (12056) ***(G-4154)***
American Casino Equipment Mfg...631 242-2440
45 W Jefryn Blvd Ste 107 Deer Park (11729) ***(G-3939)***
American Casting and Mfg Corp (PA)...800 342-0333
51 Commercial St Plainview (11803) ***(G-13035)***
American Casting and Mfg Corp...516 349-7010
65 S Terminal Dr Plainview (11803) ***(G-13036)***
American Challenge Enterprises...631 595-7171
1804 Plaza Ave Ste 6 New Hyde Park (11040) ***(G-8515)***
American Chimney Supplies Inc...631 434-2020
129 Oser Ave Ste B Hauppauge (11788) ***(G-5764)***
American Cigar...718 969-0008
6940 Fresh Meadow Ln Fresh Meadows (11365) ***(G-5194)***
American City Bus Journals Inc...716 541-1654
465 Main St Ste 100 Buffalo (14203) ***(G-2694)***
American Cleaning Solutions, Long Island City *Also called American Wax Company Inc* ***(G-7377)***
American Comfort Direct LLC...201 364-8309
708 3rd Ave Fl 6 New York (10017) ***(G-8825)***
American Conveyor, Brooklyn *Also called Crownbrook ACC LLC* ***(G-1734)***
American Country Quilts & Lin...631 283-5466
134 Mariner Dr Unit C Southampton (11968) ***(G-14949)***
American Craft Jewelers Inc (PA)...718 972-0945
3611 14th Ave Ste 522 Brooklyn (11218) ***(G-1520)***
American Crmic Process RES LLC...315 828-6268
835 Mcivor Rd Phelps (14532) ***(G-12974)***
American Culture, Greenlawn *Also called All Cultures Inc* ***(G-5620)***
American Culture Hair Inc...631 242-3142
159 E 2nd St Huntington Station (11746) ***(G-6429)***
American Diagnostic Corp...631 273-6155
55 Commerce Dr Hauppauge (11788) ***(G-5765)***
American Dies Inc...718 387-1900
37 Provost St Brooklyn (11222) ***(G-1521)***
American Douglas Metals Inc...716 856-3170
99 Bud Mil Dr Buffalo (14206) ***(G-2695)***
American Dsplay Die Ctters Inc...212 645-1274
121 Varick St Rm 301 New York (10013) ***(G-8826)***
American Electronic Products...631 924-1299
86 Horseblock Rd Unit F Yaphank (11980) ***(G-16704)***
American Epoxy and Metal Inc...718 828-7828
83 Cushman Rd Scarsdale (10583) ***(G-14636)***
American Express Publishing, New York *Also called Time Inc Affluent Media Group* ***(G-11840)***
American Felt & Filter Co Inc...845 561-3560
361 Walsh Ave New Windsor (12553) ***(G-8635)***
American Filtration Tech Inc...585 359-4130
100 Thruway Park Dr West Henrietta (14586) ***(G-16228)***
American Glass Light, Newburgh *Also called Sandy Littman Inc* ***(G-12245)***
American Graphic Design Awards...212 696-4380
89 5th Ave Ste 901 New York (10003) ***(G-8827)***
American Healthcare Supply Inc...212 674-3636
304 Park Ave S New York (10010) ***(G-8828)***
American Heritage Magazine, New York *Also called Nsgv Inc* ***(G-11004)***
American Hlth Formulations Inc (HQ)...631 392-1756
45 Adams Ave Hauppauge (11788) ***(G-5766)***
American Home Mfg LLC (HQ)...212 643-0680
302 5th Ave Fl 5 New York (10001) ***(G-8829)***
American Hormones Inc...845 471-7272
69 W Cedar St Ste 2 Poughkeepsie (12601) ***(G-13325)***
American Hose & Hydralics, Bronx *Also called American Refuse Supply Inc* ***(G-1219)***
American Hsptals Patient Guide...518 346-1099
1890 Maxon Rd Ext Schenectady (12308) ***(G-14649)***
American Icon Industries Inc...845 561-1299
392 N Montgomery St Ste 2 Newburgh (12550) ***(G-12213)***

ALPHABETIC SECTION
Ametek CTS Us Inc (PA)

American Images Inc 716 825-8888
25 Imson St Buffalo (14210) *(G-2696)*

American Inst Chem Engineers (PA) 646 495-1355
120 Wall St Fl 23 New York (10005) *(G-8830)*

American Institute Physics Inc 516 576-2410
Hntngton Qad Ste 1n1-2 Melville (11747) *(G-8002)*

American Intl Media LLC 845 359-4225
11 Martine Ave Ste 870 White Plains (10606) *(G-16420)*

American Intl Trimming 718 369-9643
80 39th St Brooklyn (11232) *(G-1522)*

American Intrmdal Cont Mfg LLC 631 774-6790
150 Motor Pkwy Ste 401 Hauppauge (11788) *(G-5767)*

American Jewish Committee 212 891-1400
561 Fashion Ave Fl 16 New York (10018) *(G-8831)*

American Jewish Congress Inc (PA) 212 879-4500
825 3rd Ave Fl 181800 New York (10022) *(G-8832)*

American Juice Company LLC 347 620-0252
224 W 35th St Fl 11 New York (10001) *(G-8833)*

American Lckr SEC Systems Inc 716 699-2773
12 Martha St Ellicottville (14731) *(G-4444)*

American Leather Specialties 800 556-6488
87 34th St Unit 1 Brooklyn (11232) *(G-1523)*

American Linear Manufacturers (PA) 516 333-1351
629 Main St Westbury (11590) *(G-16314)*

American Lpg Systems, Huntington *Also called United Data Systems Inc (G-6423)*

American Marking Systems, Fulton *Also called Krengel Manufacturing Co Inc (G-5226)*

American Material Processing 315 318-0017
126 Bankrupt Rd Phoenix (13135) *(G-12988)*

American Metal, Rome *Also called Nash Metalware Co Inc (G-14260)*

American Metal Spinning Pdts 631 454-6276
21 Eads St West Babylon (11704) *(G-16134)*

American Metalcraft Marine 315 686-9891
690 Riverside Dr Clayton (13624) *(G-3552)*

American Minerals Inc (HQ) 646 747-4222
21 W 46th St Fl 14 New York (10036) *(G-8834)*

American Mtal Stmping Spinning 718 384-1500
72 N 15th St Brooklyn (11222) *(G-1524)*

American Office Supply Inc 516 294-9444
400 Post Ave Ste 105 Westbury (11590) *(G-16315)*

American Originals Corporation 212 836-4155
1156 Avenue Of The Americ New York (10036) *(G-8835)*

American Orthotic Lab Co Inc 718 961-6487
924 118th St College Point (11356) *(G-3639)*

American Package Company Inc 718 389-4444
226 Franklin St Brooklyn (11222) *(G-1525)*

American Packaging Corporation 585 254-2002
1555 Lyell Ave Rochester (14606) *(G-13625)*

American Packaging Corporation 585 537-4650
100 Apc Dr Churchville (14428) *(G-3506)*

American Packaging Corporation 585 254-9500
777 Driving Park Ave Rochester (14613) *(G-13626)*

American Physical Society 631 591-4025
1 Research Rd Ridge (11961) *(G-13521)*

American Precision Inds Inc (HQ) 716 691-9100
45 Hazelwood Dr Amherst (14228) *(G-214)*

American Precision Inds Inc 716 652-3600
270 Quaker Rd East Aurora (14052) *(G-4193)*

American Precision Inds Inc 585 496-5755
95 North St Arcade (14009) *(G-376)*

American Pride Fasteners LLC 631 940-8292
195 S Fehr Way Bay Shore (11706) *(G-656)*

American Print Solutions Inc 718 246-7800
561 President St Brooklyn (11215) *(G-1526)*

American Print Solutions Inc (PA) 718 208-2309
2233 Nostrand Ave Ste 7 Brooklyn (11210) *(G-1527)*

American Printing & Envelope, New York *Also called Apec Paper Industries Ltd (G-8882)*

American Printing and Off Sups, Kingston *Also called Robert Tabatznik Assoc Inc (G-6916)*

American Printing Eqp & Sup, Elmont *Also called Awt Supply Corp (G-4517)*

American Products, Rochester *Also called American Time Mfg Ltd (G-13629)*

American Profile Magazine, New York *Also called Publishing Group America Inc (G-11274)*

American Puff Corp 516 379-1300
225 Buffalo Ave Freeport (11520) *(G-5143)*

American Quality Embroidery (PA) 631 467-3200
740 Koehler Ave Ronkonkoma (11779) *(G-14306)*

American Quality Technology 607 777-9488
6 Emma St Binghamton (13905) *(G-861)*

American Racing Headers Inc 631 608-1427
880 Grand Blvd Deer Park (11729) *(G-3940)*

American Refrigeration Inc (HQ) 212 699-4000
142 W 57th St Fl 17 New York (10019) *(G-8836)*

American Refuse Supply Inc 718 893-8157
521 Longfellow Ave Bronx (10474) *(G-1219)*

American Regent Inc 631 924-4000
5 Ramsey Rd Shirley (11967) *(G-14826)*

American Regent Laboratories, Shirley *Also called American Regent Inc (G-14826)*

American Rock Salt Company LLC (PA) 585 991-6878
3846 Retsof Rd Retsof (14539) *(G-13480)*

American Sealing Technology 631 254-0019
31 Prospect Pl Deer Park (11729) *(G-3941)*

American Signcrafters, Hicksville *Also called Tj Signs Unlimited LLC (G-6137)*

American Signcrafters, Islip *Also called T J Signs Unlimited LLC (G-6551)*

American Silk Mills, New York *Also called Gerli & Co Inc (G-9913)*

American Spacer Technologies 518 828-1339
6 Joslen Heights Rd Hudson (12534) *(G-6338)*

American Specialty Mfg Co 585 544-5600
272 Hudson Ave Rochester (14605) *(G-13627)*

American Sports Media 585 924-4250
106 Cobblestone Court Dr # 323 Victor (14564) *(G-15829)*

American Sports Media LLC (PA) 585 377-9636
2604 Elmwood Ave Ste 343 Rochester (14618) *(G-13628)*

American Spray-On Corp 212 929-2100
5 Hanover Sq Fl 5 # 5 New York (10004) *(G-8837)*

American Standard Mfg Inc 518 868-2512
106 Industrial Park Ln Central Bridge (12035) *(G-3353)*

American Std Shmtl Sup Corp 718 888-9350
13324 36th Rd Flushing (11354) *(G-4985)*

American Steel Gate Corp 718 291-4050
10510 150th St Jamaica (11435) *(G-6624)*

American Sugar Refining Inc 914 376-3386
1 Federal St Yonkers (10705) *(G-16735)*

American T Shirts Inc 212 563-7125
225 W 39th St Fl 6 New York (10018) *(G-8838)*

American Target Marketing Inc 518 725-4369
11 Cayadutta St Gloversville (12078) *(G-5450)*

American Tchncal Ceramics Corp (HQ) 631 622-4700
1 Norden Ln Huntington Station (11746) *(G-6430)*

American Techical Ceramics 631 622-4758
11 Stepar Pl Huntington Station (11746) *(G-6431)*

American Technical Ceramics 631 622-4700
17 Stepar Pl Huntington Station (11746) *(G-6432)*

American Time Mfg Ltd 585 266-5120
1600 N Clinton Ave Ste 1 Rochester (14621) *(G-13629)*

American Torque Inc 718 526-2433
10522 150th St Jamaica (11435) *(G-6625)*

American Towman Expeditions, Warwick *Also called American Towman Network Inc (G-15948)*

American Towman Network Inc 845 986-4546
7 West St Warwick (10990) *(G-15948)*

American Trans-Coil Corp 516 922-9640
69 Hamilton Ave Ste 3 Oyster Bay (11771) *(G-12809)*

American Trim Mfg Inc 518 239-8151
4750 State Hwy 145 Durham (12422) *(G-4183)*

American Turf Monthly, Great Neck *Also called Star Sports Corp (G-5593)*

American Vintage Wine Biscuit 718 361-1003
409 E 74th St Apt 1a New York (10021) *(G-8839)*

American Visual Display, Farmingdale *Also called American Visuals Inc (G-4720)*

American Visuals Inc 631 694-6104
90 Gazza Blvd Farmingdale (11735) *(G-4720)*

American Wax Company Inc 718 392-8080
3930 Review Ave Long Island City (11101) *(G-7377)*

American Wire Tie Inc (PA) 716 337-2412
2073 Franklin St North Collins (14111) *(G-12383)*

American Wood Column Corp 718 782-3163
913 Grand St Brooklyn (11211) *(G-1528)*

American Woods & Veneers Works 718 937-2195
4735 27th St Long Island City (11101) *(G-7378)*

American-Swiss Products Co Inc 585 292-1720
1987 W Jefferson Rd Pittsford (14534) *(G-13008)*

Americana Vineyards & Winery 607 387-6801
4367 E Covert Rd Interlaken (14847) *(G-6480)*

Americarb Inc 419 281-5800
6100 Niagara Falls Blvd Niagara Falls (14304) *(G-12259)*

Americarb International Corp 419 281-5800
6100 Niagara Falls Blvd Niagara Falls (14304) *(G-12260)*

Americo Group Inc 212 563-2700
498 7th Ave Fl 8 New York (10018) *(G-8840)*

Americo Group Inc (PA) 212 563-2700
1411 Broadway Fl 2 New York (10018) *(G-8841)*

Amerikom Group Inc 212 675-1329
247 W 30th St Rm 6w New York (10001) *(G-8842)*

Ameritool Mfg Inc 315 668-2172
64 Corporate Park Dr Central Square (13036) *(G-3390)*

Amertac Holdings Inc (PA) 610 336-1330
25 Robert Pitt Dr Monsey (10952) *(G-8284)*

Ames Advanced Materials Corp (HQ) 518 792-5808
50 Harrison Ave South Glens Falls (12803) *(G-14933)*

Ames Companies Inc 607 739-4544
114 Smith Rd Pine Valley (14872) *(G-13006)*

Ames Companies Inc 607 369-9595
196 Clifton St Unadilla (13849) *(G-15660)*

Ames Goldsmith Corp 518 792-7435
21 Rogers St Glens Falls (12801) *(G-5414)*

Amesburytruth, Rochester *Also called Truth Hardware Corporation (G-14180)*

Ameta International Co Ltd 416 992-8036
2221 Kenmore Ave Ste 108 Buffalo (14207) *(G-2697)*

Ametal International, Brooklyn *Also called Kon Tat Group Corporation (G-2081)*

Ametek Inc 631 467-8400
903 S 2nd St Ronkonkoma (11779) *(G-14307)*

Ametek Inc 607 763-4700
33 Lewis Rd Ste 6 Binghamton (13905) *(G-862)*

Ametek CTS Us Inc (PA) 631 467-8400
903 S 2nd St Ronkonkoma (11779) *(G-14308)*

ALPHABETIC

(PA)=Parent Co (HQ)=Headquarters (DH)=Div Headquarters
2019 Harris
New York Manufacturers Directory
825

Ametek Inc 585 263-7700
255 Union St N Rochester (14605) *(G-13630)*
Ametek Power Instruments, Rochester *Also called Ametek Inc (G-13630)*
Ametek Rotron, Woodstock *Also called Rotron Incorporated (G-16687)*
Ametek Rotron, Woodstock *Also called Rotron Incorporated (G-16688)*
AMG Global, New York *Also called Enchante Lites LLC (G-9673)*
AMG Global LLC, New York *Also called AMG JV LLC (G-8843)*
AMG JV LLC (HQ) 212 602-1818
15 W 34th St Fl 8 New York (10001) *(G-8843)*
Amherst Bee, Williamsville *Also called Bee Publications Inc (G-16569)*
Amherst Media Inc 716 874-4450
175 Rano St Ste 200 Buffalo (14207) *(G-2698)*
Amherst Stnless Fbrication LLC 716 691-7012
60 John Glenn Dr Amherst (14228) *(G-215)*
AMI Brands, Mamaroneck *Also called Brands Within Reach LLC (G-7735)*
Amica Magazine, New York *Also called Rizzoli Intl Publications Inc (G-11400)*
Amicale Cashmere, New York *Also called Oakhurst Partners LLC (G-11024)*
Amiram Dror Inc (PA) 212 979-9505
226 India St Brooklyn (11222) *(G-1529)*
Amish Structure 607 257-1070
32 North St Dryden (13053) *(G-4148)*
Amj DOT LLC 718 775-3288
1726 E 7th St Brooklyn (11223) *(G-1530)*
Amneal Pharmaceuticals LLC 908 231-1911
50 Horseblock Rd Brookhaven (11719) *(G-1427)*
Amneal Pharmaceuticals LLC 631 952-0214
50 Horseblock Rd Brookhaven (11719) *(G-1428)*
Amneal Pharmaceuticals NY LLC (HQ) 908 947-3120
50 Horseblock Rd Brookhaven (11719) *(G-1429)*
Amnews Corporation 212 932-7400
2340 Frdrick Duglass Blvd New York (10027) *(G-8844)*
Amnewyork 212 239-5555
330 W 34th St Fl 17 New York (10001) *(G-8845)*
Amoseastern Apparel Inc (PA) 212 921-1859
49 W 38th St Fl 7 New York (10018) *(G-8846)*
AMP-Line Corp 845 623-3288
3 Amethyst Ct West Nyack (10994) *(G-16263)*
Ampac Paper LLC (HQ) 845 713-6600
30 Coldenham Rd Walden (12586) *(G-15890)*
Ampacet Corporation (PA) 914 631-6600
660 White Plains Rd # 360 Tarrytown (10591) *(G-15474)*
Ampaco, Brooklyn *Also called American Package Company Inc (G-1525)*
Ampex Casting Corporation 212 719-1318
23 W 47th St Unit 3 New York (10036) *(G-8847)*
Amphenol Aerospace France Inc 800 678-0141
191 Delaware Ave Sidney (13838) *(G-14849)*
Amphenol Aerospace Industrial, Sidney *Also called Amphenol Corporation (G-14850)*
Amphenol Cables On Demand Corp 607 321-2115
20 Valley St Endicott (13760) *(G-4581)*
Amphenol Corporation 607 563-5364
40-60 Delaware Ave Sidney (13838) *(G-14850)*
Amphenol Corporation 607 563-5011
40-60 Delaware Ave Sidney (13838) *(G-14851)*
Amphenol Intrconnect Pdts Corp (HQ) 607 754-4444
20 Valley St Endicott (13760) *(G-4582)*
Ample Hills Creamery Inc (PA) 347 725-4061
305 Nevins St Brooklyn (11215) *(G-1531)*
Ample Hills Creamery Inc 718 809-1678
623 Vanderbilt Ave Brooklyn (11238) *(G-1532)*
Ample Hills Holdings Inc 347 725-4061
305 Nevins St Brooklyn (11215) *(G-1533)*
Amplience Inc 917 410-7189
135 W 29th St Rm 404 New York (10001) *(G-8848)*
Amplitech Inc 631 521-7738
620 Johnson Ave Ste 2 Bohemia (11716) *(G-978)*
Amplitech Group Inc 631 521-7831
620 Johnson Ave Ste 2 Bohemia (11716) *(G-979)*
Ampro International Inc 845 278-4910
30 Coventry Ln Brewster (10509) *(G-1157)*
Amri, Albany *Also called Albany Molecular Research Inc (G-35)*
Amri, Rensselaer *Also called Albany Molecular Research Inc (G-13472)*
Amri Rensselaer, Rensselaer *Also called Albany Molecular Research Inc (G-13471)*
Amron Electronics Inc 631 737-1234
160 Gary Way Ronkonkoma (11779) *(G-14309)*
AMS Star Structures Inc 914 584-0898
453 S Broadway Nyack (10960) *(G-12499)*
Amscan Everyday Warehouse, Chester *Also called Amscan Inc (G-3468)*
Amscan Inc 845 469-9116
47 Elizabeth Dr Chester (10918) *(G-3468)*
Amscan Inc 845 782-0490
108 Route 17k Newburgh (12550) *(G-12214)*
Amsco Inc 716 823-4213
925 Bailey Ave Buffalo (14206) *(G-2699)*
Amsco School Publications Inc 212 886-6500
315 Hudson St Fl 5 New York (10013) *(G-8849)*
Amscor Inc 800 825-9800
119 Lamar St West Babylon (11704) *(G-16135)*
Amstead Press Corp 347 416-2373
225 W 37th St Fl 16 New York (10018) *(G-8850)*
Amsterdam Oil Heat, Amsterdam *Also called J H Buhrmaster Company Inc (G-341)*
Amsterdam Pharmacy, New York *Also called Shrineeta Pharmacy Inc (G-11572)*
Amsterdam Printing & Litho Inc 518 792-6501
428 Corinth Rd Queensbury (12804) *(G-13415)*
Amsterdam Printing & Litho Inc 518 842-6000
166 Wallins Corners Rd Amsterdam (12010) *(G-325)*
Amsterdam Printing & Litho Inc 518 842-6000
166 Wallins Corners Rd Amsterdam (12010) *(G-326)*
Amsterdam Printing & Litho Inc 518 792-6501
428 Corinth Rd Queensbury (12804) *(G-13416)*
Amstutze Woodworking (PA) 518 946-8206
246 Springfield Rd Upper Jay (12987) *(G-15674)*
Amt Incorporated 518 284-2910
883 Chestnut St Sharon Springs (13459) *(G-14797)*
Amtek Research LLC 416 400-2906
1711 Cudaback Ave # 3865 Niagara Falls (14303) *(G-12261)*
Amtek Research LLC 212 537-6462
1711 Cudaback Ave # 3865 Niagara Falls (14303) *(G-12262)*
Amy Pak Publishing Inc 585 964-8188
3997 Roosevelt Hwy Holley (14470) *(G-6226)*
An Excelsior Elevator Corp 516 408-3070
640 Main St Unit 2 Westbury (11590) *(G-16316)*
An Group Inc 631 549-4090
17 Scott Dr Melville (11747) *(G-8003)*
An-Cor Industrial Plastics Inc 716 695-3141
900 Niagara Falls Blvd North Tonawanda (14120) *(G-12411)*
Anabec Inc 716 759-1674
9393 Main St Clarence (14031) *(G-3524)*
Anacor Pharmaceuticals Inc (HQ) 212 733-2323
235 E 42nd St New York (10017) *(G-8851)*
Anage Inc 212 944-6533
530 Fashion Ave Frnt 5 New York (10018) *(G-8852)*
Analog Digital Technology LLC 585 698-1845
95 Mount Read Blvd # 149 Rochester (14611) *(G-13631)*
Analysis & Design Aplicat Co, Melville *Also called Siemens Product Life Mgmt Sftw (G-8063)*
Analysts In Media (aim) Inc 212 488-1777
55 Broad St Fl 9 New York (10004) *(G-8853)*
Analytics Intell, New York *Also called Informa Solutions Inc (G-10212)*
Anand Printing Machinery Inc 631 667-3079
188 W 16th St Deer Park (11729) *(G-3942)*
Anandamali Inc 212 343-8964
35 N Moore St New York (10013) *(G-8854)*
Anaren Inc (HQ) 315 432-8909
6635 Kirkville Rd East Syracuse (13057) *(G-4318)*
Anaren Microwave Inc 315 432-8909
6635 Kirkville Rd East Syracuse (13057) *(G-4319)*
Anasia Inc 718 588-1407
1175 Jerome Ave Bronx (10452) *(G-1220)*
Anastasia Furs International (PA) 212 868-9241
224 W 30th St Rm 204 New York (10001) *(G-8855)*
Anatoli Inc 845 334-9000
43 Basin Rd Ste 11 West Hurley (12491) *(G-16256)*
Anbriella Sand & Gravel Corp 631 586-2111
145 S 4th St Bay Shore (11706) *(G-657)*
Anchor Canvas LLC 631 265-5602
556 W Jericho Tpke Smithtown (11787) *(G-14894)*
Anchor Commerce Trading Corp 516 881-3485
53 Dutchess Blvd Atlantic Beach (11509) *(G-455)*
Anchor Glass Container Corp 607 737-1933
151 E Mccanns Blvd Elmira Heights (14903) *(G-4509)*
Anchor Tech Products Corp 914 592-0240
4 Vernon Ln Ste 2 Elmsford (10523) *(G-4529)*
Ancon Gear & Instrument Corp (PA) 631 694-5255
29 Seabro Ave Amityville (11701) *(G-264)*
Andela Products, Richfield Springs *Also called Andela Tool & Machine Inc (G-13492)*
Andela Tool & Machine Inc 315 858-0055
493 State Route 28 Richfield Springs (13439) *(G-13492)*
Andersens Spring & Wldg Corp 516 785-7337
2374 Merrick Rd Bellmore (11710) *(G-784)*
Anderson Equipment Company 716 877-1992
2140 Military Rd Tonawanda (14150) *(G-15522)*
Anderson Instrument Co Inc (HQ) 518 922-5315
156 Auriesville Rd Fultonville (12072) *(G-5234)*
Anderson Precision Inc 716 484-1148
20 Livingston Ave Jamestown (14701) *(G-6698)*
Andes Gold Corporation 212 541-2495
405 Lexington Ave New York (10174) *(G-8856)*
Andex Corp 585 328-3790
69 Deep Rock Rd Rochester (14624) *(G-13632)*
Andigo New Media Inc 212 727-8445
150 W 25th St Rm 900 New York (10001) *(G-8857)*
Andike Millwork Inc (PA) 718 894-1796
5818 64th St Fl 2 Maspeth (11378) *(G-7821)*
Andin International Inc., New York *Also called Jotaly Inc (G-10367)*
Andor Design Corp 516 364-1619
20 Pond View Dr Syosset (11791) *(G-15208)*
Andrea Electronics Corporation (PA) 631 719-1800
620 Johnson Ave Ste 1b Bohemia (11716) *(G-980)*
Andrea Strongwater 212 873-0905
465 W End Ave New York (10024) *(G-8858)*
Andrea Systems LLC 631 390-3140
140 Finn Ct Farmingdale (11735) *(G-4721)*
Andreas Protein Cakery Inc 646 801-9826
229 E 85th St Unit 332 New York (10028) *(G-8859)*

Andrew J George 518 462-4662
457 Madison Ave Albany (12210) ***(G-41)***

Andrew M Schwartz LLC 212 391-7070
71 Gansevoort St Ste 2a New York (10014) ***(G-8860)***

Andritz Inc 518 745-2988
13 Pruyns Island Dr Glens Falls (12801) ***(G-5415)***

Androme Leather Inc 518 773-7945
21 Foster St Gloversville (12078) ***(G-5451)***

Andros Bowman Products LLC 540 217-4100
151 West Ave Lyndonville (14098) ***(G-7679)***

Andros Manufacturing Corp 585 663-5700
30 Hojack Park Rochester (14612) ***(G-13633)***

Andujar Asbestos and Lead 716 228-6757
473 4th St Buffalo (14201) ***(G-2700)***

Andy & Evan Industries Inc 212 967-7908
1071 Ave Of The Amer # 804 New York (10018) ***(G-8861)***

Andy & Evan Shirt Co., The, New York *Also called Andy & Evan Industries Inc* ***(G-8861)***

Angel Media and Publishing 845 727-4949
26 Snake Hill Rd West Nyack (10994) ***(G-16264)***

Angel Textiles Inc 212 532-0900
519 8th Ave Fl 21 New York (10018) ***(G-8862)***

Angel Tips Nail Salon 718 225-8300
25473 Horace Harding Expy Little Neck (11362) ***(G-7217)***

Angel-Made In Heaven Inc (PA) 212 869-5678
525 Fashion Ave Rm 1710 New York (10018) ***(G-8863)***

Angel-Made In Heaven Inc 718 832-4778
116 26th St Brooklyn (11232) ***(G-1534)***

Angelic Gourmet, Naples *Also called Naples Vly Mrgers Acqstons LLC* ***(G-8473)***

Angelica Forest Products Inc 585 466-3205
54 Closser Ave Angelica (14709) ***(G-366)***

Angelica Spring Company Inc 585 466-7892
99 West Ave Angelica (14709) ***(G-367)***

Angie Washroom, New Windsor *Also called Larcent Enterprises Inc* ***(G-8648)***

Angiodynamics Inc 518 761-6867
603 Queensbury Ave Queensbury (12804) ***(G-13417)***

Angiodynamics Inc 518 975-1400
603 Queensbury Ave Queensbury (12804) ***(G-13418)***

Angiodynamics Inc 518 792-4112
10 Glens Fls Technical Pa Glens Falls (12801) ***(G-5416)***

Angiodynamics Inc 518 742-4430
543 Queensbury Ave Queensbury (12804) ***(G-13419)***

Angiodynamics Inc (PA) 518 795-1400
14 Plaza Dr Latham (12110) ***(G-7063)***

Angiodynamics Inc 706 846-3126
10 Glens Falls Tech Park Glens Falls (12801) ***(G-5417)***

Angiogenex Inc (PA) 347 468-6799
425 Madison Ave Ste 902 New York (10017) ***(G-8864)***

Angiotech Biocoatings Corp 585 321-1130
336 Summit Point Dr Henrietta (14467) ***(G-6030)***

Ango Home, New York *Also called Feldman Company Inc* ***(G-9792)***

Angola Penny Saver Inc 716 549-1164
19 Center St Angola (14006) ***(G-368)***

Angus Buffers & Biochemicals, Niagara Falls *Also called Angus Chemical Company* ***(G-12263)***

Angus Chemical Company 716 283-1434
2236 Liberty Dr Niagara Falls (14304) ***(G-12263)***

Anheuser-Busch LLC 315 638-0365
2780 Brundage Rd Baldwinsville (13027) ***(G-549)***

Anheuser-Busch LLC 315 638-0365
2885 Belgium Rd Baldwinsville (13027) ***(G-550)***

Anheuser-Busch LLC 212 573-8800
250 Park Ave Fl 2 New York (10177) ***(G-8865)***

Anheuser-Busch Companies LLC 718 589-2610
510 Food Center Dr Bronx (10474) ***(G-1221)***

Anheuser-Busch Inbev Fin Inc 212 573-8800
250 Park Ave New York (10177) ***(G-8866)***

Anheuser-Busch Inbev Svcs LLC 314 765-4729
250 Park Ave Fl 2 New York (10177) ***(G-8867)***

Anhui Skyworth LLC 917 940-6903
44 Kensington Ct Hempstead (11550) ***(G-6005)***

Aniiwe Inc 347 683-1891
774 Rockaway Ave Apt 3k Brooklyn (11212) ***(G-1535)***

Anima Group LLC 917 913-2053
435 E 79th St Ph H New York (10075) ***(G-8868)***

Anima Mundi Herbals LLC 415 279-5727
2323 Borden Ave Long Island City (11101) ***(G-7379)***

Animal Fair Media Inc 212 629-0392
545 8th Ave Rm 401 New York (10018) ***(G-8869)***

Animal Pantry 631 673-3666
741 W Jericho Tpke Huntington (11743) ***(G-6391)***

Anju Sylogent LLC (HQ) 480 326-2358
251 W 19th St New York (10011) ***(G-8870)***

Anka Tool & Die Inc 845 268-4116
150 Wells Ave Congers (10920) ***(G-3709)***

Ankom Development LLC 315 986-1937
2052 Oneil Rd Macedon (14502) ***(G-7692)***

Ankom Technology Corp 315 986-8090
2052 Oneil Rd Macedon (14502) ***(G-7693)***

Anmar Acquisition LLC (HQ) 585 352-7777
35 Vantage Point Dr Rochester (14624) ***(G-13634)***

Ann Gish Inc (PA) 212 969-9200
4 W 20th St New York (10011) ***(G-8871)***

Anna B Inc 516 680-6609
55 Great Jones St Apt 6 New York (10012) ***(G-8872)***

Anna Sui Corp (PA) 212 941-8406
484 Broome St New York (10013) ***(G-8873)***

Anna Young Assoc Ltd 516 546-4400
100 Doxsee Dr Freeport (11520) ***(G-5144)***

Anne Taintor Inc 718 483-9312
137 Montague St Brooklyn (11201) ***(G-1536)***

Annese & Associates Inc 716 972-0076
500 Corporate Pkwy # 106 Buffalo (14226) ***(G-2701)***

Annies Ice 585 593-5605
35 Herman Ave Wellsville (14895) ***(G-16111)***

Annointed Buty Ministries LLC 646 867-3796
1697 E 54th St Brooklyn (11234) ***(G-1537)***

Annuals Publishing Co Inc 212 505-0950
10 E 23rd St Ste 510 New York (10010) ***(G-8874)***

Anorad Corporation 631 344-6600
100 Precision Dr Ste 1 Shirley (11967) ***(G-14827)***

Another 99 Cent Paradise 718 786-4578
4206 Greenpoint Ave Sunnyside (11104) ***(G-15201)***

Ansa Systems of USA Inc 718 835-3743
145 Hook Creek Blvd B6a1 Valley Stream (11581) ***(G-15772)***

Ansen Corporation (PA) 315 393-3573
100 Chimney Point Dr Ogdensburg (13669) ***(G-12570)***

Ansen Corporation 315 393-3573
100 Chimney Point Dr Ogdensburg (13669) ***(G-12571)***

Ansun Graphics Inc 315 437-6869
6392 Deere Rd Ste 4 Syracuse (13206) ***(G-15243)***

Answer Company, The, New York *Also called Answer Printing Inc* ***(G-8875)***

Answer Printing Inc 212 922-2922
505 8th Ave Rm 1101 New York (10018) ***(G-8875)***

Antab Mch Sprfinishing Lab Inc 585 865-8290
46 Latta Rd Rochester (14612) ***(G-13635)***

Antenna & Radome Res Assoc (PA) 631 231-8400
15 Harold Ct Bay Shore (11706) ***(G-658)***

Anterios Inc 212 303-1683
60 E 42nd St Ste 1160 New York (10165) ***(G-8876)***

Anthony Gigi Inc 860 984-1943
45 Ramsey Rd Unit 28 Shirley (11967) ***(G-14828)***

Anthony L & S LLC (PA) 212 386-7245
500 Fashion Ave Fl 16b New York (10018) ***(G-8877)***

Anthony L&S Footwear Group, New York *Also called Anthony L & S LLC* ***(G-8877)***

Anthony Lawrence of New York 212 206-8820
3233 47th Ave Long Island City (11101) ***(G-7380)***

Anthony Manno & Co Inc 631 445-1834
307 Skidmore Rd Ste 2 Deer Park (11729) ***(G-3943)***

Anthony Manufacturing Inc 631 957-9424
34 Gear Ave Lindenhurst (11757) ***(G-7161)***

Anthony River Inc 315 475-1315
116 Granger St Syracuse (13202) ***(G-15244)***

Anthony Road Wine Co Inc 315 536-2182
1020 Anthony Rd Penn Yan (14527) ***(G-12948)***

Anthroposophic Press Inc (PA) 518 851-2054
15 Greenridge Dr Clifton Park (12065) ***(G-3563)***

Antico Casale Usa LLC 914 760-1100
1244 Clintonville St 2c Whitestone (11357) ***(G-16533)***

Antimony New York LLC 917 232-1836
120 E 34th St Apt 7g New York (10016) ***(G-8878)***

Antiques & Collectible Autos 716 825-3990
35 Dole St Buffalo (14210) ***(G-2702)***

Anton Community Newspapers, Mineola *Also called Long Island Cmnty Nwsppers Inc* ***(G-8235)***

Antonicelli Vito Race Car 716 684-2205
3883 Broadway St Buffalo (14227) ***(G-2703)***

Antwerp Diamond Distributors 212 319-3300
581 5th Ave Fl 5 New York (10017) ***(G-8879)***

Antwerp Sales Intl Inc 212 354-6515
576 5th Ave New York (10036) ***(G-8880)***

Anvil Knitwear, Inc., New York *Also called Gildan Apparel USA Inc* ***(G-9919)***

Anyas Licorice Inc 917 935-1916
1027 Grand St Brooklyn (11211) ***(G-1538)***

Anyelas Vineyards LLC 315 685-3797
2433 W Lake Rd Skaneateles (13152) ***(G-14866)***

Anyvision US Inc 606 901-4894
152 Madison Ave Fl 20 New York (10016) ***(G-8881)***

Aos, Valley Stream *Also called Automated Office Systems Inc* ***(G-15773)***

APC Paper Company Inc 315 384-4225
100 Remington Ave Norfolk (13667) ***(G-12356)***

APC-Mge, New York *Also called Schneider Electric It Corp* ***(G-11509)***

Apec Paper Industries Ltd 212 730-0088
189 W 89th St Apt 5w New York (10024) ***(G-8882)***

Apex Airtronics Inc (PA) 718 485-8560
2465 Atlantic Ave Brooklyn (11207) ***(G-1539)***

Apex Aridyne Corp 516 239-4400
168 Doughty Blvd Inwood (11096) ***(G-6484)***

Apex Real Holdings Inc 877 725-2150
1640 40th St Ste A Brooklyn (11218) ***(G-1540)***

Apex Signal Corporation 631 567-1100
110 Wilbur Pl Bohemia (11716) ***(G-981)***

Apex Texicon Inc (PA) 516 239-4400
295 Madison Ave New York (10017) ***(G-8883)***

Apexx Omni-Graphics Inc 718 326-3330
5829 64th St Maspeth (11378) *(G-7822)*
Apf Management Company LLC 914 665-5400
60 Fullerton Ave Yonkers (10704) *(G-16736)*
Apf Manufacturing Company LLC (PA) 914 963-6300
60 Fullerton Ave Yonkers (10704) *(G-16737)*
Apf Munn Master Frame Makers, Yonkers *Also called Apf Manufacturing Company LLC (G-16737)*
Apg Neuros, Plattsburgh *Also called Apgn Inc (G-13106)*
Apgn Inc 518 324-4150
160 Banker Rd Plattsburgh (12901) *(G-13106)*
Aphrodities 718 224-1774
2007 Francis Lewis Blvd Whitestone (11357) *(G-16534)*
API, Central Islip *Also called Autronic Plastics Inc (G-3357)*
API Delevan, East Aurora *Also called American Precision Inds Inc (G-4193)*
API Heat Transf Thermasys Corp (HQ) 716 684-6700
2777 Walden Ave Buffalo (14225) *(G-2704)*
API Heat Transfer Company (PA) 716 684-6700
2777 Walden Ave Ste 1 Buffalo (14225) *(G-2705)*
API Heat Transfer Inc 585 496-5755
91 North St Arcade (14009) *(G-377)*
API Industries Inc (PA) 845 365-2200
2 Glenshaw St Orangeburg (10962) *(G-12668)*
API Industries Inc 845 365-2200
2 Glenshaw St Orangeburg (10962) *(G-12669)*
Apicella Jewelers Inc 212 840-2024
40 W 39th St Fl 4 New York (10018) *(G-8884)*
Apogee Power Usa Inc 202 746-2890
7 Verne Pl Hartsdale (10530) *(G-5742)*
Apogee Retail NY 516 731-1727
3041 Hempstead Tpke Levittown (11756) *(G-7130)*
Apogee Translite Inc 631 254-6975
593 Acorn St Ste B Deer Park (11729) *(G-3944)*
Apollo Apparel Group LLC 212 398-6585
1407 Brdway Ste 2000-200 New York (10018) *(G-8885)*
Apollo Display Tech Corp (PA) 631 580-4360
87 Raynor Ave Ste 1 Ronkonkoma (11779) *(G-14310)*
Apollo Investment Fund VII LP 212 515-3200
9 W 57th St Fl 43 New York (10019) *(G-8886)*
Apollo Jeans, New York *Also called Apollo Apparel Group LLC (G-8885)*
Apollo Lighting and Hasco Ltg, Mount Vernon *Also called Luminatta Inc (G-8419)*
Apollo Management V LP 914 467-6510
1 Manhattanville Rd # 201 Purchase (10577) *(G-13386)*
Apollo Optical Systems Inc 585 272-6170
925 John St West Henrietta (14586) *(G-16229)*
Apollo Orthotics Corp 516 333-3223
320 Westbury Ave Carle Place (11514) *(G-3261)*
Apollo Steel Corporation 716 283-8758
4800 Tomson Ave Niagara Falls (14304) *(G-12264)*
Apollo Windows & Doors Inc 718 386-3326
1003 Metropolitan Ave Brooklyn (11211) *(G-1541)*
Apothecus Pharmaceutical Corp (PA) 516 624-8200
220 Townsend Sq Oyster Bay (11771) *(G-12810)*
Appairent Technologies Inc (PA) 585 214-2460
150 Lucius Gordon Dr West Henrietta (14586) *(G-16230)*
Apparatus Mfg Inc 845 471-5116
13 Commerce St Poughkeepsie (12603) *(G-13326)*
Apparatus Studio 646 527-9732
122 W 30th St Fl 4 New York (10001) *(G-8887)*
Apparel Group Ltd 212 328-1200
35 W 36th St Rm 10w New York (10018) *(G-8888)*
Apparel Partnership Group LLC 212 302-7722
250 W 39th St Rm 701 New York (10018) *(G-8889)*
Apparel Production Inc 212 278-8362
270 W 39th St Rm 1701 New York (10018) *(G-8890)*
Appfigures Inc 212 343-7900
133 Chrystie St Fl 3 New York (10002) *(G-8891)*
Applause Coating LLC 631 231-5223
8b Grand Blvd Brentwood (11717) *(G-1127)*
Apple, Port Washington *Also called US Juice Partners LLC (G-13312)*
Apple & Eve LLC (HQ) 516 621-1122
2 Seaview Blvd Ste 100 Port Washington (11050) *(G-13243)*
Apple Commuter Inc 917 299-0066
54 Lake Dr New Hyde Park (11040) *(G-8516)*
Apple Core Electronics Inc 718 628-4068
991 Flushing Ave Brooklyn (11206) *(G-1542)*
Apple Digital Printing, Long Island City *Also called Apple Enterprises Inc (G-7381)*
Apple Enterprises Inc 718 361-2200
1308 43rd Ave Long Island City (11101) *(G-7381)*
Apple Healing & Relaxation 718 278-1089
3114 Broadway Long Island City (11106) *(G-7382)*
Apple Imprints Apparel Inc 716 893-1130
2336 Bailey Ave Buffalo (14211) *(G-2706)*
Apple Intercom and Elec Inc 914 633-5101
271 North Ave Ste A2 New Rochelle (10801) *(G-8590)*
Apple Med Urgent Care PC 914 523-5965
504 Gramatan Ave Mount Vernon (10552) *(G-8377)*
Apple Press 914 723-6660
23 Harrison Blvd Ste 2 White Plains (10604) *(G-16421)*
Apple Rubber Products Inc (PA) 716 684-6560
310 Erie St Lancaster (14086) *(G-7007)*
Apple Rubber Products Inc 716 684-7649
204 Cemetery Rd Lancaster (14086) *(G-7008)*
Apple Security Solutions, New Rochelle *Also called Apple Intercom and Elec Inc (G-8590)*
Application Resources Inc 516 636-6200
15 Cutternill Rd Ste 529 Great Neck (11021) *(G-5534)*
Application Security Inc (HQ) 212 912-4100
55 Broad St Rm 10a New York (10004) *(G-8892)*
Applied Coatings Holding Corp (PA) 585 482-0300
1653 E Main St Ste 1 Rochester (14609) *(G-13636)*
Applied Concepts Inc 315 696-6676
397 State Route 281 Tully (13159) *(G-15647)*
Applied Energy Solutions LLC 585 538-3270
1 Technology Pl Caledonia (14423) *(G-3153)*
Applied Image Inc 585 482-0300
1653 E Main St Ste 1 Rochester (14609) *(G-13637)*
Applied Materials Inc 518 245-1400
10 Stonebreak Rd Ste 2 Ballston Spa (12020) *(G-577)*
Applied Materials Inc 845 227-5000
2531 Route 52 Hopewell Junction (12533) *(G-6282)*
Applied Minerals Inc (PA) 212 226-4265
55 Washington St Ste 301 Brooklyn (11201) *(G-1543)*
Applied Power Systems Inc 516 935-2230
124 Charlotte Ave Hicksville (11801) *(G-6059)*
Applied Safety LLC 718 608-6292
4349 10th St Ste 311 Long Island City (11101) *(G-7383)*
Applied Technology Mfg Corp 607 687-2200
71 Temple St Owego (13827) *(G-12795)*
Applied Terminal Systems, Auburn *Also called Daikin Applied Americas Inc (G-475)*
Applince Installation Svc Corp (PA) 716 884-7425
3190 Genesee St Buffalo (14225) *(G-2707)*
Apprenda Inc 518 383-2130
433 River St Ste 4001 Troy (12180) *(G-15600)*
Apprise Mobile, New York *Also called Theirapp LLC (G-11810)*
Appsbidder Inc 917 880-4269
55 Clark St 772 Brooklyn (11201) *(G-1544)*
April Printing Co Inc 212 685-7455
1201 Broadway Ste 711 New York (10001) *(G-8893)*
APS American Polymers Svcs Inc 212 362-7711
104 W 40th St Rm 500 New York (10018) *(G-8894)*
APS Enterprise Software Inc 631 784-7720
775 Park Ave Huntington (11743) *(G-6392)*
Apsco Sports Enterprises Inc 718 965-9500
50th St & 1st Av Bg 57 F5 Brooklyn (11232) *(G-1545)*
Aptar Congers, Congers *Also called Aptargroup Inc (G-3710)*
Aptargroup Inc 845 639-3700
250 N Route 303 Congers (10920) *(G-3710)*
Apx Arstan Products, Hicksville *Also called Arstan Products International (G-6061)*
Apx Technologies Inc 516 433-1313
264 Duffy Ave Hicksville (11801) *(G-6060)*
Aquarii Inc 315 672-8807
17 Genesee St Camillus (13031) *(G-3194)*
Aquarium Pump & Piping Systems 631 567-5555
528 Chester Rd Sayville (11782) *(G-14625)*
Aquifer Drilling & Testing Inc (HQ) 516 616-6026
75 E 2nd St Mineola (11501) *(G-8204)*
AR & AR Jewelry Inc 212 764-7916
31 W 47th St Fl 15 New York (10036) *(G-8895)*
AR Publishing Company Inc 212 482-0303
55 Broad St Rm 20b New York (10004) *(G-8896)*
Arabella Textiles LLC 212 679-0611
303 5th Ave Rm 1402 New York (10016) *(G-8897)*
Arbe Machinery Inc 631 756-2477
54 Allen Blvd Farmingdale (11735) *(G-4722)*
Arbeit Bros Inc 212 736-9761
345 7th Ave Fl 20 New York (10001) *(G-8898)*
Arbor Valley Flooring, Salamanca *Also called Norton-Smith Hardwoods Inc (G-14529)*
Arborn Printing & Graphics, Mamaroneck *Also called Division Den-Bar Enterprises (G-7742)*
ARC OF CHEMUNG, THE, Elmira *Also called Chemung Cnty Chpter Nysarc Inc (G-4477)*
ARC Remanufacturing Inc 718 728-0701
1940 42nd St Long Island City (11105) *(G-7384)*
ARC Systems Inc 631 582-8020
2090 Joshuas Path Hauppauge (11788) *(G-5768)*
ARC TEC Wldg & Fabrication Inc 718 982-9274
15 Harrison Ave Staten Island (10302) *(G-15044)*
Arca Ink LLC 518 798-0100
30 Bluebird Rd South Glens Falls (12803) *(G-14934)*
Arcade Glass Works, Chaffee *Also called Hart To Hart Industries Inc (G-3404)*
Arcade Herald, Arcade *Also called Neighbor To Neighbor News Inc (G-387)*
Arcadia Chem Preservative LLC 516 466-5258
100 Great Neck Rd Apt 5b Great Neck (11021) *(G-5535)*
Arcadia Mfg Group Inc (PA) 518 434-6213
80 Cohoes Ave Green Island (12183) *(G-5602)*
Arcadia Mfg Group Inc 518 434-6213
1032 Broadway Menands (12204) *(G-8081)*
Arcangel Inc 347 771-0789
209 W 38th St Rm 1001 New York (10018) *(G-8899)*
Arch Globl Prcsion Rchster LLC 585 254-7000
1390 Mount Read Blvd Rochester (14606) *(G-13638)*
Archaelogy Magazine 718 472-3050
3636 33rd St Ste 301 Long Island City (11106) *(G-7385)*
Archer-Daniels-Midland Company 716 849-7333
250 Ganson St Buffalo (14203) *(G-2708)*

Archer-Daniels-Midland Company.......518 828-4691
201 State Route 23b Hudson (12534) ***(G-6339)***
Archer-Daniels-Midland Company.......518 828-4691
Ste B Rr 23 Hudson (12534) ***(G-6340)***
Archer-Daniels-Midland Company.......585 346-2311
3401 Rochester Rd Lakeville (14480) ***(G-6984)***
Archie Comic Publications Inc.......914 381-5155
629 Fifth Ave Ste 100 Pelham (10803) ***(G-12932)***
Archie Comics Publishers, Pelham *Also called Archie Comic Publications Inc* ***(G-12932)***
Archimedes Products Inc.......631 589-1215
21 Flcyds Run Bohemia (11716) ***(G-982)***
Architctral Dsign Elements LLC.......718 218-7800
52 Box St Brooklyn (11222) ***(G-1546)***
Architctral Mllwk Installation.......631 499-0755
590 Elwood Rd East Northport (11731) ***(G-4260)***
Architctral Shetmetal Pdts Inc.......518 381-6144
1329 Amsterdam Rd Scotia (12302) ***(G-14738)***
Architects Newspaper LLC.......212 966-0630
21 Murray St Fl 5 New York (10007) ***(G-8900)***
Architectural Coatings Inc.......718 418-9584
538 Johnson Ave Brooklyn (11237) ***(G-1547)***
Architectural Dctg Co LLC.......845 483-1340
130 Salt Point Tpke Poughkeepsie (12603) ***(G-13327)***
Architectural Enhancements Inc.......845 343-9663
135 Crotty Rd Middletown (10941) ***(G-8137)***
Architectural Fiberglass Corp.......631 842-4772
1395 Marconi Blvd Copiague (11726) ***(G-3750)***
Architectural Glass Inc.......845 831-3116
71 Maple St Apt 2 Beacon (12508) ***(G-754)***
Architectural Sign Group Inc.......516 326-1800
145 Meacham Ave Elmont (11003) ***(G-4516)***
Architectural Textiles USA Inc.......212 213-6972
36 E 23rd St Ste F New York (10010) ***(G-8901)***
Architex International, New York *Also called Architectural Textiles USA Inc* ***(G-8901)***
Archive360 Inc.......212 731-2438
165 Broadway Fl 23 New York (10006) ***(G-8902)***
Archrock Inc.......716 763-1553
305 E Fairmount Ave Ste 4 Lakewood (14750) ***(G-6988)***
Arcom Automatics LLC.......315 422-1230
185 Ainsley Dr Syracuse (13210) ***(G-15245)***
Arcom Labs, Syracuse *Also called Arrow-Communication Labs Inc* ***(G-15247)***
Arconic Fstening Systems Rings, Kingston *Also called Huck International Inc* ***(G-6902)***
Arconic Inc (PA).......212 836-2758
390 Park Ave Fl 12 New York (10022) ***(G-8903)***
Arconic Inc.......716 358-6451
2632 S Work St Ste 24 Falconer (14733) ***(G-4671)***
Arconic Inc.......315 764-4011
45 County Route 42 Massena (13662) ***(G-7900)***
Arctic Glacier Newburgh Inc.......718 456-2013
335 Moffat St Brooklyn (11237) ***(G-1548)***
Arctic Glacier Newburgh Inc (HQ).......845 561-0549
225 Lake St Newburgh (12550) ***(G-12215)***
Arctix, Locust Valley *Also called Alpha 6 Distributions LLC* ***(G-7345)***
Arcworks, Rochester *Also called Monroe Cnty Chapter Nysarc Inc* ***(G-13952)***
Arcy Plastic Laminates Inc (PA).......518 235-0753
555 Patroon Creek Blvd Albany (12206) ***(G-42)***
Ardagh Metal Packaging USA Inc.......607 584-3300
379 Broome Corporate Pkwy Conklin (13748) ***(G-3724)***
Ardent Mills LLC.......518 447-1700
101 Normanskill St Albany (12202) ***(G-43)***
Ardex Cosmetics of America.......518 283-6700
744 Pawling Ave Troy (12180) ***(G-15601)***
Area Development Magazine, Westbury *Also called Halcyon Business Publications* ***(G-16338)***
Area Inc.......212 924-7084
58 E 11th St Fl 2 New York (10003) ***(G-8904)***
Area Warehouse, New York *Also called Area Inc* ***(G-8904)***
Aremco Products Inc.......845 268-0039
707 Executive Blvd Ste B Valley Cottage (10989) ***(G-15752)***
Arena Graphics Inc.......516 767-5108
52 Main St Frnt Port Washington (11050) ***(G-13244)***
Arena Sports Center, Port Washington *Also called Arena Graphics Inc* ***(G-13244)***
Ares Box LLC.......718 858-8760
63 Flushing Ave Unit 224 Brooklyn (11205) ***(G-1549)***
Ares Printing and Packg Corp.......718 858-8760
Brooklyn Navy Yard Bldg Brooklyn (11205) ***(G-1550)***
Argee America Inc.......212 768-9840
1410 Broadway Rm 1204 New York (10018) ***(G-8905)***
Argee Sportswear, New York *Also called Argee America Inc* ***(G-8905)***
Argencord Machine Corp Inc.......631 842-8990
10 Reith St Copiague (11726) ***(G-3751)***
Argo Envelope Corp.......718 729-2700
4310 21st St Long Island City (11101) ***(G-7386)***
Argo General Machine Work Inc.......718 392-4605
3816 11th St Long Island City (11101) ***(G-7387)***
Argo Lithographers Inc.......718 729-2700
4310 21st St Long Island City (11101) ***(G-7388)***
Argon Corp (PA).......516 487-5314
160 Great Neck Rd Great Neck (11021) ***(G-5536)***
Argon Medical Devices Inc.......585 321-1130
336 Summit Point Dr Henrietta (14467) ***(G-6031)***

Argos Inc.......845 528-0576
58 Seifert Ln Putnam Valley (10579) ***(G-13401)***
Argosy Composite Advanced Mate.......212 268-0003
225 W 34th St Ste 1106 New York (10122) ***(G-8906)***
Arh, Deer Park *Also called American Racing Headers Inc* ***(G-3940)***
Aric Signs & Awnings Inc.......516 350-0409
153 Baldwin Rd Hempstead (11550) ***(G-6006)***
Ariel Optics Inc.......585 265-4820
261 David Pkwy Ontario (14519) ***(G-12647)***
Ariel Tian LLC.......212 457-1266
253 W 35th St Fl 8 Flr 8 Forest Hills (11375) ***(G-5072)***
Ariela and Associates Intl LLC (PA).......212 683-4131
1359 Broadway Fl 21 New York (10018) ***(G-8907)***
Aries Precision Products, Rochester *Also called Estebania Enterprises Inc* ***(G-13793)***
Ariesun Inc.......866 274-3049
160 W 3rd St Mount Vernon (10550) ***(G-8378)***
Arimed Orthotics Prosthetics (PA).......718 875-8754
302 Livingston St Brooklyn (11217) ***(G-1551)***
Arise At Marshall Farms Inc.......315 687-6727
1972 New Boston Rd Chittenango (13037) ***(G-3501)***
Arista Coffee Inc.......347 531-0813
5901 55th St Maspeth (11378) ***(G-7823)***
Arista Flag Corporation.......845 246-7700
157 W Saugerties Rd Saugerties (12477) ***(G-14603)***
Arista Innovations Inc.......516 746-2262
131 Liberty Ave Mineola (11501) ***(G-8205)***
Arista Printing, Mineola *Also called Arista Innovations Inc* ***(G-8205)***
Arista Steel Designs Corp.......718 965-7077
788 3rd Ave Brooklyn (11232) ***(G-1552)***
Aristocrat Lighting Inc.......718 522-0003
104 Halleck St Brooklyn (11231) ***(G-1553)***
Arizona Beverage Company LLC (HQ).......516 812-0300
60 Crossways Park Dr W # 400 Woodbury (11797) ***(G-16613)***
Arizona Beverages USA, Woodbury *Also called Arizona Beverage Company LLC* ***(G-16613)***
Ark Sciences Inc.......646 943-1520
1601 Veterans Hwy Ste 315 Islandia (11749) ***(G-6521)***
Arkay Packaging Corporation (PA).......631 273-2000
100 Marcus Blvd Ste 2 Hauppauge (11788) ***(G-5769)***
Arkema Inc.......585 243-6359
3289 Genesee St Piffard (14533) ***(G-12995)***
Arkwin Industries Inc (HQ).......516 333-2640
686 Main St Westbury (11590) ***(G-16317)***
Arlan Damper Corporation.......631 589-7431
1598 Lakeland Ave Bohemia (11716) ***(G-983)***
Arlee Group, New York *Also called Arlee Home Fashions Inc* ***(G-8908)***
Arlee Home Fashions Inc (PA).......212 689-0020
36 E 31st St Rm 800 New York (10016) ***(G-8908)***
Arlee Lighting Corp.......516 595-8558
125 Doughty Blvd Inwood (11096) ***(G-6485)***
Arlon Viscor Ltd.......914 461-1300
1133 Westchester Ave White Plains (10604) ***(G-16422)***
Arlyn Scales, East Rockaway *Also called Circuits & Systems Inc* ***(G-4293)***
Arm & Hammer, Schenectady *Also called Church & Dwight Co Inc* ***(G-14662)***
Arm Construction Company Inc.......646 235-6520
10001 27th Ave East Elmhurst (11369) ***(G-4217)***
Arm Rochester Inc.......585 354-5077
138 Joseph Ave Rochester (14605) ***(G-13639)***
Arma Container Corp.......631 254-1200
65 N Industry Ct Deer Park (11729) ***(G-3945)***
Armacel Armor Corporation.......805 384-1144
745 5th Ave Fl 7 New York (10151) ***(G-8909)***
Armadillo Bar & Grill, Kingston *Also called Tortilla Heaven Inc* ***(G-6924)***
Armento Architectural Arts, Kenmore *Also called Armento Incorporated* ***(G-6857)***
Armento Incorporated.......716 875-2423
1011 Military Rd Kenmore (14217) ***(G-6857)***
Armitron Watch Div, Little Neck *Also called E Gluck Corporation* ***(G-7218)***
Armor Dynamics Inc.......845 658-9200
138 Maple Hill Rd Kingston (12401) ***(G-6888)***
Armor Machining Services, Inc........716 825-0190
343 Elk St Buffalo (14210) ***(G-2709)***
Armor Tile, Buffalo *Also called Engineered Composites Inc* ***(G-2819)***
Armour Bearer Group Inc.......646 812-4487
424 Beach 65th St Arverne (11692) ***(G-413)***
Armstrong Mold Corporation (PA).......315 437-1517
6910 Manlius Center Rd East Syracuse (13057) ***(G-4320)***
Armstrong Mold Corporation.......315 437-1517
5860 Fisher Rd East Syracuse (13057) ***(G-4321)***
Armstrong Pumps Inc.......716 693-8813
93 East Ave North Tonawanda (14120) ***(G-12412)***
Armstrong Transmitter Corp.......315 673-1269
4835 N Street Rd Marcellus (13108) ***(G-7792)***
Arnan Development Corp (PA).......607 432-8391
6459 State Highway 23 Oneonta (13820) ***(G-12625)***
Arnell Inc.......516 486-7098
73 High St Hempstead (11550) ***(G-6007)***
Arnold Magnetic Tech Corp (HQ).......585 385-9010
770 Linden Ave Rochester (14625) ***(G-13640)***
Arnold Printing Corp.......607 272-7800
604 W Green St Ithaca (14850) ***(G-6557)***
Arnold Taylor Printing Inc.......516 781-0564
2218 Brody Ln Bellmore (11710) ***(G-785)***

ALPHABETIC

Arnold-Davis LLC 607 772-1201
187 Indl Pk Dr Binghamton (13904) ***(G-863)***
Arnolds Meat Food Products 718 384-8071
274 Heyward St Brooklyn (11206) ***(G-1554)***
Arnouse Digital Devices Corp 516 673-4444
1983 Marcus Ave Ste 104 New Hyde Park (11042) ***(G-8517)***
Arnprior Rpid Mfg Slutions Inc (PA) 585 617-6301
2400 Mount Read Blvd # 112 Rochester (14615) ***(G-13641)***
Arnprior Rpid Mfg Slutions Inc 585 617-6301
2400 Mount Read Blvd # 1124 Rochester (14615) ***(G-13642)***
Aro-Graph Corporation 315 463-8693
847 North Ave Syracuse (13206) ***(G-15246)***
Aro-Graph Displays, Syracuse *Also called Aro-Graph Corporation* ***(G-15246)***
Aromafloria, Huntington Station *Also called California Fragrance Company* ***(G-6435)***
Aromasong Usa Inc 718 838-9669
35 Frost St Brooklyn (11211) ***(G-1555)***
Aron Streit Inc 212 475-7000
171 Route 303 Orangeburg (10962) ***(G-12670)***
Aronowitz Metal Works 845 356-1660
5 Edwin Ln Monsey (10952) ***(G-8285)***
Arper USA Inc 212 647-8900
476 Broadway Ste 2f New York (10013) ***(G-8910)***
Array Marketing Group Inc (HQ) 212 750-3367
200 Madison Ave Ste 2121 New York (10016) ***(G-8911)***
Arringement International Inc 347 323-7974
16015 45th Ave Flushing (11358) ***(G-4986)***
Arro Manufacturing LLC 716 763-6203
4687 Gleason Rd Lakewood (14750) ***(G-6989)***
Arro Tool & Die Inc 716 763-6203
4687 Gleason Rd Lakewood (14750) ***(G-6990)***
Arrow Grinding Inc 716 693-3333
525 Vicke St Tonaw Ctr Tonawanda (14150) ***(G-15523)***
Arrow Leather Finishing Inc 518 762-3121
228 Pleasant Ave Johnstown (12095) ***(G-6823)***
Arrow-Communication Labs Inc 315 422-1230
185 Ainsley Dr Syracuse (13210) ***(G-15247)***
Arrowear Athletic Apparel, Lynbrook *Also called Valley Stream Sporting Gds Inc* ***(G-7677)***
Arrowhead Spring Vineyards LLC 716 434-8030
4746 Townline Rd Lockport (14094) ***(G-7285)***
Arrowpak, Richmond Hill *Also called Baralan Usa Inc* ***(G-13497)***
Arsenal Holdings LLC (PA) 212 398-9139
885 3rd Ave Rm 2403 New York (10022) ***(G-8912)***
Arstan Products International 516 433-1313
264 Duffy Ave Hicksville (11801) ***(G-6061)***
Art Asiapacific Publishing LLC 212 255-6003
410 W 24th St Apt 14a New York (10011) ***(G-8913)***
Art Bedi-Makky Foundry Corp 718 383-4191
227 India St Ste 31 Brooklyn (11222) ***(G-1556)***
Art Boards, Brooklyn *Also called Patrick Mackin Custom Furn* ***(G-2307)***
Art Digital Technologies LLC 646 649-4820
85 Debevoise Ave Brooklyn (11222) ***(G-1557)***
Art Essentials of New York (PA) 845 368-1100
25 Church Rd Airmont (10952) ***(G-11)***
Art Foam, Lindenhurst *Also called Strux Corp* ***(G-7196)***
Art Industries of New York 212 633-9200
601 W 26th St Rm 1425 New York (10001) ***(G-8914)***
Art of Platinum, The, New York *Also called Leon Mege Inc* ***(G-10553)***
Art Parts Signs Inc 585 381-2134
100 Lincoln Pkwy East Rochester (14445) ***(G-4280)***
Art People Inc 212 431-4865
594 Broadway Rm 1102 New York (10012) ***(G-8915)***
Art Precision Metal Products 631 842-8889
1465 S Strong Ave Copiague (11726) ***(G-3752)***
Art Resources Transfer Inc 212 255-2919
526 W 26th St Rm 614 New York (10001) ***(G-8916)***
Art Scroll Printing Corp 212 929-2413
230 W 41st St Bsmt 1 New York (10036) ***(G-8917)***
Art-Craft Optical Company Inc 585 546-6640
57 Goodway Dr S Rochester (14623) ***(G-13643)***
Art-TEC Jewelry Designs Ltd (PA) 212 719-2941
48 W 48th St Ste 401 New York (10036) ***(G-8918)***
Artcraft Building Services 845 895-3893
85 Old Hoagerburgh Rd Wallkill (12589) ***(G-15902)***
Artemis Inc 631 232-2424
36 Central Ave Hauppauge (11788) ***(G-5770)***
Artemis Studios Inc 718 788-6022
34 35th St Ste 2b Brooklyn (11232) ***(G-1558)***
Arthur Brown W Mfg Co 631 243-5594
49 E Industry Ct Ste I Deer Park (11729) ***(G-3946)***
Arthur Gluck Shirtmakers Inc 212 755-8165
871 E 24th St Brooklyn (11210) ***(G-1559)***
Arthur Invitation, New York *Also called Exotic Print and Paper Inc* ***(G-9753)***
Arthur Lauer Inc 845 255-7871
47 Steves Ln Gardiner (12525) ***(G-5291)***
Articulate 646 706-7596
717 Daniels Ln 419 Sagaponack (11962) ***(G-14504)***
Articulate Global Inc 800 861-4880
244 5th Ave Ste 2960 New York (10001) ***(G-8919)***
Artifex Press LLC 212 414-1482
109 W 27th St New York (10001) ***(G-8920)***
Artina Group Inc 914 592-1850
250 Clearbrook Rd Ste 245 Elmsford (10523) ***(G-4530)***

Artisan Bags, Childwold *Also called Leather Artisan* ***(G-3499)***
Artisan Custom Interiors, West Hempstead *Also called Artisan Woodworking Ltd* ***(G-16212)***
Artisan Machining Inc 631 589-1416
49 Remington Blvd Ronkonkoma (11779) ***(G-14311)***
Artisan Management Group Inc 716 569-4094
39 Venman St Frewsburg (14738) ***(G-5206)***
Artisan Meats, Canandaigua *Also called Grossglockner Inc* ***(G-3223)***
Artisan Woodworking Ltd 516 486-0818
163 Hempstead Tpke West Hempstead (11552) ***(G-16212)***
Artisanal Brands Inc 914 441-3591
42 Forest Ln Bronxville (10708) ***(G-1423)***
Artistic Frame Corp (PA) 212 289-2100
979 3rd Ave Ste 1705 New York (10022) ***(G-8921)***
Artistic Group, The, New York *Also called Artistic Typography Corp* ***(G-8923)***
Artistic Iron Works Inc 631 665-4285
94 Saxon Ave Ste A Bay Shore (11706) ***(G-659)***
Artistic Products LLC 631 435-0200
345 Oser Ave Hauppauge (11788) ***(G-5771)***
Artistic Ribbon Novelty Co Inc 212 255-4224
22 W 21st St Fl 3 New York (10010) ***(G-8922)***
Artistic Typography Corp (PA) 212 463-8880
151 W 30th St Fl 8 New York (10001) ***(G-8923)***
Artistry In Wood of Syracuse 315 431-4022
6804 Manlius Center Rd # 2 East Syracuse (13057) ***(G-4322)***
Artists, Doo Wop, Deer Park *Also called New Wop Records* ***(G-4015)***
Artkraft Sign, New York *Also called Artkraft Strauss LLC* ***(G-8924)***
Artkraft Strauss LLC 212 265-5155
130 W 57th St Apt 5e New York (10019) ***(G-8924)***
Artnews Ltd (PA) 212 398-1690
110 Greene St Ph 2 New York (10012) ***(G-8925)***
Artnewsletter, New York *Also called Artnews Ltd* ***(G-8925)***
Artone Furniture By Design, Jamestown *Also called Artone LLC* ***(G-6699)***
Artone LLC 716 664-2232
1089 Allen St Jamestown (14701) ***(G-6699)***
Artsaics Studios Inc 631 254-2558
1006 Grand Blvd Deer Park (11729) ***(G-3947)***
Artscroll Printing Corp (PA) 212 929-2413
53 W 23rd St Fl 4 New York (10010) ***(G-8926)***
Artube, Great Neck *Also called Iridium Industries Inc* ***(G-5563)***
Artyarns 914 428-0333
70 Westmoreland Ave White Plains (10606) ***(G-16423)***
Artys Sprnklr Svc Instllation 516 538-4371
234 E Meadow Ave Unit B East Meadow (11554) ***(G-4246)***
Aruba Networks Inc 732 343-1305
556 W 22nd St New York (10011) ***(G-8927)***
Arumai Technologies Inc (PA) 914 217-0038
175 King St Armonk (10504) ***(G-401)***
Arusha Tanzanite, Great Neck *Also called Le Vian Corp* ***(G-5568)***
Aruvil International Inc (PA) 212 447-5020
185 Madison Ave Rm 1701 New York (10016) ***(G-8928)***
Arvos Inc 785 243-3300
3020 Truax Rd Wellsville (14895) ***(G-16112)***
Arvos Inc (HQ) 585 593-2700
3020 Truax Rd Wellsville (14895) ***(G-16113)***
Aryzta LLC 310 417-4700
64 Chester St Rochester (14611) ***(G-13644)***
Aryzta LLC 585 235-8160
235 Buffalo Rd Rochester (14611) ***(G-13645)***
Asa Manufacturing Inc 718 853-3033
3611 14th Ave Brooklyn (11218) ***(G-1560)***
Asahi Shimbun America Inc 212 398-0257
620 8th Ave New York (10018) ***(G-8929)***
ASAP Rack Rental Inc 718 499-4495
33 35th St St5 Brooklyn (11232) ***(G-1561)***
Ascension Industries Inc (PA) 716 693-9381
1254 Erie Ave North Tonawanda (14120) ***(G-12413)***
Ascent Pharmaceuticals Inc (HQ) 631 851-0550
400 S Technology Dr Central Islip (11722) ***(G-3356)***
Asco Castings Inc (PA) 212 719-9800
3100 47th Ave Ste G Long Island City (11101) ***(G-7389)***
Ascribe Inc 585 413-0298
383 Buell Rd Rochester (14624) ***(G-13646)***
Asence Inc 347 335-2606
65 Broadway Fl 7 New York (10006) ***(G-8930)***
Asept Pak Inc 518 651-2026
64 West St Malone (12953) ***(G-7719)***
Ashco Management Inc 212 960-8428
1937 Mcdonald Ave Brooklyn (11223) ***(G-1562)***
Ashko Group LLC 212 594-6050
10 W 33rd St Rm 1019 New York (10001) ***(G-8931)***
Ashland Water Technologies, Brooklyn *Also called Solenis LLC* ***(G-2498)***
Ashland Water Technologies, Liverpool *Also called Solenis LLC* ***(G-7262)***
Ashley Resin Corp 718 851-8111
1171 59th St Brooklyn (11219) ***(G-1563)***
Ashly Audio Inc 585 872-0010
847 Holt Rd Ste 1 Webster (14580) ***(G-16074)***
Ashton-Potter USA Ltd 716 633-2000
10 Curtwright Dr Williamsville (14221) ***(G-16568)***
Asi Sign Systems, New York *Also called Modulex New York Inc* ***(G-10831)***
Asi Sign Systems Inc 646 742-1320
192 Lexington Ave Rm 1002 New York (10016) ***(G-8932)***

Asi Sign Systems Inc ...716 775-0104
2957 Alt Blvd Grand Island (14072) *(G-5495)*
Asian Global Trading Corp ...718 786-0998
3613 36th Ave Ste 2 Long Island City (11106) *(G-7390)*
Asite LLC ...203 545-3089
245 W 29th St Rm 1601 New York (10001) *(G-8933)*
Ask Chemicals Hi-Tech LLC ...607 587-9146
6329 Rte 21 Alfred Station (14803) *(G-185)*
Asm, Central Bridge *Also called American Standard Mfg Inc (G-3353)*
Asm Mechanical Systems, Ridgewood *Also called Aabco Sheet Metal Co Inc (G-13527)*
Asm USA Inc ...212 925-2906
73 Spring St Rm 309 New York (10012) *(G-8934)*
Asn Inc ...718 894-0800
6020 59th Pl Ste 2 Maspeth (11378) *(G-7824)*
Asp Industries Inc ...585 254-9130
9 Evelyn St Rochester (14606) *(G-13647)*
Aspect Printing Inc ...347 789-4284
904 E 51st St Brooklyn (11203) *(G-1564)*
Aspen Research Group Ltd ...212 425-9588
17 State St Fl 15 New York (10004) *(G-8935)*
Aspex Incorporated ...212 966-0410
161 Hudson St Apt 1a New York (10013) *(G-8936)*
Aspire One Communications LLC ...201 281-2998
245 Main St Ste 8 Cornwall (12518) *(G-3830)*
Aspire One Communications Inc ...845 534-6110
246 Main St Cornwall (12518) *(G-3831)*
Assa Abloy Entrance Systems US ...315 492-6600
28 Corporate Cir Ste 1 East Syracuse (13057) *(G-4323)*
Assembly Equipment Division, Rochester *Also called High Speed Hammer Company Inc (G-13869)*
Assessment Technologies Inc ...646 530-8666
1350 Ave Of The Americas New York (10019) *(G-8937)*
Associated Brands Inc ...585 798-3475
4001 Salt Works Rd Medina (14103) *(G-7970)*
Associated Drapery & Equipment ...516 671-5245
3 Kosnitz Dr Unit 111 Monroe (10950) *(G-8263)*
Associated Lightning Rod Co ...845 373-8309
6020 Route 22 Millerton (12546) *(G-8192)*
Associated Publishing Co, Buffalo *Also called Mac Innes Enterprises Inc (G-2931)*
Associated Publishing Company (HQ) ...325 676-4032
61 John Muir Dr Buffalo (14228) *(G-2710)*
Association For Cmpt McHy Inc (PA) ...212 869-7440
2 Penn Plz Rm 701 New York (10121) *(G-8938)*
Assouline Publishing Inc (PA) ...212 989-6769
3 Park Ave Fl 27 New York (10016) *(G-8939)*
Aston Leather Inc ...212 481-2760
153 W 27th St Ste 406 New York (10001) *(G-8940)*
Astor-Honor Division, New York *Also called Beauty Fashion Inc (G-9032)*
Astra Products Inc ...631 464-4747
6 Bethpage Rd Copiague (11726) *(G-3753)*
Astra Tool & Instrument Mfg ...914 747-3863
369 Bradhurst Ave Hawthorne (10532) *(G-5983)*
Astro Chemical Company Inc ...518 399-5338
3 Mill Rd Ballston Lake (12019) *(G-565)*
Astro Electroplating Inc ...631 968-0656
171 4th Ave Bay Shore (11706) *(G-660)*
Astro Label & Tag Ltd ...718 435-4474
5820 Fort Hamilton Pkwy Brooklyn (11219) *(G-1565)*
Astrodyne Inc ...516 536-5755
18 Neil Ct Oceanside (11572) *(G-12532)*
Astron Candle Manufacturing Co ...718 728-3330
1125 30th Ave Long Island City (11102) *(G-7391)*
Astronics Corporation (PA) ...716 805-1599
130 Commerce Way East Aurora (14052) *(G-4194)*
Astucci US Ltd ...718 752-9700
4369 9th St Long Island City (11101) *(G-7392)*
Astucci US Ltd (PA) ...212 725-3171
385 5th Ave Rm 1100 New York (10016) *(G-8941)*
Asur Jewelry Inc ...718 472-1687
4709 30th St Ste 403 Long Island City (11101) *(G-7393)*
At Copy Inc ...718 624-6136
25 Flatbush Ave Brooklyn (11217) *(G-1566)*
AT&T Corp ...212 317-7048
767 5th Ave Fl 12a New York (10153) *(G-8942)*
Atalla Handbags Inc ...718 965-5500
559 79th St Brooklyn (11209) *(G-1567)*
Atc, Huntington Station *Also called American Tchncal Ceramics Corp (G-6430)*
Atc Plastics LLC ...212 375-2515
555 Madison Ave Fl 5 New York (10022) *(G-8943)*
Atco EZ Dock, Auburn *Also called Auburn Tank & Manufacturing Co (G-466)*
Atd Precision Machining, Rochester *Also called Allstate Tool and Die Inc (G-13618)*
Atech-Seh Metal Fabricator ...716 895-8888
330 Greene St Buffalo (14206) *(G-2711)*
Ateco Products, Bay Shore *Also called Sumner Industries Inc (G-729)*
Atelier Viollet Corp ...718 782-1727
505 Driggs Ave Brooklyn (11211) *(G-1568)*
Ateliers Tamalet Corp ...929 325-7976
349 5th Ave New York (10016) *(G-8944)*
Ateres Book Binding, Brooklyn *Also called Ateres Publishing & Bk Bindery (G-1569)*
Ateres Publishing & Bk Bindery ...718 935-9355
845 Bedford Ave Brooklyn (11205) *(G-1569)*
Ateret LLC ...212 819-0777
22 W 48th St New York (10036) *(G-8945)*
Aterian Investment Partners LP (PA) ...212 547-2806
11 E 44th St Rm 1803 New York (10017) *(G-8946)*
Aterra Exploration LLC ...212 315-0030
230 W 56th St Apt 53d New York (10019) *(G-8947)*
Athalon Sportgear Inc ...212 268-8070
10 W 33rd St Rm 1012 New York (10001) *(G-8948)*
Athenex Inc (PA) ...716 427-2950
1001 Main St Ste 600 Buffalo (14203) *(G-2712)*
Athenex Pharma Solutions LLC ...877 463-7823
11342 Main St Clarence (14031) *(G-3525)*
Athenex Pharmaceutical Div LLC (PA) ...877 463-7823
1001 Main St Ste 600 Buffalo (14203) *(G-2713)*
Athletic Cap Co Inc ...718 398-1300
123 Fields Ave Staten Island (10314) *(G-15045)*
Athlon Spt Communications Inc ...212 478-1910
60 E 42nd St Ste 820 New York (10165) *(G-8949)*
ATI, Brooklyn *Also called Anne Taintor Inc (G-1536)*
ATI Specialty Materials, Lockport *Also called Tdy Industries LLC (G-7334)*
ATI Trading Inc ...718 888-7918
13631 41st Ave Ste 5a Flushing (11355) *(G-4987)*
Atis Colojet, Ronkonkoma *Also called Maharlika Holdings LLC (G-14373)*
Atk Gasl Inc ...631 737-6100
77 Raynor Ave Ronkonkoma (11779) *(G-14312)*
Atlantic Business Products, New York *Also called Facsimile Cmmncations Inds Inc (G-9770)*
Atlantic Color Corp ...631 345-3800
14 Ramsey Rd Shirley (11967) *(G-14829)*
Atlantic Electronic Tech LLC ...800 296-2177
285 5th Ave Apt 2b Brooklyn (11215) *(G-1570)*
Atlantic Electronic Technology, Brooklyn *Also called Atlantic Electronic Tech LLC (G-1570)*
Atlantic Engineer Products LLC ...518 822-1800
239 State Route 23b Hudson (12534) *(G-6341)*
Atlantic Er Inc ...516 294-3200
180 Atlantic Ave New Hyde Park (11040) *(G-8518)*
Atlantic Essential Pdts Inc ...631 434-8333
7 Oser Ave Ste 1 Hauppauge (11788) *(G-5772)*
Atlantic Farm & Food Inc ...718 441-3152
11415 Atlantic Ave Richmond Hill (11418) *(G-13496)*
Atlantic Industrial Tech Inc ...631 234-3131
90 Precision Dr Shirley (11967) *(G-14830)*
Atlantic Monthly Group Inc ...202 266-7000
60 Madison Ave New York (10010) *(G-8950)*
Atlantic Pork & Provisions Inc ...718 272-9550
14707 94th Ave Jamaica (11435) *(G-6626)*
Atlantic Precious Metal Cast ...718 937-7100
4132 27th St Long Island City (11101) *(G-7394)*
Atlantic Projects Company Inc ...518 878-2065
5 Southside Dr Ste 11s Clifton Park (12065) *(G-3564)*
Atlantic Recording Corp (HQ) ...212 707-2000
1633 Broadway Lowr 2c1 New York (10019) *(G-8951)*
Atlantic Records, New York *Also called Atlantic Recording Corp (G-8951)*
Atlantic Specialty Co Inc ...845 356-2502
20 Jeffrey Pl Monsey (10952) *(G-8286)*
Atlantic Stairs Corp ...718 417-8818
284a Meserole St Brooklyn (11206) *(G-1571)*
Atlantic States Distributing ...518 427-6364
1325 Broadway Menands (12204) *(G-8082)*
Atlantic States Kitchens Baths, Menands *Also called Atlantic States Distributing (G-8082)*
Atlantic Transformer Inc ...716 795-3258
1674 Quaker Rd Barker (14012) *(G-599)*
Atlantic Trophy Co Inc ...212 684-6020
866 Avenue Of The America New York (10001) *(G-8952)*
Atlantic Ultraviolet Corp ...631 234-3275
375 Marcus Blvd Hauppauge (11788) *(G-5773)*
Atlantic, The, New York *Also called Atlantic Monthly Group Inc (G-8950)*
Atlantis Energy Systems Inc (PA) ...845 486-4052
7 Industry St Poughkeepsie (12603) *(G-13328)*
Atlantis Energy Systems Inc (PA) ...916 438-2930
7 Industry St Poughkeepsie (12603) *(G-13329)*
Atlantis Equipment Corporation ...518 733-5910
16941 Ny 22 Stephentown (12168) *(G-15154)*
Atlantis Solar and Wind, Potsdam *Also called Atlantis Solar Inc (G-13317)*
Atlantis Solar Inc ...916 226-9183
2302 River Rd Potsdam (13676) *(G-13317)*
Atlas & Company LLC ...212 234-3100
355 Lexington Ave Fl 6 New York (10017) *(G-8953)*
Atlas Bituminous Co Inc ...315 457-2394
173 Farrell Rd Syracuse (13209) *(G-15248)*
Atlas Coatings Corp ...718 402-2000
820 E 140th St Bronx (10454) *(G-1222)*
Atlas Coatings Group Corp (PA) ...718 469-8787
4808 Farragut Rd Brooklyn (11203) *(G-1572)*
Atlas Concrete Batching Corp ...718 523-3000
9511 147th Pl Jamaica (11435) *(G-6627)*
Atlas Copco Comptec LLC (HQ) ...518 765-3344
46 School Rd Voorheesville (12186) *(G-15879)*
Atlas Fence & Railing Co Inc ...718 767-2200
15149 7th Ave Whitestone (11357) *(G-16535)*
Atlas Fence Co, Whitestone *Also called Atlas Fence & Railing Co Inc (G-16535)*
Atlas Industries, Newburgh *Also called Consolidated Spring LLC (G-12219)*

ALPHABETIC

(PA)=Parent Co (HQ)=Headquarters (DH)=Div Headquarters
2019 Harris
New York Manufacturers Directory
831

Atlas Metal Industries Inc ALPHABETIC SECTION

Atlas Metal Industries Inc ...607 776-2048
17 Wheeler Ave Hammondsport (14840) **(G-5702)**
Atlas Music Publishing LLC (PA) ...646 502-5170
6 E 39th St Ste 1104 New York (10016) **(G-8954)**
Atlas Print Solutions Inc ...212 949-8775
589 8th Ave Fl 4 New York (10018) **(G-8955)**
Atlas Recycling LLC ...212 925-3280
25 Howard St Fl 2 New York (10013) **(G-8956)**
Atlas Switch Co Inc ...516 222-6280
969 Stewart Ave Garden City (11530) **(G-5251)**
Atlas Transit Mix Corp ...718 523-3000
9511 147th Pl Jamaica (11435) **(G-6628)**
Atlaz International Ltd ...516 239-1854
298 Lawrence Ave Unit 1 Lawrence (11559) **(G-7102)**
Atmost Refrigeration Co Inc (PA) ...518 828-2180
793 Route 66 Hudson (12534) **(G-6342)**
Atomic Information Systems ...716 713-5402
1580 State Highway 357 Unadilla (13849) **(G-15661)**
Atomicdbonline.com, Unadilla *Also called Atomic Information Systems* **(G-15661)**
Atr Jewelry Inc ...212 819-0075
71 W 47th St Ste 402 New York (10036) **(G-8957)**
Ats, Mahopac *Also called Advanced Tchncal Solutions Inc* **(G-7707)**
Attends Healthcare Inc ...212 338-5100
200 Park Ave New York (10166) **(G-8958)**
Attias Oven Corp ...718 499-0145
926 3rd Ave Brooklyn (11232) **(G-1573)**
Attica Millwork Inc ...585 591-2333
71 Market St Attica (14011) **(G-458)**
Attica Package Company Inc ...585 591-0510
45 Windsor St Attica (14011) **(G-459)**
Attitudes Footwear Inc ...212 754-9113
1040 1st Ave Ste 232 New York (10022) **(G-8959)**
ATW Group, New York *Also called Great Universal Corp* **(G-9982)**
Atwater Estate Vineyards LLC ...607 546-8463
5055 State Route 414 Burdett (14818) **(G-3140)**
Atwater Foods, Lyndonville *Also called Shoreline Fruit LLC* **(G-7681)**
Atwood Tool & Machine Inc ...607 648-6543
39 Kattelville Rd Chenango Bridge (13745) **(G-3465)**
Auburn Armature, East Syracuse *Also called Power-Flo Technologies Inc* **(G-4362)**
Auburn Armature, Rochester *Also called Power-Flo Technologies Inc* **(G-14029)**
Auburn Bearing & Mfg Inc ...315 986-7600
4 State Route 350 Macedon (14502) **(G-7694)**
Auburn Custom Millwork Inc ...315 253-3843
4022 Technology Park Blvd Auburn (13021) **(G-463)**
Auburn Foundry Inc ...315 253-4441
15 Wadsworth St Auburn (13021) **(G-464)**
Auburn Leathercrafters, Auburn *Also called Finger Lakes Lea Crafters LLC* **(G-478)**
Auburn Publishing Co ...315 253-5311
25 Dill St Auburn (13021) **(G-465)**
Auburn Tank & Manufacturing Co ...315 255-2788
24 Mcmaster St Auburn (13021) **(G-466)**
Auburn Vacuum Forming Co Inc ...315 253-2440
40 York St Auburn (13021) **(G-467)**
Auburn-Watson Corp (PA) ...716 876-8000
3295 Walden Ave Depew (14043) **(G-4079)**
Aucapina Cabinets Inc ...718 609-9054
5737 57th Dr Maspeth (11378) **(G-7825)**
Audible Difference Inc ...212 662-4848
110 8th St Brooklyn (11215) **(G-1574)**
Audible Difference Inc (PA) ...212 662-4848
110 8th St Brooklyn (11215) **(G-1575)**
Audible Difference Lnc, Brooklyn *Also called Audible Difference Inc* **(G-1575)**
Audio Technology New York Inc ...718 369-7528
129 31st St Brooklyn (11232) **(G-1576)**
Audio Video Invasion Inc ...516 345-2636
53 Werman Ct Plainview (11803) **(G-13037)**
Audio-Sears Corp ...607 652-7305
2 South St Stamford (12167) **(G-15029)**
Audiology, Brooklyn *Also called Audio Technology New York Inc* **(G-1576)**
Audiosavings Inc ...888 445-1555
600 Bayview Ave Ste 200 Inwood (11096) **(G-6486)**
Audubon Machinery Corporation (PA) ...716 564-5165
814 Wurlitzer Dr North Tonawanda (14120) **(G-12414)**
Aufhauser Corp Canada, Plainview *Also called Aufhauser Manufacturing Corp* **(G-13039)**
Aufhauser Corporation (PA) ...516 694-8696
39 West Mall Plainview (11803) **(G-13038)**
Aufhauser Manufacturing Corp ...516 694-8696
39 West Mall Plainview (11803) **(G-13039)**
Augury Inc ...866 432-0976
263 W 38th St Fl 16 New York (10018) **(G-8960)**
August Graphics, Bronx *Also called D B F Associates* **(G-1250)**
August Silk Inc (PA) ...212 643-2400
499 7th Ave Fl 5s New York (10018) **(G-8961)**
August Silk Inc ...212 643-2400
499 7th Ave Fl 5s New York (10018) **(G-8962)**
August Studios ...718 706-6487
4008 22nd St Fl 3 Long Island City (11101) **(G-7395)**
August Thomsen Corp ...516 676-7100
36 Sea Cliff Ave Glen Cove (11542) **(G-5361)**
Augusta Studios, Long Island City *Also called August Studios* **(G-7395)**
Aura Detergent LLC (PA) ...718 824-2162
1746 Crosby Ave Bronx (10461) **(G-1223)**
Aura Essence, Brooklyn *Also called Candle In The Window Inc* **(G-1672)**
Aurafin Oroamerica, New York *Also called Richline Group Inc* **(G-11390)**
Auraspace Inc ...212 905-6100
41 E 11th St Fl 6 New York (10003) **(G-8963)**
Auratic Inc ...914 413-8154
41 Madison Ave Ste 1402 New York (10010) **(G-8964)**
Aureonic ...518 791-9331
13 Whispering Pines Rd Gansevoort (12831) **(G-5242)**
Aurora Indus Machining Inc ...716 826-7911
3380 N Benzing Rd Orchard Park (14127) **(G-12699)**
Aurora Machine, Rochester *Also called Alkemy Machine LLC* **(G-13613)**
Aurora Sef, Peekskill *Also called RMS Packaging Inc* **(G-12924)**
Aurora Shoe Company, King Ferry *Also called Lake View Manufacturing LLC* **(G-6881)**
Aurora Stone Group LLC ...315 471-6869
114 Marcy St East Syracuse (13057) **(G-4324)**
Aurora Technical Services Ltd ...716 652-1463
11970 Parker Rd East Aurora (14052) **(G-4195)**
Aurubis Buffalo Inc ...716 879-6700
600 Military Rd Buffalo (14207) **(G-2714)**
Aurubis Buffalo Inc (HQ) ...716 879-6700
70 Sayre St Buffalo (14207) **(G-2715)**
Ausco Inc ...516 944-9882
425 Smith St Ste 1 Farmingdale (11735) **(G-4723)**
Austin Air Systems Limited ...716 856-3700
500 Elk St Buffalo (14210) **(G-2716)**
Austin Industries Inc (PA) ...585 589-1353
3871 Oak Orchard Rd Albion (14411) **(G-155)**
Austin Mohawk and Company LLC ...315 793-3000
2175 Beechgrove Pl Utica (13501) **(G-15678)**
Austin Nichols & Co Inc (HQ) ...519 561-5225
250 Park Ave New York (10177) **(G-8965)**
Autel North America, Farmingdale *Also called Autel US Inc* **(G-4724)**
Autel US Inc (HQ) ...631 923-2620
175 Central Ave Ste 200 Farmingdale (11735) **(G-4724)**
Auterra Inc ...518 382-9600
2135 Technology Dr Schenectady (12308) **(G-14650)**
Authentic Brands Group LLC (PA) ...212 760-2410
1411 Broadway Fl 4 New York (10018) **(G-8966)**
Authentic Parts, Holbrook *Also called Ingham Industries Inc* **(G-6189)**
Authority On Transportation, Dix Hills *Also called Authority Transportation Inc* **(G-4120)**
Authority Transportation Inc ...888 933-1268
167 Oakfield Ave Dix Hills (11746) **(G-4120)**
Auto Body Services LLC ...631 431-4640
400 W Hoffman Ave Lindenhurst (11757) **(G-7162)**
Auto Data Labels, Deer Park *Also called Auto Data Systems Inc* **(G-3948)**
Auto Data Systems Inc (PA) ...631 667-2382
44 W Jefryn Blvd Ste K Deer Park (11729) **(G-3948)**
Auto Market Publications Inc ...631 667-0500
1641 Deer Park Ave Ste 5 Deer Park (11729) **(G-3949)**
Auto Sport Designs Inc ...631 425-1555
203 W Hills Rd Huntington Station (11746) **(G-6433)**
Auto-Mat Company Inc ...516 938-7373
69 Hazel St Hicksville (11801) **(G-6062)**
Auto-Mate Technologies LLC ...631 727-8886
34 Hinda Blvd Riverhead (11901) **(G-13564)**
Autodyne Manufacturing Co Inc ...631 957-5858
200 N Strong Ave Lindenhurst (11757) **(G-7163)**
Automated & MGT Solutions LLC ...518 833-0315
743 Columbia Tpke East Greenbush (12061) **(G-4227)**
Automated Biomass Systems LLC ...607 849-7800
2235 Clarks Corners Rd Marathon (13803) **(G-7788)**
Automated Bldg MGT Systems Inc (PA) ...516 216-5603
54 Cherry Ln Floral Park (11001) **(G-4956)**
Automated Building Controls ...914 381-2860
629 N Barry Ave Mamaroneck (10543) **(G-7734)**
Automated Cells & Eqp Inc ...607 936-1341
9699 Enterprise Dr Painted Post (14870) **(G-12835)**
Automated Control Logic Inc ...914 769-8880
578 Commerce St Thornwood (10594) **(G-15501)**
Automated Dynamics, Niskayuna *Also called ADC Acquisition Company* **(G-12352)**
Automated Elevator Systems ...845 595-1063
659 Jersey Ave Greenwood Lake (10925) **(G-5647)**
Automated Office Systems Inc ...516 396-5555
71 S Central Ave Valley Stream (11580) **(G-15773)**
Automated Systems Group, Rochester *Also called Micro Instrument Corp* **(G-13939)**
Automatic Bar Machining Co, Webster *Also called Kathleen B Mead* **(G-16089)**
Automatic Connector Inc ...631 543-5000
375 Oser Ave Hauppauge (11788) **(G-5774)**
Automation Correct LLC ...315 299-3589
405 Parrish Ln Syracuse (13205) **(G-15249)**
Automation Evolution LLC ...585 241-6010
800 Salt Rd Webster (14580) **(G-16075)**
Automation Papers Inc ...315 432-0565
6361 Thompson Rd Stop 1 Syracuse (13206) **(G-15250)**
Automation Source Technologies (PA) ...631 643-1678
21 Otis St Unit B West Babylon (11704) **(G-16136)**
Automationcorrect.com, Syracuse *Also called Automation Correct LLC* **(G-15249)**
Automecha International Ltd (PA) ...607 843-2235
48 S Canal St Oxford (13830) **(G-12807)**

Automotion Parking Systems LLC 516 565-5600
411 Hempstead Tpke # 200 West Hempstead (11552) *(G-16213)*
Automotive LLC 248 728-8642
4320 Federal Dr Batavia (14020) *(G-611)*
Automotive Accessories Group 212 736-8100
505 8th Ave Rm 12a05 New York (10018) *(G-8967)*
Automotive Leather Group LLC 516 627-4000
17 Barstow Rd Ste 206 Great Neck (11021) *(G-5537)*
Automtive Uphl Cnvertible Tops 914 961-4242
170 Marbledale Rd Tuckahoe (10707) *(G-15642)*
Autostat Corporation 516 379-9447
209 Nassau Rd 11 Roosevelt (11575) *(G-14434)*
Autronic Plastics Inc 516 333-7577
1150 Motor Pkwy Central Islip (11722) *(G-3357)*
Auven Therapeutics MGT LP 212 616-4000
1325 Avenue Of The Americ New York (10019) *(G-8968)*
AV Therapeutics Inc 917 497-5523
20 E 68th St Ste 204 New York (10065) *(G-8969)*
Avalanche Fabrication Inc 585 545-4000
6314 Dean Pkwy Ontario (14519) *(G-12648)*
Avalanche Studios New York Inc 212 993-6447
536 Broadway New York (10012) *(G-8970)*
Avalin LLC 212 842-2286
221 W 37th St Fl 3 New York (10018) *(G-8971)*
Avalon Copy Centers Amer Inc (PA) 315 471-3333
901 N State St Syracuse (13208) *(G-15251)*
Avalon Copy Centers Amer Inc 716 995-7777
741 Main St Buffalo (14203) *(G-2717)*
Avalon Document Services, Syracuse *Also called Avalon Copy Centers Amer Inc (G-15251)*
Avalon Document Services, Buffalo *Also called Avalon Copy Centers Amer Inc (G-2717)*
Avalonbay Communities Inc 516 484-7766
1100 Avalon Sq Glen Cove (11542) *(G-5362)*
Avanel Industries Inc 516 333-0990
121 Hopper St Westbury (11590) *(G-16318)*
Avant Garde Screen Printing Co, Flushing *Also called Albert Siy (G-4982)*
Avante 516 782-4888
35 Hicks Ln Great Neck (11024) *(G-5538)*
Avanti Advanced Mfg Corp 716 791-9001
673 Ontario St Buffalo (14207) *(G-2718)*
Avanti Control Systems Inc 518 921-4368
1 Hamilton St Fl 2 Gloversville (12078) *(G-5452)*
Avanti Furniture Corp 516 293-8220
497 Main St Farmingdale (11735) *(G-4725)*
Avanti Press Inc 212 414-1025
6 W 18th St Ste 6l New York (10011) *(G-8972)*
Avanti U S A Ltd 716 695-5800
412 Young St Tonawanda (14150) *(G-15524)*
Avaya Services Inc 866 462-8292
2 Penn Plz Rm 702 New York (10121) *(G-8973)*
Avco Industries Inc 631 851-1555
120 Windsor Pl Central Islip (11722) *(G-3358)*
Avcom of Virginia Inc 585 924-4560
590 Fishers Station Dr Victor (14564) *(G-15830)*
Aventura Technologies Inc (PA) 631 300-4000
48 Mall Dr Commack (11725) *(G-3680)*
Avenue Magazine, New York *Also called Manhattan Media LLC (G-10686)*
Avenue Mosaic Company (PA) 216 245-6306
307 W 38th St Unit Ph-21 New York (10018) *(G-8974)*
Avenue Therapeutics Inc 781 652-4500
2 Gansevoort St Fl 9 New York (10014) *(G-8975)*
Avery Biomedical Devices Inc 631 864-1600
61 Mall Dr Ste 1 Commack (11725) *(G-3681)*
Avery Dennison Corporation 626 304-2000
218 W 40th St Fl 8 New York (10018) *(G-8976)*
Avf Group Inc (HQ) 951 360-7111
2775 Broadway St Ste 200 Cheektowaga (14227) *(G-3435)*
AVI, Plainview *Also called Audio Video Invasion Inc (G-13037)*
AVI-Spl Employee 212 840-4801
8 W 38th St Rm 1101 New York (10018) *(G-8977)*
Avid Technology Inc 212 983-2424
90 Park Ave New York (10016) *(G-8978)*
Avitto Leather Goods Inc 212 219-7501
424 W Broadway Frnt A New York (10012) *(G-8979)*
Avm Printing Inc 631 351-1331
43 Corporate Dr Hauppauge (11788) *(G-5775)*
AVM Software Inc (HQ) 646 381-2468
122 E 42nd St Rm 2600 New York (10168) *(G-8980)*
Avon Press, Hauppauge *Also called Avon Reproductions Inc (G-5776)*
Avon Reproductions Inc 631 273-2400
175 Engineers Rd Hauppauge (11788) *(G-5776)*
Avr Optics, Rochester *Also called Avro Inc (G-13648)*
Avro Inc 585 445-7588
3635 Buffalo Rd Ste 2 Rochester (14624) *(G-13648)*
Avs Gem Stone Corp 212 944-6380
48 W 48th St Ste 1010 New York (10036) *(G-8981)*
AVS Laminates Inc 631 286-2136
99 Bellport Ave Bellport (11713) *(G-799)*
Avstar Fuel Systems Inc 315 255-1955
15 Brookfield Pl Auburn (13021) *(G-468)*
AVX Corporation 716 372-6611
1695 Seneca Ave Olean (14760) *(G-12592)*
AW Mack Manufacturing Co Inc 845 452-4050
1098 Dutchess Tpke Poughkeepsie (12603) *(G-13330)*
Award Publishing Limited 212 246-0405
40 W 55th St Apt 9b New York (10019) *(G-8982)*
Awning Man, The, Yonkers *Also called Fabric Concepts For Industry (G-16757)*
Awning Mart Inc 315 699-5928
5665 State Route 31 Cicero (13039) *(G-3514)*
Awr Energy Inc 585 469-7750
35 Melody Ln Plattsburgh (12901) *(G-13107)*
Awt Supply Corp 516 437-9105
153 Meacham Ave Elmont (11003) *(G-4517)*
Axim Biotechnologies Inc 212 751-0001
5 Rockefeller Plz Fl 20 Flr 20 New York (10111) *(G-8983)*
Axis Denim, New York *Also called Axis Na LLC (G-8984)*
Axis Na LLC (PA) 212 840-4005
70 W 40th St Fl 11 New York (10018) *(G-8984)*
Axle Express 518 347-2220
729 Broadway Schenectady (12305) *(G-14651)*
Axle Teknology LLC (PA) 631 423-3044
226 New York Ave Ste 301 Huntington (11743) *(G-6393)*
Axtell Bradtke Lumber Co 607 265-3850
113 Beals Pond Rd Masonville (13804) *(G-7814)*
Aycan Medical Systems LLC 585 271-3078
693 East Ave Ste 102 Rochester (14607) *(G-13649)*
AZ Yashir Bapaz Inc 212 947-7357
134 W 37th St New York (10018) *(G-8985)*
Az-Light Inc 716 837-5533
3349 Sheridan Dr Buffalo (14226) *(G-2719)*
Azibi Ltd 212 869-6550
270 W 39th St Rm 1501 New York (10018) *(G-8986)*
Aztec Industries Inc 631 585-1331
200 13th Ave Unit 5 Ronkonkoma (11779) *(G-14313)*
Aztec Mfg of Rochester 585 352-8152
19 Hickory Ln Spencerport (14559) *(G-14975)*
Aztec Tool Co Inc 631 243-1144
180 Rodeo Dr Edgewood (11717) *(G-4396)*
Azurrx Biopharma Inc 646 699-7855
760 Parkside Ave Ste 304 Brooklyn (11226) *(G-1577)*
B & B Forest Products Ltd 518 622-0811
251 Route 145 Cairo (12413) *(G-3146)*
B & B Jewelry Mfg Co, New York *Also called Barber Brothers Jewelry Mfg (G-9013)*
B & B Lumber Company Inc (PA) 866 282-0582
4800 Solvay Rd Jamesville (13078) *(G-6763)*
B & B Precision Components Inc 631 273-3321
301 Christopher St # 303 Ronkonkoma (11779) *(G-14314)*
B & B Precision Mfg Inc (PA) 585 226-6226
310 W Main St Avon (14414) *(G-517)*
B & B Sheet Metal Inc 718 433-2501
2540 50th Ave Long Island City (11101) *(G-7396)*
B & B Sweater Mills Inc (PA) 718 456-8693
1160 Flushing Ave Brooklyn (11237) *(G-1578)*
B & D Enterprises of Utica (PA) 315 735-3311
2 Campion Rd Ste 7 New Hartford (13413) *(G-8501)*
B & F Architectural Support Gr 212 279-6488
450 7th Ave Ste 307 New York (10123) *(G-8987)*
B & H Electronics Corp 845 782-5000
308 Museum Village Rd Monroe (10950) *(G-8264)*
B & H Precision Fabricators 631 563-9620
95 Davinci Dr Bohemia (11716) *(G-984)*
B & J Lumber Co Inc 518 677-3845
1075 State Route 22 Cambridge (12816) *(G-3177)*
B & K Components Ltd 323 776-4277
2100 Old Union Rd Buffalo (14227) *(G-2720)*
B & K Dye Cutting Inc 718 497-5216
245 Varet St Brooklyn (11206) *(G-1579)*
B & P Jays Inc 716 668-8408
19 N Hill Dr Buffalo (14224) *(G-2721)*
B & R Industries Inc 631 736-2275
12 Commercial Blvd Medford (11763) *(G-7938)*
B & R Promotional Products 212 563-0040
34 W 120th St Apt 1 New York (10027) *(G-8988)*
B & R Sheet 718 558-5544
10652 157th St Jamaica (11433) *(G-6629)*
B & R Tool Inc 718 948-2729
955 Rensselaer Ave Staten Island (10309) *(G-15046)*
B & W Heat Treating Company 716 876-8184
2780 Kenmore Ave Tonawanda (14150) *(G-15525)*
B & Z Technologies LLC 631 675-9666
7 Technology Dr East Setauket (11733) *(G-4298)*
B C America, New York *Also called Intertex USA Inc (G-10253)*
B C Manufacturing Inc 585 482-1080
100 Thruway Park Dr West Henrietta (14586) *(G-16231)*
B C T, Holbrook *Also called Speedcard Inc (G-6210)*
B D B Typewriter Supply Works 718 232-4800
6215 14th Ave Brooklyn (11219) *(G-1580)*
B F G Elcpltg and Mfg Co 716 362-0888
3949 Jeffrey Blvd Blasdell (14219) *(G-924)*
B H Aircraft Company Inc (PA) 631 580-9747
2230 Smithtown Ave Ronkonkoma (11779) *(G-14315)*
B H M Metal Products Co 845 292-5297
Horseshoe Lake Rd Kauneonga Lake (12749) *(G-6849)*
B J Long Co, Rochester *Also called R V Dow Enterprises Inc (G-14067)*

ALPHABETIC

B K Integrity, New York *Also called Golden Integrity Inc* ***(G-9955)***
B K Jewelry Contractor Inc....212 398-9093
71 W 47th St Fl 11 New York (10036) ***(G-8989)***
B M P, Medina *Also called Bmp America Inc* ***(G-7973)***
B M Printing, Brooklyn *Also called Bestmade Printing LLC* ***(G-1605)***
B P I, West Henrietta *Also called Brinkman Precision Inc* ***(G-16233)***
B P Nash Co Inc....315 445-1310
5841 Butternut Dr East Syracuse (13057) ***(G-4325)***
B Q P Inc....518 793-4999
6 Collins Dr Queensbury (12804) ***(G-13420)***
B S C, Binghamton *Also called Binghamton Simulator Co Inc* ***(G-868)***
B S J Limited....212 764-4600
1400 Broadway Ste 1702 New York (10018) ***(G-8990)***
B S J Limited (PA)....212 221-8403
1375 Broadway Rm 507 New York (10018) ***(G-8991)***
B Smith Furs Inc....212 967-5290
224 W 30th St Rm 402 New York (10001) ***(G-8992)***
B Tween LLC....212 819-9040
1412 Broadway Rm 1400 New York (10018) ***(G-8993)***
B V M Associates....631 254-6220
999-32 Montrell 414 Shirley (11967) ***(G-14831)***
B&B Albany Pallet Company LLC....315 492-1786
4800 Solvay Rd Jamesville (13078) ***(G-6764)***
B&K Precision Corporation....631 369-2665
31 Oakwood Dr Manorville (11949) ***(G-7782)***
B-Reel Films Inc....917 388-3836
401 Broadway Fl 24 New York (10013) ***(G-8994)***
B/E Aerospace Inc....631 563-6400
355 Knickerbocker Ave Bohemia (11716) ***(G-985)***
B/E Aerospace Inc....631 589-0877
355 Knickerbocker Ave Bohemia (11716) ***(G-986)***
B2b Cleaning Services, Yonkers *Also called Rumsey Corp* ***(G-16797)***
B3cg Interconnect Usa Inc....450 491-4040
18 Northern Ave 100 Plattsburgh (12903) ***(G-13108)***
B601 V2 Inc....646 391-6431
315 5th Ave Rm 903 New York (10016) ***(G-8995)***
Ba Sports Nutrition LLC....718 357-7402
1720 Whitestone Expy # 101 Whitestone (11357) ***(G-16536)***
Baar & Beards, New York *Also called Gce International Inc* ***(G-9891)***
Babbit Bearings, Syracuse *Also called Babbitt Bearings Inc* ***(G-15252)***
Babbitt Bearings Inc (PA)....315 479-6603
734 Burnet Ave Syracuse (13203) ***(G-15252)***
Babbitt Bearings Incorporated....315 479-6603
734 Burnet Ave Syracuse (13203) ***(G-15253)***
Babcock Co Inc....607 776-3341
36 Delaware Ave Bath (14810) ***(G-640)***
Babula Construction Inc....716 681-0886
5136 William St Lancaster (14086) ***(G-7009)***
Baby Central LLC....718 372-2229
2436 Mcdonald Ave Brooklyn (11223) ***(G-1581)***
Baby Signature Inc (PA)....212 686-1700
251 5th Ave Fl 2l New York (10016) ***(G-8996)***
Baby Uv/Kids Uv Inc (PA)....917 301-9020
11 Hawks Nest Rd Stony Brook (11790) ***(G-15163)***
Babydoll, New York *Also called Mag Brands LLC* ***(G-10660)***
Babyfair Inc....212 736-7989
34 W 33rd St Rm 818 New York (10001) ***(G-8997)***
Babyganics, Westbury *Also called Kas Direct LLC* ***(G-16347)***
Babylon Iron Works Inc....631 643-3311
205 Edison Ave West Babylon (11704) ***(G-16137)***
Babysafe Usa LLC....877 367-4141
251 County Road 17 Afton (13730) ***(G-7)***
Backstage LLC (PA)....212 493-4243
45 Main St Ste 416 Brooklyn (11201) ***(G-1582)***
Backtech Inc....973 279-0838
2 Peter Cooper Rd Apt Mf New York (10010) ***(G-8998)***
Baco Controls Inc (PA)....315 635-2500
8431 Loop Rd Baldwinsville (13027) ***(G-551)***
Baco Enterprises Inc (PA)....718 589-6225
1190 Longwood Ave Bronx (10474) ***(G-1224)***
Bactolac Pharmaceutical Inc....631 951-4908
7 Oser Ave Ste 1 Hauppauge (11788) ***(G-5777)***
Bader Enterprise Inc....718 965-9434
115 27th St Brooklyn (11232) ***(G-1583)***
Badge Machine Products Inc....585 394-0330
2491 Brickyard Rd Canandaigua (14424) ***(G-3211)***
Badger Technologies Inc....585 869-7101
5829 County Road 41 Farmington (14425) ***(G-4909)***
Badger Technologies Inc (PA)....585 869-7101
5829 County Road 41 Farmington (14425) ***(G-4910)***
Badgley Mischka Licensing LLC....212 921-1585
550 7th Ave Fl 22 New York (10018) ***(G-8999)***
Bae Systems Controls Inc (HQ)....607 770-2000
1098 Clark St Endicott (13760) ***(G-4583)***
Bae Systems Info & Elec Sys....631 912-1525
450 Pulaski Rd Greenlawn (11740) ***(G-5621)***
Bae Systems PLC....631 261-7000
1 Hazeltine Way Greenlawn (11740) ***(G-5622)***
Bag Arts Ltd....212 684-7020
20 W 36th St Rm 5r New York (10018) ***(G-9000)***
Bag Arts The Art Packaging LLC....212 684-7020
20 W 36th St Fl 5 New York (10018) ***(G-9001)***
Bag Bazaar Ltd....212 689-3508
1 E 33rd St Fl 6 New York (10016) ***(G-9002)***
Bagel Club, Bayside *Also called A T A Bagel Shoppe Inc* ***(G-741)***
Bagel Club Inc....718 423-6106
20521 35th Ave Bayside (11361) ***(G-743)***
Bagel Grove Inc....315 724-8015
7 Burrstone Rd Utica (13502) ***(G-15679)***
Bagel Land....585 442-3080
1896 Monroe Ave Rochester (14618) ***(G-13650)***
Bagel Oasis, Flushing *Also called Triboro Bagel Co Inc* ***(G-5055)***
Bagel Shoppe, The, Fishkill *Also called Enterprise Bagels Inc* ***(G-4945)***
Bagelovers Inc....607 844-3683
42 Elm St Dryden (13053) ***(G-4149)***
Bagelry, Cedarhurst *Also called M & M Bagel Corp* ***(G-3333)***
Bagels On The Square, Staten Island *Also called Carmine Street Bagels Inc* ***(G-15061)***
Bags Unlimited Inc....585 436-6282
7 Canal St Rochester (14608) ***(G-13651)***
Bagznyc Corp....212 643-8202
19 W 34th St Rm 318 New York (10001) ***(G-9003)***
Baikal Inc (PA)....212 239-4650
341 W 38th St Fl 3 New York (10018) ***(G-9004)***
Bailey Boonville Mills Inc....315 942-2131
123 Mill St Boonville (13309) ***(G-1114)***
Bailey Manufacturing Co LLC....716 965-2731
10987 Bennett State Rd Forestville (14062) ***(G-5085)***
Bainbridge & Knight LLC....212 986-5100
801 2nd Ave Fl 19 New York (10017) ***(G-9005)***
Baird Mold Making Inc....631 667-0322
195 N Fehr Way Ste C Bay Shore (11706) ***(G-661)***
Bairnco Corporation (HQ)....914 461-1300
1133 Westchester Ave N-222 White Plains (10604) ***(G-16424)***
Bajan Group Inc....518 464-2884
950 New Loudon Rd Ste 280 Latham (12110) ***(G-7064)***
Bak USA Technologies Corp....716 248-2704
425 Michigan Ave Buffalo (14203) ***(G-2722)***
Bake-Rite International Inc....518 395-3340
412 Warren St Schenectady (12305) ***(G-14652)***
Baker Commodities, Ellenburg Depot *Also called Ellenburg Recyclers* ***(G-4436)***
Baker Commodities Inc....585 482-1880
2268 Browncroft Blvd Rochester (14625) ***(G-13652)***
Baker Logging & Firewood....585 374-5733
8781 Grlnghuse Atlanta Rd Naples (14512) ***(G-8470)***
Baker Products Inc....212 459-2323
5 Oakley Rd White Plains (10606) ***(G-16425)***
Baker Tool & Die....716 694-2025
48 Industrial Dr North Tonawanda (14120) ***(G-12415)***
Baker Tool & Die & Die....716 694-2025
48 Industrial Dr North Tonawanda (14120) ***(G-12416)***
Bakers of All Nations, Mineola *Also called Ericeira Inc* ***(G-8220)***
Bakers Pride Oven Co Inc....914 576-0200
145 Huguenot St Ste Mz1 New Rochelle (10801) ***(G-8591)***
Bakery & Coffee Shop....315 287-1829
274 W Main St Gouverneur (13642) ***(G-5486)***
Bakery Innovative Tech Corp....631 758-3081
139 N Ocean Ave Patchogue (11772) ***(G-12861)***
Balajee Enterprises Inc....212 629-6150
150 W 30th St Frnt 2 New York (10001) ***(G-9006)***
Balance Enterprises Inc....516 822-3183
12 W Cherry St Hicksville (11801) ***(G-6063)***
Balanced Tech Corp....212 768-8330
37 W 37th St Fl 10 New York (10018) ***(G-9007)***
Balchem Corporation (PA)....845 326-5600
52 Sunrise Park Rd New Hampton (10958) ***(G-8497)***
Baldwin Machine Works Inc....631 842-9110
20 Grant Ave 2040 Copiague (11726) ***(G-3754)***
Baldwin Ribbon & Stamping Corp....718 335-6700
3956 63rd St Woodside (11377) ***(G-16645)***
Baldwin Richardson Foods Co....315 986-2727
3268 Blue Heron Dr Macedon (14502) ***(G-7695)***
Balint Tool, Brooklyn *Also called Tools & Stamping Corp* ***(G-2570)***
Baliva Concrete Products Inc....585 328-8442
245 Paul Rd Rochester (14624) ***(G-13653)***
Ball Chain Mfg Co Inc (PA)....914 664-7500
741 S Fulton Ave Mount Vernon (10550) ***(G-8379)***
Ball Metal Beverage Cont Corp....845 692-3800
95 Ballard Rd Middletown (10941) ***(G-8138)***
Ball Metal Beverage Cont Corp....518 587-6030
11 Adams Rd Saratoga Springs (12866) ***(G-14570)***
Ball Metal Beverage Cont Div, Middletown *Also called Ball Metal Beverage Cont Corp* ***(G-8138)***
Ball Metal Beverage Cont Div, Saratoga Springs *Also called Ball Metal Beverage Cont Corp* ***(G-14570)***
Ballantrae Lithographers Inc....914 592-3275
96 Wayside Dr White Plains (10607) ***(G-16426)***
Balticare Inc (PA)....646 380-9470
501 Fashion Ave Rm 414 New York (10018) ***(G-9008)***
Bam Enterprises Inc (PA)....716 773-7634
2937 Alt Blvd Grand Island (14072) ***(G-5496)***
Bam Sales LLC (PA)....212 781-3000
1407 Broadway Rm 2018 New York (10018) ***(G-9009)***

Bamberger Polymers Intl Corp...516 622-3600
2 Jericho Plz Ste 109 Jericho (11753) *(G-6780)*
Bamboo Global Industries...973 943-1878
339 E 58th St Apt 7e New York (10022) *(G-9010)*
Bandaroos, New York *Also called L D Weiss Inc (G-10493)*
Bandier Corp...212 242-5400
960 Park Ave Apt 11b New York (10028) *(G-9011)*
Bandit International Ltd...718 402-2100
600 E 132nd St Bronx (10454) *(G-1225)*
Bands N Bows...718 984-4316
34 Fieldway Ave Staten Island (10308) *(G-15047)*
Bangla Patrika Inc...718 482-9923
3806 31st St 2 Long Island City (11101) *(G-7397)*
Bank Displays.com, Deer Park *Also called L Miller Design Inc (G-3998)*
Bank-Miller Co Inc...914 227-9357
333 Fifth Ave Pelham (10803) *(G-12933)*
Banner Metalcraft Inc...631 563-7303
300 Trade Zone Dr Ronkonkoma (11779) *(G-14316)*
Banner Smoked Fish Inc...718 449-1992
2715 W 15th St Brooklyn (11224) *(G-1584)*
Banner Transmission & Eng Co...516 221-9459
4 Cabriolet Ln Melville (11747) *(G-8004)*
Banner Transmissions, Melville *Also called Banner Transmission & Eng Co (G-8004)*
Bannerboy Corporation...646 691-6524
20 Jay St Ste 432 Brooklyn (11201) *(G-1585)*
Bara Fashions, Brooklyn *Also called Matchables Inc (G-2178)*
Baralan Usa Inc (HQ)...718 849-5768
12019 89th Ave Richmond Hill (11418) *(G-13497)*
Barbara Matera Ltd...212 475-5006
890 Broadway Fl 5 New York (10003) *(G-9012)*
Barber & Deline Enrgy Svcs LLC...315 696-8961
10 Community Dr Tully (13159) *(G-15648)*
Barber & Deline LLC...607 749-2619
995 State Route 11a Tully (13159) *(G-15649)*
Barber Brothers Jewelry Mfg...212 819-0666
580 5th Ave Ste 725 New York (10036) *(G-9013)*
Barber Welding Inc...315 834-6645
2517 Rte 31 W Weedsport (13166) *(G-16110)*
Barbera Transduser Systems...718 816-3025
21 Louis St Staten Island (10304) *(G-15048)*
Barc Usa Inc...516 719-1052
5 Delaware Dr Ste 2 New Hyde Park (11042) *(G-8519)*
Barclay Brown Corp...718 376-7166
47 Lancaster Ave Brooklyn (11223) *(G-1586)*
Barclay Tagg Racing...631 404-8269
86 Geranium Ave Floral Park (11001) *(G-4957)*
Bardwil Industries Inc (PA)...212 944-1870
4 Bryant Park Fl 4 Flr 4 New York (10018) *(G-9014)*
Bardwil Linens, New York *Also called Bardwil Industries Inc (G-9014)*
Bare Beauty Laser Hair Removal...718 278-2273
5 E 57th St Fl 6 New York (10022) *(G-9015)*
Bare Escentuals Inc...646 537-0070
1140 3rd Ave New York (10065) *(G-9016)*
Bare Minerals, New York *Also called Bare Escentuals Inc (G-9016)*
Bare Wire Div, Jordan *Also called Omega Wire Inc (G-6842)*
Bare Wire Div, Camden *Also called Omega Wire Inc (G-3191)*
Bare Wire Division, Camden *Also called Owi Corporation (G-3192)*
Bare Wire Division, Camden *Also called International Wire Group Inc (G-3189)*
Bargold Storage Systems LLC...718 247-7000
4141 38th St Long Island City (11101) *(G-7398)*
Bari Engineering Corp...212 966-2080
240 Bowery New York (10012) *(G-9017)*
Bari-Jay Fashions Inc (PA)...212 921-1551
230 W 38th St Fl 12 New York (10018) *(G-9018)*
Barilla America Ny Inc...585 226-5600
100 Horseshoe Blvd Avon (14414) *(G-518)*
Barker Brothers Incorporated...718 456-6400
1666 Summerfield St Ste 1 Ridgewood (11385) *(G-13530)*
Barker Steel LLC...518 465-6221
126 S Port Rd Albany (12202) *(G-44)*
Barnaby Prints Inc (PA)...845 477-2501
673 Jersey Ave Greenwood Lake (10925) *(G-5648)*
Barnes Group Inc...315 457-9200
1225 State Fair Blvd Syracuse (13209) *(G-15254)*
Barnes Metal Finishing Inc...585 798-4817
3932 Salt Works Rd Medina (14103) *(G-7971)*
Barney & Dickenson Inc (PA)...607 729-1536
520 Prentice Rd Vestal (13850) *(G-15809)*
Baroka Creations Inc...212 768-0527
36 W 47th St Ste 1402 New York (10036) *(G-9019)*
Baron Packaging, Hauppauge *Also called J & M Packaging Inc (G-5852)*
Barone Offset Printing Corp...212 989-5500
89 Lake Ridge Cv Mohegan Lake (10547) *(G-8257)*
Barra & Trumbore Inc...845 626-5442
40 Old Mine Rd Kerhonkson (12446) *(G-6867)*
Barrage...212 586-9390
401 W 47th St Frnt A New York (10036) *(G-9020)*
Barrasso & Sons Trucking Inc...631 581-0360
160 Floral Park St Islip Terrace (11752) *(G-6552)*
Barrera Jose & Maria Co Ltd...212 239-1994
29 W 36th St Fl 8 New York (10018) *(G-9021)*
Barrett Bronze Inc...914 699-6060
115 Miller Pl Mount Vernon (10550) *(G-8380)*
Barrett Paving Materials Inc...315 353-6611
Rr 56 Norwood (13668) *(G-12495)*
Barrett Paving Materials Inc...315 652-4585
4530 Wetzel Rd Liverpool (13090) *(G-7222)*
Barrett Paving Materials Inc...315 737-9471
363 Rasbach Rd Clayville (13322) *(G-3554)*
Barrett Paving Materials Inc...315 737-8310
1223 Albany Rd Clayville (13322) *(G-3555)*
Barrett Paving Materials Inc...607 723-5367
14 Brandywine St Binghamton (13901) *(G-864)*
Barrett Paving Materials Inc...315 788-2037
26572 State Route 37 Watertown (13601) *(G-16001)*
Barrie House Coffee & Tea, Elmsford *Also called Bh Coffee Company LLC (G-4532)*
Barrier Brewing Company LLC...516 316-4429
612 W Walnut St Long Beach (11561) *(G-7357)*
Barron Games Intl Co LLC...716 630-0054
84 Aero Dr Ste 5 Buffalo (14225) *(G-2723)*
Barron Metal Products Inc...914 965-1232
286 Nepperhan Ave Yonkers (10701) *(G-16738)*
Barrons Educational Series Inc (PA)...631 434-3311
250 Wireless Blvd Hauppauge (11788) *(G-5778)*
Barry Industries Inc...212 242-5200
36 W 17th St Frnt 1 New York (10011) *(G-9022)*
Barry Steel Fabrication Inc (PA)...716 433-2144
30 Simonds St Lockport (14094) *(G-7286)*
Barry Supply Co Div, New York *Also called Barry Industries Inc (G-9022)*
Barson Composites Corporation (PA)...516 752-7882
160 Bethpage Sweet Old Bethpage (11804) *(G-12581)*
Bart Ostrander Trckg Log Corp...518 661-6535
1556 State Highway 30 Mayfield (12117) *(G-7919)*
Bartell Machinery Systems LLC (HQ)...315 336-7600
6321 Elmer Hill Rd Rome (13440) *(G-14246)*
Bartholomew Mazza Ltd Inc...212 935-4530
22 W 48th St Ste 805 New York (10036) *(G-9023)*
Bartizan Data Systems LLC...914 965-7977
217 Riverdale Ave Yonkers (10705) *(G-16739)*
Bartolomeo Publishing Inc...631 420-4949
100 Cabot St Unit A West Babylon (11704) *(G-16138)*
Bartolotta Furniture, Auburn *Also called Matteo & Antonio Bartolotta (G-490)*
Barton International, Glens Falls *Also called Barton Mines Company LLC (G-5418)*
Barton Mines Company LLC (PA)...518 798-5462
6 Warren St Glens Falls (12801) *(G-5418)*
Barton Tool Inc...716 665-2801
1864 Lyndon Blvd Falconer (14733) *(G-4672)*
Base Systems Inc...845 278-1991
1606 Route 22 Brewster (10509) *(G-1158)*
BASF Corporation...914 737-2554
1057 Lower South St Peekskill (10566) *(G-12917)*
BASF Corporation...914 785-2000
500 White Plains Rd Tarrytown (10591) *(G-15475)*
BASF Corporation...518 465-6534
70 Riverside Ave Rensselaer (12144) *(G-13473)*
BASF Corporation...631 689-0200
361 Sheep Pasture Rd East Setauket (11733) *(G-4299)*
BASF The Chemical Company, East Setauket *Also called BASF Corporation (G-4299)*
Basil S Kadhim...888 520-5192
280 Madison Ave Rm 912 New York (10016) *(G-9024)*
Basileus Company LLC...315 963-3516
8104 Cazenovia Rd Manlius (13104) *(G-7774)*
Basilio's, Canastota *Also called Salarinos Italian Foods Inc (G-3247)*
Basiloff LLC...646 671-0353
179 Bennett Ave Apt 7f New York (10040) *(G-9025)*
Basin Holdings LLC (PA)...212 695-7376
200 Park Ave Fl 58b New York (10166) *(G-9026)*
Bass Oil & Chemical Llc...718 628-4444
136 Morgan Ave Brooklyn (11237) *(G-1587)*
Bass Oil Company Inc...718 628-4444
136 Morgan Ave Brooklyn (11237) *(G-1588)*
Batampte Pickle Products Inc (PA)...718 251-2100
77 Brooklyn Terminal Mkt Brooklyn (11236) *(G-1589)*
Batavia Enclosures Inc...585 344-1797
636 Main St Arcade (14009) *(G-378)*
Batavia Legal Printing Inc...585 768-2100
7 Bank St Le Roy (14482) *(G-7113)*
Batavia Precision Glass LLC...585 343-6050
231 Currier Ave Buffalo (14212) *(G-2724)*
Batavia Press LLC...585 343-4429
3817 W Main Street Rd Batavia (14020) *(G-612)*
Bates Industries, South Glens Falls *Also called Mdi East Inc (G-14937)*
Bates Jackson Engraving Co Inc...716 854-3000
17 Elm St 21 Buffalo (14203) *(G-2725)*
Bator Bintor Inc...347 546-6503
42 Delevan St Brooklyn (11231) *(G-1590)*
Battenfeld Grease Oil Corp NY...716 695-2100
1174 Erie Ave North Tonawanda (14120) *(G-12417)*
Battenfeld-American Inc...716 822-8410
1575 Clinton St Buffalo (14206) *(G-2726)*
Battery Energy Storage Systems...518 256-7029
291 River St Ste 318 Troy (12180) *(G-15602)*

ALPHABETIC

Battery Research and Tstg Inc 315 342-2373
1313 County Route 1 Oswego (13126) *(G-12775)*
Battsco LLC 516 586-6544
190 Lauman Ln Unit A Hicksville (11801) *(G-6064)*
Bauble Bar Inc 646 846-2044
16 Madison Sq W Fl 5 New York (10010) *(G-9027)*
Bauerschmidt & Sons Inc 718 528-3500
11920 Merrick Blvd Jamaica (11434) *(G-6630)*
Baum Christine and John Corp 585 621-8910
1577 W Ridge Rd Rochester (14615) *(G-13654)*
Baum Essex, New York *Also called Essex Manufacturing Inc (G-9712)*
Baums Castorine Company Inc 315 336-8154
200 Matthew St Rome (13440) *(G-14247)*
Bausch & Lomb Holdings Inc (HQ) 585 338-6000
450 Lexington Ave New York (10017) *(G-9028)*
Bausch & Lomb Incorporated (HQ) 585 338-6000
1400 N Goodman St Rochester (14609) *(G-13655)*
Bausch & Lomb Incorporated 585 338-6000
1 Bausch And Lomb Pl Rochester (14604) *(G-13656)*
Bausch & Lomb Incorporated 585 338-6000
1400 N Goodman St Rochester (14609) *(G-13657)*
Baxter Healthcare Corporation 800 356-3454
711 Park Ave Medina (14103) *(G-7972)*
Baxter International Inc 845 457-9370
500 Neelytown Rd Montgomery (12549) *(G-8308)*
Bay Horse Innovations Nyinc 607 898-3337
130 Cayuga St Groton (13073) *(G-5649)*
Bay Sales Company, New York *Also called Salmco Jewelry Corp (G-11471)*
Bayit Home Automation Corp 973 988-2638
2299 Mcdonald Ave Brooklyn (11223) *(G-1591)*
Bayshore Electric Motors 631 475-1397
33 Suffolk Ave Patchogue (11772) *(G-12862)*
Bayshore Motors, Patchogue *Also called Bayshore Electric Motors (G-12862)*
Bayshore Wire Products Corp 631 451-8825
480 Mill Rd Coram (11727) *(G-3796)*
Bayside Beepers & Cellular 718 343-3888
25607 Hillside Ave Glen Oaks (11004) *(G-5386)*
Bazaar 212 903-5497
300 W 57th St Fl 25 New York (10019) *(G-9029)*
BC Communications Inc 631 549-8833
211 Depot Rd Huntington Station (11746) *(G-6434)*
BC Systems Inc 631 751-9370
200 N Belle Mead Ave # 2 Setauket (11733) *(G-14792)*
BCM, Mount Vernon *Also called Ball Chain Mfg Co Inc (G-8379)*
BCM Electronics Manuf Services 631 580-9516
3279 Veterans Memorial Ronkonkoma (11779) *(G-14317)*
Bco Industries Western NY Inc 716 877-2800
77 Oriskany Dr Tonawanda (14150) *(G-15526)*
Bcp Ingredients Inc (HQ) 845 326-5600
52 Sunrise Park Rd New Hampton (10958) *(G-8498)*
Bcs Access Systems Us LLC 315 258-3469
2150 Crane Brook Dr Auburn (13021) *(G-469)*
Bd Initiative-Hlthcare Wrkr SA, Nyack *Also called Becton Dickinson and Company (G-12500)*
Bd Projects, New York *Also called Architects Newspaper LLC (G-8900)*
Bdg Media Inc 917 551-6510
315 Park Ave S Fl 12 New York (10010) *(G-9030)*
Bdm, Syosset *Also called Buffalo Dental Mfg Co Inc (G-15210)*
Bdp Industries Inc (PA) 518 695-6851
354 State Route 29 Greenwich (12834) *(G-5636)*
BDR Creative Concepts Inc 516 942-7768
141 Central Ave Ste B Farmingdale (11735) *(G-4726)*
Bdtrims, Brooklyn *Also called Rus Auto Parts Inc (G-2427)*
Be The Media, New Hyde Park *Also called Natural E Creative LLC (G-8551)*
Beaba USA, New York *Also called Peek A Boo USA Inc (G-11135)*
Beacon, Babylon *Also called A C J Communications Inc (G-523)*
Beacon Adhesives Inc 914 699-3400
125 S Macquesten Pkwy Mount Vernon (10550) *(G-8381)*
Beacon Chemical, Mount Vernon *Also called Beacon Adhesives Inc (G-8381)*
Beacon Newspapers, Hempstead *Also called Nassau County Publications (G-6022)*
Beacon Press Inc 212 691-5050
32 Cushman Rd White Plains (10606) *(G-16427)*
Beacon Press News, Wappingers Falls *Also called Wappingers Falls Shopper Inc (G-15938)*
Beacon Spch Lnge Pthlgy Phys 516 626-1635
1441 Old Northern Blvd Roslyn (11576) *(G-14443)*
Beacon Therapy Services, Roslyn *Also called Beacon Spch Lnge Pthlgy Phys (G-14443)*
Beal Blocks, New York *Also called B & R Promotional Products (G-8988)*
BEAM Manufacturing Corp 631 253-2724
107 Otis St Unit A West Babylon (11704) *(G-16139)*
Bean King International LLC 845 268-3135
36 N Route 9w Congers (10920) *(G-3711)*
Bear Metal Works Inc 716 824-4350
39 Scoville Ave Buffalo (14206) *(G-2727)*
Bear Port Publishing Company 877 337-8577
45 W 21st St 3b New York (10010) *(G-9031)*
Beardslee Realty 516 747-5557
290 E Jericho Tpke Mineola (11501) *(G-8206)*
Bears Management Group Inc 585 624-5694
7577 E Main St Lima (14485) *(G-7149)*
Bears Playgrounds, Lima *Also called Bears Management Group Inc (G-7149)*
Beastons Budget Printing 585 244-2721
1260 Scttsvlle Rd Ste 300 Rochester (14624) *(G-13658)*
Beauty America LLC 917 744-1430
10 Bond St Ste 296 Great Neck (11021) *(G-5539)*
Beauty Fashion Inc 212 840-8800
8 W 38th St Frnt 2 New York (10018) *(G-9032)*
Beaver Creek Industries Inc 607 545-6382
11530 White Rd Canaseraga (14822) *(G-3238)*
Beaver Mountain Log Homes Inc 607 467-2700
200 Beaver Mountain Dr Hancock (13783) *(G-5709)*
Bebitz USA Inc 516 280-8378
2 Reiter Ave Hicksville (11801) *(G-6065)*
Bebop Books, New York *Also called Lee & Low Books Incorporated (G-10537)*
BEC Acquisition Co, Melville *Also called Tech Software LLC (G-8070)*
Becca Inc 646 568-6250
142 W 36th St Fl 15 New York (10018) *(G-9033)*
Becca Cosmetics, New York *Also called Becca Inc (G-9033)*
Beck Vault Company 315 337-7590
6648 Shank Ave Rome (13440) *(G-14248)*
Beck, Don, Corfu *Also called Delaval Inc (G-3806)*
Becker Electronics Inc 631 619-9100
50 Alexander Ct Ste 2 Ronkonkoma (11779) *(G-14318)*
Beckmann Converting Inc (PA) 518 842-0073
14 Park Dr Amsterdam (12010) *(G-327)*
Becks Classic Mfg Inc 631 435-3800
50 Emjay Blvd Ste 7 Brentwood (11717) *(G-1128)*
Becton Dickinson and Company 845 353-3371
1 Main St Apt 3307 Nyack (10960) *(G-12500)*
Bedessee Imports Ltd 718 272-1300
140 Varick Ave Brooklyn (11237) *(G-1592)*
Bedford Freeman & Worth (HQ) 212 576-9400
1 New York Plz Ste 4500 New York (10004) *(G-9034)*
Bedford Freeman & Worth 212 375-7000
1 New York Plz Ste 4500 New York (10004) *(G-9035)*
Bedford Communications Inc 212 807-8220
1410 Broadway Frnt 2 New York (10018) *(G-9036)*
Bedford Downing Glass 718 418-6409
220 Ingraham St Ste 2 Brooklyn (11237) *(G-1593)*
Bedford Precision Parts Corp 914 241-2211
290 Adams St Bedford Hills (10507) *(G-772)*
Bedford Pund Rdge Rcord Review, Katonah *Also called Record Review LLC (G-6846)*
Bedford Wdwrk Instllations Inc 914 764-9434
200 Pound Ridge Rd Bedford (10506) *(G-768)*
Bedrock Communications 212 532-4150
152 Madison Ave Rm 802 New York (10016) *(G-9037)*
Bedrock Landscaping Mtls Corp (PA) 631 587-4950
454 Sunrise Hwy Babylon (11704) *(G-525)*
Bedrock Plus, Babylon *Also called Bedrock Landscaping Mtls Corp (G-525)*
Bee Green Industries Inc 516 334-3525
322 Westbury Ave Carle Place (11514) *(G-3262)*
Bee Publications Inc 716 632-4700
5564 Main St Williamsville (14221) *(G-16569)*
Beebie Printing & Art Agcy Inc 518 725-4528
40 E Pine St Gloversville (12078) *(G-5453)*
Beech Grove Technology Inc 845 223-6844
11 Sandy Pines Blvd Hopewell Junction (12533) *(G-6283)*
Beech-Nut Nutrition Company (HQ) 518 839-0300
1 Nutritious Pl Amsterdam (12010) *(G-328)*
Beecher Emssn Sltn Tchnlgs LLC (PA) 607 796-0149
1250 Schweizer Rd Horseheads (14845) *(G-6305)*
Beehive Press Inc 718 654-1200
3742 Boston Rd Bronx (10469) *(G-1226)*
Beer Marketers Insights Inc 845 507-0040
49 E Maple Ave Suffern (10901) *(G-15186)*
Beetins Wholesale Inc 718 524-0899
125 Ravenhurst Ave Staten Island (10310) *(G-15049)*
Beetnpath LLC 607 319-5585
950 Danby Rd Ste 180 Ithaca (14850) *(G-6558)*
Beets Love Production LLC 585 270-2471
1150 Lee Rd Rochester (14606) *(G-13659)*
Behance, New York *Also called Adobe Systems Incorporated (G-8740)*
Beila Group Inc 212 260-1948
285 Mott St New York (10012) *(G-9038)*
Beis Moshiach Inc 718 778-8000
744 Eastern Pkwy Brooklyn (11213) *(G-1594)*
Beitals Aquarium Sales & Svc, Pearl River *Also called C B Management Services Inc (G-12895)*
Beka World LP 905 821-1050
258 Sonwil Dr Buffalo (14225) *(G-2728)*
Bekaert Corporation 716 830-1321
6000 N Bailey Ave Ste 9 Amherst (14226) *(G-216)*
Bektrom Foods Inc (PA) 516 802-3800
6800 Jericho Tpke 207w Syosset (11791) *(G-15209)*
Bel Aire Offset Corp 718 539-8333
1853 College Point Blvd College Point (11356) *(G-3640)*
Bel Aire Printing, College Point *Also called Bel Aire Offset Corp (G-3640)*
Bel Transformer Inc (HQ) 516 239-5777
500 Bayview Ave Inwood (11096) *(G-6487)*
Bel-Bee Products Incorporated 845 353-0300
100 Snake Hill Rd Ste 1 West Nyack (10994) *(G-16265)*
Belangers Gravel & Stone Inc 585 728-3906
10184 State Route 21 Wayland (14572) *(G-16070)*

Belden Inc ... 607 796-5600
224 N Main St Ste 4 Horseheads (14845) *(G-6306)*
Belden Manufacturing Inc ... 607 238-0998
1813 Us Route 11 Kirkwood (13795) *(G-6939)*
Belfair Draperies, Long Island City *Also called Anthony Lawrence of New York* *(G-7380)*
Belgian Boys USA, Farmingdale *Also called Merb LLC* *(G-4820)*
Bell-Pac, Liverpool *Also called Bellotti Packaging Inc* *(G-7223)*
Bella Figura Letterpress ... 866 699-6040
509 W Fayette St Syracuse (13204) *(G-15255)*
Bella International Inc ... 716 484-0102
111 W 2nd St Ste 4000 Jamestown (14701) *(G-6700)*
Bellataire Diamonds Inc ... 212 687-8881
19 W 44th St Fl 15 New York (10036) *(G-9039)*
Belle Maison USA Ltd ... 718 805-0200
8950 127th St Richmond Hill (11418) *(G-13498)*
Bellerophon Publications Inc ... 212 627-9977
205 Lexington Ave Fl 17 New York (10016) *(G-9040)*
Bellini Collections, New York *Also called Formart Corp* *(G-9824)*
Bellmore Steel Products Corp ... 516 785-9667
2282 Bellmore Ave Bellmore (11710) *(G-786)*
Bello LLC ... 516 623-8800
178 Hanse Ave Freeport (11520) *(G-5145)*
Bellotti Packaging Inc ... 315 433-0131
5089 Constitution Ln Liverpool (13088) *(G-7223)*
Bellwethe Hard Cider ... 607 387-9464
9070 State Route 89 Trumansburg (14886) *(G-15637)*
Belmay Holding Corporation ... 914 376-1515
1 Odell Plz Ste 123 Yonkers (10701) *(G-16740)*
Belmet Products Inc (PA) ... 718 542-8220
1350 Garrison Ave Bronx (10474) *(G-1227)*
Belrix Industries Inc ... 716 821-5964
3590 Jeffrey Blvd Buffalo (14219) *(G-2729)*
Belsito Communications Inc ... 845 534-9700
1 Ardmore St New Windsor (12553) *(G-8636)*
Belt Dewatering Press, Greenwich *Also called Bdp Industries Inc* *(G-5636)*
Belt Maintenance Systems, Buffalo *Also called Rlp Holdings Inc* *(G-3039)*
Belton Industries, Brooklyn *Also called Filta Clean Co Inc* *(G-1880)*
Beltone Corporation ... 716 565-1015
7474 Transit Rd Williamsville (14221) *(G-16570)*
Beltran Associates Inc ... 718 252-2996
1133 E 35th St Ste 1 Brooklyn (11210) *(G-1595)*
Beltran Technologies Inc ... 718 338-3311
1133 E 35th St Brooklyn (11210) *(G-1596)*
Beluga Inc (PA) ... 212 594-5511
463 7th Ave Fl 4 New York (10018) *(G-9041)*
Bematech, Bethpage *Also called Logic Controls Inc* *(G-845)*
Bemco of Western Ny Inc ... 716 823-8400
122 Roberts Ave Buffalo (14206) *(G-2730)*
Ben Weitsman of Albany LLC ... 518 462-4444
300 Smith Blvd Albany (12202) *(G-45)*
Ben-Sak Textile Inc ... 212 279-5122
307 W 38th St Frnt 9 New York (10018) *(G-9042)*
Benartex LLC ... 212 840-3250
132 W 36th St Rm 401 New York (10018) *(G-9043)*
Benchemark Printing Inc ... 518 393-1361
1890 Maxon Rd Ext Schenectady (12308) *(G-14653)*
Benchers Unlimited, Brooklyn *Also called Issacs Yisroel* *(G-2016)*
Benchmark Books, Tarrytown *Also called Marshall Cavendish Corp* *(G-15481)*
Benchmark Education Co LLC (PA) ... 914 637-7200
145 Huguenot St Fl 8 New Rochelle (10801) *(G-8592)*
Benchmark Furniture Mfg ... 718 257-4707
300 Dewitt Ave Brooklyn (11236) *(G-1597)*
Benchmark Graphics Ltd ... 212 683-1711
9 E 37th St Fl 5 New York (10016) *(G-9044)*
Benchmark Media Systems Inc ... 315 437-6300
203 E Hampton Pl Ste 2 Syracuse (13206) *(G-15256)*
Benedictine Hospital, Kingston *Also called Healthalliance Hospital* *(G-6901)*
Benemy Welding & Fabrication ... 315 548-8500
8 Pleasant Ave Phelps (14532) *(G-12975)*
Benetton Services, New York *Also called Ramsbury Property Us Inc* *(G-11322)*
Benetton Trading Usa Inc (PA) ... 212 593-0290
601 5th Ave Fl 4 New York (10017) *(G-9045)*
Benfield Control Systems Inc ... 914 948-6660
25 Lafayette Ave White Plains (10603) *(G-16428)*
Benishty Brothers Corp ... 646 339-9991
233 Mosher Ave Woodmere (11598) *(G-16640)*
Benjamin Moore & Co ... 518 736-1723
Union Ave Ext Johnstown (12095) *(G-6824)*
Benjamin Printing Inc ... 315 788-7922
60 E Church St Adams (13605) *(G-2)*
Benjamin Sheridan Corporation (HQ) ... 585 657-6161
7629 State Route 5 And 20 Bloomfield (14469) *(G-947)*
Benlee Enterprises LLC ... 212 730-7330
3100 47th Ave Unit 2 Long Island City (11101) *(G-7399)*
Bennett Die & Tool Inc ... 607 739-5629
130 Wygant Rd Horseheads (14845) *(G-6307)*
Bennett Die & Tool Inc ... 607 273-2836
113 Brewery Ln Ithaca (14850) *(G-6559)*
Bennett Manufacturing Co Inc ... 716 937-9161
13315 Railroad St Alden (14004) *(G-168)*
Bennett Multimedia Inc ... 718 629-1454
1087 Utica Ave Brooklyn (11203) *(G-1598)*
Bennett Printing Corporation ... 718 629-1454
1087 Utica Ave Brooklyn (11203) *(G-1599)*
Bennett Stair Company Inc ... 518 384-1554
1021 State Route 50 Ballston Lake (12019) *(G-566)*
Bensak, New York *Also called Ben-Sak Textile Inc* *(G-9042)*
Benson Industries Inc ... 212 779-3230
192 Lexington Ave Rm 502 New York (10016) *(G-9046)*
Benson Mills Inc (PA) ... 718 236-6743
140 58th St Ste 7j Brooklyn (11220) *(G-1600)*
Benson Steel Fabricators, Saugerties *Also called Kenbenco Inc* *(G-14609)*
Bentley Cravats, New York *Also called W B Bow Tie Corp* *(G-12060)*
Bentley Manufacturing Inc (PA) ... 212 714-1800
10 W 33rd St Rm 220 New York (10001) *(G-9047)*
Bentley Mills Inc ... 212 463-0606
91 5th Ave Rm 800 New York (10003) *(G-9048)*
Bentones Enterprises, New York *Also called Hjn Inc* *(G-10107)*
Benway-Haworth-Lwlr-Iacosta He ... 518 432-4070
21 Everett Rd Albany (12205) *(G-46)*
Benzsay & Harrison Inc ... 518 895-2311
Railroad Ave Delanson (12053) *(G-4067)*
Beowawe Binary LLC ... 646 829-3900
1095 Avenue Of The Ave New York (10036) *(G-9049)*
Bereza Iron Works Inc ... 585 254-6311
87 Dewey Ave Rochester (14608) *(G-13660)*
Berger & Wild LLC ... 646 415-8459
401 Broadway Ste 302 New York (10013) *(G-9050)*
Berjen Metal Industries Ltd ... 631 673-7979
645 New York Ave Unit 1 Huntington (11743) *(G-6394)*
Berkman Bros Inc ... 718 782-1827
538 Johnson Ave Brooklyn (11237) *(G-1601)*
Berkshire Business Forms Inc ... 518 828-2600
829 Route 66 Hudson (12534) *(G-6343)*
Berkshire Transformer (PA) ... 631 467-5328
77 Windsor Pl Ste 18 Central Islip (11722) *(G-3359)*
Berkshire Weaving, New York *Also called Richloom Fabrics Group Inc* *(G-11392)*
Bernan Associates, New York *Also called Kraus Organization Limited* *(G-10481)*
Bernard Chaus Inc (HQ) ... 212 354-1280
530 7th Ave Fl 18 New York (10018) *(G-9051)*
Bernard Chaus Inc ... 646 562-4700
515 7th Ave Ste 18 New York (10018) *(G-9052)*
Bernard Hall ... 585 425-3340
10 Perinton Hills Mall Fairport (14450) *(G-4625)*
Bernette Apparel LLC ... 212 279-5526
42 W 39th St Fl 2 New York (10018) *(G-9053)*
Bernhard Arnold & Company Inc (PA) ... 212 907-1500
551 5th Ave Fl 3 New York (10176) *(G-9054)*
Bernstein Display, New York *Also called Leo D Bernstein & Sons Inc* *(G-10548)*
Berry Global Inc ... 315 986-2161
112 Main St Macedon (14502) *(G-7696)*
Berry Global Inc ... 315 484-0397
1500 Milton Ave Solvay (13209) *(G-14916)*
Berry Industrial Group Inc (PA) ... 845 353-8338
30 Main St Nyack (10960) *(G-12501)*
Berry Jewelry Company, New York *Also called MJM Jewelry Corp* *(G-10826)*
Berry Jewelry Company, Brooklyn *Also called MJM Jewelry Corp* *(G-2218)*
Berry Plastics Corporation ... 315 986-6270
200 Main St Macedon (14502) *(G-7697)*
Berry Specialty Tapes LLC ... 631 727-6000
1852 Old Country Rd Riverhead (11901) *(G-13565)*
Bertelsmann Inc (HQ) ... 212 782-1000
1745 Broadway Fl 20 New York (10019) *(G-9055)*
Bertelsmann Pubg Group Inc (HQ) ... 212 782-1000
1540 Broadway Fl 24 New York (10036) *(G-9056)*
Beryllium Manufacturing, Copiague *Also called Worldwide Arntcal Cmpnents Inc* *(G-3795)*
Besam Entrance Solutions, East Syracuse *Also called Assa Abloy Entrance Systems US* *(G-4323)*
Bescor Video Accessories Ltd ... 631 420-1717
244 Route 109 Farmingdale (11735) *(G-4727)*
Besicorp Ltd (PA) ... 845 336-7700
1151 Flatbush Rd Kingston (12401) *(G-6889)*
Besstech, Troy *Also called Battery Energy Storage Systems* *(G-15602)*
Best Adhesives Company Inc ... 718 417-3800
4702 Metropolitan Ave Ridgewood (11385) *(G-13531)*
Best Boilers Inc ... 718 372-4210
2402 Neptune Ave Brooklyn (11224) *(G-1602)*
Best Brands Consumer Pdts Inc (PA) ... 212 684-7456
20 W 33rd St Fl 5 New York (10001) *(G-9057)*
Best Bread, Port Chester *Also called Good Bread Bakery* *(G-13201)*
Best Concrete Mix Corp ... 718 463-5500
3510 College Point Blvd Flushing (11354) *(G-4988)*
Best Foods Baking Group, Tonawanda *Also called Bimbo Bakeries Usa Inc* *(G-15527)*
Best Mdlr HMS Afrbe P Q& S In ... 631 204-0049
495 County Road 39 Southampton (11968) *(G-14950)*
Best Medical Wear Ltd ... 718 858-5544
34 Franklin Ave Ste 301 Brooklyn (11205) *(G-1603)*
Best Pallet & Crate LLC ... 518 438-2945
22 Railroad Ave Albany (12205) *(G-47)*

ALPHABETIC

(PA)=Parent Co (HQ)=Headquarters (DH)=Div Headquarters
2019 Harris
New York Manufacturers Directory
837

Best Priced Products Inc 914 345-3800
250 Clearbrook Rd Ste 240 Elmsford (10523) ***(G-4531)***
Best Time Processor LLC 917 455-4126
8746 Van Wyck Expy Richmond Hill (11418) ***(G-13499)***
Best Tinsmith Supply Inc 518 863-2541
4 Zetta Dr Northville (12134) ***(G-12476)***
Best Way Tools By Anderson Inc 631 586-4702
171 Brook Ave Deer Park (11729) ***(G-3950)***
Bestec Concept Inc 718 937-5848
140 58th St Ste 8d Brooklyn (11220) ***(G-1604)***
Bestline International RES Inc 518 631-2177
224 State St Schenectady (12305) ***(G-14654)***
Bestmade Printing LLC 718 384-0719
205 Keap St Apt 2 Brooklyn (11211) ***(G-1605)***
Bestwall LLC 518 561-3500
327 Margaret St Plattsburgh (12901) ***(G-13109)***
Bestwall LLC 518 346-6151
801 Corporation Park Schenectady (12302) ***(G-14655)***
Bestway Enterprises Inc (PA) 607 753-8261
3877 Luker Rd Cortland (13045) ***(G-3860)***
Bestway of New York Inc 607 753-8261
3877 Luker Rd Cortland (13045) ***(G-3861)***
Bestype Digital Imaging LLC 212 966-6886
285 W Broadway Frnt A New York (10013) ***(G-9058)***
Beta Transformer Tech Corp (HQ) 631 244-7393
40 Orville Dr Ste 2 Bohemia (11716) ***(G-987)***
Betapast Holdings LLC 631 582-6740
110 Nicon Ct Hauppauge (11788) ***(G-5779)***
Betatronix Inc 631 582-6740
125 Comac St Ronkonkoma (11779) ***(G-14319)***
Beth Kobliner Company LLC 212 501-8407
1995 Broadway Ste 1800 New York (10023) ***(G-9059)***
Beth Ward Studios LLC 646 922-7575
133 W 25th St Rm 8e New York (10001) ***(G-9060)***
Beths Farm Kitchen 518 799-3414
504 Rte 46 Stuyvesant Falls (12174) ***(G-15183)***
Betmar, New York *Also called Bollman Hat Company* ***(G-9118)***
Betsy & Adam Ltd (PA) 212 302-3750
525 Fashion Ave Fl 21 New York (10018) ***(G-9061)***
Better Baked Foods LLC 716 326-4651
25 Jefferson St Westfield (14787) ***(G-16392)***
Better Candy Company, Brooklyn *Also called Bader Enterprise Inc* ***(G-1583)***
Better Fresh Corp 718 628-3682
41 Varick Ave Brooklyn (11237) ***(G-1606)***
Better Power Inc 585 475-1321
508 White Spruce Blvd Rochester (14623) ***(G-13661)***
Better Wire Products Inc 716 883-3377
680 New Babcock St Buffalo (14206) ***(G-2731)***
Betterbee, Greenwich *Also called Northast Ctr For Bekeeping LLC* ***(G-5643)***
Betterbee Inc 518 314-0575
8 Meader Rd Greenwich (12834) ***(G-5637)***
Bettertex Inc 212 431-3373
450 Broadway New York (10013) ***(G-9062)***
Bettertex Interioirs, New York *Also called Bettertex Inc* ***(G-9062)***
Beverage Media Group Inc (PA) 212 571-3232
152 Madison Ave Rm 600 New York (10016) ***(G-9063)***
Beverage Works Incorporated 718 834-0500
70 Hamilton Ave 8 Brooklyn (11231) ***(G-1607)***
Beverage Works Nj Inc 631 293-3501
16 Dubon Ct Farmingdale (11735) ***(G-4728)***
Beverage Works Ny Inc 718 812-2034
70 Hamilton Ave 8 Brooklyn (11231) ***(G-1608)***
Bevilacque Group LLC 212 414-8858
19 Norwood Rd Port Washington (11050) ***(G-13245)***
Bevilacque Group LLC By Profor, Port Washington *Also called Bevilacque Group LLC* ***(G-13245)***
Beyer Graphics Inc 631 543-3900
30 Austin Blvd Ste A Commack (11725) ***(G-3682)***
Beyond Beauty Basics LLC 516 731-7100
3359 Hempstead Tpke Levittown (11756) ***(G-7131)***
Beyond Better Foods LLC 212 888-1120
101 Lincoln Ave Frnt 2 Bronx (10454) ***(G-1228)***
Beyond Design Inc 607 865-7487
807 Pines Brook Rd Walton (13856) ***(G-15910)***
Beyond Loom Inc (PA) 212 575-3100
262 W 38th St Rm 203 New York (10018) ***(G-9064)***
Beyondly Inc 646 658-3665
20 W 20th St Ste 1004 New York (10011) ***(G-9065)***
Beyondspring Inc 646 305-6387
28 Liberty St Fl 39 New York (10005) ***(G-9066)***
Beyondspring Phrmceuticals Inc 646 305-6387
28 Liberty St Fl 39 New York (10005) ***(G-9067)***
Bfc Print Network Inc (PA) 716 838-4532
455 Commerce Dr Ste 6 Amherst (14228) ***(G-217)***
Bfg Manufacturing Services Inc 716 362-0888
3949 Jeffrey Blvd Buffalo (14219) ***(G-2732)***
Bfg Marine Inc 631 586-5500
200 Candlewood Rd Bay Shore (11706) ***(G-662)***
Bfgg Investors Group LLC 585 424-3456
1900 University Ave Rochester (14610) ***(G-13662)***
Bfma Holding Corporation 607 753-6746
37 Huntington St Cortland (13045) ***(G-3862)***
Bg Bindery Inc 631 767-4242
5877 57th St Maspeth (11378) ***(G-7826)***
Bga Technology LLC 631 750-4600
116 Wilbur Pl Bohemia (11716) ***(G-988)***
Bh Brand Inc 212 239-1635
10 W 33rd St Rm 218 New York (10001) ***(G-9068)***
Bh Coffee Company LLC (PA) 914 377-2500
4 Warehouse Ln Ste 121 Elmsford (10523) ***(G-4532)***
BH Multi Com Corp (PA) 212 944-0020
15 W 46th St Fl 6 New York (10036) ***(G-9069)***
Bharat Electronics Limited 516 248-4021
53 Hilton Ave Garden City (11530) ***(G-5252)***
Bhi Elevator Cabs Inc 516 431-5665
74 Alabama Ave Island Park (11558) ***(G-6512)***
Bi Nutraceuticals Inc 631 232-1105
120 Hoffman Ln Central Islip (11749) ***(G-3360)***
Bianca Group Ltd 212 768-3011
244 W 39th St Fl 4 New York (10018) ***(G-9070)***
Bibo International LLC 617 304-2242
130 Water St Apt 4g New York (10005) ***(G-9071)***
Bick & Heintz Inc 315 733-7577
1101 Stark St Utica (13502) ***(G-15680)***
Bicker Inc 212 688-0085
50 Broad St Ste 301 New York (10004) ***(G-9072)***
Bidpress LLC 267 973-8876
659 Washington St Apt 5r New York (10014) ***(G-9073)***
Bielecky Bros Inc (PA) 718 424-4764
5022 72nd St Woodside (11377) ***(G-16646)***
Bielka Inc 212 980-6841
141 E 56th St Apt 6f New York (10022) ***(G-9074)***
Bien Cuit LLC 718 852-0200
120 Smith St Brooklyn (11201) ***(G-1609)***
Big Apple Elevtr Srv & Consult 212 279-0700
247 W 30th St New York (10001) ***(G-9075)***
Big Apple Sign Corp 631 342-0303
3 Oval Dr Islandia (11749) ***(G-6522)***
Big Apple Sign Corp (PA) 212 629-3650
247 W 35th St Rm 400 New York (10001) ***(G-9076)***
Big Apple Visual Group, Islandia *Also called Big Apple Sign Corp* ***(G-6522)***
BIG APPLE VISUAL GROUP, New York *Also called Big Apple Sign Corp* ***(G-9076)***
Big Apple Welding Supply 718 439-3959
236 47th St Brooklyn (11220) ***(G-1610)***
Big Bear, Buffalo *Also called Stephen M Kiernan* ***(G-3076)***
Big Data Bizviz LLC 716 803-2367
1075 East And West Rd West Seneca (14224) ***(G-16294)***
Big Fish Entertainment LLC 646 797-4955
1411 Broadway Fl 16 New York (10018) ***(G-9077)***
Big Geyser Inc (PA) 718 821-2200
5765 48th St Maspeth (11378) ***(G-7827)***
Big Heart Pet Brands 716 891-6566
243 Urban St Buffalo (14211) ***(G-2733)***
Big Idea Brands LLC 212 938-0270
1410 Broadway Frnt 4 New York (10018) ***(G-9078)***
Big Indie - Beautiful Boy LLC (PA) 917 464-5599
41 Plochmann Ln Woodstock (12498) ***(G-16684)***
Big John's Beef Jerky, Saratoga Springs *Also called Big Johns Adirondack Inc* ***(G-14571)***
Big Johns Adirondack Inc 518 587-3680
45 N Milton Rd Saratoga Springs (12866) ***(G-14571)***
Big Shine Energy, Newburgh *Also called Big Shine Worldwide Inc* ***(G-12216)***
Big Shine Worldwide Inc 845 444-5255
300 Corporate Blvd Newburgh (12550) ***(G-12216)***
Big White Wall Holding Inc 917 281-2649
41 E 11th St Fl 11 New York (10003) ***(G-9079)***
Bigbee Steel and Tank Company 518 273-0801
958 19th St Watervliet (12189) ***(G-16041)***
Bigname Commerce LLC 631 693-1070
5300 New Horizons Blvd Amityville (11701) ***(G-265)***
Bignay Inc 786 346-1673
315 E 86th St Apt 21ge New York (10028) ***(G-9080)***
Bigrow Paper Mfg Corp 718 624-4439
930 Bedford Ave Brooklyn (11205) ***(G-1611)***
Bigrow Paper Product, Brooklyn *Also called Bigrow Paper Mfg Corp* ***(G-1611)***
Bigsky Technologies LLC 585 270-5282
1600 N Clinton Ave Ste 11 Rochester (14621) ***(G-13663)***
Bigwood Systems Inc 607 257-0915
35 Thornwood Dr Ste 400 Ithaca (14850) ***(G-6560)***
Bilbee Controls Inc 518 622-3033
628 Main St Cairo (12413) ***(G-3147)***
Bilco Industries Inc 917 783-5008
214 W 39th St Rm 301 New York (10018) ***(G-9081)***
Bilinski Sausage Mfg Co, Cohoes *Also called Schonwetter Enterprises Inc* ***(G-3620)***
Bill Lake Homes Construction 518 673-2424
188 Flanders Rd Sprakers (12166) ***(G-14987)***
Bill Shea Enterprises Inc 585 343-2284
8825 Alexander Rd Batavia (14020) ***(G-613)***
Billanti Casting Co Inc 516 775-4800
299 S 11th St New Hyde Park (11040) ***(G-8520)***
Billanti Jewelry Casting, New Hyde Park *Also called Billanti Casting Co Inc* ***(G-8520)***
Billie-Ann Plastics Pkg Corp 718 497-3409
360 Troutman St Brooklyn (11237) ***(G-1612)***
Billing Blocks Inc 718 442-5006
147 North Ave Staten Island (10314) ***(G-15050)***

Billing Coding and Prtg Inc 718 827-9409
455 Grant Ave Brooklyn (11208) *(G-1613)*
Billion Tower Intl LLC 212 220-0608
989 6th Ave Fl 8 New York (10018) *(G-9082)*
Billion Tower USA LLC 212 220-0608
989 Avenue Of The America New York (10018) *(G-9083)*
Billsboro Winery 315 789-9538
4760 State Route 14 Geneva (14456) *(G-5317)*
Billy Beez Usa LLC 315 741-5099
9090 Destiy Usa Dr L301 Syracuse (13204) *(G-15257)*
Billy Beez Usa LLC (PA) 646 606-2249
3 W 35th St Fl 3 New York (10001) *(G-9084)*
Billy Beez Usa LLC 845 915-4709
1282 Palisades Center Dr West Nyack (10994) *(G-16266)*
Biltron Automotive Products 631 928-8613
509 Bicycle Path Unit Q Port Jeff STA (11776) *(G-13212)*
Bimbo Bakeries 631 274-4906
955 Grand Blvd Deer Park (11729) *(G-3951)*
Bimbo Bakeries 518 463-2221
78 N Manning Blvd Albany (12206) *(G-48)*
Bimbo Bakeries USA, Bay Shore *Also called Bimbo Foods Bakeries Inc (G-665)*
Bimbo Bakeries Usa Inc 716 692-9140
1960 Niagara Falls Blvd Tonawanda (14150) *(G-15527)*
Bimbo Bakeries Usa Inc 518 993-3300
And Dygert Rd Rr 5 Nelliston (13410) *(G-8481)*
Bimbo Bakeries Usa Inc 718 601-1561
5625 Broadway Frnt 2 Bronx (10463) *(G-1229)*
Bimbo Bakeries Usa Inc 845 255-4345
27 N Putt Corners Rd New Paltz (12561) *(G-8575)*
Bimbo Bakeries Usa Inc 516 877-2850
12 E Jericho Tpke Mineola (11501) *(G-8207)*
Bimbo Bakeries Usa Inc 716 372-8444
111 N 2nd St Olean (14760) *(G-12593)*
Bimbo Bakeries Usa Inc 631 951-5183
14 Spence St Bay Shore (11706) *(G-663)*
Bimbo Bakeries Usa Inc 516 887-1024
669 Sunrise Hwy Spc 4 Lynbrook (11563) *(G-7661)*
Bimbo Bakeries Usa Inc 315 379-9069
19 Miner St Ste D Canton (13617) *(G-3254)*
Bimbo Bakeries Usa Inc 518 563-1320
67 S Peru St Plattsburgh (12901) *(G-13110)*
Bimbo Bakeries Usa Inc 718 463-6300
5754 Page Pl Maspeth (11378) *(G-7828)*
Bimbo Bakeries Usa Inc 518 489-4053
40 Fuller Rd Albany (12205) *(G-49)*
Bimbo Bakeries Usa Inc 203 531-2311
30 Inez Dr Bay Shore (11706) *(G-664)*
Bimbo Bakeries Usa Inc 716 706-0450
2900 Commerce Pkwy Lancaster (14086) *(G-7010)*
Bimbo Bakeries Usa Inc 845 568-0943
98 Scobie Dr Newburgh (12550) *(G-12217)*
Bimbo Bakeries Usa Inc 800 856-8544
1624 Castle Gardens Rd Vestal (13850) *(G-15810)*
Bimbo Bakeries Usa Inc 315 782-4189
1100 Water St Watertown (13601) *(G-16002)*
Bimbo Bakeries Usa Inc 845 294-5282
9 Police Dr Goshen (10924) *(G-5476)*
Bimbo Foods Bakeries Inc (HQ) 631 273-6000
40 Harold Ct Bay Shore (11706) *(G-665)*
Bin Optics 604 257-3200
20 Thornwood Dr Ste 100 Ithaca (14850) *(G-6561)*
Binah Magazines Corp 718 305-5200
207 Foster Ave Brooklyn (11230) *(G-1614)*
Bindle and Keep 917 740-5002
47 Hall St Ste 109 Brooklyn (11205) *(G-1615)*
Binghamton Burial Vault Co Inc 607 722-4931
1114 Porter Ave Binghamton (13901) *(G-865)*
Binghamton Knitting Co Inc 607 722-6941
11 Alice St Binghamton (13904) *(G-866)*
Binghamton Precast & Sup Corp 607 722-0334
18 Phelps St Binghamton (13901) *(G-867)*
Binghamton Press, Vestal *Also called Gannett Co Inc (G-15816)*
Binghamton Simulator Co Inc 607 321-2980
151 Court St Binghamton (13901) *(G-868)*
Bino Products LLC 212 689-6008
236 5th Ave Fl 8 New York (10001) *(G-9085)*
Binoptics LLC (HQ) 607 257-3200
9 Brown Rd Ithaca (14850) *(G-6562)*
Bio Nutrition, Oceanside *Also called Only Natural Inc (G-12549)*
Bio Service, Woodside *Also called Firecom Inc (G-16655)*
Bio-Botanica Inc (PA) 631 231-0987
75 Commerce Dr Hauppauge (11788) *(G-5780)*
Bio-Chem Barrier Systems LLC 631 261-2682
11 W Scudder Pl Northport (11768) *(G-12464)*
Bio-Nutritional Products, White Plains *Also called Meta-Therm Corp (G-16476)*
Biobat Inc (PA) 718 270-1011
450 Clarkson Ave Msc129 Brooklyn (11203) *(G-1616)*
Biochemical Diagnostics Inc 631 595-9200
180 Heartland Blvd Edgewood (11717) *(G-4397)*
Biocontinuum Group Inc 212 406-1060
116 Chambers St New York (10007) *(G-9086)*
Biodesign Inc of New York (PA) 845 454-6610
1 Sunset Rdg Carmel (10512) *(G-3274)*
Biodex Medical Systems Inc (PA) 631 924-9000
20 Ramsey Rd Shirley (11967) *(G-14832)*
Biodex Medical Systems Inc 631 924-3146
49 Natcon Dr Shirley (11967) *(G-14833)*
Biodigitalpc, New Hyde Park *Also called Arnouse Digital Devices Corp (G-8517)*
Biofeedback Instrument Corp 212 222-5665
255 W 98th St Apt 3d New York (10025) *(G-9087)*
Bioinformatics Publishing, New York *Also called Genomeweb LLC (G-9906)*
Bioivt LLC (PA) 516 483-1196
123 Frost St Ste 115 Westbury (11590) *(G-16319)*
Biolitec Inc 413 525-0600
110 E 42nd St Rm 1800 New York (10017) *(G-9088)*
Biologique Recherche, New York *Also called Distribio USA LLC (G-9540)*
Biomed Pharmaceuticals Inc 914 592-0525
4 Skyline Dr Ste 5 Hawthorne (10532) *(G-5984)*
Biomedical & Industrial, Farmingdale *Also called Netech Corporation (G-4836)*
Bionic Eye Technologies Inc 845 505-5254
4 Willow Lake Dr Fishkill (12524) *(G-4943)*
Biopool Us Inc 716 483-3851
2823 Girts Rd Jamestown (14701) *(G-6701)*
Biorem Environmental Inc 585 924-2220
100 Rawson Rd Ste 230 Victor (14564) *(G-15831)*
Bioresearch Inc (PA) 212 734-5315
4 Sunset Ln Pound Ridge (10576) *(G-13375)*
Biosoil Farm Inc 518 344-4920
204 Glenville Industrial Glenville (12302) *(G-5444)*
Biospecifics Technologies Corp (PA) 516 593-7000
35 Wilbur St Lynbrook (11563) *(G-7662)*
Biospherix Ltd 315 387-3414
25 Union St Parish (13131) *(G-12860)*
Biospherix Medical, Parish *Also called Biospherix Ltd (G-12860)*
Biotech Energy Inc 800 340-1387
100 Clinton Point Dr Plattsburgh (12901) *(G-13111)*
Biotech Energy Systems, Plattsburgh *Also called Biotech Energy Inc (G-13111)*
Biotemper 516 302-7985
516 Mineola Ave Carle Place (11514) *(G-3263)*
Biotemper Plus, Carle Place *Also called Biotemper (G-3263)*
Biotie Therapies Inc 650 244-4850
420 Saw Mill River Rd Ardsley (10502) *(G-394)*
Bioworks Inc (PA) 585 924-4362
100 Rawson Rd Ste 205 Victor (14564) *(G-15832)*
Birch Coffee, Long Island City *Also called Birch Guys LLC (G-7400)*
Birch Guys LLC 917 763-0751
4035 23rd St Long Island City (11101) *(G-7400)*
Birch Machine & Tool Inc 716 735-9802
80 Telegraph Rd Middleport (14105) *(G-8131)*
Birdair Inc (HQ) 716 633-9500
65 Lawrence Bell Dr # 100 Amherst (14221) *(G-218)*
Birds Eye Foods Inc 716 988-3218
Mechanic St South Dayton (14138) *(G-14927)*
Birdsigns Inc 201 388-7613
16 W 19th St Apt 3e New York (10011) *(G-9089)*
Birkett Mills (PA) 315 536-3311
163 Main St Ste 2 Penn Yan (14527) *(G-12949)*
Birkett Mills 315 536-4112
163 Main St Ste 3 Penn Yan (14527) *(G-12950)*
Birnbaum & Bullock Ltd 212 242-2914
151 W 25th St Rm 2a New York (10001) *(G-9090)*
Birthstone Enterprises, New York *Also called Alchemy Simya Inc (G-8786)*
Bishop Print Shop Inc 607 965-8155
9 East St Edmeston (13335) *(G-4425)*
Bisley Inc 212 675-3055
1140 Broadway Rm 902 New York (10001) *(G-9091)*
Bisley North America, New York *Also called Bisley Inc (G-9091)*
Bison Bag Co Inc 716 434-4380
5404 Crown Dr Lockport (14094) *(G-7287)*
Bison Iron & Step, Buffalo *Also called M K Ulrich Construction Inc (G-2930)*
Bison Products, Buffalo *Also called Upstate Niagara Coop Inc (G-3113)*
Bison Steel Incorporated 716 683-0900
2 Main St Ste 103 Depew (14043) *(G-4080)*
Bissel-Babcock Millwork Inc 716 761-6976
3866 Kendrick Rd Sherman (14781) *(G-14815)*
Bistate Oil Management Corp 212 935-4110
10 E 40th St Rm 2710 New York (10016) *(G-9092)*
Bistrian Cement Corporation 631 324-1123
225 Springs Fireplace Rd East Hampton (11937) *(G-4232)*
Bittner Company LLC 585 214-1790
75 Goodway Dr Ste 3 Rochester (14623) *(G-13664)*
Bitzer Scroll Inc 315 463-2101
6055 Court Street Rd Syracuse (13206) *(G-15258)*
Bizbash Masterplanner, New York *Also called Bizbash Media Inc (G-9093)*
Bizbash Media Inc (PA) 646 638-3602
115 W 27th St Fl 8 New York (10001) *(G-9093)*
BJ Magazines Inc 212 367-9705
200 Varick St New York (10014) *(G-9094)*
BJG Services LLC 516 592-5692
237 W 35th St Ste 505 New York (10001) *(G-9095)*
BK Associates Intl Inc 607 432-1499
127 Commerce Rd Oneonta (13820) *(G-12626)*
Bk Printing Inc 315 565-5396
6507 Basile Rowe East Syracuse (13057) *(G-4326)*

ALPHABETIC

(PA)=Parent Co (HQ)=Headquarters (DH)=Div Headquarters
2019 Harris
New York Manufacturers Directory
839

Bklynfavors Party Print...718 277-0233
49 Sheridan Ave Brooklyn (11208) *(G-1617)*
Black & Decker (us) Inc...914 235-6300
2 Powers Ln Brewster (10509) *(G-1159)*
Black & Decker (us) Inc...716 884-6220
881 W Delavan Ave Buffalo (14209) *(G-2734)*
Black & Decker (us) Inc...631 952-2008
180 Oser Ave Ste 100 Hauppauge (11788) *(G-5781)*
Black & Decker Corporation...718 335-1042
5615 Queens Blvd Woodside (11377) *(G-16647)*
Black Bear Company Inc...718 784-7330
90 E Hawthorne Ave Valley Stream (11580) *(G-15774)*
Black Bear Fuels Oil, Harris *Also called Jus-Sar Fuel Inc (G-5722)*
Black Book Photography Inc...212 979-6700
740 Broadway Ste 202 New York (10003) *(G-9096)*
Black Book, The, New York *Also called Black Book Photography Inc (G-9096)*
Black Enterprise, New York *Also called Earl G Graves Pubg Co Inc (G-9605)*
Black Hound, Brooklyn *Also called Amiram Dror Inc (G-1529)*
Black Millwork, Spring Valley *Also called Regal Windows & Doors LLC (G-15006)*
Black River Brewing Co Inc...315 755-2739
500 Newell St Watertown (13601) *(G-16003)*
Black River Generations LLC...315 773-2314
4515 2nd St Fort Drum (13602) *(G-5091)*
Black River Woodworking LLC...315 376-8405
4773 State Route 410 Castorland (13620) *(G-3298)*
Blackbirds Brooklyn LLC...917 362-4080
597 Sackett St Brooklyn (11217) *(G-1618)*
Blackbook, New York *Also called McCarthy LLC (G-10740)*
Blackbook Media Corp...212 334-1800
32 Union Sq E Ste 4l New York (10003) *(G-9097)*
Blackbox Biometrics Inc...585 329-3399
125 Tech Park Dr Ste 1131 Rochester (14623) *(G-13665)*
Blackburn Truck Bodies LLC...315 448-3236
6216 Thompson Rd Ste 3 Syracuse (13206) *(G-15259)*
Blackheart Records, Brooklyn *Also called Lagunatic Music & Filmworks (G-2091)*
Blackstone Advanced Tech LLC...716 665-5410
86 Blackstone Ave Jamestown (14701) *(G-6702)*
Blackstone Group, New York *Also called Grand Slam Holdings LLC (G-9971)*
Blackswirl, New York *Also called Robert Ehrlich (G-11407)*
Blades...212 477-1059
659 Broadway New York (10012) *(G-9098)*
Blading Services Unlimited LLC...315 875-5313
40 Madison Blvd Canastota (13032) *(G-3240)*
Blair Cnstr Fabrication Sp...315 253-2321
13 Brae Ridge Rd Auburn (13021) *(G-470)*
Blair Industries Inc (PA)...631 924-6600
3671 Horseblock Rd Medford (11763) *(G-7939)*
Blair-Hsm, Medford *Also called HSM Machine Works Inc (G-7953)*
Blanche P Field LLC...212 355-6616
155 E 56th St Ph New York (10022) *(G-9099)*
Blasch Precision Ceramics Inc (PA)...518 436-1263
580 Broadway Ste 1 Menands (12204) *(G-8083)*
Blaser Production Inc...845 294-3200
31 Hatfield Ln Goshen (10924) *(G-5477)*
Blaser Swisslube Holding Corp (HQ)...845 294-3200
31 Hatfield Ln Goshen (10924) *(G-5478)*
Blatt Searle & Company Ltd (PA)...212 730-7717
4121 28th St Long Island City (11101) *(G-7401)*
Blc Textiles Inc...844 500-7900
330 Old Country Rd # 201 Mineola (11501) *(G-8208)*
Bleecker Pastry Tartufo Inc...718 937-9830
3722 13th St Long Island City (11101) *(G-7402)*
Bleezarde Publishing Inc...518 756-2030
164 Main St Ravena (12143) *(G-13452)*
Blend Smoothie Bar...845 568-7366
25 Creamery Dr New Windsor (12553) *(G-8637)*
Bli International Inc...631 940-9000
75 N Industry Ct Deer Park (11729) *(G-3952)*
Blinds To Go, Hartsdale *Also called TLC Vision (usa) Corporation (G-5746)*
Blinds To Go (us) Inc...718 477-9523
2845 Richmond Ave Staten Island (10314) *(G-15051)*
Blindtek Designer Systems Inc...914 347-7100
1 Hayes St Elmsford (10523) *(G-4533)*
Bliss Foods Inc...212 732-8888
275 Greenwich St Frnt 2 New York (10007) *(G-9100)*
Bliss Foods Inc...212 732-8888
275 Greenwich St Frnt 2 New York (10007) *(G-9101)*
Bliss Machine Inc...585 492-5128
260 North St Arcade (14009) *(G-379)*
Bliss-Poston The Second Wind...212 481-1055
928 Broadway Ste 403 New York (10010) *(G-9102)*
Bloch Industries LLC...585 334-9600
140 Commerce Dr Rochester (14623) *(G-13666)*
Blondie S Bakeshop Inc...631 424-4545
90 Washington Dr Centerport (11721) *(G-3347)*
Blood Moon Productions Ltd...718 556-9410
75 Saint Marks Pl Staten Island (10301) *(G-15052)*
Blooming Grove Stair Co (PA)...845 783-4245
1 Stair Way Monroe (10950) *(G-8265)*
Blooming Grove Stair Co...845 791-4016
309 E Broadway Monticello (12701) *(G-8320)*
Bloomsburg Carpet Inds Inc...212 688-7447
11 E 26th St Frnt New York (10010) *(G-9103)*
Bloomsbury Publishing Inc...212 419-5300
1385 Brdwy Fl 5 Flr 5 New York (10018) *(G-9104)*
Bloomsbury USA, New York *Also called Bloomsbury Publishing Inc (G-9104)*
Blu Sand LLC...212 564-1147
333 W 39th St Rm 704 New York (10018) *(G-9105)*
Blue and White Publishing Inc...215 431-3339
425 Riverside Dr Apt 3c New York (10025) *(G-9106)*
Blue Box, Brooklyn *Also called Pink Box Accessories LLC (G-2319)*
Blue Boy, Staten Island *Also called Rgm Signs Inc (G-15129)*
Blue Chip Mold Inc...585 647-1790
95 Lagrange Ave Rochester (14613) *(G-13667)*
Blue Duck Trading Ltd...212 268-3122
463 7th Ave Rm 806 New York (10018) *(G-9107)*
Blue Horizon Media Inc (PA)...212 661-7878
11 Park Pl Rm 1508 New York (10007) *(G-9108)*
Blue Manufacturing Co Inc...607 796-2463
3852 Watkins Rd Millport (14864) *(G-8195)*
Blue Marble Ice Cream LLC...718 858-5551
220 36th St Unit 33 Brooklyn (11232) *(G-1619)*
Blue Ocean Food Trading LLC...718 689-4291
154 42nd St Brooklyn (11232) *(G-1620)*
Blue Pig Ice Cream Factory...914 271-3850
121 Maple St Croton On Hudson (10520) *(G-3912)*
Blue Skies...631 392-1140
859 Long Island Ave Deer Park (11729) *(G-3953)*
Blue Sky Plastic Production...718 366-3966
305 Johnson Ave Brooklyn (11206) *(G-1621)*
Blue Star Beverages Corp...718 381-3535
1099 Flushing Ave Brooklyn (11237) *(G-1622)*
Blue Star Products Inc...631 952-3204
355 Marcus Blvd Ste 2 Hauppauge (11788) *(G-5782)*
Blue Stone Press, High Falls *Also called Ulster County Press Office (G-6141)*
Blue Tee Corp (PA)...212 598-0880
387 Park Ave S Fl 5 New York (10016) *(G-9109)*
Blue Toad Hard Cider...585 424-5508
120 Mushroom Blvd Rochester (14623) *(G-13668)*
Blue Tortilla LLC...631 451-0100
1070 Middle Country Rd # 4 Selden (11784) *(G-14760)*
Blue Wolf Group LLC (HQ)...866 455-9653
11 E 26th St Fl 21 New York (10010) *(G-9110)*
Bluebar Oil Co Inc...315 245-4328
8446 Mill Pond Way Blossvale (13308) *(G-963)*
Blueberry Knitting Inc (PA)...718 599-6520
138 Ross St Brooklyn (11211) *(G-1623)*
Bluebird Mobility, Williamsville *Also called Bluebird Transportation LLC (G-16571)*
Bluebird Transportation LLC...716 395-0000
5477 Main St Williamsville (14221) *(G-16571)*
Blueprint Cleanse, New York *Also called Zoe Sakoutis LLC (G-12181)*
Bluesoho (PA)...646 805-2583
160 Varick St Fl 2 New York (10013) *(G-9111)*
Blum & Fink Inc...212 695-2606
158 W 29th St Fl 12 New York (10001) *(G-9112)*
BMA Media Services Inc...585 385-2060
1655 Lyell Ave Rochester (14606) *(G-13669)*
BMC, Broadalbin *Also called Broadalbin Manufacturing Corp (G-1187)*
BMC LLC...716 681-7755
3155 Broadway St Buffalo (14227) *(G-2735)*
Bmg Chrysalis, New York *Also called Bmg Rights Management (us) LLC (G-9113)*
Bmg Printing and Promotion LLC...631 231-9200
170 Wilbur Pl Ste 700 Bohemia (11716) *(G-989)*
Bmg Rights Management (us) LLC (HQ)...212 561-3000
1 Park Ave Fl 18 New York (10016) *(G-9113)*
Bmg Systems...716 432-5160
4779 Transit Rd 169 Depew (14043) *(G-4081)*
Bmp America Inc...585 798-0950
11625 Maple Ridge Rd Medina (14103) *(G-7973)*
Bms Manufacturing Co Inc...607 535-2426
2857 County Line Rd Watkins Glen (14891) *(G-16058)*
BNC Innovative Woodworking...718 277-2800
555 Liberty Ave Brooklyn (11207) *(G-1624)*
Bnei Aram Soba Inc...718 645-4460
1616 Ocean Pkwy Brooklyn (11223) *(G-1625)*
BNH Lead Examiner Corp...718 807-1365
199 Lee Ave Ste 481 Brooklyn (11211) *(G-1626)*
Bnm Product Service...631 750-1586
1561 Lincoln Ave Holbrook (11741) *(G-6172)*
Bnns Co Inc...212 302-1844
71 W 47th St Ste 600-601 New York (10036) *(G-9114)*
BNo Intl Trdg Co Inc...716 487-1900
505 Chautauqua Ave Jamestown (14701) *(G-6703)*
Bnz Tech, East Setauket *Also called B & Z Technologies LLC (G-4298)*
Bo-Mer Plastics LLC...315 252-7216
13 Pulaski St Auburn (13021) *(G-471)*
Boa Handcuff Company, Huntington *Also called Boa Security Technologies Corp (G-6395)*
Boa Security Technologies Corp...516 576-0295
586 New York Ave Unit 3 Huntington (11743) *(G-6395)*
Boardman Simons Publishing (PA)...212 620-7200
55 Broad St Fl 26 New York (10004) *(G-9115)*
Bob Murphy Inc...607 729-3553
3127 Vestal Rd Vestal (13850) *(G-15811)*

Bob's Signs, Syracuse *Also called Wizard Equipment Inc* ***(G-15459)***
Bobley-Harmann Corporation........516 433-3800
200 Trade Zone Dr Unit 2 Ronkonkoma (11779) ***(G-14320)***
Bobrick Washroom Equipment Inc........518 877-7444
200 Commerce Dr Clifton Park (12065) ***(G-3565)***
Boces Business Office........607 763-3300
435 Glenwood Rd Binghamton (13905) ***(G-869)***
Bock Family Holdings Inc (HQ)........212 921-5688
525 Fashion Ave Rm 1000 New York (10018) ***(G-9116)***
Body Builders Inc........718 492-7997
5518 3rd Ave Brooklyn (11220) ***(G-1627)***
Bodyarmor, Whitestone *Also called Ba Sports Nutrition LLC* ***(G-16536)***
Bodycote Syracuse Heat Treatin........315 451-0000
4629 Crossroads Park Dr Liverpool (13088) ***(G-7224)***
Bodycote Thermal Proc Inc........585 436-7876
620 Buffalo Rd Rochester (14611) ***(G-13670)***
Boehm Surgical Instrument Corp........585 436-6584
966 Chili Ave Ste 3 Rochester (14611) ***(G-13671)***
Boeing Company........201 259-9400
304 Park Ave S New York (10010) ***(G-9117)***
Boeing Medcl Trtmnt Mltry Arcr, Norwich *Also called Chenango Concrete Corp* ***(G-12478)***
Boilermatic Welding Inds Inc (PA)........631 654-1341
17 Peconic Ave Medford (11763) ***(G-7940)***
Boka Printing Inc........607 725-3235
12 Hall St Binghamton (13903) ***(G-870)***
Bollman Hat Company........212 981-9836
411 5th Ave Fl 2 New York (10016) ***(G-9118)***
Bolton Point Wtr Trtmnt Plant........607 277-0660
1402 E Shore Dr Ithaca (14850) ***(G-6563)***
Bomac Inc........315 433-9181
6477 Ridings Rd Syracuse (13206) ***(G-15260)***
BOMB MAGAZINE, Brooklyn *Also called New Art Publications Inc* ***(G-2256)***
Bombardier Corp Track, Plattsburgh *Also called Bombardier Trnsp Holdings USA* ***(G-13113)***
Bombardier Mass Transit Corp........518 566-0150
71 Wall St Plattsburgh (12901) ***(G-13112)***
Bombardier Transportation........607 324-0216
1 William K Jackson Ln Hornell (14843) ***(G-6294)***
Bombardier Trnsp Holdings USA........607 776-4791
7940 State Route 415 Bath (14810) ***(G-641)***
Bombardier Trnsp Holdings USA........518 566-5067
71 Wall St Plattsburgh (12901) ***(G-13113)***
Bombay Kitchen Foods Inc........516 767-7401
76 S Bayles Ave Port Washington (11050) ***(G-13246)***
Bon Bons Chocolatier, Huntington *Also called Lady-N-Th-wndow Chocolates Inc* ***(G-6403)***
Boncraft Inc........716 662-9720
777 E Park Dr Tonawanda (14150) ***(G-15528)***
Bonded Concrete Inc (PA)........518 273-5800
303 Watervliet Shaker Rd Watervliet (12189) ***(G-16042)***
Bonded Concrete Inc........518 674-2854
Rr 43 West Sand Lake (12196) ***(G-16284)***
Bonduelle USA Inc........585 434-0399
100 Corporate Woods # 210 Rochester (14623) ***(G-13672)***
Bonduelle USA Inc........585 948-5252
40 Stevens St Oakfield (14125) ***(G-12523)***
Bondy Printing Corp........631 242-1510
267 W Main St Bay Shore (11706) ***(G-666)***
Bonelli Foods LLC........212 346-0942
139 Fulton St Rm 314 New York (10038) ***(G-9119)***
Bonide Products Inc........315 736-8231
6301 Sutliff Rd Oriskany (13424) ***(G-12751)***
Bonjour For Kids, New York *Also called Consolidated Childrens AP Inc* ***(G-9381)***
Bonk Sam Unforms Civilian Cap........718 585-0665
131 Rose Feiss Blvd Fl 2 Bronx (10454) ***(G-1230)***
Bonnie J, New York *Also called Sanoy Inc* ***(G-11484)***
Bonnier Publishing Usa Inc........212 321-0237
251 Park Ave S Fl 12 New York (10010) ***(G-9120)***
Bono Sawdust Co, Corona *Also called Bono Sawdust Supply Co Inc* ***(G-3839)***
Bono Sawdust Supply Co Inc........718 446-1374
3330 127th Pl Corona (11368) ***(G-3839)***
Bonsal American Inc........585 343-4741
102 Cedar St Batavia (14020) ***(G-614)***
Bonsal American Inc........631 208-8073
931 Burman Blvd Calverton (11933) ***(G-3162)***
Bonura and Sons Iron Works........718 381-4100
957 Lorraine Dr Franklin Square (11010) ***(G-5115)***
Book1one LLC........585 458-2101
655 Driving Park Ave Rochester (14613) ***(G-13673)***
Booklinks Publishing Svcs LLC........718 852-2116
55 Washington St Ste 253c Brooklyn (11201) ***(G-1628)***
Booklyn Artists Alliance Inc........718 383-9621
140 58th St Bldg B-7g Brooklyn (11220) ***(G-1629)***
Boom Creative Development, New York *Also called Boom LLC* ***(G-9121)***
Boom LLC........646 218-0752
800 3rd Ave Fl 2 New York (10022) ***(G-9121)***
Boonville Herald Inc........315 942-4449
105 E Schuyler St Boonville (13309) ***(G-1115)***
Boonville Manufacturing Corp........315 942-4368
13485 State Route 12 Boonville (13309) ***(G-1116)***
Boonvlle Hrald Adrndack Turist, Boonville *Also called Boonville Herald Inc* ***(G-1115)***
Boosey and Hawkes Inc (PA)........212 358-5300
229 W 28th St Fl 11 New York (10001) ***(G-9122)***
Borabora Fruit Juices Inc........914 438-8744
255 Milton Xrds Highland (12528) ***(G-6142)***
Borden & Riley Paper Co Inc........718 454-9494
18410 Jamaica Ave Ste W3 Hollis (11423) ***(G-6231)***
Borgattis Ravioli Egg Noodles........718 367-3799
632 E 187th St Bronx (10458) ***(G-1231)***
Borghese Inc (PA)........212 659-5318
3 E 54th St Fl 20 New York (10022) ***(G-9123)***
Borgwarner Inc........607 257-6700
800 Warren Rd Ithaca (14850) ***(G-6564)***
Borgwarner Inc........607 257-1800
780 Warren Rd Ithaca (14850) ***(G-6565)***
Borgwarner Ithaca LLC........607 257-6700
800 Warren Rd Ithaca (14850) ***(G-6566)***
Borgwarner Morse TEC Inc........607 266-5111
780 Warren Rd Ithaca (14850) ***(G-6567)***
Borgwarner Morse TEC LLC (HQ)........607 257-6700
800 Warren Rd Ithaca (14850) ***(G-6568)***
Borgwarner Morse TEC LLC........607 257-6700
3690 Luker Rd Cortland (13045) ***(G-3863)***
Bornomala USA Inc........347 753-2355
3766 72nd St Fl 3 Jackson Heights (11372) ***(G-6618)***
Boro Park Cutting Tool Corp........718 720-0610
106b Wakefield Ave Staten Island (10314) ***(G-15053)***
Boro Park Signs, Brooklyn *Also called Sign Group Inc* ***(G-2468)***
Bos-Hatten Inc........716 662-7030
50 Cobham Dr Orchard Park (14127) ***(G-12700)***
Boss Precision Ltd........585 352-7070
2440 S Union St Spencerport (14559) ***(G-14976)***
Boss Sauce, Rochester *Also called American Specialty Mfg Co* ***(G-13627)***
Boston Valley Pottery Inc (PA)........716 649-7490
6860 S Abbott Rd Orchard Park (14127) ***(G-12701)***
Boston Valley Terra Cotta, Orchard Park *Also called Boston Valley Pottery Inc* ***(G-12701)***
Botify Corporation........617 576-2005
119 W 24th St New York (10011) ***(G-9124)***
Botkier Ny LLC........212 343-2782
19 W 34th St Fl 7 New York (10001) ***(G-9125)***
Bottling Group LLC........315 788-6751
1035 Bradley St Watertown (13601) ***(G-16004)***
Bottling Group LLC........800 789-2626
1111 Westchester Ave White Plains (10604) ***(G-16429)***
Bottling Group LLC (HQ)........914 767-6000
1111 Westchester Ave White Plains (10604) ***(G-16430)***
Boucheron Joaillerie USA Inc........212 715-7330
460 Park Ave Fl 12 New York (10022) ***(G-9126)***
Boulay Fabrication Inc........315 677-5247
Rr 20 Box West La Fayette (13084) ***(G-6945)***
Boulevard Arts Inc........917 968-8693
1133 Broadway Ste 1523 New York (10010) ***(G-9127)***
Boulevard Printing........716 837-3800
1330 Niagara Falls Blvd # 2 Tonawanda (14150) ***(G-15529)***
Boundless Spatial Inc........646 831-5531
222 Broadway Fl 19 New York (10038) ***(G-9128)***
Boundless Technologies, Phelps *Also called Z-Axis Inc* ***(G-12984)***
Bourghol Brothers Inc........845 268-9752
73 Lake Rd Congers (10920) ***(G-3712)***
Bourne Co, New York *Also called Bourne Music Publishers* ***(G-9129)***
Bourne Music Publishers........212 391-4300
35 W 45th St Fl 2 New York (10036) ***(G-9129)***
Bow Industrial Corporation........518 561-0190
178 W Service Rd Champlain (12919) ***(G-3406)***
Bowe Industries Inc (PA)........718 441-6464
8836 77th Ave Glendale (11385) ***(G-5392)***
Bowe Industries Inc........718 441-6464
8836 77th Ave Glendale (11385) ***(G-5393)***
Bowen Products Corporation........315 498-4481
5084 S Onondaga Rd Nedrow (13120) ***(G-8478)***
Bowne Business Solutions, New York *Also called Donnelley Financial LLC* ***(G-9556)***
Bowne Enterprise Solutions, New York *Also called Donnelley Financial LLC* ***(G-9555)***
Boxcar Press Incorporated........315 473-0930
509 W Fayette St Ste 135 Syracuse (13204) ***(G-15261)***
Boyd Printing Company, Latham *Also called William Boyd Printing Co Inc* ***(G-7098)***
Boydell & Brewer Inc........585 275-0419
668 Mount Hope Ave Rochester (14620) ***(G-13674)***
Boylan Bottling Co Inc........800 289-7978
6 E 43rd St Fl 18 New York (10017) ***(G-9130)***
BP Beyond Printing Inc........516 328-2700
117 Fulton Ave Hempstead (11550) ***(G-6008)***
BP Digital Imaging LLC........607 753-0022
87 Main St Cortland (13045) ***(G-3864)***
BP Magazine, Buffalo *Also called Green Apple Courage Inc* ***(G-2858)***
Bpe Studio Inc........212 868-9896
270 W 38th St Rm 702 New York (10018) ***(G-9131)***
Bqp, Glens Falls *Also called Brennans Quick Print Inc* ***(G-5419)***
Bracci Ironworks Inc........718 629-2374
1440 Utica Ave Brooklyn (11203) ***(G-1630)***
Brach Knitting Mills Inc........845 651-4450
12 Roosevelt Ave Florida (10921) ***(G-4968)***
Brach Machine Inc........585 343-9134
4814 Ellicott Street Rd Batavia (14020) ***(G-615)***
Bradford Publications Inc........716 373-2500
639 W Norton Dr Olean (14760) ***(G-12594)***

ALPHABETIC

Bradley Marketing Group Inc 212 967-6100
1431 Broadway Fl 12 New York (10018) *(G-9132)*
Braga Woodworks 845 342-4636
19 Montgomery St Middletown (10940) *(G-8139)*
Bragley Mfg Co Inc 718 622-7469
924 Bergen St Brooklyn (11238) *(G-1631)*
Bragley Shipg Carrying Cases, Brooklyn *Also called Bragley Mfg Co Inc (G-1631)*
Braided Oak Spirits LLC 845 381-1525
12 Roberts St Middletown (10940) *(G-8140)*
Brainpop Group, New York *Also called Brainpop LLC (G-9133)*
Brainpop LLC 212 574-6017
71 W 23rd St Fl 17 New York (10010) *(G-9133)*
Brainwave Toys-New York, New York *Also called Vogel Applied Technologies (G-12051)*
Brakewell Stl Fabricators Inc 845 469-9131
55 Leone Ln Chester (10918) *(G-3469)*
Bral Nader Fine Jewelry Inc 800 493-1222
576 5th Ave New York (10036) *(G-9134)*
Bramson House Inc 516 764-5006
151 Albany Ave Freeport (11520) *(G-5146)*
Brand Box USA LLC 607 584-7682
1 Chamberlain St Binghamton (13904) *(G-871)*
Brands Within Reach LLC 847 720-9090
141 Halstead Ave Ste 201 Mamaroneck (10543) *(G-7735)*
Brandt Equipment LLC 718 994-0800
4461 Bronx Blvd Bronx (10470) *(G-1232)*
Brandt Industries, Bronx *Also called Brandt Equipment LLC (G-1232)*
Brandys Mold and Tool Ctr Ltd (PA) 585 334-8333
10 Riverton Way West Henrietta (14586) *(G-16232)*
Brannkey Inc (PA) 212 371-1515
1385 Broadway Fl 14 New York (10018) *(G-9135)*
Brannock Device Co Inc 315 475-9862
116 Luther Ave Liverpool (13088) *(G-7225)*
Branson Ultrasonics Corp 585 624-8000
475 Quaker Meeting Hse Rd Honeoye Falls (14472) *(G-6262)*
Brasilans Press Pblcations Inc 212 764-6161
60 W 46th St Rm 302 New York (10036) *(G-9136)*
Brauen Constrution 585 492-0042
1087 Chaffee Rd Arcade (14009) *(G-380)*
Braun Bros Brushes Inc 631 667-2179
35 4th St Valley Stream (11581) *(G-15775)*
Braun Brush Company, Albertson *Also called Braun Industries Inc (G-146)*
Braun Horticulture Inc 716 282-6101
3302 Highland Ave Niagara Falls (14305) *(G-12265)*
Braun Industries Inc (PA) 516 741-6000
43 Albertson Ave Albertson (11507) *(G-146)*
Brayley Tool & Machine Inc 585 342-7190
1685 Lyell Ave Rochester (14606) *(G-13675)*
Braze Inc 504 327-7269
318 W 39th St Fl 5 New York (10018) *(G-9137)*
Braze Alloy Inc 718 815-5757
3075 Richmond Ter Staten Island (10303) *(G-15054)*
Brazen Street LLC 516 305-7951
734 Pennsylvania Ave Brooklyn (11207) *(G-1632)*
Bread & Butter, New York *Also called Tphg 419 Ltd (G-11879)*
Bread Factory LLC 914 637-8150
30 Grove Ave New Rochelle (10801) *(G-8593)*
Breed Enterprises Inc 585 388-0126
34 Water St Fairport (14450) *(G-4626)*
Bren-Trnics Batteries Intl Inc 631 499-5155
10 Brayton Ct Commack (11725) *(G-3683)*
Bren-Trnics Batteries Intl LLC 631 499-5155
10 Brayton Ct Commack (11725) *(G-3684)*
Bren-Tronics Inc 631 499-5155
10 Brayton Ct Commack (11725) *(G-3685)*
Brennans Quick Print Inc 518 793-4999
6 Collins Dr Glens Falls (12804) *(G-5419)*
Brenseke George Wldg Ir Works 631 271-4870
915 Long Island Ave Ste A Deer Park (11729) *(G-3954)*
Brenseke's, Deer Park *Also called Brenseke George Wldg Ir Works (G-3954)*
Breton Industries Inc (PA) 518 842-3030
1 Sam Stratton Rd Amsterdam (12010) *(G-329)*
Brewer & Newell Printing, Rochester *Also called Forward Enterprises Inc (G-13814)*
Brewer-Cantelmo Co Inc 212 244-4600
55 W 39th St Rm 205 New York (10018) *(G-9138)*
Brewerton Special Tee's, Brewerton *Also called Irene Cerone (G-1151)*
Brewery Ommegang Ltd 607 286-4144
656 County Highway 33 Cooperstown (13326) *(G-3742)*
Brewster Coachworks, Lagrangeville *Also called Graphics Slution Providers Inc (G-6956)*
Brewster Transit Mix Corp (PA) 845 279-3738
31 Fields Ln Brewster (10509) *(G-1160)*
Brewster Transit Mix Corp 845 279-3738
Fields Ln Brewster (10509) *(G-1161)*
Brick & Ballerstein Inc 718 497-1400
1085 Irving Ave Ridgewood (11385) *(G-13532)*
Brick-It Inc 631 244-3993
17 Central Ave Hauppauge (11788) *(G-5783)*
Brickit 631 727-8977
17 Central Ave Hauppauge (11788) *(G-5784)*
Bridal Guide, New York *Also called Rfp LLC (G-11381)*
Bridge Components Inc 716 731-1184
2122 Cory Dr Sanborn (14132) *(G-14540)*
Bridge Enterprises Inc 718 625-6622
544 Park Ave Brooklyn (11205) *(G-1633)*
Bridge Fulfillment Inc 718 625-6622
445 Park Ave 204 Brooklyn (11205) *(G-1634)*
Bridge Metal Industries LLC 914 663-9200
717 S 3rd Ave Mount Vernon (10550) *(G-8382)*
Bridge Printing Inc 212 243-5390
4710 32nd Pl Fl 2 Long Island City (11101) *(G-7403)*
Bridge Records Inc 914 654-9270
200 Clinton Ave New Rochelle (10801) *(G-8594)*
Bridgehampton Steel & Wldg Inc 631 537-2486
27 Foster Ave Bridgehampton (11932) *(G-1179)*
Bridgeport Metalcraft Inc 315 623-9597
567 County Route 23 Constantia (13044) *(G-3739)*
Bridgestone APM Company 419 423-9552
6350 Inducon Dr E Sanborn (14132) *(G-14541)*
Brigadoon Software Inc (PA) 845 624-0909
119 Rockland Ctr 250 Nanuet (10954) *(G-8459)*
Brigantine Inc 212 354-8550
225 W 37th St New York (10018) *(G-9139)*
Brigar X-Press Solutions Inc 518 438-7817
5 Sand Creek Rd Ste 100 Albany (12205) *(G-50)*
Brigden Memorials, Albion *Also called Woodside Granite Industries (G-164)*
Briggs & Stratton Corporation 315 495-0100
4245 Highbridge Rd Sherrill (13461) *(G-14818)*
Briggs & Stratton Corporation 315 495-0100
5375 N Main St Munnsville (13409) *(G-8457)*
Bright Chair Co, Middletown *Also called Princeton Upholstery Co Inc (G-8172)*
Bright Kids Nyc Inc 917 539-4575
225 Broadway Ste 1504 New York (10007) *(G-9140)*
Bright Line Eting Slutions LLC 585 245-2956
41 Lake Lacoma Dr Pittsford (14534) *(G-13009)*
Bright Way Supply Inc 718 833-2882
6302 Fort Hamilton Pkwy Brooklyn (11219) *(G-1635)*
Brightline Ventures I LLC 212 626-6829
1120 Avenue Of The Americ New York (10036) *(G-9141)*
Brighton Design, Tonawanda *Also called Brighton Tool & Die Designers (G-15530)*
Brighton Tool & Die Designers (PA) 716 876-0879
463 Brighton Rd Tonawanda (14150) *(G-15530)*
Brijon, Ronkonkoma *Also called Lanco Corporation (G-14368)*
Brilliant Jewelers/Mjj Inc 212 353-2326
902 Broadway Fl 18 New York (10010) *(G-9142)*
Brilliant Stars Collection Inc 516 365-9000
150 Great Neck Rd Ste 400 Great Neck (11021) *(G-5540)*
Brinkman Intl Group Inc (PA) 585 429-5000
167 Ames St Rochester (14611) *(G-13676)*
Brinkman Precision Inc 585 429-5001
100 Park Centre Dr West Henrietta (14586) *(G-16233)*
Brinkman Products Inc 585 235-4545
167 Ames St Rochester (14611) *(G-13677)*
Brio USA 585 319-5599
85 Mushroom Blvd Rochester (14623) *(G-13678)*
Bristol Boarding Inc 585 271-7860
1149 Highland Ave Rochester (14620) *(G-13679)*
Bristol Core Inc 585 919-0302
5310 North St Canandaigua (14424) *(G-3212)*
Bristol Gift Co Inc 845 496-2821
8 North St Washingtonville (10992) *(G-15963)*
Bristol Instruments Inc 585 924-2620
770 Canning Pkwy Victor (14564) *(G-15833)*
Bristol Metals Inc 585 657-7665
7817 State Route 5 And 20 Bloomfield (14469) *(G-948)*
Bristol Seamless Ring Corp 212 874-2645
209 W 86th St Apt 817 New York (10024) *(G-9143)*
Bristol-Myers Squibb Company (PA) 212 546-4000
430 E 29th St Fl 14 New York (10016) *(G-9144)*
Bristol-Myers Squibb Company 315 432-2000
6000 Thompson Rd East Syracuse (13057) *(G-4327)*
Bristol-Myers Squibb Company 516 832-2191
1000 Stewart Ave Garden City (11530) *(G-5253)*
Bristol/White Plains 914 681-1800
305 North St White Plains (10605) *(G-16431)*
British American Publishing 518 786-6000
19 British American Blvd Latham (12110) *(G-7065)*
British Science Corporation (PA) 212 980-8700
100 Wheeler Ave Staten Island (10314) *(G-15055)*
Brittish American Envmtl, Clifton Park *Also called Microb Phase Services (G-3571)*
Broadalbin Manufacturing Corp 518 883-5313
8 Pine St Broadalbin (12025) *(G-1187)*
Broadcast Manager Inc 212 509-1200
65 Broadway Ste 602 New York (10006) *(G-9145)*
Broadnet Technologies Inc 315 443-3694
2-212 Center For Science Syracuse (13244) *(G-15262)*
Broadway Knitting Mills Inc 716 692-4421
1333 Strad Ave Ste 216 North Tonawanda (14120) *(G-12418)*
Broadway National, Ronkonkoma *Also called Broadway Neon Sign Corp (G-14322)*
Broadway National Group LLC 800 797-4467
1900 Ocean Ave Ronkonkoma (11779) *(G-14321)*
Broadway National Sign & Ltg, Ronkonkoma *Also called Broadway National Group LLC (G-14321)*
Broadway Neon Sign Corp 908 241-4177
1900 Ocean Ave Ronkonkoma (11779) *(G-14322)*

Broadway Technology LLC (PA) 646 912-6450
28 Liberty St Fl 50 New York (10005) **(G-9146)**
Brock Awnings Ltd 631 765-5200
211 E Montauk Hwy Ste 1 Hampton Bays (11946) **(G-5708)**
Broda Machine Co Inc 716 297-3221
8745 Packard Rd Niagara Falls (14304) **(G-12266)**
Broder Mfg Inc 718 366-1667
566 Johnson Ave Brooklyn (11237) **(G-1636)**
Brodock Press Inc (PA) 315 735-9577
502 Court St Ste G Utica (13502) **(G-15681)**
Broetje Automation-Usa Inc 716 204-8640
165 Lawrence Bell Dr # 116 Williamsville (14221) **(G-16572)**
Broken Threads Inc 212 730-4351
147 W 35th St Ste 501 New York (10001) **(G-9147)**
Bronx Design Group, The, Bronx *Also called G&J Graphics Inc* **(G-1277)**
Bronx New Way Corp 347 431-1385
113 E Kingsbridge Rd Bronx (10468) **(G-1233)**
Bronx Times Reporter, Brooklyn *Also called Community News Group LLC* **(G-1710)**
Bronx Wstchester Tempering Inc 914 663-9400
160 S Macquesten Pkwy Mount Vernon (10550) **(G-8383)**
Bronxville Review, New Rochelle *Also called Gannett Co Inc* **(G-8606)**
Brook & Whittle Limited 716 691-4348
215 John Glenn Dr Amherst (14228) **(G-219)**
Brook & Whittle Limited 716 853-1688
215 John Glenn Dr Buffalo (14228) **(G-2736)**
Brook North Farms Inc 315 834-9390
89 York St Auburn (13021) **(G-472)**
Brooke Maya Inc 212 268-2626
124 W 36th St Fl 7 New York (10018) **(G-9148)**
Brookhaven Instruments Corp 631 758-3200
750 Blue Point Rd Holtsville (11742) **(G-6237)**
Brooklyn Bangers LLC 718 875-3535
111 Atlantic Ave Ste 1r Brooklyn (11201) **(G-1637)**
Brooklyn Brew Shop LLC 718 874-0119
81 Prospect St Brooklyn (11201) **(G-1638)**
Brooklyn Casing Co Inc 718 522-0866
412 3rd St Brooklyn (11215) **(G-1639)**
Brooklyn Circus (PA) 718 858-0919
150 Nevins St Brooklyn (11217) **(G-1640)**
Brooklyn Cstm Met Fbrction Inc 718 499-1573
48 Prospect Park Sw Brooklyn (11215) **(G-1641)**
Brooklyn Denim Co 718 782-2600
85 N 3rd St Brooklyn (11249) **(G-1642)**
Brooklyn Heights Press, Brooklyn *Also called Brooklyn Journal Publications* **(G-1644)**
Brooklyn Industries LLC 718 788-5250
328 7th Ave Brooklyn (11215) **(G-1643)**
Brooklyn Journal Publications 718 422-7400
16 Court St 30 Brooklyn (11241) **(G-1644)**
Brooklyn Rail Inc 718 349-8427
99 Commercial St Apt 15 Brooklyn (11222) **(G-1645)**
Brooklyn Remembers Inc 718 491-1705
9201 4th Ave Brooklyn (11209) **(G-1646)**
Brooklyn Roasting Works LLC 718 855-1000
45 Washington St Brooklyn (11201) **(G-1647)**
Brooklyn Signs LLC 718 252-7575
6404 14th Ave Brooklyn (11219) **(G-1648)**
Brooklyn Sweet Spot Inc 718 522-2577
366 Myrtle Ave Ste A Brooklyn (11205) **(G-1649)**
Brooklyn Winery LLC (PA) 347 763-1506
213 N 8th St Brooklyn (11211) **(G-1650)**
Brooklyns Best Pasta Co Inc 917 881-3007
7520 Avenue V Brooklyn (11234) **(G-1651)**
Brooklynwrap Fresh Wraps, Brooklyn *Also called Brooklynwrap Inc* **(G-1652)**
Brooklynwrap Inc 718 258-8088
4714 Avenue N Brooklyn (11234) **(G-1652)**
Brooks Bottling Co LLC 607 432-1782
5560 State Highway 7 Oneonta (13820) **(G-12627)**
Brooks Litho Digital Group Inc 631 789-4500
35 W Jefryn Blvd Ste A Deer Park (11729) **(G-3955)**
Brooks Woodworking Inc 914 666-2029
15 Kensico Dr Mount Kisco (10549) **(G-8338)**
Brookside Lumber Inc 315 497-0937
4191 Duryea St Moravia (13118) **(G-8332)**
Brookvale Records Inc 631 587-7722
31 Brookvale Ave West Babylon (11704) **(G-16140)**
Broom Tioga Boces, Binghamton *Also called Boces Business Office* **(G-869)**
Bross Quality Paving 845 532-7116
4 Kossar Pl Ellenville (12428) **(G-4437)**
Brotherhood Americas 845 496-3661
100 Brotherhood Plaza Dr Washingtonville (10992) **(G-15964)**
Brothers Roofing Supplies Co 718 779-0280
10514 Astoria Blvd East Elmhurst (11369) **(G-4218)**
Brothers-In-Lawn Property 716 279-6191
176 Vulcan Tonawanda (14150) **(G-15531)**
Brown Printing Company 212 782-7800
1500 Broadway Ste 505 New York (10036) **(G-9149)**
Brown Publishing Network Inc 212 682-3330
122 E 42nd St Rm 2810 New York (10168) **(G-9150)**
Brownstone Publishers Inc 212 473-8200
149 5th Ave Fl 10 New York (10010) **(G-9151)**
Brucci Ltd 914 965-0707
861 Nepperhan Ave Yonkers (10703) **(G-16741)**
Bruce Pierce 716 731-9310
2386 Lockport Rd Sanborn (14132) **(G-14542)**
Brueton Industries Inc (PA) 516 379-3400
146 Hanse Ave Ste 1 Freeport (11520) **(G-5147)**
Brumis Imports Inc 646 845-6000
42 W 39th St Fl 4 New York (10018) **(G-9152)**
Brunner International Inc 585 798-6000
3959 Bates Rd Medina (14103) **(G-7974)**
Bruno & Canio Ltd 845 624-3060
130 Blauvelt Rd Nanuet (10954) **(G-8460)**
Bruno Associates, Altamont *Also called Rsb Associates Inc* **(G-202)**
Bruno Associates, Fort Edward *Also called Rfb Associates Inc* **(G-5100)**
Brunschwig & Fils LLC (HQ) 800 538-1880
245 Central Ave Bethpage (11714) **(G-840)**
Brushtech (disc) Inc 518 563-8420
4 Matt Ave Plattsburgh (12901) **(G-13114)**
Bruynswick Sales Inc 845 789-2049
14 Bruynswick Rd New Paltz (12561) **(G-8576)**
Bryant Machine & Development 716 894-8282
63 Stanley St Buffalo (14206) **(G-2737)**
Bryant Machine Co Inc 716 894-8282
63 Stanley St Buffalo (14206) **(G-2738)**
Bryant Manufacturing Wny Inc 716 894-8282
63 Stanley St Buffalo (14206) **(G-2739)**
Brzozka Industries Inc 631 588-8164
790 Broadway Ave Holbrook (11741) **(G-6173)**
BSC Associates LLC 607 321-2980
151 Court St Binghamton (13901) **(G-872)**
BSD Aluminum Foil LLC 347 689-3875
260 Hewest St Brooklyn (11211) **(G-1653)**
BSD Top Direct Inc 646 468-0156
68 Route 109 West Babylon (11704) **(G-16141)**
Bso Energy Corp 212 520-1827
125 Park Ave Ste 2507 New York (10017) **(G-9153)**
Bst United Corp 631 777-2110
59 Central Ave Ste 19 Farmingdale (11735) **(G-4729)**
Bsu Inc 607 272-8100
445 E State St Ithaca (14850) **(G-6569)**
Bsv Enterprises, Rochester *Also called BSV Metal Finishers Inc* **(G-13680)**
BSV Metal Finishers Inc 585 747-7070
750 Saint Paul St Rochester (14605) **(G-13680)**
Bti, Depew *Also called Buffalo Tungsten Inc* **(G-4084)**
Btween US, New York *Also called B Tween LLC* **(G-8993)**
Buckeye Corrugated Inc 585 924-1600
797 Old Dutch Rd Victor (14564) **(G-15834)**
Buckle Down, Farmingdale *Also called Custom Sitecom LLC* **(G-4746)**
Buckley Qc Fasteners Inc 716 662-1490
3874 California Rd Orchard Park (14127) **(G-12702)**
Bucksense Inc 877 710-2825
140 West St Fl 2 New York (10007) **(G-9154)**
Bud Barger Assoc Inc 631 696-6703
3 Mount Mckinley Ave Farmingville (11738) **(G-4923)**
Bud Ravioli Center Inc 718 356-4600
3817 Richmond Ave Staten Island (10312) **(G-15056)**
Budd Woodwork Inc 718 389-1110
54 Franklin St Brooklyn (11222) **(G-1654)**
Buffalo Abrasives Inc (PA) 716 693-3856
960 Erie Ave North Tonawanda (14120) **(G-12419)**
Buffalo Armory LLC 716 935-6346
1050 Military Rd Buffalo (14217) **(G-2740)**
Buffalo Blends Inc (PA) 716 825-4422
1400 William St Buffalo (14206) **(G-2741)**
Buffalo Circuits Inc 716 662-2113
105 Mid County Dr Orchard Park (14127) **(G-12703)**
Buffalo Compressed Air Inc 716 783-8673
2727 Broadway St Ste 3a Cheektowaga (14227) **(G-3436)**
Buffalo Crushed Stone Inc (HQ) 716 826-7310
500 Como Park Blvd Buffalo (14227) **(G-2742)**
Buffalo Crushed Stone Inc 716 566-9636
Rr 16 Franklinville (14737) **(G-5122)**
Buffalo Crushed Stone Inc 607 587-8102
638 State Route 244 Alfred Station (14803) **(G-186)**
Buffalo Crushed Stone Inc 716 632-6963
91 Barton Rd Clarence (14031) **(G-3526)**
Buffalo Dental Mfg Co Inc 516 496-7200
159 Lafayette Dr Syosset (11791) **(G-15210)**
Buffalo Envelope Company, Depew *Also called Buffalo Envelope Inc* **(G-4082)**
Buffalo Envelope Inc 716 686-0100
2914 Walden Ave Ste 300 Depew (14043) **(G-4082)**
Buffalo Filter LLC 716 835-7000
5900 Genesee St Lancaster (14086) **(G-7011)**
Buffalo Finishing Company, Ithaca *Also called F M Abdulky Inc* **(G-6577)**
Buffalo Finishing Works Inc 716 893-5266
1255 Niagara St Buffalo (14213) **(G-2743)**
Buffalo Games LLC 716 827-8393
220 James E Casey Dr Buffalo (14206) **(G-2744)**
Buffalo Gear Inc 716 731-2100
3635 Lockport Rd Sanborn (14132) **(G-14543)**
Buffalo Hardwood Floor Center, Buffalo *Also called Mm of East Aurora LLC* **(G-2949)**
Buffalo Hearg & Speech 716 558-1105
1026 Union Rd West Seneca (14224) **(G-16295)**

ALPHABETIC

Buffalo Law Journal 716 541-1600
　465 Main St Ste 100 Buffalo (14203) *(G-2745)*
Buffalo Lining & Fabricating 716 883-6500
　73 Gillette Ave Buffalo (14214) *(G-2746)*
Buffalo Machine Tls of Niagara 716 201-1310
　4935 Lockport Rd Lockport (14094) *(G-7288)*
Buffalo Metal Casting Co Inc 716 874-6211
　1875 Elmwood Ave Buffalo (14207) *(G-2747)*
Buffalo Metal Fabricating Corp 716 892-7800
　50 Wecker St Buffalo (14215) *(G-2748)*
Buffalo Metal Finishing Co (PA) 716 883-2751
　135 Dart St Buffalo (14213) *(G-2749)*
Buffalo News Inc 716 849-4401
　1 News Plz Buffalo (14203) *(G-2750)*
Buffalo Newspress Inc 716 852-1600
　200 Broadway St Buffalo (14204) *(G-2751)*
Buffalo Polymer Processors Inc 716 537-3153
　42 Edgewood Dr Holland (14080) *(G-6218)*
Buffalo Power Electronics Ctr 716 651-1600
　166 Taylor Dr Ste 1 Depew (14043) *(G-4083)*
Buffalo Provisions Co Inc 718 292-4300
　4009 76th St Elmhurst (11373) *(G-4462)*
Buffalo Pumps Inc (HQ) 716 693-1850
　874 Oliver St North Tonawanda (14120) *(G-12420)*
Buffalo Rocket, Buffalo Also called Rocket Communications Inc *(G-3042)*
Buffalo Snowmelter, North Tonawanda Also called Roemac Industrial Sales Inc *(G-12448)*
Buffalo Spree Publishing Inc (PA) 716 783-9119
　1738 Elmwood Ave Ste 103 Buffalo (14207) *(G-2752)*
Buffalo Standard Printing Corp 716 835-9454
　3620 Harlem Rd Ste 5 Buffalo (14215) *(G-2753)*
Buffalo Structural Steel Inc 814 827-1350
　60 Bryant Woods S Buffalo (14228) *(G-2754)*
Buffalo Tungsten Inc 716 683-9170
　2 Main St Depew (14043) *(G-4084)*
Buflovak LLC (PA) 716 895-2100
　750 E Ferry St Buffalo (14211) *(G-2755)*
Building Management Assoc Inc 718 542-4779
　998 E 167th St Ofc Bronx (10459) *(G-1234)*
Bulkley Dunton (HQ) 212 863-1800
　1 Penn Plz Ste 2814 New York (10119) *(G-9155)*
Bull Street LLC 212 495-9855
　19 W 69th St Apt 201 New York (10023) *(G-9156)*
Bullet Industries Inc 585 352-0836
　7 Turner Dr Spencerport (14559) *(G-14977)*
Bullett Media LLC 212 242-2123
　419 Lafayette St Fl 6 New York (10003) *(G-9157)*
Bullex Inc (HQ) 518 689-2023
　20 Corporate Cir Ste 3 Albany (12203) *(G-51)*
Bullex Inc 518 689-2023
　20 Corporate Cir Ste 3 Albany (12203) *(G-52)*
Bullex Digital Safety, Albany Also called Bullex Inc *(G-51)*
Bullex Digital Safety, Albany Also called Bullex Inc *(G-52)*
Bullitt Group, Bohemia Also called Bullitt Mobile LLC *(G-990)*
Bullitt Mobile LLC 631 424-1749
　80 Orville Dr Ste 100 Bohemia (11716) *(G-990)*
Bullock Boys LLC 518 783-6161
　400 Old Loudon Rd Latham (12110) *(G-7066)*
Buna Besta Tortillas 347 987-3995
　219 Johnson Ave Brooklyn (11206) *(G-1655)*
Buncee LLC 631 591-1390
　170 Montauk Hwy Speonk Speonk (11972) *(G-14984)*
Bunge Limited Finance Corp 914 684-2800
　50 Main St White Plains (10606) *(G-16432)*
Bunger Sayville, Sayville Also called Bungers Surf Shop *(G-14626)*
Bungers Surf Shop 631 244-3646
　247 W Main St Sayville (11782) *(G-14626)*
Buperiod PBC 917 406-9804
　5414 6th Ave 2 Brooklyn (11220) *(G-1656)*
Burdick Publications Inc 315 685-9500
　2352 E Lake Rd Skaneateles (13152) *(G-14867)*
Bureau of National Affairs Inc 212 687-4530
　25 W 43rd St Ste 1007 New York (10036) *(G-9158)*
Burgess Products Division, New York Mills Also called Fountainhead Group Inc *(G-12186)*
Burgess-Manning Inc (HQ) 716 662-6540
　50 Cobham Dr Orchard Park (14127) *(G-12704)*
Burke & Bannayan 585 723-1010
　2465 W Ridge Rd Ste 2 Rochester (14626) *(G-13681)*
Burke Frging Heat Treating Inc 585 235-6060
　30 Sherer St Rochester (14611) *(G-13682)*
Burlen Corp 212 684-0052
　6 E 32nd St Fl 10 New York (10016) *(G-9159)*
Burnett Process Inc (HQ) 585 254-8080
　545 Colfax St Rochester (14606) *(G-13683)*
Burnett Process Inc 585 277-1623
　545 Colfax St Rochester (14606) *(G-13684)*
Burnham Polymeric Inc 518 792-3040
　1408 Route 9 Fort Edward (12828) *(G-5094)*
Burnhams, The, Fort Edward Also called Burnham Polymeric Inc *(G-5094)*
Burns Archive Photographic Dis 212 889-1938
　140 E 38th St Frnt 1 New York (10016) *(G-9160)*
Burnt Hills Fabricators Inc 518 885-1115
　318 Charlton Rd B Ballston Spa (12020) *(G-578)*

Burnt Mill Smithing 585 293-2380
　127 Burnt Mill Rd Churchville (14428) *(G-3507)*
Burr & Son Inc 315 446-1550
　119 Seeley Rd Syracuse (13224) *(G-15263)*
Burrows Paper Corporation 315 823-2300
　730 E Mill St Little Falls (13365) *(G-7208)*
Burrows Paper Corporation 315 823-2300
　489 W Main St Little Falls (13365) *(G-7209)*
Burrows Paper Mill, Little Falls Also called Burrows Paper Corporation *(G-7208)*
Burt Millwork Corporation 718 257-4601
　85 Fairview Dr Albertson (11507) *(G-147)*
Burt Rigid Box Inc 607 433-2510
　58 Browne St Oneonta (13820) *(G-12628)*
Burt Rigid Box Inc (PA) 607 433-2510
　58 Browne St Oneonta (13820) *(G-12629)*
Burton Corporation 802 862-4500
　21 Lawrence Paquette Dr Champlain (12919) *(G-3407)*
Burton Industries Inc 631 643-6660
　243 Wyandanch Ave Ste A West Babylon (11704) *(G-16142)*
Burton Snowboards, Champlain Also called Burton Corporation *(G-3407)*
Busch Products Inc 315 474-8422
　110 Baker St Syracuse (13206) *(G-15264)*
Bush Industries Inc (PA) 716 665-2000
　1 Mason Dr Jamestown (14701) *(G-6704)*
Bushwick Bakery Corp 917 460-5994
　127 Central Ave Ste A Brooklyn (11221) *(G-1657)*
Bushwick Bottling LLC 929 666-3618
　465 Johnson Ave Brooklyn (11237) *(G-1658)*
Bushwick Kitchen LLC 917 297-1045
　630 Flushing Ave Fl 5 Brooklyn (11206) *(G-1659)*
Business Advisory Services 718 337-3740
　1104 Bay 25th St Far Rockaway (11691) *(G-4698)*
Business Card Express Inc 631 669-3400
　300 Farmingdale Rd West Babylon (11704) *(G-16143)*
Business Directory Inc 718 486-8099
　137 Division Ave Ste A Brooklyn (11211) *(G-1660)*
Business Expert Press LLC 212 661-8810
　222 E 46th St Rm 203 New York (10017) *(G-9161)*
Business First of New York (HQ) 716 854-5822
　465 Main St Ste 100 Buffalo (14203) *(G-2756)*
Business First of New York 518 640-6800
　40 British American Blvd Latham (12110) *(G-7067)*
Business Integrity Inc (HQ) 718 238-2008
　79 Madison Ave Fl 2 New York (10016) *(G-9162)*
Business Journal, Syracuse Also called CNY Business Review Inc *(G-15281)*
Business Journals 212 790-5100
　1166 Ave Of The America New York (10036) *(G-9163)*
Business Management Systems 914 245-8558
　1675 W 9th St Apt 4d Brooklyn (11223) *(G-1661)*
Business Never Stops LLC 888 479-3111
　13404 97th Ave Ste 2 South Richmond Hill (11419) *(G-14945)*
Business Review, Latham Also called Business First of New York *(G-7067)*
Bust Inc 212 675-1707
　253 36th St Unit 3 Brooklyn (11232) *(G-1662)*
Bust Magazine, Brooklyn Also called Bust Inc *(G-1662)*
Bustle Digital Group, New York Also called Bdg Media Inc *(G-9030)*
Butterck McCall Vogue Pattern, New York Also called McCall Pattern Company *(G-10739)*
Butterfly 7, Brooklyn Also called Cioccolato 7 LLC *(G-1693)*
Butternuts Beer and Ale LLC 607 263-5070
　4021 State Highway 51 Garrattsville (13342) *(G-5302)*
Butterwood Desserts Inc 716 652-0131
　1863 Davis Rd West Falls (14170) *(G-16208)*
Buttons & Trimcom Inc 212 868-1971
　519 8th Ave Rm 26 New York (10018) *(G-9164)*
Buxton Machine and Tool Co Inc 716 876-2312
　2181 Elmwood Ave Buffalo (14216) *(G-2757)*
Buxton Medical Equipment Corp 631 957-4500
　1178 Route 109 Lindenhurst (11757) *(G-7164)*
BW Elliott Mfg Co LLC 607 772-0404
　11 Beckwith Ave Binghamton (13901) *(G-873)*
Bwog, New York Also called Blue and White Publishing Inc *(G-9106)*
Bws Specialty Fabrication, Orchard Park Also called Quality Industrial Services *(G-12742)*
By Robert James 212 253-2121
　74 Orchard St New York (10002) *(G-9165)*
Bycmac Corp 845 255-0884
　144 Main St Gardiner (12525) *(G-5292)*
Byelocorp Scientific Inc (PA) 212 785-2580
　76 Perry St New York (10014) *(G-9166)*
Byer California 212 944-8989
　1407 Broadway Rm 807 New York (10018) *(G-9167)*
Byk USA Inc 845 469-5800
　48 Leone Ln Chester (10918) *(G-3470)*
Bylada Foods LLC 845 623-1300
　250 W Nyack Rd Ste 110 West Nyack (10994) *(G-16267)*
Byliner Inc 415 680-3608
　27 W 24th St Ste 202 New York (10010) *(G-9168)*
Byram Concrete & Supply LLC 914 682-4477
　145 Virginia Rd White Plains (10603) *(G-16433)*
Byrne Dairy Inc (PA) 315 475-2121
　2394 Us Route 11 La Fayette (13084) *(G-6946)*
Bys Publishing LLC 315 655-9431
　118 Albany St Cazenovia (13035) *(G-3316)*

Byte Consulting Inc 646 500-8606
295 Madison Ave Fl 35 New York (10017) *(G-9169)*
Bytheway Publishing Services 607 334-8365
365 Follett Hill Rd Norwich (13815) *(G-12477)*
Bz Media LLC 631 421-4158
225 Broadhollow Rd 211e Melville (11747) *(G-8005)*
C & A Atelier, Richmond Hill *Also called Carlos & Alex Atelier Inc (G-13500)*
C & A Service Inc (PA) 516 354-1200
65 S Tyson Ave Floral Park (11001) *(G-4958)*
C & C Athletic Inc 845 713-4670
11 Myrtle Ave Walden (12586) *(G-15891)*
C & C Bindery Co Inc 631 752-7078
25 Central Ave Unit B Farmingdale (11735) *(G-4730)*
C & C Custom Metal Fabricators 631 235-9646
2 N Hoffman Ln Hauppauge (11788) *(G-5785)*
C & C Metal Fabrications Inc 315 598-7607
159 Hubbard St Fulton (13069) *(G-5212)*
C & C Ready-Mix Corporation (PA) 607 797-5108
3112 Vestal Rd Vestal (13850) *(G-15812)*
C & C Ready-Mix Corporation 607 687-1690
3818 Rt 17 C Owego (13827) *(G-12796)*
C & D Assembly Inc 607 898-4275
107 Corona Ave Groton (13073) *(G-5650)*
C & F Fabricators & Erectors 607 432-3520
Rr 7 Colliersville (13747) *(G-3671)*
C & F Iron Works Inc 914 592-2450
14 N Payne St Ste 1 Elmsford (10523) *(G-4534)*
C & F Steel Corp 914 592-3928
14 N Payne St Ste 2 Elmsford (10523) *(G-4535)*
C & G of Kingston Inc 845 331-0148
25 Cornell St Kingston (12401) *(G-6890)*
C & G Video Systems Inc (PA) 315 452-1490
7778 Tirrell Hill Cir Liverpool (13090) *(G-7226)*
C & H Machining Inc 631 582-6737
281 Knickerbocker Ave Bohemia (11716) *(G-991)*
C & H Precision Tools Inc 631 758-3806
194 Morris Ave Ste 20 Holtsville (11742) *(G-6238)*
C & M Circuits Inc 631 589-0208
50 Orville Dr Bohemia (11716) *(G-992)*
C & M Products Inc 315 471-3303
1209 N Salina St Ste 1 Syracuse (13208) *(G-15265)*
C & R De Santis Inc 718 447-5076
2645 Forest Ave Ste 2 Staten Island (10303) *(G-15057)*
C & T Tool & Instrument Co 718 429-1253
4125 58th St Woodside (11377) *(G-16648)*
C A M Graphics Co Inc 631 842-3400
24 Central Dr Farmingdale (11735) *(G-4731)*
C B I, Oriskany *Also called Caldwell Bennett Inc (G-12752)*
C B Management Services Inc 845 735-2300
73 S Pearl St Pearl River (10965) *(G-12895)*
C B S Food Products Corp 718 452-2500
770 Chauncey St Brooklyn (11207) *(G-1663)*
C C Industries Inc 518 581-7633
344 Burgoyne Rd Saratoga Springs (12866) *(G-14572)*
C C M, Wolcott *Also called Carballo Contract Machining (G-16609)*
C D A Inc 631 473-1595
66 Southern Blvd Ste A Nesconset (11767) *(G-8483)*
C E King & Sons Inc 631 324-4944
10 Saint Francis Pl East Hampton (11937) *(G-4233)*
C F Peters Corp 718 416-7800
7030 80th St Ste 2 Glendale (11385) *(G-5394)*
C G & Son Machining Inc 315 964-2430
87 Nichols Rd Williamstown (13493) *(G-16564)*
C H Evans Brewing Co 518 447-9000
19 Quackenbush Sq Albany (12207) *(G-53)*
C H Thompson Company Inc 607 724-1094
69-93 Eldredge St Binghamton (13902) *(G-874)*
C Howard Company Inc 631 286-7940
1007 Station Rd Bellport (11713) *(G-800)*
C I G, New York *Also called Cambridge Info Group Inc (G-9185)*
C J & C Sheet Metal Corp 631 376-9425
433 Falmouth Rd West Babylon (11704) *(G-16144)*
C J Logging Equipment Inc 315 942-5431
8730 Industrial Dr Boonville (13309) *(G-1117)*
C J Winter Machine Tech (HQ) 585 429-5000
167 Ames St Rochester (14611) *(G-13685)*
C K Printing 718 965-0388
267 41st St Brooklyn (11232) *(G-1664)*
C L Precision Machine & Tl Co 718 651-8475
5015 70th St Woodside (11377) *(G-16649)*
C M E Corp 315 451-7101
1005 W Fayette St Ste 3c Syracuse (13204) *(G-15266)*
C M Insurance Company Inc 716 689-5409
205 Crosspoint Pkwy Getzville (14068) *(G-5343)*
C O P R A Inc 917 224-1727
215 E Broadway Apt 2r New York (10002) *(G-9170)*
C P Chemical Co Inc 914 428-2517
25 Home St White Plains (10606) *(G-16434)*
C Q Communications Inc 516 681-2922
17 W John St Unit 1 Hicksville (11801) *(G-6066)*
C R Bard Inc 518 793-2531
289 Bay Rd Queensbury (12804) *(G-13421)*
C R Bard Inc 518 793-2531
289 Bay Rd Glens Falls (12804) *(G-5420)*
C R C Manufacturing Inc 585 254-8820
37 Curlew St Rochester (14606) *(G-13686)*
C S I G Inc 845 383-3800
721 Broadway Ste 270 Kingston (12401) *(G-6891)*
C S L, North Creek *Also called Creative Stage Lighting Co Inc (G-12391)*
C S Welding, Ontario *Also called Cs Automation Inc (G-12650)*
C Speed LLC 315 453-1043
316 Commerce Blvd Liverpool (13088) *(G-7227)*
C T A Digital Inc 718 963-9845
36 Taaffe Pl Brooklyn (11205) *(G-1665)*
C T A Digital Inc (PA) 845 513-0433
326 State Route 208 Monroe (10950) *(G-8266)*
C To C Design & Print Inc 631 885-4020
1850 Pond Rd Unit B Ronkonkoma (11779) *(G-14323)*
C V D, Central Islip *Also called Cvd Equipment Corporation (G-3365)*
C W Sheet Metal, Maspeth *Also called Nelson Air Device Corporation (G-7862)*
C&A Aromatics, Floral Park *Also called Citrus and Allied Essences Ltd (G-4960)*
C&C Automatics Inc 315 331-1436
127 W Shore Blvd Newark (14513) *(G-12193)*
C&C Diecuts, Farmingdale *Also called C & C Bindery Co Inc (G-4730)*
C&T Tool & Instrmnt, Woodside *Also called C & T Tool & Instrument Co (G-16648)*
C-Air International, Valley Stream *Also called Parnasa International Inc (G-15789)*
C-Flex Bearing Co Inc 315 895-7454
104 Industrial Dr Frankfort (13340) *(G-5104)*
C.H.thompson Finishing, Binghamton *Also called Tcmf Inc (G-918)*
C/O Court Sq Capitl Partners, New York *Also called Mdi Holdings LLC (G-10747)*
C/O M&M Fowarding, Tonawanda *Also called Fiber Laminations Limited (G-15540)*
C/O Pdell Ndell Fine Winberger, New York *Also called Mom Dad Publishing Inc (G-10834)*
Ca Inc (HQ) 800 225-5224
520 Madison Ave Fl 22 New York (10022) *(G-9171)*
Ca Inc 800 225-5224
1 Ca Plz Ste 100 Islandia (11749) *(G-6523)*
Cab Plastics, Brooklyn *Also called Cab Signs Inc (G-1666)*
Cab Signs Inc 718 479-2424
38 Livonia Ave Brooklyn (11212) *(G-1666)*
Cab-Network Inc 516 334-8666
1500 Shames Dr Unit B Westbury (11590) *(G-16320)*
Cabba Printing Incorporated 212 319-4747
133 E 55th St New York (10022) *(G-9172)*
Cabezon Design Group Inc 718 488-9868
197 Waverly Ave Brooklyn (11205) *(G-1667)*
Cabinet Factory Inc 718 351-8922
2333 Highland Blvd Staten Island (10306) *(G-15058)*
Cabinet Shapes Corp 718 784-6255
3721 12th St Long Island City (11101) *(G-7404)*
Cabinetry By Tbr Inc 516 365-8500
1492 Northern Blvd Manhasset (11030) *(G-7764)*
Cabinets By Stanley Inc 718 222-5861
46 Hall St Brooklyn (11205) *(G-1668)*
Cable Management Solutions Inc 631 674-0004
291 Skip Ln Bay Shore (11706) *(G-667)*
Cables and Chips Inc (PA) 212 619-3132
121 Fulton St Fl 4 New York (10038) *(G-9173)*
Cables Unlimited Inc 631 563-6363
3 Old Dock Rd Yaphank (11980) *(G-16705)*
Caboodle Printing Inc 716 693-6000
1975 Wehrle Dr Ste 120 Williamsville (14221) *(G-16573)*
Cabot Coach Builders Inc 516 625-4000
77 Carriage Ln Roslyn Heights (11577) *(G-14453)*
Cabriole Designs Inc 212 593-4528
315 E 91st St Ste 3 New York (10128) *(G-9174)*
Cachet Industries Inc 212 944-2188
463 Fashion Ave Rm 601 New York (10018) *(G-9175)*
Caddell Burns Manufacturing Co 631 757-1772
247 Asharoken Ave Northport (11768) *(G-12465)*
Caddell Dry Dock & Repr Co Inc 718 442-2112
1515 Richmond Ter Staten Island (10310) *(G-15059)*
Caddell Ship Yards, Staten Island *Also called Caddell Dry Dock & Repr Co Inc (G-15059)*
Caddy Concepts Inc 516 570-6279
15 Cuttermill Rd Great Neck (11021) *(G-5541)*
CAF Usa Inc 607 737-3004
300 E 18th St Elmira Heights (14903) *(G-4510)*
Cafe Kubal 315 278-2812
202 Lockwood Rd Syracuse (13214) *(G-15267)*
Cafe Spice Gct Inc 845 863-0910
677 Little Britain Rd New Windsor (12553) *(G-8638)*
Cahoon Farms Inc 315 594-8081
10951 Lummisville Rd Wolcott (14590) *(G-16608)*
Cai Inc (PA) 212 819-0008
430 E 56th St New York (10022) *(G-9176)*
Cai Design Inc 212 401-9973
240 W 37th St Rm 303 New York (10018) *(G-9177)*
Caithness Equities Corporation (PA) 212 599-2112
565 5th Ave Fl 29 New York (10017) *(G-9178)*
Calchem Corporation (PA) 631 423-5696
2001 Ocean Ave Ronkonkoma (11779) *(G-14324)*
Caldwell Bennett Inc 315 337-8540
6152 County Seat Rd Oriskany (13424) *(G-12752)*

ALPHABETIC

Caldwell Cor, Fairport *Also called Mastercraft Decorators Inc* ***(G-4641)***

Calfonex Company ... 845 778-2212
121 Orchard St Walden (12586) ***(G-15892)***

Calgon Carbon Corporation ... 716 531-9113
830 River Rd North Tonawanda (14120) ***(G-12421)***

Calia Consultants, Staten Island *Also called Calia Technical Inc* ***(G-15060)***

Calia Technical Inc ... 718 447-3928
420 Jefferson Blvd Staten Island (10312) ***(G-15060)***

Caliber Imging Diagnostics Inc (PA) ... 585 239-9800
50 Methodist Hill Dr Rochester (14623) ***(G-13687)***

Calibrated Instruments Inc ... 914 741-5700
306 Aerie Ct Manhasset (11030) ***(G-7765)***

Calibration Technologies Inc ... 631 676-6133
30 Woodland Blvd Centereach (11720) ***(G-3343)***

Calico Cottage Inc ... 631 841-2100
210 New Hwy Amityville (11701) ***(G-266)***

California Fragrance Company ... 631 424-4023
171 E 2nd St Huntington Station (11746) ***(G-6435)***

California Petro Trnspt Corp ... 212 302-5151
114 W 47th St New York (10036) ***(G-9179)***

California US Holdings Inc ... 212 726-6500
417 5th Ave Lbby 7th New York (10016) ***(G-9180)***

Caliper Studio Inc ... 718 302-2427
75 Scott Ave Brooklyn (11237) ***(G-1669)***

Call Forwarding Technologies ... 516 621-3600
55 Northern Blvd Ste 3b Greenvale (11548) ***(G-5628)***

Callahan & Nannini Quarry Inc ... 845 496-4323
276 Clove Rd Salisbury Mills (12577) ***(G-14539)***

Callanan Industries Inc ... 315 697-9569
6375 Tuttle Rd Canastota (13032) ***(G-3241)***

Callanan Industries Inc (HQ) ... 518 374-2222
8 Southwoods Blvd Ste 4 Albany (12211) ***(G-54)***

Callanan Industries Inc ... 845 457-3158
215 Montgomery Rd Montgomery (12549) ***(G-8309)***

Callanan Industries Inc ... 845 331-6868
737 Flatbush Rd Kingston (12401) ***(G-6892)***

Callanan Industries Inc ... 518 785-5666
9 Fonda Rd Latham (12110) ***(G-7068)***

Callanan Industries Inc ... 518 382-5354
145 Cordell Rd Schenectady (12303) ***(G-14656)***

Callaway Arts & Entrmt Inc ... 646 465-4667
41 Union Sq W Ste 1101 New York (10003) ***(G-9181)***

Callaway Digital Arts Inc ... 212 675-3050
41 Union Sq W Ste 1101 New York (10003) ***(G-9182)***

Callidus Software Inc ... 212 554-7300
152 W 57th St Fl 8 New York (10019) ***(G-9183)***

Calmetrics, Holbrook *Also called Micromatter Tech Inc USA* ***(G-6201)***

Calmetrics Inc ... 631 580-2522
1340 Lincoln Ave Ste 6 Holbrook (11741) ***(G-6174)***

Calpac Incorporated ... 631 789-0502
44 Seabro Ave Amityville (11701) ***(G-267)***

Calspan Corporation (HQ) ... 716 631-6955
4455 Genesee St Buffalo (14225) ***(G-2758)***

Calspan Corporation ... 716 236-1040
2041 Niagara Falls Blvd Niagara Falls (14304) ***(G-12267)***

Calspan Flight Research Center, Niagara Falls *Also called Calspan Corporation* ***(G-12267)***

Calspan Holdings LLC (PA) ... 716 631-6955
4455 Genesee St Buffalo (14225) ***(G-2759)***

Caltex International Ltd ... 315 425-1040
60 Presidential Plz # 1405 Syracuse (13202) ***(G-15268)***

Calvary Design Team Inc (PA) ... 585 347-6127
855 Publishers Pkwy Webster (14580) ***(G-16076)***

Calvary Robotics, Webster *Also called Calvary Design Team Inc* ***(G-16076)***

Calvin Klein Inc ... 212 292-9000
654 Madison Ave New York (10065) ***(G-9184)***

CAM Machinery Co, Brooklyn *Also called S & S Machinery Corp* ***(G-2432)***

CAM Touchview Products Inc ... 631 842-3400
51 Division St Sag Harbor (11963) ***(G-14497)***

Cama Graphics Inc ... 718 707-9747
3200 Skillman Ave Ste B Long Island City (11101) ***(G-7405)***

Cambridge Info Group Inc (PA) ... 301 961-6700
888 7th Ave Ste 1701 New York (10106) ***(G-9185)***

Cambridge Kitchens Mfg Inc ... 516 935-5100
280 Duffy Ave Unit 1 Hicksville (11801) ***(G-6067)***

Cambridge Manufacturing LLC ... 516 326-1350
1700 Jericho Tpke New Hyde Park (11040) ***(G-8521)***

Cambridge Resources, Brooklyn *Also called Coda Resources Ltd* ***(G-1703)***

Cambridge Security Seals LLC ... 845 520-4111
1 Cambridge Plz Pomona (10970) ***(G-13185)***

Cambridge University Press ... 212 337-5000
165 Broadway Fl 20 New York (10006) ***(G-9186)***

Cambridge Whos Who Pubg Inc (PA) ... 516 833-8440
498 Rxr Plz Fl 4 Uniondale (11556) ***(G-15663)***

Cambridge-Pacific Inc ... 518 677-5988
891 State Rd 22 Cambridge (12816) ***(G-3178)***

Camco, Ronkonkoma *Also called Gliptone Manufacturing Inc* ***(G-14345)***

Camden House, Rochester *Also called Boydell & Brewer Inc* ***(G-13674)***

Camden News Inc ... 315 245-1849
39 Main St Camden (13316) ***(G-3185)***

Camden Wire Co Inc ... 315 245-3800
12 Masonic Ave Camden (13316) ***(G-3186)***

Camellia Foods, Buffalo *Also called Camellia General Provision Co* ***(G-2760)***

Camellia General Provision Co ... 716 893-5352
1333 Genesee St Buffalo (14211) ***(G-2760)***

Camelot Print & Copy Centers, Latham *Also called Kjckd Inc* ***(G-7078)***

Cameo Metal Products Inc ... 718 788-1106
127 12th St Brooklyn (11215) ***(G-1670)***

Cameo Process Corp ... 914 948-0082
15 Stewart Pl Apt 7g White Plains (10603) ***(G-16435)***

Cameron Bridge Works LLC ... 607 734-9456
1051 S Main St Elmira (14904) ***(G-4474)***

Cameron Mfg & Design Inc (PA) ... 607 739-3606
727 Blostein Blvd Horseheads (14845) ***(G-6308)***

Camfil Usa Inc ... 315 468-3849
6060 Tarbell Rd Syracuse (13206) ***(G-15269)***

Caminus Corporation (HQ) ... 212 515-3600
340 Madison Ave Fl 8 New York (10173) ***(G-9187)***

Campanellis Poultry Farm Inc ... 845 482-2222
4 Perry Rd Bethel (12720) ***(G-835)***

Campbell Alliance Group Inc ... 212 377-2740
335 Madison Ave Fl 17 New York (10017) ***(G-9188)***

Campbell's Print Shop, Bronx *Also called Linda Campbell* ***(G-1318)***

Campus Course Paks Inc ... 516 877-3967
1 South Ave Fl 1 Garden City (11530) ***(G-5254)***

Campus Crafts Inc ... 585 328-6780
160 Murray St Rochester (14606) ***(G-13688)***

Camso Manufacturing Usa Ltd (HQ) ... 518 561-7528
1 Martina Cir Plattsburgh (12901) ***(G-13115)***

Canaan Printing Inc ... 718 729-3100
20007 46th Ave Bayside (11361) ***(G-744)***

Canada Goose Inc ... 888 276-6297
601 W 26th St Rm 1745 New York (10001) ***(G-9189)***

Canada Goose Inc ... 888 668-0625
601 W 26th St Rm 1745 New York (10001) ***(G-9190)***

Canada Goose Us Inc (HQ) ... 888 276-6297
300 International Dr Williamsville (14221) ***(G-16574)***

Canal Asphalt Inc ... 914 667-8500
645 S Columbus Ave Mount Vernon (10550) ***(G-8384)***

Canali USA Inc (HQ) ... 212 767-0205
415 W 13th St Fl 2 New York (10014) ***(G-9191)***

Canandaigua Msgnr Incorported (PA) ... 585 394-0770
73 Buffalo St Canandaigua (14424) ***(G-3213)***

Canandaigua Quick Print, Canandaigua *Also called Carges Entps of Canandaigua* ***(G-3214)***

Canandaigua Technology Center, Canandaigua *Also called Pactiv LLC* ***(G-3230)***

Canarm Ltd ... 800 267-4427
808 Commerce Park Dr Ogdensburg (13669) ***(G-12572)***

Canarsie Courier Inc ... 718 257-0600
1142 E 92nd St 44 Brooklyn (11236) ***(G-1671)***

Canary Connect Inc ... 212 390-8576
222 Broadway Fl 19 New York (10038) ***(G-9192)***

Canastota Publishing Co Inc ... 315 697-9010
130 E Center St Canastota (13032) ***(G-3242)***

Candex Solutions Inc ... 215 650-3214
420 Lexington Ave Rm 300 New York (10170) ***(G-9193)***

Candid Litho Printing Ltd (PA) ... 212 431-3800
210 Route 109 Farmingdale (11735) ***(G-4732)***

Candid Worldwide LLC (HQ) ... 212 799-5300
210 Route 109 Farmingdale (11735) ***(G-4733)***

Candle In The Window Inc ... 718 852-5743
43 Hall St Ste C10 Brooklyn (11205) ***(G-1672)***

Candlelight Cabinetry Inc ... 716 434-2114
24 Michigan St Lockport (14094) ***(G-7289)***

Candles By Foster ... 914 739-9226
810 South St Peekskill (10566) ***(G-12918)***

Candlesticks Inc ... 212 947-8900
112 W 34th St Fl 18 New York (10120) ***(G-9194)***

Candy Kraft, Altamont *Also called Robert Pikcilingis* ***(G-201)***

Candy Land, Rome *Also called Noras Candy Shop* ***(G-14262)***

Candy Man, Wilmington *Also called Adirondack Chocolate Co Ltd* ***(G-16600)***

Candy Planet Division, New York *Also called Toymax Inc* ***(G-11878)***

Cane Simple, New York *Also called Cane Sugar LLC* ***(G-9195)***

Cane Sugar LLC ... 212 329-2695
950 3rd Ave Ste 2200 New York (10022) ***(G-9195)***

Canfield & Tack Inc ... 585 235-7710
925 Exchange St Rochester (14608) ***(G-13689)***

Canfield Aerospace & Mar Inc ... 631 648-1050
90 Remington Blvd Ronkonkoma (11779) ***(G-14325)***

Canfield Electronics Inc (PA) ... 631 585-4100
6 Burton Pl Lindenhurst (11757) ***(G-7165)***

Canfield Machine & Tool LLC ... 315 593-8062
121 Howard Rd Fulton (13069) ***(G-5213)***

Cannizzaro Seal & Engraving Co ... 718 513-6125
435 Avenue U Brooklyn (11223) ***(G-1673)***

Cannoli Factory Inc ... 631 643-2700
75 Wyandanch Ave Wyandanch (11798) ***(G-16693)***

Cannon Co, Brooklyn *Also called Attias Oven Corp* ***(G-1573)***

Cannon Industries Inc (PA) ... 585 254-8080
525 Lee Rd Rochester (14606) ***(G-13690)***

Cannonsville Lumber Inc ... 607 467-3380
199 Old Route 10 Deposit (13754) ***(G-4106)***

Canopy Books LLC (PA) ... 516 354-4888
28 N Wisconsin Ave 2-1 Massapequa (11758) ***(G-7879)***

Canopy Canopy Canopy Inc ... 347 529-5182
264 Canal St Ste 3w New York (10013) ***(G-9196)***

ALPHABETIC SECTION Caroda Inc

Cant Live Without It LLC 844 517-9355
28 W 23rd St Fl 5 New York (10010) *(G-9197)*
Canton Bio-Medical Inc (PA) 518 283-5963
11 Sicho Rd Poestenkill (12140) *(G-13179)*
Canton Noodle Corporation 212 226-3276
101 Mott St New York (10013) *(G-9198)*
Canvas Products Company Inc 516 742-1058
234 Herricks Rd Mineola (11501) *(G-8209)*
Canyon Publishing Inc 212 334-0227
55 John St Ste 6 New York (10038) *(G-9199)*
Cap USA Jerseyman Harlem Inc (PA) 212 222-7942
112 W 125th St New York (10027) *(G-9200)*
Capco Marketing 315 699-1687
8417 Oswego Rd 177 Baldwinsville (13027) *(G-552)*
Capco Wai Shing LLC 212 268-1976
132 W 36th St Rm 509 New York (10018) *(G-9201)*
Capital Concrete Inc 716 648-8001
5690 Camp Rd Hamburg (14075) *(G-5673)*
Capital District Stairs Inc 518 383-2449
45 Dunsbach Rd Halfmoon (12065) *(G-5661)*
Capital Dst Print & Imaging 518 456-6773
2075 Central Ave Schenectady (12304) *(G-14657)*
Capital E Financial Group 212 319-6550
598 Madison Ave Fl 9 New York (10022) *(G-9202)*
Capital Gold Corporation (PA) 212 668-0842
601 Lexington Ave Fl 36 New York (10022) *(G-9203)*
Capital Kit Cab & Door Mfrs 718 886-0303
1425 128th St College Point (11356) *(G-3641)*
Capital Ktchens Cab Doors Mfrs, College Point *Also called Capital Kit Cab & Door Mfrs* *(G-3641)*
Capital Mercury Shirtmakers Co, New York *Also called Gce International Inc* *(G-9892)*
Capital Programs Inc 212 842-4640
420 Lexington Ave Lbby 6 New York (10170) *(G-9204)*
Capital Reg Wkly Newsppr Group 518 674-2841
29 Sheer Rd Averill Park (12018) *(G-513)*
Capital Region Wkly Newspapers 518 877-7160
645 Albany Shaker Rd Albany (12211) *(G-55)*
Capital Sawmill Service 518 479-0729
4119 Us Highway 20 Nassau (12123) *(G-8476)*
Capital Stone LLC 518 382-7588
2241 Central Ave Schenectady (12304) *(G-14658)*
Capital Stone Saratoga LLC 518 226-8677
4295 Route 50 Saratoga Springs (12866) *(G-14573)*
Capitol Awning & Shade Co, Jamaica *Also called Capitol Awning Co Inc* *(G-6631)*
Capitol Awning Co Inc 212 505-1717
10515 180th St Jamaica (11433) *(G-6631)*
Capitol City Specialties Co 518 486-8935
10 Burdick Dr Albany (12205) *(G-56)*
Capitol Cups Inc 518 627-0051
1030 Riverfront Ctr Amsterdam (12010) *(G-330)*
Capitol Eq 2 LLC 518 886-8341
376 Broadway Ste 27 Saratoga Springs (12866) *(G-14574)*
Capitol Newspaper, Albany *Also called Newspaper Times Union* *(G-104)*
Capitol Plastic Products Inc 518 627-0051
1030 Riverfront Ctr Amsterdam (12010) *(G-331)*
Capitol Poly Corp 718 855-6000
101 Spencer St Brooklyn (11205) *(G-1674)*
Capitol Restoration Corp 516 783-1425
2473 Belmond Ave North Bellmore (11710) *(G-12373)*
Caplugs, Buffalo *Also called Protective Industries Inc* *(G-3017)*
Caplugs, Buffalo *Also called Protective Industries Inc* *(G-3018)*
Caps Teamwear Inc 585 663-1750
65 Milburn St Rochester (14607) *(G-13691)*
Capstone Printing, New York *Also called Kallen Corp* *(G-10399)*
Capstream Technologies LLC 716 945-7100
16 Main St Salamanca (14779) *(G-14524)*
Captain USA, New York *Also called CPT Usa LLC* *(G-9414)*
Caputo Bakery Inc 718 875-6871
329 Court St Ste 1 Brooklyn (11231) *(G-1675)*
Caputo's Bake Shop, Brooklyn *Also called Caputo Bakery Inc* *(G-1675)*
Capy Machine Shop Inc (PA) 631 694-6916
114 Spagnoli Rd Melville (11747) *(G-8006)*
Car Doctor Motor Sports LLC 631 537-1548
610 Scuttle Hole Rd Water Mill (11976) *(G-15968)*
Car Doctor, The, Water Mill *Also called Car Doctor Motor Sports LLC* *(G-15968)*
Car Engineering and Mfg, Victor *Also called Charles A Rogers Entps Inc* *(G-15835)*
Car-Freshner Corporation (HQ) 315 788-6250
21205 Little Tree Dr Watertown (13601) *(G-16005)*
Car-Freshner Corporation 315 788-6250
22569 Fisher Cir Watertown (13601) *(G-16006)*
Car-Go Industries Inc (PA) 718 472-1443
5007 49th St Woodside (11377) *(G-16650)*
Caraustar Industries Inc 716 874-0393
25 Dewberry Ln Buffalo (14227) *(G-2761)*
Caravan International Corp 212 223-7190
641 Lexington Ave Fl 13 New York (10022) *(G-9205)*
Caravella Food Corp 646 552-0455
16611 Cryders Ln Whitestone (11357) *(G-16537)*
Carballo Contract Machining 315 594-2511
6205 Lake Ave Wolcott (14590) *(G-16609)*
Carbaugh Tool Company Inc 607 739-3293
126 Philo Rd W Elmira (14903) *(G-4475)*
Carbert Music Inc 212 725-9277
126 E 38th St New York (10016) *(G-9206)*
Carbide-Usa LLC 607 331-9353
100 Home St Elmira (14904) *(G-4476)*
Carbon Activated Corporation 716 662-2005
336 Stonehenge Dr Orchard Park (14127) *(G-12705)*
Carbon Activated Corporation 716 677-6661
3774 Hoover Rd Blasdell (14219) *(G-925)*
Carbon Copies, Cortland *Also called BP Digital Imaging LLC* *(G-3864)*
Carbon Graphite Materials Inc 716 792-7979
115 Central Ave Brocton (14716) *(G-1195)*
Carbonfree Chemicals Spe I LLC 914 421-4900
1 N Lexington Ave White Plains (10601) *(G-16436)*
Card Pak Start Up, East Hampton *Also called Luria Communications Inc* *(G-4240)*
Card Printing.us, Monsey *Also called Tele-Pak Inc* *(G-8302)*
Cardinal Boiler and Tank, Brooklyn *Also called Cardinal Tank Corp* *(G-1676)*
Cardinal Data/Lark Graphics, Albany *Also called Andrew J George* *(G-41)*
Cardinal Tank Corp 718 625-4350
700 Hicks St Brooklyn (11231) *(G-1676)*
Cardinali Bakery, Carle Place *Also called Gennaris Itln French Bky Inc* *(G-3265)*
Cardish Machine Works Inc 518 273-2329
7 Elm St Watervliet (12189) *(G-16043)*
Cardona Industries USA Ltd (PA) 516 466-5200
505 Northern Blvd Ste 213 Great Neck (11021) *(G-5542)*
Cardullo, J Iron Works, Bay Shore *Also called Jerry Cardullo Iron Works Inc* *(G-692)*
Carduner Sales Company, Farmingville *Also called Bud Barger Assoc Inc* *(G-4923)*
Care Enterprises Inc 631 472-8155
435 Renee Dr Bayport (11705) *(G-735)*
Care/of, New York *Also called Noho Health Inc* *(G-10985)*
Careconnector 919 360-2987
177 Concord St Apt 2a Brooklyn (11201) *(G-1677)*
Careers and The Disabled, Melville *Also called Equal Opprtnity Pblcations Inc* *(G-8019)*
Carefree Kitchens Inc 631 567-2120
925 Lincoln Ave Ste 1 Holbrook (11741) *(G-6175)*
Carestream Health Inc 585 627-1800
1669 Lake Ave Rochester (14652) *(G-13692)*
Carges Entps of Canandaigua 585 394-2600
330 S Main St Canandaigua (14424) *(G-3214)*
Cargill Incorporated 585 345-1160
8849 Wortendyke Rd Batavia (14020) *(G-616)*
Cargill Incorporated 716 665-6570
1029 Poland Center Rd Kennedy (14747) *(G-6866)*
Cargill Incorporated 315 287-0241
19 Starbuck St Gouverneur (13642) *(G-5487)*
Cargill Incorporated 518 854-7417
4186 State Route 29 Salem (12865) *(G-14536)*
Cargill Incorporated 315 622-3533
7700 Maltage Dr Liverpool (13090) *(G-7228)*
Caribbean Fashion Group Inc 212 706-8851
1410 Broadway Rm 3202 New York (10018) *(G-9207)*
Caribbean Foods Delight Inc 845 398-3000
117 Route 303 Ste B Tappan (10983) *(G-15466)*
Caribe Bakery, Bronx *Also called 527 Franco Bakery Corporation* *(G-1197)*
Carl Fischer LLC (PA) 212 777-0900
48 Wall St 28 New York (10005) *(G-9208)*
Carl Safina Center Inc 808 888-9440
80 N Country Rd Setauket (11733) *(G-14793)*
Carl Zeiss Inc (HQ) 914 747-1800
1 Zeiss Dr Thornwood (10594) *(G-15502)*
Carl Zeiss Microscopy LLC 914 747-1800
1 Zeiss Dr Thornwood (10594) *(G-15503)*
Carl Zeiss Sbe LLC 914 747-1132
1 Zeiss Dr Thornwood (10594) *(G-15504)*
Carlara Group Ltd 914 769-2020
467 Bedford Rd Pleasantville (10570) *(G-13173)*
Carleton Technologies Inc (HQ) 716 662-0006
10 Cobham Dr Orchard Park (14127) *(G-12706)*
Carlisle Construction Mtls LLC 386 753-0786
9 Hudson Crossing Dr Montgomery (12549) *(G-8310)*
Carlo Monte Designs Inc 212 935-5611
17 E 48th St Fl 8 New York (10017) *(G-9209)*
Carlos & Alex Atelier Inc 718 441-8911
10010 91st Ave Fl 2 Richmond Hill (11418) *(G-13500)*
Carlson Wood Products Inc (PA) 716 287-2923
1705 Bates Rd Sinclairville (14782) *(G-14864)*
Carlson, L A Co, East Greenbush *Also called Leonard Carlson* *(G-4230)*
Carlton Ice Cream Co, Brooklyn *Also called Macedonia Ltd* *(G-2149)*
Carmen Mark Valvo Swimwear, Farmingdale *Also called Swimwear Anywhere Inc* *(G-4886)*
Carmine Street Bagels Inc 212 691-3041
107 Park Dr N Staten Island (10314) *(G-15061)*
Carnel Printing and Copying, Great Neck *Also called Carnels Printing Inc* *(G-5543)*
Carnels Printing Inc 516 883-3355
21 Schenck Ave Apt 3ba Great Neck (11021) *(G-5543)*
Carnival, New York *Also called Cookies Inc* *(G-9393)*
Carob Industries Inc 631 225-0900
215 W Hoffman Ave Lindenhurst (11757) *(G-7166)*
Caroda Inc 212 630-9986
254 W 35th St New York (10001) *(G-9210)*

(PA)=Parent Co (HQ)=Headquarters (DH)=Div Headquarters
2019 Harris
New York Manufacturers Directory
847

Carol For Eva Graham Inc 212 889-8686
366 5th Ave Rm 815 New York (10001) *(G-9211)*
Carol Group Ltd 212 505-2030
150 W 30th St Rm 902 New York (10001) *(G-9212)*
Carol Peretz 516 248-6300
49 Windsor Ave Ste 103 Mineola (11501) *(G-8210)*
Carol Peretz Workshop, Mineola *Also called Carol Peretz (G-8210)*
Carol Vail, Salem *Also called Carolina Eastern-Vail Inc (G-14537)*
Carolina Amato Inc 212 768-9095
270 W 38th St Rm 902 New York (10018) *(G-9213)*
Carolina Eastern-Vail Inc 518 854-9785
4134 State Route 22 Salem (12865) *(G-14537)*
Carolina Herrera Ltd (HQ) 212 944-5757
501 Fashion Ave Fl 17 New York (10018) *(G-9214)*
Carolina Precision Plas LLC 631 981-0743
115 Comac St Ronkonkoma (11779) *(G-14326)*
Carolinas Desserts Inc 914 779-4000
1562 Central Park Ave Yonkers (10710) *(G-16742)*
Carols Polar Parlor 315 468-3404
3800 W Genesee St Syracuse (13219) *(G-15270)*
Carolyn Ray Inc 914 476-0619
578 Nepperhan Ave Ste C10 Yonkers (10701) *(G-16743)*
Caron Distribution Center, New York *Also called National Spinning Co Inc (G-10886)*
Carousel ADS, Brooklyn *Also called Drns Corp (G-1795)*
Carpenter Industries Inc 315 463-4284
1 General Motors Dr # 10 Syracuse (13206) *(G-15271)*
Carpenter Manufacturing Co 315 682-9176
110 Fairgrounds Dr Manlius (13104) *(G-7775)*
Carpentier Industries LLC 585 385-5550
119 Despatch Dr East Rochester (14445) *(G-4281)*
Carpet Fabrications Intl 914 381-6060
628 Waverly Ave Ste 1 Mamaroneck (10543) *(G-7736)*
Carr Communications Group LLC 607 748-0481
513 Prentice Rd Vestal (13850) *(G-15813)*
Carr Jewelers, Latham *Also called Carr Manufacturing Jewelers (G-7069)*
Carr Manufacturing Jewelers 518 783-6093
22 West Ln Latham (12110) *(G-7069)*
Carr Printing, Vestal *Also called Carr Communications Group LLC (G-15813)*
Carrera Casting Corp 212 382-3296
64 W 48th St Fl 2 New York (10036) *(G-9215)*
Carrier Corporation 315 463-5744
6390 Fly Rd East Syracuse (13057) *(G-4328)*
Carrier Corporation 315 432-6000
Carrier Pkwy Tr 20 Syracuse (13221) *(G-15272)*
Carrier Corporation 315 432-6000
Carrier Global Account Syracuse (13221) *(G-15273)*
Carrier Corporation 315 432-6000
Kinne St East Syracuse (13057) *(G-4329)*
Carrier Corporation 315 432-3844
Carrier Pkwy Bldg Tr 20 East Syracuse (13057) *(G-4330)*
Carrier News, Hicksville *Also called All Island Media Inc (G-6057)*
Carrmet Industries, Farmingdale *Also called Joe P Industries Inc (G-4794)*
Carry Hot Inc 212 279-7535
545 W 45th St Rm 501 New York (10036) *(G-9216)*
Carry-All Canvas Bag Co Inc 718 375-4230
1983 Coney Island Ave Brooklyn (11223) *(G-1678)*
Carta Usa LLC 585 436-3012
1600 Lexington Ave # 116 Rochester (14606) *(G-13693)*
Carter Enterprises LLC (PA) 718 853-5052
4610 12th Ave Brooklyn (11219) *(G-1679)*
Carter Street Bakery Inc 585 749-7104
580 Child St Rochester (14606) *(G-13694)*
Carthage Fibre Drum Inc (PA) 315 493-2730
14 Hewitt Dr Carthage (13619) *(G-3286)*
Carthage Specialty Pprbd Inc 315 493-2120
30 Champion St Carthage (13619) *(G-3287)*
Cartiheal Inc 917 703-6992
575 5th Ave Fl 14 New York (10017) *(G-9217)*
Carts Mobile Food Eqp Corp 718 788-5540
113 8th St Brooklyn (11215) *(G-1680)*
Carvart Glass Inc (PA) 212 675-0030
1441 Broadway Fl 28 New York (10018) *(G-9218)*
Carver Creek Enterprises Inc 585 657-7511
2524 Cannan Rd Bloomfield (14469) *(G-949)*
Carver Sand & Gravel, Schoharie *Also called Masick Soil Conservation Co (G-14732)*
Carver Sand & Gravel LLC (PA) 518 355-6034
494 Western Tpke Ste 1 Altamont (12009) *(G-196)*
Carvin French Jewelers Inc 212 755-6474
515 Madison Ave Rm 5c New York (10022) *(G-9219)*
Cas, Cheektowaga *Also called Culinary Arts Specialties Inc (G-3439)*
Cas Biosciences LLC 844 227-2467
1501 Broadway Fl 12 New York (10036) *(G-9220)*
Casa Collection Inc 718 694-0272
106 Ferris St Brooklyn (11231) *(G-1681)*
Casa Innovations Inc 718 965-6600
155 Bay Ridge Ave Brooklyn (11220) *(G-1682)*
Casa Larga Vineyards (PA) 585 223-4210
27 Emerald Hill Cir Fairport (14450) *(G-4627)*
Casa Larga Vineyards 585 223-4210
2287 Turk Hill Rd Fairport (14450) *(G-4628)*
Casa Redimix Concrete Corp 718 589-1555
886 Edgewater Rd Bronx (10474) *(G-1235)*

Casablanca Foods LLC 212 317-1111
1617 3rd Ave Unit 287447 New York (10128) *(G-9221)*
Casablanca Records, New York *Also called Tm Music Inc (G-11853)*
Cascade Helmets Holdings Inc 315 453-3073
4697 Crssrads Pk Dr Ste 1 Liverpool (13088) *(G-7229)*
Cascade Mountain Winery & Rest 845 373-9021
835 Cascade Rd Amenia (12501) *(G-205)*
Cascade Technical Services LLC (HQ) 516 596-6300
30 N Prospect Ave Lynbrook (11563) *(G-7663)*
Cascade Technical Services LLC 518 355-2201
2846 Curry Rd Ste B Schenectady (12303) *(G-14659)*
Cascades New York Inc 716 285-3681
4001 Packard Rd Niagara Falls (14303) *(G-12268)*
Cascades New York Inc 718 340-2100
5515 Grand Ave Maspeth (11378) *(G-7829)*
Cascades New York Inc 518 346-6151
801 Corporation Park Schenectady (12302) *(G-14660)*
Cascades Tssue Group-Sales Inc 518 238-1900
148 Hudson River Rd Waterford (12188) *(G-15973)*
Cascades Tssue Group-Sales Inc (HQ) 819 363-5100
148 Hudson River Rd Waterford (12188) *(G-15974)*
Casco Security, Rochester *Also called Custom Sound and Video (G-13730)*
Case Brothers Inc 716 925-7172
370 Quinn Rd Limestone (14753) *(G-7157)*
Case Group LLC 518 720-3100
195 Cohoes Ave Green Island (12183) *(G-5603)*
Case Window and Door, Green Island *Also called Case Group LLC (G-5603)*
Casey Machine Co Inc 716 651-0150
74 Ward Rd Lancaster (14086) *(G-7012)*
Cassinelli Food Products Inc 718 274-4881
3112 23rd Ave Long Island City (11105) *(G-7406)*
Cassini Parfums Ltd 212 753-7540
3 W 57th St Fl 8 New York (10019) *(G-9222)*
Cast-All Corporation (PA) 516 741-4025
229 Liberty Ave Mineola (11501) *(G-8211)*
Cast-All Corporation 516 741-4025
229 Liberty Ave Mineola (11501) *(G-8212)*
Castek Inc (HQ) 914 636-1000
20 Jones St New Rochelle (10801) *(G-8595)*
Castel Grisch Winery, Montour Falls *Also called Malina Management Company Inc (G-8326)*
Castella Imports Inc (PA) 631 231-5500
120 Wilshire Blvd Ste A Edgewood (11717) *(G-4398)*
Castelli America LLC 716 782-2101
5151 Fairbanks Rd Ashville (14710) *(G-415)*
Casters Custom Sawing 315 387-5104
6323 Us Route 11 Sandy Creek (13145) *(G-14558)*
Castino Corporation 845 229-0341
1300 Route 9g Hyde Park (12538) *(G-6468)*
Castle Brands Inc (PA) 646 356-0200
122 E 42nd St Rm 5000 New York (10168) *(G-9223)*
Castle Connolly Medical Ltd 212 367-8400
42 W 24th St Fl 2 New York (10010) *(G-9224)*
Castle Fuels Corporation 914 381-6600
440 Mamaroneck Ave Harrison (10528) *(G-5723)*
Castle Harvester Co Inc 585 526-5884
3165 Seneca Castle Rd Seneca Castle (14547) *(G-14772)*
Castle Harvstr Met Fabricators, Seneca Castle *Also called Castle Harvester Co Inc (G-14772)*
Castle Power Solutions LLC 518 743-1000
22 Hudson Falls Rd Ste D South Glens Falls (12803) *(G-14935)*
Castle Reagh Print Craft, Freeport *Also called Castlereagh Printcraft Inc (G-5148)*
Castlereagh Printcraft Inc 516 623-1728
320 Buffalo Ave Freeport (11520) *(G-5148)*
Castoleum Corporation 914 664-5877
240 E 7th St Mount Vernon (10550) *(G-8385)*
Casttle Harbor, Plainview *Also called Hot Line Industries Inc (G-13061)*
Casual Friday Inc 585 544-9470
1561 Lyell Ave Rochester (14606) *(G-13695)*
Casuals Etc Inc 212 838-1319
16 E 52nd St Fl 4 New York (10022) *(G-9225)*
Caswell Inc 315 946-1213
7696 State Route 31 Lyons (14489) *(G-7682)*
Catalina Products Corp (PA) 718 336-8288
2455 Mcdonald Ave Brooklyn (11223) *(G-1683)*
Catalyst Group Design, New York *Also called Catalyst Group Inc (G-9226)*
Catalyst Group Inc 212 243-7777
345 7th Ave Rm 1100 New York (10001) *(G-9226)*
Catapult 323 839-6204
1140 Broadway Rm 704 New York (10001) *(G-9227)*
Cataract Hose Co 914 941-9019
6 Waller Ave Ossining (10562) *(G-12769)*
Cataract Hose Co No 2, Ossining *Also called Cataract Hose Co (G-12769)*
Cataract Steel Industries, Niagara Falls *Also called Costanzos Welding Inc (G-12274)*
Catch Ventures Inc 347 620-4351
30 W 63rd St Apt 14o New York (10023) *(G-9228)*
Cathay Global Co Inc 718 229-0920
5815 215th St Bayside Hills (11364) *(G-752)*
Cathay Home Inc (PA) 212 213-0988
230 5th Ave Ste 215 New York (10001) *(G-9229)*
Cathay Resources Inc 516 922-2839
38 Cord Pl East Norwich (11732) *(G-4271)*

ALPHABETIC SECTION

Cathedral Candle Co 315 422-9119
510 Kirkpatrick St Syracuse (13208) *(G-15274)*
Cathedral Corporation (PA) 315 338-0021
632 Ellsworth Rd Rome (13441) *(G-14249)*
Catherine Deane, New York *Also called Arcangel Inc (G-8899)*
Catherine Stein Designs Inc 212 840-1188
411 5th Ave Rm 600 New York (10016) *(G-9230)*
Catholic Courier, Rochester *Also called Rochester Catholic Press (G-14082)*
Catholic New York, New York *Also called Ecclesiastical Communications (G-9620)*
Catholic News Publishing Co 914 632-7771
420 Railroad Way Mamaroneck (10543) *(G-7737)*
Catholic Sun, The, Syracuse *Also called Syracuse Catholic Press Assn (G-15435)*
Cathy Daniels Ltd (PA) 212 354-8000
501 Fashion Ave Rm 400 New York (10018) *(G-9231)*
Catskill Castings Co, Bloomville *Also called G Haynes Holdings Inc (G-961)*
Catskill Craftsmen 607 652-7321
15 W End Ave Stamford (12167) *(G-15030)*
Catskill Delaware Publications (PA) 845 887-5200
5 Lower Main St Callicoon (12723) *(G-3160)*
Catskill Mountain News, Arkville *Also called Catskill Mountain Publishing (G-400)*
Catskill Mountain Publishing 845 586-2601
43414 State Hwy 28 Arkville (12406) *(G-400)*
Catsmo LLC 845 895-2296
25 Myers Rd Wallkill (12589) *(G-15903)*
Cattaraugus Containers Inc 716 676-2000
21 Elm St 23 Franklinville (14737) *(G-5123)*
Cava Spiliadis USA 212 247-8214
200 W 57th St Ste 908 New York (10019) *(G-9232)*
Cayuga Crushed Stone Inc 607 533-4273
87 Portland Point Rd Lansing (14882) *(G-7055)*
Cayuga Press Cortland Inc 888 229-8421
4707 Dey Rd Liverpool (13088) *(G-7230)*
Cayuga Tool and Die Inc 607 533-7400
182 Newman Rd Groton (13073) *(G-5651)*
Cayuga Wooden Boatworks Inc 315 253-7447
381 Enfield Main Rd Ithaca (14850) *(G-6570)*
Cazar Printing & Advertising 718 446-4606
4215 102nd St Corona (11368) *(G-3840)*
CB Products, Floral Park *Also called CB Publishing LLC (G-4959)*
CB Publishing LLC 516 354-4888
50 Carnation Ave Bldg 2-1 Floral Park (11001) *(G-4959)*
CBA Group LLC 607 779-7522
33 Broome Corporate Pkwy Conklin (13748) *(G-3725)*
Cbe/New York, Plainview *Also called Conrad Blasius Equipment Co (G-13044)*
CBM Fabrications Inc 518 399-8023
15 Westside Dr Ballston Lake (12019) *(G-567)*
Cbord Group Inc (HQ) 607 257-2410
950 Danby Rd Ste 100c Ithaca (14850) *(G-6571)*
CCA Holding Inc 716 446-8800
300 Corporate Pkwy Amherst (14226) *(G-220)*
CCC Publications Inc 718 306-1008
12020 Flatlands Ave Brooklyn (11207) *(G-1684)*
CCL Label Inc 716 852-2155
685 Howard St Buffalo (14206) *(G-2762)*
Ccmi Inc 315 781-3270
88 Middle St Geneva (14456) *(G-5318)*
Ccn International Inc 315 789-4400
200 Lehigh St Geneva (14456) *(G-5319)*
CCS Machinery Inc 631 968-0900
2175 Union Blvd Bay Shore (11706) *(G-668)*
CCT (us) Inc 716 297-7509
2221 Niagara Falls Blvd # 5 Niagara Falls (14304) *(G-12269)*
Cct Inc 212 532-3355
60 Madison Ave Ste 1209 New York (10010) *(G-9233)*
Ccz Ready Mix Concrete Corp 516 579-7352
2 Loring Rd Levittown (11756) *(G-7132)*
Cda Machine Inc 585 671-5959
514 Vosburg Rd Webster (14580) *(G-16077)*
CDF Indstrial Pckg Sltions Inc 716 672-2984
134 Clinton Ave Fredonia (14063) *(G-5125)*
Cdj Stamping Inc 585 224-8120
146 Halstead St Ste 123 Rochester (14610) *(G-13696)*
Cdl Manufacturing Inc 585 589-2533
15661 Telegraph Rd Albion (14411) *(G-156)*
Cdml Computer Services Ltd 718 428-9063
5343 198th St Fresh Meadows (11365) *(G-5195)*
Cds Productions Inc 518 385-8255
108 Erie Blvd Ste 400 Schenectady (12305) *(G-14661)*
CEC Elevator Cab Corp 718 328-3632
540 Manida St Bronx (10474) *(G-1236)*
Cedar West Inc (PA) 631 467-1444
1700 Ocean Ave Ste 1 Ronkonkoma (11779) *(G-14327)*
Cegid Corporation 212 757-9038
274 Madison Ave Rm 1400 New York (10016) *(G-9234)*
Cego Custom Shirts, New York *Also called Sifonya Inc (G-11581)*
Cei, Oneonta *Also called Custom Electronics Inc (G-12637)*
Ceipal LLC 585 351-2934
722 Weiland Rd Rochester (14626) *(G-13697)*
Ceipal LLC 585 584-1316
687 Lee Rd Ste 208a Rochester (14606) *(G-13698)*
CEIT Corp 518 825-0649
625 State Route 3 Unit 2 Plattsburgh (12901) *(G-13116)*

Cell-Nique Corporation 203 856-8550
22 Hamilton Way Castleton On Hudson (12033) *(G-3295)*
Cellec Technologies Inc 585 454-9166
125 Tech Park Dr Ste 2111 Rochester (14623) *(G-13699)*
Cellect Plastics LLC 518 568-7036
12 New St Saint Johnsville (13452) *(G-14517)*
Cellectis Inc 347 809-5980
430 E 29th St Ste 810 New York (10016) *(G-9235)*
Cellgen Inc 516 889-9300
55 Commercial St Freeport (11520) *(G-5149)*
Cellu Tissue - Long Island LLC 631 232-2626
555 N Research Pl Central Islip (11722) *(G-3361)*
Celmet Co 585 647-1760
105 Norton St Newark (14513) *(G-12194)*
Celonis Inc 941 615-9670
1820 Avenue M Unit 544 Brooklyn (11230) *(G-1685)*
Cem Machine Inc (PA) 315 493-4258
571 W End Ave Carthage (13619) *(G-3288)*
Cemac Foods Corp 914 835-0526
8 Cayuga Trl Harrison (10528) *(G-5724)*
Cemecon Inc 607 562-2363
315 Daniel Zenker Dr Horseheads (14845) *(G-6309)*
Cementex Latex Corp 212 741-1770
121 Varick St Frnt 2 New York (10013) *(G-9236)*
Cemento,, West Monroe *Also called Robinson Concrete Inc (G-16262)*
Cemex Cement Inc 212 317-6000
590 Madison Ave Fl 41 New York (10022) *(G-9237)*
Cemoi Inc (PA) 212 583-4920
5 Penn Plz Ste 2325 New York (10001) *(G-9238)*
Cenere, New York *Also called Precision International Co Inc (G-11229)*
Cenibra Inc 212 818-8242
1251 Ave Of The Americas New York (10020) *(G-9239)*
Ceno Technologies Inc 716 885-5050
1234 Delaware Ave Buffalo (14209) *(G-2763)*
Centar Fuel Co Inc 516 538-2424
700 Nassau Blvd West Hempstead (11552) *(G-16214)*
Centennial Media LLC 646 527-7320
10th Floor 40 Worth St Flr 10 New York (10013) *(G-9240)*
Center For Inquiry Inc (PA) 716 636-4869
3965 Rensch Rd Amherst (14228) *(G-221)*
Center For Prosthetic 845 336-7762
144 Pine St Ste 110 Kingston (12401) *(G-6893)*
Center Line Studios Inc 845 534-7143
261 Otterkill Rd New Windsor (12553) *(G-8639)*
Center Line Studios Inc (PA) 845 534-7143
112 Forge Hill Rd New Windsor (12553) *(G-8640)*
Center Sheet Metal Inc 718 378-4476
1371 E Bay Ave Bronx (10474) *(G-1237)*
Center State Propane LLC (PA) 315 841-4044
1130 Mason Rd Waterville (13480) *(G-16038)*
Centerless Technology Inc 585 436-2240
45 Wells St Rochester (14611) *(G-13700)*
Centerra Wine Company, Canandaigua *Also called Constellation Brands US Oprs (G-3217)*
Centinel Spice LLC (PA) 212 583-9700
505 Park Ave Fl 14 New York (10022) *(G-9241)*
Central Adirondack Textiles, Boonville *Also called S M S C Inc (G-1121)*
Central Apparel Group Ltd 212 868-6505
16 W 36th St Rm 1202 New York (10018) *(G-9242)*
Central Asphalt, Oriskany *Also called Suit-Kote Corporation (G-12763)*
Central Asphalt, Watkins Glen *Also called Suit-Kote Corporation (G-16061)*
Central Cnfrnce of Amrcn Rbbis 212 972-3636
355 Lexington Ave Fl 18 New York (10017) *(G-9243)*
Central Dover Development 917 709-3266
247 Dover Furnace Rd Dover Plains (12522) *(G-4143)*
Central Garden & Pet Company 631 451-8021
1100 Middle Country Rd Selden (11784) *(G-14761)*
Central Islip Pharmacy Inc 631 234-6039
1629 Islip Ave Central Islip (11722) *(G-3362)*
Central Kitchen Corp 631 283-1029
871 County Road 39 Southampton (11968) *(G-14951)*
Central Marking Equipment, Syracuse *Also called C M E Corp (G-15266)*
Central Mills Inc 212 764-9011
1400 Broadway Rm 1605 New York (10018) *(G-9244)*
Central Nat Pulp & Ppr Sls Inc 914 696-9000
3 Manhattanville Rd Purchase (10577) *(G-13387)*
Central Park Active Wear, New York *Also called Central Apparel Group Ltd (G-9242)*
Central Rede Sign Co Inc 716 213-0797
317 Wheeler St Tonawanda (14150) *(G-15532)*
Central Semiconductor Corp 631 435-1110
145 Adams Ave Hauppauge (11788) *(G-5786)*
Central Textiles Inc 212 213-8740
10 E 40th St Rm 3410 New York (10016) *(G-9245)*
Central Timber Co Inc 518 638-6338
9088 State Route 22 Granville (12832) *(G-5518)*
Central Timber Research/Devt, Granville *Also called Central Timber Co Inc (G-5518)*
Central Time Clock Inc 718 784-4900
523 50th Ave Long Island City (11101) *(G-7407)*
Centre De Conformite ICC Inc 716 283-0002
2150 Liberty Dr Ste 1 Niagara Falls (14304) *(G-12270)*
Centre Interiors Wdwkg Co Inc 718 323-1343
10001 103rd Ave Ozone Park (11417) *(G-12822)*

(PA)=Parent Co (HQ)=Headquarters (DH)=Div Headquarters

Centric Brands Inc (PA) 323 890-1800
350 5th Ave Lbby 6 New York (10118) ***(G-9246)***
Centric Denim Usa LLC (HQ) 646 839-7000
350 5th Ave Lbby 9 New York (10118) ***(G-9247)***
Centric West LLC (HQ) 646 839-7000
350 5th Ave Fl 5 New York (10118) ***(G-9248)***
Centrisource Inc 716 871-1105
777 E Park Dr Tonawanda (14150) ***(G-15533)***
Centro Inc 212 791-9450
841 Broadway Fl 6 New York (10003) ***(G-9249)***
Centroid Inc 516 349-0070
111 E Ames Ct Unit 1 Plainview (11803) ***(G-13040)***
Century Awning Concepts, Mount Vernon *Also called Kingston Building Products LLC* ***(G-8415)***
Century Direct LLC 212 763-0600
15 Enter Ln Islandia (11749) ***(G-6524)***
Century Grand Inc 212 925-3838
302 Grand St New York (10002) ***(G-9250)***
Century Metal Parts Corp 631 667-0800
230 S Fehr Way Bay Shore (11706) ***(G-669)***
Century Mold Company Inc (PA) 585 352-8600
25 Vantage Point Dr Rochester (14624) ***(G-13701)***
Century Mold Mexico LLC (HQ) 585 352-8600
25 Vantage Point Dr Rochester (14624) ***(G-13702)***
Century Pharmacy Three, New York *Also called Century Grand Inc* ***(G-9250)***
Century Ready Mix Inc 631 888-2200
615 Cord Ave West Babylon (11704) ***(G-16145)***
Century Tom Inc 347 654-3179
10416 150th St Jamaica (11435) ***(G-6632)***
Century-Tech Inc 718 326-9400
32 Intersection St Hempstead (11550) ***(G-6009)***
Century-Tech Inc 516 493-9800
32 Intersection St Hempstead (11550) ***(G-6010)***
Ceo Cast Inc 212 732-4300
211 E 43rd St Rm 400 New York (10017) ***(G-9251)***
Ceoentano, Buffalo *Also called Rosina Food Products Inc* ***(G-3045)***
Cep Technologies Corporation (PA) 914 968-4100
763 Saw Mill River Rd Yonkers (10710) ***(G-16744)***
Ceramica V. A. R. M., New Rochelle *Also called Ceramica Varm* ***(G-8596)***
Ceramica Varm (PA) 914 381-6215
479 5th Ave New Rochelle (10801) ***(G-8596)***
Ceres Technologies Inc 845 247-4701
5 Tower Dr Saugerties (12477) ***(G-14604)***
Cerion Energy Inc 585 271-5630
1 Blossom Rd Rochester (14610) ***(G-13703)***
Cerion LLC 585 271-5630
1 Blossom Rd Rochester (14610) ***(G-13704)***
Ceros Inc (PA) 347 744-9250
40 W 25th St Fl 12 New York (10010) ***(G-9252)***
Cerovene Inc 845 359-1101
10 Corporate Dr Orangeburg (10962) ***(G-12671)***
Cerovene Inc (PA) 845 267-2055
612 Corporate Way Ste 10 Valley Cottage (10989) ***(G-15753)***
Certainteed Corporation 716 823-3684
231 Ship Canal Pkwy Lackawanna (14218) ***(G-6948)***
Certainteed Corporation 716 827-7560
231 Ship Canal Pkwy Buffalo (14218) ***(G-2764)***
Certified Flameproofing Corp 631 265-4824
17 N Ingelore Ct Smithtown (11787) ***(G-14895)***
Certified Health Products Inc 718 339-7498
67 35th St Unit 12 Brooklyn (11232) ***(G-1686)***
Certified Prcsion McHining Inc 631 244-3671
70 Knickerbocker Ave # 4 Bohemia (11716) ***(G-993)***
Ces Industries Inc 631 782-7088
95 Hoffman Ln Ste S Islandia (11749) ***(G-6525)***
Cetek Inc 845 452-3510
19 Commerce St Poughkeepsie (12603) ***(G-13331)***
Cettel Studio of New York Inc 518 494-3622
636 Atateka Dr Chestertown (12817) ***(G-3490)***
Cfe, Brooklyn *Also called Carts Mobile Food Eqp Corp* ***(G-1680)***
Cffco USA Inc 718 747-1118
55 Jericho Tpke Ste 302 Jericho (11753) ***(G-6781)***
Cfg Group, New York *Also called Caribbean Fashion Group Inc* ***(G-9207)***
CFI, Perry *Also called Creative Food Ingredients Inc* ***(G-12967)***
Cfo Publishing LLC (PA) 212 459-3004
50 Broad St Frnt New York (10004) ***(G-9253)***
Cfp Purchasing Inc 705 806-0383
4760 197th St Flushing (11358) ***(G-4989)***
CFS Enterprises Inc 718 585-0500
650 E 132nd St Bronx (10454) ***(G-1238)***
CFS Steel Company, Bronx *Also called CFS Enterprises Inc* ***(G-1238)***
Cgi Technologies Solutions Inc 212 682-7411
655 3rd Ave Ste 700 New York (10017) ***(G-9254)***
Cgm, Brocton *Also called Carbon Graphite Materials Inc* ***(G-1195)***
Cgs Fabrication LLC 585 347-6127
855 Publishers Pkwy Webster (14580) ***(G-16078)***
Cgw Corp (PA) 631 472-6600
102 S Gillette Ave Bayport (11705) ***(G-736)***
Chad Pierson 518 251-0186
Chad Pierson Bakers Mills (12811) ***(G-537)***
Chad Pierson Logging & Trckg, Bakers Mills *Also called Chad Pierson* ***(G-537)***
Chain Store Age Magazine 212 756-5000
425 Park Ave New York (10022) ***(G-9255)***
Chaindom Enterprises Inc 212 719-4778
48 W 48th St Ste 200 New York (10036) ***(G-9256)***
Chakra Communications Inc 607 748-7491
32 Washington Ave Endicott (13760) ***(G-4584)***
Chakra Communications Inc 716 505-7300
80 W Drullard Ave Lancaster (14086) ***(G-7013)***
Challenge Graphics Svcs Inc (PA) 631 586-0171
22 Connor Ln Deer Park (11729) ***(G-3956)***
Cham Cold Brew LLC 646 926-0206
300 Park Ave Fl 12 New York (10022) ***(G-9257)***
Chamberlin Rubber Company Inc 585 427-7780
3333 Brighton Henrietta Rochester (14623) ***(G-13705)***
Chambord LLC 718 859-1110
4302 Farragut Rd Brooklyn (11203) ***(G-1687)***
Chameleon Color Cards Ltd 716 625-9452
6530 S Transit Rd Lockport (14094) ***(G-7290)***
Chameleon Gems Inc 516 829-3333
98 Cuttermill Rd Ste 398n Great Neck (11021) ***(G-5544)***
Champion America Inc 716 626-1616
2491 Wehrle Dr Williamsville (14221) ***(G-16575)***
Champion Cutting Tool Corp 516 536-8200
11-15 Saint Marks Ave Rockville Centre (11570) ***(G-14230)***
Champion Home Builders Inc 315 841-4122
951 Rte 12 S Sangerfield (13455) ***(G-14559)***
Champion Materials Inc (PA) 315 493-2654
502 S Washington St Carthage (13619) ***(G-3289)***
Champion Millwork Inc 315 463-0711
140 Hiawatha Pl Syracuse (13208) ***(G-15275)***
Champion Photochemistry Inc 585 760-6444
1669 Lake Ave Rochester (14615) ***(G-13706)***
Champion Zipper Corp 212 239-0414
447 W 36th St Fl 2 New York (10018) ***(G-9258)***
Champlain Hanger, Rouses Point *Also called Champlain Plastics Inc* ***(G-14467)***
Champlain Hudson Power Ex Inc 518 465-0710
600 Broadway Fl 3 Albany (12207) ***(G-57)***
Champlain Plastics Inc 518 297-3700
87 Pillsbury Rd Rouses Point (12979) ***(G-14467)***
Champlain Valley Mil Corp Inc 518 963-7650
19 Myers Way Willsboro (12996) ***(G-16597)***
Champs Sports, Hicksville *Also called Foot Locker Retail Inc* ***(G-6087)***
Chams, New York *Also called North American Mills Inc* ***(G-10992)***
Chamtek Mfg Inc 585 328-4900
123 Louise St Rochester (14606) ***(G-13707)***
Chan & Chan (usa) Corp 718 388-9633
2 Rewe St Brooklyn (11211) ***(G-1688)***
Chan Kee Dried Bean Curd Inc 718 622-0820
71 Steuben St Brooklyn (11205) ***(G-1689)***
Changdu Technology (usa) Co 917 340-1976
1417 Horseshoe Dr North Bellmore (11710) ***(G-12374)***
Changes, Glendale *Also called Bowe Industries Inc* ***(G-5392)***
Channel Manufacturing Inc (PA) 516 944-6271
55 Channel Dr Port Washington (11050) ***(G-13247)***
Chanse Petroleum Corporation (PA) 212 682-3789
828 5th Ave Apt 1f New York (10065) ***(G-9259)***
Chapin International Inc 585 343-3140
700 Ellicott St Batavia (14020) ***(G-617)***
Chapin Manufacturing Inc (PA) 585 343-3140
700 Ellicott St Ste 3 Batavia (14020) ***(G-618)***
Chapman Skateboard Co Inc 631 321-4773
87 N Industry Ct Ste A Deer Park (11729) ***(G-3957)***
Charing Cross Music Inc 212 541-7571
3 Columbus Cir Ste 1720 New York (10019) ***(G-9260)***
Charis & Mae Inc 212 641-0816
31 W 34th St Fl 8 New York (10001) ***(G-9261)***
Charl Industries Inc 631 234-0100
225 Engineers Rd Hauppauge (11788) ***(G-5787)***
Charles A Rogers Entps Inc 585 924-6400
51 Victor Heights Pkwy Victor (14564) ***(G-15835)***
Charles Freihofer Baking Co 518 463-2221
1 Prospect Rd Albany (12206) ***(G-58)***
Charles H Beckley Inc (PA) 718 665-2218
749 E 137th St Bronx (10454) ***(G-1239)***
Charles Henricks Inc 212 243-5800
70 W 36th St Rm 500 New York (10018) ***(G-9262)***
Charles Krypell Inc 212 752-3313
22 W 48th St Ste 801-803 New York (10036) ***(G-9263)***
Charles P Rogers Brass Beds (PA) 212 675-4400
26 W 17th St New York (10011) ***(G-9264)***
Charles P Rogers Brass Ir Bed, New York *Also called Charles P Rogers Brass Beds* ***(G-9264)***
Charles Perrella Inc 845 348-4777
78 S Broadway Nyack (10960) ***(G-12502)***
Charles Richter, Wallkill *Also called Richter Metalcraft Corporation* ***(G-15907)***
Charles Ross & Son Company (PA) 631 234-0500
710 Old Willets Path Hauppauge (11788) ***(G-5788)***
Charles Vaillant Inc 212 752-4832
37 W 57th St Ste 803 New York (10019) ***(G-9265)***
Charlotte Neuville Design LLC 646 530-4570
882 3rd Ave Brooklyn (11232) ***(G-1690)***
Charlton Precision Products 845 338-2351
461 Sawkill Rd Kingston (12401) ***(G-6894)***

ALPHABETIC SECTION

Charm Mfg Co Inc..607 565-8161
251 State Route 17c Waverly (14892) *(G-16063)*
Charm Pools, Waverly Also called Charm Mfg Co Inc *(G-16063)*
Charming Fashion Inc..212 730-2872
247 W 38th St Rm 1400 New York (10018) *(G-9266)*
Chart Industries Inc..716 691-0202
260 Creekside Dr Ste 100 Amherst (14228) *(G-222)*
Charter Ventures LLC..212 868-0222
135 W 36th St Rm 1800 New York (10018) *(G-9267)*
Chartwell Pharma Nda B2 Holdin.......................845 268-5000
77 Brenner Dr Congers (10920) *(G-3713)*
Chartwell Pharmaceuticals LLC.........................845 268-5000
77 Brenner Dr Congers (10920) *(G-3714)*
Chartwell Rx LLC..845 268-5000
77 Brenner Dr Congers (10920) *(G-3715)*
Chase Corporation...631 827-0476
7 Harbour Point Dr Northport (11768) *(G-12466)*
Chase Instrument Co, West Babylon Also called Peyser Instrument Corporation *(G-16181)*
Chase Media Group...914 962-3871
1520 Front St Yorktown Heights (10598) *(G-16814)*
Chase Partners, Northport Also called Chase Corporation *(G-12466)*
Chase Press, Yorktown Heights Also called Shop Smart Central Inc *(G-16823)*
Chassix Automotive Corp....................................585 815-1700
4320 Federal Dr Batavia (14020) *(G-619)*
Chateau Imports Ltd..516 841-6343
8 Maple St Ste 10 Port Washington (11050) *(G-13248)*
Chateau La Fayette Reneau, Hector Also called Lafayette Chateau *(G-6000)*
Chatham Courier, The, Hudson Also called Johnson Acquisition Corp *(G-6360)*
Chautauqua Circuits Inc......................................716 366-5771
855 Main St Dunkirk (14048) *(G-4163)*
Chautauqua Iron Works, Mayville Also called Kleinfelder John *(G-7921)*
Chautauqua Machine Spc LLC............................716 782-3276
1880 Open Meadows Rd Ashville (14710) *(G-416)*
Chautauqua Sign Co Inc......................................716 665-2222
2164 Allen Street Ext Falconer (14733) *(G-4673)*
Chautauqua Wine Company Inc.........................716 934-9463
2627 Chapin Rd Silver Creek (14136) *(G-14860)*
Chautauqua Woods Corporation.........................716 366-3808
134 Franklin Ave Dunkirk (14048) *(G-4164)*
Chautqua Prcsion Machining Inc.........................716 763-3752
1287 Hunt Rd Ashville (14710) *(G-417)*
Check Group LLC...212 221-4700
1385 Broadway Fl 16 New York (10018) *(G-9268)*
Check-Mate Industries Inc..................................631 491-1777
370 Wyandanch Ave West Babylon (11704) *(G-16146)*
Check-O-Matic Inc...845 781-7675
13 D A Weider Blvd # 101 Monroe (10950) *(G-8267)*
Checklist Boards Corporation.............................585 586-0152
763 Linden Ave Ste 2 Rochester (14625) *(G-13708)*
Chefs Delight Packing Co....................................718 388-8581
94 N 8th St Brooklyn (11249) *(G-1691)*
Chelsea Plastics Inc..212 924-4530
200 Lexington Ave Rm 914 New York (10016) *(G-9269)*
Chem-Tainer Industries Inc (PA).........................631 422-8300
361 Neptune Ave West Babylon (11704) *(G-16147)*
Chem-Tek Systems Inc..631 253-3010
208 S Fehr Way Bay Shore (11706) *(G-670)*
Chembio Diagnostic Systems Inc........................631 924-1135
3661 Horseblock Rd Ste A Medford (11763) *(G-7941)*
Chembio Diagnostics Inc (PA).............................631 924-1135
3661 Horseblock Rd Ste C Medford (11763) *(G-7942)*
Chemclean Corporation......................................718 525-4500
13045 180th St Jamaica (11434) *(G-6633)*
Chemcolloid Laboratories Inc............................516 747-2666
55 Herricks Rd New Hyde Park (11040) *(G-8522)*
Chemistry Department, Oswego Also called Energy Nuclear Operations *(G-12777)*
Chemlube International LLC (PA).......................914 381-5800
500 Mmaroneck Ave Ste 306 Harrison (10528) *(G-5725)*
Chemlube Marketing Inc.....................................914 381-5800
500 Mamaroneck Ave Harrison (10528) *(G-5726)*
Chemours Company Fc LLC...............................716 278-5100
3181 Buffalo Ave Niagara Falls (14303) *(G-12271)*
Chemprene Inc..845 831-2800
483 Fishkill Ave Beacon (12508) *(G-755)*
Chemprene Holding Inc.....................................845 831-2800
483 Fishkill Ave Beacon (12508) *(G-756)*
Chemtrade Chemicals US LLC...........................315 430-7650
1421 Willis Ave Syracuse (13204) *(G-15276)*
Chemtrade Chemicals US LLC...........................315 478-2323
344 W Genesee St Ste 100 Syracuse (13202) *(G-15277)*
Chemung Cnty Chpter Nysarc Inc (HQ)............607 734-6151
711 Sullivan St Elmira (14901) *(G-4477)*
Chenango Concrete Corp....................................607 334-2545
County Rd 32 E River Rd Norwich (13815) *(G-12478)*
Chenango Concrete Corp (PA)...........................518 294-9964
145 Podpadic Rd Richmondville (12149) *(G-13518)*
Chenango Union Printing Inc..............................607 334-2112
15 American Ave Norwich (13815) *(G-12479)*
Chenango Valley Tech Inc...................................607 674-4115
328 Route 12b Sherburne (13460) *(G-14803)*
Chentronics Corporation.....................................607 334-5531
115 County Rd 45 Norwich (13815) *(G-12480)*

Chepaume Industries LLC...................................315 829-6400
6201 Cooper St Vernon (13476) *(G-15803)*
Chequedcom Inc...888 412-0699
513 Broadway Ste 1 Saratoga Springs (12866) *(G-14575)*
Cheri Mon Baby LLC...212 354-5511
1412 Broadway Rm 1608 New York (10018) *(G-9270)*
Cheribundi Inc (PA)..800 699-0460
500 Technology Farm Dr # 11 Geneva (14456) *(G-5320)*
Cherry Creek Woodcraft Inc (PA)......................716 988-3211
1 Cherry St South Dayton (14138) *(G-14928)*
Cherry Lane Lithographing Corp.......................516 293-9294
15 E Bethpage Rd Unit A Plainview (11803) *(G-13041)*
Cherry Lane Magazine LLC................................212 561-3000
1745 Broadway 19 New York (10019) *(G-9271)*
Chesky Records Inc...212 586-7799
1650 Broadway Ste 900 New York (10019) *(G-9272)*
Chester Printing Service, Middletown Also called Triad Printing Inc *(G-8180)*
Chester West County Press................................914 684-0006
29 W 4th St Mount Vernon (10550) *(G-8386)*
Chester-Jensen Company...................................610 876-6276
124 S Main St Cattaraugus (14719) *(G-3312)*
Chesu Inc...239 564-2803
81 Newtown Ln East Hampton (11937) *(G-4234)*
Chf Industries Inc (PA).......................................212 951-7800
1 Park Ave Fl 9 New York (10016) *(G-9273)*
Chia Company, New York Also called Chia Usa LLC *(G-9274)*
Chia Usa LLC..212 226-7512
379 W Broadway New York (10012) *(G-9274)*
Chicago Watermark Company, New York Also called Donald Bruhnke *(G-9547)*
Chicken Hawk Racing Inc...................................845 758-0700
54 Elizabeth St Ste 10 Red Hook (12571) *(G-13457)*
Chicone Builders LLC..607 535-6540
302 W South St Montour Falls (14865) *(G-8325)*
Chief, The, New York Also called New York Cvl Srvc Emplys Pblsh *(G-10934)*
Child Nutrition Prog Dept Ed..............................212 371-1000
1011 1st Ave Fl 6 New York (10022) *(G-9275)*
Child's Work-Child's Play, Melville Also called Guidance Group Inc *(G-8029)*
Childrens Progress Inc......................................212 730-0905
108 W 39th St Rm 1305 New York (10018) *(G-9276)*
Chim-Cap Corp..800 262-9622
120 Schmitt Blvd Farmingdale (11735) *(G-4734)*
Chimney Doctors Americas Corp.......................631 868-3586
738a Montauk Hwy Bayport (11705) *(G-737)*
China Daily Distribution Corp (HQ)...................212 537-8888
1500 Broadway Ste 2800 New York (10036) *(G-9277)*
China Huaren Organic Pdts Inc.........................212 232-0120
100 Wall St Fl 15 New York (10005) *(G-9278)*
China Imprint LLC..585 563-3391
750 Saint Paul St Rochester (14605) *(G-13709)*
China Industrial Steel Inc..................................646 328-1502
110 Wall St Fl 11 New York (10005) *(G-9279)*
China Lithium Technologies (PA)......................212 391-2688
15 W 39th St Fl 14 New York (10018) *(G-9280)*
China N E Petro Holdings Ltd............................212 307-3568
445 Park Ave New York (10022) *(G-9281)*
China Newsweek Corporation...........................212 481-2510
15 E 40th St Fl 11 New York (10016) *(G-9282)*
China Ruitai Intl Holdings Ltd...........................718 740-2278
8710 Clover Pl Hollis (11423) *(G-6232)*
China Ting Fashion Group (usa) (HQ)...............212 716-1600
525 7th Ave Rm 1606 New York (10018) *(G-9283)*
China Xd Plastics Company Ltd........................212 747-1118
500 5th Ave Ste 938 New York (10110) *(G-9284)*
Chinese Medical Report Inc...............................718 359-5676
3907 Prince St Ste 5b Flushing (11354) *(G-4990)*
Chip It All Ltd...631 473-2040
366 Sheep Pasture Rd Port Jefferson (11777) *(G-13220)*
Chipita America Inc...845 292-2540
1243 Old Route 17 Ferndale (12734) *(G-4931)*
Chiplogic Inc..631 617-6317
14a Old Dock Rd Yaphank (11980) *(G-16706)*
Chiptek, Arcade Also called Gowanda - Bti LLC *(G-384)*
Chivvis Enterprises Inc......................................631 842-9055
10 Grant St Copiague (11726) *(G-3755)*
Chloe International Inc.......................................212 730-6661
525 Fashion Ave Rm 1601 New York (10018) *(G-9285)*
Chlor Alkali Products & Vinyls, Niagara Falls Also called Olin Chlor Alkali Logistics *(G-12320)*
Chobani LLC (HQ)..607 337-1246
147 State Highway 320 Norwich (13815) *(G-12481)*
Chobani LLC...607 847-6181
669 County Road 25 New Berlin (13411) *(G-8487)*
Chobani Idaho LLC..208 432-2248
147 State Highway 320 Norwich (13815) *(G-12482)*
Chocnyc LLC...917 804-4848
4996 Broadway New York (10034) *(G-9286)*
Choco-Logo, Buffalo Also called Dilese International Inc *(G-2801)*
Chocolat Moderne LLC......................................212 229-4797
27 W 20th St Ste 904 New York (10011) *(G-9287)*
Chocolate Delivery Systems, Buffalo Also called N Make Mold Inc *(G-2960)*
Chocolate Delivery Systems Inc (PA)...............716 877-3146
1800 Elmwood Ave Buffalo (14207) *(G-2765)*

Chocolate Lady LLC — 516 532-0551
14 Blue Heron Ln Port Jervis (12771) *(G-13225)*
Chocolate Pizza Company Inc — 315 673-4098
3774 Lee Mulroy Rd Marcellus (13108) *(G-7793)*
Chocolatier Magazine, New York Also called Haymarket Group Ltd *(G-10051)*
Chocolations LLC — 914 777-3600
607 E Boston Post Rd Mamaroneck (10543) *(G-7738)*
Chocomize Inc — 631 506-6085
3010 41st Ave Long Island City (11101) *(G-7408)*
Chocovision Corporation — 845 473-4970
331 Main St Poughkeepsie (12601) *(G-13332)*
Chohehco LLC — 315 420-4624
78 State St Skaneateles (13152) *(G-14868)*
Choice Magazine Listening Inc — 516 883-8280
85 Channel Dr Ste 3 Port Washington (11050) *(G-13249)*
Chomerics Div, Fairport Also called Parker-Hannifin Corporation *(G-4647)*
Chopt Creative Salad Co LLC (PA) — 646 233-2923
853 Broadway Ste 606 New York (10003) *(G-9288)*
Christi Plastics Inc — 585 436-8510
215 Tremont St Rochester (14608) *(G-13710)*
Christian Bus Endeavors Inc (PA) — 315 788-8560
210 Court St Ste 10 Watertown (13601) *(G-16007)*
Christian Casey LLC (PA) — 212 500-2200
1440 Broadway Frnt 3 New York (10018) *(G-9289)*
Christian Casey LLC — 212 500-2200
1440 Broadway Frnt 3 New York (10018) *(G-9290)*
Christian Dior Perfumes LLC (HQ) — 212 931-2200
19 E 57th St New York (10022) *(G-9291)*
Christian Fabrication LLC — 315 822-0135
122 South St West Winfield (13491) *(G-16305)*
Christian Press Inc — 718 886-4400
14317 Franklin Ave Flushing (11355) *(G-4991)*
Christian Siriano Holdings LLC — 212 695-5494
5 W 54th St New York (10019) *(G-9292)*
Christiana Millwork Inc (PA) — 315 492-9099
4755 Jamesville Rd Jamesville (13078) *(G-6765)*
Christina Sales Inc — 212 391-0710
1441 Broadway New York (10018) *(G-9293)*
Christiny, Wantagh Also called Christopher Anthony Pubg Co *(G-15920)*
Christo Vac, Cornwall Also called Costume Armour Inc *(G-3832)*
Christophe Danhier, New York Also called Danhier Co LLC *(G-9465)*
Christopher Anthony Pubg Co — 516 826-9205
2225 Wantagh Ave Wantagh (11793) *(G-15920)*
Christopher Designs Inc — 212 382-1013
50 W 47th St Ste 1507 New York (10036) *(G-9294)*
Christos Inc — 212 921-0025
318 W 39th St Fl 12 New York (10018) *(G-9295)*
Chroma Communications Inc — 631 289-8871
2030 Route 112 Medford (11763) *(G-7943)*
Chroma Logic — 716 736-2458
6651 Wiley Rd Ripley (14775) *(G-13562)*
Chromagraphics Press Inc — 631 367-6160
3 Martha Dr Melville (11747) *(G-8007)*
Chromalloy American LLC (HQ) — 845 230-7355
330 Blaisdell Rd Orangeburg (10962) *(G-12672)*
Chromalloy Gas Turbine LLC — 845 359-2462
330 Blaisdell Rd Orangeburg (10962) *(G-12673)*
Chromalloy Gas Turbine LLC — 845 692-8912
105 Tower Dr Middletown (10941) *(G-8141)*
Chromalloy Middletown, Middletown Also called Chromalloy Gas Turbine LLC *(G-8141)*
Chromalloy New York, Orangeburg Also called Chromalloy Gas Turbine LLC *(G-12673)*
Chromosense LLC — 646 541-2302
476 N Ridge St Rye Brook (10573) *(G-14490)*
Chronicle Express — 315 536-4422
138 Main St Penn Yan (14527) *(G-12951)*
Chronicle, The, Glens Falls Also called Oak Lone Publishing Co *(G-5437)*
Chudnow Manufacturing Co Inc — 516 593-4222
3055 New St Oceanside (11572) *(G-12533)*
Chula Girls, New York Also called Detour Apparel Inc *(G-9512)*
Church & Dwight Co Inc — 518 887-5109
706 Ennis Rd Schenectady (12306) *(G-14662)*
Church Bulletin Inc — 631 249-4994
200 Dale St West Babylon (11704) *(G-16148)*
Church Communities NY Inc — 518 589-5103
2255 Platte Clove Rd Elka Park (12427) *(G-4433)*
Church Communities NY Inc — 518 589-5103
Platte Clove Rd Elka Park (12427) *(G-4434)*
Church Publishing Incorporated (HQ) — 212 592-1800
445 5th Ave Frnt 1 New York (10016) *(G-9296)*
Chutes and Compactors of NY — 718 494-2247
1011 Westwood Ave Staten Island (10314) *(G-15062)*
CHv Printed Company — 516 997-1101
1905 Hempstead Tpke B East Meadow (11554) *(G-4247)*
Chyronhego Corporation (HQ) — 631 845-2000
5 Hub Dr Melville (11747) *(G-8008)*
CIC International Ltd — 212 213-0089
1118 42nd St Brooklyn (11219) *(G-1692)*
Ciccarelli Custom Taylor, Long Island City Also called Primo Coat Corp *(G-7560)*
Cid Technologies, Liverpool Also called Thermo Cidtec Inc *(G-7267)*
CIDC Corp — 718 342-5820
5605 Cooper Ave Glendale (11385) *(G-5395)*

Cidega American Trim, Durham Also called Advanced Yarn Technologies Inc *(G-4182)*
Cigar Box Studios Inc — 845 236-9283
24 Riverview Dr Marlboro (12542) *(G-7812)*
Cigar Oasis LLC — 516 520-5258
79 Heisser Ct Farmingdale (11735) *(G-4735)*
Cilyox Inc — 716 853-3809
345 Broadway St Buffalo (14204) *(G-2766)*
Ciment St-Laurent Inc — 518 943-4040
6446 Route 9w Catskill (12414) *(G-3302)*
Cinch Technologies Inc — 212 266-0022
7 World Trade Ctr New York (10007) *(G-9297)*
Cinderella Press Ltd — 212 431-3130
327 Canal St 3 New York (10013) *(G-9298)*
Cine Design Group LLC — 646 747-0734
15 Park Row Lbby L New York (10038) *(G-9299)*
Cine Magnetics Inc — 914 667-6707
524 S Columbus Ave Mount Vernon (10550) *(G-8387)*
Cinedeck, New York Also called Cine Design Group LLC *(G-9299)*
Cinedigm Software — 212 206-9001
45 W 36th St Fl 7 New York (10018) *(G-9300)*
Ciner Manufacturing Co Inc — 212 947-3770
20 W 37th St Fl 10 New York (10018) *(G-9301)*
Cintube Ltd — 518 324-3333
139 Distribution Way Plattsburgh (12901) *(G-13117)*
Cioccolato 7 LLC — 347 240-7115
336 Malcolm X Blvd G Brooklyn (11233) *(G-1693)*
Circle 5 Deli Corp — 718 525-5687
13440 Guy R Brewer Blvd Jamaica (11434) *(G-6634)*
Circle Peak Capital MGT LLC (PA) — 646 230-8812
1325 Ave Of The Americas New York (10019) *(G-9302)*
Circle Press Inc (PA) — 212 924-4277
121 Varick St Fl 4 New York (10013) *(G-9303)*
Circo File Corp — 516 922-1848
69 Hamilton Ave Ste 1 Oyster Bay (11771) *(G-12811)*
Circor Aerospace Inc — 631 737-1900
425 Rabro Dr Ste 1 Hauppauge (11788) *(G-5789)*
Circuits & Systems Inc — 516 593-4301
59 2nd St East Rockaway (11518) *(G-4293)*
Cirrus Healthcare Products LLC (PA) — 631 692-7600
60 Main St Cold Spring Harbor (11724) *(G-3629)*
Cisco Systems Inc — 212 714-4000
1 Penn Plz Ste 3306 New York (10119) *(G-9304)*
CIT Aerospace LLC — 212 461-5200
11 W 42nd St New York (10036) *(G-9305)*
Citadel Electrical Sup Co Inc — 646 705-0333
21 Rockland Park Ave Tappan (10983) *(G-15467)*
Citation Healthcare Labels LLC (HQ) — 631 293-4646
55 Engineers Rd Hauppauge (11788) *(G-5790)*
Citic Intl (usa) Travel Inc — 718 888-9577
13633 37th Ave Ste 2a Flushing (11354) *(G-4992)*
Citigroup Inc — 212 816-6000
388 Greenwich St New York (10013) *(G-9306)*
Citisource Industries Inc — 212 683-1033
244 5th Ave Ste 229 New York (10001) *(G-9307)*
Citixsys Technologies Inc — 212 745-1365
1 Rockefeller Plz Fl 11 New York (10020) *(G-9308)*
Citizen , The, Auburn Also called Auburn Publishing Co *(G-465)*
Citizen Publishing Corp — 845 627-1414
119 Main St Ste 2 Nanuet (10954) *(G-8461)*
Citros Building Materials Co — 718 779-0727
10514 Astoria Blvd East Elmhurst (11369) *(G-4219)*
Citrus and Allied Essences, Floral Park Also called C & A Service Inc *(G-4958)*
Citrus and Allied Essences Ltd (PA) — 516 354-1200
65 S Tyson Ave Floral Park (11001) *(G-4960)*
City and State Ny LLC — 212 268-0442
61 Broadway Rm 1315 New York (10006) *(G-9309)*
City Bakery Inc (PA) — 212 366-1414
3 W 18th St Frnt 1 New York (10011) *(G-9310)*
City Casting Corp — 212 938-0511
151 W 46th St Fl 5 New York (10036) *(G-9311)*
City Cooling Enterprises Inc — 718 331-7400
1624 61st St Brooklyn (11204) *(G-1694)*
City Evolutionary — 718 861-7585
336 Barretto St Bronx (10474) *(G-1240)*
City Fashion, The, Brooklyn Also called Amj DOT LLC *(G-1530)*
City Gear Inc — 914 450-4746
213 Taxter Rd Irvington (10533) *(G-6503)*
City Hats, New York Also called Beila Group Inc *(G-9038)*
City Jeans Inc — 718 239-5353
845 White Plins Rd Frnt 1 Bronx (10473) *(G-1241)*
City Mason Corp — 718 658-3796
10417 148th St Jamaica (11435) *(G-6635)*
City Newspaper — 585 244-3329
250 N Goodman St Ste 1 Rochester (14607) *(G-13711)*
City of Jamestown — 716 483-7545
200 E 3rd St Ste 4 Jamestown (14701) *(G-6705)*
City of Kingston — 845 331-2490
91 E Strand St Kingston (12401) *(G-6895)*
City of New York — 718 965-8787
4014 1st Ave Fl 3 Brooklyn (11232) *(G-1695)*
City of New York — 718 236-2693
5602 19th Ave Brooklyn (11204) *(G-1696)*

City of Olean ... 716 376-5694
174 S 19th St Olean (14760) *(G-12595)*
City of Oneonta ... 607 433-3470
110 East St Oneonta (13820) *(G-12630)*
City Pattern Shop Inc ... 315 463-5239
4052 New Court Ave Syracuse (13206) *(G-15278)*
City Post Express Inc ... 718 995-8690
17518 147th Ave Jamaica (11434) *(G-6636)*
City Real Estate Book Inc ... 516 593-2949
9831 S Franklin Ave Valley Stream (11580) *(G-15776)*
City Signs Inc ... 718 375-5933
1940 Mcdonald Ave Brooklyn (11223) *(G-1697)*
City Sites Sportswear Inc (PA) ... 718 375-2990
2421 Mcdonald Ave Brooklyn (11223) *(G-1698)*
City Sports Inc ... 212 730-2009
64 W 48th St Frnt B New York (10036) *(G-9312)*
City Sports Imaging Inc ... 212 481-3600
20 E 46th St Rm 200 New York (10017) *(G-9313)*
City Store Gates Mfg Corp ... 718 939-9700
1520 129th St College Point (11356) *(G-3642)*
Citypharma Inc ... 917 832-6035
7316 Roosevelt Ave Jackson Heights (11372) *(G-6619)*
Cityscape Ob/Gyn PLLC ... 212 683-3595
38 E 32nd St Fl 4 New York (10016) *(G-9314)*
Citywire Americas, New York *Also called Citywire LLC (G-9315)*
Citywire LLC ... 646 503-2216
1350 Ave Of The Am Frnt 4 New York (10019) *(G-9315)*
Cives Corporation ... 315 287-2200
8 Church St Gouverneur (13642) *(G-5488)*
Cives Corporation ... 315 543-2321
14331 Mill St Harrisville (13648) *(G-5740)*
Cives Steel Company Nthrn Div, Gouverneur *Also called Cives Corporation (G-5488)*
Civil Svc Rtred Employees Assn ... 718 937-0290
3427 Steinway St Ste 1 Long Island City (11101) *(G-7409)*
CJ Component Products LLC ... 631 567-3733
624 Tower Mews Oakdale (11769) *(G-12514)*
CJ Indstries A Div Smrset Inds, Gloversville *Also called Somerset Industries Inc (G-5466)*
CJ Jewelry Inc ... 212 719-2464
2 W 47th St Ste 1106 New York (10036) *(G-9316)*
CJ Motor Sports, Boonville *Also called C J Logging Equipment Inc (G-1117)*
Cjk Manufacturing LLC ... 585 663-6370
160 Commerce Dr Rochester (14623) *(G-13712)*
Cjn Machinery Corp ... 631 244-8030
917 Lincoln Ave Ste 13 Holbrook (11741) *(G-6176)*
CK Coatings ... 585 502-0425
57 North St Ste 150 Le Roy (14482) *(G-7114)*
Clad Industries LLC ... 585 413-4359
1704 Wayneport Rd Ste 1 Macedon (14502) *(G-7698)*
Clad Metal Specialties Inc ... 631 666-7750
1516 5th Industrial Ct Bay Shore (11706) *(G-671)*
Claddagh Electronics Ltd ... 718 784-0571
1032 47th Rd Long Island City (11101) *(G-7410)*
Clapper Hollow Designs Inc ... 518 234-9561
369 N Grand St Cobleskill (12043) *(G-3600)*
Clara Papa ... 315 733-2660
1323 Blandina St 1 Utica (13501) *(G-15682)*
Clarence Resins and Chemicals ... 716 406-9804
9585 Keller Rd Clarence Center (14032) *(G-3543)*
Clarion Publications Inc ... 585 243-3530
38 Main St Geneseo (14454) *(G-5313)*
Clark Botanicals Inc ... 914 826-4319
9 Paradise Rd Bronxville (10708) *(G-1424)*
Clark Concrete Co Inc (PA) ... 315 478-4101
434 E Brighton Ave Syracuse (13210) *(G-15279)*
Clark Laboratories Inc (HQ) ... 716 483-3851
2823 Girts Rd Jamestown (14701) *(G-6706)*
Clark Specialty Co Inc ... 607 776-3193
7185 State Route 54 Bath (14810) *(G-642)*
Clark Trucking Co Div, Syracuse *Also called Clark Concrete Co Inc (G-15279)*
Clarke Hess Communication RES ... 631 698-3350
3243 Route 112 Ste 1 Medford (11763) *(G-7944)*
Clarkson N Potter Inc ... 212 782-9000
1745 Broadway New York (10019) *(G-9317)*
Clarsons Corp ... 585 235-8775
215 Tremont St Ste 8 Rochester (14608) *(G-13713)*
Classic & Performance Spc ... 716 759-1800
80 Rotech Dr Lancaster (14086) *(G-7014)*
Classic Album ... 718 388-2818
343 Lorimer St Brooklyn (11206) *(G-1699)*
Classic Album LLC ... 718 388-2818
343 Lorimer St Brooklyn (11206) *(G-1700)*
Classic Auto Crafts Inc ... 518 966-8003
6501 State Route 32 Greenville (12083) *(G-5635)*
Classic Automation LLC (PA) ... 585 241-6010
800 Salt Rd Webster (14580) *(G-16079)*
Classic Awnings Inc ... 716 649-0390
1 Elmview Ave Hamburg (14075) *(G-5674)*
Classic Awnings and Tent Co, Hamburg *Also called Classic Awnings Inc (G-5674)*
Classic Brass Inc ... 716 763-1400
2051 Stoneman Cir Lakewood (14750) *(G-6991)*
Classic Business Solutions ... 212 563-9100
42 W 38th St Rm 1204 New York (10018) *(G-9318)*
Classic Cabinets ... 845 357-4331
375 Spook Rock Rd Suffern (10901) *(G-15187)*
Classic Collections Fine Art ... 914 591-4500
20 Haarlem Ave Ste 408 White Plains (10603) *(G-16437)*
Classic Color Graphics Inc (PA) ... 516 822-9090
268 N Broadway Unit 8 Hicksville (11801) *(G-6068)*
Classic Color Graphics Inc ... 516 822-9090
87 Broadway Hicksville (11801) *(G-6069)*
Classic Creations Inc ... 516 498-1991
1 Linden Pl Ste 409 Great Neck (11021) *(G-5545)*
Classic Designer Workshop Inc ... 212 730-8480
265 W 37th St Rm 703 New York (10018) *(G-9319)*
Classic Flavors Fragrances Inc ... 212 777-0004
878 W End Ave Apt 12b New York (10025) *(G-9320)*
Classic Hosiery Inc ... 845 342-6661
33 Mulberry St Ste 4 Middletown (10940) *(G-8142)*
Classic Labels Inc ... 631 467-2300
217 River Ave Patchogue (11772) *(G-12863)*
Classic Medallics Inc ... 718 392-5410
520 S Fulton Ave Mount Vernon (10550) *(G-8388)*
Classic Sofa Ltd ... 212 620-0485
130 E 63rd St Ph B New York (10065) *(G-9321)*
Classic Tool Design Inc ... 845 562-8700
31 Walnut St New Windsor (12553) *(G-8641)*
Classic Tube, Lancaster *Also called Classic & Performance Spc (G-7014)*
Classified Advertising, Troy *Also called Want-Ad Digest Inc (G-15634)*
Classique Perfumes Inc ... 718 657-8200
139 01 Archer Ave Jamaica (11435) *(G-6637)*
Classpass Inc (PA) ... 888 493-5953
275 7th Ave Fl 11 New York (10001) *(G-9322)*
Classroom Inc ... 212 545-8400
245 5th Ave Fl 20 New York (10016) *(G-9323)*
Clayton Dubilier & Rice Fun (PA) ... 212 407-5200
375 Park Ave Fl 18 New York (10152) *(G-9324)*
Clayville Ice Co Inc ... 315 839-5405
2514 Foundry Pl Clayville (13322) *(G-3556)*
Clean All of Syracuse LLC ... 315 472-9189
838 Erie Blvd W Syracuse (13204) *(G-15280)*
Clean Beauty Collective Inc ... 212 269-1387
45 W 45th St Fl 2 New York (10036) *(G-9325)*
Clean Gas Systems Inc ... 631 467-1600
368 Veterans Memorial Hwy 3a Commack (11725) *(G-3686)*
Clean Room Depot Inc ... 631 589-3033
1730 Church St Holbrook (11741) *(G-6177)*
Cleaning Tech Group LLC ... 716 665-2340
9 N Main St Jamestown (14701) *(G-6707)*
Cleanroom Systems Inc ... 315 452-7400
7000 Performance Dr North Syracuse (13212) *(G-12398)*
Cleanse TEC ... 718 346-9111
1000 Linwood St Brooklyn (11208) *(G-1701)*
Clear Cast Technologies Inc (PA) ... 914 945-0848
99 N Water St Ossining (10562) *(G-12770)*
Clear View Bag Company Inc ... 518 458-7153
5 Burdick Dr Albany (12205) *(G-59)*
Clearcove Systems Inc ... 585 734-3012
7910 Rae Blvd Victor (14564) *(G-15836)*
Clearlake Land Co Inc ... 315 848-2427
Hanks Rd Star Lake (13690) *(G-15035)*
Clearstep Technologies LLC ... 315 952-3628
213 Emann Dr Camillus (13031) *(G-3195)*
Clearview Glass & Mirror, Monroe *Also called G & M Clearview Inc (G-8270)*
Clearview Social Inc ... 801 414-7675
77 Goodell St Ste 430 Buffalo (14203) *(G-2767)*
Clearwater Paper Corporation ... 315 287-1200
4921 State Highway 58 Gouverneur (13642) *(G-5489)*
Clearwood Custom Carpentry and ... 315 432-8422
617 W Manlius St Ste 1 East Syracuse (13057) *(G-4331)*
Cleary Custom Cabinets Inc ... 516 939-2475
794 S Broadway Hicksville (11801) *(G-6070)*
Clemente Latham Concrete, Latham *Also called Callanan Industries Inc (G-7068)*
Clemente Latham Concrete Corp ... 518 374-2222
1245 Kings Rd Schenectady (12303) *(G-14663)*
Clemente Latham North Div, Schenectady *Also called Clemente Latham Concrete Corp (G-14663)*
Clements Burrville Sawmill ... 315 782-4549
18181 Van Allen Rd N Watertown (13601) *(G-16008)*
Clerio Vision Inc ... 617 216-7881
312 Susquehanna Rd Rochester (14618) *(G-13714)*
Cleveland Biolabs Inc (PA) ... 716 849-6810
73 High St Buffalo (14203) *(G-2768)*
Cleveland Polymer Tech LLC (PA) ... 518 326-9146
1691 Van Antwerp Rd Schenectady (12309) *(G-14664)*
Clever Devices Ltd (PA) ... 516 433-6100
300 Crossways Park Dr Woodbury (11797) *(G-16614)*
Clever Goats Media LLC ... 917 512-0340
40 Exchange Pl Ste 1602 New York (10005) *(G-9326)*
Click It Inc ... 631 686-2900
85 Corporate Dr Hauppauge (11788) *(G-5791)*
Clifford H Jones Inc ... 716 693-2444
608 Young St Tonawanda (14150) *(G-15534)*
Cliffstar LLC (HQ) ... 716 366-6100
1 Cliffstar Dr Dunkirk (14048) *(G-4165)*

ALPHABETIC

Climatronics Corp (HQ) 541 471-7111
606 Johnson Ave Ste 28 Bohemia (11716) ***(G-994)***
Climax Packaging Inc 315 376-8000
7840 State Route 26 Lowville (13367) ***(G-7649)***
Climax Paperboard, Carthage *Also called Carthage Specialty Pprbd Inc* ***(G-3287)***
Clinique Laboratories LLC (HQ) 212 572-4200
767 5th Ave Fl 41 New York (10153) ***(G-9327)***
Clinique Laboratories, Inc., New York *Also called Clinique Laboratories LLC* ***(G-9327)***
Clinique Services Inc (HQ) 212 572-4200
767 5th Ave Fl Conc6 New York (10153) ***(G-9328)***
Clinton Signs Inc 585 482-1620
1407 Empire Blvd Webster (14580) ***(G-16080)***
Clinton Vineyards Inc 845 266-5372
450 Schultzville Rd Clinton Corners (12514) ***(G-3590)***
Clintons Ditch Coop Co Inc 315 699-2695
8478 Pardee Rd Cicero (13039) ***(G-3515)***
Clintrak Clinical Labeling S (PA) 888 479-3900
2800 Veterans Hwy Bohemia (11716) ***(G-995)***
Clo-Shure Intl Inc (PA) 212 268-5029
224 W 35th St Ste 1000 New York (10001) ***(G-9329)***
Clopay Ames True Temper (HQ) 212 957-5096
712 5th Ave New York (10019) ***(G-9330)***
Closet Systems Group, The, Brooklyn *Also called Designs By Robert Scott Inc* ***(G-1770)***
Cloud Printing 212 775-0888
66 W Broadway Frnt E New York (10007) ***(G-9331)***
Cloud Rock Group LLC 516 967-6023
525 Bryant Ave Roslyn (11576) ***(G-14444)***
Cloud Toronto Inc 408 569-4542
1967 Wehrle Dr Ste 1 Williamsville (14221) ***(G-16576)***
Cloudparc Inc 954 665-5962
122 W 27th St Fl 10 New York (10001) ***(G-9332)***
Cloudscale365 Inc (PA) 888 608-6245
30 Jericho Executive Plz Jericho (11753) ***(G-6782)***
Cloudsense Inc 917 880-6195
1325 Avenue Of The Flr 28 New York (10019) ***(G-9333)***
Clover Wire Forming Co Inc 914 375-0400
1021 Saw Mill River Rd Yonkers (10710) ***(G-16745)***
Clovis Point, Queens Village *Also called East End Vineyards LLC* ***(G-13405)***
Clp Holdings LLC (PA) 917 846-5094
575 Madison Ave Ste 1006 New York (10022) ***(G-9334)***
Clp Pb LLC (PA) 212 340-8100
1290 Ave Of The Amrcas New York (10104) ***(G-9335)***
Clpa Embroidery 516 409-0002
2635 Pettit Ave Bellmore (11710) ***(G-787)***
Clyde Duneier Inc (PA) 212 398-1122
415 Madison Ave Fl 6 New York (10017) ***(G-9336)***
Cmb Wireless Group LLC (PA) 631 750-4700
116 Wilbur Pl Bohemia (11716) ***(G-996)***
Cmc-Kuhnke Inc 518 694-3310
90 State St Ste 601 Albany (12207) ***(G-60)***
CMI Microclimates, Hammondsport *Also called Custom Manufacturing Inc* ***(G-5703)***
Cmnty Corporation 646 712-9949
228 E 45th St Ste 9e New York (10017) ***(G-9337)***
Cmp Adaptive Equipment Supply, Syosset *Also called Crosley Medical Products Inc* ***(G-15213)***
Cmp Advnced Mech Sltons NY LLC 607 352-1712
90 Bevier St Binghamton (13904) ***(G-875)***
Cmp Export Co Inc 518 434-3147
413 N Pearl St Albany (12207) ***(G-61)***
Cmp Industries LLC (PA) 518 434-3147
413 N Pearl St Albany (12207) ***(G-62)***
Cmp Industries LLC 518 434-3147
413 N Pearl St Albany (12207) ***(G-63)***
Cmp Media, New York *Also called Ubm LLC* ***(G-11930)***
Cmp New York, Binghamton *Also called Cmp Advnced Mech Sltons NY LLC* ***(G-875)***
CMS Heat Transfer Division Inc 631 968-0084
273 Knickerbocker Ave Bohemia (11716) ***(G-997)***
CMX Media LLC 917 793-5831
1271 Av Of The Americas New York (10020) ***(G-9338)***
CN Group Incorporated 914 358-5690
76 Mamaroneck Ave White Plains (10601) ***(G-16438)***
Cnc Manufacturing Corp 718 728-6800
3214 49th St Long Island City (11103) ***(G-7411)***
Cnc Systems 2000 Inc 585 265-0160
6368 Dean Pkwy Ontario (14519) ***(G-12649)***
Cnhi LLC 585 798-1400
541-543 Main St Medina (14103) ***(G-7975)***
Cnhi LLC 716 693-1000
473 3rd St Ste 201 Niagara Falls (14301) ***(G-12272)***
Cnhi LLC 716 282-2311
473 3rd St Ste 201 Niagara Falls (14301) ***(G-12273)***
Cnhi LLC 716 439-9222
135 Main St Ste 1 Lockport (14094) ***(G-7291)***
Cni Meat & Produce Inc 516 599-5929
500 W Merrick Rd Valley Stream (11580) ***(G-15777)***
Cntry Cross Communications LLC 386 758-9696
106 W 3rd St Ste 106 # 106 Jamestown (14701) ***(G-6708)***
Cnv Architectural Coatings Inc 718 418-9584
538 Johnson Ave Brooklyn (11237) ***(G-1702)***
CNY Business Review Inc 315 472-3104
269 W Jefferson St Syracuse (13202) ***(G-15281)***
CNy Business Solutions 315 733-5031
502 Court St Ste 206 Utica (13502) ***(G-15683)***
Cnyshirts 315 432-1789
6392 Deere Rd Ste 1 Syracuse (13206) ***(G-15282)***
Co-Op City News, New Rochelle *Also called Hagedorn Communications Inc* ***(G-8609)***
Co-Optics America Lab Inc 607 432-0557
297 River Street Svc Rd Service Oneonta (13820) ***(G-12631)***
Co-Optics Groups, The, Oneonta *Also called Co-Optics America Lab Inc* ***(G-12631)***
Coach Inc 718 760-0624
90 Queens Blvd Elmhurst (11373) ***(G-4463)***
Coach Leatherware Intl 212 594-1850
516 W 34th St Bsmt 5 New York (10001) ***(G-9339)***
Coach Services Inc 212 594-1850
10 Hudson Yards New York (10001) ***(G-9340)***
Coalition On Positive Health 212 633-2500
1751 Park Ave Fl 4 New York (10035) ***(G-9341)***
Coast To Coast Circuits Inc 585 254-2980
205 Lagrange Ave Rochester (14613) ***(G-13715)***
Coastal Pipeline Products Corp 631 369-4000
55 Twomey Ave Calverton (11933) ***(G-3163)***
Coastal Publications Inc 631 725-1700
22 Division St Sag Harbor (11963) ***(G-14498)***
Coastel Cable Tools Inc 315 471-5361
344 E Brighton Ave Syracuse (13210) ***(G-15283)***
Coastel Cable Tools Intl, Syracuse *Also called Coastel Cable Tools Inc* ***(G-15283)***
Coated Abrasive Division, Watervliet *Also called Saint-Gobain Abrasives Inc* ***(G-16049)***
Coating Technology Inc 585 546-7170
800 Saint Paul St Rochester (14605) ***(G-13716)***
Cobbe Industries Inc 716 287-2661
1397 Harris Hollow Rd Gerry (14740) ***(G-5340)***
Cobblestone Frm Winery Vinyrd 315 549-1004
5102 State Route 89 Romulus (14541) ***(G-14280)***
Cobey Inc (PA) 716 362-9550
1 Ship Canal Pkwy Buffalo (14218) ***(G-2769)***
Cobham, Plainview *Also called Aeroflex Plainview Inc* ***(G-13033)***
Cobham Holdings (us) Inc 716 662-0006
10 Cobham Dr Orchard Park (14127) ***(G-12707)***
Cobham Holdings Inc (HQ) 716 662-0006
10 Cobham Dr Orchard Park (14127) ***(G-12708)***
Cobham Management Services Inc 716 662-0006
10 Centre Dr Orchard Park (14127) ***(G-12709)***
Cobham Mission Systems Div, Orchard Park *Also called Cobham Management Services Inc* ***(G-12709)***
Cobham Semiconductor Solutions, Plainview *Also called Aeroflex Incorporated* ***(G-13032)***
Cobico Productions Inc 347 417-5883
344 E 50th St Apt 1b New York (10022) ***(G-9342)***
Cobleskill Concrete Ready Mix, Amsterdam *Also called Cobleskill Red E Mix & Supply* ***(G-332)***
Cobleskill Red E Mix & Supply 518 234-2015
774 State Highway 5s Amsterdam (12010) ***(G-332)***
Cobleskill Stone Products Inc 518 299-3066
395 Falke Rd Prattsville (12468) ***(G-13378)***
Cobleskill Stone Products Inc 518 295-7121
163 Eastern Ave Schoharie (12157) ***(G-14731)***
Cobleskill Stone Products Inc (PA) 518 234-0221
112 Rock Rd Cobleskill (12043) ***(G-3601)***
Cobleskill Stone Products Inc 607 432-8321
57 Ceperley Ave Oneonta (13820) ***(G-12632)***
Cobleskill Stone Products Inc 607 637-4271
1565 Green Flats Rd Hancock (13783) ***(G-5710)***
Cobra Manufacturing Corp 845 514-2505
68 Leggs Mills Rd Lake Katrine (12449) ***(G-6972)***
Cobra Operating Industries LLC 607 639-1700
37 Main St Afton (13730) ***(G-8)***
Cobra Systems Inc 845 338-6675
2669 New York 32 Bloomington (12411) ***(G-959)***
Coca-Cola, Horseheads *Also called Rochester Coca Cola Bottling* ***(G-6327)***
Coca-Cola, Rochester *Also called Rochester Coca Cola Bottling* ***(G-14083)***
Coca-Cola Bottling Company 518 483-0422
15 Ida Pkwy Malone (12953) ***(G-7720)***
Coca-Cola Btlg Co Buffalo Inc 716 874-4610
200 Milens Rd Tonawanda (14150) ***(G-15535)***
Coca-Cola Btlg Co of NY Inc 845 562-3037
10 Heampstead Rd New Windsor (12553) ***(G-8642)***
Coca-Cola Btlg Co of NY Inc 518 459-2010
38 Warehouse Row Albany (12205) ***(G-64)***
Coca-Cola Btlg Co of NY Inc 718 416-7575
5840 Borden Ave Maspeth (11378) ***(G-7830)***
Coca-Cola Btlg Co of NY Inc 315 457-9221
298 Farrell Rd Syracuse (13209) ***(G-15284)***
Coca-Cola Btlg Co of NY Inc 631 434-3535
375 Wireless Blvd Hauppauge (11788) ***(G-5792)***
Coca-Cola Btlg Co of NY Inc 718 420-6800
400 Western Ave Staten Island (10303) ***(G-15063)***
Coca-Cola Btlg Co of NY Inc 914 789-1580
115 Fairview Pk Dr Ste 1 Elmsford (10523) ***(G-4536)***
Coca-Cola Refreshments USA Inc 718 401-5200
977 E 149th St Bronx (10455) ***(G-1242)***
Coca-Cola Refreshments USA Inc 315 785-8907
22614 County Route 51 Watertown (13601) ***(G-16009)***

Coca-Cola Refreshments USA Inc....914 592-0806
3 Skyline Dr Hawthorne (10532) *(G-5985)*
Coccadotts Inc....518 438-4937
1179 Central Ave Albany (12205) *(G-65)*
Cochecton Mills Inc (PA)....845 932-8282
30 Depot Rd Cochecton (12726) *(G-3605)*
Cockpit Usa Inc....212 575-1616
15 W 39th St Fl 12 New York (10018) *(G-9343)*
Cockpit Usa Inc....908 558-9704
15 W 39th St Fl 12 New York (10018) *(G-9344)*
Coco Architectureal Grilles....631 482-9449
173 Allen Blvd Farmingdale (11735) *(G-4736)*
Coco Rico Southeast, Bronx *Also called Good-O-Beverage Inc (G-1284)*
Coda Media Inc....917 478-2565
108 W 39th St Rm 1000 New York (10018) *(G-9345)*
Coda Resources Ltd (PA)....718 649-1666
960 Alabama Ave Brooklyn (11207) *(G-1703)*
Coda Story, New York *Also called Coda Media Inc (G-9345)*
Codesters Inc....646 232-1025
900 Broadway Ste 903 New York (10003) *(G-9346)*
Codinos Limited Inc....518 372-3308
704 Corporation Park # 5 Schenectady (12302) *(G-14665)*
Cody Printing Corp....718 651-8854
3728 56th St Woodside (11377) *(G-16651)*
Coe Displays Inc....718 937-5658
4301 22nd St Ste 603 Long Island City (11101) *(G-7412)*
Coecles Hbr Marina & Boat Yard....631 749-0856
68 Cartwright Rd Shelter Island (11964) *(G-14800)*
Coffee Holding Co Inc (PA)....718 832-0800
3475 Victory Blvd Ste 4 Staten Island (10314) *(G-15064)*
Coffee Holding Company Inc....718 832-0800
4425 1st Ave Brooklyn (11232) *(G-1704)*
Coffing, Getzville *Also called Columbus McKinnon Corporation (G-5345)*
Cofire Paving Corporation....718 463-1403
12030 28th Ave Flushing (11354) *(G-4993)*
Cognigen Acquisition, Buffalo *Also called Cognigen Corporation (G-2770)*
Cognigen Corporation....716 633-3463
1780 Wehrle Dr Ste 110 Buffalo (14221) *(G-2770)*
Cognitiveflow Sensor Tech....631 513-9369
9 Melville Ct Stony Brook (11790) *(G-15164)*
Cognotion Inc....347 692-0640
1407 Broadway Fl 24 New York (10018) *(G-9347)*
Cohber Press Inc (PA)....585 475-9100
1000 John St West Henrietta (14586) *(G-16234)*
Cohens Bakery Inc....716 892-8149
1132 Broadway St Buffalo (14212) *(G-2771)*
Coil Craft Inc (PA)....718 369-1210
10324 99th St Ozone Park (11417) *(G-12823)*
Coil Stamping Inc....631 588-3040
1340 Lincoln Ave Ste 1 Holbrook (11741) *(G-6178)*
Coinmach Service Corp....516 349-8555
303 Sunnyside Blvd # 70 Plainview (11803) *(G-13042)*
Colad Group LLC....716 961-1776
693 Seneca St Fl 5 Buffalo (14210) *(G-2772)*
Colarusso Blacktop Co, Hudson *Also called A Colarusso and Son Inc (G-6336)*
Colburns AC Rfrgn....716 569-3695
17 White Dr Frewsburg (14738) *(G-5207)*
Cold Mix Manufacturing Corp....718 463-1444
65 Edison Ave Mount Vernon (10550) *(G-8389)*
Cold Springs R & D Inc....315 413-1237
1207 Van Vleck Rd Ste A Syracuse (13209) *(G-15285)*
Colden Closet LLC....716 713-6125
1375 Boies Rd East Aurora (14052) *(G-4196)*
Coldstream Group Inc (PA)....914 698-5959
420 Railroad Way Mamaroneck (10543) *(G-7739)*
Colgat-Plmolive Centl Amer Inc (HQ)....212 310-2000
300 Park Ave New York (10022) *(G-9348)*
Colgate-Palmolive Company (PA)....212 310-2000
300 Park Ave Fl 3 New York (10022) *(G-9349)*
Colgate-Palmolive Company....718 506-3961
21818 100th Ave Queens Village (11429) *(G-13404)*
Colgate-Palmolive Nj Inc....212 310-2000
300 Park Ave Fl 8 New York (10022) *(G-9350)*
Coliseum, New York *Also called Plugg LLC (G-11212)*
Collection Xiix Ltd (PA)....212 686-8990
1370 Broadway Fl 17 New York (10018) *(G-9351)*
College Calendar Company....315 768-8242
148 Clinton St Whitesboro (13492) *(G-16526)*
Collegebound Teen Magazine, Staten Island *Also called Ramholtz Publishing Inc (G-15124)*
Collegeville Imagineering, Bay Shore *Also called Rubies Costume Company Inc (G-719)*
Collinite Corporation....315 732-2282
1520 Lincoln Ave Utica (13502) *(G-15684)*
Collinite Wax, Utica *Also called Collinite Corporation (G-15684)*
Collins Pet & Garden Center, Malone *Also called Scotts Feed Inc (G-7725)*
Colonial Electric, Farmingdale *Also called Colonial Precision Machinery (G-4737)*
Colonial Group LLC....516 349-8010
150 Express St Ste 2 Plainview (11803) *(G-13043)*
Colonial Label, Patchogue *Also called Depot Label Company Inc (G-12864)*
Colonial Label Systems Inc....631 254-0111
50 Corbin Ave Ste L Bay Shore (11706) *(G-672)*
Colonial Precision Machinery....631 249-0738
134 Rome St Farmingdale (11735) *(G-4737)*
Colonial Rapid, Bay Shore *Also called Colonial Label Systems Inc (G-672)*
Colonial Redi Record Corp....718 972-7433
1225 36th St Brooklyn (11218) *(G-1705)*
Colonial Tag & Label Co Inc....516 482-0508
425 Northern Blvd Ste 36 Great Neck (11021) *(G-5546)*
Colonial Tanning Corporation (PA)....518 725-7171
8 Wilson St 810 Gloversville (12078) *(G-5454)*
Colonial Wire & Cable Co Inc (PA)....631 234-8500
40 Engineers Rd Hauppauge (11788) *(G-5793)*
Colonial Wire Cable Co NJ Inc (PA)....631 234-8500
40 Engineers Rd Hauppauge (11788) *(G-5794)*
Colonie Block and Supply Co....518 869-8411
124 Lincoln Ave Colonie (12205) *(G-3677)*
Colonie Plastics Corp....631 434-6969
188 Candlewood Rd Bay Shore (11706) *(G-673)*
Colony Holdings Intl LLC....212 868-2800
131 W 35th St Fl 6 New York (10001) *(G-9352)*
Color Card LLC....631 232-1300
1065 Islip Ave Central Islip (11722) *(G-3363)*
Color Carton Corp....718 665-0840
341 Canal Pl Bronx (10451) *(G-1243)*
Color Craft Finishing Corp....631 563-3230
30 Floyds Run Ste A Bohemia (11716) *(G-998)*
Color Fx, New York *Also called Joseph Industries Inc (G-10364)*
Color Industries LLC....718 392-8301
3002 48th Ave Ste H Long Island City (11101) *(G-7413)*
Color Pro Sign, Schenectady *Also called Ray Sign Inc (G-14707)*
Color Story, Yonkers *Also called Leser Enterprises Ltd (G-16778)*
Color Unlimited Inc....212 802-7547
244 5th Ave Frnt New York (10001) *(G-9353)*
Color-Aid Corporation....212 673-5500
38 La Fayette St Ste 2 Hudson Falls (12839) *(G-6376)*
Colorfast....212 929-2440
121 Varick St Fl 9 New York (10013) *(G-9354)*
Colorfully Yours Inc....631 242-8600
11 Grant Ave Bay Shore (11706) *(G-674)*
Colorpak, Melville *Also called Poly-Pak Industries Inc (G-8057)*
Colors In Optics Ltd....718 845-0300
120 Broadway G New Hyde Park (11040) *(G-8523)*
Colorspec Coatings Intl Inc....631 472-8251
1716 Church St Holbrook (11741) *(G-6179)*
Colortex Inc....212 564-2000
1202 Lexington Ave 115 New York (10028) *(G-9355)*
Columbia, Macedon *Also called Water Technologies Inc (G-7705)*
Columbia Button Nailhead Corp....718 386-3414
306 Stagg St 316 Brooklyn (11206) *(G-1706)*
Columbia Cabinets LLC (PA)....212 972-7550
20 Maple Ave Ste F Armonk (10504) *(G-402)*
Columbia Cabinets LLC....518 283-1700
489 Broadway Saratoga Springs (12866) *(G-14576)*
Columbia Daily Spectator....212 854-9550
2875 Broadway Ste 303 New York (10025) *(G-9356)*
Columbia Dentoform Corporation (PA)....718 482-1569
3110 37th Ave Ste 307 Long Island City (11101) *(G-7414)*
Columbia Pool Accessories Inc....718 993-0389
111 Bruckner Blvd Bronx (10454) *(G-1244)*
Columbia Records Inc....212 833-8000
25 Madison Ave Fl 19 New York (10010) *(G-9357)*
Columbia Seal N Sew, Brooklyn *Also called Dlx Industries Inc (G-1784)*
Columbia Univ Publications, New York *Also called Trust of Colum Unive In The Ci (G-11906)*
Columbia University Press (HQ)....212 459-0600
61 W 62nd St Fl 3 New York (10023) *(G-9358)*
Columbia University Press....212 459-0600
61 W 62nd St Fl 3 New York (10023) *(G-9359)*
Columbia University Press....212 459-0600
61 W 62nd St Fl 3 New York (10023) *(G-9360)*
Columbus Accessories, New York *Also called Columbus Trading Corp (G-9361)*
Columbus Baking Co, Syracuse *Also called George Retzos (G-15334)*
Columbus McKinnon, Getzville *Also called C M Insurance Company Inc (G-5343)*
Columbus McKinnon Corporation (PA)....716 689-5400
205 Crosspoint Pkwy Getzville (14068) *(G-5344)*
Columbus McKinnon Corporation....716 689-5400
205 Crosspoint Pkwy Getzville (14068) *(G-5345)*
Columbus McKinnon Corporation....716 689-5400
205 Crosspoint Pkwy Getzville (14068) *(G-5346)*
Columbus McKinnon Corporation....716 689-5400
205 Crosspoint Pkwy Getzville (14068) *(G-5347)*
Columbus McKnnon- Lift TEC Div, Getzville *Also called Columbus McKinnon Corporation (G-5347)*
Columbus Trading Corp....212 564-1780
120 W 31st St Rm 600 New York (10001) *(G-9361)*
Columbus Woodworking Inc....607 674-4546
164 Casey Cheese Fctry Rd Sherburne (13460) *(G-14804)*
Comairco Equipment Inc (HQ)....716 656-0211
3250 Union Rd Cheektowaga (14227) *(G-3437)*
Comander Terminals LLC....516 922-7600
1 Commander Sq Oyster Bay (11771) *(G-12812)*
Comax Aromatics Corporation....631 249-0505
130 Baylis Rd Melville (11747) *(G-8009)*

A L P H A B E T I C

(PA)=Parent Co (HQ)=Headquarters (DH)=Div Headquarters

Comax Flavors, Melville *Also called Comax Manufacturing Corp* ***(G-8010)***
Comax Manufacturing Corp (PA)...631 249-0505
130 Baylis Rd Melville (11747) ***(G-8010)***
Combe Incorporated (PA)...914 694-5454
1101 Westchester Ave White Plains (10604) ***(G-16439)***
Combine Graphics Corp...212 695-4044
10714 Queens Blvd Forest Hills (11375) ***(G-5073)***
Comboland Packing Corp...718 858-4200
2 Cumberland St Brooklyn (11205) ***(G-1707)***
Comco Plastics Inc...718 849-9000
11 Stepar Pl Huntington Station (11746) ***(G-6436)***
Comely International Trdg Inc...212 683-1240
303 5th Ave Rm 1903 New York (10016) ***(G-9362)***
Comerford Collection, Bridgehampton *Also called Comerford Hennessy At Home Inc* ***(G-1180)***
Comerford Hennessy At Home Inc...631 537-6200
2442 Main St Bridgehampton (11932) ***(G-1180)***
Comet Flasher Inc (PA)...716 821-9595
1 Babcock St Buffalo (14210) ***(G-2773)***
Comet Intl Trdg Co Inc...731 599-2430
993 Flatbush Ave Ste 4-A Brooklyn (11226) ***(G-1708)***
Comfort Care Textiles Inc (HQ)...631 543-0531
368 Veterans Memorial Hwy # 5 Commack (11725) ***(G-3687)***
Comfortex Corporation (HQ)...518 273-3333
21 Elm St Watervliet (12189) ***(G-16044)***
Comfortex Window Fashions, Watervliet *Also called Comfortex Corporation* ***(G-16044)***
Comgraph Sales Service...716 601-7243
7491 Clinton St Elma (14059) ***(G-4449)***
Comint Apparel Group LLC (PA)...212 947-7474
463 7th Ave Fl 4 New York (10018) ***(G-9363)***
Command Components Corporation...631 666-4411
6 Cherry St Bay Shore (11706) ***(G-675)***
Command Systems Division, Farmingdale *Also called Telephonics Corporation* ***(G-4893)***
Comme-Ci Comme-CA AP Group...631 300-1035
380 Rabo Dr Hauppauge (11788) ***(G-5795)***
Commentary Inc...212 891-1400
165 E 56th St Fl 16 New York (10022) ***(G-9364)***
Commentary Magazine, New York *Also called American Jewish Committee* ***(G-8831)***
Commerce Offset Ltd...914 769-6671
657 Commerce St Thornwood (10594) ***(G-15505)***
Commerce Spring Corp...631 293-4844
143 Allen Blvd Farmingdale (11735) ***(G-4738)***
Commercehub Inc (HQ)...518 810-0700
201 Fuller Rd Fl 6 Albany (12203) ***(G-66)***
Commercial Communications LLC...845 343-9078
14 Montgomery St Middletown (10940) ***(G-8143)***
Commercial Concrete, Westbury *Also called New York Ready Mix Inc* ***(G-16359)***
Commercial Display Design LLC...607 336-7353
120 Kemper Ln Norwich (13815) ***(G-12483)***
Commercial Fabrics Inc...716 694-0641
908 Niagara Falls Blvd North Tonawanda (14120) ***(G-12422)***
Commercial Gaskets New York...212 244-8130
247 W 38th St Rm 409 New York (10018) ***(G-9365)***
Commercial Press Inc...315 274-0028
6589 Us Highway 11 Canton (13617) ***(G-3255)***
Commercial Print & Imaging...716 597-0100
4778 Main St Buffalo (14226) ***(G-2774)***
Commitment 2000 Inc...716 439-1206
105 Msgr Valente Dr Buffalo (14206) ***(G-2775)***
Committee For Color & Trends, New York *Also called Cct Inc* ***(G-9233)***
Commodity Resource Corporation...585 538-9500
2773 Caledonia Leroy Rd Caledonia (14423) ***(G-3154)***
Commodore, Bloomfield *Also called Dolco LLC* ***(G-952)***
Commodore Chocolatier USA Inc...845 561-3960
482 Broadway Newburgh (12550) ***(G-12218)***
Commodore Machine Co Inc...585 657-6916
26 Maple Ave Bloomfield (14469) ***(G-950)***
Commodore Manufacutring Corp...718 788-2600
3913 2nd Ave Brooklyn (11232) ***(G-1709)***
Commodore Tool, Brooklyn *Also called Commodore Manufacutring Corp* ***(G-1709)***
Common Sense Marketing Inc...516 282-1214
100 Herricks Rd Mineola (11501) ***(G-8213)***
Common Sense Natural Soap, Cambridge *Also called Robert Racine* ***(G-3183)***
Common Sense Natural Soap...518 677-0224
7 Pearl St Cambridge (12816) ***(G-3179)***
Commonweal Foundation Inc...212 662-4200
475 Riverside Dr Rm 405 New York (10115) ***(G-9366)***
COMMONWEAL MAGAZINE, New York *Also called Commonweal Foundation Inc* ***(G-9366)***
Commonwealth Home Fashion Inc...514 384-8290
31 Station Rd Willsboro (12996) ***(G-16598)***
Commonwealth Toy Novelty Inc (PA)...212 242-4070
980 Ave Of The Amer # 301 New York (10018) ***(G-9367)***
Communication Power Corp...631 434-7306
80 Davids Dr Ste 3 Hauppauge (11788) ***(G-5796)***
Communications Systems Div, Farmingdale *Also called Telephonics Corporation* ***(G-4891)***
Community Cpons Frnchising Inc...516 277-1968
100 Carney St Ste 2 Glen Cove (11542) ***(G-5363)***
Community Directory, Brooklyn *Also called Business Directory Inc* ***(G-1660)***
Community Glass Inc...607 737-8860
139 W 17th St Elmira (14903) ***(G-4478)***
Community Magazine, Brooklyn *Also called Bnei Aram Soba Inc* ***(G-1625)***
Community Media Group Inc...315 789-3333
218 Genesee St Geneva (14456) ***(G-5321)***
Community Media Group LLC (PA)...518 439-4949
125 Adams St Delmar (12054) ***(G-4077)***
Community Media LLC...212 229-1890
515 Canal St Fl 1 New York (10013) ***(G-9368)***
Community News Group LLC (PA)...718 260-2500
1 Metrotech Ctr Fl 10 Brooklyn (11201) ***(G-1710)***
Community Newspaper Group LLC...607 432-1000
102 Chestnut St Oneonta (13820) ***(G-12633)***
Community Newspaper Group LLC...518 565-4114
170 Margaret St Plattsburgh (12901) ***(G-13118)***
Community Newspapers, Moravia *Also called Republican Registrar Inc* ***(G-8334)***
Community Playthings, Chester *Also called Community Products LLC* ***(G-3471)***
Community Playthings, Elka Park *Also called Church Communities NY Inc* ***(G-4433)***
Community Playthings, Elka Park *Also called Church Communities NY Inc* ***(G-4434)***
COMMUNITY PLAYTHINGS AND RIFTO, Rifton *Also called Community Products LLC* ***(G-13559)***
Community Products LLC (PA)...845 658-8799
101 Woodcrest Dr Rifton (12471) ***(G-13559)***
Community Products LLC...845 658-7720
359 Gibson Hill Rd Chester (10918) ***(G-3471)***
Community Products LLC...845 572-3433
24 Elizabeth Dr Chester (10918) ***(G-3472)***
Community Products LLC...845 658-8351
2032 Route 213 St Rifton (12471) ***(G-13560)***
Community Products LLC...518 589-5103
2255 Platte Clove Rd Elka Park (12427) ***(G-4435)***
Compac Development Corporation...631 881-4903
110 Plant Ave Ste 1 Hauppauge (11788) ***(G-5797)***
Compar Manufacturing Corp...212 304-2777
308 Dyckman St New York (10034) ***(G-9369)***
Compass Printing Plus (PA)...518 523-3308
42 Main St Saranac Lake (12983) ***(G-14561)***
Competicion Mower Repair...516 280-6584
75 Windsor Ave Mineola (11501) ***(G-8214)***
Complemar Print LLC...716 875-7238
3034 Genesee St Buffalo (14225) ***(G-2776)***
Complete Fiber Solutions Inc...718 828-8900
1459 Bassett Ave Bronx (10461) ***(G-1245)***
Complete Orthopedic Svcs Inc...516 357-9113
2094 Front St East Meadow (11554) ***(G-4248)***
Complete Publishing Solutions...212 242-7321
350 W 51st St Apt 13b New York (10019) ***(G-9370)***
Complete SEC & Contrls Inc...631 421-7200
100 Hillwood Dr Huntington Station (11746) ***(G-6437)***
Complex Biosystems Inc...315 464-8007
8417 Oswego Rd 201 Baldwinsville (13027) ***(G-553)***
Complex Magazine, New York *Also called CMX Media LLC* ***(G-9338)***
Complex Media Inc (PA)...917 793-5831
229 W 43rd St Fl 10 New York (10036) ***(G-9371)***
Complystream, New York *Also called Thinktrek Inc* ***(G-11816)***
Composite Forms Inc...914 937-1808
7 Merritt St Port Chester (10573) ***(G-13194)***
Composite Materials Division, New York *Also called Mitsubishi Chemical Amer Inc* ***(G-10825)***
Compositech Ltd...516 835-1458
4 Fairbanks Blvd Woodbury (11797) ***(G-16615)***
Compoz A Puzzle Inc...516 883-2311
2 Secatoag Ave Port Washington (11050) ***(G-13250)***
Comprehensive Dental Tech...607 467-4456
Rr 1 Box 69 Hancock (13783) ***(G-5711)***
Comps Inc...516 676-0400
3 School St Ste 101b Glen Cove (11542) ***(G-5364)***
Compucolor Associates Inc...516 358-0000
2200 Marcus Ave Ste C New Hyde Park (11042) ***(G-8524)***
Computer Conversions Corp...631 261-3300
6 Dunton Ct East Northport (11731) ***(G-4261)***
Computer Instruments Corp...516 876-8400
963a Brush Hollow Rd Westbury (11590) ***(G-16321)***
Computerized Metal Bending Ser...631 249-1177
91 Cabot St Unit A West Babylon (11704) ***(G-16149)***
Comsec Ventures International...518 523-1600
17 Tamarack Ave Lake Placid (12946) ***(G-6975)***
Comstock Food, Leicester *Also called Seneca Foods Corporation* ***(G-7129)***
Comstock Foods Division, South Dayton *Also called Birds Eye Foods Inc* ***(G-14927)***
Comtech PST Corp (HQ)...631 777-8900
105 Baylis Rd Melville (11747) ***(G-8011)***
Comtech Telecom Corp (PA)...631 962-7000
68 S Service Rd Ste 230 Melville (11747) ***(G-8012)***
Con Rel Auto Electric Inc...518 356-1646
3637 Carman Rd Schenectady (12303) ***(G-14666)***
Con-Tees Custom Printing Ltd...914 664-0251
514 Union Ave Mount Vernon (10550) ***(G-8390)***
Conax Technologies LLC (PA)...716 684-4500
2300 Walden Ave Buffalo (14225) ***(G-2777)***
Concept Components, Bohemia *Also called McGuigan Inc* ***(G-1057)***
Concept One Accessories, New York *Also called Uspa Accessories LLC* ***(G-11981)***
Concept Printing and Promotion, Nyack *Also called Concept Printing Inc* ***(G-12503)***
Concept Printing Inc...845 353-4040
40 Lydecker St Nyack (10960) ***(G-12503)***

Conceptronic, Central Islip *Also called Cvd Equipment Corporation* ***(G-3366)***
Concepts In Wood of CNY 315 463-8084
4021 New Court Ave Syracuse (13206) ***(G-15286)***
Concepts Nyc Inc 212 244-1033
20 W 33rd St Fl 9 New York (10001) ***(G-9372)***
Concinnity Division, Melville *Also called I W Industries Inc* ***(G-8036)***
Conco Division, Lynbrook *Also called Russell Industries Inc* ***(G-7673)***
Concord Express Cargo Inc 718 276-7200
17214 119th Ave Jamaica (11434) ***(G-6638)***
Concord Jewelry Mfg Co LLC 212 719-4030
64 W 48th St Ste 1004 New York (10036) ***(G-9373)***
Concord Jwlry Mfrs, New York *Also called Concord Jewelry Mfg Co LLC* ***(G-9373)***
Concord Settings, New York *Also called Kaprielian Enterprises Inc* ***(G-10406)***
Concorde Apparel Company LLC (PA) 212 307-7848
55 W 39th St Fl 11 New York (10018) ***(G-9374)***
Concrete Designs Inc 607 738-0309
2770 County Route 60 Elmira (14901) ***(G-4479)***
Concrete Mixer Supplycom Inc (PA) 716 375-5565
1721 Cornell Dr Olean (14760) ***(G-12596)***
Conde Nast Entertainment LLC 212 286-2860
1 World Trade Ctr New York (10007) ***(G-9375)***
Conde Nast Publications, New York *Also called Advance Magazine Publs Inc* ***(G-8747)***
Conde Nast Publications Div, New York *Also called Advance Magazine Publs Inc* ***(G-8748)***
Conde Pumps Div, Sherrill *Also called Westmoor Ltd* ***(G-14825)***
Condeco Software Inc 408 508-7330
1350 Broadway Rm 1712 New York (10018) ***(G-9376)***
Condor Electronics Corp 585 235-1500
295 Mount Read Blvd Rochester (14611) ***(G-13717)***
Cone Buddy System Inc 585 427-9940
3495 Winton Pl Ste E290 Rochester (14623) ***(G-13718)***
Conesus Lake Association Inc 585 346-6864
5828 Big Tree Rd Lakeville (14480) ***(G-6985)***
Confer Plastics Inc 800 635-3213
97 Witmer Rd North Tonawanda (14120) ***(G-12423)***
Conference Board Inc (PA) 212 759-0900
845 3rd Ave Fl 2 New York (10022) ***(G-9377)***
Confiant Inc 646 397-4198
833 Broadway Apt 2 New York (10003) ***(G-9378)***
Conformer Products Inc 516 504-6300
60 Cuttermill Rd Ste 411 Great Neck (11021) ***(G-5547)***
Confrtrnity of Prescious Blood 718 436-1120
5300 Fort Hamilton Pkwy Brooklyn (11219) ***(G-1711)***
Congress For Jewish Culture 212 505-8040
1133 Broadway Ste 1019 New York (10010) ***(G-9379)***
Conic Systems Inc 845 856-4053
11 Rebel Ln Port Jervis (12771) ***(G-13226)***
Conmed Andover Medical Inc (HQ) 315 797-8375
525 French Rd Ste 3 Utica (13502) ***(G-15685)***
Conmed Corporation 315 797-8375
525 French Rd Utica (13502) ***(G-15686)***
Conmed Corporation (PA) 315 797-8375
525 French Rd Utica (13502) ***(G-15687)***
Connection Mold Inc 585 458-6463
585 Ling Rd Rochester (14612) ***(G-13719)***
Connectiva Systems Inc (PA) 646 722-8741
19 W 44th St Ste 611 New York (10036) ***(G-9380)***
Connex Grinding & Machining 315 946-4340
65 Clyde Rd Lyons (14489) ***(G-7683)***
Connie Cleaners, Great Neck *Also called Connie French Cleaners Inc* ***(G-5548)***
Connie French Cleaners Inc 516 487-1343
801 Middle Neck Rd Great Neck (11024) ***(G-5548)***
Connie's T Shirt Shop, East Northport *Also called Island Silkscreen Inc* ***(G-4265)***
Connies Laundry 716 822-2800
1494 S Park Ave Buffalo (14220) ***(G-2778)***
Connover Packaging Inc 585 377-2510
119 Despatch Dr East Rochester (14445) ***(G-4282)***
Conopco Inc 585 647-8322
28 Mansfield St Rochester (14606) ***(G-13720)***
Conrad Blasius Equipment Co 516 753-1200
199 Newtown Rd Plainview (11803) ***(G-13044)***
Consoldted Precision Pdts Corp 315 687-0014
901 E Genesee St Chittenango (13037) ***(G-3502)***
Consolidated Barricades Inc 518 922-7944
179 Dillenbeck Rd Fultonville (12072) ***(G-5235)***
Consolidated Childrens AP Inc (HQ) 212 239-8615
100 W 33rd St Ste 1105 New York (10001) ***(G-9381)***
Consolidated Color Press Inc 212 929-8197
307 7th Ave Rm 607 New York (10001) ***(G-9382)***
Consolidated Container Co LLC 585 262-6470
18 Champeney Ter Rochester (14605) ***(G-13721)***
Consolidated Container Co LLC 585 343-9351
14 Hall St Batavia (14020) ***(G-620)***
Consolidated Edison Co NY Inc 914 933-2936
511 Theodore Fremd Ave Rye (10580) ***(G-14478)***
Consolidated Fashion Corp 212 719-3000
225 W 39th St Fl 12 New York (10018) ***(G-9383)***
Consolidated Loose Leaf Inc (PA) 212 924-5800
989 Avnue Of The Americas New York (10018) ***(G-9384)***
Consolidated Spring LLC 845 391-8855
11 Spring St Newburgh (12550) ***(G-12219)***
Constas Printing Corporation 315 474-2176
1120 Burnet Ave Syracuse (13203) ***(G-15287)***
Constellation Brands Inc (PA) 585 678-7100
207 High Point Dr # 100 Victor (14564) ***(G-15837)***
Constellation Brands Inc 585 393-4880
3325 Marvin Sands Dr Canandaigua (14424) ***(G-3215)***
Constellation Brands Smo LLC 585 396-7161
111 8th Ave New York (10011) ***(G-9385)***
Constellation Brands US Oprs 585 396-7600
116 Buffalo St Canandaigua (14424) ***(G-3216)***
Constellation Brands US Oprs (HQ) 585 396-7600
235 N Bloomfield Rd Canandaigua (14424) ***(G-3217)***
Constellium 212 675-5087
830 3rd Ave Rm 901 New York (10022) ***(G-9386)***
Construction Parts Whse Inc 315 445-1310
5841 Butternut Dr East Syracuse (13057) ***(G-4332)***
Construction Technology Inc (PA) 914 747-8900
17 Green Ln Chappaqua (10514) ***(G-3420)***
Consumer Flavoring Extract Co 718 435-0201
921 Mcdonald Ave Brooklyn (11218) ***(G-1712)***
Consumer Reports Inc (PA) 914 378-2000
101 Truman Ave Yonkers (10703) ***(G-16746)***
CONSUMERS UNION, Yonkers *Also called Consumer Reports Inc* ***(G-16746)***
Contactive Inc 646 476-9059
137 Varick St Ste 605 New York (10013) ***(G-9387)***
Container Tstg Solutions LLC 716 487-3300
17 Tiffany Ave Jamestown (14701) ***(G-6709)***
Container Tstg Solutions LLC (PA) 716 487-3300
17 Lester St Sinclairville (14782) ***(G-14865)***
Contech Engnered Solutions LLC 716 870-9091
34 Birdsong Pkwy Orchard Park (14127) ***(G-12710)***
Contemporary Visions LLC (PA) 845 926-5469
151 Airport Dr Wappingers Falls (12590) ***(G-15928)***
Contempra Design Inc 718 984-8586
20 Grille Ct Staten Island (10309) ***(G-15065)***
Conti Auto Body Corp 516 921-6435
44 Jericho Tpke Syosset (11791) ***(G-15211)***
Continental Access, Amityville *Also called Continental Instruments LLC* ***(G-268)***
Continental Buchanan LLC 703 480-3800
350 Broadway Buchanan (10511) ***(G-2672)***
Continental Cordage Corp (HQ) 315 655-9800
75 Burton St Cazenovia (13035) ***(G-3317)***
Continental Instruments LLC 631 842-9400
355 Bayview Ave Amityville (11701) ***(G-268)***
Continental Knitting Mills 631 242-5330
156 Brook Ave Deer Park (11729) ***(G-3958)***
Continental Kraft Corp 516 681-9090
100 Jericho Quadrangle # 219 Jericho (11753) ***(G-6783)***
Continental Latex Corp 718 783-7883
1489 Shore Pkwy Apt 1g Brooklyn (11214) ***(G-1713)***
Continental Lift Truck Inc 718 738-4738
12718 Foch Blvd South Ozone Park (11420) ***(G-14944)***
Continental Quilting Co Inc 718 499-9100
3000 Marcus Ave Ste 3e6 New Hyde Park (11042) ***(G-8525)***
Continuity Publishing Inc 212 869-4170
15 W 39th St Fl 9 New York (10018) ***(G-9388)***
Continuity Software Inc 646 216-8628
5 Penn Plz Fl 23 New York (10001) ***(G-9389)***
Continuum Intl Pubg Group Inc 646 649-4215
15 W 26th St Fl 8 New York (10010) ***(G-9390)***
Contract Pharmacal Corp 631 231-4610
110 Plant Ave Hauppauge (11788) ***(G-5798)***
Contract Pharmacal Corp 631 231-4610
1324 Motor Pkwy Hauppauge (11749) ***(G-5799)***
Contract Pharmacal Corp 631 231-4610
250 Kennedy Dr Hauppauge (11788) ***(G-5800)***
Contract Pharmacal Corp 631 231-4610
145 Oser Ave Hauppauge (11788) ***(G-5801)***
Contract Pharmacal Corp 631 231-4610
160 Commerce Dr Hauppauge (11788) ***(G-5802)***
Contract Pharmacal Corp 631 231-4610
150 Commerce Dr Hauppauge (11788) ***(G-5803)***
Contract Phrmctcals Ltd Nagara 716 887-3400
100 Forest Ave Buffalo (14213) ***(G-2779)***
Control Elec Div Fil-Coil, Sayville *Also called Esc Control Electronics LLC* ***(G-14627)***
Control Electropolishing Corp 718 858-6634
109 Walworth St Brooklyn (11205) ***(G-1714)***
Control Global Solutions, Halfmoon *Also called Ebeling Associates Inc* ***(G-5662)***
Control Logic Corporation 607 965-6423
2533 State Highway 80 West Burlington (13482) ***(G-16206)***
Control Research Inc 631 225-1111
385 Bayview Ave Unit C Amityville (11701) ***(G-269)***
Controlled Castings Corp 516 349-1718
31 Commercial Ct Plainview (11803) ***(G-13045)***
Convenience Store News 214 217-7800
770 Broadway Fl 5 New York (10003) ***(G-9391)***
Convergent Audio Tech Inc 585 359-2700
85 High Tech Dr Rush (14543) ***(G-14471)***
Convergent Cnnctivity Tech Inc 845 651-5250
1751 State Route 17a Florida (10921) ***(G-4969)***
Convergent Med MGT Svcs LLC 718 921-6159
7513 3rd Ave Brooklyn (11209) ***(G-1715)***
Conversion Labs Inc (PA) 866 351-5907
1460 Broadway New York (10036) ***(G-9392)***

A L P H A B E T I C

Converter Design Inc (PA) — 518 745-7138
25 Murdock Ave Glens Falls (12801) *(G-5421)*
Conway Dressing For Success, Elmsford Also called Conway Import Co Inc *(G-4537)*
Conway Import Co Inc — 914 592-1312
4 Warehouse Ln Ste 142 Elmsford (10523) *(G-4537)*
Coocoo SMS Inc — 646 459-4260
356 New York Ave Ste 1 Huntington (11743) *(G-6396)*
Cookie Connection Inc — 315 422-2253
705 Park Ave Syracuse (13204) *(G-15288)*
Cookie Factory, Bronx Also called Golden Glow Cookie Co Inc *(G-1283)*
Cookiebaker LLC — 716 878-8000
1 Robert Rich Way Buffalo (14213) *(G-2780)*
Cookies Inc — 646 452-5552
1 E 33rd St Fl 6 New York (10016) *(G-9393)*
Cookies United LLC — 631 581-4000
141 Freeman Ave Islip (11751) *(G-6545)*
Cooking With Chef Michelle LLC — 516 662-2324
4603 Middle Country Rd Calverton (11933) *(G-3164)*
Cooks Intl Ltd Lblty Co — 212 741-4407
7 World Trade Ctr Fl 46 New York (10007) *(G-9394)*
Cooper & Clement Inc — 315 454-8135
1840 Lemoyne Ave Syracuse (13208) *(G-15289)*
Cooper Crouse Hinds Elec Pdts, Syracuse Also called Cooper Crouse-Hinds LLC *(G-15290)*
Cooper Crouse-Hinds LLC (HQ) — 315 477-7000
1201 Wolf St Syracuse (13208) *(G-15290)*
Cooper Industries LLC — 315 477-7000
Wolf & 7th North St Syracuse (13208) *(G-15291)*
Cooper Lighting LLC — 516 470-1000
100 Andrews Rd Ste 1 Hicksville (11801) *(G-6071)*
Cooper Molded Products, Syracuse Also called Cooper Industries LLC *(G-15291)*
Cooper Power Systems LLC — 716 375-7100
1648 Dugan Rd Olean (14760) *(G-12597)*
Cooper Turbocompressor Inc (HQ) — 716 896-6600
3101 Broadway St Buffalo (14227) *(G-2781)*
Cooperfriedman Elc Sup Co Inc — 718 269-4906
2219 41st Ave Long Island City (11101) *(G-7415)*
Coopers Cave Ale Co S-Corp — 518 792-0007
2 Sagamore St Glens Falls (12801) *(G-5422)*
Cooperstown Bat Company Inc — 607 547-2415
118 Main St Cooperstown (13326) *(G-3743)*
Cooperstown Brewing Co LLC — 607 286-9330
41 Browne St Oneonta (13820) *(G-12634)*
Coopersurgical Inc — 716 693-6230
825 Wurlitzer Dr North Tonawanda (14120) *(G-12424)*
Coopervision Inc — 585 385-6810
180 Thruway Park Dr West Henrietta (14586) *(G-16235)*
Coopervision Inc — 585 889-3301
711 North Rd Scottsville (14546) *(G-14749)*
Coopervision Inc — 585 385-6810
209 High Point Dr Victor (14564) *(G-15838)*
Coopervision Inc (HQ) — 585 385-6810
209 High Point Dr Ste 100 Victor (14564) *(G-15839)*
Copeland Coating Company Inc — 518 766-2932
3600 Us Highway 20 Nassau (12123) *(G-8477)*
Copen International Limited, New York Also called Cai Inc *(G-9176)*
Copen United LLC — 212 819-0008
37 W 39th St Fl 6 New York (10018) *(G-9395)*
Copesetic Inc — 315 684-7780
62 E Main St Morrisville (13408) *(G-8336)*
Copia Interactive LLC — 212 481-0520
105 Madison Ave New York (10016) *(G-9396)*
Copper John Corporation — 315 258-9269
173 State St Auburn (13021) *(G-473)*
Copper Ridge Oil Inc — 716 372-4021
111 W 2nd St Ste 404 Jamestown (14701) *(G-6710)*
Copra, New York Also called C O P R A Inc *(G-9170)*
Copy Cat — 718 934-2192
3177 Coney Island Ave A Brooklyn (11235) *(G-1716)*
Copy Corner Inc — 718 388-4545
200 Division Ave Brooklyn (11211) *(G-1717)*
Copy Room Inc — 212 371-8600
885 3rd Ave Lowr 2ll New York (10022) *(G-9397)*
Copy Stop Inc — 914 428-5188
50 Main St Ste 32 White Plains (10606) *(G-16440)*
Copy X/Press Ltd — 631 585-2200
700 Union Pkwy Ste 5 Ronkonkoma (11779) *(G-14328)*
Copy4les Inc — 212 487-9778
146 W 29th St Rm 9w New York (10001) *(G-9398)*
Copyright Reprographics, New York Also called Cabba Printing Incorporated *(G-9172)*
Cora Materials Corp — 516 488-6300
30 Nassau Terminal Rd New Hyde Park (11040) *(G-8526)*
Cora Matrls, New Hyde Park Also called Cora Materials Corp *(G-8526)*
Coral Blood Service — 800 483-4888
525 Executive Blvd # 285 Elmsford (10523) *(G-4538)*
Coral Cast LLC — 516 349-1300
31 Commercial Ct Plainview (11803) *(G-13046)*
Coral Color Process Ltd — 631 543-5200
50 Mall Dr Commack (11725) *(G-3688)*
Coral Graphic Services Inc (HQ) — 516 576-2100
840 S Broadway Hicksville (11801) *(G-6072)*
Coral Graphic Services Inc — 516 576-2100
840 S Broadway Hicksville (11801) *(G-6073)*

Coral Graphic Svce, Hicksville Also called Coral Graphic Services Inc *(G-6072)*
Coral Management Corp — 718 893-9286
923 Bryant Ave Bronx (10474) *(G-1246)*
Corbertex LLC — 212 971-0008
1412 Broadway Rm 1100 New York (10018) *(G-9399)*
Corbett Hill Gravel Products, Jamestown Also called Jamestown Macadam Inc *(G-6730)*
Corbett Stves Pttern Works Inc — 585 546-7109
80 Lowell St Rochester (14605) *(G-13722)*
Core Bamboo, New York Also called Brumis Imports Inc *(G-9152)*
Core Group Displays Inc — 845 876-5109
41 Pitcher Rd Rhinebeck (12572) *(G-13485)*
Core Swx LLC — 516 595-7488
91b Commercial St Plainview (11803) *(G-13047)*
Core Welding, Sanborn Also called Bruce Pierce *(G-14542)*
Coremet Trading Inc — 212 964-3600
160 Brdwy Ste 1107 New York (10038) *(G-9400)*
Corey Creek Vineyards, Cutchogue Also called Vedell North Fork LLC *(G-3924)*
Corey Rugs, Great Neck Also called Rosecore Division *(G-5585)*
Corinne McCormack Inc — 212 868-7919
7 W 36th St Fl 9 New York (10018) *(G-9401)*
Corinthian Cast Stone Inc — 631 920-2340
115 Wyandanch Ave Wyandanch (11798) *(G-16694)*
Corium Corporation (PA) — 914 381-0100
147 Palmer Ave Mamaroneck (10543) *(G-7740)*
Corkhill Grp, Jamaica Also called Corkhill Manufacturing Co Inc *(G-6639)*
Corkhill Manufacturing Co Inc — 718 528-7413
13121 Merrick Blvd Jamaica (11434) *(G-6639)*
Corman USA Inc — 718 727-7455
1140 Bay St Ste 2c Staten Island (10305) *(G-15066)*
Corneal Design Corporation — 301 670-7076
3288 Plank Rd Lima (14485) *(G-7150)*
Cornell Beverages Inc — 718 381-3000
105 Harrison Pl Brooklyn (11237) *(G-1718)*
Cornell Laboratory Ornithology, Ithaca Also called Cornell University *(G-6573)*
Cornell University — 607 277-2338
512 E State St Ithaca (14850) *(G-6572)*
Cornell University — 607 254-2473
159 Sapsucker Woods Rd Ithaca (14850) *(G-6573)*
Cornell University Press, Ithaca Also called Cornell University *(G-6572)*
Corning Consumer Products Co, Corning Also called Corning Vitro Corporation *(G-3818)*
Corning Incorporated (PA) — 607 974-9000
1 Riverfront Plz Corning (14831) *(G-3809)*
Corning Incorporated — 607 974-9000
Decker Bldg Corning (14831) *(G-3810)*
Corning Incorporated — 607 974-1274
905 Addison Rd Painted Post (14870) *(G-12836)*
Corning Incorporated — 607 974-9000
1 Riverfront Plz Corning (14831) *(G-3811)*
Corning Incorporated — 315 379-3200
334 County Route 16 Canton (13617) *(G-3256)*
Corning Incorporated — 607 433-3100
275 River St Oneonta (13820) *(G-12635)*
Corning Incorporated — 607 248-1200
Hp-Ab-01-A9b Corning (14831) *(G-3812)*
Corning Incorporated — 646 521-9600
767 5th Ave Ste 2301 New York (10153) *(G-9402)*
Corning Incorporated — 607 974-6729
9261 Addison Rd Painted Post (14870) *(G-12837)*
Corning Incorporated — 607 962-6036
103 Canada Rd Painted Post (14870) *(G-12838)*
Corning Incorporated — 607 974-4488
1 W Market St Ste 601 Corning (14830) *(G-3813)*
Corning Incorporated — 607 974-8496
1 Museum Way Corning (14830) *(G-3814)*
Corning International Corp (HQ) — 607 974-9000
1 Riverfront Plz Corning (14831) *(G-3815)*
Corning Optcal Cmmncations LLC — 607 974-7543
22 W 3rd St Corning (14830) *(G-3816)*
Corning Rubber Company Inc — 631 738-0041
1744 Julia Goldbach Ave Ronkonkoma (11779) *(G-14329)*
Corning Specialty Mtls Inc — 607 974-9000
1 Riverfront Plz Corning (14831) *(G-3817)*
Corning Tropel Corporation — 585 377-3200
60 Oconnor Rd Fairport (14450) *(G-4629)*
Corning Vitro Corporation — 607 974-8605
1 Riverfront Plz Corning (14830) *(G-3818)*
Corning Wax, Ronkonkoma Also called Corning Rubber Company Inc *(G-14329)*
Cornwall Local, Cornwall Also called News of The Highlands Inc *(G-3836)*
Corona Plumbing & Htg Sup Inc — 718 424-4133
10466 Roosevelt Ave Corona (11368) *(G-3841)*
Corona Ready Mix Inc — 718 271-5940
5025 97th Pl Corona (11368) *(G-3842)*
Coronado — 718 386-7425
349 Covert St Brooklyn (11237) *(G-1719)*
Coronet Kitchen & Bath, Ronkonkoma Also called Dak Mica and Wood Products *(G-14332)*
Coronet Parts Mfg Co Inc (PA) — 718 649-1750
883 Elton St Brooklyn (11208) *(G-1720)*
Coronet Parts Mfg Co Inc — 718 649-1750
901 Elton St Fl 1 Brooklyn (11208) *(G-1721)*
Corpkit Legal Supplies, Islip Also called Rike Enterprises Inc *(G-6550)*

Cort Contracting 845 758-1190
188 W Market St Red Hook (12571) *(G-13458)*
Cortland, Cortland *Also called Actuant Corporation* *(G-3858)*
Cortland Asphalt Products, Cortland *Also called McConnaughay Technologies* *(G-3884)*
Cortland Cable Company Inc 607 753-8276
44 River St Cortland (13045) *(G-3865)*
Cortland Company Inc (HQ) 607 753-8276
44 River St Cortland (13045) *(G-3866)*
Cortland Line Mfg LLC 607 756-2851
3736 Kellogg Rd Cortland (13045) *(G-3867)*
Cortland Machine and Tool Co 607 756-5852
60 Grant St Cortland (13045) *(G-3868)*
Cortland Plastics Intl LLC 607 662-0120
211 S Main St Cortland (13045) *(G-3869)*
Cortland Ready Mix, Cortland *Also called Saunders Concrete Co Inc* *(G-3893)*
Cortland Ready Mix Inc 607 753-3063
6 Locust Ave Ofc Rte 13 Cortland (13045) *(G-3870)*
Cortland Standard Printing Co 607 756-5665
110 Main St Cortland (13045) *(G-3871)*
Cortland-Ithaca Subn Shopper, Freeville *Also called Freeville Publishing Co Inc* *(G-5191)*
Corzane Cabinets, Farmingdale *Also called Kazac Inc* *(G-4799)*
Cos TEC Manufacturing Corp 631 589-7170
390 Knickerbocker Ave # 1 Bohemia (11716) *(G-999)*
Cosa Xentaur Corporation (PA) 631 345-3434
84 Horseblock Rd Unit G Yaphank (11980) *(G-16707)*
Cosco Enterprises Inc 718 383-4488
1930 Troutman St Ridgewood (11385) *(G-13533)*
Cosco Interprises Inc 718 417-8995
1930 Troutman St Ste 1 Ridgewood (11385) *(G-13534)*
Cosco Soap & Detergent, Ridgewood *Also called Cosco Enterprises Inc* *(G-13533)*
Cosco Soap and Detergent, Ridgewood *Also called Cosco Interprises Inc* *(G-13534)*
Cosense Inc 516 364-9161
125 Coachman Pl W Syosset (11791) *(G-15212)*
Cosmetic World, New York *Also called Ledes Group Inc* *(G-10536)*
Cosmetics Plus Ltd 516 768-7250
23 Deep Wood Ln Amagansett (11930) *(G-203)*
Cosmic Enterprise 718 342-6257
147 Rockaway Ave Ste A Brooklyn (11233) *(G-1722)*
Cosmicoat of Wny Inc 716 772-2644
8419 East Ave Gasport (14067) *(G-5305)*
Cosmo Electronic Machine Corp 631 249-2535
113 Gazza Blvd Farmingdale (11735) *(G-4739)*
Cosmo Optics, Albany *Also called Ion Optics Inc* *(G-86)*
Cosmopolitan Magazine 212 649-2000
300 W 57th St Fl 38 New York (10019) *(G-9403)*
Cosmos Communications Inc 718 482-1800
1105 44th Dr Long Island City (11101) *(G-7416)*
Cosmos Electronic Machine Corp (PA) 631 249-2535
140 Schmitt Blvd Farmingdale (11735) *(G-4740)*
Cossitt Concrete Products Inc 315 824-2700
6543 Middleport Rd Hamilton (13346) *(G-5698)*
Costanza Ready Mix Inc 516 783-4444
1345 Newbridge Rd North Bellmore (11710) *(G-12375)*
Costanzos Bakery Inc 716 656-9093
30 Innsbruck Dr Buffalo (14227) *(G-2782)*
Costanzos Welding Inc (PA) 716 282-0845
22nd Allen St Niagara Falls (14302) *(G-12274)*
Costello Bros Petroleum Corp (PA) 914 237-3189
990 Mclean Ave Ste 3 Yonkers (10704) *(G-16747)*
Costello Tagliapietra, New York *Also called CTS LLC* *(G-9430)*
Costume Armour Inc 845 534-9120
2 Mill St Stop 1 Cornwall (12518) *(G-3832)*
Costume Culture By Franco LLC 718 821-7100
7017 83rd St Glendale (11385) *(G-5396)*
Cote Hardwood Products Inc (PA) 607 898-5737
4725 Cat Path Rd Locke (13092) *(G-7281)*
Cote Wood Products, Locke *Also called Cote Hardwood Products Inc* *(G-7281)*
Coto Technology, New York *Also called Kearney-National Inc* *(G-10427)*
Cotswolt Industries, New York *Also called Central Textiles Inc* *(G-9245)*
Cott Beverages, Dunkirk *Also called Cliffstar LLC* *(G-4165)*
Cotton Emporium Inc (PA) 718 894-3365
8000 Cooper Ave Ste 8 Glendale (11385) *(G-5397)*
Cotton Well Drilling Co Inc 716 672-2788
Center Rd Sheridan (14135) *(G-14814)*
Cottonwood Metals Inc 646 807-8674
1625 Sycamore Ave Ste A Bohemia (11716) *(G-1000)*
Cottrell Paper Company Inc 518 885-1702
1135 Rock City Rd Rock City Falls (12863) *(G-14222)*
Coty Inc 212 389-7000
350 5th Ave Ste 2700 New York (10118) *(G-9404)*
Coty Inc (PA) 212 389-7300
350 5th Ave Ste 2700 New York (10118) *(G-9405)*
Coty US LLC (HQ) 212 389-7000
350 5th Ave New York (10118) *(G-9406)*
Coty US LLC 212 389-7000
726 Eab Plz Uniondale (11556) *(G-15664)*
Coughlin Printing Group, Watertown *Also called Christian Bus Endeavors Inc* *(G-16007)*
Councel For Sclar Hmnism Cscop, Amherst *Also called Center For Inquiry Inc* *(G-221)*
Counter Evolution 212 647-7505
37 W 17th St New York (10011) *(G-9407)*
Countertop Creations, Rochester *Also called Frank J Martello* *(G-13816)*
Countertops & Cabinets Inc 315 433-1038
4073 New Court Ave Syracuse (13206) *(G-15292)*
Countess Corporation 212 869-7070
225 W 37th St Fl 12 New York (10018) *(G-9408)*
Countess Mara Inc 212 768-7300
120 W 45th St Fl 37 New York (10036) *(G-9409)*
Country Coin-Op, Newport *Also called Reynolds Drapery Service Inc* *(G-12256)*
Country Folks 585 343-9721
123 N Spruce St Batavia (14020) *(G-621)*
Country Life LLC 631 231-1031
101 Corporate Dr Hauppauge (11788) *(G-5804)*
Country Living, New York *Also called Hearst Corporation* *(G-10069)*
Country Side Sand & Gravel (HQ) 716 988-3271
Taylor Hollow Rd Collins (14034) *(G-3672)*
Country Side Sand & Gravel 716 988-3271
8458 Route 62 South Dayton (14138) *(G-14929)*
County Draperies Inc 845 342-9009
64 Genung St Middletown (10940) *(G-8144)*
County Energy Corp 718 626-7000
65 S 11th St Apt 1e Brooklyn (11249) *(G-1723)*
County Fabricators 914 741-0219
175 Marble Ave Pleasantville (10570) *(G-13174)*
County Line Stone Co Inc 716 542-5435
4515 Crittenden Rd Akron (14001) *(G-17)*
Courbee, Westbury *Also called Lotus Apparel Designs Inc* *(G-16352)*
Courier Life Publications, Brooklyn *Also called Courier-Life Inc* *(G-1724)*
Courier Observer, Canton *Also called St Lawrence County Newspapers* *(G-3258)*
Courier Printing Corp 607 467-2191
24 Laurel Bank Ave Ste 2 Deposit (13754) *(G-4107)*
Courier-Life Inc 718 260-2500
1 Metrotech Ctr Brooklyn (11201) *(G-1724)*
Courser Inc 607 739-3861
802 County Road 64 # 100 Elmira (14903) *(G-4480)*
Courtaulds Textiles Ltd 212 946-8000
358 5th Ave Fl 6 New York (10001) *(G-9410)*
Courtlandt Boot Jack Co Inc 718 445-6200
3334 Prince St Flushing (11354) *(G-4994)*
Cousin's Furniture, Deer Park *Also called Cousins Furniture & Hm Imprvs* *(G-3959)*
Cousins Furniture & Hm Imprvs 631 254-3752
515 Acorn St Deer Park (11729) *(G-3959)*
Couture Inc 212 921-1166
16 W 37th St Frnt 1 New York (10018) *(G-9411)*
Couture Press 310 734-4831
200 Park Ave New York (10166) *(G-9412)*
Couture Timber Harvesting 607 836-4719
2760 Phelps Rd Mc Graw (13101) *(G-7926)*
Cove Point Holdings LLC (PA) 212 599-3388
60 E 42nd St Rm 3210 New York (10165) *(G-9413)*
Coventry Manufacturing Co Inc (PA) 914 668-2212
115 E 3rd St Mount Vernon (10550) *(G-8391)*
Coventya Inc (HQ) 216 351-1500
132 Clear Rd Oriskany (13424) *(G-12753)*
Coventya Inc 315 768-6635
132 Clear Rd Oriskany (13424) *(G-12754)*
Covergrip Corporation 855 268-3747
16 Douglas Ln Manorville (11949) *(G-7783)*
Covington Sound 646 256-7486
2705 Kingsbridge Ter Bronx (10463) *(G-1247)*
Cowee Forest Products Inc 518 658-2233
28 Taylor Ave Berlin (12022) *(G-830)*
Cox & Company Inc 212 366-0200
1664 Old Country Rd Plainview (11803) *(G-13048)*
Coyote Moon LLC (PA) 315 686-5600
17371 County Route 3 Clayton (13624) *(G-3553)*
Coyote Moon Vineyards, Clayton *Also called Coyote Moon LLC* *(G-3553)*
Coyote Motorsports, Spencerport *Also called Bullet Industries Inc* *(G-14977)*
Cpac Inc (HQ) 585 382-3223
2364 State Route 20a Leicester (14481) *(G-7126)*
Cpac Equipment Inc 585 382-3223
2364 State Route 20a Leicester (14481) *(G-7127)*
CPI, New York *Also called Capital Programs Inc* *(G-9204)*
CPI Aerostructures Inc 631 586-5200
91 Heartland Blvd Edgewood (11717) *(G-4399)*
CPI Industries Inc 631 909-3434
275 Dayton Ave Manorville (11949) *(G-7784)*
CPI of Falconer Inc 716 664-4444
1890 Lyndon Blvd Falconer (14733) *(G-4674)*
Cpp - Guaymas 315 687-0014
901 E Genesee St Chittenango (13037) *(G-3503)*
Cpp - Steel Treaters 315 736-3081
100 Furnace St Oriskany (13424) *(G-12755)*
Cpp Global, Ronkonkoma *Also called Carolina Precision Plas LLC* *(G-14326)*
Cpp-Syracuse Inc (HQ) 315 687-0014
901 E Genesee St Chittenango (13037) *(G-3504)*
CPS Creative, New York *Also called Complete Publishing Solutions* *(G-9370)*
CPT Usa LLC (PA) 212 575-1616
15 W 39th St Fl 12 New York (10018) *(G-9414)*
Cq Magazine, Hicksville *Also called C Q Communications Inc* *(G-6066)*
Cq Traffic Control Devices LLC 518 767-0057
1521 Us Rte 9w Selkirk (12158) *(G-14767)*

ALPHABETIC

Cq Traffic Control Products, Selkirk *Also called Cq Traffic Control Devices LLC* ***(G-14767)***
Crabtree Publishing Inc....212 496-5040
350 5th Ave Ste 3304 New York (10118) ***(G-9415)***
Craft Atlantic, New York *Also called Craftatlantic LLC* ***(G-9417)***
Craft Clerical Clothes Inc....212 764-6122
247 W 37th St Rm 1700 New York (10018) ***(G-9416)***
Craft Custom Woodwork Co Inc....718 821-2162
5949 56th Ave Maspeth (11378) ***(G-7831)***
Craft Packaging Inc....718 633-4045
1274 49th St Ste 350 Brooklyn (11219) ***(G-1725)***
Craft Robe Co., New York *Also called Craft Clerical Clothes Inc* ***(G-9416)***
Craft-Tech Mfg Corp....631 563-4949
1750 Artic Ave Bohemia (11716) ***(G-1001)***
Craftatlantic LLC....646 726-4205
115 Greenwich Ave New York (10014) ***(G-9417)***
Craftech....518 828-5011
5 Dock St Chatham (12037) ***(G-3427)***
Craftech Industries Inc....518 828-5001
8 Dock St Hudson (12534) ***(G-6344)***
Crafters Workshop Inc....914 345-2838
116 S Central Ave Ste 1 Elmsford (10523) ***(G-4539)***
Craftmaster Flavor Technology....631 789-8607
23 Albany Ave Amityville (11701) ***(G-270)***
Craftsman Manufacturing Co In....585 426-5780
1279 Mount Read Blvd Rochester (14606) ***(G-13723)***
Craftsmen Woodworkers Ltd....718 326-3350
5865 Maspeth Ave Maspeth (11378) ***(G-7832)***
Craftsmen/Access Unlimited, Binghamton *Also called Thomas F Egan* ***(G-919)***
Craig Envelope Corp....718 786-4277
220 Miller Pl Hicksville (11801) ***(G-6074)***
Craigs Station Cheese, Pavilion *Also called Wny Cheese Enterprise LLC* ***(G-12890)***
Crain Communications Inc....212 210-0100
685 3rd Ave New York (10017) ***(G-9418)***
Crains New York Business....212 210-0250
711 3rd Ave New York (10017) ***(G-9419)***
Crainville Block Co, Queensbury *Also called Glens Falls Ready Mix Inc* ***(G-13426)***
Crandall Filling Machinery Inc....716 897-3486
80 Gruner Rd Buffalo (14227) ***(G-2783)***
Crane Equipment & Service Inc (HQ)....716 689-5400
140 John Jmes Adubon Pkwy Amherst (14228) ***(G-223)***
Cranesville Block Co Inc (PA)....518 684-6154
1250 Riverfront Ctr Amsterdam (12010) ***(G-333)***
Cranesville Block Co Inc....315 732-2135
895 Catherine St Utica (13501) ***(G-15688)***
Cranesville Block Co Inc....845 292-1585
1794 State Route 52 Liberty (12754) ***(G-7143)***
Cranesville Block Co Inc....845 896-5687
70 Route 9 Fishkill (12524) ***(G-4944)***
Cranesville Block Co Inc....315 773-2296
23903 Cemetery Rd Felts Mills (13638) ***(G-4930)***
Cranesville Block Co Inc....845 331-1775
637 E Chester St Kingston (12401) ***(G-6896)***
Cranesville Block Co Inc....315 384-4000
8405 State Highway 56 Norfolk (13667) ***(G-12357)***
Cranesville Concrete, Norfolk *Also called Cranesville Block Co Inc* ***(G-12357)***
Cranesville Concrete Co, Utica *Also called Cranesville Block Co Inc* ***(G-15688)***
Cranesville Concrete Co, Liberty *Also called Cranesville Block Co Inc* ***(G-7143)***
Cranesville Ready-Mix, Amsterdam *Also called Cranesville Block Co Inc* ***(G-333)***
Cranial Technologies Inc....914 472-0975
495 Central Park Ave Scarsdale (10583) ***(G-14637)***
Crater Service Group Inc....585 482-7770
111 Humboldt St Rochester (14609) ***(G-13724)***
Crawford Print Shop Inc....607 359-4970
6120 Herrington Rd Addison (14801) ***(G-5)***
Craz Woodworking Assoc Inc....631 205-1890
24 Sawgrass Dr Bellport (11713) ***(G-801)***
Crazy Cowboy Brewing Co LLC....516 812-0576
60 Crossways Park Dr W # 400 Woodbury (11797) ***(G-16616)***
Crazy Hatter, Holtsville *Also called Screen The World Inc* ***(G-6244)***
Cream Bebe....917 578-2088
694 Myrtle Ave Ste 220 Brooklyn (11205) ***(G-1726)***
Create Prosthetics, Lake Placid *Also called Peak Performance Design LLC* ***(G-6977)***
Create-A-Card Inc....631 584-2273
16 Brasswood Rd Saint James (11780) ***(G-14510)***
Creation Baumann USA Inc....516 764-7431
114 N Centre Ave Rockville Centre (11570) ***(G-14231)***
Creations In Canvas, Croton On Hudson *Also called Dalee Bookbinding Co Inc* ***(G-3913)***
Creations In Lucite Inc....718 871-2000
165 Franklin Ave Apt 5 Brooklyn (11205) ***(G-1727)***
Creative Compositions, Amityville *Also called Jeffrey John* ***(G-291)***
Creative Costume Co....212 564-5552
3804 Rivers Pointe Way Liverpool (13090) ***(G-7231)***
Creative Counter Tops Inc....845 471-6480
17 Van Kleeck Dr Poughkeepsie (12601) ***(G-13333)***
Creative Custom Shades, Brooklyn *Also called Custom Lampshades Inc* ***(G-1742)***
Creative Design and Mch Inc....845 778-9001
197 Stone Castle Rd Rock Tavern (12575) ***(G-14224)***
Creative Food Ingredients Inc....585 237-2213
1 Lincoln Ave Perry (14530) ***(G-12967)***
Creative Forms Inc....212 431-7540
80 Varick St Apt 10a New York (10013) ***(G-9420)***
Creative Gold LLC....718 686-2225
1425 37th St Ste 5 Brooklyn (11218) ***(G-1728)***
Creative Home Furnishings (PA)....631 582-8000
250 Creative Dr Central Islip (11722) ***(G-3364)***
Creative Laminates Inc....315 463-7580
4003 Eastbourne Dr Syracuse (13206) ***(G-15293)***
Creative Magazine Inc....516 378-0800
31 Merrick Ave Ste 60 Merrick (11566) ***(G-8095)***
Creative Metal Fabricators....631 567-2266
360 Knickerbocker Ave # 13 Bohemia (11716) ***(G-1002)***
Creative Models & Prototypes....516 433-6828
160 Lauman Ln Unit A Hicksville (11801) ***(G-6075)***
Creative Orthotics & Prosthet (HQ)....607 734-7215
1300 College Ave Ste 1 Elmira (14901) ***(G-4481)***
Creative Orthotics Prosthetics, Ithaca *Also called Hanger Prsthetcs & Ortho Inc* ***(G-6580)***
Creative Orthotics Prosthetics....607 771-4672
65 Pennsylvania Ave 207 Binghamton (13903) ***(G-876)***
Creative Orthotics Prosthetics....607 431-2526
37 Associate Dr Oneonta (13820) ***(G-12636)***
Creative Printing Corp....212 226-3870
70 W 36th St Rm 500 New York (10018) ***(G-9421)***
Creative Prntng, New York *Also called Creative Printing Corp* ***(G-9421)***
Creative Scents USA Inc....718 522-5901
183 Wilson St Ste 106 Brooklyn (11211) ***(G-1729)***
Creative Solutions Group Inc (PA)....914 771-4200
555 Tuckahoe Rd Yonkers (10710) ***(G-16748)***
Creative Stage Lighting Co Inc....518 251-3302
149 State Route 28n North Creek (12853) ***(G-12391)***
Creative Stone & Cabinets....631 772-6548
448 Middle Country Rd # 1 Selden (11784) ***(G-14762)***
Creative Tools & Supply Inc....212 279-7077
135 W 29th St Rm 205 New York (10001) ***(G-9422)***
Creative Yard Designs Inc....315 706-6143
8329 Us Route 20 Manlius (13104) ***(G-7776)***
Creatron Services Inc....516 437-5119
504 Cherry Ln Floral Park (11001) ***(G-4961)***
Credit Union Journal Inc (PA)....212 803-8200
1 State St Fl 26 New York (10004) ***(G-9423)***
Crepe Team, The, Brooklyn *Also called Crepini LLC* ***(G-1730)***
Crepini LLC....347 422-0829
5600 1st Ave Brooklyn (11220) ***(G-1730)***
Crescent Duck Farm Inc....631 722-8700
10 Edgar Ave Aquebogue (11931) ***(G-374)***
Crescent Manufacturing, North Collins *Also called Crescent Marketing Inc* ***(G-12384)***
Crescent Marketing Inc (PA)....716 337-0145
10285 Eagle Dr North Collins (14111) ***(G-12384)***
Crest Haven Precast Inc....518 483-4750
4925 State Route 11 Burke (12917) ***(G-3142)***
Crest Lock Co Inc....718 345-9898
342 Herzl St Brooklyn (11212) ***(G-1731)***
Crest Mills, New York *Also called Jbl Trading LLC* ***(G-10316)***
Cri Graphic, Amityville *Also called Control Research Inc* ***(G-269)***
Crisada Inc....718 729-9730
3913 23rd St Long Island City (11101) ***(G-7417)***
Crisray Printing Corp....631 293-3770
50 Executive Blvd Ste A Farmingdale (11735) ***(G-4741)***
Cristina, Hempstead *Also called King Cracker Corp* ***(G-6017)***
Criterion Bell & Specialty....718 788-2600
4312 2nd Ave Brooklyn (11232) ***(G-1732)***
Critical Imaging LLC....315 732-5020
2428 Chenango Rd Utica (13502) ***(G-15689)***
Critical Link LLC....315 425-4045
6712 Brooklawn Pkwy # 203 Syracuse (13211) ***(G-15294)***
Crocs Inc....845 928-3002
498 Red Apple Ct Central Valley (10917) ***(G-3394)***
Crocs Medical Apparel, New York *Also called Icer Scrubs LLC* ***(G-10168)***
Cromwell Group, Mamaroneck *Also called Corium Corporation* ***(G-7740)***
Cronin Enterprises Inc....914 345-9600
70 E Main St Ste 2 Elmsford (10523) ***(G-4540)***
Crosby Company....716 852-3522
183 Pratt St Buffalo (14204) ***(G-2784)***
Croscill Home Fashions, New York *Also called Mistdoda Inc* ***(G-10824)***
Crosley Medical Products Inc....631 595-2547
19 Kathleen Dr Syosset (11791) ***(G-15213)***
Crosman Corporation (HQ)....585 657-6161
7629 State Route 5 And 20 Bloomfield (14469) ***(G-951)***
Crosman Corporation....585 398-3920
1360 Rural Rte 8 Farmington (14425) ***(G-4911)***
Cross Border Transactions LLC (PA)....646 767-7342
580 White Plains Rd # 660 Tarrytown (10591) ***(G-15476)***
Cross Bronx Optical....917 667-6611
961 E 174th St Bronx (10460) ***(G-1248)***
Cross Country Mfg Inc....607 656-4103
2355 Rte 206 Greene (13778) ***(G-5613)***
Cross Filtration Ltd Lblty Co....315 412-1539
87 W Cayuga St Moravia (13118) ***(G-8333)***
Crosstex International Inc (HQ)....631 582-6777
10 Ranick Rd Hauppauge (11788) ***(G-5805)***
Crosstex International Inc....631 582-6777
2095 Express Dr N Hauppauge (11788) ***(G-5806)***
Crosswinds Farm & Creamery....607 327-0363
6762 Log City Rd Ovid (14521) ***(G-12790)***

Croton Watch Co Inc 800 443-7639
250 W Nyack Rd Ste 114 West Nyack (10994) *(G-16268)*
Crowd Media Inc 212 497-1100
245 5th Ave Rm 1102 New York (10016) *(G-9424)*
Crowley Fabg Machining Co Inc (PA) 607 484-0299
403 N Nanticoke Ave Endicott (13760) *(G-4585)*
Crowley Foods, Binghamton *Also called HP Hood LLC (G-890)*
Crowley Foods Inc (HQ) 800 637-0019
93 Pennsylvania Ave Binghamton (13903) *(G-877)*
Crowley Tar Products Co Inc (PA) 212 682-1200
305 Madison Ave Ste 1035 New York (10165) *(G-9425)*
Crown Aircraft Lighting Inc 718 767-3410
1021 Clintonville St # 4 Whitestone (11357) *(G-16538)*
Crown Cork & Seal Usa Inc 845 343-9586
21 Industrial Pl Middletown (10940) *(G-8145)*
Crown Delta Corporation 914 245-8910
1550 Front St Yorktown Heights (10598) *(G-16815)*
Crown Die Casting Corp 914 667-5400
268 W Lincoln Ave Mount Vernon (10550) *(G-8392)*
Crown Equipment Corporation 516 822-5100
5 Charlotte Ave Ste 1 Hicksville (11801) *(G-6076)*
Crown Hill Stone Inc 716 326-4601
59 Franklin St Westfield (14787) *(G-16393)*
Crown Jewelers Intl Inc 212 420-7800
168 7th Ave S New York (10014) *(G-9426)*
Crown Lift Trucks, Hicksville *Also called Crown Equipment Corporation (G-6076)*
Crown Medical Products, Suffern *Also called Advanced Medical Mfg Corp (G-15184)*
Crown Mill Work Corp 845 371-2200
33 Murray Hill Dr Nanuet (10954) *(G-8462)*
Crown Novelty Works Inc 631 253-0949
42 Elkland Rd Melville (11747) *(G-8013)*
Crown Sign Systems Inc 914 375-2118
2 South St Mount Vernon (10550) *(G-8393)*
Crown Tank Company LLC 855 276-9682
60 Electric Pkwy Horseheads (14845) *(G-6310)*
Crown Woodworking Corp 718 974-6415
583 Montgomery St Brooklyn (11225) *(G-1733)*
Crownbrook ACC LLC (PA) 718 626-0760
478 Albany Ave 113 Brooklyn (11203) *(G-1734)*
CRS Nuclear Services LLC 716 810-0688
840 Aero Dr Ste 150 Cheektowaga (14225) *(G-3438)*
CRS Remanufacturing Co Inc 718 739-1720
9440 158th St Jamaica (11433) *(G-6640)*
Crucible Industries LLC 800 365-1180
575 State Fair Blvd Syracuse (13209) *(G-15295)*
Cruise Industry News, New York *Also called Mathisen Ventures Inc (G-10728)*
Crumbrubber Technology Inc 718 468-3988
18740 Hollis Ave Hollis (11423) *(G-6233)*
Crunched Inc 415 484-9909
41 E 11th St New York (10003) *(G-9427)*
Crusader Candle Co Inc 718 625-0005
325 Nevins St Ste 327329 Brooklyn (11215) *(G-1735)*
Cruzin Management Inc (HQ) 212 641-8700
401 Park Ave S Fl 7 New York (10016) *(G-9428)*
Crye Precision LLC 718 246-3838
63 Flushing Ave Brooklyn (11205) *(G-1736)*
Cryomech Inc 315 455-2555
113 Falso Dr Syracuse (13211) *(G-15296)*
Cryovac Inc 585 436-3211
1525 Brooks Ave Rochester (14624) *(G-13725)*
Crystal Ceres Industries Inc 716 283-0445
2250 Liberty Dr Niagara Falls (14304) *(G-12275)*
Crystal Fusion Tech Inc 631 253-9800
185 W Montauk Hwy Lindenhurst (11757) *(G-7167)*
Crystal Is Inc (HQ) 518 271-7375
70 Cohoes Ave Ste 1b Green Island (12183) *(G-5604)*
Crystal Linton Technologies 585 444-8784
2180 Brigh Henri Town Lin Rochester (14623) *(G-13726)*
Crystal Rock LLC 716 626-7460
100 Stradtman St Ste 1 Buffalo (14206) *(G-2785)*
Crystalizations Systems Inc 631 467-0090
1401 Lincoln Ave Holbrook (11741) *(G-6180)*
Crystalonics Inc 631 981-6140
2805 Veterans Mem Hwy 14 Ronkonkoma (11779) *(G-14330)*
Crystalonics of New York Inc 631 981-6140
2805 Vets Memorial Ronkonkoma (11779) *(G-14331)*
Cs Automation Inc 315 524-5123
518 Berg Rd Ontario (14519) *(G-12650)*
CS Business Systems Inc (PA) 716 886-6521
1236 Main St Buffalo (14209) *(G-2786)*
CSC Serviceworks, Inc., Plainview *Also called CSC SW Holdco Inc (G-13049)*
CSC SW Holdco Inc (HQ) 516 349-8555
303 Sunnyside Blvd # 70 Plainview (11803) *(G-13049)*
Csco LLC 212 375-6180
1407 Broadway Rm 1503 New York (10018) *(G-9429)*
Csi, Falconer *Also called Reynolds Packaging McHy Inc (G-4690)*
Csi International Inc 800 441-2895
1001 Main St Niagara Falls (14301) *(G-12276)*
CSP Technologies Inc (HQ) 518 627-0051
1031 Riverfront Ctr Amsterdam (12010) *(G-334)*
Csrea, Long Island City *Also called Civil Svc Rtred Employees Assn (G-7409)*
Csw Inc 585 247-4010
70 Pixley Industrial Pkwy Rochester (14624) *(G-13727)*
CT Industrial Supply Co Inc 718 417-3226
305 Ten Eyck St Brooklyn (11206) *(G-1737)*
CT Publications Co 718 592-2196
1120 154th St Whitestone (11357) *(G-16539)*
Ctac Holdings LLC 212 924-2280
68 35th Street Brooklyn Brooklyn (11232) *(G-1738)*
CTB Enterprise LLC 631 563-0088
1170 Lincoln Ave Unit 7 Holbrook (11741) *(G-6181)*
CTI Software Inc 631 253-3550
44 W Jefryn Blvd Ste P Deer Park (11729) *(G-3960)*
CTS LLC 212 278-0058
211 E 18th St Apt 4d New York (10003) *(G-9430)*
CTX Printing, Cambridge *Also called Cambridge-Pacific Inc (G-3178)*
Cuba Specialty Mfg Co Inc 585 567-4176
81 S Genesee St Fillmore (14735) *(G-4937)*
Cubic Trnsp Systems Inc 212 255-1810
245 W 17th St Fl 8 New York (10011) *(G-9431)*
Cubitek Inc 631 665-6900
95 Emjay Blvd Ste 2 Brentwood (11717) *(G-1129)*
Cuccio-Zanetti Inc 518 587-1363
455 Middle Grove Rd Middle Grove (12850) *(G-8115)*
Cuddeback Machining Inc 585 392-5889
18 Draffin Rd Hilton (14468) *(G-6156)*
Cuffs Planning & Models Ltd 914 632-1883
317 Beechmont Dr New Rochelle (10804) *(G-8597)*
Culicover & Shapiro Inc 516 597-4888
270 Duffy Ave Ste K Hicksville (11801) *(G-6077)*
Culin/Colella Inc 914 698-7727
632 Center Ave Mamaroneck (10543) *(G-7741)*
Culinary Arts Specialties Inc 716 656-8943
2268 Union Rd Cheektowaga (14227) *(G-3439)*
Cult Records LLC 718 395-2077
263 Bowery Apt 3 New York (10002) *(G-9432)*
Cultureiq Inc (PA) 212 755-8633
7 Penn Plz Ste 1112 New York (10001) *(G-9433)*
Cumberland Packing Corp (PA) 718 858-4200
2 Cumberland St Brooklyn (11205) *(G-1739)*
Cummins - Allison Corp 718 263-2482
8002 Kew Gardens Rd # 402 Kew Gardens (11415) *(G-6871)*
Cummins Inc 716 456-2676
4720 Baker St Lakewood (14750) *(G-6992)*
Cummins Inc 716 456-2111
4720 Baker St Lakewood (14750) *(G-6993)*
Cummins Northeast LLC 315 437-2296
6193 Eastern Ave Syracuse (13211) *(G-15297)*
Cummins-Wagner-Siewert LLC (HQ) 585 482-9640
175 Akron St Rochester (14609) *(G-13728)*
Cuore Technology, Cheektowaga *Also called Leo Schultz (G-3451)*
Cupcake Contessas Corporation 516 307-1222
1242 Julia Ln North Bellmore (11710) *(G-12376)*
Cupid Foundations Inc (PA) 212 686-6224
475 Park Ave S Manhattan New York (10022) *(G-9434)*
CUPID INTIMATES, New York *Also called Cupid Foundations Inc (G-9434)*
Curaegis Technologies Inc (PA) 585 254-1100
1999 Mount Read Blvd # 3 Rochester (14615) *(G-13729)*
Curbell Medical Products Inc 716 667-2520
20 Centre Dr Orchard Park (14127) *(G-12711)*
Curbell Medical Products Inc (HQ) 716 667-2520
7 Cobham Dr Orchard Park (14127) *(G-12712)*
Cureatr Inc 212 203-3927
222 Broadway Fl 20 New York (10038) *(G-9435)*
Curran Manufacturing Corp (PA) 631 273-1010
200 Oser Ave Hauppauge (11788) *(G-5807)*
Curran Manufacturing Corp 631 273-1010
210 Oser Ave Hauppauge (11788) *(G-5808)*
Curran Renewable Energy LLC 315 769-2000
20 Commerce Dr Massena (13662) *(G-7901)*
Currant Company LLC 845 266-8999
59 Walnut Ln Staatsburg (12580) *(G-15022)*
Currantc, Staatsburg *Also called Currant Company LLC (G-15022)*
Current Applications Inc 315 788-4689
275 Bellew Ave S Watertown (13601) *(G-16010)*
Current Controls Inc 585 593-1544
353 S Brooklyn Ave Wellsville (14895) *(G-16114)*
Curriculum Associates LLC 978 313-1355
55 Prospect St Brooklyn (11201) *(G-1740)*
Currier Plastics Inc 315 255-1779
101 Columbus St Auburn (13021) *(G-474)*
Curtin-Hebert Co Inc 518 725-7157
11 Forest St Gloversville (12078) *(G-5455)*
Curtin-Hebert Machines, Gloversville *Also called Curtin-Hebert Co Inc (G-5455)*
Curtis Instruments Inc (PA) 914 666-2971
200 Kisco Ave Mount Kisco (10549) *(G-8339)*
Curtis L Maclean L C (HQ) 716 898-7800
50 Thielman Dr Buffalo (14206) *(G-2787)*
Curtis PMC Division, Mount Kisco *Also called Curtis Instruments Inc (G-8339)*
Curtis Prtg Co The Del Press 518 477-4820
711 Columbia Tpke East Greenbush (12061) *(G-4228)*
Curtis Screw Co Inc 716 898-7800
50 Thielman Dr Buffalo (14206) *(G-2788)*

A L P H A B E T I C

Curtis/Palmer Hydroelectric LP 518 654-6297
15 Pine St Corinth (12822) **(G-3808)**
Curtiss-Wrght Intgrted Sensing, Farmingdale *Also called Curtiss-Wright Controls* **(G-4742)**
Curtiss-Wright Controls 631 756-4740
175 Central Ave Ste 100 Farmingdale (11735) **(G-4742)**
Curtiss-Wright Electro- 585 596-3482
37 Coats St Ste 200 Wellsville (14895) **(G-16115)**
Curtiss-Wright Flow Ctrl Corp (HQ) 631 293-3800
1966 Broadhollow Rd Ste E Farmingdale (11735) **(G-4743)**
Curtiss-Wright Flow Ctrl Corp 631 293-3800
1966 Broadhollow Rd Ste E Farmingdale (11735) **(G-4744)**
Cusimano, Michael, Rochester *Also called Empire Fabricators Inc* **(G-13779)**
Custom 101 Prints Inc 718 708-4425
3601 Bronxwood Ave Bronx (10469) **(G-1249)**
Custom Bags Unlimited, Hamburg *Also called Kragel Co Inc* **(G-5685)**
Custom Brewcrafters Inc 585 624-4386
300 Village Square Blvd Honeoye Falls (14472) **(G-6263)**
Custom Canvas Manufacturing Co 716 852-6372
775 Seneca St Buffalo (14210) **(G-2789)**
Custom CAS Inc 718 726-3575
2631 1st St Long Island City (11102) **(G-7418)**
Custom Coatings, Farmingdale *Also called Time-Cap Laboratories Inc* **(G-4896)**
Custom Controls 315 253-4785
2804 Skillett Rd Scipio Center (13147) **(G-14736)**
Custom Cool, Bronx *Also called S & V Restaurant Eqp Mfrs Inc* **(G-1377)**
Custom Countertops Inc (PA) 716 685-2871
3192 Walden Ave Depew (14043) **(G-4085)**
Custom Design Kitchens Inc 518 355-4446
1700 Duanesburg Rd Duanesburg (12056) **(G-4155)**
Custom Design Metals Inc 631 563-2444
1612 Locust Ave Ste C Bohemia (11716) **(G-1003)**
Custom Display Manufacture 516 783-6491
1686 Logan St North Bellmore (11710) **(G-12377)**
Custom Door & Mirror Inc 631 414-7725
148 Milbar Blvd Farmingdale (11735) **(G-4745)**
Custom Eco Friendly Bags, Roslyn *Also called Custom Eco Friendly LLC* **(G-14445)**
Custom Eco Friendly LLC (PA) 347 227-0229
50 Spruce Dr Roslyn (11576) **(G-14445)**
Custom Electronics Inc 607 432-3880
87 Browne St Oneonta (13820) **(G-12637)**
Custom European Imports Inc 845 357-5718
100 Sterling Mine Rd Sloatsburg (10974) **(G-14892)**
Custom Fixtures Inc 718 965-1141
129 13th St Brooklyn (11215) **(G-1741)**
Custom Frame & Molding Co 631 491-9091
97 Lamar St 101 West Babylon (11704) **(G-16150)**
Custom House Engravers Inc 631 567-3004
104 Keyland Ct Bohemia (11716) **(G-1004)**
Custom Klean Corp 315 865-8101
8890 Boak Rd E Holland Patent (13354) **(G-6224)**
Custom Lampshades Inc 718 254-0500
544 Park Ave Ste 503 Brooklyn (11205) **(G-1742)**
Custom Laser Inc (PA) 716 434-8600
6747 Akron Rd Lockport (14094) **(G-7292)**
Custom Lucite Creations Inc 718 871-2000
165 Franklin Ave Apt 5 Brooklyn (11205) **(G-1743)**
Custom Manufacturing Inc 607 569-2738
93 Lake St Hammondsport (14840) **(G-5703)**
Custom Metal Fabrication, West Babylon *Also called Custom Metal Incorporated* **(G-16151)**
Custom Metal Incorporated 631 643-4075
72 Otis St West Babylon (11704) **(G-16151)**
Custom Mix Inc 516 797-7090
31 Clark Blvd Massapequa Park (11762) **(G-7889)**
Custom Molding Solutions Inc 585 293-1702
456 Sanford Rd N Churchville (14428) **(G-3508)**
Custom Nutraceuticals LLC (PA) 631 755-1388
80 Orville Dr Ste 112 Bohemia (11716) **(G-1005)**
Custom Patches Inc 845 679-6320
1760 Glasco Tpke Woodstock (12498) **(G-16685)**
Custom Power System, Sayville *Also called Fil-Coil (fc) Corp* **(G-14628)**
Custom Power Systems, Central Islip *Also called Berkshire Transformer* **(G-3359)**
Custom Prtrs Guilderland Inc 518 456-2811
2210 Western Ave Guilderland (12084) **(G-5654)**
Custom Service Solutions Inc 585 637-3760
1900 Transit Way Brockport (14420) **(G-1190)**
Custom Sheet Metal Corp 315 463-9105
1 General Motors Dr Ste 5 Syracuse (13206) **(G-15298)**
Custom Shipping Products Inc 716 355-4437
8661 Knowlton Rd Clymer (14724) **(G-3599)**
Custom Sitecom LLC 631 420-4238
470 Smith St Farmingdale (11735) **(G-4746)**
Custom Sound and Video 585 424-5000
40 Rutter St Rochester (14606) **(G-13730)**
Custom Sports Lab Inc 212 832-1648
515 Madison Ave Rm 1204 New York (10022) **(G-9436)**
Custom Sportswear Corp 914 666-9200
375 Adams St Bedford Hills (10507) **(G-773)**
Custom Stair & Millwork Co 315 839-5793
6 Gridley Pl Sauquoit (13456) **(G-14621)**
Custom Studio Division, Tappan *Also called Nationwide Custom Services* **(G-15469)**
Custom Wood Inc 718 927-4700
770 E 94th St Brooklyn (11236) **(G-1744)**
Custom Woodcraft LLC 315 843-4234
2525 Perry Schumaker Rd Munnsville (13409) **(G-8458)**
Custom Woodwork Ltd 631 727-5260
205 Marcy Ave Riverhead (11901) **(G-13566)**
Customize Elite Socks LLC 212 533-8551
156 2nd Ave Apt 2c New York (10003) **(G-9437)**
Customshow Inc 800 255-5303
216 E 45th St Fl 17 New York (10017) **(G-9438)**
Cutting Edge Metal Works 631 981-8333
12 Long Island Ave Holtsville (11742) **(G-6239)**
Cuzins Duzin Corp 347 724-6200
8420 Austin St Apt 3a Kew Gardens (11415) **(G-6872)**
Cvd Equipment Corporation 845 246-3631
1117 Kings Hwy Saugerties (12477) **(G-14605)**
Cvd Equipment Corporation (PA) 631 981-7081
355 S Technology Dr Central Islip (11722) **(G-3365)**
Cvd Equipment Corporation 631 582-4365
355 S Technology Dr Central Islip (11722) **(G-3366)**
Cw Fasteners & Zippers Corp 212 594-3203
142 W 36th St Fl 5 New York (10018) **(G-9439)**
Cw Metals Inc 917 416-7906
3421 Greenpoint Ave Long Island City (11101) **(G-7419)**
Cws Powder Coatings Company LP 845 398-2911
2234 Bradley Hill Rd # 12 Blauvelt (10913) **(G-934)**
Cy Fashion Corp 212 730-8600
525 7th Ave Rm 811 New York (10018) **(G-9440)**
Cy Plastics Works Inc 585 229-2555
8601 Main St Honeoye (14471) **(G-6260)**
Cyber Knit, New York *Also called Lifestyle Design Usa Ltd* **(G-10565)**
Cyberlimit Inc 212 840-9597
257 W 38th St Fl 6 New York (10018) **(G-9441)**
Cybersports Inc (PA) 315 737-7150
11 Avery Pl Utica (13502) **(G-15690)**
Cyclone Air Power Inc 718 447-3038
12 Van St Staten Island (10310) **(G-15067)**
Cyclotherm of Watertown Inc 315 782-1100
787 Pearl St Watertown (13601) **(G-16011)**
Cygnet Studio Inc 646 450-4550
251 W 39th St Fl 17 New York (10018) **(G-9442)**
Cygnus Automation Inc 631 981-0909
1605 9th Ave Bohemia (11716) **(G-1006)**
Cyncal Steel Fabricators Inc 631 254-5600
225 Pine Aire Dr Bay Shore (11706) **(G-676)**
Cynosure Inc 516 594-3333
400 Karin Ln Hicksville (11801) **(G-6078)**
Cynthia Rowley Inc (PA) 212 242-3803
376 Bleecker St New York (10014) **(G-9443)**
Cynthia Steffe, New York *Also called Bernard Chaus Inc* **(G-9052)**
Cypress Bioscience Inc 858 452-2323
110 E 59th St Fl 33 New York (10022) **(G-9444)**
Cypress Semiconductor Corp 631 261-1358
34 Rowley Dr Northport (11768) **(G-12467)**
Cytec Industries Inc 716 372-9650
1405 Buffalo St Olean (14760) **(G-12598)**
Cytec Solvay Group, Olean *Also called Cytec Industries Inc* **(G-12598)**
Cz USA Dwf Dan Wesson Firearm, Norwich *Also called Dan Wesson Corp* **(G-12484)**
D & A Offset Services Inc 212 924-0612
185 Varick St Ste 3 New York (10014) **(G-9445)**
D & C Cleaning Inc 631 789-5659
1095 Campagnoli Ave Copiague (11726) **(G-3756)**
D & D Motor Systems Inc 315 701-0861
215 Park Ave Syracuse (13204) **(G-15299)**
D & D Printing, Buffalo *Also called Dan Trent Company Inc* **(G-2792)**
D & D Window Tech Inc (PA) 212 308-2822
979 3rd Ave Lbby 132 New York (10022) **(G-9446)**
D & E Industrial, Akron *Also called Re-Al Industrial Corp* **(G-22)**
D & G Sheet Metal Co Inc 718 326-9111
5400 Grand Ave Maspeth (11378) **(G-7833)**
D & G Welding Inc 716 873-3088
249 Hertel Ave Buffalo (14207) **(G-2790)**
D & H Amazing Deals Inc (PA) 347 318-3805
1233 39th St Brooklyn (11218) **(G-1745)**
D & I Finishing Inc 631 471-3034
1560 Ocean Ave Ste 7 Bohemia (11716) **(G-1007)**
D & L Electronic Die, Farmingdale *Also called Cosmo Electronic Machine Corp* **(G-4739)**
D & L Manufacturing, Bronx *Also called L & D Manufacturing Corp* **(G-1311)**
D & M Custom Cabinets Inc 516 678-2818
2994 Long Beach Rd Oceanside (11572) **(G-12534)**
D & M Enterprises Incorporated 914 937-6430
1 Mill St Ste 2 Port Chester (10573) **(G-13195)**
D & R Silk Screening Ltd 631 234-7464
201 Creative Dr Central Islip (11722) **(G-3367)**
D & S Supplies Inc 718 721-5256
2067 21st St Astoria (11105) **(G-422)**
D & V Enterprises Inc 917 983-9250
119 Woodlake Dr W Woodbury (11797) **(G-16617)**
D & W Design Inc (PA) 845 343-3366
62 Industrial Pl Middletown (10940) **(G-8146)**
D & W Diesel Inc 518 437-1300
51 Sicker Rd Ste 3 Latham (12110) **(G-7070)**
D & W Enterprises LLC 585 590-6727
10775 W Shelby Rd Medina (14103) **(G-7976)**

ALPHABETIC SECTION
Damianou Sportswear Inc

D and D Sheet Metal Corp ... 718 465-7585
9510 218th St Ste 4 Jamaica (11429) *(G-6641)*
D B F Associates ... 718 328-0005
1150 E 156th St Bronx (10474) *(G-1250)*
D Bag Lady Inc ... 585 425-8095
183 Perinton Pkwy Fairport (14450) *(G-4630)*
D Best Glass & Mirror, Brooklyn *Also called D Best Service Co Inc (G-1746)*
D Best Service Co Inc ... 718 972-6133
729 Church Ave Brooklyn (11218) *(G-1746)*
D C C, New York *Also called Digital Color Concepts Inc (G-9526)*
D C I Plasma Center Inc (PA) ... 914 241-1646
71 S Bedford Rd Mount Kisco (10549) *(G-8340)*
D C I Technical Inc ... 516 355-0464
475 Franklin Ave Fl 2 Franklin Square (11010) *(G-5116)*
D C M, West Babylon *Also called Display Components Mfg Inc (G-16153)*
D D & L Inc ... 607 729-9131
3 Alice St Binghamton (13904) *(G-878)*
D F Stauffer Biscuit Co Inc ... 585 968-2700
8670 Farnsworth Rd Cuba (14727) *(G-3917)*
D G M Graphics Inc ... 516 223-2220
55 Merrick Ave Merrick (11566) *(G-8096)*
D J Crowell Co Inc ... 716 684-3343
2815 Town Line Rd Alden (14004) *(G-169)*
D J Night Ltd ... 212 302-9050
225 W 37th St Fl 6 New York (10018) *(G-9447)*
D K Machine Inc ... 518 747-0626
48 Sullivan Pkwy Fort Edward (12828) *(G-5095)*
D K P Wood Railings & Stairs ... 631 665-8656
1971 Union Blvd Bay Shore (11706) *(G-677)*
D M J Casting Inc ... 212 719-1951
62 W 47th St Ste 508 New York (10036) *(G-9448)*
D Maldari & Sons Inc ... 718 499-3555
557 3rd Ave Brooklyn (11215) *(G-1747)*
D N Gannon Fabricating Inc ... 315 463-7466
404 Wavel St Syracuse (13206) *(G-15300)*
D R Cornue Woodworks ... 315 655-9463
3206 Us Route 20 Cazenovia (13035) *(G-3318)*
D R M Management Inc (PA) ... 716 668-0333
3430 Transit Rd Depew (14043) *(G-4086)*
D R S Inc (PA) ... 212 819-0237
64 W 48th St Ste 1302 New York (10036) *(G-9449)*
D R S Watch Materials ... 212 819-0470
64 W 48th St Ste 1302 New York (10036) *(G-9450)*
D S I, Poestenkill *Also called Dynamic Systems Inc (G-13180)*
D Squared Technologies Inc ... 516 932-7319
71 Birchwood Park Dr Jericho (11753) *(G-6784)*
D T B, Bohemia *Also called Dayton T Brown Inc (G-1011)*
D T I, Rochester *Also called Dimension Technologies Inc (G-13742)*
D V S Iron & Aluminum Works ... 718 768-7961
117 14th St Brooklyn (11215) *(G-1748)*
D W Haber & Son Inc ... 718 993-6405
825 E 140th St Bronx (10454) *(G-1251)*
D W S Associates Inc ... 631 667-6666
89 N Industry Ct Deer Park (11729) *(G-3961)*
D W S Printing, Deer Park *Also called D W S Associates Inc (G-3961)*
D&H, Brooklyn *Also called D & H Amazing Deals Inc (G-1745)*
D'Addario & Company Inc, Brooklyn *Also called DAddario & Company Inc (G-1749)*
D-Best Equipment Corp ... 516 358-0965
77 Hempstead Gardens Dr West Hempstead (11552) *(G-16215)*
D-C Theatricks ... 716 847-0180
747 Main St Buffalo (14203) *(G-2791)*
D-K Manufacturing Corp ... 315 592-4327
551 W 3rd St S Fulton (13069) *(G-5214)*
D-Lite Donuts ... 718 626-5953
4519 Broadway Astoria (11103) *(G-423)*
D.A.M. Construction, Company, Arverne *Also called Darrell Mitchell (G-414)*
D3 Led LLC ... 917 757-9671
566 7th Ave Rm 504 New York (10018) *(G-9451)*
D3 NY, New York *Also called D3 Led LLC (G-9451)*
D3 Repro Group ... 347 507-1075
3401 38th Ave Long Island City (11101) *(G-7420)*
Da Electric ... 347 270-3422
6 E Clarke Pl Bronx (10452) *(G-1252)*
Dab-O-Matic Corp (PA) ... 914 699-7070
896 S Columbus Ave Mount Vernon (10550) *(G-8394)*
Dabby-Reid Ltd ... 212 356-0040
347 W 36th St Rm 701 New York (10018) *(G-9452)*
Dacobe Enterprises LLC ... 315 368-0093
325 Lafayette St Utica (13502) *(G-15691)*
DAddario & Company Inc ... 631 439-3300
99 Marcus Dr Melville (11747) *(G-8014)*
DAddario & Company Inc ... 718 599-6660
1000 Dean St Ste 410 Brooklyn (11238) *(G-1749)*
DAddario & Company Inc (PA) ... 631 439-3300
595 Smith St Farmingdale (11735) *(G-4747)*
DAF Office Networks Inc ... 315 699-7070
6121 Jemola Runne Cicero (13039) *(G-3516)*
DAgostino Iron Works Inc ... 585 235-8850
10 Deep Rock Rd Rochester (14624) *(G-13731)*
Daheshist Publishing Co Ltd ... 212 581-8360
1775 Broadway 501 New York (10019) *(G-9453)*

Dahill Distributors Inc ... 347 371-9453
975 Dahill Rd Brooklyn (11204) *(G-1750)*
Dahlstrom Roll Form, Jamestown *Also called Lakeside Capital Corporation (G-6735)*
Daige Products Inc ... 516 621-2100
1 Albertson Ave Ste 3 Albertson (11507) *(G-148)*
Daikin Applied Americas Inc ... 315 253-2771
4900 Technology Park Blvd Auburn (13021) *(G-475)*
Dail Cornell Sun, The, Ithaca *Also called Daily Cornell Sun (G-6574)*
Daily Beast Company LLC (HQ) ... 212 445-4600
7 Hanover Sq New York (10004) *(G-9454)*
Daily Cornell Sun ... 607 273-0746
139 W State St Ithaca (14850) *(G-6574)*
Daily Freeman ... 845 331-5000
79 Hurley Ave Kingston (12401) *(G-6897)*
Daily Gazette Company (PA) ... 518 374-4141
2345 Maxon Rd Ext Schenectady (12308) *(G-14667)*
Daily Gazette Company ... 518 395-3060
2345 Maxon Rd Ext Schenectady (12308) *(G-14668)*
Daily Jeans, Woodbury *Also called D & V Enterprises Inc (G-16617)*
Daily Mail & Greene Cnty News (HQ) ... 518 943-2100
1 Hudson City Ctr Ste 202 Hudson (12534) *(G-6345)*
Daily Media, Rochester *Also called Daily Record (G-13732)*
Daily Messenger, Canandaigua *Also called Canandaigua Msgnr Incorporated (G-3213)*
Daily News LP (HQ) ... 212 210-2100
4 New York Plz Fl 6 New York (10004) *(G-9455)*
Daily Newsppr For Torah Jewry, Brooklyn *Also called Hamodia Corp (G-1963)*
Daily Orange Corporation ... 315 443-2314
744 Ostrom Ave Syracuse (13244) *(G-15301)*
Daily Racing Form Inc (HQ) ... 212 366-7600
708 3rd Ave Fl 12 New York (10017) *(G-9456)*
Daily Racing Form LLC ... 212 514-2180
75 Broad St New York (10004) *(G-9457)*
Daily Record (PA) ... 585 232-2035
16 W Main St Ste G9 Rochester (14614) *(G-13732)*
Daily Sun New York, New York *Also called Daily World Press Inc (G-9458)*
Daily Voice, Armonk *Also called Main Street Connect LLC (G-407)*
Daily Wear Sportswear Corp (PA) ... 718 972-0533
2308 Mcdonald Ave Brooklyn (11223) *(G-1751)*
Daily World Press Inc ... 212 922-9201
228 E 45th St Rm 700 New York (10017) *(G-9458)*
Dailycandy Inc ... 646 230-8719
584 Broadway Rm 510 New York (10012) *(G-9459)*
Daimler Buses North Amer Inc ... 315 768-8101
165 Base Rd Oriskany (13424) *(G-12756)*
Dainty Home, New York *Also called Baby Signature Inc (G-8996)*
Dairy Conveyor Corp (PA) ... 845 278-7878
38 Mount Ebo Rd S Brewster (10509) *(G-1162)*
Dairy Delite, Farmingdale *Also called Noga Dairies Inc (G-4837)*
Dairy Farmers America Inc ... 816 801-6440
5001 Brittonfield Pkwy East Syracuse (13057) *(G-4333)*
Dairy Farmers America Inc ... 585 409-2200
5140 Agi Business Pk Dr W Batavia (14020) *(G-622)*
Daisy Brand Confectionery, Bronx *Also called Scaccianoce Inc (G-1382)*
Daisy Memory Products, Roslyn *Also called Dynamic Photography Inc (G-14446)*
Dak Mica and Wood Products ... 631 467-0749
2147 5th Ave Ronkonkoma (11779) *(G-14332)*
Dakota Software Corporation ... 216 765-7100
7641 Pine Tree Dr Victor (14564) *(G-15840)*
Dakota Systems Mfg Corp ... 631 249-5811
1885 New Hwy Ste 2 Farmingdale (11735) *(G-4748)*
Dakota Wall, Farmingdale *Also called Dakota Systems Mfg Corp (G-4748)*
Dakotah, Central Islip *Also called Creative Home Furnishings (G-3364)*
Dakott LLC ... 888 805-6795
244 Madison Ave Ste 211 New York (10016) *(G-9460)*
Dal-Tile Corporation ... 718 894-9574
5840 55th Dr Maspeth (11378) *(G-7834)*
Dal-Tile Corporation ... 914 835-1801
31 Oakland Ave Harrison (10528) *(G-5727)*
Dalcom USA Ltd ... 516 466-7733
11 Middle Neck Rd Ste 301 Great Neck (11021) *(G-5549)*
Dale Press Inc ... 718 543-6200
5676 Riverdale Ave # 311 Bronx (10471) *(G-1253)*
Dalee Bookbinding Co Inc ... 914 965-1660
10 Croton Lake Rd Croton On Hudson (10520) *(G-3913)*
Dalfon, Great Neck *Also called Dalcom USA Ltd (G-5549)*
Dalma Dress Mfg Co Inc ... 212 391-8296
3 Carman Rd Greenvale (11548) *(G-5629)*
Dalrymple Grav & Contg Co Inc (HQ) ... 607 739-0391
2105 S Broadway Pine City (14871) *(G-12999)*
Dalrymple Grav & Contg Co Inc ... 607 529-3235
Chemung Flats Rd Chemung (14825) *(G-3463)*
Dalrymple Holding Corp (PA) ... 607 737-6200
2105 S Broadway Pine City (14871) *(G-13000)*
Daly Meghan ... 347 699-3259
78 5th Ave Brooklyn (11217) *(G-1752)*
Damascus Bakery Inc (PA) ... 718 855-1456
56 Gold St Brooklyn (11201) *(G-1753)*
Damianou Sportswear Inc ... 718 204-5600
6001 31st Ave Ste 2 Woodside (11377) *(G-16652)*

ALPHABETIC

(PA)=Parent Co (HQ)=Headquarters (DH)=Div Headquarters
2019 Harris
New York Manufacturers Directory
863

Damn Good Foods Inc 518 664-1414
1002 Hudson Ave Stillwater (12170) ***(G-15157)***
Damn Good Jerkey, Stillwater *Also called Damn Good Foods Inc* ***(G-15157)***
Dampits International Inc 212 581-3047
425 W 57th St New York (10019) ***(G-9461)***
Dan Ann Associates, Kirkwood *Also called Belden Manufacturing Inc* ***(G-6939)***
Dan Kane Plating Co Inc 212 675-4947
357 W 36th St New York (10018) ***(G-9462)***
Dan Trent Company Inc 716 822-1422
1728 Clinton St Buffalo (14206) ***(G-2792)***
Dan Wesson Corp 607 336-1174
65 Borden Ave Norwich (13815) ***(G-12484)***
Dana Michele LLC 917 757-7777
3 E 84th St New York (10028) ***(G-9463)***
Danaher Corporation 516 443-9432
445 E 14th St Apt 3f New York (10009) ***(G-9464)***
Danbury Pharma LLC 631 393-6333
220 Smith St Farmingdale (11735) ***(G-4749)***
Dandelion Energy Inc 603 781-2663
15 Metrotech Ctr Fl 19 Brooklyn (11201) ***(G-1754)***
DAndrea Inc 516 496-2200
115 Eileen Way Ste 106 Syosset (11791) ***(G-15214)***
Danet Inc 718 266-4444
8518 17th Ave Fl 2 Brooklyn (11214) ***(G-1755)***
DAngelo Home Collections Inc 917 267-8920
39 Warwick Tpke Warwick (10990) ***(G-15949)***
Danhier Co LLC 212 563-7683
380 Rector Pl Apt 3d New York (10280) ***(G-9465)***
Dani Accessories Inc 631 692-4505
204 Lawrence Hill Rd Cold Spring Harbor (11724) ***(G-3630)***
Dani II Inc (PA) 212 869-5999
231 W 39th St Rm 1002 New York (10018) ***(G-9466)***
Danice Stores Inc 212 665-0389
305 W 125th St New York (10027) ***(G-9467)***
Daniel & Lois Lyndaker Logging 315 346-6527
10460 Monnat School Rd Castorland (13620) ***(G-3299)***
Daniel Demarco and Assoc Inc 631 598-7000
25 Greene Ave Amityville (11701) ***(G-271)***
Daniel M Friedman & Assoc Inc 212 695-5545
19 W 34th St Fl 4 New York (10001) ***(G-9468)***
Daniel O Reich Incorporated 718 748-6000
7518 3rd Ave Brooklyn (11209) ***(G-1756)***
Danisco US Inc 585 256-5200
3490 Winton Pl Rochester (14623) ***(G-13733)***
Danisco US Inc 585 277-4300
1700 Lexington Ave Rochester (14606) ***(G-13734)***
Danner, Eg Mfg, Central Islip *Also called Eugene G Danner Mfg Inc* ***(G-3368)***
Dannon Company, LLC, White Plains *Also called Danone Us LLC* ***(G-16442)***
Danny & Nicole, New York *Also called Kelly Grace Corp* ***(G-10428)***
Danny Macaroons Inc 260 622-8463
2191 3rd Ave Ste 3 New York (10035) ***(G-9469)***
Danone Nutricia Early 914 872-8556
100 Hillside Ave White Plains (10603) ***(G-16441)***
Danone Us LLC (HQ) 914 872-8400
1 Maple Ave White Plains (10605) ***(G-16442)***
Danray Textiles Corp (PA) 212 354-5213
270 W 39th St Fl 5 New York (10018) ***(G-9470)***
Dans Paper Inc 631 537-0500
158 County Road 39 Southampton (11968) ***(G-14952)***
Dansville Logging & Lumber 585 335-5879
10903 State Route 36 Dansville (14437) ***(G-3925)***
Dantex Trimming & Textile Co, New York *Also called Danray Textiles Corp* ***(G-9470)***
Dapper Dads Inc 917 903-8045
45 Rochester Ave Brooklyn (11233) ***(G-1757)***
Darby Dental Supply 516 688-6421
105 Executive Ct Jericho (11753) ***(G-6785)***
Darco Manufacturing Inc 315 432-8905
6756 Thompson Rd Syracuse (13211) ***(G-15302)***
DArcy Printing and Lithog 212 924-1554
121 Varick St Fl 9 New York (10013) ***(G-9471)***
Dark Star Lithograph Corp 845 634-3780
9 Perth Ln New City (10956) ***(G-8490)***
Dark Storm Industries LLC 631 967-3170
4116 Sunrise Hwy Oakdale (11769) ***(G-12515)***
Darling Ingredients Inc 716 895-0655
2000 William St Buffalo (14206) ***(G-2793)***
Darman Manufacturing Coinc 315 724-9632
1410 Lincoln Ave Utica (13502) ***(G-15692)***
Darrell Mitchell 646 659-7075
704 Beach 67th St Arverne (11692) ***(G-414)***
Dart Awning Inc 516 544-2082
365 S Main St Freeport (11520) ***(G-5150)***
Dart Communications, New Hartford *Also called Dartcom Incorporated* ***(G-8502)***
Dartcom Incorporated 315 790-5456
2 Oxford Xing Ste 1 New Hartford (13413) ***(G-8502)***
Das Yidishe Licht Inc 718 387-3166
66 Middleton St Apt 1 Brooklyn (11206) ***(G-1758)***
Dash Printing Inc 212 643-8534
153 W 27th St New York (10001) ***(G-9472)***
Dashlane Inc 212 596-7510
156 5th Ave Ste 504 New York (10010) ***(G-9473)***
Dason Company Div, New York *Also called D R S Inc* ***(G-9449)***
Data Control Inc 585 265-2980
277 David Pkwy Ontario (14519) ***(G-12651)***
Data Device Corporation (HQ) 631 567-5600
105 Wilbur Pl Bohemia (11716) ***(G-1008)***
Data Display USA Inc 631 218-2130
1330 Lincoln Ave Ste 2 Holbrook (11741) ***(G-6182)***
Data Flow Inc 631 436-9200
6 Balsam Dr Medford (11763) ***(G-7945)***
Data Implementation Inc 212 979-2015
5 E 22nd St Apt 14t New York (10010) ***(G-9474)***
Data Key Communication LLC 315 445-2347
7573 Hunt Ln Fayetteville (13066) ***(G-4927)***
Data Max, New York *Also called Datamax International Inc* ***(G-9476)***
Data Palette Info Svcs LLC 718 433-1060
35 Marino Ave Port Washington (11050) ***(G-13251)***
Data-Pac Mailing Systems Corp 585 671-0210
1217 Bay Rd Ste 12 Webster (14580) ***(G-16081)***
Datacom Systems Inc 315 463-9541
9 Adler Dr East Syracuse (13057) ***(G-4334)***
Datadog Inc (PA) 866 329-4466
620 8th Ave Fl 45 New York (10018) ***(G-9475)***
Datagraphic Business Systems 516 485-9069
79 Emjay Blvd Brentwood (11717) ***(G-1130)***
Datalink Computer Products 914 666-2358
165 E Main St 175 Mount Kisco (10549) ***(G-8341)***
Datamax International Inc 212 693-0933
132 Nassau St Rm 511 New York (10038) ***(G-9476)***
Datasonic Inc 516 248-7330
1413 Cleveland Ave East Meadow (11554) ***(G-4249)***
Datatran Labs Inc 845 856-4313
11 Rebel Ln Port Jervis (12771) ***(G-13227)***
Datesweiser, Buffalo *Also called Knoll Inc* ***(G-2908)***
Datorib Inc 631 698-6222
974 Middle Country Rd Selden (11784) ***(G-14763)***
Datum Alloys Inc 607 239-6274
407 Airport Rd Endicott (13760) ***(G-4586)***
Dave & Johnny Ltd 212 302-9050
225 W 37th St Fl 6 New York (10018) ***(G-9477)***
Dave Sandel Cranes Inc 631 325-5588
56 S Country Rd Westhampton (11977) ***(G-16401)***
Davel Systems Inc 718 382-6024
1314 Avenue M Brooklyn (11230) ***(G-1759)***
Davenport, Rochester *Also called Brinkman Products Inc* ***(G-13677)***
Daves Electric Motors & Pumps 212 982-2930
282 E 7th St Apt 1 New York (10009) ***(G-9478)***
Daves Precision Machine Shop 845 626-7263
56 Webster Ave Kerhonkson (12446) ***(G-6868)***
David & Young Co Inc 212 594-6034
366 5th Ave Rm 707 New York (10001) ***(G-9479)***
David F De Marco 315 536-0882
929 Davy Rd Penn Yan (14527) ***(G-12952)***
David Fehlman 315 455-8888
6729 Pickard Dr Syracuse (13211) ***(G-15303)***
David Flatt Furniture Ltd 718 937-7944
3842 Review Ave Ste 2 Long Island City (11101) ***(G-7421)***
David Friedman and Sons, New York *Also called David Friedman Chain Co Inc* ***(G-9480)***
David Friedman Chain Co Inc 212 684-1760
10 E 38th St Fl 6 New York (10016) ***(G-9480)***
David Helsing 607 796-2681
2077 Grand Central Ave Horseheads (14845) ***(G-6311)***
David Howell & Company, Bedford Hills *Also called David Howell Product Design* ***(G-774)***
David Howell Product Design 914 666-4080
405 Adams St Bedford Hills (10507) ***(G-774)***
David Isseks & Sons Inc 212 966-8694
298 Broome St New York (10002) ***(G-9481)***
David Johnson 315 493-4735
Deer River Rd Carthage (13619) ***(G-3290)***
David King Linen Inc 718 241-7298
295 5th Ave Ste 1202 New York (10016) ***(G-9482)***
David Kucera Inc 845 255-1044
42 Steves Ln Gardiner (12525) ***(G-5293)***
David Peyser Sportswear Inc (PA) 631 231-7788
90 Spence St Bay Shore (11706) ***(G-678)***
David Peyser Sportswear Inc 212 695-7716
4 Bryant Park Fl 12 Flr 12 New York (10018) ***(G-9483)***
David S Diamonds Inc 212 921-8029
546 5th Ave Fl 7 New York (10036) ***(G-9484)***
David Sutherland Showrooms - N (PA) 212 871-9717
D&D Building 979 3rd New York (10022) ***(G-9485)***
David Weeks Studio 212 966-3433
38 Walker St Frnt 1 New York (10013) ***(G-9486)***
David Weisz & Sons USA LLC 212 840-4747
20 W 47th St Ste 601 New York (10036) ***(G-9487)***
David Yurman Enterprises LLC 914 539-4444
125 Westchester Ave # 1060 White Plains (10601) ***(G-16443)***
David Yurman Enterprises LLC (PA) 212 896-1550
24 Vestry St New York (10013) ***(G-9488)***
David Yurman Enterprises LLC 845 928-8660
484 Evergreen Ct Central Valley (10917) ***(G-3395)***
David Yurman Retail LLC 877 226-1400
712 Madison Ave New York (10065) ***(G-9489)***
Davidson Grinding Corp 631 563-3982
220 Mccormick Dr Bohemia (11716) ***(G-1009)***

Davidson Publishing, New York *Also called Boardman Simons Publishing* ***(G-9115)***
Davies Office Refurbishing Inc (PA).......518 426-7188
40 Loudonville Rd Albany (12204) ***(G-67)***
Davinci Designs Inc.......631 595-1095
20 Lucon Dr Unit A Deer Park (11729) ***(G-3962)***
Davinci Dsgns Distinctive Furn, Deer Park *Also called Davinci Designs Inc* ***(G-3962)***
Davis.......716 833-4678
283 Minnesota Ave Buffalo (14215) ***(G-2794)***
Davis Aircraft Products Co Inc.......631 563-1500
1150 Walnut Ave Ste 1 Bohemia (11716) ***(G-1010)***
Davis International Inc.......585 421-8175
388 Mason Rd Fairport (14450) ***(G-4631)***
Davis Logging & Lumber.......315 245-1040
1450 Curtiss Rd Camden (13316) ***(G-3187)***
Davis Trailer World LLC.......585 538-6640
1640 Main St York (14592) ***(G-16813)***
Davis Trlr World & Cntry Mall, York *Also called Davis Trailer World LLC* ***(G-16813)***
Davler Media Group LLC (PA).......212 315-0800
213 W 35th St Rm 1201 New York (10001) ***(G-9490)***
Davos Brands LLC.......212 779-1911
381 Park Ave S Rm 1015 New York (10016) ***(G-9491)***
Dawn Food Products Inc.......716 830-8214
160 Lawrence Bell Dr # 120 Williamsville (14221) ***(G-16577)***
Dawn Paper Co Inc (PA).......516 596-9110
4 Leonard Dr East Rockaway (11518) ***(G-4294)***
Dawn Printing Company, East Rockaway *Also called Dawn Paper Co Inc* ***(G-4294)***
Dawnex Industries Inc.......718 384-0199
861 Park Ave Brooklyn (11206) ***(G-1760)***
Dawson Doors, Jamestown *Also called Dawson Metal Company Inc* ***(G-6711)***
Dawson Metal Company Inc.......716 664-3811
825 Allen St Jamestown (14701) ***(G-6711)***
Daxor Corporation (PA).......212 330-8500
350 5th Ave Ste 4740 New York (10118) ***(G-9492)***
Day Automation Systems Inc (PA).......585 924-4630
7931 Rae Blvd Victor (14564) ***(G-15841)***
Day One Lighting, Suffern *Also called E-Ffinergy Group LLC* ***(G-15189)***
Dayleen Intimates Inc.......914 969-5900
540 Nepperhan Ave Yonkers (10701) ***(G-16749)***
Daylight Technology USA Inc.......973 255-8100
5971 59th St Maspeth (11378) ***(G-7835)***
Dayton Industries Inc.......718 542-8144
1350 Garrison Ave Bronx (10474) ***(G-1254)***
Dayton Rogers New York LLC.......585 349-4040
150 Fedex Way Rochester (14624) ***(G-13735)***
Dayton T Brown Inc (PA).......631 589-6300
1175 Church St Bohemia (11716) ***(G-1011)***
Dbase LLC.......607 729-0234
100 Emerson Pkwy Binghamton (13905) ***(G-879)***
Dbg Media.......718 599-6828
358 Classon Ave Brooklyn (11238) ***(G-1761)***
Dbs Interiors Corp.......631 491-3013
81 Otis St West Babylon (11704) ***(G-16152)***
DC Contracting & Building Corp.......631 385-1117
136 Railroad St Huntington Station (11746) ***(G-6438)***
DC Fabrication & Welding Inc.......845 295-0215
17 Radcliff Rd Ferndale (12734) ***(G-4932)***
Dcl Furniture Manufacturing.......516 248-2683
96 Windsor Ave Mineola (11501) ***(G-8215)***
Ddc Technologies Inc.......516 594-1533
311 Woods Ave Oceanside (11572) ***(G-12535)***
De Ans Pork Products Inc (PA).......718 788-2464
899 4th Ave Brooklyn (11232) ***(G-1762)***
De Iorio's Bakery, Utica *Also called Deiorio Foods Inc* ***(G-15693)***
De Luxe Packaging Corp.......416 754-4633
63 North St Saugerties (12477) ***(G-14606)***
De Marco Vineyards, Penn Yan *Also called David F De Marco* ***(G-12952)***
De Meo Brothers Hair, New York *Also called De Meo Brothers Inc* ***(G-9493)***
De Meo Brothers Inc (PA).......212 268-1400
129 W 29th St Fl 5 New York (10001) ***(G-9493)***
De Originals Ltd.......516 474-6544
22 Laurel Ln Old Westbury (11568) ***(G-12590)***
De Santis Holster and Lea Gds, Amityville *Also called Helgen Industries Inc* ***(G-283)***
Dead Ringer LLC.......585 355-4685
2100 Brghton Hnrtta St375 Rochester (14623) ***(G-13736)***
Deakon Homes and Interiors.......518 271-0342
16 Industrial Park Rd Troy (12180) ***(G-15603)***
Deal, New York *Also called Dnp Electronics America LLC* ***(G-9543)***
Deal International Inc.......585 288-4444
110 Halstead St Ste 1 Rochester (14610) ***(G-13737)***
Dean Foods Company.......315 452-5001
6867 Schuyler Rd East Syracuse (13057) ***(G-4335)***
Dean Manufacturing Inc.......607 770-1300
413 Commerce Rd Vestal (13850) ***(G-15814)***
Dean Trading Corp.......718 485-0600
200 Junius St Brooklyn (11212) ***(G-1763)***
Deanco Digital Printing LLC.......212 371-2025
4545 39th St Sunnyside (11104) ***(G-15202)***
Deangelis Ltd.......212 348-8225
262 Glen Head Rd Glen Head (11545) ***(G-5379)***
Deans Paving Inc.......315 736-7601
6002 Cavanaugh Rd Marcy (13403) ***(G-7796)***
Dearfoams Div, New York *Also called RG Barry Corporation* ***(G-11382)***
Death Wish Coffee Company LLC.......518 400-1050
100 Saratoga Village Blvd # 3 Ballston Spa (12020) ***(G-579)***
Debmar-Mercury.......212 669-5025
75 Rockefeller Plz # 1600 New York (10019) ***(G-9494)***
Deborah Connolly & Associates, New York *Also called Arabella Textiles LLC* ***(G-8897)***
Debra Fisher, Valley Stream *Also called Ready To Assemble Company Inc* ***(G-15794)***
Debrucque Cleveland Tramrail S.......315 697-5160
3 Technology Blvd Canastota (13032) ***(G-3243)***
Decal Makers Inc.......516 221-7200
2477 Merrick Rd Bellmore (11710) ***(G-788)***
Decal Techniques Inc.......631 491-1800
40 Corbin Ave Ste I Bay Shore (11706) ***(G-679)***
Deck Bros Inc.......716 852-0262
222 Chicago St Buffalo (14204) ***(G-2795)***
Decker Forest Products Inc.......607 563-2345
New York State Rte 8 Sidney (13838) ***(G-14852)***
Decorated Cookie Company LLC.......315 487-2111
314 Lakeside Rd Syracuse (13209) ***(G-15304)***
Decorative Hardeware.......914 238-5251
180 Hunts Ln Chappaqua (10514) ***(G-3421)***
Decree Signs & Graphics Inc.......973 278-3603
91 Tulip Ave Apt Kd1 Floral Park (11001) ***(G-4962)***
Dedeco International Sales Inc (PA).......845 887-4840
11617 State Route 97 Long Eddy (12760) ***(G-7361)***
Deedee Desserts LLC.......716 627-2330
6969 Southwestern Blvd Lake View (14085) ***(G-6982)***
Deejays, Monsey *Also called DJS Nyc Inc* ***(G-8287)***
Deer Park Driveshaft & Hose.......631 667-4091
85 Brook Ave Ste C Deer Park (11729) ***(G-3963)***
Deer Park Drv Shaft & Hose Co, Deer Park *Also called Deer Park Driveshaft & Hose* ***(G-3963)***
Deer Park Macaroni Co Inc (PA).......631 667-4600
1882 Deer Park Ave Deer Park (11729) ***(G-3964)***
Deer Park Macaroni Co Inc.......631 667-4600
1882 Deer Park Ave Deer Park (11729) ***(G-3965)***
Deer Park Ravioli & Macaroni, Deer Park *Also called Deer Park Macaroni Co Inc* ***(G-3965)***
Deer Park Sand & Gravel Corp.......631 586-2323
145 S 4th St Bay Shore (11706) ***(G-680)***
Deer Pk Stair Bldg Mllwk Inc.......631 363-5000
51 Kennedy Ave Blue Point (11715) ***(G-964)***
Deer Run Enterprises Inc.......585 346-0850
3772 W Lake Rd Geneseo (14454) ***(G-5314)***
Deer Run Winery, Geneseo *Also called Deer Run Enterprises Inc* ***(G-5314)***
Deerfield Millwork Inc.......631 726-9663
58 Deerfield Rd Unit 2 Water Mill (11976) ***(G-15969)***
Dees Audio & Vision.......585 719-9256
347 Seneca Pkwy Rochester (14613) ***(G-13738)***
Defelsko Corporation.......315 393-4450
800 Proctor Ave Ogdensburg (13669) ***(G-12573)***
Definition Press Inc.......212 777-4490
141 Greene St New York (10012) ***(G-9495)***
Defran Systems Inc.......212 727-8342
1 Penn Plz Ste 1700 New York (10119) ***(G-9496)***
Degennaro Fuel Service LLC.......518 239-6350
242 County Route 357 Medusa (12120) ***(G-7993)***
Deiorio Foods Inc (PA).......315 732-7612
2200 Bleecker St Utica (13501) ***(G-15693)***
Dejana Trck Utility Eqp Co LLC (HQ).......631 544-9000
490 Pulaski Rd Kings Park (11754) ***(G-6882)***
Dejana Trck Utility Eqp Co LLC.......631 549-0944
743 Park Ave Huntington (11743) ***(G-6397)***
Dejana Truck & Utility Eqp Co, Huntington *Also called Dejana Trck Utility Eqp Co LLC* ***(G-6397)***
Delaney Books Inc.......516 921-8888
212 Michael Dr Syosset (11791) ***(G-15215)***
Delaney Machine Products Ltd.......631 225-1032
150 S Alleghany Ave Ste A Lindenhurst (11757) ***(G-7168)***
Delaval Inc.......585 599-4696
850 Main Rd Corfu (14036) ***(G-3806)***
Delaware County Times Inc.......607 746-2176
56 Main St Delhi (13753) ***(G-4072)***
Delaware Manufacturing Inds, North Tonawanda *Also called Dmic Inc* ***(G-12425)***
Delaware Valley Forge Co Inc.......716 447-9140
247 Rano St Buffalo (14207) ***(G-2796)***
Delaware Valley Forge Inc.......716 447-9140
241 Rano St Buffalo (14207) ***(G-2797)***
Delbia Do Company Inc (PA).......718 585-2226
2550 Park Ave Bronx (10451) ***(G-1255)***
Delbia Do Company Inc.......718 585-2226
11 Canal Pl Bronx (10451) ***(G-1256)***
Delcath Systems Inc (PA).......212 489-2100
1633 Broadway Fl 22c New York (10019) ***(G-9497)***
Delectable, New York *Also called Vinous Group LLC* ***(G-12036)***
Delfingen Us-New York Inc.......716 215-0300
2221 Niagara Falls Blvd # 12 Niagara Falls (14304) ***(G-12277)***
Delford Industries Inc.......845 342-3901
82 Washington St 84 Middletown (10940) ***(G-8147)***
Delft Printing Inc.......716 683-1100
1000 Commerce Pkwy Lancaster (14086) ***(G-7015)***

ALPHABETIC

Delicias Andinas Food Corp 718 416-2922
  5750 Maspeth Ave Flushing (11378) *(G-4995)*
Delicioso Coco Helado Inc 718 292-1930
  849 Saint Anns Ave Bronx (10456) *(G-1257)*
Delicious Foods Inc 718 446-9352
  11202 Roosevelt Ave Corona (11368) *(G-3843)*
Dell Communications Inc 212 989-3434
  109 W 27th St Frnt 2 New York (10001) *(G-9498)*
Dell Graphics, New York Also called Dell Communications Inc *(G-9498)*
Dell's Maraschino Cherries Co, Brooklyn Also called Dells Cherries LLC *(G-1765)*
Della Systems Inc 631 580-0010
  951 S 2nd St Ronkonkoma (11779) *(G-14333)*
Dellas Graphics, Rochester Also called Canfield & Tack Inc *(G-13689)*
Dellet Industries Inc 718 965-0101
  1 43rd St Ste L8 Brooklyn (11232) *(G-1764)*
Dells Cherries LLC 718 624-4380
  175 Dikeman St Ste 177 Brooklyn (11231) *(G-1765)*
Dells Cherries LLC 718 624-4380
  81 Ferris St Brooklyn (11231) *(G-1766)*
Delocon Wholesale Inc 716 592-2711
  270 W Main St Springville (14141) *(G-15015)*
Deloka LLC 315 946-6910
  150 Dunn Rd Lyons (14489) *(G-7684)*
Delphi Amherst Test Operations, Amherst Also called Delphi Automotive LLP *(G-224)*
Delphi Automotive LLP 716 438-4886
  4326 Ridge Lea Rd Amherst (14226) *(G-224)*
Delphi Powertrain Systems LLC 585 359-6000
  5500 W Henrietta Rd West Henrietta (14586) *(G-16236)*
Delphi Powertrain Systems LLC 585 359-6000
  5500 W Henrietta Rd West Henrietta (14586) *(G-16237)*
Delphi Powertrain Systems LLC 585 359-6000
  5500 W Henrietta Rd West Henrietta (14586) *(G-16238)*
Delphi Thermal Systems 716 439-2454
  350 Upper Mountain Rd Lockport (14094) *(G-7293)*
Delphi Thrmal Lckport Model Sp, Lockport Also called Mahle Behr USA Inc *(G-7314)*
Delphi-T Compressor Engrg Ctr, Amherst Also called Mahle Indstrbeteiligungen GMBH *(G-237)*
Delroyd Worm Gear, Niagara Falls Also called Nuttall Gear L L C *(G-12317)*
Delsur Parts 631 630-1606
  112 Pheasant Cir Brentwood (11717) *(G-1131)*
Delta Lock Company LLC 631 238-7035
  366 Central Ave Bohemia (11716) *(G-1012)*
Delta Polymers Inc 631 254-6240
  130 S 2nd St Bay Shore (11706) *(G-681)*
Delta Press Inc 212 989-3445
  2426 Lucas Tpke High Falls (12440) *(G-6140)*
Delta Sheet Metal Corp 718 429-5805
  3935 Skillman Ave Long Island City (11104) *(G-7422)*
Deluxe Corporation 845 362-4054
  9 Lincoln Ave Spring Valley (10977) *(G-14988)*
Deluxe Machine & Tool Co, Batavia Also called Bill Shea Enterprises Inc *(G-613)*
Deluxe Packaging Corp 845 246-6090
  63 North St Saugerties (12477) *(G-14607)*
Deluxe Passport Express, Brooklyn Also called Deluxe Travel Store Inc *(G-1767)*
Deluxe Travel Store Inc 718 435-8111
  5014 12th Ave Brooklyn (11219) *(G-1767)*
Demartini Oil Equipment Svc 518 463-5752
  214 River Rd Glenmont (12077) *(G-5411)*
Deming Electro-Plating Corp 585 968-2355
  5 Woodruff St Cuba (14727) *(G-3918)*
Democrat & Chronicle, Rochester Also called Gannett Co Inc *(G-13822)*
Democrat & Chronicle, Farmington Also called Gannett Co Inc *(G-4914)*
Demos Medical Publishing LLC 516 889-1791
  11 W 42nd St Ste 15c New York (10036) *(G-9499)*
Deniz Information Systems 212 750-5199
  208 E 51st St Ste 129 New York (10022) *(G-9500)*
Denmar Electric 845 624-4430
  202 Main St Nanuet (10954) *(G-8463)*
Dennies Manufacturing Inc 585 393-4646
  2543 State Route 21 Canandaigua (14424) *(G-3218)*
Dennis Basso Couture Inc 212 794-4500
  825 Madison Ave New York (10065) *(G-9501)*
Dennis Basso Furs, New York Also called Dennis Basso Couture Inc *(G-9501)*
Dennis Publishing Inc 646 717-9500
  55 W 39th St Fl 5 New York (10018) *(G-9502)*
Denny Machine Co Inc 716 873-6865
  20 Norris St Buffalo (14207) *(G-2798)*
Dennys Drive Shaft Service 716 875-6640
  1189 Military Rd Kenmore (14217) *(G-6858)*
Dental Tribune America LLC 212 244-7181
  116 W 23rd St Ste 500 New York (10011) *(G-9503)*
DenTek Oral Care Inc (HQ) 865 983-1300
  660 White Plains Rd # 250 Tarrytown (10591) *(G-15477)*
Denton Advertising Inc 631 586-4333
  1650 Sycamore Ave Ste 28 Bohemia (11716) *(G-1013)*
Denton Publications Inc (PA) 518 873-6368
  14 Hand Ave Elizabethtown (12932) *(G-4430)*
Denton Publications Inc 518 561-9680
  21 Mckinley Ave Ste 3 Plattsburgh (12901) *(G-13119)*
Denton Stoneworks Inc 516 746-1500
  94 Denton Ave Garden City Park (11040) *(G-5285)*

Denvin Inc 718 232-3389
  6520 New Utrecht Ave Brooklyn (11219) *(G-1768)*
Department of Sanitation, Brooklyn Also called City of New York *(G-1696)*
Depco Inc 631 582-1995
  20 Newton Pl Hauppauge (11788) *(G-5809)*
Dependable Acme Threaded Pdts 516 338-4700
  167 School St Westbury (11590) *(G-16322)*
Dependable Lithographers Inc 718 472-4200
  3200 Skillman Ave Long Island City (11101) *(G-7423)*
Dependable Tool & Die Co Inc 315 453-5696
  129 Dwight Park Cir # 2 Syracuse (13209) *(G-15305)*
Depot Label Company Inc 631 467-2952
  217 River Ave Patchogue (11772) *(G-12864)*
Depp Glass Inc 718 784-8500
  4140 38th St Long Island City (11101) *(G-7424)*
Depuy Synthes Inc 607 271-2500
  35 Airport Rd Horseheads (14845) *(G-6312)*
Der Blatt Inc 845 783-1148
  6 Taitch Ct Unit 112 Monroe (10950) *(G-8268)*
Der Yid Inc 718 797-3900
  84 Bay St Brooklyn (11231) *(G-1769)*
Der Yid Publication, Brooklyn Also called Der Yid Inc *(G-1769)*
Deraffele Mfg Co Inc 914 636-6850
  2525 Palmer Ave Ste 4 New Rochelle (10801) *(G-8598)*
Derby Fashion Center, Conklin Also called S & T Knitting Co Inc *(G-3732)*
Derecktor Shipyards, Mamaroneck Also called Robert E Derecktor Inc *(G-7756)*
Dereon/24 K Style, New York Also called Rvc Enterprises LLC *(G-11451)*
Derm-Buro Inc (PA) 516 694-8300
  229 Newtown Rd Plainview (11803) *(G-13050)*
Dermatech Labs Inc 631 225-1700
  165 S 10th St Lindenhurst (11757) *(G-7169)*
Dern Moore Machine Company Inc 716 433-6243
  151 S Niagara St Lockport (14094) *(G-7294)*
Derosa Fabrications Inc 631 563-0640
  250 Knickerbocker Ave Bohemia (11716) *(G-1014)*
Derrick Corporation (PA) 716 683-9010
  590 Duke Rd Buffalo (14225) *(G-2799)*
Derrick Corporation 716 685-4892
  2540 Walden Ave Cheektowaga (14225) *(G-3440)*
Derrick Equipment, Buffalo Also called Derrick Corporation *(G-2799)*
Design Archives Inc 212 768-0617
  1460 Broadway New York (10036) *(G-9504)*
Design Craft Division, Jamestown Also called Larson Metal Manufacturing Co *(G-6736)*
Design Distributors Inc 631 242-2000
  300 Marcus Blvd Deer Park (11729) *(G-3966)*
Design Interiors, Brooklyn Also called Atlantic Stairs Corp *(G-1571)*
Design Lithographers Inc 212 645-8900
  519 8th Ave Ste 3 New York (10018) *(G-9505)*
Design Research Ltd 212 228-7675
  243 Centre St New York (10013) *(G-9506)*
Design Solutions LI Inc 631 656-8700
  711 Middle Country Rd Saint James (11780) *(G-14511)*
Design Source By Lg Inc 212 274-0022
  115 Bowery Frnt 1 New York (10002) *(G-9507)*
Design Works Craft Inc (PA) 631 244-5749
  70 Orville Dr Ste 1 Bohemia (11716) *(G-1015)*
Design/OI Inc 631 474-5536
  200 Wilson St Unit D2 Port Jeff STA (11776) *(G-13213)*
Designatronics Incorporated (PA) 516 328-3300
  250 Duffy Ave Unit A Hicksville (11801) *(G-6079)*
Designatronics Incorporated 516 328-3300
  250 Duffy Ave Unit A Hicksville (11801) *(G-6080)*
Designer Epoxy Finishes Inc 646 943-6044
  445 Broadhollow Rd Ste 25 Melville (11747) *(G-8015)*
Designer Glass, College Point Also called Gmd Industries Inc *(G-3645)*
Designers Folding Box Corp 716 853-5141
  84 Tennessee St Buffalo (14204) *(G-2800)*
Designlogocom Inc 212 564-0200
  15 W 37th St Lbby A New York (10018) *(G-9508)*
Designplex LLC 845 358-6647
  107 Cedar Hill Ave Nyack (10960) *(G-12504)*
Designs By Hc, New York Also called Horo Creations LLC *(G-10124)*
Designs By Novello Inc 914 934-7711
  505 N Main St Port Chester (10573) *(G-13196)*
Designs By Robert Scott Inc 718 609-2535
  810 Humboldt St Ste 3 Brooklyn (11222) *(G-1770)*
Designs For Vision Inc 631 585-3300
  4000 Veterans Mem Hwy Bohemia (11716) *(G-1016)*
Designway Ltd 212 254-2220
  27 E 21st St Fl 7 New York (10010) *(G-9509)*
Desiron, New York Also called F&M Ornamental Designs LLC *(G-9763)*
Desiron, New York Also called F&M Ornamental Designs LLC *(G-9764)*
Desktop Publishing Concepts 631 752-1934
  855 Conklin St Ste T Farmingdale (11735) *(G-4750)*
Desku Group Inc 646 436-1464
  7206 7th Ave Brooklyn (11209) *(G-1771)*
Desmi-Afti Inc 716 662-0632
  227 Thorn Ave Bldg C Orchard Park (14127) *(G-12713)*
Dessin/Fournir Inc 212 758-0844
  232 E 59th St Fl 2 New York (10022) *(G-9510)*
Dessy Creations, New York Also called A & M Rosenthal Entps Inc *(G-8688)*

Desu Machinery Corporation 716 681-5798
200 Gould Ave Depew (14043) *(G-4087)*
Detekion Security Systems Inc 607 729-7179
200 Plaza Dr Ste 1 Vestal (13850) *(G-15815)*
Detny Footwear Inc 212 423-1040
1 River Pl Apt 1224 New York (10036) *(G-9511)*
Detour Apparel Inc (PA) 212 221-3265
530 7th Ave Rm 608 New York (10018) *(G-9512)*
Detox Water, Brooklyn *Also called Superleaf LLC (G-2539)*
Deunall Corporation 516 667-8875
147 Blacksmith Rd E Levittown (11756) *(G-7133)*
Deutsch Relays 631 342-1700
55 Engineers Rd Hauppauge (11788) *(G-5810)*
Deux Lux Inc 212 620-0801
37 W 20th St Ste 1204 New York (10011) *(G-9513)*
Deva Concepts LLC 212 343-0344
75 Spring St Fl 8 New York (10012) *(G-9514)*
Devacurl, New York *Also called Deva Concepts LLC (G-9514)*
Devil Dog Manufacturing Co Inc (PA) 845 647-4411
23 Market St Ellenville (12428) *(G-4438)*
Devin Mfg Inc 585 496-5770
40 Edward St Arcade (14009) *(G-381)*
Devonian Stone New York Inc 607 655-2600
463 Atwell Hill Rd Windsor (13865) *(G-16604)*
Dew Graphics, New York *Also called DEW Graphics Inc (G-9515)*
DEW Graphics Inc 212 727-8820
519 8th Ave Fl 18 New York (10018) *(G-9515)*
Dewey Machine & Tool Inc 607 749-3930
49 James St Homer (13077) *(G-6253)*
Dewitt Plastics Inc 315 255-1209
28 Aurelius Ave Auburn (13021) *(G-476)*
Dezawy LLC 917 436-8820
55 W 116th St Ste 327 New York (10026) *(G-9516)*
Df Mavens Inc 347 813-4705
2420 49th St Astoria (11103) *(G-424)*
DFA New York LLC 212 523-0021
318 W 39th St Fl 10 New York (10018) *(G-9517)*
DH Machine Tool Services, Marathon *Also called Gallery of Machines LLC (G-7789)*
Dhs Systems LLC (HQ) 845 359-6066
560 Route 303 Ste 206 Orangeburg (10962) *(G-12674)*
Di Borghese Castello LLC 631 734-5111
17150 County Road 48 Cutchogue (11935) *(G-3921)*
Di Domenico Packaging Co Inc 718 727-5454
304 Bertram Ave Staten Island (10312) *(G-15068)*
Di Fiore and Sons Custom Wdwkg 718 278-1663
4202 Astoria Blvd Long Island City (11103) *(G-7425)*
Di Highway Sign Structure Corp 315 736-8312
40 Greenman Ave New York Mills (13417) *(G-12185)*
Di Sanos Creative Canvas Inc 315 894-3137
113 W Main St Frankfort (13340) *(G-5105)*
DI ZUKUNFT, New York *Also called Congress For Jewish Culture (G-9379)*
Dia 212 675-4097
535 W 22nd St Fl 4 New York (10011) *(G-9518)*
Dialase Inc 212 575-8833
36 W 47th St Ste 709 New York (10036) *(G-9519)*
Diam International, Yonkers *Also called Creative Solutions Group Inc (G-16748)*
Diamex Inc 212 575-8145
580 5th Ave Ste 625 New York (10036) *(G-9520)*
Diamond Boutique 516 444-3373
77 Main St Port Washington (11050) *(G-13252)*
Diamond Constellation Corp 212 819-0324
37 W 47th St Ste 506 New York (10036) *(G-9521)*
Diamond Coring & Cutting Inc 718 381-4545
5919 55th St Maspeth (11378) *(G-7836)*
Diamond Dimensions, Mount Vernon *Also called Aaron Group LLC (G-8372)*
Diamond Distributors Inc (PA) 212 921-9188
608 5th Ave Fl 10 New York (10020) *(G-9522)*
Diamond Inscription Tech 646 366-7944
36 W 47th St Ste 1008 New York (10036) *(G-9523)*
Diamond Packaging Holdings LLC 585 334-8030
111 Commerce Dr Rochester (14623) *(G-13739)*
Diamond Precast Products Inc 631 874-3777
170 Railroad Ave Center Moriches (11934) *(G-3338)*
Diamond Saw Works Inc (PA) 716 496-7417
12290 Olean Rd Chaffee (14030) *(G-3402)*
Diana Kane Incorporated 718 638-6520
229 5th Ave Ste B Brooklyn (11215) *(G-1772)*
Diane Artemis Studios, Brooklyn *Also called Artemis Studios Inc (G-1558)*
Diane Studios Inc (PA) 718 788-6007
34 35th St Ste 2b Brooklyn (11232) *(G-1773)*
Diane Von Furstenberg The Shop, New York *Also called Dvf Studio LLC (G-9589)*
Dianos Kathryn Designs 212 267-1584
376 Broadway Apt 13b New York (10013) *(G-9524)*
Dib Managmnt Inc 718 439-8190
251 53rd St Brooklyn (11220) *(G-1774)*
Dicamillo Marble and Granite 845 878-0078
20 Jon Barrett Rd Patterson (12563) *(G-12880)*
Dice America Inc 585 869-6200
7676 Netlink Dr Victor (14564) *(G-15842)*
Dick Bailey Printers, Brooklyn *Also called Dick Bailey Service Inc (G-1775)*
Dick Bailey Service Inc 718 522-4363
25 Chapel St Ste 602 Brooklyn (11201) *(G-1775)*
Dicks Concrete Co Inc (PA) 845 374-5966
1053 County Route 37 New Hampton (10958) *(G-8499)*
Dico Products, Utica *Also called Divine Brothers Company (G-15698)*
Dico Products Corporation 315 797-0470
200 Seward Ave Utica (13502) *(G-15694)*
Didco Inc 212 997-5022
8570 67th Ave Rego Park (11374) *(G-13461)*
Die-Matic Products LLC 516 433-7900
130 Express St Plainview (11803) *(G-13051)*
Diegraphics Group, Rochester *Also called Csw Inc (G-13727)*
Diehl Development Inc 585 494-2920
5922 N Lake Rd Bergen (14416) *(G-819)*
Diehl Sand & Gravel, Bergen *Also called Diehl Development Inc (G-819)*
Diemax of Rochester Inc 585 288-3912
1555 Lyell Ave Ste 141 Rochester (14606) *(G-13740)*
Diemolding Corporation (PA) 315 363-4710
100 Donald Hicks Dew Dr Wampsville (13163) *(G-15917)*
Diemolding Corporation 315 363-4710
N Court St Wampsville (13163) *(G-15918)*
Dietooling, Wampsville *Also called Diemolding Corporation (G-15918)*
DIEU DONNE, Brooklyn *Also called Donne Dieu Paper Mill Inc (G-1788)*
Digicom International Inc 631 249-8999
145 Rome St Farmingdale (11735) *(G-4751)*
Digiday, New York *Also called Dm2 Media LLC (G-9542)*
Digifab Systems Inc 212 944-9882
1412 Broadway Ste 2100 New York (10018) *(G-9525)*
Digiorange Inc 718 787-1500
5620 1st Ave Ste 4 Brooklyn (11220) *(G-1776)*
Digitac Inc (PA) 732 215-4020
2076 Ocean Pkwy Brooklyn (11223) *(G-1777)*
Digital Analysis Corporation 315 685-0760
716 Visions Dr Skaneateles (13152) *(G-14869)*
Digital Associates LLC 631 983-6075
50 Karl Ave Ste 303 Smithtown (11787) *(G-14896)*
Digital Color Concepts Inc (PA) 212 989-4888
30 W 21st St Fl 5 New York (10010) *(G-9526)*
Digital Evolution Inc (PA) 212 732-2722
200 N End Ave Apt 20e New York (10282) *(G-9527)*
Digital Fabrication Wkshp Inc 518 249-6500
99 S 3rd St Ste 2 Hudson (12534) *(G-6346)*
Digital Governance Division, New York *Also called Evidon Inc (G-9740)*
Digital Home Creations Inc 585 576-7070
350 Shadowbrook Dr Webster (14580) *(G-16082)*
Digital Imaging Tech LLC 518 885-4400
425 Eastline Rd D Ballston Spa (12020) *(G-580)*
Digital Imiging Technologies, Ballston Spa *Also called Dit Prints Incorporated (G-581)*
Digital Instruments Inc 716 874-5848
580 Ensminger Rd Tonawanda (14150) *(G-15536)*
Digital Matrix Corp 516 481-7990
34 Sarah Dr Ste B Farmingdale (11735) *(G-4752)*
Digital One USA Inc 718 396-4890
7230 Roosevelt Ave Flushing (11372) *(G-4996)*
Digital Page LLC 518 446-9129
75 Benjamin St Albany (12202) *(G-68)*
Digital United Color Prtg Inc 845 986-9846
33 South St Warwick (10990) *(G-15950)*
Digital X-Press, Albany *Also called Brigar X-Press Solutions Inc (G-50)*
Digitech Printers, New York *Also called Balajee Enterprises Inc (G-9006)*
Digitronik Labs Inc 585 360-0043
181 Saint Paul St Apt 6d Rochester (14604) *(G-13741)*
Dijifi LLC 646 519-2447
1166 Manhattan Ave # 100 Brooklyn (11222) *(G-1778)*
Dilese International Inc 716 855-3500
141 Broadway St Buffalo (14203) *(G-2801)*
Diligent Board Member Svcs LLC 212 741-8181
310 5th Ave Fl 7 New York (10001) *(G-9528)*
Diligent Corporation (PA) 212 741-8181
1385 Brdwy Fl 19 Flr 19 New York (10018) *(G-9529)*
Dillmeier Enterprises Inc 800 325-0596
106 7th St Ste 201 Garden City (11530) *(G-5255)*
Dillner Precast Inc (PA) 631 421-9130
14 Meadow Ln Lloyd Harbor (11743) *(G-7279)*
Dillner Precast Inc 631 421-9130
200 W 9th St Huntington Station (11746) *(G-6439)*
Dimaio Millwork Corporation 914 476-1937
12 Bright Pl Yonkers (10705) *(G-16750)*
Dimanco Inc (PA) 315 797-0470
200 Seward Ave Utica (13502) *(G-15695)*
Dimar Manufacturing Corp 716 759-0351
10123 Main St Clarence (14031) *(G-3527)*
Dimarzio Inc 718 442-6655
1388 Richmond Ter Staten Island (10310) *(G-15069)*
Dime Trading Inc 718 797-0303
787 Kent Ave Brooklyn (11205) *(G-1779)*
Dimension Development Corp 718 361-8825
3630 37th St Fl 1 Long Island City (11101) *(G-7426)*
Dimension Fabricators Inc 518 374-1936
2000 7th St Scotia (12302) *(G-14739)*
Dimension Technologies Inc 585 436-3530
315 Mount Read Blvd Ste 5 Rochester (14611) *(G-13742)*
Dimensional Mills, Hudson Falls *Also called Dwa Pallet Inc (G-6378)*

ALPHABETIC

(PA)=Parent Co (HQ)=Headquarters (DH)=Div Headquarters
2019 Harris
New York Manufacturers Directory
867

Dimensional Mills Inc 518 746-1047
337 Main St Hudson Falls (12839) ***(G-6377)***
Dimoda Designs Inc 212 355-8166
48 W 48th St Ste 403 New York (10036) ***(G-9530)***
Dine Rite Seating Products Inc 631 226-8899
165 E Hoffman Ave Unit 3 Lindenhurst (11757) ***(G-7170)***
Dinette Depot Ltd 516 515-9623
350 Dewitt Ave Brooklyn (11207) ***(G-1780)***
Dining Furniture, Brooklyn *Also called Dinette Depot Ltd* ***(G-1780)***
Dinos Sausage & Meat Co Inc 315 732-2661
722 Catherine St Utica (13501) ***(G-15696)***
Dinosaw Inc (PA) 518 828-9942
340 Power Ave Hudson (12534) ***(G-6347)***
Dionics-Usa Inc 516 997-7474
96b Urban Ave Westbury (11590) ***(G-16323)***
Dipaolo Baking Co Inc 585 303-5013
598 Plymouth Ave N Rochester (14608) ***(G-13743)***
Direct 2 Market Solutions, Rochester *Also called Selby Marketing Associates Inc* ***(G-14120)***
Direct Alliance, New York *Also called T & R Knitting Mills Inc* ***(G-11767)***
Direct Mktg Edctl Fndation Inc 212 790-1512
1333 Broadway Rm 301 New York (10018) ***(G-9531)***
Direct Print Inc (PA) 212 987-6003
77 E 125th St New York (10035) ***(G-9532)***
Directory Major Malls Inc 845 348-7000
20 N Broadway Ste 2 Nyack (10960) ***(G-12505)***
Direkt Force LLC 716 652-3022
455 Olean Rd Ste 3 East Aurora (14052) ***(G-4197)***
Dirt T Shirts Inc 845 336-4230
444 Old Neighborhood Rd Kingston (12401) ***(G-6898)***
Dirty Lemon Beverages LLC (PA) 877 897-7784
95 Grand St Apt 5 New York (10013) ***(G-9533)***
Dis, Islandia *Also called Duetto Integrated Systems Inc* ***(G-6527)***
Dis, New York *Also called Deniz Information Systems* ***(G-9500)***
Disc Graphics Inc 631 300-1129
30 Gilpin Ave Hauppauge (11788) ***(G-5811)***
Disc Graphics Inc (PA) 631 234-1400
10 Gilpin Ave Hauppauge (11788) ***(G-5812)***
Discountclocks.com, Long Island City *Also called Central Time Clock Inc* ***(G-7407)***
Discover Casting Inc 212 302-5060
17 W 45th St Ste 701 New York (10036) ***(G-9534)***
Discover Magazine, New York *Also called Discover Media LLC* ***(G-9535)***
Discover Media LLC 212 624-4800
90 5th Ave Ste 1100 New York (10011) ***(G-9535)***
Dispatch Graphics Inc 212 307-5943
344 W 38th St Fl 4r New York (10018) ***(G-9536)***
Dispatch Letter Service, New York *Also called Dispatch Graphics Inc* ***(G-9536)***
Dispersion Technology Inc 914 241-4777
364 Adams St Bedford Hills (10507) ***(G-775)***
Display Components Mfg Inc 631 420-0600
267 Edison Ave West Babylon (11704) ***(G-16153)***
Display Fireworks, Canandaigua *Also called Young Explosives Corp* ***(G-3237)***
Display Logic USA Inc 631 406-1922
40 Oser Ave Ste 4 Hauppauge (11788) ***(G-5813)***
Display Marketing Group Inc 631 348-4450
170 Oval Dr Ste B Islandia (11749) ***(G-6526)***
Display Presentations Ltd 631 951-4050
16 Court St Fl 14 Brooklyn (11241) ***(G-1781)***
Display Producers Inc 718 904-1200
40 Winding Brook Rd New Rochelle (10804) ***(G-8599)***
Display Shop Inc (PA) 646 202-9494
261 Madison Ave Fl 9 New York (10016) ***(G-9537)***
Display Technologies LLC (HQ) 718 321-3100
1111 Marcus Ave Ste M68 New Hyde Park (11042) ***(G-8527)***
Displays & Beyond Inc 718 805-7786
8816 77th Ave Glendale (11385) ***(G-5398)***
Displays By Rioux Inc 315 458-3639
6090 E Taft Rd North Syracuse (13212) ***(G-12399)***
Dissent Magazine 212 316-3120
120 Wall St Fl 31 New York (10005) ***(G-9538)***
Distech Systems Inc (HQ) 585 254-7020
1000 University Ave # 400 Rochester (14607) ***(G-13744)***
Distinction Magazine Inc 631 843-3522
235 Pinelawn Rd Melville (11747) ***(G-8016)***
Distinctive Printing Inc 212 727-3000
225 W 37th St Fl 16 New York (10018) ***(G-9539)***
Distribio USA LLC 212 989-6077
261 5th Ave Rm 2000 New York (10016) ***(G-9540)***
Dit Prints Incorporated 518 885-4400
27 Kent St Ste 53 Ballston Spa (12020) ***(G-581)***
Diva Farms Ltd 315 735-4397
1301 Broad St Utica (13501) ***(G-15697)***
Diversified Envelope Ltd 585 615-4697
95 Mount Read Blvd # 103 Rochester (14611) ***(G-13745)***
Diversified Manufacturing Inc 716 681-7670
4401 Walden Ave Lancaster (14086) ***(G-7016)***
Diversify Apparel, New York *Also called Babyfair Inc* ***(G-8997)***
Diversion Magazine, New York *Also called Hearst Business Publishing Inc* ***(G-10057)***
Diversity Best Practices, New York *Also called Working Mother Media Inc* ***(G-12134)***
Divine Art Furniture Inc 718 834-0111
43 Hall St Ste C9 Brooklyn (11205) ***(G-1782)***
Divine Bros, Utica *Also called Dimanco Inc* ***(G-15695)***
Divine Brothers Company 315 797-0470
200 Seward Ave Utica (13502) ***(G-15698)***
Divine Phoenix LLC 585 737-1482
2985 Benson Rd Skaneateles (13152) ***(G-14870)***
Divine Phoenix Books, Skaneateles *Also called Divine Phoenix LLC* ***(G-14870)***
Division Den-Bar Enterprises 914 381-2220
745 W Boston Post Rd Mamaroneck (10543) ***(G-7742)***
Division of Emergency Services, Holbrook *Also called M C Products* ***(G-6197)***
Dixon Tool and Manufacturing 585 235-1352
240 Burrows St Rochester (14606) ***(G-13746)***
Diyzeitung, Brooklyn *Also called News Report Inc* ***(G-2267)***
Dj Acquisition Management Corp 585 265-3000
6364 Dean Pkwy Ontario (14519) ***(G-12652)***
Dj Expression, Brooklyn *Also called Fuzion Creations Intl LLC* ***(G-1912)***
Dj Pirrone Industries Inc 518 864-5496
8865 Mariaville Rd Pattersonville (12137) ***(G-12888)***
Dj Publishing Inc 516 767-2500
25 Willowdale Ave Port Washington (11050) ***(G-13253)***
DJS Nyc Inc 845 445-8618
15 S Remsen St Monsey (10952) ***(G-8287)***
DK, Fulton *Also called D-K Manufacturing Corp* ***(G-5214)***
DK Publishing 212 366-2000
345 Hudson St New York (10014) ***(G-9541)***
Dkm Ad Art, Buffalo *Also called Dkm Sales LLC* ***(G-2802)***
Dkm Sales LLC 716 893-7777
1352 Genesee St Buffalo (14211) ***(G-2802)***
Dkny, New York *Also called Donna Karan Company LLC* ***(G-9551)***
Dkny Jeans, New York *Also called Donna Karan Company LLC* ***(G-9549)***
Dkny Underwear, New York *Also called Wacoal America Inc* ***(G-12063)***
Dl Manufacturing Inc 315 432-8977
340 Gateway Park Dr North Syracuse (13212) ***(G-12400)***
Dlc Comprehensive Medical PC 718 857-1200
979 Fulton St Brooklyn (11238) ***(G-1783)***
Dlh Energy Service LLC 716 410-0028
4422 W Fairmount Ave Lakewood (14750) ***(G-6994)***
Dli, Cazenovia *Also called Knowles Cazenovia Inc* ***(G-3320)***
Dlr Enterprises LLC 315 813-2911
104 E Seneca St Sherrill (13461) ***(G-14819)***
Dlx Industries Inc 718 272-9420
225 25th St Brooklyn (11232) ***(G-1784)***
Dm2 Media LLC 646 419-4357
1 Liberty Plz Fl 8 New York (10006) ***(G-9542)***
DMD Machining Technology Inc 585 659-8180
17231 Roosevelt Hwy Kendall (14476) ***(G-6856)***
DMEF/EDGE, New York *Also called Direct Mktg Edctl Fndation Inc* ***(G-9531)***
Dmic Inc 716 743-4360
3776 Commerce Ct North Tonawanda (14120) ***(G-12425)***
Dnp Electronics America LLC 212 503-1060
335 Madison Ave Fl 3 New York (10017) ***(G-9543)***
Doar Inc 516 872-8140
170 Earle Ave Lynbrook (11563) ***(G-7664)***
Dobrin Industries Inc (PA) 800 353-2229
210 Walnut St Ste 22 Lockport (14094) ***(G-7295)***
Dock Hardware Incorporated 585 266-7920
24 Seneca Ave Ste 4 Rochester (14621) ***(G-13747)***
Doco Quick Print Inc 315 782-6623
808 Huntington St Watertown (13601) ***(G-16012)***
Doctor Pavers 516 342-6016
34 Redleaf Ln Commack (11725) ***(G-3689)***
Doctor Print Inc (PA) 631 873-4560
18 Commerce Dr Ste 1 Hauppauge (11788) ***(G-5814)***
Doctorow Communications Inc 845 708-5166
180 Phillips Hill Rd # 5 New City (10956) ***(G-8491)***
Document Journal Inc 646 586-3099
264 Canal St New York (10013) ***(G-9544)***
Document Strategies LLC 585 506-9000
185 Gibbs St Rochester (14605) ***(G-13748)***
Doery Awning Co, Lawrence *Also called TG Peppe Inc* ***(G-7110)***
Dog Good Products LLC 212 789-7000
1407 Broadway Fl 41 New York (10018) ***(G-9545)***
Dog Guard, Troy *Also called Sunward Electronics Inc* ***(G-15629)***
Doheny Nice and Easy 518 793-1733
150 Broad St Glens Falls (12801) ***(G-5423)***
Doheny's Mobil, Glens Falls *Also called Doheny Nice and Easy* ***(G-5423)***
Dohnsco Inc 516 773-4800
19 Gracewood Dr Manhasset (11030) ***(G-7766)***
Dolby Laboratories Inc 212 767-1700
1350 6th Ave Fl 28 New York (10019) ***(G-9546)***
Dolce Vite International LLC 713 962-5767
386 12th St Brooklyn (11215) ***(G-1785)***
Dolco LLC 585 657-7777
26 Maple Ave Bloomfield (14469) ***(G-952)***
Dollar Popular Inc 914 375-0361
473 S Broadway Yonkers (10705) ***(G-16751)***
Dolmen 912 596-1537
216 Broome Corporate Pkwy Conklin (13748) ***(G-3726)***
Dolomite Group, Walworth *Also called Rochester Asphalt Materials* ***(G-15915)***
Dolomite Products Company Inc (HQ) 315 524-1998
1150 Penfield Rd Rochester (14625) ***(G-13749)***

Dolomite Products Company Inc.....607 324-3636
7610 County Road 65 Hornell (14843) *(G-6295)*
Dolomite Products Company Inc.....585 586-2568
746 Whalen Rd Penfield (14526) *(G-12940)*
Dolomite Products Company Inc.....585 768-7295
8250 Golf Rd Le Roy (14482) *(G-7115)*
Dolomite Products Company Inc.....585 352-0460
2540 S Union St Spencerport (14559) *(G-14978)*
Doma Marketing Inc.....516 684-1111
28 Haven Ave Ste 226 Port Washington (11050) *(G-13254)*
Domain, Brooklyn *Also called Sweater Brand Inc (G-2545)*
Domani Fashions Corp.....718 797-0505
86 S 1st St Brooklyn (11249) *(G-1786)*
Domestic Casing Co.....718 522-1902
410 3rd Ave Brooklyn (11215) *(G-1787)*
Dominic De Nigris Inc.....718 597-4460
3255 E Tremont Ave Frnt Bronx (10461) *(G-1258)*
Dominique Intimate Apparel, Yonkers *Also called Dayleen Intimates Inc (G-16749)*
Domino Foods Inc.....800 729-4840
1 Federal St Yonkers (10705) *(G-16752)*
Domino Sugar, Yonkers *Also called Domino Foods Inc (G-16752)*
Domoteck Interiors Inc.....718 433-4300
2430 Brooklyn Queens Expy # 1 Woodside (11377) *(G-16653)*
Don Alleson Athletic, Geneva *Also called Alleson of Rochester Inc (G-5316)*
Don Beck Inc.....585 493-3040
5249 State Route 39 Castile (14427) *(G-3292)*
Donald Bruhnke.....212 600-1260
455 W 37th St Apt 1018 New York (10018) *(G-9547)*
Donald Snyder Jr.....315 265-4485
528 Allen Falls Rd Potsdam (13676) *(G-13318)*
Donald Snyder Jr Logging, Potsdam *Also called Donald Snyder Jr (G-13318)*
Donald Stefan.....716 492-1110
3428 W Yorkshire Rd Chaffee (14030) *(G-3403)*
Donmar Printing Co.....516 280-2239
90 2nd St Ste 2 Mineola (11501) *(G-8216)*
Donna Degan, New York *Also called Leslie Stuart Co Inc (G-10555)*
Donna Distefano Ltd (PA).....212 594-3757
37 W 20th St Ste 1106 New York (10011) *(G-9548)*
Donna Karan Company LLC.....212 372-6500
240 W 40th St Bsmt 2 New York (10018) *(G-9549)*
Donna Karan Company LLC.....212 789-1500
240 W 40th St Bsmt New York (10018) *(G-9550)*
Donna Karan Company LLC.....716 297-0752
1900 Military Rd Niagara Falls (14304) *(G-12278)*
Donna Karan Company LLC (HQ).....212 789-1500
240 W 40th St New York (10018) *(G-9551)*
Donna Karan International Inc (HQ).....212 789-1500
240 W 40th St New York (10018) *(G-9552)*
Donna Karan International Inc.....212 768-5800
240 W 40th St Bsmt New York (10018) *(G-9553)*
Donna Morgan LLC.....212 575-2550
132 W 36th St Rm 801 New York (10018) *(G-9554)*
Donne Dieu Paper Mill Inc.....212 226-0573
63 Flushing Ave Unit 112 Brooklyn (11205) *(G-1788)*
Donnelley Financial LLC (HQ).....212 425-0298
55 Water St Fl 11 New York (10041) *(G-9555)*
Donnelley Financial LLC.....212 351-9000
555 5th Ave Fl 4 New York (10017) *(G-9556)*
Donorwall Inc.....212 766-9670
125 Maiden Ln Rm 205 New York (10038) *(G-9557)*
Donver Incorporated.....716 945-1910
4185 Killbuck Rd Kill Buck (14748) *(G-6878)*
Door Dam, Wassaic *Also called Presray Corporation (G-15966)*
Doortec Archtctural Met GL LLC.....718 567-2730
234 46th St Brooklyn (11220) *(G-1789)*
Dor-A-Mar Canvas Products Co.....631 750-9202
182 Cherry Ave West Sayville (11796) *(G-16288)*
Doral Apparel Group Inc.....917 208-5652
498 Fashion Ave Fl 10 New York (10018) *(G-9558)*
Doral Refining Corp.....516 223-3684
533 Atlantic Ave Freeport (11520) *(G-5151)*
Doreen Interiors Ltd.....212 255-9008
76 Nottingham Rd New Hyde Park (11040) *(G-8528)*
Dorel Hat Co (PA).....845 831-5231
1 Main St Beacon (12508) *(G-757)*
Doremus FP LLC.....212 366-3800
228 E 45th St Fl 10 New York (10017) *(G-9559)*
Dorgan Welding Service.....315 462-9030
1378 White Rd Phelps (14532) *(G-12976)*
Doric Vault of Wny Inc.....716 828-1776
73 Gilbert St Buffalo (14206) *(G-2803)*
Doris Panos Designs Ltd.....631 245-0580
130 Old East Neck Rd Melville (11747) *(G-8017)*
Dorling Kindersley Publishing.....212 213-4800
375 Hudson St New York (10014) *(G-9560)*
Dorm Co., Cheektowaga *Also called Dorm Company Corporation (G-3441)*
Dorm Company Corporation.....502 551-6195
575 Kennedy Rd Ste 2 Cheektowaga (14227) *(G-3441)*
Dormitory Authority - State NY.....631 434-1487
998 Crooked Hill Rd # 26 Brentwood (11717) *(G-1132)*
Dorose Albums, East Elmhurst *Also called Dorose Novelty Co Inc (G-4220)*
Dorose Novelty Co Inc.....718 451-3088
3107 103rd St East Elmhurst (11369) *(G-4220)*
Dorset Farms Inc.....631 734-6010
38355 Main Rd Peconic (11958) *(G-12914)*
Dorsey Metrology Intl Inc.....845 229-2929
53 Oakley St Poughkeepsie (12601) *(G-13334)*
Dortronics Systems Inc.....631 725-0505
1668 Bhmpton Sag Hbr Tpke Sag Harbor (11963) *(G-14499)*
Dory Enterprises Inc.....607 565-7079
184 Sr 17c Waverly (14892) *(G-16064)*
DOT Publishing.....315 593-2510
117 Cayuga St Fulton (13069) *(G-5215)*
Dotto Wagner.....315 342-8020
185 E Seneca St Oswego (13126) *(G-12776)*
Double Take Fashions Inc.....718 832-9000
1407 Broadway Rm 712 New York (10018) *(G-9561)*
Doug Lambertson Od.....718 698-9300
2555 Richmond Ave Ste 4 Staten Island (10314) *(G-15070)*
Dougs Machine Shop Inc.....585 905-0004
2304 Brickyard Rd Canandaigua (14424) *(G-3219)*
Dovelin Printing Company Inc.....718 302-3951
43 Hall St Ste C2 Brooklyn (11205) *(G-1790)*
Dover Enterprises, Syracuse *Also called Burr & Son Inc (G-15263)*
Dover Global Holdings Inc (HQ).....212 922-1640
280 Park Ave New York (10017) *(G-9562)*
Dover Marine Mfg & Sup Co Inc.....631 667-4300
98 N Industry Ct Deer Park (11729) *(G-3967)*
Dow Jones & Company Inc (HQ).....609 627-2999
1211 Avenue Of The Americ New York (10036) *(G-9563)*
Dow Jones & Company Inc.....212 597-5983
1211 Avenue Of The Americ New York (10036) *(G-9564)*
Dow Jones Aer Company Inc.....212 416-2000
1211 Av Of The Am Lwr C3r New York (10036) *(G-9565)*
Dowa International Corp.....212 697-3217
370 Lexington Ave Rm 1002 New York (10017) *(G-9566)*
Dowd - Witbeck Printing Corp.....518 274-2421
599 Pawling Ave Troy (12180) *(G-15604)*
Downtown Express Newspaper, New York *Also called Community Media LLC (G-9368)*
Downtown Interiors Inc.....212 337-0230
250 Hudson St Lbby 1 New York (10013) *(G-9567)*
Downtown Media Group LLC.....646 723-4510
12 W 27th St Ste 1000 New York (10001) *(G-9568)*
Downtown Music LLC.....212 625-2980
485 Broadway Fl 3 New York (10013) *(G-9569)*
Doyle & Roth Mfg Co Inc (PA).....212 269-7840
39 Broad St Ste 710 New York (10004) *(G-9570)*
Doyle Sails, Huntington Station *Also called Melbourne C Fisher Yacht Sails (G-6451)*
DP Murphy Co Inc.....631 673-9400
945 Grand Blvd Deer Park (11729) *(G-3968)*
Dpr Food Service, Deer Park *Also called Deer Park Macaroni Co Inc (G-3964)*
Dr Jacobs Naturals LLC.....718 265-1522
2615 Coney Island Ave 2nd Brooklyn (11223) *(G-1791)*
Dr Jayscom.....888 437-5297
853 Broadway Ste 1900 New York (10003) *(G-9571)*
Dr Mineral, Westbury *Also called Mineralbious Corp (G-16357)*
Dr Print, Hauppauge *Also called Doctor Print Inc (G-5814)*
Dr Reddys Laboratories NY Inc.....518 827-7702
1974 State Route 145 Middleburgh (12122) *(G-8129)*
Dra Imaging PC.....845 296-1057
169 Myers Corners Rd # 250 Wappingers Falls (12590) *(G-15929)*
Drag Specialties, Ballston Spa *Also called Lemans Corporation (G-588)*
Dragon Steel Products, New York *Also called Dragon Trading Inc (G-9572)*
Dragon Trading Inc.....212 717-1496
211 E 70th St Apt 20d New York (10021) *(G-9572)*
Draper Associates Incorporated.....212 255-2727
121 Varick St Rm 203 New York (10013) *(G-9573)*
Drapery Industries Inc.....585 232-2992
175 Humboldt St Ste 222 Rochester (14610) *(G-13750)*
Drasgow Inc.....585 786-3603
4150 Poplar Tree Rd Gainesville (14066) *(G-5240)*
Dray Enterprises Inc.....585 768-2201
1 Church St Le Roy (14482) *(G-7116)*
Dream Fabric Printing, Warwick *Also called Dream Green Productions (G-15951)*
Dream Green Productions.....917 267-8920
39 Warwick Tpke Warwick (10990) *(G-15951)*
Dream Statuary Inc.....718 647-2024
251 Cleveland St Brooklyn (11208) *(G-1792)*
Dreams To Print.....718 483-8020
10101 Foster Ave Brooklyn (11236) *(G-1793)*
Dreamwave LLC.....212 594-4250
34 W 33rd St Fl 2 New York (10001) *(G-9574)*
Drescher Paper Box Inc.....716 854-0288
10425 Keller Rd Clarence (14031) *(G-3528)*
Dresdiam Inc.....212 819-2217
36 W 47th St Ste 1008 New York (10036) *(G-9575)*
Dresser-Argus Inc.....718 643-1540
36 Bridge St Brooklyn (11201) *(G-1794)*
Dresser-Rand (delaware) LLC (HQ).....607 937-2011
100 E Chemung St Painted Post (14870) *(G-12839)*
Dresser-Rand Company.....585 596-3100
37 Coats St Wellsville (14895) *(G-16116)*

A L P H A B E T I C

Dresser-Rand Group Inc 716 375-3000
500 Paul Clark Dr Olean (14760) *(G-12599)*
Dressy Tessy Inc (PA) 212 869-0750
1410 Broadway Rm 502 New York (10018) *(G-9576)*
Drew Philips Corp (PA) 212 354-0095
231 W 39th St New York (10018) *(G-9577)*
Dreyfus Ashby Inc (HQ) 212 818-0770
630 3rd Ave Fl 15 New York (10017) *(G-9578)*
DRG New York Holdings Corp (PA) 914 668-9000
700 S Fulton Ave Mount Vernon (10550) *(G-8395)*
Dri Relays Inc (HQ) 631 342-1700
60 Commerce Dr Hauppauge (11788) *(G-5815)*
Drillco Equipment Co Inc 718 777-5986
3452 11th St Long Island City (11106) *(G-7427)*
Drillco National Group Inc (PA) 718 726-9801
2432 44th St Long Island City (11103) *(G-7428)*
Drimark 516 484-6200
999 S Oyster Bay Rd Bethpage (11714) *(G-841)*
Drive / Devilbiss Healthcare, Port Washington *Also called Medical Depot Inc (G-13285)*
Drive Medical Spv LLC 516 998-4600
99 Seaview Blvd Port Washington (11050) *(G-13255)*
Drive Shaft Shop Inc 631 348-1818
210 Blydenburg Rd Unit A Hauppauge (11749) *(G-5816)*
Drns Corp 718 369-4530
140 58th St Ste 3f Brooklyn (11220) *(G-1795)*
Dropcar Operating Company Inc (HQ) 646 342-1595
1412 Broadway Ste 2100 New York (10018) *(G-9579)*
Drt Power Systems LLC 585 247-5940
500 Mile Crossing Blvd Rochester (14624) *(G-13751)*
Drum Ready-Mix, Felts Mills *Also called Cranesville Block Co Inc (G-4930)*
Drummond Framing Inc 212 647-1701
38 W 21st St Fl 10 New York (10010) *(G-9580)*
Dryden & Palmer Co, Canajoharie *Also called Gravymaster Inc (G-3207)*
Dryve LLC 646 279-3648
4515 Waldo Ave Bronx (10471) *(G-1259)*
DSI Group Inc 800 553-2202
5713 49th St Maspeth (11378) *(G-7837)*
DSM Nutritional Products LLC 518 372-5155
2105 Technology Dr Schenectady (12308) *(G-14669)*
DSM Nutritional Products LLC 518 372-5155
300 Tech Park Glenville (12302) *(G-5445)*
Dsr International Corp 631 427-2600
107 Northern Blvd Ste 401 Great Neck (11021) *(G-5550)*
Dt Industry, New York *Also called Dressy Tessy Inc (G-9576)*
Du Monde Trading Inc 212 944-1306
1407 Brrdwy Rm 1905 New York (10018) *(G-9581)*
Du Serv Development Co, Troy *Also called George M Dujack (G-15606)*
Dual Print & Mail LLC (HQ) 716 775-8001
3235 Grand Island Blvd Grand Island (14072) *(G-5497)*
Dual Print & Mail LLC 716 684-3825
340 Nagel Dr Cheektowaga (14225) *(G-3442)*
Duall Finishing Inc 716 827-1707
53 Hopkins St Buffalo (14220) *(G-2804)*
Dualtron Manufacturing, West Babylon *Also called Vandilay Industries Inc (G-16202)*
Ducduc LLC (PA) 212 226-1868
200 Lexington Ave Rm 715 New York (10016) *(G-9582)*
Ducduc Nyc, New York *Also called Ducduc LLC (G-9582)*
Duck Flats Pharma 315 689-3407
245 E Main St Elbridge (13060) *(G-4428)*
Duck River Textiles Inc (PA) 212 679-2980
295 5th Ave New York (10016) *(G-9583)*
Duck Walk Vinyards 631 726-7555
231 Montauk Hwy Water Mill (11976) *(G-15970)*
Ducommun Aerostructures NY Inc 518 731-2791
171 Stacey Rd Coxsackie (12051) *(G-3906)*
Ducon Technologies Inc (PA) 631 694-1700
5 Penn Plz Ste 2403 New York (10001) *(G-9584)*
Ducon Technologies Inc 631 420-4900
19 Engineers Ln Farmingdale (11735) *(G-4753)*
Duetto Integrated Systems Inc 631 851-0102
85 Hoffman Ln Ste Q Islandia (11749) *(G-6527)*
Dufour Pastry Kitchens Inc 718 402-8800
251 Locust Ave Bronx (10454) *(G-1260)*
Duke Company 607 347-4455
7 Hall Rd Ithaca (14850) *(G-6575)*
Duke Concrete Products Inc 518 793-7743
50 Duke Dr Queensbury (12804) *(G-13422)*
Duke of Iron Inc 631 543-3600
1039 W Jericho Tpke Smithtown (11787) *(G-14897)*
Dulcette Technologies LLC 631 752-8700
2 Hicks St Lindenhurst (11757) *(G-7171)*
Dun-Rite Spclized Carriers LLC 718 991-1100
1561 Southern Blvd Bronx (10460) *(G-1261)*
Duncan & Son Carpentry Inc 914 664-4311
1 W Prospect Ave Mount Vernon (10550) *(G-8396)*
Dundas-Jafine Inc 716 681-9690
11099 Broadway St Alden (14004) *(G-170)*
Dundee Foods LLC (PA) 585 377-7700
815 Whitney Rd W Fairport (14450) *(G-4632)*
Dundeespirits, Fairport *Also called Dundee Foods LLC (G-4632)*
Dundy Glass & Mirror Corp 718 723-5800
12252 Montauk St Springfield Gardens (11413) *(G-15014)*
Dune Inc 212 925-6171
200 Lexington Ave Rm 200 # 200 New York (10016) *(G-9585)*
Dunkirk Construction Products 716 366-5220
852 Main St Dunkirk (14048) *(G-4166)*
Dunkirk Metal Products Wny LLC (PA) 716 366-2555
3575 Chadwick Dr Dunkirk (14048) *(G-4167)*
Dunkirk Specialty Steel LLC 716 366-1000
830 Brigham Rd Dunkirk (14048) *(G-4168)*
Dunlap Machine LLC 315 926-1013
4205 Sunset Dr Marion (14505) *(G-7800)*
Dunlea Whl GL & Mirror Inc 914 664-5277
147 S Macquesten Pkwy Mount Vernon (10550) *(G-8397)*
Dunmore Corporation 845 279-5061
3633 Danbury Rd Brewster (10509) *(G-1163)*
Dunn Paper - Natural Dam Inc 315 287-1200
4921 St Rt 58 Gouverneur (13642) *(G-5490)*
Dupli Envelope & Graphics, Syracuse *Also called Dupli Graphics Corporation (G-15306)*
Dupli Graphics Corporation (HQ) 315 234-7286
6761 Thompson Rd Syracuse (13211) *(G-15306)*
Dupli Graphics Corporation 315 422-4732
Dupli Park Dr Syracuse (13218) *(G-15307)*
Dupont, Buffalo *Also called E I Du Pont De Nemours & Co (G-2807)*
Dura Architectural Signage, Long Island City *Also called Dura Engraving Corporation (G-7429)*
Dura Engraving Corporation 718 706-6400
4815 32nd Pl Long Island City (11101) *(G-7429)*
Dura Foam Inc 718 894-2488
6302 59th Ave Maspeth (11378) *(G-7838)*
Dura Spec Inc 718 526-3053
1239 Village Ct North Baldwin (11510) *(G-12362)*
Dura-Mill Inc 518 899-2255
16 Stonebreak Rd Ballston Spa (12020) *(G-582)*
Dural Door Company Inc 718 729-1333
3128 Greenpoint Ave Long Island City (11101) *(G-7430)*
Durall Dolly LLC 802 728-7122
48 Spencer St Brooklyn (11205) *(G-1796)*
Duran Jewelry Inc 212 431-1959
36 W 47th St Ste 1205 New York (10036) *(G-9586)*
Duranm Inc 914 774-3367
101 Dale Ave Cortlandt Manor (10567) *(G-3899)*
Durasol Systems Inc (HQ) 845 610-1100
445 Bellvale Rd Chester (10918) *(G-3473)*
Durata Therapeutics Inc 646 871-6400
7 Times Sq Ste 3502 New York (10036) *(G-9587)*
Durez Corporation 716 286-0100
5000 Packard Rd Niagara Falls (14304) *(G-12279)*
Duro Dyne Corporation (HQ) 631 249-9000
81 Spence St Bay Shore (11706) *(G-682)*
Duro Dyne Machinery Corp 631 249-9000
81 Spence St Bay Shore (11706) *(G-683)*
Duro-Shed Inc (PA) 585 344-0800
721 Center Rd Buffalo (14224) *(G-2805)*
Dutch Spirits LLC 518 398-1022
98 Ryan Rd Pine Plains (12567) *(G-13005)*
Dutch's Spirits, Pine Plains *Also called Dutch Spirits LLC (G-13005)*
Dutchess Plumbing & Heating 845 889-8255
28 Reservoir Rd Staatsburg (12580) *(G-15023)*
Dutchess Wines LLC 845 876-1319
39 Lorraine Dr Rhinebeck (12572) *(G-13486)*
Dutchland Plastics LLC 315 280-0247
102 E Seneca St Sherrill (13461) *(G-14820)*
Dutchtreat, Buffalo *Also called Pdi Cone Co Inc (G-2994)*
Duvel Mortgage USA Inc 607 267-6121
656 County Highway 33 Cooperstown (13326) *(G-3744)*
Duxiana Dux Bed 212 755-2600
235 E 58th St New York (10022) *(G-9588)*
Duzmor Painting Inc 585 768-4760
7959 E Main Rd Le Roy (14482) *(G-7117)*
Dvash Foods Inc 845 578-1959
2 Brewer Rd Monsey (10952) *(G-8288)*
Dvf Studio LLC (PA) 212 741-6607
440 W 14th St New York (10014) *(G-9589)*
Dvf Studio LLC (PA) 646 576-8009
252 W 37th St Fl 14 New York (10018) *(G-9590)*
Dvmax, New York *Also called Sneakers Software Inc (G-11631)*
Dwa Pallet Inc 518 746-1047
337 Main St Hudson Falls (12839) *(G-6378)*
Dweck Industries Inc (PA) 718 615-1695
2455 Mcdonald Ave Fl 2 Brooklyn (11223) *(G-1797)*
Dweck Industries Inc 718 615-1695
2247 E 16th St Fl 2 Brooklyn (11229) *(G-1798)*
Dwell Life Inc 212 382-2010
60 Broad St Fl 24 New York (10004) *(G-9591)*
Dwell Store The, New York *Also called Dwell Life Inc (G-9591)*
Dwm International Inc 646 290-7448
37-18 Nthrn Blvd Ste 516 Long Island City (11101) *(G-7431)*
Dwnld Inc 484 483-6572
601394 Broadway Fl 6 Flr 6 New York (10013) *(G-9592)*
Dwyer Farm LLC 914 456-2742
40 Bowman Ln Walden (12586) *(G-15893)*
Dyco Electronics, Hornell *Also called Dyco Manufacturing LLC (G-6297)*

Dyco Electronics Inc 607 324-2030
7775 Industrial Park Rd Hornell (14843) ***(G-6296)***
Dyco Manufacturing LLC 607 324-2030
7775 Industrial Park Rd Hornell (14843) ***(G-6297)***
Dyenamix Inc 212 941-6642
359 Broadway Frnt 2 New York (10013) ***(G-9593)***
Dylix Corporation 719 773-2985
347 Lang Blvd Grand Island (14072) ***(G-5498)***
Dyna-Empire Inc 516 222-2700
1075 Stewart Ave Garden City (11530) ***(G-5256)***
Dyna-Tech Quality Inc 585 458-9970
1570 Emerson St Rochester (14606) ***(G-13752)***
Dyna-Vac Equipment Inc 315 865-8084
8963 State Route 365 Stittville (13469) ***(G-15160)***
Dynabrade Inc (PA) 716 631-0100
8989 Sheridan Dr Clarence (14031) ***(G-3529)***
Dynak Inc 585 271-2255
530 Savage Rd Churchville (14428) ***(G-3509)***
Dynamasters Inc 585 458-9970
1570 Emerson St Rochester (14606) ***(G-13753)***
Dynamic Decisions Inc (PA) 908 755-5000
18519 64th Ave Fresh Meadows (11365) ***(G-5196)***
Dynamic Dies Inc 585 247-4010
70 Pixley Industria Pkwy Rochester (14624) ***(G-13754)***
Dynamic Health Labs Inc 718 858-0100
110 Bridge St Ste 2 Brooklyn (11201) ***(G-1799)***
Dynamic Hybirds Inc 315 426-8110
1201 E Fayette St Ste 11 Syracuse (13210) ***(G-15308)***
Dynamic Intl Mfrs & Distrs Inc 347 993-1914
78 Lafayette Ave Ste 201 Suffern (10901) ***(G-15188)***
Dynamic Laboratories Inc 631 231-7474
30 Haynes Ct Ronkonkoma (11779) ***(G-14334)***
Dynamic Labs, Ronkonkoma *Also called Dynamic Laboratories Inc* ***(G-14334)***
Dynamic Packaging Inc 718 388-0800
1567 39th St Brooklyn (11218) ***(G-1800)***
Dynamic Pak, Syracuse *Also called Weather Products Corporation* ***(G-15455)***
Dynamic Photography Inc 516 381-2951
48 Flamingo Rd N Roslyn (11576) ***(G-14446)***
Dynamic Printing, Central Islip *Also called Richard Ruffner* ***(G-3383)***
Dynamic Screenprinting 518 487-4256
12 Vatrano Rd Albany (12205) ***(G-69)***
Dynamic Sealing Tech Inc 716 376-0708
301 W Franklin St Olean (14760) ***(G-12600)***
Dynamic Systems Inc (PA) 518 283-5350
323 Rte 355 Poestenkill (12140) ***(G-13180)***
Dynamica Inc 212 818-1900
930 5th Ave Apt 3f New York (10021) ***(G-9594)***
Dynamo Development Inc 212 385-1552
860 Broadway Fl 5 New York (10003) ***(G-9595)***
Dynasty Belts Inc 516 625-6280
161 Railroad Ave New Hyde Park (11040) ***(G-8529)***
Dynasty Chemical Corp 518 463-1146
444 N Pearl St Menands (12204) ***(G-8084)***
Dynasty Metal Works Inc 631 284-3719
787 Raynor Ave Riverhead (11901) ***(G-13567)***
Dynasty Stainless Steel & Meta 718 205-6623
5985 Maurice Ave Maspeth (11378) ***(G-7839)***
Dynatabs LLC 718 376-6084
1600 Ocean Pkwy Apt 1f Brooklyn (11230) ***(G-1801)***
Dynax Corporation 914 764-0202
79 Westchester Ave Pound Ridge (10576) ***(G-13376)***
Dyno Nobel Inc 845 338-2144
161 Ulster Ave Ulster Park (12487) ***(G-15658)***
Dynocoat Inc 631 244-9344
1738 Church St Holbrook (11741) ***(G-6183)***
Dyson-Kissner-Moran Corp (PA) 212 661-4600
2515 South Rd Ste 5 Poughkeepsie (12601) ***(G-13335)***
Dz9 Power LLC 877 533-5530
408 Wayne St Olean (14760) ***(G-12601)***
E & D Specialty Stands Inc 716 337-0161
2081 Franklin St North Collins (14111) ***(G-12385)***
E & F Home Fashions Inc (PA) 718 968-9719
2154 E 71st St Brooklyn (11234) ***(G-1802)***
E & G Press, Catskill *Also called Hill Crest Press* ***(G-3304)***
E & J Iron Works Inc 718 665-6040
801 E 136th St Bronx (10454) ***(G-1262)***
E & O Mari Inc 845 562-4400
256 Broadway Newburgh (12550) ***(G-12220)***
E & R Machine Inc 716 434-6639
211 Grand St Lockport (14094) ***(G-7296)***
E & T Plastic Mfg Co Inc (PA) 718 729-6226
4545 37th St Long Island City (11101) ***(G-7432)***
E & W Manufacturing Co Inc 516 367-8571
15 Pine Dr Woodbury (11797) ***(G-16618)***
E and V Energy Corporation 315 786-2067
22925 State Route 12 Watertown (13601) ***(G-16013)***
E B Atlas Steel Corp 716 876-0900
120 Tonawanda St Buffalo (14207) ***(G-2806)***
E B B Graphics Inc 516 750-5510
75 State St Westbury (11590) ***(G-16324)***
E B Industries LLC (PA) 631 293-8565
90 Carolyn Blvd Farmingdale (11735) ***(G-4754)***
E B Industries LLC 631 293-8565
90 Carolyn Blvd Farmingdale (11735) ***(G-4755)***
E B Trottnow Machine Spc 716 694-0600
8955 Woodside Dr Eden (14057) ***(G-4387)***
E C C Corp 518 873-6494
7 Church St Elizabethtown (12932) ***(G-4431)***
E C Lyons, Bronx *Also called Edward C Lyons Company Inc* ***(G-1265)***
E C Sumereau & Sons, Huntington Station *Also called John Larocca & Son Inc* ***(G-6449)***
E D I, Yonkers *Also called Electronic Devices Inc* ***(G-16755)***
E D I Window Systems, Binghamton *Also called D D & L Inc* ***(G-878)***
E F Iron Works & Construction 631 242-4766
241 N Fehr Way Ste 3 Bay Shore (11706) ***(G-684)***
E F Lippert Co Inc 716 373-1100
4451 S Nine Mile Rd Allegany (14706) ***(G-189)***
E F Thresh Inc 315 437-7301
6000 Galster Rd East Syracuse (13057) ***(G-4336)***
E G M Restaurant Equipment Mfg 718 782-9800
688 Flushing Ave Brooklyn (11206) ***(G-1803)***
E G S, Port Washington *Also called E Global Solutions Inc* ***(G-13256)***
E Global Solutions Inc 516 767-5138
8 Haven Ave Ste 221 Port Washington (11050) ***(G-13256)***
E Gluck Corporation (PA) 718 784-0700
6015 Little Neck Pkwy Little Neck (11362) ***(G-7218)***
E Graphics Corporation 718 486-9767
160 Havemeyer St Brooklyn (11211) ***(G-1804)***
E H Hurwitz & Associates 718 884-3766
3000 Kingsbridge Ave Bronx (10463) ***(G-1263)***
E I Du Pont De Nemours & Co 716 876-4420
3115 River Rd Buffalo (14207) ***(G-2807)***
E I Du Pont De Nemours & Co 718 761-0043
10 Teleport Dr Staten Island (10311) ***(G-15071)***
E J E Research Div, Buffalo *Also called Adco Circuits Inc* ***(G-2685)***
E J Manufacturing Inc 516 313-9380
2935 Charlotte Dr Merrick (11566) ***(G-8097)***
E J Willis Company Inc 315 891-7602
37 N Main St Middleville (13406) ***(G-8186)***
E L Smith Printing Co Inc 201 373-0111
3 Lisa Ct New City (10956) ***(G-8492)***
E M I, Rome *Also called Enviromaster International LLC* ***(G-14250)***
E M T Manufacturing Inc 516 333-1917
273 Cherry Pl East Meadow (11554) ***(G-4250)***
E P Sewing Pleating Inc 212 967-2575
327 W 36th St Frnt 2 New York (10018) ***(G-9596)***
E S M, Amherst *Also called Esm Group Inc* ***(G-226)***
E S P Metal Crafts Inc 718 381-2443
379 Harman St Brooklyn (11237) ***(G-1805)***
E Schreiber Inc 212 382-0280
580 5th Ave Fl 32a New York (10036) ***(G-9597)***
E T C, New York *Also called Casuals Etc Inc* ***(G-9225)***
E Tetz & Sons Inc (PA) 845 692-4486
130 Crotty Rd Middletown (10941) ***(G-8148)***
E W Smith Publishing Co 845 562-1218
36 Meriline Ave New Windsor (12553) ***(G-8643)***
E W Williams Publications 212 661-1516
370 Lexington Ave Rm 1409 New York (10017) ***(G-9598)***
E Z Entry Doors Inc 716 434-3440
5299 Enterprise Dr Lockport (14094) ***(G-7297)***
E&I Printing 212 206-0506
145 W 55th St Apt 12a New York (10019) ***(G-9599)***
E&M Power, Binghamton *Also called Mechanical Pwr Conversion LLC* ***(G-903)***
E&T Plastics, Long Island City *Also called E & T Plastic Mfg Co Inc* ***(G-7432)***
E-Beam Services Inc (PA) 516 622-1422
270 Duffy Ave Ste H Hicksville (11801) ***(G-6081)***
E-Ffinergy Group LLC 845 547-2424
355 Spook Rock Rd Suffern (10901) ***(G-15189)***
E-Front, New York *Also called Efront Financial Solutions Inc* ***(G-9633)***
E-One Inc 716 646-6790
4760 Camp Rd Hamburg (14075) ***(G-5675)***
E-Play Brands LLC 212 563-2646
25 W 39th St Lbby A New York (10018) ***(G-9600)***
E-Quest Lighting, East Setauket *Also called Vision Quest Lighting Inc* ***(G-4314)***
E-Systems Group LLC (HQ) 607 775-1100
100 Progress Pkwy Conklin (13748) ***(G-3727)***
E-Won Industrial Co Inc 212 750-9610
625 Main St Apt 1532 New York (10044) ***(G-9601)***
E-Z Global Wholesale Inc 888 769-7888
925 E 14th St Brooklyn (11230) ***(G-1806)***
E-Z Red Co, Deposit *Also called Walter R Tucker Entps Ltd* ***(G-4112)***
E-Z-Em Inc (HQ) 609 524-2864
155 Pinelawn Rd Ste 230n Melville (11747) ***(G-8018)***
E-Zoil Products Inc 716 213-0106
234 Fillmore Ave Tonawanda (14150) ***(G-15537)***
E.J. McKenica & Sons, Buffalo *Also called Edwin J McKenica & Sons Inc* ***(G-2813)***
E/One Utility Systems, Schenectady *Also called Environment-One Corporation* ***(G-14672)***
EAC Holdings of NY Corp 716 822-2500
701 Willet Rd Buffalo (14218) ***(G-2808)***
Ead Cases 845 343-2111
43 Smith St Middletown (10940) ***(G-8149)***
Eag Electric Inc 201 376-5103
496 Mosel Ave Staten Island (10304) ***(G-15072)***

(PA)=Parent Co (HQ)=Headquarters (DH)=Div Headquarters
2019 Harris
New York Manufacturers Directory
871

Eagle Art Publishing Inc....212 685-7411
475 Park Ave S Rm 2800 New York (10016) *(G-9602)*
Eagle Bridge Machine & Tl Inc....518 686-4541
135 State Route 67 Eagle Bridge (12057) *(G-4184)*
Eagle Business Systems, Bohemia *Also called Clintrak Clinical Labeling S (G-995)*
Eagle Comtronics Inc....315 451-3313
7665 Henry Clay Blvd Liverpool (13088) *(G-7232)*
Eagle Crest Vineyard LLC....585 346-5760
7107 Vineyard Rd Conesus (14435) *(G-3708)*
Eagle Envelope Company (HQ)....607 387-3195
8091 Trumansburg Rd Trumansburg (14886) *(G-15638)*
Eagle Fashions U S A, Brooklyn *Also called Eagle Finishing (G-1807)*
Eagle Finishing....718 497-7875
49 Wyckoff Ave Brooklyn (11237) *(G-1807)*
Eagle Graphics Inc....585 244-5006
149 Anderson Ave Rochester (14607) *(G-13755)*
Eagle Instruments Inc....914 939-6843
35 Grove St Port Chester (10573) *(G-13197)*
Eagle Lace Dyeing Corp....212 947-2712
335 W 35th St Fl 2 New York (10001) *(G-9603)*
Eagle Media Partners LP (PA)....315 434-8889
2501 James St Ste 100 Syracuse (13206) *(G-15309)*
Eagle Newspapers, Syracuse *Also called Eagle Media Partners LP (G-15309)*
Eagle Regalia Co Inc....845 425-2245
747 Chestnut Ridge Rd # 101 Spring Valley (10977) *(G-14989)*
Eagle Telephonics Inc....631 471-3600
3880 Veterans Mem Hwy Bohemia (11716) *(G-1017)*
Eagle Welding Machine....315 594-1845
13458 Ridge Rd Wolcott (14590) *(G-16610)*
Eagle Zinc Co Div, New York *Also called T L Diamond & Company Inc (G-11768)*
Eagles Nest Holdings LLC (PA)....513 874-5270
455 E 86th St New York (10028) *(G-9604)*
Earl G Graves Pubg Co Inc (HQ)....212 242-8000
260 Madison Ave Ste 11 New York (10016) *(G-9605)*
Earlville Paper Box Co Inc....315 691-2131
19 Clyde St Earlville (13332) *(G-4188)*
Earring King Jewelry Mfg Inc....718 544-7947
62 W 47th St Ste 1202 New York (10036) *(G-9606)*
Earth Enterprises Inc....212 741-3999
250 W 40th St Fl 15 New York (10018) *(G-9607)*
Earth Spectrum, New York *Also called Spectrum Prtg Lithography Inc (G-11665)*
Easco Boiler, Bronx *Also called A L Eastmond & Sons Inc (G-1201)*
Easco Boiler Corp....718 378-3000
1175 Leggett Ave Bronx (10474) *(G-1264)*
Easel, New York *Also called Ksk International Inc (G-10484)*
Easi, Flushing *Also called Easy Analytic Software Inc (G-4997)*
East Aurora Advertiser, East Aurora *Also called Grant Hamilton (G-4201)*
East Branch Winery Inc (PA)....607 292-3999
5503 Dutch St Dundee (14837) *(G-4156)*
East Cast Clor Compounding Inc....631 491-9000
15 Kean St West Babylon (11704) *(G-16154)*
East Cast Envlope Graphics LLC....718 326-2424
5615 55th Dr Maspeth (11378) *(G-7840)*
East Cast Orthtics Prosthetics....716 856-5192
505 Delaware Ave Buffalo (14202) *(G-2809)*
East Coast Business Forms Inc....631 231-9300
320 Lake Ave Ste 2 Saint James (11780) *(G-14512)*
East Coast Copacking, Brooklyn *Also called Pressed Juice LLC (G-2339)*
East Coast Cultures LLC....917 261-3010
906 State Route 28 Kingston (12401) *(G-6899)*
East Coast Cycle LLC....631 780-5360
80 Smith St Ste 1 Farmingdale (11735) *(G-4756)*
East Coast Embroidery Ltd....631 254-3878
74 Brook Ave Ste 1 Deer Park (11729) *(G-3969)*
East Coast Envmtl Group Inc....516 352-1946
136 Allen Blvd Farmingdale (11735) *(G-4757)*
East Coast Intl Tire Inc....718 386-9088
5746 Flushing Ave Bldg C Maspeth (11378) *(G-7841)*
East Coast Mines & Material, East Quogue *Also called East Coast Mines Ltd (G-4277)*
East Coast Mines Ltd....631 653-5445
2 Lewis Rd East Quogue (11942) *(G-4277)*
East Coast Molders Inc....516 240-6000
3001 New St Ste F Oceanside (11572) *(G-12536)*
East Coast Orthoic & Pros Cor (PA)....516 248-5566
75 Burt Dr Deer Park (11729) *(G-3970)*
East Coast Orthoic & Pros Cor....212 923-2161
3927 Broadway New York (10032) *(G-9608)*
East Coast Spring Mix Inc....845 355-1215
211 Lynch Ave New Hampton (10958) *(G-8500)*
East Coast Thermographers Inc....718 321-3211
1558 127th St Ste 1 College Point (11356) *(G-3643)*
East Coast Tool & Mfg....716 826-5183
1 Alliance Dr Buffalo (14218) *(G-2810)*
East End....716 532-2622
1995 Lenox Rd Collins (14034) *(G-3673)*
East End Country Kitchens Inc....631 727-2258
121 Edwards Ave Calverton (11933) *(G-3165)*
East End Sign Design Inc....631 399-2574
1425 Montauk Hwy Mastic (11950) *(G-7911)*
East End Vineyards LLC....718 468-0500
21548 Jamaica Ave Queens Village (11428) *(G-13405)*
East Hampton Ind News Inc....631 324-2500
74 Montauk Hwy Unit 19 East Hampton (11937) *(G-4235)*
East Hampton Independent The, East Hampton *Also called East Hampton Ind News Inc (G-4235)*
East Hampton Star Inc....631 324-0002
153 Main St East Hampton (11937) *(G-4236)*
East Hill Creamery LLC....585 237-3622
346 Main St S Perry (14530) *(G-12968)*
East Hills Instrument Inc....516 621-8686
60 Shames Dr Westbury (11590) *(G-16325)*
East Hudson Watershed Corp....845 319-6349
2 Route 164 Patterson (12563) *(G-12881)*
East Main Associates....585 624-1990
7520 E Main St Lima (14485) *(G-7151)*
East Meet East Inc....646 481-0033
32 W 39th St Fl 4 New York (10018) *(G-9609)*
East Pattern & Model Corp (PA)....585 461-3240
769 Trabold Rd Rochester (14624) *(G-13756)*
East Pattern & Model Corp....585 461-3240
80 Saginaw Dr Rochester (14623) *(G-13757)*
East Penn Manufacturing Co....631 321-7161
790 Railroad Ave Babylon (11704) *(G-526)*
East Ridge Quick Print....585 266-4911
1249 Ridgeway Ave Ste Y Rochester (14615) *(G-13758)*
East Side Machine Inc....585 265-4560
625 Phillips Rd Webster (14580) *(G-16083)*
East To West Architectral Pdts....631 433-9690
103 Tinton Pl Ste 1a East Northport (11731) *(G-4262)*
East West Global Sourcing Inc....917 887-2286
425 Neptune Ave Apt 22a Brooklyn (11224) *(G-1808)*
East/West Industries Inc....631 981-5900
2002 Orville Dr N Ronkonkoma (11779) *(G-14335)*
Eastco Manufacturing Corp....914 738-5667
323 Fifth Ave Pelham (10803) *(G-12934)*
Eastend Enforcement Products....631 878-8424
50 Dillmont Dr Smithtown (11787) *(G-14898)*
Eastern Air Products LLC....716 391-1866
41 Ward Rd Lancaster (14086) *(G-7017)*
Eastern Castings Co....518 677-5610
2 Pearl St Cambridge (12816) *(G-3180)*
Eastern Color Imaging, Bohemia *Also called Eastern Color Stripping Inc (G-1018)*
Eastern Color Stripping Inc....631 563-3700
666 Lanson St Bohemia (11716) *(G-1018)*
Eastern Company....315 468-6251
3000 Milton Ave Solvay (13209) *(G-14917)*
Eastern Concepts Ltd....718 472-3377
4125 39th St Sunnyside (11104) *(G-15203)*
Eastern Enterprise Corp....718 727-8600
465 Bay St Ste 2 Staten Island (10304) *(G-15073)*
Eastern Exterior Wall....631 589-3880
869 Lincoln Ave Bohemia (11716) *(G-1019)*
Eastern Feather & Down Corp....718 387-4100
1027 Metropolitan Ave Brooklyn (11211) *(G-1809)*
Eastern Finding Corp....516 747-6640
116 County Courthouse Rd New Hyde Park (11040) *(G-8530)*
Eastern Hills Printing (PA)....716 741-3300
9195 Main St Clarence (14031) *(G-3530)*
Eastern Industrial Steel Corp (PA)....845 639-9749
4 Fringe Ct New City (10956) *(G-8493)*
Eastern Jewelry Mfg Co Inc....212 840-0001
48 W 48th St Ste 707 New York (10036) *(G-9610)*
Eastern Jungle Gym Inc (PA)....845 878-9800
30 Commerce Dr Carmel (10512) *(G-3275)*
Eastern Machine and Electric....716 284-8271
1041 Niagara Ave Niagara Falls (14305) *(G-12280)*
Eastern Manufacturing Inc....716 741-4572
9530 Cobblestone Dr Clarence (14031) *(G-3531)*
Eastern Metal of Elmira Inc (PA)....607 734-2295
1430 Sullivan St Elmira (14901) *(G-4482)*
Eastern Niagra Radiology....716 882-6544
899 Main St Buffalo (14203) *(G-2811)*
Eastern Offset, Albany *Also called Northeast Commercial Prtg Inc (G-106)*
Eastern Precision Machining....631 286-4758
11 Farber Dr Ste I Bellport (11713) *(G-802)*
Eastern Precision Mfg....845 358-1951
76 S Franklin St 78 Nyack (10960) *(G-12506)*
Eastern Silk Mills Inc....212 730-1300
148 W 37th St Fl 3 New York (10018) *(G-9611)*
Eastern Silver of Boro Park....718 854-5600
4901 16th Ave Brooklyn (11204) *(G-1810)*
Eastern Storefronts & Mtls Inc....631 471-7065
1739 Julia Goldbach Ave Ronkonkoma (11779) *(G-14336)*
Eastern Strategic Materials....212 332-1619
45 Rockefeller Plz # 2000 New York (10111) *(G-9612)*
Eastern Unit Exch Rmnfacturing....718 739-7113
186 Beech St Floral Park (11001) *(G-4963)*
Eastern Welding Inc....631 727-0306
274 Mill Rd Riverhead (11901) *(G-13568)*
Easterncctv (usa) LLC (PA)....516 870-3779
50 Commercial St Plainview (11803) *(G-13052)*
Eastland Electronics Co Inc....631 580-3800
700 Union Pkwy Ste 9 Ronkonkoma (11779) *(G-14337)*

Eastman Chemical Company ...585 722-2905
2255 Mount Read Blvd Rochester (14615) *(G-13759)*
Eastman Kodak Company ...585 722-2187
233 Olde Harbour Trl Rochester (14612) *(G-13760)*
Eastman Kodak Company (PA) ...585 724-4000
343 State St Rochester (14650) *(G-13761)*
Eastman Kodak Company ...585 724-5600
1669 Lake Ave Bldg 31-4 Rochester (14652) *(G-13762)*
Eastman Kodak Company ...585 722-9695
1818 W Jefferson Rd Pittsford (14534) *(G-13010)*
Eastman Kodak Company ...585 726-6261
39 Kaywood Dr Rochester (14626) *(G-13763)*
Eastman Kodak Company ...585 724-4000
2600 Manitou Rd Rochester (14650) *(G-13764)*
Eastman Kodak Company ...800 698-3324
343 State St Rochester (14650) *(G-13765)*
Eastman Kodak Company ...585 722-4385
1999 Lake Ave 6/83/RI Rochester (14650) *(G-13766)*
Eastman Kodak Company ...585 588-5598
300 Weiland Road Rochester (14650) *(G-13767)*
Eastman Kodak Company ...585 726-7000
343 State St Rochester (14650) *(G-13768)*
Eastman Kodak Company ...585 722-4007
336 Initiative Dr Rochester (14624) *(G-13769)*
Eastman Kodak Company ...585 588-3896
100 Latona Rd Gate 340 Rochester (14652) *(G-13770)*
Eastman Kodak Company ...585 724-4000
343 State St Rochester (14650) *(G-13771)*
Eastman Machine Company ...716 856-2200
779 Washington St Buffalo (14203) *(G-2812)*
Eastman Park Micrographics Inc ...866 934-4376
100 Latona Rd Bldg 318 Rochester (14652) *(G-13772)*
Eastnets Americas Corp ...212 631-0666
450 7th Ave Ste 1509 New York (10123) *(G-9613)*
Easton Pharmaceuticals Inc ...347 284-0192
736 Center St Ste 5 Lewiston (14092) *(G-7139)*
Eastport Feeds Inc ...631 325-0077
140 E Moriches Blvd Eastport (11941) *(G-4384)*
Eastside Orthotics Prosthetics, New York *Also called Manhattan Eastside Dev Corp (G-10685)*
Eastside Oxide Co ...607 734-1253
211 Judson St Elmira (14901) *(G-4483)*
Eastwood Litho Inc ...315 437-2626
4020 New Court Ave Syracuse (13206) *(G-15310)*
Easy Analytic Software Inc (PA) ...718 740-7930
7359 196th St Flushing (11366) *(G-4997)*
Easy Book Publishing Inc ...518 459-6281
260 Osborne Rd Ste 3 Albany (12211) *(G-70)*
Easy H2b, Hudson *Also called Micosta Enterprises Inc (G-6364)*
Eaten Lightened, Bronx *Also called Beyond Better Foods LLC (G-1228)*
Eating Evolved Inc ...516 510-2601
10 Technology Dr Unit 4 East Setauket (11733) *(G-4300)*
Eatingevolved LLC ...631 675-2440
10 Technology Dr Unit 4 Setauket (11733) *(G-14794)*
Eaton Brothers Corp ...716 649-8250
3530 Lakeview Rd Hamburg (14075) *(G-5676)*
Eaton Corporation ...516 353-3017
280 Bellmore Rd East Meadow (11554) *(G-4251)*
Eaton Corporation ...315 579-2872
125 E Jefferson St Syracuse (13202) *(G-15311)*
Eaton Crouse-Hinds ...315 477-7000
1201 Wolf St Syracuse (13208) *(G-15312)*
Eatons Crouse Hinds Business ...315 477-7000
1201 Wolf St Syracuse (13208) *(G-15313)*
Eaw Electronic Systems Inc ...845 471-5290
900 Dutchess Tpke Ste 3 Poughkeepsie (12603) *(G-13336)*
Eazy Locks LLC ...718 327-7770
1914 Mott Ave Far Rockaway (11691) *(G-4699)*
Eazylift Albany LLC ...518 452-6929
836 Troy Schenectady Rd Latham (12110) *(G-7071)*
EB Acquisitions LLC ...212 355-3310
444 Madison Ave Ste 501 New York (10022) *(G-9614)*
Eb Couture Ltd ...212 912-0190
110 W 34th St Rm 1002 New York (10001) *(G-9615)*
EB&I Marketing, Skaneateles *Also called Burdick Publications Inc (G-14867)*
Ebc Technologies LLC ...631 729-8182
200 Motor Pkwy Ste D26 Hauppauge (11788) *(G-5817)*
Ebeling Associates Inc (PA) ...518 688-8700
9 Corporate Dr Ste 1 Halfmoon (12065) *(G-5662)*
Ebenezer Railcar Services Inc ...716 674-5650
1005 Indian Church Rd West Seneca (14224) *(G-16296)*
Eberhardt Enterprises Inc ...585 458-7681
1325 Mount Read Blvd Rochester (14606) *(G-13773)*
EBM, Westbury *Also called Executive Business Media Inc (G-16329)*
EBM Care Inc ...212 500-5000
317 Madison Ave New York (10017) *(G-9616)*
Ebner Publishing International ...646 742-0740
37 W 26th St Rm 412 New York (10010) *(G-9617)*
Eboost, New York *Also called Vitalize Labs LLC (G-12046)*
Ebrevia Inc ...203 870-3000
12 E 49th St Fl 11 New York (10017) *(G-9618)*

Ebsco Industries Inc ...585 398-2000
5815 County Road 41 Farmington (14425) *(G-4912)*
EBY Electro Inc ...516 576-7777
210 Express St Plainview (11803) *(G-13053)*
EC Wood & Company Inc ...718 388-2287
110 E Industry Ct Deer Park (11729) *(G-3971)*
Eccella Corporation ...718 612-0451
75 Broad St Rm 2900 New York (10004) *(G-9619)*
Ecclesiastical Communications ...212 688-2399
1011 1st Ave Fl 6 New York (10022) *(G-9620)*
Ecclesiastical Press, Edmeston *Also called Bishop Print Shop Inc (G-4425)*
Ecco Bay Sportswear, New York *Also called Cathy Daniels Ltd (G-9231)*
Echo Appellate Press Inc ...516 432-3601
30 W Park Ave Ste 200 Long Beach (11561) *(G-7358)*
Echo Group Inc ...917 608-7440
62 W 39th St Ste 1005 New York (10018) *(G-9621)*
Eci, Norwich *Also called Electron Coil Inc (G-12485)*
Eck Plastic Arts Inc ...607 722-3227
87 Prospect Ave Binghamton (13901) *(G-880)*
Ecker Window Corp ...914 776-0000
1 Odell Plz Yonkers (10701) *(G-16753)*
Ecko Fin & Tooling Inc ...716 487-0200
221 Hopkins Ave Ste 2 Jamestown (14701) *(G-6712)*
Eclectic Cntract Furn Inds Inc ...212 967-5504
450 Fashion Ave Ste 2710 New York (10123) *(G-9622)*
Eclipse Collection Jewelers (PA) ...212 764-6883
7 W 45th St Rm 1401 New York (10036) *(G-9623)*
Eco-Bat America LLC ...845 692-4414
65 Ballard Rd Middletown (10941) *(G-8150)*
Ecolab Inc ...716 683-6298
3719 Union Rd Ste 121 Cheektowaga (14225) *(G-3443)*
Ecological Laboratories Inc (PA) ...516 823-3441
4 Waterford Rd Island Park (11558) *(G-6513)*
Econocraft Worldwide Mfg Inc ...914 966-2280
56 Worth St Frnt Unit Yonkers (10701) *(G-16754)*
Econometric Software Inc ...516 938-5254
15 Gloria Pl Plainview (11803) *(G-13054)*
Economist Intelligence Unit NA ...212 554-0600
750 3rd Ave Fl 5 New York (10017) *(G-9624)*
Economist Magazine, The, New York *Also called Economist Newspaper NA Inc (G-9625)*
Economist Newspaper NA Inc (HQ) ...212 554-0676
750 3rd Ave Fl 5 New York (10017) *(G-9625)*
Economy Pump & Motor Repr Inc ...718 433-2600
3652 36th St Astoria (11106) *(G-425)*
Ecoplast & Packaging LLC ...718 996-0800
4619 Surf Ave Brooklyn (11224) *(G-1811)*
Ecosmartplastics, Bohemia *Also called Repellem Consumer Pdts Corp (G-1082)*
ECR International Inc (PA) ...315 797-1310
2201 Dwyer Ave Utica (13501) *(G-15699)*
ECR International Inc ...716 366-5500
85 Middle Rd Dunkirk (14048) *(G-4169)*
Ecs Global, Brooklyn *Also called Energy Conservation & Sup Inc (G-1836)*
Ecto Tech Automation, Buffalo *Also called Multisorb Technologies Inc (G-2958)*
Ecuador News Inc ...718 205-7014
6403 Roosevelt Ave Fl 2 Woodside (11377) *(G-16654)*
Ed Beach Forest Management ...607 538-1745
2042 Scott Rd Bloomville (13739) *(G-960)*
Ed Levin Inc ...518 677-8595
52 W Main St Cambridge (12816) *(G-3181)*
Ed Levin Jewelry, Cambridge *Also called Ed Levin Inc (G-3181)*
Ed Negron Fine Woodworking ...718 246-1016
43 Hall St Fl 5 Brooklyn (11205) *(G-1812)*
Edco Sales, Syracuse *Also called Camfil Usa Inc (G-15269)*
Edco Supply Corporation ...718 788-8108
323 36th St Brooklyn (11232) *(G-1813)*
Eden Tool & Die Inc ...716 992-4240
2721 Hemlock Rd Eden (14057) *(G-4388)*
Edesia World Wide LLC ...646 705-3505
1485 5th Ave New York (10035) *(G-9626)*
Edge Display Group Entp Inc ...631 498-1373
35 Sawgrass Dr Ste 2 Bellport (11713) *(G-803)*
Edgewood Industries Inc ...516 227-2447
635 Commercial Ave Garden City (11530) *(G-5257)*
Edgian Press Inc ...516 931-2114
10 Bethpage Rd Hicksville (11801) *(G-6082)*
Edible Arragement, Babylon *Also called Nsj Group Ltd (G-530)*
Edible Arrangement Store 1373, Hicksville *Also called Noaspence Inc (G-6114)*
Edison Power & Light Co Inc ...718 522-0002
204 Van Dyke St 207 Brooklyn (11231) *(G-1814)*
Edison Price Lighting Inc (PA) ...718 685-0700
4150 22nd St Long Island City (11101) *(G-7433)*
Edison Price Lighting Inc ...718 685-0700
4105 21st St Long Island City (11101) *(G-7434)*
Edith Lances Corp ...212 683-1990
247 W 35th St Fl 2 New York (10001) *(G-9627)*
Editions De Prfums Madison LLC (HQ) ...646 666-0527
654 Madison Ave Rm 1609 New York (10065) *(G-9628)*
Edlaw Pharmaceuticals Inc ...631 454-6888
195 Central Ave Ste B Farmingdale (11735) *(G-4758)*
EDM Mfg ...631 669-1966
141 John St Ste 600 Babylon (11702) *(G-527)*

ALPHABETIC

(PA)=Parent Co (HQ)=Headquarters (DH)=Div Headquarters
2019 Harris
New York Manufacturers Directory
873

Edo Crprtion-Fiber Science Div, Bohemia *Also called Edo LLC* ***(G-1020)***
Edo LLC (HQ)....631 630-4000
1500 New Horizons Blvd Amityville (11701) ***(G-272)***
Edo LLC....631 218-1413
5852 Johnson Ave Bohemia (11716) ***(G-1020)***
Edo LLC....631 630-4200
1500 New Horizons Blvd Amityville (11701) ***(G-273)***
Edo LLC....631 630-4000
1500 New Horizons Blvd Amityville (11701) ***(G-274)***
EDP Renewables North Amer LLC....518 426-1650
1971 Western Ave 230 Albany (12203) ***(G-71)***
Edr Industries Inc....516 868-1928
100 Commercial St Freeport (11520) ***(G-5152)***
Edrington Group Usa LLC (PA)....212 352-6000
27 W 23rd St Fl 4 New York (10010) ***(G-9629)***
Edroy Products Co Inc....845 358-6600
245 N Midland Ave Nyack (10960) ***(G-12507)***
Edsal Machine Products Inc (PA)....718 439-9163
126 56th St Brooklyn (11220) ***(G-1815)***
Edsim Leather Co Inc (PA)....212 695-8500
131 W 35th St Fl 14 New York (10001) ***(G-9630)***
Educational Networks Inc....866 526-0200
104 W 40th St Rm 1810 New York (10018) ***(G-9631)***
Edward C Lyons Company Inc....718 515-5361
3646 White Plains Rd Frnt Bronx (10467) ***(G-1265)***
Edward C Muller Corp....718 881-7270
3646 White Plains Rd Frnt Bronx (10467) ***(G-1266)***
Edward C. Lyons, Bronx *Also called Edward C Muller Corp* ***(G-1266)***
Edwards Graphic Co Inc....718 548-6858
3801 Hudson Manor Ter 4s Bronx (10463) ***(G-1267)***
Edwards Vacuum LLC (HQ)....800 848-9800
6416 Inducon Dr W Sanborn (14132) ***(G-14544)***
Edwin J McKenica & Sons Inc....716 823-4646
1200 Clinton St Buffalo (14206) ***(G-2813)***
Edwin Mellen Press Inc....716 754-2796
442 Center St Lewiston (14092) ***(G-7140)***
Eeboo Corporation....212 222-0823
170 W 74th St Apt 102 New York (10023) ***(G-9632)***
Eeg Enterprises Inc....516 293-7472
586 Main St Farmingdale (11735) ***(G-4759)***
Efam Enterprises LLC....718 204-1760
3731 29th St Long Island City (11101) ***(G-7435)***
Effective Slling Solutions LLC....716 771-8503
1898 Hanley Dr Lake View (14085) ***(G-6983)***
Efficiency Printing Co Inc....914 949-8611
126 S Lexington Ave White Plains (10606) ***(G-16444)***
Efj Inc....518 234-4799
128 Macarthur Ave Cobleskill (12043) ***(G-3602)***
Efron Designs Ltd....718 482-8440
2121 41st Ave Ste 5b Long Island City (11101) ***(G-7436)***
Efront Financial Solutions Inc....212 220-0660
11 E 44th St Fl 15 New York (10017) ***(G-9633)***
Efs Designs LLC....718 852-9511
610 Smith St Ste 3 Brooklyn (11231) ***(G-1816)***
Eft Analytics Inc....212 290-2300
350 5th Ave Ste 4810 New York (10118) ***(G-9634)***
Eg Indsturies, Rochester *Also called Ernie Green Industries Inc* ***(G-13792)***
Eg Industries, Rochester *Also called Ernie Green Industries Inc* ***(G-13790)***
Eg Industries, Rochester *Also called Ernie Green Industries Inc* ***(G-13791)***
Egg Low Farms Inc....607 674-4653
35 W State St Sherburne (13460) ***(G-14805)***
Egli Machine Company Inc....607 563-3663
240 State Highway 7 Sidney (13838) ***(G-14853)***
Egmont US Inc....212 685-0102
443 Park Ave S Rm 806 New York (10016) ***(G-9635)***
Ehrlich Enterprises Inc....631 956-0690
82 Wyandanch Ave Unit C Wyandanch (11798) ***(G-16695)***
Ehs Group LLC....914 937-6162
69 Townsend St Port Chester (10573) ***(G-13198)***
Ei, Endicott *Also called Endicott Interconnect Tech Inc* ***(G-4588)***
El Electronics Inc....516 334-0870
1800 Shames Dr Westbury (11590) ***(G-16326)***
Eidosmedia Inc....646 795-2100
14 Wall St Ste 6c New York (10005) ***(G-9636)***
Eileens Special Cheesecake....212 966-5585
17 Cleveland Pl Frnt A New York (10012) ***(G-9637)***
Eis Inc....585 426-5330
40 Hytec Cir Rochester (14606) ***(G-13774)***
Eiseman-Ludmar Co Inc....516 932-6990
56 Bethpage Dr Hicksville (11801) ***(G-6083)***
Eisen Bros, Brooklyn *Also called National Die & Button Mould Co* ***(G-2245)***
Ej Group Inc....315 699-2601
6177 S Bay Rd Cicero (13039) ***(G-3517)***
Eko-Blu, New York *Also called N Y Winstons Inc* ***(G-10870)***
Ekostinger Inc....585 739-0450
140 Despatch Dr East Rochester (14445) ***(G-4283)***
Eks Manufacturing Inc....917 217-0784
577 Wortman Ave Brooklyn (11208) ***(G-1817)***
El Diario LLC....212 807-4600
1 Metrotech Ctr Fl 1801 Brooklyn (11201) ***(G-1818)***
EL Erman International Ltd....212 444-9440
1205 E 29th St Brooklyn (11210) ***(G-1819)***
El Greco Woodworking Inc (PA)....716 483-0315
106 E 1st St Ste 1 Jamestown (14701) ***(G-6713)***
El-Don Battery Post Inc....716 627-3697
4109 Saint Francis Dr Hamburg (14075) ***(G-5677)***
El-Gen LLC....631 218-3400
7 Shirley St Unit 1 Bohemia (11716) ***(G-1021)***
El-La Design Inc....212 382-1080
209 W 38th St Rm 901 New York (10018) ***(G-9638)***
Ela, New York *Also called Electric Lighting Agencies* ***(G-9640)***
Elab Smokers Boutique....585 865-4513
4373 Lake Ave Rochester (14612) ***(G-13775)***
Elam Materials Inc....585 658-2248
1 Conlon Ave Mount Morris (14510) ***(G-8366)***
Elam Sand & Gravel Corp (PA)....585 657-8000
8222 State Route 5 And 20 Bloomfield (14469) ***(G-953)***
Elan Upholstery Inc....631 563-0650
120b Wilbur Pl Ste B Bohemia (11716) ***(G-1022)***
Elana Laderos Ltd....212 764-0840
230 W 38th St Fl 15 New York (10018) ***(G-9639)***
Elanco Animal Health, New Hyde Park *Also called Eli Lilly and Company* ***(G-8532)***
Elantas Pdg Inc....716 372-9650
1405 Buffalo St Olean (14760) ***(G-12602)***
Elara Brands, Jericho *Also called Elara Fdsrvice Disposables LLC* ***(G-6786)***
Elara Fdsrvice Disposables LLC....877 893-3244
420 Jericho Tpke Ste 320 Jericho (11753) ***(G-6786)***
Elastomers Inc....716 633-4883
2095 Wehrle Dr Williamsville (14221) ***(G-16578)***
Elco Manufacturing Co Inc (PA)....516 767-3577
26 Ivy Way Port Washington (11050) ***(G-13257)***
Elderlee Incorporated (HQ)....315 789-6670
729 Cross Rd Oaks Corners (14518) ***(G-12527)***
Eldorado Coffee Distributors, Maspeth *Also called Eldorado Coffee Roasters Ltd* ***(G-7842)***
Eldorado Coffee Roasters Ltd....718 418-4100
5675 49th St Maspeth (11378) ***(G-7842)***
Eleanors Best....845 809-5621
15 Peacock Way Garrison (10524) ***(G-5303)***
Electomechanical Componets, Auburn *Also called Emcom Inc* ***(G-477)***
Electrcal Instrumentation Ctrl....518 861-5789
1253 Youngs Rd Delanson (12053) ***(G-4068)***
Electric City Concrete Co Inc (HQ)....518 887-5560
774 State Highway 5s Amsterdam (12010) ***(G-335)***
Electric Lighting Agencies (PA)....212 645-4580
36 W 25th St Fl 6 New York (10010) ***(G-9640)***
Electric Motor Specialties, Jamestown *Also called Electric Motor Specialty Inc* ***(G-6714)***
Electric Motor Specialty, Jamestown *Also called Sunset Ridge Holdings Inc* ***(G-6753)***
Electric Motor Specialty Inc....716 487-1458
490 Crescent St Jamestown (14701) ***(G-6714)***
Electric Motors and Pumps Inc....718 935-9118
466 Carroll St Brooklyn (11215) ***(G-1820)***
Electric Swtchbard Sltions LLC....718 643-1105
270 Park Ave New Hyde Park (11040) ***(G-8531)***
Electrical Controls Link....585 924-7010
100 Rawson Rd Ste 220 Victor (14564) ***(G-15843)***
Electro Abrasives LLC....716 822-2500
701 Willet Rd Buffalo (14218) ***(G-2814)***
Electro Alloy Recovery Inc....631 879-7530
130 Knickerbocker Ave M Bohemia (11716) ***(G-1023)***
Electro Form Corp....607 722-6404
128 Bevier St Binghamton (13904) ***(G-881)***
Electro Industries, Westbury *Also called El Electronics Inc* ***(G-16326)***
Electro Plating Service Inc....914 948-3777
127 Oakley Ave White Plains (10601) ***(G-16445)***
Electro Waste Systems, Bohemia *Also called Electro Alloy Recovery Inc* ***(G-1023)***
ELECTRO-HARMONIX, Long Island City *Also called New Sensor Corporation* ***(G-7538)***
Electro-Metrics Corporation....518 762-2600
231 Enterprise Rd Johnstown (12095) ***(G-6825)***
Electro-Optical Products Corp....718 456-6000
6240 Forest Ave Fl 2 Ridgewood (11385) ***(G-13535)***
Electrochem Solutions Inc (HQ)....716 759-5800
10000 Wehrle Dr Clarence (14031) ***(G-3532)***
Electron Coil Inc....607 336-7414
141 Barr Rd Norwich (13815) ***(G-12485)***
Electron Top Mfg Co Inc....718 846-7400
12615 89th Ave Richmond Hill (11418) ***(G-13501)***
Electronic Arts Inc....212 672-0722
1515 Broadway Rm 3601 New York (10036) ***(G-9641)***
Electronic Coating Tech Inc (PA)....518 688-2048
1 Mustang Dr Ste 4 Cohoes (12047) ***(G-3610)***
Electronic Devices Inc (HQ)....914 965-4400
21 Gray Oaks Ave Yonkers (10710) ***(G-16755)***
Electronic Die Corp....718 455-3200
19th St Fl 2 Flr 2 Brooklyn (11232) ***(G-1821)***
Electronic Machine Parts LLC....631 434-3700
400 Oser Ave Ste 2000 Hauppauge (11788) ***(G-5818)***
Electronic Printing Inc....631 218-2200
1200 Prime Pl Hauppauge (11788) ***(G-5819)***
Electronic Systems Inc....631 589-4389
1742 Church St Holbrook (11741) ***(G-6184)***
Electronic Tech Briefs, New York *Also called Abp International Inc* ***(G-8712)***
Electronics & Innovation Ltd....585 214-0598
150 Research Blvd Rochester (14623) ***(G-13776)***

Electronics Systems Division, Hauppauge *Also called Parker-Hannifin Corporation* ***(G-5909)***
Electrosurgical Instrument Co, Rochester *Also called Ftt Medical Inc* ***(G-13819)***
Electrotech Service Eqp Corp.........718 626-7700
2450 46th St Astoria (11103) ***(G-426)***
Elegance Coating Ltd.........386 668-8379
33 W Service Rd 100 Champlain (12919) ***(G-3408)***
Elegant Desserts By Metro Inc.........718 388-1323
868 Kent Ave Brooklyn (11205) ***(G-1822)***
Elegant Headwear Co Inc.........212 695-8520
10 W 33rd St Rm 1122 New York (10001) ***(G-9642)***
Elegant Jewelers Mfg Co Inc.........212 869-4951
31 W 47th St Ste 301 New York (10036) ***(G-9643)***
Elegant Linen Inc.........718 492-0297
200 60th St Brooklyn (11220) ***(G-1823)***
Elegant Sportswear, Brooklyn *Also called K & S Childrens Wear Inc* ***(G-2062)***
Element K, Rochester *Also called Skillsoft Corporation* ***(G-14130)***
Element St Johns Corp.........917 349-2139
764 Saint Johns Pl Brooklyn (11216) ***(G-1824)***
Elementar Americas Inc.........856 787-0022
119 Comac St Ronkonkoma (11779) ***(G-14338)***
Elementis Srl Inc (HQ).........845 692-3914
15 Big Pond Rd Huguenot (12746) ***(G-6385)***
Eleni's Cookies, Long Island City *Also called Elenis Nyc Inc* ***(G-7437)***
Elenis Nyc Inc (PA).........718 361-8136
4725 34th St Ste 305 Long Island City (11101) ***(G-7437)***
Elepath Inc.........347 417-4975
110 Kent Ave 9 Brooklyn (11249) ***(G-1825)***
Elephants Custom Furniture Inc.........917 509-3581
67 Van Dam St Brooklyn (11222) ***(G-1826)***
Elevator Accessories Mfg.........914 739-7004
1035 Howard St 37 Peekskill (10566) ***(G-12919)***
Elevator Interiors Inc.........315 218-7186
1116 S Salina St Syracuse (13202) ***(G-15314)***
Elevator Ventures Corporation.........212 375-1900
9720 99th St Ozone Park (11416) ***(G-12824)***
Elevondata Labs Inc.........470 222-5438
1350 Ave Of The Amrcs 2nd New York (10019) ***(G-9644)***
Eli Lilly and Company.........516 622-2244
1979 Marcus Ave New Hyde Park (11042) ***(G-8532)***
Elias Artmetal Inc.........516 873-7501
70 E 2nd St Mineola (11501) ***(G-8217)***
Elias Fragrances Inc (PA).........718 693-6400
3 Hunter Dr Rye Brook (10573) ***(G-14491)***
Elie Balleh Couture, New York *Also called Eb Couture Ltd* ***(G-9615)***
Elie Tahari Ltd.........212 398-2622
501 5th Ave Fl 2 New York (10017) ***(G-9645)***
Elie Tahari Ltd.........212 398-2622
510 5th Ave Fl 3 New York (10036) ***(G-9646)***
Elie Tahari Ltd.........631 329-8883
1 Main St East Hampton (11937) ***(G-4237)***
Elie Tahari Ltd.........212 763-2000
1114 Ave Of The Americas New York (10036) ***(G-9647)***
Elie Tahari Ltd.........973 671-6300
510 5th Ave Lbby A New York (10036) ***(G-9648)***
Elima-Draft Incorporated.........631 375-2830
20 Hopewell Dr Stony Brook (11790) ***(G-15165)***
Elis Bread (eli Zabar) Inc (PA).........212 772-2011
1064 Madison Ave Apt 5 New York (10028) ***(G-9649)***
Elite Cellular Accessories Inc.........877 390-2502
61 E Industry Ct Deer Park (11729) ***(G-3972)***
Elite Coffee Roasters, East Amherst *Also called Elite Roasters Inc* ***(G-4189)***
Elite Daily Inc.........212 402-9097
53 W 23rd St Fl 12 New York (10010) ***(G-9650)***
Elite Machine Inc.........585 289-4733
3 Merrick Cir Manchester (14504) ***(G-7760)***
Elite Parfums Ltd (HQ).........212 983-2640
551 5th Ave Rm 1500 New York (10176) ***(G-9651)***
Elite Precise Manufacturer LLC.........518 993-3040
55 Willett St Fort Plain (13339) ***(G-5102)***
Elite Roasters Inc (PA).........716 626-0307
8600 Transit Rd Ste 1b East Amherst (14051) ***(G-4189)***
Elite Semi Conductor Products.........631 884-8400
860 N Richmond Ave Lindenhurst (11757) ***(G-7172)***
Elite Traveler LLC.........646 430-7900
441 Lexington Ave Fl 3 New York (10017) ***(G-9652)***
Elite Traveler Magazine, New York *Also called Universal Cmmncations of Miami* ***(G-11958)***
Elitsac Inc.........585 493-2628
103 S Main St Castile (14427) ***(G-3293)***
Elitsac Lumber, Castile *Also called Elitsac Inc* ***(G-3293)***
Elizabeth Arden, New York *Also called Unilever United States Inc* ***(G-11945)***
Elizabeth Arden Inc.........845 810-2175
214 Red Apple Ct Central Valley (10917) ***(G-3396)***
Elizabeth Eakins Inc (PA).........212 628-1950
654 Madison Ave Rm 1409 New York (10065) ***(G-9653)***
Elizabeth Fillmore LLC.........212 647-0863
27 W 20th St Ste 705 New York (10011) ***(G-9654)***
Elizabeth Gillett Ltd.........212 629-7993
260 W 36th St Rm 802 New York (10018) ***(G-9655)***
Elizabeth Gillett Designs, New York *Also called Elizabeth Gillett Ltd* ***(G-9655)***
Elizabeth Wilson.........516 486-2157
579 Edgemere Ave Uniondale (11553) ***(G-15665)***
Elizabeth Wood.........315 492-5470
4900 Broad Rd Syracuse (13215) ***(G-15315)***
Elizabeth's, Uniondale *Also called Elizabeth Wilson* ***(G-15665)***
Ella Design, New York *Also called Lai Apparel Design Inc* ***(G-10509)***
Elle Magazine, New York *Also called Hearst Corporation* ***(G-10064)***
Ellenburg Recyclers.........518 594-3900
5005 State Route 11 Ellenburg Depot (12935) ***(G-4436)***
Ellicottville Distillery LLC.........716 597-6121
5462 Robbins Rd Ellicottville (14731) ***(G-4445)***
Ellicottville Kitchen Eqp, Salamanca *Also called Strategies North America Inc* ***(G-14534)***
Elliot Industries Inc.........716 287-3100
Leach Rd Ellington (14732) ***(G-4448)***
Elliot Lauren, New York *Also called I S C A Corp* ***(G-10160)***
Elliot Lucca, New York *Also called Indonesian Imports Inc* ***(G-10200)***
Elliot Mann Nyc Inc.........212 260-0658
324 E 9th St Frnt A New York (10003) ***(G-9656)***
Elliquence LLC.........516 277-9000
2455 Grand Ave Baldwin (11510) ***(G-538)***
Ellis Products Corp (PA).........516 791-3732
628 Golf Dr Valley Stream (11581) ***(G-15778)***
Ellison Bronze Inc.........716 665-6522
125 W Main St Falconer (14733) ***(G-4675)***
Ellman International, Hicksville *Also called Cynosure Inc* ***(G-6078)***
Elm Graphics Inc.........315 737-5984
9694 Mallory Rd New Hartford (13413) ***(G-8503)***
Elm Ready Mix, Westbury *Also called Elm Transit Mix Corporation* ***(G-16327)***
Elm Transit Mix Corporation.........516 333-6144
482 Grand Blvd Westbury (11590) ***(G-16327)***
Elma Press, Elma *Also called Frederick Coon Inc* ***(G-4450)***
Elmar Industries Inc.........716 681-5650
200 Gould Ave Depew (14043) ***(G-4088)***
Elmat Quality Printing Ltd.........516 569-5722
79 Columbia Ave Cedarhurst (11516) ***(G-3331)***
Elmgang Enterprises I Inc.........212 868-4142
354 W 38th St Frnt New York (10018) ***(G-9657)***
Elmgrove Technologies Div, Rochester *Also called Photonamics Inc* ***(G-14020)***
Elmira Heat Treating Inc.........607 734-1577
407 S Kinyon St Elmira (14904) ***(G-4484)***
Elmira Star-Gazette, Elmira *Also called Star-Gazette Fund Inc* ***(G-4503)***
Elmont North Little League.........516 775-8210
1532 Clay St Elmont (11003) ***(G-4518)***
Elmsford Sheet Metal Works Inc.........914 739-6300
23 Arlo Ln Cortlandt Manor (10567) ***(G-3900)***
Elo Touch Solutions Inc.........585 427-2802
2245 Brdgtn Hnrtta Twn Ln Rochester (14623) ***(G-13777)***
Elodina Inc.........646 402-5202
222 Broadway Fl 19 New York (10038) ***(G-9658)***
Elramida Holdings Inc.........646 280-0503
2555 E 29th St Brooklyn (11235) ***(G-1827)***
Elrene Home Fashions, New York *Also called Josie Accessories Inc* ***(G-10366)***
Elsag North America LLC.........877 773-5724
7 Sutton Pl Ste A Brewster (10509) ***(G-1164)***
Elsevier Inc (HQ).........212 989-5800
230 Park Ave Fl 8 New York (10169) ***(G-9659)***
Eltee Tool & Die Co.........607 748-4301
404 E Franklin St Endicott (13760) ***(G-4587)***
Elton El Mantle Inc.........315 432-9067
6072 Court Street Rd Syracuse (13206) ***(G-15316)***
Eluminocity US Inc.........651 528-1165
80 Pine St Fl 24 New York (10005) ***(G-9660)***
Elvo, Mount Kisco *Also called Zumbach Electronics Corp* ***(G-8362)***
Elwood International Inc.........631 842-6600
89 Hudson St Copiague (11726) ***(G-3757)***
Elwood Specialty Products Inc.........716 877-6622
2180 Elmwood Ave Buffalo (14216) ***(G-2815)***
Elwood, William J, Copiague *Also called Elwood International Inc* ***(G-3757)***
Ely Beach Solar LLC.........718 796-9400
5030 Broadway Ste 819 New York (10034) ***(G-9661)***
EM Pfaff & Son Inc.........607 739-3691
204 E Franklin St Horseheads (14845) ***(G-6313)***
Em-Kay Molds Inc.........716 895-6180
398 Ludington St Buffalo (14206) ***(G-2816)***
Ema Jewelry Inc.........212 575-8989
246 W 38th St Fl 6 New York (10018) ***(G-9662)***
Emagin Corporation (PA).........845 838-7900
2070 Route 52 Bldg 334 Hopewell Junction (12533) ***(G-6284)***
Embassy Apparel Inc.........212 768-8330
37 W 37th St Fl 10 New York (10018) ***(G-9663)***
Embassy Dinettes Inc.........631 253-2292
78 E Industry Ct Deer Park (11729) ***(G-3973)***
Embassy Industries Inc.........631 435-0209
315 Oser Ave Ste 1 Hauppauge (11788) ***(G-5820)***
Embassy Millwork Inc.........518 839-0965
3 Sam Stratton Rd Amsterdam (12010) ***(G-336)***
Ember Media Corporation.........212 695-1919
224 W 35th St 1502 New York (10001) ***(G-9664)***
Emblaze Systems Inc (HQ).........212 371-1100
424 Madison Ave Fl 16 New York (10017) ***(G-9665)***
Embroidery Screen Prtg Netwrk, Vestal *Also called Spst Inc* ***(G-15822)***

ALPHABETIC

EMC Corporation 212 564-6866
2 Penn Plz Fl 24 New York (10121) ***(G-9666)***
EMC Tech Inc 716 488-9071
1984 Allen Street Ext Falconer (14733) ***(G-4676)***
Emco Chemical (usa) Corp 718 797-3652
334 Douglass St Brooklyn (11217) ***(G-1828)***
Emco Electric Services LLC 212 420-9766
526 W 26th St Rm 1012 New York (10001) ***(G-9667)***
Emco Finishing Products Inc 716 483-1176
470 Crescent St Jamestown (14701) ***(G-6715)***
Emcom Inc 315 255-5300
62 Columbus St Ste 4 Auburn (13021) ***(G-477)***
Emcom Industries Inc 716 852-3711
235 Genesee St Buffalo (14204) ***(G-2817)***
Emcs LLC 716 523-2002
4414 Manor Ln Hamburg (14075) ***(G-5678)***
Emda Inc 631 243-6363
81 Westbury Ave Plainview (11803) ***(G-13055)***
Emdroidme, Poughkeepsie *Also called Sciane Enterprises Inc* ***(G-13366)***
Emerald Holdings Inc 718 797-4404
63 Flushing Ave Unit 201 Brooklyn (11205) ***(G-1829)***
Emerald Knitting, Brooklyn *Also called Emerald Holdings Inc* ***(G-1829)***
Emergency Beacon Corp 914 576-2700
15 River St New Rochelle (10801) ***(G-8600)***
Emergent Power Inc (HQ) 201 441-3590
968 Albany Shaker Rd Latham (12110) ***(G-7072)***
Emerson & Oliver LLC 585 775-9929
44 Elton St Rochester (14607) ***(G-13778)***
Emerson Control Techniques, Grand Island *Also called Nidec Indus Automtn USA LLC* ***(G-5507)***
Emerson Electric Co 212 244-2490
1250 Broadway Ste 2300 New York (10001) ***(G-9668)***
Emes Motor Inc 718 387-2445
876 Metropolitan Ave Brooklyn (11211) ***(G-1830)***
Emhart Glass Manufacturing Inc 607 734-3671
74 Kahler Rd Horseheads (14845) ***(G-6314)***
EMI Music Publishing, New York *Also called Screen Gems-EMI Music Inc* ***(G-11523)***
Emilia Interiors Inc (PA) 718 629-4202
867 E 52nd St Brooklyn (11203) ***(G-1831)***
Emilior Phrm Compounding Inc 855 426-6768
2510 Westchester Ave # 207 Bronx (10461) ***(G-1268)***
Emily and Ashley, New York *Also called Greenbeads Llc* ***(G-9984)***
Emitled Inc 516 531-3533
2300 Shames Dr Westbury (11590) ***(G-16328)***
Emkay Bordeaux, Arcade *Also called Emkay Trading Corp* ***(G-382)***
Emkay Candle Company, Syracuse *Also called Muench-Kreuzer Candle Company* ***(G-15377)***
Emkay Trading Corp (PA) 914 592-9000
250 Clearbrook Rd Ste 127 Elmsford (10523) ***(G-4541)***
Emkay Trading Corp 585 492-3800
58 Church St Arcade (14009) ***(G-382)***
Emmi USA Inc 845 268-9990
100 Dutch Hill Rd Ste 220 Orangeburg (10962) ***(G-12675)***
Emoji, New York *Also called Leng Universal Inc* ***(G-10545)***
Emory Machine & Tool Co Inc 585 436-9610
6176 Hunters Dr Farmington (14425) ***(G-4913)***
Emp, Hauppauge *Also called Electronic Machine Parts LLC* ***(G-5818)***
Emphascience 585 348-9415
115 Sullys Trl Ste 6 Pittsford (14534) ***(G-13011)***
Empire Air Hvac, Brooklyn *Also called Empire Air Systems LLC* ***(G-1832)***
Empire Air Specialties Inc 518 689-4440
40 Kraft Ave Albany (12205) ***(G-72)***
Empire Air Systems LLC 718 377-1549
2535 65th St Brooklyn (11204) ***(G-1832)***
Empire Archtctural Systems Inc 518 773-5109
125 Belzano Rd Johnstown (12095) ***(G-6826)***
Empire Brewing Company Inc 315 925-8308
120 Walton St Syracuse (13202) ***(G-15317)***
Empire Building Products Inc 518 695-6094
12 Spring St Schuylerville (12871) ***(G-14733)***
Empire Business Forms Inc (PA) 845 562-7780
128 S Robinson Ave 2 Newburgh (12550) ***(G-12221)***
Empire Cheese Inc 585 968-1552
4520 County Road 6 Cuba (14727) ***(G-3919)***
Empire Coachworks Intl LLC 732 257-7981
475 Haverstraw Rd Suffern (10901) ***(G-15190)***
Empire Coffee Company Inc 914 934-1100
106 Purdy Ave Port Chester (10573) ***(G-13199)***
Empire Devleopment 716 789-2097
5889 Magnolia Stedman Rd Mayville (14757) ***(G-7920)***
Empire Division Inc 315 476-6273
201 Kirkpatrick St # 207 Syracuse (13208) ***(G-15318)***
Empire Fabricators Inc 585 235-3050
95 Saginaw Dr Rochester (14623) ***(G-13779)***
Empire Industrial Burner Svc 631 242-4619
550 Brook Ave Deer Park (11729) ***(G-3974)***
Empire Industrial Systems Corp (PA) 631 242-4619
40 Corbin Ave Bay Shore (11706) ***(G-685)***
Empire Innovation Group LLC 716 852-5000
410 Main St Ste 5 Buffalo (14202) ***(G-2818)***
Empire Metal Fabricators Inc 585 288-2140
1385 Empire Blvd Ste 3 Rochester (14609) ***(G-13780)***
Empire Metal Finishing Inc 718 545-6700
2469 46th St Astoria (11103) ***(G-427)***
Empire National, Brooklyn *Also called A To Z Kosher Meat Products Co* ***(G-1458)***
Empire Open Mri 914 961-1777
1915 Central Park Ave # 25 Yonkers (10710) ***(G-16756)***
Empire Optical Inc 585 454-4470
1249 Ridgeway Ave Ste P Rochester (14615) ***(G-13781)***
Empire Plastics Inc 607 754-9132
2011 E Main St Endwell (13760) ***(G-4616)***
Empire Precision Plastics, Rochester *Also called Epp Team Inc* ***(G-13788)***
Empire Press Co (PA) 718 756-9500
550 Empire Blvd Brooklyn (11225) ***(G-1833)***
Empire Publishing Inc 516 829-4000
1525 Central Ave Ste 1 Far Rockaway (11691) ***(G-4700)***
Empire Signs, East Elmhurst *Also called Liberty Awnings & Signs Inc* ***(G-4223)***
Empire State Metal Pdts Inc 718 847-1617
10110 Jamaica Ave Richmond Hill (11418) ***(G-13502)***
Empire State Weeklies Inc 585 671-1533
46 North Ave Webster (14580) ***(G-16084)***
Empire Steel Works Inc 516 561-3500
110a New South Rd Hicksville (11801) ***(G-6084)***
Empire Transit Mix Inc 718 384-3000
430 Maspeth Ave Brooklyn (11211) ***(G-1834)***
Empire Ventilation Eqp Co Inc (PA) 718 728-2143
9 Industrial Dr Florida (10921) ***(G-4970)***
Empro Niagara Inc 716 433-2769
5027 Ridge Rd Lockport (14094) ***(G-7298)***
Ems Development Corporation (HQ) 631 924-4736
95 Horseblock Rd Unit 2 Yaphank (11980) ***(G-16708)***
Ems Development Corporation 631 345-6200
95 Horseblock Rd Unit 2a Yaphank (11980) ***(G-16709)***
Ems Technologies Inc 607 723-3676
71 Frederick St Binghamton (13901) ***(G-882)***
Emsaru USA Corp 212 459-9355
608 5th Ave Ste 500 New York (10020) ***(G-9669)***
Emsig Manufacturing Corp (PA) 718 784-7717
263 W 38th St Fl 5 New York (10018) ***(G-9670)***
Emsig Manufacturing Corp 518 828-7301
160 Fairview Ave Ste 916 Hudson (12534) ***(G-6348)***
Emsig Manufacturing Corp 718 784-7717
263 W 38th St Fl 5 New York (10018) ***(G-9671)***
Emtron Hybrids Inc 631 924-9668
86 Horseblock Rd Unit G Yaphank (11980) ***(G-16710)***
Emulso Corp 716 854-2889
2750 Kenmore Ave Tonawanda (14150) ***(G-15538)***
Emunas Sales Inc 718 621-3138
947 E 27th St Brooklyn (11210) ***(G-1835)***
Emusiccom Inc (PA) 212 201-9240
215 Lexington Ave Fl 18 New York (10016) ***(G-9672)***
Emvi Chocolate, Broadalbin *Also called Emvi Inc* ***(G-1188)***
Emvi Inc 518 883-5111
111 Bellen Rd Ste 2 Broadalbin (12025) ***(G-1188)***
En Tech Corp 845 398-0776
375 Western Hwy Tappan (10983) ***(G-15468)***
Enable Labs, Troy *Also called Vita Rara Inc* ***(G-15631)***
Enbi Indiana Inc 585 647-1627
1661 Lyell Ave Rochester (14606) ***(G-13782)***
Enchante Lites LLC (HQ) 212 602-1818
15 W 34th St Fl 8 New York (10001) ***(G-9673)***
Encore Electronics Inc 518 584-5354
4400 Route 50 Saratoga Springs (12866) ***(G-14577)***
Encore Refining and Recycleing 631 319-1910
1120 Lincoln Ave Holbrook (11741) ***(G-6185)***
Encore Retail Systems Inc (PA) 718 385-3443
180 E Prospect Ave Mamaroneck (10543) ***(G-7743)***
Encysive Pharmaceuticals Inc (HQ) 212 733-2323
235 E 42nd St New York (10017) ***(G-9674)***
Endava Inc (HQ) 212 920-7240
441 Lexington Ave Rm 702 New York (10017) ***(G-9675)***
Endeavor Printing LLC 718 570-2720
3704 29th St Long Island City (11101) ***(G-7438)***
Endicott Interconnect Tech Inc 866 820-4820
1701 North St Endicott (13760) ***(G-4588)***
Endicott Precision Inc 607 754-7076
1328-30 Campville Rd Endicott (13760) ***(G-4589)***
Endicott Research Group Inc 607 754-9187
2601 Wayne St Endicott (13760) ***(G-4590)***
Endoscopic Procedure Center, Syracuse *Also called Elizabeth Wood* ***(G-15315)***
Endovor Inc 214 679-7385
1330 1st Ave Apt 1119 New York (10021) ***(G-9676)***
Endovor LLC 214 679-7385
525 E 68th St A1027 New York (10065) ***(G-9677)***
Endurance LLC 212 719-2500
530 7th Ave Rm 902 New York (10018) ***(G-9678)***
Endurart Inc 212 473-7000
132 Nassau St Rm 1100 New York (10038) ***(G-9679)***
Enecon Corporation (PA) 516 349-0022
6 Platinum Ct Medford (11763) ***(G-7946)***
Eneflux Armtek Magnetics Inc (HQ) 516 576-3434
6 Platinum Ct Medford (11763) ***(G-7947)***
Ener-G-Rotors Inc 518 372-2608
17 Fern Ave Schenectady (12306) ***(G-14670)***

ALPHABETIC SECTION

Energy Brands Inc (HQ) 212 545-6000
260 Madison Ave Fl 10 New York (10016) *(G-9680)*
Energy Conservation & Sup Inc 718 855-5888
55 Washington St Ste 324 Brooklyn (11201) *(G-1836)*
Energy Harvesters LLC 617 325-9852
63 Garden Dr Rochester (14609) *(G-13783)*
Energy Intelligence Group Inc (PA) 212 532-1112
270 Madison Ave Fl 19 New York (10016) *(G-9681)*
Energy Materials Corporation 315 247-0880
1999 Lake Ave Rochester (14650) *(G-13784)*
Energy Nuclear Operations 315 342-0055
268 Lake Rd Oswego (13126) *(G-12777)*
Energy Panel Structures Inc 315 923-7777
10269 Old Route 31 Clyde (14433) *(G-3592)*
Energy Panel Structures Inc 585 343-1777
10269 Old Route 31 Clyde (14433) *(G-3593)*
Energy Panel Structures Inc 518 355-6708
364 Burdeck St Schenectady (12306) *(G-14671)*
Enertiv Inc 646 350-3525
320 W 37th St Ste 1500 New York (10018) *(G-9682)*
Enetics Inc 585 924-5010
830 Canning Pkwy Victor (14564) *(G-15844)*
Engagement Technology LLC 914 591-7600
33 W Main St Ste 303 Elmsford (10523) *(G-4542)*
Engelack Gem Corporation 212 719-3094
36 W 47th St Ste 601 New York (10036) *(G-9683)*
Engineered Air Products, Lancaster Also called Eastern Air Products LLC *(G-7017)*
Engineered Composites Inc 716 362-0295
55 Roberts Ave Buffalo (14206) *(G-2819)*
Engineered Lifting Tech, Orchard Park Also called Kinedyne Inc *(G-12724)*
Engineered Metal Products Inc 631 842-3780
10 Reith St Copiague (11726) *(G-3758)*
Engineered Plastics Inc 800 682-2525
300 International Dr # 100 Williamsville (14221) *(G-16579)*
Engineered Polymer Systems Div, Marion Also called Parker-Hannifin Corporation *(G-7804)*
Engineered Products Oper Epo, Rochester Also called Pulsafeeder Inc *(G-14054)*
Engineering Educational Eqp Co, New Paltz Also called Kevco Industries *(G-8578)*
Engineering Maint Pdts Inc 516 624-9774
250 Berry Hill Rd Oyster Bay (11771) *(G-12813)*
Engineering Mfg & Tech, East Meadow Also called E M T Manufacturing Inc *(G-4250)*
Engineering Mfg Tech LLC 607 754-7111
101 Delaware Ave Endicott (13760) *(G-4591)*
Engrav-O-Type Press Inc 585 262-7590
30 Bermar Park Ste 2 Rochester (14624) *(G-13785)*
Enhance A Colour Corp 212 490-3620
211 E 43rd St Rm 700 New York (10017) *(G-9684)*
Enhanced Tool Inc 716 691-5200
90 Pineview Dr Amherst (14228) *(G-225)*
Eni Mks Products Group 585 427-8300
100 Highpower Rd Rochester (14623) *(G-13786)*
Eni Technology Inc (HQ) 585 427-8300
100 Highpower Rd Rochester (14623) *(G-13787)*
Enivate - Aerospace Division, Orchard Park Also called ITT Enidine Inc *(G-12720)*
Enjoy, Scarsdale Also called Japan America Learning Ctr Inc *(G-14639)*
Enjoy City North Inc 607 584-5061
100 Emerson Pkwy Binghamton (13905) *(G-883)*
Enlighten Air Inc 917 656-1248
23 E 81st St Apt 10 New York (10028) *(G-9685)*
Enplas America Inc 646 892-7811
299 Park Ave Fl 4 a New York (10171) *(G-9686)*
Enrg Inc 716 873-2939
155 Chandler St 5 Buffalo (14207) *(G-2820)*
Ensil Technical Services Inc 716 282-1020
1901 Maryland Ave Niagara Falls (14305) *(G-12281)*
Entermarket 914 437-7268
280 N Bedford Rd Ste 305 Mount Kisco (10549) *(G-8342)*
Enterprise Bagels Inc 845 896-3823
986 Main St Ste 3 Fishkill (12524) *(G-4945)*
Enterprise Folding Box Co Inc 716 876-6421
75 Isabelle St Buffalo (14207) *(G-2821)*
Enterprise Press Inc 212 741-2111
627 Greenwich St New York (10014) *(G-9687)*
Enterprise Tech Group Inc 914 588-0327
3 Church St New Rochelle (10801) *(G-8601)*
Enterprise Wood Products Inc 718 853-9243
4712 18th Ave Brooklyn (11204) *(G-1837)*
Entertainment Weekly Inc (HQ) 212 522-5600
135 W 50th St Frnt 3 New York (10020) *(G-9688)*
Entertron Industries Inc 716 772-7216
99 Robinson Pl Lockport (14094) *(G-7299)*
Enticing Lingerie Inc 718 998-8625
166 Gravesend Neck Rd Brooklyn (11223) *(G-1838)*
Entraintant Inc 212 946-4724
1 World Trade Ctr Fl 85 New York (10007) *(G-9689)*
Enumeral Biomedical Corp 347 227-4787
1370 Broadway Fl 5 New York (10018) *(G-9690)*
Envent Systems Inc 646 294-6980
62 Harmon Ave Pelham (10803) *(G-12935)*
Enviro Service & Supply Corp 347 838-6500
45b Marble Loop Staten Island (10309) *(G-15074)*
Enviroform Recycled Pdts Inc 315 789-1810
287 Gambee Rd Geneva (14456) *(G-5322)*
Enviromaster International LLC 315 336-3716
5780 Success Dr Rome (13440) *(G-14250)*
Environment-One Corporation 518 346-6161
2773 Balltown Rd Schenectady (12309) *(G-14672)*
Environmental Closures, Mineola Also called Geotechnical Drilling Inc *(G-8224)*
Environmental Temp Systems LLC 516 640-5818
111 Roosevelt Ave Ste C Mineola (11501) *(G-8218)*
Envy Publishing Group Inc 212 253-9874
118 E 25th St Bsmt Ll New York (10010) *(G-9691)*
Enyce, New York Also called 5 Star Apparel LLC *(G-8681)*
Enzo Diagnostics, Farmingdale Also called Enzo Life Sciences Inc *(G-4760)*
Enzo Life Sciences Inc (HQ) 631 694-7070
10 Executive Blvd Farmingdale (11735) *(G-4760)*
Enzo Life Sciences Intl Inc 610 941-0430
10 Executive Blvd Farmingdale (11735) *(G-4761)*
Enzo Manzoni LLC 212 464-7000
2896 W 12th St Brooklyn (11224) *(G-1839)*
Eon Collections 212 695-1263
247 W 35th St Rm 401 New York (10001) *(G-9692)*
Eon Labs Inc (HQ) 516 478-9700
1999 Marcus Ave Ste 300 New Hyde Park (11042) *(G-8533)*
Ephesus Lighting, Syracuse Also called Eaton Corporation *(G-15311)*
Epi Printing & Finishing, Rochester Also called Engrav-O-Type Press Inc *(G-13785)*
Epic Beauty Co LLC 212 327-3059
929 Park Ave 5 New York (10028) *(G-9693)*
Epic Pharma LLC 718 276-8600
22715 N Conduit Ave Laurelton (11413) *(G-7099)*
Epicor Software Corporation 805 496-6789
2165 Technology Dr Schenectady (12308) *(G-14673)*
Epl, Long Island City Also called Edison Price Lighting Inc *(G-7433)*
Epner Technology Inc 718 782-8722
25 Division Pl Brooklyn (11222) *(G-1840)*
Epner Technology Incorporated (PA) 718 782-5948
279 Frost St Brooklyn (11222) *(G-1841)*
Epner Technology Incorporated 718 782-8722
78 Kingsland Ave Brooklyn (11222) *(G-1842)*
Epoch Microelectronics Inc 914 332-8570
420 Columbus Ave Ste 204 Valhalla (10595) *(G-15741)*
Eponym Inc 646 918-4586
85 N 3rd St 112 Brooklyn (11249) *(G-1843)*
Epost International Inc 212 352-9390
483 10th Ave New York (10018) *(G-9694)*
Epp Team Inc 585 454-4995
500 Lee Rd Ste 400 Rochester (14606) *(G-13788)*
Eps Iron Works Inc 516 294-5840
38 Windsor Ave Ste 101 Mineola (11501) *(G-8219)*
Epuffer Inc 718 374-6030
2348 80th St Fl 1 Brooklyn (11214) *(G-1844)*
Equal Opprtnity Pblcations Inc 631 421-9421
445 Broadhollow Rd # 425 Melville (11747) *(G-8019)*
Equicenter Inc 585 742-2522
3247 Rush Mendon Rd Honeoye Falls (14472) *(G-6264)*
Equicheck LLC 631 987-6356
20 Medford Ave Ste 7 Patchogue (11772) *(G-12865)*
Equilend Holdings LLC (PA) 212 901-2200
225 Liberty St Fl 10 New York (10281) *(G-9695)*
Equilibrium Brewery LLC 201 245-0292
22 Henry St Middletown (10940) *(G-8151)*
Equine Imaging LLC (PA) 414 326-0665
20 Tibbits Ln Port Washington (11050) *(G-13258)*
Equinox Aegis LLC 212 316-9078
80 Riverside Blvd New York (10069) *(G-9696)*
Equipment Apparel LLC 212 502-1890
19 W 34th St Fl 8 New York (10001) *(G-9697)*
Equityarcade LLC 678 232-1301
33 Nassau Ave Brooklyn (11222) *(G-1845)*
Equivital Inc 646 513-4169
19 W 34th St Rm 1018 New York (10001) *(G-9698)*
ER Butler & Co Inc (PA) 212 925-3565
55 Prince St Frnt A New York (10012) *(G-9699)*
Erbessd Reliability LLC 518 874-2700
2c Glens Falls Tech Park Glens Falls (12801) *(G-5424)*
Erbessd Reliability Instrs, Glens Falls Also called Erbessd Reliability LLC *(G-5424)*
Ercole Nyc Inc (PA) 212 675-2218
142 26th St Brooklyn (11232) *(G-1846)*
Erdle Perforating Holdings Inc (PA) 585 247-4700
100 Pixley Indus Pkwy Rochester (14624) *(G-13789)*
Ergun Inc 631 721-0049
10 Mineola Ave Unit B Roslyn Heights (11577) *(G-14454)*
Erhard & Gilcher Inc 315 474-1072
235 Cortland Ave Syracuse (13202) *(G-15319)*
Eric S Turner & Company Inc 914 235-7114
3335 Centre Ave New Rochelle (10801) *(G-8602)*
Eric Signature, New York Also called Harrison Sportswear Inc *(G-10041)*
Eric Winterling Inc 212 629-7686
20 W 20th St Fl 5 New York (10011) *(G-9700)*
Ericeira Inc 516 294-4034
54 E Jericho Tpke Mineola (11501) *(G-8220)*
Erickson Beamon Ltd 212 643-4810
498 Fashion Ave Rm 2406 New York (10018) *(G-9701)*
Erie Engineered Products Inc 716 206-0204
3949 Walden Ave Lancaster (14086) *(G-7018)*

Erika T Schwartz MD PC
724 5th Ave Fl 10 New York (10019) *(G-9702)* 212 873-3420

Erin Snow Ltd 212 675-7762
140 E 56th St Apt 3a New York (10022) *(G-9703)*

Ernie Green Industries Inc 585 295-8951
85 Pixley Industrial Pkwy Rochester (14624) *(G-13790)*

Ernie Green Industries Inc 585 647-2300
1667 Emerson St Rochester (14606) *(G-13791)*

Ernie Green Industries Inc 585 647-2300
460 Buffalo Rd Ste 220 Rochester (14611) *(G-13792)*

Ernst Publishing Co, Albany *Also called Ucc Guide Inc* *(G-137)*

Ert Software Inc 845 358-5721
4 Pine Glen Dr Blauvelt (10913) *(G-935)*

Ertel Alsop, Kingston *Also called Stavo Industries Inc* *(G-6920)*

Ertel Engineering Co, Kingston *Also called Stavo Industries Inc* *(G-6921)*

Es Beta Inc 631 582-6740
125 Comac St Ronkonkoma (11779) *(G-14339)*

Esc Control Electronics LLC 631 467-5328
98 Lincoln Ave Sayville (11782) *(G-14627)*

Eschen Prosthetic & Orthotic L 212 606-1262
510 E 73rd St Ste 201 New York (10021) *(G-9704)*

Eschen Prsthetic Orthotic Labs 516 871-0029
299 Duffy Ave Hicksville (11801) *(G-6085)*

Escholar LLC 914 989-2900
222 Bloomingdale Rd # 107 White Plains (10605) *(G-16446)*

Esense LLC 718 887-9779
4402 23rd St Ste 114 Long Island City (11101) *(G-7439)*

Eser Realty Corp (PA) 718 383-0565
62 Greenpoint Ave 64 Brooklyn (11222) *(G-1847)*

Esi, Holbrook *Also called Electronic Systems Inc* *(G-6184)*

ESi Cases & Accessories Inc 212 883-8838
44 E 32nd St Rm 601 New York (10016) *(G-9705)*

Eskay Metal Fabricating, Buffalo *Also called Schuler-Subra Inc* *(G-3058)*

Eskayel Inc 347 703-8084
75 S 6th St Brooklyn (11249) *(G-1848)*

Esm Group Inc (HQ) 716 446-8914
300 Corporate Pkwy 118n Amherst (14226) *(G-226)*

Esm Group Inc 724 265-1766
300 Corporate Pkwy 118n Buffalo (14226) *(G-2822)*

Esm II Inc (HQ) 716 446-8888
300 Corporate Pkwy 118n Amherst (14226) *(G-227)*

Esm Special Metals & Tech Inc 716 446-8914
300 Corporate Pkwy 118n Amherst (14226) *(G-228)*

Espey Mfg & Electronics Corp (PA) 518 584-4100
233 Ballston Ave Saratoga Springs (12866) *(G-14578)*

Espostos Fnest Qlty Ssage Pdts, New York *Also called Elmgang Enterprises I Inc* *(G-9657)*

Esquire Magazine, New York *Also called Hearst Corporation* *(G-10066)*

Esquire Mechanical Corp 718 625-4006
79 Sandford St Brooklyn (11205) *(G-1849)*

Ess Bee Industries Inc 718 894-5202
95 Evergreen Ave Brooklyn (11206) *(G-1850)*

Essar Americas 212 292-2600
277 Park Ave 47th New York (10172) *(G-9706)*

Essar Steel Minnesota LLC (PA) 212 292-2600
150 E 52nd St Fl 27 New York (10022) *(G-9707)*

Essence Communications Inc (PA) 212 522-1212
241 37th St Fl 1 Brooklyn (11232) *(G-1851)*

Essence Magazine, Brooklyn *Also called Essence Communications Inc* *(G-1851)*

Essence Ventures LLC 212 522-1212
225 Liberty St Fl 9 New York (10281) *(G-9708)*

Essential Homme Magazine, New York *Also called Essential Publications US LLC* *(G-9709)*

Essential Publications US LLC 646 707-0898
14 E 4th St Rm 604 New York (10012) *(G-9709)*

Essential Ribbons Inc 212 967-4173
53 W 36th St Rm 405 New York (10018) *(G-9710)*

Essequattro USA Inc 917 862-0005
1 Little West 12th St New York (10014) *(G-9711)*

Essex Box & Pallet Co Inc 518 834-7279
49 Industrial Park Rd Keeseville (12944) *(G-6850)*

Essex Industries 518 942-6671
17 Pilfershire Rd Mineville (12956) *(G-8253)*

Essex Manufacturing Inc 212 239-0080
350 5th Ave Ste 2400 New York (10118) *(G-9712)*

Essex Works Ltd 718 495-4575
446 Riverdale Ave Brooklyn (11207) *(G-1852)*

Essie Cosmetics Ltd 212 818-1500
575 5th Ave New York (10017) *(G-9713)*

Essilor Laboratories Amer Inc 845 365-6700
165 Route 303 Orangeburg (10962) *(G-12676)*

Essity Prof Hygiene N Amer LLC 518 692-8434
72 County Route 53 Greenwich (12834) *(G-5638)*

Essity Prof Hygiene N Amer LLC 518 583-2785
49 Geyser Rd Saratoga Springs (12866) *(G-14579)*

ESSITY PROFESSIONAL HYGIENE NORTH AMERICA LLC, Saratoga Springs *Also called Essity Prof Hygiene N Amer LLC* *(G-14579)*

Estebania Enterprises Inc 585 529-9330
15 Mcardle St Ste A Rochester (14611) *(G-13793)*

Estee Lauder, New York *Also called Prescriptives Inc* *(G-11234)*

Estee Lauder Companies Inc 917 606-3240
9 W 22nd St New York (10010) *(G-9714)*

Estee Lauder Companies Inc 212 572-4200
110 E 59th St Fl 37 New York (10022) *(G-9715)*

Estee Lauder Companies Inc 212 756-4800
655 Madison Ave Fl 15 New York (10065) *(G-9716)*

Estee Lauder Companies Inc 646 762-7718
28 W 23rd St New York (10010) *(G-9717)*

Estee Lauder Companies Inc 631 694-2601
80 Ruland Rd Ste 3 Melville (11747) *(G-8020)*

Estee Lauder Companies Inc (PA) 212 572-4200
767 5th Ave Fl 1 New York (10153) *(G-9718)*

Estee Lauder Companies Inc 212 572-4200
7 Corporate Center Dr Melville (11747) *(G-8021)*

Estee Lauder Companies Inc 646 602-7590
65 Bleecker St Frnt 1 New York (10012) *(G-9719)*

Estee Lauder Inc 631 531-1000
125 Pinelawn Rd Melville (11747) *(G-8022)*

Estee Lauder International Inc (HQ) 212 572-4200
767 5th Ave Fl Conc6 New York (10153) *(G-9720)*

Estiator, New York *Also called Interhellenic Publishing Inc* *(G-10241)*

ET Oakes Corporation 631 232-0002
686 Old Willets Path Hauppauge (11788) *(G-5821)*

ET Precision Optics Inc 585 254-2560
33 Curlew St Rochester (14606) *(G-13794)*

Etcetera Wallpapers, Glen Cove *Also called Sunnyside Decorative Prints Co* *(G-5377)*

Eternal Fortune Fashion LLC 212 965-5322
135 W 36th St Fl 3 New York (10018) *(G-9721)*

Eternal Line 845 856-1999
1237 State Route 42 Sparrow Bush (12780) *(G-14972)*

Eternal Love Parfums Corp 516 921-6100
485 Underhill Blvd # 207 Syosset (11791) *(G-15216)*

Eternal Love Perfumes, Syosset *Also called Eternal Love Parfums Corp* *(G-15216)*

Ethis Communications Inc 212 791-1440
44 Church St Ste 200 White Plains (10601) *(G-16447)*

Etna Products Co Inc (PA) 212 989-7591
99 Madison Ave Fl 11 New York (10016) *(G-9722)*

Etna Tool & Die Corporation 212 475-4350
42 Bond St Frnt A New York (10012) *(G-9723)*

Eton Institute 855 334-3688
1 Rockefeller Plz Fl 11 New York (10020) *(G-9724)*

Eton International, New York *Also called Basil S Kadhim* *(G-9024)*

Ets, Mineola *Also called Environmental Temp Systems LLC* *(G-8218)*

Eu Design LLC 212 420-7788
73 Spring St Rm 506 New York (10012) *(G-9725)*

Eugene Biro Corp 212 997-0146
581 5th Ave Fl 3 New York (10017) *(G-9726)*

Eugene G Danner Mfg Inc 631 234-5261
160 Oval Dr Central Islip (11749) *(G-3368)*

Eugenia Selective Living Inc 631 277-1461
122 Freeman Ave Islip (11751) *(G-6546)*

Euphorbia Productions Ltd 212 533-1700
632 Broadway Fl 9 New York (10012) *(G-9727)*

Euphrates Inc 518 762-3488
230 Enterprise Rd Johnstown (12095) *(G-6827)*

Euro Bands Inc 212 719-9777
247 W 37th St Ste 700 New York (10018) *(G-9728)*

Euro Fine Paper Inc 516 238-5253
220 Nassau Blvd Garden City (11530) *(G-5258)*

Euro Gear (usa) Inc 518 578-1775
1 Cumberland Ave Plattsburgh (12901) *(G-13120)*

Euro Marmol Gran 631 940-9165
2 Saxwood St Ste G Deer Park (11729) *(G-3975)*

Euro Pacific Precious Metals 212 481-0310
152 Madison Ave Rm 1003 New York (10016) *(G-9729)*

Euro Woodworking Inc 718 246-9172
303 Park Ave Fl 8 Brooklyn (11205) *(G-1853)*

Euroco Costumes Inc 212 629-9665
254 W 35th St Fl 15 New York (10001) *(G-9730)*

Euromed Inc 845 359-4039
25 Corporate Dr Orangeburg (10962) *(G-12677)*

Europadisk LLC 718 407-7300
2402 Queens Plz S Long Island City (11101) *(G-7440)*

European Marble Works Co Inc 718 387-9778
54 Nassau Blvd Garden City (11530) *(G-5259)*

Europrojects Intl Inc 917 262-0795
152 W 25th St Fl 8b New York (10001) *(G-9731)*

Eurotex Inc 716 205-8861
4600 Witmer Rd Niagara Falls (14305) *(G-12282)*

Eurotex North America, Niagara Falls *Also called Eurotex Inc* *(G-12282)*

Ev-Box North America Inc 646 930-6305
335 Madison Ave Fl 4 New York (10017) *(G-9732)*

Eva Fehren, New York *Also called Gorga Fehren Fine Jewelry LLC* *(G-9959)*

Evado Filip 917 774-8666
159 Bleecker St New York (10012) *(G-9733)*

Evangelist, The, Albany *Also called Albany Catholic Press Assoc* *(G-32)*

Evans & Paul LLC 516 576-0800
140 Dupont St Plainview (11803) *(G-13056)*

Evans Chemetics LP 315 539-9221
228 E Main St Waterloo (13165) *(G-15991)*

Evans Manufacturing LLC 631 439-3300
595 Smith St Farmingdale (11735) *(G-4762)*

Eve Sales Corp 718 589-6800
945 Close Ave Bronx (10473) *(G-1269)*

Evelo Inc 917 251-8743
327 Beach 101st St Rockaway Park (11694) *(G-14228)*
Evenhouse Printing 716 649-2666
4783 Southwestern Blvd Hamburg (14075) *(G-5679)*
Evening Telegram, Herkimer *Also called Gatehouse Media LLC (G-6039)*
Evening Tribune, Hornell *Also called Gatehouse Media LLC (G-6299)*
Event Journal Inc 516 470-1811
366 N Broadway Ste 209 Jericho (11753) *(G-6787)*
Event Services Corporation 315 488-9357
6171 Airport Rd Solvay (13209) *(G-14918)*
Ever-Nu-Metal Products Inc 646 423-5833
471 20th St Brooklyn (11215) *(G-1854)*
Everblock Systems LLC (PA) 844 422-5625
790 Madison Ave Rm 506 New York (10065) *(G-9734)*
Evercore Partners Svcs E LLC 212 857-3100
55 E 52nd St New York (10055) *(G-9735)*
Everest Bbn Inc 212 268-7979
42 Broadway Ste 1736 New York (10004) *(G-9736)*
Everfab Inc 716 655-1550
12928 Big Tree Rd East Aurora (14052) *(G-4198)*
Evergreen, New York *Also called Integrated Copyright Group (G-10230)*
Evergreen Corp Central NY 315 454-4175
235 Cortland Ave Syracuse (13202) *(G-15320)*
Evergreen Manufacturing, Syracuse *Also called Evergreen Corp Central NY (G-15320)*
Evergreen Slate Company Inc 518 642-2530
2027 County Route 23 Middle Granville (12849) *(G-8109)*
Everlast Seals and Supply LLC 718 388-7373
41 Montrose Ave Brooklyn (11206) *(G-1855)*
Everlast Sports Mfg Corp (HQ) 212 239-0990
42 W 39th St New York (10018) *(G-9737)*
Everlast Worldwide Inc (HQ) 212 239-0990
42 W 39th St Fl 3 New York (10018) *(G-9738)*
Everlasting Memories 716 833-1111
3701 Mckinley Pkwy # 210 Blasdell (14219) *(G-926)*
Everplans, New York *Also called Beyondly Inc (G-9065)*
Eversan Inc 315 736-3967
34 Main St Ste 3 Whitesboro (13492) *(G-16527)*
Everstone Industries LLC 347 777-8150
242 W 122nd St Apt 4b New York (10027) *(G-9739)*
Everybodys Carribbean Magazine, Brooklyn *Also called Herman Hall Communications (G-1975)*
Evidon Inc (HQ) 917 262-2530
10 E 39th St Fl 8 New York (10016) *(G-9740)*
Evocate Media LLC 646 361-3014
100 W 139th St Apt 34a New York (10030) *(G-9741)*
Evolution Impressions Inc 585 473-6600
160 Commerce Dr Rochester (14623) *(G-13795)*
Evolution Spirits Inc 917 543-7880
401 Park Ave S New York (10016) *(G-9742)*
Evonik Corporation 518 233-7090
7 Schoolhouse Ln Waterford (12188) *(G-15975)*
Ewatchfactory Corp (PA) 212 564-8318
390 5th Ave Rm 910 New York (10018) *(G-9743)*
Ewt Holdings III Corp (HQ) 212 644-5900
666 5th Ave Fl 36 New York (10103) *(G-9744)*
Ex El Enterprises Ltd 212 489-4500
630 Fort Washington Ave New York (10040) *(G-9745)*
Ex-It Medical Devices Inc 212 653-0637
1330 Ave Of The Americas New York (10019) *(G-9746)*
Exact Machining & Mfg 585 334-7090
305 Commerce Dr Ste 7 Rochester (14623) *(G-13796)*
Exact Solutions Inc 212 707-8627
139 Fulton St Rm 511 New York (10038) *(G-9747)*
Exacta LLC 716 406-2303
8955 Williams Ct Clarence Center (14032) *(G-3544)*
Excel Aluminum Products Inc 315 471-0925
563 N Salina St Syracuse (13208) *(G-15321)*
Excel Conveyor LLC 718 474-0001
350 Beach 79th St Ste 1 Rockaway Beach (11693) *(G-14225)*
Excel Graphics Services Inc 212 929-2183
519 8th Ave Fl 18 New York (10018) *(G-9748)*
Excel Industries Inc 716 542-5468
11737 Main St Clarence (14031) *(G-3533)*
Excel Paint Applicators Inc 347 221-1968
555 Doughty Blvd Inwood (11096) *(G-6488)*
Excel Technology Inc 212 355-3400
780 3rd Ave New York (10017) *(G-9749)*
Excelco Developments Inc 716 934-2651
65 Main St Silver Creek (14136) *(G-14861)*
Excelco/Newbrook Inc 716 934-2644
16 Mechanic St Silver Creek (14136) *(G-14862)*
Excell Print & Promotions Inc 914 437-8668
50 Main St Ste 100 White Plains (10606) *(G-16448)*
Excelled Sheepskin & Lea Coat (PA) 212 594-5843
1359 Broadway Fl 9 New York (10018) *(G-9750)*
Excellent Art Mfg Corp 718 388-7075
531 Bayview Ave Inwood (11096) *(G-6489)*
Excellent Photocopies, Brooklyn *Also called Excellent Printing Inc (G-1857)*
Excellent Poly Inc 718 768-6555
820 4th Ave Brooklyn (11232) *(G-1856)*
Excellent Printing Inc 718 384-7272
165 Hooper St Brooklyn (11211) *(G-1857)*
Excelsior Graphics Inc 212 730-6200
485 Madison Ave Fl 13 New York (10022) *(G-9751)*
Excelsior Mlt-Cltural Inst Inc 706 627-4285
13340 Roosevelt Ave 7g Flushing (11354) *(G-4998)*
Excelsior Publications 607 746-7600
133 Main St Delhi (13753) *(G-4073)*
Excelsior Wood Products LLC 845 339-6630
401b Sawkill Rd Kingston (12401) *(G-6900)*
Excelsus Solutions LLC 585 533-0003
12 Pixley Industrial Pkwy # 40 Rochester (14624) *(G-13797)*
Exceltech Inc 718 423-7262
5317 Hollis Court Blvd Fresh Meadows (11365) *(G-5197)*
Exchange My Mail Inc 516 605-1835
30 Jericho Executive Plz 100c Jericho (11753) *(G-6788)*
Executive Business Media Inc 516 334-3030
825 Old Country Rd Westbury (11590) *(G-16329)*
Executive Machines Inc 718 965-6600
882 3rd Ave Unit 8 Brooklyn (11232) *(G-1858)*
Executive Mirror Doors Inc 631 234-1090
1 Comac Loop Unit 7 Ronkonkoma (11779) *(G-14340)*
Executive Sign Corp 212 397-4050
43 Boulevard Cornwall On Hudson (12520) *(G-3838)*
Executive Sign Corporation 212 397-4050
347 W 36th St Rm 902 New York (10018) *(G-9752)*
Exelis, Amityville *Also called Harris Corporation (G-280)*
Exergy LLC 516 832-9300
320 Endo Blvd Unit 1 Garden City (11530) *(G-5260)*
Exfo Burleigh Pdts Group Inc 585 301-1530
181 S Main St Ste 10 Canandaigua (14424) *(G-3220)*
Exhibit Corporation America 718 937-2600
4623 Crane St Ste 3 Long Island City (11101) *(G-7441)*
Exhibit Portables, Long Island City *Also called Exhibit Corporation America (G-7441)*
Exhibits & More 585 924-4040
7615 Omnitech Pl Ste 4a Victor (14564) *(G-15845)*
Exide Batteries, Batavia *Also called Exide Technologies (G-623)*
Exide Technologies 585 344-0656
4330 Commerce Dr Batavia (14020) *(G-623)*
Exigo Precision Inc 585 254-5818
190 Murray St Rochester (14606) *(G-13798)*
Exotic Print and Paper Inc 212 807-0465
15 E 13th St New York (10003) *(G-9753)*
Expedi-Printing Inc 516 513-0919
41 Red Brook Rd Great Neck (11024) *(G-5551)*
Expedient Heat Treating Corp 716 433-1177
61 Dale Dr North Tonawanda (14120) *(G-12426)*
Experiment LLC 212 889-1659
260 5th Ave Fl 3 New York (10001) *(G-9754)*
Experiment Publishing LLC 212 889-1273
220 E 23rd St Ste 600 New York (10010) *(G-9755)*
Expert Industries Inc 718 434-6060
848 E 43rd St Brooklyn (11210) *(G-1859)*
Expert Machine Services Inc 718 786-1200
3944a 28th St Long Island City (11101) *(G-7442)*
Expert Metal Slitters Corp 718 361-2735
3740 12th St Long Island City (11101) *(G-7443)*
Expo Furniture Designs Inc 516 674-1420
1 Garvies Point Rd Glen Cove (11542) *(G-5365)*
Expo Lighting Design, Glen Cove *Also called Expo Furniture Designs Inc (G-5365)*
Expositor Newspapers Inc 585 427-2468
2535 Brighton Henrietta Rochester (14623) *(G-13799)*
Express Building Supply Inc 516 608-0379
3550 Lawson Blvd Oceanside (11572) *(G-12537)*
Express Checkout LLC 646 512-2068
110 E 1st St Apt 20 New York (10009) *(G-9756)*
Express Concrete Inc 631 273-4224
1250 Suffolk Ave Brentwood (11717) *(G-1133)*
Express Mart, Watertown *Also called Petre Alii Petroleum (G-16032)*
Express Press, Rochester *Also called Clarsons Corp (G-13713)*
Express Seal Div, Lancaster *Also called Apple Rubber Products Inc (G-7007)*
Express Tag & Label, Brooklyn *Also called Jerry Tomaselli (G-2036)*
Expresseal, Lancaster *Also called Apple Rubber Products Inc (G-7008)*
Expression Embroidery, Jamaica *Also called Expressions Punching & Digitiz (G-6642)*
Expressions Punching & Digitiz 718 291-1177
9315 179th Pl Jamaica (11433) *(G-6642)*
Expressive Scent, Brooklyn *Also called Jacmax Industries LLC (G-2029)*
Exquisite Glass & Stone Inc 718 937-9266
3117 12th St Astoria (11106) *(G-428)*
Extek Inc 585 533-1672
7500 W Henrietta Rd Rush (14543) *(G-14472)*
Exten II LLC 716 895-2214
127 Elm St East Aurora (14052) *(G-4199)*
Extreme Auto Accessories Corp (PA) 718 978-6722
235 Liberty Ave Mineola (11501) *(G-8221)*
Extreme Group Holdings LLC (HQ) 212 833-8000
550 Madison Ave Fl 6 New York (10022) *(G-9757)*
Extreme Molding LLC 518 326-9319
25 Gibson St Ste 2 Watervliet (12189) *(G-16045)*
Extreme Shale Performance LLC 814 688-7956
2285 County Route 60 Elmira (14901) *(G-4485)*
Extreme Spices Inc (PA) 917 496-4081
5634 56th St Ste 36 Maspeth (11378) *(G-7843)*

ALPHABETIC

Extreme Streetwear, Batavia *Also called Alicia F Herdlein* ***(G-608)***
Exxelia-Raf Tabtronics LLC 585 243-4331
2854 Genesee St Piffard (14533) ***(G-12996)***
EY Industries Inc 718 624-9122
63 Flushing Ave Unit 331 Brooklyn (11205) ***(G-1860)***
Eye Shadow, New York *Also called Stony Apparel Corp* ***(G-11716)***
Eyeglass Service Industries 914 666-3150
777 Bedford Rd Bedford Hills (10507) ***(G-776)***
Eyelock Corporation 855 393-5625
321 W 44th St Ste 702 New York (10036) ***(G-9758)***
Eyelock LLC (HQ) 855 393-5625
321 W 44th St Ste 702 New York (10036) ***(G-9759)***
Eyenovia Inc 917 289-1117
501 5th Ave Rm 1404 New York (10017) ***(G-9760)***
Eyeworks Inc 585 454-4470
1249 Ridgeway Ave Ste M Rochester (14615) ***(G-13800)***
EZ Lift Garage Door Service, Spring Valley *Also called EZ Lift Operator Corp* ***(G-14990)***
EZ Lift Operator Corp 845 356-1676
111 S Main St Spring Valley (10977) ***(G-14990)***
EZ Newsletter LLC 412 943-7777
1449 Bay Ridge Ave 2 Brooklyn (11219) ***(G-1861)***
EZ Systems US Inc 929 295-0699
215 Water St Gf Brooklyn (11201) ***(G-1862)***
Ezcontacts.com, Brooklyn *Also called Provision Supply LLC* ***(G-2359)***
F & B Photo Offset Co Inc (PA) 516 431-5433
4 California Pl N Island Park (11558) ***(G-6514)***
F & D Printing, Staten Island *Also called F & D Services Inc* ***(G-15075)***
F & D Services Inc 718 984-1635
34 E Augusta Ave Staten Island (10308) ***(G-15075)***
F & H Metal Finishing Co Inc 585 798-2151
700 Genesee St Medina (14103) ***(G-7977)***
F & J Designs Inc 212 302-8755
526 Fashion Ave Fl 8 New York (10018) ***(G-9761)***
F & M Precise Metals Co, Farmingdale *Also called Pirnat Precise Metals Inc* ***(G-4850)***
F & R Enterprises Inc (PA) 315 841-8189
1594 State Route 315 Waterville (13480) ***(G-16039)***
F & T Graphics Inc 631 643-1000
690 Old Willets Path Hauppauge (11788) ***(G-5822)***
F & V Distribution Company LLC 516 812-0393
1 Arizona Plz Woodbury (11797) ***(G-16619)***
F A Alpine Windows Mfg 845 469-5700
1683 State Route 17m Chester (10918) ***(G-3474)***
F C W Division, Uniondale *Also called Hearst Business Media* ***(G-15669)***
F Cappiello Dairy Pdts Inc 518 374-5064
115 Van Guysling Ave Schenectady (12305) ***(G-14674)***
F E Hale Mfg Co 315 894-5490
120 Benson Pl Frankfort (13340) ***(G-5106)***
F H Stickles & Son Inc 518 851-9048
2590 Rr 9 Livingston (12541) ***(G-7275)***
F I S, Oriskany *Also called Fiber Instrument Sales Inc* ***(G-12757)***
F J Remey Co Inc 516 741-5112
121 Willis Ave Mineola (11501) ***(G-8222)***
F K Williams Division, North Tonawanda *Also called Gardei Industries LLC* ***(G-12429)***
F L Demeter Inc 516 487-5187
12 N Gate Rd Great Neck (11023) ***(G-5552)***
F Logic, Hastings On Hudson *Also called Flogic Inc* ***(G-5748)***
F M Abdulky Inc (PA) 607 272-7373
527 W Seneca St Ithaca (14850) ***(G-6576)***
F M Abdulky Inc 607 272-7373
527 W Seneca St Ithaca (14850) ***(G-6577)***
F M C Aricultural Chem Group, Middleport *Also called FMC Corporation* ***(G-8132)***
F M C Peroxygen Chemicals Div, Tonawanda *Also called FMC Corporation* ***(G-15541)***
F M EDM Inc 716 655-1784
210 Pennsylvania Ave East Aurora (14052) ***(G-4200)***
F M Group Inc 845 589-0102
100 Wells Ave Congers (10920) ***(G-3716)***
F M Howell & Company (PA) 607 734-6291
79 Pennsylvania Ave Elmira (14904) ***(G-4486)***
F M L Industries Inc 607 749-7273
10 Hudson St Homer (13077) ***(G-6254)***
F Olivers LLC 585 244-2585
747 Park Ave Rochester (14607) ***(G-13801)***
F P H Communications 212 528-1728
225 Broadway Ste 2008 New York (10007) ***(G-9762)***
F R A M Technologies Inc 718 338-6230
3048 Bedford Ave Brooklyn (11210) ***(G-1863)***
F W Roberts Mfg Co Inc 716 434-3555
73 Lock St Lockport (14094) ***(G-7300)***
F X Graphix Inc 716 871-1511
3043 Delaware Ave Buffalo (14217) ***(G-2823)***
F&M Ornamental Designs LLC 212 353-2600
200 Lexington Ave Rm 702 New York (10016) ***(G-9763)***
F&M Ornamental Designs LLC (PA) 908 241-7776
200 Lexington Ave Rm 702 New York (10016) ***(G-9764)***
F+w Media Inc 212 447-1400
1140 Broadway Fl 14 New York (10001) ***(G-9765)***
F-O-R Software LLC 212 231-9506
757 3rd Ave Fl 20 New York (10017) ***(G-9766)***
F-O-R Software LLC (PA) 914 220-8800
10 Bank St Ste 880 White Plains (10606) ***(G-16449)***
F-O-R Software LLC 212 724-3920
100 Park Ave Rm 1600 New York (10017) ***(G-9767)***
F3 Foods, New York *Also called Freshly Inc* ***(G-9849)***
F5 Networks Inc 888 882-7535
600 Lexington Ave Fl 5 New York (10022) ***(G-9768)***
Fab Industries Corp (HQ) 516 498-3200
98 Cuttermill Rd Ste 412 Great Neck (11021) ***(G-5553)***
Fabbian USA Corp 973 882-3824
307 W 38th St Rm 1103 New York (10018) ***(G-9769)***
Fabric Concepts For Industry 914 375-2565
354 Ashburton Ave Yonkers (10701) ***(G-16757)***
Fabric Quilters Unlimited Inc 516 333-2866
1400 Shames Dr Westbury (11590) ***(G-16330)***
Fabric Resources Intl Ltd (PA) 516 829-4550
9 Park Pl Great Neck (11021) ***(G-5554)***
Fabrication Enterprises Inc 914 591-9300
250 Clearbrook Rd Ste 240 Elmsford (10523) ***(G-4543)***
Faces Magazine Inc (PA) 201 843-4004
46 Violet Ave Poughkeepsie (12601) ***(G-13337)***
Faces Magazine Inc 845 454-7420
40 Violet Ave Poughkeepsie (12601) ***(G-13338)***
Facilamatic Instrument Corp 516 825-6300
39 Clinton Ave Valley Stream (11580) ***(G-15779)***
Facilities, New York *Also called Bedrock Communications* ***(G-9037)***
Facilities Exchange, New York *Also called FX INC* ***(G-9865)***
Facsimile Cmmncations Inds Inc (PA) 212 741-6400
134 W 26th St Fl 3 New York (10001) ***(G-9770)***
Factory East 718 280-1558
723 Kent Ave Brooklyn (11249) ***(G-1864)***
Factory Nyc, Brooklyn *Also called Factory East* ***(G-1864)***
Factory Wheel Warehouse Inc 516 605-2131
30 W Ames Ct Plainview (11803) ***(G-13057)***
Fad Inc 631 385-2460
630 New York Ave Ste B Huntington (11743) ***(G-6398)***
Fad Treasures, Huntington *Also called Fad Inc* ***(G-6398)***
Fader Inc 212 741-7100
71 W 23rd St Ste 1300 New York (10010) ***(G-9771)***
Fage USA Dairy Industry Inc 518 762-5912
1 Opportunity Dr Johnstown (12095) ***(G-6828)***
Fage USA Holdings (HQ) 518 762-5912
1 Opportunity Dr Johnstown (12095) ***(G-6829)***
Fage USA Yogurt Mfg Plant, Johnstown *Also called Fage USA Dairy Industry Inc* ***(G-6828)***
Fahrenheit NY Inc 212 354-6554
315 W 39th St Rm 803 New York (10018) ***(G-9772)***
Fahy-Williams Publishing Inc 315 781-6820
171 Reed St Geneva (14456) ***(G-5323)***
Fair-Rite Products Corp (PA) 845 895-2055
1 Commercial Row Wallkill (12589) ***(G-15904)***
Fairbanks Mfg LLC 845 341-0002
79 Industrial Pl Middletown (10940) ***(G-8152)***
Fairbanks Morse Engine 608 364-8465
1666 Division St Palmyra (14522) ***(G-12850)***
Fairchild Publications Inc (HQ) 212 630-4000
475 5th Ave New York (10017) ***(G-9773)***
Fairchild Publishing LLC 212 286-3897
4 Times Sq Fl 17 New York (10036) ***(G-9774)***
Fairmount Press 212 255-2300
70 W 36th St Rm 500 New York (10018) ***(G-9775)***
Fairview Bell and Intercom 718 627-8621
502 Gravesend Neck Rd B Brooklyn (11223) ***(G-1865)***
Fairview Paper Box Corp 585 786-5230
200 Allen St Warsaw (14569) ***(G-15944)***
Fait Usa Inc 215 674-5310
350 5th Ave Fl 41 New York (10118) ***(G-9776)***
Falcon Chair and Table Inc 716 664-7136
121 S Work St Falconer (14733) ***(G-4677)***
Falcon Perspectives Inc 718 706-9168
28 Vernon Blvd Ste 45 Long Island City (11101) ***(G-7444)***
Falcone Food Distribution, Brooklyn *Also called Falcones Cookie Land Ltd* ***(G-1866)***
Falconer Electronics Inc (PA) 716 665-4176
421 W Everett St Falconer (14733) ***(G-4678)***
Falcones Cookie Land Ltd (PA) 718 236-4200
1648 61st St Brooklyn (11204) ***(G-1866)***
Falconstor Software Inc (PA) 631 777-5188
2 Huntington Quadrangle Melville (11747) ***(G-8023)***
Falk Precision Inc 315 437-4545
5917 Fisher Rd East Syracuse (13057) ***(G-4337)***
Falke's Quarry, Prattsville *Also called Cobleskill Stone Products Inc* ***(G-13378)***
Fallon Inc 718 326-7226
5930 56th Rd Maspeth (11378) ***(G-7844)***
Falls Manufacturing Inc (PA) 518 672-7189
95 Main St Philmont (12565) ***(G-12986)***
Falso Industries Inc 315 463-0266
4100 New Court Ave Syracuse (13206) ***(G-15322)***
Falso Metal Fabricating, Syracuse *Also called Falso Industries Inc* ***(G-15322)***
Falvo Manufacturing Co Inc 315 724-7925
20 Harbor Point Rd Utica (13502) ***(G-15700)***
Fam Creations 212 869-4833
7 W 45th St Ste 1404 New York (10036) ***(G-9777)***
Fambus Inc 607 785-3700
2800 Watson Blvd Endicott (13760) ***(G-4592)***

Fame Construction Inc...718 626-1000
2388 Brklyn Queens Expy W Astoria (11103) **(G-429)**
Family Fuel Co Inc...718 232-2009
1571 W 10th St Brooklyn (11204) **(G-1867)**
Family Hearing Center...845 897-3059
18 Westage Dr Ste 16 Fishkill (12524) **(G-4946)**
Family Publications Ltd...212 947-2177
325 W 38th St Rm 804 New York (10018) **(G-9778)**
Family Publishing Group Inc...914 381-7474
141 Halstead Ave Mamaroneck (10543) **(G-7744)**
Famous Box Scooter Co...631 943-2013
75 Rogers Ct West Babylon (11704) **(G-16155)**
Famous Doughnuts Inc...716 834-6356
3043 Main St Buffalo (14214) **(G-2824)**
Fancy, New York *Also called Thing Daemon Inc* **(G-11815)**
Fancy Flamingo LLC...516 209-7306
450 W 17th St Apt 528 New York (10011) **(G-9779)**
Fancy Window & Door, Brooklyn *Also called Fancy Windows & Doors Mfg Corp* **(G-1868)**
Fancy Windows & Doors Mfg Corp...718 366-7800
312 Ten Eyck St Brooklyn (11206) **(G-1868)**
Fanshawe Foods LLC...212 757-3130
5 Columbus Cir New York (10019) **(G-9780)**
Fantasia Jewelry Inc...212 921-9590
42 W 39th St Fl 14 New York (10018) **(G-9781)**
Fantasy Glass Compan...845 786-5818
61 Beach Rd Stony Point (10980) **(G-15171)**
Fantasy Sports Media Group Inc...416 917-6002
27 W 20th St Ste 900 New York (10011) **(G-9782)**
Fantasy Sports Network, New York *Also called Fantasy Sports Media Group Inc* **(G-9782)**
Fanvision Entertainment LLC (PA)...917 297-7428
33 W 17th St Ste 901 New York (10011) **(G-9783)**
Fao Printing, Brooklyn *Also called Phillip Tissicher* **(G-2314)**
Far East Industries Inc (PA)...718 687-2482
118 Stephan Marc Ln New Hyde Park (11040) **(G-8534)**
Far Eastern Coconut Company...631 851-8800
200 Corporate Plz 201a Central Islip (11749) **(G-3369)**
Far Rockaway Drugs Inc...718 471-2500
1727 Seagirt Blvd Far Rockaway (11691) **(G-4701)**
Faradyne Motors LLC...315 331-5985
2077 Division St Palmyra (14522) **(G-12851)**
Farber Plastics Inc...516 378-4860
162 Hanse Ave Freeport (11520) **(G-5153)**
Farber Trucking Corp...516 378-4860
162 Hanse Ave Freeport (11520) **(G-5154)**
Farmers Hub LLC (HQ)...914 380-2945
8 Francine Ct White Plains (10607) **(G-16450)**
Farmingdale Iron Works Inc...631 249-5995
105 Florida St Farmingdale (11735) **(G-4763)**
Farney Lumber Corporation...315 346-6013
7194 Brewery Rd Lowville (13367) **(G-7650)**
Faro Industries Inc...585 647-6000
340 Lyell Ave Rochester (14606) **(G-13802)**
Farrand Controls Division, Valhalla *Also called Ruhle Companies Inc* **(G-15747)**
Farrant Screw Machine Products...585 457-3213
Gulf Rd Java Village (14083) **(G-6772)**
Farrington Packaging Corp...315 733-4600
2007 Beechgrove Pl Utica (13501) **(G-15701)**
Farthing Press Inc...716 852-4674
260 Oak St Buffalo (14203) **(G-2825)**
Fashion Accents LLC...401 331-6626
366 5th Ave Rm 802 New York (10001) **(G-9784)**
Fashion Ave Sweater Knits LLC...212 302-8282
525 7th Ave Fl 4 New York (10018) **(G-9785)**
Fashion Avenue Knits Inc...718 456-9000
1400 Broadway Rm 2401 New York (10018) **(G-9786)**
Fashion Calendar International...212 289-0420
153 E 87th St Apt 6a New York (10128) **(G-9787)**
Fashion Chef, The, Brooklyn *Also called Charlotte Neuville Design LLC* **(G-1690)**
Fashion Ribbon Co Inc (PA)...718 482-0100
3401 38th Ave Long Island City (11101) **(G-7445)**
Fashiondex Inc...914 271-6121
153 W 27th St Ste 701 New York (10001) **(G-9788)**
Fasprint...518 483-4631
20 Finney Blvd Malone (12953) **(G-7721)**
Fast By Gast Inc...716 773-1536
120 Industrial Dr Grand Island (14072) **(G-5499)**
Fast Company Magazine, New York *Also called Mansueto Ventures LLC* **(G-10696)**
Fastener Dimensions Inc...718 847-6321
9403 104th St Ozone Park (11416) **(G-12825)**
Faster-Form Corp...800 327-3676
1 Faster Form Cir Ste 1 # 1 New Hartford (13413) **(G-8504)**
Fastnet Software Intl Inc...888 740-7790
459 Elwood Rd East Northport (11731) **(G-4263)**
Fastsigns, Buffalo *Also called Fletcher Enterprises Inc* **(G-2828)**
Fastsigns, Staten Island *Also called Vez Inc* **(G-15151)**
Fastsigns...518 456-7446
1593 Central Ave Albany (12205) **(G-73)**
Father Sam's Bakery, Buffalo *Also called Commitment 2000 Inc* **(G-2775)**
Faucets and More Incorporated...734 328-2387
5318a 16th Ave Ste 106 Brooklyn (11204) **(G-1869)**
Faulkner Truss Company Inc...315 536-8894
1830 King Hill Rd Dresden (14441) **(G-4147)**
Faviana International Inc (PA)...212 594-4422
320 W 37th St Fl 10 New York (10018) **(G-9789)**
Favorite Plastic Corp...718 253-7000
1465 Utica Ave Brooklyn (11234) **(G-1870)**
Faye Bernard Loungewear...718 951-7245
2604 Avenue M Brooklyn (11210) **(G-1871)**
Fayette Street Coatings Inc...315 488-5401
1 Burr Dr Liverpool (13088) **(G-7233)**
FB Laboratories Inc...631 750-0000
70 Commerce Dr Hauppauge (11788) **(G-5823)**
FB Sale LLC...315 986-9999
1688 Wayneport Rd Macedon (14502) **(G-7699)**
FBC Chemical Corporation...716 681-1581
4111 Walden Ave Lancaster (14086) **(G-7019)**
Fbm Galaxy Inc...315 463-5144
6741 Old Collamer Rd East Syracuse (13057) **(G-4338)**
Fcmp Inc...716 692-4623
230 Fire Tower Dr Tonawanda (14150) **(G-15539)**
Fcr LLC...845 926-1071
508 Fishkill Ave Beacon (12508) **(G-758)**
Fearby Enterprises, Medina *Also called F & H Metal Finishing Co Inc* **(G-7977)**
Federal Contract MGT Svcs, Brooklyn *Also called It Commodity Sourcing Inc* **(G-2017)**
Federal Envelope Inc...212 243-8380
22 W 32nd St New York (10001) **(G-9790)**
Federal Pump Corporation...718 451-2000
250 E 73rd St Apt 18c New York (10021) **(G-9791)**
Federal Sample Card Corp...718 458-1344
4520 83rd St Elmhurst (11373) **(G-4464)**
Federal Sheet Metal Works Inc...315 735-4730
1416 Dudley Ave Utica (13501) **(G-15702)**
Fedex Ground Package Sys Inc...800 463-3339
82 Gateway Dr Plattsburgh (12901) **(G-13121)**
Fedex Office & Print Svcs Inc...718 982-5223
2456 Richmond Ave Ste C Staten Island (10314) **(G-15076)**
Fei Communications Inc...516 794-4500
55 Charles Lindbergh Blvd Uniondale (11553) **(G-15666)**
Fei Products LLC (PA)...716 693-6230
825 Wurlitzer Dr North Tonawanda (14120) **(G-12427)**
Fei-Zyfer Inc...714 933-4045
55 Charles Lindbergh Blvd Uniondale (11553) **(G-15667)**
Feinkind Inc...800 289-6136
17 Algonquin Dr Irvington (10533) **(G-6504)**
Feinstein Iron Works Inc...516 997-8300
990 Brush Hollow Rd Westbury (11590) **(G-16331)**
Felber Metal Fabricators, Holbrook *Also called Brzozka Industries Inc* **(G-6173)**
Felchar Manufacturing Corp (HQ)...607 723-3106
196 Corporate Dr Binghamton (13904) **(G-884)**
Feldheim Publishers, Nanuet *Also called Philipp Feldheim Inc* **(G-8467)**
Feldman Company Inc...212 966-1303
241 W 37th St Rm 1001 New York (10018) **(G-9792)**
Feldman Jewelry Creations Inc...718 438-8895
4821 16th Ave Brooklyn (11204) **(G-1872)**
Feldman Manufacturing Corp...718 433-1700
3010 41st Ave Ste 3fl Long Island City (11101) **(G-7446)**
Feldmeier Equipment Inc (PA)...315 823-2000
6800 Townline Rd Syracuse (13211) **(G-15323)**
Feldware Inc...718 372-0486
250 Avenue W Brooklyn (11223) **(G-1873)**
Felicetti Concrete Products...716 284-5740
4129 Hyde Park Blvd Niagara Falls (14305) **(G-12283)**
Felix Roma & Sons Inc...607 748-3336
2 S Page Ave Endicott (13760) **(G-4593)**
Felix Schoeller North Amer Inc...315 298-8425
179 County Route 2a Pulaski (13142) **(G-13379)**
Felluss Recording...212 727-8055
36 E 23rd St Rm 9l New York (10010) **(G-9793)**
Felton Machine Co Inc...716 215-9001
2221 Niagara Falls Blvd Niagara Falls (14304) **(G-12284)**
Feminist Press Inc...212 817-7915
365 5th Ave Ste 5406 New York (10016) **(G-9794)**
Femtech Women Powered Software...516 328-2631
1230 Hempstead Tpke Franklin Square (11010) **(G-5117)**
Fenbar Prcision Machinists Inc...914 769-5506
633 Commerce St Thornwood (10594) **(G-15506)**
Fence Plaza Corp...718 469-2200
1601 Nostrand Ave Brooklyn (11226) **(G-1874)**
Fenix Furniture Co...631 273-3500
35 Drexel Dr Bay Shore (11706) **(G-686)**
Fennell Industries LLC (PA)...607 733-6693
108 Stephens Pl Elmira (14901) **(G-4487)**
Fennell Spring Company LLC...607 739-3541
295 Hemlock St Horseheads (14845) **(G-6315)**
Fenton Mobility Products Inc...716 484-7014
26 Center St Randolph (14772) **(G-13447)**
Fera Pharmaceuticals LLC...516 277-1449
134 Birch Hill Rd Locust Valley (11560) **(G-7346)**
Feraco Industries...631 547-8120
3 Plumb Ct Huntington Station (11746) **(G-6440)**
Ferguson Enterprises Inc...800 437-1146
200 Atlantic Ave New Hyde Park (11040) **(G-8535)**
Fermer Precision Inc...315 822-6371
114 Johnson Rd Ilion (13357) **(G-6474)**

ALPHABETIC

Ferrara Bakery & Cafe Inc (PA) 212 226-6150
195 Grand St New York (10013) ***(G-9795)***
Ferrara Bros LLC (HQ) 718 939-3030
12005 31st Ave Flushing (11354) ***(G-4999)***
Ferrara Manufacturing, New York *Also called Rogers Group Inc* ***(G-11423)***
Ferrara Manufacturing Company, New York *Also called HC Contracting Inc* ***(G-10054)***
Ferraro Manufacturing Company 631 752-1509
150 Central Ave Farmingdale (11735) ***(G-4764)***
Ferris USA LLC 617 895-8102
18 W 108th St Apt 4a New York (10025) ***(G-9796)***
Ferro Corporation 585 586-8770
603 W Commercial St East Rochester (14445) ***(G-4284)***
Ferro Corporation 315 536-3357
1789 Transelco Dr Penn Yan (14527) ***(G-12953)***
Ferro Electronic Mtl Systems, Penn Yan *Also called Ferro Electronics Materials* ***(G-12954)***
Ferro Electronic Mtl Systems, Penn Yan *Also called Ferro Electronics Materials* ***(G-12955)***
Ferro Electronics Materials 716 278-9400
4511 Hyde Park Blvd Niagara Falls (14305) ***(G-12285)***
Ferro Electronics Materials (HQ) 315 536-3357
1789 Transelco Dr Penn Yan (14527) ***(G-12954)***
Ferro Electronics Materials 315 536-3357
1789 Transelco Dr Penn Yan (14527) ***(G-12955)***
Ferro Fabricators Inc 718 703-0007
1117 38th St Brooklyn (11218) ***(G-1875)***
Ferro Machine Co Inc 845 398-3641
70 S Greenbush Rd Orangeburg (10962) ***(G-12678)***
Festival Bakers, Bronx *Also called Waldorf Bakers Inc* ***(G-1417)***
Fevertree USA Inc 718 852-5577
77 Front St Fl 2 Brooklyn (11201) ***(G-1876)***
Feyem USA Inc 845 363-6253
7 Sutton Pl Brewster (10509) ***(G-1165)***
Ffc Holding Corp Subsidiaries (PA) 716 366-5400
1 Ice Cream Dr Dunkirk (14048) ***(G-4170)***
FG Galassi Moulding Co Inc 845 258-2100
699 Pulaski Hwy Goshen (10924) ***(G-5479)***
Fgi, Amsterdam *Also called Fiber Glass Industries Inc* ***(G-337)***
Fiber Foot Appliances Inc 631 465-9199
34 Sarah Dr Ste A Farmingdale (11735) ***(G-4765)***
Fiber Glass Industries Inc (PA) 518 842-4000
69 Edson St Amsterdam (12010) ***(G-337)***
Fiber Instrument Sales Inc (PA) 315 736-2206
161 Clear Rd Oriskany (13424) ***(G-12757)***
Fiber Laminations Limited 716 692-1825
600 Main St Tonawanda (14150) ***(G-15540)***
Fiber Optics Schott America, Auburn *Also called Schott Corporation* ***(G-499)***
Fiber USA Corp 718 888-1512
13620 38th Ave Ste 11f Flushing (11354) ***(G-5000)***
Fiber-Seal of New York Inc (PA) 212 888-5580
979 3rd Ave Ste 903 New York (10022) ***(G-9797)***
Fiberall Corp 516 371-5200
449 Sheridan Blvd Inwood (11096) ***(G-6490)***
Fiberdyne Labs Inc 315 895-8470
127 Business Park Dr Frankfort (13340) ***(G-5107)***
Fiberone LLC 315 434-8877
5 Technology Pl Ste 4 East Syracuse (13057) ***(G-4339)***
Fiberwave Corporation 718 802-9011
140 58th St Ste 37 Brooklyn (11220) ***(G-1877)***
Fibre Case & Novelty Co Inc (PA) 212 254-6060
270 Lafayette St Ste 1510 New York (10012) ***(G-9798)***
Fibre Materials Corp 516 349-1660
40 Dupont St Plainview (11803) ***(G-13058)***
Fibrix LLC 716 683-4100
3307 Walden Ave Depew (14043) ***(G-4089)***
Fibron Products Inc 716 886-2378
170 Florida St Buffalo (14208) ***(G-2826)***
Fidelus Technologies LLC 212 616-7800
240 W 35th St Fl 6 New York (10001) ***(G-9799)***
Fidesa US Corporation 212 269-9000
17 State St Unit 122 New York (10004) ***(G-9800)***
Field Company, Brooklyn *Also called Field Wares LLC* ***(G-1878)***
Field Trip Jerky, Brooklyn *Also called Provisionaire & Co LLC* ***(G-2360)***
Field Wares LLC 508 380-6545
53 Bridge St Apt 410 Brooklyn (11201) ***(G-1878)***
Fieldbrook Foods Corporation (HQ) 716 366-5400
1 Ice Cream Dr Dunkirk (14048) ***(G-4171)***
Fieldtex Products Inc 585 427-2940
3055 Brighton Henrietta Rochester (14623) ***(G-13803)***
Fierce Fun Toys LLC 646 322-7172
100 Riverside Dr Ste 2 New York (10024) ***(G-9801)***
Fifty Door Partners LLC (PA) 845 562-3332
509 Temple Hill Rd New Windsor (12553) ***(G-8644)***
Fika, New York *Also called Pachanga Inc* ***(G-11087)***
Fil Doux Inc 212 202-1459
227 5th Ave Brooklyn (11215) ***(G-1879)***
Fil-Coil (fc) Corp (PA) 631 467-5328
98 Lincoln Ave Sayville (11782) ***(G-14628)***
Fil-Coil International LLC 631 467-5328
98 Lincoln Ave Sayville (11782) ***(G-14629)***
Filestream Inc 516 759-4100
257 Buckram Rd Locust Valley (11560) ***(G-7347)***
Filling Equipment Co Inc 718 445-2111
1539 130th St College Point (11356) ***(G-3644)***
Fillmore Greenhouses Inc 585 567-2678
11589 State Route 19a Portageville (14536) ***(G-13314)***
Filmpak Extrusion LLC 631 293-6767
125 Spagnoli Rd Melville (11747) ***(G-8024)***
Films Media Group, New York *Also called Infobase Publishing Company* ***(G-10207)***
Filta Clean Co Inc 718 495-3800
107 Georgia Ave Brooklyn (11207) ***(G-1880)***
Filter Tech Inc (PA) 315 682-8815
113 Fairgrounds Dr Manlius (13104) ***(G-7777)***
Filtros Ltd 585 586-8770
603 W Commercial St East Rochester (14445) ***(G-4285)***
Filtros Plant, East Rochester *Also called Filtros Ltd* ***(G-4285)***
Fin-Tech360, Whitestone *Also called Financial Technologies 360 Inc* ***(G-16540)***
Fina Cabinet Corp 718 409-2900
20 N Macquesten Pkwy Mount Vernon (10550) ***(G-8398)***
Final Dimension Inc 718 786-0100
57-401 59th St Fl 1 Flr 1 Maspeth (11378) ***(G-7845)***
Final Touch Printing Inc 845 352-2677
29 Decatur Ave Unit 1 Spring Valley (10977) ***(G-14991)***
Finals, The, Port Jervis *Also called Swimwear Anywhere Inc* ***(G-13238)***
Finance Manager, East Setauket *Also called Mml Software Ltd* ***(G-4305)***
Financial Technologies 360 Inc 862 200-1164
15436 24th Ave Whitestone (11357) ***(G-16540)***
Financial Times Newspaper, New York *Also called FT Publications Inc* ***(G-9857)***
Financial Times, The, New York *Also called FT Publications Inc* ***(G-9856)***
Findmine Inc 925 787-6181
137 Varick St Fl 2 New York (10013) ***(G-9802)***
Fine and Raw Chocolate 718 366-3633
288 Seigel St Brooklyn (11206) ***(G-1881)***
Fine Arts Furniture Inc 212 744-9139
3872 13th St Long Island City (11101) ***(G-7447)***
Fine Cut Diamonds Corporation 212 575-8780
580 5th Ave Ste 709 New York (10036) ***(G-9803)***
Fine Sheer Industries Inc (PA) 212 594-4224
350 5th Ave Ste 4710 New York (10118) ***(G-9804)***
Fine Sounds Group Inc (PA) 212 364-0219
214 Lafayette St New York (10012) ***(G-9805)***
Fineline Thermographers Inc 718 643-1100
544 Park Ave Ste 308 Brooklyn (11205) ***(G-1882)***
Finer Touch Printing Corp 516 944-8000
4 Yennicock Ave Port Washington (11050) ***(G-13259)***
Finesse Accessories, Plainview *Also called Mgd Brands Inc* ***(G-13075)***
Finesse Creations Inc 718 692-2100
3004 Avenue J Brooklyn (11210) ***(G-1883)***
Finest Cc Corp 917 574-4525
3111 E Tremont Ave Bronx (10461) ***(G-1270)***
Finestar, Long Island City *Also called Efam Enterprises LLC* ***(G-7435)***
Finger Food Products Inc 716 297-4888
6400 Inducon Dr W Sanborn (14132) ***(G-14545)***
Finger Lakes Cheese Trail 607 857-5726
4970 County Road 14 Odessa (14869) ***(G-12567)***
Finger Lakes Chemicals Inc (PA) 585 454-4760
420 Saint Paul St Rochester (14605) ***(G-13804)***
Finger Lakes Conveyors Inc 315 539-9246
2359 State Route 414 E Waterloo (13165) ***(G-15992)***
Finger Lakes Distilling 607 546-5510
4676 State Route 414 Burdett (14818) ***(G-3141)***
Finger Lakes Extrusion Corp 585 905-0632
2437 State Route 21 Canandaigua (14424) ***(G-3221)***
Finger Lakes Lea Crafters LLC 315 252-4107
42 Washington St Auburn (13021) ***(G-478)***
Finger Lakes Media Inc 607 243-7600
45 Water St Dundee (14837) ***(G-4157)***
Finger Lakes Radiology LLC 315 787-5399
196 North St Geneva (14456) ***(G-5324)***
Finger Lakes Timber Co Inc 585 346-2990
6274 Decker Rd Livonia (14487) ***(G-7278)***
Finger Lakes Times, Geneva *Also called Community Media Group Inc* ***(G-5321)***
Finger Lakes Trellis Supply 315 904-4007
4041a Railroad Ave Williamson (14589) ***(G-16558)***
Finger Lakes/Castle, Rochester *Also called Finger Lakes Chemicals Inc* ***(G-13804)***
Finger Lkes Stirs Cabinets LLC 315 638-3150
7496 Kingdom Rd Baldwinsville (13027) ***(G-554)***
Fingerlakes Construction, Clyde *Also called Energy Panel Structures Inc* ***(G-3592)***
Fingerlakes Construction, Clyde *Also called Energy Panel Structures Inc* ***(G-3593)***
Fingerlakes Construction, Schenectady *Also called Energy Panel Structures Inc* ***(G-14671)***
Fingerprint America Inc 518 435-1609
1843 Central Ave Albany (12205) ***(G-74)***
Finish Line Technologies Inc (PA) 631 666-7300
50 Wireless Blvd Hauppauge (11788) ***(G-5824)***
Finishing Line, The, Le Roy *Also called Duzmor Painting Inc* ***(G-7117)***
Finzer Holding LLC 315 597-1147
2085 Division St Palmyra (14522) ***(G-12852)***
Finzer Roller New York, Palmyra *Also called Finzer Holding LLC* ***(G-12852)***
Fiora Italy, Valley Cottage *Also called Innovative Jewelry Inc* ***(G-15756)***
Fire Apparatus Service Tech 716 753-3538
7895 Lyons Rd Sherman (14781) ***(G-14816)***
Fire Curtain Technologies, Canandaigua *Also called Murcadom Corporation* ***(G-3226)***
Fire Fox Security Corp 917 981-9280
2070 72nd St Apt B1 Brooklyn (11204) ***(G-1884)***

Fire Islanq Fuel 631 772-1482
106 Parkwood Dr Shirley (11967) ***(G-14834)***
Fire Island News, Bronx *Also called Five Islands Publishing Inc* ***(G-1271)***
Fire Island Sea Clam Co Inc 631 589-2199
132 Atlantic Ave West Sayville (11796) ***(G-16289)***
Fire Island Tide Publication 631 567-7470
40 Main St Sayville (11782) ***(G-14630)***
Fire Island Tide The, Sayville *Also called Fire Island Tide Publication* ***(G-14630)***
Firecom Inc (PA) 718 899-6100
3927 59th St Woodside (11377) ***(G-16655)***
Firefighters Journal 718 391-0283
2420 Jackson Ave Long Island City (11101) ***(G-7448)***
Firetronics Inc (PA) 516 997-5151
50 Jericho Tpke Jericho (11753) ***(G-6789)***
Fireworks By Grucci Inc 631 286-0088
20 Pinehurst Dr Bellport (11713) ***(G-804)***
First Choice News Inc 212 477-2044
639 1/2 Broadway New York (10012) ***(G-9806)***
First Displays Inc 347 642-5972
2415 43rd Ave Fl 2 Long Island City (11101) ***(G-7449)***
First Due Fire Equipment Inc 845 222-1329
130 W Ramapo Rd Garnerville (10923) ***(G-5300)***
First Games Publr Netwrk Inc 212 983-0501
420 Lexington Ave Rm 412 New York (10170) ***(G-9807)***
First Impressions Finishing 631 467-2244
132 Remington Blvd Ronkonkoma (11779) ***(G-14341)***
First Light Farm & Creamery, East Bethany *Also called Sandvoss Farms LLC* ***(G-4213)***
First Line Printing Inc 718 606-0860
3728 56th St Woodside (11377) ***(G-16656)***
First Love Fashions LLC 212 256-1089
1407 Broadway Rm 2010 New York (10018) ***(G-9808)***
First Manufacturing Co Inc (HQ) 516 763-0400
3800 Oceanside Rd W Oceanside (11572) ***(G-12538)***
First Presbyterian Church 315 252-3861
112 South St Auburn (13021) ***(G-479)***
First Qlty Packg Solutions LLC (PA) 516 829-3030
80 Cuttermill Rd Ste 500 Great Neck (11021) ***(G-5555)***
First Quality Hygienic Inc 516 829-3030
80 Cuttermill Rd Ste 500 Great Neck (11021) ***(G-5556)***
First Quality Products Inc (HQ) 516 829-4949
80 Cuttermill Rd Ste 500 Great Neck (11021) ***(G-5557)***
First Sbf Holding Inc (PA) 845 425-9882
9 Pinecrest Rd Ste 101 Valley Cottage (10989) ***(G-15754)***
First View, New York *Also called Viewfinder Inc* ***(G-12032)***
First2print Inc 212 868-6886
494 8th Ave Fl 12 New York (10001) ***(G-9809)***
Firth Rixson Inc (HQ) 585 328-1383
181 Mckee Rd Rochester (14611) ***(G-13805)***
Firth Rixson Monroe, Rochester *Also called Firth Rixson Inc* ***(G-13805)***
Fisau, Brooklyn *Also called Business Management Systems* ***(G-1661)***
Fischer Diamonds Inc 212 869-1990
1212 Avenue Of The Americ New York (10036) ***(G-9810)***
Fischler Diamonds Inc 212 921-8196
580 5th Ave Ste 3100 New York (10036) ***(G-9811)***
Fischler Hockey Service 212 749-4152
200 W 109th St Apt C5 New York (10025) ***(G-9812)***
Fish & Crown Ltd (PA) 212 707-9603
42 W 39th St New York (10018) ***(G-9813)***
Fisher-Price, East Aurora *Also called Mattel Inc* ***(G-4206)***
Fishers Storage Sheds 585 382-9580
7854 Alverson Rd Leicester (14481) ***(G-7128)***
Fishing Valley LLC 716 523-6158
7217 N Canal Rd Lockport (14094) ***(G-7301)***
Fisonic Corp 212 732-3777
4402 23rd St Long Island City (11101) ***(G-7450)***
Fisonic Corp (PA) 716 763-0295
31-00 47th Ave Ste 106 New York (10023) ***(G-9814)***
Fisonic Technology, New York *Also called Fisonic Corp* ***(G-9814)***
Fitch Group, New York *Also called Francis Emory Fitch Inc* ***(G-9838)***
Fitsmo LLC 585 519-1956
108 Packetts Gln Fairport (14450) ***(G-4633)***
Fitzgerald Publishing Co Inc 914 793-5016
1853 Central Park Ave # 8 Yonkers (10710) ***(G-16758)***
Fitzpatrick and Weller Inc 716 699-2393
12 Mill St Ellicottville (14731) ***(G-4446)***
Fitzsimmons Systems Inc 315 214-7010
53 Nelson St Cazenovia (13035) ***(G-3319)***
Five Boro Doors Mouldings Inc 718 865-9371
3569 Maple Ct Oceanside (11572) ***(G-12539)***
Five Boro Holding LLC 718 431-9500
1425 37th St Ste 3 Brooklyn (11218) ***(G-1885)***
Five Burroughs Brewing Co 718 355-8575
215 47th St Brooklyn (11220) ***(G-1886)***
Five Corners Repair Inc 585 322-7369
6653 Hardys Rd Bliss (14024) ***(G-946)***
Five Islands Publishing Inc 631 583-5345
8 Fort Charles Pl Bronx (10463) ***(G-1271)***
Five Star Awnings Inc 718 860-6070
5923 Decatur St Ridgewood (11385) ***(G-13536)***
Five Star Creations Inc 845 783-1187
4 Preshburg Blvd Unit 302 Monroe (10950) ***(G-8269)***
Five Star Industries Inc 716 674-2589
114 Willowdale Dr West Seneca (14224) ***(G-16297)***
Five Star Millwork LLC 845 920-0247
6 E Dexter Plz Pearl River (10965) ***(G-12896)***
Five Star Printing, Jamaica *Also called Ssrja LLC* ***(G-6678)***
Five Star Prtg & Mailing Svcs 212 929-0300
225 W 37th St Fl 16 New York (10018) ***(G-9815)***
Five Star Tool Co Inc 585 328-9580
125 Elmgrove Park Rochester (14624) ***(G-13806)***
Fixtures 2000 Inc 631 236-4100
400 Oser Ave Ste 350 Hauppauge (11788) ***(G-5825)***
Fiz Beverages, Rochester *Also called Load/N/Go Beverage Corp* ***(G-13915)***
Flado Enterprises Inc 716 668-6400
1380 French Rd Ste 6 Depew (14043) ***(G-4090)***
Flagpoles Incorporated 631 751-5500
95 Gnarled Hollow Rd East Setauket (11733) ***(G-4301)***
Flair Display Inc 718 324-9330
3920 Merritt Ave Bronx (10466) ***(G-1272)***
Flair Printers, Brooklyn *Also called Printing Sales Group Limited* ***(G-2351)***
Flame Control Coatings LLC 716 282-1399
4120 Hyde Park Blvd Niagara Falls (14305) ***(G-12286)***
Flanagans Creative Disp Inc 845 858-2542
55 Jersey Ave Port Jervis (12771) ***(G-13228)***
Flanders Precisionaire NY 518 751-5640
1 Vapor Trl Hudson (12534) ***(G-6349)***
Flare Multi Copy, Brooklyn *Also called Flare Multicopy Corp* ***(G-1887)***
Flare Multicopy Corp 718 258-8860
1840 Flatbush Ave Brooklyn (11210) ***(G-1887)***
Flashflo Manufacturing Inc 716 826-9500
88 Hopkins St Buffalo (14220) ***(G-2827)***
Flatcut LLC 212 542-5732
68 Jay St Ste 901 Brooklyn (11201) ***(G-1888)***
Flaum Appetizing, Brooklyn *Also called M & M Food Products Inc* ***(G-2142)***
Flavor League, Brooklyn *Also called Flavor Paper Ltd* ***(G-1889)***
Flavor Paper Ltd 718 422-0230
216 Pacific St Brooklyn (11201) ***(G-1889)***
Flavormatic Industries LLC 845 297-9100
90 Brentwood Dr Wappingers Falls (12590) ***(G-15930)***
Flavors Holdings Inc (HQ) 212 572-8677
35 E 62nd St New York (10065) ***(G-9816)***
Fleaheart Inc 718 521-4958
61 Greenpoint Ave Ste 403 Brooklyn (11222) ***(G-1890)***
Fleetcom Inc 914 776-5582
1081 Yonkers Ave Yonkers (10704) ***(G-16759)***
Fleetwood Cabinet Co Inc (PA) 516 379-2139
673 Livonia Ave Brooklyn (11207) ***(G-1891)***
Fleischman Vinegar, North Rose *Also called Fleischmanns Vinegar Co Inc* ***(G-12394)***
Fleischmanns Vinegar Co Inc 315 587-4414
4754 State Route 414 North Rose (14516) ***(G-12394)***
Fletcher Enterprises Inc 716 837-7446
4913 Genesee St Buffalo (14225) ***(G-2828)***
Fleurette, New York *Also called Blum & Fink Inc* ***(G-9112)***
Flex Enterprises Inc 585 742-1000
820 Canning Pkwy Victor (14564) ***(G-15846)***
Flex Supply, Farmingdale *Also called Custom Door & Mirror Inc* ***(G-4745)***
Flex Tubing, Canandaigua *Also called Finger Lakes Extrusion Corp* ***(G-3221)***
Flex-Hose Company Inc 315 437-1903
6801 Crossbow Dr East Syracuse (13057) ***(G-4340)***
Flexbar Machine Corporation 631 582-8440
250 Gibbs Rd Islandia (11749) ***(G-6528)***
Flexfit Llc 516 932-8800
350 Karin Ln Unit A Hicksville (11801) ***(G-6086)***
Flexible Lifeline Systems Inc 716 896-4949
100 Stradtman St Buffalo (14206) ***(G-2829)***
Flexim Americas Corporation (HQ) 631 492-2300
250 Executive Dr Ste V Edgewood (11717) ***(G-4400)***
Flexlume Sign Corporation 716 884-2020
1464 Main St Buffalo (14209) ***(G-2830)***
Flextrade Systems Inc (PA) 516 627-8993
111 Great Neck Rd Ste 314 Great Neck (11021) ***(G-5558)***
Flickinger Glassworks Inc 718 875-1531
175 Van Dyke St Ste 321ap Brooklyn (11231) ***(G-1892)***
Flightline Electronics Inc (HQ) 585 924-4000
7625 Omnitech Pl Victor (14564) ***(G-15847)***
Flik International/Compass 212 450-4750
450 Lexington Ave New York (10017) ***(G-9817)***
Flint Group Incorporated 585 458-1223
1128 Lexington Ave Bldg 3 Rochester (14606) ***(G-13807)***
Flint Ink North America Div, Rochester *Also called Flint Group Incorporated* ***(G-13807)***
Flirtatious, New York *Also called Soho Apparel Ltd* ***(G-11636)***
Flo-Tech Orthotic & Prosthetic 607 387-3070
7325 Halseyville Rd Trumansburg (14886) ***(G-15639)***
Float Tech Inc 518 266-0964
216 River St Ste 1 Troy (12180) ***(G-15605)***
Flogic Inc 914 478-1352
25 Chestnut Dr Hastings On Hudson (10706) ***(G-5748)***
Flomatic Corporation 518 761-9797
15 Pruyns Island Dr Glens Falls (12801) ***(G-5425)***
Flomatic Valves, Glens Falls *Also called Flomatic Corporation* ***(G-5425)***
Florelle Tissue Corporation 647 997-7405
1 Bridge St Brownville (13615) ***(G-2671)***

ALPHABETIC

Florida North Inc 518 868-2888
134 Vanderwerken Rd Sloansville (12160) ***(G-14891)***
Flour Power Bakery Cafe 917 747-6895
87 Debruce Rd Livingston Manor (12758) ***(G-7276)***
Flow Control LLC (HQ) 914 323-5700
1 International Dr Rye Brook (10573) ***(G-14492)***
Flow Dental, Deer Park *Also called Flow X Ray Corporation* ***(G-3976)***
Flow Society, New York *Also called Big Idea Brands LLC* ***(G-9078)***
Flow X Ray Corporation 631 242-9729
100 W Industry Ct Deer Park (11729) ***(G-3976)***
Flow-Safe Inc 716 662-2585
3865 Taylor Rd Orchard Park (14127) ***(G-12714)***
Flower City Printing Inc (PA) 585 663-9000
1725 Mount Read Blvd Rochester (14606) ***(G-13808)***
Flower City Printing Inc 585 512-1235
1001 Lee Rd Rochester (14606) ***(G-13809)***
Flower Cy Tissue Mills Co Inc (PA) 585 458-9200
700 Driving Park Ave Rochester (14613) ***(G-13810)***
Flowmedica Inc 800 772-6446
603 Queensbury Ave Queensbury (12804) ***(G-13423)***
Flownet LLC 716 685-4036
580 Lake Ave Lancaster (14086) ***(G-7020)***
Floymar Manufacturing, Wyandanch *Also called Ehrlich Enterprises Inc* ***(G-16695)***
Flp Group LLC 315 252-7583
301 Clark St Auburn (13021) ***(G-480)***
Fluid Handling LLC 716 897-2800
175 Standard Pkwy Cheektowaga (14227) ***(G-3444)***
Fluid Handling LLC (HQ) 716 897-2800
175 Standard Pkwy Cheektowaga (14227) ***(G-3445)***
Fluid Mechanisms Hauppauge Inc 631 234-0100
225 Engineers Rd Hauppauge (11788) ***(G-5826)***
Fluid Metering Inc (HQ) 516 922-6050
5 Aerial Way Ste 500 Syosset (11791) ***(G-15217)***
Fluorologic Inc 585 248-2796
33 Bishops Ct Pittsford (14534) ***(G-13012)***
Flushing Boiler & Welding Co 718 463-1266
8720 Ditmas Ave Brooklyn (11236) ***(G-1893)***
Flushing Iron Weld Inc 718 359-2208
13125 Maple Ave Flushing (11355) ***(G-5001)***
Flushing Pharmacy Inc 718 260-8999
414 Flushing Ave Ste 1 Brooklyn (11205) ***(G-1894)***
Flushing Terminal, Flushing *Also called Tilcon New York Inc* ***(G-5053)***
Fluxdata Incorporated 800 425-0176
176 Anderson Ave Ste F304 Rochester (14607) ***(G-13811)***
Fly Creek Cder Mill Orchrd Inc 607 547-9692
288 Goose St Fly Creek (13337) ***(G-5064)***
Fly-Tyers Carry-All LLC 607 821-1460
112 Meade Rd Charlotteville (12036) ***(G-3425)***
Flycell Inc 212 400-1212
80 Pine St Fl 29 New York (10005) ***(G-9818)***
Flynn's Xerox, New York *Also called Flynns Inc* ***(G-9819)***
Flynns Inc (PA) 212 339-8700
115 W 30th St New York (10001) ***(G-9819)***
FM Brush Co Inc 718 821-5939
7002 72nd Pl Glendale (11385) ***(G-5399)***
FMC Corporation 716 735-3761
100 Niagara St Middleport (14105) ***(G-8132)***
FMC Corporation 716 879-0400
78 Sawyer Ave Ste 1 Tonawanda (14150) ***(G-15541)***
FMC Fashion Division, Oceanside *Also called First Manufacturing Co Inc* ***(G-12538)***
Foam Products Inc 718 292-4830
360 Southern Blvd Bronx (10454) ***(G-1273)***
Focus Point Windows & Doors, Long Beach *Also called Air Tite Manufacturing Inc* ***(G-7356)***
Fog Creek Software Inc 866 364-2733
75 Broad St Fl 19 New York (10004) ***(G-9820)***
Folder Factory Inc 540 477-3852
5300 New Horizons Blvd Amityville (11701) ***(G-275)***
Folders.com, Amityville *Also called Folder Factory Inc* ***(G-275)***
Folene Packaging LLC 917 626-6740
2509 Avenue M Brooklyn (11210) ***(G-1895)***
Foley Graphics, Yorktown Heights *Also called Foleys Graphic Center Inc* ***(G-16816)***
Foleys Graphic Center Inc 914 245-3625
1661 Front St Ste 3 Yorktown Heights (10598) ***(G-16816)***
Folia Water Inc 412 802-5083
175 Varick St New York (10014) ***(G-9821)***
Folio Graphics Co Inc 718 763-2076
2759 E 66th St Brooklyn (11234) ***(G-1896)***
Folstaf Company, The, Charlotteville *Also called Fly-Tyers Carry-All LLC* ***(G-3425)***
Fonar Corporation (PA) 631 694-2929
110 Marcus Dr Melville (11747) ***(G-8025)***
Fontrick Door Inc 585 345-6032
9 Apollo Dr Batavia (14020) ***(G-624)***
Foo Yuan Food Products Co Inc 212 925-2840
2301 Borden Ave Long Island City (11101) ***(G-7451)***
Food Basket USA Company Ltd 631 231-8999
30 Inez Dr Bay Shore (11706) ***(G-687)***
Food Gems Ltd 718 296-7788
8423 Rockaway Blvd Ozone Park (11416) ***(G-12826)***
Foot Locker Retail Inc 516 827-5306
358 Broadway Mall Hicksville (11801) ***(G-6087)***
For A Safer America, Amsterdam *Also called Keep America Beautiful Inc* ***(G-344)***
Forbes Precision Inc 585 865-7069
100 Boxart St Ste 105 Rochester (14612) ***(G-13812)***
Forbes Products, Dansville *Also called GPM Associates LLC* ***(G-3926)***
Force Digital Media Inc 631 243-0243
39 W Jefryn Blvd Ste 2 Deer Park (11729) ***(G-3977)***
Force Dynamics Inc 607 546-5023
4995 Voorheis Rd Trumansburg (14886) ***(G-15640)***
Ford Gum & Machine Company Inc (PA) 716 542-4561
18 Newton Ave Akron (14001) ***(G-18)***
Ford Regulator Valve Corp 718 497-3255
199 Varet St Brooklyn (11206) ***(G-1897)***
Fordham Marble Co Inc 914 682-6699
45 Crane Ave White Plains (10603) ***(G-16451)***
Forecast Consoles Inc 631 253-9000
681 Old Willets Path Hauppauge (11788) ***(G-5827)***
Forerunner Technologies Inc (PA) 631 337-2100
150 Executive Dr Ste M Edgewood (11717) ***(G-4401)***
Forest Hills Courier, Bayside *Also called Schneps Publications Inc* ***(G-749)***
Forest Iron Works Inc 516 671-4229
3 Elm St Ste A Locust Valley (11560) ***(G-7348)***
Forest Laboratories LLC (HQ) 212 421-7850
909 3rd Ave Fl 23 New York (10022) ***(G-9822)***
Forest Laboratories LLC 212 421-7850
45 Adams Ave Hauppauge (11788) ***(G-5828)***
Forest Laboratories LLC 631 858-6010
500 Commack Rd Commack (11725) ***(G-3690)***
Forest Labs 631 755-1185
210 Sea Ln Farmingdale (11735) ***(G-4766)***
Forest Medical LLC 315 434-9000
6700 Old Collamer Rd # 114 East Syracuse (13057) ***(G-4341)***
Forest Research Institute Inc 631 858-5200
49 Mall Dr Commack (11725) ***(G-3691)***
Forest Uniforms, New York *Also called Urban Textiles Inc* ***(G-11970)***
Forever Grown Diamonds Inc 212 354-2827
22 W 48th St Ste 402 New York (10036) ***(G-9823)***
Forge Metal Finishing Inc 585 730-7340
383 Buell Rd Rochester (14624) ***(G-13813)***
Forkey Construction & Fabg Inc 607 849-4879
3690 Luker Rd Cortland (13045) ***(G-3872)***
Form A Rockland Plastics Inc 315 848-3300
7152 Main St Cranberry Lake (12927) ***(G-3907)***
Form-Tec Inc 516 867-0200
216 N Main St Ste E Freeport (11520) ***(G-5155)***
Formac Welding Inc 631 421-5525
42 W Hills Rd Huntington Station (11746) ***(G-6441)***
Formart Corp 212 819-1819
312 5th Ave Fl 6 New York (10001) ***(G-9824)***
Formatix Corp 631 467-3399
9 Colt Ct Ronkonkoma (11779) ***(G-14342)***
Formats Unlimited Inc 631 249-9200
19 W Jefryn Blvd Ste 2 Deer Park (11729) ***(G-3978)***
Formcraft Display Products 914 632-1410
42 Beverly Rd New Rochelle (10804) ***(G-8603)***
Formed Plastics Inc 516 334-2300
207 Stonehinge Ln Carle Place (11514) ***(G-3264)***
Formosa Polymer Corporation 718 326-1769
5641 55th Ave Maspeth (11378) ***(G-7846)***
Forms For You Division, Newburgh *Also called Empire Business Forms Inc* ***(G-12221)***
Foro Marble Co Inc 718 852-2322
166 2nd Ave Brooklyn (11215) ***(G-1898)***
Forrest Engravg, New Rochelle *Also called Forrest Engraving Co Inc* ***(G-8604)***
Forrest Engraving Co Inc 845 228-0200
92 1st St New Rochelle (10801) ***(G-8604)***
Forsyth Industries Inc 716 652-1070
1195 Colvin Blvd Buffalo (14223) ***(G-2831)***
Forsythe Cosmetic Group Ltd 516 239-4200
10 Niagara Ave Freeport (11520) ***(G-5156)***
Forsythe Licensing, Freeport *Also called Forsythe Cosmetic Group Ltd* ***(G-5156)***
Fort Miller Group Inc 518 695-5000
688 Wilbur Ave Greenwich (12834) ***(G-5639)***
Fort Miller Service Corp (PA) 518 695-5000
688 Wilbur Ave Greenwich (12834) ***(G-5640)***
Fort Orange Press Inc 518 489-3233
11 Sand Creek Rd Albany (12205) ***(G-75)***
Forte Network 631 390-9050
75 Lockfield Rd East Northport (11731) ***(G-4264)***
Forte Security Group, East Northport *Also called Forte Network* ***(G-4264)***
Fortech Inc 315 478-2048
223 4th North St Syracuse (13208) ***(G-15324)***
Fortech Div, Syracuse *Also called Fortech Inc* ***(G-15324)***
Forteq North America Inc 585 427-9410
150 Park Centre Dr West Henrietta (14586) ***(G-16239)***
Fortitude Industries Inc 607 324-1500
7200 County Route 70a Hornell (14843) ***(G-6298)***
Fortress Biotech Inc (PA) 781 652-4500
2 Gansevoort St Fl 9 New York (10014) ***(G-9825)***
Fortune Poly Products Inc 718 361-0767
17910 93rd Ave Jamaica (11433) ***(G-6643)***
Fortune Sign 646 383-8682
1334 39th St Brooklyn (11218) ***(G-1899)***
Forum Publishing Co 631 754-5000
383 E Main St Centerport (11721) ***(G-3348)***

ALPHABETIC SECTION

Forum South, The, Howard Beach *Also called Vpj Publication Inc* **(G-6333)**
Forward Enterprises Inc 585 235-7670
   250 Cumberland St Ste 100 Rochester (14605) **(G-13814)**
Forwear, New York *Also called A and J Apparel Corp* **(G-8690)**
Foseco Inc 914 345-4760
   777 Old Saw Mill River Rd Tarrytown (10591) **(G-15478)**
Fossil Industries Inc 631 254-9200
   44 W Jefryn Blvd Ste A Deer Park (11729) **(G-3979)**
Foster - Gordon Manufacturing 631 589-6776
   55 Knickerbocker Ave G Bohemia (11716) **(G-1024)**
Foster Reeve & Associates Inc (PA) 718 609-0090
   1155 Manhattan Ave # 1011 Brooklyn (11222) **(G-1900)**
Foster Refrigerators Entp 518 671-6036
   300 Fairview Ave Hudson (12534) **(G-6350)**
Fotis Oneonta Italian Bakery 607 432-3871
   42 River St Oneonta (13820) **(G-12638)**
Fotofiles, Vestal *Also called Truebite Inc* **(G-15824)**
Fougera Pharmaceuticals Inc (HQ) 631 454-7677
   60 Baylis Rd Melville (11747) **(G-8026)**
Fougera Pharmaceuticals Inc 631 454-7677
   55 Cantiague Rock Rd Hicksville (11801) **(G-6088)**
Foundation Center Inc (PA) 212 620-4230
   1 Financial Sq Fl 24 New York (10005) **(G-9826)**
Foundtion For A Mndful Soc Inc (PA) 902 431-8062
   228 Park Ave S New York (10003) **(G-9827)**
Fountain Tile Outlet Inc 718 927-4555
   609 Fountain Ave Ste A Brooklyn (11208) **(G-1901)**
Fountainhead Group Inc (PA) 315 736-0037
   23 Garden St New York Mills (13417) **(G-12186)**
Fountainhead Group Inc 708 598-7100
   3 Graden St New York Mills (13417) **(G-12187)**
Four &TWenty Blackbirds, Brooklyn *Also called Blackbirds Brooklyn LLC* **(G-1618)**
Four Brothers Italian Bakery 914 741-5434
   332 Elwood Ave Hawthorne (10532) **(G-5986)**
Four Directions Inc 315 829-8388
   4677 State Route 5 Vernon (13476) **(G-15804)**
Four Fat Fowl Inc 518 733-5230
   324 State Route 43 Stop B Stephentown (12168) **(G-15155)**
Four K Machine Shop Inc 516 997-0752
   54 Brooklyn Ave Westbury (11590) **(G-16332)**
Four M Studios, New York *Also called Time Inc* **(G-11838)**
Four M Studios 212 557-6600
   125 Park Ave Fl 20 New York (10017) **(G-9828)**
Four M Studios 212 557-6600
   125 Park Ave Fl 20 New York (10017) **(G-9829)**
Four M Studios 212 499-2000
   805 3rd Ave Fl 22 New York (10022) **(G-9830)**
Four M Studios 515 284-2157
   805 3rd Ave Fl 29 New York (10022) **(G-9831)**
Four Paws Products Ltd 631 436-7421
   3125 Vtrans Mem Hwy Ste 1 Ronkonkoma (11779) **(G-14343)**
Four Quarter, Westbury *Also called Cab-Network Inc* **(G-16320)**
Four S Showcase Manufacturing 718 649-4900
   1044 Linwood St Brooklyn (11208) **(G-1902)**
Four Sasors Multi-Services Inc 347 843-6262
   3525 Decatur Ave Apt 2k Bronx (10467) **(G-1274)**
Four Seasons Buildings Pdts, Holbrook *Also called Latium USA Trading LLC* **(G-6193)**
Four Seasons Fashion Mfg Inc 212 947-6820
   270 W 39th St Fl 12 New York (10018) **(G-9832)**
Four Square Tool, Conklin *Also called Toolroom Express Inc* **(G-3735)**
Four Star, New York *Also called Vanity Room Inc* **(G-11993)**
Four Wheel Drive, Staten Island *Also called Cyclone Air Power Inc* **(G-15067)**
Four-Way Pallet Corp 631 351-3401
   191 E 2nd St Huntington Station (11746) **(G-6442)**
Fourteen Arnold Ave Corp 315 272-1700
   14 Arnold Ave Utica (13502) **(G-15703)**
Fourtys Ny Inc 212 382-0301
   231 W 39th St Rm 806 New York (10018) **(G-9833)**
Fowler Route Co Inc 917 653-4640
   25 Sunnyside Dr Yonkers (10705) **(G-16760)**
Fownes Brothers & Co Inc (PA) 212 683-0150
   16 E 34th St Fl 5 New York (10016) **(G-9834)**
Fownes Brothers & Co Inc 518 752-4411
   204 County Highway 157 Gloversville (12078) **(G-5456)**
Fox 416 Corp 718 385-4600
   416 Thatford Ave Brooklyn (11212) **(G-1903)**
Fox Run Vineyards Inc 315 536-4616
   670 State Route 14 Penn Yan (14527) **(G-12956)**
Fox Unlimited Inc 212 736-3071
   345 7th Ave Rm 2b New York (10001) **(G-9835)**
Fox's U-Bet Syrups, Brooklyn *Also called Fox 416 Corp* **(G-1903)**
Foxhill Press Inc 212 995-9620
   37 E 7th St Ste 2 New York (10003) **(G-9836)**
Fppf Chemical Co Inc (PA) 716 856-9607
   117 W Tupper St Ste 1 Buffalo (14201) **(G-2832)**
Fra-Rik Formica Fabg Co Inc 718 597-3335
   1464 Blondell Ave Fl 2 Bronx (10461) **(G-1275)**
Fradan Manufacturing Corp 914 632-3653
   499 5th Ave New Rochelle (10801) **(G-8605)**
Fragrance Acquisitions LLC 845 534-9172
   1900 Corporate Blvd Newburgh (12550) **(G-12222)**

Fralo, Syracuse *Also called Roth Global Plastics Inc* **(G-15410)**
Frame Shoppe & Art Gallery 516 365-6014
   447 Plandome Rd Manhasset (11030) **(G-7767)**
Frame Shoppe & Gallery, Manhasset *Also called Frame Shoppe & Art Gallery* **(G-7767)**
Frame Works America Inc 631 288-1300
   146 Mill Rd Westhampton Beach (11978) **(G-16403)**
Framerica Corporation 631 650-1000
   2 Todd Ct Yaphank (11980) **(G-16711)**
Framing Technology Inc 585 464-8470
   137 Syke St Rochester (14611) **(G-13815)**
Francepress LLC (PA) 646 202-9828
   115 E 57th St Fl 11 New York (10022) **(G-9837)**
Franchet Metal Craft Inc 718 658-6400
   17832 93rd Ave Jamaica (11433) **(G-6644)**
Francis Emory Fitch Inc (HQ) 212 619-3800
   229 W 28th St New York (10001) **(G-9838)**
Franco Apparel Group Inc 212 967-7272
   1407 Broadway New York (10018) **(G-9839)**
Franco Apparel Group Team, New York *Also called Franco Apparel Group Inc* **(G-9839)**
Franetta, New York *Also called Beyond Loom Inc* **(G-9064)**
Frank Billanti Casting Co Inc 212 221-0440
   42 W 38th St Rm 204 New York (10018) **(G-9840)**
Frank Blancato Inc 212 768-1495
   64 W 48th St Fl 16 New York (10036) **(G-9841)**
Frank J Martello 585 235-2780
   1227 Maple St Rochester (14611) **(G-13816)**
Frank Lowe Rbr & Gasket Co Inc 631 777-2707
   44 Ramsey Rd Shirley (11967) **(G-14835)**
Frank Merriwell Inc 516 921-8888
   212 Michael Dr Syosset (11791) **(G-15218)**
Frank Murken Products, Schenectady *Also called Tattersall Industries LLC* **(G-14720)**
Frank Wardynski & Sons Inc 716 854-6083
   336 Peckham St Buffalo (14206) **(G-2833)**
Frank Wines Inc 646 765-6637
   345 E 80th St Apt 8b New York (10075) **(G-9842)**
Franklin Electric Co Inc 718 244-7744
   17501 Rockaway Blvd # 309 Jamaica (11434) **(G-6645)**
Franklin Manufacturing Div, Hauppauge *Also called Embassy Industries Inc* **(G-5820)**
Franklin Packaging Inc (PA) 631 582-8900
   96 Sea Cove Rd Northport (11768) **(G-12468)**
Franklin Poly Film Inc 718 492-3523
   1149 56th St Brooklyn (11219) **(G-1904)**
Franklin Report LLC 212 639-9100
   201 E 69th St Apt 14j New York (10021) **(G-9843)**
Franklin's Printing, Cheektowaga *Also called Hugh F McPherson Inc* **(G-3450)**
Franklin-Douglas Inc 516 883-0121
   52 Main St Side Port Washington (11050) **(G-13260)**
Franks Cushions Inc 718 848-1216
   6302 59th Ave Maspeth (11378) **(G-7847)**
Franz Fischer Inc 718 821-1300
   1267 Flushing Ave Brooklyn (11237) **(G-1905)**
Frasier and Jones, Syracuse *Also called Frazer & Jones Co* **(G-15325)**
Fratellis LLC 607 722-5663
   20 Campbell Rd Binghamton (13905) **(G-885)**
Frazer & Jones Co 315 468-6251
   3000 Milton Ave Syracuse (13209) **(G-15325)**
Frazer & Jones Division, Solvay *Also called Eastern Company* **(G-14917)**
Frazer Computing Inc 315 379-3500
   6196 Us Highway 11 Canton (13617) **(G-3257)**
Frazier Industrial Company 315 539-9256
   1291 Waterloo Geneva Rd Waterloo (13165) **(G-15993)**
Fred A Nudd Corporation (PA) 315 524-2531
   1743 State Route 104 Ontario (14519) **(G-12653)**
Fred Lawrence Co, Bay Shore *Also called Lanwood Industries Inc* **(G-694)**
Fred M Lawrence Co Inc (PA) 718 786-7227
   45 Drexel Dr Bay Shore (11706) **(G-688)**
Fred M Velepec Co Inc 718 821-6636
   7172 70th St Glendale (11385) **(G-5400)**
Fred Santucci Inc 716 483-1411
   121 Jackson Ave E Jamestown (14701) **(G-6716)**
Fred Schulz Inc 845 724-3409
   4 Jordan Ct Poughquag (12570) **(G-13374)**
Frederick Coon Inc 716 683-6812
   5751 Clinton St Elma (14059) **(G-4450)**
Frederick Cowan & Company Inc 631 369-0360
   144 Beach Rd Wading River (11792) **(G-15884)**
Frederick Machine Repair Inc 716 332-0104
   405 Ludington St Buffalo (14206) **(G-2834)**
Fredonia Pennysaver Inc (PA) 716 679-1509
   276 W Main St Ste 1 Fredonia (14063) **(G-5126)**
Free Trader, Elizabethtown *Also called Denton Publications Inc* **(G-4430)**
Free Trader, Plattsburgh *Also called Denton Publications Inc* **(G-13119)**
Freeda Vitamins Inc (PA) 718 433-4337
   4725 34th St Ste 303 Long Island City (11101) **(G-7452)**
Freedom Mfg LLC 518 584-0441
   3 Duplainville Rd Apt C Saratoga Springs (12866) **(G-14580)**
Freedom Rains Inc 646 710-4512
   230 W 39th St Fl 7 New York (10018) **(G-9844)**
Freedom Run Winery Inc 716 433-4136
   5138 Lower Mountain Rd Lockport (14094) **(G-7302)**

(PA)=Parent Co (HQ)=Headquarters (DH)=Div Headquarters

Freeman Technology Inc.....732 829-8345
2355 Bell Blvd Apt 2h Bayside (11360) *(G-745)*
Freeport Baldwin Leader, Garden City *Also called L & M Publications Inc (G-5264)*
Freeport Paper Industries Inc.....631 851-1555
120 Windsor Pl Central Islip (11722) *(G-3370)*
Freeport Screen & Stamping.....516 379-0330
31 Hanse Ave Freeport (11520) *(G-5157)*
Freetime Magazine Inc.....585 473-2266
1255 University Ave # 270 Rochester (14607) *(G-13817)*
Freeville Publishing Co Inc.....607 844-9119
9 Main St Freeville (13068) *(G-5191)*
Freeze Divisional Centl Mills, New York *Also called Central Mills Inc (G-9244)*
Freeze-Dry Foods Inc.....585 589-6399
111 West Ave Ste 2 Albion (14411) *(G-157)*
Freihofer's Bakery Outlet, Nelliston *Also called Bimbo Bakeries Usa Inc (G-8481)*
Freihofer's Bakery Outlet, New Paltz *Also called Bimbo Bakeries Usa Inc (G-8575)*
French & Itln Furn Craftsmen.....718 599-5000
999 Grand St Brooklyn (11211) *(G-1906)*
French Accnt Rugs & Tapestries.....212 686-6097
36 E 31st St Frnt B New York (10016) *(G-9845)*
French Associates Inc.....718 387-9880
7339 172nd St Fresh Meadows (11366) *(G-5198)*
French Atmosphere Inc (PA).....516 371-9100
421 7th Ave 525 New York (10001) *(G-9846)*
French Itln Furn Craftsmen Cor, Brooklyn *Also called French & Itln Furn Craftsmen (G-1906)*
French Morning LLC.....646 290-7463
27 W 20th St Ste 800 New York (10011) *(G-9847)*
French Pdts Frnch Pickle Works, Fresh Meadows *Also called French Associates Inc (G-5198)*
Frequency Electronics Inc (PA).....516 794-4500
55 Charles Lindbergh Blvd # 2 Uniondale (11553) *(G-15668)*
Frequency Selective Networks.....718 424-7500
12 N Cottage St Valley Stream (11580) *(G-15780)*
Fresenius Kabi Usa LLC.....716 773-0053
3159 Staley Rd Grand Island (14072) *(G-5500)*
Fresenius Kabi USA LLC.....716 773-0800
3159 Staley Rd Grand Island (14072) *(G-5501)*
Fresh Bake Pizza Co, Depew *Also called D R M Management Inc (G-4086)*
Fresh Fanatic Inc.....516 521-6574
88 Washington Ave Brooklyn (11205) *(G-1907)*
Fresh Ice Cream Company LLC.....347 603-6021
630 Flushing Ave 4 Brooklyn (11206) *(G-1908)*
Fresh Prints LLC.....917 826-2752
134 E 70th St New York (10021) *(G-9848)*
Freshly Inc (PA).....844 373-7459
115 E 23rd St Fl 7 New York (10010) *(G-9849)*
Freshop Inc.....585 738-6035
3246 Monroe Ave Ste 1 Rochester (14618) *(G-13818)*
Freshway Distributors, Hicksville *Also called Kozy Shack Enterprises LLC (G-6100)*
Frew Run Gravel Products Inc.....716 569-4712
984 Frew Run Rd Frewsburg (14738) *(G-5208)*
Frey Concrete Inc.....716 213-5832
3949 Frest Pk Way Ste 400 North Tonawanda (14120) *(G-12428)*
Frey Concrete Incoprorated, Orchard Park *Also called United Materials LLC (G-12748)*
Frey Sand & Gravel, North Tonawanda *Also called Frey Concrete Inc (G-12428)*
Fridge Magazine Inc.....212 997-7673
108 W 39th St Fl 4 New York (10018) *(G-9850)*
Friendly Fuel Incorporated.....518 581-7036
54 Church St Saratoga Springs (12866) *(G-14581)*
Friendly Star Fuel Inc.....718 369-8801
889 3rd Ave Brooklyn (11232) *(G-1909)*
Friendship Dairies LLC.....585 973-3031
6701 County Road 20 Friendship (14739) *(G-5210)*
Frieslndcmpina Ingrdnts N Amer.....607 746-0196
40196 State Hwy 10 Delhi Delhi (13753) *(G-4074)*
Frigo Design, Brewerton *Also called Ae Fund Inc (G-1149)*
Frisch Plastics Corp.....973 685-5936
7 Joyce Rd Hartsdale (10530) *(G-5743)*
Frito-Lay North America Inc.....607 775-7000
10 Spud Ln Binghamton (13904) *(G-886)*
Fritters & Buns Inc.....845 227-6609
236 Blue Hill Rd Hopewell Junction (12533) *(G-6285)*
Froebe Group LLC.....646 649-2150
154 W 27th St Rm 4 New York (10001) *(G-9851)*
Fronhofer Tool Company Inc.....518 692-2496
4197 County Rd 48 Cossayuna (12823) *(G-3905)*
Frontier Ht-Dip Glvanizing Inc.....716 875-2091
1740 Elmwood Ave Buffalo (14207) *(G-2835)*
Frontier Hydraulics Corp.....716 694-2070
1738 Elmwood Ave Ste 2 Buffalo (14207) *(G-2836)*
Frontiers Unlimited Inc.....631 283-4663
52 Jagger Ln Southampton (11968) *(G-14953)*
Fross Industries Inc.....716 297-0652
3315 Haseley Dr Niagara Falls (14304) *(G-12287)*
Frost Publications Inc.....845 726-3232
55 Laurel Hill Dr Westtown (10998) *(G-16413)*
Frozen Food Digest Inc.....212 557-8600
271 Madison Ave Ste 805 New York (10016) *(G-9852)*
Frozen Pastry Products Corp.....845 364-9833
41 Lincoln Ave Spring Valley (10977) *(G-14992)*
Frp Apparel Group LLC.....212 695-8000
110 W 40th St Fl 26 New York (10018) *(G-9853)*
Fruit St Hlth Pub Beneft Corp.....347 960-6400
85 Broad St Fl 18 New York (10004) *(G-9854)*
Fruitcrown Products Corp (PA).....631 694-5800
250 Adams Blvd Farmingdale (11735) *(G-4767)*
Fsr Beauty Ltd.....212 447-0036
411 5th Ave Rm 804 New York (10016) *(G-9855)*
FT Publications Inc (HQ).....212 641-6500
330 Hudson St New York (10013) *(G-9856)*
FT Publications Inc.....212 641-2420
330 Hudson St New York (10013) *(G-9857)*
FT Seismic Support Inc.....607 527-8595
5596 Mills Rd Campbell (14821) *(G-3203)*
Fts Systems Inc (HQ).....845 687-5300
3538 Main St Stone Ridge (12484) *(G-15161)*
Ftt Manufacturing, Rochester *Also called Ppi Corp (G-14031)*
Ftt Medical Inc.....585 444-0980
275 Commerce Dr Rochester (14623) *(G-13819)*
Ftt Mfg, Rochester *Also called Ppi Corp (G-14032)*
Fuccillo Ford Nelliston Inc.....518 993-5555
6500 State Hwy 5 Nelliston (13410) *(G-8482)*
Fuda Group (usa) Corporation.....646 751-7488
48 Wall St Fl 11 New York (10005) *(G-9858)*
Fuel Data Systems Inc.....800 447-7870
772 Greenville Tpke Middletown (10940) *(G-8153)*
Fuel Efficiency LLC.....315 923-2511
101 Davis Pkwy Clyde (14433) *(G-3594)*
Fuel Energy Services USA Ltd.....607 846-2650
250 Ltta Brook Indus Pkwy Horseheads (14845) *(G-6316)*
Fuel Soul.....516 379-0810
188 Merrick Rd Merrick (11566) *(G-8098)*
Fuel Watchman Sales & Service.....718 665-6100
364 Jackson Ave Bronx (10454) *(G-1276)*
Fujitsu Ntwrk Cmmnications Inc.....845 731-2000
2 Blue Hill Plz Ste 1609 Pearl River (10965) *(G-12897)*
Fulcrum Acoustic LLC.....866 234-0678
25 Circle St Ste 104 Rochester (14607) *(G-13820)*
Fulcrum Promos, New York *Also called Fulcrum Promotions & Prtg LLC (G-9859)*
Fulcrum Promotions & Prtg LLC.....203 909-6362
135 W 41st St New York (10036) *(G-9859)*
Full Circle Home LLC.....212 432-0001
131 W 35th St Fl 8 New York (10001) *(G-9860)*
Full Circle Studios LLC.....716 875-7740
710 Main St Buffalo (14202) *(G-2837)*
Full Motion Beverage Inc (PA).....631 585-1100
998 Old Country Rd Plainview (11803) *(G-13059)*
Full Timer, Bronx *Also called Fuel Watchman Sales & Service (G-1276)*
Fuller Sportswear Co Inc.....516 773-3353
10 Grenfell Dr Great Neck (11020) *(G-5559)*
Fuller Tool Incorporated.....315 891-3183
225 Platform Rd Newport (13416) *(G-12255)*
Fulmont Ready-Mix Company Inc (PA).....518 887-5560
774 State Highway 5s Amsterdam (12010) *(G-338)*
Fulton Boiler Works Inc (PA).....315 298-5121
3981 Port St Pulaski (13142) *(G-13380)*
Fulton Boiler Works Inc.....315 298-5121
972 Centerville Rd Pulaski (13142) *(G-13381)*
Fulton China LLC.....315 298-0112
3981 Port St Pulaski (13142) *(G-13382)*
Fulton Companies, Pulaski *Also called Fulton Volcanic Inc (G-13384)*
Fulton Daily News, Fulton *Also called DOT Publishing (G-5215)*
Fulton Heating Solutions Inc.....315 298-5121
972 Centerville Rd Pulaski (13142) *(G-13383)*
Fulton Newspapers Inc.....315 598-6397
67 S 2nd St Fulton (13069) *(G-5216)*
Fulton Patriot, Fulton *Also called Fulton Newspapers Inc (G-5216)*
Fulton Tool Co Inc.....315 598-2900
802 W Broadway Ste 1 Fulton (13069) *(G-5217)*
Fulton Volcanic Inc (PA).....315 298-5121
3981 Port St Pulaski (13142) *(G-13384)*
Fultonville Machine & Tool Co.....518 853-4441
73 Union St Fultonville (12072) *(G-5236)*
Fun Industries of NY.....631 845-3805
111 Milbar Blvd Farmingdale (11735) *(G-4768)*
Fun Media Inc.....646 472-0135
1001 Ave Of The Americas New York (10018) *(G-9861)*
Fung Wong Bakery Inc.....212 267-4037
30 Mott St Frnt New York (10013) *(G-9862)*
Fung Wong Bakery Shop, New York *Also called Fung Wong Bakery Inc (G-9862)*
Fungilab Inc.....631 750-6361
89 Cabot Ct Ste K Hauppauge (11788) *(G-5829)*
Furniture By Craftmaster Ltd.....631 750-0658
1595 Ocean Ave Ste A9 Bohemia (11716) *(G-1025)*
Furniture Doctor Inc.....585 657-6941
7007 State Route 5 And 20 Bloomfield (14469) *(G-954)*
Furniture Dsign By Knossos Inc.....718 729-0404
2430 Bklyn Qns Expy Ste 3 Woodside (11377) *(G-16657)*
Furniture World, New Rochelle *Also called Towse Publishing Co (G-8629)*
Fuse Electronics Inc.....607 352-3222
1223 Us Route 11 Kirkwood (13795) *(G-6940)*
Fusion Brands America Inc., New York *Also called Clean Beauty Collective Inc (G-9325)*

ALPHABETIC SECTION Gamma Products Inc

Fusion Connect Inc (PA).......212 201-2400
420 Lexington Ave Rm 1718 New York (10170) ***(G-9863)***
Fusion Pro Performance Ltd.......917 833-0761
16 W 36th St Rm 1205 New York (10018) ***(G-9864)***
Futon City Discounters Inc.......315 437-1328
6361 Thompson Rd Syracuse (13206) ***(G-15326)***
Future Diagnostics LLC.......347 434-6700
266 47th St Brooklyn (11220) ***(G-1910)***
Future Screw Machine Pdts Inc.......631 765-1610
41155 County Road 48 Southold (11971) ***(G-14968)***
Future Spray Finishing Co.......631 242-6252
78 Brook Ave Ste A Deer Park (11729) ***(G-3980)***
Future Star Digatech.......718 666-0350
713 Monroe St Brooklyn (11221) ***(G-1911)***
Futurebiotics, Hauppauge *Also called FB Laboratories Inc* ***(G-5823)***
Futurebiotics LLC.......631 273-6300
70 Commerce Dr Hauppauge (11788) ***(G-5830)***
Fuzion Creations Intl LLC.......718 369-8800
140 58th St Ste A Brooklyn (11220) ***(G-1912)***
FX INC.......212 244-2240
1 Penn Plz Ste 6238 New York (10119) ***(G-9865)***
G & C Welding Co Inc.......516 883-3228
39 Annette Dr Port Washington (11050) ***(G-13261)***
G & G C Machine & Tool Co Inc.......516 873-0999
18 Sylvester St Westbury (11590) ***(G-16333)***
G & J Rdymx & Masnry Sup Inc.......718 454-0800
18330 Jamaica Ave Hollis (11423) ***(G-6234)***
G & M Clearview Inc.......845 781-4877
112 Spring St Monroe (10950) ***(G-8270)***
G & M Dege Inc.......631 475-1450
250 Orchard Rd Bldg 1 East Patchogue (11772) ***(G-4273)***
G & P Printing Inc.......212 274-8092
142 Baxter St New York (10013) ***(G-9866)***
G A Braun Inc (PA).......315 475-3123
79 General Irwin Blvd North Syracuse (13212) ***(G-12401)***
G A Braun Inc.......315 475-3123
461 E Brighton Ave Syracuse (13210) ***(G-15327)***
G A Richards & Co Inc.......516 334-5412
18 Sylvester St Westbury (11590) ***(G-16334)***
G and G Service.......518 785-9247
21 Nelson Ave Latham (12110) ***(G-7073)***
G B International Trdg Co Ltd.......607 785-0938
408 Airport Rd Endicott (13760) ***(G-4594)***
G Bopp USA Inc.......845 296-1065
4 Bill Horton Way Wappingers Falls (12590) ***(G-15931)***
G C Casting, Oneonta *Also called American Blade Mfg LLC* ***(G-12624)***
G C Controls Inc.......607 656-4117
1408 County Road 2 Greene (13778) ***(G-5614)***
G C Hanford Manufacturing Co (PA).......315 476-7418
304 Oneida St Syracuse (13202) ***(G-15328)***
G C Mobile Svces, Cortlandt Manor *Also called Gc Mobile Services Inc* ***(G-3901)***
G E Inspection Technologies LP.......315 554-2000
721 Visions Dr Skaneateles (13152) ***(G-14871)***
G F Labels LLC.......518 798-6643
10 Ferguson Ln Queensbury (12804) ***(G-13424)***
G Haynes Holdings Inc.......607 538-1160
51971 State Highway 10 Bloomville (13739) ***(G-961)***
G I Certified Inc.......212 397-1945
623 W 51st St New York (10019) ***(G-9867)***
G L 7 Sales Plus Ltd.......631 696-8290
125 Middle Country Rd F Coram (11727) ***(G-3797)***
G M I, Hornell *Also called Gray Manufacturing Inds LLC* ***(G-6300)***
G Marks Hdwr Liquidating Corp.......631 225-5400
333 Bayview Ave Amityville (11701) ***(G-276)***
G N R Co, Smithtown *Also called G N R Plastics Inc* ***(G-14899)***
G N R Plastics Inc.......631 724-8758
11 Wandering Way Smithtown (11787) ***(G-14899)***
G Pesso & Sons Inc.......718 224-9130
20320 35th Ave Bayside (11361) ***(G-746)***
G R M, Bellmore *Also called Rush Gold Manufacturing Ltd* ***(G-793)***
G S Communications USA Inc.......718 389-7371
179 Greenpoint Ave Brooklyn (11222) ***(G-1913)***
G Schirmer Inc (HQ).......212 254-2100
180 Madison Ave Ste 2400 New York (10016) ***(G-9868)***
G Schirmer Inc.......845 469-4699
2 Old Rt 17 Chester (10918) ***(G-3475)***
G Sicuranza Ltd.......516 759-0259
4 East Ave Glen Cove (11542) ***(G-5366)***
G T Machine & Tool, Long Island City *Also called Theodosiou Inc* ***(G-7614)***
G Tech Natureal Gasses Systems, Buffalo *Also called Gas Tchnlogy Enrgy Cncepts LLC* ***(G-2841)***
G W Canfield & Son Inc.......315 735-5522
600 Plant St Utica (13502) ***(G-15704)***
G W Manufacturing, Ridgewood *Also called Gw Manufacturing* ***(G-13538)***
G Z G Rest & Kit Met Works.......718 788-8621
120 13th St Brooklyn (11215) ***(G-1914)***
G&G Led LLC.......800 285-6780
10 Corprate Dr Clifton Pa Clifton Park Clifton Park (12065) ***(G-3566)***
G&J Graphics Inc.......718 409-9874
2914 Westchester Ave Bronx (10461) ***(G-1277)***
G&W Industries, New York *Also called Gw Acquisition LLC* ***(G-10011)***
G-Forces, Plainview *Also called Derm-Buro Inc* ***(G-13050)***
G-III Apparel Group, New York *Also called G-III Leather Fashions Inc* ***(G-9872)***
G-III Apparel Group Ltd (PA).......212 403-0500
512 7th Ave Fl 35 New York (10018) ***(G-9869)***
G-III Apparel Group Ltd.......212 403-0500
512 Fashion Ave Fl 35 New York (10018) ***(G-9870)***
G-III Apparel Group Ltd.......212 840-7272
512 7th Ave Fl 35 New York (10018) ***(G-9871)***
G-III Leather Fashions Inc.......212 403-0500
512 7th Ave Fl 35 New York (10018) ***(G-9872)***
G-S Plastic Optics, Rochester *Also called Germanow-Simon Corporation* ***(G-13832)***
G18 Corporation.......212 869-0010
215 W 40th St Fl 9 New York (10018) ***(G-9873)***
G4i, Rensselaer *Also called Great 4 Image Inc* ***(G-13474)***
Gabani Inc.......631 283-4930
81 Lee Ave Southampton (11968) ***(G-14954)***
Gabila & Sons Mfg Inc.......631 789-2220
100 Wartburg Ave Copiague (11726) ***(G-3759)***
Gabila Food Products Inc.......631 789-2220
100 Wartburg Ave Copiague (11726) ***(G-3760)***
Gabila's Knishes, Copiague *Also called Gabila & Sons Mfg Inc* ***(G-3759)***
Gabriella Importers Inc.......212 579-3945
305 W 87th St New York (10024) ***(G-9874)***
Gabrielle Andra.......212 366-9624
305 W 21st St New York (10011) ***(G-9875)***
Gac Express Inc.......718 438-2227
1310 52nd St Brooklyn (11219) ***(G-1915)***
Gad Systems, Lawrence *Also called John J Richardson* ***(G-7103)***
Gadabout USA Wheelchairs Inc.......585 338-2110
892 E Ridge Rd Rochester (14621) ***(G-13821)***
Gaddis Engineering, Glen Cove *Also called Gaddis Industrial Equipment* ***(G-5367)***
Gaddis Industrial Equipment.......516 759-3100
140 Pratt Oval Glen Cove (11542) ***(G-5367)***
Gaebel Enterprises, East Syracuse *Also called Gei International Inc* ***(G-4342)***
Gagne Associates Inc.......800 800-5954
41 Commercial Dr Johnson City (13790) ***(G-6808)***
Gailer Stamping Diecutting LLC.......212 243-5662
3718 Nthrn Blvd 324 Fl 3 Long Island City (11101) ***(G-7453)***
GAI Manufacturing Co LLC (HQ).......718 292-9000
50 E 153rd St Bronx (10451) ***(G-1278)***
Galas Framing Services.......718 706-0007
4224 Orchard St Fl 4 Long Island City (11101) ***(G-7454)***
Galax, Monsey *Also called Ta Chen International Inc* ***(G-8300)***
Galaxy Knitting Mills, Long Island City *Also called In Toon Amkor Fashions Inc* ***(G-7474)***
Galaxy Software LLC.......631 244-8405
927 Montauk Hwy Unit 229 Oakdale (11769) ***(G-12516)***
Galian Handbags, New York *Also called Rodem Incorporated* ***(G-11418)***
Galison Publishing LLC.......212 354-8840
70 W 36th St Fl 11 New York (10018) ***(G-9876)***
Galiva Inc.......903 600-5755
236 Broadway Ste 214 Brooklyn (11211) ***(G-1916)***
Gallagher Printing Inc.......716 873-2434
2518 Delaware Ave Buffalo (14216) ***(G-2838)***
Gallant Graphics Ltd.......845 868-1166
242 Attlebury Hill Rd Stanfordville (12581) ***(G-15033)***
Galle & Zinter Inc.......716 833-4212
3405 Harlem Rd Buffalo (14225) ***(G-2839)***
Galle Mamorial, Buffalo *Also called Galle & Zinter Inc* ***(G-2839)***
Gallery 57 Dental.......212 246-8700
24 W 57th St Ste 701 New York (10019) ***(G-9877)***
Gallery of Machines LLC.......607 849-6028
20 Front St Marathon (13803) ***(G-7789)***
Galli Shirts and Sports AP.......845 226-7305
246 Judith Dr Stormville (12582) ***(G-15179)***
Galmer Ltd.......718 392-4609
4301 21st St Ste 130b Long Island City (11101) ***(G-7455)***
Galmer Silversmiths, Long Island City *Also called Galmer Ltd* ***(G-7455)***
Galt Industries Inc.......212 758-0770
121 E 71st St Frnt A New York (10021) ***(G-9878)***
Gamble & Gamble Inc (PA).......716 731-3239
5890 West St Sanborn (14132) ***(G-14546)***
GAME Sportswear Ltd (PA).......914 962-1701
1401 Front St Yorktown Heights (10598) ***(G-16817)***
Game Time LLC.......914 557-9662
1407 Broadway Rm 400 New York (10018) ***(G-9879)***
Gameclub Inc.......415 359-5742
46 W 65th St Apt 1a New York (10023) ***(G-9880)***
Games For Change Inc.......212 242-4922
205 E 42nd St Fl 20 New York (10017) ***(G-9881)***
Gametime Sportswear Plus LLC.......315 724-5893
1206 Belle Ave Utica (13501) ***(G-15705)***
Gamma Enterprises LLC.......631 755-1080
113 Alder St West Babylon (11704) ***(G-16156)***
Gamma Instrument Co Inc.......516 486-5526
34 Sarah Dr Ste B Farmingdale (11735) ***(G-4769)***
Gamma Lab, West Babylon *Also called Gamma Enterprises LLC* ***(G-16156)***
Gamma North Corporation.......716 902-5100
13595 Broadway St Alden (14004) ***(G-171)***
Gamma Products Inc.......845 562-3332
509 Temple Hill Rd New Windsor (12553) ***(G-8645)***

ALPHABETIC

Gan Kavod Inc — ALPHABETIC SECTION

Gan Kavod Inc 315 797-3114
2050 Tilden Ave New Hartford (13413) *(G-8505)*
Ganesh Foods, Waterloo Also called Gharana Industries LLC *(G-15994)*
Gangi Distributors Inc 718 442-5745
135 Mcclean Ave Staten Island (10305) *(G-15077)*
Gannett Co Inc 585 232-7100
245 E Main St Rochester (14604) *(G-13822)*
Gannett Co Inc 585 924-3406
6300 Collett Rd Farmington (14425) *(G-4914)*
Gannett Co Inc 914 278-9315
92 North Ave New Rochelle (10801) *(G-8606)*
Gannett Co Inc 607 798-1234
4421 Vestal Pkwy E Vestal (13850) *(G-15816)*
Gannett Co Inc 607 352-2702
10 Gannett Dr Johnson City (13790) *(G-6809)*
Gannett NY Production Facility, Johnson City Also called Gannett Co Inc *(G-6809)*
Gannett Stllite Info Ntwrk Inc 914 965-5000
1 Odell Plz Yonkers (10701) *(G-16761)*
Gannett Stllite Info Ntwrk Inc 585 798-1400
413 Main St Medina (14103) *(G-7978)*
Gannett Stllite Info Ntwrk LLC 845 578-2300
1 Crosfield Ave West Nyack (10994) *(G-16269)*
Gannett Stllite Info Ntwrk LLC 845 454-2000
85 Civic Center Plz Poughkeepsie (12601) *(G-13339)*
Gannett Stllite Info Ntwrk LLC 914 381-3400
700 Waverly Ave Mamaroneck (10543) *(G-7745)*
Gannett Suburban Newspapers, Mamaroneck Also called Gannett Stllite Info Ntwrk LLC *(G-7745)*
Gar Wood Custom Boats 518 494-2966
20 Duell Hill Rd Brant Lake (12815) *(G-1124)*
Garan Incorporated (HQ) 212 563-1292
200 Madison Ave Fl 4 New York (10016) *(G-9882)*
Garan Manufacturing Corp (HQ) 212 563-2000
200 Madison Ave Fl 4 New York (10016) *(G-9883)*
Garb-El Products Co, Buffalo Also called 240 Michigan Street Inc *(G-2675)*
Garb-O-Liner Inc 914 235-1585
64 Drake Ave New Rochelle (10805) *(G-8607)*
Garco, Penfield Also called Robinson Tools LLC *(G-12944)*
Garco Manufacturing Corp Inc 718 287-3330
4802 Farragut Rd Brooklyn (11203) *(G-1917)*
Gardall Safe Corporation 315 432-9115
219 Lamson St Ste 1 Syracuse (13206) *(G-15329)*
Gardei Industries LLC (PA) 716 693-7100
1087 Erie Ave North Tonawanda (14120) *(G-12429)*
Gardei Manufacturing, North Tonawanda Also called Pioneer Printers Inc *(G-12442)*
Garden State Shavings Inc 845 544-2835
16 Almond Tree Ln Warwick (10990) *(G-15952)*
Gardner Dnver Oberdorfer Pumps 315 437-0361
5900 Firestone Dr Syracuse (13206) *(G-15330)*
Gardner The Train Doctor, North Rose Also called Gargraves Trackage Corporation *(G-12395)*
Garelick Farms LLC 518 283-0820
504 Third Avenue Ext East Greenbush (12061) *(G-4229)*
Gargraves Trackage Corporation (PA) 315 483-6577
8967 Ridge Rd North Rose (14516) *(G-12395)*
Garland Technology LLC (PA) 716 242-8500
199 Delaware Ave Buffalo (14202) *(G-2840)*
Garlock Sealing Tech LLC 315 597-4811
1666 Division St Palmyra (14522) *(G-12853)*
Garment Care Systems LLC 518 674-1826
55 Blue Heron Dr Averill Park (12018) *(G-514)*
Garrett J Cronin 914 761-9299
1 Stuart Way White Plains (10607) *(G-16452)*
Gary Gelbfish MD 718 258-3004
2502 Avenue I Brooklyn (11210) *(G-1918)*
Gary Plastic, Bronx Also called Viele Manufacturing Corp *(G-1416)*
Gary Plastic Packaging Corp (PA) 718 893-2200
1340 Viele Ave Bronx (10474) *(G-1279)*
Gary Roth & Associates Ltd 516 333-1000
1400 Old Country Rd # 305 Westbury (11590) *(G-16335)*
Gary Stock Corporation 914 276-2700
597 Rte 22 Croton Falls (10519) *(G-3911)*
Garyline, Bronx Also called Gary Plastic Packaging Corp *(G-1279)*
Garys Loft 212 244-0970
28 W 36th St New York (10018) *(G-9884)*
Gas Field Specialists Inc 716 378-6422
224 N Main St Horseheads (14845) *(G-6317)*
Gas Recovery Systems LLC (HQ) 914 421-4903
1 N Lexington Ave Ste 620 White Plains (10601) *(G-16453)*
Gas Recovery Systems Illinois, White Plains Also called Gas Recovery Systems LLC *(G-16453)*
Gas Tchnlogy Enrgy Cncepts LLC 716 831-9695
201 Dutton Ave Buffalo (14211) *(G-2841)*
Gas Turbine Controls Corp 914 693-0830
6 Skyline Dr Ste 150 Hawthorne (10532) *(G-5987)*
Gasoft Equipment Inc 845 863-1010
231 Dubois St Newburgh (12550) *(G-12223)*
Gasport Welding & Fabg Inc 716 772-7205
8430 Telegraph Rd Gasport (14067) *(G-5306)*
Gasser & Sons Inc (PA) 631 543-6600
440 Moreland Rd Commack (11725) *(G-3692)*

Gassho Body & Mind Inc 518 695-9991
76 Broad St Schuylerville (12871) *(G-14734)*
Gatecomusa, Flushing Also called Yellow E House Inc *(G-5061)*
Gatehouse Media LLC (HQ) 585 598-0030
175 Sullys Trl Ste 300 Pittsford (14534) *(G-13013)*
Gatehouse Media LLC 315 792-5000
350 Willowbrook Office Pa Utica (13501) *(G-15706)*
Gatehouse Media LLC 607 776-2121
10 W Steuben St Bath (14810) *(G-643)*
Gatehouse Media LLC 315 866-2220
111 Green St Herkimer (13350) *(G-6039)*
Gatehouse Media LLC 607 936-4651
34 W Pulteney St Corning (14830) *(G-3819)*
Gatehouse Media LLC 585 394-0770
73 Buffalo St Canandaigua (14424) *(G-3222)*
Gatehouse Media LLC 607 324-1425
32 Broadway Mall Hornell (14843) *(G-6299)*
Gatehuse Media PA Holdings Inc (HQ) 585 598-0030
175 Sullys Trl Fl 3 Pittsford (14534) *(G-13014)*
Gateway Prtg & Graphics Inc 716 823-3873
3970 Big Tree Rd Hamburg (14075) *(G-5680)*
Gatherer's Gourmet Granola, Delmar Also called Sanzdranz LLC *(G-4078)*
Gatti Tool & Mold Inc 585 328-1350
997 Beahan Rd Rochester (14624) *(G-13823)*
Gaughan Construction Corp 718 850-9577
13034 90th Ave Richmond Hill (11418) *(G-13503)*
Gavin Mfg Corp 631 467-0040
25 Central Ave Unit A Farmingdale (11735) *(G-4770)*
Gay Sheet Metal Dies Inc 716 877-0208
301 Hinman Ave Buffalo (14216) *(G-2842)*
Gaylord Archival, North Syracuse Also called Gaylord Bros Inc *(G-12402)*
Gaylord Bros Inc 315 457-5070
7282 William Barry Blvd North Syracuse (13212) *(G-12402)*
Gaymar Industries Inc 800 828-7341
10 Centre Dr Orchard Park (14127) *(G-12715)*
Gazette & Press, Rye Also called Mason & Gore Inc *(G-14485)*
Gazette Press Inc 914 963-8300
2 Clinton Ave Rye (10580) *(G-14479)*
Gb Aero Engine LLC 914 925-9600
555 Theodore Fremd Ave Rye (10580) *(G-14480)*
Gb Group Inc 212 594-3748
Umpire State Bldg 1808 New York (10021) *(G-9885)*
Gbf, Tonawanda Also called Green Buffalo Fuel LLC *(G-15544)*
Gbg Denim Usa, LLC, New York Also called Centric Denim Usa LLC *(G-9247)*
Gbg National Brands Group LLC 646 839-7000
350 5th Ave Lbby 9 New York (10118) *(G-9886)*
Gbg Socks LLC 646 839-7000
350 5th Ave Lbby 9 New York (10118) *(G-9887)*
Gbg USA Inc 646 839-7083
350 5th Ave Fl 7 New York (10118) *(G-9888)*
Gbg USA Inc 212 615-3400
261 W 35th St Fl 15 New York (10001) *(G-9889)*
Gc Mobile Services Inc 914 736-9730
32 William Puckey Dr Cortlandt Manor (10567) *(G-3901)*
Gce International Inc (PA) 212 704-4800
1385 Broadway Fl 21 New York (10018) *(G-9890)*
Gce International Inc 212 868-0500
350 5th Ave Ste 616 New York (10118) *(G-9891)*
Gce International Inc 773 263-1210
1359 Broadway Rm 2000 New York (10018) *(G-9892)*
GCM Metal Industries Inc 718 386-4059
454 Troutman St Brooklyn (11237) *(G-1919)*
Gcns Technology Group Inc (PA) 347 713-8160
597 Rutland Rd Brooklyn (11203) *(G-1920)*
Gcom Software Inc (PA) 518 869-1671
24 Madison Avenue Ext Albany (12203) *(G-76)*
Gds Publishing Inc 212 796-2000
40 Wall St Fl 5 New York (10005) *(G-9893)*
GE Aviation Systems LLC 631 467-5500
1000 Macarthur Mem Hwy Bohemia (11716) *(G-1026)*
GE Aviation Systems LLC 513 243-9104
1000 Macarthur Mem Hwy Bohemia (11716) *(G-1027)*
GE Global Research 518 387-5000
1 Research Cir Niskayuna (12309) *(G-12353)*
GE Healthcare Fincl Svcs Inc 212 713-2000
299 Park Ave Fl 3 New York (10171) *(G-9894)*
GE Healthcare Inc 516 626-2799
80 Seaview Blvd Ste E Port Washington (11050) *(G-13262)*
GE Mds LLC (HQ) 585 242-9600
175 Science Pkwy Rochester (14620) *(G-13824)*
GE Plastics 518 475-5011
1 Noryl Ave Selkirk (12158) *(G-14768)*
GE Polymershapes 516 433-4092
120 Andrews Rd Hicksville (11801) *(G-6089)*
Gear Motions Incorporated 716 885-1080
1120 Niagara St Buffalo (14213) *(G-2843)*
Gear Motions Incorporated (PA) 315 488-0100
1750 Milton Ave Syracuse (13209) *(G-15331)*
Geddes Bakery Co Inc 315 437-8084
421 S Main St North Syracuse (13212) *(G-12403)*
Gefa Instrument Corp 516 420-4419
205 Bethpage Sweet Old Bethpage (11804) *(G-12584)*

Gehring Textiles, Dolgeville *Also called Gehring Tricot Corporation* ***(G-4133)***
Gehring Tricot Corporation (PA)..........315 429-8551
68 Ransom St Dolgeville (13329) ***(G-4133)***
Gehring Tricot Corporation..........315 429-8551
68 Ransom St Ste 272 Dolgeville (13329) ***(G-4134)***
Gei International Inc (PA)..........315 463-9261
100 Ball St East Syracuse (13057) ***(G-4342)***
Geier Bindery Co, Farmingdale *Also called Mid Island Group* ***(G-4824)***
Gelber & Mundy Jewelry Co Inc..........516 482-1585
5 Bond St Frnt 2 Great Neck (11021) ***(G-5560)***
Gelber Mundy of Great Neck, Great Neck *Also called Gelber & Mundy Jewelry Co Inc* ***(G-5560)***
Geliko LLC..........212 876-5620
1601 3rd Ave Apt 16a New York (10128) ***(G-9895)***
Gem, Schenectady *Also called Green Enviro Machine LLC* ***(G-14685)***
Gem Manufacturing Inc..........585 235-1670
853 West Ave Bldg 17a Rochester (14611) ***(G-13825)***
Gem Metal Spinning & Stamping..........718 729-7014
517 47th Rd Long Island City (11101) ***(G-7456)***
Gem Reproduction Services Corp..........845 298-0172
1299 Route 9 Ste 105 Wappingers Falls (12590) ***(G-15932)***
Gemcor Automation LLC..........716 674-9300
100 Gemcor Dr West Seneca (14224) ***(G-16298)***
Gemini Manufactures..........716 633-0306
160 Holtz Dr Cheektowaga (14225) ***(G-3446)***
Gemini Pharmaceuticals Inc..........631 543-3334
87 Modular Ave Ste 1 Commack (11725) ***(G-3693)***
Gemoro Inc..........212 768-8844
48 W 48th St Ste 1102 New York (10036) ***(G-9896)***
Gemprint Corporation..........212 997-0007
580 5th Ave Bsmt Ll05 New York (10036) ***(G-9897)***
Gemson Graphics Inc..........516 873-8400
820 Willis Ave Ste 2c Albertson (11507) ***(G-149)***
Gemtrol Inc..........716 894-0716
1800 Broadway St Bldg 1c Buffalo (14212) ***(G-2844)***
Gemveto Jewelry Company Inc..........212 755-2522
18 E 48th St Rm 501 New York (10017) ***(G-9898)***
Gen Publishing Inc..........914 834-3880
140 Huguenot St Fl 3 New Rochelle (10801) ***(G-8608)***
Gen-West Associates LLC..........315 255-1779
101 Columbus St Auburn (13021) ***(G-481)***
Genco John..........716 483-5446
71 River St Jamestown (14701) ***(G-6717)***
Genencor Division Danisco US, Rochester *Also called Danisco US Inc* ***(G-13733)***
Genencor International, Rochester *Also called Danisco US Inc* ***(G-13734)***
Genencor International Inc..........585 256-5200
3490 Winton Pl Rochester (14623) ***(G-13826)***
General Art Company Inc..........212 255-1298
14 E 38th St Fl 6 New York (10016) ***(G-9899)***
General Art Framing, New York *Also called General Art Company Inc* ***(G-9899)***
General Bearing Corporation (HQ)..........845 358-6000
44 High St West Nyack (10994) ***(G-16270)***
General Business Supply Inc..........518 720-3939
2550 9th Ave Watervliet (12189) ***(G-16046)***
General Chemical, Syracuse *Also called Chemtrade Chemicals US LLC* ***(G-15276)***
General Cinema Bevs of Ohio..........914 767-6000
1 Pepsi Way Ste 1 # 1 Somers (10589) ***(G-14919)***
General Coatings Tech Inc (PA)..........718 821-1232
24 Woodward Ave Ridgewood (11385) ***(G-13537)***
General Composites Inc..........518 963-7333
39 Myers Way Willsboro (12996) ***(G-16599)***
General Control Systems Inc..........518 270-8045
60 Cohoes Ave Ste 101 Green Island (12183) ***(G-5605)***
General Cryogenic Tech LLC..........516 334-8200
400 Shames Dr Westbury (11590) ***(G-16336)***
General Cutting Inc..........631 580-5011
90 13th Ave Unit 10 Ronkonkoma (11779) ***(G-14344)***
General Diaries Corporation..........516 371-2244
56 John St Inwood (11096) ***(G-6491)***
General Die and Die Cutng Inc..........516 665-3584
11 Finch Ct Massapequa Park (11762) ***(G-7890)***
General Electric Company..........315 456-3304
5990 E Molloy Rd Syracuse (13211) ***(G-15332)***
General Electric Company..........315 554-2000
721 Visions Dr Skaneateles (13152) ***(G-14872)***
General Electric Company..........518 385-4022
1 River Rd Bldg 55 Schenectady (12305) ***(G-14675)***
General Electric Company..........518 385-2211
1 River Rd Bldg 33 Schenectady (12305) ***(G-14676)***
General Electric Company..........518 459-4110
11 Anderson Dr Albany (12205) ***(G-77)***
General Electric Company..........203 373-2756
1 River Rd Bldg 43 Schenectady (12345) ***(G-14677)***
General Electric Company..........518 385-3716
1 River Rd Schenectady (12345) ***(G-14678)***
General Electric Company..........518 746-5750
446 Lock 8 Way 8th Hudson Falls (12839) ***(G-6379)***
General Electric Company..........518 385-2211
1 River Rd Bldg 37 Schenectady (12345) ***(G-14679)***
General Electric Company..........518 387-5000
1 Research Cir Schenectady (12309) ***(G-14680)***
General Electric Company..........518 385-7620
2690 Balltown Rd Bldg 600 Niskayuna (12309) ***(G-12354)***
General Electric Company..........518 385-3439
705 Corporation Park Schenectady (12302) ***(G-14681)***
General Electric Intl Inc..........518 385-2211
1 River Rd Bldg 53202j Schenectady (12345) ***(G-14682)***
General Fibre Products Corp..........516 358-7500
170 Nassau Terminal Rd New Hyde Park (11040) ***(G-8536)***
General Fire-Proof Door Corp..........718 893-5500
913 Edgewater Rd Bronx (10474) ***(G-1280)***
General Galvanizing Sup Co Inc (PA)..........718 589-4300
652 Whittier St Fl Mezz Bronx (10474) ***(G-1281)***
General Led Corp..........516 280-2854
206 E Jericho Tpke Mineola (11501) ***(G-8223)***
General Led Holdings LLC..........212 629-6830
19 W 36th St Fl 6 New York (10018) ***(G-9900)***
General Media Strategies Inc..........212 586-4141
521 5th Ave Fl 17 New York (10175) ***(G-9901)***
General Microwave Corporation (HQ)..........516 802-0900
227a Michael Dr Syosset (11791) ***(G-15219)***
General Mills Inc..........716 856-6060
54 S Michigan Ave Buffalo (14203) ***(G-2845)***
General Mills Inc..........716 856-6060
315 Ship Canal Pkwy Buffalo (14218) ***(G-2846)***
General Motors LLC..........315 764-2000
56 Chevrolet Rd Massena (13662) ***(G-7902)***
General Motors LLC..........716 879-5000
2995 River Rd 2 Buffalo (14207) ***(G-2847)***
General Mtr Cmponents Holdings, Lockport *Also called GM Components Holdings LLC* ***(G-7306)***
General Oil Equipment Co Inc (PA)..........716 691-7012
60 John Glenn Dr Amherst (14228) ***(G-229)***
General Plating LLC..........585 423-0830
850 Saint Paul St Ste 10 Rochester (14605) ***(G-13827)***
General Refining & Smelting..........516 538-4747
106 Taft Ave Hempstead (11550) ***(G-6011)***
General Refining Corporation..........516 538-4747
59 Madison Ave Hempstead (11550) ***(G-6012)***
General Semiconductor Inc..........631 300-3818
150 Motor Pkwy Ste 101 Hauppauge (11788) ***(G-5831)***
General Specialties, Shokan *Also called Mack Wood Working* ***(G-14846)***
General Splice Corporation..........914 271-5131
Hwy 129 Croton On Hudson (10520) ***(G-3914)***
General Sportwear Company Inc (PA)..........212 764-5820
230 W 38th St Fl 4 New York (10018) ***(G-9902)***
General Trade Mark La..........718 979-7261
31 Hylan Blvd Apt 14c Staten Island (10305) ***(G-15078)***
General Vy-Coat LLC..........718 266-6002
1636 Coney Island Ave 2b Brooklyn (11230) ***(G-1921)***
General Welding & Fabg Inc (PA)..........716 652-0033
991 Maple Rd Elma (14059) ***(G-4451)***
General Welding & Fabg Inc..........585 697-7660
60 Saginaw Dr Ste 4 Rochester (14623) ***(G-13828)***
Generation Power LLC..........315 234-2451
238 W Division St Syracuse (13204) ***(G-15333)***
Generic Compositors, Stamford *Also called Stone Crest Industries Inc* ***(G-15032)***
Generic Pharmaceutical Svcs..........631 348-6900
1324 Motor Pkwy Ste 114 Hauppauge (11749) ***(G-5832)***
Generics Bidco I LLC..........256 859-4011
1 Ram Ridge Rd Chestnut Ridge (10977) ***(G-3492)***
Genesee Building Products LLC..........585 548-2726
7982 Byron Stafford Rd Stafford (14143) ***(G-15026)***
Genesee County Express, Hornell *Also called Seneca Media Inc* ***(G-6302)***
Genesee Manufacturing Co Inc..........585 266-3201
566 Hollenbeck St Rochester (14621) ***(G-13829)***
Genesee Metal Products Inc..........585 968-6000
106 Railroad Ave Wellsville (14895) ***(G-16117)***
Genesee Metal Stampings Inc..........585 475-0450
975 John St West Henrietta (14586) ***(G-16240)***
Genesee Plant, Piffard *Also called Arkema Inc* ***(G-12995)***
Genesee Reserve Buffalo LLC..........716 824-3116
300 Bailey Ave Buffalo (14210) ***(G-2848)***
Genesis Digital Imaging Inc..........310 305-7358
150 Verona St Rochester (14608) ***(G-13830)***
Genesis Electl Motor, Woodside *Also called Genesis Electrical Motors* ***(G-16658)***
Genesis Electrical Motors..........718 274-7030
6010 32nd Ave Woodside (11377) ***(G-16658)***
Genesis Machining Corp..........516 377-1197
725 Brooklyn Ave North Baldwin (11510) ***(G-12363)***
Genesis Mannequins USA II Inc..........212 505-6600
151 W 25th St Fl 4 New York (10001) ***(G-9903)***
Genetic Engineering News, New Rochelle *Also called Gen Publishing Inc* ***(G-8608)***
Geneva Granite Co Inc (PA)..........315 789-8142
272 Border City Rd Geneva (14456) ***(G-5325)***
Geneva Printing Company Inc..........315 789-8191
40 Castle St Geneva (14456) ***(G-5326)***
Geneva Watch Company Inc (HQ)..........212 221-1177
1407 Broadway Rm 400 New York (10018) ***(G-9904)***
Genie Fastener Mfg Co, Bohemia *Also called Treo Industries Inc* ***(G-1097)***
Genie Instant Printing Center, New York *Also called Genie Instant Printing Co Inc* ***(G-9905)***
Genie Instant Printing Co Inc..........212 575-8258
37 W 43rd St New York (10036) ***(G-9905)***

ALPHABETIC

Genius Media Group Inc 509 670-7502
92 3rd St Brooklyn (11231) ***(G-1922)***
Gennaris Itln French Bky Inc 516 997-8968
465 Westbury Ave Carle Place (11514) ***(G-3265)***
Genoa Sand & Gravel Lnsg 607 533-4551
390 Peruville Rd Freeville (13068) ***(G-5192)***
Genomeweb LLC 212 651-5636
40 Fulton St Rm 1002 New York (10038) ***(G-9906)***
Genpak Industries Inc 518 798-9511
26 Republic Plz Middletown (10940) ***(G-8154)***
Genpak LLC 845 343-7971
Republic Plz Middletown (10940) ***(G-8155)***
Gentner Precision Components 315 597-5734
406 Stafford Rd Palmyra (14522) ***(G-12854)***
Genzyme Corporation 212 698-0300
521 W 57th St Fl 5 New York (10019) ***(G-9907)***
Genzyme Genetics, New York *Also called Genzyme Corporation* ***(G-9907)***
Geo Publishing, New York *Also called Emblaze Systems Inc* ***(G-9665)***
Geoffrey Beene Inc 212 371-5570
37 W 57th St Frnt 2 New York (10019) ***(G-9908)***
Geometric Circuits Inc 631 249-0230
920 Lincoln Ave Unit 1 Holbrook (11741) ***(G-6186)***
Geonex International Corp 212 473-4555
200 Park Ave S Ste 920 New York (10003) ***(G-9909)***
Geopump Inc 585 798-6666
213 State St Medina (14103) ***(G-7979)***
Geordie Magee Uphl & Canvas 315 676-7679
Weber Rd Brewerton (13029) ***(G-1150)***
George Basch Co Inc 516 378-8100
1554 Peapond Rd North Bellmore (11710) ***(G-12378)***
George Chilson Logging 607 732-1558
54 Franklin St Elmira (14904) ***(G-4488)***
George Industries LLC (PA) 607 748-3371
1 S Page Ave Endicott (13760) ***(G-4595)***
George Knitting Mills Corp 212 242-3300
116 W 23rd St Fl 4 New York (10011) ***(G-9910)***
George Lake Distilling Company 518 639-1025
2 Pinecroft Dr Queensbury (12804) ***(G-13425)***
George Lederman Inc 212 753-4556
515 Madison Ave Rm 1218 New York (10022) ***(G-9911)***
George M Dujack 518 279-1303
80 Town Office Rd Troy (12180) ***(G-15606)***
George Ponte Inc 914 243-4202
500 E Main St Jefferson Valley (10535) ***(G-6776)***
George Raum Manufacturing, Central Islip *Also called Gmr Manufacturing Inc* ***(G-3371)***
George Retzos 315 422-2913
502 Pearl St Syracuse (13203) ***(G-15334)***
Georgia-Pacific, Plattsburgh *Also called Bestwall LLC* ***(G-13109)***
Georgia-Pacific, Schenectady *Also called Bestwall LLC* ***(G-14655)***
Georgia-Pacific Corrugared LLC 585 343-3800
4 Etreadeasy Ave Batavia (14020) ***(G-625)***
Georgia-Pacific LLC 845 986-2011
17 Forester Ave Warwick (10990) ***(G-15953)***
Georgia-Pacific LLC 631 924-7401
319 Yaphank Ave Yaphank (11980) ***(G-16712)***
Georgie Kaye, New York *Also called Georgy Creative Fashions Inc* ***(G-9912)***
Georgy Creative Fashions Inc 212 279-4885
249 W 29th St New York (10001) ***(G-9912)***
Geospatial Systems Inc (HQ) 585 427-8310
150 Lucius Gordon Dr # 211 West Henrietta (14586) ***(G-16241)***
Geosync Microwave Inc 631 760-5567
320 Oser Ave Hauppauge (11788) ***(G-5833)***
Geotec, Westbury *Also called Tishcon Corp* ***(G-16379)***
Geotech Associates Ltd 631 286-0251
20 Stiriz Rd Brookhaven (11719) ***(G-1430)***
Geotechnical Drilling Inc 516 616-6055
75 E 2nd St Mineola (11501) ***(G-8224)***
Geoweb3d Inc 607 323-1114
4104 Vestal Rd Ste 202 Vestal (13850) ***(G-15817)***
Gerald McGlone 518 482-2613
17 Zoar Ave Colonie (12205) ***(G-3678)***
Geri-Gentle Corporation (PA) 917 804-7807
3841 Ocean View Ave Brooklyn (11224) ***(G-1923)***
Geritrex LLC 914 668-4003
40 Commercial Ave Middletown (10941) ***(G-8156)***
Geritrex Holdings Inc (PA) 914 668-4003
144 E Kingsbridge Rd Mount Vernon (10550) ***(G-8399)***
Gerli & Co Inc 212 213-1919
41 Madison Ave Ste 4101 New York (10010) ***(G-9913)***
German Machine & Assembly Inc 585 546-4200
226 Jay St Rochester (14608) ***(G-13831)***
Germanium Corp America Inc 315 853-4900
34 Robinson Rd Clinton (13323) ***(G-3585)***
Germanow-Simon Corporation 585 232-1440
408 Saint Paul St Rochester (14605) ***(G-13832)***
Gernatt Asphalt Products Inc (PA) 716 532-3371
13870 Taylor Hollow Rd Collins (14034) ***(G-3674)***
Gernatt Asphalt Products Inc 716 496-5111
Benz Dr Springville (14141) ***(G-15016)***
Gernatt Companies, Collins *Also called Gernatt Asphalt Products Inc* ***(G-3674)***
Gerome Technologies Inc 518 463-1324
85 Broadway Ste 1 Menands (12204) ***(G-8085)***

Gerson & Gerson Inc (PA) 212 244-6775
100 W 33rd St Ste 911 New York (10001) ***(G-9914)***
Gertrude Hawk Chocolates Inc
21182 Salmon Run Mall Loo Watertown (13601) ***(G-16014)***
Ges Ges 631 291-9624
89 Cabot Ct Ste A Hauppauge (11788) ***(G-5834)***
Get Real Surfaces Inc (PA) 845 337-4483
121 Washington St Poughkeepsie (12601) ***(G-13340)***
Getec Inc 845 292-0800
624 Harris Rd Ferndale (12734) ***(G-4933)***
Getinge Group Logistics Ameri 585 475-1400
1777 E Henrietta Rd Rochester (14623) ***(G-13833)***
Getinge Usa Inc (HQ) 800 475-9040
1777 E Henrietta Rd Rochester (14623) ***(G-13834)***
Getting The Word Out Inc 518 891-9352
36 Church St Apt 106 Saranac Lake (12983) ***(G-14562)***
Gevril, Valley Cottage *Also called First Sbf Holding Inc* ***(G-15754)***
GF Packaging LLC (PA) 716 692-2705
2727 Broadway St Ste 3 Cheektowaga (14227) ***(G-3447)***
Gfb Fashions Ltd 212 239-9230
463 Fashion Ave Rm 1502 New York (10018) ***(G-9915)***
Gfh Orthotic & Prosthetic Labs 631 467-3725
161 Keyland Ct Bohemia (11716) ***(G-1028)***
Gfl Amenities, Brooklyn *Also called Gfl USA Inc* ***(G-1924)***
Gfl USA Inc 917 297-8701
81 Prospect St Brooklyn (11201) ***(G-1924)***
Gg Design and Printing 718 321-3220
93 Henry St Frnt 1 New York (10002) ***(G-9916)***
Ggp Publishing Inc 914 834-8896
105 Calvert St Ste 201 Harrison (10528) ***(G-5728)***
GH Bass & Co (HQ) 646 768-4600
512 7th Ave Fl 28 New York (10018) ***(G-9917)***
Gh Induction Atmospheres LLC 585 368-2120
35 Industrial Park Cir Rochester (14624) ***(G-13835)***
Ghani Textiles Inc 718 859-4561
2459 Coyle St Fl 2 Brooklyn (11235) ***(G-1925)***
Gharana Industries LLC 315 651-4004
61 Swift St Waterloo (13165) ***(G-15994)***
Ghostek LLC 855 310-3439
140 58th St Ste 2g Brooklyn (11220) ***(G-1926)***
Giagni Enterprises LLC 914 699-6500
550 S Columbus Ave Mount Vernon (10550) ***(G-8400)***
Giagni International Corp 914 699-6500
548 S Columbus Ave Mount Vernon (10550) ***(G-8401)***
Gibar Inc 315 452-5656
7838 Brewerton Rd Cicero (13039) ***(G-3518)***
Gibraltar Industries Inc (PA) 716 826-6500
3556 Lake Shore Rd # 100 Buffalo (14219) ***(G-2849)***
Gift Valleys.com, Ronkonkoma *Also called Bobley-Harmann Corporation* ***(G-14320)***
Gifts Software Inc 904 438-6000
360 Lexington Ave Rm 601 New York (10017) ***(G-9918)***
Gig-It, New York *Also called 212 Db Corp* ***(G-8670)***
Gild-Rite Inc 631 752-9000
51 Carolyn Blvd Farmingdale (11735) ***(G-4771)***
Gildan Apparel USA Inc (HQ) 212 476-0341
48 W 38th St Fl 8 New York (10018) ***(G-9919)***
Gilded Otter Brewing Co 845 256-1700
3 Main St New Paltz (12561) ***(G-8577)***
Giliberto Designs Inc 212 695-0216
142 W 36th St Fl 8 New York (10018) ***(G-9920)***
Gillette Creamery, Albany *Also called Phyljohn Distributors Inc* ***(G-115)***
Gillies Coffee Company 718 499-7766
150 19th St Brooklyn (11232) ***(G-1927)***
Gillinder Brothers Inc 845 856-5375
39 Erie St 55 Port Jervis (12771) ***(G-13229)***
Gillinder Glass, Port Jervis *Also called Gillinder Brothers Inc* ***(G-13229)***
Gilmores Sound Advice Inc 212 265-4445
599 11th Ave Fl 5 New York (10036) ***(G-9921)***
Gim Electronics Corp 516 942-3382
270 Duffy Ave Ste H Hicksville (11801) ***(G-6090)***
Gimbel & Associates, Garden City *Also called H&E Service Corp* ***(G-5261)***
Gina Group LLC 212 947-2445
10 W 33rd St Ph 3 New York (10001) ***(G-9922)***
Gina Hosiery, New York *Also called Gina Group LLC* ***(G-9922)***
Ginny Lee Cafe, Lodi *Also called Wagner Vineyards & Brewing Co* ***(G-7355)***
Giovane Ltd 212 332-7373
592 5th Ave Ste L New York (10036) ***(G-9923)***
Giovane Piranesi, New York *Also called Giovane Ltd* ***(G-9923)***
Giovanni Bakery Corp 212 695-4296
476 9th Ave New York (10018) ***(G-9924)***
Giovanni Food Co Inc (PA) 315 457-2373
8800 Sixty Rd Baldwinsville (13027) ***(G-555)***
Giuliante Machine Tool Inc 914 835-0008
12 John Walsh Blvd Peekskill (10566) ***(G-12920)***
Giulietta LLC 212 334-1859
649 Morgan Ave Ste 3h Brooklyn (11222) ***(G-1928)***
Giumenta Corp (PA) 718 832-1200
42 2nd Ave Brooklyn (11215) ***(G-1929)***
Giumenta Corp 718 832-1200
42 2nd Ave Brooklyn (11215) ***(G-1930)***
Givaudan Fragrances Corp 212 649-8800
40 W 57th St Fl 11 New York (10019) ***(G-9925)***

Givi Inc.....212 586-5029
16 W 56th St Fl 4 New York (10019) **(G-9926)**
Gizmo Products Inc.....585 301-0970
2257 County Road 4 Bldg 3 Stanley (14561) **(G-15034)**
GKN Aerospace Monitor Inc.....562 619-8558
1000 New Horizons Blvd Amityville (11701) **(G-277)**
GL & RL Logging Inc.....518 883-3936
713 Union Mills Rd Broadalbin (12025) **(G-1189)**
GL&v USA Inc.....518 747-2444
27 Allen St Hudson Falls (12839) **(G-6380)**
Glaceau, New York *Also called Energy Brands Inc* **(G-9680)**
Glacee Skincare LLC.....212 690-7632
611 W 136th St Apt 4 New York (10031) **(G-9927)**
Gladding Braided Products LLC.....315 653-7211
110 County Road 13a South Otselic (13155) **(G-14943)**
Glamour Magazine.....212 286-2860
4 Times Sq Fl 16 New York (10036) **(G-9928)**
Glamourpuss Nyc LLC.....212 722-1370
1305 Madison Ave New York (10128) **(G-9929)**
Glaro Inc.....631 234-1717
735 Calebs Path Ste 1 Hauppauge (11788) **(G-5835)**
Glasbau Hahn America LLC.....845 566-3331
15 Little Brook Ln Ste 2 Newburgh (12550) **(G-12224)**
Glasgow Products Inc.....516 374-5937
886 Lakeside Dr Woodmere (11598) **(G-16641)**
Glass Apps LLC (PA).....310 987-1536
11 Times Sq Ste 15 New York (10036) **(G-9930)**
Glass Menagerie Inc.....845 754-8344
1756 Rte 209 Westbrookville (12785) **(G-16307)**
Glassbox US Inc.....917 378-2933
234 5th Ave Ste 207 New York (10001) **(G-9931)**
Glasses USA LLC.....212 784-6094
954 Lexington Ave Ste 537 New York (10021) **(G-9932)**
Glassesusa.com, New York *Also called Glasses USA LLC* **(G-9932)**
Glassfab Inc.....585 262-4000
257 Ormond St Rochester (14605) **(G-13836)**
Glasson Sculpture Works.....845 255-2969
23 Shaft Rd Gardiner (12525) **(G-5294)**
Glassview LLC (PA).....646 844-4922
25 E 67th St Ph A New York (10065) **(G-9933)**
Glasteel Parts & Services Inc (HQ).....585 235-1010
1000 West Ave Rochester (14611) **(G-13837)**
Glaxosmithkline LLC.....845 341-7590
3 Tyler St Montgomery (12549) **(G-8311)**
Glaxosmithkline LLC.....845 797-3259
6 Alpert Dr Wappingers Falls (12590) **(G-15933)**
Glaxosmithkline LLC.....585 738-9025
1177 Winton Rd S Rochester (14618) **(G-13838)**
Glaxosmithkline LLC.....716 913-5679
17 Mahogany Dr Buffalo (14221) **(G-2850)**
Glaxosmithkline LLC.....518 239-6901
3169 Route 145 East Durham (12423) **(G-4216)**
Glaxosmithkline LLC.....518 852-9637
108 Woodfield Blvd Mechanicville (12118) **(G-7931)**
Glaxosmthkline Cnsmr Heathcare, East Durham *Also called Glaxosmithkline LLC* **(G-4216)**
Gleaner Company Ltd.....718 657-0788
9205 172nd St Fl 2 Jamaica (11433) **(G-6646)**
Gleason Corporation (PA).....585 473-1000
1000 University Ave Rochester (14607) **(G-13839)**
Gleason Works (HQ).....585 473-1000
1000 University Ave Rochester (14607) **(G-13840)**
Gleason-Avery, Auburn *Also called John G Rubino Inc* **(G-486)**
Glen Plaza Marble & Gran Inc.....516 671-1100
75 Glen Cove Ave Ste A Glen Cove (11542) **(G-5368)**
Glenda Inc.....718 442-8981
1732 Victory Blvd Staten Island (10314) **(G-15079)**
Glendale Architectural WD Pdts.....718 326-2700
7102 80th St Glendale (11385) **(G-5401)**
Glendale Products, Glendale *Also called Glendale Architectural WD Pdts* **(G-5401)**
Glenn Foods Inc (PA).....516 377-1400
371 S Main St Ste 119-405 Freeport (11520) **(G-5158)**
Glenn Horowitz Bookseller Inc.....212 691-9100
20 W 55th St Ph New York (10019) **(G-9934)**
Glenn Wayne Bakery, Bohemia *Also called Glenn Wayne Wholesale Bky Inc* **(G-1029)**
Glenn Wayne Wholesale Bky Inc.....631 289-9200
1800 Artic Ave Bohemia (11716) **(G-1029)**
Glenny's, Freeport *Also called Glenn Foods Inc* **(G-5158)**
Glenora Farm Inc.....607 243-8383
340 Dundee Glenora Rd Dundee (14837) **(G-4158)**
Glenora Farms, Dundee *Also called Glenora Farm Inc* **(G-4158)**
Glenora Wine Cellars Inc.....607 243-9500
5435 State Route 14 Dundee (14837) **(G-4159)**
Glenridge Fabricators Inc.....718 456-2297
7945 77th Ave Glendale (11385) **(G-5402)**
Glens Falls Newspapers Inc.....518 792-3131
76 Lawrence St Glens Falls (12801) **(G-5426)**
Glens Falls Printing LLC.....518 793-0555
51 Hudson Ave Glens Falls (12801) **(G-5427)**
Glens Falls Ready Mix Inc.....518 793-1695
112 Big Boom Rd Queensbury (12804) **(G-13426)**
Glenwood Cast Stone Inc.....718 859-6500
4106 Glenwood Rd Brooklyn (11210) **(G-1931)**
Glenwood Mason Supply, Brooklyn *Also called Glenwood Cast Stone Inc* **(G-1931)**
Glenwood Masonry Products, Brooklyn *Also called Superior Block Corp* **(G-2536)**
Gli-Dex Sales Corp.....716 692-6501
855 Wurlitzer Dr North Tonawanda (14120) **(G-12430)**
Glidden Machine & Tool, North Tonawanda *Also called Gli-Dex Sales Corp* **(G-12430)**
Glidden Professional Paint Ctr, Rochester *Also called PPG Architectural Finishes Inc* **(G-14030)**
Gliptone Manufacturing Inc.....631 285-7250
1740 Julia Goldbach Ave Ronkonkoma (11779) **(G-14345)**
Glissade New York LLC.....631 756-4800
399 Smith St Farmingdale (11735) **(G-4772)**
Glissen Chemical Co Inc (PA).....718 436-4200
1321 58th St Brooklyn (11219) **(G-1932)**
Glitner Ticketing, Levittown *Also called Glitnir Ticketing Inc* **(G-7134)**
Glitnir Ticketing Inc.....516 390-5168
3 Snapdragon Ln Levittown (11756) **(G-7134)**
Glitter, New York *Also called Magic Numbers Inc* **(G-10668)**
Glk Foods LLC.....585 289-4414
11 Clark St Shortsville (14548) **(G-14847)**
Gllusa, Farmingdale *Also called Green Logic Led Elec Sup Inc* **(G-4775)**
Global Abrasive Products Inc (PA).....716 438-0047
62 Mill St Lockport (14094) **(G-7303)**
Global Alliance For Tb.....212 227-7540
40 Wall St Fl 24 New York (10005) **(G-9935)**
Global Alumina Services Co.....212 309-8060
277 Park Ave Fl 40 New York (10172) **(G-9936)**
Global Applctions Solution LLC.....212 741-9595
125 Park Ave Fl 25 New York (10017) **(G-9937)**
Global Brands Inc.....845 358-1212
1031 Route 9w S Nyack (10960) **(G-12508)**
Global Creations, New York *Also called Global Gem Corporation* **(G-9941)**
Global Entity Media Inc.....631 580-7772
2090 5th Ave Ste 2 Ronkonkoma (11779) **(G-14346)**
Global Finance Magazine.....212 524-3223
7 E 20th St New York (10003) **(G-9938)**
Global Finance Magazine., New York *Also called Global Finance Media Inc* **(G-9939)**
Global Finance Magazine., New York *Also called Global Finance Magazine* **(G-9938)**
Global Finance Media Inc.....212 447-7900
7 E 20th St Fl 2 New York (10003) **(G-9939)**
Global Financial Shared Svcs, Seneca Falls *Also called Xylem Inc* **(G-14790)**
Global Fire Corporation.....888 320-1799
244 5th Ave Ste 2238 New York (10001) **(G-9940)**
Global Food Source & Co Inc.....914 320-9615
114 Carpenter Ave Tuckahoe (10707) **(G-15643)**
Global Gem Corporation.....212 350-9936
425 Madison Ave Rm 400 New York (10017) **(G-9941)**
Global Glass Corp.....516 681-2309
134 Woodbury Rd Hicksville (11801) **(G-6091)**
Global Gold Inc (PA).....212 239-4657
1410 Broadway Fl 8 New York (10018) **(G-9942)**
Global Gold Corporation (PA).....914 925-0020
555 Theodore Fremd Ave C208 Rye (10580) **(G-14481)**
Global Graphics Inc.....718 939-4967
3711 Prince St Ste D Flushing (11354) **(G-5002)**
Global Grind Digital.....212 840-9399
512 Fashion Ave Fl 42 New York (10018) **(G-9943)**
Global Hanger & Display Inc.....631 475-5900
14 Hewlett Ave East Patchogue (11772) **(G-4274)**
Global Instrumentation LLC.....315 682-0272
8104 Cazenovia Rd Ste 2/3 Manlius (13104) **(G-7778)**
Global Lighting Inc.....914 591-4095
201 Saw Mill River Rd 3 Yonkers (10701) **(G-16762)**
Global Marine Power Inc.....631 208-2933
221 Scott Ave Calverton (11933) **(G-3166)**
Global Market Development Inc.....631 667-1000
200 Executive Dr Ste G Edgewood (11717) **(G-4402)**
Global Payment Tech Inc.....516 887-0700
20 E Sunrise Hwy Valley Stream (11581) **(G-15781)**
Global Payment Tech Inc (PA).....631 563-2500
170 Wilbur Pl Ste 600 Bohemia (11716) **(G-1030)**
Global Plastics LP.....800 417-4605
21 Downing St Frnt 1 New York (10014) **(G-9944)**
Global Precision Inds Inc.....585 254-0010
955 Millstead Way Rochester (14624) **(G-13841)**
Global Precision Products, Rush *Also called Gpp Post-Closing Inc* **(G-14474)**
Global Resources Sg Inc.....212 686-1411
267 5th Ave Rm 506 New York (10016) **(G-9945)**
Global Security Tech LLC.....917 838-4507
123 Grove Ave Ste 222 Cedarhurst (11516) **(G-3332)**
Global Steel Products Corp (HQ).....631 586-3455
95 Marcus Blvd Deer Park (11729) **(G-3981)**
Global Technologies Inc (PA).....631 243-7924
81 E Jefryn Blvd Ste D Deer Park (11729) **(G-3982)**
Global Textile, New York *Also called Himatsingka America Inc* **(G-10102)**
Global Tissue Group Inc (PA).....631 924-3019
870 Expressway Dr S Medford (11763) **(G-7948)**
Global Video LLC (HQ).....516 222-2600
1000 Woodbury Rd Ste 1 Woodbury (11797) **(G-16620)**
Globalfoundries US 2 LLC (HQ).....512 457-3900
2070 Route 52 Hopewell Junction (12533) **(G-6286)**

ALPHABETIC

Globalfoundries US Inc 512 457-3900
2070 Route 52 Hopewell Junction (12533) ***(G-6287)***
Globalfoundries US Inc 518 305-9013
400 Stone Break Rd Ext Malta (12020) ***(G-7730)***
Globalfoundries US Inc 408 462-3900
107 Hermes Rd Ballston Spa (12020) ***(G-583)***
Globalquest Solutions Inc 716 601-3524
2813 Wehrle Dr Ste 3 Buffalo (14221) ***(G-2851)***
Globe Electronic Hardware Inc 718 457-0303
3424 56th St Woodside (11377) ***(G-16659)***
Globe Metallurgical Inc 716 804-0862
3807 Highland Ave Niagara Falls (14305) ***(G-12288)***
Globe Specialty Metals, Niagara Falls *Also called Globe Metallurgical Inc* ***(G-12288)***
Globe-Tex, New Rochelle *Also called HB Athletic Inc* ***(G-8613)***
Globe-Tex Apparal, New York *Also called Tbhl International LLC* ***(G-11787)***
Globmarble LLC 347 717-4088
2201 Neptune Ave Ste 5 Brooklyn (11224) ***(G-1933)***
Globus Cork Inc 347 963-4059
741 E 136th St Bronx (10454) ***(G-1282)***
Gloede Neon Signs Ltd Inc 845 471-4366
97 N Clinton St Poughkeepsie (12601) ***(G-13341)***
Glopak USA Corp (PA) 844 445-6725
35 Engel St Ste B Hicksville (11801) ***(G-6092)***
Gloria Apparel Inc 212 947-0869
500 Fashion Ave 8 New York (10018) ***(G-9946)***
Glowa Manufacturing Inc 607 770-0811
6 Emma St Binghamton (13905) ***(G-887)***
Gluck Orgelbau Inc 212 233-2684
170 Park Row Apt 20a New York (10038) ***(G-9947)***
Gluten Free Bake Shop Inc 845 782-5307
19 Industry Dr Mountainville (10953) ***(G-8455)***
Glycobia Inc 607 339-0051
33 Thornwood Dr Ste 104 Ithaca (14850) ***(G-6578)***
Glyph Production Technologies, Cortland *Also called Technologies Application LLC* ***(G-3896)***
GM Components Holdings LLC 716 439-2237
200 Upper Mountain Rd Lockport (14094) ***(G-7304)***
GM Components Holdings LLC 585 647-7000
1000 Lexington Ave Rochester (14606) ***(G-13842)***
GM Components Holdings LLC 716 439-2463
200 Upper Mountain Rd Lockport (14094) ***(G-7305)***
GM Components Holdings LLC 716 439-2011
200 Upper Mountain Rd # 7 Lockport (14094) ***(G-7306)***
GM Components Holdings LLC 716 439-2402
200 Upper Mountain Rd # 10 Lockport (14094) ***(G-7307)***
GM Insulation Corp 516 354-6000
1345 Rosser Ave Elmont (11003) ***(G-4519)***
GM Palmer Inc 585 492-2990
51 Edward St Arcade (14009) ***(G-383)***
GM Pre Cast Products, Jamestown *Also called Suhor Industries Inc* ***(G-6751)***
GM Printing, Long Island City *Also called Grand Meridian Printing Inc* ***(G-7460)***
GMC Mercantile Corp 212 498-9488
231 W 39th St Rm 612 New York (10018) ***(G-9948)***
Gmch Lockport, Lockport *Also called GM Components Holdings LLC* ***(G-7305)***
Gmch Lockport Ptc, Lockport *Also called GM Components Holdings LLC* ***(G-7304)***
Gmch Rochester, Rochester *Also called GM Components Holdings LLC* ***(G-13842)***
Gmd Industries Inc 718 445-8779
12920 18th Ave College Point (11356) ***(G-3645)***
Gmp LLC 914 939-0571
47 Purdy Ave Port Chester (10573) ***(G-13200)***
Gmr Manufacturing Inc 631 582-2600
101 Windsor Pl Unit D Central Islip (11722) ***(G-3371)***
Gms Hicks Street Corporation 718 858-1010
214 Hicks St Brooklyn (11201) ***(G-1934)***
Gn Printing 718 784-1713
4216 34th Ave Long Island City (11101) ***(G-7457)***
Gncc Capital Inc (PA) 702 951-9793
244 5th Ave Ste 2525 New York (10001) ***(G-9949)***
GNI Commerce Inc 347 275-1155
458 Neptune Ave Apt 11f Brooklyn (11224) ***(G-1935)***
Gnosis Chocolate Inc 646 688-5549
4003 27th St Long Island City (11101) ***(G-7458)***
Go Blue Technologies Ltd 631 404-6285
325 August Rd North Babylon (11703) ***(G-12360)***
Go Go Apple Inc 646 264-8909
4126 Benham St Elmhurst (11373) ***(G-4465)***
Go Mobo, New York *Also called Mobo Systems Inc* ***(G-10828)***
Gocare247, Brooklyn *Also called Mdcare911 LLC* ***(G-2183)***
Goddard Design Co 718 599-0170
51 Nassau Ave Ste 1b Brooklyn (11222) ***(G-1936)***
Godiva Chocolatier Inc (HQ) 212 984-5900
333 W 34th St Fl 6 New York (10001) ***(G-9950)***
Godiva Chocolatier Inc 718 271-3603
9015 Queens Blvd Ste 2045 Elmhurst (11373) ***(G-4466)***
Goergen-Mackwirth Co Inc 716 874-4800
765 Hertel Ave Buffalo (14207) ***(G-2852)***
Gogo Squeez, New York *Also called Materne North America Corp* ***(G-10727)***
Gold & Diamonds Wholesale Outl 718 438-7888
4417 5th Ave Brooklyn (11220) ***(G-1937)***
Gold Coast Gazette, Glen Cove *Also called Kch Publications Inc* ***(G-5369)***
Gold Mark Mfg Co, Brooklyn *Also called Goldmark Inc* ***(G-1939)***
Gold Medal Packing Inc 315 337-1911
8301 Old River Rd Oriskany (13424) ***(G-12758)***
Gold Pride Press Inc 585 224-8800
12 Pixley Industrial Pkwy # 40 Rochester (14624) ***(G-13843)***
Goldarama Company Inc 212 730-7299
56 W 45th St Ste 1504 New York (10036) ***(G-9951)***
Goldberg Prosthetic & Orthotic 631 689-6606
9 Technology Dr East Setauket (11733) ***(G-4302)***
Goldberger Company LLC (PA) 212 924-1194
36 W 25th St Fl 14 New York (10010) ***(G-9952)***
Goldberger International, New York *Also called Goldberger Company LLC* ***(G-9952)***
Golden Argosy LLC (PA) 212 268-0003
225 W 34th St Ste 1106 New York (10122) ***(G-9953)***
Golden Artist Colors Inc 607 847-6154
188 Bell Rd New Berlin (13411) ***(G-8488)***
Golden Bridge Group Inc 718 335-8882
7416 Grand Ave Elmhurst (11373) ***(G-4467)***
Golden Eagle Marketing LLC 212 726-1242
244 5th Ave New York (10001) ***(G-9954)***
Golden Egret LLC 516 922-2839
38 Cord Pl East Norwich (11732) ***(G-4272)***
Golden Glow Cookie Co Inc 718 379-6223
1844 Givan Ave Bronx (10469) ***(G-1283)***
Golden Group International Ltd 845 440-1025
305 Quaker Rd Patterson (12563) ***(G-12882)***
Golden Integrity Inc 212 764-6753
37 W 47th St Ste 1601 New York (10036) ***(G-9955)***
Golden Leaves Knitwear Inc 718 875-8235
43 Hall St Ste B3 Brooklyn (11205) ***(G-1938)***
Golden Legacy Ilstrd Histry, Yonkers *Also called Fitzgerald Publishing Co Inc* ***(G-16758)***
Golden Renewable Energy LLC 914 920-9800
700 Nepperhan Ave Yonkers (10703) ***(G-16763)***
Golden Taste Inc 845 356-4133
318 Roosevelt Ave Spring Valley (10977) ***(G-14993)***
Goldmark Inc 718 438-0295
3611 14th Ave Ste B01 Brooklyn (11218) ***(G-1939)***
Goldmark Products Inc 631 777-3343
855 Conklin St Ste D Farmingdale (11735) ***(G-4773)***
Goldmont Enterprises Inc 212 947-3633
7603 Caldwell Ave Middle Village (11379) ***(G-8121)***
Goldsmith, Binghamton *Also called Mellem Corporation* ***(G-904)***
Goldstar Lighting LLC 646 543-6811
1407 Broadway Fl 30 New York (10018) ***(G-9956)***
Golf Directories USA Inc 516 365-5351
39 Orchard St Ste 7 Manhasset (11030) ***(G-7768)***
Golf Odyssey, New York *Also called Maven Marketing LLC* ***(G-10731)***
Golfing Magazine 516 822-5446
22 W Nicholai St Ste 200 Hicksville (11801) ***(G-6093)***
Golos Printing Inc 607 732-1896
110 E 9th St Elmira Heights (14903) ***(G-4511)***
Golub Corporation 518 943-3903
320 W Bridge St Catskill (12414) ***(G-3303)***
Golub Corporation 518 899-6063
3 Hemphill Pl Ste 116 Malta (12020) ***(G-7731)***
Golub Corporation 315 363-0679
142 Genesee St Oneida (13421) ***(G-12609)***
Golub Corporation 607 336-2588
5631 State Highway 12 Norwich (13815) ***(G-12486)***
Golub Corporation 518 583-3697
3045 Route 50 Saratoga Springs (12866) ***(G-14582)***
Golub Corporation 518 822-0076
351 Fairview Ave Ste 3 Hudson (12534) ***(G-6351)***
Golub Corporation 607 235-7240
33 Chenango Bridge Rd Binghamton (13901) ***(G-888)***
Golub Corporation 845 344-0327
511 Schutt Road Ext Middletown (10940) ***(G-8157)***
Gone South Concrete Block Inc 315 598-2141
2809 State Route 3 Fulton (13069) ***(G-5218)***
Good Bread Bakery 914 939-3900
33 New Broad St Ste 1 Port Chester (10573) ***(G-13201)***
Good Earth Inc 716 684-8111
5960 Broadway St Lancaster (14086) ***(G-7021)***
Good Earth Organics Corp (PA) 716 684-8111
5960 Broadway St Lancaster (14086) ***(G-7022)***
Good Health Healthcare Newsppr 585 421-8109
106 Cobblestone Court Dr Victor (14564) ***(G-15848)***
Good Home Co Inc 212 352-1509
132 W 24th St New York (10011) ***(G-9957)***
Good Show Sportswear, New York *Also called Good Show Sportwear Inc* ***(G-9958)***
Good Show Sportwear Inc 212 334-8751
132 Mulberry St 3 New York (10013) ***(G-9958)***
Good-O-Beverage Inc 718 328-6400
1801 Boone Ave Bronx (10460) ***(G-1284)***
Gooding & Associates Inc 631 749-3313
15 Dinah Rock Rd Shelter Island (11964) ***(G-14801)***
Gooding Co Inc 716 266-6252
5568 Davison Rd Lockport (14094) ***(G-7308)***
Goodman Main Stopper Mfg Co 718 875-5140
523 Atlantic Ave Brooklyn (11217) ***(G-1940)***
Goodnature Products Inc (PA) 716 855-3325
3860 California Rd Orchard Park (14127) ***(G-12716)***
Goodrich Corporation 315 838-1200
104 Otis St Rome (13441) ***(G-14251)***

Goodwill Inds of Greater NY..........914 621-0781
80 Route 6 Unit 605 Baldwin Place (10505) *(G-546)*
Goodwill Inds Wstn NY Inc..........716 633-3305
4311 Transit Rd Williamsville (14221) *(G-16580)*
Gorbel Inc (PA)..........585 924-6262
600 Fishers Run Fishers (14453) *(G-4940)*
Gorden Automotive Equipment..........716 674-2700
60 N America Dr West Seneca (14224) *(G-16299)*
Gordon Fire Equipment LLC..........845 691-5700
3199 Us Highway 9w Highland (12528) *(G-6143)*
Gordon S Anderson Mfg Co..........845 677-3304
215 N Mabbettsville Rd Millbrook (12545) *(G-8188)*
Gorga Fehren Fine Jewelry LLC..........646 861-3595
153 E 88th St New York (10128) *(G-9959)*
Goshen Quarry, Goshen *Also called Tilcon New York Inc (G-5484)*
Got Power Inc..........631 767-9493
5 Campus Ln Ronkonkoma (11779) *(G-14347)*
Got Wood LLC..........315 440-8857
28 North St Cleveland (13042) *(G-3561)*
Gotenna Inc..........415 894-2616
81 Willoughby St Ste 302 Brooklyn (11201) *(G-1941)*
Gotham City Industries Inc..........914 713-0979
372 Fort Hill Rd Scarsdale (10583) *(G-14638)*
Gotham Diamonds, New York *Also called American Originals Corporation (G-8835)*
Gotham Energy 360 LLC..........917 338-1023
48 Wall St Fl 5 New York (10005) *(G-9960)*
Gotham Ink & Color Co Inc..........845 947-4000
19 Holt Dr Stony Point (10980) *(G-15172)*
Gotham T-Shirt Corp..........516 676-0900
211 Glen Cove Ave Unit 5 Sea Cliff (11579) *(G-14755)*
Gotham Veterinary Center PC..........212 222-1900
700 Columbus Ave Frnt 5 New York (10025) *(G-9961)*
Gothic Cabinet Craft Inc (PA)..........347 881-1420
5877 57th St Maspeth (11378) *(G-7848)*
Gottlieb & Sons Inc..........212 575-1907
21 W 47th St Fl 4 New York (10036) *(G-9962)*
Gottlieb Jewelery Mfg, New York *Also called Gottlieb & Sons Inc (G-9962)*
Gottlieb Schwartz Family..........718 761-2010
724 Collfield Ave Staten Island (10314) *(G-15080)*
Goulds Pumps (ipg) LLC..........315 568-2811
240 Fall St Seneca Falls (13148) *(G-14773)*
Goulds Pumps Incorporated, Seneca Falls *Also called Goulds Pumps LLC (G-14774)*
Goulds Pumps LLC (HQ)..........315 568-2811
240 Fall St Seneca Falls (13148) *(G-14774)*
Goulds Pumps LLC..........315 568-2811
280 Fall St Seneca Falls (13148) *(G-14775)*
Gourmet Boutique LLC (PA)..........718 977-1200
14402 158th St Jamaica (11434) *(G-6647)*
Gourmet Connection, Baldwinsville *Also called Capco Marketing (G-552)*
Gourmet Crafts Inc..........718 372-0505
152 Highlawn Ave Brooklyn (11223) *(G-1942)*
Gourmet Factory Inc..........631 231-4548
55 Corporate Dr Hauppauge (11788) *(G-5836)*
Gourmet Nut Inc..........877 830-9030
3611 14th Ave Ste 654 Brooklyn (11218) *(G-1943)*
Gourmet Toast Corp..........718 852-4536
345 Park Ave Brooklyn (11205) *(G-1944)*
Gourmia, Brooklyn *Also called Steelstone Group LLC (G-2519)*
Government Data Publication..........347 789-8719
1661 Mcdonald Ave Brooklyn (11230) *(G-1945)*
Gowanda - Bti LLC..........716 492-4081
7426a Tanner Pkwy Arcade (14009) *(G-384)*
Goya Foods Inc..........716 549-0076
200 S Main St Angola (14006) *(G-369)*
Goya Foods Great Lakes, Angola *Also called Goya Foods Inc (G-369)*
Goyard Inc (HQ)..........212 813-0005
20 E 63rd St New York (10065) *(G-9963)*
Goyard Miami LLC (HQ)..........212 813-0005
20 E 63rd St New York (10065) *(G-9964)*
Goyard NM Beverly Hills LLC..........212 355-3872
20 E 63rd St New York (10065) *(G-9965)*
Goyard US, New York *Also called Goyard Inc (G-9963)*
Gpc International Inc (PA)..........631 752-9600
510 Broadhollow Rd # 205 Melville (11747) *(G-8027)*
Gpi Equipment Company, Jefferson Valley *Also called George Ponte Inc (G-6776)*
GPM Associates LLC..........585 335-3940
10 Forbes St Dansville (14437) *(G-3926)*
GPM Associates LLC..........585 359-1770
45 High Tech Dr Ste 100 Rush (14543) *(G-14473)*
Gpp Post-Closing Inc..........585 334-4640
90 High Tech Dr Rush (14543) *(G-14474)*
Gpsi, Hauppauge *Also called Generic Pharmaceutical Svcs (G-5832)*
Gpt, Bohemia *Also called Global Payment Tech Inc (G-1030)*
Gq Magazine..........212 286-2860
4 Times Sq Fl 9 New York (10036) *(G-9966)*
Grace Associates Inc..........718 767-9000
470 West St Harrison (10528) *(G-5729)*
Grace Ryan & Magnus Mllwk LLC..........914 665-0902
17 N Bleeker St Mount Vernon (10550) *(G-8402)*
Grace Wheeler..........716 483-1254
118 E 1st St Jamestown (14701) *(G-6718)*

Gradian Health Systems Inc..........212 537-0340
915 Broadway Ste 1001 New York (10010) *(G-9967)*
Gradient Lens Corporation..........585 235-2620
207 Tremont St Ste 1 Rochester (14608) *(G-13844)*
Grado Group Inc..........718 556-4200
66 Willow Ave Staten Island (10305) *(G-15081)*
Grado Laboratories Inc..........718 435-5340
4614 7th Ave Ste 1 Brooklyn (11220) *(G-1946)*
Gradual LLC..........347 293-0974
1040 46th Ave Fl 2 Long Island City (11101) *(G-7459)*
Grafconect Corp..........212 714-1795
575 8th Ave Rm 1902 New York (10018) *(G-9968)*
Graham Corporation (PA)..........585 343-2216
20 Florence Ave Batavia (14020) *(G-626)*
Grainful, Ithaca *Also called Beetnpath LLC (G-6558)*
Gramco Inc (PA)..........716 592-2845
299 Waverly St Springville (14141) *(G-15017)*
Gramercy Jewelry Mfg Corp..........212 268-0461
35 W 45th St Fl 5 New York (10036) *(G-9969)*
Granada Electronics Inc..........718 387-1157
485 Kent Ave Brooklyn (11249) *(G-1947)*
Grand Central Publishing (HQ)..........212 364-1200
1290 Ave Of The Americas New York (10104) *(G-9970)*
Grand Island Animal Hospital..........716 773-7645
2323 Whitehaven Rd Grand Island (14072) *(G-5502)*
Grand Island Research & Dev, Grand Island *Also called Grand Island Animal Hospital (G-5502)*
Grand Knitting Mills Inc (PA)..........631 226-5000
7050 New Horizons Blvd # 1 Amityville (11701) *(G-278)*
GRAND MARNIER, New York *Also called Marnier-Lapostolle Inc (G-10715)*
Grand Meridian Printing Inc..........718 937-3888
3116 Hunters Point Ave Long Island City (11101) *(G-7460)*
Grand Prix Litho Inc..........631 242-4182
101 Colin Dr Unit 5 Holbrook (11741) *(G-6187)*
Grand Processing Inc..........718 388-0600
1050 Grand St Brooklyn (11211) *(G-1948)*
Grand Slam Holdings LLC (HQ)..........212 583-5000
345 Park Ave Bsmt Lb4 New York (10154) *(G-9971)*
Grand Slam Safety LLC..........315 766-7008
9793 S Bridge St Croghan (13327) *(G-3908)*
Grandeur Creations Inc..........212 643-1277
146 W 29th St Rm 9e New York (10001) *(G-9972)*
Grandma Browns Beans Inc..........315 963-7221
5837 Scenic Ave Mexico (13114) *(G-8108)*
Grandma Maes Cntry Nturals LLC..........212 348-8171
340 E 93rd St Apt 30h New York (10128) *(G-9973)*
Grandview Block & Supply Co..........518 346-7981
1705 Hamburg St Schenectady (12304) *(G-14683)*
Grandview Concrete Corp..........518 346-7981
1705 Hamburg St Schenectady (12304) *(G-14684)*
Granite & Marble Works Inc..........518 584-2800
8 Commerce Park Dr Gansevoort (12831) *(G-5243)*
Granite Tops Inc..........914 699-2909
716 S Columbus Ave Mount Vernon (10550) *(G-8403)*
Granite Works LLC..........607 565-7012
133 William Donnelly Waverly (14892) *(G-16065)*
Granny's Kitchens, Frankfort *Also called Maplehurst Bakeries LLC (G-5109)*
Grant Hamilton (PA)..........716 652-0320
710 Main St East Aurora (14052) *(G-4201)*
Grant's Interest Rate Observer, New York *Also called Grants Financial Publishing (G-9975)*
Grant-Noren..........845 726-4281
83 Ridge Rd Westtown (10998) *(G-16414)*
Grantoo LLC..........646 356-0460
60 Broad St Ste 3502 New York (10004) *(G-9974)*
Grants Financial Publishing..........212 809-7994
2 Wall St Ste 603 New York (10005) *(G-9975)*
Granville Glass & Granite..........518 812-0492
131 Revere Rd Hudson Falls (12839) *(G-6381)*
Graph-Tex Inc..........607 756-7791
46 Elm St Cortland (13045) *(G-3873)*
Graph-Tex Inc (PA)..........607 756-1875
24 Court St Cortland (13045) *(G-3874)*
Graphalloy, Yonkers *Also called Graphite Metallizing Corp (G-16764)*
Graphic Cntrls Acqisition Corp (HQ)..........716 853-7500
400 Exchange St Buffalo (14204) *(G-2853)*
Graphic Concepts, Plainview *Also called Steval Graphics Concepts Inc (G-13090)*
Graphic Connections, Geneva *Also called Tramwell Inc (G-5334)*
Graphic Controls Holdings Inc (HQ)..........716 853-7500
400 Exchange St Buffalo (14204) *(G-2854)*
Graphic Design U S A, New York *Also called American Graphic Design Awards (G-8827)*
Graphic Fabrications Inc..........516 763-3222
488a Sunrise Hwy Rockville Centre (11570) *(G-14232)*
Graphic For Industry, New York *Also called Graphics For Industry Inc (G-9977)*
Graphic Image Associates LLC..........631 249-9600
305 Spagnoli Rd Melville (11747) *(G-8028)*
Graphic Lab Inc..........212 682-1815
228 E 45th St Fl 4 New York (10017) *(G-9976)*
Graphic Management Partners, Port Chester *Also called Gmp LLC (G-13200)*
Graphic Printing..........718 701-4433
2376 Jerome Ave Bronx (10468) *(G-1285)*

ALPHABETIC

Graphic Signs & Awnings Ltd 718 227-6000
165 Industrial Loop Ste 1 Staten Island (10309) ***(G-15082)***
Graphicomm Inc 716 283-0830
7703 Niagara Falls Blvd Niagara Falls (14304) ***(G-12289)***
Graphics 247 Corp 718 729-2470
4402 23rd St Ste 113 Long Island City (11101) ***(G-7461)***
Graphics For Industry Inc 212 889-6202
307 W 36th St Fl 10 New York (10018) ***(G-9977)***
Graphics Plus Printing Inc 607 299-0500
215 S Main St Cortland (13045) ***(G-3875)***
Graphics Service Bureau Inc (PA) 212 684-3600
3030 47th Ave Long Island City (11101) ***(G-7462)***
Graphics Slution Providers Inc (PA) 845 677-5088
115 Barmore Rd Lagrangeville (12540) ***(G-6956)***
Graphis Inc 212 532-9387
389 5th Ave Rm 1105 New York (10016) ***(G-9978)***
Graphite Metallizing Corp (PA) 914 968-8400
1050 Nepperhan Ave Yonkers (10703) ***(G-16764)***
Graphitek Inc 518 686-5966
4883 State Route 67 Hoosick Falls (12090) ***(G-6275)***
Graphtex A Div of Htc, Utica *Also called Human Technologies Corporation* ***(G-15711)***
Grasers Dental Ceramics 716 649-5100
5020 Armor Duells Rd # 2 Orchard Park (14127) ***(G-12717)***
Gratitude & Company Inc 607 277-3188
215 N Cayuga St Ste 71 Ithaca (14850) ***(G-6579)***
Graver Technologies LLC 585 624-1330
300 W Main St Honeoye Falls (14472) ***(G-6265)***
Gravity East Village Inc 212 388-9788
515 E 5th St New York (10009) ***(G-9979)***
Gravymaster Inc 203 453-1893
101 Erie Blvd Canajoharie (13317) ***(G-3207)***
Gray Glass Inc 718 217-2943
21744 98th Ave Ste C Queens Village (11429) ***(G-13406)***
Gray Manufacturing Inds LLC 607 281-1325
6258 Ice House Rd Hornell (14843) ***(G-6300)***
Grayers America Inc 310 953-2742
304 Bleecker St New York (10014) ***(G-9980)***
Grayhawk Leasing LLC (HQ) 914 767-6000
1 Pepsi Way Somers (10589) ***(G-14920)***
Graymont Materials Inc 518 561-5200
111 Quarry Rd Plattsburgh (12901) ***(G-13122)***
Graywood Companies Inc (PA) 585 254-7000
1390 Mount Read Blvd Rochester (14606) ***(G-13845)***
Grc, Hempstead *Also called General Refining & Smelting* ***(G-6011)***
Great 4 Image Inc 518 424-2058
5 Forest Hills Blvd Rensselaer (12144) ***(G-13474)***
Great Adirondack Yarn Company 518 843-3381
950 County Highway 126 Amsterdam (12010) ***(G-339)***
Great American Awning & Patio 518 899-2300
43 Round Lake Rd Ballston Spa (12020) ***(G-584)***
Great American Bicycle LLC 518 584-8100
41 Geyser Rd Saratoga Springs (12866) ***(G-14583)***
Great American Dessert Co LLC 718 894-3494
5842 Maurice Ave Maspeth (11378) ***(G-7849)***
Great American Industries Inc (HQ) 607 729-9331
300 Plaza Dr Vestal (13850) ***(G-15818)***
Great American Tool Co Inc 716 646-5700
7223 Boston State Rd Hamburg (14075) ***(G-5681)***
Great Arrow Graphics, Buffalo *Also called Massimo Friedman Inc* ***(G-2938)***
Great ATL Pr-Cast Con Statuary 718 948-5677
225 Ellis St Staten Island (10307) ***(G-15083)***
Great Brands of Europe Inc 914 872-8804
100 Hillside Ave Fl 3 White Plains (10603) ***(G-16454)***
Great China Empire, New York *Also called Gce International Inc* ***(G-9890)***
Great Dane Parent LLC (PA) 518 810-0700
201 Fuller Rd Fl 6 Albany (12203) ***(G-78)***
Great Eastern Color Lith (PA) 845 454-7420
46 Violet Ave Poughkeepsie (12601) ***(G-13342)***
Great Eastern Pasta Works LLC 631 956-0889
385 Sheffield Ave West Babylon (11704) ***(G-16157)***
Great Gates Etc, New York *Also called North Eastern Fabricators Inc* ***(G-10993)***
Great Impressions, South Dayton *Also called Cherry Creek Woodcraft Inc* ***(G-14928)***
Great Jones Lumber Corp 212 254-5560
45 Great Jones St New York (10012) ***(G-9981)***
Great Lakes Cheese NY Inc 315 232-4511
23 Phelps St Adams (13605) ***(G-3)***
Great Lakes Gear Co Inc 716 694-0715
126 E Niagara St Ste 2 Tonawanda (14150) ***(G-15542)***
Great Lakes Metal Treating 716 694-1240
300 E Niagara St Tonawanda (14150) ***(G-15543)***
Great Lakes Orthpd Labs Inc 716 878-7307
1031 Main St Buffalo (14203) ***(G-2855)***
Great Lakes Plastics Co Inc 716 896-3100
2371 Broadway St Buffalo (14212) ***(G-2856)***
Great Lakes Pressed Steel Corp 716 885-4037
1400 Niagara St Buffalo (14213) ***(G-2857)***
Great Lakes Specialites 716 672-4622
9491 Route 60 Fredonia (14063) ***(G-5127)***
Great Lakes Technologies, Liverpool *Also called Scapa North America* ***(G-7261)***
Great Northern Printing Co, Potsdam *Also called Randy Sixberry* ***(G-13322)***
Great Rock Automation Inc 631 270-1508
99 Rome St Farmingdale (11735) ***(G-4774)***
Great Universal Corp 917 302-0065
1441 Broadway Ste 6066 New York (10018) ***(G-9982)***
Great Wall Corp 212 704-4372
4727 36th St Long Island City (11101) ***(G-7463)***
Great Western Malting Co 800 496-7732
16 Beeman Way Champlain (12919) ***(G-3409)***
Greatbatch Medical, Alden *Also called Integer Holdings Corporation* ***(G-173)***
Greatbatch Medical, Clarence *Also called Precimed Inc* ***(G-3539)***
Greater Niagara Bldg Ctr Inc 716 299-0543
9540 Niagara Falls Blvd Niagara Falls (14304) ***(G-12290)***
Greater Niagara Newspaper, Medina *Also called Gannett Stllite Info Ntwrk Inc* ***(G-7978)***
Greek Nat Hrald Dily Nwsppr In, Long Island City *Also called National Herald Inc* ***(G-7533)***
Green Apple Courage Inc 716 614-4673
374 Delaware Ave Ste 240 Buffalo (14202) ***(G-2858)***
Green Beam Led Inc 718 439-6262
4601b 1st Ave Brooklyn (11232) ***(G-1949)***
Green Buffalo Fuel LLC 716 768-0600
720 Riverview Blvd Tonawanda (14150) ***(G-15544)***
Green Conveyor & Mch Group LLC 607 692-7050
8308 Rte 79 Whitney Point (13862) ***(G-16555)***
Green Earth Enterprise, New York *Also called Earth Enterprises Inc* ***(G-9607)***
Green Energy Concepts Inc 845 238-2574
37 Elkay Dr Ste 51 Chester (10918) ***(G-3476)***
Green Enviro Machine LLC 407 461-6412
2366 Algonquin Rd Schenectady (12309) ***(G-14685)***
Green Girl Prtg & Msgnr Inc 212 575-0357
44 W 39th St New York (10018) ***(G-9983)***
Green Island Power Authority 518 273-0661
20 Clinton St Green Island (12183) ***(G-5606)***
Green Logic Led Elec Sup Inc (PA) 516 280-2854
75 Marine St Farmingdale (11735) ***(G-4775)***
Green Mountain Graphics, Sunnyside *Also called Eastern Concepts Ltd* ***(G-15203)***
Green Prosthetics & Orthotics 716 484-1088
1290 E 2nd St Jamestown (14701) ***(G-6719)***
Green Renewable Inc 518 658-2233
28 Taylor Ave Berlin (12022) ***(G-831)***
Green Valley Foods LLC 315 926-4280
3736 S Main St Marion (14505) ***(G-7801)***
Green Wave International Inc 718 499-3371
5423 1st Ave Brooklyn (11220) ***(G-1950)***
Green Zone Food Service Inc 917 709-1728
9906 Christie Ave 3a Corona (11368) ***(G-3844)***
Greenbeads Llc 212 327-2765
220 E 72nd St Apt 17d New York (10021) ***(G-9984)***
Greenbeam Led, Brooklyn *Also called Green Beam Led Inc* ***(G-1949)***
Greenbush Tape & Label Inc 518 465-2389
40 Broadway Unit 31 Albany (12202) ***(G-79)***
Greene Brass & Alum Fndry LLC 607 656-4204
51971 State Highway 10 Bloomville (13739) ***(G-962)***
Greene Brass & Aluminum Fndry, Greene *Also called American Blade Mfg LLC* ***(G-5612)***
Greene Lumber Co LP 607 278-6101
16991 State Highway 23 Davenport (13750) ***(G-3928)***
Greene Technologies Inc 607 656-4166
Grand & Clinton St Greene (13778) ***(G-5615)***
Greenebuild LLC 917 562-0556
390a Lafayette Ave Brooklyn (11238) ***(G-1951)***
Greenfield Die Casting Corp 516 623-9230
99 Doxsee Dr Freeport (11520) ***(G-5159)***
Greenfield Industries Inc 516 623-9230
99 Doxsee Dr Freeport (11520) ***(G-5160)***
Greenfield Manufacturing Inc 518 581-2368
25 Freedom Way Saratoga Springs (12866) ***(G-14584)***
Greenfield Martin Clothiers, Brooklyn *Also called Martin Greenfield Clothiers* ***(G-2174)***
Greengale Publishing, New York *Also called Niche Media Holdings LLC* ***(G-10961)***
Greenkissny Inc 914 304-4323
75 S Broadway White Plains (10601) ***(G-16455)***
Greenleaf Cabinet Makers LLC 315 432-4600
6691 Pickard Dr Syracuse (13211) ***(G-15335)***
Greenmaker Industries LLC 866 684-7800
885 Conklin St Farmingdale (11735) ***(G-4776)***
Greenpac Mill LLC (HQ) 716 299-0560
4400 Royal Ave Niagara Falls (14303) ***(G-12291)***
Greentree Pharmacy Inc 718 768-2700
291 7th Ave Brooklyn (11215) ***(G-1952)***
Greenvale Bagel Inc 516 221-8221
3060 Merrick Rd Wantagh (11793) ***(G-15921)***
Greenville Local, Ravena *Also called Bleezarde Publishing Inc* ***(G-13452)***
Greenway Cabinetry Inc 516 877-0009
485 Willis Ave Williston Park (11596) ***(G-16594)***
Greenwood Winery LLC 315 432-8132
6475 Collamer Rd East Syracuse (13057) ***(G-4343)***
Gregg Sadwick, Rochester *Also called Jml Optical Industries LLC* ***(G-13894)***
Gregson-Clark, Caledonia *Also called Rhett M Clark Inc* ***(G-3157)***
Greif Inc 716 836-4200
2122 Colvin Blvd Tonawanda (14150) ***(G-15545)***
Greno Industries Inc 518 393-4195
2820 Amsterdam Rd Scotia (12302) ***(G-14740)***
Gresham Computing, New York *Also called Gresham Technologies (us) Inc* ***(G-9985)***
Gresham Technologies (us) Inc 646 943-5955
11 Park Pl Frnt 3 New York (10007) ***(G-9985)***

Grey House Publishing Inc.......845 483-3535
84 Patrick Ln Stop 3 Poughkeepsie (12603) ***(G-13343)***
Grey House Publishing Inc (PA).......518 789-8700
4919 Route 22 Amenia (12501) ***(G-206)***
Grey State Apparel LLC.......212 255-4216
305 7th Ave Ste 13a New York (10001) ***(G-9986)***
Greyhouse Publshng, Poughkeepsie *Also called Grey House Publishing Inc* ***(G-13343)***
Greyline Signs Inc.......716 947-4526
6631 Schuyler Dr Derby (14047) ***(G-4113)***
Greyston Bakery Inc.......914 375-1510
104 Alexander St Yonkers (10701) ***(G-16765)***
Grid Typographic Services Inc.......212 627-0303
27 W 24th St Ste 9c New York (10010) ***(G-9987)***
Grid Typographic Svces, New York *Also called Grid Typographic Services Inc* ***(G-9987)***
Griffin Chemical Company LLC.......716 693-2465
889 Erie Ave Ste 1 North Tonawanda (14120) ***(G-12431)***
Griffin Manufacturing Company.......585 265-1991
1656 Ridge Rd Webster (14580) ***(G-16085)***
Griffon Corporation (PA).......212 957-5000
712 5th Ave Fl 18 New York (10019) ***(G-9988)***
Grillbot LLC.......646 258-5639
1562 1st Ave Ste 251 New York (10028) ***(G-9989)***
Grillmaster Inc.......718 272-9191
15314 83rd St Howard Beach (11414) ***(G-6330)***
Grimble Bakery, Bronx *Also called Miss Grimble Associates Inc* ***(G-1333)***
Grind.......646 558-3250
1216 Broadway Fl 2 New York (10001) ***(G-9990)***
Grinnell Designs Ltd.......212 391-5277
260 W 39th St Rm 302 New York (10018) ***(G-9991)***
Grit Energy Services Inc (PA).......212 701-4500
100 Wall St Fl 11 New York (10005) ***(G-9992)***
Grohe America Inc.......212 206-8820
160 5th Ave Fl 4 New York (10010) ***(G-9993)***
Grolier International Inc (HQ).......212 343-6100
557 Broadway New York (10012) ***(G-9994)***
Grom Columbus LLC.......212 974-3444
1796 Broadway New York (10019) ***(G-9995)***
Grossglockner Inc.......585 266-4960
2640 Brickyard Rd Canandaigua (14424) ***(G-3223)***
Grosso Materials Inc.......845 361-5211
90 Collabar Rd Montgomery (12549) ***(G-8312)***
Group Commerce Inc (PA).......646 346-0598
902 Broadway Fl 6 New York (10010) ***(G-9996)***
Group Enterainment LLC.......212 868-5233
115 W 29th St Rm 1102 New York (10001) ***(G-9997)***
Group International LLC.......718 475-8805
14711 34th Ave Flushing (11354) ***(G-5003)***
Groupe 16sur20 LLC (PA).......212 625-1620
198 Bowery New York (10012) ***(G-9998)***
Grover Cleveland Press Inc.......716 564-2222
2676 Sweet Home Rd Amherst (14228) ***(G-230)***
Grow Computer Inc.......646 535-2037
448 15th St Apt 1r Brooklyn (11215) ***(G-1953)***
Grownbeans Inc.......212 989-3486
110 Bank St Apt 2j New York (10014) ***(G-9999)***
Growth Products Ltd.......914 428-1316
80 Lafayette Ave White Plains (10603) ***(G-16456)***
Grphics Grafek, Syracuse *Also called Matt Industries Inc* ***(G-15368)***
Gruber Display Co Inc.......718 882-8220
3920g Merritt Ave Bronx (10466) ***(G-1286)***
Grumman Field Support Services.......516 575-0574
S Oyster Bay Rd Bethpage (11714) ***(G-842)***
Gruner + Jahr Prtg & Pubg Co.......212 463-1000
110 5th Ave Fl 7 New York (10011) ***(G-10000)***
Gruner + Jahr USA Group Inc (PA).......866 323-9336
1745 Broadway Fl 16 New York (10019) ***(G-10001)***
Gruner Jahr USA Publishing Div, New York *Also called Gruner + Jahr USA Group Inc* ***(G-10001)***
Grunt Apparel Inc.......646 878-6171
105 Duane St Apt 7c New York (10007) ***(G-10002)***
Gryphon Sensors LLC.......315 452-8882
5801 E Taft Rd North Syracuse (13212) ***(G-12404)***
Gs Communications USA, Brooklyn *Also called G S Communications USA Inc* ***(G-1913)***
Gsa Upstate NY (PA).......631 244-5744
755 Montauk Hwy Oakdale (11769) ***(G-12517)***
Gsb Digital, Long Island City *Also called Graphics Service Bureau Inc* ***(G-7462)***
Gschwind Group, Patchogue *Also called Suffolk McHy & Pwr Tl Corp* ***(G-12877)***
Gscp Emax Acquisition LLC.......212 902-1000
85 Broad St New York (10004) ***(G-10003)***
GSE Composites Inc.......631 389-1300
110 Oser Ave Hauppauge (11788) ***(G-5837)***
Gsn Government Security News, Massapequa Park *Also called World Business Media LLC* ***(G-7896)***
Gsp Components Inc.......585 436-3377
1190 Brooks Ave Rochester (14624) ***(G-13846)***
Gt Innovations LLC.......585 739-7659
7674 Swamp Rd Bergen (14416) ***(G-820)***
Gt Machine & Tool, Long Island City *Also called Cnc Manufacturing Corp* ***(G-7411)***
Gt Parts & Services, Clifton Park *Also called Worldwide Gas Turbine Pdts Inc* ***(G-3581)***
Gti America Inc.......716 332-6151
1207 Del Ave Unit 214 Buffalo (14209) ***(G-2859)***
Gti Graphic Technology Inc (PA).......845 562-7066
211 Dupont Ave Newburgh (12550) ***(G-12225)***
Guaranteed Printing Svc Co Inc.......212 929-2410
4710 33rd St Long Island City (11101) ***(G-7464)***
Guardian Booth LLC.......844 992-6684
29 Roosevelt Ave Ste 301 Spring Valley (10977) ***(G-14994)***
Guardian Concrete Inc.......518 372-0080
2140 Maxon Rd Ext Schenectady (12308) ***(G-14686)***
Guardian Concrete Steps, Schenectady *Also called Guardian Concrete Inc* ***(G-14686)***
Guardian Industries LLC.......315 787-7000
50 Forge Ave Geneva (14456) ***(G-5327)***
Guardian News & Media LLC.......917 900-4663
315 W 36th St Fl 8 New York (10018) ***(G-10004)***
Guardian Systems Tech Inc.......716 481-5597
659 Oakwood Ave East Aurora (14052) ***(G-4202)***
Guernica.......914 414-7318
63 3rd Pl Apt 4r Brooklyn (11231) ***(G-1954)***
Guernica Magazine, Brooklyn *Also called Guernica* ***(G-1954)***
Guess Inc.......716 298-3561
1826 Military Rd Spc 113 Niagara Falls (14304) ***(G-12292)***
Guest Informat LLC.......212 557-3010
110 E 42nd St Rm 1714 New York (10017) ***(G-10005)***
Guest of A Guest Inc.......212 206-0397
113 Jane St New York (10014) ***(G-10006)***
Guesthouse Division, Brooklyn *Also called R H Guest Incorporated* ***(G-2376)***
Guidance Channel, Woodbury *Also called Global Video LLC* ***(G-16620)***
Guidance Group Inc.......631 619-2600
40 Aero Rd Ste 2 Bohemia (11716) ***(G-1031)***
Guidance Group Inc.......631 756-4618
1 Huntington Quad 1n03 Melville (11747) ***(G-8029)***
Guild Diamond Products Inc (PA).......212 871-0007
1212 Avenue Of The Americ New York (10036) ***(G-10007)***
Guilderland Printing, Guilderland *Also called Custom Prtrs Guilderland Inc* ***(G-5654)***
Guilford Press, New York *Also called Guilford Publications Inc* ***(G-10008)***
Guilford Press, New York *Also called Guilford Publications Inc* ***(G-10009)***
Guilford Publications Inc.......212 431-9800
7 Penn Plz Ste 1200 New York (10001) ***(G-10008)***
Guilford Publications Inc.......800 365-7006
370 7th Ave Ste 1200 New York (10001) ***(G-10009)***
Guitar Specialist Inc.......914 401-9052
307 Rte 22 Goldens Bridge (10526) ***(G-5475)***
Guldenschuh Logging & Lbr LLC.......585 538-4750
143 Wheatland Center Rd Caledonia (14423) ***(G-3155)***
Gullo Machine & Tool Inc.......585 657-7318
4 E Main St Bloomfield (14469) ***(G-955)***
Gumbusters of New York, Brooklyn *Also called Metro Products & Services LLC* ***(G-2201)***
Gun Week, Buffalo *Also called Second Amendment Foundation* ***(G-3061)***
Gunlocke Company LLC (HQ).......585 728-5111
1 Gunlocke Dr Wayland (14572) ***(G-16071)***
Guosa Life Sciences Inc.......718 813-7806
708 3rd Ave Fl 6 New York (10017) ***(G-10010)***
Gupp Signs Inc.......585 244-5070
340 Lake Ave Rochester (14608) ***(G-13847)***
Gurley Precision Instrs Inc.......518 272-6300
514 Fulton St Troy (12180) ***(G-15607)***
Gustbuster Ltd.......631 391-9000
855 Conklin St Ste O Farmingdale (11735) ***(G-4777)***
Gutchess Freedom Inc.......716 492-2824
10699 Maple Grove Rd Freedom (14065) ***(G-5131)***
Gutchess Lumber Co Inc (PA).......607 753-3393
890 Mclean Rd Cortland (13045) ***(G-3876)***
Gutchess Lumber Co Inc.......716 492-2824
10699 Maple Grove Rd Freedom (14065) ***(G-5132)***
Guthrie Heli-ARC Inc.......585 548-5053
6276 Clinton Street Rd Bergen (14416) ***(G-821)***
Gutts Corporation of America, Irvington *Also called Guttz Corporation of America* ***(G-6505)***
Guttz Corporation of America.......914 591-9600
50 S Buckhout St Ste 104 Irvington (10533) ***(G-6505)***
Guyson Corporation of USa (HQ).......518 587-7894
13 Grande Blvd Saratoga Springs (12866) ***(G-14585)***
Gw Acquisition LLC.......212 736-4848
1370 Broadway Rm 1100 New York (10018) ***(G-10011)***
GW Lisk Company Inc.......315 548-2165
1369 Phelps Junction Rd Phelps (14532) ***(G-12977)***
Gw Manufacturing.......718 386-8078
24a Woodward Ave Ridgewood (11385) ***(G-13538)***
Gym Store Inc.......718 366-7804
5889 57th St Maspeth (11378) ***(G-7850)***
GYM STORE.COM, Maspeth *Also called Gym Store Inc* ***(G-7850)***
H & H Furniture Co.......718 850-5252
11420 101st Ave Jamaica (11419) ***(G-6648)***
H & H Hulls Inc.......518 828-1339
35 Industrial Tract Anx Hudson (12534) ***(G-6352)***
H & H Laboratories Inc (PA).......718 624-8041
61 4th St Brooklyn (11231) ***(G-1955)***
H & H Laboratories Inc.......718 624-8041
409 Hoyt St Brooklyn (11231) ***(G-1956)***
H & H Metal Specialty Inc.......716 665-2110
153 Hopkins Ave Jamestown (14701) ***(G-6720)***
H & H Technologies Inc.......631 567-3526
10 Colt Ct Ronkonkoma (11779) ***(G-14348)***

ALPHABETIC

(PA)=Parent Co (HQ)=Headquarters (DH)=Div Headquarters

2019 Harris
New York Manufacturers Directory

895

H & M Leasing Corp 631 225-5246
1245 Marconi Blvd Copiague (11726) **(G-3761)**
H & R Precision, Farmingdale *Also called Precision Envelope Co Inc* **(G-4856)**
H & S Edible Products Corp 914 413-3489
119 Fulton Ln Mount Vernon (10550) **(G-8404)**
H & T Goldman Corporation 800 822-0272
2 W 46th St Ste 607 New York (10036) **(G-10012)**
H A Guden Company Inc 631 737-2900
99 Raynor Ave Ronkonkoma (11779) **(G-14349)**
H and B Digital, New York *Also called A & M LLC* **(G-8687)**
H B Millwork Inc (PA) 631 289-8086
500 Long Island Ave Medford (11763) **(G-7949)**
H B Millwork Inc 631 924-4195
9 Old Dock Rd Yaphank (11980) **(G-16713)**
H Best Ltd 212 354-2400
1411 Broadway Fl 8 New York (10018) **(G-10013)**
H C Kionka & Co Inc 212 227-3155
15 Maiden Ln Ste 908 New York (10038) **(G-10014)**
H C Young Tool & Machine Co 315 463-0663
3700 New Court Ave Syracuse (13206) **(G-15336)**
H D M Labs Inc 516 431-8357
153 Kingston Blvd Island Park (11558) **(G-6515)**
H F Brown Machine Co Inc 315 732-6129
708 State St Utica (13502) **(G-15707)**
H F Cary & Sons 607 598-2563
70 Reniff Rd Lockwood (14859) **(G-7344)**
H F W Communications Inc (HQ) 315 703-7979
6437 Collamer Rd Ste 1 East Syracuse (13057) **(G-4344)**
H Freund Woodworking Co Inc 516 334-3774
589 Main St Westbury (11590) **(G-16337)**
H G Maybeck Co Inc 718 297-4410
17930 93rd Ave Ste 2 Jamaica (11433) **(G-6649)**
H Group LLC 212 719-5500
462 7th Ave Fl 9 New York (10018) **(G-10015)**
H H B Bakery of Little Neck 718 631-7004
24914 Horace Harding Expy Flushing (11362) **(G-5004)**
H K Technologies Inc 718 255-1898
4332 22nd St Ste 405 Long Island City (11101) **(G-7465)**
H Klein & Sons Inc 516 746-0163
95 Searing Ave Ste 2 Mineola (11501) **(G-8225)**
H L Robinson Sand & Gravel (PA) 607 659-5153
535 Ithaca Rd Candor (13743) **(G-3252)**
H M W, Brewster *Also called Hudson Machine Works Inc* **(G-1168)**
H Rindustries 516 487-3825
393 Jericho Tpke Mineola (11501) **(G-8226)**
H Risch Inc 585 442-0110
44 Saginaw Dr Rochester (14623) **(G-13848)**
H S Assembly Inc 585 266-4287
570 Hollandback Rochester (14605) **(G-13849)**
H T L & S Ltd 718 435-4474
5820 Fort Hamilton Pkwy Brooklyn (11219) **(G-1957)**
H T Specialty Inc 585 458-4060
70 Bermar Park Rochester (14624) **(G-13850)**
H THEOPHILE, New York *Also called Kathmando Valley Preservation* **(G-10417)**
H W Naylor Co Inc 607 263-5145
121 Main St Morris (13808) **(G-8335)**
H W Wilson Company Inc 718 588-8635
950 University Ave Bronx (10452) **(G-1287)**
H&E Service Corp 646 472-1936
400 Garden Cy Plz Ste 405 Garden City (11530) **(G-5261)**
H&F Products Inc 845 651-6100
51 Forest Rd Ste 360 Monroe (10950) **(G-8271)**
H&L Computers Inc 516 873-8088
13523 Northern Blvd Flushing (11354) **(G-5005)**
H2 At Hammerman, New York *Also called Hammerman Bros Inc* **(G-10026)**
H2gear Fashions LLC 347 787-7508
1065 Shepherd Ave Brooklyn (11208) **(G-1958)**
H2o Solutions Inc 518 527-0915
61 Major Dickinson Ave Stillwater (12170) **(G-15158)**
Haagen-Dazs, Farmingdale *Also called Nestle Healthcare Ntrtn Inc* **(G-4835)**
Haanen Packard Machinery Inc (PA) 518 747-2330
16 Allen St Hudson Falls (12839) **(G-6382)**
Haba USA 800 468-6873
4407 Jordan Rd Skaneateles (13152) **(G-14873)**
Habasit America Inc 716 824-8484
1400 Clinton St Buffalo (14206) **(G-2860)**
Habco Corp 631 789-1400
41 Ranick Dr E Amityville (11701) **(G-279)**
Habco Sales, Amityville *Also called Habco Corp* **(G-279)**
Habermaass Corporation 315 685-8919
4407 Jordan Rd Skaneateles (13152) **(G-14874)**
Habitat Magazine, New York *Also called Carol Group Ltd* **(G-9212)**
Hachette Book Group Inc (HQ) 800 759-0190
1290 Ave Of The Americas New York (10104) **(G-10016)**
Hachette Book Group USA 212 364-1200
237 Park Ave New York (10017) **(G-10017)**
Hacker Boat Company Inc (PA) 518 543-6731
8 Delaware Ave Silver Bay (12874) **(G-14859)**
Haculla Nyc Inc 718 886-3163
6805 Fresh Meadow Ln Fresh Meadows (11365) **(G-5199)**
Haddad Bros Inc (PA) 212 563-2117
28 W 36th St Rm 1026 New York (10018) **(G-10018)**
Haddad Bros Inc 718 377-5505
1200 Mcdonald Ave Brooklyn (11230) **(G-1959)**
Haddad Hosiery LLC 212 251-0022
34 W 33rd St Rm 401 New York (10001) **(G-10019)**
Hades Manufacturing Corp 631 249-4244
140 Finn Ct Farmingdale (11735) **(G-4778)**
Hadfield Inc 631 981-4314
840 S 2nd St Ronkonkoma (11779) **(G-14350)**
Hadley Exhibits Inc (PA) 716 874-3666
1700 Elmwood Ave Buffalo (14207) **(G-2861)**
Hadleys Fab-Weld Inc 315 926-5101
4202 Sunset Dr Marion (14505) **(G-7802)**
Hadp LLC 518 831-6824
602 Potential Pkwy Scotia (12302) **(G-14741)**
Hagadah Passover Bakery 718 638-1589
814 Bergen St Brooklyn (11238) **(G-1960)**
Hagedorn Communications Inc (PA) 914 636-7400
662 Main St Ste 1 New Rochelle (10801) **(G-8609)**
Hagedorn Communications Inc 914 636-7400
20 W 22nd St Ste 906 New York (10010) **(G-10020)**
Hagner Industries Inc 716 873-5720
95 Botsford Pl Buffalo (14216) **(G-2862)**
Hahns Old Fashioned Cake Co 631 249-3456
75 Allen Blvd Farmingdale (11735) **(G-4779)**
Haig Graphic Communications, Hauppauge *Also called Haig Press Inc* **(G-5838)**
Haig Press Inc 631 582-5800
690 Old Willets Path Hauppauge (11788) **(G-5838)**
Haights Cross Operating Co (HQ) 914 289-9400
10 New King St Ste 102 White Plains (10604) **(G-16457)**
Hailo Network Usa Inc 646 561-8552
568 Broadway Fl 11 New York (10012) **(G-10021)**
Hain Blueprint Inc 212 414-5741
1111 Marcus Ave Ste 100 New Hyde Park (11042) **(G-8537)**
Hain Celestial Group Inc (PA) 516 587-5000
1111 Marcus Ave Ste 100 New Hyde Park (11042) **(G-8538)**
Hain Refrigerated Foods Inc 425 485-2476
1111 Marcus Ave Ste 100 New Hyde Park (11042) **(G-8539)**
Haines Equipment Inc 607 566-8531
20 Carrington St Avoca (14809) **(G-516)**
Hair Color Research Group Inc 718 445-6026
13320 Whitestone Expy Flushing (11354) **(G-5006)**
Hair Ventures LLC (PA) 718 664-7689
94 Fargo Ln Irvington (10533) **(G-6506)**
Hairstory, Irvington *Also called Hair Ventures LLC* **(G-6506)**
Haitian Times Inc 718 230-8700
80 Lakeside Dr New Rochelle (10801) **(G-8610)**
Hakson Safety Wears Inc 613 667-3015
111 Colgate Ave Buffalo (14220) **(G-2863)**
Halcyon Business Publications 800 735-2732
400 Post Ave Ste 304 Westbury (11590) **(G-16338)**
Haldey Phrm Compounding, Bronx *Also called Emilior Phrm Compounding Inc* **(G-1268)**
Hale Electrical Dist Svcs Inc 716 818-7595
12088 Big Tree Rd Wales Center (14169) **(G-15901)**
Haley Concrete Inc (PA) 716 492-0849
10413 Delevan Elton Rd Delevan (14042) **(G-4070)**
Haleys Comet Seafood Corp 212 571-1828
605 3rd Ave Fl 34 New York (10158) **(G-10022)**
Halfmoon Town Water Department 518 233-7489
8 Brookwood Rd Waterford (12188) **(G-15976)**
Halfway House LLC 518 873-2198
7158 Us Route 9 Elizabethtown (12932) **(G-4432)**
Hallagan Manufacturing Co Inc 315 331-4640
500 Hoffman St Newark (14513) **(G-12195)**
Hallmark Hlth Care Sltions LLC 516 513-0959
200 Motor Pkwy Ste D26 Hauppauge (11788) **(G-5839)**
Hallock Fabricating Corp 631 727-2441
324 Doctors Path Riverhead (11901) **(G-13569)**
Halm Instrument Co Inc 516 676-6700
180 Glen Head Rd Glen Head (11545) **(G-5380)**
Halmark Architectural Finshg 718 272-1831
353 Stanley Ave Brooklyn (11207) **(G-1961)**
Halmode Apparel Inc 212 819-9114
1400 Brdwy 11th & Fl 16 New York (10018) **(G-10023)**
Halmode Petite Div, New York *Also called Halmode Apparel Inc* **(G-10023)**
Halo Associates 212 691-9549
289 Bleecker St Fl 5 New York (10014) **(G-10024)**
Halo Optical Products Inc 518 773-4256
9 Phair St Ste 1 Gloversville (12078) **(G-5457)**
Halpern Tool Corp (PA) 914 633-0038
111 Plain Ave New Rochelle (10801) **(G-8611)**
Hamil America Inc 212 244-2645
42 W 39th St Fl 15 New York (10018) **(G-10025)**
Hamilton County News, Amsterdam *Also called William J Kline & Son Inc* **(G-364)**
Hamilton Design Kit Homes, Queensbury *Also called Northern Design & Bldg Assoc* **(G-13435)**
Hamilton Marketing Corporation 585 395-0678
5211 Lake Rd S Brockport (14420) **(G-1191)**
Hamilton Printing Company Inc 518 732-2161
22 Hamilton Ave Troy (12180) **(G-15608)**
Hamlet Products Inc 914 665-0307
221 N Macquesten Pkwy Mount Vernon (10550) **(G-8405)**

Hamlin Bottle & Can Return Inc ... 585 259-1301
3423 Redman Rd Brockport (14420) *(G-1192)*
Hammer Packaging Corp (PA) ... 585 424-3880
200 Lucius Gordon Dr West Henrietta (14586) *(G-16242)*
Hammerman Bros Inc ... 212 956-2800
50 W 57th St Fl 12 New York (10019) *(G-10026)*
Hammond & Irving Inc (PA) ... 315 253-6265
254 North St Auburn (13021) *(G-482)*
Hammond Manufacturing Co Inc ... 716 630-7030
475 Cayuga Rd Cheektowaga (14225) *(G-3448)*
Hamodia Corp ... 718 338-5637
324 Avenue I Brooklyn (11230) *(G-1962)*
Hamodia Corp ... 718 853-9094
207 Foster Ave Brooklyn (11230) *(G-1963)*
Hampshire Chemical Corp ... 315 539-9221
228 E Main St Waterloo (13165) *(G-15995)*
Hampshire Jewels, New York *Also called Emsaru USA Corp (G-9669)*
Hampshire Lithographers, New York *Also called Advantage Quick Print Inc (G-8758)*
Hampshire Sub II Inc (HQ) ... 631 321-0923
114 W 41st St Fl 5 New York (10036) *(G-10027)*
Hampton Art LLC ... 631 924-1335
19 Scouting Blvd Medford (11763) *(G-7950)*
Hampton Press Incorporated ... 646 638-3800
307 7th Ave Rm 506 New York (10001) *(G-10028)*
Hampton Sand Corp ... 631 325-5533
1 High St Westhampton (11977) *(G-16402)*
Hampton Shipyards Inc ... 631 653-6777
7 Carter Ln East Quogue (11942) *(G-4278)*
Hampton Technologies LLC ... 631 924-1335
19 Scouting Blvd Medford (11763) *(G-7951)*
Hampton Transport Inc ... 631 716-4445
3655 Route 112 Coram (11727) *(G-3798)*
Hamptons Magazine, Southampton *Also called Hamptons Media LLC (G-14956)*
Hamptons Magazine ... 631 283-7125
67 Hampton Rd Unit 5 Southampton (11968) *(G-14955)*
Hamptons Media LLC ... 631 283-6900
67 Hampton Rd Unit 5 Southampton (11968) *(G-14956)*
Hamtronics Inc ... 585 392-9430
39 Willnick Cir Rochester (14626) *(G-13851)*
Han-Kraft Uniform Headwear, Buffalo *Also called Hankin Brothers Cap Co (G-2864)*
Hana Pastries Inc ... 718 369-7593
34 35th St Unit 9 Brooklyn (11232) *(G-1964)*
Hana Sheet Metal Inc ... 914 377-0773
9 Celli Pl 11 Yonkers (10701) *(G-16766)*
Hana Sportswear Inc ... 315 639-6332
321 Lakeview Dr Dexter (13634) *(G-4115)*
Hanan Products Company Inc ... 516 938-1000
196 Miller Pl Hicksville (11801) *(G-6094)*
Hanco Metal Products Inc ... 212 787-5992
25 Jay St Brooklyn (11201) *(G-1965)*
Hancock Quarry/Asphalt, Hancock *Also called Cobleskill Stone Products Inc (G-5710)*
Hancor Inc ... 607 565-3033
1 Wm Donnelly Ind Pkwy Waverly (14892) *(G-16066)*
Hand Care Inc ... 516 747-5649
42 Sugar Maple Dr Roslyn (11576) *(G-14447)*
Hand Held Products Inc (HQ) ... 315 554-6000
700 Visions Dr Skaneateles Falls (13153) *(G-14879)*
Hand Held Products Inc ... 315 554-6000
700 Visions Dr Skaneateles Falls (13153) *(G-14880)*
Handcraft Cabinetry Inc ... 914 681-9437
230 Ferris Ave Ste 1 White Plains (10603) *(G-16458)*
Handcraft Manufacturing Corp (PA) ... 212 251-0022
34 W 33rd St Rm 401 New York (10001) *(G-10029)*
Handmade Frames Inc ... 718 782-8364
1013 Grand St Ste 2 Brooklyn (11211) *(G-1966)*
Handone Studios Inc ... 585 421-8175
388 Mason Rd Fairport (14450) *(G-4634)*
Handsome Dans LLC (PA) ... 917 965-2499
186 1st Ave New York (10009) *(G-10030)*
Handy & Harman Ltd (HQ) ... 212 520-2300
590 Madison Ave Rm 3202 New York (10022) *(G-10031)*
Handy Laundry Products Corp (PA) ... 845 701-1111
382 Route 59 Ste 318 Airmont (10952) *(G-12)*
Handy Tool & Mfg Co Inc ... 718 478-9203
1205 Rockaway Ave Brooklyn (11236) *(G-1967)*
Hanes Supply Inc ... 518 438-0139
156 Railroad Ave Ste 3 Albany (12205) *(G-80)*
Hanesbrands Inc ... 212 576-9300
260 Madison Ave Fl 6 New York (10016) *(G-10032)*
Hanet Plastics Usa Inc ... 518 324-5850
139 Distribution Way Plattsburgh (12901) *(G-13123)*
Hanford Pharmaceuticals, Syracuse *Also called G C Hanford Manufacturing Co (G-15328)*
Hanger Inc ... 518 435-0840
1315 Central Ave Albany (12205) *(G-81)*
Hanger Inc ... 518 438-4546
6620 Fly Rd Ste 203 East Syracuse (13057) *(G-4345)*
Hanger Inc ... 718 575-5504
11835 Queens Blvd Ste Ll3 Forest Hills (11375) *(G-5074)*
Hanger Inc ... 516 678-3650
556 Merrick Rd Ste 101 Rockville Centre (11570) *(G-14233)*
Hanger Clinic, Elmira *Also called Hanger Prsthetcs & Ortho Inc (G-4489)*
Hanger Clinic, Oneonta *Also called Creative Orthotics Prosthetics (G-12636)*
Hanger Prosthectics Orthotics, Forest Hills *Also called Hanger Inc (G-5074)*
Hanger Prsthetcs & Ortho Inc ... 631 751-6966
2500 Route 347 3 Stony Brook (11790) *(G-15166)*
Hanger Prsthetcs & Ortho Inc ... 516 338-4466
5502 Brush Hollow Rd Westbury (11590) *(G-16339)*
Hanger Prsthetcs & Ortho Inc ... 607 277-6620
310 Taughannock Blvd 1a Ithaca (14850) *(G-6580)*
Hanger Prsthetcs & Ortho Inc ... 607 776-8013
47 W Steuben St Bath (14810) *(G-644)*
Hanger Prsthetcs & Ortho Inc ... 607 771-4672
65 Pennsylvania Ave Binghamton (13903) *(G-889)*
Hanger Prsthetcs & Ortho Inc ... 315 472-5200
910 Erie Blvd E Ste 3 Syracuse (13210) *(G-15337)*
Hanger Prsthetcs & Ortho Inc ... 607 795-1220
1300 College Ave Ste 1 Elmira (14901) *(G-4489)*
Hanger Prsthetcs & Ortho Inc ... 607 334-3320
6142 State Highway 12 # 14 Norwich (13815) *(G-12487)*
Hanger Prsthetcs & Ortho Inc ... 315 789-4810
787 State Route 5 And 20 Geneva (14456) *(G-5328)*
Hania By Anya Cole LLC ... 212 302-3550
16 W 56th St Fl 4 New York (10019) *(G-10033)*
Hankin Brothers Cap Co ... 716 892-8840
1910 Genesee St Buffalo (14211) *(G-2864)*
Hanna Altinis Co Inc ... 718 706-1134
3601 48th Ave Long Island City (11101) *(G-7466)*
Hannay Reels Inc ... 518 797-3791
553 State Route 143 Westerlo (12193) *(G-16389)*
Hansa Plastics Inc ... 631 269-9050
8 Meadow Glen Rd Kings Park (11754) *(G-6883)*
Hansa Usa LLC ... 646 412-6407
18 E 48th St Fl 3 New York (10017) *(G-10034)*
Hansae Co Ltd ... 212 354-6690
501 Fashion Ave Rm 208 New York (10018) *(G-10035)*
Hansen & Hansen Qulty Prtg Div, Syracuse *Also called Syracuse Computer Forms Inc (G-15436)*
Hansen Metal Fabrications, Farmington *Also called Hansen Steel (G-4915)*
Hansen Steel ... 585 398-2020
6021 County Road 41 Farmington (14425) *(G-4915)*
Hanson Aggregates East LLC ... 716 372-1574
4419 S Nine Mile Rd Allegany (14706) *(G-190)*
Hanson Aggregates East LLC ... 585 798-0762
Glenwood Ave Medina (14103) *(G-7980)*
Hanson Aggregates East LLC ... 716 372-1574
4419 S 9 Mile Rd Falconer (14733) *(G-4679)*
Hanson Aggregates East LLC ... 585 343-1787
5870 Main Rd Stafford (14143) *(G-15027)*
Hanson Aggregates East LLC ... 315 536-9391
131 Garfield Ave Penn Yan (14527) *(G-12957)*
Hanson Aggregates East LLC ... 315 493-3721
County Rt 47 Great Bend (13643) *(G-5526)*
Hanson Aggregates New York LLC ... 716 665-4620
2237 Allen St Jamesville (13078) *(G-6766)*
Hanson Aggregates New York LLC ... 716 665-4620
2237 Allen Street Ext Jamestown (14701) *(G-6721)*
Hanson Aggregates New York LLC ... 585 638-5841
6895 Ellicott Street Rd Pavilion (14525) *(G-12889)*
Hanson Aggregates New York LLC ... 315 469-5501
4800 Jamesville Rd Jamesville (13078) *(G-6767)*
Hanson Aggregates New York LLC ... 607 276-5881
546 Clark Rd Almond (14804) *(G-193)*
Hanson Aggregates PA Inc ... 315 858-1100
237 Kingdom Rd Jordanville (13361) *(G-6844)*
Hanson Aggregates PA Inc ... 518 568-2444
7904 St Hwy 5 Saint Johnsville (13452) *(G-14518)*
Hanson Aggregates PA LLC ... 585 624-3800
2049 County Rd 6 Honeoye Falls (14472) *(G-6266)*
Hanson Aggregates PA LLC ... 585 624-1220
2049 Honeoye Falls 6 Rd Honeoye Falls (14472) *(G-6267)*
Hanson Aggregates PA LLC ... 315 469-5501
4800 Jamesville Rd Jamesville (13078) *(G-6768)*
Hanson Aggregates PA LLC ... 315 685-3321
Rr 321 Skaneateles (13152) *(G-14875)*
Hanson Aggregates PA LLC ... 315 782-2300
25133 Nys Rt 3 Watertown (13601) *(G-16015)*
Hanson Aggregates PA LLC ... 315 821-7222
1780 State Route 12b Oriskany Falls (13425) *(G-12767)*
Hanson Aggregates PA LLC ... 315 393-3743
701 Cedar St Ogdensburg (13669) *(G-12574)*
Hanson Aggregates PA LLC ... 315 789-6202
2026 County Rd Ste 6 Oaks Corners (14518) *(G-12528)*
Hanson Aggregates PA LLC ... 585 436-3250
1535 Scottsville Rd Rochester (14623) *(G-13852)*
Hanson Ready Mix Concrete, Almond *Also called Hanson Aggregates New York LLC (G-193)*
Hanson Sign Companies, Falconer *Also called Hanson Sign Screen Prcess Corp (G-4680)*
Hanson Sign Screen Prcess Corp ... 716 661-3900
82 Carter St Falconer (14733) *(G-4680)*
Hanyan & Higgins Company Inc ... 315 769-8838
9772 State Highway 56 Massena (13662) *(G-7903)*
Happy Fella, New York *Also called Hf Mfg Corp (G-10090)*
Happy Sock, New York *Also called United Retail II (G-11954)*
Happy Software LLC ... 518 584-4668
11 Federal St Saratoga Springs (12866) *(G-14586)*

ALPHABETIC

Harbec Inc ALPHABETIC SECTION

Harbec Inc 585 265-0010
  358 Timothy Ln Ontario (14519) *(G-12654)*
Harbor Elc Fabrication Tls Inc 914 636-4400
  29 Portman Rd New Rochelle (10801) *(G-8612)*
Harbor Point Mineral Pdts Inc 315 797-1300
  71 Wurz Ave Utica (13502) *(G-15708)*
Harbor Wldg & Fabrication Corp 631 667-1880
  30 Railroad Ave Copiague (11726) *(G-3762)*
Harbors Maine Lobster LLC 516 775-2400
  969 Lakeville Rd New Hyde Park (11040) *(G-8540)*
Harborside Press 631 470-4967
  94 N Woodhull Rd Huntington (11743) *(G-6399)*
Harbour Roads, Albany Also called Kal-Harbour Inc *(G-90)*
Hard Manufacturing Co Inc 716 893-1800
  230 Grider St Buffalo (14215) *(G-2865)*
Hard Ten, Brooklyn Also called Dreams To Print *(G-1793)*
Hard Ten Clothing Inc 212 302-1321
  231 W 39th St Rm 606 New York (10018) *(G-10036)*
Harden Furniture LLC (PA) 315 675-3600
  8550 Mill Pond Way Mc Connellsville (13401) *(G-7925)*
Hardinge Inc (HQ) 607 734-2281
  1 Hardinge Dr Elmira (14903) *(G-4490)*
Hargrave Development 716 877-7880
  84 Shepard Ave Kenmore (14217) *(G-6859)*
Hargraves Bus MGT Consulting, Kenmore Also called Hargrave Development *(G-6859)*
Haring, J V & Son, Staten Island Also called J V Haring & Son *(G-15094)*
Harmac Medical Products Inc (PA) 716 897-4500
  2201 Bailey Ave Buffalo (14211) *(G-2866)*
Harmon and Castella Printing 845 471-9163
  164 Garden St Poughkeepsie (12601) *(G-13344)*
Harmonic Drive LLC 631 231-6630
  89 Cabot Ct Ste A Hauppauge (11788) *(G-5840)*
Harney & Sons Tea Corp (PA) 518 789-2100
  5723 Route 22 Millerton (12546) *(G-8193)*
Harold Wood Co Inc 716 873-1535
  329 Hinman Ave Buffalo (14216) *(G-2867)*
Harome Designs LLC 631 864-1900
  75 Modular Ave Commack (11725) *(G-3694)*
Harper International Corp 716 276-9900
  4455 Genesee St Ste 123 Buffalo (14225) *(G-2868)*
Harper International Corp 716 276-9900
  99 Sheldon Ave Depew (14043) *(G-4091)*
Harper Products Ltd 516 997-2330
  117 State St Westbury (11590) *(G-16340)*
Harper's Bazaar, New York Also called Hearst Corporation *(G-10068)*
Harpercollins 212 207-7000
  195 Broadway New York (10007) *(G-10037)*
Harpercollins Publishers LLC (HQ) 212 207-7000
  195 Broadway Fl 2 New York (10007) *(G-10038)*
Harpercollins Publishers LLC 212 553-4200
  233 Broadway Rm 1001 New York (10279) *(G-10039)*
Harpers Magazine Foundation 212 420-5720
  666 Broadway Fl 11 New York (10012) *(G-10040)*
Harris, Rome Also called Peraton Inc *(G-14266)*
Harris Assembly Group, Binghamton Also called Arnold-Davis LLC *(G-863)*
Harris Corporation 585 244-5830
  1680 University Ave Rochester (14610) *(G-13853)*
Harris Corporation 585 269-6600
  400 Initiative Dr Rochester (14624) *(G-13854)*
Harris Corporation 585 269-5001
  800 Lee Rd Bldg 601 Rochester (14606) *(G-13855)*
Harris Corporation 413 263-6200
  800 Lee Rd Rochester (14606) *(G-13856)*
Harris Corporation 631 630-4000
  1500 New Horizons Blvd Amityville (11701) *(G-280)*
Harris Corporation 585 269-5000
  2696 Manitou Rd Bldg 101 Rochester (14624) *(G-13857)*
Harris Corporation 585 244-5830
  570 Culver Rd Rochester (14609) *(G-13858)*
Harris Corporation 585 244-5830
  50 Carlson Rd Rochester (14610) *(G-13859)*
Harris Corporation 718 767-1100
  1902 Whitestone Expy # 204 Whitestone (11357) *(G-16541)*
Harris Corporation 585 244-5830
  1350 Jefferson Rd Rochester (14623) *(G-13860)*
Harris Globl Cmmunications Inc 585 244-5830
  1350 Jefferson Rd Rochester (14623) *(G-13861)*
Harris Logging Inc 518 792-1083
  39 Mud Pond Rd Queensbury (12804) *(G-13427)*
Harris Machine, Newark Also called Van Laeken Richard *(G-12211)*
Harris Rf Communications, Rochester Also called Harris Corporation *(G-13860)*
Harrison Bakery West 315 422-1468
  1306 W Genesee St Syracuse (13204) *(G-15338)*
Harrison Sportswear Inc 212 391-1051
  260 W 39th St Fl 7 New York (10018) *(G-10041)*
Harry N Abrams Incorporated 212 206-7715
  195 Broadway Fl 9 New York (10007) *(G-10042)*
Harry Winston Inc (HQ) 212 399-1000
  717 5th Ave Fl 9 New York (10022) *(G-10043)*
Harry's Razor Company, New York Also called Harrys Inc *(G-10044)*
Harrys Inc (PA) 888 212-6855
  75 Varick St Fl 9 New York (10013) *(G-10044)*

Hart Energy Publishing Lllp 212 621-4621
  110 William St Fl 18 New York (10038) *(G-10045)*
Hart Reproduction Services 212 704-0556
  242 W 36th St Rm 801 New York (10018) *(G-10046)*
Hart Rifle Barrel Inc 315 677-9841
  1680 Jamesville Ave Syracuse (13210) *(G-15339)*
Hart Specialties Inc 631 226-5600
  5000 New Horizons Blvd Amityville (11701) *(G-281)*
Hart Sports Inc 631 385-1805
  4 Roxanne Ct Huntington Station (11746) *(G-6443)*
Hart To Hart Industries Inc 716 492-2709
  13520 Chaffee Curriers Rd Chaffee (14030) *(G-3404)*
Hartchrom Inc 518 880-0411
  25 Gibson St Ste 1 Watervliet (12189) *(G-16047)*
Hartford Hwy Dept 315 724-0654
  Rr 12 New Hartford (13413) *(G-8506)*
Hartford Town Park System, New Hartford Also called Hartford Hwy Dept *(G-8506)*
Hartman Enterprises Inc 315 363-7300
  455 Elizabeth St Oneida (13421) *(G-12610)*
Harvard University Press 212 337-0280
  150 5th Ave Ste 632 New York (10011) *(G-10047)*
Harvard Woven Label, New York Also called Imperial-Harvard Label Co *(G-10186)*
Harvest Homes Inc 518 895-2341
  1331 Cole Rd Delanson (12053) *(G-4069)*
Harvest Technologies Inc 518 899-7124
  36 Featherfoil Way Ballston Spa (12020) *(G-585)*
Harvy Canes, Flushing Also called Harvy Surgical Supply Corp *(G-5007)*
Harvy Surgical Supply Corp 718 939-1122
  3435 Collins Pl Flushing (11354) *(G-5007)*
Harwitt Industries Inc 516 623-9787
  61 S Main St Unit A Freeport (11520) *(G-5161)*
Hasco Componets 516 328-9292
  906 Jericho Tpke New Hyde Park (11040) *(G-8541)*
Haskell Jewels Ltd (PA) 212 764-3332
  390 5th Ave Fl 2 New York (10018) *(G-10048)*
Haskell Machine & Tool Inc 607 749-2421
  5 S Fulton St Homer (13077) *(G-6255)*
Hastings Hide Inc 516 295-2400
  372 Doughty Blvd Inwood (11096) *(G-6492)*
Hastings Tile & Bath Inc (PA) 631 285-3330
  711 Koehler Ave Ste 8 Ronkonkoma (11779) *(G-14351)*
Hat Attack I Bujibaja, Bronx Also called Hat Attack Inc *(G-1288)*
Hat Attack Inc (PA) 718 994-1000
  4643 Bullard Ave Ste A Bronx (10470) *(G-1288)*
Hat Depot, Brooklyn Also called Room At The Top Inc *(G-2414)*
Hat Factory Furniture Co 914 788-6288
  1000 N Division St Ste 8 Peekskill (10566) *(G-12921)*
Hatfield Metal Fab Inc 845 454-9078
  16 Hatfield Ln Poughkeepsie (12603) *(G-13345)*
Hathaway Prcess Instrmentation, Amherst Also called Allied Motion Systems Corp *(G-210)*
Hatherleigh Company Ltd 607 538-1092
  62545 State Highway 10 Hobart (13788) *(G-6163)*
Haun Welding Supply Inc 607 846-2289
  1100 Sullivan St Elmira (14901) *(G-4491)*
Haun Welding Supply Inc 315 592-5012
  214 N 4th St Fulton (13069) *(G-5219)*
Hauppauge Computer Works Inc (HQ) 631 434-1600
  909 Motor Pkwy Hauppauge (11788) *(G-5841)*
Hauppauge Digital Inc (PA) 631 434-1600
  909 Motor Pkwy Hauppauge (11788) *(G-5842)*
Hauppuge Cmpt Dgtal Erope Sarl, Hauppauge Also called Hauppauge Computer Works Inc *(G-5841)*
Haute By Blair Stanley LLC 212 557-7868
  330 E 38th St Apt 23e New York (10016) *(G-10049)*
Havaianas, New York Also called Alpargatas Usa Inc *(G-8807)*
Have Your Cake Kitchen LLC 646 820-8074
  291 Union St Phb Brooklyn (11231) *(G-1968)*
Haverstraw Quarry, Haverstraw Also called Tilcon New York Inc *(G-5982)*
Hawk-I Security Inc 631 656-1056
  355 Oser Ave Hauppauge (11788) *(G-5843)*
Hawkins Fabrics Inc (PA) 518 773-9550
  328 N Perry St Johnstown (12095) *(G-6830)*
Hawthorne Garden Company (HQ) 516 883-6550
  800 Port Washington Blvd Port Washington (11050) *(G-13263)*
Hawthorne Gardening Co., Port Washington Also called Hawthorne Garden Company *(G-13263)*
Hawver Display Inc (PA) 585 544-2290
  140 Carter St Rochester (14621) *(G-13862)*
Hayman-Chaffey Designs Inc 212 889-7771
  137 E 25th St New York (10010) *(G-10050)*
Haymarket Group Ltd 212 239-0855
  12 W 37th St 9 New York (10018) *(G-10051)*
Haymarket Media Inc (HQ) 646 638-6000
  275 7th Ave Fl 10 New York (10001) *(G-10052)*
Haynes Roberts Inc 212 989-1901
  601 W 26th St Rm 1655 New York (10001) *(G-10053)*
Hazlitt 1852 Vineyards, Hector Also called Hazlitts 1852 Vineyards Inc *(G-5999)*
Hazlitts 1852 Vineyards Inc 607 546-9463
  5712 State Route 414 Hector (14841) *(G-5999)*
Hazlow Electronics Inc 585 325-5323
  49 Saint Bridgets Dr Rochester (14605) *(G-13863)*

HB Athletic Inc (PA) 914 560-8422
56 Harrison St Ste 305 New Rochelle (10801) **(G-8613)**
Hbs, Grea. Neck *Also called Toni Industries Inc* **(G-5596)**
Hc Brill Co Inc 716 685-4000
3765 Walden Ave Lancaster (14086) **(G-7023)**
HC Contracting Inc 212 643-9292
318 W 39th St Fl 4 New York (10018) **(G-10054)**
Hci Engineering 315 336-3450
5880 Bartlett Rd Rome (13440) **(G-14252)**
Hdm Hydraulics LLC 716 694-8004
125 Fire Tower Dr Tonawanda (14150) **(G-15546)**
Heads & Tails Lure Co 607 739-7900
283 Hibbard Rd Horseheads (14845) **(G-6318)**
Health Care Compliance (HQ) 516 478-4100
30 Jericho Executive Plz 400c Jericho (11753) **(G-6790)**
Health Care Originals Inc 585 471-8215
1 Pleasant St Ste 442 Rochester (14604) **(G-13864)**
Health Care Products 631 789-8228
369 Bayview Ave Amityville (11701) **(G-282)**
Health Matters America Inc 716 235-8772
2501 Broadway St Ste 2 Buffalo (14227) **(G-2869)**
Healthalliance Hospital 845 338-2500
105 Marys Ave Kingston (12401) **(G-6901)**
Healthee Endeavors Inc 718 653-5499
3565c Boston Rd Bronx (10469) **(G-1289)**
Healthone Pharmacy Inc 718 495-9015
119 Pennsylvania Ave Brooklyn (11207) **(G-1969)**
Healthway Home Products Inc 315 298-2904
3420 Maple Ave Pulaski (13142) **(G-13385)**
Healthway Products Company 315 207-1410
249a Mitchell St Oswego (13126) **(G-12778)**
Healthy Basement Systems LLC 516 650-9046
79 Cedarhurst Ave Medford (11763) **(G-7952)**
Healthy Brand Oil Corp (PA) 718 937-0806
5215 11th St Ste A Long Island City (11101) **(G-7467)**
Healthy N Fit Intl Inc (PA) 800 338-5200
7 Sutton Pl Ste A Brewster (10509) **(G-1166)**
Healthy Way of Life Magazine 718 616-1681
1529 Voorhies Ave Brooklyn (11235) **(G-1970)**
Heany Industries Inc 585 889-2700
249 Briarwood Ln Scottsville (14546) **(G-14750)**
Hearing Aid Office, The, Albany *Also called Benway-Haworth-Lwlr-Iacosta He* **(G-46)**
Hearing Spech Ctr of Rochester 585 286-9373
1170 Ridge Rd Ste 2 Webster (14580) **(G-16086)**
Hearst Bus Communications Inc (PA) 212 649-2000
300 W 57th St Fl 2 New York (10019) **(G-10055)**
Hearst Business Media (HQ) 516 227-1300
50 Charles Lindbergh Blvd # 103 Uniondale (11553) **(G-15669)**
Hearst Business Media Corp 631 650-6151
3500 Sunrise Hwy Ste 100 Great River (11739) **(G-5601)**
Hearst Business Media Corp 631 650-4441
300 W 57th St Fl 2 New York (10019) **(G-10056)**
Hearst Business Publishing Inc 212 969-7500
888 7th Ave Fl 2 New York (10106) **(G-10057)**
Hearst Communications Inc (HQ) 212 649-2000
300 W 57th St New York (10019) **(G-10058)**
Hearst Communications Inc 212 247-1014
828 9th Ave New York (10019) **(G-10059)**
Hearst Communications Inc (HQ) 212 649-2000
300 W 57th St New York (10019) **(G-10060)**
Hearst Corporation (PA) 212 649-2000
300 W 57th St Fl 42 New York (10019) **(G-10061)**
Hearst Corporation 212 649-3100
300 W 57th St Fl 29 New York (10019) **(G-10062)**
Hearst Corporation 212 903-5366
224 W 57th St Frnt 1 New York (10019) **(G-10063)**
Hearst Corporation 212 767-5800
1633 Broadway Fl 44 New York (10019) **(G-10064)**
Hearst Corporation 516 382-4580
810 7th Ave New York (10019) **(G-10065)**
Hearst Corporation 518 454-5694
645 Albany Shaker Rd Albany (12211) **(G-82)**
Hearst Corporation 212 649-4271
300 W 57th St Fl 21 New York (10019) **(G-10066)**
Hearst Corporation 212 204-4300
1440 Broadway Fl 13 New York (10018) **(G-10067)**
Hearst Corporation 212 903-5000
300 W 57th St Fl 42 New York (10019) **(G-10068)**
Hearst Corporation 212 649-3204
300 W 57th St Fl 32 New York (10019) **(G-10069)**
Hearst Corporation 212 649-2275
300 W 57th St Fl 42 New York (10019) **(G-10070)**
Hearst Digital Studios Inc 212 969-7552
300 W 57th St New York (10019) **(G-10071)**
Hearst Enterprises, New York *Also called Hearst Corporation* **(G-10061)**
Hearst Entertainment, New York *Also called Hearst Digital Studios Inc* **(G-10071)**
Hearst Holdings Inc (HQ) 212 649-2000
300 W 57th St New York (10019) **(G-10072)**
Hearst Interactive Media, New York *Also called Hearst Communications Inc* **(G-10060)**
Heart of Tea 917 725-3164
419 Lafayette St Fl 2f New York (10003) **(G-10073)**
Hearth Cabinets and More Ltd 315 641-1197
4483 Buckley Rd Liverpool (13088) **(G-7234)**
Heartland Commerce Inc 845 920-0800
1 Blue Hill Plz Ste 16 Pearl River (10965) **(G-12898)**
Hearts of Palm LLC 212 944-6660
1411 Broadway Fl 23 New York (10018) **(G-10074)**
Hearts of Palm LLC (PA) 212 944-6660
1411 Broadway Fl 25 New York (10018) **(G-10075)**
Heartwood Specialties Inc 607 654-0102
10249 Gibson Rd Hammondsport (14840) **(G-5704)**
Heary Bros Lghtning Protection 716 941-6141
11291 Moore Rd Springville (14141) **(G-15018)**
Heat USA II LLC 212 564-4328
35 E 21st St New York (10010) **(G-10076)**
Heath Manufacturing Company 800 444-3140
700 Ellicott St Batavia (14020) **(G-627)**
Heath Outdoors Products, Batavia *Also called Heath Manufacturing Company* **(G-627)**
Heatherdell RB Hammers, Blauvelt *Also called Rbhammers Corp* **(G-939)**
Heating & Burner Supply Inc 718 665-0006
479 Walton Ave Bronx (10451) **(G-1290)**
Hebeler LLC (PA) 716 873-9300
2000 Military Rd Tonawanda (14150) **(G-15547)**
Hebeler Process Solutions LLC 716 873-9300
2000 Military Rd Tonawanda (14150) **(G-15548)**
Hecht & Sohn Glass Co Inc 718 782-8295
406 Willoughby Ave Brooklyn (11205) **(G-1971)**
Hector Pt Sr Rehab Svc Pllc 518 371-5554
1 Wall St Clifton Park (12065) **(G-3567)**
Hedges and Gardens, East Hampton *Also called Irony Limited Inc* **(G-4238)**
Heed LLC 646 708-7111
462 Fashion Ave Fl 5 New York (10018) **(G-10077)**
Hefti, New Rochelle *Also called Harbor Elc Fabrication Tls Inc* **(G-8612)**
Heidelberg Group Inc 315 866-0999
3056 State Hwy Rte 28 N Herkimer (13350) **(G-6040)**
Heindl Printers, Rochester *Also called Louis Heindl & Son Inc* **(G-13917)**
Heineck Associates Inc 631 207-2347
28 Curtis Ave Bellport (11713) **(G-805)**
Heintz & Weber Co Inc 716 852-7171
150 Reading St Buffalo (14220) **(G-2870)**
Heinz Mr 718 761-3997
146 Melvin Ave Staten Island (10314) **(G-15084)**
Heleo.com, New York *Also called Helium Media Inc* **(G-10078)**
Helgen Industries Inc 631 841-6300
431 Bayview Ave Amityville (11701) **(G-283)**
Heliojet Cleaning Tech Inc 585 768-8710
57 North St Ste 120 Le Roy (14482) **(G-7118)**
Helium Media Inc 917 596-4081
165 Duane St Apt 7b New York (10013) **(G-10078)**
Hellas Stone Inc 718 545-4716
3344 9th St Astoria (11106) **(G-430)**
Heller Performance Polymers, New York *Also called Atc Plastics LLC* **(G-8943)**
Helmel Engineering Pdts Inc 716 297-8644
6520 Lockport Rd Niagara Falls (14305) **(G-12293)**
Helmer Avenue, West Winfield *Also called Precisionmatics Co Inc* **(G-16306)**
Helmont Mills Inc (HQ) 516 568-7913
15 Lion Ave Saint Johnsville (13452) **(G-14519)**
Helvetica Press Incorporated 212 737-1857
244 5th Ave New York (10001) **(G-10079)**
Hemisphere Novelties Inc 914 378-4100
167 Saw Mill River Rd 3c Yonkers (10701) **(G-16767)**
Hempstead Sentinel Inc 516 486-5000
55 Chasner St Hempstead (11550) **(G-6013)**
Hemstrought's Bakeries, New Hartford *Also called B & D Enterprises of Utica* **(G-8501)**
Henderson Products Inc 315 785-0994
22686 Fisher Rd Ste A Watertown (13601) **(G-16016)**
Henderson Truck Equipment, Watertown *Also called Henderson Products Inc* **(G-16016)**
Hendrickson Custom Cabinetry 718 401-0137
132 Saint Anns Ave Fl 2 Bronx (10454) **(G-1291)**
Hengyuan Copper USA Inc 718 357-6666
14107 20th Ave Ste 506 Whitestone (11357) **(G-16542)**
Hennig Custom Woodwork Corp 516 536-3460
2497 Long Beach Rd Oceanside (11572) **(G-12540)**
Hennig Custom Woodworking, Oceanside *Also called Hennig Custom Woodwork Corp* **(G-12540)**
Henpecked Husband Farms Corp 631 728-2800
1212 Speonk Riverhead Rd Speonk (11972) **(G-14985)**
Henry Design Studios Inc 516 801-2760
129 Birch Hill Rd Ste 2 Locust Valley (11560) **(G-7349)**
Henry Dunay Designs Inc 212 768-9700
10 W 46th St Ste 1200 New York (10036) **(G-10080)**
Henry Holt and Company LLC 646 307-5095
175 5th Ave Ste 400 New York (10010) **(G-10081)**
Henry Morgan 718 317-5013
433 Tennyson Dr Staten Island (10312) **(G-15085)**
Henry Newman LLC 607 273-8512
312 4th St Ithaca (14850) **(G-6581)**
Henry Schein Fincl Svcs LLC (HQ) 631 843-5500
135 Duryea Rd Melville (11747) **(G-8030)**
Henry Schein International Inc, Melville *Also called Henry Schein Fincl Svcs LLC* **(G-8030)**
Henry Segal Co, Woodmere *Also called Shane Tex Inc* **(G-16642)**
Henrys Deals Inc 347 821-4685
1002 Quentin Rd Ste 2009 Brooklyn (11223) **(G-1972)**

ALPHABETIC

(PA)=Parent Co (HQ)=Headquarters (DH)=Div Headquarters
2019 Harris
New York Manufacturers Directory
899

Herald Newspapers Company Inc (HQ).....315 470-0011
220 S Warren St Syracuse (13202) *(G-15340)*
Herald Publishing Company LLC.....315 470-2022
4 Times Sq Fl 23 New York (10036) *(G-10082)*
Herald Statesman, Yonkers *Also called Gannett Stllite Info Ntwrk Inc (G-16761)*
Herbert Jaffe Inc.....718 392-1956
4011 Skillman Ave Long Island City (11104) *(G-7468)*
Hercules, Huntington Station *Also called I A S National Inc (G-6447)*
Hercules Candy Co.....315 463-4339
720 W Manlius St East Syracuse (13057) *(G-4346)*
Hercules Gift & Gourmet, East Syracuse *Also called Hercules Candy Co (G-4346)*
Hercules Group Inc.....212 813-8000
27 Seaview Blvd Port Washington (11050) *(G-13264)*
Hercules Heat Treating Corp.....718 625-1266
101 Classon Ave 113 Brooklyn (11205) *(G-1973)*
Hercules International Inc.....631 423-6900
95 W Hills Rd Huntington Station (11746) *(G-6444)*
Herff Jones LLC.....607 936-2366
262 W 2nd St Corning (14830) *(G-3820)*
Hergo Ergonomic Support (PA).....718 894-0639
5601 55th Ave Maspeth (11378) *(G-7851)*
Heritage Contract Flooring LLC.....716 853-1555
29 Depot St Buffalo (14206) *(G-2871)*
Heritage Packaging, Victor *Also called W Stuart Smith Inc (G-15876)*
Heritage Printing Center.....518 563-8240
94 Margaret St Plattsburgh (12901) *(G-13124)*
Heritage Wide Plank Flooring, Riverhead *Also called Custom Woodwork Ltd (G-13566)*
Herkimer Cheese, Ilion *Also called Original Hrkmer Cnty Chese Inc (G-6477)*
Herkimer Diamond Mines Inc.....315 891-7355
800 Mohawk St Herkimer (13350) *(G-6041)*
Herkimer Tool & Equipment Co, Herkimer *Also called Herkimer Tool & Machining Corp (G-6042)*
Herkimer Tool & Machining Corp.....315 866-2110
125 Marginal Rd Herkimer (13350) *(G-6042)*
Herman H Sticht Company Inc.....718 852-7602
45 Main St Ste 401 Brooklyn (11201) *(G-1974)*
Herman Hall Communications.....718 941-1879
1630 Nostrand Ave Brooklyn (11226) *(G-1975)*
Herman Kay, New York *Also called Mystic Inc (G-10869)*
Herman Kay Company Ltd.....212 239-2025
463 7th Ave Fl 12 New York (10018) *(G-10083)*
Hermann Gerdens Inc.....631 841-3132
1725 N Strongs Rd Copiague (11726) *(G-3763)*
Hermann J Wiemer Vineyard.....607 243-7971
3962 Rte 14 Dundee (14837) *(G-4160)*
Hermosa Corp.....315 768-4320
102 Main St New York Mills (13417) *(G-12188)*
Heron Hill Vineyards Inc (PA).....607 868-4241
9301 County Route 76 Hammondsport (14840) *(G-5705)*
Heron Hill Winery, Hammondsport *Also called Heron Hill Vineyards Inc (G-5705)*
Herr Manufacturing Co Inc.....716 754-4341
17 Pearce Ave Tonawanda (14150) *(G-15549)*
Herris Gourmet Inc.....917 578-2308
536 Grand St Brooklyn (11211) *(G-1976)*
Herrmann Group LLC.....716 876-9798
2320 Elmwood Ave Kenmore (14217) *(G-6860)*
Hersco-Arch Products, Long Island City *Also called Hersco-Orthotic Labs Corp (G-7469)*
Hersco-Orthotic Labs Corp.....718 391-0416
3928 Crescent St Long Island City (11101) *(G-7469)*
Hershel Horowitz Corp.....212 719-1710
50 W 47th St Ste 2011 New York (10036) *(G-10084)*
Hershey Kiss 203 Inc.....516 503-3740
3536 Bunker Ave Wantagh (11793) *(G-15922)*
Hertling Trousers Inc.....718 784-6100
236 Greenpoint Ave Brooklyn (11222) *(G-1977)*
Hes Inc.....607 359-2974
6303 Symonds Hill Rd Addison (14801) *(G-6)*
Hesperus Nauticals Inc (HQ).....516 974-3016
115 N Broadway Ste 206 Hicksville (11801) *(G-6095)*
Hess Corporation (PA).....212 997-8500
1185 Ave Of The Amer New York (10036) *(G-10085)*
Hess Energy Exploration Ltd (HQ).....732 750-6500
1185 Ave Of The Americas New York (10036) *(G-10086)*
Hess Explrtion Prod Hldngs Ltd (HQ).....732 750-6000
1185 Ave Of The Americas New York (10036) *(G-10087)*
Hess Oil Virgin Island Corp.....212 997-8500
1185 Ave Of The Amer 39 New York (10036) *(G-10088)*
Hess Pipeline Corporation.....212 997-8500
1185 Ave Of The Amer 39 New York (10036) *(G-10089)*
Hexion Inc.....518 792-8040
64 Fernan Rd South Glens Falls (12803) *(G-14936)*
Hey Doll, New York *Also called Lesilu Productions Inc (G-10554)*
Hf Mfg Corp (PA).....212 594-9142
1460 Broadway New York (10036) *(G-10090)*
Hf Technologies LLC.....585 254-5030
810 Martin Rd Hamlin (14464) *(G-5700)*
HFC Prestige Intl US LLC.....212 389-7800
350 5th Ave New York (10118) *(G-10091)*
Hfi, New York *Also called Home Fashions Intl LLC (G-10120)*
Hgi Skydyne, Port Jervis *Also called Hornet Group Inc (G-13230)*
Hh Liquidating Corp.....646 282-2500
110 E 59th St Fl 34 New York (10022) *(G-10092)*
HHS Pharmaceuticals Inc.....347 674-1670
107 Hamilton Pl New York (10031) *(G-10093)*
Hl Speed Envelope Co Inc.....718 617-1600
560 S 3rd Ave Ste 1 Mount Vernon (10550) *(G-8406)*
Hl Tech Signs of NY Inc.....516 794-7880
415 E Meadow Ave East Meadow (11554) *(G-4252)*
Hl Wines, New York *Also called Frank Wines Inc (G-9842)*
Hi-Lites, Watkins Glen *Also called Skylark Publications Ltd (G-16060)*
Hi-Med, Old Bethpage *Also called Hitemco Med Applications Inc (G-12585)*
Hi-Tech Advanced Solutions Inc.....718 926-3488
10525 65th Ave Apt 4h Forest Hills (11375) *(G-5075)*
Hi-Tech Cnc Machining Corp.....914 668-5090
13 Elm Ave Mount Vernon (10550) *(G-8407)*
Hi-Tech Industries NY Inc.....607 217-7361
23 Ozalid Rd Johnson City (13790) *(G-6810)*
Hi-Tech Metals Inc.....718 894-1212
5920 56th Ave Maspeth (11378) *(G-7852)*
Hi-Tech Packg World-Wide LLC.....845 947-1912
110 Corporate Dr New Windsor (12553) *(G-8646)*
Hi-Tech Pharmacal - An Akorn, Amityville *Also called Hi-Tech Pharmacal Co Inc (G-284)*
Hi-Tech Pharmacal - An Akorn, Amityville *Also called Hi-Tech Pharmacal Co Inc (G-285)*
Hi-Tech Pharmacal Co Inc (HQ).....631 789-8228
369 Bayview Ave Amityville (11701) *(G-284)*
Hi-Tech Pharmacal Co Inc.....631 789-8228
26 Edison St Amityville (11701) *(G-285)*
Hi-Temp Brazing Inc.....631 491-4917
539 Acorn St Deer Park (11729) *(G-3983)*
Hi-Temp Fabrication Inc.....716 852-5655
15 Lawrence Bell Dr Buffalo (14221) *(G-2872)*
Hi-Tron Semiconductor Corp.....631 231-1500
85 Engineers Rd Hauppauge (11788) *(G-5844)*
Hibert Publishing LLC.....914 381-7474
222 Purchase St Rye (10580) *(G-14482)*
Hibu Inc (HQ).....516 730-1900
90 Merrick Ave Ste 530 East Meadow (11554) *(G-4253)*
Hickey Freeman Tailored CL Inc (HQ).....585 467-7240
1155 N Clinton Ave Rochester (14621) *(G-13865)*
Hickory Hollow Wind Cellars, Dundee *Also called Hickory Road Land Co LLC (G-4161)*
Hickory Road Land Co LLC.....607 243-9114
5289 Route 14 Dundee (14837) *(G-4161)*
Hicksville Machine Works Corp.....516 931-1524
761 S Broadway Hicksville (11801) *(G-6096)*
Hig Capital, Williamsville *Also called Ashton-Potter USA Ltd (G-16568)*
Higgins Supl Co, Mc Graw *Also called Higgins Supply Company Inc (G-7927)*
Higgins Supply Company Inc.....607 836-6474
18-25 South St Mc Graw (13101) *(G-7927)*
High End Print Solutions Inc.....585 325-5320
250 Cumberland St Ste 100 Rochester (14605) *(G-13866)*
High Energy U. S. A., New York *Also called Kidz World Inc (G-10442)*
High Falls Brewing Company LLC (HQ).....585 546-1030
445 Saint Paul St Rochester (14605) *(G-13867)*
High Falls Operating Co LLC.....585 546-1030
445 Saint Paul St Rochester (14605) *(G-13868)*
High Frequency Tech Co Inc.....631 242-3020
1531 Smithtown Ave Ste 1 Bohemia (11716) *(G-1032)*
High Line Lube LLC.....914 684-0170
374 Central Ave White Plains (10606) *(G-16459)*
High Performance Sftwr USA Inc.....866 616-4958
145 Hook Creek Blvd Valley Stream (11581) *(G-15782)*
High Point Design LLC.....212 354-2400
1411 Broadway Fl 8 New York (10018) *(G-10094)*
High Prfmce Plymr Cmposits Div, Medford *Also called Enecon Corporation (G-7946)*
High Quality Video Inc (PA).....212 686-9534
12 W 27th St Fl 7 New York (10001) *(G-10095)*
High Ridge News LLC.....718 548-7412
5818 Broadway Bronx (10463) *(G-1292)*
High Speed Hammer Company Inc.....585 266-4287
313 Norton St Rochester (14621) *(G-13869)*
High Voltage Inc.....518 329-3275
31 County Route 7a Copake (12516) *(G-3746)*
Highcrest Investors LLC (HQ).....212 702-4323
445 Hamilton Ave Ste 1210 New York (10153) *(G-10096)*
Higher Power Industries Inc.....914 709-9800
11 Sunny Slope Ter Yonkers (10703) *(G-16768)*
Highland Injection Molding.....716 945-2424
175 Rochester St Salamanca (14779) *(G-14525)*
Highland Museum & Lighthouse.....508 487-1121
111 M Simons Rd Cairo (12413) *(G-3148)*
Highland Organization Corp.....631 991-3240
435 Unit 23 Brook Ave Deer Park (11729) *(G-3984)*
Highland Valley Supply Inc.....845 849-2863
30 Airport Dr Wappingers Falls (12590) *(G-15934)*
Highlander Realty Inc.....914 235-8073
70 Church St New Rochelle (10805) *(G-8614)*
Highline Media LLC.....859 692-2100
375 Park Ave New York (10152) *(G-10097)*
Highrange Fuels Inc.....914 930-8300
96 Oregon Rd Cortlandt Manor (10567) *(G-3902)*
Highside Inc.....917 525-3340
531 W 143rd St Apt 3c New York (10031) *(G-10098)*

Highway Garage 518 568-2837
110 State Highway 331 Saint Johnsville (13452) *(G-14520)*
Highway Toll ADM LLC 516 684-9584
66 Powerhouse Rd Ste 301 Roslyn Heights (11577) *(G-14455)*
Hill Crest Press 518 943-0671
138 Grandview Ave Catskill (12414) *(G-3304)*
Hill Knitting Mills Inc 718 846-5000
10005 92nd Ave Ste Mgmt Richmond Hill (11418) *(G-13504)*
Hillary Merchant Inc 646 575-9242
2 Wall St Ste 807 New York (10005) *(G-10099)*
Hillburn Granite Company Inc 845 357-8900
166 Sixth St Hillburn (10931) *(G-6153)*
Hilliard Corporation (PA) 607 733-7121
100 W 4th St Elmira (14901) *(G-4492)*
Hilliard Corporation 607 733-7121
1420 College Ave Elmira (14901) *(G-4493)*
Hills Pet Products Inc (HQ) 212 310-2000
300 Park Ave New York (10022) *(G-10100)*
Hillside Iron Works, Waterford *Also called Maximum Security Products Corp* *(G-15977)*
Hillside Printing Inc 718 658-6719
16013 Hillside Ave Jamaica (11432) *(G-6650)*
Hilltop Slate Inc 518 642-1453
Rr 22 Box A Middle Granville (12849) *(G-8110)*
Hilltown Pork Inc (PA) 518 781-4050
12948 State Route 22 Canaan (12029) *(G-3206)*
Hilord Chemical Corporation 631 234-7373
70 Engineers Rd Hauppauge (11788) *(G-5845)*
Himatsingka America Inc (HQ) 212 824-2949
261 5th Ave Rm 1400 New York (10016) *(G-10101)*
Himatsingka America Inc 212 252-0802
261 5th Ave Rm 501 New York (10016) *(G-10102)*
Hinge Inc 502 445-3111
137 5th Ave Fl 5 New York (10010) *(G-10103)*
Hinspergers Poly Industries 585 798-6625
430 W Oak Orchard St Medina (14103) *(G-7981)*
Hipotronics Inc (HQ) 845 279-8091
1650 Route 22 Brewster (10509) *(G-1167)*
Hippo Industries, Oyster Bay *Also called Engineering Maint Pdts Inc* *(G-12813)*
Hippocrene Books Inc (PA) 212 685-4371
171 Madison Ave Rm 1605 New York (10016) *(G-10104)*
Hipshot Products Inc 607 532-9404
8248 State Route 96 Interlaken (14847) *(G-6481)*
Hirsch Optical Corp 516 752-2211
91 Carolyn Blvd Farmingdale (11735) *(G-4780)*
His Productions USA Inc 212 594-3737
15 Broad St Apt 3030 New York (10005) *(G-10105)*
His Vision Inc 585 254-0022
1260 Lyell Ave Rochester (14606) *(G-13870)*
HISPANICA INTERNATIONAL DELIGH, New York *Also called Life On Earth Inc* *(G-10563)*
Historic TW Inc (HQ) 212 484-8000
75 Rockefeller Plz New York (10019) *(G-10106)*
History Publishing Company LLC 845 398-8161
173 Route 9w Palisades (10964) *(G-12846)*
Hisun Led, Flushing *Also called Hisun Optoelectronics Co Ltd* *(G-5008)*
Hisun Optoelectronics Co Ltd 718 886-6966
4109 College Point Blvd Flushing (11355) *(G-5008)*
Hitachi Cable America Inc (HQ) 914 694-9200
2 Manhattanville Rd # 301 Purchase (10577) *(G-13388)*
Hitachi Metals America Ltd 914 694-9200
2 Manhattanville Rd # 301 Purchase (10577) *(G-13389)*
Hitachi Metals America Ltd (HQ) 914 694-9200
2 Manhattanville Rd # 301 Purchase (10577) *(G-13390)*
Hitemco, Old Bethpage *Also called Barson Composites Corporation* *(G-12583)*
Hitemco Med Applications Inc 516 752-7882
160 Sweet Hollow Rd Old Bethpage (11804) *(G-12585)*
Hje Company Inc 518 792-8733
820 Quaker Rd Queensbury (12804) *(G-13428)*
Hjn Inc (PA) 212 398-9564
16 W 46th St Fl 9 New York (10036) *(G-10107)*
HK Metal Trading Ltd 212 868-3333
450 Fashion Ave Ste 2300 New York (10123) *(G-10108)*
Hks Printing Company Inc 212 675-2529
115 E 27th St New York (10016) *(G-10109)*
Hlw Acres LLC 585 591-0795
1727 Exchange Street Rd Attica (14011) *(G-460)*
Hlw Acres Poultry Processing, Attica *Also called Hlw Acres LLC* *(G-460)*
Hmi Metal Powders, Clayville *Also called Homogeneous Metals Inc* *(G-3558)*
Hmi Metal Powders 315 839-5421
2395 Main St Clayville (13322) *(G-3557)*
Hmo Beverage Corporation 917 371-6100
68 33rd St Unit 4 Brooklyn (11232) *(G-1978)*
HMS Productions LLC (PA) 212 719-9190
72 Jericho Tpke Mineola (11501) *(G-8227)*
Hn Precision-Ny, Rochester *Also called Nationwide Precision Pdts Corp* *(G-13964)*
Hnc Enterprises LLC 904 448-9387
10624 Avenue D Brooklyn (11236) *(G-1979)*
Hnh, New York *Also called Handy & Harman Ltd* *(G-10031)*
Hni Corporation 212 683-2232
200 Lexington Ave Rm 1112 New York (10016) *(G-10110)*
HNST Mold Inspections LLC (PA) 845 215-9258
87 S Nauraushaun Rd Pearl River (10965) *(G-12899)*
Hobart Corporation 631 864-3440
71 Mall Dr Ste 1 Commack (11725) *(G-3695)*
Hobart Corporation 585 427-9000
3495 Winton Pl Rochester (14623) *(G-13871)*
Hockey Facility 518 452-7396
830 Albany Shaker Rd Albany (12211) *(G-83)*
Hodgins Engraving Co Inc 585 343-4444
3817 W Main Street Rd Batavia (14020) *(G-628)*
Hoehn Inc 518 463-8900
159 Chestnut St Albany (12210) *(G-84)*
Hoehn.us, Albany *Also called Hoehn Inc* *(G-84)*
Hoercher Industries Inc 585 398-2982
A1 Country Club Rd Ste 1 East Rochester (14445) *(G-4286)*
Hoffman & Hoffman 315 536-4773
489 State Route 54 Penn Yan (14527) *(G-12958)*
Hoffmann-La Roche Inc 973 890-2291
430 E 29th St New York (10016) *(G-10111)*
Hogan Flavors & Fragrances 212 598-4310
130 E 18th St Frnt New York (10003) *(G-10112)*
Hogan Fragrances International, New York *Also called Hogan Flavors & Fragrances* *(G-10112)*
Hogil Pharmaceutical Corp 914 681-1800
237 Mmaroneck Ave Ste 207 White Plains (10605) *(G-16460)*
Hohenforst Splitting Co Inc 518 725-0012
152 W Fulton St Gloversville (12078) *(G-5458)*
Hohl Machine & Conveyor Co Inc 716 882-7210
1580 Niagara St Buffalo (14213) *(G-2873)*
Hohlveyor, Buffalo *Also called Hohl Machine & Conveyor Co Inc* *(G-2873)*
Hohmann & Barnard Inc (HQ) 631 234-0600
30 Rasons Ct Hauppauge (11788) *(G-5846)*
Hohmann & Barnard Inc 518 357-9757
310 Wayto Rd Schenectady (12303) *(G-14687)*
Hola Publishing Co 718 424-3129
2932 Northern Blvd Long Island City (11101) *(G-7470)*
Holbrooke By Sberry, New York *Also called Holbrooke Inc* *(G-10113)*
Holbrooke Inc 646 397-4674
444 E 20th St Apt 1b New York (10009) *(G-10113)*
Holcim (us) Inc 518 828-8478
4303 Us Route 9 Hudson (12534) *(G-6353)*
Holdens Screen Supply Corp 212 627-2727
121 Varick St New York (10013) *(G-10114)*
Holiday House Publishing, New York *Also called Bicker Inc* *(G-9072)*
Holland & Sherry Inc (PA) 212 542-8410
330 E 59th St Ph New York (10022) *(G-10115)*
Holland & Sherry Intr Design, New York *Also called Holland & Sherry Inc* *(G-10115)*
Hollander HM Fshons Hldngs LLC 212 575-0400
440 Park Ave S Fl 10 New York (10016) *(G-10116)*
Hollander Sleep Products LLC 212 575-0400
440 Park Ave S New York (10016) *(G-10117)*
Hollingsworth & Vose Company 518 695-8000
3235 County Rte 113 Greenwich (12834) *(G-5641)*
Holloween Adventures, New York *Also called Masquerade LLC* *(G-10723)*
Hollywood Advertising Banners 631 842-3000
539 Oak St Copiague (11726) *(G-3764)*
Hollywood Banners, Copiague *Also called Hollywood Advertising Banners* *(G-3764)*
Hollywood Banners Inc 631 842-3000
539 Oak St Copiague (11726) *(G-3765)*
Hollywood Signs Inc 917 577-7333
388 3rd Ave Brooklyn (11215) *(G-1980)*
Holmes Group The Inc 212 333-2300
271 W 47th St Apt 23a New York (10036) *(G-10118)*
Holstein World, East Syracuse *Also called H F W Communications Inc* *(G-4344)*
Holy Cow Kosher LLC 347 788-8620
750 Chestnut Ridge Rd Spring Valley (10977) *(G-14995)*
Holyoke Fittings Inc 718 649-0710
850 Stanley Ave Brooklyn (11208) *(G-1981)*
Home Fashions Intl LLC (PA) 212 689-3579
295 5th Ave Ste 1520 New York (10016) *(G-10119)*
Home Fashions Intl LLC 212 684-0091
295 5th Ave Ste 1520 New York (10016) *(G-10120)*
Home Ideal Inc 718 762-8998
4528 159th St Flushing (11358) *(G-5009)*
Home Lighting & Accessories, New City *Also called Doctorow Communications Inc* *(G-8491)*
Home Maide Inc 845 837-1700
1 Short St Harriman (10926) *(G-5719)*
Home Reporter & Sunset News, Brooklyn *Also called Home Reporter Inc* *(G-1982)*
Home Reporter Inc 718 238-6600
8723 3rd Ave Brooklyn (11209) *(G-1982)*
Home4u Inc 347 262-7214
152 Skillman St Apt 8 Brooklyn (11205) *(G-1983)*
Homegrown For Good LLC 857 540-6361
29 Beechwood Ave New Rochelle (10801) *(G-8615)*
Homer Iron Works LLC 607 749-3963
5130 Us Route 11 Homer (13077) *(G-6256)*
Homer Logging Contractor 607 753-8553
6176 Sunnyside Dr Homer (13077) *(G-6257)*
Homes Land Eastrn Long Island, Southampton *Also called Frontiers Unlimited Inc* *(G-14953)*
Homesell Inc 718 514-0346
4010 Hylan Blvd Staten Island (10308) *(G-15086)*

ALPHABETIC

Homogeneous Metals Inc 315 839-5421
2395 Main St Clayville (13322) ***(G-3558)***
Honeoye Falls Distillery LLC (PA) 201 780-4618
168 W Main St Honeoye Falls (14472) ***(G-6268)***
Honeybee Rbtics Cft Mechanisms, Brooklyn *Also called Honeybee Robotics Ltd* ***(G-1984)***
Honeybee Robotics Ltd (HQ) 212 966-0661
Suit Bldg 128 Brooklyn (11205) ***(G-1984)***
Honeywell Authorized Dealer, Floral Park *Also called Automated Bldg MGT Systems Inc* ***(G-4956)***
Honeywell Imaging and Mobility, Skaneateles Falls *Also called Hand Held Products Inc* ***(G-14879)***
Honeywell International Inc 518 270-0200
3 Tibbits Ave Troy (12183) ***(G-15595)***
Honeywell International Inc 315 554-6643
700 Visions Dr Skaneateles Falls (13153) ***(G-14881)***
Honeywell International Inc 716 631-2197
307 Cayuga Rd Ste 160 Cheektowaga (14225) ***(G-3449)***
Honeywell International Inc 516 577-2661
2 Corporate Center Dr # 100 Melville (11747) ***(G-8031)***
Honeywell International Inc 516 577-2000
2 Corporate Center Dr # 100 Melville (11747) ***(G-8032)***
Honeywell International Inc 516 577-2813
2 Corporate Center Dr # 100 Melville (11747) ***(G-8033)***
Honeywell International Inc 845 342-4400
13 Bedford Ave Middletown (10940) ***(G-8158)***
Honeywell International Inc 212 964-5111
263 Old Country Rd Melville (11747) ***(G-8034)***
Honeywell International Inc 516 577-2000
2 Corporate Center Dr # 100 Melville (11747) ***(G-8035)***
Honeywell International Inc 315 463-7208
7000 Airways Park Dr # 4 East Syracuse (13057) ***(G-4347)***
Honeywell International Inc 631 471-2202
1859 Lakeland Ave Lake Ronkonkoma (11779) ***(G-6980)***
Honeywell Scanning & Mobility, Skaneateles Falls *Also called Hand Held Products Inc* ***(G-14880)***
Honor Brand Feeds, Narrowsburg *Also called Narrowsburg Feed & Grain Co* ***(G-8474)***
Honora, New York *Also called Brannkey Inc* ***(G-9135)***
Hood Industries Inc 716 836-0301
580 Tifft St Buffalo (14220) ***(G-2874)***
Hooek Produktion Inc 212 367-9111
147 W 26th St Fl 6 New York (10001) ***(G-10121)***
Hoosier Magnetics Inc 315 323-5832
110 Denny St Ogdensburg (13669) ***(G-12575)***
Hope International Productions 212 247-3188
315 W 57th St Apt 6h New York (10019) ***(G-10122)***
Hopes Windows Inc 716 665-5124
84 Hopkins Ave Jamestown (14701) ***(G-6722)***
Hopewell Precision Inc 845 221-2737
19 Ryan Rd Hopewell Junction (12533) ***(G-6288)***
Hoptron Brewtique 631 438-0296
22 W Main St Ste 11 Patchogue (11772) ***(G-12866)***
Horace J Metz 716 873-9103
2385 Elmwood Ave Kenmore (14217) ***(G-6861)***
Horizon Apparel Mfg Inc 516 361-4878
115 Bayside Dr Atlantic Beach (11509) ***(G-456)***
Horizon Floors I LLC 212 509-9686
11 Broadway Lbby 5 New York (10004) ***(G-10123)***
Horizons Magazine, Brooklyn *Also called Targum Press USA Inc* ***(G-2556)***
Horne Organization Inc (PA) 914 572-1330
15 Arthur Pl Yonkers (10701) ***(G-16769)***
Horne Products Inc 631 293-0773
144 Verdi St Farmingdale (11735) ***(G-4781)***
Hornet Group Inc 845 858-6400
100 River Rd Port Jervis (12771) ***(G-13230)***
Horning Greenhouses, Penn Yan *Also called Ivan Horning* ***(G-12959)***
Horns & Halos Cft Brewing LLC 585 507-7248
3154 State St Caledonia (14423) ***(G-3156)***
Horo Creations LLC 212 719-4818
71 W 47th St Ste 404 New York (10036) ***(G-10124)***
Horseheads Printing, Horseheads *Also called David Helsing* ***(G-6311)***
Hosel & Ackerson Inc (PA) 212 575-1490
570 Fashion Ave Rm 805 New York (10018) ***(G-10125)***
Hoshizaki Nrtheastern Dist Ctr 516 605-1411
150 Dupont St Ste 100 Plainview (11803) ***(G-13060)***
Hoskie Co Inc 718 628-8672
132 Harrison Pl Brooklyn (11237) ***(G-1985)***
Hosmer Inc 888 467-9463
6999 State Route 89 Ovid (14521) ***(G-12791)***
Hosmer's Winery, Ovid *Also called Hosmer Inc* ***(G-12791)***
Hospira Inc 716 684-9400
2501 Walden Ave Buffalo (14225) ***(G-2875)***
Hospitality Graphic Systems 212 563-9334
500 10th Ave New York (10018) ***(G-10126)***
Hospitality Graphics Inc 212 643-6700
545 8th Ave Rm 401 New York (10018) ***(G-10127)***
Hospitality Inc 212 268-1930
247 W 35th St 4 New York (10001) ***(G-10128)***
Hot Cashews, New York *Also called Just Bottoms & Tops Inc* ***(G-10383)***
Hot Kiss Inc 212 730-0404
1407 Brdwy Ste 2000 New York (10018) ***(G-10129)***

Hot Line Industries Inc (PA) 516 764-0400
28 South Mall Plainview (11803) ***(G-13061)***
Hot Sox Company Incorporated (PA) 212 957-2000
95 Madison Ave Fl 15 New York (10016) ***(G-10130)***
Hotel Business, Islandia *Also called Icd Publications Inc* ***(G-6530)***
Hotelexpert, New York *Also called Tyme Global Technologies LLC* ***(G-11923)***
Houghton Mifflin Clarion Books, New York *Also called Houghton Mifflin Harcourt Pubg* ***(G-10131)***
Houghton Mifflin Harcourt Pubg 212 420-5800
3 Park Ave Fl 18 New York (10016) ***(G-10131)***
Houghton Mifflin Harcourt Pubg 914 747-2709
28 Claremont Ave Thornwood (10594) ***(G-15507)***
Houles USA Inc 212 935-3900
979 3rd Ave Ste 1200 New York (10022) ***(G-10132)***
Hound & Gatos Pet Foods Corp 212 618-1917
14 Wall St Fl 20 New York (10005) ***(G-10133)***
Hourglass Interactive LLC 954 254-2853
1 Union Sq S Apt 20j New York (10003) ***(G-10134)***
House O'Weenies, Bronx *Also called Marathon Enterprises Inc* ***(G-1321)***
House of Heydenryk Jr Inc 212 206-9611
601 W 26th St Rm 305 New York (10001) ***(G-10135)***
House of Heydenryk The, New York *Also called House of Heydenryk Jr Inc* ***(G-10135)***
House of Portfolios Co Inc (PA) 212 206-7323
37 W 26th St Rm 305 New York (10010) ***(G-10136)***
House of Portfolios Co Inc 212 206-7323
48 W 21st St New York (10010) ***(G-10137)***
House of Serengeti, White Plains *Also called Farmers Hub LLC* ***(G-16450)***
House of Stone Inc 845 782-7271
1015 State Route 17m Monroe (10950) ***(G-8272)***
House of The Foaming Case Inc 718 454-0101
110 08 Dunkirk St Saint Albans (11412) ***(G-14507)***
House Pearl Fashions (us) Ltd 212 840-3183
1410 Broadway Rm 1501 New York (10018) ***(G-10138)***
Hovee Inc 646 249-6200
722 Saint Nicholas Ave New York (10031) ***(G-10139)***
Hover-Davis Inc (HQ) 585 352-9590
100 Paragon Dr Rochester (14624) ***(G-13872)***
Howard Charles Inc 917 902-6934
180 Froehlich Farm Blvd Woodbury (11797) ***(G-16621)***
Howard Formed Steel Pdts Div, Bronx *Also called Truxton Corp* ***(G-1408)***
Howard J Moore Company Inc 631 351-8467
210 Terminal Dr Ste B Plainview (11803) ***(G-13062)***
Howden Fan Company, Depew *Also called Howden North America Inc* ***(G-4093)***
Howden North America Inc (HQ) 803 741-2700
2475 George Urban Blvd # 120 Depew (14043) ***(G-4092)***
Howden North America Inc 716 817-6900
2475 George Urban Blvd # 120 Depew (14043) ***(G-4093)***
Howdens, Depew *Also called Howden North America Inc* ***(G-4092)***
Howe Machine & Tool Corp 516 931-5687
236 Park Ave Bethpage (11714) ***(G-843)***
Howell Packaging, Elmira *Also called F M Howell & Company* ***(G-4486)***
Howmedica Osteonics Corp 518 783-1880
2 Northway Ln Latham (12110) ***(G-7074)***
Howmedica Osteonics Corp 516 484-0897
95 Seaview Blvd Ste 201 Port Washington (11050) ***(G-13265)***
HP Hood LLC 607 295-8134
25 Hurlbut St Arkport (14807) ***(G-399)***
HP Hood LLC 315 363-3870
252 Genesee St Oneida (13421) ***(G-12611)***
HP Hood LLC 315 658-2132
20700 State Route 411 La Fargeville (13656) ***(G-6942)***
HP Hood LLC 518 218-9097
816 Burdeck St Schenectady (12306) ***(G-14688)***
HP Hood LLC 315 829-3339
19 Ward St Vernon (13476) ***(G-15805)***
HP Hood LLC 607 772-6580
93 Pennsylvania Ave Binghamton (13903) ***(G-890)***
HP Inc 650 857-1501
5 Computer Dr S Albany (12205) ***(G-85)***
HP Inc 650 857-1501
556 W 22nd St Fl 8 New York (10011) ***(G-10140)***
Hpce, Pearl River *Also called Hunts Point Clean Energy LLC* ***(G-12902)***
Hpi Co Inc (PA) 718 851-2753
1656 41st St Brooklyn (11218) ***(G-1986)***
Hpk Industries LLC 315 724-0196
1208 Broad St Utica (13501) ***(G-15709)***
HRA Poster Project, Brooklyn *Also called City of New York* ***(G-1695)***
Hrd Metal Products Inc 631 243-6700
120 E Jefryn Blvd Ste A Deer Park (11729) ***(G-3985)***
Hri Metals LLC 518 822-1013
1233 Us Route 9 Hudson (12534) ***(G-6354)***
Hs Homeworx LLC 646 870-0406
18 E 74th St Fl 5 New York (10021) ***(G-10141)***
HSM Machine Works Inc (PA) 631 924-6600
3671 Horseblock Rd Medford (11763) ***(G-7953)***
HSM Packaging Corporation 315 476-7996
4529 Crown Rd Liverpool (13090) ***(G-7235)***
HSN, New York *Also called Macfadden Cmmnctions Group LLC* ***(G-10647)***
Htf Components Inc 914 703-6795
134 Bowbell Rd White Plains (10607) ***(G-16461)***

Hti Recycling LLC (PA) 716 433-9294
490 Ohio St Lockport (14094) ***(G-7309)***
Hubbard Tool and Die Corp 315 337-7840
Rome Indus Ctr Bldg 5 Rome (13440) ***(G-14253)***
Hubbell Inc 845 586-2707
46124 State Highway 30 # 2 Margaretville (12455) ***(G-7798)***
Hubbell Galvanising, Yorkville *Also called O W Hubbell & Sons Inc* ***(G-16828)***
Hubbell Galvanizing Inc 315 736-8311
5124 Commercial Dr Yorkville (13495) ***(G-16827)***
Hubco Inc 716 683-5940
2885 Commerce Dr Alden (14004) ***(G-172)***
Hubray Inc 800 645-2855
2045 Grand Ave North Baldwin (11510) ***(G-12364)***
Huck International Inc 845 331-7300
1 Corporate Dr Kingston (12401) ***(G-6902)***
Huckleberry Inc 631 630-5450
655 Old Willets Path Hauppauge (11788) ***(G-5847)***
Hudson Cabinetry Design, Peekskill *Also called Hat Factory Furniture Co* ***(G-12921)***
Hudson Dying & Finishing LLC 518 752-4389
68 Harrison St Gloversville (12078) ***(G-5459)***
Hudson Eastern Industries Inc 917 295-5818
1118 143rd Pl Whitestone (11357) ***(G-16543)***
Hudson Envelope Corporation (PA) 212 473-6666
135 3rd Ave New York (10003) ***(G-10142)***
Hudson Fabrics LLC 518 671-6100
128 2nd Street Ext Hudson (12534) ***(G-6355)***
Hudson Industries Corporation 518 762-4638
100 Maple Ave Johnstown (12095) ***(G-6831)***
Hudson Machine Works Inc 845 279-1413
30 Branch Rd Brewster (10509) ***(G-1168)***
Hudson Mirror LLC 914 930-8906
710 Washington St Peekskill (10566) ***(G-12922)***
Hudson News Inc 212 971-6800
250 Greenwich St New York (10007) ***(G-10143)***
Hudson Park Press Inc 212 929-8898
232 Madison Ave Rm 1400 New York (10016) ***(G-10144)***
Hudson Power Transmission Co 718 622-3869
241 Halsey St Brooklyn (11216) ***(G-1987)***
Hudson Printing Co Inc 718 937-8600
747 3rd Ave Lbby 3 New York (10017) ***(G-10145)***
Hudson Scenic Studio Inc (PA) 914 375-0900
130 Fernbrook St Yonkers (10705) ***(G-16770)***
Hudson Software Corporation 914 773-0400
3 W Main St Ste 106 Elmsford (10523) ***(G-4544)***
Hudson Technologies Company (HQ) 845 735-6000
1 Blue Hill Plz Ste 1541 Pearl River (10965) ***(G-12900)***
Hudson Valley Baking Co, Mamaroneck *Also called Richard Engdal Baking Corp* ***(G-7755)***
Hudson Valley Black Press 845 562-1313
343 Broadway Newburgh (12550) ***(G-12226)***
Hudson Valley Chocolatier Inc (PA) 845 831-8240
269 Main St Beacon (12508) ***(G-759)***
Hudson Valley Coatings LLC 845 398-1778
175 N Route 9w Ste 12 Congers (10920) ***(G-3717)***
Hudson Valley Creamery LLC 518 851-2570
2986 Us Route 9 Hudson (12534) ***(G-6356)***
Hudson Valley Foie Gras LLC 845 292-2500
80 Brooks Rd Ferndale (12734) ***(G-4934)***
Hudson Valley Lighting Inc 845 561-0300
151 Airport Dr Wappingers Falls (12590) ***(G-15935)***
Hudson Valley Magazine, Fishkill *Also called Suburban Publishing Inc* ***(G-4952)***
Hudson Valley Office Furn Inc 845 565-6673
7 Wisner Ave Newburgh (12550) ***(G-12227)***
Hudson Valley Paper Works Inc 845 569-8883
8 Lander St 15 Newburgh (12550) ***(G-12228)***
Hudson Valley Steel Products 845 565-2270
5231 Route 9w Newburgh (12550) ***(G-12229)***
Hudson Valley Tech Dev Ctr Inc 845 391-8214
180 South St Highland (12528) ***(G-6144)***
Hudsonyards Studios LLC, New York *Also called Hys LLC* ***(G-10157)***
Huersch Marketing Group LLC 518 874-1045
70 Cohoes Ave Ste 4 Green Island (12183) ***(G-5607)***
Huffington Post, The, New York *Also called Thehuffingtonpostcom Inc* ***(G-11809)***
Hugh F McPherson Inc 716 668-6107
70 Innsbruck Dr Cheektowaga (14227) ***(G-3450)***
Hugo Boss Usa Inc (HQ) 212 940-0600
55 Water St Fl 48 New York (10041) ***(G-10146)***
Huhtamaki Inc 315 593-5311
100 State St Fulton (13069) ***(G-5220)***
Hulley Holding Company Inc (PA) 716 332-3982
2500 Elmwood Ave Kenmore (14217) ***(G-6862)***
Hulley Woodworking Company, Kenmore *Also called Hulley Holding Company Inc* ***(G-6862)***
Hum Limited Liability Corp 631 525-2174
70 Deer Valley Dr Nesconset (11767) ***(G-8484)***
Human Condition Safety Inc 646 867-0644
61 Broadway Fl 31 New York (10006) ***(G-10147)***
Human Electronics Inc 315 724-9850
155 Genesee St Utica (13501) ***(G-15710)***
Human Life Foundation Inc 212 685-5210
271 Madison Ave Ste 1005 New York (10016) ***(G-10148)***
Human Technologies Corporation 315 735-3532
2260 Dwyer Ave Utica (13501) ***(G-15711)***
Humana Press Inc 212 460-1500
233 Spring St Fl 6 New York (10013) ***(G-10149)***
Humanscale Corporation (PA) 212 725-4749
1114 Ave Of Americas 15 New York (10036) ***(G-10150)***
Humanware USA Inc (PA) 800 722-3393
1 Ups Way Champlain (12919) ***(G-3410)***
Humboldt Woodworking 718 707-0022
3836 11th St Long Island City (11101) ***(G-7471)***
Humor Rainbow Inc 646 402-9113
555 W 18th St New York (10011) ***(G-10151)***
Hunt Country Furniture Inc (PA) 845 832-6601
19 Dog Tail Corners Rd Wingdale (12594) ***(G-16606)***
Hunt Country Vineyards 315 595-2812
4021 Italy Hill Rd Branchport (14418) ***(G-1123)***
Hunter Displays, East Patchogue *Also called Hunter Metal Industries Inc* ***(G-4275)***
Hunter Douglas Inc (HQ) 845 664-7000
1 Blue Hill Plz Ste 1569 Pearl River (10965) ***(G-12901)***
Hunter Douglas Inc 212 588-0564
979 3rd Ave New York (10022) ***(G-10152)***
Hunter Machine Inc 585 924-7480
6551 Anthony Dr Victor (14564) ***(G-15849)***
Hunter Metal Industries Inc 631 475-5900
14 Hewlett Ave East Patchogue (11772) ***(G-4275)***
Huntington Ice & Cube Corp (PA) 718 456-2013
335 Moffat St Brooklyn (11237) ***(G-1988)***
Huntington Ingalls Inc 518 884-3834
33 Cady Hill Blvd Saratoga Springs (12866) ***(G-14587)***
Huntington Services Inc 516 795-8500
727 N Broadway Ste A4 Massapequa (11758) ***(G-7880)***
Huntington Welding & Iron 631 423-3331
139 W Pulaski Rd Huntington Station (11746) ***(G-6445)***
Huntington Woodworking Inc 631 271-7897
691 E Jericho Tpke Huntington Station (11746) ***(G-6446)***
Hunts Point Clean Energy LLC 203 451-5143
401 N Middletown Rd Pearl River (10965) ***(G-12902)***
Huron Tl Cutter Grinding Inc 631 420-7000
2045 Wellwood Ave Farmingdale (11735) ***(G-4782)***
Hurryworks LLC 516 998-4600
990 Seaview Blvd Port Washington (11050) ***(G-13266)***
Hustler Powerboats, Calverton *Also called Global Marine Power Inc* ***(G-3166)***
Hutchinson Industries Inc 716 852-1435
92 Msgr Valente Dr Buffalo (14206) ***(G-2876)***
Hutnick Rehab, Bohemia *Also called Gfh Orthotic & Prosthetic Labs* ***(G-1028)***
Hvr Mso LLC 833 345-6974
2678 South Rd Ste 202 Poughkeepsie (12601) ***(G-13346)***
Hw Holdings Inc (HQ) 212 399-1000
718 5th Ave New York (10019) ***(G-10153)***
Hw Specialties Co Inc 631 589-0745
210 Knickerbocker Ave B Bohemia (11716) ***(G-1033)***
Hy Cert Services Inc 631 231-7005
122 Cain Dr Brentwood (11717) ***(G-1134)***
Hy-Grade Metal Products Corp 315 475-4221
906 Burnet Ave Syracuse (13203) ***(G-15341)***
Hy-Tech Mold Inc 585 247-2450
60 Elmgrove Park Rochester (14624) ***(G-13873)***
Hybrid Cases, Holbrook *Also called Roadie Products Inc* ***(G-6206)***
Hyde Park, Poughkeepsie *Also called Architectural Dctg Co LLC* ***(G-13327)***
Hyde Park Brewing Co Inc 845 229-8277
4076 Albany Post Rd Hyde Park (12538) ***(G-6469)***
Hydramec Inc 585 593-5190
4393 River St Scio (14880) ***(G-14735)***
Hydrive Energy 914 925-9100
350 Theodore Fremd Ave Rye (10580) ***(G-14483)***
Hydro-Air Components Inc 716 827-6510
100 Rittling Blvd Buffalo (14220) ***(G-2877)***
Hydroacoustics Inc 585 359-1000
999 Lehigh Station Rd # 100 Henrietta (14467) ***(G-6032)***
Hydrogen Technology Corp 800 315-9554
915 Broadway Ste 801 New York (10010) ***(G-10154)***
Hygrade 718 488-9000
30 Warsoff Pl Brooklyn (11205) ***(G-1989)***
Hygrade Fuel Inc 516 741-0723
260 Columbus Pkwy Mineola (11501) ***(G-8228)***
Hyman Podrusnick Co Inc 718 853-4502
212 Foster Ave Brooklyn (11230) ***(G-1990)***
Hyperbaric Technologies Inc 518 842-3030
1 Sam Stratton Rd Amsterdam (12010) ***(G-340)***
Hyperlaw Inc 212 873-6982
17 W 70th St Apt 4 New York (10023) ***(G-10155)***
Hyperline Systems Inc 613 736-8500
9322 3rd Ave Ste 406 Brooklyn (11209) ***(G-1991)***
Hypoxico Inc 212 972-1009
50 Lexington Ave Ste 249 New York (10010) ***(G-10156)***
Hypres Inc (PA) 914 592-1190
175 Clearbrook Rd Elmsford (10523) ***(G-4545)***
Hys LLC (HQ) 212 716-6600
80 Broad St New York (10004) ***(G-10157)***
Hytech Tool & Die Inc 716 488-2796
2202 Washington St Jamestown (14701) ***(G-6723)***
I & I Systems 845 753-9126
66 Table Rock Rd Tuxedo Park (10987) ***(G-15656)***
I & S of NY Inc 716 373-7001
4174 Route 417 Allegany (14706) ***(G-191)***

ALPHABETIC

I 2 Print Inc 718 937-8800
  3819 24th St Long Island City (11101) *(G-7472)*
I 3 Manufacturing Services Inc 607 238-7077
  100 Eldredge St Binghamton (13901) *(G-891)*
I A S National Inc 631 423-6900
  95 W Hills Rd Huntington Station (11746) *(G-6447)*
I C S, New York Also called Integrated Graphics Inc *(G-10231)*
I D E Processes Corporation (PA) 718 544-1177
  106 81st Ave Kew Gardens (11415) *(G-6873)*
I D Machine Inc 607 796-2549
  1580 Lake St Elmira (14901) *(G-4494)*
I D Tel Corp 718 876-6000
  55 Canal St Staten Island (10304) *(G-15087)*
I Do Machining, Elmira Also called I D Machine Inc *(G-4494)*
I E D Corp 631 348-0424
  88 Bridge Rd Islandia (11749) *(G-6529)*
I E M, Troy Also called Interntnal Elctronic Mchs Corp *(G-15610)*
I Fix Screen 631 421-1938
  203 Centereach Mall Centereach (11720) *(G-3344)*
I J White Corporation 631 293-3788
  20 Executive Blvd Farmingdale (11735) *(G-4783)*
I L C, Bohemia Also called Ilc Industries LLC *(G-1036)*
I Love Accessories Inc 212 239-1875
  10 W 33rd St Rm 210 New York (10001) *(G-10158)*
I Meglio Corp 631 617-6900
  151 Alkier St Brentwood (11717) *(G-1135)*
I N K T Inc 212 957-2700
  250 W 54th St Fl 9 New York (10019) *(G-10159)*
I On Youth 716 832-6509
  115 Godfrey St Buffalo (14215) *(G-2878)*
I Rauchs Sons Inc 718 507-8844
  3220 112th St East Elmhurst (11369) *(G-4221)*
I S C A Corp (PA) 212 719-5123
  512 7th Ave Fl 7 New York (10018) *(G-10160)*
I Shalom & Co Inc 212 532-7911
  411 5th Ave Fl 4 New York (10016) *(G-10161)*
I Spiewak & Sons Inc 212 695-1620
  225 W 37th St Fl 15l New York (10018) *(G-10162)*
I Trade Technology Ltd 845 357-4943
  3 Rustic Dr Airmont (10952) *(G-13)*
I Trade Technology Ltd 615 348-7233
  400 Rella Blvd Ste 165 Suffern (10901) *(G-15191)*
I Triple E Spectrum, New York Also called Magazine I Spectrum E *(G-10661)*
I W Industries Inc (PA) 631 293-9494
  35 Melville Park Rd Melville (11747) *(G-8036)*
I W M, Dryden Also called Integrated Water Management *(G-4150)*
I'M Nuts, Hewlett Also called Yes Were Nuts Ltd *(G-6055)*
I-Evolve Techonology Services (PA) 801 566-5268
  501 John James Audubon Pk Amherst (14228) *(G-231)*
I3 Assembly LLC 607 238-7077
  100 Eldredge St Binghamton (13901) *(G-892)*
I3 Electronics Inc (PA) 607 238-7077
  100 Eldredge St Binghamton (13901) *(G-893)*
I3 Electronics Inc 607 238-7077
  Huron Campus 1500 1700 Endicott (13760) *(G-4596)*
IA Construction Corporation 716 933-8787
  Rr 305 Box S Portville (14770) *(G-13316)*
Iaas , The, Flushing Also called Intercultural Alliance Artists *(G-5011)*
IAC Search LLC (HQ) 212 314-7300
  555 W 18th St New York (10011) *(G-10163)*
Iac/Interactivecorp (PA) 212 314-7300
  555 W 18th St New York (10011) *(G-10164)*
Iadc Inc 718 238-0623
  845 Father Capodanno Blvd Staten Island (10305) *(G-15088)*
IaMmaliamills LLC 805 845-2137
  32 33rd St Unit 13 Brooklyn (11232) *(G-1992)*
Iat Interactive LLC 914 273-2233
  333 N Bedford Rd Ste 110 Mount Kisco (10549) *(G-8343)*
Iba Industrial Inc 631 254-6800
  151 Heartland Blvd Edgewood (11717) *(G-4403)*
IBC/ Worldwide, New Hyde Park Also called Interntnal Bus Cmmncations Inc *(G-8542)*
Ibio Inc 302 355-0650
  600 Madison Ave Ste 1601 New York (10022) *(G-10165)*
IBM, New York Also called International Bus Mchs Corp *(G-10243)*
IBM, Armonk Also called International Bus Mchs Corp *(G-404)*
IBM, Hopewell Junction Also called International Bus Mchs Corp *(G-6289)*
IBM, Armonk Also called International Bus Mchs Corp *(G-405)*
IBM World Trade Corporation (HQ) 914 765-1900
  1 New Orchard Rd Ste 1 # 1 Armonk (10504) *(G-403)*
Ibrands International LLC 212 354-1330
  230 W 39th St New York (10018) *(G-10166)*
Ic Optics, New Hyde Park Also called Colors In Optics Ltd *(G-8523)*
Icarus Enterprises Inc 917 969-4461
  568 Broadway Fl 11 New York (10012) *(G-10167)*
Icd Publications Inc (PA) 631 246-9300
  1377 Motor Pkwy Ste 410 Islandia (11749) *(G-6530)*
Ice Air LLC 914 668-4700
  80 Hartford Ave Mount Vernon (10553) *(G-8408)*
Ice Cream Man Inc 518 692-8382
  417 State Route 29 Greenwich (12834) *(G-5642)*

Ice Cube Inc (PA) 613 254-0071
  171 E Industry Ct Ste B Deer Park (11729) *(G-3986)*
Icell Inc 516 590-0007
  133 Fulton Ave Hempstead (11550) *(G-6014)*
Icer Scrubs LLC 212 221-4700
  1385 Broadway Fl 16 New York (10018) *(G-10168)*
Icer Sports LLC 212 221-4700
  1385 Broadway Fl 16 New York (10018) *(G-10169)*
Ices Queen, Brooklyn Also called Primo Frozen Desserts Inc *(G-2343)*
Icestone LLC 718 624-4900
  63 Flushing Ave Unit 283b Brooklyn (11205) *(G-1993)*
ICM, North Syracuse Also called Interntnal Cntrls Msrmnts Corp *(G-12406)*
ICM Controls Corp 315 233-5266
  7313 William Barry Blvd North Syracuse (13212) *(G-12405)*
Icon Design LLC 585 768-6040
  9 Lent Ave Le Roy (14482) *(G-7119)*
Icon Enterprises Intl Inc 718 752-9764
  2653 Stony St Mohegan Lake (10547) *(G-8258)*
Icon-TV, Mohegan Lake Also called Icon Enterprises Intl Inc *(G-8258)*
Iconix Inc 516 513-1420
  40 Oser Ave Ste 4 Hauppauge (11788) *(G-5848)*
ICP, Depew Also called Pcb Group Inc *(G-4100)*
Icpme-Ithaca Center, Ithaca Also called International Center For Postg *(G-6585)*
Icy Hot Lingerie, New York Also called Sensual Inc *(G-11544)*
Icynene US Acquisition Corp (HQ) 800 758-7325
  438 Main St Ste 100 Buffalo (14202) *(G-2879)*
ID Signsystems Inc 585 266-5750
  410 Atlantic Ave Rochester (14609) *(G-13874)*
Idalia Solar Technologies LLC 212 792-3913
  270 Lafayette St Ste 1402 New York (10012) *(G-10170)*
Idc, West Babylon Also called Isolation Dynamics Corp *(G-16158)*
Ideal Accessories, New York Also called Ideal Fastener Corporation *(G-10172)*
Ideal Burial Vault Company 585 599-2242
  1166 Vision Pkwy Corfu (14036) *(G-3807)*
Ideal Creations Inc 212 563-5928
  10 W 33rd St Rm 708 New York (10001) *(G-10171)*
Ideal Fastener Corporation 212 244-0260
  246 W 38th St Rm 502 New York (10018) *(G-10172)*
Ideal Manufacturing Inc 585 872-7190
  80 Bluff Dr East Rochester (14445) *(G-4287)*
Ideal Signs Inc 718 292-9196
  538 Wales Ave Bronx (10455) *(G-1293)*
Ideal Snacks Corporation 845 292-7000
  89 Mill St Liberty (12754) *(G-7144)*
Ideal Stair Parts, Little Falls Also called Ideal Wood Products Inc *(G-7210)*
Ideal Wood Products Inc 315 823-1124
  225 W Main St Little Falls (13365) *(G-7210)*
Identfication Data Imaging LLC 516 484-6500
  26 Harbor Park Dr Port Washington (11050) *(G-13267)*
Identifycom Inc 212 235-0000
  120 W 45th St Ste 2701 New York (10036) *(G-10173)*
Identity Ink & Custom Tee, Kenmore Also called Herrmann Group LLC *(G-6860)*
Ideoli Group Inc 212 705-8769
  938 Port Washington Blvd # 1 Port Washington (11050) *(G-13268)*
Idesco Corp 212 889-2530
  37 W 26th St Fl 10 New York (10010) *(G-10174)*
Idex Health & Science LLC 585 244-7220
  55 Science Pkwy Rochester (14620) *(G-13875)*
Idg, New York Also called International Direct Group Inc *(G-10246)*
Idg LLC 315 797-1000
  31 Faass Ave Utica (13502) *(G-15712)*
Idg Technetwork, New York Also called International Data Group Inc *(G-10244)*
IDI, Port Washington Also called Identfication Data Imaging LLC *(G-13267)*
Idl, Ronkonkoma Also called Ingenious Designs LLC *(G-14353)*
Idonethis, New York Also called West Internet Trading Company *(G-12095)*
IEC Electronics Corp (PA) 315 331-7742
  105 Norton St Newark (14513) *(G-12196)*
IEC Electronics Corp 585 647-1760
  1365 Emerson Sq Rochester (14606) *(G-13876)*
IEC Electronics Wire Cable Inc 585 924-9010
  105 Norton St Newark (14513) *(G-12197)*
IEC Holden Corporation 518 213-3991
  51 Distribution Way Plattsburgh (12901) *(G-13125)*
Ieh Corporation 718 492-4440
  140 58th St Ste 8e Brooklyn (11220) *(G-1994)*
Iep Energy Holding LLC 212 702-4300
  767 5th Ave Ste 4600 New York (10153) *(G-10175)*
Iet Labs Inc (PA) 516 334-5959
  1 Expressway Plz Ste 120 Roslyn Heights (11577) *(G-14456)*
Iff, New York Also called Interntnal Flvors Frgrnces Inc *(G-10251)*
Ifg Corp 212 629-9600
  1372 Brdwy 12ae 12 Ae New York (10018) *(G-10176)*
Ifg Corp 212 239-8615
  463 7th Ave Fl 4 New York (10018) *(G-10177)*
Igambit Inc (PA) 631 670-6777
  1050 W Jericho Tpke Ste A Smithtown (11787) *(G-14900)*
Igk Equestrian, Auburn Also called Brook North Farms Inc *(G-472)*
Ignelzi Interiors Inc 718 464-0279
  9805 217th St Queens Village (11429) *(G-13407)*

ALPHABETIC SECTION

Igniter Systems Inc 716 542-5511
12600 Clarence Center Rd Akron (14001) *(G-19)*
Igt Global Solutions Corp 518 382-2900
1 Broadway Ctr Fl 2 Schenectady (12305) *(G-14689)*
Ihd Motorsports LLC 979 690-1669
1152 Upper Front St Binghamton (13905) *(G-894)*
Iheartcommunications Inc 585 454-4884
100 Chestnut St Ste 1700 Rochester (14604) *(G-13877)*
Iheartcommunications Inc 212 603-4660
1133 Ave Americas Fl 34 New York (10036) *(G-10178)*
Ihi Inc (HQ) 212 599-8100
150 E 52nd St Fl 24 New York (10022) *(G-10179)*
Iim Global, Long Beach Also called Innovation In Motion Inc *(G-7359)*
Iimak, Amherst Also called International Imaging Mtls Inc *(G-232)*
Ik Supply, Farmingdale Also called International Key Supply LLC *(G-4788)*
Ikeddi Enterprises Inc (PA) 212 302-7644
1407 Brdwy Ste 2900 New York (10018) *(G-10180)*
Ikeddi Enterprises Inc 212 302-7644
1407 Broadway Rm 1805 New York (10018) *(G-10181)*
Ilab America Inc 631 615-5053
45 Hemlock St Selden (11784) *(G-14764)*
Ilc Holdings Inc (HQ) 631 567-5600
105 Wilbur Pl Bohemia (11716) *(G-1034)*
Ilc Industries Inc 631 567-5600
105 Wilbur Pl Bohemia (11716) *(G-1035)*
Ilc Industries LLC (HQ) 631 567-5600
105 Wilbur Pl Bohemia (11716) *(G-1036)*
Iles Formula Inc (PA) 315 834-2478
40 Harrison St Apt 17h New York (10013) *(G-10182)*
Ilico Jewelry Inc 516 482-0201
98 Cuttermill Rd Ste 396 Great Neck (11021) *(G-5561)*
Ilion Plastics Inc 315 894-4868
27 Pleasant Ave Ilion (13357) *(G-6475)*
Illinois Tool Works Inc 860 435-2574
5979 N Elm Ave Millerton (12546) *(G-8194)*
Illinois Tool Works Inc 716 681-8222
4471 Walden Ave Lancaster (14086) *(G-7024)*
Illinois Tool Works Inc 607 770-4945
33 Lewis Rd Binghamton (13905) *(G-895)*
Iluv, Port Washington Also called Jwin Electronics Corp *(G-13275)*
Ima Life North America Inc 716 695-6354
2175 Military Rd Tonawanda (14150) *(G-15550)*
Imacor Inc 516 393-0970
821 Franklin Ave Ste 301 Garden City (11530) *(G-5262)*
Image Iron Works Inc 718 592-8276
5050 98th St Corona (11368) *(G-3845)*
Image Press, The, Cicero Also called Add Associates Inc *(G-3513)*
Image Sales & Marketing Inc 516 238-7023
106 Thornwood Rd Massapequa Park (11762) *(G-7891)*
Image Tech 716 635-0167
96 Donna Lea Blvd Buffalo (14221) *(G-2880)*
Image Typography Inc 631 218-6932
751 Coates Ave Ste 31 Holbrook (11741) *(G-6188)*
Image360 ..... 585 272-1234
275 Marketplace Dr Rochester (14623) *(G-13878)*
Images Scientific Instruments, Staten Island Also called Images Si Inc *(G-15089)*
Images Si Inc 718 966-3694
109 Woods Of Arden Rd Staten Island (10312) *(G-15089)*
Imaginant Inc 585 264-0480
3800 Monroe Ave Ste 29 Pittsford (14534) *(G-13015)*
Imaging and Sensing Technology, Horseheads Also called Mirion Technologies Ist Corp *(G-6321)*
Imbitive Tech Amer Corp 888 843-2323
1623 Military Rd Ste 1011 Niagara Falls (14304) *(G-12294)*
Imbitive Technologies Corp (PA) 888 843-2323
1623 Military Rd Ste 1011 Niagara Falls (14304) *(G-12295)*
Imbtec America, Niagara Falls Also called Imbitive Tech Amer Corp *(G-12294)*
IMC Teddy Food Service 631 789-8881
50 Ranick Dr E Amityville (11701) *(G-286)*
Imco Inc 585 352-7810
15 Turner Dr Spencerport (14559) *(G-14979)*
Imek Media LLC 212 422-9000
32 Broadway Ste 511 New York (10004) *(G-10183)*
Imena Jewelry Manufacturer Inc 212 827-0073
2 W 45th St Ste 1000 New York (10036) *(G-10184)*
Imerys Fsed Mnrl Ngara FLS Inc 716 286-1250
4901 Hyde Park Blvd Niagara Falls (14305) *(G-12296)*
Imerys Fsed Mnrl Ngara FLS Inc (HQ) 716 286-1250
2000 College Ave Niagara Falls (14305) *(G-12297)*
Imerys Steelcasting Usa Inc (HQ) 716 278-1634
4111 Witmer Rd Niagara Falls (14305) *(G-12298)*
Imerys Usa Inc 315 287-0780
16a Main St Hailesboro Rd Gouverneur (13642) *(G-5491)*
IMG The Daily 212 541-5640
432 W 45th St Fl 5 New York (10036) *(G-10185)*
Immco Diagnostics Inc 716 691-0091
640 Ellicott St Fl 3 Buffalo (14203) *(G-2881)*
Impact Journals LLC 800 922-0957
6666 E Quaker St Ste 1 Orchard Park (14127) *(G-12718)*
Impact Tech A Skrsky Innvtions, Rochester Also called Sikorsky Aircraft Corporation *(G-14129)*

Impala Press Ltd 631 588-4262
931 S 2nd St Ronkonkoma (11779) *(G-14352)*
Imperia Masonry Supply Corp (PA) 914 738-0900
57 Canal Rd Pelham (10803) *(G-12936)*
Imperial Color, Brentwood Also called Lauricella Press Inc *(G-1140)*
Imperial Damper & Louver Co 718 731-3800
907 E 141st St Bronx (10454) *(G-1294)*
Imperial Frames & Albums LLC 718 832-9793
8200 21st Ave Brooklyn (11214) *(G-1995)*
Imperial Instrmnt & Mach, Westbury Also called Imperial Instrument Corp *(G-16341)*
Imperial Instrument Corp 516 739-6644
18 Sylvester St Westbury (11590) *(G-16341)*
Imperial Polymers Inc 718 387-4741
534 Grand St Brooklyn (11211) *(G-1996)*
Imperial Pools Inc (PA) 518 786-1200
33 Wade Rd Latham (12110) *(G-7075)*
Imperial-Harvard Label Co 212 736-8420
236 W 40th St Fl 3 New York (10018) *(G-10186)*
Imperium Partners Group LLC 212 433-1360
509 Madison Ave New York (10022) *(G-10187)*
Impladent Ltd (PA) 718 465-1810
19845 Foothill Ave Jamaica (11423) *(G-6651)*
Import-Export Corporation 718 707-0880
3814 30th St Long Island City (11101) *(G-7473)*
Impremedia LLC (PA) 212 807-4600
1 Metrotech Ctr Fl 18 Brooklyn (11201) *(G-1997)*
Impress Graphic Technologies 516 781-0845
141 Linden Ave Westbury (11590) *(G-16342)*
Impressart 631 940-9530
100 Executive Dr Ste D Edgewood (11717) *(G-4404)*
Impressions Inc 212 594-5954
36 W 37th St Rm 400 New York (10018) *(G-10188)*
Impressions International Inc 585 442-5240
410 Alexander St Ste 2 Rochester (14607) *(G-13879)*
Impressions Prtg & Graphics, New York Also called Designlogocom Inc *(G-9508)*
Impressive Imprints 716 692-0905
601 Division St North Tonawanda (14120) *(G-12432)*
Impressive Imprints Inc 631 293-6161
195 Central Ave Ste N Farmingdale (11735) *(G-4784)*
Imprint Branded Content LLC 212 888-8073
34 W 27th St Rm 501 New York (10001) *(G-10189)*
Imprinted Sportswear, Camillus Also called Steve Poli Sales *(G-3197)*
IMR Test Labs, Lansing Also called Metal Improvement Company LLC *(G-7056)*
Imrex LLC (PA) 516 479-3675
55 Sandy Hill Rd Oyster Bay (11771) *(G-12814)*
In Mocean Group LLC (PA) 212 944-0317
463 Fashion Ave Fl 21 New York (10018) *(G-10190)*
In Room Plus Inc 716 838-9433
2495 Main St Ste 217 Buffalo (14214) *(G-2882)*
In Toon Amkor Fashions Inc 718 937-4546
4809 34th St Long Island City (11101) *(G-7474)*
In-House Inc 718 445-9007
1535 126th St Ste 3 College Point (11356) *(G-3646)*
In-Step Marketing Inc Inc 212 797-3450
39 Broadway Fl 32 New York (10006) *(G-10191)*
In2green LLC 914 693-5054
14 Bellair Dr Hastings On Hudson (10706) *(G-5749)*
Incentivate Health LLC 518 469-8491
60 Railroad Pl Ste 101 Saratoga Springs (12866) *(G-14588)*
Incitec Pivot Limited 212 238-3010
120 Broadway Fl 32 New York (10271) *(G-10192)*
Incodema Inc 607 277-7070
407 Cliff St Ithaca (14850) *(G-6582)*
Incodema3d LLC 607 269-4390
407 Cliff St Ithaca (14850) *(G-6583)*
Incon Gems Inc 212 221-8560
2 W 46th St Ste 603 New York (10036) *(G-10193)*
Incredible Scents Inc 516 656-3300
1 Plaza Rd Ste 202 Greenvale (11548) *(G-5630)*
Incro Marketing USA Corp (PA) 917 365-5552
157 Columbus Ave New York (10023) *(G-10194)*
Incycle Software Corp (PA) 212 626-2608
1120 Ave Of The Americas New York (10036) *(G-10195)*
Indegy Inc 866 801-5394
1460 Broadway New York (10036) *(G-10196)*
Independence Harley-Davidson, Binghamton Also called Ihd Motorsports LLC *(G-894)*
Independent Baptist Voice, Conklin Also called Newspaper Publisher LLC *(G-3730)*
Independent Field Svc LLC (PA) 315 559-9243
6744 Pickard Dr Syracuse (13211) *(G-15342)*
Independent Home Products LLC 718 541-1256
59 Hempstead Gardens Dr West Hempstead (11552) *(G-16216)*
Index Incorporated 440 632-5400
415 Concord Ave Bronx (10455) *(G-1295)*
Index Magazine 212 243-1428
526 W 26th St Rm 920 New York (10001) *(G-10197)*
India Abroad Publications Inc 212 929-1727
102 Madison Ave Frnt B New York (10016) *(G-10198)*
Indian Ladder Farmstead Brewer 518 577-1484
287 Altamont Rd Altamont (12009) *(G-197)*
Indian Larry Legacy 718 609-9184
400 Union Ave Brooklyn (11211) *(G-1998)*

(PA)=Parent Co (HQ)=Headquarters (DH)=Div Headquarters

Indian Springs Mfg Co Inc 315 635-6101
2095 W Genesee Rd Baldwinsville (13027) ***(G-556)***

Indian Valley, Binghamton *Also called Ivi Services Inc* ***(G-897)***

Indian Water Treatment Plant, Ossining *Also called Ossining Village of Inc* ***(G-12773)***

Indigo Home Inc 212 684-4146
230 5th Ave Ste 1916 New York (10001) ***(G-10199)***

Indigo Rein, New York *Also called Jrg Apparel Group Company Ltd* ***(G-10372)***

Indikon Company, New Hartford *Also called Riverhawk Company LP* ***(G-8510)***

Indira Cesarine, New York *Also called Untitled Media* ***(G-11964)***

Indira Foods Inc 718 343-1500
25503 Hillside Ave # 255 Floral Park (11004) ***(G-4966)***

Indium Corporation of America (PA) 800 446-3486
34 Robinson Rd Clinton (13323) ***(G-3586)***

Indium Corporation of America 315 793-8200
1676 Lincoln Ave Utica (13502) ***(G-15713)***

Indium Corporation of America 315 381-2330
111 Business Park Dr Utica (13502) ***(G-15714)***

Indonesian Imports Inc (PA) 888 800-5899
339 5th Ave Fl 2 New York (10016) ***(G-10200)***

Indulge Desserts Holdings LLC (PA) 212 231-8600
666 5th Ave Fl 27 New York (10103) ***(G-10201)***

Indus Precision Manufacturing 845 268-0782
50 N Harrison Ave Ste 9 Congers (10920) ***(G-3718)***

Industrial Cables, Chester *Also called Nexans Energy USA Inc* ***(G-3478)***

Industrial Electronic Hardware 718 492-4440
140 58th St Ste 8e Brooklyn (11220) ***(G-1999)***

Industrial Fabricating Corp (PA) 315 437-3353
6201 E Molloy Rd East Syracuse (13057) ***(G-4348)***

Industrial Fabricating Corp 315 437-8234
4 Collamer Cir East Syracuse (13057) ***(G-4349)***

Industrial Finishing Products 718 342-4871
820 Remsen Ave Brooklyn (11236) ***(G-2000)***

Industrial Indxing Systems Inc 585 924-9181
626 Fishers Run Victor (14564) ***(G-15850)***

Industrial Machine Repair 607 272-0717
1144 Taughannock Blvd Ithaca (14850) ***(G-6584)***

Industrial Mch Gear Works LLC 516 695-4442
77 Woodland Ave Rockville Centre (11570) ***(G-14234)***

Industrial Municipal Equipment (PA) 631 665-6712
146 Concourse E Brightwaters (11718) ***(G-1186)***

Industrial Oil Tank Service 315 736-6080
120 Dry Rd Oriskany (13424) ***(G-12759)***

Industrial Paint Services Corp 607 687-0107
60 W Main St 62 Owego (13827) ***(G-12797)***

Industrial Paper Tube Inc 718 893-5000
1335 E Bay Ave Bronx (10474) ***(G-1296)***

Industrial Precision Pdts Inc 315 343-4421
350 Mitchell St Oswego (13126) ***(G-12779)***

Industrial Raw Materials LLC 212 688-8080
39 West Mall Plainview (11803) ***(G-13063)***

Industrial Raw Materials LLC 212 688-8080
112 W 56th St New York (10019) ***(G-10202)***

Industrial SEC Systems Contrls, Garden City *Also called Issco Corporation* ***(G-5263)***

Industrial Services of Wny 716 799-7788
7221 Niagara Falls Blvd Niagara Falls (14304) ***(G-12299)***

Industrial Support Inc 716 662-2954
36 Depot St Buffalo (14206) ***(G-2883)***

Industrial Test Eqp Co Inc 516 883-6423
2 Manhasset Ave Port Washington (11050) ***(G-13269)***

Industrial Tool & Die Co Inc 518 273-7383
14 Industrial Park Rd Troy (12180) ***(G-15609)***

Industrial Wax, Plainview *Also called Industrial Raw Materials LLC* ***(G-13063)***

Industrial Welding & Fabg Co, Jamestown *Also called Wilston Enterprises Inc* ***(G-6762)***

Industrial Welding & Fabg Co, Jamestown *Also called Fred Santucci Inc* ***(G-6716)***

Industry Forecast, Mount Kisco *Also called Jerome Levy Forecasting Center* ***(G-8345)***

Inertia Switch Inc 845 359-8300
70 S Greenbush Rd Orangeburg (10962) ***(G-12679)***

Inex Inc 716 537-2270
9229 Olean Rd Holland (14080) ***(G-6219)***

Infant Formula Laboratory Svc 718 257-3000
711 Livonia Ave Brooklyn (11207) ***(G-2001)***

Inficon Inc (HQ) 315 434-1100
2 Technology Pl East Syracuse (13057) ***(G-4350)***

Inficon Holding AG 315 434-1100
2 Technology Pl East Syracuse (13057) ***(G-4351)***

Infimed, Liverpool *Also called Varex Imaging Corporation* ***(G-7269)***

Infimed Inc (PA) 315 453-4545
121 Metropolitan Park Dr Liverpool (13088) ***(G-7236)***

Infimed Inc 585 383-1710
15 Fisher Rd Pittsford (14534) ***(G-13016)***

Infinite Software Solutions 718 982-1315
1110 South Ave Ste 303 Staten Island (10314) ***(G-15090)***

Infinity Augmented Reality Inc 917 677-2084
228 Park Ave S 61130 New York (10003) ***(G-10203)***

Infinity Sourcing Services LLC 212 868-2900
224 W 35th St Ste 902 New York (10001) ***(G-10204)***

Infirmary Nyc 504 606-6280
1720 2nd Ave New York (10128) ***(G-10205)***

Infitec Inc 315 433-1150
6500 Badgley Rd East Syracuse (13057) ***(G-4352)***

Inflation Systems Inc 914 381-8070
500 Ogden Ave Mamaroneck (10543) ***(G-7746)***

Influence Graphics, Long Island City *Also called Sizzal LLC* ***(G-7593)***

Info Label Inc 518 664-0791
12 Enterprise Ave Halfmoon (12065) ***(G-5663)***

Info Quick Solutions 315 463-1400
7460 Morgan Rd Liverpool (13090) ***(G-7237)***

Infobase Holdings Inc (HQ) 212 967-8800
132 W 31st St Fl 17 New York (10001) ***(G-10206)***

Infobase Publishing Company (PA) 212 967-8800
132 W 31st St Fl 17 New York (10001) ***(G-10207)***

Infomir LLC 631 482-6636
2626 E 14th St Ste 101f Brooklyn (11235) ***(G-2002)***

Infor Global Solutions Inc (HQ) 646 336-1700
641 Avenue Of Americas New York (10011) ***(G-10208)***

Inform Studio Inc 718 401-6149
480 Austin Pl Frnt E Bronx (10455) ***(G-1297)***

Informa Business Media Inc (HQ) 212 204-4200
605 3rd Ave New York (10158) ***(G-10209)***

Informa Business Media Inc 914 949-8500
707 Westchester Ave # 101 White Plains (10604) ***(G-16462)***

Informa Media Inc (HQ) 212 204-4200
605 3rd Ave Fl 22 New York (10158) ***(G-10210)***

Informa Media Inc 212 204-4200
1166 Ave Of The Americas New York (10036) ***(G-10211)***

Informa Solutions Inc 516 543-3733
45 Rockefeller Plz # 2000 New York (10111) ***(G-10212)***

Informa Uk Ltd 646 957-8966
52 Vanderbilt Ave Fl 7 New York (10017) ***(G-10213)***

Informatica LLC 212 845-7650
810 7th Ave Ste 1100c New York (10019) ***(G-10214)***

Informerly Inc 646 238-7137
35 Essex St New York (10002) ***(G-10215)***

Infoservices International 631 549-1805
1 Saint Marks Pl Cold Spring Harbor (11724) ***(G-3631)***

Infrared Components Corp 315 732-1544
2306 Bleecker St Utica (13501) ***(G-15715)***

Ingenious Designs LLC 631 254-3376
2060 9th Ave Ronkonkoma (11779) ***(G-14353)***

Ingersoll-Rand Company 716 896-6600
3101 Broadway St Buffalo (14227) ***(G-2884)***

Ingham Industries Inc 631 242-2493
1363 Lincoln Ave Ste 1 Holbrook (11741) ***(G-6189)***

Ingleside Machine Co Inc 585 924-3046
1120 Hook Rd Farmington (14425) ***(G-4916)***

Inglis Co Inc 315 475-1315
116 Granger St Syracuse (13202) ***(G-15343)***

Ink Publishing Corporation 347 294-1220
68 Jay St Ste 315 Brooklyn (11201) ***(G-2003)***

Ink Well 718 253-9736
1440 Coney Island Ave Brooklyn (11230) ***(G-2004)***

Ink-It Printing Inc 718 229-5590
1535 126th St Ste 1 College Point (11356) ***(G-3647)***

Ink-It Prtg Inc/Angle Offset, College Point *Also called Ink-It Printing Inc* ***(G-3647)***

Inkkas LLC 646 845-9803
38 E 29th St Rm 6r New York (10016) ***(G-10216)***

Inland Paper Products Corp 718 827-8150
444 Liberty Ave Brooklyn (11207) ***(G-2005)***

Inland Printing Company Inc 516 367-4700
36 Orchard Dr Woodbury (11797) ***(G-16622)***

Inland Vacuum Industries Inc (PA) 585 293-3330
35 Howard Ave Churchville (14428) ***(G-3510)***

Innex Industries Inc 585 247-3575
6 Marway Dr Rochester (14624) ***(G-13880)***

Innofun Digital Entrmt LLC 347 708-0078
19 W 34th St Rm 1018 New York (10001) ***(G-10217)***

Innogenix Inc 631 450-4704
8200 New Horizons Blvd Amityville (11701) ***(G-287)***

Innotech Graphic Eqp Corp 845 268-6900
614 Corporate Way Ste 5 Valley Cottage (10989) ***(G-15755)***

Innova Interiors Inc 718 401-2122
780 E 134th St Fl 2 Bronx (10454) ***(G-1298)***

Innovant Inc (PA) 631 348-1900
135 Oval Dr Islandia (11749) ***(G-6531)***

Innovant Inc 212 929-4883
37 W 20th St Ste 1101 New York (10011) ***(G-10218)***

Innovant Group, Islandia *Also called Innovant Inc* ***(G-6531)***

Innovation Associates Inc 607 798-9376
530 Columbia Dr Ste 101 Johnson City (13790) ***(G-6811)***

Innovation In Motion Inc 407 878-7561
780 Long Beach Blvd Long Beach (11561) ***(G-7359)***

Innovation MGT Group Inc 800 889-0987
999 Montauk Hwy Shirley (11967) ***(G-14836)***

Innovative Automation Inc 631 439-3300
595 Smith St Farmingdale (11735) ***(G-4785)***

Innovative Cleaning Solutions 716 731-4408
2990 Carney Dr Sanborn (14132) ***(G-14547)***

Innovative Designs LLC 212 695-0892
141 W 36th St Fl 8 New York (10018) ***(G-10219)***

Innovative Industries LLC 718 784-7300
4322 22nd St Ste 205 Long Island City (11101) ***(G-7475)***

Innovative Jewelry Inc (PA) 718 408-8950
707 Executive Blvd Ste D Valley Cottage (10989) ***(G-15756)***

Innovative Labs LLC 631 231-5522
85 Commerce Dr Hauppauge (11788) *(G-5849)*
Innovative Municipal Pdts US 800 387-5777
454 River Rd Glenmont (12077) *(G-5412)*
Innovative Plastics Corp (PA) 845 359-7500
400 Route 303 Orangeburg (10962) *(G-12680)*
Innovative Power Products Inc 631 563-0088
1170 Lincoln Ave Unit 7 Holbrook (11741) *(G-6190)*
Innovative Surface Solutions, Glenmont *Also called Innovative Municipal Pdts US (G-5412)*
Innovative Systems of New York 516 541-7410
201 Rose St Massapequa Park (11762) *(G-7892)*
Innovative Video Tech Inc 631 388-5700
355 Oser Ave Hauppauge (11788) *(G-5850)*
Innroad Inc 631 458-1437
519 8th Ave Fl 15 New York (10018) *(G-10220)*
Ino-Tex LLC 212 400-2205
135 W 36th St Fl 6 New York (10018) *(G-10221)*
Inolife Tchnlgies Oprtions Inc 212 386-5575
11 E 86th St Ste 19b New York (10028) *(G-10222)*
Inori Jewels 347 703-5078
580 5th Ave New York (10036) *(G-10223)*
Inova LLC 866 528-2804
2 Van Buren Blvd Bldg 19 Guilderland Center (12085) *(G-5656)*
Inova LLC 518 861-3400
6032 Depot Rd Altamont (12009) *(G-198)*
Inpro Corporation 716 332-4699
250 Cooper Ave Ste 102 Tonawanda (14150) *(G-15551)*
Inprotopia Corporation 917 338-7501
401 W 110th St Apt 2001 New York (10025) *(G-10224)*
Inquiring Minds Inc (PA) 845 246-5775
65 S Partition St Saugerties (12477) *(G-14608)*
Inscape (new York) Inc (HQ) 716 665-6210
221 Lister Ave 1 Falconer (14733) *(G-4681)*
Inscape Architectural Interiors, Falconer *Also called Inscape (new York) Inc (G-4681)*
Inscape Inc 716 665-6210
221 Lister Ave Falconer (14733) *(G-4682)*
Insert Outsert Experts, The, Lockport *Also called Gooding Co Inc (G-7308)*
Insight Unlimited Inc 914 861-2090
660 Quaker Rd Chappaqua (10514) *(G-3422)*
Insight Venture Partners IV 212 230-9200
1114 Avenue Of The Americ New York (10036) *(G-10225)*
Insomnia Cookies On The Hill, New York *Also called U Serve Brands Inc (G-11927)*
Inspired Entertainment Inc (PA) 646 565-3861
250 W 57th St Ste 2223 New York (10107) *(G-10226)*
Instant Again LLC 585 436-8003
1277 Mount Read Blvd # 2 Rochester (14606) *(G-13881)*
Instant Monogramming Inc 585 654-5550
1150 University Ave Ste 5 Rochester (14607) *(G-13882)*
Instant Printing Service, Ithaca *Also called Madison Printing Corp (G-6592)*
Instant Stream Inc 917 438-7182
1271 Ave Of The Americas New York (10020) *(G-10227)*
Instant Verticals Inc 631 501-0001
330 Broadhollow Rd Farmingdale (11735) *(G-4786)*
Instantwhip of Buffalo Inc 716 892-7031
2117 Genesee St Buffalo (14211) *(G-2885)*
Institute of Electrical and El 212 705-8900
3 Park Ave Fl 17 New York (10016) *(G-10228)*
Instrumentation Laboratory Co 845 680-0028
526 Route 303 Orangeburg (10962) *(G-12681)*
Insty Trints, Kenmore *Also called Horace J Metz (G-6861)*
Insty-Prints, Niagara Falls *Also called Graphicomm Inc (G-12289)*
Insty-Prints of Buffalo Inc (PA) 716 853-6483
265 Franklin St Buffalo (14202) *(G-2886)*
Insulating Coatings Corp 607 723-1727
27 Link Dr Ste D Binghamton (13904) *(G-896)*
Insultech, North Tonawanda *Also called Shannon Entps Wstn NY Inc (G-12450)*
Int Trading USA LLC 212 760-2338
261 W 35th St Ste 1100 New York (10001) *(G-10229)*
Intech 21 Inc 516 626-7221
21 Harbor Park Dr Port Washington (11050) *(G-13270)*
Inteco Intimates, New York *Also called Intimateco LLC (G-10256)*
Integer Holdings Corporation 716 937-5100
11900 Walden Ave Alden (14004) *(G-173)*
Integer Holdings Corporation 716 759-5200
4098 Barton Rd Clarence (14031) *(G-3534)*
Integra Microsystem 1988 Inc 718 609-6099
61 Greenpoint Ave Ste 412 Brooklyn (11222) *(G-2006)*
Integrated Control Corp 631 673-5100
748 Park Ave Huntington (11743) *(G-6400)*
Integrated Copyright Group 615 329-3999
1745 Broadway 19 New York (10019) *(G-10230)*
Integrated Graphics Inc (PA) 212 592-5600
7 W 36th St Fl 12 New York (10018) *(G-10231)*
Integrated Indus Resources, Lockport *Also called GM Components Holdings LLC (G-7307)*
Integrated Liner Tech Inc (PA) 518 621-7422
45 Discovery Dr Rensselaer (12144) *(G-13475)*
Integrated Medical Devices 315 457-4200
549 Electronics Pkwy # 200 Liverpool (13088) *(G-7238)*
Integrated Solar Tech LLC 914 249-9364
181 Westchester Ave # 409 Port Chester (10573) *(G-13202)*
Integrated Tech Support Svcs 718 454-2497
18616 Jordan Ave Saint Albans (11412) *(G-14508)*

Integrated Water Management 607 844-4276
289 Cortland Rd Dryden (13053) *(G-4150)*
Integrated Wood Components Inc 607 467-1739
791 Airport Rd Deposit (13754) *(G-4108)*
Integrity Tool Incorporated 315 524-4409
6485 Furnace Rd Ontario (14519) *(G-12655)*
Integrted Work Envronments LLC 716 725-5088
6346 Everwood Ct N East Amherst (14051) *(G-4190)*
Integument Technologies Inc 716 873-1199
72 Pearce Ave Tonawanda (14150) *(G-15552)*
Intek Precision 585 293-0853
539 Attridge Rd Churchville (14428) *(G-3511)*
INTEL Corporation 408 765-8080
55 Dodge Rd Getzville (14068) *(G-5348)*
Intelibs Inc 877 213-2640
1500 Stony Brook Rd Ste 3 Stony Brook (11794) *(G-15167)*
Intellicheck Inc (PA) 516 992-1900
535 Broadhollow Rd B51 Melville (11747) *(G-8037)*
Intellidyne LLC 516 676-0777
303 Sunnyside Blvd # 75 Plainview (11803) *(G-13064)*
Intelligen Power Systems LLC 212 750-0373
301 Winding Rd Old Bethpage (11804) *(G-12586)*
Intelligence Newsletter, New York *Also called Intellignc The Ftr Cmptng Nwsl (G-10232)*
Intelligent Ctrl Systems LLC 516 340-1011
208 Route 109 Ste 211 Farmingdale (11735) *(G-4787)*
Intelligent Traffic Systems 631 567-5994
140 Keyland Ct Unit 1 Bohemia (11716) *(G-1037)*
Intellignc The Ftr Cmptng Nwsl 212 222-1123
360 Central Park W New York (10025) *(G-10232)*
Intellimetal Inc 585 424-3260
2025 Brighton Henrietta Rochester (14623) *(G-13883)*
Intellitravel Media Inc (HQ) 646 695-6700
530 Fashion Ave Rm 201 New York (10018) *(G-10233)*
Intentions Jewelry LLC 845 226-4650
83 Miller Hill Dr Lagrangeville (12540) *(G-6957)*
Inter Craft Custom Furniture 718 278-2573
1431 Astoria Blvd Astoria (11102) *(G-431)*
Inter Metal Fabricators Inc 718 852-4000
161 Dikeman St Brooklyn (11231) *(G-2007)*
Inter Molds Inc 631 667-8580
26 Cleveland Ave Bay Shore (11706) *(G-689)*
Inter Pacific Consulting Corp 718 460-2787
14055 34th Ave Apt 3n Flushing (11354) *(G-5010)*
Inter Parfums Inc (PA) 212 983-2640
551 5th Ave New York (10176) *(G-10234)*
Inter Parfums Usa LLC 212 983-2640
551 5th Ave Rm 1500 New York (10176) *(G-10235)*
Inter State Laminates Inc 518 283-8355
44 Main St Poestenkill (12140) *(G-13181)*
Inter-Fence Co Inc 718 939-9700
1520 129th St College Point (11356) *(G-3648)*
Interactive Instruments Inc 518 347-0955
704 Corporation Park # 1 Scotia (12302) *(G-14742)*
Interaxissourcingcom Inc 212 905-6001
41 E 11th St Fl 11 New York (10003) *(G-10236)*
Interbrand LLC 212 840-9595
1 W 37th St Fl 9 New York (10018) *(G-10237)*
Intercept Pharmaceuticals Inc (PA) 646 747-1000
10 Hudson Yards Fl 37 New York (10001) *(G-10238)*
Intercos America Inc 845 732-3900
11 Centerock Rd West Nyack (10994) *(G-16271)*
Intercos America Inc 845 732-3910
120 Brookhill Dr West Nyack (10994) *(G-16272)*
Intercotton Company Inc 212 265-3809
888 7th Ave Fl 29 New York (10106) *(G-10239)*
Intercultural Alliance Artists 917 406-1202
4510 165th St Flushing (11358) *(G-5011)*
Interdgital Communications LLC 631 622-4000
2 Huntington Quad Ste 4s Melville (11747) *(G-8038)*
Interdynamics 914 241-1423
100 S Bedford Rd Ste 300 Mount Kisco (10549) *(G-8344)*
Interface Performance Mtls 315 346-3100
9635 Main St Beaver Falls (13305) *(G-766)*
Interface Performance Mtls Inc 315 592-8100
2885 State Route 481 Fulton (13069) *(G-5221)*
Interface Performance Mtls Inc 518 686-3400
12 Davis St Hoosick Falls (12090) *(G-6276)*
Interface Products Co Inc 631 242-4605
215 N Fehr Way Ste C Bay Shore (11706) *(G-690)*
Interfaceflor LLC 212 686-8284
330 5th Ave Fl 12 New York (10001) *(G-10240)*
Interhellenic Publishing Inc 212 967-5016
421 7th Ave Ste 810 New York (10001) *(G-10241)*
Interior Metals 718 439-7324
255 48th St Brooklyn (11220) *(G-2008)*
Interior Solutions of Wny LLC 716 332-0372
472 Franklin St Buffalo (14202) *(G-2887)*
Interiors By Robert, Richmond Hill *Also called Terbo Ltd (G-13516)*
Interiors-Pft Inc 212 244-9600
3200 Skillman Ave Fl 3 Long Island City (11101) *(G-7476)*
International Aids Vaccine Ini 646 381-8066
140 58th St Brooklyn (11220) *(G-2009)*

ALPHABETIC

International Aids Vccne Inttv (PA) — 212 847-1111
125 Broad St Fl 9th New York (10004) *(G-10242)*

International Bus Mchs Corp — 212 324-5000
55 Broad St Fl 27 New York (10004) *(G-10243)*

International Bus Mchs Corp — 914 345-5219
1 New Orchard Rd Ste 1 # 1 Armonk (10504) *(G-404)*

International Bus Mchs Corp — 800 426-4968
10 North Dr Hopewell Junction (12533) *(G-6289)*

International Bus Mchs Corp — 914 499-2000
20 Old Post Rd Armonk (10504) *(G-405)*

International Business Times, New York Also called Newsweek Media Group Inc *(G-10957)*

International Casein Corp Cal — 516 466-4363
111 Great Neck Rd Ste 218 Great Neck (11021) *(G-5562)*

International Center For Postg — 607 257-5860
179 Graham Rd Ste E Ithaca (14850) *(G-6585)*

International Climbing Mchs — 607 288-4001
630 Elmira Rd Ithaca (14850) *(G-6586)*

International Data Group Inc — 212 331-7883
117 E 55th St Ste 204 New York (10022) *(G-10244)*

International Design Assoc Ltd — 212 687-0333
747 3rd Ave Rm 218 New York (10017) *(G-10245)*

International Direct Group Inc — 212 921-9036
525 7th Ave Rm 208 New York (10018) *(G-10246)*

International Fiber Corp — 716 693-4040
50 Bridge St North Tonawanda (14120) *(G-12433)*

International Fire-Shield Inc — 315 255-1006
194 Genesee St Auburn (13021) *(G-483)*

International Fireproof Door — 718 783-1310
1005 Greene Ave Brooklyn (11221) *(G-2010)*

International Identity LLC — 787 864-0379
824 Park Ave Apt 1c Brooklyn (11206) *(G-2011)*

International Imaging Mtls Inc (PA) — 716 691-6333
310 Commerce Dr Amherst (14228) *(G-232)*

International Inspirations Ltd (PA) — 212 465-8500
358 5th Ave Rm 501 New York (10001) *(G-10247)*

International Key Supply LLC — 631 983-6096
32 Gazza Blvd Farmingdale (11735) *(G-4788)*

International Leisure Pdts Inc — 631 254-2155
191 Rodeo Dr Edgewood (11717) *(G-4405)*

International Mdse Svcs Inc — 914 699-4000
336 S Fulton Ave Fl 1 Mount Vernon (10553) *(G-8409)*

International Metals Trdg LLC — 866 923-0182
25 Melville Park Rd # 114 Melville (11747) *(G-8039)*

International MGT Netwrk — 646 401-0032
445 Park Ave Fl 9 New York (10022) *(G-10248)*

International Mtls & Sups Inc — 518 834-9899
56 Industrial Park Rd Keeseville (12944) *(G-6851)*

International Newspaper Prntng, Glen Head Also called International Newsppr Prtg Co *(G-5381)*

International Newsppr Prtg Co — 516 626-6095
18 Carlisle Dr Glen Head (11545) *(G-5381)*

International Office — 212 334-4617
110 Greene St Ste 1206 New York (10012) *(G-10249)*

International Ord Tech Inc — 716 664-1100
101 Harrison St Jamestown (14701) *(G-6724)*

International Paper Company — 518 585-6761
568 Shore Airport Rd Ticonderoga (12883) *(G-15511)*

International Paper Company — 585 663-1000
200 Boxart St Rochester (14612) *(G-13884)*

International Paper Company — 845 986-6409
1422 Long Meadow Rd Tuxedo Park (10987) *(G-15657)*

International Paper Company — 607 775-1550
1240 Conklin Rd Conklin (13748) *(G-3728)*

International Paper Company — 315 797-5120
50 Harbor Point Rd Utica (13502) *(G-15716)*

International Paper Company — 716 852-2144
100 Bud Mil Dr Buffalo (14206) *(G-2888)*

International Paper Company — 518 372-6461
803 Corporation Park Glenville (12302) *(G-5446)*

International Robotics Inc — 914 630-1060
2001 Palmer Ave Ste Ll1 Larchmont (10538) *(G-7057)*

International Society For Medl — 520 820-8594
520 White Plains Rd Tarrytown (10591) *(G-15479)*

International Stone Accessrs — 718 522-5399
703 Myrtle Ave Brooklyn (11205) *(G-2012)*

International Stone Gallery, Lockport Also called 6478 Ridge Road LLC *(G-7283)*

International Time Products — 516 931-0005
410 Jericho Tpke Ste 110 Jericho (11753) *(G-6791)*

International Tool & Mch Inc — 585 654-6955
121 Lincoln Ave Rochester (14611) *(G-13885)*

International Wire Group, Camden Also called Camden Wire Co Inc *(G-3186)*

International Wire Group (PA) — 315 245-3800
12 Masonic Ave Camden (13316) *(G-3188)*

International Wire Group Inc (HQ) — 315 245-2000
12 Masonic Ave Camden (13316) *(G-3189)*

Internationl Studios Inc — 212 819-1616
108 W 39th St Rm 1300 New York (10018) *(G-10250)*

Internodal International Inc — 631 765-0037
54800 Route 25 Southold (11971) *(G-14969)*

Interntnal Auto Voluntary Untd — 718 743-8732
1956 Bay Ridge Ave Fl 2 Brooklyn (11204) *(G-2013)*

Interntnl Bus Cmmncations Inc (PA) — 516 352-4505
1981 Marcus Ave Ste C105 New Hyde Park (11042) *(G-8542)*

Interntnal Cntrls Msrmnts Corp (PA) — 315 233-5266
7313 William Barry Blvd North Syracuse (13212) *(G-12406)*

Interntnal Elctronic Mchs Corp — 518 268-1636
850 River St Troy (12180) *(G-15610)*

Interntnal Flvors Frgrnces Inc (PA) — 212 765-5500
521 W 57th St New York (10019) *(G-10251)*

Interntnal Pblctons Mdia Group, New York Also called Interntnl Publcatns Media Grup *(G-10252)*

Interntnl Publcatns Media Grup — 917 604-9602
708 3rd Ave 145 New York (10017) *(G-10252)*

Interntonal Consmr Connections — 516 481-3438
5 Terminal Rd Unit A West Hempstead (11552) *(G-16217)*

Interparts International Inc (PA) — 516 576-2000
190 Express St Plainview (11803) *(G-13065)*

Interplex Nas Electronics, College Point Also called Nas CP Corp *(G-3657)*

Intersource Management Group (PA) — 518 372-6798
7 Corporate Dr Ste 3 Halfmoon (12065) *(G-5664)*

Intersource Management Group — 518 372-6798
144 Erie Blvd Schenectady (12305) *(G-14690)*

Interstate Litho Corp — 631 232-6025
151 Alkier St Brentwood (11717) *(G-1136)*

Interstate Window Corporation — 631 231-0800
345 Crooked Hill Rd Ste 1 Brentwood (11717) *(G-1137)*

Interstate Wood & Vinyl Pdts, Amityville Also called Interstate Wood Products Inc *(G-288)*

Interstate Wood Products Inc — 631 842-4488
1084 Sunrise Hwy Amityville (11701) *(G-288)*

Intersurgical Incorporated (PA) — 315 451-2900
6757 Kinne St East Syracuse (13057) *(G-4353)*

Intertex USA Inc — 212 279-3601
131 W 35th St Fl 10 New York (10001) *(G-10253)*

Interview New York — 857 928-4120
77 Bleecker St New York (10012) *(G-10254)*

Inteva Products LLC — 248 655-8886
30 Rockefeller Plz New York (10112) *(G-10255)*

Intex Company Inc (PA) — 516 223-0200
80 Commercial St Freeport (11520) *(G-5162)*

Intimateco LLC — 212 239-4411
463 7th Ave Rm 602 New York (10018) *(G-10256)*

Intra-Cellular Therapies Inc (PA) — 646 440-9333
430 E 29th St Ste 900 New York (10016) *(G-10257)*

Intralinks Holdings Inc (HQ) — 212 543-7700
150 E 42nd St Fl 8 New York (10017) *(G-10258)*

Intrapac International Corp — 518 561-2030
4 Plant St Plattsburgh (12901) *(G-13126)*

Intraworlds Inc — 631 602-5333
222 Broadway Fl 19 New York (10038) *(G-10259)*

Intrepid Control Service Inc — 718 886-8771
2904 Francis Lewis Blvd Flushing (11358) *(G-5012)*

Intri-Cut Inc — 716 691-5200
90 Pineview Dr Amherst (14228) *(G-233)*

Intrigue Concepts Inc — 800 424-8170
8 Gilbert Pl Ste 8 # 8 Roosevelt (11575) *(G-14435)*

Intriguing Threads Apparel Inc (PA) — 212 768-8733
552 Fashion Ave Rm 603 New York (10018) *(G-10260)*

Intrinsiq Materials Inc — 585 301-4432
1200 Ridgeway Ave Ste 110 Rochester (14615) *(G-13886)*

Intstrux LLC — 646 688-2782
15 W 39th St Fl 13 New York (10018) *(G-10261)*

Intuition Publishing Limited — 212 838-7115
40 E 34th St Rm 1101 New York (10016) *(G-10262)*

Invagen Pharmaceuticals Inc — 631 949-6367
550 S Research Pl Central Islip (11722) *(G-3372)*

Invagen Pharmaceuticals Inc (HQ) — 631 231-3233
7 Oser Ave Ste 4 Hauppauge (11788) *(G-5851)*

Investars, New York Also called Netelogic Inc *(G-10911)*

Investment News — 212 210-0100
711 3rd Ave Fl 3 New York (10017) *(G-10263)*

Investors Business Daily Inc — 212 626-7676
140 E 45th St Ste 19b New York (10017) *(G-10264)*

Invid Tech, Hauppauge Also called Innovative Video Tech Inc *(G-5850)*

Invision Inc (HQ) — 212 557-5554
25 W 43rd St Ste 609 New York (10036) *(G-10265)*

Inwood Material — 516 371-1842
1 Sheridan Blvd Inwood (11096) *(G-6493)*

INX International Ink Co — 716 366-6010
3257 Middle Rd Dunkirk (14048) *(G-4172)*

Ion Optics Inc — 518 339-6853
75 Benjamin St Albany (12202) *(G-86)*

Ion-Tof Usa Inc — 845 352-8082
100 Red Schoolhouse Rd A-1 Spring Valley (10977) *(G-14996)*

Ip Med Inc — 516 766-3800
3571 Hargale Rd Oceanside (11572) *(G-12541)*

IPC/Razor LLC (PA) — 212 551-4500
277 Park Ave Fl 39 New York (10172) *(G-10266)*

Ipcc, Flushing Also called Inter Pacific Consulting Corp *(G-5010)*

Ipe, Orchard Park Also called Bos-Hatten Inc *(G-12700)*

Ippolita, New York Also called Ale Viola LLC *(G-8789)*

Ipsidy Inc (PA) — 407 951-8640
780 Long Beach Blvd Long Beach (11561) *(G-7360)*

Iquit Cig LLC — 718 475-1422
4014 13th Ave Brooklyn (11218) *(G-2014)*

Ir Media Group (usa) Inc 212 425-9649
25 Broadway Fl 9 New York (10004) *(G-10267)*
Iradj Moini Couture Ltd 212 594-9242
403 W 46th St New York (10036) *(G-10268)*
Irene Cerone 315 668-2899
9600 Brewerton Rd Brewerton (13029) *(G-1151)*
Iridesse Inc 212 230-6000
600 Madison Ave Fl 5 New York (10022) *(G-10269)*
Iridium Industries Inc 516 504-9700
17 Barstow Rd Ste 302 Great Neck (11021) *(G-5563)*
Iriniri Designs Ltd 845 469-7934
1358 Kings Hwy Sugar Loaf (10981) *(G-15200)*
Irish America Inc 212 725-2993
875 Americas Rm 2100 New York (10001) *(G-10270)*
Irish America Magazine, New York *Also called Irish America Inc (G-10270)*
Irish Echo Newspaper Corp 212 482-4818
165 Madison Ave Rm 302 New York (10016) *(G-10271)*
Irish Tribune Inc 212 684-3366
875 Avenue Of The Amerrm2 Rm 2100 New York (10001) *(G-10272)*
Irish Voice Newspaper, New York *Also called Irish Tribune Inc (G-10272)*
Iron Art Inc 914 592-7977
14 N Payne St Elmsford (10523) *(G-4546)*
Iron Flamingo Brewery, Corning *Also called Rising Sons 6 Brewing Coinc (G-3824)*
Iron Horse Graphics Ltd 631 537-3400
112 Maple Ln Bridgehampton (11932) *(G-1181)*
Iron Smoke Whiskey LLC 585 388-7584
111 Parce Ave Ste 5 Fairport (14450) *(G-4635)*
Ironshore Holdings Inc 315 457-1052
290 Elwood Davis Rd Liverpool (13088) *(G-7239)*
Irony Limited Inc (PA) 631 329-4065
53 Sag Harbor Tpke East Hampton (11937) *(G-4238)*
Iroquois Rock Products Inc (HQ) 585 381-7010
1150 Penfield Rd Rochester (14625) *(G-13887)*
Irpenscom 585 507-7997
4 Katsura Ct Penfield (14526) *(G-12941)*
Irtronics Instruments Inc 914 693-6291
132 Forest Blvd Ardsley (10502) *(G-395)*
Irv Inc 212 334-4507
475 Park Ave S Fl 11 New York (10016) *(G-10273)*
Irv & Vic Sportswear Co, Yonkers *Also called Robert Viggiani (G-16796)*
Irv Schroder & Sons Inc 518 828-0194
2906 Atlantic Ave Stottville (12172) *(G-15181)*
Irving Consumer Products Inc (HQ) 518 747-4151
1 Eddy St Fort Edward (12828) *(G-5096)*
Irving Farm Coffee Co Inc (PA) 212 206-0707
151 W 19th St Fl 6 New York (10011) *(G-10274)*
Irving Tissue Div, Fort Edward *Also called Irving Consumer Products Inc (G-5096)*
Irving Woodlands LLC 607 723-4862
53 Shaw Rd Conklin (13748) *(G-3729)*
Irx Therapeutics Inc 347 442-0640
140 58th St Brooklyn (11220) *(G-2015)*
Isfel Co Inc (PA) 212 736-6216
110 W 34th St Rm 1101 New York (10001) *(G-10275)*
Ish Precision Machine Corp (PA) 718 436-8858
190 Earle Ave Lynbrook (11563) *(G-7665)*
Isimulate LLC 877 947-2831
43 New Scotland Ave Albany (12208) *(G-87)*
Isine Inc (PA) 631 913-4400
105 Maxess Rd Ste 124 Melville (11747) *(G-8040)*
Isis/Koppermann, New York *Also called Isisnet LLC (G-10276)*
Isisnet LLC 212 239-1205
53 W 36th St Rm 502 New York (10018) *(G-10276)*
Island Audio Engineering 631 543-2372
7 Glenmere Ct Commack (11725) *(G-3696)*
Island Automated Gate Co LLC 631 425-0196
125 W Hills Rd Huntington Station (11746) *(G-6448)*
Island Chimney Service, Bohemia *Also called Ace Cntracting Consulting Corp (G-971)*
Island Circuits International 516 625-5555
1318 130th St Fl 2 College Point (11356) *(G-3649)*
Island Components Group Inc 631 563-4224
101 Colin Dr Unit 4 Holbrook (11741) *(G-6191)*
Island Custom Stairs Inc 631 205-5335
23 Scouting Blvd Unit C Medford (11763) *(G-7954)*
Island Industries Corp 631 451-8825
480 Mill Rd Coram (11727) *(G-3799)*
Island Instrument Corp 631 243-0550
65 Burt Dr Deer Park (11729) *(G-3987)*
Island Interiors, West Babylon *Also called Dbs Interiors Corp (G-16152)*
Island Lite Louvers Inc 631 608-4250
35 Albany Ave Amityville (11701) *(G-289)*
Island Machine Inc 518 562-1232
86 Boynton Ave Plattsburgh (12901) *(G-13127)*
Island Marketing Corp 516 739-0500
95 Searing Ave Ste 2 Mineola (11501) *(G-8229)*
Island Nameplate Inc 845 651-4005
124 S Main St Florida (10921) *(G-4971)*
Island Ordnance Systems LLC 516 746-2100
267 E Jericho Tpke Ste 2 Mineola (11501) *(G-8230)*
Island Precision, Ronkonkoma *Also called Roger Latari (G-14408)*
Island Publications, Melville *Also called Distinction Magazine Inc (G-8016)*
Island Pyrochemical Inds Corp (PA) 516 746-2100
267 E Jericho Tpke Ste 2 Mineola (11501) *(G-8231)*
Island Ready Mix Inc 631 874-3777
170 Railroad Ave Center Moriches (11934) *(G-3339)*
Island Recycling Corp 631 234-6688
228 Blydenburg Rd Central Islip (11749) *(G-3373)*
Island Research and Dev Corp 631 471-7100
200 13th Ave Unit 12 Ronkonkoma (11779) *(G-14354)*
Island Silkscreen Inc 631 757-4567
328 Larkfield Rd East Northport (11731) *(G-4265)*
Island Stairs Corp 347 645-0560
178 Industrial Loop Staten Island (10309) *(G-15091)*
Island Street Lumber Co Inc 716 692-4127
11 Felton St North Tonawanda (14120) *(G-12434)*
Island Technology, Ronkonkoma *Also called Island Research and Dev Corp (G-14354)*
Islandaire, Saint James *Also called RE Hansen Industries Inc (G-14514)*
Islandia Mri Associates PC 631 234-2828
200 Corporate Plz Ste 203 Central Islip (11749) *(G-3374)*
Islechem LLC 716 773-8401
2801 Long Rd Grand Island (14072) *(G-5503)*
Islip Bulletin, Patchogue *Also called John Lor Publishing Ltd (G-12868)*
Islip Miniture Golf 631 940-8900
500 E Main St Bay Shore (11706) *(G-691)*
ISO Plastics Corp 914 663-8300
160 E 1st St Mount Vernon (10550) *(G-8410)*
Isolation Dynamics Corp 631 491-5670
66 Otis St Unit A West Babylon (11704) *(G-16158)*
Isolation Systems Inc 716 694-6390
889 Erie Ave Ste 1 North Tonawanda (14120) *(G-12435)*
Isolation Technology Inc 631 253-3314
73 Nancy St Unit A West Babylon (11704) *(G-16159)*
Isonics Corporation 212 356-7400
535 8th Ave Fl 3 New York (10018) *(G-10277)*
Isp Optics Corporation (HQ) 914 591-3070
50 S Buckhout St Irvington (10533) *(G-6507)*
Israeli Yellow Pages 718 520-1000
12510 Queens Blvd Ste 14 Kew Gardens (11415) *(G-6874)*
Issacs Yisroel 718 851-7430
4424 18th Ave Brooklyn (11204) *(G-2016)*
Issco Corporation (PA) 212 732-8748
111 Cherry Valley Ave # 410 Garden City (11530) *(G-5263)*
Ist Conax Nuclear, Buffalo *Also called Mirion Tech Conax Nuclear Inc (G-2948)*
It Commodity Sourcing Inc 718 677-1577
1640 E 22nd St Brooklyn (11210) *(G-2017)*
It's About Time, Mount Kisco *Also called Iat Interactive LLC (G-8343)*
It's About Time Publishing, Mount Kisco *Also called Laurtom Inc (G-8349)*
Itac Label & Tag Corp 718 625-2148
179 Lexington Ave Brooklyn (11216) *(G-2018)*
Italian Marble & Granite Inc 716 741-1800
8526 Roll Rd Clarence Center (14032) *(G-3545)*
Itc Mfg Group Inc 212 684-3696
109 W 38th St Rm 701 New York (10018) *(G-10278)*
Itelinso, Cold Spring Harbor *Also called Infoservices International (G-3631)*
Ithaca Beer Company Inc 607 272-1305
122 Ithaca Beer Dr Ithaca (14850) *(G-6587)*
Ithaca Ice Company, The, Ithaca *Also called Henry Newman LLC (G-6581)*
Ithaca Journal News Co Inc 607 272-2321
123 W State St Ste 1 Ithaca (14850) *(G-6588)*
Ithaca Peripherals, Ithaca *Also called Transact Technologies Inc (G-6613)*
Ithaca Pregancy Center 607 753-3909
4 Church St Cortland (13045) *(G-3877)*
Ithaca Times, Ithaca *Also called New Ski Inc (G-6600)*
Itin Scale Co Inc 718 336-5900
4802 Glenwood Rd Brooklyn (11234) *(G-2019)*
ITR Industries Inc (PA) 914 964-7063
441 Saw Mill River Rd Yonkers (10701) *(G-16771)*
Its Our Time, New York *Also called Fashion Avenue Knits Inc (G-9786)*
Itss, Saint Albans *Also called Integrated Tech Support Svcs (G-14508)*
ITT Accounts Payable, Seneca Falls *Also called Goulds Pumps LLC (G-14775)*
ITT Aerospace Controls LLC 914 641-2000
4 W Red Oak Ln White Plains (10604) *(G-16463)*
ITT Corp 716 662-1900
7 Centre Dr Orchard Park (14127) *(G-12719)*
ITT Corporation 585 269-7109
4847 Main St Hemlock (14466) *(G-6004)*
ITT Corporation 866 448-8372
2881 E Bayard Street Ext Seneca Falls (13148) *(G-14776)*
ITT Corporation 315 568-2811
240 Fall St Seneca Falls (13148) *(G-14777)*
ITT Engineered Valves LLC (HQ) 662 257-6982
240 Fall St Seneca Falls (13148) *(G-14778)*
ITT Enidine Inc (HQ) 716 662-1900
7 Centre Dr Orchard Park (14127) *(G-12720)*
ITT Goulds Pumps Inc 914 641-2129
240 Fall St Seneca Falls (13148) *(G-14779)*
ITT Inc (PA) 914 641-2000
1133 Westchester Ave N-100 White Plains (10604) *(G-16464)*
ITT Industries Holdings Inc (HQ) 914 641-2000
1133 Westchester Ave N-100 White Plains (10604) *(G-16465)*
ITT International Holdings Inc (HQ) 914 641-2000
1133 Westchester Ave White Plains (10604) *(G-16466)*
ITT LLC (HQ) 914 641-2000
1133 Westchester Ave N-100 White Plains (10604) *(G-16467)*

ALPHABETIC

(PA)=Parent Co (HQ)=Headquarters (DH)=Div Headquarters
2019 Harris
New York Manufacturers Directory
909

ITT LLC ALPHABETIC SECTION

ITT LLC 315 568-4733
240 Fall St Seneca Falls (13148) ***(G-14780)***
ITT LLC 315 258-4904
1 Goulds Dr Auburn (13021) ***(G-484)***
ITT LLC 914 641-2000
2881 E Bayard Street Ext Seneca Falls (13148) ***(G-14781)***
ITT Monitoring Control, Seneca Falls *Also called ITT LLC* ***(G-14780)***
ITT Water Technology, Auburn *Also called ITT LLC* ***(G-484)***
Itts Industrial Inc 718 605-6934
165 Industrial Loop Ste C Staten Island (10309) ***(G-15092)***
Ivalua Inc 650 930-9710
195 Montague St Brooklyn (11201) ***(G-2020)***
Ivan Horning 315 536-3028
848 State Route 14a Penn Yan (14527) ***(G-12959)***
Iver Printing Inc 718 275-2070
124 N 12th St New Hyde Park (11040) ***(G-8543)***
Ives Farm Market 315 592-4880
2652 Rr 176 Fulton (13069) ***(G-5222)***
Ives Slaughterhouse, Fulton *Also called Ives Farm Market* ***(G-5222)***
Ivi Services Inc 607 729-5111
5 Pine Camp Dr Binghamton (13904) ***(G-897)***
Ivy Classic Industries Inc 914 632-8200
40 Plain Ave New Rochelle (10801) ***(G-8616)***
Ivy Enterprises Inc (HQ) 516 621-9779
25 Harbor Park Dr Port Washington (11050) ***(G-13271)***
Iwc New York Btq, New York *Also called Richemont North America Inc* ***(G-11386)***
Iwci, Deposit *Also called Integrated Wood Components Inc* ***(G-4108)***
Iwe, East Amherst *Also called Integrted Work Envronments LLC* ***(G-4190)***
Iweb Design Inc 805 243-8305
1491 Metro Ave Ste 3i Bronx (10462) ***(G-1299)***
Izi Creations, New York *Also called Adamor Inc* ***(G-8733)***
Izquierdo Studios Ltd 212 807-9757
34 W 28th St 6 New York (10001) ***(G-10279)***
Izun Pharmaceuticals Corp (PA) 212 618-6357
1 Rockefeller Plz Fl 11 New York (10020) ***(G-10280)***
J & A Usa Inc 631 243-3336
335 Crooked Hill Rd Brentwood (11717) ***(G-1138)***
J & C Finishing 718 456-1087
1067 Wyckoff Ave Ridgewood (11385) ***(G-13539)***
J & D Walter Distributors Inc 518 449-1606
6 Old River Rd Glenmont (12077) ***(G-5413)***
J & D Walter Wholesale Distrg, Glenmont *Also called J & D Walter Distributors Inc* ***(G-5413)***
J & E Talit Inc 718 850-1333
13011 Atlantic Ave Fl 2 Richmond Hill (11418) ***(G-13505)***
J & F Advertising, Carle Place *Also called Market Place Publications* ***(G-3270)***
J & G Machine & Tool Co Inc 315 310-7130
4510 Smith Rd Marion (14505) ***(G-7803)***
J & H Creations Inc 212 465-0962
19 W 36th St Fl 3 New York (10018) ***(G-10281)***
J & J Bronze & Aluminum Cast 718 383-2111
249 Huron St Brooklyn (11222) ***(G-2021)***
J & J Log & Lumber Corp 845 832-6535
528 Old State Route 22 Dover Plains (12522) ***(G-4144)***
J & J Printing Inc (PA) 315 458-7411
500 Cambridge Ave Syracuse (13208) ***(G-15344)***
J & J Swiss Precision Inc 631 243-5584
160 W Industry Ct Ste F Deer Park (11729) ***(G-3988)***
J & J Tl Die Mfg & Stampg Corp 845 228-0242
594 Horsepound Rd Carmel (10512) ***(G-3276)***
J & L Precision Co Inc 585 768-6388
9222 Summit Street Rd Le Roy (14482) ***(G-7120)***
J & M Packaging Inc 631 608-3069
21 Newton Rd Hauppauge (11788) ***(G-5852)***
J & M Textile Co Inc 212 268-8000
505 8th Ave Rm 701 New York (10018) ***(G-10282)***
J & N Computer Services Inc 585 388-8780
1387 Fairport Rd Ste 900j Fairport (14450) ***(G-4636)***
J & R Unique Giftware 718 821-0398
5863 56th St Maspeth (11378) ***(G-7853)***
J & S Licata Bros Inc 718 805-6924
8931 129th St Richmond Hill (11418) ***(G-13506)***
J & S Logging Inc 315 262-2112
3860 State Highway 56 South Colton (13687) ***(G-14925)***
J & T Metal Products Co Inc 631 226-7400
89 Eads St West Babylon (11704) ***(G-16160)***
J & X Production Inc 718 200-1228
327 W 36th St 7f New York (10018) ***(G-10283)***
J A G Diamond Manufacturers 212 575-0660
580 5th Ave Ste 905b New York (10036) ***(G-10284)***
J A T Printing Inc 631 427-1155
46 Gerard St Unit 2 Huntington (11743) ***(G-6401)***
J A Yansick Lumber Co Inc 585 492-4312
16 Rule Dr Arcade (14009) ***(G-385)***
J B S, Scotia *Also called Jbs LLC* ***(G-14743)***
J B Tool & Die Co Inc 516 333-1480
629 Main St Westbury (11590) ***(G-16343)***
J C Industries Inc 631 420-1920
89 Eads St West Babylon (11704) ***(G-16161)***
J D Calato Manufacturing Co (PA) 716 285-3546
4501 Hyde Park Blvd Niagara Falls (14305) ***(G-12300)***
J D Cousins Inc 716 824-1098
667 Tifft St Buffalo (14220) ***(G-2889)***
J D Handling Systems Inc 518 828-9676
1346 State Route 9h Ghent (12075) ***(G-5357)***
J D Steward Inc 718 358-0169
4537 162nd St Flushing (11358) ***(G-5013)***
J Davis Manufacturing Co Inc 315 337-7574
222 Erie Blvd E Rome (13440) ***(G-14254)***
J E T, Ronkonkoma *Also called Jet Redi Mix Concrete Inc* ***(G-14358)***
J Edlin Interiors Ltd 212 243-2111
122 W 27th St Fl 2 New York (10001) ***(G-10285)***
J F B & Sons Lithographers 631 467-1444
1700 Ocean Ave Lake Ronkonkoma (11779) ***(G-6981)***
J F M Sheet Metal Inc 631 737-8494
2090 Pond Rd Ronkonkoma (11779) ***(G-14355)***
J F Machining Company Inc 716 791-3910
2382 Balmer Rd Ransomville (14131) ***(G-13451)***
J Gimbel Inc 718 296-5200
275 Hempstead Tpke Ste A West Hempstead (11552) ***(G-16218)***
J H Buhrmaster Company Inc 518 843-1700
164 W Main St Amsterdam (12010) ***(G-341)***
J H Buscher Inc 716 667-2003
227 Thorn Ave Ste 30 Orchard Park (14127) ***(G-12721)***
J H C Fabrications Inc (PA) 718 649-0065
595 Berriman St Brooklyn (11208) ***(G-2022)***
J H M Engineering 718 871-1810
4014 8th Ave Brooklyn (11232) ***(G-2023)***
J H Rhodes Company Inc 315 829-3600
10 Ward St Vernon (13476) ***(G-15806)***
J H Robotics Inc 607 729-3758
109 Main St Johnson City (13790) ***(G-6812)***
J I Intrntnal Contact Lens Lab 718 997-1212
6352 Saunders St Ste A Rego Park (11374) ***(G-13462)***
J Ironwork, Brooklyn *Also called Railings By New Star Brass* ***(G-2380)***
J J Creations Inc 718 392-2828
4742 37th St Long Island City (11101) ***(G-7477)***
J Jamner Surgical Instrs Inc 914 592-9051
40 Saw Mill River Rd # 12 Hawthorne (10532) ***(G-5988)***
J K Fertility, Yonkers *Also called J Kendall LLC* ***(G-16772)***
J Kendall LLC 646 739-4956
71 Belvedere Dr Yonkers (10705) ***(G-16772)***
J Lowy Co 718 338-7324
940 E 19th St Brooklyn (11230) ***(G-2024)***
J Lowy Lea Skullcaps Mfg Co, Brooklyn *Also called J Lowy Co* ***(G-2024)***
J M Canty Inc 716 625-4227
6100 Donner Rd Lockport (14094) ***(G-7310)***
J M Haley Corp 631 845-5200
151 Toledo St Ste 1 Farmingdale (11735) ***(G-4789)***
J M L Productions Inc 718 643-1674
162 Spencer St Brooklyn (11205) ***(G-2025)***
J M P Display Fixture Co Inc 718 649-0333
760 E 96th St Brooklyn (11236) ***(G-2026)***
J M R Plastics Corporation 718 898-9825
5847 78th St Middle Village (11379) ***(G-8122)***
J Mackenzie Ltd 585 321-1770
234 Wallace Way Rochester (14624) ***(G-13888)***
J N White Associates Inc 585 237-5191
129 N Center St Perry (14530) ***(G-12969)***
J P Installations Warehouse 914 576-3188
29 Portman Rd New Rochelle (10801) ***(G-8617)***
J P Printing Inc (PA) 516 293-6110
331 Main St Farmingdale (11735) ***(G-4790)***
J P R Pharmacy Inc 718 327-0600
529 Beach 20th St Far Rockaway (11691) ***(G-4702)***
J Pahura Contractors 585 589-5793
415 East Ave Albion (14411) ***(G-158)***
J Percoco Industries Inc 631 312-4572
1546 Ocean Ave Ste 4 Bohemia (11716) ***(G-1038)***
J Percy For Mrvin Rchards Ltd (HQ) 212 944-5300
512 Fashion Ave New York (10018) ***(G-10286)***
J Petrocelli Wine Cellars LLC 631 765-1100
39390 Route 25 Peconic (11958) ***(G-12915)***
J R Cooperage Co Inc 718 387-1664
125 Division Pl Brooklyn (11222) ***(G-2027)***
J R Gold Designs Ltd 212 922-9292
555 5th Ave Fl 19 New York (10017) ***(G-10287)***
J R Nites (PA) 212 354-9670
1400 Broadway Rm 601 New York (10018) ***(G-10288)***
J R Products Inc 716 633-7565
9680 County Rd Clarence Center (14032) ***(G-3546)***
J R S Precision Machining 631 737-1330
40 Raynor Ave Ste 2 Ronkonkoma (11779) ***(G-14356)***
J Rivera, Bohemia *Also called Pro Torque* ***(G-1079)***
J Sussman Inc 718 297-0228
10910 180th St Jamaica (11433) ***(G-6652)***
J T D Stamping Co Inc 631 643-4144
403 Wyandanch Ave West Babylon (11704) ***(G-16162)***
J T Printing 21 ....718 484-3939
165 Industrial Loop Ste E Staten Island (10309) ***(G-15093)***
J T Systematic 607 754-0929
39 Valley St Endwell (13760) ***(G-4617)***
J V Haring & Son 718 720-1947
1277 Clove Rd Ste 2 Staten Island (10301) ***(G-15094)***
J V Precision Inc 518 851-3200
3031 Us Route 9 Hudson (12534) ***(G-6357)***

J Valdi, New York *Also called Lgb Inc (G-10559)*
J Vogler Enterprise LLC..........585 247-1625
15 Evelyn St Rochester (14606) **(G-13889)**
J W Stevens Co Inc..........315 472-6311
6059 Corporate Dr East Syracuse (13057) **(G-4354)**
J&R Fuel of LI Inc..........631 234-1959
97 W Suffolk Ave Central Islip (11722) **(G-3375)**
J&T Macquesten Realty, Mount Vernon *Also called Dunlea Whl GL & Mirror Inc (G-8397)*
J-K Prosthetics & Orthotics..........914 699-2077
699 N Macquesten Pkwy Mount Vernon (10552) **(G-8411)**
J.hoaglund, New York *Also called THE Design Group Inc (G-11808)*
J.N. White Designs, Perry *Also called J N White Associates Inc (G-12969)*
J3 Printing Inc..........516 304-6103
11214 Colfax St Queens Village (11429) **(G-13408)**
J9 Technologies Inc..........412 586-5038
25 Broadway Fl 9 New York (10004) **(G-10289)**
Jaab Precision Inc..........631 218-3725
180 Gary Way Ronkonkoma (11779) **(G-14357)**
Jab Concrete Supply Corp..........718 842-5250
1465 Bronx River Ave Bronx (10472) **(G-1300)**
Jabil Circuit Inc..........845 471-9237
2455 South Rd Poughkeepsie (12601) **(G-13347)**
Jabo Agricultural Inc..........631 475-1800
9 Northwood Ln Patchogue (11772) **(G-12867)**
Jac Usa Inc..........212 841-7430
45 Broadway Ste 1810 New York (10006) **(G-10290)**
Jack J Florio Jr..........716 434-9123
36b Main St Lockport (14094) **(G-7311)**
Jack L Popkin & Co Inc..........718 361-6700
12510 84th Rd Kew Gardens (11415) **(G-6875)**
Jack Luckner Steel Shelving Co..........718 363-0500
5454 43rd St Maspeth (11378) **(G-7854)**
Jack Merkel Inc..........631 234-2600
1720 Express Dr S Hauppauge (11788) **(G-5853)**
Jack W Miller..........585 538-2399
2339 North Rd Scottsville (14546) **(G-14751)**
Jackel Inc..........908 359-2039
1359 Broadway Fl 17 New York (10018) **(G-10291)**
Jackel International, New York *Also called Jackel Inc (G-10291)*
Jackie's Girls, New York *Also called Waterbury Garment LLC (G-12080)*
Jacks and Jokers 52 LLC..........917 740-2595
215 E 68th St Apt 5o New York (10065) **(G-10292)**
Jacks Gourmet LLC..........718 954-4681
1000 Dean St Ste 214 Brooklyn (11238) **(G-2028)**
Jackson Dakota Inc..........718 786-8600
979 3rd Ave Ste 501 New York (10022) **(G-10293)**
Jackson Dakota Inc (PA)..........212 838-9444
979 3rd Ave Ste 503 New York (10022) **(G-10294)**
Jacksons Welding LLC..........607 756-2725
215 N Homer Ave Cortland (13045) **(G-3878)**
Jacksons Welding Service & Sls, Cortland *Also called Jacksons Welding LLC (G-3878)*
Jaclyn Inc..........212 736-5657
330 5th Ave Rm 1305 New York (10001) **(G-10295)**
Jacmax Industries LLC..........718 439-3743
473 Wortman Ave Brooklyn (11208) **(G-2029)**
Jacmel Jewelry Inc (PA)..........718 349-4300
1385 Broadway Fl 8 New York (10018) **(G-10296)**
Jacob Dresdner Co, New York *Also called Dresdiam Inc (G-9575)*
Jacob Hidary Foundation Inc..........212 736-6540
10 W 33rd St Rm 900 New York (10001) **(G-10297)**
Jacob Inc..........646 450-3067
287 Keap St Brooklyn (11211) **(G-2030)**
Jacobi Industries, Medford *Also called Jacobi Tool & Die Mfg Inc (G-7955)*
Jacobi Tool & Die Mfg Inc..........631 736-5394
131 Middle Island Rd Medford (11763) **(G-7955)**
Jacobs & Cohen Inc..........212 714-2702
255 W 36th St Fl 9 New York (10018) **(G-10298)**
Jacobs Juice Corp..........646 255-2860
388 Avenue X Apt 2h Brooklyn (11223) **(G-2031)**
Jacobs Manufacturing, Hogansburg *Also called Jacobs Tobacco Company (G-6165)*
Jacobs Press Inc..........315 252-4861
87 Columbus St Auburn (13021) **(G-485)**
Jacobs Tobacco Company..........518 358-4948
344 Frogtown Rd Hogansburg (13655) **(G-6165)**
Jacobs Woodworking LLC..........315 427-8999
801 W Fayette St Syracuse (13204) **(G-15345)**
Jacoby Enterprises LLC..........718 435-0289
1615 54th St Brooklyn (11204) **(G-2032)**
Jacques Torres Chocolate, Brooklyn *Also called Mrchocolatecom LLC (G-2235)*
Jad Corp of America..........718 762-8900
2048 119th St College Point (11356) **(G-3650)**
Jadak Technologies Inc..........315 701-0678
7279 William Barry Blvd North Syracuse (13212) **(G-12407)**
Jado Sewing Machines Inc..........718 784-2314
4008 22nd St Long Island City (11101) **(G-7478)**
Jaf Converters Inc..........631 842-3131
60 Marconi Blvd Copiague (11726) **(G-3766)**
Jag Footwear ACC & Ret Corp..........800 999-1877
1411 Broadway Fl 20 New York (10018) **(G-10299)**
Jag Lighting..........917 226-3575
6105 56th Dr Maspeth (11378) **(G-7855)**
Jag Manufacturing Inc..........518 762-9558
26 Grecco Dr Johnstown (12095) **(G-6832)**
Jags Manufacturing Network Inc..........631 750-6367
13403 Lincoln Ave Holbrook (11741) **(G-6192)**
Jaguar Casting Co Inc..........212 869-0197
100 United Nations Plz 38a New York (10017) **(G-10300)**
Jaguar Industries Inc..........845 947-1800
89 Broadway Haverstraw (10927) **(G-5979)**
Jaguar Jewelry Casting NY Inc..........212 768-4848
48 W 48th St Ste 500 New York (10036) **(G-10301)**
Jaidan Industries Inc..........516 944-3650
16 Capi Ln Port Washington (11050) **(G-13272)**
Jain Irrigation Inc..........315 755-4400
740 Water St Watertown (13601) **(G-16017)**
Jakes Sneakers Inc..........718 233-1132
845 Classon Ave Brooklyn (11238) **(G-2033)**
Jakob Schlaepfer Inc..........212 221-2323
37 W 26th St Rm 208 New York (10010) **(G-10302)**
Jal Signs Inc..........516 536-7280
540 Merrick Rd Baldwin (11510) **(G-539)**
Jalex Industries Ltd..........631 491-5072
86 Nancy St West Babylon (11704) **(G-16163)**
Jam Industries Inc..........585 458-9830
9 Marway Cir Rochester (14624) **(G-13890)**
Jam Paper, New York *Also called Hudson Envelope Corporation (G-10142)*
Jam Printing Publishing Inc..........914 345-8400
11 Clearbrook Rd Ste 133 Elmsford (10523) **(G-4547)**
Jamaica Electroplating, North Baldwin *Also called Dura Spec Inc (G-12362)*
Jamaica Iron Works Inc..........718 657-4849
10847 Merrick Blvd Jamaica (11433) **(G-6653)**
Jamaica Lamp Corp..........718 776-5039
21220 Jamaica Ave Queens Village (11428) **(G-13409)**
Jamaican Weekly Gleaner, Jamaica *Also called Gleaner Company Ltd (G-6646)*
Jamar Precision Products Co..........631 254-0234
5 Lucon Dr Deer Park (11729) **(G-3989)**
Jamco Aerospace Inc..........631 586-7900
121a E Industry Ct Deer Park (11729) **(G-3990)**
James A Staley Co Inc..........845 878-3344
5 Bowen Ct Carmel (10512) **(G-3277)**
James B Crowell & Sons Inc..........845 895-3464
242 Lippincott Rd Wallkill (12589) **(G-15905)**
James Conolly Printing Co..........585 426-4150
72 Marway Cir Rochester (14624) **(G-13891)**
James D Rubino Inc..........631 244-8730
20 Jules Ct Ste 5 Bohemia (11716) **(G-1039)**
James King Woodworking Inc..........518 761-6091
656 County Line Rd Queensbury (12804) **(G-13429)**
James L Taylor Mfg Co (PA)..........845 452-3780
130 Salt Point Tpke Poughkeepsie (12603) **(G-13348)**
James L Taylor Mfg Co..........845 452-3780
130 Salt Point Tpke Poughkeepsie (12603) **(G-13349)**
James L. Taylor Mfg., Poughkeepsie *Also called James L Taylor Mfg Co (G-13348)*
James Morgan Publishing (PA)..........212 655-5470
5 Penn Plz Ste 2300 New York (10001) **(G-10303)**
James Morris..........315 824-8519
6697 Airport Rd Hamilton (13346) **(G-5699)**
James Richard Specialty Chem..........914 478-7500
24 Ridge St Hastings On Hudson (10706) **(G-5750)**
James Thompson & Company Inc (PA)..........212 686-4242
463 7th Ave Rm 1603 New York (10018) **(G-10304)**
James Town Macadam Inc..........716 665-4504
1946 New York Ave Falconer (14733) **(G-4683)**
James Wire Die Co..........315 894-3233
138 West St Ilion (13357) **(G-6476)**
James Woerner Inc..........631 454-9330
130 Allen Blvd Farmingdale (11735) **(G-4791)**
Jamesport Vineyards, Jamesport *Also called North House Vineyards Inc (G-6693)*
Jamestown Advanced Pdts Corp..........716 483-3406
2855 Girts Rd Jamestown (14701) **(G-6725)**
Jamestown Awning Inc..........716 483-1435
313 Steele St Jamestown (14701) **(G-6726)**
Jamestown Bronze Works Inc..........716 665-2302
174 Hopkins Ave Jamestown (14701) **(G-6727)**
Jamestown Cont of Rochester..........585 254-9190
82 Edwards Deming Dr Rochester (14606) **(G-13892)**
Jamestown Container Corp (PA)..........716 665-4623
14 Deming Dr Falconer (14733) **(G-4684)**
Jamestown Engine Plant, Lakewood *Also called Cummins Inc (G-6992)*
Jamestown Fab Stl & Sup Inc..........716 665-2227
1034 Allen St Jamestown (14701) **(G-6728)**
Jamestown Iron Works Inc..........716 665-2818
2022 Allen Street Ext Falconer (14733) **(G-4685)**
Jamestown Kitchen & Bath Inc..........716 665-2299
1085 E 2nd St Jamestown (14701) **(G-6729)**
Jamestown Macadam Inc (PA)..........716 664-5108
74 Walden Ave Jamestown (14701) **(G-6730)**
Jamestown Metal Products LLC..........716 665-5313
178 Blackstone Ave Jamestown (14701) **(G-6731)**
Jamestown Plastics Inc (PA)..........716 792-4144
8806 Highland Ave Brocton (14716) **(G-1196)**
Jamestown Public Works, Jamestown *Also called City of Jamestown (G-6705)*

ALPHABETIC

Jamestown Scientific Inds LLC....716 665-3224
1300 E 2nd St Jamestown (14701) **(G-6732)**
Janco Press Inc....631 563-3003
20 Floyds Run Bohemia (11716) **(G-1040)**
Jane Bakes Inc....845 920-1100
40 S Main St Pearl River (10965) **(G-12903)**
Jane Bohan Inc....212 529-6090
611 Broadway New York (10012) **(G-10305)**
Jane Knitting Kit, New York *Also called Janes Designer Yrn Pttrns Inc* **(G-10306)**
Jane Lewis....607 722-0584
82 Castle Creek Rd Binghamton (13901) **(G-898)**
Janed Enterprises....631 694-4494
48 Allen Blvd Unit B Farmingdale (11735) **(G-4792)**
Janel Corporation (PA)....516 256-8143
303 Merrick Rd Ste 400 Lynbrook (11563) **(G-7666)**
Janes Designer Yrn Pttrns Inc....347 260-3071
1745 Broadway Ste 1750 New York (10019) **(G-10306)**
Janice Moses Represents....212 898-4898
99 Battery Pl Apt 10d New York (10280) **(G-10307)**
Janlynn Corporation, The, Bohemia *Also called Spectrum Crafts Inc* **(G-1091)**
Japan America Learning Ctr Inc (PA)....914 723-7600
81 Montgomery Ave Scarsdale (10583) **(G-14639)**
Japan Printing & Graphics Inc....212 406-2905
160 Broadway Lbby D New York (10038) **(G-10308)**
Jaquith Industries Inc....315 478-5700
600 E Brighton Ave Syracuse (13210) **(G-15346)**
Jar Metals Inc....845 425-8901
50 2nd Ave Nanuet (10954) **(G-8464)**
Jaracz Jr Joseph Paul....716 533-1377
64 Ferndale Dr Orchard Park (14127) **(G-12722)**
Jarets Stuffed Cupcakes....607 658-9096
116 Oak Hill Ave Endicott (13760) **(G-4597)**
Jarit Surgical Instruments, Hawthorne *Also called J Jamner Surgical Instrs Inc* **(G-5988)**
Jarvik Heart Inc....212 397-3911
333 W 52nd St Ste 700 New York (10019) **(G-10309)**
Jasani Designs Usa Inc....212 257-6465
25 W 43rd St Ste 1014 New York (10036) **(G-10310)**
Jasco Cutting Tools, Rochester *Also called Graywood Companies Inc* **(G-13845)**
Jasco Heat Treating Inc....585 388-0071
75 Macedon Center Rd Fairport (14450) **(G-4637)**
Jasco Tools, Rochester *Also called Arch Globl Prcsion Rchster LLC* **(G-13638)**
Jason & Jean Products Inc....718 271-8300
104 Corona Ave Corona (11368) **(G-3846)**
Jason Ladanye Guitar Piano & H....518 527-3973
605 Park Ave Albany (12208) **(G-88)**
Jason Manufacturing Company, Rochester *Also called Three R Enterprises Inc* **(G-14169)**
Jasper Transport LLC....315 729-5760
1680 Flat St Penn Yan (14527) **(G-12960)**
Javcon Machine Inc....631 586-1890
255 Skidmore Rd Deer Park (11729) **(G-3991)**
Javin Machine Corp....631 643-3322
31 Otis St West Babylon (11704) **(G-16164)**
Javlyn Process Systems LLC....585 424-5580
3136 Winton Rd S Ste 102 Rochester (14623) **(G-13893)**
Jax Coco USA LLC....347 688-8198
5 Penn Plz Ste 2300 New York (10001) **(G-10311)**
Jax Signs and Neon Inc....607 727-3420
108 Odell Ave Endicott (13760) **(G-4598)**
Jaxi's Sportswear, Brooklyn *Also called Jaxis Inc* **(G-2034)**
Jaxis Inc (PA)....212 302-7611
1365 38th St Brooklyn (11218) **(G-2034)**
Jaxson Rollforming Inc....631 842-7775
145 Dixon Ave Ste 1 Amityville (11701) **(G-290)**
Jay Bags Inc....845 459-6500
55 Union Rd Ste 107 Spring Valley (10977) **(G-14997)**
Jay Little Oil Well Servi....716 925-8905
5460 Nichols Run Limestone (14753) **(G-7158)**
Jay Moulding Corporation....518 237-4200
7 Bridge Ave Ste 1 Cohoes (12047) **(G-3611)**
Jay Strongwater Holdings LLC (HQ)....646 657-0558
12 W 21st St Fl 11 New York (10010) **(G-10312)**
Jay Turoff....718 856-7300
681 Coney Island Ave Brooklyn (11218) **(G-2035)**
Jay-Aimee Designs Inc....718 609-0333
1 Great Neck Rd Ste 1 # 1 Great Neck (11021) **(G-5564)**
Jay-Art Nvelties/Tower Grafics, Brooklyn *Also called Jay Turoff* **(G-2035)**
Jaya Apparel Group LLC....212 764-4980
1384 Broadway Fl 18 New York (10018) **(G-10313)**
Jayden Star LLC....212 686-0400
385 5th Ave Rm 507 New York (10016) **(G-10314)**
Jaymar Jewelry Co Inc....212 564-4788
69 5th Ave Apt 8d New York (10003) **(G-10315)**
Jays Furniture Products Inc....716 876-8854
321 Ramsdell Ave Buffalo (14216) **(G-2890)**
JB Star, New York *Also called Jewels By Star Ltd* **(G-10330)**
Jbf Stainless LLC....315 569-2800
148 Industrial Park Dr Frankfort (13340) **(G-5108)**
Jbl Trading LLC....347 394-5592
3 W 35th St Fl 5 New York (10001) **(G-10316)**
Jbren Corp....716 332-5928
107 Dorothy St Buffalo (14206) **(G-2891)**
Jbs LLC....518 346-0001
6 Maple Ave Scotia (12302) **(G-14743)**
JC California Inc....212 334-4380
359 Broadway Fl 3 New York (10013) **(G-10317)**
JC Crystal Inc....212 594-0858
260 W 35th St Fl 10 New York (10001) **(G-10318)**
Jcdecaux Mallscape LLC (HQ)....646 834-1200
350 5th Ave Fl 73 New York (10118) **(G-10319)**
JD Granary LLC....607 627-6294
7 Railroad St Smyrna (13464) **(G-14912)**
JD Tool Inc....607 786-3129
205 Harrison Ave Endicott (13760) **(G-4599)**
Jds Graphics, New York *Also called JDS Graphics Inc* **(G-10320)**
JDS Graphics Inc....973 330-3300
226 W 37th St Fl 10 New York (10018) **(G-10320)**
Jdt International LLC....212 400-7570
276 5th Ave Rm 704 New York (10001) **(G-10321)**
JE Miller Inc....315 437-6811
747 W Manlius St East Syracuse (13057) **(G-4355)**
JE Monahan Fabrications LLC....518 761-0414
559 Queensbury Ave 1/2 Queensbury (12804) **(G-13430)**
Jeam Imports, Brooklyn *Also called Executive Machines Inc* **(G-1858)**
Jean Philippe Fragrances LLC....212 983-2640
551 5th Ave Rm 1500 New York (10176) **(G-10322)**
Jeanjer LLC....212 944-1330
1400 Broadway Fl 15 New York (10018) **(G-10323)**
Jeans Inc....646 223-1122
1357 Broadway Ste 411 New York (10018) **(G-10324)**
Jed Lights Inc (HQ)....516 812-5001
10 Connor Ln Deer Park (11729) **(G-3992)**
Jeff Cooper Inc....516 333-8200
288 Westbury Ave Carle Place (11514) **(G-3266)**
Jefferson Concrete Corp....315 788-4171
22850 County Route 51 Watertown (13601) **(G-16018)**
Jeffersonville Volunteer....845 482-3110
49 Callicoon Center Rd Jeffersonville (12748) **(G-6779)**
Jeffrey D Menoff....716 665-1468
785 Fairmount Ave Jamestown (14701) **(G-6733)**
Jeffrey John....631 842-2850
25 Elm Pl Amityville (11701) **(G-291)**
Jeffrey Spring Modern Art, Astoria *Also called Modern Art Foundry Inc* **(G-436)**
Jekerda Sales, East Williston *Also called North American Pipe Corp* **(G-4382)**
Jem Container Corp....800 521-0145
151 Fairchild Ave Ste 1 Plainview (11803) **(G-13066)**
Jem Sign Corp (PA)....516 867-4466
470 S Franklin St Hempstead (11550) **(G-6015)**
Jem Threading Specialties Inc....718 665-3341
1059 Washington Ave Bronx (10456) **(G-1301)**
Jem Tool & Die Corp....631 539-8734
81 Paris Ct West Islip (11795) **(G-16259)**
JEm Wdwkg & Cabinets Inc....518 828-5361
250 Falls Rd Hudson (12534) **(G-6358)**
Jemcap Servicing LLC....212 213-9353
360 Madison Ave Rm 1902 New York (10017) **(G-10325)**
Jenalex Creative Marketing Inc....212 935-2266
116 E 57th St Fl 3 New York (10022) **(G-10326)**
Jenlor Ltd....315 637-9080
523 E Genesee St Fayetteville (13066) **(G-4928)**
Jenmar Door & Glass Inc....718 767-7900
15038 12th Ave Whitestone (11357) **(G-16544)**
Jenna Concrete Corporation....718 842-5250
1465 Bronx River Ave Bronx (10472) **(G-1302)**
Jenna Harlem River Inc....718 842-5997
1465 Bronx River Ave Bronx (10472) **(G-1303)**
Jenray Products Inc....914 375-5596
252 Lake Ave Fl 2a Yonkers (10701) **(G-16773)**
Jentsch & Co Inc....716 852-4111
107 Dorothy St Buffalo (14206) **(G-2892)**
JEnvie Sport Inc....212 967-2322
241 W 37th St Rm 1007 New York (10018) **(G-10327)**
Jeric Knit Wear....631 979-8827
61 Hofstra Dr Smithtown (11787) **(G-14901)**
Jerome Levy Forecasting Center....914 244-8617
69 S Moger Ave Ste 202 Mount Kisco (10549) **(G-8345)**
Jerome Stvens Phrmcuticals Inc....631 567-1113
60 Davinci Dr Bohemia (11716) **(G-1041)**
Jerry Cardullo Iron Works Inc....631 242-8881
101 Spence St Bay Shore (11706) **(G-692)**
Jerry Miller I.D. Shoes, Buffalo *Also called Jerry Miller Molded Shoes Inc* **(G-2893)**
Jerry Miller Molded Shoes Inc (PA)....716 881-3920
36 Mason St Buffalo (14213) **(G-2893)**
Jerry Sorbara Furs Inc....212 594-3897
39 W 32nd St Rm 1400 New York (10001) **(G-10328)**
Jerry Tomaselli....718 965-1400
141 32nd St Brooklyn (11232) **(G-2036)**
Jerry's Bagels & Bakery, Valley Stream *Also called Jerrys Bagels* **(G-15783)**
Jerrys Bagels....516 791-0063
951 Rosedale Rd Valley Stream (11581) **(G-15783)**
Jersey Express Inc....716 834-6151
3080 Main St Buffalo (14214) **(G-2894)**
Jescar Enterprises Inc....845 352-5850
213 Airport Executive Par Nanuet (10954) **(G-8465)**

ALPHABETIC SECTION John Langenbacher Co Inc

Jesco Lighting Inc 718 366-3211
15 Harbor Park Dr Port Washington (11050) *(G-13273)*
Jesco Lighting Group LLC (PA) 718 366-3211
15 Harbor Park Dr Port Washington (11050) *(G-13274)*
Jesse Joeckel 631 668-2772
65 Tuthill Rd Montauk (11954) *(G-8304)*
Jessel Marking Equipment, Syracuse *Also called New York Marking Devices Corp (G-15381)*
Jessica Michelle, New York *Also called Orchid Manufacturing Co Inc (G-11059)*
Jet Redi Mix Concrete Inc 631 580-3640
2101 Pond Rd Ste 1 Ronkonkoma (11779) *(G-14358)*
Jet Sew Corporation 315 896-2683
8119 State Route 12 Barneveld (13304) *(G-602)*
Jet-Black Sealers Inc 716 891-4197
555 Ludwig Ave Buffalo (14227) *(G-2895)*
Jets Lefrois Corp 585 637-5003
56 High St Brockport (14420) *(G-1193)*
Jets Lefrois Foods, Brockport *Also called Jets Lefrois Corp (G-1193)*
Jette Group, Bay Shore *Also called Cable Management Solutions Inc (G-667)*
Jetwrx Rotable Services, Elmira *Also called Jrsmm LLC (G-4495)*
Jewelers Machinist Co Inc 631 661-5020
400 Columbus Ave Babylon (11704) *(G-528)*
Jewelers Solder Supply Inc 718 637-1256
1362 54th St Brooklyn (11219) *(G-2037)*
Jewelry Arts Manufacturing 212 382-3583
151 W 46th St Fl 12 New York (10036) *(G-10329)*
Jewelry By Sarah Belle 518 793-1626
10394 State Route 149 Fort Ann (12827) *(G-5089)*
Jewels By Star Ltd 212 308-3490
555 5th Ave Fl 7 New York (10017) *(G-10330)*
Jeweltex Mfg Corp 212 921-8188
48 W 48th St Ste 507 New York (10036) *(G-10331)*
Jewish Heritage For Blind 718 338-4999
1655 E 24th St Brooklyn (11229) *(G-2038)*
Jewish Journal 718 630-9350
7014 13th Ave Brooklyn (11228) *(G-2039)*
Jewish Press Inc 718 330-1100
4915 16th Ave Brooklyn (11204) *(G-2040)*
Jewish Week Inc (PA) 212 921-7822
1501 Broadway Ste 505 New York (10036) *(G-10332)*
Jewler's Solder Sheet & Wire, Brooklyn *Also called Jewelers Solder Supply Inc (G-2037)*
Jeypore Group, New York *Also called Incon Gems Inc (G-10193)*
JF Machine Shop Inc 631 491-7273
89 Otis St Unit A West Babylon (11704) *(G-16165)*
Jf Rafter The Lexington Co, Eden *Also called John F Rafter Inc (G-4389)*
Jfe Engineering Corporation 212 310-9320
350 Park Ave Fl 27th New York (10022) *(G-10333)*
Jfe Steel America Inc (HQ) 212 310-9320
600 3rd Ave Fl 12 New York (10016) *(G-10334)*
Jfs Inc 646 264-1200
531 W 26th St Unit 531 # 531 New York (10001) *(G-10335)*
JG Innovative Industries Inc 718 784-7300
8002 Kew Gardens Rd # 5002 Kew Gardens (11415) *(G-6876)*
JGM Wholesale Bakery Inc 631 396-0131
296 Route 109 Farmingdale (11735) *(G-4793)*
Jgx LLC 212 575-1244
1407 Broadway Rm 1416 New York (10018) *(G-10336)*
Jhc Labresin, Brooklyn *Also called J H C Fabrications Inc (G-2022)*
Jill Fagin Enterprises Inc (PA) 212 674-9383
39 E 12th St Apt 612 New York (10003) *(G-10337)*
Jillery, New York *Also called Jill Fagin Enterprises Inc (G-10337)*
Jim Henson Company Inc 212 794-2400
3718 Northern Blvd # 400 Long Island City (11101) *(G-7479)*
Jim Henson Productions, Long Island City *Also called Jim Henson Company Inc (G-7479)*
Jim Quinn 518 356-0398
12 Morningside Dr Schenectady (12303) *(G-14691)*
Jim Quinn and Associates, Schenectady *Also called Jim Quinn (G-14691)*
Jim Romas Bakery Inc 607 748-7425
202 N Nanticoke Ave Endicott (13760) *(G-4600)*
Jim Wachtler Inc 212 755-4367
1212 Avenue Of The New York (10036) *(G-10338)*
Jimco Lamp & Manufacturing Co 631 218-2152
181 Freeman Ave Islip (11751) *(G-6547)*
Jimco Lamp Company, Islip *Also called Jimco Lamp & Manufacturing Co (G-6547)*
Jimeale Incorporated 917 686-5383
130 Church St Ste 163 New York (10007) *(G-10339)*
Jimmy Crystal New York Co Ltd 212 594-0858
47 W 37th St Fl 3 New York (10018) *(G-10340)*
Jimmy Sales, Brooklyn *Also called Tie King Inc (G-2567)*
Jinglebell Inc 914 219-5395
190 Byram Lake Rd Armonk (10504) *(G-406)*
JINGLENOG DBA, Armonk *Also called Jinglebell Inc (G-406)*
Jiranimo Industries Ltd 212 921-5106
49a W 37th St New York (10018) *(G-10341)*
Jj Basics LLC (PA) 212 768-4779
525 7th Ave Rm 307 New York (10018) *(G-10342)*
JJ Cassone Bakery Inc 914 939-1568
202 S Regent St Port Chester (10573) *(G-13203)*
Jj Fantasia Inc 212 868-1198
38 W 32nd St New York (10001) *(G-10343)*
JK Manufacturing Inc 212 683-3535
115 Forest Ave Unit 22 Locust Valley (11560) *(G-7350)*
Jlt Lancaster Clamps Div, Poughkeepsie *Also called James L Taylor Mfg Co (G-13349)*
JM Manufacturer Inc 212 869-0626
241 W 37th St Rm 924 New York (10018) *(G-10344)*
JM Murray Center Inc (PA) 607 756-9913
823 State Route 13 Ste 1 Cortland (13045) *(G-3879)*
JM Murray Center Inc 607 756-0246
4057 West Rd Cortland (13045) *(G-3880)*
JM Originals Inc 845 647-3003
70 Berme Rd Ellenville (12428) *(G-4439)*
JM Studio Inc 646 546-5514
247 W 35th St Fl 3 New York (10001) *(G-10345)*
Jma Wireless, Liverpool *Also called John Mezzalingua Assoc LLC (G-7240)*
Jmg Fuel Inc 631 579-4319
3 Fowler Ave Ronkonkoma (11779) *(G-14359)*
Jml Optical Industries LLC 585 248-8900
820 Linden Ave Rochester (14625) *(G-13894)*
Jml Quarries Inc 845 932-8206
420 Bernas Rd Cochecton (12726) *(G-3606)*
JMS Ices Inc 718 448-0853
501 Port Richmond Ave Staten Island (10302) *(G-15095)*
Jn Marina, New York *Also called Marina Jewelry Co Inc (G-10703)*
Jo Mart Chocolates, Brooklyn *Also called Jo-Mart Candies Corp (G-2041)*
Jo-Mart Candies Corp 718 375-1277
2917 Avenue R Brooklyn (11229) *(G-2041)*
Jo-Vin Decorators Inc 718 441-9350
9423 Jamaica Ave Woodhaven (11421) *(G-16636)*
Joan Boyce Ltd (PA) 212 867-7474
19 W 44th St Ste 417 New York (10036) *(G-10346)*
Joanna Mastroianni, New York *Also called Elana Laderos Ltd (G-9639)*
Jobs Weekly Inc 716 648-5627
31 Buffalo St Ste 2 Hamburg (14075) *(G-5682)*
Jobson Medical Information LLC (PA) 212 274-7000
440 9th Ave Fl 14 New York (10001) *(G-10347)*
Jockey International Inc 212 840-4900
1411 Broadway Rm 1010 New York (10018) *(G-10348)*
Jockey Store, New York *Also called Jockey International Inc (G-10348)*
Joe Benbasset Inc (PA) 212 594-8440
213 W 35th St Fl 11 New York (10001) *(G-10349)*
Joe Fresh, New York *Also called Jfs Inc (G-10335)*
Joe Moro 607 272-0591
214 Fayette St Ithaca (14850) *(G-6589)*
Joe P Industries Inc 631 293-7889
6 Commerce Dr Farmingdale (11735) *(G-4794)*
Joe Pietryka Incorporated (PA) 845 855-1201
85 Charles Colman Blvd Pawling (12564) *(G-12892)*
Joe's Jerky, Sherrill *Also called Patla Enterprises Inc (G-14821)*
Joed Press 212 243-3620
242 W 36th St Fl 8 New York (10018) *(G-10350)*
Joel Kiryas Meat Market Corp 845 782-9194
51 Forest Rd Ste 345 Monroe (10950) *(G-8273)*
Joel Zelcer 917 525-6790
102 S 8th St Brooklyn (11249) *(G-2042)*
Joes Jeans, New York *Also called Centric West LLC (G-9248)*
John A Eberly Inc 315 449-3034
136 Beattie St Syracuse (13224) *(G-15347)*
John A Vassilaros & Son Inc 718 886-4140
2905 120th St Flushing (11354) *(G-5014)*
John Augulíaro Printing Co 718 382-5283
2533 Mcdonald Ave Brooklyn (11223) *(G-2043)*
John Bossone, Glendale *Also called New Day Woodwork Inc (G-5404)*
John C Dolph Company Inc 732 329-2333
200 Von Roll Dr Schenectady (12306) *(G-14692)*
John Crane Inc 315 593-6237
2314 County Route 4 Fulton (13069) *(G-5223)*
John Deere Authorized Dealer, Fulton *Also called Gone South Concrete Block Inc (G-5218)*
John E Potente & Sons Inc 516 935-8585
114 Woodbury Rd Unit 1 Hicksville (11801) *(G-6097)*
John F Krell Jr 315 492-3201
4046 W Seneca Trpk Syracuse (13215) *(G-15348)*
John F Rafter Inc 716 992-3425
2746 W Church St Eden (14057) *(G-4389)*
John G Rubino Inc 315 253-7396
45 Aurelius Ave Auburn (13021) *(G-486)*
John Gailer Inc 212 243-5662
3718 Northern Blvd Ste 3 Long Island City (11101) *(G-7480)*
John Hassall LLC (HQ) 516 334-6200
609 Cantiague Rock Rd # 1 Westbury (11590) *(G-16344)*
John Hassall LLC 323 869-0150
609 Cantiague Rock Rd # 1 Westbury (11590) *(G-16345)*
John J Mazur Inc 631 242-4554
94 E Jefryn Blvd Ste K Deer Park (11729) *(G-3993)*
John J Richardson 516 538-6339
12 Bernard St Lawrence (11559) *(G-7103)*
John Kochis Custom Designs 212 244-6046
237 W 35th St Ste 502 New York (10001) *(G-10351)*
John Kristiansen New York Inc 212 388-1097
665 Broadway Frnt New York (10012) *(G-10352)*
John Langenbacher Co Inc 718 328-0141
888 Longfellow Ave Bronx (10474) *(G-1304)*

ALPHABETIC

(PA)=Parent Co (HQ)=Headquarters (DH)=Div Headquarters
2019 Harris
New York Manufacturers Directory 913

John Larocca & Son Inc ALPHABETIC SECTION

John Larocca & Son Inc......631 423-5256
290 Broadway Huntington Station (11746) ***(G-6449)***
John Lor Publishing Ltd......631 475-1000
20 Medford Ave Ste 1 Patchogue (11772) ***(G-12868)***
John Mezzalingua Assoc LLC (PA)......315 431-7100
7645 Henry Clay Blvd Liverpool (13088) ***(G-7240)***
John N Fehlinger Co Inc (PA)......212 233-5656
20 Vesey St Rm 1000 New York (10007) ***(G-10353)***
John Patrick, Germantown *Also called On The Double Inc* ***(G-5339)***
John Prior......516 520-9801
2545 Hempstead Tpke # 402 East Meadow (11554) ***(G-4254)***
John R Robinson Inc......718 786-6088
3805 30th St Long Island City (11101) ***(G-7481)***
John Ramsey Elec Svcs LLC......585 298-9596
7940 Rae Blvd Victor (14564) ***(G-15851)***
John Szoke Editions, New York *Also called John Szoke Graphics Inc* ***(G-10354)***
John Szoke Graphics Inc......212 219-8300
24 W 57th St Ste 304 New York (10019) ***(G-10354)***
John T Montecalvo Inc......631 325-1492
1233 Speonk River Head Rd Speonk (11972) ***(G-14986)***
John V Agugliaro Printing, Brooklyn *Also called John Auguliaro Printing Co* ***(G-2043)***
John Vespa Inc (PA)......315 788-6330
19626 Overlook Dr Watertown (13601) ***(G-16019)***
John Wiley & Sons Inc......845 457-6250
46 Wavey Willow Ln Montgomery (12549) ***(G-8313)***
Johnnie Ryan Co Inc......716 282-1606
3084 Niagara St Niagara Falls (14303) ***(G-12301)***
Johnny Bienstock Music......212 779-7977
126 E 38th St New York (10016) ***(G-10355)***
Johnny Mica Inc......631 225-5213
116 E Hoffman Ave Lindenhurst (11757) ***(G-7173)***
Johnny's Ideal Prntng Co, Hudson *Also called Johnnys Ideal Printing Co* ***(G-6359)***
Johnnys Ideal Printing Co......518 828-6666
352 Warren St Hudson (12534) ***(G-6359)***
Johnnys Machine Shop......631 338-9733
81 Mahan St West Babylon (11704) ***(G-16166)***
Johns Manville Corporation......518 565-3000
1 Kaycee Loop Rd Plattsburgh (12901) ***(G-13128)***
Johns Ravioli Company Inc......914 576-7030
15 Drake Ave New Rochelle (10805) ***(G-8618)***
Johnson & Hoffman LLC......516 742-3333
40 Voice Rd Carle Place (11514) ***(G-3267)***
Johnson Acquisition Corp (HQ)......518 828-1616
364 Warren St Hudson (12534) ***(G-6360)***
Johnson Bros Lumber, Cazenovia *Also called PDJ Inc* ***(G-3324)***
Johnson Contrls Authorized Dlr, Bronx *Also called Pronto Gas Heating Sups Inc* ***(G-1366)***
Johnson Contrls Authorized Dlr, North Baldwin *Also called Split Systems Corp* ***(G-12367)***
Johnson Controls......585 288-6200
90 Goodway Dr Ste 1 Rochester (14623) ***(G-13895)***
Johnson Controls......518 952-6040
1399 Vischer Ferry Rd Clifton Park (12065) ***(G-3568)***
Johnson Controls......845 774-4120
4 Commerce Dr S Ste 3 Harriman (10926) ***(G-5720)***
Johnson Controls......607 338-5100
6731 Collamer Rd Ste 4 East Syracuse (13057) ***(G-4356)***
Johnson Controls Inc......585 924-9346
90 Goodway Dr Ste 1 Rochester (14623) ***(G-13896)***
Johnson Controls Inc......518 884-8313
339 Brownell Rd Ballston Spa (12020) ***(G-586)***
Johnson Controls Inc......518 694-4822
130 Railroad Ave Albany (12205) ***(G-89)***
Johnson Controls Inc......585 671-1930
237 Birch Ln Webster (14580) ***(G-16087)***
Johnson Controls Inc......914 593-5200
8 Skyline Dr Ste 115 Hawthorne (10532) ***(G-5989)***
Johnson Controls Inc......716 688-7340
130 John Muir Dr Ste 100 Buffalo (14228) ***(G-2896)***
Johnson Controls Inc......585 724-2232
1669 Lake Ave Bldg 333 Rochester (14652) ***(G-13897)***
Johnson Manufacturing Company......716 881-3030
1489 Niagara St Buffalo (14213) ***(G-2897)***
Johnson Mch & Fibr Pdts Co Inc......716 665-2003
142 Hopkins Ave Jamestown (14701) ***(G-6734)***
Johnson Newspaper Corporation......518 483-4700
469 E Main St Ste 2 Malone (12953) ***(G-7722)***
Johnson Outdoors Inc......607 779-2200
625 Conklin Rd Binghamton (13903) ***(G-899)***
Johnson S Sand Gravel Inc......315 771-1450
23284 County Route 3 La Fargeville (13656) ***(G-6943)***
Johnston Dandy Company......315 455-5773
100 Dippold Ave Syracuse (13208) ***(G-15349)***
Johnston Precision Inc......315 253-4181
7 Frank Smith St Auburn (13021) ***(G-487)***
Joldeson One Aerospace Inds, Ozone Park *Also called Joldeson One Aerospace Inds* ***(G-12827)***
Joldeson One Aerospace Inds......718 848-7396
10002 103rd Ave Ozone Park (11417) ***(G-12827)***
Jolibe Atelier LLC......917 319-5908
325 W 38th St Studio New York (10018) ***(G-10356)***
Jolin Machining Corp......631 589-1305
1561 Smithtown Ave Bohemia (11716) ***(G-1042)***
Jomar Industries Inc......845 357-5773
382 Route 59 Ste 352 Airmont (10952) ***(G-14)***
Jomart Associates Inc......212 627-2153
170 Oval Dr Ste A Islandia (11749) ***(G-6532)***
Jomat New York Inc......718 369-7641
4100 1st Ave Ste 3 Brooklyn (11232) ***(G-2044)***
Jon Barry Company Division, Brooklyn *Also called Kwik Ticket Inc* ***(G-2085)***
Jon Lyn Ink Inc......516 546-2312
255 Sunrise Hwy Ste 1 Merrick (11566) ***(G-8099)***
Jon Teri Sports Inc (PA)......212 398-0657
241 W 37th St Frnt 2 New York (10018) ***(G-10357)***
Jonas Louis Paul Studios Inc......518 851-2211
304 Miller Rd Hudson (12534) ***(G-6361)***
Jonathan Brose......716 417-8978
51 Canal St Lockport (14094) ***(G-7312)***
Jonathan David Publishers Inc......718 456-8611
6822 Eliot Ave Middle Village (11379) ***(G-8123)***
Jonathan Lord Corp......631 563-4445
87 Carlough Rd Unit A Bohemia (11716) ***(G-1043)***
Jonathan Meizler LLC......212 213-2977
57 Orchard St New York (10002) ***(G-10358)***
Jonathan Metal & Glass Ltd......718 846-8000
17818 107th Ave Jamaica (11433) ***(G-6654)***
Jonathan Michael Coat Corp......212 239-9230
463 Fashion Ave Rm 1502 New York (10018) ***(G-10359)***
Jonathan Michael Coats, New York *Also called Gfb Fashions Ltd* ***(G-9915)***
Jonden Manufacturing Co Inc......516 442-4895
3069 Lawson Blvd Oceanside (11572) ***(G-12542)***
Jones Humdinger......607 771-6501
204 Hayes Rd Binghamton (13905) ***(G-900)***
Jones Jeanswear Group, New York *Also called One Jeanswear Group Inc* ***(G-11042)***
Jones New York, New York *Also called Nine West Holdings Inc* ***(G-10975)***
Jones New York, New York *Also called Nine West Holdings Inc* ***(G-10977)***
Jones New York, New York *Also called Nine West Holdings Inc* ***(G-10979)***
Jones New York, New York *Also called Authentic Brands Group LLC* ***(G-8966)***
Jonice Industires......516 640-4283
95 Angevine Ave Hempstead (11550) ***(G-6016)***
Jordache Enterprises Inc......212 944-1330
1400 Broadway Rm 1415 New York (10018) ***(G-10360)***
Jordache Enterprises Inc (PA)......212 643-8400
1400 Broadway Rm 1400 # 1400 New York (10018) ***(G-10361)***
Jordache Woodworking Corp......718 349-3373
276 Greenpoint Ave # 1303 Brooklyn (11222) ***(G-2045)***
Jordan Box Co, Syracuse *Also called Jordon Box Company Inc* ***(G-15350)***
Jordan Machine Inc......585 647-3585
1241 Ridgeway Ave Ste I Rochester (14615) ***(G-13898)***
Jordan Panel Systems Corp (PA)......631 754-4900
196 Laurel Rd Unit 2 East Northport (11731) ***(G-4266)***
Jordan Scott Designs Ltd......212 947-4250
25 W 36th St Fl 12 New York (10018) ***(G-10362)***
Jordon Box Company Inc......315 422-3419
140 Dickerson St Syracuse (13202) ***(G-15350)***
Jordon Controls, Rochester *Also called Rotork Controls Inc* ***(G-14104)***
Jos H Lowenstein and Sons Inc (PA)......718 388-5410
420 Morgan Ave Brooklyn (11222) ***(G-2046)***
Joseph (uk) Inc......212 570-0077
1061 Madison Ave Grnd New York (10028) ***(G-10363)***
Joseph A Filippazzo Software......718 987-1626
106 Lovell Ave Staten Island (10314) ***(G-15096)***
Joseph Fedele......718 448-3658
1950b Richmond Ter Staten Island (10302) ***(G-15097)***
Joseph Industries Inc (PA)......212 764-0010
1410 Broadway Rm 1201 New York (10018) ***(G-10364)***
Joseph Paul......718 693-4269
1064 Rogers Ave Apt 5 Brooklyn (11226) ***(G-2047)***
Joseph Shalhoub & Son Inc......718 871-6300
1258 Prospect Ave Brooklyn (11218) ***(G-2048)***
Joseph Struhl Co Inc......516 741-3660
195 Atlantic Ave New Hyde Park (11040) ***(G-8544)***
Joseph Treu Successors Inc......212 691-7026
104 W 27th St Rm 5b New York (10001) ***(G-10365)***
Joseph Zakon Winery Ltd......718 604-1430
586 Montgomery St Brooklyn (11225) ***(G-2049)***
Joseph's Cloak, New York *Also called Americo Group Inc* ***(G-8841)***
Josh Packaging Inc......631 822-1660
245 Marcus Blvd Ste 1 Hauppauge (11788) ***(G-5854)***
Josie Accessories Inc......212 889-6376
261 5th Ave Fl 10 New York (10016) ***(G-10366)***
Jotaly Inc......212 886-6000
1385 Broadway Fl 12 New York (10018) ***(G-10367)***
Journal and Republican, Lowville *Also called Lowville Newspaper Corporation* ***(G-7653)***
Journal News......914 694-5000
1133 Westchester Ave N-110 White Plains (10604) ***(G-16468)***
Journal News......845 578-2324
200 N Route 303 West Nyack (10994) ***(G-16273)***
Journal Register Company......518 584-4242
20 Lake Ave Saratoga Springs (12866) ***(G-14589)***
Journal Register Company (PA)......212 257-7212
5 Hanover Sq Fl 25 New York (10004) ***(G-10368)***
Jovani Fashion Ltd......212 279-0222
1370 Broadway Fl 4 New York (10018) ***(G-10369)***

Joy Edward Company 315 474-3360
105 Enderberry Cir Syracuse (13224) *(G-15351)*
Joy of Learning 718 443-6463
992 Gates Ave Brooklyn (11221) *(G-2050)*
Joy Process Mechanical, Syracuse *Also called Joy Edward Company (G-15351)*
Joya LLC 718 852-6979
19 Vanderbilt Ave Brooklyn (11205) *(G-2051)*
Joya Studio, Brooklyn *Also called Joya LLC (G-2051)*
Joyce Center, Manhasset *Also called Advanced Prosthetics Orthotics (G-7763)*
Joyce Trimming Inc 212 719-3110
109 W 38th St New York (10018) *(G-10370)*
Joyva Corp (PA) 718 497-0170
53 Varick Ave Brooklyn (11237) *(G-2052)*
JP Filling Inc 845 534-4793
20 Industry Dr Mountainville (10953) *(G-8456)*
JP Signs 518 569-3907
9592 State Route 9 Chazy (12921) *(G-3432)*
Jpl Designs Ltd 212 689-7096
343 E 30th St Apt 3k New York (10016) *(G-10371)*
Jpm Fine Woodworking LLC 516 236-7605
103 Estate Dr Jericho (11753) *(G-6792)*
Jpmorgan Chase Bank Nat Assn 718 767-3592
13207 14th Ave College Point (11356) *(G-3651)*
Jpw Riggers & Erectors, Syracuse *Also called Jpw Structural Contracting Inc (G-15352)*
Jpw Structural Contracting Inc 315 432-1111
6376 Thompson Rd Syracuse (13206) *(G-15352)*
Jq Woodworking Inc 516 766-3424
3085 New St Oceanside (11572) *(G-12543)*
Jr Engineering Enterprise LLC 716 909-2693
2141 Bedell Rd Grand Island (14072) *(G-5504)*
Jrb Machine-Tool Inc 716 206-0355
11 Embry Pl Lancaster (14086) *(G-7025)*
Jre Test, Victor *Also called John Ramsey Elec Svcs LLC (G-15851)*
Jrg Apparel Group Company Ltd 212 997-0900
1407 Broadway Rm 817 New York (10018) *(G-10372)*
Jrlon Inc 315 597-4067
4344 Fox Rd Palmyra (14522) *(G-12855)*
JRs Fuels Inc 518 622-9939
8037 Route 32 Cairo (12413) *(G-3149)*
JRS Pharma LP (HQ) 845 878-8300
2981 Route 22 Ste 1 Patterson (12563) *(G-12883)*
Jrsmm LLC 607 331-1549
1316 College Ave Elmira (14901) *(G-4495)*
JS Blank & Co Inc 212 689-4835
112 Madison Ave Fl 7 New York (10016) *(G-10373)*
Jsc Design, New York *Also called Badgley Mischka Licensing LLC (G-8999)*
Jsc Designs Ltd 212 302-1001
550 Fashion Ave Fl 22 New York (10018) *(G-10374)*
JSD Communications Inc 914 588-1841
10 Colonel Thomas Ln Bedford (10506) *(G-769)*
JSM Vinyl Products Inc 516 775-4520
44 Orchid Ln New Hyde Park (11040) *(G-8545)*
Jsp, Bohemia *Also called Jerome Stvens Phrmcuticals Inc (G-1041)*
Jsr Ultrasonics Division, Pittsford *Also called Imaginant Inc (G-13015)*
Jt Precision Inc 716 795-3860
8701 Haight Rd Barker (14012) *(G-600)*
Jt Roselle Lighting & Sup Inc 914 666-3700
333 N Bedford Rd Ste 120 Mount Kisco (10549) *(G-8346)*
JT Systems Inc 315 622-1980
8132 Oswego Rd Liverpool (13090) *(G-7241)*
Jta USA Inc 718 722-0902
63 Flushing Ave Unit 339 Brooklyn (11205) *(G-2053)*
Jtekt Torsen North America 585 464-5000
2 Jetview Dr Rochester (14624) *(G-13899)*
Juan Motors, Palmyra *Also called Faradyne Motors LLC (G-12851)*
Judaica Press Inc 718 972-6202
123 Ditmas Ave Brooklyn (11218) *(G-2054)*
Judi Boisson American Country, Southampton *Also called American Country Quilts & Lin (G-14949)*
Judis Lampshades Inc 917 561-3921
1495 E 22nd St Brooklyn (11210) *(G-2055)*
Judith Lewis Printer Inc 516 997-7777
1915 Ladenburg Dr Westbury (11590) *(G-16346)*
Judith N Graham Inc 914 921-5446
64 Halls Ln Rye (10580) *(G-14484)*
Judys Group Inc 212 921-0515
226 W 37th St Fl 7 New York (10018) *(G-10375)*
Juices Enterprises Inc 718 953-1860
1142 Nostrand Ave Brooklyn (11225) *(G-2056)*
Julia Knit Inc 718 848-1900
8050 Pitkin Ave Ozone Park (11417) *(G-12828)*
Julian A McDermott Corporation 718 456-3606
1639 Stephen St Ridgewood (11385) *(G-13540)*
Julian Freirich Company Inc (PA) 718 361-9111
4601 5th St Long Island City (11101) *(G-7482)*
Julians Recipe LLC 888 640-8880
128 Norman Ave Brooklyn (11222) *(G-2057)*
Julius Cohen Jewelers Inc 212 371-3050
169 Richardson St Brooklyn (11222) *(G-2058)*
Julius Klein Group 212 719-1811
580 5th Ave Ste 500 New York (10036) *(G-10376)*
Julius Lowy Frame Restoring Co 212 861-8585
232 E 59th St 4fn New York (10022) *(G-10377)*
Jumo, New York *Also called Medikidz Usa Inc (G-10759)*
Jump Design Group Inc 212 869-3300
1400 Broadway Fl 2 New York (10018) *(G-10378)*
Jump Design Group, The, New York *Also called Jump Design Group Inc (G-10378)*
Jump Ramp Games Inc 212 500-1456
307 W 38th St Rm 1101 New York (10018) *(G-10379)*
Jumprope Inc 347 927-5867
121 W 27th St Ste 1204 New York (10001) *(G-10380)*
June Jacobs Labs LLC 212 471-4830
460 Park Ave Fl 16 New York (10022) *(G-10381)*
Junior Achevement of Eastrn NY 518 783-4336
8 Stanley Cir Ste 8 # 8 Latham (12110) *(G-7076)*
Juniors Cheesecake Inc (PA) 718 852-5257
386 Flatbush Avenue Ext Brooklyn (11201) *(G-2059)*
Juniper Elbow Co Inc (PA) 718 326-2546
7215 Metropolitan Ave Middle Village (11379) *(G-8124)*
Juniper Industries, Middle Village *Also called Juniper Elbow Co Inc (G-8124)*
Juniper Industries Florida Inc 718 326-2546
7215 Metropolitan Ave Middle Village (11379) *(G-8125)*
Junk In My Trunk Inc 631 420-5865
266 Route 109 Farmingdale (11735) *(G-4795)*
Juno Chefs 845 294-5400
1 6 1/2 Station Rd Goshen (10924) *(G-5480)*
Jupiter Creations Inc 917 493-9393
330 7th Ave Ste 901 New York (10001) *(G-10382)*
Juris Publishing Inc 631 351-5430
52 Elm St Ste 7 Huntington (11743) *(G-6402)*
Jurist Company Inc 212 243-8008
1105 44th Dr Long Island City (11101) *(G-7483)*
Jus By Julie LLC (PA) 718 266-3906
2184 Mcdonald Ave Brooklyn (11223) *(G-2060)*
Jus-Sar Fuel Inc 845 791-8900
884 Old Route 17 Harris (12742) *(G-5722)*
Just Beverages LLC 480 388-1133
31 Broad St Glens Falls (12801) *(G-5428)*
Just Bottoms & Tops Inc (PA) 212 564-3202
1412 Broadway Rm 1808 New York (10018) *(G-10383)*
Just Brass Inc 212 724-5447
215 W 90th St Apt 9a New York (10024) *(G-10384)*
Just For Men Div, New York *Also called Jeanjer LLC (G-10323)*
Just Goods Inc 917 294-0043
311 W 43rd St Fl 12 New York (10036) *(G-10385)*
Just In Time Cnc Machinin 585 247-3850
13 Marway Dr Rochester (14624) *(G-13900)*
Just In Time Cnc Machining 585 335-2010
88 Ossian St Dansville (14437) *(G-3927)*
Just In Time Company, Endwell *Also called J T Systematic (G-4617)*
Just Lamps of New York Inc 716 626-2240
334 Harris Hill Rd Apt 1 Buffalo (14221) *(G-2898)*
Just Press Print LLC 585 783-1300
304 Whitney St Rochester (14606) *(G-13901)*
Just Right Carbines LLC 585 261-5331
231 Saltonstall St Canandaigua (14424) *(G-3224)*
Just Wood Pallets Inc 718 644-7013
78 Vails Gate Heights Dr New Windsor (12553) *(G-8647)*
Justa Company 718 932-6139
3464 9th St Long Island City (11106) *(G-7484)*
Justin Ashley Designs Inc 718 707-0200
4301 21st St Ste 212a Long Island City (11101) *(G-7485)*
Justin Gregory Inc 631 249-5187
94 E Jefryn Blvd Ste E Deer Park (11729) *(G-3994)*
Justperfectmsp Ltd 877 201-0005
48 W 48th St Ste 401 New York (10036) *(G-10386)*
Justyna Kaminska NY Inc 917 423-5527
1261 Broadway Rm 406 New York (10001) *(G-10387)*
Juvly Aesthetics Inc 614 686-3627
18 E 41st St Rm 406 New York (10017) *(G-10388)*
Jvl Ventures LLC 212 365-7555
230 Park Ave Rm 2829 New York (10169) *(G-10389)*
JW Burg Machine & Tool Inc 716 434-0015
7430 Rapids Rd Clarence Center (14032) *(G-3547)*
JW Consulting Inc 845 325-7070
20 Chevron Rd Unit 201 Monroe (10950) *(G-8274)*
Jwin Electronics Corp (PA) 516 626-7188
2 Harbor Park Dr Port Washington (11050) *(G-13275)*
K & B Signs, Mount Vernon *Also called K & B Stamping Co Inc (G-8412)*
K & B Stamping Co Inc 914 664-8555
29 Mount Vernon Ave Mount Vernon (10550) *(G-8412)*
K & B Woodworking Inc 518 634-7253
133 Rolling Meadow Rd Cairo (12413) *(G-3150)*
K & E Fabricating Company Inc 716 829-1829
40 Stanley St Buffalo (14206) *(G-2899)*
K & H Industries Inc (PA) 716 312-0088
160 Elmview Ave Hamburg (14075) *(G-5683)*
K & H Industries Inc 716 312-0088
160 Elmview Ave Hamburg (14075) *(G-5684)*
K & H Precision Products Inc 585 624-4894
45 Norton St Honeoye Falls (14472) *(G-6269)*
K & R Allied Inc 718 625-6610
39 Pearl St Fl 2 Brooklyn (11201) *(G-2061)*

ALPHABETIC

K & S & East, Pelham *Also called Eastco Manufacturing Corp* ***(G-12934)***
K & S Childrens Wear Inc 718 624-0006
204 Wallabout St Brooklyn (11206) ***(G-2062)***
K Barthelmes Mfg Co Inc 585 328-8140
61 Brooklea Dr Rochester (14624) ***(G-13902)***
K C Technical Services, Bohemia *Also called Cos TEC Manufacturing Corp* ***(G-999)***
K D Dance, Bronx *Also called KD Dids Inc* ***(G-1305)***
K D M Die Company Inc 716 828-9000
620 Elk St Buffalo (14210) ***(G-2900)***
K Displays 718 854-6045
1363 47th St Brooklyn (11219) ***(G-2063)***
K Dymond Industries Inc 631 828-0826
16 Commercial Blvd Medford (11763) ***(G-7956)***
K F I Inc 516 546-2904
33 Debevoise Ave Roosevelt (11575) ***(G-14436)***
K Hein Machines Inc 607 748-1546
341 Vestal Pkwy E Vestal (13850) ***(G-15819)***
K Industries Inc (PA) 631 897-2125
1107 Station Rd Ste 5a Bellport (11713) ***(G-806)***
K M Drive Line Inc 718 599-0628
966 Grand St Brooklyn (11211) ***(G-2064)***
K P I Plastics, Howes Cave *Also called W Kintz Plastics Inc* ***(G-6334)***
K P Signs, North Bellmore *Also called KP Industries Inc* ***(G-12379)***
K Road Power Management LLC (PA) 212 351-0535
330 Madison Ave Fl 25 New York (10017) ***(G-10390)***
K Sidrane Inc 631 393-6974
24 Baiting Place Rd Farmingdale (11735) ***(G-4796)***
K T A V Publishing House Inc 201 963-9524
527 Empire Blvd Brooklyn (11225) ***(G-2065)***
K T P Design Co Inc 212 481-6613
118 E 28th St Rm 707 New York (10016) ***(G-10391)***
K Z Precision, Lancaster *Also called Kz Precision Inc* ***(G-7026)***
K&G of Syracuse Inc 315 446-1921
2500 Erie Blvd E Syracuse (13224) ***(G-15353)***
K&Ns Foods Usa LLC 315 598-8080
607 Phillips St Fulton (13069) ***(G-5224)***
K-Binet Inc 845 348-1149
624 Route 303 Blauvelt (10913) ***(G-936)***
K-D Stone Inc 518 642-2082
Rr 22 Middle Granville (12849) ***(G-8111)***
K-Technologies Inc 716 828-4444
4090 Jeffrey Blvd Buffalo (14219) ***(G-2901)***
K.E.Y.S. Publishers, Brooklyn *Also called Kwesi Legesse LLC* ***(G-2084)***
K2 International Corp 212 947-1734
22 W 32nd St Fl 9 New York (10001) ***(G-10392)***
K2 Plastics Inc 585 494-2727
8210 Buffalo Rd Bergen (14416) ***(G-822)***
Kabar Manufacturing Corp (HQ) 631 694-6857
140 Schmitt Blvd Farmingdale (11735) ***(G-4797)***
Kabar Manufacturing Corp 631 694-1036
113 Gazza Blvd Farmingdale (11735) ***(G-4798)***
Kabbalah Centre, Richmond Hill *Also called Research Centre of Kabbalah* ***(G-13509)***
Kabco Pharmaceuticals Inc 631 842-3600
2000 New Horizons Blvd Amityville (11701) ***(G-292)***
Kabrics 607 962-6344
2737 Forest Hill Dr Corning (14830) ***(G-3821)***
Kadant Inc 518 793-8801
436 Quaker Rd Glens Falls (12804) ***(G-5429)***
Kaddis Manufacturing Corp 585 624-3070
1175 Bragg St Honeoye Falls (14472) ***(G-6270)***
Kadmon Corporation LLC (PA) 212 308-6000
450 E 29th St Fl 5 New York (10016) ***(G-10393)***
Kadmon Holdings Inc 212 308-6000
450 E 29th St New York (10016) ***(G-10394)***
Kaffeto Gourmet, Tarrytown *Also called Altaro Corp* ***(G-15473)***
Kafko (us) Corp 877 721-7665
787 Watervliet Shaker Rd Latham (12110) ***(G-7077)***
Kahn-Lucas-Lancaster Inc 212 239-2407
112 W 34th St Ste 600 New York (10120) ***(G-10395)***
Kaitery Furs Ltd 718 204-1396
2529 49th St Long Island City (11103) ***(G-7486)***
Kal Manufacturing Corporation 585 265-4310
657 Basket Rd Webster (14580) ***(G-16088)***
Kal-Harbour Inc 518 266-0690
11 Villa Rd Albany (12204) ***(G-90)***
Kalati Company Inc 516 423-9132
10 Bond St Ste 1 Great Neck (11021) ***(G-5565)***
Kale Factory Inc 917 363-6361
790 Washington Ave Brooklyn (11238) ***(G-2066)***
Kaleidoscope Imaging Inc 212 631-9947
251 W 39th St Fl 4 New York (10018) ***(G-10396)***
Kaleko Bros 212 819-0100
62 W 47th St Ste 1504 New York (10036) ***(G-10397)***
Kalel Partners LLC 347 561-7804
7012 170th St Ste 101 Flushing (11365) ***(G-5015)***
Kalikow Brothers LP 212 643-0315
34 W 33rd St Fl 4n New York (10001) ***(G-10398)***
Kallen Corp 212 242-1470
99 Hudson St New York (10013) ***(G-10399)***
Kaltec Food Packaging Inc 845 856-9888
36 Center St 40 Port Jervis (12771) ***(G-13231)***
Kaltech Food Packaging Inc 845 856-1210
3640 Center St Port Jervis (12771) ***(G-13232)***
Kaltex America Inc 212 971-0575
350 5th Ave Ste 7100 New York (10118) ***(G-10400)***
Kaltex North America Inc (HQ) 212 894-3200
350 5th Ave Ste 7100 New York (10118) ***(G-10401)***
Kamali Automotive Group Inc 516 627-4000
17 Barstow Rd Ste 206 Great Neck (11021) ***(G-5566)***
Kamali Group Inc 516 627-4000
17 Barstow Rd Ste 206 Great Neck (11021) ***(G-5567)***
Kamali Leather LLC 518 762-2522
204 Harrison St Johnstown (12095) ***(G-6833)***
Kaman Automation Inc 585 254-8840
1000 University Ave Rochester (14607) ***(G-13903)***
Kamerys Wholesale Meats Inc 716 372-6756
322 E Riverside Dr Olean (14760) ***(G-12603)***
Kamwo Meridian Herbs LLC 212 966-6370
211 Grand St New York (10013) ***(G-10402)***
Kan Pak LLC 620 440-2319
105 Horizon Park Dr Penn Yan (14527) ***(G-12961)***
Kane-M Inc 973 777-2797
135 W 29th St Rm 1003 New York (10001) ***(G-10403)***
Kaneka America LLC 212 705-4340
546 5th Ave Fl 21 New York (10036) ***(G-10404)***
Kangaroo Crossing, Manlius *Also called Mayberry Shoe Company Inc* ***(G-7780)***
Kannalife Sciences Inc 516 669-3219
4 Knoll Ct Lloyd Harbor (11743) ***(G-7280)***
Kantek Inc 516 594-4600
3460a Hampton Rd Oceanside (11572) ***(G-12544)***
Kantian Skincare LLC 631 780-4711
496 Smithtown Byp Smithtown (11787) ***(G-14902)***
Kaplan Inc 212 752-1840
444 Madison Ave Ste 803 New York (10022) ***(G-10405)***
Kaprielian Enterprises Inc 212 645-6623
207 W 25th St Fl 8 New York (10001) ***(G-10406)***
Kaps-All Packaging Systems 631 574-8778
200 Mill Rd Riverhead (11901) ***(G-13570)***
Kapstone Container Corporation 518 842-2450
28 Park Dr Amsterdam (12010) ***(G-342)***
Karbra Company 212 736-9300
460 Park Ave Rm 401 New York (10022) ***(G-10407)***
Karen Kane Inc 212 827-0980
1441 Broadway Fl 33 New York (10018) ***(G-10408)***
Karey Kassl Corp 516 349-8484
180 Terminal Dr Plainview (11803) ***(G-13067)***
Karey Products, Plainview *Also called Karey Kassl Corp* ***(G-13067)***
Karishma Fashions Inc 718 565-5404
3708 74th St Jackson Heights (11372) ***(G-6620)***
Karlyn Industries Inc 845 351-2249
16 Spring St Southfields (10975) ***(G-14966)***
Karo Sheet Metal Inc 718 542-8420
229 Russell St Brooklyn (11222) ***(G-2067)***
Karosheet Metal, Brooklyn *Also called Karo Sheet Metal Inc* ***(G-2067)***
Karp Associates Inc (PA) 631 768-8300
260 Spagnoli Rd Melville (11747) ***(G-8041)***
Karp Overseas Corporation 718 784-2105
5454 43rd St Maspeth (11378) ***(G-7856)***
Karr Graphics Corp 212 645-6000
2219 41st Ave Ste 2a Long Island City (11101) ***(G-7487)***
Kart, Maspeth *Also called Jack Luckner Steel Shelving Co* ***(G-7854)***
Kartell Us Inc 212 966-6665
39 Greene St New York (10013) ***(G-10409)***
Kas Direct LLC 516 934-0541
1600 Stewart Ave Ste 411 Westbury (11590) ***(G-16347)***
Kas-Kel, Fonda *Also called Kasson & Keller Inc* ***(G-5065)***
Kas-Ray Industries Inc 212 620-3144
122 W 26th St New York (10001) ***(G-10410)***
Kaseya US Sales LLC 415 694-5700
26 W 17th St Fl 9 New York (10011) ***(G-10411)***
Kasisto Inc 917 734-4750
43 W 24th St Rm 8b New York (10010) ***(G-10412)***
Kasper Group LLC (HQ) 212 354-4311
1412 Broadway Fl 5 New York (10018) ***(G-10413)***
Kasper Group LLC 212 354-4311
1412 Broadway New York (10018) ***(G-10414)***
Kassis Superior Sign Co Inc 315 463-7446
6699 Old Thompson Rd Syracuse (13211) ***(G-15354)***
Kasson & Keller Inc 518 853-3421
60 School St Fonda (12068) ***(G-5065)***
Kastor Consulting Inc 718 224-9109
3919 218th St Bayside (11361) ***(G-747)***
Kat Nap Products, Brooklyn *Also called Steinbock-Braff Inc* ***(G-2520)***
Kate Spade & Company LLC (HQ) 212 354-4900
2 Park Ave Fl 8 New York (10016) ***(G-10415)***
Kates Paperie Ltd 212 966-3904
188 Lafayette St Frnt A New York (10013) ***(G-10416)***
Katherine Blizniak (PA) 716 674-8545
525 Bullis Rd West Seneca (14224) ***(G-16300)***
Kathleen B Mead 585 247-0146
393 Coastal View Dr Webster (14580) ***(G-16089)***
Kathmando Valley Preservation 212 727-0074
36 W 25th St Fl 17 New York (10010) ***(G-10417)***

Katikati Inc 585 678-1764
150 Lucius Gordon Dr West Henrietta (14586) *(G-16243)*
Katz Americas, Sanborn *Also called Katz Group Americas Inc (G-14548)*
Katz Gluten Free, Mountainville *Also called Gluten Free Bake Shop Inc (G-8455)*
Katz Group Americas Inc (HQ) 716 995-3059
3685 Lockport Rd Sanborn (14132) *(G-14548)*
Katz Martell Fashion Trdg Intl 212 840-0070
1385 Broadway Rm 1401 New York (10018) *(G-10418)*
Kaufman Brothers Printing 212 563-1854
327 W 36th St Rm 403 New York (10018) *(G-10419)*
Kawasaki Rail Car Inc (HQ) 914 376-4700
29 Wells Ave Bldg 4 Yonkers (10701) *(G-16774)*
Kawasho Foods USA Inc 212 841-7400
45 Broadway Fl 18 New York (10006) *(G-10420)*
Kay See Dental Mfg Co 816 842-2817
777 Avenue Of The New York (10001) *(G-10421)*
Kay-Ray Industries, New York *Also called Kas-Ray Industries Inc (G-10410)*
Kaylon Industries LLC 315 303-2119
15 Downer St Baldwinsville (13027) *(G-557)*
Kaymil Printing Company Inc 212 594-3718
140 W 30th St Frnt New York (10001) *(G-10422)*
Kaymil Ticket Company, New York *Also called Kaymil Printing Company Inc (G-10422)*
Kayo of California 212 354-6336
525 Fashion Ave Rm 309 New York (10018) *(G-10423)*
Kays Caps Inc (PA) 518 273-6079
65 Arch St Troy (12183) *(G-15596)*
Kazac Inc 631 249-7299
55 Allen Blvd Ste C Farmingdale (11735) *(G-4799)*
KB Millwork Inc 516 280-2183
36 Grey Ln Levittown (11756) *(G-7135)*
Kbc, Bronx *Also called Kirschner Brush LLC (G-1309)*
Kbl Healthcare LP 212 319-5555
757 3rd Ave Fl 20 New York (10017) *(G-10424)*
Kbs Communications LLC 212 765-7124
331 W 57th St Ste 148 New York (10019) *(G-10425)*
Kc Tag Co 518 842-6666
108 Edson St Amsterdam (12010) *(G-343)*
Kch Publications Inc 516 671-2360
57 Glen St Ste 1 Glen Cove (11542) *(G-5369)*
Kcp Holdco Inc (PA) 212 265-1500
603 W 50th St New York (10019) *(G-10426)*
KD Dids Inc 718 402-2012
140 E 144th St Bronx (10451) *(G-1305)*
KDI Paragon, Lagrangeville *Also called Paragon Aquatics (G-6960)*
KDO Industries Inc 631 608-4612
32 Ranick Dr W Amityville (11701) *(G-293)*
Ke Durasol Awnings Inc 845 610-1100
445 Bellvale Rd Chester (10918) *(G-3477)*
Kearney-National Inc (HQ) 212 661-4600
565 5th Ave Fl 4 New York (10017) *(G-10427)*
Keck Group Inc (PA) 845 988-5757
314 State Route 94 S Warwick (10990) *(G-15954)*
Kedco Inc 516 454-7800
564 Smith St Farmingdale (11735) *(G-4800)*
Kedco Wine Storage Systems, Farmingdale *Also called Kedco Inc (G-4800)*
Keebler Company 585 948-8010
2999 Judge Rd Oakfield (14125) *(G-12524)*
Keegan Ales LLC 845 331-2739
20 Saint James St Kingston (12401) *(G-6903)*
Keeler Services 607 776-5757
47 W Steuben St Ste 4 Bath (14810) *(G-645)*
Keeners East End Litho Inc 631 324-8565
10 Prospect Blvd East Hampton (11937) *(G-4239)*
Keep America Beautiful Inc 518 842-4388
1 Prospect St Amsterdam (12010) *(G-344)*
Keep Healthy Inc 631 651-9090
1019 Fort Salonga Rd Northport (11768) *(G-12469)*
Kefa Industries Group Inc 718 568-9297
9219 63rd Dr Rego Park (11374) *(G-13463)*
Kehr-Buffalo Wire Frame Co Inc 716 897-2288
127 Kehr St Buffalo (14211) *(G-2902)*
Keith Lewis Studio Inc 845 339-5629
35 Rifton Ter Rifton (12471) *(G-13561)*
Keller Bros & Miller Inc 716 854-2374
401 Franklin St Buffalo (14202) *(G-2903)*
Keller Technology Corporation (PA) 716 693-3840
2320 Military Rd Tonawanda (14150) *(G-15553)*
Kelley Farm & Garden Inc 518 234-2332
239 W Main St Cobleskill (12043) *(G-3603)*
Kelly Foundry & Machine Co 315 732-8313
300 Hubbell St Ste 308 Utica (13501) *(G-15717)*
Kelly Grace Corp (PA) 212 704-9603
49 W 37th St Fl 10 New York (10018) *(G-10428)*
Kelly Window Systems Inc 631 420-8500
460 Smith St Farmingdale (11735) *(G-4801)*
Kelmar Systems Inc 631 421-1230
284 Broadway Huntington Station (11746) *(G-6450)*
Kelson Products Inc 716 825-2585
3300 N Benzing Rd Orchard Park (14127) *(G-12723)*
Kelta Inc (PA) 631 789-5000
141 Rodeo Dr Edgewood (11717) *(G-4406)*
Keltron Connector Co., Ronkonkoma *Also called Keltron Electronics (de Corp) (G-14360)*
Keltron Electronics (de Corp) 631 567-6300
3385 Vtrans Mem Hwy Ste E Ronkonkoma (11779) *(G-14360)*
Kem Medical Products Corp (PA) 631 454-6565
400 Broadhollow Rd Ste 2 Farmingdale (11735) *(G-4802)*
Kemco Sales LLC 203 762-1902
119 Despatch Dr East Rochester (14445) *(G-4288)*
Kemet Properties LLC 718 654-8079
1179 E 224th St Bronx (10466) *(G-1306)*
Kemp Metal Products Inc 516 997-8860
2300 Shames Dr Westbury (11590) *(G-16348)*
Kemp Technologies Inc (PA) 631 345-5292
1540 Broadway Fl 23 New York (10036) *(G-10429)*
Ken-Ton Open Mri PC 716 876-7000
2882 Elmwood Ave Kenmore (14217) *(G-6863)*
Kenal Services Corp 315 788-9226
1109 Water St Watertown (13601) *(G-16020)*
Kenan International Trading 718 672-4922
10713 Northern Blvd Corona (11368) *(G-3847)*
Kenbenco Inc 845 246-3066
437 Route 212 Saugerties (12477) *(G-14609)*
Kendall Circuits Inc 631 473-3636
5507-10 Nesconset Hwy 105 Mount Sinai (11766) *(G-8368)*
Kendi Iron Works Inc (PA) 718 821-2722
236 Johnson Ave Brooklyn (11206) *(G-2068)*
Kendor Music Inc 716 492-1254
21 Grove St Delevan (14042) *(G-4071)*
Kenmar Shirts Inc (PA) 718 824-3880
1415 Blondell Ave Bronx (10461) *(G-1307)*
Kennedy Valve Division, Elmira *Also called McWane Inc (G-4497)*
Kennel Klub, Utica *Also called Clara Papa (G-15682)*
Kenneth Cole Productions LP (HQ) 212 265-1500
603 W 50th St New York (10019) *(G-10430)*
Kenneth Cole Productions Inc (HQ) 212 265-1500
603 W 50th St New York (10019) *(G-10431)*
Kenneth J Lane Inc 212 868-1780
20 W 37th St Fl 9 New York (10018) *(G-10432)*
Kenney Manufacturing Displays 631 231-5563
12 Grand Blvd Brentwood (11717) *(G-1139)*
Kenny Mfg, Brentwood *Also called Kenney Manufacturing Displays (G-1139)*
Kennyetto Graphics Inc 518 883-6360
137 E State St Ext Gloversville (12078) *(G-5460)*
Kens Service & Sales Inc 716 683-1155
11500 Clinton St Elma (14059) *(G-4452)*
Kensington & Sons LLC 646 430-8298
270 Lafayette St Ste 200 New York (10012) *(G-10433)*
Kensington Publishing Corp 212 407-1500
119 W 40th St Fl 21 New York (10018) *(G-10434)*
Kenstan Lock & Hardware Co Inc 631 423-1977
101 Commercial St Ste 100 Plainview (11803) *(G-13068)*
Kenstan Lock Co., Plainview *Also called Kenstan Lock & Hardware Co Inc (G-13068)*
Kent Associates Inc 212 675-0722
99 Battery Pl Apt 11p New York (10280) *(G-10435)*
Kent Chemical Corporation 212 521-1700
460 Park Ave Fl 7 New York (10022) *(G-10436)*
Kent Gage & Tool Company, Poughkeepsie *Also called Stanfordville Mch & Mfg Co Inc (G-13368)*
Kent Nutrition Group Inc 315 788-0032
810 Waterman Dr Watertown (13601) *(G-16021)*
Kenwell Corporation 315 592-4263
871 Hannibal St Fulton (13069) *(G-5225)*
Kenwin Sales Corp 516 933-7553
86 W Industry Ct Deer Park (11729) *(G-3995)*
Kenyon Press Inc 607 674-9066
1 Kenyon Press Dr Sherburne (13460) *(G-14806)*
Keon Optics Inc 845 429-7103
30 John F Kennedy Dr Stony Point (10980) *(G-15173)*
Kepco Inc (PA) 718 461-7000
13138 Sanford Ave Flushing (11355) *(G-5016)*
Kepco Inc 718 461-7000
13140 Maple Ave Flushing (11355) *(G-5017)*
Kepco Inc 718 461-7000
13138 Sanford Ave Flushing (11355) *(G-5018)*
Kerner and Merchant 315 463-8023
104 Johnson St East Syracuse (13057) *(G-4357)*
Kernow North America 585 586-3590
5 Park Forest Dr Pittsford (14534) *(G-13017)*
Kerns Manufacturing Corp (PA) 718 784-4044
3714 29th St Long Island City (11101) *(G-7488)*
Kerry Bfnctnal Ingredients Inc (HQ) 608 363-1200
158 State Highway 320 Norwich (13815) *(G-12488)*
Kerry Bio-Science, Norwich *Also called Kerry Bfnctnal Ingredients Inc (G-12488)*
Keryakos Inc 518 344-7092
1080 Catalyn St Fl 2 Schenectady (12303) *(G-14693)*
Kesser Wine, Brooklyn *Also called Joseph Zakon Winery Ltd (G-2049)*
Kessler Thermometer Corp 631 841-5500
40 Gleam St West Babylon (11704) *(G-16167)*
Kesso Foods Inc 718 777-5303
7720 21st Ave East Elmhurst (11370) *(G-4222)*
Ketcham Medicine Cabinets 631 615-6151
3505 Vtrans Mem Hwy Ste L Ronkonkoma (11779) *(G-14361)*
Ketcham Pump Co Inc 718 457-0800
3420 64th St Woodside (11377) *(G-16660)*

ALPHABETIC

Ketchum Manufacturing Co Inc 518 696-3331
11 Town Shed Rd Lake Luzerne (12846) ***(G-6974)***
Keuka Brewing Co LLC 607 868-4648
8572 Briglin Rd Hammondsport (14840) ***(G-5706)***
Keuka Studios Inc 585 624-5960
1011 Rush Henrietta Townl Rush (14543) ***(G-14475)***
Keurig Dr Pepper Inc 315 589-4911
4363 State Route 104 Williamson (14589) ***(G-16559)***
Keurig Dr Pepper Inc 914 846-2300
55 Hunter Ln Elmsford (10523) ***(G-4548)***
Keurig Dr Pepper Inc 718 246-6200
212 Wolcott St Brooklyn (11231) ***(G-2069)***
Kevco Industries 845 255-7407
6 Millbrook Rd New Paltz (12561) ***(G-8578)***
Kevin Freeman 631 447-5321
414 S Service Rd Ste 119 Patchogue (11772) ***(G-12869)***
Kevin J Kassman 585 529-4245
1408 Buffalo Rd Rochester (14624) ***(G-13904)***
Kevin Regan Logging Ltd 315 245-3890
1011 Hillsboro Rd Camden (13316) ***(G-3190)***
Key Brand Entertainment Inc 212 966-5400
104 Franklin St New York (10013) ***(G-10437)***
Key Cast Stone Company Inc 631 789-2145
113 Albany Ave Amityville (11701) ***(G-294)***
Key Computer Svcs of Chelsea 212 206-8060
227 E 56th St New York (10022) ***(G-10438)***
Key Container Corp 631 582-3847
135 Hollins Ln East Islip (11730) ***(G-4244)***
Key Digital Systems Inc 914 667-9700
521 E 3rd St Mount Vernon (10553) ***(G-8413)***
Key Foods, Valley Stream *Also called Cni Meat & Produce Inc* ***(G-15777)***
Key High Vacuum Products Inc 631 584-5959
36 Southern Blvd Nesconset (11767) ***(G-8485)***
Key Signals 631 433-2962
47 Tuthill Point Rd East Moriches (11940) ***(G-4257)***
Key Tech Finishing 716 832-1232
2929 Main St Ste 2 Buffalo (14214) ***(G-2904)***
Keyes Machine Works Inc 585 426-5059
147 Park Ave Gates (14606) ***(G-5310)***
Keymark Corporation 518 853-3421
1188 Cayadutta St Fonda (12068) ***(G-5066)***
Keynote Systems Corporation 716 564-1332
2810 Sweet Home Rd Buffalo (14228) ***(G-2905)***
Keystone Corporation (PA) 716 832-1232
144 Milton St Buffalo (14210) ***(G-2906)***
Keystone Electronics Corp (PA) 516 328-7500
2040 Jericho Tpke New Hyde Park (11040) ***(G-8546)***
KG Motors Inc 607 562-2877
202 Daniel Zenker Dr Big Flats (14814) ***(G-855)***
Khk Usa Inc 516 248-3850
259 Elm Pl Ste 2 Mineola (11501) ***(G-8232)***
Ki Pro Performance, New York *Also called Fusion Pro Performance Ltd* ***(G-9864)***
Kicks Closet Sportswear Inc 347 577-0857
1031 Southern Blvd Frnt 2 Bronx (10459) ***(G-1308)***
Kids, New York *Also called Bagznyc Corp* ***(G-9003)***
Kids Discover, New York *Also called Mark Levine* ***(G-10706)***
Kids Discover LLC 212 677-4457
192 Lexington Ave Rm 1003 New York (10016) ***(G-10439)***
Kidtellect Inc 617 803-1456
222 Broadway Level19 New York (10038) ***(G-10440)***
Kidz Concepts LLC 212 398-1110
1412 Broadway Fl 3 New York (10018) ***(G-10441)***
Kidz Toyz Inc 914 261-4453
280 N Bedford Rd Ste 203 Mount Kisco (10549) ***(G-8347)***
Kidz World Inc 212 563-4949
226 W 37th St Fl 12 New York (10018) ***(G-10442)***
Kik Us Inc 519 505-7616
161 Bowery Apt 6 New York (10002) ***(G-10443)***
Kilian Manufacturing Corp (HQ) 315 432-0700
1728 Burnet Ave Syracuse (13206) ***(G-15355)***
Killer Motor Sports, New York *Also called Vertana Group LLC* ***(G-12017)***
Kiltronx Enviro Systems LLC 917 971-7177
330 Motor Pkwy Ste 201 Hauppauge (11788) ***(G-5855)***
Kim Eugenia Inc 212 674-1345
347 W 36th St Rm 502 New York (10018) ***(G-10444)***
Kim Jae Printing Co Inc 212 691-6289
249 Parkside Dr Roslyn Heights (11577) ***(G-14457)***
Kim Seybert Inc (PA) 212 564-7850
37 W 37th St Fl 9 New York (10018) ***(G-10445)***
Kimball Office Inc 212 753-6161
215 Park Ave S Fl 3 New York (10003) ***(G-10446)***
Kimber Mfg Inc 914 965-0753
16 Harrison Ave Yonkers (10705) ***(G-16775)***
Kimber Mfg Inc (PA) 914 964-0771
1 Lawton St Yonkers (10705) ***(G-16776)***
Kimber Mfg Inc 406 758-2222
1120 Saw Mill River Rd Yonkers (10710) ***(G-16777)***
Kimberley Diamond, New York *Also called H C Kionka & Co Inc* ***(G-10014)***
Kimberly-Clark Corporation 212 554-4252
1285 Ave Of The Americas New York (10019) ***(G-10447)***
Kimbri Liquor, Mohegan Lake *Also called Shopping Center Wine & Liquor* ***(G-8259)***
Kinaneco Inc (PA) 315 468-6201
2925 Milton Ave Syracuse (13209) ***(G-15356)***
Kinaneco Printing Systems, Syracuse *Also called Kinaneco Inc* ***(G-15356)***
Kinatek, Niskayuna *Also called Kinematic Technologies Inc* ***(G-12355)***
Kind Group LLC (PA) 212 645-0800
19 W 44th St Ste 811 New York (10036) ***(G-10448)***
Kindling Inc 212 400-6296
440 Park Ave S Fl 14 New York (10016) ***(G-10449)***
Kinecosystem, New York *Also called Kik Us Inc* ***(G-10443)***
Kinedyne Inc 716 667-6833
3566 S Benzing Rd Orchard Park (14127) ***(G-12724)***
Kineflow Division, Rochester *Also called Cummins-Wagner-Siewert LLC* ***(G-13728)***
Kinematic Technologies Inc 518 346-7686
1129 Glenmeadow Ct Niskayuna (12309) ***(G-12355)***
Kinemotive Corporation 631 249-6440
222 Central Ave Ste 1 Farmingdale (11735) ***(G-4803)***
Kinetic Fuel Technology Inc 716 745-1461
1205 Balmer Rd Youngstown (14174) ***(G-16836)***
Kinetic Laboratories, Youngstown *Also called Kinetic Fuel Technology Inc* ***(G-16836)***
Kinetic Marketing Inc 212 620-0600
1133 Broadway Ste 221 New York (10010) ***(G-10450)***
Kinfolk Store, Brooklyn *Also called Kinfolk Studios Inc* ***(G-2071)***
Kinfolk Store, The, Brooklyn *Also called Kinfolk Studios Inc* ***(G-2070)***
Kinfolk Studios Inc 770 617-5592
94 Wythe Ave Brooklyn (11249) ***(G-2070)***
Kinfolk Studios Inc (PA) 347 799-2946
90 Wythe Ave Brooklyn (11249) ***(G-2071)***
King Album Inc 631 253-9500
20 Kean St West Babylon (11704) ***(G-16168)***
King Cracker Corp 516 539-9251
307 Peninsula Blvd Hempstead (11550) ***(G-6017)***
King Displays Inc 212 629-8455
333 W 52nd St New York (10019) ***(G-10451)***
King Lithographers Inc (PA) 914 667-4200
245 S 4th Ave Mount Vernon (10550) ***(G-8414)***
King Paving, Albany *Also called King Road Materials Inc* ***(G-91)***
King Research Inc 718 788-0122
114 12th St Ste 1 Brooklyn (11215) ***(G-2072)***
King Road Materials Inc (HQ) 518 381-9995
8 Southwoods Blvd Albany (12211) ***(G-91)***
King Road Materials Inc 518 382-5354
145 Cordell Rd Schenectady (12303) ***(G-14694)***
King Road Materials Inc 518 382-5354
Cordell Rd Albany (12212) ***(G-92)***
King Sales Inc 718 301-9862
284 Wallabout St Brooklyn (11206) ***(G-2073)***
King Steel Iron Work Corp 718 384-7500
2 Seneca Ave Brooklyn (11237) ***(G-2074)***
Kingboard Holdings Limited 705 844-1993
120 Broadway Fl 32 New York (10271) ***(G-10452)***
Kingform Cap Company Inc 516 822-2501
121 New South Rd Hicksville (11801) ***(G-6098)***
Kings Cnty Brwers Cllctive LLC 917 207-2739
381 Troutman St Brooklyn (11237) ***(G-2075)***
Kings Film & Sheet Inc 718 624-7510
482 Baltic St Brooklyn (11217) ***(G-2076)***
Kings Material, Brooklyn *Also called US Concrete Inc* ***(G-2612)***
Kings Park Asphalt Corporation 631 269-9774
201 Moreland Rd Ste 2 Hauppauge (11788) ***(G-5856)***
Kings Park Ready Mix Corp 631 269-4330
140 Old Northport Rd E Kings Park (11754) ***(G-6884)***
Kings Quarry, Adams Center *Also called R G King General Construction* ***(G-4)***
Kings Quartet Corp 845 986-9090
270 Kings Hwy Warwick (10990) ***(G-15955)***
Kings Ready Mix, Roslyn Heights *Also called US Concrete Inc* ***(G-14461)***
Kings Ready Mix Inc 718 853-4644
703 3rd Ave Fl 2 Flr 2 Roslyn Heights (11577) ***(G-14458)***
Kings Specialty Co, Brooklyn *Also called Kings Film & Sheet Inc* ***(G-2076)***
Kingsbury Printing Co Inc 518 747-6606
813 Bay Rd Queensbury (12804) ***(G-13431)***
Kingston Building Products LLC 914 665-0707
11 Brookdale Pl Ste 101 Mount Vernon (10550) ***(G-8415)***
Kingston Hoops Summer 845 401-6830
68 Glen St Kingston (12401) ***(G-6904)***
Kingston Pharma LLC 315 705-4019
5 County Route 42 Massena (13662) ***(G-7904)***
Kingston Pharmaceuticals, Massena *Also called Kingston Pharma LLC* ***(G-7904)***
Kingston Wste Wtr Trment Plant, Kingston *Also called City of Kingston* ***(G-6895)***
Kingstreet Sounds, New York *Also called His Productions USA Inc* ***(G-10105)***
Kinplex Corp (PA) 631 242-4800
200 Heartland Blvd Edgewood (11717) ***(G-4407)***
Kinplex Corp 631 242-4800
200 Heartland Blvd Edgewood (11717) ***(G-4408)***
Kinro Manufacturing Inc (HQ) 817 483-7791
200 Mmaroneck Ave Ste 301 White Plains (10601) ***(G-16469)***
Kinshofer Usa Inc 716 731-4333
6420 Inducon Dr W Ste G Sanborn (14132) ***(G-14549)***
Kintex Inc 716 297-0652
3315 Haseley Dr Niagara Falls (14304) ***(G-12302)***

Kionix Inc 607 257-1080
36 Thornwood Dr Ithaca (14850) *(G-6590)*

Kirays & Joel Meat Market, Monroe *Also called Joel Kiryas Meat Market Corp* *(G-8273)*

Kirschner Brush LLC 718 292-1809
605 E 132nd St Frnt 3 Bronx (10454) *(G-1309)*

Kirtas Inc 585 924-5999
749 Phillips Rd Ste 300 Victor (14564) *(G-15852)*

Kirtas Inc 585 924-2420
7620 Omnitech Pl Victor (14564) *(G-15853)*

Kiss My Face, Gardiner *Also called Bycmac Corp* *(G-5292)*

Kissle, Jamaica *Also called Whitney Foods Inc* *(G-6691)*

Kistler Instrument Corporation 716 691-5100
75 John Glenn Dr Amherst (14228) *(G-234)*

Kitchen Cabinet Co, Poughkeepsie *Also called Modern Cabinet Company Inc* *(G-13355)*

Kitchen Design Center, Sauquoit *Also called Custom Stair & Millwork Co* *(G-14621)*

Kitchen Specialty Craftsmen 607 739-0833
2366 Corning Rd Elmira (14903) *(G-4496)*

Kiton Building Corp 212 486-3224
4 E 54th St New York (10022) *(G-10453)*

Kittinger Company Inc 716 876-1000
4675 Transit Rd Buffalo (14221) *(G-2907)*

Kittredge & Sons Inc 978 567-0998
3315 Haseley Dr Niagara Falls (14304) *(G-12303)*

Kittywalk Systems Inc 516 627-8418
10 Farmview Rd Port Washington (11050) *(G-13276)*

Kj Astoria Gourmet Inc 718 545-6900
3720 Broadway Astoria (11103) *(G-432)*

KJ MEAT DIRECT, Monroe *Also called JW Consulting Inc* *(G-8274)*

Kjckd Inc (PA) 518 435-9696
630 Columbia St Ext Ste 2 Latham (12110) *(G-7078)*

KKR Millennium GP LLC 212 750-8300
9 W 57th St Ste 4150 New York (10019) *(G-10454)*

KKR Ntral Rsources Fund I-A LP 212 750-8300
9 W 57th St Ste 4200 New York (10019) *(G-10455)*

Kkw Corp 631 589-5454
90 Bourne Blvd Sayville (11782) *(G-14631)*

KLA-Tencor Corporation 845 897-1723
20 Corporate Park Rd C Hopewell Junction (12533) *(G-6290)*

Klara Technologies Inc 844 215-5272
1 State St Fl 25 New York (10004) *(G-10456)*

Klauber Brothers Inc (PA) 212 686-2531
253 W 35th St Fl 11 New York (10001) *(G-10457)*

Kld Labs Inc 631 549-4222
55 Cabot Ct Hauppauge (11788) *(G-5857)*

Klearbar Inc 516 684-9892
8 Graywood Rd Port Washington (11050) *(G-13277)*

Klee Corp 585 272-0320
340 Jefferson Rd Rochester (14623) *(G-13905)*

Kleen Stik Industries Inc 718 984-5031
44 Lenzie St Staten Island (10312) *(G-15098)*

Kleer-Fax Inc 631 225-1100
750 New Horizons Blvd Amityville (11701) *(G-295)*

Klees Car Wash and Detailing, Rochester *Also called Klee Corp* *(G-13905)*

Klein & Company, Massapequa *Also called R Klein Jewelry Co Inc* *(G-7884)*

Klein & Sons Logging Inc 845 292-6682
3114 State Route 52 Wht Sphr Spgs (12787) *(G-16557)*

Klein Cutlery LLC 585 928-2500
7971 Refinery Rd Bolivar (14715) *(G-1111)*

Klein Reinforcing Services Inc 585 352-9433
11 Turner Dr Spencerport (14559) *(G-14980)*

Kleinfelder John 716 753-3163
5239 W Lake Rd Mayville (14757) *(G-7921)*

Klemmt Orthopaedic Services, Johnson City *Also called Klemmt Orthotics & Prosthetics* *(G-6813)*

Klemmt Orthotics & Prosthetics 607 770-4400
130 Oakdale Rd Johnson City (13790) *(G-6813)*

Klg Usa LLC 845 856-5311
20 W King St Port Jervis (12771) *(G-13233)*

Kling Magnetics Inc 518 392-4000
343 State Route 295 Chatham (12037) *(G-3428)*

Klutz (HQ) 650 687-2600
568 Broadway Rm 503 New York (10012) *(G-10458)*

Klutz Store, New York *Also called Klutz* *(G-10458)*

Klx Aerospace Solutions, Cornwall *Also called Klx Inc* *(G-3833)*

Klx Inc 845 534-0401
45 Quaker Ave Ste 203 Cornwall (12518) *(G-3833)*

KMA Corporation 518 743-1330
153 Maple St Ste 5 Glens Falls (12801) *(G-5430)*

Kms Contracting Inc 718 495-6500
86 Georgia Ave Brooklyn (11207) *(G-2077)*

Knf Clean Room Products Corp 631 588-7000
1800 Ocean Ave Ronkonkoma (11779) *(G-14362)*

Kng Construction Co Inc 212 595-1451
19 Silo Ln Warwick (10990) *(G-15956)*

Knickerbocker Partition Corp (PA) 516 546-0550
260 Spagnoli Rd Melville (11747) *(G-8042)*

Knight Life Entertainment 646 733-8911
674 Lincoln Pl Apt 9 Brooklyn (11216) *(G-2078)*

Knight Sttlement Sand Grav LLC 607 776-2048
7291 County Route 15 Bath (14810) *(G-646)*

Knightly Endeavors 845 340-0949
319 Wall St Ste 2 Kingston (12401) *(G-6905)*

Knise & Krick Inc 315 422-3516
324 Pearl St Syracuse (13203) *(G-15357)*

Knit Resource Center Ltd 212 221-1990
250 W 39th St Rm 207 New York (10018) *(G-10459)*

Knitty City, New York *Also called A Thousand Cranes Inc* *(G-8698)*

Knj Fabricators LLC 347 234-6985
4341 Wickham Ave Bronx (10466) *(G-1310)*

Knogo, Ronkonkoma *Also called Sentry Technology Corporation* *(G-14410)*

Knoll Inc 716 891-1700
1700 Broadway St Buffalo (14212) *(G-2908)*

Knoll Inc 212 343-4124
1330 Ave Of The A New York (10019) *(G-10460)*

Knoll Printing & Packaging Inc 516 621-0100
149 Eileen Way Syosset (11791) *(G-15220)*

Knoll Textile, New York *Also called Knoll Inc* *(G-10460)*

Knoll Worldwide, Syosset *Also called Knoll Printing & Packaging Inc* *(G-15220)*

Knorr Brake Company LLC 518 561-1387
613 State Route 3 Unit 1 Plattsburgh (12901) *(G-13129)*

Knorr Brake Holding Corp (HQ) 315 786-5356
748 Starbuck Ave Watertown (13601) *(G-16022)*

Knorr Brake Truck Systems Co (HQ) 315 786-5200
748 Starbuck Ave Watertown (13601) *(G-16023)*

Knothe Apparel Group, New York *Also called Sleepwear Holdings Inc* *(G-11618)*

Knowles Cazenovia Inc (HQ) 315 655-8710
2777 Us Route 20 Cazenovia (13035) *(G-3320)*

Knowlton Technologies LLC 315 782-0600
213 Factory St Watertown (13601) *(G-16024)*

Knucklehead Embroidery Inc 607 797-2725
800 Valley Plz Ste 4 Johnson City (13790) *(G-6814)*

Ko Fro Foods Inc 718 972-6480
4418 18th Ave 4420 Brooklyn (11204) *(G-2079)*

Ko-Sure Food Distributors, Brooklyn *Also called Taam Tov Foods Inc* *(G-2551)*

Kobalt Music Pubg Amer Inc (HQ) 212 247-6204
2 Gansevoort St Fl 6 New York (10014) *(G-10461)*

Kobe Steel USA Holdings Inc (HQ) 212 751-9400
535 Madison Ave Fl 5 New York (10022) *(G-10462)*

Koch Metal Spinning Co Inc 716 835-3631
74 Jewett Ave Buffalo (14214) *(G-2909)*

Koch Supply & Trading LP 212 319-4895
667 Madison Ave Fl 22 New York (10065) *(G-10463)*

Kodak Alaris Inc (HQ) 585 290-2891
336 Initiative Dr Rochester (14624) *(G-13906)*

Kodak Gallery - Cohber, West Henrietta *Also called Cohber Press Inc* *(G-16234)*

Kodak Graphic Communications 585 724-4000
343 State St Rochester (14650) *(G-13907)*

Kodansha USA Inc 917 322-6200
451 Park Ave S Fl 7 New York (10016) *(G-10464)*

Kodiak Cutting Tools LLC 800 892-1006
2700 Bellevue Ave Syracuse (13219) *(G-15358)*

Kodiak Studios Inc 718 769-5399
3030 Emmons Ave Apt 3t Brooklyn (11235) *(G-2080)*

Koehler Instrument Company Inc (PA) 631 589-3800
85 Corporate Dr Holtsville (11742) *(G-6240)*

Koehler-Gibson Mkg & Graphics, Buffalo *Also called Koehlr-Gibson Mkg Graphics Inc* *(G-2910)*

Koehlr-Gibson Mkg Graphics Inc 716 838-5960
875 Englewood Ave Buffalo (14223) *(G-2910)*

Koenig Iron Works Inc 718 433-0900
814 37th Ave Long Island City (11101) *(G-7489)*

Koeppels Kustom Kitchens Inc 518 489-0092
16 Van Rensselaer Rd Albany (12205) *(G-93)*

Kohlberg Sports Group Inc (HQ) 914 241-7430
111 Radio Circle Dr Mount Kisco (10549) *(G-8348)*

Kohler Awning Inc 716 685-3333
2600 Walden Ave Buffalo (14225) *(G-2911)*

Koke Inc 800 535-5303
582 Queensbury Ave Queensbury (12804) *(G-13432)*

Kokin Inc 212 643-8225
247 W 38th St Rm 701 New York (10018) *(G-10465)*

Kokoroko Bakery, Woodside *Also called Kokoroko Corporation* *(G-16661)*

Kokoroko Corporation 718 433-4321
4755 47th St Woodside (11377) *(G-16661)*

Kollage Work Too Ltd 212 695-1821
261 W 35th St Ste 302 New York (10001) *(G-10466)*

Komar Layering LLC (HQ) 212 725-1500
16 E 34th St Fl 10 New York (10016) *(G-10467)*

Komar Luxury Brands 646 472-0060
16 E 34th St Fl 10 New York (10016) *(G-10468)*

Kon Tat Group Corporation 718 207-5022
1491 E 34th St Brooklyn (11234) *(G-2081)*

Konar Precision Mfg Inc 631 242-4466
62 S 2nd St Ste F Deer Park (11729) *(G-3996)*

Kondor Technologies Inc 631 471-8832
206 Christopher St Ronkonkoma (11779) *(G-14363)*

Konecranes Inc 585 359-4450
1020 Lehigh Station Rd # 4 Henrietta (14467) *(G-6033)*

Kong Kee Food Corp 718 937-2746
4831 Van Dam St Long Island City (11101) *(G-7490)*

Konica Mnolta Sups Mfg USA Inc 845 294-8400
51 Hatfield Ln Goshen (10924) *(G-5481)*

Konrad Design, Farmingdale *Also called T A Tool & Molding Inc* ***(G-4888)***
Konrad Prosthetics & Orthotics (PA) 516 485-9164
596 Jennings Ave West Hempstead (11552) ***(G-16219)***
Konstantin D FRAnk& Sons Vini 607 868-4884
9749 Middle Rd Hammondsport (14840) ***(G-5707)***
Koon Enterprises LLC 718 886-3163
6805 Fresh Madow Ln Ste B Fresh Meadows (11365) ***(G-5200)***
Koonichi Inc 718 886-8338
6805 Fresh Madow Ln Ste B Fresh Meadows (11365) ***(G-5201)***
Koppers Choclat Specialty Inc 917 834-2290
501 Madison Ave Rm 402 New York (10022) ***(G-10469)***
Koppert Cress USA LLC 631 779-3640
2975 Sound Ave Riverhead (11901) ***(G-13571)***
Korangy Publishing Inc (PA) 212 260-1332
450 W 31st St Fl 4 New York (10001) ***(G-10470)***
Kore Infrastructure LLC (PA) 646 532-9060
4 High Pine Glen Cove (11542) ***(G-5370)***
Korea Central Daily News Inc (HQ) 718 361-7700
4327 36th St Long Island City (11101) ***(G-7491)***
Korea Times New York Inc (HQ) 718 784-4526
3710 Skillman Ave Long Island City (11101) ***(G-7492)***
Korea Times New York Inc 718 729-5555
3710 Skillman Ave Long Island City (11101) ***(G-7493)***
Korea Times New York Inc 718 961-7979
15408 Nthrn Blvd Ste 2b Flushing (11354) ***(G-5019)***
Korean New York Daily, The, Flushing *Also called New York IL Bo Inc* ***(G-5028)***
Korean Yellow Pages 718 461-0073
14809 Northern Blvd Flushing (11354) ***(G-5020)***
Koregon Enterprises Inc 450 218-6836
102 W Service Rd Champlain (12919) ***(G-3411)***
Korin Japanese Trading Corp 212 587-7021
57 Warren St Frnt A New York (10007) ***(G-10471)***
Koring Bros Inc 888 233-1292
30 Pine St New Rochelle (10801) ***(G-8619)***
Koshii Maxelum America Inc 845 471-0500
12 Van Kleeck Dr Poughkeepsie (12601) ***(G-13350)***
Kossars On Grand LLC 212 473-4810
367 Grand St New York (10002) ***(G-10472)***
Koster Keunen Waxes, Sayville *Also called Kkw Corp* ***(G-14631)***
Koster Keunen Waxes Ltd 631 589-0400
90 Bourne Blvd Sayville (11782) ***(G-14632)***
Kotel Importers Inc 212 245-6200
22 W 48th St Ste 607 New York (10036) ***(G-10473)***
Kourosh, College Point *Also called Lahoya Enterprise Inc* ***(G-3652)***
Kovatch Mobile Equipment Corp 518 785-0900
68 Sicker Rd Latham (12110) ***(G-7079)***
Kowa American Corporation (HQ) 212 303-7800
55 E 59th St Fl 19 New York (10022) ***(G-10474)***
Kozinn+sons Merchant Tailors 212 643-1916
150 W 55th St 4c New York (10019) ***(G-10475)***
Kozy Shack Enterprises LLC (HQ) 516 870-3000
83 Ludy St Hicksville (11801) ***(G-6099)***
Kozy Shack Enterprises LLC 516 870-3000
50 Ludy St Hicksville (11801) ***(G-6100)***
KP Industries Inc 516 679-3161
2481 Charles Ct Ste 1 North Bellmore (11710) ***(G-12379)***
KPP Ltd 516 338-5201
200 Robbins Ln Unit C2 Jericho (11753) ***(G-6793)***
Kps Capital Partners LP (PA) 212 338-5100
485 Lexington Ave Fl 31 New York (10017) ***(G-10476)***
Kraft Hat Manufacturers Inc 845 735-6200
7 Veterans Pkwy Pearl River (10965) ***(G-12904)***
Kraft Heinz Foods Company 607 865-7131
261 Delaware St Walton (13856) ***(G-15911)***
Kraft Heinz Foods Company 315 376-6575
7388 Utica Blvd Lowville (13367) ***(G-7651)***
Kraft Heinz Foods Company 607 527-4584
8596 Main St Campbell (14821) ***(G-3204)***
Kraft Heinz Foods Company 585 226-4400
140 Spring St Avon (14414) ***(G-519)***
Kraftees, Oswego *Also called Patrick Kraft* ***(G-12786)***
Kragel Co Inc 716 648-1344
23 Lake St Hamburg (14075) ***(G-5685)***
Krainz Creations Inc 212 583-1555
589 5th Ave New York (10017) ***(G-10477)***
Kraman Iron Works Inc 212 460-8400
410 E 10th St New York (10009) ***(G-10478)***
Kramartron Precision Inc 845 368-3668
2 Spook Rock Rd Unit 107 Tallman (10982) ***(G-15462)***
Krasner Group Inc (PA) 212 268-4100
40 W 37th St Ph A New York (10018) ***(G-10479)***
Kraus & Sons Inc 212 620-0408
355 S End Ave Apt 10j New York (10280) ***(G-10480)***
Kraus Organization Limited (PA) 212 686-5411
181 Hudson St Ste 2a New York (10013) ***(G-10481)***
Kraus USA Inc 800 775-0703
12 Harbor Park Dr Port Washington (11050) ***(G-13278)***
Kravitz Design Inc (PA) 212 625-1644
13 Crosby St Rm 401 New York (10013) ***(G-10482)***
Krengel Manufacturing Co Inc 212 227-1901
121 Fulton Ave Fl 2 Fulton (13069) ***(G-5226)***
Kreon Inc 516 470-9522
999 S Oyster Bay Rd # 105 Bethpage (11714) ***(G-844)***
Krepe Kraft Inc 716 826-7086
1801 Elmwood Ave Buffalo (14207) ***(G-2912)***
Krepe-Kraft, Buffalo *Also called Krepe Kraft Inc* ***(G-2912)***
Kris-Tech Wire Company Inc (PA) 315 339-5268
80 Otis St Rome (13441) ***(G-14255)***
Kronenberger Mfg Corp 585 385-2340
115 Despatch Dr East Rochester (14445) ***(G-4289)***
Kronos Incorporated 518 459-5545
16 Sage Est Ste 206 Albany (12204) ***(G-94)***
Krug Precision Inc 516 944-9350
7 Carey Pl Port Washington (11050) ***(G-13279)***
Kryten Iron Works Inc 914 345-0990
3 Browns Ln Ste 201 Hawthorne (10532) ***(G-5990)***
KSA Manufacturing LLC 315 488-0809
5050 Smoral Rd Camillus (13031) ***(G-3196)***
Kse Sportsman Media Inc (PA) 212 852-6600
1040 Ave Of The Americas New York (10018) ***(G-10483)***
Ksk International Inc (PA) 212 354-7770
450 Park Ave Ste 2703 New York (10022) ***(G-10484)***
Ksm Group Ltd 716 751-6006
2905 Beebe Rd Newfane (14108) ***(G-12252)***
Kt Group Inc 212 760-2500
13 W 36th St Fl 3 New York (10018) ***(G-10485)***
Ktk Thermal Technologies Inc 585 678-9025
1657 E Park Dr Macedon (14502) ***(G-7700)***
Kubota Authorized Dealer, Mendon *Also called Saxby Implement Corp* ***(G-8094)***
Kuno Steel Products Corp 516 938-8500
132 Duffy Ave Hicksville (11801) ***(G-6101)***
Kuraray America Inc 212 986-2230
33 Maiden Ln Fl 6 New York (10038) ***(G-10486)***
Kurrier Inc 718 389-3018
145 Java St Brooklyn (11222) ***(G-2082)***
Kurt Gaum Inc 212 719-2836
580 5th Ave Ste 303 New York (10036) ***(G-10487)***
Kurtskraft Inc 516 944-4449
437 Port Washington Blvd Port Washington (11050) ***(G-13280)***
Kurtz Truck Equipment Inc 607 849-3468
1085 Mcgraw Marathon Rd Marathon (13803) ***(G-7790)***
Kurz and Zobel Inc 585 254-9060
688 Colfax St Rochester (14606) ***(G-13908)***
Kush Oasis Enterprises LLC 516 513-1316
228 Martin Dr Syosset (11791) ***(G-15221)***
Kussmaul Electronics Co Inc 631 218-0298
170 Cherry Ave West Sayville (11796) ***(G-16290)***
Kustom Collabo, Brooklyn *Also called Vsg International LLC* ***(G-2636)***
Kustom Korner 716 646-0173
5140 Camp Rd Hamburg (14075) ***(G-5686)***
Kw Distributors Group Inc 718 843-3500
9018 Liberty Ave Ozone Park (11417) ***(G-12829)***
Kw Kitchen Design, Ozone Park *Also called Kw Distributors Group Inc* ***(G-12829)***
Kwadair LLC 646 824-2511
137 Kent St Brooklyn (11222) ***(G-2083)***
Kwesi Legesse LLC 347 581-9872
203 Remsen Ave Brooklyn (11212) ***(G-2084)***
Kwik Kut Manufacturing Co, Mohawk *Also called Mary F Morse* ***(G-8255)***
Kwik Ticket Inc (PA) 718 421-3800
4101 Glenwood Rd Brooklyn (11210) ***(G-2085)***
Kwong CHI Metal Fabrication 718 369-6429
166 41st St Brooklyn (11232) ***(G-2086)***
Kww Productions Corp 212 398-8181
1410 Broadway Fl 24 New York (10018) ***(G-10488)***
Kybod Group LLC 408 306-1657
305 E 40th St Apt 5k New York (10016) ***(G-10489)***
Kyle Editing LLC 212 675-3464
48 W 25th St Fl 5 New York (10010) ***(G-10490)***
Kyle R Lawrence Electric Inc 315 502-4181
101 Hyde Pkwy Palmyra (14522) ***(G-12856)***
Kyntec Corporation 716 810-6956
2100 Old Union Rd Buffalo (14227) ***(G-2913)***
Kyocera Precision Tools Inc 607 687-0012
1436 Taylor Rd Owego (13827) ***(G-12798)***
Kyra Communications Corp 516 783-6244
3864 Bayberry Ln Seaford (11783) ***(G-14758)***
Kz Precision Inc 716 683-3202
1 Mason Pl Lancaster (14086) ***(G-7026)***
L & D Acquisition LLC 585 531-9000
1 Lake Niagara Ln Naples (14512) ***(G-8471)***
L & D Manufacturing Corp 718 665-5226
366 Canal Pl Frnt Bronx (10451) ***(G-1311)***
L & J Interiors Inc 631 218-0838
35 Orville Dr Ste 3 Bohemia (11716) ***(G-1044)***
L & K Graphics Inc 631 667-2269
1917 Deer Park Ave Deer Park (11729) ***(G-3997)***
L & L Overhead Garage Doors (PA) 718 721-2518
3125 45th St Long Island City (11103) ***(G-7494)***
L & M Optical Disc LLC 718 649-3500
65 W 36th St Fl 11 New York (10018) ***(G-10491)***
L & M Publications Inc 516 378-3133
2 Endo Blvd Garden City (11530) ***(G-5264)***
L & M Uniserv Corp 718 854-3700
4416 18th Ave Pmb 133 Brooklyn (11204) ***(G-2087)***
L & M West, New York *Also called L & M Optical Disc LLC* ***(G-10491)***

L & S Metals Inc...716 692-6865
111 Witmer Rd North Tonawanda (14120) *(G-12436)*
L A Burdick Chocolates...212 796-0143
5 E 20th St New York (10003) *(G-10492)*
L A R Electronics Corp...716 285-0555
2733 Niagara St Niagara Falls (14303) *(G-12304)*
L A S Replacement Parts Inc...718 583-4700
1645 Webster Ave Bronx (10457) *(G-1312)*
L American Ltd...716 372-9480
222 Homer St Olean (14760) *(G-12604)*
L and S Packing Co...631 845-1717
101 Central Ave Farmingdale (11735) *(G-4804)*
L D Flecken Inc...631 777-4881
11 Old Dock Rd Unit 11 # 11 Yaphank (11980) *(G-16714)*
L D Weiss Inc (PA)...212 697-3023
320 E 42nd St Apt 3106 New York (10017) *(G-10493)*
L F Fashion Orient Intl Co Ltd...917 667-3398
32 W 40th St Apt 2l New York (10018) *(G-10494)*
L F International Inc...212 756-5000
425 Park Ave Fl 5 New York (10022) *(G-10495)*
L I C Screen Printing Inc...516 546-7289
2949 Joyce Ln Merrick (11566) *(G-8100)*
L I F Publishing Corp (PA)...631 345-5200
14 Ramsey Rd Shirley (11967) *(G-14837)*
L I Stamp, Ridgewood *Also called Long Island Stamp & Seal Co* *(G-13542)*
L J Valente Inc...518 674-3750
8957 Ny Highway 66 Averill Park (12018) *(G-515)*
L K Manufacturing Corp...631 243-6910
56 Eads St West Babylon (11704) *(G-16169)*
L K Printing, White Plains *Also called Copy Stop Inc* *(G-16440)*
L K Printing Corp...914 761-1944
50 Main St Ste 32 White Plains (10606) *(G-16470)*
L LLC...716 885-3918
106 Soldiers Pl Buffalo (14222) *(G-2914)*
L M N Printing Company Inc...516 285-8526
23 W Merrick Rd Ste A Valley Stream (11580) *(G-15784)*
L M R, New York *Also called Lefrak Entertainment Co Ltd* *(G-10540)*
L Miller Design Inc...631 242-1163
100 E Jefryn Blvd Ste F Deer Park (11729) *(G-3998)*
L N D Incorporated...516 678-6141
3230 Lawson Blvd Oceanside (11572) *(G-12545)*
L P R Precision Parts & Tls Co...631 293-7334
108 Rome St Ste 1 Farmingdale (11735) *(G-4805)*
L P Transportation, Selkirk *Also called Palpross Incorporated* *(G-14770)*
L S I, East Aurora *Also called Luminescent Systems Inc* *(G-4204)*
L S Sign Co Inc...718 469-8600
1030 Wyckoff Ave Ridgewood (11385) *(G-13541)*
L S Z Inc...914 948-4040
30 Glenn St Ste 309 White Plains (10603) *(G-16471)*
L V D, Akron *Also called Strippit Inc* *(G-23)*
L VII Resilient LLC...631 987-5819
108 Cherry Ln Medford (11763) *(G-7957)*
L W S Inc...631 580-0472
125 Gary Way Ste 1 Ronkonkoma (11779) *(G-14364)*
L Y Z Creations Ltd Inc...718 768-2977
78 18th St Brooklyn (11232) *(G-2088)*
L& JG Stickley Incorporated (PA)...315 682-5500
1 Stickley Dr Manlius (13104) *(G-7779)*
L&M Specialty Fabrication...585 283-4847
3816 Oak Orchard Rd Albion (14411) *(G-159)*
L'Etoile Jewelers, Lynbrook *Also called Master Craft Jewelry Co Inc* *(G-7668)*
L-3 Cmmnctons Ntronix Holdings...212 697-1111
600 3rd Ave Fl 34 New York (10016) *(G-10496)*
L-3 Narda-Miteq, Hauppauge *Also called L3 Technologies Inc* *(G-5859)*
L-3 Narda-Miteq, Hauppauge *Also called L3 Technologies Inc* *(G-5862)*
L3 Communication, New York *Also called L3 Foreign Holdings Inc* *(G-10497)*
L3 Foreign Holdings Inc (HQ)...212 697-1111
600 3rd Ave Fl 32 New York (10016) *(G-10497)*
L3 Technologies Inc (PA)...212 697-1111
600 3rd Ave Fl 34 New York (10016) *(G-10498)*
L3 Technologies Inc...631 231-1700
435 Moreland Rd Hauppauge (11788) *(G-5858)*
L3 Technologies Inc...631 436-7400
100 Davids Dr Hauppauge (11788) *(G-5859)*
L3 Technologies Inc...631 289-0363
49 Rider Ave Patchogue (11772) *(G-12870)*
L3 Technologies Inc...631 231-3994
435 Moreland Rd Hauppauge (11788) *(G-5860)*
L3 Technologies Inc...631 231-1700
435 Moreland Rd Hauppauge (11788) *(G-5861)*
L3 Technologies Inc...631 436-7400
330 Oser Ave Hauppauge (11788) *(G-5862)*
La Bella Strings, Newburgh *Also called E & O Mari Inc* *(G-12220)*
La Calenita Bakery & Cafeteria...718 205-8273
4008 83rd St Elmhurst (11373) *(G-4468)*
La Cola 1 Inc...917 509-6669
529 W 42nd St Apt 5b New York (10036) *(G-10499)*
La Cremeria...212 226-6758
178 Mulberry St New York (10012) *(G-10500)*
La Escondida Inc...845 562-1387
129 Lake St Newburgh (12550) *(G-12230)*
La Fina Design Inc...212 689-6725
42 W 38th St Rm 1200 New York (10018) *(G-10501)*
La Flor Products Company Inc (PA)...631 851-9601
25 Hoffman Ave Hauppauge (11788) *(G-5863)*
La Flor Spices, Hauppauge *Also called La Flor Products Company Inc* *(G-5863)*
La Forge Francaise Ltd Inc...631 591-0572
100 Kroemer Ave Riverhead (11901) *(G-13572)*
La Lame Inc...212 921-9770
215 W 40th St Fl 5 New York (10018) *(G-10502)*
La Lame Importers, New York *Also called La Lame Inc* *(G-10502)*
La Mar Lighting Co Inc...631 777-7700
485 Smith St Farmingdale (11735) *(G-4806)*
La Prima Bakery Inc (PA)...718 584-4442
765 E 182nd St Bronx (10460) *(G-1313)*
La Raza, Brooklyn *Also called Impremedia LLC* *(G-1997)*
La Strada Dance Footwear Inc...631 242-1401
770 Grand Blvd Ste 1 Deer Park (11729) *(G-3999)*
La Voz Hispana, New York *Also called Nick Lugo Inc* *(G-10963)*
La-Mar Fashions, Deer Park *Also called Continental Knitting Mills* *(G-3958)*
Lab Crafters Inc...631 471-7755
2085 5th Ave Ronkonkoma (11779) *(G-14365)*
Lab-Aids Inc...631 737-1133
17 Colt Ct Ronkonkoma (11779) *(G-14366)*
Labarba-Q LLC...845 806-6227
32 Highland Ave Warwick (10990) *(G-15957)*
Labatt USA LLC...716 604-1050
79 Perry St Ste 1 Buffalo (14203) *(G-2915)*
Labco of Palmyra Inc...315 597-5202
904 Canandaigua Rd Palmyra (14522) *(G-12857)*
Label Gallery Inc...607 334-3244
1 Lee Ave 11 Norwich (13815) *(G-12489)*
Label Source Inc...212 244-1403
321 W 35th St New York (10001) *(G-10503)*
Labella Pasta Inc...845 331-9130
906 State Route 28 Kingston (12401) *(G-6906)*
Labels I-G, New York *Also called Labels Inter-Global Inc* *(G-10504)*
Labels Inter-Global Inc...212 398-0006
109 W 38th St Rm 701 New York (10018) *(G-10504)*
Labels X Press, Buffalo *Also called Magazines & Brochures Inc* *(G-2933)*
Labels, Stickers and More, Bayport *Also called Stickershopcom Inc* *(G-739)*
Labeltex Mills Inc...212 279-6165
1430 Broadway Rm 1510 New York (10018) *(G-10505)*
Labgrafix Printing Inc...516 280-8300
43 Rocklyn Ave Unit B Lynbrook (11563) *(G-7667)*
Labhar - Friedman, New York *Also called L F International Inc* *(G-10495)*
Labortory For Laser Energetics, Rochester *Also called University of Rochester* *(G-14190)*
Labrador Stone Inc...570 465-2120
11 Dutchess Rd Binghamton (13901) *(G-901)*
Lackawanna Hot Rolled Plant, Blasdell *Also called Republic Steel Inc* *(G-928)*
Lactalis American Group Inc...716 827-2622
2375 S Park Ave Buffalo (14220) *(G-2916)*
Lactalis American Group Inc (HQ)...716 823-6262
2376 S Park Ave Buffalo (14220) *(G-2917)*
Lady Brass Co Inc...516 887-8040
1717 Broadway Unit 2 Hewlett (11557) *(G-6047)*
Lady Burd Exclusive Cosmt Inc (PA)...631 454-0444
44 Executive Blvd Ste 1 Farmingdale (11735) *(G-4807)*
Lady Burd Private Label Cosmt, Farmingdale *Also called Lady Burd Exclusive Cosmt Inc* *(G-4807)*
Lady Ester Lingerie Corp...212 689-1729
33 E 33rd St Rm 800 New York (10016) *(G-10506)*
Lady Linda Cakes, Bronx *Also called Operative Cake Corp* *(G-1348)*
Lady-N-Th-wndow Chocolates Inc...631 549-1059
319 Main St Huntington (11743) *(G-6403)*
Ladybird Bakery Inc...718 499-8108
1112 8th Ave Brooklyn (11215) *(G-2089)*
Lafarge Building Materials Inc...518 756-5000
Rr Ravena (12143) *(G-13453)*
Lafarge North America Inc...716 651-9235
6125 Genesee St Lancaster (14086) *(G-7027)*
Lafarge North America Inc...716 854-5791
575 Ohio St Buffalo (14203) *(G-2918)*
Lafarge North America Inc...716 772-2621
400 Hinman Rd Lockport (14094) *(G-7313)*
Lafarge North America Inc...914 930-3027
350 Broadway Buchanan (10511) *(G-2673)*
Lafarge North America Inc...518 756-5000
1916 Route 9 W Ravena (12143) *(G-13454)*
Lafarge North America Inc...716 876-8788
4001 River Rd Tonawanda (14150) *(G-15554)*
Lafayette Chateau...607 546-2062
Rr 414 Hector (14841) *(G-6000)*
Lafayette Mirror & Glass Co...718 768-0660
2300 Marcus Ave New Hyde Park (11042) *(G-8547)*
Lafayette Pub Inc...212 925-4242
332 Lafayette St New York (10012) *(G-10507)*
Lagardere North America Inc (HQ)...212 477-7373
60 E 42nd St Ste 1940 New York (10165) *(G-10508)*
Lagasse Works Inc...315 946-9202
5 Old State Route 31 Lyons (14489) *(G-7685)*

ALPHABETIC

Lage Industries Corporation 718 342-3400
9814 Ditmas Ave Brooklyn (11236) *(G-2090)*
Lagoner Farms Inc 315 904-4109
6895 Lake Ave Williamson (14589) *(G-16560)*
Lagunatic Music & Filmworks 212 353-9600
456 Johnson Ave 202 Brooklyn (11237) *(G-2091)*
Lahoya Enterprise Inc 718 886-8799
1842 College Point Blvd College Point (11356) *(G-3652)*
Lahr Plastics, Fairport *Also called Lahr Recycling & Resins Inc (G-4638)*
Lahr Recycling & Resins Inc 585 425-8608
164 Daley Rd Fairport (14450) *(G-4638)*
Lai Apparel Design Inc 212 382-1075
209 W 38th St Rm 901 New York (10018) *(G-10509)*
Lai International Inc 763 780-0060
1 Tibbits Ave Green Island (12183) *(G-5608)*
Laird Telemedia 845 339-9555
2000 Sterling Rd Mount Marion (12456) *(G-8363)*
Lake Champlain Weekly, Plattsburgh *Also called Studley Printing & Publishing (G-13160)*
Lake Country Media, Albion *Also called Albion-Holley Pennysaver Inc (G-154)*
Lake Country Woodworkers Ltd 585 374-6353
12 Clark St Naples (14512) *(G-8472)*
Lake Image Systems Inc 585 321-3630
205 Summit Point Dr Ste 2 Henrietta (14467) *(G-6034)*
Lake Immunogenics Inc 585 265-1973
348 Berg Rd Ontario (14519) *(G-12656)*
Lake Placid Advertisers Wkshp 518 523-3359
Cold Brook Plz Lake Placid (12946) *(G-6976)*
Lake Region Medical Inc 716 662-5025
3902 California Rd Orchard Park (14127) *(G-12725)*
Lake View Manufacturing LLC 315 364-7892
1690 State Route 90 N King Ferry (13081) *(G-6881)*
Lakeland Industries Inc (PA) 631 981-9700
3555 Vtrans Mem Hwy Ste C Ronkonkoma (11779) *(G-14367)*
Lakelands Concrete, Lima *Also called East Main Associates (G-7151)*
Lakelands Concrete Pdts Inc 585 624-1990
7520 E Main St Lima (14485) *(G-7152)*
Lakeshore Carbide Inc 716 462-4349
1959 Maple Rd Buffalo (14221) *(G-2919)*
Lakeshore Pennysaver, Fredonia *Also called Fredonia Pennysaver Inc (G-5126)*
Lakeside Capital Corporation 716 664-2555
402 Chandler St Ste 2 Jamestown (14701) *(G-6735)*
Lakeside Cider Mill Farm Inc 518 399-8359
336 Schauber Rd Ballston Lake (12019) *(G-568)*
Lakeside Concrete Services Inc 716 681-7510
89 Brandel Ave Lancaster (14086) *(G-7028)*
Lakeside Container Corp (PA) 518 561-6150
299 Arizona Ave Plattsburgh (12903) *(G-13130)*
Lakeside Industries Inc 716 386-3031
2 Lakeside Dr Bemus Point (14712) *(G-818)*
Lakeside Precision Inc 716 366-5030
208 Dove St Dunkirk (14048) *(G-4173)*
Lakestar Semi Inc (PA) 212 974-6254
888 7th Ave Ste 3300 New York (10106) *(G-10510)*
Lakewood Vineyards Inc 607 535-9252
4024 State Route 14 Watkins Glen (14891) *(G-16059)*
Lali Jewelry Inc 212 944-2277
50 W 47th St Ste 1610 New York (10036) *(G-10511)*
Lali Jewels, New York *Also called Lali Jewelry Inc (G-10511)*
Lalique Boutique, New York *Also called Lalique North America Inc (G-10512)*
Lalique North America Inc 212 355-6550
609 Madison Ave New York (10022) *(G-10512)*
Lam Research Corporation 845 896-0606
300 Westage Bus Ctr Dr # 190 Fishkill (12524) *(G-4947)*
Lamar Plastics Packaging Ltd 516 378-2500
216 N Main St Ste F Freeport (11520) *(G-5163)*
Lambro Industries Inc (PA) 631 842-8088
115 Albany Ave Amityville (11701) *(G-296)*
Laminated Window Products Inc 631 242-6883
211 N Fehr Way Bay Shore (11706) *(G-693)*
Lamm Industries Inc 718 368-0181
2513 E 21st St Brooklyn (11235) *(G-2092)*
Lamontage, New York *Also called Mgk Group Inc (G-10788)*
Lamoreaux Landing Wl 607 582-6162
9224 State Route 414 Lodi (14860) *(G-7353)*
Lamothermic Corp 845 278-6118
391 Route 312 Brewster (10509) *(G-1169)*
Lamparts Co Inc 914 723-8986
160 E 3rd St Ste 2 Mount Vernon (10550) *(G-8416)*
Lams Foods Inc 718 217-0476
9723 218th St Queens Village (11429) *(G-13410)*
Lancaster Knives Inc (PA) 716 683-5050
165 Court St Lancaster (14086) *(G-7029)*
Lancaster Quality Pork Inc 718 439-8822
5600 1st Ave Ste 6 Brooklyn (11220) *(G-2093)*
Lancaster Tanks and Steel Pdts, Buffalo *Also called Jbren Corp (G-2891)*
Lance Valves 716 681-5825
15 Enterprise Dr Lancaster (14086) *(G-7030)*
Lanco Corporation 631 231-2300
2905 Vtrans Mem Hwy Ste 3 Ronkonkoma (11779) *(G-14368)*
Lanco Manufacturing Co 516 292-8953
384 Hempstead Tpke West Hempstead (11552) *(G-16220)*
Land and Sea Trailer Shop, Coram *Also called G L 7 Sales Plus Ltd (G-3797)*
Land n Sea Inc (PA) 212 444-6000
1375 Broadway Fl 2 New York (10018) *(G-10513)*
Land OLakes Inc 516 681-2980
50 Ludy St Hicksville (11801) *(G-6102)*
Land Packaging Corp 914 472-5976
7 Black Birch Ln Scarsdale (10583) *(G-14640)*
Land Self Prtction Systems Div, Buffalo *Also called Northrop Grumman Intl Trdg Inc (G-2975)*
Landies Candies Co Inc 716 834-8212
2495 Main St Ste 350 Buffalo (14214) *(G-2920)*
Landlord Guard Inc 212 695-6505
1 Maiden Ln Fl 7 New York (10038) *(G-10514)*
Landmark Group Inc 845 358-0350
709 Executive Blvd Ste A Valley Cottage (10989) *(G-15757)*
Landpro Equipment LLC (PA) 716 665-3110
1756 Lindquist Dr Falconer (14733) *(G-4686)*
Lane Enterprises Inc 607 776-3366
16 May St Bath (14810) *(G-647)*
Lane Enterprises Inc 518 885-4385
825 State Route 67 Ballston Spa (12020) *(G-587)*
Lane Metal Products, Bath *Also called Lane Enterprises Inc (G-647)*
Lanel, Floral Park *Also called Creatron Services Inc (G-4961)*
Lanes Flr Cvrngs Intriors Inc 212 532-5200
30 W 26th St Fl 11r New York (10010) *(G-10515)*
Langer Biomechanics Inc 800 645-5520
2905 Vtrans Mem Hwy Ste 2 Ronkonkoma (11779) *(G-14369)*
Language and Graphics Inc 212 315-5266
350 W 57th St Apt 14i New York (10019) *(G-10516)*
Lanier Clothes, New York *Also called Oxford Industries Inc (G-11076)*
Lannett Company, Carmel *Also called Silarx Pharmaceuticals Inc (G-3281)*
Lanoves Inc 718 384-1880
72 Anthony St Brooklyn (11222) *(G-2094)*
Lanwood Industries Inc 718 786-3000
45 Drexel Dr Bay Shore (11706) *(G-694)*
Lanza Corp 914 937-6360
404 Willett Ave Port Chester (10573) *(G-13204)*
Lapp Management Corp 607 243-5141
3700 Route 14 Himrod (14842) *(G-6160)*
Larcent Enterprises Inc 845 562-3332
509 Temple Hill Rd New Windsor (12553) *(G-8648)*
Laregence Inc 212 736-2548
34 W 27th St Fl 2 New York (10001) *(G-10517)*
Largo Music Inc 212 756-5080
425 Park Ave Ste 501 New York (10022) *(G-10518)*
Larkin Anya Ltd 718 361-1827
4310 23rd St Ste 2b Long Island City (11101) *(G-7495)*
Larosa Cupcakes 347 866-3920
314 Lake Ave Staten Island (10303) *(G-15099)*
Larry Kings Corporation 718 481-8741
13708 250th St Rosedale (11422) *(G-14440)*
Larson Metal Manufacturing Co 716 665-6807
1831 Mason Dr Jamestown (14701) *(G-6736)*
LArte Del Gelato Gruppo Inc 718 383-6600
3100 47th Ave Long Island City (11101) *(G-7496)*
Larte Del Gelato Inc 212 366-0570
75 9th Ave Frnt 38 New York (10011) *(G-10519)*
Laseoptics Corp 716 462-5078
300 International Dr # 100 Buffalo (14221) *(G-2921)*
Laser & Electron Beam Inc 603 626-6080
77 7th Ave Apt 3h New York (10011) *(G-10520)*
Laser and Varicose Vein Trtmnt 718 667-1777
500 Seaview Ave Ste 240 Staten Island (10305) *(G-15100)*
Laser Printer Checks Corp 845 782-5837
7 Vayoel Moshe Ct # 101 Monroe (10950) *(G-8275)*
Lasermax Inc 585 272-5420
3495 Winton Pl Ste A37 Rochester (14623) *(G-13909)*
Lasermaxdefense, Rochester *Also called Lasermax Inc (G-13909)*
Lasertech Crtridge RE-Builders 518 373-1246
7 Longwood Dr Clifton Park (12065) *(G-3569)*
Last Magazine, The, New York *Also called Berger & Wild LLC (G-9050)*
Last N Last, New Rochelle *Also called Paint Over Rust Products Inc (G-8621)*
Last Resort, The, Rouses Point *Also called Sandys Deli Inc (G-14470)*
Last Straw Inc 516 371-2727
22 Lawrence Ln Unit 1 Lawrence (11559) *(G-7104)*
Lasticks Aerospace Inc 631 242-8484
35 Washington Ave Ste E Bay Shore (11706) *(G-695)*
Latchable Inc 646 833-0604
450 W 33rd St Fl 12 New York (10001) *(G-10521)*
Latham International Inc (PA) 518 783-7776
787 Watervliet Shaker Rd Latham (12110) *(G-7080)*
Latham International Inc 518 346-5292
706 Corporation Park 1 Schenectady (12302) *(G-14695)*
Latham International Mfg Corp 800 833-3800
787 Watervliet Shaker Rd Latham (12110) *(G-7081)*
Latham Manufacturing, Schenectady *Also called Latham International Inc (G-14695)*
Latham Manufacturing, Latham *Also called Latham Pool Products Inc (G-7083)*
Latham Pool Products, Latham *Also called Latham International Mfg Corp (G-7081)*
Latham Pool Products Inc (PA) 518 951-1000
787 Watervliet Shaker Rd Latham (12110) *(G-7082)*
Latham Pool Products Inc 260 432-8731
787 Watervliet Shaker Rd Latham (12110) *(G-7083)*

Latham Seamless Gutters, Altamont *Also called Alfred B Parella* **(G-194)**
Latham Software Sciences Inc....518 785-1100
678 Troy Schenectady Rd # 104 Latham (12110) **(G-7084)**
Latina Media Ventures LLC (PA)....212 642-0200
625 Madison Ave Frnt 3 New York (10022) **(G-10522)**
Latium USA Trading LLC (PA)....631 563-4000
5005 Veterans Mem Hwy Holbrook (11741) **(G-6193)**
Latorre Orthopedic Laboratory....518 786-8655
960 Troy Schenectady Rd Latham (12110) **(G-7085)**
Laufer Wind Group LLC....212 792-3912
270 Lafayette St Ste 1402 New York (10012) **(G-10523)**
Laundress Inc....212 209-0074
247 W 30th St Ste 7l New York (10001) **(G-10524)**
Laura Star Service Center, Averill Park *Also called Garment Care Systems LLC* **(G-514)**
Lauricella Press Inc....516 931-5906
81 Emjay Blvd Brentwood (11717) **(G-1140)**
Laurtom Inc....914 273-2233
333 N Bedford Rd Ste 100 Mount Kisco (10549) **(G-8349)**
Laurus Development Inc....716 823-1202
3556 Lake Shore Rd # 121 Buffalo (14219) **(G-2922)**
Lavanya, Jackson Heights *Also called Karishma Fashions Inc* **(G-6620)**
Law360, New York *Also called Portfolio Media Inc* **(G-11221)**
Lawdy Miss Clawdy, Pound Ridge *Also called Lloyd Price Icon Food Brands* **(G-13377)**
Lawn Elements Inc....631 656-9711
1150 Lincoln Ave Ste 4 Holbrook (11741) **(G-6194)**
Lawson M Whiting Inc....315 986-3064
15 State Route 350 Macedon (14502) **(G-7701)**
Lawton Electric Co, Ogdensburg *Also called Lawtons Electric Motor Service* **(G-12576)**
Lawtons Electric Motor Service....315 393-2728
148 Cemetery Rd Ogdensburg (13669) **(G-12576)**
Layton Manufacturing Corp (PA)....718 498-6000
864 E 52nd St Brooklyn (11203) **(G-2095)**
Lazare Kaplan Intl Inc (PA)....212 972-9700
19 W 44th St Fl 16 New York (10036) **(G-10525)**
Lazarek Inc....315 343-1242
209 Erie St Oswego (13126) **(G-12780)**
Lazer Incorporated (PA)....336 744-8047
1465 Jefferson Rd Ste 110 Rochester (14623) **(G-13910)**
Lazer Marble & Granite Corp....718 859-9644
1053 Dahill Rd Brooklyn (11204) **(G-2096)**
Lazer Photo Engraving, Rochester *Also called Lazer Incorporated* **(G-13910)**
Lazo Setter Company, New York *Also called Mataci Inc* **(G-10725)**
Lb Furniture Industries LLC....518 828-1501
99 S 3rd St Hudson (12534) **(G-6362)**
Lb Laundry Inc....347 399-8030
4431 Kissena Blvd Flushing (11355) **(G-5021)**
Lcdrives Corp....860 712-8926
65 Main St Pytn Hl 3204 Rm 3204 Peyton Hall Potsdam (13676) **(G-13319)**
Lco Destiny LLC....315 782-3302
1 Fisher Cir Watertown (13601) **(G-16025)**
LD McCauley LLC....716 662-6744
3875 California Rd Orchard Park (14127) **(G-12726)**
LDB Interior Textiles, New York *Also called E W Williams Publications* **(G-9598)**
LDI Lighting Inc (PA)....718 384-4490
240 Broadway Ste C Brooklyn (11211) **(G-2097)**
LDI Lighting Inc....718 384-4490
193 Williamsburg St W A Brooklyn (11211) **(G-2098)**
Le Book Publishing Inc (HQ)....212 334-5252
580 Broadway Rm 1001 New York (10012) **(G-10526)**
Le Chocolate of Rockland LLC....845 533-4125
1 Ramapo Ave Suffern (10901) **(G-15192)**
Le Creuset, Riverhead *Also called Schiller Stores Inc* **(G-13583)**
Le Hook Rouge LLC....212 947-6272
275 Conover St Ste 3q-3p Brooklyn (11231) **(G-2099)**
Le Lab, Valley Stream *Also called Lelab Dental Laboratory Inc* **(G-15785)**
Le Labo Fragrances, Brooklyn *Also called Le Labo Holding LLC* **(G-2100)**
Le Labo Holding LLC (HQ)....646 490-6200
122 N 6th St Fl 2 Brooklyn (11249) **(G-2100)**
Le Labo Holding LLC....646 719-1740
80 39th St Fl Ground Brooklyn (11232) **(G-2101)**
Le Paveh Ltd....212 736-6110
23 W 47th St Ste 501 New York (10036) **(G-10527)**
Le Roy Pennysaver, Le Roy *Also called Dray Enterprises Inc* **(G-7116)**
Le Vian Corp (PA)....516 466-7200
235 Great Neck Rd Great Neck (11021) **(G-5568)**
Le Vian Corp....516 466-7200
10 W 46th St New York (10036) **(G-10528)**
Lea & Viola Inc....646 918-6866
525 Fashion Ave Rm 1401 New York (10018) **(G-10529)**
Leader Herald, The, Gloversville *Also called William B Collins Company* **(G-5473)**
Leader Printing Inc....516 546-1544
2272 Babylon Tpke Merrick (11566) **(G-8101)**
Leader Sheet Metal Inc....347 271-4961
759 E 133rd St 2 Bronx (10454) **(G-1314)**
Leader, The, Corning *Also called Gatehouse Media LLC* **(G-3819)**
Leadership Connect, New York *Also called Leadership Directories Inc* **(G-10530)**
Leadership Directories Inc (PA)....212 627-4140
1407 Broadway Rm 318 New York (10018) **(G-10530)**
Leadertex Group, New York *Also called Leadertex Intl Inc* **(G-10531)**
Leadertex Intl Inc....212 563-2242
135 W 36th St Fl 12 New York (10018) **(G-10531)**
Leape Resources,, Alexander *Also called Lenape Energy Inc* **(G-179)**
Learn360, New York *Also called Infobase Holdings Inc* **(G-10206)**
Learningateway LLC....212 920-7969
106 Saint James Pl Brooklyn (11238) **(G-2102)**
Learningexpress LLC....646 274-6454
224 W 29th St Fl 3 New York (10001) **(G-10532)**
Leather Artisan....518 359-3102
9740 State Highway 3 Childwold (12922) **(G-3499)**
Leather Craftsmen Inc (PA)....631 752-9000
6 Dubon Ct Farmingdale (11735) **(G-4808)**
Leather Indexes Corp....516 827-1900
174a Miller Pl Hicksville (11801) **(G-6103)**
Leather Outlet....518 668-0328
1656 State Route 9 Lake George (12845) **(G-6964)**
Leatherstocking Mobile Home PA....315 839-5691
2089 Doolittle Rd Sauquoit (13456) **(G-14622)**
Leblon Cachaca, New York *Also called Leblon LLC* **(G-10534)**
Leblon Holdings LLC....212 741-2675
33 Irving Pl Fl 3 New York (10003) **(G-10533)**
Leblon LLC....954 649-0148
33 Irving Pl Fl 3 New York (10003) **(G-10534)**
Leblon LLC....786 281-5672
266 W 26th St Ste 801 New York (10001) **(G-10535)**
Lebron Equipment Supply, New York *Also called 3835 Lebron Rest Eqp & Sup Inc* **(G-8679)**
Lechler Laboratories Inc....845 426-6800
100 Red Schoolhse Rd C2 Spring Valley (10977) **(G-14998)**
Lechler Labs, Chestnut Ridge *Also called Mehron Inc* **(G-3493)**
Lechler Labs, Spring Valley *Also called Lechler Laboratories Inc* **(G-14998)**
Lecreuset of America, Central Valley *Also called Schiller Stores Inc* **(G-3397)**
Led Lumina USA LLC....631 750-4433
116 Wilbur Pl Bohemia (11716) **(G-1045)**
Led Next, Westbury *Also called Emitled Inc* **(G-16328)**
Led Waves, Brooklyn *Also called Light Waves Concept Inc* **(G-2121)**
Led Waves Inc....347 416-6182
4100 1st Ave Ste 3n Brooklyn (11232) **(G-2103)**
Ledan Inc....631 239-1226
6 Annetta Ave Northport (11768) **(G-12470)**
Ledan Design Group, Northport *Also called Ledan Inc* **(G-12470)**
Ledes Group Inc....212 840-8800
85 5th Ave Fl 12 New York (10003) **(G-10536)**
Lee & Low Books Incorporated....212 779-4400
95 Madison Ave Rm 1205 New York (10016) **(G-10537)**
Lee Dyeing Company NC Inc....518 736-5232
328 N Perry St Johnstown (12095) **(G-6834)**
Lee Enterprises Incorporated....518 792-3131
76 Lawrence St Glens Falls (12801) **(G-5431)**
Lee Newspapers Inc....518 673-3237
6113 State Highway 5 Palatine Bridge (13428) **(G-12842)**
Lee Printing Inc....718 237-1651
188 Lee Ave Brooklyn (11211) **(G-2104)**
Lee Publications Inc (PA)....518 673-3237
6113 State Highway 5 Palatine Bridge (13428) **(G-12843)**
Lee Spring Company Div, New York *Also called Unimex Corporation* **(G-11946)**
Lee Spring Company LLC (HQ)....718 362-5183
140 58th St Ste 3c Brooklyn (11220) **(G-2105)**
Lee Spring LLC (PA)....718 236-2222
140 58th St Ste 3c Brooklyn (11220) **(G-2106)**
Lee World Industries LLC (PA)....212 265-8866
150 Broadway Ste 1608 New York (10038) **(G-10538)**
Lee Yuen Fung Trading Co Inc (PA)....212 594-9595
125 W 29th St Fl 5 New York (10001) **(G-10539)**
Leesa Designs Ltd....631 261-3991
31 Glenn Cres Centerport (11721) **(G-3349)**
Leetech Manufacturing Inc....631 563-1442
105 Carlough Rd Unit C Bohemia (11716) **(G-1046)**
Lefrak Entertainment Co Ltd....212 586-3600
40 W 57th St Fl 4 New York (10019) **(G-10540)**
Legacy Manufacturing, Bronx *Also called Legacy USA LLC* **(G-1315)**
Legacy USA LLC....718 292-5333
415 Concord Ave Bronx (10455) **(G-1315)**
Legacy Valve LLC....914 403-5075
14 Railroad Ave Valhalla (10595) **(G-15742)**
Legal Servicing LLC....716 565-9300
2801 Wehrle Dr Ste 5 Williamsville (14221) **(G-16581)**
Legal Strategies Inc....516 377-3940
1795 Harvard Ave Merrick (11566) **(G-8102)**
Legendary Auto Interiors Ltd....315 331-1212
121 W Shore Blvd Newark (14513) **(G-12198)**
Legge System, Peekskill *Also called Walter G Legge Company Inc* **(G-12928)**
Leggiadro International Inc (PA)....212 997-8766
8 W 36th St Fl 9 New York (10018) **(G-10541)**
Legion Lighting Co Inc....718 498-1770
221 Glenmore Ave Brooklyn (11207) **(G-2107)**
Legno Veneto USA....716 651-9169
3283 Walden Ave Depew (14043) **(G-4094)**
Lehigh Cement Company (HQ)....518 792-1137
313 Warren St Glens Falls (12801) **(G-5432)**
Lehigh Cement Company....518 943-5940
120 Alpha Rd Catskill (12414) **(G-3305)**

(PA)=Parent Co (HQ)=Headquarters (DH)=Div Headquarters
2019 Harris
New York Manufacturers Directory
923

Lehigh Northeast Cement, Glens Falls Also called Lehigh Cement Company (G-5432)

Lehmann Printing Company Inc 212 929-2395
247 W 37th St Rm 2a New York (10018) *(G-10542)*

Lehneis Orthotics Prosthetic 516 790-1897
517 Route 111 Ste 300 Hauppauge (11788) *(G-5864)*

Lehneis Orthotics Prosthetic 631 369-3115
518 E Main St Riverhead (11901) *(G-13573)*

Leica Microsystems Inc 716 686-3000
3362 Walden Ave Depew (14043) *(G-4095)*

Leidel Corporation (PA) 631 244-0900
95 Orville Dr Bohemia (11716) *(G-1047)*

Leigh Scott Enterprises Inc 718 343-5440
24802 Union Tpke Bellerose (11426) *(G-781)*

Leiter Sukkahs Inc 718 436-0303
1346 39th St Brooklyn (11218) *(G-2108)*

Lela Rose, New York Also called Stitch & Couture Inc (G-11713)

Lelab Dental Laboratory Inc 516 561-5050
550 W Merrick Rd Ste 8 Valley Stream (11580) *(G-15785)*

Lemans Corporation 518 885-7500
10 Mccrea Hill Rd Ballston Spa (12020) *(G-588)*

Lemetric Hair Centers Inc 212 986-5620
124 E 40th St Rm 601 New York (10016) *(G-10543)*

Lemode Concepts Inc 631 841-0796
19 Elm Pl Amityville (11701) *(G-297)*

Lemode Plumbing & Heating 718 545-3336
3455 11th St Astoria (11106) *(G-433)*

Lemon Brothers Foundation Inc 347 920-2749
23b Debs Pl Bronx (10475) *(G-1316)*

Lemoyne Machine Products Corp 315 454-0708
106 Evelyn Ter Syracuse (13208) *(G-15359)*

Lemral Knitwear Inc 718 210-0175
70 Franklin Ave Brooklyn (11205) *(G-2109)*

Lenape Energy Inc (PA) 585 344-1200
9489 Alexander Rd Alexander (14005) *(G-179)*

Lenape Resources Inc 585 344-1200
9489 Alexander Rd Alexander (14005) *(G-180)*

Lenaro Paper Co Inc 631 439-8800
31 Windsor Pl Central Islip (11722) *(G-3376)*

Lenco, Amityville Also called Saraga Industries Corp (G-315)

Lencore Acoustics Corp (PA) 516 682-9292
1 Crossways Park Dr W Woodbury (11797) *(G-16623)*

Lencore Acoustics Corp 315 384-9114
1 S Main St Norfolk (13667) *(G-12358)*

Lending Trimming Co Inc 212 242-7502
179 Christopher St New York (10014) *(G-10544)*

Leng Universal Inc 212 398-6800
530 7th Ave Rm 1101 New York (10018) *(G-10545)*

Lennons Litho Inc 315 866-3156
234 Kast Hill Rd Herkimer (13350) *(G-6043)*

Lenny & Bill LLC 516 997-5757
717 Main St Westbury (11590) *(G-16349)*

Lenon Models Inc 212 229-1581
236 W 27th St Rm 900 New York (10001) *(G-10546)*

Lenore Marshall Inc 212 947-5945
231 W 29th St Frnt 1 New York (10001) *(G-10547)*

Lens Lab 718 379-2020
2124 Bartow Ave Bronx (10475) *(G-1317)*

Lens Lab Express 718 921-5488
482 86th St Brooklyn (11209) *(G-2110)*

Lens Lab Express of Graham Ave 718 486-0117
28 Graham Ave Brooklyn (11206) *(G-2111)*

Lens Lab Express Southern Blvd 718 626-5184
3097 Steinway St Ste 301 Astoria (11103) *(G-434)*

Lens Triptar Co Inc 585 473-4470
439 Monroe Ave Ste 1 Rochester (14607) *(G-13911)*

Lenz, Peconic Also called Dorset Farms Inc (G-12914)

Leo D Bernstein & Sons Inc (PA) 212 337-9578
151 W 25th St Frnt 1 New York (10001) *(G-10548)*

Leo Diamond, The, New York Also called Leo Schachter Diamonds LLC (G-10552)

Leo Ingwer Inc 212 719-1342
62 W 47th St Ste 1004 New York (10036) *(G-10549)*

Leo International Inc 718 290-8005
471 Sutter Ave Brooklyn (11207) *(G-2112)*

Leo P Callahan Inc 607 797-7314
229 Lwer Stlla Ireland Rd Binghamton (13905) *(G-902)*

Leo Paper Inc 917 305-0708
286 5th Ave Fl 6 New York (10001) *(G-10550)*

Leo Schachter & Co Inc 212 688-2000
529 5th Ave New York (10017) *(G-10551)*

Leo Schachter Diamonds LLC 212 688-2000
50 W 47th St Ste 2100 New York (10036) *(G-10552)*

Leo Schultz 716 969-0945
1144 Maryvale Dr Cheektowaga (14225) *(G-3451)*

Leon Mege Inc 212 768-3868
151 W 46th St Ste 901 New York (10036) *(G-10553)*

Leonard Bus Sales Inc 607 467-3100
730 Ellsworth Rd Rome (13441) *(G-14256)*

Leonard Carlson 518 477-4710
90 Waters Rd East Greenbush (12061) *(G-4230)*

Leonard Oakes Estate Winery 585 318-4418
10609 Ridge Rd Medina (14103) *(G-7982)*

Leonardo Printing Corp 914 664-7890
529 E 3rd St Mount Vernon (10553) *(G-8417)*

Leonardo Prntng, Mount Vernon Also called Leonardo Printing Corp (G-8417)

Lep, Hawthorne Also called Ludl Electronic Products Ltd (G-5992)

Leprino Foods Company 570 888-9658
400 Leprino Ave Waverly (14892) *(G-16067)*

Leroux Fuels 518 563-3653
994 Military Tpke Plattsburgh (12901) *(G-13131)*

Leroy Plastics Inc 585 768-8158
20 Lent Ave Le Roy (14482) *(G-7121)*

Les Ateliers Tamalet, New York Also called Ateliers Tamalet Corp (G-8944)

Les Chateaux De France Inc 516 239-6795
1 Craft Ave Inwood (11096) *(G-6494)*

Lesanne Life Sciences LLC 914 234-0860
47 Brook Farm Rd Bedford (10506) *(G-770)*

Leser Enterprises Ltd 212 644-8921
1767 Central Park Ave Yonkers (10710) *(G-16778)*

Lesieur Cristal Inc 646 604-4314
1034 44th Dr Fl 2 Long Island City (11101) *(G-7497)*

Lesilu Productions Inc 212 947-6419
60 W 38th St Rm 302 New York (10018) *(G-10554)*

Leslie Stuart Co Inc 212 629-4551
149 W 36th St Fl 8 New York (10018) *(G-10555)*

Lesly Enterprise & Associates 631 988-1301
29 Columbo Dr Deer Park (11729) *(G-4000)*

Lessoilcom 516 319-5052
672 Dogwood Ave Franklin Square (11010) *(G-5118)*

Letigre, New York Also called Lt2 LLC (G-10623)

Letterama Inc (PA) 516 349-0800
111 Cabot St West Babylon (11704) *(G-16170)*

Lettergraphics, Bridgeport Also called Syracuse Letter Company Inc (G-1184)

Level Wear, Cheektowaga Also called Accolade USA Inc (G-3434)

Levi Shabtai 212 302-7393
1 W 47th St New York (10036) *(G-10556)*

Levi Strauss & Co 917 213-6263
13432 Blossom Ave Flushing (11355) *(G-5022)*

Leviton Manufacturing Co Inc (PA) 631 812-6000
201 N Service Rd Melville (11747) *(G-8043)*

Levitt Industrial Textile, Deer Park Also called Kenwin Sales Corp (G-3995)

Levolor Inc (HQ) 845 664-7000
1 Blue Hill Plz Pearl River (10965) *(G-12905)*

Levolor Window Furnishings Inc, Pearl River Also called Levolor Inc (G-12905)

Levon Graphics Corp 631 753-2022
500 Brook Ave Deer Park (11729) *(G-4001)*

Levy Group Inc (PA) 212 398-0707
1333 Broadway Fl 9 New York (10018) *(G-10557)*

Lewis & Myers Inc (PA) 585 494-1410
7307 S Lake Rd Bergen (14416) *(G-823)*

Lewis Avenue LLC 718 669-0579
172 5th Ave 111 Brooklyn (11217) *(G-2113)*

Lewis Machine Co Inc 718 625-0799
209 Congress St Brooklyn (11201) *(G-2114)*

Lewis Sand & Gravel, Lewis Also called Upstone Materials Inc (G-7137)

Lewis, S J Machine Co, Brooklyn Also called Lewis Machine Co Inc (G-2114)

Lexan Industries Inc 631 434-7586
15 Harold Ct Bay Shore (11706) *(G-696)*

Lexar Global LLC 845 352-9700
711 Executive Blvd Ste K Valley Cottage (10989) *(G-15758)*

Lexington Machining LLC 585 235-0880
677 Buffalo Rd Rochester (14611) *(G-13912)*

Lexington Machining LLC (PA) 585 235-0880
677 Buffalo Rd Rochester (14611) *(G-13913)*

Lexis Nexis Mathew Bender, Menands Also called Lexis Publishing (G-8086)

Lexis Publishing 518 487-3000
1275 Broadway Menands (12204) *(G-8086)*

Lf Outerwear LLC 212 239-2025
463 7th Ave Fl 12 New York (10018) *(G-10558)*

Lgb Inc 212 278-8280
1410 Broadway Rm 3205 New York (10018) *(G-10559)*

Lgn Materials & Solutions 888 414-0005
149 Esplanade Mount Vernon (10553) *(G-8418)*

Lhv Precast Inc 845 336-8880
540 Ulster Landing Rd Kingston (12401) *(G-6907)*

LI Community Newspapers Inc 516 747-8282
132 E 2nd St Mineola (11501) *(G-8233)*

LI Fireproof Door, Whitestone Also called Lif Industries Inc (G-16545)

LI Pipe Supply, Garden City Also called Long Island Pipe Supply Inc (G-5267)

LI Script LLC 631 321-3850
333 Crossways Park Dr Woodbury (11797) *(G-16624)*

Libbys Bakery Cafe LLC 603 918-8825
92 Montcalm St Ticonderoga (12883) *(G-15512)*

Liberty Apparel Company Inc (PA) 718 625-4000
1407 Broadway Rm 1500 New York (10018) *(G-10560)*

Liberty Awnings & Signs Inc 347 203-1470
7705 21st Ave East Elmhurst (11370) *(G-4223)*

Liberty Brass Turning Co Inc 718 784-2911
1200 Shames Dr Unit C Westbury (11590) *(G-16350)*

Liberty Controls Inc 718 461-0600
1505 132nd St Fl 2 College Point (11356) *(G-3653)*

Liberty Displays Inc 716 743-1757
4230b Ridge Lea Rd # 110 Amherst (14226) *(G-235)*

Liberty Fabrication Inc 718 495-5735
226 Glenmore Ave Brooklyn (11207) *(G-2115)*

Liberty Food and Fuel 315 299-4039
1131 N Salina St Syracuse (13208) ***(G-15360)***
Liberty Install Inc 631 651-5655
100 Centershore Rd Centerport (11721) ***(G-3350)***
Liberty Iron Works, Liberty *Also called Neversink Steel Corp* ***(G-7146)***
Liberty Label Mfg Inc 631 737-2365
21 Peachtree Ct Holbrook (11741) ***(G-6195)***
Liberty Machine & Tool 315 699-3242
7908 Ontario Ave Cicero (13039) ***(G-3519)***
Liberty Panel & Home Center, Brooklyn *Also called Liberty Panel Center Inc* ***(G-2116)***
Liberty Panel Center Inc (PA) 718 647-2763
1009 Liberty Ave Brooklyn (11208) ***(G-2116)***
Liberty Pipe Incorporated 516 747-2472
128 Liberty Ave Mineola (11501) ***(G-8234)***
Liberty Pumps Inc 800 543-2550
7000 Appletree Ave Bergen (14416) ***(G-824)***
Liberty Ready Mix Inc 718 526-1700
9533 150th St Jamaica (11435) ***(G-6655)***
LIBRARY OF AMERICA, New York *Also called Literary Classics of US* ***(G-10578)***
Licenders (PA) 212 759-5200
939 8th Ave New York (10019) ***(G-10561)***
Lickity Splits 585 345-6091
238 East Ave Batavia (14020) ***(G-629)***
Liddabit Sweets 917 912-1370
330 Wythe Ave Apt 2g Brooklyn (11249) ***(G-2117)***
Liddell Corporation 716 297-8557
4600 Witmer Ind Est 5 Niagara Falls (14305) ***(G-12305)***
Lidestri Food and Drink, Fairport *Also called Lidestri Foods Inc* ***(G-4639)***
Lidestri Foods Inc (PA) 585 377-7700
815 Whitney Rd W Fairport (14450) ***(G-4639)***
Lids Corporation 518 459-7060
131 Colonie Ctr Spc 429 Albany (12205) ***(G-95)***
Lieb Cellars LLC 631 298-1942
35 Cox Neck Rd Mattituck (11952) ***(G-7914)***
Lieb Cellars Tasting Room, Mattituck *Also called Lieb Cellars LLC* ***(G-7914)***
Liebe NY, Perry *Also called R J Liebe Athletic Company* ***(G-12970)***
Lif Distributing Inc 631 630-6900
155 Oval Dr Islandia (11749) ***(G-6533)***
Lif Industries Inc (PA) 516 390-6800
5 Harbor Park Dr Ste 1 Port Washington (11050) ***(G-13281)***
Lif Industries Inc 718 767-8800
1105 Clintonville St Whitestone (11357) ***(G-16545)***
Lifc Corp 516 426-5737
101 Haven Ave Port Washington (11050) ***(G-13282)***
Life Earth Company 310 751-0627
200 W 113th St Apt 2d New York (10026) ***(G-10562)***
Life Juice Brands LLC 585 944-7982
115 Brook Rd Pittsford (14534) ***(G-13010)***
Life Medical Technologies LLC 845 894-2121
2070 Rte 52 21a Bldg 320a Hopewell Junction (12533) ***(G-6291)***
Life On Earth Inc (PA) 866 928-5070
575 Lexington Ave Fl 4 New York (10022) ***(G-10563)***
Life Pill Laboratories LLC 914 682-2146
50 Main St Ste 100 White Plains (10606) ***(G-16472)***
Life Plus Style, New York *Also called International Design Assoc Ltd* ***(G-10245)***
Life Style Design Group 212 391-8666
1441 Broadway Fl 7 New York (10018) ***(G-10564)***
Life Technologies Corporation 716 774-6700
3175 Staley Rd Grand Island (14072) ***(G-5505)***
Life Watch Technology Inc 917 669-2428
42-10 Polen St Ste 412 Flushing (11355) ***(G-5023)***
Lifegas, Cohoes *Also called Linde Gas North America LLC* ***(G-3612)***
Lifegas, Syracuse *Also called Linde Gas North America LLC* ***(G-15362)***
Lifelink Monitoring Corp (PA) 845 336-2098
3201 Route 212 Bearsville (12409) ***(G-764)***
Lifesake Division, New Hartford *Also called Faster-Form Corp* ***(G-8504)***
Lifescan Inc 516 557-2693
15 Tardy Ln N Wantagh (11793) ***(G-15923)***
Lifestyle Design Usa Ltd 212 279-9400
315 W 39th St Rm 1400 New York (10018) ***(G-10565)***
Lifestyle-Trimco (PA) 718 257-9101
323 Malta St Brooklyn (11207) ***(G-2118)***
Lifestyle-Trimco Viaggo, Brooklyn *Also called Lifestyle-Trimco* ***(G-2118)***
Lifetime Brands Inc (PA) 516 683-6000
1000 Stewart Ave Garden City (11530) ***(G-5265)***
Lifetime Chimney Supply LLC 516 576-8144
171 E Ames Ct Plainview (11803) ***(G-13069)***
Lifetime Stainless Steel Corp 585 924-9393
7387 Ny 96 850 Victor (14564) ***(G-15854)***
Lifewatch Inc 800 716-1433
1344 Broadway Ste 106 Hewlett (11557) ***(G-6048)***
Lifewatch Personal Mergency, Hewlett *Also called Lifewatch Inc* ***(G-6048)***
Lifeway Network Inc 718 779-8075
8510 61st Rd Rego Park (11374) ***(G-13464)***
Liffey Sheet Metal Corp 347 381-1134
4555 36th St Long Island City (11101) ***(G-7498)***
Lift Safe - Fuel Safe Inc 315 423-7702
212 W Seneca Tpke Syracuse (13205) ***(G-15361)***
Liftforward Inc (PA) 917 693-4993
180 Maiden Ln Fl 10 New York (10038) ***(G-10566)***
Light Blue USA LLC 718 475-2515
1421 Locust Ave Brooklyn (11230) ***(G-2119)***
Light Dental Labs Inc 516 785-7730
250 N Syracuse Ave Massapequa (11758) ***(G-7881)***
Light Fabrications, Rochester *Also called Eis Inc* ***(G-13774)***
Light House Hill Marketing 212 354-1338
38 W 39th St Fl 4l New York (10018) ***(G-10567)***
Light Inc 212 629-3255
530 Fashion Ave Rm 1002 New York (10018) ***(G-10568)***
Light Phone Inc (PA) 415 595-0044
49 Bogart St Apt 44 Brooklyn (11206) ***(G-2120)***
Light Waves Concept Inc 212 677-6400
4100 1st Ave Brooklyn (11232) ***(G-2121)***
Lightbulb Press Inc 212 485-8800
39 W 28th St New York (10001) ***(G-10569)***
Lighthouse Components 917 993-6820
14 Wall St New York (10005) ***(G-10570)***
Lighting By Dom Yonkers Inc 914 968-8700
253 S Broadway Yonkers (10705) ***(G-16779)***
Lighting Collaborative Inc 212 253-7220
275 Park Ave Apt 6k Brooklyn (11205) ***(G-2122)***
Lighting Holdings Intl LLC (PA) 845 306-1850
4 Manhattanville Rd Purchase (10577) ***(G-13391)***
Lighting N Beyond LLC 718 669-9142
628 Ste 303 Blauvelt (10913) ***(G-937)***
Lighting Products Division, Skaneateles Falls *Also called Welch Allyn Inc* ***(G-14884)***
Lighting Sculptures Inc 631 242-3387
66 N Industry Ct Deer Park (11729) ***(G-4002)***
Lighting Services Inc (PA) 845 942-2800
2 Holt Dr Stony Point (10980) ***(G-15174)***
Lightspin Technologies Inc 301 656-7600
616 Lowell Dr Endwell (13760) ***(G-4618)***
Lik LLC 516 848-5135
6 Bluff Point Rd Northport (11768) ***(G-12471)***
Lilac Quarries LLC 607 867-4016
1702 State Highway 8 Mount Upton (13809) ***(G-8371)***
Lilly Collection, New York *Also called Lily & Taylor Inc* ***(G-10571)***
Lillys Homestyle Bakeshop Inc 718 491-2904
6210 9th Ave Brooklyn (11220) ***(G-2123)***
Lily & Taylor Inc 212 564-5459
247 W 37th St Frnt 6 New York (10018) ***(G-10571)***
Lime Energy Co 704 892-4442
1a Elk Terminal Buffalo (14204) ***(G-2923)***
Limo-Print.com, Central Islip *Also called Color Card LLC* ***(G-3363)***
Lin Jin Feng 718 232-3039
7718 18th Ave Brooklyn (11214) ***(G-2124)***
Lincdoc LLC 585 563-1669
401 Main St East Rochester (14445) ***(G-4290)***
Linco Printing Inc 718 937-5141
5022 23rd St Long Island City (11101) ***(G-7499)***
Lincware, East Rochester *Also called Lincdoc LLC* ***(G-4290)***
Linda Campbell 718 994-4026
4420 Richardson Ave Bronx (10470) ***(G-1318)***
Linda Richards, New York *Also called Linrich Designs Inc* ***(G-10573)***
Linda Tool & Die Corporation 718 522-2066
163 Dwight St Brooklyn (11231) ***(G-2125)***
Linde Gas North America LLC 518 713-2015
10 Arrowhead Ln Cohoes (12047) ***(G-3612)***
Linde Gas North America LLC 315 431-4081
147 Midler Park Dr Syracuse (13206) ***(G-15362)***
Linde LLC 716 847-0748
101 Katherine St Buffalo (14210) ***(G-2924)***
Linde LLC 518 439-8187
76 W Yard Rd Feura Bush (12067) ***(G-4935)***
Linde LLC 716 773-7552
3279 Grand Island Blvd Grand Island (14072) ***(G-5506)***
Linde Merchant Production Inc 315 593-1360
370 Owens Rd Fulton (13069) ***(G-5227)***
Linden Cookies Inc 845 268-5050
25 Brenner Dr Congers (10920) ***(G-3719)***
Linden Forms & Systems Inc 212 219-1100
40 S 6th St Brooklyn (11249) ***(G-2126)***
Linden Meyr Munroe Inc 518 471-5111
20 Hemlock St Latham (12110) ***(G-7086)***
Lindenhurst Fabricators Inc 631 226-3737
117 S 13th St Lindenhurst (11757) ***(G-7174)***
Linder New York LLC 646 678-5819
195 Chrystie St Rm 900 New York (10002) ***(G-10572)***
Lindley Wood Works Inc 607 523-7786
9625 Morgan Creek Rd Lindley (14858) ***(G-7207)***
Lindsay Lyn Accessories Div, New York *Also called Jaclyn Inc* ***(G-10295)***
Line By Line Design Inc (PA) 716 655-4680
425 Olean Rd East Aurora (14052) ***(G-4203)***
Line Ward Corporation 716 675-7373
157 Seneca Creek Rd Buffalo (14224) ***(G-2925)***
Linear Lighting Corporation 718 361-7552
3130 Hunters Point Ave Long Island City (11101) ***(G-7500)***
Linear Signs Inc 631 532-5330
275 W Hoffman Ave Ste 1 Lindenhurst (11757) ***(G-7175)***
Linita Design & Mfg Corp 716 566-7753
1951 Hamburg Tpke Ste 24 Lackawanna (14218) ***(G-6949)***

ALPHABETIC

(PA)=Parent Co (HQ)=Headquarters (DH)=Div Headquarters
2019 Harris
New York Manufacturers Directory
925

Link Control Systems Inc ALPHABETIC SECTION

Link Control Systems Inc 631 471-3950
16 Colt Ct Ronkonkoma (11779) **(G-14370)**
Linli Color, West Babylon *Also called East Cast Clor Compounding Inc* **(G-16154)**
Lino International Inc 516 482-7100
111 Great Neck Rd 300a Great Neck (11021) **(G-5569)**
Lino Metal, Great Neck *Also called Lino International Inc* **(G-5569)**
Lino Press Inc 718 665-2625
652 Southern Blvd Bronx (10455) **(G-1319)**
Linrich Designs Inc 212 382-2257
256 W 38th St Fl 8 New York (10018) **(G-10573)**
Lintex Linens Inc 212 679-8046
295 5th Ave Ste 1703 New York (10016) **(G-10574)**
Linzer Products Corp (HQ) 631 253-3333
248 Wyandanch Ave West Babylon (11704) **(G-16171)**
Lion & Bear Distributors, Jericho *Also called Satnam Distributors LLC* **(G-6801)**
Lion Die-Cutting Co Inc 718 383-8841
95 Dobbin St Ste 1 Brooklyn (11222) **(G-2127)**
Lion In The Sun Park Slope Ltd 718 369-4006
232 7th Ave Brooklyn (11215) **(G-2128)**
Lionel Habas Associates Inc 212 860-8454
1601 3rd Ave Apt 22d New York (10128) **(G-10575)**
Lipe Automation, Liverpool *Also called Ironshore Holdings Inc* **(G-7239)**
Lippincott Massie McQuilkin L 212 352-2055
27 W 20th St Ste 305 New York (10011) **(G-10576)**
Liptis Pharmaceuticals USA Inc 845 627-0260
110 Red Schoolhouse Rd Spring Valley (10977) **(G-14999)**
Liquid Industries Inc 716 628-2999
7219 New Jersey Ave Niagara Falls (14305) **(G-12306)**
Liquid Knits Inc 718 706-6600
3200 Skillman Ave Fl 2 Long Island City (11101) **(G-7501)**
Liquid Management Partners LLC 516 775-5050
3000 Marcus Ave Ste 1w9 New Hyde Park (11042) **(G-8548)**
Liquitane, Rochester *Also called Consolidated Container Co LLC* **(G-13721)**
Liquitane, Batavia *Also called Consolidated Container Co LLC* **(G-620)**
Lisk Coils, Phelps *Also called GW Lisk Company Inc* **(G-12977)**
List & Beisler GMBH 646 866-6960
311 W 43rd St Fl 12 New York (10036) **(G-10577)**
Listec Video Corp (PA) 631 273-3029
90 Oser Ave Hauppauge (11788) **(G-5865)**
Liston Manufacturing Inc 716 695-2111
421 Payne Ave North Tonawanda (14120) **(G-12437)**
Litchfield Fabrics of NC (PA) 518 773-9500
111 Woodside Ave Gloversville (12078) **(G-5461)**
Lite Brite Manufacturing Inc 718 855-9797
575 President St Brooklyn (11215) **(G-2129)**
Lite FM Radio, New York *Also called Iheartcommunications Inc* **(G-10178)**
Lite-Makers Inc 718 739-9300
10715 180th St Jamaica (11433) **(G-6656)**
Litelab Corp 718 361-6829
540 54th Ave Long Island City (11101) **(G-7502)**
Litelab Corp (PA) 716 856-4300
251 Elm St Buffalo (14203) **(G-2926)**
Literary Classics of US 212 308-3360
14 E 60th St Ste 1101 New York (10022) **(G-10578)**
Litho Dynamics Inc 914 769-1759
17 Saw Mill River Rd Hawthorne (10532) **(G-5991)**
Lithomatic Business Forms Inc 212 255-6700
233 W 18th St Frnt A New York (10011) **(G-10579)**
Litmor Publications, Garden City *Also called Litmor Publishing Corp* **(G-5266)**
Litmor Publishing Corp (PA) 516 931-0012
821 Franklin Ave Ste 208 Garden City (11530) **(G-5266)**
Little Bird Chocolates Inc 646 620-6395
25 Fairchild Ave Ste 200 Plainview (11803) **(G-13070)**
Little Bird Kitchen, Plainview *Also called Little Bird Chocolates Inc* **(G-13070)**
Little Eric Shoes On Madison 212 717-1513
1118 Madison Ave New York (10028) **(G-10580)**
Little Trees, Watertown *Also called Car-Freshner Corporation* **(G-16005)**
Little Valley Sand & Gravel 716 938-6676
8984 New Albion Rd Little Valley (14755) **(G-7221)**
Little Wolf Cabinet Shop Inc 212 734-1116
1583 1st Ave Frnt 1 New York (10028) **(G-10581)**
Littlebits Electronics Inc (PA) 917 464-4577
601 W 26th St Rm M274 New York (10001) **(G-10582)**
Live Oak Media, Pine Plains *Also called ABRA Media Inc* **(G-13004)**
Live Vote II Inc 646 343-9053
105 W 86th St 322 New York (10024) **(G-10583)**
Liveright Publishing Corp 212 354-5500
500 5th Ave Fl 6 New York (10110) **(G-10584)**
Livermoore Logging, Cassadaga *Also called Wrights Hardwoods Inc* **(G-3291)**
Livetiles Corp (PA) 917 472-7887
60 Madison Ave Fl 8 New York (10010) **(G-10585)**
Livid Magazine 929 340-7123
1055 Bedford Ave Apt 4c Brooklyn (11216) **(G-2130)**
Living Doors Inc 631 924-5393
22 Scouting Blvd Ste 3 Medford (11763) **(G-7958)**
Living Media, Long Island City *Also called Thomson Press (india) Limited* **(G-7616)**
Living Well Innovations Inc 646 517-3200
115 Engineers Rd Hauppauge (11788) **(G-5866)**
Livingston County News 585 243-1234
122 Main St Geneseo (14454) **(G-5315)**
Livingston Lighting and Power, Scottsville *Also called Power and Cnstr Group Inc* **(G-14752)**
Liz Claiborne Coats, New York *Also called Levy Group Inc* **(G-10557)**
Liz Lange, Brooklyn *Also called Zoomers Inc* **(G-2670)**
Lizotte Logging Inc 518 359-2200
50 Haymeadow Rd Tupper Lake (12986) **(G-15650)**
Ljmm Inc 845 454-5876
188 Washington St Poughkeepsie (12601) **(G-13351)**
Lk Industries Inc 716 941-9202
9731 Center St Glenwood (14069) **(G-5448)**
LLC Major Major 212 354-8550
1407 Broadway Fl 10 New York (10018) **(G-10586)**
Llcs Publishing Corp 718 569-2703
2071 Flatbush Ave Ste 189 Brooklyn (11234) **(G-2131)**
Lloyd Price Icon Food Brands 914 764-8624
95 Horseshoe Hill Rd Pound Ridge (10576) **(G-13377)**
Lloyds Fashions Inc (PA) 631 435-3353
335 Crooked Hill Rd Brentwood (11717) **(G-1141)**
Lmg National Publishing Inc (HQ) 585 598-6874
350 Willowbrook Office Pa Fairport (14450) **(G-4640)**
Lmgi, Liverpool *Also called Lockheed Martin Global Inc* **(G-7243)**
LMI, Bergen *Also called Lewis & Myers Inc* **(G-823)**
Lmr Group Inc 212 730-9221
463 7th Ave Fl 4 New York (10018) **(G-10587)**
Lmt Technology Solutions 585 784-7470
4 Commercial St Ste 400 Rochester (14614) **(G-13914)**
Lnd, Oceanside *Also called L N D Incorporated* **(G-12545)**
LNK International Inc 631 435-3500
22 Arkay Dr Hauppauge (11788) **(G-5867)**
LNK International Inc 631 435-3500
100 Ricefield Ln Hauppauge (11788) **(G-5868)**
LNK International Inc 631 435-3500
325 Kennedy Dr Hauppauge (11788) **(G-5869)**
LNK International Inc 631 543-3787
145 Ricefield Ln Hauppauge (11788) **(G-5870)**
LNK International Inc 631 435-3500
40 Arkay Dr Hauppauge (11788) **(G-5871)**
LNK International Inc 631 231-4020
55 Arkay Dr Hauppauge (11788) **(G-5872)**
Lo & Sons Inc 917 775-4025
55 Prospect St Brooklyn (11201) **(G-2132)**
Lo-Co Fuel Corp 631 929-5086
10 Stephen Dr Wading River (11792) **(G-15885)**
Load/N/Go Beverage Corp (PA) 585 218-4019
355 Portland Ave Rochester (14605) **(G-13915)**
Loar Group Inc (PA) 212 210-9348
450 Lexington Ave Fl 31 New York (10017) **(G-10588)**
Local Media Group Inc 845 341-1100
40 Mulberry St Middletown (10940) **(G-8159)**
Local Media Group Inc (HQ) 845 341-1100
40 Mulberry St Middletown (10940) **(G-8160)**
Local Media Group Inc 845 341-1100
60 Brookline Ave Middletown (10940) **(G-8161)**
Local Media Group Inc 845 794-3712
479 Broadway Monticello (12701) **(G-8321)**
Local Media Group Inc 845 340-4910
34 John St Kingston (12401) **(G-6908)**
Local Media Group Holdings LLC (HQ) 585 598-0030
175 Sullys Trl Ste 300 Pittsford (14534) **(G-13019)**
Local News, Oswego *Also called Dotto Wagner* **(G-12776)**
Locations Magazine 212 288-4745
124 E 79th St New York (10075) **(G-10589)**
Lock 1 Distilling Company LLC 315 934-4376
17 Culvert St Phoenix (13135) **(G-12989)**
Locker Masters Inc 518 288-3203
10329 State Route 22 Granville (12832) **(G-5519)**
Lockheed Martin Corporation 716 297-1000
2221 Niagara Falls Blvd Niagara Falls (14304) **(G-12307)**
Lockheed Martin Corporation 212 953-1510
420 Lexington Ave Rm 2601 New York (10170) **(G-10590)**
Lockheed Martin Corporation 315 793-5800
8373 Seneca Tpke New Hartford (13413) **(G-8507)**
Lockheed Martin Corporation 516 228-2000
55 Charles Lindbergh Blvd # 1 Uniondale (11553) **(G-15670)**
Lockheed Martin Corporation 607 751-2000
1801 State Route 17 Owego (13827) **(G-12799)**
Lockheed Martin Corporation 315 456-0123
497 Electronics Pkwy # 5 Liverpool (13088) **(G-7242)**
Lockheed Martin Corporation 315 456-6604
6060 Tarbell Rd Syracuse (13206) **(G-15363)**
Lockheed Martin Corporation 212 697-1105
600 3rd Ave Fl 35 New York (10016) **(G-10591)**
Lockheed Martin Global Inc (HQ) 315 456-2982
497 Electronics Pkwy # 5 Liverpool (13088) **(G-7243)**
Lockheed Martin Integrtd Systm 315 456-3333
497 Electronics Pkwy Syracuse (13221) **(G-15364)**
Lockheed Martin Overseas 315 456-0123
497 Electronics Pkwy # 7 Liverpool (13088) **(G-7244)**
Lockhouse Distillery 716 768-4898
41 Columbia St Ste 200 Buffalo (14204) **(G-2927)**
Lockwood Trade Journal Co Inc 212 391-2060
3743 Crescent St Fl 2 Long Island City (11101) **(G-7503)**

Lodi Down & Feather, New York *Also called Sleepable Sofas Ltd (G-11617)*
Lodolce Machine Co Inc 845 246-7017
  196 Malden Tpke Saugerties (12477) *(G-14610)*
Logic Controls Inc 516 248-0400
  999 S Oyster Bay Rd Bethpage (11714) *(G-845)*
Logical Control Solutions Inc 585 424-5340
  829 Phillips Rd Ste 100 Victor (14564) *(G-15855)*
Logical Operations Inc 585 350-7000
  3535 Winton Pl Rochester (14623) *(G-13916)*
Logitek Inc 631 567-1100
  110 Wilbur Pl Bohemia (11716) *(G-1048)*
Logo 212 846-2568
  1515 Broadway New York (10036) *(G-10592)*
Logo Print Company 607 324-5403
  135 Seneca St Hornell (14843) *(G-6301)*
Logomax Inc 631 420-0484
  242 Route 109 Ste B Farmingdale (11735) *(G-4809)*
Lois Kitchen LLC 216 308-9335
  206 Avenue A Apt 2a New York (10009) *(G-10593)*
Lokai Holdings LLC 646 979-3474
  36 E 31st St Rm 602 New York (10016) *(G-10594)*
Lola, New York *Also called Alyk Inc (G-8815)*
Lollipop Tree Inc 845 471-8733
  181 York St Auburn (13021) *(G-488)*
Lollytogs Ltd (PA) 212 502-6000
  100 W 33rd St Ste 1012 New York (10001) *(G-10595)*
Lomak Petroleum, Mayville *Also called Range Rsurces - Appalachia LLC (G-7923)*
Lombardi Design & Mfg, Freeport *Also called Anna Young Assoc Ltd (G-5144)*
Lomin Construction Company 516 759-5734
  328 Glen Cove Rd Glen Head (11545) *(G-5382)*
Lomir Inc 518 483-7697
  213 W Main St Malone (12953) *(G-7723)*
Lomir Biomedical Inc, Malone *Also called Lomir Inc (G-7723)*
London Paris Ltd 718 564-4793
  4211 13th Ave Brooklyn (11219) *(G-2133)*
London Theater News Ltd 212 517-8608
  12 E 86th St Apt 620 New York (10028) *(G-10596)*
Long Blockchain Corp (PA) 855 542-2832
  12 Dubon Ct Ste 1 Farmingdale (11735) *(G-4810)*
Long Ireland Brewing LLC 631 403-4303
  723 Pulaski St Riverhead (11901) *(G-13574)*
Long Island Advance, Patchogue *Also called Patchogue Advance Inc (G-12873)*
Long Island Analytical Labs 631 472-3400
  110 Colin Dr Holbrook (11741) *(G-6196)*
Long Island Brand Bevs LLC 855 542-2832
  3788 Review Ave Long Island City (11101) *(G-7504)*
Long Island Business News 631 737-1700
  2150 Smithtown Ave Ste 7 Ronkonkoma (11779) *(G-14371)*
Long Island Catholic Newspaper 516 594-1212
  50 N Park Ave Rockville Centre (11570) *(G-14235)*
Long Island Cmnty Nwsppers Inc (PA) 516 482-4490
  132 E 2nd St Mineola (11501) *(G-8235)*
Long Island Cmnty Nwsppers Inc 631 427-7000
  322 Main St Huntington (11743) *(G-6404)*
Long Island Compost Corp 516 334-6600
  100 Urban Ave Westbury (11590) *(G-16351)*
Long Island Fireproof Door, Port Washington *Also called Lif Industries Inc (G-13281)*
Long Island Geotech 631 473-1044
  6 Berkshire Ct Port Jefferson (11777) *(G-13221)*
Long Island Golfer Magazine, Hicksville *Also called Golfing Magazine (G-6093)*
Long Island Green Guys 631 664-4306
  26 Silverbrook Dr Riverhead (11901) *(G-13575)*
Long Island Metalform Inc 631 242-9088
  12 Lucon Dr Deer Park (11729) *(G-4003)*
Long Island Pipe Supply Inc (PA) 516 222-8008
  586 Commercial Ave Garden City (11530) *(G-5267)*
Long Island Pipe Supply Inc 718 456-7877
  5858 56th St Flushing (11378) *(G-5024)*
Long Island Pipe Supply Inc 518 270-2159
  75 Cohoes Ave Troy (12183) *(G-15597)*
Long Island Pipe Supply Inc (PA) 516 222-8008
  586 Commercial Ave Garden City (11530) *(G-5268)*
Long Island Precast Inc 631 286-0240
  20 Stiriz Rd Brookhaven (11719) *(G-1431)*
Long Island Press, Farmingdale *Also called Morey Publishing (G-4830)*
Long Island Radiant Heat, Mastic Beach *Also called Vincent Genovese (G-7912)*
Long Island Ready Mix 516 485-5260
  75 Chasner St Hempstead (11550) *(G-6018)*
Long Island Stamp & Seal Co 718 628-8550
  5431 Myrtle Ave Ste 2 Ridgewood (11385) *(G-13542)*
Long Island Tool & Die Inc 631 225-0600
  1445 S Strong Ave Copiague (11726) *(G-3767)*
Long Islander Newspapers LLC 631 427-7000
  14 Wall St Ste A Huntington (11743) *(G-6405)*
Long Islands Best Inc 855 542-3785
  1650 Sycamore Ave Ste 4b Bohemia (11716) *(G-1049)*
Long Islndr Nrth/Sth Pblctns, Huntington *Also called Long Island Cmnty Nwsppers Inc (G-6404)*
Long Lumber and Supply Corp 518 439-1661
  2100 New Scotland Rd Slingerlands (12159) *(G-14889)*
Long Paige, New York *Also called Jiranimo Industries Ltd (G-10341)*

Longo Cabinets, Lindenhurst *Also called Longo Commercial Cabinets Inc (G-7176)*
Longo Commercial Cabinets Inc 631 225-4290
  829 N Richmond Ave Lindenhurst (11757) *(G-7176)*
Longo New York Inc 212 929-7128
  444 W 17th St New York (10011) *(G-10597)*
Longstem Organizers Inc 914 777-2174
  380 E Main St Jefferson Valley (10535) *(G-6777)*
Longtail Studios Inc 646 443-8146
  180 Varick St Rm 820 New York (10014) *(G-10598)*
Loobrica International Corp 347 997-0296
  41 Darnell Ln Staten Island (10309) *(G-15101)*
Look By M Inc 212 213-4019
  838 Avenue Of The America New York (10001) *(G-10599)*
Lookbooks Media Inc 646 737-3360
  208 W 30th St Rm 802 New York (10001) *(G-10600)*
Loom Concepts LLC 212 813-9586
  767 Lexington Ave Rm 405 New York (10065) *(G-10601)*
Loominus Handwoven, Woodstock *Also called Marsha Fleisher (G-16686)*
Loomis Root Inc 716 564-7668
  135 Pineview Dr Amherst (14228) *(G-236)*
Loomstate LLC 212 219-2300
  270 Bowery Fl 3 New York (10012) *(G-10602)*
Looney Tunes CD Store, West Babylon *Also called Brookvale Records Inc (G-16140)*
Looseleaf Law Publications Inc 718 359-5559
  4308 162nd St Flushing (11358) *(G-5025)*
Loosesleeve Law Publications, Flushing *Also called Warodean Corporation (G-5059)*
Lopez Restorations Inc (PA) 718 383-1555
  394 Mcguinness Blvd Ste 4 Brooklyn (11222) *(G-2134)*
Lopopolo Iron Works Inc 718 339-0572
  2495 Mcdonald Ave Brooklyn (11223) *(G-2135)*
Loral Space & Commnctns Holdng 212 697-1105
  600 5th Ave Fl 16 New York (10020) *(G-10603)*
Loral Space Communications Inc (PA) 212 697-1105
  600 5th Ave Fl 16 New York (10020) *(G-10604)*
Loral Spacecom Corporation (HQ) 212 697-1105
  565 5th Ave Fl 19 New York (10017) *(G-10605)*
LOreal Usa Inc 212 818-1500
  575 5th Ave Bsmt New York (10017) *(G-10606)*
LOreal Usa Inc 917 606-9554
  435 Hudson St New York (10014) *(G-10607)*
LOreal Usa Inc 212 389-4201
  10 Hudson Yards Fl 27 New York (10001) *(G-10608)*
LOreal USA Products Inc (HQ) 212 818-1500
  10 Hudson Yards New York (10001) *(G-10609)*
Lorelei Orthotics Prosthetics 212 727-2011
  30 E 40th St Rm 905 New York (10016) *(G-10610)*
Loreman's, Keeseville *Also called Loremanss Embroidery Engrav (G-6852)*
Loremanss Embroidery Engrav 518 834-9205
  1599 Front St Keeseville (12944) *(G-6852)*
Lorena Canals USA Inc 844 567-3622
  104 Burnside Dr Hastings On Hudson (10706) *(G-5751)*
Lori Silverman Shoes, White Plains *Also called Lsil & Co Inc (G-16473)*
Lornamead Inc 646 745-3643
  175 Cooper Ave Tonawanda (14150) *(G-15555)*
Lornamead Inc (HQ) 716 874-7190
  1359 Broadway Fl 17 New York (10018) *(G-10611)*
Los Angles Tmes Cmmnctions LLC 212 418-9600
  780 3rd Ave Fl 40 New York (10017) *(G-10612)*
Los Olivos Ltd 631 773-6439
  105 Bi County Blvd Farmingdale (11735) *(G-4811)*
Lost Worlds Inc 212 923-3423
  920 Riverside Dr Apt 68 New York (10032) *(G-10613)*
Losurdo Creamery, Heuvelton *Also called Losurdo Foods Inc (G-6044)*
Losurdo Foods Inc 518 842-1500
  78 Sam Stratton Rd Amsterdam (12010) *(G-345)*
Losurdo Foods Inc 315 344-2444
  34 Union St Heuvelton (13654) *(G-6044)*
Lots O' Luv, Syosset *Also called Bektrom Foods Inc (G-15209)*
Lotta Luv Beauty LLC 646 786-2847
  1359 Broadway Fl 17 New York (10018) *(G-10614)*
Lotus Apparel Designs Inc 646 236-9363
  661 Oakwood Ct Westbury (11590) *(G-16352)*
Lotus Awnings Enterprises Inc 718 965-4824
  157 11th St Brooklyn (11215) *(G-2136)*
Lotus Thread, New York *Also called Nasserati Inc (G-10875)*
Lou Sally Fashions Corp (HQ) 212 354-9670
  1400 Broadway Rm 601 New York (10018) *(G-10615)*
Lou Sally Fashions Corp 212 354-1283
  1400 Broadway Frnt 3 New York (10018) *(G-10616)*
Loudon Ltd 631 757-4447
  281 Larkfield Rd East Northport (11731) *(G-4267)*
Loughlin Manufacturing Corp 631 585-4422
  1601 9th Ave Bohemia (11716) *(G-1050)*
Louis Heindl & Son Inc 585 454-5080
  306 Central Ave Rochester (14605) *(G-13917)*
Louis Iannettoni 315 454-3231
  1841 Lemoyne Ave Syracuse (13208) *(G-15365)*
Louis Schwartz 845 356-6624
  28 Lawrence St Spring Valley (10977) *(G-15000)*
Louis Vuitton North Amer Inc 212 644-2574
  1000 3rd Ave New York (10022) *(G-10617)*
Louise Blouin Media, New York *Also called Ltb Media (usa) Inc (G-10624)*

Loungehouse LLC ... 646 524-2965
34 W 33rd St Fl 11 New York (10001) *(G-10618)*
Lourdes Industries Inc (PA) ... 631 234-6600
65 Hoffman Ave Hauppauge (11788) *(G-5873)*
Lourdes Systems Inc ... 631 234-7077
21 Newton Pl Hauppauge (11788) *(G-5874)*
Love & Quiches Desserts, Freeport *Also called Saj of Freeport Corp (G-5180)*
Love Bright Jewelry Inc ... 516 620-2509
3446 Frederick St Oceanside (11572) *(G-12546)*
Love Unlimited NY Inc ... 718 359-8500
762 Summa Ave Westbury (11590) *(G-16353)*
Lovebrightjewelry.com, Oceanside *Also called Love Bright Jewelry Inc (G-12546)*
Lovee Doll & Toy Co Inc ... 212 242-1545
39 W 38th St Rm 4w New York (10018) *(G-10619)*
Lovejoy Chaplet Corporation ... 518 686-5232
12 River St Hoosick Falls (12090) *(G-6277)*
Lovingly LLC ... 845 977-0775
1399 Route 52 Ste 100 Fishkill (12524) *(G-4948)*
Low-Cost Mfg Co Inc ... 516 627-3282
318 Westbury Ave Carle Place (11514) *(G-3268)*
Lowel-Light Manufacturing Inc ... 718 921-0600
140 58th St Ste 8c Brooklyn (11220) *(G-2137)*
Lowville Farmers Coop Inc ... 315 376-6587
5500 Shady Ave Lowville (13367) *(G-7652)*
Lowville Newspaper Corporation ... 315 376-3525
7567 S State St Lowville (13367) *(G-7653)*
Loy L Press Inc ... 716 634-5966
3959 Union Rd Buffalo (14225) *(G-2928)*
Loyaltyplant Inc (PA) ... 551 221-2701
70 23 Juno St Forest Hills (11375) *(G-5076)*
LPI Envelope, Bay Shore *Also called 3dflam Inc (G-650)*
Lr Acquisition LLC ... 212 301-8765
1407 Broadway Rm 1207 New York (10018) *(G-10620)*
Lr Paris, New York *Also called Lr Paris LLC (G-10621)*
Lr Paris LLC (PA) ... 212 634-9372
345 7th Ave Fl 7 New York (10001) *(G-10621)*
Lrc Electronics, Horseheads *Also called Belden Inc (G-6306)*
Ls Power Equity Partners LP (PA) ... 212 615-3456
1700 Broadway Fl 35 New York (10019) *(G-10622)*
Lsc Peripherals Incorporated ... 631 244-0707
415 Central Ave Ste F Bohemia (11716) *(G-1051)*
LSI Computer Systems ... 631 271-0400
1235 Walt Whitman Rd Melville (11747) *(G-8044)*
LSI Lightron Inc ... 845 562-5500
500 Hudson Valley Ave New Windsor (12553) *(G-8649)*
Lsil & Co Inc ... 914 761-0998
2 Greene Ln White Plains (10605) *(G-16473)*
Lt Apparel Group, New York *Also called Lollytogs Ltd (G-10595)*
Lt2 LLC ... 212 684-1510
250 Park Ave S Fl 10 New York (10003) *(G-10623)*
Ltb Media (usa) Inc ... 212 447-9555
77 Water St Ste 702 New York (10005) *(G-10624)*
LTS Inc ... 845 494-2940
37 Ramland Rd 2 Orangeburg (10962) *(G-12682)*
Lu Biscuits, White Plains *Also called Great Brands of Europe Inc (G-16454)*
Lubbu Inc ... 917 693-9600
20 Payne Ave Sag Harbor (11963) *(G-14500)*
Lucas Dental Equipment Co Inc ... 631 244-2807
360 Knickerbocker Ave # 4 Bohemia (11716) *(G-1052)*
Lucas Electric ... 516 809-8619
3524 Merrick Rd Seaford (11783) *(G-14759)*
Lucas Vineyards Inc ... 607 532-4825
3862 County Road 150 Interlaken (14847) *(G-6482)*
Lucia Group Inc ... 631 392-4900
45 W Jefryn Blvd Ste 108 Deer Park (11729) *(G-4004)*
Lucida Surfaces USA, Tallman *Also called Lucida Usa LLC (G-15463)*
Lucida Usa LLC ... 845 877-7008
321 Route 59 Unit 327 Tallman (10982) *(G-15463)*
Lucideon ... 518 382-0082
2210 Technology Dr Schenectady (12308) *(G-14696)*
Lucinas Gourmet Food Inc ... 646 835-9784
3646 37th St Long Island City (11101) *(G-7505)*
Lucky Lous Inc ... 631 672-1932
24 State St Lake Grove (11755) *(G-6967)*
Lucky Magazine ... 212 286-6220
4 Times Sq Fl 22 New York (10036) *(G-10625)*
Lucky Peach LLC ... 212 228-0031
60 E 11th St Fl 5 New York (10003) *(G-10626)*
Ludl Electronic Products Ltd ... 914 769-6111
171 Brady Ave Hawthorne (10532) *(G-5992)*
Ludlow Music Inc ... 212 594-9795
266 W 37th St Fl 17 New York (10018) *(G-10627)*
Lugo Nutrition Inc ... 302 573-2503
51 N Broadway Ste 2 Nyack (10960) *(G-12509)*
Luitpold Pharmaceuticals Inc (HQ) ... 631 924-4000
5 Ramsey Rd Shirley (11967) *(G-14838)*
Luitpold Pharmaceuticals Inc ... 631 924-4000
5 Ramsey Rd Shirley (11967) *(G-14839)*
Lukas Lighting Inc ... 800 841-4011
4020 22nd St Ste 11 Long Island City (11101) *(G-7506)*
Luke's Copy Shop, Staten Island *Also called R & L Press of SI Inc (G-15122)*
Lukoil Americas Corporation (HQ) ... 212 421-4141
505 5th Ave Fl 9 New York (10017) *(G-10628)*
Lukoil North America LLC (HQ) ... 212 421-4141
505 5th Ave Fl 9 New York (10017) *(G-10629)*
Luluvise Inc ... 914 309-7812
229 W 116th St Apt 5a New York (10026) *(G-10630)*
Lumazu LLC ... 518 623-3372
141 Garnet Lake Rd Warrensburg (12885) *(G-15940)*
Lumazu LLC (PA) ... 518 623-3372
484 S Johnsburg Rd Warrensburg (12885) *(G-15941)*
Lumetrics Inc ... 585 214-2455
1565 Jefferson Rd Ste 420 Rochester (14623) *(G-13918)*
Luminary Publishing Inc ... 845 334-8600
314 Wall St Kingston (12401) *(G-6909)*
Luminati Aerospace LLC ... 631 574-2616
400 David Ct Calverton (11933) *(G-3167)*
Luminatta Inc ... 914 664-3600
717 S 3rd Ave Mount Vernon (10550) *(G-8419)*
Luminescent Systems Inc (HQ) ... 716 655-0800
130 Commerce Way East Aurora (14052) *(G-4204)*
Luna Luz, New York *Also called Azibi Ltd (G-8986)*
Luria Communications Inc ... 631 329-4922
31 Shorewood Dr Fl 1 East Hampton (11937) *(G-4240)*
Lust For Life Footwear LLC ... 646 732-9742
48 S Main St Pearl River (10965) *(G-12906)*
Luvente, Long Island City *Also called Benlee Enterprises LLC (G-7399)*
Lux Accessories, New York *Also called International Inspirations Ltd (G-10247)*
Lux Mundi Corp ... 631 244-4596
10 Colt Ct Ronkonkoma (11779) *(G-14372)*
Luxcore Networks Inc (PA) ... 212 618-1724
14 Wall St Fl 20 New York (10005) *(G-10631)*
Luxe Imagine Consulting LLC ... 212 273-9770
261 W 35th St Ste 404 New York (10001) *(G-10632)*
Luxerdame Co Inc ... 718 752-9800
4315 Queens St Ste A Long Island City (11101) *(G-7507)*
Luxfer Magtech Inc ... 631 727-8600
680 Elton St Riverhead (11901) *(G-13576)*
Luxury Daily, New York *Also called Napean LLC (G-10874)*
Lvl Xiii Brands Inc ... 646 530-2795
315 W 39th St Rm 1201 New York (10018) *(G-10633)*
Lwa Works Inc ... 518 271-8360
2622 7th Ave Ste 50s Watervliet (12189) *(G-16048)*
Lycian Stage Lighting, Chester *Also called Ric-Lo Productions Ltd (G-3481)*
Lydall Performance Mtl Inc ... 518 273-6320
68 George St Green Island (12183) *(G-5609)*
Lydall Performance Mtls Inc ... 518 273-6320
68 George St Green Island (12183) *(G-5610)*
Lyn Jo Enterprises Ltd ... 716 753-2776
Rr 394 Box 147 Mayville (14757) *(G-7922)*
Lyn Jo Kitchens Inc ... 718 336-6060
1679 Mcdonald Ave Brooklyn (11230) *(G-2138)*
Lynch Knitting Mills Inc ... 718 821-3436
538 Johnson Ave Brooklyn (11237) *(G-2139)*
Lyndaker Timber Harvesting LLC ... 315 346-1328
10204 State Route 812 Castorland (13620) *(G-3300)*
Lynmar Printing Corp ... 631 957-8500
8600 New Horizons Blvd Amityville (11701) *(G-298)*
Lyntronics Inc ... 631 205-1061
7 Old Dock Rd Unit 1 Yaphank (11980) *(G-16715)*
Lynx Product Group LLC ... 716 751-3100
650 Lake St Wilson (14172) *(G-16601)*
Lyophilization Systems Inc ... 845 338-0456
14 Hickory Hill Rd New Paltz (12561) *(G-8579)*
M & C Furniture ... 718 422-2136
375 Park Ave Brooklyn (11205) *(G-2140)*
M & D Fire Door, Brooklyn *Also called M & D Installers Inc (G-2141)*
M & D Installers Inc (PA) ... 718 782-6978
70 Flushing Ave Ste 1 Brooklyn (11205) *(G-2141)*
M & D Millwork LLC ... 631 789-1439
178 New Hwy Amityville (11701) *(G-299)*
M & E Mfg Co Inc ... 845 331-7890
19 Progress St Kingston (12401) *(G-6910)*
M & H Research and Dev Corp ... 607 734-2346
471 Post Creek Rd Beaver Dams (14812) *(G-765)*
M & J Custom Lampshade Company, Brooklyn *Also called Mjk Enterprises LLC (G-2217)*
M & L Steel & Ornamental Iron ... 718 816-8660
27 Housman Ave Staten Island (10303) *(G-15102)*
M & M Bagel Corp ... 516 295-1222
507 Central Ave Cedarhurst (11516) *(G-3333)*
M & M Canvas & Awnings Inc ... 631 424-5370
180 Oval Dr Islandia (11749) *(G-6534)*
M & M Food Products Inc ... 718 821-1970
286 Scholes St Brooklyn (11206) *(G-2142)*
M & M Molding Corp ... 631 582-1900
250 Creative Dr Central Islip (11722) *(G-3377)*
M & M Signs & Awnings, Islandia *Also called M & M Canvas & Awnings Inc (G-6534)*
M & R Design, New York *Also called Mrinalini Inc (G-10852)*
M & R Woodworking & Finishing ... 718 486-5480
49 Withers St Brooklyn (11211) *(G-2143)*
M & S Precision Machine Co LLC ... 518 747-1193
27 Casey Rd Queensbury (12804) *(G-13433)*

M & S Quality Co Ltd 212 302-8757
26 W 47th St Ste 502 New York (10036) *(G-10634)*
M & S Schmalberg Inc 212 244-2090
242 W 36th St Rm 700 New York (10018) *(G-10635)*
M & W Aluminum Products Inc 315 414-0005
321 Wavel St Syracuse (13206) *(G-15366)*
M &L Industry of NY Inc 845 827-6255
583 State Route 32 Ste 1u Highland Mills (10930) *(G-6151)*
M A C, Elmsford *Also called Magnetic Analysis Corporation (G-4549)*
M A M Knitting Mills Corp 800 570-0093
43 Hall St Brooklyn (11205) *(G-2144)*
M A Moslow & Bros Inc 716 896-2950
375 Norfolk Ave Buffalo (14215) *(G-2929)*
M A R A Metals Ltd 718 786-7868
2520 40th Ave Long Island City (11101) *(G-7508)*
M and J Hair Center Inc 516 872-1010
1103 Stewart Ave Ste 100 Garden City (11530) *(G-5269)*
M B C Metal Inc 718 384-6713
68 Lombardy St Brooklyn (11222) *(G-2145)*
M B M Manufacturing Inc 718 769-4148
331 Rutledge St Ste 203 Brooklyn (11211) *(G-2146)*
M C Kitchen & Bath, Brooklyn *Also called M & C Furniture (G-2140)*
M C Packaging Corp Plant, Babylon *Also called M C Packaging Corporation (G-529)*
M C Packaging Corporation (PA) 631 694-3012
120-200 Adams Blvd Farmingdale (11735) *(G-4812)*
M C Packaging Corporation 631 643-3763
300 Governor Ave Babylon (11704) *(G-529)*
M C Products 631 471-4070
1330 Lincoln Ave Ste 2 Holbrook (11741) *(G-6197)*
M D I, Shirley *Also called Modular Devices Inc (G-14841)*
M D I Industries, Deer Park *Also called MD International Industries (G-4009)*
M D L, New York *Also called Meryl Diamond Ltd (G-10779)*
M F L B Inc 631 254-8300
7 Grant Ave Bay Shore (11706) *(G-697)*
M F Manufacturing Enterprises 516 822-5135
2 Ballad Ln Hicksville (11801) *(G-6104)*
M Factory USA Inc (HQ) 917 410-7878
32 33rd St Unit 5 Brooklyn (11232) *(G-2147)*
M G New York Inc 212 371-5566
14 E 60th St Ste 400 New York (10022) *(G-10636)*
M H Mandelbaum Orthotic 631 473-8668
116 Oakland Ave Port Jefferson (11777) *(G-13222)*
M H Manufacturing Incorporated 212 461-6900
50 W 47th St New York (10036) *(G-10637)*
M H Stryke Co Inc 631 242-2660
181 E Industry Ct Ste A Deer Park (11729) *(G-4005)*
M Heskia Company Inc 212 768-1845
98 Cutter Rd Ste 125 New York (10036) *(G-10638)*
M Hidary & Co Inc 212 736-6540
10 W 33rd St Rm 900 New York (10001) *(G-10639)*
M I, Hauppauge *Also called Mason Industries Inc (G-5881)*
M I I, Mamaroneck *Also called Marval Industries Inc (G-7748)*
M I T Poly-Cart Corp 212 724-7290
211 Central Park W New York (10024) *(G-10640)*
M J K, Brooklyn *Also called Mjk Cutting Inc (G-2216)*
M J M Tooling Corp 718 292-3590
1059 Washington Ave Bronx (10456) *(G-1320)*
M K S, Rochester *Also called Mks Medical Electronics (G-13950)*
M K Ulrich Construction Inc 716 893-5777
1601 Harlem Rd Buffalo (14206) *(G-2930)*
M L A, New York *Also called Modern Language Assn Amer Inc (G-10829)*
M L Design Inc (PA) 212 233-0213
77 Ludlow St Frnt 1 New York (10002) *(G-10641)*
M M Tool and Manufacturing 845 691-4140
175 Chapel Hill Rd Highland (12528) *(G-6145)*
M M Welding 315 363-3980
558 Lenox Ave Oneida (13421) *(G-12612)*
M Manastrip-M Corporation 518 664-2089
821 Main St Clifton Park (12065) *(G-3570)*
M O S S Communications, Franklin Square *Also called Movin On Sounds and SEC Inc (G-5119)*
M P I, Tarrytown *Also called Micro Powders Inc (G-15483)*
M P X, Melville *Also called Military Parts Exchange LLC (G-8047)*
M R C, Buffalo *Also called Tchnologies N MRC Ameerica LLC (G-3087)*
M R C Industries Inc 516 328-6900
99 Seaview Blvd Ste 210 Port Washington (11050) *(G-13283)*
M S B International Ltd (PA) 212 302-5551
1412 Broadway Rm 1210 New York (10018) *(G-10642)*
M S Riviera Inc 212 391-0206
42 W 48th St Fl 4 New York (10036) *(G-10643)*
M Santoliquido Corp 914 375-6674
925 Saw Mill River Rd Yonkers (10710) *(G-16780)*
M Shanken Communications Inc (PA) 212 684-4224
825 8th Ave Fl 33 New York (10019) *(G-10644)*
M Squared Graphics, Oyster Bay *Also called Miroddi Imaging Inc (G-12816)*
M T D Corporation 631 491-3905
41 Otis St West Babylon (11704) *(G-16172)*
M T M Printing Co Inc 718 353-3297
2321 College Point Blvd College Point (11356) *(G-3654)*
M V Sport, Bay Shore *Also called Mv Corp Inc (G-703)*
M W Microwave Corp 516 295-1814
45 Auerbach Ln Lawrence (11559) *(G-7105)*
M&A Metals, Brooklyn *Also called Interior Metals (G-2008)*
M&C Associates LLC 631 467-8760
700 Vets Memrl Hwy 335 Hauppauge (11788) *(G-5875)*
M&F Stringing LLC 914 664-1600
2 Cortlandt St Mount Vernon (10550) *(G-8420)*
M&G Duravent Inc 518 463-7284
10 Jupiter Ln Albany (12205) *(G-96)*
M&H Soaring, Beaver Dams *Also called M & H Research and Dev Corp (G-765)*
M&M Printing Inc 516 796-3020
245 Westbury Ave Carle Place (11514) *(G-3269)*
M/Wbe, Brooklyn *Also called Active World Solutions Inc (G-1480)*
M2 Apparel, New York *Also called M2 Fashion Group Holdings Inc (G-10645)*
M2 Fashion Group Holdings Inc 917 208-2948
153 E 87th St Apt 10d New York (10128) *(G-10645)*
M2 Race Systems Inc 607 882-9078
53 Enfield Main Rd Ithaca (14850) *(G-6591)*
Mac Artspray Finishing Corp 718 649-3800
799 Sheffield Ave Brooklyn (11207) *(G-2148)*
Mac Crete Corporation 718 932-1803
3412 10th St Long Island City (11106) *(G-7509)*
Mac Donuts of New York, Long Island City *Also called Mac Crete Corporation (G-7509)*
Mac Innes Enterprises Inc 325 676-4032
61 John Muir Dr Buffalo (14228) *(G-2931)*
Mac Swed Inc 212 684-7730
20 W 36th St Rm 5l New York (10018) *(G-10646)*
Mac-Artspray Finshg, Brooklyn *Also called Mac Artspray Finishing Corp (G-2148)*
Macabee Foods LLC 845 623-1300
250 W Nyack Rd Ste 110 West Nyack (10994) *(G-16274)*
Macadoodles 607 652-9019
26 River St Stamford (12167) *(G-15031)*
Macaran Printed Products, Cohoes *Also called W N Vanalstine & Sons Inc (G-3624)*
Macauto Usa Inc 585 342-2060
80 Excel Dr Rochester (14621) *(G-13919)*
Macedonia Ltd 718 462-3596
34 E 29th St Brooklyn (11226) *(G-2149)*
Macfadden Cmmnctions Group LLC 212 979-4800
333 7th Ave Fl 11 New York (10001) *(G-10647)*
Machias Furniture Factory Inc (PA) 716 353-8687
3638 Route 242 Machias (14101) *(G-7706)*
Machida Incorporated 845 365-0600
40 Ramland Rd S Ste 1 Orangeburg (10962) *(G-12683)*
Machina Deus Lex Inc 917 577-0972
15921 Grand Central Pkwy Jamaica (11432) *(G-6657)*
Machine Clothing Company, New York *Also called Billion Tower Intl LLC (G-9082)*
Machine Components Corp 516 694-7222
70 Newtown Rd Plainview (11803) *(G-13071)*
Machine Technology Inc 845 454-4030
104 Bushwick Rd Poughkeepsie (12603) *(G-13352)*
Machinecraft Inc 585 436-1070
1645 Lyell Ave Ste 125 Rochester (14606) *(G-13920)*
Machinery Mountings Inc 631 851-0480
41 Sarah Dr Hauppauge (11788) *(G-5876)*
Machinit Inc 631 454-9297
400 Smith St Farmingdale (11735) *(G-4813)*
Machoonjdgroup 856 345-4689
18 Victorian Ln Medford (11763) *(G-7959)*
Macinnes Tool Corporation 585 467-1920
1700 Hudson Ave Ste 3 Rochester (14617) *(G-13921)*
Mack Studios Displays Inc 315 252-7542
5500 Technology Park Blvd Auburn (13021) *(G-489)*
Mack Wood Working 845 657-6625
2792 State Route 28 Shokan (12481) *(G-14846)*
Mackenzie-Childs LLC (PA) 315 364-6118
3260 State Route 90 Aurora (13026) *(G-511)*
Maclean Curtis, Buffalo *Also called Curtis L Maclean L C (G-2787)*
Macmillan Audio 646 600-7856
175 5th Ave New York (10010) *(G-10648)*
Macmillan College Pubg Co Inc 212 702-2000
866 3rd Ave Frnt 2 New York (10022) *(G-10649)*
Macmillan Holdings LLC 212 576-9428
1 New York Plz Ste 4500 New York (10004) *(G-10650)*
Macmillan Publishers Inc 646 307-5151
175 5th Ave Ste 400 New York (10010) *(G-10651)*
Macmillan Publishing Group LLC (HQ) 212 674-5145
175 5th Ave New York (10010) *(G-10652)*
Macneil Polymers Inc (PA) 716 681-7755
3155 Broadway St Buffalo (14227) *(G-2932)*
Maco Bag Corporation 315 226-1000
412 Van Buren St Newark (14513) *(G-12199)*
Macro Tool & Machine Company 845 223-3824
1397 Route 55 Lagrangeville (12540) *(G-6958)*
Macrolink Inc 631 924-8200
25 Scouting Blvd Ste 1 Medford (11763) *(G-7960)*
Mad Scntsts Brwing Prtners LLC 347 766-2739
40 Van Dyke St Brooklyn (11231) *(G-2150)*
Madame Alexander Doll 2018 LLC 917 576-8381
600 3rd Ave Fl 2 New York (10016) *(G-10653)*
Madame Alexander Doll Co LLC 212 244-4500
112 W 34th St Ste 1207 New York (10120) *(G-10654)*
Madden Zone, New York *Also called Steven Madden Ltd (G-11709)*

ALPHABETIC

(PA)=Parent Co (HQ)=Headquarters (DH)=Div Headquarters
2019 Harris
New York Manufacturers Directory
929

Made Close LLC.....917 837-1357
141 Meserole Ave Brooklyn (11222) ***(G-2151)***
Made Fresh Daily.....212 285-2253
226 Front St New York (10038) ***(G-10655)***
Madhat Inc.....518 947-0732
149 Sullivan St Apt 3e New York (10012) ***(G-10656)***
Madison & Dunn.....585 563-7760
850 Saint Paul St Ste 29 Rochester (14605) ***(G-13922)***
Madison County Distillery LLC.....315 391-6070
2420 Rte 20 Cazenovia (13035) ***(G-3321)***
Madison Electric.....718 358-4121
21916 Linden Blvd Cambria Heights (11411) ***(G-3176)***
Madison Lifestyle Ny LLC (PA).....212 725-4002
1412 Broadway Rm 1610 New York (10018) ***(G-10657)***
Madison Manufacturing, Hamilton *Also called James Morris* ***(G-5699)***
Madison Mfg & Mch Inc.....315 922-4476
3882 Sanderson Rd Erieville (13061) ***(G-4621)***
Madison Printing Corp.....607 273-3535
704 W Buffalo St Ithaca (14850) ***(G-6592)***
Madison Square Press, New York *Also called Annuals Publishing Co Inc* ***(G-8874)***
Madjek Inc.....631 842-4475
185 Dixon Ave Amityville (11701) ***(G-300)***
Madoff Energy III LLC.....212 744-1918
319 Lafayette St New York (10012) ***(G-10658)***
Madonna, New York *Also called Haddad Bros Inc* ***(G-10018)***
Maehr Industries Inc.....631 924-1661
14 Sawgrass Dr Bellport (11713) ***(G-807)***
Mafco Consolidated Group Inc (HQ).....212 572-8600
35 E 62nd St New York (10065) ***(G-10659)***
Mag Brands LLC.....212 629-9600
463 7th Ave Fl 4 New York (10018) ***(G-10660)***
Mag Inc.....607 257-6970
20 Eastlake Rd Ithaca (14850) ***(G-6593)***
Magazine Group, New York *Also called Thomas Publishing Company LLC* ***(G-11820)***
Magazine I Spectrum E.....212 419-7555
3 Park Ave Fl 17 New York (10016) ***(G-10661)***
Magazines & Brochures Inc.....716 875-9699
2205 Kenmore Ave Ste 107 Buffalo (14207) ***(G-2933)***
Magcrest Packaging Inc.....845 425-0451
5 Highview Rd Monsey (10952) ***(G-8289)***
Mageba USA LLC.....212 317-1991
575 Lexington Ave Fl 4 New York (10022) ***(G-10662)***
Magee Canvas & Trailer Sales, Brewerton *Also called Geordie Magee Uphl & Canvas* ***(G-1150)***
Magellan Aerospace Bethel Inc.....203 798-9373
9711 50th Ave Corona (11368) ***(G-3848)***
Magellan Aerospace NY Inc (HQ).....718 699-4000
9711 50th Ave Corona (11368) ***(G-3849)***
Magellan Aerospace NY Inc.....631 589-2440
25 Aero Rd Bohemia (11716) ***(G-1053)***
Magellan Aerospace Processing.....631 694-1818
165 Field St West Babylon (11704) ***(G-16173)***
Mager & Gougelman Inc (PA).....212 661-3939
345 E 37th St Rm 316 New York (10016) ***(G-10663)***
Mager & Gougelman Inc.....212 661-3939
230 Hilton Ave Ste 112 Hempstead (11550) ***(G-6019)***
Mager & Gougelman Inc.....516 489-0202
230 Hilton Ave Ste 112 Hempstead (11550) ***(G-6020)***
Maggio Data Forms.....631 348-0343
1735 Express Dr S Hauppauge (11788) ***(G-5877)***
Maggy Boutique Ltd.....212 997-5222
530 Fashion Ave Fl 6 New York (10018) ***(G-10664)***
Maggy London, New York *Also called Maggy Boutique Ltd* ***(G-10664)***
Maggy London Blouse Div, New York *Also called Maggy London International Ltd* ***(G-10665)***
Maggy London International Ltd (PA).....212 944-7199
530 Fashion Ave Fl 16 New York (10018) ***(G-10665)***
Magic Brands International LLC.....212 563-4999
31 W 34th St Rm 401 New York (10001) ***(G-10666)***
Magic Maestro Music, New York *Also called Simon & Simon LLC* ***(G-11596)***
Magic Novelty Co Inc (PA).....212 304-2777
308 Dyckman St New York (10034) ***(G-10667)***
Magic Numbers Inc.....646 839-8578
29 Little West 12th St New York (10014) ***(G-10668)***
Magic Reed.....914 630-4006
723 Larchmont Acres Apt D Larchmont (10538) ***(G-7058)***
Magic Tank LLC.....877 646-2442
80 Maiden Ln Rm 2204 New York (10038) ***(G-10669)***
Magic Tech Co Ltd.....516 539-7944
401 Hempstead Tpke West Hempstead (11552) ***(G-16221)***
Magic Touch Icewares Intl.....212 794-2852
220 E 72nd St Apt 11g New York (10021) ***(G-10670)***
Magna Products Corp.....585 647-2280
777 Mount Read Blvd Rochester (14606) ***(G-13923)***
Magnaworks Technology Inc.....631 218-3431
36 Carlough Rd Unit H Bohemia (11716) ***(G-1054)***
Magnesium Technologies Corp.....905 689-7361
266 Elmwood Ave Buffalo (14222) ***(G-2934)***
Magnet Wire Division, Edgewood *Also called Weico Wire & Cable Inc* ***(G-4424)***
Magnet-Ndctive Systems Ltd USA.....585 924-4000
7625 Omnitech Pl Victor (14564) ***(G-15856)***
Magnetic Aids Inc.....845 863-1400
201 Ann St Newburgh (12550) ***(G-12231)***
Magnetic Analysis Corporation (PA).....914 530-2000
103 Fairview Pk Dr Ste 2 Elmsford (10523) ***(G-4549)***
Magnetic Technologies Corp (HQ).....585 385-9010
770 Linden Ave Rochester (14625) ***(G-13924)***
Magnetic Technology, Rochester *Also called Arnold Magnetic Tech Corp* ***(G-13640)***
Magnificat Inc.....914 502-1820
86 Main St Ste 303 Yonkers (10701) ***(G-16781)***
Magniflood Inc.....631 226-1000
7200 New Horizons Blvd Amityville (11701) ***(G-301)***
Magnum Creation Inc.....212 642-0993
23 W 47th St Fl 5 New York (10036) ***(G-10671)***
Magnum Shielding Corporation.....585 381-9957
3800 Monroe Ave Ste 14f Pittsford (14534) ***(G-13020)***
Magnus Precision Mfg Inc.....315 548-8032
1912 State Route 96 Phelps (14532) ***(G-12978)***
Magnus Sands Point Shop, Port Washington *Also called Robert Bartholomew Ltd* ***(G-13301)***
Magpump LLC.....585 444-9812
235 Middle Rd Ste 600 Henrietta (14467) ***(G-6035)***
Magsoft Corporation.....518 877-8390
2715 State Route 9 # 102 Ballston Spa (12020) ***(G-589)***
Magtrol Inc.....716 668-5555
70 Gardenville Pkwy W Buffalo (14224) ***(G-2935)***
Maharam Fabric Corporation.....631 582-3434
74 Horseblock Rd Yaphank (11980) ***(G-16716)***
Maharlika Holdings LLC.....631 319-6203
111 Trade Zone Ct Unit A Ronkonkoma (11779) ***(G-14373)***
Mahin Impressions Inc.....212 871-9777
30 W Main St Ste 301 Riverhead (11901) ***(G-13577)***
Mahle Behr USA Inc.....716 439-2011
350 Upper Mountain Rd Lockport (14094) ***(G-7314)***
Mahle Indstrbeteiligungen GMBH.....716 319-6700
4236 Ridge Lea Rd Amherst (14226) ***(G-237)***
Mahle Industries Incorporated.....248 735-3623
4236 Ridge Lea Rd Amherst (14226) ***(G-238)***
Maia Systems LLC.....718 206-0100
8344 Parsons Blvd Ste 101 Jamaica (11432) ***(G-6658)***
Maidenform LLC.....201 436-9200
260 Madison Ave Fl 6 New York (10016) ***(G-10672)***
Mailers-Pblsher Wlfare Tr Fund.....212 869-5986
1501 Broadway New York (10036) ***(G-10673)***
Main Street Connect LLC.....203 803-4110
200 Business Park Dr # 209 Armonk (10504) ***(G-407)***
Main Street Sweets.....914 332-5757
35 Main St Tarrytown (10591) ***(G-15480)***
Mainly Monograms Inc.....845 624-4923
260 W Nyack Rd Ste 1 West Nyack (10994) ***(G-16275)***
Maio Fuel Company LP.....914 683-1154
46 Fairview Ave White Plains (10603) ***(G-16474)***
Maison Goyard, New York *Also called Goyard Miami LLC* ***(G-9964)***
Maiyet Inc.....212 343-9999
16 Crosby St Apt Corp New York (10013) ***(G-10674)***
Maizteca Foods Inc.....718 641-3933
13005 Liberty Ave South Richmond Hill (11419) ***(G-14946)***
Majestic Curtains LLC.....718 898-0774
4410 Ketcham St Apt 2g Elmhurst (11373) ***(G-4469)***
Majestic Home Imprvs Distr.....718 853-5079
5902 Fort Hamilton Pkwy Brooklyn (11219) ***(G-2152)***
Majestic Mold & Tool Inc.....315 695-2079
177 Volney St Phoenix (13135) ***(G-12990)***
Majestic Rayon Corporation.....212 929-6443
116 W 23rd St Fl 4 New York (10011) ***(G-10675)***
Majesty Brands LLC.....212 283-3400
469 7th Ave Rm 1301 New York (10018) ***(G-10676)***
Major-IPC Inc.....845 292-2200
53 Webster Ave Liberty (12754) ***(G-7145)***
Makamah Enterprises Inc.....631 231-0200
89 Cabot Ct Ste C Hauppauge (11788) ***(G-5878)***
Makarenko Studios Inc.....914 968-7673
2984 Saddle Ridge Dr Yorktown Heights (10598) ***(G-16818)***
Makari, New York *Also called Victoria Albi International* ***(G-12028)***
Make-Waves Instrument Corp (PA).....716 681-7524
4172 Vinewood Dr Buffalo (14221) ***(G-2936)***
Makerbot Industries LLC (HQ).....347 334-6800
1 Metrotech Ctr Fl 21 Brooklyn (11201) ***(G-2153)***
Makers Nutrition LLC (PA).....631 456-5397
315 Oser Ave Ste 3 Hauppauge (11788) ***(G-5879)***
Makiplastic.....716 772-2222
4904 Gasport Rd Gasport (14067) ***(G-5307)***
Maks Pharma & Diagnostics Inc.....631 270-1528
2365 Milburn Ave Bldg 2 Baldwin (11510) ***(G-540)***
Malcon Inc.....914 666-7146
405 Adams St Bedford Hills (10507) ***(G-777)***
Male Power Apparel, Hauppauge *Also called Comme-Ci Comme-CA AP Group* ***(G-5795)***
Maler Technologies Inc.....212 391-2070
337 E 81st St Bsmt New York (10028) ***(G-10677)***
Malhame Publs & Importers Inc.....631 694-8600
180 Orville Dr Unit A Bohemia (11716) ***(G-1055)***
Malia Mills, Brooklyn *Also called IaMmaliamills LLC* ***(G-1992)***
Malia Mills Inc.....212 354-4200
32 33rd St Unit 13 Brooklyn (11232) ***(G-2154)***
Malibu Cabinets, Suffern *Also called American Best Cabinets Inc* ***(G-15185)***

Malin + Goetz Inc (PA) 212 244-7771
330 7th Ave Ste 2100 New York (10001) *(G-10678)*
Malina Management Company Inc 607 535-9614
3620 County Road 16 Montour Falls (14865) *(G-8326)*
Malisa Branko Inc 631 225-9741
95 Garfield Ave Copiague (11726) *(G-3768)*
Mall Inc 315 751-9490
4876 Bethel Rd Cazenovia (13035) *(G-3322)*
Mallery Lumber LLC 607 637-2236
158 Labarre St Hancock (13783) *(G-5712)*
Mallinckrodt Pharmaceuticals, Hobart *Also called Specgx LLC (G-6164)*
Mallory & Church LLC 212 868-7888
552 Fashion Ave Rm 202 New York (10018) *(G-10679)*
Malone Concrete Products Div, Malone *Also called Upstone Materials Inc (G-7729)*
Malone Industrial Press Inc 518 483-5880
10 Stevens St Malone (12953) *(G-7724)*
Malone News, Malone *Also called Johnson Newspaper Corporation (G-7722)*
Malone Welding, Montour Falls *Also called Robert M Brown (G-8327)*
Malouf Colette Inc 212 941-9588
594 Broadway Rm 1216 New York (10012) *(G-10680)*
Maloya Laser Inc 631 543-2327
65a Mall Dr Ste 1 Commack (11725) *(G-3697)*
Malyn Industrial Ceramics Inc 716 741-1510
8640 Roll Rd Clarence Center (14032) *(G-3548)*
Mam Knitg, Brooklyn *Also called M A M Knitting Mills Corp (G-2144)*
Mam Molding Inc 607 433-2121
147 River St Oneonta (13820) *(G-12639)*
Mam USA Corporation 914 269-2500
2700 Westchester Ave # 315 Purchase (10577) *(G-13392)*
Mamco, Oneonta *Also called Mold-A-Matic Corporation (G-12641)*
Mamitas Ices Ltd 718 738-3238
10411 100th St Ozone Park (11417) *(G-12830)*
Mamma Says, Ferndale *Also called Chipita America Inc (G-4931)*
Man of World 212 915-0017
25 W 39th St Fl 5 New York (10018) *(G-10681)*
Man Products Inc 631 789-6500
99 Milbar Blvd Unit 1 Farmingdale (11735) *(G-4814)*
Mana Products Inc (PA) 718 361-2550
3202 Queens Blvd Fl 6 Long Island City (11101) *(G-7510)*
Mana Products Inc 718 361-5204
3202 Queens Blvd Fl 6 Long Island City (11101) *(G-7511)*
Manacraft Precision Inc 914 654-0967
945 Spring Rd Pelham (10803) *(G-12937)*
Manchester Newspaper Inc (PA) 518 642-1234
14 E Main St Granville (12832) *(G-5520)*
Manchester Wood Inc 518 642-9518
1159 County Route 24 Granville (12832) *(G-5521)*
Manchu New York Inc 212 921-5050
530 Fashion Ave Rm 1906 New York (10018) *(G-10682)*
Manchu Times Fashion Inc 212 921-5050
530 Sventh Ave Ste 1906 New York (10018) *(G-10683)*
Mancum Graphics, New York *Also called Mc Squared Nyc Inc (G-10738)*
Mandalay Food Products Inc 718 230-3370
640 Dean St Brooklyn (11238) *(G-2155)*
Mandarin Soy Sauce Inc 845 343-1505
4 Sands Station Rd Middletown (10940) *(G-8162)*
MANe Enterprises Inc 718 472-4955
4929 30th Pl Long Island City (11101) *(G-7512)*
Mango Usa Inc 718 998-6050
5620 1st Ave Ste 1 Brooklyn (11220) *(G-2156)*
Manhasset Tool & Die Co Inc 716 684-6066
4270 Walden Ave Lancaster (14086) *(G-7031)*
Manhattan Cabinetry, Island Park *Also called A-1 Manhattan Custom Furn Inc (G-6511)*
Manhattan Cabinets, Island Park *Also called A-1 Manhattan Custom Furn Inc (G-6510)*
Manhattan Cabinets Inc 212 548-2436
1349 2nd Ave New York (10021) *(G-10684)*
Manhattan Comfort Inc (PA) 908 888-0818
1482 Carroll St Brooklyn (11213) *(G-2157)*
Manhattan Cooling Towers Inc 212 279-1045
1142 46th Rd Long Island City (11101) *(G-7513)*
Manhattan Display Inc 718 392-1365
1215 Jackson Ave Ste B Long Island City (11101) *(G-7514)*
Manhattan Eastside Dev Corp 212 305-3275
622 W 168th St Ste Vc333 New York (10032) *(G-10685)*
Manhattan Map Co, New York *Also called Yale Robbins Inc (G-12158)*
Manhattan Media LLC (PA) 212 268-8600
535 5th Ave Fl 23 New York (10017) *(G-10686)*
Manhattan Milling & Drying Co 516 496-1041
78 Pond Rd Woodbury (11797) *(G-16625)*
Manhattan Neon Sign Corp 212 714-0430
640 W 28th St Fl 2 New York (10001) *(G-10687)*
Manhattan Poly Bag Corporation 917 689-7549
1228 47th St Brooklyn (11219) *(G-2158)*
Manhattan Scientifics Inc (PA) 212 541-2405
405 Lexington Ave Fl 26 New York (10174) *(G-10688)*
Manhattan Shade & Glass Co Inc (PA) 212 288-5616
37 Pond Park Rd Great Neck (11023) *(G-5570)*
Manhattan Shade & Glass Co Inc 212 288-5616
135 Ricefield Ln Hauppauge (11788) *(G-5880)*
Manhattan Signs, Floral Park *Also called Decree Signs & Graphics Inc (G-4962)*
Manhattan Special Bottling 718 388-4144
342 Manhattan Ave Brooklyn (11211) *(G-2159)*
Manhattan Times Inc 212 569-5800
5030 Broadway Ste 801 New York (10034) *(G-10689)*
Manhole Brrier SEC Systems Inc 516 741-1032
8002 Kew Gardens Rd # 901 Kew Gardens (11415) *(G-6877)*
Manifestation-Glow Press Inc 718 380-5259
7740 164th St Fresh Meadows (11366) *(G-5202)*
Manifold Center, The, Medford *Also called B & R Industries Inc (G-7938)*
Manitou Concrete 585 424-6040
1260 Jefferson Rd Rochester (14623) *(G-13925)*
Mann Consultants LLC 914 763-0512
67 Chapel Rd Waccabuc (10597) *(G-15881)*
Mann Publications Inc 212 840-6266
450 Fashion Ave Ste 2306 New York (10123) *(G-10690)*
Mannesmann Corporation 212 258-4000
601 Lexington Ave Fl 56 New York (10022) *(G-10691)*
Manning Lewis Div Rubicon Inds 908 687-2400
848 E 43rd St Brooklyn (11210) *(G-2160)*
Mannix, Brentwood *Also called Interstate Window Corporation (G-1137)*
Manny Grunberg Inc 212 302-6173
62 W 47th St Ste 703 New York (10036) *(G-10692)*
Mannys Cheesecake Inc 315 732-0639
1221 Pleasant St Utica (13501) *(G-15718)*
Manor Electric Supply Corp 718 648-8003
2737 Ocean Ave Brooklyn (11229) *(G-2161)*
Manrico Cashmere, New York *Also called Manrico Usa Inc (G-10693)*
Manrico Usa Inc 212 794-4200
922 Madison Ave New York (10021) *(G-10693)*
Manrico Usa Inc (PA) 212 794-4200
922 Madison Ave New York (10021) *(G-10694)*
Mansfield Press Inc 212 265-5411
599 11th Ave Fl 3 New York (10036) *(G-10695)*
Mansueto Ventures LLC 212 389-5300
7 World Trade Ctr Fl 29 New York (10007) *(G-10696)*
Mantel & Mantel Stamping Corp 631 467-1916
802 S 4th St Ronkonkoma (11779) *(G-14374)*
Manth Mfg Inc 716 693-6525
131 Fillmore Ave Tonawanda (14150) *(G-15556)*
Manth-Brownell Inc 315 687-7263
1120 Fyler Rd Kirkville (13082) *(G-6934)*
Manufacturers Indexing Pdts 631 271-0956
53 Gristmill Ln Halesite (11743) *(G-5658)*
Manufacturers Tool & Die Co 585 352-1080
3 Turner Dr Spencerport (14559) *(G-14981)*
Manufacturing, Lockport *Also called Hti Recycling LLC (G-7309)*
Manufacturing & Tech Entp Ctr, Highland *Also called Hudson Valley Tech Dev Ctr Inc (G-6144)*
Manufacturing Facility, Middletown *Also called President Cont Group II LLC (G-8171)*
Manufacturing Resources Inc 631 481-0041
2392 Innovation Way # 4 Rochester (14624) *(G-13926)*
Manufacturing Solutions Inc 585 235-3320
850 Saint Paul St Ste 11 Rochester (14605) *(G-13927)*
Manzella Knitting 716 825-0808
3345 N Benzing Rd Orchard Park (14127) *(G-12727)*
Manzione Enterprises, Brooklyn *Also called Manzione Ready Mix Corp (G-2162)*
Manzione Ready Mix Corp 718 628-3837
46 Knickerbocker Ave Brooklyn (11237) *(G-2162)*
Mapeasy Inc 631 537-6213
54 Industrial Rd Wainscott (11975) *(G-15889)*
Maple Grove and Enterprises, Arcade *Also called Maple Grove Corp (G-386)*
Maple Grove Corp 585 492-5286
7075 Route 98 Arcade (14009) *(G-386)*
Maple Hill Creamery LLC (PA) 518 758-7777
285 Allendale Rd W Stuyvesant (12173) *(G-15182)*
Maple Hill Creamery LLC 518 758-7777
5 Hudson St Kinderhook (12106) *(G-6880)*
Maplehurst Bakeries LLC 315 735-5000
178 Industrial Park Dr Frankfort (13340) *(G-5109)*
Mapleland Farms LLC 518 854-7669
647 Bunker Hill Rd Salem (12865) *(G-14538)*
Maplewood Ice Co Inc 518 499-2345
9785 State Route 4 Whitehall (12887) *(G-16523)*
Mar-A-Thon Filters Inc 631 957-4774
369 41st St Lindenhurst (11757) *(G-7177)*
Maracle Industrial Finshg Co 585 387-9077
93 Kilbourn Rd Rochester (14618) *(G-13928)*
Maramont Corporation (PA) 718 439-8900
5600 1st Ave Brooklyn (11220) *(G-2163)*
Marathon Boat Group Inc 607 849-3211
1 Grumman Way Marathon (13803) *(G-7791)*
Marathon Enterprises Inc 718 665-2560
787 E 138th St Bronx (10454) *(G-1321)*
Marathon Roofing Products Inc 716 685-3340
3310 N Benzing Rd Orchard Park (14127) *(G-12728)*
Marble Knits Inc 718 237-7990
544 Park Ave Ste 3 Brooklyn (11205) *(G-2164)*
Marble Knitting Mills, Brooklyn *Also called Marble Knits Inc (G-2164)*
Marble Works Inc 914 376-3653
681 Saw Mill River Rd Yonkers (10710) *(G-16782)*
Marc Kaufman Furs, New York *Also called Mksf Inc (G-10827)*

A
L
P
H
A
B
E
T
I
C

Marcal Printing Inc 516 942-9500
85 N Broadway Hicksville (11801) ***(G-6105)***
Marcasiano Inc 212 614-9412
296 Elizabeth St Apt 2f New York (10012) ***(G-10697)***
Marcel Finishing Corp 718 381-2889
4 David Ct Plainview (11803) ***(G-13072)***
Marcellus Energy Services LLC 607 236-0038
3 Mill St Ste 6 Candor (13743) ***(G-3253)***
Marchesa Accesories, New York *Also called Akh Group LLC* ***(G-8780)***
Marco Hi-Tech JV LLC (PA) 212 798-8100
475 Park Ave S Fl 10 New York (10016) ***(G-10698)***
Marco Manufacturing Inc 845 485-1571
55 Page Park Dr Poughkeepsie (12603) ***(G-13353)***
Marco Moore Inc 212 575-2090
825 Northern Blvd Ste 201 Great Neck (11021) ***(G-5571)***
Marcon Electronic Systems LLC 516 633-6396
152 Westend Ave Freeport (11520) ***(G-5164)***
Marcon Services 516 223-8019
152 Westend Ave Freeport (11520) ***(G-5165)***
Marconi Intl USA Co Ltd 212 391-2626
214 W 39th St Rm 703 New York (10018) ***(G-10699)***
Marcovicci-Wenz Engineering 631 467-9040
33 Comac Loop Unit 10 Ronkonkoma (11779) ***(G-14375)***
Marcus Goldman Inc 212 431-0707
37 W 39th St Rm 1201 New York (10018) ***(G-10700)***
Marcy Business Forms Inc 718 935-9100
1468 40th St Brooklyn (11218) ***(G-2165)***
Marcy Printing Inc 718 935-9100
777 Kent Ave Ste A Brooklyn (11205) ***(G-2166)***
Mardek LLC 585 735-9333
73 N Wilmarth Rd Pittsford (14534) ***(G-13021)***
Mardon Tool & Die Co Inc 585 254-4545
19 Lois St Rochester (14606) ***(G-13929)***
Marex Aquisition Corp 585 458-3940
1385 Emerson St Rochester (14606) ***(G-13930)***
Mari Strings Inc 212 799-6781
14 W 71st St New York (10023) ***(G-10701)***
Maria Dionisio Welding Inc 631 956-0815
71 W Montauk Hwy Lindenhurst (11757) ***(G-7178)***
Mariah Metal Products Inc 516 938-9783
89 Tec St Hicksville (11801) ***(G-6106)***
Marie Claire Magazine, New York *Also called Marie Claire USA* ***(G-10702)***
Marie Claire USA 212 841-8493
300 W 57th St Fl 34 New York (10019) ***(G-10702)***
Marietta Corporation (HQ) 607 753-6746
37 Huntington St Cortland (13045) ***(G-3881)***
Marietta Corporation 607 753-0982
106 Central Ave Cortland (13045) ***(G-3882)***
Marietta Corporation 323 589-8181
37 Huntington St Cortland (13045) ***(G-3883)***
Marigold Signs Inc 516 433-7446
485 S Broadway Ste 34 Hicksville (11801) ***(G-6107)***
Marina Holding Corp 718 646-9283
3939 Emmons Ave Brooklyn (11235) ***(G-2167)***
Marina Ice Cream 718 235-3000
888 Jamaica Ave Brooklyn (11208) ***(G-2168)***
Marina Jewelry Co Inc 212 354-5027
42 W 48th St Ste 804 New York (10036) ***(G-10703)***
Marine & Indus Hydraulics Inc 914 698-2036
329 Center Ave Mamaroneck (10543) ***(G-7747)***
Marine Boiler & Welding Inc 718 378-1900
1428 Sheridan Expy Bronx (10459) ***(G-1322)***
Marinos Italian Ices, Richmond Hill *Also called Olympic Ice Cream Co Inc* ***(G-13507)***
Maripharm Laboratories 716 984-6520
2045 Niagara Falls Blvd Niagara Falls (14304) ***(G-12308)***
Maritime Activity Reports (PA) 212 477-6700
118 E 25th St Fl 2 New York (10010) ***(G-10704)***
Maritime Broadband Inc 347 404-6041
1143 47th Ave Long Island City (11101) ***(G-7515)***
Mark - 10 Corporation 631 842-9200
11 Dixon Ave Copiague (11726) ***(G-3769)***
Mark Dri Products Inc 516 484-6200
999 S Oyster Bay Rd # 312 Bethpage (11714) ***(G-846)***
Mark Ecko Enterprises, New York *Also called Mee Accessories LLC* ***(G-10762)***
Mark F Rosenhaft N A O 516 374-1010
538 Central Ave Cedarhurst (11516) ***(G-3334)***
Mark I Publications Inc 718 205-8000
7119 80th St Ste 8201 Glendale (11385) ***(G-5403)***
Mark King Jewelry Inc 212 921-0746
62 W 47th St Ste 310r New York (10036) ***(G-10705)***
Mark Levine 212 677-4457
149 5th Ave Fl 10 New York (10010) ***(G-10706)***
Mark Nelson Designs LLC 646 422-7020
404 E 55th St Fl 4 New York (10022) ***(G-10707)***
Mark Peri International 516 208-6824
3516 Hargale Rd Oceanside (11572) ***(G-12547)***
Mark Posner 718 258-6241
1950 52nd St Brooklyn (11204) ***(G-2169)***
Mark Robinson Inc 212 223-3515
18 E 48th St Rm 1102 New York (10017) ***(G-10708)***
Mark T Westinghouse 518 678-3262
138 Grandview Ave Catskill (12414) ***(G-3306)***
Markar Architectural Products 716 685-4104
68 Ward Rd Lancaster (14086) ***(G-7032)***
Marken LLP 631 396-7454
123 Smith St Farmingdale (11735) ***(G-4815)***
Market Factory Inc 212 625-9988
45 W 27th St Frnt 1 New York (10001) ***(G-10709)***
Market Logic Software Inc 646 405-1041
80 Pine St Fl 24 New York (10005) ***(G-10710)***
Market Partners International 212 447-0855
232 Madison Ave Rm 1400 New York (10016) ***(G-10711)***
Market Place Publications 516 997-7909
234 Silverlake Blvd Ste 2 Carle Place (11514) ***(G-3270)***
Marketer's Forum Magazine, Centerport *Also called Forum Publishing Co* ***(G-3348)***
Marketfax Information Services, Hastings On Hudson *Also called Alternative Technology Corp* ***(G-5747)***
Marketing Action Xecutives Inc 212 971-9155
50 W 96th St Apt 7b New York (10025) ***(G-10712)***
Marketing Group International 631 754-8095
1 Stargazer Ct Northport (11768) ***(G-12472)***
Marketplace Slutions Group LLC 631 868-0111
48 Nimbus Rd Ste 303 Holbrook (11741) ***(G-6198)***
Marketplace, The, Chester *Also called Advertiser Publications Inc* ***(G-3467)***
Marketresearchcom Inc 212 807-2600
641 Ave Of The America New York (10011) ***(G-10713)***
Markin Tubing LP (PA) 585 495-6211
1 Markin Ln Wyoming (14591) ***(G-16699)***
Markin Tubing LP 585 495-6211
400 Ingham Ave Buffalo (14218) ***(G-2937)***
Markin Tubing Division, Buffalo *Also called Markin Tubing LP* ***(G-2937)***
Markin Tubing Inc 585 495-6211
Pearl Creek Rd Wyoming (14591) ***(G-16700)***
Markowitz Jewelry Co Inc 845 774-1175
53 Forest Rd Ste 104 Monroe (10950) ***(G-8276)***
Markpericom 516 208-6824
3516 Hargale Rd Oceanside (11572) ***(G-12548)***
Marks Corpex Banknote Co (PA) 631 968-0277
1440 5th Ave Bay Shore (11706) ***(G-698)***
Marks USA, Amityville *Also called G Marks Hdwr Liquidating Corp* ***(G-276)***
Marksmen Manufacturing Corp 800 305-6942
355 Marcus Blvd Deer Park (11729) ***(G-4006)***
Marktech International Corp (PA) 518 956-2980
3 Northway Ln N Ste 1 Latham (12110) ***(G-7087)***
Marktech Optoelectronics, Latham *Also called Marktech International Corp* ***(G-7087)***
Markwik Corp 516 470-1990
309 W John St Hicksville (11801) ***(G-6108)***
Marlborough Jewels Inc 718 768-2000
67 35th St Unit 2 Brooklyn (11232) ***(G-2170)***
Marley Spoon Inc 646 934-6970
601 W 26th St Rm 900 New York (10001) ***(G-10714)***
Marlou Garments Inc 516 739-7100
2115 Jericho Tpke New Hyde Park (11040) ***(G-8549)***
Marlow Printing Co Inc 718 625-4948
667 Kent Ave Brooklyn (11249) ***(G-2171)***
Marly Home Industries USA Inc 718 388-3030
181 Lombardy St Brooklyn (11222) ***(G-2172)***
Marmach Machine Inc 585 768-8800
11 Lent Ave Le Roy (14482) ***(G-7122)***
Marnier-Lapostolle Inc 212 207-4350
183 Madison Ave New York (10016) ***(G-10715)***
Marotta Dental Studio Inc 631 249-7520
130 Finn Ct Farmingdale (11735) ***(G-4816)***
Marovato Industries Inc 718 389-0800
108 Dobbin St Brooklyn (11222) ***(G-2173)***
Marplex Furniture Corporation 914 969-7755
167 Saw Mill Rver Rd Fl 1 Flr 1 Yonkers (10701) ***(G-16783)***
Marquardt Switches Inc (HQ) 315 655-8050
2711 Us Route 20 Cazenovia (13035) ***(G-3323)***
Marretti USA Inc 212 255-5565
101 Ave Of The Am Fl 9 New York (10013) ***(G-10716)***
Marros Equipment & Trucks 315 539-8702
2354 State Route 414 Waterloo (13165) ***(G-15996)***
Mars Fashions Inc 718 402-2200
780 E 134th St Fl 5 Bronx (10454) ***(G-1323)***
Marsal & Sons, Lindenhurst *Also called Middleby Corporation* ***(G-7180)***
Marsha Fleisher 845 679-6500
18 Tinker St Woodstock (12498) ***(G-16686)***
Marshall Cavendish Corp 914 332-8888
99 White Plains Rd Tarrytown (10591) ***(G-15481)***
Marshall Ingredients LLC 800 796-9353
5786 Limekiln Rd Wolcott (14590) ***(G-16611)***
Marsid Group Ltd 516 334-1603
245 Westbury Ave Carle Place (11514) ***(G-3271)***
Marsid Press, Carle Place *Also called Marsid Group Ltd* ***(G-3271)***
MARsid-M&m Group, The, Carle Place *Also called M&M Printing Inc* ***(G-3269)***
Mart-Tex Athletics Inc 631 454-9583
180 Allen Blvd Farmingdale (11735) ***(G-4817)***
Martens Country Kit Pdts LLC 315 776-8821
1323 Towpath Rd Port Byron (13140) ***(G-13188)***
Martha & Marley Spoon, New York *Also called Marley Spoon Inc* ***(G-10714)***
Martha Stewart Living (HQ) 212 827-8000
601 W 26th St Rm 900 New York (10001) ***(G-10717)***

Martha Stewart Living Omni LLC 212 827-8000
20 W 43rd St New York (10036) *(G-10718)*
Martin Dental Studio, Watertown *Also called Martins Dental Studio (G-16026)*
Martin Greenfield Clothiers 718 497-5480
239 Varet St Brooklyn (11206) *(G-2174)*
Martin Orna Ir Works II Inc 516 354-3923
266 Elmont Rd Elmont (11003) *(G-4520)*
Martinelli Holdings LLC 302 504-1361
4 Ellsworth Ave Apt 2 Harrison (10528) *(G-5730)*
Martinelli Publications, Yonkers *Also called Yonkers Time Publishing Co (G-16811)*
Martinez Specialties Inc 607 898-3053
205 Bossard Rd Groton (13073) *(G-5652)*
Martins Dental Studio 315 788-0800
162 Sterling St Watertown (13601) *(G-16026)*
Marval Industries Inc 914 381-2400
315 Hoyt Ave Mamaroneck (10543) *(G-7748)*
Marvel Dairy Whip Inc 516 889-4232
258 Lido Blvd Lido Beach (11561) *(G-7148)*
Marvel Entertainment LLC (HQ) 212 576-4000
135 W 50th St Fl 7 New York (10020) *(G-10719)*
Marvel Equipment Corp Inc 718 383-6597
215 Eagle St Brooklyn (11222) *(G-2175)*
Marvellissima Intl Ltd 212 682-7306
333 E 46th St Apt 20a New York (10017) *(G-10720)*
Marx Myles Graphic Services, New York *Also called X Myles Mar Inc (G-12148)*
Mary Ann Liebert Inc 914 740-2100
140 Huguenot St Fl 3 New Rochelle (10801) *(G-8620)*
Mary Bright Inc 212 677-1970
269 E 10th St Apt 7 New York (10009) *(G-10721)*
Mary F Morse 315 866-2741
125 Columbia St Ste 1 Mohawk (13407) *(G-8255)*
Marzullo Electric LLC 315 455-1050
103 Oliva Dr Syracuse (13211) *(G-15367)*
Mas Cutting Inc 212 869-0826
257 W 39th St Rm 11e New York (10018) *(G-10722)*
Masick Soil Conservation Co 518 827-5354
4860 State Route 30 Schoharie (12157) *(G-14732)*
Mason & Gore Inc 914 921-1025
2 Clinton Ave Rye (10580) *(G-14485)*
Mason Carvings Inc 716 484-7884
2871 Ivystone Dr Jamestown (14701) *(G-6737)*
Mason Contract Products LLC 516 328-6900
85 Denton Ave New Hyde Park (11040) *(G-8550)*
Mason Industries Inc (PA) 631 348-0282
350 Rabro Dr Hauppauge (11788) *(G-5881)*
Mason Industries Inc 631 348-0282
33 Ranick Rd Ste 1 Hauppauge (11788) *(G-5882)*
Mason Medical Products, Port Washington *Also called M R C Industries Inc (G-13283)*
Mason Transparent Package Inc 718 792-6000
1180 Commerce Ave Bronx (10462) *(G-1324)*
Mason Woodworks LLC 917 363-7052
127 Chester Ave Brooklyn (11218) *(G-2176)*
Masonville Stone Incorporated 607 265-3597
12999 State Highway 8 Masonville (13804) *(G-7815)*
Maspeth Press Inc 718 429-2363
6620 Grand Ave Maspeth (11378) *(G-7857)*
Maspeth Steel Fabricators Inc 718 361-9192
5215 11th St Ste 21 Long Island City (11101) *(G-7516)*
Maspeth Welding Inc 718 497-5430
5930 54th St Maspeth (11378) *(G-7858)*
Masquerade LLC 212 673-4546
104 4th Ave New York (10003) *(G-10723)*
Mass Appeal Magazine 718 858-0979
261 Vandervoort Ave Brooklyn (11211) *(G-2177)*
Mass Mdsg Self Selection Eqp 631 234-3300
35 Orville Dr Ste 2 Bohemia (11716) *(G-1056)*
Massapequa Post 516 798-5100
1045b Park Blvd Massapequa Park (11762) *(G-7893)*
Massapqua Prcsion McHining Ltd 631 789-1485
30 Seabro Ave Amityville (11701) *(G-302)*
Massena Metals Inc 315 769-3846
86 S Racquette River Rd Massena (13662) *(G-7905)*
Massena Ready Mix, Massena *Also called Upstone Materials Inc (G-7910)*
Massimo Friedman Inc 716 836-0408
2495 Main St Ste 457 Buffalo (14214) *(G-2938)*
Masten Enterprises LLC (PA) 845 932-8206
420 Bernas Rd Cochecton (12726) *(G-3607)*
Master & Dynamics, New York *Also called New Audio LLC (G-10917)*
Master Art Corp 845 362-6430
131 Clinton Ln Ste E Spring Valley (10977) *(G-15001)*
Master Craft Finishers Inc 631 586-0540
30 W Jefryn Blvd Ste 1 Deer Park (11729) *(G-4007)*
Master Craft Jewelry Co Inc 516 599-1012
150 Vincent Ave Lynbrook (11563) *(G-7668)*
Master Image Printing Inc 914 347-4400
75 N Central Ave Ste 202 Elmsford (10523) *(G-4550)*
Master Juvenile Products Inc 845 647-8400
70 Berme Rd Ellenville (12428) *(G-4440)*
Master Machine Incorporated 716 487-2555
155 Blackstone Ave Jamestown (14701) *(G-6738)*
Master-Halco Inc 631 585-8150
19 Zorn Blvd Yaphank (11980) *(G-16717)*
Mastercraft Decorators Inc 585 223-5150
320 Macedon Center Rd Fairport (14450) *(G-4641)*
Mastercraft Manufacturing Co 718 729-5620
3715 11th St Long Island City (11101) *(G-7517)*
Masterdisk Corporation 212 541-5022
134 S Central Ave Ste C Elmsford (10523) *(G-4551)*
Mastro Concrete Inc 718 528-6788
15433 Brookville Blvd Rosedale (11422) *(G-14441)*
Mastro Graphic Arts Inc 585 436-7570
67 Deep Rock Rd Rochester (14624) *(G-13931)*
Mata Fashions LLC 917 716-7894
222 W 37th St Fl 4 New York (10018) *(G-10724)*
Mataci Inc 212 502-1899
247 W 35th St Fl 15 New York (10001) *(G-10725)*
Match Eyewear LLC 516 877-0170
1600 Shames Dr Westbury (11590) *(G-16354)*
Matchables Inc 718 389-9318
106 Green St Ste G1 Brooklyn (11222) *(G-2178)*
Matel LLC 646 825-6760
90 Park Ave Fl 18 New York (10016) *(G-10726)*
Material Measuring Corporation 516 334-6167
121 Hopper St Westbury (11590) *(G-16355)*
Material Process Systems Inc 718 302-3081
87 Richardson St Ste 2 Brooklyn (11211) *(G-2179)*
Materials Design Workshop 718 893-1954
830 Barry St Bronx (10474) *(G-1325)*
Materion Advanced Materials (HQ) 800 327-1355
2978 Main St Buffalo (14214) *(G-2939)*
Materion Advanced Materials 800 327-1355
42 Mount Ebo Rd S Brewster (10509) *(G-1170)*
Materion Brewster LLC 845 279-0900
42 Mount Ebo Rd S Brewster (10509) *(G-1171)*
Materne North America Corp (HQ) 212 675-7881
20 W 22nd St Fl 12 New York (10010) *(G-10727)*
Matheson Tri-Gas Inc 518 203-5003
15 Green Mountain Dr Cohoes (12047) *(G-3613)*
Mathisen Ventures Inc 212 986-1025
441 Lexington Ave Rm 809 New York (10017) *(G-10728)*
Matic Industries Inc 718 886-5470
1540 127th St College Point (11356) *(G-3655)*
Matov Industries Inc 718 392-5060
1011 40th Ave Long Island City (11101) *(G-7518)*
Matrix Machining Corp 631 643-6690
69 B Nancy St Unitb West Babylon (11704) *(G-16174)*
Matrix Railway Corp 631 643-1483
69 Nancy St Unit A West Babylon (11704) *(G-16175)*
Matrix Steel Company Inc 718 381-6800
50 Bogart St Brooklyn (11206) *(G-2180)*
Matrixcare Inc 518 583-6400
575 8th Ave Fl 15 New York (10018) *(G-10729)*
Matrox Graphics Inc 518 561-4417
625 State Route 3 1/2 Plattsburgh (12901) *(G-13132)*
Matt Industries Inc (PA) 315 472-1316
6761 Thompson Rd Syracuse (13211) *(G-15368)*
Mattel Inc 716 714-8514
609 Girard Ave East Aurora (14052) *(G-4205)*
Mattel Inc 310 252-2000
636 Girard Ave East Aurora (14052) *(G-4206)*
Matteo & Antonio Bartolotta 315 252-2220
282 State St Auburn (13021) *(G-490)*
Matteson Logging Inc 585 593-3037
2808 Beech Hill Rd Wellsville (14895) *(G-16118)*
Mattessich Iron LLC 315 409-8496
1484 New State Route 31 Memphis (13112) *(G-8076)*
Matthew Shively LLC 914 937-3531
40 Merritt St Port Chester (10573) *(G-13205)*
Matthew-Lee Corporation 631 226-0100
149 Pennsylvania Ave Lindenhurst (11757) *(G-7179)*
Matthews Hats 718 859-4683
99 Kenilworth Pl Fl 1 Brooklyn (11210) *(G-2181)*
Mauceri Sign & Awning Co, Jamaica *Also called Mauceri Sign Inc (G-6659)*
Mauceri Sign Inc 718 656-7700
16725 Rockaway Blvd Jamaica (11434) *(G-6659)*
Maurice Max Inc 212 334-6573
49 W 27th St Fl 5 New York (10001) *(G-10730)*
Maury's Cookie Dough, New York *Also called City Bakery Inc (G-9310)*
Mausner Equipment Co Inc 631 689-7358
8 Heritage Ln Setauket (11733) *(G-14795)*
Maven Marketing LLC (PA) 615 510-3248
349 5th Ave Fl 8 New York (10016) *(G-10731)*
Maverik Lacrosse LLC 516 213-3050
535 W 24th St Fl 5 New York (10011) *(G-10732)*
Maviano Corp 845 494-2598
21 Robert Pitt Dr Ste 207 Monsey (10952) *(G-8290)*
Max 200 Performance Dog Eqp 315 776-9588
2113 State Route 31 Port Byron (13140) *(G-13189)*
Max Brenner Union Square LLC 646 467-8803
841 Broadway New York (10003) *(G-10733)*
Max Kahan Inc 212 575-4646
20 W 47th St Ste 300 New York (10036) *(G-10734)*
Maxi Companies Inc 315 446-1002
4317 E Genesee St De Witt (13214) *(G-3930)*

ALPHABETIC

Maxim Hygiene Products Inc (PA) 516 621-3323
121 E Jericho Tpke Mineola (11501) **(G-8236)**
Maximum Security Products Corp 518 233-1800
3 Schoolhouse Ln Waterford (12188) **(G-15977)**
Maxine Denker Inc (PA) 212 689-1440
212 Manhattan St Staten Island (10307) **(G-15103)**
Maxivision, Brooklyn *Also called Bestec Concept Inc* **(G-1604)**
Maxsecure Systems Inc 800 657-4336
300 International Dr # 100 Buffalo (14221) **(G-2940)**
Maxsun Corporation (PA) 718 418-6800
5711 49th St Maspeth (11378) **(G-7859)**
Maxsun Furnishings, Maspeth *Also called Maxsun Corporation* **(G-7859)**
Maxwell Bakery Inc 718 498-2200
2700 Atlantic Ave Brooklyn (11207) **(G-2182)**
May Ship Repair Contg Corp 718 442-9700
3075 Richmond Ter Ste 3 Staten Island (10303) **(G-15104)**
May Tool & Die Inc 716 695-1033
9 Hackett Dr Tonawanda (14150) **(G-15557)**
Maybelline Inc 212 885-1310
575 5th Ave Bsmt Fl New York (10017) **(G-10735)**
Mayberry Shoe Company Inc 315 692-4086
131 W Seneca St Ste B Manlius (13104) **(G-7780)**
Maybrook Asphalt, Montgomery *Also called Tilcon New York Inc* **(G-8318)**
Mayer Bros Apple Products Inc (PA) 716 668-1787
3300 Transit Rd West Seneca (14224) **(G-16301)**
Mayfair Machine Company Inc 631 981-6644
128 Remington Blvd Ronkonkoma (11779) **(G-14376)**
Mayflower Splint Co 631 549-5131
16 Arbor Ln Dix Hills (11746) **(G-4121)**
Mayim Chaim Beverages, Bronx *Also called New York Bottling Co Inc* **(G-1340)**
Maz Systems Inc (PA) 855 629-3444
127 W 26th St Ste 500 New York (10001) **(G-10736)**
Mazerna USA, Nanuet *Also called Jescar Enterprises Inc* **(G-8465)**
Mazza Classics Incorporated 631 390-9060
117 Gazza Blvd Farmingdale (11735) **(G-4818)**
Mazza Co, The, North Baldwin *Also called W & B Mazza & Sons Inc* **(G-12371)**
Mazzella Blasting Mat Co, Bronx *Also called T M International LLC* **(G-1399)**
MB Food Processing Inc 845 436-5001
5190 S Fallsburg Main St South Fallsburg (12779) **(G-14931)**
MB Plastics Inc (PA) 718 523-1180
130 Stony Hollow Rd Greenlawn (11740) **(G-5623)**
MBA Orthotics Inc 631 392-4755
60 Corbin Ave Unit 60g Bay Shore (11706) **(G-699)**
Mbh Furniture Innovations Inc 845 354-8202
28 Lincoln Ave Spring Valley (10977) **(G-15002)**
Mbny LLC (PA) 646 467-8810
260 5th Ave Fl 9 New York (10001) **(G-10737)**
Mbss, Kew Gardens *Also called Manhole Brrier SEC Systems Inc* **(G-6877)**
Mc Coy Tops and Covers, Woodside *Also called Mc Coy Tops and Interiors Inc* **(G-16662)**
Mc Coy Tops and Interiors Inc 718 458-5800
6914 49th Ave Woodside (11377) **(G-16662)**
Mc Gregor Vineyard Winery, Dundee *Also called East Branch Winery Inc* **(G-4156)**
Mc Ivor Manufacturing Inc 716 825-1808
400 Ingham Ave Buffalo (14218) **(G-2941)**
Mc Squared Nyc Inc 212 947-2260
121 Varick St Frnt B New York (10013) **(G-10738)**
McAllisters Precision Wldg Inc 518 221-3455
47 Broadway Menands (12204) **(G-8087)**
McAlpin Industries Inc (PA) 585 266-3060
255 Hollenbeck St Rochester (14621) **(G-13932)**
McAlpin Industries Inc 585 544-5335
265 Hollenbeck St Rochester (14621) **(G-13933)**
McArdle Solutions, New York *Also called McPc Inc* **(G-10746)**
McAuliffe Paper Inc 315 453-2222
100 Commerce Blvd Liverpool (13088) **(G-7245)**
McBooks Press Inc 607 272-2114
520 N Meadow St 2 Ithaca (14850) **(G-6594)**
McCall Pattern Company (HQ) 212 465-6800
120 Broadway Fl 34 New York (10271) **(G-10739)**
McCarthy LLC 646 862-5354
32 Union Sq E New York (10003) **(G-10740)**
McCarthy Tire and Auto Ctr, Menands *Also called McCarthy Tire Svc Co NY Inc* **(G-8088)**
McCarthy Tire Svc Co NY Inc 518 449-5185
980 Broadway Menands (12204) **(G-8088)**
McClary Media Inc 800 453-6397
1 Venner Rd Amsterdam (12010) **(G-346)**
McConnaughay Technologies 607 753-1100
1911 Lorings Crossing Rd Cortland (13045) **(G-3884)**
McCullagh Coffee, Buffalo *Also called S J McCullagh Inc* **(G-3053)**
McD Metals LLC 518 456-9694
20 Corporate Cir Ste 2 Albany (12203) **(G-97)**
McDermott Light & Signal, Ridgewood *Also called Julian A McDermott Corporation* **(G-13540)**
McDonough Hardwoods Ltd 315 829-3449
6426 Skinner Rd Vernon Center (13477) **(G-15807)**
McDowell Research Co Inc (HQ) 315 332-7100
2000 Technology Pkwy Newark (14513) **(G-12200)**
McEwan Trucking & Grav Produc 716 609-1828
11696 Route 240 East Concord (14055) **(G-4214)**
McG Electronics Inc 631 586-5125
12 Burt Dr Deer Park (11729) **(G-4008)**
McG Graphics Inc 631 499-0730
101 Village Hill Dr Dix Hills (11746) **(G-4122)**
McG Surge Protection, Deer Park *Also called McG Electronics Inc* **(G-4008)**
McGraw Wood Products LLC (PA) 607 836-6465
1 Charles St Mc Graw (13101) **(G-7928)**
McGraw-Hill Education Inc (PA) 646 766-2000
2 Penn Plz Fl 20 New York (10121) **(G-10741)**
McGraw-Hill School Education H (PA) 646 766-2000
2 Penn Plz Fl 20 New York (10121) **(G-10742)**
McGraw-Hill School Educatn LLC 646 766-2060
2 Penn Plz Fl 20 New York (10121) **(G-10743)**
McGuigan Inc 631 750-6222
210 Knickerbocker Ave Bohemia (11716) **(G-1057)**
McHone Industries Inc 716 945-3380
110 Elm St Salamanca (14779) **(G-14526)**
McIntosh Box & Pallet Co Inc 716 825-4122
11 Hubbard St Buffalo (14206) **(G-2942)**
McIntosh Box & Pallet Co Inc 315 789-8750
40 Doran Ave Geneva (14456) **(G-5329)**
McIntosh Box & Pallet Co Inc 315 675-8511
741 State Route 49 Bernhards Bay (13028) **(G-833)**
McIntosh Box & Pallet Co Inc 315 446-9350
200 6th St Rome (13440) **(G-14257)**
McKee Foods Corporation 631 979-9364
111 Serene Pl Hauppauge (11788) **(G-5883)**
McKeon Rolling Stl Door Co Inc (PA) 631 803-3000
44 Sawgrass Dr Bellport (11713) **(G-808)**
MCM Natural Stone Inc 585 586-6510
860 Linden Ave Ste 1 Rochester (14625) **(G-13934)**
McM Products USA Inc (PA) 646 756-4090
681 5th Ave Fl 10 New York (10022) **(G-10744)**
McMahon Group LLC (PA) 212 957-5300
545 W 45th St New York (10036) **(G-10745)**
McMahon Publishing Group, New York *Also called McMahon Group LLC* **(G-10745)**
McPc Inc 212 583-6000
731 Lexington Ave New York (10022) **(G-10746)**
McQuilling Partners Inc (PA) 516 227-5718
1035 Stewart Ave Ste 100 Garden City (11530) **(G-5270)**
McWane Inc 607 734-2211
1021 E Water St Elmira (14901) **(G-4497)**
MD International Industries 631 254-3100
120 E Jefryn Blvd Ste Aa Deer Park (11729) **(G-4009)**
Md-Reports, Staten Island *Also called Infinite Software Solutions* **(G-15090)**
Mdcare911 LLC 917 640-4869
30 Main St Apt 5c Brooklyn (11201) **(G-2183)**
Mdi, Hauppauge *Also called Metal Dynamics Intl Corp* **(G-5888)**
Mdi East Inc 518 747-8730
22 Hudson Falls Rd Ste 6 South Glens Falls (12803) **(G-14937)**
Mdi Holdings LLC 212 559-1127
399 Park Ave Fl 14 New York (10022) **(G-10747)**
Mdj Sales Associates Inc 914 420-5897
27 Doris Rd Mamaroneck (10543) **(G-7749)**
Mdr Printing Corp 516 627-3221
125 Plandome Rd Manhasset (11030) **(G-7769)**
Mds Hot Bagels Deli Inc 718 438-5650
127 Church Ave Brooklyn (11218) **(G-2184)**
ME & Ro Inc (PA) 212 431-8744
241 Elizabeth St Frnt A New York (10012) **(G-10748)**
Me-J, New York *Also called Mej Beats LLC* **(G-10766)**
Meade Machine Co Inc 315 923-1703
31 Ford St Clyde (14433) **(G-3595)**
Meades Welding and Fabricating 631 581-1555
331 Islip Ave Islip (11751) **(G-6548)**
Mealplan Corp 909 706-8398
203 E 4th St Apt 6 New York (10009) **(G-10749)**
Measupro Inc (PA) 845 425-8777
1 Alpine Ct Spring Valley (10977) **(G-15003)**
Measurement Incorporated 914 682-1969
7-11 S Broadway Ste 402 White Plains (10601) **(G-16475)**
Mecca Printing, Buffalo *Also called B & P Jays Inc* **(G-2721)**
Mechanical Displays Inc 718 258-5588
4420 Farragut Rd Brooklyn (11203) **(G-2185)**
Mechanical Pwr Conversion LLC 607 766-9620
6 Emma St Binghamton (13905) **(G-903)**
Mechanical Rubber Pdts Co Inc 845 986-2271
77 Forester Ave Ste 1 Warwick (10990) **(G-15958)**
Mechanical Specialties Co, Binghamton *Also called Ms Machining Inc* **(G-907)**
Mechanical Technology Inc (PA) 518 218-2550
325 Washington Avenue Ext Albany (12205) **(G-98)**
Mecho Systems 718 729-8373
3708 34th St Long Island City (11101) **(G-7519)**
Mechon Beiss Uvas 718 436-1489
1130 40th St Brooklyn (11218) **(G-2186)**
Mechoshade Systems Inc (HQ) 718 729-2020
4203 35th St Long Island City (11101) **(G-7520)**
Med Reviews LLC 212 239-5860
1370 Broadway Fl 5 New York (10018) **(G-10750)**
Med Services Inc 631 218-6450
100 Knickerbocker Ave C Bohemia (11716) **(G-1058)**

ALPHABETIC SECTION — Merco Tape, Hillburn

Med-Eng LLC 315 713-0103
103 Tulloch Dr Ogdensburg (13669) *(G-12577)*
Medallion Associates Inc 212 929-9130
37 W 20th St Fl 4 New York (10011) *(G-10751)*
Medallion Security Door & Win, New Hyde Park Also called Texas Home Security Inc *(G-8566)*
Medco, Edgewood Also called Merit Electronic Design Co Inc *(G-4409)*
Medco Machine LLC 315 986-2109
2320 Walworth Marion Rd Walworth (14568) *(G-15914)*
Medek Laboratories Inc 845 943-4988
63 First Ave Monroe (10950) *(G-8277)*
Meder Textile Co Inc 516 883-0409
20 Lynn Rd Port Washington (11050) *(G-13284)*
Medforce Technologies Inc 845 426-0459
2 Executive Blvd Ste 410 Suffern (10901) *(G-15193)*
Medi-Physics, Port Washington Also called GE Healthcare Inc *(G-13262)*
Medi-Ray Inc 877 898-3003
150 Marbledale Rd Tuckahoe (10707) *(G-15644)*
Medi-Tech International Corp (PA) 800 333-0109
26 Court St Ste 1301 Brooklyn (11242) *(G-2187)*
Media Press Corp 212 791-6347
55 John St 520 New York (10038) *(G-10752)*
Media Technologies Ltd 631 467-7900
220 Sonata Ct Eastport (11941) *(G-4385)*
Media Transcripts Inc 212 362-1481
41 W 83rd St Apt 2b New York (10024) *(G-10753)*
Media Trust LLC (PA) 212 802-1162
404 Park Ave S Fl 2 New York (10016) *(G-10754)*
Mediaplanet Publishing Hse Inc (HQ) 646 922-1400
350 7th Ave Fl 18 New York (10001) *(G-10755)*
Mediapost Communications LLC 212 204-2000
1460 Broadway Fl 12 New York (10036) *(G-10756)*
Medical Acoustics LLC 716 218-7353
640 Ellicott St Ste 407 Buffalo (14203) *(G-2943)*
Medical Action Industries Inc 631 231-4600
150 Motor Pkwy Ste 205 Hauppauge (11788) *(G-5884)*
Medical Coaches Incorporated (PA) 607 432-1333
399 County Highway 58 Oneonta (13820) *(G-12640)*
Medical Daily Inc 646 867-7100
7 Hanover Sq Fl 6 New York (10004) *(G-10757)*
Medical Depot Inc (PA) 516 998-4600
99 Seaview Blvd Ste 210 Port Washington (11050) *(G-13285)*
Medical Information Systems 516 621-7200
2 Seaview Blvd Ste 104 Port Washington (11050) *(G-13286)*
Medical Technology Products 631 285-6640
33a Smith St Greenlawn (11740) *(G-5624)*
Medicine Rules Inc 631 334-5395
2 Constance Ct East Setauket (11733) *(G-4303)*
Medidata Solutions Inc (PA) 212 918-1800
350 Hudson St Fl 9 New York (10014) *(G-10758)*
Mediflex, Islandia Also called Flexbar Machine Corporation *(G-6528)*
Medikidz Usa Inc 646 895-9319
205 Lexington Ave Rm 1601 New York (10016) *(G-10759)*
Medima LLC 716 741-0400
5727 Strickler Rd Clarence (14031) *(G-3535)*
Medima Metals, Clarence Also called Medima LLC *(G-3535)*
Medina Journal Register, Medina Also called Cnhi LLC *(G-7975)*
Medina Millworks LLC 585 798-2969
10694 Ridge Rd Medina (14103) *(G-7983)*
Medipoint Inc 516 294-8822
72 E 2nd St Mineola (11501) *(G-8237)*
Medipoint International, Mineola Also called Medipoint Inc *(G-8237)*
Medisca Inc (HQ) 514 333-7811
661 State Route 3 Unit C Plattsburgh (12901) *(G-13133)*
Medisonic Inc 516 653-2345
57 Watermill Ln Ste 296 Great Neck (11021) *(G-5572)*
Mediterranean Thick Yogurt, East Elmhurst Also called Kesso Foods Inc *(G-4222)*
Mediterrean Dyro Company 718 786-4888
1102 38th Ave Long Island City (11101) *(G-7521)*
Meditub Incorporated 866 633-4882
11 Wedgewood Ln Lawrence (11559) *(G-7106)*
Medius North America, New York Also called Medius Software Inc *(G-10760)*
Medius Software Inc 877 295-0058
12 E 49th St Fl 11 New York (10017) *(G-10760)*
Medizine Operating LLC (PA) 212 695-2223
750 3rd Ave Fl 6 New York (10017) *(G-10761)*
Medline Industries Inc 845 344-3301
3301 Route 6 Middletown (10940) *(G-8163)*
Medsafe Systems Inc 516 883-8222
46 Orchard Farm Rd Port Washington (11050) *(G-13287)*
Medsim-Eagle Simulation Inc 607 658-9354
811 North St Endicott (13760) *(G-4601)*
Medsource Technologies LLC 716 662-5025
3902 California Rd Orchard Park (14127) *(G-12729)*
Medsurg Direct, Plainview Also called Peter Digioia *(G-13081)*
Medtech Products Inc (HQ) 914 524-6810
660 White Plains Rd Tarrytown (10591) *(G-15482)*
Medtek Skin Care Inc (PA) 518 745-7264
206 Glen St Ste 5 Glens Falls (12801) *(G-5433)*
Mee Accessories LLC (PA) 917 262-1000
475 10th Ave Fl 9 New York (10018) *(G-10762)*
Meeco Sullivan LLC 800 232-3625
3 Chancellor Ln Warwick (10990) *(G-15959)*
Meegenius Inc 212 283-7285
151 W 25th St Fl 3 New York (10001) *(G-10763)*
Meeker Sales Corp 718 384-5400
551 Sutter Ave Brooklyn (11207) *(G-2188)*
Mega Apparel International, Merrick Also called Mega Sourcing Inc *(G-8103)*
Mega Graphics Inc 914 962-1402
1725 Front St Ste 1 Yorktown Heights (10598) *(G-16819)*
Mega Power Sports Corporation 212 627-3380
1123 Broadway Ph New York (10010) *(G-10764)*
Mega Sourcing Inc (PA) 646 682-0304
1929 Edward Ln Merrick (11566) *(G-8103)*
Mega Tool & Mfg Corp 607 734-8398
1023 Caton Ave Elmira (14904) *(G-4498)*
Megohmer Vbrating Reed Standco, Brooklyn Also called Herman H Sticht Company Inc *(G-1974)*
Mehron Inc 845 426-1700
100 Red Schoolhouse Rd C2 Chestnut Ridge (10977) *(G-3493)*
Meiragtx Holdings PLC (PA) 646 490-2965
430 E 29th St Fl 10 New York (10016) *(G-10765)*
Meisel-Peskin Co Inc (PA) 718 497-1840
349 Scholes St 353 Brooklyn (11206) *(G-2189)*
Mej Beats LLC 516 707-6655
180 E 64th St New York (10065) *(G-10766)*
Mekanism Inc 212 226-2772
80 Broad St Fl 35 New York (10004) *(G-10767)*
Mekatronics Incorporated 516 883-6805
85 Channel Dr Ste 2 Port Washington (11050) *(G-13288)*
Mel Bernie and Company Inc 212 889-8570
384 5th Ave Fl 4 New York (10018) *(G-10768)*
Melbourne C Fisher Yacht Sails 631 673-5055
1345 New York Ave Ste 2 Huntington Station (11746) *(G-6451)*
Melcher Media Inc 212 727-2322
124 W 13th St New York (10011) *(G-10769)*
Meliorum Technologies Inc 585 313-0616
620 Park Ave 145 Rochester (14607) *(G-13935)*
Melissa, Interlaken Also called Hipshot Products Inc *(G-6481)*
Melita Corp 718 392-7280
3330 14th St Astoria (11106) *(G-435)*
Melland Gear Instr of Huppauge 631 234-0100
225 Engineers Rd Hauppauge (11788) *(G-5885)*
Mellem Corporation 607 723-0001
31 Lewis St Ste 1 Binghamton (13901) *(G-904)*
Mellen Press, The, Lewiston Also called PSR Press Ltd *(G-7142)*
Mellen Pressroom & Bindery, Lewiston Also called 450 Ridge St Inc *(G-7138)*
Melmont Fine Pringng/Graphics 516 939-2253
6 Robert Ct Ste 24 Bethpage (11714) *(G-847)*
Meloon Foundries LLC 315 454-3231
1841 Lemoyne Ave Syracuse (13208) *(G-15369)*
Melto Metal Products Co Inc 516 546-8866
37 Hanse Ave Freeport (11520) *(G-5166)*
Meltz Lumber Co of Mellenville 518 672-7021
483 Route 217 Hudson (12534) *(G-6363)*
Melwood Partners Inc 631 923-0134
102 Marcus Dr Melville (11747) *(G-8045)*
Memory Md Inc 917 318-0215
205 E 42nd St Fl 14 New York (10017) *(G-10770)*
Memory Protection Devices Inc 631 249-0001
200 Broadhollow Rd Ste 4 Farmingdale (11735) *(G-4819)*
Menpin Supply Corp 718 415-4168
1229 60th St Brooklyn (11219) *(G-2190)*
Menrose USA LLC 718 221-5540
605 Montgomery St Brooklyn (11225) *(G-2191)*
Mens Journal, New York Also called Straight Arrow Publishing Co *(G-11717)*
Mens Journal LLC 212 484-1616
1290 Ave Of The Americas New York (10104) *(G-10771)*
Mensch Mill & Lumber Corp (PA) 718 359-7500
1261 Commerce Ave Bronx (10462) *(G-1326)*
Mensch Supply, Bronx Also called Mensch Mill & Lumber Corp *(G-1326)*
Mentholatum Company (HQ) 716 677-2500
707 Sterling Dr Orchard Park (14127) *(G-12730)*
Menucha Publishers Inc 718 232-0856
1221 38th St Brooklyn (11218) *(G-2192)*
Mer Gems Corp 212 714-9129
62 W 47th St Ste 614 New York (10036) *(G-10772)*
Merb LLC 631 393-3621
140 Carolyn Blvd Farmingdale (11735) *(G-4820)*
Mercado Global Inc 718 838-9908
254 36th St Unit 41 Brooklyn (11232) *(G-2193)*
Mercer Milling Co 315 701-1334
4698 Crossroads Park Dr Liverpool (13088) *(G-7246)*
Mercer Rubber Co 631 348-0282
350 Rabro Dr Hauppauge (11788) *(G-5886)*
Mercer's Dairy, Boonville Also called Quality Dairy Farms Inc *(G-1120)*
Merchandiser Inc 315 462-6411
70 Stephens St Clifton Springs (14432) *(G-3582)*
Merchant Service Pymnt Access 212 561-5516
626 Rxr Plz Uniondale (11556) *(G-15671)*
Merco Hackensack Inc 845 357-3699
201 Route 59 Ste D2 Hillburn (10931) *(G-6154)*
Merco Tape, Hillburn Also called Merco Hackensack Inc *(G-6154)*

(PA)=Parent Co (HQ)=Headquarters (DH)=Div Headquarters

Mercury Apparel, West Nyack *Also called Mainly Monograms Inc* ***(G-16275)***
Mercury Envelope Co Inc...516 678-6744
100 Merrick Rd Ste 204e Rockville Centre (11570) ***(G-14236)***
Mercury Envelope Printing, Rockville Centre *Also called Mercury Envelope Co Inc* ***(G-14236)***
Mercury Lock and Door Service...718 542-7048
529 C Wortham St Bronx (10474) ***(G-1327)***
Mercury Paint Corporation (PA)...718 469-8787
4808 Farragut Rd Brooklyn (11203) ***(G-2194)***
Mercury Pen Company Inc...518 899-9653
245 Eastline Rd Ballston Lake (12019) ***(G-569)***
Mercury Plastics Corp...718 498-5400
989 Utica Ave 995 Brooklyn (11203) ***(G-2195)***
Mercury Print Productions Inc (PA)...585 458-7900
2332 Innovation Way 4 Rochester (14624) ***(G-13936)***
Meredith Corporate Solutions, New York *Also called Four M Studios* ***(G-9830)***
Meredith Hispanic Ventures, New York *Also called Four M Studios* ***(G-9831)***
Mergence Studios Ltd...212 288-5616
135 Ricefield Ln Hauppauge (11788) ***(G-5887)***
Mergent Inc...212 413-7700
444 Madison Ave Ste 502 New York (10022) ***(G-10773)***
Meridian Adhesives Group LLC (PA)...212 771-1717
100 Park Ave Fl 31 New York (10017) ***(G-10774)***
Meridian Manufacturing Inc...518 885-0450
27 Kent St Ste 103a Ballston Spa (12020) ***(G-590)***
Meridian Technologies Inc...516 285-1000
700 Elmont Rd Elmont (11003) ***(G-4521)***
Merit Electronic Design Co Inc...631 667-9699
190 Rodeo Dr Edgewood (11717) ***(G-4409)***
Meritool LLC...716 699-6005
4496 Route 353 Salamanca (14779) ***(G-14527)***
Merkos Bookstore, Brooklyn *Also called Merkos Llnyonei Chinuch Inc* ***(G-2196)***
Merkos Llnyonei Chinuch Inc...718 778-0226
291 Kingston Ave Brooklyn (11213) ***(G-2196)***
Merrill Communications, New York *Also called Merrill New York Company Inc* ***(G-10778)***
Merrill Communications LLC...212 620-5600
1345 Ave Of The Amrcs 1 New York (10105) ***(G-10775)***
Merrill Corporation...917 934-7300
25 W 45th St Ste 900 New York (10036) ***(G-10776)***
Merrill Corporation...212 620-5600
1345 Ave Of The Ave Fl 17 Flr 17 New York (10105) ***(G-10777)***
Merrill New York Company Inc...212 229-6500
246 W 54th St New York (10019) ***(G-10778)***
Merrill Press, Buffalo *Also called Complemar Print LLC* ***(G-2776)***
Merrimac Leasing, Johnstown *Also called Lee Dyeing Company NC Inc* ***(G-6834)***
Merritt Estate Winery Inc...716 965-4800
2264 King Rd Forestville (14062) ***(G-5086)***
Merritt Machinery LLC...716 434-5558
10 Simonds St Lockport (14094) ***(G-7315)***
Meryl Diamond Ltd (PA)...212 730-0333
1375 Broadway Fl 9 New York (10018) ***(G-10779)***
Merz Metal & Machine Corp...716 893-7786
237 Chelsea Pl Buffalo (14211) ***(G-2944)***
Merzon Leather Co Inc...718 782-6260
810 Humboldt St Ste 2 Brooklyn (11222) ***(G-2197)***
Mesh LLC...646 839-7000
350 5th Ave Lbby 9 New York (10118) ***(G-10780)***
Mesoblast Inc...212 880-2060
505 5th Ave Fl 3 New York (10017) ***(G-10781)***
Mesorah Publications Ltd...718 921-9000
4401 2nd Ave Brooklyn (11232) ***(G-2198)***
Messenger Post Media, Canandaigua *Also called Wolfe Publications Inc* ***(G-3236)***
Messenger Press...518 885-9231
1826 Amsterdam Rd Ballston Spa (12020) ***(G-591)***
Messex Group Inc...646 229-2582
244 5th Ave Ste D256 New York (10001) ***(G-10782)***
Mestel Brothers Stairs & Rails...516 496-4127
11 Gary Rd Ste 102 Syosset (11791) ***(G-15222)***
Met Weld International LLC...518 765-2318
5727 Ostrander Rd Altamont (12009) ***(G-199)***
Meta Pharmacy Systems Inc...516 488-6189
401 Franklin Ave Ste 106 Garden City (11530) ***(G-5271)***
Meta-Therm Corp...914 697-4840
70 W Red Oak Ln White Plains (10604) ***(G-16476)***
Metadure Parts & Sales Inc...631 249-2141
165 Gazza Blvd Farmingdale (11735) ***(G-4821)***
Metal Cladding Inc...716 434-5513
230 S Niagara St Lockport (14094) ***(G-7316)***
Metal Coated Fibers Inc...518 280-8514
679 Mariaville Rd Schenectady (12306) ***(G-14697)***
Metal Concepts...845 592-1863
9 Hanna Ln 12 Beacon (12508) ***(G-760)***
Metal Container Corporation...845 567-1500
1000 Breunig Rd New Windsor (12553) ***(G-8650)***
Metal Crafts Inc...718 443-3333
650 Berriman St Brooklyn (11208) ***(G-2199)***
Metal Dynamics Intl Corp...631 231-1153
25 Corporate Dr Hauppauge (11788) ***(G-5888)***
Metal Fab LLC...607 775-3200
13 Spud Ln Binghamton (13904) ***(G-905)***
Metal Improvement Company LLC...631 567-2610
210 Candlewood Rd Bay Shore (11706) ***(G-700)***
Metal Improvement Company LLC...607 533-7000
131 Woodsedge Dr Lansing (14882) ***(G-7056)***
Metal Man Restoration...914 662-4218
254 E 3rd St Fl 1 Mount Vernon (10553) ***(G-8421)***
Metal Man Services, Watertown *Also called Kenal Services Corp* ***(G-16020)***
Metal Products Intl LLC...716 215-1930
7510 Porter Rd Ste 4 Niagara Falls (14304) ***(G-12309)***
Metal Solutions Inc...315 732-6271
1821 Broad St Ste 5 Utica (13501) ***(G-15719)***
Metal Stampings, Honeoye Falls *Also called Stever-Locke Industries Inc* ***(G-6274)***
Metal Tek Products...516 586-4514
100 Express St Plainview (11803) ***(G-13073)***
Metal Works of NY Inc...718 525-9440
11603 Merrick Blvd Jamaica (11434) ***(G-6660)***
Metalcraft By N Barzel, Brooklyn *Also called Metal Crafts Inc* ***(G-2199)***
Metalcraft Marine Us Inc...315 501-4015
583 E Broadway St Cape Vincent (13618) ***(G-3259)***
Metalico Aluminum Recovery Inc...315 463-9500
6223 Thompson Rd Syracuse (13206) ***(G-15370)***
Metallic Ladder Mfg Corp...716 358-6201
41 S Washington St Randolph (14772) ***(G-13448)***
Metalline Fire Door Co Inc (PA)...718 583-2320
4110 Park Ave Bronx (10457) ***(G-1328)***
Metallized Carbon Corporation (PA)...914 941-3738
19 S Water St Ossining (10562) ***(G-12771)***
Metallogix Design Fabrication...315 738-4554
1305 Conkling Ave Utica (13501) ***(G-15720)***
Metalocke Industries Inc...718 267-9200
3202 57th St Woodside (11377) ***(G-16663)***
Metals Building Products...844 638-2527
5005 Veterans Mem Hwy Holbrook (11741) ***(G-6199)***
Metalsigma Usa Inc...212 731-4346
350 5th Ave New York (10118) ***(G-10783)***
Metalsmith Inc...631 467-1500
1340 Lincoln Ave Ste 13 Holbrook (11741) ***(G-6200)***
Metalworks Inc...718 319-0011
1303 Herschell St Bronx (10461) ***(G-1329)***
Metcar Products, Ossining *Also called Metallized Carbon Corporation* ***(G-12771)***
Meteor Express Inc...718 551-9177
16801 Rockaway Blvd # 202 Jamaica (11434) ***(G-6661)***
Methods Tooling & Mfg Inc...845 246-7100
635 Glasco Tpke Mount Marion (12456) ***(G-8364)***
Metpar Corp...516 333-2600
95 State St Westbury (11590) ***(G-16356)***
Metro Center Western New York, Buffalo *Also called William S Hein & Co Inc* ***(G-3132)***
Metro City Group Inc...516 781-2500
2283 Bellmore Ave Bellmore (11710) ***(G-789)***
Metro Creative Graphics Inc (PA)...212 947-5100
519 8th Ave Fl 18 New York (10018) ***(G-10784)***
Metro Door Inc (HQ)...800 669-3667
2929 Express Dr N 300b Islandia (11749) ***(G-6535)***
Metro Duct Systems Inc...718 278-4294
1219 Astoria Blvd Apt 2 Long Island City (11102) ***(G-7522)***
Metro Dynamics Scie...631 842-4300
20 Nancy St Unit A West Babylon (11704) ***(G-16176)***
Metro Fuel LLC...212 836-9608
800 3rd Ave Fl 28 New York (10022) ***(G-10785)***
Metro Group Inc (PA)...718 729-7200
5023 23rd St Long Island City (11101) ***(G-7523)***
Metro Group Inc...716 434-4055
8 South St Lockport (14094) ***(G-7317)***
Metro Grouping, Long Island City *Also called Metro Group Inc* ***(G-7523)***
Metro Iron Corp...631 842-5929
4 Seabro Ave Amityville (11701) ***(G-303)***
Metro Kitchens Corp...718 434-1166
1040 E 45th St Brooklyn (11203) ***(G-2200)***
Metro Lube (PA)...718 947-1167
9110 Metropolitan Ave Rego Park (11374) ***(G-13465)***
Metro Machining & Fabricating...718 545-0104
3234 61st St Woodside (11377) ***(G-16664)***
Metro Mattress Corp...716 205-2300
2212 Military Rd Niagara Falls (14304) ***(G-12310)***
Metro Nespaper, New York *Also called Seabay Media Holdings LLC* ***(G-11525)***
Metro New York, New York *Also called Sb New York Inc* ***(G-11496)***
Metro Products & Services LLC (PA)...866 846-8486
1424 74th St Brooklyn (11228) ***(G-2201)***
Metro Service Center, Elmsford *Also called Westinghouse A Brake Tech Corp* ***(G-4577)***
Metro Service Solutions, Islandia *Also called Metro Door Inc* ***(G-6535)***
METRO STORAGE CENTER, Getzville *Also called William S Hein & Co Inc* ***(G-5356)***
Metro Tel Communications, Staten Island *Also called I D Tel Corp* ***(G-15087)***
Metrofab Pipe Incorporated...516 349-7373
15 Fairchild Ct Plainview (11803) ***(G-13074)***
Metropltan Data Sltons MGT Inc...516 586-5520
279 Conklin St Farmingdale (11735) ***(G-4822)***
Metropolis Magazine, New York *Also called Bellerophon Publications Inc* ***(G-9040)***
Metropolitan Granite & MBL Inc...585 342-7020
860 Maple St Ste 100 Rochester (14611) ***(G-13937)***
Metropolitan Packg Mfg Corp...718 383-2700
68 Java St Brooklyn (11222) ***(G-2202)***
Metropolitan Signs Inc...315 638-1448
3760 Patchett Rd Baldwinsville (13027) ***(G-558)***

Metrosource Publishing Inc 212 691-5127
498 Fashion Ave Fl 10 New York (10018) *(G-10786)*
Mettowee Lumber & Plastics Co 518 642-1100
82 Church St Granville (12832) *(G-5522)*
Mexico Independent Inc (PA) 315 963-3763
260 Washington St Watertown (13601) *(G-16027)*
Meyco Products Inc (PA) 631 421-9800
1225 Walt Whitman Rd Melville (11747) *(G-8046)*
Mezmeriz Inc 607 216-8140
33 Thornwood Dr Ste 100 Ithaca (14850) *(G-6595)*
Mf Digital, Deer Park *Also called Formats Unlimited Inc (G-3978)*
Mg Imaging 212 704-4073
229 W 28th St Rm 300 New York (10001) *(G-10787)*
Mgd Brands Inc 516 545-0150
30 Commercial Ct Plainview (11803) *(G-13075)*
Mgi, Hauppauge *Also called Mini Graphics Inc (G-5893)*
Mgi, Northport *Also called Marketing Group International (G-12472)*
Mgk Group Inc 212 989-2732
979 3rd Ave Ste 1811 New York (10022) *(G-10788)*
Mgr Equipment Corp 516 239-3030
22 Gates Ave Inwood (11096) *(G-6495)*
Mgs Group, The, Rome *Also called MGS Manufacturing Inc (G-14258)*
MGS Manufacturing Inc (PA) 315 337-3350
122 Otis St Rome (13441) *(G-14258)*
Mht Lighting, Staten Island *Also called North American Mfg Entps Inc (G-15109)*
Mhxco Foam Company LLC 518 843-8400
120 Edson St Amsterdam (12010) *(G-347)*
Miami Media LLC (HQ) 212 268-8600
72 Madison Ave Fl 11 New York (10016) *(G-10789)*
Mibro Group 716 631-5713
4039 Genesee St Buffalo (14225) *(G-2945)*
Mica America, Bay Shore *Also called Fenix Furniture Co (G-686)*
Mica International Ltd 516 378-3400
126 Albany Ave Freeport (11520) *(G-5167)*
Mica World, Huntington Station *Also called Huntington Woodworking Inc (G-6446)*
Micatu Inc 888 705-8836
315 Daniel Zenker Dr # 202 Horseheads (14845) *(G-6319)*
Micelli Chocalate Mold Co, West Babylon *Also called Sweet Tooth Enterprises LLC (G-16199)*
Michael Andrews Bespoke, New York *Also called Michael Andrews LLC (G-10790)*
Michael Andrews LLC 212 677-1755
680 Broadway Fl Mezz New York (10012) *(G-10790)*
Michael Benalt Inc 845 628-1008
100 Buckshollow Rd Mahopac (10541) *(G-7708)*
Michael Bernstein Design Assoc 718 456-9277
361 Stagg St Fl 4 Brooklyn (11206) *(G-2203)*
Michael Bondanza Inc 212 869-0043
10 E 38th St Fl 6 New York (10016) *(G-10791)*
Michael Feldman Inc 718 433-1700
3010 41st Ave Ste 3 Long Island City (11101) *(G-7524)*
Michael Fiore Ltd 516 561-8238
126 E Fairview Ave Valley Stream (11580) *(G-15786)*
Michael K Lennon Inc 631 288-5200
851 Riverhead Rd Westhampton Beach (11978) *(G-16404)*
Michael Karp Music Inc 212 840-3285
59 W 71st St Apt 7a New York (10023) *(G-10792)*
Michael Kors, New York *Also called Herman Kay Company Ltd (G-10083)*
Michael Neuman, Rye *Also called Western Oil and Gas JV Inc (G-14489)*
Michael P Mmarr 315 623-9380
1358 State Route 49 Constantia (13044) *(G-3740)*
Michael Stuart Inc 718 821-0704
199 Cook St Brooklyn (11206) *(G-2204)*
Michael Todd Stevens 585 436-9957
95 Mount Read Blvd # 125 Rochester (14611) *(G-13938)*
Michaelian & Kohlberg Inc 212 431-9009
225 E 59th St New York (10022) *(G-10793)*
Michbi Doors Inc 631 231-9050
75 Emjay Blvd Brentwood (11717) *(G-1142)*
Mickelberry Communications Inc (PA) 212 832-0303
405 Park Ave New York (10022) *(G-10794)*
Micosta Enterprises Inc 518 822-9708
3007 County Route 20 Hudson (12534) *(G-6364)*
Micro Contacts Inc (PA) 516 433-4830
1 Enterprise Pl Unit E Hicksville (11801) *(G-6109)*
Micro Contract Manufacturing 631 738-7874
27 Scouting Blvd Unit E Medford (11763) *(G-7961)*
Micro Essential Laboratory 718 338-3618
4224 Avenue H Brooklyn (11210) *(G-2205)*
Micro Graphics, Lockport *Also called Jack J Florio Jr (G-7311)*
Micro Instrument Corp 585 458-3150
1199 Emerson St Rochester (14606) *(G-13939)*
Micro Photo Acoustics Inc 631 750-6035
105 Comac St Ronkonkoma (11779) *(G-14377)*
Micro Powders Inc (PA) 914 332-6400
580 White Plains Rd # 400 Tarrytown (10591) *(G-15483)*
Micro Publishing Inc 212 533-9180
71 W 23rd St Lbby A New York (10010) *(G-10795)*
Micro Semicdtr Researches LLC (PA) 646 863-6070
310 W 52nd St Apt 12b New York (10019) *(G-10796)*
Micro Systems Specialists Inc 845 677-6150
3280 Franklin Ave Fl 2 Millbrook (12545) *(G-8189)*
Micro Threaded Products Inc 585 288-0080
325 Mount Read Blvd Ste 4 Rochester (14611) *(G-13940)*
Micro-Tech Machine Inc 315 331-6671
301 W Shore Blvd Newark (14513) *(G-12201)*
Microb Phase Services 518 877-8948
14 Nottingham Way S Clifton Park (12065) *(G-3571)*
Microcad Trning Consulting Inc 617 923-0500
1110 Route 55 Ste 209 Lagrangeville (12540) *(G-6959)*
Microcad Trning Consulting Inc 631 291-9484
77 Arkay Dr Ste C2 Hauppauge (11788) *(G-5889)*
Microchip Technology Inc 631 233-3280
80 Arkay Dr Ste 100 Hauppauge (11788) *(G-5890)*
Microchip Technology Inc 607 785-5992
3301 Country Club Rd Endicott (13760) *(G-4602)*
Microera Printers Inc 585 783-1300
304 Whitney St Rochester (14606) *(G-13941)*
Microfoam, Utica *Also called Idg LLC (G-15712)*
Microgen Systems Inc 585 214-2426
3 Railroad St Ste D Fairport (14450) *(G-4642)*
Micromatter Tech Inc USA 631 580-2522
1340 Lincoln Ave Ste 6 Holbrook (11741) *(G-6201)*
Micromem Technologies 212 672-1806
245 Park Ave Fl 24 New York (10167) *(G-10797)*
Micromod Automation Inc 585 321-9200
3 Townline Cir Ste 4 Rochester (14623) *(G-13942)*
Micromod Automtn & Contrls Inc 585 321-9209
3 Townline Cir Ste 4 Rochester (14623) *(G-13943)*
Micromold Products Inc 914 969-2850
7 Odell Plz 133 Yonkers (10701) *(G-16784)*
Micron Inds Rochester Inc 585 247-6130
31 Industrial Park Cir Rochester (14624) *(G-13944)*
Micropage, New York *Also called Micro Publishing Inc (G-10795)*
MICROPEN DIVISION, Honeoye Falls *Also called Micropen Technologies Corp (G-6271)*
Micropen Technologies Corp 585 624-2610
93 Papermill St Honeoye Falls (14472) *(G-6271)*
Microsoft Corporation 914 323-2150
125 Westchester Ave White Plains (10601) *(G-16477)*
Microsoft Corporation 631 760-2340
160 Walt Whitman Rd 1006b Huntington Station (11746) *(G-6452)*
Microsoft Corporation 212 245-2100
11 Times Sq Fl 9 New York (10036) *(G-10798)*
Microsoft Corporation 516 380-1531
2929 Expressway Dr N # 300 Hauppauge (11749) *(G-5891)*
Microstrategy Incorporated 888 537-8135
5 Penn Plz Ste 901 New York (10001) *(G-10799)*
Microwave Filter Company Inc (PA) 315 438-4700
6743 Kinne St East Syracuse (13057) *(G-4358)*
Mid Atlantic Graphics Corp 631 345-3800
14 Ramsey Rd Shirley (11967) *(G-14840)*
Mid Enterprise Inc 631 924-3933
809 Middle Country Rd Middle Island (11953) *(G-8118)*
Mid Hdson Wkshp For The Dsbled 845 471-3820
188 Washington St Poughkeepsie (12601) *(G-13354)*
Mid Island Die Cutting Corp 631 293-0180
77 Schmitt Blvd Farmingdale (11735) *(G-4823)*
Mid Island Group 631 293-0180
77 Schmitt Blvd Farmingdale (11735) *(G-4824)*
Mid York Weekly & Pennysaver 315 792-4990
221 Oriskany St E Utica (13501) *(G-15721)*
Mid-Hudson Concrete Pdts Inc 845 265-3141
3504 Route 9 Cold Spring (10516) *(G-3625)*
Mid-Island Bindery Inc 631 293-0180
77 Schmitt Blvd Farmingdale (11735) *(G-4825)*
Mid-State Ready Mix, Central Square *Also called Torrington Industries Inc (G-3392)*
Mid-York Press Inc 607 674-4491
2808 State Highway 80 Sherburne (13460) *(G-14807)*
Midas Mdici Group Holdings Inc (PA) 212 792-0920
445 Park Ave Frnt 5 New York (10022) *(G-10800)*
Midbury Industries Inc 516 868-0600
86 E Merrick Rd Freeport (11520) *(G-5168)*
Middle Ages Brewing Company 315 476-4250
120 Wilkinson St Ste 3 Syracuse (13204) *(G-15371)*
Middleby Corporation 631 226-6688
175 E Hoffman Ave Lindenhurst (11757) *(G-7180)*
Middletown Press (PA) 845 343-1895
20 W Main St 26 Middletown (10940) *(G-8164)*
Midgley Printing Corp 315 475-1864
433 W Onondaga St Ste B Syracuse (13202) *(G-15372)*
Midland Farms Inc (PA) 518 436-7038
375 Broadway Menands (12204) *(G-8089)*
Midland Machinery Co Inc 716 692-1200
101 Cranbrook Road Ext Exd Tonawanda (14150) *(G-15558)*
Midstate Printing Corp 315 475-4101
4707 Dey Rd Liverpool (13088) *(G-7247)*
Midstate Spring Inc 315 437-2623
4054 New Court Ave Syracuse (13206) *(G-15373)*
Midura Jewels Inc 213 265-8090
36 W 47th St Ste 809i New York (10036) *(G-10801)*
Miggins Screw Products Inc 845 279-2307
66 Putnam Ave Brewster (10509) *(G-1172)*
Mighty Quinns Barbeque LLC 973 777-8340
103 2nd Ave Frnt 1 New York (10003) *(G-10802)*

ALPHABETIC

(PA)=Parent Co (HQ)=Headquarters (DH)=Div Headquarters
2019 Harris
New York Manufacturers Directory
937

Miguelina Inc ALPHABETIC SECTION

Miguelina Inc 212 925-0320
325 W 37th St Fl 2 New York (10018) **(G-10803)**
Mikael Aghal LLC 212 596-4010
49 W 38th St Fl 4 New York (10018) **(G-10804)**
Mikam Graphics LLC 212 684-9393
1440 Broadway Fl 22 New York (10018) **(G-10805)**
Mike's Custom Cabinets, Constantia *Also called Michael P Mmarr* **(G-3740)**
Miken Companies Inc 716 668-6311
75 Boxwood Ln Buffalo (14227) **(G-2946)**
Mil & Mir Steel Products Co 718 328-7596
1210 Randall Ave Bronx (10474) **(G-1330)**
Mil-Spec. Enterprises, Brooklyn *Also called Carter Enterprises LLC* **(G-1679)**
Milaaya Embroideries, New York *Also called Milaaya Inc* **(G-10806)**
Milaaya Inc 212 764-6386
147 W 35th St Ste 602 New York (10001) **(G-10806)**
Milan Provision Co Inc 718 899-7678
10815 Roosevelt Ave Corona (11368) **(G-3850)**
Milanese Commercial Door LLC 518 658-0398
28 Taylor Ave Berlin (12022) **(G-832)**
Milano Granite and Marble Corp 718 477-7200
3521 Victory Blvd Staten Island (10314) **(G-15105)**
Milburn Printing, Bohemia *Also called Mpe Graphics Inc* **(G-1060)**
Miles Machine Inc 716 484-6026
85 Jones And Gifford Ave Jamestown (14701) **(G-6739)**
Milestone Construction Corp 718 459-8500
9229 Queens Blvd Ste C2 Rego Park (11374) **(G-13466)**
Milex Precision Inc 631 595-2393
66 S 2nd St Ste G Bay Shore (11706) **(G-701)**
Milgo Industrial, Brooklyn *Also called M B C Metal Inc* **(G-2145)**
Milgo Industrial Inc (PA) 718 388-6476
68 Lombardy St Brooklyn (11222) **(G-2206)**
Milgo Industrial Inc 718 387-0406
514 Varick Ave Brooklyn (11222) **(G-2207)**
Milgo/Bufkin, Brooklyn *Also called Milgo Industrial Inc* **(G-2206)**
Military Parts Exchange LLC 631 243-1700
145 Pinelawn Rd Ste 240n Melville (11747) **(G-8047)**
Milkboy, Brooklyn *Also called Menrose USA LLC* **(G-2191)**
Mill Services, Cobleskill *Also called Efj Inc* **(G-3602)**
Mill, The, Corning *Also called Ryers Creek Corp* **(G-3825)**
Mill-Max Mfg Corp 516 922-6000
190 Pine Hollow Rd Oyster Bay (11771) **(G-12815)**
Millbrook Vineyard, Millbrook *Also called Millbrook Winery Inc* **(G-8190)**
Millbrook Winery Inc 845 677-8383
26 Wing Rd Millbrook (12545) **(G-8190)**
Millco Woodworking LLC 585 526-6844
1710 Railroad Pl Hall (14463) **(G-5671)**
Millennium Antenna Corp 315 798-9374
1001 Broad St Ste 401 Utica (13501) **(G-15722)**
Millennium Medical Publishing 212 995-2211
611 Broadway Rm 310 New York (10012) **(G-10807)**
Millennium Productions Inc 212 944-6203
265 W 37th St 11 New York (10018) **(G-10808)**
Millennium Rmnfctred Toner Inc 718 585-9887
7 Bruckner Blvd Bronx (10454) **(G-1331)**
Millennium Signs & Display Inc 516 292-8000
90 W Graham Ave Hempstead (11550) **(G-6021)**
Millennium Stl Rack Rntals Inc (PA) 718 965-4736
253 Bond St Brooklyn (11217) **(G-2208)**
Miller & Berkowitz Ltd 212 244-5459
345 7th Ave Fl 20 New York (10001) **(G-10809)**
Miller & Veit Inc 212 247-2275
22 W 48th St Ste 703 New York (10036) **(G-10810)**
Miller Blaker Inc 718 665-0500
620 E 132nd St Bronx (10454) **(G-1332)**
Miller Mechanical Services Inc 518 792-0430
55-57 Walnut St Glens Falls (12801) **(G-5434)**
Miller Metal Fabricating Inc 585 359-3400
315 Commerce Dr Rochester (14623) **(G-13945)**
Miller Mohr Display Inc 631 941-2769
12 Technology Dr Unit 6 East Setauket (11733) **(G-4304)**
Miller Place Printing Inc 631 473-1158
451 Route 25a Unit 11 Miller Place (11764) **(G-8191)**
Miller Printing & Litho Inc 518 842-0001
97 Guy Park Ave Amsterdam (12010) **(G-348)**
Miller Stuart, Hauppauge *Also called Compac Development Corporation* **(G-5797)**
Miller Technology Inc 631 694-2224
61 Gazza Blvd Farmingdale (11735) **(G-4826)**
Miller Truck Rental, Scottsville *Also called Jack W Miller* **(G-14751)**
Miller's Ready Mix, Gloversville *Also called Stephen Miller Gen Contrs Inc* **(G-5467)**
Millercoors LLC 585 385-0670
1000 Pittsford Victor Rd Pittsford (14534) **(G-13022)**
Millers Bulk Food and Bakery 585 798-9700
10858 Ridge Rd Medina (14103) **(G-7984)**
Millers Millworks Inc 585 494-1420
29 N Lake Ave Bergen (14416) **(G-825)**
Millers Presentation Furniture, Bergen *Also called Millers Millworks Inc* **(G-825)**
Milli Home, New York *Also called Global Resources Sg Inc* **(G-9945)**
Milligan & Higgins Div, Johnstown *Also called Hudson Industries Corporation* **(G-6831)**
Milliore Fashion Inc 212 302-0001
250 W 39th St Rm 506 New York (10018) **(G-10811)**
Millivac Instruments Inc 518 355-8300
2818 Curry Rd Schenectady (12303) **(G-14698)**
Millrock Technology Inc 845 339-5700
39 Kieffer Ln Ste 2 Kingston (12401) **(G-6911)**
Mills, William J & Company, Greenport *Also called 125-127 Main Street Corp* **(G-5625)**
Millwood Inc 518 233-1475
430 Hudson River Rd Waterford (12188) **(G-15978)**
Millwright Wdwrk Installetion 631 587-2635
991 Peconic Ave West Babylon (11704) **(G-16177)**
Milmar Food Group, Goshen *Also called Juno Chefs* **(G-5480)**
Milmar Food Group II LLC 845 294-5400
1 6 1/2 Station Rd Goshen (10924) **(G-5482)**
Milne Mfg Inc 716 772-2536
8411 State St Gasport (14067) **(G-5308)**
Milnot Holding Corporation 518 839-0300
1 Nutritious Pl Amsterdam (12010) **(G-349)**
Milso Industries Inc 631 234-1133
25 Engineers Rd Hauppauge (11788) **(G-5892)**
Milton Merl & Associates Inc 212 634-9292
647 W 174th St Bsmt B New York (10033) **(G-10812)**
Miltons of New York Inc 212 997-3359
110 W 40th St Rm 1001 New York (10018) **(G-10813)**
Milward Alloys Inc 716 434-5536
500 Mill St Lockport (14094) **(G-7318)**
Mima S Bakery, Brooklyn *Also called Vito & Sons Bakery* **(G-2631)**
Mimeocom Inc (PA) 212 847-3000
3 Park Ave Fl 22 New York (10016) **(G-10814)**
Mimi So International LLC 212 300-8600
22 W 48th St Ste 902 New York (10036) **(G-10815)**
Mimi So New York, New York *Also called Mimi So International LLC* **(G-10815)**
Min Ho Designs Inc 212 838-3667
425 Madison Ave Rm 1703 New York (10017) **(G-10816)**
Min New York, New York *Also called Salonclick LLC* **(G-11472)**
Min-Max Machine Ltd 631 585-4378
1971 Pond Rd Ronkonkoma (11779) **(G-14378)**
Mind Designs Inc (PA) 631 563-3644
5 Gregory Ct Farmingville (11738) **(G-4924)**
Mindbodygreen LLC 347 529-6952
45 Main St Ste 422 Brooklyn (11201) **(G-2209)**
Mine Defense Systems, Amityville *Also called Edo LLC* **(G-272)**
Mineo & Sapio Meats Inc 716 884-2398
410 Connecticut St Buffalo (14213) **(G-2947)**
Mineralbious Corp 516 498-9715
28 Northcote Rd Westbury (11590) **(G-16357)**
Minerals Technologies Inc (PA) 212 878-1800
622 3rd Ave Rm 3800 New York (10017) **(G-10817)**
Minero & Sapio Sausage, Buffalo *Also called Mineo & Sapio Meats Inc* **(G-2947)**
Mines Press Inc 914 788-1800
231 Croton Ave Cortlandt Manor (10567) **(G-3903)**
Ming Pao (new York) Inc 718 786-2888
4331 33rd St Fl 2 Long Island City (11101) **(G-7525)**
Ming Pao (new York) Inc 212 334-2220
265 Canal St Ste 403 New York (10013) **(G-10818)**
Ming Pao (new York) Inc (HQ) 718 786-2888
4331 33rd St Long Island City (11101) **(G-7526)**
Ming Pao Daily News, New York, Long Island City *Also called Ming Pao (new York) Inc* **(G-7525)**
Ming Pay N Y, Long Island City *Also called Ming Pao (new York) Inc* **(G-7526)**
Mini Circuits, Brooklyn *Also called Scientific Components Corp* **(G-2453)**
Mini Circuits Lab, Deer Park *Also called Scientific Components Corp* **(G-4042)**
Mini Graphics Inc 516 223-6464
140 Commerce Dr Hauppauge (11788) **(G-5893)**
Mini-Circuits, Brooklyn *Also called Scientific Components Corp* **(G-2452)**
Mini-Circuits Fort Wayne LLC 718 934-4500
13 Neptune Ave Brooklyn (11235) **(G-2210)**
Mini-Max Dntl Repr Eqpmnts Inc 631 242-0322
25 W Jefryn Blvd Ste B Deer Park (11729) **(G-4010)**
Minico Industries Inc 631 595-1455
66a S 2nd St Ste A Bay Shore (11706) **(G-702)**
Minimill Technologies Inc 315 692-4557
5792 Widewaters Pkwy # 1 Syracuse (13214) **(G-15374)**
Minisink Rubber, Warwick *Also called Mechanical Rubber Pdts Co Inc* **(G-15958)**
Minitec Framing Systems LLC 585 924-4690
5602 County Road 41 Farmington (14425) **(G-4917)**
Mink Mart Inc 212 868-2785
345 7th Ave Fl 9 New York (10001) **(G-10819)**
Minority Reporter Inc (PA) 585 225-3628
19 Borrowdale Dr Rochester (14626) **(G-13946)**
Mint-X Products Corporation 877 646-8224
2048 119th St College Point (11356) **(G-3656)**
Minted Green Inc 845 458-1845
85 Regina Rd Airmont (10952) **(G-15)**
Minute Man Printing Company, White Plains *Also called Garrett J Cronin* **(G-16452)**
Minuteman Press, Manhasset *Also called Mdr Printing Corp* **(G-7769)**
Minuteman Press, Port Washington *Also called Kurtskraft Inc* **(G-13280)**
Minuteman Press, Hewlett *Also called Torsaf Printers Inc* **(G-6051)**
Minuteman Press, Glen Oaks *Also called Wynco Press One Inc* **(G-5388)**
Minuteman Press, Deer Park *Also called L & K Graphics Inc* **(G-3997)**
Minuteman Press, Huntington *Also called J A T Printing Inc* **(G-6401)**

Minuteman Press, East Syracuse *Also called Seaboard Graphic Services LLC* ***(G-4369)***
Minuteman Press, Hauppauge *Also called Huckleberry Inc* ***(G-5847)***
Minuteman Press, Bellerose *Also called Leigh Scott Enterprises Inc* ***(G-781)***
Minuteman Press, Adams *Also called Benjamin Printing Inc* ***(G-2)***
Minuteman Press, Rockville Centre *Also called Graphic Fabrications Inc* ***(G-14232)***
Minuteman Press, Elmsford *Also called Cronin Enterprises Inc* ***(G-4540)***
Minuteman Press, Rochester *Also called Baum Christine and John Corp* ***(G-13654)***
Minuteman Press, Selden *Also called Datorib Inc* ***(G-14763)***
Minuteman Press, Rochester *Also called Multiple Imprssons of Rchester* ***(G-13960)***
Minuteman Press, Fairport *Also called Bernard Hall* ***(G-4625)***
Minuteman Press, Farmingdale *Also called J P Printing Inc* ***(G-4790)***
Minuteman Press, Merrick *Also called Jon Lyn Ink Inc* ***(G-8099)***
Minuteman Press, East Northport *Also called Loudon Ltd* ***(G-4267)***
Minuteman Press Inc....845 623-2277
121 W Nyack Rd Ste 3 Nanuet (10954) ***(G-8466)***
Minuteman Press Intl Inc....718 343-5440
24814 Union Tpke Jamaica (11426) ***(G-6662)***
Minutemen Precision Mch & Tl, Ronkonkoma *Also called Minutemen Precsn McHning Tool* ***(G-14379)***
Minutemen Precsn McHning Tool....631 467-4900
135 Raynor Ave Ronkonkoma (11779) ***(G-14379)***
Miny Group Inc....212 925-6722
148 Lafayette St Fl 2 New York (10013) ***(G-10820)***
Minyanville Media Inc....212 991-6200
708 3rd Ave Fl 6 New York (10017) ***(G-10821)***
Mip, Halesite *Also called Manufacturers Indexing Pdts* ***(G-5658)***
Mirage Moulding & Supply, Farmingdale *Also called Mirage Moulding Mfg Inc* ***(G-4827)***
Mirage Moulding Mfg Inc....631 843-6168
160 Milbar Blvd Farmingdale (11735) ***(G-4827)***
Mirandy Products Ltd....516 489-6800
1078 Grand Ave South Hempstead (11550) ***(G-14942)***
Mirion Tech Conax Nuclear Inc....716 681-1973
402 Sonwil Dr Buffalo (14225) ***(G-2948)***
Mirion Tech Imaging LLC....607 562-4300
315 Daniel Zenker Dr Horseheads (14845) ***(G-6320)***
Mirion Tech Imging Systems Div, Horseheads *Also called Mirion Tech Imaging LLC* ***(G-6320)***
Mirion Technologies Ist Corp (HQ)....607 562-4300
315 Daniel Zenker Dr # 204 Horseheads (14845) ***(G-6321)***
Miroddi Imaging Inc (PA)....516 624-6898
27 Centre View Dr Oyster Bay (11771) ***(G-12816)***
Mirror-Tech Manufacturing Co....914 965-1232
286 Nepperhan Ave Yonkers (10701) ***(G-16785)***
Mirrorlite Superscript, Peekskill *Also called Hudson Mirror LLC* ***(G-12922)***
Miscellnous Ir Fabricators Inc....518 355-1822
1404 Dunnsville Rd Schenectady (12306) ***(G-14699)***
Mishpacha Magazine Inc....718 686-9339
5809 16th Ave Brooklyn (11204) ***(G-2211)***
Mison Concepts Inc....516 933-8000
485 S Broadway Ste 33 Hicksville (11801) ***(G-6110)***
Misonix Inc (PA)....631 694-9555
1938 New Hwy Farmingdale (11735) ***(G-4828)***
Miss Grimble Associates Inc....718 665-2253
909 E 135th St Bronx (10454) ***(G-1333)***
Miss Group (PA)....212 391-2535
1410 Broadway Rm 703 New York (10018) ***(G-10822)***
Miss Group, The, Brooklyn *Also called MISS Sportswear Inc* ***(G-2213)***
Miss Group, The, Brooklyn *Also called MISS Sportswear Inc* ***(G-2214)***
Miss Jessies LLC....718 643-9016
441 Broadway Fl 2 New York (10013) ***(G-10823)***
Miss Jessies Products, New York *Also called Miss Jessies LLC* ***(G-10823)***
MISS Sportswear Inc....212 391-2535
117 9th St Brooklyn (11215) ***(G-2212)***
MISS Sportswear Inc (PA)....212 391-2535
117 9th St Brooklyn (11215) ***(G-2213)***
MISS Sportswear Inc....718 369-6012
117 9th St Brooklyn (11215) ***(G-2214)***
Mission Crane Service Inc (PA)....718 937-3333
4700 33rd St Long Island City (11101) ***(G-7527)***
Mission Critical Energy Inc....716 276-8465
1801 N French Rd Getzville (14068) ***(G-5349)***
Missiontex Inc....718 532-9053
236 Greenpoint Ave Ste 12 Brooklyn (11222) ***(G-2215)***
Mistdoda Inc (HQ)....919 735-7111
261 5th Ave Fl 25 New York (10016) ***(G-10824)***
Mitchell Electronics Corp....914 699-3800
85 W Grand St Mount Vernon (10552) ***(G-8422)***
Mitchell Machine Tool LLC....585 254-7520
190 Murray St Rochester (14606) ***(G-13947)***
Mitchell Prtg & Mailing Inc (PA)....315 343-3531
1 Burkle St Oswego (13126) ***(G-12781)***
Mitchell Stone Products LLC....518 359-7029
161 Main St Tupper Lake (12986) ***(G-15651)***
Mitchell's Speedway Press, Oswego *Also called Speedway Press Inc* ***(G-12788)***
Mitco Manufacturing....800 338-8908
605 Locust St Garden City (11530) ***(G-5272)***
Mitegen LLC....607 266-8877
95 Brown Rd Ste 1034 Ithaca (14850) ***(G-6596)***
Mitel Networks Inc....877 654-3573
300 State St Ste 100 Rochester (14614) ***(G-13948)***
Mitsubishi Chemical Amer Inc (PA)....212 223-3043
655 3rd Ave Fl 15 New York (10017) ***(G-10825)***
Mitsubishi Elc Pwr Pdts Inc....516 962-2813
55 Marcus Dr Melville (11747) ***(G-8048)***
Mitsui Chemicals America Inc (HQ)....914 253-0777
800 Westchester Ave N607 Rye Brook (10573) ***(G-14493)***
Mitten Manufacturing Inc....315 437-7564
5960 Court Street Rd Syracuse (13206) ***(G-15375)***
Mix N Mac LLC....845 381-5536
280 Route 211 E Middletown (10940) ***(G-8165)***
Mixture Screen Printing....845 561-2857
1607 Route 300 100 Newburgh (12550) ***(G-12232)***
Mizkan America Inc....585 798-5720
711 Park Ave Medina (14103) ***(G-7985)***
Mizkan America Inc....585 765-9171
247 West Ave Lyndonville (14098) ***(G-7680)***
Mizkan Americas Inc....315 483-6944
7673 Sodus Center Rd Sodus (14551) ***(G-14913)***
MJB Printing Corp....631 581-0177
280 Islip Ave Islip (11751) ***(G-6549)***
Mjj Brilliant, New York *Also called Brilliant Jewelers/Mjj Inc* ***(G-9142)***
Mjk Cutting Inc....718 384-7613
117 9th St Brooklyn (11215) ***(G-2216)***
Mjk Enterprises LLC....917 653-9042
34 35th St Brooklyn (11232) ***(G-2217)***
MJM Jewelry Corp (PA)....212 354-5014
29 W 38th St Rm 1601 New York (10018) ***(G-10826)***
MJM Jewelry Corp....718 596-1600
400 3rd Ave Brooklyn (11215) ***(G-2218)***
Mjs Woodworking, Bohemia *Also called J Percoco Industries Inc* ***(G-1038)***
Mkj Communications Corp....212 206-0072
850 3rd Ave Ste 402 Brooklyn (11232) ***(G-2219)***
Mks Instruments Inc....585 292-7472
100 Highpower Rd Rochester (14623) ***(G-13949)***
Mks Medical Electronics....585 292-7400
100 Highpower Rd Rochester (14623) ***(G-13950)***
Mksf Inc....212 563-3877
212 W 30th St New York (10001) ***(G-10827)***
Mkt329 Inc....631 249-5500
565 Broadhollow Rd Ste 5 Farmingdale (11735) ***(G-4829)***
MLS Sales....516 681-2736
226 10th St Bethpage (11714) ***(G-848)***
Mm of East Aurora LLC....716 651-9663
3801 Harlem Rd Buffalo (14215) ***(G-2949)***
MMC Enterprises Corp....800 435-1088
175 Commerce Dr Ste E Hauppauge (11788) ***(G-5894)***
MMC Magnetics Corp....631 435-9888
175 Commerce Dr Ste E Hauppauge (11788) ***(G-5895)***
Mml Software Ltd....631 941-1313
45 Research Way Ste 207 East Setauket (11733) ***(G-4305)***
MMS H& F Inc....718 785-6663
8745 144th St Jamaica (11435) ***(G-6663)***
Mnn Holding Company LLC....404 558-5251
155 Water St Ste 616 Brooklyn (11201) ***(G-2220)***
MNS Fuel Corp....516 735-3835
2154 Pond Rd Ronkonkoma (11779) ***(G-14380)***
Mobile Fleet Inc (PA)....631 206-2920
10 Commerce Dr Hauppauge (11788) ***(G-5896)***
Mobile Media Inc (PA)....845 744-8080
24 Center St Pine Bush (12566) ***(G-12997)***
Mobile Mini Inc....315 732-4555
2222 Oriskany St W Ste 3 Utica (13502) ***(G-15723)***
Mobile Mini Inc....631 543-4900
1158 Jericho Tpke Commack (11725) ***(G-3698)***
Mobileapp Systems LLC....716 667-2780
4 Grand View Trl Buffalo (14217) ***(G-2950)***
Mobius Labs Inc....518 961-2600
37 Vischer Ferry Rd Rexford (12148) ***(G-13481)***
Mobo Systems Inc....212 260-0895
26 Broadway Fl 24 New York (10004) ***(G-10828)***
Mod Printing, Islip *Also called MJB Printing Corp* ***(G-6549)***
Mod-A-Can Inc (PA)....516 931-8545
178 Miller Pl Hicksville (11801) ***(G-6111)***
Mod-Pac Corp (PA)....716 898-8480
1801 Elmwood Ave Ste 1 Buffalo (14207) ***(G-2951)***
Mod-Pac Corp....716 447-9013
1801 Elmwood Ave Ste 1 Buffalo (14207) ***(G-2952)***
Modern Art Foundry Inc....718 728-2030
1870 41st St Astoria (11105) ***(G-436)***
Modern Block LLC....315 923-7443
2440 Wyne Zandra Rose Vly Clyde (14433) ***(G-3596)***
Modern Cabinet Company Inc....845 473-4900
17 Van Kleeck Dr Poughkeepsie (12601) ***(G-13355)***
Modern Coating and Research....315 597-3517
400 E Main St Palmyra (14522) ***(G-12858)***
Modern Craft Bar Rest Equip, Lindenhurst *Also called Modern Craft Bar Rest Equip* ***(G-7181)***
Modern Craft Bar Rest Equip....631 226-5647
165 E Hoffman Ave Unit 3 Lindenhurst (11757) ***(G-7181)***
Modern Decal Co....315 622-2778
8146 Soule Rd Liverpool (13090) ***(G-7248)***
Modern Farmer Media Inc....518 828-7447
403 Warren St Hudson (12534) ***(G-6365)***

ALPHABETIC

Modern Itln Bky of W Babylon......631 589-7300
301 Locust Ave Oakdale (11769) *(G-12518)*
Modern Language Assn Amer Inc......646 576-5000
85 Broad St Fl 5 New York (10004) *(G-10829)*
Modern Mechanical Fab Inc......518 298-5177
100 Walnut St Ste 7 Champlain (12919) *(G-3412)*
Modern Metal Fabricators Inc......518 966-4142
799 Cr 111 Hannacroix (12087) *(G-5716)*
Modern Packaging Inc......631 595-2437
505 Acorn St Deer Park (11729) *(G-4011)*
Modern Plastic Bags Mfg Inc......718 237-2985
63 Flushing Ave Unit 303 Brooklyn (11205) *(G-2221)*
Modern Publishing, New York *Also called Unisystems Inc (G-11951)*
Modern-TEC Manufacturing Inc......716 625-8700
4935 Lockport Rd Lockport (14094) *(G-7319)*
Modo Eyewear, New York *Also called Modo Retail LLC (G-10830)*
Modo Retail LLC......212 965-4900
252 Mott St New York (10012) *(G-10830)*
Modu-Craft Inc (PA)......716 694-0709
276 Creekside Dr Tonawanda (14150) *(G-15559)*
Modu-Craft Inc......716 694-0709
337 Payne Ave North Tonawanda (14120) *(G-12438)*
Modular Devices Inc......631 345-3100
1 Roned Rd Shirley (11967) *(G-14841)*
Modular Medical Corp......718 829-2626
1513 Olmstead Ave Bronx (10462) *(G-1334)*
Modulex New York Inc......646 742-1320
192 Lexington Ave Rm 1002 New York (10016) *(G-10831)*
Modulightor Inc......212 371-0336
246 E 58th St New York (10022) *(G-10832)*
Modutank Inc......718 392-1112
4104 35th Ave Long Island City (11101) *(G-7528)*
Moes Wear Apparel Inc......718 940-1597
1020 E 48th St Ste 8 Brooklyn (11203) *(G-2222)*
Moffitt Fan Corporation......585 768-7010
54 Church St Le Roy (14482) *(G-7123)*
Moga Trading Company Inc......718 760-2966
57 Granger St Corona (11368) *(G-3851)*
Mogen David Winegroup, Westfield *Also called Wine Group Inc (G-16400)*
Mohawk Cabinet Company Inc......518 725-0645
137 E State St Gloversville (12078) *(G-5462)*
Mohawk Electro Techniques Inc......315 896-2661
7677 Cameron Hill Rd Barneveld (13304) *(G-603)*
Mohawk Fabric Company Inc......518 842-3090
96 Guy Park Ave Amsterdam (12010) *(G-350)*
Mohawk Fine Papers Inc (PA)......518 237-1740
465 Saratoga St Cohoes (12047) *(G-3614)*
Mohawk Fine Papers Inc......518 237-1741
465 Saratoga St Cohoes (12047) *(G-3615)*
Mohawk Innovative Tech Inc (PA)......518 862-4290
1037 Watervliet Shaker Rd Albany (12205) *(G-99)*
Mohawk Metal Mfg & Sls......315 853-7663
4901 State Route 233 Westmoreland (13490) *(G-16407)*
Mohawk Resources Ltd......518 842-1431
65 Vrooman Ave Amsterdam (12010) *(G-351)*
Mohawk River Leather Works......518 853-3900
32 Broad St Fultonville (12072) *(G-5237)*
Mohawk Sign Systems Inc......518 842-5303
5 Dandreano Dr Amsterdam (12010) *(G-352)*
Mohawk Valley Knt McHy Co Inc......315 736-3038
561 Main St New York Mills (13417) *(G-12189)*
Mohawk Valley Manufacturing......315 797-0851
2237 Broad St Frankfort (13340) *(G-5110)*
Mohawk Valley Mill, Little Falls *Also called Burrows Paper Corporation (G-7209)*
Mohawk Valley Printing Co, Herkimer *Also called Lennons Litho Inc (G-6043)*
Moira New Hope Food Pantry......518 529-6524
2341 County Route 5 Moira (12957) *(G-8261)*
Mokai Manufacturing Inc......845 566-8287
13 Jeanne Dr Newburgh (12550) *(G-12233)*
Molabs Inc......310 721-6828
32 Little West 12th St New York (10014) *(G-10833)*
Mold-A-Matic Corporation......607 433-2121
147 River St Oneonta (13820) *(G-12641)*
Mold-Rite Plastics LLC......518 561-1812
1 Plant St Plattsburgh (12901) *(G-13134)*
Moldcraft Inc......716 684-1126
240 Gould Ave Depew (14043) *(G-4096)*
Moldedtanks.com, Bay Shore *Also called Chem-Tek Systems Inc (G-670)*
Moldova Pickles & Salads Inc......718 284-2220
1060 E 46th St Brooklyn (11203) *(G-2223)*
Moldtech Inc......716 685-3344
1900 Commerce Pkwy Lancaster (14086) *(G-7033)*
Moleclar Insght Phrmctcals Inc (HQ)......914 789-2800
777 N Broadway Ste 101 Sleepy Hollow (10591) *(G-14886)*
Molecular Glasses Inc......585 210-2861
1667 Lake Ave Ste 278b Rochester (14615) *(G-13951)*
Moley Magnetics Inc......716 434-4023
5202 Commerce Dr Lockport (14094) *(G-7320)*
Mom Dad Publishing Inc......646 476-9170
59 Maiden Ln Fl 27 New York (10038) *(G-10834)*
MOMENTIVE, Waterford *Also called Mpm Holdings Inc (G-15984)*
Momentive, Waterford *Also called Mpm Silicones LLC (G-15986)*
Momentive Performance LLC (HQ)......281 325-3536
260 Hudson River Rd Waterford (12188) *(G-15979)*
Momentive Performance Mtls Inc......614 986-2495
260 Hudson River Rd Waterford (12188) *(G-15980)*
Momentive Performance Mtls Inc......914 784-4807
769 Old Saw Mill River Rd Tarrytown (10591) *(G-15484)*
Momentive Performance Mtls Inc (HQ)......518 237-3330
260 Hudson River Rd Waterford (12188) *(G-15981)*
Momentive Prfmce Mtls Holdings, Waterford *Also called Momentive Prfmce Mtls Holdings (G-15982)*
Momentive Prfmce Mtls Holdings......518 237-3330
260 Hudson River Rd Waterford (12188) *(G-15982)*
Momentummedia Sports Pubg, Ithaca *Also called Mag Inc (G-6593)*
Momn Pops Inc......845 567-0640
13 Orr Hatch Cornwall (12518) *(G-3834)*
Momofuku 171 First Avenue LLC......212 777-7773
171 1st Ave New York (10003) *(G-10835)*
Monacelli Press LLC......212 229-9925
236 W 27th St Rm 4a New York (10001) *(G-10836)*
Monaghan Medical Corporation (PA)......518 561-7330
5 Latour Ave Ste 1600 Plattsburgh (12901) *(G-13135)*
Monaghan Medical Corporation......315 472-2136
327 W Fayette St Ste 214 Syracuse (13202) *(G-15376)*
Monarch Electric Products Inc......718 583-7996
4077 Park Ave Fl 5 Bronx (10457) *(G-1335)*
Monarch Graphics Inc......631 232-1300
1065 Islip Ave Central Islip (11722) *(G-3378)*
Monarch Metal Fabrication Inc......631 563-8967
1625 Sycamore Ave Ste A Bohemia (11716) *(G-1059)*
Monarch Plastics Inc......716 569-2175
225 Falconer St Frewsburg (14738) *(G-5209)*
Monasani Signs Inc......631 266-2635
22 Compton St East Northport (11731) *(G-4268)*
Mondelez Global LLC......845 567-4701
800 Corporate Blvd Newburgh (12550) *(G-12234)*
Mondelez Global LLC......585 345-3300
4303 Federal Dr Batavia (14020) *(G-630)*
Mondo Publishing Inc (PA)......212 268-3560
980 Avenue Of The America New York (10018) *(G-10837)*
Moneast Inc......845 298-8898
1708 Route 9 Ste 3 Wappingers Falls (12590) *(G-15936)*
Monelle Jewelry......212 977-9535
608 5th Ave Ste 504 New York (10020) *(G-10838)*
Moneypaper Inc......914 925-0022
411 Theodore Fremd Ave # 132 Rye (10580) *(G-14486)*
Monfefo LLC......347 779-2600
630 Flushing Ave 5q Brooklyn (11206) *(G-2224)*
Mongiello Sales Inc......845 436-4200
250 Hilldale Rd Hurleyville (12747) *(G-6466)*
Mongodb Inc (PA)......646 727-4092
1633 Broadway Fl 38 New York (10019) *(G-10839)*
Mongru Neckwear Inc......718 706-0406
1010 44th Ave Fl 2 Long Island City (11101) *(G-7529)*
Monitor Controls, Hauppauge *Also called Monitor Elevator Products LLC (G-5897)*
Monitor Elevator Products LLC......631 543-4334
125 Ricefield Ln Hauppauge (11788) *(G-5897)*
Monkey Rum, New York *Also called Evolution Spirits Inc (G-9742)*
Mono-Systems Inc......716 821-1344
180 Hopkins St Buffalo (14220) *(G-2953)*
Monofrax LLC......716 483-7200
1870 New York Ave Falconer (14733) *(G-4687)*
Monolithic Coatings Inc......914 621-2765
916 Highway Route 20 Sharon Springs (13459) *(G-14798)*
Monroe Cable Company Inc......845 692-2800
14 Commercial Ave Middletown (10941) *(G-8166)*
Monroe Cnty Chapter Nysarc Inc......585 698-1320
1651 Lyell Ave Rochester (14606) *(G-13952)*
Monroe County Auto Svcs Inc (PA)......585 764-3741
1505 Lyell Ave Rochester (14606) *(G-13953)*
Monroe Fluid Technology Inc......585 392-3434
36 Draffin Rd Hilton (14468) *(G-6157)*
Monroe Industries Inc......585 226-8230
5611 Tec Dr Avon (14414) *(G-520)*
Monroe Piping & Shtmtl LLC (PA)......585 482-0200
68 Humboldt St Rochester (14609) *(G-13954)*
Monroe Plating Div, Rochester *Also called McAlpin Industries Inc (G-13933)*
Monroe Stair Products Inc (PA)......845 783-4245
1 Stair Way Monroe (10950) *(G-8278)*
Monroe Stair Products Inc......845 791-4016
309 E Broadway Monticello (12701) *(G-8322)*
Monroe Table Company Inc......716 945-7700
255 Rochester St Ste 15 Salamanca (14779) *(G-14528)*
Montauk Brewing Company Inc......631 668-8471
62 S Erie Ave Montauk (11954) *(G-8305)*
Montauk Inlet Seafood Inc......631 668-3419
E Lake Dr Ste 540-541 Montauk (11954) *(G-8306)*
Monte Press Inc......718 325-4999
4808 White Plains Rd Bronx (10470) *(G-1336)*
Monteforte Bakery, Richmond Hill *Also called J & S Licata Bros Inc (G-13506)*
Montero International Inc......212 695-1787
149 Sullivan Ln Unit 1 Westbury (11590) *(G-16358)*

Montezuma Winery LLC 315 568-8190
2981 Us Route 20 Seneca Falls (13148) *(G-14782)*
Montfort Brothers Inc 845 896-6694
44 Elm St Fishkill (12524) *(G-4949)*
Monthly Gift Inc 888 444-9661
401 Park Ave S New York (10016) *(G-10840)*
Monticello Black Top Corp 845 434-7280
80 Patio Dr Thompsonville (12784) *(G-15500)*
Montly Gift, New York *Also called Monthly Gift Inc (G-10840)*
Montrose Equipment Sales Inc 718 388-7446
202 N 10th St Brooklyn (11211) *(G-2225)*
Moo Goong Hwa, Corona *Also called Kenan International Trading (G-3847)*
Moog - Isp, Niagara Falls *Also called Moog Inc (G-12311)*
Moog Inc (PA) 716 652-2000
400 Jamison Rd Elma (14059) *(G-4453)*
Moog Inc 716 687-4954
300 Jamison Rd East Aurora (14052) *(G-4207)*
Moog Inc 716 805-8100
7021 Seneca St East Aurora (14052) *(G-4208)*
Moog Inc 716 731-6300
6686 Walmore Rd Niagara Falls (14304) *(G-12311)*
Moog Inc 716 687-4778
160 Jamison Rd Elma (14059) *(G-4454)*
Moog Inc 716 687-5486
500 Jamison Rd Plt20 Elma (14059) *(G-4455)*
Moog Space and Defense Group, Elma *Also called Moog Inc (G-4455)*
Moon Gates Company 718 426-0023
3243 104th St East Elmhurst (11369) *(G-4224)*
Moon, Wm, Catskill *Also called William Moon Iron Works Inc (G-3309)*
Mooney-Keehley Inc 585 271-1573
38 Saginaw Dr Rochester (14623) *(G-13955)*
Mooradian Hydraulics & Eqp Co (PA) 518 766-3866
1190 Route 9 Castleton On Hudson (12033) *(G-3296)*
Moore Business Forms, Lakewood *Also called R R Donnelley & Sons Company (G-6996)*
Moore Business Forms, Grand Island *Also called R R Donnelley & Sons Company (G-5510)*
Moore Printing Company Inc 585 394-1533
9 Coy St Canandaigua (14424) *(G-3225)*
Moore Research Center, Grand Island *Also called RR Donnelley & Sons Company (G-5511)*
Mooseberry Soap Co LLC 315 332-8913
513 W Union St Ste B Newark (14513) *(G-12202)*
Moran Shipyard Corporation (HQ) 718 981-5600
2015 Richmond Ter Staten Island (10302) *(G-15106)*
Morco, Plainview *Also called Howard J Moore Company Inc (G-13062)*
Morco Products Corp 718 853-4005
556 39th St Brooklyn (11232) *(G-2226)*
Morcon Inc (PA) 518 677-8511
879 State Rd 22 Cambridge (12816) *(G-3182)*
Mordechai Collection, New York *Also called Ada Gems Corp (G-8731)*
Morehouse Publishing, New York *Also called Church Publishing Incorporated (G-9296)*
Moreland Hose & Belting Corp 631 563-7071
4118 Sunrise Hwy Oakdale (11769) *(G-12519)*
Morelle Products Ltd 212 391-8070
211 E 18th St Apt 4d New York (10003) *(G-10841)*
Moresca Clothing and Costume 845 331-6012
361 Union Center Rd Ulster Park (12487) *(G-15659)*
Morey Publishing 516 284-3300
20 Hempstead Tpke Unit B Farmingdale (11735) *(G-4830)*
Morgik Metal Designs 212 463-0304
145 Hudson St Frnt 4 New York (10013) *(G-10842)*
Morgood Tools Inc 585 436-8828
940 Millstead Way Rochester (14624) *(G-13956)*
Morito/Kane-M, New York *Also called Kane-M Inc (G-10403)*
Morningstar Concrete Products 716 693-4020
528 Young St Tonawanda (14150) *(G-15560)*
Morningstar Foods, Delhi *Also called Saputo Dairy Foods Usa LLC (G-4075)*
Moro Corporation 607 724-4241
23 Griswold St Binghamton (13904) *(G-906)*
Moro Design, Ithaca *Also called Joe Moro (G-6589)*
Morris Brothers Sign Svc Inc 212 675-9130
37 W 20th St Ste 708 New York (10011) *(G-10843)*
Morris Fine Furniture Workshop, Brooklyn *Also called Walter P Sauer LLC (G-2638)*
Morris Golf Ventures 631 283-0559
Sebonac Inlet Rd Southampton (11968) *(G-14957)*
Morris Kitchen Inc 646 413-5186
30 Chester Ct Brooklyn (11225) *(G-2227)*
Morris Machining Service Inc 585 527-8100
95 Mount Read Blvd Rochester (14611) *(G-13957)*
Morris Products Inc 518 743-0523
53 Carey Rd Queensbury (12804) *(G-13434)*
Morse Systems, Ithaca *Also called Borgwarner Ithaca LLC (G-6566)*
Mortech Industries Inc 845 628-6138
961 Route 6 Mahopac (10541) *(G-7709)*
Mortgage Press Ltd 516 409-1400
1220 Wantagh Ave Wantagh (11793) *(G-15924)*
Morton Buildings Inc 585 786-8191
5616 Route 20a E Warsaw (14569) *(G-15945)*
Morton Salt Inc 585 493-2511
45 Ribaud Ave Silver Springs (14550) *(G-14863)*
Mosaic Microsystems LLC 585 314-7441
500 Lee Rd Ste 200 Rochester (14606) *(G-13958)*
Mosby Holdings Corp (HQ) 212 309-8100
125 Park Ave New York (10017) *(G-10844)*
Moschos Furs Inc 212 244-0255
345 7th Ave Rm 1501 New York (10001) *(G-10845)*
Moscot Wholesale Corp 212 647-1550
69 W 14th St Fl 2 New York (10011) *(G-10846)*
Moser Baer Technologies Inc 585 749-0480
6 Camborne Cir Fairport (14450) *(G-4643)*
Motema Music LLC 212 860-6969
8 W 127th St Apt 2 New York (10027) *(G-10847)*
Mother Nature & Partners, Brooklyn *Also called Mnn Holding Company LLC (G-2220)*
Moti Inc 718 436-4280
4118 13th Ave Brooklyn (11219) *(G-2228)*
Motion Message Inc 631 924-9500
22 Sawgrass Dr Ste 4 Bellport (11713) *(G-809)*
Motivair Corporation 716 691-9222
85 Woodridge Dr Amherst (14228) *(G-239)*
Motor Components LLC 607 737-8011
2243 Corning Rd Elmira Heights (14903) *(G-4512)*
Motorad of America, Niagara Falls *Also called Transcedar Industries Ltd (G-12343)*
Motorola Solutions Inc 518 348-0833
7 Deer Run Holw Halfmoon (12065) *(G-5665)*
Motorola Solutions Inc 518 869-9517
251 New Karner Rd Albany (12205) *(G-100)*
Mott's, Williamson *Also called Keurig Dr Pepper Inc (G-16559)*
Motts, Elmsford *Also called Motts LLP (G-4552)*
Motts LLP (HQ) 972 673-8088
55 Hunter Ln Elmsford (10523) *(G-4552)*
Mount Kisco Transfer Stn Inc 914 666-6350
10 Lincoln Pl Mount Kisco (10549) *(G-8350)*
Mount Vernon Iron Works Inc 914 668-7064
130 Miller Pl Mount Vernon (10550) *(G-8423)*
Mount Vernon Machine Inc 845 268-9400
614 Corporate Way Ste 8 Valley Cottage (10989) *(G-15759)*
Mountain and Isles LLC 212 354-1890
525 7th Ave Fl 22 New York (10018) *(G-10848)*
Mountain Forest Products Inc 518 597-3674
3281 Nys Route 9n Crown Point (12928) *(G-3916)*
Mountain Side Farms Inc 718 526-3442
15504 Liberty Ave Jamaica (11433) *(G-6664)*
Mountain T-Shirts Inc 518 943-4533
8 W Bridge St Catskill (12414) *(G-3307)*
Mountain T-Shirts & Sign Works, Catskill *Also called Mountain T-Shirts Inc (G-3307)*
Movin On Sounds and SEC Inc 516 489-2350
636 Hempstead Tpke Franklin Square (11010) *(G-5119)*
Movinads & Signs LLC 518 378-3000
1771 Route 9 Halfmoon (12065) *(G-5666)*
Moznaim Co, Brooklyn *Also called Moznaim Publishing Co Inc (G-2229)*
Moznaim Publishing Co Inc 718 853-0525
4304 12th Ave Brooklyn (11219) *(G-2229)*
Mozzarella Fresca Incorporated 559 752-4823
2376 S Park Ave Buffalo (14220) *(G-2954)*
MP Caroll Inc 716 683-8520
4822 Genesee St Cheektowaga (14225) *(G-3452)*
Mp Displays LLC 845 268-4113
704 Executive Blvd Ste 1 Valley Cottage (10989) *(G-15760)*
Mp Studio Inc 212 302-5666
147 W 35th St Ste 1603 New York (10001) *(G-10849)*
MP&sm, Rochester *Also called Monroe Piping & Shtmtl LLC (G-13954)*
Mpdraw LLC 212 228-8383
109 Ludlow St New York (10002) *(G-10850)*
Mpdw Inc (PA) 925 631-6878
158 W 29th St Fl 12 New York (10001) *(G-10851)*
Mpe Graphics Inc 631 582-8900
120 Wilbur Pl Ste A Bohemia (11716) *(G-1060)*
Mpi Consulting Incorporated 631 253-2377
87 Jersey St West Babylon (11704) *(G-16178)*
Mpi Incorporated 845 471-7630
165 Smith St Stop 3 Poughkeepsie (12601) *(G-13356)*
Mpl Inc 607 266-0480
41 Dutch Mill Rd Ithaca (14850) *(G-6597)*
Mpl Metal Inc 718 338-4952
1560 Troy Ave Brooklyn (11203) *(G-2230)*
Mpm Holdings Inc 518 237-3330
260 Hudson River Rd Waterford (12188) *(G-15983)*
Mpm Holdings Inc (PA) 518 237-3330
260 Hudson River Rd Waterford (12188) *(G-15984)*
Mpm Intermediate Holdings Inc (HQ) 518 237-3330
260 Hudson River Rd Waterford (12188) *(G-15985)*
Mpm Silicones LLC 518 233-3330
260 Hudson River Rd Waterford (12188) *(G-15986)*
Mr Disposable Inc 718 388-8574
101 Richardson St Ste 2 Brooklyn (11211) *(G-2231)*
Mr Glass Tempering LLC 718 576-3826
38 15th St Brooklyn (11215) *(G-2232)*
Mr Pierogi LLC 718 499-7821
126 12th St Brooklyn (11215) *(G-2233)*
Mr Sign, East Northport *Also called Monasani Signs Inc (G-4268)*
Mr Sign, Brooklyn *Also called Penn Signs Inc (G-2310)*
Mr Sign Usa Inc 718 218-3321
1920 Atlantic Ave Brooklyn (11233) *(G-2234)*

ALPHABETIC

Mr Smoothie....845 296-1686
207 South Ave Ste F102 Poughkeepsie (12601) ***(G-13357)***
Mr Steam, Long Island City *Also called Sussman-Automatic Corporation* ***(G-7611)***
MRC Bearings, Jamestown *Also called SKF USA Inc* ***(G-6747)***
MRC Global (us) Inc....607 739-8575
224 N Main St Bldg 13-1 Horseheads (14845) ***(G-6322)***
Mrchocolatecom LLC....718 875-9772
66 Water St Ste 2 Brooklyn (11201) ***(G-2235)***
Mri Northtowns Group PC....716 836-4646
199 Park Club Ln Ste 300 Buffalo (14221) ***(G-2955)***
Mrinalini Inc....646 510-2747
469 7th Ave Rm 1254 New York (10018) ***(G-10852)***
Mrp Supports LLC....716 332-7673
3310 N Benzing Rd Orchard Park (14127) ***(G-12731)***
Mrs John L Strong & Co LLC....212 838-3775
699 Madison Ave Fl 5 New York (10065) ***(G-10853)***
Mrt Textile Inc....800 674-1073
350 5th Ave New York (10118) ***(G-10854)***
Ms Machining Inc....607 723-1105
2 William St Binghamton (13904) ***(G-907)***
Ms Paper Products Co Inc....718 624-0248
930 Bedford Ave Brooklyn (11205) ***(G-2236)***
Ms Spares LLC....607 223-3024
8055 Evesborough Dr Clay (13041) ***(G-3551)***
Ms. Michelles, Calverton *Also called Cooking With Chef Michelle LLC* ***(G-3164)***
Msdivisions, Middletown *Also called Commercial Communications LLC* ***(G-8143)***
Msi Inc....845 639-6683
329 Strawtown Rd New City (10956) ***(G-8494)***
Msi-Molding Solutions Inc....315 736-2412
6247 State Route 233 Rome (13440) ***(G-14259)***
MSP Technologycom LLC....631 424-7542
77 Bankside Dr Centerport (11721) ***(G-3351)***
MSQ Corporation....718 465-0900
21504 Hempstead Ave Queens Village (11429) ***(G-13411)***
Mssi, Millbrook *Also called Micro Systems Specialists Inc* ***(G-8189)***
Mt Fuel Corp....631 445-2047
9 Bayles Ave Stony Brook (11790) ***(G-15168)***
Mt Morris Shopper Inc....585 658-3520
85 N Main St Mount Morris (14510) ***(G-8367)***
MTI, Albany *Also called Mechanical Technology Inc* ***(G-98)***
MTI, New York *Also called Minerals Technologies Inc* ***(G-10817)***
MTI Instruments Inc....518 218-2550
325 Washington Ave 3 Albany (12206) ***(G-101)***
MTK Electronics Inc....631 924-7666
1 National Blvd Medford (11763) ***(G-7962)***
Mtm Publishing Inc....212 242-6930
435 W 23rd St New York (10011) ***(G-10855)***
Mtwli Precision Corp....631 244-3767
1605 Sycamore Ave Unit B Bohemia (11716) ***(G-1061)***
Mtz Enterprises Inc....347 834-2716
870 39th St Brooklyn (11232) ***(G-2237)***
Mud Puddle Books Inc....212 647-9168
36 W 25th St Fl 5 New York (10010) ***(G-10856)***
Mudpuppy, New York *Also called Galison Publishing LLC* ***(G-9876)***
Muench-Kreuzer Candle Company (PA)....315 471-4515
617 Hiawatha Blvd E Syracuse (13208) ***(G-15377)***
Mulitex Usa Inc....212 398-0440
215 W 40th St Fl 7 New York (10018) ***(G-10857)***
Muller Quaker Dairy, Batavia *Also called Dairy Farmers America Inc* ***(G-622)***
Muller Tool Inc....716 895-3658
74 Anderson Rd Buffalo (14225) ***(G-2956)***
Mullers Cider House LLC....585 287-5875
1344 University Ave # 180 Rochester (14607) ***(G-13959)***
Mullican Flooring LP....716 537-2642
209 Vermont St Holland (14080) ***(G-6220)***
Multi Packaging Solutions Inc....516 488-2000
325 Duffy Ave Unit 1 Hicksville (11801) ***(G-6112)***
Multi Packaging Solutions Inc (HQ)....646 885-0005
150 E 52nd St Fl 28 New York (10022) ***(G-10858)***
Multi Packg Solutions Intl Ltd (HQ)....646 885-0005
885 3rd Ave Fl 28 New York (10022) ***(G-10859)***
Multi Tech Electric....718 606-2695
2526 50th St Woodside (11377) ***(G-16665)***
Multi-Health Systems Inc....800 456-3003
Indus Pkwy Ste 70660 60 Cheektowaga (14227) ***(G-3453)***
Multifold Die Ctng Finshg Corp....631 232-1235
120 Ricefield Ln Ste B Hauppauge (11788) ***(G-5898)***
Multimatic Products Inc....800 767-7633
900 Marconi Ave Ronkonkoma (11779) ***(G-14381)***
Multimedia Plus Inc....212 982-3229
853 Broadway Ste 1605 New York (10003) ***(G-10860)***
Multimedia Services Inc....607 936-3186
11136 River Rd 40 Corning (14830) ***(G-3822)***
Multiple Imprssons of Rchester (PA)....585 546-1160
41 Chestnut St Rochester (14604) ***(G-13960)***
Multisorb Tech Intl LLC (PA)....716 824-8900
325 Harlem Rd Buffalo (14224) ***(G-2957)***
Multisorb Technologies Inc....716 656-1402
10 French Rd Buffalo (14227) ***(G-2958)***
Multitone Finishing Co Inc....516 485-1043
56 Hempstead Gardens Dr West Hempstead (11552) ***(G-16222)***
Multiwire Laboratories Ltd....607 257-3378
95 Brown Rd 1018266a Ithaca (14850) ***(G-6598)***
Munn Works LLC....914 665-6100
150 N Macquesten Pkwy Mount Vernon (10550) ***(G-8424)***
Munschauer Inc....716 895-8888
330 Greene St Buffalo (14206) ***(G-2959)***
Munson Machinery Company Inc....315 797-0090
210 Seward Ave Utica (13502) ***(G-15724)***
Murcadom Corporation....585 412-2176
5711 Thomas Rd Canandaigua (14424) ***(G-3226)***
Murphy Manufacturing Co Inc....585 223-0100
38 West Ave Fairport (14450) ***(G-4644)***
Murray Bresky Consultants Ltd (PA)....845 436-5001
5190 Main St South Fallsburg (12779) ***(G-14932)***
Murray Logging LLC....518 834-7372
1535 Route 9 Keeseville (12944) ***(G-6853)***
Murray's Chicken, South Fallsburg *Also called Murray Bresky Consultants Ltd* ***(G-14932)***
Music & Sound Retailer Inc....516 767-2500
25 Willowdale Ave Port Washington (11050) ***(G-13289)***
Music Sales, New York *Also called G Schirmer Inc* ***(G-9868)***
Music Sales, Chester *Also called G Schirmer Inc* ***(G-3475)***
Music Sales Corporation (PA)....212 254-2100
180 Madison Ave Ste 2400 New York (10016) ***(G-10861)***
Mustang Bio Inc....781 652-4500
2 Gansevoort St Fl 9 New York (10014) ***(G-10862)***
Mustang-Major Tool & Die Co....716 992-9200
3243 N Boston Rd Eden (14057) ***(G-4390)***
Mustard Tin....315 769-8409
6100 Saint Lawrence Ctr Massena (13662) ***(G-7906)***
Mutual Engraving Company Inc....516 489-0534
497 Hempstead Ave West Hempstead (11552) ***(G-16223)***
Mutual Harware, Long Island City *Also called Mutual Sales Corp* ***(G-7530)***
Mutual Library Bindery Inc....315 455-6638
6295 E Molloy Rd Ste 3 East Syracuse (13057) ***(G-4359)***
Mutual Sales Corp....718 361-8373
545 49th Ave Long Island City (11101) ***(G-7530)***
Muzet Inc....315 452-0050
104 S Main St Syracuse (13212) ***(G-15378)***
Mv Corp Inc....631 273-8020
88 Spence St Ste 90 Bay Shore (11706) ***(G-703)***
Mwi Inc (PA)....585 424-4200
1269 Brighton Henrietta T Rochester (14623) ***(G-13961)***
Mwsi Inc (PA)....914 347-4200
12 Skyline Dr Ste 230 Hawthorne (10532) ***(G-5993)***
Mx Solar USA LLC....732 356-7300
100 Wall St Ste 1000 New York (10005) ***(G-10863)***
My Apparel, New York *Also called El-La Design Inc* ***(G-9638)***
My Hanky Inc....646 321-0869
680 81st St Apt 4d Brooklyn (11228) ***(G-2238)***
My Life My Health, Flushing *Also called Life Watch Technology Inc* ***(G-5023)***
My Most Favorite Food....212 580-5130
247 W 72nd St Frnt 1 New York (10023) ***(G-10864)***
My Publisher Inc....212 935-5215
845 3rd Ave Rm 1410 New York (10022) ***(G-10865)***
Myers Group LLC (PA)....973 761-6414
257 W 38th St New York (10018) ***(G-10866)***
Mylan Health Management LLC....917 262-2950
405 Lexington Ave New York (10174) ***(G-10867)***
Myles Tool Company Inc....716 731-1300
6300 Inducon Corporate Dr Sanborn (14132) ***(G-14550)***
Mymee Inc....917 476-4122
110 E 25th St New York (10010) ***(G-10868)***
Mypublisher Inc (HQ)....914 773-4312
8 Westchester Plz Ste 145 Elmsford (10523) ***(G-4553)***
Mystery Scene Magazine, New York *Also called Kbs Communications LLC* ***(G-10425)***
Mystic Display Co Inc....718 485-2651
909 Remsen Ave Brooklyn (11236) ***(G-2239)***
Mystic Inc (PA)....212 239-2025
463 7th Ave Fl 12 New York (10018) ***(G-10869)***
MZB Accessories LLC....718 472-7500
2976 Northern Blvd Fl 4 Long Island City (11101) ***(G-7531)***
N & G of America Inc....516 428-3414
28 W Lane Dr Plainview (11803) ***(G-13076)***
N & L Fuel Corp....718 863-3538
2014 Blackrock Ave Bronx (10472) ***(G-1337)***
N & L Instruments Inc....631 471-4000
90 13th Ave Unit 1 Ronkonkoma (11779) ***(G-14382)***
N A Alumil Corporation....718 355-9393
4401 21st St Ste 203 Long Island City (11101) ***(G-7532)***
N A P, Brooklyn *Also called Nap Industries Inc* ***(G-2243)***
N A R Associates Inc....845 557-8713
128 Rte 55 Barryville (12719) ***(G-607)***
N A S C O, Watertown *Also called Northern Awning & Sign Company* ***(G-16030)***
N C Iron Works Inc....718 633-4660
1117 60th St Brooklyn (11219) ***(G-2240)***
N E Controls LLC....315 626-2480
7048 Interstate Island Rd Syracuse (13209) ***(G-15379)***
N I Boutique, Long Island City *Also called Nazim Izzak Inc* ***(G-7534)***
N I T, New York *Also called Network Infrstructure Tech Inc* ***(G-10913)***
N Make Mold Inc....716 877-3146
85 River Rock Dr Ste 202 Buffalo (14207) ***(G-2960)***

N R S I, Syosset *Also called National Rding Styles Inst Inc (G-15225)*
N Sketch Build Inc 800 975-0597
982 Main St Ste 4-130 Fishkill (12524) *(G-4950)*
N V Magazine, New York *Also called Envy Publishing Group Inc (G-9691)*
N Y B P Inc 585 624-2541
1355 Pittsford Mendon Rd Mendon (14506) *(G-8093)*
N Y Bijoux Corp 212 244-9585
33 Sands Point Rd Port Washington (11050) *(G-13290)*
N Y Contract Seating Inc 718 417-9298
5560 60th St Maspeth (11378) *(G-7860)*
N Y Elli Design Corp 718 228-0014
5001 Metropolitan Ave 1 Ridgewood (11385) *(G-13543)*
N Y Western Concrete Corp 585 343-6850
638 E Main St Batavia (14020) *(G-631)*
N Y Winstons Inc 212 665-3166
5 W 86th St Apt 9e New York (10024) *(G-10870)*
N3a Corporation 516 284-6799
345 Doughty Blvd Inwood (11096) *(G-6496)*
Nabisco, Newburgh *Also called Mondelez Global LLC (G-12234)*
Nabisco, Batavia *Also called Mondelez Global LLC (G-630)*
Nadcor, Plattsburgh *Also called North American Door Corp (G-13137)*
Nae, Central Islip *Also called North American Enclosures Inc (G-3381)*
Nafco, Newark *Also called North American Filter Corp (G-12203)*
Nagad Cabinets Inc 718 382-7200
1039 Mcdonald Ave Brooklyn (11230) *(G-2241)*
Nagle Fuel Corporation 212 304-4618
265 Nagle Ave New York (10034) *(G-10871)*
Nak International Corp (PA) 516 334-6245
131 Jericho Tpke Ste 204 Jericho (11753) *(G-6794)*
Nakano Foods, Medina *Also called Mizkan America Inc (G-7985)*
Nakano Foods, Lyndonville *Also called Mizkan America Inc (G-7680)*
Nalco Company LLC 518 796-1985
6 Butler Pl 2 Saratoga Springs (12866) *(G-14590)*
Nalge Nunc International Corp (HQ) 585 498-2661
1600 Lexington Ave # 107 Rochester (14606) *(G-13962)*
Name Base Inc 212 545-1400
172 Lexington Ave Apt 1 New York (10016) *(G-10872)*
Nameplate Mfrs of Amer 631 752-0055
65 Toledo St Farmingdale (11735) *(G-4831)*
NAMSNET, Long Island City *Also called Toweriq Inc (G-7618)*
Nanette Lepore, Brooklyn *Also called Nlhe LLC (G-2270)*
Nanette Lepore, New York *Also called Robespierre Inc (G-11410)*
Nanette Lepore Showroom, New York *Also called Robespierre Inc (G-11409)*
Nanit, New York *Also called Udisense Inc (G-11931)*
Nano Vibronix Inc 516 374-8330
601 Chestnut St Cedarhurst (11516) *(G-3335)*
Nanobionovum LLC 518 581-1171
117 Grand Ave Saratoga Springs (12866) *(G-14591)*
Nanomas Technologies Inc 607 821-4208
1093 Clark St Endicott (13760) *(G-4603)*
Nanoprobes Inc 631 205-9490
95 Horseblock Rd Unit 1 Yaphank (11980) *(G-16718)*
Nanopv Corporation 609 851-3666
7526 Morgan Rd Liverpool (13090) *(G-7249)*
Nanorx Inc 914 671-0224
6 Devoe Pl Chappaqua (10514) *(G-3423)*
Nanotronics Imaging Inc 212 401-6209
63 Flushing Ave Unit 128 Brooklyn (11205) *(G-2242)*
Nanovibronix Inc 914 233-3004
525 Executive Blvd Elmsford (10523) *(G-4554)*
Nantier Ball Minoustchine Pubg, New York *Also called NBM Publishing Inc (G-10900)*
Nantucket Allserve Inc 914 612-4000
55 Hunter Ln Elmsford (10523) *(G-4555)*
Nantucket Nectars, Elmsford *Also called Nantucket Allserve Inc (G-4555)*
Nanz Company, The, New York *Also called Nanz Custom Hardware Inc (G-10873)*
Nanz Custom Hardware Inc (PA) 212 367-7000
20 Vandam St Fl 5l New York (10013) *(G-10873)*
Nanz Custom Hardware Inc 212 367-7000
105 E Jefryn Blvd Deer Park (11729) *(G-4012)*
Naomi Manufacturing, Island Park *Also called Nathan Berrie & Sons Inc (G-6516)*
Nap Industries, Brooklyn *Also called Marlow Printing Co Inc (G-2171)*
Nap Industries Inc 718 625-4948
667 Kent Ave Brooklyn (11249) *(G-2243)*
Napco Security Tech Inc (PA) 631 842-9400
333 Bayview Ave Amityville (11701) *(G-304)*
Napean LLC 917 968-6757
401 Broadway Ste 1408 New York (10013) *(G-10874)*
Naples Vly Mrgers Acqstons LLC 585 490-1339
154 N Main St Naples (14512) *(G-8473)*
Narda Satellite Networks, Hauppauge *Also called L3 Technologies Inc (G-5861)*
Narratively Inc 203 536-0332
30 John St Brooklyn (11201) *(G-2244)*
Narrowsburg Feed & Grain Co 845 252-3936
Fifth And Main St Narrowsburg (12764) *(G-8474)*
Nas CP Corp (HQ) 718 961-6757
1434 110th St Apt 4a College Point (11356) *(G-3657)*
Nas Quick Sign Inc 716 876-7599
1628 Elmwood Ave Buffalo (14207) *(G-2961)*

Nas-Tra Automotive Inds Inc 631 225-1225
3 Sidney Ct Lindenhurst (11757) *(G-7182)*
Nasco Enterprises Inc 516 921-9696
95 Woodcrest Dr Syosset (11791) *(G-15223)*
Nasdaq Omx, New York *Also called Omx (us) Inc (G-11040)*
Nash Metalware Co Inc 315 339-5794
200 Railroad St Rome (13440) *(G-14260)*
Nash Printing Inc 516 935-4567
101 Dupont St Ste 2 Plainview (11803) *(G-13077)*
Nasiff Associates Inc 315 676-2346
841 County Route 37 Central Square (13036) *(G-3391)*
Nassau Auto Remanufacturer 516 485-4500
2477 Charles Ct North Bellmore (11710) *(G-12380)*
Nassau Auto Remanufacturers, North Bellmore *Also called Nassau Auto Remanufacturer (G-12380)*
Nassau Candy Distributors Inc (HQ) 516 433-7100
530 W John St Hicksville (11801) *(G-6113)*
Nassau Candy Specialty, Hicksville *Also called Nassau Candy Distributors Inc (G-6113)*
Nassau Chromium Plating Co Inc 516 746-6666
122 2nd St Mineola (11501) *(G-8238)*
Nassau County Publications 516 481-5400
5 Centre St Hempstead (11550) *(G-6022)*
Nassau Suffolk Brd of Womens 631 666-8835
145 New York Ave Bay Shore (11706) *(G-704)*
Nassau Tool Works Inc 631 328-7031
1479 N Clinton Ave Bay Shore (11706) *(G-705)*
Nasserati Inc 212 947-8100
225 W 39th St Fl 6 New York (10018) *(G-10875)*
Nastel Technologies Inc (PA) 631 761-9100
88 Sunnyside Blvd Ste 101 Plainview (11803) *(G-13078)*
Nastra Automotive, Lindenhurst *Also called Nas-Tra Automotive Inds Inc (G-7182)*
Nat Nast Company Inc (PA) 212 575-1186
1370 Broadway Rm 900 New York (10018) *(G-10876)*
Natech Plastics Inc 631 580-3506
85 Remington Blvd Ronkonkoma (11779) *(G-14383)*
Nathan Berrie & Sons Inc 516 432-8500
3956 Long Beach Rd Island Park (11558) *(G-6516)*
Nathan Love LLC 212 925-7111
407 Broome St Rm 6r New York (10013) *(G-10877)*
Nathan Printing Express Inc 914 472-0914
740 Central Park Ave Scarsdale (10583) *(G-14641)*
Nathan Steel Corp 315 797-1335
36 Wurz Ave Utica (13502) *(G-15725)*
Nation Company LLC 212 209-5400
520 8th Ave Rm 2100 New York (10018) *(G-10878)*
Nation Magazine 212 209-5400
33 Irving Pl Fl 8 New York (10003) *(G-10879)*
Nation, The, New York *Also called Nation Company LLC (G-10878)*
National Advertising & Prtg 212 629-7650
231 W 29th St Rm 1408 New York (10001) *(G-10880)*
National Catholic Wkly Review, New York *Also called America Press Inc (G-8822)*
National Computer & Electronic 631 242-7222
367 Bay Shore Rd Ste D Deer Park (11729) *(G-4013)*
National Contract Industries 212 249-0045
510 E 86th St Apt 16b New York (10028) *(G-10881)*
National Die & Button Mould Co 201 939-7800
1 Kent Ave Brooklyn (11249) *(G-2245)*
National Elev Cab & Door Corp 718 478-5900
5315 37th Ave Woodside (11377) *(G-16666)*
National Equipment Corporation (PA) 718 585-0200
600 Mmaroneck Ave Ste 400 Harrison (10528) *(G-5731)*
National Equipment Corporation 718 585-0200
801 E 141st St Bronx (10454) *(G-1338)*
National Flag & Display Co Inc (PA) 212 228-6600
30 E 21st St Apt 2b New York (10010) *(G-10882)*
National Ggraphic Partners LLC 212 656-0726
485 Lexington Ave Fl 3 New York (10017) *(G-10883)*
National Grape Coop Assn Inc (PA) 716 326-5200
80 State St Westfield (14787) *(G-16394)*
National Health Prom Assoc 914 421-2525
711 Westchester Ave # 301 White Plains (10604) *(G-16478)*
National Herald Inc 718 784-5255
3710 30th St Long Island City (11101) *(G-7533)*
National Learning Corp (PA) 516 921-8888
212 Michael Dr Syosset (11791) *(G-15224)*
National Maint Contg Corp 716 285-1583
5600 Niagara Falls Blvd Niagara Falls (14304) *(G-12312)*
National Pad & Paper, Syracuse *Also called Automation Papers Inc (G-15250)*
National Paper Converting Inc 607 687-6049
207 Corporate Dr Owego (13827) *(G-12800)*
National Parachute Industries 908 782-1646
78 White Rd Extensio Palenville (12463) *(G-12844)*
National Parachute Industry, Palenville *Also called National Parachute Industries (G-12844)*
National Pipe & Plastics Inc (PA) 607 729-9381
3421 Vestal Rd Vestal (13850) *(G-15820)*
National Prfmce Solutions Inc 718 833-4767
1043 78th St Brooklyn (11228) *(G-2246)*
National Prosthetic Orthot 718 767-8400
21441 42nd Ave Ste 3a Bayside (11361) *(G-748)*
National Ramp, Valley Cottage *Also called Landmark Group Inc (G-15757)*
National Rding Styles Inst Inc 516 921-5500
179 Lafayette Dr Syosset (11791) *(G-15225)*

(PA)=Parent Co (HQ)=Headquarters (DH)=Div Headquarters
2019 Harris
New York Manufacturers Directory
943

National Reproductions Inc 212 619-3800
229 W 28th St Fl 9 New York (10001) *(G-10884)*
National Review Inc (PA) 212 679-7330
19 W 44th St Ste 1701 New York (10036) *(G-10885)*
NATIONAL REVIEW ONLINE, New York *Also called National Review Inc (G-10885)*
National Security Systems Inc 516 627-2222
511 Manhasset Woods Rd Manhasset (11030) *(G-7770)*
National Spinning Co Inc 212 382-6400
1212 Ave Of The Americ St New York (10036) *(G-10886)*
National Steel Rule Die Inc 718 402-1396
441 Southern Blvd Bronx (10455) *(G-1339)*
National Time Recording Eqp Co 212 227-3310
64 Reade St Fl 2 New York (10007) *(G-10887)*
National Tobacco Company LP 212 253-8185
257 Park Ave S Fl 7 New York (10010) *(G-10888)*
National Vac Envmtl Svcs Corp 518 743-0563
80 Park Rd Glens Falls (12804) *(G-5435)*
National Wire & Metal Tech Inc 716 661-9180
22 Carolina St Jamestown (14701) *(G-6740)*
Nationwide Circuits Inc 585 328-0791
1444 Emerson St Rochester (14606) *(G-13963)*
Nationwide Coils Inc (PA) 914 277-7396
24 Foxwood Cir Mount Kisco (10549) *(G-8351)*
Nationwide Custom Services 845 365-0414
77 Main St Tappan (10983) *(G-15469)*
Nationwide Dairy Inc 347 689-8148
792 E 93rd St Brooklyn (11236) *(G-2247)*
Nationwide Displays, Central Islip *Also called Nationwide Exhibitor Svcs Inc (G-3379)*
Nationwide Exhibitor Svcs Inc 631 467-2034
110 Windsor Pl Central Islip (11722) *(G-3379)*
Nationwide Lifts, Queensbury *Also called S & H Enterprises Inc (G-13440)*
Nationwide Precision Pdts Corp 585 272-7100
200 Tech Park Dr Rochester (14623) *(G-13964)*
Nationwide Sales and Service 631 491-6625
303 Smith St Ste 4 Farmingdale (11735) *(G-4832)*
Nationwide Tarps Incorporated (PA) 518 843-1545
50 Willow St Amsterdam (12010) *(G-353)*
Native Amercn Enrgy Group Inc (PA) 718 408-2323
7211 Austin St Ste 288 Forest Hills (11375) *(G-5077)*
Native Textiles Inc (PA) 212 951-5100
411 5th Ave Rm 901 New York (10016) *(G-10889)*
Natori Company Incorporated (PA) 212 532-7796
180 Madison Ave Fl 18 New York (10016) *(G-10890)*
Natori Company Incorporated 212 532-7796
180 Madison Ave Fl 19 New York (10016) *(G-10891)*
Natori Company, The, New York *Also called Natori Company Incorporated (G-10891)*
Natural Dreams LLC 718 760-4202
5312 104th St Corona (11368) *(G-3852)*
Natural E Creative LLC 516 488-1143
1110 Jericho Tpke New Hyde Park (11040) *(G-8551)*
Natural Image Hair Concepts, Garden City *Also called M and J Hair Center Inc (G-5269)*
Natural Lab Inc 718 321-8848
13538 39th Ave Ste 4 Flushing (11354) *(G-5026)*
Natural Matters Inc 212 337-3077
300 W 12th St New York (10014) *(G-10892)*
Natural Organics Labs Inc 631 957-5600
9500 New Horizons Blvd Amityville (11701) *(G-305)*
Natural Stone & Cabinet Inc 718 388-2988
1365 Halsey St Brooklyn (11237) *(G-2248)*
Naturally Free Food Inc 631 361-9710
35 Roundabout Rd Smithtown (11787) *(G-14903)*
Naturally Serious, New York *Also called Peter Thomas Roth Labs LLC (G-11170)*
Nature America Inc (HQ) 212 726-9200
1 New York Plz Ste 4500 New York (10004) *(G-10893)*
Nature Only Inc 917 922-6539
10420 Queens Blvd Apt 3b Forest Hills (11375) *(G-5078)*
Nature Publishing Co 212 726-9200
345 Park Ave S New York (10010) *(G-10894)*
Nature Publishing Group, New York *Also called Nature America Inc (G-10893)*
Natures Bounty (ny) Inc 631 567-9500
90 Orville Dr Bohemia (11716) *(G-1062)*
Natures Bounty (ny) Inc (HQ) 631 200-2000
2100 Smithtown Ave Ronkonkoma (11779) *(G-14384)*
Natures Bounty Co 631 244-2021
2100 Smithtown Ave Ronkonkoma (11779) *(G-14385)*
Natures Bounty Co 631 588-3492
4320 Veterans Mem Hwy Holbrook (11741) *(G-6202)*
Natures Value Inc (PA) 631 846-2500
468 Mill Rd Coram (11727) *(G-3800)*
Natures Warehouse 800 215-4372
55 Main St Philadelphia (13673) *(G-12985)*
Naturpathica Holistic Hlth Inc 631 329-8792
74 Montauk Hwy Unit 23 East Hampton (11937) *(G-4241)*
Natus Medical Incorporated 631 457-4430
150 Motor Pkwy Ste 106 Hauppauge (11788) *(G-5899)*
Nautica International Inc (HQ) 212 541-5757
40 W 57th St New York (10019) *(G-10895)*
Nautica Opco LLC (HQ) 212 541-5757
40 W 57th St Fl 3 New York (10019) *(G-10896)*
Nautica Vf, New York *Also called Nautica Opco LLC (G-10896)*
Nautical Marine Paint Corp 718 462-7000
4802 Farragut Rd Brooklyn (11203) *(G-2249)*
Nautical Paint, Brooklyn *Also called Nautical Marine Paint Corp (G-2249)*
Nautilusthink Inc 646 239-6858
360 W 36th St Apt 7s New York (10018) *(G-10897)*
Navas Designs Inc 818 988-9050
200 E 58th St Apt 17b New York (10022) *(G-10898)*
Navatar Group Inc (HQ) 212 863-9655
90 Broad St Ste 1703 New York (10004) *(G-10899)*
Navilyst Medical Inc 800 833-9973
10 Glens Fls Technical Pa Glens Falls (12801) *(G-5436)*
Navitar Inc 585 359-4000
200 Commerce Dr Rochester (14623) *(G-13965)*
Navy Plum LLC 845 641-7441
47 Plum Rd Monsey (10952) *(G-8291)*
Nazim Izzak Inc 212 920-5546
4402 23rd St Ste 517 Long Island City (11101) *(G-7534)*
Nb Elctrcal Enclsures Mfrs Inc 718 272-8792
902 903 Shepherd Ave Brooklyn (11208) *(G-2250)*
Nbets Corporation 516 785-1259
1901 Wantagh Ave Wantagh (11793) *(G-15925)*
NBM Publishing Inc 646 559-4681
160 Brdway Ste 700 E Wing New York (10038) *(G-10900)*
Nbn Technologies LLC 585 355-5556
136 Wilshire Rd Rochester (14618) *(G-13966)*
Nbs, Amityville *Also called New Business Solutions Inc (G-306)*
Nbty Inc 631 200-2062
4320 Veterans Mem Hwy Holbrook (11741) *(G-6203)*
Nbty Manufacturing LLC (HQ) 631 567-9500
2100 Smithtown Ave Ronkonkoma (11779) *(G-14386)*
NC Audience Exchange LLC 212 416-3400
1211 Ave Of The Americas New York (10036) *(G-10901)*
Ncc Ny LLC 718 943-7000
1840 Mcdonald Ave Brooklyn (11223) *(G-2251)*
Nceec, Deer Park *Also called National Computer & Electronic (G-4013)*
Nci, New York *Also called National Contract Industries (G-10881)*
Nci Group Inc 315 339-1245
6168 State Route 233 Rome (13440) *(G-14261)*
Nci Panel Systems, Montgomery *Also called Northeast Cnstr Inds Inc (G-8314)*
NCM Publishers Inc 212 691-9100
200 Varick St Rm 608 New York (10014) *(G-10902)*
NCR Corporation 607 273-5310
950 Danby Rd Ithaca (14850) *(G-6599)*
NCR Corporation 516 876-7200
30 Jericho Executive Plz Jericho (11753) *(G-6795)*
ND Labs Inc 516 612-4900
202 Merrick Rd Lynbrook (11563) *(G-7669)*
Ne & Ws Inc 718 326-4699
6085 60th St Maspeth (11378) *(G-7861)*
NEa Manufacturing Corp 516 371-4200
345 Doughty Blvd Inwood (11096) *(G-6497)*
Necd, Woodside *Also called National Elev Cab & Door Corp (G-16666)*
Necessary Objects Ltd (PA) 212 334-9888
3030 47th Ave Fl 6 Long Island City (11101) *(G-7535)*
Neenah Northeast LLC 315 376-3571
5492 Bostwick St Lowville (13367) *(G-7654)*
Nefab Packaging North East LLC 518 346-9105
203 Glenville Indus Park Scotia (12302) *(G-14744)*
Nefco, Copiague *Also called North East Finishing Co Inc (G-3771)*
Negys New Land Vinyrd Winery 315 585-4432
623 Lerch Rd Ste 1 Geneva (14456) *(G-5330)*
Neighbor Newspapers 631 226-2636
565 Broadhollow Rd Ste 3 Farmingdale (11735) *(G-4833)*
Neighbor To Neighbor News Inc 585 492-2525
223 Main St Arcade (14009) *(G-387)*
Neil Savalia Inc 212 869-0123
15 W 47th St Ste 903 New York (10036) *(G-10903)*
Neilson International Inc 631 454-0400
144 Allen Blvd Ste B Farmingdale (11735) *(G-4834)*
Nelco Laboratories Inc 631 242-0082
154 Brook Ave Deer Park (11729) *(G-4014)*
Nell-Joy Industries Inc (PA) 631 842-8989
8 Reith St Ste 10 Copiague (11726) *(G-3770)*
Nelson Air Device Corporation 718 729-3801
4628 54th Ave Maspeth (11378) *(G-7862)*
Nelson Holdings Ltd (PA) 607 772-1794
71 Frederick St Binghamton (13901) *(G-908)*
Nelson Prsthtics Orthotics Lab, Cheektowaga *Also called Prosthetics By Nelson Inc (G-3456)*
Nemaris Inc 646 794-8648
475 Park Ave S Fl 11 New York (10016) *(G-10904)*
Neo Cabinetry LLC 718 403-0456
400 Liberty Ave Brooklyn (11207) *(G-2252)*
Neo Plastics LLC 646 542-1499
1007 Sheffield Ave Brooklyn (11207) *(G-2253)*
Neo Ray Lighting Products, Hicksville *Also called Cooper Lighting LLC (G-6071)*
Neometrics, Hauppauge *Also called Natus Medical Incorporated (G-5899)*
Neon 212 727-5628
1400 Broadway Rm 300 New York (10018) *(G-10905)*
Neopost USA Inc 631 435-9100
415 Oser Ave Ste K Hauppauge (11788) *(G-5900)*
Nepco, Warrensburg *Also called Northeastern Products Corp (G-15942)*

Nepenthes America Inc 212 343-4262
2219 41st Ave 401 Long Island City (11101) *(G-7536)*
Neptune Machine Inc 718 852-4100
521 Carroll St Brooklyn (11215) *(G-2254)*
Neptune Soft Water Inc 315 446-5151
1201 E Fayette St Ste 6 Syracuse (13210) *(G-15380)*
Nerak Systems Inc 914 763-8259
4 Stage Door Rd Fishkill (12524) *(G-4951)*
Nervecom Inc 212 625-9914
199 Lafayette St Apt 3b New York (10012) *(G-10906)*
Nervve Technologies Inc (PA) 716 800-2250
450 Park Ave Fl 30 New York (10022) *(G-10907)*
Nes Bearing Company Inc 716 372-6532
1601 Johnson St Olean (14760) *(G-12605)*
Nes Costume, New York *Also called Nes Jewelry Inc (G-10908)*
Nes Jewelry Inc (PA) 212 502-0025
10 W 33rd St Fl 9 New York (10001) *(G-10908)*
Nesher Printing Inc 212 760-2521
30 E 33rd St Frnt A New York (10016) *(G-10909)*
Nessen Lighting, The, Mamaroneck *Also called Coldstream Group Inc (G-7739)*
Nestle Healthcare Ntrtn Inc 516 249-5085
565 Broadhollow Rd Farmingdale (11735) *(G-4835)*
Nestle Purina Factory, Dunkirk *Also called Nestle Purina Petcare Company (G-4174)*
Nestle Purina Petcare Company 716 366-8080
3800 Middle Rd Dunkirk (14048) *(G-4174)*
Nestle Usa Inc 914 272-4021
1311 Mmroneck Ave Ste 350 White Plains (10605) *(G-16479)*
Nestle Usa Inc 212 688-2490
520 Madison Ave New York (10022) *(G-10910)*
NET & Die Inc 315 592-4311
24 Foster St Fulton (13069) *(G-5228)*
Netech Corporation 631 531-0100
110 Toledo St Farmingdale (11735) *(G-4836)*
Netegrity Inc (HQ) 631 342-6000
1 Ca Plz Central Islip (11749) *(G-3380)*
Netologic Inc 212 269-3796
17 State St Fl 38 New York (10004) *(G-10911)*
Netsuite Inc 646 652-5700
8 W 40th St 5f New York (10018) *(G-10912)*
Nettle Meadow Farm, Warrensburg *Also called Lumazu LLC (G-15941)*
Network Infrstructure Tech Inc 212 404-7340
90 John St Fl 7 New York (10038) *(G-10913)*
Neumann Jutta New York Inc 212 982-7048
355 E 4th St New York (10009) *(G-10914)*
Neurotrope Inc 973 242-0005
205 E 42nd St Fl 17 New York (10017) *(G-10915)*
Neva Slip, Inwood *Also called Excellent Art Mfg Corp (G-6489)*
Neversink Steel Corp 845 292-4611
12 Asthalter Rd Liberty (12754) *(G-7146)*
Neverware Inc (PA) 516 302-3223
112 W 27th St Ste 201 New York (10001) *(G-10916)*
Neville Mfg Svc & Dist Inc (PA) 716 834-3038
2320 Clinton St Cheektowaga (14227) *(G-3454)*
New Age Ironworks Inc 718 277-1895
183 Van Siclen Ave Brooklyn (11207) *(G-2255)*
New Age Precision Tech Inc 631 471-4000
151 Remington Blvd Ronkonkoma (11779) *(G-14387)*
New American, Brooklyn *Also called Afro Times Newspaper (G-1493)*
New Art Publications Inc 718 636-9100
80 Hanson Pl Ste 703 Brooklyn (11217) *(G-2256)*
New Art Signs Co Inc 718 443-0900
78 Plymouth Dr N Glen Head (11545) *(G-5383)*
New Atlantic Ready Mix Corp 718 812-0739
18330 Jamaica Ave Hollis (11423) *(G-6235)*
New Audio LLC 212 213-6060
132 W 31st St Rm 701 New York (10001) *(G-10917)*
New Avon LLC 716 572-4842
433 Thorncliff Rd Buffalo (14223) *(G-2962)*
New Avon LLC (HQ) 212 282-6000
1 Liberty Plz Fl 25 New York (10006) *(G-10918)*
New Balance Underwear, New York *Also called Balanced Tech Corp (G-9007)*
New Bgnnngs Win Door Dstrs LLC 845 214-0698
28 Willowbrook Hts Poughkeepsie (12603) *(G-13358)*
New Buffalo Shirt Factory Inc 716 436-5839
1979 Harlem Rd Buffalo (14212) *(G-2963)*
New Business Solutions Inc 631 789-1500
31 Sprague Ave Amityville (11701) *(G-306)*
New City Press Inc 845 229-0335
202 Comforter Blvd Hyde Park (12538) *(G-6470)*
New Classic Inc 718 609-1100
4143 37th St Long Island City (11101) *(G-7537)*
New Concepts of New York LLC 212 695-4999
89 19th St 91 Brooklyn (11232) *(G-2257)*
New Cov Manufacturing, West Henrietta *Also called Semans Enterprises Inc (G-16250)*
New Day Woodwork Inc 718 275-1721
8861 76th Ave Glendale (11385) *(G-5404)*
New Deal Printing Corp (PA) 718 729-5800
420 E 55th St Apt Grdp New York (10022) *(G-10919)*
New Dimension Awards Inc (PA) 718 236-8200
6505 11th Ave Brooklyn (11219) *(G-2258)*
New Dimension Trophies, Brooklyn *Also called New Dimension Awards Inc (G-2258)*
New Dimensions Office Group 718 387-0995
540 Morgan Ave Brooklyn (11222) *(G-2259)*
New Dimensions Research Corp 631 694-1356
260 Spagnoli Rd Melville (11747) *(G-8049)*
New Directions Publishing 212 255-0230
80 8th Ave Fl 19 New York (10011) *(G-10920)*
New Dynamics Corporation 845 692-0022
15 Fortune Rd W Middletown (10941) *(G-8167)*
New Eagle Silo Corp 585 492-1300
7648 Hurdville Rd Arcade (14009) *(G-388)*
New Energy Systems Group 917 573-0302
116 W 23rd St Fl 5 New York (10011) *(G-10921)*
New England Barns Inc 631 445-1461
45805 Route 25 Southold (11971) *(G-14970)*
New England Orthotic & Prost 212 682-9313
235 E 38th St New York (10016) *(G-10922)*
New England Reclamation Inc 914 949-2000
20 Haarlem Ave White Plains (10603) *(G-16480)*
New ERA Cap Co Inc 716 604-9000
160 Delaware Ave Buffalo (14202) *(G-2964)*
New ERA Cap Co Inc (PA) 716 604-9000
160 Delaware Ave Buffalo (14202) *(G-2965)*
New ERA Cap Co Inc 716 549-0445
8061 Erie Rd Derby (14047) *(G-4114)*
New Fine Chemicals Inc 631 321-8151
35 W Hoffman Ave Lindenhurst (11757) *(G-7183)*
New Generation Lighting Inc 212 966-0328
144 Bowery Frnt 1 New York (10013) *(G-10923)*
New Goldstar 1 Printing Corp 212 343-3909
63 Orchard St New York (10002) *(G-10924)*
New Hampton Creations Inc 212 244-7474
237 W 35th St Ste 502 New York (10001) *(G-10925)*
New Hope Media LLC 646 366-0830
108 W 39th St Rm 805 New York (10018) *(G-10926)*
New Hope Mills Inc 315 252-2676
181 York St Auburn (13021) *(G-491)*
New Hope Mills Mfg Inc (PA) 315 252-2676
181 York St Auburn (13021) *(G-492)*
New Horizon Graphics Inc 631 231-8055
1200 Prime Pl Hauppauge (11788) *(G-5901)*
New Horizons Bakery, Binghamton *Also called Fratellis LLC (G-885)*
New Jersey Pulverizing Co Inc (PA) 516 921-9595
4 Rita St Syosset (11791) *(G-15226)*
New Kit On The Block 631 757-5655
100 Knickerbocker Ave K Bohemia (11716) *(G-1063)*
New Living Inc 631 751-8819
99 Waverly Ave Apt 6d Patchogue (11772) *(G-12871)*
New Market Products LLC 607 292-6226
9671 Back St Wayne (14893) *(G-16073)*
New Media Investment Group Inc (PA) 212 479-3160
1345 Avenue Of The Americ New York (10105) *(G-10927)*
New Mount Pleasant Bakery 518 374-7577
941 Crane St Schenectady (12303) *(G-14700)*
New Paltz Times, New Paltz *Also called Ulster Publishing Co Inc (G-8583)*
New Press 212 629-8802
120 Wall St Fl 31 New York (10005) *(G-10928)*
New Primecare 516 822-4031
1184 Broadway Hewlett (11557) *(G-6049)*
New Republic 212 989-8200
1 Union Sq W New York (10003) *(G-10929)*
New Rosen Printing, Buffalo *Also called Cilyox Inc (G-2766)*
New Scale Technologies Inc 585 924-4450
121 Victor Heights Pkwy Victor (14564) *(G-15857)*
New Sensor Corporation (PA) 718 937-8300
5501 2nd St Long Island City (11101) *(G-7538)*
New Ski Inc 607 277-7000
109 N Cayuga St Ste A Ithaca (14850) *(G-6600)*
New Skin, Tarrytown *Also called Medtech Products Inc (G-15482)*
New Star Bakery 718 961-8868
4121a Kissena Blvd Flushing (11355) *(G-5027)*
New Style Signs Limited Inc 212 242-7848
171 Madison Ave Rm 204 New York (10016) *(G-10930)*
New Triad For Collaborative 212 873-9610
205 W 86th St Apt 911 New York (10024) *(G-10931)*
New Vision Industries Inc 607 687-7700
1239 Campville Rd Endicott (13760) *(G-4604)*
New Windsor Waste Water Plant 845 561-2550
145 Caesars Ln New Windsor (12553) *(G-8651)*
New Wop Records 631 617-9732
317 W 14th St Deer Park (11729) *(G-4015)*
New World Records, Brooklyn *Also called Recorded Anthlogy of Amrcn Mus (G-2390)*
New York Accessory Group Inc (PA) 212 532-7911
411 5th Ave Fl 4 New York (10016) *(G-10932)*
New York Air Brake, Watertown *Also called Knorr Brake Truck Systems Co (G-16023)*
New York Air Brake LLC 315 786-5576
781 Pearl St Watertown (13601) *(G-16028)*
New York Air Brake LLC (HQ) 315 786-5219
748 Starbuck Ave Watertown (13601) *(G-16029)*
New York Barbell, Elmira *Also called TDS Fitness Equipment Corp (G-4505)*
New York Binding Co Inc 718 729-2454
2121 41st Ave Ste A Long Island City (11101) *(G-7539)*
New York Blood Pressure, Mendon *Also called N Y B P Inc (G-8093)*

A L P H A B E T I C

(PA)=Parent Co (HQ)=Headquarters (DH)=Div Headquarters
2019 Harris
New York Manufacturers Directory
945

New York Bottling Co Inc 718 963-3232
626 Whittier St Bronx (10474) *(G-1340)*
New York Christan Times Inc 718 638-6397
1061 Atlantic Ave Brooklyn (11238) *(G-2260)*
New York Computer Consulting 516 921-1932
14 Pheasant Ln Woodbury (11797) *(G-16626)*
New York CT Loc246 Seiu Wel BF 212 233-0616
217 Broadway New York (10007) *(G-10933)*
New York Cutting & Gumming Co 212 563-4146
265 Ballard Rd Middletown (10941) *(G-8168)*
New York Cvl Srvc Emplys Pblsh 212 962-2690
277 Broadway Ste 1506 New York (10007) *(G-10934)*
New York Daily Challenge Inc (PA) 718 636-9500
1195 Atlantic Ave Fl 2 Brooklyn (11216) *(G-2261)*
New York Daily News, New York *Also called Daily News LP (G-9455)*
New York Daily News 212 248-2100
4 New York Plz Fl 6 New York (10004) *(G-10935)*
New York Digital Corporation 631 630-9798
33 Walt Whitman Rd # 117 Huntington Station (11746) *(G-6453)*
New York Digital Print Center 718 767-1953
15050 14th Rd Ste 1 Whitestone (11357) *(G-16546)*
New York Division, Owego *Also called Kyocera Precision Tools Inc (G-12798)*
New York Elegance Entps Inc 212 685-3088
385 5th Ave Rm 709 New York (10016) *(G-10936)*
New York Embroidery & Monogram, Hicksville *Also called NY Embroidery Inc (G-6116)*
New York Enrgy Synthetics Inc 212 634-4787
375 Park Ave Ste 2607 New York (10152) *(G-10937)*
New York Enterprise Report, New York *Also called Rsl Media LLC (G-11443)*
New York Eye, Amityville *Also called Hart Specialties Inc (G-281)*
New York Familypublications, Mamaroneck *Also called Family Publishing Group Inc (G-7744)*
New York Fan Coil LLC 646 580-1344
7 Chesapeake Bay Rd Coram (11727) *(G-3801)*
New York Findings Corp 212 925-5745
70 Bowery Unit 8 New York (10013) *(G-10938)*
New York Fshion Week Guide LLC 646 757-9119
387 Park Ave S Fl 5 New York (10016) *(G-10939)*
New York Hospital Disposable 718 384-1620
101 Richardson St Ste 1 Brooklyn (11211) *(G-2262)*
New York IL Bo Inc 718 961-1538
4522 162nd St Fl 2 Flushing (11358) *(G-5028)*
New York Imaging Service Inc 716 834-8022
255 Cooper Ave Tonawanda (14150) *(G-15561)*
New York Industrial Works Inc 718 292-0615
796 E 140th St Bronx (10454) *(G-1341)*
New York Laser & Aesthetics 516 627-7777
1025 Nthrn Blvd Ste 206 Roslyn (11576) *(G-14448)*
New York Law Journal, New York *Also called Alm Media LLC (G-8805)*
New York Legal Publishing 518 459-1100
120 Broadway Ste 1a Menands (12204) *(G-8090)*
New York Manufactured Products 585 254-9353
6 Cairn St Rochester (14611) *(G-13967)*
New York Manufacturing Corp 585 254-9353
6 Cairn St Rochester (14611) *(G-13968)*
New York Marking Devices Corp 585 454-5188
700 Clinton Ave S Ste 2 Rochester (14620) *(G-13969)*
New York Marking Devices Corp (PA) 315 463-8641
2207 Teall Ave Syracuse (13206) *(G-15381)*
New York Media LLC 212 508-0700
75 Varick St Ste 1404 New York (10013) *(G-10940)*
New York Packaging Corp 516 746-0600
135 Fulton Ave New Hyde Park (11040) *(G-8552)*
New York Packaging II LLC 516 746-0600
135 Fulton Ave Garden City Park (11040) *(G-5286)*
New York Pasta Authority Inc 347 787-2130
640 Parkside Ave Brooklyn (11226) *(G-2263)*
New York Poplin LLC 718 768-3296
4611 1st Ave Brooklyn (11232) *(G-2264)*
New York Post, Brooklyn *Also called Nyp Holdings Inc (G-2282)*
New York Post, New York *Also called Nyp Holdings Inc (G-11018)*
New York Press Inc 212 268-8600
72 Madison Ave Fl 11 New York (10016) *(G-10941)*
New York Qrtrly Foundation Inc 917 843-8825
322 76th St Brooklyn (11209) *(G-2265)*
New York Quarries Inc 518 756-3138
305 Rte 111 Alcove (12007) *(G-165)*
New York Ravioli Pasta Co Inc 516 270-2852
12 Denton Ave S New Hyde Park (11040) *(G-8553)*
New York Ready Mix Inc 516 338-6969
120 Rushmore St Westbury (11590) *(G-16359)*
New York Review of Books, New York *Also called Nyrev Inc (G-11019)*
New York Rhbilitative Svcs LLC 516 239-0990
214 E Sunrise Hwy Valley Stream (11581) *(G-15787)*
New York Running Co, New York *Also called PRC Liquidating Company (G-11227)*
New York Skateboards, Deer Park *Also called Chapman Skateboard Co Inc (G-3957)*
New York Spring Water Inc 212 777-4649
517 W 36th St New York (10018) *(G-10942)*
New York State Assoc 518 434-2281
453 New Karner Rd Albany (12205) *(G-102)*
New York State Foam Enrgy LLC 845 534-4656
2 Commercial Dr Cornwall (12518) *(G-3835)*
New York State Tool Co Inc 315 737-8985
3343 Oneida St Chadwicks (13319) *(G-3400)*
New York Steel Services Co 718 291-7770
18009 Liberty Ave Jamaica (11433) *(G-6665)*
New York Sweater Company Inc 845 629-9533
141 W 36th St Rm 17 New York (10018) *(G-10943)*
New York Tank Co, Watervliet *Also called Bigbee Steel and Tank Company (G-16041)*
New York Times Co Mag Group, New York *Also called Gruner + Jahr Prtg & Pubg Co (G-10000)*
New York Times Company (PA) 212 556-1234
620 8th Ave New York (10018) *(G-10944)*
New York Times Company 718 281-7000
1 New York Times Plz Flushing (11354) *(G-5029)*
New York Times Company 212 556-1200
620 8th Ave Fl 9 New York (10018) *(G-10945)*
New York Times Company 212 556-4300
620 8th Ave Bsmt 1 New York (10018) *(G-10946)*
New York Trading Co, New York *Also called E-Won Industrial Co Inc (G-9601)*
New York Typing & Printing Co 718 268-7900
10816 72nd Ave Forest Hills (11375) *(G-5079)*
New York University 212 998-4300
7 E 12th St Ste 800 New York (10003) *(G-10947)*
New York Vanity and Mfg Co 718 417-1010
10 Henry St Freeport (11520) *(G-5169)*
New York1 News Operations 212 379-3311
75 9th Ave Frnt 6 New York (10011) *(G-10948)*
Newbay Media LLC (HQ) 212 378-0400
28 E 28th St Fl 12 New York (10016) *(G-10949)*
Newburgh Brewing Company LLC 845 569-2337
88 S Colden St Newburgh (12550) *(G-12235)*
Newburgh Distribution Corp (PA) 845 561-6330
463 Temple Hill Rd New Windsor (12553) *(G-8652)*
Newburgh Envelope Corp 845 566-4211
1720 Route 300 Newburgh (12550) *(G-12236)*
Newcastle Fabrics Corp 718 388-6600
86 Beadel St Brooklyn (11222) *(G-2266)*
Newchem Inc 315 331-7680
407 Cliff St Ithaca (14850) *(G-6601)*
Newco Products Division, Ballston Spa *Also called Dura-Mill Inc (G-582)*
Newcut, Ithaca *Also called Newchem Inc (G-6601)*
Newkirk Products Inc (HQ) 518 862-3200
15 Corporate Cir Albany (12203) *(G-103)*
Newline Products Inc 972 881-3318
509 Temple Hill Rd New Windsor (12553) *(G-8653)*
Newmat Northeast Corp 631 253-9277
81b Mahan St West Babylon (11704) *(G-16179)*
Newport Business Solutions Inc 631 319-6129
61 Keyland Ct Bohemia (11716) *(G-1064)*
Newport Corporation 585 248-4246
705 Saint Paul St Rochester (14605) *(G-13970)*
Newport Graphics Inc 212 924-2600
121 Varick St Rm 302 New York (10013) *(G-10950)*
Newport Rochester Inc 585 262-1325
705 Saint Paul St Rochester (14605) *(G-13971)*
News Communications Inc (PA) 212 689-2500
501 Madison Ave Fl 23 New York (10022) *(G-10951)*
News Corporation (PA) 212 416-3400
1211 Ave Of The Americas New York (10036) *(G-10952)*
News India Times, New York *Also called News India USA Inc (G-10954)*
News India Times, New York *Also called News India Usa LLC (G-10953)*
News India Usa LLC 212 675-7515
37 W 20th St Ste 1109 New York (10011) *(G-10953)*
News India USA Inc 212 675-7515
37 W 20th St Ste 1109 New York (10011) *(G-10954)*
News Now Waverly 607 296-6769
446 Broad St Apt 2 Waverly (14892) *(G-16068)*
News of The Highlands Inc (PA) 845 534-7771
35 Hasbrouck Ave Cornwall (12518) *(G-3836)*
News Report Inc 718 851-6607
1281 49th St Ste 3 Brooklyn (11219) *(G-2267)*
News Review, The, Mattituck *Also called Times Review Newspaper Corp (G-7918)*
News/Sprts Microwave Rentl Inc 619 670-0572
415 Madison Ave Fl 11 New York (10017) *(G-10955)*
Newsday LLC (PA) 631 843-4050
235 Pinelawn Rd Melville (11747) *(G-8050)*
Newsday LLC 631 843-3135
25 Deshon Dr Melville (11747) *(G-8051)*
Newsday Media Group, Melville *Also called Newsday LLC (G-8050)*
Newspaper Delivery Solutions 718 370-1111
309 Bradley Ave Staten Island (10314) *(G-15107)*
Newspaper Publisher LLC 607 775-0472
1035 Conklin Rd Conklin (13748) *(G-3730)*
Newspaper Times Union 518 454-5676
645 Albany Shaker Rd Albany (12211) *(G-104)*
Newsweek LLC 646 867-7100
7 Hanover Sq Fl 5 New York (10004) *(G-10956)*
Newsweek Media Group Inc (PA) 646 867-7100
7 Hanover Sq Fl 5 New York (10004) *(G-10957)*
Newtex Industries Inc (PA) 585 924-9135
8050 Victor Mendon Rd Victor (14564) *(G-15858)*
Newtown Finishing, Brooklyn *Also called Newcastle Fabrics Corp (G-2266)*

Newyork Pedorthic Associates 718 236-7700
2102 63rd St Brooklyn (11204) *(G-2268)*
Nex-Gen Ready Mix Corp 347 231-0073
530 Faile St Bronx (10474) *(G-1342)*
Nexans Energy USA Inc 845 469-2141
25 Oakland Ave Chester (10918) *(G-3478)*
Nexbev Industries LLC 646 648-1255
600 Bradley Hill Rd Ste 2 Blauvelt (10913) *(G-938)*
Nexgen Enviro Systems Inc 631 226-2930
190 E Hoffman Ave Ste D Lindenhurst (11757) *(G-7184)*
Nexis 3 LLC 585 285-4120
1681 Lyell Ave Rochester (14606) *(G-13972)*
Nexstar Holding Corp 716 929-9000
275 Northpointe Pkwy Amherst (14228) *(G-240)*
Next Advance Inc (PA) 518 674-3510
2113 Ny 7 Ste 1 Troy (12180) *(G-15611)*
Next Big Sound Inc 646 657-9837
125 Park Ave Fl 19 New York (10017) *(G-10958)*
Next Magazine, New York *Also called Rnd Enterprises Inc (G-11403)*
Next Potential LLC 401 742-5190
278 E 10th St Apt 5b New York (10009) *(G-10959)*
Next Step Magazine, The, Victor *Also called Next Step Publishing Inc (G-15859)*
Next Step Publishing Inc 585 742-1260
2 W Main St Ste 200 Victor (14564) *(G-15859)*
Nextpotential, New York *Also called Next Potential LLC (G-10959)*
Nfe Management LLC 212 798-6100
1345 Ave Of The Americas New York (10105) *(G-10960)*
Nfk International, Brooklyn *Also called Slava Industries Incorporated (G-2483)*
Niabraze LLC 716 447-1082
675 Ensminger Rd Tonawanda (14150) *(G-15562)*
Niagara Blower Company (HQ) 800 426-5169
91 Sawyer Ave Tonawanda (14150) *(G-15563)*
Niagara Chocolates, Buffalo *Also called Sweetworks Inc (G-3082)*
Niagara Cooler Inc 716 434-1235
6605 Slyton Settlement Rd Lockport (14094) *(G-7321)*
Niagara Development & Mfg Div, Niagara Falls *Also called Fross Industries Inc (G-12287)*
Niagara Falls Plant, Niagara Falls *Also called Tulip Molded Plastics Corp (G-12344)*
Niagara Fiberboard Inc 716 434-8881
140 Van Buren St Lockport (14094) *(G-7322)*
Niagara Fiberglass Inc 716 822-3921
88 Okell St Buffalo (14220) *(G-2966)*
Niagara Gazette, Niagara Falls *Also called Cnhi LLC (G-12273)*
Niagara Gear Corporation 716 874-3131
941 Military Rd Buffalo (14217) *(G-2967)*
Niagara Label Company Inc 716 542-3000
12715 Lewis Rd Akron (14001) *(G-20)*
Niagara Lasalle Corporation 716 827-7010
110 Hopkins St Buffalo (14220) *(G-2968)*
Niagara Precision Inc 716 439-0956
233 Market St Lockport (14094) *(G-7323)*
Niagara Punch & Die Corp 716 896-7619
176 Gruner Rd Buffalo (14227) *(G-2969)*
Niagara Refining LLC 716 706-1400
5661 Transit Rd Depew (14043) *(G-4097)*
Niagara Sample Book Co Inc 716 284-6151
1717 Mackenna Ave Niagara Falls (14303) *(G-12313)*
Niagara Scientific Inc 315 437-0821
6743 Kinne St East Syracuse (13057) *(G-4360)*
Niagara Sheets LLC 716 692-1129
7393 Shawnee Rd North Tonawanda (14120) *(G-12439)*
Niagara Thermo Products, Niagara Falls *Also called Kintex Inc (G-12302)*
Niagara Transformer Corp 716 896-6500
1747 Dale Rd Buffalo (14225) *(G-2970)*
Niagara Tying Service Inc 716 825-0066
176 Dingens St Buffalo (14206) *(G-2971)*
Nibble Inc Baking Co 518 334-3950
451 Broadway Apt 5 Troy (12180) *(G-15612)*
Nibmor Project LLC 718 374-5091
11 Middle Neck Rd Great Neck (11021) *(G-5573)*
Nice-Pak Products Inc (PA) 845 365-2772
2 Nice Pak Park Orangeburg (10962) *(G-12684)*
Nice-Pak Products Inc 845 353-6090
100 Brookhill Dr West Nyack (10994) *(G-16276)*
Niche Design Inc 212 777-2101
310 Fishkill Ave Unit 11 Beacon (12508) *(G-761)*
Niche Media Holdings LLC (HQ) 702 990-2500
257 Park Ave S Fl 5 New York (10010) *(G-10961)*
Niche Modern, Beacon *Also called Niche Design Inc (G-761)*
Nicholas Dfine Furn Decorators 914 245-8982
546 E 170th St 48 Bronx (10456) *(G-1343)*
Nicholas Kirkwood LLC (PA) 646 559-5239
807 Washington St New York (10014) *(G-10962)*
Nicholson Steam Trap, Walden *Also called Spence Engineering Company Inc (G-15897)*
Nick Lugo Inc 212 348-2100
159 E 116th St Fl 2 New York (10029) *(G-10963)*
Nickel City Studios Photo Jour 716 200-0956
45 Linwood Ave Buffalo (14209) *(G-2972)*
Nickelodeon Magazines Inc (HQ) 212 541-1949
1633 Broadway Fl 7 New York (10019) *(G-10964)*
Nicoform Inc 585 454-5530
72 Cascade Dr Ste 12 Rochester (14614) *(G-13973)*
Nicolia Concrete Products Inc 631 669-0700
640 Muncy St Lindenhurst (11757) *(G-7185)*
Nicolia of Long Island, Lindenhurst *Also called Nicolia Concrete Products Inc (G-7185)*
Nicolia Ready Mix Inc (PA) 631 669-7000
615 Cord Ave Lindenhurst (11757) *(G-7186)*
Nicolia Ready Mix Inc 631 669-7000
615 Cord Ave Lindenhurst (11757) *(G-7187)*
Nicolo Raineri 212 925-6128
82 Bowery New York (10013) *(G-10965)*
Nicolo Raineri Jeweler, New York *Also called Nicolo Raineri (G-10965)*
Nicolock Paving Stones LLC (HQ) 631 669-0700
612 Muncy St Lindenhurst (11757) *(G-7188)*
Nidec Indus Automtn USA LLC 716 774-1193
359 Lang Blvd Bldg B Grand Island (14072) *(G-5507)*
Nidec Motor Corporation 315 434-9303
6268 E Molloy Rd East Syracuse (13057) *(G-4361)*
Niebylski Bakery Inc 718 721-5152
2364 Steinway St Astoria (11105) *(G-437)*
Nift Group Inc 504 505-1144
14 Woodbine St Brooklyn (11221) *(G-2269)*
Nifty Bar Grinding & Cutting 585 381-0450
450 Whitney Rd Penfield (14526) *(G-12942)*
Nightingale Corp 905 896-3434
750 Ensminger Rd Ste 108 Tonawanda (14150) *(G-15564)*
Nightingale Food Entps Inc 347 577-1630
2306 1st Ave New York (10035) *(G-10966)*
Nijon Tool Co Inc 631 242-3434
12 Evergreen Pl 12 # 12 Deer Park (11729) *(G-4016)*
Nike Inc 212 226-5433
21 Mercer St Frnt A New York (10013) *(G-10967)*
Nike Inc 631 242-3014
102 The Arches Cir Deer Park (11729) *(G-4017)*
Nike Inc 631 960-0184
2675 Sunrise Hwy Islip Terrace (11752) *(G-6553)*
Nike Inc 716 298-5615
1886 Military Rd Niagara Falls (14304) *(G-12314)*
Nikish Software Corp 631 754-1618
12 Whispering Fields Dr Northport (11768) *(G-12473)*
Nikkei America Inc (HQ) 212 261-6200
1325 Avenue Of The Americ New York (10019) *(G-10968)*
Nikkei America Holdings Inc (HQ) 212 261-6200
1325 Avenue Of The Americ New York (10019) *(G-10969)*
Nikon Instruments Inc (HQ) 631 547-4200
1300 Walt Whitman Rd Fl 2 Melville (11747) *(G-8052)*
Nilda Desserts, Poughkeepsie *Also called Ljmm Inc (G-13351)*
Nildas Desserts Limited 845 454-5876
188 Washington St Poughkeepsie (12601) *(G-13359)*
Nimbletv Inc 646 502-7010
450 Fashion Ave Fl 43 New York (10123) *(G-10970)*
Ninas Custard 716 636-0345
2577 Millersport Hwy Getzville (14068) *(G-5350)*
Nine Pin Ciderworks LLC 518 449-9999
929 Broadway Albany (12207) *(G-105)*
Nine West Holdings Inc 212 642-3860
1411 Broadway Fl 38 New York (10018) *(G-10971)*
Nine West Holdings Inc 212 642-3860
1411 Broadway New York (10018) *(G-10972)*
Nine West Holdings Inc 212 391-5000
1411 Broadway Fl 15 New York (10018) *(G-10973)*
Nine West Holdings Inc 212 221-6376
1411 Broadway Fl 38 New York (10018) *(G-10974)*
Nine West Holdings Inc 212 575-2571
1441 Broadway Fl 20 New York (10018) *(G-10975)*
Nine West Holdings Inc 212 642-3860
1411 Broadway Fl 15 New York (10018) *(G-10976)*
Nine West Holdings Inc 212 642-3860
575 Fashion Ave Frnt 1 New York (10018) *(G-10977)*
Nine West Holdings Inc 212 822-1300
1441 Broadway New York (10018) *(G-10978)*
Nine West Holdings Inc 215 785-4000
1441 Broadway Fl 10 New York (10018) *(G-10979)*
Nireco America, Port Jervis *Also called Datatran Labs Inc (G-13227)*
Nirvana Inc 315 942-4900
1 Nirvana Plz Forestport (13338) *(G-5083)*
Nirx Medical Technologies LLC 516 676-6479
15 Cherry Ln Glen Head (11545) *(G-5384)*
Nite Train R, Champlain *Also called Koregon Enterprises Inc (G-3411)*
Nitram Energy Inc 716 662-6540
50 Cobham Dr Orchard Park (14127) *(G-12732)*
Nitro Manufacturing LLC 716 646-9900
440 Shirley Rd North Collins (14111) *(G-12386)*
Nitro Manufacturing LLC 716 646-9900
106 Evans St Ste E Hamburg (14075) *(G-5687)*
Nitro Wheels Inc 716 337-0709
4440 Shirley Rd North Collins (14111) *(G-12387)*
Nixon Gear, Syracuse *Also called Gear Motions Incorporated (G-15331)*
Njf Publishing Corp 631 345-5200
14 Ramsey Rd Shirley (11967) *(G-14842)*
Njr Medical Devices 440 258-8204
390 Oak Ave Cedarhurst (11516) *(G-3336)*
Nk Electric LLC 914 271-0222
22 Scenic Dr Croton On Hudson (10520) *(G-3915)*

ALPHABETIC

(PA)=Parent Co (HQ)=Headquarters (DH)=Div Headquarters

NK Medical Products Inc (PA) — 716 759-7200
 80 Creekside Dr Amherst (14228) *(G-241)*
Nlhe LLC — 212 594-0012
 141 Flushing Ave 906 Brooklyn (11205) *(G-2270)*
Nlr Counter Tops LLC — 347 295-0410
 902 E 92nd St New York (10128) *(G-10980)*
Nmcc, Niagara Falls Also called National Maint Contg Corp *(G-12312)*
No Longer Empty Inc — 202 413-4262
 122 W 27th St Fl 10 New York (10001) *(G-10981)*
Noah Enterprises Ltd (PA) — 212 736-2888
 520 8th Ave Lbby 2 New York (10018) *(G-10982)*
Noaspence Inc — 516 433-7848
 1040 S Broadway Unit 6 Hicksville (11801) *(G-6114)*
Nobilium, Albany Also called Cmp Industries LLC *(G-63)*
Noble Checks Inc — 212 537-6241
 1682 43rd St Apt 2 Brooklyn (11204) *(G-2271)*
Noble Pine Products Co Inc — 914 664-5877
 240 E 7th St Mount Vernon (10550) *(G-8425)*
Noble Vintages, Fredonia Also called Woodbury Vineyards Inc *(G-5130)*
Noble Wood Shavings, Sherrill Also called Dlr Enterprises LLC *(G-14819)*
Nochairs Inc — 917 748-8731
 325 W 38th St Rm 310 New York (10018) *(G-10983)*
Noco Incorporated (PA) — 716 833-6626
 2440 Sheridan Dr Ste 202 Tonawanda (14150) *(G-15565)*
Nodus Noodle Corporation — 718 309-3725
 4504 Queens Blvd Sunnyside (11104) *(G-15204)*
Noel Assoc — 516 371-5420
 114 Henry St Ste A Inwood (11096) *(G-6498)*
Noetic Partners Inc — 212 836-4351
 445 Park Ave Frnt 1 New York (10022) *(G-10984)*
Noga Dairies Inc — 516 293-5448
 175 Price Pkwy Farmingdale (11735) *(G-4837)*
Noho Health Inc — 877 227-3631
 9 Great Jones St Apt 4 New York (10012) *(G-10985)*
Noir Jewelry LLC — 212 465-8500
 358 5th Ave Rm 501 New York (10001) *(G-10986)*
Nola Speaker, Holbrook Also called Accent Speaker Technology Ltd *(G-6167)*
Nomad Editions LLC — 212 918-0992
 123 Ellison Ave Bronxville (10708) *(G-1425)*
None, College Point Also called City Store Gates Mfg Corp *(G-3642)*
Noodle Education Inc — 646 289-7800
 59 Charles St Suite200 New York (10014) *(G-10987)*
Norampac New York City Inc — 718 340-2100
 5515 Grand Ave Maspeth (11378) *(G-7863)*
Noras Candy Shop — 315 337-4530
 321 N Doxtator St Rome (13440) *(G-14262)*
Norazza Inc (PA) — 716 706-1160
 3938 Broadway St Buffalo (14227) *(G-2973)*
Norcorp Inc — 914 666-1310
 400 E Main St Mount Kisco (10549) *(G-8352)*
Nordic Interior Inc — 718 456-7000
 26 Court St Ste 2211 Brooklyn (11242) *(G-2272)*
Nordic Press Inc — 212 686-3356
 243 E 34th St New York (10016) *(G-10988)*
Nordon Inc (PA) — 585 546-6200
 691 Exchange St Rochester (14608) *(G-13974)*
Nordon Inc. — 585 546-6200
 1600 Lexington Ave 235a Rochester (14606) *(G-13975)*
Nordon Inc — 585 546-6200
 711 Exchange St Rochester (14608) *(G-13976)*
Noresco Industrial Group Inc — 516 759-3355
 3 School St Ste 103 Glen Cove (11542) *(G-5371)*
Norfalco LLC — 416 775-1431
 330 Madison Ave Fl 7 New York (10017) *(G-10989)*
Norlite LLC — 518 235-0030
 628 Saratoga St Cohoes (12047) *(G-3616)*
Norlite Corporation, Cohoes Also called Norlite LLC *(G-3616)*
Noroc Enterprises Inc — 718 585-3230
 415 Concord Ave Bronx (10455) *(G-1344)*
Norse Energy Corp USA — 716 568-2048
 3556 Lake Shore Rd # 700 Buffalo (14219) *(G-2974)*
Norsk Titanium US Inc (HQ) — 949 735-9463
 44 Martina Cir Plattsburgh (12901) *(G-13136)*
Nortek Powder Coating LLC — 315 337-2339
 5900 Success Dr Rome (13440) *(G-14263)*
North America Pastel Artists — 718 463-4701
 13303 41st Ave Apt 1a Flushing (11355) *(G-5030)*
North American Bear Co Inc — 212 388-0700
 1261 Broadway Rm 815 New York (10001) *(G-10990)*
North American Breweries Inc (HQ) — 585 546-1030
 445 Saint Paul St Rochester (14605) *(G-13977)*
North American Carbide, Orchard Park Also called Transport National Dev Inc *(G-12746)*
North American Carbide of NY, Orchard Park Also called Transport National Dev Inc *(G-12747)*
North American DF Inc (PA) — 718 698-2500
 4591 Hylan Blvd Staten Island (10312) *(G-15108)*
North American Door Corp — 518 566-0161
 1471 Military Tpke Plattsburgh (12901) *(G-13137)*
North American Enclosures Inc — 631 234-9500
 85 Jetson Ln Ste B Central Islip (11722) *(G-3381)*
North American Filter Corp (PA) — 800 265-8943
 200 W Shore Blvd Newark (14513) *(G-12203)*

North American Graphics Inc — 212 725-2200
 150 Varick St Rm 303 New York (10013) *(G-10991)*
North American Hoganas Inc — 716 285-3451
 5950 Packard Rd Niagara Falls (14304) *(G-12315)*
North American MBL Systems Inc — 718 898-8700
 3354 62nd St Woodside (11377) *(G-16667)*
North American Mfg Entps Inc (PA) — 718 524-4370
 1961 Richmond Ter Staten Island (10302) *(G-15109)*
North American Mfg Entps Inc — 718 524-4370
 1961 Richmond Ter Staten Island (10302) *(G-15110)*
North American Mills Inc — 212 695-6146
 1370 Broadway Rm 1101 New York (10018) *(G-10992)*
North American Pipe Corp — 516 338-2863
 156 High St East Williston (11596) *(G-4382)*
North American Service Group, Ballston Spa Also called North American Svcs Group LLC *(G-592)*
North American Signs Buffalo, Buffalo Also called Nas Quick Sign Inc *(G-2961)*
North American Slate Inc — 518 642-1702
 50 Columbus St Granville (12832) *(G-5523)*
North American Svcs Group LLC (HQ) — 518 885-1820
 1240 Saratoga Rd Ballston Spa (12020) *(G-592)*
North Americas Breweries, Rochester Also called High Falls Brewing Company LLC *(G-13867)*
North Amrcn Brwries Hldngs LLC (PA) — 585 546-1030
 445 Saint Paul St Rochester (14605) *(G-13978)*
North Atlantic Industries Inc — 631 567-1100
 50 Orville Dr Ste 3 Bohemia (11716) *(G-1065)*
North Atlantic Industries Inc (PA) — 631 567-1100
 110 Wilbur Pl Bohemia (11716) *(G-1066)*
North Atlantic Trading Co, New York Also called National Tobacco Company LP *(G-10888)*
North Bronx Retinal & Ophthlmi — 347 535-4932
 3725 Henry Hudson Pkwy Bronx (10463) *(G-1345)*
North Coast Outfitters Ltd — 631 727-5580
 1015 E Main St Ste 1 Riverhead (11901) *(G-13578)*
NORTH COUNTRY BEHAVIORAL HEALT, Saranac Lake Also called Northern New York Rural *(G-14563)*
North Country Books Inc — 315 735-4877
 220 Lafayette St Utica (13502) *(G-15726)*
North Country Dairy, North Lawrence Also called Upstate Niagara Coop Inc *(G-12393)*
North Country This Week — 315 265-1000
 19 Depot St Ste 1 Potsdam (13676) *(G-13320)*
North County News, Yorktown Heights Also called Northern Tier Publishing Corp *(G-16820)*
North Delaware Printing Inc — 716 692-0576
 645 Delaware St Ste 1 Tonawanda (14150) *(G-15566)*
North E Rggers Erectors NY Inc — 518 842-6377
 178 Clizbe Ave Amsterdam (12010) *(G-354)*
North East Finishing Co Inc — 631 789-8000
 245 Ralph Ave Copiague (11726) *(G-3771)*
North East Fuel Group Inc — 718 984-6774
 51 Stuyvesant Ave Staten Island (10312) *(G-15111)*
North Eastern Fabricators Inc — 718 542-0450
 910 Park Ave Ph Ph New York (10075) *(G-10993)*
North Eastern Rescue Vehicles — 315 414-9999
 10 Dwight Park Dr Ste 1 Syracuse (13209) *(G-15382)*
North End Paper Co Inc — 315 593-8100
 702 Hannibal St Fulton (13069) *(G-5229)*
North Face, Central Valley Also called Vf Outdoor LLC *(G-3398)*
NORTH FIELD, Island Park Also called Northfeld Precision Instr Corp *(G-6517)*
North Fork Wood Works Inc — 631 255-4028
 5175 Route 48 Mattituck (11952) *(G-7915)*
North Hills Signal Proc Corp — 631 244-7393
 40 Orville Dr Bohemia (11716) *(G-1067)*
North House Vineyards Inc — 631 779-2817
 1216 Main Rd Rte 25a Jamesport (11947) *(G-6693)*
North Hudson Woodcraft Corp — 315 429-3105
 152 N Helmer Ave Dolgeville (13329) *(G-4135)*
North Pk Innovations Group Inc (PA) — 716 699-2031
 6442 Route 242 E Ellicottville (14731) *(G-4447)*
North Point Technologies — 607 238-1114
 520 Columbia Dr Ste 105 Johnson City (13790) *(G-6815)*
North Point Technology LLC — 866 885-3377
 816 Buffalo St Endicott (13760) *(G-4605)*
North Salina Cigar Store, Syracuse Also called Saakshi Inc *(G-15412)*
North Shore Farms Two Ltd — 516 280-6880
 330 E Jericho Tpke Mineola (11501) *(G-8239)*
North Shore Home Improver — 631 474-2824
 200 Wilson St Port Jeff STA (11776) *(G-13214)*
North Shore Monuments Inc — 516 759-2156
 667 Cedar Swamp Rd Ste 5 Glen Head (11545) *(G-5385)*
North Shore Neon Sign Co Inc — 718 937-4848
 4649 54th Ave Flushing (11378) *(G-5031)*
North Shore News Group, Smithtown Also called Smithtown News Inc *(G-14909)*
North Shore Orthtics Prsthtics — 631 928-3040
 591 Bicycle Path Ste D Port Jeff STA (11776) *(G-13215)*
North Shore Pallet Inc — 631 673-4700
 191 E 2nd St Huntington Station (11746) *(G-6454)*
North Six Inc — 212 463-7227
 159 Bleecker St Frnt A New York (10012) *(G-10994)*
North Star Knitting Mills Inc — 718 894-4848
 7030 80th St Glendale (11385) *(G-5405)*

North Sunshine LLC..........307 027-1634
616 Corporate Way Ste 2-3 Valley Cottage (10989) ***(G-15761)***
North-East Machine Inc..........518 746-1837
4160 State Route 4 Hudson Falls (12839) ***(G-6383)***
North-South Books Inc..........212 706-4545
600 3rd Ave Fl 2 New York (10016) ***(G-10995)***
Northamerican Breweries, Rochester *Also called North American Breweries Inc* ***(G-13977)***
Northast Coml Win Trtments Inc..........845 331-0148
25 Cornell St Kingston (12401) ***(G-6912)***
Northast Ctr For Bekeeping LLC..........800 632-3379
8 Meader Rd Greenwich (12834) ***(G-5643)***
Northeast Cnstr Inds Inc..........845 565-1000
657 Rte 17 K S St Ste 2 Montgomery (12549) ***(G-8314)***
Northeast Commercial Prtg Inc (PA)..........518 459-5047
1237 Central Ave Ste 3 Albany (12205) ***(G-106)***
Northeast Concrete Pdts Inc..........518 563-0700
1024 Military Tpke Plattsburgh (12901) ***(G-13138)***
Northeast Conveyors Inc..........585 768-8912
7620 Evergreen St Lima (14485) ***(G-7153)***
Northeast Data..........845 331-5554
619 State Route 28 Kingston (12401) ***(G-6913)***
Northeast Doulas..........845 621-0654
23 Hilltop Dr Mahopac (10541) ***(G-7710)***
Northeast Fabricators LLC..........607 865-4031
30-35 William St Walton (13856) ***(G-15912)***
Northeast Group..........518 563-8214
12 Nepco Way Plattsburgh (12903) ***(G-13139)***
Northeast Group, The, Plattsburgh *Also called Northeast Prtg & Dist Co Inc* ***(G-13141)***
Northeast Hardware Specialties..........516 487-6868
393 Jericho Tpke Ste 103 Mineola (11501) ***(G-8240)***
Northeast Mesa LLC (PA)..........845 878-9344
10 Commerce Dr Carmel (10512) ***(G-3278)***
Northeast Metrology Corp..........716 827-3770
4490 Broadway Depew (14043) ***(G-4098)***
Northeast Pallet & Cont Co Inc..........518 271-0535
1 Mann Ave Bldg 300 Troy (12180) ***(G-15613)***
Northeast Promotional Group In..........518 793-1024
75 Main St South Glens Falls (12803) ***(G-14938)***
Northeast Prtg & Dist Co Inc..........514 577-3545
163 Idaho Ave Plattsburgh (12903) ***(G-13140)***
Northeast Prtg & Dist Co Inc (PA)..........518 563-8214
12 Nepco Way Plattsburgh (12903) ***(G-13141)***
Northeast Solite Corporation (PA)..........845 246-2646
1135 Kings Hwy Saugerties (12477) ***(G-14611)***
Northeast Solite Corporation..........845 246-2177
962 Kings Hwy Mount Marion (12456) ***(G-8365)***
Northeast Stitches & Ink Inc..........518 798-5549
95 Main St South Glens Falls (12803) ***(G-14939)***
Northeast Toner Inc..........518 899-5545
26 Walden Gln Fl 2 Ballston Lake (12019) ***(G-570)***
Northeast Treaters Inc..........518 945-2660
796 Schoharie Tpke Athens (12015) ***(G-451)***
Northeast Treaters NY LLC..........518 945-2660
796 Schoharie Tpke Athens (12015) ***(G-452)***
Northeast Windows Usa Inc..........516 378-6577
1 Kees Pl Merrick (11566) ***(G-8104)***
Northeastern Air Quality Inc..........518 857-3641
730 3rd St Albany (12206) ***(G-107)***
Northeastern Fuel Corp..........917 560-6241
51 Stuyvesant Ave Staten Island (10312) ***(G-15112)***
Northeastern Products Corp (PA)..........518 623-3161
115 Sweet Rd Warrensburg (12885) ***(G-15942)***
Northeastern Sealcoat Inc..........585 544-4372
470 Hollenbeck St Bldg 3 Rochester (14621) ***(G-13979)***
Northeastern Sign Corp..........315 265-6657
102 Cold Brook Dr South Colton (13687) ***(G-14926)***
Northeastern Transparts Inc..........716 833-0792
5727 S Park Ave Hamburg (14075) ***(G-5688)***
Northeastern Water Jet Inc..........518 843-4988
4 Willow St Amsterdam (12010) ***(G-355)***
Northern Air Systems Inc (PA)..........585 594-5050
3605 Buffalo Rd Rochester (14624) ***(G-13980)***
Northern Air Technology Inc (PA)..........585 594-5050
3605 Buffalo Rd Rochester (14624) ***(G-13981)***
Northern Awning & Sign Company..........315 782-8515
22891 County Route 51 Watertown (13601) ***(G-16030)***
Northern Biodiesel Inc..........585 545-4534
317 State Route 104 Ontario (14519) ***(G-12657)***
Northern Bituminous Mix Inc..........315 598-2141
32 Silk Rd Fulton (13069) ***(G-5230)***
Northern Design & Bldg Assoc..........518 747-2200
100 Park Rd Queensbury (12804) ***(G-13435)***
Northern Design Inc..........716 652-7071
12990 Old Big Tree Rd East Aurora (14052) ***(G-4209)***
Northern Forest Pdts Co Inc..........315 942-6955
9833 Crolius Dr Boonville (13309) ***(G-1118)***
Northern Goose Polar Project, New York *Also called Freedom Rains Inc* ***(G-9844)***
Northern King Lures Inc (PA)..........585 865-3373
167 Armstrong Rd Rochester (14616) ***(G-13982)***
Northern Lifts Elevator Co LLC (PA)..........518 644-2831
45 Indian Brook Hollow Rd Bolton Landing (12814) ***(G-1112)***
Northern Lights Candles, Wellsville *Also called Northern Lights Entps Inc* ***(G-16119)***
Northern Lights Entps Inc..........585 593-1200
3474 Andover Rd Wellsville (14895) ***(G-16119)***
Northern Machining Inc..........315 384-3189
2a N Main St Norfolk (13667) ***(G-12359)***
Northern Metalworks Corp..........646 523-1689
15 King Ave Selden (11784) ***(G-14765)***
Northern New York Rural..........518 891-9460
126 Kiwassa Rd Saranac Lake (12983) ***(G-14563)***
Northern NY Newspapers Corp..........315 782-1000
260 Washington St Watertown (13601) ***(G-16031)***
Northern Ready Mix LLC (HQ)..........315 336-7900
6131 E Taft Rd North Syracuse (13212) ***(G-12408)***
Northern Ready-Mix Inc, North Syracuse *Also called Northern Ready Mix LLC* ***(G-12408)***
Northern Tier Cnc Inc (PA)..........518 236-4702
733 Woods Falls Rd Mooers Forks (12959) ***(G-8331)***
Northern Tier Publishing Corp..........914 962-4748
1520 Front St Yorktown Heights (10598) ***(G-16820)***
Northern Timber Harvesting LLC..........585 233-7330
6042 State Route 21 Alfred Station (14803) ***(G-187)***
NORTHERN WESTCHESTER HOSPITAL, Mount Kisco *Also called Norcorp Inc* ***(G-8352)***
Northfeld Precision Instr Corp..........516 431-1112
4400 Austin Blvd Island Park (11558) ***(G-6517)***
Northknight Logistics Inc..........716 283-3090
7724 Buffalo Ave Niagara Falls (14304) ***(G-12316)***
Northland Filter Intl LLC..........315 207-1410
249a Mitchell St Oswego (13126) ***(G-12782)***
Northpoint Digital LLC..........212 819-1700
1540 Broadway Fl 41 New York (10036) ***(G-10996)***
Northpoint Trading Inc (PA)..........212 481-8001
347 5th Ave New York (10016) ***(G-10997)***
Northport Printing, West Babylon *Also called Bartolomeo Publishing Inc* ***(G-16138)***
Northrock Industries Inc..........631 924-6130
31 Crossway E Bohemia (11716) ***(G-1068)***
Northrop Grumman Corporation..........703 280-2900
660 Grumman Rd W Bethpage (11714) ***(G-849)***
Northrop Grumman Intl Trdg Inc..........716 626-7233
1740 Wehrle Dr Buffalo (14221) ***(G-2975)***
Northrop Grumman Systems Corp..........516 575-0574
925 S Oyster Bay Rd Bethpage (11714) ***(G-850)***
Northrop Grumman Systems Corp..........716 626-4600
1740 Wehrle Dr Buffalo (14221) ***(G-2976)***
Northrop Grumman Systems Corp..........631 423-1014
70 Dewey St Huntington (11743) ***(G-6406)***
Northrop Grumman Systems Corp..........315 336-0500
Rr 26 Box N Rome (13440) ***(G-14264)***
Northside Media Group LLC (HQ)..........917 318-6513
55 Washington St Ste 652 Brooklyn (11201) ***(G-2273)***
Northside Media Group LLC..........917 318-6513
55 Washington St Ste 652 Brooklyn (11201) ***(G-2274)***
Northtown Imaging, Buffalo *Also called Mri Northtowns Group PC* ***(G-2955)***
Northwest Company LLC (PA)..........516 484-6996
49 Bryant Ave Roslyn (11576) ***(G-14449)***
Northwest Urgent Care..........646 870-6406
2628 Broadway New York (10025) ***(G-10998)***
Northwest Wine Services, Riverhead *Also called Railex Wine Services LLC* ***(G-13581)***
Northwind Graphics..........518 899-9651
2453 State Route 9 Ballston Spa (12020) ***(G-593)***
Norton Pulpstones Incorporated..........716 433-9400
120 Church St Lockport (14094) ***(G-7324)***
Norton, Ww & Company,, New York *Also called Liveright Publishing Corp* ***(G-10584)***
Norton-Smith Hardwoods Inc (PA)..........716 945-0346
25 Morningside Ave Salamanca (14779) ***(G-14529)***
Norwesco Inc..........607 687-8081
263 Corporate Dr Owego (13827) ***(G-12801)***
Norwich Manufacturing Division, Binghamton *Also called Felchar Manufacturing Corp* ***(G-884)***
Norwich Pharma Services, Norwich *Also called Norwich Pharmaceuticals Inc* ***(G-12490)***
Norwich Pharmaceuticals Inc..........607 335-3000
6826 State Highway 12 Norwich (13815) ***(G-12490)***
Norwood Quar Btmnous Con Plnts, Norwood *Also called Barrett Paving Materials Inc* ***(G-12495)***
Norwood Screw Machine Parts..........516 481-6644
200 E 2nd St Ste 2 Mineola (11501) ***(G-8241)***
Not For Profit Chari, Bronx *Also called Lemon Brothers Foundation Inc* ***(G-1316)***
Noteworthy Company, The, Amsterdam *Also called Noteworthy Industries Inc* ***(G-356)***
Noteworthy Industries Inc..........518 842-2662
336 Forest Ave Amsterdam (12010) ***(G-356)***
Noticia Hispanoamericana Inc..........516 223-5678
636 Seaman Ave North Baldwin (11510) ***(G-12365)***
Noto Industrial Corp..........631 736-7600
11 Thomas St Coram (11727) ***(G-3802)***
Notubes.com, Big Flats *Also called KG Motors Inc* ***(G-855)***
Nova Inc..........212 967-1139
362 5th Ave Ste 1001 New York (10001) ***(G-10999)***
Nova Health Systems Inc..........315 798-9018
1001 Broad St Ste 3 Utica (13501) ***(G-15727)***
Nova Optical, Orangeburg *Also called Essilor Laboratories Amer Inc* ***(G-12676)***
Nova Pack, Philmont *Also called Pvc Container Corporation* ***(G-12987)***
Nova Packaging Ltd Inc..........914 232-8406
7 Sunrise Ave Katonah (10536) ***(G-6845)***

ALPHABETIC

Nova Science Publishers Inc...631 231-7269
400 Oser Ave Ste 1600 Hauppauge (11788) ***(G-5902)***
Novamed-Usa Inc...914 789-2100
4 Westchester Plz Ste 137 Elmsford (10523) ***(G-4556)***
Novartis AG...617 435-0469
18 Driftwood Dr Port Washington (11050) ***(G-13291)***
Novartis Corporation...718 276-8600
22715 N Conduit Ave Laurelton (11413) ***(G-7100)***
Novartis Pharmaceuticals Corp...888 669-6682
230 Park Ave New York (10169) ***(G-11000)***
Novartis Pharmaceuticals Corp...718 276-8600
22715 N Conduit Ave Laurelton (11413) ***(G-7101)***
Novatech Inc...716 892-6682
190 Gruner Rd Cheektowaga (14227) ***(G-3455)***
Novel Box Company Ltd...718 965-2222
659 Berriman St Brooklyn (11208) ***(G-2275)***
Novelis Corporation...315 342-1036
448 County Route 1a Oswego (13126) ***(G-12783)***
Novelis Corporation...315 349-0121
72 Alcan W Entrance Rd Oswego (13126) ***(G-12784)***
Novelis Inc...315 349-0121
448 County Route 1a Oswego (13126) ***(G-12785)***
Novelty Crystal Corp (PA)...718 458-6700
3015 48th Ave Long Island City (11101) ***(G-7540)***
Novelty Scenic Studios Inc, Monroe *Also called Associated Drapery & Equipment* ***(G-8263)***
Noven Pharmaceuticals Inc...212 682-4420
350 5th Ave Ste 3700 New York (10118) ***(G-11001)***
Novita Fabrics Furnishing Corp...516 299-4500
207 Elm Pl Ste 2 Mineola (11501) ***(G-8242)***
Novoye Rsskoye Slovo Pubg Corp...646 460-4566
2614 Voorhies Ave Brooklyn (11235) ***(G-2276)***
Novum Medical Products Inc...716 759-7200
80 Creekside Dr Amherst (14228) ***(G-242)***
Nppi, Vestal *Also called National Pipe & Plastics Inc* ***(G-15820)***
Nr Fragrances & Cosmetics Inc...212 686-4006
1220 Broadway Rm 700 New York (10001) ***(G-11002)***
Nrd LLC...716 773-7634
2937 Alt Blvd Grand Island (14072) ***(G-5508)***
Nsgv Inc...212 367-3167
90 5th Ave New York (10011) ***(G-11003)***
Nsgv Inc...212 367-3100
90 5th Ave New York (10011) ***(G-11004)***
Nsh, Menands *Also called Simmons Machine Tool Corp* ***(G-8091)***
Nsi Industries LLC...800 841-2505
50 S Macquesten Pkwy Mount Vernon (10550) ***(G-8426)***
Nsj Group Ltd...631 893-9300
80 W Main St Ste A Babylon (11702) ***(G-530)***
NSM Surveillance, New York *Also called News/Sprts Microwave Rentl Inc* ***(G-10955)***
Nsusa, Deer Park *Also called Nutra Solutions USA Inc* ***(G-4019)***
NTI Global, Amsterdam *Also called Nationwide Tarps Incorporated* ***(G-353)***
Nu - Communitek LLC...516 433-3553
108 New South Rd Ste A Hicksville (11801) ***(G-6115)***
Nu Life Restorations of L I...516 489-5200
51 Valley Rd Old Westbury (11568) ***(G-12591)***
Nu Ways Inc...585 254-7510
655 Pullman Ave Rochester (14615) ***(G-13983)***
Nu-Chem Laboratories, Bellport *Also called Optisource International Inc* ***(G-810)***
Nu-Life Long Island, Old Westbury *Also called Nu Life Restorations of L I* ***(G-12591)***
Nu2 Systems LLC...914 719-7272
155 Lafayette Ave White Plains (10603) ***(G-16481)***
Nubian Heritage...631 265-3551
367 Old Willets Path Hauppauge (11788) ***(G-5903)***
Nucare Pharmacy & Surgical, New York *Also called Nucare Pharmacy West LLC* ***(G-11006)***
Nucare Pharmacy & Surgical, New York *Also called Nucare Pharmacy Inc* ***(G-11005)***
Nucare Pharmacy Inc...212 426-9300
1789 1st Ave New York (10128) ***(G-11005)***
Nucare Pharmacy West LLC...212 462-2525
250 9th Ave New York (10001) ***(G-11006)***
Nuclear Diagnostic Pdts NY Inc...516 575-4201
130 Commercial St Plainview (11803) ***(G-13079)***
Nucor Steel Auburn Inc...315 253-4561
25 Quarry Rd Auburn (13021) ***(G-493)***
Nugent Printing Company, Oceanside *Also called The Nugent Organization Inc* ***(G-12561)***
Nulux Inc...718 383-1112
1717 Troutman St Ridgewood (11385) ***(G-13544)***
Numed Pharmaceuticals, Brooklyn *Also called Ys Marketing Inc* ***(G-2667)***
Numerix LLC (PA)...212 302-2220
99 Park Ave Fl 5 New York (10016) ***(G-11007)***
Nupro Technologies LLC...412 422-5922
23 Coach St Ste 2a Canandaigua (14424) ***(G-3227)***
Nutec Components Inc...631 242-1224
81 E Jefryn Blvd Ste A Deer Park (11729) ***(G-4018)***
Nutech Biosciences Inc...315 505-6500
537 Fitch St Oneida (13421) ***(G-12613)***
Nutek Disposables Inc...516 829-3030
80 Cuttermill Rd Ste 500 Great Neck (11021) ***(G-5574)***
Nutra Solutions USA Inc...631 392-1900
1019 Grand Blvd Deer Park (11729) ***(G-4019)***
Nutra-Scientifics LLC...917 238-8510
108 Overlook Rd Pomona (10970) ***(G-13186)***
Nutra-Vet Research Corp...845 473-1900
201 Smith St Poughkeepsie (12601) ***(G-13360)***
Nutraceutical Wellness LLC...888 454-3320
28 W 27th St Fl 2 New York (10001) ***(G-11008)***
Nutrafol, New York *Also called Nutraceutical Wellness LLC* ***(G-11008)***
Nutraqueen LLC...347 368-6568
138 E 34th St Apt 2f New York (10016) ***(G-11009)***
Nutrascience Labs Inc...631 247-0660
70 Carolyn Blvd Farmingdale (11735) ***(G-4838)***
Nutratech Labs Inc...315 695-2256
406 State Route 264 Phoenix (13135) ***(G-12991)***
Nutrifast LLC...347 671-3181
244 5th Ave Ste W249 New York (10001) ***(G-11010)***
Nutritional Designs, Lynbrook *Also called ND Labs Inc* ***(G-7669)***
Nuttall Gear L L C (HQ)...716 298-4100
2221 Niagara Falls Blvd # 17 Niagara Falls (14304) ***(G-12317)***
Nuvite Chemical Compounds Corp...718 383-8351
213 Freeman St 215 Brooklyn (11222) ***(G-2277)***
NY 1 Art Gallery Inc...917 698-0626
32 3rd St New Hyde Park (11040) ***(G-8554)***
NY Cabinet Factory Inc...718 256-6541
6901 14th Ave Brooklyn (11228) ***(G-2278)***
NY Cutting Inc...646 434-1355
3 Chestnut St Ste 1 Suffern (10901) ***(G-15194)***
NY Denim Inc...212 764-6668
1407 Broadway Rm 1021 New York (10018) ***(G-11011)***
NY Embroidery Inc...516 822-6456
25 Midland Ave Hicksville (11801) ***(G-6116)***
NY Froyo LLC...516 312-4588
324 W 19th St Deer Park (11729) ***(G-4020)***
NY Iron Inc...718 302-9000
3131 48th Ave Ste 2 Long Island City (11101) ***(G-7541)***
NY Orthopedic Usa Inc...718 852-5330
63 Flushing Ave Unit 333 Brooklyn (11205) ***(G-2279)***
NY Phrmacy Compounding Ctr Inc...201 403-5151
3715 23rd Ave Astoria (11105) ***(G-438)***
NY Print Partners, Sunnyside *Also called Deanco Digital Printing LLC* ***(G-15202)***
NY Tempering LLC...718 326-8989
6021 Flushing Ave Maspeth (11378) ***(G-7864)***
NY Tilemakers...989 278-8453
331 Grand St Brooklyn (11211) ***(G-2280)***
Nyahb Inc...845 352-5300
161 Route 59 Ste 101 Monsey (10952) ***(G-8292)***
Nyc Bronx Inc...917 417-0509
2490 Grand Concourse Bronx (10458) ***(G-1346)***
Nyc Community Media LLC...212 229-1890
1 Metrotech Ctr N Fl 10 Brooklyn (11201) ***(G-2281)***
Nyc Design Co, New York *Also called M S B International Ltd* ***(G-10642)***
Nyc District Council Ubcja...212 366-7500
395 Hudson St Lbby 3 New York (10014) ***(G-11012)***
Nyc Idol Apparel Inc...212 997-9797
214 W 39th St Rm 807 New York (10018) ***(G-11013)***
Nyc Knitwear Inc...212 840-1313
525 Fashion Ave Rm 701 New York (10018) ***(G-11014)***
Nyc Thermography, New York *Also called Hart Reproduction Services* ***(G-10046)***
Nyc Trade Printers Corp...718 606-0610
3245 62nd St Woodside (11377) ***(G-16668)***
Nycom Business Solutions Inc...516 345-6000
804 Hempstead Tpke Franklin Square (11010) ***(G-5120)***
Nycon Diamond & Tools Corp...855 937-6922
55 Knickerbocker Ave A Bohemia (11716) ***(G-1069)***
Nyemac Inc...631 668-1303
Paradise Ln Montauk (11954) ***(G-8307)***
Nyi Building Products Inc (PA)...518 458-7500
5 Southside Dr Ste 204 Clifton Park (12065) ***(G-3572)***
Nykon Inc...315 483-0504
8175 Stell Rd Sodus (14551) ***(G-14914)***
Nylon LLc...212 226-6454
110 Greene St Ste 607 New York (10012) ***(G-11015)***
Nylon Magazine, New York *Also called Nylon LLc* ***(G-11015)***
Nylon Media Inc (PA)...212 226-6454
110 Greene St Ste 607 New York (10012) ***(G-11016)***
Nylonshop, New York *Also called Nylon Media Inc* ***(G-11016)***
Nyman Jewelry Inc (PA)...212 944-1976
66 W 9th St New York (10011) ***(G-11017)***
Nyp Holdings Inc...718 260-2500
1 Metrotech Ctr N Fl 10 Brooklyn (11201) ***(G-2282)***
Nyp Holdings Inc (HQ)...212 997-9272
1211 Ave Of The Americas New York (10036) ***(G-11018)***
Nyrev Inc...212 757-8070
435 Hudson St Rm 300 New York (10014) ***(G-11019)***
Nys Nyu-Cntr Intl Cooperation...212 998-3680
418 Lafayette St New York (10003) ***(G-11020)***
NYSASBO, Albany *Also called New York State Assoc* ***(G-102)***
Nysco Products LLC...718 792-9000
211 Saw Mill River Rd Hawthorne (10532) ***(G-5994)***
Nyt Capital LLC (HQ)...212 556-1234
620 8th Ave New York (10018) ***(G-11021)***
Nytimes Corporate...212 556-1234
620 8th Ave Fl 17 New York (10018) ***(G-11022)***
O & S Machine & Tool Co Inc...716 941-5542
8143 State Rd Colden (14033) ***(G-3633)***

O Brien Gere Mfg Inc......315 437-6100
7600 Morgan Rd Ste 1 Liverpool (13090) *(G-7250)*
O C Choppers, Newburgh *Also called Orange County Choppers Inc (G-12237)*
O P I Industries, Ronkonkoma *Also called Paramount Equipment Inc (G-14395)*
O Rama Light Inc......518 539-9000
22 Hudson Falls Rd Ste 52 South Glens Falls (12803) *(G-14940)*
O Tex, Rochester *Also called Robert J Faraone (G-14076)*
O Val Nick Music Co Inc......212 873-2179
254 W 72nd St Apt 1a New York (10023) *(G-11023)*
O W Hubbell & Sons Inc......315 736-8311
5124 Commercial Dr Yorkville (13495) *(G-16828)*
O'Bryan Bros, New York *Also called Komar Layering LLC (G-10467)*
O'Neil Construction, Glen Head *Also called Lomin Construction Company (G-5382)*
O-At-Ka Milk Products Coop Inc (PA)......585 343-0536
700 Ellicott St Batavia (14020) *(G-632)*
O-Neh-Da Vineyard, Conesus *Also called Eagle Crest Vineyard LLC (G-3708)*
Oak Lone Publishing Co Inc......518 792-1126
15 Ridge St Glens Falls (12801) *(G-5437)*
Oak Valley Logging Inc......518 622-8249
558 Frank Hitchcock Rd Cairo (12413) *(G-3151)*
Oak-Bark Corporation......518 372-5691
37 Maple Ave Scotia (12302) *(G-14745)*
Oak-Mitsui Inc......518 686-8060
1 Mechanic St Bldg 2 Hoosick Falls (12090) *(G-6278)*
Oak-Mitsui Technologies LLC......518 686-4961
80 1st St Hoosick Falls (12090) *(G-6279)*
Oakdale Industrial Elec Corp......631 737-4090
1995 Pond Rd Ronkonkoma (11779) *(G-14388)*
Oakhurst Partners LLC......212 502-3220
148 Madison Ave Fl 13 New York (10016) *(G-11024)*
Oaklee International Inc......631 436-7900
125 Raynor Ave Ronkonkoma (11779) *(G-14389)*
Oakwood Publishing Co......516 482-7720
10 Bond St Ste 1 Great Neck (11021) *(G-5575)*
Oasis Cosmetic Labs Inc......631 758-0038
182 Long Island Ave Holtsville (11742) *(G-6241)*
Oberdorfer Pumps Inc......315 437-0361
5900 Firestone Dr Syracuse (13206) *(G-15383)*
Oberon, New York *Also called Tabrisse Collections Inc (G-11773)*
Obout Software Inc......212 380-3500
728 Ocean View Ave Apt A1 Brooklyn (11235) *(G-2283)*
Observer Daily Sunday Newsppr......716 366-3000
10 E 2nd St Dunkirk (14048) *(G-4175)*
Observer Dispatch, Utica *Also called Gatehouse Media LLC (G-15706)*
Observer Media LLC......212 755-2400
1 Whitehall St Fl 7 New York (10004) *(G-11025)*
Ocala Group LLC......516 233-2750
1981 Marcus Ave Ste 227 New Hyde Park (11042) *(G-8555)*
Occidental Chemical Corp......716 278-7795
4700 Buffalo Ave Niagara Falls (14304) *(G-12318)*
Occidental Chemical Corp......716 773-8100
2801 Long Rd Grand Island (14072) *(G-5509)*
Occidental Chemical Corp......716 278-7794
56 Street & Energy Blvd Niagara Falls (14302) *(G-12319)*
Occidental Chemical Corp......716 694-3827
3780 Commerce Ct Ste 600 North Tonawanda (14120) *(G-12440)*
Occidental Energy Mktg Inc......212 632-4950
1230 Av Of The Amrcs 80 New York (10020) *(G-11026)*
Occunomix International LLC......631 741-1940
585 Bicycle Path Ste 52 Port Jeff STA (11776) *(G-13216)*
Ocean Cardiac Monitoring......631 777-3700
38 W 17th St Deer Park (11729) *(G-4021)*
Ocean Park Drugs & Surgical, Far Rockaway *Also called Far Rockaway Drugs Inc (G-4701)*
Ocean Printing, Ronkonkoma *Also called Copy X/Press Ltd (G-14328)*
Ocean Waves Swim LLC......212 967-4481
19 W 34th St Fl 11 New York (10001) *(G-11027)*
Oceanconnect Marine Inc (HQ)......203 328-3117
330 Madison Ave New York (10017) *(G-11028)*
Oceans Cuisine Ltd......631 209-9200
367 Sheffield Ct Ridge (11961) *(G-13522)*
Oceanside-Island Park Herald, Lawrence *Also called Richner Communications Inc (G-7108)*
Oci USA Inc (PA)......646 589-6180
660 Madison Ave Fl 19 New York (10065) *(G-11029)*
Ocip Holding LLC (PA)......646 589-6180
660 Madison Ave Fl 19 New York (10065) *(G-11030)*
Ocs Industries, Glendale *Also called CIDC Corp (G-5395)*
Octave Music Group Inc (HQ)......212 991-6540
850 3rd Ave Ste 15th New York (10022) *(G-11031)*
Octopus Advanced Systems Inc......914 771-6110
27 Covington Rd Yonkers (10710) *(G-16786)*
Odegard Inc......212 545-0069
3030 47th Ave Ste 700 Long Island City (11101) *(G-7542)*
Oden Machinery Inc (PA)......716 874-3000
600 Ensminger Rd Tonawanda (14150) *(G-15567)*
ODY Accessories Inc......212 239-0580
1239 Broadway New York (10001) *(G-11032)*
Odyssey Controls Inc......585 548-9800
6256 Clinton Street Rd Bergen (14416) *(G-826)*
Odyssey Mag Pubg Group Inc......212 545-4800
4 New York Plz New York (10004) *(G-11033)*
Oehlers Wldg & Fabrication Inc......716 821-1800
242 Elk St Buffalo (14210) *(G-2977)*
OEM Solutions Inc......716 864-9324
4995 Rockhaven Dr Clarence (14031) *(G-3536)*
Oerlikon Blzers Cating USA Inc......716 270-2228
6000 N Bailey Ave Ste 9 Amherst (14226) *(G-243)*
Oerlikon Blzers Cating USA Inc......716 270-2228
6000 N Bailey Ave Ste 9 Amherst (14226) *(G-244)*
Oerlikon Blzers Cating USA Inc......716 564-8557
6000 N Bailey Ave Ste 3 Buffalo (14226) *(G-2978)*
Oerlikon Metco (us) Inc......716 270-2228
6000 N Bailey Ave Amherst (14226) *(G-245)*
Oestreich Metal Works Inc......315 463-4268
6131 Court Street Rd Syracuse (13206) *(G-15384)*
Office Grabs LLC......347 678-3993
1245 50th St Apt 4d Brooklyn (11219) *(G-2284)*
Office Grabs NY Inc......212 444-1331
1303 53rd St 105 Brooklyn (11219) *(G-2285)*
Officegrabscom, Brooklyn *Also called Office Grabs LLC (G-2284)*
Official Offset Corporation......631 957-8500
8600 New Horizons Blvd Amityville (11701) *(G-307)*
Official Press, The, New York *Also called Hks Printing Company Inc (G-10109)*
Ogd V-Hvac Inc......315 858-1002
174 Pumkinhook Rd Van Hornesville (13475) *(G-15802)*
Ogden Newspapers Inc......716 487-1111
15 W 2nd St Jamestown (14701) *(G-6741)*
Ogi Limited, New York *Also called Osnat Gad Inc (G-11066)*
Ogilvie Press, Lancaster *Also called Rmf Printing Technologies Inc (G-7045)*
Ogosport LLC......718 554-0777
63 Flushing Ave Unit 137 Brooklyn (11205) *(G-2286)*
Ogulnick Uniforms, New York *Also called Tailored Sportsman LLC (G-11776)*
OH How Cute Inc......347 838-6031
38 Androvette St Staten Island (10309) *(G-15113)*
Ohio Baking Company Inc......315 724-2033
10585 Cosby Manor Rd Utica (13502) *(G-15728)*
Ohserase Manufacturing LLC......518 358-9309
26 Eagle Dr Akwesasne (13655) *(G-26)*
Ohserase Manufacturing LLC......518 358-9309
393 Frogtown Rd Hogansburg (13655) *(G-6166)*
Oil and Lubricant Depot LLC......718 258-9220
61 Ranick Dr S Amityville (11701) *(G-308)*
Oil Depot, The, Amityville *Also called Oil and Lubricant Depot LLC (G-308)*
Oil Solutions Intl Inc......631 608-8889
35 Mill St Amityville (11701) *(G-309)*
Okcupid, New York *Also called Humor Rainbow Inc (G-10151)*
Okey Enterprises Inc......212 213-2640
347 5th Ave Rm 1005 New York (10016) *(G-11034)*
Okra Energy LLC......206 495-7574
99 Jane St Apt 5d New York (10014) *(G-11035)*
Olan Laboratories Inc......631 582-2082
20 Newton Pl Hauppauge (11788) *(G-5904)*
Old Castle Precast, Middle Island *Also called Afco Precast Sales Corp (G-8116)*
Old Dutch Mustard Co Inc (PA)......516 466-0522
98 Cuttermill Rd Ste 260s Great Neck (11021) *(G-5576)*
Old Dutchmans Wrough Iron Inc......716 688-2034
2800 Millersport Hwy Getzville (14068) *(G-5351)*
Old Williamsburgh Candle Corp......718 566-1500
321 Route 59 Tallman (10982) *(G-15464)*
Old World Mouldings Inc......631 563-8660
821 Lincoln Ave Bohemia (11716) *(G-1070)*
Oldcastle Apg Northeast Inc......585 924-2103
735 Wangum Rd Fishers (14453) *(G-4941)*
Oldcastle Building Envelope (HQ)......212 957-5400
1350 Ave Of The Americas New York (10019) *(G-11036)*
Oldcastle Buildingenvelope Inc......631 234-2200
895 Motor Pkwy Hauppauge (11788) *(G-5905)*
Oldcastle Materials Inc......585 424-6410
1260 Jefferson Rd Rochester (14623) *(G-13984)*
Oldcastle Precast Inc......518 767-2116
100 S County Rte 101 South Bethlehem (12161) *(G-14924)*
Oldcastle Precast Inc......518 767-2112
123 County Route 101 Selkirk (12158) *(G-14769)*
Oldcastle Precast Bldg Systems, Selkirk *Also called Oldcastle Precast Inc (G-14769)*
Olde Chtqua Vneyards Ltd Lblty......716 792-2749
6654 W Main Rd Portland (14769) *(G-13315)*
Olean Advanced Products, Olean *Also called AVX Corporation (G-12592)*
Olean Waste Water Treatment, Olean *Also called City of Olean (G-12595)*
Oledworks LLC (PA)......585 287-6802
1645 Lyell Ave Ste 140 Rochester (14606) *(G-13985)*
Olin Chlor Alkali Logistics......716 278-6411
2400 Buffalo Ave Niagara Falls (14303) *(G-12320)*
Olive Branch Foods LLC......631 343-7070
3124 Express Dr S Islandia (11749) *(G-6536)*
Olive Led Lighting Inc......718 746-0830
1310 111th St College Point (11356) *(G-3658)*
OLIVEA MATHEWS, New York *Also called Pride & Joys Inc (G-11239)*
Oliver Gear, Buffalo *Also called Gear Motions Incorporated (G-2843)*
Oliver Gear Inc......716 885-1080
1120 Niagara St Buffalo (14213) *(G-2979)*
Olmstead Machine Inc......315 587-9864
10399 Warehouse Ave North Rose (14516) *(G-12396)*

ALPHABETIC

(PA)=Parent Co (HQ)=Headquarters (DH)=Div Headquarters
2019 Harris
New York Manufacturers Directory
951

Olmstead Products Corp 516 681-3700
1 Jefry Ln Hicksville (11801) *(G-6117)*
Olollo Inc 877 701-0110
43 Hall St Ste B8 Brooklyn (11205) *(G-2287)*
Olson Sign Company Inc 518 370-2118
1750 Valley Rd Ext Schenectady (12302) *(G-14701)*
Olson Signs & Graphics, Schenectady *Also called Olson Sign Company Inc (G-14701)*
Olympia Company, Elmsford *Also called Olympia Sports Company Inc (G-4557)*
Olympia Sports Company Inc 914 347-4737
500 Executive Blvd # 170 Elmsford (10523) *(G-4557)*
Olympic Ice Cream Co Inc 718 849-6200
12910 91st Ave Richmond Hill (11418) *(G-13507)*
Olympic Jewelry Inc 212 768-7004
62 W 47th St Ste 509 New York (10036) *(G-11037)*
Olympic Manufacturing Inc 631 231-8900
195 Marcus Blvd Hauppauge (11788) *(G-5906)*
Olympic Press Inc 212 242-4934
950 3rd Ave Fl 7 New York (10022) *(G-11038)*
Olympic Software & Consulting 631 351-0655
290 Broadhollow Rd 130e Melville (11747) *(G-8053)*
Omc Inc 718 731-5001
4010 Park Ave Bronx (10457) *(G-1347)*
Omega Consolidated Corporation 585 392-9262
101 Heinz St Hilton (14468) *(G-6158)*
Omega Furniture Manufacturing 315 463-7428
102 Wavel St Syracuse (13206) *(G-15385)*
Omega Heater Company Inc 631 588-8820
2059 9th Ave Ronkonkoma (11779) *(G-14390)*
Omega Tool Measuring Mchs Inc (PA) 585 598-7800
101 Perinton Pkwy Fairport (14450) *(G-4645)*
Omega Wire Inc 315 337-4300
900 Railroad St Rome (13440) *(G-14265)*
Omega Wire Inc 315 689-7115
24 N Beaver St Jordan (13080) *(G-6842)*
Omega Wire Inc (HQ) 315 245-3800
12 Masonic Ave Camden (13316) *(G-3191)*
Omg Cleaners Inc 718 282-2011
565 Coney Island Ave Brooklyn (11218) *(G-2288)*
Omg Desserts Inc 585 698-1561
1227 Ridgeway Ave Ste J Rochester (14615) *(G-13986)*
Omicron Technologies Inc 631 434-7697
1736 Church St Holbrook (11741) *(G-6204)*
Omni-ID Usa Inc 585 697-9913
1200 Ridgeway Ave Ste 106 Rochester (14615) *(G-13987)*
Omniafiltra LLC 315 346-7300
9567 Main St Beaver Falls (13305) *(G-767)*
Omnicare Anesthesia PC (PA) 718 433-0044
3636 33rd St Ste 211 Astoria (11106) *(G-439)*
Omnimusic, Port Washington *Also called Franklin-Douglas Inc (G-13260)*
Omntec Mfg Inc 631 981-2001
1993 Pond Rd Ronkonkoma (11779) *(G-14391)*
Omp Printing & Graphics, Clinton *Also called Tenney Media Group (G-3589)*
Omrix Biopharmaceuticals Inc 908 218-0707
1 Rckfller Ctr Ste 2322 New York (10020) *(G-11039)*
Omt, Yorkville *Also called Oriskany Mfg Tech LLC (G-16830)*
Omx (us) Inc 646 428-2800
140 Broadway Fl 25 New York (10005) *(G-11040)*
On Demand Books LLC 212 966-2222
939 Lexington Ave New York (10065) *(G-11041)*
On Line Power Technologies 914 968-4440
113 Sunnyside Dr Yonkers (10705) *(G-16787)*
On Montauk, Montauk *Also called Nyemac Inc (G-8307)*
On Semiconductor Corporation 585 784-5770
1964 Lake Ave Rochester (14615) *(G-13988)*
On The Double Inc 518 431-3571
178 Viewmont Rd Germantown (12526) *(G-5339)*
On The Job Embroidery & AP 914 381-3556
154 E Boston Post Rd # 1 Mamaroneck (10543) *(G-7750)*
On The Mark Digital Printing & 716 823-3373
5758 S Park Ave Hamburg (14075) *(G-5689)*
On The Spot Binding Inc 718 497-2200
4805 Metropolitan Ave Ridgewood (11385) *(G-13545)*
On Time Plastics Inc 516 442-4280
121 Henry St Freeport (11520) *(G-5170)*
Once Again Nut Butter Collectv (PA) 585 468-2535
12 S State St Nunda (14517) *(G-12497)*
Ondrivesus Corp 516 771-6777
216 N Main St Bldg B2 Freeport (11520) *(G-5171)*
One In A Million Inc 516 829-1111
51 Franklin Ave Valley Stream (11580) *(G-15788)*
One Jeanswear Group Inc (HQ) 212 575-2571
1441 Broadway New York (10018) *(G-11042)*
One Step Up Kids, New York *Also called Kidz Concepts LLC (G-10441)*
One Step Up Ltd (PA) 212 398-1110
1412 Broadway Fl 3 New York (10018) *(G-11043)*
One Story Inc 917 816-3659
232 3rd St Ste A108 Brooklyn (11215) *(G-2289)*
One Tree Dist 315 701-2924
200 Midler Park Dr Syracuse (13206) *(G-15386)*
One-Blue LLC 212 223-4380
1350 Broadway Rm 1406 New York (10018) *(G-11044)*
Oneida Air Systems Inc 315 476-5151
1001 W Fayette St Ste 2a Syracuse (13204) *(G-15387)*
Oneida Concrete Products, Buffalo *Also called Oneida Sales & Service Inc (G-2980)*
Oneida Dispatch, Oneida *Also called Oneida Publications Inc (G-12618)*
Oneida Foundries Inc 315 363-4570
559 Fitch St Oneida (13421) *(G-12614)*
Oneida International Inc 315 361-3000
163-181 Kenwood Ave Oneida (13421) *(G-12615)*
Oneida Molded Plastics LLC (PA) 315 363-7980
104 S Warner St Oneida (13421) *(G-12616)*
Oneida Molded Plastics LLC 315 363-7990
104 S Warner St Oneida (13421) *(G-12617)*
Oneida Publications Inc 315 363-5100
730 Lenox Ave Oneida (13421) *(G-12618)*
Oneida Sales & Service Inc 716 822-8205
155 Commerce Dr Buffalo (14218) *(G-2980)*
Oneida Silversmiths Inc 315 361-3000
163 Kenwood Ave 181 Oneida (13421) *(G-12619)*
Oneonta Asphalt, Oneonta *Also called Cobleskill Stone Products Inc (G-12632)*
Oneonta City Wtr Trtmnt Plant, Oneonta *Also called City of Oneonta (G-12630)*
Oneonta Fence 607 433-6707
2 Washburn St Oneonta (13820) *(G-12642)*
Ongweoweh Corp (PA) 607 266-7070
5 Barr Rd Ithaca (14850) *(G-6602)*
Onia LLC (PA) 646 701-0008
10 E 40th St Fl 37 New York (10016) *(G-11045)*
Only Hearts Ltd (PA) 212 268-0886
134 W 37th St Fl 9 New York (10018) *(G-11046)*
Only Natural Inc 516 897-7001
3580 Oceanside Rd Unit 5 Oceanside (11572) *(G-12549)*
Onondaga Nation 315 469-3230
3951 State Route 11 Nedrow (13120) *(G-8479)*
Ontario Knife Company 716 676-5527
26 Empire St Franklinville (14737) *(G-5124)*
Ontario Label Graphics Inc 716 434-8505
6444 Ridge Rd Lockport (14094) *(G-7325)*
Ontario Plastics Inc 585 663-2644
2503 Dewey Ave Rochester (14616) *(G-13989)*
Ony Biotech Inc 716 636-9096
1576 Sweet Home Rd Amherst (14228) *(G-246)*
Ony Inc Baird Researchpark 716 636-9096
1576 Sweet Home Rd Buffalo (14228) *(G-2981)*
Onyx Solar Group LLC 917 951-9732
79 Madison Ave Fl 8 New York (10016) *(G-11047)*
Opd, Depew *Also called Leica Microsystems Inc (G-4095)*
Open & Shut Doors, Brentwood *Also called Michbi Doors Inc (G-1142)*
Open Text Inc 585 424-1950
1225 Jefferson Rd Ste A30 Rochester (14623) *(G-13990)*
Open-Xchange Inc 914 332-5720
303 S Broadway Ste 224 Tarrytown (10591) *(G-15485)*
Openfin Inc 917 450-8822
25 Broadway Fl 9 New York (10004) *(G-11048)*
Openroad Integrated Media Inc 212 691-0900
180 Maiden Ln Ste 2803 New York (10038) *(G-11049)*
Operateit Inc 631 259-4777
2805 Vtrans Mem Hwy Ste 2 Ronkonkoma (11779) *(G-14392)*
Operative Cake Corp 718 278-5600
711 Brush Ave Bronx (10465) *(G-1348)*
Operative Media Inc (HQ) 212 994-8930
6 E 32nd St Fl 3 New York (10016) *(G-11050)*
Ophthotech Corporation 212 845-8200
1 Penn Plz Ste 3520 New York (10119) *(G-11051)*
Opposuits USA Inc 917 438-8878
228 E 45th St Ste 9e New York (10017) *(G-11052)*
Oprah Magazine, New York *Also called Hearst Corporation (G-10063)*
Optical Gaging Products Div, Rochester *Also called Quality Vision Intl Inc (G-14061)*
Opticool Solutions LLC 585 347-6127
855 Publishers Pkwy Webster (14580) *(G-16090)*
Opticool Technologies, Webster *Also called Opticool Solutions LLC (G-16090)*
Optics Technology Inc 585 586-0950
3800 Monroe Ave Ste 3 Pittsford (14534) *(G-13023)*
Optika Eyes Ltd 631 567-8852
153 Main St Unit 1 Sayville (11782) *(G-14633)*
Optimax Systems Inc (PA) 585 265-1020
6367 Dean Pkwy Ontario (14519) *(G-12658)*
Optimized Devices Inc 914 769-6100
220 Marble Ave Pleasantville (10570) *(G-13175)*
Optimum Applied Systems Inc 845 471-3333
16 Victory Ln Ste 5 Poughkeepsie (12603) *(G-13361)*
Optimum Window Mfg Corp 845 647-1900
28 Canal St Ellenville (12428) *(G-4441)*
Optionline LLC 516 218-3225
100 Hilton Ave Apt 23 Garden City (11530) *(G-5273)*
Options Publishing, New York *Also called Triumph Learning LLC (G-11902)*
Optipro Systems LLC 585 265-0160
6368 Dean Pkwy Ontario (14519) *(G-12659)*
Optisource International Inc 631 924-8360
40 Sawgrass Dr Ste 1 Bellport (11713) *(G-810)*
Optogenics of Syracuse Inc 315 446-3000
2840 Erie Blvd E Syracuse (13224) *(G-15388)*
Opus Technology Corporation 631 271-1883
10 Gwynne Rd Melville (11747) *(G-8054)*

Oracle America Inc 518 427-9353
7 Southwoods Blvd Ste 1 Albany (12211) ***(G-108)***
Oracle America Inc 585 317-4648
345 Woodcliff Dr Ste 1 Fairport (14450) ***(G-4646)***
Oracle Corporation 212 508-7700
120 Park Ave Fl 26 New York (10017) ***(G-11053)***
Orafol Americas Inc 585 272-0290
200 Park Centre Dr West Henrietta (14586) ***(G-16244)***
Orafol Americas Inc 585 272-0309
200 Park Centre Dr Henrietta (14467) ***(G-6036)***
Oramaax Dental Products Inc 516 771-8514
216 N Main St Ste A Freeport (11520) ***(G-5172)***
Orange County Choppers Inc 845 522-5200
14 Crossroads Ct Newburgh (12550) ***(G-12237)***
Orange County Ironworks LLC 845 769-3000
36 Maybrook Rd Montgomery (12549) ***(G-8315)***
Orange Die Cutting Corp 845 562-0900
1 Favoriti Ave Newburgh (12550) ***(G-12238)***
Orange Packaging, Newburgh *Also called Orange Die Cutting Corp* ***(G-12238)***
Orangenius Inc 631 742-0648
79 Madison Ave Fl 4 New York (10016) ***(G-11054)***
Orbcomm Inc 703 433-6396
125 Business Park Dr Utica (13502) ***(G-15729)***
Orbis Brynmore Lithographics 212 987-2100
1735 2nd Ave Frnt 1 New York (10128) ***(G-11055)***
Orbit Industries LLC 914 244-1500
116 Radio Circle Dr # 302 Mount Kisco (10549) ***(G-8353)***
Orbit International Corp (PA) 631 435-8300
80 Cabot Ct Hauppauge (11788) ***(G-5907)***
Orbit International Corp 631 435-8300
80 Cabot Ct Hauppauge (11788) ***(G-5908)***
Orbital Holdings Inc 951 360-7100
2775 Broadway St Ste 200 Buffalo (14227) ***(G-2982)***
Orcam Inc 800 713-3741
16 Madison Sq W Fl 11 New York (10010) ***(G-11056)***
Orchard Apparel Group Ltd 212 268-8701
212 W 35th St Fl 7 New York (10001) ***(G-11057)***
Orchard Platform Advisors LLC 888 217-2718
55 W 21st St Fl 2 New York (10010) ***(G-11058)***
Orchard Sausages Inc 718 381-9388
340 Johnson Ave Brooklyn (11206) ***(G-2290)***
Orchid Manufacturing Co Inc 212 840-5700
77 W 55th St Apt 4k New York (10019) ***(G-11059)***
Ordergroove Inc 866 253-1261
75 Broad St Fl 23 New York (10004) ***(G-11060)***
Orenova Group LLC 914 517-3000
10 New King St Ste 106 White Plains (10604) ***(G-16482)***
Orens Daily Roast Inc (PA) 212 348-5400
12 E 46th St Fl 6 New York (10017) ***(G-11061)***
Orffeo Printing & Imaging Inc 716 681-5757
99 Cambria St Lancaster (14086) ***(G-7034)***
Orfit Industries America, Jericho *Also called SC Medical Overseas Inc* ***(G-6802)***
Organic Peak, Mineola *Also called Maxim Hygiene Products Inc* ***(G-8236)***
Orics Industries Inc 718 461-8613
240 Smith St Farmingdale (11735) ***(G-4839)***
Origin Press Inc 516 746-2262
131 Liberty Ave Mineola (11501) ***(G-8243)***
Original Crunch Roll Fctry LLC 716 402-5030
90 Sylvan Pkwy Amherst (14228) ***(G-247)***
Original Dream Statuary, Brooklyn *Also called Dream Statuary Inc* ***(G-1792)***
Original Hrkmer Cnty Chese Inc 315 895-7428
2745 State Route 51 Ilion (13357) ***(G-6477)***
Oriskany Arms Inc 315 737-2196
175 Clear Rd Oriskany (13424) ***(G-12760)***
Oriskany Manufacturing LLC 315 732-4962
2 Wurz Ave Yorkville (13495) ***(G-16829)***
Oriskany Mfg Tech LLC 315 732-4962
2 Wurz Ave Yorkville (13495) ***(G-16830)***
Orlandi Inc (PA) 631 756-0110
131 Executive Blvd Farmingdale (11735) ***(G-4840)***
Orlandi Inc 631 756-0110
121 Executive Blvd Farmingdale (11735) ***(G-4841)***
Orlandi Scented Products, Farmingdale *Also called Orlandi Inc* ***(G-4840)***
Orleans Custom Packing Inc 585 314-8227
101 Cadbury Way Holley (14470) ***(G-6227)***
Orleans Pallet Company Inc 585 589-0781
227 West Ave Albion (14411) ***(G-160)***
Ormec Systems Corp (PA) 585 385-3520
19 Linden Park Rochester (14625) ***(G-13991)***
Ornametal Inc 845 562-5151
216 S William St Newburgh (12550) ***(G-12239)***
Oro Avanti Inc (PA) 516 487-5185
250 Kings Point Rd Great Neck (11024) ***(G-5577)***
Orolia Usa Inc (HQ) 585 321-5800
1565 Jefferson Rd Ste 460 Rochester (14623) ***(G-13992)***
Orpheo USA Corp 212 464-8255
315 Madison Ave Rm 2601 New York (10017) ***(G-11062)***
Ortex Home Textile Inc 718 241-7298
523 E 82nd St Brooklyn (11236) ***(G-2291)***
Ortex Home Textiles, Brooklyn *Also called Ortex Home Textile Inc* ***(G-2291)***
Ortho Medical Products (PA) 212 879-3700
315 E 83rd St New York (10028) ***(G-11063)***
Ortho Rite Inc 914 235-9100
434 Waverly Ave Mamaroneck (10543) ***(G-7751)***
Ortho-Clinical Diagnostics Inc 585 453-4771
100 Latona Rd Bldg 313 Rochester (14626) ***(G-13993)***
Ortho-Clinical Diagnostics Inc 585 453-5200
2402 Innovation Way # 3 Rochester (14624) ***(G-13994)***
Ortho-Clinical Diagnostics Inc 716 631-1281
15 Limestone Dr Williamsville (14221) ***(G-16582)***
Ortho-Clinical Diagnostics Inc 585 453-3000
1000 Lee Rd Rochester (14626) ***(G-13995)***
Ortho/Rochester Tech, Rochester *Also called Ortho-Clinical Diagnostics Inc* ***(G-13994)***
Orthocon Inc 914 357-2600
1 Bridge St Ste 121 Irvington (10533) ***(G-6508)***
Orthocraft Inc 718 951-1700
1477 E 27th St Brooklyn (11210) ***(G-2292)***
Orthogonal 585 254-2775
1999 Lake Ave Rochester (14650) ***(G-13996)***
Orthopedic Arts Laboratory Inc 718 858-2400
141 Atlantic Ave Apt 1 Brooklyn (11201) ***(G-2293)***
Orthopedic Treatment Facility 718 898-7326
4906 Queens Blvd Woodside (11377) ***(G-16669)***
Orthotics & Prosthetics Dept 585 341-9299
4901 Lac De Ville Blvd Rochester (14618) ***(G-13997)***
Orthstar Enterprises Inc 607 562-2100
119 Sing Sing Rd Horseheads (14845) ***(G-6323)***
Orza Bakery Inc 914 965-5736
261 New Main St Ste 263 Yonkers (10701) ***(G-16788)***
Os33 Inc 708 336-3466
16 W 22nd St Fl 6 New York (10010) ***(G-11064)***
Osaka Gas Energy America Corp 914 253-5500
1 N Lexington Ave Ste 504 White Plains (10601) ***(G-16483)***
Oscar Heyman & Bros Inc (PA) 212 593-0400
501 Madison Ave Fl 15 New York (10022) ***(G-11065)***
OSI Pharmaceuticals LLC 631 847-0175
500 Bi County Blvd # 118 Farmingdale (11735) ***(G-4842)***
OSI Pharmaceuticals LLC (HQ) 631 962-2000
1 Bioscience Way Dr Farmingdale (11735) ***(G-4843)***
OSI Specialties, Tarrytown *Also called Momentive Performance Mtls Inc* ***(G-15484)***
Osmose Holdings Inc 716 882-5905
2475 George Urban Blvd # 160 Depew (14043) ***(G-4099)***
Osnat Gad Inc 212 957-0535
608 5th Ave Ste 609 New York (10020) ***(G-11066)***
Oso Industries Inc 917 709-2050
1205 Manhattan Ave Brooklyn (11222) ***(G-2294)***
Osprey Boat 631 331-4153
96 Mount Sinai Ave Mount Sinai (11766) ***(G-8369)***
Osprey Publishing Inc 212 419-5300
1385 Broadway Fl 5 New York (10018) ***(G-11067)***
Ossining Bakery Lmp Inc 914 941-2654
50 N Highland Ave Ossining (10562) ***(G-12772)***
Ossining Village of Inc 914 202-9668
25 Fowler Ave Ossining (10562) ***(G-12773)***
Osteohealth, Shirley *Also called Luitpold Pharmaceuticals Inc* ***(G-14838)***
Oswald Manufacturing Co Inc 516 883-8850
65 Channel Dr Port Washington (11050) ***(G-13292)***
Otex Protective Inc 585 232-7160
2180 Brighton Henrietta Rochester (14623) ***(G-13998)***
Other Half Brewing Co 347 987-3527
195 Centre St Brooklyn (11231) ***(G-2295)***
Other Press LLC 212 414-0054
267 5th Ave Fl 6 New York (10016) ***(G-11068)***
Otis Bedding Mfg Co Inc (PA) 716 825-2599
80 James E Casey Dr Buffalo (14206) ***(G-2983)***
Otis Elevator Company 315 736-0167
5172 Commercial Dr Yorkville (13495) ***(G-16831)***
Otis Elevator Company 917 339-9600
1 Penn Plz Ste 410 New York (10119) ***(G-11069)***
Otis Products Inc (PA) 315 348-4300
6987 Laura St Lyons Falls (13368) ***(G-7689)***
Otis Technology, Lyons Falls *Also called Otis Products Inc* ***(G-7689)***
Otiwti, Fairport *Also called Qualitrol Company LLC* ***(G-4653)***
Otsego Ready Mix Inc 607 432-3400
2 Wells Ave Oneonta (13820) ***(G-12643)***
Ottaway Newspapers Inc 845 343-2181
40 Mulberry St Middletown (10940) ***(G-8169)***
Ougra Inc 646 342-4575
3100 47th Ave Unit 4 Long Island City (11101) ***(G-7543)***
Our Daily Eats LLC 518 810-8412
10 Burdick Dr Ste 1 Albany (12205) ***(G-109)***
Our Own Candle Company Inc (PA) 716 769-5000
10349 Main St Findley Lake (14736) ***(G-4939)***
Our Terms Fabricators Inc 631 752-1517
48 Cabot St West Babylon (11704) ***(G-16180)***
Ourem Iron Works Inc 914 476-4856
498 Nepperhan Ave Ste 5 Yonkers (10701) ***(G-16789)***
Out of Print, New York *Also called Sputnick 84 LLC* ***(G-11686)***
Outdoor Group LLC 877 503-5483
1325 John St West Henrietta (14586) ***(G-16245)***
Outreach Publishing Corp 718 773-0525
546 Montgomery St Brooklyn (11225) ***(G-2296)***
Ovation Instore, Maspeth *Also called DSI Group Inc* ***(G-7837)***

ALPHABETIC

Oved Mens LLC 212 563-4999
31 W 34th St Fl 4 New York (10001) *(G-11070)*
Overhead Door Corporation 518 828-7652
1 Hudson Ave Hudson (12534) *(G-6366)*
Overlook Press, The, New York Also called Peter Mayer Publishers Inc *(G-11169)*
Overnight Labels Inc 631 242-4240
151 W Industry Ct Ste 15 Deer Park (11729) *(G-4022)*
Overnight Mountings Inc 516 865-3000
1400 Plaza Ave New Hyde Park (11040) *(G-8556)*
Overture Media Inc 917 446-7455
411 Lafayette St Ste 638 New York (10003) *(G-11071)*
Ovid Therapeutics Inc 646 661-7661
1460 Broadway Fl 4 New York (10036) *(G-11072)*
Ovitz Corporation 585 474-4695
150 Lucius Gordon Dr # 123 West Henrietta (14586) *(G-16246)*
OWayne Enterprises Inc 718 326-2200
4901 Maspeth Ave Maspeth (11378) *(G-7865)*
Owego Pennysaver Press Inc 607 687-2434
181 Front St Owego (13827) *(G-12802)*
Owens Corning Sales LLC 518 475-3600
1277 Feura Bush Rd Feura Bush (12067) *(G-4936)*
Owens Table Mixers LLC 650 303-7342
250 Mercer St Apt C616 New York (10012) *(G-11073)*
Owens-Brockway Glass Cont Inc 315 258-3211
7134 County House Rd Auburn (13021) *(G-494)*
Owi Corporation 315 245-4305
12 Masonic Ave Camden (13316) *(G-3192)*
Owl Books Div, New York Also called Henry Holt and Company LLC *(G-10081)*
Owl Wire & Cable LLC 315 697-2011
3127 Seneca Tpke Canastota (13032) *(G-3244)*
Owletts Saw Mills 607 525-6340
4214 Cook Rd Woodhull (14898) *(G-16638)*
Own Instrument Inc 914 668-6546
250 E 7th St Mount Vernon (10550) *(G-8427)*
Oxair Ltd 716 298-8288
8320 Quarry Rd Niagara Falls (14304) *(G-12321)*
Oxbo International Corporation (HQ) 585 548-2665
7275 Batavia Byron Rd Byron (14422) *(G-3145)*
Oxford Book Company Inc 212 227-2120
9 Pine St New York (10005) *(G-11074)*
Oxford Cleaners 212 734-0006
847 Lexington Ave Frnt New York (10065) *(G-11075)*
Oxford Industries Inc 212 247-7712
600 5th Ave Fl 12 New York (10020) *(G-11076)*
Oxford Industries Inc 212 840-2288
25 W 39th St New York (10018) *(G-11077)*
Oxford University Press LLC (HQ) 212 726-6000
198 Madison Ave Fl 8 New York (10016) *(G-11078)*
Oxford University Press LLC 212 726-6000
198 Madison Ave Fl 8 New York (10016) *(G-11079)*
Oxford University Press USA, New York Also called Oxford University Press LLC *(G-11078)*
Oxo International Inc 212 242-3333
601 W 26th St Rm 1050 New York (10001) *(G-11080)*
Oxygen Inc (PA) 516 433-1144
6 Midland Ave Hicksville (11801) *(G-6118)*
Oxygen Generating Systems Intl, North Tonawanda Also called Audubon Machinery Corporation *(G-12414)*
Oyster Bay Brewing Company 516 802-5546
36 Audrey Ave Oyster Bay (11771) *(G-12817)*
Oyster Bay Pump Works Inc 516 933-4500
78 Midland Ave Unit 1 Hicksville (11801) *(G-6119)*
Oz Baking Company Ltd 516 466-5114
114 Middle Neck Rd Great Neck (11021) *(G-5578)*
Ozipko Enterprises Inc 585 424-6740
125 White Spruce Blvd Rochester (14623) *(G-13999)*
Ozmodyl Ltd 212 226-0622
233 Broadway Rm 707 New York (10279) *(G-11081)*
Ozteck Industries Inc 516 883-8857
65 Channel Dr Port Washington (11050) *(G-13293)*
P & B Woodworking Inc 845 744-2508
2415 State Route 52 Pine Bush (12566) *(G-12998)*
P & C Gas Measurements Service 716 257-3412
9505 Tannery Rd Cattaraugus (14719) *(G-3313)*
P & C Service, Cattaraugus Also called P & C Gas Measurements Service *(G-3313)*
P & F Bakers Inc 516 931-6821
640 S Broadway Hicksville (11801) *(G-6120)*
P & F Industries Inc (PA) 631 694-9800
445 Broadhollow Rd # 100 Melville (11747) *(G-8055)*
P & F Industries of NY Corp 718 894-3501
6006 55th Dr Maspeth (11378) *(G-7866)*
P & H Machine Shop Inc 585 247-5500
40 Industrial Park Cir Rochester (14624) *(G-14000)*
P & H Thermotech Inc 585 624-1310
1883 Heath Markham Rd Lima (14485) *(G-7154)*
P & I Sportswear Inc 718 934-4587
384 5th Ave New York (10018) *(G-11082)*
P & L Development LLC 516 986-1700
200 Hicks St Westbury (11590) *(G-16360)*
P & L Development LLC 516 986-1700
275 Grand Blvd Unit 1 Westbury (11590) *(G-16361)*
P & L Development LLC (PA) 516 986-1700
200 Hicks St Westbury (11590) *(G-16362)*
P & M LLC 631 842-2200
50 Ranick Dr E Amityville (11701) *(G-310)*
P & R Industries Inc (PA) 585 266-6725
1524 N Clinton Ave Rochester (14621) *(G-14001)*
P & R Industries Inc 585 544-1811
1524 N Clinton Ave Rochester (14621) *(G-14002)*
P & W Press Inc 646 486-3417
20 W 22nd St Ste 710 New York (10010) *(G-11083)*
P and F Machine Industries, Maspeth Also called P & F Industries of NY Corp *(G-7866)*
P B & H Moulding Corporation 315 455-1756
7121 Woodchuck Hill Rd Fayetteville (13066) *(G-4929)*
P C I, Bohemia Also called Precision Charts Inc *(G-1077)*
P C I Manufacturing Div, Westbury Also called Procomponents Inc *(G-16368)*
P C I Paper Conversions Inc (PA) 315 437-1641
3584 Walters Rd Syracuse (13209) *(G-15389)*
P C I Paper Conversions Inc 315 703-8300
6761 Thompson Rd Syracuse (13211) *(G-15390)*
P C I Paper Conversions Inc 315 634-3317
6761 Thompson Rd Syracuse (13211) *(G-15391)*
P C I Paper Conversions Inc 315 437-1641
6761 Thompson Rd Syracuse (13211) *(G-15392)*
P C Rfrs Radiology 212 586-5700
3630 37th St Frnt Long Island City (11101) *(G-7544)*
P C T, Amsterdam Also called Power and Composite Tech LLC *(G-357)*
P D A Panache, Bohemia Also called Pda Panache Corp *(G-1073)*
P D I, Brooklyn Also called Promotional Development Inc *(G-2357)*
P D R Inc 516 829-5300
101 Dupont St Plainview (11803) *(G-13080)*
P E Guerin (PA) 212 243-5270
23 Jane St New York (10014) *(G-11084)*
P E Machine Works, Plainview Also called Port Everglades Machine Works *(G-13083)*
P G I, Forest Hills Also called Preston Glass Industries Inc *(G-5080)*
P G M, Rochester Also called Precision Grinding & Mfg Corp *(G-14035)*
P G Media, New York Also called Parents Guide Network Corp *(G-11110)*
P H Custom Woodworking Corp 917 801-1444
830 Barry St Fl 2nd Bronx (10474) *(G-1349)*
P J D Publications Ltd 516 626-0650
1315 Jericho Tpke New Hyde Park (11040) *(G-8557)*
P J R Industries Inc 716 825-9300
1951 Hamburg Tpke Ste 17 Buffalo (14218) *(G-2984)*
P K G Equipment Incorporated 585 436-4650
367 Paul Rd Rochester (14624) *(G-14003)*
P L X, Deer Park Also called Plx Inc *(G-4026)*
P M Belts Usa Inc 800 762-3580
131 32nd St Brooklyn (11232) *(G-2297)*
P M I, Saint James Also called Polymers Merona Inc *(G-14513)*
P M Plastics Inc 716 662-1255
1 Bank St Ste 1 # 1 Orchard Park (14127) *(G-12733)*
P P I Business Forms Inc 716 825-1241
94 Spaulding St Buffalo (14220) *(G-2985)*
P Pascal Coffee Roasters, Yonkers Also called P Pascal Inc *(G-16790)*
P Pascal Inc 914 969-7933
960 Nepperhan Ave Yonkers (10703) *(G-16790)*
P R B Metal Products Inc 631 467-1800
200 Christopher St Ronkonkoma (11779) *(G-14393)*
P S M Group Inc 716 532-6686
17 Main St Forestville (14062) *(G-5087)*
P S Pibbs Inc 718 445-8046
13315 32nd Ave Flushing (11354) *(G-5032)*
P T E Inc 516 775-3839
36 Ontario Rd Floral Park (11001) *(G-4964)*
P T I, Tuckahoe Also called Packaging Tech & Insptn LLC *(G-15645)*
P Tool & Die Co Inc 585 889-1340
3535 Union St North Chili (14514) *(G-12382)*
P V C Molding Technologies 315 331-1212
122 W Shore Blvd Newark (14513) *(G-12204)*
P&F, Melville Also called P & F Industries Inc *(G-8055)*
P&G Metal Components Corp 716 896-7900
54 Gruner Rd Buffalo (14227) *(G-2986)*
P&G Steel Inc 716 896-7900
54 Gruner Rd Buffalo (14227) *(G-2987)*
P&I, Pper P I Daily P I People, New York Also called Pensions & Investments *(G-11150)*
P-Ryton Corp 718 937-7052
504 50th Ave Long Island City (11101) *(G-7545)*
P.A.t, Bohemia Also called Precision Assembly Tech Inc *(G-1076)*
P1 Generator Windings LLC (PA) 518 930-2879
2165 Technology Dr Schenectady (12308) *(G-14702)*
P8h Inc 212 343-1142
81 Prospect St 7 Brooklyn (11201) *(G-2298)*
PA Pellets LLC (HQ) 814 848-9970
1 Fischers Rd Ste 160 Pittsford (14534) *(G-13024)*
Paal Technologies Inc 631 319-6262
152 Remington Blvd Ste 1 Ronkonkoma (11779) *(G-14394)*
Pace Editions Inc (PA) 212 421-3237
32 E 57th St Fl 3 New York (10022) *(G-11085)*
Pace Editions Inc 212 675-7431
44 W 18th St Fl 5 New York (10011) *(G-11086)*
Pace Polyethylene Mfg Co Inc (PA) 914 381-3000
46 Calvert St Harrison (10528) *(G-5732)*
Pace Prints, New York Also called Pace Editions Inc *(G-11085)*

Pace Up Pharmaceuticals LLC 631 450-4495
200 Bangor St Lindenhurst (11757) *(G-7189)*
Pace Walkers of America Inc 631 444-2147
105 Washington Ave Port Jefferson (11777) *(G-13223)*
Pace Window & Door, Victor *Also called Pace Window and Door Corp (G-15860)*
Pace Window and Door Corp (PA) 585 924-8350
7224 State Route 96 Victor (14564) *(G-15860)*
Pacemaker Packaging Corp 718 458-1188
7200 51st Rd Woodside (11377) *(G-16670)*
Pachanga Inc 212 832-0022
824 10th Ave New York (10019) *(G-11087)*
Pacific Alliance Usa Inc 336 500-8184
350 5th Ave Lbby 9 New York (10118) *(G-11088)*
Pacific Alliance Usa Inc (HQ) 646 839-7000
1450 Broadway Fl 21 New York (10018) *(G-11089)*
Pacific City International 646 309-1250
265 W 37th St New York (10018) *(G-11090)*
Pacific Concepts, New York *Also called Ewatchfactory Corp (G-9743)*
Pacific Designs Intl Inc 718 364-2867
2743 Webster Ave Bronx (10458) *(G-1350)*
Pacific Die Cast Inc 845 778-6374
827 Route 52 Ste 2 Walden (12586) *(G-15894)*
Pacific Poly Product Corp 718 786-7129
3934 Crescent St Long Island City (11101) *(G-7546)*
Pacific Worldwide Inc 212 502-3360
20 W 33rd St Fl 11 New York (10001) *(G-11091)*
Pack America Corp (HQ) 212 508-6666
108 W 39th St Fl 16 New York (10018) *(G-11092)*
Package One Inc (PA) 518 344-5425
414 Union St Schenectady (12305) *(G-14703)*
Package Pavement Company Inc 845 221-2224
3530 Route 52 Stormville (12582) *(G-15180)*
Package Print Technologies 716 871-9905
1831 Niagara St Buffalo (14207) *(G-2988)*
Packaging Avantage/Marietta La, Cortland *Also called Marietta Corporation (G-3883)*
Packaging Corporation America 315 457-6780
4471 Steelway Blvd S Liverpool (13090) *(G-7251)*
Packaging Dynamics Ltd 631 563-4499
35 Carlough Rd Ste 2 Bohemia (11716) *(G-1071)*
Packaging Tech & Insptn LLC 914 337-2005
145 Main St Tuckahoe (10707) *(G-15645)*
Pacline Conveyors Inc 716 932-7858
15 Charlotte Rd Buffalo (14225) *(G-2989)*
Pacs Switchgear LLC (PA) 516 465-7100
1211 Stewart Ave Bethpage (11714) *(G-851)*
Pactiv Corporation 518 743-3100
6 Haskell Ave Glens Falls (12801) *(G-5438)*
Pactiv LLC 518 562-6101
74 Weed St Plattsburgh (12901) *(G-13142)*
Pactiv LLC 315 457-6780
4471 Steelway Blvd S Liverpool (13090) *(G-7252)*
Pactiv LLC 585 394-5125
2651 Brickyard Rd Canandaigua (14424) *(G-3228)*
Pactiv LLC 518 793-2524
18 Peck Ave Glens Falls (12801) *(G-5439)*
Pactiv LLC 847 482-2000
5310 North St Canandaigua (14424) *(G-3229)*
Pactiv LLC 518 562-6120
74 Weed St Plattsburgh (12901) *(G-13143)*
Pactiv LLC 585 248-1213
1169 Pittsford Victor Rd Pittsford (14534) *(G-13025)*
Pactiv LLC 585 393-3149
5250 North St Canandaigua (14424) *(G-3230)*
Paddle8, Brooklyn *Also called P8h Inc (G-2298)*
Paddock Chevrolet Golf Dome 716 504-4059
175 Brompton Rd Tonawanda (14150) *(G-15568)*
Paddy Lee Fashions Inc 718 786-6020
4709 36th St Fl 2nd Long Island City (11101) *(G-7547)*
Paesana, Farmingdale *Also called L and S Packing Co (G-4804)*
Page Front Group Inc 716 823-8222
2703 S Park Ave Lackawanna (14218) *(G-6950)*
Pageant Media US Limited 646 891-2110
200 Park Ave S Fl 16 New York (10003) *(G-11093)*
Paint Over Rust Products Inc 914 636-0700
38 Portman Rd New Rochelle (10801) *(G-8621)*
Pak 21, Brooklyn *Also called Apex Real Holdings Inc (G-1540)*
Paklab, Hauppauge *Also called Universal Packg Systems Inc (G-5966)*
Pal Aluminum Inc (PA) 516 937-1990
230 Duffy Ave Unit B Hicksville (11801) *(G-6121)*
Pal Aluminum Inc 718 262-0091
10620 180th St Jamaica (11433) *(G-6666)*
Pal Industries, Hicksville *Also called Pal Aluminum Inc (G-6121)*
Pal Industries, Jamaica *Also called Pal Aluminum Inc (G-6666)*
Pal Manufacturing Corp 516 937-1990
230 Duffy Ave Unit B Hicksville (11801) *(G-6122)*
Paladino Prtg & Graphics Inc 718 279-6000
20009 32nd Ave Flushing (11361) *(G-5033)*
Palagonia Bakery Co Inc 718 272-5400
508 Junius St Brooklyn (11212) *(G-2299)*
Palagonia Italian Bread, Brooklyn *Also called Palagonia Bakery Co Inc (G-2299)*
Palagrave Macmillan, New York *Also called Macmillan Publishing Group LLC (G-10652)*
Paleteria Fernandez Inc 914 315-1598
350 Mamaroneck Ave Mamaroneck (10543) *(G-7752)*
Paleteria Fernandez Inc (PA) 914 939-3694
33 N Main St Port Chester (10573) *(G-13206)*
Paletot Ltd 212 268-3774
499 Fashion Ave Rm 25s New York (10018) *(G-11094)*
Palgrave Macmillan Ltd 646 307-5028
175 5th Ave Frnt 4 New York (10010) *(G-11095)*
Palisades Paper Inc 845 354-0333
13 Jackson Ave Spring Valley (10977) *(G-15004)*
Pall Biomedical Inc 516 484-3600
25 Harbor Park Dr Port Washington (11050) *(G-13294)*
Pall Corporation (HQ) 516 484-5400
25 Harbor Park Dr Port Washington (11050) *(G-13295)*
Pall Corporation 607 753-6041
3643 State Route 281 Cortland (13045) *(G-3885)*
Pall Corporation 607 753-6041
3669 State Route 281 Cortland (13045) *(G-3886)*
Pall Corporation 516 484-2818
25 Harbor Park Dr Port Washington (11050) *(G-13296)*
Pall Corporation 607 753-6041
839 State Route 13 Ste 12 Cortland (13045) *(G-3887)*
Pall Life Sciences, Port Washington *Also called Pall Corporation (G-13296)*
Pall Medical, Port Washington *Also called Pall Biomedical Inc (G-13294)*
Pall Trinity Micro, Cortland *Also called Pall Corporation (G-3885)*
Pall's Advnced Sprtons Systems, Cortland *Also called Pall Corporation (G-3887)*
Palladia Inc 212 206-3669
105 W 17th St New York (10011) *(G-11096)*
Palladium Times, Oswego *Also called Sample News Group LLC (G-12787)*
Pallet Division Inc 585 328-3780
40 Silver St Rochester (14611) *(G-14004)*
Pallet Services Inc (PA) 716 873-7700
4055 Casillo Pkwy Clarence (14031) *(G-3537)*
Pallet Services Inc 585 647-4020
1681 Lyell Ave Rochester (14606) *(G-14005)*
Pallets Inc 518 747-4177
99 1/2 East St Fort Edward (12828) *(G-5097)*
Pallets R US Inc 631 758-2360
555 Woodside Ave Bellport (11713) *(G-811)*
Pallette Stone Corporation 518 584-2421
269 Ballard Rd Gansevoort (12831) *(G-5244)*
Palma Tool & Die Company Inc 716 681-4464
40 Ward Rd Lancaster (14086) *(G-7035)*
Palmbay Ltd 718 424-3388
4459 Kissena Blvd Apt 6h Flushing (11355) *(G-5034)*
Palmer Industries Inc 607 754-8741
2320 Lewis St Endicott (13760) *(G-4606)*
Palmer Industries Inc (PA) 607 754-2957
509 Paden St Endicott (13760) *(G-4607)*
Palpross Incorporated 845 469-2188
Maple Ave Rr 396 Selkirk (12158) *(G-14770)*
Paltalk, New York *Also called AVM Software Inc (G-8980)*
Palumbo Block Co Inc 845 832-6100
365 Dover Furnace Rd Dover Plains (12522) *(G-4145)*
Pama Enterprises Inc 516 504-6300
60 Cuttermill Rd Ste 411 Great Neck (11021) *(G-5579)*
Pan American Leathers Inc (PA) 978 741-4150
347 W 36th St Rm 1204 New York (10018) *(G-11097)*
Pan American Roller Inc 914 762-8700
5 Broad Ave Ossining (10562) *(G-12774)*
Panagraphics Inc 716 312-8088
30 Quail Run Orchard Park (14127) *(G-12734)*
Panelogic Inc 607 962-6319
366 Baker Street Ext Corning (14830) *(G-3823)*
Pangea Brands LLC (PA) 617 638-0001
6 W 20th St Fl 3 New York (10011) *(G-11098)*
Pangea Brands LLC 617 638-0001
6 W 20th St Fl 3 New York (10011) *(G-11099)*
Panoply Media LLC (HQ) 646 382-5423
15 Metrotech Ctr Fl 8 Brooklyn (11201) *(G-2300)*
Panther Graphics Inc (PA) 585 546-7163
465 Central Ave Rochester (14605) *(G-14006)*
Pap Chat Inc 516 350-1888
3105 Quentin Rd Brooklyn (11234) *(G-2301)*
Papa Bubble 212 966-2599
380 Broome St Frnt A New York (10013) *(G-11100)*
Paper Box Corp 212 226-7490
1751 2nd Ave Apt 10a New York (10128) *(G-11101)*
Paper House Productions Inc 845 246-7261
160 Malden Tpke Bldg 2 Saugerties (12477) *(G-14612)*
Paper Magazine, New York *Also called Paper Publishing Company Inc (G-11103)*
Paper Magic Group Inc 631 521-3682
345 7th Ave Fl 6 New York (10001) *(G-11102)*
Paper Publishing Company Inc 212 226-4405
15 E 32nd St New York (10016) *(G-11103)*
Papercutz Inc 646 559-4681
160 Broadway Rm 700e New York (10038) *(G-11104)*
Paperworks, Baldwinsville *Also called Specialized Packg Group Inc (G-561)*
Paperworks Industries Inc 913 621-0922
2900 Mclane Rd Baldwinsville (13027) *(G-559)*
Paperworld Inc 516 221-2702
3054 Lee Pl Bellmore (11710) *(G-790)*

(PA)=Parent Co (HQ)=Headquarters (DH)=Div Headquarters
2019 Harris
New York Manufacturers Directory
955

Par Pharmaceutical, Chestnut Ridge *Also called Generics Bidco I LLC* ***(G-3492)***
Par Pharmaceutical Inc (HQ) 845 573-5500
1 Ram Ridge Rd Chestnut Ridge (10977) ***(G-3494)***
Par Phrmceutical Companies Inc (HQ) 845 573-5500
1 Ram Ridge Rd Chestnut Ridge (10977) ***(G-3495)***
Par Sterile Products LLC (HQ) 845 573-5500
6 Ram Ridge Rd Chestnut Ridge (10977) ***(G-3496)***
Par Technology Corporation (PA) 315 738-0600
8383 Seneca Tpke Ste 2 New Hartford (13413) ***(G-8508)***
Par-Foam Products Inc 716 855-2066
239 Van Rensselaer St Buffalo (14210) ***(G-2990)***
Parabit Systems Inc 516 378-4800
2677 Grand Ave Bellmore (11710) ***(G-791)***
PARABOLA, New York *Also called Society For The Study* ***(G-11634)***
Parace Bionics LLC 877 727-2231
100 Park Ave Rm 1600 New York (10017) ***(G-11105)***
Parachute Publishing LLC 212 337-6743
322 8th Ave Ste 702 New York (10001) ***(G-11106)***
Parade Magazine, New York *Also called Parade Publications Inc* ***(G-11107)***
Parade Publications Inc (HQ) 212 450-7000
711 3rd Ave New York (10017) ***(G-11107)***
Paradigm Group LLC 718 860-1538
1357 Lafayette Ave Frnt 1 Bronx (10474) ***(G-1351)***
Paradigm Mktg Consortium Inc 516 496-0000
350 Michael Dr Syosset (11791) ***(G-15227)***
Paradigm Spine LLC 888 273-9897
505 Park Ave Fl 14 New York (10022) ***(G-11108)***
Paradise Plastics LLC 718 788-3733
116 39th St Brooklyn (11232) ***(G-2302)***
Paradiso Cnsld Entps LLC 585 924-3937
1115 E Main St Unit 58 Rochester (14609) ***(G-14007)***
Paragon Aquatics 845 452-5500
1351 Route 55 Unit 1 Lagrangeville (12540) ***(G-6960)***
Paragon Publishing Inc 718 302-2093
97 Harrison Ave Brooklyn (11206) ***(G-2303)***
Paragon Steel Rule Dies Inc 585 254-3395
979 Mount Read Blvd Rochester (14606) ***(G-14008)***
Paramount Cord & Brackets 212 325-9100
6 Tournament Dr White Plains (10605) ***(G-16484)***
Paramount Equipment Inc 631 981-4422
201 Christopher St Ronkonkoma (11779) ***(G-14395)***
Paramount Graphix 845 367-5003
26 Hill St Port Jervis (12771) ***(G-13234)***
Paramount Textiles Inc 212 966-1040
34 Walker St New York (10013) ***(G-11109)***
Paratore Signs Inc 315 455-5551
1551 Brewerton Rd Syracuse (13208) ***(G-15393)***
Paratus Industries Inc 716 826-2000
6659 E Quaker St Orchard Park (14127) ***(G-12735)***
Pardazzio Uomo, Westbury *Also called Montero International Inc* ***(G-16358)***
Parents Guide Network Corp 212 213-8840
419 Park Ave S Rm 505 New York (10016) ***(G-11110)***
Pareteum Corporation (PA) 212 984-1096
1185 Ave Of The Americas New York (10036) ***(G-11111)***
Parfums Boucheron Jewelry, New York *Also called Boucheron Joaillerie USA Inc* ***(G-9126)***
Parfuse Corp 516 997-8888
65 Kinkel St Westbury (11590) ***(G-16363)***
Parijat Jewels Inc 212 302-2549
15 W 47th St Ste 1811 New York (10036) ***(G-11112)***
Paris Art Label Co Inc 631 467-2300
217 River Ave Patchogue (11772) ***(G-12872)***
Paris Review Foundation Inc 212 343-1333
544 W 27th St Fl 3 New York (10001) ***(G-11113)***
Paris Wedding Center Corp (PA) 347 368-4085
42-53 42 55 Main St Flushing (11355) ***(G-5035)***
Paris Wedding Center Corp 212 267-8088
45 E Broadway Fl 2 New York (10002) ***(G-11114)***
Park Assist LLC 646 666-7525
57 W 38th St Fl 11 New York (10018) ***(G-11115)***
Park Ave Bldg & Roofg Sups LLC 718 403-0100
2120 Atlantic Ave Brooklyn (11233) ***(G-2304)***
Park Avenue Imprints LLC (PA) 716 822-5737
2955 S Park Ave Buffalo (14218) ***(G-2991)***
Park Avenue Nutrition, Richmond Hill *Also called Womens Health Care PC* ***(G-13517)***
Park Avenue Sportswear Ltd (PA) 718 369-0520
820 4th Ave Brooklyn (11232) ***(G-2305)***
Park Electrochemical Corp (PA) 631 465-3600
48 S Service Rd Ste 300 Melville (11747) ***(G-8056)***
Park Enterprises Rochester Inc 585 546-4200
226 Jay St Rochester (14608) ***(G-14009)***
Park Slope Copy Center 718 783-0268
123 7th Ave Brooklyn (11215) ***(G-2306)***
Park West Jewelery Inc 646 329-6145
565 W End Ave Apt 8b New York (10024) ***(G-11116)***
Park's Department, Williamsville *Also called Town of Amherst* ***(G-16591)***
Park-Ohio Inds Trsry Co Inc (HQ) 212 966-3310
80 State St Albany (12207) ***(G-110)***
Parkchester Dps LLC 718 823-4411
2000 E Tremont Ave Bronx (10462) ***(G-1352)***
Parker Machine Company Inc 518 747-0675
28 Sullivan Pkwy Fort Edward (12828) ***(G-5098)***
Parker Warby Retail Inc (PA) 646 517-5223
161 Ave Of The Amer Fl 6f New York (10013) ***(G-11117)***
Parker-Hannifin Aerospace, Clyde *Also called Parker-Hannifin Corporation* ***(G-3597)***
Parker-Hannifin Corporation 716 686-6400
4087 Walden Ave Lancaster (14086) ***(G-7036)***
Parker-Hannifin Corporation 631 231-3737
124 Columbia St Clyde (14433) ***(G-3597)***
Parker-Hannifin Corporation 716 685-4040
4087 Walden Ave Lancaster (14086) ***(G-7037)***
Parker-Hannifin Corporation 631 231-3737
300 Marcus Blvd Hauppauge (11788) ***(G-5909)***
Parker-Hannifin Corporation 585 425-7000
83 Estates Dr W Fairport (14450) ***(G-4647)***
Parker-Hannifin Corporation 315 926-4211
3967 Buffalo St Marion (14505) ***(G-7804)***
Parker-Hannifin Corporation 716 685-4040
4087 Walden Ave Lancaster (14086) ***(G-7038)***
Parkmatic Car Prkg Systems LLC (PA) 516 224-7700
47-10 A 32nd Pl Long Island City (11101) ***(G-7548)***
Parkmatic Car Prkg Systems LLC 800 422-5438
2025 130th St College Point (11356) ***(G-3659)***
Parkside Candy Co Inc (PA) 716 833-7540
3208 Main St Ste 1 Buffalo (14214) ***(G-2992)***
Parkside Printing Co Inc 516 933-5423
4 Tompkins Ave Jericho (11753) ***(G-6796)***
Parlec LLC 585 425-4400
101 Perinton Pkwy Fl 1 Fairport (14450) ***(G-4648)***
Parlor City Paper Box Co Inc 607 772-0600
2 Eldredge St Binghamton (13901) ***(G-909)***
Parlor Labs Inc 866 801-7323
515 W 19th St New York (10011) ***(G-11118)***
Parnasa International Inc 516 394-0400
181 S Franklin Ave # 400 Valley Stream (11581) ***(G-15789)***
Parrinello Printing Inc 716 633-7780
84 Aero Dr Buffalo (14225) ***(G-2993)***
Parrington Instruments 518 373-8420
12 Droms Rd Rexford (12148) ***(G-13482)***
Parsley Apparel Corp 631 981-7181
2153 Pond Rd Ronkonkoma (11779) ***(G-14396)***
Parsons & Whittemore Inc 914 937-9009
4 International Dr # 300 Port Chester (10573) ***(G-13207)***
Parsons Whittemore Entps Corp (PA) 914 937-9009
4 International Dr # 300 Port Chester (10573) ***(G-13208)***
Parsons-Meares Ltd 212 242-3378
2107 41st Ave Ste 1l Long Island City (11101) ***(G-7549)***
Partech Inc (HQ) 315 738-0600
8383 Seneca Tpke Ste 2 New Hartford (13413) ***(G-8509)***
Partlow Corporation 518 922-5315
156 Auriesville Rd Fultonville (12072) ***(G-5238)***
Partlow West, Fultonville *Also called Partlow Corporation* ***(G-5238)***
Pasabahce USA 212 683-1600
41 Madison Ave Fl 7 New York (10010) ***(G-11119)***
Pascale Madonna, Long Island City *Also called Fashion Ribbon Co Inc* ***(G-7445)***
Pass & Seymour Inc (HQ) 315 468-6211
50 Boyd Ave Syracuse (13209) ***(G-15394)***
Pass Em-Entries Inc (PA) 718 392-0100
3914 Crescent St Long Island City (11101) ***(G-7550)***
Passive-Plus Inc 631 425-0938
48 Elm St Huntington (11743) ***(G-6407)***
Passport Brands Inc (PA) 646 459-2625
240 Madison Ave Fl 8 New York (10016) ***(G-11120)***
Passport Magazine, New York *Also called Q Communications Inc* ***(G-11288)***
Passur Aerospace Inc 631 589-6800
35 Orville Dr Ste 1 Bohemia (11716) ***(G-1072)***
Pasta People, West Babylon *Also called Great Eastern Pasta Works LLC* ***(G-16157)***
Pastosa Ravioli, Staten Island *Also called Bud Ravioli Center Inc* ***(G-15056)***
Pat & Rose Dress Inc 212 279-1357
327 W 36th St Rm 3a New York (10018) ***(G-11121)***
Patchogue Advance Inc 631 475-1000
20 Medford Ave Ste 1 Patchogue (11772) ***(G-12873)***
Patco Group, Maspeth *Also called Patco Tapes Inc* ***(G-7867)***
Patco Tapes Inc 718 497-1527
5927 56th St Maspeth (11378) ***(G-7867)***
Patdan Fuel Corporation 718 326-3668
7803 68th Rd Middle Village (11379) ***(G-8126)***
Pathfinder 103 Inc 315 363-4260
229 Park Ave Oneida (13421) ***(G-12620)***
Pathfinder Industries Inc 315 593-2483
117 N 3rd St Fulton (13069) ***(G-5231)***
Pati Inc 718 244-6788
Jfk Intl Airprt Hngar 16 Jamaica (11430) ***(G-6667)***
Patience Brewster Inc 315 685-8336
3872 Jordan Rd Skaneateles (13152) ***(G-14876)***
Patient Portal Tech Inc (PA) 315 638-2030
8276 Willett Pkwy Ste 200 Baldwinsville (13027) ***(G-560)***
Patient-Wear LLC 914 740-7770
3940 Merritt Ave Bronx (10466) ***(G-1353)***
Patla Enterprises Inc 315 367-0237
190 E State St Sherrill (13461) ***(G-14821)***
Patmian LLC 212 758-0770
655 Madison Ave Fl 24 New York (10065) ***(G-11122)***
Patricia Underwood, New York *Also called Paletot Ltd* ***(G-11094)***

Patrick Rohan 718 781-2573
9 Green St Monticello (12701) **(G-8323)**
Patrick Kraft (PA) 315 343-9376
262 W Seneca St Oswego (13126) **(G-12786)**
Patrick Mackin Custom Furn 718 237-2592
612 Degraw St Brooklyn (11217) **(G-2307)**
Patrick Ryans Modern Press 518 434-2921
1 Colonie St Albany (12207) **(G-111)**
Patsy Strocchia & Sons Iron Wo 516 625-8800
175 I U Willets Rd Ste 4 Albertson (11507) **(G-150)**
Patterson Blacktop Corp 845 628-3425
1181 Route 6 Carmel (10512) **(G-3279)**
Patterson Blacktop Corp (HQ) 914 949-2000
20 Haarlem Ave White Plains (10603) **(G-16485)**
Patterson Materials Corp 845 832-6000
322 Walsh Ave New Windsor (12553) **(G-8654)**
Patterson Materials Corp (HQ) 914 949-2000
20 Haarlem Ave White Plains (10603) **(G-16486)**
Patuga LLC 716 204-7220
7954 Transit Rd 316 Williamsville (14221) **(G-16583)**
Paul Bunyan Products Inc 315 696-6164
890 Mclean Rd Cortland (13045) **(G-3888)**
Paul David Enterprises Inc 646 667-5530
19 W 34th St Rm 1018 New York (10001) **(G-11123)**
Paul De Lima Coffee Company, Liverpool *Also called Paul De Lima Company Inc* **(G-7253)**
Paul De Lima Company Inc (PA) 315 457-3725
7546 Morgan Rd Ste 1 Liverpool (13090) **(G-7253)**
Paul De Lima Company Inc 315 457-3725
8550 Pardee Rd Cicero (13039) **(G-3520)**
Paul Delima Coffee Company 315 457-3725
8550 Pardee Rd Cicero (13039) **(G-3521)**
Paul J Mitchell Logging Inc 518 359-7029
15 Mitchell Ln Tupper Lake (12986) **(G-15652)**
Paul Michael Group Inc 631 585-5700
460 Hawkins Ave Ronkonkoma (11779) **(G-14397)**
Paul T Freund Corporation (PA) 315 597-4873
216 Park Dr Palmyra (14522) **(G-12859)**
Paula Dorf Cosmetics Inc 212 582-0073
850 7th Ave Ste 801 New York (10019) **(G-11124)**
Paula Varsalona Ltd 212 570-9100
552 Fashion Ave Rm 602 New York (10018) **(G-11125)**
Paulin Investment Company 631 957-8500
8600 New Horizons Blvd Amityville (11701) **(G-311)**
Paulpac LLC 631 283-7610
104 Foster Xing Southampton (11968) **(G-14958)**
Pauls Rods & Restos Inc 631 665-7637
131 Brook Ave Ste 13 Deer Park (11729) **(G-4023)**
Paumanok Vineyards Ltd 631 722-8800
1074 Main Rd Rte 25 Aquebogue (11931) **(G-375)**
Pavana USA Inc 646 833-8811
10 W 33rd St Rm 408 New York (10001) **(G-11126)**
Pavco Asphalt Inc 631 289-3223
615 Furrows Rd Holtsville (11742) **(G-6242)**
Pavmed Inc 212 401-1951
60 E 42nd St Fl 46 New York (10165) **(G-11127)**
Pawling Corporation (PA) 845 855-1000
157 Charles Colman Blvd Pawling (12564) **(G-12893)**
Pawling Corporation 845 373-9300
32 Nelson Hill Rd Wassaic (12592) **(G-15965)**
Pawling Engineered Pdts Inc 845 855-1000
157 Charles Colman Blvd Pawling (12564) **(G-12894)**
Pawling Engineered Products, Pawling *Also called Pawling Corporation* **(G-12893)**
Paxton Metal Craft Division, Peekskill *Also called Elevator Accessories Mfg* **(G-12919)**
Paya Printing of NY Inc 516 625-8346
87 Searingtown Rd Albertson (11507) **(G-151)**
Pb Industries, Homer *Also called Solidus Industries Inc* **(G-6259)**
Pb Mapinfo Corporation 518 285-6000
1 Global Vw Troy (12180) **(G-15614)**
Pb08 Inc 347 866-7353
40 Bloomingdale Rd Hicksville (11801) **(G-6123)**
Pbi Media Inc., New York *Also called Access Intelligence LLC* **(G-8719)**
PBL Industries Corp 631 979-4266
49 Dillmont Dr Smithtown (11787) **(G-14904)**
PBR Graphics Inc 518 458-2909
20 Railroad Ave Ste 1 Albany (12205) **(G-112)**
PC Solutions & Consulting 607 735-0466
407 S Walnut St Elmira (14904) **(G-4499)**
Pca/Syracuse, 384, Liverpool *Also called Packaging Corporation America* **(G-7251)**
Pcamerica, Pearl River *Also called Heartland Commerce Inc* **(G-12898)**
Pcb Coach Builders Corp 718 897-7606
6334 Austin St Rego Park (11374) **(G-13467)**
Pcb Group Inc 716 684-0001
3425 Walden Ave Depew (14043) **(G-4100)**
Pcb Piezotronics Inc 716 684-0001
3425 Walden Ave Depew (14043) **(G-4101)**
Pcb Piezotronics Inc 716 684-0003
3425 Walden Ave Depew (14043) **(G-4102)**
PCI Industries Corp 914 662-2700
550 Franklin Ave Mount Vernon (10550) **(G-8428)**
Pcx Aerostructures LLC 631 467-2632
60 Milbar Blvd Farmingdale (11735) **(G-4844)**
Pda Panache Corp 631 776-0523
70 Knickerbocker Ave # 7 Bohemia (11716) **(G-1073)**
Pdf Seal Incorporated 631 595-7035
503 Acorn St Deer Park (11729) **(G-4024)**
Pdi, New York *Also called Props Displays & Interiors* **(G-11266)**
Pdi Cone Co Inc 716 825-8750
69 Leddy St Buffalo (14210) **(G-2994)**
Pdj Components Inc 845 469-9191
35 Brookside Ave Chester (10918) **(G-3479)**
PDJ Inc 315 655-8824
2550 E Ballina Rd Cazenovia (13035) **(G-3324)**
Pdk Labs Inc 631 273-2630
145 Ricefield Ln Hauppauge (11788) **(G-5910)**
PDM Studios Inc 716 694-8337
510 Main St Tonawanda (14150) **(G-15569)**
PDQ Manufacturing Co Inc 845 889-3123
29 Hilee Rd Rhinebeck (12572) **(G-13487)**
PDQ Printing, New Paltz *Also called PDQ Shipping Services* **(G-8580)**
PDQ Shipping Services 845 255-5500
8 New Paltz Plz 299 New Paltz (12561) **(G-8580)**
Peace Times Weekly Inc 718 762-6500
14527 33rd Ave Flushing (11354) **(G-5036)**
Peaceful Valley Maple Farm (PA) 518 762-0491
116 Lagrange Rd Johnstown (12095) **(G-6835)**
Peachtree Enterprises Inc 212 989-3445
2219 41st Ave Ste 4a Long Island City (11101) **(G-7551)**
Peak Motion Inc 716 534-4925
11190 Main St Clarence (14031) **(G-3538)**
Peak Performance Design LLC 518 302-9198
7 Old Military Rd Lake Placid (12946) **(G-6977)**
Peaks Coffee Company 315 565-1900
3264 Rte 20 Cazenovia (13035) **(G-3325)**
Peanut Butter & Co Inc 212 757-3130
119 W 57th St Ste 300 New York (10019) **(G-11128)**
Pearl Erwin Inc (PA) 212 889-7410
389 5th Ave Rm 1100 New York (10016) **(G-11129)**
Pearl Leather Finishers Inc (PA) 518 762-4543
11 Industrial Pkwy 21 Johnstown (12095) **(G-6836)**
Pearl Leather Group LLC 516 627-4047
17 Barstow Rd Ste 206 Great Neck (11021) **(G-5580)**
Pearl River Pastries LLC 845 735-5100
389 W Nyack Rd West Nyack (10994) **(G-16277)**
Pearl River Pastry Chocolates, West Nyack *Also called Pearl River Pastries LLC* **(G-16277)**
Pearl Technologies Inc 315 365-3742
13297 Seneca St Savannah (13146) **(G-14623)**
Pearltek, New York *Also called Robin Stanley Inc* **(G-11411)**
Pearson Education Inc 845 340-8700
317 Wall St Kingston (12401) **(G-6914)**
Pearson Education Inc 212 782-3337
1185 Avenue Of The Americ New York (10036) **(G-11130)**
Pearson Education Inc 212 366-2000
375 Hudson St New York (10014) **(G-11131)**
Pearson Education Inc 201 236-7000
59 Brookhill Dr West Nyack (10994) **(G-16278)**
Pearson Education Holdings Inc (HQ) 201 236-6716
330 Hudson St Fl 9 New York (10013) **(G-11132)**
Pearson Inc (HQ) 212 641-2400
1330 Hudson St New York (10013) **(G-11133)**
Pearson Longman LLC 917 981-2200
51 Madison Ave Fl 27 New York (10010) **(G-11134)**
Pearson Longman LLC (HQ) 212 641-2400
10 Bank St Ste 1030 White Plains (10606) **(G-16487)**
Peck & Hale LLC 631 589-2510
180 Division Ave West Sayville (11796) **(G-16291)**
Pecker Iron Works LLC 914 665-0100
137 Ruxton Rd Mount Kisco (10549) **(G-8354)**
Peckham Industries Inc (PA) 914 949-2000
20 Haarlem Ave Ste 200 White Plains (10603) **(G-16488)**
Peckham Industries Inc 518 943-0155
7065 Us Highway 9w Catskill (12414) **(G-3308)**
Peckham Industries Inc 518 893-2176
430 Coy Rd Greenfield Center (12833) **(G-5619)**
Peckham Industries Inc 518 945-1120
Uninn St Athens (12015) **(G-453)**
Peckham Materials, Carmel *Also called Patterson Blacktop Corp* **(G-3279)**
Peckham Materials Corp 845 562-5370
322 Walsh Ave Newburgh (12553) **(G-12240)**
Peckham Materials Corp (HQ) 914 686-2045
20 Haarlem Ave Ste 200 White Plains (10603) **(G-16489)**
Peckham Materials Corp 518 747-3353
438 Vaughn Rd Hudson Falls (12839) **(G-6384)**
Peckham Materials Corp 518 945-1120
2 Union St Ext Athens (12015) **(G-454)**
Peckham Materials Corp 518 494-2313
5983 State Route 9 Chestertown (12817) **(G-3491)**
Peckham Road Corp 518 792-3157
375 Bay Rd Ste 101 Queensbury (12804) **(G-13436)**
Peco Conduit Fittings, Orangeburg *Also called Producto Electric Corp* **(G-12688)**
Peco Pallet Inc (HQ) 914 376-5444
2 Bridge St Ste 210 Irvington (10533) **(G-6509)**
Peconic B Shopper, Southold *Also called Academy Printing Services Inc* **(G-14967)**

ALPHABETIC

(PA)=Parent Co (HQ)=Headquarters (DH)=Div Headquarters
2019 Harris
New York Manufacturers Directory
957

Peconic Ironworks Ltd 631 204-0323
33 Flying Point Rd # 108 Southampton (11968) *(G-14959)*
Peconic Plastics Inc 631 653-3676
6062 Old Country Rd Quogue (11959) *(G-13446)*
Pecoraro Dairy Products Inc (PA) 718 388-2379
287 Leonard St Brooklyn (11211) *(G-2308)*
Pedifix Inc 845 277-2850
301 Fields Ln Brewster (10509) *(G-1173)*
Pedre Corp (PA) 212 868-2935
270 Duffy Ave Ste G Hicksville (11801) *(G-6124)*
Pedre Watch, Hicksville *Also called Pedre Corp (G-6124)*
Peek A Boo USA Inc 201 533-8700
555 8th Ave Rm 403 New York (10018) *(G-11135)*
Peelle Company (PA) 631 231-6000
373 Smithtown Byp 311 Hauppauge (11788) *(G-5911)*
Peer International Corp (HQ) 212 265-3910
152 W 57th St Fl 10 New York (10019) *(G-11136)*
Peer Software Incorporated (PA) 631 979-1770
1363 Veterans Hwy Ste 44 Hauppauge (11788) *(G-5912)*
Peer-Southern Productions Inc (HQ) 212 265-3910
152 W 57th St Fl 10 New York (10019) *(G-11137)*
Peerless Envelopes & Prtg Co, Brooklyn *Also called H T L & S Ltd (G-1957)*
Peerless Instrument Co Inc 631 396-6500
1966 Broadhollow Rd Ste D Farmingdale (11735) *(G-4845)*
Peerless Mfg Co 716 539-7400
50 Cobham Dr Orchard Park (14127) *(G-12736)*
Peerless-Winsmith Inc 716 592-9311
172 Eaton St Springville (14141) *(G-15019)*
Peermusic III Ltd (PA) 212 265-3910
152 W 57th St Fl 10 New York (10019) *(G-11138)*
Peermusic Ltd (HQ) 212 265-3910
152 W 57th St Fl 10 New York (10019) *(G-11139)*
Pegasus Books NY Ltd 646 343-9502
148 W 37th St Fl 13 New York (10018) *(G-11140)*
Pegasystems Inc 212 626-6550
1120 Ave Of The Americas New York (10036) *(G-11141)*
Peggy Jennings Designs, New York *Also called PJ Designs Inc (G-11203)*
Pei Genesis International, Farmingville *Also called Pei/Genesis Inc (G-4925)*
Pei/Genesis Inc 631 256-1747
2410 N Ocean Ave Ste 401 Farmingville (11738) *(G-4925)*
Peking Food LLC 718 628-8080
47 Stewart Ave Brooklyn (11237) *(G-2309)*
Peko Precision Products Inc 585 301-1386
70 Holworthy St Rochester (14606) *(G-14010)*
Pelican Bay Ltd 718 729-9300
3901 22nd St Long Island City (11101) *(G-7552)*
Pelican Products Co Inc (PA) 718 860-3220
1049 Lowell St Bronx (10459) *(G-1354)*
Pelkowski Precast Corp 631 269-5727
294a Old Northport Rd Kings Park (11754) *(G-6885)*
Pella Corporation 607 223-2023
800 Valley Plz Ste 5 Johnson City (13790) *(G-6816)*
Pella Corporation 607 231-8550
800 Valley Plz Ste 5 Johnson City (13790) *(G-6817)*
Pella Corporation 607 238-2812
800 Valley Plz Ste 5 Johnson City (13790) *(G-6818)*
Pella Corporation 516 385-3622
77 Albertson Ave Ste 2 Albertson (11507) *(G-152)*
Pella Corporation 607 238-2812
800 Valley Plz Ste 5 Johnson City (13790) *(G-6819)*
Pella Corporation 516 385-3622
77 Albertson Ave Ste 2 Albertson (11507) *(G-153)*
Pella Corporation 607 231-8550
800 Valley Plz Ste 5 Johnson City (13790) *(G-6820)*
Pella Corporation 631 208-0710
901 Burman Blvd Calverton (11933) *(G-3168)*
Pella Window Door, Johnson City *Also called Pella Corporation (G-6816)*
Pella Window Door, Johnson City *Also called Pella Corporation (G-6817)*
Pella Window Door, Johnson City *Also called Pella Corporation (G-6818)*
Pella Window Door, Albertson *Also called Pella Corporation (G-152)*
Pella Window Door, Johnson City *Also called Pella Corporation (G-6819)*
Pella Window Door, Albertson *Also called Pella Corporation (G-153)*
Pella Window Door, Johnson City *Also called Pella Corporation (G-6820)*
Pellegrini Vineyards LLC 631 734-4111
23005 Main Rd Cutchogue (11935) *(G-3922)*
Pellets LLC 716 693-1750
63 Industrial Dr Ste 3 North Tonawanda (14120) *(G-12441)*
Pellicano Specialty Foods Inc 716 822-2366
195 Reading St Buffalo (14220) *(G-2995)*
Peloton Interactive Inc 866 679-9129
140 W 23rd St Frnt 1 New York (10011) *(G-11142)*
Peloton Interactive Inc (PA) 866 650-1996
125 W 25th St Fl 11 New York (10001) *(G-11143)*
Pems Tool & Machine Inc 315 823-3595
125 Southern Ave Little Falls (13365) *(G-7211)*
Pemystifying Diital, Woodbury *Also called Photo Industry Inc (G-16628)*
Penasack Machine Company Inc 585 589-7044
49 Sanford St Albion (14411) *(G-161)*
Pencoa, Westbury *Also called Harper Products Ltd (G-16340)*
Penetradar Corporation 716 731-2629
2509 Niagara Falls Blvd Niagara Falls (14304) *(G-12322)*
Penetron International Ltd 631 941-9700
45 Research Way Ste 203 East Setauket (11733) *(G-4306)*
Penfli Industries Inc 212 947-6080
11 Woodland Pl Great Neck (11021) *(G-5581)*
Penguin Putnam Inc 212 366-2000
375 Hudson St Bsmt 1 New York (10014) *(G-11144)*
Penguin Random House LLC 212 782-1000
1540 Broadway New York (10036) *(G-11145)*
Penguin Random House LLC (HQ) 212 782-9000
1745 Broadway New York (10019) *(G-11146)*
Penguin Random House LLC 212 572-6162
1745 Broadway Frnt 3 New York (10019) *(G-11147)*
Penguin Random House LLC 212 782-9000
1745 Broadway Frnt 3 New York (10019) *(G-11148)*
Penguin Random House LLC 212 366-2377
80 State St Albany (12207) *(G-113)*
Penhouse Media Group Inc (PA) 212 702-6000
11 Penn Plz Fl 12 New York (10001) *(G-11149)*
Peninsula Plastics Ltd 716 854-3050
161 Marine Dr Apt 6e Buffalo (14202) *(G-2996)*
Penn & Fletcher Inc 212 239-6868
2107 41st Ave Fl 5 Long Island City (11101) *(G-7553)*
Penn Can Asphalt Materials, Lyons *Also called Penn Can Equipment Corporation (G-7686)*
Penn Can Equipment Corporation 315 378-0337
300 Cole Rd Lyons (14489) *(G-7686)*
Penn Enterprises Inc 845 446-0765
845 Washington Rd West Point (10996) *(G-16283)*
Penn Signs Inc 718 797-1112
1920 Atlantic Ave Brooklyn (11233) *(G-2310)*
Penn State Metal Fabri 718 786-8814
810 Humboldt St Ste 9 Brooklyn (11222) *(G-2311)*
Pennant Foods, Rochester *Also called Aryzta LLC (G-13645)*
Pennant Ingredients Inc (HQ) 585 235-8160
64 Chester St Rochester (14611) *(G-14011)*
Penner Elbow Company Inc 718 526-9000
4700 76th St Elmhurst (11373) *(G-4470)*
Pennsauken Packing Company LLC 585 377-7700
815 Whitney Rd W Fairport (14450) *(G-4649)*
Penny Express, Avon *Also called Penny Lane Printing Inc (G-521)*
Penny Lane Printing Inc 585 226-8111
1471 Rte 15 Avon (14414) *(G-521)*
Penny Saver News, Edgewood *Also called S G New York LLC (G-4414)*
Pennysaver Group Inc 914 966-1400
80 Alexander St Yonkers (10701) *(G-16791)*
Pennysaver News, Bohemia *Also called S G New York LLC (G-1084)*
Pennysaver/Town Crier, Edgewood *Also called All Island Media Inc (G-4395)*
Pennysavers Rw Publications, Elma *Also called R W Publications Div of Wtrhs (G-4457)*
Pensions & Investments 212 210-0763
711 3rd Ave New York (10017) *(G-11150)*
Pensrus, Staten Island *Also called Henry Morgan (G-15085)*
Penta-Tech Coated Products LLC 315 986-4098
1610 Commons Pkwy Macedon (14502) *(G-7702)*
Pentair Water Pool and Spa Inc 845 452-5500
341 Route 55 Lagrangeville (12540) *(G-6961)*
Pentaplastics, Bohemia *Also called Leidel Corporation (G-1047)*
Penthouse Group, The, Freeport *Also called Penthouse Manufacturing Co Inc (G-5173)*
Penthouse Manufacturing Co Inc 516 379-1300
225 Buffalo Ave Freeport (11520) *(G-5173)*
Penton Information Services, New York *Also called Informa Business Media Inc (G-10209)*
Penton Media - Aviation Week, New York *Also called Informa Media Inc (G-10210)*
Peoples Choice M R I 716 681-7377
125 Galileo Dr Buffalo (14221) *(G-2997)*
Pep Realty, New York *Also called Atlas Recycling LLC (G-8956)*
Pepe Creations Inc 212 391-1514
2 W 45th St Ste 1003 New York (10036) *(G-11151)*
Peppermints Salon Inc 718 357-6304
15722 Powells Cove Blvd Whitestone (11357) *(G-16547)*
Pepsi Beverages Co 518 782-2150
421 Old Niskayuna Rd Latham (12110) *(G-7088)*
Pepsi Beverages Company, Watertown *Also called Bottling Group LLC (G-16004)*
Pepsi Beverages Company, White Plains *Also called Bottling Group LLC (G-16429)*
Pepsi Beverages Company, White Plains *Also called Bottling Group LLC (G-16430)*
Pepsi Bottle and Group, Somers *Also called General Cinema Bevs of Ohio (G-14919)*
Pepsi Bottling Ventures LLC 631 772-6144
4141 Parklane Ave Ste 600 Patchogue (11772) *(G-12874)*
Pepsi Bottling Ventures LLC 631 226-9000
550 New Horizons Blvd Amityville (11701) *(G-312)*
Pepsi Btlg Group Globl Fin LLC (HQ) 914 767-6000
1 Pepsi Way Ste 1 # 1 Somers (10589) *(G-14921)*
Pepsi-Cola, Patchogue *Also called Pepsi Bottling Ventures LLC (G-12874)*
Pepsi-Cola Bottling Co NY Inc 914 699-2600
601 S Fulton Ave Mount Vernon (10550) *(G-8429)*
Pepsi-Cola Bottling Co NY Inc (PA) 718 392-1000
11202 15th Ave College Point (11356) *(G-3660)*
Pepsi-Cola Bottling Co NY Inc 718 892-1570
650 Brush Ave Bronx (10465) *(G-1355)*
Pepsi-Cola Bottling Group (HQ) 914 767-6000
1111 Westchester Ave White Plains (10604) *(G-16490)*
Pepsi-Cola Metro Btlg Co Inc (HQ) 914 767-6000
1111 Westchester Ave White Plains (10604) *(G-16491)*

Pepsi-Cola Metro Btlg Co Inc 914 253-2000
700 Anderson Hill Rd Purchase (10577) ***(G-13393)***
Pepsi-Cola Metro Btlg Co Inc 518 834-7811
1524 Route 9 Keeseville (12944) ***(G-6854)***
Pepsi-Cola Newburgh Btlg Inc 845 562-5400
1 Pepsi Way Newburgh (12550) ***(G-12241)***
Pepsi-Cola Operating Company (HQ) 914 767-6000
1111 Westchester Ave White Plains (10604) ***(G-16492)***
Pepsi-Cola Sales and Dist Inc (HQ) 914 253-2000
700 Anderson Hill Rd Purchase (10577) ***(G-13394)***
Pepsico, White Plains *Also called Pepsi-Cola Metro Btlg Co Inc* ***(G-16491)***
Pepsico, Newburgh *Also called Pepsi-Cola Newburgh Btlg Inc* ***(G-12241)***
Pepsico, Latham *Also called Pepsi Beverages Co* ***(G-7088)***
Pepsico, Keeseville *Also called Pepsi-Cola Metro Btlg Co Inc* ***(G-6854)***
Pepsico, White Plains *Also called Pepsi-Cola Bottling Group* ***(G-16490)***
Pepsico, Amityville *Also called Pepsi Bottling Ventures LLC* ***(G-312)***
Pepsico 419 252-0247
3 Skyline Dr Hawthorne (10532) ***(G-5995)***
Pepsico 914 801-1500
100 Summit Lake Dr # 103 Valhalla (10595) ***(G-15743)***
Pepsico Inc (PA) 914 253-2000
700 Anderson Hill Rd Purchase (10577) ***(G-13395)***
Pepsico Inc 914 253-2000
1111 Westchester Ave White Plains (10604) ***(G-16493)***
Pepsico Inc 914 742-4500
100 E Stevens Ave Valhalla (10595) ***(G-15744)***
Pepsico Inc 914 253-2000
Anderson Hill Rd Purchase (10577) ***(G-13396)***
Pepsico Inc 914 253-3474
150 Airport Rd Hngr V White Plains (10604) ***(G-16494)***
Pepsico Inc 914 253-2713
700 Anderson Hill Rd Purchase (10577) ***(G-13397)***
Pepsico Inc 914 767-6976
1111 Westchester Ave White Plains (10604) ***(G-16495)***
Pepsico Capital Resources Inc 914 253-2000
700 Anderson Hill Rd Purchase (10577) ***(G-13398)***
Pepsico Sales Inc 914 253-2000
700 Anderson Hill Rd Purchase (10577) ***(G-13399)***
Per Annum Inc 212 647-8700
555 8th Ave Rm 202 New York (10018) ***(G-11152)***
Peraflex Hose Inc 716 876-8806
155 Great Arrow Ave Ste 4 Buffalo (14207) ***(G-2998)***
Peralta Metal Works Inc 718 649-8661
602 Atkins Ave Brooklyn (11208) ***(G-2312)***
Peraton Inc 315 838-7000
474 Phoenix Dr Rome (13441) ***(G-14266)***
Peregrine Industries Inc 631 838-2870
40 Wall St New York (10005) ***(G-11153)***
Pereira & ODell LLC 212 897-1000
5 Crosby St Rm 5h New York (10013) ***(G-11154)***
Perfect Form Manufacturing LLC 585 500-5923
1325 John St West Henrietta (14586) ***(G-16247)***
Perfect Forms and Systems Inc 631 462-1100
35 Riverview Ter Smithtown (11787) ***(G-14905)***
Perfect Gear & Instrument (HQ) 516 328-3330
250 Duffy Ave Hicksville (11801) ***(G-6125)***
Perfect Gear & Instrument 516 873-6122
125 Railroad Ave Garden City Park (11040) ***(G-5287)***
Perfect Poly Inc 631 265-0539
1 Gina Ct Nesconset (11767) ***(G-8486)***
Perfect Print Inc 718 832-5280
220 36th St Unit 2a Brooklyn (11232) ***(G-2313)***
Perfect Publications, Brooklyn *Also called Joseph Paul* ***(G-2047)***
Perfect Shoulder Company Inc 914 699-8100
2 Cortlandt St Mount Vernon (10550) ***(G-8430)***
Perfection Gear Inc 716 592-9310
172 Eaton St Springville (14141) ***(G-15020)***
Perfex Corporation 315 826-3600
32 Case St Poland (13431) ***(G-13184)***
Perforated Screen Surfaces 866 866-8690
216 Broome Corporate Pkwy Conklin (13748) ***(G-3731)***
Performance Advantage Co Inc 716 683-7413
6 W Main St Lowr Rear Lancaster (14086) ***(G-7039)***
Performance Custom Trailer 518 504-4021
230 Lockhart Mountain Rd Lake George (12845) ***(G-6965)***
Performance Designed By Peters 585 223-9062
7 Duxbury Hts Fairport (14450) ***(G-4650)***
Performance Diesel Service LLC 315 854-5269
24 Latour Ave Plattsburgh (12901) ***(G-13144)***
Performance Lacrosse Group Inc (HQ) 315 453-3073
4697 Crossroads Park Dr Liverpool (13088) ***(G-7254)***
Performance Mfg Inc 716 735-3500
80 Telegraph Rd Middleport (14105) ***(G-8133)***
Performance Precision Mfg LLC 518 993-3033
55 Willett St Fort Plain (13339) ***(G-5103)***
Performance Sourcing Group Inc (PA) 914 636-2100
109 Montgomery Ave Scarsdale (10583) ***(G-14642)***
Performance Systems Contg Inc 607 277-6240
124 Brindley St Ithaca (14850) ***(G-6603)***
Performance Technologies Inc (HQ) 585 256-0200
3500 Winton Pl Ste 4 Rochester (14623) ***(G-14012)***
Performance Wire & Cable Inc 315 245-2594
9482 State Route 13 Camden (13316) ***(G-3193)***
Perfume Amrcana Whlesalers Inc 212 683-8029
11 W 30th St Betwe Broad Between New York (10001) ***(G-11155)***
Perfumers Workshop Intl Ltd (PA) 212 644-8950
350 7th Ave Rm 802 New York (10001) ***(G-11156)***
Peri, Pearl River *Also called Piezo Electronics Research* ***(G-12907)***
Peri-Facts Academy 585 275-6037
601 Elmwood Ave Rochester (14642) ***(G-14013)***
Perimondo LLC 212 749-0721
331 W 84th St Apt 2 New York (10024) ***(G-11157)***
Periodical Services Co Inc 518 822-9300
351 Fairview Ave Ste 300 Hudson (12534) ***(G-6367)***
Perkins International Inc (HQ) 309 675-1000
672 Delaware Ave Buffalo (14209) ***(G-2999)***
Perma Glow Ltd Inc 212 575-9677
48 W 48th St Ste 301 New York (10036) ***(G-11158)***
Perma Tech Inc 716 854-0707
363 Hamburg St Buffalo (14204) ***(G-3000)***
Permanent Observer Mission 212 883-0140
320 E 51st St New York (10022) ***(G-11159)***
Permanent Press, Sag Harbor *Also called Second Chance Press Inc* ***(G-14503)***
Permit Fashion Group Inc 212 912-0988
27 Chauncey Pl Woodbury (11797) ***(G-16627)***
Perretta Graphics Corp 845 473-0550
46 Violet Ave Poughkeepsie (12601) ***(G-13362)***
Perrigo Company 718 960-9900
1625 Bathgate Ave Bronx (10457) ***(G-1356)***
Perrigo New York Inc 718 901-2800
455 Claremont Pkwy Bronx (10457) ***(G-1357)***
Perrigo New York Inc (HQ) 718 960-9900
1700 Bathgate Ave Bronx (10457) ***(G-1358)***
Perrone Aerospace, Fultonville *Also called Perrone Leather LLC* ***(G-5239)***
Perrone Leather LLC (PA) 518 853-4300
182a Riverside Dr Fultonville (12072) ***(G-5239)***
Perrottas Bakery Inc 518 283-4711
766 Pawling Ave Troy (12180) ***(G-15615)***
Perry Ellis America, New York *Also called Perry Ellis Menswear LLC* ***(G-11162)***
Perry Ellis International Inc 212 536-5400
1126 Avenue Of The Americ New York (10036) ***(G-11160)***
Perry Ellis International Inc 212 536-5499
42 W 39th St Fl 4 New York (10018) ***(G-11161)***
Perry Ellis Menswear LLC (HQ) 212 221-7500
1120 Avenue Of The Americ New York (10036) ***(G-11162)***
Perry Plastics Inc 718 747-5600
3050 Whitestone Expy # 300 Flushing (11354) ***(G-5037)***
Perry Street Software Inc 415 935-1429
489 5th Ave Rm 2900 New York (10017) ***(G-11163)***
Perrys Ice Cream Company Inc 716 542-5492
1 Ice Cream Plz Akron (14001) ***(G-21)***
Persch Service Print Inc (PA) 716 366-2677
11 W 3rd St Dunkirk (14048) ***(G-4176)***
Perseus Books Group, New York *Also called Clp Pb LLC* ***(G-9335)***
Persistent Systems LLC 212 561-5895
303 5th Ave Rm 306 New York (10016) ***(G-11164)***
Personal Graphics Corporation 315 853-3421
5123 State Route 233 Westmoreland (13490) ***(G-16408)***
Perugina Div, New York *Also called Nestle Usa Inc* ***(G-10910)***
Pervi Precision Company Inc 631 589-5557
220 Knickerbocker Ave # 1 Bohemia (11716) ***(G-1074)***
PES Group, Brooklyn *Also called Project Energy Savers LLC* ***(G-2356)***
Pesce Bakery, Saugerties *Also called Pesces Bakery Inc* ***(G-14613)***
Pesces Bakery Inc 845 246-4730
20 Pesce Ct Saugerties (12477) ***(G-14613)***
Pesselnik & Cohen Inc 212 925-0287
82 Bowery Unit 10 New York (10013) ***(G-11165)***
Pet Authority, Brooklyn *Also called Dynamic Health Labs Inc* ***(G-1799)***
Pet Proteins LLC 888 293-1029
347 W 36th St Rm 1204 New York (10018) ***(G-11166)***
Petcap Press Corporation 718 609-0910
3200 Skillman Ave Ste F Long Island City (11101) ***(G-7554)***
Pete Levin Music Inc 845 247-9211
598 Schoolhouse Rd Saugerties (12477) ***(G-14614)***
Peter Atman Inc 212 644-8882
6 E 45th St Rm 1100 New York (10017) ***(G-11167)***
Peter C Herman Inc 315 926-4100
5395 Skinner Rd Marion (14505) ***(G-7805)***
Peter Digioia 516 644-5517
7 Sherwood Dr Plainview (11803) ***(G-13081)***
Peter Kwasny Inc 727 641-1462
400 Oser Ave Ste 1650 Hauppauge (11788) ***(G-5913)***
Peter Lang Publishing Inc (HQ) 212 647-7700
29 Broadway Rm 1800 New York (10006) ***(G-11168)***
Peter Mayer Publishers Inc 212 673-2210
141 Wooster St Fl 4 New York (10012) ***(G-11169)***
Peter Papastrat 607 723-8112
193 Main St Binghamton (13905) ***(G-910)***
Peter Pauper Press Inc 914 681-0144
202 Mmaroneck Ave Ste 400 White Plains (10601) ***(G-16496)***
Peter Productions Devivi Inc 315 568-8484
2494 Kingdom Rd Waterloo (13165) ***(G-15997)***

A L P H A B E T I C

Peter Thomas Roth Labs LLC (PA) 212 581-5800
460 Park Ave Fl 16 New York (10022) ***(G-11170)***
Peters LLC....607 637-5470
5259 Peas Eddy Rd Hancock (13783) ***(G-5713)***
Petit Printing Corp....716 871-9490
42 Hunters Gln Getzville (14068) ***(G-5352)***
Petnet Solutions Inc....865 218-2000
660 1st Ave Rm 140 New York (10016) ***(G-11171)***
Petre Alii Petroleum 315 785-1037
1268 Arsenal St Watertown (13601) ***(G-16032)***
Petrillo's Bakery, Fairport *Also called Scaife Enterprises Inc* ***(G-4656)***
Petro Inc....516 686-1717
3 Fairchild Ct Plainview (11803) ***(G-13082)***
Petro Inc....516 686-1900
477 W John St Hicksville (11801) ***(G-6126)***
Petrune, Ithaca *Also called Petrunia LLC* ***(G-6604)***
Petrunia LLC....607 277-1930
126 E State St Ithaca (14850) ***(G-6604)***
Petteys Lumber....518 792-5943
10247 State Route 149 Fort Ann (12827) ***(G-5090)***
Pexip Inc (HQ)....703 338-3544
240 W 35th St Ste 300 New York (10001) ***(G-11172)***
Peyser Instrument Corporation....631 841-3600
40 Gleam St West Babylon (11704) ***(G-16181)***
Pezera Associates, Calverton *Also called East End Country Kitchens Inc* ***(G-3165)***
Pfannenberg Inc 716 685-6866
68 Ward Rd Lancaster (14086) ***(G-7040)***
Pfannenberg Manufacturing LLC....716 685-6866
68 Ward Rd Lancaster (14086) ***(G-7041)***
Pfaudler Inc (HQ)....585 235-1000
1000 West Ave Rochester (14611) ***(G-14014)***
Pfaudler US Inc....585 235-1000
1000 West Ave Rochester (14611) ***(G-14015)***
Pfeil & Holing Inc....718 545-4600
5815 Northern Blvd Woodside (11377) ***(G-16671)***
Pfisterer Lapp LLC 585 768-6221
130 Gilbert St Le Roy (14482) ***(G-7124)***
Pfizer HCP Corporation (HQ)....212 733-2323
235 E 42nd St New York (10017) ***(G-11173)***
Pfizer Inc (PA) 212 733-2323
235 E 42nd St New York (10017) ***(G-11174)***
Pfizer Inc....518 297-6611
64 Maple St Rouses Point (12979) ***(G-14468)***
Pfizer Inc....914 437-5868
4 Martine Ave White Plains (10606) ***(G-16497)***
Pfizer Inc....937 746-3603
150 E 42nd St Fl 38 New York (10017) ***(G-11175)***
Pfizer Inc....212 733-6276
150 E 42nd St Bsmt 2 New York (10017) ***(G-11176)***
Pfizer Inc....212 733-2323
235 E 42nd St New York (10017) ***(G-11177)***
Pfizer Overseas LLC....212 733-2323
235 E 42nd St New York (10017) ***(G-11178)***
Pgs Millwork Inc (PA) 518 828-2608
32 Hickory Ln Hudson (12534) ***(G-6368)***
PH David J Rossi 585 455-1160
50 Celtic Ln Rochester (14626) ***(G-14016)***
Phaidon Press Inc 212 652-5400
65 Bleecker St Fl 8 New York (10012) ***(G-11179)***
Phantom Laboratory Inc 518 692-1190
2727 State Route 29 Greenwich (12834) ***(G-5644)***
Phantom Laboratory, The, Greenwich *Also called Phantom Laboratory Inc* ***(G-5644)***
Pharbest Pharmaceuticals Inc 631 249-5130
14 Engineers Ln Ste 1 Farmingdale (11735) ***(G-4846)***
Pharma-Smart International Inc 585 427-0730
Rochester Tech Park 773 E Rochester (14624) ***(G-14017)***
Pharmaceutic Labs LLC....518 608-1060
15 Walker Way Albany (12205) ***(G-114)***
Pharmaderm, Melville *Also called Fougera Pharmaceuticals Inc* ***(G-8026)***
Pharmadva LLC....585 469-1410
36 King St Rochester (14608) ***(G-14018)***
Pharmalife Inc....631 249-4040
130 Gazza Blvd Farmingdale (11735) ***(G-4847)***
Pharmasmart, Rochester *Also called Pharma-Smart International Inc* ***(G-14017)***
Pharmavantage LLC....631 321-8171
15 Lakeland Ave Babylon (11702) ***(G-531)***
PHASE IL MARKETING DBA, Amherst *Also called Nexstar Holding Corp* ***(G-240)***
PHC Restoration Holdings LLC....212 643-0517
147 W 29th St Ste 4e New York (10001) ***(G-11180)***
Phelinger Tool & Die Corp 716 685-1780
1254 Town Line Rd Alden (14004) ***(G-174)***
Phelps Cement Products Inc....315 548-9415
5 S Newark St Phelps (14532) ***(G-12979)***
Pheonix Custom Furniture Ltd....212 727-2648
2107 41st Ave Fl 2 Long Island City (11101) ***(G-7555)***
Philcom Ltd 716 875-8005
1144 Military Rd Buffalo (14217) ***(G-3001)***
Philip Crangi, New York *Also called PHC Restoration Holdings LLC* ***(G-11180)***
Philip Morris Intl Inc (PA)....917 663-2000
120 Park Ave Fl 6 New York (10017) ***(G-11181)***
Philipp Feldheim Inc (PA) 845 356-2282
208 Airport Executive Par Nanuet (10954) ***(G-8467)***
Philippe Adec Paris, New York *Also called Morelle Products Ltd* ***(G-10841)***
Philips Elec N Amer Corp 607 776-3692
7265 State Route 54 Bath (14810) ***(G-648)***
Philips Healthcare, Latham *Also called Philips Medical Systems Mr* ***(G-7089)***
Philips Lighting N Amer Corp....646 265-7170
267 5th Ave New York (10016) ***(G-11182)***
Philips Medical Systems Mr (HQ)....518 782-1122
450 Old Niskayuna Rd Latham (12110) ***(G-7089)***
Phillip J Ortiz Manufacturing....845 226-7030
44 Railroad Ave Hopewell Junction (12533) ***(G-6292)***
Phillip Tissicher....718 282-3310
1688 Utica Ave Brooklyn (11234) ***(G-2314)***
Phillips-Van Heusen Europe....212 381-3500
200 Madison Ave Bsmt 1 New York (10016) ***(G-11183)***
Philpac Corporation (PA)....716 875-8005
1144 Military Rd Buffalo (14217) ***(G-3002)***
Phoenix Envmtl Svcs Corp....718 381-8100
7314 88th St Glendale (11385) ***(G-5406)***
Phoenix Graphics Inc....585 232-4040
464 State St 470 Rochester (14608) ***(G-14019)***
Phoenix Laboratories Inc....516 822-1230
200 Adams Blvd Farmingdale (11735) ***(G-4848)***
Phoenix Material Handling, Phoenix *Also called Phoenix Welding & Fabg Inc* ***(G-12992)***
Phoenix Mch Pdts of Hauppauge....631 234-0100
225 Engineers Rd Hauppauge (11788) ***(G-5914)***
Phoenix Metal Designs Inc 516 597-4100
100 Hinsdale St Brooklyn (11207) ***(G-2315)***
Phoenix Metal Products Inc....516 546-4200
100 Bennington Ave Freeport (11520) ***(G-5174)***
Phoenix Usa LLC 646 351-6598
315 W 33rd St Apt 30h New York (10001) ***(G-11184)***
Phoenix Venture Fund LLC....212 759-1909
70 E 55th St Fl 10 New York (10022) ***(G-11185)***
Phoenix Welding & Fabg Inc 315 695-2223
10 County Route 6 Phoenix (13135) ***(G-12992)***
Phoenix Wood Wrights Ltd....631 727-9691
132 Kroemer Ave 3 Riverhead (11901) ***(G-13579)***
Photo Industry Inc....516 364-0016
7600 Jericho Tpke Ste 301 Woodbury (11797) ***(G-16628)***
Photo Medic Equipment Inc 631 242-6600
3 Saxwood St Ste E Deer Park (11729) ***(G-4025)***
Photograve Corporation 718 667-4825
1140 S Railroad Ave Staten Island (10306) ***(G-15114)***
Photon Gear Inc....585 265-3360
245 David Pkwy Ontario (14519) ***(G-12660)***
Photon Vision Systems Inc (PA) 607 749-2689
1 Technology Pl Homer (13077) ***(G-6258)***
Photonamics Inc....585 247-8990
558 Elmgrove Rd Rochester (14606) ***(G-14020)***
Photonic Controls LLC 607 562-4585
500 1st Ctr Ste 2 Horseheads (14845) ***(G-6324)***
Photonics Industries Intl Inc (PA) 631 218-2240
1800 Ocean Ave Unit A Ronkonkoma (11779) ***(G-14398)***
Photonix Technologies Inc....607 786-4600
48 Washington Ave Endicott (13760) ***(G-4608)***
Phototherapeutix, Glens Falls *Also called Medtek Skin Care Inc* ***(G-5433)***
Phyljohn Distributors Inc....518 459-2775
6 Interstate Ave Albany (12205) ***(G-115)***
Phymetrix Inc....631 627-3950
28 Scouting Blvd Ste C Medford (11763) ***(G-7963)***
Physical Review, Ridge *Also called American Physical Society* ***(G-13521)***
Physicalmind Institute 212 343-2150
84 Wooster St Ste 605 New York (10012) ***(G-11186)***
Phytofilter Technologies Inc....518 507-6399
9 Kirby Rd Apt 19 Saratoga Springs (12866) ***(G-14592)***
Piaggio Group Americas Inc....212 380-4400
257 Park Ave S Fl 4 New York (10010) ***(G-11187)***
Piano Software Inc 646 350-1999
1 World Trade Ctr Ste 46d New York (10007) ***(G-11188)***
Piazzas Ice Cream Ice Hse Inc....718 818-8811
41 Housman Ave Staten Island (10303) ***(G-15115)***
Pibbs Industries, Flushing *Also called P S Pibbs Inc* ***(G-5032)***
Pic A Poc Enterprises Inc 631 981-2094
53 Union Ave Ronkonkoma (11779) ***(G-14399)***
Pic Nic LLC....914 245-6500
51 Mahopac Ave Amawalk (10501) ***(G-204)***
Picador USA....646 307-5629
175 5th Ave New York (10010) ***(G-11189)***
Picasso Coach Builders, Rego Park *Also called Pcb Coach Builders Corp* ***(G-13467)***
Piccini Industries Ltd 845 365-0614
37 Ramland Rd Orangeburg (10962) ***(G-12685)***
Piccini Mnm Inc 845 741-6770
35 Highland Ave West Nyack (10994) ***(G-16279)***
PICKETT BUILDING MATERIALS, Oneonta *Also called Arnan Development Corp* ***(G-12625)***
Pico Direct LLC....212 947-8969
70 Post Dr Roslyn (11576) ***(G-14450)***
Picone Meat Specialties Ltd 914 381-3002
180 Jefferson Ave Mamaroneck (10543) ***(G-7753)***
Picone's Sausage, Mamaroneck *Also called Picone Meat Specialties Ltd* ***(G-7753)***
Pictoure Inc....212 641-0098
110 Wall St New York (10005) ***(G-11190)***

Picture Perfect Framing 718 851-1884
1758 50th St Brooklyn (11204) *(G-2316)*
Pidyon Controls Inc (PA) 212 683-9523
141 W 24th St Apt 4 New York (10011) *(G-11191)*
Pie, Webster *Also called Practical Instrument Elec Inc (G-16092)*
Piemonte Company, Woodside *Also called Piemonte Home Made Ravioli Co (G-16672)*
Piemonte Home Made Ravioli Co (PA) 718 429-1972
3436 65th St Woodside (11377) *(G-16672)*
Piemonte Home Made Ravioli Co 212 226-0475
190 Grand St New York (10013) *(G-11192)*
Pier-Tech Inc 516 442-5420
7 Hampton Rd Oceanside (11572) *(G-12550)*
Pierce Arrow Draperies, Buffalo *Also called Pierce Arrow Drapery Mfg (G-3003)*
Pierce Arrow Drapery Mfg 716 876-3023
1685 Elmwood Ave Ste 312 Buffalo (14207) *(G-3003)*
Pierce Industries LLC 585 458-0888
465 Paul Rd Ste A Rochester (14624) *(G-14021)*
Pierce Steel Fabricators 716 372-7652
430 N 7th St Olean (14760) *(G-12606)*
Pierrepont Visual Graphics 585 305-9672
15 Elser Ter Rochester (14611) *(G-14022)*
Pietro Demarco Importers Inc 914 969-3201
1185 Saw Mill River Rd Yonkers (10710) *(G-16792)*
Piezo Electronics Research 845 735-9349
30 Walter St Pearl River (10965) *(G-12907)*
Pii Holdings Inc (HQ) 716 876-9951
2150 Elmwood Ave Buffalo (14207) *(G-3004)*
Pilates Designs LLC 718 721-5929
3517 31st St Astoria (11106) *(G-440)*
Pilgrim Foods Co, Great Neck *Also called Old Dutch Mustard Co Inc (G-5576)*
Pilgrim Surf & Supply 718 218-7456
68 N 3rd St Brooklyn (11249) *(G-2317)*
Pilkington North America Inc 315 438-3341
6412 Deere Rd Ste 1 Syracuse (13206) *(G-15395)*
Piller Power Systems Inc (HQ) 845 695-6658
45 Wes Warren Dr Middletown (10941) *(G-8170)*
Pillow Perfections Ltd Inc 718 383-2259
252 Norman Ave Ste 101 Brooklyn (11222) *(G-2318)*
Pilot Inc (PA) 212 951-1133
421 W 24th St Apt 4c New York (10011) *(G-11193)*
Pilot Inc 212 951-1133
110 E 25th St New York (10010) *(G-11194)*
Pilot Products Inc 718 728-2141
2413 46th St Long Island City (11103) *(G-7556)*
Pin Pharma Inc 212 543-2583
3960 Broadway Fl 2 New York (10032) *(G-11195)*
Pincharming Inc 516 663-5115
215 Brixton Rd Garden City (11530) *(G-5274)*
Pindar Vineyards LLC 631 734-6200
37645 Route 25 Peconic (11958) *(G-12916)*
Pinder International Inc (PA) 631 273-0324
1140 Motor Pkwy Ste A Hauppauge (11788) *(G-5915)*
Pine Barrens Printing, Westhampton Beach *Also called Michael K Lennon Inc (G-16404)*
Pine Bush Printing Co Inc 518 456-2431
2005 Western Ave Albany (12203) *(G-116)*
Pine Hill Fabricators 716 823-2474
2731 Seneca St Buffalo (14224) *(G-3005)*
Pine Tree Farms Inc 607 532-4312
3714 Cayuga St Interlaken (14847) *(G-6483)*
Pingmd Inc 212 632-2665
136 Madison Ave Fl 6 New York (10016) *(G-11196)*
Pink Inc 212 352-8282
23 E 10th St Apt 1b New York (10003) *(G-11197)*
Pink and Palmer, Rye *Also called Judith N Graham Inc (G-14484)*
Pink Box Accessories LLC 718 435-2821
940 40th St Brooklyn (11219) *(G-2319)*
Pink Crush LLC 718 788-6978
1410 Broadway Rm 1002 New York (10018) *(G-11198)*
Pinnacle Manufacturing Co Inc 585 343-5664
56 Harvester Ave Batavia (14020) *(G-633)*
Pinos Press Inc 315 935-0110
201 E Jefferson St Syracuse (13202) *(G-15396)*
Pinpoint Systems Intl Inc (PA) 631 775-2100
10 Pinehurst Dr Bellport (11713) *(G-812)*
Pins and Lanes, Lowville *Also called Qubicaamf Worldwide LLC (G-7655)*
Pins N Needles 212 535-6222
1045 Lexington Ave Apt 2n New York (10021) *(G-11199)*
Pintail Coffee Inc 631 396-0808
1776 New Hwy Farmingdale (11735) *(G-4849)*
Pintrill LLC 718 782-1000
231 Grand St Brooklyn (11211) *(G-2320)*
Pioneer Printers Inc 716 693-7100
1087 Erie Ave North Tonawanda (14120) *(G-12442)*
Pioneer Window Holdings Inc (PA) 516 822-7000
15 Frederick Pl Hicksville (11801) *(G-6127)*
Pioneer Window Holdings Inc 518 762-5526
200 Union Ave Johnstown (12095) *(G-6837)*
Pioneer Windows Manufacturing, Hicksville *Also called Pioneer Window Holdings Inc (G-6127)*
PIP Inc 518 861-0133
968 Albany Shaker Rd Latham (12110) *(G-7090)*
PIP Printing, Oceanside *Also called Ahw Printing Corp (G-12531)*
PIP Printing, Latham *Also called PIP Inc (G-7090)*
PIP Printing, Lynbrook *Also called Pro Printing (G-7670)*
PIP Printing, Syosset *Also called Vivona Business Printers Inc (G-15233)*
PIP Printing, White Plains *Also called Alamar Printing Inc (G-16417)*
PIP Printing, Hicksville *Also called Marcal Printing Inc (G-6105)*
Piper Plastics Corp 631 842-6889
102 Ralph Ave Copiague (11726) *(G-3772)*
Piper Plastics Corp 631 842-6889
105 Ralph Ave Copiague (11726) *(G-3773)*
Pirnat Precise Metals Inc 631 293-9169
127 Marine St Farmingdale (11735) *(G-4850)*
Pirod Inc 631 231-7660
15 Oser Ave Hauppauge (11788) *(G-5916)*
Piroke Trade Inc 646 515-1537
1430 35th St Fl 2 Brooklyn (11218) *(G-2321)*
Pit Stop Motorsports, Forestville *Also called P S M Group Inc (G-5087)*
Pitney Bowes Inc 212 564-7548
637 W 27th St Fl 8 New York (10001) *(G-11200)*
Pitney Bowes Inc 203 356-5000
90 Park Ave Rm 1110 New York (10016) *(G-11201)*
Pitney Bowes Inc 518 283-0345
350 Jordan Rd Ste 1 Troy (12180) *(G-15616)*
Pitney Bowes Inc 516 822-0900
200 Robbins Ln Unit B2 Jericho (11753) *(G-6797)*
Pivot Punch Corporation 716 625-8000
6550 Campbell Blvd Lockport (14094) *(G-7326)*
Pivot Records LLC 718 417-1213
600 Johnson Ave Brooklyn (11237) *(G-2322)*
Piwik Pro LLC 888 444-0049
222 Broadway Fl 19 New York (10038) *(G-11202)*
Pixacore, New York *Also called Intstrux LLC (G-10261)*
Pixos Print 585 500-4600
75 Goodway Dr Rochester (14623) *(G-14023)*
Pixy Dust, Amagansett *Also called Cosmetics Plus Ltd (G-203)*
Pizza Blends LLC 518 356-6650
1411 Rottrdm Indstl Park Schenectady (12306) *(G-14704)*
Pj Decorators Inc 516 735-9693
257 Pontiac Pl East Meadow (11554) *(G-4255)*
PJ Designs Inc 212 355-3100
100 E 50th St Ste 38a New York (10022) *(G-11203)*
Pk Metals, Coram *Also called Suffolk Indus Recovery Corp (G-3805)*
Pk30 System LLC 212 473-8050
3607 Atwood Rd Stone Ridge (12484) *(G-15162)*
Pkg Group 212 965-0112
560 Broadway Rm 406 New York (10012) *(G-11204)*
Pl Developments, Westbury *Also called P & L Development LLC (G-16362)*
Pl Developments New York, Westbury *Also called P & L Development LLC (G-16361)*
Place Vendome Holding Co Inc 212 696-0765
230 5th Ave Ste 1107 New York (10001) *(G-11205)*
Placid Baker 518 326-2657
250 Broadway Troy (12180) *(G-15617)*
Placid Industries, Elmira *Also called Sepac Inc (G-4502)*
Pladis Limited, White Plains *Also called Star Brands North America Inc (G-16506)*
Plain Digital Inc 914 310-0280
235 Garth Rd Apt D6a Scarsdale (10583) *(G-14643)*
Planar Optics Inc 585 671-0100
858 Hard Rd Webster (14580) *(G-16091)*
Planet Embroidery 718 381-4827
6695 Forest Ave Ridgewood (11385) *(G-13546)*
Plant Office, Wyoming *Also called Texas Brine Company LLC (G-16701)*
Plant-Tech2o Inc 516 483-7845
30 Chasner St Hempstead (11550) *(G-6023)*
Plascal Corp 516 249-2200
361 Eastern Pkwy Farmingdale (11735) *(G-4851)*
Plascoline Inc 917 410-5754
275 Madison Ave Fl 14th New York (10016) *(G-11206)*
Plaslok Corp 716 681-7755
3155 Broadway St Buffalo (14227) *(G-3006)*
Plastic & Reconstructive Svcs 914 584-5605
333 N Bedford Rd Mount Kisco (10549) *(G-8355)*
Plastic Solutions Inc 631 234-9013
158 Schenck Ave Bayport (11705) *(G-738)*
Plastic Sys/Gr Bflo Inc 716 835-7555
465 Cornwall Ave Buffalo (14215) *(G-3007)*
Plastic Works 914 576-2050
26 Garden St New Rochelle (10801) *(G-8622)*
Plastic-Craft Products Corp 845 358-3010
744 W Nyack Rd West Nyack (10994) *(G-16280)*
Plasticware LLC (PA) 845 267-0790
13 Wilsher Dr Monsey (10952) *(G-8293)*
Plasticweld Systems, Newfane *Also called Vante Inc (G-12254)*
Plasticycle Corporation (PA) 914 997-6882
245 Main St Ste 430 White Plains (10601) *(G-16498)*
Plastifold Industries Division, Brooklyn *Also called Visitainer Corp (G-2629)*
Plastirun Corporation 631 273-2626
70 Emjay Blvd Bldg A Brentwood (11717) *(G-1143)*
Plastitel Usa Inc 450 687-0600
641 Ridge Rd Chazy (12921) *(G-3433)*
Plastpac Inc 908 272-7200
32 Walton St Brooklyn (11206) *(G-2323)*

ALPHABETIC

Platform Experts Inc.....646 843-7100
2938 Quentin Rd Brooklyn (11229) ***(G-2324)***
Platina, New York *Also called Alexander Primak Jewelry Inc* ***(G-8793)***
Platinum Carting Corp.....631 649-4322
1806 Carleton Ave Bay Shore (11706) ***(G-706)***
Platinum Printing & Graphics.....631 249-3325
70 Carolyn Blvd Ste C Farmingdale (11735) ***(G-4852)***
Platinum Sales Promotion Inc.....718 361-0200
3514a Crescent St Long Island City (11106) ***(G-7557)***
Plattco Corporation (PA).....518 563-4640
7 White St Plattsburgh (12901) ***(G-13145)***
Plattco Corporation.....518 563-4640
18 White St Plattsburgh (12901) ***(G-13146)***
Platter's Chocolates, North Tonawanda *Also called Roger L Urban Inc* ***(G-12449)***
Plattsburgh Press-Republican, Plattsburgh *Also called Community Newspaper Group LLC* ***(G-13118)***
Plattsburgh Quarry, Plattsburgh *Also called Graymont Materials Inc* ***(G-13122)***
Plattsburgh Sheet Metal Inc.....518 561-4930
95 Sailly Ave Plattsburgh (12901) ***(G-13147)***
Play-It Productions Inc.....212 695-6530
735 Port Washington Blvd Port Washington (11050) ***(G-13297)***
Playbill Incorporated (PA).....212 557-5757
729 7th Ave Fl 4 New York (10019) ***(G-11207)***
Playbill Incorporated.....718 335-4033
3715 61st St Woodside (11377) ***(G-16673)***
Playfitness Corp.....917 497-5443
27 Palisade St Staten Island (10305) ***(G-15116)***
Playground NY Inc.....505 920-7236
55 Hope St Apt 212 Brooklyn (11211) ***(G-2325)***
Playlife LLC.....646 207-9082
297 Church St Fl 5 New York (10013) ***(G-11208)***
Plaza Bracelte Mounting, New Hyde Park *Also called Satco Castings Service Inc* ***(G-8561)***
Plaza Group Creation, New York *Also called Jordan Scott Designs Ltd* ***(G-10362)***
Pleasure Chest Sales Ltd.....212 242-2158
156 7th Ave S New York (10014) ***(G-11209)***
Pleatco LLC.....516 609-0200
28 Garvies Point Rd Glen Cove (11542) ***(G-5372)***
Plectica LLC.....917 304-7052
175 Varick St New York (10014) ***(G-11210)***
Plexi Craft Quality Products.....212 924-3244
200 Lexington Ave Rm 914 New York (10016) ***(G-11211)***
Pliant LLC.....315 986-6286
200 Main St Macedon (14502) ***(G-7703)***
Pliotron Company America LLC.....716 298-4457
4650 Witmer Indus Est Niagara Falls (14305) ***(G-12323)***
Plt, Rochester *Also called Precision Laser Technology LLC* ***(G-14036)***
Plug Power Inc.....585 474-3993
1200 Ridgeway Ave Ste 123 Rochester (14615) ***(G-14024)***
Plug Power Inc (PA).....518 782-7700
968 Albany Shaker Rd Latham (12110) ***(G-7091)***
Plugg LLC.....212 840-6655
1410 Broadway Frnt 2 New York (10018) ***(G-11212)***
Plura Broadcast Inc (PA).....516 997-5675
67 Grand Ave Massapequa (11758) ***(G-7882)***
Plures Technologies Inc (PA).....585 905-0554
4070 County Road 16 Canandaigua (14424) ***(G-3231)***
Pluribus Products Inc.....718 852-1614
1 Overlook Ave Bayville (11709) ***(G-753)***
Pluslux LLC.....516 371-4400
461 Doughty Blvd Inwood (11096) ***(G-6499)***
Plx Inc (PA).....631 586-4190
25 W Jefryn Blvd Ste A Deer Park (11729) ***(G-4026)***
PM, Rochester *Also called Professional Machine LLC* ***(G-14051)***
Pmb Precision Products Inc.....631 491-6753
725 Mount Ave West Babylon (11704) ***(G-16182)***
Pmd, Victor *Also called Progressive Mch & Design LLC* ***(G-15862)***
PMF, Brooklyn *Also called Precision Mtal Fabricators Inc* ***(G-2335)***
PMG, Ronkonkoma *Also called Paul Michael Group Inc* ***(G-14397)***
PMI Global Services Inc.....917 663-2000
120 Park Ave Fl 6 New York (10017) ***(G-11213)***
PMI Industries LLC.....585 464-8050
350 Buell Rd Rochester (14624) ***(G-14025)***
Pmrnyc, Brooklyn *Also called Total Metal Resource* ***(G-2575)***
PNC Sports.....516 665-2244
1880 Deer Park Ave Deer Park (11729) ***(G-4027)***
Pneumercator Company Inc.....631 293-8450
1785 Express Dr N Hauppauge (11788) ***(G-5917)***
Pni Capital Partners.....516 466-7120
1400 Old Country Rd # 103 Westbury (11590) ***(G-16364)***
Podravka International USA.....212 661-0125
420 Lexington Ave Rm 2034 New York (10170) ***(G-11214)***
Poerformance Design, Fairport *Also called Performance Designed By Peters* ***(G-4650)***
Poetry Mailing List Marsh Hawk.....516 766-1891
2823 Rockaway Ave Oceanside (11572) ***(G-12551)***
Poets House Inc.....212 431-7920
10 River Ter New York (10282) ***(G-11215)***
Point Canvas Company Inc.....607 692-4381
5952 State Route 26 Whitney Point (13862) ***(G-16556)***
Point Electric Div, Blauvelt *Also called Swivelier Company Inc* ***(G-941)***
Point Industrial, Bemus Point *Also called Lakeside Industries Inc* ***(G-818)***
Point of Sale Outfitters, Geneva *Also called R M Reynolds* ***(G-5331)***
Pointman LLC (PA).....716 842-1439
403 Main St Ste 200 Buffalo (14203) ***(G-3008)***
Pointwise Information Service.....315 457-4111
223 1st St Liverpool (13088) ***(G-7255)***
Pol-Tek Industries Ltd.....716 823-1502
2300 Clinton St Buffalo (14227) ***(G-3009)***
Pole-Tech Co Inc.....631 689-5525
97 Gnarled Hollow Rd East Setauket (11733) ***(G-4307)***
Poletech Flagpole Manufaturer, East Setauket *Also called Pole-Tech Co Inc* ***(G-4307)***
Polich Tallix Inc.....845 567-9464
39 Edmunds Ln Walden (12586) ***(G-15895)***
Policy ADM Solutions Inc.....914 332-4320
505 White Plains Rd Tarrytown (10591) ***(G-15486)***
Polish American Journal, Orchard Park *Also called Panagraphics Inc* ***(G-12734)***
Political Risk Services, The, East Syracuse *Also called The PRS Group Inc* ***(G-4373)***
POLITICAL SCIENCE QUARTERLY, New York *Also called Academy of Political Science* ***(G-8716)***
Polkadot Usa Inc.....914 835-3697
33 Country Rd Mamaroneck (10543) ***(G-7754)***
Pollack Graphics Inc.....212 727-8400
601 W 26th St Ste M204 New York (10001) ***(G-11216)***
Pollardwater, New Hyde Park *Also called Ferguson Enterprises Inc* ***(G-8535)***
Polly Treating, New York *Also called Xinya International Trading Co* ***(G-12152)***
Polo Ralph Lauren Hosiery Div, New York *Also called Hot Sox Company Incorporated* ***(G-10130)***
Polska Gazeta, Brooklyn *Also called Spring Publishing Corporation* ***(G-2505)***
Poly Can, Carthage *Also called David Johnson* ***(G-3290)***
Poly Craft Industries Corp.....631 630-6731
40 Ranick Rd Hauppauge (11788) ***(G-5918)***
Poly Scientific R&D Corp.....631 586-0400
70 Cleveland Ave Bay Shore (11706) ***(G-707)***
Poly-Flex Corp (PA).....631 586-9500
250 Executive Dr Ste S Edgewood (11717) ***(G-4410)***
Poly-Pak Industries Inc (PA).....631 293-6767
125 Spagnoli Rd Melville (11747) ***(G-8057)***
Polycast Industries Inc.....631 595-2530
130 S 2nd St Bay Shore (11706) ***(G-708)***
Polygen Pharmaceuticals Inc.....631 392-4044
41 Mercedes Way Unit 17 Edgewood (11717) ***(G-4411)***
Polymag Inc.....631 286-4111
685 Station Rd Ste 2 Bellport (11713) ***(G-813)***
Polymag Tek Inc.....585 235-8390
215 Tremont St Ste 2 Rochester (14608) ***(G-14026)***
Polymer Conversions Inc.....716 662-8550
5732 Big Tree Rd Orchard Park (14127) ***(G-12737)***
Polymer Engineered Pdts Inc.....585 426-1811
23 Moonlanding Rd Rochester (14624) ***(G-14027)***
Polymer Slutions Group Fin LLC (PA).....212 771-1717
100 Park Ave Fl 31 New York (10017) ***(G-11217)***
Polymers Merona Inc.....631 862-8010
347 Lake Ave Ste 4 Saint James (11780) ***(G-14513)***
Polyplastic Forms Inc.....631 249-5011
49 Gazza Blvd Farmingdale (11735) ***(G-4853)***
Polyseal Packaging Corp.....718 792-5530
1178 E 180th St Bronx (10460) ***(G-1359)***
Polyset Company Inc.....518 664-6000
65 Hudson Ave Mechanicville (12118) ***(G-7932)***
Polyshot Corporation.....585 292-5010
75 Lucius Gordon Dr West Henrietta (14586) ***(G-16248)***
Polytech Pool Mfg Inc.....718 492-8991
262 48th St 262 Brooklyn (11220) ***(G-2326)***
Polytex Inc.....716 549-5100
1305 Eden Evans Center Rd Angola (14006) ***(G-370)***
Pompian Manufacturing Co Inc.....914 476-7076
280 Nepperhan Ave Yonkers (10701) ***(G-16793)***
Poncio Signs.....718 543-4851
3007 Albany Cres Bronx (10463) ***(G-1360)***
Ponder, New York *Also called Parlor Labs Inc* ***(G-11118)***
Ponti Rossi Inc.....347 506-9616
186 Franklin St Apt C16 Brooklyn (11222) ***(G-2327)***
Pony Farm Press & Graphics.....607 432-9020
330 Pony Farm Rd Oneonta (13820) ***(G-12644)***
Pooran Pallet Inc.....718 938-7970
319 Barretto St Bronx (10474) ***(G-1361)***
Pop A2z, New York *Also called Sky Frame & Art Inc* ***(G-11613)***
Pop Nyc, New York *Also called Popnyc 1 LLC* ***(G-11218)***
Pop Printing Incorporated.....212 808-7800
288 Hamilton Ave Brooklyn (11231) ***(G-2328)***
Popnyc 1 LLC.....646 684-4600
75 Saint Nicholas Pl 2e New York (10032) ***(G-11218)***
Poppin Inc.....212 391-7200
16 Madison Sq W Fl 3 New York (10010) ***(G-11219)***
Popular Mechanics, New York *Also called Hearst Corporation* ***(G-10065)***
Popular Pattern, New York *Also called Stephen Singer Pattern Co Inc* ***(G-11706)***
Porcelain Refinishing Corp.....516 352-4841
19905 32nd Ave Flushing (11358) ***(G-5038)***
Pork King Sausage Inc.....718 542-2810
F22 Hunts Point Co Op Mkt Bronx (10474) ***(G-1362)***

Porous Materials Inc 607 257-5544
20 Dutch Mill Rd Ithaca (14850) *(G-6605)*
Port Authority of NY & NJ..718 390-2534
2777 Goethals Rd N Fl 2 Staten Island (10303) *(G-15117)*
Port Everglades Machine Works...516 367-2280
57 Colgate Dr Plainview (11803) *(G-13083)*
Port Jackson Media, Amsterdam *Also called McClary Media Inc (G-346)*
Port Jervis Machine Corp..845 856-6210
176 1/2 Jersey Ave Port Jervis (12771) *(G-13235)*
Portequip Work Stations, Niagara Falls *Also called Stephenson Custom Case Company (G-12338)*
Portfab LLC...718 542-3600
45 Ranick Dr E Amityville (11701) *(G-313)*
Portfolio Decisionware Inc...212 947-1326
235 W 48th St New York (10036) *(G-11220)*
Portfolio Media Inc...646 783-7100
111 W 19th St Fl 5 New York (10011) *(G-11221)*
Portville Sand & Gravel Div, Portville *Also called IA Construction Corporation (G-13316)*
Portware LLC (HQ)..212 425-5233
233 Broadway Fl 24 New York (10279) *(G-11222)*
Poseidon Systems LLC...585 239-6025
200 Canal View Blvd # 300 Rochester (14623) *(G-14028)*
Posillico Materials LLC...631 249-1872
1750 New Hwy Farmingdale (11735) *(G-4854)*
Posimech Inc..631 924-5959
15 Scouting Blvd Unit 3 Medford (11763) *(G-7964)*
Positive Print Litho Offset..212 431-4850
121 Varick St Rm 204 New York (10013) *(G-11223)*
Post Journal..716 487-1111
412 Murray Ave Jamestown (14701) *(G-6742)*
Post Road..203 545-2122
101 E 16th St Apt 4b New York (10003) *(G-11224)*
Post Standard, The, Syracuse *Also called Herald Newspapers Company Inc (G-15340)*
Post Star, Glens Falls *Also called Lee Enterprises Incorporated (G-5431)*
Post-Journal, The, Jamestown *Also called Ogden Newspapers Inc (G-6741)*
Potential Poly Bag Inc...718 258-0800
1253 Coney Island Ave Brooklyn (11230) *(G-2329)*
Potsdam Specialty Paper Inc..315 265-4000
547a Sissonville Rd Potsdam (13676) *(G-13321)*
Potsdam Stone Concrete, Plattsburgh *Also called Upstone Materials Inc (G-13166)*
Potter Lumber Co Inc...716 373-1260
3786 Potter Rd Allegany (14706) *(G-192)*
Potters Industries LLC...315 265-4920
56 Reynolds Rd Norwood (13668) *(G-12496)*
Poughkeepsie Journal, Poughkeepsie *Also called Gannett Stllite Info Ntwrk LLC (G-13339)*
Poultry Dist, Brooklyn *Also called Vineland Kosher Poultry Inc (G-2625)*
Powa Technologies Inc...347 344-7848
1 Bryant Park Ste 39 New York (10036) *(G-11225)*
Power and Cnstr Group Inc...585 889-6020
86 River Rd Scottsville (14546) *(G-14752)*
Power and Composite Tech LLC...518 843-6825
200 Wallins Corners Rd Amsterdam (12010) *(G-357)*
Power Connector Inc...631 563-7878
140 Wilbur Pl Ste 4 Bohemia (11716) *(G-1075)*
Power Gneration Indus Engs Inc..315 633-9389
8927 Tyler Rd Bridgeport (13030) *(G-1182)*
Power Line Constructors Inc...315 853-6183
24 Robinson Rd Clinton (13323) *(G-3587)*
Power Metrics Intl Inc..718 524-4370
1961 Richmond Ter Staten Island (10302) *(G-15118)*
Power Scrub It Inc...516 997-2500
75 Urban Ave Westbury (11590) *(G-16365)*
Power-Flo Technologies Inc...315 399-5801
6500 New Venture Gear Dr East Syracuse (13057) *(G-4362)*
Power-Flo Technologies Inc...585 426-4607
62 Marway Cir Rochester (14624) *(G-14029)*
Powerflow Inc...716 892-1014
1714 Broadway St Buffalo (14212) *(G-3010)*
Powerhouse Books, Brooklyn *Also called Powerhouse Cultural Entrmt Inc (G-2330)*
Powerhouse Cultural Entrmt Inc..212 604-9074
126a Front St Brooklyn (11201) *(G-2330)*
Powermate Cellular...718 833-9400
140 58th St Ste 1d Brooklyn (11220) *(G-2331)*
Powers Fasteners, Brewster *Also called Black & Decker (us) Inc (G-1159)*
Powertex Inc (PA)...518 297-4000
1 Lincoln Blvd Ste 101 Rouses Point (12979) *(G-14469)*
Powertex Bulk Shipg Solutions, Rouses Point *Also called Powertex Inc (G-14469)*
Powr-UPS Corp...631 345-5700
1 Roned Rd Shirley (11967) *(G-14843)*
Poz Publishing, New York *Also called Smart & Strong LLC (G-11621)*
Ppc Broadband Inc (HQ)..315 431-7200
6176 E Molloy Rd East Syracuse (13057) *(G-4363)*
PPG Architectural Finishes Inc..585 271-1363
566 Clinton Ave S Rochester (14620) *(G-14030)*
Ppi Corp...585 880-7277
275 Commerce Dr Rochester (14623) *(G-14031)*
Ppi Corp...585 243-0300
275 Commerce Dr Rochester (14623) *(G-14032)*
Ppr Direct Marketing LLC (PA)..718 965-8600
74 20th St Brooklyn (11232) *(G-2332)*

PR & Stone & Tile Inc..718 383-1115
17 Beadel St Brooklyn (11222) *(G-2333)*
Practical Instrument Elec Inc..585 872-9350
34 May St Ste 3 Webster (14580) *(G-16092)*
Practicepro Software Systems...516 222-0010
666 Old Country Rd Bsmt Garden City (11530) *(G-5275)*
Prager Metis Cpas LLC..212 972-7555
225 W 34th St Ste 1800 New York (10122) *(G-11226)*
Pragmatics Technology Inc...845 795-5071
14 Old Indian Trl Milton (12547) *(G-8196)*
Pratt With ME Hmi Met Powders, Clayville *Also called Hmi Metal Powders (G-3557)*
Praxair Inc...716 879-2000
175 E Park Dr Tonawanda (14150) *(G-15570)*
Praxair Inc...716 649-1600
5322 Scranton Rd Hamburg (14075) *(G-5690)*
Praxair Inc...518 482-4360
120 Railroad Ave Albany (12205) *(G-117)*
Praxair Inc...716 286-4600
4501 Royal Ave Niagara Falls (14303) *(G-12324)*
Praxair Inc...845 359-4200
542 Route 303 Orangeburg (10962) *(G-12686)*
Praxair Inc...716 879-4000
135 E Park Dr Tonawanda (14150) *(G-15571)*
Praxair Distribution Inc...315 457-5821
4560 Morgan Pl Liverpool (13090) *(G-7256)*
Praxair Distribution Inc...315 735-6153
9432 State Route 49 Marcy (13403) *(G-7797)*
Praxair Surface Tech Inc..845 398-8322
560 Route 303 Orangeburg (10962) *(G-12687)*
Praxis Powder Technology Inc...518 812-0112
604 Queensbury Ave Queensbury (12804) *(G-13437)*
PRC Liquidating Company...212 823-9626
10 Columbus Cir New York (10019) *(G-11227)*
Pre Cycled Inc...845 278-7611
1689 Route 22 Brewster (10509) *(G-1174)*
Pre-Tech Plastics Inc...518 942-5950
3085 Plank Rd Mineville (12956) *(G-8254)*
Precare Corp...631 524-5171
150 Marcus Blvd Hauppauge (11788) *(G-5919)*
Precare Corp (PA)...631 667-1055
150 Marcus Blvd Hauppauge (11788) *(G-5920)*
Precimed Inc...716 759-5600
10000 Wehrle Dr Clarence (14031) *(G-3539)*
Precious Plate Inc..716 283-0690
2124 Liberty Dr Niagara Falls (14304) *(G-12325)*
Precipart Corporation...631 694-3100
120 Finn Ct Ste 2 Farmingdale (11735) *(G-4855)*
Precise Optics, Deer Park *Also called Photo Medic Equipment Inc (G-4025)*
Precise Punch Corporation..716 625-8000
6550 Campbell Blvd Lockport (14094) *(G-7327)*
Precise Tool & Mfg Inc...585 247-0700
9 Coldwater Cres Rochester (14624) *(G-14033)*
Preciseled Inc..516 418-5337
52 Railroad Ave Valley Stream (11580) *(G-15790)*
Precision Abrasives Corp...716 826-5833
3176 Abbott Rd Orchard Park (14127) *(G-12738)*
Precision Arms Inc..845 225-1130
421 Route 52 Carmel (10512) *(G-3280)*
Precision Assembly Tech Inc..631 699-9400
160 Wilbur Pl Ste 500 Bohemia (11716) *(G-1076)*
Precision Built Tops LLC...607 336-5417
89 Borden Ave Norwich (13815) *(G-12491)*
Precision Charts Inc...631 244-8295
130 Wilbur Pl Bohemia (11716) *(G-1077)*
Precision Cnc..631 847-3999
71 E Jefryn Blvd Deer Park (11729) *(G-4028)*
Precision Co., Menands *Also called McAllisters Precision Wldg Inc (G-8087)*
Precision Cosmetics Mfg Co..914 667-1200
519 S 5th Ave Ste 6 Mount Vernon (10550) *(G-8431)*
PRECISION CUSTOM COATINGS LLC, New York *Also called Precision Custom Coatings LLC (G-11228)*
Precision Custom Coatings LLC...212 868-5770
234 W 39th St New York (10018) *(G-11228)*
Precision Dental Cabinets Inc (PA)..631 543-3870
900 W Jericho Tpke Smithtown (11787) *(G-14906)*
Precision Dental Ceramics of B..716 681-4133
5204 Genesee St Bowmansville (14026) *(G-1122)*
Precision Design Systems Inc..585 426-4500
1645 Lyell Ave Ste 136 Rochester (14606) *(G-14034)*
Precision Diamond Cutters Inc...212 719-4438
1410 E 22nd St Brooklyn (11210) *(G-2334)*
Precision Diecutting Inc..315 776-8465
1381 Spring Lake Rd Port Byron (13140) *(G-13190)*
Precision Eforming LLC...607 753-7730
839 State Route 13 Ste 1 Cortland (13045) *(G-3889)*
Precision Elctro Mnrl Pmco Inc..716 284-2484
150 Portage Rd Niagara Falls (14303) *(G-12326)*
Precision Electronics Inc..631 842-4900
1 Di Tomas Ct Copiague (11726) *(G-3774)*
Precision Engraving Company, Amityville *Also called Precision Signscom Inc (G-314)*
Precision Envelope Co Inc...631 694-3990
110 Schmitt Blvd 7a Farmingdale (11735) *(G-4856)*

A L P H A B E T I C

(PA)=Parent Co (HQ)=Headquarters (DH)=Div Headquarters
2019 Harris
New York Manufacturers Directory
963

Precision Extrusion Inc 518 792-1199
12 Glens Fls Technical Pa Glens Falls (12801) ***(G-5440)***
Precision Fabrication LLC 585 591-3449
40 S Pearl St Attica (14011) ***(G-461)***
Precision Filters Inc (PA) 607 277-3550
240 Cherry St Ithaca (14850) ***(G-6606)***
Precision Furniture, Bronx *Also called Precision Orna Ir Works Inc **(G-1363)***
Precision Gear Incorporated 718 321-7200
11207 14th Ave College Point (11356) ***(G-3661)***
Precision Grinding & Mfg Corp (PA) 585 458-4300
1305 Emerson St Rochester (14606) ***(G-14035)***
Precision International Co Inc 212 268-9090
201 E 28th St 9n New York (10016) ***(G-11229)***
Precision Label Corporation 631 270-4490
175 Marine St Farmingdale (11735) ***(G-4857)***
Precision Laser Technology LLC 585 458-6208
1001 Lexington Ave Ste 4 Rochester (14606) ***(G-14036)***
Precision Locker, Jamestown *Also called Rollform of Jamestown Inc **(G-6745)***
Precision Machine Parts, Valatie *Also called Weiss Industries Inc **(G-15740)***
Precision Machine Tech LLC 585 467-1840
85 Excel Dr Rochester (14621) ***(G-14037)***
Precision Machining and Mfg 845 647-5380
190 Port Ben Rd Wawarsing (12489) ***(G-16069)***
Precision Magnetics LLC 585 385-9010
770 Linden Ave Rochester (14625) ***(G-14038)***
Precision Mechanisms Corp 516 333-5955
50 Bond St Westbury (11590) ***(G-16366)***
Precision Metals Corp 631 586-5032
221 Skip Ln Bay Shore (11706) ***(G-709)***
Precision Mtal Fabricators Inc 718 832-9805
236 39th St Brooklyn (11232) ***(G-2335)***
Precision N Amer Fd McHy LLC 518 462-3387
60 Commerce Ave Ste 42 Albany (12206) ***(G-118)***
Precision Orna Ir Works Inc 718 379-5200
1838 Adee Ave Bronx (10469) ***(G-1363)***
Precision Packaging Pdts Inc 585 638-8200
88 Nesbitt Dr Holley (14470) ***(G-6228)***
Precision Pharma Services Inc 631 752-7314
155 Duryea Rd Melville (11747) ***(G-8058)***
Precision Photo-Fab Inc 716 821-9393
4020 Jeffrey Blvd Buffalo (14219) ***(G-3011)***
Precision Plus Vacuum Parts 716 297-2039
6416 Inducon Dr W Sanborn (14132) ***(G-14551)***
Precision Polish LLC 315 894-3792
144 Adams St Frankfort (13340) ***(G-5111)***
Precision Process Inc (PA) 716 731-1587
2111 Liberty Dr Niagara Falls (14304) ***(G-12327)***
Precision Product Inc 718 852-7127
18 Steuben St Brooklyn (11205) ***(G-2336)***
Precision Ready Mix Inc 718 658-5600
14707 Liberty Ave Jamaica (11435) ***(G-6668)***
Precision Signscom Inc 631 841-7500
243 Dixon Ave Amityville (11701) ***(G-314)***
Precision Spclty Fbrctions LLC 716 824-2108
51 N Gates Ave Buffalo (14218) ***(G-3012)***
Precision Systems Mfg Inc 315 451-3480
4855 Executive Dr Liverpool (13088) ***(G-7257)***
Precision Techniques Inc 718 991-1440
25 Holt Dr Stony Point (10980) ***(G-15175)***
Precision Tool and Mfg 518 678-3130
314 Pennsylvania Ave Palenville (12463) ***(G-12845)***
Precision Valve & Automtn Inc (PA) 518 371-2684
1 Mustang Dr Ste 3 Cohoes (12047) ***(G-3617)***
Precisionmatics Co Inc 315 822-6324
1 Helmer Ave West Winfield (13491) ***(G-16306)***
Predator Mountainwear Inc 315 727-3241
324 Fire Lane 15 Auburn (13021) ***(G-495)***
Preebro Printing 718 633-7300
5319 Fort Hamilton Pkwy Brooklyn (11219) ***(G-2337)***
Preferred Fragrance, Newburgh *Also called Fragrance Acquisitions LLC **(G-12222)***
Preferred Wholesale, New York *Also called R-S Restaurant Eqp Mfg Corp **(G-11314)***
Prejean Winery Inc 315 536-7524
2634 State Route 14 Penn Yan (14527) ***(G-12962)***
Preload Concrete Structures 631 231-8100
60 Commerce Dr Hauppauge (11788) ***(G-5921)***
Premco Inc 914 636-7095
11 Beechwood Ave New Rochelle (10801) ***(G-8623)***
Premier, Richmond Hill *Also called 131-11 Atlantic RE Inc **(G-13494)***
Premier Brands America Inc (PA) 914 667-6200
31 South St Ste 2s1 Mount Vernon (10550) ***(G-8432)***
Premier Brands of America Inc 718 325-3000
555 E 242nd St Bronx (10470) ***(G-1364)***
Premier Brands of America Inc 718 325-3000
120 Pearl St Mount Vernon (10550) ***(G-8433)***
Premier Cabinet Wholesalers, Rochester *Also called Rochester Countertop Inc **(G-14085)***
Premier Care Industries, Hauppauge *Also called Precare Corp **(G-5919)***
Premier Care Industries, Hauppauge *Also called Precare Corp **(G-5920)***
Premier Finishing Inc 716 484-6271
85 Jones And Gifford Ave Jamestown (14701) ***(G-6743)***
Premier Hardwood Products Inc 315 492-1786
4800 Solvay Rd Jamesville (13078) ***(G-6769)***
Premier Heart LLC 516 883-3383
110 Main St Port Washington (11050) ***(G-13298)***
Premier Ingridients Inc 516 641-6763
3 Johnstone Rd Great Neck (11021) ***(G-5582)***
Premier Ink Systems Inc 845 782-5802
2 Commerce Dr S Harriman (10926) ***(G-5721)***
Premier Jewelry Designs LLC 212 391-8778
25 W 45th St Ste 305 New York (10036) ***(G-11230)***
Premier Knits Ltd 718 323-8264
9735 133rd Ave Ozone Park (11417) ***(G-12831)***
Premier Machining Tech Inc 716 608-1311
2100 Old Union Rd Buffalo (14227) ***(G-3013)***
Premier Metals Group 585 436-4020
11 Cairn St Rochester (14611) ***(G-14039)***
Premier Packaging Corporation 585 924-8460
6 Framark Dr Victor (14564) ***(G-15861)***
Premier Paint Roller Co LLC 718 441-7700
13111 Atlantic Ave Richmond Hill (11418) ***(G-13508)***
Premier Sign Systems LLC 585 235-0390
10 Excel Dr Rochester (14621) ***(G-14040)***
Premier Skirting Products Inc 516 239-6581
241 Mill St Lawrence (11559) ***(G-7107)***
Premier Skrting Tblecloths Too, Lawrence *Also called Premier Skirting Products Inc **(G-7107)***
Premier Store Fixtures, Hauppauge *Also called Fixtures 2000 Inc **(G-5825)***
Premier Supplies, New York *Also called Print By Premier LLC **(G-11245)***
Premier Systems LLC 631 587-9700
41 John St Ste 6 Babylon (11702) ***(G-532)***
Premier Woodcraft Ltd 610 383-6624
277 Martine Ave 214 White Plains (10601) ***(G-16499)***
Premier Woodworking Inc 631 236-4100
400 Oser Ave Hauppauge (11788) ***(G-5922)***
Premiere Living Products LLC 631 873-4337
22 Branwood Dr Dix Hills (11746) ***(G-4123)***
Premium 5 Kids LLC 212 563-4999
31 W 34th St New York (10001) ***(G-11231)***
Premium Assure Inc 605 252-9999
1726 Mcdonald Ave Ste 201 Brooklyn (11230) ***(G-2338)***
Premium Bldg Components Inc 518 885-0194
831 Rt 67 Bldg 46 Ballston Spa (12020) ***(G-594)***
Premium Mulch & Materials Inc 631 320-3666
482 Mill Rd Coram (11727) ***(G-3803)***
Premium Ocean LLC 917 231-1061
1271 Ryawa Ave Bronx (10474) ***(G-1365)***
Premium Processing Corp 631 232-1105
30 Kittiwake Ln Babylon (11702) ***(G-533)***
Premium Shirts Lerma Mexico, New York *Also called American T Shirts Inc **(G-8838)***
Premium Sweets USA Inc 718 739-6000
16803 Hillside Ave Jamaica (11432) ***(G-6669)***
Premium Wine Group LLC 631 298-1900
35 Cox Neck Rd Mattituck (11952) ***(G-7916)***
Premium Woodworking LLC 631 485-3133
108 Lamar St West Babylon (11704) ***(G-16183)***
Prepac Designs Inc 914 524-7800
25 Abner Pl Yonkers (10704) ***(G-16794)***
Preparatory Magazine Group 718 761-4800
1200 South Ave Ste 202 Staten Island (10314) ***(G-15119)***
Preplay Inc 917 297-7428
33 W 17th St Ste 901 New York (10011) ***(G-11232)***
Presbrey- Leland Memorials, Valhalla *Also called Presbrey-Leland Inc **(G-15745)***
Presbrey-Leland Inc 914 949-2264
250 Lakeview Ave Valhalla (10595) ***(G-15745)***
Prescribing Reference Inc 646 638-6000
275 7th Ave Fl 10 New York (10001) ***(G-11233)***
Prescriptives Inc (HQ) 212 572-4400
767 5th Ave New York (10153) ***(G-11234)***
Preserving Chrstn Publications (PA) 315 942-6617
12614 State Route 46 Boonville (13309) ***(G-1119)***
President Cont Group II LLC 845 516-1600
290 Ballard Rd Middletown (10941) ***(G-8171)***
Presray Corporation 845 373-9300
32 Nelson Hill Rd Wassaic (12592) ***(G-15966)***
Press Express 914 592-3790
400 Executive Blvd # 146 Elmsford (10523) ***(G-4558)***
Press Glass Na Inc (PA) 212 631-3044
1345 Ave Of The Flr 2 New York (10105) ***(G-11235)***
Press of Manorville & Moriches, Southampton *Also called Southampton Town Newspapers **(G-14962)***
Press Room New York Division, New York *Also called Circle Press Inc **(G-9303)***
Pressed Juice LLC (PA) 646 573-9157
205 Clinton Ave Apt 12a Brooklyn (11205) ***(G-2339)***
Presser Kosher Baking Corp 718 375-5088
1720 Avenue M Brooklyn (11230) ***(G-2340)***
Presstek Printing 585 266-2770
20 Balfour Dr Rochester (14621) ***(G-14041)***
Presstek Printing LLC 585 467-8140
521 E Ridge Rd Rochester (14621) ***(G-14042)***
Presstek Printing LLC 585 266-2770
20 Balfour Dr Rochester (14621) ***(G-14043)***
Pressure Washer Sales, Holland Patent *Also called Custom Klean Corp **(G-6224)***
Prestacycle Llc 518 588-5546
689 Riverview Rd Rexford (12148) ***(G-13483)***

ALPHABETIC SECTION

Prestel Publishing LLC 212 995-2720
900 Broadway Ste 603 New York (10003) *(G-11236)*
Presti Ready Mix Concrete Inc 516 378-6006
210 E Merrick Rd Freeport (11520) *(G-5175)*
Presti Stone and Mason, Freeport Also called Presti Ready Mix Concrete Inc *(G-5175)*
Prestige Box Corporation (PA) 516 773-3115
115 Cuttermill Rd Great Neck (11021) *(G-5583)*
PRESTIGE BRANDS, Tarrytown Also called Prestige Consmr Healthcare Inc *(G-15488)*
Prestige Brands Intl LLC 914 524-6800
660 White Plains Rd Tarrytown (10591) *(G-15487)*
Prestige Consmr Healthcare Inc (PA) 914 524-6800
660 White Plains Rd Tarrytown (10591) *(G-15488)*
Prestige Envelope & Lithograph 631 521-7043
1745 Merrick Ave Ste 2 Merrick (11566) *(G-8105)*
Prestige Global NY Sls Corp 212 776-4322
102 W 38th St Fl 8 New York (10018) *(G-11237)*
Prestige Hangers Str Fixs Corp 718 522-6777
1026 55th St Brooklyn (11219) *(G-2341)*
Prestige Litho & Graphics, Merrick Also called Prestige Envelope & Lithograph *(G-8105)*
Prestige Printing Company, Brooklyn Also called 6727 11th Ave Corp (PA) *(G-1444)*
Prestigeline Inc 631 273-3636
5 Inez Dr Bay Shore (11706) *(G-710)*
Preston Glass Industries Inc 718 997-8888
10420 Queens Blvd Apt 17a Forest Hills (11375) *(G-5080)*
Prestone Press LLC 347 468-7900
4750 30th St Long Island City (11101) *(G-7558)*
Prestone Printing Company, Long Island City Also called Prestone Press LLC *(G-7558)*
Pretty Fuel Inc 315 823-4063
29 W Lansing St Little Falls (13365) *(G-7212)*
Prevost Car (us) Inc 518 957-2052
260 Banker Rd Plattsburgh (12901) *(G-13148)*
Prg Integrated Solutions, Armonk Also called Production Resource Group LLC *(G-408)*
Price Chopper Operating Co 518 562-3565
19 Centre Dr Plattsburgh (12901) *(G-13149)*
Price Chopper Operating Co 518 456-5115
2080 Western Ave Ste 160 Guilderland (12004) *(G-5655)*
Price Chopper Pharmacy, Catskill Also called Golub Corporation *(G-3303)*
Price Chopper Pharmacy, Oneida Also called Golub Corporation *(G-12609)*
Price Chopper Pharmacy, Norwich Also called Golub Corporation *(G-12486)*
Price Chopper Pharmacy, Hudson Also called Golub Corporation *(G-6351)*
Price Chopper Pharmacy, Middletown Also called Golub Corporation *(G-8157)*
Price Chopper Pharmacy 184, Malta Also called Golub Corporation *(G-7731)*
Price Chopper Pharmacy 234, Binghamton Also called Golub Corporation *(G-888)*
Pricet Printing 315 655-0369
3852 Charles Rd Cazenovia (13035) *(G-3326)*
Pricing Engine Inc 917 549-3289
175 Varick St Fl 4 New York (10014) *(G-11238)*
Pride & Joys Inc 212 594-9820
1400 Broadway Rm 503 New York (10018) *(G-11239)*
Pride Lines Ltd 631 225-0033
651 W Hoffman Ave Lindenhurst (11757) *(G-7190)*
Pride Pak Inc 905 828-2149
11531 Maple Ridge Rd Medina (14103) *(G-7986)*
Prim Hall Enterprises Inc 518 561-7408
11 Spellman Rd Plattsburgh (12901) *(G-13150)*
Prima Asphalt and Concrete 631 289-3223
615 Furrows Rd Holtsville (11742) *(G-6243)*
Prima Satchel Inc 929 367-7770
51 Forest Rd Ste 302 Monroe (10950) *(G-8279)*
Primary Wave Publishing LLC 212 661-6990
116 E 16th St Fl 9 New York (10003) *(G-11240)*
Prime Cook (wttc) Inc (PA) 646 881-0068
15038 Jewel Ave Flushing (11367) *(G-5039)*
Prime Electric Motors Inc 718 784-1124
4850 33rd St Long Island City (11101) *(G-7559)*
Prime Food Processing Corp 718 963-2323
300 Vandervoort Ave Brooklyn (11211) *(G-2342)*
Prime Garments Inc 212 354-7294
66 Randall Ave Rockville Centre (11570) *(G-14237)*
Prime Materials Recovery Inc 315 697-5251
51 Madison Blvd Canastota (13032) *(G-3245)*
Prime Pack LLC 732 253-7734
303 5th Ave Rm 1007 New York (10016) *(G-11241)*
Prime Pharmaceutical, New York Also called Prime Pack LLC *(G-11241)*
Prime Research Solutions LLC 917 836-7941
7328 136th St Flushing (11367) *(G-5040)*
Prime Time, Garden City Also called Richner Communications Inc *(G-5278)*
Prime Tool & Die LLC 607 334-5435
6277 County Road 32 Norwich (13815) *(G-12492)*
Prime Turbine Parts LLC 518 306-7306
77 Railroad Pl Saratoga Springs (12866) *(G-14593)*
Prime View USA Inc 212 730-4905
36 W 44th St Ste 812 New York (10036) *(G-11242)*
Prime Wood Products 518 792-1407
1288 Vaughn Rd Queensbury (12804) *(G-13438)*
Primelite Manufacturing Corp 516 868-4411
407 S Main St Freeport (11520) *(G-5176)*
Primesouth Inc 585 567-4191
11537 Route 19 Fillmore (14735) *(G-4938)*

Primo Coat Corp 718 349-2070
4315 Queens St Fl 3 Long Island City (11101) *(G-7560)*
Primo Frozen Desserts Inc 718 252-2312
1633 Utica Ave Brooklyn (11234) *(G-2343)*
Primo Plastics Inc 718 349-1000
162 Russell St Brooklyn (11222) *(G-2344)*
Primoplast Inc 631 750-0680
1555 Ocean Ave Ste E Bohemia (11716) *(G-1078)*
Prince Minerals, New York Also called American Minerals Inc *(G-8834)*
Prince Rubber & Plas Co Inc (PA) 225 272-1653
137 Arthur St Buffalo (14207) *(G-3014)*
Prince Seating Corp 718 363-2300
1355 Atlantic Ave Brooklyn (11216) *(G-2345)*
Princess Marcella Borghese, New York Also called Borghese Inc *(G-9123)*
Princess Music Publishing Co 212 586-0240
1650 Broadway Ste 701 New York (10019) *(G-11243)*
Princetel Inc 914 579-2410
200 Saw Mill River Rd Hawthorne (10532) *(G-5996)*
Princeton Label & Packaging 609 490-0800
217 River Ave Patchogue (11772) *(G-12875)*
Princeton Upholstery Co Inc (PA) 845 343-2196
51 Railroad Ave Middletown (10940) *(G-8172)*
Principia Partners LLC 212 480-2270
140 Broadway Fl 46 New York (10005) *(G-11244)*
Princton Archtctural Press LLC (HQ) 518 671-6100
202 Warren St Hudson (12534) *(G-6369)*
Print & Graphics Group 518 371-4649
12 Fire Rd Clifton Park (12065) *(G-3573)*
Print Better Inc 347 348-1841
5939 Myrtle Ave Ridgewood (11385) *(G-13547)*
Print By Premier LLC 212 947-1365
470 Fashion Ave Fl 8 New York (10018) *(G-11245)*
Print Center Inc 718 643-9559
3 Harbor Rd Ste 21 Cold Spring Harbor (11724) *(G-3632)*
Print City Corp 212 487-9778
165 W 29th St New York (10001) *(G-11246)*
Print Cottage LLC 516 369-1749
1138 Lakeshore Dr Massapequa Park (11762) *(G-7894)*
Print Early LLC 718 915-7368
821 Prospect Ave Apt 1a Westbury (11590) *(G-16367)*
Print House Inc 718 443-7500
538 Johnson Ave Brooklyn (11237) *(G-2346)*
Print It Here 516 308-7785
185 Jerusalem Ave Massapequa (11758) *(G-7883)*
Print It Inc 845 371-2227
59 Route 59 Ste 141 Monsey (10952) *(G-8294)*
Print Mall 718 437-7700
4122 16th Ave Brooklyn (11204) *(G-2347)*
Print Management Group Inc 212 213-1555
33 E 33rd St Fl 3 New York (10016) *(G-11247)*
Print Market Inc 631 940-8181
66 E Jefryn Blvd Ste 1 Deer Park (11729) *(G-4029)*
Print Masters, Mount Vernon Also called Con-Tees Custom Printing Ltd *(G-8390)*
Print Media Inc 212 563-4040
350 7th Ave Fl 12 New York (10001) *(G-11248)*
Print On Demand Initiative Inc 585 239-6044
1240 Jefferson Rd Rochester (14623) *(G-14044)*
Print Seforim Bzul Inc 718 679-1011
8 Lynch St Apt 6r Brooklyn (11206) *(G-2348)*
Print Shoppe 315 792-9585
311 Turner St Ste 310 Utica (13501) *(G-15730)*
Print Solutions Plus Inc 315 234-3801
7325 Oswego Rd Liverpool (13090) *(G-7258)*
Print-O-Rama Copy Center, Merrick Also called Leader Printing Inc *(G-8101)*
Printcorp Inc 631 696-0641
2050 Ocean Ave Ronkonkoma (11779) *(G-14400)*
Printech Business Systems Inc 212 290-2542
519 8th Ave Fl 3 New York (10018) *(G-11249)*
Printed Deals, Rochester Also called Valassis Communications Inc *(G-14197)*
Printed Image 716 821-1880
1906 Clinton St Buffalo (14206) *(G-3015)*
Printer Components Inc (HQ) 585 924-5190
100 Photikon Dr Ste 2 Fairport (14450) *(G-4651)*
Printers 3, Hauppauge Also called Avm Printing Inc *(G-5775)*
Printers 3 Inc 631 351-1331
43 Corporate Dr Ste 2 Hauppauge (11788) *(G-5923)*
Printery 516 922-3250
43 W Main St Oyster Bay (11771) *(G-12818)*
Printery 315 253-7403
55 Arterial W Auburn (13021) *(G-496)*
Printex Packaging Corporation 631 234-4300
555 Raymond Dr Islandia (11749) *(G-6537)*
Printfacility Inc 212 349-4009
225 Broadway Fl 3 New York (10007) *(G-11250)*
Printhouse, The, Brooklyn Also called Print House Inc *(G-2346)*
Printing, Hempstead Also called Reliable Press II Inc *(G-6025)*
Printing Emporium, Merrick Also called D G M Graphics Inc *(G-8096)*
Printing Express, Jamaica Also called Hillside Printing Inc *(G-6650)*
Printing Factory LLC 718 451-0500
1940 Utica Ave Brooklyn (11234) *(G-2349)*
Printing House of W S Miller, Oyster Bay Also called Printery *(G-12818)*

Printing Max New York Inc 718 692-1400
2282 Flatbush Ave Brooklyn (11234) ***(G-2350)***
Printing Plus, Rochester *Also called Ozipko Enterprises Inc* ***(G-13999)***
Printing Prmtnal Solutions LLC 315 474-1110
2320 Milton Ave Ste 5 Syracuse (13209) ***(G-15397)***
Printing Promotional Solutions, Syracuse *Also called Printing Prmtnal Solutions LLC* ***(G-15397)***
Printing Resources Inc 518 482-2470
100 Fuller Rd Ste 1 Albany (12205) ***(G-119)***
Printing Sales Group Limited 718 258-8860
1856 Flatbush Ave Brooklyn (11210) ***(G-2351)***
Printing Spectrum Inc 631 689-1010
12 Research Way Ste 1 East Setauket (11733) ***(G-4308)***
Printing X Press Ions 631 242-1992
5 Dix Cir Dix Hills (11746) ***(G-4124)***
Printinghouse Press Ltd 212 719-0990
10 E 39th St Rm 700 New York (10016) ***(G-11251)***
Printroc Inc 585 461-2556
620 South Ave Rochester (14620) ***(G-14045)***
Printutopia 718 788-1545
393 Prospect Ave Brooklyn (11215) ***(G-2352)***
Printworks Printing & Design 315 433-8587
5982 E Molloy Rd Syracuse (13211) ***(G-15398)***
Printz and Patternz LLC 518 944-6020
1550 Altamont Ave Schenectady (12303) ***(G-14705)***
Printz Pttrnz Scrn-Prnting EMB, Schenectady *Also called Printz and Patternz LLC* ***(G-14705)***
Priscilla Quart Co Firts 516 365-2755
160 Plandome Rd Fl 2 Manhasset (11030) ***(G-7771)***
Prism Solar Technologies Inc (HQ) 845 883-4200
180 South St Highland (12528) ***(G-6146)***
Prismatic Dyeing & Finshg Inc 845 561-1800
40 Wisner Ave Newburgh (12550) ***(G-12242)***
Private Lbel Fods Rchester Inc 585 254-9205
1686 Lyell Ave Rochester (14606) ***(G-14046)***
Private Portfolio, New York *Also called Coty US LLC* ***(G-9406)***
Pro Drones Usa LLC 718 530-3558
115 E 57th St Fl 11 New York (10022) ***(G-11252)***
Pro Metal of NY Corp 516 285-0440
814 W Merrick Rd Valley Stream (11580) ***(G-15791)***
Pro Pack, Eagle Bridge *Also called Professional Packg Svcs Inc* ***(G-4185)***
Pro Printers of Greene County, Catskill *Also called Mark T Westinghouse* ***(G-3306)***
Pro Printing 516 561-9700
359 Merrick Rd Lynbrook (11563) ***(G-7670)***
Pro Publica Inc 212 514-5250
155 Ave Of The Americas New York (10013) ***(G-11253)***
Pro Torque 631 218-8700
1440 Church St Bohemia (11716) ***(G-1079)***
Pro-Gear Co Inc 716 684-3811
1120 Niagara St Buffalo (14213) ***(G-3016)***
Pro-Line Solutions Inc 914 664-0002
18 Sargent Pl Mount Vernon (10550) ***(G-8434)***
Pro-TEC V I P, Gloversville *Also called Protech (llc)* ***(G-5463)***
Pro-Tech Catings Solutions Inc 631 707-9400
250 Executive Dr Ste H Edgewood (11717) ***(G-4412)***
Pro-Tech Sno Pusher, Rochester *Also called Pro-Tech Wldg Fabrication Inc* ***(G-14047)***
Pro-Tech Wldg Fabrication Inc 585 436-9855
711 West Ave Rochester (14611) ***(G-14047)***
Pro-Teck Coating Inc 716 537-2619
7785 Olean Rd Holland (14080) ***(G-6221)***
Pro-Tek Packaging Group, Ronkonkoma *Also called Oaklee International Inc* ***(G-14389)***
Pro-Value Distribution Inc 585 783-1461
1547 Lyell Ave Ste 3 Rochester (14606) ***(G-14048)***
Proactive Medical Products LLC 845 205-6004
270 Washington St Mount Vernon (10553) ***(G-8435)***
Procab, Woodridge *Also called Professional Cab Detailing Co* ***(G-16643)***
Procomponents Inc (PA) 516 683-0909
900 Merchants Concourse Westbury (11590) ***(G-16368)***
Procter & Gamble Company 646 885-4201
120 W 45th St Fl 3 New York (10036) ***(G-11254)***
Product Development Intl LLC 212 279-6170
215 W 40th St Fl 8 New York (10018) ***(G-11255)***
Product Integration & Mfg Inc 585 436-6260
55 Fessenden St Rochester (14611) ***(G-14049)***
Product Station Inc 516 942-4220
366 N Broadway Ste 410 Jericho (11753) ***(G-6798)***
Productand Design Inc 718 858-2440
63 Flushing Ave Unit 322 Brooklyn (11205) ***(G-2353)***
Production Metal Cutting Inc 585 458-7136
1 Curlew St Rochester (14606) ***(G-14050)***
Production Milling Company 914 666-0792
364 Adams St Ste 5 Bedford Hills (10507) ***(G-778)***
Production Resource Group LLC (PA) 877 774-7088
200 Business Park Dr # 109 Armonk (10504) ***(G-408)***
Production Resource Group LLC 845 567-5700
539 Temple Hill Rd New Windsor (12553) ***(G-8655)***
Producto Corporation 716 484-7131
2980 Turner Rd Jamestown (14701) ***(G-6744)***
Producto Electric Corp 845 359-4900
11 Kings Hwy Orangeburg (10962) ***(G-12688)***
Professional Buty Holdings Inc 631 787-8576
150 Motor Pkwy Ste 401 Hauppauge (11788) ***(G-5924)***
Professional Cab Detailing Co 845 436-7282
Navograrsky Rd Woodridge (12789) ***(G-16643)***
Professional Disposables Inc 845 365-1700
2 Nice Pak Park Orangeburg (10962) ***(G-12689)***
Professional Health Imaging, Wantagh *Also called R M F Health Management L L C* ***(G-15926)***
Professional Machine LLC 508 966-5171
1390 Mount Read Blvd Rochester (14606) ***(G-14051)***
Professional Manufacturers 631 586-2440
475 Brook Ave Deer Park (11729) ***(G-4030)***
Professional Medical Devices 914 835-0614
10 Century Trl Harrison (10528) ***(G-5733)***
Professional Packg Svcs Inc 518 677-5100
62 Owlkill Rd Eagle Bridge (12057) ***(G-4185)***
Professional Pavers Corp 718 784-7853
6605 Woodhaven Blvd Bsmt Rego Park (11374) ***(G-13468)***
Professional Remodelers Inc 516 565-9300
340 Hempstead Ave Unit A West Hempstead (11552) ***(G-16224)***
Professional Solutions Print 631 231-9300
300 Wheeler Rd Ste 303 Hauppauge (11788) ***(G-5925)***
Professional Tape Corporation 516 656-5519
100 Pratt Oval Glen Cove (11542) ***(G-5373)***
Professional Technologies, Rome *Also called Professional Technology Inc* ***(G-14267)***
Professional Technology Inc 315 337-4156
5433 Lowell Rd Rome (13440) ***(G-14267)***
Professnal Spt Pblications Inc (PA) 212 697-1460
519 8th Ave New York (10018) ***(G-11256)***
Professnal Spt Pblications Inc 516 327-9500
570 Elmont Rd Elmont (11003) ***(G-4522)***
Professnal Spt Pblications Inc 516 327-9500
570 Elmont Rd Ste 202 Elmont (11003) ***(G-4523)***
Proficient Surgical Eqp Inc 516 487-1175
99 Seaview Blvd Ste 1c Port Washington (11050) ***(G-13299)***
Profile, New York *Also called Eternal Fortune Fashion LLC* ***(G-9721)***
Profile Printing & Graphics (PA) 631 273-2727
275 Marcus Blvd Hauppauge (11788) ***(G-5926)***
Profoot Inc 718 965-8600
74 20th St Fl 2 Brooklyn (11232) ***(G-2354)***
Proforma, Westfield *Also called A Trusted Name Inc* ***(G-16391)***
Proformance Foods Inc 703 869-3413
44 Dobbin St Fl 1 Brooklyn (11222) ***(G-2355)***
Progenics Pharmaceuticals Inc (PA) 646 975-2500
1 World Trade Ctr Fl 47s New York (10007) ***(G-11257)***
Proginet Corporation 516 535-3600
200 Garden Cy Plz Ste 220 Garden City (11530) ***(G-5276)***
PROGRESS INDUSTRIES SALES, Utica *Also called Fourteen Arnold Ave Corp* ***(G-15703)***
Progressive Color Graphics 212 292-8787
122 Station Rd Great Neck (11023) ***(G-5584)***
Progressive Fibre Products Co 212 566-2720
160 Broadway Rm 1105 New York (10038) ***(G-11258)***
Progressive Graphics & Prtg 315 331-3635
1171 E Union St Newark (14513) ***(G-12205)***
Progressive Hardware Co Inc 631 445-1826
63 Brightside Ave East Northport (11731) ***(G-4269)***
Progressive Mch & Design LLC (PA) 585 924-5250
727 Rowley Rd Victor (14564) ***(G-15862)***
Progressive Orthotics Ltd (PA) 631 732-5556
280 Middle Country Rd G Selden (11784) ***(G-14766)***
Progressive Orthotics Ltd 631 447-3860
285 Sills Rd Bldg 8c East Patchogue (11772) ***(G-4276)***
Progressive Products LLC 914 417-6022
4 International Dr # 224 Rye Brook (10573) ***(G-14494)***
Progressive Tool Company Inc 607 748-8294
3221 Lawndale St Endwell (13760) ***(G-4619)***
Progressus Company Inc 516 255-0245
100 Merrick Rd Ste 510w Rockville Centre (11570) ***(G-14238)***
Prohibition Distillery LLC 917 685-8989
10 Union St Roscoe (12776) ***(G-14439)***
Project Energy Savers LLC 718 596-4231
68 Jay St Ste 516 Brooklyn (11201) ***(G-2356)***
Project Visual, Islandia *Also called Zahk Sales Inc* ***(G-6541)***
Prokosch and Sonn Sheet Metal 845 562-4211
772 South St Newburgh (12550) ***(G-12243)***
Prolink Industries Inc 212 354-5690
1407 Broadway Rm 3605 New York (10018) ***(G-11259)***
Prolocksusa, Hauppauge *Also called Olan Laboratories Inc* ***(G-5904)***
Promats Athletics, Delhi *Also called Sportsfield Specialties Inc* ***(G-4076)***
Prometheus Books Inc 716 691-2158
59 John Glenn Dr Amherst (14228) ***(G-248)***
Prometheus International Inc 718 472-0700
4502 11th St Long Island City (11101) ***(G-7561)***
Promosuite, New York *Also called Broadcast Manager Inc* ***(G-9145)***
Promotional Development Inc 718 485-8550
909 Remsen Ave Brooklyn (11236) ***(G-2357)***
Promotional Sales Books LLC 212 675-0364
30 W 26th St Frnt New York (10010) ***(G-11260)***
Prompt Bindery Co Inc 212 675-5181
350 W 38th St New York (10018) ***(G-11261)***
Prompt Printing Inc 631 454-6524
160 Rome St Farmingdale (11735) ***(G-4858)***
Pronovias USA Inc 212 897-6393
14 E 52nd St New York (10022) ***(G-11262)***

Pronto Gas Heating Sups Inc 718 292-0707
431 E 165th St Fl 2 Bronx (10456) *(G-1366)*
Pronto Jewelry Inc 212 719-9455
23 W 47th St New York (10036) *(G-11263)*
Pronto Printer 914 737-0800
2085 E Main St Ste 3 Cortlandt Manor (10567) *(G-3904)*
Pronto Tool & Die Co Inc 631 981-8920
50 Remington Blvd Ronkonkoma (11779) *(G-14401)*
Proof 7 Ltd 212 680-1843
121 Varick St Rm 301 New York (10013) *(G-11264)*
Proof Industries Inc 631 694-7663
125 Rome St Farmingdale (11735) *(G-4859)*
Proof Magazine, New York *Also called Rough Draft Publishing LLC (G-11436)*
Propak Inc 518 677-5100
70 Owlkill Rd Eagle Bridge (12057) *(G-4186)*
Proper Chemical Ltd 631 420-8000
280 Smith St Farmingdale (11735) *(G-4860)*
Proper Cloth LLC 646 964-4221
495 Broadway Fl 6 New York (10012) *(G-11265)*
Props Displays & Interiors 212 620-3840
132 W 18th St New York (10011) *(G-11266)*
Props For Today, Long Island City *Also called Interiors-Pft Inc (G-7476)*
Prospect News Inc 212 374-2800
6 Maiden Ln Fl 9 New York (10038) *(G-11267)*
Prosthetic Rehabilitation Ctr (PA) 845 565-8255
2 Winding Ln Newburgh (12550) *(G-12244)*
Prosthetics By Nelson Inc (PA) 716 894-6666
2959 Genesee St Cheektowaga (14225) *(G-3456)*
Protec Friction Supply, Mount Kisco *Also called Rpb Distributors LLC (G-8358)*
Protech (llc) 518 725-7785
11 Cayadutta St Gloversville (12078) *(G-5463)*
Protective Industries Inc (HQ) 716 876-9951
2150 Elmwood Ave Buffalo (14207) *(G-3017)*
Protective Industries Inc 716 876-9855
2150 Elmwood Ave Buffalo (14207) *(G-3018)*
Protective Industries Inc 716 876-9951
2510 Elmwood Ave Buffalo (14217) *(G-3019)*
Protective Lining Corp 718 854-3838
601 39th St Brooklyn (11232) *(G-2358)*
Protective Power Systms & Cntr 845 721-1875
2092 Rt 9 G Staatsburg Staatsburg (12580) *(G-15024)*
Protein Sciences Corporation 203 686-0800
401 N Middletown Rd Pearl River (10965) *(G-12908)*
Protex International Corp 631 563-4250
366 Central Ave Bohemia (11716) *(G-1080)*
Proto Machine Inc 631 392-1159
60 Corbin Ave Ste D Bay Shore (11706) *(G-711)*
Protocase Incorporated 866 849-3911
210 S 8th St Lewiston (14092) *(G-7141)*
Protofast Holding Corp 631 753-2549
182 N Oak St Copiague (11726) *(G-3775)*
Prototype Manufacturing Corp 716 695-1700
836 Wurlitzer Dr North Tonawanda (14120) *(G-12443)*
Provident Fuel Inc 516 224-4427
4 Stillwell Ln Woodbury (11797) *(G-16629)*
Provision Supply LLC (PA) 347 623-0237
1153 55th St Brooklyn (11219) *(G-2359)*
Provisionaire & Co LLC 646 681-8600
630 Flushing Ave Fl 4 Brooklyn (11206) *(G-2360)*
Provisions 5 Corp 718 809-5292
119 S 3rd St Ste D201 New Hyde Park (11040) *(G-8558)*
Prsa, New York *Also called Public Relations Soc Amer Inc (G-11273)*
Prweek/Prescribing Reference, New York *Also called Haymarket Media Inc (G-10052)*
Pry Care Products, Mount Vernon *Also called Pro-Line Solutions Inc (G-8434)*
Prz Technologies Inc 716 683-1300
5490 Broadway St Lancaster (14086) *(G-7042)*
Ps38 LLC 212 302-1108
209 W 38th St Fl 5 New York (10018) *(G-11268)*
Ps38 LLC 212 819-1123
545 8th Ave Rm 350 New York (10018) *(G-11269)*
Psb Ltd 585 654-7078
543 Atlantic Ave Ste 2 Rochester (14609) *(G-14052)*
Psg Innovations Inc 917 299-8986
924 Kilmer Ln Valley Stream (11581) *(G-15792)*
PSI Transit Mix Corp 631 382-7930
34 E Main St Smithtown (11787) *(G-14907)*
Pspi, Potsdam *Also called Potsdam Specialty Paper Inc (G-13321)*
Pspi, Elmont *Also called Professnal Spt Pblications Inc (G-4523)*
PSR Press Ltd 716 754-2266
415 Ridge St Lewiston (14092) *(G-7142)*
Psychology Today, New York *Also called Sussex Publishers LLC (G-11752)*
Psychonomic Society Inc 512 381-1494
233 Spring St Fl 7 New York (10013) *(G-11270)*
Ptc Precision LLC 607 748-8294
3221 Lawndale St Endwell (13760) *(G-4620)*
Pti-Pacific Inc 212 414-8495
166 5th Ave Fl 4t New York (10010) *(G-11271)*
Pts Financial Technology LLC 844 825-7634
1001 Ave Of The Americas New York (10018) *(G-11272)*
Public Relations Soc Amer Inc (PA) 212 460-1400
120 Wall St Fl 21 New York (10005) *(G-11273)*
Public School, New York *Also called Ps38 LLC (G-11268)*
Public School, New York *Also called Ps38 LLC (G-11269)*
Publimax Printing Corp 718 366-7133
6615 Traffic Ave Ridgewood (11385) *(G-13548)*
Publishers Clearing House LLC 516 249-4063
265 Spagnoli Rd Ste 1 Melville (11747) *(G-8059)*
Publishers Weekly, New York *Also called Pwxyz LLC (G-11287)*
Publishing Group America Inc 646 658-0550
60 E 42nd St Ste 1146 New York (10165) *(G-11274)*
Publishing Medical Journals, Orchard Park *Also called Impact Journals LLC (G-12718)*
Publishing Synthesis Ltd 212 219-0135
39 Crosby St Apt 2n New York (10013) *(G-11275)*
Publishing Trends, New York *Also called Market Partners International (G-10711)*
Puccio Design International 516 248-6426
54 Nassau Blvd Garden City (11530) *(G-5277)*
Puccio European Marble & Onyx, Garden City *Also called Puccio Design International (G-5277)*
Puccio Marble and Onyx, Garden City *Also called European Marble Works Co Inc (G-5259)*
Pugliese Vineyards Inc 631 734-4057
34515 Main Rd Rte 25 Cutchogue (11935) *(G-3923)*
Pullman Mfg Corporation 585 334-1350
77 Commerce Dr Rochester (14623) *(G-14053)*
Pulmuone Foods Usa Inc 845 365-3300
30 Rockland Park Ave Tappan (10983) *(G-15470)*
Pulsafeeder Inc (HQ) 585 292-8000
2883 Brghton Hnrietta Twn Rochester (14623) *(G-14054)*
Pulsar Technology Systems Inc 718 361-9292
2720 42nd Rd Long Island City (11101) *(G-7562)*
Pulse Plastics Products Inc 718 328-5224
1156 E 165th St Bronx (10459) *(G-1367)*
Pumilia's Pizza Shell, Waterville *Also called F & R Enterprises Inc (G-16039)*
Pumpcrete Corporation 716 667-7867
7126 Ellicott Rd Orchard Park (14127) *(G-12739)*
Pura Fruta LLC 415 279-5727
2323 Borden Ave Long Island City (11101) *(G-7563)*
Pure Acoustics Inc 718 788-4411
18 Fuller Pl Brooklyn (11215) *(G-2361)*
Pure Functional Foods Inc 315 294-0733
267 State Route 89 Savannah (13146) *(G-14624)*
Pure Ghee Inc (PA) 718 224-7399
5701 225th St Flushing (11364) *(G-5041)*
Pure Golds Family Corp 516 483-5600
1 Brooklyn Rd Hempstead (11550) *(G-6024)*
Pure Green LLC 800 306-9122
439 Centre Island Rd Oyster Bay (11771) *(G-12819)*
Pure Kemika LLC 718 745-2200
2156 Legion St Bellmore (11710) *(G-792)*
Pure Planet Waters LLC 718 676-7900
4809 Avenue N Ste 185 Brooklyn (11234) *(G-2362)*
Pure Trade Us Inc 212 256-1600
347 5th Ave Rm 604 New York (10016) *(G-11276)*
Purebase Networks Inc 646 670-8964
37 Wall St Apt 9a New York (10005) *(G-11277)*
Purely Maple LLC 203 997-9309
902 Broadway Fl 6 New York (10010) *(G-11278)*
Pureology Research LLC 212 984-4360
565 5th Ave New York (10017) *(G-11279)*
Purine Pharma LLC 315 705-4030
144 E Kingsbridge Rd Mount Vernon (10550) *(G-8436)*
Purinepharma LLC 732 485-1400
5 County Route 42 Massena (13662) *(G-7907)*
Purity Ice Cream Co Inc 607 272-1545
700 Cascadilla St Ste A Ithaca (14850) *(G-6607)*
Purity Products Inc 516 767-1967
200 Terminal Dr Plainview (11803) *(G-13084)*
Purvi Enterprises Incorporated 347 808-9448
5556 44th St Maspeth (11378) *(G-7868)*
Putnam Cnty News Recorder LLC 845 265-2468
3 Stone St Cold Spring (10516) *(G-3626)*
Putnam Rolling Ladder Co Inc (PA) 212 226-5147
32 Howard St New York (10013) *(G-11280)*
Putnam Rolling Ladder Co Inc 718 381-8219
444 Jefferson St Brooklyn (11237) *(G-2363)*
PVA, Cohoes *Also called Precision Valve & Automtn Inc (G-3617)*
Pvc Container Corporation 518 672-7721
370 Stevers Crossing Rd Philmont (12565) *(G-12987)*
Pvc Industries Inc 518 877-8670
107 Pierce Rd Clifton Park (12065) *(G-3574)*
Pvh Corp (PA) 212 381-3500
200 Madison Ave Bsmt 1 New York (10016) *(G-11281)*
Pvh Corp 845 561-0233
1073 State Route 94 New Windsor (12553) *(G-8656)*
Pvh Corp 631 254-8200
1358 The Arches Cir Deer Park (11729) *(G-4031)*
Pvh Corp 212 549-6000
285 Madison Ave Fl 2 New York (10017) *(G-11282)*
Pvh Corp 212 381-3800
200 Madison Ave Bsmt 1 New York (10016) *(G-11283)*
Pvh Corp 212 502-6300
404 5th Ave Fl 4 New York (10018) *(G-11284)*
Pvh Corp 212 719-2600
205 W 39th St Fl 4 New York (10018) *(G-11285)*
Pvh Europe, New York *Also called Phillips-Van Heusen Europe (G-11183)*

ALPHABETIC

(PA)=Parent Co (HQ)=Headquarters (DH)=Div Headquarters
2019 Harris
New York Manufacturers Directory
967

Pvi Solar Inc...212 280-2100
599 11th Ave Bby New York (10036) ***(G-11286)***
PVS Chemical Solutions, Buffalo *Also called PVS Technologies Inc* ***(G-3021)***
PVS Chemical Solutions Inc...716 825-5762
55 Lee St Buffalo (14210) ***(G-3020)***
PVS Technologies Inc...716 825-5762
55 Lee St Buffalo (14210) ***(G-3021)***
Pwxyz LLC...212 377-5500
71 W 23rd St Ste 1608 New York (10010) ***(G-11287)***
Pylantis New York LLC...310 429-5911
102 E Cortland St Groton (13073) ***(G-5653)***
Pyragon Inc...585 697-0444
95 Mount Read Blvd Ste 14 Rochester (14611) ***(G-14055)***
Pyrotek Incorporated...607 756-3050
641 State Route 13 Cortland (13045) ***(G-3890)***
Pyrotek Incorporated...716 731-3221
2040 Cory Dr Sanborn (14132) ***(G-14552)***
Pyx Enterprise, Brooklyn *Also called Pyx Inc* ***(G-2364)***
Pyx Inc...718 469-4253
143 E 29th St Brooklyn (11226) ***(G-2364)***
Q Communications Inc...212 594-6520
247 W 35th St Rm 1200 New York (10001) ***(G-11288)***
Q Ed Creations...212 391-1155
2 W 46th St Ste 1408 New York (10036) ***(G-11289)***
Q Omni Inc...914 962-2726
1994 Commerce St Yorktown Heights (10598) ***(G-16821)***
Q Squared Design LLC...212 686-8860
1133 Broadway Ste 1424 New York (10010) ***(G-11290)***
Q.E.d, Rochester *Also called QED Technologies Intl Inc* ***(G-14056)***
Qca, Rochester *Also called Quality Contract Assemblies* ***(G-14060)***
QED Technologies Intl Inc...585 256-6540
1040 University Ave Rochester (14607) ***(G-14056)***
Qes Solutions Inc (PA)...585 783-1455
1547 Lyell Ave Rochester (14606) ***(G-14057)***
Qhi Group Incorporated...646 512-5727
40 Wall St Ste 2866 New York (10005) ***(G-11291)***
Qioptiq, Inc....585 223-2370
78 Schuyler Baldwin Dr Fairport (14450) ***(G-4652)***
Qlc, Long Island City *Also called Quadlogic Controls Corporation* ***(G-7565)***
Qlogix Entertainment LLC...215 459-6315
600 W 113th St 7b4 New York (10025) ***(G-11292)***
Qls Solutions Group Inc...716 852-2203
701 Seneca St Ste 600 Buffalo (14210) ***(G-3022)***
Qmc Technologies Inc...716 681-0810
4388 Broadway Depew (14043) ***(G-4103)***
Qmi, Mount Vernon *Also called Giagni Enterprises LLC* ***(G-8400)***
Qna Tech, Ridge *Also called Quality and Asrn Tech Corp* ***(G-13523)***
Qos Enterprises LLC...585 454-0550
282 Hollenbeck St Rochester (14621) ***(G-14058)***
Qpbc Inc...718 685-1900
1306 38th Ave Long Island City (11101) ***(G-7564)***
Qps Die Cutters Finishers Corp...718 966-1811
140 Alverson Ave Staten Island (10309) ***(G-15120)***
Qrs Technologies Inc...315 457-5300
549 Electronics Pkwy Liverpool (13088) ***(G-7259)***
Qsf Inc...585 247-6200
140 Cherry Rd Gates (14624) ***(G-5311)***
Qsr Medical Communications, Westhampton Beach *Also called Shugar Publishing* ***(G-16405)***
Qssi, Walden *Also called Pacific Die Cast Inc* ***(G-15894)***
Qta Machining Inc...716 862-8108
876 Bailey Ave Buffalo (14206) ***(G-3023)***
Qtalk Publishing LLC...877 549-1841
1 E Broadway Fl 4 New York (10038) ***(G-11293)***
Quad/Graphics Inc...518 581-4000
56 Duplainville Rd Saratoga Springs (12866) ***(G-14594)***
Quad/Graphics Inc...212 672-1300
135 W 50th St Fl 8 New York (10020) ***(G-11294)***
Quad/Graphics Inc...212 206-5535
60 5th Ave Lowr Level New York (10011) ***(G-11295)***
Quad/Graphics Inc...212 741-1001
375 Hudson St New York (10014) ***(G-11296)***
Quadlogic Controls Corporation...212 930-9300
3300 Northern Blvd Fl 2 Long Island City (11101) ***(G-7565)***
Quadra Flex Corp...607 758-7066
1955 State Route 13 Cortland (13045) ***(G-3891)***
Quadra Flex Quality Labels, Cortland *Also called Quadra Flex Corp* ***(G-3891)***
Quadrangle Quick Print, Melville *Also called Quadrangle Quickprints Ltd* ***(G-8060)***
Quadrangle Quickprints Ltd...631 694-4464
1 Huntington Quad Ll04 Melville (11747) ***(G-8060)***
Quadrant Biosciences Inc...315 614-2325
505 Irving Ave Ste 3100ab Syracuse (13210) ***(G-15399)***
Quadristi LLC...585 279-3318
275 Mount Read Blvd Rochester (14611) ***(G-14059)***
Quaker Bonnet Inc...716 885-7208
54 Irving Pl Buffalo (14201) ***(G-3024)***
Quaker Boy Inc (PA)...716 662-3979
5455 Webster Rd Orchard Park (14127) ***(G-12740)***
Quaker Boy Turkey Calls, Orchard Park *Also called Quaker Boy Inc* ***(G-12740)***
Quaker Millwork & Lumber Inc...716 662-3388
77 S Davis St Orchard Park (14127) ***(G-12741)***
Qualbuys LLC...855 884-3274
6800 Jericho Tpke 120w Syosset (11791) ***(G-15228)***
Qualicoat Inc...585 293-2650
14 Sanford Rd N Churchville (14428) ***(G-3512)***
Qualified Manufacturing Corp...631 249-4440
15 Amber Ct East Islip (11730) ***(G-4245)***
Qualitea Imports Inc...917 624-6750
74 Lafayette Ave Suffern (10901) ***(G-15195)***
Qualitrol Company LLC (HQ)...586 643-3717
1385 Fairport Rd Fairport (14450) ***(G-4653)***
Quality and Asrn Tech Corp...646 450-6762
18 Marginwood Dr Ridge (11961) ***(G-13523)***
Quality Bindery Service Inc...716 883-5185
501 Amherst St Buffalo (14207) ***(G-3025)***
Quality Candle Mfg Co Inc...631 842-8475
121 Cedar St Copiague (11726) ***(G-3776)***
Quality Carpet One Floor & HM...718 941-4200
214 Ditmas Ave Brooklyn (11218) ***(G-2365)***
Quality Castings Inc...732 409-3203
3100 47th Ave Ste 2120b Long Island City (11101) ***(G-7566)***
Quality Circle Products Inc...914 736-6600
2108 Albany Post Rd Montrose (10548) ***(G-8329)***
Quality Components Framing Sys...315 768-1167
44 Mohawk St Bldg 10 Whitesboro (13492) ***(G-16528)***
Quality Contract Assemblies...585 663-9030
100 Boxart St Ste 251 Rochester (14612) ***(G-14060)***
Quality Dairy Farms Inc...315 942-2611
13584 State Route 12 Boonville (13309) ***(G-1120)***
Quality Embedments Mfg Co, New York *Also called Endurart Inc* ***(G-9679)***
Quality Enclosures Inc (PA)...631 234-0115
101 Windsor Pl Unit H Central Islip (11722) ***(G-3382)***
Quality Fence, Merrick *Also called Quality Lineals Usa Inc* ***(G-8106)***
Quality Foam Inc...718 381-3644
137 Gardner Ave Brooklyn (11237) ***(G-2366)***
Quality Fuel 1 Corporation...631 392-4090
1235 Deer Park Ave North Babylon (11703) ***(G-12361)***
Quality Graphics Tri State...845 735-2523
171 Center St Pearl River (10965) ***(G-12909)***
Quality Guides...716 326-3163
39 E Main St Westfield (14787) ***(G-16395)***
Quality HM Brands Holdings LLC (PA)...718 292-2024
125 Rose Feiss Blvd Bronx (10454) ***(G-1368)***
Quality Impressions Inc...646 613-0002
4334 32nd Pl Ste 3 Long Island City (11101) ***(G-7567)***
Quality Industrial Services...716 667-7703
75 Bank St Orchard Park (14127) ***(G-12742)***
Quality King Distributors Inc...631 439-2027
201 Comac St Ronkonkoma (11779) ***(G-14402)***
Quality Life Inc...718 939-5787
2047 129th St College Point (11356) ***(G-3662)***
Quality Lineals Usa Inc...516 378-6577
105 Bennington Ave Ste 1 Freeport (11520) ***(G-5177)***
Quality Lineals Usa Inc (PA)...516 378-6577
1 Kees Pl Merrick (11566) ***(G-8106)***
Quality Machining Service Inc...315 736-5774
70 Sauquoit St New York Mills (13417) ***(G-12190)***
Quality Manufacturing Sys LLC...716 763-0988
1995 Stoneman Cir Lakewood (14750) ***(G-6995)***
Quality Metal Stamping LLC (PA)...516 255-9000
100 Merrick Rd Ste 310w Rockville Centre (11570) ***(G-14239)***
Quality Millwork Corp...718 892-2250
425 Devoe Ave Bronx (10460) ***(G-1369)***
Quality Nature Inc...718 484-4666
8225 5th Ave Ste 215 Brooklyn (11209) ***(G-2367)***
Quality Offset LLC...347 342-4660
4750 30th St Long Island City (11101) ***(G-7568)***
Quality One Wireless LLC...631 233-3337
2127 Lakeland Ave Unit 2 Ronkonkoma (11779) ***(G-14403)***
Quality Patterns Inc...212 704-0355
246 W 38th St Fl 9 New York (10018) ***(G-11297)***
Quality Plus, Rochester *Also called Rapid Precision Machining Inc* ***(G-14069)***
Quality Quick Signs, Depew *Also called Flado Enterprises Inc* ***(G-4090)***
Quality Ready Mix Inc...516 437-0100
1824 Gilford Ave New Hyde Park (11040) ***(G-8559)***
Quality Saw & Knife Inc...631 491-4747
115 Otis St West Babylon (11704) ***(G-16184)***
Quality Stainless Fabrication, Gates *Also called Qsf Inc* ***(G-5311)***
Quality Stainless Steel NY Inc (PA)...718 748-1785
865 63rd St Brooklyn (11220) ***(G-2368)***
Quality Stair Builders Inc...631 694-0711
95 Schmitt Blvd Farmingdale (11735) ***(G-4861)***
Quality Strapping Inc...718 418-1111
55 Meadow St Brooklyn (11206) ***(G-2369)***
Quality Vision International, Rochester *Also called Quality Vision Services Inc* ***(G-14062)***
Quality Vision Intl Inc (PA)...585 544-0450
850 Hudson Ave Rochester (14621) ***(G-14061)***
Quality Vision Services Inc...585 544-0450
1175 North St Rochester (14621) ***(G-14062)***
Quality Woodworking Corp...718 875-3437
260 Butler St Brooklyn (11217) ***(G-2370)***
Qualtech Tool & Machine Inc...585 223-9227
1000 Turk Hill Rd Ste 292 Fairport (14450) ***(G-4654)***

Qualtronic Devices Inc 631 360-0859
130 Oakside Dr Smithtown (11787) *(G-14908)*
Quanta Electronics Inc 631 961-9953
48 Fran Ln Centereach (11720) *(G-3345)*
Quantum Asset Recovery 716 393-2712
482 Niagara Falls Blvd Buffalo (14223) *(G-3026)*
Quantum Knowledge LLC 631 727-6111
356 Reeves Ave Riverhead (11901) *(G-13580)*
Quantum Logic Corp 516 746-1380
91 5th Ave New Hyde Park (11040) *(G-8560)*
Quantum Mechanics Ny LLC 917 519-7077
40 Hennessey Dr Huntington (11743) *(G-6408)*
Quantum Medical Imaging LLC 631 567-5800
150 Verona St Rochester (14608) *(G-14063)*
Quantum Sails Rochester LLC 585 342-5200
1461 Hudson Ave Rochester (14621) *(G-14064)*
Quartet Financial Systems Inc (PA) 845 358-6071
1412 Broadway Rm 2300 New York (10018) *(G-11298)*
Quarto Group Inc (HQ) 212 779-0700
276 5th Ave Rm 205 New York (10001) *(G-11299)*
Quattro Frameworks Inc 718 361-2620
4310 23rd St Ste 307 Long Island City (11101) *(G-7569)*
Qubicaamf Worldwide LLC 315 376-6541
7412 Utica Blvd Lowville (13367) *(G-7655)*
Queen Ann Macaroni Mfg Co Inc 718 256-1061
7205 18th Ave Brooklyn (11204) *(G-2371)*
Queen Ann Ravioli, Brooklyn *Also called Queen Ann Macaroni Mfg Co Inc (G-2371)*
Queen City Malting LLC 716 481-1313
644 N Forest Rd Buffalo (14221) *(G-3027)*
Queen City Manufacturing Inc 716 877-1102
333 Henderson Ave Buffalo (14217) *(G-3028)*
Queenaire Technologies Inc 315 393-5454
9483 State Highway 37 Ogdensburg (13669) *(G-12578)*
Queens Central News, Camden *Also called Camden News Inc (G-3185)*
Queens Chronicle, Glendale *Also called Mark I Publications Inc (G-5403)*
Queens Ldgr/Grenpoint Star Inc 718 639-7000
6960 Grand Ave Fl 2 Maspeth (11378) *(G-7869)*
Queens Ready Mix Inc 718 526-4919
14901 95th Ave Jamaica (11435) *(G-6670)*
Queens Times, Whitestone *Also called CT Publications Co (G-16539)*
Queens Tribune, Whitestone *Also called Tribco LLC (G-16550)*
Quest Bead & Cast Inc 212 354-1737
49 W 37th St Fl 16 New York (10018) *(G-11300)*
Quest Beads, New York *Also called Quest Bead & Cast Inc (G-11300)*
Quest Magazine, New York *Also called Quest Media Llc (G-11301)*
Quest Manufacturing Inc 716 312-8000
5600 Camp Rd Hamburg (14075) *(G-5691)*
Quest Manufacturing Inc 716 312-8000
5600 Camp Rd Hamburg (14075) *(G-5692)*
Quest Media Llc 646 840-3404
920 3rd Ave Fl 6 New York (10022) *(G-11301)*
Queue Solutions LLC 631 750-6440
250 Knickerbocker Ave Bohemia (11716) *(G-1081)*
Quick Frzen Foods Annual Prcss, New York *Also called Frozen Food Digest Inc (G-9852)*
Quick Guide, New York *Also called Guest Informat LLC (G-10005)*
Quick Roll Leaf Mfg Co Inc (PA) 845 457-1500
118 Bracken Rd Montgomery (12549) *(G-8316)*
Quick Sign F X 516 249-6531
6 Powell St Farmingdale (11735) *(G-4862)*
Quick Turn Around Machining, Buffalo *Also called Qta Machining Inc (G-3023)*
Quicker Printer Inc 607 734-8622
210 W Gray St Elmira (14901) *(G-4500)*
Quickprint 585 394-2600
330 S Main St Canandaigua (14424) *(G-3232)*
Quikrete Companies LLC 716 213-2027
11 N Steelawanna Ave Lackawanna (14218) *(G-6951)*
Quikrete Companies LLC 315 673-2020
4993 Limeledge Rd Ste 560 Marcellus (13108) *(G-7794)*
Quikrete-Buffalo, Lackawanna *Also called Quikrete Companies LLC (G-6951)*
Quilted Koala Ltd 800 223-5678
1384 Broadway Ste 15 New York (10018) *(G-11302)*
Quinn and Co of NY Ltd 212 868-1900
48 W 38th St Ph New York (10018) *(G-11303)*
Quintel Usa Inc 585 420-8364
1200 Ridgeway Ave Ste 132 Rochester (14615) *(G-14065)*
Quip Nyc Inc 917 331-3993
45 Main St Ste 616 Brooklyn (11201) *(G-2372)*
Quist Industries Ltd 718 243-2800
204 Van Dyke St Ste 320a Brooklyn (11231) *(G-2373)*
Quogue Capital LLC 212 554-4475
1285 Ave Of The Ave Fl 35 Flr 35 New York (10019) *(G-11304)*
Quoin LLC 914 967-9400
555 Theodore Fremd Ave B302 Rye (10580) *(G-14487)*
Quoizel Inc 631 436-4402
590 Old Willets Path # 1 Hauppauge (11788) *(G-5927)*
Quorum Group LLC 585 798-8888
11601 Maple Ridge Rd Medina (14103) *(G-7987)*
Quotable Cards Inc 212 420-7552
611 Broadway Rm 615 New York (10012) *(G-11305)*
Quva Pharma Inc 973 224-7795
135 Central Park W New York (10023) *(G-11306)*
Qworldstar Inc 212 768-4500
200 Park Ave S Fl 8 New York (10003) *(G-11307)*
R & A Industrial Products 716 823-4300
30 Cornelia St Buffalo (14210) *(G-3029)*
R & B Fabrication Inc 315 640-9901
7282 State Route 31 Cicero (13039) *(G-3522)*
R & B Machinery Corp 716 894-3332
400 Kennedy Rd Ste 3 Buffalo (14227) *(G-3030)*
R & F Boards & Dividers Inc 718 331-1529
1678 57th St Brooklyn (11204) *(G-2374)*
R & F Handmade Paints Inc 845 331-3112
84 Ten Broeck Ave Kingston (12401) *(G-6915)*
R & F Marketing, New York *Also called Place Vendome Holding Co Inc (G-11205)*
R & H Baking Co Inc 718 852-1768
19 5th St Brooklyn (11231) *(G-2375)*
R & J Displays Inc 631 491-3500
96 Otis St West Babylon (11704) *(G-16185)*
R & J Graphics Inc 631 293-6611
45 Central Ave Farmingdale (11735) *(G-4863)*
R & J Sheet Metal Distributors 518 433-1525
156 Orange St Albany (12210) *(G-120)*
R & L Press Inc 718 447-8557
896 Forest Ave Staten Island (10310) *(G-15121)*
R & L Press of SI Inc 718 667-3258
2461 Hylan Blvd Staten Island (10306) *(G-15122)*
R & M Graphics of New York 212 929-0294
121 Varick St Fl 9 New York (10013) *(G-11308)*
R & M Industries Inc 212 366-6414
111 Broadway Rm 1112 New York (10006) *(G-11309)*
R & M Richards Inc (PA) 212 921-8820
1400 Broadway Fl 9 New York (10018) *(G-11310)*
R & M Thermofoil Doors Inc 718 206-4991
14830 94th Ave Jamaica (11435) *(G-6671)*
R & R Grosbard Inc 212 575-0077
1156 Avenue Of The Amrcs New York (10036) *(G-11311)*
R & S Machine Center Inc 518 563-4016
4398 Route 22 Plattsburgh (12901) *(G-13151)*
R and J Sheet Metal, Albany *Also called R & J Sheet Metal Distributors (G-120)*
R C Henderson Stair Builders 516 876-9898
100 Summa Ave Westbury (11590) *(G-16369)*
R C Kolstad Water Corp 585 216-2230
73 Lake Rd Ontario (14519) *(G-12661)*
R D A Container Corporation 585 247-2323
70 Cherry Rd Gates (14624) *(G-5312)*
R D Drive and Shop, Little Falls *Also called R D S Mountain View Trucking (G-7213)*
R D Printing Associates Inc 631 390-5964
1865 New Hwy Ste 1 Farmingdale (11735) *(G-4864)*
R D R Industries Inc 315 866-5020
146 W Main St Mohawk (13407) *(G-8256)*
R D S Mountain View Trucking 315 823-4265
1600 State Route 5s Little Falls (13365) *(G-7213)*
R D Specialties Inc 585 265-0220
560 Salt Rd Webster (14580) *(G-16093)*
R E F Precision Products 631 242-4471
517 Acorn St Ste A Deer Park (11729) *(G-4032)*
R F Giardina Co 516 922-1364
200 Lexington Ave Apt 3a Oyster Bay (11771) *(G-12820)*
R G Flair Co Inc 631 586-7311
199 S Fehr Way Bay Shore (11706) *(G-712)*
R G Glass, New York *Also called RG Glass Creations Inc (G-11383)*
R G King General Construction 315 583-3560
13018 County Route 155 Adams Center (13606) *(G-4)*
R Goldsmith 718 239-1396
1974 Mayflower Ave Bronx (10461) *(G-1370)*
R H Crown Co Inc 518 762-4589
100 N Market St Johnstown (12095) *(G-6838)*
R H Guest Incorporated 718 675-7600
1300 Church Ave Brooklyn (11226) *(G-2376)*
R Hochman Papers Incorporated 516 466-6414
1000 Dean St Ste 315 Brooklyn (11238) *(G-2377)*
R I C, Ontario *Also called Rochester Industrial Ctrl Inc (G-12664)*
R I R Communications Systems 718 706-9957
20 Nuvern Ave Mount Vernon (10550) *(G-8437)*
R J Liebe Athletic Company 585 237-6111
200 Main St N Perry (14530) *(G-12970)*
R J Reynolds Tobacco Company 716 871-1553
275 Cooper Ave Ste 116 Tonawanda (14150) *(G-15572)*
R J S Direct Marketing Inc 631 667-5768
561 Acorn St Ste E Deer Park (11729) *(G-4033)*
R J Valente Gravel Inc (PA) 518 432-4470
1 Madison St Troy (12180) *(G-15618)*
R J Valente Gravel Inc 518 279-1001
3349 Rte 2 Cropseyville (12052) *(G-3909)*
R J Valente Gravel Inc 518 432-4470
315 Partition St Ext Rensselaer (12144) *(G-13476)*
R K B Opto-Electronics Inc (PA) 315 455-6636
6677 Moore Rd Syracuse (13211) *(G-15400)*
R Klein Jewelry Co Inc 516 482-3260
39 Brockmeyer Dr Massapequa (11758) *(G-7884)*
R L C Electronics Inc 914 241-1334
83 Radio Circle Dr Mount Kisco (10549) *(G-8356)*
R M F Health Management L L C 718 854-5400
3361 Park Ave Wantagh (11793) *(G-15926)*

A L P H A B E T I C

R M Reynolds 315 789-7365
504 Exchange St Geneva (14456) *(G-5331)*
R P Fedder Corp (PA) 585 288-1600
740 Driving Park Ave B Rochester (14613) *(G-14066)*
R P M, Deer Park *Also called Rinaldi Precision Machine (G-4036)*
R P M Industries Inc 315 255-1105
26 Aurelius Ave Auburn (13021) *(G-497)*
R P M Machine Co 585 671-3744
755 Gravel Rd Webster (14580) *(G-16094)*
R P O, West Henrietta *Also called Rochester Precision Optics LLC (G-16249)*
R R Donnelley & Sons Company 716 763-2613
112 Winchester Rd Lakewood (14750) *(G-6996)*
R R Donnelley & Sons Company 716 773-0647
300 Lang Blvd Grand Island (14072) *(G-5510)*
R R Donnelley & Sons Company 518 438-9722
4 Executive Park Dr Ste 2 Albany (12203) *(G-121)*
R R Donnelley & Sons Company 646 755-8125
250 W 26th St Rm 402 New York (10001) *(G-11312)*
R S T Cable and Tape Inc 631 981-0096
2130 Pond Rd Ste B Ronkonkoma (11779) *(G-14404)*
R Schleider Contracting Corp 631 269-4249
135 Old Northport Rd Kings Park (11754) *(G-6886)*
R Steiner Technologies Inc 585 425-5912
180 Perinton Pkwy Fairport (14450) *(G-4655)*
R T C A, Elmsford *Also called Radon Testing Corp of America (G-4559)*
R T F Manufacturing, Hudson *Also called Atmost Refrigeration Co Inc (G-6342)*
R V Dow Enterprises Inc 585 454-5862
466 Central Ave Rochester (14605) *(G-14067)*
R V H Estates Inc 914 664-9888
138 Mount Vernon Ave Mount Vernon (10550) *(G-8438)*
R W Publications Div of Wtrhs (PA) 716 714-5620
6091 Seneca St Bldg C Elma (14059) *(G-4456)*
R W Publications Div of Wtrhs 716 714-5620
6091 Seneca St Bldg C Elma (14059) *(G-4457)*
R&A Prods, Buffalo *Also called R & A Industrial Products (G-3029)*
R&S Machine, Plattsburgh *Also called R & S Machine Center Inc (G-13151)*
R&S Steel LLC 315 281-0123
412 Canal St Rome (13440) *(G-14268)*
R-Co Products Corporation 800 854-7657
1855 Big Tree Rd Lakewood (14750) *(G-6997)*
R-Pac International Corp (PA) 212 465-1818
132 W 36th St Fl 7 New York (10018) *(G-11313)*
R-S Restaurant Eqp Mfg Corp (PA) 212 925-0335
272 Bowery New York (10012) *(G-11314)*
R-Tronics, Rome *Also called J Davis Manufacturing Co Inc (G-14254)*
RA Newhouse Inc (PA) 516 248-6670
110 Liberty Ave Mineola (11501) *(G-8244)*
Racing Industries Inc 631 905-0100
901 Scott Ave Calverton (11933) *(G-3169)*
Radax Industries Inc 585 265-2055
700 Basket Rd Ste A Webster (14580) *(G-16095)*
Radiancy Inc (HQ) 845 398-1647
40 Ramland Rd S Ste 200 Orangeburg (10962) *(G-12690)*
Radiant Pro Ltd 516 763-5678
245 Merrick Rd Oceanside (11572) *(G-12552)*
Radiation Shielding Systems 888 631-2278
415 Spook Rock Rd Suffern (10901) *(G-15196)*
Radicle Farm Company, New York *Also called Radicle Farm LLC (G-11315)*
Radicle Farm LLC 315 226-3294
394 Broadway Fl 5 New York (10013) *(G-11315)*
Radiology Film Reading Svcs, Long Island City *Also called P C Rfrs Radiology (G-7544)*
Radloop, Poughkeepsie *Also called Hvr Mso LLC (G-13346)*
Radnor-Wallace (PA) 516 767-2131
921 Port Washington Blvd # 1 Port Washington (11050) *(G-13300)*
Radon Testing Corp of America (PA) 914 345-3380
2 Hayes St Elmsford (10523) *(G-4559)*
Raff Enterprises 518 218-7883
12 Petra Ln Ste 6 Albany (12205) *(G-122)*
Rag & Bone Industries LLC (PA) 212 278-8214
425 W 13th St Fl 3 New York (10014) *(G-11316)*
Rago Foundations LLC (PA) 718 728-8436
1815 27th Ave Astoria (11102) *(G-441)*
Ragozin Data 212 674-3123
4402 11th St Ste 613 Long Island City (11101) *(G-7570)*
Rags Knitwear Ltd 718 782-8417
850 Metropolitan Ave Brooklyn (11211) *(G-2378)*
Raharney Capital LLC 212 220-9084
325 Gold St Fl 502 Brooklyn (11201) *(G-2379)*
Railex Wine Services LLC (PA) 631 369-7000
889 Harrison Ave Riverhead (11901) *(G-13581)*
Railings By New Star Brass 516 358-1153
26 Cobeck Ct Brooklyn (11223) *(G-2380)*
Railworks Corporation 904 296-5055
83 Central Ave Farmingdale (11735) *(G-4865)*
Railworks Transit Systems Inc (HQ) 212 502-7900
5 Penn Plz New York (10001) *(G-11317)*
Rain Catchers Seamless Gutters 516 520-1956
39 Park Ln Bethpage (11714) *(G-852)*
Rainbeau Ridge Farm 914 234-2197
49 Davids Way Bedford Hills (10507) *(G-779)*
Rainbow Custom Counter Tops, Staten Island *Also called Joseph Fedele (G-15097)*

Rainbow Leather Inc 718 939-8762
1415 112th St College Point (11356) *(G-3663)*
Rainbow Lettering 607 732-5751
1329 College Ave Elmira (14901) *(G-4501)*
Rainbow Plastics Inc 718 218-7288
371 Vandervoort Ave Brooklyn (11211) *(G-2381)*
Rainbow Poly Bag Co Inc 718 386-3500
179 Morgan Ave Brooklyn (11237) *(G-2382)*
Rainbow Powder Coating Corp 631 586-4019
86 E Industry Ct Deer Park (11729) *(G-4034)*
Rainforest Apothecary, Long Island City *Also called Anima Mundi Herbals LLC (G-7379)*
Rainforest Apparel LLC 212 840-0880
1385 Broadway Fl 24 New York (10018) *(G-11318)*
Rainforest Inc 212 575-7620
54 W 40th St New York (10018) *(G-11319)*
Raith America Inc 518 874-3000
300 Jordan Rd Troy (12180) *(G-15619)*
Rajbhog Foods Inc 718 358-5105
4123 Murray St Flushing (11355) *(G-5042)*
RAK Finishing Corp 718 416-4242
15934 83rd St Howard Beach (11414) *(G-6331)*
Raleigh and Drake Pbc 212 625-8212
110 E 25th St Fl 3 New York (10010) *(G-11320)*
Raloid Tool Co Inc 518 664-4261
Hc 146 Mechanicville (12118) *(G-7933)*
Ralph Lauren Corporation (PA) 212 318-7000
650 Madison Ave Fl C1 New York (10022) *(G-11321)*
Ralph Martinelli 914 345-3055
100 Clearbrook Rd Ste 170 Elmsford (10523) *(G-4560)*
Ralph Payne 718 222-4200
475 Van Buren St Ste 11c Brooklyn (11221) *(G-2383)*
Ralph's Ices, Staten Island *Also called JMS Ices Inc (G-15095)*
Ralphs Famous Italian Ices 718 605-5052
4212c Hylan Blvd Staten Island (10308) *(G-15123)*
Ralphs Ices of Levittown 516 520-0618
3831 Carrel Blvd Oceanside (11572) *(G-12553)*
Ram Fabricating LLC 315 437-6654
412 Wavel St Syracuse (13206) *(G-15401)*
Ram Machining LLC 585 426-1007
1645 Lyell Ave Ste 158 Rochester (14606) *(G-14068)*
Ram Precision Tool Inc 716 759-8722
139 Gunnville Rd Lancaster (14086) *(G-7043)*
Ram Transformer Technologies 914 632-3988
11 Beechwood Ave New Rochelle (10801) *(G-8624)*
Rambachs International Bakery 518 563-1721
65 S Peru St Plattsburgh (12901) *(G-13152)*
Ramco Arts, Sodus *Also called Nykon Inc (G-14914)*
Ramholtz Publishing Inc 718 761-4800
1200 South Ave Ste 202 Staten Island (10314) *(G-15124)*
Ramick Welding, Farmingdale *Also called W R P Welding Ltd (G-4904)*
Ramler International Ltd 516 353-3106
485 Underhill Blvd # 100 Syosset (11791) *(G-15229)*
Ramsbury Property Us Inc (HQ) 212 223-6250
601 5th Ave Fl 4 New York (10017) *(G-11322)*
Ramsey Electronics, Victor *Also called Avcom of Virginia Inc (G-15830)*
Ramsey Electronics LLC 585 924-4560
590 Fishers Station Dr Victor (14564) *(G-15863)*
Ramsey Solutions LLC 888 329-1055
228 Park Ave S Ste 29075 New York (10003) *(G-11323)*
Ramy Brook LLC 212 744-2789
231 W 39th St Rm 720 New York (10018) *(G-11324)*
Ran Mar Enterprises Ltd 631 666-4754
143 Anchor Ln Bay Shore (11706) *(G-713)*
Rand & Paseka Mfg Co Inc 516 867-1500
10 Hanse Ave Freeport (11520) *(G-5178)*
Rand Machine Products, Inc. 716 665-5217
2072 Allen Street Ext Falconer (14733) *(G-4688)*
Rand Mfg, Schenectady *Also called Rand Products Manufacturing Co (G-14706)*
Rand Products Manufacturing Co 518 374-9871
1602 Van Vranken Ave Schenectady (12308) *(G-14706)*
Randa Accessories Lea Gds LLC 212 354-5100
417 5th Ave Fl 11 New York (10016) *(G-11325)*
Randall Loeffler Inc 212 226-8787
588 Broadway Rm 1203 New York (10012) *(G-11326)*
Randob Labs Ltd 845 534-2197
45 Quaker Ave Ste 207 Cornwall (12518) *(G-3837)*
Randolph Dimension Corporation 716 358-6901
216 Main St Ste 216 Randolph (14772) *(G-13449)*
Randy Sixberry 315 265-6211
6 Main St Ste 101 Potsdam (13676) *(G-13322)*
Range Repair Warehouse 585 235-0980
421 Penbrooke Dr Ste 2 Penfield (14526) *(G-12943)*
Range Rsrces - Appalachia LLC 716 753-3385
100 E Chautauqua St Mayville (14757) *(G-7923)*
Ranger Design Us Inc 800 565-5321
6377 Dean Pkwy Ontario (14519) *(G-12662)*
Ranney Precision 716 731-6418
6421 Wendt Dr Niagara Falls (14304) *(G-12328)*
Ranney Precision Machining, Niagara Falls *Also called Ranney Precision (G-12328)*
Rap Genius, Brooklyn *Also called Genius Media Group Inc (G-1922)*
Rapa Independent North America 518 561-0513
124 Connecticut Rd Plattsburgh (12903) *(G-13153)*

Raphael, Peconic *Also called J Petrocelli Wine Cellars LLC* ***(G-12915)***
Rapid Fan & Blower Inc 718 786-2060
2314 39th Ave Long Island City (11101) ***(G-7571)***
Rapid Intellect Group Inc 518 929-3210
77b Church St Chatham (12037) ***(G-3429)***
Rapid Precision Machining Inc 585 467-0780
50 Lafayette Rd Rochester (14609) ***(G-14069)***
Rapid Print and Marketing Inc 585 924-1520
8 High St Victor (14564) ***(G-15864)***
Rapid Rays Printing & Copying 716 852-0550
300 Broadway St Buffalo (14204) ***(G-3031)***
Rapid Removal LLC 716 665-4663
1599 Route 394 Falconer (14733) ***(G-4689)***
Rapid Reproductions LLC 607 843-2221
4511 State Hwy 12 Oxford (13830) ***(G-12808)***
Rapid Service Engraving Co 716 896-4555
1593 Genesee St Buffalo (14211) ***(G-3032)***
Rapid-Lite Fixture Corporation 347 599-2600
249 Huron St Brooklyn (11222) ***(G-2384)***
Rapistak Corporation 716 822-2804
2025 Electric Ave Blasdell (14219) ***(G-927)***
Rapp Signs Inc 607 656-8167
3979 State Route 206 Greene (13778) ***(G-5616)***
Rare Editions, New York *Also called Star Childrens Dress Co Inc* ***(G-11695)***
Rare Form Brewing Company 518 313-9256
90 Congress St Troy (12180) ***(G-15620)***
Rasco Graphics Inc 212 206-0447
519 8th Ave Fl 18 New York (10018) ***(G-11327)***
Rasp Incorporated 518 747-8020
8 Dukes Way Gansevoort (12831) ***(G-5245)***
Ratan Ronkonkoma 631 588-6800
3055 Veterans Mem Hwy Ronkonkoma (11779) ***(G-14405)***
Rational Enterprises, Albany *Also called Rational Retention LLC* ***(G-123)***
Rational Retention LLC (PA) 518 489-3000
2 Tower Pl Ste 13 Albany (12203) ***(G-123)***
Rational Retention LLC 518 489-3000
2 Tower Pl Ste 13 Albany (12203) ***(G-124)***
Rauch Industries Inc 704 867-5333
828 S Broadway Tarrytown (10591) ***(G-15489)***
Raulli and Sons Inc (PA) 315 479-6693
213 Teall Ave Syracuse (13210) ***(G-15402)***
Raulli and Sons Inc 315 474-1370
660 Burnet Ave Syracuse (13203) ***(G-15403)***
Raulli and Sons Inc 315 479-2515
920 Canal St Syracuse (13210) ***(G-15404)***
Raulli Iron Works Inc 315 337-8070
133 Mill St Rome (13440) ***(G-14269)***
Rave Inc 716 695-1110
940 River Rd North Tonawanda (14120) ***(G-12444)***
Raven New York LLC 212 584-9690
450 W 15th St New York (10011) ***(G-11328)***
Ravioli Store Inc 718 729-9300
4344 21st St Long Island City (11101) ***(G-7572)***
Ravioli Store, The, Long Island City *Also called Pelican Bay Ltd* ***(G-7552)***
Raw Indulgence Ltd 866 498-4671
44 Executive Blvd Ste 205 Elmsford (10523) ***(G-4561)***
Raw Revolution, Elmsford *Also called Raw Indulgence Ltd* ***(G-4561)***
Rawlings Sporting Goods Co Inc 315 429-8511
52 Mckinley Ave Dolgeville (13329) ***(G-4136)***
Rawpothecary Inc 917 783-7770
630 Flushing Ave Brooklyn (11206) ***(G-2385)***
Raxon Fabrics Corp (HQ) 212 532-6816
261 5th Ave New York (10016) ***(G-11329)***
Ray Gold Shade Inc 718 377-8892
16 Wellington Ct Brooklyn (11230) ***(G-2386)***
Ray Griffiths Inc 212 689-7209
303 5th Ave Rm 1901 New York (10016) ***(G-11330)***
Ray Medica Inc 952 885-0500
505 Park Ave Ste 1400 New York (10022) ***(G-11331)***
Ray Sign Inc 518 377-1371
28 Colonial Ave Schenectady (12304) ***(G-14707)***
Ray Theta Inc 646 757-4956
31 W 34th St Fl 7 New York (10001) ***(G-11332)***
Rayana Designs Inc 718 786-2040
2520 40th Ave Long Island City (11101) ***(G-7573)***
Rayco Manufacturing Co Inc 516 431-2006
10715 180th St Jamaica (11433) ***(G-6672)***
Rayco Manufacturing Div, Jamaica *Also called Rayco Manufacturing Co Inc* ***(G-6672)***
Rayco of Schenectady Inc 518 212-5113
4 Sam Stratton Rd Amsterdam (12010) ***(G-358)***
Raydon Precision Bearing Co 516 887-2582
75 Merrick Rd Lynbrook (11563) ***(G-7671)***
Raydoor Inc 212 421-0641
134 W 29th St Rm 909 New York (10001) ***(G-11333)***
Raymond Corporation (HQ) 607 656-2311
22 S Canal St Greene (13778) ***(G-5617)***
Raymond Corporation 315 643-5000
6533 Chrysler Ln East Syracuse (13057) ***(G-4364)***
Raymond Sales Corporation (HQ) 607 656-2311
22 S Canal St Greene (13778) ***(G-5618)***
Rays Italian Bakery Inc 516 825-9170
45 Railroad Ave Valley Stream (11580) ***(G-15793)***
Rays Restaurant & Bakery Inc 718 441-7707
12325 Jamaica Ave Jamaica (11418) ***(G-6673)***
Raytech Corp Asbestos Personal 516 747-0300
190 Willis Ave Mineola (11501) ***(G-8245)***
RB Converting Inc 607 777-1325
28 Track Dr Binghamton (13904) ***(G-911)***
RB Diamond Inc 212 398-4560
22 W 48th St Ste 904 New York (10036) ***(G-11334)***
RB Woodcraft Inc 315 474-2429
1860 Erie Blvd E Ste 1 Syracuse (13210) ***(G-15405)***
RB Wyatt Mfg Co Inc 718 209-9682
2518 Ralph Ave Brooklyn (11234) ***(G-2387)***
Rbhammers Corp 845 353-5042
500 Bradley Hill Rd Blauvelt (10913) ***(G-939)***
Rbw Studio LLC 212 388-1621
67 34th St Unit 5 Brooklyn (11232) ***(G-2388)***
RC Entps Bus & Trck Inc 518 568-5753
5895 State Highway 29 Saint Johnsville (13452) ***(G-14521)***
Rce Manufacturing LLC 631 856-9005
10 Brayton Ct Commack (11725) ***(G-3699)***
RCM Design Division, New York *Also called S Rothschild & Co Inc* ***(G-11459)***
RD Intrntnl Style 212 382-2360
275 W 39th St Fl 7 New York (10018) ***(G-11335)***
Rd2 Construction & Dem LLC 718 980-1650
63 Trossach Rd Staten Island (10304) ***(G-15125)***
Rda Holding Co (PA) 914 238-1000
750 3rd Ave New York (10017) ***(G-11336)***
Rdd Pharma Inc 302 319-9970
3 Columbus Cir Fl 15 New York (10019) ***(G-11337)***
Rdi, Edgewood *Also called Iba Industrial Inc* ***(G-4403)***
Rdi Inc (PA) 914 773-1000
333 N Bedford Rd Ste 135 Mount Kisco (10549) ***(G-8357)***
Rdi Electronics, Mount Kisco *Also called Rdi Inc* ***(G-8357)***
RE 99 Cents Inc 718 639-2325
4905 Roosevelt Ave Woodside (11377) ***(G-16674)***
RE Hansen Industries Inc (PA) 631 471-2900
500 Middle Country Rd A Saint James (11780) ***(G-14514)***
Re-Al Industrial Corp 716 542-4556
5391 Crittenden Rd Akron (14001) ***(G-22)***
Read Manufacturing Company Inc 631 567-4487
330 Dante Ct Holbrook (11741) ***(G-6205)***
Reader's Digest, New York *Also called Trusted Media Brands Inc* ***(G-11907)***
Readers Dgest Yung Fmilies Inc 914 238-1000
Readers Digest Rd Pleasantville (10570) ***(G-13176)***
Readers Digest Assn Incthe 414 423-0100
16 E 34th St Fl 14 New York (10016) ***(G-11338)***
Readers Digest Sls & Svcs Inc 914 238-1000
Readers Digest Rd Pleasantville (10570) ***(G-13177)***
Ready Check Glo Inc 516 547-1849
23 Bruce Ln Ste E East Northport (11731) ***(G-4270)***
Ready Egg Farms Inc 607 674-4653
35 W State St Sherburne (13460) ***(G-14808)***
Ready To Assemble Company Inc 516 825-4397
115 S Corona Ave Valley Stream (11580) ***(G-15794)***
Real Bark Mulch LLC 518 747-3650
1380 Towpath Ln Fort Edward (12828) ***(G-5099)***
Real Co Inc 347 433-8549
616 Corporate Way Valley Cottage (10989) ***(G-15762)***
Real Deal, The, New York *Also called Korangy Publishing Inc* ***(G-10470)***
Real Design Inc 315 429-3071
187 S Main St Dolgeville (13329) ***(G-4137)***
Real Est Book of Long Island 516 364-5000
575 Underhill Blvd # 110 Syosset (11791) ***(G-15230)***
Real Estate Media Inc 212 929-6976
120 Broadway Fl 5 New York (10271) ***(G-11339)***
Real Wood Tiles, Buffalo *Also called Fibron Products Inc* ***(G-2826)***
Reality Ai, New York *Also called Reality Analytics Inc* ***(G-11340)***
Reality Analytics Inc (PA) 347 363-2200
157 Columbus Ave New York (10023) ***(G-11340)***
Realtimetraderscom 716 632-6600
1325 N Forest Rd Ste 240 Buffalo (14221) ***(G-3033)***
Rear View Safety Inc 855 815-3842
1797 Atlantic Ave Brooklyn (11233) ***(G-2389)***
Reason Software Company Inc 646 664-1038
228 Park Ave S Unit 74122 New York (10003) ***(G-11341)***
REB Lybss Inc 845 238-5633
44 Virginia Ave Monroe (10950) ***(G-8280)***
Recommunity, Beacon *Also called Fcr LLC* ***(G-758)***
Recon Construction Corp 718 939-1305
1108 Shore Rd Little Neck (11363) ***(G-7219)***
Record 518 270-1200
20 Lake Ave Saratoga Springs (12866) ***(G-14595)***
Record Advertiser 716 693-1000
435 River Rd North Tonawanda (14120) ***(G-12445)***
Record Review LLC 914 244-0533
16 The Pkwy Fl 3 Katonah (10536) ***(G-6846)***
Recorded Anthlogy of Amrcn Mus 212 290-1695
20 Jay St Ste 1001 Brooklyn (11201) ***(G-2390)***
Recorder, The, Amsterdam *Also called Tri-Village Publishers Inc* ***(G-361)***
Recycled Brooklyn Group LLC 917 902-0662
236 Van Brunt St Brooklyn (11231) ***(G-2391)***
Red Line Networx Screen Prtg, Brooklyn *Also called Body Builders Inc* ***(G-1627)***

Red Newt Cellars Inc
ALPHABETIC SECTION

Red Newt Cellars Inc 607 546-4100
3675 Tichenor Rd Hector (14841) *(G-6001)*
Red Oak Software Inc 585 454-3170
3349 Monroe Ave Ste 175 Rochester (14618) *(G-14070)*
Red Onyx Industrial Pdts LLC 516 459-6035
23 Green St Ste 310 Huntington (11743) *(G-6409)*
Red Tail Moulding & Mllwk LLC 516 852-4613
23 Frowein Rd Ste 1 Center Moriches (11934) *(G-3340)*
Red Tail Ridge Inc 315 536-4580
846 State Route 14 Penn Yan (14527) *(G-12963)*
Red Tail Ridge Winery, Penn Yan *Also called Red Tail Ridge Inc (G-12963)*
Red White & Blue Entps Corp 718 565-8080
3443 56th St Woodside (11377) *(G-16675)*
Redbook Magazine 212 649-3331
224 W 57th St Lbby Fl22 New York (10019) *(G-11342)*
Redcom Laboratories Inc 585 924-6567
1 Redcom Ctr Victor (14564) *(G-15865)*
Reddi Car Corp 631 589-3141
174 Greeley Ave Sayville (11782) *(G-14634)*
Redding Reloading Equipment, Cortland *Also called Redding-Hunter Inc (G-3892)*
Redding-Hunter Inc 607 753-3331
1089 Starr Rd Cortland (13045) *(G-3892)*
Redi Bag USA, Garden City Park *Also called New York Packaging II LLC (G-5286)*
Redi Records Payroll 718 854-6990
1225 36th St Brooklyn (11218) *(G-2392)*
Redi-Bag USA, New Hyde Park *Also called New York Packaging Corp (G-8552)*
Redken 5th Avenue NYC LLC 212 818-1500
575 5th Ave Fl 23 New York (10017) *(G-11343)*
Redken 5th Avenue Nyc LLC 212 984-5113
565 5th Ave New York (10017) *(G-11344)*
Redland Foods Corp 716 288-9061
40 Sonwil Dr Cheektowaga (14225) *(G-3457)*
Redspring Communications Inc 518 587-0547
125 High Rock Ave Saratoga Springs (12866) *(G-14596)*
Reebok International Ltd 718 370-0471
2655 Richmond Ave Staten Island (10314) *(G-15126)*
Reed Business Information, New York *Also called Relx Inc (G-11355)*
Reed Systems Ltd 845 647-3660
17 Edwards Pl Ellenville (12428) *(G-4442)*
Reefer Tek Llc 347 590-1067
885a E 149th St Fl 2 Bronx (10455) *(G-1371)*
Reelcology Inc 845 258-1880
39 Transport Ln Pine Island (10969) *(G-13002)*
Reelex Packaging Solutions Inc 845 878-7878
39 Jon Barrett Rd Patterson (12563) *(G-12884)*
Reenergy Black River, Fort Drum *Also called Black River Generations LLC (G-5091)*
Reenergy Black River LLC 315 773-2314
4515 Ephrtes River Vly Rd Fort Drum (13602) *(G-5092)*
Reentry Games Inc 646 421-0080
215 E 5th St New York (10003) *(G-11345)*
Reese Manufacturing Inc 631 842-3780
16 Reith St Copiague (11726) *(G-3777)*
Refill Services LLC 607 369-5864
16 Winkler Rd Sidney (13838) *(G-14854)*
Refined Sugars Inc 914 963-2400
1 Federal St Yonkers (10705) *(G-16795)*
REFINEDKIND PET PRODUCTS, Irvington *Also called Feinkind Inc (G-6504)*
Refinery 29 Inc (PA) 212 966-3112
225 Broadway Fl 23 New York (10007) *(G-11346)*
Reflex Offset Inc 516 746-4142
305 Suburban Ave Deer Park (11729) *(G-4035)*
Reflexite Precision Tech Ctr, Henrietta *Also called Orafol Americas Inc (G-6036)*
Regal Commodities, Purchase *Also called Regal Trading Inc (G-13400)*
Regal Emblem Co Inc 212 925-8833
250 W Broadway Fl 2 New York (10013) *(G-11347)*
Regal Jewelry Inc 212 382-1695
39 W 32nd St Rm 1004 New York (10001) *(G-11348)*
Regal Screen Printing Intl 845 356-8181
42 Grove St Spring Valley (10977) *(G-15005)*
Regal Tip, Niagara Falls *Also called J D Calato Manufacturing Co (G-12300)*
Regal Trading Inc 914 694-6100
2975 Westchester Ave # 210 Purchase (10577) *(G-13400)*
Regal Windows & Doors LLC 201 934-0100
254 Old Nyack Tpke Spring Valley (10977) *(G-15006)*
Regan Arts LLC 646 488-6610
65 Bleecker St Fl 8 New York (10012) *(G-11349)*
Rege Inc 845 565-7772
110 Corporate Dr New Windsor (12553) *(G-8657)*
Regence Picture Frames Inc 718 779-0888
12 Cherry Ln Lynbrook (11563) *(G-7672)*
Regeneron Pharmaceuticals Inc (PA) 914 847-7000
777 Old Saw Mill River Rd # 10 Tarrytown (10591) *(G-15490)*
Regeneron Pharmaceuticals Inc 518 488-6000
81 Columbia Tpke Rensselaer (12144) *(G-13477)*
Regenlab USA LLC 800 220-9082
575 Madison Ave Ste 1006 New York (10022) *(G-11350)*
Regenron Hlthcare Slutions Inc 914 847-7000
745 Old Saw Mill River Rd Tarrytown (10591) *(G-15491)*
Regina Press, Bohemia *Also called Malhame Publs & Importers Inc (G-1055)*
Regional MGT & Consulting Inc 718 599-3718
79 Bridgewater St Brooklyn (11222) *(G-2393)*
Register Graphics Inc 716 358-2921
220 Main St Randolph (14772) *(G-13450)*
Rehab Tech, Syracuse *Also called Rehablitation Tech of Syracuse (G-15406)*
Rehabilitation International 212 420-1500
15350 89th Ave Apt 1101 Jamaica (11432) *(G-6674)*
Rehablitation Tech of Syracuse 315 426-9920
1101 Erie Blvd E Ste 209 Syracuse (13210) *(G-15406)*
Reich Paper, Brooklyn *Also called Daniel O Reich Incorporated (G-1756)*
Reichert Inc 716 686-4500
3362 Walden Ave Depew (14043) *(G-4104)*
Reichert Technologies, Depew *Also called Reichert Inc (G-4104)*
Reilly Windows & Doors, Calverton *Also called Pella Corporation (G-3168)*
Reimann & Georger Corporation 716 895-1156
1849 Harlem Rd Buffalo (14212) *(G-3034)*
Reinhold Brothers Inc 212 867-8310
799 Park Ave New York (10021) *(G-11351)*
Reino Manufacturing Co Inc 914 636-8990
34 Circuit Rd New Rochelle (10805) *(G-8625)*
Reis D Furniture Mfg 516 248-5676
327 Sagamore Ave Ste 2 Mineola (11501) *(G-8246)*
Reisman Bros Bakery Inc 718 331-1975
110 Avenue O Brooklyn (11204) *(G-2394)*
Reismans Bros. Bakery, Brooklyn *Also called Reisman Bros Bakery Inc (G-2394)*
Relavis Corporation 212 995-2900
40 Wall St Ste 3300 New York (10005) *(G-11352)*
Release Coatings New York Inc 585 593-2335
125 S Brooklyn Ave Wellsville (14895) *(G-16120)*
Reliable Autmtc Sprnklr Co Inc (PA) 800 431-1588
103 Fairview Pk Dr Ste 1 Elmsford (10523) *(G-4562)*
Reliable Brothers Inc 518 273-6732
185 Cohoes Ave Green Island (12183) *(G-5611)*
Reliable Elec Mt Vernon Inc 914 668-4440
519 S 5th Ave Mount Vernon (10550) *(G-8439)*
Reliable Press II Inc 718 840-5812
73 Sealey Ave Hempstead (11550) *(G-6025)*
Reliable Welding & Fabrication 631 758-2637
214 W Main St Patchogue (11772) *(G-12876)*
Reliance Fluid Tech LLC 716 332-0988
3943 Buffalo Ave Niagara Falls (14303) *(G-12329)*
Reliance Gayco, Kingston *Also called Universal Metal Fabricators (G-6927)*
Reliance Machining Inc 718 784-0314
4335 Vernon Blvd Long Island City (11101) *(G-7574)*
Reliance Mica Co Inc 718 788-0282
336 Beach 149th St Rockaway Park (11694) *(G-14229)*
Reliant Security 917 338-2200
450 Fashion Ave Ste 503 New York (10123) *(G-11353)*
Relmada Therapeutics Inc 646 677-3853
750 3rd Ave Fl 9 New York (10017) *(G-11354)*
Relx Inc (HQ) 212 309-8100
230 Park Ave Ste 700 New York (10169) *(G-11355)*
Relx Inc 212 463-6644
249 W 17th St New York (10011) *(G-11356)*
Relx Inc 212 633-3900
655 6th Ave New York (10010) *(G-11357)*
REM Printing Inc 518 438-7338
55 Railroad Ave Albany (12205) *(G-125)*
Rem-Tronics Inc 716 934-2697
659 Brigham Rd Dunkirk (14048) *(G-4177)*
Remains Lighting, Brooklyn *Also called Aesthonics Inc (G-1492)*
Remains Lighting 212 675-8051
130 W 28th St Frnt 1 New York (10001) *(G-11358)*
Remarkable Liquids LLC 518 861-5351
6032 Depot Rd Altamont (12009) *(G-200)*
Remarkety Inc (PA) 800 570-7564
81 Prospect St Brooklyn (11201) *(G-2395)*
Rembar Company LLC 914 693-2620
67 Main St Dobbs Ferry (10522) *(G-4130)*
Remedies Surgical Supplies 718 599-5301
331 Rutledge St Ste 204 Brooklyn (11211) *(G-2396)*
Remedy Intelligent Staffing, New York *Also called Medizine Operating LLC (G-10761)*
Remee Products Corp (PA) 845 651-4431
1751 State Route 17a Florida (10921) *(G-4972)*
Remfo, Florida *Also called Remee Products Corp (G-4972)*
Remington Arms Company LLC 315 895-3482
14 Hoefler Ave Ilion (13357) *(G-6478)*
Remodeling News, Bedford *Also called JSD Communications Inc (G-769)*
Remsen Fuel Inc 718 984-9551
4668 Amboy Rd Staten Island (10312) *(G-15127)*
Remsen Graphics Corp 718 643-7500
52 Court St 2 Brooklyn (11201) *(G-2397)*
Ren Tool & Manufacturing Co 518 377-2123
1801 Chrisler Ave Schenectady (12303) *(G-14708)*
Renaissance Bijou Ltd 212 869-1969
20 W 47th St Ste 18 New York (10036) *(G-11359)*
Renaissance Global, New York *Also called Renaissnce Crpt Tapestries Inc (G-11360)*
Renaissance Import, Lockport *Also called Candlelight Cabinetry Inc (G-7289)*
Renaissnce Crpt Tapestries Inc 212 696-0080
200 Lexington Ave Rm 1006 New York (10016) *(G-11360)*
Renaldos Sales & Service Ctr 716 337-3760
1770 Milestrip Rd North Collins (14111) *(G-12388)*
Renanssance The Book, Port Chester *Also called Albumx Corp (G-13192)*

Renco Group Inc (PA) 212 541-6000
1 Rockefeller Plz Fl 29 New York (10020) ***(G-11361)***
Renco Group of Companies, Inc., New York *Also called Renco Group Inc* ***(G-11361)***
Renco Manufacturing Inc 718 392-8877
1040 45th Ave Fl 2 Long Island City (11101) ***(G-7575)***
Rene Portier Inc 718 853-7896
3611 14th Ave Ste 6 Brooklyn (11218) ***(G-2398)***
Renegade Nation Ltd 212 868-9000
434 Av Of The Amercs Fl 6 New York (10011) ***(G-11362)***
Renegade Nation Online LLC 212 868-9000
434 Ave Of The Americas # 6 New York (10011) ***(G-11363)***
Renewable Energy Inc 718 690-2691
6 Cornell Ln Little Neck (11363) ***(G-7220)***
Rennen International, Mineola *Also called Extreme Auto Accessories Corp* ***(G-8221)***
Renold Inc 716 326-3121
100 Bourne St Westfield (14787) ***(G-16396)***
Renovatio Med & Surgical Sups, Buffalo *Also called Yr Blanc & Co LLC* ***(G-3137)***
Rentschler Biotechnologie GMBH 631 656-7137
400 Oser Ave Ste 1650 Hauppauge (11788) ***(G-5928)***
REO Welding Inc 518 238-1022
5 New Cortland St Cohoes (12047) ***(G-3618)***
Repapers Corporation (PA) 305 691-1635
268 N Broadway Unit 9 Hicksville (11801) ***(G-6128)***
Repellem Consumer Pdts Corp 631 273-3992
1626 Locust Ave Ste 6 Bohemia (11716) ***(G-1082)***
Repertoire International De Ll 212 817-1990
365 5th Ave Fl 3 New York (10016) ***(G-11364)***
Repro Med Systems Inc 845 469-2042
24 Carpenter Rd Ste 1 Chester (10918) ***(G-3480)***
Repsol Oil & Gas Usa LLC 607 562-4000
337 Daniel Zenker Dr Horseheads (14845) ***(G-6325)***
Republic Clothing Corporation 212 719-3000
1411 Broadway Fl 37 New York (10018) ***(G-11365)***
Republic Clothing Group, New York *Also called Republic Clothing Corporation* ***(G-11365)***
Republic Clothing Group Inc 212 719-3000
1411 Broadway Fl 37 New York (10018) ***(G-11366)***
Republic Construction Co Inc 914 235-3654
305 North Ave New Rochelle (10801) ***(G-8626)***
Republic Steel Inc 716 827-2800
3049 Lake Shore Rd Blasdell (14219) ***(G-928)***
Republican Registrar Inc 315 497-1551
6 Central St Moravia (13118) ***(G-8334)***
Request Inc 518 899-1254
14 Corporate Dr Ste 6 Halfmoon (12065) ***(G-5667)***
Request Jeans, New York *Also called US Design Group Ltd* ***(G-11974)***
Request Multimedia, Halfmoon *Also called Request Inc* ***(G-5667)***
Request Serious Play LLC 518 899-1254
14 Corporate Dr Halfmoon (12065) ***(G-5668)***
Rescuestuff Inc 718 318-7570
962 Washington St Peekskill (10566) ***(G-12923)***
Research Centre of Kabbalah 718 805-0380
8384 115th St Richmond Hill (11418) ***(G-13509)***
Research Frontiers Inc (PA) 516 364-1902
240 Crossways Park Dr Woodbury (11797) ***(G-16630)***
Reserve Confections Chocolate, Spring Valley *Also called Reserve Confections Inc* ***(G-15007)***
Reserve Confections Inc 845 371-7744
3 Perlman Dr Ste 105 Spring Valley (10977) ***(G-15007)***
Reserve Gas Company, Alden *Also called Alden Aurora Gas Company Inc* ***(G-167)***
Reserve Gas Company Inc 716 937-9484
13441 Railroad St Alden (14004) ***(G-175)***
Reservoir Media Management Inc (PA) 212 675-0541
225 Varick St Fl 6 New York (10014) ***(G-11367)***
Residential Fences Corp 631 205-9758
1760 Middle Country Rd Ridge (11961) ***(G-13524)***
Resonance Technologies Inc 631 237-4901
109 Comac St Ronkonkoma (11779) ***(G-14406)***
Resonant Legal Media LLC 212 687-7100
1040 Av Of The Amrcs 18 New York (10018) ***(G-11368)***
Resonant Legal Media LLC (PA) 800 781-3591
1 Penn Plz Ste 1514 New York (10119) ***(G-11369)***
Resource Capital Funds LP 631 692-9111
2 Jericho Plz Ste 103 Jericho (11753) ***(G-6799)***
Resource PTRlm&ntrochmcl Intl 212 537-3856
3 Columbus Cir Fl 15 New York (10019) ***(G-11370)***
Response Care Inc 585 671-4144
38 Commercial St Webster (14580) ***(G-16096)***
Responselink Inc 518 424-7776
31 Dussault Dr Latham (12110) ***(G-7092)***
Responselink of Albany, Latham *Also called Responselink Inc* ***(G-7092)***
Restaurant 570 8th Avenue LLC 646 722-8191
213 W 40th St Fl 3 New York (10018) ***(G-11371)***
Restonic, Buffalo *Also called Royal Bedding Co Buffalo Inc* ***(G-3049)***
Restorsea LLC 212 828-8878
641 Lexington Ave Fl 27 New York (10022) ***(G-11372)***
Retailer, Lockport *Also called Metro Group Inc* ***(G-7317)***
Retailer, The, Port Washington *Also called Music & Sound Retailer Inc* ***(G-13289)***
Retia Medical LLC (PA) 914 594-1986
7 Dana Rd Ste 121 Valhalla (10595) ***(G-15746)***
Retrophin LLC 646 564-3680
777 3rd Ave Fl 22 New York (10017) ***(G-11373)***

Reuse Action Incorporated 716 949-0900
279 Northampton St Buffalo (14208) ***(G-3035)***
Reuter Pallet Pkg Sys Inc 845 457-9937
272 Neelytown Rd Montgomery (12549) ***(G-8317)***
Reuters Loan Pricing Corp 212 833-9200
3 Times Sq Fl 3 # 3 New York (10036) ***(G-11374)***
Revival Industries Inc 315 868-1085
126 Old Forge Rd Ilion (13357) ***(G-6479)***
Revival Sash & Door LLC (PA) 973 500-4242
135 E 57th St Bldg 15125 New York (10022) ***(G-11375)***
Revivn Public Benefit Corp 347 762-8193
63 Flushing Ave Unit 231 Brooklyn (11205) ***(G-2399)***
Revlon Inc (PA) 212 527-4000
1 New York Plz New York (10004) ***(G-11376)***
Revlon Consumer Products Corp (HQ) 212 527-4000
1 New York Plz New York (10004) ***(G-11377)***
Revman International Inc (HQ) 212 894-3100
350 5th Ave 70th New York (10118) ***(G-11378)***
Revolutionwear Inc 617 669-9191
1745 Broadway Fl 17 New York (10019) ***(G-11379)***
Rexford Services Inc 716 366-6671
4849 W Lake Rd Dunkirk (14048) ***(G-4178)***
Reynolds Book Bindery LLC 607 772-8937
37 Milford St Binghamton (13904) ***(G-912)***
Reynolds Drapery Service Inc 315 845-8632
7440 Main St Newport (13416) ***(G-12256)***
Reynolds Manufacturing Inc 607 562-8936
3298 State Rte 352 Big Flats (14814) ***(G-856)***
Reynolds Metals Company LLC (HQ) 212 518-5400
390 Park Ave New York (10022) ***(G-11380)***
Reynolds Packaging McHy Inc 716 358-6451
2632 S Work St Ste 24 Falconer (14733) ***(G-4690)***
Reynolds Shipyard Corporation 718 981-2800
200 Edgewater St Staten Island (10305) ***(G-15128)***
Reynolds Tech Fabricators Inc 315 437-0532
6895 Kinne St East Syracuse (13057) ***(G-4365)***
Rf Communications, Rochester *Also called Harris Corporation* ***(G-13858)***
Rf Inter Science Co, Patchogue *Also called Kevin Freeman* ***(G-12869)***
Rfb Associates Inc 518 271-0551
35 Sullivan Pkwy Fort Edward (12828) ***(G-5100)***
Rfg, New York *Also called M S Riviera Inc* ***(G-10643)***
Rfn Inc 516 764-5100
40 Drexel Dr Bay Shore (11706) ***(G-714)***
Rfp LLC 212 838-7733
228 E 45th St Fl 11 New York (10017) ***(G-11381)***
Rft, New York *Also called Rainforest Inc* ***(G-11319)***
RG, Buffalo *Also called Roberts-Gordon LLC* ***(G-3040)***
RG Apparel Group, New York *Also called Excelled Sheepskin & Lea Coat* ***(G-9750)***
RG Barry Corporation 212 244-3145
9 E 37th St Fl 11 New York (10016) ***(G-11382)***
RG Glass Creations Inc 212 675-0030
1441 Broadway Ste 28 New York (10018) ***(G-11383)***
RGH Associates Inc 631 643-1111
86 Nancy St West Babylon (11704) ***(G-16186)***
Rgm Signs Inc 718 442-0598
1234 Castleton Ave Staten Island (10310) ***(G-15129)***
Rheonix Inc (PA) 607 257-1242
10 Brown Rd Ste 103 Ithaca (14850) ***(G-6608)***
Rhett M Clark Inc 585 538-9570
3213 Lehigh St Caledonia (14423) ***(G-3157)***
Rhino Trunk & Case Inc 585 244-4553
565 Blossom Rd Ste J Rochester (14610) ***(G-14071)***
Rhoda Lee Inc 212 840-5700
77 W 55th St Apt 4k New York (10019) ***(G-11384)***
Rhosey LLC 718 382-1226
1677 Mcdonald Ave Brooklyn (11230) ***(G-2400)***
Ribble Lumber Inc 315 536-6221
249 1/2 Lake St Penn Yan (14527) ***(G-12964)***
Ribz LLC 212 764-9595
1407 Broadway Rm 1402 New York (10018) ***(G-11385)***
Ric-Lo Productions Ltd 845 469-2285
1144 Kings Hwy Chester (10918) ***(G-3481)***
Rich Brilliant Willing, Brooklyn *Also called Rbw Studio LLC* ***(G-2388)***
Rich Holdings Inc 716 878-8000
1 Robert Rich Way Buffalo (14213) ***(G-3036)***
Rich Products Corporation (PA) 716 878-8000
1 Robert Rich Way Buffalo (14213) ***(G-3037)***
Richard Anthony Corp 914 922-7141
1500 Front St Ste 12 Yorktown Heights (10598) ***(G-16822)***
Richard Anthony Custom Mllwk, Yorktown Heights *Also called Richard Anthony Corp* ***(G-16822)***
Richard Bauer Logging 585 343-4149
3936 Cookson Rd Alexander (14005) ***(G-181)***
Richard C Owen Publishers Inc 914 232-3903
243 Route 100 Somers (10589) ***(G-14922)***
Richard Engdal Baking Corp 914 777-9600
421 Waverly Ave Mamaroneck (10543) ***(G-7755)***
Richard Manno & Company Inc 631 643-2200
42 Lamar St West Babylon (11704) ***(G-16187)***
Richard Manufacturing Co Inc 718 254-0958
63 Flushing Ave Unit 327 Brooklyn (11205) ***(G-2401)***

ALPHABETIC

Richard Rothbard Inc
ALPHABETIC SECTION

Richard Rothbard Inc 845 355-2300
1866 Route 284 Slate Hill (10973) ***(G-14885)***
Richard Ruffner 631 234-4600
69 Carleton Ave Central Islip (11722) ***(G-3383)***
Richard Stacey Rs Automation, Albion *Also called Rs Automation* ***(G-162)***
Richard Stewart 518 632-5363
4495 State Rte 149 Hartford (12838) ***(G-5741)***
Richards & West Inc 585 461-4088
501 W Commercial St Ste 1 East Rochester (14445) ***(G-4291)***
Richards Logging LLC 518 359-2775
201 State Route 3 Tupper Lake (12986) ***(G-15653)***
Richards Machine Tool Co Inc 716 683-3380
36 Nichter Rd Lancaster (14086) ***(G-7044)***
Richards Screw Machine, West Babylon *Also called RGH Associates Inc* ***(G-16186)***
Richardson Brands Company (HQ) 800 839-8938
101 Erie Blvd Canajoharie (13317) ***(G-3208)***
Richardson Foods, Canajoharie *Also called Richardson Brands Company* ***(G-3208)***
Richemont North America Inc 212 355-7052
535 Madison Ave New York (10022) ***(G-11386)***
Richemont North America Inc 212 644-9500
729 Madison Ave New York (10065) ***(G-11387)***
Richer's Bakery, Flushing *Also called H H B Bakery of Little Neck* ***(G-5004)***
Richlar Custom Foam Div, East Syracuse *Also called Richlar Industries Inc* ***(G-4366)***
Richlar Industries Inc 315 463-5144
6741 Old Collamer Rd East Syracuse (13057) ***(G-4366)***
Richline Group Inc 212 643-2908
245 W 29th St Rm 900 New York (10001) ***(G-11388)***
Richline Group Inc 212 764-8454
1385 Broadway Fl 12 New York (10018) ***(G-11389)***
Richline Group Inc 914 699-0000
1385 Broadway Fl 12 New York (10018) ***(G-11390)***
Richloom Fabrics Corp (PA) 212 685-5400
261 5th Ave Fl 12 New York (10016) ***(G-11391)***
Richloom Fabrics Group Inc (PA) 212 685-5400
261 5th Ave Fl 12 New York (10016) ***(G-11392)***
Richmond Ready Mix Corp 917 731-8400
328 Park St Staten Island (10306) ***(G-15130)***
Richmond Ready Mix Corp II 917 731-8400
291 Chelsea Rd Staten Island (10314) ***(G-15131)***
Richner Communications Inc (PA) 516 569-4000
2 Endo Blvd Garden City (11530) ***(G-5278)***
Richner Communications Inc 516 569-4000
379 Central Ave Lawrence (11559) ***(G-7108)***
Richs Sttches EMB Screenprint 845 621-2175
407 Route 6 Mahopac (10541) ***(G-7711)***
Richter Charles Metal STMp&sp 845 895-2025
80 Cottage St Wallkill (12589) ***(G-15906)***
Richter Metalcraft Corporation 845 895-2025
80 Cottage St Wallkill (12589) ***(G-15907)***
Rick-Mic Industries Inc 631 563-8389
1951 Ocean Ave Ste 6 Ronkonkoma (11779) ***(G-14407)***
Rid Lom Precision Mfg 585 594-8600
50 Regency Oaks Blvd Rochester (14624) ***(G-14072)***
Ridge Cabinet & Showcase Inc 585 663-0560
1545 Mount Read Blvd # 2 Rochester (14606) ***(G-14073)***
Ridgewood Times Prtg & Pubg 718 821-7500
6071 Woodbine St Fl 1 Ridgewood (11385) ***(G-13549)***
Riefler Concrete Products LLC 716 649-3260
5690 Camp Rd Hamburg (14075) ***(G-5693)***
Rigidized Metals Corporation 716 849-4703
658 Ohio St Buffalo (14203) ***(G-3038)***
Rigidized-Metal, Buffalo *Also called Rigidized Metals Corporation* ***(G-3038)***
Rij Pharmaceutical Corporation 845 692-5799
40 Commercial Ave Middletown (10941) ***(G-8173)***
Rike Enterprises Inc 631 277-8338
46 Taft Ave Islip (11751) ***(G-6550)***
Riley Gear Corporation 716 694-0900
61 Felton St North Tonawanda (14120) ***(G-12446)***
RILM, New York *Also called Repertoire International De LI* ***(G-11364)***
Rimco Plastics Corp 607 739-3864
316 Colonial Dr Horseheads (14845) ***(G-6326)***
Rims Like New Inc 845 537-0396
507 Union School Rd Middletown (10941) ***(G-8174)***
Rina, Plattsburgh *Also called Rapa Independent North America* ***(G-13153)***
Rinaldi Precision Machine 631 242-4141
43 Crossway Dr Deer Park (11729) ***(G-4036)***
Ring Division Producto Machine, Jamestown *Alsc called Producto Corporation* ***(G-6744)***
Ringlead Inc 310 906-0545
200 Broadhollow Rd # 400 Melville (11747) ***(G-8061)***
Rings Wire Inc 212 741-9779
246 W 38th St Rm 501 New York (10018) ***(G-11393)***
Rini Tank & Truck Service 718 384-6606
327 Nassau Ave Brooklyn (11222) ***(G-2402)***
Rino, Freeport *Also called Ondrivesus Corp* ***(G-5171)***
Riot New Media Group Inc 604 700-4896
147 Prince St Ste 1 Brooklyn (11201) ***(G-2403)***
Rip Van Wafels Inc 415 529-5403
67 West St Ste 705 Brooklyn (11222) ***(G-2404)***
Ripak Aerospace Processing, West Babylon *Also called Magellan Aerospace Processing* ***(G-16173)***
Ripi Precision Co Inc (PA) 631 694-2453
92 Toledo St Farmingdale (11735) ***(G-4866)***
Ripley Machine & Tool Co Inc 716 736-3205
9825 E Main Rd Ripley (14775) ***(G-13563)***
Riri USA Inc 212 268-3866
350 5th Ave Ste 6700 New York (10118) ***(G-11394)***
Risa Management Corp 718 361-2606
5501 43rd St Fl 3 Maspeth (11378) ***(G-7870)***
Risa's, Maspeth *Also called Risa Management Corp* ***(G-7870)***
Rising Sons 6 Brewing Coinc 607 368-4836
196 Baker St Corning (14830) ***(G-3824)***
Rising Stars Soccer Club CNY 315 381-3096
4980 State Route 233 Westmoreland (13490) ***(G-16409)***
Rision Inc 212 987-2628
306 E 78th St Apt 1b New York (10075) ***(G-11395)***
Risk Management Magazine, New York *Also called Risk Society Management Pubg* ***(G-11396)***
Risk Society Management Pubg 212 286-9364
655 3rd Ave Fl 2 New York (10017) ***(G-11396)***
RIT Printing Corp 631 586-6220
250 N Fairway Bay Shore (11706) ***(G-715)***
Rita Medical Systems, Glens Falls *Also called Angiodynamics Inc* ***(G-5417)***
Ritchie Brothers Slate Co, Middle Granville *Also called Vermont Natural Stoneworks* ***(G-8114)***
Ritchie Corp 212 768-0083
263 W 38th St Fl 13 New York (10018) ***(G-11397)***
Ritnoa Inc 212 660-2148
24019 Jamaica Ave Fl 2 Bellerose (11426) ***(G-782)***
Rittlewood Holding Co, New York *Also called Rda Holding Co* ***(G-11336)***
Riva Jewelry Manufacturing Inc 718 361-3100
140 58th St Ste 8b Brooklyn (11220) ***(G-2405)***
River Valley Paper Company 330 631-8320
2801 Court St Syracuse (13208) ***(G-15407)***
Riverdale Press, The, Bronx *Also called Dale Press Inc* ***(G-1253)***
Riverfront Costume Design 716 693-2501
200 River Rd North Tonawanda (14120) ***(G-12447)***
Riverhawk Company LP 315 624-7171
215 Clinton Rd New Hartford (13413) ***(G-8510)***
Riverside Automation, Rochester *Also called Riverview Associates Inc* ***(G-14074)***
Riverside Iron LLC 315 535-4864
26 Water St Gouverneur (13642) ***(G-5492)***
Riverside Machinery Company (PA) 718 492-7400
140 53rd St Brooklyn (11232) ***(G-2406)***
Riverside Machinery Company 718 492-7400
132 54th St Brooklyn (11220) ***(G-2407)***
Rivertowns Enterprise, Dobbs Ferry *Also called W H White Publications Inc* ***(G-4132)***
Riverview Associates Inc 585 235-5980
1040 Jay St Rochester (14611) ***(G-14074)***
Riverview Industries Inc 845 265-5284
3012 Route 9 Ste 1 Cold Spring (10516) ***(G-3627)***
Riverwood Signs By Dandev Desi 845 229-0282
7 Maple Ln Hyde Park (12538) ***(G-6471)***
Rizzoli Intl Publications Inc (HQ) 212 387-3400
300 Park Ave S Fl 4 New York (10010) ***(G-11398)***
Rizzoli Intl Publications Inc 212 387-3572
300 Park Ave S Fl 3 New York (10010) ***(G-11399)***
Rizzoli Intl Publications Inc 212 308-2000
300 Park Ave Frnt 4 New York (10022) ***(G-11400)***
RJ Harvey Instrument Corp 845 359-3943
11 Jane St Tappan (10983) ***(G-15471)***
Rj Millworkers Inc 607 433-0525
12 Lewis St Oneonta (13820) ***(G-12645)***
RJ Precision LLC 585 768-8030
6662 Main Rd Stafford (14143) ***(G-15028)***
Rj Welding & Fabricating Inc 315 523-1288
2300 Wheat Rd Clifton Springs (14432) ***(G-3583)***
Rjd Associates, New York *Also called Robert J Deluca Associates* ***(G-11408)***
Rjm2 Ltd 212 944-1660
241 W 37th St Rm 926 New York (10018) ***(G-11401)***
Rjs Machine Works Inc 716 826-1778
1611 Electric Ave Lackawanna (14218) ***(G-6952)***
Rk Pharma Inc 646 884-3765
401 Milltown Rd Bldg Pearl River (10965) ***(G-12910)***
Rle Industries LLC 973 276-1444
1175 York Ave Apt 15e New York (10065) ***(G-11402)***
Rlp Holdings Inc 716 852-0832
1049 Military Rd Buffalo (14217) ***(G-3039)***
Rls Holdings Inc 716 418-7274
11342 Main St Clarence (14031) ***(G-3540)***
Rm Bakery LLC 718 472-3036
220 Coster St Bronx (10474) ***(G-1372)***
Rmb Embroidery Service 585 271-5560
176 Anderson Ave Ste F110 Rochester (14607) ***(G-14075)***
Rmd Holding Inc 845 628-0030
593 Route 6 Mahopac (10541) ***(G-7712)***
Rmf Print Management Group 716 683-4351
786 Terrace Blvd Ste 3 Depew (14043) ***(G-4105)***
Rmf Printing Technologies Inc 716 683-7500
50 Pearl St Lancaster (14086) ***(G-7045)***
Rmi Printing, New York *Also called Rosen Mandell & Immerman Inc* ***(G-11431)***
RMS Medical Products, Chester *Also called Repro Med Systems Inc* ***(G-3480)***

ALPHABETIC SECTION
Rochling Advent Tool & Mold LP

RMS Packaging Inc 914 205-2070
1050 Lower South St Peekskill (10566) *(G-12924)*
Rmw Filtration Products Co LLC 631 226-9412
230 Lambert Ave Copiague (11726) *(G-3778)*
Rnd Enterprises Inc 212 627-0165
446 W 33rd St New York (10001) *(G-11403)*
Road Cases USA Inc 631 563-0633
1625 Sycamore Ave Ste A Bohemia (11716) *(G-1083)*
Roadie Products Inc 631 567-8588
1121 Lincoln Ave Unit 20 Holbrook (11741) *(G-6206)*
Roadrunner Records Inc (PA) 212 274-7500
1290 Avenue Of The Americ New York (10104) *(G-11404)*
Roanwell Corporation 718 401-0288
2564 Park Ave Bronx (10451) *(G-1373)*
Roar Beverages LLC 631 683-5565
125 W Shore Rd Huntington (11743) *(G-6410)*
Roar Biomedical Inc 631 591-2749
4603 Middle Country Rd Calverton (11933) *(G-3170)*
Rob Herschenfeld Design Inc 718 456-6801
304 Boerum St Brooklyn (11206) *(G-2408)*
Rob Salamida Company Inc 607 729-4868
71 Pratt Ave Ste 1 Johnson City (13790) *(G-6821)*
Robat Inc 518 812-6244
1 Fairchild Sq Ste 114 Clifton Park (12065) *(G-3575)*
Robeco/Ascot Products Inc 516 243-1521
100 Ring Rd W Garden City (11530) *(G-5279)*
Robell Research Inc 212 755-6577
635 Madison Ave Fl 13 New York (10022) *(G-11405)*
Robert & William Inc (PA) 631 727-5780
224 Griffing Ave Riverhead (11901) *(G-13582)*
Robert Abady Dog Food Co Ltd 845 473-1900
201 Smith St Poughkeepsie (12601) *(G-13363)*
Robert Bartholomew Ltd 516 767-2970
15 Main St Port Washington (11050) *(G-13301)*
Robert Bosch LLC 315 733-3312
2118 Beechgrove Pl Utica (13501) *(G-15731)*
Robert Cohen 718 789-0996
10540 Rockaway Blvd Ste A Ozone Park (11417) *(G-12832)*
Robert Danes Danes Inc (PA) 212 226-1351
481 Greenwich St Apt 5b New York (10013) *(G-11406)*
Robert E Derecktor Inc 914 698-0962
311 E Boston Post Rd Mamaroneck (10543) *(G-7756)*
Robert Ehrlich 516 353-4617
75 Saint Marks Pl New York (10003) *(G-11407)*
Robert Greenburg (PA) 845 586-2226
Cross Rd Margaretville (12455) *(G-7799)*
Robert J Deluca Associates 845 357-3212
260 Riverside Dr Apt 8a New York (10025) *(G-11408)*
Robert J Faraone 585 232-7160
1600 N Clinton Ave Rochester (14621) *(G-14076)*
Robert King Music, New York *Also called Alphonse Lduc - Rbert King Inc (G-8809)*
Robert Lighting & Energy, New York *Also called Rle Industries LLC (G-11402)*
Robert M Brown 607 426-6250
150 Mill St Montour Falls (14865) *(G-8327)*
Robert M Vault 315 243-1447
1360 Lestina Beach Rd Bridgeport (13030) *(G-1183)*
Robert Miller Associates LLC 718 392-1640
2219 41st Ave Ste 505 Long Island City (11101) *(G-7576)*
Robert Pikcilingis 518 355-1860
2575 Western Ave Altamont (12009) *(G-201)*
Robert Racine (PA) 518 677-0224
41 N Union St Cambridge (12816) *(G-3183)*
Robert Strahan Custom Wdwkg 718 349-3570
810 Humboldt St Ste 9 Brooklyn (11222) *(G-2409)*
Robert Strahan Woodworks, Brooklyn *Also called Robert Strahan Custom Wdwkg (G-2409)*
Robert Tabatznik Assoc Inc (PA) 845 336-4555
867 Flatbush Rd Kingston (12401) *(G-6916)*
Robert Viggiani 914 423-4046
37 Vredenburgh Ave Ste B Yonkers (10704) *(G-16796)*
Robert W Butts Logging Co 518 643-2897
420 Mannix Rd Peru (12972) *(G-12972)*
Robert-Masters Corp 718 545-1030
3217 61st St Woodside (11377) *(G-16676)*
Roberts Nichols Fire Apparatus 518 431-1945
84 Island View Rd Cohoes (12047) *(G-3619)*
Roberts Office Furn Cncpts Inc 315 451-9185
7327 Henry Clay Blvd Liverpool (13088) *(G-7260)*
Roberts-Gordon LLC (HQ) 716 852-4400
1250 William St Buffalo (14206) *(G-3040)*
Robespierre Inc 212 764-8810
214 W 39th St Ph Ste 602 New York (10018) *(G-11409)*
Robespierre Inc (PA) 212 594-0012
225 W 35th St Ste 801 New York (10001) *(G-11410)*
Robin Industries Ltd 718 218-9616
56 N 3rd St Brooklyn (11249) *(G-2410)*
Robin Stanley Inc 212 871-0007
1212 Avenue Of The Americ New York (10036) *(G-11411)*
Robinson Concrete Inc (PA) 315 253-6666
3486 Franklin Street Rd Auburn (13021) *(G-498)*
Robinson Concrete Inc 315 676-4333
2735 State Route 49 West Monroe (13167) *(G-16262)*
Robinson Concrete Inc 315 492-6200
3537 Apulia Rd Jamesville (13078) *(G-6770)*
Robinson Concrete Inc 315 676-4662
7020 Corporate Park Dr Brewerton (13029) *(G-1152)*
Robinson Knife 716 685-6300
2615 Walden Ave Buffalo (14225) *(G-3041)*
Robinson Tools LLC 585 586-5432
477 Whitney Rd Penfield (14526) *(G-12944)*
Robly Digital Marketing LLC 917 238-0730
93 Leonard St Apt 6 New York (10013) *(G-11412)*
Robo Self Serve, Williamsville *Also called Schmitt Sales Inc (G-16585)*
Robocom Systems International, Farmingdale *Also called Robocom Us LLC (G-4867)*
Robocom Us LLC (HQ) 631 861-2045
1111 Broadhollow Rd # 100 Farmingdale (11735) *(G-4867)*
Roboshop Inc 315 437-6454
226 Midler Park Dr Syracuse (13206) *(G-15408)*
Robot Fruit Inc 631 423-7250
40 Radcliff Dr Huntington (11743) *(G-6411)*
Robs Cycle Supply 315 292-6878
613 Wolf St Syracuse (13208) *(G-15409)*
Robs Really Good LLC 516 671-4411
100 Roslyn Ave Sea Cliff (11579) *(G-14756)*
Roccera LLC 585 426-0887
771 Elmgrove Rd Bldg No2 Rochester (14624) *(G-14077)*
Rocco Bormioli Glass Co Inc (PA) 212 719-0606
41 Madison Ave Ste 1603 New York (10010) *(G-11413)*
Roche Tcrc Inc 800 626-3553
420 E 29th St Fl 15 Flr 15 New York (10016) *(G-11414)*
Rochester 100 Inc 585 475-0200
40 Jefferson Rd Rochester (14623) *(G-14078)*
Rochester Asphalt Materials (HQ) 585 381-7010
1150 Penfield Rd Rochester (14625) *(G-14079)*
Rochester Asphalt Materials 315 524-4619
1200 Atlantic Ave Walworth (14568) *(G-15915)*
Rochester Asphalt Materials 585 924-7360
5929 Loomis Rd Farmington (14425) *(G-4918)*
Rochester Atomated Systems Inc 585 594-3222
40 Regency Oaks Blvd Rochester (14624) *(G-14080)*
Rochester Business Journal 585 546-8303
16 W Main St Ste 341 Rochester (14614) *(G-14081)*
Rochester Catholic Press (PA) 585 529-9530
1150 Buffalo Rd Rochester (14624) *(G-14082)*
Rochester Coca Cola Bottling 607 739-5678
210 Industrial Park Rd Horseheads (14845) *(G-6327)*
Rochester Coca Cola Bottling 585 546-3900
123 Upper Falls Blvd Rochester (14605) *(G-14083)*
Rochester Colonial Mfg Corp (PA) 585 254-8191
1794 Lyell Ave Rochester (14606) *(G-14084)*
Rochester Countertop Inc (PA) 585 338-2260
3300 Monroe Ave Ste 212 Rochester (14618) *(G-14085)*
Rochester Democrat & Chronicle 585 232-7100
55 Exchange Blvd Rochester (14614) *(G-14086)*
Rochester Gear Inc 585 254-5442
213 Norman St Rochester (14613) *(G-14087)*
Rochester Golf Week, Rochester *Also called Expositor Newspapers Inc (G-13799)*
Rochester Industrial Ctrl Inc (PA) 315 524-4555
6400 Furnace Rd Ontario (14519) *(G-12663)*
Rochester Industrial Ctrl Inc 315 524-4555
6345 Furnace Rd Ontario (14519) *(G-12664)*
Rochester Insulated Glass Inc 585 289-3611
73 Merrick Cir Manchester (14504) *(G-7761)*
Rochester Lumber Company 585 924-7171
6080 Collett Rd Farmington (14425) *(G-4919)*
Rochester Magnet, East Rochester *Also called Carpentier Industries LLC (G-4281)*
Rochester Midland Corporation (PA) 585 336-2200
155 Paragon Dr Rochester (14624) *(G-14088)*
Rochester Orthopedic Labs (PA) 585 272-1060
300 Airpark Dr Ste 100 Rochester (14624) *(G-14089)*
Rochester Overnight Pltg LLC 585 328-4590
2 Cairn St Rochester (14611) *(G-14090)*
Rochester Photonics Corp 585 387-0674
115 Canal Landing Blvd Rochester (14626) *(G-14091)*
Rochester Precision Optics LLC 585 292-5450
850 John St West Henrietta (14586) *(G-16249)*
Rochester Screen Printing, Rochester *Also called Michael Todd Stevens (G-13938)*
Rochester Seal Pro LLC 585 594-3818
53 Northwind Way Rochester (14624) *(G-14092)*
Rochester Silver Works LLC 585 477-9501
100 Latona Rd Bldg 110 Rochester (14652) *(G-14093)*
Rochester Silver Works LLC 585 743-1610
240 Aster St Rochester (14615) *(G-14094)*
Rochester Stampings Inc 585 467-5241
400 Trade Ct Rochester (14624) *(G-14095)*
Rochester Steel Treating Works 585 546-3348
962 E Main St Rochester (14605) *(G-14096)*
Rochester Structural LLC 585 436-1250
961 Lyell Ave Bldg 5 Rochester (14606) *(G-14097)*
Rochester Technology Park, Rochester *Also called Tech Park Food Services LLC (G-14161)*
Rochester Tool and Mold Inc 585 464-9336
515 Lee Rd Rochester (14606) *(G-14098)*
Rochester Tube Fabricators 585 254-0290
1128 Lexington Ave 5d Rochester (14606) *(G-14099)*
Rochling Advent Tool & Mold LP 585 254-2000
999 Ridgeway Ave Rochester (14615) *(G-14100)*

ALPHABETIC

Rock Hill Bakehouse Ltd 518 743-1627
21 Saratoga Rd Gansevoort (12831) ***(G-5246)***
Rock Iroquois Products Inc 585 637-6834
5251 Sweden Walker Rd Brockport (14420) ***(G-1194)***
Rock Mountain Farms Inc 845 647-9084
11 Spring St Ellenville (12428) ***(G-4443)***
Rock Stream Vineyards 607 243-8322
162 Fir Tree Point Rd Rock Stream (14878) ***(G-14223)***
Rockaloid, Piermont *Also called Rockland Colloid Corp* ***(G-12994)***
Rockaway Stairs Ltd 718 945-0047
1011 Bay 24th St Far Rockaway (11691) ***(G-4703)***
Rocket Communications, Buffalo *Also called Gallagher Printing Inc* ***(G-2838)***
Rocket Communications Inc 716 873-2594
2507 Delaware Ave Buffalo (14216) ***(G-3042)***
Rocket Fuel Inc 212 594-8888
401 Park Ave S Fl 5 New York (10016) ***(G-11415)***
Rocket Tech Fuel Corp 516 810-8947
20 Corbin Ave Bay Shore (11706) ***(G-716)***
Rocking The Boat Inc 718 466-5799
812 Edgewater Rd Bronx (10474) ***(G-1374)***
Rockland Colloid Corp (PA) 845 359-5559
44 Franklin St Piermont (10968) ***(G-12994)***
Rockland County Times, Nanuet *Also called Citizen Publishing Corp* ***(G-8461)***
Rockland Insulated Wire Cable 845 429-3103
87 Broadway Haverstraw (10927) ***(G-5980)***
Rockland Manufacturing Co 845 358-6000
44 High St West Nyack (10994) ***(G-16281)***
Rockland Review Publishing, West Nyack *Also called Angel Media and Publishing* ***(G-16264)***
Rockmills Steel Products Corp 718 366-8300
5912 54th St Maspeth (11378) ***(G-7871)***
Rockport Pa LLC 212 482-8580
505 5th Ave Fl 26 New York (10017) ***(G-11416)***
Rockville Pro, Inwood *Also called Audiosavings Inc* ***(G-6486)***
Rockwell Automation Inc 585 487-2700
1000 Pittsford Victor Rd # 17 Pittsford (14534) ***(G-13026)***
Rockwell Video Solutions LLC 631 745-0582
10 Koral Dr Southampton (11968) ***(G-14960)***
Rodac USA Corp 716 741-3931
5605 Kraus Rd Clarence (14031) ***(G-3541)***
Rodale Electronics, Hauppauge *Also called Rodale Wireless Inc* ***(G-5929)***
Rodale Inc 212 697-2040
733 3rd Ave Fl 15 New York (10017) ***(G-11417)***
Rodale Wireless Inc 631 231-0044
20 Oser Ave Ste 2 Hauppauge (11788) ***(G-5929)***
Rodan, Hicksville *Also called Oxygen Inc* ***(G-6118)***
Rodem Incorporated 212 779-7122
120 W 29th St Frnt A New York (10001) ***(G-11418)***
Rodgard Corporation 716 852-1435
92 Msgr Valente Dr Buffalo (14206) ***(G-3043)***
Roemac Industrial Sales Inc 716 692-7332
27 Fredericka St North Tonawanda (14120) ***(G-12448)***
Roessel & Co Inc 585 458-5560
199 Lagrange Ave Rochester (14613) ***(G-14101)***
Roffe Accessories Inc 212 213-1440
833 Broadway Apt 4 New York (10003) ***(G-11419)***
Rogan LLC 212 680-1407
330 Bowery New York (10012) ***(G-11420)***
Rogan LLC (PA) 646 496-9339
270 Bowery 3 New York (10012) ***(G-11421)***
Roger & Sons Inc (PA) 212 226-4734
268 Bowery Frnt 6 New York (10012) ***(G-11422)***
Roger L Urban Inc (PA) 716 693-5391
908 Niagara Falls Blvd # 107 North Tonawanda (14120) ***(G-12449)***
Roger Latari 631 580-2422
30 Raynor Ave Ste 1 Ronkonkoma (11779) ***(G-14408)***
Roger Michael Press Inc (PA) 732 752-0800
499 Van Brunt St Ste 6b Brooklyn (11231) ***(G-2411)***
Rogers Enterprises, Rochester *Also called Dock Hardware Incorporated* ***(G-13747)***
Rogers Group Inc 212 643-9292
318 W 39th St Fl 4 New York (10018) ***(G-11423)***
Rogers Industrial Spring, Buffalo *Also called Kehr-Buffalo Wire Frame Co Inc* ***(G-2902)***
Rohlfs Stined Leaded GL Studio 914 699-4848
783 S 3rd Ave Mount Vernon (10550) ***(G-8440)***
Rohrbach Brewing Company Inc 585 594-9800
3859 Buffalo Rd Rochester (14624) ***(G-14102)***
Rokon Tech LLC 718 429-0729
5223 74th St Elmhurst (11373) ***(G-4471)***
Roli Retreads Inc 631 694-7670
212 E Carmans Rd Unit A Farmingdale (11735) ***(G-4868)***
Roli Tire and Auto Repair, Farmingdale *Also called Roli Retreads Inc* ***(G-4868)***
Roli USA Inc 412 600-4840
100 5th Ave New York (10011) ***(G-11424)***
Rolite Mfg Inc 716 683-0259
10 Wendling Ct Lancaster (14086) ***(G-7046)***
Roll Lock Truss, Waddington *Also called Structural Wood Corporation* ***(G-15882)***
Rollers Inc 716 837-0700
2495 Main St Ste 359 Buffalo (14214) ***(G-3044)***
Rollers Unlimited, Syracuse *Also called David Fehlman* ***(G-15303)***
Rollform of Jamestown Inc 716 665-5310
181 Blackstone Ave Jamestown (14701) ***(G-6745)***
Rollhaus Seating Products Inc 718 729-9111
4310 21st St Long Island City (11101) ***(G-7577)***
Rolling Gate Supply Corp 718 366-5258
7919 Cypress Ave Glendale (11385) ***(G-5407)***
Rolling Star Manufacturing Inc 315 896-4767
125 Liberty Ln Barneveld (13304) ***(G-604)***
Rolling Stone, New York *Also called Wenner Media LLC* ***(G-12094)***
Rolling Stone Magazine 212 484-1616
1290 Ave Of The Amer Fl 2 New York (10104) ***(G-11425)***
Rollo Mio Artisan Bakery, Bronx *Also called Rm Bakery LLC* ***(G-1372)***
Rollson Inc 631 423-9578
10 Smugglers Cv Huntington (11743) ***(G-6412)***
Roly Door Sales Inc 716 877-1515
5659 Herman Hill Rd Hamburg (14075) ***(G-5694)***
Roma Bakery Inc 516 825-9170
45 Railroad Ave Valley Stream (11580) ***(G-15795)***
Roma Industries LLC 212 268-0723
12 W 37th St Fl 10 New York (10018) ***(G-11426)***
Roma Ray Bakery, Valley Stream *Also called Rays Italian Bakery Inc* ***(G-15793)***
Romac Electronics Inc 516 349-7900
155 E Ames Ct Unit 1 Plainview (11803) ***(G-13085)***
Roman Iron Works Inc 516 621-1103
15 Plaza Rd Greenvale (11548) ***(G-5631)***
Roman Stone Construction Co 631 667-0566
85 S 4th St Bay Shore (11706) ***(G-717)***
Romance & Co Inc 212 382-0337
2 W 47th St Ste 1111 New York (10036) ***(G-11427)***
Romantic Times Inc 718 237-1097
9 Ridgewood Pl Brooklyn (11237) ***(G-2412)***
Romantic Times Magazine, Brooklyn *Also called Romantic Times Inc* ***(G-2412)***
Romar Contracting Inc 845 778-2737
630 State Route 52 Walden (12586) ***(G-15896)***
Romark Diagnostics, Tappan *Also called RJ Harvey Instrument Corp* ***(G-15471)***
Rome Fastener, New York *Also called Rings Wire Inc* ***(G-11393)***
Rome Fastener Sales Corp (PA) 212 741-9779
246 W 38th St Rm 501 New York (10018) ***(G-11428)***
Rome Main Street Alliance Inc 315 271-8356
506 N James St Rome (13440) ***(G-14270)***
Rome Sign & Display Co 315 336-0550
510 Erie Blvd W Rome (13440) ***(G-14271)***
Rome Specialty Company Inc 315 337-8200
501 W Embargo St Rome (13440) ***(G-14272)***
Romir Enterprises, New York *Also called Mer Gems Corp* ***(G-10772)***
Romold Inc 585 529-4440
5 Moonlanding Rd Rochester (14624) ***(G-14103)***
Rona Precision Inc 631 737-4034
142 Remington Blvd Ste 2 Ronkonkoma (11779) ***(G-14409)***
Rona Precision Mfg, Ronkonkoma *Also called Rona Precision Inc* ***(G-14409)***
Ronan Paints, Bronx *Also called T J Ronan Paint Corp* ***(G-1398)***
Ronbar Laboratories Inc 718 937-6755
5202 Van Dam St Long Island City (11101) ***(G-7578)***
Roner Inc (PA) 718 392-6020
3553 24th St Long Island City (11106) ***(G-7579)***
Roner Inc 718 392-6020
1433 31st Ave Long Island City (11106) ***(G-7580)***
Ronmar, Flushing *Also called United Steel Products Inc* ***(G-5058)***
Ronni Nicole Group LLC 212 764-1000
1400 Broadway Rm 2102 New York (10018) ***(G-11429)***
Roode Hoek & Co Inc 718 522-5921
55 Ferris St Brooklyn (11231) ***(G-2413)***
Roofing Consultant, Buffalo *Also called Tiedemann Waldemar Inc* ***(G-3095)***
Room At The Top Inc 718 257-0766
632 Hegeman Ave Brooklyn (11207) ***(G-2414)***
Roome Technologies Inc 585 229-4437
4796 Honeoye Business Par Honeoye (14471) ***(G-6261)***
Rooster Hill Vineyards, Penn Yan *Also called Hoffman & Hoffman* ***(G-12958)***
Ropack USA Inc 631 482-7777
49 Mall Dr Commack (11725) ***(G-3700)***
Rosco Inc (PA) 718 526-2601
9021 144th Pl Jamaica (11435) ***(G-6675)***
Rosco Collision Avoidance Inc 718 526-2601
9021 144th Pl Jamaica (11435) ***(G-6676)***
Rosco Div, Rome *Also called Rome Specialty Company Inc* ***(G-14272)***
Roscoe Brothers Inc 607 844-3750
15 Freeville Rd Dryden (13053) ***(G-4151)***
Rose Cumming, New York *Also called Dessin/Fournir Inc* ***(G-9510)***
Rose Fence Inc (PA) 516 223-0777
345 W Sunrise Hwy Freeport (11520) ***(G-5179)***
Rose Fence Inc 516 790-2308
356 Bay Ave Halesite (11743) ***(G-5659)***
Rose Fence Inc 516 223-0777
345 Sunrise Hwy Baldwin (11510) ***(G-541)***
Rose Gourmet, Brooklyn *Also called Rhosey LLC* ***(G-2400)***
Rose Graphics LLC 516 547-6142
109 Kean St West Babylon (11704) ***(G-16188)***
Rose Solomon Co 718 855-1788
63 Flushing Ave Unit 330 Brooklyn (11205) ***(G-2415)***
Rose Trunk Mfg Co Inc 516 766-6686
3935 Sally Ln Oceanside (11572) ***(G-12554)***
Rose-Ann Division, New York *Also called Texport Fabrics Corp* ***(G-11805)***

Rosecore Division 516 504-4530
11 Grace Ave Ste 100 Great Neck (11021) *(G-5585)*
Rosedub, South Fallsburg *Also called Allied Wine Corp (G-14930)*
Rosemont Press Incorporated (PA) 212 239-4770
253 Church St Apt 2 New York (10013) *(G-11430)*
Rosemont Press Incorporated 212 239-4770
35 W Jefryn Blvd Ste A Deer Park (11729) *(G-4037)*
Rosen Mandell & Immerman Inc 212 691-2277
121 Varick St Rm 301 New York (10013) *(G-11431)*
Rosen Publishing Group Inc 212 777-3017
29 E 21st St Fl 2 New York (10010) *(G-11432)*
Rosenau Beck Inc 212 279-6202
135 W 36th St Rm 10l New York (10018) *(G-11433)*
Rosenbaum Foot, Brooklyn *Also called Newyork Pedorthic Associates (G-2268)*
Rosenwach Group, The, Astoria *Also called Rosenwach Tank Co Inc (G-442)*
Rosenwach Tank Co, Astoria *Also called Sitecraft Inc (G-444)*
Rosenwach Tank Co Inc (PA) 212 972-4411
4302 Ditmars Blvd Astoria (11105) *(G-442)*
Rosetti Handbags and ACC (HQ) 646 839-7945
350 5th Ave Lbby 9 New York (10118) *(G-11434)*
Rosina Food Products Inc 716 668-0123
170 French Rd Buffalo (14227) *(G-3045)*
Rosina Holding Inc (PA) 716 668-0123
170 French Rd Buffalo (14227) *(G-3046)*
Roslyn Bread Company Inc 516 625-1470
190 Mineola Ave Roslyn Heights (11577) *(G-14459)*
Ross Communications Associates 631 393-5089
200 Broadhollow Rd # 207 Melville (11747) *(G-8062)*
Ross Electronics Ltd 718 569-6643
12 Maple Ave Haverstraw (10927) *(G-5981)*
Ross JC Inc 716 439-1161
6722 Lincoln Ave Lockport (14094) *(G-7328)*
Ross L Sports Screening Inc 716 824-5350
2756 Seneca St Buffalo (14224) *(G-3047)*
Ross Metal Fabricators Div, Hauppauge *Also called Charles Ross & Son Company (G-5788)*
Ross Metal Fabricators Inc 631 586-7000
225 Marcus Blvd Deer Park (11729) *(G-4038)*
Ross Valve Mfg 518 274-0961
75 102nd St Troy (12180) *(G-15621)*
Rossi Tool & Dies Inc 845 267-8246
161 Route 303 Valley Cottage (10989) *(G-15763)*
Rosy Blue Inc (HQ) 212 687-8838
529 5th Ave Fl 12 New York (10017) *(G-11435)*
Rota File Corporation 516 496-7200
159 Lafayette Dr Syosset (11791) *(G-15231)*
Rota Pack Inc 631 274-1037
34 Sarah Dr Ste B Farmingdale (11735) *(G-4869)*
Rota Tool, Syosset *Also called Rota File Corporation (G-15231)*
Rotation Dynamics Corporation 585 352-9023
3581 Big Ridge Rd Spencerport (14559) *(G-14982)*
Roth Clothing Co Inc (PA) 718 384-4927
300 Penn St Brooklyn (11211) *(G-2416)*
Roth Design & Consulting Inc 718 209-0193
132 Bogart St Brooklyn (11206) *(G-2417)*
Roth Global Plastics Inc 315 475-0100
1 General Motors Dr Syracuse (13206) *(G-15410)*
Roth's Metal Works, Brooklyn *Also called Roth Design & Consulting Inc (G-2417)*
Rothe Welding Inc 845 246-3051
1455 Route 212 Saugerties (12477) *(G-14615)*
Roto Salt Company Inc 315 536-3742
118 Monell St Penn Yan (14527) *(G-12965)*
Rotork Controls Inc 585 328-1550
675 Mile Crossing Blvd Rochester (14624) *(G-14104)*
Rotork Controls Inc (HQ) 585 247-2304
675 Mile Crossing Blvd Rochester (14624) *(G-14105)*
Rotron Incorporated (HQ) 845 679-2401
55 Hasbrouck Ln Woodstock (12498) *(G-16687)*
Rotron Incorporated 845 679-2401
9 Hasbrouck Ln Woodstock (12498) *(G-16688)*
Rotronic Instrument Corp 631 427-3898
160 E Main St Ste 1 Huntington (11743) *(G-6413)*
Rotronic Instrument Corp (HQ) 631 348-6844
135 Engineers Rd Ste 150 Hauppauge (11788) *(G-5930)*
Rottkamp Tennis Inc 631 421-0040
100 Broadway Huntington Station (11746) *(G-6455)*
Rough Brothers Holding Co (HQ) 716 826-6500
3556 Lake Shore Rd # 100 Buffalo (14219) *(G-3048)*
Rough Draft Publishing LLC 212 741-4773
1916 Old Chelsea Sta New York (10113) *(G-11436)*
Rough Guides US Ltd 212 414-3635
345 Hudson St Fl 4 New York (10014) *(G-11437)*
Round Top Knit & Screening 518 622-3600
Rr 31 Round Top (12473) *(G-14466)*
Roust USA, New York *Also called Russian Standard Vodka USA Inc (G-11450)*
Rovel Manufacturing Co Inc 516 365-2752
52 Wimbledon Dr Roslyn (11576) *(G-14451)*
Row, The, New York *Also called Tr Apparel LLC (G-11881)*
Roxanne Assoulin, New York *Also called Maurice Max Inc (G-10730)*
Roxter Lighting, Long Island City *Also called Matov Industries Inc (G-7518)*
Royal Adhesives & Sealants LLC 315 451-1755
3584 Walters Rd Rsd Syracuse (13209) *(G-15411)*
Royal Apparel, Hauppauge *Also called Summit Apparel Inc (G-5951)*
Royal Bedding Co Buffalo Inc 716 895-1414
201 James E Casey Dr Buffalo (14206) *(G-3049)*
Royal Clothing Corp 718 436-5841
1316 48th St Apt 1 Brooklyn (11219) *(G-2418)*
Royal Copenhagen Inc (PA) 845 454-4442
63 Page Park Dr Poughkeepsie (12603) *(G-13364)*
Royal Crown Financial 718 234-7237
1028 Dahill Rd Brooklyn (11204) *(G-2419)*
Royal Custom Cabinets 315 376-6042
6149 Patty St Lowville (13367) *(G-7656)*
Royal Engraving, Brooklyn *Also called Tripi Engraving Co Inc (G-2586)*
Royal Fireworks Printing Co 845 726-3333
First Ave Unionville (10988) *(G-15673)*
Royal Industries Inc (PA) 718 369-3046
225 25th St Brooklyn (11232) *(G-2420)*
Royal Jewelry Mfg Inc (PA) 212 302-2500
825 Northern Blvd Fl 2 Great Neck (11021) *(G-5586)*
Royal Kedem Wine, Marlboro *Also called Royal Wine Corporation (G-7813)*
Royal Kosher Foods LLC 347 221-1867
1464 45th St Ste 1a Brooklyn (11219) *(G-2421)*
Royal Line The, Brooklyn *Also called Royal Industries Inc (G-2420)*
Royal Marble & Granite Inc 516 536-5900
3295 Royal Ave Oceanside (11572) *(G-12555)*
Royal Media Group, New York *Also called Royal News Corp (G-11439)*
Royal Metal Products Inc 518 966-4442
463 West Rd Surprise (12176) *(G-15207)*
Royal Miracle Corp 212 921-5797
2 W 46th St Rm 9209 New York (10036) *(G-11438)*
Royal Molds Inc 718 382-7686
1634 Marine Pkwy Brooklyn (11234) *(G-2422)*
Royal News Corp 212 564-8972
8 W 38th St Rm 901 New York (10018) *(G-11439)*
Royal Paint Roller Corp 516 367-4370
1 Harvard Dr Woodbury (11797) *(G-16631)*
Royal Paint Roller Mfg, Woodbury *Also called Royal Paint Roller Corp (G-16631)*
Royal Plastics Corp 718 647-7500
2840 Atlantic Ave Ste 1 Brooklyn (11207) *(G-2423)*
Royal Press, Staten Island *Also called C & R De Santis Inc (G-15057)*
Royal Press, White Plains *Also called L K Printing Corp (G-16470)*
Royal Products, Hauppauge *Also called Curran Manufacturing Corp (G-5807)*
Royal Products, Hauppauge *Also called Curran Manufacturing Corp (G-5808)*
Royal Promotion Group Inc 212 246-3780
119 W 57th St Ste 906 New York (10019) *(G-11440)*
Royal Sweet Bakery Inc 718 567-7770
119 49th St Brooklyn (11232) *(G-2424)*
Royal Tees Inc 845 357-9448
29 Lafayette Ave Suffern (10901) *(G-15197)*
Royal Windows and Doors, Bay Shore *Also called Royal Windows Mfg Corp (G-718)*
Royal Windows Mfg Corp 631 435-8888
1769 5th Ave Unit A Bay Shore (11706) *(G-718)*
Royal Wine Corporation 845 236-4000
1519 Route 9w Marlboro (12542) *(G-7813)*
Royale Limousine Manufacturers, Roslyn Heights *Also called Cabot Coach Builders Inc (G-14453)*
Royalton Millwork & Design 716 439-4092
7526 Tonawanda Creek Rd Lockport (14094) *(G-7329)*
Royalty Network Inc (PA) 212 967-4300
224 W 30th St Rm 1007 New York (10001) *(G-11441)*
Royce Associates A Ltd Partnr 516 367-6298
366 N Broadway Ste 400 Jericho (11753) *(G-6800)*
Rozal Industries Inc 631 420-4277
151 Marine St Farmingdale (11735) *(G-4870)*
Rp55 Inc 212 840-4035
230 W 39th St Fl 7 New York (10018) *(G-11442)*
Rpb Distributors LLC 914 244-3600
45 Kensico Dr Mount Kisco (10549) *(G-8358)*
Rpc Inc 347 873-3935
165 Emporia Ave Elmont (11003) *(G-4524)*
RPC Car Service, Elmont *Also called Rpc Inc (G-4524)*
RPC Photonics Inc 585 272-2840
330 Clay Rd Rochester (14623) *(G-14106)*
Rpf Associates Inc 631 462-7446
2155 Jericho Tpke Ste A Commack (11725) *(G-3701)*
Rpg, New York *Also called Royal Promotion Group Inc (G-11440)*
RPM Displays, Auburn *Also called R P M Industries Inc (G-497)*
RPS Holdings Inc 607 257-7778
99 Eastlake Rd Ithaca (14850) *(G-6609)*
RR Donnelley & Sons Company 716 773-0300
300 Lang Blvd Grand Island (14072) *(G-5511)*
Rs Automation 585 589-0199
4015 Oak Orchard Rd Albion (14411) *(G-162)*
RS Precision Industries Inc 631 420-0424
295 Adams Blvd Farmingdale (11735) *(G-4871)*
Rsb Associates Inc 518 281-5067
488 Picard Rd Altamont (12009) *(G-202)*
Rsl Media LLC 212 307-6760
1001 Ave Of The Ave Fl 11 Flr 11 New York (10018) *(G-11443)*
RSM Electron Power Inc (PA) 631 586-7600
221 W Industry Ct Deer Park (11729) *(G-4039)*

ALPHABETIC

RSM Electron Power Inc 631 586-7600
100 Engineers Rd Ste 100 # 100 Hauppauge (11788) ***(G-5931)***
Rsquared Ny Inc 631 521-8700
100 Heartland Blvd Edgewood (11717) ***(G-4413)***
RSR, Middletown *Also called Eco-Bat America LLC* ***(G-8150)***
Rt Machined Specialties 716 731-2055
2221 Niagara Falls Blvd Niagara Falls (14304) ***(G-12330)***
Rt Solutions LLC 585 245-3456
80 Linden Oaks Ste 210 Rochester (14625) ***(G-14107)***
RTD Manufacturing Inc 315 337-3151
6273 State Route 233 Rome (13440) ***(G-14273)***
Rtr Bag & Co Ltd 212 620-0011
27 W 20th St New York (10011) ***(G-11444)***
Rtt News 716 632-3400
1325 N Forest Rd Ste 240 Williamsville (14221) ***(G-16584)***
Rubber Stamp X Press 631 423-1322
7 Bradford Pl Huntington Station (11747) ***(G-6456)***
Rubber Stamps Inc 212 675-1180
174 Herricks Rd Mineola (11501) ***(G-8247)***
Rubberform Recycled Pdts LLC 716 478-0404
75 Michigan St Lockport (14094) ***(G-7330)***
Rubicon Industries Corp (PA) 718 434-4700
848 E 43rd St Brooklyn (11210) ***(G-2425)***
Rubie's Distribution Center, Bay Shore *Also called Rubies Costume Company Inc* ***(G-720)***
Rubies Costume Company Inc (PA) 718 846-1008
12008 Jamaica Ave Richmond Hill (11418) ***(G-13510)***
Rubies Costume Company Inc 631 777-3300
158 Candlewood Rd Bay Shore (11706) ***(G-719)***
Rubies Costume Company Inc 718 441-0834
12017 Jamaica Ave Richmond Hill (11418) ***(G-13511)***
Rubies Costume Company Inc 631 951-3688
1 Holloween Hwy Bay Shore (11706) ***(G-720)***
Rubies Costume Company Inc 516 333-3473
601 Cantiague Rock Rd Westbury (11590) ***(G-16370)***
Rubies Costume Company Inc 631 435-7912
158 Candlewood Rd Bay Shore (11706) ***(G-721)***
Rubies Costume Company Inc 516 326-1500
158 Candlewood Rd Bay Shore (11706) ***(G-722)***
Rubies Costume Company Inc 718 846-1008
1 Rubie Plz Richmond Hill (11418) ***(G-13512)***
Rubies Masquerade Company LLC (PA) 718 846-1008
1 Rubie Plz Richmond Hill (11418) ***(G-13513)***
Rubinstein Jewelry Mfg Co 718 784-8650
3100 47th Ave Long Island City (11101) ***(G-7581)***
Ruby Engineering LLC 646 391-4600
354 Sackett St Brooklyn (11231) ***(G-2426)***
Ruby Newco LLC 212 852-7000
1211 Ave Of The Americas New York (10036) ***(G-11445)***
Ruby Road, New York *Also called Hearts of Palm LLC* ***(G-10074)***
Ruby Road, New York *Also called Hearts of Palm LLC* ***(G-10075)***
Ruckel Manufacturing Co, Brooklyn *Also called EY Industries Inc* ***(G-1860)***
Rudolf Friedman Inc 212 869-5070
42 W 48th St Ste 1102 New York (10036) ***(G-11446)***
Rudy Stempel & Family Sawmill 518 872-0431
73 Stemple Rd East Berne (12059) ***(G-4212)***
Ruga Grinding & Mfg Corp 631 924-5067
84 Horseblock Rd Unit A Yaphank (11980) ***(G-16719)***
Rugby Magazine, White Plains *Also called American Intl Media LLC* ***(G-16420)***
Ruggeri Manufacturing, Rochester *Also called Van Thomas Inc* ***(G-14199)***
Ruhle Companies Inc 914 287-4000
99 Wall St Valhalla (10595) ***(G-15747)***
Rui Xing International Trdg Co 516 298-2667
89 Jerusalem Ave Hicksville (11801) ***(G-6129)***
Rule Breaker Snacks, Brooklyn *Also called Have Your Cake Kitchen LLC* ***(G-1968)***
Rumsey Corp 914 751-3640
15 Rumsey Rd Yonkers (10705) ***(G-16797)***
Rumson Acquisition LLC (PA) 718 349-4300
1385 Broadway Fl 9 New York (10018) ***(G-11447)***
Run It Systems, New York *Also called Marcus Goldman Inc* ***(G-10700)***
Runs Capital Inc 212 618-1201
14 Wall St Fl 203420 New York (10005) ***(G-11448)***
Runs Inc 212 618-1201
14 Wall St Fl 203420 New York (10005) ***(G-11449)***
Rural Hill Sand and Grav Corp 315 846-5212
10262 County Route 79 Woodville (13650) ***(G-16689)***
Rus Auto Parts Inc 800 410-2669
508 Coney Island Ave Brooklyn (11218) ***(G-2427)***
Rus Industries Inc 716 284-7828
3255 Lockport Rd Niagara Falls (14305) ***(G-12331)***
Rush Gold Manufacturing Ltd 516 781-3155
2400 Merrick Rd Bellmore (11710) ***(G-793)***
Rush Gravel Corp 585 533-1740
130 Kavanaugh Rd Honeoye Falls (14472) ***(G-6272)***
Rush Machinery Inc 585 554-3070
4761 State Route 364 Rushville (14544) ***(G-14477)***
Russco Metal Spinning Co Inc 516 872-6055
1020 Archer Pl Baldwin (11510) ***(G-542)***
Russell Bass 607 637-5253
59 Saw Mill Rd Hancock (13783) ***(G-5714)***
Russell Bass & Son Lumber, Hancock *Also called Russell Bass* ***(G-5714)***
Russell Industries Inc 516 536-5000
40 Horton Ave Lynbrook (11563) ***(G-7673)***
Russell Plastics Tech Co Inc 631 963-8602
521 W Hoffman Ave Lindenhurst (11757) ***(G-7191)***
Russian Bazaar, Brooklyn *Also called Danet Inc* ***(G-1755)***
Russian Daily, Brooklyn *Also called Novoye Rsskoye Slovo Pubg Corp* ***(G-2276)***
Russian Mix Inc 347 385-7198
2225 Benson Ave Apt 74 Brooklyn (11214) ***(G-2428)***
Russian Standard Vodka USA Inc (PA) 212 679-1894
232 Madison Ave Fl 16 New York (10016) ***(G-11450)***
Russkaya Reklama Inc 718 769-3000
2699 Coney Island Ave Brooklyn (11235) ***(G-2429)***
Russo's Gluten Free Gourmet, Shirley *Also called Anthony Gigi Inc* ***(G-14828)***
Rutcarele Inc 347 830-5353
3449 110th St Corona (11368) ***(G-3853)***
Rv Printing 631 567-8658
39 Portside Dr Holbrook (11741) ***(G-6207)***
Rvc Enterprises LLC (PA) 212 391-4600
1384 Broadway Fl 17 New York (10018) ***(G-11451)***
Rw Gate Company (PA) 518 874-4750
79 102nd St Troy (12180) ***(G-15622)***
Rw Gate Company 518 874-4750
75 102nd St Troy (12180) ***(G-15623)***
Rw Manufacturing Company, East Rochester *Also called Richards & West Inc* ***(G-4291)***
Rwb Controls Inc 716 897-4341
471 Connecticut St Buffalo (14213) ***(G-3050)***
RWS Manufacturing Inc 518 361-1657
22 Ferguson Ln Queensbury (12804) ***(G-13439)***
Ry-Gan Printing, Rochester *Also called Whitestone Dev Group LLC* ***(G-14208)***
Ryan Gems Inc 212 697-0149
20 E 46th St Rm 200 New York (10017) ***(G-11452)***
Ryan Printing, Hilton *Also called William J Ryan* ***(G-6159)***
Ryan Printing Inc 845 535-3235
300 Corporate Dr Ste 6 Blauvelt (10913) ***(G-940)***
Ryba General Merchandise Inc 718 522-2028
63 Flushing Ave Unit 332 Brooklyn (11205) ***(G-2430)***
Ryba Software Inc 718 264-9352
7359 186th St Fresh Meadows (11366) ***(G-5203)***
Rye Record 914 713-3213
14 Elm Pl Ste 200 Rye (10580) ***(G-14488)***
Ryers Creek Corp 607 523-6617
1330 Mill Dr Corning (14830) ***(G-3825)***
Ryland Peters & Small Inc 646 791-5410
341 E 116th St New York (10029) ***(G-11453)***
S & B Fashion Inc 718 482-1386
4315 Queens St Ste B Long Island City (11101) ***(G-7582)***
S & B Machine Works Inc 516 997-2666
111 New York Ave Westbury (11590) ***(G-16371)***
S & C Bridal LLC (PA) 212 789-7000
1407 Broadway Fl 41 New York (10018) ***(G-11454)***
S & C Bridals LLC 213 624-4477
1407 Broadway Fl 41 New York (10018) ***(G-11455)***
S & D Welding Corp 631 454-0383
229 Edison Ave Ste A West Babylon (11704) ***(G-16189)***
S & H Enterprises Inc 888 323-8755
10b Holden Ave Queensbury (12804) ***(G-13440)***
S & H Machine Company Inc 716 834-1194
83 Clyde Ave Buffalo (14215) ***(G-3051)***
S & H Uniform Corp 914 937-6800
1 Aqueduct Rd White Plains (10606) ***(G-16500)***
S & J Sheet Metal Supply 718 384-0800
70 Grand Ave Brooklyn (11205) ***(G-2431)***
S & J Trading Inc 718 347-1323
8030 263rd St Floral Park (11004) ***(G-4967)***
S & K Counter Tops Inc 716 662-7986
4708 Duerr Rd Orchard Park (14127) ***(G-12743)***
S & L Aerospace Metals LLC 718 326-1821
12012 28th Ave Flushing (11354) ***(G-5043)***
S & M Ring Corp 212 382-0900
1080 Channel Dr Hewlett (11557) ***(G-6050)***
S & R Tool Inc 585 346-2029
6066 Stone Hill Rd Lakeville (14480) ***(G-6986)***
S & S Enterprises, Jamestown *Also called Genco John* ***(G-6717)***
S & S Fashions Inc 718 328-0001
941 Longfellow Ave Bronx (10474) ***(G-1375)***
S & S Machinery Corp (PA) 718 492-7400
140 53rd St Brooklyn (11232) ***(G-2432)***
S & S Machinery Corp 718 492-7400
132 54th St Brooklyn (11220) ***(G-2433)***
S & S Manufacturing Co Inc (PA) 212 444-6000
1375 Broadway Fl 2 New York (10018) ***(G-11456)***
S & S Prtg Die-Cutting Co Inc 718 388-8990
488 Morgan Ave Ste A Brooklyn (11222) ***(G-2434)***
S & S Soap Co Inc 718 585-2900
815 E 135th St Bronx (10454) ***(G-1376)***
S & T Knitting Co Inc (PA) 607 722-7558
1010 Conklin Rd Conklin (13748) ***(G-3732)***
S & T Machine Inc 718 272-2484
970 E 92nd St Fl 1 Brooklyn (11236) ***(G-2435)***
S & V Custom Furniture Mfg 516 746-8299
75 Windsor Ave Unit E Mineola (11501) ***(G-8248)***
S & V Knits Inc 631 752-1595
117 Marine St Farmingdale (11735) ***(G-4872)***

S & V Restaurant Eqp Mfrs Inc 718 220-1140
4320 Park Ave Bronx (10457) *(G-1377)*
S & W Knitting Mills Inc 718 237-2416
703 Bedford Ave Fl 3 Brooklyn (11206) *(G-2436)*
S & W Ladies Wear 718 431-2800
3611 14th Ave Ste 601 Brooklyn (11218) *(G-2437)*
S & W Metal Trading Corp 212 719-5070
1601 E 7th St Brooklyn (11230) *(G-2438)*
S A Baxter LLC (PA) 845 469-7995
37 Elkay Dr Ste 33 Chester (10918) *(G-3482)*
S A W, Kingston *Also called Spiegel Woodworks Inc (G-6918)*
S and G Imaging, Walworth *Also called Software & General Services Co (G-15916)*
S B B, Syracuse *Also called Sullivan Bazinet Bongio Inc (G-15432)*
S B Manufacturing LLC 845 352-3700
161 Route 59 Monsey (10952) *(G-8295)*
S B Whistler & Sons Inc 585 798-3000
11023 W Center Street Ext Medina (14103) *(G-7988)*
S Broome and Co Inc 718 663-6800
3300 47th Ave Fl 1 Long Island City (11101) *(G-7583)*
S D C, Armonk *Also called Surgical Design Corp (G-410)*
S D I, Binghamton *Also called Sensor & Decontamination Inc (G-914)*
S D S of Long Island, Bay Shore *Also called M F L B Inc (G-697)*
S D Z Metal Spinning Stamping 718 778-3600
1807 Pacific St Brooklyn (11233) *(G-2439)*
S Donadic Inc 718 361-9888
4525 39th St Sunnyside (11104) *(G-15205)*
S E A Supls, Plainview *Also called S E A Supplies Ltd (G-13086)*
S E A Supplies Ltd 516 694-6677
1670 Old Country Rd # 104 Plainview (11803) *(G-13086)*
S G I 917 386-0385
40 E 52nd St Frnt A New York (10022) *(G-11457)*
S G New York LLC 631 698-8400
1 Rodeo Dr Edgewood (11717) *(G-4414)*
S G New York LLC (PA) 631 665-4000
2950 Vtrans Mem Hwy Ste 1 Bohemia (11716) *(G-1084)*
S Hellerman Inc (PA) 718 622-2995
242 Green St Brooklyn (11222) *(G-2440)*
S I Communications Inc 914 725-2500
8 Harwood Ct Scarsdale (10583) *(G-14644)*
S J B Fabrication 716 895-0281
430 Kennedy Rd Buffalo (14227) *(G-3052)*
S J McCullagh Inc (PA) 716 856-3473
245 Swan St Buffalo (14204) *(G-3053)*
S K Circuits Inc (PA) 703 376-8718
340 Rosewood Cir Canastota (13032) *(G-3246)*
S Kashi & Sons Inc 212 869-9393
175 Great Neck Rd Ste 204 Great Neck (11021) *(G-5587)*
S L C Industries Incorporated 607 775-2299
63 Barlow Rd Binghamton (13904) *(G-913)*
S L Fashions Group, New York *Also called Lou Sally Fashions Corp (G-10615)*
S M I, New York *Also called Specialty Minerals Inc (G-11661)*
S M S C Inc 315 942-4394
101 Water St Boonville (13309) *(G-1121)*
S P Books Inc 212 431-5011
99 Spring St Fl 3 New York (10012) *(G-11458)*
S P Industries Inc 845 255-5000
815 Rte 208 Gardiner (12525) *(G-5295)*
S R & R Industries Inc 845 692-8329
45 Enterprise Pl Middletown (10941) *(G-8175)*
S R Instruments Inc (PA) 716 693-5977
600 Young St Tonawanda (14150) *(G-15573)*
S R Sloan Inc (PA) 315 736-7730
8111 Halsey Rd Whitesboro (13492) *(G-16529)*
S Rothschild & Co Inc (PA) 212 354-8550
1407 Broadway Fl 10 New York (10018) *(G-11459)*
S S I, Rochester *Also called Schlegel Systems Inc (G-14115)*
S S Precision Gear & Instr 718 457-7474
4512 104th St Corona (11368) *(G-3854)*
S Scharf Inc 516 541-9552
278 N Richmond Ave Massapequa (11758) *(G-7885)*
S T J Orthotic Svces, Lindenhurst *Also called Stj Orthotic Services Inc (G-7195)*
S Z Design & Prints, Monsey *Also called Sz - Design & Print Inc (G-8299)*
S&B Alternative Fuels Inc 631 585-6637
1232 Stony Brook Rd Lake Grove (11755) *(G-6968)*
S&D Welding, West Babylon *Also called S & D Welding Corp (G-16189)*
S&G Optical, Long Island City *Also called 21st Century Optics Inc (G-7362)*
S'Well Bottle, New York *Also called Cant Live Without It LLC (G-9197)*
S.W.H. Precision Industries, Hauppauge *Also called Makamah Enterprises Inc (G-5878)*
S1 Biopharma Inc 201 839-0941
7 World Trade Ctr 250g New York (10007) *(G-11460)*
S2 Sportswear Inc 347 335-0713
4100 1st Ave Ste 5n Brooklyn (11232) *(G-2441)*
S3j Electronics LLC 716 206-1309
2000 Commerce Pkwy Lancaster (14086) *(G-7047)*
SA Day Buffalo Flux Facility, Buffalo *Also called Johnson Manufacturing Company (G-2897)*
Saab Defense and SEC USA LLC 315 445-5009
5717 Enterprise Pkwy East Syracuse (13057) *(G-4367)*
Saad Collection Inc (PA) 212 937-0341
1165 Broadway Ste 305 New York (10001) *(G-11461)*

Saakshi Inc 315 475-3988
851 N Salina St Syracuse (13208) *(G-15412)*
Sabbsons International Inc 718 360-1947
474 50th St Brooklyn (11220) *(G-2442)*
Sabic Innovative Plas US LLC 518 475-5011
1 Noryl Ave Selkirk (12158) *(G-14771)*
Sabic Innovative Plastics 713 448-7474
1 Gail Ct East Greenbush (12061) *(G-4231)*
Sabila Corp (PA) 845 981-7128
480 Liberty Corners Rd Pine Island (10969) *(G-13003)*
Sabin Metal Corporation (PA) 631 329-1695
300 Pantigo Pl Ste 102 East Hampton (11937) *(G-4242)*
Sabin Metal Corporation 585 538-2194
1647 Wheatland Center Rd Scottsville (14546) *(G-14753)*
Sabin Robbins, New York *Also called Eagles Nest Holdings LLC (G-9604)*
Sabin Robbins Paper Company 513 874-5270
455 E 86th St New York (10028) *(G-11462)*
Sabra Dipping Company LLC (PA) 914 372-3900
777 Westchester Ave Fl 3 White Plains (10604) *(G-16501)*
Sabre Energy Services LLC 518 514-1572
1891 New Scotland Rd Slingerlands (12159) *(G-14890)*
Sabre Enterprises Inc 315 430-3127
6799 Townline Rd Syracuse (13211) *(G-15413)*
Saccomize Inc 818 287-3000
1554 Stillwell Ave Bronx (10461) *(G-1378)*
Sacks and Company New York (PA) 212 741-1000
119 W 57th St Ste 512 New York (10019) *(G-11463)*
Sadowsky Guitars Ltd 718 433-1990
2107 41st Ave Fl 4 Long Island City (11101) *(G-7584)*
Saes Memry, New Hartford *Also called Saes Smart Materials Inc (G-8511)*
Saes Smart Materials Inc 315 266-2026
4355 Middle Settlement Rd New Hartford (13413) *(G-8511)*
Safavieh Inc 516 945-1900
40 Harbor Park Dr Port Washington (11050) *(G-13302)*
Safcore LLC 917 627-5263
23 Van Dam St Brooklyn (11222) *(G-2443)*
Safe Circuits Inc 631 586-3682
15 Shoreham Dr W Dix Hills (11746) *(G-4125)*
Safe Flight Instrument Corp 914 946-9500
20 New King St White Plains (10604) *(G-16502)*
Safe Passage International Inc 585 292-4910
333 Metro Park Ste F204 Rochester (14623) *(G-14108)*
Safe Seat USA Inc 516 586-8240
1670 Old Country Rd # 116 Plainview (11803) *(G-13087)*
Safe Skies LLC (PA) 888 632-5027
954 3rd Ave Ste 504 New York (10022) *(G-11464)*
Safe-Dent Enterprises LLC 845 362-0141
4 Orchard Hill Dr Monsey (10952) *(G-8296)*
Safeguard Inc 631 929-3273
578 Sound Ave Wading River (11792) *(G-15886)*
Safespan Platform Systems Inc 716 694-1100
237 Fillmore Ave Tonawanda (14150) *(G-15574)*
Safetec of America Inc 716 895-1822
887 Kensington Ave Buffalo (14215) *(G-3054)*
Safety-Kleen Systems Inc 716 855-2212
60 Katherine St Buffalo (14210) *(G-3055)*
Sag Harbor, New York *Also called Life Style Design Group (G-10564)*
Sag Harbor Express 631 725-1700
35 Main St Sag Harbor (11963) *(G-14501)*
Sag Harbor Industries Inc (PA) 631 725-0440
1668 Bhmpton Sag Hbr Tpke Sag Harbor (11963) *(G-14502)*
Saga International Recycl LLC 718 621-5900
6623 13th Ave Brooklyn (11219) *(G-2444)*
Sage Audio Video Tech LLC 212 213-1523
53 W 36th St Rm 605 New York (10018) *(G-11465)*
Sage Knitwear Inc 718 628-7902
103 Jersey St Unit D West Babylon (11704) *(G-16190)*
Sagelife Parenting LLC 315 299-5713
235 Harrison St Ste 2 Syracuse (13202) *(G-15414)*
Sagemylife, Syracuse *Also called Sagelife Parenting LLC (G-15414)*
Sahadi Fine Foods Inc 718 369-0100
4215 1st Ave Brooklyn (11232) *(G-2445)*
Sahlen Packing Company Inc 716 852-8677
318 Howard St Buffalo (14206) *(G-3056)*
Sailorbags, Rochester *Also called Paradiso Cnsld Entps LLC (G-14007)*
Saint Gobain Grains & Powders 716 731-8200
6600 Walmore Rd Niagara Falls (14304) *(G-12332)*
Saint Honore Pastry Shop Inc 516 767-2555
993 Port Washington Blvd Port Washington (11050) *(G-13303)*
Saint Laurie, New York *Also called Kozinn+sons Merchant Tailors (G-10475)*
Saint Martins Press, New York *Also called Bedford Freeman & Worth (G-9035)*
Saint-Gbain Advnced Crmics LLC 716 691-2000
168 Creekside Dr Amherst (14228) *(G-249)*
Saint-Gbain Advnced Crmics LLC (HQ) 716 278-6066
23 Acheson Dr Niagara Falls (14303) *(G-12333)*
Saint-Gobain Abrasives Inc 518 266-2200
2600 10th Ave Watervliet (12189) *(G-16049)*
Saint-Gobain Adfors Amer Inc (HQ) 716 775-3900
1795 Baseline Rd Grand Island (14072) *(G-5512)*
Saint-Gobain Adfors Amer Inc 585 589-4401
14770 East Ave Albion (14411) *(G-163)*

ALPHABETIC

(PA)=Parent Co (HQ)=Headquarters (DH)=Div Headquarters
2019 Harris
New York Manufacturers Directory
979

Saint-Gobain Dynamics Inc 716 278-6007
23 Acheson Dr Niagara Falls (14303) ***(G-12334)***

Saint-Gobain Performance Plas, Poestenkill *Also called Canton Bio-Medical Inc* ***(G-13179)***

Saint-Gobain Prfmce Plas Corp 518 642-2200
1 Sealants Park Granville (12832) ***(G-5524)***

Saint-Gobain Prfmce Plas Corp 518 686-7301
14 Mccaffrey St Hoosick Falls (12090) ***(G-6280)***

Saint-Gobain Prfmce Plas Corp 518 283-5963
11 Sicho Rd Poestenkill (12140) ***(G-13182)***

Saint-Gobain Prfmce Plas Corp 518 686-7301
1 Liberty St Hoosick Falls (12090) ***(G-6281)***

Saint-Gobain Strl Ceramics 716 278-6233
23 Acheson Dr Niagara Falls (14303) ***(G-12335)***

Saint-Gobain-Paris France, Grand Island *Also called Saint-Gobain Adfors Amer Inc* ***(G-5512)***

Saj of Freeport Corp 516 623-8800
178 Hanse Ave Freeport (11520) ***(G-5180)***

Sakonnet Technology LLC 212 849-9267
11 E 44th St Fl 1000 New York (10017) ***(G-11466)***

Salamanca Daily Reporter, Salamanca *Also called Sun-Times Media Group Inc* ***(G-14535)***

Salamanca Lumber Company Inc 716 945-4810
59 Rochester St Salamanca (14779) ***(G-14530)***

Salamanca Penny Saver, Salamanca *Also called Salamanca Press Penny Saver* ***(G-14531)***

Salamanca Press Penny Saver 716 945-1500
36 River St Salamanca (14779) ***(G-14531)***

Salarinos Italian Foods Inc 315 697-9766
110 James St Canastota (13032) ***(G-3247)***

Sale 121 Corp 240 855-8988
1324 Lexington Ave # 111 New York (10128) ***(G-11467)***

Salentica Corp 212 672-1777
245 Park Ave Fl 39 New York (10167) ***(G-11468)***

Salerno Packaging Inc (HQ) 518 563-3636
14 Gus Lapham Ln Plattsburgh (12901) ***(G-13154)***

Salerno Plastic Film and Bags, Plattsburgh *Also called Salerno Packaging Inc* ***(G-13154)***

Sales & Marketing Office, Syracuse *Also called Monaghan Medical Corporation* ***(G-15376)***

Sales Department, Floral Park *Also called Allomatic Products Company* ***(G-4955)***

Sales Hacker Inc 516 660-2836
505 E 14th St Apt 5h New York (10009) ***(G-11469)***

Sales Office, Northport *Also called Cypress Semiconductor Corp* ***(G-12467)***

Sales Tax Asset Rceivable Corp 212 788-5874
255 Greenwich St Fl 6 New York (10007) ***(G-11470)***

Salisbury Sportswear Inc 516 221-9519
2523 Marine Pl Bellmore (11710) ***(G-794)***

Salit Specialty Rebar Inc 716 299-1990
1050 Military Rd Buffalo (14217) ***(G-3057)***

Salko Kitchens Inc 845 565-4420
256 Walsh Ave New Windsor (12553) ***(G-8658)***

Sally Sherman Foods, Mount Vernon *Also called UFS Industries Inc* ***(G-8452)***

Salmco Jewelry Corp 212 695-8792
22 W 32nd St Fl 16 New York (10001) ***(G-11471)***

Salmon Crek Cabinetry Inc 315 589-5419
6687 Salmon Creek Rd Williamson (14589) ***(G-16561)***

Salmon River News, Watertown *Also called Mexico Independent Inc* ***(G-16027)***

Salonclick LLC 718 643-6793
117 Crosby St New York (10012) ***(G-11472)***

Salsburg Dimensional Stone 631 653-6790
18 Pine St Brookhaven (11719) ***(G-1432)***

Salty Road Inc 347 673-3925
190 Bedford Ave 404 Brooklyn (11249) ***(G-2446)***

Salutem Group LLC 347 620-2640
44 Wall St Fl 12 New York (10005) ***(G-11473)***

Salvador Colletti Blank 718 217-6725
25141 Van Zandt Ave Douglaston (11362) ***(G-4139)***

Salvin Company, Kingston *Also called Vincent Conigliaro* ***(G-6931)***

Sam A Lupo & Sons Inc (PA) 800 388-5352
1219 Campville Rd Endicott (13760) ***(G-4609)***

Sam Bonk Uniform, Bronx *Also called Bonk Sam Uniforms Civilian Cap* ***(G-1230)***

Sam Hee International Inc 212 594-7815
213 W 35th St Ste 503 New York (10001) ***(G-11474)***

Sam NY, New York *Also called Andrew M Schwartz LLC* ***(G-8860)***

Sam Salem & Son LLC 212 695-6020
302 5th Ave Fl 4 New York (10001) ***(G-11475)***

Samaki Inc 845 858-1012
62 Jersey Ave Port Jervis (12771) ***(G-13236)***

Samco LLC 518 725-4705
122 S Main St Gloversville (12078) ***(G-5464)***

Samco Scientific Corporation, Rochester *Also called Samco Scientific LLC* ***(G-14109)***

Samco Scientific LLC 800 522-3359
75 Panorama Creek Dr Rochester (14625) ***(G-14109)***

Samoss Group Ltd (PA) 212 239-6677
213 W 35th St Rm 1301 New York (10001) ***(G-11476)***

Sampla Belting North Amer LLC 716 667-7450
61 N Gates Ave Lackawanna (14218) ***(G-6953)***

Sample News Group LLC 315 343-3800
140 W 1st St Oswego (13126) ***(G-12787)***

Sampsons Prsthtic Orthotic Lab, Schenectady *Also called Sampsons Prsthtic Orthotic Lab* ***(G-14709)***

Sampsons Prsthtic Orthotic Lab 518 374-6011
1737 State St Schenectady (12304) ***(G-14709)***

Samscreen Inc 607 722-3979
216 Broome Corporate Pkwy Conklin (13748) ***(G-3733)***

Samson Technologies Corp (HQ) 631 784-2200
278 Duffy Ave Unit B Hicksville (11801) ***(G-6130)***

Samuel B Collection Inc 516 466-1826
98 Cuttermill Rd Great Neck (11021) ***(G-5588)***

Samuel Broome Uniform ACC, Long Island City *Also called S Broome and Co Inc* ***(G-7583)***

Samuel French Inc (PA) 212 206-8990
235 Park Ave S Fl 5 New York (10003) ***(G-11477)***

Samuel H Moss, New York *Also called Samoss Group Ltd* ***(G-11476)***

Samuel Schulman Furs Inc 212 736-5550
150 W 30th St Fl 13 New York (10001) ***(G-11478)***

Samuel Son & Co Inc 716 856-6500
250 Lake Ave Ste 3 Blasdell (14219) ***(G-929)***

San Francisco Chronicle, New York *Also called Hearst Communications Inc* ***(G-10058)***

San Jae Educational Resou 845 364-5458
9 Chamberlain Ct Pomona (10970) ***(G-13187)***

San Signs & Awnings, Yonkers *Also called M Santoliquido Corp* ***(G-16780)***

Sanaa Spices, Maspeth *Also called Extreme Spices Inc* ***(G-7843)***

Sanctuary Brands LLC (PA) 212 704-4014
70 W 40th St Fl 5 New York (10018) ***(G-11479)***

Sand Hill Industries Inc 518 885-7991
12 Grove St Ballston Spa (12020) ***(G-595)***

Sandberg & Sikorski, New York *Also called A Jaffe Inc* ***(G-8697)***

Sandbox Brands Inc 212 647-8877
26 W 17th St Lbby New York (10011) ***(G-11480)***

Sandle Custom Bearing Corp 585 593-7000
1110 State Route 19 Wellsville (14895) ***(G-16121)***

Sandow Media LLC 646 805-0200
101 Park Ave Fl 4 New York (10178) ***(G-11481)***

Sandstone Technologies Corp (PA) 585 785-5537
2117 Buffalo Rd 245 Rochester (14624) ***(G-14110)***

Sandstone Technologies Corp 585 785-5537
2117 Buffalo Rd Unit 245 Rochester (14624) ***(G-14111)***

Sandvoss Farms LLC 585 297-7044
10198 East Rd East Bethany (14054) ***(G-4213)***

Sandy Dalal Ltd 212 532-5822
220 Central Park S 10f New York (10019) ***(G-11482)***

Sandy Duftler Designs Ltd 516 379-3084
775 Brooklyn Ave Ste 105 North Baldwin (11510) ***(G-12366)***

Sandy Littman Inc 845 562-1112
420 N Montgomery St Newburgh (12550) ***(G-12245)***

Sandys Bumper Mart Inc 315 472-8149
120 Wall St Syracuse (13204) ***(G-15415)***

Sandys Deli Inc 518 297-6951
90 Montgomery St Rouses Point (12979) ***(G-14470)***

Sanford Printing Inc 718 461-1202
13335 41st Rd Flushing (11355) ***(G-5044)***

Sanford Stone LLC 607 467-1313
185 Latham Rd Deposit (13754) ***(G-4109)***

Sangster Foods Inc 212 993-9129
225 Parkside Ave Apt 3p Brooklyn (11226) ***(G-2447)***

Sanguine Gas Exploration LLC 212 582-8555
152 W 57th St Fl 4100 New York (10019) ***(G-11483)***

Sanjay Pallets Inc 347 590-2485
424 Coster St Bronx (10474) ***(G-1379)***

Sanmina Corporation 607 689-5000
1200 Taylor Rd Owego (13827) ***(G-12803)***

Sanoy Inc 212 695-6384
19 W 36th St Fl 11 New York (10018) ***(G-11484)***

Sanrex Corporation 516 625-1313
50 Seaview Blvd Ste 2 Port Washington (11050) ***(G-13304)***

Santa Fe Manufacturing Corp 631 234-0100
225 Engineers Rd Hauppauge (11788) ***(G-5932)***

Santee Print Works (PA) 212 997-1570
58 W 40th St Fl 11 New York (10018) ***(G-11485)***

Santucci Custom Lighting 866 853-1929
2943 Lumbard Rd Clinton (13323) ***(G-3588)***

Sanzdranz LLC (PA) 518 894-8625
83 Dumbarton Dr Delmar (12054) ***(G-4078)***

Sanzdranz LLC 518 894-8625
388 Broadway Schenectady (12305) ***(G-14710)***

Sapienza Bake Shop, Elmont *Also called Sapienza Pastry Inc* ***(G-4525)***

Sapienza Pastry Inc 516 352-5232
1376 Hempstead Tpke Elmont (11003) ***(G-4525)***

Sapphire Systems Inc (HQ) 212 905-0100
405 Lexington Ave Fl 49 New York (10174) ***(G-11486)***

Sappi North America Inc 914 696-5544
925 Westchester Ave # 115 White Plains (10604) ***(G-16503)***

Saptalis Pharmaceuticals LLC (PA) 631 231-2751
45 Davids Dr Hauppauge (11788) ***(G-5933)***

Saputo Dairy Foods Usa LLC 607 746-2141
40236 State Highway 10 Delhi (13753) ***(G-4075)***

Sara Lee Courtaulds USA, New York *Also called Courtaulds Textiles Ltd* ***(G-9410)***

Sarabeth's Bakery, Bronx *Also called Sbk Preserves Inc* ***(G-1381)***

Sarabeths Kitchen LLC 718 589-2900
1161 E 156th St Bronx (10474) ***(G-1380)***

Saraga Industries Corp 631 842-4049
690 Albany Ave Unit D Amityville (11701) ***(G-315)***

Saratoga Chips LLC 877 901-6950
63 Putnam St Ste 202 Saratoga Springs (12866) ***(G-14597)***

Saratoga Horseworks Ltd 518 843-6756
57 Edson St Amsterdam (12010) ***(G-359)***

Saratoga Lighting Holdings LLC 212 906-7800
535 Madison Ave Fl 4 New York (10022) ***(G-11487)***
Saratoga Spring Water Company 518 584-6363
11 Geyser Rd Saratoga Springs (12866) ***(G-14598)***
Saratogian USA Today, Saratoga Springs *Also called Journal Register Company* ***(G-14589)***
Saraval Industries 516 768-9033
348 N Midland Ave Nyack (10960) ***(G-12510)***
Sargent Manufacturing Inc 212 722-7000
120 E 124th St New York (10035) ***(G-11488)***
Sargento Foods Inc 920 893-8484
498 7th Ave New York (10018) ***(G-11489)***
Sarina Accessories LLC 212 239-8106
15 W 36th St Fl 5 New York (10018) ***(G-11490)***
Sarkisians Jewelry Co 212 869-1060
17 W 45th St Ste 201 New York (10036) ***(G-11491)***
Sartek Industries Inc (PA) 631 473-3555
17 N Belle Mead Ave Ste 1 East Setauket (11733) ***(G-4309)***
Sarug Inc 718 339-2791
2055 Mcdonald Ave Brooklyn (11223) ***(G-2448)***
SAS Industries Inc 631 727-1441
939 Wading River Manor Rd Manorville (11949) ***(G-7785)***
Sas Maintenance Services Inc 718 837-2124
8435 Bay 16th St Ste A Brooklyn (11214) ***(G-2449)***
Satco Castings Service Inc 516 354-1500
1400 Plaza Ave New Hyde Park (11040) ***(G-8561)***
Satco Lighting, Edgewood *Also called Satco Products Inc* ***(G-4415)***
Satco Products Inc (PA) 631 243-2022
110 Heartland Blvd Edgewood (11717) ***(G-4415)***
Satellite Incorporated 212 221-6687
43 W 46th St Ste 503 New York (10036) ***(G-11492)***
Satin Fine Foods Inc 845 469-1034
32 Leone Ln Chester (10918) ***(G-3483)***
Satispie LLC 716 982-4600
155 Balta Dr Rochester (14623) ***(G-14112)***
Satnam Distributors LLC 516 802-0600
200 Robbins Ln Unit B Jericho (11753) ***(G-6801)***
Saturn Industries Inc (PA) 518 828-9956
157 Union Tpke Hudson (12534) ***(G-6370)***
Satya Jewelry, New York *Also called Sube Inc* ***(G-11732)***
Saunders Concrete, Etna *Also called W F Saunders & Sons Inc* ***(G-4623)***
Saunders Concrete Co Inc 607 756-7905
6 Locust Ave Cortland (13045) ***(G-3893)***
Sausbiers Awning Shop Inc 518 828-3748
43 8th St Hudson (12534) ***(G-6371)***
SAV Thermo Inc 631 249-9444
133 Cabot St West Babylon (11704) ***(G-16191)***
Savaco Inc 716 751-9455
2905 Beebe Rd Newfane (14108) ***(G-12253)***
Savage & Son Installations LLC 585 342-7533
676 Pullman Ave Rochester (14615) ***(G-14113)***
Save Around, Binghamton *Also called Enjoy City North Inc* ***(G-883)***
Save Mor Copy Center, Brooklyn *Also called At Copy Inc* ***(G-1566)***
Save More Beverage Corp 518 371-2520
1512 Route 9 Ste 1 Halfmoon (12065) ***(G-5669)***
Save O Seal Corporation Inc 914 592-3031
90 E Main St Elmsford (10523) ***(G-4563)***
Savenergy Inc 516 239-1958
645 South St Unit A Garden City (11530) ***(G-5280)***
Saveur Magazine 212 219-7400
304 Park Ave S Fl 8 New York (10010) ***(G-11493)***
Savoritefactory, New York *Also called Q Ed Creations* ***(G-11289)***
Savwatt Usa Inc (PA) 646 478-2676
475 Park Ave S Fl 30 New York (10016) ***(G-11494)***
Saw Mill Pediatrics Pllc 914 449-6064
95 Locust Rd Pleasantville (10570) ***(G-13178)***
Saxby Implement Corp (PA) 585 624-2938
180 Mendon Victor Rd Mendon (14506) ***(G-8094)***
Saxon Glass Technologies Inc 607 587-9630
200 N Main St Ste 114 Alfred (14802) ***(G-184)***
Saxton Corporation 518 732-7705
1320 Route 9 Castleton On Hudson (12033) ***(G-3297)***
Sayeda Manufacturing Corp 631 345-2525
20 Scouting Blvd Medford (11763) ***(G-7965)***
Sb Corporation 212 822-3166
114 W 41st St Fl 4 New York (10036) ***(G-11495)***
Sb Molds LLC 845 352-3700
161 Route 59 Ste 203a Monsey (10952) ***(G-8297)***
Sb New York Inc (HQ) 212 457-7790
120 Broadway New York (10271) ***(G-11496)***
Sbb Inc 315 422-2376
1 Gm Dr Ste 5 East Syracuse (13057) ***(G-4368)***
Sbcontract.com, Farmingdale *Also called Metadure Parts & Sales Inc* ***(G-4821)***
Sbi Enterprises, Ellenville *Also called Master Juvenile Products Inc* ***(G-4440)***
Sbi Enterprises, Ellenville *Also called JM Originals Inc* ***(G-4439)***
Sbk Preserves Inc 800 773-7378
1161 E 156th St Bronx (10474) ***(G-1381)***
SC Building Solutions LLC 800 564-1152
53 W 23rd St Fl 12 New York (10010) ***(G-11497)***
SC Medical Overseas Inc 516 935-8500
350 Jericho Tpke Ste 302 Jericho (11753) ***(G-6802)***
SC Supply Chain Management LLC 212 344-3322
90 Broad St Ste 1504 New York (10004) ***(G-11498)***
SC Textiles Inc 631 944-6262
434 New York Ave Huntington (11743) ***(G-6414)***
Scaccianoce Inc 718 991-4462
1165 Burnett Pl Bronx (10474) ***(G-1382)***
Scaife Enterprises Inc 585 454-5231
4 Chillon Ct Fairport (14450) ***(G-4656)***
Scalamandre Silks, Hauppauge *Also called Scalamandre Wallpaper Inc* ***(G-5934)***
Scalamandre Silks Inc (PA) 212 980-3888
979 3rd Ave Ste 202 New York (10022) ***(G-11499)***
Scalamandre Wallpaper Inc 631 467-8800
350 Wireless Blvd Hauppauge (11788) ***(G-5934)***
Scale-Tronix Inc 914 948-8117
4341 State Street Rd Skaneateles (13152) ***(G-14877)***
Scan-A-Chrome Color Inc 631 532-6146
555 Oak St Copiague (11726) ***(G-3779)***
Scancorp Inc 315 454-5596
1840 Lemoyne Ave Syracuse (13208) ***(G-15416)***
Scanga Woodworking Corp 845 265-9115
22 Corporate Park W Cold Spring (10516) ***(G-3628)***
Scapa North America 315 413-1111
1111 Vine St Liverpool (13088) ***(G-7261)***
Scara-Mix Inc 718 442-7357
2537 Richmond Ter Staten Island (10303) ***(G-15132)***
Scarano Boat Building Inc 518 463-3401
194 S Port Rd Albany (12202) ***(G-126)***
Scarano Boatbuilding Inc 518 463-3401
194 S Port Rd Albany (12202) ***(G-127)***
Scarguard Labs LLC 516 482-8050
15 Barstow Rd Great Neck (11021) ***(G-5589)***
Scarsdale Inquirer, Scarsdale *Also called S I Communications Inc* ***(G-14644)***
Scehenvus Fire Dist 607 638-9017
40 Main St Schenevus (12155) ***(G-14730)***
Scehenvus Gram Hose Co, Schenevus *Also called Scehenvus Fire Dist* ***(G-14730)***
Scent 2 Market, Yonkers *Also called Belmay Holding Corporation* ***(G-16740)***
Scent-A-Vision Inc 631 424-4905
171 E 2nd St Huntington Station (11746) ***(G-6457)***
Scepter Inc 315 568-4225
11 Lamb Rd Seneca Falls (13148) ***(G-14783)***
Scepter Publishers Inc 212 354-0670
56 Harrison St Ste 401 New Rochelle (10801) ***(G-8627)***
Scerri Quality Wood Floors, New York *Also called Wood Floor Expo Inc* ***(G-12132)***
Sch Dpx Corporation 917 405-5377
22 W 21st St Ste 700 New York (10010) ***(G-11500)***
Schaefer Entps Deposit Inc (PA) 607 467-4990
315 Old Route 10 Deposit (13754) ***(G-4110)***
Schaefer Logging Inc 607 467-4990
315 Old Route 10 Deposit (13754) ***(G-4111)***
Schaefer Machine Co Inc 516 248-6880
100 Hudson St Mineola (11501) ***(G-8249)***
Schaller & Webber, New York *Also called Schaller Manufacturing Corp* ***(G-11502)***
Schaller & Weber, New York *Also called Schaller Manufacturing Corp* ***(G-11501)***
Schaller Manufacturing Corp (PA) 718 721-5480
1654 2nd Ave Apt 2n New York (10028) ***(G-11501)***
Schaller Manufacturing Corp 212 879-3047
1654 2nd Ave Apt 2n New York (10028) ***(G-11502)***
Scharf and Breit Inc 516 282-0287
2 Hillside Ave Ste F Williston Park (11596) ***(G-16595)***
Schatz Bearing Corporation 845 452-6000
10 Fairview Ave Poughkeepsie (12601) ***(G-13365)***
Schenck Corporation (HQ) 631 242-4010
535 Acorn St Deer Park (11729) ***(G-4040)***
Schenck Trebel Corp (HQ) 631 242-4010
535 Acorn St Deer Park (11729) ***(G-4041)***
SCHENECTADY HERALD PRINTING CO, Troy *Also called Dowd - Witbeck Printing Corp* ***(G-15604)***
Schenectady Steel Co Inc 518 355-3220
18 Mariaville Rd Schenectady (12306) ***(G-14711)***
Schiller Stores Inc 845 928-4316
869 Adirondack Way Central Valley (10917) ***(G-3397)***
Schiller Stores Inc (PA) 631 208-9400
509 Tanger Mall Dr Riverhead (11901) ***(G-13583)***
Schilling Forge Inc 315 454-4421
606 Factory Ave Syracuse (13208) ***(G-15417)***
Schindler Elevator Corporation 212 708-1000
620 12th Ave Fl 4 New York (10036) ***(G-11503)***
Schindler Elevator Corporation 800 225-3123
1211 6th Ave Ste 2950 New York (10036) ***(G-11504)***
Schlegel Electronic Mtls Inc (PA) 585 295-2030
1600 Lexington Ave # 236 Rochester (14606) ***(G-14114)***
Schlegel Systems Inc (HQ) 585 427-7200
1555 Jefferson Rd Rochester (14623) ***(G-14115)***
Schless Bottles Inc (PA) 718 236-2790
4616 16th Ave Brooklyn (11204) ***(G-2450)***
Schlumberger Foundation Inc 212 350-9400
601 Lexington Ave Fl 57 New York (10022) ***(G-11505)***
Schlumberger Technology Corp 607 378-0105
224 N Main St Bldg S Horseheads (14845) ***(G-6328)***
Schmersal Inc 914 347-4775
15 Skyline Dr Ste 230 Hawthorne (10532) ***(G-5997)***
Schmitt Sales Inc 716 632-8595
5095 Main St Williamsville (14221) ***(G-16585)***

ALPHABETIC

(PA)=Parent Co (HQ)=Headquarters (DH)=Div Headquarters
2019 Harris
New York Manufacturers Directory
981

Schneeman Studio Limited ... 212 244-3330
330 W 38th St Rm 505 New York (10018) *(G-11506)*
Schneider Amalco Inc ... 917 470-9674
600 3rd Ave Fl 2 New York (10016) *(G-11507)*
Schneider Brothers Corporation ... 315 458-8369
7371 Eastman Rd Syracuse (13212) *(G-15418)*
Schneider Elc Systems USA Inc ... 214 527-3099
7 E 8th St New York (10003) *(G-11508)*
Schneider Electric It Corp ... 646 335-0216
520 8th Ave Rm 2103 New York (10018) *(G-11509)*
Schneider Electric Usa Inc ... 646 335-0220
112 W 34th St Ste 908 New York (10120) *(G-11510)*
Schneider Electric Usa Inc ... 585 377-1313
441 Penbrooke Dr Ste 9 Penfield (14526) *(G-12945)*
Schneider M Soap & Chemical Co ... 718 389-1000
1930 Troutman St Ridgewood (11385) *(G-13550)*
Schneider Mills Inc ... 828 632-0801
1430 Broadway Rm 1202 New York (10018) *(G-11511)*
Schneider Optics Inc (HQ) ... 631 761-5000
285 Oser Ave Hauppauge (11788) *(G-5935)*
Schneps Publications Inc (PA) ... 718 224-5863
3815 Bell Blvd Ste 38 Bayside (11361) *(G-749)*
Schoen Trimming & Cord Co Inc ... 212 255-3949
151 W 25th St Fl 10 New York (10001) *(G-11512)*
Schoharie Quarry/Asphalt, Schoharie *Also called Cobleskill Stone Products Inc* *(G-14731)*
Scholastic Copy Center, New York *Also called Scholastic Inc* *(G-11515)*
Scholastic Corporation (PA) ... 212 343-6100
557 Broadway Lbby 1 New York (10012) *(G-11513)*
Scholastic Inc (HQ) ... 800 724-6527
557 Broadway Lbby 1 New York (10012) *(G-11514)*
Scholastic Inc ... 212 343-6100
557 Broadway Lbby 1 New York (10012) *(G-11515)*
Scholastic Inc ... 212 343-7100
568 Broadway Rm 809 New York (10012) *(G-11516)*
Scholastic U.S.A., New York *Also called Scholastic Inc* *(G-11514)*
Scholium International Inc. ... 516 883-8032
151 Cow Neck Rd Port Washington (11050) *(G-13305)*
Schonbek, Plattsburgh *Also called Swarovski Lighting Ltd* *(G-13161)*
Schonbek Shipping Bldg, Plattsburgh *Also called Swarovski Lighting Ltd* *(G-13162)*
Schonwetter Enterprises Inc ... 518 237-0171
41 Lark St Cohoes (12047) *(G-3620)*
School Guide Publications, Mamaroneck *Also called Catholic News Publishing Co* *(G-7737)*
School of Management, Binghamton *Also called Suny At Binghamton* *(G-916)*
Schoolnet Inc (HQ) ... 646 496-9000
525 Fashion Ave Fl 4 New York (10018) *(G-11517)*
Schott Corporation (HQ) ... 914 831-2200
555 Taxter Rd Ste 470 Elmsford (10523) *(G-4564)*
Schott Corporation ... 315 255-2791
62 Columbus St Auburn (13021) *(G-499)*
Schott Gemtron Corporation ... 423 337-3522
555 Taxter Rd Ste 470 Elmsford (10523) *(G-4565)*
Schott Lithotec USA Corp ... 845 463-5300
555 Taxter Rd Ste 470 Elmsford (10523) *(G-4566)*
Schott North America Inc (HQ) ... 914 831-2200
555 Taxter Rd Ste 470 Elmsford (10523) *(G-4567)*
Schott Solar Pv Inc ... 888 457-6527
555 Taxter Rd Ste 470 Elmsford (10523) *(G-4568)*
Schrader Meat Market ... 607 869-6328
1937 Summerville Rd Romulus (14541) *(G-14281)*
Schroeder Machine Div, East Syracuse *Also called Niagara Scientific Inc* *(G-4360)*
Schuler-Haas Electric Corp ... 607 936-3514
598 Ritas Way Painted Post (14870) *(G-12840)*
Schuler-Subra Inc ... 716 893-3100
83 Doat St Buffalo (14211) *(G-3058)*
Schulz Interiors, Poughquag *Also called Fred Schulz Inc* *(G-13374)*
Schulze Vineyards & Winery LLC ... 716 778-8090
2090 Coomer Rd Burt (14028) *(G-3144)*
Schuster & Richard Lab, College Point *Also called Schuster & Richard Labortories* *(G-3664)*
Schuster & Richard Labortories ... 718 358-8607
1420 130th St College Point (11356) *(G-3664)*
Schutt Cider Mill ... 585 872-2924
1063 Plank Rd Webster (14580) *(G-16097)*
Schutte-Buffalo Hammer Mill, Buffalo *Also called Schutte-Buffalo Hammermill LLC* *(G-3059)*
Schutte-Buffalo Hammermill LLC ... 716 855-1202
61 Depot St Buffalo (14206) *(G-3059)*
Schwab Corp (HQ) ... 585 381-4900
900 Linden Ave Rochester (14625) *(G-14116)*
Schwabel Fabricating Co Inc (PA) ... 716 876-2086
349 Sawyer Ave Tonawanda (14150) *(G-15575)*
Schwartz Textile LLC ... 718 499-8243
160 7th St Brooklyn (11215) *(G-2451)*
Schweitzer-Mauduit Intl Inc ... 518 329-4222
2424 Route 82 Ancram (12502) *(G-365)*
SCI Bore Inc ... 212 674-7128
70 Irving Pl Apt 5c New York (10003) *(G-11518)*
Sciane Enterprises Inc ... 845 452-2400
2600 South Rd Ste 37 Poughkeepsie (12601) *(G-13366)*
Sciarra Laboratories Inc ... 516 933-7853
48509 S Broadway Hicksville (11801) *(G-6131)*
Sciegen Pharmaceuticals Inc (PA) ... 631 434-2723
330 Oser Ave Hauppauge (11788) *(G-5936)*
Scienta Pharmaceuticals LLC ... 845 589-0774
612 Corporate Way Ste 9 Valley Cottage (10989) *(G-15764)*
Scientific American Library, New York *Also called Bedford Freeman & Worth* *(G-9034)*
Scientific Components Corp (PA) ... 718 934-4500
13 Neptune Ave Brooklyn (11235) *(G-2452)*
Scientific Components Corp ... 631 243-4901
161 E Industry Ct Deer Park (11729) *(G-4042)*
Scientific Components Corp ... 718 368-2060
2450 Knapp St Brooklyn (11235) *(G-2453)*
Scientific Industries Inc (PA) ... 631 567-4700
80 Orville Dr Ste 102 Bohemia (11716) *(G-1085)*
Scientific Plastics Inc ... 212 967-1199
243 W 30th St Fl 8 New York (10001) *(G-11519)*
Scientific Polymer Products ... 585 265-0413
6265 Dean Pkwy Ontario (14519) *(G-12665)*
Scientific Solutions Globl LLC ... 516 543-3376
326 Westbury Ave Carle Place (11514) *(G-3272)*
Scientific Tool Co Inc (PA) ... 315 431-4243
101 Arterial Rd Syracuse (13206) *(G-15419)*
Scientifics Direct Inc ... 716 773-7500
532 Main St Tonawanda (14150) *(G-15576)*
Scissor Online, Bolivar *Also called Klein Cutlery LLC* *(G-1111)*
Sciterra LLC ... 646 883-3724
244 5th Ave Ste L280 New York (10001) *(G-11520)*
Scj Associates Inc ... 585 359-0600
60 Commerce Dr Rochester (14623) *(G-14117)*
SCM, New York *Also called SC Supply Chain Management LLC* *(G-11498)*
SCM, Suffern *Also called Super Conductor Materials Inc* *(G-15198)*
Scomac Inc. ... 585 494-2200
8629 Buffalo Rd Bergen (14416) *(G-827)*
Scooby Dog Food, Utica *Also called Scooby Rendering & Inc* *(G-15732)*
Scooby Rendering & Inc ... 315 793-1014
1930 Oriskany St W Utica (13502) *(G-15732)*
Scoops R US Incorporated ... 212 730-7959
1514 Broadway New York (10036) *(G-11521)*
Scorpion Security Products Inc ... 607 724-9999
330 N Jensen Rd Vestal (13850) *(G-15821)*
Scotia Beverages Inc ... 518 370-3621
701 Corporation Park Schenectady (12302) *(G-14712)*
Scott Rotary Seals, Olean *Also called Dynamic Sealing Tech Inc* *(G-12600)*
Scott Silverstein Llc ... 212 781-1818
242 W 38th St New York (10018) *(G-11522)*
Scotti Graphics Inc ... 212 367-9602
3200 Skillman Ave Fl 1 Long Island City (11101) *(G-7585)*
Scotts Company LLC ... 631 478-6843
65 Engineers Rd Hauppauge (11788) *(G-5937)*
Scotts Feed Inc ... 518 483-3110
245 Elm St Malone (12953) *(G-7725)*
Screen Gems Inc ... 845 561-0036
41 Windsor Hwy New Windsor (12553) *(G-8659)*
Screen Gems-EMI Music Inc (HQ) ... 212 786-8000
150 5th Ave Fl 7 New York (10011) *(G-11523)*
Screen Team Inc ... 718 786-2424
3402c Review Ave Long Island City (11101) *(G-7586)*
Screen The World Inc ... 631 475-0023
658 Blue Point Rd Holtsville (11742) *(G-6244)*
Screw Compressor Tech Inc ... 716 827-6600
158 Ridge Rd Buffalo (14218) *(G-3060)*
Script-Master Div, New York *Also called Brewer-Cantelmo Co Inc* *(G-9138)*
Scriven Duplicating Service ... 518 233-8180
100 Eastover Rd Troy (12182) *(G-15624)*
Scriven Press, Troy *Also called Scriven Duplicating Service* *(G-15624)*
Scroll Media Inc ... 617 395-8904
235 W 102nd St Apt 14i New York (10025) *(G-11524)*
Scully Sanitation ... 315 899-8996
11146 Skaneateles Tpke West Edmeston (13485) *(G-16207)*
Scy Manufacturing Inc ... 516 986-3083
600 Bayview Ave Ste 200 Inwood (11096) *(G-6500)*
SD Christie Associates Inc ... 914 734-1800
424 Central Ave Ste 5 Peekskill (10566) *(G-12925)*
SD Eagle Global Inc. ... 516 822-1778
2 Kay St Jericho (11753) *(G-6803)*
SD Times, Melville *Also called Bz Media LLC* *(G-8005)*
SDC, Saugerties *Also called Stainless Design Concepts Ltd* *(G-14617)*
Sdi, Sunnyside *Also called S Donadic Inc* *(G-15205)*
Sdi Cable, Bohemia *Also called Security Dynamics Inc* *(G-1086)*
SDJ Machine Shop Inc ... 585 458-1236
1215 Mount Read Blvd # 1 Rochester (14606) *(G-14118)*
Sdp/Si, Hicksville *Also called Designatronics Incorporated* *(G-6079)*
Sdr Technology Inc ... 716 583-1249
1613 Lindan Dr Alden (14004) *(G-176)*
Se-Mar Electric Co Inc ... 716 674-7404
101 South Ave West Seneca (14224) *(G-16302)*
Sea Breeze Fish & Seafood of S (PA) ... 718 984-0447
240 Page Ave Staten Island (10307) *(G-15133)*
Sea Isle Custom Rod Builders ... 516 868-8855
495 Guy Lombardo Ave Freeport (11520) *(G-5181)*
Sea Mats, Malone *Also called Seaway Mats Inc* *(G-7726)*
Sea Waves Inc (PA) ... 516 766-4201
2425 Long Beach Rd Oceanside (11572) *(G-12556)*

ALPHABETIC SECTION

Seneca Stone Corporation (HQ)

Seabay Media Holdings LLC (PA) 212 457-7790
120 Broadway Fl 6 New York (10271) *(G-11525)*
Seaboard Electronics, New Rochelle *Also called Highlander Realty Inc (G-8614)*
Seaboard Graphic Services LLC 315 652-4200
6881 Schuyler Rd East Syracuse (13057) *(G-4369)*
Seal & Design Inc 315 432-8021
6741 Thompson Rd Syracuse (13211) *(G-15420)*
Seal Reinforced Fiberglass Inc (PA) 631 842-2230
19 Bethpage Rd Copiague (11726) *(G-3780)*
Seal Reinforced Fiberglass Inc 631 842-2230
23 Bethpage Rd Copiague (11726) *(G-3781)*
Sealmaster, Buffalo *Also called Jet-Black Sealers Inc (G-2895)*
Sealtest Dairy Products, Rochester *Also called Upstate Niagara Coop Inc (G-14193)*
Sealy Mattress Co Albany Inc 518 880-1600
30 Veterans Memorial Dr Troy (12183) *(G-15598)*
Sean John, New York *Also called Christian Casey LLC (G-9289)*
Sean John Clothing, New York *Also called Christian Casey LLC (G-9290)*
Sean John Clothing Inc 212 500-2200
1710 Broadway Frnt 1 New York (10019) *(G-11526)*
Sean John Clothing Inc (PA) 212 500-2200
1440 Broadway Frnt 3 New York (10018) *(G-11527)*
Seanair Machine Co Inc 631 694-2820
95 Verdi St Farmingdale (11735) *(G-4873)*
Searles Graphics Inc (PA) 631 345-2202
56 Old Dock Rd Yaphank (11980) *(G-16720)*
Seasons Soyfood Inc 718 797-9896
605 Degraw St Brooklyn (11217) *(G-2454)*
Seating Inc 800 468-2475
60 N State St Nunda (14517) *(G-12498)*
Seaward Candies 585 638-6761
3588 N Main Street Rd Holley (14470) *(G-6229)*
Seaway Mats Inc 518 483-2560
252 Park St Malone (12953) *(G-7726)*
Seaway Timber Harvesting Inc (PA) 315 769-5970
15121 State Highway 37 Massena (13662) *(G-7908)*
Sebby Clothing, New York *Also called Comint Apparel Group LLC (G-9363)*
Second Amendment Foundation 716 885-6408
267 Linwood Ave Ste A Buffalo (14209) *(G-3061)*
Second Chance Press Inc 631 725-1101
4170 Noyac Rd Sag Harbor (11963) *(G-14503)*
Second Generation Wood Stairs 718 370-0085
2581 Richmond Ter Ste 3 Staten Island (10303) *(G-15134)*
Secret Celebrity Licensing LLC 212 812-9277
1431 Broadway Fl 10 New York (10018) *(G-11528)*
Secs Inc (PA) 914 667-5600
550 S Columbus Ave Mount Vernon (10550) *(G-8441)*
Secs Inc 914 667-5600
550 S Columbus Ave Mount Vernon (10550) *(G-8442)*
Sector Microwave Inds Inc 631 242-2245
999 Grand Blvd Deer Park (11729) *(G-4043)*
Securax, Bohemia *Also called Protex International Corp (G-1080)*
Secure International 716 206-2500
100 W Drullard Ave Ste 3 Lancaster (14086) *(G-7048)*
Secured Services Inc (PA) 866 419-3900
110 William St Fl 14 New York (10038) *(G-11529)*
Secureit Tactical Inc (PA) 800 651-8835
6691 Commerce Blvd Syracuse (13211) *(G-15421)*
Securities Data Publishing Inc (PA) 212 631-1411
11 Penn Plz Fl 17 New York (10001) *(G-11530)*
Security Defense System 718 769-7900
15038 12th Ave Whitestone (11357) *(G-16548)*
Security Dynamics Inc 631 392-1701
217 Knickerbocker Ave # 4 Bohemia (11716) *(G-1086)*
Security Letter 212 348-1553
166 E 96th St Apt 3b New York (10128) *(G-11531)*
Security Offset Services Inc 631 944-6031
11 Grandview St Huntington (11743) *(G-6415)*
Seedlings Lf Scnce Ventures LLC 917 913-8511
230 E 15th St Apt 1a New York (10003) *(G-11532)*
Seeley Machine Inc 518 798-9510
75 Big Boom Rd Queensbury (12804) *(G-13441)*
Seeley Machine & Fabrication, Queensbury *Also called Seeley Machine Inc (G-13441)*
Seetin Design Group Inc 718 486-5610
57 Grand Street Ext Brooklyn (11211) *(G-2455)*
Sefaira Inc 855 733-2472
135 E 57th St Fl 6 New York (10022) *(G-11533)*
Sefi Fabricator, Amityville *Also called IMC Teddy Food Service (G-286)*
Sefi Fabricators, Amityville *Also called P & M LLC (G-310)*
Segovia Technology Co 212 868-4412
33 Irving Pl Fl 7 New York (10003) *(G-11534)*
Seibel Modern Mfg & Wldg Corp 716 683-1536
38 Palmer Pl Lancaster (14086) *(G-7049)*
Seidlin Consulting 212 496-2043
580 W End Ave New York (10024) *(G-11535)*
Seifert Graphics Inc 315 736-2744
6133 Judd Rd Oriskany (13424) *(G-12761)*
Seifert Transit Graphics, Oriskany *Also called Seifert Graphics Inc (G-12761)*
Seisenbacher Inc 585 730-4960
175 Humboldt St Ste 250 Rochester (14610) *(G-14119)*
Seize Sur Vingt, New York *Also called Groupe 16sur20 LLC (G-3998)*
Sekas International Ltd 212 629-6095
345 7th Ave Fl 9 New York (10001) *(G-11536)*
Selby Marketing Associates Inc (PA) 585 377-0750
1001 Lexington Aveste 800 Rochester (14606) *(G-14120)*
Select Controls Inc 631 567-9010
45 Knickerbocker Ave # 3 Bohemia (11716) *(G-1087)*
Select Door, North Java *Also called Select Interior Door Ltd (G-12392)*
Select Fabricators Inc 585 393-0650
5310 North St Ste 5 Canandaigua (14424) *(G-3233)*
Select Industries New York Inc 800 723-5333
450 Fashion Ave Ste 3002 New York (10123) *(G-11537)*
Select Information Exchange 212 496-6435
175 W 79th St 3a New York (10024) *(G-11538)*
Select Interior Door Ltd 585 535-9900
2074 Perry Rd North Java (14113) *(G-12392)*
Select Jewelry Inc 718 784-3626
4728 37th St Fl 3 Long Island City (11101) *(G-7587)*
Select Products Holdings LLC (PA) 631 421-6000
1 Arnold Dr Unit 3 Huntington (11743) *(G-6416)*
Select-A-Form Inc 631 981-3076
4717 Veterans Mem Hwy Holbrook (11741) *(G-6208)*
Select-Tech Inc 845 895-8111
3050 State Route 208 Wallkill (12589) *(G-15908)*
Selective Beauty Corporation 585 336-7600
315 Bleecker St 109 New York (10014) *(G-11539)*
Selectrode Industries Inc (PA) 631 547-5470
230 Broadway Huntington Station (11746) *(G-6458)*
Selflock Screw Products Co Inc 315 541-4464
461 E Brighton Ave Syracuse (13210) *(G-15422)*
Sellas Life Sciences Group Inc (PA) 917 438-4353
15 W 38th St Fl 10 New York (10018) *(G-11540)*
Sellco Industries Inc 607 756-7594
58 Grant St Cortland (13045) *(G-3894)*
Selux Corporation 845 691-7723
5 Lumen Ln Highland (12528) *(G-6147)*
Semans Enterprises Inc 585 444-0097
25 Hendrix Rd Ste E West Henrietta (14586) *(G-16250)*
Semco Ceramics Inc 315 782-3000
363 Eastern Blvd Watertown (13601) *(G-16033)*
Semec Corp 518 825-0160
20 Gateway Dr Plattsburgh (12901) *(G-13155)*
Semi-Linear Inc 212 243-2108
1123 Broadway Ste 718 New York (10010) *(G-11541)*
Semitronics Corp (HQ) 516 223-0200
80 Commercial St Freeport (11520) *(G-5182)*
Semrock, Rochester *Also called Semrok Inc (G-14121)*
Semrok Inc 585 594-7050
3625 Buffalo Rd Ste 6 Rochester (14624) *(G-14121)*
Semtex Industrial, Freeport *Also called Intex Company Inc (G-5162)*
Sendec Corp 585 425-5965
151 Perinton Pkwy Fairport (14450) *(G-4657)*
Sendyne Corp 212 966-0663
250 W Broadway Fl 6 New York (10013) *(G-11542)*
Seneca Ceramics Corp 315 781-0100
835 Mcivor Rd Phelps (14532) *(G-12980)*
Seneca County Area Shopper 607 532-4333
1885 State Route 96a Ovid (14521) *(G-12792)*
Seneca Falls Capital Inc (PA) 315 568-5804
314 Fall St Seneca Falls (13148) *(G-14784)*
Seneca Falls Machine, Seneca Falls *Also called Seneca Falls Capital Inc (G-14784)*
Seneca Falls Machine Tool Co 315 568-5804
314 Fall St Seneca Falls (13148) *(G-14785)*
Seneca Falls Technology Group, Seneca Falls *Also called Seneca Falls Machine Tool Co (G-14785)*
Seneca FLS Spc & Logistics Co (PA) 315 568-4139
50 Johnston St Seneca Falls (13148) *(G-14786)*
Seneca Foods Corporation (PA) 315 926-8100
3736 S Main St Marion (14505) *(G-7806)*
Seneca Foods Corporation 315 781-8733
100 Gambee Rd Geneva (14456) *(G-5332)*
Seneca Foods Corporation 315 926-0531
3709 Mill St Marion (14505) *(G-7807)*
Seneca Foods Corporation 315 926-4277
3732 S Main St Marion (14505) *(G-7808)*
Seneca Foods Corporation 585 658-2211
5705 Rte 36 Leicester (14481) *(G-7129)*
Seneca Manufacturing Company 716 945-4400
175 Rochester St Salamanca (14779) *(G-14532)*
Seneca Media Inc (PA) 607 324-1425
32 Broadway Mall Hornell (14843) *(G-6302)*
Seneca Media Inc 585 593-5300
159 N Main St Wellsville (14895) *(G-16122)*
Seneca Nation Enterprise 716 934-7430
11482 Route 20 Irving (14081) *(G-6501)*
Seneca Resources Company LLC 716 630-6750
165 Lawrence Bell Dr Williamsville (14221) *(G-16586)*
Seneca Signs LLC 315 446-9420
102 Headson Dr Syracuse (13214) *(G-15423)*
Seneca Stone Corporation 315 549-8253
Cty Rd 121 Hoster Cors Rd Fayette (13065) *(G-4926)*
Seneca Stone Corporation (HQ) 607 737-6200
2105 S Broadway Pine City (14871) *(G-13001)*

ALPHABETIC

Seneca TEC Inc 585 381-2645
73 Country Corner Ln Fairport (14450) ***(G-4658)***
Seneca Truck & Trailer Inc 315 781-1100
2200 State Route 14 Geneva (14456) ***(G-5333)***
Seneca West Printing Inc 716 675-8010
860 Center Rd West Seneca (14224) ***(G-16303)***
Senera Co Inc 516 639-3774
834 Glenridge Ave Valley Stream (11581) ***(G-15796)***
Sensational Collection Inc (PA) 212 840-7388
1410 Broadway Rm 505 New York (10018) ***(G-11543)***
Sensio America 877 501-5337
800 Route 146 Ste 175 Clifton Park (12065) ***(G-3576)***
Sensio America LLC (PA) 877 501-5337
800 Route 146 Ste 175 Clifton Park (12065) ***(G-3577)***
Sensitron Semiconductor, Deer Park *Also called RSM Electron Power Inc* ***(G-4039)***
Sensitron Semiconductor, Hauppauge *Also called RSM Electron Power Inc* ***(G-5931)***
Sensor & Decontamination Inc 301 526-8389
892 Powderhouse Rd Binghamton (13903) ***(G-914)***
Sensor Films Incorporated 585 738-3500
687 Rowley Rd Victor (14564) ***(G-15866)***
Sensormatic Electronics LLC 845 365-3125
10 Corporate Dr Orangeburg (10962) ***(G-12691)***
Sensual Inc 212 869-1450
463 7th Ave New York (10018) ***(G-11544)***
Sentine Printing Inc 516 334-7400
75 State St Westbury (11590) ***(G-16372)***
Sentinel Printing, Hempstead *Also called Hempstead Sentinel Inc* ***(G-6013)***
Sentinel Printing Services Inc 845 562-1218
36 Meriline Ave New Windsor (12553) ***(G-8660)***
Sentinel Products Corp 518 568-7036
12 New St Saint Johnsville (13452) ***(G-14522)***
Sentinel, The, New Windsor *Also called E W Smith Publishing Co* ***(G-8643)***
Sentry Automatic Sprinkler 631 723-3095
735 Flanders Rd Riverhead (11901) ***(G-13584)***
Sentry Devices Corp 631 491-3191
33 Rustic Gate Ln Dix Hills (11746) ***(G-4126)***
Sentry Funding Partnership, Ronkonkoma *Also called Sentry Technology Corporation* ***(G-14411)***
Sentry Metal Blast Inc 716 285-5241
553 West Ave Lockport (14094) ***(G-7331)***
Sentry Metal Services, Lockport *Also called Sentry Metal Blast Inc* ***(G-7331)***
Sentry Technology Corporation 631 739-2000
1881 Lakeland Ave Ronkonkoma (11779) ***(G-14410)***
Sentry Technology Corporation (PA) 800 645-4224
1881 Lakeland Ave Ronkonkoma (11779) ***(G-14411)***
Sepac Inc 607 732-2030
1580 Lake St Ste 1 Elmira (14901) ***(G-4502)***
Sepco-Sturges Electronics, Dryden *Also called Sturges Elec Pdts Co Inc* ***(G-4152)***
Sephardic Yellow Pages 718 998-0299
2150 E 4th St Brooklyn (11223) ***(G-2456)***
Sepsa North America, Ballston Spa *Also called Albatros North America Inc* ***(G-575)***
September Associates, Oakdale *Also called Steel-Brite Ltd* ***(G-12522)***
Sequa Corporation 201 343-1122
330 Blaisdell Rd Orangeburg (10962) ***(G-12692)***
Serge Duct Designs Inc 718 783-7799
535 Dean St Apt 124 Brooklyn (11217) ***(G-2457)***
Seri Systems Inc 585 272-5515
172 Metro Park Rochester (14623) ***(G-14122)***
Sermoneta Gloves, New York *Also called Shadal LLC* ***(G-11551)***
Serraview America Inc 800 903-3716
2 Wall St Fl 10 New York (10005) ***(G-11545)***
Service Advertising Group Inc 718 361-6161
4216 34th Ave Long Island City (11101) ***(G-7588)***
Service Canvas Co Inc 716 853-0558
149 Swan St Unit 155 Buffalo (14203) ***(G-3062)***
Service Education Incorporated 585 264-9240
790 Canning Pkwy Ste 1 Victor (14564) ***(G-15867)***
Service Filtration Corp 716 877-2608
225 E Park Dr Tonawanda (14150) ***(G-15577)***
Service Machine & Tool Company 607 732-0413
206 E Mccanns Blvd Elmira Heights (14903) ***(G-4513)***
Service Mfg Group Inc (PA) 716 893-1482
400 Scajaquada St Buffalo (14211) ***(G-3063)***
Service Mfg Group Inc 716 893-1482
400 Scajaquada St Buffalo (14211) ***(G-3064)***
Servicenow Inc 914 318-1168
60 E 42nd St Ste 1230 New York (10165) ***(G-11546)***
Servo Reeler System, Queens Village *Also called Xedit Corp* ***(G-13413)***
Servotec Usa LLC 518 671-6120
1 Industrial Tract Anx # 3 Hudson (12534) ***(G-6372)***
Servotronics Inc (PA) 716 655-5990
1110 Maple Rd Elma (14059) ***(G-4458)***
Serway Bros Inc (PA) 315 337-0601
Plant 2 Rome Indus Ctr Rome (13440) ***(G-14274)***
Serway Cabinet Trends, Rome *Also called Serway Bros Inc* ***(G-14274)***
Sesco Industries Inc 718 939-5137
11019 15th Ave College Point (11356) ***(G-3665)***
Setauket Manufacturing Co 631 231-7272
202 Christopher St Ronkonkoma (11779) ***(G-14412)***
Seton Identification Products, Williamsville *Also called Tricor Direct Inc* ***(G-16592)***
Settapani Bakery, Brooklyn *Also called Settepani Inc* ***(G-2458)***
Settepani Inc (PA) 718 349-6524
602 Lorimer St Brooklyn (11211) ***(G-2458)***
Setterstix Inc 716 257-3451
261 S Main St Cattaraugus (14719) ***(G-3314)***
Setton Farms, Commack *Also called Settons Intl Foods Inc* ***(G-3702)***
Settons Intl Foods Inc (PA) 631 543-8090
85 Austin Blvd Commack (11725) ***(G-3702)***
Seven Springs Gravel Pdts LLC 585 343-4336
8479 Seven Springs Rd Batavia (14020) ***(G-634)***
Seven Stories Press Inc 212 226-8760
140 Watts St New York (10013) ***(G-11547)***
Seventeen Magazine, New York *Also called Hearst Corporation* ***(G-10067)***
Seville Central Mix Corp (PA) 516 868-3000
157 Albany Ave Freeport (11520) ***(G-5183)***
Seville Central Mix Corp 516 293-6190
495 Wining Rd Old Bethpage (11804) ***(G-12587)***
Seville Central Mix Corp 516 239-8333
101 Johnson Rd Lawrence (11559) ***(G-7109)***
Seviroli Foods Inc (PA) 516 222-6220
601 Brook St Garden City (11530) ***(G-5281)***
Sew True, New York *Also called Champion Zipper Corp* ***(G-9258)***
Sextet Fabrics Inc 516 593-0608
21 Ryder Pl Ste 4 East Rockaway (11518) ***(G-4295)***
Sfoglini LLC 646 872-1035
630 Flushing Ave Fl 2 Brooklyn (11206) ***(G-2459)***
Sg Blocks Inc (PA) 615 585-2639
195 Montague St Fl 14 Brooklyn (11201) ***(G-2460)***
Sg Nyc LLC 310 210-1837
28 W 27th St Fl 12 New York (10001) ***(G-11548)***
SGD North America 212 753-4200
900 3rd Ave Fl 4 New York (10022) ***(G-11549)***
SGD Pharma Packaging Inc 212 223-7100
900 3rd Ave Fl 4 New York (10022) ***(G-11550)***
Sgg, Long Island City *Also called Stanley Creations Inc* ***(G-7599)***
SGS, Phoenix *Also called Southern Graphic Systems LLC* ***(G-12993)***
Sgt Dresser-Rand, Wellsville *Also called Siemens Government Tech Inc* ***(G-16123)***
Sh Leather Novelty Company 718 387-7742
123 Clymer St Bsmt Brooklyn (11249) ***(G-2461)***
Shaant Industries Inc 716 366-3654
134 Franklin Ave Dunkirk (14048) ***(G-4179)***
Shad Industries Inc 631 504-6028
7 Old Dock Rd Unit 1 Yaphank (11980) ***(G-16721)***
Shadal LLC 212 319-5946
609 Madison Ave Ste 611 New York (10022) ***(G-11551)***
Shade & Shutter Systems of NY 631 208-0275
260 Hampton Rd Southampton (11968) ***(G-14961)***
Shade Tree Greetings Inc 585 442-4580
704 Clinton Ave S Rochester (14620) ***(G-14123)***
Shadow Lake Golf & Racquet CLB, Rochester *Also called Dolomite Products Company Inc* ***(G-13749)***
Shadowtv Inc 212 445-2540
630 9th Ave Ste 202 New York (10036) ***(G-11552)***
Shafer & Sons 315 853-5285
4932 State Route 233 Westmoreland (13490) ***(G-16410)***
Shah Diamonds Inc 212 888-9393
22 W 48th St Ste 600 New York (10036) ***(G-11553)***
Shahin Designs Ltd 212 737-7225
766 Madison Ave Fl 3 New York (10065) ***(G-11554)***
Shake Inc 650 544-5479
175 Varick St Fl 4 New York (10014) ***(G-11555)***
Shake-N-Go Fashion Inc 516 944-7777
83 Harbor Rd Port Washington (11050) ***(G-13306)***
Shake-N-Go Fashion Inc (PA) 516 944-7777
85 Harbor Rd Port Washington (11050) ***(G-13307)***
Shako Inc 315 437-1294
6191 E Molloy Rd East Syracuse (13057) ***(G-4370)***
Shakuff LLC 212 675-0383
34 35th St Unit 29 Brooklyn (11232) ***(G-2462)***
Shalam Imports Inc (PA) 718 686-6271
1552 Dahill Rd Ste B Brooklyn (11204) ***(G-2463)***
Shalamex, Brooklyn *Also called Shalam Imports Inc* ***(G-2463)***
Shamrock Plastic Corporation 585 328-6040
95 Mount Read Blvd Rochester (14611) ***(G-14124)***
Shamrock Plastics & Tool Inc 585 328-6040
95 Mount Read Blvd # 149 Rochester (14611) ***(G-14125)***
Shamron Mills Ltd 212 354-0430
484 River St Troy (12180) ***(G-15625)***
Shane & Shawn, New York *Also called Detny Footwear Inc* ***(G-9511)***
Shane Tex Inc 516 486-7522
717 Longacre Ave Woodmere (11598) ***(G-16642)***
Shanghai Harmony AP Intl LLC 646 569-5680
3 Wykagyl Ter New Rochelle (10804) ***(G-8628)***
Shanghai Stove Inc 718 599-4583
78 Gerry St 82 Brooklyn (11206) ***(G-2464)***
Shanker Industries Realty Inc (PA) 631 940-9889
301 Suburban Ave Deer Park (11729) ***(G-4044)***
Shannon Entps Wstn NY Inc 716 693-7954
75 Main St North Tonawanda (14120) ***(G-12450)***
Shanu Gems Inc 212 921-4470
1212 Ave Of The Americas New York (10036) ***(G-11556)***

Shapeways Inc (PA)......914 356-5816
419 Park Ave S Fl 9 New York (10016) ***(G-11557)***
Shapeways Inc......646 470-3576
3002 48th Ave Ste 2 Long Island City (11101) ***(G-7589)***
Shapiro Bernstein & Co Inc......212 588-0878
488 Madison Ave Fl 1201 New York (10022) ***(G-11558)***
Shapiro William NY Univ Med Ctr, New York *Also called William H Shapiro* ***(G-12112)***
Shar-Mar Machine Company......631 567-8040
1648 Locust Ave Ste F Bohemia (11716) ***(G-1088)***
Sharedbook Inc......646 442-8840
110 William St Fl 30 New York (10038) ***(G-11559)***
Sharodine Inc......516 767-3548
18 Haven Ave Frnt 2 Port Washington (11050) ***(G-13308)***
Sharon Manufacturing Co Inc......631 242-8870
540 Brook Ave Deer Park (11729) ***(G-4045)***
Sharonana Enterprises Inc......631 875-5619
52 Sharon Dr Coram (11727) ***(G-3804)***
Sharp Printing Inc......716 731-3994
3477 Lockport Rd Sanborn (14132) ***(G-14553)***
Shawmut Woodworking & Sup Inc......212 920-8900
3 E 54th St Fl 8 New York (10022) ***(G-11560)***
Shawmutdesign and Construction, New York *Also called Shawmut Woodworking & Sup Inc* ***(G-11560)***
Sheets, The, Long Island City *Also called Ragozin Data* ***(G-7570)***
Shehawken Archery Co Inc......607 967-8333
40 S Main St Bainbridge (13733) ***(G-534)***
Shelby Crushed Stone Inc......585 798-4501
10830 Blair Rd Medina (14103) ***(G-7989)***
Sheldon Slate Products Co Inc......518 642-1280
Fox Rd Middle Granville (12849) ***(G-8112)***
Sheldrake Point Vineyard LLC......607 532-8967
7448 County Road 153 Ovid (14521) ***(G-12793)***
Sheldrake Point Winery, Ovid *Also called Sheldrake Point Vineyard LLC* ***(G-12793)***
Shell Ann Printing, Stony Point *Also called Stony Point Graphics Ltd* ***(G-15176)***
Shell Containers Inc (ny)......516 352-4505
1981 Marcus Ave Ste C105 New Hyde Park (11042) ***(G-8562)***
Shell Pipe Line Corporation......212 740-8786
4116 Broadway New York (10033) ***(G-11561)***
Shelley Promotions Inc......212 924-4987
87 5th Ave New York (10003) ***(G-11562)***
Shelter Enterprises Inc......518 237-4100
8 Saratoga St Cohoes (12047) ***(G-3621)***
Shelter Island Cmnty Nwspapers, Shelter Island *Also called Shelter Island Reporter Inc* ***(G-14802)***
Shelter Island Reporter Inc......631 749-1000
50 N Ferry Rd Shelter Island (11964) ***(G-14802)***
Shenfeld Studio Tile, Syracuse *Also called Shenfield Studio LLC* ***(G-15424)***
Shenfield Studio LLC......315 436-8869
6361 Thompson Rd Stop 12 Syracuse (13206) ***(G-15424)***
Shengkun North America Inc......212 217-2460
262 W 38th St Rm 903 New York (10018) ***(G-11563)***
Shennong Pharmaceuticals Inc......347 422-2200
110 Wall St New York (10005) ***(G-11564)***
Shenzhen Xnhdingsheng Tech Ltd......510 506-5753
4112a Main St 2fd09 Flushing (11355) ***(G-5045)***
Shepherds Flat, New York *Also called Caithness Equities Corporation* ***(G-9178)***
Shepherds Pl LLC......516 647-8151
31 Keller St Valley Stream (11580) ***(G-15797)***
Sheppard Grain Enterprises LLC......315 548-9271
1615 Maryland Rd Phelps (14532) ***(G-12981)***
Sherburne Metal Sales Inc (PA)......607 674-4441
40 S Main St Sherburne (13460) ***(G-14809)***
Sherco Services LLC......516 676-3028
2 Park Pl Ste A Glen Cove (11542) ***(G-5374)***
Sheridan House Inc......914 725-5431
230 Nelson Rd Scarsdale (10583) ***(G-14645)***
Sherrill Manufacturing Inc......315 280-0727
102 E Seneca St Sherrill (13461) ***(G-14822)***
Sherwin Commerce, New York *Also called AT&T Corp* ***(G-8942)***
Shhhmouse, Brooklyn *Also called Digiorange Inc* ***(G-1776)***
Shield Press Inc......212 431-7489
9 Lispenard St Fl 1 New York (10013) ***(G-11565)***
Shield Security Doors Ltd......202 468-3308
169 Columbia Hts Apt 6b Brooklyn (11201) ***(G-2465)***
Shimada Shoji (hk) Limited......212 268-0465
165 W 46th St Ste 709 New York (10036) ***(G-11566)***
Shindo Usa Inc......212 868-9311
162 W 36th St New York (10018) ***(G-11567)***
Shine Foods USA Inc......516 784-9674
7824 266th St Glen Oaks (11004) ***(G-5387)***
Shining Creations Inc......845 358-4911
40 S Main St Ste 1 New City (10956) ***(G-8495)***
Shinn Vineyard, Mattituck *Also called Shinn Winery LLC* ***(G-7917)***
Shinn Winery LLC......631 804-0367
2000 Oregon Rd Mattituck (11952) ***(G-7917)***
Shipman Print Solutions, Niagara Falls *Also called Shipman Printing Inds Inc* ***(G-12336)***
Shipman Printing Inds Inc......716 504-7700
2424 Niagara Falls Blvd Niagara Falls (14304) ***(G-12336)***
Shipman Printing Inds Inc......716 504-7700
6120 Lendell Dr Sanborn (14132) ***(G-14554)***
Shipmtes/Printmates Holdg Corp (PA)......518 370-1158
705 Corporation Park # 2 Scotia (12302) ***(G-14746)***
Shipprite Software Inc......315 733-6191
1312 Genesee St Utica (13502) ***(G-15733)***
Shira Accessories Ltd......212 594-4455
28 W 36th St Fl 6 New York (10018) ***(G-11568)***
Shirl-Lynn of New York (PA)......315 363-5898
266 Wilson St Oneida (13421) ***(G-12621)***
Shiro Limited......212 780-0007
928 Broadway Ste 806 New York (10010) ***(G-11569)***
Shirt Shack, Spring Valley *Also called Regal Screen Printing Intl* ***(G-15005)***
Shiseido Americas Corporation (HQ)......212 805-2300
900 3rd Ave Fl 15 New York (10022) ***(G-11570)***
Shiseido Cosmetics, New York *Also called Shiseido Americas Corporation* ***(G-11570)***
Shop Sky Inc......347 686-4616
10471 128th St South Richmond Hill (11419) ***(G-14947)***
Shop Smart Central Inc......914 962-3871
1520 Front St Yorktown Heights (10598) ***(G-16823)***
Shopping Center Wine & Liquor......914 528-1600
3008 E Main St Mohegan Lake (10547) ***(G-8259)***
Shore Line Momogramming & EMB, Mamaroneck *Also called Shore Line Monogramming Inc* ***(G-7757)***
Shore Line Monogramming Inc......914 698-8000
115 Hoyt Ave Mamaroneck (10543) ***(G-7757)***
Shore Products Co, Auburn *Also called T Shore Products Ltd* ***(G-502)***
Shoreline Fruit LLC......585 765-2639
10190 Route 18 Lyndonville (14098) ***(G-7681)***
Shoreline Publishing Inc......914 738-7869
629 Fifth Ave Ste B01 Pelham (10803) ***(G-12938)***
Short Jj Associates Inc (PA)......315 986-3511
1645 Wayneport Rd Macedon (14502) ***(G-7704)***
Short Run Forms Inc......631 567-7171
171 Keyland Ct Bohemia (11716) ***(G-1089)***
Showeray Co (PA)......718 965-3633
1857 E 8th St Brooklyn (11223) ***(G-2466)***
Shred Center......716 664-3052
20 Carroll St Jamestown (14701) ***(G-6746)***
Shredder Essentials, Brooklyn *Also called Casa Innovations Inc* ***(G-1682)***
Shrineeta Pharmacy......212 234-7959
1749 Amsterdam Ave Frnt New York (10031) ***(G-11571)***
Shrineeta Pharmacy Inc......212 234-7959
1743 Amsterdam Ave New York (10031) ***(G-11572)***
Shugar Publishing......631 288-4404
99b Main St Westhampton Beach (11978) ***(G-16405)***
Shyam Ahuja Limited......212 644-5910
201 E 56th St Frnt A New York (10022) ***(G-11573)***
Shyk International Corp......212 663-3302
258 Riverside Dr Apt 7b New York (10025) ***(G-11574)***
Shykat Promotions......866 574-2757
10561 Creek Rd Forestville (14062) ***(G-5088)***
Si Funeral Services, Fairport *Also called Suhor Industries Inc* ***(G-4663)***
Si Group Inc (HQ)......518 347-4200
2750 Balltown Rd Schenectady (12309) ***(G-14713)***
Si Group Inc......518 347-4200
1000 Main St Rotterdam Junction (12150) ***(G-14462)***
Si Group Inc......518 347-4200
Rr 5 Box South Rotterdam Junction (12150) ***(G-14463)***
Si Group Global Manufacturing, Rotterdam Junction *Also called Si Group Inc* ***(G-14462)***
Sl Partners Inc......516 433-1415
15 E Carl St Unit 1 Hicksville (11801) ***(G-6132)***
Sick Inc......585 347-2000
855 Publishers Pkwy Webster (14580) ***(G-16098)***
Sidco Filter Corporation......585 289-3100
58 North Ave Manchester (14504) ***(G-7762)***
Sidco Food Distribution Corp......718 733-3939
2324 Webster Ave Bronx (10458) ***(G-1383)***
Side Hill Farmers Coop Inc......315 447-4693
8275 State Route 13 Canastota (13032) ***(G-3248)***
Side Hustle Music Group LLC......800 219-4003
600 3rd Ave Fl 2 New York (10016) ***(G-11575)***
Sidney Favorite Printing Div, Sidney *Also called Tri-Town News Inc* ***(G-14855)***
Siegel & Stockman Inc......212 633-1508
126 W 25th St Frnt 1 New York (10001) ***(G-11576)***
Siegfrieds Call Inc......845 765-2275
20 Kent St 109 Beacon (12508) ***(G-762)***
Siemens Corporation......202 434-7800
527 Madison Ave Fl 8 New York (10022) ***(G-11577)***
Siemens Electro Industrial Sa......212 258-4000
527 Madison Ave Fl 8 New York (10022) ***(G-11578)***
Siemens Government Tech Inc......585 593-1234
37 Coats St Wellsville (14895) ***(G-16123)***
Siemens Hlthcare Dgnostics Inc......914 631-0475
511 Benedict Ave Tarrytown (10591) ***(G-15492)***
Siemens Industry Inc......716 568-0983
85 Northpointe Pkwy Amherst (14228) ***(G-250)***
Siemens Industry Inc......716 568-0983
85 Northpointe Pkwy Ste 8 Buffalo (14228) ***(G-3065)***
Siemens Industry Inc......585 797-2300
50 Methodist Hill Dr # 1500 Rochester (14623) ***(G-14126)***
Siemens Industry Inc......631 231-3600
155 Plant Ave Hauppauge (11788) ***(G-5938)***

ALPHABETIC

(PA)=Parent Co (HQ)=Headquarters (DH)=Div Headquarters
2019 Harris
New York Manufacturers Directory
985

Siemens Mobility Inc (HQ) 916 717-8174
1 Penn Plz Frnt 11 New York (10119) ***(G-11579)***
Siemens Product Life Mgmt Sftw 585 389-8699
345 Woodcliff Dr Fairport (14450) ***(G-4659)***
Siemens Product Life Mgmt Sftw 631 549-2300
60 Broadhollow Rd Melville (11747) ***(G-8063)***
Siemens USA Holdings Inc 212 258-4000
527 Madison Ave Fl 8 New York (10022) ***(G-11580)***
Sierra Processing LLC 518 433-0020
2 Moyer Ave Schenectady (12306) ***(G-14714)***
Sierson Crane Inc 315 723-6914
4822 State Route 233 Westmoreland (13490) ***(G-16411)***
Sierson Welding Inc 315 724-3903
12 Partyka Rd Westmoreland (13490) ***(G-16412)***
Sifonya Inc 212 620-4512
303 Park Ave S Frnt 2 New York (10010) ***(G-11581)***
Siga Technologies Inc (PA) 212 672-9100
31 E 62nd St New York (10065) ***(G-11582)***
Sigelock Systems LLC (PA) 888 744-3562
3205 Lawson Blvd Oceanside (11572) ***(G-12557)***
Sigma Intl Gen Med Apprtus LLC 585 798-3901
711 Park Ave Medina (14103) ***(G-7990)***
Sigma Manufacturing Inds Inc 718 842-9180
1361 E Bay Ave Bronx (10474) ***(G-1384)***
Sigma Worldwide LLC (PA) 646 217-0629
65 W 83rd St Apt 5 New York (10024) ***(G-11583)***
Sigmacare, New York *Also called Matrixcare Inc* ***(G-10729)***
Sigmamotor Inc 716 735-3115
3 N Main St Middleport (14105) ***(G-8134)***
Sigmund Cohn Corp 914 664-5300
121 S Columbus Ave Mount Vernon (10553) ***(G-8443)***
Sign & Signs 718 941-6200
785 Coney Island Ave Brooklyn (11218) ***(G-2467)***
Sign A Rama Inc 631 952-3324
663 Old Willets Path C Hauppauge (11788) ***(G-5939)***
Sign A Rama of Syracuse 315 446-9420
3060 Erie Blvd E Ste 1 Syracuse (13224) ***(G-15425)***
Sign Center Inc 212 967-2113
15 W 39th St Fl 7 New York (10018) ***(G-11584)***
Sign City of New York Inc 718 661-1118
13212 11th Ave College Point (11356) ***(G-3666)***
Sign Company 212 967-2113
15 W 39th St Fl 7 New York (10018) ***(G-11585)***
Sign Company, The, New York *Also called Sign Center Inc* ***(G-11584)***
Sign Depot Distribution, Huntington Station *Also called BC Communications Inc* ***(G-6434)***
Sign Design, Port Chester *Also called Lanza Corp* ***(G-13204)***
Sign Design Group New York Inc 718 392-0779
3326 Northern Blvd Long Island City (11101) ***(G-7590)***
Sign Expo, New York *Also called Signexpo Enterprises Inc* ***(G-11588)***
Sign Group Inc 718 438-7103
5215 New Utrecht Ave Brooklyn (11219) ***(G-2468)***
Sign Here Enterprises LLC 914 328-3111
28 N Central Ave Rear Hartsdale (10530) ***(G-5744)***
Sign Impressions Inc 585 723-0420
2590 W Ridge Rd Ste 6 Rochester (14626) ***(G-14127)***
Sign Language Custom WD Signs, Perry *Also called Sign Language Inc* ***(G-12971)***
Sign Language Inc 585 237-2620
6491 State Route 20a Perry (14530) ***(G-12971)***
Sign Men 718 227-7446
389 Wild Ave Ste G Staten Island (10314) ***(G-15135)***
Sign Shop Inc 631 226-4145
1272 Montauk Hwy Ste A Copiague (11726) ***(G-3782)***
Sign Studio Inc 518 266-0877
1 Ingalls Ave Troy (12180) ***(G-15626)***
Sign Works Incorporated 914 592-0700
150 Clearbrook Rd Ste 118 Elmsford (10523) ***(G-4569)***
Sign World Inc 212 619-9000
1194 Utica Ave Brooklyn (11203) ***(G-2469)***
Sign-A-Rama, Hartsdale *Also called Sign Here Enterprises LLC* ***(G-5744)***
Sign-A-Rama, Baldwin *Also called Jal Signs Inc* ***(G-539)***
Sign-A-Rama, Mount Kisco *Also called Westchester Signs Inc* ***(G-8359)***
Sign-A-Rama, Syracuse *Also called Sign A Rama of Syracuse* ***(G-15425)***
Sign-A-Rama, Huntington Station *Also called Z-Car-D Corp* ***(G-6465)***
Sign-A-Rama, Bellmore *Also called Speedy Sign A Rama USA Inc* ***(G-795)***
Sign-A-Rama, Hicksville *Also called Marigold Signs Inc* ***(G-6107)***
Sign-A-Rama, New Hyde Park *Also called Three Gems Inc* ***(G-8567)***
Sign-A-Rama, Hauppauge *Also called Sign A Rama Inc* ***(G-5939)***
Signa Chemistry Inc (PA) 212 933-4101
400 Madison Ave Fl 21 New York (10017) ***(G-11586)***
Signal Graphics Printing, Wappingers Falls *Also called Gem Reproduction Services Corp* ***(G-15932)***
Signal Transformer, Inwood *Also called Bel Transformer Inc* ***(G-6487)***
Signature Diamond Entps LLC 212 869-5115
15 W 47th St Ste 203 New York (10036) ***(G-11587)***
Signature Industries Inc 516 679-5177
32 Saint Johns Pl Freeport (11520) ***(G-5184)***
Signature Metal MBL Maint LLC 718 292-8280
791 E 132nd St Bronx (10454) ***(G-1385)***
Signature Name Plate Co Inc 585 321-9960
292 Commerce Dr Rochester (14623) ***(G-14128)***
Signatures, New York *Also called Light House Hill Marketing* ***(G-10567)***
Signexpo Enterprises Inc (PA) 212 925-8585
127 W 26th St Rm 401 New York (10001) ***(G-11588)***
Signpost Inc 877 334-2837
127 W 26th St Fl 2 New York (10001) ***(G-11589)***
Signs & Decal Corp 718 486-6400
410 Morgan Ave Brooklyn (11211) ***(G-2470)***
Signs By Sunrise, Jamaica *Also called Tru-Art Sign Co Inc* ***(G-6685)***
Signs By Tomorrow, Commack *Also called Rpf Associates Inc* ***(G-3701)***
Signs Inc 518 483-4759
2 Boyer Ave Malone (12953) ***(G-7727)***
Signs Ink Ltd 914 739-9059
3255 Crompond Rd Yorktown Heights (10598) ***(G-16824)***
Signs New York, Brooklyn *Also called Brooklyn Signs LLC* ***(G-1648)***
Signs Now, Rochester *Also called Image360* ***(G-13878)***
Signs of Success Ltd 516 295-6000
247 Merrick Rd Ste 101 Lynbrook (11563) ***(G-7674)***
Sigro Precision, West Babylon *Also called BEAM Manufacturing Corp* ***(G-16139)***
Sihi Pumps Inc (HQ) 716 773-6450
303 Industrial Dr Grand Island (14072) ***(G-5513)***
Sikorsky Aircraft Corporation 585 424-1990
300 Canal View Blvd Rochester (14623) ***(G-14129)***
Silar Laboratories Division, Scotia *Also called Oak-Bark Corporation* ***(G-14745)***
Silarx Pharmaceuticals Inc (HQ) 845 352-4020
1033 Stoneleigh Ave Carmel (10512) ***(G-3281)***
Silgan Containers Mfg Corp 315 946-4826
8673 Lyons Marengo Rd Lyons (14489) ***(G-7687)***
Silgan Plastics LLC 315 536-5690
40 Powell Ln Penn Yan (14527) ***(G-12966)***
Silicon Carbide Products Inc 607 562-8599
361 Daniel Zenker Dr Horseheads (14845) ***(G-6329)***
Silicone Products & Technology 716 684-1155
4471 Walden Ave Lancaster (14086) ***(G-7050)***
Silipos Holding LLC (PA) 716 283-0700
7049 Williams Rd Niagara Falls (14304) ***(G-12337)***
Silk Screen Art Inc 518 762-8423
1 School St Johnstown (12095) ***(G-6839)***
Silly Phillie Creations Inc 718 492-6300
140 58th St Ste 6f Brooklyn (11220) ***(G-2471)***
Silva Cabinetry Inc 914 737-7697
12 White St Ste C Buchanan (10511) ***(G-2674)***
Silvatrim Corp 212 675-0933
324 W 22nd St New York (10011) ***(G-11590)***
Silvatrim Corporation America, New York *Also called Silvatrim Corp* ***(G-11590)***
Silver Bell Baking Co 718 335-9539
6406 Admiral Ave Middle Village (11379) ***(G-8127)***
Silver City Group Inc 315 363-0344
27577 W Seneca St Sherrill (13461) ***(G-14823)***
Silver City Metals, Sherrill *Also called Silver City Group Inc* ***(G-14823)***
Silver Creek Carpet, New York *Also called Bloomsburg Carpet Inds Inc* ***(G-9103)***
Silver Griffin Inc 518 272-7771
691 Hoosick Rd Troy (12180) ***(G-15627)***
Silver Oak Pharmacy Inc 718 922-3400
5105 Church Ave Brooklyn (11203) ***(G-2472)***
Silverlight Digital LLC 646 650-5330
15 E 32nd St Fl 3 New York (10016) ***(G-11591)***
Silverman & Gorf Inc 718 625-1309
60 Franklin Ave Brooklyn (11205) ***(G-2473)***
Silverstone Shtmtl Fbrications 718 422-0380
66 Huntington St Brooklyn (11231) ***(G-2474)***
Silvertique Fine Jewelry, New York *Also called Goldarama Company Inc* ***(G-9951)***
Sima Technologies LLC 412 828-9130
345 Oser Ave Hauppauge (11788) ***(G-5940)***
Simcha Candle Co Inc 845 783-0406
244 Mac Arthur Ave New Windsor (12553) ***(G-8661)***
Simco Leather Corporation 518 762-7100
99 Pleasant Ave Johnstown (12095) ***(G-6840)***
Similarweb Inc 347 685-5422
50 W 17th St Fl 9 New York (10011) ***(G-11592)***
Simka Diamond Corp 212 921-4420
580 5th Ave Ste 709 New York (10036) ***(G-11593)***
Simmons Fabricating Svc Inc 845 635-3755
1558 Main St Pleasant Valley (12569) ***(G-13172)***
Simmons Machine Tool Corp (PA) 518 462-5431
1700 Broadway Menands (12204) ***(G-8091)***
Simmons-Boardman Pubg Corp (HQ) 212 620-7200
55 Broad St Fl 26 New York (10004) ***(G-11594)***
Simon & Schuster Inc 212 698-7000
1230 Ave Of The Americas New York (10020) ***(G-11595)***
Simon & Simon LLC 202 419-0490
1745 Broadway Fl 17 New York (10019) ***(G-11596)***
Simon Defense Inc 516 217-6000
1 Trade Zone Dr Unit 15 Ronkonkoma (11779) ***(G-14413)***
Simon Liu Inc 718 567-2011
280 24th St Brooklyn (11232) ***(G-2475)***
Simon S Decorating Inc 718 339-2931
1670 E 19th St Brooklyn (11229) ***(G-2476)***
Simon Schuster Digital Sls Inc 212 698-4391
51 W 52d St New York (10019) ***(G-11597)***
Simple Brewer 845 490-0182
346 Route 202 Somers (10589) ***(G-14923)***

ALPHABETIC SECTION SLC, Auburn

Simple Elegance New York, Brooklyn *Also called Sabbsons International Inc (G-2442)*
Simple Elegance New York Inc.......718 360-1947
474 50th St Brooklyn (11220) *(G-2477)*
Simplex Manufacturing Co Inc.......315 252-7524
105 Dunning Ave Auburn (13021) *(G-500)*
Simplicity Bandsaw Inc.......716 557-8805
3674 Main St Hinsdale (14743) *(G-6162)*
Simply Amazing Enterprises Inc.......631 503-6452
68 S Service Rd Ste 1 Melville (11747) *(G-8064)*
Simply Lite Foods, Commack *Also called Simply Natural Foods LLC (G-3703)*
Simply Natural Foods LLC.......631 543-9600
74 Mall Dr Commack (11725) *(G-3703)*
Simpore Inc.......585 748-5980
150 Lucius Gordon Dr # 110 West Henrietta (14586) *(G-16251)*
Simrex Corporation.......716 206-0174
1223 William St Buffalo (14206) *(G-3066)*
Sims Group USA Holdings Corp.......718 786-6031
3027 Greenpoint Ave Long Island City (11101) *(G-7591)*
Sims Metal Management, New York *Also called Smm - North America Trade Corp (G-11627)*
Sims Steel Corporation.......631 587-8670
650 Muncy St Lindenhurst (11757) *(G-7192)*
Simtec Industries Corporation.......631 293-0080
65 Marine St Ste A Farmingdale (11735) *(G-4874)*
Simulaids Inc.......845 679-2475
16 Simulaids Dr Saugerties (12477) *(G-14616)*
Sinapi's Italian Ice, Hawthorne *Also called Four Brothers Italian Bakery (G-5986)*
Sincerus LLC.......800 419-2804
2478 Mcdonald Ave Brooklyn (11223) *(G-2478)*
Sinclair International Company (PA).......518 798-2361
85 Boulevard Queensbury (12804) *(G-13442)*
Sinclair Technologies Inc (HQ).......716 874-3682
5811 S Park Ave 3 Hamburg (14075) *(G-5695)*
Sing Ah Poultry.......718 625-7253
114 Sackett St Brooklyn (11231) *(G-2479)*
Sing Tao Daily, New York *Also called Sing Tao Newspapers NY Ltd (G-11598)*
Sing Tao Newspapers NY Ltd.......212 431-9030
5317 8th Ave Brooklyn (11220) *(G-2480)*
Sing Tao Newspapers NY Ltd.......718 821-0123
905 Flushing Ave Fl 2 Brooklyn (11206) *(G-2481)*
Sing Tao Newspapers NY Ltd (PA).......212 699-3800
188 Lafayette St New York (10013) *(G-11598)*
Sing Trix.......212 352-1500
118 W 22nd St Fl 3 New York (10011) *(G-11599)*
Singlecut Beersmiths LLC.......718 606-0788
1933 37th St Astoria (11105) *(G-443)*
Sinn- Tech Industries Inc.......631 643-1171
48 Gleam St West Babylon (11704) *(G-16192)*
Sinnara, Maspeth *Also called Purvi Enterprises Incorporated (G-7868)*
Sino Printing Inc.......212 334-6896
30 Allen St Frnt A New York (10002) *(G-11600)*
Sir Industries Inc.......631 234-2444
208 Blydenburg Rd Unit C Hauppauge (11749) *(G-5941)*
Sir Kensington's, New York *Also called Kensington & Sons LLC (G-10433)*
Sir Speedy, Bay Shore *Also called Bondy Printing Corp (G-666)*
Sir Speedy, Rochester *Also called Beastons Budget Printing (G-13658)*
Sir Speedy, Westbury *Also called E B B Graphics Inc (G-16324)*
Sir Speedy, Plainview *Also called Nash Printing Inc (G-13077)*
Sir Speedy, Wappingers Falls *Also called Moneast Inc (G-15936)*
Sir Speedy, Pleasantville *Also called Carlara Group Ltd (G-13173)*
Sir Speedy, Westbury *Also called Sentine Printing Inc (G-16372)*
Sir Speedy, Lake Placid *Also called Lake Placid Advertisers Wkshp (G-6976)*
Sir Speedy, Plainview *Also called P D R Inc (G-13080)*
Sirianni Hardwoods Inc.......607 962-4688
912 Addison Rd Painted Post (14870) *(G-12841)*
Siskind Group Inc.......212 840-0880
1385 Broadway Fl 24 New York (10018) *(G-11601)*
Sister Sister Inc (PA).......212 629-9600
463 7th Ave Fl 4 New York (10018) *(G-11602)*
Sita Finishing Inc.......718 417-5295
207 Starr St Ste 1 Brooklyn (11237) *(G-2482)*
Sita Knitting, Brooklyn *Also called Sita Finishing Inc (G-2482)*
Sitecraft Inc.......718 729-4900
4302 Ditmars Blvd Astoria (11105) *(G-444)*
Sitewatch Technology LLC.......207 778-3246
22 Sunset Ave East Quogue (11942) *(G-4279)*
Siw Inc.......631 888-0130
271 Skip Ln Bay Shore (11706) *(G-723)*
Sixnet LLC.......518 877-5173
331 Ushers Rd Ste 14 Ballston Lake (12019) *(G-571)*
Sixnet Holdings LLC.......518 877-5173
331 Ushers Rd Ste 10 Ballston Lake (12019) *(G-572)*
Sixpoint Brewery, Brooklyn *Also called Mad Scntsts Brwing Prtners LLC (G-2150)*
Sixteen Markets Inc.......347 759-1024
110 Wall St Ste 1502 New York (10005) *(G-11603)*
Sixthscents Paper Products Ltd.......212 627-5066
37-18 Nthrn Blvd Ste 418 Long Island City (11101) *(G-7592)*
Sixthscents Products, Long Island City *Also called Sixthscents Paper Products Ltd (G-7592)*
Sizzal LLC.......212 354-6123
1105 44th Rd Fl 2 Long Island City (11101) *(G-7593)*

Sj Associates Inc (PA).......516 942-3232
500 N Broadway Ste 159 Jericho (11753) *(G-6804)*
Sjm Interface, New York *Also called Sign Company (G-11585)*
Sk Capital Partners II LP (PA).......212 826-2700
400 Park Ave Ste 820 New York (10022) *(G-11604)*
Sk Energy Shots, New York *Also called Street King LLC (G-11719)*
Sk Titan Holdings LLC (HQ).......212 826-2700
400 Park Ave New York (10022) *(G-11605)*
Skae Power Solutions LLC (PA).......845 365-9103
348 Route 9w Palisades (10964) *(G-12847)*
Skaffles Group LLC.......212 944-9494
1400 Broadway Fl 26 New York (10018) *(G-11606)*
Skandacor Direct Inc.......585 265-9020
545 Basket Rd Webster (14580) *(G-16099)*
Skd Distribution Corp.......718 525-6000
28 Westchester Ave Jericho (11753) *(G-6805)*
Skd Tactical Inc.......845 897-2889
291 Main St Highland Falls (10928) *(G-6149)*
Skechers Factory Outlet 315, Bronx *Also called Skechers USA Inc (G-1386)*
Skechers USA Inc.......718 585-3024
651 River Ave Bronx (10451) *(G-1386)*
Skelton Screw Products Co, Westbury *Also called All Type Screw Machine Pdts (G-16313)*
Sketch Studio Trading Inc.......212 244-2875
221 W 37th St Ste 600 New York (10018) *(G-11607)*
SKF Aeroengine North America, Falconer *Also called SKF USA Inc (G-4691)*
SKF Aeroengine North America, Falconer *Also called SKF USA Inc (G-4692)*
SKF USA Inc.......716 661-2869
1 Maroco St Falconer (14733) *(G-4691)*
SKF USA Inc.......716 661-2600
402 Chandler St Jamestown (14701) *(G-6747)*
SKF USA Inc.......716 661-2600
1 Maroco St Falconer (14733) *(G-4692)*
Skil-Care Corporation.......914 963-2040
29 Wells Ave Bldg 4 Yonkers (10701) *(G-16798)*
Skills Alliance Inc.......646 492-5300
135 W 29th St Rm 201 New York (10001) *(G-11608)*
Skillsoft Corporation.......585 240-7500
500 Canal View Blvd Rochester (14623) *(G-14130)*
Skimovex USA, Orchard Park *Also called Burgess-Manning Inc (G-12704)*
Skin Atelier Inc.......845 294-1202
1997 Route 17m Goshen (10924) *(G-5483)*
Skin Dynamic, Long Island City *Also called P-Ryton Corp (G-7545)*
Skin Prints Inc.......845 920-8756
63 Walter St Pearl River (10965) *(G-12911)*
Skincare Products Inc.......917 837-5255
118 E 57th St New York (10022) *(G-11609)*
Skinprint, Goshen *Also called Skin Atelier Inc (G-5483)*
Skip Hop Inc.......646 902-9874
50 W 23rd St Fl 10 New York (10010) *(G-11610)*
Skip Hop Holdings Inc (HQ).......212 868-9850
50 W 23rd St Fl 10 New York (10010) *(G-11611)*
Skooba Design, Rochester *Also called Three Point Ventures LLC (G-14168)*
Sky Aerospace Products, Westbury *Also called John Hassall LLC (G-16345)*
Sky Art Media Inc.......917 355-9022
114 E 25th St Fl 11 New York (10010) *(G-11612)*
Sky Frame & Art Inc (PA).......212 925-7856
141 W 28th St Fl 12 New York (10001) *(G-11613)*
Sky Geek, Lagrangeville *Also called Styles Aviation Inc (G-6962)*
Sky Laundromat Inc.......718 639-7070
8615 Ava Pl Apt 4e Jamaica (11432) *(G-6677)*
Skydyne Company.......845 858-6400
100 River Rd Port Jervis (12771) *(G-13237)*
Skye's The Limit, New York *Also called Alfred Dunner Inc (G-8795)*
Skyguard, Hauppauge *Also called Vehicle Manufacturers Inc (G-5968)*
Skyhorse Publishing Inc (PA).......212 643-6816
307 W 36th St Fl 11 New York (10018) *(G-11614)*
Skylark Publications Ltd.......607 535-9866
217 N Franklin St Watkins Glen (14891) *(G-16060)*
Skyler Brand Ventures LLC.......646 979-5904
590 Madison Ave Fl 19 New York (10022) *(G-11615)*
Skyline Custom Cabinetry Inc.......631 393-2983
200 Verdi St Unit A Farmingdale (11735) *(G-4875)*
Skyline LLC.......631 403-4131
16 Hulse Rd Ste 1 East Setauket (11733) *(G-4310)*
Skyline New York, Hauppauge *Also called Watson Productions LLC (G-5973)*
Skyop LLC.......585 598-4737
5297 Parkside Dr Ste 440c Canandaigua (14424) *(G-3234)*
Skystem LLC.......877 778-3320
100 W 92nd St Apt 20d New York (10025) *(G-11616)*
Skytravel (usa) LLC.......518 888-2610
20 Talon Dr Schenectady (12309) *(G-14715)*
Slant/Fin Corporation (PA).......516 484-2600
100 Forest Dr Greenvale (11548) *(G-5632)*
Slantco Manufacturing Inc (HQ).......516 484-2600
100 Forest Dr Greenvale (11548) *(G-5633)*
Slanto Manufacturing Inc.......516 759-5721
40 Garvies Point Rd Glen Cove (11542) *(G-5375)*
Slava Industries Incorporated (PA).......718 499-4850
555 16th St Brooklyn (11215) *(G-2483)*
SLC, Auburn *Also called Auburn Custom Millwork Inc (G-463)*

ALPHABETIC

(PA)=Parent Co (HQ)=Headquarters (DH)=Div Headquarters
2019 Harris
New York Manufacturers Directory
987

Sleep Improvement Center Inc.....516 536-5799
178 Sunrise Hwy Fl 2 Rockville Centre (11570) ***(G-14240)***
Sleep Master, Syracuse *Also called Futon City Discounters Inc* ***(G-15326)***
Sleepable Sofas Ltd.....973 546-4502
600 3rd Ave Fl 15 New York (10016) ***(G-11617)***
Sleeping Partners Home Fashion, Brooklyn *Also called Sleeping Partners Intl Inc* ***(G-2484)***
Sleeping Partners Intl Inc.....212 254-1515
140 58th St Ste 3e Brooklyn (11220) ***(G-2484)***
Sleepwear Holdings Inc.....516 466-4738
1372 Broadway Fl 18 New York (10018) ***(G-11618)***
Sleepy Head Inc.....718 237-9655
230 3rd St Brooklyn (11215) ***(G-2485)***
Slidebean Incorporated.....866 365-0588
25 Broadway New York (10004) ***(G-11619)***
Slim Line Case Co Inc.....585 546-3639
64 Spencer St Rochester (14608) ***(G-14131)***
Slims Bagels Unlimited Inc (PA).....718 229-1140
22118 Horace Harding Expy Oakland Gardens (11364) ***(G-12526)***
Sliperfection, New York *Also called Lady Ester Lingerie Corp* ***(G-10506)***
Sln Group Inc.....718 677-5969
2172 E 26th St Brooklyn (11229) ***(G-2486)***
Sloane Design Inc.....212 539-0184
226 52nd St Brooklyn (11220) ***(G-2487)***
Slosson Eductl Publications.....716 652-0930
538 Buffalo Rd East Aurora (14052) ***(G-4210)***
Slyde Inc.....917 331-2114
474 48th Ave Apt 18a Long Island City (11109) ***(G-7594)***
SM News Plus Incorporated.....212 888-0153
346 E 59th St Frnt 1 New York (10022) ***(G-11620)***
Small Business Advisors Inc.....516 374-1387
2005 Park St Atlantic Beach (11509) ***(G-457)***
Smart & Strong LLC.....212 938-2051
212 W 35th St Fl 8 New York (10001) ***(G-11621)***
Smart High Voltage Solutions.....631 563-6724
390 Knickerbocker Ave # 6 Bohemia (11716) ***(G-1090)***
Smart Space Products LLC (PA).....877 777-2441
244 5th Ave Ste 2487 New York (10001) ***(G-11622)***
Smart Systems Inc.....607 776-5380
320 E Washington St Bath (14810) ***(G-649)***
Smart USA Inc (PA).....631 969-1111
1440 5th Ave Bay Shore (11706) ***(G-724)***
Smart Weigh, Spring Valley *Also called Measupro Inc* ***(G-15003)***
Smartoners Inc (PA).....718 975-0197
289 Keap St Ste A Brooklyn (11211) ***(G-2488)***
Smartpill Corporation.....716 882-0701
847 Main St Buffalo (14203) ***(G-3067)***
Smartys Corner.....607 239-5276
501 W Main St Endicott (13760) ***(G-4610)***
SMC, Conklin *Also called E-Systems Group LLC* ***(G-3727)***
SMC Diode Solutions LLC.....631 965-0869
101 Sunnyside Blvd Plainview (11803) ***(G-13088)***
Smg Control Systems, Buffalo *Also called Service Mfg Group Inc* ***(G-3064)***
Smg Metal Products LLC.....716 633-6439
390 Cayuga Rd Cheektowaga (14225) ***(G-3458)***
SMI, Salamanca *Also called Snyder Manufacturing Inc* ***(G-14533)***
Smidgens Inc.....585 624-1486
7336 Community Dr Lima (14485) ***(G-7155)***
Smile Specialists.....877 337-6135
236 E 36th St New York (10016) ***(G-11623)***
Smith & Watson.....212 686-6444
200 Lexington Ave Rm 805 New York (10016) ***(G-11624)***
Smith Control Systems Inc.....518 828-7646
1839 Route 9h Hudson (12534) ***(G-6373)***
Smith Graphics Inc.....631 420-4180
40 Florida St Farmingdale (11735) ***(G-4876)***
Smith International Inc.....585 265-2330
1915 Lake Rd Ontario (14519) ***(G-12666)***
Smith International Inc.....212 350-9400
601 Lexington Ave Fl 57 New York (10022) ***(G-11625)***
Smith Metal Works Newark Inc.....315 331-1651
1000 E Union St Newark (14513) ***(G-12206)***
Smith Sand & Gravel Inc.....315 673-4124
4782 Shepard Rd Marcellus (13108) ***(G-7795)***
Smith Service Corps, Ontario *Also called Smith International Inc* ***(G-12666)***
Smith Street Bread Co LLC.....718 797-9712
17 5th St Brooklyn (11231) ***(G-2489)***
Smith Tool & Die Inc.....607 674-4165
714 Pleasant Valley Rd Sherburne (13460) ***(G-14810)***
Smith, E W Publishing, New Windsor *Also called Sentinel Printing Services Inc* ***(G-8660)***
Smithers Tools & Mch Pdts Inc.....845 876-3063
3718 Route 9g Rhinebeck (12572) ***(G-13488)***
Smithtown Concrete Products.....631 265-1815
441 Middle Country Rd Saint James (11780) ***(G-14515)***
Smithtown News Inc.....631 265-2100
1 Brooksite Dr Smithtown (11787) ***(G-14909)***
Sml Acquisition LLC.....914 592-3130
33 W Main St Ste 505 Elmsford (10523) ***(G-4570)***
Sml Brothers Holding Corp.....718 402-2000
820 E 140th St Bronx (10454) ***(G-1387)***
Sml USA Inc (PA).....212 736-8800
5 Penn Plz Ste 1500 New York (10001) ***(G-11626)***
Smm - North America Trade Corp.....212 604-0710
16 W 22nd St Fl 10 New York (10010) ***(G-11627)***
Smokey Joes, Oceanside *Also called Yale Trouser Corporation* ***(G-12566)***
Smooth Industries Incorporated.....212 869-1080
1411 Broadway Rm 3000 New York (10018) ***(G-11628)***
Smooth Magazine.....212 925-1150
55 John St Ste 800 New York (10038) ***(G-11629)***
Smoothbore International Inc.....315 754-8124
13881 Westbury Cutoff Rd Red Creek (13143) ***(G-13455)***
Smoothies Strawberry Nysf.....315 406-4250
581 State Fair Blvd Syracuse (13209) ***(G-15426)***
SMS, Huntington Station *Also called Super Sweep Inc* ***(G-6459)***
Smsc, Hauppauge *Also called Standard Microsystems Corp* ***(G-5948)***
Snake Tray, Bay Shore *Also called Snake Tray International LLC* ***(G-725)***
Snake Tray International LLC.....631 674-0004
291 Skip Ln Bay Shore (11706) ***(G-725)***
Snapp Too Enterprise.....718 224-5252
3312 211th St Flushing (11361) ***(G-5046)***
Snapple Beverage Corp (del) (HQ).....914 612-4000
900 King St Rye Brook (10573) ***(G-14495)***
Snapple Distributors, Staten Island *Also called Gangi Distributors Inc* ***(G-15077)***
Snapple Distributors, Ronkonkoma *Also called American Bottling Company* ***(G-14305)***
Sneaker News Inc.....347 687-1588
41 Elizabeth St Ste 301 New York (10013) ***(G-11630)***
Sneakers Software Inc.....800 877-9221
519 8th Ave Rm 812 New York (10018) ***(G-11631)***
Sneaky Chef Foods LLC.....914 301-3277
520 White Plains Rd Tarrytown (10591) ***(G-15493)***
Snow Craft Co Inc.....516 739-1399
200 Fulton Ave New Hyde Park (11040) ***(G-8563)***
Snowman.....212 239-8818
404 5th Ave Fl 7 New York (10018) ***(G-11632)***
Snr Cctv Systems Division, East Setauket *Also called Sartek Industries Inc* ***(G-4309)***
Sns Machinery, Brooklyn *Also called Riverside Machinery Company* ***(G-2406)***
Snyder Industries Inc (PA).....716 694-1240
340 Wales Ave Tonawanda (14150) ***(G-15578)***
Snyder Logging.....315 265-1462
528 Allen Falls Rd Potsdam (13676) ***(G-13323)***
Snyder Manufacturing Inc.....716 945-0354
255 Rochester St Unit 1 Salamanca (14779) ***(G-14533)***
Snyder Neon & Plastic Signs, Colonie *Also called Snyders Neon Displays Inc* ***(G-3679)***
Snyders Neon Displays Inc.....518 857-4100
5 Highland Ave Colonie (12205) ***(G-3679)***
Sobi, Brooklyn *Also called Social Bicycles Inc* ***(G-2490)***
Soc America Inc.....631 472-6666
3505 Veterans Memorial Hw Ronkonkoma (11779) ***(G-14414)***
Social Bicycles Inc (PA).....917 746-7624
55 Prospect St Ste 304 Brooklyn (11201) ***(G-2490)***
Social Register Association.....646 612-7314
14 Wall St Ste 3f New York (10005) ***(G-11633)***
Social Science Electronic Pubg.....585 442-8170
1239 University Ave Rochester (14607) ***(G-14132)***
Society Awards, Long Island City *Also called Dwm International Inc* ***(G-7431)***
Society For The Study.....212 822-8806
20 W 20th St Fl 2 New York (10011) ***(G-11634)***
Sockbin.....917 519-1119
718 Avenue U Brooklyn (11223) ***(G-2491)***
Socket Products Mfg Corp.....631 232-9870
175 Bridge Rd Islandia (11749) ***(G-6538)***
Socks and More of NY Inc.....718 769-1785
1605 Avenue Z Fl 1 Brooklyn (11235) ***(G-2492)***
Sofanou, Niagara Falls *Also called Delfingen Us-New York Inc* ***(G-12277)***
Soft Sheen Products Inc (HQ).....212 818-1500
575 5th Ave New York (10017) ***(G-11635)***
Soft-Noze Usa Inc.....315 732-2726
2216 Broad St Frankfort (13340) ***(G-5112)***
Soft-Tex International Inc.....800 366-2324
428 Hudson River Rd Waterford (12188) ***(G-15987)***
Soft-Tex Manufacturing Co, Waterford *Also called Soft-Tex International Inc* ***(G-15987)***
Softcard, New York *Also called Jvl Ventures LLC* ***(G-10389)***
Softlink International.....914 574-8197
297 Knollwood Rd Ste 301 White Plains (10607) ***(G-16504)***
Software & General Services Co.....315 986-4184
1365 Fairway 5 Cir Walworth (14568) ***(G-15916)***
Soggy Doggy Productions LLC.....877 504-4811
50 Chestnut Ave Larchmont (10538) ***(G-7059)***
Sogimex, New York *Also called Myers Group LLC* ***(G-10866)***
Soho and Tribeca Map, New York *Also called Ozmodyl Ltd* ***(G-11081)***
Soho Apparel Ltd.....212 840-1109
525 Fashion Ave Fl 6 New York (10018) ***(G-11636)***
Soho Editions Inc.....914 591-5100
2641 Deer St Mohegan Lake (10547) ***(G-8260)***
Soho Guilds, Kew Gardens *Also called A & B Color Corp (del)* ***(G-6869)***
Soho Letterpress Inc.....718 788-2518
68 35th St Unit 6 Brooklyn (11232) ***(G-2493)***
Soho Press Inc.....212 260-1900
853 Broadway Ste 1402 New York (10003) ***(G-11637)***
Sokolin LLC (PA).....631 537-4434
445 Sills Rd Unit K Yaphank (11980) ***(G-16722)***
Sokolin Wine, Yaphank *Also called Sokolin LLC* ***(G-16722)***

Sol Markowitz, Monroe *Also called C T A Digital Inc (G-8266)*
Sola Home Expo Inc.....718 646-3383
172 Neptune Ave Brooklyn (11235) **(G-2494)**
Solabia USA Inc.....212 847-2397
28 W 44th St New York (10036) **(G-11638)**
Solar Energy Systems LLC (PA).....718 389-1545
1205 Manhattan Ave # 1210 Brooklyn (11222) **(G-2495)**
Solar Metrology LLC.....845 247-4701
1340 Lincoln Ave Ste 6 Holbrook (11741) **(G-6209)**
Solar Screen Co Inc.....718 592-8222
5311 105th St Corona (11368) **(G-3855)**
Solar Thin Films Inc (PA).....212 629-8260
445 Central Ave Unit 366 Cedarhurst (11516) **(G-3337)**
Solarelectricway, Brooklyn *Also called Solarwaterway Inc (G-2496)*
Solarpath Inc.....201 490-4499
415 Madison Ave Fl 14 New York (10017) **(G-11639)**
Solarpath Sun Solutions, New York *Also called Solarpath Inc (G-11639)*
Solarwaterway Inc.....888 998-5337
254 36th St Ste C453 Brooklyn (11232) **(G-2496)**
Solarz Bros Printing Corp.....718 383-1330
231 Norman Ave Ste 105 Brooklyn (11222) **(G-2497)**
Solenis LLC.....718 383-1717
761 Humboldt St Brooklyn (11222) **(G-2498)**
Solenis LLC.....315 461-4730
911 Old Liverpool Rd Liverpool (13088) **(G-7262)**
Soleo Health, Hawthorne *Also called Biomed Pharmaceuticals Inc (G-5984)*
Solepoxy Inc.....716 372-6300
211 W Franklin St Olean (14760) **(G-12607)**
Solex Catsmo Fine Foods, Wallkill *Also called Catsmo LLC (G-15903)*
Solid Cell Inc.....585 426-5000
771 Elmgrove Rd Rochester (14624) **(G-14133)**
Solid Sealing Technology Inc.....518 874-3600
44 Dalliba Ave Ste 240 Watervliet (12189) **(G-16050)**
Solid Surface Acrylics LLC.....716 743-1870
800 Walck Rd Ste 14 North Tonawanda (14120) **(G-12451)**
Solid Surfaces Inc.....585 292-5340
1 Townline Cir Rochester (14623) **(G-14134)**
Solid-Look Corporation.....917 683-1780
4628 243rd St Douglaston (11362) **(G-4140)**
Solidus Industries Inc.....607 749-4540
6849 N Glen Haven Rd Homer (13077) **(G-6259)**
Solivaira Specialties Inc.....716 693-4009
4 Detroit St North Tonawanda (14120) **(G-12452)**
Solmac Inc.....716 630-7061
1975 Wehrle Dr Ste 130 Williamsville (14221) **(G-16587)**
Solo, Brooklyn *Also called Air Skate & Air Jump Corp (G-1496)*
Solstarny, New York *Also called Solstars Inc (G-11640)*
Solstars Inc.....212 605-0430
575 Madison Ave Ste 1006 New York (10022) **(G-11640)**
Solstiss Inc.....212 719-9194
561 Fashion Ave Fl 16 New York (10018) **(G-11641)**
Soludos LLC.....212 219-1101
520 Broadway Fl 5 New York (10012) **(G-11642)**
Solutia Business Entps Inc.....314 674-1000
111 8th Ave New York (10011) **(G-11643)**
Solvaira Specialties Inc (PA).....716 693-4040
50 Bridge St North Tonawanda (14120) **(G-12453)**
Solvaira Specialty LP (PA).....716 693-4040
50 Bridge St North Tonawanda (14120) **(G-12454)**
Solvaira Specialty LP.....716 693-4040
50 Bridge St North Tonawanda (14120) **(G-12455)**
Solve Advisors Inc.....646 699-5041
265 Sunrise Hwy Ste 22 Rockville Centre (11570) **(G-14241)**
Solvents Company Inc.....631 595-9300
9 Cornell St Kingston (12401) **(G-6917)**
Somers Stain Glass Inc.....631 586-7772
108 Brook Ave Ste A Deer Park (11729) **(G-4046)**
Somerset Dyeing & Finishing.....518 773-7383
68 Harrison St Gloversville (12078) **(G-5465)**
Somerset Industries Inc (PA).....518 773-7383
68 Harrison St Gloversville (12078) **(G-5466)**
Somerset Manufacturers Inc.....516 626-3832
36 Glen Cove Rd Roslyn Heights (11577) **(G-14460)**
Somerset Production Co LLC.....716 932-6480
338 Harris Hill Rd # 102 Buffalo (14221) **(G-3068)**
Somerville Acquisitions Co Inc.....845 856-5261
15 Big Pond Rd Huguenot (12746) **(G-6386)**
Somerville Tech Group Inc.....908 782-9500
15 Big Pond Rd Huguenot (12746) **(G-6387)**
Sommer and Sons Printing Inc.....716 822-4311
2222 S Park Ave Buffalo (14220) **(G-3069)**
Somml Health Inc.....518 880-2170
43 New Scotland Ave Mc25 Albany (12208) **(G-128)**
Sonaal Industries Inc.....718 383-3860
210 Kingsland Ave Brooklyn (11222) **(G-2499)**
Sonaer Inc.....631 756-4780
68 Lamar St Unit D West Babylon (11704) **(G-16193)**
Sonicor Inc.....631 920-6555
82 Otis St West Babylon (11704) **(G-16194)**
Soniquence LLC.....516 267-6400
2473 Grand Ave Baldwin (11510) **(G-543)**

Sonneman-A Way of Light, Wappingers Falls *Also called Contemporary Visions LLC (G-15928)*
Sono-Tek Corporation (PA).....845 795-2020
2012 Route 9w Stop 3 Milton (12547) **(G-8197)**
Sonoco Products Company.....518 392-2000
87 Center St Chatham (12037) **(G-3430)**
Sonoco-Crellin Intl Inc (HQ).....518 392-2000
87 Center St Chatham (12037) **(G-3431)**
Sonomed Inc.....516 354-0900
1979 Marcus Ave Ste C105 New Hyde Park (11042) **(G-8564)**
Sonomed Escalon, New Hyde Park *Also called Sonomed Inc (G-8564)*
Sonotec US Inc.....631 415-4758
190 Blydenburg Rd Islandia (11749) **(G-6539)**
Sonus-USA, Webster *Also called Hearing Spech Ctr of Rochester (G-16086)*
Sony Broadband Entertainment (HQ).....212 833-6800
550 Madison Ave Fl 6 New York (10022) **(G-11644)**
Sony Corporation of America (HQ).....212 833-8000
25 Madison Ave Fl 27 New York (10010) **(G-11645)**
Sony Dadc US Inc.....212 833-8800
550 Madison Ave New York (10022) **(G-11646)**
Sony Music Entertainment, New York *Also called Sony Music Holdings Inc (G-11649)*
Sony Music Entertainment, New York *Also called Sony Corporation of America (G-11645)*
Sony Music Entertainment.....212 833-8000
25 Madison Ave Fl 19 New York (10010) **(G-11647)**
Sony Music Entertainment Inc.....212 833-5057
79 5th Ave Fl 16 New York (10003) **(G-11648)**
Sony Music Holdings, New York *Also called Sony Music Entertainment (G-11647)*
Sony Music Holdings Inc (HQ).....212 833-8000
25 Madison Ave Fl 26 New York (10010) **(G-11649)**
Sony Style, New York *Also called Sony Dadc US Inc (G-11646)*
Sony/Atv Music Publishing LLC (HQ).....212 833-7730
25 Madison Ave Fl 24 New York (10010) **(G-11650)**
Sopark Corp (PA).....716 822-0434
3300 S Park Ave Buffalo (14218) **(G-3070)**
Soper Designs, New York *Also called Kurt Gaum Inc (G-10487)*
Sorfin Yoshimura Ltd.....516 802-4600
100 Crossways Park Dr W # 215 Woodbury (11797) **(G-16632)**
Soroc Technology Corp.....716 849-5913
1051 Clinton St Buffalo (14206) **(G-3071)**
Sorrento Lactalis, Buffalo *Also called Lactalis American Group Inc (G-2917)*
Sorrento Lactalis Inc.....716 823-6262
2375 S Park Ave Buffalo (14220) **(G-3072)**
SOS International LLC.....212 742-2410
426 W Broadway Apt 6a New York (10012) **(G-11651)**
Sotek Inc.....716 821-5961
3590 Jeffrey Blvd Blasdell (14219) **(G-930)**
Soterix Medical Inc.....888 990-8327
237 W 35th St Ste 1401 New York (10001) **(G-11652)**
Soterix Medical Technologies, New York *Also called Soterix Medical Inc (G-11652)*
Sound & Communication, Port Washington *Also called Testa Communications Inc (G-13311)*
Sound Communications Inc.....516 767-2500
25 Willowdale Ave Port Washington (11050) **(G-13309)**
Sound Source Inc.....585 271-5370
161 Norris Dr Rochester (14610) **(G-14135)**
Sound Video Systems Wny LLC.....716 684-8200
1720 Military Rd Buffalo (14217) **(G-3073)**
Soundcoat Company Inc (HQ).....631 242-2200
1 Burt Dr Deer Park (11729) **(G-4047)**
Source Envelope Inc.....866 284-0707
104 Allen Blvd Ste I Farmingdale (11735) **(G-4877)**
Source Media, New York *Also called Credit Union Journal Inc (G-9423)*
Source Media LLC (HQ).....212 803-8200
1 State St Fl 27 New York (10004) **(G-11653)**
Source Technologies.....718 708-0305
9728 3rd Ave Brooklyn (11209) **(G-2500)**
South Bridge Press Inc.....212 233-4047
122 W 26th St Fl 3 New York (10001) **(G-11654)**
South Brooklyn Book Company, New York *Also called Welcome Rain Publishers LLC (G-12089)*
South Central Boyz.....718 496-7270
2568 Bedford Ave Apt 1a Brooklyn (11226) **(G-2501)**
South of The Highway, Southampton *Also called Dans Paper Inc (G-14952)*
South Seneca Vinyl LLC.....315 585-6050
1585 Yale Farm Rd Romulus (14541) **(G-14282)**
South Shore Ice Co Inc.....516 379-2056
89 E Fulton Ave Roosevelt (11575) **(G-14437)**
South Shore Ready Mix Inc.....516 872-3049
116 E Hawthorne Ave Valley Stream (11580) **(G-15798)**
South Shore Tribune Inc.....516 431-5628
4 California Pl N Island Park (11558) **(G-6518)**
Southampton Town Newspapers (PA).....631 283-4100
135 Windmill Ln Southampton (11968) **(G-14962)**
Southampton Town Newspapers.....631 288-1100
12 Mitchell Rd Westhampton Beach (11978) **(G-16406)**
Southbay Fuel Injectors.....516 442-4707
566 Merrick Rd Ste 3 Rockville Centre (11570) **(G-14242)**
Southco Inc.....585 624-2545
250 East St Honeoye Falls (14472) **(G-6273)**
Southern Adirondack Honey Co., Greenwich *Also called Betterbee Inc (G-5637)*

ALPHABETIC

(PA)=Parent Co (HQ)=Headquarters (DH)=Div Headquarters
2019 Harris
New York Manufacturers Directory
989

Southern Adrndck Fbr Prdcrs CP 518 692-2700
2532 State Route 40 Greenwich (12834) *(G-5645)*
Southern Graphic Systems LLC 315 695-7079
67 County Route 59 Phoenix (13135) *(G-12993)*
Southern Standard Cartons, Great Neck *Also called Standard Group (G-5591)*
Southern Standard Cartoons, Great Neck *Also called Standard Group LLC (G-5592)*
Southern Tier Pennysaver, Jamestown *Also called Spartan Publishing Inc (G-6748)*
Southern Tier Plastics Inc 607 723-2601
Kirkwood Industrial Park Binghamton (13902) *(G-915)*
Southside Precast Products, Buffalo *Also called P J R Industries Inc (G-2984)*
Soutine Inc 212 496-1450
104 W 70th St Frnt 1 New York (10023) *(G-11655)*
Sovereign Brands LLC (PA) 212 343-8366
81 Greene St Apt 2 New York (10012) *(G-11656)*
Sovereign Servicing System LLC 914 779-1400
1 Stone Pl Ste 200 Bronxville (10708) *(G-1426)*
Sp Scientific, Gardiner *Also called S P Industries Inc (G-5295)*
Spa Sciara, Mount Kisco *Also called Plastic & Reconstructive Svcs (G-8355)*
Space 150 .... 612 332-6458
20 Jay St Ste 928 Brooklyn (11201) *(G-2502)*
Space Age Plstic Fbrcators Inc 718 324-4062
4519 White Plains Rd Bronx (10470) *(G-1388)*
Space Coast Semiconductor Inc 631 414-7131
1111 Broadhollow Rd Fl 3 Farmingdale (11735) *(G-4878)*
Space Sign 718 961-1112
1525 132nd St College Point (11356) *(G-3667)*
Space-Craft Worldwide Inc 631 603-3000
47 Wireless Blvd Hauppauge (11788) *(G-5942)*
Spaeth Design Inc 718 606-9685
6006 37th Ave Woodside (11377) *(G-16677)*
Spandage, Brooklyn *Also called Medi-Tech International Corp (G-2187)*
Spanish Artisan Wine Group LLC 914 414-6982
370 Cushman Rd Patterson (12563) *(G-12885)*
Spanish Artisan Wine Group Ltd, Patterson *Also called Spanish Artisan Wine Group LLC (G-12885)*
Spanish Tele Dirctry Hola 912, Long Island City *Also called Hola Publishing Co (G-7470)*
Spanjer Corp 347 448-8033
3856 11th St Long Island City (11101) *(G-7595)*
Spanjer Signs, Long Island City *Also called Spanjer Corp (G-7595)*
Spano's Bread, Utica *Also called Ohio Baking Company Inc (G-15728)*
Sparclean MBL Refinishing Inc 718 445-2351
6915 64th Pl Ridgewood (11385) *(G-13551)*
Spark Creations Inc 212 575-8385
10 W 46th St Fl 9 New York (10036) *(G-11657)*
Sparkle Light Manufacturing, Yonkers *Also called Lighting By Dom Yonkers Inc (G-16779)*
Sparrow Mining Co (PA) 718 519-6600
3743 White Plains Rd Bronx (10467) *(G-1389)*
Sparta Commercial Services Inc (PA) 212 239-2666
555 5th Ave Fl 14 New York (10017) *(G-11658)*
Spartacist Publishing Co 212 732-7860
48 Warren St New York (10007) *(G-11659)*
Spartan Brands Inc (PA) 212 340-0320
451 Park Ave S Fl 5 New York (10016) *(G-11660)*
Spartan Instruments, West Babylon *Also called Pmb Precision Products Inc (G-16182)*
Spartan Publishing Inc 716 664-7373
2 Harding Ave Jamestown (14701) *(G-6748)*
Spaulding & Rogers Mfg Inc 518 768-2070
3252 New Scotland Rd Voorheesville (12186) *(G-15880)*
Spaulding Law Printing Inc 315 422-4805
231 Walton St Ste 103 Syracuse (13202) *(G-15427)*
Speaqua Corp 858 334-9042
46 W Jefryn Blvd Deer Park (11729) *(G-4048)*
Specgx LLC 607 538-9124
172 Railroad Ave Hobart (13788) *(G-6164)*
Special Circle Inc 516 595-9988
123 Shelter Rock Rd New Hyde Park (11040) *(G-8565)*
Special Metals Corporation 716 366-5663
100 Willowbrook Ave Dunkirk (14048) *(G-4180)*
Special Metals Corporation 315 798-2900
4317 Middle Settlement Rd New Hartford (13413) *(G-8512)*
Special Tees 718 980-0987
250 Buel Ave Staten Island (10305) *(G-15136)*
Specialists Ltd 212 941-7696
4740 Metropolitan Ave Ridgewood (11385) *(G-13552)*
Speciality Quality Packaging, Schenectady *Also called Sqp Inc (G-14716)*
Specialized Packg Group Inc (HQ) 315 638-4355
2900 Mclane Rd Baldwinsville (13027) *(G-561)*
Specialized Packg Radisson LLC 315 638-4355
8800 Sixty Rd Baldwinsville (13027) *(G-562)*
Specialized Printed Forms Inc 585 538-2381
352 Center St Caledonia (14423) *(G-3158)*
Specialty Bldg Solutions Inc 631 393-6918
Eads St Ste 165a West Babylon (11704) *(G-16195)*
Specialty Fabricators 631 256-6982
4120 Sunrise Hwy Oakdale (11769) *(G-12520)*
Specialty Ink Co Inc (PA) 631 586-3666
40 Harbour Dr Blue Point (11715) *(G-965)*
Specialty Microwave Corp 631 737-2175
120 Raynor Ave Ronkonkoma (11779) *(G-14415)*
Specialty Minerals Inc 518 585-7982
35 Highland St Ticonderoga (12883) *(G-15513)*
Specialty Minerals Inc (HQ) 212 878-1800
622 3rd Ave Fl 38 New York (10017) *(G-11661)*
Specialty Model & Mold Inc 631 475-0840
2231 5th Ave Ste 22 Ronkonkoma (11779) *(G-14416)*
Specialty Products Inc 866 869-4335
15 Frowein Rd Bldg E2 Center Moriches (11934) *(G-3341)*
Specialty Quality Packg LLC 914 580-3200
602 Potential Pkwy Scotia (12302) *(G-14747)*
Specialty Services 585 728-5650
2631e Naples St Wayland (14572) *(G-16072)*
Specialty Signs Co Inc 212 243-8521
15 W 39th St Fl 7 New York (10018) *(G-11662)*
Specialty Silicone Pdts Inc 518 885-8826
3 Mccrea Hill Rd Ballston Spa (12020) *(G-596)*
Specialty Steel Fabg Corp 718 893-6326
544 Casanova St Bronx (10474) *(G-1390)*
Specialty Steel of America., Bronx *Also called Specialty Steel Fabg Corp (G-1390)*
Specialty Wldg & Fabg NY Inc (PA) 315 426-1807
1025 Hiawatha Blvd E Syracuse (13208) *(G-15428)*
Specified Air Solutions LLC (HQ) 716 852-4400
1250 William St Buffalo (14206) *(G-3074)*
Specilty Bus Mchs Holdings LLC 212 587-9600
260 W 35th St Fl 11 New York (10001) *(G-11663)*
Spectacle Brewing LLC 845 942-8776
55 W Rr Ave Ste 25 Garnerville (10923) *(G-5301)*
Spectacle Optical Inc 646 706-1015
9801 67th Ave Apt 7f Rego Park (11374) *(G-13469)*
Spectaculars, Westhampton Beach *Also called Frame Works America Inc (G-16403)*
Spectra Vista Corporation 845 471-7007
29 Firemens Way Stop 3 Poughkeepsie (12603) *(G-13367)*
Spectracom Corporation (HQ) 585 321-5800
1565 Jefferson Rd Ste 460 Rochester (14623) *(G-14136)*
Spectral Systems LLC (PA) 845 896-2200
35 Corporate Park Rd Hopewell Junction (12533) *(G-6293)*
Spectron Glass & Electronics 631 582-5600
595 Old Willets Path A Hauppauge (11788) *(G-5943)*
Spectron Systems Technology (PA) 631 582-5600
595 Old Willets Path A Hauppauge (11788) *(G-5944)*
Spectronics Corporation 516 333-4840
956 Brush Hollow Rd Westbury (11590) *(G-16373)*
Spectrum, Oceanside *Also called Kantek Inc (G-12544)*
Spectrum Apparel Inc 212 239-2025
463 Fashion Ave Fl 12 New York (10018) *(G-11664)*
Spectrum Brands Inc 631 232-1200
2100 Pacific St Hauppauge (11788) *(G-5945)*
Spectrum Cable Corporation 585 235-7714
295 Mount Read Blvd Ste 2 Rochester (14611) *(G-14137)*
Spectrum Catalysts Inc 631 560-3683
69 Windsor Pl Central Islip (11722) *(G-3384)*
Spectrum Crafts Inc 631 244-5749
70 Orville Dr Ste 1 Bohemia (11716) *(G-1091)*
Spectrum On Broadway 718 932-5388
6106 34th Ave Woodside (11377) *(G-16678)*
Spectrum Prtg Lithography Inc 212 255-3131
505 8th Ave Rm 1802 New York (10018) *(G-11665)*
Spectrum Signs Inc 631 756-1010
6106 34th Ave Woodside (11377) *(G-16679)*
Spectrum Thin Films Inc 631 901-1010
135 Marcus Blvd Hauppauge (11788) *(G-5946)*
Speedcard Inc 631 472-1904
133 Glenmere Way Holbrook (11741) *(G-6210)*
Speedpro Imaging, East Syracuse *Also called Bk Printing Inc (G-4326)*
Speedway LLC 631 738-2536
2825 Middle Country Rd Lake Grove (11755) *(G-6969)*
Speedway Press Inc (HQ) 315 343-3531
1 Burkle St Oswego (13126) *(G-12788)*
Speedways Conveyors Inc 716 893-2222
1210 E Ferry St Buffalo (14211) *(G-3075)*
Speedy Enterprise of USA Corp 718 463-3000
4120 162nd St Flushing (11358) *(G-5047)*
Speedy Sign A Rama USA Inc 516 783-1075
2956 Merrick Rd Bellmore (11710) *(G-795)*
Speedzone Inc 631 750-1973
937 Montauk Hwy Oakdale (11769) *(G-12521)*
Speedzone Raceway Hobbies, Oakdale *Also called Speedzone Inc (G-12521)*
Spektrix Inc 646 741-5110
115 W 30th St Rm 501 New York (10001) *(G-11666)*
Spellman Hgh-Voltage Elec Corp (PA) 631 630-3000
475 Wireless Blvd Hauppauge (11788) *(G-5947)*
Spellman High Vltage Elec Corp 914 686-3600
1 Commerce Park Valhalla (10595) *(G-15748)*
Spence Engineering Company Inc 845 778-5566
150 Coldenham Rd Walden (12586) *(G-15897)*
Spencer AB Inc 646 831-3728
265 W 37th St Rm 2388 New York (10018) *(G-11667)*
Sperry Advertising, South Glens Falls *Also called Northeast Stitches & Ink Inc (G-14939)*
Spex, Rochester *Also called Precision Machine Tech LLC (G-14037)*
Speyside Holdings LLC 845 928-2221
911 State Route 32 Highland Mills (10930) *(G-6152)*

Spf Holdings II LLC (HQ)....212 750-8300
9 W 57th St Ste 4200 New York (10019) ***(G-11668)***
Spfm Corp (PA)....718 788-6800
162 2nd Ave Brooklyn (11215) ***(G-2503)***
Spforms, Caledonia *Also called Specialized Printed Forms Inc* ***(G-3158)***
Sph Group Holdings LLC (HQ)....212 520-2300
590 Madison Ave Fl 32 New York (10022) ***(G-11669)***
Spic and Span Company....914 524-6823
660 White Plains Rd # 250 Tarrytown (10591) ***(G-15494)***
Spiegel Woodworks Inc....845 336-8090
418 Old Neighborhood Rd Kingston (12401) ***(G-6918)***
Spin Holdco Inc (HQ)....516 349-8555
303 Sunnyside Blvd # 70 Plainview (11803) ***(G-13089)***
Spin Magazine Media....212 231-7400
276 5th Ave Rm 800 New York (10001) ***(G-11670)***
Spin-Rite Corporation....585 266-5200
30 Dubelbeiss Ln Rochester (14622) ***(G-14138)***
Spinco Metal Products Inc....315 331-6285
1 Country Club Dr Newark (14513) ***(G-12207)***
Spinergy, Rochester *Also called BMA Media Services Inc* ***(G-13669)***
Spirent Inc (HQ)....631 208-0680
303 Griffing Ave Riverhead (11901) ***(G-13585)***
Spirit Music Group Inc (HQ)....212 533-7672
235 W 23rd St Fl 4 New York (10011) ***(G-11671)***
Splacer Inc....646 853-9789
33 W 17th St Fl 6 New York (10011) ***(G-11672)***
Splice Technologies Inc....631 924-8108
625 North St Manorville (11949) ***(G-7786)***
Split Rock Trading Co Inc....631 929-3261
22 Creek Rd Wading River (11792) ***(G-15887)***
Split Systems Corp (PA)....516 223-5511
1593 Grand Ave North Baldwin (11510) ***(G-12367)***
Spongebath LLC....917 475-1347
2334 28th St Apt 2r Astoria (11105) ***(G-445)***
Sport Athleisure Ltd....212 868-6505
16 W 36th St Rm 1205 New York (10018) ***(G-11673)***
Sports Illustrated For Kids....212 522-1212
1271 Ave Of The Americas New York (10020) ***(G-11674)***
Sports Pblications Prod NY LLC....212 366-7700
708 3rd Ave Fl 12 New York (10017) ***(G-11675)***
Sports Products America LLC....212 594-5511
34 W 33rd St Fl 2 New York (10001) ***(G-11676)***
Sports Reporter Inc....212 737-2750
527 3rd Ave Ste 327 New York (10016) ***(G-11677)***
Sportsdepot Inc....516 543-5018
891 Hayes St Baldwin (11510) ***(G-544)***
Sportsfield Specialties Inc (PA)....607 746-8911
41155 State Highway 10 Delhi (13753) ***(G-4076)***
Sportsgrid Inc....646 849-4085
404 5th Ave Fl 3 New York (10018) ***(G-11678)***
Sportsmaster Apparel, Troy *Also called Standard Manufacturing Co Inc* ***(G-15628)***
Sportswear Unlimited, Bedford Hills *Also called Custom Sportswear Corp* ***(G-773)***
Spotlight Newspaper, Delmar *Also called Community Media Group LLC* ***(G-4077)***
Spotlight Publications LLC....914 345-9473
100 Clearbrook Rd Ste 170 Elmsford (10523) ***(G-4571)***
Spray Market, The, Brooklyn *Also called Spfm Corp* ***(G-2503)***
Spray Moret LLC....917 213-9592
1411 Broadway Fl 8 New York (10018) ***(G-11679)***
Spray Nine Corporation....800 477-7299
309 W Montgomery St Johnstown (12095) ***(G-6841)***
Spray-Tech Finishing Inc....716 664-6317
443 Buffalo St Jamestown (14701) ***(G-6749)***
Sprayground, New York *Also called Spray Moret LLC* ***(G-11679)***
Spread-Mmms LLC....917 727-8116
545 Prospect Pl Apt 10d Brooklyn (11238) ***(G-2504)***
Spring Inc....646 732-0323
41 E 11th St Fl 11 New York (10003) ***(G-11680)***
Spring Publishing Corporation....718 782-0881
419 Manhattan Ave Brooklyn (11222) ***(G-2505)***
Spring Street Design Group, New York *Also called Vetta Jewelry Inc* ***(G-12020)***
Springer Adis Us LLC (HQ)....212 460-1500
233 Spring St Fl 6 New York (10013) ***(G-11681)***
Springer Business Media, New York *Also called Springer Scnce + Bus Media LLC* ***(G-11685)***
Springer Customer Svc Ctr LLC....212 460-1500
233 Spring St Fl 6 New York (10013) ***(G-11682)***
Springer Healthcare LLC....212 460-1500
233 Spring St Fl 6 New York (10013) ***(G-11683)***
Springer Publishing Co LLC....212 431-4370
11 W 42nd St Ste 15a New York (10036) ***(G-11684)***
Springer Scnce + Bus Media LLC (HQ)....212 460-1500
233 Spring St Fl 6 New York (10013) ***(G-11685)***
Springfield Control Systems....718 631-0870
4056 Douglaston Pkwy Douglaston (11363) ***(G-4141)***
Springfield Oil Services Inc (PA)....914 315-6812
550 Mmaroneck Ave Ste 503 Harrison (10528) ***(G-5734)***
Springville Mfg Co Inc....716 592-4957
8798 North St Springville (14141) ***(G-15021)***
SPS Medical Supply Corp (HQ)....585 359-0130
6789 W Henrietta Rd Rush (14543) ***(G-14476)***
SPS Medical Supply Corp....585 968-2377
31 Water St Ste 1 Cuba (14727) ***(G-3920)***
Spst Inc....607 798-6952
119b Rano Blvd Vestal (13850) ***(G-15822)***
Sputnick 84 LLC....844 667-7468
1745 Broadway Frnt 3 New York (10019) ***(G-11686)***
SPX Cooling Technologies Inc....914 697-5030
30 Glenn St Ste 403 White Plains (10603) ***(G-16505)***
SPX Corporation....914 366-7402
220 White Plains Rd Tarrytown (10591) ***(G-15495)***
SPX Corporation....631 467-2632
70 Raynor Ave Ronkonkoma (11779) ***(G-14417)***
SPX Corporation....585 436-5550
135 Mount Read Blvd Rochester (14611) ***(G-14139)***
SPX Flow Technology, Rochester *Also called SPX Flow Us LLC* ***(G-14140)***
SPX Flow Us LLC (HQ)....585 436-5550
135 Mount Read Blvd Rochester (14611) ***(G-14140)***
SPX Flow Us LLC....716 692-3000
105 Crosspoint Pkwy Getzville (14068) ***(G-5353)***
SPX Precision Components, Ronkonkoma *Also called SPX Corporation* ***(G-14417)***
Sqp, Scotia *Also called Specialty Quality Packg LLC* ***(G-14747)***
Sqp Inc....518 831-6800
602 Potential Pkwy Schenectady (12302) ***(G-14716)***
Square One Coating Systems LLC....315 790-5921
170 Base Rd Oriskany (13424) ***(G-12762)***
Square One Publishers Inc....516 535-2010
115 Herricks Rd Garden City Park (11040) ***(G-5288)***
Square Stamping Mfg Corp....315 896-2641
108 Old Remsen Rd Barneveld (13304) ***(G-605)***
Squeaky Clean, Brooklyn *Also called National Prfmce Solutions Inc* ***(G-2246)***
SRC Liquidation Company....716 631-3900
435 Lawrence Bell Dr # 4 Williamsville (14221) ***(G-16588)***
Srctec LLC....315 452-8700
5801 E Taft Rd Ste 6 Syracuse (13212) ***(G-15429)***
Sriracha2go, New York *Also called Kybod Group LLC* ***(G-10489)***
Srlh Holdings Inc (HQ)....929 529-7951
15 Big Pond Rd Huguenot (12746) ***(G-6388)***
SRP, New York *Also called Structured Retail Products* ***(G-11724)***
SRP Apparel Group Inc....212 764-4810
525 7th Ave Rm 1808 New York (10018) ***(G-11687)***
Srtech Industry Corp....718 496-7001
12019 Ketch Ct College Point (11356) ***(G-3668)***
SS&c Financial Services LLC (HQ)....914 670-3600
1 South Rd Harrison (10528) ***(G-5735)***
Ssa Trading Ltd....646 465-9500
226 W 37th St Fl 6 New York (10018) ***(G-11688)***
Ssac Inc....800 843-8848
8242 Loop Rd Baldwinsville (13027) ***(G-563)***
Ssf Production LLC....518 324-3407
194 Pleasant Ridge Rd Plattsburgh (12901) ***(G-13156)***
SSG Fashions Ltd....212 221-0933
27 E 37th St Frnt 1 New York (10016) ***(G-11689)***
Ssjjj Manufacturing LLC (PA)....516 498-3200
98 Cuttermill Rd Ste 412 Great Neck (11021) ***(G-5590)***
SSP, Syracuse *Also called Selflock Screw Products Co Inc* ***(G-15422)***
Ssrja LLC....718 725-7020
10729 180th St Jamaica (11433) ***(G-6678)***
St James Printing Inc....631 981-2095
656 Rosevale Ave Ronkonkoma (11779) ***(G-14418)***
St John....718 720-8367
229 Morrison Ave Staten Island (10310) ***(G-15137)***
St John....718 771-4541
1700 Saint Johns Pl Brooklyn (11233) ***(G-2506)***
St Lawrence Cement Co, Catskill *Also called Ciment St-Laurent Inc* ***(G-3302)***
St Lawrence County Newspapers (HQ)....315 393-1003
1 Main St Ste 103 Canton (13617) ***(G-3258)***
St Lawrence Lumber Inc....315 649-2990
27140 County Route 57 Three Mile Bay (13693) ***(G-15509)***
St Raymond Monument Co....718 824-3600
2727 Lafayette Ave Bronx (10465) ***(G-1391)***
St Silicones Corporation....518 406-3208
821 Main St Clifton Park (12065) ***(G-3578)***
St Silicones Inc....518 664-0745
95 N Central Ave Mechanicville (12118) ***(G-7934)***
St Tropez Inc....800 366-6383
530 Broadway Fl 10 New York (10012) ***(G-11690)***
Stack Electronics, Deer Park *Also called Veja Electronics Inc* ***(G-4058)***
Stafford Labs Orthotics/Prosth....845 692-5227
189 Monhagen Ave Middletown (10940) ***(G-8176)***
Stag Brothers Cast Stone Co....718 629-0975
909 E 51st St Brooklyn (11203) ***(G-2507)***
Stainless Design Concepts Ltd....845 246-3631
1117 Kings Hwy Saugerties (12477) ***(G-14617)***
Stainless Metals Inc....718 784-1454
6001 31st Ave Ste 1 Woodside (11377) ***(G-16680)***
Stairworld Inc....718 441-9722
10114 Jamaica Ave Richmond Hill (11418) ***(G-13514)***
Stallion Inc (PA)....718 706-0111
3620 34th St Long Island City (11106) ***(G-7596)***
Stallion Technologies Inc....315 622-1176
4324 Loveland Dr Liverpool (13090) ***(G-7263)***
Stamp, Rhinebeck *Also called Smithers Tools & Mch Pdts Inc* ***(G-13488)***
Stamp Rite Tool & Die Inc....718 752-0334
4311 35th St Long Island City (11101) ***(G-7597)***

ALPHABETIC

(PA)=Parent Co (HQ)=Headquarters (DH)=Div Headquarters
2019 Harris
New York Manufacturers Directory
991

Stampcrete Decorative Concrete, Liverpool *Also called Stampcrete International Ltd* ***(G-7264)***
Stampcrete International Ltd....315 451-2837
325 Commerce Blvd Liverpool (13088) ***(G-7264)***
Stamped Fittings Inc....607 733-9988
217 Lenox Ave Elmira Heights (14903) ***(G-4514)***
Stamper Technology Inc....585 247-8370
232 Wallace Way Rochester (14624) ***(G-14141)***
Standard Analytics Io Inc....917 882-5422
7 World Trade Ctr 46th New York (10007) ***(G-11691)***
Standard Bots Company....646 876-2687
33 Wellington Rd Locust Valley (11560) ***(G-7351)***
Standard Diversified Inc (HQ)....302 824-7062
155 Mineola Blvd Mineola (11501) ***(G-8250)***
Standard Group (PA)....718 335-5500
1010 Nthrn Blvd Ste 236 Great Neck (11021) ***(G-5591)***
Standard Group LLC (HQ)....718 507-6430
1010 Nthrn Blvd Ste 236 Great Neck (11021) ***(G-5592)***
Standard Industrial Works Inc....631 888-0130
271 Skip Ln Bay Shore (11706) ***(G-726)***
Standard Industries Inc (PA)....212 821-1600
9 W 57th St Fl 30 New York (10019) ***(G-11692)***
Standard Manufacturing Co Inc (PA)....518 235-2200
750 2nd Ave Troy (12182) ***(G-15628)***
Standard Microsystems Corp (HQ)....631 435-6000
80 Arkay Dr Ste 100 Hauppauge (11788) ***(G-5948)***
Standard Motor Products Inc (PA)....718 392-0200
3718 Northern Blvd # 600 Long Island City (11101) ***(G-7598)***
Standard Paper Box Machine Co....718 328-3300
347 Coster St Fl 2 Bronx (10474) ***(G-1392)***
Standard Portable, Mayville *Also called Lyn Jo Enterprises Ltd* ***(G-7922)***
Standard Products Division, Wassaic *Also called Pawling Corporation* ***(G-15965)***
Standard Screen Supply Corp (PA)....212 627-2727
121 Varick St Rm 200 New York (10013) ***(G-11693)***
Standard Wedding Band Co....516 294-0954
951 Franklin Ave Garden City (11530) ***(G-5282)***
Standing Stone Vineyards....607 582-6051
9934 State Route 414 Hector (14841) ***(G-6002)***
Standwill Packaging Inc....631 752-1236
220 Sherwood Ave Farmingdale (11735) ***(G-4879)***
Stanfordville Mch & Mfg Co Inc (PA)....845 868-2266
29 Victory Ln Poughkeepsie (12603) ***(G-13368)***
Stanley Creations Inc....718 361-6100
3100 47th Ave Ste 4105 Long Island City (11101) ***(G-7599)***
Stanley Home Products, Leicester *Also called Cpac Inc* ***(G-7126)***
Stanley Industrial Eqp LLC....315 656-8733
8094 Saintsville Rd Kirkville (13082) ***(G-6935)***
Stanley Paper Co Inc....518 489-1131
1 Terminal St Albany (12206) ***(G-129)***
Stanmark Jewelry Inc....212 730-2557
64 W 48th St Ste 1303 New York (10036) ***(G-11694)***
Stanson Automated LLC....866 505-7826
145 Saw Mill River Rd # 2 Yonkers (10701) ***(G-16799)***
Staplex Company Inc....718 768-3333
777 5th Ave Brooklyn (11232) ***(G-2508)***
Star Brands North America Inc (HQ)....914 355-9750
10 Bank St Ste 1011 White Plains (10606) ***(G-16506)***
Star Childrens Dress Co Inc (PA)....212 279-1524
1250 Broadway Fl 18 New York (10001) ***(G-11695)***
Star Communications, Hauppauge *Also called Star Quality Printing Inc* ***(G-5949)***
Star Community Pubg Group LLC, Melville *Also called Star Community Publishing* ***(G-8065)***
Star Community Publishing....631 843-4050
235 Pinelawn Rd Melville (11747) ***(G-8065)***
Star Composition Services Inc....212 684-4001
170 Hewes St Brooklyn (11211) ***(G-2509)***
Star Desk Pad Co Inc....914 963-9400
60 Mclean Ave Yonkers (10705) ***(G-16800)***
Star Headlight Lantern Co Inc (PA)....585 226-9500
455 Rochester St Avon (14414) ***(G-522)***
Star Kay White Inc (PA)....845 268-2600
151 Wells Ave Congers (10920) ***(G-3720)***
Star Mold Co Inc....631 694-2283
125 Florida St Farmingdale (11735) ***(G-4880)***
Star Mountain Coffee, Jamaica *Also called Star Mountain JFK Inc* ***(G-6679)***
Star Mountain JFK Inc....718 553-6787
Federal Cir Bldg 141 Jamaica (11430) ***(G-6679)***
Star Poly Bag Inc (PA)....718 384-3130
200 Liberty Ave Brooklyn (11207) ***(G-2510)***
Star Poly Bag Inc....718 384-5342
96 Snediker Ave Brooklyn (11207) ***(G-2511)***
Star Press Pearl River Inc....845 268-2294
614 Corporate Way Ste 8 Valley Cottage (10989) ***(G-15765)***
Star Quality Printing Inc....631 273-1900
270 Oser Ave Hauppauge (11788) ***(G-5949)***
Star Ready Mix East Inc....631 289-8787
225 Springs Fireplace Rd East Hampton (11937) ***(G-4243)***
Star Ready Mix Inc....631 289-8787
172 Peconic Ave Medford (11763) ***(G-7966)***
Star Seal of New York, Gasport *Also called Cosmicoat of Wny Inc* ***(G-5305)***
Star Sports Corp....516 773-4075
747 Middle Neck Rd # 103 Great Neck (11024) ***(G-5593)***
Star Tubing Corp....716 483-1703
53 River St Jamestown (14701) ***(G-6750)***
Star Wire Mesh Fabricators....212 831-4133
518 E 119th St New York (10035) ***(G-11696)***
Star-Gazette Fund Inc....607 734-5151
310 E Church St Elmira (14901) ***(G-4503)***
Starbrook Incorporated....212 514-5212
141 Neptune Ave A Brooklyn (11235) ***(G-2512)***
Starcraft Press Inc....718 383-6700
4402 11th St Ste 311 Long Island City (11101) ***(G-7600)***
Starcyl USA Corp....877 782-7295
348 State Route 11 Champlain (12919) ***(G-3413)***
Starfire Holding Corporation (PA)....914 614-7000
767 5th Ave Fl 47 New York (10153) ***(G-11697)***
Starfire Printing, Holbrook *Also called Image Typography Inc* ***(G-6188)***
Starfire Printing Inc....631 736-1495
28 Washington Ave Holtsville (11742) ***(G-6245)***
Starfire Swords Ltd Inc....607 589-7244
74 Railroad Ave Spencer (14883) ***(G-14974)***
Starfire Systems Inc....518 899-9336
8 Sarnowski Dr Glenville (12302) ***(G-5447)***
Starfuels Inc (HQ)....914 289-4800
50 Main St White Plains (10606) ***(G-16507)***
Stargate Computer Corp....516 474-4799
24 Harmony Dr Port Jeff STA (11776) ***(G-13217)***
Stark Aquarium Products Co Inc....718 445-5357
2914 122nd St Flushing (11354) ***(G-5048)***
Stark Fish, Flushing *Also called Stark Aquarium Products Co Inc* ***(G-5048)***
Starkey & Henricks, New York *Also called Charles Henricks Inc* ***(G-9262)***
Starlight Paint Factory, Bronx *Also called Starlite Pnt & Varnish Co Inc* ***(G-1393)***
Starline Usa Inc....716 773-0100
3036 Alt Blvd Grand Island (14072) ***(G-5514)***
Starliner Shipping & Travel....718 385-1515
5305 Church Ave Ste 1 Brooklyn (11203) ***(G-2513)***
Starlite Media LLC (PA)....212 909-7700
118 E 28th St Rm 601 New York (10016) ***(G-11698)***
Starlite Pnt & Varnish Co Inc....718 292-6420
724 E 140th St Bronx (10454) ***(G-1393)***
Staroba Plastics Inc....716 537-3153
42 Edgewood Dr Holland (14080) ***(G-6222)***
Stasi Industries Inc....516 334-2742
501 Winding Rd Old Bethpage (11804) ***(G-12588)***
Statebook LLC....845 383-1991
185 Fair St Ste 2 Kingston (12401) ***(G-6919)***
Staten Island Advance, Staten Island *Also called Advance Publications Inc* ***(G-15040)***
Staten Island Parent Magazine....718 761-4800
16 Shenandoah Ave Ste 2 Staten Island (10314) ***(G-15138)***
Staten Island Stair Inc....718 317-9276
439 Sharrotts Rd Staten Island (10309) ***(G-15139)***
Statewide Fireproof Door Co....845 268-6043
178 Charles Blvd Valley Cottage (10989) ***(G-15766)***
Station Hill of Barrytown....845 758-5293
120 Station Hill Rd Barrytown (12507) ***(G-606)***
Stature Electric, Watertown *Also called Allied Motion Technologies Inc* ***(G-16000)***
Stature Electric Inc....716 242-7535
495 Commerce Dr Amherst (14228) ***(G-251)***
Staub Machine Company Inc....716 649-4211
206 Lake St Hamburg (14075) ***(G-5696)***
Staub Square, Hamburg *Also called Staub Machine Company Inc* ***(G-5696)***
Stavo Industries Inc (PA)....845 331-4552
132 Flatbush Ave Kingston (12401) ***(G-6920)***
Stavo Industries Inc....845 331-5389
132 Flatbush Ave Kingston (12401) ***(G-6921)***
Stealth Archtctral Windows Inc....718 821-6666
232 Varet St Brooklyn (11206) ***(G-2514)***
Stealth Inc....718 252-7900
1129 E 27th St Brooklyn (11210) ***(G-2515)***
Stealth Window, Brooklyn *Also called Stealth Archtctral Windows Inc* ***(G-2514)***
Steamline Machine, Fairport *Also called Streamline Precision Inc* ***(G-4662)***
Steamworks, Lockport *Also called Jonathan Brose* ***(G-7312)***
Stebe Shcjhjff....839 383-9833
18 Lynbrook Rd Poughkeepsie (12603) ***(G-13369)***
Stedman Energy Inc....716 789-3018
4411 Canterbury Dr Mayville (14757) ***(G-7924)***
Steel & Obrien Mfg Inc....585 492-5800
7869 Route 98 Arcade (14009) ***(G-389)***
Steel City Salt LLC....716 532-0000
13870 Taylor Hollow Rd Collins (14034) ***(G-3675)***
Steel Craft, Brooklyn *Also called Steelcraft Manufacturing Co* ***(G-2516)***
Steel Craft Rolling Door....631 608-8662
5 Di Tomas Ct Copiague (11726) ***(G-3783)***
Steel Excel Inc (HQ)....914 461-1300
1133 Westchester Ave White Plains (10604) ***(G-16508)***
Steel Partners Holdings LP (PA)....212 520-2300
590 Madison Ave Rm 3202 New York (10022) ***(G-11699)***
Steel Sales Inc....607 674-6363
8085 New York St Hwy 12 Sherburne (13460) ***(G-14811)***
Steel Tech SA LLC....845 786-3691
7 Hillside Dr Thiells (10984) ***(G-15499)***
Steel Work Inc....585 232-1555
340 Oak St Rochester (14608) ***(G-14142)***

ALPHABETIC SECTION
Stone Bridge Iron and Stl Inc

Steel-Brite Ltd 631 589-4044
2 Dawn Dr Oakdale (11769) ***(G-12522)***
Steelcraft Manufacturing Co 718 277-2404
352 Pine St Brooklyn (11208) ***(G-2516)***
Steeldeck Ny Inc 718 599-3700
141 Banker St Brooklyn (11222) ***(G-2517)***
Steele Truss and Panel LLC 518 562-4663
112 Trade Rd Plattsburgh (12901) ***(G-13157)***
Steele Truss Company Inc 518 562-4663
118 Trade Rd Plattsburgh (12901) ***(G-13158)***
Steelflex Electro Corp 516 226-4466
145 S 13th St Lindenhurst (11757) ***(G-7193)***
Steelmasters Inc 718 498-2854
135 Liberty Ave Brooklyn (11212) ***(G-2518)***
Steelstone Group LLC 888 552-0033
1425 37th St Brooklyn (11218) ***(G-2519)***
Steelways Inc 845 562-0860
401 S Water St Newburgh (12553) ***(G-12246)***
Steelways Shipyard, Newburgh *Also called Steelways Inc* ***(G-12246)***
Steering Columns Galore Inc 845 278-5762
8 Vine Rd Mahopac (10541) ***(G-7713)***
Steezys LLC 646 276-5333
80 8th Ave 202 New York (10011) ***(G-11700)***
Stefan & Sons Welding, Chaffee *Also called Donald Stefan* ***(G-3403)***
Stefan Furs Inc 212 594-2788
150 W 30th St Fl 15 New York (10001) ***(G-11701)***
Stefan Sydor Optics Inc 585 271-7300
31 Jetview Dr Rochester (14624) ***(G-14143)***
Steffen Publishing Inc 315 865-4100
9584 Main St Holland Patent (13354) ***(G-6225)***
Steigercraft, Bellport *Also called AVS Laminates Inc* ***(G-799)***
Stein Fibers Ltd (PA) 518 489-5700
4 Computer Dr W Ste 200 Albany (12205) ***(G-130)***
Stein Industries Inc 631 789-2222
22 Sprague Ave Amityville (11701) ***(G-316)***
Steinbock-Braff Inc 718 972-6500
3611 14th Ave Brooklyn (11218) ***(G-2520)***
Steindl Cast Stone Co Inc 718 296-8530
9107 76th St Woodhaven (11421) ***(G-16637)***
Steiner Doors, Brooklyn *Also called A G M Deco Inc* ***(G-1456)***
Steiner Technologies Inc 585 425-5910
180 Perinton Pkwy Fairport (14450) ***(G-4660)***
Steinway Inc (HQ) 718 721-2600
1 Steinway Pl Long Island City (11105) ***(G-7601)***
Steinway and Sons (HQ) 718 721-2600
1 Steinway Pl Long Island City (11105) ***(G-7602)***
Steinway Awning II LLC (PA) 718 729-2965
4230 24th St Astoria (11101) ***(G-446)***
Steinway Awnings, Astoria *Also called Steinway Awning II LLC* ***(G-446)***
Steinway Hall, Long Island City *Also called Steinway Inc* ***(G-7601)***
Steinway Musical Instrs Inc (HQ) 781 894-9770
1133 Avenue Of The Americ New York (10036) ***(G-11702)***
Steinway Pasta & Gelati Inc 718 246-5414
146 Albany Ave Lindenhurst (11757) ***(G-7194)***
Stellar Alliance, New York *Also called Alen Sands York Associates Ltd* ***(G-8790)***
Stellar Printing Inc 718 361-1600
3838 9th St Long Island City (11101) ***(G-7603)***
Stemcultures LLC 518 621-0848
1 Discovery Dr Rensselaer (12144) ***(G-13478)***
Stemline Therapeutics Inc 646 502-2311
750 Lexington Ave Fl 11 New York (10022) ***(G-11703)***
Stensul Inc (PA) 212 380-8620
150 W 25th St Fl 3 New York (10001) ***(G-11704)***
Stephan & Company ACC Ltd (PA) 212 481-3888
10 E 38th St Fl 9 New York (10016) ***(G-11705)***
Stephen Bader Company Inc 518 753-4456
10 Charles St Valley Falls (12185) ***(G-15770)***
Stephen Dweck, New York *Also called Rumson Acquisition LLC* ***(G-11447)***
Stephen Dweck Industries, Brooklyn *Also called Dweck Industries Inc* ***(G-1797)***
Stephen J Lipkins Inc 631 249-8866
855 Conklin St Ste A Farmingdale (11735) ***(G-4881)***
Stephen M Kiernan 716 836-6300
701 Seneca St Ste 300 Buffalo (14210) ***(G-3076)***
Stephen Miller Gen Contrs Inc 518 661-5601
301 Riceville Rd Gloversville (12078) ***(G-5467)***
Stephen Singer Pattern Co Inc 212 947-2902
340 W 39th St Fl 4 New York (10018) ***(G-11706)***
Stephenson Custom Case Company 905 542-8762
1623 Military Rd Niagara Falls (14304) ***(G-12338)***
Stephenson Lumber Company Inc 518 548-7521
Rr 8 Speculator (12164) ***(G-14973)***
Stepping Stones One Day Signs 518 237-5774
105 Broad St Waterford (12188) ***(G-15988)***
Steps Plus Inc 315 432-0885
6375 Thompson Rd Syracuse (13206) ***(G-15430)***
Stereo Advantage Inc 716 656-7161
45 Boxwood Ln Cheektowaga (14227) ***(G-3459)***
Steri-Pharma LLC 315 473-7180
429 S West St Syracuse (13202) ***(G-15431)***
Sterilator Company, Cuba *Also called SPS Medical Supply Corp* ***(G-3920)***
Steriliz LLC 585 415-5411
150 Linden Oaks Ste B Rochester (14625) ***(G-14144)***
Steris Corporation 877 887-1788
40 Melville Park Rd Ste 1 Melville (11747) ***(G-8066)***
Steris Corporation 845 469-4087
23 Elizabeth Dr Chester (10918) ***(G-3484)***
Sterling Industries Inc 631 753-3070
410 Eastern Pkwy Farmingdale (11735) ***(G-4882)***
Sterling Molded Products Inc 845 344-4546
9-17 Oliver Ave Middletown (10940) ***(G-8177)***
Sterling North America Inc 631 243-6933
270 Oser Ave Hauppauge (11788) ***(G-5950)***
Sterling Pierce Company Inc 516 593-1170
395 Atlantic Ave East Rockaway (11518) ***(G-4296)***
Sterling Possessions Ltd 212 594-0418
251 W 39th St New York (10018) ***(G-11707)***
Sterling Shelf Liners Inc 631 676-5175
836 Grundy Ave Holbrook (11741) ***(G-6211)***
Sterling Sound Inc 212 604-9433
88 10th Ave Frnt 6 New York (10011) ***(G-11708)***
Sterling Toggle Inc 631 491-0500
99 Mahan St West Babylon (11704) ***(G-16196)***
Stern & Stern Industries Inc 607 324-4485
188 Thacher St Hornell (14843) ***(G-6303)***
Sterrx LLC 518 324-7879
141 Idaho Ave Plattsburgh (12903) ***(G-13159)***
Stetron International Inc (PA) 716 854-3443
90 Broadway St Ste 1 Buffalo (14203) ***(G-3077)***
Steuben Courier Advocate, Bath *Also called Gatehouse Media LLC* ***(G-643)***
Steuben Foods Incorporated (PA) 718 291-3333
1150 Maple Rd Elma (14059) ***(G-4459)***
Steuben Foods Incorporated 716 655-4000
1150 Maple Rd Elma (14059) ***(G-4460)***
Steval Graphics Concepts Inc 516 576-0220
7 Fairchild Ct Ste 200 Plainview (11803) ***(G-13090)***
Steve & Andys Organics Inc 718 499-7933
630 Flushing Ave Brooklyn (11206) ***(G-2521)***
STEVE MADDEN, Long Island City *Also called Steven Madden Ltd* ***(G-7604)***
Steve Poli Sales 315 487-0394
102 Farmington Dr Camillus (13031) ***(G-3197)***
Steven Coffey Pallet S Inc 585 261-6783
3376 Edgemere Dr Rochester (14612) ***(G-14145)***
Steven John Opticians 718 543-3336
5901 Riverdale Ave Bronx (10471) ***(G-1394)***
Steven Kraus Associates Inc 631 923-2033
9 Private Rd Huntington (11743) ***(G-6417)***
Steven Madden Ltd (PA) 718 446-1800
5216 Barnett Ave Long Island City (11104) ***(G-7604)***
Steven Madden Ltd 212 695-5545
19 W 34th St Fl 4 New York (10001) ***(G-11709)***
Stevens Bandes Graphics Corp 212 675-1128
333 Hudson St Fl 3 New York (10013) ***(G-11710)***
Stevenson Printing Co Inc 516 676-1233
1 Brewster St Ste 2 Glen Cove (11542) ***(G-5376)***
Stever-Locke Industries Inc 585 624-3450
179 N Main St Honeoye Falls (14472) ***(G-6274)***
Steves Original Furs Inc 212 967-8007
345 7th Ave Fl 9 New York (10001) ***(G-11711)***
Stewart Tobori & Chang Div, New York *Also called Harry N Abrams Incorporated* ***(G-10042)***
Stewarts Processing Corp (PA) 518 581-1200
2907 State Route 9 Ballston Spa (12020) ***(G-597)***
Stewarts Shops Corp 518 499-9376
60 Poultney St Whitehall (12887) ***(G-16524)***
Stf, Cedarhurst *Also called Solar Thin Films Inc* ***(G-3337)***
STf Services Inc 315 463-8506
26 Corporate Cir Ste 2 East Syracuse (13057) ***(G-4371)***
STI-Co Industries Inc 716 662-2680
11 Cobham Dr Ste A Orchard Park (14127) ***(G-12744)***
Stickershopcom Inc 631 563-4323
582 Middle Rd Bayport (11705) ***(G-739)***
Sticky Socks LLC 212 541-5927
200 W 60th St Apt 7g New York (10023) ***(G-11712)***
Stidd Systems Inc 631 477-2400
220 Carpenter St Greenport (11944) ***(G-5626)***
Stiegelbauer Associates Inc (PA) 718 624-0835
Bldg 280 Brooklyn (11205) ***(G-2522)***
Stilltheone Distillery LLC 914 217-0347
500 Mmaroneck Ave Ste 205 Harrison (10528) ***(G-5736)***
Stillwater Wood & Iron 518 664-4501
114 N Hudson Ave Stillwater (12170) ***(G-15159)***
Stitch & Couture Inc (PA) 212 947-9204
224 W 30th St Fl 14 New York (10001) ***(G-11713)***
Stj Orthotic Services Inc (PA) 631 956-0181
920 Wellwood Ave Ste B Lindenhurst (11757) ***(G-7195)***
Stk Electronics Inc 315 655-8476
2747 Rte 20 Cazenovia (13035) ***(G-3327)***
Stock Drive Products Div, Hicksville *Also called Designatronics Incorporated* ***(G-6080)***
Stoffel Polygon Systems Inc 914 961-2000
199 Marbledale Rd Tuckahoe (10707) ***(G-15646)***
Stone & Terrazzo World Inc 718 361-6899
5132 35th St Long Island City (11101) ***(G-7605)***
Stone and Bath Gallery 718 438-4500
868 39th St Brooklyn (11232) ***(G-2523)***
Stone Bridge Iron and Stl Inc 518 695-3752
426 Purinton Rd Gansevoort (12831) ***(G-5247)***

ALPHABETIC

Stone Crafters International, Brooklyn *Also called PR & Stone & Tile Inc (G-2333)*
Stone Crest Industries Inc......607 652-2665
152 Starheim Rd Stamford (12167) *(G-15032)*
Stone Expo & Cabinetry LLC......516 292-2988
7 Terminal Rd West Hempstead (11552) *(G-16225)*
Stone Glo Products, Bronx *Also called TWI-Laq Industries Inc (G-1410)*
Stone House Associates Inc......212 221-7447
37 W 47th St Ste 910 New York (10036) *(G-11714)*
Stone Well Bodies & Mch Inc......315 497-3512
625 Sill Rd Genoa (13071) *(G-5338)*
Stonegate Stabless......518 746-7133
106 Reynolds Rd Fort Edward (12828) *(G-5101)*
Stones Homemade Candies Inc......315 343-8401
145 W Bridge St Oswego (13126) *(G-12789)*
Stonesong Press LLC......212 929-4600
270 W 39th St Rm 201 New York (10018) *(G-11715)*
Stoney Croft Converters Inc......718 608-9800
364 Sharrotts Rd Staten Island (10309) *(G-15140)*
Stony Apparel Corp......212 391-0022
1407 Broadway Rm 3300 New York (10018) *(G-11716)*
Stony Brook Mfg Co Inc (PA)......631 369-9530
652 Scott Ave Calverton (11933) *(G-3171)*
Stony Brook University......631 632-6434
310 Administration Bldg Stony Brook (11794) *(G-15169)*
Stony Manufacturing Inc......716 652-6730
591 Pound Rd Elma (14059) *(G-4461)*
Stony Point Graphics Ltd......845 786-3322
79 S Liberty Dr Stony Point (10980) *(G-15176)*
Stop Entertainment Inc......212 242-7867
408 Rye Hill Rd Monroe (10950) *(G-8281)*
Stop N Shop LLC......518 512-9657
911 Central Ave Ste 149 Albany (12206) *(G-131)*
Storage Sheds, Westmoreland *Also called Shafer & Sons (G-16410)*
Storflex Fixture, Corning *Also called Storflex Holdings Inc (G-3826)*
Storflex Holdings Inc......607 962-2137
392 Pulteney St Corning (14830) *(G-3826)*
Stork H & E Turbo Blading Inc......607 277-4968
334 Comfort Rd Ithaca (14850) *(G-6610)*
Stormberg Brand, Valley Cottage *Also called Stromberg Brand Corporation (G-15767)*
Storybooks Forever......716 822-7845
4 Magnolia Ave Buffalo (14220) *(G-3078)*
Strada Soft Inc......718 556-6940
20 Clifton Ave Staten Island (10305) *(G-15141)*
Strahl & Pitsch Inc......631 669-0175
230 Great East Neck Rd West Babylon (11704) *(G-16197)*
Straight Arrow Publishing Co......212 484-1616
1290 Ave Of The Amer Fl 2 New York (10104) *(G-11717)*
Strassburg Medical LLC......716 433-9368
525 Wheatfield St North Tonawanda (14120) *(G-12456)*
Stratconglobal Inc......212 989-2355
685 3rd Ave Fl 4 New York (10017) *(G-11718)*
Strategic Signage Sourcing LLC......518 450-1093
2 Gilbert Rd Saratoga Springs (12866) *(G-14599)*
Strategies North America Inc......716 945-6053
150 Elm St Salamanca (14779) *(G-14534)*
Strathmore Directories Ltd......516 997-2525
26 Bond St Westbury (11590) *(G-16374)*
Strathmore Publications, Westbury *Also called Strathmore Directories Ltd (G-16374)*
Strativa Pharmaceuticals......201 802-4000
1 Ram Ridge Rd Spring Valley (10977) *(G-15008)*
Strato Transit Components LLC......518 686-4541
155 State Route 67 Eagle Bridge (12057) *(G-4187)*
Stratusoft, Great Neck *Also called Application Resources Inc (G-5534)*
Straus Communications......845 782-4000
20 West Ave Ste 201 Chester (10918) *(G-3485)*
Straus Newspaper, Chester *Also called Straus Communications (G-3485)*
Straus Newspapers Inc......845 782-4000
20 West Ave Chester (10918) *(G-3486)*
Strauss Eye Prosthetics Inc......585 424-1350
360 White Spruce Blvd Rochester (14623) *(G-14146)*
Strawtown Jewerly, New City *Also called Shining Creations Inc (G-8495)*
Stream Police, New York *Also called Instant Stream Inc (G-10227)*
Streamline Precision Inc......585 421-9050
205 Turk Hill Park Fairport (14450) *(G-4661)*
Streamline Precision Inc......585 421-9050
1000 Turk Hill Rd Ste 205 Fairport (14450) *(G-4662)*
Streck's Machinery, Watervliet *Also called Strecks Inc (G-16051)*
Strecks Inc......518 273-4410
800 1st St Watervliet (12189) *(G-16051)*
Street Beat Sportswear Inc (PA)......718 302-1500
462 Kent Ave Fl 2 Brooklyn (11249) *(G-2524)*
Street King LLC......212 400-2200
575 Madison Ave Fl 24 New York (10022) *(G-11719)*
Street Smart Designs Inc......646 865-0056
29 W 35th St Fl 6 New York (10001) *(G-11720)*
Streetcred Nyc LLC......646 675-0073
1006 6th Ave Fl 3 New York (10018) *(G-11721)*
Streit Matzoh Co, Orangeburg *Also called Aron Streit Inc (G-12670)*
Striata Inc......212 918-4677
48 Wall St Ste 1100 New York (10005) *(G-11722)*
Strictly Business, Plattsburgh *Also called Northeast Group (G-13139)*
Strider Global LLC......212 726-1302
261 W 28th St Apt 6a New York (10001) *(G-11723)*
Striker Orthopedics......585 381-1773
7 Linden Park Rochester (14625) *(G-14147)*
Strippit Inc (HQ)......716 542-4511
12975 Clarence Center Rd Akron (14001) *(G-23)*
Strocchia Iron Works, Albertson *Also called Patsy Strocchia & Sons Iron Wo (G-150)*
Stroehmann Bakeries 33, Maspeth *Also called Bimbo Bakeries Usa Inc (G-7828)*
Stroehmann Bakeries 56, Olean *Also called Bimbo Bakeries Usa Inc (G-12593)*
Stroehmann Bakeries 72, Goshen *Also called Bimbo Bakeries Usa Inc (G-5476)*
Stroehmann Bakeries 90, Vestal *Also called Bimbo Bakeries Usa Inc (G-15810)*
Stromberg Brand Corporation......914 739-7410
12 Ford Products Rd Valley Cottage (10989) *(G-15767)*
Strong Forge & Fabrication......585 343-5251
20 Liberty St Batavia (14020) *(G-635)*
Strong Group Inc......516 766-6300
222 Atlantic Ave Unit B Oceanside (11572) *(G-12558)*
Strong Hospital, Rochester *Also called Orthotics & Prosthetics Dept (G-13997)*
Strong Ventures, New York *Also called Mrs John L Strong & Co LLC (G-10853)*
Structural Ceramics Division, Niagara Falls *Also called Saint-Gbain Advnced Crmics LLC (G-12333)*
Structural Ceramics Group, Niagara Falls *Also called Saint-Gobain Dynamics Inc (G-12334)*
Structural Industries Inc......631 471-5200
2950 Veterans Memorial Hw Bohemia (11716) *(G-1092)*
Structural Wood Corporation......315 388-4442
243 Lincoln Ave Waddington (13694) *(G-15882)*
Structured 3d Inc......346 704-2614
188 Dixon Ave Amityville (11701) *(G-317)*
Structured Retail Products......212 224-3692
225 Park Ave S Fl 8 New York (10003) *(G-11724)*
Structuredweb Inc......201 325-3110
20 W 20th St Ste 402 New York (10011) *(G-11725)*
Struthers Electronics, Bay Shore *Also called Lexan Industries Inc (G-696)*
Strux Corp......516 768-3969
100 Montauk Hwy Lindenhurst (11757) *(G-7196)*
STS Refill America LLC......516 934-8008
399 W John St Unit A Hicksville (11801) *(G-6133)*
STS Steel Inc......518 370-2693
301 Nott St Bldg 304 Schenectady (12305) *(G-14717)*
Stu-Art Supplies, North Baldwin *Also called Hubray Inc (G-12364)*
Stuart Communications Inc......845 252-7414
93 Erie Ave Narrowsburg (12764) *(G-8475)*
Stuart Mold & Manufacturing......716 488-9765
560 N Work St Falconer (14733) *(G-4693)*
Stuart Spector Designs Ltd......845 246-6124
1450 Route 212 Saugerties (12477) *(G-14618)*
Stuart Tool & Die Inc......716 488-1975
600 N Work St Falconer (14733) *(G-4694)*
Stuart-Dean Co Inc......718 472-1326
4350 10th St Long Island City (11101) *(G-7606)*
Stubbs Printing Inc......315 769-8641
271 E Orvis St Ste B Massena (13662) *(G-7909)*
Stucki Embroidery Works Inc (PA)......845 657-2308
Rr 28 Box W Boiceville (12412) *(G-1110)*
Studco Building Systems US LLC......585 545-3000
1700 Boulter Indus Park Webster (14580) *(G-16100)*
Student Lifeline Inc......516 327-0800
922 Hempstead Tpke Franklin Square (11010) *(G-5121)*
Student Safety Books, Franklin Square *Also called Student Lifeline Inc (G-5121)*
Studio 21 LA Inc......718 965-6579
13 42nd St Fl 5 Brooklyn (11232) *(G-2525)*
Studio 22 Print......212 679-2656
20 Park Ave New York (10016) *(G-11726)*
Studio 26, New York *Also called R R Donnelley & Sons Company (G-11312)*
Studio 40 Inc......212 420-8631
810 Humboldt St Ste 4 Brooklyn (11222) *(G-2526)*
Studio Associates of New York......212 268-1163
242 W 30th St Rm 604 New York (10001) *(G-11727)*
Studio Fun International Inc......914 238-1000
44 S Broadway Fl 7 White Plains (10601) *(G-16509)*
Studio One Leather Design Inc......212 760-1701
270 W 39th St Rm 505 New York (10018) *(G-11728)*
Studio Silversmiths Inc......718 418-6785
6315 Traffic Ave Ridgewood (11385) *(G-13553)*
Studley Printing & Publishing......518 563-1414
4701 State Route 9 Plattsburgh (12901) *(G-13160)*
Stuff Magazine......212 302-2626
1040 Ave Of The Amrcas New York (10018) *(G-11729)*
Stuhrling Original LLC......718 840-5760
449 20th St Brooklyn (11215) *(G-2527)*
Sturdy Store Displays Inc......718 389-9919
110 Beard St Brooklyn (11231) *(G-2528)*
Sturges Elec Pdts Co Inc......607 844-8604
23 North St Dryden (13053) *(G-4152)*
Sturges Electronics LLC......607 844-8604
23 North St Dryden (13053) *(G-4153)*
Sturges Manufacturing Co Inc......315 732-6159
2030 Sunset Ave Utica (13502) *(G-15734)*
Stutzman Management Corp......800 735-2013
11 Saint Joseph St Lancaster (14086) *(G-7051)*

Style Plus Hosiery Mills, Valley Stream *Also called Ellis Products Corp* ***(G-15778)***
Stylebuilt Accessories Inc (PA)....917 439-0578
45 Rose Ln East Rockaway (11518) ***(G-4297)***
Stylebuilt Acesries, East Rockaway *Also called Stylebuilt Accessories Inc* ***(G-4297)***
Styleclick Inc (HQ)....212 329-0300
810 7th Ave Fl 18 New York (10019) ***(G-11730)***
Stylecraft Interiors Inc....516 487-2133
22 Watermill Ln Great Neck (11021) ***(G-5594)***
Stylemaster, Richmond Hill *Also called Belle Maison USA Ltd* ***(G-13498)***
Styles Aviation Inc (PA)....845 677-8185
30 Airway Dr Ste 2 Lagrangeville (12540) ***(G-6962)***
Styles Manufacturing Corp....516 763-5303
3571 Hargale Rd Oceanside (11572) ***(G-12559)***
Stylesprit, New York *Also called Entrainant Inc* ***(G-9689)***
Stylist Pleating Corp....718 384-8181
107 Vanderveer St Apt 3b Brooklyn (11207) ***(G-2529)***
Stylistic Press Inc....212 675-0797
99 Battery Pl Apt 11p New York (10280) ***(G-11731)***
Sube Inc....212 243-6930
146 W 29th St Rm 4e New York (10001) ***(G-11732)***
Substrate LLC....212 913-9600
539 46th Ave Long Island City (11101) ***(G-7607)***
Suburban Marketing Assoc, Elmsford *Also called Ralph Martinelli* ***(G-4560)***
Suburban News, Spencerport *Also called Westside News Inc* ***(G-14983)***
Suburban Publishing Inc (PA)....845 463-0542
1 Summit Ct Ste 200a Fishkill (12524) ***(G-4952)***
Suburban Publishing Inc....914 345-0601
100 Clearbrook Rd Ste 170 Elmsford (10523) ***(G-4572)***
Success Apparel LLC....212 502-1890
19 W 34th St Fl 7 New York (10001) ***(G-11733)***
Successware Inc....716 565-2338
8860 Main St 102 Williamsville (14221) ***(G-16589)***
Sue & Sam Co Inc (PA)....718 436-1672
720 39th St 720 # 720 Brooklyn (11232) ***(G-2530)***
Suez Energy Astoria LLC....718 274-7700
17-10 Steinway St Flushing (11375) ***(G-5049)***
Suffolk Cement Precast Inc (PA)....631 727-4432
1813 Middle Rd Calverton (11933) ***(G-3172)***
Suffolk Cement Products Inc....631 727-2317
1843 Middle Rd Calverton (11933) ***(G-3173)***
Suffolk Community Council Inc (PA)....631 434-9277
819 Grand Blvd Ste 1 Deer Park (11729) ***(G-4049)***
Suffolk Copy Center Inc....631 665-0570
26 W Main St Bay Shore (11706) ***(G-727)***
Suffolk Granite Manufacturing....631 226-4774
25 Gear Ave Lindenhurst (11757) ***(G-7197)***
Suffolk Indus Recovery Corp....631 732-6403
3542 Route 112 Coram (11727) ***(G-3805)***
Suffolk McHy & Pwr Tl Corp (PA)....631 289-7153
12 Waverly Ave Patchogue (11772) ***(G-12877)***
Suffolk Monument Mfg, Lindenhurst *Also called Suffolk Granite Manufacturing* ***(G-7197)***
Suffolk Printing, Bay Shore *Also called Suffolk Copy Center Inc* ***(G-727)***
Sugar Foods Corporation (PA)....212 753-6900
950 3rd Ave Fl 21 New York (10022) ***(G-11734)***
Sugar Shack Desert Company Inc....518 523-7540
2567 Main St Lake Placid (12946) ***(G-6978)***
Sugarbear Cupcakes....917 698-9005
14552 159th St Jamaica (11434) ***(G-6680)***
Suhor Industries Inc (PA)....585 377-5100
72 Oconnor Rd Fairport (14450) ***(G-4663)***
Suhor Industries Inc....716 483-6818
584 Buffalo St Jamestown (14701) ***(G-6751)***
Suit-Kote Corporation (PA)....607 753-1100
1911 Lorings Crossing Rd Cortland (13045) ***(G-3895)***
Suit-Kote Corporation....315 735-8501
191 Dry Rd Oriskany (13424) ***(G-12763)***
Suit-Kote Corporation....607 535-2743
20 Fairgrounds Ln Watkins Glen (14891) ***(G-16061)***
Suit-Kote Corporation....585 268-7127
5628 Tuckers Corners Rd Belmont (14813) ***(G-817)***
Suit-Kote Corporation....716 664-3750
57 Lister St Jamestown (14701) ***(G-6752)***
Suit-Kote Corporation....716 683-8850
505 Como Park Blvd Buffalo (14227) ***(G-3079)***
Suite Solutions Inc....716 929-3050
100 Corporate Pkwy # 338 Amherst (14226) ***(G-252)***
Sukkah Center, Brooklyn *Also called Y & A Trading Inc* ***(G-2661)***
Sullivan Bazinet Bongio Inc....315 437-6500
1 General Motors Dr Ste 5 Syracuse (13206) ***(G-15432)***
Sullivan Concrete Inc....845 888-2235
420 Bernas Rd Cochecton (12726) ***(G-3608)***
Sullivan County Democrat, Callicoon *Also called Catskill Delaware Publications* ***(G-3160)***
Sullivan St Bky - Hlls Kit Inc....212 265-5580
533 W 47th St New York (10036) ***(G-11735)***
Sullivan Structures, Cochecton *Also called Sullivan Concrete Inc* ***(G-3608)***
Suma Industries Inc....646 436-5202
345 E 52nd St Apt 9d New York (10022) ***(G-11736)***
Sumax Cycle Products Inc....315 768-1058
122 Clear Rd Oriskany (13424) ***(G-12764)***
Sumer Gold Ltd....212 354-8677
33 W 46th St Fl 4 New York (10036) ***(G-11737)***
Sumitomo Elc USA Holdings Inc (HQ)....212 490-6610
600 5th Ave Fl 18 New York (10020) ***(G-11738)***
Summit Aerospace Inc....718 433-1326
4301 21st St Ste 203 Long Island City (11101) ***(G-7608)***
Summit Apparel Inc (PA)....631 213-8299
91 Cabot Ct Hauppauge (11788) ***(G-5951)***
Summit Communications....914 273-5504
28 Half Mile Rd Armonk (10504) ***(G-409)***
Summit Fincl Disclosure LLC....212 913-0510
216 E 45th St Fl 15 New York (10017) ***(G-11739)***
Summit Instrument Corp....516 433-0140
99 Engineers Dr Hicksville (11801) ***(G-6134)***
Summit Laser Products, Holbrook *Also called Summit Technologies LLC* ***(G-6212)***
Summit Lubricants Inc....585 815-0798
4d Treadeasy Ave Batavia (14020) ***(G-636)***
Summit Manufacturing LLC (HQ)....631 952-1570
100 Spence St Bay Shore (11706) ***(G-728)***
Summit MSP LLC....716 433-1014
6042 Old Beattie Rd Lockport (14094) ***(G-7332)***
Summit Plastics, Bay Shore *Also called Summit Manufacturing LLC* ***(G-728)***
Summit Print & Mail LLC....716 433-1014
6042 Old Beattie Rd Lockport (14094) ***(G-7333)***
Summit Professional Networks....212 557-7480
469 Fashion Ave Fl 10 New York (10018) ***(G-11740)***
Summit Research Laboratories, Huguenot *Also called Somerville Acquisitions Co Inc* ***(G-6386)***
Summit Technologies LLC....631 590-1040
723 Broadway Ave Holbrook (11741) ***(G-6212)***
Summit Vitamins, Hauppauge *Also called American Hlth Formulations Inc* ***(G-5766)***
Summitreheis, Huguenot *Also called Elementis Srl Inc* ***(G-6385)***
Sumner Industries Inc....631 666-7290
309 Orinoco Dr Bay Shore (11706) ***(G-729)***
Sun Microsystems, Albany *Also called Oracle America Inc* ***(G-108)***
Sun Ming Jan Inc....718 418-8221
145 Noll St Brooklyn (11206) ***(G-2531)***
Sun Printing Incorporated....607 337-3034
57 Borden Ave 65 Norwich (13815) ***(G-12493)***
Sun Scientific Inc....914 479-5108
145 Palisade St Dobbs Ferry (10522) ***(G-4131)***
Sun Source, New York *Also called Jacobs & Cohen Inc* ***(G-10298)***
Sun Valley Printing, Binghamton *Also called Jane Lewis* ***(G-898)***
Sun-Times Media Group Inc....716 945-1644
36 River St Salamanca (14779) ***(G-14535)***
Suna Bros Inc....212 869-5670
10 W 46th St Fl 5 New York (10036) ***(G-11741)***
Sunbelt Industries Inc (PA)....315 823-2947
540 E Mill St Little Falls (13365) ***(G-7214)***
Sunbilt Solar Pdts By Sussman....718 297-0228
10910 180th St Jamaica (11433) ***(G-6681)***
Sunburst Studios Inc....718 768-6360
584 3rd Ave Brooklyn (11215) ***(G-2532)***
Sunbuster, Farmingdale *Also called Gustbuster Ltd* ***(G-4777)***
Sundance Industries Inc....845 795-5809
36 Greentree Ln Milton (12547) ***(G-8198)***
Sunday Record, The, Saratoga Springs *Also called Record* ***(G-14595)***
Sundial Brands....631 842-8800
1 Adams Blvd Farmingdale (11735) ***(G-4883)***
Sundial Brands LLC....631 842-8800
11 Ranick Dr S Amityville (11701) ***(G-318)***
Sundial Creations, Amityville *Also called Sundial Group LLC* ***(G-320)***
Sundial Fragrances & Flavors....631 842-8800
11 Ranick Dr S Amityville (11701) ***(G-319)***
Sundial Group LLC....631 842-8800
11 Ranick Dr S Amityville (11701) ***(G-320)***
Sundown Ski & Sport Shop Inc (PA)....631 737-8600
3060 Middle Country Rd Lake Grove (11755) ***(G-6970)***
Sunfeather Herbal Soap, Potsdam *Also called Sunfeather Natural Soap Co Inc* ***(G-13324)***
Sunfeather Natural Soap Co Inc....315 265-1776
1551 State Highway 72 Potsdam (13676) ***(G-13324)***
Sunham Home Fashions LLC (PA)....212 695-1218
136 Madison Ave Fl 16 New York (10016) ***(G-11742)***
Sunlight US Co., Inc., Buffalo *Also called Rough Brothers Holding Co* ***(G-3048)***
Sunny Names, New York *Also called Sunynams Fashions Ltd* ***(G-11746)***
Sunny Scuba Inc (PA)....212 333-4915
454 9th Ave New York (10018) ***(G-11743)***
Sunny Sports, New York *Also called Sunny Scuba Inc* ***(G-11743)***
Sunnycrest Inc (PA)....315 252-7214
58 Prospect St Auburn (13021) ***(G-501)***
Sunnyside Decorative Prints Co....516 671-1935
67 Robinson Ave Glen Cove (11542) ***(G-5377)***
Sunoco Inc....315 593-0500
376 Owens Rd Fulton (13069) ***(G-5232)***
Sunquest Pharmaceuticals Inc....855 478-6779
385 W John St Ste 1 Hicksville (11801) ***(G-6135)***
Sunrise Door Solutions....631 464-4139
1215 Sunrise Hwy Copiague (11726) ***(G-3784)***
Sunrise Installation, Copiague *Also called Sunrise Door Solutions* ***(G-3784)***
Sunrise Jewelers of NY Inc....516 541-1302
1220 Sunrise Hwy Massapequa (11758) ***(G-7886)***

ALPHABETIC

Sunrise Snacks Rockland Inc (PA)....845 352-2676
3 Sunrise Dr Monsey (10952) ***(G-8298)***
Sunrise Tile Inc....718 939-0538
13309 35th Ave Flushing (11354) ***(G-5050)***
Sunset Ridge Holdings Inc....716 487-1458
490-496 Crescent St Jamestown (14701) ***(G-6753)***
Sunshine Diamond Cutter Inc....212 221-1028
38 W 48th St Ste 905 New York (10036) ***(G-11744)***
Sunward Electronics Inc....518 687-0030
258 Broadway Ste 2a Troy (12180) ***(G-15629)***
Sunwin Global Industry Inc....646 370-6196
295 5th Ave Ste 515 New York (10016) ***(G-11745)***
Sunwire Electric Corp....718 456-7500
70 Wyckoff Ave Apt 4h Brooklyn (11237) ***(G-2533)***
Suny At Binghamton....607 777-2316
Vestal Pkwy E Binghamton (13901) ***(G-916)***
Sunynams Fashions Ltd....212 268-5200
270 W 38th St Fl 2 New York (10018) ***(G-11746)***
Supdates, New York *Also called Bull Street LLC* ***(G-9156)***
Super Conductor Materials Inc....845 368-0240
391 Spook Rock Rd Suffern (10901) ***(G-15198)***
Super Express USA Pubg Corp....212 227-5800
8410 101st St Apt 4l Richmond Hill (11418) ***(G-13515)***
Super Moderna/Magic Master, New Hyde Park *Also called Joseph Struhl Co Inc* ***(G-8544)***
Super Neon Light Co Inc....718 236-5667
7813 16th Ave Brooklyn (11214) ***(G-2534)***
Super Price Chopper Inc....716 893-3323
1580 Genesee St Buffalo (14211) ***(G-3080)***
Super Steelworks Corporation....718 386-4770
12 Lucon Dr Deer Park (11729) ***(G-4050)***
Super Stud Building Products, Long Island City *Also called Superior Metals & Processing* ***(G-7609)***
Super Sweep Inc (PA)....631 223-8205
20 Railroad St Unit 1 Huntington Station (11746) ***(G-6459)***
Super Web Inc....631 643-9100
97 Lamar St West Babylon (11704) ***(G-16198)***
Super-Trim Inc....212 255-2370
30 W 24th St Fl 4 New York (10010) ***(G-11747)***
Superboats Inc....631 226-1761
694 Roosevelt Ave Lindenhurst (11757) ***(G-7198)***
Superflex Ltd....718 768-1400
152 44th St Brooklyn (11232) ***(G-2535)***
Supergen Products LLC....315 573-7887
320 Hoffman St Newark (14513) ***(G-12208)***
Superior Aggragates Supply LLC....516 333-2923
612 Muncy St Lindenhurst (11757) ***(G-7199)***
Superior Bat Company, Jamestown *Also called Grace Wheeler* ***(G-6718)***
Superior Block Corp....718 421-0900
761 E 42nd St Brooklyn (11210) ***(G-2536)***
Superior Confections Inc....718 698-3300
1150 South Ave Staten Island (10314) ***(G-15142)***
Superior Decorators Inc....718 381-4793
7416 Cypress Hills St Glendale (11385) ***(G-5408)***
Superior Elec Enclosure Inc....718 797-9090
16 Spencer St Brooklyn (11205) ***(G-2537)***
Superior Energy Services Inc....716 483-0100
1720 Foote Avenue Ext Jamestown (14701) ***(G-6754)***
Superior Exteriors of Buffalo....716 873-1000
57 Insbrook Ct East Amherst (14051) ***(G-4191)***
Superior Fiber Mills Inc....718 782-7500
181 Lombardy St Brooklyn (11222) ***(G-2538)***
Superior Furs Inc....516 365-4123
1697 Northern Blvd Manhasset (11030) ***(G-7772)***
Superior Glove Works USA Ltd....716 626-9500
2345 Walden Ave Ste 600 Cheektowaga (14225) ***(G-3460)***
Superior Metal & Woodwork Inc....631 465-9004
70 Central Ave Farmingdale (11735) ***(G-4884)***
Superior Metals & Processing....718 545-7500
801 26th Ave Long Island City (11102) ***(G-7609)***
Superior Model Form Co, Middle Village *Also called Goldmont Enterprises Inc* ***(G-8121)***
Superior Motion Controls Inc....516 420-2921
40 Smith St Farmingdale (11735) ***(G-4885)***
Superior Packaging, Farmingdale *Also called Mkt329 Inc* ***(G-4829)***
Superior Plastic Slipcovers, Glendale *Also called Superior Decorators Inc* ***(G-5408)***
Superior Print On Demand....607 240-5231
165 Charles St Vestal (13850) ***(G-15823)***
Superior Printing Ink Co Inc....716 877-0250
777 E Park Dr Tonawanda (14150) ***(G-15579)***
Superior Stl Door Trim Co Inc....716 665-3256
154 Fairmount Ave Jamestown (14701) ***(G-6755)***
Superior Technology Inc....585 352-6556
200 Paragon Dr Rochester (14624) ***(G-14148)***
Superior Tool Company, North Tonawanda *Also called Ameri-Cut Tool Grinding Inc* ***(G-12410)***
Superior Walls of Hudson Vly, Poughkeepsie *Also called Superior Wlls of Hdson Vly Inc* ***(G-13370)***
Superior Walls Upstate NY Inc....585 624-9390
7574 E Main St Lima (14485) ***(G-7156)***
Superior Washer & Gasket Corp (PA)....631 273-8282
170 Adams Ave Hauppauge (11788) ***(G-5952)***
Superior Welding....631 676-2751
331 Dante Ct Ste G Holbrook (11741) ***(G-6213)***
Superior Wlls of Hdson Vly Inc....845 485-4033
68 Violet Ave Poughkeepsie (12601) ***(G-13370)***
Superior Wood Turnings....716 483-1254
118 E 1st St Jamestown (14701) ***(G-6756)***
Superite Gear Instr of Hppauge (PA)....631 234-0100
225 Engineers Rd Hauppauge (11788) ***(G-5953)***
Superleaf LLC....888 887-4318
212 7th St 1 Brooklyn (11215) ***(G-2539)***
Supermarket Equipment Depo Inc....718 665-6200
1135 Bronx River Ave Bronx (10472) ***(G-1395)***
Supermedia LLC....212 513-9700
2 Penn Plz Fl 22 New York (10121) ***(G-11748)***
Superpower Inc....518 346-1414
450 Duane Ave Ste 1 Schenectady (12304) ***(G-14718)***
Supersmile, New York *Also called Robell Research Inc* ***(G-11405)***
Supply & Demand, New York *Also called Drew Philips Corp* ***(G-9577)***
Supply Technologies NY , Inc., Albany *Also called Park-Ohio Inds Trsry Co Inc* ***(G-110)***
Supplynet Inc (PA)....800 826-0279
706 Executive Blvd Ste B Valley Cottage (10989) ***(G-15768)***
Suppositoria Laboratory, Bronx *Also called Perrigo New York Inc* ***(G-1358)***
Supreme Boilers Inc....718 342-2220
9221 Ditmas Ave Brooklyn (11236) ***(G-2540)***
Supreme Chocolatier LLC....718 761-9600
1150 South Ave Fl 1 Staten Island (10314) ***(G-15143)***
Supreme Fire Proof Door Co....718 665-4224
391 Rider Ave Bronx (10451) ***(G-1396)***
Supreme Leather Products, Spring Valley *Also called Louis Schwartz* ***(G-15000)***
Supreme Poly Plastics Inc....718 456-9300
299 Meserole St Brooklyn (11206) ***(G-2541)***
Supreme Poultry Inc....718 472-0300
3788 Review Ave Long Island City (11101) ***(G-7610)***
Supreme Screw Products Inc....718 293-6600
10 Skyline Dr Unit B Plainview (11803) ***(G-13091)***
Supreme Steel Inc....631 884-1320
690 N Jefferson Ave Lindenhurst (11757) ***(G-7200)***
Supresta US LLC (HQ)....914 674-9434
420 Saw Mill River Rd Ardsley (10502) ***(G-396)***
Sure Fit Inc....212 395-9340
58 W 40th St Rm 2a New York (10018) ***(G-11749)***
Sure Flow Equipment Inc....800 263-8251
250 Cooper Ave Ste 102 Tonawanda (14150) ***(G-15580)***
Sure Iron Works, Brooklyn *Also called Kms Contracting Inc* ***(G-2077)***
Sure-Kol Refrigerator Co Inc....718 625-0601
490 Flushing Ave Brooklyn (11205) ***(G-2542)***
Surepure Inc....917 368-8480
405 Lexington Ave Fl 25 New York (10174) ***(G-11750)***
Surescan Corporation....607 321-0042
100 Eldredge St Binghamton (13901) ***(G-917)***
Surf-Tech Manufacturing Corp....631 589-1194
28 Colt Ct Ronkonkoma (11779) ***(G-14419)***
Surface Finish Technology....607 732-2909
215 Judson St Elmira (14901) ***(G-4504)***
Surface Magazine....646 805-0200
134 W 26th St Frnt 1 New York (10001) ***(G-11751)***
Surface Publishing, New York *Also called Surface Magazine* ***(G-11751)***
Surgical Design Corp....914 273-2445
3 Macdonald Ave Armonk (10504) ***(G-410)***
Surmet Ceramics Corporation....716 875-4091
699 Hertel Ave Ste 290 Buffalo (14207) ***(G-3081)***
Surmotech LLC....585 742-1220
7676 Netlink Dr Victor (14564) ***(G-15868)***
Surprise Plastics Inc....718 492-6355
124 57th St Brooklyn (11220) ***(G-2543)***
Surtic Mining Company LLC....718 434-0477
1825 Foster Ave Brooklyn (11230) ***(G-2544)***
Surving Studios....845 355-1430
17 Millsburg Rd Middletown (10940) ***(G-8178)***
Survival Inc....631 385-5060
90 Washington Dr Ste C Centerport (11721) ***(G-3352)***
Sussex Publishers LLC (PA)....212 260-7210
115 E 23rd St Fl 9 New York (10010) ***(G-11752)***
Sussman-Automatic Corporation (PA)....347 609-7652
4320 34th St Long Island City (11101) ***(G-7611)***
Sutter Machine Tool and Die, Bronx *Also called M J M Tooling Corp* ***(G-1320)***
Sutton Place Software Inc....631 421-1737
13 Tappen Dr Melville (11747) ***(G-8067)***
Svyz Trading Corp....718 220-1140
4320 Park Ave Bronx (10457) ***(G-1397)***
Swagelok Western NY....585 359-8470
10 Thruway Park Dr West Henrietta (14586) ***(G-16252)***
Swain Technology Inc....585 889-2786
963 North Rd Scottsville (14546) ***(G-14754)***
Swamp Island Dessert Co, West Falls *Also called Butterwood Desserts Inc* ***(G-16208)***
Swank Inc....212 867-2600
90 Park Ave Rm 1302 New York (10016) ***(G-11753)***
Swanson Lumber....716 499-1726
5273 N Hill Rd Gerry (14740) ***(G-5341)***
Swaps Monitor Publications Inc....212 742-8550
29 Broadway Rm 1315 New York (10006) ***(G-11754)***

Swarovski Lighting Ltd (PA) 518 563-7500
61 Industrial Blvd Plattsburgh (12901) *(G-13161)*
Swarovski Lighting Ltd 518 324-6378
1483 Military Tpke Ste B Plattsburgh (12901) *(G-13162)*
Swarovski North America Ltd 212 695-1502
1 Penn Plz Frnt 4 New York (10119) *(G-11755)*
Swatfame Inc 212 944-8022
530 Fashion Ave Rm 1204 New York (10018) *(G-11756)*
Swatt Baking Co, Olean *Also called L American Ltd (G-12604)*
Sweater Brand Inc 718 797-0505
86 S 1st St Brooklyn (11249) *(G-2545)*
Swedish Hill Vineyard Inc 607 403-0029
4565 State Route 414 Romulus (14541) *(G-14283)*
Swedish Hill Winery, Romulus *Also called Swedish Hill Vineyard Inc (G-14283)*
Sweet Melodys LLC 716 580-3227
8485 Transit Rd East Amherst (14051) *(G-4192)*
Sweet Mouth Inc 800 433-7758
244 5th Ave Ste L243 New York (10001) *(G-11757)*
Sweet Tooth Enterprises LLC 631 752-2888
135 Dale St West Babylon (11704) *(G-16199)*
Sweeteners Plus Inc 585 728-3770
5768 Sweeteners Blvd Lakeville (14480) *(G-6987)*
Sweetwater Energy Inc 585 647-5760
500 Lee Rd Ste 200 Rochester (14606) *(G-14149)*
Sweetworks Inc (PA) 716 634-4545
3500 Genesee St Buffalo (14225) *(G-3082)*
Swift Fulfillment Services 516 593-1198
290 Broadway Lynbrook (11563) *(G-7675)*
Swift Glass Co Inc 607 733-7166
131 22nd St Elmira Heights (14903) *(G-4515)*
Swift Multigraphics LLC 585 442-8000
55 Southwood Ln Rochester (14618) *(G-14150)*
Swift River Associates Inc 716 875-0902
4051 River Rd Tonawanda (14150) *(G-15581)*
Swimline Corp (PA) 631 254-2155
191 Rodeo Dr Edgewood (11717) *(G-4416)*
Swimline International Corp 631 254-2155
191 Rodeo Dr Edgewood (11717) *(G-4417)*
Swimwear Anywhere Inc (PA) 631 420-1400
85 Sherwood Ave Farmingdale (11735) *(G-4886)*
Swimwear Anywhere Inc 845 858-4141
21 Minisink Ave Port Jervis (12771) *(G-13238)*
Swing Frame, Freeport *Also called Access Display Group Inc (G-5136)*
Swirl Bliss LLC 516 867-9475
1777 Grand Ave North Baldwin (11510) *(G-12368)*
Swirls Twirls Incorporated 516 541-9400
4116 Sunrise Hwy Massapequa (11758) *(G-7887)*
Swiss Specialties Inc 631 567-8800
15 Crescent Ct Wading River (11792) *(G-15888)*
Swiss Tool Corporation 631 842-7766
100 Court St Copiague (11726) *(G-3785)*
Swissbit Na Inc 914 935-1400
18 Willett Ave 202 Port Chester (10573) *(G-13209)*
Swisse Cheeks, Brooklyn *Also called Silly Phillie Creations Inc (G-2471)*
Swissmar Inc 905 764-1121
6391 Walmore Rd Niagara Falls (14304) *(G-12339)*
Swissway Inc 631 351-5350
123 W Hills Rd Huntington Station (11746) *(G-6460)*
Switch Beverage Company LLC 203 202-7383
2 Seaview Blvd Fl 3 Port Washington (11050) *(G-13310)*
Switches and Sensors Inc 631 924-2167
86 Horseblock Rd Unit J Yaphank (11980) *(G-16723)*
Switching Power Inc 631 981-7231
3601 Veterans Mem Hwy Ronkonkoma (11779) *(G-14420)*
Switzer, Buffalo *Also called Precision Photo-Fab Inc (G-3011)*
Swivelier Company Inc 845 353-1455
600 Bradley Hill Rd Ste 3 Blauvelt (10913) *(G-941)*
Swremote, Buffalo *Also called Pointman LLC (G-3008)*
Sycamore Hill Designs Inc 585 820-7322
7585 Modock Rd Victor (14564) *(G-15869)*
Sylhan LLC (PA) 631 243-6600
210 Rodeo Dr Edgewood (11717) *(G-4418)*
Symantec Corporation 646 487-6000
1 Penn Plz Ste 5420 New York (10119) *(G-11758)*
Symbio Technologies LLC 914 576-1205
333 Mamaroneck Ave White Plains (10605) *(G-16510)*
Symbol Technologies LLC (HQ) 631 737-6851
1 Zebra Plz Holtsville (11742) *(G-6246)*
Symbol Technologies LLC 631 738-2400
110 Orville Dr Bohemia (11716) *(G-1093)*
Symbol Technologies LLC 631 218-3907
25 Andrea Rd Holbrook (11741) *(G-6214)*
Symbol Technologies Delaware, Holtsville *Also called Symbol Technologies LLC (G-6246)*
Symmetry Medical Inc 845 368-4573
201 Route 59 Bldg E Hillburn (10931) *(G-6155)*
Symphony Talent LLC (PA) 212 999-9000
19 W 34th St Rm 1000 New York (10001) *(G-11759)*
Symrise Inc 646 459-5000
505 Park Ave Fl 15 New York (10022) *(G-11760)*
Symwave Inc (HQ) 949 542-4400
80 Arkay Dr Hauppauge (11788) *(G-5954)*
Synced Inc 917 565-5591
120 Walker St Ste 4 New York (10013) *(G-11761)*
Synco Technologies Inc 212 255-2031
54 W 21st St Rm 602 New York (10010) *(G-11762)*
Synergx Systems Inc (HQ) 516 433-4700
3927 59th St Woodside (11377) *(G-16681)*
Synergy Digital 718 643-2742
43 Hall St Brooklyn (11205) *(G-2546)*
Synergy Flavors NY Company LLC 585 232-6648
86 White St Rochester (14608) *(G-14151)*
Synergy Pharmaceuticals Inc (HQ) 212 227-8611
420 Lexington Ave Rm 2500 New York (10170) *(G-11763)*
Synergy Pharmaceuticals Inc (PA) 212 297-0020
420 Lexington Ave Rm 2012 New York (10170) *(G-11764)*
Synergy Resources Inc 631 665-2050
320 Carleton Ave Ste 6200 Central Islip (11722) *(G-3385)*
Synergy Tooling Systems Inc (PA) 716 834-4457
287 Commerce Dr Amherst (14228) *(G-253)*
Syntec Optics, Rochester *Also called Syntec Technologies Inc (G-14152)*
Syntec Optics, Rochester *Also called Syntec Technologies Inc (G-14153)*
Syntec Technologies Inc (PA) 585 768-2513
515 Lee Rd Rochester (14606) *(G-14152)*
Syntec Technologies Inc 585 464-9336
515 Lee Rd Rochester (14606) *(G-14153)*
Syntel Inc 212 785-9810
1 Exchange Plz Ste 2001 New York (10006) *(G-11765)*
Synthes USA, Horseheads *Also called Depuy Synthes Inc (G-6312)*
Synthetic Textiles Inc (PA) 716 842-2598
398 Broadway St Buffalo (14204) *(G-3083)*
Syntho Pharmaceuticals Inc 631 755-9898
230 Sherwood Ave Farmingdale (11735) *(G-4887)*
Syraco Products Inc 315 476-5306
1054 S Clinton St Syracuse (13202) *(G-15433)*
Syracusa Sand and Gravel Inc 585 924-7146
1389 Malone Rd Victor (14564) *(G-15870)*
Syracuse Casing Co Inc 315 475-0309
528 Erie Blvd W Syracuse (13204) *(G-15434)*
Syracuse Catholic Press Assn 315 422-8153
421 S Warren St Fl 2 Syracuse (13202) *(G-15435)*
Syracuse Computer Forms Inc 315 478-0108
216 Burnet Ave Syracuse (13203) *(G-15436)*
Syracuse Corrugated Box Corp 315 437-9901
302 Stoutenger St East Syracuse (13057) *(G-4372)*
Syracuse Cultural Workers Prj 315 474-1132
400 Lodi St Syracuse (13203) *(G-15437)*
Syracuse Hvac, Syracuse *Also called John F Krell Jr (G-15348)*
Syracuse Industrial Sls Co Ltd 315 478-5751
1850 Lemoyne Ave Syracuse (13208) *(G-15438)*
Syracuse Label & Surround Prtg, Syracuse *Also called Syracuse Label Co Inc (G-15439)*
Syracuse Label Co Inc 315 422-1037
200 Stewart Dr Syracuse (13212) *(G-15439)*
Syracuse Letter Company Inc 315 476-8328
1179 Oak Ln Bridgeport (13030) *(G-1184)*
Syracuse Midstate Spring, Syracuse *Also called Midstate Spring Inc (G-15373)*
Syracuse New Times, Syracuse *Also called All Times Publishing LLC (G-15238)*
Syracuse New Times, Syracuse *Also called A Zimmer Ltd (G-15237)*
Syracuse Plastics LLC 315 637-9881
7400 Morgan Rd Liverpool (13090) *(G-7265)*
Syracuse Prosthetic Center Inc 315 476-9697
1124 E Fayette St Syracuse (13210) *(G-15440)*
Syracuse Stamping Company, Syracuse *Also called Syraco Products Inc (G-15433)*
Syracuse Technical Center, Syracuse *Also called Chemtrade Chemicals US LLC (G-15277)*
Syracuse University Press Inc 315 443-5534
621 Skytop Rd Ste 110 Syracuse (13244) *(G-15441)*
Syrasoft LLC 315 708-0341
6 Canton St Baldwinsville (13027) *(G-564)*
System of AME Binding 631 390-8560
95 Hoffman Ln Central Islip (11749) *(G-3386)*
Systems Drs C3 Inc (HQ) 716 631-6200
485 Cayuga Rd Buffalo (14225) *(G-3084)*
Systems Trading Inc 718 261-8900
48 S Svc Rd Ste Ll90 Melville (11747) *(G-8068)*
Sz - Design & Print Inc 845 659-2273
33 Rita Ave Monsey (10952) *(G-8299)*
T & C Power Conversion Inc 585 482-5551
132 Humboldt St Rochester (14610) *(G-14154)*
T & K Printing, Brooklyn *Also called T&K Printing Inc (G-2550)*
T & L Automatics Inc 585 647-3717
770 Emerson St Rochester (14613) *(G-14155)*
T & L Trading Co 718 782-5550
17 Meserole St Brooklyn (11206) *(G-2547)*
T & M Plating Inc 212 967-1110
357 W 36th St Fl 7 New York (10018) *(G-11766)*
T & R Knitting Mills Inc (PA) 718 497-4017
8000 Cooper Ave Ste 6 Glendale (11385) *(G-5409)*
T & R Knitting Mills Inc 212 840-8665
214 W 39th St New York (10018) *(G-11767)*
T & Smoothie Inc 631 804-6653
499 N Service Rd Ste 83 Patchogue (11772) *(G-12878)*
T A S Sales Service LLC 518 234-4919
105 Kenyon Rd Cobleskill (12043) *(G-3604)*

A L P H A B E T I C

T A Tool & Molding Inc 631 293-0172
185 Marine St Farmingdale (11735) ***(G-4888)***
T C Dunham Paint Company Inc 914 969-4202
761 Nepperhan Ave Yonkers (10703) ***(G-16801)***
T C I, Whitesboro *Also called Telecommunication Concepts* ***(G-16530)***
T C Peters Printing Co Inc 315 724-4149
2336 W Whitesboro St Utica (13502) ***(G-15735)***
T C Timber, Skaneateles *Also called Habermaass Corporation* ***(G-14874)***
T E Q, Huntington Station *Also called Tequipment Inc* ***(G-6462)***
T Eason Land Surveyor 631 474-2200
27 Poplar St Port Jeff STA (11776) ***(G-13218)***
T G M Products Inc 631 491-0515
90 Wyandanch Ave Unit E Wyandanch (11798) ***(G-16696)***
T G S Inc 516 629-6905
6 Wildwood Ct Locust Valley (11560) ***(G-7352)***
T J Ronan Paint Corp 718 292-1100
749 E 135th St Bronx (10454) ***(G-1398)***
T J Signs Unlimited LLC (PA) 631 273-4800
171 Freeman Ave Islip (11751) ***(G-6551)***
T Jn Electric 917 560-0981
116 Cortlandt Rd Mahopac (10541) ***(G-7714)***
T Jn Electric Inc 845 628-6970
901 Route 6 Mahopac (10541) ***(G-7715)***
T L Diamond & Company Inc (PA) 212 249-6660
116 E 68th St Apt 5a New York (10065) ***(G-11768)***
T L F Graphics Inc (PA) 585 272-5500
235 Metro Park Rochester (14623) ***(G-14156)***
T L X, Plainview *Also called Xpress Printing Inc* ***(G-13103)***
T Lemme Mechanical Inc 518 436-4136
1074 Broadway Menands (12204) ***(G-8092)***
T M Design Screen Printing, Rochester *Also called Todd Walbridge* ***(G-14171)***
T M I of New York, Brooklyn *Also called Technipoly Manufacturing Inc* ***(G-2559)***
T M I Plastics Industries Inc 718 383-0363
28 Wythe Ave Brooklyn (11249) ***(G-2548)***
T M International LLC 718 842-0949
413 Faile St 15 Bronx (10474) ***(G-1399)***
T M Machine Inc 716 822-0817
176 Reading St Buffalo (14220) ***(G-3085)***
T M W Diamonds Mfg Co (PA) 212 869-8444
15 W 47th St Ste 302 New York (10036) ***(G-11769)***
T Mix Inc 646 379-6814
6217 5th Ave Brooklyn (11220) ***(G-2549)***
T O Dey Service Corp 212 683-6300
151 W 46th St Fl 3 New York (10036) ***(G-11770)***
T O Gronlund Company Inc 212 679-3535
200 Lexington Ave Rm 1515 New York (10016) ***(G-11771)***
T R P Machine Inc 631 567-9620
35 Davinci Dr Ste B Bohemia (11716) ***(G-1094)***
T Rj Shirts Inc 347 642-3071
3050 90th St East Elmhurst (11369) ***(G-4225)***
T RS Great American Rest 516 294-1680
17 Hillside Ave Williston Park (11596) ***(G-16596)***
T S B A Group Inc (PA) 718 565-6000
3830 Woodside Ave Sunnyside (11104) ***(G-15206)***
T S O General Corp 631 952-5320
81 Emjay Blvd Unit 1 Brentwood (11717) ***(G-1144)***
T S P Corp 585 768-6769
78 One Half Lake St Le Roy (14482) ***(G-7125)***
T S Pink Corp 607 432-1100
139 Pony Farm Rd Oneonta (13820) ***(G-12646)***
T Shore Products Ltd 315 252-9174
5 Eagle Dr Auburn (13021) ***(G-502)***
T T I, Oriskany *Also called Terahertz Technologies Inc* ***(G-12765)***
T V Trade Media Inc 212 288-3933
216 E 75th St Apt 1w New York (10021) ***(G-11772)***
T&B Bakery Corp 646 642-4300
5870 56th St Maspeth (11378) ***(G-7872)***
T&K Printing Inc 718 439-9454
262 44th St Brooklyn (11232) ***(G-2550)***
T-Base Communications USA Inc 315 713-0013
806 Commerce Park Dr Ogdensburg (13669) ***(G-12579)***
T-Company LLC 646 290-6365
16 Monitor Rd Smithtown (11787) ***(G-14910)***
T-Rex Supply Corporation 516 308-0505
1 Fulton Ave Ste 120 Hempstead (11550) ***(G-6026)***
T-S-K Electronics Inc 716 693-3916
908 Niagara Falls Blvd # 201 North Tonawanda (14120) ***(G-12457)***
T-Shirt Graphics, Ballston Spa *Also called Sand Hill Industries Inc* ***(G-595)***
Ta Chen International Inc 845 352-5300
17 Main St Ste 217 Monsey (10952) ***(G-8300)***
Taam Tov Foods Inc 718 788-8880
188 28th St Brooklyn (11232) ***(G-2551)***
Taber Acquisition Corp 716 694-4000
455 Bryant St North Tonawanda (14120) ***(G-12458)***
Taber Industries, North Tonawanda *Also called Taber Acquisition Corp* ***(G-12458)***
Tabi Inc 347 701-1051
488 Onderdonk Ave Apt 1l Flushing (11385) ***(G-5051)***
Table Tops Paper Corp 718 831-6440
47 Hall St Ste C-2 Brooklyn (11205) ***(G-2552)***
Tablecloths For Granted Ltd 518 370-5481
510 Union St Schenectady (12305) ***(G-14719)***
Tables Manufacturing, Edgewood *Also called Kinplex Corp* ***(G-4408)***
Tablet Newspaper, The, Brooklyn *Also called Tablet Publishing Company Inc* ***(G-2553)***
Tablet Publishing Company Inc 718 965-7333
1712 10th Ave Brooklyn (11215) ***(G-2553)***
Tabrisse Collections Inc 212 921-1014
1412 Broadway New York (10018) ***(G-11773)***
TAC Screw Products Inc 585 663-5840
170 Bennington Dr Rochester (14616) ***(G-14157)***
Tackle Factory, Fillmore *Also called Cuba Specialty Mfg Co Inc* ***(G-4937)***
Taconic, Petersburg *Also called Tonoga Inc* ***(G-12973)***
Tacr, Middletown *Also called Turbine Arfoil Cating Repr LLC* ***(G-8181)***
Tactair Fluid Controls Inc 315 451-3928
4806 W Taft Rd Liverpool (13088) ***(G-7266)***
Tactica International Inc (PA) 212 575-0500
11 W 42nd St New York (10036) ***(G-11774)***
Tag Dental Implant Solutions, Valley Stream *Also called Total Dntl Implant Sltions LLC* ***(G-15800)***
Tag Envelope Co Inc 718 389-6844
1419 128th St College Point (11356) ***(G-3669)***
Tag Flange & Machining Inc 516 536-1300
3375 Royal Ave Oceanside (11572) ***(G-12560)***
Tag Manufacturing, Brooklyn *Also called Schwartz Textile LLC* ***(G-2451)***
Tahari Arthur S Levine, New York *Also called Tahari ASL LLC* ***(G-11775)***
Tahari ASL LLC 212 763-2800
1114 Ave Of The Americas New York (10036) ***(G-11775)***
Tai Seng 718 399-6311
106 Lexington Ave Brooklyn (11238) ***(G-2554)***
Tailorbyrd, New York *Also called Sanctuary Brands LLC* ***(G-11479)***
Tailored Coatings Inc 716 893-4869
1800 Brdwy St Bldg 2a Buffalo (14212) ***(G-3086)***
Tailored Sportsman LLC 646 366-8733
230 W 38th St Fl 6 New York (10018) ***(G-11776)***
Takeform Architectural Graphics, Medina *Also called Quorum Group LLC* ***(G-7987)***
Talas, Brooklyn *Also called Technical Library Service Inc* ***(G-2558)***
Talisman Industries LLC 908 433-7116
237 Flatbush Ave Apt 3 New York (10007) ***(G-11777)***
Talmu NY LLC 347 434-6700
266 47th St Brooklyn (11220) ***(G-2555)***
Tam Ceramics Group of Ny LLC 716 278-9400
4511 Hyde Park Blvd Niagara Falls (14305) ***(G-12340)***
Tam Ceramics LLC 716 278-9480
4511 Hyde Park Blvd Niagara Falls (14305) ***(G-12341)***
Tambetti Inc 212 751-9584
48 W 48th St Ste 501 New York (10036) ***(G-11778)***
Tami Great Food Corp 845 352-7901
22 Briarcliff Dr Monsey (10952) ***(G-8301)***
Tamka Sport LLC 718 224-7820
225 Beverly Rd Douglaston (11363) ***(G-4142)***
Tamperproof Screw Company Inc 516 931-1616
30 Laurel St Hicksville (11801) ***(G-6136)***
Tamsen Z LLC 212 292-6412
350 Park Ave Fl 4 New York (10022) ***(G-11779)***
Tanagro Jewelry Corp 212 753-2817
36 W 44th St Ste 1101 New York (10036) ***(G-11780)***
Tandy Leather Factory Inc 845 480-3588
298 Main St Nyack (10960) ***(G-12511)***
Tangent Machine & Tool Corp 631 249-3088
108 Gazza Blvd Farmingdale (11735) ***(G-4889)***
Tangram Company LLC 631 758-0460
125 Corporate Dr Holtsville (11742) ***(G-6247)***
Tannens 718 292-4646
363 E 149th St Bronx (10455) ***(G-1400)***
Tao Group LLC 646 625-4818
355 W 16th St New York (10011) ***(G-11781)***
Tap2play LLC 914 960-6232
110 W 40th St Rm 1902 New York (10018) ***(G-11782)***
Tape Printers Inc 631 249-5585
155 Allen Blvd Ste A Farmingdale (11735) ***(G-4890)***
Tape Systems Inc 914 668-3700
630 S Columbus Ave Mount Vernon (10550) ***(G-8444)***
Tape-It Inc 631 243-4100
233 N Fehr Way Bay Shore (11706) ***(G-730)***
Tapemaker Supply Company LLC 914 693-3407
22 Sherbrooke Rd Hartsdale (10530) ***(G-5745)***
Tapestries Etc, New York *Also called Vander Heyden Woodworking* ***(G-11990)***
Tapestry Inc 212 615-2082
515 W 33rd St New York (10001) ***(G-11783)***
Tapestry Inc (PA) 212 594-1850
10 Hudson Yards New York (10001) ***(G-11784)***
Tappan Wire & Cable Inc (HQ) 845 353-9000
100 Bradley Hill Rd Blauvelt (10913) ***(G-942)***
Taqa Entertainment, Valley Stream *Also called Taste and See Entrmt Inc* ***(G-15799)***
Tara Rific Screen Printing Inc 718 583-6864
4197 Park Ave Bronx (10457) ***(G-1401)***
Target Rock, Farmingdale *Also called Curtiss-Wright Flow Ctrl Corp* ***(G-4743)***
Targetprocess Inc (PA) 877 718-2617
1325 Millersport Hwy Amherst (14221) ***(G-254)***
Targum Press USA Inc 248 355-2266
1946 59th St Brooklyn (11204) ***(G-2556)***
Taro Manufacturing Company Inc 315 252-9430
114 Clark St Auburn (13021) ***(G-503)***

Tarrytown Bakery Inc 914 631-0209
150 Wildey St Tarrytown (10591) *(G-15496)*
Tarsia Technical Industries 631 231-8322
93 Marcus Blvd Hauppauge (11788) *(G-5955)*
Tarsier Ltd 646 880-8680
1365 York Ave Apt 23e New York (10021) *(G-11785)*
Taste and See Entrmt Inc 516 285-3010
255 Dogwood Rd Valley Stream (11580) *(G-15799)*
Tate's Bake Shop, East Moriches *Also called Tates Wholesale LLC* *(G-4258)*
Tates Wholesale LLC 631 780-6511
62 Pine St East Moriches (11940) *(G-4258)*
Tatra Mfg Corporation 631 691-1184
30 Railroad Ave Copiague (11726) *(G-3786)*
Tattersall Industries LLC 518 381-4270
2125 Technology Dr Schenectady (12308) *(G-14720)*
Taumel Assembly Systems, Patterson *Also called Taumel Metalforming Corp* *(G-12886)*
Taumel Metalforming Corp 845 878-3100
25 Jon Barrett Rd Patterson (12563) *(G-12886)*
Taylor & Francis Group LLC 212 216-7800
52 Vanderbilt Ave Fl 11 New York (10017) *(G-11786)*
Taylor Brothers Inc 607 625-2828
6 Jacobs Rd Apalachin (13732) *(G-372)*
Taylor Communications Inc 937 221-1303
155 Pinelawn Rd Ste 120s Melville (11747) *(G-8069)*
Taylor Communications Inc 718 361-1000
3200 Skillman Ave Fl 3 Long Island City (11101) *(G-7612)*
Taylor Communications Inc 718 352-0220
1600 Stewart Ave Ste 301 Westbury (11590) *(G-16375)*
Taylor Concrete Products Inc 315 788-2191
20475 Old Rome Rd Watertown (13601) *(G-16034)*
Taylor Copy Services, Syracuse *Also called Constas Printing Corporation* *(G-15287)*
Taylor Devices Inc (PA) 716 694-0800
90 Taylor Dr North Tonawanda (14120) *(G-12459)*
Taylor Made Group LLC (HQ) 518 725-0681
93 South Blvd Gloversville (12078) *(G-5468)*
Taylor Metalworks Inc 716 662-3113
3925 California Rd Orchard Park (14127) *(G-12745)*
Taylor Precision Machining 607 535-3101
3921 Dug Rd Montour Falls (14865) *(G-8328)*
Taylor Products Inc (PA) 518 773-9312
66 Kingsboro Ave Gloversville (12078) *(G-5469)*
Taylor Tank Company Inc 718 434-1300
848 E 43rd St Brooklyn (11210) *(G-2557)*
Tb, Rochester *Also called Turner Bellows Inc* *(G-14181)*
Tbhl International LLC 212 799-2007
252 W 38th St Fl 11 New York (10018) *(G-11787)*
Tc Transcontinental USA Inc 818 993-4767
67 Irving Pl Fl 2 New York (10003) *(G-11788)*
Tchnologies N MRC Ameerica LLC 716 822-4300
25 Roberts Ave Buffalo (14206) *(G-3087)*
Tcmf Inc 607 724-1094
69-93 Eldredge St Binghamton (13901) *(G-918)*
TCS Electronics Inc 585 337-4301
1124 Corporate Dr Farmington (14425) *(G-4920)*
TCS Industries Inc 585 426-1160
400 Trabold Rd Rochester (14624) *(G-14158)*
Tdg Operations LLC 212 779-4300
200 Lexington Ave Rm 1314 New York (10016) *(G-11789)*
Tdk USA Corporation (HQ) 516 535-2600
455 Rxr Plz Uniondale (11556) *(G-15672)*
Tdo Sandblasting, Roosevelt *Also called Tropical Driftwood Originals* *(G-14438)*
TDS Fitness Equipment Corp 607 733-6789
160 Home St Elmira (14904) *(G-4505)*
TDS Foundry Corporation 607 733-6789
160 Home St Elmira (14904) *(G-4506)*
TDS Woodcraft, Staten Island *Also called TDS Woodworking Inc* *(G-15144)*
TDS Woodworking Inc 718 442-5298
104 Port Richmond Ave Staten Island (10302) *(G-15144)*
Tdy Industries LLC 716 433-4411
695 Ohio St Lockport (14094) *(G-7334)*
Te Connectivity Corporation 585 785-2500
2245 Brighton Henrta Twn Rochester (14623) *(G-14159)*
Te Neues Publishing Company (PA) 212 627-9090
350 7th Ave Rm 301 New York (10001) *(G-11790)*
Tea & Coffee Trade Journal, Long Island City *Also called Lockwood Trade Journal Co Inc* *(G-7503)*
Tea Life LLC 516 365-7711
73 Plandome Rd Manhasset (11030) *(G-7773)*
Teachergaming LLC 866 644-9323
809 W 181st St 231 New York (10033) *(G-11791)*
Teachley LLC 347 552-1272
25 Broadway Fl 13 New York (10004) *(G-11792)*
Teale Machine Company Inc 585 244-6700
1425 University Ave Rochester (14607) *(G-14160)*
Tealeafs 716 688-8022
5416 Main St Williamsville (14221) *(G-16590)*
Team Builders Inc 718 979-1005
88 New Dorp Plz S Ste 303 Staten Island (10306) *(G-15145)*
Team Builders Management, Staten Island *Also called Team Builders Inc* *(G-15145)*
Team Fabrication Inc 716 655-4038
1055 Davis Rd West Falls (14170) *(G-16209)*

Tebbens Steel LLC 631 208-8330
800 Burman Blvd Calverton (11933) *(G-3174)*
TEC - Crete Transit Mix Corp 718 657-6880
4673 Metropolitan Ave Ridgewood (11385) *(G-13554)*
TEC Glass & Inst LLC 315 926-7639
4211 Sunset Dr Marion (14505) *(G-7809)*
Tech Lube, Yaphank *Also called Tribology Inc* *(G-16724)*
Tech Park Food Services LLC 585 295-1250
789 Elmgrove Rd Rochester (14624) *(G-14161)*
Tech Products Inc 718 442-4900
105 Willow Ave Staten Island (10305) *(G-15146)*
Tech Software LLC 516 986-3050
270 Spagnoli Rd Ste 102 Melville (11747) *(G-8070)*
Tech Valley Printing, Watervliet *Also called General Business Supply Inc* *(G-16046)*
Techgrass 646 719-2000
77 Water St New York (10005) *(G-11793)*
Technic Inc 516 349-0700
111 E Ames Ct Unit 2 Plainview (11803) *(G-13092)*
Technical Library Service Inc 212 219-0770
330 Morgan Ave Brooklyn (11211) *(G-2558)*
Technical Packaging Inc 516 223-2300
2365 Milburn Ave Baldwin (11510) *(G-545)*
Technical Service Industries 212 719-9800
17506 Devonshire Rd 5n Jamaica (11432) *(G-6682)*
Technical Wldg Fabricators LLC 518 463-2229
27 Thatcher St Albany (12207) *(G-132)*
Techniflo Corporation 716 741-3500
9730 County Rd Clarence Center (14032) *(G-3549)*
Technimetal Precision Inds 631 231-8900
195 Marcus Blvd Hauppauge (11788) *(G-5956)*
Technipoly Manufacturing Inc 718 383-0363
20 Wythe Ave Brooklyn (11249) *(G-2559)*
Technologies Application LLC 607 275-0345
3736 Kellogg Rd Cortland (13045) *(G-3896)*
Technology Desking Inc 212 257-6998
39 Broadway Rm 1640 New York (10006) *(G-11794)*
Technomag Inc 631 246-6142
12 Technology Dr Unit 5 East Setauket (11733) *(G-4311)*
Technopaving New York Inc 631 351-6472
270 Broadway Huntington Station (11746) *(G-6461)*
Tecmotiv (usa) Inc 905 669-5911
1500 James Ave Niagara Falls (14305) *(G-12342)*
Tecnofil Chenango SAC 607 674-4441
40 S Main St Sherburne (13460) *(G-14812)*
Tecnolux Incorporated 718 369-3900
103 14th St Brooklyn (11215) *(G-2560)*
Tectonic Flooring USA LLC 212 686-2700
1140 1st Ave Frnt 1 New York (10065) *(G-11795)*
Tectran Inc 800 776-5549
2345 Walden Ave Ste 100 Cheektowaga (14225) *(G-3461)*
Tectran Mfg Inc (HQ) 800 776-5549
2345 Walden Ave Ste 1 Buffalo (14225) *(G-3088)*
Ted Westbrook 716 625-4443
4736 Mapleton Rd Lockport (14094) *(G-7335)*
Tee Pee Auto Sales Corp 516 338-9333
52 Swan St Westbury (11590) *(G-16376)*
Tee Pee Fence & Rail, Jamaica *Also called Tee Pee Fence and Railing* *(G-6683)*
Tee Pee Fence and Railing 718 658-8323
9312 179th Pl Jamaica (11433) *(G-6683)*
Tee Pee Signs, Hempstead *Also called Jem Sign Corp* *(G-6015)*
Teen Vogue, New York *Also called Conde Nast Entertainment LLC* *(G-9375)*
Teena Creations Inc 516 867-1500
10 Hanse Ave Freeport (11520) *(G-5185)*
Tegna Inc 716 849-2222
259 Delaware Ave Buffalo (14202) *(G-3089)*
Tek Precision Co Ltd 631 242-0330
205 W Industry Ct Deer Park (11729) *(G-4051)*
Teka Fine Line Brushes Inc 718 692-2928
3691 Bedford Ave Brooklyn (11229) *(G-2561)*
Teka Precision Inc 845 753-1900
251 Mountainview Ave Nyack (10960) *(G-12512)*
Teknic Inc 585 784-7454
115 Victor Heights Pkwy Victor (14564) *(G-15871)*
Tel Tech International 516 393-5174
200 Broadhollow Rd # 207 Melville (11747) *(G-8071)*
Tel Technology Center Amer LLC (HQ) 512 424-4200
255 Fuller Rd Ste 244 Albany (12203) *(G-133)*
Tel-Tru Inc 585 232-1440
392 Saint Paul St Rochester (14605) *(G-14162)*
Tel-Tru Inc (PA) 585 295-0225
408 Saint Paul St Rochester (14605) *(G-14163)*
Tel-Tru Manufacturing Company, Rochester *Also called Tel-Tru Inc* *(G-14163)*
Tele-Pak Inc 845 426-2300
421 Route 59 Ste 7 Monsey (10952) *(G-8302)*
Tele-Vue Optics Inc 845 469-4551
32 Elkay Dr Chester (10918) *(G-3487)*
Telebyte Inc (PA) 631 423-3232
355 Marcus Blvd Ste 2 Hauppauge (11788) *(G-5957)*
Telechemische Inc 845 561-3237
222 Dupont Ave Newburgh (12550) *(G-12247)*
Telecommunication Concepts 315 736-8523
329 Oriskany Blvd Whitesboro (13492) *(G-16530)*

ALPHABETIC

Teledyne Lecroy Inc (HQ) **ALPHABETIC SECTION**

Teledyne Lecroy Inc (HQ) 845 425-2000
700 Chestnut Ridge Rd Chestnut Ridge (10977) ***(G-3497)***
Teledyne Optech Inc 585 427-8310
1046 University Ave # 149 Rochester (14607) ***(G-14164)***
Telemergency Ltd 914 629-4222
3 Quincy Ln White Plains (10605) ***(G-16511)***
Telephone Sales & Service Co (PA) 212 233-8505
132 W Broadway New York (10013) ***(G-11796)***
Telephonics Corporation 631 755-7659
815 Broadhollow Rd Farmingdale (11735) ***(G-4891)***
Telephonics Corporation 631 549-6000
770 Park Ave Huntington (11743) ***(G-6418)***
Telephonics Corporation (HQ) 631 755-7000
815 Broadhollow Rd Farmingdale (11735) ***(G-4892)***
Telephonics Corporation 631 755-7000
815 Broadhollow Rd Farmingdale (11735) ***(G-4893)***
Telephonics Corporation 631 755-7000
770 Park Ave Huntington (11743) ***(G-6419)***
Telephonics Corporation 631 470-8800
780 Park Ave Huntington (11743) ***(G-6420)***
Telephonics Tlsi Corp 631 470-8854
780 Park Ave Huntington (11743) ***(G-6421)***
Telesca-Heyman Inc 212 534-3442
304 E 94th St 6 New York (10128) ***(G-11797)***
Teller Printing Corp 718 486-3662
317 Division Ave Brooklyn (11211) ***(G-2562)***
Telmar Information Services (PA) 212 725-3000
711 3rd Ave Rm 1500 New York (10017) ***(G-11798)***
Telog Instruments Inc 585 742-3000
830 Canning Pkwy Victor (14564) ***(G-15872)***
Telxon Corporation (HQ) 631 738-2400
1 Zebra Plz Holtsville (11742) ***(G-6248)***
Tempco Glass Fabrication LLC 718 461-6888
13110 Maple Ave Flushing (11355) ***(G-5052)***
Temper Corporation (PA) 518 853-3467
544 Persse Rd Fonda (12068) ***(G-5067)***
Temper Corporation 518 853-3467
544 Persse Rd Fonda (12068) ***(G-5068)***
Temple Bar, New York *Also called Lafayette Pub Inc* ***(G-10507)***
Temple St Clair LLC 212 219-8664
594 Broadway Rm 306 New York (10012) ***(G-11799)***
Tempo Industries Inc 516 334-6900
90 Hopper St Westbury (11590) ***(G-16377)***
Tempo Paris, New York *Also called 6th Avenue Showcase Inc* ***(G-8684)***
Temptu Inc 718 937-9503
522 46th Ave Ste B Long Island City (11101) ***(G-7613)***
Temrex Corporation (PA) 516 868-6221
300 Buffalo Ave Freeport (11520) ***(G-5186)***
Temrick Inc 631 567-8860
1605 Sycamore Ave Unit B Bohemia (11716) ***(G-1095)***
Tenby LLC 646 863-5890
344 W 38th St Fl 3 New York (10018) ***(G-11800)***
Tenney Media Group (PA) 315 853-5569
28 Robinson Rd Clinton (13323) ***(G-3589)***
Tennyson Machine Co Inc 914 668-5468
535 S 5th Ave Mount Vernon (10550) ***(G-8445)***
Tens Machine Company Inc 631 981-3321
800 Grundy Ave Holbrook (11741) ***(G-6215)***
Tensa Software 914 686-5376
66 Greenvale Cir White Plains (10607) ***(G-16512)***
Tensator Group, Bay Shore *Also called Tensator Inc* ***(G-731)***
Tensator Inc 631 666-0300
260 Spur Dr S Bay Shore (11706) ***(G-731)***
Tent and Table Com LLC 716 570-0258
2845 Bailey Ave Buffalo (14215) ***(G-3090)***
Tentina Window Fashions Inc 631 957-9585
1186 Route 109 Lindenhurst (11757) ***(G-7201)***
Tequipment Inc 516 922-3508
7 Norden Ln Huntington Station (11746) ***(G-6462)***
Terahertz Technologies Inc 315 736-3642
169 Clear Rd Oriskany (13424) ***(G-12765)***
Terani Couture, New York *Also called Countess Corporation* ***(G-9408)***
Terbo Ltd 718 847-2860
8905 130th St Richmond Hill (11418) ***(G-13516)***
Termatec Molding Inc 315 483-4150
28 Foley Dr Sodus (14551) ***(G-14915)***
Terphane Holdings LLC (HQ) 585 657-5800
2754 W Park Dr Bloomfield (14469) ***(G-956)***
Terphane Inc., Bloomfield *Also called Terphane LLC* ***(G-957)***
Terphane LLC 585 657-5800
2754 W Park Dr Bloomfield (14469) ***(G-957)***
Terra Engry Resource Tech Inc (PA) 212 286-9197
99 Park Ave Ph A New York (10016) ***(G-11801)***
Terranua US Corp 212 852-9028
535 5th Ave Fl 4 New York (10017) ***(G-11802)***
Terrapin Station Ltd 716 874-6677
1172 Hertel Ave Buffalo (14216) ***(G-3091)***
Terrells Potato Chip Co Inc 315 437-2786
218 Midler Park Dr Syracuse (13206) ***(G-15442)***
Tesla Motors Inc 212 206-1204
10 Columbus Cir Ste 102d New York (10019) ***(G-11803)***
Tessy Plastics Corp (PA) 315 689-3924
700 Visions Dr Skaneateles (13152) ***(G-14878)***
Tessy Plastics Corp 315 689-3924
488 State Route 5 Elbridge (13060) ***(G-4429)***
Testa Communications Inc 516 767-2500
25 Willowdale Ave Port Washington (11050) ***(G-13311)***
Testori Interiors Inc 518 298-4400
107 Lwrnce Paqtte Indstrl Champlain (12919) ***(G-3414)***
Teva Pharmaceuticals Usa Inc 212 259-2030
145 W 57th St New York (10019) ***(G-11804)***
Texas Brine Company LLC 585 495-6228
1346 Saltvale Rd Wyoming (14591) ***(G-16701)***
Texas Home Security Inc (PA) 516 747-2100
50 Rose Pl New Hyde Park (11040) ***(G-8566)***
Texport Fabrics Corp 212 226-6066
495 Broadway Fl 7 New York (10012) ***(G-11805)***
Texray, New York *Also called Z-Ply Corp* ***(G-12167)***
TG Peppe Inc 516 239-7852
299 Rockaway Tpke Unit B Lawrence (11559) ***(G-7110)***
Tg Polymers Inc 585 670-9427
667 Hills Pond Rd Webster (14580) ***(G-16101)***
Tg Therapeutics Inc 212 554-4484
2 Gansevoort St Fl 9 New York (10014) ***(G-11806)***
Tgp Flying Cloud Holdings LLC 646 829-3900
565 5th Ave Fl 27 New York (10017) ***(G-11807)***
Thales Laser SA 585 223-2370
78 Schuyler Baldwin Dr Fairport (14450) ***(G-4664)***
Thalian, New York *Also called F & J Designs Inc* ***(G-9761)***
Thalle Industries Inc (PA) 914 762-3415
51 Route 100 Briarcliff Manor (10510) ***(G-1177)***
Thatcher Company New York Inc 315 589-9330
4135 Rte 104 Williamson (14589) ***(G-16562)***
Thats My Girl Inc (PA) 212 695-0020
80 39th St Ste 501 Brooklyn (11232) ***(G-2563)***
Thayer Tool & Die Inc 716 782-4841
1718 Blckvlle Watts Flts Ashville (14710) ***(G-418)***
The Caldwell Manufacturing Co (PA) 585 352-3790
2605 Manitou Rd Ste 100 Rochester (14624) ***(G-14165)***
The Caldwell Manufacturing Co 585 352-2803
Holland Industrial Park Victor (14564) ***(G-15873)***
The Centro Company Inc 914 533-2200
215 Silver Spring Rd South Salem (10590) ***(G-14948)***
The Chocolate Shop 716 882-5055
871 Niagara St Buffalo (14213) ***(G-3092)***
THE Design Group Inc 212 681-1548
240 Madison Ave Fl 8 New York (10016) ***(G-11808)***
The Earth Times Foundation 718 297-0488
195 Adams St Apt 6j Brooklyn (11201) ***(G-2564)***
The Fisherman, Shirley *Also called L I F Publishing Corp* ***(G-14837)***
The Fisherman, Shirley *Also called Njf Publishing Corp* ***(G-14842)***
The Gramecy Group 518 348-1325
4 Gramecy Ct Clifton Park (12065) ***(G-3579)***
The Hacker Quarterly, Saint James *Also called 2600 Enterprises Inc* ***(G-14509)***
The Kingsbury Printing Co Inc 518 747-6606
632 County Line Rd Queensbury (12804) ***(G-13443)***
The Nugent Organization Inc 212 645-6600
3433 Ocean Harbor Dr Oceanside (11572) ***(G-12561)***
The Observer, Dundee *Also called Finger Lakes Media Inc* ***(G-4157)***
The Observer, Dunkirk *Also called Observer Daily Sunday Newsppr* ***(G-4175)***
The Printing Company, Albany *Also called Printing Resources Inc* ***(G-119)***
The PRS Group Inc (PA) 315 431-0511
5800 Hrtge Lndng Dr Ste E East Syracuse (13057) ***(G-4373)***
The River Reporter, Narrowsburg *Also called Stuart Communications Inc* ***(G-8475)***
The Sandhar Corp 718 523-0819
16427 Highland Ave Jamaica (11432) ***(G-6684)***
The Smoke House of Catskills 845 246-8767
724 Route 212 Saugerties (12477) ***(G-14619)***
The Spirited Shipper, Long Island City *Also called Platinum Sales Promotion Inc* ***(G-7557)***
Theautopartsshop.com, Hauppauge *Also called Ebc Technologies LLC* ***(G-5817)***
Thego, Calverton *Also called Acme Marine Hoist Inc* ***(G-3161)***
Thego Corporation 631 776-2472
2 Mooring Dr Bellport (11713) ***(G-814)***
Thehuffingtonpostcom Inc (HQ) 212 245-7844
770 Broadway Fl 4 New York (10003) ***(G-11809)***
Theirapp LLC 212 896-1255
950 3rd Ave Ste 190 New York (10022) ***(G-11810)***
Themis Chimney Inc 718 937-4716
190 Morgan Ave Brooklyn (11237) ***(G-2565)***
Theodore A Rapp Associates 845 469-2100
728 Craigville Rd Chester (10918) ***(G-3488)***
Theodosiou Inc 718 728-6800
3214 49th St Long Island City (11103) ***(G-7614)***
Theory LLC 212 762-2300
1114 Avenue Of The Americ New York (10036) ***(G-11811)***
Theory LLC 212 879-0265
1157 Madison Ave New York (10028) ***(G-11812)***
Theory LLC 631 204-0231
98 Main St Southampton (11968) ***(G-14963)***
Therese The Childrens Collectn 518 346-2315
301 Nott St Schenectady (12305) ***(G-14721)***
Therm Incorporated 607 272-8500
1000 Hudson Street Ext Ithaca (14850) ***(G-6611)***
Thermacon Tank Insulation, Jericho *Also called Vertarib Inc* ***(G-6806)***

Thermal Foams/Syracuse Inc (PA)......716 874-6474
2101 Kenmore Ave Buffalo (14207) **(G-3093)**
Thermal Foams/Syracuse Inc......315 699-8734
6173 S Bay Rd Cicero (13039) **(G-3523)**
Thermal Process Cnstr Co......631 293-6400
19 Engineers Ln Farmingdale (11735) **(G-4894)**
Thermal Tech Doors Inc (PA)......516 745-0100
576 Brook St Garden City (11530) **(G-5283)**
Thermo Cidtec Inc......315 451-9410
101 Commerce Blvd Liverpool (13088) **(G-7267)**
Thermo Fisher Scientific Inc......585 899-7780
1935 Penfield Rd Penfield (14526) **(G-12946)**
Thermo Fisher Scientific Inc......716 774-6700
3175 Staley Rd Grand Island (14072) **(G-5515)**
Thermo Fisher Scientific Inc......585 458-8008
1999 Mnt Rd Blvd 1-3 Rochester (14615) **(G-14166)**
Thermo Fisher Scientific Inc......585 899-7610
75 Panorama Creek Dr Rochester (14625) **(G-14167)**
Thermoaura Inc......518 813-4997
132b Railroad Ave Ste B Albany (12205) **(G-134)**
Thermold Corporation......315 697-3924
7059 Harp Rd Canastota (13032) **(G-3249)**
Thermopatch Corporation (PA)......315 446-8110
2204 Erie Blvd E Syracuse (13224) **(G-15443)**
Thermotech Corp......716 823-3311
3 Bradford St Buffalo (14210) **(G-3094)**
Theskimm Inc......646 213-4754
50 W 23rd St Ste 501 New York (10010) **(G-11813)**
Thestreet Inc (PA)......212 321-5000
14 Wall St Fl 15 New York (10005) **(G-11814)**
Thewave Communications LLC......646 973-8294
3933 White Plains Rd Bronx (10466) **(G-1402)**
Thewritedeal, New York *Also called Dezawy LLC* **(G-9516)**
Thing Daemon Inc......917 746-9895
57 Bond St New York (10012) **(G-11815)**
Think Green Junk Removal Inc......845 297-7771
29 Meadow Wood Ln Wappingers Falls (12590) **(G-15937)**
Think Tank, New York *Also called City and State Ny LLC* **(G-9309)**
Thinktrek Inc......212 884-8399
420 Lexington Ave Rm 300 New York (10170) **(G-11816)**
Thirsty Owl Wine Company......607 869-5805
6861 State Route 89 Ovid (14521) **(G-12794)**
Thistle Hill Weavers......518 284-2729
143 Baxter Rd Cherry Valley (13320) **(G-3466)**
Thom McGinnes Excavating Plbg, Le Roy *Also called T S P Corp* **(G-7125)**
Thomas C Wilson, Long Island City *Also called Thomas C Wilson LLC* **(G-7615)**
Thomas C Wilson LLC......718 729-3360
2111 44th Ave Long Island City (11101) **(G-7615)**
Thomas Electronics Inc (PA)......315 923-2051
208 Davis Pkwy Clyde (14433) **(G-3598)**
Thomas Enterprise Solutions, New York *Also called Thomas Publishing Company LLC* **(G-11818)**
Thomas F Egan......607 669-4822
570 Hance Rd Binghamton (13903) **(G-919)**
Thomas Group Inc......212 947-6400
131 Varick St Rm 1016 New York (10013) **(G-11817)**
Thomas Group, The, New York *Also called Thomas Group Inc* **(G-11817)**
Thomas Jefferson Press, Port Jefferson *Also called Pace Walkers of America Inc* **(G-13223)**
Thomas Matthews Wdwkg Ltd......631 287-3657
15 Powell Ave Southampton (11968) **(G-14964)**
Thomas Matthews Wdwkg Ltd (PA)......631 287-2023
225 Ocean View Pkwy Southampton (11968) **(G-14965)**
Thomas Publishing Company LLC (PA)......212 695-0500
5 Penn Plz Fl 9 New York (10001) **(G-11818)**
Thomas Publishing Company LLC......212 695-0500
5 Penn Plz Fl 9 New York (10001) **(G-11819)**
Thomas Publishing Company LLC......212 695-0500
5 Penn Plz Fl 8 New York (10001) **(G-11820)**
Thomas Publishing Company LLC......212 695-0500
5 Penn Plz Fl 9 New York (10001) **(G-11821)**
Thomas R Schul TEC GL & Inst, Marion *Also called TEC Glass & Inst LLC* **(G-7809)**
Thomas Sasson Co Inc......212 697-4998
555 5th Ave Rm 1900 New York (10017) **(G-11822)**
Thompson Ferrier LLC......212 244-2212
230 5th Ave Ste 1004 New York (10001) **(G-11823)**
Thompson Overhead Door Co Inc......718 788-2470
47 16th St Brooklyn (11215) **(G-2566)**
Thomson Industries Inc (PA)......716 691-9100
45 Hazelwood Dr Amherst (14228) **(G-255)**
Thomson Press (india) Limited......646 318-0369
4 Court Sq Fl 3rm2 Long Island City (11101) **(G-7616)**
Thomson Reuters Corporation......212 393-9461
500 Pearl St New York (10007) **(G-11824)**
Thomson Reuters Corporation (HQ)......646 223-4000
3 Times Sq New York (10036) **(G-11825)**
Thornwillow Press Ltd......212 980-0738
57 W 58th St Ste 11e New York (10019) **(G-11826)**
Thornwood Products Ltd......914 769-9161
401 Claremont Ave Ste 7 Thornwood (10594) **(G-15508)**
Thousand Island Ready Mix Con......315 686-3203
38760 State Route 180 La Fargeville (13656) **(G-6944)**
Thousand Islands Printing Co......315 482-2581
45501 St Rt 12 Alexandria Bay (13607) **(G-182)**
Thousand Islands Sun, Alexandria Bay *Also called Thousand Islands Printing Co* **(G-182)**
Thousand Islands Winery LLC......315 482-9306
43298 Seaway Ave Ste 1 Alexandria Bay (13607) **(G-183)**
Thread Check Inc......631 231-1515
390 Oser Ave Ste 2 Hauppauge (11788) **(G-5958)**
Thread LLC (PA)......212 414-8844
26 W 17th St Rm 301 New York (10011) **(G-11827)**
Three Brothers Winery, Geneva *Also called Negys New Land Vinyrd Winery* **(G-5330)**
Three Five III-V Materials Inc......212 213-8290
19 W 21st St Rm 203 New York (10010) **(G-11828)**
Three Gems Inc......516 248-0388
2201 Hillside Ave New Hyde Park (11040) **(G-8567)**
Three Point Ventures LLC......585 697-3444
3495 Winton Pl Ste E120 Rochester (14623) **(G-14168)**
Three R Enterprises Inc......585 254-5050
447 Adirondack St Rochester (14606) **(G-14169)**
Three Star Offset Printing......516 867-8223
188 N Main St Freeport (11520) **(G-5187)**
Three Star Supply, Jamaica *Also called City Mason Corp* **(G-6635)**
Three V, Brooklyn *Also called 3v Company Inc* **(G-1440)**
Three Village Times, Mineola *Also called Westbury Times* **(G-8252)**
Thuro Metal Products Inc (PA)......631 435-0444
21-25 Grand Blvd N Brentwood (11717) **(G-1145)**
Thyssenkrupp Materials NA Inc......212 972-8800
489 5th Ave Fl 20 New York (10017) **(G-11829)**
Thyssenkrupp Materials NA Inc......585 279-0000
1673 Lyell Ave Rochester (14606) **(G-14170)**
TI Group Auto Systems LLC......315 568-7042
240 Fall St Seneca Falls (13148) **(G-14787)**
Tia Lattrell......845 373-9494
13 Powder House Rd Amenia (12501) **(G-207)**
Tibana Finishing Inc......718 417-5375
1630 Cody Ave Ridgewood (11385) **(G-13555)**
Tibco Software Inc......646 495-2600
120 W 45th St Fl 18 New York (10036) **(G-11830)**
Tibro Water Technologies Ltd......647 426-3415
106 E Seneca St Unit 25 Sherrill (13461) **(G-14824)**
Tic TAC Toes Mfg Corp......518 773-8187
1 Hamilton St Gloversville (12078) **(G-5470)**
Tickle Hill Winery......607 546-7740
3831 Ball Diamond Rd Hector (14841) **(G-6003)**
Ticonderoga Mch & Wldg Corp......518 585-7444
55 Race Track Rd Ticonderoga (12883) **(G-15514)**
Ticonium Division, Albany *Also called Cmp Industries LLC* **(G-62)**
Ticoniun, Albany *Also called Cmp Export Co Inc* **(G-61)**
Tie King Inc (PA)......718 768-8484
243 44th St Brooklyn (11232) **(G-2567)**
Tie King Inc......212 714-9611
42 W 38th St Rm 1200 New York (10018) **(G-11831)**
Tiedemann Waldemar Inc......716 875-5665
1720 Military Rd Ste 2 Buffalo (14217) **(G-3095)**
Tien Wah Press, New York *Also called Twp America Inc* **(G-11921)**
Tiffen Co, The, Hauppauge *Also called Tiffen Company LLC* **(G-5959)**
Tiffen Company LLC......631 273-2500
80 Oser Ave Hauppauge (11788) **(G-5959)**
Tiffen Company LLC (PA)......631 273-2500
90 Oser Ave Hauppauge (11788) **(G-5960)**
Tiga Holdings Inc......845 838-3000
74 Dennings Ave Beacon (12508) **(G-763)**
Tiger 21 LLC......212 360-1700
1995 Broadway Fl 6 New York (10023) **(G-11832)**
Tiger J LLC......212 465-9300
1430 Broadway Rm 1900 New York (10018) **(G-11833)**
Tiger Supply Inc......631 293-2700
99 Sherwood Ave Farmingdale (11735) **(G-4895)**
Tii Industries Inc......631 789-5000
1385 Akron St Copiague (11726) **(G-3787)**
Tii Technologies Inc (HQ)......516 364-9300
141 Rodeo Dr Edgewood (11717) **(G-4419)**
Tika Mobile Inc (PA)......646 650-5545
902 Broadway Fl 6 New York (10010) **(G-11834)**
Tikamobile, New York *Also called Tika Mobile Inc* **(G-11834)**
Tiki Industries Inc......516 779-3629
8 Tree Haven Ln Riverhead (11901) **(G-13586)**
Tilaros Bakery Inc......716 488-3209
32 Willard St Ste 34 Jamestown (14701) **(G-6757)**
Tilcon New York Inc......845 778-5591
272 Berea Rd Walden (12586) **(G-15898)**
Tilcon New York Inc......845 638-3594
66 Scratchup Rd Haverstraw (10927) **(G-5982)**
Tilcon New York Inc......845 480-3249
3466 College Point Blvd Flushing (11354) **(G-5053)**
Tilcon New York Inc......845 615-0216
2 Quarry Rd Goshen (10924) **(G-5484)**
Tilcon New York Inc......845 457-3158
215 Montgomery Rd Montgomery (12549) **(G-8318)**
Tilcon New York Inc......845 942-0602
Fort Of Elm Tomkins Cove (10986) **(G-15516)**
Tilcon New York Inc......845 358-3100
1 Crusher Rd West Nyack (10994) **(G-16282)**

ALPHABETIC

Tillsonburg Company USA Inc 267 994-8096
37 W 39th St Rm 1101 New York (10018) ***(G-11835)***
Tim Cretin Logging & Sawmill 315 946-4476
3607 Wayne Center Rd Lyons (14489) ***(G-7688)***
Timber Frames Inc 585 374-6405
5557 State Route 64 Canandaigua (14424) ***(G-3235)***
Timberbuilt Inc 716 337-0012
10821 Schaffstall Dr North Collins (14111) ***(G-12389)***
Time Base Consoles, Edgewood *Also called Time Base Corporation* ***(G-4420)***
Time Base Corporation (PA) 631 293-4068
170 Rodeo Dr Edgewood (11717) ***(G-4420)***
Time Home Entertainment Inc 212 522-1212
1271 Ave Of The Americas New York (10020) ***(G-11836)***
Time Inc 212 522-1212
1271 Avenue Of The Americ New York (10020) ***(G-11837)***
Time Inc (HQ) 212 522-1212
225 Liberty St Ste C2 New York (10281) ***(G-11838)***
Time Inc 212 522-0361
1271 Ave Of The Amer Sb7 New York (10020) ***(G-11839)***
Time Inc Affluent Media Group (HQ) 212 382-5600
1120 Ave Of The Americas New York (10036) ***(G-11840)***
Time Inc Affluent Media Group (HQ) 212 382-5600
1120 Ave Of The Americas New York (10036) ***(G-11841)***
Time Out America LLC 646 432-3000
1540 Broadway Fl 42 New York (10036) ***(G-11842)***
Time Out New York Partners LP 646 432-3000
475 10th Ave Fl 12 New York (10018) ***(G-11843)***
Time Precision, Carmel *Also called Precision Arms Inc* ***(G-3280)***
Time Release Sciences Inc 716 823-4580
205 Dingens St Buffalo (14206) ***(G-3096)***
Time Square Lighting, Stony Point *Also called Times Square Stage Ltg Co Inc* ***(G-15177)***
Time To Know Inc 212 230-1210
655 3rd Ave Fl 21 New York (10017) ***(G-11844)***
Time Warner Companies Inc (HQ) 212 484-8000
1 Time Warner Ctr Bsmt B New York (10019) ***(G-11845)***
Time-Cap Laboratories Inc 631 753-9090
7 Michael Ave Farmingdale (11735) ***(G-4896)***
Timeless Decor LLC 315 782-5759
22419 Fisher Rd Watertown (13601) ***(G-16035)***
Timeless Fashions LLC 212 730-9328
100 United Nations Plz New York (10017) ***(G-11846)***
Timeless Frames, Watertown *Also called Lco Destiny LLC* ***(G-16025)***
Timely Signs Inc 516 285-5339
2135 Linden Blvd Elmont (11003) ***(G-4526)***
Timely Signs of Kingston Inc 845 331-8710
154 Clinton Ave Fl 1 Kingston (12401) ***(G-6922)***
Times Beacon Record Newspapers (PA) 631 331-1154
185 Route 25a Ste 4 East Setauket (11733) ***(G-4312)***
Times Center, The, New York *Also called New York Times Company* ***(G-10946)***
Times Herald, The, Olean *Also called Bradford Publications Inc* ***(G-12594)***
Times Herald-Record, Middletown *Also called Local Media Group Inc* ***(G-8161)***
Times Herald-Record, Monticello *Also called Local Media Group Inc* ***(G-8321)***
Times Herald-Record, Kingston *Also called Local Media Group Inc* ***(G-6908)***
Times News Weekly, Ridgewood *Also called Ridgewood Times Prtg & Pubg* ***(G-13549)***
Times Review Newspaper Corp 631 354-8031
7780 Main Rd Mattituck (11952) ***(G-7918)***
Times Square Stage Ltg Co Inc 845 947-3034
5 Holt Dr Stony Point (10980) ***(G-15177)***
Times Square Studios Ltd 212 930-7720
1500 Broadway Fl 2 New York (10036) ***(G-11847)***
Timesdigest, New York *Also called New York Times Company* ***(G-10945)***
Timing Group LLC 646 878-2600
237 W 37th St Ste 1100 New York (10018) ***(G-11848)***
Timothy L Simpson 518 234-1401
5819 State Route 145 Sharon Springs (13459) ***(G-14799)***
Tin Box Company of America Inc (PA) 631 845-1600
216 Sherwood Ave Farmingdale (11735) ***(G-4897)***
Tin Inc 607 775-1550
1240 Conklin Rd Conklin (13748) ***(G-3734)***
Tint World 631 458-1999
3165 Route 112 Medford (11763) ***(G-7967)***
Tio Foods LLC 917 946-1160
120 E 23rd St Fl 5 New York (10010) ***(G-11849)***
Tio Gazpacho, New York *Also called Tio Foods LLC* ***(G-11849)***
Tioga County Courier 607 687-0108
59 Church St Owego (13827) ***(G-12804)***
Tioga County Waste Wood Recycl, Owego *Also called Wholesale Mulch & Sawdust Inc* ***(G-12806)***
Tioga Hardwoods Inc (PA) 607 657-8686
12685 State Route 38 Berkshire (13736) ***(G-828)***
Tioga Tool Inc (PA) 607 785-6005
160 Glendale Dr Endicott (13760) ***(G-4611)***
Tips & Dies Inc 315 337-4161
505 Rome Industrial Park Rome (13440) ***(G-14275)***
Tirado Distillery Inc 718 620-2244
1646 Hering Ave Bronx (10461) ***(G-1403)***
Tire Conversion Tech Inc 518 372-1600
874 Albany Shaker Rd Latham (12110) ***(G-7093)***
Tis Ansonia LLC 518 272-4920
70 Cohoes Rd Watervliet (12189) ***(G-16052)***
Tishcon Corp (PA) 516 333-3056
30 New York Ave Westbury (11590) ***(G-16378)***
Tishcon Corp 516 333-3056
37 Brooklyn Ave Westbury (11590) ***(G-16379)***
Tishcon Corp 516 333-3050
41 New York Ave Westbury (11590) ***(G-16380)***
Tishcon Corp 516 333-3050
36 New York Ave Westbury (11590) ***(G-16381)***
Titan Controls Inc 516 358-2407
122 W 27th St Fl 5 New York (10001) ***(G-11850)***
Titan Steel Corp 315 656-7046
6333 N Kirkville Rd Kirkville (13082) ***(G-6936)***
Titan Technology Group, New York *Also called Ttg LLC* ***(G-11910)***
Titanium Dem Remediation Group 716 433-4100
4907 I D A Park Dr Lockport (14094) ***(G-7336)***
Titanx Engine Cooling Inc 716 665-7129
2258 Allen Street Ext Jamestown (14701) ***(G-6758)***
Titchener Iron Works Division, Binghamton *Also called Moro Corporation* ***(G-906)***
Titherington Design & Mfg 518 324-2205
102 Sharron Ave Unit 1 Plattsburgh (12901) ***(G-13163)***
Title of Work, New York *Also called Jonathan Meizler LLC* ***(G-10358)***
Tito Moldmaker Co, New York *Also called Vasquez Tito* ***(G-11999)***
Titus Mountain Sand & Grav LLC 518 483-3740
17 Junction Rd Malone (12953) ***(G-7728)***
Tiziana Therapeutics Inc 646 396-4970
420 Lexington Ave # 2525 New York (10170) ***(G-11851)***
Tj Powder Coaters LLC 607 724-4779
24 Broad St Binghamton (13904) ***(G-920)***
Tj Signs Unlimited LLC 631 273-4800
327 New South Rd Hicksville (11801) ***(G-6137)***
Tjb Sunshine Enterprises 518 384-6483
6 Redwood Dr Ballston Lake (12019) ***(G-573)***
Tkm Technologies Inc 631 474-4700
623 Bicycle Path Ste 5 Port Jeff STA (11776) ***(G-13219)***
TLC Vision (usa) Corporation 914 395-3949
150 Central Park Ave Hartsdale (10530) ***(G-5746)***
TLC-Lc Inc (PA) 212 756-8900
115 E 57th St Bsmt New York (10022) ***(G-11852)***
TLC-The Light Connection Inc 315 736-7384
132 Base Rd Oriskany (13424) ***(G-12766)***
Tlf Graphics, Rochester *Also called T L F Graphics Inc* ***(G-14156)***
Tli Import Inc 917 578-4568
151 2nd Ave Brooklyn (11215) ***(G-2568)***
Tlsi Incorporated 631 470-8880
780 Park Ave Huntington (11743) ***(G-6422)***
Tm Music Inc 212 471-4000
9 E 63rd St Apt 2-3 New York (10065) ***(G-11853)***
TMC Usa LLC (PA) 518 587-8920
60 Railroad Pl Ste 501 Saratoga Springs (12866) ***(G-14600)***
Tmp Technologies Inc (PA) 716 895-6100
1200 Northland Ave Buffalo (14215) ***(G-3097)***
Tmp Technologies Inc 585 495-6231
6110 Lamb Rd Wyoming (14591) ***(G-16702)***
Tms Development, Westbury *Also called Vescom Structural Systems Inc* ***(G-16386)***
Tms International LLC 315 253-8925
25 Quarry Rd Auburn (13021) ***(G-504)***
Tms Structures Inc 646 740-7646
1745 Broadway Fl 17 New York (10019) ***(G-11854)***
Tntpaving 607 372-4911
1077 Taft Ave Endicott (13760) ***(G-4612)***
To Dey, New York *Also called T O Dey Service Corp* ***(G-11770)***
Tobay Printing Co Inc 631 842-3300
1361 Marconi Blvd Copiague (11726) ***(G-3788)***
Tobeyco Manufacturing Co Inc 607 962-2446
165 Cedar St Corning (14830) ***(G-3827)***
Tocare LLC 718 767-0618
15043b 14th Ave Fl 1 Whitestone (11357) ***(G-16549)***
Today Media, Harrison *Also called Martinelli Holdings LLC* ***(G-5730)***
Todaysgentleman.com, Oceanside *Also called Adf Accessories Inc* ***(G-12530)***
Todd Enterprises, West Babylon *Also called Chem-Tainer Industries Inc* ***(G-16147)***
Todd Enterprises Inc 516 773-8087
747 Middle Neck Rd # 103 Great Neck (11024) ***(G-5595)***
Todd Systems Inc 914 963-3400
50 Ash St Yonkers (10701) ***(G-16802)***
Todd Walbridge 585 254-3018
1916 Lyell Ave Rochester (14606) ***(G-14171)***
Todt Hill Audiological Svcs 718 816-1952
78 Todt Hill Rd Ste 202 Staten Island (10314) ***(G-15147)***
Toga Manufacturing Inc (HQ) 631 242-4800
200 Heartland Blvd Edgewood (11717) ***(G-4421)***
Toho Company Limited 212 391-9058
1501 Broadway Ste 2005 New York (10036) ***(G-11855)***
Toho Shoji (new York) Inc 212 868-7466
990 Avenue Of The America New York (10018) ***(G-11856)***
Token, Brooklyn *Also called 3phase Industries LLC* ***(G-1438)***
Tokenize Inc 585 981-9919
125 Tech Park Dr 2137b Rochester (14623) ***(G-14172)***
Tokens, Staten Island *Also called Maxine Denker Inc* ***(G-15103)***
Tokion Magazine, New York *Also called Downtown Media Group LLC* ***(G-9568)***
Tokyo Electron America Inc 518 289-3100
2 Bayberry Dr Malta (12020) ***(G-7732)***

Tokyo Electron America Inc.......518 292-4200
255 Fuller Rd Ste 214 Albany (12203) *(G-135)*
Toledo Graphics Group, Farmingdale *Also called Desktop Publishing Concepts (G-4750)*
Toltec Fabrics Inc.......212 706-9310
437 5th Ave Fl 10 New York (10016) *(G-11857)*
Tom & Jerry Printcraft Forms (PA).......914 777-7468
960 Mamaroneck Ave Mamaroneck (10543) *(G-7758)*
Tom & Linda Platt Inc.......212 221-7208
55 W 39th St Rm 1701 New York (10018) *(G-11858)*
Tom Dixon, New York *Also called Design Research Ltd (G-9506)*
Tom Doherty Associates Inc.......212 388-0100
175 5th Ave Frnt 1 New York (10010) *(G-11859)*
Tom James Company.......212 593-0204
717 5th Ave New York (10022) *(G-11860)*
Tomas Maier.......212 988-8686
956 Madison Ave Frnt 1 New York (10021) *(G-11861)*
Tomia Beauty Brands LLC.......917 301-0125
38 W 21st St New York (10010) *(G-11862)*
Tomia Beauty Supply, New York *Also called Tomia Beauty Brands LLC (G-11862)*
Tomkins USA, Syracuse *Also called Tompkins Srm LLC (G-15444)*
Tommy Boy Entertainment LLC.......212 388-8300
220 E 23rd St Ste 400 New York (10010) *(G-11863)*
Tommy Hilfiger, New York *Also called Pvh Corp (G-11282)*
Tommy John Inc.......800 708-3490
100 Broadway Ste 1101 New York (10005) *(G-11864)*
Tompkins Metal Finishing Inc.......585 344-2600
6 Apollo Dr Batavia (14020) *(G-637)*
Tompkins Srm LLC.......315 422-8763
623 Oneida St Syracuse (13202) *(G-15444)*
Tompkins Weekly Inc.......607 539-7100
36 Besemer Rd Ithaca (14850) *(G-6612)*
Tomric Systems Inc.......716 854-6050
85 River Rock Dr Buffalo (14207) *(G-3098)*
Tonanwanda News, Niagara Falls *Also called Cnhi LLC (G-12272)*
Tonawanda Coke Corporation.......716 876-6222
3875 River Rd Tonawanda (14150) *(G-15582)*
Tonawanda Limb & Brace Inc.......716 695-1131
545 Delaware St Tonawanda (14150) *(G-15583)*
Tonche Timber LLC.......845 389-3489
3959 State Highway 30 Amsterdam (12010) *(G-360)*
Toner-N-More Inc.......718 232-6200
2220 65th St Ste 103 Brooklyn (11204) *(G-2569)*
Tongli Pharmaceuticals USA Inc (PA).......212 842-8837
4260 Main St Apt 6f Flushing (11355) *(G-5054)*
Toni Industries Inc.......212 921-0700
111 Great Neck Rd Ste 305 Great Neck (11021) *(G-5596)*
Tonix Pharmaceuticals Inc (HQ).......212 980-9155
509 Madison Ave Rm 306 New York (10022) *(G-11865)*
Tonix Phrmceuticals Holdg Corp (PA).......212 980-9155
509 Madison Ave Rm 306 New York (10022) *(G-11866)*
Tonner Doll Company Inc (PA).......845 339-9537
1094 Morton Blvd Kingston (12401) *(G-6923)*
Tonoga Inc (PA).......518 658-3202
95-136 Coonbrook Rd Petersburg (12138) *(G-12973)*
Tony Baird Electronics Inc.......315 422-4430
461 E Brighton Ave Syracuse (13210) *(G-15445)*
Tonys Ornamental Ir Works Inc.......315 337-3730
6757 Martin St Rome (13440) *(G-14276)*
Tooling Enterprises Inc.......716 842-0445
680 New Babcock St Ste 1 Buffalo (14206) *(G-3099)*
Toolroom Express Inc.......607 723-5373
1010 Conklin Rd Conklin (13748) *(G-3735)*
Tools & Stamping Corp.......718 392-4040
48 Eagle St Brooklyn (11222) *(G-2570)*
Tootter Inc.......212 204-7937
1470 Royce St Brooklyn (11234) *(G-2571)*
Top Fortune Usa Ltd.......516 608-2694
100 Atlantic Ave Ste 2 Lynbrook (11563) *(G-7676)*
Top Stuff, New York *Also called Isfel Co Inc (G-10275)*
Topaz Industries Inc.......631 207-0700
130 Corporate Dr Holtsville (11742) *(G-6249)*
Topiderm Inc (PA).......631 226-7979
5200 New Horizons Blvd Amityville (11701) *(G-321)*
Topix Pharmaceuticals Inc (PA).......631 226-7979
5200 New Horizons Blvd Amityville (11701) *(G-322)*
Topoo Industries Incorporated.......718 331-3755
7815 16th Ave Brooklyn (11214) *(G-2572)*
Toppan Vintage Inc (HQ).......212 596-7747
747 3rd Ave Fl 7 New York (10017) *(G-11867)*
Topps-All Products of Yonkers.......914 968-4226
148 Ludlow St Ste 2 Yonkers (10705) *(G-16803)*
Toprint Ltd.......718 439-0469
6110 7th Ave Brooklyn (11220) *(G-2573)*
Toptec Products LLC.......631 421-9800
1225 Walt Whitman Rd Melville (11747) *(G-8072)*
Tor Books, New York *Also called Tom Doherty Associates Inc (G-11859)*
Toray Holding (usa) Inc (HQ).......212 697-8150
461 5th Ave Fl 9 New York (10017) *(G-11868)*
Toray Industries Inc.......212 697-8150
600 3rd Ave Fl 5 New York (10016) *(G-11869)*
Torino Indus Fabrication Inc.......631 509-1640
4 Pinehurst Dr Bellport (11713) *(G-815)*
Torino Industrial Inc.......631 509-1640
4 Pinehurst Dr Bellport (11713) *(G-816)*
Torino Industrial Fabrication, Bellport *Also called Torino Industrial Inc (G-816)*
Tork Inc (PA).......914 664-3542
50 S Macquesten Pkwy Mount Vernon (10550) *(G-8446)*
Torotron Corporation.......718 428-6992
18508 Union Tpke Ste 101 Fresh Meadows (11366) *(G-5204)*
Torre Products Co Inc.......212 925-8989
479 Washington St New York (10013) *(G-11870)*
Torrent Ems LLC.......716 312-4099
190 Walnut St Lockport (14094) *(G-7337)*
Torrey Pines Research, Fairport *Also called Xactiv Inc (G-4668)*
Torrington Industries Inc.......315 676-4662
90 Corporate Park Dr Central Square (13036) *(G-3392)*
Torsaf Printers Inc.......516 569-5577
1313 Broadway Hewlett (11557) *(G-6051)*
Tortilla Heaven Inc.......845 339-1550
97 Abeel St Kingston (12401) *(G-6924)*
Tortilleria Chinantla Inc.......718 302-0101
975 Grand St Brooklyn (11211) *(G-2574)*
Tortilleria Oaxaca.......347 355-7336
121 Port Richmond Ave Staten Island (10302) *(G-15148)*
Tory Electric.......914 292-5036
641 Old Post Rd Bedford (10506) *(G-771)*
Tosch Products Ltd.......315 672-3040
25 Main St Camillus (13031) *(G-3198)*
Toshiba Amer Info Systems Inc (HQ).......949 583-3000
1251 Ave Of The New York (10020) *(G-11871)*
Toshiba America Inc (HQ).......212 596-0600
1251 Ave Of Ameri New York (10020) *(G-11872)*
Total Concept Graphic Inc.......212 229-2626
519 8th Ave Rm 805a New York (10018) *(G-11873)*
Total Defense Inc.......631 257-3258
1393 Veterans Memorial Hw Hauppauge (11788) *(G-5961)*
Total Dntl Implant Sltions LLC.......212 877-3777
260 W Sunrise Hwy Valley Stream (11581) *(G-15800)*
Total Energy Fabrication Corp.......580 363-1500
2 Hardscrabble Rd North Salem (10560) *(G-12397)*
Total Machine and Welding, Bronx *Also called Coral Management Corp (G-1246)*
Total Metal Resource.......718 384-7818
175 Bogart St Brooklyn (11206) *(G-2575)*
Total Piping Solutions Inc.......716 372-0160
1760 Haskell Rd Olean (14760) *(G-12608)*
Total Solution Graphics Inc.......718 706-1540
2511 49th Ave Long Island City (11101) *(G-7617)*
Total Webcasting Inc.......845 883-0909
8 Bruce St New Paltz (12561) *(G-8581)*
Toto USA Inc.......917 237-0665
20 W 22nd St Frnt 2 New York (10010) *(G-11874)*
Touch Adjust Clip Co Inc.......631 589-3077
1687 Roosevelt Ave Bohemia (11716) *(G-1096)*
Touch Tunes, New York *Also called Touchtunes Music Corporation (G-11876)*
Touchcare P LLC.......646 824-5373
111 W 19th St Fl 8 New York (10011) *(G-11875)*
Touchdown, New York *Also called Professnal Spt Pblications Inc (G-11256)*
Touchstone Technology Inc.......585 458-2690
350 Mile Crossing Blvd Rochester (14624) *(G-14173)*
Touchtunes Music Corporation (HQ).......847 419-3300
850 3rd Ave Ste 15c New York (10022) *(G-11876)*
Toura LLC.......646 652-8668
392 2nd St 2 Brooklyn (11215) *(G-2576)*
Tovie Asarese Royal Prtg Co.......716 885-7692
351 Grant St Buffalo (14213) *(G-3100)*
Tower Computers, Brewster *Also called Base Systems Inc (G-1158)*
Tower Isles Frozen Foods Ltd.......718 495-2626
2025 Atlantic Ave Brooklyn (11233) *(G-2577)*
Tower Isles Patties, Brooklyn *Also called Tower Isles Frozen Foods Ltd (G-2577)*
Tower Sales Co, Brooklyn *Also called Turoff Tower Graphics Inc (G-2593)*
Toweriq Inc.......844 626-7638
37-18 Nthrn Blvd Ste 421 Long Island City (11101) *(G-7618)*
Town Line Auto, Greenville *Also called Classic Auto Crafts Inc (G-5635)*
Town of Amherst.......716 631-7113
450 Maple Rd Williamsville (14221) *(G-16591)*
Town of Ohio.......315 392-2055
N Lake Rd Forestport (13338) *(G-5084)*
Town of Ohio Highway Garage, Forestport *Also called Town of Ohio (G-5084)*
Towne House Restorations Inc.......718 497-9200
4309 Vernon Blvd Long Island City (11101) *(G-7619)*
Townley Inc.......212 779-0544
10 W 33rd St Rm 418 New York (10001) *(G-11877)*
Townley Cosmetics, New York *Also called Townley Inc (G-11877)*
Townline Machine Co Inc.......315 462-3413
3151 Manchester Clifton Springs (14432) *(G-3584)*
Towpath Machine Corp.......315 252-0112
31 Allen St Auburn (13021) *(G-505)*
Towse Publishing Co.......914 235-3095
1333a North Ave New Rochelle (10804) *(G-8629)*
Toy Admiration Co Inc.......914 963-9400
60 Mclean Ave Yonkers (10705) *(G-16804)*
Toymax Inc (HQ).......212 633-6611
200 5th Ave New York (10010) *(G-11878)*

ALPHABETIC

Tpa Computer Corp 877 866-6044
531 Route 52 Apt 4 Carmel (10512) ***(G-3282)***

TPC Inc 315 438-8605
6780 Nthrn Blvd Ste 401 East Syracuse (13057) ***(G-4374)***

Tphg 419 Ltd 212 683-0444
419 Park Ave S Frnt A New York (10016) ***(G-11879)***

Tpi Arcade Inc 585 492-0122
7888 Route 98 Arcade (14009) ***(G-390)***

Tpi Industries LLC (HQ) 845 692-2820
265 Ballard Rd Middletown (10941) ***(G-8179)***

Tpti, Stony Brook *Also called Transistor Power Tech Inc* ***(G-15170)***

Tr Apparel LLC 310 595-4337
609 Greenwich St Fl 3 New York (10014) ***(G-11880)***

Tr Apparel LLC (HQ) 646 358-3888
609 Greenwich St Fl 3 New York (10014) ***(G-11881)***

TR Designs Inc 212 398-9300
260 W 39th St Fl 19 New York (10018) ***(G-11882)***

Trac Medical Solutions Inc 518 346-7799
2165 Technology Dr Schenectady (12308) ***(G-14722)***

Trac Regulators Inc 914 699-9352
160 S Terrace Ave Mount Vernon (10550) ***(G-8447)***

Tracey Welding Co Inc 518 756-6309
29 Riverview Dr Coeymans (12045) ***(G-3609)***

Track 7 Inc 845 544-1810
3 Forester Ave Warwick (10990) ***(G-15960)***

Traco Manufacturing Inc 585 343-2434
4300 Commerce Dr Batavia (14020) ***(G-638)***

Tracy Reese, New York *Also called TR Designs Inc* ***(G-11882)***

Trade Mark Graphics Inc 718 306-0001
4502 Avenue N Brooklyn (11234) ***(G-2578)***

Tradepaq Corporation 914 332-9174
220 White Plains Rd # 360 Tarrytown (10591) ***(G-15497)***

Trader Interntnal Publications 914 631-6856
50 Fremont Rd Sleepy Hollow (10591) ***(G-14887)***

Trader Joe's 541, New York *Also called Trader Joes Company* ***(G-11883)***

Trader Joes Company 212 529-6326
138 E 14th St New York (10003) ***(G-11883)***

Tradewins Publishing Corp 631 361-6916
528 Route 25a Ste A Saint James (11780) ***(G-14516)***

Trading Edge Ltd 347 699-7079
1923 Bleecker St Apt 1r Ridgewood (11385) ***(G-13556)***

Trading Services International 212 501-0142
133 W 72nd St Rm 601 New York (10023) ***(G-11884)***

Trafalgar Company LLC (HQ) 212 768-8800
417 5th Ave Fl 11 New York (10016) ***(G-11885)***

Traffic Lane Closures LLC 845 228-6100
1214 Route 52 Ste 1 Carmel (10512) ***(G-3283)***

Traffic Logix Corporation 866 915-6449
3 Harriet Ln Spring Valley (10977) ***(G-15009)***

Tramwell Inc 315 789-2762
70 State St Geneva (14456) ***(G-5334)***

Trane US Inc 718 721-8844
4518 Court Sq Ste 100 Long Island City (11101) ***(G-7620)***

Trane US Inc 914 593-0303
3 Westchester Plz Ste 198 Elmsford (10523) ***(G-4573)***

Trane US Inc 315 234-1500
15 Technology Pl East Syracuse (13057) ***(G-4375)***

Trane US Inc 518 785-1315
301 Old Niskayuna Rd # 1 Latham (12110) ***(G-7094)***

Trane US Inc 585 256-2500
75 Town Centre Dr Ste I Rochester (14623) ***(G-14174)***

Trane US Inc 716 626-1260
45 Earhart Dr Ste 103 Buffalo (14221) ***(G-3101)***

Trane US Inc 631 952-9477
245 Newtown Rd Ste 500 Plainview (11803) ***(G-13093)***

Trans Tech Bus, Warwick *Also called Transprttion Collaborative Inc* ***(G-15961)***

Trans-High Corporation 212 387-0500
250 W 57th St Ste 920 New York (10107) ***(G-11886)***

Trans-Lux Corporation (PA) 800 243-5544
135 E 57th St Unit 100 New York (10022) ***(G-11887)***

Transact Technologies Inc 607 257-8901
20 Bomax Dr Ithaca (14850) ***(G-6613)***

Transaction Printer Group 607 274-2500
108 Woodcrest Ter Ithaca (14850) ***(G-6614)***

Transcat Inc (PA) 585 352-7777
35 Vantage Point Dr Rochester (14624) ***(G-14175)***

Transcedar Industries Ltd 716 731-6442
6292 Walmore Rd Niagara Falls (14304) ***(G-12343)***

Transcntinental Ultra Flex Inc 718 272-9100
975 Essex St Brooklyn (11208) ***(G-2579)***

Transco Railway Products Inc 716 825-1663
Milestrip Rd Rr 179 Buffalo (14219) ***(G-3102)***

Transco Railway Products Inc 716 824-1219
Milestrip Rd Blasdell (14219) ***(G-931)***

Transcontinental Printing GP 716 626-3078
300 International Dr # 200 Amherst (14221) ***(G-256)***

Transcontinental Ross-Ellis, New York *Also called Tc Transcontinental USA Inc* ***(G-11788)***

Transistor Devices Inc 631 471-7492
125 Comac St Ronkonkoma (11779) ***(G-14421)***

Transistor Power Tech Inc (PA) 631 491-0265
38 Robert Cres Stony Brook (11790) ***(G-15170)***

Transit Air Inc 607 324-0216
1 William K Jackson Ln Hornell (14843) ***(G-6304)***

Transitair Systems, Hornell *Also called Transit Air Inc* ***(G-6304)***

Transland Sourcing LLC 718 596-5704
5 Lynch St Brooklyn (11249) ***(G-2580)***

Transpo Industries Inc (PA) 914 636-1000
20 Jones St Ste 3 New Rochelle (10801) ***(G-8630)***

Transport National Dev Inc (PA) 716 662-0270
5720 Ellis Rd Orchard Park (14127) ***(G-12746)***

Transport National Dev Inc 716 662-0270
5720 Ellis Rd Orchard Park (14127) ***(G-12747)***

Transportation Department, Bay Shore *Also called Bimbo Bakeries Usa Inc* ***(G-663)***

Transportgistics Inc 631 567-4100
28 N Country Rd Ste 103 Mount Sinai (11766) ***(G-8370)***

Transprttion Collaborative Inc 845 988-2333
7 Lake Station Rd Warwick (10990) ***(G-15961)***

Transtech Systems Inc (PA) 518 370-5558
900 Albany Shaker Rd Latham (12110) ***(G-7095)***

Trash and Vaudeville Inc 212 777-1727
96 E 7th St Frnt A New York (10009) ***(G-11888)***

Travel Leisure Magazine, New York *Also called Time Inc Affluent Media Group* ***(G-11841)***

Treauu Inc 703 731-0196
60 E 120th St Fl 2 New York (10035) ***(G-11889)***

Trebor Instrument Corp 631 423-7026
39 Balsam Dr Dix Hills (11746) ***(G-4127)***

Treehouse Private Brands Inc 716 693-4715
570 Fillmore Ave Tonawanda (14150) ***(G-15584)***

Treiman Publications Corp 607 657-8473
12724 State Route 38 Berkshire (13736) ***(G-829)***

Trek Inc (PA) 716 438-7555
190 Walnut St Lockport (14094) ***(G-7338)***

Tremont Offset Inc 718 892-7333
1500 Ericson Pl Bronx (10461) ***(G-1404)***

Trench & Marine Pump Co Inc 212 423-9098
3466 Park Ave Bronx (10456) ***(G-1405)***

Trend Pot Inc 212 431-9970
40 Exchange Pl Ste 1902 New York (10005) ***(G-11890)***

Trendsformers Ltd Liability Co 888 700-2423
150 W 56th St Apt 6406 New York (10019) ***(G-11891)***

Trensdformers, New York *Also called Trendsformers Ltd Liability Co* ***(G-11891)***

Treo Brands LLC 914 341-1850
106 Calvert St Harrison (10528) ***(G-5737)***

Treo Industries Inc 631 737-4022
35 Carlough Rd Ste 1 Bohemia (11716) ***(G-1097)***

Treyco Products Corp 716 693-6525
131 Fillmore Ave Tonawanda (14150) ***(G-15585)***

Tri City Highway Products Inc 607 722-2967
111 Bevier St Binghamton (13904) ***(G-921)***

Tri County Custom Vacuum 845 774-7595
653 State Route 17m Monroe (10950) ***(G-8282)***

Tri Kolor Printing & Sty 315 474-6753
1035 Montgomery St Syracuse (13202) ***(G-15446)***

Tri Star, Maspeth *Also called Asn Inc* ***(G-7824)***

Tri Star Label Inc 914 237-4800
630 S Columbus Ave Mount Vernon (10550) ***(G-8448)***

Tri State Awnings, Sloatsburg *Also called Custom European Imports Inc* ***(G-14892)***

Tri State Shearing Bending Inc 718 485-2200
366 Herzl St Brooklyn (11212) ***(G-2581)***

Tri Supreme Optical, Farmingdale *Also called Tri-Supreme Optical LLC* ***(G-4899)***

Tri Valley Iron Inc 845 365-1013
700 Oak Tree Rd Palisades (10964) ***(G-12848)***

Tri-Boro Shelving Inc 718 782-8527
1940 Flushing Ave Ridgewood (11385) ***(G-13557)***

Tri-City Highway Products Inc 518 294-9964
145 Podpadic Rd Richmondville (12149) ***(G-13519)***

Tri-Flex Label Corp 631 293-0411
48 Allen Blvd Unit A Farmingdale (11735) ***(G-4898)***

Tri-Force Sales LLC 732 261-5507
767 3rd Ave Rm 35b New York (10017) ***(G-11892)***

Tri-Lon Clor Lithographers Ltd 212 255-6140
233 Spring St Frnt 9th New York (10013) ***(G-11893)***

Tri-Metal Industries Inc 716 691-3323
100 Pineview Dr Amherst (14228) ***(G-257)***

Tri-Plex Packaging Corporation 212 481-6070
307 5th Ave Fl 7 New York (10016) ***(G-11894)***

Tri-Seal Holdings Inc 845 353-3300
900 Bradley Hill Rd Blauvelt (10913) ***(G-943)***

Tri-Seal International Inc (HQ) 845 353-3300
900 Bradley Hill Rd Blauvelt (10913) ***(G-944)***

Tri-Star Offset Corp 718 894-5555
6020 59th Pl Ste 3 Maspeth (11378) ***(G-7873)***

Tri-State Brick & Stone NY Inc (PA) 212 366-0300
333 7th Ave Fl 5 New York (10001) ***(G-11895)***

Tri-State Food Jobbers Inc 718 921-1211
5600 1st Ave Unit A5 Brooklyn (11220) ***(G-2582)***

Tri-State Metals LLC 914 347-8157
41 N Lawn Ave Elmsford (10523) ***(G-4574)***

Tri-State Towing Equipment NY, Westbury *Also called Tee Pee Auto Sales Corp* ***(G-16376)***

Tri-State Window Factory Corp 631 667-8600
360 Marcus Blvd Deer Park (11729) ***(G-4052)***

Tri-Supreme Optical LLC 631 249-2020
91 Carolyn Blvd Farmingdale (11735) ***(G-4899)***

Tri-Technologies Inc 914 699-2001
40 Hartford Ave Mount Vernon (10553) ***(G-8449)***

Tri-Town News Inc (PA) 607 561-3515
74 Main St Sidney (13838) ***(G-14855)***
Tri-Town Packing Corp 315 389-5101
Helena Rd Brasher Falls (13613) ***(G-1125)***
Tri-Village Publishers Inc 518 843-1100
1 Venner Rd Amsterdam (12010) ***(G-361)***
Triad Counter Corp 631 750-0615
1225 Church St Bohemia (11716) ***(G-1098)***
Triad Network Technologies 585 924-8505
75b Victor Heights Pkwy Victor (14564) ***(G-15874)***
Triad Printing Inc 845 343-2722
7 Prospect St Middletown (10940) ***(G-8180)***
Trialgraphix, New York *Also called Resonant Legal Media LLC* ***(G-11369)***
Triangle Grinding Machine Corp 631 643-3636
66 Nancy St Unit A West Babylon (11704) ***(G-16200)***
Triangle Label Tag Inc 718 875-3030
525 Dekalb Ave Brooklyn (11205) ***(G-2583)***
Triangle Rubber Co Inc 631 589-9400
50 Aero Rd Bohemia (11716) ***(G-1099)***
Trianon Collection Inc 212 921-9450
16 W 46th St Fl 10 New York (10036) ***(G-11896)***
Tribco LLC 718 357-7400
15050 14th Rd Ste 2 Whitestone (11357) ***(G-16550)***
Tribology Inc 631 345-3000
35 Old Dock Rd Yaphank (11980) ***(G-16724)***
Triboro Bagel Co Inc 718 359-9245
18312 Horace Harding Expy Flushing (11365) ***(G-5055)***
Triboro Iron Works Inc 718 361-9600
3830 31st St Long Island City (11101) ***(G-7621)***
Triborough Electric 718 321-2144
15044 11th Ave Whitestone (11357) ***(G-16551)***
Tribune Entertainment Co Del 203 866-2204
220 E 42nd St Fl 26 New York (10017) ***(G-11897)***
Tribune Media Services Inc (HQ) 518 792-9914
40 Media Dr Queensbury (12804) ***(G-13444)***
Triceutical Inc 631 249-0003
1652 Hering Ave Bronx (10461) ***(G-1406)***
Trico Manufacturing Corp 718 349-6565
196 Dupont St Brooklyn (11222) ***(G-2584)***
Tricon Machine LLC 585 671-0679
820 Coventry Dr Webster (14580) ***(G-16102)***
Tricon Piping Systems Inc 315 697-8787
2 Technology Blvd Canastota (13032) ***(G-3250)***
Tricor Direct Inc (HQ) 716 626-1616
2491 Wehrle Dr Williamsville (14221) ***(G-16592)***
Tricycle Foundation Inc 800 873-9871
89 5th Ave Ste 301 New York (10003) ***(G-11898)***
Trident Partners III, Victor *Also called Newtex Industries Inc* ***(G-15858)***
Trident Precision Mfg Inc 585 265-2010
734 Salt Rd Webster (14580) ***(G-16103)***
Trident Valve Actuator Co 914 698-2650
329 Center Ave Mamaroneck (10543) ***(G-7759)***
Trihex Manufacturing Inc 315 589-9331
6708 Pound Rd Williamson (14589) ***(G-16563)***
Tril Inc 631 645-7989
320 Pioxi St Copiague (11726) ***(G-3789)***
Trilake Three Press Corp 518 359-2462
136 Park St Tupper Lake (12986) ***(G-15654)***
Trilon Color Lithographers, New York *Also called Tri-Lon Clor Lithographers Ltd* ***(G-11893)***
Trimac Molding Services 607 967-2900
13 Pruyn St Bainbridge (13733) ***(G-535)***
Trimaster/Htech Holding LLC (HQ) 212 257-6772
590 Madison Ave Fl 27 New York (10022) ***(G-11899)***
Trimet Coal LLC 718 951-3654
1615 Avenue I Apt 420 Brooklyn (11230) ***(G-2585)***
Trimfit Inc (PA) 215 245-1122
463 7th Ave Rm 1501 New York (10018) ***(G-11900)***
Trimfit Global, New York *Also called Trimfit Inc* ***(G-11900)***
Trimmer Capacitor Company, The, Cazenovia *Also called Voltronics LLC* ***(G-3329)***
Trinic LLC 607 655-1517
40 Grossett Dr Kirkwood (13795) ***(G-6941)***
Trinity Biotech Distribution, Jamestown *Also called Biopool Us Inc* ***(G-6701)***
Trinity Biotech USA, Jamestown *Also called Clark Laboratories Inc* ***(G-6706)***
Trinity Packaging Corporation 716 668-3111
55 Innsbruck Dr Buffalo (14227) ***(G-3103)***
Trinity Packaging Corporation (HQ) 914 273-4111
357 Main St Armonk (10504) ***(G-411)***
Trinity Tools Inc 716 694-1111
261 Main St North Tonawanda (14120) ***(G-12460)***
Trio French Bakery, New York *Also called Giovanni Bakery Corp* ***(G-9924)***
Tripar Manufacturing Co Inc 631 563-0855
1620 Ocean Ave Ste 1 Bohemia (11716) ***(G-1100)***
Tripi Engraving Co Inc 718 383-6500
60 Meserole Ave Brooklyn (11222) ***(G-2586)***
TRIPLE CANOPY, New York *Also called Canopy Canopy Canopy Inc* ***(G-9196)***
Triple E Manufacturing 716 761-6996
117 Osborn St Sherman (14781) ***(G-14817)***
Triple H Construction Inc 516 280-8252
832 Bethlynn Ct East Meadow (11554) ***(G-4256)***
Triple J Bedding LLC 718 643-8005
63 Flushing Ave Unit 331 Brooklyn (11205) ***(G-2587)***
Triple Point Manufacturing 631 218-4988
1371 Church St Ste 6 Bohemia (11716) ***(G-1101)***
Triplett Machine Inc 315 548-3198
1374 Phelps Junction Rd Phelps (14532) ***(G-12982)***
Triplex Industries Inc 585 621-6920
100 Boxart St Ste 27 Rochester (14612) ***(G-14176)***
Tripp Plating Works Inc 716 894-2424
1491 William St Buffalo (14206) ***(G-3104)***
Tristate Contract Sales LLC 845 782-2614
164 Dug Rd Chester (10918) ***(G-3489)***
Triton Builders Inc 631 841-2534
645 Broadway Ste T Amityville (11701) ***(G-323)***
Triumph Actuation Systems LLC 516 378-0162
417 S Main St Freeport (11520) ***(G-5188)***
Triumph Apparel Corporation (PA) 212 302-2606
530 Fashion Ave Ste M1 New York (10018) ***(G-11901)***
Triumph Group Inc 516 997-5757
717 Main St Westbury (11590) ***(G-16382)***
Triumph Learning LLC (HQ) 212 652-0200
212 W 35th St Fl 2 New York (10001) ***(G-11902)***
Triumph Structures-Long Island, Westbury *Also called Triumph Group Inc* ***(G-16382)***
TRM Linen Inc 718 686-6075
1546 59th St Brooklyn (11219) ***(G-2588)***
Trojan Metal Fabrication Inc (PA) 631 968-5040
2215 Union Blvd Bay Shore (11706) ***(G-732)***
Trojan Powder Coating, Bay Shore *Also called Trojan Metal Fabrication Inc* ***(G-732)***
Tronic Plating Co Inc 516 293-7883
37 Potter St Farmingdale (11735) ***(G-4900)***
Tronser Inc 315 655-9528
3066 John Trush Jr Blvd Cazenovia (13035) ***(G-3328)***
Tropical Driftwood Originals 516 623-0980
499 Nassau Rd Roosevelt (11575) ***(G-14438)***
Tropp Printing Corp 212 233-4519
181 Broadway Fl 3 New York (10007) ***(G-11903)***
Tropp Prntng, New York *Also called Tropp Printing Corp* ***(G-11903)***
Trove Inc 212 268-2046
20 Jay St Ste 846 Brooklyn (11201) ***(G-2589)***
Troy Belting and Supply Co (PA) 518 272-4920
70 Cohoes Rd Watervliet (12189) ***(G-16053)***
Troy Boiler Works Inc 518 274-2650
2800 7th Ave Troy (12180) ***(G-15630)***
Troy Cabinet Manufacturing Div, Troy *Also called Deakon Homes and Interiors* ***(G-15603)***
Troy Industrial Solutions 518 272-4920
70 Cohoes Rd Watervliet (12189) ***(G-16054)***
Troy Sand & Gravel Co Inc (PA) 518 203-5115
34 Grange Rd West Sand Lake (12196) ***(G-16285)***
Troy Sand & Gravel Co Inc 518 674-2854
Rr 43 West Sand Lake (12196) ***(G-16286)***
Troy Sign & Printing 718 994-4482
4827 White Plains Rd Bronx (10470) ***(G-1407)***
Troy Sign Printing Center, Bronx *Also called Troy Sign & Printing* ***(G-1407)***
Troyer Inc 585 352-5590
4555 Lyell Rd Rochester (14606) ***(G-14177)***
Troys Landscape Supply Co Inc 518 785-1526
1266 Loudon Rd Cohoes (12047) ***(G-3622)***
Trs Packaging, Buffalo *Also called Time Release Sciences Inc* ***(G-3096)***
Tru Mold Shoes Inc 716 881-4484
42 Breckenridge St Buffalo (14213) ***(G-3105)***
Tru-Art Sign Co Inc 718 658-5068
10515 180th St Jamaica (11433) ***(G-6685)***
Tru-Tone Metal Products Inc 718 386-5960
1261 Willoughby Ave Brooklyn (11237) ***(G-2590)***
Truarc Fabrication 518 691-0430
1 Commerce Park Dr Gansevoort (12831) ***(G-5248)***
Truck-Lite Co LLC 716 665-2614
310 E Elmwood Ave Falconer (14733) ***(G-4695)***
Truck-Lite Co LLC (HQ) 716 665-6214
310 E Elmwood Ave Falconer (14733) ***(G-4696)***
Truck-Lite Sub Inc 800 888-7095
310 E Elmwood Ave Falconer (14733) ***(G-4697)***
True Type Printing Co Inc 718 706-6900
8600 New Horizons Blvd Amityville (11701) ***(G-324)***
Truebite Inc 607 785-7664
2590 Glenwood Rd Vestal (13850) ***(G-15824)***
Truebite Inc 607 786-3184
129 Squires Ave Endicott (13760) ***(G-4613)***
Trueex LLC 646 786-8526
162 5th Ave Ste 900 New York (10010) ***(G-11904)***
Trueforge Global McHy Corp 516 825-7040
100 Merrick Rd Ste 208e Rockville Centre (11570) ***(G-14243)***
Truemade Products Inc 631 981-4755
910 Marconi Ave Ronkonkoma (11779) ***(G-14422)***
Truesense Imaging Inc 585 784-5500
1964 Lake Ave Rochester (14615) ***(G-14178)***
Truform Manufacturing Corp 585 458-1090
1500 N Clinton Ave Rochester (14621) ***(G-14179)***
Truly Tubular Fitting Corp 914 664-8686
115 E 3rd St Mount Vernon (10550) ***(G-8450)***
Trunk & Trolley LLC 212 947-9001
15 W 34th St New York (10001) ***(G-11905)***
Trunk Outlet, Rochester *Also called Rhino Trunk & Case Inc* ***(G-14071)***
Trusses & Trim Division, Farmington *Also called Rochester Lumber Company* ***(G-4919)***

Trust of Colum Unive In The Ci 212 854-2793
2929 Broadway Fl 3 New York (10025) ***(G-11906)***
Trusted Media Brands Inc (HQ) 914 238-1000
750 3rd Ave Fl 3 New York (10017) ***(G-11907)***
Trusted Media Brands Inc 914 244-5244
44 S Broadway Fl 7 White Plains (10601) ***(G-16513)***
Trustfort LLC 781 787-0906
4250 Veterans Memorial Hw Holbrook (11741) ***(G-6216)***
Truth Hardware Corporation 585 627-5964
1555 Jefferson Rd Rochester (14623) ***(G-14180)***
Truxton Corp 718 842-6000
1357 Lafayette Ave Bronx (10474) ***(G-1408)***
TRW Automotive Inc 315 255-3311
2150 Crane Brook Dr Auburn (13021) ***(G-506)***
Trylon Wire & Metal Works Inc 718 542-4472
526 Tiffany St Bronx (10474) ***(G-1409)***
Tryp Times Square 212 246-8800
234 W 48th St New York (10036) ***(G-11908)***
TS Manufactoring, New York *Also called Alpine Creations Ltd* ***(G-8813)***
TS Pink, Oneonta *Also called T S Pink Corp* ***(G-12646)***
TSA Luggage Locks, New York *Also called Safe Skies LLC* ***(G-11464)***
Tsar USA LLC 646 415-7968
99 Madison Ave Fl 5 New York (10016) ***(G-11909)***
Tsi Technologies, New York *Also called Trading Services International* ***(G-11884)***
Tsm, Elmsford *Also called Tri-State Metals LLC* ***(G-4574)***
TSS Foam Industries Corp 585 538-2321
2770 W Main St Caledonia (14423) ***(G-3159)***
Tss-Transport Simulation, New York *Also called Aimsun Inc* ***(G-8776)***
Tte Filters LLC (HQ) 716 532-2234
1 Magnetic Pkwy Gowanda (14070) ***(G-5493)***
Ttg LLC 917 777-0959
115 W 30th St Rm 209 New York (10001) ***(G-11910)***
TTI, Hauppauge *Also called Tarsia Technical Industries* ***(G-5955)***
Tube Fabrication Company Inc 716 673-1871
183 E Main St Ste 10 Fredonia (14063) ***(G-5128)***
Tucano Usa Inc 212 966-9211
77 Bleecker St Apt C212 New York (10012) ***(G-11911)***
Tucker Jones House Inc 631 642-9092
1 Enterprise Dr East Setauket (11733) ***(G-4313)***
Tucker Printers Inc 585 359-3030
270 Middle Rd Henrietta (14467) ***(G-6037)***
Tudor Electrical Supply Co Inc 212 867-7550
137 W 24th St New York (10011) ***(G-11912)***
Tug Hill Vineyards 315 376-4336
4051 Yancey Rd Lowville (13367) ***(G-7657)***
Tulip Molded Plastics Corp 716 282-1261
3123 Highland Ave Niagara Falls (14305) ***(G-12344)***
Tully Products Inc 716 773-3166
2065 Baseline Rd Grand Island (14072) ***(G-5516)***
Tulmar Manufacturing Inc 315 393-7191
101 Tulloch Dr Ogdensburg (13669) ***(G-12580)***
Tumble Forms Inc (PA) 315 429-3101
1013 Barker Rd Dolgeville (13329) ***(G-4138)***
Tumblehome Boatshop 518 623-5050
684 State Route 28 Warrensburg (12885) ***(G-15943)***
Tunaverse Media Inc 631 778-8350
750 Veterans Hwy Ste 200 Hauppauge (11788) ***(G-5962)***
Tunecore Inc (PA) 646 651-1060
45 Main St Ste 705 Brooklyn (11201) ***(G-2591)***
Tunecore Inc 646 651-1060
63 Pearl St Brooklyn (11201) ***(G-2592)***
Tupper Lake Hardwoods Inc 518 359-8248
167 Pitchfork Pond Rd Tupper Lake (12986) ***(G-15655)***
Turbine Arfoil Cating Repr LLC 845 692-8912
105 Tower Dr Middletown (10941) ***(G-8181)***
Turbine Engine Comp Utica 315 768-8070
8273 Halsey Rd Whitesboro (13492) ***(G-16531)***
Turbo Express Inc 718 723-3686
16019 Rockaway Blvd Ste D Jamaica (11434) ***(G-6686)***
Turbo Machined Products LLC 315 895-3010
102 Industrial Dr Frankfort (13340) ***(G-5113)***
Turbofil Packaging Mchs LLC 914 239-3878
30 Beach St Mount Vernon (10550) ***(G-8451)***
Turbopro Inc 716 681-8651
1284 Town Line Rd Alden (14004) ***(G-177)***
Turkprime, Flushing *Also called Prime Research Solutions LLC* ***(G-5040)***
Turn On Products Inc (PA) 212 764-2121
270 W 38th St Rm 1200 New York (10018) ***(G-11913)***
Turn On Products Inc 212 764-4545
525 7th Ave Rm 1403 New York (10018) ***(G-11914)***
Turner Bellows Inc 585 235-4456
526 Child St Ste 1 Rochester (14606) ***(G-14181)***
Turner Plating, New Rochelle *Also called Eric S Turner & Company Inc* ***(G-8602)***
Turner Undgrd Instllations Inc 585 739-0238
1233 Lehigh Station Rd Henrietta (14467) ***(G-6038)***
Turning Point Tool LLC 585 288-7380
135 Dodge St Rochester (14606) ***(G-14182)***
Turoff Tower Graphics Inc 718 856-7300
681 Coney Island Ave Brooklyn (11218) ***(G-2593)***
Tusk Manufacturing Inc 631 567-3349
1371 Church St Ste 1 Bohemia (11716) ***(G-1102)***
Tuthill Corporation 631 727-1097
75 Kings Dr Riverhead (11901) ***(G-13587)***
Tuthilltown Spirits LLC 845 255-1527
14 Gristmill Ln Gardiner (12525) ***(G-5296)***
Tuv Taam Corp 718 855-2207
502 Flushing Ave Brooklyn (11205) ***(G-2594)***
TV Data, Queensbury *Also called Tribune Media Services Inc* ***(G-13444)***
TV Executive, New York *Also called T V Trade Media Inc* ***(G-11772)***
TV Guide Magazine LLC (HQ) 800 866-1400
50 Rockefeller Plz Fl 14 New York (10020) ***(G-11915)***
TV Guide Magazine Group Inc (HQ) 212 852-7500
1211 Ave Of The Americas New York (10036) ***(G-11916)***
TV Guilfoil & Associates Inc (PA) 315 453-0920
121 Dwight Park Cir Syracuse (13209) ***(G-15447)***
TVI Imports LLC 631 793-3077
178 Abbey St Massapequa Park (11762) ***(G-7895)***
Twcc Product and Sales 212 614-9364
122 5th Ave New York (10011) ***(G-11917)***
Twenty-First Century Press Inc 716 837-0800
501 Cornwall Ave Buffalo (14215) ***(G-3106)***
Twentyone Brix Winery, Portland *Also called Olde Chtqua Vneyards Ltd Lblty* ***(G-13315)***
TWI Watches LLC 718 663-3969
4014 1st Ave Brooklyn (11232) ***(G-2595)***
TWI-Laq Industries Inc 718 638-5860
1345 Seneca Ave Bronx (10474) ***(G-1410)***
Twin Counties Pro Printers Inc 518 828-3278
59 Fairview Ave Hudson (12534) ***(G-6374)***
Twin County Recycling Corp (PA) 516 827-6900
113 Magnolia Ave Westbury (11590) ***(G-16383)***
Twin Lake Chemical Inc 716 433-3824
520 Mill St Lockport (14094) ***(G-7339)***
Twin Marquis Inc (HQ) 718 386-6868
7 Bushwick Pl Brooklyn (11206) ***(G-2596)***
Twin Pane Insulated GL Co Inc 631 924-1060
86 Horseblock Rd Unit D Yaphank (11980) ***(G-16725)***
Twin Rivers Paper Company LLC 315 348-8491
Lyonsdale Rd Lyons Falls (13368) ***(G-7690)***
Twin Rivers Paper Company LLC 315 823-2300
501 W Main St Little Falls (13365) ***(G-7215)***
Twinco Mfg Co Inc 631 231-0022
30 Commerce Dr Hauppauge (11788) ***(G-5963)***
Twinkle Lighting Inc 718 225-0939
13114 40th Rd Flushing (11354) ***(G-5056)***
Twist Intimate Apparel, New York *Also called Twist Intimate Group LLC* ***(G-11918)***
Twist Intimate Group LLC (PA) 212 695-5990
35 W 35th St Rm 903 New York (10001) ***(G-11918)***
Twist It Top It 718 793-8947
10309 Metropolitan Ave Forest Hills (11375) ***(G-5081)***
Two Bills Machine & Tool Co 516 437-2585
17 Concord St Floral Park (11001) ***(G-4965)***
Two Palms Press Inc 212 965-8598
476 Broadway Ste 3f New York (10013) ***(G-11919)***
Two Worlds Arts Ltd 212 929-2210
307 Kingsland Ave Brooklyn (11222) ***(G-2597)***
Two Worlds Arts Ltd (PA) 212 929-2210
122 W 18th St New York (10011) ***(G-11920)***
Two-Four Software, New York *Also called F-O-R Software LLC* ***(G-9766)***
Two-Four Software, White Plains *Also called F-O-R Software LLC* ***(G-16449)***
Twp America Inc (HQ) 212 274-8090
299 Broadway Ste 720 New York (10007) ***(G-11921)***
TX Rx Systems Inc 716 549-4700
8625 Industrial Pkwy Angola (14006) ***(G-371)***
Tyco Simplexgrinnell 315 437-9664
6731 Collamer Rd Ste 4 East Syracuse (13057) ***(G-4376)***
Tycoon International Inc 212 563-7107
3436 W 32nd St Fl 4 Flr 4 New York (10001) ***(G-11922)***
Tyme Global Technologies LLC 212 796-1950
60 W 66th St Apt 15a New York (10023) ***(G-11923)***
Tyme Inc 646 205-1603
48 Wall St Ste 1100 New York (10005) ***(G-11924)***
Tyme Technologies Inc (PA) 212 461-2315
17 State St Fl 7 New York (10004) ***(G-11925)***
Tymetal Corp (HQ) 518 692-9930
678 Wilbur Ave Greenwich (12834) ***(G-5646)***
Tymor Park 845 724-5691
249 Duncan Rd Lagrangeville (12540) ***(G-6963)***
U All Inc 518 438-2558
9 Interstate Ave Albany (12205) ***(G-136)***
U B J, New York *Also called United Brothers Jewelry Inc* ***(G-11952)***
U E Systems Incorporated (PA) 914 592-1220
14 Hayes St Elmsford (10523) ***(G-4575)***
U K Sailmakers, Port Chester *Also called Ulmer Sales LLC* ***(G-13210)***
U S Air Tool Co Inc (PA) 631 471-3300
60 Fleetwood Ct Ronkonkoma (11779) ***(G-14423)***
U S Air Tool International, Ronkonkoma *Also called U S Air Tool Co Inc* ***(G-14423)***
U S Energy Development Corp (PA) 716 636-0401
2350 N Forest Rd Getzville (14068) ***(G-5354)***
U S Japan Publication NY Inc 212 252-8833
147 W 35th St Ste 1705 New York (10001) ***(G-11926)***
U S Orthotic Center, New York *Also called Custom Sports Lab Inc* ***(G-9436)***
U S Plychmical Overseas Corp 845 356-5530
584 Chestnut Ridge Rd # 586 Chestnut Ridge (10977) ***(G-3498)***

U S Sugar Co Inc 716 828-1170
692 Bailey Ave Buffalo (14206) *(G-3107)*
U S TEC, Victor *Also called 331 Holding Inc (G-15827)*
U S Tech Corporation 315 437-7207
6511 Basile Rowe East Syracuse (13057) *(G-4377)*
U Serve Brands Inc 877 632-6654
345 7th Ave Rm 501 New York (10001) *(G-11927)*
U X World Inc 914 375-6167
245 Saw Mill River Rd # 106 Hawthorne (10532) *(G-5998)*
U-Cut Enterprises Inc 315 492-9316
4800 Solvay Rd Jamesville (13078) *(G-6771)*
U2o Usa LLC 516 813-9500
206 Terminal Dr Plainview (11803) *(G-13094)*
Ubec, Salamanca *Also called Highland Injection Molding (G-14525)*
Ubees Inc 916 505-8470
575 5th Ave 21 New York (10017) *(G-11928)*
Ubm Inc 212 600-3000
2 Penn Plz New York (10121) *(G-11929)*
Ubm LLC (HQ) 516 562-7800
1983 Marcus Ave Ste 250 New Hyde Park (11042) *(G-8568)*
Ubm LLC 516 562-5000
2 Penn Plz Fl 15 New York (10121) *(G-11930)*
Ubm Tech, New Hyde Park *Also called Ubm LLC (G-8568)*
Uc Coatings LLC (PA) 716 833-9366
2250 Fillmore Ave Buffalo (14214) *(G-3108)*
Ucb Pharma Inc (PA) 919 767-2555
755 Jefferson Rd Rochester (14623) *(G-14183)*
Ucc Guide Inc (PA) 518 434-0909
99 Washington Ave Albany (12210) *(G-137)*
Ucr Steel Group LLC (PA) 718 764-3414
90 Trade Zone Ct Ronkonkoma (11779) *(G-14424)*
Udisense Inc 866 696-2648
315 W 36th St Fl 2 New York (10018) *(G-11931)*
Ue Music, New York *Also called Universal Edition Inc (G-11959)*
Ufc Biotechnology 716 777-3776
1576 Sweet Home Rd # 225 Amherst (14228) *(G-258)*
Ufo Contemporary Inc 212 226-5400
42 W 38th St Rm 1204 New York (10018) *(G-11932)*
Ufp New York LLC 716 496-5484
13989 E Schutt Rd Chaffee (14030) *(G-3405)*
Ufp New York LLC 518 828-2888
11 Falls Industrial Pk Rd Hudson (12534) *(G-6375)*
Ufp New York LLC (HQ) 315 253-2758
11 Allen St Auburn (13021) *(G-507)*
Ufp New York LLC 607 563-1556
13 Winkler Rd Sidney (13838) *(G-14856)*
UFS Industries Inc 718 822-1100
300 N Macquesten Pkwy Mount Vernon (10550) *(G-8452)*
Ufx Holding I Corporation (HQ) 212 644-5900
55 E 52nd St Fl 35 New York (10055) *(G-11933)*
Ufx Holding II Corporation (HQ) 212 644-5900
55 E 52nd St Fl 35 New York (10055) *(G-11934)*
UGI, Brooklyn *Also called United Gemdiam Inc (G-2602)*
Uhmac Inc 716 537-2343
136 N Main St Holland (14080) *(G-6223)*
Ui Acquisition Holding Co (PA) 607 779-7522
33 Broome Corporate Pkwy Conklin (13748) *(G-3736)*
Ui Holding Company (HQ) 607 779-7522
33 Broome Corporate Pkwy Conklin (13748) *(G-3737)*
UI Corp 201 203-4453
3812 Corporal Stone St # 2 Bayside (11361) *(G-750)*
UI Information & Insights Inc (HQ) 518 640-9200
23 British American Blvd # 2 Latham (12110) *(G-7096)*
Ullink Inc (HQ) 646 565-6675
11 Times Sq Ste 31d New York (10036) *(G-11935)*
Ulmer Sales LLC 718 885-1700
10 Midland Ave Ste 1 Port Chester (10573) *(G-13210)*
Ulrich Planfiling Eqp Corp 716 763-1815
2120 4th Ave Lakewood (14750) *(G-6998)*
Ulrich Sign Co Inc 716 434-0167
177 Oakhurst St Lockport (14094) *(G-7340)*
Ulster County Iron Works LLC 845 255-0003
64 N Putt Corners Rd New Paltz (12561) *(G-8582)*
Ulster County Press Office 845 687-4480
1209 State Route 213 High Falls (12440) *(G-6141)*
Ulster Precision Inc 845 338-0995
100 Lipton St Kingston (12401) *(G-6925)*
Ulster Publishing Co Inc (PA) 845 334-8205
322 Wall St Fl 1 Kingston (12401) *(G-6926)*
Ulster Publishing Co Inc 845 255-7005
29 S Chestnut St Ste 101 New Paltz (12561) *(G-8583)*
Ultimate Pavers Corp 917 417-2652
659 Quincy Ave Staten Island (10305) *(G-15149)*
Ultimate Prcision Met Pdts Inc 631 249-9441
200 Finn Ct Farmingdale (11735) *(G-4901)*
Ultimate Signs & Designs Inc 516 481-0800
86 Sewell St Hempstead (11550) *(G-6027)*
Ultimate Styles of America 631 254-0219
27 Garfield Ave Unit A Bay Shore (11706) *(G-733)*
Ultra Clarity Corp 719 470-1010
3101 Parkview Dr Spring Valley (10977) *(G-15010)*
Ultra Elec Flightline Systems, Victor *Also called Flightline Electronics Inc (G-15847)*
Ultra Electronics Inc, Victor *Also called Magnet-Ndctive Systems Ltd USA (G-15856)*
Ultra Electronics, Ems, Yaphank *Also called Ems Development Corporation (G-16708)*
Ultra Fine Jewelry Mfg 516 349-2848
180 Dupont St Unit C Plainview (11803) *(G-13095)*
Ultra Thin Pzza Shlls Fltbrads, Deer Park *Also called Ultra Thin Ready To Bake Pizza (G-4053)*
Ultra Thin Ready To Bake Pizza 516 679-6655
151 E Industry Ct Deer Park (11729) *(G-4053)*
Ultra Tool and Manufacturing 585 467-3700
159 Lagrange Ave Rochester (14613) *(G-14184)*
Ultra-Scan Corporation 716 832-6269
4240 Ridge Lea Rd Ste 10 Amherst (14226) *(G-259)*
Ultradian Diagnostics LLC 518 618-0046
5 University Pl A324 Rensselaer (12144) *(G-13479)*
Ultraflex Power Technologies 631 467-6814
158 Remington Blvd Ste 2 Ronkonkoma (11779) *(G-14425)*
Ultralife Corporation (PA) 315 332-7100
2000 Technology Pkwy Newark (14513) *(G-12209)*
Ultrapedics Ltd (PA) 718 748-4806
355 Ovington Ave Ste 104 Brooklyn (11209) *(G-2598)*
Ultravolt Inc 631 471-4444
1800 Ocean Ave Unit A Ronkonkoma (11779) *(G-14426)*
Ultrepet LLC 781 275-6400
136c Fuller Rd Albany (12205) *(G-138)*
Umbro Machine & Tool Co Inc 845 876-4669
3811 Route 9g Rhinebeck (12572) *(G-13489)*
Umi, New York *Also called Urban Mapping Inc (G-11969)*
Umicore Technical Materials 518 792-7700
9 Pruyns Island Dr Glens Falls (12801) *(G-5441)*
Umicore USA Inc 919 874-7171
9 Pruyns Island Dr Glens Falls (12801) *(G-5442)*
Ums Manufacturing LLC 518 562-2410
194 Pleasant Ridge Rd Plattsburgh (12901) *(G-13164)*
Unadilla Laminated Products, Sidney *Also called Unadilla Silo Company Inc (G-14857)*
Unadilla Silo Company Inc 607 369-9341
100 West Rd Sidney (13838) *(G-14857)*
Uncharted Power Inc 646 675-7783
527 W 125th St New York (10027) *(G-11936)*
Uncle Wallys LLC 631 205-0455
41 Natcon Dr Shirley (11967) *(G-14844)*
Under Armour Inc 518 761-6787
1444 State Route 9 Lake George (12845) *(G-6966)*
Underline Communications LLC 212 994-4340
12 W 27th St Fl 14 New York (10001) *(G-11937)*
Uneeda Enterprizes Inc 800 431-2494
640 Chestnut Ridge Rd Spring Valley (10977) *(G-15011)*
UNI Jewelry Inc 212 398-1818
48 W 48th St Ste 1401 New York (10036) *(G-11938)*
UNI Source Technology 514 748-8888
1320 Rt 9 Champlain (12919) *(G-3415)*
Unicel Corporation 760 741-3912
235 W Industry Ct Deer Park (11729) *(G-4054)*
Unicell Body Company Inc (PA) 716 853-8628
571 Howard St Buffalo (14206) *(G-3109)*
Unicell Body Company Inc 716 853-8628
170 Cordell Rd Schenectady (12303) *(G-14723)*
Unicell Body Company Inc 585 424-2660
1319 Brighton Henrietta Rochester (14623) *(G-14185)*
Unicenter Millwork Inc 716 741-8201
9605 Clarence Center Rd Clarence Center (14032) *(G-3550)*
Unico Special Products Inc 845 562-9255
25 Renwick St Newburgh (12550) *(G-12248)*
Unicorn Graphics, Garden City *Also called Won & Lee Inc (G-5284)*
Unidex Company, Warsaw *Also called Unidex Corporation Western NY (G-15946)*
Unidex Corporation Western NY 585 786-3170
2416 State Route 19 N Warsaw (14569) *(G-15946)*
Unifab Inc 585 235-1760
215 Tremont St Ste 31 Rochester (14608) *(G-14186)*
Unified Inc led 646 370-4650
35 W 36th St New York (10018) *(G-11939)*
Unified Media Inc 917 595-2710
180 Madison Ave Lbby L New York (10016) *(G-11940)*
Unified Solutions For Clg Inc 718 782-8800
1829 Pacific St Brooklyn (11233) *(G-2599)*
Uniflex Holdings LLC (PA) 516 932-2000
1600 Caleds Ext Ste 135 Hauppauge (11788) *(G-5964)*
Unifor Inc 212 673-3434
149 5th Ave Ste 3r New York (10010) *(G-11941)*
Uniform Express, Rochester *Also called Kevin J Kassman (G-13904)*
Uniform Namemakers Inc 716 626-5474
55 Amherst Villa Rd Buffalo (14225) *(G-3110)*
Uniformed Fire Officer Assoiat 212 293-9300
125 Maiden Ln New York (10038) *(G-11942)*
Uniforms By Park Coats Inc 718 499-1182
790 3rd Ave Brooklyn (11232) *(G-2600)*
Unifrax Corporation 716 278-3800
2351 Whirlpool St Niagara Falls (14305) *(G-12345)*
Unifrax Holding Co (HQ) 212 644-5900
55 E 52nd St Fl 35 New York (10055) *(G-11943)*
Unifrax I LLC 716 696-3000
360 Fire Tower Dr Tonawanda (14150) *(G-15586)*

ALPHABETIC

Unifrax I LLC (HQ) ALPHABETIC SECTION

Unifrax I LLC (HQ).....716 768-6500
600 Rverwalk Pkwy Ste 120 Tonawanda (14150) ***(G-15587)***
Unifuse LLC.....845 889-4000
2092 Route 9g Staatsburg (12580) ***(G-15025)***
Unike Products Inc.....347 686-4616
18230 Wexford Ter Apt 2m Jamaica (11432) ***(G-6687)***
Unilever United States Inc.....212 546-0200
390 Park Ave New York (10022) ***(G-11944)***
Unilever United States Inc.....212 546-0200
663 5th Ave Fl 8 New York (10022) ***(G-11945)***
Unilock Ltd.....716 822-6074
510 Smith St Buffalo (14210) ***(G-3111)***
Unilock New York Inc (HQ).....845 278-6700
51 International Blvd Brewster (10509) ***(G-1175)***
Unilux Advanced Mfg LLC.....518 344-7490
30 Commerce Park Rd Schenectady (12309) ***(G-14724)***
Unimar Inc.....315 699-4400
3195 Vickery Rd Syracuse (13212) ***(G-15448)***
Unimex Corporation (PA).....212 755-8800
54 E 64th St New York (10065) ***(G-11946)***
Unimex Corporation.....718 236-2222
1462 62nd St Brooklyn (11219) ***(G-2601)***
Union Standard & Un Conf McHy, Bronx *Also called National Equipment Corporation* ***(G-1338)***
Union Standard Eqp Co Div, Harrison *Also called National Equipment Corporation* ***(G-5731)***
Union Sun & Journal, Lockport *Also called Cnhi LLC* ***(G-7291)***
Unipharm Inc.....212 594-3260
350 5th Ave Ste 6701 New York (10118) ***(G-11947)***
Uniqlo USA LLC.....877 486-4756
546 Broadway New York (10012) ***(G-11948)***
Unique Designs Inc.....212 575-7701
521 5th Ave Rm 820 New York (10175) ***(G-11949)***
Unique Display Mfg Corp (PA).....516 546-3800
216 N Main St Ste D Freeport (11520) ***(G-5189)***
Unique MBL Gran Orgnztion Corp.....718 482-0440
3831 9th St Long Island City (11101) ***(G-7622)***
Unique Overseas Inc.....516 466-9792
425 Northern Blvd Ste 22 Great Neck (11021) ***(G-5597)***
Unique Packaging Corporation.....514 341-5872
11320 State Route 9 # 3807 Champlain (12919) ***(G-3416)***
Unique Petz LLC.....212 714-1800
10 W 33rd St Rm 220 New York (10001) ***(G-11950)***
Unique Quality Fabrics Inc.....845 343-3070
115 Wisner Ave Middletown (10940) ***(G-8182)***
Unisend LLC.....585 414-9575
249 Gallant Fox Ln Webster (14580) ***(G-16104)***
Unison Industries LLC.....607 335-5000
5345 State Highway 12 Norwich (13815) ***(G-12494)***
Unisource Food Eqp Systems Inc.....516 681-0537
1505 Lincoln Ave Holbrook (11741) ***(G-6217)***
Unistel LLC.....585 341-4600
860 Hard Rd Webster (14580) ***(G-16105)***
Unisystems Inc (PA).....212 826-0850
155 E 55th St Apt 203 New York (10022) ***(G-11951)***
Unit Step Company, Sanborn *Also called Gamble & Gamble Inc* ***(G-14546)***
United Baking Co Inc.....631 413-5116
16 Bronx Ave Central Islip (11722) ***(G-3387)***
United Baking Co Inc (PA).....631 205-0455
41 Natcon Dr Shirley (11967) ***(G-14845)***
United Biochemicals LLC.....716 731-5161
6351 Inducon Dr E Sanborn (14132) ***(G-14555)***
United Brothers Jewelry Inc.....212 921-2558
48 W 48th St Ste 700 New York (10036) ***(G-11952)***
United Business Forms, Long Island City *Also called United Print Group Inc* ***(G-7623)***
United Data Systems Inc.....631 549-6900
202 E Main St Ste 302 Huntington (11743) ***(G-6423)***
United Dividers, Elmira *Also called Fennell Industries LLC* ***(G-4487)***
United Farm Processing Corp (PA).....718 933-6060
4366 Park Ave Bronx (10457) ***(G-1411)***
United Gemdiam Inc.....718 851-5083
1537 52nd St Brooklyn (11219) ***(G-2602)***
United Iron Inc.....914 667-5700
6 Roslyn Pl Mount Vernon (10550) ***(G-8453)***
United Knitwear International (PA).....212 354-2920
1384 Broadway Rm 1210 New York (10018) ***(G-11953)***
United Machining Inc.....631 589-6751
1595 Smithtown Ave Ste D Bohemia (11716) ***(G-1103)***
United Materials LLC (PA).....716 683-1432
3949 Frest Pk Way Ste 400 North Tonawanda (14120) ***(G-12461)***
United Materials LLC.....716 731-2332
2186 Cory Dr Sanborn (14132) ***(G-14556)***
United Materials LLC.....716 662-0564
75 Bank St Orchard Park (14127) ***(G-12748)***
United Metal Industries Inc.....516 354-6800
1008 3rd Ave New Hyde Park (11040) ***(G-8569)***
United Pet Group, Hauppauge *Also called Spectrum Brands Inc* ***(G-5945)***
United Pickle Products Corp.....718 933-6060
4366 Park Ave Bronx (10457) ***(G-1412)***
United Pipe Nipple Co Inc.....516 295-2468
1602 Lakeview Dr Hewlett (11557) ***(G-6052)***
United Plastics Inc.....718 389-2255
640 Humboldt St Ste 1 Brooklyn (11222) ***(G-2603)***
United Print Group Inc.....718 392-4242
3636 33rd St Ste 303 Long Island City (11106) ***(G-7623)***
United Retail II.....212 966-9692
436 W Broadway New York (10012) ***(G-11954)***
United Richter Electrical Mtrs.....716 855-1945
106 Michigan Ave Buffalo (14204) ***(G-3112)***
United Rockland Holding Co Inc.....845 357-1900
9 N Airmont Rd Suffern (10901) ***(G-15199)***
United Satcom Inc.....718 359-4100
4555 Robinson St Flushing (11355) ***(G-5057)***
United Sheet Metal Corp.....718 482-1197
4602 28th St Long Island City (11101) ***(G-7624)***
United Silicone Inc.....716 681-8222
4471 Walden Ave Lancaster (14086) ***(G-7052)***
United States Gypsum Company.....585 948-5221
2750 Maple Ave Oakfield (14125) ***(G-12525)***
United Steel Products Inc.....914 968-7782
3340 127th Pl Flushing (11368) ***(G-5058)***
United Steel Products Inc.....718 478-5330
3340 127th Pl Corona (11368) ***(G-3856)***
United Structure Solution Inc.....347 227-7526
240 W 65th St Apt 26c New York (10023) ***(G-11955)***
United Sttes Brnze Sign of Fla.....516 352-5155
811 2nd Ave New Hyde Park (11040) ***(G-8570)***
United Supply Systems, Syosset *Also called Paradigm Mktg Consortium Inc* ***(G-15227)***
United Synggue Cnsrvtive Jdism (PA).....212 533-7800
120 Broadway Ste 1540 New York (10271) ***(G-11956)***
United Technologies Corp.....315 432-7849
6304 Carrier Pkwy East Syracuse (13057) ***(G-4378)***
United Technologies Corp.....866 788-5095
1212 Pittsford Victor Rd Pittsford (14534) ***(G-13027)***
United Thread Mills Corp (PA).....516 536-3900
3530 Lawson Blvd Gf Oceanside (11572) ***(G-12562)***
United Transit Mix Inc.....718 416-3400
318 Boerum St Brooklyn (11206) ***(G-2604)***
United Wind Inc.....888 313-3353
195 Plymouth St Brooklyn (11201) ***(G-2605)***
United Wire Technologies Inc.....315 623-7203
1804 State Route 49 Constantia (13044) ***(G-3741)***
United-Guardian Inc (PA).....631 273-0900
230 Marcus Blvd Hauppauge (11788) ***(G-5965)***
Unither Manufacturing LLC.....585 475-9000
755 Jefferson Rd Rochester (14623) ***(G-14187)***
Unither Manufacturing LLC.....585 274-5430
331 Clay Rd Rochester (14623) ***(G-14188)***
Unitone Communication Systems.....212 777-9090
220 E 23rd St Ste 411 New York (10010) ***(G-11957)***
Universal 3d Innovation Inc.....516 837-9423
1085 Rockaway Ave Valley Stream (11581) ***(G-15801)***
Universal Armor Systems Corp.....631 838-1836
9 Tanners Ln Levittown (11756) ***(G-7136)***
Universal Builders Supply Inc.....845 758-8801
45 Ocallaghan Ln Red Hook (12571) ***(G-13459)***
Universal Cmmncations of Miami.....212 986-5100
801 2nd Ave Lbby New York (10017) ***(G-11958)***
Universal Coolers Inc.....718 788-8621
120 13th St Brooklyn (11215) ***(G-2606)***
Universal Custom Millwork Inc.....518 330-6622
3 Sam Stratton Rd Amsterdam (12010) ***(G-362)***
Universal Designs Inc.....718 721-1111
3517 31st St Long Island City (11106) ***(G-7625)***
Universal Edition Inc.....917 213-2177
331 W 57th St Ste 380 New York (10019) ***(G-11959)***
Universal Elliot Corp.....212 736-8877
327 W 36th St Rm 700 New York (10018) ***(G-11960)***
Universal Fire Proof Door.....718 455-8442
1171 Myrtle Ave Brooklyn (11206) ***(G-2607)***
Universal Forest Products, Chaffee *Also called Ufp New York LLC* ***(G-3405)***
Universal Forest Products, Hudson *Also called Ufp New York LLC* ***(G-6375)***
Universal Forest Products, Auburn *Also called Ufp New York LLC* ***(G-507)***
Universal Instruments Corp (HQ).....800 842-9732
33 Broome Corporate Pkwy Conklin (13748) ***(G-3738)***
Universal Interiors LLC.....518 298-4400
107 Lawrence Paquette Dr Champlain (12919) ***(G-3417)***
Universal Metal Fabricators.....845 331-8248
27 Emerick St Kingston (12401) ***(G-6927)***
Universal Metal Works LLC.....315 598-7607
159 Hubbard St Fulton (13069) ***(G-5233)***
Universal Metals Inc.....516 829-0896
98 Cuttermill Rd Ste 428 Great Neck (11021) ***(G-5598)***
Universal Mus Group Hldngs Inc (HQ).....212 333-8000
1755 Broadway Fl 6 New York (10019) ***(G-11961)***
Universal Music Group Inc.....212 333-8237
825 8th Ave Fl C2b New York (10019) ***(G-11962)***
Universal Packg Systems Inc (PA).....631 543-2277
380 Townline Rd Ste 130 Hauppauge (11788) ***(G-5966)***
Universal Parent and Youth.....917 754-2426
1530 Pa Ave Apt 17e Brooklyn (11239) ***(G-2608)***
Universal Precision Corp.....585 321-9760
40 Commerce Dr Rochester (14623) ***(G-14189)***
Universal Proteins, Amityville *Also called Natural Organics Labs Inc* ***(G-305)***
Universal Ready Mix Inc.....516 746-4535
197 Atlantic Ave New Hyde Park (11040) ***(G-8571)***

Universal Remote Control Inc (PA)....914 630-4343
500 Mmaroneck Ave Ste 502 Harrison (10528) ***(G-5738)***
Universal Screening Associates....718 232-2744
6509 11th Ave Brooklyn (11219) ***(G-2609)***
Universal Shielding Corp....631 667-7900
20 W Jefryn Blvd Deer Park (11729) ***(G-4055)***
Universal Signs and Svc Inc....631 446-1121
435 Brook Ave Unit 2 Deer Park (11729) ***(G-4056)***
Universal Steel Fabricators....718 342-0782
90 Junius St Brooklyn (11212) ***(G-2610)***
Universal Step Inc....315 437-7611
5970 Butternut Dr East Syracuse (13057) ***(G-4379)***
Universal Thin Film Lab Corp....845 562-0601
232 N Plank Rd Newburgh (12550) ***(G-12249)***
Universal Tooling Corporation....716 985-4691
4533 Route 60 Gerry (14740) ***(G-5342)***
Universal Water Technology, Far Rockaway *Also called Business Advisory Services* ***(G-4698)***
Universe Publishing, New York *Also called Rizzoli Intl Publications Inc* ***(G-11399)***
University Advertising Agency, Stony Brook *Also called Stony Brook University* ***(G-15169)***
University of Rochester....585 275-3483
250 E River Rd Rochester (14623) ***(G-14190)***
University Table Cloth Company....845 371-3876
10 Centre St Spring Valley (10977) ***(G-15012)***
Uniware Houseware Corp (PA)....631 242-7400
120 Wilshire Blvd Ste B Brentwood (11717) ***(G-1146)***
Unlimited Ink Inc....631 582-0696
595 Old Willets Path B Hauppauge (11788) ***(G-5967)***
Unqork Inc....844 486-7675
85 5th Ave Fl 6 New York (10003) ***(G-11963)***
Untitled Media....212 780-0960
45 Lispenard St Apt 1w New York (10013) ***(G-11964)***
Untuckit LLC (PA)....201 214-9054
110 Greene St Ste 400 New York (10012) ***(G-11965)***
Untuckit LLC....646 724-1857
379 W Broadway Fl 2 New York (10012) ***(G-11966)***
UOP LLC....716 879-7600
175 E Park Dr Tonawanda (14150) ***(G-15588)***
Up Country, New York *Also called Du Monde Trading Inc* ***(G-9581)***
Upayori, Brooklyn *Also called Universal Parent and Youth* ***(G-2608)***
Uppercut, Suffern *Also called NY Cutting Inc* ***(G-15194)***
Upstate Cabinet Company Inc....585 429-5090
32 Marway Cir Rochester (14624) ***(G-14191)***
Upstate Door Inc....585 786-3880
26 Industrial St Warsaw (14569) ***(G-15947)***
Upstate Farms Cheese LLC....607 527-4584
8600 Main St Campbell (14821) ***(G-3205)***
Upstate Increte Incorporated....585 254-2010
49 Adelaide St Rochester (14606) ***(G-14192)***
Upstate Insulated Glass Inc....315 475-4960
47 Weber Rd Central Square (13036) ***(G-3393)***
Upstate Milk Co-Operatives, Buffalo *Also called Upstate Niagara Coop Inc* ***(G-3114)***
Upstate Niagara Coop Inc (PA)....716 892-3156
25 Anderson Rd Buffalo (14225) ***(G-3113)***
Upstate Niagara Coop Inc....716 892-2121
1730 Dale Rd Buffalo (14225) ***(G-3114)***
Upstate Niagara Coop Inc....585 458-1880
45 Fulton Ave Rochester (14608) ***(G-14193)***
Upstate Niagara Coop Inc....716 484-7178
223 Fluvanna Ave Jamestown (14701) ***(G-6759)***
Upstate Niagara Coop Inc....315 389-5111
22 County Route 52 North Lawrence (12967) ***(G-12393)***
Upstate Office Furniture, Johnson City *Also called Upstate Office Liquidators Inc* ***(G-6822)***
Upstate Office Liquidators Inc....607 722-9234
718 Azon Rd Johnson City (13790) ***(G-6822)***
Upstate Piping Products Inc....518 238-3457
95 Hudson River Rd Waterford (12188) ***(G-15989)***
Upstate Printing Inc....315 475-6140
433 W Onondaga St Syracuse (13202) ***(G-15449)***
Upstate Records Management LLC....518 834-1144
1729 Front St Keeseville (12944) ***(G-6855)***
Upstate Refractory Svcs Inc....315 331-2955
100 Erie Blvd Newark (14513) ***(G-12210)***
Upstate Tube Inc....315 488-5636
5050 Smoral Rd Camillus (13031) ***(G-3199)***
Upstone Materials Inc....518 873-2275
Rr 9 Lewis (12950) ***(G-7137)***
Upstone Materials Inc....518 891-0236
909 State Route 3 Saranac Lake (12983) ***(G-14564)***
Upstone Materials Inc (HQ)....518 561-5321
111 Quarry Rd Plattsburgh (12901) ***(G-13165)***
Upstone Materials Inc....518 483-2671
359 Elm St Malone (12953) ***(G-7729)***
Upstone Materials Inc....315 265-8036
111 Quarry Rd Plattsburgh (12901) ***(G-13166)***
Upstone Materials Inc....315 764-0251
539 S Main St Massena (13662) ***(G-7910)***
Uptek Solutions Corp....631 256-5565
130 Knickerbocker Ave A Bohemia (11716) ***(G-1104)***
Uptown, Halfmoon *Also called Save More Beverage Corp* ***(G-5669)***
Uptown Media Group LLC....212 360-5073
113 E 125th St Frnt 1 New York (10035) ***(G-11967)***
Upturn Industries Inc....607 967-2923
2-4 Whitney Way Bainbridge (13733) ***(G-536)***
Urban Apparel Group Inc....212 947-7009
226 W 37th St Fl 17 New York (10018) ***(G-11968)***
Urban Mapping Inc....415 946-8170
295 Madison Ave Rm 1010 New York (10017) ***(G-11969)***
Urban Precast LLC....845 331-6299
6 Kieffer Ln Kingston (12401) ***(G-6928)***
Urban Rose, New York *Also called French Atmosphere Inc* ***(G-9846)***
Urban Technologies Inc....716 672-2709
3451 Stone Quarry Rd Fredonia (14063) ***(G-5129)***
Urban Textiles Inc....212 777-1900
254 W 35th St Unit 13 New York (10001) ***(G-11970)***
Urban Woodworks Ltd....718 827-1570
18 Crescent St Brooklyn (11208) ***(G-2611)***
Urbandaddy Inc....212 929-7905
900 Broadway Ste 1003 New York (10003) ***(G-11971)***
Urdu Times....718 297-8700
16920 Hillside Ave Jamaica (11432) ***(G-6688)***
Urrey Lumber....518 827-4851
663 Clauverwie Rd Middleburgh (12122) ***(G-8130)***
Ursula Company Store, Waterford *Also called Ursula of Switzerland Inc* ***(G-15990)***
Ursula of Switzerland Inc (PA)....518 237-2580
31 Mohawk Ave Waterford (12188) ***(G-15990)***
Urthworx Inc....646 373-7535
320 W 106th St Apt 2f New York (10025) ***(G-11972)***
US Airports Flight Support Svc, Rochester *Also called Usairports Services Inc* ***(G-14194)***
US Allegro Inc....347 408-6601
5430 44th St Maspeth (11378) ***(G-7874)***
US Alliance Paper Inc....631 254-3030
101 Heartland Blvd Edgewood (11717) ***(G-4422)***
US Angels, New York *Also called S & C Bridals LLC* ***(G-11455)***
US Authentic LLC....914 767-0295
11 Mt Holly Rd E Katonah (10536) ***(G-6847)***
US Beverage Net Inc....315 579-2025
225 W Jefferson St Syracuse (13202) ***(G-15450)***
US China Magazine....212 663-4333
200 W 95th St Apt 21 New York (10025) ***(G-11973)***
US Concrete Inc....718 853-4644
10 Powerhouse Rd Roslyn Heights (11577) ***(G-14461)***
US Concrete Inc....718 438-6800
692 Mcdonald Ave Brooklyn (11218) ***(G-2612)***
US Design Group Ltd....212 354-4070
1385 Broadway Rm 1905 New York (10018) ***(G-11974)***
US Diagnostics Inc....866 216-5308
711 3rd Ave Rm 1502 New York (10017) ***(G-11975)***
US Drives Inc....716 731-1606
2221 Niagara Falls Blvd # 41 Niagara Falls (14304) ***(G-12346)***
US Electroplating Corp....631 293-1998
100 Field St Unit A West Babylon (11704) ***(G-16201)***
US Energy Group, New Hyde Park *Also called Use Acquisition LLC* ***(G-8572)***
US Epoxy Inc....800 332-3883
11 Old Dock Rd Unit 7 Yaphank (11980) ***(G-16726)***
US Frontline News Inc....212 922-9090
228 E 45th St Rm 700 New York (10017) ***(G-11976)***
US Global Lubricants Inc....845 271-4277
22 Hudson Dr Stony Point (10980) ***(G-15178)***
US Health Equipment Company....845 658-7576
138 Maple Hill Rd Kingston (12401) ***(G-6929)***
US Hoists Corp....631 472-3030
800 Burman Blvd Calverton (11933) ***(G-3175)***
US Home Textiles Group LLC....212 768-3030
1400 Broadway Fl 18 New York (10018) ***(G-11977)***
US Juice Partners LLC (HQ)....516 621-1122
2 Seaview Blvd Port Washington (11050) ***(G-13312)***
US News & World Report Inc (PA)....212 716-6800
120 5th Ave Fl 7 New York (10011) ***(G-11978)***
US Nonwovens Corp (PA)....631 952-0100
100 Emjay Blvd Brentwood (11717) ***(G-1147)***
US Peroxide....716 775-5585
1815 Love Rd Ste 1 Grand Island (14072) ***(G-5517)***
US Polychemical Holding Corp....845 356-5530
584 Chestnut Ridge Rd Spring Valley (10977) ***(G-15013)***
US Pump Corp....516 303-7799
707 Woodfield Rd West Hempstead (11552) ***(G-16226)***
US Salt LLC....607 535-2721
Salt Point Rd Watkins Glen (14891) ***(G-16062)***
US Sander LLC....518 875-9157
4131 Rte 20 Esperance (12066) ***(G-4622)***
US Sweeteners Corp....718 854-8714
133-48 St Brooklyn (11232) ***(G-2613)***
US Weekly LLC....212 484-1616
1290 Ave Of The Americas New York (10104) ***(G-11979)***
USA Body Inc....315 852-6123
994 Middle Lake Rd De Ruyter (13052) ***(G-3929)***
USA Custom Pad Corp (PA)....607 563-9550
16 Winkler Rd Sidney (13838) ***(G-14858)***
USA Foil Inc....631 234-5252
445 Sills Rd Yaphank (11980) ***(G-16727)***
USA Halal Foods Inc....718 291-9111
4700 Northern Blvd Long Island City (11101) ***(G-7626)***
USA Illumination Inc....845 565-8500
1126 River Rd New Windsor (12553) ***(G-8662)***

ALPHABETIC

(PA)=Parent Co (HQ)=Headquarters (DH)=Div Headquarters

USA Sealing Inc ...716 288-9952
356 Sonwil Dr Cheektowaga (14225) ***(G-3462)***
USA Sewing Inc ...315 792-8017
901 Broad St Ste 2 Utica (13501) ***(G-15736)***
USA Signs of America Inc ...631 254-6900
172 E Industry Ct Deer Park (11729) ***(G-4057)***
USA Tees.com, Brooklyn *Also called Universal Screening Associates* ***(G-2609)***
USA Today International Corp ...703 854-3400
535 Madison Ave Fl 27 New York (10022) ***(G-11980)***
Usai, New Windsor *Also called USA Illumination Inc* ***(G-8662)***
Usairports Services Inc ...585 527-6835
1295 Scottsville Rd Rochester (14624) ***(G-14194)***
Use Acquisition LLC ...516 812-6800
270 Park Ave New Hyde Park (11040) ***(G-8572)***
Used Equipment Directory, New York *Also called Informa Media Inc* ***(G-10211)***
Usheco Inc ...845 658-9200
138 Maple Hill Rd Kingston (12401) ***(G-6930)***
Ushers Machine and Tool Co Inc ...518 877-5501
180 Ushers Rd Round Lake (12151) ***(G-14464)***
Uspa Accessories LLC ...212 868-2590
1411 Broadway Fl 7 New York (10018) ***(G-11981)***
Usq Group LLC ...212 777-7751
222 Broadway Fl 19 New York (10038) ***(G-11982)***
UTC Aerospace Systems ...315 838-1200
104 Otis St Rome (13441) ***(G-14277)***
UTC Fire SEC Americas Corp Inc ...518 456-0444
10 Walker Way Ste 3 Albany (12205) ***(G-139)***
Utica Boilers, Utica *Also called ECR International Inc* ***(G-15699)***
Utica Cutlery Company ...315 733-4663
820 Noyes St Utica (13502) ***(G-15737)***
Utica Metal Products Inc ...315 732-6163
1526 Lincoln Ave Utica (13502) ***(G-15738)***
Utility Brass & Bronze Div, Brooklyn *Also called Giumenta Corp* ***(G-1929)***
Utility Canvas Inc (PA) ...845 255-9290
2686 Route 44 55 Gardiner (12525) ***(G-5297)***
Utility Engineering Co ...845 735-8900
40 Walter St Pearl River (10965) ***(G-12912)***
Utility Manufacturing Co Inc ...516 997-6300
700 Main St Westbury (11590) ***(G-16384)***
Utility Systems Tech Inc ...518 326-4142
70 Cohoes Rd Watervliet (12189) ***(G-16055)***
Utleys Incorporated ...718 956-1661
3123 61st St Woodside (11377) ***(G-16682)***
Uxc Eclipse (usa) Inc ...212 965-6400
200 W 41st St Fl 15 New York (10036) ***(G-11983)***
Uxc Eclipse USA, New York *Also called Uxc Eclipse (usa) Inc* ***(G-11983)***
V & E Kohnstamm & Co Div, Brooklyn *Also called Virginia Dare Extract Co Inc* ***(G-2626)***
V & J Graphics Inc ...315 363-1933
153 Phelps St Oneida (13421) ***(G-12622)***
V A I, Ronkonkoma *Also called Vormittag Associates Inc* ***(G-14428)***
V A P Tool & Dye ...631 587-5262
436 W 4th St West Islip (11795) ***(G-16260)***
V C N Group Ltd Inc ...516 223-4812
1 Clifton St North Baldwin (11510) ***(G-12369)***
V E Power Door Co Inc ...631 231-4500
140 Emjay Blvd Brentwood (11717) ***(G-1148)***
V E W, New York *Also called Vera Wang Group LLC* ***(G-12007)***
V Lake Industries Inc ...716 885-9141
1555 Niagara St Buffalo (14213) ***(G-3115)***
V Magazine, New York *Also called Visionaire Publishing LLC* ***(G-12043)***
Va Inc ...585 385-5930
803 Linden Ave Ste 1 Rochester (14625) ***(G-14195)***
Vaad LHafotzas Sichoes ...718 778-5436
788 Eastern Pkwy Brooklyn (11213) ***(G-2614)***
Vac Air Service Inc ...716 665-2206
1295 E 2nd St Jamestown (14701) ***(G-6760)***
Vaccinex Inc ...585 271-2700
1895 Mount Hope Ave Rochester (14620) ***(G-14196)***
Vacheron New York Btq, New York *Also called Richemont North America Inc* ***(G-11387)***
Vactronics, Bayside Hills *Also called Cathay Global Co Inc* ***(G-752)***
Vacuum Instrument Corporation (PA) ...631 737-0900
2101 9th Ave Ste A Ronkonkoma (11779) ***(G-14427)***
Vader Systems LLC ...716 688-1600
385 Crsspint Pkwy Ste 104 Getzville (14068) ***(G-5355)***
Vaire LLC ...631 271-4933
200 E 2nd St Ste 34 Huntington Station (11746) ***(G-6463)***
Valad Electric Heating Corp ...888 509-4927
65 Leonards Dr Montgomery (12549) ***(G-8319)***
Valair Inc ...716 751-9480
87 Harbor St Wilson (14172) ***(G-16602)***
Valassis Communications Inc ...585 627-4138
5 Marway Cir Ste 8 Rochester (14624) ***(G-14197)***
Valcour Brewing Company LLC ...518 324-2337
49 Ohio Rd Plattsburgh (12903) ***(G-13167)***
Valenti Distributing ...716 824-2304
84 Maple Ave Blasdell (14219) ***(G-932)***
Valenti Neckwear Co Inc ...914 969-0700
540 Nepperhan Ave Ste 564 Yonkers (10701) ***(G-16805)***
Valentin & Kalich Jwly Mfg Ltd ...212 575-9044
42 W 48th St Ste 903 New York (10036) ***(G-11984)***
Valentin Magro, New York *Also called Valentin & Kalich Jwly Mfg Ltd* ***(G-11984)***
Valentine Jewelry Mfg Co Inc ...212 382-0606
31 W 47th St Ste 602 New York (10036) ***(G-11985)***
Valentine Packaging Corp ...718 418-6000
6020 59th Pl Ste 7 Maspeth (11378) ***(G-7875)***
Valerie Bohigian ...914 631-8866
225 Hunter Ave Sleepy Hollow (10591) ***(G-14888)***
Valian Associates, Sleepy Hollow *Also called Valerie Bohigian* ***(G-14888)***
Valiant Entertainment LLC ...212 972-0361
350 7th Ave Rm 300 New York (10001) ***(G-11986)***
Valle Signs and Awnings ...516 408-3440
55 Decker St Copiague (11726) ***(G-3790)***
Valley Creek Side Inc ...315 839-5526
1960 State Route 8 Clayville (13322) ***(G-3559)***
Valley Industrial Products Inc ...631 385-9300
152 New York Ave Huntington (11743) ***(G-6424)***
Valley Industries, Gerry *Also called Cobbe Industries Inc* ***(G-5340)***
Valley Signs, Clayville *Also called Valley Creek Side Inc* ***(G-3559)***
Valley Stream Sporting Gds Inc ...516 593-7800
325 Hendrickson Ave Lynbrook (11563) ***(G-7677)***
Valmont Inc (PA) ...212 685-1653
1 W 34th St Rm 303 New York (10001) ***(G-11987)***
Valmont Site Pro 1, Hauppauge *Also called Pirod Inc* ***(G-5916)***
Valois of America Inc ...845 639-3700
250 N Route 303 Congers (10920) ***(G-3721)***
Valplast International Corp ...516 442-3923
200 Shames Dr Westbury (11590) ***(G-16385)***
Value Fragrances & Flavors Inc ...845 294-5726
7 Musket Ct Goshen (10924) ***(G-5485)***
Value Line Inc (HQ) ...212 907-1500
551 5th Ave Fl 3 New York (10176) ***(G-11988)***
Value Line Publishing LLC ...201 842-8054
551 5th Ave Fl 3 New York (10176) ***(G-11989)***
Value Spring Technology Inc ...917 705-4658
521 Harrison Ave Harrison (10528) ***(G-5739)***
Valvetech Inc ...315 548-4551
1391 Phelps Junction Rd Phelps (14532) ***(G-12983)***
Valvoline Instant Oil Change, White Plains *Also called High Line Lube LLC* ***(G-16459)***
Van Blarcom Closures Inc (PA) ...718 855-3810
156 Sanford St Brooklyn (11205) ***(G-2615)***
Van Cpeters Logging Inc ...607 637-3574
4480 Peas Eddy Rd Hancock (13783) ***(G-5715)***
Van Heusen, New Windsor *Also called Pvh Corp* ***(G-8656)***
Van Heusen, Deer Park *Also called Pvh Corp* ***(G-4031)***
Van Heusen, New York *Also called Pvh Corp* ***(G-11284)***
Van Heusen, New York *Also called Pvh Corp* ***(G-11285)***
Van Laeken Richard ...315 331-0289
2680 Parker Rd Newark (14513) ***(G-12211)***
Van Leeuwen Artisan Ice Cream ...718 701-1630
56 Dobbin St Brooklyn (11222) ***(G-2616)***
Van Reenen Tool & Die Inc ...585 288-6000
350 Commerce Dr 4 Rochester (14623) ***(G-14198)***
Van Slyke Belting LLC ...518 283-5479
606 Snyders Corners Rd Poestenkill (12140) ***(G-13183)***
Van Thomas Inc ...585 426-1414
740 Driving Park Ave G1 Rochester (14613) ***(G-14199)***
Vanberg & Dewulf Co Inc ...607 547-8184
52 Pioneer St Ste 4 Cooperstown (13326) ***(G-3745)***
Vance Metal Fabricators Inc ...315 789-5626
251 Gambee Rd Geneva (14456) ***(G-5335)***
Vanchlor Company Inc (PA) ...716 434-2624
45 Main St Lockport (14094) ***(G-7341)***
Vanchlor Company Inc ...716 434-2624
555 W Jackson St Lockport (14094) ***(G-7342)***
Vandam Inc ...212 929-0416
1111 44th Rd Fl 403 Long Island City (11101) ***(G-7627)***
Vandemark Chemical Inc (PA) ...716 433-6764
1 N Transit Rd Lockport (14094) ***(G-7343)***
Vander Heyden Woodworking ...212 242-0525
151 W 25th St Fl 8 New York (10001) ***(G-11990)***
Vandilay Industries Inc ...631 226-3064
60 Bell St Unit A West Babylon (11704) ***(G-16202)***
Vanec, Orchard Park *Also called Vibration & Noise Engrg Corp* ***(G-12749)***
Vanguard Graphics LLC ...607 272-1212
17 Hallwoods Rd Ithaca (14850) ***(G-6615)***
Vanguard Metals Inc ...631 234-6500
135 Brightside Ave Central Islip (11722) ***(G-3388)***
Vanguard Printing, Ithaca *Also called Vanguard Graphics LLC* ***(G-6615)***
Vanhouten Motorsports ...315 387-6312
27 Center Rd Lacona (13083) ***(G-6955)***
Vanilla Sky LLC ...347 738-4195
3318 Broadway Long Island City (11106) ***(G-7628)***
Vanity Fair ...212 286-6052
4 Times Sq Bsmt C1b New York (10036) ***(G-11991)***
Vanity Fair Bathmart Inc ...718 584-6700
2971 Webster Ave Bronx (10458) ***(G-1413)***
Vanity Fair Brands LP ...212 548-1548
25 W 39th St New York (10018) ***(G-11992)***
Vanity Room Inc ...212 921-7154
230 W 39th St Rm 900 New York (10018) ***(G-11993)***
Vanlab, Rochester *Also called Synergy Flavors NY Company LLC* ***(G-14151)***

ALPHABETIC SECTION
Vertana Group LLC (PA)

Vans Inc 631 724-1011
313 Smith Haven Mall Lake Grove (11755) *(G-6971)*
Vans Inc 718 349-2311
25 Franklin St Brooklyn (11222) *(G-2617)*
Vansantis Development Inc 315 461-0113
4595 Morgan Pl Liverpool (13090) *(G-7268)*
Vansridge Dairy LLC 315 364-8569
2831 Black St Scipio Center (13147) *(G-14737)*
Vantage Mfg & Assembly LLC 845 471-5290
900 Dutchess Tpke Poughkeepsie (12603) *(G-13371)*
Vante Inc 716 778-7691
3600 Coomer Rd Newfane (14108) *(G-12254)*
Varex Imaging Corporation 315 234-6853
121 Metropolitan Dr Liverpool (13088) *(G-7269)*
Varflex Corporation 315 336-4400
512 W Court St Rome (13440) *(G-14278)*
Variable Graphics LLC 212 691-2323
15 W 36th St Rm 601 New York (10018) *(G-11994)*
Varian Medical Systems, Liverpool *Also called Infimed Inc (G-7236)*
Varick Street Litho Inc 646 843-0800
149 W 27th St Fl 4 New York (10001) *(G-11995)*
Variety Gem Co Inc (PA) 212 921-1820
295 Northern Blvd Ste 208 Great Neck (11021) *(G-5599)*
Varnish Software Inc 201 857-2832
85 Broad St Fl 18 New York (10004) *(G-11996)*
Varonis Systems Inc (PA) 877 292-8767
1250 Broadway Fl 29 New York (10001) *(G-11997)*
Varsity Monitor LLC 212 691-6292
50 5th Ave Fl 3 Flr 3 New York (10011) *(G-11998)*
Vasomedical Inc (PA) 516 997-4600
137 Commercial St Ste 200 Plainview (11803) *(G-13096)*
Vasomedical Solutions Inc 516 997-4600
137 Commercial St Ste 200 Plainview (11803) *(G-13097)*
Vasquez Tito 212 944-0441
36 W 47th St Ste 206 New York (10036) *(G-11999)*
Vassilaros Coffee, Flushing *Also called John A Vassilaros & Son Inc (G-5014)*
Vaughan Designs Inc (HQ) 212 319-7070
979 3rd Ave Ste 1511 New York (10022) *(G-12000)*
Vault.com, Vault Media, New York *Also called Vaultcom Inc (G-12001)*
Vaultcom Inc (PA) 212 366-4212
132 W 31st St Rm 1501 New York (10001) *(G-12001)*
Vcp Mobility Inc 718 356-7827
4131 Richmond Ave Staten Island (10312) *(G-15150)*
Vdc Electronics Inc 631 683-5850
155 W Carver St Ste 2 Huntington (11743) *(G-6425)*
Vector Group Ltd 212 409-2800
712 5th Ave New York (10019) *(G-12002)*
Vector Magnetics LLC 607 273-8351
236 Cherry St Ithaca (14850) *(G-6616)*
Vectra Visual, Long Island City *Also called Taylor Communications Inc (G-7612)*
Vedell North Fork LLC 631 323-3526
36225 Main Rd Cutchogue (11935) *(G-3924)*
Veeco Instruments Inc 516 677-0200
100 Sunnyside Blvd Ste B Woodbury (11797) *(G-16633)*
Veeco Instruments Inc 516 349-8300
1 Terminal Dr Plainview (11803) *(G-13098)*
Veeco Instruments Inc (PA) 516 677-0200
1 Terminal Dr Plainview (11803) *(G-13099)*
Veeco Process Equipment, Plainview *Also called Veeco Instruments Inc (G-13098)*
Veeco Process Equipment Inc (HQ) 516 677-0200
1 Terminal Dr Plainview (11803) *(G-13100)*
Vega Coffee Inc 415 881-7969
325 N End Ave Apt 4b New York (10282) *(G-12003)*
Vegetable Operations, Geneva *Also called Seneca Foods Corporation (G-5332)*
Vegetable Operations, Marion *Also called Seneca Foods Corporation (G-7808)*
Vehicle Manufacturers Inc 631 851-1700
400 Oser Ave Ste 100 Hauppauge (11788) *(G-5968)*
Vehicle Safety Dept 315 458-6683
5801 E Taft Rd Ste 4 Syracuse (13212) *(G-15451)*
Vehicle Tracking Solutions LLC 631 586-7400
152 Veterans Memorial Hwy Commack (11725) *(G-3704)*
Veja Electronics Inc (PA) 631 321-6086
46 W Jefryn Blvd Ste A Deer Park (11729) *(G-4058)*
Velis Associates Inc (PA) 631 225-4220
151 S 14th St Lindenhurst (11757) *(G-7202)*
Vell Company Inc 845 365-1013
700 Oak Tree Rd Palisades (10964) *(G-12849)*
Velmex Inc 585 657-6151
7550 State Route 5 And 20 Bloomfield (14469) *(G-958)*
Velocity Pharma LLC 631 393-2905
210-220 Sea Ln Farmingdale (11735) *(G-4902)*
Velocity Print Solutions, Scotia *Also called Shipmtes/Printmates Holdg Corp (G-14746)*
Velp Scientific Inc 631 573-6002
155 Keyland Ct Bohemia (11716) *(G-1105)*
Velvet Healing By Alma Corp 347 271-4220
645 Melrose Ave Frnt 1 Bronx (10455) *(G-1414)*
Velvetop Products, Huntington Station *Also called Walsh & Hughes Inc (G-6464)*
Venco Sales Inc 631 754-0782
755 Park Ave Ste 300 Huntington (11743) *(G-6426)*
Vending Times Inc 516 442-1850
55 Maple Ave Ste 304 Rockville Centre (11570) *(G-14244)*

Vendome Group LLC 646 795-3899
237 W 35th St Fl 16 New York (10001) *(G-12004)*
Vendome Press, New York *Also called Helvetica Press Incorporated (G-10079)*
Veneer One Inc 516 536-6480
3415 Hampton Rd Oceanside (11572) *(G-12563)*
Vengo Inc 866 526-7054
999 S Oyster Bay Rd # 407 Bethpage (11714) *(G-853)*
Venice Marina, Brooklyn *Also called Marina Holding Corp (G-2167)*
Vent-A-Fume, Buffalo *Also called Vent-A-Kiln Corporation (G-3116)*
Vent-A-Kiln Corporation 716 876-2023
51 Botsford Pl Buffalo (14216) *(G-3116)*
Ventosa Vineyards LLC 315 719-0000
3440 State Route 96a Geneva (14456) *(G-5336)*
Ventrus Biosciences Inc 646 706-5208
99 Hudson St New York (10013) *(G-12005)*
Ventura Enterprise Co Inc 212 391-0170
512 Fashion Ave Fl 38 New York (10018) *(G-12006)*
Venture Economics, New York *Also called Securities Data Publishing Inc (G-11530)*
Venture Respiratory Inc 718 437-3633
1413 38th St Brooklyn (11218) *(G-2618)*
Venue Graphics Supply Inc 718 361-1690
1120 46th Rd Long Island City (11101) *(G-7629)*
Venus, New York *Also called Shah Diamonds Inc (G-11553)*
Venus Manufacturing Co Inc (PA) 315 639-3100
349 Lakeview Dr Dexter (13634) *(G-4116)*
Venus Printing Company 212 967-8900
1420 Kew Ave Hewlett (11557) *(G-6053)*
Vepo Solutions LLC 914 384-2121
3 Fairview Ct Cross River (10518) *(G-3910)*
Ver-Tech Elevator, Ozone Park *Also called Elevator Ventures Corporation (G-12824)*
Vera Wang Group LLC (PA) 212 575-6400
15 E 26th St Fl 4 New York (10010) *(G-12007)*
Veranda Magazine, New York *Also called Veranda Publications Inc (G-12008)*
Veranda Publications Inc 212 903-5206
300 W 57th St Fl 28 New York (10019) *(G-12008)*
Veratex Inc (PA) 212 683-9300
254 5th Ave Fl 3 New York (10001) *(G-12009)*
Verdonette Inc 212 719-2003
270 W 39th St Fl 5 New York (10018) *(G-12010)*
Veriled Inc 877 521-5520
100 Church St Ste 871 New York (10007) *(G-12011)*
Verint Americas Inc 631 962-9334
175 Broadhollow Rd # 100 Melville (11747) *(G-8073)*
Verint SEC Intelligence Inc 631 962-9300
175 Broadhollow Rd # 100 Melville (11747) *(G-8074)*
Verint Systems Inc (PA) 631 962-9600
175 Broadhollow Rd # 100 Melville (11747) *(G-8075)*
Verizon, New York *Also called Supermedia LLC (G-11748)*
Verla International Ltd 845 561-2440
463 Temple Hill Rd New Windsor (12553) *(G-8663)*
Vermed, Buffalo *Also called Vermont Medical Inc (G-3118)*
Vermed Inc 800 669-6905
400 Exchange St Buffalo (14204) *(G-3117)*
Vermont Medical Inc 802 463-9976
400 Exchange St Buffalo (14204) *(G-3118)*
Vermont Multicolor Slate 518 642-2400
146 State Route 22a Middle Granville (12849) *(G-8113)*
Vermont Natural Stoneworks 518 642-2460
146 State Route 22a Middle Granville (12849) *(G-8114)*
Vermont Structural Slate Co 518 499-1912
Buckley Rd Whitehall (12887) *(G-16525)*
Vernon Devices, New Rochelle *Also called Halpern Tool Corp (G-8611)*
Vernon Plating Works Inc 718 639-1124
3318 57th St Woodside (11377) *(G-16683)*
Vernon Wine & Liquor Inc 718 784-5096
5006 Vernon Blvd Long Island City (11101) *(G-7630)*
Verns Machine Co Inc 315 926-4223
4929 Steel Point Rd Marion (14505) *(G-7810)*
Verona Pharma Inc 914 797-5007
50 Main St Ste 1000 White Plains (10606) *(G-16514)*
Verris Inc 201 565-1648
99 Wall St Unit 236 New York (10005) *(G-12012)*
Versailles Drapery Upholstery 212 533-2059
4709 30th St Ste 200 Long Island City (11101) *(G-7631)*
Versailles Industries LLC 212 792-9615
485 Fashion Ave Rm 500 New York (10018) *(G-12013)*
Versaponents, Deer Park *Also called Lighting Sculptures Inc (G-4002)*
Versaponents Inc 631 242-3387
66 N Industry Ct Deer Park (11729) *(G-4059)*
Verso Inc 718 246-8160
20 Jay St Ste 1010 Brooklyn (11201) *(G-2619)*
Verso Corporation 212 599-2700
370 Lexington Ave Rm 802 New York (10017) *(G-12014)*
Verso Paper Management LP 781 320-8660
370 Lexington Ave Rm 802 New York (10017) *(G-12015)*
Verso Paper Management LP (PA) 212 599-2700
60 W 42nd Ste 1942 New York (10165) *(G-12016)*
Vertaloc, New York *Also called US Diagnostics Inc (G-11975)*
Vertana Group LLC (PA) 646 430-8226
450 Lexington Ave Fl 4 New York (10017) *(G-12017)*

ALPHABETIC

Vertarib Inc...561 683-0888
471 N Broadway Ste 196 Jericho (11753) **(G-6806)**
Vertex Innovative Solutions...315 437-6711
6671 Commerce Blvd Syracuse (13211) **(G-15452)**
Vertical Apparel, New York *Also called American Apparel Trading Corp* **(G-8823)**
Vertical Lax Inc...518 669-3699
20 Corporate Cir Ste 4 Albany (12203) **(G-140)**
Vertical Research Partners LLC...212 257-6499
52 Vanderbilt Ave Rm 200 New York (10017) **(G-12018)**
Vertiv Corporation...516 349-8500
79 Express St Fl 14 Plainview (11803) **(G-13101)**
Vescom Structural Systems Inc...516 876-8100
100 Shames Dr Unit 1 Westbury (11590) **(G-16386)**
Vespa Sand & Stone, Watertown *Also called John Vespa Inc* **(G-16019)**
Vestal Asphalt Inc (PA)...607 785-3393
201 Stage Rd Vestal (13850) **(G-15825)**
Vestal Electronic Devices LLC...607 773-8461
635 Dickson St Endicott (13760) **(G-4614)**
Veteran Air LLC...315 720-1101
7174 State Fair Blvd Syracuse (13209) **(G-15453)**
Veteran Air Filtration, Syracuse *Also called Veteran Air LLC* **(G-15453)**
Veteran Offset Printing, Rochester *Also called Veterans Offset Printing Inc* **(G-14200)**
Veterans Offset Printing Inc...585 288-2900
500 N Goodman St Rochester (14609) **(G-14200)**
Veterinary Biochemical Ltd...845 473-1900
201 Smith St Poughkeepsie (12601) **(G-13372)**
Vetra Systems Corporation...631 434-3185
275 Marcus Blvd Unit J Hauppauge (11788) **(G-5969)**
Vetroelite Inc...925 724-7900
115 W 30th St Rm 402 New York (10001) **(G-12019)**
Vetta Jewelry Inc (PA)...212 564-8250
989 Avenue Of The America New York (10018) **(G-12020)**
Vexos Inc (HQ)...855 711-3227
60 E 42nd St Ste 1250 New York (10165) **(G-12021)**
Vez Inc...718 273-7002
3801 Victory Blvd Ste 5 Staten Island (10314) **(G-15151)**
Vf Imagewear Inc...718 352-2363
333 Pratt Ave Bayside (11359) **(G-751)**
Vf Outdoor Inc...718 698-6215
2655 Richmond Ave # 1570 Staten Island (10314) **(G-15152)**
Vf Outdoor LLC...845 928-4900
461 Dune Rd Central Valley (10917) **(G-3398)**
Vf Services LLC...212 575-7820
25 W 39th St New York (10018) **(G-12022)**
Vgg Holding LLC...212 415-6700
590 Madison Ave Fl 41 New York (10022) **(G-12023)**
Vhx Corporation...347 689-1446
555 W 18th St New York (10011) **(G-12024)**
Via America Fine Jewelry Inc...212 302-1218
578 5th Ave Unit 26 New York (10036) **(G-12025)**
Viamedia Corporation...718 485-7792
2610 Atlantic Ave Brooklyn (11207) **(G-2620)**
Viana Signs Corp...516 887-2000
3520 Lawson Blvd Oceanside (11572) **(G-12564)**
Viatran Corporation (HQ)...716 564-7813
199 Fire Tower Dr Tonawanda (14150) **(G-15589)**
Vibe Magazine, New York *Also called Vibe Media Group LLC* **(G-12026)**
Vibe Media Group LLC...212 448-7300
120 Wall St Fl 21 New York (10005) **(G-12026)**
Vibra Tech Industries Inc...914 946-1916
126 Oakley Ave White Plains (10601) **(G-16515)**
Vibration & Noise Engrg Corp...716 827-4959
3374 N Benzing Rd Orchard Park (14127) **(G-12749)**
Vibration Eliminator Co Inc (PA)...631 841-4000
15 Dixon Ave Copiague (11726) **(G-3791)**
Vibro-Laser Instrs Corp LLC...518 874-2700
2c Glens Falls Tech Park Glens Falls (12801) **(G-5443)**
Vic Demayos Inc...845 626-4343
4967 Us Highway 209 Accord (12404) **(G-1)**
Vic Leak Detection, Ronkonkoma *Also called Vacuum Instrument Corporation* **(G-14427)**
Vic-Gina Printing Company Inc...914 636-0200
1299 North Ave New Rochelle (10804) **(G-8631)**
Vickers Stock Research Corp (HQ)...212 425-7500
61 Broadway Rm 1910 New York (10006) **(G-12027)**
Vicks Lithograph & Prtg Corp (PA)...315 272-2401
5166 Commercial Dr Yorkville (13495) **(G-16832)**
Vicks Lithograph & Prtg Corp...315 736-9344
5210 Commercial Dr Yorkville (13495) **(G-16833)**
Vicon Industries Inc (PA)...631 952-2288
135 Fell Ct Hauppauge (11788) **(G-5970)**
Vicron Electronic Mfg, Bronx *Also called Monarch Electric Products Inc* **(G-1335)**
Victoire Latam Asset MGT LLC, New York *Also called Capital E Financial Group* **(G-9202)**
Victor Insulators Inc...585 924-2127
280 Maple Ave Victor (14564) **(G-15875)**
Victoria Albi International...212 689-2600
1178 Broadway Fl 5 New York (10001) **(G-12028)**
Victoria Dngelo Intr Cllctions, Warwick *Also called DAngelo Home Collections Inc* **(G-15949)**
Victoria Fine Foods LLC (HQ)...718 649-1635
443 E 100th St Brooklyn (11236) **(G-2621)**
Victoria Fine Foods Holding Co (HQ)...718 649-1635
443 E 100th St Brooklyn (11236) **(G-2622)**
Victoria Plating Co Inc...718 589-1550
650 Tiffany St Bronx (10474) **(G-1415)**
Victoria Precision Inc...845 473-9309
78 Travis Rd Hyde Park (12538) **(G-6472)**
Victoria Stilwell Positevely, New York *Also called Dog Good Products LLC* **(G-9545)**
Victory Garden...212 206-7273
31 Carmine St Frnt A New York (10014) **(G-12029)**
Victory Signs Inc...315 762-0220
8915 Old State Route 13 Canastota (13032) **(G-3251)**
Victory Sports, Staten Island *Also called Glenda Inc* **(G-15079)**
Vida-Blend LLC...518 627-4138
1430 State Highway 5s Amsterdam (12010) **(G-363)**
Vidal Candies USA Inc...609 781-8169
845 3rd Ave Fl 6 New York (10022) **(G-12030)**
Videk Inc...585 377-0377
1387 Fairport Rd 1000c Fairport (14450) **(G-4665)**
Video Technology Services Inc...516 937-9700
5 Aerial Way Ste 300 Syosset (11791) **(G-15232)**
Viducci, Great Neck *Also called Classic Creations Inc* **(G-5545)**
Viele Manufacturing Corp...718 893-2200
1340 Viele Ave Bronx (10474) **(G-1416)**
View Collections Inc...212 944-4030
265 W 37th St Rm 5w New York (10018) **(G-12031)**
Viewfinder Inc...212 831-0939
101 W 23rd St Ste 2303 New York (10011) **(G-12032)**
Viewsport International Inc...585 259-1562
11 Feathery Cir Penfield (14526) **(G-12947)**
Vigneri Chocolate Inc...585 254-6160
810 Emerson St Rochester (14613) **(G-14201)**
Viking Athletics Ltd...631 957-8000
80 Montauk Hwy Ste 1 Lindenhurst (11757) **(G-7203)**
Viking Industries Inc...845 883-6325
89 S Ohioville Rd New Paltz (12561) **(G-8584)**
Viking Iron Works Inc...845 471-5010
37 Hatfield Ln Poughkeepsie (12603) **(G-13373)**
Viking Jackets & Athletic Wear, Walden *Also called C & C Athletic Inc* **(G-15891)**
Viking Mar Wldg Ship Repr LLC...718 758-4116
14 Raleigh Pl Brooklyn (11226) **(G-2623)**
Viking Technologies Ltd...631 957-8000
80 E Montauk Hwy Lindenhurst (11757) **(G-7204)**
Viking-Cives, Harrisville *Also called Cives Corporation* **(G-5740)**
Viktor Gold Enterprise Corp...212 768-8885
58 W 47th St Unit 36 New York (10036) **(G-12033)**
Vilebrequin...212 546-9220
160 Varick St Fl 2 New York (10013) **(G-12034)**
Village Decoration Ltd...315 437-2522
20 Corporate Cir East Syracuse (13057) **(G-4380)**
Village Herald...516 569-4403
379 Central Ave Lawrence (11559) **(G-7111)**
Village Lantern Baking Corp...631 225-1690
155 N Wellwood Ave Lindenhurst (11757) **(G-7205)**
Village Plaquesmith, Ththe, Bohemia *Also called Custom House Engravers Inc* **(G-1004)**
Village Print Room, Oneonta *Also called Pony Farm Press & Graphics* **(G-12644)**
Village Printing, Endicott *Also called Fambus Inc* **(G-4592)**
Village Times, The, East Setauket *Also called Times Beacon Record Newspapers* **(G-4312)**
Village Video News, West Babylon *Also called Village Video Productions Inc* **(G-16203)**
Village Video Productions Inc...631 752-9311
107 Alder St West Babylon (11704) **(G-16203)**
Village Wrought Iron Inc...315 683-5589
7756 Main St Fabius (13063) **(G-4624)**
Villager, The, Brooklyn *Also called Nyc Community Media LLC* **(G-2281)**
Villeroy & Boch Usa Inc...212 213-8149
41 Madison Ave Ste 1801 New York (10010) **(G-12035)**
Vin Mar Precision Metals Inc...631 563-6608
1465 S Strong Ave Copiague (11726) **(G-3792)**
Vin-Clair Bindery, West Haverstraw *Also called Vin-Clair Inc* **(G-16210)**
Vin-Clair Inc...845 429-4998
132 E Railroad Ave West Haverstraw (10993) **(G-16210)**
Vincent Associates, Rochester *Also called Va Inc* **(G-14195)**
Vincent Conigliaro...845 340-0489
308 State Route 28 Kingston (12401) **(G-6931)**
Vincent Genovese...631 281-8170
19 Woodmere Dr Mastic Beach (11951) **(G-7912)**
Vincent Manufacturing Co Inc...315 823-0280
560 E Mill St Little Falls (13365) **(G-7216)**
Vincent Martino Dental Lab...716 674-7800
74 Ransier Dr Buffalo (14224) **(G-3119)**
Vincents Food Corp...516 481-3544
179 Old Country Rd Carle Place (11514) **(G-3273)**
Vincys Printing Ltd...518 355-4363
1832 Curry Rd Schenectady (12306) **(G-14725)**
Vinegar Hill Asset LLC...718 469-0342
436 E 34th St Brooklyn (11203) **(G-2624)**
Vineland Kosher Poultry Inc...718 921-1347
5600 1st Ave A7 Brooklyn (11220) **(G-2625)**
Vinevrest Co, Washingtonville *Also called Brotherhood Americas* **(G-15964)**
Vinifera Wine Cellard, Hammondsport *Also called Konstantin D FRAnk& Sons Vini* **(G-5707)**
Vinous Group LLC...917 275-5184
54 W 40th St New York (10018) **(G-12036)**

Vinyl Materials Inc 631 586-9444
365 Bay Shore Rd Deer Park (11729) ***(G-4060)***
Vinyl Tech Window, Staten Island *Also called Eastern Enterprise Corp* ***(G-15073)***
Vinyl Works Inc 518 786-1200
33 Wade Rd Latham (12110) ***(G-7097)***
Vinyline Window and Door Inc 914 476-3500
636 Saw Mill River Rd Yonkers (10710) ***(G-16806)***
Viola Cabinet Corporation 716 284-6327
4205 Hyde Park Blvd Niagara Falls (14305) ***(G-12347)***
Viola Construction, Niagara Falls *Also called Viola Cabinet Corporation* ***(G-12347)***
VIP Foods Inc 718 821-5330
1080 Wyckoff Ave Ridgewood (11385) ***(G-13558)***
VIP Printing 718 641-9361
16040 95th St Howard Beach (11414) ***(G-6332)***
Viraj - USA Inc (HQ) 516 280-8380
2 Reiter Ave Hicksville (11801) ***(G-6138)***
Virgil Mountain Inc (PA) 212 378-0007
1 E 28th St Fl 4 New York (10016) ***(G-12037)***
Virginia Dare Extract Co Inc (PA) 718 788-6320
882 3rd Ave Unit 2 Brooklyn (11232) ***(G-2626)***
Viridis Learning Inc 347 420-9181
2 Gold St Apt 4005 New York (10038) ***(G-12038)***
Viropro Inc 650 300-5190
49 W 38th St Fl 11 New York (10018) ***(G-12039)***
Virtual Frameworks Inc 646 690-8207
115 5th Ave Frnt 2 New York (10003) ***(G-12040)***
Virtual Super LLC 212 685-6400
116 E 27th St Fl 3 New York (10016) ***(G-12041)***
Virtualapt Corp 917 293-3173
45 Main St Ste 613 Brooklyn (11201) ***(G-2627)***
Virtusphere Inc 607 760-2207
7 Hillside Ave Binghamton (13903) ***(G-922)***
Virtuvent Inc 855 672-8677
81 Prospect St Fl 7 Brooklyn (11201) ***(G-2628)***
Visant Secondary Holdings Corp (HQ) 914 595-8200
357 Main St Armonk (10504) ***(G-412)***
Vishay Thin Film LLC 716 283-4025
2160 Liberty Dr Niagara Falls (14304) ***(G-12348)***
Visible Systems Corporation (PA) 508 628-1510
248 Main St Ste 2 Oneida (13421) ***(G-12623)***
Visimetrics Corporation 716 871-7070
2290 Kenmore Ave Buffalo (14207) ***(G-3120)***
Vision Logic Inc 212 729-4606
300 Park Ave Fl 12 New York (10022) ***(G-12042)***
Vision Quest, Brooklyn *Also called Lens Lab Express* ***(G-2110)***
Vision Quest Lighting Inc 631 737-4800
12 Satterly Rd East Setauket (11733) ***(G-4314)***
Vision World, Bedford Hills *Also called Eyeglass Service Industries* ***(G-776)***
Vision-Sciences, Orangeburg *Also called Machida Incorporated* ***(G-12683)***
Visionaire Publishing LLC 646 434-6091
30 W 24th St New York (10010) ***(G-12043)***
Visiontron Corp 631 582-8600
720 Old Willets Path Hauppauge (11788) ***(G-5971)***
Visitainer Corp 718 636-0300
148 Classon Ave Brooklyn (11205) ***(G-2629)***
Vista Pharmacy & Surgical, Far Rockaway *Also called J P R Pharmacy Inc* ***(G-4702)***
Vista Visual Group, Lindenhurst *Also called Linear Signs Inc* ***(G-7175)***
Vistalab Technologies Inc 914 244-6226
2 Geneva Rd Brewster (10509) ***(G-1176)***
Vistec Lithography, Troy *Also called Raith America Inc* ***(G-15619)***
Vistec Lithography, Inc. 518 874-3000
125 Monroe St Watervliet (12189) ***(G-16056)***
Visual Citi Inc (PA) 631 482-3030
305 Henry St Lindenhurst (11757) ***(G-7206)***
Visual Effects Inc 718 324-0011
15929 Jamaica Ave 2 Jamaica (11432) ***(G-6689)***
Visual F-X, Brooklyn *Also called Street Beat Sportswear Inc* ***(G-2524)***
Visual ID Source Inc 516 307-9759
65 E 2nd St Mineola (11501) ***(G-8251)***
Visual Impact Graphics Inc 585 548-7118
653 Ellicott St Ste 6 Batavia (14020) ***(G-639)***
Visual Millwork & Fix Mfg Inc 718 267-7800
95 Marcus Blvd Deer Park (11729) ***(G-4061)***
Vita Rara Inc 518 369-7356
415 River St Ste 4 Troy (12180) ***(G-15631)***
Vita-Gen Laboratories LLC 631 450-4357
71s Mall Dr Commack (11725) ***(G-3705)***
Vita-Nat Inc 631 293-6000
298 Adams Blvd Farmingdale (11735) ***(G-4903)***
Vitafede (PA) 213 488-0136
25 W 26th St Fl 5 New York (10010) ***(G-12044)***
Vitakem Nutraceutical Inc 631 956-8343
811 W Jericho Tpke Smithtown (11787) ***(G-14911)***
Vital Signs & Graphics Co Inc 518 237-8372
251 Saratoga St Cohoes (12047) ***(G-3623)***
Vital Vio Inc 914 245-6048
185 Jordan Rd Ste 1 Troy (12180) ***(G-15632)***
Vitale Ready Mix Concrete, Auburn *Also called Robinson Concrete Inc* ***(G-498)***
Vitalis LLC 646 831-7338
902 Broadway Fl 6 New York (10010) ***(G-12045)***
Vitalize Labs LLC 212 966-6130
134 Spring St Ste 502 New York (10012) ***(G-12046)***
VITAMIX LABORATORIES, Commack *Also called Wellmill LLC* ***(G-3706)***
Vitane Pharmaceuticals Inc 845 267-6700
125 Wells Ave Congers (10920) ***(G-3722)***
Vitarose Corp of America 718 951-9700
2615 Nostrand Ave Ste 1 Brooklyn (11210) ***(G-2630)***
Viterion Corporation 914 333-6033
565 Taxter Rd Ste 175 Elmsford (10523) ***(G-4576)***
Vito & Sons Bakery 201 617-8501
1423 72nd St Brooklyn (11228) ***(G-2631)***
Vitobob Furniture Inc 516 676-1696
3879 13th St Long Island City (11101) ***(G-7632)***
Vitra Inc (HQ) 212 463-5700
10 Gansevoort St New York (10014) ***(G-12047)***
Vitrix Hot Glass and Crafts, Corning *Also called Vitrix Inc* ***(G-3828)***
Vitrix Inc 607 936-8707
77 W Market St Corning (14830) ***(G-3828)***
Vits International Inc 845 353-5000
200 Corporate Dr Blauvelt (10913) ***(G-945)***
Vivid Rgb Lighting LLC 718 635-0817
824 Main St Ste 1 Peekskill (10566) ***(G-12926)***
Vivona Business Printers Inc 516 496-3453
343 Jackson Ave Syosset (11791) ***(G-15233)***
Vivus Technologies LLC 585 798-6658
591 Mahar St Medina (14103) ***(G-7991)***
Vizbee Inc 650 787-1424
120 E 23rd St Fl 5 New York (10010) ***(G-12048)***
Vizio Medical Devices LLC 646 845-7382
200 Chambers St Apt 28a New York (10007) ***(G-12049)***
VJ Technologies Inc (PA) 631 589-8800
89 Carlough Rd Bohemia (11716) ***(G-1106)***
Vjt, Bohemia *Also called VJ Technologies Inc* ***(G-1106)***
Vline Inc 512 222-5464
81 Prospect St Brooklyn (11201) ***(G-2632)***
VM Choppy & Sons LLC 518 266-1444
4 Van Buren St Troy (12180) ***(G-15633)***
Vma, Poughkeepsie *Also called Vantage Mfg & Assembly LLC* ***(G-13371)***
Vnovom Svete 212 302-9480
55 Broad St Fl 20 New York (10004) ***(G-12050)***
Vogel Applied Technologies 212 677-3136
36 E 12th St Fl 7 New York (10003) ***(G-12051)***
Vogue China, New York *Also called Advance Magazine Publs Inc* ***(G-8751)***
Vogue Too Plting Stitching EMB 212 354-1022
265 W 37th St Fl 14 New York (10018) ***(G-12052)***
Voices For All LLC 518 261-1664
29 Moreland Dr Mechanicville (12118) ***(G-7935)***
Volckening Inc (PA) 718 748-0294
6700 3rd Ave Brooklyn (11220) ***(G-2633)***
Volkert Precision Tech Inc 718 464-9500
22240 96th Ave Ste 3 Queens Village (11429) ***(G-13412)***
Volpi Manufacturing USA Co Inc 315 255-1737
5 Commerce Way Auburn (13021) ***(G-508)***
Volt Tek Inc 585 377-2050
111 Parce Ave Fairport (14450) ***(G-4666)***
Voltronics LLC 410 749-2424
2777 Us Route 20 Cazenovia (13035) ***(G-3329)***
Von Musulin Patricia 212 206-8345
148 W 24th St Fl 10 New York (10011) ***(G-12053)***
Von Pok & Chang New York Inc 212 599-0556
4 E 43rd St Fl 7 New York (10017) ***(G-12054)***
Von Roll Usa Inc 203 562-2171
200 Von Roll Dr Schenectady (12306) ***(G-14726)***
Von Roll Usa Inc (HQ) 518 344-7100
200 Von Roll Dr Schenectady (12306) ***(G-14727)***
Vondom LLC 212 207-3252
979 3rd Ave Ste 1532 New York (10022) ***(G-12055)***
Voodoo Manufacturing Inc 646 893-8366
361 Stagg St Ste 408 Brooklyn (11206) ***(G-2634)***
Vormittag Associates Inc (PA) 800 824-7776
120 Comac St Ste 1 Ronkonkoma (11779) ***(G-14428)***
Vortex Ventures Inc 516 946-8345
857 Newton Ave North Baldwin (11510) ***(G-12370)***
Vosky Precision Machining Corp 631 737-3200
70 Air Park Dr Ronkonkoma (11779) ***(G-14429)***
Voss Manufacturing Inc 716 731-5062
2345 Lockport Rd Sanborn (14132) ***(G-14557)***
Voss Signs LLC 315 682-6418
112 Fairgrounds Dr Ste 2 Manlius (13104) ***(G-7781)***
Voss Usa Inc 212 995-2255
236 W 30th St Rm 900 New York (10001) ***(G-12056)***
Vox Systems, Massapequa *Also called Huntington Services Inc* ***(G-7880)***
Voyager Custom Products, Buffalo *Also called Voyager Emblems Inc* ***(G-3121)***
Voyager Emblems Inc 416 255-3421
701 Seneca St Ste D Buffalo (14210) ***(G-3121)***
Vpj Publication Inc 718 845-3221
15519 Lahn St Howard Beach (11414) ***(G-6333)***
Vpulse Inc 646 729-5675
191 Nassau Ave Brooklyn (11222) ***(G-2635)***
Vr Containment LLC 917 972-3441
17625 Union Tpke Ste 175 Fresh Meadows (11366) ***(G-5205)***
Vr Food Equipment Inc 315 531-8133
5801 County Road 41 Farmington (14425) ***(G-4921)***

ALPHABETIC

Vsg International LLC 718 300-8171
  196 Clinton Ave Apt A2 Brooklyn (11205) *(G-2636)*
Vship Co 718 706-8566
  3636 33rd St Ste 207 Astoria (11106) *(G-447)*
Vsii, Melville Also called Verint SEC Intelligence Inc *(G-8074)*
VSM Investors LLC (PA) 212 351-1600
  245 Park Ave Fl 41 New York (10167) *(G-12057)*
Vtb Holdings Inc (HQ) 914 345-2255
  100 Summit Lake Dr Valhalla (10595) *(G-15749)*
Vts Medical Systems, Melville Also called Steris Corporation *(G-8066)*
Vulcan Iron Works Inc 631 395-6846
  190 Weeks Ave Manorville (11949) *(G-7787)*
Vulcan Steam Forging Co 716 875-3680
  247 Rano St Buffalo (14207) *(G-3122)*
Vulcraft of New York Inc (HQ) 607 529-9000
  621 M St Chemung (14825) *(G-3464)*
Vulto Creamery LLC 607 865-7059
  3509 Dunk Hill Rd Walton (13856) *(G-15913)*
Vuzix Corporation (PA) 585 359-5900
  25 Hendrix Rd Ste A West Henrietta (14586) *(G-16253)*
Vvs International Inc 212 302-5410
  2 W 46th St New York (10036) *(G-12058)*
VWR Education LLC 585 359-2502
  5100 W Henrietta Rd West Henrietta (14586) *(G-16254)*
Vyera Pharmaceuticals LLC 646 356-5577
  600 3rd Ave Fl 10 New York (10016) *(G-12059)*
Vytek Inc 631 750-1770
  271 Knickerbocker Ave Bohemia (11716) *(G-1107)*
Vytl Fitness, New York Also called Crowd Media Inc *(G-9424)*
W & B Mazza & Sons Inc 516 379-4130
  2145 Marion Pl North Baldwin (11510) *(G-12371)*
W & G Manufacturing, Brooklyn Also called Sue & Sam Co Inc *(G-2530)*
W & H Stampings Inc 631 234-6161
  45 Engineers Rd Hauppauge (11788) *(G-5972)*
W & W Manufacturing Co 516 942-0011
  239 Higbie Ln West Islip (11795) *(G-16261)*
W A Baum Co Inc 631 226-3940
  620 Oak St Copiague (11726) *(G-3793)*
W B Bow Tie Corp 212 683-6130
  521 W 26th St Fl 6 New York (10001) *(G-12060)*
W D Technology Inc 914 779-8738
  42 Water St Ste B Eastchester (10709) *(G-4383)*
W Designe Inc 914 736-1058
  5 John Walsh Blvd Peekskill (10566) *(G-12927)*
W E W Container Corporation 718 827-8150
  189 Wyona St Brooklyn (11207) *(G-2637)*
W F Saunders & Sons Inc (PA) 315 469-3217
  5126 S Onondaga Rd Nedrow (13120) *(G-8480)*
W F Saunders & Sons Inc 607 257-6930
  30 Pinckney Rd Etna (13062) *(G-4623)*
W G R Z - T V Channel 2, Buffalo Also called Tegna Inc *(G-3089)*
W H Jones & Son Inc 716 875-8233
  1208 Military Rd Kenmore (14217) *(G-6864)*
W H White Publications Inc 914 725-2500
  95 Main St Dobbs Ferry (10522) *(G-4132)*
W Hubbell & Sons Inc (PA) 315 736-8311
  5124 Commercial Dr Yorkville (13495) *(G-16834)*
W J Albro Machine Works Inc 631 345-0657
  86 Horseblock Rd Unit L Yaphank (11980) *(G-16728)*
W K Z A 106.9 K I S S-F M, Jamestown Also called Cntry Cross Communications LLC *(G-6708)*
W Kintz Plastics Inc (HQ) 518 296-8513
  165 Caverns Rd Howes Cave (12092) *(G-6334)*
W M T Publications Inc 585 244-3329
  250 N Goodman St Ste 1 Rochester (14607) *(G-14202)*
W M W, Buffalo Also called West Metal Works Inc *(G-3128)*
W N R Pattern & Tool Inc 716 681-9334
  21 Pavement Rd Lancaster (14086) *(G-7053)*
W N Vanalstine & Sons Inc (PA) 518 237-1436
  18 New Cortland St Cohoes (12047) *(G-3624)*
W R P Welding Ltd 631 249-8859
  126 Toledo St Farmingdale (11735) *(G-4904)*
W Stuart Smith Inc 585 742-3310
  625 Fishers Run Victor (14564) *(G-15876)*
W W Custom Clad Inc 518 673-3322
  75 Creek St Canajoharie (13317) *(G-3209)*
W W Norton & Company Inc (PA) 212 354-5500
  500 5th Ave Fl 6 New York (10110) *(G-12061)*
W W Norton & Company Inc 212 354-5500
  500 5th Ave Lbby 1 New York (10110) *(G-12062)*
W.O.w Brand Products, North Tonawanda Also called Griffin Chemical Company LLC *(G-12431)*
Wacf Enterprise Inc 631 745-5841
  275 Asharoken Ave Northport (11768) *(G-12474)*
Wacoal America Inc 212 743-9600
  136 Madison Ave Fl 15 New York (10016) *(G-12063)*
Wacoal International Corp 212 532-6100
  136 Madison Ave Fl 15 New York (10016) *(G-12064)*
Wadadda.com, Monticello Also called Patrick Rohan *(G-8323)*
Waddington North America Inc 585 638-8200
  88 Nesbitt Dr Holley (14470) *(G-6230)*

Wadsworth Logging Inc 518 863-6870
  3095 State Highway 30 Gloversville (12078) *(G-5471)*
Waffenbauch USA 716 326-4508
  165 Academy St Westfield (14787) *(G-16397)*
Wagner Farms, Lodi Also called Lamoreaux Landing WI *(G-7353)*
Wagner Hardwoods LLC 607 594-3321
  6307 St Route 224 Cayuta (14824) *(G-3315)*
Wagner Hardwoods LLC (PA) 607 229-8198
  6052 County Road 20 Friendship (14739) *(G-5211)*
Wagner Lumber, Owego Also called Wagner Millwork Inc *(G-12805)*
Wagner Millwork Inc 607 687-5362
  4060 Gaskill Rd Owego (13827) *(G-12805)*
Wagner Nineveh Inc 607 693-2689
  224 County Rd 26 Afton (13730) *(G-9)*
Wagner Technical Services Inc 845 566-4018
  1658 Route 300 Newburgh (12550) *(G-12250)*
Wagner Vineyards LLC 607 582-6976
  9322 State Route 414 Lodi (14860) *(G-7354)*
Wagner Vineyards & Brewing Co 607 582-6574
  9322 State Route 414 Lodi (14860) *(G-7355)*
Wagners LLC (PA) 516 933-6580
  366 N Broadway Ste 402 Jericho (11753) *(G-6807)*
Waguya News, Wolcott Also called Wayuga Community Newspapers *(G-16612)*
Wainland Inc 718 626-2233
  2460 47th St Astoria (11103) *(G-448)*
Wal Machine, West Babylon Also called Mpi Consulting Incorporated *(G-16178)*
Walco Stainless, Utica Also called Utica Cutlery Company *(G-15737)*
Waldman Alexander M Diamond Co 212 921-8098
  30 W 47th St Ste 805 New York (10036) *(G-12065)*
Waldman Diamond Company, New York Also called Waldman Alexander M Diamond Co *(G-12065)*
Waldman Publishing Corporation (PA) 212 730-9590
  570 Fashion Ave Rm 800 New York (10018) *(G-12066)*
Waldorf Bakers Inc 718 665-2253
  909 E 135th St Bronx (10454) *(G-1417)*
Walking Charger, The, Rochester Also called Energy Harvesters LLC *(G-13783)*
Wall Protection Products LLC 877 943-6826
  32 Nelson Hill Rd Wassaic (12592) *(G-15967)*
Wall Street Reporter Magazine 212 363-2600
  419 Lafayette St Fl 2 New York (10003) *(G-12067)*
Wall Tool & Tape Corp 718 641-6813
  8111 101st Ave Ozone Park (11416) *(G-12833)*
Wall Tool Manufacturing, Ozone Park Also called Wall Tool & Tape Corp *(G-12833)*
Wallace Home Design Ctr 631 765-3890
  44500 County Road 48 Southold (11971) *(G-14971)*
Wallace Refiners Inc 212 391-2649
  15 W 47th St Ste 808 New York (10036) *(G-12068)*
Wallguard.com, Wassaic Also called Wall Protection Products LLC *(G-15967)*
Wallkill Lodge No 627 F&Am 845 778-7148
  61 Main St Walden (12586) *(G-15899)*
Wallkill Valley Publications 845 561-0170
  300 Stony Brook Ct Ste B Newburgh (12550) *(G-12251)*
Wallkill Valley Times, Newburgh Also called Wallkill Valley Publications *(G-12251)*
Wally Packaging, Monsey Also called Magcrest Packaging Inc *(G-8289)*
Walnut Packaging Inc 631 293-3836
  450 Smith St Farmingdale (11735) *(G-4905)*
Walnut Printing Inc 718 707-0100
  2812 41st Ave Long Island City (11101) *(G-7633)*
Walpole Woodworkers Inc 631 726-2859
  779 Montauk Hwy Water Mill (11976) *(G-15971)*
Walsh & Hughes Inc (PA) 631 427-5904
  1455 New York Ave Huntington Station (11746) *(G-6464)*
Walsh & Sons Machine Inc 845 526-0301
  15 Secor Rd Ste 5 Mahopac (10541) *(G-7716)*
Walter G Legge Company Inc 914 737-5040
  444 Central Ave Peekskill (10566) *(G-12928)*
Walter P Sauer LLC 718 937-0600
  276 Grndpint Ave Ste 8400 Brooklyn (11222) *(G-2638)*
Walter R Tucker Entps Ltd 607 467-2866
  8 Leonard Way Deposit (13754) *(G-4112)*
Walters & Walters Inc 347 202-8535
  961 E 224th St Bronx (10466) *(G-1418)*
Wan Ja Shan, Middletown Also called Mandarin Soy Sauce Inc *(G-8162)*
Wanjashan International LLC 845 343-1505
  4 Sands Station Rd Middletown (10940) *(G-8183)*
Want-Ad Digest Inc 518 279-1181
  870 Hoosick Rd Ste 1 Troy (12180) *(G-15634)*
Wantagh 5 & 10, Wantagh Also called Nbets Corporation *(G-15925)*
Wantagh Computer Center 516 826-2189
  10 Stanford Ct Wantagh (11793) *(G-15927)*
Wapons Specialists, Ridgewood Also called Specialists Ltd *(G-13552)*
Wappingers Falls Shopper Inc 845 297-3723
  84 E Main St Wappingers Falls (12590) *(G-15938)*
Warby Parker Eyewear, New York Also called Parker Warby Retail Inc *(G-11117)*
Ward Diesel Filter Systems, Horseheads Also called Beecher Emssn Sltn Tchnlgs LLC *(G-6305)*
Ward Industrial Equipment Inc (PA) 716 856-6966
  1051 Clinton St Buffalo (14206) *(G-3123)*
Ward Iron Works Limited, Buffalo Also called Ward Industrial Equipment Inc *(G-3123)*

Ward Lafrance Truck Corp 518 893-1865
26 Congress St Ste 259f Saratoga Springs (12866) ***(G-14601)***
Ward Sales Co Inc 315 476-5276
1117 W Fayette St Ste 1 Syracuse (13204) ***(G-15454)***
Ward Steel Company Inc 315 451-4566
4591 Morgan Pl Liverpool (13090) ***(G-7270)***
Warm 212 925-1200
181 Mott St Frnt 1 New York (10012) ***(G-12069)***
Warnaco Group Inc (HQ) 212 287-8000
501 Fashion Ave New York (10018) ***(G-12070)***
Warnaco Inc (HQ) 212 287-8000
501 Fashion Ave Fl 14 New York (10018) ***(G-12071)***
Warnaco Inc 718 722-3000
70 Washington St Fl 10 Brooklyn (11201) ***(G-2639)***
Warner 716 446-0663
514 Hopkins Rd Buffalo (14221) ***(G-3124)***
Warner Energy LLC (PA) 315 457-3828
7526 Morgan Rd Liverpool (13090) ***(G-7271)***
Warner Music Group Corp (HQ) 212 275-2000
1633 Broadway New York (10019) ***(G-12072)***
Warner Music Inc (HQ) 212 275-2000
1633 Broadway New York (10019) ***(G-12073)***
Warner S, New York *Also called Warnaco Inc* ***(G-12071)***
Warodean Corporation 718 359-5559
4308 162nd St Flushing (11358) ***(G-5059)***
Warren Corporation (HQ) 917 379-3434
711 5th Ave Fl 11 New York (10022) ***(G-12074)***
Warren Cutlery Corp 845 876-3444
3584 Route 9g Rhinebeck (12572) ***(G-13490)***
Warren Energy Services LLC 212 697-9660
1114 Ave Of The Americas New York (10036) ***(G-12075)***
Warren Printing Inc 212 627-5000
3718 Northern Blvd # 418 Long Island City (11101) ***(G-7634)***
Warshaw Jacobson Group, New York *Also called Irv Inc* ***(G-10273)***
Warwick Press, Warwick *Also called Digital United Color Prtg Inc* ***(G-15950)***
Warwick Valley Wine Co 845 258-4858
114 Little York Rd Warwick (10990) ***(G-15962)***
Warwick Vly Winery Distillary, Warwick *Also called Warwick Valley Wine Co* ***(G-15962)***
Wascomat of America, Inwood *Also called Pluslux LLC* ***(G-6499)***
Wash Quarters LLC 989 802-2017
680 Hoagerburgh Rd Wallkill (12589) ***(G-15909)***
Washburn Litho Envirgo Prtg, Rochester *Also called Presstek Printing LLC* ***(G-14043)***
Washburn Manufacturing Tech 607 387-3991
9828 State Route 96 Trumansburg (14886) ***(G-15641)***
Washburns Dairy Inc 518 725-0629
145 N Main St Gloversville (12078) ***(G-5472)***
Washer Solutions Inc 585 742-6388
760 Canning Pkwy Ste A Victor (14564) ***(G-15877)***
Washingtom Mills Elec Mnrls (HQ) 716 278-6600
1801 Buffalo Ave Niagara Falls (14303) ***(G-12349)***
Washington Foundries Inc 516 374-8447
1434 Vian Ave Hewlett (11557) ***(G-6054)***
Washington Mills Tonawanda Inc (HQ) 716 693-4550
1000 E Niagara St Tonawanda (14150) ***(G-15590)***
Washington Post Advg Sls Ofc, New York *Also called Wp Company LLC* ***(G-12142)***
Washington Square News, New York *Also called New York University* ***(G-10947)***
Waste Management, Palatine Bridge *Also called Lee Publications Inc* ***(G-12843)***
Wastecorp Pumps LLC (PA) 888 829-2783
345 W 85th St Apt 23 New York (10024) ***(G-12076)***
Wastequip - Consolidated, New Lebanon *Also called Wastequip Manufacturing Co LLC* ***(G-8574)***
Wastequip Manufacturing Co LLC 800 235-0734
1079 State Route 20 New Lebanon (12125) ***(G-8574)***
Watch Journal LLC 212 229-1500
110 E 25th St Fl 4 New York (10010) ***(G-12077)***
Watchanish LLC 917 558-0404
1 Rockefeller Plz Fl 11 New York (10020) ***(G-12078)***
Watchcraft Inc 347 531-0382
2214 40th Ave Ste 4 Long Island City (11101) ***(G-7635)***
Watchtime Magazine, New York *Also called Ebner Publishing International* ***(G-9617)***
Watec America Corporation 702 434-6111
720 Route 17m Ste 4 Middletown (10940) ***(G-8184)***
Water Cooling Corp 718 723-6500
24520 Merrick Blvd Rosedale (11422) ***(G-14442)***
Water Energy Systems LLC 844 822-7665
1 Maiden Ln New York (10038) ***(G-12079)***
Water Lilies, Astoria *Also called Wlf Founders Corporation* ***(G-450)***
Water Oracle 845 876-8327
41 E Market St Rhinebeck (12572) ***(G-13491)***
Water Splash Inc 800 936-3430
25 Locust St Ste 421 Champlain (12919) ***(G-3418)***
Water Street Brass Corporation 716 763-0059
4515 Gleason Rd Lakewood (14750) ***(G-6999)***
Water Technologies Inc (PA) 315 986-0000
1635 Commons Pkwy Macedon (14502) ***(G-7705)***
Water Wise of America Inc 585 232-1210
75 Bermar Park Ste 5 Rochester (14624) ***(G-14203)***
Waterbury Garment LLC 212 725-1500
16 E 34th St Fl 10 New York (10016) ***(G-12080)***
Watermark Designs Holdings Ltd 718 257-2800
350 Dewitt Ave Brooklyn (11207) ***(G-2640)***
Watertown Concrete Inc 315 788-1040
24471 State Route 12 Watertown (13601) ***(G-16036)***
Watertown Daily Times, Watertown *Also called Northern NY Newspapers Corp* ***(G-16031)***
Watkins Welding and Mch Sp Inc 914 949-6168
87 Westmoreland Ave White Plains (10606) ***(G-16516)***
Watson Adventures LLC 212 564-8293
330 W 38th St Rm 407 New York (10018) ***(G-12081)***
Watson Bowman Acme Corp 716 691-8162
95 Pineview Dr Amherst (14228) ***(G-260)***
Watson Laboratories Inc 951 493-5300
1033 Stoneleigh Ave Carmel (10512) ***(G-3284)***
Watson Productions LLC 516 334-9766
740 Old Willets Path # 400 Hauppauge (11788) ***(G-5973)***
Wave Float Rooms LLC 844 356-2876
4817 Kraus Rd Clarence (14031) ***(G-3542)***
Wave of Long Island, The, Rockaway Beach *Also called Wave Publishing Co Inc* ***(G-14226)***
Wave Publishing Co Inc 718 634-4000
8808 Rockaway Beach Blvd Rockaway Beach (11693) ***(G-14226)***
Waverly Iron Corp 631 732-2800
25 Commercial Blvd Medford (11763) ***(G-7968)***
Wavodyne Therapeutics Inc 954 632-6630
150 Lucius Gordon Dr West Henrietta (14586) ***(G-16255)***
Way Out Toys Inc 212 689-9094
230 5th Ave Ste 800 New York (10001) ***(G-12082)***
Waymor1 Inc 518 677-8511
Hc 22 Cambridge (12816) ***(G-3184)***
Wayne County Mail, Webster *Also called Empire State Weeklies Inc* ***(G-16084)***
Wayne Decorators Inc 718 529-4200
14409 Rockaway Blvd Apt 1 Jamaica (11436) ***(G-6690)***
Wayne Integrated Tech Corp 631 242-0213
160 Rodeo Dr Edgewood (11717) ***(G-4423)***
Wayne Printing Inc 914 761-2400
70 W Red Oak Ln Fl 4 White Plains (10604) ***(G-16517)***
Wayne Printing & Lithographic, White Plains *Also called Wayne Printing Inc* ***(G-16517)***
Waynes Welding Inc 315 768-6146
66 Calder Ave Yorkville (13495) ***(G-16835)***
Wayuga Community Newspapers (PA) 315 754-6229
6784 Main St Red Creek (13143) ***(G-13456)***
Wayuga Community Newspapers 315 594-2506
12039 E Main St Wolcott (14590) ***(G-16612)***
Wayuga News, Red Creek *Also called Wayuga Community Newspapers* ***(G-13456)***
Wcd Window Coverings Inc 845 336-4511
1711 Ulster Ave Lake Katrine (12449) ***(G-6973)***
WD Certified Contracting LLC 516 493-9319
112 Magnolia Ave 101-A Westbury (11590) ***(G-16387)***
We Work 877 673-6628
1 Little West 12th St New York (10014) ***(G-12083)***
Wea International Inc (HQ) 212 275-1300
75 Rockefeller Plz New York (10019) ***(G-12084)***
Wear Abouts Apparel Inc 212 827-0888
260 W 36th St Rm 602 New York (10018) ***(G-12085)***
Weather Products Corporation 315 474-8593
102 W Division St Fl 1 Syracuse (13204) ***(G-15455)***
Weather Tight Exteriors 631 375-5108
8 Woodbrook Dr Ridge (11961) ***(G-13525)***
Weatherproof, Bay Shore *Also called David Peyser Sportswear Inc* ***(G-678)***
Weaver Machine & Tool Co Inc 315 253-4422
44 York St Auburn (13021) ***(G-509)***
Weaver Wind Energy LLC 607 379-9463
7 Union St Freeville (13068) ***(G-5193)***
Web Associates Inc 716 883-3377
1255 Niagara St Buffalo (14213) ***(G-3125)***
Web Graphics, Queensbury *Also called Amsterdam Printing & Litho Inc* ***(G-13416)***
Web Seal Inc (PA) 585 546-1320
15 Oregon St Rochester (14605) ***(G-14204)***
Web-Cote Industries 914 630-1600
19 Avon Rd Larchmont (10538) ***(G-7060)***
Web-Tech Packaging Inc 716 684-4520
500 Commerce Pkwy Lancaster (14086) ***(G-7054)***
Webb-Mason Inc 716 276-8792
300 Airborne Pkwy Ste 210 Buffalo (14225) ***(G-3126)***
Weber Intl Packg Co LLC 518 561-8282
318 Cornelia St Plattsburgh (12901) ***(G-13168)***
Weber-Knapp Company (PA) 716 484-9135
441 Chandler St Jamestown (14701) ***(G-6761)***
Webinfinity Americas Inc (PA) 516 331-5180
315 Main St Unit 4 Huntington (11743) ***(G-6427)***
Webster Ontrio Wlwrth Pnnysver 585 265-3620
164 E Main St Webster (14580) ***(G-16106)***
Webster Printing Corporation 585 671-1533
46 North Ave Webster (14580) ***(G-16107)***
Wecare Organics LLC (PA) 315 689-1937
9293 Bonta Bridge Rd Jordan (13080) ***(G-6843)***
Weco Metal Products, Ontario *Also called Dj Acquisition Management Corp* ***(G-12652)***
Wedding Gown Preservation Co 607 748-7999
707 North St Endicott (13760) ***(G-4615)***
Wedel Sign Company Inc 631 727-4577
705 W Main St Riverhead (11901) ***(G-13588)***
Week Publications, The, New York *Also called Dennis Publishing Inc* ***(G-9502)***
Weekly Ajkal 718 565-2100
3707 74th St Ste 8 Jackson Heights (11372) ***(G-6621)***
Weekly Bornomal, Jackson Heights *Also called Bornomala USA Inc* ***(G-6618)***

A L P H A B E T I C

Weekly Business News Corp ALPHABETIC SECTION

Weekly Business News Corp 212 689-5888
274 Madison Ave Rm 1101 New York (10016) ***(G-12086)***

Weeks & Reichel Printing Inc 631 589-1443
131 Railroad Ave Sayville (11782) ***(G-14635)***

Wego International Floors LLC 516 487-3510
239 Great Neck Rd Great Neck (11021) ***(G-5600)***

Weico Wire & Cable Inc 631 254-2970
161 Rodeo Dr Edgewood (11717) ***(G-4424)***

Weicro Graphics Inc 631 253-3360
95 Mahan St West Babylon (11704) ***(G-16204)***

Weider Publications LLC 212 545-4800
1 Park Ave Fl 10 New York (10016) ***(G-12087)***

Weighing & Systems Tech Inc 518 274-2797
274 2nd St Troy (12180) ***(G-15635)***

Weinfeld Skull Cap Mfg Co Inc 718 854-3864
6022 14th Ave Brooklyn (11219) ***(G-2641)***

Weisbeck Publishing Printing 716 937-9226
13200 Broadway St Alden (14004) ***(G-178)***

Weisco Inc 212 575-8989
246 W 38th St Fl 6 New York (10018) ***(G-12088)***

Weiss Industries Inc 518 784-9643
27 Blossom Ln Valatie (12184) ***(G-15740)***

Weiss Instruments Inc 631 207-1200
905 Waverly Ave Holtsville (11742) ***(G-6250)***

Wel Made Enterprises Inc 631 752-1238
1630 New Hwy Farmingdale (11735) ***(G-4906)***

Welch Allyn Inc 315 685-4100
4341 State Street Rd Skaneateles Falls (13153) ***(G-14882)***

Welch Allyn Inc (HQ) 315 685-4100
4341 State Street Rd Skaneateles Falls (13153) ***(G-14883)***

Welch Allyn Inc 315 685-4347
4619 Jordan Rd Skaneateles Falls (13153) ***(G-14884)***

Welch Foods Inc A Cooperative 716 326-5252
2 S Portage St Westfield (14787) ***(G-16398)***

Welch Foods Inc A Cooperative 716 326-3131
100 N Portage St Westfield (14787) ***(G-16399)***

Welch Machine Inc 585 647-3578
961 Lyell Ave Bldg 1-6 Rochester (14606) ***(G-14205)***

Welcome Magazine Inc 716 839-3121
4511 Harlem Rd Amherst (14226) ***(G-261)***

Welcome Rain Publishers LLC 212 686-1909
230 5th Ave New York (10001) ***(G-12089)***

Weld-Built Body Co Inc 631 643-9700
276 Long Island Ave Wyandanch (11798) ***(G-16697)***

Weldcomputer Corporation 518 283-2897
105 Jordan Rd Ste 1 Troy (12180) ***(G-15636)***

Welded Tube Usa Inc 716 828-1111
2537 Hamburg Tpke Lackawanna (14218) ***(G-6954)***

Welding and Brazing Svcs Inc 607 397-1009
2761 County Highway 26 Richfield Springs (13439) ***(G-13493)***

Welding Chapter of New York 212 481-1496
44 W 28th St Fl 12 New York (10001) ***(G-12090)***

Welding Metallurgy Inc (HQ) 631 253-0500
360 Motor Pkwy Ste 100 Hauppauge (11788) ***(G-5974)***

Weldrite Closures Inc 585 429-8790
11 Sutton Pt Pittsford (14534) ***(G-13028)***

Well-Made Toy Mfg Corporation 718 381-4225
146 Soundview Dr Port Washington (11050) ***(G-13313)***

Wellmill LLC 631 465-9245
69 Mall Dr Commack (11725) ***(G-3706)***

Wellquest International Inc (PA) 212 689-9094
230 5th Ave Ste 800 New York (10001) ***(G-12091)***

Wells Rugs Inc 516 676-2056
44 Sea Cliff Ave Glen Cove (11542) ***(G-5378)***

Wells, George Ruggery, Glen Cove *Also called Wells Rugs Inc* ***(G-5378)***

Wellspring Corp (PA) 212 529-5454
54a Ludlow St New York (10002) ***(G-12092)***

Wellspring Omni Holdings Corp 212 318-9800
390 Park Ave New York (10022) ***(G-12093)***

Wellsville Daily Reporter, Wellsville *Also called Seneca Media Inc* ***(G-16122)***

Wemco Casting LLC 631 563-8050
20 Jules Ct Ste 2 Bohemia (11716) ***(G-1108)***

Wen Hwa Printing, Flushing *Also called Global Graphics Inc* ***(G-5002)***

Wendels Poultry Farm 716 592-2299
12466 Vaughn St East Concord (14055) ***(G-4215)***

Wendon Engineering, Hawthorne *Also called Princetel Inc* ***(G-5996)***

Wendt Corporation 716 391-1200
2555 Walden Ave Buffalo (14225) ***(G-3127)***

Wendys Auto Express Inc 845 624-6100
121 Main St Nanuet (10954) ***(G-8468)***

Wenig Company, The, Amityville *Also called Portfab LLC* ***(G-313)***

Wenig Corporation 718 542-3600
230 Manida St Fl 2 Bronx (10474) ***(G-1419)***

Wenner Bakery, Ronkonkoma *Also called Wenner Bread Products Inc* ***(G-14431)***

Wenner Bread Products Inc (PA) 800 869-6262
2001 Orville Dr N Ronkonkoma (11779) ***(G-14430)***

Wenner Bread Products Inc 800 869-6262
2001 Orville Dr N Ronkonkoma (11779) ***(G-14431)***

Wenner Media LLC (PA) 212 484-1616
1290 Ave Of The Amer Fl 2 New York (10104) ***(G-12094)***

Were Forms Inc 585 482-4400
500 Helendale Rd Ste 190 Rochester (14609) ***(G-14206)***

Werlatone Inc 845 278-2220
17 Jon Barrett Rd Patterson (12563) ***(G-12887)***

Werma (usa) Inc 315 414-0200
6731 Collamer Rd Ste 1 East Syracuse (13057) ***(G-4381)***

Werner Brothers Electric Inc 518 377-3056
677 Riverview Rd Rexford (12148) ***(G-13484)***

Wessie Machine Inc 315 926-4060
5229 Steel Point Rd Marion (14505) ***(G-7811)***

West End Iron Works Inc 518 456-1105
4254 Albany St Albany (12205) ***(G-141)***

West End Journal, Far Rockaway *Also called Empire Publishing Inc* ***(G-4700)***

West Falls Machine Co Inc 716 655-0440
11692 E Main Rd East Aurora (14052) ***(G-4211)***

West Falls Machine Co 1, East Aurora *Also called West Falls Machine Co Inc* ***(G-4211)***

West Herr Automotive Group, Hamburg *Also called Kustom Korner* ***(G-5686)***

West Internet Trading Company 415 484-5848
47 Great Jones St Fl 5 New York (10012) ***(G-12095)***

West Metal Works Inc 716 895-4900
68 Hayes Pl Buffalo (14210) ***(G-3128)***

West Seneca Bee Inc 716 632-4700
5564 Main St Williamsville (14221) ***(G-16593)***

Westbrook Machinery, Lockport *Also called Ted Westbrook* ***(G-7335)***

Westbury Times 516 747-8282
132 E 2nd St Mineola (11501) ***(G-8252)***

Westchester County Bus Jurnl, White Plains *Also called Westfair Communications Inc* ***(G-16521)***

Westchester Law Journal Inc 914 948-0715
199 Main St Ste 301 White Plains (10601) ***(G-16518)***

Westchester Magazine, Elmsford *Also called Suburban Publishing Inc* ***(G-4572)***

Westchester Mailing Service 914 948-1116
39 Westmoreland Ave Fl 2 White Plains (10606) ***(G-16519)***

Westchester Modular Homes Inc 845 832-9400
30 Reagans Mill Rd Wingdale (12594) ***(G-16607)***

Westchester Signs Inc 914 666-7446
145 Kisco Ave Mount Kisco (10549) ***(G-8359)***

Westchester Technologies Inc 914 736-1034
8 John Walsh Blvd Ste 311 Peekskill (10566) ***(G-12929)***

Westchester Valve & Fitting Co 914 762-6600
741 Pierce Rd Clifton Park (12065) ***(G-3580)***

Westchester Wine Warehouse LLC 914 824-1400
53 Tarrytown Rd Ste 1 White Plains (10607) ***(G-16520)***

Westchster Crankshaft Grinding, East Elmhurst *Also called Westchstr Crnkshft Grndng* ***(G-4226)***

Westchstr Crnkshft Grndng 718 651-3900
3263 110th St East Elmhurst (11369) ***(G-4226)***

Westcode Incorporated 607 766-9881
2226 Airport Rd Binghamton (13905) ***(G-923)***

Western Edition, Westhampton Beach *Also called Southampton Town Newspapers* ***(G-16406)***

Western New York Energy LLC 585 798-9693
4141 Bates Rd Medina (14103) ***(G-7992)***

Western New York Family Mag 716 836-3486
3147 Delaware Ave Ste B Buffalo (14217) ***(G-3129)***

Western Oil and Gas JV Inc 914 967-4758
7 Mccullough Pl Rye (10580) ***(G-14489)***

Western Queens Gazette, Long Island City *Also called Service Advertising Group Inc* ***(G-7588)***

Westfair Communications Inc 914 694-3600
3 Westchester Park Dr G7 White Plains (10604) ***(G-16521)***

Westfield Publication, Westfield *Also called Quality Guides* ***(G-16395)***

Westinghouse A Brake Tech Corp 518 561-0044
72 Arizona Ave Plattsburgh (12903) ***(G-13169)***

Westinghouse A Brake Tech Corp 914 347-8650
4 Warehouse Ln Ste 144 Elmsford (10523) ***(G-4577)***

Westmail Press, White Plains *Also called Westchester Mailing Service* ***(G-16519)***

Westmoor Ltd 315 363-1500
906 W Hamilton Ave Sherrill (13461) ***(G-14825)***

Westmore Litho Corp 718 361-9403
4017 22nd St Long Island City (11101) ***(G-7636)***

Westmore Litho Printing Co, Long Island City *Also called Westmore Litho Corp* ***(G-7636)***

Westpoint Home LLC (HQ) 212 930-2000
28 E 28th St Cncrse Level New York (10016) ***(G-12096)***

Westrock - Solvay Llc (HQ) 315 484-9050
53 Indl Dr Syracuse (13204) ***(G-15456)***

Westrock - Southern Cont LLC 315 487-6111
100 Southern Dr Camillus (13031) ***(G-3200)***

Westrock Cp LLC 770 448-2193
45 Campion Rd New Hartford (13413) ***(G-8513)***

Westrock Cp LLC 716 692-6510
51 Robinson St North Tonawanda (14120) ***(G-12462)***

Westrock CP LLC 315 484-9050
53 Industrial Dr Syracuse (13204) ***(G-15457)***

Westrock CP LLC 716 694-1000
51 Robinson St North Tonawanda (14120) ***(G-12463)***

Westrock Mwv LLC 212 688-5000
299 Park Ave Fl 13 New York (10171) ***(G-12097)***

Westrock Rkt LLC 631 586-6000
140 W Industry Ct Deer Park (11729) ***(G-4062)***

Westrock Rkt LLC 315 487-6111
100 Southern Dr Camillus (13031) ***(G-3201)***

Westrock Rkt Company 770 448-2193
53 Indl Dr Syracuse (13204) *(G-15458)*
Westrock Rkt Company 770 448-2193
4914 W Genesee St Camillus (13031) *(G-3202)*
Westron Corporation 516 678-2300
18 Neil Ct Oceanside (11572) *(G-12565)*
Westron Lighting, Oceanside *Also called Westron Corporation (G-12565)*
Westside News Inc 585 352-3411
1835 N Union St Spencerport (14559) *(G-14983)*
Westypo Printers Inc 914 737-7394
540 Harrison Ave Peekskill (10566) *(G-12930)*
Wet & Wild Pools & Spas, Brooklyn *Also called Polytech Pool Mfg Inc (G-2326)*
Wet Paint, New York *Also called Wetpaintcom Inc (G-12098)*
Wetherall Contracting NY Inc 718 894-7011
8312 Penelope Ave Ste 101 Middle Village (11379) *(G-8128)*
Wetlook Detailing Inc 212 390-8877
1125 Banner Ave Apt 11a Brooklyn (11235) *(G-2642)*
Wetpaintcom Inc 206 859-6300
45 W 89th St Apt 4a New York (10024) *(G-12098)*
Wew Container, Brooklyn *Also called Inland Paper Products Corp (G-2005)*
Wey Inc 212 532-3299
21 W 39th St Fl 6 New York (10018) *(G-12099)*
WF Lake Corp 518 798-9934
65 Park Rd Queensbury (12804) *(G-13445)*
Wg Sheet Metal Corp 718 235-3093
341 Amber St Brooklyn (11208) *(G-2643)*
Whalebone Creative, Montauk *Also called Jesse Joeckel (G-8304)*
Whalens Horseradish Products 518 587-6404
1710 Route 29 Galway (12074) *(G-5241)*
Wham 1180 AM, Rochester *Also called Iheartcommunications Inc (G-13877)*
Whats Next Manufacturing Inc 585 492-1014
4 Rule Dr Arcade (14009) *(G-391)*
Whentech LLC (HQ) 212 571-0042
55 E 52nd St Fl 40 New York (10055) *(G-12100)*
Where Is Utica Cof Rasting Inc 315 269-8898
92 Genesee St Utica (13502) *(G-15739)*
Whirlwind Music Distrs Inc 800 733-9473
99 Ling Rd Rochester (14612) *(G-14207)*
Whispr Group Inc 212 924-3979
6 Saint Johns Ln New York (10013) *(G-12101)*
Whitacre Engineering Company 315 622-1075
4522 Wetzel Rd Liverpool (13090) *(G-7272)*
White Coffee Corp 718 204-7900
1835 38th St Astoria (11105) *(G-449)*
White Eagle Packing Co Inc 518 374-4366
922 Congress St Schenectady (12303) *(G-14728)*
White Gate Holdings Inc (PA) 212 564-3266
22 W 38th St Fl 6 New York (10018) *(G-12102)*
White House Cabinet Shop LLC 607 674-9358
11 Knapp St Sherburne (13460) *(G-14813)*
White Label Partners LLC 917 445-6650
250 Mercer St Apt B1205 New York (10012) *(G-12103)*
White Plains Coat Apron Co Inc 914 736-2610
4 John Walsh Blvd Peekskill (10566) *(G-12931)*
White Plains Linen, Peekskill *Also called White Plains Coat Apron Co Inc (G-12931)*
White Plains Marble Inc 914 347-6000
186 E Main St Elmsford (10523) *(G-4578)*
White Workroom Inc 212 941-5910
40 W 27th St Fl 11 New York (10001) *(G-12104)*
Whiteboard Ventures Inc 855 972-6346
315 W 36th St Fl 10 New York (10018) *(G-12105)*
Whitehall Times, Granville *Also called Manchester Newspaper Inc (G-5520)*
Whitesboro Spring & Alignment (PA) 315 736-4441
247 Oriskany Blvd Whitesboro (13492) *(G-16532)*
Whitesboro Spring Svce, Whitesboro *Also called Whitesboro Spring & Alignment (G-16532)*
Whitestone Dev Group LLC 585 482-7770
111 Humboldt St Rochester (14609) *(G-14208)*
Whitestone Panetteria LLC 516 543-9788
15045 12th Rd Whitestone (11357) *(G-16552)*
Whitestone Pharmacy, Whitestone *Also called Tocare LLC (G-16549)*
Whitewall Magazine, New York *Also called Sky Art Media Inc (G-11612)*
Whitford Development Inc 631 471-7711
646 Main St Ste 301 Port Jefferson (11777) *(G-13224)*
Whiting Door Mfg Corp (PA) 716 542-5427
113 Cedar St Akron (14001) *(G-24)*
Whiting Door Mfg Corp 716 542-3070
13550 Bloomingdale Rd Akron (14001) *(G-25)*
Whitley East LLC 718 403-0050
Brooklyn Navy Yd Bg 2 Fl Brooklyn (11205) *(G-2644)*
Whitney Boin Studio Inc 914 377-4385
42 Warburton Ave Ste 1 Yonkers (10701) *(G-16807)*
Whitney Foods Inc 718 291-3333
15504 Liberty Ave Jamaica (11433) *(G-6691)*
Whitsons Food Svc Bronx Corp 631 424-2700
1800 Motor Pkwy Islandia (11749) *(G-6540)*
Whittall & Shon (PA) 212 594-2626
1201 Broadway Ste 904a New York (10001) *(G-12106)*
Wholesale, New York *Also called Ashko Group LLC (G-8931)*
Wholesale Mulch & Sawdust Inc 607 687-2637
3711 Waverly Rd Owego (13827) *(G-12806)*
Wholesale Window Warehouse, Oceanside *Also called Express Building Supply Inc (G-12537)*
Wicked Smart LLC 518 459-2855
700 5th Ave Watervliet (12189) *(G-16057)*
Wicked Spoon Inc 646 335-2890
127 W 24th St Fl 6 New York (10011) *(G-12107)*
Wickers Performance Wear, Commack *Also called Wickers Sportswear Inc (G-3707)*
Wickers Sportswear Inc (PA) 631 543-1700
88 Wyandanch Blvd Commack (11725) *(G-3707)*
Wide Flange Inc 718 492-8705
176 27th St Brooklyn (11232) *(G-2645)*
Widex International, Hauppauge *Also called Widex Usa Inc (G-5975)*
Widex Usa Inc (HQ) 718 360-1000
185 Commerce Dr Hauppauge (11788) *(G-5975)*
Widgetworks Unlimited LLC 914 666-6395
395 Millwood Rd Chappaqua (10514) *(G-3424)*
Widmer Time Recorder Company 212 227-0405
27 Park Pl Rm 219 New York (10007) *(G-12108)*
Wiggby Precision Machine Corp 718 439-6900
140 58th St Ste 56 Brooklyn (11220) *(G-2646)*
Wikoff Color Corporation 585 458-0653
686 Pullman Ave Rochester (14615) *(G-14209)*
Wil-Nic, Freeport *Also called Edr Industries Inc (G-5152)*
Wilbar International Inc 631 951-9800
50 Cabot Ct Hauppauge (11788) *(G-5976)*
Wilbedone Inc 607 756-8813
1133 State Route 222 Cortland (13045) *(G-3897)*
Wilco Industries Inc 631 676-2593
788 Marconi Ave Ronkonkoma (11779) *(G-14432)*
Wilcro Inc 716 632-4204
90 Earhart Dr Ste 19 Buffalo (14221) *(G-3130)*
Wild Turkey, New York *Also called Austin Nichols & Co Inc (G-8965)*
Wild Works Incorporated 716 891-4197
30 Railroad Ave Albany (12205) *(G-142)*
Wilda, Long Island City *Also called Import-Export Corporation (G-7473)*
Wilkesboro Road, New York *Also called Schneider Mills Inc (G-11511)*
Willard Machine 716 885-1630
73 Forest Ave Buffalo (14213) *(G-3131)*
Willco Fine Art Ltd 718 935-9567
145 Nassau St Apt 9c New York (10038) *(G-12109)*
Willemin-Macodel Inc 914 345-3504
5 Westchester Plz Elmsford (10523) *(G-4579)*
William B Collins Company 518 773-8272
8 E Fulton St Gloversville (12078) *(G-5473)*
William Boyd Printing Co Inc 518 339-5832
4 Weed Rd Ste 1 Latham (12110) *(G-7098)*
William Brooks Woodworking 718 495-9767
856 Saratoga Ave Brooklyn (11212) *(G-2647)*
William Charles Prtg Co Inc 516 349-0900
7 Fairchild Ct Ste 100 Plainview (11803) *(G-13102)*
William E William Valve Corp 718 392-1660
3852 Review Ave Long Island City (11101) *(G-7637)*
William E Williams Valve Corp 718 392-1660
3850 Review Ave Long Island City (11101) *(G-7638)*
William Goldberg Diamond Corp 212 980-4343
589 5th Ave Fl 14 New York (10017) *(G-12110)*
William H Jackson Company 718 784-4482
3629 23rd St Long Island City (11106) *(G-7639)*
William H Sadlier Inc (PA) 212 233-3646
9 Pine St New York (10005) *(G-12111)*
William H Shapiro 212 263-7037
530 1st Ave Ste 3e New York (10016) *(G-12112)*
William Harvey Studio Inc 718 599-4343
214 N 8th St Brooklyn (11211) *(G-2648)*
William J Kline & Son Inc (PA) 518 843-1100
1 Venner Rd Amsterdam (12010) *(G-364)*
William J Ryan 585 392-6200
1365 Hamlin Parma Townlne Hilton (14468) *(G-6159)*
William Kanes Mfg Corp 718 346-1515
23 Alabama Ave Brooklyn (11207) *(G-2649)*
William Moon Iron Works Inc 518 943-3861
80 Main St Catskill (12414) *(G-3309)*
William Morrow Publishing, New York *Also called Harpercollins Publishers LLC (G-10038)*
William R Shoemaker Inc 716 649-0511
399 Pleasant Ave Hamburg (14075) *(G-5697)*
William S Hein & Co Inc (PA) 716 882-2600
2350 N Forest Rd Ste 14a Getzville (14068) *(G-5356)*
William S Hein & Co Inc 716 882-2600
1575 Main St Buffalo (14209) *(G-3132)*
William Somerville Maintenance 212 534-4600
129 E 124th St New York (10035) *(G-12113)*
William Ward Logging 518 946-7826
Valley Rd Jay (12941) *(G-6775)*
Williams Tool Inc 315 737-7226
9372 Elm St Chadwicks (13319) *(G-3401)*
Williams-Sonoma Store 154, New York *Also called Williams-Sonoma Stores Inc (G-12114)*
Williams-Sonoma Stores Inc 212 633-2203
110 7th Ave New York (10011) *(G-12114)*
Williamsburg Bulletin 718 387-0123
136 Ross St Brooklyn (11211) *(G-2650)*
Williamson Law Book Co 585 924-3400
790 Canning Pkwy Ste 2 Victor (14564) *(G-15878)*

ALPHABETIC

(PA)=Parent Co (HQ)=Headquarters (DH)=Div Headquarters
2019 Harris
New York Manufacturers Directory
1017

Willis Mc Donald Co Inc....212 366-1526
44 W 62nd St Ph A New York (10023) ***(G-12115)***
Willow Creek Winery, Silver Creek *Also called Chautauqua Wine Company Inc* ***(G-14860)***
Wilmax Usa LLC....917 388-2790
315 5th Ave Rm 505 New York (10016) ***(G-12116)***
Wilmington Products USA, Roslyn *Also called Northwest Company LLC* ***(G-14449)***
Wilson & Wilson Group....212 729-4736
6514 110th St Forest Hills (11375) ***(G-5082)***
Wilson Beef Farms LLC....607 545-8308
10751 Hess Rd Canaseraga (14822) ***(G-3239)***
Wilson N Wilson Group & RES, Forest Hills *Also called Wilson & Wilson Group* ***(G-5082)***
Wilson Picture Frames, West Hempstead *Also called Interntonal Consmr Connections* ***(G-16217)***
Wilson Press LLC....315 568-9693
56 Miller St Seneca Falls (13148) ***(G-14788)***
Wilsonart Intl Holdings LLC....516 935-6980
999 S Oyster Bay Rd # 3305 Bethpage (11714) ***(G-854)***
Wilston Enterprises Inc....716 483-1411
121 Jackson Ave Jamestown (14701) ***(G-6762)***
Wilt Industries Inc....518 548-4961
2452 State Route 8 Lake Pleasant (12108) ***(G-6979)***
Win Set Technologies LLC....631 234-7077
2364 Middle Country Rd Centereach (11720) ***(G-3346)***
Win Wood Cabinetry Inc....516 304-2216
200 Forest Dr Ste 7 Greenvale (11548) ***(G-5634)***
Win-Holt Equipment Corp (PA)....516 222-0335
20 Crossways Park Dr N # 205 Woodbury (11797) ***(G-16634)***
Win-Holt Equipment Group, Woodbury *Also called Win-Holt Equipment Corp* ***(G-16634)***
Winchester Optical Company (HQ)....607 734-4251
1935 Lake St Elmira (14901) ***(G-4507)***
Windiam Usa Inc....212 542-0949
580 5th Ave Ste 2907 New York (10036) ***(G-12117)***
Window Tech Systems Inc....518 899-9000
15 Old Stonebreak Rd Ballston Spa (12020) ***(G-598)***
Window-Fix Inc....718 854-3475
331 37th St Fl 1 Brooklyn (11232) ***(G-2651)***
Windowcraft Inc....516 294-3580
77 2nd Ave Garden City Park (11040) ***(G-5289)***
Windowman Inc (usa)....718 246-2626
460 Kingsland Ave Brooklyn (11222) ***(G-2652)***
Windows Media Publishing LLC....917 732-7892
369 Remsen Ave Brooklyn (11212) ***(G-2653)***
Windowtex Inc....877 294-3580
77 2nd Ave New Hyde Park (11040) ***(G-8573)***
Windsor Technology LLC....585 461-2500
1527 Lyell Ave Rochester (14606) ***(G-14210)***
Windsor United Industries LLC....607 655-3300
10 Park St Windsor (13865) ***(G-16605)***
Wine & Spirits Magazine Inc (PA)....212 695-4660
2 W 32nd St Ste 601 New York (10001) ***(G-12118)***
Wine Group Inc....716 326-3151
85 Bourne St Westfield (14787) ***(G-16400)***
Wine Services Inc....631 722-3800
1129 Cross River Dr Ste A Riverhead (11901) ***(G-13589)***
Winerackscom Inc....845 658-7181
819 Route 32 Tillson (12486) ***(G-15515)***
Winesoft International Corp....914 400-6247
503 S Broadway Ste 220 Yonkers (10705) ***(G-16808)***
Wing Heung Noodle Inc....212 966-7496
144 Baxter St New York (10013) ***(G-12119)***
Wing Kei Noodle Inc....212 226-1644
102 Canal St New York (10002) ***(G-12120)***
Wink Acquisition Corp., New York *Also called Wink Labs Inc* ***(G-12122)***
Wink Inc....212 389-1382
606 W 28th St Fl 6 New York (10001) ***(G-12121)***
Wink Labs Inc (HQ)....916 717-0437
606 W 28th St Fl 7 New York (10001) ***(G-12122)***
Winn Manufacturing Inc....518 642-3515
12 Burtis Ave Granville (12832) ***(G-5525)***
Winner Press Inc....718 937-7715
4331 33rd St 1 Long Island City (11101) ***(G-7640)***
Winsight LLC....646 708-7309
90 Broad St Ste 402 New York (10004) ***(G-12123)***
Winson Surnamer Inc....718 729-8787
4402 11th St Ste 601 Long Island City (11101) ***(G-7641)***
Winter Water Factory....646 387-3247
191 33rd St Brooklyn (11232) ***(G-2654)***
Winterling, Eric Costumes, New York *Also called Eric Winterling Inc* ***(G-9700)***
Winters Instruments, Buffalo *Also called Winters Instruments Inc* ***(G-3133)***
Winters Instruments Inc (HQ)....281 880-8607
455 Cayuga Rd Ste 650 Buffalo (14225) ***(G-3133)***
Winters Railroad Service Inc....716 337-2668
11309 Sisson Hwy North Collins (14111) ***(G-12390)***
Winterwheat Corp....212 203-2064
11 Wall St New York (10005) ***(G-12124)***
Wired Coffee and Bagel Inc....518 506-3194
Rr 9 Malta (12020) ***(G-7733)***
Wireless Communications Inc....845 353-5921
4 Chemong Ct Nyack (10960) ***(G-12513)***
With You Designs LLC....800 413-0670
54 Elizabeth St Ste 2 Red Hook (12571) ***(G-13460)***
With You Lockets, Red Hook *Also called With You Designs LLC* ***(G-13460)***
Wizard Equipment Inc....315 414-9999
10 Dwight Park Dr Ste 3 Syracuse (13209) ***(G-15459)***
Wizer Equipment, Rochester *Also called Woerner Industries Inc* ***(G-14211)***
Wizq Inc....586 381-9048
307 5th Ave Fl 8 New York (10016) ***(G-12125)***
Wl Concepts & Production Inc....516 538-5300
1 Bennington Ave Freeport (11520) ***(G-5190)***
Wlf Founders Corporation....718 777-8899
4510 19th Ave Astoria (11105) ***(G-450)***
Wlj Printers, White Plains *Also called Westchester Law Journal Inc* ***(G-16518)***
Wm E Martin and Sons Co Inc....516 605-2444
55 Bryant Ave Ste 300 Roslyn (11576) ***(G-14452)***
Wmg Acquisition Corp (HQ)....212 275-2000
75 Rockefeller Plz New York (10019) ***(G-12126)***
Wmw Machinery Company, Deer Park *Also called World LLC* ***(G-4065)***
Wna Holley, Holley *Also called Waddington North America Inc* ***(G-6230)***
Wny Cheese Enterprise LLC....585 243-6516
1842 Craig Rd Pavilion (14525) ***(G-12890)***
Wny Enterprise LLC....585 243-6514
1840 Craig Rd Pavilion (14525) ***(G-12891)***
Wny Jobs.com, Hamburg *Also called Jobs Weekly Inc* ***(G-5682)***
Wobbleworks Inc (PA)....718 618-9904
89 5th Ave Ste 802 New York (10003) ***(G-12127)***
Wochit Inc (PA)....212 979-8343
12 E 33rd St Fl 4 New York (10016) ***(G-12128)***
Woerner Industries Inc....585 436-1934
485 Hague St Rochester (14606) ***(G-14211)***
Wok To Walk, New York *Also called Restaurant 570 8th Avenue LLC* ***(G-11371)***
Wolak Inc....315 839-5366
2360 King Rd Clayville (13322) ***(G-3560)***
Wolf X-Ray Corporation....631 242-9729
100 W Industry Ct Deer Park (11729) ***(G-4063)***
Wolfe Lumber Mill Inc....716 772-7750
8416 Ridge Rd Gasport (14067) ***(G-5309)***
Wolfe Publications Inc (PA)....585 394-0770
73 Buffalo St Canandaigua (14424) ***(G-3236)***
Wolff & Dungey Inc....315 475-2105
325 Temple St Syracuse (13202) ***(G-15460)***
Wolffer Estate Vineyard Inc....631 537-5106
139 Sagg Rd Sagaponack (11962) ***(G-14505)***
Wolffer Estate Winery, Sagaponack *Also called Wolffer Estate Vineyard Inc* ***(G-14505)***
Wolfgang B Gourmet Foods Inc....518 719-1727
117 Cauterskill Ave Catskill (12414) ***(G-3310)***
Wolo Mfg Corp....631 242-0333
1 Saxwood St Ste 1 # 1 Deer Park (11729) ***(G-4064)***
Wolski Wood Works Inc....718 577-9816
14134 78th Rd Apt 3c Flushing (11367) ***(G-5060)***
Wolters Kluwer US Inc....212 894-8920
111 8th Ave Fl 13 New York (10011) ***(G-12129)***
Women's Health Magazine, New York *Also called Rodale Inc* ***(G-11417)***
Womens E News Inc....212 244-1720
6 Barclay St Fl 6 # 6 New York (10007) ***(G-12130)***
Womens Health Care PC (PA)....718 850-0009
11311 Jamaica Ave Ste C Richmond Hill (11418) ***(G-13517)***
Womens Wear Daily, New York *Also called Fairchild Publications Inc* ***(G-9773)***
Won & Lee Inc....516 222-0712
971 Stewart Ave Garden City (11530) ***(G-5284)***
Wonder Natural Foods Corp (PA)....631 726-4433
670 Montauk Hwy Unit 2 Water Mill (11976) ***(G-15972)***
Wonder Products, Middletown *Also called Advanced Enterprises Inc* ***(G-8136)***
Wonderly Company, The, Kingston *Also called Northast Coml Win Trtments Inc* ***(G-6912)***
Wonton Food Inc....718 784-8178
5210 37th St Long Island City (11101) ***(G-7642)***
Wonton Food Inc (PA)....718 628-6868
220 Moore St 222 Brooklyn (11206) ***(G-2655)***
Wonton Food Inc....212 677-8865
183 E Broadway New York (10002) ***(G-12131)***
Wood & Hyde Leather Co Inc....518 725-7105
68 Wood St Gloversville (12078) ***(G-5474)***
Wood Design, Peekskill *Also called W Designe Inc* ***(G-12927)***
Wood Designs Deluxe Corp....917 414-4640
4090 Austin Blvd Island Park (11558) ***(G-6519)***
Wood Etc Inc....315 484-9663
1175 State Fair Blvd # 2 Syracuse (13209) ***(G-15461)***
Wood Floor Expo Inc....212 472-0671
426 E 73rd St Frnt 1 New York (10021) ***(G-12132)***
Wood Innovations of Suffolk....631 698-2345
266 Middle Island Rd # 8 Medford (11763) ***(G-7969)***
Wood Talk....631 940-3085
203 N Fehr Way Ste C Bay Shore (11706) ***(G-734)***
Wood Tex Products LLC....607 243-5141
3700 Route 14 Himrod (14842) ***(G-6161)***
Wood-Mizer Holdings Inc....315 564-5722
8604 State Route 104 Hannibal (13074) ***(G-5718)***
Wood-Tex Products, Himrod *Also called Lapp Management Corp* ***(G-6160)***
Woodards Concrete Products Inc....845 361-3471
629 Lybolt Rd Bullville (10915) ***(G-3139)***
Woodbine Products Inc....631 586-3770
110 Plant Ave Hauppauge (11788) ***(G-5977)***
Woodbury Printing Plus + Inc....845 928-6610
96 Turner Rd Central Valley (10917) ***(G-3399)***

Woodbury Systems Group Inc 516 364-2653
30 Glenn Dr Woodbury (11797) *(G-16635)*
Woodbury Vineyards Inc 716 679-9463
3215 S Roberts Rd Fredonia (14063) *(G-5130)*
Woodcock Brothers Brewing Comp 716 333-4000
638 Lake St Wilson (14172) *(G-16603)*
Wooden Boatworks 631 477-6507
190 Sterling St Unit 2 Greenport (11944) *(G-5627)*
Woodfalls Industries 518 236-7201
434 Burke Rd Plattsburgh (12901) *(G-13170)*
Woodmaster Industries, Jamaica *Also called Abbott Industries Inc (G-6622)*
Woodmotif Inc 516 564-8325
42 Chasner St Hempstead (11550) *(G-6028)*
Woodmotif Cabinetry, Hempstead *Also called Woodmotif Inc (G-6028)*
Woods Knife Corporation 516 798-4972
19 Brooklyn Ave Massapequa (11758) *(G-7888)*
Woods Machine and Tool LLC 607 699-3253
150 Howell St Nichols (13812) *(G-12351)*
Woodside Decorator, Staten Island *Also called All Signs (G-15043)*
Woodside Granite Industries 585 589-6500
13890 Ridge Rd W Albion (14411) *(G-164)*
Woodstock Times, Kingston *Also called Ulster Publishing Co Inc (G-6926)*
Woodtalk Stairs & Rails, Bay Shore *Also called Wood Talk (G-734)*
Woodtronics Inc 914 962-5205
1661 Front St Ste 3 Yorktown Heights (10598) *(G-16825)*
Woodward Industries Inc 716 692-2242
233 Fillmore Ave Ste 1 Tonawanda (14150) *(G-15591)*
Woodward/White Inc 718 509-6082
45 Main St Ste 820 Brooklyn (11201) *(G-2656)*
Woolmark Americas Inc 347 767-3160
110 E 25th St Fl 3 New York (10010) *(G-12133)*
Woolmark Company, The, New York *Also called Woolmark Americas Inc (G-12133)*
Wordingham Machine Co Inc 585 924-2294
515 Lee Rd Rochester (14606) *(G-14212)*
Wordingham Technologies, Rochester *Also called Wordingham Machine Co Inc (G-14212)*
Wordwise Inc 914 232-5366
1 Brady Ln Katonah (10536) *(G-6848)*
Working Family Solutions Inc 845 802-6182
359 Washington Avenue Ext Saugerties (12477) *(G-14620)*
Working Mother Media Inc 212 351-6400
2 Park Ave Fl 10 New York (10016) *(G-12134)*
Workman Publishing Co Inc (PA) 212 254-5900
225 Varick St Fl 9 New York (10014) *(G-12135)*
Workman Publishing Co Inc 212 254-5900
708 Broadway Fl 6 New York (10003) *(G-12136)*
Workplace Interiors LLC 585 425-7420
400 Packetts Lndg Fairport (14450) *(G-4667)*
Workshop Art Fabrication 845 331-0385
117 Tremper Ave Kingston (12401) *(G-6932)*
World Best Sporting Goods Inc 800 489-0908
225 Post Ave Westbury (11590) *(G-16388)*
World Business Media LLC 212 344-0759
4770 Sunrise Hwy Ste 105 Massapequa Park (11762) *(G-7896)*
World Cheese Co Inc 718 965-1700
178 28th St Brooklyn (11232) *(G-2657)*
World Guide Publishing 800 331-7840
1271 Ave Of The Americas New York (10020) *(G-12137)*
World Journal LLC (HQ) 718 746-8889
14107 20th Ave Fl 2 Whitestone (11357) *(G-16553)*
World Journal LLC 718 871-5000
6007 8th Ave Brooklyn (11220) *(G-2658)*
World LLC 631 940-9121
513 Acorn St Ste B Deer Park (11729) *(G-4065)*
World Maritime News 212 477-6700
118 E 25th St Fl 2 New York (10010) *(G-12138)*
World of McIntosh, New York *Also called Fine Sounds Group Inc (G-9805)*
World Screen News, New York *Also called Wsn Inc (G-12145)*
World Trading Center Inc 631 273-3330
115 Engineers Rd Fl 2 Hauppauge (11788) *(G-5978)*
Worldwide Arntcal Cmpnents Inc (PA) 631 842-3780
10 Reith St Copiague (11726) *(G-3794)*
Worldwide Arntcal Cmpnents Inc 631 842-3780
10 Reith St Copiague (11726) *(G-3795)*
Worldwide Gas Turbine Pdts Inc 518 877-7200
300 Commerce Dr Clifton Park (12065) *(G-3581)*
Worldwide Resources Inc 718 760-5000
1908 Avenue O Brooklyn (11230) *(G-2659)*
Worldwide Ticket Craft 516 538-6200
1390 Jerusalem Ave Merrick (11566) *(G-8107)*
Worm Power, Rochester *Also called Rt Solutions LLC (G-14107)*
Worth Collection Ltd (PA) 212 268-0312
520 8th Ave Rm 2301 New York (10018) *(G-12139)*
Worth Publishers Inc 212 475-6000
1 New York Plz Ste 4500 New York (10004) *(G-12140)*
Worthington Industries Inc 315 336-5500
530 Henry St Rome (13440) *(G-14279)*
Worzalla Publishing Company 212 967-7909
222 W 37th St Fl 10 New York (10018) *(G-12141)*
Wp Company LLC 212 445-5050
395 Hudson St Lbby 1 New York (10014) *(G-12142)*
Wp Lavori USA Inc (HQ) 212 244-6074
597 Broadway Fl 2 New York (10012) *(G-12143)*

WR Design Corp 212 354-9000
230 W 39th St Fl 5f New York (10018) *(G-12144)*
WR Smith & Sons Inc 845 620-9400
121 W Nyack Rd Nanuet (10954) *(G-8469)*
Wr9000, New York *Also called WR Design Corp (G-12144)*
Wrightcut EDM & Machine Inc 607 733-5018
951 Carl St Elmira (14904) *(G-4508)*
Wrights Hardwoods Inc 716 595-2345
6868 Route 60 Cassadaga (14718) *(G-3291)*
Writing Sculptures, Deer Park *Also called Versaponents Inc (G-4059)*
Wrkbook LLC 914 355-1293
19 Brookdale Ave White Plains (10603) *(G-16522)*
Wsf Industries Inc 716 692-4930
7 Hackett Dr Tonawanda (14150) *(G-15592)*
Wsn Inc 212 924-7620
1123 Broadway Ste 1207 New York (10010) *(G-12145)*
Wt Shade, New Hyde Park *Also called Windowtex Inc (G-8573)*
Www.dynatabs.com, Brooklyn *Also called Dynatabs LLC (G-1801)*
Www.picturesongold.com, Staten Island *Also called Photograve Corporation (G-15114)*
Www.poppin.com, New York *Also called Poppin Inc (G-11219)*
Wyde Lumber 845 513-5571
419 State Route 17b Monticello (12701) *(G-8324)*
Wyeth, Rouses Point *Also called Pfizer Inc (G-14468)*
Wyeth Holdings LLC 845 602-5000
401 N Middletown Rd Pearl River (10965) *(G-12913)*
Wyeth LLC (HQ) 973 660-5000
235 E 42nd St New York (10017) *(G-12146)*
Wyeth Pharmaceutical Division, Pearl River *Also called Wyeth Holdings LLC (G-12913)*
Wynco Press One Inc 516 354-6145
7839 268th St Glen Oaks (11004) *(G-5388)*
Wynn Starr Flavors Inc (PA) 845 584-3080
225 N Route 303 Ste 109 Congers (10920) *(G-3723)*
Wyrestorm Technologies LLC 518 289-1293
23 Wood Rd Round Lake (12151) *(G-14465)*
X Brand Editions 718 482-7646
4020 22nd St Ste 1 Long Island City (11101) *(G-7643)*
X Function Inc (PA) 212 231-0092
45 W 89th St Apt 4a New York (10024) *(G-12147)*
X Myles Mar Inc 212 683-2015
875 Av Of The Americas New York (10001) *(G-12148)*
X Press Screen Printing 716 679-7788
4867 W Lake Rd Dunkirk (14048) *(G-4181)*
X-Gen Pharmaceuticals Inc (PA) 607 562-2700
300 Daniel Zenker Dr Big Flats (14814) *(G-857)*
X-Gen Pharmaceuticals Inc 631 261-8188
4 York Ct Northport (11768) *(G-12475)*
X-L Envelope and Printing Inc 716 852-2135
701 Seneca St Ste 100 Buffalo (14210) *(G-3134)*
X-Press Printing & Office Sup, Mahopac *Also called Rmd Holding Inc (G-7712)*
X-Treme Ready Mix Inc 718 739-3384
17801 Liberty Ave Jamaica (11433) *(G-6692)*
X1000, Binghamton *Also called Surescan Corporation (G-917)*
Xactiv Inc 585 288-7220
71 Perinton Pkwy Fairport (14450) *(G-4668)*
Xactra Technologies Inc 585 426-2030
105 Mclaughlin Rd Ste F Rochester (14615) *(G-14213)*
Xanadu 212 465-0580
150 W 30th St Rm 702 New York (10001) *(G-12149)*
Xania Labs Inc 718 361-2550
3202 Queens Blvd Fl 6 Long Island City (11101) *(G-7644)*
Xborder Entertainment LLC 518 726-7036
568 State Route 3 Plattsburgh (12901) *(G-13171)*
Xedit Corp 718 380-1592
21831 97th Ave Queens Village (11429) *(G-13413)*
Xeku Corporation 607 761-1447
2520 Vestal Pkwy E222 Vestal (13850) *(G-15826)*
Xeleum Lighting LLC 954 617-8170
333 N Bedford Rd Ste 135 Mount Kisco (10549) *(G-8360)*
Xelic Incorporated 585 415-2764
1250 Pittsford Victor Rd # 370 Pittsford (14534) *(G-13029)*
Xentaur Corporation 631 345-3434
84 Horseblock Rd Unit G Yaphank (11980) *(G-16729)*
Xerox Corporation 585 422-4564
800 Phillips Rd Ste 20599 Webster (14580) *(G-16108)*
Xerox Corporation 212 330-1386
485 Lexington Ave Fl 10 New York (10017) *(G-12150)*
Xerox Corporation 518 434-6543
80 State St Ste 3 Albany (12207) *(G-143)*
Xerox Corporation 585 427-4500
225 Tech Park Dr Rochester (14623) *(G-14214)*
Xerox Corporation 585 264-5584
80 Linden Oaks Rochester (14625) *(G-14215)*
Xing Lin USA Intl Corp 212 947-4846
1410 Broadway Rm 3201 New York (10018) *(G-12151)*
Xinya International Trading Co 212 216-9681
115 W 30th St Rm 1109 New York (10001) *(G-12152)*
Xl Graphics Inc 212 929-8700
121 Varick St Rm 300 New York (10013) *(G-12153)*
Xli Corporation 585 436-2250
55 Vanguard Pkwy Rochester (14606) *(G-14216)*
Xomox Jewelry Inc 212 944-8428
151 W 46th St Fl 15 New York (10036) *(G-12154)*

ALPHABETIC

Xpand, New York
ALPHABETIC SECTION

Xpand, New York *Also called Whiteboard Ventures Inc* **(G-12105)**
Xpress Printing Inc....516 605-1000
7 Fairchild Ct Ste 100 Plainview (11803) **(G-13103)**
Xstatic Pro Inc....718 237-2299
901 Essex St Brooklyn (11208) **(G-2660)**
Xstelos Holdings Inc....212 729-4962
630 5th Ave Ste 2600 New York (10111) **(G-12155)**
Xto Incorporated (PA)....315 451-7807
110 Wrentham Dr Liverpool (13088) **(G-7273)**
Xylem, Cheektowaga *Also called Fluid Handling LLC* **(G-3445)**
Xylem Inc....716 862-4123
2881 E Bayard Street Ext Seneca Falls (13148) **(G-14789)**
Xylem Inc....315 258-4949
1 Goulds Dr Auburn (13021) **(G-510)**
Xylem Inc....315 239-2499
2881 E Bayard Street Ext Seneca Falls (13148) **(G-14790)**
Xylem Inc (PA)....914 323-5700
1 International Dr Rye Brook (10573) **(G-14496)**
Xylon Industries Inc....631 293-4717
79 Florida St Farmingdale (11735) **(G-4907)**
Y & A Trading Inc....718 436-6333
1365 38th St Brooklyn (11218) **(G-2661)**
Y & Z Precision Inc....516 349-8243
155 E Ames Ct Unit 4 Plainview (11803) **(G-13104)**
Y & Z Precision Machine Shop, Plainview *Also called Y & Z Precision Inc* **(G-13104)**
Y-Mabs Therapeutics Inc (PA)....917 817-2992
230 Park Ave Fl 33 New York (10169) **(G-12156)**
Yacoubian Jewelers Inc....212 302-6729
2 W 45th St Ste 1104 New York (10036) **(G-12157)**
Yale, Getzville *Also called Columbus McKinnon Corporation* **(G-5346)**
Yale Robbins Inc....212 683-5700
205 Lexington Ave Fl 12 New York (10016) **(G-12158)**
Yale Trouser Corporation....516 255-0700
3670 Oceanside Rd W Ste 6 Oceanside (11572) **(G-12566)**
Yaloz Mold & Die, Brooklyn *Also called Yaloz Mould & Die Co Inc* **(G-2662)**
Yaloz Mould & Die Co Inc....718 389-1131
239 Java St Fl 2 Brooklyn (11222) **(G-2662)**
Yam TV LLC....917 932-5418
144 W 23rd St Apt 8e New York (10011) **(G-12159)**
Yankee Corp....718 589-1377
1180 Randall Ave Bronx (10474) **(G-1420)**
Yankee Fuel Inc....631 880-8810
780 Sunrise Hwy West Babylon (11704) **(G-16205)**
Yankee Wiping Cloth, Bronx *Also called Yankee Corp* **(G-1420)**
Yarnz International Inc....212 868-5883
260 W 36th St Rm 201 New York (10018) **(G-12160)**
Yated Neeman Inc....845 369-1600
53 Olympia Ln Monsey (10952) **(G-8303)**
Yellow E House Inc....718 888-2000
18812 Northern Blvd Flushing (11358) **(G-5061)**
Yellow Pages Inc (PA)....845 639-6060
222 N Main St New City (10956) **(G-8496)**
Yellowpagecitycom....585 410-6688
280 Kenneth Dr Ste 300 Rochester (14623) **(G-14217)**
Yeohlee Inc....212 631-8099
12 W 29th St New York (10001) **(G-12161)**
Yepes Fine Furniture....718 383-0221
72 Van Dam St Brooklyn (11222) **(G-2663)**
Yes Were Nuts Ltd....516 374-1940
1215 Broadway Hewlett (11557) **(G-6055)**
Yesteryears Vintage Doors LLC....315 324-5250
66 S Main St Hammond (13646) **(G-5701)**
Yewtree Millworks Corp....914 320-5851
372 Ashburton Ave Yonkers (10701) **(G-16809)**
Yfd Cabinetry, West Haverstraw *Also called Your Furniture Designers Inc* **(G-16211)**
Yigal-Azrouel Inc (PA)....212 302-1194
500 7th Ave Fl 8 New York (10018) **(G-12162)**
Ying Ke Youth Age Group Inc....929 402-8458
1 Campbell Dr Dix Hills (11746) **(G-4128)**
Yiwen Usa Inc....212 370-0828
60 E 42nd St Ste 1030 New York (10165) **(G-12163)**
Yofah Religious Articles Inc....718 435-3288
2001 57th St Ste 1 Brooklyn (11204) **(G-2664)**
Yogibo LLC....518 456-1762
120 Washington Avenue Ext # 23 Albany (12203) **(G-144)**
Yogolicious Inc....914 236-3455
516 N State Rd Briarcliff Manor (10510) **(G-1178)**
Yohay Baking Company, Lindenhurst *Also called Alrajs Inc* **(G-7159)**
Yoland Corporation....718 499-4803
253 36th St Unit 2 Brooklyn (11232) **(G-2665)**
Yoman Madeo Fano....631 438-0246
1 S Ocean Ave Patchogue (11772) **(G-12879)**
Yomiuri International Inc....212 752-2196
747 3rd Ave Fl 28 New York (10017) **(G-12164)**
Yong Ji Productions Inc....917 559-4616
10219 44th Ave Corona (11368) **(G-3857)**
Yonkers Cabinet Inc....914 668-2133
1179 Yonkers Ave Yonkers (10704) **(G-16810)**
Yonkers Time Publishing Co....914 965-4000
40 Larkin Plz Yonkers (10701) **(G-16811)**
Yonkers Whl Beer Distrs Inc....914 963-8600
424 Riverdale Ave Yonkers (10705) **(G-16812)**
Yorganic, New York *Also called Bliss Foods Inc* **(G-9100)**
Yorganic, New York *Also called Bliss Foods Inc* **(G-9101)**
York Fuel Incorporated....718 951-0202
1760 Flatbush Ave Brooklyn (11210) **(G-2666)**
York Industries Inc....516 746-3736
303 Nassau Blvd Garden City Park (11040) **(G-5290)**
York International Corporation....718 389-4152
1130 45th Rd Long Island City (11101) **(G-7645)**
York Ladder Inc....718 784-6666
3720 12th St Long Island City (11101) **(G-7646)**
York Ladders, Long Island City *Also called AAAA York Inc* **(G-7364)**
Yorktown Printing Corp....914 962-2526
1520 Front St Yorktown Heights (10598) **(G-16826)**
Yorkville Sound Inc....716 297-2920
4625 Witmer Indus Est Niagara Falls (14305) **(G-12350)**
Yost Neon Displays Inc....716 674-6780
20 Ransier Dr West Seneca (14224) **(G-16304)**
You and ME Legwear LLC....212 279-9292
10 W 33rd St Rm 300 New York (10001) **(G-12165)**
You First Services Inc....716 204-7215
485 Cayuga Rd Buffalo (14225) **(G-3135)**
Young & Franklin Inc (HQ)....315 457-3110
942 Old Liverpool Rd Liverpool (13088) **(G-7274)**
Young & Swartz Inc....716 852-2171
39 Cherry St Buffalo (14204) **(G-3136)**
Young Explosives Corp....585 394-1783
2165 New Michigan Rd Canandaigua (14424) **(G-3237)**
Younique Clothing, New York *Also called Turn On Products Inc* **(G-11914)**
Your Furniture Designers Inc....845 947-3046
118 E Railroad Ave West Haverstraw (10993) **(G-16211)**
Your Name Professional Brand, Long Island City *Also called Mana Products Inc* **(G-7510)**
Your Way Custom Cabinets Inc....914 371-1870
20 N Macquesten Pkwy Mount Vernon (10550) **(G-8454)**
Yourhealth911.com, Brooklyn *Also called GNI Commerce Inc* **(G-1935)**
Ypis of Staten Island Inc....718 815-4557
130 Stuyvesant Pl Ste 5 Staten Island (10301) **(G-15153)**
Yr Blanc & Co LLC....716 800-3999
25 Eltham Dr Buffalo (14226) **(G-3137)**
Ys Marketing Inc....718 778-6080
2004 Mcdonald Ave Brooklyn (11223) **(G-2667)**
YS Publishing Co Inc....212 682-9360
228 E 45th St Rm 700 New York (10017) **(G-12166)**
Yugo Landau, Brooklyn *Also called Eastern Feather & Down Corp* **(G-1809)**
Yula Corporation....718 991-0900
330 Bryant Ave Bronx (10474) **(G-1421)**
Yum Yum Noodle Bar....845 679-7992
275 Fair St Ste 17 Kingston (12401) **(G-6933)**
Yurman Retail, New York *Also called David Yurman Enterprises LLC* **(G-9488)**
Z Card North America, New York *Also called In-Step Marketing Inc* **(G-10191)**
Z Works Inc....631 750-0612
1395 Lakeland Ave Ste 10 Bohemia (11716) **(G-1109)**
Z-Axis Inc....315 548-5000
1916 State Route 96 Phelps (14532) **(G-12984)**
Z-Car-D Corp....631 424-2077
403 Oakwood Rd Huntington Station (11746) **(G-6465)**
Z-Ply Corp....212 398-7011
213 W 35th St Ste 5w New York (10001) **(G-12167)**
Z-Studios Dsign Fbrication LLC....347 512-4210
30 Haven Pl Brooklyn (11233) **(G-2668)**
Zacks Enterprises Inc....800 366-4924
33 Corporate Dr Orangeburg (10962) **(G-12693)**
Zacmel Graphics LLC....631 944-6031
500 Brook Ave Ste B Deer Park (11729) **(G-4066)**
Zagwear, Orangeburg *Also called Zacks Enterprises Inc* **(G-12693)**
Zahk Sales Inc....631 851-0851
75 Hoffman Ln Ste A Islandia (11749) **(G-6541)**
Zaika Flavors of India, New Windsor *Also called Cafe Spice Gct Inc* **(G-8638)**
Zak Jewelry Tools Inc....212 768-8122
55 W 47th St Fl 2 New York (10036) **(G-12168)**
Zanetti Millwork, Middle Grove *Also called Cuccio-Zanetti Inc* **(G-8115)**
Zanzano Woodworking Inc....914 725-6025
91 Locust Ave Scarsdale (10583) **(G-14646)**
Zappala Farms AG Systems Inc....315 626-6293
11404 Schuler Rd Cato (13033) **(G-3301)**
Zappone Chrysler Jeep Ddge Inc....518 982-0610
1780 Route 9 Halfmoon (12065) **(G-5670)**
Zar Apparel Group, New York *Also called Zar Group LLC* **(G-12169)**
Zar Group LLC (PA)....212 944-2510
1450 Broadway Fl 17 New York (10018) **(G-12169)**
Zaro Bake Shop Inc (PA)....718 993-7327
138 Bruckner Blvd Bronx (10454) **(G-1422)**
Zaro's Bread Basket, Bronx *Also called Zaro Bake Shop Inc* **(G-1422)**
Zastech Inc....516 496-4777
15 Ryan St Syosset (11791) **(G-15234)**
Zazoom LLC (PA)....212 321-2100
1 Exchange Plz Ste 801 New York (10006) **(G-12170)**
Zazoom Media Group, New York *Also called Zazoom LLC* **(G-12170)**
Zebra Books, New York *Also called Kensington Publishing Corp* **(G-10434)**
Zebra Environmental Corp (PA)....516 596-6300
30 N Prospect Ave Lynbrook (11563) **(G-7678)**

1020
2019 Harris
New York Manufacturers Directory
(G-0000) Company's Geographic Section entry number

ALPHABETIC SECTION

Zebra Technologies Entp Corp 800 722-6234
  1 Zebra Plz Holtsville (11742) *(G-6251)*
Zebrowski Industries Inc 716 532-3911
  4345 Route 39 Collins (14034) *(G-3676)*
Zedge Inc 330 577-3424
  22 Cortlandt St Fl 11 New York (10007) *(G-12171)*
Zeeba Jewelry Manufacturing, New York *Also called Zeeba Jewelry Mfg Inc* *(G-12172)*
Zeeba Jewelry Mfg Inc 212 997-1009
  36 W 47th St Ste 902 New York (10036) *(G-12172)*
Zehnder Rittling, Buffalo *Also called Hydro-Air Components Inc* *(G-2877)*
Zela International Co 518 436-1833
  13 Manor St Albany (12207) *(G-145)*
Zeller Woodworks LLC 585 254-7607
  35 Norman St Rochester (14613) *(G-14218)*
Zelman & Friedman Jwly Mfg Co 718 349-3400
  4722 37th St Long Island City (11101) *(G-7647)*
Zenger Group Inc 716 871-1058
  777 E Park Dr Tonawanda (14150) *(G-15593)*
Zenger Partners LLC 716 876-2284
  1881 Kenmore Ave Kenmore (14217) *(G-6865)*
Zenith Autoparts Corp 845 344-1382
  20 Industrial Pl Middletown (10940) *(G-8185)*
Zenith Color Comm Group Inc (PA) 212 989-4400
  4710 33rd St Long Island City (11101) *(G-7648)*
Zenith Energy US Logistics (PA) 212 993-1280
  725 5th Ave Fl 19 New York (10022) *(G-12173)*
Zenith Promotions, Lawrence *Also called Last Straw Inc* *(G-7104)*
Zenith Solutions 718 575-8570
  6922 Manse St Flushing (11375) *(G-5062)*
Zeo Health Ltd 845 353-5185
  159 Route 303 Valley Cottage (10989) *(G-15769)*
Zeppelin Electric Company Inc 631 928-9467
  26 Deer Ln East Setauket (11733) *(G-4315)*
Zeptometrix Corporation (PA) 716 882-0920
  847 Main St Buffalo (14203) *(G-3138)*
Zered Inc (PA) 718 353-7464
  12717 20th Ave College Point (11356) *(G-3670)*
Zerovalent Nanometals Inc 585 298-8592
  693 East Ave Ste 103 Rochester (14607) *(G-14219)*
Zeta Machine Corp 631 471-8832
  206 Christopher St Ronkonkoma (11779) *(G-14433)*
Zeteck, New York *Also called Zetek Corporation* *(G-12174)*
Zetek Corporation 212 668-1485
  13 E 37th St Ste 701 New York (10016) *(G-12174)*
Zg Apparel Group LLC 212 944-2510
  1450 Broadway Fl 17 New York (10018) *(G-12175)*
Zia Power Inc 845 661-8388
  116 E 27th St New York (10016) *(G-12176)*
Ziebart, Rochester *Also called Monroe County Auto Svcs Inc* *(G-13953)*
Ziegler Truck & Diesl Repr Inc 315 782-7278
  22249 Fabco Rd Watertown (13601) *(G-16037)*
Zielinskis Asphalt Inc 315 306-4057
  4989 State Route 12b Oriskany Falls (13425) *(G-12768)*
Zierick Manufacturing Corp (PA) 800 882-8020
  131 Radio Circle Dr Mount Kisco (10549) *(G-8361)*
Ziff Davis Publishing LLC (HQ) 212 503-3500
  28 E 28th St Fl 10 New York (10016) *(G-12177)*
Ziff-Davis Publishing, New York *Also called Ziff Davis Publishing LLC* *(G-12177)*
Zinc Corporation America Div, New York *Also called Hh Liquidating Corp* *(G-10092)*
Zinepak LLC 212 706-8621
  349 5th Ave New York (10016) *(G-12178)*

Zings Company LLC 631 454-0339
  250 Adams Blvd Farmingdale (11735) *(G-4908)*
Zinnias Inc 718 746-8551
  24520 Grand Central Pkwy 4l Bellerose (11426) *(G-783)*
Zip Jack Custom Umbrellas, Tarrytown *Also called Zip-Jack Industries Ltd* *(G-15498)*
Zip Products Inc 585 482-0044
  565 Blossom Rd Ste E Rochester (14610) *(G-14220)*
Zip-Jack Industries Ltd 914 592-2000
  73 Carrollwood Dr Tarrytown (10591) *(G-15498)*
Zipari Inc 855 558-7884
  45 Main St Ste 406 Brooklyn (11201) *(G-2669)*
Ziptswitch, Bay Shore *Also called Adeptronics Incorporated* *(G-652)*
Zircar Ceramics Inc (PA) 845 651-6600
  100 N Main St Ste 2 Florida (10921) *(G-4973)*
Zircar Refr Composites Inc 845 651-2200
  14 Golden Hill Ter Florida (10921) *(G-4974)*
Zircar Refr Composites Inc (PA) 845 651-4481
  46 Jayne St Florida (10921) *(G-4975)*
Zircar Zirconia Inc 845 651-3040
  87 Meadow Rd Florida (10921) *(G-4976)*
Zirconia Creations Intl 212 239-3730
  134 W 29th St Rm 801 New York (10001) *(G-12179)*
Zitomer LLC 212 737-5560
  969 Madison Ave Fl 1 New York (10021) *(G-12180)*
Zmz Mfg Inc 518 234-4336
  300 Mickle Hollow Rd Warnerville (12187) *(G-15939)*
Zoe Sakoutis LLC 212 414-5741
  135 W 29th St Rm 704 New York (10001) *(G-12181)*
Zographos Designs Ltd 212 545-0227
  300 E 33rd St Apt 9m New York (10016) *(G-12182)*
Zomega Terahertz Corporation 585 347-4337
  806 Admiralty Way Webster (14580) *(G-16109)*
Zone Fabricators Inc 718 272-0200
  10780 101st St Ozone Park (11417) *(G-12834)*
Zoomers Inc (PA) 718 369-2656
  32 33rd St Brooklyn (11232) *(G-2670)*
Zoomifier Corporation 800 255-5303
  216 E 45th St Fl 17 New York (10017) *(G-12183)*
Zorlu USA Inc (PA) 212 689-4622
  295 5th Ave Ste 503 New York (10016) *(G-12184)*
Zotos International Inc 315 781-3207
  300 Forge Ave Geneva (14456) *(G-5337)*
Zuant, Valley Stream *Also called High Performance Sftwr USA Inc* *(G-15782)*
Zumbach Electronics Corp 914 241-7080
  140 Kisco Ave Mount Kisco (10549) *(G-8362)*
Zumtobel Lighting Inc (HQ) 845 691-6262
  3300 Route 9w Highland (12528) *(G-6148)*
Zwack Incorporated 518 733-5135
  15875 Ny 22 Stephentown (12168) *(G-15156)*
Zweigles Inc 585 546-1740
  651 Plymouth Ave N Rochester (14608) *(G-14221)*
Zydoc Med Transcription LLC 631 273-1963
  1455 Veterans Memorial Hw Islandia (11749) *(G-6542)*
Zyloware Corporation (PA) 914 708-1200
  8 Slater St Ste 1 Port Chester (10573) *(G-13211)*
Zyloware Eyewear, Port Chester *Also called Zyloware Corporation* *(G-13211)*
Zymtrnix Catalytic Systems Inc 607 351-2639
  526 N Campus Ithaca (14853) *(G-6617)*
Zyp Precision LLC 315 539-3667
  1098 Birdsey Rd Waterloo (13165) *(G-15998)*

PRODUCT INDEX

• Product categories are listed in alphabetical order.

A

ABRASIVES
ABRASIVES: Aluminum Oxide Fused
ABRASIVES: Coated
ABRASIVES: Grains
ACADEMIC TUTORING SVCS
ACCELERATION INDICATORS & SYSTEM COMPONENTS: Aerospace
ACCELERATORS: Electron Linear
ACCOUNTING MACHINES & CASH REGISTERS
ACID RESIST: Etching
ACIDS
ACIDS: Sulfuric, Oleum
ACOUSTICAL BOARD & TILE
ACRYLIC RESINS
ACTUATORS: Indl, NEC
ADDITIVE BASED PLASTIC MATERIALS: Plasticizers
ADHESIVES
ADHESIVES & SEALANTS
ADHESIVES & SEALANTS WHOLESALERS
ADHESIVES: Epoxy
ADVERTISING AGENCIES
ADVERTISING AGENCIES: Consultants
ADVERTISING DISPLAY PRDTS
ADVERTISING MATERIAL DISTRIBUTION
ADVERTISING REPRESENTATIVES: Electronic Media
ADVERTISING REPRESENTATIVES: Magazine
ADVERTISING REPRESENTATIVES: Media
ADVERTISING REPRESENTATIVES: Newspaper
ADVERTISING REPRESENTATIVES: Printed Media
ADVERTISING SPECIALTIES, WHOLESALE
ADVERTISING SVCS: Direct Mail
ADVERTISING SVCS: Display
ADVERTISING SVCS: Outdoor
ADVERTISING SVCS: Sample Distribution
ADVERTISING SVCS: Transit
AERIAL WORK PLATFORMS
AEROSOLS
AGENTS, BROKERS & BUREAUS: Personal Service
AGRICULTURAL EQPT: BARN, SILO, POULTRY, DAIRY/LIVESTOCK MACH
AGRICULTURAL EQPT: Fertilizng, Sprayng, Dustng/Irrigatn Mach
AGRICULTURAL EQPT: Milking Machines
AGRICULTURAL EQPT: Planting Machines
AGRICULTURAL EQPT: Spreaders, Fertilizer
AGRICULTURAL EQPT: Trailers & Wagons, Farm
AGRICULTURAL EQPT: Turf & Grounds Eqpt
AIR CLEANING SYSTEMS
AIR CONDITIONERS, AUTOMOTIVE: Wholesalers
AIR CONDITIONING & VENTILATION EQPT & SPLYS: Wholesales
AIR CONDITIONING EQPT
AIR CONDITIONING UNITS: Complete, Domestic Or Indl
AIR COOLERS: Metal Plate
AIR DUCT CLEANING SVCS
AIR MATTRESSES: Plastic
AIR POLLUTION MEASURING SVCS
AIR PREHEATERS: Nonrotating, Plate Type
AIR PURIFICATION EQPT
AIRCRAFT & AEROSPACE FLIGHT INSTRUMENTS & GUIDANCE SYSTEMS
AIRCRAFT & HEAVY EQPT REPAIR SVCS
AIRCRAFT ASSEMBLY PLANTS
AIRCRAFT CONTROL SYSTEMS: Electronic Totalizing Counters
AIRCRAFT ENGINES & ENGINE PARTS: Research & Development, Mfr
AIRCRAFT ENGINES & PARTS
AIRCRAFT EQPT & SPLYS WHOLESALERS
AIRCRAFT FLIGHT INSTRUMENT REPAIR SVCS
AIRCRAFT FLIGHT INSTRUMENTS
AIRCRAFT LIGHTING
AIRCRAFT PARTS & AUXILIARY EQPT: Assys, Subassemblies/Parts
AIRCRAFT PARTS & AUXILIARY EQPT: Body & Wing Assys & Parts
AIRCRAFT PARTS & AUXILIARY EQPT: Body Assemblies & Parts
AIRCRAFT PARTS & AUXILIARY EQPT: Gears, Power Transmission
AIRCRAFT PARTS & AUXILIARY EQPT: Landing Assemblies & Brakes
AIRCRAFT PARTS & AUXILIARY EQPT: Military Eqpt & Armament
AIRCRAFT PARTS & AUXILIARY EQPT: Refueling Eqpt, In Flight
AIRCRAFT PARTS & AUXILIARY EQPT: Seat Ejector Devices
AIRCRAFT PARTS & EQPT, NEC
AIRCRAFT SEATS
AIRCRAFT: Airplanes, Fixed Or Rotary Wing
AIRCRAFT: Gliders
AIRCRAFT: Motorized
AIRCRAFT: Research & Development, Manufacturer
ALARM SYSTEMS WHOLESALERS
ALARMS: Burglar
ALARMS: Fire
ALCOHOL: Ethyl & Ethanol
ALCOHOL: Methyl & Methanol, Synthetic
ALKALIES & CHLORINE
ALKALOIDS & OTHER BOTANICAL BASED PRDTS
ALLERGENS & ALLERGENIC EXTRACTS
ALTERNATORS & GENERATORS: Battery Charging
ALTERNATORS: Automotive
ALUMINUM
ALUMINUM ORE MINING
ALUMINUM PRDTS
ALUMINUM: Rolling & Drawing
AMMONIUM NITRATE OR AMMONIUM SULFATE
AMMUNITION
AMMUNITION: Components
AMMUNITION: Pellets & BB's, Pistol & Air Rifle
AMMUNITION: Small Arms
AMPLIFIERS
AMPLIFIERS: Parametric
AMPLIFIERS: Pulse Amplifiers
AMPLIFIERS: RF & IF Power
AMUSEMENT & RECREATION SVCS: Amusement Ride
AMUSEMENT & RECREATION SVCS: Arcades
AMUSEMENT & RECREATION SVCS: Art Gallery, Commercial
AMUSEMENT & RECREATION SVCS: Arts & Crafts Instruction
AMUSEMENT & RECREATION SVCS: Exposition Operation
AMUSEMENT & RECREATION SVCS: Gambling & Lottery Svcs
AMUSEMENT & RECREATION SVCS: Game Machines
AMUSEMENT & RECREATION SVCS: Golf Club, Membership
AMUSEMENT & RECREATION SVCS: Physical Fitness Instruction
AMUSEMENT & RECREATION SVCS: Tennis & Professionals
AMUSEMENT MACHINES: Coin Operated
AMUSEMENT PARK DEVICES & RIDES
ANALGESICS
ANALYZERS: Moisture
ANALYZERS: Network
ANESTHESIA EQPT
ANESTHETICS: Bulk Form
ANIMAL FEED & SUPPLEMENTS: Livestock & Poultry
ANIMAL FEED: Wholesalers
ANIMAL FOOD & SUPPLEMENTS: Bird Food, Prepared
ANIMAL FOOD & SUPPLEMENTS: Dog
ANIMAL FOOD & SUPPLEMENTS: Dog & Cat
ANIMAL FOOD & SUPPLEMENTS: Feed Concentrates
ANIMAL FOOD & SUPPLEMENTS: Feed Premixes
ANIMAL FOOD & SUPPLEMENTS: Feed Supplements
ANIMAL FOOD & SUPPLEMENTS: Livestock
ANIMAL FOOD & SUPPLEMENTS: Mineral feed supplements
ANIMAL FOOD & SUPPLEMENTS: Pet, Exc Dog & Cat, Canned
ANIMAL FOOD & SUPPLEMENTS: Poultry
ANODIZING SVC
ANTENNAS: Radar Or Communications
ANTENNAS: Receiving
ANTIBIOTICS
ANTIBIOTICS, PACKAGED
ANTIFREEZE
ANTIQUE FURNITURE RESTORATION & REPAIR
ANTIQUE REPAIR & RESTORATION SVCS, EXC FURNITURE & AUTOS
ANTIQUE SHOPS
ANTIQUES, WHOLESALE
APPAREL ACCESS STORES
APPAREL DESIGNERS: Commercial
APPAREL: Hand Woven
APPLIANCE CORDS: Household Electrical Eqpt
APPLIANCES, HOUSEHOLD: Kitchen, Major, Exc Refrigs & Stoves
APPLIANCES, HOUSEHOLD: Laundry Machines, Incl Coin-Operated
APPLIANCES, HOUSEHOLD: Refrigerator Cabinets, Metal Or Wood
APPLIANCES, HOUSEHOLD: Refrigs, Mechanical & Absorption
APPLIANCES: Household, Refrigerators & Freezers
APPLIANCES: Major, Cooking
APPLIANCES: Small, Electric
APPLICATIONS SOFTWARE PROGRAMMING
AQUARIUM ACCESS, METAL
AQUARIUM DESIGN & MAINTENANCE SVCS
AQUARIUMS & ACCESS: Glass
AQUARIUMS & ACCESS: Plastic
ARCHITECTURAL SVCS
ARMATURE REPAIRING & REWINDING SVC
AROMATIC CHEMICAL PRDTS
ART & ORNAMENTAL WARE: Pottery
ART DEALERS & GALLERIES
ART DESIGN SVCS
ART GOODS & SPLYS WHOLESALERS
ART MARBLE: Concrete
ART NEEDLEWORK, MADE FROM PURCHASED MATERIALS
ART RELATED SVCS
ART RESTORATION SVC
ART SPLY STORES
ARTISTS' EQPT
ARTISTS' MATERIALS, WHOLESALE
ARTISTS' MATERIALS: Frames, Artists' Canvases
ARTISTS' MATERIALS: Ink, Drawing, Black & Colored
ARTISTS' MATERIALS: Paints, Exc Gold & Bronze
ARTISTS' MATERIALS: Pastels
ARTISTS' MATERIALS: Wax
ARTS & CRAFTS SCHOOL
ARTWORK: Framed
ASBESTOS PRODUCTS
ASPHALT & ASPHALT PRDTS
ASPHALT COATINGS & SEALERS
ASPHALT MIXTURES WHOLESALERS
ASPHALT PLANTS INCLUDING GRAVEL MIX TYPE
ASSEMBLING SVC: Plumbing Fixture Fittings, Plastic
ASSOCIATIONS: Engineering
ASSOCIATIONS: Scientists'
ATOMIZERS
ATTENUATORS
AUDIO & VIDEO EQPT, EXC COMMERCIAL
AUDIO COMPONENTS
AUDIO ELECTRONIC SYSTEMS
AUDIO-VISUAL PROGRAM PRODUCTION SVCS
AUDIOLOGISTS' OFFICES
AUDITING SVCS
AUTO & HOME SUPPLY STORES: Auto & Truck Eqpt & Parts
AUTO & HOME SUPPLY STORES: Automotive Access
AUTO & HOME SUPPLY STORES: Speed Shops, Incl Race Car Splys
AUTO & HOME SUPPLY STORES: Trailer Hitches, Automotive
AUTO & HOME SUPPLY STORES: Truck Eqpt & Parts
AUTOCLAVES: Indl
AUTOCLAVES: Laboratory
AUTOMATIC REGULATING CONTROL: Building Svcs Monitoring, Auto

PRODUCT INDEX

AUTOMATIC REGULATING CONTROLS: AC & Refrigeration
AUTOMATIC REGULATING CONTROLS: Elect Air Cleaner, Automatic
AUTOMATIC REGULATING CONTROLS: Energy Cutoff, Residtl/Comm
AUTOMATIC REGULATING CONTROLS: Ice Maker
AUTOMATIC REGULATING CONTROLS: Pneumatic Relays, Air-Cond
AUTOMATIC REGULATING CONTROLS: Refrig/Air-Cond Defrost
AUTOMATIC REGULATING CTRLS: Damper, Pneumatic Or Electric
AUTOMATIC TELLER MACHINES
AUTOMATIC VENDING MACHINES: Mechanisms & Parts
AUTOMOBILE RECOVERY SVCS
AUTOMOBILES: Off-Highway, Electric
AUTOMOBILES: Wholesalers
AUTOMOTIVE & TRUCK GENERAL REPAIR SVC
AUTOMOTIVE BODY, PAINT & INTERIOR REPAIR & MAINTENANCE SVC
AUTOMOTIVE PARTS, ACCESS & SPLYS
AUTOMOTIVE PARTS: Plastic
AUTOMOTIVE PRDTS: Rubber
AUTOMOTIVE REPAIR SHOPS: Brake Repair
AUTOMOTIVE REPAIR SHOPS: Diesel Engine Repair
AUTOMOTIVE REPAIR SHOPS: Electrical Svcs
AUTOMOTIVE REPAIR SHOPS: Engine Repair
AUTOMOTIVE REPAIR SHOPS: Machine Shop
AUTOMOTIVE REPAIR SHOPS: Springs, Rebuilding & Repair
AUTOMOTIVE REPAIR SHOPS: Trailer Repair
AUTOMOTIVE REPAIR SVC
AUTOMOTIVE SPLYS & PARTS, NEW, WHOL: Testing Eqpt, Electric
AUTOMOTIVE SPLYS & PARTS, NEW, WHOLESALE: Brakes
AUTOMOTIVE SPLYS & PARTS, NEW, WHOLESALE: Clutches
AUTOMOTIVE SPLYS & PARTS, NEW, WHOLESALE: Splys
AUTOMOTIVE SPLYS & PARTS, NEW, WHOLESALE: Trim
AUTOMOTIVE SPLYS & PARTS, NEW, WHOLESALE: Wheels
AUTOMOTIVE SPLYS & PARTS, USED, WHOLESALE: Wheels
AUTOMOTIVE SPLYS & PARTS, WHOLESALE, NEC
AUTOMOTIVE SPLYS/PARTS, NEW, WHOL: Body Rpr/Paint Shop Splys
AUTOMOTIVE SVCS, EXC REPAIR & CARWASHES: Maintenance
AUTOMOTIVE SVCS, EXC REPAIR: Washing & Polishing
AUTOMOTIVE SVCS, EXC RPR/CARWASHES: High Perf Auto Rpr/Svc
AUTOMOTIVE TOPS INSTALLATION OR REPAIR: Canvas Or Plastic
AUTOMOTIVE TOWING & WRECKING SVC
AUTOMOTIVE UPHOLSTERY SHOPS
AUTOMOTIVE WELDING SVCS
AUTOMOTIVE: Bodies
AUTOMOTIVE: Seating
AUTOTRANSFORMERS: Electric
AWNING REPAIR SHOP
AWNINGS & CANOPIES
AWNINGS & CANOPIES: Awnings, Fabric, From Purchased Matls
AWNINGS & CANOPIES: Fabric
AWNINGS: Fiberglass
AWNINGS: Metal
AXLES

B

BABY FORMULA
BABY PACIFIERS: Rubber
BADGES: Identification & Insignia
BAGS & BAGGING: Knit
BAGS & CONTAINERS: Textile, Exc Sleeping
BAGS & SACKS: Shipping & Shopping
BAGS: Canvas
BAGS: Cellophane
BAGS: Duffle, Canvas, Made From Purchased Materials
BAGS: Food Storage & Frozen Food, Plastic
BAGS: Food Storage & Trash, Plastic
BAGS: Garment Storage Exc Paper Or Plastic Film
BAGS: Grocers', Made From Purchased Materials
BAGS: Knapsacks, Canvas, Made From Purchased Materials
BAGS: Laundry, Garment & Storage
BAGS: Paper

BAGS: Paper, Made From Purchased Materials
BAGS: Plastic
BAGS: Plastic & Pliofilm
BAGS: Plastic, Made From Purchased Materials
BAGS: Rubber Or Rubberized Fabric
BAGS: Shipping
BAGS: Shopping, Made From Purchased Materials
BAGS: Tea, Fabric, Made From Purchased Materials
BAGS: Textile
BAGS: Trash, Plastic Film, Made From Purchased Materials
BAGS: Wardrobe, Closet Access, Made From Purchased Materials
BAKERIES, COMMERCIAL: On Premises Baking Only
BAKERIES: On Premises Baking & Consumption
BAKERY FOR HOME SVC DELIVERY
BAKERY MACHINERY
BAKERY PRDTS, FROZEN: Wholesalers
BAKERY PRDTS: Bagels, Fresh Or Frozen
BAKERY PRDTS: Bakery Prdts, Partially Cooked, Exc frozen
BAKERY PRDTS: Bread, All Types, Fresh Or Frozen
BAKERY PRDTS: Buns, Sweet, Frozen
BAKERY PRDTS: Cakes, Bakery, Exc Frozen
BAKERY PRDTS: Cakes, Bakery, Frozen
BAKERY PRDTS: Cones, Ice Cream
BAKERY PRDTS: Cookies
BAKERY PRDTS: Cookies & crackers
BAKERY PRDTS: Cracker Meal & Crumbs
BAKERY PRDTS: Doughnuts, Exc Frozen
BAKERY PRDTS: Doughnuts, Frozen
BAKERY PRDTS: Dry
BAKERY PRDTS: Frozen
BAKERY PRDTS: Matzoth
BAKERY PRDTS: Pastries, Danish, Frozen
BAKERY PRDTS: Pastries, Exc Frozen
BAKERY PRDTS: Pies, Bakery, Frozen
BAKERY PRDTS: Rolls, Bread Type, Fresh Or Frozen
BAKERY PRDTS: Wholesalers
BAKERY: Wholesale Or Wholesale & Retail Combined
BANDAGES
BANDS: Copper & Copper Alloy
BANNERS: Fabric
BANQUET HALL FACILITIES
BAR FIXTURES: Wood
BARBECUE EQPT
BARRICADES: Metal
BARS & BAR SHAPES: Steel, Hot-Rolled
BARS, COLD FINISHED: Steel, From Purchased Hot-Rolled
BARS: Concrete Reinforcing, Fabricated Steel
BARS: Iron, Made In Steel Mills
BASEBOARDS: Metal
BASEMENT WINDOW AREAWAYS: Concrete
BASES, BEVERAGE
BASKETS: Steel Wire
BATCHING PLANTS: Cement Silos
BATH SALTS
BATHING SUIT STORES
BATHMATS, COTTON
BATHROOM ACCESS & FITTINGS: Vitreous China & Earthenware
BATHTUBS: Concrete
BATTERIES, EXC AUTOMOTIVE: Wholesalers
BATTERIES: Alkaline, Cell Storage
BATTERIES: Lead Acid, Storage
BATTERIES: Rechargeable
BATTERIES: Storage
BATTERIES: Wet
BATTERY CASES: Plastic Or Plastics Combination
BATTERY CHARGERS
BATTERY CHARGERS: Storage, Motor & Engine Generator Type
BATTERY CHARGING GENERATORS
BATTS & BATTING: Cotton
BEARINGS & PARTS Ball
BEARINGS: Ball & Roller
BEAUTY & BARBER SHOP EQPT
BEAUTY SALONS
BED & BREAKFAST INNS
BEDDING, BEDSPREADS, BLANKETS & SHEETS
BEDDING, BEDSPREADS, BLANKETS & SHEETS: Comforters & Quilts
BEDDING, FROM SILK OR MANMADE FIBER
BEDS & ACCESS STORES
BEDS: Hospital
BEDSPREADS & BED SETS, FROM PURCHASED MATERIALS

BEDSPREADS, COTTON
BEEKEEPERS' SPLYS
BEEKEEPERS' SPLYS: Bee Smokers
BEER & ALE, WHOLESALE: Beer & Other Fermented Malt Liquors
BEER, WINE & LIQUOR STORES
BEER, WINE & LIQUOR STORES: Beer, Packaged
BEER, WINE & LIQUOR STORES: Wine
BELLOWS
BELTING: Rubber
BELTING: Transmission, Rubber
BELTS: Conveyor, Made From Purchased Wire
BENCHES: Seating
BEVERAGE BASES & SYRUPS
BEVERAGE PRDTS: Brewers' Grain
BEVERAGE, NONALCOHOLIC: Iced Tea/Fruit Drink, Bottled/Canned
BEVERAGES, ALCOHOLIC: Ale
BEVERAGES, ALCOHOLIC: Applejack
BEVERAGES, ALCOHOLIC: Beer
BEVERAGES, ALCOHOLIC: Beer & Ale
BEVERAGES, ALCOHOLIC: Bourbon Whiskey
BEVERAGES, ALCOHOLIC: Brandy
BEVERAGES, ALCOHOLIC: Cocktails
BEVERAGES, ALCOHOLIC: Cordials & Premixed Cocktails
BEVERAGES, ALCOHOLIC: Distilled Liquors
BEVERAGES, ALCOHOLIC: Gin
BEVERAGES, ALCOHOLIC: Liquors, Malt
BEVERAGES, ALCOHOLIC: Near Beer
BEVERAGES, ALCOHOLIC: Neutral Spirits, Fruit
BEVERAGES, ALCOHOLIC: Rum
BEVERAGES, ALCOHOLIC: Vodka
BEVERAGES, ALCOHOLIC: Wines
BEVERAGES, MALT
BEVERAGES, NONALCOHOLIC: Bottled & canned soft drinks
BEVERAGES, NONALCOHOLIC: Carbonated
BEVERAGES, NONALCOHOLIC: Carbonated, Canned & Bottled, Etc
BEVERAGES, NONALCOHOLIC: Cider
BEVERAGES, NONALCOHOLIC: Flavoring extracts & syrups, nec
BEVERAGES, NONALCOHOLIC: Fruit Drnks, Under 100% Juice, Can
BEVERAGES, NONALCOHOLIC: Lemonade, Bottled & Canned, Etc
BEVERAGES, NONALCOHOLIC: Soft Drinks, Canned & Bottled, Etc
BEVERAGES, NONALCOHOLIC: Tea, Iced, Bottled & Canned, Etc
BEVERAGES, WINE & DISTILLED ALCOHOLIC, WHOLESALE: Liquor
BEVERAGES, WINE & DISTILLED ALCOHOLIC, WHOLESALE: Neutral Sp
BEVERAGES, WINE & DISTILLED ALCOHOLIC, WHOLESALE: Wine
BEVERAGES, WINE WHOLESALE : Wine Coolers
BICYCLE SHOPS
BICYCLES WHOLESALERS
BICYCLES, PARTS & ACCESS
BILLETS: Steel
BILLFOLD INSERTS: Plastic
BILLIARD & POOL TABLES & SPLYS
BINDING SVC: Books & Manuals
BINDING SVC: Magazines
BINDING SVC: Pamphlets
BINDING SVC: Trade
BINS: Prefabricated, Sheet Metal
BIOLOGICAL PRDTS: Bacterial Vaccines
BIOLOGICAL PRDTS: Blood Derivatives
BIOLOGICAL PRDTS: Exc Diagnostic
BIOLOGICAL PRDTS: Extracts
BIOLOGICAL PRDTS: Vaccines
BIOLOGICAL PRDTS: Vaccines & Immunizing
BIOLOGICAL PRDTS: Veterinary
BLADES: Knife
BLADES: Saw, Chain Type
BLADES: Saw, Hand Or Power
BLANKBOOKS
BLANKBOOKS & LOOSELEAF BINDERS
BLANKBOOKS: Albums
BLANKBOOKS: Albums, Record
BLANKBOOKS: Memorandum, Printed
BLANKETS & BLANKETING, COTTON
BLASTING SVC: Sand, Metal Parts

PRODUCT INDEX

BLINDS & SHADES: Vertical
BLINDS : Window
BLOCK & BRICK: Sand Lime
BLOCKS & BRICKS: Concrete
BLOCKS: Chimney Or Fireplace, Concrete
BLOCKS: Landscape Or Retaining Wall, Concrete
BLOCKS: Paving, Asphalt, Not From Refineries
BLOCKS: Paving, Concrete
BLOCKS: Paving, Cut Stone
BLOCKS: Radiation-Proof, Concrete
BLOCKS: Standard, Concrete Or Cinder
BLOWERS & FANS
BLOWERS & FANS
BLUEPRINTING SVCS
BOAT BUILDING & REPAIR
BOAT BUILDING & REPAIRING: Fiberglass
BOAT BUILDING & REPAIRING: Kayaks
BOAT BUILDING & REPAIRING: Motorized
BOAT BUILDING & REPAIRING: Non-Motorized
BOAT BUILDING & RPRG: Fishing, Small, Lobster, Crab, Oyster
BOAT DEALERS
BOAT DEALERS: Canoe & Kayak
BOAT LIFTS
BOAT REPAIR SVCS
BOAT YARD: Boat yards, storage & incidental repair
BOATS & OTHER MARINE EQPT: Plastic
BODIES: Truck & Bus
BODY PARTS: Automobile, Stamped Metal
BOILER REPAIR SHOP
BOILERS & BOILER SHOP WORK
BOILERS: Low-Pressure Heating, Steam Or Hot Water
BOLTS: Metal
BONDERIZING: Bonderizing, Metal Or Metal Prdts
BOOK STORES
BOOK STORES: College
BOOKS, WHOLESALE
BOOTHS: Spray, Sheet Metal, Prefabricated
BOOTS: Women's
BORING MILL
BOTTLE CAPS & RESEALERS: Plastic
BOTTLED WATER DELIVERY
BOTTLES: Plastic
BOTTLES: Vacuum
BOUTIQUE STORES
BOWLING EQPT & SPLYS
BOX & CARTON MANUFACTURING EQPT
BOXES & CRATES: Rectangular, Wood
BOXES & SHOOK: Nailed Wood
BOXES: Corrugated
BOXES: Filing, Paperboard Made From Purchased Materials
BOXES: Mail Or Post Office, Collection/Storage, Sheet Metal
BOXES: Packing & Shipping, Metal
BOXES: Paperboard, Folding
BOXES: Paperboard, Set-Up
BOXES: Plastic
BOXES: Solid Fiber
BOXES: Stamped Metal
BOXES: Switch, Electric
BOXES: Wooden
BRAKES & BRAKE PARTS
BRAKES: Electromagnetic
BRASS FOUNDRY, NEC
BRAZING SVCS
BRAZING: Metal
BRIC-A-BRAC
BRICK, STONE & RELATED PRDTS WHOLESALERS
BRICKS & BLOCKS: Structural
BRICKS: Concrete
BRIDAL SHOPS
BRIDGE COMPONENTS: Bridge sections, prefabricated, highway
BROADCASTING & COMMS EQPT: Antennas, Transmitting/Comms
BROADCASTING & COMMS EQPT: Rcvr-Transmitter Unt, Transceiver
BROADCASTING & COMMUNICATIONS EQPT: Cellular Radio Telephone
BROADCASTING & COMMUNICATIONS EQPT: Studio Eqpt, Radio & TV
BROADCASTING & COMMUNICATIONS EQPT: Transmitting, Radio/TV
BROKERS' SVCS
BROKERS: Automotive
BROKERS: Business
BROKERS: Food
BROKERS: Loan
BROKERS: Printing
BRONZE FOUNDRY, NEC
BROOMS
BROOMS & BRUSHES
BROOMS & BRUSHES: Hair Pencils Or Artists' Brushes
BROOMS & BRUSHES: Household Or Indl
BROOMS & BRUSHES: Paint & Varnish
BROOMS & BRUSHES: Paint Rollers
BROOMS & BRUSHES: Paintbrushes
BRUSHES
BRUSHES & BRUSH STOCK CONTACTS: Electric
BUCKLES & PARTS
BUILDING & OFFICE CLEANING SVCS
BUILDING & STRUCTURAL WOOD MBRS: Timbers, Struct, Lam Lumber
BUILDING & STRUCTURAL WOOD MEMBERS
BUILDING & STRUCTURAL WOOD MEMBERS: Arches, Laminated Lumber
BUILDING BOARD & WALLBOARD, EXC GYPSUM
BUILDING BOARD: Gypsum
BUILDING CLEANING & MAINTENANCE SVCS
BUILDING COMPONENTS: Structural Steel
BUILDING ITEM REPAIR SVCS, MISCELLANEOUS
BUILDING PRDTS & MATERIALS DEALERS
BUILDING PRDTS: Concrete
BUILDING PRDTS: Stone
BUILDING STONE, ARTIFICIAL: Concrete
BUILDINGS & COMPONENTS: Prefabricated Metal
BUILDINGS, PREFABRICATED: Wholesalers
BUILDINGS: Portable
BUILDINGS: Prefabricated, Metal
BUILDINGS: Prefabricated, Plastic
BUILDINGS: Prefabricated, Wood
BUILDINGS: Prefabricated, Wood
BULLETIN BOARDS: Wood
BUMPERS: Motor Vehicle
BURIAL VAULTS: Concrete Or Precast Terrazzo
BURLAP & BURLAP PRDTS
BURNERS: Gas, Indl
BUSES: Wholesalers
BUSHINGS & BEARINGS: Copper, Exc Machined
BUSINESS ACTIVITIES: Non-Commercial Site
BUSINESS FORMS WHOLESALERS
BUSINESS FORMS: Printed, Continuous
BUSINESS FORMS: Printed, Manifold
BUSINESS MACHINE REPAIR, ELECTRIC
BUSINESS SUPPORT SVCS
BUTADIENE: Indl, Organic, Chemical
BUTTONS

C

CABINETS & CASES: Show, Display & Storage, Exc Wood
CABINETS: Bathroom Vanities, Wood
CABINETS: Entertainment
CABINETS: Entertainment Units, Household, Wood
CABINETS: Factory
CABINETS: Filing, Metal
CABINETS: Filing, Wood
CABINETS: Kitchen, Metal
CABINETS: Kitchen, Wood
CABINETS: Office, Metal
CABINETS: Office, Wood
CABINETS: Radio & Television, Metal
CABINETS: Show, Display, Etc, Wood, Exc Refrigerated
CABLE TELEVISION
CABLE TELEVISION PRDTS
CABLE: Coaxial
CABLE: Fiber
CABLE: Fiber Optic
CABLE: Nonferrous, Shipboard
CABLE: Noninsulated
CABLE: Ropes & Fiber
CABLE: Steel, Insulated Or Armored
CAGES: Wire
CALCULATING & ACCOUNTING EQPT
CALIBRATING SVCS, NEC
CAMERAS & RELATED EQPT: Photographic
CANDLE SHOPS
CANDLES
CANDLES: Wholesalers
CANDY & CONFECTIONS: Cake Ornaments
CANDY & CONFECTIONS: Candy Bars, Including Chocolate Covered
CANDY & CONFECTIONS: Chocolate Candy, Exc Solid Chocolate
CANDY & CONFECTIONS: Fudge
CANDY & CONFECTIONS: Halvah
CANDY, NUT & CONFECTIONERY STORES: Candy
CANDY, NUT & CONFECTIONERY STORES: Confectionery
CANDY: Chocolate From Cacao Beans
CANNED SPECIALTIES
CANOPIES: Sheet Metal
CANS: Aluminum
CANS: Metal
CANVAS PRDTS
CANVAS PRDTS, WHOLESALE
CANVAS PRDTS: Convertible Tops, Car/Boat, Fm Purchased Mtrl
CANVAS PRDTS: Shades, Made From Purchased Materials
CAPACITORS: Fixed Or Variable
CAPACITORS: NEC
CAPS & PLUGS: Electric, Attachment
CAR WASH EQPT
CARBIDES
CARBON & GRAPHITE PRDTS, NEC
CARBONS: Electric
CARDBOARD PRDTS, EXC DIE-CUT
CARDBOARD: Waterproof, Made From Purchased Materials
CARDIOVASCULAR SYSTEM DRUGS, EXC DIAGNOSTIC
CARDS: Beveled
CARDS: Color
CARDS: Greeting
CARDS: Identification
CARPET DYEING & FINISHING
CARPETS & RUGS: Tufted
CARPETS, RUGS & FLOOR COVERING
CARPETS: Hand & Machine Made
CARPETS: Textile Fiber
CARRIAGES: Horse Drawn
CARRYING CASES, WHOLESALE
CARTONS: Egg, Molded Pulp, Made From Purchased Materials
CASEMENTS: Aluminum
CASES, WOOD
CASES: Attache'
CASES: Carrying
CASES: Carrying, Clothing & Apparel
CASES: Jewelry
CASES: Nonrefrigerated, Exc Wood
CASES: Packing, Nailed Or Lock Corner, Wood
CASES: Plastic
CASES: Sample Cases
CASES: Shipping, Nailed Or Lock Corner, Wood
CASH REGISTER REPAIR SVCS
CASINGS: Sheet Metal
CASKETS & ACCESS
CASKETS WHOLESALERS
CAST STONE: Concrete
CASTERS
CASTINGS GRINDING: For The Trade
CASTINGS: Aerospace Investment, Ferrous
CASTINGS: Aerospace, Aluminum
CASTINGS: Aerospace, Nonferrous, Exc Aluminum
CASTINGS: Aluminum
CASTINGS: Brass, NEC, Exc Die
CASTINGS: Bronze, NEC, Exc Die
CASTINGS: Die, Aluminum
CASTINGS: Die, Lead
CASTINGS: Die, Nonferrous
CASTINGS: Die, Zinc
CASTINGS: Ductile
CASTINGS: Gray Iron
CASTINGS: Machinery, Aluminum
CASTINGS: Machinery, Nonferrous, Exc Die or Aluminum Copper
CASTINGS: Precision
CASTINGS: Steel
CATALOG & MAIL-ORDER HOUSES
CATALOG SHOWROOMS
CATALYSTS: Chemical
CATAPULTS
CATERERS
CEILING SYSTEMS: Luminous, Commercial
CEMENT & CONCRETE RELATED PRDTS & EQPT: Bituminous
CEMENT ROCK: Crushed & Broken
CEMENT: Heat Resistant
CEMENT: High Temperature, Refractory, Nonclay

PRODUCT INDEX

CEMENT: Hydraulic
CEMENT: Masonry
CEMENT: Natural
CEMENT: Portland
CEMETERY MEMORIAL DEALERS
CERAMIC FIBER
CERAMIC FLOOR & WALL TILE WHOLESALERS
CHAIN: Welded, Made From Purchased Wire
CHAINS: Forged
CHAMBERS & CAISSONS
CHANDELIERS: Commercial
CHANDELIERS: Residential
CHARCOAL: Activated
CHASSIS: Motor Vehicle
CHEESE WHOLESALERS
CHEMICAL INDICATORS
CHEMICAL PROCESSING MACHINERY & EQPT
CHEMICAL: Sodm Compnds/Salts, Inorg, Exc Rfnd Sodm Chloride
CHEMICALS & ALLIED PRDTS WHOLESALERS, NEC
CHEMICALS & ALLIED PRDTS, WHOLESALE: Alkalines & Chlorine
CHEMICALS & ALLIED PRDTS, WHOLESALE: Anti-Corrosion Prdts
CHEMICALS & ALLIED PRDTS, WHOLESALE: Aromatic
CHEMICALS & ALLIED PRDTS, WHOLESALE: Chemical Additives
CHEMICALS & ALLIED PRDTS, WHOLESALE: Chemicals, Indl
CHEMICALS & ALLIED PRDTS, WHOLESALE: Dry Ice
CHEMICALS & ALLIED PRDTS, WHOLESALE: Essential Oils
CHEMICALS & ALLIED PRDTS, WHOLESALE: Oxygen
CHEMICALS & ALLIED PRDTS, WHOLESALE: Plastics Materials, NEC
CHEMICALS & ALLIED PRDTS, WHOLESALE: Plastics Prdts, NEC
CHEMICALS & ALLIED PRDTS, WHOLESALE: Plastics Sheets & Rods
CHEMICALS & ALLIED PRDTS, WHOLESALE: Polyurethane Prdts
CHEMICALS & ALLIED PRDTS, WHOLESALE: Salts & Polishes, Indl
CHEMICALS & ALLIED PRDTS, WHOLESALE: Spec Clean/Sanitation
CHEMICALS & ALLIED PRDTS, WHOLESALE: Syn Resin, Rub/Plastic
CHEMICALS & ALLIED PRDTS, WHOLESALE: Waxes, Exc Petroleum
CHEMICALS/ALLIED PRDTS, WHOL: Coal Tar Prdts, Prim/Intermdt
CHEMICALS: Agricultural
CHEMICALS: Alcohols
CHEMICALS: Aluminum Chloride
CHEMICALS: Aluminum Compounds
CHEMICALS: Aluminum Oxide
CHEMICALS: Brine
CHEMICALS: Calcium & Calcium Compounds
CHEMICALS: Compounds Or Salts, Iron, Ferric Or Ferrous
CHEMICALS: Fire Retardant
CHEMICALS: Formaldehyde
CHEMICALS: Fuel Tank Or Engine Cleaning
CHEMICALS: High Purity Grade, Organic
CHEMICALS: High Purity, Refined From Technical Grade
CHEMICALS: Hydrogen Peroxide
CHEMICALS: Inorganic, NEC
CHEMICALS: Isotopes, Radioactive
CHEMICALS: Lithium Compounds, Inorganic
CHEMICALS: Medicinal
CHEMICALS: Medicinal, Organic, Uncompounded, Bulk
CHEMICALS: Metal Salts/Compounds, Exc Sodium, Potassium/Alum
CHEMICALS: NEC
CHEMICALS: Organic, NEC
CHEMICALS: Phenol
CHEMICALS: Silica Compounds
CHEMICALS: Sodium Bicarbonate
CHEMICALS: Sodium/Potassium Cmpnds,Exc Bleach,Alkalies/Alum
CHEMICALS: Sulfur Chloride
CHEMICALS: Water Treatment
CHEWING GUM
CHILD DAY CARE SVCS
CHILDREN'S & INFANTS' CLOTHING STORES
CHILDREN'S WEAR STORES
CHIMES: Electric

CHIMNEY CAPS: Concrete
CHIMNEYS & FITTINGS
CHINA COOKWARE
CHLORINE
CHOCOLATE, EXC CANDY FROM BEANS: Chips, Powder, Block, Syrup
CHOCOLATE, EXC CANDY FROM PURCH CHOC: Chips, Powder, Block
CHRISTMAS TREE LIGHTING SETS: Electric
CHUCKS
CHURCHES
CHUTES & TROUGHS
CHUTES: Coal, Sheet Metal, Prefabricated
CIGAR LIGHTERS EXC PRECIOUS METAL
CIGARETTE & CIGAR PRDTS & ACCESS
CIRCUIT BOARDS, PRINTED: Television & Radio
CIRCUIT BOARDS: Wiring
CIRCUITS, INTEGRATED: Hybrid
CIRCUITS: Electronic
CIRCULAR KNIT FABRICS DYEING & FINISHING
CLAMPS & COUPLINGS: Hose
CLAY PRDTS: Architectural
CLAYS, EXC KAOLIN & BALL
CLEANING EQPT: Blast, Dustless
CLEANING EQPT: Carpet Sweepers, Exc Household Elec Vacuum
CLEANING EQPT: Commercial
CLEANING EQPT: High Pressure
CLEANING OR POLISHING PREPARATIONS, NEC
CLEANING PRDTS: Automobile Polish
CLEANING PRDTS: Degreasing Solvent
CLEANING PRDTS: Deodorants, Nonpersonal
CLEANING PRDTS: Disinfectants, Household Or Indl Plant
CLEANING PRDTS: Drycleaning Preparations
CLEANING PRDTS: Indl Plant Disinfectants Or Deodorants
CLEANING PRDTS: Laundry Preparations
CLEANING PRDTS: Metal Polish
CLEANING PRDTS: Polishing Preparations & Related Prdts
CLEANING PRDTS: Rug, Upholstery/Dry Clng Detergents/Spotters
CLEANING PRDTS: Sanitation Preparations
CLEANING PRDTS: Sanitation Preps, Disinfectants/Deodorants
CLEANING PRDTS: Shoe Polish Or Cleaner
CLEANING PRDTS: Specialty
CLEANING PRDTS: Window Cleaning Preparations
CLEANING SVCS: Industrial Or Commercial
CLIPPERS: Fingernail & Toenail
CLIPS & FASTENERS, MADE FROM PURCHASED WIRE
CLOSURES: Closures, Stamped Metal
CLOSURES: Plastic
CLOTHING & ACCESS, WOMEN, CHILD & INFANT, WHOL: Diapers
CLOTHING & ACCESS, WOMEN, CHILD & INFANT, WHOL: Scarves
CLOTHING & ACCESS, WOMEN, CHILD & INFANT, WHOLESALE: Under
CLOTHING & ACCESS, WOMEN, CHILD & INFANT, WHSLE: Sportswear
CLOTHING & ACCESS, WOMEN, CHILDREN & INFANT, WHOL: Access
CLOTHING & ACCESS, WOMEN, CHILDREN & INFANT, WHOL: Gloves
CLOTHING & ACCESS, WOMEN, CHILDREN & INFANT, WHOL: Handbags
CLOTHING & ACCESS, WOMEN, CHILDREN & INFANT, WHOL: Sweaters
CLOTHING & ACCESS, WOMEN, CHILDREN & INFANTS, WHOL: Purses
CLOTHING & ACCESS, WOMEN, CHILDREN/INFANT, WHOL: Baby Goods
CLOTHING & ACCESS, WOMEN, CHILDREN/INFANT, WHOL: Nightwear
CLOTHING & ACCESS, WOMEN, CHILDREN/INFANT, WHOL: Swimsuits
CLOTHING & ACCESS, WOMENS, CHILDREN & INFANTS, WHOL: Hats
CLOTHING & ACCESS: Costumes, Masquerade
CLOTHING & ACCESS: Costumes, Theatrical
CLOTHING & ACCESS: Cummerbunds
CLOTHING & ACCESS: Footlets
CLOTHING & ACCESS: Handicapped
CLOTHING & ACCESS: Handkerchiefs, Exc Paper
CLOTHING & ACCESS: Hospital Gowns
CLOTHING & ACCESS: Men's Miscellaneous Access

CLOTHING & ACCESS: Suspenders
CLOTHING & APPAREL STORES: Custom
CLOTHING & FURNISHINGS, MEN & BOY, WHOLESALE: Suits/Trousers
CLOTHING & FURNISHINGS, MEN'S & BOYS', WHOLESALE: Caps
CLOTHING & FURNISHINGS, MEN'S & BOYS', WHOLESALE: Fur
CLOTHING & FURNISHINGS, MEN'S & BOYS', WHOLESALE: Gloves
CLOTHING & FURNISHINGS, MEN'S & BOYS', WHOLESALE: Hats
CLOTHING & FURNISHINGS, MEN'S & BOYS', WHOLESALE: Neckwear
CLOTHING & FURNISHINGS, MEN'S & BOYS', WHOLESALE: Scarves
CLOTHING & FURNISHINGS, MEN'S & BOYS', WHOLESALE: Shirts
CLOTHING & FURNISHINGS, MEN'S & BOYS', WHOLESALE: Umbrellas
CLOTHING & FURNISHINGS, MEN'S & BOYS', WHOLESALE: Uniforms
CLOTHING & FURNISHINGS, MENS & BOYS, WHOL: Sportswear/Work
CLOTHING & FURNISHINGS, MENS & BOYS, WHOLESALE: Apprl Belts
CLOTHING ACCESS STORES: Umbrellas
CLOTHING STORES, NEC
CLOTHING STORES: Dancewear
CLOTHING STORES: Designer Apparel
CLOTHING STORES: Jeans
CLOTHING STORES: Leather
CLOTHING STORES: T-Shirts, Printed, Custom
CLOTHING STORES: Uniforms & Work
CLOTHING STORES: Unisex
CLOTHING STORES: Work
CLOTHING, WOMEN & CHILD, WHLSE: Dress, Suit, Skirt & Blouse
CLOTHING/ACCESS, WOMEN, CHILDREN/INFANT, WHOL: Apparel Belt
CLOTHING/FURNISHINGS, MEN/BOY, WHOL: Furnishings, Exc Shoes
CLOTHING: Academic Vestments
CLOTHING: Access
CLOTHING: Access, Women's & Misses'
CLOTHING: Aprons, Exc Rubber/Plastic, Women, Misses, Junior
CLOTHING: Aprons, Harness
CLOTHING: Aprons, Work, Exc Rubberized & Plastic, Men's
CLOTHING: Athletic & Sportswear, Men's & Boys'
CLOTHING: Athletic & Sportswear, Women's & Girls'
CLOTHING: Baker, Barber, Lab/Svc Ind Apparel, Washable, Men
CLOTHING: Bathing Suits & Beachwear, Children's
CLOTHING: Bathing Suits & Swimwear, Girls, Children & Infant
CLOTHING: Bathing Suits & Swimwear, Knit
CLOTHING: Bathrobes, Mens & Womens, From Purchased Materials
CLOTHING: Belts
CLOTHING: Blouses & Shirts, Girls' & Children's
CLOTHING: Blouses, Boys', From Purchased Materials
CLOTHING: Blouses, Women's & Girls'
CLOTHING: Blouses, Womens & Juniors, From Purchased Mtrls
CLOTHING: Brassieres
CLOTHING: Bridal Gowns
CLOTHING: Burial
CLOTHING: Capes & Jackets, Women's & Misses'
CLOTHING: Capes, Exc Fur/Rubber, Womens, Misses & Juniors
CLOTHING: Chemises, Camisoles/Teddies, Women, Misses/Junior
CLOTHING: Children & Infants'
CLOTHING: Children's, Girls'
CLOTHING: Clergy Vestments
CLOTHING: Coats & Jackets, Leather & Sheep-Lined
CLOTHING: Coats & Suits, Men's & Boys'
CLOTHING: Coats, Leatherette, Oiled Fabric, Etc, Mens & Boys
CLOTHING: Coats, Tailored, Mens/Boys, From Purchased Mtls
CLOTHING: Corset Access, Clasps & Stays
CLOTHING: Costumes

PRODUCT INDEX

CLOTHING: Diaper Covers, Waterproof, From Purchased Material
CLOTHING: Disposable
CLOTHING: Down-Filled, Men's & Boys'
CLOTHING: Dresses
CLOTHING: Dresses & Skirts
CLOTHING: Dresses, Knit
CLOTHING: Dressing Gowns, Mens/Womens, From Purchased Matls
CLOTHING: Foundation Garments, Women's
CLOTHING: Furs
CLOTHING: Garments, Indl, Men's & Boys'
CLOTHING: Girdles & Other Foundation Garments, Knit
CLOTHING: Girdles & Panty Girdles
CLOTHING: Gloves, Knit, Exc Dress & Semidress
CLOTHING: Gowns & Dresses, Wedding
CLOTHING: Gowns, Formal
CLOTHING: Hats & Caps, Leather
CLOTHING: Hats & Caps, NEC
CLOTHING: Hats & Caps, Uniform
CLOTHING: Hats & Headwear, Knit
CLOTHING: Hosiery, Men's & Boys'
CLOTHING: Hosiery, Pantyhose & Knee Length, Sheer
CLOTHING: Hospital, Men's
CLOTHING: Housedresses
CLOTHING: Jackets & Vests, Exc Fur & Leather, Women's
CLOTHING: Jackets, Knit
CLOTHING: Jeans, Men's & Boys'
CLOTHING: Knit Underwear & Nightwear
CLOTHING: Leather
CLOTHING: Leather & sheep-lined clothing
CLOTHING: Maternity
CLOTHING: Men's & boy's clothing, nec
CLOTHING: Men's & boy's underwear & nightwear
CLOTHING: Mens & Boys Jackets, Sport, Suede, Leatherette
CLOTHING: Millinery
CLOTHING: Neckties, Knit
CLOTHING: Neckwear
CLOTHING: Outerwear, Knit
CLOTHING: Outerwear, Lthr, Wool/Down-Filled, Men, Youth/Boy
CLOTHING: Outerwear, Women's & Misses' NEC
CLOTHING: Overcoats & Topcoats, Men/Boy, Purchased Materials
CLOTHING: Pants, Work, Men's, Youths' & Boys'
CLOTHING: Panty Hose
CLOTHING: Raincoats, Exc Vulcanized Rubber, Purchased Matls
CLOTHING: Robes & Dressing Gowns
CLOTHING: Robes & Housecoats, Children's
CLOTHING: Scarves & Mufflers, Knit
CLOTHING: Service Apparel, Women's
CLOTHING: Shawls, Knit
CLOTHING: Sheep-Lined
CLOTHING: Shirts
CLOTHING: Shirts, Dress, Men's & Boys'
CLOTHING: Shirts, Knit
CLOTHING: Shirts, Sports & Polo, Men & Boy, Purchased Mtrl
CLOTHING: Shirts, Sports & Polo, Men's & Boys'
CLOTHING: Shirts, Women's & Juniors', From Purchased Mtrls
CLOTHING: Skirts
CLOTHING: Slacks & Shorts, Dress, Men's, Youths' & Boys'
CLOTHING: Slacks, Girls' & Children's
CLOTHING: Sleeping Garments, Men's & Boys'
CLOTHING: Sleeping Garments, Women's & Children's
CLOTHING: Slipper Socks
CLOTHING: Socks
CLOTHING: Sportswear, Women's
CLOTHING: Suits & Skirts, Women's & Misses'
CLOTHING: Suits, Men's & Boys', From Purchased Materials
CLOTHING: Sweaters & Sweater Coats, Knit
CLOTHING: Sweaters, Men's & Boys'
CLOTHING: Sweatshirts & T-Shirts, Men's & Boys'
CLOTHING: Swimwear, Men's & Boys'
CLOTHING: Swimwear, Women's & Misses'
CLOTHING: T-Shirts & Tops, Knit
CLOTHING: T-Shirts & Tops, Women's & Girls'
CLOTHING: Tailored Suits & Formal Jackets
CLOTHING: Ties, Handsewn, From Purchased Materials
CLOTHING: Ties, Neck & Bow, Men's & Boys'
CLOTHING: Ties, Neck, Men's & Boys', From Purchased Material
CLOTHING: Tights & Leg Warmers
CLOTHING: Trousers & Slacks, Men's & Boys'
CLOTHING: Underwear, Knit
CLOTHING: Underwear, Men's & Boys'
CLOTHING: Underwear, Women's & Children's
CLOTHING: Uniforms & Vestments
CLOTHING: Uniforms, Ex Athletic, Women's, Misses' & Juniors'
CLOTHING: Uniforms, Men's & Boys'
CLOTHING: Uniforms, Military, Men/Youth, Purchased Materials
CLOTHING: Uniforms, Policemen's, From Purchased Materials
CLOTHING: Uniforms, Team Athletic
CLOTHING: Uniforms, Work
CLOTHING: Warm Weather Knit Outerwear, Including Beachwear
CLOTHING: Waterproof Outerwear
CLOTHING: Work Apparel, Exc Uniforms
CLOTHING: Work, Men's
CLUTCHES OR BRAKES: Electromagnetic
CLUTCHES, EXC VEHICULAR
COAL MINING SERVICES
COAL MINING SVCS: Bituminous, Contract Basis
COATING COMPOUNDS: Tar
COATING OR WRAPPING SVC: Steel Pipe
COATING SVC
COATING SVC: Aluminum, Metal Prdts
COATING SVC: Electrodes
COATING SVC: Hot Dip, Metals Or Formed Prdts
COATING SVC: Metals & Formed Prdts
COATING SVC: Metals, With Plastic Or Resins
COATING SVC: Rust Preventative
COATING SVC: Silicon
COATINGS: Air Curing
COATINGS: Epoxy
COATINGS: Polyurethane
COFFEE SVCS
COILS & TRANSFORMERS
COILS: Electric Motors Or Generators
COILS: Pipe
COIN OPERATED LAUNDRIES & DRYCLEANERS
COIN-OPERATED LAUNDRY
COKE: Calcined Petroleum, Made From Purchased Materials
COKE: Produced In Chemical Recovery Coke Ovens
COLLECTION AGENCY, EXC REAL ESTATE
COLLEGES, UNIVERSITIES & PROFESSIONAL SCHOOLS
COLLETS
COLOGNES
COLOR SEPARATION: Photographic & Movie Film
COLORS: Pigments, Inorganic
COLORS: Pigments, Organic
COMFORTERS & QUILTS, FROM MANMADE FIBER OR SILK
COMMERCIAL & INDL SHELVING WHOLESALERS
COMMERCIAL & OFFICE BUILDINGS RENOVATION & REPAIR
COMMERCIAL ART & GRAPHIC DESIGN SVCS
COMMERCIAL EQPT WHOLESALERS, NEC
COMMERCIAL EQPT, WHOLESALE: Bakery Eqpt & Splys
COMMERCIAL EQPT, WHOLESALE: Comm Cooking & Food Svc Eqpt
COMMERCIAL EQPT, WHOLESALE: Display Eqpt, Exc Refrigerated
COMMERCIAL EQPT, WHOLESALE: Mannequins
COMMERCIAL EQPT, WHOLESALE: Restaurant, NEC
COMMERCIAL EQPT, WHOLESALE: Scales, Exc Laboratory
COMMERCIAL EQPT, WHOLESALE: Store Fixtures & Display Eqpt
COMMERCIAL LAUNDRY EQPT
COMMERCIAL PRINTING & NEWSPAPER PUBLISHING COMBINED
COMMON SAND MINING
COMMUNICATION HEADGEAR: Telephone
COMMUNICATIONS CARRIER: Wired
COMMUNICATIONS EQPT & SYSTEMS, NEC
COMMUNICATIONS EQPT REPAIR & MAINTENANCE
COMMUNICATIONS EQPT WHOLESALERS
COMMUNICATIONS EQPT: Microwave
COMMUNICATIONS EQPT: Radio, Marine
COMMUNICATIONS SVCS
COMMUNICATIONS SVCS: Cellular
COMMUNICATIONS SVCS: Data
COMMUNICATIONS SVCS: Facsimile Transmission
COMMUNICATIONS SVCS: Internet Host Svcs
COMMUNICATIONS SVCS: Online Svc Providers
COMMUNICATIONS SVCS: Proprietary Online Svcs Networks
COMMUNICATIONS SVCS: Satellite Earth Stations
COMMUNICATIONS SVCS: Signal Enhancement Network Svcs
COMMUNICATIONS SVCS: Telephone, Data
COMMUNICATIONS SVCS: Telephone, Local
COMMUNICATIONS SVCS: Telephone, Voice
COMMUTATORS: Electronic
COMPACT DISCS OR CD'S, WHOLESALE
COMPACT LASER DISCS: Prerecorded
COMPACTORS: Trash & Garbage, Residential
COMPARATORS: Optical
COMPOSITION STONE: Plastic
COMPOST
COMPRESSORS, AIR CONDITIONING: Wholesalers
COMPRESSORS: Air & Gas
COMPRESSORS: Air & Gas, Including Vacuum Pumps
COMPRESSORS: Refrigeration & Air Conditioning Eqpt
COMPRESSORS: Wholesalers
COMPUTER & COMPUTER SOFTWARE STORES
COMPUTER & COMPUTER SOFTWARE STORES: Peripheral Eqpt
COMPUTER & COMPUTER SOFTWARE STORES: Software, Bus/Non-Game
COMPUTER & COMPUTER SOFTWARE STORES: Software, Computer Game
COMPUTER & OFFICE MACHINE MAINTENANCE & REPAIR
COMPUTER DISKETTES WHOLESALERS
COMPUTER FORMS
COMPUTER GRAPHICS SVCS
COMPUTER HARDWARE REQUIREMENTS ANALYSIS
COMPUTER INTERFACE EQPT: Indl Process
COMPUTER PERIPHERAL EQPT REPAIR & MAINTENANCE
COMPUTER PERIPHERAL EQPT, NEC
COMPUTER PERIPHERAL EQPT, WHOLESALE
COMPUTER PERIPHERAL EQPT: Encoders
COMPUTER PERIPHERAL EQPT: Film Reader Devices
COMPUTER PERIPHERAL EQPT: Graphic Displays, Exc Terminals
COMPUTER PERIPHERAL EQPT: Input Or Output
COMPUTER PROGRAMMING SVCS
COMPUTER PROGRAMMING SVCS: Custom
COMPUTER RELATED MAINTENANCE SVCS
COMPUTER SERVICE BUREAU
COMPUTER SOFTWARE DEVELOPMENT
COMPUTER SOFTWARE DEVELOPMENT & APPLICATIONS
COMPUTER SOFTWARE SYSTEMS ANALYSIS & DESIGN: Custom
COMPUTER STORAGE DEVICES, NEC
COMPUTER TERMINALS
COMPUTER TERMINALS: CRT
COMPUTER-AIDED DESIGN SYSTEMS SVCS
COMPUTER-AIDED ENGINEERING SYSTEMS SVCS
COMPUTERS, NEC
COMPUTERS, NEC, WHOLESALE
COMPUTERS, PERIPHERALS & SOFTWARE, WHOLESALE: Disk Drives
COMPUTERS, PERIPHERALS & SOFTWARE, WHOLESALE: Printers
COMPUTERS, PERIPHERALS & SOFTWARE, WHOLESALE: Software
COMPUTERS: Indl, Process, Gas Flow
COMPUTERS: Mainframe
COMPUTERS: Personal
CONCENTRATES, DRINK
CONCENTRATES, FLAVORING, EXC DRINK
CONCRETE CURING & HARDENING COMPOUNDS
CONCRETE MIXERS
CONCRETE PLANTS
CONCRETE PRDTS
CONCRETE PRDTS, PRECAST, NEC
CONCRETE: Asphaltic, Not From Refineries
CONCRETE: Bituminous
CONCRETE: Ready-Mixed
CONDENSERS & CONDENSING UNITS: Air Conditioner
CONDENSERS: Fixed Or Variable
CONDENSERS: Heat Transfer Eqpt, Evaporative
CONDENSERS: Motors Or Generators
CONDUITS & FITTINGS: Electric
CONDUITS: Pressed Pulp Fiber, Made From Purchased Materials

PRODUCT INDEX

CONFECTIONERY PRDTS WHOLESALERS
CONFECTIONS & CANDY
CONFINEMENT SURVEILLANCE SYS MAINTENANCE & MONITORING SVCS
CONNECTORS & TERMINALS: Electrical Device Uses
CONNECTORS: Cord, Electric
CONNECTORS: Electrical
CONNECTORS: Electronic
CONNECTORS: Solderless, Electric-Wiring Devices
CONSTRUCTION & MINING MACHINERY WHOLESALERS
CONSTRUCTION & ROAD MAINTENANCE EQPT: Drags, Road
CONSTRUCTION EQPT: Attachments
CONSTRUCTION EQPT: Attachments, Snow Plow
CONSTRUCTION EQPT: Crane Carriers
CONSTRUCTION EQPT: Cranes
CONSTRUCTION EQPT: Dozers, Tractor Mounted, Material Moving
CONSTRUCTION EQPT: Hammer Mills, Port, Incl Rock/Ore Crush
CONSTRUCTION EQPT: Rakes, Land Clearing, Mechanical
CONSTRUCTION EQPT: Rollers, Sheepsfoot & Vibratory
CONSTRUCTION EQPT: SCRAPERS, GRADERS, ROLLERS & SIMILAR EQPT
CONSTRUCTION EQPT: Wrecker Hoists, Automobile
CONSTRUCTION MATERIALS, WHOLESALE: Aggregate
CONSTRUCTION MATERIALS, WHOLESALE: Awnings
CONSTRUCTION MATERIALS, WHOLESALE: Block, Concrete & Cinder
CONSTRUCTION MATERIALS, WHOLESALE: Blocks, Building, NEC
CONSTRUCTION MATERIALS, WHOLESALE: Building Stone, Granite
CONSTRUCTION MATERIALS, WHOLESALE: Building Stone, Marble
CONSTRUCTION MATERIALS, WHOLESALE: Building, Exterior
CONSTRUCTION MATERIALS, WHOLESALE: Building, Interior
CONSTRUCTION MATERIALS, WHOLESALE: Cement
CONSTRUCTION MATERIALS, WHOLESALE: Clay, Exc Refractory
CONSTRUCTION MATERIALS, WHOLESALE: Concrete Mixtures
CONSTRUCTION MATERIALS, WHOLESALE: Door Frames
CONSTRUCTION MATERIALS, WHOLESALE: Glass
CONSTRUCTION MATERIALS, WHOLESALE: Gravel
CONSTRUCTION MATERIALS, WHOLESALE: Lime Building Prdts
CONSTRUCTION MATERIALS, WHOLESALE: Limestone
CONSTRUCTION MATERIALS, WHOLESALE: Masons' Materials
CONSTRUCTION MATERIALS, WHOLESALE: Millwork
CONSTRUCTION MATERIALS, WHOLESALE: Molding, All Materials
CONSTRUCTION MATERIALS, WHOLESALE: Paving Materials
CONSTRUCTION MATERIALS, WHOLESALE: Paving Mixtures
CONSTRUCTION MATERIALS, WHOLESALE: Prefabricated Structures
CONSTRUCTION MATERIALS, WHOLESALE: Roof, Asphalt/Sheet Metal
CONSTRUCTION MATERIALS, WHOLESALE: Roofing & Siding Material
CONSTRUCTION MATERIALS, WHOLESALE: Sand
CONSTRUCTION MATERIALS, WHOLESALE: Septic Tanks
CONSTRUCTION MATERIALS, WHOLESALE: Siding, Exc Wood
CONSTRUCTION MATERIALS, WHOLESALE: Stone, Crushed Or Broken
CONSTRUCTION MATERIALS, WHOLESALE: Tile, Clay/Other Ceramic
CONSTRUCTION MATERIALS, WHOLESALE: Windows
CONSTRUCTION MATLS, WHOL: Lumber, Rough, Dressed/Finished
CONSTRUCTION MATLS, WHOLESALE: Soil Erosion Cntrl Fabrics
CONSTRUCTION SAND MINING
CONSTRUCTION SITE PREPARATION SVCS
CONSTRUCTION: Bridge
CONSTRUCTION: Commercial & Institutional Building
CONSTRUCTION: Concrete Patio
CONSTRUCTION: Dry Cleaning Plant
CONSTRUCTION: Food Prdts Manufacturing or Packing Plant
CONSTRUCTION: Guardrails, Highway
CONSTRUCTION: Heavy Highway & Street
CONSTRUCTION: Indl Building & Warehouse
CONSTRUCTION: Indl Building, Prefabricated
CONSTRUCTION: Indl Buildings, New, NEC
CONSTRUCTION: Pharmaceutical Manufacturing Plant
CONSTRUCTION: Power & Communication Transmission Tower
CONSTRUCTION: Power Plant
CONSTRUCTION: Religious Building
CONSTRUCTION: Residential, Nec
CONSTRUCTION: Single-Family Housing
CONSTRUCTION: Single-family Housing, New
CONSTRUCTION: Steel Buildings
CONSTRUCTION: Street Surfacing & Paving
CONSTRUCTION: Tennis Court
CONSTRUCTION: Warehouse
CONSULTING SVC: Business, NEC
CONSULTING SVC: Computer
CONSULTING SVC: Educational
CONSULTING SVC: Engineering
CONSULTING SVC: Financial Management
CONSULTING SVC: Human Resource
CONSULTING SVC: Management
CONSULTING SVC: Marketing Management
CONSULTING SVC: Online Technology
CONSULTING SVC: Sales Management
CONSULTING SVCS, BUSINESS: Communications
CONSULTING SVCS, BUSINESS: Energy Conservation
CONSULTING SVCS, BUSINESS: Publishing
CONSULTING SVCS, BUSINESS: Safety Training Svcs
CONSULTING SVCS, BUSINESS: Sys Engnrg, Exc Computer/Prof
CONSULTING SVCS, BUSINESS: Systems Analysis & Engineering
CONSULTING SVCS, BUSINESS: Systems Analysis Or Design
CONSULTING SVCS, BUSINESS: Test Development & Evaluation
CONSULTING SVCS, BUSINESS: Testing, Educational Or Personnel
CONSULTING SVCS: Oil
CONSULTING SVCS: Scientific
CONTACT LENSES
CONTACTS: Electrical
CONTAINERS, GLASS: Cosmetic Jars
CONTAINERS, GLASS: Food
CONTAINERS, GLASS: Medicine Bottles
CONTAINERS: Cargo, Wood & Metal Combination
CONTAINERS: Cargo, Wood & Wood With Metal
CONTAINERS: Corrugated
CONTAINERS: Foil, Bakery Goods & Frozen Foods
CONTAINERS: Food & Beverage
CONTAINERS: Food, Folding, Made From Purchased Materials
CONTAINERS: Food, Liquid Tight, Including Milk
CONTAINERS: Food, Metal
CONTAINERS: Glass
CONTAINERS: Laminated Phenolic & Vulcanized Fiber
CONTAINERS: Liquid Tight Fiber, From Purchased Materials
CONTAINERS: Metal
CONTAINERS: Plastic
CONTAINERS: Sanitary, Food
CONTAINERS: Shipping & Mailing, Fiber
CONTAINERS: Shipping, Bombs, Metal Plate
CONTAINERS: Shipping, Wood
CONTAINERS: Wood
CONTRACT FOOD SVCS
CONTRACTOR: Framing
CONTRACTORS: Acoustical & Ceiling Work
CONTRACTORS: Acoustical & Insulation Work
CONTRACTORS: Antenna Installation
CONTRACTORS: Awning Installation
CONTRACTORS: Boiler & Furnace
CONTRACTORS: Boiler Maintenance Contractor
CONTRACTORS: Building Eqpt & Machinery Installation
CONTRACTORS: Building Sign Installation & Mntnce
CONTRACTORS: Carpentry Work
CONTRACTORS: Carpentry, Cabinet & Finish Work
CONTRACTORS: Carpentry, Cabinet Building & Installation
CONTRACTORS: Carpentry, Finish & Trim Work
CONTRACTORS: Ceramic Floor Tile Installation
CONTRACTORS: Closed Circuit Television Installation
CONTRACTORS: Commercial & Office Building
CONTRACTORS: Communications Svcs
CONTRACTORS: Concrete
CONTRACTORS: Concrete Pumping
CONTRACTORS: Concrete Repair
CONTRACTORS: Construction Site Cleanup
CONTRACTORS: Countertop Installation
CONTRACTORS: Demountable Partition Installation
CONTRACTORS: Directional Oil & Gas Well Drilling Svc
CONTRACTORS: Drywall
CONTRACTORS: Electrical
CONTRACTORS: Electronic Controls Installation
CONTRACTORS: Energy Management Control
CONTRACTORS: Excavating
CONTRACTORS: Excavating Slush Pits & Cellars Svcs
CONTRACTORS: Exterior Wall System Installation
CONTRACTORS: Fence Construction
CONTRACTORS: Fiber Optic Cable Installation
CONTRACTORS: Fire Detection & Burglar Alarm Systems
CONTRACTORS: Fire Escape Installation
CONTRACTORS: Fire Sprinkler System Installation Svcs
CONTRACTORS: Floor Laying & Other Floor Work
CONTRACTORS: Garage Doors
CONTRACTORS: Gas Field Svcs, NEC
CONTRACTORS: Gasoline Condensation Removal Svcs
CONTRACTORS: Glass, Glazing & Tinting
CONTRACTORS: Heating & Air Conditioning
CONTRACTORS: Highway & Street Construction, General
CONTRACTORS: Highway & Street Paving
CONTRACTORS: Highway Sign & Guardrail Construction & Install
CONTRACTORS: Home & Office Intrs Finish, Furnish/Remodel
CONTRACTORS: Hydraulic Eqpt Installation & Svcs
CONTRACTORS: Hydronics Heating
CONTRACTORS: Insulation Installation, Building
CONTRACTORS: Kitchen & Bathroom Remodeling
CONTRACTORS: Lighting Syst
CONTRACTORS: Machinery Installation
CONTRACTORS: Marble Installation, Interior
CONTRACTORS: Masonry & Stonework
CONTRACTORS: Mechanical
CONTRACTORS: Multi-Family Home Remodeling
CONTRACTORS: Office Furniture Installation
CONTRACTORS: Oil & Gas Building, Repairing & Dismantling Svc
CONTRACTORS: Oil & Gas Field Fire Fighting Svcs
CONTRACTORS: Oil & Gas Field Geological Exploration Svcs
CONTRACTORS: Oil & Gas Field Geophysical Exploration Svcs
CONTRACTORS: Oil & Gas Well Casing Cement Svcs
CONTRACTORS: Oil & Gas Well Drilling Svc
CONTRACTORS: Oil & Gas Wells Svcs
CONTRACTORS: Oil Field Haulage Svcs
CONTRACTORS: Oil Field Lease Tanks: Erectg, Clng/Rprg Svcs
CONTRACTORS: Oil Sampling Svcs
CONTRACTORS: Oil/Gas Well Construction, Rpr/Dismantling Svcs
CONTRACTORS: On-Site Welding
CONTRACTORS: Ornamental Metal Work
CONTRACTORS: Painting & Wall Covering
CONTRACTORS: Parking Facility Eqpt Installation
CONTRACTORS: Pipe Laying
CONTRACTORS: Plastering, Plain or Ornamental
CONTRACTORS: Plumbing
CONTRACTORS: Power Generating Eqpt Installation
CONTRACTORS: Prefabricated Fireplace Installation
CONTRACTORS: Prefabricated Window & Door Installation
CONTRACTORS: Roofing
CONTRACTORS: Roustabout Svcs
CONTRACTORS: Safety & Security Eqpt
CONTRACTORS: Sandblasting Svc, Building Exteriors
CONTRACTORS: Seismograph Survey Svcs
CONTRACTORS: Sheet Metal Work, NEC
CONTRACTORS: Sheet metal Work, Architectural
CONTRACTORS: Siding
CONTRACTORS: Single-family Home General Remodeling
CONTRACTORS: Solar Energy Eqpt
CONTRACTORS: Sound Eqpt Installation
CONTRACTORS: Stone Masonry
CONTRACTORS: Store Fixture Installation
CONTRACTORS: Store Front Construction
CONTRACTORS: Structural Iron Work, Structural
CONTRACTORS: Structural Steel Erection

PRODUCT INDEX

CONTRACTORS: Svc Station Eqpt Installation, Maint & Repair
CONTRACTORS: Svc Well Drilling Svcs
CONTRACTORS: Textile Warping
CONTRACTORS: Tile Installation, Ceramic
CONTRACTORS: Ventilation & Duct Work
CONTRACTORS: Water Intake Well Drilling Svc
CONTRACTORS: Water Well Drilling
CONTRACTORS: Water Well Servicing
CONTRACTORS: Waterproofing
CONTRACTORS: Well Chemical Treating Svcs
CONTRACTORS: Well Logging Svcs
CONTRACTORS: Window Treatment Installation
CONTRACTORS: Windows & Doors
CONTRACTORS: Wood Floor Installation & Refinishing
CONTROL CIRCUIT DEVICES
CONTROL EQPT: Electric
CONTROL EQPT: Noise
CONTROL PANELS: Electrical
CONTROLS & ACCESS: Indl, Electric
CONTROLS & ACCESS: Motor
CONTROLS: Access, Motor
CONTROLS: Automatic Temperature
CONTROLS: Electric Motor
CONTROLS: Environmental
CONTROLS: Marine & Navy, Auxiliary
CONTROLS: Numerical
CONTROLS: Relay & Ind
CONTROLS: Thermostats, Exc Built-in
CONTROLS: Voice
CONVENIENCE STORES
CONVENTION & TRADE SHOW SVCS
CONVERTERS: Data
CONVERTERS: Frequency
CONVERTERS: Phase Or Rotary, Electrical
CONVERTERS: Power, AC to DC
CONVERTERS: Torque, Exc Auto
CONVEYOR SYSTEMS: Belt, General Indl Use
CONVEYOR SYSTEMS: Bulk Handling
CONVEYOR SYSTEMS: Pneumatic Tube
CONVEYOR SYSTEMS: Robotic
CONVEYORS & CONVEYING EQPT
COOKING & FOOD WARMING EQPT: Commercial
COOKING & FOODWARMING EQPT: Coffee Brewing
COOKING & FOODWARMING EQPT: Commercial
COOKING WARE, EXC PORCELAIN ENAMELED
COOKING WARE: Cooking Ware, Porcelain Enameled
COOKWARE, STONEWARE: Coarse Earthenware & Pottery
COOKWARE: Fine Earthenware
COOLING TOWERS: Metal
COPPER ORES
COPPER PRDTS: Refined, Primary
COPPER: Rolling & Drawing
COPYRIGHT BUYING & LICENSING
CORD & TWINE
CORE WASH OR WAX
CORES: Magnetic
CORK & CORK PRDTS: Tiles
CORRESPONDENCE SCHOOLS
CORRUGATED PRDTS: Boxes, Partition, Display Items, Sheet/Pad
COSMETIC PREPARATIONS
COSMETICS & TOILETRIES
COSMETICS WHOLESALERS
COSTUME JEWELRY & NOVELTIES: Apparel, Exc Precious Metals
COSTUME JEWELRY & NOVELTIES: Bracelets, Exc Precious Metals
COSTUME JEWELRY & NOVELTIES: Costume Novelties
COSTUME JEWELRY & NOVELTIES: Earrings, Exc Precious Metals
COSTUME JEWELRY & NOVELTIES: Exc Semi & Precious
COUGH MEDICINES
COUNTER & SINK TOPS
COUNTERS & COUNTING DEVICES
COUNTERS OR COUNTER DISPLAY CASES, EXC WOOD
COUNTERS OR COUNTER DISPLAY CASES, WOOD
COUNTERS: Mechanical
COUNTING DEVICES: Controls, Revolution & Timing
COUNTING DEVICES: Electromechanical
COUNTING DEVICES: Speed Indicators & Recorders, Vehicle
COUPLINGS: Shaft
COUPON REDEMPTION SVCS
COURIER SVCS: Ground
COVERS: Automobile Seat
COVERS: Automotive, Exc Seat & Tire
COVERS: Canvas
COVERS: Hot Tub & Spa
COVERS: Slip Made Of Fabric, Plastic, Etc.
CRANE & AERIAL LIFT SVCS
CRANES & MONORAIL SYSTEMS
CRANES: Indl Plant
CRANKSHAFTS & CAMSHAFTS: Machining
CRATES: Fruit, Wood Wirebound
CREDIT BUREAUS
CROWNS & CLOSURES
CRUDE PETROLEUM & NATURAL GAS PRODUCTION
CRUDE PETROLEUM & NATURAL GAS PRODUCTION
CRUDE PETROLEUM PRODUCTION
CRUDES: Cyclic, Organic
CRYOGENIC COOLING DEVICES: Infrared Detectors, Masers
CRYSTALS
CULTURE MEDIA
CULVERTS: Metal Plate
CUPS: Plastic Exc Polystyrene Foam
CURBING: Granite Or Stone
CURTAIN & DRAPERY FIXTURES: Poles, Rods & Rollers
CURTAIN WALLS: Building, Steel
CURTAINS & BEDDING: Knit
CURTAINS & CURTAIN FABRICS: Lace
CURTAINS: Cottage Sets, From Purchased Materials
CURTAINS: Shower
CURTAINS: Window, From Purchased Materials
CUSHIONS & PILLOWS
CUSHIONS & PILLOWS: Bed, From Purchased Materials
CUSHIONS: Textile, Exc Spring & Carpet
CUSTOM COMPOUNDING OF RUBBER MATERIALS
CUT STONE & STONE PRODUCTS
CUTLERY
CUTLERY WHOLESALERS
CUTOUTS: Cardboard, Die-Cut, Made From Purchased Materials
CUTOUTS: Distribution
CUTTING SVC: Paper, Exc Die-Cut
CYCLIC CRUDES & INTERMEDIATES
CYLINDER & ACTUATORS: Fluid Power
CYLINDERS: Pressure

D

DAIRY EQPT
DAIRY PRDTS STORE: Cheese
DAIRY PRDTS STORE: Ice Cream, Packaged
DAIRY PRDTS STORES
DAIRY PRDTS WHOLESALERS: Fresh
DAIRY PRDTS: Bakers' Cheese
DAIRY PRDTS: Bottled Baby Formula
DAIRY PRDTS: Butter
DAIRY PRDTS: Canned Baby Formula
DAIRY PRDTS: Cheese
DAIRY PRDTS: Cheese, Cottage
DAIRY PRDTS: Concentrated Skim Milk
DAIRY PRDTS: Cream Substitutes
DAIRY PRDTS: Cream, Sweet
DAIRY PRDTS: Dairy Based Desserts, Frozen
DAIRY PRDTS: Dietary Supplements, Dairy & Non-Dairy Based
DAIRY PRDTS: Dips & Spreads, Cheese Based
DAIRY PRDTS: Dried & Powdered Milk & Milk Prdts
DAIRY PRDTS: Evaporated Milk
DAIRY PRDTS: Farmers' Cheese
DAIRY PRDTS: Fermented & Cultured Milk Prdts
DAIRY PRDTS: Frozen Desserts & Novelties
DAIRY PRDTS: Ice Cream & Ice Milk
DAIRY PRDTS: Ice Cream, Bulk
DAIRY PRDTS: Ice Cream, Packaged, Molded, On Sticks, Etc.
DAIRY PRDTS: Milk, Condensed & Evaporated
DAIRY PRDTS: Milk, Fluid
DAIRY PRDTS: Milk, Processed, Pasteurized, Homogenized/Btld
DAIRY PRDTS: Natural Cheese
DAIRY PRDTS: Processed Cheese
DAIRY PRDTS: Pudding Pops, Frozen
DAIRY PRDTS: Sherbets, Dairy Based
DAIRY PRDTS: Spreads, Cheese
DAIRY PRDTS: Whipped Topping, Exc Frozen Or Dry Mix
DAIRY PRDTS: Yogurt, Exc Frozen
DAIRY PRDTS: Yogurt, Frozen
DATA PROCESSING & PREPARATION SVCS
DATA PROCESSING SVCS
DATABASE INFORMATION RETRIEVAL SVCS
DECORATIVE WOOD & WOODWORK
DEFENSE SYSTEMS & EQPT
DEGREASING MACHINES
DEHYDRATION EQPT
DELAY LINES
DENTAL EQPT
DENTAL EQPT & SPLYS
DENTAL EQPT & SPLYS WHOLESALERS
DENTAL EQPT & SPLYS: Cabinets
DENTAL EQPT & SPLYS: Compounds
DENTAL EQPT & SPLYS: Cutting Instruments
DENTAL EQPT & SPLYS: Dental Materials
DENTAL EQPT & SPLYS: Enamels
DENTAL EQPT & SPLYS: Laboratory
DENTAL EQPT & SPLYS: Orthodontic Appliances
DENTAL EQPT & SPLYS: Sterilizers
DENTAL EQPT & SPLYS: Teeth, Artificial, Exc In Dental Labs
DENTAL EQPT & SPLYS: Wax
DENTISTS' OFFICES & CLINICS
DEODORANTS: Personal
DEPILATORIES, COSMETIC
DERMATOLOGICALS
DERRICKS: Oil & Gas Field
DESALTER KITS: Sea Water
DESIGN SVCS, NEC
DESIGN SVCS: Commercial & Indl
DESIGN SVCS: Computer Integrated Systems
DESIGN SVCS: Shoe
DETECTION APPARATUS: Electronic/Magnetic Field, Light/Heat
DIAGNOSTIC SUBSTANCES
DIAGNOSTIC SUBSTANCES OR AGENTS: Blood Derivative
DIAGNOSTIC SUBSTANCES OR AGENTS: In Vivo
DIAGNOSTIC SUBSTANCES OR AGENTS: Microbiology & Virology
DIAGNOSTIC SUBSTANCES OR AGENTS: Veterinary
DIAMOND MINING SVCS: Indl
DIAMOND SETTER SVCS
DIAMONDS, GEMS, WHOLESALE
DIAMONDS: Cutting & Polishing
DIAPERS: Cloth
DIAPERS: Disposable
DIE CUTTING SVC: Paper
DIE SETS: Presses, Metal Stamping
DIES & TOOLS: Special
DIES: Cutting, Exc Metal
DIES: Extrusion
DIES: Paper Cutting
DIES: Plastic Forming
DIES: Steel Rule
DIODES: Light Emitting
DIODES: Solid State, Germanium, Silicon, Etc
DIRECT SELLING ESTABLISHMENTS: Beverage Svcs
DIRECT SELLING ESTABLISHMENTS: Food Svcs
DISCOUNT DEPARTMENT STORES
DISCS & TAPE: Optical, Blank
DISHWASHING EQPT: Commercial
DISINFECTING SVCS
DISK & DRUM DRIVES & COMPONENTS: Computers
DISK DRIVES: Computer
DISPENSING EQPT & PARTS, BEVERAGE: Fountain/Other Beverage
DISPENSING EQPT & SYSTEMS, BEVERAGE: Liquor
DISPLAY CASES: Refrigerated
DISPLAY FIXTURES: Showcases, Wood, Exc Refrigerated
DISPLAY FIXTURES: Wood
DISPLAY ITEMS: Corrugated, Made From Purchased Materials
DISPLAY STANDS: Merchandise, Exc Wood
DISTILLATES: Hardwood
DOCK OPERATION SVCS, INCL BLDGS, FACILITIES, OPERS & MAINT
DOCKS: Floating, Wood
DOCKS: Prefabricated Metal
DOCUMENT EMBOSSING SVCS
DOLLIES: Mechanics'
DOLOMITE: Crushed & Broken
DOLOMITIC MARBLE: Crushed & Broken
DOMESTIC HELP SVCS
DOOR & WINDOW REPAIR SVCS
DOOR OPERATING SYSTEMS: Electric
DOORS & WINDOWS WHOLESALERS: All Materials
DOORS & WINDOWS: Screen & Storm

PRODUCT INDEX

DOORS & WINDOWS: Storm, Metal
DOORS: Dormers, Wood
DOORS: Fire, Metal
DOORS: Folding, Plastic Or Plastic Coated Fabric
DOORS: Garage, Overhead, Metal
DOORS: Garage, Overhead, Wood
DOORS: Glass
DOORS: Rolling, Indl Building Or Warehouse, Metal
DOORS: Wooden
DOWN FEATHERS
DRAPERIES & CURTAINS
DRAPERIES & DRAPERY FABRICS, COTTON
DRAPERIES: Plastic & Textile, From Purchased Materials
DRAPERY & UPHOLSTERY STORES: Draperies
DRAPES & DRAPERY FABRICS, FROM MANMADE FIBER
DRIED FRUITS WHOLESALERS
DRILL BITS
DRILLING MACHINERY & EQPT: Water Well
DRINK MIXES, NONALCOHOLIC: Cocktail
DRINKING PLACES: Alcoholic Beverages
DRINKING PLACES: Night Clubs
DRINKING PLACES: Wine Bar
DRINKING WATER COOLERS WHOLESALERS: Mechanical
DRIVE SHAFTS
DRIVES: High Speed Indl, Exc Hydrostatic
DRONES: Target, Used By Ships, Metal
DROP CLOTHS: Fabric
DRUG TESTING KITS: Blood & Urine
DRUGS & DRUG PROPRIETARIES, WHOL: Biologicals/Allied Prdts
DRUGS & DRUG PROPRIETARIES, WHOLESALE
DRUGS & DRUG PROPRIETARIES, WHOLESALE: Pharmaceuticals
DRUGS & DRUG PROPRIETARIES, WHOLESALE: Vitamins & Minerals
DRUGS ACTING ON THE CENTRAL NERVOUS SYSTEM & SENSE ORGANS
DRUGS AFFECTING NEOPLASMS & ENDOCRINE SYSTEMS
DRUGS/DRUG PROPRIETARIES, WHOL: Proprietary/Patent Medicines
DRUGS: Parasitic & Infective Disease Affecting
DRUMS: Fiber
DRYCLEANING EQPT & SPLYS: Commercial
DRYCLEANING SVC: Drapery & Curtain
DUCTING: Plastic
DUCTS: Sheet Metal
DUMPSTERS: Garbage
DYES & PIGMENTS: Organic
DYES: Synthetic Organic

E

EATING PLACES
EDUCATIONAL PROGRAMS ADMINISTRATION SVCS
EDUCATIONAL SVCS
EDUCATIONAL SVCS, NONDEGREE GRANTING: Continuing Education
ELASTOMERS
ELECTRIC MOTOR REPAIR SVCS
ELECTRIC SERVICES
ELECTRIC SVCS, NEC Power Transmission
ELECTRIC SVCS, NEC: Power Generation
ELECTRICAL APPARATUS & EQPT WHOLESALERS
ELECTRICAL APPLIANCES, TELEVISIONS & RADIOS WHOLESALERS
ELECTRICAL CONSTRUCTION MATERIALS WHOLESALERS
ELECTRICAL CURRENT CARRYING WIRING DEVICES
ELECTRICAL DISCHARGE MACHINING, EDM
ELECTRICAL EQPT & SPLYS
ELECTRICAL EQPT FOR ENGINES
ELECTRICAL EQPT REPAIR & MAINTENANCE
ELECTRICAL EQPT REPAIR SVCS
ELECTRICAL EQPT: Automotive, NEC
ELECTRICAL EQPT: Household
ELECTRICAL GOODS, WHOLESALE: Batteries, Dry Cell
ELECTRICAL GOODS, WHOLESALE: Burglar Alarm Systems
ELECTRICAL GOODS, WHOLESALE: Capacitors
ELECTRICAL GOODS, WHOLESALE: Connectors
ELECTRICAL GOODS, WHOLESALE: Electronic Parts
ELECTRICAL GOODS, WHOLESALE: Facsimile Or Fax Eqpt
ELECTRICAL GOODS, WHOLESALE: Fans, Household
ELECTRICAL GOODS, WHOLESALE: Fittings & Construction Mat
ELECTRICAL GOODS, WHOLESALE: Intercommunication Eqpt
ELECTRICAL GOODS, WHOLESALE: Light Bulbs & Related Splys
ELECTRICAL GOODS, WHOLESALE: Lighting Fittings & Access
ELECTRICAL GOODS, WHOLESALE: Lighting Fixtures, Comm & Indl
ELECTRICAL GOODS, WHOLESALE: Lighting Fixtures, Residential
ELECTRICAL GOODS, WHOLESALE: Mobile telephone Eqpt
ELECTRICAL GOODS, WHOLESALE: Motors
ELECTRICAL GOODS, WHOLESALE: Semiconductor Devices
ELECTRICAL GOODS, WHOLESALE: Signaling, Eqpt
ELECTRICAL GOODS, WHOLESALE: Sound Eqpt
ELECTRICAL GOODS, WHOLESALE: Telephone Eqpt
ELECTRICAL GOODS, WHOLESALE: Transformers
ELECTRICAL GOODS, WHOLESALE: VCR & Access
ELECTRICAL GOODS, WHOLESALE: Vacuum Cleaners, Household
ELECTRICAL GOODS, WHOLESALE: Video Eqpt
ELECTRICAL GOODS, WHOLESALE: Wire & Cable
ELECTRICAL GOODS, WHOLESALE: Wire & Cable, Electronic
ELECTRICAL INDL APPARATUS, NEC
ELECTRICAL SPLYS
ELECTRICAL SUPPLIES: Porcelain
ELECTRODES: Fluorescent Lamps
ELECTRODES: Indl Process
ELECTRODES: Thermal & Electrolytic
ELECTROMEDICAL EQPT
ELECTRON TUBES
ELECTRON TUBES: Cathode Ray
ELECTRONIC COMPONENTS
ELECTRONIC DETECTION SYSTEMS: Aeronautical
ELECTRONIC DEVICES: Solid State, NEC
ELECTRONIC EQPT REPAIR SVCS
ELECTRONIC LOADS & POWER SPLYS
ELECTRONIC PARTS & EQPT WHOLESALERS
ELECTRONIC SHOPPING
ELECTRONIC TRAINING DEVICES
ELECTROPLATING & PLATING SVC
ELEVATORS & EQPT
ELEVATORS WHOLESALERS
ELEVATORS: Installation & Conversion
ELEVATORS: Stair, Motor Powered
EMBLEMS: Embroidered
EMBOSSING SVC: Paper
EMBROIDERING & ART NEEDLEWORK FOR THE TRADE
EMBROIDERING SVC
EMBROIDERING SVC: Schiffli Machine
EMBROIDERING: Swiss Loom
EMBROIDERY ADVERTISING SVCS
EMERGENCY ALARMS
EMPLOYMENT AGENCY SVCS
ENAMELING SVC: Metal Prdts, Including Porcelain
ENAMELS
ENCLOSURES: Electronic
ENCODERS: Digital
ENERGY MEASUREMENT EQPT
ENGINE REBUILDING: Diesel
ENGINE REBUILDING: Gas
ENGINEERING SVCS
ENGINEERING SVCS: Building Construction
ENGINEERING SVCS: Electrical Or Electronic
ENGINEERING SVCS: Heating & Ventilation
ENGINEERING SVCS: Industrial
ENGINEERING SVCS: Marine
ENGINEERING SVCS: Mechanical
ENGINEERING SVCS: Pollution Control
ENGINEERING SVCS: Professional
ENGINEERING SVCS: Sanitary
ENGINEERING SVCS: Structural
ENGINES: Internal Combustion, NEC
ENGRAVING SVC, NEC
ENGRAVING SVC: Jewelry & Personal Goods
ENGRAVING SVCS
ENGRAVING: Steel line, For The Printing Trade
ENGRAVINGS: Plastic
ENTERTAINERS & ENTERTAINMENT GROUPS
ENTERTAINMENT SVCS
ENVELOPES
ENVELOPES WHOLESALERS
ENVIRONMENTAL QUALITY PROGS ADMIN, GOVT: Waste Management
ENZYMES
EPOXY RESINS
EQUIPMENT: Pedestrian Traffic Control
EQUIPMENT: Rental & Leasing, NEC
ESCALATORS: Passenger & Freight
ETCHING & ENGRAVING SVC
ETCHING SVC: Metal
ETCHING SVC: Photochemical
ETHANOLAMINES
ETHYLENE-PROPYLENE RUBBERS: EPDM Polymers
EXCAVATING EQPT
EXERCISE EQPT STORES
EXHAUST HOOD OR FAN CLEANING SVCS
EXHAUST SYSTEMS: Eqpt & Parts
EXPANSION JOINTS: Rubber
EXPLOSIVES
EXPLOSIVES, EXC AMMO & FIREWORKS WHOLESALERS
EXTENSION CORDS
EXTRACTS, FLAVORING
EXTRACTS: Dying Or Tanning, Natural
EYEGLASSES
EYEGLASSES: Sunglasses
EYES: Artificial

F

FABRIC FINISHING: Mending, Wool
FABRIC STORES
FABRICATED METAL PRODUCTS, NEC
FABRICS & CLOTH: Quilted
FABRICS: Alpacas, Mohair, Woven
FABRICS: Apparel & Outerwear, Broadwoven
FABRICS: Apparel & Outerwear, Cotton
FABRICS: Apparel & Outerwear, From Manmade Fiber Or Silk
FABRICS: Automotive, From Manmade Fiber
FABRICS: Bags & Bagging, Cotton
FABRICS: Broad Woven, Goods, Cotton
FABRICS: Broadwoven, Cotton
FABRICS: Broadwoven, Synthetic Manmade Fiber & Silk
FABRICS: Broadwoven, Wool
FABRICS: Brocade, Cotton
FABRICS: Canvas
FABRICS: Chemically Coated & Treated
FABRICS: Coated Or Treated
FABRICS: Cords
FABRICS: Corduroys, Cotton
FABRICS: Denims
FABRICS: Elastic, From Manmade Fiber Or Silk
FABRICS: Fiberglass, Broadwoven
FABRICS: Glass, Narrow
FABRICS: Glove, Lining
FABRICS: Hand Woven
FABRICS: Handkerchief, Cotton
FABRICS: Jean
FABRICS: Jersey Cloth
FABRICS: Lace & Decorative Trim, Narrow
FABRICS: Lace & Lace Prdts
FABRICS: Lace, Knit, NEC
FABRICS: Laminated
FABRICS: Linings & Interlinings, Cotton
FABRICS: Long Cloth, Cotton
FABRICS: Nonwoven
FABRICS: Nylon, Broadwoven
FABRICS: Paper, Broadwoven
FABRICS: Pile Warp or Flat Knit
FABRICS: Pile, Circular Knit
FABRICS: Pocketing Twill, Cotton
FABRICS: Polyester, Broadwoven
FABRICS: Print, Cotton
FABRICS: Resin Or Plastic Coated
FABRICS: Rubberized
FABRICS: Shirting, Cotton
FABRICS: Shoe
FABRICS: Silk, Broadwoven
FABRICS: Silk, Narrow
FABRICS: Spandex, Broadwoven
FABRICS: Specialty Including Twisted Weaves, Broadwoven
FABRICS: Stretch, Cotton
FABRICS: Surgical Fabrics, Cotton
FABRICS: Tapestry, Cotton
FABRICS: Tricot
FABRICS: Trimmings
FABRICS: Trimmings, Textile
FABRICS: Upholstery, Cotton

PRODUCT INDEX

FABRICS: Varnished Glass & Coated Fiberglass
FABRICS: Wall Covering, From Manmade Fiber Or Silk
FABRICS: Warp & Flat Knit Prdts
FABRICS: Warp Knit, Lace & Netting
FABRICS: Weft Or Circular Knit
FABRICS: Woven, Narrow Cotton, Wool, Silk
FACILITIES SUPPORT SVCS
FACSIMILE COMMUNICATION EQPT
FAMILY CLOTHING STORES
FANS, BLOWING: Indl Or Commercial
FANS, EXHAUST: Indl Or Commercial
FANS, VENTILATING: Indl Or Commercial
FARM & GARDEN MACHINERY WHOLESALERS
FARM PRDTS, RAW MATERIALS, WHOLESALE: Bristles
FARM PRDTS, RAW MATERIALS, WHOLESALE: Hides
FARM SPLY STORES
FARM SPLYS, WHOLESALE: Beekeeping Splys, Nondurable
FASTENERS: Metal
FASTENERS: Metal
FASTENERS: Notions, NEC
FASTENERS: Notions, Snaps
FASTENERS: Notions, Zippers
FAUCETS & SPIGOTS: Metal & Plastic
FEATHERS: Renovating
FELT: Acoustic
FENCE POSTS: Iron & Steel
FENCES & FENCING MATERIALS
FENCES OR POSTS: Ornamental Iron Or Steel
FENCING DEALERS
FENCING MATERIALS: Docks & Other Outdoor Prdts, Wood
FENCING MATERIALS: Plastic
FENCING MATERIALS: Wood
FENCING: Chain Link
FERRITES
FERROALLOYS
FERROMANGANESE, NOT MADE IN BLAST FURNACES
FERTILIZERS: NEC
FERTILIZERS: Nitrogenous
FERTILIZERS: Phosphatic
FIBER & FIBER PRDTS: Acrylic
FIBER & FIBER PRDTS: Fluorocarbon
FIBER & FIBER PRDTS: Organic, Noncellulose
FIBER & FIBER PRDTS: Polyester
FIBER & FIBER PRDTS: Synthetic Cellulosic
FIBER OPTICS
FIBERS: Carbon & Graphite
FILLERS & SEALERS: Wood
FILM & SHEET: Unsuppported Plastic
FILM BASE: Cellulose Acetate Or Nitrocellulose Plastics
FILM: Motion Picture
FILTERS
FILTERS & SOFTENERS: Water, Household
FILTERS: Air
FILTERS: Air Intake, Internal Combustion Engine, Exc Auto
FILTERS: General Line, Indl
FILTERS: Motor Vehicle
FILTERS: Paper
FILTRATION DEVICES: Electronic
FINANCIAL INVESTMENT ACTIVITIES, NEC: Financial Reporting
FINANCIAL INVESTMENT ADVICE
FINANCIAL SVCS
FINDINGS & TRIMMINGS Fabric, NEC
FINDINGS & TRIMMINGS Waistbands, Trouser
FINDINGS & TRIMMINGS: Apparel
FINDINGS & TRIMMINGS: Fabric
FINGERNAILS, ARTIFICIAL
FINGERPRINT EQPT
FINISHING AGENTS: Leather
FIRE ARMS, SMALL: Guns Or Gun Parts, 30 mm & Below
FIRE ARMS, SMALL: Pellet & BB guns
FIRE ARMS, SMALL: Rifles Or Rifle Parts, 30 mm & below
FIRE CONTROL OR BOMBING EQPT: Electronic
FIRE DETECTION SYSTEMS
FIRE ESCAPES
FIRE EXTINGUISHERS: Portable
FIRE OR BURGLARY RESISTIVE PRDTS
FIRE PROTECTION EQPT
FIREARMS & AMMUNITION, EXC SPORTING, WHOLESALE
FIREARMS: Small, 30mm or Less
FIREFIGHTING APPARATUS
FIREPLACE & CHIMNEY MATERIAL: Concrete
FIREPLACE EQPT & ACCESS
FIREWORKS
FIREWORKS DISPLAY SVCS

FISH & SEAFOOD PROCESSORS: Canned Or Cured
FISH & SEAFOOD PROCESSORS: Fresh Or Frozen
FISHING EQPT: Lures
FITTINGS & ASSEMBLIES: Hose & Tube, Hydraulic Or Pneumatic
FITTINGS: Pipe
FITTINGS: Pipe, Fabricated
FIXTURES & EQPT: Kitchen, Metal, Exc Cast Aluminum
FIXTURES: Bank, Metal, Ornamental
FIXTURES: Cut Stone
FLAGPOLES
FLAGS: Fabric
FLAT GLASS: Antique
FLAT GLASS: Building
FLAT GLASS: Construction
FLAT GLASS: Laminated
FLAT GLASS: Plate, Polished & Rough
FLAT GLASS: Strengthened Or Reinforced
FLAT GLASS: Tempered
FLAT GLASS: Window, Clear & Colored
FLATWARE, STAINLESS STEEL
FLAVORS OR FLAVORING MATERIALS: Synthetic
FLOOR COMPOSITION: Magnesite
FLOOR COVERING STORES
FLOOR COVERING STORES: Carpets
FLOOR COVERING: Plastic
FLOOR COVERINGS WHOLESALERS
FLOOR COVERINGS: Tile, Support Plastic
FLOORING & GRATINGS: Open, Construction Applications
FLOORING: Hard Surface
FLOORING: Hardwood
FLORISTS
FLOWER ARRANGEMENTS: Artificial
FLOWER POTS Plastic
FLOWERS: Artificial & Preserved
FLUID METERS & COUNTING DEVICES
FLUID POWER PUMPS & MOTORS
FLUID POWER VALVES & HOSE FITTINGS
FLUORO RUBBERS
FLUXES
FOAM CHARGE MIXTURES
FOAM RUBBER
FOIL & LEAF: Metal
FOIL, ALUMINUM, HOUSEHOLD, WHOLESALE
FOIL: Aluminum
FOIL: Copper
FOIL: Laminated To Paper Or Other Materials
FOOD CASINGS: Plastic
FOOD PRDTS, BREAKFAST: Cereal, Infants' Food
FOOD PRDTS, BREAKFAST: Cereal, Wheat Flakes
FOOD PRDTS, CANNED OR FRESH PACK: Fruit Juices
FOOD PRDTS, CANNED OR FRESH PACK: Vegetable Juices
FOOD PRDTS, CANNED OR FRESH PACK: Vegetable Juices
FOOD PRDTS, CANNED: Baby Food
FOOD PRDTS, CANNED: Barbecue Sauce
FOOD PRDTS, CANNED: Beans & Bean Sprouts
FOOD PRDTS, CANNED: Catsup
FOOD PRDTS, CANNED: Ethnic
FOOD PRDTS, CANNED: Fruit Juices, Concentrated
FOOD PRDTS, CANNED: Fruit Juices, Fresh
FOOD PRDTS, CANNED: Fruits
FOOD PRDTS, CANNED: Fruits
FOOD PRDTS, CANNED: Fruits & Fruit Prdts
FOOD PRDTS, CANNED: Italian
FOOD PRDTS, CANNED: Jams, Including Imitation
FOOD PRDTS, CANNED: Jams, Jellies & Preserves
FOOD PRDTS, CANNED: Maraschino Cherries
FOOD PRDTS, CANNED: Mexican, NEC
FOOD PRDTS, CANNED: Olives
FOOD PRDTS, CANNED: Puddings, Exc Meat
FOOD PRDTS, CANNED: Ravioli
FOOD PRDTS, CANNED: Sauerkraut
FOOD PRDTS, CANNED: Soup, Chicken
FOOD PRDTS, CANNED: Spaghetti & Other Pasta Sauce
FOOD PRDTS, CANNED: Tomato Sauce.
FOOD PRDTS, CANNED: Tomatoes
FOOD PRDTS, CANNED: Vegetables
FOOD PRDTS, CONFECTIONERY, WHOLESALE: Candy
FOOD PRDTS, CONFECTIONERY, WHOLESALE: Nuts, Salted/Roasted
FOOD PRDTS, CONFECTIONERY, WHOLESALE: Snack Foods
FOOD PRDTS, FISH & SEAFOOD, WHOLESALE: Fresh

FOOD PRDTS, FISH & SEAFOOD: Canned & Jarred, Etc
FOOD PRDTS, FISH & SEAFOOD: Fish, Fresh, Prepared
FOOD PRDTS, FISH & SEAFOOD: Fish, Smoked
FOOD PRDTS, FISH & SEAFOOD: Fresh/Frozen Chowder, Soup/Stew
FOOD PRDTS, FISH & SEAFOOD: Salmon, Smoked
FOOD PRDTS, FISH & SEAFOOD: Seafood, Frozen, Prepared
FOOD PRDTS, FROZEN: Breakfasts, Packaged
FOOD PRDTS, FROZEN: Dinners, Packaged
FOOD PRDTS, FROZEN: Ethnic Foods, NEC
FOOD PRDTS, FROZEN: Fruits & Vegetables
FOOD PRDTS, FROZEN: Fruits, Juices & Vegetables
FOOD PRDTS, FROZEN: NEC
FOOD PRDTS, FROZEN: Pizza
FOOD PRDTS, FROZEN: Snack Items
FOOD PRDTS, FROZEN: Vegetables, Exc Potato Prdts
FOOD PRDTS, FROZEN: Whipped Topping
FOOD PRDTS, MEAT & MEAT PRDTS, WHOLESALE: Brokers
FOOD PRDTS, MEAT & MEAT PRDTS, WHOLESALE: Fresh
FOOD PRDTS, WHOL: Canned Goods, Fruit, Veg, Seafood/Meats
FOOD PRDTS, WHOLESALE: Beverage Concentrates
FOOD PRDTS, WHOLESALE: Beverages, Exc Coffee & Tea
FOOD PRDTS, WHOLESALE: Chocolate
FOOD PRDTS, WHOLESALE: Coffee & Tea
FOOD PRDTS, WHOLESALE: Coffee, Green Or Roasted
FOOD PRDTS, WHOLESALE: Condiments
FOOD PRDTS, WHOLESALE: Cookies
FOOD PRDTS, WHOLESALE: Flour
FOOD PRDTS, WHOLESALE: Grains
FOOD PRDTS, WHOLESALE: Health
FOOD PRDTS, WHOLESALE: Juices
FOOD PRDTS, WHOLESALE: Organic & Diet
FOOD PRDTS, WHOLESALE: Pasta & Rice
FOOD PRDTS, WHOLESALE: Sandwiches
FOOD PRDTS, WHOLESALE: Sausage Casings
FOOD PRDTS, WHOLESALE: Specialty
FOOD PRDTS, WHOLESALE: Tea
FOOD PRDTS: Almond Pastes
FOOD PRDTS: Animal & marine fats & oils
FOOD PRDTS: Bran, Rice
FOOD PRDTS: Bread Crumbs, Exc Made In Bakeries
FOOD PRDTS: Breakfast Bars
FOOD PRDTS: Cane Syrup, From Purchased Raw Sugar
FOOD PRDTS: Cereals
FOOD PRDTS: Cheese Curls & Puffs
FOOD PRDTS: Chicken, Processed, Frozen
FOOD PRDTS: Chocolate Bars, Solid
FOOD PRDTS: Chocolate Coatings & Syrup
FOOD PRDTS: Coconut Oil
FOOD PRDTS: Coconut, Desiccated & Shredded
FOOD PRDTS: Coffee
FOOD PRDTS: Coffee Extracts
FOOD PRDTS: Coffee Roasting, Exc Wholesale Grocers
FOOD PRDTS: Cole Slaw, Bulk
FOOD PRDTS: Cooking Oils, Refined Vegetable, Exc Corn
FOOD PRDTS: Corn Oil Prdts
FOOD PRDTS: Cottonseed Lecithin
FOOD PRDTS: Dessert Mixes & Fillings
FOOD PRDTS: Desserts, Ready-To-Mix
FOOD PRDTS: Dough, Pizza, Prepared
FOOD PRDTS: Doughs & Batters
FOOD PRDTS: Doughs & Batters From Purchased Flour
FOOD PRDTS: Doughs, Frozen Or Refrig From Purchased Flour
FOOD PRDTS: Dressings, Salad, Raw & Cooked Exc Dry Mixes
FOOD PRDTS: Dried & Dehydrated Fruits, Vegetables & Soup Mix
FOOD PRDTS: Ducks, Processed, Fresh
FOOD PRDTS: Ducks, Processed, NEC
FOOD PRDTS: Edible Oil Prdts, Exc Corn Oil
FOOD PRDTS: Edible fats & oils
FOOD PRDTS: Egg Substitutes, Made From Eggs
FOOD PRDTS: Eggs, Processed
FOOD PRDTS: Emulsifiers
FOOD PRDTS: Flavored Ices, Frozen
FOOD PRDTS: Flour & Other Grain Mill Products
FOOD PRDTS: Flour Mixes & Doughs
FOOD PRDTS: Fruit Juices
FOOD PRDTS: Fruits & Vegetables, Pickled
FOOD PRDTS: Fruits, Dehydrated Or Dried

PRODUCT INDEX

FOOD PRDTS: Fruits, Dried Or Dehydrated, Exc Freeze-Dried
FOOD PRDTS: Gelatin Dessert Preparations
FOOD PRDTS: Gluten Meal
FOOD PRDTS: Granulated Cane Sugar
FOOD PRDTS: Horseradish, Exc Sauce
FOOD PRDTS: Ice, Blocks
FOOD PRDTS: Ice, Cubes
FOOD PRDTS: Instant Coffee
FOOD PRDTS: Jelly, Corncob
FOOD PRDTS: Juice Pops, Frozen
FOOD PRDTS: Macaroni Prdts, Dry, Alphabet, Rings Or Shells
FOOD PRDTS: Macaroni, Noodles, Spaghetti, Pasta, Etc
FOOD PRDTS: Malt
FOOD PRDTS: Mayonnaise & Dressings, Exc Tomato Based
FOOD PRDTS: Mixes, Bread & Roll From Purchased Flour
FOOD PRDTS: Mixes, Doughnut From Purchased Flour
FOOD PRDTS: Mixes, Pancake From Purchased Flour
FOOD PRDTS: Mixes, Sauces, Dry
FOOD PRDTS: Mixes, Seasonings, Dry
FOOD PRDTS: Mustard, Prepared
FOOD PRDTS: Nuts & Seeds
FOOD PRDTS: Olive Oil
FOOD PRDTS: Oriental Noodles
FOOD PRDTS: Pasta, Rice/Potatoes, Uncooked, Pkgd
FOOD PRDTS: Pasta, Uncooked, Packaged With Other Ingredients
FOOD PRDTS: Peanut Butter
FOOD PRDTS: Pickles, Vinegar
FOOD PRDTS: Pizza, Refrigerated
FOOD PRDTS: Popcorn, Popped
FOOD PRDTS: Popcorn, Unpopped
FOOD PRDTS: Potato & Corn Chips & Similar Prdts
FOOD PRDTS: Potato Chips & Other Potato-Based Snacks
FOOD PRDTS: Potatoes, Dried, Packaged With Other Ingredients
FOOD PRDTS: Poultry, Processed, NEC
FOOD PRDTS: Poultry, Slaughtered & Dressed
FOOD PRDTS: Preparations
FOOD PRDTS: Prepared Meat Sauces Exc Tomato & Dry
FOOD PRDTS: Prepared Sauces, Exc Tomato Based
FOOD PRDTS: Raw cane sugar
FOOD PRDTS: Relishes, Vinegar
FOOD PRDTS: Rice, Milled
FOOD PRDTS: Salads
FOOD PRDTS: Sandwiches
FOOD PRDTS: Sauerkraut, Bulk
FOOD PRDTS: Seasonings & Spices
FOOD PRDTS: Soup Mixes, Dried
FOOD PRDTS: Soy Sauce
FOOD PRDTS: Spices, Including Ground
FOOD PRDTS: Spreads, Sandwich, Salad Dressing Base
FOOD PRDTS: Starches
FOOD PRDTS: Sugar
FOOD PRDTS: Sugar, Beet
FOOD PRDTS: Sugar, Cane
FOOD PRDTS: Sugar, Corn
FOOD PRDTS: Sugar, Granulated Cane, Purchd Raw Sugar/Syrup
FOOD PRDTS: Syrup, Maple
FOOD PRDTS: Syrups
FOOD PRDTS: Tea
FOOD PRDTS: Tofu Desserts, Frozen
FOOD PRDTS: Tofu, Exc Frozen Desserts
FOOD PRDTS: Tortillas
FOOD PRDTS: Vegetables, Dried or Dehydrated Exc Freeze-Dried
FOOD PRDTS: Vegetables, Pickled
FOOD PRDTS: Vinegar
FOOD PRODUCTS MACHINERY
FOOD STORES: Delicatessen
FOOD STORES: Grocery, Independent
FOOD STORES: Supermarkets
FOOTWEAR, WHOLESALE: Athletic
FOOTWEAR, WHOLESALE: Shoe Access
FOOTWEAR, WHOLESALE: Shoes
FOOTWEAR: Cut Stock
FORGINGS
FORGINGS: Aircraft, Ferrous
FORGINGS: Aluminum
FORGINGS: Gear & Chain
FORGINGS: Machinery, Ferrous
FORGINGS: Nonferrous
FORGINGS: Pump & compressor, Nonferrous

FORMS: Concrete, Sheet Metal
FOUNDRIES: Aluminum
FOUNDRIES: Brass, Bronze & Copper
FOUNDRIES: Gray & Ductile Iron
FOUNDRIES: Iron
FOUNDRIES: Nonferrous
FOUNDRIES: Steel
FOUNDRIES: Steel Investment
FRAMES & FRAMING WHOLESALE
FRANCHISES, SELLING OR LICENSING
FREIGHT CONSOLIDATION SVCS
FREIGHT FORWARDING ARRANGEMENTS
FRICTION MATERIAL, MADE FROM POWDERED METAL
FRUIT & VEGETABLE MARKETS
FUEL ADDITIVES
FUEL BRIQUETTES & WAXES
FUEL BRIQUETTES OR BOULETS, MADE WITH PETROLEUM BINDER
FUEL CELL FORMS: Cardboard, Made From Purchased Materials
FUEL CELLS: Solid State
FUEL DEALERS: Wood
FUEL OIL DEALERS
FUELS: Diesel
FUELS: Ethanol
FUELS: Oil
FUNDRAISING SVCS
FUNERAL HOMES & SVCS
FUNGICIDES OR HERBICIDES
FUR APPAREL STORES
FUR CLOTHING WHOLESALERS
FUR FINISHING & LINING: For The Fur Goods Trade
FUR: Apparel
FUR: Coats
FUR: Coats & Other Apparel
FUR: Hats
FUR: Jackets
FURNACES & OVENS: Indl
FURNACES: Indl, Electric
FURNITURE & CABINET STORES: Cabinets, Custom Work
FURNITURE & CABINET STORES: Custom
FURNITURE & FIXTURES Factory
FURNITURE PARTS: Metal
FURNITURE REFINISHING SVCS
FURNITURE STOCK & PARTS: Carvings, Wood
FURNITURE STOCK & PARTS: Dimension Stock, Hardwood
FURNITURE STOCK & PARTS: Frames, Upholstered Furniture, Wood
FURNITURE STOCK & PARTS: Hardwood
FURNITURE STORES
FURNITURE STORES: Cabinets, Kitchen, Exc Custom Made
FURNITURE STORES: Custom Made, Exc Cabinets
FURNITURE STORES: Juvenile
FURNITURE STORES: Office
FURNITURE STORES: Outdoor & Garden
FURNITURE STORES: Unfinished
FURNITURE WHOLESALERS
FURNITURE, HOUSEHOLD: Wholesalers
FURNITURE, OFFICE: Wholesalers
FURNITURE, WHOLESALE: Beds & Bedding
FURNITURE, WHOLESALE: Racks
FURNITURE, WHOLESALE: Tables, Occasional
FURNITURE: Bed Frames & Headboards, Wood
FURNITURE: Bedroom, Wood
FURNITURE: Beds, Household, Incl Folding & Cabinet, Metal
FURNITURE: Bookcases, Office, Wood
FURNITURE: Box Springs, Assembled
FURNITURE: Cabinets & Filing Drawers, Office, Exc Wood
FURNITURE: Cabinets & Vanities, Medicine, Metal
FURNITURE: Chairs & Couches, Wood, Upholstered
FURNITURE: Chairs, Household Upholstered
FURNITURE: Chairs, Household Wood
FURNITURE: Chairs, Office Exc Wood
FURNITURE: Chairs, Office Wood
FURNITURE: China Closets
FURNITURE: Church
FURNITURE: Console Tables, Wood
FURNITURE: Couches, Sofa/Davenport, Upholstered Wood Frames
FURNITURE: Cribs, Metal
FURNITURE: Cut Stone
FURNITURE: Desks & Tables, Office, Wood
FURNITURE: Desks, Metal
FURNITURE: Desks, Wood
FURNITURE: Dinette Sets, Metal

FURNITURE: Dining Room, Wood
FURNITURE: Fiberglass & Plastic
FURNITURE: Foundations & Platforms
FURNITURE: Garden, Exc Wood, Metal, Stone Or Concrete
FURNITURE: Hospital
FURNITURE: Hotel
FURNITURE: Household, Metal
FURNITURE: Household, NEC
FURNITURE: Household, Upholstered On Metal Frames
FURNITURE: Household, Upholstered, Exc Wood Or Metal
FURNITURE: Household, Wood
FURNITURE: Hydraulic Barber & Beauty Shop Chairs
FURNITURE: Institutional, Exc Wood
FURNITURE: Juvenile, Wood
FURNITURE: Kitchen & Dining Room
FURNITURE: Kitchen & Dining Room, Metal
FURNITURE: Laboratory
FURNITURE: Living Room, Upholstered On Wood Frames
FURNITURE: Mattresses & Foundations
FURNITURE: Mattresses, Box & Bedsprings
FURNITURE: Mattresses, Innerspring Or Box Spring
FURNITURE: NEC
FURNITURE: Novelty, Wood
FURNITURE: Office Panel Systems, Exc Wood
FURNITURE: Office Panel Systems, Wood
FURNITURE: Office, Exc Wood
FURNITURE: Office, Wood
FURNITURE: Outdoor, Wood
FURNITURE: Pews, Church
FURNITURE: Picnic Tables Or Benches, Park
FURNITURE: Rattan
FURNITURE: Restaurant
FURNITURE: School
FURNITURE: Ship
FURNITURE: Silverware Chests, Wood
FURNITURE: Sleep
FURNITURE: Sofa Beds Or Convertible Sofas)
FURNITURE: Storage Chests, Household, Wood
FURNITURE: Tables & Table Tops, Wood
FURNITURE: Theater
FURNITURE: Unfinished, Wood
FURNITURE: Upholstered
FURNITURE: Vehicle
FURRIERS
FUSES: Electric

G

GAMES & TOYS: Airplanes
GAMES & TOYS: Baby Carriages & Restraint Seats
GAMES & TOYS: Banks
GAMES & TOYS: Child Restraint Seats, Automotive
GAMES & TOYS: Craft & Hobby Kits & Sets
GAMES & TOYS: Doll Hats
GAMES & TOYS: Dolls & Doll Clothing
GAMES & TOYS: Dolls, Exc Stuffed Toy Animals
GAMES & TOYS: Electronic
GAMES & TOYS: Game Machines, Exc Coin-Operated
GAMES & TOYS: Miniature Dolls, Collectors'
GAMES & TOYS: Puzzles
GAMES & TOYS: Scooters, Children's
GAMES & TOYS: Trains & Eqpt, Electric & Mechanical
GARBAGE CONTAINERS: Plastic
GARBAGE DISPOSALS: Household
GARBAGE DISPOSERS & COMPACTORS: Commercial
GARNET MINING SVCS
GAS & OIL FIELD EXPLORATION SVCS
GAS & OIL FIELD SVCS, NEC
GAS STATIONS
GAS: Refinery
GASES & LIQUIFIED PETROLEUM GASES
GASES: Carbon Dioxide
GASES: Flourinated Hydrocarbon
GASES: Indl
GASES: Neon
GASES: Nitrogen
GASES: Oxygen
GASKET MATERIALS
GASKETS
GASKETS & SEALING DEVICES
GASOLINE FILLING STATIONS
GASOLINE WHOLESALERS
GATES: Dam, Metal Plate
GATES: Ornamental Metal
GAUGES
GEARS

PRODUCT INDEX

GEARS & GEAR UNITS: Reduction, Exc Auto
GEARS: Power Transmission, Exc Auto
GELATIN
GEM STONES MINING, NEC: Natural
GEMSTONE & INDL DIAMOND MINING SVCS
GENERAL & INDUSTRIAL LOAN INSTITUTIONS
GENERAL MERCHANDISE, NONDURABLE, WHOLESALE
GENERATING APPARATUS & PARTS: Electrical
GENERATION EQPT: Electronic
GENERATORS: Electric
GENERATORS: Electrochemical, Fuel Cell
GENERATORS: Gas
GENERATORS: Ultrasonic
GIFT SHOP
GIFT, NOVELTY & SOUVENIR STORES: Artcraft & carvings
GIFT, NOVELTY & SOUVENIR STORES: Gifts & Novelties
GIFTS & NOVELTIES: Wholesalers
GIFTWARE: Brass
GLASS FABRICATORS
GLASS PRDTS, FROM PURCHASED GLASS: Art
GLASS PRDTS, FROM PURCHASED GLASS: Glass Beads, Reflecting
GLASS PRDTS, FROM PURCHASED GLASS: Glassware
GLASS PRDTS, FROM PURCHASED GLASS: Insulating
GLASS PRDTS, FROM PURCHASED GLASS: Mirrored
GLASS PRDTS, FROM PURCHASED GLASS: Mirrors, Framed
GLASS PRDTS, FROM PURCHASED GLASS: Mosaics
GLASS PRDTS, FROM PURCHASED GLASS: Ornaments, Christmas Tree
GLASS PRDTS, FROM PURCHASED GLASS: Sheet, Bent
GLASS PRDTS, FROM PURCHASED GLASS: Watch Crystals
GLASS PRDTS, FROM PURCHASED GLASS: Windshields
GLASS PRDTS, FROM PURCHD GLASS: Strengthened Or Reinforced
GLASS PRDTS, PRESSED OR BLOWN: Bulbs, Electric Lights
GLASS PRDTS, PRESSED OR BLOWN: Glassware, Art Or Decorative
GLASS PRDTS, PRESSED OR BLOWN: Glassware, Novelty
GLASS PRDTS, PRESSED OR BLOWN: Lens Blanks, Optical
GLASS PRDTS, PRESSED OR BLOWN: Lighting Eqpt Parts
GLASS PRDTS, PRESSED OR BLOWN: Optical
GLASS PRDTS, PRESSED OR BLOWN: Ornaments, Christmas Tree
GLASS PRDTS, PRESSED OR BLOWN: Scientific Glassware
GLASS PRDTS, PRESSED/BLOWN: Glassware, Art, Decor/Novelty
GLASS PRDTS, PURCHASED GLASS: Glassware, Scientific/Tech
GLASS PRDTS, PURCHASED GLASS: Insulating, Multiple-Glazed
GLASS PRDTS, PURCHD GLASS: Furniture Top, Cut, Beveld/Polshd
GLASS PRDTS, PURCHSD GLASS: Ornamental, Cut, Engraved/Décor
GLASS STORE: Leaded Or Stained
GLASS STORES
GLASS: Fiber
GLASS: Flat
GLASS: Leaded
GLASS: Pressed & Blown, NEC
GLASS: Stained
GLASS: Structural
GLASS: Tempered
GLASSWARE STORES
GLASSWARE WHOLESALERS
GLASSWARE: Laboratory
GLASSWARE: Laboratory & Medical
GLOBAL POSITIONING SYSTEMS & EQPT
GLOVES: Fabric
GLOVES: Leather
GLOVES: Leather, Dress Or Semidress
GLOVES: Leather, Work
GLOVES: Plastic
GLOVES: Safety
GLOVES: Work
GLOVES: Woven Or Knit, From Purchased Materials
GLUE
GOLD ORE MINING
GOLD ORES
GOLD RECOVERY FROM TAILINGS
GOLD STAMPING, EXC BOOKS

GOLF EQPT
GOURMET FOOD STORES
GOVERNMENT, EXECUTIVE OFFICES: Mayors'
GOVERNMENT, GENERAL: Administration
GRANITE: Crushed & Broken
GRANITE: Cut & Shaped
GRANITE: Dimension
GRANITE: Dimension
GRAPHIC ARTS & RELATED DESIGN SVCS
GRAPHIC LAYOUT SVCS: Printed Circuitry
GRASSES: Artificial & Preserved
GRAVE MARKERS: Concrete
GRAVEL MINING
GREASE CUPS: Metal
GREASE TRAPS: Concrete
GREENHOUSES: Prefabricated Metal
GREETING CARDS WHOLESALERS
GRINDING BALLS: Ceramic
GRINDING SVC: Precision, Commercial Or Indl
GRINDING SVCS: Ophthalmic Lens, Exc Prescription
GRINDS: Electric
GRIT: Steel
GRITS: Crushed & Broken
GROCERIES WHOLESALERS, NEC
GROCERIES, GENERAL LINE WHOLESALERS
GUARDRAILS
GUIDANCE SYSTEMS & EQPT: Space Vehicle
GUIDED MISSILES & SPACE VEHICLES
GUM & WOOD CHEMICALS
GUN STOCKS: Wood
GUNSMITHS
GUTTERS: Sheet Metal
GYPSUM PRDTS

H

HAIR & HAIR BASED PRDTS
HAIR ACCESS WHOLESALERS
HAIR CARE PRDTS
HAIR CARE PRDTS: Hair Coloring Preparations
HAIRPIN MOUNTINGS
HANDBAG STORES
HANDBAGS
HANDBAGS: Women's
HANDCUFFS & LEG IRONS
HANDLES: Brush Or Tool, Plastic
HANDLES: Wood
HANGERS: Garment, Plastic
HANGERS: Garment, Wire
HANGERS: Garment, Wire
HARDBOARD & FIBERBOARD PRDTS
HARDWARE
HARDWARE & BUILDING PRDTS: Plastic
HARDWARE & EQPT: Stage, Exc Lighting
HARDWARE CLOTH: Woven Wire, Made From Purchased Wire
HARDWARE STORES
HARDWARE STORES: Builders'
HARDWARE STORES: Pumps & Pumping Eqpt
HARDWARE STORES: Snowblowers
HARDWARE STORES: Tools
HARDWARE WHOLESALERS
HARDWARE, WHOLESALE: Bolts
HARDWARE, WHOLESALE: Builders', NEC
HARDWARE, WHOLESALE: Chains
HARDWARE, WHOLESALE: Security Devices, Locks
HARDWARE: Aircraft
HARDWARE: Builders'
HARDWARE: Cabinet
HARDWARE: Door Opening & Closing Devices, Exc Electrical
HARDWARE: Furniture
HARDWARE: Furniture, Builders' & Other Household
HARDWARE: Luggage
HARDWARE: Piano
HARNESS ASSEMBLIES: Cable & Wire
HARNESSES, HALTERS, SADDLERY & STRAPS
HEADPHONES: Radio
HEALTH AIDS: Exercise Eqpt
HEALTH SCREENING SVCS
HEARING AIDS
HEAT EMISSION OPERATING APPARATUS
HEAT EXCHANGERS
HEAT EXCHANGERS: After Or Inter Coolers Or Condensers, Etc
HEAT TREATING: Metal
HEATERS: Space, Exc Electric

HEATERS: Swimming Pool, Oil Or Gas
HEATERS: Unit, Domestic
HEATING & AIR CONDITIONING EQPT & SPLYS WHOLESALERS
HEATING & AIR CONDITIONING UNITS, COMBINATION
HEATING EQPT & SPLYS
HEATING EQPT: Complete
HEATING EQPT: Induction
HEATING SYSTEMS: Radiant, Indl Process
HEATING UNITS & DEVICES: Indl, Electric
HELICOPTERS
HELMETS: Athletic
HIGH ENERGY PARTICLE PHYSICS EQPT
HIGHWAY SIGNALS: Electric
HOBBY & CRAFT SPLY STORES
HOBBY, TOY & GAME STORES: Ceramics Splys
HOBBY, TOY & GAME STORES: Toys & Games
HOISTS
HOLDING COMPANIES: Banks
HOLDING COMPANIES: Investment, Exc Banks
HOLDING COMPANIES: Personal, Exc Banks
HOME DELIVERY NEWSPAPER ROUTES
HOME ENTERTAINMENT EQPT: Electronic, NEC
HOME FOR THE MENTALLY RETARDED
HOME FURNISHINGS WHOLESALERS
HOMEBUILDERS & OTHER OPERATIVE BUILDERS
HOMEFURNISHING STORES: Beddings & Linens
HOMEFURNISHING STORES: Cookware, Exc Aluminum
HOMEFURNISHING STORES: Lighting Fixtures
HOMEFURNISHING STORES: Mirrors
HOMEFURNISHING STORES: Vertical Blinds
HOMEFURNISHING STORES: Window Furnishings
HOMEFURNISHINGS & SPLYS, WHOLESALE: Decorative
HOMEFURNISHINGS, WHOLESALE: Bedspreads
HOMEFURNISHINGS, WHOLESALE: Blinds, Venetian
HOMEFURNISHINGS, WHOLESALE: Blinds, Vertical
HOMEFURNISHINGS, WHOLESALE: Carpets
HOMEFURNISHINGS, WHOLESALE: Curtains
HOMEFURNISHINGS, WHOLESALE: Draperies
HOMEFURNISHINGS, WHOLESALE: Kitchenware
HOMEFURNISHINGS, WHOLESALE: Linens, Table
HOMEFURNISHINGS, WHOLESALE: Pillowcases
HOMEFURNISHINGS, WHOLESALE: Rugs
HOMEFURNISHINGS, WHOLESALE: Stainless Steel Flatware
HOMEFURNISHINGS, WHOLESALE: Window Covering Parts & Access
HOMEFURNISHINGS, WHOLESALE: Wood Flooring
HOMES, MODULAR: Wooden
HOMES: Log Cabins
HONES
HORMONE PREPARATIONS
HORSE & PET ACCESSORIES: Textile
HORSE ACCESS: Harnesses & Riding Crops, Etc, Exc Leather
HOSE: Automobile, Plastic
HOSE: Fire, Rubber
HOSE: Flexible Metal
HOSE: Plastic
HOSE: Pneumatic, Rubber Or Rubberized Fabric, NEC
HOSE: Rubber
HOSE: Vacuum Cleaner, Rubber
HOSES & BELTING: Rubber & Plastic
HOSPITALS: Cancer
HOSPITALS: Medical & Surgical
HOT TUBS
HOT TUBS: Plastic & Fiberglass
HOUSEHOLD APPLIANCE STORES: Air Cond Rm Units, Self-Contnd
HOUSEHOLD APPLIANCE STORES: Fans, Electric
HOUSEHOLD APPLIANCE STORES: Garbage Disposals
HOUSEHOLD ARTICLES: Metal
HOUSEHOLD FURNISHINGS, NEC
HOUSEWARE STORES
HOUSEWARES, ELECTRIC, EXC COOKING APPLIANCES & UTENSILS
HOUSEWARES, ELECTRIC: Cooking Appliances
HOUSEWARES, ELECTRIC: Extractors, Juice
HOUSEWARES, ELECTRIC: Fryers
HOUSEWARES, ELECTRIC: Heaters, Sauna
HOUSEWARES, ELECTRIC: Heaters, Space
HOUSEWARES, ELECTRIC: Heating, Bsbrd/Wall, Radiant Heat
HOUSEWARES, ELECTRIC: Humidifiers, Household

PRODUCT INDEX

HOUSEWARES, ELECTRIC: Massage Machines, Exc Beauty/Barber
HOUSEWARES: Dishes, China
HOUSEWARES: Dishes, Earthenware
HOUSEWARES: Dishes, Plastic
HOUSEWARES: Kettles & Skillets, Cast Iron
HUMIDIFIERS & DEHUMIDIFIERS
HYDRAULIC EQPT REPAIR SVC
Hard Rubber & Molded Rubber Prdts

I

ICE
ICE CREAM & ICES WHOLESALERS
IDENTIFICATION TAGS, EXC PAPER
IGNEOUS ROCK: Crushed & Broken
IGNITION APPARATUS & DISTRIBUTORS
IGNITION SYSTEMS: High Frequency
IGNITION SYSTEMS: Internal Combustion Engine
INCINERATORS
INDICATORS: Cabin Environment
INDL & PERSONAL SVC PAPER WHOLESALERS
INDL & PERSONAL SVC PAPER, WHOL: Bags, Paper/Disp Plastic
INDL & PERSONAL SVC PAPER, WHOL: Boxes, Corrugtd/Solid Fiber
INDL & PERSONAL SVC PAPER, WHOL: Container, Paper/Plastic
INDL & PERSONAL SVC PAPER, WHOL: Cups, Disp, Plastic/Paper
INDL & PERSONAL SVC PAPER, WHOLESALE: Paperboard & Prdts
INDL & PERSONAL SVC PAPER, WHOLESALE: Press Sensitive Tape
INDL EQPT SVCS
INDL GASES WHOLESALERS
INDL MACHINERY & EQPT WHOLESALERS
INDL MACHINERY REPAIR & MAINTENANCE
INDL PATTERNS: Foundry Patternmaking
INDL PROCESS INSTRUMENT: Potentiomtrc Self-Bal, Exc XY Plot
INDL PROCESS INSTRUMENTS: Analyzers
INDL PROCESS INSTRUMENTS: Control
INDL PROCESS INSTRUMENTS: Controllers, Process Variables
INDL PROCESS INSTRUMENTS: Digital Display, Process Variables
INDL PROCESS INSTRUMENTS: Elements, Primary
INDL PROCESS INSTRUMENTS: Fluidic Devices, Circuit & Systems
INDL PROCESS INSTRUMENTS: Indl Flow & Measuring
INDL PROCESS INSTRUMENTS: Level & Bulk Measuring
INDL PROCESS INSTRUMENTS: On-Stream Gas Or Liquid Analysis
INDL PROCESS INSTRUMENTS: Temperature
INDL PROCESS INSTRUMENTS: Water Quality Monitoring/Cntrl Sys
INDL SALTS WHOLESALERS
INDL SPLYS WHOLESALERS
INDL SPLYS, WHOL: Fasteners, Incl Nuts, Bolts, Screws, Etc
INDL SPLYS, WHOLESALE: Abrasives
INDL SPLYS, WHOLESALE: Adhesives, Tape & Plasters
INDL SPLYS, WHOLESALE: Bearings
INDL SPLYS, WHOLESALE: Bins & Containers, Storage
INDL SPLYS, WHOLESALE: Brushes, Indl
INDL SPLYS, WHOLESALE: Clean Room Splys
INDL SPLYS, WHOLESALE: Fasteners & Fastening Eqpt
INDL SPLYS, WHOLESALE: Gears
INDL SPLYS, WHOLESALE: Knives, Indl
INDL SPLYS, WHOLESALE: Mill Splys
INDL SPLYS, WHOLESALE: Rubber Goods, Mechanical
INDL SPLYS, WHOLESALE: Seals
INDL SPLYS, WHOLESALE: Springs
INDL SPLYS, WHOLESALE: Tools
INDL SPLYS, WHOLESALE: Valves & Fittings
INDUCTORS
INFORMATION RETRIEVAL SERVICES
INFRARED OBJECT DETECTION EQPT
INGOT: Aluminum
INK OR WRITING FLUIDS
INK: Letterpress Or Offset
INK: Printing
INK: Screen process
INSECTICIDES
INSPECTION & TESTING SVCS

INSTR, MEASURE & CONTROL: Gauge, Oil Pressure & Water Temp
INSTRUMENTS & METERS: Measuring, Electric
INSTRUMENTS, LABORATORY: Differential Thermal Analysis
INSTRUMENTS, LABORATORY: Magnetic/Elec Properties Measuring
INSTRUMENTS, LABORATORY: Mass Spectrometers
INSTRUMENTS, LABORATORY: Protein Analyzers
INSTRUMENTS, LABORATORY: Spectrometers
INSTRUMENTS, MEASURING & CNTRL: Radiation & Testing, Nuclear
INSTRUMENTS, MEASURING & CNTRL: Testing, Abrasion, Etc
INSTRUMENTS, MEASURING & CNTRLG: Aircraft & Motor Vehicle
INSTRUMENTS, MEASURING & CNTRLG: Stress, Strain & Measure
INSTRUMENTS, MEASURING & CNTRLG: Tensile Strength Testing
INSTRUMENTS, MEASURING & CNTRLG: Thermometers/Temp Sensors
INSTRUMENTS, MEASURING & CONTROLLING: Gas Detectors
INSTRUMENTS, MEASURING & CONTROLLING: Magnetometers
INSTRUMENTS, MEASURING & CONTROLLING: Photogrammetrical
INSTRUMENTS, MEASURING & CONTROLLING: Toll Booths, Automatic
INSTRUMENTS, MEASURING & CONTROLLING: Ultrasonic Testing
INSTRUMENTS, MEASURING/CNTRL: Hydrometers, Exc Indl Process
INSTRUMENTS, MEASURING/CNTRLG: Fare Registers, St Cars/Buses
INSTRUMENTS, MEASURING/CNTRLNG: Med Diagnostic Sys, Nuclear
INSTRUMENTS, OPTICAL: Borescopes
INSTRUMENTS, OPTICAL: Elements & Assemblies, Exc Ophthalmic
INSTRUMENTS, OPTICAL: Gratings, Diffraction
INSTRUMENTS, OPTICAL: Grinding, Lens Exc Ophthalmic
INSTRUMENTS, OPTICAL: Lenses, All Types Exc Ophthalmic
INSTRUMENTS, OPTICAL: Mirrors
INSTRUMENTS, OPTICAL: Prisms
INSTRUMENTS, OPTICAL: Spyglasses
INSTRUMENTS, OPTICAL: Test & Inspection
INSTRUMENTS, SURGICAL & MEDICAL: Blood & Bone Work
INSTRUMENTS, SURGICAL & MEDICAL: Blood Pressure
INSTRUMENTS, SURGICAL & MEDICAL: Catheters
INSTRUMENTS, SURGICAL & MEDICAL: IV Transfusion
INSTRUMENTS, SURGICAL & MEDICAL: Inhalation Therapy
INSTRUMENTS, SURGICAL & MEDICAL: Inhalators
INSTRUMENTS, SURGICAL & MEDICAL: Knives
INSTRUMENTS, SURGICAL & MEDICAL: Lasers, Surgical
INSTRUMENTS, SURGICAL & MEDICAL: Muscle Exercise, Ophthalmic
INSTRUMENTS, SURGICAL & MEDICAL: Ophthalmic
INSTRUMENTS, SURGICAL & MEDICAL: Physiotherapy, Electrical
INSTRUMENTS, SURGICAL & MEDICAL: Skin Grafting
INSTRUMENTS, SURGICAL & MEDICAL: Suction Therapy
INSTRUMENTS: Analytical
INSTRUMENTS: Colonoscopes, Electromedical
INSTRUMENTS: Combustion Control, Indl
INSTRUMENTS: Electrocardiographs
INSTRUMENTS: Electrolytic Conductivity, Indl
INSTRUMENTS: Endoscopic Eqpt, Electromedical
INSTRUMENTS: Function Generators
INSTRUMENTS: Generators Tachometer
INSTRUMENTS: Indl Process Control
INSTRUMENTS: Laser, Scientific & Engineering
INSTRUMENTS: Measurement, Indl Process
INSTRUMENTS: Measuring & Controlling
INSTRUMENTS: Measuring Electricity
INSTRUMENTS: Measuring, Electrical Energy
INSTRUMENTS: Measuring, Electrical Power
INSTRUMENTS: Measuring, Electrical Quantities
INSTRUMENTS: Medical & Surgical
INSTRUMENTS: Meteorological
INSTRUMENTS: Microwave Test
INSTRUMENTS: Optical, Analytical
INSTRUMENTS: Oscillographs & Oscilloscopes
INSTRUMENTS: Pressure Measurement, Indl

INSTRUMENTS: Radar Testing, Electric
INSTRUMENTS: Radio Frequency Measuring
INSTRUMENTS: Standards & Calibration, Electrical Measuring
INSTRUMENTS: Telemetering, Indl Process
INSTRUMENTS: Temperature Measurement, Indl
INSTRUMENTS: Test, Electrical, Engine
INSTRUMENTS: Test, Electronic & Electric Measurement
INSTRUMENTS: Test, Electronic & Electrical Circuits
INSTRUMENTS: Testing, Semiconductor
INSTRUMENTS: Thermal Conductive, Indl
INSTRUMENTS: Vibration
INSTRUMENTS: Viscometer, Indl Process
INSULATION & CUSHIONING FOAM: Polystyrene
INSULATION MATERIALS WHOLESALERS
INSULATION: Felt
INSULATION: Fiberglass
INSULATORS & INSULATION MATERIALS: Electrical
INSULATORS, PORCELAIN: Electrical
INTEGRATED CIRCUITS, SEMICONDUCTOR NETWORKS, ETC
INTERCOMMUNICATIONS SYSTEMS: Electric
INTERIOR DECORATING SVCS
INTERIOR DESIGN SVCS, NEC
INTERIOR DESIGNING SVCS
INTERIOR REPAIR SVCS
INTRAVENOUS SOLUTIONS
INVERTERS: Nonrotating Electrical
INVERTERS: Rotating Electrical
INVESTMENT ADVISORY SVCS
INVESTMENT FUNDS: Open-Ended
INVESTORS: Security Speculators For Own Account
IRON & STEEL PRDTS: Hot-Rolled
IRON & STEEL: Corrugating, Cold-Rolled
IRON ORE MINING
IRON OXIDES
IRONING BOARDS
IRRADIATION EQPT: Nuclear
IRRIGATION SYSTEMS, NEC Water Distribution Or Sply Systems

J

JANITORIAL & CUSTODIAL SVCS
JANITORIAL EQPT & SPLYS WHOLESALERS
JEWELERS' FINDINGS & MATERIALS
JEWELERS' FINDINGS & MATERIALS: Castings
JEWELERS' FINDINGS & MATERIALS: Parts, Unassembled
JEWELERS' FINDINGS & MTLS: Jewel Prep, Instr, Tools, Watches
JEWELERS' FINDINGS/MTRLS: Gem Prep, Settings, Real/Imitation
JEWELRY & PRECIOUS STONES WHOLESALERS
JEWELRY APPAREL
JEWELRY FINDINGS & LAPIDARY WORK
JEWELRY FINDINGS WHOLESALERS
JEWELRY REPAIR SVCS
JEWELRY STORES
JEWELRY STORES: Precious Stones & Precious Metals
JEWELRY, PREC METAL: Mountings, Pens, Lthr, Etc, Gold/Silver
JEWELRY, PRECIOUS METAL: Bracelets
JEWELRY, PRECIOUS METAL: Cases
JEWELRY, PRECIOUS METAL: Cigar & Cigarette Access
JEWELRY, PRECIOUS METAL: Earrings
JEWELRY, PRECIOUS METAL: Medals, Precious Or Semiprecious
JEWELRY, PRECIOUS METAL: Mountings & Trimmings
JEWELRY, PRECIOUS METAL: Necklaces
JEWELRY, PRECIOUS METAL: Pearl, Natural Or Cultured
JEWELRY, PRECIOUS METAL: Pins
JEWELRY, PRECIOUS METAL: Rings, Finger
JEWELRY, PRECIOUS METAL: Rosaries/Other Sm Religious Article
JEWELRY, PRECIOUS METAL: Settings & Mountings
JEWELRY, PRECIOUS METAL: Trimmings, Canes, Umbrellas, Etc
JEWELRY, WHOLESALE
JEWELRY: Decorative, Fashion & Costume
JEWELRY: Precious Metal
JIGS & FIXTURES
JOB PRINTING & NEWSPAPER PUBLISHING COMBINED
JOB TRAINING & VOCATIONAL REHABILITATION SVCS
JOINTS: Ball Except aircraft & Auto
JOINTS: Expansion
JOINTS: Expansion, Pipe

PRODUCT INDEX

K

KEYBOARDS: Computer Or Office Machine
KEYS, KEY BLANKS
KITCHEN CABINET STORES, EXC CUSTOM
KITCHEN CABINETS WHOLESALERS
KITCHEN TOOLS & UTENSILS WHOLESALERS
KITCHEN UTENSILS: Bakers' Eqpt, Wood
KITCHEN UTENSILS: Food Handling & Processing Prdts, Wood
KITCHEN UTENSILS: Wooden
KITCHENWARE STORES
KITCHENWARE: Plastic
KNIT GOODS, WHOLESALE
KNIT OUTERWEAR DYEING & FINISHING, EXC HOSIERY & GLOVE
KNIVES: Agricultural Or Indl

L

LABELS: Cotton, Printed
LABELS: Paper, Made From Purchased Materials
LABELS: Woven
LABORATORIES, TESTING: Forensic
LABORATORIES, TESTING: Product Testing, Safety/Performance
LABORATORIES: Biological Research
LABORATORIES: Biotechnology
LABORATORIES: Commercial Nonphysical Research
LABORATORIES: Dental
LABORATORIES: Dental Orthodontic Appliance Production
LABORATORIES: Electronic Research
LABORATORIES: Medical
LABORATORIES: Noncommercial Research
LABORATORIES: Physical Research, Commercial
LABORATORIES: Testing
LABORATORIES: Testing
LABORATORY APPARATUS & FURNITURE
LABORATORY APPARATUS: Furnaces
LABORATORY APPARATUS: Pipettes, Hemocytometer
LABORATORY APPARATUS: Shakers & Stirrers
LABORATORY EQPT, EXC MEDICAL: Wholesalers
LABORATORY EQPT: Chemical
LABORATORY EQPT: Clinical Instruments Exc Medical
LABORATORY EQPT: Measuring
LABORATORY EQPT: Sterilizers
LACE GOODS & WARP KNIT FABRIC DYEING & FINISHING
LACQUERING SVC: Metal Prdts
LADDERS: Metal
LADDERS: Portable, Metal
LADDERS: Wood
LAMINATED PLASTICS: Plate, Sheet, Rod & Tubes
LAMINATING SVCS
LAMP & LIGHT BULBS & TUBES
LAMP BULBS & TUBES, ELECTRIC: For Specialized Applications
LAMP BULBS & TUBES, ELECTRIC: Light, Complete
LAMP BULBS & TUBES/PARTS, ELECTRIC: Generalized Applications
LAMP FRAMES: Wire
LAMP SHADES: Glass
LAMP SHADES: Metal
LAMP STORES
LAMPS: Arc Units, Electrotherapeutic
LAMPS: Floor, Residential
LAMPS: Fluorescent
LAMPS: Table, Residential
LAMPS: Ultraviolet
LAND SUBDIVIDERS & DEVELOPERS: Commercial
LAND SUBDIVISION & DEVELOPMENT
LANGUAGE SCHOOLS
LANTERNS
LAPIDARY WORK & DIAMOND CUTTING & POLISHING
LAPIDARY WORK: Contract Or Other
LAPIDARY WORK: Jewel Cut, Drill, Polish, Recut/Setting
LARD: From Slaughtering Plants
LASER SYSTEMS & EQPT
LASERS: Welding, Drilling & Cutting Eqpt
LAUNDRY & GARMENT SVCS, NEC: Fur Cleaning, Repairing/Storage
LAUNDRY & GARMENT SVCS, NEC: Garment Alteration & Repair
LAUNDRY EQPT: Commercial
LAUNDRY EQPT: Household
LAUNDRY SVC: Wiping Towel Sply
LAWN & GARDEN EQPT
LAWN & GARDEN EQPT STORES
LAWN & GARDEN EQPT: Tractors & Eqpt
LAWN & GARDEN EQPT: Trimmers
LAWN MOWER REPAIR SHOP
LEAD & ZINC
LEAD PENCILS & ART GOODS
LEASING & RENTAL SVCS: Cranes & Aerial Lift Eqpt
LEASING & RENTAL SVCS: Earth Moving Eqpt
LEASING & RENTAL: Computers & Eqpt
LEASING & RENTAL: Construction & Mining Eqpt
LEASING & RENTAL: Other Real Estate Property
LEASING: Laundry Eqpt
LEASING: Shipping Container
LEATHER GOODS, EXC FOOTWEAR, GLOVES, LUGGAGE/BELTING, WHOL
LEATHER GOODS: Belt Laces
LEATHER GOODS: Belting & Strapping
LEATHER GOODS: Boxes
LEATHER GOODS: Cases
LEATHER GOODS: Corners, Luggage
LEATHER GOODS: Cosmetic Bags
LEATHER GOODS: Desk Sets
LEATHER GOODS: Garments
LEATHER GOODS: Holsters
LEATHER GOODS: Key Cases
LEATHER GOODS: NEC
LEATHER GOODS: Personal
LEATHER GOODS: Transmission Belting
LEATHER GOODS: Wallets
LEATHER TANNING & FINISHING
LEATHER, LEATHER GOODS & FURS, WHOLESALE
LEATHER: Accessory Prdts
LEATHER: Artificial
LEATHER: Bag
LEATHER: Bookbinders'
LEATHER: Case
LEATHER: Colored
LEATHER: Cut
LEATHER: Die-cut
LEATHER: Embossed
LEATHER: Finished
LEATHER: Glove
LEATHER: Handbag
LEATHER: Processed
LEATHER: Upholstery
LEGAL & TAX SVCS
LEGAL OFFICES & SVCS
LEGITIMATE LIVE THEATER PRODUCERS
LENS COATING: Ophthalmic
LENSES: Plastic, Exc Optical
LESSORS: Landholding Office
LIFESAVING & SURVIVAL EQPT, EXC MEDICAL, WHOLESALE
LIGHT SENSITIVE DEVICES
LIGHTING EQPT: Flashlights
LIGHTING EQPT: Motor Vehicle, Headlights
LIGHTING EQPT: Motor Vehicle, NEC
LIGHTING EQPT: Outdoor
LIGHTING EQPT: Reflectors, Metal, For Lighting Eqpt
LIGHTING EQPT: Streetcar Fixtures
LIGHTING EQPT: Strobe Lighting Systems
LIGHTING FIXTURES WHOLESALERS
LIGHTING FIXTURES, NEC
LIGHTING FIXTURES: Airport
LIGHTING FIXTURES: Decorative Area
LIGHTING FIXTURES: Fluorescent, Commercial
LIGHTING FIXTURES: Fluorescent, Residential
LIGHTING FIXTURES: Indl & Commercial
LIGHTING FIXTURES: Motor Vehicle
LIGHTING FIXTURES: Ornamental, Commercial
LIGHTING FIXTURES: Public
LIGHTING FIXTURES: Residential
LIGHTING FIXTURES: Residential, Electric
LIGHTING FIXTURES: Street
LIGHTS: Trouble lights
LIME
LIME: Agricultural
LIMESTONE & MARBLE: Dimension
LIMESTONE: Crushed & Broken
LIMESTONE: Cut & Shaped
LIMESTONE: Dimension
LIMESTONE: Ground
LINEN SPLY SVC: Apron
LINEN SPLY SVC: Coat
LINENS & TOWELS WHOLESALERS
LINENS: Napkins, Fabric & Nonwoven, From Purchased Materials
LINENS: Tablecloths, From Purchased Materials
LINERS & COVERS: Fabric
LINERS & LINING
LINERS: Indl, Metal Plate
LINIMENTS
LININGS: Apparel, Made From Purchased Materials
LININGS: Fabric, Apparel & Other, Exc Millinery
LIP BALMS
LIPSTICK
LIQUEFIED PETROLEUM GAS DEALERS
LIQUID CRYSTAL DISPLAYS
LITHOGRAPHIC PLATES
LOCK & KEY SVCS
LOCKERS
LOCKERS: Refrigerated
LOCKS
LOCKS: Coin-Operated
LOCKS: Safe & Vault, Metal
LOCKSMITHS
LOCOMOTIVES & PARTS
LOG LOADING & UNLOADING SVCS
LOGGING
LOGGING CAMPS & CONTRACTORS
LOGGING: Timber, Cut At Logging Camp
LOGGING: Wood Chips, Produced In The Field
LOGGING: Wooden Logs
LOOSELEAF BINDERS
LOTIONS OR CREAMS: Face
LOTIONS: SHAVING
LOUDSPEAKERS
LOUVERS: Ventilating
LOZENGES: Pharmaceutical
LUBRICANTS: Corrosion Preventive
LUBRICATING EQPT: Indl
LUBRICATING OIL & GREASE WHOLESALERS
LUBRICATION SYSTEMS & EQPT
LUGGAGE & BRIEFCASES
LUGGAGE & LEATHER GOODS STORES: Leather, Exc Luggage & Shoes
LUGGAGE WHOLESALERS
LUGGAGE: Traveling Bags
LUGGAGE: Wardrobe Bags
LUMBER & BLDG MATLS DEALER, RET: Garage Doors, Sell/Install
LUMBER & BLDG MATRLS DEALERS, RET: Bath Fixtures, Eqpt/Sply
LUMBER & BLDG MTRLS DEALERS, RET: Doors, Storm, Wood/Metal
LUMBER & BLDG MTRLS DEALERS, RET: Windows, Storm, Wood/Metal
LUMBER & BUILDING MATERIAL DEALERS, RETAIL: Roofing Material
LUMBER & BUILDING MATERIALS DEALER, RET: Door & Window Prdts
LUMBER & BUILDING MATERIALS DEALER, RET: Masonry Matls/Splys
LUMBER & BUILDING MATERIALS DEALERS, RETAIL: Brick
LUMBER & BUILDING MATERIALS DEALERS, RETAIL: Countertops
LUMBER & BUILDING MATERIALS DEALERS, RETAIL: Paving Stones
LUMBER & BUILDING MATERIALS DEALERS, RETAIL: Sand & Gravel
LUMBER & BUILDING MATERIALS DEALERS, RETAIL: Tile, Ceramic
LUMBER & BUILDING MATERIALS RET DEALERS: Millwork & Lumber
LUMBER & BUILDING MATLS DEALERS, RET: Concrete/Cinder Block
LUMBER: Dimension, Hardwood
LUMBER: Fiberboard
LUMBER: Fuelwood, From Mill Waste
LUMBER: Furniture Dimension Stock, Softwood
LUMBER: Hardwood Dimension
LUMBER: Hardwood Dimension & Flooring Mills
LUMBER: Kiln Dried
LUMBER: Plywood, Hardwood
LUMBER: Plywood, Hardwood or Hardwood Faced
LUMBER: Plywood, Prefinished, Hardwood
LUMBER: Plywood, Softwood
LUMBER: Poles, Wood, Untreated
LUMBER: Siding, Dressed
LUMBER: Silo Stock, Sawn

PRODUCT INDEX

LUMBER: Treated
LUNCHROOMS & CAFETERIAS

M

MACHINE PARTS: Stamped Or Pressed Metal
MACHINE SHOPS
MACHINE TOOL ACCESS: Balancing Machines
MACHINE TOOL ACCESS: Cams
MACHINE TOOL ACCESS: Cutting
MACHINE TOOL ACCESS: Diamond Cutting, For Turning, Etc
MACHINE TOOL ACCESS: Dies, Thread Cutting
MACHINE TOOL ACCESS: Dressing/Wheel Crushing Attach, Diamond
MACHINE TOOL ACCESS: Drills
MACHINE TOOL ACCESS: Knives, Shear
MACHINE TOOL ACCESS: Milling Machine Attachments
MACHINE TOOL ACCESS: Sockets
MACHINE TOOL ACCESS: Tool Holders
MACHINE TOOL ACCESS: Tools & Access
MACHINE TOOL ATTACHMENTS & ACCESS
MACHINE TOOLS & ACCESS
MACHINE TOOLS, METAL CUTTING: Centering
MACHINE TOOLS, METAL CUTTING: Exotic, Including Explosive
MACHINE TOOLS, METAL CUTTING: Grind, Polish, Buff, Lapp
MACHINE TOOLS, METAL CUTTING: Lathes
MACHINE TOOLS, METAL CUTTING: Numerically Controlled
MACHINE TOOLS, METAL CUTTING: Tool Replacement & Rpr Parts
MACHINE TOOLS, METAL FORMING: Die Casting & Extruding
MACHINE TOOLS, METAL FORMING: Electroforming
MACHINE TOOLS, METAL FORMING: Forging Machinery & Hammers
MACHINE TOOLS, METAL FORMING: Forming, Metal Deposit
MACHINE TOOLS, METAL FORMING: Headers
MACHINE TOOLS, METAL FORMING: High Energy Rate
MACHINE TOOLS, METAL FORMING: Presses, Hyd & Pneumatic
MACHINE TOOLS, METAL FORMING: Pressing
MACHINE TOOLS, METAL FORMING: Punching & Shearing
MACHINE TOOLS, METAL FORMING: Rebuilt
MACHINE TOOLS, METAL FORMING: Spinning, Spline Rollg/Windg
MACHINE TOOLS: Metal Cutting
MACHINE TOOLS: Metal Forming
MACHINERY & EQPT, AGRICULTURAL, WHOLESALE: Dairy
MACHINERY & EQPT, AGRICULTURAL, WHOLESALE: Landscaping Eqpt
MACHINERY & EQPT, AGRICULTURAL, WHOLESALE: Lawn & Garden
MACHINERY & EQPT, INDL, WHOL: Controlling Instruments/Access
MACHINERY & EQPT, INDL, WHOL: Recording Instruments/Access
MACHINERY & EQPT, INDL, WHOLESALE: Conveyor Systems
MACHINERY & EQPT, INDL, WHOLESALE: Countersinks
MACHINERY & EQPT, INDL, WHOLESALE: Cranes
MACHINERY & EQPT, INDL, WHOLESALE: Fans
MACHINERY & EQPT, INDL, WHOLESALE: Food Manufacturing
MACHINERY & EQPT, INDL, WHOLESALE: Food Product Manufacturng
MACHINERY & EQPT, INDL, WHOLESALE: Heat Exchange
MACHINERY & EQPT, INDL, WHOLESALE: Hydraulic Systems
MACHINERY & EQPT, INDL, WHOLESALE: Indl Machine Parts
MACHINERY & EQPT, INDL, WHOLESALE: Instruments & Cntrl Eqpt
MACHINERY & EQPT, INDL, WHOLESALE: Machine Tools & Access
MACHINERY & EQPT, INDL, WHOLESALE: Measure/Test, Electric
MACHINERY & EQPT, INDL, WHOLESALE: Packaging
MACHINERY & EQPT, INDL, WHOLESALE: Paint Spray
MACHINERY & EQPT, INDL, WHOLESALE: Pneumatic Tools
MACHINERY & EQPT, INDL, WHOLESALE: Power Plant Machinery
MACHINERY & EQPT, INDL, WHOLESALE: Processing & Packaging
MACHINERY & EQPT, INDL, WHOLESALE: Robots
MACHINERY & EQPT, INDL, WHOLESALE: Safety Eqpt
MACHINERY & EQPT, INDL, WHOLESALE: Textile
MACHINERY & EQPT, INDL, WHOLESALE: Tire Recapping Machinery
MACHINERY & EQPT, INDL, WHOLESALE: Water Pumps
MACHINERY & EQPT, INDL, WHOLESALE: Woodworking
MACHINERY & EQPT, WHOLESALE: Construction, General
MACHINERY & EQPT, WHOLESALE: Crushing, Pulverizng & Screeng
MACHINERY & EQPT, WHOLESALE: Masonry
MACHINERY & EQPT, WHOLESALE: Road Construction & Maintenance
MACHINERY & EQPT: Electroplating
MACHINERY & EQPT: Farm
MACHINERY & EQPT: Gas Producers, Generators/Other Rltd Eqpt
MACHINERY & EQPT: Liquid Automation
MACHINERY & EQPT: Metal Finishing, Plating Etc
MACHINERY BASES
MACHINERY, COMMERCIAL LAUNDRY: Dryers, Incl Coin-Operated
MACHINERY, COMMERCIAL LAUNDRY: Washing, Incl Coin-Operated
MACHINERY, EQPT & SUPPLIES: Parking Facility
MACHINERY, FLOOR SANDING: Commercial
MACHINERY, FOOD PRDTS: Beverage
MACHINERY, FOOD PRDTS: Choppers, Commercial
MACHINERY, FOOD PRDTS: Confectionery
MACHINERY, FOOD PRDTS: Cutting, Chopping, Grinding, Mixing
MACHINERY, FOOD PRDTS: Dairy & Milk
MACHINERY, FOOD PRDTS: Dairy, Pasteurizing
MACHINERY, FOOD PRDTS: Food Processing, Smokers
MACHINERY, FOOD PRDTS: Juice Extractors, Fruit & Veg, Comm
MACHINERY, FOOD PRDTS: Milk Processing, NEC
MACHINERY, FOOD PRDTS: Mixers, Commercial
MACHINERY, FOOD PRDTS: Oilseed Crushing & Extracting
MACHINERY, FOOD PRDTS: Ovens, Bakery
MACHINERY, FOOD PRDTS: Packing House
MACHINERY, FOOD PRDTS: Presses, Cheese, Beet, Cider & Sugar
MACHINERY, FOOD PRDTS: Roasting, Coffee, Peanut, Etc.
MACHINERY, MAILING: Canceling
MACHINERY, MAILING: Mailing
MACHINERY, MAILING: Postage Meters
MACHINERY, METALWORKING: Assembly, Including Robotic
MACHINERY, METALWORKING: Cutting & Slitting
MACHINERY, OFFICE: Perforators
MACHINERY, OFFICE: Stapling, Hand Or Power
MACHINERY, OFFICE: Time Clocks &Time Recording Devices
MACHINERY, PACKAGING: Canning, Food
MACHINERY, PACKAGING: Carton Packing
MACHINERY, PACKAGING: Packing & Wrapping
MACHINERY, PAPER INDUSTRY: Converting, Die Cutting & Stampng
MACHINERY, PAPER INDUSTRY: Paper Mill, Plating, Etc
MACHINERY, PRINTING TRADES: Copy Holders
MACHINERY, PRINTING TRADES: Plates
MACHINERY, PRINTING TRADES: Plates, Offset
MACHINERY, PRINTING TRADES: Printing Trade Parts & Attchts
MACHINERY, PRINTING TRADES: Sticks
MACHINERY, SEWING: Sewing & Hat & Zipper Making
MACHINERY, TEXTILE: Card Cutting, Jacquard
MACHINERY, TEXTILE: Embroidery
MACHINERY, TEXTILE: Silk Screens
MACHINERY, TEXTILE: Thread Making Or Spinning
MACHINERY, WOODWORKING: Bandsaws
MACHINERY, WOODWORKING: Cabinet Makers'
MACHINERY, WOODWORKING: Furniture Makers
MACHINERY, WOODWORKING: Lathes, Wood Turning Includes Access
MACHINERY, WOODWORKING: Pattern Makers'
MACHINERY, WOODWORKING: Sanding, Exc Portable Floor Sanders
MACHINERY: Ammunition & Explosives Loading
MACHINERY: Assembly, Exc Metalworking
MACHINERY: Automotive Maintenance
MACHINERY: Automotive Related
MACHINERY: Billing
MACHINERY: Brewery & Malting
MACHINERY: Bridge Or Gate, Hydraulic
MACHINERY: Concrete Prdts
MACHINERY: Construction
MACHINERY: Cryogenic, Industrial
MACHINERY: Custom
MACHINERY: Drill Presses
MACHINERY: Electronic Component Making
MACHINERY: Engraving
MACHINERY: Extruding
MACHINERY: Fiber Optics Strand Coating
MACHINERY: Gear Cutting & Finishing
MACHINERY: General, Industrial, NEC
MACHINERY: Glassmaking
MACHINERY: Grinding
MACHINERY: Ice Cream
MACHINERY: Ice Crushers
MACHINERY: Ice Making
MACHINERY: Industrial, NEC
MACHINERY: Jewelers
MACHINERY: Marking, Metalworking
MACHINERY: Metalworking
MACHINERY: Milling
MACHINERY: Mining
MACHINERY: Optical Lens
MACHINERY: Ozone
MACHINERY: Packaging
MACHINERY: Paper Industry Miscellaneous
MACHINERY: Pharmaciutical
MACHINERY: Photographic Reproduction
MACHINERY: Plastic Working
MACHINERY: Printing Presses
MACHINERY: Recycling
MACHINERY: Riveting
MACHINERY: Road Construction & Maintenance
MACHINERY: Rubber Working
MACHINERY: Screening Eqpt, Electric
MACHINERY: Semiconductor Manufacturing
MACHINERY: Separation Eqpt, Magnetic
MACHINERY: Sheet Metal Working
MACHINERY: Specialty
MACHINERY: Textile
MACHINERY: Tire Shredding
MACHINERY: Wire Drawing
MACHINERY: Woodworking
MACHINES: Forming, Sheet Metal
MACHINISTS' TOOLS: Measuring, Precision
MACHINISTS' TOOLS: Precision
MAGAZINES, WHOLESALE
MAGNETIC INK & OPTICAL SCANNING EQPT
MAGNETIC RESONANCE IMAGING DEVICES: Nonmedical
MAGNETIC TAPE, AUDIO: Prerecorded
MAGNETOHYDRODYNAMIC DEVICES OR MHD
MAGNETS: Ceramic
MAGNETS: Permanent
MAGNIFIERS
MAIL-ORDER BOOK CLUBS
MAIL-ORDER HOUSE, NEC
MAIL-ORDER HOUSES: Book & Record Clubs
MAIL-ORDER HOUSES: Books, Exc Book Clubs
MAIL-ORDER HOUSES: Cards
MAIL-ORDER HOUSES: Clothing, Exc Women's
MAIL-ORDER HOUSES: Computer Eqpt & Electronics
MAIL-ORDER HOUSES: Cosmetics & Perfumes
MAIL-ORDER HOUSES: Fitness & Sporting Goods
MAIL-ORDER HOUSES: Food
MAIL-ORDER HOUSES: Furniture & Furnishings
MAIL-ORDER HOUSES: Gift Items
MAIL-ORDER HOUSES: Jewelry
MAIL-ORDER HOUSES: Magazines
MAILING LIST: Brokers
MAILING LIST: Compilers
MAILING SVCS, NEC
MANAGEMENT CONSULTING SVCS: Automation & Robotics
MANAGEMENT CONSULTING SVCS: Business
MANAGEMENT CONSULTING SVCS: Construction Project
MANAGEMENT CONSULTING SVCS: Distribution Channels
MANAGEMENT CONSULTING SVCS: Food & Beverage
MANAGEMENT CONSULTING SVCS: Industrial
MANAGEMENT CONSULTING SVCS: Industrial & Labor
MANAGEMENT CONSULTING SVCS: Industry Specialist
MANAGEMENT CONSULTING SVCS: New Products & Svcs
MANAGEMENT CONSULTING SVCS: Real Estate
MANAGEMENT CONSULTING SVCS: Training & Development
MANAGEMENT SERVICES
MANAGEMENT SVCS: Administrative
MANAGEMENT SVCS: Circuit, Motion Picture Theaters

PRODUCT INDEX

MANAGEMENT SVCS: Construction
MANAGEMENT SVCS: Restaurant
MANDRELS
MANHOLES COVERS: Concrete
MANICURE PREPARATIONS
MANIFOLDS: Pipe, Fabricated From Purchased Pipe
MANNEQUINS
MANUFACTURING INDUSTRIES, NEC
MAPS
MARBLE BOARD
MARBLE, BUILDING: Cut & Shaped
MARBLE: Crushed & Broken
MARINAS
MARINE HARDWARE
MARINE RELATED EQPT
MARINE SVC STATIONS
MARKERS
MARKETS: Meat & fish
MARKING DEVICES
MARKING DEVICES: Date Stamps, Hand, Rubber Or Metal
MARKING DEVICES: Embossing Seals & Hand Stamps
MARKING DEVICES: Embossing Seals, Corporate & Official
MARKING DEVICES: Figures, Metal
MARKING DEVICES: Irons, Marking Or Branding
MARKING DEVICES: Letters, Metal
MARKING DEVICES: Numbering Machines
MARKING DEVICES: Pads, Inking & Stamping
MARKING DEVICES: Postmark Stamps, Hand, Rubber Or Metal
MARKING DEVICES: Screens, Textile Printing
MASKS: Gas
MASQUERADE OR THEATRICAL COSTUMES STORES
MASTIC ROOFING COMPOSITION
MATERIALS HANDLING EQPT WHOLESALERS
MATS & MATTING, MADE FROM PURCHASED WIRE
MATS OR MATTING, NEC: Rubber
MATS, MATTING & PADS: Auto, Floor, Exc Rubber Or Plastic
MATS, MATTING & PADS: Nonwoven
MATS: Blasting, Rope
MATTRESS STORES
MEAT & FISH MARKETS: Fish
MEAT & MEAT PRDTS WHOLESALERS
MEAT CUTTING & PACKING
MEAT MARKETS
MEAT PRDTS: Bologna, From Purchased Meat
MEAT PRDTS: Boneless Meat, From Purchased Meat
MEAT PRDTS: Dried Beef, From Purchased Meat
MEAT PRDTS: Frankfurters, From Purchased Meat
MEAT PRDTS: Frozen
MEAT PRDTS: Meat By-Prdts, From Slaughtered Meat
MEAT PRDTS: Meat Extracts, From Purchased Meat
MEAT PRDTS: Pork, From Slaughtered Meat
MEAT PRDTS: Prepared Beef Prdts From Purchased Beef
MEAT PRDTS: Prepared Pork Prdts, From Purchased Meat
MEAT PRDTS: Sausage Casings, Natural
MEAT PRDTS: Sausages & Related Prdts, From Purchased Meat
MEAT PRDTS: Sausages, From Purchased Meat
MEAT PRDTS: Sausages, From Slaughtered Meat
MEAT PRDTS: Snack Sticks, Incl Jerky, From Purchased Meat
MEAT PROCESSED FROM PURCHASED CARCASSES
MED, DENTAL & HOSPITAL EQPT, WHOL: Incontinent Prdts/Splys
MEDIA BUYING AGENCIES
MEDIA: Magnetic & Optical Recording
MEDICAL & HOSPITAL EQPT WHOLESALERS
MEDICAL & HOSPITAL SPLYS: Radiation Shielding Garments
MEDICAL & SURGICAL SPLYS: Bandages & Dressings
MEDICAL & SURGICAL SPLYS: Braces, Orthopedic
MEDICAL & SURGICAL SPLYS: Canes, Orthopedic
MEDICAL & SURGICAL SPLYS: Clothing, Fire Resistant & Protect
MEDICAL & SURGICAL SPLYS: Cotton & Cotton Applicators
MEDICAL & SURGICAL SPLYS: Ear Plugs
MEDICAL & SURGICAL SPLYS: Foot Appliances, Orthopedic
MEDICAL & SURGICAL SPLYS: Gynecological Splys & Appliances
MEDICAL & SURGICAL SPLYS: Limbs, Artificial
MEDICAL & SURGICAL SPLYS: Models, Anatomical
MEDICAL & SURGICAL SPLYS: Orthopedic Appliances
MEDICAL & SURGICAL SPLYS: Personal Safety Eqpt
MEDICAL & SURGICAL SPLYS: Prosthetic Appliances
MEDICAL & SURGICAL SPLYS: Respiratory Protect Eqpt, Personal
MEDICAL & SURGICAL SPLYS: Sponges
MEDICAL & SURGICAL SPLYS: Suspensories
MEDICAL & SURGICAL SPLYS: Technical Aids, Handicapped
MEDICAL EQPT REPAIR SVCS, NON-ELECTRIC
MEDICAL EQPT: Diagnostic
MEDICAL EQPT: Electromedical Apparatus
MEDICAL EQPT: Electrotherapeutic Apparatus
MEDICAL EQPT: Heart-Lung Machines, Exc Iron Lungs
MEDICAL EQPT: Laser Systems
MEDICAL EQPT: MRI/Magnetic Resonance Imaging Devs, Nuclear
MEDICAL EQPT: PET Or Position Emission Tomography Scanners
MEDICAL EQPT: Patient Monitoring
MEDICAL EQPT: Sterilizers
MEDICAL EQPT: Ultrasonic Scanning Devices
MEDICAL EQPT: Ultrasonic, Exc Cleaning
MEDICAL EQPT: X-Ray Apparatus & Tubes, Radiographic
MEDICAL EQPT: X-Ray Apparatus & Tubes, Therapeutic
MEDICAL PHOTOGRAPHY & ART SVCS
MEDICAL, DENTAL & HOSPITAL EQPT, WHOL: Dentists' Prof Splys
MEDICAL, DENTAL & HOSPITAL EQPT, WHOL: Hosptl Eqpt/Furniture
MEDICAL, DENTAL & HOSPITAL EQPT, WHOL: Surgical Eqpt & Splys
MEDICAL, DENTAL & HOSPITAL EQPT, WHOLESALE: Diagnostic, Med
MEDICAL, DENTAL & HOSPITAL EQPT, WHOLESALE: Med Eqpt & Splys
MEDICAL, DENTAL & HOSPITAL EQPT, WHOLESALE: Medical Lab
MELAMINE RESINS: Melamine-Formaldehyde
MEMBERSHIP ORGS, BUSINESS: Growers' Marketing Advisory Svc
MEMBERSHIP ORGS, CIVIC, SOCIAL/FRAT: Educator's Assoc
MEMORY DEVICES: Magnetic Bubble
MEN'S & BOYS' CLOTHING ACCESS STORES
MEN'S & BOYS' CLOTHING STORES
MEN'S & BOYS' CLOTHING WHOLESALERS, NEC
MEN'S & BOYS' SPORTSWEAR CLOTHING STORES
MEN'S & BOYS' SPORTSWEAR WHOLESALERS
MEN'S & BOYS' UNDERWEAR WHOLESALERS
MEN'S SUITS STORES
MESSAGE CONCENTRATORS
METAL & STEEL PRDTS: Abrasive
METAL COMPONENTS: Prefabricated
METAL CUTTING SVCS
METAL FABRICATORS: Architechtural
METAL FABRICATORS: Plate
METAL FABRICATORS: Sheet
METAL FABRICATORS: Structural, Ship
METAL FINISHING SVCS
METAL RESHAPING & REPLATING SVCS
METAL SERVICE CENTERS & OFFICES
METAL SPINNING FOR THE TRADE
METAL STAMPING, FOR THE TRADE
METAL STAMPINGS: Patterned
METAL STAMPINGS: Perforated
METAL STAMPINGS: Rigidized
METAL TREATING COMPOUNDS
METAL, TITANIUM: Sponge & Granules
METAL: Heavy, Perforated
METALLIC ORES WHOLESALERS
METALS SVC CENTERS & WHOL: Structural Shapes, Iron Or Steel
METALS SVC CENTERS & WHOLESALERS: Cable, Wire
METALS SVC CENTERS & WHOLESALERS: Iron & Steel Prdt, Ferrous
METALS SVC CENTERS & WHOLESALERS: Misc Nonferrous Prdts
METALS SVC CENTERS & WHOLESALERS: Nonferrous Sheets, Etc
METALS SVC CENTERS & WHOLESALERS: Pipe & Tubing, Steel
METALS SVC CENTERS & WHOLESALERS: Sheets, Metal
METALS SVC CENTERS & WHOLESALERS: Steel
METALS SVC CENTERS & WHOLESALERS: Tin & Tin Base Metals
METALS SVC CENTERS & WHOLESALERS: Tubing, Metal
METALS: Honeycombed
METALS: Precious NEC
METALS: Precious, Secondary
METALS: Primary Nonferrous, NEC
METALWORK: Miscellaneous
METALWORK: Ornamental
METALWORKING MACHINERY WHOLESALERS
METER READERS: Remote
METERING DEVICES: Flow Meters, Impeller & Counter Driven
METERING DEVICES: Totalizing, Consumption
METERING DEVICES: Water Quality Monitoring & Control Systems
METERS: Elasped Time
METERS: Liquid
METHANOL: Natural
MICA PRDTS
MICROCIRCUITS, INTEGRATED: Semiconductor
MICROFILM EQPT
MICROMANIPULATOR
MICROPHONES
MICROPROCESSORS
MICROWAVE COMPONENTS
MICROWAVE OVENS: Household
MILITARY INSIGNIA
MILITARY INSIGNIA, TEXTILE
MILL PRDTS: Structural & Rail
MILLINERY SUPPLIES: Veils & Veiling, Bridal, Funeral, Etc
MILLING: Chemical
MILLING: Grains, Exc Rice
MILLWORK
MINE DEVELOPMENT SVCS: Nonmetallic Minerals
MINERAL ABRASIVES MINING SVCS
MINERAL MINING: Nonmetallic
MINERAL PRODUCTS
MINERAL WOOL
MINERAL WOOL INSULATION PRDTS
MINERALS: Ground Or Otherwise Treated
MINERALS: Ground or Treated
MINIATURES
MINING EXPLORATION & DEVELOPMENT SVCS
MINING SVCS, NEC: Lignite
MIRROR REPAIR SHOP
MIRRORS: Motor Vehicle
MIXING EQPT
MIXTURES & BLOCKS: Asphalt Paving
MOBILE COMMUNICATIONS EQPT
MOBILE HOMES
MOBILE HOMES WHOLESALERS
MODELS
MODELS: General, Exc Toy
MODULES: Computer Logic
MODULES: Solid State
MOLDED RUBBER PRDTS
MOLDING COMPOUNDS
MOLDINGS, ARCHITECTURAL: Plaster Of Paris
MOLDINGS: Picture Frame
MOLDS: Indl
MOLDS: Plastic Working & Foundry
MONUMENTS & GRAVE MARKERS, EXC TERRAZZO
MONUMENTS: Concrete
MONUMENTS: Cut Stone, Exc Finishing Or Lettering Only
MOPS: Floor & Dust
MORTGAGE BANKERS
MOTION PICTURE & VIDEO PRODUCTION SVCS
MOTION PICTURE & VIDEO PRODUCTION SVCS: Non-Theatrical, TV
MOTION PICTURE PRODUCTION & DISTRIBUTION
MOTION PICTURE PRODUCTION & DISTRIBUTION: Television
MOTION PICTURE PRODUCTION ALLIED SVCS
MOTION PICTURE PRODUCTION SVCS
MOTOR & GENERATOR PARTS: Electric
MOTOR HOMES
MOTOR REPAIR SVCS
MOTOR SCOOTERS & PARTS
MOTOR VEHICLE ASSEMBLY, COMPLETE: Autos, Incl Specialty
MOTOR VEHICLE ASSEMBLY, COMPLETE: Buses, All Types
MOTOR VEHICLE ASSEMBLY, COMPLETE: Cars, Armored
MOTOR VEHICLE ASSEMBLY, COMPLETE: Fire Department Vehicles
MOTOR VEHICLE ASSEMBLY, COMPLETE: Military Motor Vehicle
MOTOR VEHICLE ASSEMBLY, COMPLETE: Motor Buses
MOTOR VEHICLE ASSEMBLY, COMPLETE: Snow Plows

PRODUCT INDEX

MOTOR VEHICLE ASSEMBLY, COMPLETE: Truck & Tractor Trucks
MOTOR VEHICLE ASSEMBLY, COMPLETE: Trucks, Pickup
MOTOR VEHICLE DEALERS: Automobiles, New & Used
MOTOR VEHICLE PARTS & ACCESS: Acceleration Eqpt
MOTOR VEHICLE PARTS & ACCESS: Air Conditioner Parts
MOTOR VEHICLE PARTS & ACCESS: Axel Housings & Shafts
MOTOR VEHICLE PARTS & ACCESS: Bearings
MOTOR VEHICLE PARTS & ACCESS: Body Components & Frames
MOTOR VEHICLE PARTS & ACCESS: Cylinder Heads
MOTOR VEHICLE PARTS & ACCESS: Electrical Eqpt
MOTOR VEHICLE PARTS & ACCESS: Engines & Parts
MOTOR VEHICLE PARTS & ACCESS: Fuel Systems & Parts
MOTOR VEHICLE PARTS & ACCESS: Gears
MOTOR VEHICLE PARTS & ACCESS: Power Steering Eqpt
MOTOR VEHICLE PARTS & ACCESS: Propane Conversion Eqpt
MOTOR VEHICLE PARTS & ACCESS: Sanders, Safety
MOTOR VEHICLE PARTS & ACCESS: Tops
MOTOR VEHICLE PARTS & ACCESS: Transmission Housings Or Parts
MOTOR VEHICLE PARTS & ACCESS: Transmissions
MOTOR VEHICLE PARTS & ACCESS: Wheel rims
MOTOR VEHICLE PARTS & ACCESS: Wiring Harness Sets
MOTOR VEHICLE SPLYS & PARTS WHOLESALERS: New
MOTOR VEHICLE: Hardware
MOTOR VEHICLE: Radiators
MOTOR VEHICLE: Steering Mechanisms
MOTOR VEHICLES & CAR BODIES
MOTOR VEHICLES, WHOLESALE: Recreational, All-Terrain
MOTOR VEHICLES, WHOLESALE: Truck bodies
MOTORCYCLE ACCESS
MOTORCYCLE DEALERS
MOTORCYCLE DEALERS: Bicycles, Motorized
MOTORCYCLE PARTS: Wholesalers
MOTORCYCLES & RELATED PARTS
MOTORS: Electric
MOTORS: Generators
MOTORS: Torque
MOVIE THEATERS, EXC DRIVE-IN
MOWERS & ACCESSORIES
MULTIPLEXERS: Telephone & Telegraph
MUSEUMS & ART GALLERIES
MUSIC BROADCASTING SVCS
MUSIC COPYING SVCS
MUSIC DISTRIBUTION APPARATUS
MUSIC LICENSING & ROYALTIES
MUSIC LICENSING TO RADIO STATIONS
MUSIC RECORDING PRODUCER
MUSICAL ENTERTAINERS
MUSICAL INSTRUMENT PARTS & ACCESS, WHOLESALE
MUSICAL INSTRUMENT REPAIR
MUSICAL INSTRUMENTS & ACCESS: Carrying Cases
MUSICAL INSTRUMENTS & ACCESS: NEC
MUSICAL INSTRUMENTS & ACCESS: Pianos
MUSICAL INSTRUMENTS & ACCESS: Pipe Organs
MUSICAL INSTRUMENTS & PARTS: Brass
MUSICAL INSTRUMENTS & PARTS: String
MUSICAL INSTRUMENTS & SPLYS STORES
MUSICAL INSTRUMENTS & SPLYS STORES: Pianos
MUSICAL INSTRUMENTS WHOLESALERS
MUSICAL INSTRUMENTS: Electric & Electronic
MUSICAL INSTRUMENTS: Guitars & Parts, Electric & Acoustic
MUSICAL INSTRUMENTS: Harmonicas
MUSICAL INSTRUMENTS: Heads, Drum
MUSICAL INSTRUMENTS: Organs
MUSICAL INSTRUMENTS: Strings, Instrument

N

NAIL SALONS
NAME PLATES: Engraved Or Etched
NAMEPLATES
NATIONAL SECURITY FORCES
NATURAL BUTANE PRODUCTION
NATURAL GAS COMPRESSING SVC, On-Site
NATURAL GAS DISTRIBUTION TO CONSUMERS
NATURAL GAS LIQUIDS PRODUCTION
NATURAL GAS PRODUCTION
NATURAL GAS TRANSMISSION & DISTRIBUTION
NATURAL GASOLINE PRODUCTION
NAVIGATIONAL SYSTEMS & INSTRUMENTS
NET & NETTING PRDTS
NETS: Laundry
NEW & USED CAR DEALERS
NEWS DEALERS & NEWSSTANDS
NEWS FEATURE SYNDICATES
NEWS PICTURES GATHERING & DISTRIBUTING SVCS
NEWS SYNDICATES
NEWSPAPERS & PERIODICALS NEWS REPORTING SVCS
NEWSPAPERS, WHOLESALE
NICKEL ALLOY
NONCURRENT CARRYING WIRING DEVICES
NONFERROUS: Rolling & Drawing, NEC
NONMETALLIC MINERALS: Support Activities, Exc Fuels
NOTARIES PUBLIC
NOTEBOOKS, MADE FROM PURCHASED MATERIALS
NOTIONS: Button Blanks & Molds
NOTIONS: Pins, Straight, Steel Or Brass
NOTIONS: Studs, Shirt, Exc Precious/Semi Metal/Stone
NOVELTIES
NOVELTIES & SPECIALTIES: Metal
NOVELTIES: Paper, Made From Purchased Materials
NOVELTIES: Plastic
NOVELTY SHOPS
NOZZLES & SPRINKLERS Lawn Hose
NOZZLES: Spray, Aerosol, Paint Or Insecticide
NUCLEAR REACTORS: Military Or Indl
NURSERIES & LAWN & GARDEN SPLY STORES, RETAIL: Sod
NURSERIES & LAWN & GARDEN SPLY STORES, RETAIL: Top Soil
NURSERIES & LAWN/GARDEN SPLY STORE, RET: Lawnmowers/Tractors
NURSERY & GARDEN CENTERS
NUTS: Metal
NYLON RESINS

O

OFFICE EQPT WHOLESALERS
OFFICE EQPT, WHOLESALE: Duplicating Machines
OFFICE FIXTURES: Exc Wood
OFFICE FIXTURES: Wood
OFFICE FURNITURE REPAIR & MAINTENANCE SVCS
OFFICE SPLY & STATIONERY STORES
OFFICE SPLY & STATIONERY STORES: Office Forms & Splys
OFFICE SPLYS, NEC, WHOLESALE
OFFICES & CLINICS OF DENTISTS: Prosthodontist
OFFICES & CLINICS OF DRS, MED: Specialized Practitioners
OFFICES & CLINICS OF HEALTH PRACTITIONERS: Nutritionist
OIL & GAS FIELD MACHINERY
OIL FIELD MACHINERY & EQPT
OIL FIELD SVCS, NEC
OIL ROYALTY TRADERS
OILS & GREASES: Blended & Compounded
OILS & GREASES: Lubricating
OILS: Anise
OILS: Essential
OILS: Lubricating
OILS: Lubricating
OILS: Orange
OILS: Still
OINTMENTS
ON-LINE DATABASE INFORMATION RETRIEVAL SVCS
OPEN PIT GOLD MINING
OPERATOR: Apartment Buildings
OPHTHALMIC GOODS
OPHTHALMIC GOODS WHOLESALERS
OPHTHALMIC GOODS: Eyewear, Protective
OPHTHALMIC GOODS: Frames & Parts, Eyeglass & Spectacle
OPHTHALMIC GOODS: Frames, Lenses & Parts, Eyeglasses
OPHTHALMIC GOODS: Lenses, Ophthalmic
OPHTHALMIC GOODS: Spectacles
OPHTHALMIC GOODS: Temples & Fronts, Ophthalmic
OPTICAL GOODS STORES
OPTICAL GOODS STORES: Opticians
OPTICAL INSTRUMENTS & APPARATUS
OPTICAL INSTRUMENTS & LENSES
OPTICAL SCANNING SVCS
OPTOMETRIC EQPT & SPLYS WHOLESALERS
ORAL PREPARATIONS
ORDNANCE
ORGAN TUNING & REPAIR SVCS
ORGANIZATIONS, NEC
ORGANIZATIONS: Medical Research
ORGANIZATIONS: Professional
ORGANIZATIONS: Religious
ORGANIZATIONS: Research Institute
ORGANIZATIONS: Scientific Research Agency
ORGANIZERS, CLOSET & DRAWER Plastic
ORNAMENTS: Christmas Tree, Exc Electrical & Glass
ORTHOPEDIC SUNDRIES: Molded Rubber
OSCILLATORS
OUTLETS: Electric, Convenience
OVENS: Paint Baking & Drying

P

PACKAGE DESIGN SVCS
PACKAGED FROZEN FOODS WHOLESALERS, NEC
PACKAGING & LABELING SVCS
PACKAGING MATERIALS, INDL: Wholesalers
PACKAGING MATERIALS, WHOLESALE
PACKAGING MATERIALS: Paper
PACKAGING MATERIALS: Paper, Coated Or Laminated
PACKAGING MATERIALS: Paper, Thermoplastic Coated
PACKAGING MATERIALS: Plastic Film, Coated Or Laminated
PACKAGING MATERIALS: Polystyrene Foam
PACKAGING MATERIALS: Resinous Impregnated Paper
PACKAGING: Blister Or Bubble Formed, Plastic
PACKING & CRATING SVC
PACKING & CRATING SVCS: Containerized Goods For Shipping
PACKING MATERIALS: Mechanical
PACKING: Metallic
PADDING: Foamed Plastics
PADS: Desk, Exc Paper
PADS: Desk, Paper, Made From Purchased Materials
PADS: Mattress
PAGERS: One-way
PAINT STORE
PAINTING SVC: Metal Prdts
PAINTS & ADDITIVES
PAINTS & ALLIED PRODUCTS
PAINTS & VARNISHES: Plastics Based
PAINTS, VARNISHES & SPLYS, WHOLESALE: Paints
PALLET REPAIR SVCS
PALLETS
PALLETS & SKIDS: Wood
PALLETS: Wood & Metal Combination
PALLETS: Wooden
PANEL & DISTRIBUTION BOARDS: Electric
PANELS: Building, Wood
PANELS: Cardboard, Die-Cut, Made From Purchased Materials
PAPER & BOARD: Die-cut
PAPER CONVERTING
PAPER MANUFACTURERS: Exc Newsprint
PAPER PRDTS
PAPER PRDTS: Feminine Hygiene Prdts
PAPER PRDTS: Infant & Baby Prdts
PAPER PRDTS: Napkin Stock
PAPER PRDTS: Napkins, Sanitary, Made From Purchased Material
PAPER PRDTS: Pattern Tissue
PAPER PRDTS: Pressed Pulp Prdts
PAPER PRDTS: Sanitary
PAPER PRDTS: Sanitary Tissue Paper
PAPER PRDTS: Tampons, Sanitary, Made From Purchased Material
PAPER PRDTS: Toilet Paper, Made From Purchased Materials
PAPER PRDTS: Toweling Tissue
PAPER PRDTS: Towels, Napkins/Tissue Paper, From Purchd Mtrls
PAPER, WHOLESALE: Fine
PAPER, WHOLESALE: Printing
PAPER: Absorbent
PAPER: Adding Machine Rolls, Made From Purchased Materials
PAPER: Adhesive
PAPER: Art
PAPER: Bristols
PAPER: Building, Insulating & Packaging
PAPER: Business Form
PAPER: Card
PAPER: Chemically Treated, Made From Purchased Materials
PAPER: Cigarette
PAPER: Cloth, Lined, Made From Purchased Materials
PAPER: Coated & Laminated, NEC

PRODUCT INDEX

PAPER: Coated, Exc Photographic, Carbon Or Abrasive
PAPER: Corrugated
PAPER: Envelope
PAPER: Filter
PAPER: Kraft
PAPER: Parchment
PAPER: Printer
PAPER: Specialty
PAPER: Tissue
PAPER: Wrapping
PAPER: Wrapping & Packaging
PAPER: Writing
PAPERBOARD
PAPERBOARD CONVERTING
PAPERBOARD PRDTS: Building Insulating & Packaging
PAPERBOARD PRDTS: Container Board
PAPERBOARD PRDTS: Folding Boxboard
PAPERBOARD PRDTS: Kraft Linerboard
PAPERBOARD PRDTS: Packaging Board
PAPERBOARD: Boxboard
PAPERBOARD: Liner Board
PAPIER-MACHE PRDTS, EXC STATUARY & ART GOODS
PARACHUTES
PARKING LOTS
PARTITIONS & FIXTURES: Except Wood
PARTITIONS: Nonwood, Floor Attached
PARTITIONS: Solid Fiber, Made From Purchased Materials
PARTITIONS: Wood & Fixtures
PARTITIONS: Wood, Floor Attached
PARTS: Metal
PARTY & SPECIAL EVENT PLANNING SVCS
PASTES, FLAVORING
PATENT OWNERS & LESSORS
PATTERNS: Indl
PAVERS
PAVING MATERIALS: Prefabricated, Concrete
PAVING MIXTURES
PENCILS & PENS WHOLESALERS
PENS & PARTS: Ball Point
PENS & PARTS: Cartridges, Refill, Ball Point
PENS & PENCILS: Mechanical, NEC
PERFUME: Concentrated
PERFUME: Perfumes, Natural Or Synthetic
PERFUMES
PERLITE: Processed
PERSONAL APPEARANCE SVCS
PERSONAL CREDIT INSTITUTIONS: Consumer Finance Companies
PEST CONTROL SVCS
PET ACCESS: Collars, Leashes, Etc, Exc Leather
PET COLLARS, LEASHES, MUZZLES & HARNESSES: Leather
PET SPLYS
PET SPLYS WHOLESALERS
PETROLEUM & PETROLEUM PRDTS, WHOLESALE Engine Fuels & Oils
PETROLEUM & PETROLEUM PRDTS, WHOLESALE Fuel Oil
PETROLEUM & PETROLEUM PRDTS, WHOLESALE: Bulk Stations
PETROLEUM PRDTS WHOLESALERS
PEWTER WARE
PHARMACEUTICAL PREPARATIONS: Adrenal
PHARMACEUTICAL PREPARATIONS: Barbituric Acid
PHARMACEUTICAL PREPARATIONS: Digitalis
PHARMACEUTICAL PREPARATIONS: Druggists' Preparations
PHARMACEUTICAL PREPARATIONS: Medicines, Capsule Or Ampule
PHARMACEUTICAL PREPARATIONS: Penicillin
PHARMACEUTICAL PREPARATIONS: Pills
PHARMACEUTICAL PREPARATIONS: Powders
PHARMACEUTICAL PREPARATIONS: Procaine
PHARMACEUTICAL PREPARATIONS: Proprietary Drug PRDTS
PHARMACEUTICAL PREPARATIONS: Solutions
PHARMACEUTICAL PREPARATIONS: Tablets
PHARMACEUTICALS
PHARMACEUTICALS: Mail-Order Svc
PHARMACEUTICALS: Medicinal & Botanical Prdts
PHARMACIES & DRUG STORES
PHONOGRAPH NEEDLES
PHONOGRAPH RECORDS WHOLESALERS
PHONOGRAPH RECORDS: Prerecorded
PHOSPHATES

PHOTOCOPY MACHINES
PHOTOCOPYING & DUPLICATING SVCS
PHOTOELECTRIC DEVICES: Magnetic
PHOTOENGRAVING SVC
PHOTOFINISHING LABORATORIES
PHOTOGRAPH DEVELOPING & RETOUCHING SVCS
PHOTOGRAPHIC EQPT & SPLY: Sound Recordg/Reprod Eqpt, Motion
PHOTOGRAPHIC EQPT & SPLYS
PHOTOGRAPHIC EQPT & SPLYS WHOLESALERS
PHOTOGRAPHIC EQPT & SPLYS, WHOLESALE: Motion Picture
PHOTOGRAPHIC EQPT & SPLYS: Cameras, Aerial
PHOTOGRAPHIC EQPT & SPLYS: Cameras, Still & Motion Pictures
PHOTOGRAPHIC EQPT & SPLYS: Editing Eqpt, Motion Picture
PHOTOGRAPHIC EQPT & SPLYS: Film, Sensitized
PHOTOGRAPHIC EQPT & SPLYS: Graphic Arts Plates, Sensitized
PHOTOGRAPHIC EQPT & SPLYS: Plates, Sensitized
PHOTOGRAPHIC EQPT & SPLYS: Printing Eqpt
PHOTOGRAPHIC EQPT & SPLYS: Processing Eqpt
PHOTOGRAPHIC EQPT & SPLYS: Shutters, Camera
PHOTOGRAPHIC EQPT & SPLYS: Toners, Prprd, Not Chem Plnts
PHOTOGRAPHIC EQPT/SPLYS, WHOL: Cameras/Projectors/Eqpt/Splys
PHOTOGRAPHIC LIBRARY SVCS
PHOTOGRAPHIC PEOCESSING CHEMICALS
PHOTOGRAPHIC PROCESSING EQPT & CHEMICALS
PHOTOGRAPHIC SENSITIZED GOODS, NEC
PHOTOGRAPHIC SVCS
PHOTOGRAPHY SVCS: Commercial
PHOTOGRAPHY SVCS: Portrait Studios
PHOTOGRAPHY SVCS: Still Or Video
PHOTOTYPESETTING SVC
PHOTOVOLTAIC Solid State
PHYSICAL FITNESS CENTERS
PHYSICIANS' OFFICES & CLINICS: Medical doctors
PICTURE FRAMES: Metal
PICTURE FRAMES: Wood
PICTURE FRAMING SVCS, CUSTOM
PICTURE PROJECTION EQPT
PIECE GOODS & NOTIONS WHOLESALERS
PIECE GOODS, NOTIONS & DRY GOODS, WHOL: Textile Converters
PIECE GOODS, NOTIONS & DRY GOODS, WHOL: Textiles, Woven
PIECE GOODS, NOTIONS & DRY GOODS, WHOLESALE: Fabrics, Knit
PIECE GOODS, NOTIONS & DRY GOODS, WHOLESALE: Fabrics, Lace
PIECE GOODS, NOTIONS & DRY GOODS, WHOLESALE: Sewing Access
PIECE GOODS, NOTIONS & OTHER DRY GOODS, WHOLESALE: Buttons
PIECE GOODS, NOTIONS & OTHER DRY GOODS, WHOLESALE: Fabrics
PIECE GOODS, NOTIONS & OTHER DRY GOODS, WHOLESALE: Woven
PIECE GOODS, NOTIONS/DRY GOODS, WHOL: Drapery Mtrl, Woven
PIECE GOODS, NOTIONS/DRY GOODS, WHOL: Linen Piece, Woven
PIECE GOODS, NOTIONS/DRY GOODS, WHOL: Sewing Splys/Notions
PILLOW FILLING MTRLS: Curled Hair, Cotton Waste, Moss
PILLOWS: Sponge Rubber
PINS
PIPE & FITTING: Fabrication
PIPE & FITTINGS: Cast Iron
PIPE & FITTINGS: Pressure, Cast Iron
PIPE CLEANERS
PIPE JOINT COMPOUNDS
PIPE: Concrete
PIPE: Extruded, Aluminum
PIPE: Plastic
PIPE: Sheet Metal
PIPES & TUBES: Steel
PIPES & TUBES: Welded
PIPES: Steel & Iron
PIPES: Tobacco
PISTONS & PISTON RINGS
PLACEMATS: Plastic Or Textile

PLANING MILLS: Independent, Exc Millwork
PLANING MILLS: Millwork
PLANT CARE SVCS
PLAQUES: Clay, Plaster/Papier-Mache, Factory Production
PLAQUES: Picture, Laminated
PLASMAS
PLASTER WORK: Ornamental & Architectural
PLASTIC COLORING & FINISHING
PLASTIC PRDTS
PLASTIC PRDTS REPAIR SVCS
PLASTICIZERS, ORGANIC: Cyclic & Acyclic
PLASTICS FILM & SHEET
PLASTICS FILM & SHEET: Polyethylene
PLASTICS FILM & SHEET: Polyvinyl
PLASTICS FILM & SHEET: Vinyl
PLASTICS FINISHED PRDTS: Laminated
PLASTICS MATERIAL & RESINS
PLASTICS MATERIALS, BASIC FORMS & SHAPES WHOLESALERS
PLASTICS PROCESSING
PLASTICS SHEET: Packing Materials
PLASTICS: Blow Molded
PLASTICS: Cast
PLASTICS: Extruded
PLASTICS: Finished Injection Molded
PLASTICS: Injection Molded
PLASTICS: Molded
PLASTICS: Polystyrene Foam
PLASTICS: Thermoformed
PLATE WORK: Metalworking Trade
PLATEMAKING SVC: Color Separations, For The Printing Trade
PLATEMAKING SVC: Embossing, For The Printing Trade
PLATEMAKING SVC: Gravure, Plates Or Cylinders
PLATES
PLATES: Paper, Made From Purchased Materials
PLATES: Plastic Exc Polystyrene Foam
PLATES: Truss, Metal
PLATING & FINISHING SVC: Decorative, Formed Prdts
PLATING & POLISHING SVC
PLATING COMPOUNDS
PLATING SVC: Chromium, Metals Or Formed Prdts
PLATING SVC: Electro
PLATING SVC: Gold
PLATING SVC: NEC
PLAYGROUND EQPT
PLEATING & STITCHING FOR THE TRADE: Decorative & Novelty
PLEATING & STITCHING FOR TRADE: Permanent Pleating/Pressing
PLEATING & STITCHING SVC
PLEATING & TUCKING FOR THE TRADE
PLUGS: Electric
PLUMBING & HEATING EQPT & SPLY, WHOL: Htg Eqpt/Panels, Solar
PLUMBING & HEATING EQPT & SPLY, WHOLESALE: Hydronic Htg Eqpt
PLUMBING & HEATING EQPT & SPLYS WHOLESALERS
PLUMBING & HEATING EQPT & SPLYS, WHOL: Plumbing Fitting/Sply
PLUMBING & HEATING EQPT & SPLYS, WHOL: Plumbng/Heatng Valves
PLUMBING & HEATING EQPT & SPLYS, WHOL: Water Purif Eqpt
PLUMBING & HEATING EQPT & SPLYS, WHOLESALE: Boilers, Steam
PLUMBING & HEATING EQPT & SPLYS, WHOLESALE: Brass/Fittings
PLUMBING & HEATING EQPT & SPLYS, WHOLESALE: Sanitary Ware
PLUMBING FIXTURES
PLUMBING FIXTURES: Brass, Incl Drain Cocks, Faucets/Spigots
PLUMBING FIXTURES: Plastic
POINT OF SALE DEVICES
POLISHING SVC: Metals Or Formed Prdts
POLYESTERS
POLYETHYLENE RESINS
POLYTETRAFLUOROETHYLENE RESINS
POLYVINYL CHLORIDE RESINS
POPCORN & SUPPLIES WHOLESALERS
POSTERS
POTTERY: Laboratory & Indl
POULTRY & POULTRY PRDTS WHOLESALERS

PRODUCT INDEX

POULTRY & SMALL GAME SLAUGHTERING & PROCESSING
POULTRY SLAUGHTERING & PROCESSING
POWDER PUFFS & MITTS
POWDER: Aluminum Atomized
POWDER: Metal
POWDER: Silver
POWER GENERATORS
POWER SPLY CONVERTERS: Static, Electronic Applications
POWER SUPPLIES: All Types, Static
POWER SUPPLIES: Transformer, Electronic Type
POWER SWITCHING EQPT
POWER TOOLS, HAND: Grinders, Portable, Electric Or Pneumatic
POWER TOOLS, HAND: Guns, Pneumatic, Chip Removal
POWER TOOLS, HAND: Hammers, Portable, Elec/Pneumatic, Chip
POWER TRANSMISSION EQPT WHOLESALERS
POWER TRANSMISSION EQPT: Aircraft
POWER TRANSMISSION EQPT: Mechanical
PRECAST TERRAZZO OR CONCRETE PRDTS
PRECIOUS METALS
PRECIOUS METALS WHOLESALERS
PRECIOUS STONES & METALS, WHOLESALE
PRECIOUS STONES WHOLESALERS
PRECIPITATORS: Electrostatic
PRERECORDED TAPE, CD & RECORD STORES: Video Discs/Tapes
PRERECORDED TAPE, CD/RECORD STORES: Video Tapes, Prerecorded
PRERECORDED TAPE, COMPACT DISC & RECORD STORES
PRERECORDED TAPE, COMPACT DISC & RECORD STORES: Records
PRESSED FIBER & MOLDED PULP PRDTS, EXC FOOD PRDTS
PRESSES
PRIMARY METAL PRODUCTS
PRINT CARTRIDGES: Laser & Other Computer Printers
PRINTED CIRCUIT BOARDS
PRINTERS & PLOTTERS
PRINTERS' SVCS: Folding, Collating, Etc
PRINTERS: Computer
PRINTERS: Magnetic Ink, Bar Code
PRINTING & BINDING: Book Music
PRINTING & BINDING: Books
PRINTING & BINDING: Pamphlets
PRINTING & EMBOSSING: Plastic Fabric Articles
PRINTING & ENGRAVING: Card, Exc Greeting
PRINTING & ENGRAVING: Financial Notes & Certificates
PRINTING & ENGRAVING: Invitation & Stationery
PRINTING & ENGRAVING: Plateless
PRINTING & ENGRAVING: Poster & Decal
PRINTING & STAMPING: Fabric Articles
PRINTING & WRITING PAPER WHOLESALERS
PRINTING EQPT & SUPPLIES: Illustration & Poster Woodcuts
PRINTING INKS WHOLESALERS
PRINTING MACHINERY
PRINTING MACHINERY, EQPT & SPLYS: Wholesalers
PRINTING TRADES MACHINERY & EQPT REPAIR SVCS
PRINTING, COMMERCIAL Newspapers, NEC
PRINTING, COMMERCIAL: Announcements, NEC
PRINTING, COMMERCIAL: Bags, Plastic, NEC
PRINTING, COMMERCIAL: Business Forms, NEC
PRINTING, COMMERCIAL: Calendars, NEC
PRINTING, COMMERCIAL: Cards, Visiting, Incl Business, NEC
PRINTING, COMMERCIAL: Circulars, NEC
PRINTING, COMMERCIAL: Coupons, NEC
PRINTING, COMMERCIAL: Decals, NEC
PRINTING, COMMERCIAL: Envelopes, NEC
PRINTING, COMMERCIAL: Imprinting
PRINTING, COMMERCIAL: Invitations, NEC
PRINTING, COMMERCIAL: Labels & Seals, NEC
PRINTING, COMMERCIAL: Letterpress & Screen
PRINTING, COMMERCIAL: Literature, Advertising, NEC
PRINTING, COMMERCIAL: Magazines, NEC
PRINTING, COMMERCIAL: Periodicals, NEC
PRINTING, COMMERCIAL: Post Cards, Picture, NEC
PRINTING, COMMERCIAL: Promotional
PRINTING, COMMERCIAL: Publications
PRINTING, COMMERCIAL: Screen
PRINTING, COMMERCIAL: Stamps, Trading, NEC
PRINTING, COMMERCIAL: Stationery, NEC
PRINTING, COMMERCIAL: Tags, NEC
PRINTING, LITHOGRAPHIC: Advertising Posters
PRINTING, LITHOGRAPHIC: Calendars
PRINTING, LITHOGRAPHIC: Color
PRINTING, LITHOGRAPHIC: Decals
PRINTING, LITHOGRAPHIC: Forms & Cards, Business
PRINTING, LITHOGRAPHIC: Forms, Business
PRINTING, LITHOGRAPHIC: Letters, Circular Or Form
PRINTING, LITHOGRAPHIC: Menus
PRINTING, LITHOGRAPHIC: Offset & photolithographic printing
PRINTING, LITHOGRAPHIC: On Metal
PRINTING, LITHOGRAPHIC: Post Cards, Picture
PRINTING, LITHOGRAPHIC: Promotional
PRINTING, LITHOGRAPHIC: Publications
PRINTING, LITHOGRAPHIC: Tags
PRINTING, LITHOGRAPHIC: Tickets
PRINTING, LITHOGRAPHIC: Transfers, Decalcomania Or Dry
PRINTING: Books
PRINTING: Books
PRINTING: Broadwoven Fabrics. Cotton
PRINTING: Checkbooks
PRINTING: Commercial, NEC
PRINTING: Engraving & Plate
PRINTING: Flexographic
PRINTING: Gravure, Business Form & Card
PRINTING: Gravure, Color
PRINTING: Gravure, Forms, Business
PRINTING: Gravure, Imprinting
PRINTING: Gravure, Job
PRINTING: Gravure, Labels
PRINTING: Gravure, Rotogravure
PRINTING: Gravure, Stamps, Trading
PRINTING: Gravure, Stationery
PRINTING: Laser
PRINTING: Letterpress
PRINTING: Lithographic
PRINTING: Offset
PRINTING: Pamphlets
PRINTING: Photo-Offset
PRINTING: Photogravure
PRINTING: Photolithographic
PRINTING: Rotary Photogravure
PRINTING: Rotogravure
PRINTING: Screen, Broadwoven Fabrics, Cotton
PRINTING: Screen, Fabric
PRINTING: Screen, Manmade Fiber & Silk, Broadwoven Fabric
PRINTING: Thermography
PROFESSIONAL EQPT & SPLYS, WHOLESALE: Analytical Instruments
PROFESSIONAL EQPT & SPLYS, WHOLESALE: Engineers', NEC
PROFESSIONAL EQPT & SPLYS, WHOLESALE: Optical Goods
PROFESSIONAL EQPT & SPLYS, WHOLESALE: Scientific & Engineerg
PROFESSIONAL EQPT & SPLYS, WHOLESALE: Theatrical
PROFILE SHAPES: Unsupported Plastics
PROGRAM ADMIN, GOVT: Air, Water & Solid Waste Mgmt, Local
PROMOTION SVCS
PROPERTY DAMAGE INSURANCE
PROTECTION EQPT: Lightning
PROTECTIVE FOOTWEAR: Rubber Or Plastic
PUBLIC RELATIONS & PUBLICITY SVCS
PUBLISHERS: Art Copy
PUBLISHERS: Art Copy & Poster
PUBLISHERS: Atlases
PUBLISHERS: Book
PUBLISHERS: Book Clubs, No Printing
PUBLISHERS: Books, No Printing
PUBLISHERS: Catalogs
PUBLISHERS: Comic Books, No Printing
PUBLISHERS: Directories, NEC
PUBLISHERS: Directories, Telephone
PUBLISHERS: Guides
PUBLISHERS: Magazines, No Printing
PUBLISHERS: Maps
PUBLISHERS: Miscellaneous
PUBLISHERS: Music Book
PUBLISHERS: Music Book & Sheet Music
PUBLISHERS: Music, Book
PUBLISHERS: Music, Sheet
PUBLISHERS: Newsletter
PUBLISHERS: Newspaper
PUBLISHERS: Newspapers, No Printing
PUBLISHERS: Pamphlets, No Printing
PUBLISHERS: Periodical, With Printing
PUBLISHERS: Periodicals, Magazines
PUBLISHERS: Periodicals, No Printing
PUBLISHERS: Posters
PUBLISHERS: Sheet Music
PUBLISHERS: Shopping News
PUBLISHERS: Technical Manuals
PUBLISHERS: Technical Manuals & Papers
PUBLISHERS: Technical Papers
PUBLISHERS: Telephone & Other Directory
PUBLISHERS: Textbooks, No Printing
PUBLISHERS: Trade journals, No Printing
PUBLISHING & BROADCASTING: Internet Only
PUBLISHING & PRINTING: Art Copy
PUBLISHING & PRINTING: Book Clubs
PUBLISHING & PRINTING: Book Music
PUBLISHING & PRINTING: Books
PUBLISHING & PRINTING: Catalogs
PUBLISHING & PRINTING: Comic Books
PUBLISHING & PRINTING: Directories, NEC
PUBLISHING & PRINTING: Guides
PUBLISHING & PRINTING: Magazines: publishing & printing
PUBLISHING & PRINTING: Music, Book
PUBLISHING & PRINTING: Newsletters, Business Svc
PUBLISHING & PRINTING: Newspapers
PUBLISHING & PRINTING: Pamphlets
PUBLISHING & PRINTING: Patterns, Paper
PUBLISHING & PRINTING: Posters
PUBLISHING & PRINTING: Shopping News
PUBLISHING & PRINTING: Technical Manuals
PUBLISHING & PRINTING: Textbooks
PUBLISHING & PRINTING: Trade Journals
PUBLISHING & PRINTING: Yearbooks
PULP MILLS
PULP MILLS: Mech Pulp, Incl Groundwood & Thermomechanical
PULP MILLS: Mechanical & Recycling Processing
PULP MILLS: Soda Pulp
PUMICE
PUMP GOVERNORS: Gas Machines
PUMPS
PUMPS & PARTS: Indl
PUMPS & PUMPING EQPT REPAIR SVCS
PUMPS & PUMPING EQPT WHOLESALERS
PUMPS, HEAT: Electric
PUMPS: Domestic, Water Or Sump
PUMPS: Fluid Power
PUMPS: Measuring & Dispensing
PUMPS: Vacuum, Exc Laboratory
PUNCHES: Forming & Stamping
PURIFICATION & DUST COLLECTION EQPT
PURSES: Women's
PUSHCARTS & WHEELBARROWS

Q

QUICKLIME

R

RACE TRACK OPERATION
RACEWAYS
RACKS & SHELVING: Household, Wood
RACKS: Garment, Exc Wood
RACKS: Garment, Wood
RACKS: Pallet, Exc Wood
RADAR SYSTEMS & EQPT
RADIO & TELEVISION COMMUNICATIONS EQUIPMENT
RADIO & TELEVISION REPAIR
RADIO BROADCASTING & COMMUNICATIONS EQPT
RADIO BROADCASTING STATIONS
RADIO COMMUNICATIONS: Airborne Eqpt
RADIO RECEIVER NETWORKS
RADIO, TELEVISION & CONSUMER ELECTRONICS STORES: Eqpt, NEC
RADIO, TV & CONSUMER ELEC STORES: Automotive Sound Eqpt
RADIO, TV & CONSUMER ELECTRONICS: VCR & Access
RADIO, TV/CONSUMER ELEC STORES: Antennas, Satellite Dish
RAILINGS: Prefabricated, Metal
RAILINGS: Wood
RAILROAD CAR RENTING & LEASING SVCS
RAILROAD CAR REPAIR SVCS

PRODUCT INDEX

RAILROAD CARGO LOADING & UNLOADING SVCS
RAILROAD EQPT
RAILROAD EQPT & SPLYS WHOLESALERS
RAILROAD EQPT, EXC LOCOMOTIVES
RAILROAD EQPT: Brakes, Air & Vacuum
RAILROAD EQPT: Cars & Eqpt, Dining
RAILROAD EQPT: Cars & Eqpt, Rapid Transit
RAILROAD EQPT: Cars, Maintenance
RAILROAD EQPT: Cars, Motor
RAILROAD EQPT: Locomotives & Parts, Indl
RAILROAD RELATED EQPT: Railway Track
RAILS: Steel Or Iron
RAMPS: Prefabricated Metal
RAZORS, RAZOR BLADES
RAZORS: Electric
REAL ESTATE AGENCIES & BROKERS
REAL ESTATE AGENTS & MANAGERS
REAL ESTATE OPERATORS, EXC DEVELOPERS: Apartment Hotel
REAL ESTATE OPERATORS, EXC DEVELOPERS: Commercial/Indl Bldg
RECEIVERS: Radio Communications
RECLAIMED RUBBER: Reworked By Manufacturing Process
RECORD BLANKS: Phonographic
RECORDING HEADS: Speech & Musical Eqpt
RECORDS & TAPES: Prerecorded
RECORDS OR TAPES: Masters
RECOVERY SVC: Iron Ore, From Open Hearth Slag
RECOVERY SVCS: Metal
RECREATIONAL & SPORTING CAMPS
RECTIFIERS: Electrical Apparatus
RECTIFIERS: Solid State
RECYCLABLE SCRAP & WASTE MATERIALS WHOLESALERS
RECYCLING: Paper
REELS: Cable, Metal
REFINERS & SMELTERS: Aluminum
REFINERS & SMELTERS: Antimony, Primary
REFINERS & SMELTERS: Cobalt, Primary
REFINERS & SMELTERS: Copper
REFINERS & SMELTERS: Copper, Secondary
REFINERS & SMELTERS: Gold
REFINERS & SMELTERS: Lead, Secondary
REFINERS & SMELTERS: Nonferrous Metal
REFINERS & SMELTERS: Platinum Group Metal Refining, Primary
REFINERS & SMELTERS: Silicon, Primary, Over 99% Pure
REFINERS & SMELTERS: Silver
REFINERS & SMELTERS: Zinc, Primary, Including Slabs & Dust
REFINING LUBRICATING OILS & GREASES, NEC
REFINING: Petroleum
REFRACTORIES: Alumina Fused
REFRACTORIES: Brick
REFRACTORIES: Brick
REFRACTORIES: Clay
REFRACTORIES: Graphite, Carbon Or Ceramic Bond
REFRACTORIES: Nonclay
REFRACTORY CASTABLES
REFRACTORY MATERIALS WHOLESALERS
REFRIGERATION & HEATING EQUIPMENT
REFRIGERATION EQPT & SPLYS WHOLESALERS
REFRIGERATION EQPT: Complete
REFRIGERATION REPAIR SVCS
REFRIGERATION SVC & REPAIR
REFRIGERATORS & FREEZERS WHOLESALERS
REFUSE SYSTEMS
REGULATORS: Generator Voltage
REGULATORS: Power
REGULATORS: Transmission & Distribution Voltage
REGULATORS: Transmission & Distribution Voltage
RELAYS & SWITCHES: Indl, Electric
RELAYS: Electronic Usage
RELIGIOUS SPLYS WHOLESALERS
REMOVERS & CLEANERS
RENTAL CENTERS: General
RENTAL SVCS: Business Machine & Electronic Eqpt
RENTAL SVCS: Costume
RENTAL SVCS: Electronic Eqpt, Exc Computers
RENTAL SVCS: Eqpt, Theatrical
RENTAL SVCS: Invalid Splys
RENTAL SVCS: Live Plant
RENTAL SVCS: Pallet
RENTAL SVCS: Stores & Yards Eqpt
RENTAL SVCS: Tent & Tarpaulin

RENTAL SVCS: Work Zone Traffic Eqpt, Flags, Cones, Etc
RENTAL: Video Tape & Disc
REPEATERS: Passive
REPRODUCTION SVCS: Video Tape Or Disk
RESEARCH, DEV & TESTING SVCS, COMM: Chem Lab, Exc Testing
RESEARCH, DEVELOPMENT & TEST SVCS, COMM: Business Analysis
RESEARCH, DEVELOPMENT & TEST SVCS, COMM: Cmptr Hardware Dev
RESEARCH, DEVELOPMENT & TEST SVCS, COMM: Research, Exc Lab
RESEARCH, DEVELOPMENT & TESTING SVCS, COMM: Research Lab
RESEARCH, DEVELOPMENT & TESTING SVCS, COMMERCIAL: Medical
RESEARCH, DVLPMT & TESTING SVCS, COMM: Merger, Acq & Reorg
RESEARCH, DVLPT & TEST SVCS, COMM: Mkt Analysis or Research
RESIDENTIAL REMODELERS
RESINS: Custom Compound Purchased
RESISTORS
RESISTORS & RESISTOR UNITS
RESORT HOTELS
RESPIRATORS
RESTAURANT EQPT REPAIR SVCS
RESTAURANT EQPT: Carts
RESTAURANT EQPT: Food Wagons
RESTAURANT EQPT: Sheet Metal
RESTAURANTS:Full Svc, American
RESTAURANTS:Full Svc, Mexican
RESTAURANTS:Full Svc, Seafood
RESTAURANTS:Limited Svc, Coffee Shop
RESTAURANTS:Limited Svc, Ice Cream Stands Or Dairy Bars
RESTAURANTS:Limited Svc, Lunch Counter
RESTAURANTS:Ltd Svc, Ice Cream, Soft Drink/Fountain Stands
RESUME WRITING SVCS
RETAIL BAKERY: Bagels
RETAIL BAKERY: Bread
RETAIL BAKERY: Cookies
RETAIL LUMBER YARDS
RETAIL STORES, NEC
RETAIL STORES: Alarm Signal Systems
RETAIL STORES: Alcoholic Beverage Making Eqpt & Splys
RETAIL STORES: Aquarium Splys
RETAIL STORES: Artificial Limbs
RETAIL STORES: Audio-Visual Eqpt & Splys
RETAIL STORES: Awnings
RETAIL STORES: Cake Decorating Splys
RETAIL STORES: Canvas Prdts
RETAIL STORES: Cleaning Eqpt & Splys
RETAIL STORES: Concrete Prdts, Precast
RETAIL STORES: Cosmetics
RETAIL STORES: Electronic Parts & Eqpt
RETAIL STORES: Engine & Motor Eqpt & Splys
RETAIL STORES: Farm Eqpt & Splys
RETAIL STORES: Fiberglass Materials, Exc Insulation
RETAIL STORES: Fire Extinguishers
RETAIL STORES: Gravestones, Finished
RETAIL STORES: Hearing Aids
RETAIL STORES: Ice
RETAIL STORES: Infant Furnishings & Eqpt
RETAIL STORES: Medical Apparatus & Splys
RETAIL STORES: Mobile Telephones & Eqpt
RETAIL STORES: Monuments, Finished To Custom Order
RETAIL STORES: Motors, Electric
RETAIL STORES: Orthopedic & Prosthesis Applications
RETAIL STORES: Photocopy Machines
RETAIL STORES: Religious Goods
RETAIL STORES: Stones, Crystalline, Rough
RETAIL STORES: Telephone Eqpt & Systems
RETAIL STORES: Tents
RETAIL STORES: Water Purification Eqpt
RETAIL STORES: Welding Splys
REUPHOLSTERY & FURNITURE REPAIR
REUPHOLSTERY SVCS
RIBBONS & BOWS
RIBBONS, NEC
RIBBONS: Machine, Inked Or Carbon
RIDING APPAREL STORES
RIVETS: Metal
ROAD MATERIALS: Bituminous, Not From Refineries

ROBOTS: Assembly Line
ROCK SALT MINING
ROCKET LAUNCHERS
ROCKETS: Space & Military
RODS: Extruded, Aluminum
RODS: Plastic
RODS: Steel & Iron, Made In Steel Mills
RODS: Welding
ROLL COVERINGS: Rubber
ROLL FORMED SHAPES: Custom
ROLLED OR DRAWN SHAPES, NEC: Copper & Copper Alloy
ROLLERS & FITTINGS: Window Shade
ROLLING MILL MACHINERY
ROLLS & BLANKETS, PRINTERS': Rubber Or Rubberized Fabric
ROLLS: Rubber, Solid Or Covered
ROOFING MATERIALS: Asphalt
ROOFING MATERIALS: Sheet Metal
ROPE
ROTORS: Motor
RUBBER
RUBBER PRDTS: Automotive, Mechanical
RUBBER PRDTS: Mechanical
RUBBER PRDTS: Oil & Gas Field Machinery, Mechanical
RUBBER PRDTS: Reclaimed
RUBBER PRDTS: Silicone
RUBBER PRDTS: Sponge
RUBBER PRDTS: Wet Suits
RUBBER STRUCTURES: Air-Supported
RUGS : Hand & Machine Made
RULERS: Metal

S

SAFES & VAULTS: Metal
SAFETY EQPT & SPLYS WHOLESALERS
SAILBOAT BUILDING & REPAIR
SAILS
SALES PROMOTION SVCS
SALT
SALT & SULFUR MINING
SAMPLE BOOKS
SAND & GRAVEL
SAND MINING
SAND: Hygrade
SANDSTONE: Crushed & Broken
SANITARY SVCS: Environmental Cleanup
SANITARY SVCS: Waste Materials, Recycling
SANITARY WARE: Metal
SANITATION CHEMICALS & CLEANING AGENTS
SASHES: Door Or Window, Metal
SATCHELS
SATELLITES: Communications
SAW BLADES
SAWDUST & SHAVINGS
SAWDUST, WHOLESALE
SAWING & PLANING MILLS
SAWING & PLANING MILLS: Custom
SAWS & SAWING EQPT
SCALES & BALANCES, EXC LABORATORY
SCALES: Baby
SCALP TREATMENT SVCS
SCANNING DEVICES: Optical
SCHOOLS & EDUCATIONAL SVCS, NEC
SCIENTIFIC EQPT REPAIR SVCS
SCISSORS: Hand
SCRAP & WASTE MATERIALS, WHOLESALE: Ferrous Metal
SCRAP & WASTE MATERIALS, WHOLESALE: Metal
SCRAP & WASTE MATERIALS, WHOLESALE: Plastics Scrap
SCRAP & WASTE MATERIALS, WHOLESALE: Rags
SCREENS: Projection
SCREENS: Window, Metal
SCREENS: Woven Wire
SCREW MACHINE PRDTS
SCREW MACHINES
SCREWS: Metal
SEALANTS
SEALING COMPOUNDS: Sealing, synthetic rubber or plastic
SEARCH & DETECTION SYSTEMS, EXC RADAR
SEARCH & NAVIGATION SYSTEMS
SEATING: Bleacher, Portable
SECRETARIAL SVCS
SECURITY CONTROL EQPT & SYSTEMS
SECURITY DEVICES
SECURITY EQPT STORES

PRODUCT INDEX

SECURITY PROTECTIVE DEVICES MAINTENANCE & MONITORING SVCS
SECURITY SYSTEMS SERVICES
SEMICONDUCTOR & RELATED DEVICES: Read-Only Memory Or ROM
SEMICONDUCTOR CIRCUIT NETWORKS
SEMICONDUCTOR DEVICES: Wafers
SEMICONDUCTORS & RELATED DEVICES
SENSORS: Temperature For Motor Windings
SENSORS: Temperature, Exc Indl Process
SEPARATORS: Metal Plate
SEPTIC TANKS: Concrete
SEPTIC TANKS: Plastic
SERVICES, NEC
SERVOMOTORS: Electric
SEWAGE & WATER TREATMENT EQPT
SEWAGE TREATMENT SYSTEMS & EQPT
SEWER CLEANING EQPT: Power
SEWING CONTRACTORS
SEWING MACHINES & PARTS: Indl
SEWING, NEEDLEWORK & PIECE GOODS STORE: Needlework Gds/Sply
SEWING, NEEDLEWORK & PIECE GOODS STORES: Sewing & Needlework
SHADES: Lamp & Light, Residential
SHADES: Lamp Or Candle
SHADES: Window
SHAFTS: Flexible
SHALE MINING, COMMON
SHALE: Expanded
SHAPES & PILINGS, STRUCTURAL: Steel
SHEATHING: Paper
SHEET METAL SPECIALTIES, EXC STAMPED
SHEET MUSIC STORES
SHEET MUSIC, WHOLESALE
SHEETING: Laminated Plastic
SHEETS & STRIPS: Aluminum
SHEETS: Fabric, From Purchased Materials
SHELVES & SHELVING: Wood
SHELVING: Office & Store, Exc Wood
SHERARDIZING SVC: Metals Or Metal Prdts
SHIELDS OR ENCLOSURES: Radiator, Sheet Metal
SHIMS: Metal
SHIP BUILDING & REPAIRING: Cargo Vessels
SHIP BUILDING & REPAIRING: Cargo, Commercial
SHIP BUILDING & REPAIRING: Ferryboats
SHIP BUILDING & REPAIRING: Lighthouse Tenders
SHIP BUILDING & REPAIRING: Offshore Sply Boats
SHIP BUILDING & REPAIRING: Rigging, Marine
SHIP BUILDING & REPAIRING: Tankers
SHIPBUILDING & REPAIR
SHIPPING AGENTS
SHOCK ABSORBERS: Indl
SHOE & BOOT ACCESS
SHOE MATERIALS: Counters
SHOE MATERIALS: Plastic
SHOE MATERIALS: Quarters
SHOE MATERIALS: Sole Parts
SHOE MATERIALS: Uppers
SHOE REPAIR SHOP
SHOE STORES
SHOE STORES: Children's
SHOE STORES: Custom
SHOE STORES: Orthopedic
SHOE STORES: Women's
SHOES & BOOTS WHOLESALERS
SHOES: Athletic, Exc Rubber Or Plastic
SHOES: Ballet Slippers
SHOES: Canvas, Rubber Soled
SHOES: Infants' & Children's
SHOES: Men's
SHOES: Men's, Sandals
SHOES: Orthopedic, Men's
SHOES: Orthopedic, Women's
SHOES: Plastic Or Rubber
SHOES: Plastic Or Rubber Soles With Fabric Uppers
SHOES: Rubber Or Rubber Soled Fabric Uppers
SHOES: Women's
SHOES: Women's, Dress
SHOES: Women's, Sandals
SHOPPING CENTERS & MALLS
SHOT PEENING SVC
SHOWCASES & DISPLAY FIXTURES: Office & Store
SHOWER STALLS: Metal
SHOWER STALLS: Plastic & Fiberglass
SIDING & STRUCTURAL MATERIALS: Wood
SIGN LETTERING & PAINTING SVCS
SIGN PAINTING & LETTERING SHOP
SIGNALING APPARATUS: Electric
SIGNALING DEVICES: Sound, Electrical
SIGNALS: Railroad, Electric
SIGNALS: Traffic Control, Electric
SIGNS & ADVERTISING SPECIALTIES
SIGNS & ADVERTISING SPECIALTIES: Artwork, Advertising
SIGNS & ADVERTISING SPECIALTIES: Displays, Paint Process
SIGNS & ADVERTISING SPECIALTIES: Letters For Signs, Metal
SIGNS & ADVERTISING SPECIALTIES: Novelties
SIGNS & ADVERTISING SPECIALTIES: Scoreboards, Electric
SIGNS & ADVERTISING SPECIALTIES: Signs
SIGNS & ADVERTSG SPECIALTIES: Displays/Cutouts Window/Lobby
SIGNS, EXC ELECTRIC, WHOLESALE
SIGNS: Electrical
SIGNS: Neon
SILICA MINING
SILICON & CHROMIUM
SILICON WAFERS: Chemically Doped
SILICONE RESINS
SILICONES
SILK SCREEN DESIGN SVCS
SILVER ORES
SILVER ORES PROCESSING
SILVERSMITHS
SILVERWARE
SILVERWARE & PLATED WARE
SILVERWARE, SILVER PLATED
SIMULATORS: Electronic Countermeasure
SIMULATORS: Flight
SINKS: Vitreous China
SKIN CARE PRDTS: Suntan Lotions & Oils
SKYLIGHTS
SLAB & TILE: Precast Concrete, Floor
SLABS: Steel
SLATE PRDTS
SLATE: Dimension
SLINGS: Rope
SLIP RINGS
SLIPPERS: House
SMOKE DETECTORS
SNOW PLOWING SVCS
SOAPS & DETERGENTS
SOAPS & DETERGENTS: Textile
SOCIAL SERVICES INFORMATION EXCHANGE
SOCIAL SVCS, HANDICAPPED
SOCIAL SVCS: Individual & Family
SOFT DRINKS WHOLESALERS
SOFTWARE PUBLISHERS: Application
SOFTWARE PUBLISHERS: Business & Professional
SOFTWARE PUBLISHERS: Computer Utilities
SOFTWARE PUBLISHERS: Education
SOFTWARE PUBLISHERS: Home Entertainment
SOFTWARE PUBLISHERS: NEC
SOFTWARE PUBLISHERS: Operating Systems
SOFTWARE PUBLISHERS: Publisher's
SOFTWARE PUBLISHERS: Word Processing
SOFTWARE TRAINING, COMPUTER
SOLAR CELLS
SOLAR HEATING EQPT
SOLDERS
SOLVENTS
SONAR SYSTEMS & EQPT
SOUND EQPT: Electric
SOUND EQPT: Underwater
SOUND REPRODUCING EQPT
SPACE VEHICLE EQPT
SPARK PLUGS: Internal Combustion Engines
SPAS
SPEAKER SYSTEMS
SPECIAL EVENTS DECORATION SVCS
SPECIALTY FOOD STORES: Coffee
SPECIALTY FOOD STORES: Health & Dietetic Food
SPECIALTY FOOD STORES: Juices, Fruit Or Vegetable
SPECIALTY FOOD STORES: Tea
SPECIALTY FOOD STORES: Vitamin
SPERM BANK
SPONGES: Plastic
SPOOLS: Fiber, Made From Purchased Materials
SPOOLS: Indl
SPORTING & ATHLETIC GOODS: Bags, Golf
SPORTING & ATHLETIC GOODS: Bowling Pins
SPORTING & ATHLETIC GOODS: Bows, Archery
SPORTING & ATHLETIC GOODS: Boxing Eqpt & Splys, NEC
SPORTING & ATHLETIC GOODS: Camping Eqpt & Splys
SPORTING & ATHLETIC GOODS: Cartridge Belts
SPORTING & ATHLETIC GOODS: Driving Ranges, Golf, Electronic
SPORTING & ATHLETIC GOODS: Dumbbells & Other Weight Eqpt
SPORTING & ATHLETIC GOODS: Fishing Bait, Artificial
SPORTING & ATHLETIC GOODS: Fishing Eqpt
SPORTING & ATHLETIC GOODS: Fishing Tackle, General
SPORTING & ATHLETIC GOODS: Game Calls
SPORTING & ATHLETIC GOODS: Gymnasium Eqpt
SPORTING & ATHLETIC GOODS: Hockey Eqpt & Splys, NEC
SPORTING & ATHLETIC GOODS: Lacrosse Eqpt & Splys, NEC
SPORTING & ATHLETIC GOODS: Pools, Swimming, Exc Plastic
SPORTING & ATHLETIC GOODS: Pools, Swimming, Plastic
SPORTING & ATHLETIC GOODS: Shooting Eqpt & Splys, General
SPORTING & ATHLETIC GOODS: Skateboards
SPORTING & ATHLETIC GOODS: Skates & Parts, Roller
SPORTING & ATHLETIC GOODS: Target Shooting Eqpt
SPORTING & ATHLETIC GOODS: Team Sports Eqpt
SPORTING & ATHLETIC GOODS: Tennis Eqpt & Splys
SPORTING & REC GOODS, WHOLESALE: Camping Eqpt & Splys
SPORTING & RECREATIONAL GOODS & SPLYS WHOLESALERS
SPORTING & RECREATIONAL GOODS, WHOL: Sharpeners, Sporting
SPORTING & RECREATIONAL GOODS, WHOLESALE: Boat Access & Part
SPORTING & RECREATIONAL GOODS, WHOLESALE: Exercise
SPORTING & RECREATIONAL GOODS, WHOLESALE: Fishing
SPORTING & RECREATIONAL GOODS, WHOLESALE: Fishing Tackle
SPORTING & RECREATIONAL GOODS, WHOLESALE: Hot Tubs
SPORTING & RECREATIONAL GOODS, WHOLESALE: Skiing
SPORTING & RECREATIONAL GOODS, WHOLESALE: Watersports
SPORTING GOODS
SPORTING GOODS STORES, NEC
SPORTING GOODS STORES: Camping Eqpt
SPORTING GOODS STORES: Fishing Eqpt
SPORTING GOODS STORES: Playground Eqpt
SPORTING GOODS STORES: Skateboarding Eqpt
SPORTING GOODS STORES: Tennis Goods & Eqpt
SPORTING GOODS: Archery
SPORTING GOODS: Fishing Nets
SPORTING GOODS: Sailboards
SPORTING GOODS: Skin Diving Eqpt
SPORTING GOODS: Surfboards
SPORTING/ATHLETIC GOODS: Gloves, Boxing, Handball, Etc
SPORTS APPAREL STORES
SPORTS PROMOTION SVCS
SPOUTING: Plastic & Fiberglass Reinforced
SPRAYING & DUSTING EQPT
SPRAYING EQPT: Agricultural
SPRAYS: Artificial & Preserved
SPRINGS: Coiled Flat
SPRINGS: Leaf, Automobile, Locomotive, Etc
SPRINGS: Mechanical, Precision
SPRINGS: Precision
SPRINGS: Sash Balances
SPRINGS: Steel
SPRINGS: Wire
SPRINKLING SYSTEMS: Fire Control
STAGE LIGHTING SYSTEMS
STAINLESS STEEL
STAIRCASES & STAIRS, WOOD
STAMPED ART GOODS FOR EMBROIDERING
STAMPING SVC: Book, Gold
STAMPINGS: Automotive
STAMPINGS: Metal
STANDS & RACKS: Engine, Metal

PRODUCT INDEX

STARTERS: Motor
STATIC ELIMINATORS: Ind
STATIONARY & OFFICE SPLYS, WHOLESALE: Blank Books
STATIONARY & OFFICE SPLYS, WHOLESALE: Laser Printer Splys
STATIONARY & OFFICE SPLYS, WHOLESALE: Stationery
STATIONER'S SUNDRIES: Rubber
STATIONERY & OFFICE SPLYS WHOLESALERS
STATIONERY PRDTS
STATIONERY: Made From Purchased Materials
STATUARY & OTHER DECORATIVE PRDTS: Nonmetallic
STATUES: Nonmetal
STEAM SPLY SYSTEMS SVCS INCLUDING GEOTHERMAL
STEAM, HEAT & AIR CONDITIONING DISTRIBUTION SVC
STEEL & ALLOYS: Tool & Die
STEEL FABRICATORS
STEEL MILLS
STEEL, COLD-ROLLED: Sheet Or Strip, From Own Hot-Rolled
STEEL, COLD-ROLLED: Strip NEC, From Purchased Hot-Rolled
STEEL, HOT-ROLLED: Sheet Or Strip
STEEL: Cold-Rolled
STEEL: Galvanized
STEEL: Laminated
STENCIL BOARD: Die-Cut, Made From Purchased Materials
STENCILS
STONE: Cast Concrete
STONE: Crushed & Broken, NEC
STONE: Dimension, NEC
STONE: Quarrying & Processing, Own Stone Prdts
STONEWARE CLAY MINING
STORE FIXTURES, EXC REFRIGERATED: Wholesalers
STORE FIXTURES: Exc Wood
STORE FIXTURES: Wood
STORE FRONTS: Prefabricated, Metal
STORE FRONTS: Prefabricated, Wood
STRAPPING
STRAPS: Bindings, Textile
STRAPS: Braids, Textile
STRAPS: Cotton Webbing
STRAWS: Drinking, Made From Purchased Materials
STRINGING BEADS
STRUCTURAL SUPPORT & BUILDING MATERIAL: Concrete
STUDIOS: Artist's
STUDIOS: Sculptor's
STUDS & JOISTS: Sheet Metal
SUBSCRIPTION FULFILLMENT SVCS: Magazine, Newspaper, Etc
SUGAR SUBSTITUTES: Organic
SUNDRIES & RELATED PRDTS: Medical & Laboratory, Rubber
SUNROOMS: Prefabricated Metal
SUPERMARKETS & OTHER GROCERY STORES
SURFACE ACTIVE AGENTS
SURFACE ACTIVE AGENTS: Oils & Greases
SURGICAL & MEDICAL INSTRUMENTS WHOLESALERS
SURGICAL APPLIANCES & SPLYS
SURGICAL APPLIANCES & SPLYS
SURGICAL EQPT: See Also Instruments
SURGICAL IMPLANTS
SURVEYING SVCS: Aerial Digital Imaging
SVC ESTABLISHMENT EQPT & SPLYS WHOLESALERS
SVC ESTABLISHMENT EQPT, WHOL: Cleaning & Maint Eqpt & Splys
SVC ESTABLISHMENT EQPT, WHOLESALE: Beauty Parlor Eqpt & Sply
SVC ESTABLISHMENT EQPT, WHOLESALE: Firefighting Eqpt
SVC ESTABLISHMENT EQPT, WHOLESALE: Laundry Eqpt & Splys
SWEEPING COMPOUNDS
SWIMMING POOL ACCESS: Leaf Skimmers Or Pool Rakes
SWIMMING POOL EQPT: Filters & Water Conditioning Systems
SWIMMING POOL SPLY STORES
SWIMMING POOLS, EQPT & SPLYS: Wholesalers
SWITCHBOARDS & PARTS: Power
SWITCHES
SWITCHES: Electric Power
SWITCHES: Electric Power, Exc Snap, Push Button, Etc
SWITCHES: Electronic
SWITCHES: Electronic Applications
SWITCHES: Silicon Control
SWITCHES: Starting, Fluorescent
SWITCHES: Time, Electrical Switchgear Apparatus
SWITCHGEAR & SWITCHBOARD APPARATUS
SWITCHGEAR & SWITCHGEAR ACCESS, NEC
SWORDS
SYNTHETIC RESIN FINISHED PRDTS, NEC
SYRUPS, DRINK
SYRUPS, FLAVORING, EXC DRINK
SYSTEMS INTEGRATION SVCS
SYSTEMS INTEGRATION SVCS: Local Area Network
SYSTEMS SOFTWARE DEVELOPMENT SVCS

T

TABLE OR COUNTERTOPS, PLASTIC LAMINATED
TABLECLOTHS & SETTINGS
TABLES: Lift, Hydraulic
TABLETS & PADS: Book & Writing, Made From Purchased Material
TABLEWARE OR KITCHEN ARTICLES: Commercial, Fine Earthenware
TABLEWARE: Plastic
TAGS & LABELS: Paper
TAGS: Paper, Blank, Made From Purchased Paper
TAILORS: Custom
TALLOW: Animal
TANK REPAIR SVCS
TANK TOWERS: Metal Plate
TANKS & OTHER TRACKED VEHICLE CMPNTS
TANKS: Concrete
TANKS: Cryogenic, Metal
TANKS: Fuel, Including Oil & Gas, Metal Plate
TANKS: Lined, Metal
TANKS: Plastic & Fiberglass
TANKS: Standard Or Custom Fabricated, Metal Plate
TANKS: Storage, Farm, Metal Plate
TANKS: Water, Metal Plate
TANKS: Wood
TANNERIES: Leather
TAPE DRIVES
TAPES, ADHESIVE: MedicaL
TAPES: Audio Range, Blank
TAPES: Coated Fiberglass, Pipe Sealing Or Insulating
TAPES: Gummed, Cloth Or Paper Based, From Purchased Matls
TAPES: Magnetic
TAPES: Pressure Sensitive
TARGET DRONES
TARPAULINS
TELECOMMUNICATION SYSTEMS & EQPT
TELECOMMUNICATIONS CARRIERS & SVCS: Wired
TELEMARKETING BUREAUS
TELEMETERING EQPT
TELEPHONE ANSWERING SVCS
TELEPHONE BOOTHS, EXC WOOD
TELEPHONE EQPT INSTALLATION
TELEPHONE EQPT: Modems
TELEPHONE EQPT: NEC
TELEPHONE SVCS
TELEPHONE SWITCHING EQPT
TELEPHONE: Fiber Optic Systems
TELEPHONE: Headsets
TELEPHONE: Sets, Exc Cellular Radio
TELEVISION BROADCASTING & COMMUNICATIONS EQPT
TELEVISION BROADCASTING STATIONS
TELEVISION SETS
TELEVISION: Closed Circuit Eqpt
TEMPERING: Metal
TENT REPAIR SHOP
TENTS: All Materials
TERMINAL BOARDS
TERRA COTTA: Architectural
TEST KITS: Pregnancy
TESTERS: Battery
TESTERS: Environmental
TESTERS: Integrated Circuit
TESTERS: Physical Property
TESTERS: Water, Exc Indl Process
TEXTILE & APPAREL SVCS
TEXTILE BAGS WHOLESALERS
TEXTILE CONVERTERS: Knit Goods
TEXTILE FABRICATORS
TEXTILE FINISH: Chem Coat/Treat, Fire Resist, Manmade
TEXTILE FINISHING: Chemical Coating Or Treating
TEXTILE FINISHING: Decorative, Man Fiber & Silk, Broadwoven
TEXTILE FINISHING: Dyeing, Broadwoven, Cotton
TEXTILE FINISHING: Dyeing, Finishing & Printng, Linen Fabric
TEXTILE FINISHING: Dyeing, Manmade Fiber & Silk, Broadwoven
TEXTILE FINISHING: Embossing, Cotton, Broadwoven
TEXTILE FINISHING: Embossing, Man Fiber & Silk, Broadwoven
TEXTILE FINISHING: Silk, Broadwoven
TEXTILE FINISHING: Sponging, Cotton, Broadwoven, Trade
TEXTILE PRDTS: Hand Woven & Crocheted
TEXTILE: Finishing, Cotton Broadwoven
TEXTILE: Finishing, Raw Stock NEC
TEXTILE: Goods, NEC
TEXTILES
TEXTILES: Bagging, Jute
TEXTILES: Fibers, Textile, Rcvrd From Mill Waste/Rags
TEXTILES: Flock
TEXTILES: Linen Fabrics
TEXTILES: Mill Waste & Remnant
TEXTILES: Tops & Top Processing, Manmade Or Other Fiber
THEATRICAL LIGHTING SVCS
THEATRICAL PRODUCERS & SVCS
THEATRICAL SCENERY
THERMOMETERS: Indl
THERMOMETERS: Liquid-In-Glass & Bimetal
THERMOMETERS: Medical, Digital
THERMOPLASTIC MATERIALS
THERMOPLASTICS
THERMOSETTING MATERIALS
THIN FILM CIRCUITS
THREAD: All Fibers
THREAD: Embroidery
TICKET OFFICES & AGENCIES: Theatrical
TIES, FORM: Metal
TILE: Asphalt, Floor
TILE: Brick & Structural, Clay
TILE: Drain, Clay
TILE: Fireproofing, Clay
TILE: Mosaic, Ceramic
TILE: Stamped Metal, Floor Or Wall
TILE: Terrazzo Or Concrete, Precast
TILE: Wall & Floor, Ceramic
TILE: Wall & Floor, clay
TIMBER PRDTS WHOLESALERS
TIMING DEVICES: Electronic
TIN
TIRE & INNER TUBE MATERIALS & RELATED PRDTS
TIRE & TUBE REPAIR MATERIALS, WHOLESALE
TIRE CORD & FABRIC
TIRE INFLATORS: Hand Or Compressor Operated
TIRES & INNER TUBES
TIRES: Auto
TITANIUM MILL PRDTS
TOBACCO LEAF PROCESSING
TOBACCO: Chewing
TOBACCO: Chewing & Snuff
TOBACCO: Cigarettes
TOBACCO: Cigars
TOBACCO: Smoking
TOILET FIXTURES: Plastic
TOILET PREPARATIONS
TOILETRIES, COSMETICS & PERFUME STORES
TOILETRIES, WHOLESALE: Hair Preparations
TOILETRIES, WHOLESALE: Perfumes
TOILETRIES, WHOLESALE: Toilet Preparations
TOILETRIES, WHOLESALE: Toiletries
TOMBSTONES: Terrazzo Or Concrete, Precast
TOOL & DIE STEEL
TOOLS: Carpenters', Including Levels & Chisels, Exc Saws
TOOLS: Hand
TOOLS: Hand, Engravers'
TOOLS: Hand, Jewelers'
TOOLS: Hand, Mechanics
TOOLS: Hand, Plumbers'
TOOLS: Hand, Power
TOOTHBRUSHES: Electric
TOOTHBRUSHES: Exc Electric
TOOTHPASTES, GELS & TOOTHPOWDERS
TOWELS: Indl
TOWELS: Linen & Linen & Cotton Mixtures
TOWERS, SECTIONS: Transmission, Radio & Television
TOYS
TOYS & HOBBY GOODS & SPLYS, WHOLESALE: Arts/Crafts Eqpt/Sply

PRODUCT INDEX

TOYS & HOBBY GOODS & SPLYS, WHOLESALE: Balloons, Novelty
TOYS & HOBBY GOODS & SPLYS, WHOLESALE: Educational Toys
TOYS & HOBBY GOODS & SPLYS, WHOLESALE: Toys & Games
TOYS & HOBBY GOODS & SPLYS, WHOLESALE: Toys, NEC
TOYS & HOBBY GOODS & SPLYS, WHOLESALE: Video Games
TOYS, HOBBY GOODS & SPLYS WHOLESALERS
TOYS: Dolls, Stuffed Animals & Parts
TOYS: Electronic
TOYS: Video Game Machines
TRADE SHOW ARRANGEMENT SVCS
TRADERS: Commodity, Contracts
TRAILERS & PARTS: Boat
TRAILERS & PARTS: Truck & Semi's
TRAILERS & TRAILER EQPT
TRAILERS: Semitrailers, Truck Tractors
TRANSDUCERS: Electrical Properties
TRANSDUCERS: Pressure
TRANSFORMERS: Control
TRANSFORMERS: Distribution
TRANSFORMERS: Distribution, Electric
TRANSFORMERS: Electric
TRANSFORMERS: Electronic
TRANSFORMERS: Ignition, Domestic Fuel Burners
TRANSFORMERS: Power Related
TRANSFORMERS: Signaling Transformers, Electric
TRANSFORMERS: Specialty
TRANSLATION & INTERPRETATION SVCS
TRANSMISSIONS: Motor Vehicle
TRANSPORTATION EQPT & SPLYS, WHOLESALE: Acft/Space Vehicle
TRANSPORTATION EQPT & SPLYS WHOLESALERS, NEC
TRANSPORTATION EQUIPMENT, NEC
TRANSPORTATION: Local Passenger, NEC
TRAP ROCK: Crushed & Broken
TRAPS: Animal & Fish, Wire
TRAPS: Stem
TRAVEL AGENCIES
TRAVEL TRAILERS & CAMPERS
TRAYS: Cable, Metal Plate
TRAYS: Plastic
TROPHIES, NEC
TROPHIES, PEWTER
TROPHIES, PLATED, ALL METALS
TROPHIES, SILVER
TROPHIES: Metal, Exc Silver
TROPHY & PLAQUE STORES
TRUCK & BUS BODIES: Ambulance
TRUCK & BUS BODIES: Motor Vehicle, Specialty
TRUCK & BUS BODIES: Truck, Motor Vehicle
TRUCK BODIES: Body Parts
TRUCK GENERAL REPAIR SVC
TRUCK PAINTING & LETTERING SVCS
TRUCK PARTS & ACCESSORIES: Wholesalers
TRUCKING & HAULING SVCS: Garbage, Collect/Transport Only
TRUCKING, DUMP
TRUCKING: Except Local
TRUCKING: Local, Without Storage
TRUCKS & TRACTORS: Industrial
TRUCKS: Forklift
TRUCKS: Indl
TRUNKS
TRUSSES: Wood, Roof
TUBE & TUBING FABRICATORS
TUBES: Finned, For Heat Transfer
TUBES: Generator, Electron Beam, Beta Ray
TUBES: Paper
TUBES: Paper Or Fiber, Chemical Or Electrical Uses
TUBES: Steel & Iron
TUBES: Vacuum
TUBES: Wrought, Welded Or Lock Joint
TUBING: Flexible, Metallic
TUBING: Glass
TUBING: Plastic
TUBING: Seamless
TUNGSTEN CARBIDE
TUNGSTEN CARBIDE POWDER
TURBINE GENERATOR SET UNITS: Hydraulic, Complete
TURBINES & TURBINE GENERATOR SET UNITS: Gas, Complete
TURBINES & TURBINE GENERATOR SETS
TURBINES & TURBINE GENERATOR SETS & PARTS
TURBINES: Hydraulic, Complete
TURBINES: Steam
TURBO-GENERATORS
TYPESETTING SVC
TYPESETTING SVC: Computer
TYPOGRAPHY

U

ULTRASONIC EQPT: Cleaning, Exc Med & Dental
UMBRELLAS & CANES
UMBRELLAS: Garden Or Wagon
UNIFORM STORES
UNIVERSITY
UNSUPPORTED PLASTICS: Floor Or Wall Covering
UPHOLSTERY FILLING MATERIALS
UPHOLSTERY MATERIALS, BROADWOVEN
UPHOLSTERY WORK SVCS
URANIUM ORE MINING, NEC
USED CAR DEALERS
USED MERCHANDISE STORES: Building Materials
USED MERCHANDISE STORES: Rare Books
UTENSILS: Cast Aluminum, Cooking Or Kitchen
UTENSILS: Household, Cooking & Kitchen, Metal
UTENSILS: Household, Cooking & Kitchen, Porcelain Enameled
UTENSILS: Household, Metal, Exc Cast
UTENSILS: Household, Porcelain Enameled
UTILITY TRAILER DEALERS

V

VACUUM CLEANER STORES
VACUUM CLEANERS: Household
VACUUM CLEANERS: Indl Type
VACUUM SYSTEMS: Air Extraction, Indl
VALUE-ADDED RESELLERS: Computer Systems
VALVES
VALVES & PIPE FITTINGS
VALVES & REGULATORS: Pressure, Indl
VALVES: Aerosol, Metal
VALVES: Aircraft
VALVES: Aircraft, Control, Hydraulic & Pneumatic
VALVES: Aircraft, Fluid Power
VALVES: Control, Automatic
VALVES: Electrohydraulic Servo, Metal
VALVES: Fluid Power, Control, Hydraulic & pneumatic
VALVES: Gas Cylinder, Compressed
VALVES: Hard Rubber
VALVES: Indl
VALVES: Plumbing & Heating
VALVES: Regulating & Control, Automatic
VALVES: Water Works
VARNISHES, NEC
VEGETABLE STANDS OR MARKETS
VEHICLES: All Terrain
VEHICLES: Recreational
VENDING MACHINES & PARTS
VENTILATING EQPT: Metal
VENTILATING EQPT: Sheet Metal
VENTURE CAPITAL COMPANIES
VETERINARY PHARMACEUTICAL PREPARATIONS
VIBRATORS: Concrete Construction
VIDEO & AUDIO EQPT, WHOLESALE
VIDEO CAMERA-AUDIO RECORDERS: Household Use
VIDEO EQPT
VIDEO PRODUCTION SVCS
VIDEO REPAIR SVCS
VIDEO TAPE PRODUCTION SVCS
VINYL RESINS, NEC
VISUAL COMMUNICATIONS SYSTEMS
VITAMINS: Natural Or Synthetic, Uncompounded, Bulk
VITAMINS: Pharmaceutical Preparations

W

WALL COVERINGS WHOLESALERS
WALLBOARD: Decorated, Made From Purchased Materials
WALLPAPER & WALL COVERINGS
WALLS: Curtain, Metal
WAREHOUSE CLUBS STORES
WAREHOUSING & STORAGE FACILITIES, NEC
WAREHOUSING & STORAGE, REFRIGERATED: Frozen Or Refrig Goods
WAREHOUSING & STORAGE: General
WAREHOUSING & STORAGE: General
WAREHOUSING & STORAGE: Refrigerated
WARM AIR HEATING & AC EQPT & SPLYS, WHOLESALE Air Filters
WARM AIR HEATING/AC EQPT/SPLYS, WHOL Dehumidifiers, Exc Port
WARM AIR HEATING/AC EQPT/SPLYS, WHOL: Ventilating Eqpt/Sply
WASHCLOTHS
WASHERS: Metal
WASHERS: Plastic
WATCH STRAPS, EXC METAL
WATCHCASES
WATCHES
WATCHES & PARTS, WHOLESALE
WATER PURIFICATION EQPT: Household
WATER SUPPLY
WATER TREATMENT EQPT: Indl
WATER: Mineral, Carbonated, Canned & Bottled, Etc
WATER: Pasteurized & Mineral, Bottled & Canned
WATER: Pasteurized, Canned & Bottled, Etc
WATERPROOFING COMPOUNDS
WAVEGUIDES & FITTINGS
WAXES: Mineral, Natural
WAXES: Paraffin
WAXES: Petroleum, Not Produced In Petroleum Refineries
WEATHER STRIPS: Metal
WEAVING MILL, BROADWOVEN FABRICS: Wool Or Similar Fabric
WEDDING CHAPEL: Privately Operated
WEIGHING MACHINERY & APPARATUS
WELDING & CUTTING APPARATUS & ACCESS, NEC
WELDING EQPT
WELDING EQPT & SPLYS WHOLESALERS
WELDING EQPT: Electrical
WELDING MACHINES & EQPT: Ultrasonic
WELDING REPAIR SVC
WELDING SPLYS, EXC GASES: Wholesalers
WELDING TIPS: Heat Resistant, Metal
WELDMENTS
WHEELBARROWS
WHEELCHAIR LIFTS
WHEELCHAIRS
WHEELS & PARTS
WHEELS: Abrasive
WHEELS: Buffing & Polishing
WHEELS: Iron & Steel, Locomotive & Car
WIGS & HAIRPIECES
WIND TUNNELS
WINDINGS: Coil, Electronic
WINDMILLS: Electric Power Generation
WINDOW & DOOR FRAMES
WINDOW BLIND REPAIR SVCS
WINDOW FRAMES & SASHES: Plastic
WINDOW FRAMES, MOLDING & TRIM: Vinyl
WINDOW TRIMMING SVCS
WINDOWS: Wood
WINE & DISTILLED ALCOHOLIC BEVERAGES WHOLESALERS
WINE CELLARS, BONDED: Wine, Blended
WIRE
WIRE & CABLE: Aluminum
WIRE & WIRE PRDTS
WIRE CLOTH & WOVEN WIRE PRDTS, MADE FROM PURCHASED WIRE
WIRE FABRIC: Welded Steel
WIRE FENCING & ACCESS WHOLESALERS
WIRE MATERIALS: Copper
WIRE MATERIALS: Steel
WIRE PRDTS: Ferrous Or Iron, Made In Wiredrawing Plants
WIRE PRDTS: Steel & Iron
WIRE WHOLESALERS
WIRE: Barbed
WIRE: Barbed & Twisted
WIRE: Communication
WIRE: Mesh
WIRE: Nonferrous
WIRE: Nonferrous, Appliance Fixture
WIRE: Steel, Insulated Or Armored
WOMEN'S & CHILDREN'S CLOTHING WHOLESALERS, NEC
WOMEN'S & GIRLS' SPORTSWEAR WHOLESALERS
WOMEN'S CLOTHING STORES
WOMEN'S CLOTHING STORES: Ready-To-Wear
WOMEN'S SPECIALTY CLOTHING STORES

PRODUCT INDEX

WOMEN'S SPORTSWEAR STORES
WOOD FENCING WHOLESALERS
WOOD PRDTS: Beekeeping Splys
WOOD PRDTS: Clothespins
WOOD PRDTS: Display Forms, Boot & Shoe
WOOD PRDTS: Engraved
WOOD PRDTS: Furniture Inlays, Veneers
WOOD PRDTS: Jalousies, Glass, Wood Framed
WOOD PRDTS: Ladders & Stepladders
WOOD PRDTS: Laundry
WOOD PRDTS: Moldings, Unfinished & Prefinished
WOOD PRDTS: Mulch Or Sawdust
WOOD PRDTS: Novelties, Fiber
WOOD PRDTS: Outdoor, Structural
WOOD PRDTS: Panel Work
WOOD PRDTS: Pedestals & Statuary
WOOD PRDTS: Rulers & Rules
WOOD PRDTS: Shavings & Packaging, Excelsior
WOOD PRDTS: Shoe Trees
WOOD PRDTS: Signboards
WOOD PRDTS: Silo Staves
WOOD PRDTS: Survey Stakes
WOOD PRDTS: Trellises
WOOD PRDTS: Trophy Bases
WOOD PRDTS: Window Backs, Store Or Lunchroom, Prefabricated
WOOD PRDTS: Yard Sticks
WOOD PRODUCTS: Reconstituted
WOOD TREATING: Creosoting
WOOD TREATING: Flooring, Block
WOOD TREATING: Structural Lumber & Timber
WOODWORK & TRIM: Interior & Ornamental
WOODWORK: Carved & Turned
WOODWORK: Interior & Ornamental, NEC
WOVEN WIRE PRDTS, NEC
WRITING FOR PUBLICATION SVCS

X

X-RAY EQPT & TUBES

Y

YARN & YARN SPINNING
YARN MILLS: Twisting
YARN WHOLESALERS
YARN: Embroidery, Spun
YARN: Natural & Animal Fiber, Spun
YARN: Specialty & Novelty
YARN: Weaving, Twisting, Winding Or Spooling
YOGURT WHOLESALERS

PRODUCT SECTION

Product category — **BOXES: Folding**
Edgar & Son Paperboard ....G....... 999 999-9999
Yourtown *(G-11480)*
Ready Box Co ....E....... 999 999-9999
Anytown *(G-7097)*

City

Indicates approximate employment figure
A = Over 500 employees, B = 251-500
C = 101-250, D = 51-100, E = 20-50
F = 10-19, G = 5-9

Business phone

Geographic Section entry number where full company information appears.

See footnotes for symbols and codes identification.
• Refer to the Industrial Product Index preceding this section to locate product headings.

ABRASIVES

American Douglas Metals Inc ....F....... 716 856-3170
Buffalo *(G-2695)*
Buffalo Abrasives Inc ....E....... 716 693-3856
North Tonawanda *(G-12419)*
Dedeco International Sales Inc ......E....... 845 887-4840
Long Eddy *(G-7361)*
Dico Products Corporation ....F....... 315 797-0470
Utica *(G-15694)*
Electro Abrasives LLC ....E....... 716 822-2500
Buffalo *(G-2814)*
Imerys Fsed Mnrl Ngara FLS Inc ......G....... 716 286-1250
Niagara Falls *(G-12296)*
Imerys Fsed Mnrl Ngara FLS Inc ......E....... 716 286-1250
Niagara Falls *(G-12297)*
Meloon Foundries LLC ....E....... 315 454-3231
Syracuse *(G-15369)*
Niabraze LLC ....F....... 716 447-1082
Tonawanda *(G-15562)*
Precision Elctro Mnrl Pmco Inc ......E....... 716 284-2484
Niagara Falls *(G-12326)*
Saint-Gbain Advnced Crmics LLC ....E....... 716 691-2000
Amherst *(G-249)*
Saint-Gobain Abrasives Inc ....B....... 518 266-2200
Watervliet *(G-16049)*
Select-Tech Inc ....G....... 845 895-8111
Wallkill *(G-15908)*
Uneeda Enterprizes Inc ....C....... 800 431-2494
Spring Valley *(G-15011)*
Warren Cutlery Corp ....F....... 845 876-3444
Rhinebeck *(G-13490)*

ABRASIVES: Aluminum Oxide Fused

Washington Mills Tonawanda Inc ....E....... 716 693-4550
Tonawanda *(G-15590)*

ABRASIVES: Coated

Barton Mines Company LLC ....C....... 518 798-5462
Glens Falls *(G-5418)*
Brick-It Inc ....G....... 631 244-3993
Hauppauge *(G-5783)*
Conrad Blasius Equipment Co ......G....... 516 753-1200
Plainview *(G-13044)*
Global Abrasive Products Inc ....E....... 716 438-0047
Lockport *(G-7303)*
Precision Abrasives Corp ....E....... 716 826-5833
Orchard Park *(G-12738)*

ABRASIVES: Grains

EAC Holdings of NY Corp ....E....... 716 822-2500
Buffalo *(G-2808)*
Sunbelt Industries Inc ....F....... 315 823-2947
Little Falls *(G-7214)*
Washington Mills Elec Mnrls ....D....... 716 278-6600
Niagara Falls *(G-12349)*

ACADEMIC TUTORING SVCS

Bright Kids Nyc Inc ....E....... 917 539-4575
New York *(G-9140)*

ACCELERATION INDICATORS & SYSTEM COMPONENTS: Aerospace

Aeroflex Incorporated ....B....... 516 694-6700
Plainview *(G-13032)*
Arsenal Holdings LLC ....G....... 212 398-9139
New York *(G-8912)*
Cobham Holdings (us) Inc ....A....... 716 662-0006
Orchard Park *(G-12707)*
Cobham Holdings Inc ....E....... 716 662-0006
Orchard Park *(G-12708)*
Ihi Inc ....E....... 212 599-8100
New York *(G-10179)*
Inertia Switch Inc ....E....... 845 359-8300
Orangeburg *(G-12679)*
Woodbine Products Inc ....E....... 631 586-3770
Hauppauge *(G-5977)*

ACCELERATORS: Electron Linear

Iba Industrial Inc ....E....... 631 254-6800
Edgewood *(G-4403)*

ACCOUNTING MACHINES & CASH REGISTERS

Logic Controls Inc ....E....... 516 248-0400
Bethpage *(G-845)*

ACID RESIST: Etching

Greenfield Manufacturing Inc ....E....... 518 581-2368
Saratoga Springs *(G-14584)*

ACIDS

Evans Chemetics LP ....D....... 315 539-9221
Waterloo *(G-15991)*

ACIDS: Sulfuric, Oleum

Norfalco LLC ....F....... 416 775-1431
New York *(G-10989)*

ACOUSTICAL BOARD & TILE

Lencore Acoustics Corp ....F....... 315 384-9114
Norfolk *(G-12358)*
Mecho Systems ....F....... 718 729-8373
Long Island City *(G-7519)*
Ssf Production LLC ....F....... 518 324-3407
Plattsburgh *(G-13156)*

ACRYLIC RESINS

Creations In Lucite Inc ....G....... 718 871-2000
Brooklyn *(G-1727)*

ACTUATORS: Indl, NEC

Makerbot Industries LLC ....C....... 347 334-6800
Brooklyn *(G-2153)*
Marine & Indus Hydraulics Inc ......F....... 914 698-2036
Mamaroneck *(G-7747)*
Rotork Controls Inc ....F....... 585 328-1550
Rochester *(G-14104)*
Rotork Controls Inc ....C....... 585 247-2304
Rochester *(G-14105)*
Trident Valve Actuator Co ....F....... 914 698-2650
Mamaroneck *(G-7759)*
Young & Franklin Inc ....D....... 315 457-3110
Liverpool *(G-7274)*

ADDITIVE BASED PLASTIC MATERIALS: Plasticizers

Bamberger Polymers Intl Corp ......F....... 516 622-3600
Jericho *(G-6780)*
Dewitt Plastics Inc ....F....... 315 255-1209
Auburn *(G-476)*
Fougera Pharmaceuticals Inc ....C....... 631 454-7677
Melville *(G-8026)*
Mitsui Chemicals America Inc ......E....... 914 253-0777
Rye Brook *(G-14493)*

ADHESIVES

Adirondack Spclty Adhsives Inc ....F....... 518 869-5736
Albany *(G-29)*
Aremco Products Inc ....F....... 845 268-0039
Valley Cottage *(G-15752)*
Beacon Adhesives Inc ....E....... 914 699-3400
Mount Vernon *(G-8381)*
Best Adhesives Company Inc ....G....... 718 417-3800
Ridgewood *(G-13531)*
PPG Architectural Finishes Inc ......E....... 585 271-1363
Rochester *(G-14030)*
Ran Mar Enterprises Ltd ....F....... 631 666-4754
Bay Shore *(G-713)*
Saint Gobain Grains & Powders ....A....... 716 731-8200
Niagara Falls *(G-12332)*
Web-Cote Industries ....E....... 914 630-1600
Larchmont *(G-7060)*

ADHESIVES & SEALANTS

Able National Corp ....E....... 718 386-8801
Brooklyn *(G-1471)*
Advanced Polymer Solutions LLC ....G....... 516 621-5800
Port Washington *(G-13240)*
All Out Die Cutting Inc ....E....... 718 346-6666
Brooklyn *(G-1508)*
Angiotech Biocoatings Corp ....E....... 585 321-1130
Henrietta *(G-6030)*
Astro Chemical Company Inc ....E....... 518 399-5338
Ballston Lake *(G-565)*
Classic Labels Inc ....E....... 631 467-2300
Patchogue *(G-12863)*
Hexion Inc ....E....... 518 792-8040
South Glens Falls *(G-14936)*
Legacy USA LLC ....F....... 718 292-5333
Bronx *(G-1315)*
Meridian Adhesives Group LLC ......G....... 212 771-1717
New York *(G-10774)*
P C I Paper Conversions Inc ....D....... 315 703-8300
Syracuse *(G-15390)*
P C I Paper Conversions Inc ....E....... 315 634-3317
Syracuse *(G-15391)*
Polycast Industries Inc ....G....... 631 595-2530
Bay Shore *(G-708)*
Polyset Company Inc ....E....... 518 664-6000
Mechanicville *(G-7932)*
Royal Adhesives & Sealants LLC ....F....... 315 451-1755
Syracuse *(G-15411)*
Utility Manufacturing Co Inc ....E....... 516 997-6300
Westbury *(G-16384)*
Wild Works Incorporated ....G....... 716 891-4197
Albany *(G-142)*

ADHESIVES & SEALANTS WHOLESALERS

Nyi Building Products Inc ....F....... 518 458-7500
Clifton Park *(G-3572)*

ADHESIVES: Epoxy

US Epoxy Inc ....G....... 800 332-3883
Yaphank *(G-16726)*

ADVERTISING AGENCIES

Act Communications Group Inc ....F....... 631 669-2403
West Islip *(G-16257)*
Ad Makers Long Island Inc ....F....... 631 595-9100
Deer Park *(G-3933)*
Gatehouse Media LLC ....B....... 585 598-0030
Pittsford *(G-13013)*
Gruner + Jahr Prtg & Pubg Co ......C....... 212 463-1000
New York *(G-10000)*

ADVERTISING AGENCIES

Kinaneco Inc	E	315 468-6201
Syracuse *(G-15356)*		
Luria Communications Inc	G	631 329-4922
East Hampton *(G-4240)*		
Media Trust LLC	G	212 802-1162
New York *(G-10754)*		
Mickelberry Communications Inc	G	212 832-0303
New York *(G-10794)*		
Middletown Press	G	845 343-1895
Middletown *(G-8164)*		
Scholastic Corporation	G	212 343-6100
New York *(G-11513)*		
Service Advertising Group Inc	F	718 361-6161
Long Island City *(G-7588)*		
Stop Entertainment Inc	F	212 242-7867
Monroe *(G-8281)*		

ADVERTISING AGENCIES: Consultants

Galli Shirts and Sports AP	G	845 226-7305
Stormville *(G-15179)*		
Mason & Gore Inc	E	914 921-1025
Rye *(G-14485)*		
Whispr Group Inc	F	212 924-3979
New York *(G-12101)*		

ADVERTISING DISPLAY PRDTS

Accenta Incorporated	G	716 565-6262
Buffalo *(G-2681)*		
Arnprior Rpid Mfg Slutions Inc	C	585 617-6301
Rochester *(G-13641)*		
Arnprior Rpid Mfg Slutions Inc	C	585 617-6301
Rochester *(G-13642)*		
D3 Led LLC	E	917 757-9671
New York *(G-9451)*		
Federal Sample Card Corp	G	718 458-1344
Elmhurst *(G-4464)*		
JG Innovative Industries Inc	G	718 784-7300
Kew Gardens *(G-6876)*		
Mack Studios Displays Inc	E	315 252-7542
Auburn *(G-489)*		
Nationwide Exhibitor Svcs Inc	F	631 467-2034
Central Islip *(G-3379)*		
Promotional Development Inc	D	718 485-8550
Brooklyn *(G-2357)*		
Qps Die Cutters Finishers Corp	E	718 966-1811
Staten Island *(G-15120)*		
Swift Multigraphics LLC	G	585 442-8000
Rochester *(G-14150)*		
Tri-Plex Packaging Corporation	E	212 481-6070
New York *(G-11894)*		

ADVERTISING MATERIAL DISTRIBUTION

Penny Lane Printing Inc	D	585 226-8111
Avon *(G-521)*		
Real Est Book of Long Island	F	516 364-5000
Syosset *(G-15230)*		
Shipmtes/Printmates Holdg Corp	D	518 370-1158
Scotia *(G-14746)*		
Technomag Inc	G	631 246-6142
East Setauket *(G-4311)*		

ADVERTISING REPRESENTATIVES: Electronic Media

Business Never Stops LLC	G	888 479-3111
South Richmond Hill *(G-14945)*		
World Business Media LLC	F	212 344-0759
Massapequa Park *(G-7896)*		

ADVERTISING REPRESENTATIVES: Magazine

Icd Publications Inc	E	631 246-9300
Islandia *(G-6530)*		
McClary Media Inc	G	800 453-6397
Amsterdam *(G-346)*		

ADVERTISING REPRESENTATIVES: Media

Redbook Magazine	F	212 649-3331
New York *(G-11342)*		

ADVERTISING REPRESENTATIVES: Newspaper

Advertiser Publications Inc	F	845 783-1111
Chester *(G-3467)*		
Bradford Publications Inc	C	716 373-2500
Olean *(G-12594)*		
Community Cpons Frnchising Inc	E	516 277-1968
Glen Cove *(G-5363)*		
Fire Island Tide Publication	F	631 567-7470
Sayville *(G-14630)*		
L & M Publications Inc	E	516 378-3133
Garden City *(G-5264)*		
Local Media Group Inc	E	845 341-1100
Middletown *(G-8160)*		
Long Island Cmnty Nwsppers Inc	D	516 482-4490
Mineola *(G-8235)*		
Market Place Publications	E	516 997-7909
Carle Place *(G-3270)*		
Service Advertising Group Inc	F	718 361-6161
Long Island City *(G-7588)*		

ADVERTISING REPRESENTATIVES: Printed Media

Informa Media Inc	B	212 204-4200
New York *(G-10210)*		
Press Express	G	914 592-3790
Elmsford *(G-4558)*		

ADVERTISING SPECIALTIES, WHOLESALE

A Trusted Name Inc	F	716 326-7400
Westfield *(G-16391)*		
Ad-Vantage Printing Inc	F	718 820-0688
Kew Gardens *(G-6870)*		
All American Awards Inc	F	631 567-2025
Bohemia *(G-975)*		
Concept Printing Inc	G	845 353-4040
Nyack *(G-12503)*		
Elco Manufacturing Co Inc	F	516 767-3577
Port Washington *(G-13257)*		
In-Step Marketing Inc	F	212 797-3450
New York *(G-10191)*		
Middletown Press	G	845 343-1895
Middletown *(G-8164)*		
U All Inc	E	518 438-2558
Albany *(G-136)*		
Ward Sales Co Inc	G	315 476-5276
Syracuse *(G-15454)*		
Whispr Group Inc	F	212 924-3979
New York *(G-12101)*		

ADVERTISING SVCS: Direct Mail

Advertiser Publications Inc	F	845 783-1111
Chester *(G-3467)*		
Century Direct LLC	C	212 763-0600
Islandia *(G-6524)*		
Design Distributors Inc	D	631 242-2000
Deer Park *(G-3966)*		
Orffeo Printing & Imaging Inc	G	716 681-5757
Lancaster *(G-7034)*		
Shipmtes/Printmates Holdg Corp	D	518 370-1158
Scotia *(G-14746)*		
Syracuse Letter Company Inc	F	315 476-8328
Bridgeport *(G-1184)*		
Thomas Publishing Company LLC	B	212 695-0500
New York *(G-11818)*		

ADVERTISING SVCS: Display

Apple Imprints Apparel Inc	E	716 893-1130
Buffalo *(G-2706)*		
Exhibits & More	G	585 924-4040
Victor *(G-15845)*		
L Miller Design Inc	G	631 242-1163
Deer Park *(G-3998)*		
Mystic Display Co Inc	G	718 485-2651
Brooklyn *(G-2239)*		

ADVERTISING SVCS: Outdoor

Artkraft Strauss LLC	E	212 265-5155
New York *(G-8924)*		

ADVERTISING SVCS: Sample Distribution

Instantwhip of Buffalo Inc	E	716 892-7031
Buffalo *(G-2885)*		

ADVERTISING SVCS: Transit

Danet Inc	F	718 266-4444
Brooklyn *(G-1755)*		
Fun Media Inc	E	646 472-0135
New York *(G-9861)*		

PRODUCT SECTION

AERIAL WORK PLATFORMS

Park Ave Bldg & Roofg Sups LLC	E	718 403-0100
Brooklyn *(G-2304)*		

AEROSOLS

Fountainhead Group Inc	C	708 598-7100
New York Mills *(G-12187)*		

AGENTS, BROKERS & BUREAUS: Personal Service

Superior Print On Demand	G	607 240-5231
Vestal *(G-15823)*		
T J Signs Unlimited LLC	E	631 273-4800
Islip *(G-6551)*		

AGRICULTURAL EQPT: BARN, SILO, POULTRY, DAIRY/LIVESTOCK MACH

Vansridge Dairy LLC	E	315 364-8569
Scipio Center *(G-14737)*		

AGRICULTURAL EQPT: Fertilizng, Sprayng, Dustng/Irrigatn Mach

Jain Irrigation Inc	D	315 755-4400
Watertown *(G-16017)*		

AGRICULTURAL EQPT: Milking Machines

Westmoor Ltd	F	315 363-1500
Sherrill *(G-14825)*		

AGRICULTURAL EQPT: Planting Machines

Good Earth Organics Corp	E	716 684-8111
Lancaster *(G-7022)*		

AGRICULTURAL EQPT: Spreaders, Fertilizer

Chapin Manufacturing Inc	C	585 343-3140
Batavia *(G-618)*		

AGRICULTURAL EQPT: Trailers & Wagons, Farm

Renaldos Sales & Service Ctr	G	716 337-3760
North Collins *(G-12388)*		

AGRICULTURAL EQPT: Turf & Grounds Eqpt

Bdp Industries Inc	E	518 695-6851
Greenwich *(G-5636)*		

AIR CLEANING SYSTEMS

Acme Engineering Products Inc	E	518 236-5659
Mooers *(G-8330)*		
Flanders Precisionaire NY	G	518 751-5640
Hudson *(G-6349)*		
Veteran Air LLC	G	315 720-1101
Syracuse *(G-15453)*		

AIR CONDITIONERS, AUTOMOTIVE: Wholesalers

American Comfort Direct LLC	E	201 364-8309
New York *(G-8825)*		

AIR CONDITIONING & VENTILATION EQPT & SPLYS: Wholesales

Elima-Draft Incorporated	G	631 375-2830
Stony Brook *(G-15165)*		
Layton Manufacturing Corp	E	718 498-6000
Brooklyn *(G-2095)*		

AIR CONDITIONING EQPT

Carrier Corporation	B	315 463-5744
East Syracuse *(G-4328)*		
Carrier Corporation	B	315 432-6000
East Syracuse *(G-4329)*		
Duro Dyne Corporation	C	631 249-9000
Bay Shore *(G-682)*		
Elima-Draft Incorporated	G	631 375-2830
Stony Brook *(G-15165)*		
EMC Tech Inc	F	716 488-9071
Falconer *(G-4676)*		
Empire Air Systems LLC	F	718 377-1549
Brooklyn *(G-1832)*		

PRODUCT SECTION

AIRCRAFT PARTS & AUXILIARY EQPT: Assys, Subassemblies/Parts

Layton Manufacturing Corp .... E 718 498-6000
Brooklyn *(G-2095)*
M M Tool and Manufacturing .... G 845 691-4140
Highland *(G-6145)*
RE Hansen Industries Inc .... C 631 471-2900
Saint James *(G-14514)*
Split Systems Corp .... G 516 223-5511
North Baldwin *(G-12367)*
Transit Air Inc .... E 607 324-0216
Hornell *(G-6304)*

AIR CONDITIONING UNITS: Complete, Domestic Or Indl

AC Air Cooling Co Inc .... F 718 933-1011
Bronx *(G-1206)*
Balticare Inc .... F 646 380-9470
New York *(G-9008)*
Duro Dyne Machinery Corp .... E 631 249-9000
Bay Shore *(G-683)*
Ice Air LLC .... E 914 668-4700
Mount Vernon *(G-8408)*
JE Miller Inc .... E 315 437-6811
East Syracuse *(G-4355)*
Niagara Blower Company .... D 800 426-5169
Tonawanda *(G-15563)*
Pfannenberg Inc .... D 716 685-6866
Lancaster *(G-7040)*

AIR COOLERS: Metal Plate

Thermotech Corp .... G 716 823-3311
Buffalo *(G-3094)*

AIR DUCT CLEANING SVCS

Filta Clean Co Inc .... E 718 495-3800
Brooklyn *(G-1880)*

AIR MATTRESSES: Plastic

Diamond Packaging Holdings LLC .... G 585 334-8030
Rochester *(G-13739)*

AIR POLLUTION MEASURING SVCS

Clean Gas Systems Inc .... E 631 467-1600
Commack *(G-3686)*

AIR PREHEATERS: Nonrotating, Plate Type

Arvos Inc .... G 585 593-2700
Wellsville *(G-16113)*

AIR PURIFICATION EQPT

Aeromed Inc .... G 518 843-9144
Utica *(G-15677)*
Airgle Corporation .... E 866 501-7750
Ronkonkoma *(G-14296)*
Austin Air Systems Limited .... D 716 856-3700
Buffalo *(G-2716)*
Beecher Emssn Sltn Tchnlgs LLC ..... F 607 796-0149
Horseheads *(G-6305)*
Beltran Associates Inc .... E 718 252-2996
Brooklyn *(G-1595)*
Clean Gas Systems Inc .... E 631 467-1600
Commack *(G-3686)*
JT Systems Inc .... F 315 622-1980
Liverpool *(G-7241)*
Phytofilter Technologies Inc .... E 518 507-6399
Saratoga Springs *(G-14592)*
Sbb Inc .... G 315 422-2376
East Syracuse *(G-4368)*
Sullivan Bazinet Bongio Inc .... E 315 437-6500
Syracuse *(G-15432)*

AIRCRAFT & AEROSPACE FLIGHT INSTRUMENTS & GUIDANCE SYSTEMS

Bae Systems Controls Inc .... A 607 770-2000
Endicott *(G-4583)*
CIC International Ltd .... D 212 213-0089
Brooklyn *(G-1692)*
Emergency Beacon Corp .... F 914 576-2700
New Rochelle *(G-8600)*
Facilamatic Instrument Corp .... F 516 825-6300
Valley Stream *(G-15779)*
Kwadair LLC .... G 646 824-2511
Brooklyn *(G-2083)*
No Longer Empty Inc .... G 202 413-4262
New York *(G-10981)*

Select Fabricators Inc .... F 585 393-0650
Canandaigua *(G-3233)*

AIRCRAFT & HEAVY EQPT REPAIR SVCS

Binghamton Simulator Co Inc .... E 607 321-2980
Binghamton *(G-868)*
James A Staley Co Inc .... F 845 878-3344
Carmel *(G-3277)*

AIRCRAFT ASSEMBLY PLANTS

Altius Aviation LLC .... G 315 455-7555
Syracuse *(G-15242)*
Barclay Tagg Racing .... E 631 404-8269
Floral Park *(G-4957)*
Bombardier Trnsp Holdings USA ...... E 518 566-5067
Plattsburgh *(G-13113)*
Grumman Field Support Services ..... D 516 575-0574
Bethpage *(G-842)*
Lesly Enterprise & Associates .... E 631 988-1301
Deer Park *(G-4000)*
Lockheed Martin Corporation .... D 315 793-5800
New Hartford *(G-8507)*
Moog Inc .... B 716 687-4954
East Aurora *(G-4207)*
Northrop Grumman Systems Corp ... A 516 575-0574
Bethpage *(G-850)*
Northrop Grumman Systems Corp ... D 716 626-4600
Buffalo *(G-2976)*
Northrop Grumman Systems Corp ... G 631 423-1014
Huntington *(G-6406)*
Pro Drones Usa LLC .... F 718 530-3558
New York *(G-11252)*
Sikorsky Aircraft Corporation .... D 585 424-1990
Rochester *(G-14129)*

AIRCRAFT CONTROL SYSTEMS: Electronic Totalizing Counters

Moog Inc .... A 716 652-2000
Elma *(G-4453)*
Moog Inc .... B 716 687-5486
Elma *(G-4455)*

AIRCRAFT ENGINES & ENGINE PARTS: Research & Development, Mfr

General Electric Company .... E 518 385-7620
Niskayuna *(G-12354)*
General Electric Company .... A 518 385-4022
Schenectady *(G-14675)*

AIRCRAFT ENGINES & PARTS

Advanced Atomization Tech LLC ...... B 315 923-2341
Clyde *(G-3591)*
ARC Systems Inc .... E 631 582-8020
Hauppauge *(G-5786)*
B H Aircraft Company Inc .... C 631 580-9747
Ronkonkoma *(G-14315)*
Chromalloy American LLC .... E 845 230-7355
Orangeburg *(G-12672)*
Chromalloy Gas Turbine LLC .... E 845 359-2462
Orangeburg *(G-12673)*
Chromalloy Gas Turbine LLC .... E 845 692-8912
Middletown *(G-8141)*
Colonial Group LLC .... E 516 349-8010
Plainview *(G-13043)*
Davis Aircraft Products Co Inc .... C 631 563-1500
Bohemia *(G-1010)*
Dyna-Empire Inc .... C 516 222-2700
Garden City *(G-5256)*
Gb Aero Engine LLC .... B 914 925-9600
Rye *(G-14480)*
Honeywell International Inc .... D 518 270-0200
Troy *(G-15595)*
Honeywell International Inc .... A 315 554-6643
Skaneateles Falls *(G-14881)*
Honeywell International Inc .... G 716 631-2197
Cheektowaga *(G-3449)*
Honeywell International Inc .... E 516 577-2661
Melville *(G-8031)*
Honeywell International Inc .... E 516 577-2000
Melville *(G-8032)*
Honeywell International Inc .... E 516 577-2813
Melville *(G-8033)*
Honeywell International Inc .... G 845 342-4400
Middletown *(G-8158)*
Honeywell International Inc .... A 212 964-5111
Melville *(G-8034)*

Honeywell International Inc .... B 516 577-2000
Melville *(G-8035)*
Honeywell International Inc .... F 315 463-7208
East Syracuse *(G-4347)*
Honeywell International Inc .... G 631 471-2202
Lake Ronkonkoma *(G-6980)*
Howe Machine & Tool Corp .... E 516 931-5687
Bethpage *(G-843)*
ITT Enidine Inc .... B 716 662-1900
Orchard Park *(G-12720)*
Kerns Manufacturing Corp .... C 718 784-4044
Long Island City *(G-7488)*
Lourdes Industries Inc .... D 631 234-6600
Hauppauge *(G-5873)*
Magellan Aerospace Bethel Inc .... C 203 798-9373
Corona *(G-3848)*
Magellan Aerospace Processing ...... G 631 694-1818
West Babylon *(G-16173)*
McGuigan Inc .... E 631 750-6222
Bohemia *(G-1057)*
Nell-Joy Industries Inc .... E 631 842-8989
Copiague *(G-3770)*
SOS International LLC .... B 212 742-2410
New York *(G-11651)*
Therm Incorporated .... E 607 272-8500
Ithaca *(G-6611)*
Triumph Actuation Systems LLC ...... B 516 378-0162
Freeport *(G-5188)*
Triumph Group Inc .... B 516 997-5757
Westbury *(G-16382)*
Turbine Engine Comp Utica .... A 315 768-8070
Whitesboro *(G-16531)*
United Technologies Corp .... G 315 432-7849
East Syracuse *(G-4378)*

AIRCRAFT EQPT & SPLYS WHOLESALERS

Fastener Dimensions Inc .... E 718 847-6321
Ozone Park *(G-12825)*
Magellan Aerospace NY Inc .... C 631 589-2440
Bohemia *(G-1053)*
Styles Aviation Inc .... G 845 677-8185
Lagrangeville *(G-6962)*
Worldwide Arntcl Cmpnnts Inc .... E 631 842-3780
Copiague *(G-3794)*

AIRCRAFT FLIGHT INSTRUMENT REPAIR SVCS

Safe Flight Instrument Corp .... C 914 946-9500
White Plains *(G-16502)*

AIRCRAFT FLIGHT INSTRUMENTS

Mod-A-Can Inc .... D 516 931-8545
Hicksville *(G-6111)*
Safe Flight Instrument Corp .... C 914 946-9500
White Plains *(G-16502)*

AIRCRAFT LIGHTING

Aerospace Lighting Corporation .... D 631 563-6400
Bohemia *(G-974)*
Astronics Corporation .... C 716 805-1599
East Aurora *(G-4194)*
B/E Aerospace Inc .... E 631 563-6400
Bohemia *(G-985)*
Luminescent Systems Inc .... B 716 655-0800
East Aurora *(G-4204)*

AIRCRAFT PARTS & AUXILIARY EQPT: Assys, Subassemblies/Parts

Aero Trades Mfg Corp .... E 516 746-3360
Mineola *(G-8200)*
Air Industries Machining Corp .... C 631 328-7000
Bay Shore *(G-653)*
Arkwin Industries Inc .... C 516 333-2640
Westbury *(G-16317)*
Ausco Inc .... D 516 944-9882
Farmingdale *(G-4723)*
CPI Aerostructures Inc .... B 631 586-5200
Edgewood *(G-4399)*
Design/OI Inc .... F 631 474-5536
Port Jeff STA *(G-13213)*
Engineered Metal Products Inc .... G 631 842-3780
Copiague *(G-3758)*
Excelco Developments Inc .... B 716 934-2651
Silver Creek *(G-14861)*
Excelco/Newbrook Inc .... D 716 934-2644
Silver Creek *(G-14862)*

Employee Codes: A=Over 500 employees, B=251-500
C=101-250, D=51-100, E=20-50, F=10-19, G=5-9

AIRCRAFT PARTS & AUXILIARY EQPT: Assys, Subassemblies/Parts

GKN Aerospace Monitor Inc ....B...... 562 619-8558
  Amityville *(G-277)*
Goodrich Corporation ....C...... 315 838-1200
  Rome *(G-14251)*
Handy Tool & Mfg Co Inc ....E...... 718 478-9203
  Brooklyn *(G-1967)*
Hicksville Machine Works Corp.............F...... 516 931-1524
  Hicksville *(G-6096)*
Lai International Inc ....E...... 763 780-0060
  Green Island *(G-5608)*
Magellan Aerospace Bethel Inc ....C...... 203 798-9373
  Corona *(G-3848)*
Magellan Aerospace NY Inc ....C...... 718 699-4000
  Corona *(G-3849)*
Min-Max Machine Ltd ....F...... 631 585-4378
  Ronkonkoma *(G-14378)*
Norsk Titanium US Inc...........................G...... 949 735-9463
  Plattsburgh *(G-13136)*
Posimech Inc ....E...... 631 924-5959
  Medford *(G-7964)*
S & L Aerospace Metals LLC ....D...... 718 326-1821
  Flushing *(G-5043)*
Superior Motion Controls Inc ....E...... 516 420-2921
  Farmingdale *(G-4885)*
Tek Precision Co Ltd ....E...... 631 242-0330
  Deer Park *(G-4051)*
Wilco Industries Inc ....G...... 631 676-2593
  Ronkonkoma *(G-14432)*

AIRCRAFT PARTS & AUXILIARY EQPT: Body & Wing Assys & Parts

Aero Strctures Long Island Inc..............D...... 516 997-5757
  Westbury *(G-16311)*

AIRCRAFT PARTS & AUXILIARY EQPT: Body Assemblies & Parts

Air Industries Group ....D...... 631 881-4920
  Hauppauge *(G-5758)*
Reese Manufacturing Inc ....G...... 631 842-3780
  Copiague *(G-3777)*

AIRCRAFT PARTS & AUXILIARY EQPT: Gears, Power Transmission

Gleason Works ....A...... 585 473-1000
  Rochester *(G-13840)*
W J Albro Machine Works Inc ....G...... 631 345-0657
  Yaphank *(G-16728)*

AIRCRAFT PARTS & AUXILIARY EQPT: Landing Assemblies & Brakes

Blair Industries Inc ....E...... 631 924-6600
  Medford *(G-7939)*
Dyna-Empire Inc ....C...... 516 222-2700
  Garden City *(G-5256)*
Nassau Tool Works Inc ....E...... 631 328-7031
  Bay Shore *(G-705)*

AIRCRAFT PARTS & AUXILIARY EQPT: Military Eqpt & Armament

Armacel Armor Corporation ....E...... 805 384-1144
  New York *(G-8909)*
Dresser-Argus Inc ....G...... 718 643-1540
  Brooklyn *(G-1794)*
Edo LLC ....G...... 631 630-4000
  Amityville *(G-272)*
Metadure Parts & Sales Inc ....F...... 631 249-2141
  Farmingdale *(G-4821)*

AIRCRAFT PARTS & AUXILIARY EQPT: Refueling Eqpt, In Flight

Usairports Services Inc ....E...... 585 527-6835
  Rochester *(G-14194)*

AIRCRAFT PARTS & AUXILIARY EQPT: Seat Ejector Devices

East/West Industries Inc ....E...... 631 981-5900
  Ronkonkoma *(G-14335)*

AIRCRAFT PARTS & EQPT, NEC

AAR Allen Services Inc ....E...... 516 222-9000
  Garden City *(G-5250)*
Alken Industries Inc ....E...... 631 467-2000
  Ronkonkoma *(G-14298)*
Ancon Gear & Instrument Corp ....F...... 631 694-4255
  Amityville *(G-264)*
Astronics Corporation ....C...... 716 805-1599
  East Aurora *(G-4194)*
B & B Precision Components Inc ....E...... 631 273-3321
  Ronkonkoma *(G-14314)*
B/E Aerospace Inc ....E...... 631 563-6400
  Bohemia *(G-985)*
Canfield Aerospace & Mar Inc ....E...... 631 648-1050
  Ronkonkoma *(G-14325)*
Caravan International Corp 212 223-7190
  New York *(G-9205)*
Carleton Technologies Inc ....B...... 716 662-0006
  Orchard Park *(G-12706)*
Circor Aerospace Inc ....D...... 631 737-1900
  Hauppauge *(G-5789)*
Cox & Company Inc ....C...... 212 366-0200
  Plainview *(G-13048)*
Crown Aircraft Lighting Inc....................E...... 718 767-3410
  Whitestone *(G-16538)*
Davis Aircraft Products Co Inc ....E...... 631 563-1500
  Bohemia *(G-1010)*
Drt Power Systems LLC ....E...... 585 247-5940
  Rochester *(G-13751)*
Ducommun Aerostructures NY Inc ....B...... 518 731-2791
  Coxsackie *(G-3906)*
Eastern Precision Machining ....E...... 631 286-4758
  Bellport *(G-802)*
Ensil Technical Services Inc ....E...... 716 282-1020
  Niagara Falls *(G-12281)*
Fluid Mechanisms Hauppauge Inc ....E...... 631 234-0100
  Hauppauge *(G-5826)*
GE Aviation Systems LLC ....E...... 631 467-5500
  Bohemia *(G-1026)*
HSM Machine Works Inc ....E...... 631 924-6600
  Medford *(G-7953)*
Jac Usa Inc ....G...... 212 841-7430
  New York *(G-10290)*
Jamco Aerospace Inc ....E...... 631 586-7900
  Deer Park *(G-3990)*
Jaquith Industries Inc ....E...... 315 478-5700
  Syracuse *(G-15346)*
Joldeson One Aerospace Inds ....D...... 718 848-7396
  Ozone Park *(G-12827)*
Jrsmm LLC 607 331-1549
  Elmira *(G-4495)*
Lenny & Bill LLC ....D...... 516 997-5757
  Westbury *(G-16349)*
Loar Group Inc ....C...... 212 210-9348
  New York *(G-10588)*
Magellan Aerospace NY Inc ....C...... 631 589-2440
  Bohemia *(G-1053)*
MD International Industries....................E...... 631 254-3100
  Deer Park *(G-4009)*
Metal Dynamics Intl Corp ....G...... 631 231-1153
  Hauppauge *(G-5888)*
Milex Precision Inc ....F...... 631 595-2393
  Bay Shore *(G-701)*
Military Parts Exchange LLC ....F...... 631 243-1700
  Melville *(G-8047)*
Minutemen Precsn McHning Tool ....E...... 631 467-4900
  Ronkonkoma *(G-14379)*
Moog Inc ....A...... 716 652-2000
  Elma *(G-4453)*
Parker-Hannifin Corporation ....C...... 631 231-3737
  Clyde *(G-3597)*
Precision Cnc ....E...... 631 847-3999
  Deer Park *(G-4028)*
Ripi Precision Co Inc ....F...... 631 694-2453
  Farmingdale *(G-4866)*
Santa Fe Manufacturing Corp ....G...... 631 234-0100
  Hauppauge *(G-5932)*
Servotronics Inc ....C...... 716 655-5990
  Elma *(G-4458)*
Styles Aviation Inc 845 677-8185
  Lagrangeville *(G-6962)*
Sumner Industries Inc ....E...... 631 666-7290
  Bay Shore *(G-729)*
Tangent Machine & Tool Corp ....F...... 631 249-3088
  Farmingdale *(G-4889)*
Tens Machine Company Inc ....E...... 631 981-3321
  Holbrook *(G-6215)*
TPC Inc ....E...... 315 438-8605
  East Syracuse *(G-4374)*
Triumph Actuation Systems LLC ....D...... 516 378-0162
  Freeport *(G-5188)*
Universal Armor Systems Corp ....E...... 631 838-1836
  Levittown *(G-7136)*
UTC Aerospace Systems 315 838-1200
  Rome *(G-14277)*
Vosky Precision Machining Corp ....F...... 631 737-3200
  Ronkonkoma *(G-14429)*
Young & Franklin Inc ....D...... 315 457-3110
  Liverpool *(G-7274)*

AIRCRAFT SEATS

B/E Aerospace Inc ....E...... 631 563-6400
  Bohemia *(G-985)*
East/West Industries Inc ....E...... 631 981-5900
  Ronkonkoma *(G-14335)*

AIRCRAFT: Airplanes, Fixed Or Rotary Wing

Boeing Company ....A...... 201 259-9400
  New York *(G-9117)*

AIRCRAFT: Gliders

M & H Research and Dev Corp ....G...... 607 734-2346
  Beaver Dams *(G-765)*

AIRCRAFT: Motorized

Lockheed Martin Corporation ....E...... 716 297-1000
  Niagara Falls *(G-12307)*

AIRCRAFT: Research & Development, Manufacturer

Alliant Tchsystems Oprtons LLC ....E...... 631 737-6100
  Ronkonkoma *(G-14301)*
Atk Gasl Inc ....F...... 631 737-6100
  Ronkonkoma *(G-14312)*
Calspan Corporation ....C...... 716 631-6955
  Buffalo *(G-2758)*
Calspan Corporation ....F...... 716 236-1040
  Niagara Falls *(G-12267)*
Calspan Holdings LLC..........................F...... 716 631-6955
  Buffalo *(G-2759)*
Luminati Aerospace LLC ....F...... 631 574-2616
  Calverton *(G-3167)*
Tech Park Food Services LLC ....G...... 585 295-1250
  Rochester *(G-14161)*
Xactiv Inc ....F...... 585 288-7220
  Fairport *(G-4668)*

ALARM SYSTEMS WHOLESALERS

Lifewatch Inc ....F...... 800 716-1433
  Hewlett *(G-6048)*

ALARMS: Burglar

Datasonic Inc...G...... 516 248-7330
  East Meadow *(G-4249)*
Harris Corporation ....A...... 413 263-6200
  Rochester *(G-13856)*
Sentry Devices Corp ....F...... 631 491-3191
  Dix Hills *(G-4126)*
Unitone Communication Systems.........G...... 212 777-9090
  New York *(G-11957)*
UTC Fire SEC Americas Corp Inc ....D...... 518 456-0444
  Albany *(G-139)*

ALARMS: Fire

Fire Apparatus Service Tech.................G...... 716 753-3538
  Sherman *(G-14816)*
Toweriq Inc ....F...... 844 626-7638
  Long Island City *(G-7618)*

ALCOHOL: Ethyl & Ethanol

Sunoco Inc...G...... 315 593-0500
  Fulton *(G-5232)*

ALCOHOL: Methyl & Methanol, Synthetic

Balchem Corporation ....B...... 845 326-5600
  New Hampton *(G-8497)*
Hunts Point Clean Energy LLC.............G...... 203 451-5143
  Pearl River *(G-12902)*

ALKALIES & CHLORINE

Chemours Company Fc LLC.................E...... 716 278-5100
  Niagara Falls *(G-12271)*
FMC Corporation ....C...... 716 879-0400
  Tonawanda *(G-15541)*
Occidental Chemical Corp ....E...... 716 278-7795
  Niagara Falls *(G-12318)*
Occidental Chemical Corp ....E...... 716 773-8100
  Grand Island *(G-5509)*

PRODUCT SECTION　　　　　　　　　　　　　　　　　　　　　　　　　ANESTHETICS: Bulk Form

Occidental Chemical Corp ....C....... 716 278-7794
　Niagara Falls *(G-12319)*
Occidental Chemical Corp ....G....... 716 694-3827
　North Tonawanda *(G-12440)*
Olin Chlor Alkali Logistics ....C....... 716 278-6411
　Niagara Falls *(G-12320)*

ALKALOIDS & OTHER BOTANICAL BASED PRDTS

Bio-Botanica Inc...............................D....... 631 231-0987
　Hauppauge *(G-5780)*

ALLERGENS & ALLERGENIC EXTRACTS

Nelco Laboratories Inc ....E....... 631 242-0082
　Deer Park *(G-4014)*

ALTERNATORS & GENERATORS: Battery Charging

ARC Systems Inc ....E....... 631 582-8020
　Hauppauge *(G-5768)*

ALTERNATORS: Automotive

Con Rel Auto Electric Inc ....E....... 518 356-1646
　Schenectady *(G-14666)*
Eastern Unit Exch Rmnfacturing..............F....... 718 739-7113
　Floral Park *(G-4963)*

ALUMINUM

Alcoa USA Corp ....G....... 315 764-4011
　Massena *(G-7898)*
American Std Shtmtl Sup Corp ....F....... 718 888-9350
　Flushing *(G-4985)*
Greene Brass & Alum Fndry LLC ....G....... 607 656-4204
　Bloomville *(G-962)*

ALUMINUM ORE MINING

American Douglas Metals Inc.................F....... 716 856-3170
　Buffalo *(G-2695)*

ALUMINUM PRDTS

A-Fab Initiatives Inc ....F....... 716 877-5257
　Buffalo *(G-2680)*
Alumi-Tech LLC....................................G....... 585 663-7010
　Penfield *(G-12939)*
Amt Incorporated ....E....... 518 284-2910
　Sharon Springs *(G-14797)*
Apollo Management V LP.....................E....... 914 467-6510
　Purchase *(G-13386)*
Arconic Inc ....D....... 212 836-2758
　New York *(G-8903)*
Arconic Inc ....G....... 315 764-4011
　Massena *(G-7900)*
Constellium ....E....... 212 675-5087
　New York *(G-9386)*
Flagpoles Incorporated ....D....... 631 751-5500
　East Setauket *(G-4301)*
Itts Industrial Inc ....G....... 718 605-6934
　Staten Island *(G-15092)*
J Sussman Inc ....E....... 718 297-0228
　Jamaica *(G-6652)*
Keymark Corporation ....A....... 518 853-3421
　Fonda *(G-5066)*
Minitec Framing Systems LLC ....E....... 585 924-4690
　Farmington *(G-4917)*
North Coast Outfitters Ltd....................E....... 631 727-5580
　Riverhead *(G-13578)*
Nyahb Inc...G....... 845 352-5300
　Monsey *(G-8292)*
Pioneer Window Holdings Inc ....E....... 518 762-5526
　Johnstown *(G-6837)*
Super Sweep Inc ....F....... 631 223-8205
　Huntington Station *(G-6459)*
Swiss Tool Corporation ....E....... 631 842-7766
　Copiague *(G-3785)*

ALUMINUM: Rolling & Drawing

Alcoa Corporation ....B....... 412 315-2900
　Massena *(G-7897)*
Arconic Inc ....D....... 212 836-2758
　New York *(G-8903)*
Arconic Inc ....G....... 315 764-4011
　Massena *(G-7900)*
Mitsubishi Chemical Amer inc...............E....... 212 223-3043
　New York *(G-10825)*

N A Alumil Corporation.........................G....... 718 355-9393
　Long Island City *(G-7532)*

AMMONIUM NITRATE OR AMMONIUM SULFATE

Oci USA Inc ....G....... 646 589-6180
　New York *(G-11029)*
Ocip Holding LLC ....G....... 646 589-6180
　New York *(G-11030)*

AMMUNITION

Circor Aerospace Inc ....D....... 631 737-1900
　Hauppauge *(G-5789)*

AMMUNITION: Components

CIC International Ltd.............................D....... 212 213-0089
　Brooklyn *(G-1692)*

AMMUNITION: Pellets & BB's, Pistol & Air Rifle

Benjamin Sheridan Corporation............G....... 585 657-6161
　Bloomfield *(G-947)*
Crosman Corporation ....E....... 585 657-6161
　Bloomfield *(G-951)*
Crosman Corporation ....E....... 585 398-3920
　Farmington *(G-4911)*

AMMUNITION: Small Arms

CIC International Ltd.............................D....... 212 213-0089
　Brooklyn *(G-1692)*

AMPLIFIERS

Aguilar Amplification LLC ....E....... 212 431-9109
　New York *(G-8771)*
Amplitech Group Inc.............................G....... 631 521-7831
　Bohemia *(G-979)*
Broadcast Manager Inc ....E....... 212 509-1200
　New York *(G-9145)*
Ilab America Inc ....G....... 631 615-5053
　Selden *(G-14764)*

AMPLIFIERS: Parametric

Electronics & Innovation Ltd ....F....... 585 214-0598
　Rochester *(G-13776)*

AMPLIFIERS: Pulse Amplifiers

AMP-Line Corp.....................................F....... 845 623-3288
　West Nyack *(G-16263)*

AMPLIFIERS: RF & IF Power

Ametek CTS Us Inc ....E....... 631 467-8400
　Ronkonkoma *(G-14308)*
B & H Electronics Corp ....E....... 845 782-5000
　Monroe *(G-8264)*
Communication Power Corp.................E....... 631 434-7306
　Hauppauge *(G-5796)*
Mks Medical Electronics ....C....... 585 292-7400
　Rochester *(G-13950)*
Srtech Industry Corp ....E....... 718 496-7001
　College Point *(G-3668)*

AMUSEMENT & RECREATION SVCS: Amusement Ride

Billy Beez Usa LLC ....E....... 315 741-5099
　Syracuse *(G-15257)*
Billy Beez Usa LLC ....F....... 646 606-2249
　New York *(G-9084)*
Billy Beez Usa LLC ....E....... 845 915-4709
　West Nyack *(G-16266)*

AMUSEMENT & RECREATION SVCS: Arcades

Inspired Entertainment Inc....................F....... 646 565-3861
　New York *(G-10226)*

AMUSEMENT & RECREATION SVCS: Art Gallery, Commercial

Pace Editions Inc ....E....... 212 421-3237
　New York *(G-11085)*

AMUSEMENT & RECREATION SVCS: Arts & Crafts Instruction

Donne Dieu Paper Mill Inc....................G....... 212 226-0573
　Brooklyn *(G-1788)*

AMUSEMENT & RECREATION SVCS: Exposition Operation

Family Publications Ltd........................F....... 212 947-2177
　New York *(G-9778)*

AMUSEMENT & RECREATION SVCS: Gambling & Lottery Svcs

Inspired Entertainment Inc....................F....... 646 565-3861
　New York *(G-10226)*

AMUSEMENT & RECREATION SVCS: Game Machines

Mission Crane Service Inc ....D....... 718 937-3333
　Long Island City *(G-7527)*

AMUSEMENT & RECREATION SVCS: Golf Club, Membership

Dolomite Products Company Inc ....E....... 315 524-1998
　Rochester *(G-13749)*

AMUSEMENT & RECREATION SVCS: Physical Fitness Instruction

Playfitness Corp....................................G....... 917 497-5443
　Staten Island *(G-15116)*

AMUSEMENT & RECREATION SVCS: Tennis & Professionals

Paddock Chevrolet Golf Dome ....E....... 716 504-4059
　Tonawanda *(G-15568)*

AMUSEMENT MACHINES: Coin Operated

Mission Crane Service Inc ....D....... 718 937-3333
　Long Island City *(G-7527)*

AMUSEMENT PARK DEVICES & RIDES

Acro Industries Inc ....C....... 585 254-3661
　Rochester *(G-13600)*
Lakeside Industries Inc ....F....... 716 386-3031
　Bemus Point *(G-818)*
Macro Tool & Machine Company.........G....... 845 223-3824
　Lagrangeville *(G-6958)*

ANALGESICS

Mentholatum Company ....E....... 716 677-2500
　Orchard Park *(G-12730)*
Perrigo Company ....E....... 718 960-9900
　Bronx *(G-1356)*
Wyeth LLC ....A....... 973 660-5000
　New York *(G-12146)*

ANALYZERS: Moisture

Phymetrix Inc ....G....... 631 627-3950
　Medford *(G-7963)*

ANALYZERS: Network

Cgw Corp ....G....... 631 472-6600
　Bayport *(G-736)*
Everest Bbn Inc....................................F....... 212 268-7979
　New York *(G-9736)*
Gcns Technology Group Inc ....G....... 347 713-8160
　Brooklyn *(G-1920)*

ANESTHESIA EQPT

Gradian Health Systems Inc ....G....... 212 537-0340
　New York *(G-9967)*
Intersurgical Incorporated ....E....... 315 451-2900
　East Syracuse *(G-4353)*
Omnicare Anesthesia PC ....E....... 718 433-0044
　Astoria *(G-439)*

ANESTHETICS: Bulk Form

Ucb Pharma Inc....................................B....... 919 767-2555
　Rochester *(G-14183)*

Employee Codes: A=Over 500 employees, B=251-500
C=101-250, D=51-100, E=20-50, F=10-19, G=5-9

ANIMAL FEED & SUPPLEMENTS: Livestock & Poultry

Bailey Boonville Mills Inc............G....... 315 942-2131
Boonville *(G-1114)*
Baker Commodities Inc..............E....... 585 482-1880
Rochester *(G-13652)*
Cargill Incorporated...................D....... 585 345-1160
Batavia *(G-616)*
Cargill Incorporated...................G....... 716 665-6570
Kennedy *(G-6866)*
Cargill Incorporated...................E....... 315 287-0241
Gouverneur *(G-5487)*
Cargill Incorporated...................G....... 518 854-7417
Salem *(G-14536)*
Cargill Incorporated...................E....... 315 622-3533
Liverpool *(G-7228)*
Central Garden & Pet Company..........G....... 631 451-8021
Selden *(G-14761)*
Eastport Feeds Inc....................G....... 631 325-0077
Eastport *(G-4384)*
Harbor Point Mineral Pdts Inc........F....... 315 797-1300
Utica *(G-15708)*
Lowville Farmers Coop Inc............E....... 315 376-6587
Lowville *(G-7652)*
Scotts Feed Inc........................E....... 518 483-3110
Malone *(G-7725)*

ANIMAL FEED: Wholesalers

Kelley Farm & Garden Inc.............E....... 518 234-2332
Cobleskill *(G-3603)*
Scotts Feed Inc........................E....... 518 483-3110
Malone *(G-7725)*

ANIMAL FOOD & SUPPLEMENTS: Bird Food, Prepared

Heath Manufacturing Company........G....... 800 444-3140
Batavia *(G-627)*
Pine Tree Farms Inc...................E....... 607 532-4312
Interlaken *(G-6483)*
Wagners LLC.............................G....... 516 933-6580
Jericho *(G-6807)*

ANIMAL FOOD & SUPPLEMENTS: Dog

Dog Good Products LLC...............G....... 212 789-7000
New York *(G-9545)*
Nestle Purina Petcare Company......B....... 716 366-8080
Dunkirk *(G-4174)*
Robert Abady Dog Food Co Ltd......F....... 845 473-1900
Poughkeepsie *(G-13363)*
Scooby Rendering & Inc...............G....... 315 793-1014
Utica *(G-15732)*

ANIMAL FOOD & SUPPLEMENTS: Dog & Cat

Colgate-Palmolive Company..........A....... 212 310-2000
New York *(G-9349)*
Hills Pet Products Inc..................G....... 212 310-2000
New York *(G-10100)*
Hound & Gatos Pet Foods Corp.....G....... 212 618-1917
New York *(G-10133)*
Pet Proteins LLC.......................G....... 888 293-1029
New York *(G-11166)*

ANIMAL FOOD & SUPPLEMENTS: Feed Concentrates

Gramco Inc..............................G....... 716 592-2845
Springville *(G-15017)*

ANIMAL FOOD & SUPPLEMENTS: Feed Premixes

Commodity Resource Corporation...F....... 585 538-9500
Caledonia *(G-3154)*

ANIMAL FOOD & SUPPLEMENTS: Feed Supplements

Veterinary Biochemical Ltd............G....... 845 473-1900
Poughkeepsie *(G-13372)*

ANIMAL FOOD & SUPPLEMENTS: Livestock

JD Granary LLC........................G....... 607 627-6294
Smyrna *(G-14912)*
Kent Nutrition Group Inc..............F....... 315 788-0032
Watertown *(G-16021)*

ANIMAL FOOD & SUPPLEMENTS: Mineral feed supplements

Nutra-Vet Research Corp.............F....... 845 473-1900
Poughkeepsie *(G-13360)*

ANIMAL FOOD & SUPPLEMENTS: Pet, Exc Dog & Cat, Canned

Grandma Maes Cntry Nturals LLC..G....... 212 348-8171
New York *(G-9973)*

ANIMAL FOOD & SUPPLEMENTS: Poultry

Cochecton Mills Inc....................E....... 845 932-8282
Cochecton *(G-3605)*
Narrowsburg Feed & Grain Co......F....... 845 252-3936
Narrowsburg *(G-8474)*

ANODIZING SVC

Able Anodizing Corp...................F....... 718 252-0660
Brooklyn *(G-1470)*
C H Thompson Company Inc........D....... 607 724-1094
Binghamton *(G-874)*
Fallon Inc................................E....... 718 326-7226
Maspeth *(G-7844)*
Forge Metal Finishing Inc.............G....... 585 730-7340
Rochester *(G-13813)*
Keymark Corporation..................A....... 518 853-3421
Fonda *(G-5066)*
Tru-Tone Metal Products Inc........E....... 718 386-5960
Brooklyn *(G-2590)*
Utica Metal Products Inc.............D....... 315 732-6163
Utica *(G-15738)*

ANTENNAS: Radar Or Communications

B & Z Technologies LLC..............G....... 631 675-9666
East Setauket *(G-4298)*
Gryphon Sensors LLC.................F....... 315 452-8882
North Syracuse *(G-12404)*
Srctec LLC..............................C....... 315 452-8700
Syracuse *(G-15429)*

ANTENNAS: Receiving

Ampro International Inc...............G....... 845 278-4910
Brewster *(G-1157)*
Pyragon Inc.............................E....... 585 697-0444
Rochester *(G-14055)*
Russell Industries Inc.................E....... 516 536-5000
Lynbrook *(G-7673)*

ANTIBIOTICS

G C Hanford Manufacturing Co......C....... 315 476-7418
Syracuse *(G-15328)*
Pfizer Inc................................E....... 212 733-2323
New York *(G-11174)*
Pfizer Overseas LLC..................E....... 212 733-2323
New York *(G-11178)*

ANTIBIOTICS, PACKAGED

Durata Therapeutics Inc..............G....... 646 871-6400
New York *(G-9587)*
Forest Laboratories LLC.............C....... 631 858-6010
Commack *(G-3690)*

ANTIFREEZE

Bass Oil Company Inc.................E....... 718 628-4444
Brooklyn *(G-1588)*
Fppf Chemical Co Inc..................G....... 716 856-9607
Buffalo *(G-2832)*

ANTIQUE FURNITURE RESTORATION & REPAIR

Irony Limited Inc.......................G....... 631 329-4065
East Hampton *(G-4238)*
Nicholas Dfine Furn Decorators....F....... 914 245-8982
Bronx *(G-1343)*

ANTIQUE REPAIR & RESTORATION SVCS, EXC FURNITURE & AUTOS

A W R Group Inc.......................F....... 718 729-0412
Long Island City *(G-7363)*

ANTIQUE SHOPS

American Country Quilts & Lin......G....... 631 283-5466
Southampton *(G-14949)*
Blanche P Field LLC..................E....... 212 355-6616
New York *(G-9099)*

ANTIQUES, WHOLESALE

Two Worlds Arts Ltd...................G....... 212 929-2210
New York *(G-11920)*

APPAREL ACCESS STORES

Crye Precision LLC....................C....... 718 246-3838
Brooklyn *(G-1736)*
Jag Footwear ACC & Ret Corp.....A....... 800 999-1877
New York *(G-10299)*
Nazim Izzak Inc.........................G....... 212 920-5546
Long Island City *(G-7534)*

APPAREL DESIGNERS: Commercial

Dianos Kathryn Designs..............G....... 212 267-1584
New York *(G-9524)*

APPAREL: Hand Woven

Jeans Inc................................G....... 646 223-1122
New York *(G-10324)*

APPLIANCE CORDS: Household Electrical Eqpt

All Shore Industries Inc...............F....... 718 720-0018
Staten Island *(G-15042)*

APPLIANCES, HOUSEHOLD: Kitchen, Major, Exc Refrigs & Stoves

Ajmadison Corp........................D....... 718 532-1800
Brooklyn *(G-1497)*
Barrage..................................E....... 212 586-9390
New York *(G-9020)*
Design Solutions LI Inc................G....... 631 656-8700
Saint James *(G-14511)*
Hobart Corporation....................E....... 631 864-3440
Commack *(G-3695)*
Talmu NY LLC..........................G....... 347 434-6700
Brooklyn *(G-2555)*

APPLIANCES, HOUSEHOLD: Laundry Machines, Incl Coin-Operated

Pluslux LLC.............................G....... 516 371-4400
Inwood *(G-6499)*

APPLIANCES, HOUSEHOLD: Refrigerator Cabinets, Metal Or Wood

Ae Fund Inc.............................E....... 315 698-7650
Brewerton *(G-1149)*

APPLIANCES, HOUSEHOLD: Refrigs, Mechanical & Absorption

General Electric Company...........A....... 518 385-4022
Schenectady *(G-14675)*

APPLIANCES: Household, Refrigerators & Freezers

Acme Kitchenettes Corp.............E....... 518 828-4191
Hudson *(G-6337)*
Robin Industries Ltd...................F....... 718 218-9616
Brooklyn *(G-2410)*
Sure-Kol Refrigerator Co Inc........F....... 718 625-0601
Brooklyn *(G-2542)*

APPLIANCES: Major, Cooking

Applince Installation Svc Corp......E....... 716 884-7425
Buffalo *(G-2707)*
Bakers Pride Oven Co Inc............C....... 914 576-0200
New Rochelle *(G-8591)*
Oxo International Inc..................C....... 212 242-3333
New York *(G-11080)*
Steelstone Group LLC................G....... 888 552-0033
Brooklyn *(G-2519)*

PRODUCT SECTION

ASPHALT PLANTS INCLUDING GRAVEL MIX TYPE

APPLIANCES: Small, Electric
A & M LLC .... G 212 354-1341
  New York *(G-8687)*
Algonquin Power .... G 315 393-5595
  Ogdensburg *(G-12569)*
Fulton Volcanic Inc .... D 315 298-5121
  Pulaski *(G-13384)*
General Electric Company .... G 315 554-2000
  Skaneateles *(G-14872)*
Tactica International Inc .... E 212 575-0500
  New York *(G-11774)*
Uniware Houseware Corp .... E 631 242-7400
  Brentwood *(G-1146)*

APPLICATIONS SOFTWARE PROGRAMMING
Galaxy Software LLC .... G 631 244-8405
  Oakdale *(G-12516)*
Maven Marketing LLC .... G 615 510-3248
  New York *(G-10731)*

AQUARIUM ACCESS, METAL
Aquarium Pump & Piping Systems .... F 631 567-5555
  Sayville *(G-14625)*

AQUARIUM DESIGN & MAINTENANCE SVCS
C B Management Services Inc .... F 845 735-2300
  Pearl River *(G-12895)*

AQUARIUMS & ACCESS: Glass
C B Management Services Inc .... F 845 735-2300
  Pearl River *(G-12895)*
Stark Aquarium Products Co Inc .... E 718 445-5357
  Flushing *(G-5048)*

AQUARIUMS & ACCESS: Plastic
Aquarium Pump & Piping Systems .... F 631 567-5555
  Sayville *(G-14625)*
Eugene G Danner Mfg Inc .... E 631 234-5261
  Central Islip *(G-3368)*

ARCHITECTURAL SVCS
B & F Architectural Support Gr .... E 212 279-6488
  New York *(G-8987)*
Deerfield Millwork Inc .... F 631 726-9663
  Water Mill *(G-15969)*
Productand Design Inc .... F 718 858-2440
  Brooklyn *(G-2353)*

ARMATURE REPAIRING & REWINDING SVC
Ener-G-Rotors Inc .... G 518 372-2608
  Schenectady *(G-14670)*
Power-Flo Technologies Inc .... D 315 399-5801
  East Syracuse *(G-4362)*
Sunset Ridge Holdings Inc .... G 716 487-1458
  Jamestown *(G-6753)*

AROMATIC CHEMICAL PRDTS
C & A Service Inc .... G 516 354-1200
  Floral Park *(G-4958)*
Citrus and Allied Essences Ltd .... C 516 354-1200
  Floral Park *(G-4960)*

ART & ORNAMENTAL WARE: Pottery
American Country Quilts & Lin .... G 631 283-5466
  Southampton *(G-14949)*

ART DEALERS & GALLERIES
Frame Shoppe & Art Gallery .... G 516 365-6014
  Manhasset *(G-7767)*
Penhouse Media Group Inc .... C 212 702-6000
  New York *(G-11149)*

ART DESIGN SVCS
Dwm International Inc .... F 646 290-7448
  Long Island City *(G-7431)*
Graphics Plus Printing Inc .... E 607 299-0500
  Cortland *(G-3875)*

ART GOODS & SPLYS WHOLESALERS
Gei International Inc .... E 315 463-9261
  East Syracuse *(G-4342)*

Golden Group International Ltd .... G 845 440-1025
  Patterson *(G-12882)*

ART MARBLE: Concrete
Fordham Marble Co Inc .... F 914 682-6699
  White Plains *(G-16451)*
Milano Granite and Marble Corp .... F 718 477-7200
  Staten Island *(G-15105)*
Royal Marble & Granite Inc .... G 516 536-5900
  Oceanside *(G-12555)*

ART NEEDLEWORK, MADE FROM PURCHASED MATERIALS
Clpa Embroidery .... G 516 409-0002
  Bellmore *(G-787)*
Jomar Industries Inc .... E 845 357-5773
  Airmont *(G-14)*
Knucklehead Embroidery Inc .... G 607 797-2725
  Johnson City *(G-6814)*
Screen The World Inc .... F 631 475-0023
  Holtsville *(G-6244)*
Verdonette Inc .... G 212 719-2003
  New York *(G-12010)*

ART RELATED SVCS
Halo Associates .... G 212 691-9549
  New York *(G-10024)*

ART RESTORATION SVC
Julius Lowy Frame Restoring Co .... E 212 861-8585
  New York *(G-10377)*
Sunburst Studios Inc .... G 718 768-6360
  Brooklyn *(G-2532)*

ART SPLY STORES
Simon Liu Inc .... F 718 567-2011
  Brooklyn *(G-2475)*

ARTISTS' EQPT
Simon Liu Inc .... F 718 567-2011
  Brooklyn *(G-2475)*
Spaulding & Rogers Mfg Inc .... D 518 768-2070
  Voorheesville *(G-15880)*

ARTISTS' MATERIALS, WHOLESALE
R & F Handmade Paints Inc .... F 845 331-3112
  Kingston *(G-6915)*

ARTISTS' MATERIALS: Frames, Artists' Canvases
Clapper Hollow Designs Inc .... E 518 234-9561
  Cobleskill *(G-3600)*
Handmade Frames Inc .... F 718 782-8364
  Brooklyn *(G-1966)*
Lopez Restorations Inc .... F 718 383-1555
  Brooklyn *(G-2134)*
Timeless Decor LLC .... F 315 782-5759
  Watertown *(G-16035)*

ARTISTS' MATERIALS: Ink, Drawing, Black & Colored
Sml Brothers Holding Corp .... D 718 402-2000
  Bronx *(G-1387)*

ARTISTS' MATERIALS: Paints, Exc Gold & Bronze
Golden Artist Colors Inc .... C 607 847-6154
  New Berlin *(G-8488)*

ARTISTS' MATERIALS: Pastels
North America Pastel Artists .... G 718 463-4701
  Flushing *(G-5030)*

ARTISTS' MATERIALS: Wax
Micro Powders Inc .... E 914 332-6400
  Tarrytown *(G-15483)*

ARTS & CRAFTS SCHOOL
Slosson Eductl Publications .... F 716 652-0930
  East Aurora *(G-4210)*

ARTWORK: Framed
Handmade Frames Inc .... F 718 782-8364
  Brooklyn *(G-1966)*

ASBESTOS PRODUCTS
Andujar Asbestos and Lead .... G 716 228-6757
  Buffalo *(G-2700)*
Regional MGT & Consulting Inc .... F 718 599-3718
  Brooklyn *(G-2393)*

ASPHALT & ASPHALT PRDTS
A Colarusso and Son Inc .... E 518 828-3218
  Hudson *(G-6336)*
Atlas Bituminous Co Inc .... F 315 457-2394
  Syracuse *(G-15248)*
Barrett Paving Materials Inc .... F 315 737-9471
  Clayville *(G-3554)*
Barrett Paving Materials Inc .... G 607 723-5367
  Binghamton *(G-864)*
C & C Ready-Mix Corporation .... E 607 797-5108
  Vestal *(G-15812)*
Callanan Industries Inc .... G 845 457-3158
  Montgomery *(G-8309)*
Cobleskill Stone Products Inc .... E 607 432-8321
  Oneonta *(G-12632)*
Cobleskill Stone Products Inc .... F 607 637-4271
  Hancock *(G-5710)*
Cosmicoat of Wny Inc .... G 716 772-2644
  Gasport *(G-5305)*
Hanson Aggregates PA LLC .... E 585 624-3800
  Honeoye Falls *(G-6266)*
King Road Materials Inc .... G 518 381-9995
  Albany *(G-91)*
King Road Materials Inc .... G 518 382-5354
  Schenectady *(G-14694)*
Northern Bituminous Mix Inc .... G 315 598-2141
  Fulton *(G-5230)*
Package Pavement Company Inc .... D 845 221-2224
  Stormville *(G-15180)*
Peckham Materials Corp .... G 845 562-5370
  Newburgh *(G-12240)*
Peckham Materials Corp .... D 914 686-2045
  White Plains *(G-16489)*
Posillico Materials LLC .... F 631 249-1872
  Farmingdale *(G-4854)*
Suit-Kote Corporation .... C 607 753-1100
  Cortland *(G-3895)*
Suit-Kote Corporation .... E 716 664-3750
  Jamestown *(G-6752)*
Upstone Materials Inc .... D 518 561-5321
  Plattsburgh *(G-13165)*
Vestal Asphalt Inc .... F 607 785-3393
  Vestal *(G-15825)*

ASPHALT COATINGS & SEALERS
Barrett Paving Materials Inc .... E 315 353-6611
  Norwood *(G-12495)*
Callanan Industries Inc .... E 845 457-3158
  Montgomery *(G-8309)*
Northeastern Sealcoat Inc .... F 585 544-4372
  Rochester *(G-13979)*
Peckham Materials Corp .... E 518 747-3353
  Hudson Falls *(G-6384)*
Sheldon Slate Products Co Inc .... E 518 642-1280
  Middle Granville *(G-8112)*
Suit-Kote Corporation .... E 607 535-2743
  Watkins Glen *(G-16061)*
Tntpaving .... G 607 372-4911
  Endicott *(G-4612)*

ASPHALT MIXTURES WHOLESALERS
A Colarusso and Son Inc .... E 518 828-3218
  Hudson *(G-6336)*
County Line Stone Co Inc .... E 716 542-5435
  Akron *(G-17)*
Hanson Aggregates PA LLC .... E 585 624-1220
  Honeoye Falls *(G-6267)*

ASPHALT PLANTS INCLUDING GRAVEL MIX TYPE
Midland Machinery Co Inc .... D 716 692-1200
  Tonawanda *(G-15558)*
Patterson Blacktop Corp .... G 845 628-3425
  Carmel *(G-3279)*
Peckham Materials Corp .... E 518 747-3353
  Hudson Falls *(G-6384)*

Employee Codes: A=Over 500 employees, B=251-500
C=101-250, D=51-100, E=20-50, F=10-19, G=5-9

ASPHALT PLANTS INCLUDING GRAVEL MIX TYPE

Penn Can Equipment Corporation ....G... 315 378-0337
  Lyons *(G-7686)*
Rochester Asphalt Materials................G... 315 524-4619
  Walworth *(G-15915)*

ASSEMBLING SVC: Plumbing Fixture Fittings, Plastic

Mark Posner ....G... 718 258-6241
  Brooklyn *(G-2169)*

ASSOCIATIONS: Engineering

American Inst Chem Engineers ....D... 646 495-1355
  New York *(G-8830)*

ASSOCIATIONS: Scientists'

Association For Cmpt McHy Inc..............D... 212 869-7440
  New York *(G-8938)*

ATOMIZERS

Aloi Solutions LLC..................................E... 585 292-0920
  Rochester *(G-13619)*
Ascribe Inc...E... 585 413-0298
  Rochester *(G-13646)*
Boom LLC ....E... 646 218-0752
  New York *(G-9121)*
Chan & Chan (usa) Corp ....G... 718 388-9633
  Brooklyn *(G-1688)*
Christian Dior Perfumes LLC ....E... 212 931-2200
  New York *(G-9291)*
Deva Concepts LLC ....E... 212 343-0344
  New York *(G-9514)*
Givi Inc ....F... 212 586-5029
  New York *(G-9926)*
Hoskie Co Inc ....D... 718 628-8672
  Brooklyn *(G-1985)*
Mitten Manufacturing Inc ....E... 315 437-7564
  Syracuse *(G-15375)*
Shyam Ahuja Limited ....G... 212 644-5910
  New York *(G-11573)*
Trendsformers Ltd Liability Co...............G... 888 700-2423
  New York *(G-11891)*

ATTENUATORS

Mini-Circuits Fort Wayne LLC................B... 718 934-4500
  Brooklyn *(G-2210)*
Traffic Lane Closures LLC ....F... 845 228-6100
  Carmel *(G-3283)*

AUDIO & VIDEO EQPT, EXC COMMERCIAL

Audio Video Invasion Inc ....F... 516 345-2636
  Plainview *(G-13037)*
Audiosavings Inc ....F... 888 445-1555
  Inwood *(G-6486)*
Avcom of Virginia Inc ....D... 585 924-4560
  Victor *(G-15830)*
AVI-Spl Employee ....B... 212 840-4801
  New York *(G-8977)*
B & H Electronics Corp ....E... 845 782-5000
  Monroe *(G-8264)*
Communication Power Corp...................E... 631 434-7306
  Hauppauge *(G-5796)*
Digital Home Creations Inc ....G... 585 576-7070
  Webster *(G-16082)*
Fulcrum Acoustic LLC............................G... 866 234-0678
  Rochester *(G-13820)*
G E Inspection Technologies LP ....C... 315 554-2000
  Skaneateles *(G-14871)*
General Electric Company ....G... 315 554-2000
  Skaneateles *(G-14872)*
Key Digital Systems Inc ....E... 914 667-9700
  Mount Vernon *(G-8413)*
L3 Technologies Inc...............................A... 631 436-7400
  Hauppauge *(G-5859)*
Laird Telemedia ....C... 845 339-9555
  Mount Marion *(G-8363)*
Masterdisk Corporation..........................F... 212 541-5022
  Elmsford *(G-4551)*
Navitar Inc ....D... 585 359-4000
  Rochester *(G-13965)*
NEa Manufacturing Corp ....E... 516 371-4200
  Inwood *(G-6497)*
New Wop Records ....G... 631 617-9592
  Deer Park *(G-4015)*
Octave Music Group Inc ....G... 212 991-6540
  New York *(G-11031)*
Sage Audio Video Tech LLC ....G... 212 213-1523
  New York *(G-11465)*

Scy Manufacturing Inc...........................G... 516 986-3083
  Inwood *(G-6500)*
Sima Technologies LLC.........................G... 412 828-9130
  Hauppauge *(G-5940)*
Sony Corporation of America ....C... 212 833-8000
  New York *(G-11645)*
Sound Video Systems Wny LLC............F... 716 684-8200
  Buffalo *(G-3073)*
Tkm Technologies Inc ....G... 631 474-4700
  Port Jeff STA *(G-13219)*
Touchtunes Music Corporation ....D... 847 419-3300
  New York *(G-11876)*
Wyrestorm Technologies LLC ....F... 518 289-1293
  Round Lake *(G-14465)*

AUDIO COMPONENTS

Ashly Audio Inc ....E... 585 872-0010
  Webster *(G-16074)*

AUDIO ELECTRONIC SYSTEMS

Audio Technology New York Inc...........F... 718 369-7528
  Brooklyn *(G-1576)*
B & K Components Ltd ....D... 323 776-4277
  Buffalo *(G-2720)*
Convergent Audio Tech Inc....................E... 585 359-2700
  Rush *(G-14471)*
Gilmores Sound Advice Inc ....F... 212 265-4445
  New York *(G-9921)*
Granada Electronics Inc.........................G... 718 387-1157
  Brooklyn *(G-1947)*
Lamm Industries Inc ....G... 718 368-0181
  Brooklyn *(G-2092)*
Vincent Conigliaro ....F... 845 340-0489
  Kingston *(G-6931)*
Whirlwind Music Distrs Inc ....D... 800 733-9473
  Rochester *(G-14207)*
Yorkville Sound Inc ....G... 716 297-2920
  Niagara Falls *(G-12350)*

AUDIO-VISUAL PROGRAM PRODUCTION SVCS

ABRA Media Inc ....G... 518 398-1010
  Pine Plains *(G-13004)*
Guilford Publications Inc ....D... 212 431-9800
  New York *(G-10008)*
Hatherleigh Company Ltd ....G... 607 538-1092
  Hobart *(G-6163)*
Play-It Productions Inc ....F... 212 695-6530
  Port Washington *(G-13297)*

AUDIOLOGISTS' OFFICES

Family Hearing Center............................G... 845 897-3059
  Fishkill *(G-4946)*
Todt Hill Audiological Svcs ....G... 718 816-1952
  Staten Island *(G-15147)*

AUDITING SVCS

Advance Finance Group LLC.................D... 212 630-5900
  New York *(G-8746)*

AUTO & HOME SUPPLY STORES: Auto & Truck Eqpt & Parts

K M Drive Line Inc...................................G... 718 599-0628
  Brooklyn *(G-2064)*

AUTO & HOME SUPPLY STORES: Automotive Access

Blackburn Truck Bodies LLC................G... 315 448-3236
  Syracuse *(G-15259)*
Legendary Auto Interiors Ltd ....E... 315 331-1212
  Newark *(G-12198)*
Split Rock Trading Co Inc......................G... 631 929-3261
  Wading River *(G-15887)*
Zappala Farms AG Systems Inc ....E... 315 626-6293
  Cato *(G-3301)*

AUTO & HOME SUPPLY STORES: Speed Shops, Incl Race Car Splys

Auto Sport Designs Inc ....F... 631 425-1555
  Huntington Station *(G-6433)*
Marcovicci-Wenz Engineering ....G... 631 467-9040
  Ronkonkoma *(G-14375)*
Troyer Inc...F... 585 352-5590
  Rochester *(G-14177)*

AUTO & HOME SUPPLY STORES: Trailer Hitches, Automotive

General Welding & Fabg Inc ....F... 585 697-7660
  Rochester *(G-13828)*

AUTO & HOME SUPPLY STORES: Truck Eqpt & Parts

Agri Services Co ....G... 716 937-6618
  Alden *(G-166)*
Bick & Heintz Inc ....F... 315 733-7577
  Utica *(G-15680)*
Dejana Trck Utility Eqp Co LLC ....C... 631 544-9000
  Kings Park *(G-6882)*
General Welding & Fabg Inc ....G... 716 652-0033
  Elma *(G-4451)*

AUTOCLAVES: Indl

Wsf Industries Inc ....E... 716 692-4930
  Tonawanda *(G-15592)*

AUTOCLAVES: Laboratory

SPS Medical Supply Corp ....F... 585 968-2377
  Cuba *(G-3920)*
Vivus Technologies LLC ....E... 585 798-6658
  Medina *(G-7991)*

AUTOMATIC REGULATING CONTROL: Building Svcs Monitoring, Auto

Building Management Assoc Inc...........E... 718 542-4779
  Bronx *(G-1234)*
Johnson Controls Inc ....C... 585 724-2232
  Rochester *(G-13897)*
Reuse Action Incorporated ....G... 716 949-0900
  Buffalo *(G-3035)*
Unisend LLC..E... 585 414-9575
  Webster *(G-16104)*
Virtual Super LLC ....E... 212 685-6400
  New York *(G-12041)*

AUTOMATIC REGULATING CONTROLS: AC & Refrigeration

Bitzer Scroll Inc ....D... 315 463-2101
  Syracuse *(G-15258)*
Care Enterprises Inc ....G... 631 472-8155
  Bayport *(G-735)*
Siemens Industry Inc ....D... 716 568-0983
  Amherst *(G-250)*

AUTOMATIC REGULATING CONTROLS: Elect Air Cleaner, Automatic

Biorem Environmental Inc ....E... 585 924-2220
  Victor *(G-15831)*

AUTOMATIC REGULATING CONTROLS: Energy Cutoff, Residtl/Comm

Black River Generations LLC ....E... 315 773-2314
  Fort Drum *(G-5091)*
Eastern Strategic Materials...................E... 212 332-1619
  New York *(G-9612)*
Johnson Controls Inc ....E... 914 593-5200
  Hawthorne *(G-5989)*

AUTOMATIC REGULATING CONTROLS: Ice Maker

Henderson Products Inc ....E... 315 785-0994
  Watertown *(G-16016)*

AUTOMATIC REGULATING CONTROLS: Pneumatic Relays, Air-Cond

A K Allen Co Inc ....C... 516 747-5450
  Melville *(G-7996)*

AUTOMATIC REGULATING CONTROLS: Refrig/Air-Cond Defrost

Carrier Corporation.................................B... 315 432-6000
  Syracuse *(G-15272)*
Svyz Trading Corp ....K... 718 220-1140
  Bronx *(G-1397)*

PRODUCT SECTION

AUTOMOTIVE SPLYS & PARTS, NEW, WHOLESALE: Splys

AUTOMATIC REGULATING CTRLS: Damper, Pneumatic Or Electric

Air Louver & Damper Inc ....F...... 718 392-3232
  Long Island City (G-7369)
Airflex Industrial Inc ....E...... 631 752-1234
  Farmingdale (G-4710)

AUTOMATIC TELLER MACHINES

International Mdse Svcs Inc ....G...... 914 699-4000
  Mount Vernon (G-8409)
Jpmorgan Chase Bank Nat Assn ....G...... 718 767-3592
  College Point (G-3651)
K&G of Syracuse Inc ....G...... 315 446-1921
  Syracuse (G-15353)
Mid Enterprise Inc ....G...... 631 924-3933
  Middle Island (G-8118)
Parabit Systems Inc ....E...... 516 378-4800
  Bellmore (G-791)
Stanson Automated LLC ....F...... 866 505-7826
  Yonkers (G-16799)

AUTOMATIC VENDING MACHINES: Mechanisms & Parts

Global Payment Tech Inc ....F...... 516 887-0700
  Valley Stream (G-15781)
Global Payment Tech Inc ....E...... 631 563-2500
  Bohemia (G-1030)

AUTOMOBILE RECOVERY SVCS

Nova Inc ....G...... 212 967-1139
  New York (G-10999)

AUTOMOBILES: Off-Highway, Electric

Bombardier Trnsp Holdings USA ....D...... 607 776-4791
  Bath (G-641)

AUTOMOBILES: Wholesalers

Split Rock Trading Co Inc ....G...... 631 929-3261
  Wading River (G-15887)

AUTOMOTIVE & TRUCK GENERAL REPAIR SVC

Dennys Drive Shaft Service ....G...... 716 875-6640
  Kenmore (G-6858)
Homer Iron Works LLC ....G...... 607 749-3963
  Homer (G-6256)
James Woerner Inc ....G...... 631 454-9330
  Farmingdale (G-4791)
Whitesboro Spring & Alignment ....F...... 315 736-4441
  Whitesboro (G-16532)

AUTOMOTIVE BODY, PAINT & INTERIOR REPAIR & MAINTENANCE SVC

Conti Auto Body Corp ....G...... 516 921-6435
  Syosset (G-15211)

AUTOMOTIVE PARTS, ACCESS & SPLYS

Actasys Inc ....G...... 914 432-2336
  Watervliet (G-16040)
Allomatic Products Company ....G...... 516 775-0330
  Floral Park (G-4955)
Alloy Metal Products LLC ....F...... 315 676-2405
  Central Square (G-3389)
American Auto ACC Incrporation ....E...... 718 886-6600
  Flushing (G-4984)
American Refuse Supply Inc ....G...... 718 893-8157
  Bronx (G-1219)
Anchor Commerce Trading Corp ....G...... 516 881-3485
  Atlantic Beach (G-455)
Axle Express ....E...... 518 347-2220
  Schenectady (G-14651)
Bigbee Steel and Tank Company ....E...... 518 273-0801
  Watervliet (G-16041)
Borgwarner Inc ....F...... 607 257-6700
  Ithaca (G-6564)
Borgwarner Inc ....E...... 607 257-1800
  Ithaca (G-6565)
Borgwarner Ithaca LLC ....B...... 607 257-6700
  Ithaca (G-6566)
Borgwarner Morse TEC Inc ....D...... 607 266-5111
  Ithaca (G-6567)
Borgwarner Morse TEC LLC ....C...... 607 257-6700
  Ithaca (G-6568)

Borgwarner Morse TEC LLC ....D...... 607 257-6700
  Cortland (G-3863)
Car-Go Industries Inc ....G...... 718 472-1443
  Woodside (G-16650)
Cubic Trnsp Systems Inc ....F...... 212 255-1810
  New York (G-9431)
Cummins Inc ....A...... 716 456-2111
  Lakewood (G-6993)
Custom Sitecom LLC ....F...... 631 420-4238
  Farmingdale (G-4746)
Delphi Automotive LLP ....G...... 716 438-4886
  Amherst (G-224)
Delphi Powertrain Systems LLC ....C...... 585 359-6000
  West Henrietta (G-16236)
Delphi Powertrain Systems LLC ....B...... 585 359-6000
  West Henrietta (G-16237)
Delphi Powertrain Systems LLC ....E...... 585 359-6000
  West Henrietta (G-16238)
Delphi Thermal Systems ....F...... 716 439-2454
  Lockport (G-7293)
Dmic Inc ....G...... 716 743-4360
  North Tonawanda (G-12425)
Electronic Machine Parts LLC ....F...... 631 434-3700
  Hauppauge (G-5818)
Exten II LLC ....F...... 716 895-2214
  East Aurora (G-4199)
Fast By Gast Inc ....G...... 716 773-1536
  Grand Island (G-5499)
General Motors LLC ....A...... 716 879-5000
  Buffalo (G-2847)
General Motors LLC ....B...... 315 764-2000
  Massena (G-7902)
GM Components Holdings LLC ....B...... 585 647-7000
  Rochester (G-13842)
GM Components Holdings LLC ....B...... 716 439-2463
  Lockport (G-7305)
GM Components Holdings LLC ....B...... 716 439-2011
  Lockport (G-7306)
Interntnal Auto Voluntary Untd ....G...... 718 743-8732
  Brooklyn (G-2013)
ITT Enidine Inc ....B...... 716 662-1900
  Orchard Park (G-12720)
Jtekt Torsen North America ....F...... 585 464-5000
  Rochester (G-13899)
Karlyn Industries Inc ....F...... 845 351-2249
  Southfields (G-14966)
Kerns Manufacturing Corp ....C...... 718 784-4044
  Long Island City (G-7488)
Lee World Industries LLC ....F...... 212 265-8866
  New York (G-10538)
Magtrol Inc ....E...... 716 668-5555
  Buffalo (G-2935)
Mahle Behr USA Inc ....B...... 716 439-2011
  Lockport (G-7314)
Mahle Industries Incorporated ....F...... 248 735-3623
  Amherst (G-238)
Nas-Tra Automotive Inds Inc ....C...... 631 225-1225
  Lindenhurst (G-7182)
Par-Foam Products Inc ....C...... 716 855-2066
  Buffalo (G-2990)
Parker-Hannifin Corporation ....D...... 716 685-4040
  Lancaster (G-7037)
Performance Designed By Peters ......F...... 585 223-9062
  Fairport (G-4650)
Phillip J Ortiz Manufacturing ....G...... 845 226-7030
  Hopewell Junction (G-6292)
Powerflow Inc ....D...... 716 892-1014
  Buffalo (G-3010)
Pro-Value Distribution Inc ....G...... 585 783-1461
  Rochester (G-14048)
Rosco Inc ....C...... 718 526-2601
  Jamaica (G-6675)
Specialty Silicone Pdts Inc ....D...... 518 885-8826
  Ballston Spa (G-596)
Tesla Motors Inc ....A...... 212 206-1204
  New York (G-11803)
Troyer Inc ....F...... 585 352-5590
  Rochester (G-14177)
TRW Automotive Inc ....B...... 315 255-3311
  Auburn (G-506)
Whiting Door Mfg Corp ....B...... 716 542-5427
  Akron (G-24)
Wolo Mfg Corp ....E...... 631 242-0333
  Deer Park (G-4064)
Yomiuri International Inc ....G...... 212 752-2196
  New York (G-12164)

AUTOMOTIVE PARTS: Plastic

CN Group Incorporated ....A...... 914 358-5690
  White Plains (G-16438)

Fiber Laminations Limited ....F...... 716 692-1825
  Tonawanda (G-15540)
Koonichi Inc ....G...... 718 886-8338
  Fresh Meadows (G-5201)
Macauto Usa Inc ....E...... 585 342-2060
  Rochester (G-13919)
Rus Auto Parts Inc ....G...... 800 410-2669
  Brooklyn (G-2427)
Tint World ....G...... 631 458-1999
  Medford (G-7967)

AUTOMOTIVE PRDTS: Rubber

Vehicle Manufacturers Inc ....E...... 631 851-1700
  Hauppauge (G-5968)

AUTOMOTIVE REPAIR SHOPS: Brake Repair

Whitesboro Spring & Alignment ....F...... 315 736-4441
  Whitesboro (G-16532)

AUTOMOTIVE REPAIR SHOPS: Diesel Engine Repair

Jack W Miller ....G...... 585 538-2399
  Scottsville (G-14751)

AUTOMOTIVE REPAIR SHOPS: Electrical Svcs

Gerome Technologies Inc ....D...... 518 463-1324
  Menands (G-8085)

AUTOMOTIVE REPAIR SHOPS: Engine Repair

Jack Merkel Inc ....G...... 631 234-2600
  Hauppauge (G-5853)

AUTOMOTIVE REPAIR SHOPS: Machine Shop

Bullet Industries Inc ....G...... 585 352-0836
  Spencerport (G-14977)
Meade Machine Co Inc ....G...... 315 923-1703
  Clyde (G-3595)
Vytek Inc ....F...... 631 750-1770
  Bohemia (G-1107)

AUTOMOTIVE REPAIR SHOPS: Springs, Rebuilding & Repair

Andersens Spring & Wldg Corp ....G...... 516 785-7337
  Bellmore (G-784)

AUTOMOTIVE REPAIR SHOPS: Trailer Repair

General Welding & Fabg Inc ....F...... 585 697-7660
  Rochester (G-13828)

AUTOMOTIVE REPAIR SVC

Banner Transmission & Eng Co ....F...... 516 221-9459
  Melville (G-8004)
Cyclone Air Power Inc ....G...... 718 447-3038
  Staten Island (G-15067)

AUTOMOTIVE SPLYS & PARTS, NEW, WHOL: Testing Eqpt, Electric

Katikati Inc ....G...... 585 678-1764
  West Henrietta (G-16243)

AUTOMOTIVE SPLYS & PARTS, NEW, WHOLESALE: Brakes

Interparts International Inc ....E...... 516 576-2000
  Plainview (G-13065)

AUTOMOTIVE SPLYS & PARTS, NEW, WHOLESALE: Clutches

Rpb Distributors LLC ....G...... 914 244-3600
  Mount Kisco (G-8358)

AUTOMOTIVE SPLYS & PARTS, NEW, WHOLESALE: Splys

Extreme Auto Accessories Corp ....F...... 718 978-6722
  Mineola (G-8221)

Employee Codes: A=Over 500 employees, B=251-500
C=101-250, D=51-100, E=20-50, F=10-19, G=5-9

AUTOMOTIVE SPLYS & PARTS, NEW, WHOLESALE: Trim

Legendary Auto Interiors Ltd ....E....... 315 331-1212
  Newark *(G-12198)*

AUTOMOTIVE SPLYS & PARTS, NEW, WHOLESALE: Wheels

Factory Wheel Warehouse Inc ....G....... 516 605-2131
  Plainview *(G-13057)*

AUTOMOTIVE SPLYS & PARTS, USED, WHOLESALE: Wheels

Factory Wheel Warehouse Inc ....G....... 516 605-2131
  Plainview *(G-13057)*

AUTOMOTIVE SPLYS & PARTS, WHOLESALE, NEC

Auto-Mat Company Inc ....E....... 516 938-7373
  Hicksville *(G-6062)*
Axle Teknology LLC ....G....... 631 423-3044
  Huntington *(G-6393)*
Deer Park Driveshaft & Hose ....G....... 631 667-4091
  Deer Park *(G-3963)*
Depot Label Company Inc ....G....... 631 467-2952
  Patchogue *(G-12864)*
Noresco Industrial Group Inc ....E....... 516 759-3355
  Glen Cove *(G-5371)*
Qpbc Inc ....E....... 718 685-1900
  Long Island City *(G-7564)*
Split Rock Trading Co Inc ....G....... 631 929-3261
  Wading River *(G-15887)*
Tint World ....G....... 631 458-1999
  Medford *(G-7967)*

AUTOMOTIVE SPLYS/PARTS, NEW, WHOL: Body Rpr/Paint Shop Splys

Auto Body Services LLC ....F....... 631 431-4640
  Lindenhurst *(G-7162)*

AUTOMOTIVE SVCS, EXC REPAIR & CARWASHES: Maintenance

Roli Retreads Inc ....E....... 631 694-7670
  Farmingdale *(G-4868)*

AUTOMOTIVE SVCS, EXC REPAIR: Washing & Polishing

Saccomize Inc ....G....... 818 287-3000
  Bronx *(G-1378)*

AUTOMOTIVE SVCS, EXC RPR/CARWASHES: High Perf Auto Rpr/Svc

Riverview Industries Inc ....G....... 845 265-5284
  Cold Spring *(G-3627)*

AUTOMOTIVE TOPS INSTALLATION OR REPAIR: Canvas Or Plastic

Quantum Sails Rochester LLC ....G....... 585 342-5200
  Rochester *(G-14064)*

AUTOMOTIVE TOWING & WRECKING SVC

American Towman Network Inc ....F....... 845 986-4546
  Warwick *(G-15948)*

AUTOMOTIVE UPHOLSTERY SHOPS

Sausbiers Awning Shop Inc ....G....... 518 828-3748
  Hudson *(G-6371)*

AUTOMOTIVE WELDING SVCS

Big Apple Welding Supply ....G....... 718 439-3959
  Brooklyn *(G-1610)*
Chautauqua Machine Spc LLC ....F....... 716 782-3276
  Ashville *(G-416)*
Waynes Welding Inc ....E....... 315 768-6146
  Yorkville *(G-16835)*

AUTOMOTIVE: Bodies

Antiques & Collectible Autos ....G....... 716 825-3990
  Buffalo *(G-2702)*

Conti Auto Body Corp ....G....... 516 921-6435
  Syosset *(G-15211)*
Empire Coachworks Intl LLC ....D....... 732 257-7981
  Suffern *(G-15190)*

AUTOMOTIVE: Seating

Johnson Controls Inc ....D....... 518 884-8313
  Ballston Spa *(G-586)*
Johnson Controls Inc ....G....... 518 694-4822
  Albany *(G-89)*
Johnson Controls Inc ....E....... 585 671-1930
  Webster *(G-16087)*
Johnson Controls Inc ....C....... 585 724-2232
  Rochester *(G-13897)*

AUTOTRANSFORMERS: Electric

General Electric Company ....A....... 518 385-4022
  Schenectady *(G-14675)*
General Electric Company ....E....... 518 385-7620
  Niskayuna *(G-12354)*

AWNING REPAIR SHOP

Kohler Awning Inc ....E....... 716 685-3333
  Buffalo *(G-2911)*
TG Peppe Inc ....G....... 516 239-7852
  Lawrence *(G-7110)*

AWNINGS & CANOPIES

Five Star Awnings Inc ....F....... 718 860-6070
  Ridgewood *(G-13536)*
Hart To Hart Industries Inc ....G....... 716 492-2709
  Chaffee *(G-3404)*
Lotus Awnings Enterprises Inc ....F....... 718 965-4824
  Brooklyn *(G-2136)*
Superior Exteriors of Buffalo ....F....... 716 873-1000
  East Amherst *(G-4191)*
Vitarose Corp of America ....G....... 718 951-9700
  Brooklyn *(G-2630)*

AWNINGS & CANOPIES: Awnings, Fabric, From Purchased Matls

125-127 Main Street Corp ....F....... 631 477-1500
  Greenport *(G-5625)*
Abble Awning Co Inc ....G....... 516 822-1200
  Bethpage *(G-837)*
Acme Awning Co Inc ....F....... 718 409-1881
  Bronx *(G-1210)*
Awning Mart Inc ....G....... 315 699-5928
  Cicero *(G-3514)*
Brock Awnings Ltd ....F....... 631 765-5200
  Hampton Bays *(G-5708)*
C E King & Sons Inc ....G....... 631 324-4944
  East Hampton *(G-4233)*
Canvas Products Company Inc ....F....... 516 742-1058
  Mineola *(G-8209)*
Capitol Awning Co Inc ....F....... 212 505-1717
  Jamaica *(G-6631)*
Classic Awnings Inc ....F....... 716 649-0390
  Hamburg *(G-5674)*
Di Sanos Creative Canvas Inc ....G....... 315 894-3137
  Frankfort *(G-5105)*
Dor-A-Mar Canvas Products Co ....F....... 631 750-9202
  West Sayville *(G-16288)*
Durasol Systems Inc ....D....... 845 610-1100
  Chester *(G-3473)*
Fabric Concepts For Industry ....F....... 914 375-2565
  Yonkers *(G-16757)*
Jamestown Awning Inc ....G....... 716 483-1435
  Jamestown *(G-6726)*
Kohler Awning Inc ....E....... 716 685-3333
  Buffalo *(G-2911)*
M & M Canvas & Awnings Inc ....G....... 631 424-5370
  Islandia *(G-6534)*
Mauceri Sign Inc ....F....... 718 656-7700
  Jamaica *(G-6659)*
Northern Awning & Sign Company ....G....... 315 782-8515
  Watertown *(G-16030)*
Perma Tech Inc ....E....... 716 854-0707
  Buffalo *(G-3000)*
Sausbiers Awning Shop Inc ....G....... 518 828-3748
  Hudson *(G-6371)*
Steinway Awning II LLC ....G....... 718 729-2965
  Astoria *(G-446)*
TG Peppe Inc ....G....... 516 239-7852
  Lawrence *(G-7110)*

AWNINGS & CANOPIES: Fabric

Kingston Building Products LLC ....G....... 914 665-0707
  Mount Vernon *(G-8415)*
Lanza Corp ....G....... 914 937-6360
  Port Chester *(G-13204)*

AWNINGS: Fiberglass

Acme Awning Co Inc ....F....... 718 409-1881
  Bronx *(G-1210)*
Space Sign ....F....... 718 961-1112
  College Point *(G-3667)*
Vitarose Corp of America ....G....... 718 951-9700
  Brooklyn *(G-2630)*

AWNINGS: Metal

Dart Awning Inc ....G....... 516 544-2082
  Freeport *(G-5150)*
Kenan International Trading ....G....... 718 672-4922
  Corona *(G-3847)*
Space Sign ....F....... 718 961-1112
  College Point *(G-3667)*

AXLES

Axle Teknology LLC ....G....... 631 423-3044
  Huntington *(G-6393)*
Temper Corporation ....G....... 518 853-3467
  Fonda *(G-5068)*

BABY FORMULA

Baby Central LLC ....G....... 718 372-2229
  Brooklyn *(G-1581)*

BABY PACIFIERS: Rubber

Mam USA Corporation ....F....... 914 269-2500
  Purchase *(G-13392)*

BADGES: Identification & Insignia

Identfication Data Imaging LLC ....G....... 516 484-6500
  Port Washington *(G-13267)*

BAGS & BAGGING: Knit

Nochairs Inc ....G....... 917 748-8731
  New York *(G-10983)*

BAGS & CONTAINERS: Textile, Exc Sleeping

Carry Hot Inc ....F....... 212 279-7535
  New York *(G-9216)*

BAGS & SACKS: Shipping & Shopping

Kapstone Container Corporation ....D....... 518 842-2450
  Amsterdam *(G-342)*

BAGS: Canvas

Aka Sport Inc ....F....... 631 858-9888
  Dix Hills *(G-4118)*
H G Maybeck Co Inc ....E....... 718 297-4410
  Jamaica *(G-6649)*
Spray Moret LLC ....G....... 917 213-9592
  New York *(G-11679)*

BAGS: Cellophane

Aladdin Packaging LLC ....D....... 631 273-4747
  Hauppauge *(G-5759)*

BAGS: Duffle, Canvas, Made From Purchased Materials

Select Fabricators Inc ....F....... 585 393-0650
  Canandaigua *(G-3233)*

BAGS: Food Storage & Frozen Food, Plastic

Pactiv LLC ....C....... 585 394-5125
  Canandaigua *(G-3228)*

BAGS: Food Storage & Trash, Plastic

Bag Arts The Art Packaging LLC ....G....... 212 684-7020
  New York *(G-9001)*
Mint-X Products Corporation ....F....... 877 646-8224
  College Point *(G-3656)*
Pactiv LLC ....C....... 518 793-2524
  Glens Falls *(G-5439)*

PRODUCT SECTION

BAGS: Garment Storage Exc Paper Or Plastic Film

Apex Real Holdings Inc .... G 877 725-2150
Brooklyn *(G-1540)*

BAGS: Grocers', Made From Purchased Materials

333 J & M Food Corp .... F 718 381-1493
Ridgewood *(G-13526)*
Bag Arts The Art Packaging LLC .... G 212 684-7020
New York *(G-9001)*
Lin Jin Feng .... G 718 232-3039
Brooklyn *(G-2124)*

BAGS: Knapsacks, Canvas, Made From Purchased Materials

Johnson Outdoors Inc .... C 607 779-2200
Binghamton *(G-899)*

BAGS: Laundry, Garment & Storage

Handy Laundry Products Corp .... G 845 701-1111
Airmont *(G-12)*

BAGS: Paper

American Packaging Corporation .... C 585 254-9500
Rochester *(G-13626)*
APC Paper Company Inc .... D 315 384-4225
Norfolk *(G-12356)*
R P Fedder Corp .... E 585 288-1600
Rochester *(G-14066)*
Uniflex Holdings LLC .... F 516 932-2000
Hauppauge *(G-5964)*

BAGS: Paper, Made From Purchased Materials

Polyseal Packaging Corp .... E 718 792-5530
Bronx *(G-1359)*

BAGS: Plastic

Adart Polyethylene Bag Mfg .... G 516 932-1001
Plainview *(G-13030)*
American Packaging Corporation .... G 585 254-2002
Rochester *(G-13625)*
American Packaging Corporation .... C 585 254-9500
Rochester *(G-13626)*
Berry Global Inc .... C 315 986-2161
Macedon *(G-7696)*
Centre De Conformite ICC Inc .... E 716 283-0002
Niagara Falls *(G-12270)*
Clear View Bag Company Inc .... C 518 458-7153
Albany *(G-59)*
D Bag Lady Inc .... G 585 425-8095
Fairport *(G-4630)*
Ecoplast & Packaging LLC .... G 718 996-0800
Brooklyn *(G-1811)*
Edco Supply Corporation .... D 718 788-8108
Brooklyn *(G-1813)*
H G Maybeck Co Inc .... E 718 297-4410
Jamaica *(G-6649)*
Ivi Services Inc .... D 607 729-5111
Binghamton *(G-897)*
Jay Bags Inc .... G 845 459-6500
Spring Valley *(G-14997)*
JM Murray Center Inc .... C 607 756-9913
Cortland *(G-3879)*
JM Murray Center Inc .... C 607 756-0246
Cortland *(G-3880)*
Kemco Sales LLC .... F 203 762-1902
East Rochester *(G-4288)*
Nova Packaging Ltd Inc .... E 914 232-8406
Katonah *(G-6845)*
Select Fabricators Inc .... F 585 393-0650
Canandaigua *(G-3233)*
Tai Seng .... G 718 399-6311
Brooklyn *(G-2554)*
Tg Polymers Inc .... G 585 670-9427
Webster *(G-16101)*
Trinity Packaging Corporation .... E 716 668-3111
Buffalo *(G-3103)*
W E W Container Corporation .... E 718 827-8150
Brooklyn *(G-2637)*

BAGS: Plastic & Pliofilm

Maco Bag Corporation .... C 315 226-1000
Newark *(G-12199)*
Modern Plastic Bags Mfg Inc .... G 718 237-2985
Brooklyn *(G-2221)*
Uniflex Holdings LLC .... F 516 932-2000
Hauppauge *(G-5964)*

BAGS: Plastic, Made From Purchased Materials

Alco Plastics Inc .... E 716 683-3020
Lancaster *(G-7005)*
Allied Converters Inc .... E 914 235-1585
New Rochelle *(G-8589)*
Amby International Inc .... G 718 645-0964
Brooklyn *(G-1517)*
API Industries Inc .... B 845 365-2200
Orangeburg *(G-12668)*
API Industries Inc .... C 845 365-2200
Orangeburg *(G-12669)*
Bags Unlimited Inc .... E 585 436-6282
Rochester *(G-13651)*
Bison Bag Co Inc .... D 716 434-4380
Lockport *(G-7287)*
Capitol Poly Corp .... E 718 855-6000
Brooklyn *(G-1674)*
Connover Packaging Inc .... G 585 377-2510
East Rochester *(G-4282)*
Excellent Poly Inc .... F 718 768-6555
Brooklyn *(G-1856)*
Filmpak Extrusion LLC .... D 631 293-6767
Melville *(G-8024)*
Fortune Poly Products Inc .... F 718 361-0767
Jamaica *(G-6643)*
Franklin Poly Film Inc .... F 718 492-3523
Brooklyn *(G-1904)*
Josh Packaging Inc .... E 631 822-1660
Hauppauge *(G-5854)*
Magcrest Packaging Inc .... G 845 425-0451
Monsey *(G-8289)*
Manhattan Poly Bag Corporation .... E 917 689-7549
Brooklyn *(G-2158)*
Mason Transparent Package Inc .... E 718 792-6000
Bronx *(G-1324)*
Metropolitan Packg Mfg Corp .... E 718 383-2700
Brooklyn *(G-2202)*
Nap Industries Inc .... D 718 625-4948
Brooklyn *(G-2243)*
New York Packaging Corp .... D 516 746-0600
New Hyde Park *(G-8552)*
New York Packaging II LLC .... E 516 746-0600
Garden City Park *(G-5286)*
Noteworthy Industries Inc .... C 518 842-2662
Amsterdam *(G-356)*
Pacific Poly Product Corp .... F 718 786-7129
Long Island City *(G-7546)*
Pack America Corp .... G 212 508-6666
New York *(G-11092)*
Paradise Plastics LLC .... E 718 788-3733
Brooklyn *(G-2302)*
Paramount Equipment Inc .... E 631 981-4422
Ronkonkoma *(G-14395)*
Poly Craft Industries Corp .... E 631 630-6731
Hauppauge *(G-5918)*
Poly-Pak Industries Inc .... B 631 293-6767
Melville *(G-8057)*
Polyseal Packaging Corp .... E 718 792-5530
Bronx *(G-1359)*
Primo Plastics Inc .... E 718 349-1000
Brooklyn *(G-2344)*
Rainbow Poly Bag Co Inc .... E 718 386-3500
Brooklyn *(G-2382)*
Rege Inc .... F 845 565-7772
New Windsor *(G-8657)*
Rtr Bag & Co Ltd .... G 212 620-0011
New York *(G-11444)*
Salerno Packaging Inc .... F 518 563-3636
Plattsburgh *(G-13154)*
Star Poly Bag Inc .... F 718 384-3130
Brooklyn *(G-2510)*
Star Poly Bag Inc .... F 718 384-5342
Brooklyn *(G-2511)*
Supreme Poly Plastics Inc .... F 718 456-9300
Brooklyn *(G-2541)*
T M I Plastics Industries Inc .... F 718 383-0363
Brooklyn *(G-2548)*
Technipoly Manufacturing Inc .... F 718 383-0363
Brooklyn *(G-2559)*
Trinity Packaging Corporation .... F 914 273-4111
Armonk *(G-411)*
United Plastics Inc .... G 718 389-2255
Brooklyn *(G-2603)*

BAGS: Rubber Or Rubberized Fabric

Adam Scott Designs Inc .... E 212 420-8866
New York *(G-8732)*
Chamberlin Rubber Company Inc .... E 585 427-7780
Rochester *(G-13705)*

BAGS: Shipping

Shalam Imports Inc .... F 718 686-6271
Brooklyn *(G-2463)*

BAGS: Shopping, Made From Purchased Materials

Ampac Paper LLC .... G 845 713-6600
Walden *(G-15890)*
Custom Eco Friendly LLC .... F 347 227-0229
Roslyn *(G-14445)*
Rtr Bag & Co Ltd .... G 212 620-0011
New York *(G-11444)*

BAGS: Tea, Fabric, Made From Purchased Materials

Health Matters America Inc .... F 716 235-8772
Buffalo *(G-2869)*

BAGS: Textile

Ace Drop Cloth Canvas Pdts Inc .... E 718 731-1550
Bronx *(G-1208)*
GPM Associates LLC .... G 585 359-1770
Rush *(G-14473)*
GPM Associates LLC .... G 585 335-3940
Dansville *(G-3926)*
Ivi Services Inc .... D 607 729-5111
Binghamton *(G-897)*
Jag Manufacturing Inc .... E 518 762-9558
Johnstown *(G-6832)*
Kragel Co Inc .... G 716 648-1344
Hamburg *(G-5685)*
Kush Oasis Enterprises LLC .... G 516 513-1316
Syosset *(G-15221)*
Mgk Group Inc .... E 212 989-2732
New York *(G-10788)*
Paulpac LLC .... G 631 283-7610
Southampton *(G-14958)*
Prima Satchel Inc .... G 929 367-7770
Monroe *(G-8279)*

BAGS: Trash, Plastic Film, Made From Purchased Materials

Garb-O-Liner Inc .... G 914 235-1585
New Rochelle *(G-8607)*
Golden Group International Ltd .... G 845 440-1025
Patterson *(G-12882)*
Jad Corp of America .... E 718 762-8900
College Point *(G-3650)*
Repellem Consumer Pdts Corp .... F 631 273-3992
Bohemia *(G-1082)*

BAGS: Wardrobe, Closet Access, Made From Purchased Materials

Colden Closet LLC .... G 716 713-6125
East Aurora *(G-4196)*

BAKERIES, COMMERCIAL: On Premises Baking Only

40 Street Baking Inc .... G 212 683-4700
Brooklyn *(G-1441)*
A & M Appel Distributing Inc .... G 516 735-1172
Massapequa *(G-7876)*
A Angonoa Inc .... C 718 762-4466
College Point *(G-3634)*
American Vintage Wine Biscuit .... G 718 361-1003
New York *(G-8839)*
Aphrodites .... G 718 224-1774
Whitestone *(G-16534)*
Aryzta LLC .... C 585 235-8160
Rochester *(G-13645)*
Aryzta LLC .... D 310 417-4700
Rochester *(G-13644)*

Employee Codes: A=Over 500 employees, B=251-500
C=101-250, D=51-100, E=20-50, F=10-19, G=5-9

BAKERIES, COMMERCIAL: On Premises Baking Only

Better Baked Foods LLC .... D 716 326-4651
  Westfield *(G-16392)*
Bimbo Bakeries .... G 631 274-4906
  Deer Park *(G-3951)*
Bimbo Bakeries .... F 518 463-2221
  Albany *(G-48)*
Bimbo Bakeries Usa Inc .... E 518 993-3300
  Nelliston *(G-8481)*
Bimbo Bakeries Usa Inc .... G 718 601-1561
  Bronx *(G-1229)*
Bimbo Bakeries Usa Inc .... F 845 255-4345
  New Paltz *(G-8575)*
Bimbo Bakeries Usa Inc .... E 631 951-5183
  Bay Shore *(G-663)*
Bimbo Bakeries Usa Inc .... F 518 563-1320
  Plattsburgh *(G-13110)*
Bimbo Foods Bakeries Inc .... C 631 273-6000
  Bay Shore *(G-665)*
Bread Factory LLC .... E 914 637-8150
  New Rochelle *(G-8593)*
Bushwick Bakery Corp .... G 917 460-5994
  Brooklyn *(G-1657)*
Chambord LLC .... E 718 859-1110
  Brooklyn *(G-1687)*
Cohens Bakery Inc .... E 716 892-8149
  Buffalo *(G-2771)*
Fratellis LLC .... E 607 722-5663
  Binghamton *(G-885)*
Gennaris Itln French Bky Inc .... E 516 997-8968
  Carle Place *(G-3265)*
Gourmet Toast Corp .... G 718 852-4536
  Brooklyn *(G-1944)*
H & S Edible Products Corp .... E 914 413-3489
  Mount Vernon *(G-8404)*
Hagadah Passover Bakery .... E 718 638-1589
  Brooklyn *(G-1960)*
Hana Pastries Inc .... G 718 369-7593
  Brooklyn *(G-1964)*
Herris Gourmet Inc .... G 917 578-2308
  Brooklyn *(G-1976)*
J & S Licata Bros Inc .... F 718 805-6924
  Richmond Hill *(G-13506)*
Jarets Stuffed Cupcakes .... G 607 658-9096
  Endicott *(G-4597)*
King Cracker Corp .... F 516 539-9251
  Hempstead *(G-6017)*
La Calenita Bakery & Cafeteria ...... G 718 205-8273
  Elmhurst *(G-4468)*
Larosa Cupcakes .... G 347 866-3920
  Staten Island *(G-15099)*
Maplehurst Bakeries LLC .... B 315 735-5000
  Frankfort *(G-5109)*
Melita Corp .... C 718 392-7280
  Astoria *(G-435)*
New Mount Pleasant Bakery .... E 518 374-7577
  Schenectady *(G-14700)*
New Star Bakery .... E 718 961-8868
  Flushing *(G-5027)*
Nibble Inc Baking Co .... G 518 334-3950
  Troy *(G-15612)*
Nightingale Food Entps Inc .... G 347 577-1630
  New York *(G-10966)*
Operative Cake Corp .... E 718 278-5600
  Bronx *(G-1348)*
Ossining Bakery Lmp Inc .... G 914 941-2654
  Ossining *(G-12972)*
Oz Baking Company Ltd .... G 516 466-5114
  Great Neck *(G-5578)*
Palagonia Bakery Co Inc .... G 718 272-5400
  Brooklyn *(G-2299)*
Peking Food LLC .... E 718 628-8080
  Brooklyn *(G-2309)*
Rays Italian Bakery Inc .... F 516 825-9170
  Valley Stream *(G-15793)*
Rm Bakery LLC .... E 718 472-3036
  Bronx *(G-1372)*
Roma Bakery Inc .... F 516 825-9170
  Valley Stream *(G-15795)*
Saint Honore Pastry Shop Inc .... G 516 767-2555
  Port Washington *(G-13303)*
Saj of Freeport Corp .... C 516 623-8800
  Freeport *(G-5180)*
Silver Bell Baking Co .... G 718 335-9539
  Middle Village *(G-8127)*
Smith Street Bread Co LLC .... G 718 797-9712
  Brooklyn *(G-2489)*
Sugarbear Cupcakes .... G 917 698-9005
  Jamaica *(G-6680)*
Sullivan St Bky - Hlls Kit Inc .... E 212 265-5580
  New York *(G-11735)*

Tphg 419 Ltd .... F 212 683-0444
  New York *(G-11879)*
Uncle Wallys LLC .... E 631 205-0455
  Shirley *(G-14844)*
Village Lantern Baking Corp .... G 631 225-1690
  Lindenhurst *(G-7205)*
Vito & Sons Bakery .... F 201 617-8501
  Brooklyn *(G-2631)*
Waldorf Bakers Inc .... F 718 665-2253
  Bronx *(G-1417)*
Whitestone Panetteria LLC .... G 516 543-9788
  Whitestone *(G-16552)*
Zaro Bake Shop Inc .... C 718 993-7327
  Bronx *(G-1422)*

BAKERIES: On Premises Baking & Consumption

B & D Enterprises of Utica .... D 315 735-3311
  New Hartford *(G-8501)*
Bagel Land .... E 585 442-3080
  Rochester *(G-13650)*
Caputo Bakery Inc .... G 718 875-6871
  Brooklyn *(G-1675)*
Costanzos Bakery Inc .... C 716 656-9093
  Buffalo *(G-2782)*
Dipaolo Baking Co Inc .... D 585 303-5013
  Rochester *(G-13743)*
Ferrara Bakery & Cafe Inc .... D 212 226-6150
  New York *(G-9795)*
Geddes Bakery Co Inc .... E 315 437-8084
  North Syracuse *(G-12403)*
Gennaris Itln French Bky Inc .... E 516 997-8968
  Carle Place *(G-3265)*
JJ Cassone Bakery Inc .... B 914 939-1568
  Port Chester *(G-13203)*
L American Ltd .... F 716 372-9480
  Olean *(G-12604)*
New Hope Mills Mfg Inc .... E 315 252-2676
  Auburn *(G-492)*
New Mount Pleasant Bakery .... E 518 374-7577
  Schenectady *(G-14700)*
Niebylski Bakery Inc .... G 718 721-5152
  Astoria *(G-437)*
Ohio Baking Company Inc .... E 315 724-2033
  Utica *(G-15728)*
Perrottas Bakery Inc .... E 518 283-4711
  Troy *(G-15615)*
Pesces Bakery Inc .... G 845 246-4730
  Saugerties *(G-14613)*
Presser Kosher Baking Corp .... E 718 375-5088
  Brooklyn *(G-2340)*
Saint Honore Pastry Shop Inc .... G 516 767-2555
  Port Washington *(G-13303)*
Sapienza Pastry Inc .... E 516 352-5232
  Elmont *(G-4525)*
Settepani Inc .... E 718 349-6524
  Brooklyn *(G-2458)*
T Shore Products Ltd .... G 315 252-9174
  Auburn *(G-502)*
Tarrytown Bakery Inc .... F 914 631-0209
  Tarrytown *(G-15496)*
Wenner Bread Products Inc .... B 800 869-6262
  Ronkonkoma *(G-14430)*
Wenner Bread Products Inc .... E 800 869-6262
  Ronkonkoma *(G-14431)*

BAKERY FOR HOME SVC DELIVERY

Circle 5 Deli Corp .... G 718 525-5687
  Jamaica *(G-6634)*

BAKERY MACHINERY

Unisource Food Eqp Systems Inc .... E 516 681-0537
  Holbrook *(G-6217)*

BAKERY PRDTS, FROZEN: Wholesalers

Fratellis LLC .... E 607 722-5663
  Binghamton *(G-885)*
Modern Itln Bky of W Babylon .... C 631 589-7300
  Oakdale *(G-12518)*

BAKERY PRDTS: Bagels, Fresh Or Frozen

999 Bagels Inc .... G 718 915-0742
  Brooklyn *(G-1448)*
A T A Bagel Shoppe Inc .... G 718 352-4948
  Bayside *(G-741)*
Bagel Club Inc .... F 718 423-6106
  Bayside *(G-743)*

Bagel Grove Inc .... E 315 724-8015
  Utica *(G-15679)*
Bagel Land .... E 585 442-3080
  Rochester *(G-13650)*
Bagelovers Inc .... F 607 844-3683
  Dryden *(G-4149)*
Enterprise Bagels Inc .... F 845 896-3823
  Fishkill *(G-4945)*
FB Sale LLC .... G 315 986-9999
  Macedon *(G-7699)*
Greenvale Bagel Inc .... E 516 221-8221
  Wantagh *(G-15921)*
M & M Bagel Corp .... F 516 295-1222
  Cedarhurst *(G-3333)*
Mds Hot Bagels Deli Inc 718 438-5650
  Brooklyn *(G-2184)*

BAKERY PRDTS: Bakery Prdts, Partially Cooked, Exc frozen

New Hope Mills Mfg Inc .... E 315 252-2676
  Auburn *(G-492)*
T&B Bakery Corp .... G 646 642-4300
  Maspeth *(G-7872)*

BAKERY PRDTS: Bread, All Types, Fresh Or Frozen

Addeo Bakers Inc .... F 718 367-8316
  Bronx *(G-1212)*
Aladdin Bakers Inc 718 499-1818
  Brooklyn *(G-1498)*
Bimbo Bakeries Usa Inc .... C 718 463-6300
  Maspeth *(G-7828)*
Commitment 2000 Inc .... E 716 439-1206
  Buffalo *(G-2775)*
Dipaolo Baking Co Inc .... D 585 303-5013
  Rochester *(G-13743)*
George Retzos .... G 315 422-2913
  Syracuse *(G-15334)*
Giovanni Bakery Corp .... F 212 695-4296
  New York *(G-9924)*
Harrison Bakery West .... E 315 422-1468
  Syracuse *(G-15338)*
L American Ltd .... F 716 372-9480
  Olean *(G-12604)*
La Prima Bakery Inc .... F 718 584-4442
  Bronx *(G-1313)*
Modern Itln Bky of W Babylon .... C 631 589-7300
  Oakdale *(G-12518)*
Ohio Baking Company Inc .... E 315 724-2033
  Utica *(G-15728)*
Rock Hill Bakehouse Ltd .... E 518 743-1627
  Gansevoort *(G-5246)*
Roslyn Bread Company Inc .... E 516 625-1470
  Roslyn Heights *(G-14459)*
Tarrytown Bakery Inc .... F 914 631-0209
  Tarrytown *(G-15496)*
Wenner Bread Products Inc .... B 800 869-6262
  Ronkonkoma *(G-14430)*
Wenner Bread Products Inc .... E 800 869-6262
  Ronkonkoma *(G-14431)*

BAKERY PRDTS: Buns, Sweet, Frozen

Liddabit Sweets .... G 917 912-1370
  Brooklyn *(G-2117)*

BAKERY PRDTS: Cakes, Bakery, Exc Frozen

Always Baked Fresh .... G 631 648-0811
  Holbrook *(G-6171)*
Charlotte Neuville Design LLC .... G 646 530-4570
  Brooklyn *(G-1690)*
Chocnyc LLC .... G 917 804-4848
  New York *(G-9286)*
Coccadotts Inc .... F 518 438-4937
  Albany *(G-65)*
Cupcake Contessas Corporation ... G 516 307-1222
  North Bellmore *(G-12376)*
Ferrara Bakery & Cafe Inc .... D 212 226-6150
  New York *(G-9795)*
Great American Dessert Co LLC ... D 718 894-3494
  Maspeth *(G-7849)*
Hahns Old Fashioned Cake Co ..... F 631 249-3456
  Farmingdale *(G-4779)*
Jonathan Lord Corp .... F 631 563-4445
  Bohemia *(G-1043)*
McKee Foods Corporation .... A 631 979-9364
  Hauppauge *(G-5883)*

Placid Baker ....G.... 518 326-2657
Troy (G-15617)
Scaife Enterprises Inc ....F.... 585 454-5231
Fairport (G-4656)

BAKERY PRDTS: Cakes, Bakery, Frozen

Culinary Arts Specialties Inc ....D.... 716 656-8943
Cheektowaga (G-3439)
LArte Del Gelato Gruppo Inc....F.... 718 383-6600
Long Island City (G-7496)

BAKERY PRDTS: Cones, Ice Cream

Alrajs Inc....E.... 631 225-0300
Lindenhurst (G-7159)
Cone Buddy System Inc....F.... 585 427-9940
Rochester (G-13718)
Larte Del Gelato Inc....G.... 212 366-0570
New York (G-10519)
Pdi Cone Co Inc ....D.... 716 825-8750
Buffalo (G-2994)

BAKERY PRDTS: Cookies

212kiddish Inc....G.... 718 705-7227
Brooklyn (G-1434)
AAA Noodle Products Mfg ....G.... 212 431-4090
New York (G-8703)
Chipita America Inc ....E.... 845 292-2540
Ferndale (G-4931)
Cooking With Chef Michelle LLC....G.... 516 662-2324
Calverton (G-3164)
D F Stauffer Biscuit Co Inc....E.... 585 968-2700
Cuba (G-3917)
Decorated Cookie Company LLC....E.... 315 487-2111
Syracuse (G-15304)
Elenis Nyc Inc....E.... 718 361-8136
Long Island City (G-7437)
Falcones Cookie Land Ltd ....E.... 718 236-4200
Brooklyn (G-1866)
Golden Glow Cookie Co Inc....E.... 718 379-6223
Bronx (G-1283)
Kaltec Food Packaging Inc ....E.... 845 856-9888
Port Jervis (G-13231)
Keebler Company ....F.... 585 948-8010
Oakfield (G-12524)
Linden Cookies Inc....E.... 845 268-5050
Congers (G-3719)
Lloyd Price Icon Food Brands....F.... 914 764-8624
Pound Ridge (G-13377)
Mannys Cheesecake Inc....G.... 315 732-0639
Utica (G-15718)
Quaker Bonnet Inc....G.... 716 885-7208
Buffalo (G-3024)
Treehouse Private Brands Inc ....C.... 716 693-4715
Tonawanda (G-15584)
United Baking Co Inc....C.... 631 205-0455
Shirley (G-14845)
Wonton Food Inc....C.... 718 628-6868
Brooklyn (G-2655)

BAKERY PRDTS: Cookies & crackers

Butterwood Desserts Inc....E.... 716 652-0131
West Falls (G-16208)
Cookies United LLC....C.... 631 581-4000
Islip (G-6545)
Danny Macaroons Inc....G.... 260 622-8463
New York (G-9469)
Great Brands of Europe Inc ....G.... 914 872-8804
White Plains (G-16454)
Jonathan Lord Corp....F.... 631 563-4445
Bohemia (G-1043)
Ladybird Bakery Inc....G.... 718 499-8108
Brooklyn (G-2089)
New Mount Pleasant Bakery ....E.... 518 374-7577
Schenectady (G-14700)
Pepsico Inc....A.... 914 253-2000
Purchase (G-13395)
Sapienza Pastry Inc ....E.... 516 352-5232
Elmont (G-4525)
U Serve Brands Inc....F.... 877 632-6654
New York (G-11927)
United Baking Co Inc....F.... 631 413-5116
Central Islip (G-3387)
Zaro Bake Shop Inc ....C.... 718 993-7327
Bronx (G-1422)

BAKERY PRDTS: Cracker Meal & Crumbs

Wonton Food Inc....E.... 718 784-8178
Long Island City (G-7642)

BAKERY PRDTS: Doughnuts, Exc Frozen

3rd Avenue Doughnut Inc ....F.... 718 748-3294
Brooklyn (G-1439)
Alicias Bakery Inc ....G.... 914 235-4689
New Rochelle (G-8588)
Bimbo Bakeries Usa Inc....E.... 203 531-2311
Bay Shore (G-664)
Cuzins Duzin Corp....G.... 347 724-6200
Kew Gardens (G-6872)
D-Lite Donuts ....G.... 718 626-5953
Astoria (G-423)
Famous Doughnuts Inc....G.... 716 834-6356
Buffalo (G-2824)

BAKERY PRDTS: Doughnuts, Frozen

Maplehurst Bakeries LLC....B.... 315 735-5000
Frankfort (G-5109)

BAKERY PRDTS: Dry

17 Bakers LLC....F.... 844 687-6836
Williamsville (G-16565)
Aryzta LLC....C.... 585 235-8160
Rochester (G-13645)
Creative Food Ingredients Inc ....C.... 585 237-2213
Perry (G-12967)
My Most Favorite Food....G.... 212 580-5130
New York (G-10864)

BAKERY PRDTS: Frozen

Bello LLC....C.... 516 623-8800
Freeport (G-5145)
Butterwood Desserts Inc....E.... 716 652-0131
West Falls (G-16208)
Deiorio Foods Inc....C.... 315 732-7612
Utica (G-15693)
Dufour Pastry Kitchens Inc....E.... 718 402-8800
Bronx (G-1260)
Fratellis LLC....E.... 607 722-5663
Binghamton (G-885)
Ko Fro Foods Inc ....E.... 718 972-6480
Brooklyn (G-2079)
Rich Holdings Inc....D.... 716 878-8000
Buffalo (G-3036)
Rich Products Corporation ....A.... 716 878-8000
Buffalo (G-3037)
Wenner Bread Products Inc....B.... 800 869-6262
Ronkonkoma (G-14430)
Wenner Bread Products Inc....E.... 800 869-6262
Ronkonkoma (G-14431)

BAKERY PRDTS: Matzoth

Aron Streit Inc....E.... 212 475-7000
Orangeburg (G-12670)

BAKERY PRDTS: Pastries, Danish, Frozen

Pearl River Pastries LLC ....E.... 845 735-5100
West Nyack (G-16277)

BAKERY PRDTS: Pastries, Exc Frozen

Alrajs Inc....E.... 631 225-0300
Lindenhurst (G-7159)
Cannoli Factory Inc....E.... 631 643-2700
Wyandanch (G-16693)

BAKERY PRDTS: Pies, Bakery, Frozen

Circle Peak Capital MGT LLC....E.... 646 230-8812
New York (G-9302)
Micosta Enterprises Inc....G.... 518 822-9708
Hudson (G-6364)

BAKERY PRDTS: Rolls, Bread Type, Fresh Or Frozen

Kossars On Grand LLC ....F.... 212 473-4810
New York (G-10472)

BAKERY PRDTS: Wholesalers

A & M Appel Distributing Inc....G.... 516 735-1172
Massapequa (G-7876)
Aron Streit Inc ....E.... 212 475-7000
Orangeburg (G-12670)
B & D Enterprises of Utica ....D.... 315 735-3311
New Hartford (G-8501)
Cannoli Factory Inc....E.... 631 643-2700
Wyandanch (G-16693)

Costanzos Bakery Inc....C.... 716 656-9093
Buffalo (G-2782)
Damascus Bakery Inc....D.... 718 855-1456
Brooklyn (G-1753)
Fratellis LLC ....E.... 607 722-5663
Binghamton (G-885)
Hahns Old Fashioned Cake Co....F.... 631 249-3456
Farmingdale (G-4779)
King Cracker Corp....F.... 516 539-9251
Hempstead (G-6017)
Mac Crete Corporation ....F.... 718 932-1803
Long Island City (G-7509)
Modern Itln Bky of W Babylon....C.... 631 589-7300
Oakdale (G-12518)
Ohio Baking Company Inc ....E.... 315 724-2033
Utica (G-15728)
Operative Cake Corp ....E.... 718 278-5600
Bronx (G-1348)
Roslyn Bread Company Inc ....E.... 516 625-1470
Roslyn Heights (G-14459)
Wenner Bread Products Inc....E.... 800 869-6262
Ronkonkoma (G-14431)

BAKERY: Wholesale Or Wholesale & Retail Combined

527 Franco Bakery Corporation ....G.... 718 993-4200
Bronx (G-1197)
Above The Rest Baking Corp ....D.... 718 313-9222
Bronx (G-1205)
Amiram Dror Inc....F.... 212 979-9505
Brooklyn (G-1529)
Andreas Protein Cakery Inc....G.... 646 801-9826
New York (G-8859)
B & D Enterprises of Utica ....D.... 315 735-3311
New Hartford (G-8501)
Bakery & Coffee Shop ....G.... 315 287-1829
Gouverneur (G-5486)
Bien Cuit LLC ....E.... 718 852-0200
Brooklyn (G-1609)
Bimbo Bakeries Usa Inc....G.... 716 692-9140
Tonawanda (G-15527)
Bimbo Bakeries Usa Inc....E.... 516 877-2850
Mineola (G-8207)
Bimbo Bakeries Usa Inc....C.... 716 372-8444
Olean (G-12593)
Bimbo Bakeries Usa Inc....F.... 516 887-1024
Lynbrook (G-7661)
Bimbo Bakeries Usa Inc....F.... 315 379-9069
Canton (G-3254)
Bimbo Bakeries Usa Inc....F.... 518 489-4053
Albany (G-49)
Bimbo Bakeries Usa Inc....F.... 716 706-0450
Lancaster (G-7010)
Bimbo Bakeries Usa Inc....D.... 845 568-0943
Newburgh (G-12217)
Bimbo Bakeries Usa Inc....C.... 315 782-4189
Watertown (G-16002)
Blackbirds Brooklyn LLC ....E.... 917 362-4080
Brooklyn (G-1618)
Blondie S Bakeshop Inc....G.... 631 424-4545
Centerport (G-3347)
Caputo Bakery Inc ....G.... 718 875-6871
Brooklyn (G-1675)
Carmine Street Bagels Inc ....F.... 212 691-3041
Staten Island (G-15061)
Carolinas Desserts Inc ....G.... 914 779-4000
Yonkers (G-16742)
Carter Street Bakery Inc....G.... 585 749-7104
Rochester (G-13694)
City Bakery Inc....E.... 212 366-1414
New York (G-9310)
Cookie Connection Inc....G.... 315 422-2253
Syracuse (G-15288)
Costanzos Bakery Inc....C.... 716 656-9093
Buffalo (G-2782)
Daly Meghan....F.... 347 699-3259
Brooklyn (G-1752)
Damascus Bakery Inc....D.... 718 855-1456
Brooklyn (G-1753)
Delicias Andinas Food Corp ....E.... 718 416-2922
Flushing (G-4995)
Eileens Special Cheesecake....G.... 212 966-5585
New York (G-9637)
Ericeira Inc....G.... 516 294-4034
Mineola (G-8220)
Felix Roma & Sons Inc ....D.... 607 748-3336
Endicott (G-4593)
Flour Power Bakery Cafe ....G.... 917 747-6895
Livingston Manor (G-7276)

PRODUCT

Employee Codes: A=Over 500 employees, B=251-500
C=101-250, D=51-100, E=20-50, F=10-19, G=5-9
2019 Harris
New York Manufacturers Directory
1059

BAKERY: Wholesale Or Wholesale & Retail Combined

Food Gems Ltd .... E 718 296-7788
  Ozone Park (G-12826)
Fotis Oneonta Italian Bakery .... G 607 432-3871
  Oneonta (G-12638)
Fung Wong Bakery Inc .... E 212 267-4037
  New York (G-9862)
Gabila & Sons Mfg Inc .... E 631 789-2220
  Copiague (G-3759)
Geddes Bakery Co Inc .... E 315 437-8084
  North Syracuse (G-12403)
Glenn Wayne Wholesale Bky Inc .... D 631 289-9200
  Bohemia (G-1029)
Gluten Free Bake Shop Inc .... E 845 782-5307
  Mountainville (G-8455)
Golden Glow Cookie Co Inc .... E 718 379-6223
  Bronx (G-1283)
Good Bread Bakery .... F 914 939-3900
  Port Chester (G-13201)
H H B Bakery of Little Neck .... E 718 631-7004
  Flushing (G-5004)
Have Your Cake Kitchen LLC .... G 646 820-8074
  Brooklyn (G-1968)
Heidelberg Group Inc .... E 315 866-0999
  Herkimer (G-6040)
Hum Limited Liability Corp .... G 631 525-2174
  Nesconset (G-8484)
Jane Bakes Inc .... E 845 920-1100
  Pearl River (G-12903)
Jerrys Bagels .... E 516 791-0063
  Valley Stream (G-15783)
JGM Wholesale Bakery Inc .... E 631 396-0131
  Farmingdale (G-4793)
Jim Romas Bakery Inc .... E 607 748-7425
  Endicott (G-4600)
JJ Cassone Bakery Inc .... B 914 939-1568
  Port Chester (G-13203)
Kokoroko Corporation .... G 718 433-4321
  Woodside (G-16661)
Ladybird Bakery Inc .... E 718 499-8108
  Brooklyn (G-2089)
Lillys Homestyle Bakeshop Inc .... D 718 491-2904
  Brooklyn (G-2123)
Ljmm Inc .... E 845 454-5876
  Poughkeepsie (G-13351)
Made Close LLC .... G 917 837-1357
  Brooklyn (G-2151)
Maxwell Bakery Inc .... E 718 498-2200
  Brooklyn (G-2182)
Millers Bulk Food and Bakery .... G 585 798-9700
  Medina (G-7984)
Miss Grimble Associates Inc .... F 718 665-2253
  Bronx (G-1333)
Niebylski Bakery Inc .... E 718 721-5152
  Astoria (G-437)
Nildas Desserts Limited .... F 845 454-5876
  Poughkeepsie (G-13359)
Perrottas Bakery Inc .... G 518 283-4711
  Troy (G-15615)
Pesces Bakery Inc .... E 845 246-4730
  Saugerties (G-14613)
Presser Kosher Baking Corp .... E 718 375-5088
  Brooklyn (G-2340)
Quaker Bonnet Inc .... G 716 885-7208
  Buffalo (G-3024)
R & H Baking Co Inc .... E 718 852-1768
  Brooklyn (G-2375)
Rambachs International Bakery .... F 518 563-1721
  Plattsburgh (G-13152)
Rays Restaurant & Bakery Inc .... G 718 441-7707
  Jamaica (G-6673)
Reisman Bros Bakery Inc .... F 718 331-1975
  Brooklyn (G-2394)
Richard Engdal Baking Corp .... F 914 777-9600
  Mamaroneck (G-7755)
Royal Sweet Bakery Inc .... E 718 567-7770
  Brooklyn (G-2424)
Sapienza Pastry Inc .... E 516 352-5232
  Elmont (G-4525)
Secure International .... G 716 206-2500
  Lancaster (G-7048)
Settepani Inc .... E 718 349-6524
  Brooklyn (G-2458)
Slims Bagels Unlimited Inc .... E 718 229-1140
  Oakland Gardens (G-12526)
Soutine Inc .... E 212 496-1450
  New York (G-11655)
Stebe Shcjhjff .... F 839 383-9833
  Poughkeepsie (G-13369)
Tates Wholesale LLC .... C 631 780-6511
  East Moriches (G-4258)
Tilaros Bakery Inc .... G 716 488-3209
  Jamestown (G-6757)
Triboro Bagel Co Inc .... E 718 359-9245
  Flushing (G-5055)

BANDAGES

Medi-Tech International Corp .... G 800 333-0109
  Brooklyn (G-2187)

BANDS: Copper & Copper Alloy

Milward Alloys Inc .... E 716 434-5536
  Lockport (G-7318)

BANNERS: Fabric

Ace Banner & Flag Company .... F 212 620-9111
  New York (G-8724)
Arista Flag Corporation .... F 845 246-7700
  Saugerties (G-14603)
Big Apple Sign Corp .... D 212 629-3650
  New York (G-9076)
Big Apple Sign Corp .... E 631 342-0303
  Islandia (G-6522)
Dkm Sales LLC .... E 716 893-7777
  Buffalo (G-2802)
Hollywood Banners Inc .... E 631 842-3000
  Copiague (G-3765)
Kraus & Sons Inc .... F 212 620-0408
  New York (G-10480)
Sellco Industries Inc .... E 607 756-7594
  Cortland (G-3894)

BANQUET HALL FACILITIES

Casa Larga Vineyards 585 223-4210
  Fairport (G-4627)

BAR FIXTURES: Wood

Modern Craft Bar Rest Equip .... G 631 226-5647
  Lindenhurst (G-7181)

BARBECUE EQPT

Korin Japanese Trading Corp .... E 212 587-7021
  New York (G-10471)
Podravka International USA .... F 212 661-0125
  New York (G-11214)

BARRICADES: Metal

Consolidated Barricades Inc .... G 518 922-7944
  Fultonville (G-5235)
Inpro Corporation .... G 716 332-4699
  Tonawanda (G-15551)

BARS & BAR SHAPES: Steel, Hot-Rolled

Vell Company Inc .... G 845 365-1013
  Palisades (G-12849)

BARS, COLD FINISHED: Steel, From Purchased Hot-Rolled

Niagara Lasalle Corporation .... D 716 827-7010
  Buffalo (G-2968)

BARS: Concrete Reinforcing, Fabricated Steel

Agl Industries Inc .... E 718 326-7597
  Maspeth (G-7816)
Arista Steel Designs Corp .... G 718 965-7077
  Brooklyn (G-1552)
Baco Enterprises Inc .... D 718 589-6225
  Bronx (G-1224)
Barker Steel LLC .... G 518 465-6221
  Albany (G-44)
City Evolutionary .... G 718 861-7585
  Bronx (G-1240)
DAgostino Iron Works Inc .... G 585 235-8850
  Rochester (G-13731)
Designs By Novello Inc .... G 914 934-7711
  Port Chester (G-13196)
Dimension Fabricators Inc .... E 518 374-1936
  Scotia (G-14739)
Ferro Fabricators Inc .... F 718 703-0007
  Brooklyn (G-1875)
GCM Metal Industries Inc .... F 718 386-4059
  Brooklyn (G-1919)
Harbor Wldg & Fabrication Corp .... F 631 667-1880
  Copiague (G-3762)
Klein Reinforcing Services Inc .... F 585 352-9423
  Spencerport (G-14980)
New York Steel Services Co .... G 718 291-7770
  Jamaica (G-6665)
Siw Inc .... F 631 888-0130
  Bay Shore (G-723)
Steel Sales Inc .... E 607 674-6363
  Sherburne (G-14811)
Torino Industrial Inc .... F 631 509-1640
  Bellport (G-816)
Wide Flange Inc .... F 718 492-8705
  Brooklyn (G-2645)

BARS: Iron, Made In Steel Mills

Crucible Industries LLC .... B 800 365-1180
  Syracuse (G-15295)
Tri Valley Iron Inc .... F 845 365-1013
  Palisades (G-12848)

BASEBOARDS: Metal

Slanto Manufacturing Inc .... E 516 759-5721
  Glen Cove (G-5375)

BASEMENT WINDOW AREAWAYS: Concrete

Healthy Basement Systems LLC .... F 516 650-9046
  Medford (G-7952)

BASES, BEVERAGE

Better Fresh Corp .... G 718 628-3682
  Brooklyn (G-1606)
Life On Earth Inc .... F 866 928-5070
  New York (G-10563)
Tealeafs .... G 716 688-8022
  Williamsville (G-16590)
Wynn Starr Flavors Inc .... D 845 584-3080
  Congers (G-3723)

BASKETS: Steel Wire

Braun Horticulture Inc .... G 716 282-6101
  Niagara Falls (G-12265)

BATCHING PLANTS: Cement Silos

New Eagle Silo Corp .... G 585 492-1300
  Arcade (G-388)

BATH SALTS

Aromasong Usa Inc .... F 718 838-9669
  Brooklyn (G-1555)

BATHING SUIT STORES

Malia Mills Inc .... F 212 354-4200
  Brooklyn (G-2154)
Shirl-Lynn of New York .... G 315 363-5898
  Oneida (G-12621)

BATHMATS, COTTON

Michael Stuart Inc .... E 718 821-0704
  Brooklyn (G-2204)

BATHROOM ACCESS & FITTINGS: Vitreous China & Earthenware

AMG JV LLC .... G 212 602-1818
  New York (G-8843)
Gamma Products Inc .... D 845 562-3332
  New Windsor (G-8645)
Larcent Enterprises Inc .... E 845 562-3332
  New Windsor (G-8648)
Stone and Bath Gallery .... G 718 438-4500
  Brooklyn (G-2523)

BATHTUBS: Concrete

Meditub Incorporated .... F 866 633-4882
  Lawrence (G-7106)

BATTERIES, EXC AUTOMOTIVE: Wholesalers

El-Don Battery Post Inc .... G 716 627-3697
  Hamburg (G-5677)

BATTERIES: Alkaline, Cell Storage

Bren-Trnics Batteries Intl LLC .... E 631 499-5155
  Commack (G-3684)

PRODUCT SECTION

Ultralife Corporation ....B....... 315 332-7100
  Newark *(G-12209)*

BATTERIES: Lead Acid, Storage

Exide Technologies ....G....... 585 344-0656
  Batavia *(G-623)*
Johnson Controls Inc ....C....... 585 724-2232
  Rochester *(G-13897)*

BATTERIES: Rechargeable

Bren-Trnics Batteries Intl Inc ....G....... 631 499-5155
  Commack *(G-3683)*
Synergy Digital ....F....... 718 643-2742
  Brooklyn *(G-2546)*

BATTERIES: Storage

Amco Intl Mfg & Design Inc ....E....... 718 388-8668
  Brooklyn *(G-1518)*
Battery Energy Storage Systems ....G....... 518 256-7029
  Troy *(G-15602)*
Battery Research and Tstg Inc ....F....... 315 342-2373
  Oswego *(G-12775)*
Battsco LLC ....G....... 516 586-6544
  Hicksville *(G-6064)*
Bren-Tronics Inc. ....C....... 631 499-5155
  Commack *(G-3685)*
Cellec Technologies Inc ....G....... 585 454-9166
  Rochester *(G-13699)*
China Lithium Technologies ....G....... 212 391-2688
  New York *(G-9280)*
El-Don Battery Post Inc ....G....... 716 627-3697
  Hamburg *(G-5677)*
New Energy Systems Group ....C....... 917 573-0302
  New York *(G-10921)*
W & W Manufacturing Co ....F....... 516 942-0011
  West Islip *(G-16261)*

BATTERIES: Wet

Bren-Tronics Inc. ....C....... 631 499-5155
  Commack *(G-3685)*
Electrochem Solutions Inc ....D....... 716 759-5800
  Clarence *(G-3532)*
Shad Industries Inc ....G....... 631 504-6028
  Yaphank *(G-16721)*

BATTERY CASES: Plastic Or Plastics Combination

Memory Protection Devices Inc ....F....... 631 249-0001
  Farmingdale *(G-4819)*

BATTERY CHARGERS

Applied Energy Solutions LLC ....E....... 585 538-3270
  Caledonia *(G-3153)*
China Lithium Technologies ....G....... 212 391-2688
  New York *(G-9280)*
Eluminocity US Inc ....G....... 651 528-1165
  New York *(G-9660)*
Kussmaul Electronics Co Inc ....E....... 631 218-0298
  West Sayville *(G-16290)*
Walter R Tucker Entps Ltd ....E....... 607 467-2866
  Deposit *(G-4112)*

BATTERY CHARGERS: Storage, Motor & Engine Generator Type

Apogee Power Usa Inc ....F....... 202 746-2890
  Hartsdale *(G-5742)*
Vdc Electronics Inc ....F....... 631 683-5850
  Huntington *(G-6425)*

BATTERY CHARGING GENERATORS

Eluminocity US Inc ....G....... 651 528-1165
  New York *(G-9660)*

BATTS & BATTING: Cotton

Ino-Tex LLC ....G....... 212 400-2205
  New York *(G-10221)*
Rovel Manufacturing Co Inc ....G....... 516 365-2752
  Roslyn *(G-14451)*
Superior Fiber Mills Inc ....E....... 718 782-7500
  Brooklyn *(G-2538)*
Vincent Manufacturing Co Inc ....F....... 315 823-0280
  Little Falls *(G-7216)*

BEARINGS & PARTS Ball

A Hyatt Ball Co Ltd ....G....... 518 747-0272
  Fort Edward *(G-5093)*
General Bearing Corporation ....C....... 845 358-6000
  West Nyack *(G-16270)*
Kilian Manufacturing Corp ....D....... 315 432-0700
  Syracuse *(G-15355)*
Mageba USA LLC ....E....... 212 317-1991
  New York *(G-10662)*
Nes Bearing Company Inc ....E....... 716 372-6532
  Olean *(G-12605)*
Schatz Bearing Corporation ....D....... 845 452-6000
  Poughkeepsie *(G-13365)*
SKF USA Inc ....D....... 716 661-2869
  Falconer *(G-4691)*
SKF USA Inc ....D....... 716 661-2600
  Falconer *(G-4692)*
SKF USA Inc ....D....... 716 661-2600
  Jamestown *(G-6747)*

BEARINGS: Ball & Roller

American Refuse Supply Inc ....G....... 718 893-8157
  Bronx *(G-1219)*
David Fehlman ....G....... 315 455-8888
  Syracuse *(G-15303)*
Lemoyne Machine Products Corp ....G....... 315 454-0708
  Syracuse *(G-15359)*
Raydon Precision Bearing Co ....G....... 516 887-2582
  Lynbrook *(G-7671)*
Sandle Custom Bearing Corp ....G....... 585 593-7000
  Wellsville *(G-16121)*

BEAUTY & BARBER SHOP EQPT

Accurate Pnt Powdr Coating Inc ....F....... 585 235-1650
  Rochester *(G-13597)*
Adults and Children With Learn ....E....... 516 593-8230
  East Rockaway *(G-4292)*
Advanced Assembly Services Inc ....G....... 716 217-8144
  Lancaster *(G-7001)*
Blackbox Biometrics Inc ....E....... 585 329-3399
  Rochester *(G-13665)*
Brooklyn Industries LLC ....G....... 718 788-5250
  Brooklyn *(G-1643)*
Callanan Industries Inc ....G....... 518 382-5354
  Schenectady *(G-14656)*
East Penn Manufacturing Co ....G....... 631 321-7161
  Babylon *(G-526)*
Freedom Mfg LLC ....F....... 518 584-0441
  Saratoga Springs *(G-14580)*
Goodwill Inds of Greater NY ....C....... 914 621-0781
  Baldwin Place *(G-546)*
Goodwill Inds Wstn NY Inc ....F....... 716 633-3305
  Williamsville *(G-16580)*
Innovative Industries LLC ....G....... 718 784-7300
  Long Island City *(G-7475)*
J & A Usa Inc ....G....... 631 243-3336
  Brentwood *(G-1138)*
Jags Manufacturing Network Inc ....G....... 631 750-6367
  Holbrook *(G-6192)*
Nitro Manufacturing LLC ....F....... 716 646-9900
  Hamburg *(G-5687)*
Ohserase Manufacturing LLC ....E....... 518 358-9309
  Akwesasne *(G-26)*
Ohserase Manufacturing LLC ....G....... 518 358-9309
  Hogansburg *(G-6166)*
Oledworks LLC ....E....... 585 287-6802
  Rochester *(G-13985)*
P S Pibbs Inc ....D....... 718 445-8046
  Flushing *(G-5032)*
Paperworks Industries Inc ....F....... 913 621-0922
  Baldwinsville *(G-559)*
Paratus Industries Inc ....E....... 716 826-2000
  Orchard Park *(G-12735)*
PCI Industries Corp ....E....... 914 662-2700
  Mount Vernon *(G-8428)*
Qualbuys LLC ....G....... 855 884-3274
  Syosset *(G-15228)*
S B Manufacturing LLC ....F....... 845 352-3700
  Monsey *(G-8295)*

BEAUTY SALONS

Lemetric Hair Centers Inc ....F....... 212 986-5620
  New York *(G-10543)*

BED & BREAKFAST INNS

Malina Management Company Inc ....E....... 607 535-9614
  Montour Falls *(G-8326)*

BEEKEEPERS' SPLYS: Bee Smokers

Newspaper Publisher LLC ....F....... 607 775-0472
  Conklin *(G-3730)*

BEDDING, BEDSPREADS, BLANKETS & SHEETS

Cathay Home Inc ....E....... 212 213-0988
  New York *(G-9229)*
Indigo Home Inc ....G....... 212 684-4146
  New York *(G-10199)*
Jdt International LLC ....G....... 212 400-7570
  New York *(G-10321)*
Northpoint Trading Inc ....F....... 212 481-8001
  New York *(G-10997)*
Richloom Fabrics Group Inc ....E....... 212 685-5400
  New York *(G-11392)*
Sunham Home Fashions LLC ....D....... 212 695-1218
  New York *(G-11742)*

BEDDING, BEDSPREADS, BLANKETS & SHEETS: Comforters & Quilts

Alen Sands York Associates Ltd ....F....... 212 563-6305
  New York *(G-8790)*
EY Industries Inc ....F....... 718 624-9122
  Brooklyn *(G-1860)*
Kaltex North America Inc ....E....... 212 894-3200
  New York *(G-10401)*
Revman International Inc ....E....... 212 894-3100
  New York *(G-11378)*

BEDDING, FROM SILK OR MANMADE FIBER

Chf Industries Inc ....E....... 212 951-7800
  New York *(G-9273)*
Westpoint Home LLC ....A....... 212 930-2000
  New York *(G-12096)*

BEDS & ACCESS STORES

Charles P Rogers Brass Beds ....F....... 212 675-4400
  New York *(G-9264)*
Duxiana Dux Bed ....G....... 212 755-2600
  New York *(G-9588)*
Metro Mattress Corp ....E....... 716 205-2300
  Niagara Falls *(G-12310)*

BEDS: Hospital

Hard Manufacturing Co Inc ....E....... 716 893-1800
  Buffalo *(G-2865)*
NK Medical Products Inc ....G....... 716 759-7200
  Amherst *(G-241)*
Novum Medical Products Inc ....F....... 716 759-7200
  Amherst *(G-242)*
VSM Investors LLC ....G....... 212 351-1600
  New York *(G-12057)*

BEDSPREADS & BED SETS, FROM PURCHASED MATERIALS

Belle Maison USA Ltd ....E....... 718 805-0200
  Richmond Hill *(G-13498)*
Bramson House Inc ....C....... 516 764-5006
  Freeport *(G-5146)*
C & G of Kingston Inc ....D....... 845 331-0148
  Kingston *(G-6890)*
County Draperies Inc ....E....... 845 342-9009
  Middletown *(G-8144)*
Fabric Quilters Unlimited Inc ....E....... 516 333-2866
  Westbury *(G-16330)*
Himatsingka America Inc ....E....... 212 824-2949
  New York *(G-10101)*
Jo-Vin Decorators Inc ....E....... 718 441-9350
  Woodhaven *(G-16636)*
Wayne Decorators Inc ....G....... 718 529-4200
  Jamaica *(G-6690)*

BEDSPREADS, COTTON

Mason Contract Products LLC ....D....... 516 328-6900
  New Hyde Park *(G-8550)*

BEEKEEPERS' SPLYS

Northast Ctr For Bekeeping LLC ....F....... 800 632-3379
  Greenwich *(G-5643)*

BEEKEEPERS' SPLYS: Bee Smokers

Ubees Inc ....F....... 916 505-8470
  New York *(G-11928)*

Employee Codes: A=Over 500 employees, B=251-500
C=101-250, D=51-100, E=20-50, F=10-19, G=5-9

2019 Harris
New York Manufacturers Directory

BEER & ALE, WHOLESALE: Beer & Other Fermented Malt Liquors

BEER & ALE, WHOLESALE: Beer & Other Fermented Malt Liquors

- Constellation Brands Inc ....D...... 585 678-7100
  Victor *(G-15837)*
- Load/N/Go Beverage Corp ....F...... 585 218-4019
  Rochester *(G-13915)*
- Save More Beverage Corp ....G...... 518 371-2520
  Halfmoon *(G-5669)*

BEER, WINE & LIQUOR STORES

- Lucas Vineyards Inc ....F...... 607 532-4825
  Interlaken *(G-6482)*

BEER, WINE & LIQUOR STORES: Beer, Packaged

- Load/N/Go Beverage Corp ....F...... 585 218-4019
  Rochester *(G-13915)*
- Save More Beverage Corp ....G...... 518 371-2520
  Halfmoon *(G-5669)*
- Valcour Brewing Company LLC ....E...... 518 324-2337
  Plattsburgh *(G-13167)*

BEER, WINE & LIQUOR STORES: Wine

- Casa Larga Vineyards ....E...... 585 223-4210
  Fairport *(G-4627)*
- Coyote Moon LLC ....F...... 315 686-5600
  Clayton *(G-3553)*
- J Petrocelli Wine Cellars LLC ....E...... 631 765-1100
  Peconic *(G-12915)*
- Negys New Land Vinyrd Winery ....G...... 315 585-4432
  Geneva *(G-5330)*
- Olde Chtqua Vneyards Ltd Lblty ....F...... 716 792-2749
  Portland *(G-13315)*
- Standing Stone Vineyards ....G...... 607 582-6051
  Hector *(G-6002)*

BELLOWS

- Kinemotive Corporation ....E...... 631 249-6440
  Farmingdale *(G-4803)*
- Nicoform Inc ....E...... 585 454-5530
  Rochester *(G-13973)*

BELTING: Rubber

- Van Slyke Belting LLC ....G...... 518 283-5479
  Poestenkill *(G-13183)*

BELTING: Transmission, Rubber

- Sampla Belting North Amer LLC ....E...... 716 667-7450
  Lackawanna *(G-6953)*

BELTS: Conveyor, Made From Purchased Wire

- Chemprene Inc ....C...... 845 831-2800
  Beacon *(G-755)*
- Chemprene Holding Inc ....C...... 845 831-2800
  Beacon *(G-756)*
- Habasit America Inc ....D...... 716 824-8484
  Buffalo *(G-2860)*

BENCHES: Seating

- Jays Furniture Products Inc ....E...... 716 876-8854
  Buffalo *(G-2890)*
- Jcdecaux Mallscape LLC ....E...... 646 834-1200
  New York *(G-10319)*

BEVERAGE BASES & SYRUPS

- Agua Enerviva LLC ....F...... 516 597-5440
  Bethpage *(G-839)*
- Boylan Bottling Co Inc ....E...... 800 289-7978
  New York *(G-9230)*
- Buffalo Blends Inc ....F...... 716 825-4422
  Buffalo *(G-2741)*
- Flavormatic Industries LLC ....E...... 845 297-9100
  Wappingers Falls *(G-15930)*

BEVERAGE PRDTS: Brewers' Grain

- Kings Cnty Brwers Cllctive LLC ....F...... 917 207-2739
  Brooklyn *(G-2075)*

BEVERAGE, NONALCOHOLIC: Iced Tea/Fruit Drink, Bottled/Canned

- Arizona Beverage Company LLC ....G...... 516 812-0300
  Woodbury *(G-16613)*
- Cell-Nique Corporation ....G...... 203 856-8550
  Castleton On Hudson *(G-3295)*
- Cham Cold Brew LLC ....G...... 646 926-0206
  New York *(G-9257)*
- F & V Distribution Company LLC ....G...... 516 812-0393
  Woodbury *(G-16619)*
- Hain Celestial Group Inc ....C...... 516 587-5000
  New Hyde Park *(G-8538)*
- Heart of Tea ....F...... 917 725-3164
  New York *(G-10073)*
- Long Blockchain Corp ....G...... 855 542-2832
  Farmingdale *(G-4810)*
- Long Island Brand Bevs LLC ....D...... 855 542-2832
  Long Island City *(G-7504)*

BEVERAGES, ALCOHOLIC: Ale

- Empire Brewing Company Inc ....D...... 315 925-8308
  Syracuse *(G-15317)*
- Rising Sons 6 Brewing Co inc ....G...... 607 368-4836
  Corning *(G-3824)*

BEVERAGES, ALCOHOLIC: Applejack

- Honeoye Falls Distillery LLC ....F...... 201 780-4618
  Honeoye Falls *(G-6268)*

BEVERAGES, ALCOHOLIC: Beer

- Anheuser-Busch LLC ....C...... 315 638-0365
  Baldwinsville *(G-550)*
- Anheuser-Busch LLC ....C...... 212 573-8800
  New York *(G-8865)*
- Anheuser-Busch Companies LLC ....G...... 718 589-2610
  Bronx *(G-1221)*
- Anheuser-Busch Inbev Fin Inc ....F...... 212 573-8800
  New York *(G-8866)*
- Brazen Street LLC ....E...... 516 305-7951
  Brooklyn *(G-1632)*
- Brewery Ommegang Ltd ....F...... 607 286-4144
  Cooperstown *(G-3742)*
- Constellation Brands Inc ....D...... 585 678-7100
  Victor *(G-15837)*
- Coopers Cave Ale Co S-Corp ....F...... 518 792-0007
  Glens Falls *(G-5422)*
- Cooperstown Brewing Co LLC ....F...... 607 286-9330
  Oneonta *(G-12634)*
- Custom Brewcrafters Inc ....F...... 585 624-4386
  Honeoye Falls *(G-6263)*
- Five Burroughs Brewing Co ....G...... 718 355-8575
  Brooklyn *(G-1886)*
- Gilded Otter Brewing Co ....D...... 845 256-1700
  New Paltz *(G-8577)*
- High Falls Brewing Company LLC ....C...... 585 546-1030
  Rochester *(G-13867)*
- Hoptron Brewtique ....G...... 631 438-0296
  Patchogue *(G-12866)*
- Hyde Park Brewing Co Inc ....E...... 845 229-8277
  Hyde Park *(G-6469)*
- Indian Ladder Farmstead Brewer ....G...... 518 577-1484
  Altamont *(G-197)*
- Ithaca Beer Company Inc ....E...... 607 272-1305
  Ithaca *(G-6587)*
- Keegan Ales LLC ....F...... 845 331-2739
  Kingston *(G-6903)*
- Keuka Brewing Co LLC ....G...... 607 868-4648
  Hammondsport *(G-5706)*
- Labatt USA LLC ....D...... 716 604-1050
  Buffalo *(G-2915)*
- Lock 1 Distilling Company LLC ....G...... 315 934-4376
  Phoenix *(G-12989)*
- Long Ireland Brewing Co ....G...... 631 403-4303
  Riverhead *(G-13574)*
- Mad Scntsts Brwing Prtners LLC ....E...... 347 766-2739
  Brooklyn *(G-2150)*
- Middle Ages Brewing Company ....G...... 315 476-4250
  Syracuse *(G-15371)*
- Millercoors LLC ....E...... 585 385-0670
  Pittsford *(G-13022)*
- Montauk Brewing Company Inc ....F...... 631 668-8471
  Montauk *(G-8305)*
- Newburgh Brewing Company LLC ....F...... 845 569-2337
  Newburgh *(G-12235)*
- North American Breweries Inc ....F...... 585 546-1030
  Rochester *(G-13977)*
- North Amrcn Brwries Hldngs LLC ....E...... 585 546-1030
  Rochester *(G-13978)*
- Oyster Bay Brewing Company ....F...... 516 802-5546
  Oyster Bay *(G-12817)*
- Rare Form Brewing Company ....G...... 518 313-9256
  Troy *(G-15620)*
- Remarkable Liquids LLC ....D...... 518 861-5351
  Altamont *(G-200)*
- Rohrbach Brewing Company Inc ....D...... 585 594-9800
  Rochester *(G-14102)*
- Spectacle Brewing LLC ....F...... 845 942-8776
  Garnerville *(G-5301)*
- Vanberg & Dewulf Co LLC ....G...... 607 547-8184
  Cooperstown *(G-3745)*
- Woodcock Brothers Brewing Comp ....F...... 716 333-4000
  Wilson *(G-16603)*
- Yonkers Whl Beer Distrs Inc ....G...... 914 963-8600
  Yonkers *(G-16812)*

BEVERAGES, ALCOHOLIC: Beer & Ale

- Anheuser-Busch LLC ....G...... 315 638-0365
  Baldwinsville *(G-549)*
- Anheuser-Busch Inbev Svcs LLC ....G...... 314 765-4729
  New York *(G-8867)*
- Barrier Brewing Company LLC ....G...... 516 316-4429
  Long Beach *(G-7357)*
- Black River Brewing Co Inc ....G...... 315 755-2739
  Watertown *(G-16003)*
- Butternuts Beer and Ale LLC ....G...... 607 263-5070
  Garrattsville *(G-5302)*
- C H Evans Brewing Co ....F...... 518 447-9000
  Albany *(G-53)*
- Duvel Mortgage USA Inc ....G...... 607 267-6121
  Cooperstown *(G-3744)*
- Equilibrium Brewery LLC ....G...... 201 245-0292
  Middletown *(G-8151)*
- Other Half Brewing Co ....G...... 347 987-3527
  Brooklyn *(G-2295)*
- Simple Brewer ....E...... 845 490-0182
  Somers *(G-14923)*
- Valcour Brewing Company LLC ....E...... 518 324-2337
  Plattsburgh *(G-13167)*
- Wagner Vineyards & Brewing Co ....E...... 607 582-6574
  Lodi *(G-7355)*

BEVERAGES, ALCOHOLIC: Bourbon Whiskey

- Iron Smoke Whiskey LLC ....G...... 585 388-7584
  Fairport *(G-4635)*

BEVERAGES, ALCOHOLIC: Brandy

- Cruzin Management Inc ....E...... 212 641-8700
  New York *(G-9428)*

BEVERAGES, ALCOHOLIC: Cocktails

- Dutch Spirits LLC ....F...... 518 398-1022
  Pine Plains *(G-13005)*

BEVERAGES, ALCOHOLIC: Cordials & Premixed Cocktails

- Infirmary Nyc ....G...... 504 606-6280
  New York *(G-10205)*

BEVERAGES, ALCOHOLIC: Distilled Liquors

- Adirondack Distilling Company ....G...... 315 316-0387
  Utica *(G-15675)*
- Austin Nichols & Co Inc ....E...... 519 561-5225
  New York *(G-8965)*
- Braided Oak Spirits LLC ....F...... 845 381-1525
  Middletown *(G-8140)*
- Constellation Brands Inc ....D...... 585 678-7100
  Victor *(G-15837)*
- Ellicottville Distillery LLC ....G...... 716 597-6121
  Ellicottville *(G-4445)*
- Finger Lakes Distilling ....F...... 607 546-5510
  Burdett *(G-3141)*
- George Lake Distilling Company ....G...... 518 639-1025
  Queensbury *(G-13425)*
- Leblon LLC ....G...... 954 649-0148
  New York *(G-10534)*
- Leblon LLC ....E...... 786 281-5672
  New York *(G-10535)*
- Lockhouse Distillery ....G...... 716 768-4898
  Buffalo *(G-2927)*
- Marnier-Lapostolle Inc ....D...... 212 207-4350
  New York *(G-10715)*
- Prohibition Distillery LLC ....G...... 917 685-8989
  Roscoe *(G-14439)*

Sovereign Brands LLC ....G...... 212 343-8366
New York *(G-11656)*
Stilltheone Distillery LLC ....G...... 914 217-0347
Harrison *(G-5736)*
Tirado Distillery Inc..................G...... 718 620-2244
Bronx *(G-1403)*
Tuthilltown Spirits LLC ....F 845 255-1527
Gardiner *(G-5296)*

BEVERAGES, ALCOHOLIC: Gin

21st Century Spirits Corp..................G...... 718 499-0606
Brooklyn *(G-1435)*
Madison County Distillery LLC ....G...... 315 391-6070
Cazenovia *(G-3321)*

BEVERAGES, ALCOHOLIC: Liquors, Malt

Castle Brands Inc..................E 646 356-0200
New York *(G-9223)*
Marnier-Lapostolle Inc..................D 212 207-4350
New York *(G-10715)*
Vernon Wine & Liquor Inc ....G...... 718 784-5096
Long Island City *(G-7630)*

BEVERAGES, ALCOHOLIC: Near Beer

Horns & Halos Cft Brewing LLC ....E 585 507-7248
Caledonia *(G-3156)*

BEVERAGES, ALCOHOLIC: Neutral Spirits, Fruit

Davos Brands LLC..................F...... 212 779-1911
New York *(G-9491)*
Dutch Spirits LLC..................F 518 398-1022
Pine Plains *(G-13005)*

BEVERAGES, ALCOHOLIC: Rum

Castle Brands Inc..................E 646 356-0200
New York *(G-9223)*
Cruzin Management Inc..................E 212 641-8700
New York *(G-9428)*
Evolution Spirits Inc ....G...... 917 543-7880
New York *(G-9742)*
Leblon Holdings LLC..................E 212 741-2675
New York *(G-10533)*

BEVERAGES, ALCOHOLIC: Vodka

Russian Standard Vodka USA Inc ....G...... 212 679-1894
New York *(G-11450)*

BEVERAGES, ALCOHOLIC: Wines

Allied Wine Corp ....F 845 796-4160
South Fallsburg *(G-14930)*
Americana Vineyards & Winery..................F 607 387-6801
Interlaken *(G-6480)*
Anthony Road Wine Co Inc..................F 315 536-2182
Penn Yan *(G-12948)*
Anyelas Vineyards LLC ....F 315 685-3797
Skaneateles *(G-14866)*
Arrowhead Spring Vineyards LLC..................G...... 716 434-8030
Lockport *(G-7285)*
Atwater Estate Vineyards LLC ....E 607 546-8463
Burdett *(G-3140)*
Bellwethe Hard Cider..................F 607 387-9464
Trumansburg *(G-15637)*
Billsboro Winery ....G...... 315 789-9538
Geneva *(G-5317)*
Brooklyn Winery LLC ....F 347 763-1506
Brooklyn *(G-1650)*
Brotherhood Americas ....E 845 496-3661
Washingtonville *(G-15964)*
Casa Larga Vineyards ....E 585 223-4210
Fairport *(G-4627)*
Casa Larga Vineyards ....G...... 585 223-4210
Fairport *(G-4628)*
Cascade Mountain Winery & Rest..................F 845 373-9021
Amenia *(G-205)*
Cava Spiliadis USA..................E 212 247-8214
New York *(G-9232)*
Chautauqua Wine Company Inc ....G...... 716 934-9463
Silver Creek *(G-14860)*
Clinton Vineyards Inc ....G...... 845 266-5372
Clinton Corners *(G-3590)*
Cobblestone Frm Winery Vinyrd ....F 315 549-1004
Romulus *(G-14280)*
Constellation Brands US Oprs ....A 585 396-7600
Canandaigua *(G-3216)*
Constellation Brands US Oprs ....B 585 396-7600
Canandaigua *(G-3217)*
Coyote Moon LLC ....F 315 686-5600
Clayton *(G-3553)*
David F De Marco..................G...... 315 536-0882
Penn Yan *(G-12952)*
Deer Run Enterprises Inc ....G...... 585 346-0850
Geneseo *(G-5314)*
Di Borghese Castello LLC..................F 631 734-5111
Cutchogue *(G-3921)*
Dorset Farms Inc..................F 631 734-6010
Peconic *(G-12914)*
Duck Walk Vinyards..................E 631 726-7555
Water Mill *(G-15970)*
Dutchess Wines LLC ....G...... 845 876-1319
Rhinebeck *(G-13486)*
Eagle Crest Vineyard LLC ....G...... 585 346-5760
Conesus *(G-3708)*
East Branch Winery Inc..................G...... 607 292-3999
Dundee *(G-4156)*
East End Vineyards LLC ....G...... 718 468-0500
Queens Village *(G-13405)*
Fly Creek Cder Mill Orchrd Inc ....G...... 607 547-9692
Fly Creek *(G-5064)*
Fox Run Vineyards Inc ....F 315 536-4616
Penn Yan *(G-12956)*
Frank Wines Inc ....G...... 646 765-6637
New York *(G-9842)*
Freedom Run Winery Inc..................G...... 716 433-4136
Lockport *(G-7302)*
Gabriella Importers Inc..................F 212 579-3945
New York *(G-9874)*
Glenora Farm Inc ....G...... 607 243-8383
Dundee *(G-4158)*
Glenora Wine Cellars Inc..................E 607 243-9500
Dundee *(G-4159)*
Greenwood Winery LLC ....E 315 432-8132
East Syracuse *(G-4343)*
Hazlitts 1852 Vineyards Inc..................E 607 546-9463
Hector *(G-5999)*
Hermann J Wiemer Vineyard ....G...... 607 243-7971
Dundee *(G-4160)*
Heron Hill Vineyards Inc..................E 607 868-4241
Hammondsport *(G-5705)*
Hoffman & Hoffman ....G...... 315 536-4773
Penn Yan *(G-12958)*
Hosmer Inc..................F 888 467-9463
Ovid *(G-12791)*
Hunt Country Vineyards..................E 315 595-2812
Branchport *(G-1123)*
J Petrocelli Wine Cellars LLC ....E 631 765-1100
Peconic *(G-12915)*
Joseph Zakon Winery Ltd ....G...... 718 604-1430
Brooklyn *(G-2049)*
Konstantin D FRAnk& Sons Vini ....E 607 868-4884
Hammondsport *(G-5707)*
L & D Acquisition LLC ....F 585 531-9000
Naples *(G-8471)*
Lafayette Chateau..................E 607 546-2062
Hector *(G-6000)*
Lakewood Vineyards Inc..................F 607 535-9252
Watkins Glen *(G-16059)*
Lamoreaux Landing WI ....D 607 582-6162
Lodi *(G-7353)*
Leonard Oakes Estate Winery ....G...... 585 318-4418
Medina *(G-7982)*
Lieb Cellars LLC..................E 631 298-1942
Mattituck *(G-7914)*
Lucas Vineyards Inc ....F 607 532-4825
Interlaken *(G-6482)*
Malina Management Company Inc ....E 607 535-9614
Montour Falls *(G-8326)*
Merritt Estate Winery Inc..................F 716 965-4800
Forestville *(G-5086)*
Millbrook Winery Inc..................F 845 677-8383
Millbrook *(G-8190)*
Montezuma Winery LLC ....G...... 315 568-8190
Seneca Falls *(G-14782)*
Negys New Land Vinyrd Winery ....G...... 315 585-4432
Geneva *(G-5330)*
North House Vineyards Inc..................G...... 631 779-2817
Jamesport *(G-6693)*
Olde Chtqua Vneyards Ltd Lblty ....F 716 792-2749
Portland *(G-13315)*
Paumanok Vineyards Ltd ....E...... 631 722-8800
Aquebogue *(G-375)*
Pellegrini Vineyards LLC..................G 631 734-4111
Cutchogue *(G-3922)*
Pindar Vineyards LLC..................E 631 734-6200
Peconic *(G-12916)*
Prejean Winery Inc..................F 315 536-7524
Penn Yan *(G-12962)*
Premium Wine Group LLC ....E 631 298-1900
Mattituck *(G-7916)*
Pugliese Vineyards Inc..................G...... 631 734-4057
Cutchogue *(G-3923)*
Railex Wine Services LLC ....E 631 369-7000
Riverhead *(G-13581)*
Red Newt Cellars Inc ....F 607 546-4100
Hector *(G-6001)*
Red Tail Ridge Inc..................F 315 536-4580
Penn Yan *(G-12963)*
Rock Stream Vineyards..................G...... 607 243-8322
Rock Stream *(G-14223)*
Royal Wine Corporation ....F 845 236-4000
Marlboro *(G-7813)*
Schulze Vineyards & Winery LLC..................F 716 778-8090
Burt *(G-3144)*
Sheldrake Point Vineyard LLC..................F 607 532-8967
Ovid *(G-12793)*
Shinn Winery LLC ....G...... 631 804-0367
Mattituck *(G-7917)*
Sokolin LLC..................E 631 537-4434
Yaphank *(G-16722)*
Spanish Artisan Wine Group LLC ....G...... 914 414-6982
Patterson *(G-12885)*
Standing Stone Vineyards ....G...... 607 582-6051
Hector *(G-6002)*
Swedish Hill Vineyard Inc ....D 607 403-0029
Romulus *(G-14283)*
Thirsty Owl Wine Company ....G...... 607 869-5805
Ovid *(G-12794)*
Thousand Islands Winery LLC ....E 315 482-9306
Alexandria Bay *(G-183)*
Trader Joes Company ....E 212 529-6326
New York *(G-11883)*
Tug Hill Vineyards..................G...... 315 376-4336
Lowville *(G-7657)*
Vedell North Fork LLC..................G...... 631 323-3526
Cutchogue *(G-3924)*
Ventosa Vineyards LLC ....G...... 315 719-0000
Geneva *(G-5336)*
Wagner Vineyards LLC..................G...... 607 582-6976
Lodi *(G-7354)*
Wagner Vineyards & Brewing Co ....E 607 582-6574
Lodi *(G-7355)*
Warwick Valley Wine Co..................F 845 258-4858
Warwick *(G-15962)*
Westchester Wine Warehouse LLC..................F 914 824-1400
White Plains *(G-16520)*
Wine Group Inc..................D 716 326-3151
Westfield *(G-16400)*
Wolffer Estate Vineyard Inc ....E 631 537-5106
Sagaponack *(G-14505)*
Woodbury Vineyards Inc..................G...... 716 679-9463
Fredonia *(G-5130)*

BEVERAGES, MALT

Crazy Cowboy Brewing Co LLC ....E 516 812-0576
Woodbury *(G-16616)*
High Falls Operating Co LLC..................A 585 546-1030
Rochester *(G-13868)*

BEVERAGES, NONALCOHOLIC: Bottled & canned soft drinks

3v Company Inc ....E 718 858-7333
Brooklyn *(G-1440)*
American Bottling Company..................F 516 714-0002
Ronkonkoma *(G-14305)*
Beverage Works Nj Inc..................E 631 293-3501
Farmingdale *(G-4728)*
Beverage Works Ny Inc ....E 718 812-2034
Brooklyn *(G-1608)*
Big Geyser Inc..................C 718 821-2200
Maspeth *(G-7827)*
Borabora Fruit Juices Inc..................G...... 914 438-8744
Highland *(G-6142)*
Bottling Group LLC..................F 914 767-6000
White Plains *(G-16430)*
Brands Within Reach LLC ....E 847 720-9090
Mamaroneck *(G-7735)*
Cliffstar LLC ....A 716 366-6100
Dunkirk *(G-4165)*
Coca-Cola Bottling Company ....E 518 483-0422
Malone *(G-7720)*
Coca-Cola Btlg Co Buffalo Inc..................C 716 874-4610
Tonawanda *(G-15535)*
Coca-Cola Btlg Co of NY Inc..................F 845 562-3037
New Windsor *(G-8642)*

PRODUCT

Employee Codes: A=Over 500 employees, B=251-500
C=101-250, D=51-100, E=20-50, F=10-19, G=5-9

BEVERAGES, NONALCOHOLIC: Bottled & canned soft drinks

Coca-Cola Btlg Co of NY Inc .... E 718 416-7575
  Maspeth *(G-7830)*
Coca-Cola Btlg Co of NY Inc .... F 315 457-9221
  Syracuse *(G-15284)*
Coca-Cola Btlg Co of NY Inc .... E 631 434-3535
  Hauppauge *(G-5792)*
Coca-Cola Btlg Co of NY Inc .... F 718 420-6800
  Staten Island *(G-15063)*
Coca-Cola Btlg Co of NY Inc .... F 914 789-1580
  Elmsford *(G-4536)*
Coca-Cola Refreshments USA Inc .... E 315 785-8907
  Watertown *(G-16009)*
Coca-Cola Refreshments USA Inc .... G 914 592-0806
  Hawthorne *(G-5985)*
Doheny Nice and Easy .... G 518 793-1733
  Glens Falls *(G-5423)*
Fancy Flamingo LLC .... G 516 209-7306
  New York *(G-9779)*
Gangi Distributors Inc .... F 718 442-5745
  Staten Island *(G-15077)*
Grayhawk Leasing LLC .... G 914 767-6000
  Somers *(G-14920)*
N Y Winstons Inc .... G 212 665-3166
  New York *(G-10870)*
Owens Table Mixers LLC .... G 650 303-7342
  New York *(G-11073)*
Pepsi-Cola Operating Company .... E 914 767-6000
  White Plains *(G-16492)*
Pepsico Inc .... A 914 253-2000
  Purchase *(G-13395)*
Pepsico Capital Resources Inc .... G 914 253-2000
  Purchase *(G-13398)*
Shopping Center Wine & Liquor .... G 914 528-1600
  Mohegan Lake *(G-8259)*
Snapp Too Enterprise .... G 718 224-5252
  Flushing *(G-5046)*
Street King LLC .... G 212 400-2200
  New York *(G-11719)*
Unilever United States Inc .... G 212 546-0200
  New York *(G-11944)*
Unilever United States Inc .... C 212 546-0200
  New York *(G-11945)*

BEVERAGES, NONALCOHOLIC: Carbonated

Pepsi Beverages Co .... G 518 782-2150
  Latham *(G-7088)*
Pepsi Bottling Ventures LLC .... D 631 772-6144
  Patchogue *(G-12874)*
Pepsi Bottling Ventures LLC .... E 631 226-9000
  Amityville *(G-312)*
Pepsi Btlg Group Globl Fin LLC .... G 914 767-6000
  Somers *(G-14921)*
Pepsi-Cola Bottling Group .... G 914 767-6000
  White Plains *(G-16490)*
Pepsi-Cola Metro Btlg Co Inc .... B 518 834-7811
  Keeseville *(G-6854)*
Pepsi-Cola Newburgh Btlg Inc .... C 845 562-5400
  Newburgh *(G-12241)*
Pepsico .... F 419 252-0247
  Hawthorne *(G-5995)*
Pepsico .... E 914 801-1500
  Valhalla *(G-15743)*
Pepsico Inc .... B 914 742-4500
  Valhalla *(G-15744)*
Pepsico Inc .... A 914 253-2000
  Purchase *(G-13396)*
Pepsico Inc .... E 914 253-3474
  White Plains *(G-16494)*
Pepsico Inc .... F 914 253-2713
  Purchase *(G-13397)*

BEVERAGES, NONALCOHOLIC: Carbonated, Canned & Bottled, Etc

Beverage Works Incorporated .... G 718 834-0500
  Brooklyn *(G-1607)*
Blue Star Beverages Corp .... G 718 381-3535
  Brooklyn *(G-1622)*
Bottling Group LLC .... B 800 789-2626
  White Plains *(G-16429)*
Chateau Imports Ltd .... G 516 841-6343
  Port Washington *(G-13248)*
Chohehco LLC .... G 315 420-4624
  Skaneateles *(G-14868)*
Fevertree USA Inc .... F 718 852-5577
  Brooklyn *(G-1876)*
Green Zone Food Service Inc .... G 917 709-1728
  Corona *(G-3844)*
Hmo Beverage Corporation .... G 917 371-6100
  Brooklyn *(G-1978)*
Hydrive Energy .... G 914 925-9100
  Rye *(G-14483)*
Juices Enterprises Inc .... G 718 953-1860
  Brooklyn *(G-2056)*
Liquid Management Partners LLC .... F 516 775-5050
  New Hyde Park *(G-8548)*
Nexbev Industries LLC .... F 646 648-1255
  Blauvelt *(G-938)*
Save More Beverage Corp .... G 518 371-2520
  Halfmoon *(G-5669)*
Switch Beverage Company LLC .... F 203 202-7383
  Port Washington *(G-13310)*
Treo Brands LLC .... G 914 341-1850
  Harrison *(G-5737)*

BEVERAGES, NONALCOHOLIC: Cider

Lakeside Cider Mill Farm Inc .... G 518 399-8359
  Ballston Lake *(G-568)*
Mullers Cider House LLC .... G 585 287-5875
  Rochester *(G-13959)*
Nine Pin Ciderworks LLC .... F 518 449-9999
  Albany *(G-105)*
Schutt Cider Mill .... F 585 872-2924
  Webster *(G-16097)*

BEVERAGES, NONALCOHOLIC: Flavoring extracts & syrups, nec

Citrus and Allied Essences Ltd .... C 516 354-1200
  Floral Park *(G-4960)*
Comax Manufacturing Corp .... D 631 249-0505
  Melville *(G-8010)*
Danisco US Inc .... D 585 277-4300
  Rochester *(G-13734)*
Delbia Do Company Inc .... E 718 585-2226
  Bronx *(G-1255)*
Delbia Do Company Inc .... F 718 585-2226
  Bronx *(G-1256)*
DSM Nutritional Products LLC .... C 518 372-5155
  Schenectady *(G-14669)*
DSM Nutritional Products LLC .... C 518 372-5155
  Glenville *(G-5445)*
Interntnal Flvors Frgrnces Inc .... C 212 765-5500
  New York *(G-10251)*
Keurig Dr Pepper Inc .... C 315 589-4911
  Williamson *(G-16559)*
Natural Organics Labs Inc .... B 631 957-5600
  Amityville *(G-305)*
Pepsico Inc .... A 914 253-2000
  Purchase *(G-13395)*
Star Kay White Inc .... D 845 268-2600
  Congers *(G-3720)*
Synergy Flavors NY Company LLC ...... G 585 232-6648
  Rochester *(G-14151)*
Torre Products Co Inc .... G 212 925-8989
  New York *(G-11870)*

BEVERAGES, NONALCOHOLIC: Fruit Drnks, Under 100% Juice, Can

A Health Obsession LLC .... E 347 850-4587
  Brooklyn *(G-1457)*
Ba Sports Nutrition LLC .... C 718 357-7402
  Whitestone *(G-16536)*
Cheribundi Inc .... E 800 699-0460
  Geneva *(G-5320)*
Nantucket Allserve Inc .... B 914 612-4000
  Elmsford *(G-4555)*
Purely Maple LLC .... F 203 997-9309
  New York *(G-11278)*

BEVERAGES, NONALCOHOLIC: Lemonade, Bottled & Canned, Etc

Dirty Lemon Beverages LLC .... G 877 897-7784
  New York *(G-9533)*

BEVERAGES, NONALCOHOLIC: Soft Drinks, Canned & Bottled, Etc

Austin Nichols & Co Inc .... E 519 561-5225
  New York *(G-8965)*
Bottling Group LLC .... E 315 788-6751
  Watertown *(G-16004)*
Boylan Bottling Co Inc .... E 800 289-7978
  New York *(G-9130)*
Clintons Ditch Coop Co Inc .... C 315 699-2695
  Cicero *(G-3515)*
Coca-Cola Btlg Co of NY Inc .... F 518 459-2010
  Albany *(G-64)*
Coca-Cola Refreshments USA Inc .... E 718 401-5200
  Bronx *(G-1242)*
Cornell Beverages Inc .... F 718 381-3000
  Brooklyn *(G-1718)*
Energy Brands Inc .... E 212 545-6000
  New York *(G-9680)*
General Cinema Bevs of Ohio .... A 914 767-6000
  Somers *(G-14919)*
Good-O-Beverage Inc .... F 718 328-6400
  Bronx *(G-1284)*
Johnnie Ryan Co Inc .... F 716 282-1606
  Niagara Falls *(G-12301)*
Keurig Dr Pepper Inc .... C 315 589-4911
  Williamson *(G-16559)*
Keurig Dr Pepper Inc .... D 914 846-2300
  Elmsford *(G-4548)*
Keurig Dr Pepper Inc .... G 718 246-6200
  Brooklyn *(G-2069)*
La Cola 1 Inc .... G 917 509-6669
  New York *(G-10499)*
Life Earth Company .... G 310 751-0627
  New York *(G-10562)*
Load/N/Go Beverage Corp .... F 585 218-4019
  Rochester *(G-13915)*
Manhattan Special Bottling .... F 718 388-4144
  Brooklyn *(G-2159)*
Monfefo LLC .... G 347 779-2600
  Brooklyn *(G-2224)*
New York Bottling Co Inc .... F 718 963-3232
  Bronx *(G-1340)*
Pepsi-Cola Bottling Co NY Inc .... C 914 699-2600
  Mount Vernon *(G-8429)*
Pepsi-Cola Bottling Co NY Inc .... A 718 392-1000
  College Point *(G-3660)*
Pepsi-Cola Bottling Co NY Inc .... D 718 892-1570
  Bronx *(G-1355)*
Pepsi-Cola Metro Btlg Co Inc .... G 914 767-6000
  White Plains *(G-16491)*
Pepsi-Cola Metro Btlg Co Inc .... E 914 253-2000
  Purchase *(G-13393)*
Pepsi-Cola Sales and Dist Inc .... G 914 253-2000
  Purchase *(G-13394)*
Pepsico Sales Inc .... G 914 253-2000
  Purchase *(G-13399)*
Rochester Coca Cola Bottling .... E 607 739-5678
  Horseheads *(G-6327)*
Rochester Coca Cola Bottling .... D 585 546-3900
  Rochester *(G-14083)*
Royal Crown Financial .... G 718 234-7237
  Brooklyn *(G-2419)*
Scotia Beverages Inc .... A 518 370-3621
  Schenectady *(G-14712)*
Snapple Beverage Corp (del) .... D 914 612-4000
  Rye Brook *(G-14495)*
Stewarts Processing Corp .... D 518 581-1200
  Ballston Spa *(G-597)*

BEVERAGES, NONALCOHOLIC: Tea, Iced, Bottled & Canned, Etc

East Coast Cultures LLC .... F 917 261-3010
  Kingston *(G-6899)*

BEVERAGES, WINE & DISTILLED ALCOHOLIC, WHOLESALE: Liquor

Austin Nichols & Co Inc .... E 519 561-5225
  New York *(G-8965)*
Cruzin Management Inc .... E 212 641-8700
  New York *(G-9428)*
Marnier-Lapostolle Inc .... D 212 207-4350
  New York *(G-10715)*

BEVERAGES, WINE & DISTILLED ALCOHOLIC, WHOLESALE: Neutral Sp

Spanish Artisan Wine Group LLC .... G 914 414-6982
  Patterson *(G-12885)*

BEVERAGES, WINE & DISTILLED ALCOHOLIC, WHOLESALE: Wine

Coyote Moon LLC .... F 315 686-5600
  Clayton *(G-3553)*
Royal Wine Corporation .... F 845 236-4000
  Marlboro *(G-7813)*

PRODUCT SECTION

BEVERAGES, WINE WHOLESALE : Wine Coolers

Hootron Brewtique .... G 631 438-0296
  Patchogue *(G-12866)*

BICYCLE SHOPS

Bignay Inc .... G 786 346-1673
  New York *(G-9080)*

BICYCLES WHOLESALERS

East Coast Cycle LLC .... G 631 780-5360
  Farmingdale *(G-4756)*

BICYCLES, PARTS & ACCESS

Bignay Inc .... G 786 346-1673
  New York *(G-9080)*
East Coast Cycle LLC .... G 631 780-5360
  Farmingdale *(G-4756)*
Evelo Inc .... G 917 251-8743
  Rockaway Park *(G-14228)*
Great American Bicycle LLC .... E 518 584-8100
  Saratoga Springs *(G-14583)*
KG Motors Inc .... E 607 562-2877
  Big Flats *(G-855)*
Prestacycle Llc .... G 518 588-5546
  Rexford *(G-13483)*
Social Bicycles Inc .... E 917 746-7624
  Brooklyn *(G-2490)*

BILLETS: Steel

Homogeneous Metals Inc .... D 315 839-5421
  Clayville *(G-3558)*

BILLFOLD INSERTS: Plastic

Quality Lineals Usa Inc .... D 516 378-6577
  Merrick *(G-8106)*

BILLIARD & POOL TABLES & SPLYS

A Hyatt Ball Co Ltd .... G 518 747-0272
  Fort Edward *(G-5093)*
International Leisure Pdts Inc .... E 631 254-2155
  Edgewood *(G-4405)*

BINDING SVC: Books & Manuals

514 Adams Corporation .... G 516 352-6948
  Franklin Square *(G-5114)*
A-Quick Bindery LLC .... G 631 491-1110
  West Babylon *(G-16126)*
Agrecolor Inc .... F 516 741-8700
  Mineola *(G-8202)*
Argo Lithographers Inc .... E 718 729-2700
  Long Island City *(G-7388)*
Arista Innovations Inc .... E 516 746-2262
  Mineola *(G-8205)*
Baum Christine and John Corp .... G 585 621-8910
  Rochester *(G-13654)*
Beastons Budget Printing .... G 585 244-2721
  Rochester *(G-13658)*
Benchemark Printing Inc .... D 518 393-1361
  Schenectady *(G-14653)*
Bernard Hall .... G 585 425-3340
  Fairport *(G-4625)*
Beyer Graphics Inc .... D 631 543-3900
  Commack *(G-3682)*
Bg Bindery Inc .... G 631 767-4242
  Maspeth *(G-7826)*
Boncraft Inc .... D 716 662-9720
  Tonawanda *(G-15528)*
Bondy Printing Corp .... G 631 242-1510
  Bay Shore *(G-666)*
Brodock Press Inc .... D 315 735-9577
  Utica *(G-15681)*
Brooks Litho Digital Group Inc .... G 631 789-4500
  Deer Park *(G-3955)*
Carlara Group Ltd .... G 914 769-2020
  Pleasantville *(G-13173)*
Carnels Printing Inc .... G 516 883-3355
  Great Neck *(G-5543)*
Castlereagh Printcraft Inc .... D 516 623-1728
  Freeport *(G-5148)*
Chakra Communications Inc .... E 607 748-7491
  Endicott *(G-4584)*
Challenge Graphics Svcs Inc .... E 631 586-0171
  Deer Park *(G-3956)*

Classic Album .... E 718 388-2818
  Brooklyn *(G-1699)*
Cohber Press Inc .... D 585 475-9100
  West Henrietta *(G-16234)*
Copy Corner Inc .... G 718 388-4545
  Brooklyn *(G-1717)*
Cosmos Communications Inc .... C 718 482-1800
  Long Island City *(G-7416)*
D G M Graphics Inc .... F 516 223-2220
  Merrick *(G-8096)*
David Helsing .... G 607 796-2681
  Horseheads *(G-6311)*
Dependable Lithographers Inc .... F 718 472-4200
  Long Island City *(G-7423)*
Dispatch Graphics Inc .... F 212 307-5943
  New York *(G-9536)*
Division Den-Bar Enterprises .... G 914 381-2220
  Mamaroneck *(G-7742)*
Dowd - Witbeck Printing Corp .... F 518 274-2421
  Troy *(G-15604)*
DP Murphy Co Inc .... D 631 673-9400
  Deer Park *(G-3968)*
E B B Graphics Inc .... F 516 750-5510
  Westbury *(G-16324)*
E L Smith Printing Co Inc .... G 201 373-0111
  New City *(G-8492)*
Eastwood Litho Inc .... G 315 437-2626
  Syracuse *(G-15310)*
Erhard & Gilcher Inc .... G 315 474-1072
  Syracuse *(G-15319)*
Flare Multicopy Corp .... E 718 258-8860
  Brooklyn *(G-1887)*
Flp Group Llc .... E 315 252-7583
  Auburn *(G-480)*
Foleys Graphic Center Inc .... E 914 245-3625
  Yorktown Heights *(G-16816)*
Fulton Newspapers Inc .... G 315 598-6397
  Fulton *(G-5216)*
Gateway Prtg & Graphics Inc .... E 716 823-3873
  Hamburg *(G-5680)*
Gazette Press Inc .... E 914 963-8300
  Rye *(G-14479)*
Graphicomm Inc .... G 716 283-0830
  Niagara Falls *(G-12289)*
Haig Press Inc .... E 631 582-5800
  Hauppauge *(G-5838)*
Hudson Printing Co Inc .... E 718 937-8600
  New York *(G-10145)*
In-House Inc .... F 718 445-9007
  College Point *(G-3646)*
Interstate Litho Corp .... D 631 232-6025
  Brentwood *(G-1136)*
Jack J Florio Jr .... G 716 434-9123
  Lockport *(G-7311)*
James Conolly Printing Co .... E 585 426-4150
  Rochester *(G-13891)*
Jane Lewis .... G 607 722-0584
  Binghamton *(G-898)*
Johnnys Ideal Printing Co .... G 518 828-6666
  Hudson *(G-6359)*
Jon Lyn Ink Inc .... G 516 546-2312
  Merrick *(G-8099)*
Kaufman Brothers Printing .... E 212 563-1854
  New York *(G-10419)*
King Lithographers Inc .... E 914 667-4200
  Mount Vernon *(G-8414)*
Louis Heindl & Son Inc .... E 585 454-5080
  Rochester *(G-13917)*
Loy L Press Inc .... E 716 634-5966
  Buffalo *(G-2928)*
Melcher Media Inc .... F 212 727-2322
  New York *(G-10769)*
Mercury Print Productions Inc .... C 585 458-7900
  Rochester *(G-13936)*
Midgley Printing Corp .... G 315 475-1864
  Syracuse *(G-15372)*
Moneast Inc .... G 845 298-8898
  Wappingers Falls *(G-15936)*
Multiple Imprssons of Rchester .... G 585 546-1160
  Rochester *(G-13960)*
Newport Graphics Inc .... E 212 924-2600
  New York *(G-10950)*
Prestige Envelope & Lithograph .... F 631 521-7043
  Merrick *(G-8105)*
Printing Resources Inc .... E 518 482-2470
  Albany *(G-119)*
Pro Printing .... G 516 561-9700
  Lynbrook *(G-7670)*
Progressive Graphics & Prtg .... G 315 331-3635
  Newark *(G-12205)*

BIOLOGICAL PRDTS: Bacterial Vaccines

Prompt Bindery Co Inc .... F 212 675-5181
  New York *(G-11261)*
Psychonomic Society Inc .... E 512 381-1494
  New York *(G-11270)*
Quad/Graphics Inc .... A 518 581-4000
  Saratoga Springs *(G-14594)*
Reynolds Book Bindery LLC .... F 607 772-8937
  Binghamton *(G-912)*
Richard Ruffner .... F 631 234-4600
  Central Islip *(G-3383)*
Rmd Holding Inc .... G 845 628-0030
  Mahopac *(G-7712)*
Roger Michael Press Inc .... D 732 752-0800
  Brooklyn *(G-2411)*
Rosemont Press Incorporated .... E 212 239-4770
  New York *(G-11430)*
Rosen Mandell & Immerman Inc .... E 212 691-2277
  New York *(G-11431)*
S L C Industries Incorporated .... F 607 775-2299
  Binghamton *(G-913)*
Sentine Printing Inc .... G 516 334-7400
  Westbury *(G-16372)*
Shipman Printing Inds Inc .... E 716 504-7700
  Niagara Falls *(G-12336)*
Spectrum Prtg Lithography Inc .... E 212 255-3131
  New York *(G-11665)*
Thomas Group Inc .... F 212 947-6400
  New York *(G-11817)*
Tobay Printing Co Inc .... E 631 842-3300
  Copiague *(G-3788)*
Tom & Jerry Printcraft Forms .... E 914 777-7468
  Mamaroneck *(G-7758)*
Tri-Lon Clor Lithographers Ltd .... E 212 255-6140
  New York *(G-11893)*
Vicks Lithograph & Prtg Corp .... C 315 272-2401
  Yorkville *(G-16832)*
Vin-Clair Inc .... G 845 429-4998
  West Haverstraw *(G-16210)*
Webster Printing Corporation .... F 585 671-1533
  Webster *(G-16107)*
Westchester Mailing Service .... E 914 948-1116
  White Plains *(G-16519)*
William Charles Prtg Co Inc .... E 516 349-0900
  Plainview *(G-13102)*
Wilson Press LLC .... E 315 568-9693
  Seneca Falls *(G-14788)*
Won & Lee Inc .... E 516 222-0712
  Garden City *(G-5284)*
Wynco Press One Inc .... G 516 354-6145
  Glen Oaks *(G-5388)*
X Myles Mar Inc .... E 212 683-2015
  New York *(G-12148)*
Zenger Partners LLC .... F 716 876-2284
  Kenmore *(G-6865)*

BINDING SVC: Magazines

Copy Room Inc .... F 212 371-8600
  New York *(G-9397)*

BINDING SVC: Pamphlets

Mid-Island Bindery Inc .... E 631 293-0180
  Farmingdale *(G-4825)*

BINDING SVC: Trade

Dime Trading Inc .... G 718 797-0303
  Brooklyn *(G-1779)*
Gold Pride Press Inc .... E 585 224-8800
  Rochester *(G-13843)*
Piroke Trade Inc .... G 646 515-1537
  Brooklyn *(G-2321)*
Quality Bindery Service Inc .... E 716 883-5185
  Buffalo *(G-3025)*
Whitford Development Inc .... F 631 471-7711
  Port Jefferson *(G-13224)*

BINS: Prefabricated, Sheet Metal

Golden Group International Ltd .... G 845 440-1025
  Patterson *(G-12882)*
H & M Leasing Corp .... G 631 225-5246
  Copiague *(G-3761)*

BIOLOGICAL PRDTS: Bacterial Vaccines

Ip Med Inc .... G 516 766-3800
  Oceanside *(G-12541)*

BIOLOGICAL PRDTS: Blood Derivatives

Instrumentation Laboratory Co ....C....... 845 680-0028
  Orangeburg *(G-12681)*

BIOLOGICAL PRDTS: Exc Diagnostic

Acorda Therapeutics Inc ....C....... 914 347-4300
  Ardsley *(G-392)*
Advance Biofactures Corp ....E....... 516 593-7000
  Lynbrook *(G-7658)*
AG Biotech Inc ....G....... 585 346-0020
  Livonia *(G-7277)*
Albany Molecular Research Inc...........G....... 518 512-2234
  Albany *(G-34)*
Albany Molecular Research Inc...........B....... 518 512-2000
  Albany *(G-35)*
Cypress Bioscience Inc ....F....... 858 452-2323
  New York *(G-9444)*
Ecological Laboratories Inc ....D....... 516 823-3441
  Island Park *(G-6513)*
Kadmon Holdings Inc ....D....... 212 308-6000
  New York *(G-10394)*
Meiragtx Holdings PLC ....E....... 646 490-2965
  New York *(G-10765)*
Nanoprobes Inc ....F....... 631 205-9490
  Yaphank *(G-16718)*
Omrix Biopharmaceuticals Inc ....C....... 908 218-0707
  New York *(G-11039)*
Rentschler Biotechnologie GMBH ....G....... 631 656-7137
  Hauppauge *(G-5928)*
Roar Biomedical Inc ....G....... 631 591-2749
  Calverton *(G-3170)*
Synergy Pharmaceuticals Inc ....G....... 212 227-8611
  New York *(G-11763)*
Vyera Pharmaceuticals LLC ....E....... 646 356-5577
  New York *(G-12059)*
Wyeth Holdings LLC ....D....... 845 602-5000
  Pearl River *(G-12913)*
Wyeth LLC ....A....... 973 660-5000
  New York *(G-12146)*
Zeptometrix Corporation ....D....... 716 882-0920
  Buffalo *(G-3138)*

BIOLOGICAL PRDTS: Extracts

Akshar Extracts Inc ....G....... 631 588-9727
  Ronkonkoma *(G-14297)*

BIOLOGICAL PRDTS: Vaccines

AV Therapeutics Inc ....E....... 917 497-5523
  New York *(G-8969)*
International Aids Vaccine Ini ....D....... 646 381-8066
  Brooklyn *(G-2009)*
International Aids Vccne Inttv ....D....... 212 847-1111
  New York *(G-10242)*

BIOLOGICAL PRDTS: Vaccines & Immunizing

Siga Technologies Inc ....E....... 212 672-9100
  New York *(G-11582)*

BIOLOGICAL PRDTS: Veterinary

Bioivt LLC ....D....... 516 483-1196
  Westbury *(G-16319)*

BLADES: Knife

Ontario Knife Company ....D....... 716 676-5527
  Franklinville *(G-5124)*

BLADES: Saw, Chain Type

Quality Saw & Knife Inc ....F....... 631 491-4747
  West Babylon *(G-16184)*

BLADES: Saw, Hand Or Power

Niabraze LLC ....F....... 716 447-1082
  Tonawanda *(G-15562)*

BLANKBOOKS

Dalee Bookbinding Co Inc ....F....... 914 965-1660
  Croton On Hudson *(G-3913)*

BLANKBOOKS & LOOSELEAF BINDERS

Classic Album ....E....... 718 388-2818
  Brooklyn *(G-1699)*

Colad Group LLC ....D....... 716 961-1776
  Buffalo *(G-2772)*
Folder Factory Inc ....F....... 540 477-3852
  Amityville *(G-275)*
Foster - Gordon Manufacturing ....G....... 631 589-6776
  Bohemia *(G-1024)*
GPM Associates LLC ....E....... 585 335-3940
  Dansville *(G-3926)*
Leather Indexes Corp ....D....... 516 827-1900
  Hicksville *(G-6103)*
Roger Michael Press Inc ....D....... 732 752-0800
  Brooklyn *(G-2411)*

BLANKBOOKS: Albums

Albumx Corp ....D....... 914 939-6878
  Port Chester *(G-13192)*
Classic Album LLC ....D....... 718 388-2818
  Brooklyn *(G-1700)*
Dorose Novelty Co Inc ....F....... 718 451-3088
  East Elmhurst *(G-4220)*
King Album Inc ....E....... 631 253-9500
  West Babylon *(G-16168)*
Lanwood Industries Inc ....E....... 718 786-3000
  Bay Shore *(G-694)*
Leather Craftsmen Inc ....D....... 631 752-9000
  Farmingdale *(G-4808)*
Mypublisher Inc ....E....... 914 773-4312
  Elmsford *(G-4553)*

BLANKBOOKS: Albums, Record

Brookvale Records Inc ....F....... 631 587-7722
  West Babylon *(G-16140)*
Motema Music LLC ....G....... 212 860-6969
  New York *(G-10847)*
Renegade Nation Ltd ....F....... 212 868-9000
  New York *(G-11362)*
Simon & Simon LLC ....G....... 202 419-0490
  New York *(G-11596)*
Tm Music Inc ....F....... 212 471-4000
  New York *(G-11853)*
Tommy Boy Entertainment LLC ....F....... 212 388-8300
  New York *(G-11863)*
Wmg Acquisition Corp ....F....... 212 275-2000
  New York *(G-12126)*

BLANKBOOKS: Memorandum, Printed

General Diaries Corporation ....F....... 516 371-2244
  Inwood *(G-6491)*
Quotable Cards Inc ....G....... 212 420-7552
  New York *(G-11305)*

BLANKETS & BLANKETING, COTTON

In2green LLC ....G....... 914 693-5054
  Hastings On Hudson *(G-5749)*
Northwest Company LLC ....C....... 516 484-6996
  Roslyn *(G-14449)*

BLASTING SVC: Sand, Metal Parts

Carpenter Industries Inc ....F....... 315 463-4284
  Syracuse *(G-15271)*
Tropical Driftwood Originals ....G....... 516 623-0980
  Roosevelt *(G-14438)*

BLINDS & SHADES: Vertical

Blindtek Designer Systems Inc ....F....... 914 347-7100
  Elmsford *(G-4533)*
J Gimbel Inc ....E....... 718 296-5200
  West Hempstead *(G-16218)*
KPP Ltd ....F....... 516 338-5201
  Jericho *(G-6793)*
Vertical Research Partners LLC ....F....... 212 257-6499
  New York *(G-12018)*

BLINDS : Window

Blinds To Go (us) Inc ....E....... 718 477-9523
  Staten Island *(G-15051)*
Comfortex Corporation ....E....... 518 273-3333
  Watervliet *(G-16044)*
D & D Window Tech Inc ....G....... 212 308-2822
  New York *(G-9446)*
Drapery Industries Inc ....F....... 585 232-2992
  Rochester *(G-13750)*
Fabric Quilters Unlimited Inc ....E....... 516 333-2866
  Westbury *(G-16330)*
Hunter Douglas Inc ....D....... 845 664-7000
  Pearl River *(G-12901)*

Hunter Douglas Inc ....C....... 212 588-0564
  New York *(G-10152)*
Instant Verticals Inc ....F....... 631 501-0001
  Farmingdale *(G-4786)*
Levolor Inc ....B....... 845 664-7000
  Pearl River *(G-12905)*
Nu Ways Inc ....G....... 585 254-7510
  Rochester *(G-13983)*
Tentina Window Fashions Inc ....C....... 631 957-9585
  Lindenhurst *(G-7201)*
TLC Vision (usa) Corporation ....G....... 914 395-3949
  Hartsdale *(G-5746)*

BLOCK & BRICK: Sand Lime

Everblock Systems LLC ....G....... 844 422-5625
  New York *(G-9734)*

BLOCKS & BRICKS: Concrete

All American Concrete Corp ....G....... 718 497-3301
  Brooklyn *(G-1506)*
Chenango Concrete Corp ....F....... 607 334-2545
  Norwich *(G-12478)*
Dicks Concrete Co Inc ....E....... 845 374-5966
  New Hampton *(G-8499)*
Edgewood Industries Inc ....D....... 516 227-2447
  Garden City *(G-5257)*
Fort Miller Service Corp ....F....... 518 695-5000
  Greenwich *(G-5640)*
Grace Associates Inc ....G....... 718 767-9000
  Harrison *(G-5729)*
Hanson Aggregates New York LLC .....G....... 607 276-5881
  Almond *(G-193)*
Jenna Concrete Corporation ....E....... 718 842-5250
  Bronx *(G-1302)*
Jenna Harlem River Inc ....G....... 718 842-5997
  Bronx *(G-1303)*
Modern Block LLC ....G....... 315 923-7443
  Clyde *(G-3596)*
Superior Block Corp ....F....... 718 421-0900
  Brooklyn *(G-2536)*
Unilock New York Inc ....G....... 845 278-6700
  Brewster *(G-1175)*

BLOCKS: Chimney Or Fireplace, Concrete

Ace Cntracting Consulting Corp ....G....... 631 567-4752
  Bohemia *(G-971)*
Chimney Doctors Americas Corp ....G....... 631 868-3586
  Bayport *(G-737)*
Great American Awning & Patio ....F....... 518 899-2300
  Ballston Spa *(G-584)*

BLOCKS: Landscape Or Retaining Wall, Concrete

Creative Yard Designs Inc ....G....... 315 706-6143
  Manlius *(G-7776)*
Everblock Systems LLC ....G....... 844 422-5625
  New York *(G-9734)*
Northeast Mesa LLC ....G....... 845 878-9344
  Carmel *(G-3278)*
Troys Landscape Supply Co Inc ....F....... 518 785-1526
  Cohoes *(G-3622)*

BLOCKS: Paving, Asphalt, Not From Refineries

Kings Park Asphalt Corporation ....G....... 631 269-9774
  Hauppauge *(G-5856)*

BLOCKS: Paving, Concrete

Nicolia Concrete Products Inc ....D....... 631 669-0700
  Lindenhurst *(G-7185)*
Unilock Ltd ....E....... 716 822-6074
  Buffalo *(G-3111)*

BLOCKS: Paving, Cut Stone

Unilock New York Inc ....G....... 845 278-6700
  Brewster *(G-1175)*

BLOCKS: Radiation-Proof, Concrete

Radiation Shielding Systems ....F....... 888 631-2278
  Suffern *(G-15196)*

BLOCKS: Standard, Concrete Or Cinder

Barrasso & Sons Trucking Inc ....E....... 631 581-0360
  Islip Terrace *(G-6552)*

PRODUCT SECTION   BOLTS: Metal

Colonie Block and Supply Co ....G 518 869-8411
  Colonie *(G-3677)*
Cranesville Block Co Inc ....E 518 684-6154
  Amsterdam *(G-333)*
Cranesville Block Co Inc ....E 315 773-2296
  Felts Mills *(G-4930)*
Crest Haven Precast Inc ....G 518 483-4750
  Burke *(G-3142)*
Duke Concrete Products Inc ....E 518 793-7743
  Queensbury *(G-13422)*
Felicetti Concrete Products ....G 716 284-5740
  Niagara Falls *(G-12283)*
Gone South Concrete Block Inc ....E 315 598-2141
  Fulton *(G-5218)*
Grandview Block & Supply Co ....E 518 346-7981
  Schenectady *(G-14683)*
Imperia Masonry Supply Corp ....E 914 738-0900
  Pelham *(G-12936)*
Lafarge North America Inc ....E 518 756-5000
  Ravena *(G-13454)*
Montfort Brothers Inc ....E 845 896-6694
  Fishkill *(G-4949)*
Morningstar Concrete Products ....F 716 693-4020
  Tonawanda *(G-15560)*
New York Ready Mix Inc ....G 516 338-6969
  Westbury *(G-16359)*
Oldcastle Apg Northeast Inc ....E 585 924-2103
  Fishers *(G-4941)*
Palumbo Block Co Inc ....E 845 832-6100
  Dover Plains *(G-4145)*
Phelps Cement Products Inc ....E 315 548-9415
  Phelps *(G-12979)*
Riefler Concrete Products LLC ....C 716 649-3260
  Hamburg *(G-5693)*
Smithtown Concrete Products ....F 631 265-1815
  Saint James *(G-14515)*
Suffolk Cement Products Inc ....E 631 727-2317
  Calverton *(G-3173)*
Taylor Concrete Products Inc ....E 315 788-2191
  Watertown *(G-16034)*

BLOWERS & FANS

Air Crafters Inc ....C 631 471-7788
  Ronkonkoma *(G-14295)*
American Filtration Tech Inc ....F 585 359-4130
  West Henrietta *(G-16228)*
Applied Safety LLC ....G 718 608-6292
  Long Island City *(G-7383)*
Buffalo Filter LLC ....D 716 835-7000
  Lancaster *(G-7011)*
Camfil Usa Inc ....F 315 468-3849
  Syracuse *(G-15269)*
Daikin Applied Americas Inc ....D 315 253-2771
  Auburn *(G-475)*
Delphi Powertrain Systems LLC ....B 585 359-6000
  West Henrietta *(G-16237)*
Ducon Technologies Inc ....F 631 694-1700
  New York *(G-9584)*
Ducon Technologies Inc ....E 631 420-4900
  Farmingdale *(G-4753)*
Dundas-Jafine Inc ....E 716 681-9690
  Alden *(G-170)*
Filtros Ltd ....E 585 586-8770
  East Rochester *(G-4285)*
Healthway Products Company ....E 315 207-1410
  Oswego *(G-12778)*
North American Filter Corp ....D 800 265-8943
  Newark *(G-12203)*
Parker-Hannifin Corporation ....D 716 685-4040
  Lancaster *(G-7037)*
Standard Motor Products Inc ....B 718 392-0200
  Long Island City *(G-7598)*
Vent-A-Kiln Corporation ....G 716 876-2023
  Buffalo *(G-3116)*

BLOWERS & FANS

Moffitt Fan Corporation ....E 585 768-7010
  Le Roy *(G-7123)*
Rotron Incorporated ....B 845 679-2401
  Woodstock *(G-16687)*
Rotron Incorporated ....E 845 679-2401
  Woodstock *(G-16688)*

BLUEPRINTING SVCS

A Esteban & Company Inc ....E 212 989-7000
  New York *(G-8691)*
Foleys Graphic Center Inc ....E 914 245-3625
  Yorktown Heights *(G-16816)*

BOAT BUILDING & REPAIR

American Metalcraft Marine ....G 315 686-9891
  Clayton *(G-3552)*
Cayuga Wooden Boatworks Inc ....E 315 253-7447
  Ithaca *(G-6570)*
Coecles Hbr Marina & Boat Yard ....F 631 749-0856
  Shelter Island *(G-14800)*
Eastern Welding Inc ....G 631 727-0306
  Riverhead *(G-13568)*
Global Marine Power Inc ....E 631 208-2933
  Calverton *(G-3166)*
Hacker Boat Company Inc ....E 518 543-6731
  Silver Bay *(G-14859)*
Hampton Shipyards Inc ....E 631 653-6777
  East Quogue *(G-4278)*
Jag Manufacturing Inc ....E 518 762-9558
  Johnstown *(G-6832)*
Katherine Blizniak ....G 716 674-8545
  West Seneca *(G-16300)*
May Ship Repair Contg Corp ....E 718 442-9700
  Staten Island *(G-15104)*
Metalcraft Marine Us Inc ....F 315 501-4015
  Cape Vincent *(G-3259)*
Mokai Manufacturing Inc ....G 845 566-8287
  Newburgh *(G-12233)*
Scarano Boat Building Inc ....E 518 463-3401
  Albany *(G-126)*
Scarano Boatbuilding Inc ....E 518 463-3401
  Albany *(G-127)*
Wooden Boatworks ....G 631 477-6507
  Greenport *(G-5627)*

BOAT BUILDING & REPAIRING: Fiberglass

Fantasy Glass Compan ....G 845 786-5818
  Stony Point *(G-15171)*
Gar Wood Custom Boats ....G 518 494-2966
  Brant Lake *(G-1124)*
Superboats Inc ....G 631 226-1761
  Lindenhurst *(G-7198)*
Tumblehome Boatshop ....G 518 623-5050
  Warrensburg *(G-15943)*

BOAT BUILDING & REPAIRING: Kayaks

Ashco Management Inc ....F 212 960-8428
  Brooklyn *(G-1562)*

BOAT BUILDING & REPAIRING: Motorized

Marathon Boat Group Inc ....F 607 849-3211
  Marathon *(G-7791)*

BOAT BUILDING & REPAIRING: Non-Motorized

Rocking The Boat Inc ....F 718 466-5799
  Bronx *(G-1374)*

BOAT BUILDING & RPRG: Fishing, Small, Lobster, Crab, Oyster

AVS Laminates Inc ....E 631 286-2136
  Bellport *(G-799)*
Robert E Derecktor Inc ....D 914 698-0962
  Mamaroneck *(G-7756)*

BOAT DEALERS

Global Marine Power Inc ....E 631 208-2933
  Calverton *(G-3166)*
Marathon Boat Group Inc ....F 607 849-3211
  Marathon *(G-7791)*
Marina Holding Corp ....F 718 646-9283
  Brooklyn *(G-2167)*
Superboats Inc ....G 631 226-1761
  Lindenhurst *(G-7198)*

BOAT DEALERS: Canoe & Kayak

Johnson Outdoors Inc ....C 607 779-2200
  Binghamton *(G-899)*

BOAT LIFTS

Kleinfelder John ....G 716 753-3163
  Mayville *(G-7921)*

BOAT REPAIR SVCS

Cayuga Wooden Boatworks Inc ....E 315 253-7447
  Ithaca *(G-6570)*

Robert E Derecktor Inc ....D 914 698-0962
  Mamaroneck *(G-7756)*
Superboats Inc ....G 631 226-1761
  Lindenhurst *(G-7198)*

BOAT YARD: Boat yards, storage & incidental repair

Robert E Derecktor Inc ....D 914 698-0962
  Mamaroneck *(G-7756)*

BOATS & OTHER MARINE EQPT: Plastic

Global Marine Power Inc ....E 631 208-2933
  Calverton *(G-3166)*

BODIES: Truck & Bus

Able Weldbuilt Industries Inc ....F 631 643-9700
  Deer Park *(G-3931)*
Bay Horse Innovations Nyinc ....G 607 898-3337
  Groton *(G-5649)*
Blackburn Truck Bodies LLC ....E 315 448-3236
  Syracuse *(G-15259)*
Conti Auto Body Corp ....G 516 921-6435
  Syosset *(G-15211)*
Daimler Buses North Amer Inc ....A 315 768-8101
  Oriskany *(G-12756)*
Donver Incorporated ....F 716 945-1910
  Kill Buck *(G-6878)*
Premium Bldg Components Inc ....E 518 885-0194
  Ballston Spa *(G-594)*

BODY PARTS: Automobile, Stamped Metal

Albert Kemperle Inc ....E 718 629-1084
  Brooklyn *(G-1499)*
Automotive LLC ....F 248 728-8642
  Batavia *(G-611)*
Kustom Korner ....E 716 646-0173
  Hamburg *(G-5686)*
M & W Aluminum Products Inc ....F 315 414-0005
  Syracuse *(G-15366)*
Qpbc Inc ....E 718 685-1900
  Long Island City *(G-7564)*
Racing Industries Inc ....E 631 905-0100
  Calverton *(G-3169)*
Utica Metal Products Inc ....D 315 732-6163
  Utica *(G-15738)*

BOILER REPAIR SHOP

A L Eastmond & Sons Inc ....D 718 378-3000
  Bronx *(G-1201)*
Empire Industrial Systems Corp ....F 631 242-4619
  Bay Shore *(G-685)*
Flushing Boiler & Welding Co ....G 718 463-1266
  Brooklyn *(G-1893)*
Troy Boiler Works Inc ....E 518 274-2650
  Troy *(G-15630)*

BOILERS & BOILER SHOP WORK

Marine Boiler & Welding Inc ....F 718 378-1900
  Bronx *(G-1322)*
Supreme Boilers Inc ....G 718 342-2220
  Brooklyn *(G-2540)*

BOILERS: Low-Pressure Heating, Steam Or Hot Water

Best Boilers Inc ....F 718 372-4210
  Brooklyn *(G-1602)*
ECR International Inc ....D 315 797-1310
  Utica *(G-15699)*
ECR International Inc ....C 716 366-5500
  Dunkirk *(G-4169)*
Great Rock Automation Inc ....F 631 270-1508
  Farmingdale *(G-4774)*
Rockmills Steel Products Corp ....F 718 366-8300
  Maspeth *(G-7871)*
Unilux Advanced Mfg LLC ....E 518 344-7490
  Schenectady *(G-14724)*

BOLTS: Metal

Baco Enterprises Inc ....D 718 589-6225
  Bronx *(G-1224)*
Jem Threading Specialties Inc ....G 718 665-3341
  Bronx *(G-1301)*
Marksmen Manufacturing Corp ....E 800 305-6942
  Deer Park *(G-4006)*

BOLTS: Metal

PRODUCT SECTION

Park-Ohio Inds Trsry Co Inc ....F 212 966-3310
  Albany *(G-110)*
Simon Defense Inc ....G 516 217-6000
  Ronkonkoma *(G-14413)*

BONDERIZING: Bonderizing, Metal Or Metal Prdts

Clad Metal Specialties Inc ....F 631 666-7750
  Bay Shore *(G-671)*

BOOK STORES

Barrons Educational Series Inc ....C 631 434-3311
  Hauppauge *(G-5778)*
Penguin Random House LLC ....A 212 572-6162
  New York *(G-11147)*
Penguin Random House LLC ....G 212 366-2377
  Albany *(G-113)*
Rizzoli Intl Publications Inc ....E 212 387-3400
  New York *(G-11398)*
Romantic Times Inc ....F 718 237-1097
  Brooklyn *(G-2412)*
Royal Fireworks Printing Co ....F 845 726-3333
  Unionville *(G-15673)*
Samuel French Inc ....E 212 206-8990
  New York *(G-11477)*
Second Chance Press Inc ....G 631 725-1101
  Sag Harbor *(G-14503)*
Sharedbook Inc ....E 646 442-8840
  New York *(G-11559)*
Society For The Study ....G 212 822-8806
  New York *(G-11634)*
Soho Press Inc ....G 212 260-1900
  New York *(G-11637)*
Thornwillow Press Ltd ....G 212 980-0738
  New York *(G-11826)*
William S Hein & Co Inc ....C 716 882-2600
  Getzville *(G-5356)*

BOOK STORES: College

Patrick Kraft ....G 315 343-9376
  Oswego *(G-12786)*

BOOKS, WHOLESALE

Anthroposophic Press Inc ....G 518 851-2054
  Clifton Park *(G-3563)*
Columbia University Press ....E 212 459-0600
  New York *(G-9360)*
Kensington Publishing Corp ....D 212 407-1500
  New York *(G-10434)*
Kodansha USA Inc ....G 917 322-6200
  New York *(G-10464)*
Living Well Innovations Inc ....G 646 517-3200
  Hauppauge *(G-5866)*
Macmillan Publishers Inc ....A 646 307-5151
  New York *(G-10651)*
Macmillan Publishing Group LLC ....B 212 674-5145
  New York *(G-10652)*
Moznaim Publishing Co Inc ....G 718 853-0525
  Brooklyn *(G-2229)*
North Country Books Inc ....G 315 735-4877
  Utica *(G-15726)*
North-South Books Inc ....E 212 706-4545
  New York *(G-10995)*
Rizzoli Intl Publications Inc ....E 212 387-3400
  New York *(G-11398)*
S P Books Inc ....G 212 431-5011
  New York *(G-11458)*
Samuel French Inc ....E 212 206-8990
  New York *(G-11477)*
Scholium International Inc ....G 516 883-8032
  Port Washington *(G-13305)*
Swift Fulfillment Services ....G 516 593-1198
  Lynbrook *(G-7675)*
Te Neues Publishing Company ....F 212 627-9090
  New York *(G-11790)*
W W Norton & Company Inc ....G 212 354-5500
  New York *(G-12061)*

BOOTHS: Spray, Sheet Metal, Prefabricated

Auto Body Services LLC ....F 631 431-4640
  Lindenhurst *(G-7162)*

BOOTS: Women's

Jag Footwear ACC & Ret Corp ....A 800 999-1877
  New York *(G-10299)*
Lsil & Co Inc ....G 914 761-0998
  White Plains *(G-16473)*

S & W Ladies Wear ....G 718 431-2800
  Brooklyn *(G-2437)*
Steven Madden Ltd ....D 212 695-5545
  New York *(G-11709)*

BORING MILL

Graywood Companies Inc ....E 585 254-7000
  Rochester *(G-13845)*
RTD Manufacturing Inc ....G 315 337-3151
  Rome *(G-14273)*

BOTTLE CAPS & RESEALERS: Plastic

Berry Global Inc ....C 315 986-2161
  Macedon *(G-7696)*
Berry Global Inc ....C 315 484-0397
  Solvay *(G-14916)*

BOTTLED WATER DELIVERY

Mayer Bros Apple Products Inc ....D 716 668-1787
  West Seneca *(G-16301)*

BOTTLES: Plastic

Alphamed Bottles Inc ....E 631 524-5577
  Central Islip *(G-3355)*
Alpla Inc ....G 607 250-8101
  Cortland *(G-3859)*
Capitol Plastic Products Inc ....C 518 627-0051
  Amsterdam *(G-331)*
Chapin International Inc ....C 585 343-3140
  Batavia *(G-617)*
Chapin Manufacturing Inc ....C 585 343-3140
  Batavia *(G-618)*
Cortland Plastics Intl LLC ....E 607 662-0120
  Cortland *(G-3869)*
David Johnson ....F 315 493-4735
  Carthage *(G-3290)*
Intrapac International Corp ....C 518 561-2030
  Plattsburgh *(G-13126)*
Kybod Group LLC ....G 408 306-1657
  New York *(G-10489)*
Monroe Cnty Chapter Nysarc Inc ....G 585 698-1320
  Rochester *(G-13952)*
Nalge Nunc International Corp ....A 585 498-2661
  Rochester *(G-13962)*
Pvc Container Corporation ....C 518 672-7721
  Philmont *(G-12987)*
Samco Scientific LLC ....C 800 522-3359
  Rochester *(G-14109)*
Schless Bottles Inc ....F 718 236-2790
  Brooklyn *(G-2450)*

BOTTLES: Vacuum

Cant Live Without It LLC ....D 844 517-9355
  New York *(G-9197)*

BOUTIQUE STORES

Elab Smokers Boutique ....G 585 865-4513
  Rochester *(G-13775)*

BOWLING EQPT & SPLYS

Joe Moro ....G 607 272-0591
  Ithaca *(G-6589)*
Mac Swed Inc ....F 212 684-7730
  New York *(G-10646)*

BOX & CARTON MANUFACTURING EQPT

Standard Paper Box Machine Co ....E 718 328-3300
  Bronx *(G-1392)*

BOXES & CRATES: Rectangular, Wood

J & M Packaging Inc ....F 631 608-3069
  Hauppauge *(G-5852)*
Northeast Pallet & Cont Co Inc ....F 518 271-0535
  Troy *(G-15613)*
R D A Container Corporation ....E 585 247-2323
  Gates *(G-5312)*

BOXES & SHOOK: Nailed Wood

Great Lakes Specialites ....E 716 672-4622
  Fredonia *(G-5127)*
McGraw Wood Products LLC ....E 607 836-6465
  Mc Graw *(G-7928)*
McIntosh Box & Pallet Co Inc ....D 315 675-8511
  Bernhards Bay *(G-833)*

McIntosh Box & Pallet Co Inc ....E 315 446-9350
  Rome *(G-14257)*
Philpac Corporation ....E 716 875-8005
  Buffalo *(G-3002)*
Reuter Pallet Pkg Sys Inc ....G 845 457-9937
  Montgomery *(G-8317)*

BOXES: Corrugated

Action Paper Co Inc ....G 718 665-1652
  Bronx *(G-1211)*
Arma Container Corp ....E 631 254-1200
  Deer Park *(G-3945)*
Bellotti Packaging Inc ....F 315 433-0131
  Liverpool *(G-7223)*
Bestwall LLC ....C 518 346-6151
  Schenectady *(G-14655)*
Buckeye Corrugated Inc ....D 585 924-1600
  Victor *(G-15834)*
Cattaraugus Containers Inc ....E 716 676-2000
  Franklinville *(G-5123)*
Fennell Industries LLC ....E 607 733-6693
  Elmira *(G-4487)*
General Fibre Products Corp ....D 516 358-7500
  New Hyde Park *(G-8536)*
International Paper Company ....C 585 663-1000
  Rochester *(G-13884)*
International Paper Company ....C 607 775-1550
  Conklin *(G-3728)*
International Paper Company ....D 518 372-6461
  Glenville *(G-5446)*
J & M Packaging Inc ....F 631 608-3069
  Hauppauge *(G-5852)*
Jamestown Cont of Rochester ....D 585 254-9190
  Rochester *(G-13892)*
Jamestown Container Corp ....D 716 665-4623
  Falconer *(G-4684)*
Kapstone Container Corporation ....D 518 842-2450
  Amsterdam *(G-342)*
Lakeside Container Corp ....F 518 561-6150
  Plattsburgh *(G-13130)*
Mkt329 Inc ....E 631 249-5500
  Farmingdale *(G-4829)*
Niagara Sheets LLC ....D 716 692-1129
  North Tonawanda *(G-12439)*
Norampac New York City Inc ....C 718 340-2100
  Maspeth *(G-7863)*
Packaging Corporation America ....C 315 457-6780
  Liverpool *(G-7251)*
Pactiv LLC ....G 315 457-6780
  Liverpool *(G-7252)*
Philpac Corporation ....E 716 875-8005
  Buffalo *(G-3002)*
President Cont Group II LLC ....G 845 516-1600
  Middletown *(G-8171)*
Prestige Box Corporation ....E 516 773-3115
  Great Neck *(G-5583)*
Professional Packg Svcs Inc ....E 518 677-5100
  Eagle Bridge *(G-4185)*
R D A Container Corporation ....E 585 247-2323
  Gates *(G-5312)*
Seneca FLS Spc & Logistics Co ....D 315 568-4139
  Seneca Falls *(G-14786)*
Syracuse Corrugated Box Corp ....F 315 437-9901
  East Syracuse *(G-4372)*
Technical Packaging Inc ....F 516 223-2300
  Baldwin *(G-545)*
Tin Inc ....D 607 775-1550
  Conklin *(G-3734)*
Westrock - Southern Cont LLC ....C 315 487-6111
  Camillus *(G-3200)*
Westrock Cp LLC ....C 770 448-2193
  New Hartford *(G-8513)*
Westrock Cp LLC ....C 716 692-6510
  North Tonawanda *(G-12462)*
Westrock CP LLC ....C 716 694-1000
  North Tonawanda *(G-12463)*
Westrock Rkt LLC ....C 631 586-6000
  Deer Park *(G-4062)*

BOXES: Filing, Paperboard Made From Purchased Materials

Paul T Freund Corporation ....D 315 597-4873
  Palmyra *(G-12859)*

BOXES: Mail Or Post Office, Collection/Storage, Sheet Metal

Maloya Laser Inc ....E 631 543-2327
  Commack *(G-3697)*

PRODUCT SECTION
BROADCASTING & COMMUNICATIONS EQPT: Studio Eqpt, Radio & TV

BOXES: Packing & Shipping, Metal

Alpine Paper Box Co Inc ....E 718 345-4040
  Brooklyn *(G-1514)*

BOXES: Paperboard, Folding

Abbot & Abbot Box Corp ....F 888 930-5972
  Long Island City *(G-7365)*
Alpha Packaging Industries Inc ....E 718 267-4115
  Long Island City *(G-7374)*
Arkay Packaging Corporation ....E 631 273-2000
  Hauppauge *(G-5769)*
Burt Rigid Box Inc ....D 607 433-2510
  Oneonta *(G-12628)*
Cattaraugus Containers Inc ....E 716 676-2000
  Franklinville *(G-5123)*
Climax Packaging Inc ....C 315 376-8000
  Lowville *(G-7649)*
Color Carton Corp ....D 718 665-0840
  Bronx *(G-1243)*
Designers Folding Box Corp ....E 716 853-5141
  Buffalo *(G-2800)*
Disc Graphics Inc ....C 631 300-1129
  Hauppauge *(G-5811)*
Disc Graphics Inc ....C 631 234-1400
  Hauppauge *(G-5812)*
F M Howell & Company ....D 607 734-6291
  Elmira *(G-4486)*
Flower City Printing Inc ....C 585 663-9000
  Rochester *(G-13808)*
Gavin Mfg Corp ....E 631 467-0040
  Farmingdale *(G-4770)*
Gaylord Bros Inc ....E 315 457-5070
  North Syracuse *(G-12402)*
HSM Packaging Corporation ....D 315 476-7996
  Liverpool *(G-7235)*
Knoll Printing & Packaging Inc ....E 516 621-0100
  Syosset *(G-15220)*
M C Packaging Corporation ....E 631 643-3763
  Babylon *(G-529)*
Multi Packg Solutions Intl Ltd ....F 646 885-0005
  New York *(G-10859)*
Novel Box Company Ltd ....E 718 965-2222
  Brooklyn *(G-2275)*
Paper Box Corp ....D 212 226-7490
  New York *(G-11101)*
Premier Packaging Corporation ....E 585 924-8460
  Victor *(G-15861)*
Prestige Box Corporation ....E 516 773-3115
  Great Neck *(G-5583)*
Specialized Packg Group Inc ....G 315 638-4355
  Baldwinsville *(G-561)*
Specialized Packg Radisson LLC .....C 315 638-4355
  Baldwinsville *(G-562)*
Standard Group ....E 718 335-5500
  Great Neck *(G-5591)*
Standard Group LLC ....C 718 507-6430
  Great Neck *(G-5592)*
Viking Industries Inc ....D 845 883-6325
  New Paltz *(G-8584)*
Visitainer Corp ....E 718 636-0300
  Brooklyn *(G-2629)*

BOXES: Paperboard, Set-Up

A Fleisig Paper Box Corp ....F 212 226-7490
  New York *(G-8693)*
American Package Company Inc .....E 718 389-4444
  Brooklyn *(G-1525)*
Brick & Ballerstein Inc ....D 718 497-1400
  Ridgewood *(G-13532)*
Burt Rigid Box Inc ....D 607 433-2510
  Oneonta *(G-12628)*
Cascades New York Inc ....D 718 340-2100
  Maspeth *(G-7829)*
Drescher Paper Box Inc ....E 716 854-0288
  Clarence *(G-3528)*
Earlville Paper Box Co Inc ....E 315 691-2131
  Earlville *(G-4188)*
F M Howell & Company ....D 607 734-6291
  Elmira *(G-4486)*
Fairview Paper Box Corp ....E 585 786-5230
  Warsaw *(G-15944)*
Jordon Box Company Inc ....E 315 422-3419
  Syracuse *(G-15350)*
Lionel Habas Associates Inc ....F 212 860-8454
  New York *(G-10575)*
Parlor City Paper Box Co Inc ....D 607 772-0600
  Binghamton *(G-909)*
Prestige Box Corporation ....E 516 773-3115
  Great Neck *(G-5583)*

Propak Inc ....G 518 677-5100
  Eagle Bridge *(G-4186)*
Pure Trade Us Inc ....E 212 256-1600
  New York *(G-11276)*
Seneca FLS Spc & Logistics Co .....D 315 568-4139
  Seneca Falls *(G-14786)*

BOXES: Plastic

American Package Company Inc .....E 718 389-4444
  Brooklyn *(G-1525)*
Hornet Group Inc ....D 845 858-6400
  Port Jervis *(G-13230)*
Novel Box Company Ltd ....E 718 965-2222
  Brooklyn *(G-2275)*
Philcom Ltd ....E 716 875-8005
  Buffalo *(G-3001)*
Printex Packaging Corporation ....D 631 234-4300
  Islandia *(G-6537)*
R P M Industries Inc ....E 315 255-1105
  Auburn *(G-497)*
Rui Xing International Trdg Co ....G 516 298-2667
  Hicksville *(G-6129)*

BOXES: Solid Fiber

Burt Rigid Box Inc ....D 607 433-2510
  Oneonta *(G-12628)*
Specialized Packg Radisson LLC ...C 315 638-4355
  Baldwinsville *(G-562)*

BOXES: Stamped Metal

Novel Box Company Ltd ....E 718 965-2222
  Brooklyn *(G-2275)*

BOXES: Switch, Electric

Cables and Chips Inc ....E 212 619-3132
  New York *(G-9173)*

BOXES: Wooden

Abbot & Abbot Box Corp ....F 888 930-5972
  Long Island City *(G-7365)*
M &L Industry of NY Inc ....G 845 827-6255
  Highland Mills *(G-6151)*
Quality Woodworking Corp ....F 718 875-3437
  Brooklyn *(G-2370)*

BRAKES & BRAKE PARTS

Interparts International Inc ....E 516 576-2000
  Plainview *(G-13065)*
Rpb Distributors LLC ....G 914 244-3600
  Mount Kisco *(G-8358)*

BRAKES: Electromagnetic

Magtrol Inc ....E 716 668-5555
  Buffalo *(G-2935)*

BRASS FOUNDRY, NEC

Eastern Finding Corp ....F 516 747-6640
  New Hyde Park *(G-8530)*

BRAZING SVCS

Kittredge & Sons Inc ....G 978 567-0998
  Niagara Falls *(G-12303)*
Parfuse Corp ....E 516 997-8888
  Westbury *(G-16363)*
W R P Welding Ltd ....G 631 249-8859
  Farmingdale *(G-4904)*
Welding and Brazing Svcs Inc ....G 607 397-1009
  Richfield Springs *(G-13493)*

BRAZING: Metal

Hi-Temp Brazing Inc ....E 631 491-4917
  Deer Park *(G-3983)*
Milgo Industrial Inc ....D 718 388-6476
  Brooklyn *(G-2206)*
Milgo Industrial Inc ....G 718 387-0406
  Brooklyn *(G-2207)*

BRIC-A-BRAC

Five Star Creations Inc ....E 845 783-1187
  Monroe *(G-8269)*

BRICK, STONE & RELATED PRDTS WHOLESALERS

Barrasso & Sons Trucking Inc ....E 631 581-0360
  Islip Terrace *(G-6552)*
Clemente Latham Concrete Corp ...D 518 374-2222
  Schenectady *(G-14663)*
East Coast Mines Ltd ....E 631 653-5445
  East Quogue *(G-4277)*
Hampton Sand Corp ....G 631 325-5533
  Westhampton *(G-16402)*
Hanson Aggregates PA LLC ....E 585 624-3800
  Honeoye Falls *(G-6266)*
Imperia Masonry Supply Corp ....E 914 738-0900
  Pelham *(G-12936)*
Peckham Materials Corp ....E 518 494-2313
  Chestertown *(G-3491)*
Phelps Cement Products Inc ....E 315 548-9415
  Phelps *(G-12979)*

BRICKS & BLOCKS: Structural

Everblock Systems LLC ....G 844 422-5625
  New York *(G-9734)*
Semco Ceramics Inc ....G 315 782-3000
  Watertown *(G-16033)*

BRICKS: Concrete

Brickit ....E 631 727-8977
  Hauppauge *(G-5784)*

BRIDAL SHOPS

Vera Wang Group LLC ....C 212 575-6400
  New York *(G-12007)*

BRIDGE COMPONENTS: Bridge sections, prefabricated, highway

Apollo Steel Corporation ....F 716 283-8758
  Niagara Falls *(G-12264)*
Port Authority of NY & NJ ....D 718 390-2534
  Staten Island *(G-15117)*

BROADCASTING & COMMS EQPT: Antennas, Transmitting/Comms

Century Metal Parts Corp ....E 631 667-0800
  Bay Shore *(G-669)*
Edo LLC ....G 631 630-4000
  Amityville *(G-272)*
Fei-Zyfer Inc ....G 714 933-4045
  Uniondale *(G-15667)*
Gti America Inc ....G 716 332-6151
  Buffalo *(G-2859)*
John Mezzalingua Assoc LLC ....A 315 431-7100
  Liverpool *(G-7240)*
Millennium Antenna Corp ....F 315 798-9374
  Utica *(G-15722)*
Sinclair Technologies Inc ....E 716 874-3682
  Hamburg *(G-5695)*
STI-Co Industries Inc ....E 716 662-2680
  Orchard Park *(G-12744)*

BROADCASTING & COMMS EQPT: Rcvr-Transmitter Unt, Transceiver

Magnet-Ndctive Systems Ltd USA ...E 585 924-4000
  Victor *(G-15856)*

BROADCASTING & COMMUNICATIONS EQPT: Cellular Radio Telephone

Advanced Comm Solutions ....G 914 693-5076
  Ardsley *(G-393)*
Bullitt Mobile LLC ....D 631 424-1749
  Bohemia *(G-990)*
Ghostek LLC ....F 855 310-3439
  Brooklyn *(G-1926)*
Nycom Business Solutions Inc ....G 516 345-6000
  Franklin Square *(G-5120)*

BROADCASTING & COMMUNICATIONS EQPT: Studio Eqpt, Radio & TV

Big Fish Entertainment LLC ....C 646 797-4955
  New York *(G-9077)*
Hopewell Precision Inc ....E 845 221-2737
  Hopewell Junction *(G-6288)*

Employee Codes: A=Over 500 employees, B=251-500
C=101-250, D=51-100, E=20-50, F=10-19, G=5-9

2019 Harris
New York Manufacturers Directory

1069

BROADCASTING & COMMUNICATIONS EQPT: Studio Eqpt, Radio & TV

Times Square Studios Ltd..............C....... 212 930-7720
 New York *(G-11847)*

BROADCASTING & COMMUNICATIONS EQPT: Transmitting, Radio/TV

Armstrong Transmitter Corp..............F....... 315 673-1269
 Marcellus *(G-7792)*

BROKERS' SVCS

Remsen Graphics Corp..............G....... 718 643-7500
 Brooklyn *(G-2397)*

BROKERS: Automotive

Monroe County Auto Svcs Inc..............E....... 585 764-3741
 Rochester *(G-13953)*

BROKERS: Business

Spanish Artisan Wine Group LLC..............G....... 914 414-6982
 Patterson *(G-12885)*

BROKERS: Food

Quinn and Co of NY Ltd..............D....... 212 868-1900
 New York *(G-11303)*

BROKERS: Loan

Mml Software Ltd..............E....... 631 941-1313
 East Setauket *(G-4305)*

BROKERS: Printing

Alabaster Group Inc..............G....... 516 867-8223
 Freeport *(G-5138)*
Melmont Fine Pringng/Graphics..............G....... 516 939-2253
 Bethpage *(G-847)*
Prestige Envelope & Lithograph..............F....... 631 521-7043
 Merrick *(G-8105)*

BRONZE FOUNDRY, NEC

American Blade Mfg LLC..............G....... 607 656-4204
 Greene *(G-5612)*
American Blade Mfg LLC..............F....... 607 432-4518
 Oneonta *(G-12624)*
Argos Inc..............E....... 845 528-0576
 Putnam Valley *(G-13401)*

BROOMS

K & R Allied Inc..............F....... 718 625-6610
 Brooklyn *(G-2061)*

BROOMS & BRUSHES

Braun Industries Inc..............F....... 516 741-6000
 Albertson *(G-146)*
Cpac Inc..............E....... 585 382-3223
 Leicester *(G-7126)*
Excel Paint Applicators Inc..............E....... 347 221-1968
 Inwood *(G-6488)*
Full Circle Home LLC..............G....... 212 432-0001
 New York *(G-9860)*
Perfex Corporation..............F....... 315 826-3600
 Poland *(G-13184)*

BROOMS & BRUSHES: Hair Pencils Or Artists' Brushes

Teka Fine Line Brushes Inc..............G....... 718 692-2928
 Brooklyn *(G-2561)*

BROOMS & BRUSHES: Household Or Indl

Abtex Corporation..............E....... 315 536-7403
 Dresden *(G-4146)*
Braun Bros Brushes Inc..............G....... 631 667-2179
 Valley Stream *(G-15775)*
Brushtech (disc) Inc..............F....... 518 563-8420
 Plattsburgh *(G-13114)*
Culicover & Shapiro Inc..............G....... 516 597-4888
 Hicksville *(G-6077)*
FM Brush Co Inc..............C....... 718 821-5939
 Glendale *(G-5399)*
Volckening Inc..............E....... 718 748-0294
 Brooklyn *(G-2633)*
Young & Swartz Inc..............F....... 716 852-2171
 Buffalo *(G-3136)*

BROOMS & BRUSHES: Paint & Varnish

Linzer Products Corp..............C....... 631 253-3333
 West Babylon *(G-16171)*

BROOMS & BRUSHES: Paint Rollers

131-11 Atlantic RE Inc..............D....... 718 441-7700
 Richmond Hill *(G-13494)*
Pan American Roller Inc..............F....... 914 762-8700
 Ossining *(G-12774)*
Premier Paint Roller Co LLC..............F....... 718 441-7700
 Richmond Hill *(G-13508)*
Royal Paint Roller Corp..............E....... 516 367-4370
 Woodbury *(G-16631)*

BROOMS & BRUSHES: Paintbrushes

E & W Manufacturing Co Inc..............E....... 516 367-8571
 Woodbury *(G-16618)*
Kirschner Brush LLC..............F....... 718 292-1809
 Bronx *(G-1309)*

BRUSHES

Walter R Tucker Entps Ltd..............E....... 607 467-2866
 Deposit *(G-4112)*

BRUSHES & BRUSH STOCK CONTACTS: Electric

Graphite Metallizing Corp..............C....... 914 968-8400
 Yonkers *(G-16764)*

BUCKLES & PARTS

Maxine Denker Inc..............G....... 212 689-1440
 Staten Island *(G-15103)*

BUILDING & OFFICE CLEANING SVCS

Rumsey Corp..............G....... 914 751-3640
 Yonkers *(G-16797)*

BUILDING & STRUCTURAL WOOD MBRS: Timbers, Struct, Lam Lumber

Empire Building Products Inc..............G....... 518 695-6094
 Schuylerville *(G-14733)*
New England Barns Inc..............E....... 631 445-1461
 Southold *(G-14970)*

BUILDING & STRUCTURAL WOOD MEMBERS

Architctral Mllwk Installation..............E....... 631 499-0755
 East Northport *(G-4260)*
Harvest Homes Inc..............E....... 518 895-2341
 Delanson *(G-4069)*
Timber Frames Inc..............G....... 585 374-6405
 Canandaigua *(G-3235)*
Ufp New York LLC..............E....... 607 563-1556
 Sidney *(G-14856)*
Unadilla Silo Company Inc..............D....... 607 369-9341
 Sidney *(G-14857)*

BUILDING & STRUCTURAL WOOD MEMBERS: Arches, Laminated Lumber

Stephenson Lumber Company Inc..............G....... 518 548-7521
 Speculator *(G-14973)*

BUILDING BOARD & WALLBOARD, EXC GYPSUM

Continental Buchanan LLC..............D....... 703 480-3800
 Buchanan *(G-2672)*

BUILDING BOARD: Gypsum

Continental Buchanan LLC..............D....... 703 480-3800
 Buchanan *(G-2672)*

BUILDING CLEANING & MAINTENANCE SVCS

Broadway National Group LLC..............D....... 800 797-4467
 Ronkonkoma *(G-14321)*
JM Murray Center Inc..............C....... 607 756-9913
 Cortland *(G-3879)*
JM Murray Center Inc..............C....... 607 756-0246
 Cortland *(G-3880)*

Richard Ruffner..............F....... 631 234-4600
 Central Islip *(G-3383)*

BUILDING COMPONENTS: Structural Steel

Castle Harvester Co Inc..............G....... 585 526-5884
 Seneca Castle *(G-14772)*
D N Gannon Fabricating Inc..............G....... 315 463-7466
 Syracuse *(G-15300)*
International Metals Trdg LLC..............G....... 866 923-0182
 Melville *(G-8039)*
Kuno Steel Products Corp..............F....... 516 938-8500
 Hicksville *(G-6101)*
Marovato Industries Inc..............F....... 718 389-0800
 Brooklyn *(G-2173)*
R&S Steel LLC..............F....... 315 281-0123
 Rome *(G-14268)*
Schenectady Steel Co Inc..............E....... 518 355-3220
 Schenectady *(G-14711)*
Stone Bridge Iron and Stl Inc..............D....... 518 695-3752
 Gansevoort *(G-5247)*
STS Steel Inc..............D....... 518 370-2693
 Schenectady *(G-14717)*
Titan Steel Corp..............F....... 315 656-7046
 Kirkville *(G-6936)*
Torino Indus Fabrication Inc..............G....... 631 509-1640
 Bellport *(G-815)*
Ward Steel Company Inc..............E....... 315 451-4566
 Liverpool *(G-7270)*
Wilston Enterprises Inc..............F....... 716 483-1411
 Jamestown *(G-6762)*

BUILDING ITEM REPAIR SVCS, MISCELLANEOUS

ER Butler & Co Inc..............E....... 212 925-3565
 New York *(G-9699)*
Otis Elevator Company..............E....... 917 339-9600
 New York *(G-11069)*

BUILDING PRDTS & MATERIALS DEALERS

Arnan Development Corp..............D....... 607 432-8391
 Oneonta *(G-12625)*
Cossitt Concrete Products Inc..............F....... 315 824-2700
 Hamilton *(G-5698)*
Delocon Wholesale Inc..............F....... 716 592-2711
 Springville *(G-15015)*
Elitsac Inc..............F....... 585 493-2628
 Castile *(G-3293)*
Gone South Concrete Block Inc..............E....... 315 598-2141
 Fulton *(G-5218)*
Imperia Masonry Supply Corp..............E....... 914 738-0900
 Pelham *(G-12936)*
Phelps Cement Products Inc..............E....... 315 548-9415
 Phelps *(G-12979)*
Structural Wood Corporation..............E....... 315 388-4442
 Waddington *(G-15882)*

BUILDING PRDTS: Concrete

Access Products Inc..............G....... 800 679-4022
 Buffalo *(G-2682)*
Apollo Management V LP..............E....... 914 467-6510
 Purchase *(G-13386)*
Duke Company..............G....... 607 347-4455
 Ithaca *(G-6575)*
Hanson Aggregates East LLC..............G....... 716 372-1574
 Allegany *(G-190)*
Murcadom Corporation..............F....... 585 412-2176
 Canandaigua *(G-3226)*
Standard Industries Inc..............G....... 212 821-1600
 New York *(G-11692)*

BUILDING PRDTS: Stone

Icestone LLC..............E....... 718 624-4900
 Brooklyn *(G-1993)*
Roto Salt Company Inc..............E....... 315 536-3742
 Penn Yan *(G-12965)*

BUILDING STONE, ARTIFICIAL: Concrete

Crown Hill Stone Inc..............E....... 716 326-4601
 Westfield *(G-16393)*

BUILDINGS & COMPONENTS: Prefabricated Metal

All American Building..............G....... 607 797-7123
 Binghamton *(G-859)*

PRODUCT SECTION

Austin Mohawk and Company LLC ...... E 315 793-3000
  Utica *(G-15678)*
Birdair Inc ...... D 716 633-9500
  Amherst *(G-218)*
Deraffele Mfg Co Inc ...... E 914 636-6850
  New Rochelle *(G-9598)*
Man Products Inc ...... E 631 789-6500
  Farmingdale *(G-4814)*
Metals Building Products 844 638-2527
  Holbrook *(G-6199)*
Overhead Door Corporation ...... D 518 828-7652
  Hudson *(G-6366)*
Walpo!e Woodworkers Inc ...... G 631 726-2859
  Water Mill *(G-15971)*

BUILDINGS, PREFABRICATED: Wholesalers

Shafer & Sons ...... G 315 853-5285
  Westmoreland *(G-16410)*

BUILDINGS: Portable

Mobile Mini Inc ...... F 315 732-4555
  Utica *(G-15723)*
Mobile Mini Inc ...... E 631 543-4900
  Commack *(G-3698)*
Morton Buildings Inc ...... E 585 786-8191
  Warsaw *(G-15945)*
Nci Group Inc ...... D 315 339-1245
  Rome *(G-14261)*
Universal Shielding Corp ...... E 631 667-7900
  Deer Park *(G-4055)*

BUILDINGS: Prefabricated, Metal

Energy Panel Structures Inc ...... G 315 923-7777
  Clyde *(G-3592)*
Energy Panel Structures Inc ...... G 585 343-1777
  Clyde *(G-3593)*
Energy Panel Structures Inc ...... G 518 355-6708
  Schenectady *(G-14671)*

BUILDINGS: Prefabricated, Plastic

Euro Woodworking Inc ...... G 718 246-9172
  Brooklyn *(G-1853)*

BUILDINGS: Prefabricated, Wood

Cort Contracting ...... F 845 758-1190
  Red Hook *(G-13458)*
Duro-Shed Inc ...... E 585 344-0800
  Buffalo *(G-2805)*
Eastern Exterior Wall ...... E 631 589-3880
  Bohemia *(G-1019)*
Energy Panel Structures Inc ...... G 315 923-7777
  Clyde *(G-3592)*
Energy Panel Structures Inc ...... G 585 343-1777
  Clyde *(G-3593)*
Energy Panel Structures Inc ...... G 518 355-6708
  Schenectady *(G-14671)*
Fishers Storage Sheds ...... G 585 382-9580
  Leicester *(G-7128)*
Walpole Woodworkers Inc ...... G 631 726-2859
  Water Mill *(G-15971)*

BUILDINGS: Prefabricated, Wood

Lapp Management Corp ...... G 607 243-5141
  Himrod *(G-6160)*
Roscoe Brothers Inc ...... F 607 844-3750
  Dryden *(G-4151)*
Shafer & Sons ...... G 315 853-5285
  Westmoreland *(G-16410)*
Shelter Enterprises Inc ...... D 518 237-4100
  Cohoes *(G-3621)*
Wood Tex Products LLC ...... D 607 243-5141
  Himrod *(G-6161)*

BULLETIN BOARDS: Wood

Aarco Products Inc ...... F 631 924-5461
  Yaphank *(G-16703)*

BUMPERS: Motor Vehicle

4bumpers Llc ...... F 212 721-9600
  New York *(G-8680)*

BURIAL VAULTS: Concrete Or Precast Terrazzo

Beck Vault Company ...... G 315 337-7590
  Rome *(G-14248)*
Doric Vault of Wny Inc ...... F 716 828-1776
  Buffalo *(G-2803)*
Ideal Burial Vault Company ...... G 585 599-2242
  Corfu *(G-3807)*
Robert M Vault 315 243-1447
  Bridgeport *(G-1183)*
Suhor Industries Inc ...... F 585 377-5100
  Fairport *(G-4663)*
Suhor Industries Inc ...... G 716 483-6818
  Jamestown *(G-6751)*

BURLAP & BURLAP PRDTS

James Thompson & Company Inc ...... E 212 686-4242
  New York *(G-10304)*

BURNERS: Gas, Indl

Dyson-Kissner-Moran Corp ...... E 212 661-4600
  Poughkeepsie *(G-13335)*
Frederick Cowan & Company Inc ...... F 631 369-0360
  Wading River *(G-15884)*

BUSES: Wholesalers

Leonard Bus Sales Inc ...... G 607 467-3100
  Rome *(G-14256)*

BUSHINGS & BEARINGS: Copper, Exc Machined

Amt Incorporated ...... E 518 284-2910
  Sharon Springs *(G-14797)*

BUSINESS ACTIVITIES: Non-Commercial Site

Adirondack Leather Pdts Inc ...... F 607 547-5798
  Fly Creek *(G-5063)*
Ajmadison Corp ...... D 718 532-1800
  Brooklyn *(G-1497)*
Aka Sport Inc ...... F 631 858-9888
  Dix Hills *(G-4118)*
American Comfort Direct LLC ...... E 201 364-8309
  New York *(G-8825)*
Anne Taintor Inc ...... G 718 483-9312
  Brooklyn *(G-1536)*
Arm Construction Company Inc ...... G 646 235-6520
  East Elmhurst *(G-4217)*
Aspire One Communications Inc ...... G 845 534-6110
  Cornwall *(G-3831)*
Aureonic ...... G 518 791-9331
  Gansevoort *(G-5242)*
Bart Ostrander Trckg Log Corp ...... G 518 661-6535
  Mayfield *(G-7919)*
Birdsigns Inc ...... G 201 388-7613
  New York *(G-9089)*
Buperiod PBC ...... F 917 406-9804
  Brooklyn *(G-1656)*
Catch Ventures Inc ...... F 347 620-4051
  New York *(G-9228)*
Cfp Purchasing Inc ...... G 705 806-0383
  Flushing *(G-4989)*
Cloud Rock Group LLC ...... G 516 967-6023
  Roslyn *(G-14444)*
D & V Enterprises Inc ...... F 917 983-9250
  Woodbury *(G-16617)*
Dapper Dads Inc ...... G 917 903-8045
  Brooklyn *(G-1757)*
Dezawy LLC ...... F 917 436-8820
  New York *(G-9516)*
Eccella Corporation ...... G 718 612-0451
  New York *(G-9619)*
Edesia World Wide LLC ...... G 646 705-3505
  New York *(G-9626)*
Envent Systems Inc ...... G 646 294-6980
  Pelham *(G-12935)*
Evocate Media LLC ...... F 646 361-3014
  New York *(G-9741)*
Excell Print & Promotions Inc ...... G 914 437-8668
  White Plains *(G-16448)*
Fitsmo LLC ...... G 585 519-1956
  Fairport *(G-4633)*
Fresh Prints LLC ...... F 917 826-2752
  New York *(G-9848)*
Garrett J Cronin ...... G 914 761-9299
  White Plains *(G-16452)*
Gorga Fehren Fine Jewelry LLC ...... G 646 861-3595
  New York *(G-9959)*
Greene Brass & Alum Fndry LLC ...... G 607 656-4204
  Bloomville *(G-962)*
Have Your Cake Kitchen LLC ...... G 646 820-8074
  Brooklyn *(G-1968)*
HHS Pharmaceuticals Inc ...... F 347 674-1670
  New York *(G-10093)*
Highside Inc ...... G 917 525-3340
  New York *(G-10098)*
Hourglass Interactive LLC ...... F 954 254-2853
  New York *(G-10134)*
Hovee Inc ...... G 646 249-6200
  New York *(G-10139)*
Hs Homeworx LLC ...... G 646 870-0406
  New York *(G-10141)*
Hum Limited Liability Corp ...... G 631 525-2174
  Nesconset *(G-8484)*
Inscape (new York) Inc ...... D 716 665-6210
  Falconer *(G-4681)*
Joel Zelcer ...... F 917 525-6790
  Brooklyn *(G-2042)*
Jr Engineering Enterprise LLC ...... G 716 909-2693
  Grand Island *(G-5504)*
L VII Resilient LLC ...... F 631 987-5819
  Medford *(G-7957)*
Labrador Stone Inc ...... G 570 465-2120
  Binghamton *(G-901)*
Latchable Inc ...... E 646 833-0604
  New York *(G-10521)*
Magcrest Packaging Inc ...... G 845 425-0451
  Monsey *(G-8289)*
Murcadom Corporation ...... F 585 412-2176
  Canandaigua *(G-3226)*
New York Qrtrly Foundation Inc ...... F 917 843-8825
  Brooklyn *(G-2265)*
On Line Power Technologies ...... G 914 968-4440
  Yonkers *(G-16787)*
Pap Chat Inc ...... G 516 350-1888
  Brooklyn *(G-2301)*
Patrick Rohan ...... F 718 781-2573
  Monticello *(G-8323)*
Patuga LLC ...... G 716 204-7220
  Williamsville *(G-16583)*
Phoenix Usa LLC ...... G 646 351-6598
  New York *(G-11184)*
Pilot Inc ...... G 212 951-1133
  New York *(G-11193)*
Pilot Inc ...... G 212 951-1133
  New York *(G-11194)*
Pink Box Accessories LLC ...... G 718 435-2821
  Brooklyn *(G-2319)*
Plain Digital Inc ...... G 914 310-0280
  Scarsdale *(G-14643)*
Playfitness Corp ...... G 917 497-5443
  Staten Island *(G-15116)*
Playground NY Inc ...... F 505 920-7236
  Brooklyn *(G-2325)*
Playlife LLC ...... G 646 207-9082
  New York *(G-11208)*
Ready Check Glo Inc ...... G 516 547-1849
  East Northport *(G-4270)*
Ready To Assemble Company Inc ...... E 516 825-4397
  Valley Stream *(G-15794)*
Rision Inc ...... G 212 987-2628
  New York *(G-11395)*
Roscoe Brothers Inc ...... F 607 844-3750
  Dryden *(G-4151)*
Scan-A-Chrome Color Inc ...... G 631 532-6146
  Copiague *(G-3779)*
Sensor & Decontamination Inc ...... F 301 526-8389
  Binghamton *(G-914)*
Slyde Inc ...... F 917 331-2114
  Long Island City *(G-7594)*
South Central Boyz ...... G 718 496-7270
  Brooklyn *(G-2501)*
Special Circle Inc ...... F 516 595-9988
  New Hyde Park *(G-8565)*
Streetcred Nyc LLC ...... G 646 675-0073
  New York *(G-11721)*
Surtic Mining Company LLC ...... G 718 434-0477
  Brooklyn *(G-2544)*
Tg Polymers Inc ...... G 585 670-9427
  Webster *(G-16101)*
Treauu Inc ...... G 703 731-0196
  New York *(G-11889)*
Urthworx Inc ...... G 646 373-7535
  New York *(G-11972)*
Verris Inc ...... G 201 565-1648
  New York *(G-12012)*
Vertical Lax Inc ...... G 518 669-3699
  Albany *(G-140)*
Viewsport International Inc ...... G 585 259-1562
  Penfield *(G-12947)*

Employee Codes: A=Over 500 employees, B=251-500
C=101-250, D=51-100, E=20-50, F=10-19, G=5-9

BUSINESS ACTIVITIES: Non-Commercial Site — PRODUCT SECTION

Virtuvent Inc .... G 855 672-8677
  Brooklyn *(G-2628)*
Vortex Ventures Inc .... G 516 946-8345
  North Baldwin *(G-12370)*
Wrkbook LLC .... F 914 355-1293
  White Plains *(G-16522)*

BUSINESS FORMS WHOLESALERS

American Print Solutions Inc .... G 718 208-2309
  Brooklyn *(G-1527)*
Composite Forms Inc .... F 914 937-1808
  Port Chester *(G-13194)*
Empire Business Forms Inc .... F 845 562-7780
  Newburgh *(G-12221)*

BUSINESS FORMS: Printed, Continuous

Five Boro Holding LLC .... F 718 431-9500
  Brooklyn *(G-1885)*
Linden Forms & Systems Inc .... E 212 219-1100
  Brooklyn *(G-2126)*
Syracuse Computer Forms Inc .... E 315 478-0108
  Syracuse *(G-15436)*

BUSINESS FORMS: Printed, Manifold

Abra-Ka-Data Systems Ltd .... E 631 667-5550
  Deer Park *(G-3932)*
Amsterdam Printing & Litho Inc .... F 518 842-6000
  Amsterdam *(G-325)*
Amsterdam Printing & Litho Inc .... F 518 842-6000
  Amsterdam *(G-326)*
Bmg Printing and Promotion LLC .... G 631 231-9200
  Bohemia *(G-989)*
Gateway Prtg & Graphics Inc .... E 716 823-3873
  Hamburg *(G-5680)*
Maggio Data Forms .... C 631 348-0343
  Hauppauge *(G-5877)*
Marcy Business Forms Inc .... G 718 935-9100
  Brooklyn *(G-2165)*
P P I Business Forms Inc .... F 716 825-1241
  Buffalo *(G-2985)*
Resonant Legal Media LLC .... G 800 781-3591
  New York *(G-11369)*
Richard Ruffner .... F 631 234-4600
  Central Islip *(G-3383)*
RR Donnelley & Sons Company .... D 716 773-0300
  Grand Island *(G-5511)*
Select-A-Form Inc .... D 631 981-3076
  Holbrook *(G-6208)*
Taylor Communications Inc .... F 937 221-1303
  Melville *(G-8069)*
Taylor Communications Inc .... F 718 352-0220
  Westbury *(G-16375)*
Williamson Law Book Co .... F 585 924-3400
  Victor *(G-15878)*

BUSINESS MACHINE REPAIR, ELECTRIC

National Time Recording Eqp Co .... F 212 227-3310
  New York *(G-10887)*
Neopost USA Inc .... E 631 435-9100
  Hauppauge *(G-5900)*
Xerox Corporation .... C 585 427-4500
  Rochester *(G-14214)*
Yellow E House Inc .... G 718 888-2000
  Flushing *(G-5061)*

BUSINESS SUPPORT SVCS

Cabezon Design Group Inc .... G 718 488-9868
  Brooklyn *(G-1667)*
Diamond Inscription Tech .... F 646 366-7944
  New York *(G-9523)*

BUTADIENE: Indl, Organic, Chemical

Unified Solutions For Clg Inc .... F 718 782-8800
  Brooklyn *(G-2599)*

BUTTONS

Buttons & Trimcom Inc .... F 212 868-1971
  New York *(G-9164)*
E-Won Industrial Co Inc .... E 212 750-9610
  New York *(G-9601)*
Empire State Metal Pdts Inc .... F 718 847-1617
  Richmond Hill *(G-13502)*
Emsig Manufacturing Corp .... F 718 784-7717
  New York *(G-9670)*
Emsig Manufacturing Corp .... F 518 828-7301
  Hudson *(G-6348)*
Emsig Manufacturing Corp .... E 718 784-7717
  New York *(G-9671)*
Eu Design LLC .... G 212 420-7788
  New York *(G-9725)*
Joyce Trimming Inc .... G 212 719-3110
  New York *(G-10370)*
Kraus & Sons Inc .... F 212 620-0408
  New York *(G-10480)*
National Die & Button Mould Co .... E 201 939-7800
  Brooklyn *(G-2245)*
Shimada Shoji (hk) Limited .... E 212 268-0465
  New York *(G-11566)*

CABINETS & CASES: Show, Display & Storage, Exc Wood

260 Oak Street Inc .... G 877 852-4676
  Buffalo *(G-2676)*
Able Steel Equipment Co Inc .... E 718 361-9240
  Long Island City *(G-7366)*
S & K Counter Tops Inc .... E 716 662-7986
  Orchard Park *(G-12743)*

CABINETS: Bathroom Vanities, Wood

Glissade New York LLC .... E 631 756-4800
  Farmingdale *(G-4772)*
Nagad Cabinets Inc .... G 718 382-7200
  Brooklyn *(G-2241)*
New York Vanity and Mfg Co .... E 718 417-1010
  Freeport *(G-5169)*
Tristate Contract Sales LLC .... G 845 782-2614
  Chester *(G-3489)*

CABINETS: Entertainment

Dbs Interiors Corp .... F 631 491-3013
  West Babylon *(G-16152)*
Time Base Corporation .... E 631 293-4068
  Edgewood *(G-4420)*
W Designe Inc .... E 914 736-1058
  Peekskill *(G-12927)*

CABINETS: Entertainment Units, Household, Wood

Handcraft Cabinetry Inc .... G 914 681-9437
  White Plains *(G-16458)*

CABINETS: Factory

T O Gronlund Company Inc .... F 212 679-3535
  New York *(G-11771)*
Thornwood Products Ltd .... E 914 769-9161
  Thornwood *(G-15508)*
Wood Etc Inc .... E 315 484-9663
  Syracuse *(G-15461)*

CABINETS: Filing, Metal

Schwab Corp .... E 585 381-4900
  Rochester *(G-14116)*

CABINETS: Filing, Wood

Red White & Blue Entps Corp .... G 718 565-8080
  Woodside *(G-16675)*

CABINETS: Kitchen, Metal

American Best Cabinets Inc .... E 845 369-6666
  Suffern *(G-15185)*
Hellas Stone Inc .... G 718 545-4716
  Astoria *(G-430)*
Majestic Home Imprvs Distr .... G 718 853-5079
  Brooklyn *(G-2152)*
Manhattan Cabinets Inc .... E 212 548-2436
  New York *(G-10684)*
Methods Tooling & Mfg Inc .... G 845 246-7100
  Mount Marion *(G-8364)*
Steelcraft Manufacturing Co .... F 718 277-2404
  Brooklyn *(G-2516)*

CABINETS: Kitchen, Wood

A-1 Manhattan Custom Furn Inc .... E 212 750-9800
  Island Park *(G-6510)*
Able Kitchen .... F 877 268-1264
  Cedarhurst *(G-3330)*
Acme Kitchenettes Corp .... E 518 828-4191
  Hudson *(G-6337)*
Aka Enterprises .... E 716 474-4579
  Wyoming *(G-16698)*
Aki Cabinets Inc .... E 718 721-2541
  Astoria *(G-420)*
Andike Millwork Inc .... G 718 894-1796
  Maspeth *(G-7821)*
Artone LLC .... D 716 664-2232
  Jamestown *(G-6699)*
Atlantic States Distributing .... G 518 427-6364
  Menands *(G-8082)*
Auburn-Watson Corp .... F 716 876-8000
  Depew *(G-4079)*
Aucapina Cabinets Inc .... G 718 609-9054
  Maspeth *(G-7825)*
Bauerschmidt & Sons Inc .... D 718 528-3500
  Jamaica *(G-6630)*
Bloch Industries LLC .... D 585 334-9600
  Rochester *(G-13666)*
Cabinet Factory Inc .... F 718 351-8922
  Staten Island *(G-15058)*
Cabinet Shapes Corp .... E 718 784-6255
  Long Island City *(G-7404)*
Cabinetry By Tbr Inc .... E 516 365-8500
  Manhasset *(G-7764)*
Cabinets By Stanley Inc .... E 718 222-5861
  Brooklyn *(G-1668)*
Cambridge Kitchens Mfg Inc .... F 516 935-5100
  Hicksville *(G-6067)*
Candlelight Cabinetry Inc .... E 716 434-2114
  Lockport *(G-7289)*
Capital Kit Cab & Door Mfrs .... E 718 886-0303
  College Point *(G-3641)*
Carefree Kitchens Inc .... G 631 567-2120
  Holbrook *(G-6175)*
Carlos & Alex Atelier Inc .... E 718 441-8911
  Richmond Hill *(G-13500)*
Casa Collection Inc .... G 718 694-0272
  Brooklyn *(G-1681)*
Catskill Craftsmen Inc .... F 607 652-7321
  Stamford *(G-15030)*
Central Kitchen Corp .... F 631 283-1029
  Southampton *(G-14951)*
Chicone Builders LLC .... G 607 535-6540
  Montour Falls *(G-8325)*
Classic Cabinets .... F 845 357-4331
  Suffern *(G-15187)*
Clearwood Custom Carpentry and .... E 315 432-8422
  East Syracuse *(G-4331)*
Cleary Custom Cabinets Inc .... F 516 939-2475
  Hicksville *(G-6070)*
Columbia Cabinets LLC .... G 212 972-7550
  Armonk *(G-402)*
Columbia Cabinets LLC .... E 518 283-1700
  Saratoga Springs *(G-14576)*
Craft Custom Woodwork Co Inc .... F 718 821-2162
  Maspeth *(G-7831)*
Creative Stone & Cabinets .... E 631 772-6548
  Selden *(G-14762)*
Custom CAS Inc .... E 718 726-3575
  Long Island City *(G-7418)*
Custom Woodcraft LLC .... F 315 843-4234
  Munnsville *(G-8458)*
D & M Custom Cabinets Inc .... F 516 678-2818
  Oceanside *(G-12534)*
Dak Mica and Wood Products .... G 631 467-0749
  Ronkonkoma *(G-14332)*
Dbs Interiors Corp .... F 631 491-3013
  West Babylon *(G-16152)*
Deakon Homes and Interiors .... F 518 271-0342
  Troy *(G-15603)*
Di Fiore and Sons Custom Wdwkg .... G 718 278-1663
  Long Island City *(G-7425)*
East End Country Kitchens Inc .... F 631 727-2258
  Calverton *(G-3165)*
EC Wood & Company Inc .... F 718 388-2287
  Deer Park *(G-3971)*
EM Pfaff & Son Inc .... F 607 739-3691
  Horseheads *(G-6313)*
Enterprise Wood Products Inc .... G 718 853-9243
  Brooklyn *(G-1837)*
Fina Cabinet Corp .... F 718 409-2900
  Mount Vernon *(G-8398)*
Finger Lkes Stirs Cabinets LLC .... G 315 638-3150
  Baldwinsville *(G-554)*
Fra-Rik Formica Fabg Co Inc .... F 718 597-3335
  Bronx *(G-1275)*
Greenway Cabinetry Inc .... F 516 877-0009
  Williston Park *(G-16594)*
Hearth Cabinets and More Ltd .... G 315 641-1197
  Liverpool *(G-7234)*
Hendrickson Custom Cabinetry .... F 718 401-0137
  Bronx *(G-1291)*

PRODUCT SECTION

CAMERAS & RELATED EQPT: Photographic

Home Ideal Inc	G	718 762-8998
Flushing (G-5009)		
Huntington Woodworking Inc	G	631 271-7897
Huntington Station (G-6446)		
Ignelzi Interiors Inc	E	718 464-0279
Queens Village (G-13407)		
J Percoco Industries Inc	G	631 312-4572
Bohemia (G-1038)		
JEm Wdwkg & Cabinets Inc	F	518 828-5361
Hudson (G-6358)		
Jordache Woodworking Corp	F	718 349-3373
Brooklyn (G-2045)		
K-Binet Inc	G	845 348-1149
Blauvelt (G-936)		
Kw Distributors Group Inc	F	718 843-3500
Ozone Park (G-12829)		
Longo Commercial Cabinets Inc	E	631 225-4290
Lindenhurst (G-7176)		
Lyn Jo Kitchens Inc	G	718 336-6060
Brooklyn (G-2138)		
Material Process Systems Inc	F	718 302-3081
Brooklyn (G-2179)		
Matteo & Antonio Bartolotta	F	315 252-2220
Auburn (G-490)		
McGraw Wood Products LLC	E	607 836-6465
Mc Graw (G-7928)		
Methods Tooling & Mfg Inc	E	845 246-7100
Mount Marion (G-8364)		
Metro Kitchens Corp	F	718 434-1166
Brooklyn (G-2200)		
Michael Bernstein Design Assoc	E	718 456-9277
Brooklyn (G-2203)		
Michael P Mmarr	F	315 623-9380
Constantia (G-3740)		
Millco Woodworking LLC	F	585 526-6844
Hall (G-5671)		
Modern Cabinet Company Inc	E	845 473-4900
Poughkeepsie (G-13355)		
N Y Elli Design Corp	F	718 228-0014
Ridgewood (G-13543)		
Neo Cabinetry LLC	F	718 403-0456
Brooklyn (G-2252)		
Nexis 3 LLC	E	585 285-4120
Rochester (G-13972)		
NY Cabinet Factory Inc	F	718 256-6541
Brooklyn (G-2278)		
Pgs Millwork Inc	D	518 828-2608
Hudson (G-6368)		
Piccini Industries Ltd	E	845 365-0614
Orangeburg (G-12685)		
Precision Dental Cabinets Inc	F	631 543-3870
Smithtown (G-14906)		
Premier Woodcraft Ltd	E	610 383-6624
White Plains (G-16499)		
Premium Woodworking LLC	G	631 485-3133
West Babylon (G-16183)		
R & M Thermofoil Doors Inc	G	718 206-4991
Jamaica (G-6671)		
Ralph Payne	G	718 222-4200
Brooklyn (G-2383)		
Red White & Blue Entps Corp	G	718 565-8080
Woodside (G-16675)		
Ribble Lumber Inc	G	315 536-6221
Penn Yan (G-12964)		
Royal Custom Cabinets	G	315 376-6042
Lowville (G-7656)		
S & V Custom Furniture Mfg	F	516 746-8299
Mineola (G-8248)		
S Donadic Inc	D	718 361-9888
Sunnyside (G-15205)		
Salko Kitchens Inc	F	845 565-4420
New Windsor (G-8658)		
Salmon Creek Cabinetry Inc	E	315 589-5419
Williamson (G-16561)		
Serway Bros Inc	E	315 337-0601
Rome (G-14274)		
Silva Cabinetry Inc	E	914 737-7697
Buchanan (G-2674)		
Skyline Custom Cabinetry Inc	G	631 393-2983
Farmingdale (G-4875)		
Stone Expo & Cabinetry LLC	F	516 292-2988
West Hempstead (G-16225)		
Upstate Cabinet Company Inc	F	585 429-5090
Rochester (G-14191)		
Viola Cabinet Corporation	F	716 284-6327
Niagara Falls (G-12347)		
W Designe Inc	E	914 736-1058
Peekskill (G-12927)		
White House Cabinet Shop LLC	F	607 674-9358
Sherburne (G-14813)		
William Brooks Woodworking	F	718 495-9767
Brooklyn (G-2647)		
Win Wood Cabinetry Inc	G	516 304-2216
Greenvale (G-5634)		
Wood Etc Inc	F	315 484-9663
Syracuse (G-15461)		
Yonkers Cabinet Inc	F	914 668-2133
Yonkers (G-16810)		
Your Furniture Designers Inc	G	845 947-3046
West Haverstraw (G-16211)		
Your Way Custom Cabinets Inc	G	914 371-1870
Mount Vernon (G-8454)		

CABINETS: Office, Metal

Gothic Cabinet Craft Inc	D	347 881-1420
Maspeth (G-7848)		
Natural Stone & Cabinet Inc	G	718 388-2988
Brooklyn (G-2248)		
Riverfront Costume Design	G	716 693-2501
North Tonawanda (G-12447)		

CABINETS: Office, Wood

A G Master Crafts Ltd	F	516 745-6262
Garden City (G-5249)		
Chicone Builders LLC	G	607 535-6540
Montour Falls (G-8325)		
Commercial Display Design LLC	F	607 336-7353
Norwich (G-12483)		
Concepts In Wood of CNY	E	315 463-8084
Syracuse (G-15286)		
Craft Custom Woodwork Co Inc	F	718 821-2162
Maspeth (G-7831)		
Culin/Colella Inc	G	914 698-7727
Mamaroneck (G-7741)		
Fina Cabinet Corp	F	718 409-2900
Mount Vernon (G-8398)		
Gothic Cabinet Craft Inc	D	347 881-1420
Maspeth (G-7848)		
Materials Design Workshop	F	718 893-1954
Bronx (G-1325)		
N Y Elli Design Corp	F	718 228-0014
Ridgewood (G-13543)		
Poppin Inc	D	212 391-7200
New York (G-11219)		
Riverfront Costume Design	G	716 693-2501
North Tonawanda (G-12447)		
Stylecraft Interiors Inc	F	516 487-2133
Great Neck (G-5594)		
Three R Enterprises Inc	F	585 254-5050
Rochester (G-14169)		
Wood Etc Inc	F	315 484-9663
Syracuse (G-15461)		

CABINETS: Radio & Television, Metal

CIDC Corp	F	718 342-5820
Glendale (G-5395)		

CABINETS: Show, Display, Etc, Wood, Exc Refrigerated

Custom Design Kitchens Inc	F	518 355-4446
Duanesburg (G-4155)		
E F Thresh Inc	G	315 437-7301
East Syracuse (G-4336)		
Fleetwood Cabinet Co Inc	G	516 379-2139
Brooklyn (G-1891)		
Johnny Mica Inc	G	631 225-5213
Lindenhurst (G-7173)		
Telesca-Heyman Inc	F	212 534-3442
New York (G-11797)		

CABLE TELEVISION

Hearst Holdings Inc	F	212 649-2000
New York (G-10072)		
Historic TW Inc	E	212 484-8000
New York (G-10106)		
Time Warner Companies Inc	D	212 484-8000
New York (G-11845)		

CABLE TELEVISION PRDTS

Arcom Automatics LLC	G	315 422-1230
Syracuse (G-15245)		
Arrow-Communication Labs Inc	B	315 422-1230
Syracuse (G-15247)		
Belden Inc	B	607 796-5600
Horseheads (G-6306)		
Eagle Comtronics Inc	C	315 451-3313
Liverpool (G-7232)		
Eeg Enterprises Inc	F	516 293-7472
Farmingdale (G-4759)		

CABLE: Coaxial

Hyperline Systems Inc	G	613 736-8500
Brooklyn (G-1991)		

CABLE: Fiber

Cables and Chips Inc	E	212 619-3132
New York (G-9173)		
Fiber Instrument Sales Inc	C	315 736-2206
Oriskany (G-12757)		
Fiberone LLC	F	315 434-8877
East Syracuse (G-4339)		
Laseoptics Corp	F	716 462-5078
Buffalo (G-2921)		
Triad Network Technologies	E	585 924-8505
Victor (G-15874)		

CABLE: Fiber Optic

Complete Fiber Solutions Inc	G	718 828-8900
Bronx (G-1245)		
Corning Incorporated	G	607 974-6729
Painted Post (G-12837)		
Corning Incorporated	A	607 974-9000
Corning (G-3809)		
Corning Incorporated	E	607 248-1200
Corning (G-3812)		
Corning Specialty Mtls Inc	G	607 974-9000
Corning (G-3817)		
Fiberdyne Labs Inc	D	315 895-8470
Frankfort (G-5107)		
TLC-The Light Connection Inc	D	315 736-7384
Oriskany (G-12766)		

CABLE: Nonferrous, Shipboard

Monroe Cable Company Inc	C	845 692-2800
Middletown (G-8166)		

CABLE: Noninsulated

Cortland Cable Company Inc	E	607 753-8276
Cortland (G-3865)		
J Davis Manufacturing Co Inc	E	315 337-7574
Rome (G-14254)		
Nexans Energy USA Inc	C	845 469-2141
Chester (G-3478)		
Reelcology Inc	F	845 258-1880
Pine Island (G-13002)		
Ultra Clarity Corp	G	719 470-1010
Spring Valley (G-15010)		
Weico Wire & Cable Inc	E	631 254-2970
Edgewood (G-4424)		

CABLE: Ropes & Fiber

Cortland Company Inc	D	607 753-8276
Cortland (G-3866)		

CABLE: Steel, Insulated Or Armored

Dragon Trading Inc	G	212 717-1496
New York (G-9572)		
Dsr International Corp	F	631 427-2600
Great Neck (G-5550)		

CAGES: Wire

Renco Group Inc	G	212 541-6000
New York (G-11361)		

CALCULATING & ACCOUNTING EQPT

Hand Held Products Inc	B	315 554-6000
Skaneateles Falls (G-14879)		
Merchant Service Pymnt Access	G	212 561-5516
Uniondale (G-15671)		

CALIBRATING SVCS, NEC

Phymetrix Inc	G	631 627-3950
Medford (G-7963)		
Quality Vision Services Inc	D	585 544-0450
Rochester (G-14062)		

CAMERAS & RELATED EQPT: Photographic

Bescor Video Accessories Ltd	F	631 420-1717
Farmingdale (G-4727)		
Core Swx LLC	F	516 595-7488
Plainview (G-13047)		

CAMERAS & RELATED EQPT: Photographic

Easterncctv (usa) LLC ....F 516 870-3779
  Plainview (G-13052)
Fanvision Entertainment LLC ....G 917 297-7428
  New York (G-9783)
Lake Image Systems Inc ....F 585 321-3630
  Henrietta (G-6034)
Rear View Safety Inc ....E 855 815-3842
  Brooklyn (G-2389)
Rosco Collision Avoidance Inc ....G 718 526-2601
  Jamaica (G-6676)
Watec America Corporation ....E 702 434-6111
  Middletown (G-8184)

CANDLE SHOPS

Candles By Foster ....G 914 739-9226
  Peekskill (G-12918)
Northern Lights Entps Inc ....C 585 593-1200
  Wellsville (G-16119)

CANDLES

A & L Asset Management Ltd ....C 718 566-1500
  Brooklyn (G-1450)
Astron Candle Manufacturing Co ....G 718 728-3330
  Long Island City (G-7391)
Betterbee Inc ....F 518 314-0575
  Greenwich (G-5637)
Candle In The Window Inc ....F 718 852-5743
  Brooklyn (G-1672)
Candles By Foster ....G 914 739-9226
  Peekskill (G-12918)
Cathedral Candle Co ....D 315 422-9119
  Syracuse (G-15274)
Crusader Candle Co Inc ....E 718 625-0005
  Brooklyn (G-1735)
Hs Homeworx LLC ....G 646 870-0406
  New York (G-10141)
International Design Assoc Ltd ....G 212 687-0333
  New York (G-10245)
Joya LLC ....F 718 852-6979
  Brooklyn (G-2051)
Kkw Corp ....E 631 589-5454
  Sayville (G-14631)
Lux Mundi Corp ....G 631 244-4596
  Ronkonkoma (G-14372)
Muench-Kreuzer Candle Company ....D 315 471-4515
  Syracuse (G-15377)
Northern Lights Entps Inc ....C 585 593-1200
  Wellsville (G-16119)
Old Williamsburgh Candle Corp ....C 718 566-1500
  Tallman (G-15464)
Quality Candle Mfg Co Inc ....F 631 842-8475
  Copiague (G-3776)
Simcha Candle Co Inc ....G 845 783-0406
  New Windsor (G-8661)
Thompson Ferrier LLC ....G 212 244-2212
  New York (G-11823)
TV Guilfoil & Associates Inc ....G 315 453-0920
  Syracuse (G-15447)

CANDLES: Wholesalers

Candle In The Window Inc ....F 718 852-5743
  Brooklyn (G-1672)

CANDY & CONFECTIONS: Cake Ornaments

Naples Vly Mrgers Acqstons LLC ....G 585 490-1339
  Naples (G-8473)
OH How Cute Inc ....G 347 838-6031
  Staten Island (G-15113)
Pfeil & Holing Inc ....D 718 545-4600
  Woodside (G-16671)

CANDY & CONFECTIONS: Candy Bars, Including Chocolate Covered

Chocolate Delivery Systems Inc ....E 716 877-3146
  Buffalo (G-2765)
Eatingevolved LLC ....F 631 675-2440
  Setauket (G-14794)
Fine and Raw Chocolate ....G 718 366-3633
  Brooklyn (G-1881)
N Make Mold Inc ....E 716 877-3146
  Buffalo (G-2960)
Vigneri Chocolate Inc ....G 585 254-6160
  Rochester (G-14201)

CANDY & CONFECTIONS: Chocolate Candy, Exc Solid Chocolate

Aigner Chocolates ....F 718 544-1850
  Forest Hills (G-5070)
Amiram Dror Inc ....F 212 979-9505
  Brooklyn (G-1529)
Chocolate Pizza Company Inc ....F 315 673-4098
  Marcellus (G-7793)
Robert Pikcilingis ....F 518 355-1860
  Altamont (G-201)

CANDY & CONFECTIONS: Fudge

Alrajs Inc ....E 631 225-0300
  Lindenhurst (G-7159)

CANDY & CONFECTIONS: Halvah

Joyva Corp ....D 718 497-0170
  Brooklyn (G-2052)

CANDY, NUT & CONFECTIONERY STORES: Candy

5th Avenue Chocolatiere Ltd ....G 212 935-5454
  Freeport (G-5134)
Adirondack Chocolate Co Ltd ....F 518 946-7270
  Wilmington (G-16600)
Amiram Dror Inc ....F 212 979-9505
  Brooklyn (G-1529)
Commodore Chocolatier USA Inc ....G 845 561-3960
  Newburgh (G-12218)
Ford Gum & Machine Company Inc ....D 716 542-4561
  Akron (G-18)
Godiva Chocolatier Inc ....E 212 984-5900
  New York (G-9950)
Hercules Candy Co ....G 315 463-4339
  East Syracuse (G-4346)
Hudson Valley Chocolatier Inc ....F 845 831-8240
  Beacon (G-759)
Jo-Mart Candies Corp ....F 718 375-1277
  Brooklyn (G-2041)
Lady-N-Th-wndow Chocolates Inc ....F 631 549-1059
  Huntington (G-6403)
Noras Candy Shop ....F 315 337-4530
  Rome (G-14262)
Parkside Candy Co Inc ....F 716 833-7540
  Buffalo (G-2992)
Roger L Urban Inc ....E 716 693-5391
  North Tonawanda (G-12449)
Seaward Candies ....G 585 638-6761
  Holley (G-6229)
The Chocolate Shop ....G 716 882-5055
  Buffalo (G-3092)

CANDY, NUT & CONFECTIONERY STORES: Confectionery

Noaspence Inc ....G 516 433-7848
  Hicksville (G-6114)

CANDY: Chocolate From Cacao Beans

Adirondack Chocolate Co Ltd ....F 518 946-7270
  Wilmington (G-16600)
Aigner Chocolates ....F 718 544-1850
  Forest Hills (G-5070)
Chocolate Pizza Company Inc ....F 315 673-4098
  Marcellus (G-7793)
Godiva Chocolatier Inc ....E 212 984-5900
  New York (G-9950)
Roger L Urban Inc ....E 716 693-5391
  North Tonawanda (G-12449)
Superior Confections Inc ....D 718 698-3300
  Staten Island (G-15142)

CANNED SPECIALTIES

Global Food Source & Co Inc ....G 914 320-9615
  Tuckahoe (G-15643)
Goya Foods Inc ....D 716 549-0076
  Angola (G-369)
Grandma Browns Beans Inc ....F 315 963-7221
  Mexico (G-8108)
Kawasho Foods USA Inc ....F 212 841-7400
  New York (G-10420)

CANOPIES: Sheet Metal

Austin Mohawk and Company LLC ....E 315 793-3000
  Utica (G-15678)

PRODUCT SECTION

CANS: Aluminum

Anheuser-Busch Companies LLC ....G 718 589-2610
  Bronx (G-1221)
Ball Metal Beverage Cont Corp ....C 845 692-3800
  Middletown (G-8138)
Reynolds Metals Company LLC ....C 212 518-5400
  New York (G-11380)

CANS: Metal

Ardagh Metal Packaging USA Inc ....C 607 584-3300
  Conklin (G-3724)
Ball Metal Beverage Cont Corp ....E 518 587-6030
  Saratoga Springs (G-14570)
Brakewell Stl Fabricators Inc ....E 845 469-9131
  Chester (G-3469)
Crown Cork & Seal Usa Inc ....E 845 343-9586
  Middletown (G-8145)
Erie Engineered Products Inc ....E 716 206-0204
  Lancaster (G-7018)
Hornet Group Inc ....E 845 858-6400
  Port Jervis (G-13230)
J C Industries Inc ....E 631 420-1920
  West Babylon (G-16161)
Metal Container Corporation ....E 845 567-1500
  New Windsor (G-8650)
Seneca Foods Corporation ....D 315 926-0531
  Marion (G-7807)

CANVAS PRDTS

Ace Canvas & Tent Corp ....F 631 648-0614
  Ronkonkoma (G-14288)
Anchor Canvas LLC ....G 631 265-5602
  Smithtown (G-14894)
Broadway Neon Sign Corp ....F 908 241-4177
  Ronkonkoma (G-14322)
Custom European Imports Inc ....E 845 357-5718
  Sloatsburg (G-14892)
Jag Manufacturing Inc ....E 518 762-9558
  Johnstown (G-6832)
Ke Durasol Awnings Inc ....E 845 610-1100
  Chester (G-3477)
Nationwide Tarps Incorporated ....D 518 843-1545
  Amsterdam (G-353)
Point Canvas Company Inc ....G 607 692-4381
  Whitney Point (G-16556)
Service Canvas Co Inc ....F 716 853-0558
  Buffalo (G-3062)
Utility Canvas Inc ....G 845 255-9290
  Gardiner (G-5297)
Y & A Trading Inc ....F 718 436-6333
  Brooklyn (G-2661)

CANVAS PRDTS, WHOLESALE

Awning Mart Inc ....G 315 699-5928
  Cicero (G-3514)
Brock Awnings Ltd ....F 631 765-5200
  Hampton Bays (G-5708)
Point Canvas Company Inc ....G 607 692-4381
  Whitney Point (G-16556)

CANVAS PRDTS: Convertible Tops, Car/Boat, Fm Purchased Mtrl

Automtve Uphl Cnvertible Tops ....G 914 961-4242
  Tuckahoe (G-15642)
Mc Coy Tops and Interiors Inc ....G 718 458-5800
  Woodside (G-16662)
Quantum Sails Rochester LLC ....G 585 342-5200
  Rochester (G-14064)

CANVAS PRDTS: Shades, Made From Purchased Materials

Jo-Vin Decorators Inc ....E 718 441-9350
  Woodhaven (G-16636)
Laminated Window Products Inc ....F 631 242-6883
  Bay Shore (G-693)

CAPACITORS: Fixed Or Variable

General Electric Company ....B 518 746-5750
  Hudson Falls (G-6379)

CAPACITORS: NEC

American Tchncal Ceramics Corp ....B 631 622-4700
  Huntington Station (G-6430)
American Techical Ceramics ....B 631 622-4758
  Huntington Station (G-6431)

PRODUCT SECTION

American Technical Ceramics ....B 631 622-4700
  Huntington Station *(G-6432)*
AVX Corporation ....D 716 372-6611
  Olean *(G-12592)*
Custom Electronics Inc ....D 607 432-3880
  Oneonta *(G-12637)*
Electron Coil Inc ....D 607 336-7414
  Norwich *(G-12485)*
Ems Development Corporation ....D 631 345-6200
  Yaphank *(G-16709)*
Hipotronics Inc ....C 845 279-8091
  Brewster *(G-1167)*
Integer Holdings Corporation ....E 716 937-5100
  Alden *(G-173)*
Kemet Properties LLC ....G 718 654-8079
  Bronx *(G-1306)*
Knowles Cazenovia Inc ....C 315 655-8710
  Cazenovia *(G-3320)*
MTK Electronics Inc..............................E 631 924-7666
  Medford *(G-7962)*
Passive-Plus Inc...................................F 631 425-0938
  Huntington *(G-6407)*
Russell Industries Inc...........................G 516 536-5000
  Lynbrook *(G-7673)*
Stk Electronics Inc ....E 315 655-8476
  Cazenovia *(G-3327)*
Strux Corp ....E 516 768-3969
  Lindenhurst *(G-7196)*
Tronser Inc ....G 315 655-9528
  Cazenovia *(G-3328)*
Viking Technologies Ltd ....E 631 957-8000
  Lindenhurst *(G-7204)*
Voltronics LLC ....E 410 749-2424
  Cazenovia *(G-3329)*

CAPS & PLUGS: Electric, Attachment

Delfingen Us-New York Inc ....E 716 215-0300
  Niagara Falls *(G-12277)*
Leviton Manufacturing Co Inc ....B 631 812-6000
  Melville *(G-8043)*

CAR WASH EQPT

Econocraft Worldwide Mfg Inc ....G 914 966-2280
  Yonkers *(G-16754)*
Hercules International Inc ....E 631 423-6900
  Huntington Station *(G-6444)*
I A S National Inc ....E 631 423-6900
  Huntington Station *(G-6447)*
Klee Corp ....G 585 272-0320
  Rochester *(G-13905)*
Liquid Industries Inc ....G 716 628-2999
  Niagara Falls *(G-12306)*
Metro Lube ....G 718 947-1167
  Rego Park *(G-13465)*
Wetlook Detailing Inc............................G 212 390-8877
  Brooklyn *(G-2642)*

CARBIDES

Carbide-Usa LLC..................................G 607 331-9353
  Elmira *(G-4476)*
Lakeshore Carbide Inc ....G 716 462-4349
  Buffalo *(G-2919)*
Transport National Dev Inc ....E 716 662-0270
  Orchard Park *(G-12747)*

CARBON & GRAPHITE PRDTS, NEC

Americarb Inc.......................................D 419 281-5800
  Niagara Falls *(G-12259)*
Americarb International Corp ....G 419 281-5800
  Niagara Falls *(G-12260)*
Carbon Graphite Materials Inc.............G 716 792-7979
  Brocton *(G-1195)*
Carbonfree Chemicals Spe I LLC ....E 914 421-4900
  White Plains *(G-16436)*
Go Blue Technologies Ltd ....G 631 404-6285
  North Babylon *(G-12360)*
Hh Liquidating Corp ....A 646 282-2500
  New York *(G-10092)*
Mwi Inc ....D 585 424-4200
  Rochester *(G-13961)*
Pyrotek Incorporated............................E 716 731-3221
  Sanborn *(G-14552)*
Xactiv Inc ....F 585 288-7220
  Fairport *(G-4668)*

CARBONS: Electric

Metallized Carbon Corporation.............C 914 941-3738
  Ossining *(G-12771)*

CARDBOARD PRDTS, EXC DIE-CUT

M C Packaging Corporation ....C 631 694-3012
  Farmingdale *(G-4812)*
M C Packaging Corporation ....E 631 643-3763
  Babylon *(G-529)*

CARDBOARD: Waterproof, Made From Purchased Materials

Ums Manufacturing LLC ....F 518 562-2410
  Plattsburgh *(G-13164)*

CARDIOVASCULAR SYSTEM DRUGS, EXC DIAGNOSTIC

Bristol-Myers Squibb Company ....A 212 546-4000
  New York *(G-9144)*
Mesoblast Inc ....G 212 880-2060
  New York *(G-10781)*
Pfizer Inc ....A 212 733-2323
  New York *(G-11174)*

CARDS: Beveled

Foster - Gordon Manufacturing ....G 631 589-6776
  Bohemia *(G-1024)*

CARDS: Color

Mooney-Keehley Inc ....G 585 271-1573
  Rochester *(G-13955)*
Tele-Pak Inc ....E 845 426-2300
  Monsey *(G-8302)*

CARDS: Greeting

1/2 Off Cards Wantagh Inc ....G 516 809-9832
  Wantagh *(G-15919)*
Anne Taintor Inc...................................G 718 483-9312
  Brooklyn *(G-1536)*
Avanti Press Inc ....E 212 414-1025
  New York *(G-8972)*
Massimo Friedman Inc ....E 716 836-0408
  Buffalo *(G-2938)*
Paper House Productions Inc..............E 845 246-7261
  Saugerties *(G-14612)*
Paper Magic Group Inc........................B 631 521-3682
  New York *(G-11102)*
Quotable Cards Inc ....G 212 420-7552
  New York *(G-11305)*
Shade Tree Greetings Inc ....F 585 442-4580
  Rochester *(G-14123)*

CARDS: Identification

Allsafe Technologies Inc ....D 716 691-0400
  Amherst *(G-212)*
Alpha Incorporated...............................G 718 765-1614
  Brooklyn *(G-1512)*
Global Security Tech LLC ....F 917 838-4507
  Cedarhurst *(G-3332)*
Iadc Inc ....F 718 238-0623
  Staten Island *(G-15088)*
Metropltan Data Sltons MGT Inc..........F 516 586-5520
  Farmingdale *(G-4822)*
Multi Packaging Solutions Inc ....E 646 885-0005
  New York *(G-10858)*

CARPET DYEING & FINISHING

Eskayel Inc ....G 347 703-8084
  Brooklyn *(G-1848)*

CARPETS & RUGS: Tufted

Interfaceflor LLC ....E 212 686-8284
  New York *(G-10240)*

CARPETS, RUGS & FLOOR COVERING

Aladdin Manufacturing Corp.................C 212 561-8715
  New York *(G-8781)*
Bentley Mills Inc ....E 212 463-0606
  New York *(G-9048)*
Bloomsburg Carpet Inds Inc ....G 212 688-7447
  New York *(G-9103)*
Carpet Fabrications Intl ....E 914 381-6060
  Mamaroneck *(G-7736)*
Excellent Art Mfg Corp ....F 718 388-7075
  Inwood *(G-6489)*
Jbl Trading LLC ....G 347 394-5592
  New York *(G-10316)*
Kalati Company Inc..............................G 516 423-9132
  Great Neck *(G-5565)*
Lanes Flr Cvrngs Intriors Inc ....E 212 532-5200
  New York *(G-10515)*
Loom Concepts LLC ....G 212 813-9586
  New York *(G-10601)*
Lorena Canals USA Inc ....G 844 567-3622
  Hastings On Hudson *(G-5751)*
Michaelian & Kohlberg Inc ....G 212 431-9009
  New York *(G-10793)*
Northpoint Trading Inc ....G 212 481-8001
  New York *(G-10997)*
Odegard Inc ....G 212 545-0069
  Long Island City *(G-7542)*
Pawling Corporation.............................G 845 373-9300
  Wassaic *(G-15965)*
Quality Carpet One Floor & HM ....G 718 941-4200
  Brooklyn *(G-2365)*
Rosecore Division.................................F 516 504-4530
  Great Neck *(G-5585)*
Shyam Ahuja Limited ....G 212 644-5910
  New York *(G-11573)*
Sunrise Tile Inc ....G 718 939-0538
  Flushing *(G-5050)*
Tdg Operations LLC ....G 212 779-4300
  New York *(G-11789)*
Tiger 21 LLC ....G 212 360-1700
  New York *(G-11832)*
Wells Rugs Inc ....G 516 676-2056
  Glen Cove *(G-5378)*

CARPETS: Hand & Machine Made

Elizabeth Eakins Inc ....F 212 628-1950
  New York *(G-9653)*
Tsar USA LLC ....F 646 415-7968
  New York *(G-11909)*

CARPETS: Textile Fiber

Scalamandre Silks Inc ....D 212 980-3888
  New York *(G-11499)*

CARRIAGES: Horse Drawn

Tectran Inc ....G 800 776-5549
  Cheektowaga *(G-3461)*

CARRYING CASES, WHOLESALE

Bristol Boarding Inc..............................G 585 271-7860
  Rochester *(G-13679)*
Sigma Worldwide LLC ....G 646 217-0629
  New York *(G-11583)*

CARTONS: Egg, Molded Pulp, Made From Purchased Materials

Tri-Seal International Inc ....G 845 353-3300
  Blauvelt *(G-944)*

CASEMENTS: Aluminum

Rohlfs Stined Leaded GL Studio ....E 914 699-4848
  Mount Vernon *(G-8440)*

CASES, WOOD

Bragley Mfg Co Inc ....E 718 622-7469
  Brooklyn *(G-1631)*

CASES: Attache'

Dlx Industries Inc ....D 718 272-9420
  Brooklyn *(G-1784)*
Randa Accessories Lea Gds LLC.........D 212 354-5100
  New York *(G-11325)*
Trafalgar Company LLC ....G 212 768-8800
  New York *(G-11885)*

CASES: Carrying

Ead Cases ....F 845 343-2111
  Middletown *(G-8149)*
Fieldtex Products Inc ....C 585 427-2940
  Rochester *(G-13803)*
Merzon Leather Co Inc ....C 718 782-6260
  Brooklyn *(G-2197)*
Sigma Worldwide LLC ....G 646 217-0629
  New York *(G-11583)*
Three Point Ventures LLC ....F 585 697-3444
  Rochester *(G-14168)*

CASES: Carrying, Clothing & Apparel

CASES: Carrying, Clothing & Apparel
212 Biz LLC .... G 212 391-4444
  New York *(G-8669)*
Calvin Klein Inc .... E 212 292-9000
  New York *(G-9184)*
Donna Morgan LLC .... E 212 575-2550
  New York *(G-9554)*

CASES: Jewelry
Ada Gems Corp .... G 212 719-0100
  New York *(G-8731)*
Astucci US Ltd .... G 212 725-3171
  New York *(G-8941)*
Bauble Bar Inc .... E 646 846-2044
  New York *(G-9027)*
K Displays .... F 718 854-6045
  Brooklyn *(G-2063)*
Unique Packaging Corporation .... G 514 341-5872
  Champlain *(G-3416)*

CASES: Nonrefrigerated, Exc Wood
R H Guest Incorporated .... G 718 675-7600
  Brooklyn *(G-2376)*

CASES: Packing, Nailed Or Lock Corner, Wood
Falvo Manufacturing Co Inc .... F 315 724-7925
  Utica *(G-15700)*
Technical Packaging Inc .... F 516 223-2300
  Baldwin *(G-545)*

CASES: Plastic
Bragley Mfg Co Inc .... E 718 622-7469
  Brooklyn *(G-1631)*
Displays By Rioux Inc .... G 315 458-3639
  North Syracuse *(G-12399)*
Hamlet Products Inc .... F 914 665-0307
  Mount Vernon *(G-8405)*
Sigma Worldwide LLC .... G 646 217-0629
  New York *(G-11583)*

CASES: Sample Cases
Fibre Case & Novelty Co Inc .... G 212 254-6060
  New York *(G-9798)*
Progressive Fibre Products Co .... E 212 566-2720
  New York *(G-11258)*

CASES: Shipping, Nailed Or Lock Corner, Wood
Bristol Boarding Inc .... G 585 271-7860
  Rochester *(G-13679)*
McIntosh Box & Pallet Co Inc .... F 315 789-8750
  Geneva *(G-5329)*

CASH REGISTER REPAIR SVCS
Precision Laser Technology LLC .... F 585 458-6208
  Rochester *(G-14036)*
SPX Flow Us LLC .... D 585 436-5550
  Rochester *(G-14140)*

CASINGS: Sheet Metal
Craft-Tech Mfg Corp .... G 631 563-4949
  Bohemia *(G-1001)*

CASKETS & ACCESS
Milso Industries Inc .... F 631 234-1133
  Hauppauge *(G-5892)*
North Hudson Woodcraft Corp .... E 315 429-3105
  Dolgeville *(G-4135)*

CASKETS WHOLESALERS
Milso Industries Inc .... F 631 234-1133
  Hauppauge *(G-5892)*

CAST STONE: Concrete
Steindl Cast Stone Co Inc .... G 718 296-8530
  Woodhaven *(G-16637)*

CASTERS
Dimanco Inc .... G 315 797-0470
  Utica *(G-15695)*

Workshop Art Fabrication .... F 845 331-0385
  Kingston *(G-6932)*

CASTINGS GRINDING: For The Trade
Grind .... G 646 558-3250
  New York *(G-9990)*

CASTINGS: Aerospace Investment, Ferrous
Brinkman Precision Inc .... D 585 429-5001
  West Henrietta *(G-16233)*
Cpp-Syracuse Inc .... E 315 687-0014
  Chittenango *(G-3504)*
Worldwide Resources Inc .... F 718 760-5000
  Brooklyn *(G-2659)*

CASTINGS: Aerospace, Aluminum
Broetje Automation-Usa Inc .... C 716 204-8640
  Williamsville *(G-16572)*
E M T Manufacturing Inc .... F 516 333-1917
  East Meadow *(G-4250)*
Eastern Strategic Materials .... F 212 332-1619
  New York *(G-9612)*

CASTINGS: Aerospace, Nonferrous, Exc Aluminum
Summit Aerospace Inc .... G 718 433-1326
  Long Island City *(G-7608)*

CASTINGS: Aluminum
Airflex Industrial Inc .... E 631 752-1234
  Farmingdale *(G-4710)*
Armstrong Mold Corporation .... E 315 437-1517
  East Syracuse *(G-4320)*
Armstrong Mold Corporation .... D 315 437-1517
  East Syracuse *(G-4321)*
Eastern Castings Co .... F 518 677-5610
  Cambridge *(G-3180)*
Hitachi Metals America Ltd .... E 914 694-9200
  Purchase *(G-13390)*
J & J Bronze & Aluminum Cast .... E 718 383-2111
  Brooklyn *(G-2021)*
Milward Alloys Inc .... E 716 434-5536
  Lockport *(G-7318)*
Taylor Metalworks Inc .... C 716 662-3113
  Orchard Park *(G-12745)*

CASTINGS: Brass, NEC, Exc Die
Discover Casting Inc .... F 212 302-5060
  New York *(G-9534)*

CASTINGS: Bronze, NEC, Exc Die
Art Bedi-Makky Foundry Corp .... G 718 383-4191
  Brooklyn *(G-1556)*
J & J Bronze & Aluminum Cast .... E 718 383-2111
  Brooklyn *(G-2021)*
Modern Art Foundry Inc .... E 718 728-2030
  Astoria *(G-436)*

CASTINGS: Die, Aluminum
Albest Metal Stamping Corp .... D 718 388-6000
  Brooklyn *(G-1500)*
Crown Die Casting Corp .... E 914 667-5400
  Mount Vernon *(G-8392)*
Greene Brass & Alum Fndry LLC .... G 607 656-4204
  Bloomville *(G-962)*
Greenfield Industries Inc .... D 516 623-9230
  Freeport *(G-5160)*
ITT Corporation .... D 315 568-2811
  Seneca Falls *(G-14777)*
ITT LLC .... D 914 641-2000
  Seneca Falls *(G-14781)*
Louis Iannettoni .... D 315 454-3231
  Syracuse *(G-15365)*
Pinnacle Manufacturing Co Inc .... E 585 343-5664
  Batavia *(G-633)*
Tpi Arcade Inc .... D 585 492-0122
  Arcade *(G-390)*

CASTINGS: Die, Lead
American Casting and Mfg Corp .... D 800 342-0333
  Plainview *(G-13035)*
American Casting and Mfg Corp .... G 516 349-7010
  Plainview *(G-13036)*

CASTINGS: Die, Nonferrous
Albest Metal Stamping Corp .... D 718 388-6000
  Brooklyn *(G-1500)*
AM Cast Inc .... F 631 750-1644
  Bohemia *(G-977)*
Crown Die Casting Corp .... E 914 667-5400
  Mount Vernon *(G-8392)*
Crown Novelty Works Inc .... G 631 253-0949
  Melville *(G-8013)*
Mar-A-Thon Filters Inc .... G 631 957-4774
  Lindenhurst *(G-7177)*

CASTINGS: Die, Zinc
Cast-All Corporation .... E 516 741-4025
  Mineola *(G-8212)*
Cast-All Corporation .... E 516 741-4025
  Mineola *(G-8211)*
Greenfield Die Casting Corp .... E 516 623-9230
  Freeport *(G-5159)*
Pinnacle Manufacturing Co Inc .... E 585 343-5664
  Batavia *(G-633)*

CASTINGS: Ductile
Hitachi Metals America Ltd .... E 914 694-9200
  Purchase *(G-13390)*
Jamestown Iron Works Inc .... F 716 665-2818
  Falconer *(G-4685)*
Noresco Industrial Group Inc .... E 516 759-3355
  Glen Cove *(G-5371)*

CASTINGS: Gray Iron
Auburn Foundry Inc .... E 315 253-4441
  Auburn *(G-464)*
Oneida Foundries Inc .... E 315 363-4570
  Oneida *(G-12614)*

CASTINGS: Machinery, Aluminum
Auto-Mate Technologies LLC .... F 631 727-8886
  Riverhead *(G-13564)*
Corbett Stves Pttern Works Inc .... E 585 546-7109
  Rochester *(G-13722)*
Ppi Corp .... D 585 243-0300
  Rochester *(G-14032)*

CASTINGS: Machinery, Nonferrous, Exc Die or Aluminum Copper
Plattco Corporation .... E 518 563-4640
  Plattsburgh *(G-13145)*
Zierick Manufacturing Corp .... D 800 882-8020
  Mount Kisco *(G-8361)*

CASTINGS: Precision
Buffalo Metal Casting Co Inc .... E 716 874-6211
  Buffalo *(G-2747)*
Controlled Castings Corp .... E 516 349-1718
  Plainview *(G-13045)*
General Motors LLC .... B 315 764-2000
  Massena *(G-7902)*
Lamothermic Corp .... D 845 278-6118
  Brewster *(G-1169)*
Miller Technology Inc .... G 631 694-2224
  Farmingdale *(G-4826)*
Quality Castings Inc .... E 732 409-3203
  Long Island City *(G-7566)*

CASTINGS: Steel
A & V Castings Inc .... G 212 997-0042
  New York *(G-8689)*

CATALOG & MAIL-ORDER HOUSES
Avcom of Virginia Inc .... D 585 924-4560
  Victor *(G-15830)*
Iac/Interactivecorp .... A 212 314-7300
  New York *(G-10164)*
Kate Spade & Company LLC .... B 212 354-4900
  New York *(G-10415)*
Lechler Laboratories Inc .... E 845 426-6800
  Spring Valley *(G-14998)*
Rda Holding Co .... E 914 238-1000
  New York *(G-11336)*
Valmont Inc .... F 212 685-1653
  New York *(G-11987)*

PRODUCT SECTION   CHEMICALS & ALLIED PRDTS, WHOLESALE: Chemical Additives

CATALOG SHOWROOMS

Studio 21 LA Inc ....E 718 965-6579
  Brooklyn *(G-2525)*

CATALYSTS: Chemical

Ames Goldsmith Corp ....F 518 792-7435
  Glens Falls *(G-5414)*
Next Potential LLC ....G 401 742-5190
  New York *(G-10959)*
Signa Chemistry Inc ....F 212 933-4101
  New York *(G-11586)*
UOP LLC ....E 716 879-7600
  Tonawanda *(G-15588)*

CATAPULTS

Catapult ....G 323 839-6204
  New York *(G-9227)*
Laser & Electron Beam Inc ....G 603 626-6080
  New York *(G-10520)*

CATERERS

Delicious Foods Inc ....F 718 446-9352
  Corona *(G-3843)*
Lifc Corp ....G 516 426-5737
  Port Washington *(G-13282)*
Soutine Inc ....G 212 496-1450
  New York *(G-11655)*

CEILING SYSTEMS: Luminous, Commercial

Green Beam Led Inc ....G 718 439-6262
  Brooklyn *(G-1949)*

CEMENT & CONCRETE RELATED PRDTS & EQPT: Bituminous

Presti Ready Mix Concrete Inc ....G 516 378-6006
  Freeport *(G-5175)*

CEMENT ROCK: Crushed & Broken

Schaefer Entps Deposit Inc ....E 607 467-4990
  Deposit *(G-4110)*

CEMENT: Heat Resistant

Roccera LLC ....F 585 426-0887
  Rochester *(G-14077)*

CEMENT: High Temperature, Refractory, Nonclay

Silicon Carbide Products Inc ....E 607 562-8599
  Horseheads *(G-6329)*

CEMENT: Hydraulic

Lafarge North America Inc ....E 716 651-9235
  Lancaster *(G-7027)*
Lafarge North America Inc ....G 716 854-5791
  Buffalo *(G-2918)*
Lafarge North America Inc ....E 716 772-2621
  Lockport *(G-7313)*
Lafarge North America Inc ....D 914 930-3027
  Buchanan *(G-2673)*
Lafarge North America Inc ....E 518 756-5000
  Ravena *(G-13454)*
Lafarge North America Inc ....F 716 876-8788
  Tonawanda *(G-15554)*
Upstone Materials Inc ....G 518 873-2275
  Lewis *(G-7137)*

CEMENT: Masonry

Ciment St-Laurent Inc ....C 518 943-4040
  Catskill *(G-3302)*
Lafarge Building Materials Inc ....F 518 756-5000
  Ravena *(G-13453)*

CEMENT: Natural

Euro Gear (usa) Inc ....G 518 578-1775
  Plattsburgh *(G-13120)*
Hanson Aggregates New York LLC ..F 716 665-4620
  Jamesville *(G-6766)*

CEMENT: Portland

Holcim (us) Inc ....G 518 328-8478
  Hudson *(G-6353)*

Lehigh Cement Company ....C 518 792-1137
  Glens Falls *(G-5432)*
Pallette Stone Corporation ....E 518 584-2421
  Gansevoort *(G-5244)*

CEMETERY MEMORIAL DEALERS

Glen Plaza Marble & Gran Inc ....G 516 671-1100
  Glen Cove *(G-5368)*
North Shore Monuments Inc ....G 516 759-2156
  Glen Head *(G-5385)*

CERAMIC FIBER

Argosy Composite Advanced Mate ..F 212 268-0003
  New York *(G-8906)*
Cetek Inc ....E 845 452-3510
  Poughkeepsie *(G-13331)*
Enrg Inc ....F 716 873-2939
  Buffalo *(G-2820)*
Heany Industries Inc ....D 585 889-2700
  Scottsville *(G-14750)*
Starfire Systems Inc ....F 518 899-9336
  Glenville *(G-5447)*
Ufx Holding I Corporation ....F 212 644-5900
  New York *(G-11933)*
Ufx Holding II Corporation ....F 212 644-5900
  New York *(G-11934)*
Unifrax Holding Co ....F 212 644-5900
  New York *(G-11943)*
Unifrax I LLC ....C 716 768-6500
  Tonawanda *(G-15587)*
Unifrax I LLC ....C 716 696-3000
  Tonawanda *(G-15586)*

CERAMIC FLOOR & WALL TILE WHOLESALERS

Dal-Tile Corporation 718 894-9574
  Maspeth *(G-7834)*
Dal-Tile Corporation ....G 914 835-1801
  Harrison *(G-5727)*

CHAIN: Welded, Made From Purchased Wire

All-Lifts Incorporated ....E 518 465-3461
  Albany *(G-38)*
Columbus McKinnon Corporation ...C 716 689-5400
  Getzville *(G-5344)*
Columbus McKinnon Corporation ...C 716 689-5400
  Getzville *(G-5345)*
Columbus McKinnon Corporation ...C 716 689-5400
  Getzville *(G-5346)*

CHAINS: Forged

Dragon Trading Inc ....G 212 717-1496
  New York *(G-9572)*
Extreme Shale Performance LLC ....G 814 688-7956
  Elmira *(G-4485)*

CHAMBERS & CAISSONS

Hyperbaric Technologies Inc ....G 518 842-3030
  Amsterdam *(G-340)*

CHANDELIERS: Commercial

Global Lighting Inc ....G 914 591-4095
  Yonkers *(G-16762)*
Lite-Makers Inc ....E 718 739-9300
  Jamaica *(G-6656)*
Santucci Custom Lighting ....F 866 853-1929
  Clinton *(G-3588)*

CHANDELIERS: Residential

Swarovski Lighting Ltd ....B 518 324-6378
  Plattsburgh *(G-13162)*

CHARCOAL: Activated

Calgon Carbon Corporation ....G 716 531-9113
  North Tonawanda *(G-12421)*
Carbon Activated Corporation ....G 716 662-2005
  Orchard Park *(G-12705)*

CHASSIS: Motor Vehicle

Wendys Auto Express Inc ....G 845 624-6100
  Nanuet *(G-8468)*

CHEESE WHOLESALERS

Alps Provision Co Inc ....E 718 721-4477
  Astoria *(G-421)*

CHEMICAL INDICATORS

LTS Inc ....F 845 494-2940
  Orangeburg *(G-12682)*

CHEMICAL PROCESSING MACHINERY & EQPT

Charles Ross & Son Company ....D 631 234-0500
  Hauppauge *(G-5788)*
Maharlika Holdings LLC ....F 631 319-6203
  Ronkonkoma *(G-14373)*
National Equipment Corporation ....F 718 585-0200
  Harrison *(G-5731)*
National Equipment Corporation ....E 718 585-0200
  Bronx *(G-1338)*
Spectrum Catalysts Inc ....G 631 560-3683
  Central Islip *(G-3384)*
Stainless Design Concepts Ltd ......E 845 246-3631
  Saugerties *(G-14617)*
Surepure Inc ....G 917 368-8480
  New York *(G-11750)*
West Metal Works Inc ....F 716 895-4900
  Buffalo *(G-3128)*

CHEMICAL: Sodm Compnds/Salts, Inorg, Exc Rfnd Sodm Chloride

Chemtrade Chemicals US LLC ....G 315 478-2323
  Syracuse *(G-15277)*

CHEMICALS & ALLIED PRDTS WHOLESALERS, NEC

Aithaca Chemical Corp ....F 516 229-2330
  Uniondale *(G-15662)*
Caswell Inc ....F 315 946-1213
  Lyons *(G-7682)*
Chemlube International LLC ....F 914 381-5800
  Harrison *(G-5725)*
Chemlube Marketing Inc ....F 914 381-5800
  Harrison *(G-5726)*
Ecological Laboratories Inc ....D 516 823-3441
  Island Park *(G-6513)*
FBC Chemical Corporation ....G 716 681-1581
  Lancaster *(G-7019)*
Finger Lakes Chemicals Inc ....E 585 454-4760
  Rochester *(G-13804)*
Island Pyrochemical Inds Corp ......C 516 746-2100
  Mineola *(G-8231)*
Jad Corp of America ....E 718 762-8900
  College Point *(G-3650)*
Nalco Company LLC ....E 518 796-1985
  Saratoga Springs *(G-14590)*
Poly Scientific R&D Corp ....E 631 586-0400
  Bay Shore *(G-14720)*
Tattersall Industries LLC ....E 518 381-4270
  Schenectady *(G-14720)*
Thatcher Company New York Inc ...E 315 589-9330
  Williamson *(G-16562)*
Water Wise of America Inc ....F 585 232-1210
  Rochester *(G-14203)*

CHEMICALS & ALLIED PRDTS, WHOLESALE: Alkalines & Chlorine

Arcadia Chem Preservative LLC .....G 516 466-5258
  Great Neck *(G-5535)*

CHEMICALS & ALLIED PRDTS, WHOLESALE: Anti-Corrosion Prdts

Engineering Maint Pdts Inc ....F 516 624-9774
  Oyster Bay *(G-12813)*

CHEMICALS & ALLIED PRDTS, WHOLESALE: Aromatic

Classic Flavors Fragrances Inc ....G 212 777-0004
  New York *(G-9320)*

CHEMICALS & ALLIED PRDTS, WHOLESALE: Chemical Additives

Mitsui Chemicals America Inc ....E 914 253-0777
  Rye Brook *(G-14493)*

CHEMICALS & ALLIED PRDTS, WHOLESALE: Chemical Additives

PRODUCT SECTION

Specialty Minerals Inc ....E....... 212 878-1800
New York *(G-11661)*

CHEMICALS & ALLIED PRDTS, WHOLESALE: Chemicals, Indl

Dynasty Chemical Corp ....E....... 518 463-1146
Menands *(G-8084)*
Umicore USA Inc ....E....... 919 874-7171
Glens Falls *(G-5442)*

CHEMICALS & ALLIED PRDTS, WHOLESALE: Dry Ice

South Shore Ice Co Inc ....F....... 516 379-2056
Roosevelt *(G-14437)*

CHEMICALS & ALLIED PRDTS, WHOLESALE: Essential Oils

Flavormatic Industries LLC ....E....... 845 297-9100
Wappingers Falls *(G-15930)*

CHEMICALS & ALLIED PRDTS, WHOLESALE: Oxygen

Praxair Distribution Inc ....G....... 315 457-5821
Liverpool *(G-7256)*

CHEMICALS & ALLIED PRDTS, WHOLESALE: Plastics Materials, NEC

Ampac Paper LLC ....G....... 845 713-6600
Walden *(G-15890)*
Josh Packaging Inc ....E....... 631 822-1660
Hauppauge *(G-5854)*
Marval Industries Inc ....D....... 914 381-2400
Mamaroneck *(G-7748)*

CHEMICALS & ALLIED PRDTS, WHOLESALE: Plastics Prdts, NEC

Albea Cosmetics America Inc ....E....... 212 371-5100
New York *(G-8784)*
Autronic Plastics Inc ....D....... 516 333-7577
Central Islip *(G-3357)*
Broder Mfg Inc ....G....... 718 366-1667
Brooklyn *(G-1636)*
Vinyl Materials Inc ....E....... 631 586-9444
Deer Park *(G-4060)*

CHEMICALS & ALLIED PRDTS, WHOLESALE: Plastics Sheets & Rods

Astra Products Inc ....G....... 631 464-4747
Copiague *(G-3753)*

CHEMICALS & ALLIED PRDTS, WHOLESALE: Polyurethane Prdts

Vincent Manufacturing Co Inc ....F....... 315 823-0280
Little Falls *(G-7216)*

CHEMICALS & ALLIED PRDTS, WHOLESALE: Salts & Polishes, Indl

R Schleider Contracting Corp ....G....... 631 269-4249
Kings Park *(G-6886)*

CHEMICALS & ALLIED PRDTS, WHOLESALE: Spec Clean/Sanitation

Prestige Consmr Healthcare Inc ....D....... 914 524-6800
Tarrytown *(G-15488)*

CHEMICALS & ALLIED PRDTS, WHOLESALE: Syn Resin, Rub/Plastic

Clarence Resins and Chemicals ....G....... 716 406-9804
Clarence Center *(G-3543)*

CHEMICALS & ALLIED PRDTS, WHOLESALE: Waxes, Exc Petroleum

Collinite Corporation ....G....... 315 732-2282
Utica *(G-15684)*

CHEMICALS/ALLIED PRDTS, WHOL: Coal Tar Prdts, Prim/Intermdt

Castoleum Corporation ....F....... 914 664-5877
Mount Vernon *(G-8385)*

CHEMICALS: Agricultural

Agrochem Inc ....E....... 518 226-4850
Saratoga Springs *(G-14569)*
E I Du Pont De Nemours & Co ....C....... 718 761-0043
Staten Island *(G-15071)*
FMC Corporation ....E....... 716 735-3761
Middleport *(G-8132)*

CHEMICALS: Alcohols

Full Motion Beverage Inc ....G....... 631 585-1100
Plainview *(G-13059)*

CHEMICALS: Aluminum Chloride

Vanchlor Company Inc ....F....... 716 434-2624
Lockport *(G-7341)*
Vanchlor Company Inc ....F....... 716 434-2624
Lockport *(G-7342)*

CHEMICALS: Aluminum Compounds

Benzsay & Harrison Inc ....G....... 518 895-2311
Delanson *(G-4067)*
Somerville Acquisitions Co Inc ....F....... 845 856-5261
Huguenot *(G-6386)*
Somerville Tech Group Inc ....D....... 908 782-9500
Huguenot *(G-6387)*

CHEMICALS: Aluminum Oxide

Meliorum Technologies Inc ....G....... 585 313-0616
Rochester *(G-13935)*

CHEMICALS: Brine

Texas Brine Company LLC ....G....... 585 495-6228
Wyoming *(G-16701)*

CHEMICALS: Calcium & Calcium Compounds

Minerals Technologies Inc ....E....... 212 878-1800
New York *(G-10817)*

CHEMICALS: Compounds Or Salts, Iron, Ferric Or Ferrous

North American Hoganas Inc ....E....... 716 285-3451
Niagara Falls *(G-12315)*

CHEMICALS: Fire Retardant

Flame Control Coatings LLC ....E....... 716 282-1399
Niagara Falls *(G-12286)*
Gordon Fire Equipment LLC ....G....... 845 691-5700
Highland *(G-6143)*
International Fire-Shield Inc ....F....... 315 255-1006
Auburn *(G-483)*
Kent Chemical Corporation ....E....... 212 521-1700
New York *(G-10436)*
Safeguard Inc ....F....... 631 929-3273
Wading River *(G-15886)*
Supresta US LLC ....E....... 914 674-9434
Ardsley *(G-396)*

CHEMICALS: Formaldehyde

Hexion Inc ....E....... 518 792-8040
South Glens Falls *(G-14936)*
Oak-Bark Corporation ....E....... 518 372-5691
Scotia *(G-14745)*

CHEMICALS: Fuel Tank Or Engine Cleaning

Amtek Research LLC ....E....... 416 400-2906
Niagara Falls *(G-12261)*

CHEMICALS: High Purity Grade, Organic

Molecular Glasses Inc ....G....... 585 210-2861
Rochester *(G-13951)*

CHEMICALS: High Purity, Refined From Technical Grade

Aithaca Chemical Corp ....F....... 516 229-2330
Uniondale *(G-15662)*
Germanium Corp America Inc ....F....... 315 853-4900
Clinton *(G-3585)*
Incitec Pivot Limited ....G....... 212 238-3010
New York *(G-10192)*

CHEMICALS: Hydrogen Peroxide

US Peroxide ....G....... 716 775-5585
Grand Island *(G-5517)*

CHEMICALS: Inorganic, NEC

Akzo Nobel Chemicals LLC ....C....... 914 674-5008
Dobbs Ferry *(G-4129)*
Amtek Research LLC ....E....... 416 400-2906
Niagara Falls *(G-12261)*
Amtek Research LLC ....E....... 212 537-6462
Niagara Falls *(G-12262)*
Anchor Commerce Trading Corp ....G....... 516 881-3485
Atlantic Beach *(G-455)*
Arkema Inc ....C....... 585 243-6359
Piffard *(G-12995)*
Auterra Inc ....E....... 518 382-9600
Schenectady *(G-14650)*
Byk USA Inc ....E....... 845 469-5800
Chester *(G-3470)*
Carbon Activated Corporation ....E....... 716 677-6661
Blasdell *(G-925)*
Cerion Energy Inc ....E....... 585 271-5630
Rochester *(G-13703)*
Cerion LLC ....E....... 585 271-5630
Rochester *(G-13704)*
Chemours Company Fc LLC ....E....... 716 278-5100
Niagara Falls *(G-12271)*
Chemtrade Chemicals US LLC ....E....... 315 430-7650
Syracuse *(G-15276)*
Danisco US Inc ....D....... 585 277-4300
Rochester *(G-13734)*
Dynasty Chemical Corp ....E....... 518 463-1146
Menands *(G-8084)*
Element St Johns Corp ....G....... 917 349-2139
Brooklyn *(G-1824)*
Elementis Srl Inc ....C....... 845 692-3914
Huguenot *(G-6385)*
Emco Chemical (usa) Corp ....E....... 718 797-3652
Brooklyn *(G-1828)*
Esm Group Inc ....F....... 716 446-8914
Amherst *(G-226)*
Esm Group Inc ....G....... 724 265-1766
Buffalo *(G-2822)*
Esm Special Metals & Tech Inc ....E....... 716 446-8914
Amherst *(G-228)*
Ferro Corporation ....E....... 585 586-8770
East Rochester *(G-4284)*
Ferro Corporation ....C....... 315 536-3357
Penn Yan *(G-12953)*
Ferro Electronics Materials ....C....... 716 278-9400
Niagara Falls *(G-12285)*
FMC Corporation ....E....... 716 735-3761
Middleport *(G-8132)*
Hampshire Chemical Corp ....D....... 315 539-9221
Waterloo *(G-15995)*
Innovative Municipal Pdts US ....E....... 800 387-5777
Glenmont *(G-5412)*
Kowa American Corporation ....E....... 212 303-7800
New York *(G-10474)*
Lawn Elements Inc ....F....... 631 656-9711
Holbrook *(G-6194)*
Moog Inc ....D....... 716 731-6300
Niagara Falls *(G-12311)*
Multisorb Tech Intl LLC ....G....... 716 824-8900
Buffalo *(G-2957)*
Multisorb Technologies Inc ....E....... 716 656-1402
Buffalo *(G-2958)*
Poly Scientific R&D Corp ....E....... 631 586-0400
Bay Shore *(G-707)*
Polyset Company Inc ....E....... 518 664-6000
Mechanicville *(G-7932)*
S E A Supplies Ltd ....F....... 516 694-6677
Plainview *(G-13086)*
Scientific Polymer Products ....G....... 585 265-0413
Ontario *(G-12665)*
Specialty Minerals Inc ....G....... 518 585-7982
Ticonderoga *(G-15513)*
Specialty Minerals Inc ....E....... 212 878-1800
New York *(G-11661)*

PRODUCT SECTION

CHIMNEYS & FITTINGS

Srlh Holdings Inc ....C 929 529-7951
  Huguenot *(G-6388)*
Tangram Company LLC ....E 631 758-0460
  Holtsville *(G-6247)*
Thatcher Company New York Inc ....E 315 589-9330
  Williamson *(G-16562)*
Vandemark Chemical Inc ....D 716 433-6764
  Lockport *(G-7343)*
Washingtom Mills Elec Mnrls ....D 716 278-6600
  Niagara Falls *(G-12349)*

CHEMICALS: Isotopes, Radioactive

Isonics Corporation ....G 212 356-7400
  New York *(G-10277)*

CHEMICALS: Lithium Compounds, Inorganic

Alpha-En Corporation ....F 914 418-2000
  Yonkers *(G-16732)*

CHEMICALS: Medicinal

Biobat Inc ....G 718 270-1011
  Brooklyn *(G-1616)*
Biotemper ....G 516 302-7985
  Carle Place *(G-3263)*
Proper Chemical Ltd ....G 631 420-8000
  Farmingdale *(G-4860)*

CHEMICALS: Medicinal, Organic, Uncompounded, Bulk

Asept Pak Inc ....E 518 651-2026
  Malone *(G-7719)*
Good Earth Inc ....G 716 684-8111
  Lancaster *(G-7021)*

CHEMICALS: Metal Salts/Compounds, Exc Sodium, Potassium/Alum

PVS Technologies Inc ....E 716 825-5762
  Buffalo *(G-3021)*

CHEMICALS: NEC

Akzo Nobel Chemicals LLC ....G 716 778-8554
  Burt *(G-3143)*
Akzo Nobel Chemicals LLC ....C 914 674-5008
  Dobbs Ferry *(G-4129)*
Anabec Inc ....G 716 759-1674
  Clarence *(G-3524)*
Ask Chemicals Hi-Tech LLC ....C 607 587-9146
  Alfred Station *(G-185)*
Balchem Corporation ....B 845 326-5600
  New Hampton *(G-8497)*
Barson Composites Corporation ....E 516 752-7882
  Old Bethpage *(G-12583)*
Bcp Ingredients Inc ....D 845 326-5600
  New Hampton *(G-8498)*
Bonide Products Inc ....C 315 736-8231
  Oriskany *(G-12751)*
C & A Service Inc ....G 516 354-1200
  Floral Park *(G-4958)*
Calfonex Company ....F 845 778-2212
  Walden *(G-15892)*
Citrus and Allied Essences Ltd ....C 516 354-1200
  Floral Park *(G-4960)*
Classic Flavors Fragrances Inc ....G 212 777-0004
  New York *(G-9320)*
Danisco US Inc ....D 585 256-5200
  Rochester *(G-13733)*
Fitzsimmons Systems Inc ....F 315 214-7010
  Cazenovia *(G-3319)*
Hampshire Chemical Corp ....D 315 539-9221
  Waterloo *(G-15995)*
I A S National Inc ....E 631 423-6900
  Huntington Station *(G-6447)*
Indium Corporation of America ....E 315 793-8200
  Utica *(G-15713)*
Instrumentation Laboratory Co ....C 845 680-0028
  Orangeburg *(G-12681)*
Kaneka America LLC ....D 212 705-4340
  New York *(G-10404)*
Micro Powders Inc ....E 914 332-6400
  Tarrytown *(G-15483)*
Momentive Performance LLC ....G 281 325-3536
  Waterford *(G-15979)*
Momentive Performance Mtls Inc ....D 914 784-4807
  Tarrytown *(G-15484)*
Monroe Fluid Technology Inc ....E 585 392-3434
  Hilton *(G-6157)*
Nalco Company LLC ....E 518 796-1985
  Saratoga Springs *(G-14590)*
New Fine Chemicals Inc ....G 631 321-8151
  Lindenhurst *(G-7183)*
Pure Kemika LLC ....G 718 745-2200
  Bellmore *(G-792)*
PVS Chemical Solutions Inc ....D 716 825-5762
  Buffalo *(G-3020)*
Reddi Car Corp ....G 631 589-3141
  Sayville *(G-14634)*
Rochester Midland Corporation ....C 585 336-2200
  Rochester *(G-14088)*
Royce Associates A Ltd Partnr ....G 516 367-6298
  Jericho *(G-6800)*
Specialty Minerals Inc ....E 212 878-1800
  New York *(G-11661)*
Tam Ceramics LLC ....D 716 278-9480
  Niagara Falls *(G-12341)*
Tangram Company LLC ....E 631 758-0460
  Holtsville *(G-6247)*
US Polychemical Holding Corp ....E 845 356-5530
  Spring Valley *(G-15013)*
Utility Manufacturing Co Inc ....E 516 997-6300
  Westbury *(G-16384)*
Venue Graphics Supply Inc ....E 718 361-1690
  Long Island City *(G-7629)*
Wyeth Holdings LLC ....D 845 602-5000
  Pearl River *(G-12913)*
Yiwen Usa Inc ....F 212 370-0828
  New York *(G-12163)*

CHEMICALS: Organic, NEC

Akzo Nobel Chemicals LLC ....G 716 778-8554
  Burt *(G-3143)*
Akzo Nobel Functional Chem LLC ......D 845 276-8200
  Brewster *(G-1155)*
Ames Goldsmith Corp ....F 518 792-7435
  Glens Falls *(G-5414)*
Arcadia Chem Preservative LLC ....G 516 466-5258
  Great Neck *(G-5535)*
Arkema Inc ....C 585 243-6359
  Piffard *(G-12995)*
Bamboo Global Industries ....G 973 943-1878
  New York *(G-9010)*
BASF Corporation ....B 914 737-2554
  Peekskill *(G-12917)*
BASF Corporation ....F 914 785-2000
  Tarrytown *(G-15475)*
BASF Corporation ....B 518 465-6534
  Rensselaer *(G-13473)*
BASF Corporation ....C 631 689-0200
  East Setauket *(G-4299)*
Caltex International Ltd ....E 315 425-1040
  Syracuse *(G-15268)*
China Ruitai Intl Holdings Ltd ....G 718 740-2278
  Hollis *(G-6232)*
Danisco US Inc ....D 585 256-5200
  Rochester *(G-13733)*
Enviro Service & Supply Corp ....F 347 838-6500
  Staten Island *(G-15074)*
Evonik Corporation ....E 518 233-7090
  Waterford *(G-15975)*
Genencor International Inc ....G 585 256-5200
  Rochester *(G-13826)*
Hampshire Chemical Corp ....D 315 539-9221
  Waterloo *(G-15995)*
Henpecked Husband Farms Corp ....G 631 728-2800
  Speonk *(G-14985)*
International Mtls & Sups Inc ....G 518 834-9899
  Keeseville *(G-6851)*
Islechem LLC ....E 716 773-8401
  Grand Island *(G-5503)*
Jos H Lowenstein and Sons Inc ....D 718 388-5410
  Brooklyn *(G-2046)*
Marval Industries Inc ....D 914 381-2400
  Mamaroneck *(G-7748)*
Poly Scientific R&D Corp ....E 631 586-0400
  Bay Shore *(G-707)*
Polymer Slutions Group Fin LLC ....G 212 771-1717
  New York *(G-11217)*
Rose Solomon Co ....E 718 855-1788
  Brooklyn *(G-2415)*
Royce Associates A Ltd Partnr ....G 516 367-6298
  Jericho *(G-6800)*
Solvents Company Inc ....F 631 595-9300
  Kingston *(G-6917)*
Telechemische Inc ....G 845 561-3237
  Newburgh *(G-12247)*
Twin Lake Chemical Inc ....F 716 433-3824
  Lockport *(G-7339)*
United Biochemicals LLC ....E 716 731-5161
  Sanborn *(G-14555)*

CHEMICALS: Phenol

Si Group Inc ....C 518 347-4200
  Schenectady *(G-14713)*
Si Group Inc ....C 518 347-4200
  Rotterdam Junction *(G-14462)*

CHEMICALS: Silica Compounds

Precision Elctro Mnrl Pmco Inc ....E 716 284-2484
  Niagara Falls *(G-12326)*

CHEMICALS: Sodium Bicarbonate

Church & Dwight Co Inc ....F 518 887-5109
  Schenectady *(G-14662)*

CHEMICALS: Sodium/Potassium Cmpnds, Exc Bleach, Alkalies/Alum

Tibro Water Technologies Ltd ....F 647 426-3415
  Sherrill *(G-14824)*

CHEMICALS: Sulfur Chloride

PVS Chemical Solutions Inc ....D 716 825-5762
  Buffalo *(G-3020)*
Sabre Energy Services LLC ....F 518 514-1572
  Slingerlands *(G-14890)*

CHEMICALS: Water Treatment

Coventya Inc ....D 216 351-1500
  Oriskany *(G-12753)*
Crystal Fusion Tech Inc ....F 631 253-9800
  Lindenhurst *(G-7167)*
Cytec Industries Inc ....D 716 372-9650
  Olean *(G-12598)*
Ecological Laboratories Inc ....E 516 823-3441
  Island Park *(G-6513)*
Halfmoon Town Water Department .....G 518 233-7489
  Waterford *(G-15976)*
Solenis LLC ....E 718 383-1717
  Brooklyn *(G-2498)*
Solenis LLC ....C 315 461-4730
  Liverpool *(G-7262)*
Water Wise of America Inc ....F 585 232-1210
  Rochester *(G-14203)*

CHEWING GUM

Ford Gum & Machine Company Inc ....D 716 542-4561
  Akron *(G-18)*
Sweetworks Inc ....C 716 634-4545
  Buffalo *(G-3082)*

CHILD DAY CARE SVCS

Parents Guide Network Corp ....E 212 213-8840
  New York *(G-11110)*

CHILDREN'S & INFANTS' CLOTHING STORES

Slims Bagels Unlimited Inc ....E 718 229-1140
  Oakland Gardens *(G-12526)*

CHILDREN'S WEAR STORES

JM Originals Inc ....C 845 647-3003
  Ellenville *(G-4439)*
S & C Bridal LLC ....F 212 789-7000
  New York *(G-11454)*
S & C Bridals LLC ....G 213 624-4477
  New York *(G-11455)*

CHIMES: Electric

Analog Digital Technology LLC ....G 585 698-1845
  Rochester *(G-13631)*
Ingham Industries Inc ....G 631 242-2493
  Holbrook *(G-6189)*

CHIMNEY CAPS: Concrete

American Chimney Supplies Inc ....G 631 434-2020
  Hauppauge *(G-5764)*

CHIMNEYS & FITTINGS

American Chimney Supplies Inc ....G 631 434-2020
  Hauppauge *(G-5764)*

CHIMNEYS & FITTINGS

Chimney Doctors Americas Corp .... G 631 868-3586
  Bayport *(G-737)*

CHINA COOKWARE

Prime Cook (wttc) Inc .... G 646 881-0068
  Flushing *(G-5039)*
Swissmar Inc .... G 905 764-1121
  Niagara Falls *(G-12339)*

CHLORINE

Indian Springs Mfg Co Inc .... F 315 635-6101
  Baldwinsville *(G-556)*

CHOCOLATE, EXC CANDY FROM BEANS: Chips, Powder, Block, Syrup

5th Avenue Chocolatiere Ltd .... G 212 935-5454
  Freeport *(G-5134)*
Associated Brands Inc .... B 585 798-3475
  Medina *(G-7970)*
Big Heart Pet Brands .... E 716 891-6566
  Buffalo *(G-2733)*
Eating Evolved Inc .... G 516 510-2601
  East Setauket *(G-4300)*
Gnosis Chocolate Inc .... G 646 688-5549
  Long Island City *(G-7458)*
Hershey Kiss 203 Inc .... G 516 503-3740
  Wantagh *(G-15922)*
Jo-Mart Candies Corp .... F 718 375-1277
  Brooklyn *(G-2041)*
Joyva Corp .... D 718 497-0170
  Brooklyn *(G-2052)*
Lanco Corporation .... C 631 231-2300
  Ronkonkoma *(G-14368)*
Momn Pops Inc .... E 845 567-0640
  Cornwall *(G-3834)*
Noras Candy Shop .... F 315 337-4530
  Rome *(G-14262)*
Robert Pikcilingis .... F 518 355-1860
  Altamont *(G-201)*
Settons Intl Foods Inc .... D 631 543-8090
  Commack *(G-3702)*
Simply Natural Foods LLC .... C 631 543-9600
  Commack *(G-3703)*
The Chocolate Shop .... G 716 882-5055
  Buffalo *(G-3092)*

CHOCOLATE, EXC CANDY FROM PURCH CHOC: Chips, Powder, Block

5th Avenue Chocolatiere LLC .... E 516 868-8070
  Freeport *(G-5133)*
Chocolate Lady LLC .... G 516 532-0551
  Port Jervis *(G-13225)*
Commodore Chocolatier USA Inc .... F 845 561-3960
  Newburgh *(G-12218)*
Ctac Holdings LLC .... E 212 924-2280
  Brooklyn *(G-1738)*
Dilese International Inc .... F 716 855-3500
  Buffalo *(G-2801)*
Dolce Vite International LLC .... F 713 962-5767
  Brooklyn *(G-1785)*
Doma Marketing Inc .... G 516 684-1111
  Port Washington *(G-13254)*
Emvi Inc .... G 518 883-5111
  Broadalbin *(G-1188)*
Godiva Chocolatier Inc .... E 718 271-3603
  Elmhurst *(G-4466)*
Greenwood Winery LLC .... E 315 432-8132
  East Syracuse *(G-4343)*
Lady-N-Th-wndow Chocolates Inc .... F 631 549-1059
  Huntington *(G-6403)*
Le Chocolate of Rockland LLC .... E 845 533-4125
  Suffern *(G-15192)*
Menrose USA LLC .... E 718 221-5540
  Brooklyn *(G-2191)*
Nibmor Project LLC .... F 718 374-5091
  Great Neck *(G-5573)*
Reserve Confections Inc .... F 845 371-7744
  Spring Valley *(G-15007)*
Rip Van Wafels Inc .... E 415 529-5403
  Brooklyn *(G-2404)*
Sweetworks Inc .... F 716 634-4545
  Buffalo *(G-3082)*
Yes Were Nuts Ltd .... E 516 374-1940
  Hewlett *(G-6055)*

CHRISTMAS TREE LIGHTING SETS: Electric

Rbw Studio LLC .... E 212 388-1621
  Brooklyn *(G-2388)*

CHUCKS

Northfeld Precision Instr Corp .... E 516 431-1112
  Island Park *(G-6517)*

CHURCHES

Christian Press Inc 718 886-4400
  Flushing *(G-4991)*

CHUTES & TROUGHS

Sargent Manufacturing Inc 212 722-7000
  New York *(G-11488)*

CHUTES: Coal, Sheet Metal, Prefabricated

Fenton Mobility Products Inc 716 484-7014
  Randolph *(G-13447)*

CIGAR LIGHTERS EXC PRECIOUS METAL

Arcadia Mfg Group Inc .... E 518 434-6213
  Green Island *(G-5602)*
Arcadia Mfg Group Inc .... E 518 434-6213
  Menands *(G-8081)*

CIGARETTE & CIGAR PRDTS & ACCESS

Iquit Cig LLC .... G 718 475-1422
  Brooklyn *(G-2014)*
Saakshi Inc .... G 315 475-3988
  Syracuse *(G-15412)*

CIRCUIT BOARDS, PRINTED: Television & Radio

Buffalo Circuits Inc .... G 716 662-2113
  Orchard Park *(G-12703)*
Kendall Circuits Inc .... E 631 473-3636
  Mount Sinai *(G-8368)*
Sanmina Corporation .... B 607 689-5000
  Owego *(G-12803)*
TCS Electronics Inc .... E 585 337-4301
  Farmington *(G-4920)*

CIRCUIT BOARDS: Wiring

Coast To Coast Circuits Inc .... E 585 254-2980
  Rochester *(G-13715)*
Nationwide Circuits Inc .... E 585 328-0791
  Rochester *(G-13963)*
Stever-Locke Industries Inc .... G 585 624-3450
  Honeoye Falls *(G-6274)*

CIRCUITS, INTEGRATED: Hybrid

Crystalonics Inc .... F 631 981-6140
  Ronkonkoma *(G-14330)*
Emtron Hybrids Inc .... F 631 924-9668
  Yaphank *(G-16710)*
General Microwave Corporation .... F 516 802-0900
  Syosset *(G-15219)*

CIRCUITS: Electronic

A K Allen Co Inc .... C 516 747-5450
  Melville *(G-7996)*
A R V Precision Mfg Inc .... G 631 293-9643
  Farmingdale *(G-4705)*
Accessories For Electronics .... E 631 847-0158
  South Hempstead *(G-14941)*
Adco Circuits Inc .... G 716 668-6600
  Buffalo *(G-2685)*
Advance Circuit Technology Inc .... E 585 328-2000
  Rochester *(G-13604)*
Aeroflex Plainview Inc .... B 516 694-6700
  Plainview *(G-13033)*
Aeroflex Plainview Inc .... G 631 231-9100
  Hauppauge *(G-5756)*
All Shore Industries Inc .... F 718 720-0018
  Staten Island *(G-15042)*
Alloy Machine & Tool Co Inc .... G 516 593-3445
  Lynbrook *(G-7660)*
American Quality Technology .... F 607 777-9488
  Binghamton *(G-861)*
Anaren Inc .... B 315 432-8909
  East Syracuse *(G-4318)*

B H M Metal Products Co .... G 845 292-5297
  Kauneonga Lake *(G-6849)*
Canfield Electronics Inc .... F 631 585-4100
  Lindenhurst *(G-7165)*
Celmet Co .... G 585 647-1760
  Newark *(G-12194)*
Chiplogic Inc .... F 631 617-6317
  Yaphank *(G-16706)*
Cloud Toronto Inc .... F 408 569-4542
  Williamsville *(G-16576)*
Dynamic Hybirds Inc .... G 315 426-8110
  Syracuse *(G-15308)*
Eastland Electronics Co Inc .... G 631 580-3800
  Ronkonkoma *(G-14337)*
Fei Communications Inc .... E 516 794-4500
  Uniondale *(G-15666)*
Hudson Valley Tech Dev Ctr Inc .... F 845 391-8214
  Highland *(G-6144)*
Hypres Inc .... E 914 592-1190
  Elmsford *(G-4545)*
IEC Electronics Corp .... B 315 331-7742
  Newark *(G-12196)*
Imrex LLC .... B 516 479-3675
  Oyster Bay *(G-12814)*
Island Circuits International .... G 516 625-5555
  College Point *(G-3649)*
Island Research and Dev Corp .... D 631 471-7100
  Ronkonkoma *(G-14354)*
Jenlor Ltd .... F 315 637-9080
  Fayetteville *(G-4928)*
Keltron Electronics (de Corp) .... F 631 567-6300
  Ronkonkoma *(G-14360)*
Logitek Inc .... D 631 567-1100
  Bohemia *(G-1048)*
Mekatronics Incorporated .... E 516 883-6805
  Port Washington *(G-13288)*
Meridian Technologies Inc .... E 516 285-1000
  Elmont *(G-4521)*
Merit Electronic Design Co Inc .... C 631 667-9699
  Edgewood *(G-4409)*
Mid Hdson Wkshp For The Dsbled .... E 845 471-3820
  Poughkeepsie *(G-13354)*
Mirion Technologies Ist Corp .... D 607 562-4300
  Horseheads *(G-6321)*
Nelson Holdings Ltd .... G 607 772-1794
  Binghamton *(G-908)*
Oakdale Industrial Elec Corp .... F 631 737-4090
  Ronkonkoma *(G-14388)*
Opus Technology Corporation .... F 631 271-1883
  Melville *(G-8054)*
Pcb Piezotronics Inc .... B 716 684-0003
  Depew *(G-4102)*
Polycast Industries Inc .... G 631 595-2530
  Bay Shore *(G-708)*
Precision Assembly Tech Inc .... E 631 699-9400
  Bohemia *(G-1076)*
Premier Systems LLC .... G 631 587-9700
  Babylon *(G-532)*
Quality Contract Assemblies .... G 585 663-9030
  Rochester *(G-14060)*
R L C Electronics Inc .... D 914 241-1334
  Mount Kisco *(G-8356)*
Rdi Inc 914 773-1000
  Mount Kisco *(G-8357)*
Rem-Tronics Inc .... D 716 934-2697
  Dunkirk *(G-4177)*
Rochester Industrial Ctrl Inc .... D 315 524-4555
  Ontario *(G-12664)*
Rochester Industrial Ctrl Inc .... D 315 524-4555
  Ontario *(G-12663)*
Safe Circuits Inc .... G 631 586-3682
  Dix Hills *(G-4125)*
Scientific Components Corp .... B 718 368-2060
  Brooklyn *(G-2453)*
Sonaer Inc .... D 631 756-4780
  West Babylon *(G-16193)*
Sopark Corp .... D 716 822-0434
  Buffalo *(G-3070)*
Stetron International Inc .... F 716 854-3443
  Buffalo *(G-3077)*
Surmotech LLC .... D 585 742-1220
  Victor *(G-15868)*
T-S-K Electronics Inc .... G 716 693-3916
  North Tonawanda *(G-12457)*
Te Connectivity Corporation .... E 585 785-2500
  Rochester *(G-14159)*
Telephonics Corporation .... E 631 549-6000
  Huntington *(G-6418)*
Telephonics Corporation .... A 631 755-7000
  Farmingdale *(G-4892)*

PRODUCT SECTION

CLOTHING & ACCESS, WOMEN, CHILD & INFANT, WHOL: Scarves

Tlsi Incorporated.................................D....... 631 470-8880
  Huntington *(G-6422)*
Torotron Corporation.............................G....... 718 428-6992
  Fresh Meadows *(G-5204)*
Trading Services International............F....... 212 501-0142
  New York *(G-11884)*
Unison Industries LLC..........................B....... 607 335-5000
  Norwich *(G-12494)*
Vestal Electronic Devices LLC............F....... 607 773-8461
  Endicott *(G-4614)*
Xedit Corp..G....... 718 380-1592
  Queens Village *(G-13413)*

CIRCULAR KNIT FABRICS DYEING & FINISHING

A-One Moving & Storage Inc.................E....... 718 266-6002
  Brooklyn *(G-1465)*
Gehring Tricot Corporation....................C....... 315 429-8551
  Dolgeville *(G-4134)*
Lifestyle Design Usa Ltd.......................G....... 212 279-9400
  New York *(G-10565)*

CLAMPS & COUPLINGS: Hose

United Metal Industries Inc...................G....... 516 354-6800
  New Hyde Park *(G-8569)*

CLAY PRDTS: Architectural

Jq Woodworking Inc...............................G....... 516 766-3424
  Oceanside *(G-12543)*
Lenon Models Inc...................................G....... 212 229-1581
  New York *(G-10546)*

CLAYS, EXC KAOLIN & BALL

Applied Minerals Inc..............................F....... 212 226-4265
  Brooklyn *(G-1543)*

CLEANING EQPT: Blast, Dustless

Cleaning Tech Group LLC.....................E....... 716 665-2340
  Jamestown *(G-6707)*
Guyson Corporation of USa..................E....... 518 587-7894
  Saratoga Springs *(G-14585)*

CLEANING EQPT: Carpet Sweepers, Exc Household Elec Vacuum

American Comfort Direct LLC...............E....... 201 364-8309
  New York *(G-8825)*

CLEANING EQPT: Commercial

Oxford Cleaners.....................................G....... 212 734-0006
  New York *(G-11075)*

CLEANING EQPT: High Pressure

Custom Klean Corp................................F....... 315 865-8101
  Holland Patent *(G-6224)*
Heliojet Cleaning Tech Inc....................F....... 585 768-8710
  Le Roy *(G-7118)*
Power Scrub It Inc.................................F....... 516 997-2500
  Westbury *(G-16365)*

CLEANING OR POLISHING PREPARATIONS, NEC

American Wax Company Inc.................E....... 718 392-8080
  Long Island City *(G-7377)*
Car-Freshner Corporation.....................D....... 315 788-6250
  Watertown *(G-16006)*
Chemclean Corporation.........................E....... 718 525-4500
  Jamaica *(G-6633)*
Clean All of Syracuse LLC....................G....... 315 472-9189
  Syracuse *(G-15280)*
Collinite Corporation...............................G....... 315 732-2282
  Utica *(G-15684)*
FBC Chemical Corporation....................G....... 716 681-1581
  Lancaster *(G-7019)*
George Basch Co Inc.............................F....... 516 378-8100
  North Bellmore *(G-12378)*
Grillbot LLC...G....... 646 258-5639
  New York *(G-9989)*
Mdi Holdings LLC...................................A....... 212 559-1127
  New York *(G-10747)*
Nuvite Chemical Compounds Corp......F....... 718 383-8351
  Brooklyn *(G-2277)*
Progressive Products LLC....................G....... 914 417-6022
  Rye Brook *(G-14494)*

Spic and Span Company........................F....... 914 524-6823
  Tarrytown *(G-15494)*
Spray Nine Corporation.........................D....... 800 477-7299
  Johnstown *(G-6841)*
Topps-All Products of Yonkers.............F....... 914 968-4226
  Yonkers *(G-16803)*
U S Plychmical Overseas Corp.............E....... 845 356-5530
  Chestnut Ridge *(G-3498)*

CLEANING PRDTS: Automobile Polish

Jescar Enterprises Inc..........................G....... 845 352-5850
  Nanuet *(G-8465)*

CLEANING PRDTS: Degreasing Solvent

Solvents Company Inc..........................F....... 631 595-9300
  Kingston *(G-6917)*

CLEANING PRDTS: Deodorants, Nonpersonal

Car-Freshner Corporation.....................C....... 315 788-6250
  Watertown *(G-16005)*

CLEANING PRDTS: Disinfectants, Household Or Indl Plant

Castoleum Corporation...........................F....... 914 664-5877
  Mount Vernon *(G-8385)*
King Research Inc..................................E....... 718 788-0122
  Brooklyn *(G-2072)*
Noble Pine Products Co Inc..................F....... 914 664-5877
  Mount Vernon *(G-8425)*
Safe Seat USA Inc................................F....... 516 586-8240
  Plainview *(G-13087)*
Spongebath LLC.....................................G....... 917 475-1347
  Astoria *(G-445)*

CLEANING PRDTS: Drycleaning Preparations

Connie French Cleaners Inc.................G....... 516 487-1343
  Great Neck *(G-5548)*
Omg Cleaners Inc..................................G....... 718 282-2011
  Brooklyn *(G-2288)*
Wedding Gown Preservation Co..........D....... 607 748-7999
  Endicott *(G-4615)*

CLEANING PRDTS: Indl Plant Disinfectants Or Deodorants

Mirandy Products Ltd............................E....... 516 489-6800
  South Hempstead *(G-14942)*

CLEANING PRDTS: Laundry Preparations

Connies Laundry.....................................G....... 716 822-2800
  Buffalo *(G-2778)*
Laundress Inc...F....... 212 209-0074
  New York *(G-10524)*
Lb Laundry Inc.......................................G....... 347 399-8030
  Flushing *(G-5021)*

CLEANING PRDTS: Metal Polish

Conrad Blasius Equipment Co..............G....... 516 753-1200
  Plainview *(G-13044)*

CLEANING PRDTS: Polishing Preparations & Related Prdts

Royce Associates A Ltd Partnr............G....... 516 367-6298
  Jericho *(G-6800)*

CLEANING PRDTS: Rug, Upholstery/Dry Clng Detergents/Spotters

Greenmaker Industries LLC..................F....... 866 684-7800
  Farmingdale *(G-4776)*

CLEANING PRDTS: Sanitation Preparations

Adirondack Waste MGT Inc..................G....... 518 585-2224
  Ticonderoga *(G-15510)*
City of New York....................................C....... 718 236-2693
  Brooklyn *(G-1696)*
Simply Amazing Enterprises Inc..........G....... 631 503-6452
  Melville *(G-8064)*
TWI-Laq Industries Inc..........................E....... 718 638-5860
  Bronx *(G-1410)*

CLEANING PRDTS: Sanitation Preps, Disinfectants/Deodorants

Scully Sanitation....................................G....... 315 899-8996
  West Edmeston *(G-16207)*
Walter G Legge Company Inc...............G....... 914 737-5040
  Peekskill *(G-12928)*

CLEANING PRDTS: Shoe Polish Or Cleaner

Premier Brands America Inc.................C....... 914 667-6200
  Mount Vernon *(G-8432)*
Premier Brands of America Inc............E....... 718 325-3000
  Mount Vernon *(G-8433)*
Premier Brands of America Inc............E....... 718 325-3000
  Bronx *(G-1364)*

CLEANING PRDTS: Specialty

Caltex International Ltd.........................E....... 315 425-1040
  Syracuse *(G-15268)*
Cpac Inc..E....... 585 382-3223
  Leicester *(G-7126)*
Crescent Marketing Inc.........................C....... 716 337-0145
  North Collins *(G-12384)*
Enviro Service & Supply Corp..............F....... 347 838-6500
  Staten Island *(G-15074)*
Finger Lakes Chemicals Inc.................E....... 585 454-4760
  Rochester *(G-13804)*
Four Sasons Multi-Services Inc...........C....... 347 843-6262
  Bronx *(G-1274)*
Gliptone Manufacturing Inc..................F....... 631 285-7250
  Ronkonkoma *(G-14345)*
Griffin Chemical Company LLC............G....... 716 693-2465
  North Tonawanda *(G-12431)*
HFC Prestige Intl US LLC....................A....... 212 389-7800
  New York *(G-10091)*
Sensor & Decontamination Inc............F....... 301 526-8389
  Binghamton *(G-914)*

CLEANING PRDTS: Window Cleaning Preparations

Tjb Sunshine Enterprises......................F....... 518 384-6483
  Ballston Lake *(G-573)*

CLEANING SVCS: Industrial Or Commercial

Wellspring Omni Holdings Corp...........A....... 212 318-9800
  New York *(G-12093)*

CLIPPERS: Fingernail & Toenail

Revlon Consumer Products Corp........B....... 212 527-4000
  New York *(G-11377)*

CLIPS & FASTENERS, MADE FROM PURCHASED WIRE

Hohmann & Barnard Inc........................E....... 631 234-0600
  Hauppauge *(G-5846)*
Hohmann & Barnard Inc........................E....... 518 357-9757
  Schenectady *(G-14687)*

CLOSURES: Closures, Stamped Metal

Van Blarcom Closures Inc....................C....... 718 855-3810
  Brooklyn *(G-2615)*

CLOSURES: Plastic

Industrial Paper Tube Inc......................F....... 718 893-5000
  Bronx *(G-1296)*
Van Blarcom Closures Inc....................C....... 718 855-3810
  Brooklyn *(G-2615)*

CLOTHING & ACCESS, WOMEN, CHILD & INFANT, WHOL: Diapers

First Quality Hygienic Inc.....................G....... 516 829-3030
  Great Neck *(G-5556)*

CLOTHING & ACCESS, WOMEN, CHILD & INFANT, WHOL: Scarves

Ace & Jig LLC..G....... 347 227-0318
  Brooklyn *(G-1475)*
Gce International Inc............................D....... 212 704-4800
  New York *(G-9890)*
Lr Paris LLC...F....... 212 634-9372
  New York *(G-10621)*

Employee Codes: A=Over 500 employees, B=251-500
C=101-250, D=51-100, E=20-50, F=10-19, G=5-9

CLOTHING & ACCESS, WOMEN, CHILD & INFANT, WHOLESALE: Under

Apparel Partnership Group LLC .... G 212 302-7722
New York (G-8889)
Authentic Brands Group LLC .... C 212 760-2410
New York (G-8966)
Mrt Textile Inc .... G 800 674-1073
New York (G-10854)
Nautica Opco LLC .... B 212 541-5757
New York (G-10896)

CLOTHING & ACCESS, WOMEN, CHILD & INFANT, WHSLE: Sportswear

Bandit International Ltd .... F 718 402-2100
Bronx (G-1225)
Kidz Concepts LLC .... D 212 398-1110
New York (G-10441)
Sensational Collection Inc .... G 212 840-7388
New York (G-11543)

CLOTHING & ACCESS, WOMEN, CHILDREN & INFANT, WHOL: Access

Embassy Apparel Inc .... F 212 768-8330
New York (G-9663)
Fad Inc .... E 631 385-2460
Huntington (G-6398)

CLOTHING & ACCESS, WOMEN, CHILDREN & INFANT, WHOL: Gloves

Fownes Brothers & Co Inc .... E 212 683-0150
New York (G-9834)
Fownes Brothers & Co Inc .... E 518 752-4411
Gloversville (G-5456)

CLOTHING & ACCESS, WOMEN, CHILDREN & INFANT, WHOL: Handbags

Accessries Direct Intl USA Inc .... E 646 448-8200
New York (G-8722)
Goyard Inc .... G 212 813-0005
New York (G-9963)
Goyard Miami LLC .... G 212 813-0005
New York (G-9964)
Quilted Koala Ltd .... F 800 223-5678
New York (G-11302)
Street Smart Designs Inc .... G 646 865-0056
New York (G-11720)

CLOTHING & ACCESS, WOMEN, CHILDREN & INFANT, WHOL: Sweaters

B & B Sweater Mills Inc .... F 718 456-8693
Brooklyn (G-1578)
Bock Family Holdings Inc .... E 212 921-5688
New York (G-9116)
Keryakos Inc .... F 518 344-7092
Schenectady (G-14693)

CLOTHING & ACCESS, WOMEN, CHILDREN & INFANTS, WHOL: Purses

Formart Corp .... F 212 819-1819
New York (G-9824)

CLOTHING & ACCESS, WOMEN, CHILDREN/INFANT, WHOL: Baby Goods

Sunwin Global Industry Inc .... G 646 370-6196
New York (G-11745)

CLOTHING & ACCESS, WOMEN, CHILDREN/INFANT, WHOL: Nightwear

Komar Luxury Brands .... G 646 472-0060
New York (G-10468)

CLOTHING & ACCESS, WOMEN, CHILDREN/INFANT, WHOL: Swimsuits

Christina Sales Inc .... F 212 391-0710
New York (G-9293)

CLOTHING & ACCESS, WOMENS, CHILDREN & INFANTS, WHOL: Hats

Mega Power Sports Corporation .... G 212 627-3380
New York (G-10764)

CLOTHING & ACCESS: Costumes, Masquerade

Lr Paris LLC .... F 212 634-9372
New York (G-10621)
Masquerade LLC .... F 212 673-4546
New York (G-10723)
Rubies Masquerade Company LLC ...... G 718 846-1008
Richmond Hill (G-13513)

CLOTHING & ACCESS: Costumes, Theatrical

Barbara Matera Ltd .... D 212 475-5006
New York (G-9012)
Costume Armour Inc .... F 845 534-9120
Cornwall (G-3832)
D-C Theatricks .... G 716 847-0180
Buffalo (G-2791)
Euroco Costumes Inc .... G 212 629-9665
New York (G-9730)
Izquierdo Studios Ltd .... F 212 807-9757
New York (G-10279)
Parsons-Meares Ltd .... D 212 242-3378
Long Island City (G-7549)
Schneeman Studio Limited .... G 212 244-3330
New York (G-11506)

CLOTHING & ACCESS: Cummerbunds

Westchester Wine Warehouse LLC ...... F 914 824-1400
White Plains (G-16520)

CLOTHING & ACCESS: Footlets

Jersey Express Inc .... F 716 834-6151
Buffalo (G-2894)

CLOTHING & ACCESS: Handicapped

Brooklyn Denim Co .... F 718 782-2600
Brooklyn (G-1642)
Eb Couture Ltd .... E 212 912-0190
New York (G-9615)
Kww Productions Corp .... F 212 398-8181
New York (G-10488)
M2 Fashion Group Holdings Inc .... G 917 208-2948
New York (G-10645)
Ribz LLC .... F 212 764-9595
New York (G-11385)
Timeless Fashions LLC .... G 212 730-9328
New York (G-11846)

CLOTHING & ACCESS: Handkerchiefs, Exc Paper

Gce International Inc .... D 212 704-4800
New York (G-9890)
My Hanky Inc .... F 646 321-0869
Brooklyn (G-2238)

CLOTHING & ACCESS: Hospital Gowns

New York Hospital Disposable .... E 718 384-1620
Brooklyn (G-2262)
Shamron Mills Ltd .... G 212 354-0430
Troy (G-15625)

CLOTHING & ACCESS: Men's Miscellaneous Access

Accessries Direct Intl USA Inc .... E 646 448-8200
New York (G-8722)
Adf Accessories Inc .... G 516 450-5755
Oceanside (G-12530)
Apollo Apparel Group LLC .... F 212 398-6585
New York (G-8885)
Bh Brand Inc .... E 212 239-1635
New York (G-9068)
Carter Enterprises LLC .... E 718 853-5052
Brooklyn (G-1679)
Dreamwave LLC .... F 212 594-4250
New York (G-9574)
Foot Locker Retail Inc .... E 516 827-5306
Hicksville (G-6087)
Hoehn Inc .... F 518 463-8900
Albany (G-84)

Hudson Dying & Finishing LLC .... E 518 752-4389
Gloversville (G-5459)
I Shalom & Co Inc .... C 212 532-7911
New York (G-10161)
Intercotton Company Inc .... G 212 265-3809
New York (G-10239)
Jimeale Incorporated .... G 917 686-5383
New York (G-10339)
Jolibe Atelier LLC .... F 917 319-5908
New York (G-10356)
Jonathan Meizler LLC .... G 212 213-2977
New York (G-10358)
Joseph Industries Inc .... E 212 764-0010
New York (G-10364)
L D Weiss Inc .... G 212 697-3023
New York (G-10493)
Linder New York LLC .... F 646 678-5819
New York (G-10572)
Meryl Diamond Ltd .... D 212 730-0333
New York (G-10779)
Mountain and Isles LLC .... F 212 354-1890
New York (G-10848)
New York Accessory Group Inc .... E 212 532-7911
New York (G-10932)
NY 1 Art Gallery Inc .... G 917 698-0626
New Hyde Park (G-8554)
Onia LLC .... E 646 701-0008
New York (G-11045)
Ppr Direct Marketing LLC .... G 718 965-8600
Brooklyn (G-2332)
Rjm2 Ltd .... G 212 944-1660
New York (G-11401)
Robert Miller Associates LLC .... F 718 392-1640
Long Island City (G-7576)
Rosetti Handbags and ACC .... E 646 839-7945
New York (G-11434)
Swank Inc .... B 212 867-2600
New York (G-11753)
Trash and Vaudeville Inc .... G 212 777-1727
New York (G-11888)
Ufo Contemporary Inc .... F 212 226-5400
New York (G-11932)
Unified Inc led .... F 646 370-4650
New York (G-11939)

CLOTHING & ACCESS: Suspenders

Perry Ellis Menswear LLC .... C 212 221-7500
New York (G-11162)
Randa Accessories Lea Gds LLC .... D 212 354-5100
New York (G-11325)
Trafalgar Company LLC .... G 212 768-8800
New York (G-11885)

CLOTHING & APPAREL STORES: Custom

Crye Precision LLC .... C 718 246-3838
Brooklyn (G-1736)
Knucklehead Embroidery Inc .... G 607 797-2725
Johnson City (G-6814)
Peter Papastrat .... G 607 723-8112
Binghamton (G-910)

CLOTHING & FURNISHINGS, MEN & BOY, WHOLESALE: Suits/Trousers

Hugo Boss Usa Inc .... D 212 940-0600
New York (G-10146)

CLOTHING & FURNISHINGS, MEN'S & BOYS', WHOLESALE: Caps

Grunt Apparel Inc .... G 646 878-6171
New York (G-10002)

CLOTHING & FURNISHINGS, MEN'S & BOYS', WHOLESALE: Fur

Georgy Creative Fashions Inc .... G 212 279-4885
New York (G-9912)

CLOTHING & FURNISHINGS, MEN'S & BOYS', WHOLESALE: Gloves

Fownes Brothers & Co Inc .... E 212 683-0150
New York (G-9834)
Fownes Brothers & Co Inc .... E 518 752-4411
Gloversville (G-5456)

PRODUCT SECTION

CLOTHING: Athletic & Sportswear, Men's & Boys'

CLOTHING & FURNISHINGS, MEN'S & BOYS', WHOLESALE: Hats

Ideal Creations Inc .... E 212 563-5928
  New York *(G-10171)*
Mega Power Sports Corporation .... G 212 627-3380
  New York *(G-10764)*

CLOTHING & FURNISHINGS, MEN'S & BOYS', WHOLESALE: Neckwear

Mongru Neckwear Inc .... E 718 706-0406
  Long Island City *(G-7529)*
Roffe Accessories Inc .... E 212 213-1440
  New York *(G-11419)*

CLOTHING & FURNISHINGS, MEN'S & BOYS', WHOLESALE: Scarves

Gce International Inc .... D 212 704-4800
  New York *(G-9890)*

CLOTHING & FURNISHINGS, MEN'S & BOYS', WHOLESALE: Shirts

Hard Ten Clothing Inc .... G 212 302-1321
  New York *(G-10036)*
Just Brass Inc .... G 212 724-5447
  New York *(G-10384)*

CLOTHING & FURNISHINGS, MEN'S & BOYS', WHOLESALE: Umbrellas

Adam Scott Designs Inc .... E 212 420-8866
  New York *(G-8732)*

CLOTHING & FURNISHINGS, MEN'S & BOYS', WHOLESALE: Uniforms

Custom Sportswear Corp .... G 914 666-9200
  Bedford Hills *(G-773)*

CLOTHING & FURNISHINGS, MENS & BOYS, WHOL: Sportswear/Work

Bilco Industries Inc .... F 917 783-5008
  New York *(G-9081)*
Nautica Opco LLC .... B 212 541-5757
  New York *(G-10896)*

CLOTHING & FURNISHINGS, MENS & BOYS, WHOLESALE: Apprl Belts

Dynasty Belts Inc .... E 516 625-6280
  New Hyde Park *(G-8529)*
New Classic Inc .... F 718 609-1100
  Long Island City *(G-7537)*

CLOTHING ACCESS STORES: Umbrellas

Zip-Jack Industries Ltd .... E 914 592-2000
  Tarrytown *(G-15498)*

CLOTHING STORES, NEC

1 Atelier LLC .... G 917 916-2968
  New York *(G-8664)*
Fad Inc .... E 631 385-2460
  Huntington *(G-6398)*
Kcp Holdco Inc .... F 212 265-1500
  New York *(G-10426)*
Kenneth Cole Productions Inc .... B 212 265-1500
  New York *(G-10431)*
Marsha Fleisher .... F 845 679-6500
  Woodstock *(G-16686)*
Tr Apparel LLC .... G 646 358-3888
  New York *(G-11881)*

CLOTHING STORES: Dancewear

Shirl-Lynn of New York .... F 315 363-5898
  Oneida *(G-12621)*

CLOTHING STORES: Designer Apparel

Randall Loeffler Inc .... E 212 226-8787
  New York *(G-11326)*

CLOTHING STORES: Jeans

Brooklyn Denim Co .... F 718 782-2600
  Brooklyn *(G-1642)*

Centric Denim Usa LLC .... F 646 839-7000
  New York *(G-9247)*
Joseph (uk) Inc .... G 212 570-0077
  New York *(G-10363)*

CLOTHING STORES: Leather

Leather Artisan .... G 518 359-3102
  Childwold *(G-3499)*
Lost Worlds Inc .... G 212 923-3423
  New York *(G-10613)*

CLOTHING STORES: T-Shirts, Printed, Custom

JP Signs .... G 518 569-3907
  Chazy *(G-3432)*
Randy Sixberry .... G 315 265-6211
  Potsdam *(G-13322)*

CLOTHING STORES: Uniforms & Work

All American Awards Inc .... F 631 567-2025
  Bohemia *(G-975)*
Vans Inc .... F 631 724-1011
  Lake Grove *(G-6971)*

CLOTHING STORES: Unisex

David Peyser Sportswear Inc .... E 212 695-7716
  New York *(G-9483)*

CLOTHING STORES: Work

Protech (llc) .... E 518 725-7785
  Gloversville *(G-5463)*

CLOTHING, WOMEN & CHILD, WHLSE: Dress, Suit, Skirt & Blouse

Billy Beez Usa LLC .... F 315 741-5099
  Syracuse *(G-15257)*
Billy Beez Usa LLC .... F 646 606-2249
  New York *(G-9084)*
Billy Beez Usa LLC .... E 845 915-4709
  West Nyack *(G-16266)*

CLOTHING/ACCESS, WOMEN, CHILDREN/INFANT, WHOL: Apparel Belt

New Classic Inc .... F 718 609-1100
  Long Island City *(G-7537)*

CLOTHING/FURNISHINGS, MEN/BOY, WHOL: Furnishings, Exc Shoes

Embassy Apparel Inc .... F 212 768-8330
  New York *(G-9663)*

CLOTHING: Academic Vestments

Tr Apparel LLC .... E 310 595-4337
  New York *(G-11880)*
Tr Apparel LLC .... G 646 358-3888
  New York *(G-11881)*

CLOTHING: Access

David & Young Co Inc .... G 212 594-6034
  New York *(G-9479)*
J & C Finishing .... E 718 456-1087
  Ridgewood *(G-13539)*
JC California Inc .... G 212 334-4380
  New York *(G-10317)*
Patient-Wear LLC .... G 914 740-7770
  Bronx *(G-1353)*
S & B Fashion Inc .... G 718 482-1386
  Long Island City *(G-7582)*
Twcc Product and Sales .... E 212 614-9364
  New York *(G-11917)*

CLOTHING: Access, Women's & Misses'

1 Atelier LLC .... G 917 916-2968
  New York *(G-8664)*
5th & Ocean Clothing Inc .... C 716 604-9000
  Buffalo *(G-2677)*
Accessries Direct Intl USA Inc .... E 646 448-8200
  New York *(G-8722)*
Authentic Brands Group LLC .... C 212 760-2410
  New York *(G-8966)*
Bag Bazaar Ltd .... E 212 689-3508
  New York *(G-9002)*

Bh Brand Inc .... E 212 239-1635
  New York *(G-9068)*
Botkier Ny LLC .... G 212 343-2782
  New York *(G-9125)*
Carolina Amato Inc .... G 212 768-9095
  New York *(G-9213)*
Collection Xiix Ltd .... F 212 686-8990
  New York *(G-9351)*
DFA New York LLC .... E 212 523-0021
  New York *(G-9517)*
Elliot Mann Nyc Inc .... E 212 260-0658
  New York *(G-9656)*
Fad Inc .... E 631 385-2460
  Huntington *(G-6398)*
Giulietta LLC .... G 212 334-1859
  Brooklyn *(G-1928)*
Hoehn Inc .... F 518 463-8900
  Albany *(G-84)*
I Shalom & Co Inc .... C 212 532-7911
  New York *(G-10161)*
Krasner Group Inc .... E 212 268-4100
  New York *(G-10479)*
Ksk International Inc .... E 212 354-7770
  New York *(G-10484)*
L D Weiss Inc .... E 212 697-3023
  New York *(G-10493)*
New Concepts of New York LLC .... E 212 695-4999
  Brooklyn *(G-2257)*
New York Accessory Group Inc .... C 212 532-7911
  New York *(G-10932)*
ODY Accessories Inc .... E 212 239-0580
  New York *(G-11032)*
Petrunia LLC .... G 607 277-1930
  Ithaca *(G-6604)*
Popnyc 1 LLC .... G 646 684-4600
  New York *(G-11218)*
Uspa Accessories LLC .... C 212 868-2590
  New York *(G-11981)*
White Gate Holdings Inc .... G 212 564-3266
  New York *(G-12102)*

CLOTHING: Aprons, Exc Rubber/Plastic, Women, Misses, Junior

Elizabeth Wilson .... G 516 486-2157
  Uniondale *(G-15665)*
Republic Clothing Group Inc .... C 212 719-3000
  New York *(G-11366)*
Richard Manufacturing Co Inc .... G 718 254-0958
  Brooklyn *(G-2401)*

CLOTHING: Aprons, Harness

Breton Industries Inc .... C 518 842-3030
  Amsterdam *(G-329)*

CLOTHING: Aprons, Work, Exc Rubberized & Plastic, Men's

Richard Manufacturing Co Inc .... G 718 254-0958
  Brooklyn *(G-2401)*

CLOTHING: Athletic & Sportswear, Men's & Boys'

Adpro Sports LLC .... D 716 854-5116
  Buffalo *(G-2687)*
Bandit International Ltd .... F 718 402-2100
  Bronx *(G-1225)*
Beluga Inc .... E 212 594-5511
  New York *(G-9041)*
Benetton Trading Usa Inc .... G 212 593-0290
  New York *(G-9045)*
Bilco Industries Inc .... F 917 783-5008
  New York *(G-9081)*
Billion Tower USA LLC .... G 212 220-0608
  New York *(G-9083)*
Broken Threads Inc .... G 212 730-4351
  New York *(G-9147)*
Caps Teamwear Inc .... G 585 663-1750
  Rochester *(G-13691)*
Caribbean Fashion Group Inc .... G 212 706-8851
  New York *(G-9207)*
Central Mills Inc .... C 212 764-9011
  New York *(G-9244)*
City Jeans Inc .... G 718 239-5353
  Bronx *(G-1241)*
Continental Knitting Mills .... G 631 242-5330
  Deer Park *(G-3958)*
David Peyser Sportswear Inc .... C 631 231-7788
  Bay Shore *(G-678)*

Employee Codes: A=Over 500 employees, B=251-500
C=101-250, D=51-100, E=20-50, F=10-19, G=5-9

CLOTHING: Athletic & Sportswear, Men's & Boys'

David Peyser Sportswear Inc .... E 212 695-7716
  New York (G-9483)
Endurance LLC .... E 212 719-2500
  New York (G-9678)
Eternal Fortune Fashion LLC .... G 212 965-5322
  New York (G-9721)
Ferris USA LLC .... G 617 895-8102
  New York (G-9796)
Feyem USA Inc .... G 845 363-6253
  Brewster (G-1165)
Gametime Sportswear Plus LLC .... G 315 724-5893
  Utica (G-15705)
General Sportwear Company Inc .... C 212 764-5820
  New York (G-9902)
Groupe 16sur20 LLC .... F 212 625-1620
  New York (G-9998)
Haculla Nyc Inc .... F 718 886-3163
  Fresh Meadows (G-5199)
Hansae Co Ltd .... G 212 354-6690
  New York (G-10035)
Hf Mfg Corp .... D 212 594-9142
  New York (G-10090)
Icer Sports LLC .... F 212 221-4700
  New York (G-10169)
Jacob Hidary Foundation Inc .... F 212 736-6540
  New York (G-10297)
Joseph (uk) Inc .... G 212 570-0077
  New York (G-10363)
Kicks Closet Sportswear Inc .... G 347 577-0857
  Bronx (G-1308)
Kidz World Inc .... F 212 563-4949
  New York (G-10442)
London Paris Ltd .... G 718 564-4793
  Brooklyn (G-2133)
Luxe Imagine Consulting LLC .... G 212 273-9770
  New York (G-10632)
M Hidary & Co Inc .... D 212 736-6540
  New York (G-10639)
Mann Consultants LLC .... E 914 763-0512
  Waccabuc (G-15881)
Mee Accessories LLC .... B 917 262-1000
  New York (G-10762)
Miss Group .... G 212 391-2535
  New York (G-10822)
Nautica International Inc .... D 212 541-5757
  New York (G-10895)
Nautica Opco LLC .... B 212 541-5757
  New York (G-10896)
Nine West Holdings Inc .... G 212 575-2571
  New York (G-10975)
North American Mills Inc .... F 212 695-6146
  New York (G-10992)
On The Double Inc .... G 518 431-3571
  Germantown (G-5339)
One Step Up Ltd .... D 212 398-1110
  New York (G-11043)
P & I Sportswear Inc .... G 718 934-4587
  New York (G-11082)
Ps38 LLC .... F 212 819-1123
  New York (G-11269)
Pvh Corp .... G 212 381-3800
  New York (G-11283)
Ralph Lauren Corporation .... B 212 318-7000
  New York (G-11321)
Ramsbury Property Us Inc .... F 212 223-6250
  New York (G-11322)
Rp55 Inc .... G 212 840-4035
  New York (G-11442)
S & S Fashions Inc .... G 718 328-0001
  Bronx (G-1375)
Sandy Dalal Ltd .... G 212 532-5822
  New York (G-11482)
Sb Corporation .... G 212 822-3166
  New York (G-11495)
Siskind Group Inc .... F 212 840-0880
  New York (G-11601)
Sister Sister Inc .... G 212 629-9600
  New York (G-11602)
Sport Athleisure Ltd .... F 212 868-6505
  New York (G-11673)
Sterling Possessions Ltd .... G 212 594-0418
  New York (G-11707)
Tbhl International LLC .... F 212 799-2007
  New York (G-11787)
Tibana Finishing Inc .... E 718 417-5375
  Ridgewood (G-13555)
Tillsonburg Company USA Inc .... E 267 994-8096
  New York (G-11835)
Under Armour Inc .... E 518 761-6787
  Lake George (G-6966)

Warnaco Group Inc .... E 212 287-8000
  New York (G-12070)
Warnaco Inc .... B 212 287-8000
  New York (G-12071)

CLOTHING: Athletic & Sportswear, Women's & Girls'

Adpro Sports LLC .... D 716 854-5116
  Buffalo (G-2687)
Alleson of Rochester Inc .... D 585 272-0606
  Rochester (G-13614)
Alpha 6 Distributions LLC .... F 516 801-8290
  Locust Valley (G-7345)
Amber Bever Inc .... G 212 391-4911
  Brooklyn (G-1516)
Anna Sui Corp .... E 212 941-8406
  New York (G-8873)
Avalin LLC .... F 212 842-2286
  New York (G-8971)
B Tween LLC .... F 212 819-9040
  New York (G-8993)
Bam Sales LLC .... F 212 781-3000
  New York (G-9009)
Bandier Corp .... G 212 242-5400
  New York (G-9011)
Bilco Industries Inc .... F 917 783-5008
  New York (G-9081)
Caribbean Fashion Group Inc .... G 212 706-8851
  New York (G-9207)
Casuals Etc Inc .... D 212 838-1319
  New York (G-9225)
Continental Knitting Mills .... G 631 242-5330
  Deer Park (G-3958)
Dianos Kathryn Designs .... G 212 267-1584
  New York (G-9524)
Doral Apparel Group Inc .... G 917 208-5652
  New York (G-9558)
Dr Jayscom .... G 888 437-5297
  New York (G-9571)
First Love Fashions LLC .... F 212 256-1089
  New York (G-9808)
H2gear Fashions LLC .... G 347 787-7508
  Brooklyn (G-1958)
Hearts of Palm LLC .... E 212 944-6660
  New York (G-10074)
Hearts of Palm LLC .... E 212 944-6660
  New York (G-10075)
Jaya Apparel Group LLC .... E 212 764-4980
  New York (G-10313)
Katz Martell Fashion Trdg Intl .... G 212 840-0070
  New York (G-10418)
Kicks Closet Sportswear Inc .... G 347 577-0857
  Bronx (G-1308)
Lai Apparel Design Inc .... E 212 382-1075
  New York (G-10509)
Leslie Stuart Co Inc .... F 212 629-4551
  New York (G-10555)
Liquid Knits Inc .... F 718 706-6600
  Long Island City (G-7501)
Mango Usa Inc .... E 718 998-6050
  Brooklyn (G-2156)
Marconi Intl USA Co Ltd .... G 212 391-2626
  New York (G-10699)
Mars Fashions Inc .... E 718 402-2200
  Bronx (G-1323)
MISS Sportswear Inc .... G 212 391-2535
  Brooklyn (G-2212)
MISS Sportswear Inc .... G 212 391-2535
  Brooklyn (G-2213)
MISS Sportswear Inc .... F 718 369-6012
  Brooklyn (G-2214)
Nine West Holdings Inc .... G 212 221-6376
  New York (G-10974)
Nine West Holdings Inc .... G 215 785-4000
  New York (G-10979)
Nine West Holdings Inc .... G 212 575-2571
  New York (G-10975)
On The Double Inc .... G 518 431-3571
  Germantown (G-5339)
One Step Up Ltd .... D 212 398-1110
  New York (G-11043)
P & I Sportswear Inc .... G 718 934-4587
  New York (G-11082)
Penfli Industries Inc .... F 212 947-6080
  Great Neck (G-5581)
Sensational Collection Inc .... G 212 840-7388
  New York (G-11543)
Shanghai Harmony AP Intl LLC .... E 646 569-5680
  New Rochelle (G-8628)

Shirl-Lynn of New York .... F 315 363-5898
  Oneida (G-12621)
Sport Athleisure Ltd .... F 212 868-6505
  New York (G-11673)
Stony Apparel Corp .... G 212 391-0022
  New York (G-11716)
Swatfame Inc .... G 212 944-8022
  New York (G-11756)
Tillsonburg Company USA Inc .... E 267 994-8096
  New York (G-11835)
Z-Ply Corp .... E 212 398-7011
  New York (G-12167)
Zg Apparel Group LLC .... E 212 944-2510
  New York (G-12175)

CLOTHING: Baker, Barber, Lab/Svc Ind Apparel, Washable, Men

HC Contracting Inc .... D 212 643-9292
  New York (G-10054)

CLOTHING: Bathing Suits & Beachwear, Children's

Warnaco Group Inc .... E 212 287-8000
  New York (G-12070)

CLOTHING: Bathing Suits & Swimwear, Girls, Children & Infant

6 Shore Road LLC .... G 212 274-9666
  New York (G-8683)
Baby Uv/Kids Uv Inc .... F 917 301-9020
  Stony Brook (G-15163)
Candlesticks Inc .... F 212 947-8900
  New York (G-9194)
In Mocean Group LLC .... D 212 944-0317
  New York (G-10190)
Oxygen Inc .... G 516 433-1144
  Hicksville (G-6118)

CLOTHING: Bathing Suits & Swimwear, Knit

IaMmaliamills LLC .... G 805 845-2137
  Brooklyn (G-1992)
Tomas Maier .... G 212 988-8686
  New York (G-11861)
Vilebrequin .... G 212 546-9220
  New York (G-12034)

CLOTHING: Bathrobes, Mens & Womens, From Purchased Materials

Natori Company Incorporated .... D 212 532-7796
  New York (G-10890)
Sketch Studio Trading Inc .... G 212 244-2875
  New York (G-11607)

CLOTHING: Belts

Barrera Jose & Maria Co Ltd .... E 212 239-1994
  New York (G-9021)
Centric Brands Inc .... D 323 890-1800
  New York (G-9246)
Courtlandt Boot Jack Co Inc .... E 718 445-6200
  Flushing (G-4994)
Daniel M Friedman & Assoc Inc ...... E 212 695-5545
  New York (G-9468)
Dynasty Belts Inc .... E 516 625-6280
  New Hyde Park (G-8529)
Gbg USA Inc .... D 646 839-7083
  New York (G-9888)
Gbg USA Inc .... E 212 615-3400
  New York (G-9889)
Nassau Suffolk Brd of Womens ...... E 631 666-8835
  Bay Shore (G-704)
New Classic Inc .... F 718 609-1100
  Long Island City (G-7537)
P M Belts Usa Inc .... E 800 762-3580
  Brooklyn (G-2297)
Perry Ellis Menswear LLC .... C 212 221-7500
  New York (G-11162)
Randa Accessories Lea Gds LLC .... D 212 354-5100
  New York (G-11325)
Sandy Duftler Designs Ltd .... F 516 379-3084
  North Baldwin (G-12366)
Sh Leather Novelty Company .... F 718 387-7742
  Brooklyn (G-2461)
Tapestry Inc .... B 212 594-1850
  New York (G-11784)

PRODUCT SECTION

CLOTHING: Children & Infants'

Trafalgar Company LLC .... G 212 768-8800
New York *(G-11885)*
Universal Elliot Corp .... G 212 736-8877
New York *(G-11960)*
Xinya International Trading Co .... G 212 216-9681
New York *(G-12152)*

CLOTHING: Blouses & Shirts, Girls' & Children's

Cheri Mon Baby LLC .... G 212 354-5511
New York *(G-9270)*
Gw Acquisition LLC .... E 212 736-4848
New York *(G-10011)*
Sports Products America LLC .... E 212 594-5511
New York *(G-11676)*

CLOTHING: Blouses, Boys', From Purchased Materials

Jacks and Jokers 52 LLC .... G 917 740-2595
New York *(G-10292)*
Nat Nast Company Inc .... E 212 575-1186
New York *(G-10876)*

CLOTHING: Blouses, Women's & Girls'

Accessries Direct Intl USA Inc .... E 646 448-8200
New York *(G-8722)*
Apparel Group Ltd .... E 212 328-1200
New York *(G-8888)*
August Silk Inc .... E 212 643-2400
New York *(G-8961)*
August Silk Inc .... G 212 643-2400
New York *(G-8962)*
Bernard Chaus Inc .... D 212 354-1280
New York *(G-9051)*
Bernard Chaus Inc .... C 646 562-4700
New York *(G-9052)*
Cyberlimit Inc .... F 212 840-9597
New York *(G-9441)*
Cynthia Rowley Inc .... F 212 242-3803
New York *(G-9443)*
Embassy Apparel Inc .... F 212 768-8330
New York *(G-9663)*
Feyem USA Inc .... G 845 363-6253
Brewster *(G-1165)*
Fourtys Ny Inc .... F 212 382-0301
New York *(G-9833)*
Gildan Apparel USA Inc .... D 212 476-0341
New York *(G-9919)*
Glamourpuss Nyc LLC .... G 212 722-1370
New York *(G-9929)*
Grey State Apparel LLC .... E 212 255-4216
New York *(G-9986)*
Icer Sports LLC .... F 212 221-4700
New York *(G-10169)*
Kate Spade & Company LLC .... B 212 354-4900
New York *(G-10415)*
Krasner Group Inc .... G 212 268-4100
New York *(G-10479)*
Ksk International Inc .... E 212 354-7770
New York *(G-10484)*
Lea & Viola Inc .... G 646 918-6866
New York *(G-10529)*
Liberty Apparel Company Inc .... E 718 625-4000
New York *(G-10560)*
Lt2 LLC .... E 212 684-1510
New York *(G-10623)*
M S B International Ltd .... F 212 302-5551
New York *(G-10642)*
Maggy London International Ltd .... C 212 944-7199
New York *(G-10665)*
Mega Sourcing Inc .... G 646 682-0304
Merrick *(G-8103)*
Mulitex Usa Inc .... G 212 398-0440
New York *(G-10857)*
Nyc Knitwear Inc .... E 212 840-1313
New York *(G-11014)*
Orchid Manufacturing Co Inc .... F 212 840-5700
New York *(G-11059)*
Plugg LLC .... F 212 840-6655
New York *(G-11212)*
Ramy Brook LLC .... E 212 744-2789
New York *(G-11324)*
Raven New York LLC .... G 212 584-9690
New York *(G-11328)*
Robert Danes Danes Inc .... G 212 226-1351
New York *(G-11406)*
Saad Collection Inc .... G 212 937-0341
New York *(G-11461)*

Soho Apparel Ltd .... G 212 840-1109
New York *(G-11636)*
Spencer AB Inc .... G 646 831-3728
New York *(G-11667)*
Tibana Finishing Inc .... E 718 417-5375
Ridgewood *(G-13555)*
Triumph Apparel Corporation .... E 212 302-2606
New York *(G-11901)*
Turn On Products Inc .... D 212 764-2121
New York *(G-11913)*
Ursula Of Switzerland Inc .... E 518 237-2580
Waterford *(G-15990)*
Vanity Room Inc .... F 212 921-7154
New York *(G-11993)*
Ventura Enterprise Co Inc .... E 212 391-0170
New York *(G-12006)*
Yeohlee Inc .... F 212 631-8099
New York *(G-12161)*

CLOTHING: Blouses, Womens & Juniors, From Purchased Mtrls

18 Rocks LLC .... E 631 465-9990
Melville *(G-7995)*
79 Metro Ltd .... G 212 944-4030
New York *(G-8685)*
Agi Brooks Production Co Inc .... F 212 268-1533
New York *(G-8768)*
Alexander Wang Incorporated .... D 212 532-3103
New York *(G-8794)*
Amerex Corporation .... G 212 221-3151
New York *(G-8819)*
Anna Sui Corp .... E 212 941-8406
New York *(G-8873)*
Donna Karan Company LLC .... C 212 789-1500
New York *(G-9550)*
Donna Karan Company LLC .... B 212 789-1500
New York *(G-9551)*
Donna Karan International Inc .... F 212 789-1500
New York *(G-9552)*
Donna Karan International Inc .... G 212 768-5800
New York *(G-9553)*
Elie Tahari Ltd .... G 212 398-2622
New York *(G-9645)*
Elie Tahari Ltd .... D 212 763-2000
New York *(G-9647)*
Fuller Sportswear Co Inc .... G 516 773-3353
Great Neck *(G-5559)*
Gabrielle Andra .... G 212 366-9624
New York *(G-9875)*
Geoffrey Beene Inc .... E 212 371-5570
New York *(G-9908)*
International Direct Group Inc .... E 212 921-9036
New York *(G-10246)*
Jeanjer LLC .... A 212 944-1330
New York *(G-10323)*
Land n Sea Inc .... D 212 444-6000
New York *(G-10513)*
Necessary Objects Ltd .... E 212 334-9888
Long Island City *(G-7535)*
Orchard Apparel Group Ltd .... G 212 268-8701
New York *(G-11057)*
Paddy Lee Fashions Inc .... F 718 786-6020
Long Island City *(G-7547)*
Pat & Rose Dress Inc .... D 212 279-1357
New York *(G-11121)*
Permit Fashion Group Inc .... G 212 912-0988
Woodbury *(G-16627)*
Phillips-Van Heusen Europe .... F 212 381-3500
New York *(G-11183)*
Pvh Corp .... D 212 381-3500
New York *(G-11281)*
Pvh Corp .... G 212 549-6000
New York *(G-11282)*
Pvh Corp .... G 212 719-2600
New York *(G-11285)*
Rhoda Lee Inc .... D 212 840-5700
New York *(G-11384)*
S & S Manufacturing Co Inc .... D 212 444-6000
New York *(G-11456)*
Stitch & Couture Inc .... E 212 947-9204
New York *(G-11713)*
Tahari ASL LLC .... B 212 763-2800
New York *(G-11775)*
Turn On Products Inc .... F 212 764-4545
New York *(G-11914)*

CLOTHING: Brassieres

Cupid Foundations Inc .... C 212 686-6224
New York *(G-9434)*

East Coast Molders Inc .... C 516 240-6000
Oceanside *(G-12536)*
Edith Lances Corp .... E 212 683-1990
New York *(G-9627)*
New York Elegance Entps Inc .... F 212 685-3088
New York *(G-10936)*
Valmont Inc .... F 212 685-1653
New York *(G-11987)*
Warnaco Inc .... B 212 287-8000
New York *(G-12071)*
Warnaco Inc .... F 718 722-3000
Brooklyn *(G-2639)*

CLOTHING: Bridal Gowns

Anna B Inc .... G 516 680-6609
New York *(G-8872)*
B S J Limited .... E 212 764-4600
New York *(G-8990)*
B S J Limited .... E 212 221-8403
New York *(G-8991)*
Nasserati Inc .... G 212 947-8100
New York *(G-10875)*
Shane Tex Inc .... F 516 486-7522
Woodmere *(G-16642)*
Stitch & Couture Inc .... E 212 947-9204
New York *(G-11713)*
Thread LLC .... G 212 414-8844
New York *(G-11827)*
Vera Wang Group LLC .... E 212 575-6400
New York *(G-12007)*

CLOTHING: Burial

Rose Solomon Co .... E 718 855-1788
Brooklyn *(G-2415)*

CLOTHING: Capes & Jackets, Women's & Misses'

Alicia Adams Alpaca Inc .... G 845 868-3366
Millbrook *(G-8187)*
Uniqlo USA LLC .... F 877 486-4756
New York *(G-11948)*

CLOTHING: Capes, Exc Fur/Rubber, Womens, Misses & Juniors

Adrienne Landau Designs Inc .... F 212 695-8362
New York *(G-8742)*

CLOTHING: Chemises, Camisoles/Teddies, Women, Misses/Junior

Lady Ester Lingerie Corp .... E 212 689-1729
New York *(G-10506)*
Mrt Textile Inc .... G 800 674-1073
New York *(G-10854)*

CLOTHING: Children & Infants'

Andy & Evan Industries Inc .... G 212 967-7908
New York *(G-8861)*
Gce International Inc .... F 212 868-0500
New York *(G-9891)*
Grand Knitting Mills Inc .... E 631 226-5000
Amityville *(G-278)*
Great Universal Corp .... E 917 302-0065
New York *(G-9982)*
Haddad Bros Inc .... E 718 377-5505
Brooklyn *(G-1959)*
Haddad Bros Inc .... F 212 563-2117
New York *(G-10018)*
JM Originals Inc .... C 845 647-3003
Ellenville *(G-4439)*
Manchu New York Inc .... G 212 921-5050
New York *(G-10682)*
Michael Stuart Inc .... E 718 821-0704
Brooklyn *(G-2204)*
S & C Bridal LLC .... F 212 789-7000
New York *(G-11454)*
S & C Bridals LLC .... G 213 624-4477
New York *(G-11455)*
Silly Phillie Creations Inc .... F 718 492-6300
Brooklyn *(G-2471)*
Skip Hop Inc .... E 646 902-9874
New York *(G-11610)*
Skip Hop Holdings Inc .... G 212 868-9850
New York *(G-11611)*
Thats My Girl Inc .... G 212 695-0020
Brooklyn *(G-2563)*

Employee Codes: A=Over 500 employees, B=251-500
C=101-250, D=51-100, E=20-50, F=10-19, G=5-9

CLOTHING: Children's, Girls'

Aerobic Wear Inc....G....631 673-1830
Huntington Station *(G-6428)*
Domani Fashions Corp....G....718 797-0505
Brooklyn *(G-1786)*
Franco Apparel Group Inc....D....212 967-7272
New York *(G-9839)*
Gerson & Gerson Inc....C....212 244-6775
New York *(G-9914)*
Gw Acquisition LLC....E....212 736-4848
New York *(G-10011)*
Haddad Bros Inc....E....718 377-5505
Brooklyn *(G-1959)*
Isfel Co Inc....G....212 736-6216
New York *(G-10275)*
Jeanjer LLC....A....212 944-1330
New York *(G-10323)*
JM Originals Inc....C....845 647-3003
Ellenville *(G-4439)*
Jomat New York Inc....E....718 369-7641
Brooklyn *(G-2044)*
Kahn-Lucas-Lancaster Inc....D....212 239-2407
New York *(G-10395)*
Land n Sea Inc....D....212 444-6000
New York *(G-10513)*
Liberty Apparel Company Inc....E....718 625-4000
New York *(G-10560)*
Lollytogs Ltd....D....212 502-6000
New York *(G-10595)*
M Hidary & Co Inc....D....212 736-6540
New York *(G-10639)*
Michael Stuart Inc....E....718 821-0704
Brooklyn *(G-2204)*
Miltons of New York Inc....G....212 997-3359
New York *(G-10813)*
Nyc Bronx Inc....G....917 417-0509
Bronx *(G-1346)*
Pink Crush LLC....G....718 788-6978
New York *(G-11198)*
Pti-Pacific Inc....G....212 414-8495
New York *(G-11271)*
Rogers Group Inc....E....212 643-9292
New York *(G-11423)*
S Rothschild & Co Inc....C....212 354-8550
New York *(G-11459)*
Sch Dpx Corporation....G....917 405-5377
New York *(G-11500)*
Swatfame Inc....G....212 944-8022
New York *(G-11756)*
Therese The Childrens Collectn....G....518 346-2315
Schenectady *(G-14721)*
Yigal-Azrouel Inc....E....212 302-1194
New York *(G-12162)*
Z-Ply Corp....E....212 398-7011
New York *(G-12167)*

CLOTHING: Clergy Vestments

Davis....G....716 833-4678
Buffalo *(G-2794)*
Roth Clothing Co Inc....G....718 384-4927
Brooklyn *(G-2416)*
Warner....G....716 446-0663
Buffalo *(G-3124)*

CLOTHING: Coats & Jackets, Leather & Sheep-Lined

Andrew M Schwartz LLC....G....212 391-7070
New York *(G-8860)*
Cockpit Usa Inc....F....212 575-1616
New York *(G-9343)*
Excelled Sheepskin & Lea Coat....F....212 594-5843
New York *(G-9750)*
J Percy For Mrvin Rchards Ltd....E....212 944-5300
New York *(G-10286)*
Lost Worlds Inc....G....212 923-3423
New York *(G-10613)*

CLOTHING: Coats & Suits, Men's & Boys'

Adrian Jules Ltd....D....585 342-5886
Rochester *(G-13603)*
Advance Apparel Intl Inc....G....212 944-0984
New York *(G-8745)*
Allytex LLC....G....518 376-7539
Ballston Spa *(G-576)*
Centric Brands Inc....D....323 890-1800
New York *(G-9246)*
Check Group LLC....D....212 221-4700
New York *(G-9268)*
Christian Casey LLC....E....212 500-2200
New York *(G-9289)*
Christian Casey LLC....E....212 500-2200
New York *(G-9290)*
Concorde Apparel Company LLC....G....212 307-7848
New York *(G-9374)*
Excelled Sheepskin & Lea Coat....F....212 594-5843
New York *(G-9750)*
G-III Apparel Group Ltd....B....212 403-0500
New York *(G-9869)*
G-III Apparel Group Ltd....F....212 840-7272
New York *(G-9871)*
Giliberto Designs Inc....E....212 695-0216
New York *(G-9920)*
Great 4 Image Inc....E....518 424-2058
Rensselaer *(G-13474)*
Hana Sportswear Inc....E....315 639-6332
Dexter *(G-4115)*
Hickey Freeman Tailored CL Inc....E....585 467-7240
Rochester *(G-13865)*
Hugo Boss Usa Inc....D....212 940-0600
New York *(G-10146)*
J & X Production Inc....F....718 200-1228
New York *(G-10283)*
L F Fashion Orient Intl Co Ltd....G....917 667-3398
New York *(G-10494)*
Lvl Xiii Brands Inc....F....646 530-2795
New York *(G-10633)*
M Hidary & Co Inc....D....212 736-6540
New York *(G-10639)*
Manchu New York Inc....G....212 921-5050
New York *(G-10682)*
Mv Corp Inc....C....631 273-8020
Bay Shore *(G-703)*
Opposuits USA Inc....E....917 438-8878
New York *(G-11052)*
Pat & Rose Dress Inc....D....212 279-1357
New York *(G-11121)*
Proper Cloth LLC....G....646 964-4221
New York *(G-11265)*
Ps38 LLC....G....212 302-1108
New York *(G-11268)*
Therese The Childrens Collectn....G....518 346-2315
Schenectady *(G-14721)*
Wp Lavori USA Inc....G....212 244-6074
New York *(G-12143)*
Yong Ji Productions Inc....E....917 559-4616
Corona *(G-3857)*

CLOTHING: Coats, Leatherette, Oiled Fabric, Etc, Mens & Boys

House Pearl Fashions (us) Ltd....F....212 840-3183
New York *(G-10138)*

CLOTHING: Coats, Tailored, Mens/Boys, From Purchased Mtls

Blue Duck Trading Ltd....G....212 268-3122
New York *(G-9107)*

CLOTHING: Corset Access, Clasps & Stays

Higgins Supply Company Inc....D....607 836-6474
Mc Graw *(G-7927)*

CLOTHING: Costumes

Costume Culture By Franco LLC....G....718 821-7100
Glendale *(G-5396)*
Creative Costume Co....G....212 564-5552
Liverpool *(G-7231)*
Cygnet Studio Inc....F....646 450-4550
New York *(G-9442)*
Eric Winterling Inc....E....212 629-7686
New York *(G-9700)*
John Kristiansen New York Inc....F....212 388-1097
New York *(G-10352)*
Kidz Concepts LLC....D....212 398-1110
New York *(G-10441)*
Kiton Building Corp....E....212 486-3224
New York *(G-10453)*
Koon Enterprises LLC....G....718 886-3163
Fresh Meadows *(G-5200)*
Moresca Clothing and Costume....F....845 331-6012
Ulster Park *(G-15659)*
Prolink Industries Inc....F....212 354-5690
New York *(G-11259)*
Rubies Costume Company Inc....B....718 846-1008
Richmond Hill *(G-13510)*
Rubies Costume Company Inc....D....631 777-3300
Bay Shore *(G-719)*
Rubies Costume Company Inc....C....718 441-0834
Richmond Hill *(G-13511)*
Rubies Costume Company Inc....C....631 951-3688
Bay Shore *(G-720)*
Rubies Costume Company Inc....E....516 333-3473
Westbury *(G-16370)*
Rubies Costume Company Inc....F....631 435-7912
Bay Shore *(G-721)*
Rubies Costume Company Inc....E....516 326-1500
Bay Shore *(G-722)*
Rubies Costume Company Inc....C....718 846-1008
Richmond Hill *(G-13512)*
South Central Boyz....G....718 496-7270
Brooklyn *(G-2501)*

CLOTHING: Diaper Covers, Waterproof, From Purchased Material

Hercules Group Inc....E....212 813-8000
Port Washington *(G-13264)*

CLOTHING: Disposable

A Lunt Design Inc....F....716 662-0781
Orchard Park *(G-12695)*
Dvf Studio LLC....D....212 741-6607
New York *(G-9589)*
Dvf Studio LLC....G....646 576-8009
New York *(G-9590)*
HB Athletic Inc....F....914 560-8422
New Rochelle *(G-8613)*
Hpk Industries LLC....F....315 724-0196
Utica *(G-15709)*
Lakeland Industries Inc....C....631 981-9700
Ronkonkoma *(G-14367)*
Rainforest Apparel LLC....G....212 840-0880
New York *(G-11318)*

CLOTHING: Down-Filled, Men's & Boys'

Nyc Idol Apparel Inc....G....212 997-9797
New York *(G-11013)*

CLOTHING: Dresses

18 Rocks LLC....E....631 465-9990
Melville *(G-7995)*
Agi Brooks Production Co Inc....F....212 268-1533
New York *(G-8768)*
Allison Che Fashion Inc....F....212 391-1433
New York *(G-8800)*
Amj DOT LLC....G....718 775-3288
Brooklyn *(G-1530)*
Anna Sui Corp....E....212 941-8406
New York *(G-8873)*
August Silk Inc....E....212 643-2400
New York *(G-8961)*
August Silk Inc....G....212 643-2400
New York *(G-8962)*
Christian Siriano Holdings LLC....G....212 695-5494
New York *(G-9292)*
Csco LLC....E....212 375-6180
New York *(G-9429)*
CTS LLC....G....212 278-0058
New York *(G-9430)*
Cynthia Rowley Inc....F....212 242-3803
New York *(G-9443)*
Dalma Dress Mfg Co Inc....E....212 391-8296
Greenvale *(G-5629)*
Damianou Sportswear Inc....D....718 204-5600
Woodside *(G-16652)*
Dave & Johnny Ltd....E....212 302-9050
New York *(G-9477)*
Donna Karan Company LLC....C....212 789-1500
New York *(G-9550)*
Donna Karan Company LLC....C....716 297-0752
Niagara Falls *(G-12278)*
Donna Karan Company LLC....B....212 789-1500
New York *(G-9551)*
Donna Karan International Inc....F....212 789-1500
New York *(G-9552)*
Donna Karan International Inc....G....212 768-5800
New York *(G-9553)*
Faviana International Inc....E....212 594-4422
New York *(G-9789)*
Four Seasons Fashion Mfg Inc....E....212 947-6820
New York *(G-9832)*
G-III Apparel Group Ltd....E....212 403-0500
New York *(G-9870)*

Geoffrey Beere Inc .... E 212 371-5570
  New York (G-9908)
Haddad Bros Inc 718 377-5505
  Brooklyn (G-1959)
Halmode Apparel Inc .... A 212 819-9114
  New York (G-10023)
Haute By Blair Stanley LLC .... G 212 557-7868
  New York (G-10049)
I S C A Corp .... F 212 719-5123
  New York (G-10160)
Icer Scrubs LLC .... F 212 221-4700
  New York (G-10168)
Infinity Sourcing Services LLC .... G 212 868-2900
  New York (G-10204)
J R Nites 212 354-9670
  New York (G-10288)
Jiranimo Industries Ltd .... F 212 921-5106
  New York (G-10341)
Jon Teri Sports Inc .... E 212 398-0657
  New York (G-10357)
Judys Group Inc .... E 212 921-0515
  New York (G-10375)
Jump Design Group Inc .... C 212 869-3300
  New York (G-10378)
Kasper Group LLC .... C 212 354-4311
  New York (G-10414)
Krasner Group Inc .... G 212 268-4100
  New York (G-10479)
L F Fashion Orient Intl Co Ltd .... G 917 667-3398
  New York (G-10494)
Lmr Group Inc .... G 212 730-9221
  New York (G-10587)
Lou Sally Fashions Corp .... E 212 354-9670
  New York (G-10615)
Lcu Sally Fashions Corp .... E 212 354-1283
  New York (G-10616)
Milliore Fashion Inc 212 302-0001
  New York (G-10811)
Necessary Objects Ltd .... E 212 334-9888
  Long Island City (G-7535)
Nine West Holdings Inc 212 391-5000
  New York (G-10973)
Pat & Rose Dress Inc .... D 212 279-1357
  New York (G-11121)
Plugg LLC .... F 212 840-6655
  New York (G-11212)
Product Development Intl LLC .... G 212 279-6170
  New York (G-11255)
Quality Patterns Inc .... D 212 704-0355
  New York (G-11297)
R & M Richards Inc .... D 212 921-8820
  New York (G-11310)
Raven New York LLC .... G 212 584-9690
  New York (G-11328)
Rogan LLC .... G 212 680-1407
  New York (G-11420)
Rogan LLC .... E 646 496-9339
  New York (G-11421)
Ronni Nicole Group LLC .... E 212 764-1000
  New York (G-11429)
Sg Nyc LLC .... E 310 210-1837
  New York (G-11548)
Spencer AB Inc .... G 646 831-3728
  New York (G-11667)
SSG Fashions Ltd .... G 212 221-0933
  New York (G-11689)
Tabrisse Collections Inc .... F 212 921-1014
  New York (G-11773)
Tahari ASL LLC .... B 212 763-2800
  New York (G-11775)
Texport Fabrics Corp .... F 212 223-6066
  New York (G-11805)
Therese The Childrens Collectn .... G 518 346-2315
  Schenectady (G-14721)
Tom & Linda Platt Inc .... F 212 221-7208
  New York (G-11858)
Turn On Products Inc .... F 212 764-4545
  New York (G-11914)
Vanity Room Inc .... F 212 921-7154
  New York (G-11993)
Wear Abouts Apparel Inc .... F 212 827-0888
  New York (G-12085)
Worth Collection Ltd .... E 212 268-0312
  New York (G-12139)
Yeohlee Inc .... F 212 631-8099
  New York (G-12161)

CLOTHING: Dresses & Skirts

Betsy & Adam Ltd .... E 212 302-3750
  New York (G-9061)

CLOTHING: Dresses, Knit

Summit Apparel Inc .... E 631 213-8299
  Hauppauge (G-5951)
Winter Water Factory .... G 646 387-3247
  Brooklyn (G-2654)

CLOTHING: Dressing Gowns, Mens/Womens, From Purchased Matls

Mata Fashions LLC .... G 917 716-7894
  New York (G-10724)

CLOTHING: Foundation Garments, Women's

Deunall Corporation .... C 516 667-8875
  Levittown (G-7133)
E P Sewing Pleating Inc .... E 212 967-2575
  New York (G-9596)
Rago Foundations LLC .... E 718 728-8436
  Astoria (G-441)

CLOTHING: Furs

Anastasia Furs International .... G 212 868-9241
  New York (G-8855)
Avante .... G 516 782-4888
  Great Neck (G-5538)
B Smith Furs Inc .... F 212 967-5290
  New York (G-8992)
Dennis Basso Couture Inc .... F 212 794-4500
  New York (G-9501)
Georgy Creative Fashions Inc .... G 212 279-4885
  New York (G-9912)
Miller & Berkowitz Ltd .... F 212 244-5459
  New York (G-10809)
Sekas International Ltd .... F 212 629-6095
  New York (G-11536)
Stefan Furs Inc .... G 212 594-2788
  New York (G-11701)

CLOTHING: Garments, Indl, Men's & Boys

Beardslee Realty 516 747-5557
  Mineola (G-8206)
Classic Designer Workshop Inc .... G 212 730-8480
  New York (G-9319)
Kse Sportsman Media Inc .... D 212 852-6600
  New York (G-10483)
Stealth Inc .... F 718 252-7900
  Brooklyn (G-2515)

CLOTHING: Girdles & Other Foundation Garments, Knit

Maidenform LLC .... F 201 436-9200
  New York (G-10672)

CLOTHING: Girdles & Panty Girdles

Burlen Corp .... F 212 684-0052
  New York (G-9159)

CLOTHING: Gloves, Knit, Exc Dress & Semidress

Hawkins Fabrics Inc .... E 518 773-9550
  Johnstown (G-6830)

CLOTHING: Gowns & Dresses, Wedding

A & M Rosenthal Entps Inc .... E 646 638-9600
  New York (G-8688)
Alvina Vlenta Couture Collectn .... F 212 921-7058
  New York (G-8814)
Arcangel Inc .... G 347 771-0789
  New York (G-8899)
Birnbaum & Bullock Ltd .... G 212 242-2914
  New York (G-9090)
Cachet Industries Inc .... E 212 944-2188
  New York (G-9175)
Christos Inc .... E 212 921-0025
  New York (G-9295)
Couture Inc .... G 212 921-1166
  New York (G-9411)
Elana Laderos Ltd .... F 212 764-0840
  New York (G-9639)
Everlasting Memories .... G 716 833-1111
  Blasdell (G-926)
Kelly Grace Corp .... C 212 704-9603
  New York (G-10428)
Paris Wedding Center Corp .... F 347 368-4085
  Flushing (G-5035)
Paris Wedding Center Corp .... E 212 267-8088
  New York (G-11114)
Parsley Apparel Corp .... E 631 981-7181
  Ronkonkoma (G-14396)
Paula Varsalona Ltd .... F 212 570-9100
  New York (G-11125)

CLOTHING: Gowns, Formal

Bari-Jay Fashions Inc .... E 212 921-1551
  New York (G-9018)
Crisada Inc .... G 718 729-9730
  Long Island City (G-7417)
D J Night Ltd .... E 212 302-9050
  New York (G-9447)
Elizabeth Fillmore LLC .... E 212 647-0863
  New York (G-9654)
Jovani Fashion Ltd .... G 212 279-0222
  New York (G-10369)
Lily & Taylor Inc .... F 212 564-5459
  New York (G-10571)
Pronovias USA Inc .... E 212 897-6393
  New York (G-11262)
Ursula of Switzerland Inc .... E 518 237-2580
  Waterford (G-15990)

CLOTHING: Hats & Caps, Leather

J Lowy Co .... G 718 338-7324
  Brooklyn (G-2024)

CLOTHING: Hats & Caps, NEC

A-1 Skull Cap Corp .... E 718 633-9333
  Brooklyn (G-1463)
Athletic Cap Co Inc .... E 718 398-1300
  Staten Island (G-15045)
Flexfit Llc .... D 516 932-8800
  Hicksville (G-6086)
Kraft Hat Manufacturers Inc .... D 845 735-6200
  Pearl River (G-12904)
Paletot Ltd .... F 212 268-3774
  New York (G-11094)
Weinfeld Skull Cap Mfg Co Inc .... G 718 854-3864
  Brooklyn (G-2641)

CLOTHING: Hats & Caps, Uniform

Bonk Sam Uniforms Civilian Cap .... E 718 585-0665
  Bronx (G-1230)
Hankin Brothers Cap Co .... F 716 892-8840
  Buffalo (G-2864)
Kays Caps Inc .... G 518 273-6079
  Troy (G-15596)
Kingform Cap Company Inc .... D 516 822-2501
  Hicksville (G-6098)
New ERA Cap Co Inc .... B 716 604-9000
  Buffalo (G-2964)
New ERA Cap Co Inc 716 604-9000
  Buffalo (G-2965)
New ERA Cap Co Inc .... F 716 549-0445
  Derby (G-4114)

CLOTHING: Hats & Headwear, Knit

Gce International Inc .... D 212 704-4800
  New York (G-9890)
Lids Corporation .... G 518 459-7060
  Albany (G-95)

CLOTHING: Hosiery, Men's & Boys'

Haddad Hosiery LLC .... G 212 251-0022
  New York (G-10019)
High Point Design LLC .... F 212 354-2400
  New York (G-10094)
Lr Acquisition LLC .... F 212 301-8765
  New York (G-10620)
You and ME Legwear LLC .... F 212 279-9292
  New York (G-12165)

CLOTHING: Hosiery, Pantyhose & Knee Length, Sheer

Ellis Products Corp .... G 516 791-3732
  Valley Stream (G-15778)
Gina Group LLC .... E 212 947-2445
  New York (G-9922)
Hot Sox Company Incorporated .... E 212 957-2000
  New York (G-10130)
Trimfit Inc .... E 215 245-1122
  New York (G-11900)

CLOTHING: Hospital, Men's

Company		Phone
Adar Medical Uniform LLC	F	718 935-1197
Brooklyn *(G-1481)*		
Norcorp Inc	E	914 666-1310
Mount Kisco *(G-8352)*		

CLOTHING: Housedresses

Company		Phone
Millennium Productions Inc	F	212 944-6203
New York *(G-10808)*		

CLOTHING: Jackets & Vests, Exc Fur & Leather, Women's

Company		Phone
Donna Karan International Inc	F	212 789-1500
New York *(G-9552)*		
Donna Karan International Inc	G	212 768-5800
New York *(G-9553)*		
Levy Group Inc	C	212 398-0707
New York *(G-10557)*		
Standard Manufacturing Co Inc	D	518 235-2200
Troy *(G-15628)*		
Tiger J LLC	E	212 465-9300
New York *(G-11833)*		

CLOTHING: Jackets, Knit

Company		Phone
Freedom Rains Inc	G	646 710-4512
New York *(G-9844)*		
J & D Walter Distributors Inc	F	518 449-1606
Glenmont *(G-5413)*		

CLOTHING: Jeans, Men's & Boys'

Company		Phone
Guess Inc	E	716 298-3561
Niagara Falls *(G-12292)*		
Messex Group Inc	G	646 229-2582
New York *(G-10782)*		
One Jeanswear Group Inc	B	212 575-2571
New York *(G-11042)*		

CLOTHING: Knit Underwear & Nightwear

Company		Phone
In Toon Amkor Fashions Inc	E	718 937-4546
Long Island City *(G-7474)*		
Jockey International Inc	E	212 840-4900
New York *(G-10348)*		
Maidenform LLC	F	201 436-9200
New York *(G-10672)*		
Native Textiles Inc	G	212 951-5100
New York *(G-10889)*		

CLOTHING: Leather

Company		Phone
Avanti U S A Ltd	F	716 695-5800
Tonawanda *(G-15524)*		
G-III Apparel Group Ltd	B	212 403-0500
New York *(G-9869)*		
Georgy Creative Fashions Inc	G	212 279-4885
New York *(G-9912)*		
Louis Schwartz	G	845 356-6624
Spring Valley *(G-15000)*		
Studio One Leather Design Inc	F	212 760-1701
New York *(G-11728)*		

CLOTHING: Leather & sheep-lined clothing

Company		Phone
Cockpit Usa Inc	F	908 558-9704
New York *(G-9344)*		
G-III Leather Fashions Inc	E	212 403-0500
New York *(G-9872)*		

CLOTHING: Maternity

Company		Phone
Medi-Tech International Corp	G	800 333-0109
Brooklyn *(G-2187)*		
Zoomers Inc	E	718 369-2656
Brooklyn *(G-2670)*		

CLOTHING: Men's & boy's clothing, nec

Company		Phone
Apogee Retail NY	G	516 731-1727
Levittown *(G-7130)*		
By Robert James	G	212 253-2121
New York *(G-9165)*		
Eon Collections	E	212 695-1263
New York *(G-9692)*		

CLOTHING: Men's & boy's underwear & nightwear

Company		Phone
Apparel Partnership Group LLC	G	212 302-7722
New York *(G-8889)*		
Candlesticks Inc	F	212 947-8900
New York *(G-9194)*		
Christian Casey LLC	E	212 500-2200
New York *(G-9289)*		
Christian Casey LLC	E	212 500-2200
New York *(G-9290)*		
Revolutionwear Inc	G	617 669-9191
New York *(G-11379)*		
Tommy John Inc	E	800 708-3490
New York *(G-11864)*		
Waterbury Garment LLC	E	212 725-1500
New York *(G-12080)*		

CLOTHING: Mens & Boys Jackets, Sport, Suede, Leatherette

Company		Phone
Broadway Knitting Mills Inc	G	716 692-4421
North Tonawanda *(G-12418)*		
G-III Apparel Group Ltd	B	212 403-0500
New York *(G-9869)*		
Standard Manufacturing Co Inc	D	518 235-2200
Troy *(G-15628)*		

CLOTHING: Millinery

Company		Phone
Albrizio Inc	G	212 719-5290
Brooklyn *(G-1501)*		
Lenore Marshall Inc	G	212 947-5945
New York *(G-10547)*		
Lloyds Fashions Inc	G	631 435-3353
Brentwood *(G-1141)*		

CLOTHING: Neckties, Knit

Company		Phone
Mongru Neckwear Inc	E	718 706-0406
Long Island City *(G-7529)*		

CLOTHING: Neckwear

Company		Phone
Emunas Sales Inc	F	718 621-3138
Brooklyn *(G-1835)*		
JS Blank & Co Inc	E	212 689-4835
New York *(G-10373)*		
MANe Enterprises Inc	D	718 472-4955
Long Island City *(G-7512)*		
Mongru Neckwear Inc	E	718 706-0406
Long Island City *(G-7529)*		
Roffe Accessories Inc		212 213-1440
New York *(G-11419)*		
S Broome and Co Inc	D	718 663-6800
Long Island City *(G-7583)*		
Valenti Neckwear Co Inc	G	914 969-0700
Yonkers *(G-16805)*		
Warnaco Inc	B	212 287-8000
New York *(G-12071)*		
Wetherall Contracting NY Inc	F	718 894-7011
Middle Village *(G-8128)*		

CLOTHING: Outerwear, Knit

Company		Phone
Alpha Knitting Mills Inc	F	718 628-6300
Brooklyn *(G-1513)*		
Andrea Strongwater	G	212 873-0905
New York *(G-8858)*		
Asian Global Trading Corp	F	718 786-0998
Long Island City *(G-7390)*		
Bock Family Holdings Inc	G	212 921-5688
New York *(G-9116)*		
Dressy Tessy Inc	G	212 869-0750
New York *(G-9576)*		
E I Du Pont De Nemours & Co	E	716 876-4420
Buffalo *(G-2807)*		
Emerald Holdings Inc	G	718 797-4404
Brooklyn *(G-1829)*		
Fashion Avenue Knits Inc	F	718 456-9000
New York *(G-9786)*		
Gabani Inc	G	631 283-4930
Southampton *(G-14954)*		
GAME Sportswear Ltd	E	914 962-1701
Yorktown Heights *(G-16817)*		
Gildan Apparel USA Inc	G	212 476-0341
New York *(G-9919)*		
Hamil America Inc	F	212 244-2645
New York *(G-10025)*		
Hania By Anya Cole LLC	G	212 302-3550
New York *(G-10033)*		
Lynch Knitting Mills Inc	F	718 821-3436
Brooklyn *(G-2139)*		
Machinit Inc	G	631 454-9297
Farmingdale *(G-4813)*		
Mars Fashions Inc		718 402-2200
Bronx *(G-1323)*		
Mdj Sales Associates Inc	G	914 420-5897
Mamaroneck *(G-7749)*		
Native Textiles Inc	G	212 951-5100
New York *(G-10889)*		
North Star Knitting Mills Inc	G	718 894-4848
Glendale *(G-5405)*		
S & V Knits Inc	E	631 752-1595
Farmingdale *(G-4872)*		
T & R Knitting Mills Inc	F	212 840-8665
New York *(G-11767)*		

CLOTHING: Outerwear, Lthr, Wool/Down-Filled, Men, Youth/Boy

Company		Phone
Brigantine Inc		212 354-8550
New York *(G-9139)*		
Herman Kay Company Ltd		212 239-2025
New York *(G-10083)*		
I Spiewak & Sons Inc		212 695-1620
New York *(G-10162)*		
Maiyet Inc	G	212 343-9999
New York *(G-10674)*		
Rainforest Inc	F	212 575-7620
New York *(G-11319)*		
Vf Outdoor Inc	E	718 698-6215
Staten Island *(G-15152)*		
Vf Outdoor LLC	E	845 928-4900
Central Valley *(G-3398)*		

CLOTHING: Outerwear, Women's & Misses' NEC

Company		Phone
525 America LLC	G	212 921-5688
New York *(G-8682)*		
6th Avenue Showcase Inc		212 382-0400
New York *(G-8684)*		
A & B Finishing Inc	E	718 522-4702
Brooklyn *(G-1449)*		
Accessory Street LLC	F	212 686-8990
New York *(G-8721)*		
Ally Nyc Corp		212 447-7277
New York *(G-8804)*		
Angel-Made In Heaven Inc	G	718 832-4778
Brooklyn *(G-1534)*		
Bagznyc Corp	F	212 643-8202
New York *(G-9003)*		
Bank-Miller Co Inc	E	914 227-9357
Pelham *(G-12933)*		
Bock Family Holdings Inc	G	212 921-5688
New York *(G-9116)*		
Canada Goose Inc	G	888 668-0625
New York *(G-9190)*		
Canada Goose Us Inc	G	888 276-6297
Williamsville *(G-16574)*		
Candlesticks Inc	F	212 947-8900
New York *(G-9194)*		
Carolina Herrera Ltd		212 944-5757
New York *(G-9214)*		
Central Mills Inc	C	212 764-9011
New York *(G-9244)*		
China Ting Fashion Group (usa)	G	212 716-1600
New York *(G-9283)*		
Comint Apparel Group LLC	F	212 947-7474
New York *(G-9363)*		
Consolidated Fashion Corp	G	212 719-3000
New York *(G-9383)*		
Cynthia Rowley Inc	F	212 242-3803
New York *(G-9443)*		
Dalma Dress Mfg Co Inc	E	212 391-8296
Greenvale *(G-5629)*		
Dana Michele LLC		917 757-7777
New York *(G-9463)*		
Dani II Inc	F	212 869-5999
New York *(G-9466)*		
Donna Karan International Inc	F	212 789-1500
New York *(G-9552)*		
Donna Karan International Inc	G	212 768-5800
New York *(G-9553)*		
Elie Tahari Ltd		212 398-2622
New York *(G-9646)*		
Emerald Holdings Inc	G	718 797-4404
Brooklyn *(G-1829)*		
Emerson & Oliver LLC	G	585 775-9929
Rochester *(G-13778)*		
Falls Manufacturing Inc	G	518 672-7189
Philmont *(G-12986)*		
Four Seasons Fashion Mfg Inc	E	212 947-6820
New York *(G-9832)*		
G-III Apparel Group Ltd	B	212 403-0500
New York *(G-9869)*		

PRODUCT SECTION

CLOTHING: Shirts

G-III Leather Fashions Inc .... E 212 403-0500
New York (G-9872)
GAME Sportswear Ltd .... E 914 962-1701
Yorktown Heights (G-16817)
Gloria Apparel Inc .... F 212 947-0869
New York (G-9946)
Golden Leaves Knitwear Inc .... E 718 875-8235
Brooklyn (G-1938)
Hana Sportswear Inc .... E 315 639-6332
Dexter (G-4115)
Herman Kay Company Ltd .... C 212 239-2025
New York (G-10083)
Hot Line Industries Inc .... F 516 764-0400
Plainview (G-13061)
House Pearl Fashions (us) Ltd .... F 212 840-3183
New York (G-10138)
Int Trading USA LLC .... C 212 760-2338
New York (G-10229)
Jesse Joeckel .... G 631 668-2772
Montauk (G-8304)
Jomat New York Inc .... E 718 369-7641
Brooklyn (G-2044)
Just Bottoms & Tops Inc .... F 212 564-3202
New York (G-10383)
Kasper Group LLC .... F 212 354-4311
New York (G-10413)
Lahoya Enterprise Inc .... E 718 886-8799
College Point (G-3652)
Land n Sea Inc .... D 212 444-6000
New York (G-10513)
Lemral Knitwear Inc .... D 718 210-0175
Brooklyn (G-2109)
Lgb Inc .... E 212 278-8280
New York (G-10559)
Liberty Apparel Company Inc .... E 718 625-4000
New York (G-10560)
Light Inc .... G 212 629-3255
New York (G-10568)
Luxe Imagine Consulting LLC .... G 212 273-9770
New York (G-10632)
M A M Knitting Mills Corp .... E 800 570-0093
Brooklyn (G-2144)
Maggy Boutique Ltd .... E 212 997-5222
New York (G-10664)
Maiyet Inc .... G 212 343-9999
New York (G-10674)
Manchu New York Inc .... G 212 921-5050
New York (G-10682)
Manchu Times Fashion Inc .... G 212 921-5050
New York (G-10683)
Marina Holding Corp .... F 718 646-9283
Brooklyn (G-2167)
Miguelina Inc .... F 212 925-0320
New York (G-10803)
Miltons of New York Inc .... G 212 997-3359
New York (G-10813)
Moes Wear Apparel Inc .... F 718 940-1597
Brooklyn (G-2222)
Mv Corp Inc .... C 631 273-8020
Bay Shore (G-703)
Mystic Inc .... C 212 239-2025
New York (G-10869)
Only Hearts Ltd .... E 212 268-0886
New York (G-11046)
Pacific Alliance Usa Inc .... G 336 500-8184
New York (G-11088)
Pacific Alliance Usa Inc .... D 646 839-7000
New York (G-11089)
Pat & Rose Dress Inc .... D 212 279-1357
New York (G-11121)
Primo Coat Corp .... E 718 349-2070
Long Island City (G-7560)
Pti-Pacific Inc .... G 212 414-8495
New York (G-11271)
Pvh Corp .... D 212 502-6300
New York (G-11284)
RD Intrntnl Style .... G 212 382-2360
New York (G-11335)
Republic Clothing Corporation .... E 212 719-3000
New York (G-11365)
Rogers Group Inc .... E 212 643-9292
New York (G-11423)
Rvc Enterprises LLC .... F 212 391-4600
New York (G-11451)
S & V Knits Inc .... E 631 752-1595
Farmingdale (G-4872)
S & W Knitting Mills Inc .... E 718 237-2416
Brooklyn (G-2436)
Smooth Industries Incorporated .... E 212 869-1080
New York (G-11628)

SRP Apparel Group Inc .... G 212 764-4810
New York (G-11687)
Standard Manufacturing Co Inc .... D 518 235-2200
Troy (G-15628)
Sunynams Fashions Ltd .... G 212 268-5200
New York (G-11746)
Survival Inc .... G 631 385-5060
Centerport (G-3352)
Tbhl International LLC .... F 212 799-2007
New York (G-11787)
THE Design Group Inc .... F 212 681-1548
New York (G-11808)
Vf Imagewear Inc .... E 718 352-2363
Bayside (G-751)
Vf Outdoor LLC .... E 845 928-4900
Central Valley (G-3398)
Warnaco Group Inc .... E 212 287-8000
New York (G-12070)
Yigal-Azrouel Inc .... E 212 302-1194
New York (G-12162)
Zar Group LLC .... G 212 944-2510
New York (G-12169)
Zia Power Inc .... E 845 661-8388
New York (G-12176)

CLOTHING: Overcoats & Topcoats, Men/Boy, Purchased Materials

Ralph Lauren Corporation .... B 212 318-7000
New York (G-11321)

CLOTHING: Pants, Work, Men's, Youths' & Boys'

Ace Drop Cloth Canvas Pdts Inc .... E 718 731-1550
Bronx (G-1208)

CLOTHING: Panty Hose

Brach Knitting Mills Inc .... F 845 651-4450
Florida (G-4968)
Classic Hosiery Inc .... E 845 342-6661
Middletown (G-8142)
Fine Sheer Industries Inc .... F 212 594-4224
New York (G-9804)

CLOTHING: Raincoats, Exc Vulcanized Rubber, Purchased Matls

Essex Manufacturing Inc .... D 212 239-0080
New York (G-9712)
Levy Group Inc .... C 212 398-0707
New York (G-10557)
Mpdw Inc .... G 925 631-6878
New York (G-10851)

CLOTHING: Robes & Dressing Gowns

Authentic Brands Group LLC .... C 212 760-2410
New York (G-8966)
Komar Luxury Brands .... G 646 472-0060
New York (G-10468)
Lady Ester Lingerie Corp .... E 212 689-1729
New York (G-10506)
Nautica Opco LLC .... B 212 541-5757
New York (G-10896)
Palmbay Ltd .... G 718 424-3388
Flushing (G-5034)

CLOTHING: Robes & Housecoats, Children's

Waterbury Garment LLC .... E 212 725-1500
New York (G-12080)

CLOTHING: Scarves & Mufflers, Knit

180s LLC .... E 410 534-6320
New York (G-8666)

CLOTHING: Service Apparel, Women's

Bestec Concept Inc .... G 718 937-5848
Brooklyn (G-1604)
Chloe International Inc .... F 212 730-6661
New York (G-9285)
Fashion Ave Sweater Knits LLC .... D 212 302-8282
New York (G-9785)
GMC Mercantile Corp .... F 212 498-9488
New York (G-9948)
HC Contracting Inc .... D 212 643-9292
New York (G-10054)

Jsc Designs Ltd .... E 212 302-1001
New York (G-10374)
Lotus Apparel Designs Inc .... G 646 236-9363
Westbury (G-16352)
Mag Brands LLC .... D 212 629-9600
New York (G-10660)
RAK Finishing Corp .... E 718 416-4242
Howard Beach (G-6331)

CLOTHING: Shawls, Knit

Lloyds Fashions Inc .... D 631 435-3353
Brentwood (G-1141)

CLOTHING: Sheep-Lined

US Authentic LLC .... G 914 767-0295
Katonah (G-6847)

CLOTHING: Shirts

Andy & Evan Industries Inc .... G 212 967-7908
New York (G-8861)
August Silk Inc .... E 212 643-2400
New York (G-8961)
August Silk Inc .... E 212 643-2400
New York (G-8962)
Bowe Industries Inc .... D 718 441-6464
Glendale (G-5392)
Bowe Industries Inc .... D 718 441-6464
Glendale (G-5393)
Check Group LLC .... D 212 221-4700
New York (G-9268)
Christian Casey LLC .... E 212 500-2200
New York (G-9289)
Christian Casey LLC .... E 212 500-2200
New York (G-9290)
Colony Holdings Intl LLC .... E 212 868-2800
New York (G-9352)
Cyberlimit Inc .... F 212 840-9597
New York (G-9441)
Donna Karan International Inc .... F 212 789-1500
New York (G-9552)
Donna Karan International Inc .... E 212 768-5800
New York (G-9553)
Garan Incorporated .... E 212 563-1292
New York (G-9882)
Garan Manufacturing Corp .... E 212 563-2000
New York (G-9883)
Gbg National Brands Group LLC .... G 646 839-7000
New York (G-9886)
Grayers America Inc .... E 310 953-2742
New York (G-9980)
Groupe 16sur20 LLC .... F 212 625-1620
New York (G-9998)
Haddad Bros Inc .... F 212 563-2117
New York (G-10018)
Interbrand LLC .... G 212 840-9595
New York (G-10237)
Jordache Enterprises Inc .... D 212 944-1330
New York (G-10360)
Jordache Enterprises Inc .... C 212 643-8400
New York (G-10361)
Just Brass Inc .... G 212 724-5447
New York (G-10384)
Lt2 LLC .... E 212 684-1510
New York (G-10623)
M S B International Ltd .... F 212 302-5551
New York (G-10642)
Mega Sourcing Inc .... G 646 682-0304
Merrick (G-8103)
Miltons of New York Inc .... G 212 997-3359
New York (G-10813)
Mulitex Usa Inc .... G 212 398-0440
New York (G-10857)
Oxford Industries Inc .... F 212 840-2288
New York (G-11077)
Perry Ellis Menswear LLC .... C 212 221-7500
New York (G-11162)
Roffe Accessories Inc .... E 212 213-1440
New York (G-11419)
Saad Collection Inc .... G 212 937-0341
New York (G-11461)
Schwartz Textile LLC .... E 718 499-8243
Brooklyn (G-2451)
Sifonya Inc .... G 212 620-4512
New York (G-11581)
Whittall & Shon .... G 212 594-2626
New York (G-12106)
Yale Trouser Corporation .... F 516 255-0700
Oceanside (G-12566)

CLOTHING: Shirts, Dress, Men's & Boys'

CLOTHING: Shirts, Dress, Men's & Boys'

Americo Group Inc ....E...... 212 563-2700
  New York *(G-8840)*
Americo Group Inc ....E...... 212 563-2700
  New York *(G-8841)*
Arthur Gluck Shirtmakers Inc ....F...... 212 755-8165
  Brooklyn *(G-1559)*
Gce International Inc ....D...... 773 263-1210
  New York *(G-9892)*
Great Universal Corp ....E...... 917 302-0065
  New York *(G-9982)*
Phillips-Van Heusen Europe ....F...... 212 381-3500
  New York *(G-11183)*
Pvh Corp ....D...... 212 381-3500
  New York *(G-11281)*
Pvh Corp ....G...... 845 561-0233
  New Windsor *(G-8656)*
Pvh Corp ....G...... 631 254-8200
  Deer Park *(G-4031)*
Pvh Corp ....E...... 212 549-6000
  New York *(G-11282)*
Pvh Corp ....G...... 212 719-2600
  New York *(G-11285)*
Ralph Lauren Corporation ....B...... 212 318-7000
  New York *(G-11321)*
Warnaco Inc ....B...... 212 287-8000
  New York *(G-12071)*
Warnaco Inc ....F...... 718 722-3000
  Brooklyn *(G-2639)*

CLOTHING: Shirts, Knit

KD Dids Inc ....E...... 718 402-2012
  Bronx *(G-1305)*
Ralph Lauren Corporation ....B...... 212 318-7000
  New York *(G-11321)*
Warnaco Inc ....F...... 718 722-3000
  Brooklyn *(G-2639)*

CLOTHING: Shirts, Sports & Polo, Men & Boy, Purchased Mtrl

Ibrands International LLC ....F...... 212 354-1330
  New York *(G-10166)*
Sue & Sam Co Inc ....E...... 718 436-1672
  Brooklyn *(G-2530)*

CLOTHING: Shirts, Sports & Polo, Men's & Boys'

Grunt Apparel Inc ....G...... 646 878-6171
  New York *(G-10002)*
Oved Mens LLC ....E...... 212 563-4999
  New York *(G-11070)*
Perry Ellis International Inc ....F...... 212 536-5400
  New York *(G-11160)*
Perry Ellis International Inc ....G...... 212 536-5499
  New York *(G-11161)*

CLOTHING: Shirts, Women's & Juniors', From Purchased Mtrls

Brach Knitting Mills Inc ....F...... 845 651-4450
  Florida *(G-4968)*
Jordache Enterprises Inc ....D...... 212 944-1330
  New York *(G-10360)*
Jordache Enterprises Inc ....C...... 212 643-8400
  New York *(G-10361)*

CLOTHING: Skirts

Alfred Dunner Inc ....B...... 212 478-4300
  New York *(G-8795)*
Anna Sui Corp ....E...... 212 941-8406
  New York *(G-8873)*
Bruno & Canio Ltd ....E...... 845 624-3060
  Nanuet *(G-8460)*
Carolina Herrera Ltd ....E...... 212 944-5757
  New York *(G-9214)*
Geoffrey Beene Inc ....E...... 212 371-5570
  New York *(G-9908)*
Hampshire Sub II Inc ....D...... 631 321-0923
  New York *(G-10027)*
Kayo of California ....G...... 212 354-6336
  New York *(G-10423)*
Nyc Idol Apparel Inc ....G...... 212 997-9797
  New York *(G-11013)*
Pat & Rose Dress Inc ....D...... 212 279-1357
  New York *(G-11121)*
Permit Fashion Group Inc ....G...... 212 912-0988
  Woodbury *(G-16627)*

Rhoda Lee Inc ....D...... 212 840-5700
  New York *(G-11384)*
Tenby LLC ....C...... 646 863-5890
  New York *(G-11800)*
Turn On Products Inc ....F...... 212 764-4545
  New York *(G-11914)*

CLOTHING: Slacks & Shorts, Dress, Men's, Youths' & Boys'

Montero International Inc ....G...... 212 695-1787
  Westbury *(G-16358)*

CLOTHING: Slacks, Girls' & Children's

Garan Incorporated ....C...... 212 563-1292
  New York *(G-9882)*
Garan Manufacturing Corp ....G...... 212 563-2000
  New York *(G-9883)*
Jordache Enterprises Inc ....D...... 212 944-1330
  New York *(G-10360)*
Jordache Enterprises Inc ....C...... 212 643-8400
  New York *(G-10361)*

CLOTHING: Sleeping Garments, Men's & Boys'

Sleepwear Holdings Inc ....C...... 516 466-4738
  New York *(G-11618)*

CLOTHING: Sleeping Garments, Women's & Children's

Allure Fashions Inc ....G...... 516 829-2470
  Great Neck *(G-5532)*
Candlesticks Inc ....F...... 212 947-8900
  New York *(G-9194)*
Kokin Inc ....E...... 212 643-8225
  New York *(G-10465)*
Komar Luxury Brands ....G...... 646 472-0060
  New York *(G-10468)*
Natori Company Incorporated ....D...... 212 532-7796
  New York *(G-10890)*
Waterbury Garment LLC ....E...... 212 725-1500
  New York *(G-12080)*

CLOTHING: Slipper Socks

Palmbay Ltd ....G...... 718 424-3388
  Flushing *(G-5034)*

CLOTHING: Socks

Ace Drop Cloth Canvas Pdts Inc ....E...... 718 731-1550
  Bronx *(G-1208)*
Ashko Group LLC ....F...... 212 594-6050
  New York *(G-8931)*
Customize Elite Socks LLC ....G...... 212 533-8551
  New York *(G-9437)*
Fine Sheer Industries Inc ....F...... 212 594-4224
  New York *(G-9804)*
Galiva Inc ....G...... 903 600-5755
  Brooklyn *(G-1916)*
Gbg Socks LLC ....E...... 646 839-7000
  New York *(G-9887)*
Gina Group LLC ....E...... 212 947-2445
  New York *(G-9922)*
La Strada Dance Footwear Inc ....G...... 631 242-1401
  Deer Park *(G-3999)*
Majesty Brands LLC ....G...... 212 283-3400
  New York *(G-10676)*
New Hampton Creations Inc ....G...... 212 244-7474
  New York *(G-10925)*
Sockbin ....G...... 917 519-1119
  Brooklyn *(G-2491)*
Socks and More of NY Inc ....G...... 718 769-1785
  Brooklyn *(G-2492)*
Sticky Socks LLC ....G...... 212 541-5927
  New York *(G-11712)*
Strassburg Medical LLC ....G...... 716 433-9368
  North Tonawanda *(G-12456)*
Trimfit Inc ....E...... 215 245-1122
  New York *(G-11900)*
United Retail II ....G...... 212 966-9692
  New York *(G-11954)*

CLOTHING: Sportswear, Women's

31 Phillip Lim LLC ....E...... 212 354-6540
  New York *(G-8678)*
American Apparel Trading Corp ....G...... 212 764-5990
  New York *(G-8823)*

Angel-Made In Heaven Inc ....F...... 212 869-5678
  New York *(G-8863)*
Argee America Inc ....G...... 212 768-9840
  New York *(G-8905)*
AZ Yashir Bapaz Inc ....G...... 212 947-7357
  New York *(G-8985)*
Bandit International Ltd ....F...... 718 402-2100
  Bronx *(G-1225)*
Bernard Chaus Inc ....D...... 212 354-1280
  New York *(G-9051)*
Bernard Chaus Inc ....C...... 646 562-4700
  New York *(G-9052)*
Cai Design Inc ....F...... 212 401-9973
  New York *(G-9177)*
Cathy Daniels Ltd ....E...... 212 354-8000
  New York *(G-9231)*
Central Apparel Group Ltd ....G...... 212 868-6505
  New York *(G-9242)*
City Sites Sportswear Inc ....E...... 718 375-2990
  Brooklyn *(G-1698)*
Daily Wear Sportswear Corp ....G...... 718 972-0533
  Brooklyn *(G-1751)*
Danice Stores Inc ....F...... 212 665-0389
  New York *(G-9467)*
Double Take Fashions Inc ....G...... 718 832-9000
  New York *(G-9561)*
Drew Philips Corp ....G...... 212 354-0095
  New York *(G-9577)*
El-La Design Inc ....G...... 212 382-1080
  New York *(G-9638)*
F & J Designs Inc ....G...... 212 302-8755
  New York *(G-9761)*
French Atmosphere Inc ....F...... 516 371-9100
  New York *(G-9846)*
Halmode Apparel Inc ....A...... 212 819-9114
  New York *(G-10023)*
Ikeddi Enterprises Inc ....F...... 212 302-7644
  New York *(G-10180)*
Ikeddi Enterprises Inc ....G...... 212 302-7644
  New York *(G-10181)*
Intriguing Threads Apparel Inc ....F...... 212 768-8733
  New York *(G-10260)*
J & E Talit Inc ....G...... 718 850-1333
  Richmond Hill *(G-13505)*
Jaxis Inc ....G...... 212 302-7611
  Brooklyn *(G-2034)*
JEnvie Sport Inc ....G...... 212 967-2322
  New York *(G-10327)*
Joe Benbasset Inc ....E...... 212 594-8440
  New York *(G-10349)*
Jonden Manufacturing Co Inc ....F...... 516 442-4895
  Oceanside *(G-12542)*
Karen Kane Inc ....F...... 212 827-0980
  New York *(G-10408)*
Kayo of California ....G...... 212 354-6336
  New York *(G-10423)*
Leggiadro International Inc ....G...... 212 997-8766
  New York *(G-10541)*
Life Style Design Group ....E...... 212 391-8666
  New York *(G-10564)*
Marcasiano Inc ....G...... 212 614-9412
  New York *(G-10697)*
Meryl Diamond Ltd ....D...... 212 730-0333
  New York *(G-10779)*
Millennium Productions Inc ....F...... 212 944-6203
  New York *(G-10808)*
Morelle Products Ltd ....G...... 212 391-8070
  New York *(G-10841)*
Nine West Holdings Inc ....G...... 212 642-3860
  New York *(G-10971)*
Nine West Holdings Inc ....G...... 212 642-3860
  New York *(G-10977)*
Nlhe LLC ....E...... 212 594-0012
  Brooklyn *(G-2270)*
Noah Enterprises Ltd ....E...... 212 736-2888
  New York *(G-10982)*
Park Avenue Sportswear Ltd ....F...... 718 369-0520
  Brooklyn *(G-2305)*
Pride & Joys Inc ....G...... 212 594-9820
  New York *(G-11239)*
Pvh Corp ....G...... 212 381-3500
  New York *(G-11283)*
Ramsbury Property Us Inc ....F...... 212 223-6250
  New York *(G-11322)*
Rene Portier Inc ....G...... 718 853-7896
  Brooklyn *(G-2398)*
Ritchie Corp ....F...... 212 768-0083
  New York *(G-11397)*
Robespierre Inc ....G...... 212 764-8810
  New York *(G-11409)*

PRODUCT SECTION

Robespierre Inc .... C 212 594-0012
 New York *(G-11410)*
S & S Manufacturing Co Inc .... D 212 444-6000
 New York *(G-11456)*
S2 Sportswear Inc .... F 347 335-0713
 Brooklyn *(G-2441)*
Salisbury Sportswear Inc .... E 516 221-9519
 Bellmore *(G-794)*
Siskind Group Inc .... F 212 840-0880
 New York *(G-11601)*
Snowman .... G 212 239-8818
 New York *(G-11632)*
Ssa Trading Ltd .... F 646 465-9500
 New York *(G-11688)*
SSG Fashions Ltd .... G 212 221-0933
 New York *(G-11689)*
St John .... G 718 720-8367
 Staten Island *(G-15137)*
St John .... G 718 771-4541
 Brooklyn *(G-2506)*
Sterling Possessions Ltd .... G 212 594-0418
 New York *(G-11707)*
Street Beat Sportswear Inc .... F 718 302-1500
 Brooklyn *(G-2524)*
Tiger J LLC .... E 212 465-9300
 New York *(G-11833)*
TR Designs Inc .... E 212 398-9300
 New York *(G-11882)*
Turn On Products Inc .... D 212 764-2121
 New York *(G-11913)*
Urban Apparel Group Inc .... E 212 947-7009
 New York *(G-11968)*

CLOTHING: Suits & Skirts, Women's & Misses'

Bindle and Keep .... G 917 740-5002
 Brooklyn *(G-1615)*
Opposuits USA Inc .... E 917 438-8878
 New York *(G-11052)*
R & M Richards Inc .... D 212 921-8820
 New York *(G-11310)*

CLOTHING: Suits, Men's & Boys', From Purchased Materials

Bindle and Keep .... G 917 740-5002
 Brooklyn *(G-1615)*
Canali USA Inc .... E 212 767-0205
 New York *(G-9191)*
Donna Karan Company LLC .... C 212 789-1500
 New York *(G-9550)*
Donna Karan Company LLC .... B 212 789-1500
 New York *(G-9551)*
Kozinn+sons Merchant Tailors .... E 212 643-1916
 New York *(G-10475)*
Martin Greenfield Clothiers .... C 718 497-5480
 Brooklyn *(G-2174)*
Michael Andrews LLC .... F 212 677-1755
 New York *(G-10790)*
Primo Coat Corp .... E 718 349-2070
 Long Island City *(G-7560)*
Roth Clothing Co Inc .... G 718 384-4927
 Brooklyn *(G-2416)*
Royal Clothing Corp .... G 718 436-5841
 Brooklyn *(G-2418)*
Tom James Company .... F 212 593-0204
 New York *(G-11860)*

CLOTHING: Sweaters & Sweater Coats, Knit

79 Metro Ltd .... G 212 944-4030
 New York *(G-8685)*
A & B Finishing Inc .... E 718 522-4702
 Brooklyn *(G-1449)*
Accurate Knitting Corp .... G 646 552-2216
 Brooklyn *(G-1472)*
B & B Sweater Mills Inc .... F 718 456-8693
 Brooklyn *(G-1578)*
Binghamton Knitting Co Inc .... E 607 722-6941
 Binghamton *(G-866)*
Blueberry Knitting Inc .... G 718 599-6520
 Brooklyn *(G-1623)*
Charter Ventures LLC .... F 212 868-0222
 New York *(G-9267)*
Domani Fashions Corp .... G 718 797-0505
 Brooklyn *(G-1786)*
Golden Leaves Knitwear Inc .... E 718 875-8235
 Brooklyn *(G-1938)*
Great Adirondack Yarn Company .... F 518 843-3381
 Amsterdam *(G-339)*

Jeric Knit Wear .... G 631 979-8827
 Smithtown *(G-14901)*
Jj Basics LLC .... E 212 768-4779
 New York *(G-10342)*
Julia Knit Inc .... G 718 848-1900
 Ozone Park *(G-12828)*
K & S Childrens Wear Inc .... E 718 624-0006
 Brooklyn *(G-2062)*
Keryakos Inc .... F 518 344-7092
 Schenectady *(G-14693)*
Knit Resource Center Ltd .... G 212 221-1990
 New York *(G-10459)*
M A M Knitting Mills Corp .... G 800 570-0093
 Brooklyn *(G-2144)*
M B M Manufacturing Inc .... F 718 769-4148
 Brooklyn *(G-2146)*
Manrico Usa Inc .... G 212 794-4200
 New York *(G-10693)*
Marble Knits Inc .... E 718 237-7990
 Brooklyn *(G-2164)*
Matchables Inc .... F 718 389-9318
 Brooklyn *(G-2178)*
New York Sweater Company Inc .... E 845 629-9533
 New York *(G-10943)*
Phillips-Van Heusen Europe .... F 212 381-3500
 New York *(G-11183)*
Premier Knits Ltd .... F 718 323-8264
 Ozone Park *(G-12831)*
Pvh Corp .... D 212 381-3500
 New York *(G-11281)*
Pvh Corp .... G 212 549-6000
 New York *(G-11282)*
Rags Knitwear Ltd .... F 718 782-8417
 Brooklyn *(G-2378)*
S & T Knitting Co Inc .... E 607 722-7558
 Conklin *(G-3732)*
S & W Knitting Mills Inc .... E 718 237-2416
 Brooklyn *(G-2436)*
Sage Knitwear Inc .... G 718 628-7902
 West Babylon *(G-16190)*
Sarug Inc .... D 718 339-2791
 Brooklyn *(G-2448)*
Sweater Brand Inc .... G 718 797-0505
 Brooklyn *(G-2545)*
T & R Knitting Mills Inc .... E 718 497-4017
 Glendale *(G-5409)*
United Knitwear International .... G 212 354-2920
 New York *(G-11953)*
WR Design Corp .... E 212 354-9000
 New York *(G-12144)*

CLOTHING: Sweaters, Men's & Boys'

Bernette Apparel LLC .... F 212 279-5526
 New York *(G-9053)*
Cotton Emporium Inc .... G 718 894-3365
 Glendale *(G-5397)*
Just Bottoms & Tops Inc .... F 212 564-3202
 New York *(G-10383)*
Komar Luxury Brands .... G 646 472-0060
 New York *(G-10468)*
M A M Knitting Mills Corp .... E 800 570-0093
 Brooklyn *(G-2144)*
S & W Knitting Mills Inc .... E 718 237-2416
 Brooklyn *(G-2436)*
Scharf and Breit Inc .... E 516 282-0287
 Williston Park *(G-16595)*
Schwartz Textile LLC .... E 718 499-8243
 Brooklyn *(G-2451)*
Uniqlo USA LLC .... F 877 486-4756
 New York *(G-11948)*

CLOTHING: Sweatshirts & T-Shirts, Men's & Boys'

Kt Group Inc .... G 212 760-2500
 New York *(G-10485)*

CLOTHING: Swimwear, Men's & Boys'

Comme-Ci Comme-CA AP Group .... E 631 300-1035
 Hauppauge *(G-5795)*
Swimwear Anywhere Inc .... E 845 858-4141
 Port Jervis *(G-13238)*

CLOTHING: Swimwear, Women's & Misses'

Christina Sales Inc .... F 212 391-0710
 New York *(G-9293)*
Comme-Ci Comme-CA AP Group .... E 631 300-1035
 Hauppauge *(G-5795)*

Feldman Manufacturing Corp .... D 718 433-1700
 Long Island City *(G-7446)*
Malia Mills Inc .... F 212 354-4200
 Brooklyn *(G-2154)*
Michael Feldman Inc .... D 718 433-1700
 Long Island City *(G-7524)*
Ocean Waves Swim LLC .... G 212 967-4481
 New York *(G-11027)*
Sea Waves Inc .... G 516 766-4201
 Oceanside *(G-12556)*
Swimwear Anywhere Inc .... D 631 420-1400
 Farmingdale *(G-4886)*
Swimwear Anywhere Inc .... E 845 858-4141
 Port Jervis *(G-13238)*
Venus Manufacturing Co Inc .... D 315 639-3100
 Dexter *(G-4116)*

CLOTHING: T-Shirts & Tops, Knit

American T Shirts Inc .... E 212 563-7125
 New York *(G-8838)*
Central Mills Inc .... C 212 764-9011
 New York *(G-9244)*
Elegant Headwear Co Inc .... G 212 695-8520
 New York *(G-9642)*
J & E Talit Inc .... G 718 850-1333
 Richmond Hill *(G-13505)*
Jfs Inc .... F 646 264-1200
 New York *(G-10335)*
Mann Consultants LLC .... E 914 763-0512
 Waccabuc *(G-15881)*

CLOTHING: T-Shirts & Tops, Women's & Girls'

Alfred Dunner Inc .... B 212 478-4300
 New York *(G-8795)*
Bowe Industries Inc .... D 718 441-6464
 Glendale *(G-5392)*
Garan Incorporated .... C 212 563-1292
 New York *(G-9882)*
Garan Manufacturing Corp .... G 212 563-2000
 New York *(G-9883)*
Gce International Inc .... D 212 704-4800
 New York *(G-9890)*
Hansae Co Ltd .... G 212 354-6690
 New York *(G-10035)*
T Rj Shirts Inc .... G 347 642-3071
 East Elmhurst *(G-4225)*

CLOTHING: Tailored Suits & Formal Jackets

Crisada Inc .... G 718 729-9730
 Long Island City *(G-7417)*
John Kochis Custom Designs .... G 212 244-6046
 New York *(G-10351)*
Shane Tex Inc .... F 516 486-7522
 Woodmere *(G-16642)*

CLOTHING: Ties, Handsewn, From Purchased Materials

Ralph Lauren Corporation .... B 212 318-7000
 New York *(G-11321)*
Tie King Inc .... G 212 714-9611
 New York *(G-11831)*

CLOTHING: Ties, Neck & Bow, Men's & Boys'

Tie King Inc .... E 718 768-8484
 Brooklyn *(G-2567)*

CLOTHING: Ties, Neck, Men's & Boys', From Purchased Material

Countess Mara Inc .... G 212 768-7300
 New York *(G-9409)*
Mallory & Church LLC .... G 212 868-7888
 New York *(G-10679)*
Perry Ellis Menswear LLC .... C 212 221-7500
 New York *(G-11162)*
Randa Accessories Lea Gds LLC .... D 212 354-5100
 New York *(G-11325)*
W B Bow Tie Corp .... F 212 683-6130
 New York *(G-12060)*

CLOTHING: Tights & Leg Warmers

Look By M Inc .... G 212 213-4019
 New York *(G-10599)*

Employee Codes: A=Over 500 employees, B=251-500
C=101-250, D=51-100, E=20-50, F=10-19, G=5-9

CLOTHING: Trousers & Slacks, Men's & Boys'

PRODUCT SECTION

CLOTHING: Trousers & Slacks, Men's & Boys'

Adrian Jules Ltd ....D 585 342-5886
  Rochester *(G-13603)*
Check Group LLC ....D 212 221-4700
  New York *(G-9268)*
Christian Casey LLC ....E 212 500-2200
  New York *(G-9289)*
Christian Casey LLC ....E 212 500-2200
  New York *(G-9290)*
Groupe 16sur20 LLC ....F 212 625-1620
  New York *(G-9998)*
Hertling Trousers Inc ....E 718 784-6100
  Brooklyn *(G-1977)*
Hugo Boss Usa Inc ....D 212 940-0600
  New York *(G-10146)*
Int Trading USA LLC ....C 212 760-2338
  New York *(G-10229)*
Jordache Enterprises Inc ....E 212 944-1330
  New York *(G-10360)*
Jordache Enterprises Inc ....C 212 643-8400
  New York *(G-10361)*
M Hidary & Co Inc ....D 212 736-6540
  New York *(G-10639)*
M S B International Ltd ....F 212 302-5551
  New York *(G-10642)*
Miltons of New York Inc ....G 212 997-3359
  New York *(G-10813)*
Mulitex Usa Inc ....G 212 398-0440
  New York *(G-10857)*
Pat & Rose Dress Inc ....D 212 279-1357
  New York *(G-11121)*
Perry Ellis International Inc ....F 212 536-5400
  New York *(G-11160)*
Primo Coat Corp ....E 718 349-2070
  Long Island City *(G-7560)*
Ralph Lauren Corporation ....B 212 318-7000
  New York *(G-11321)*
Sean John Clothing Inc ....E 212 500-2200
  New York *(G-11526)*
Sean John Clothing Inc ....E 212 500-2200
  New York *(G-11527)*

CLOTHING: Underwear, Knit

Balanced Tech Corp ....E 212 768-8330
  New York *(G-9007)*

CLOTHING: Underwear, Men's & Boys'

Becks Classic Mfg Inc ....D 631 435-3800
  Brentwood *(G-1128)*
Check Group LLC ....D 212 221-4700
  New York *(G-9268)*
Comme-Ci Comme-CA AP Group ....G 631 300-1035
  Hauppauge *(G-5795)*
Twist Intimate Group LLC ....G 212 695-5990
  New York *(G-11918)*
Warnaco Group Inc ....E 212 287-8000
  New York *(G-12070)*
Warnaco Inc ....B 212 287-8000
  New York *(G-12071)*
Warnaco Inc ....F 718 722-3000
  Brooklyn *(G-2639)*
Wickers Sportswear Inc ....G 631 543-1700
  Commack *(G-3707)*

CLOTHING: Underwear, Women's & Children's

Enticing Lingerie Inc ....E 718 998-8625
  Brooklyn *(G-1838)*
Intimateco LLC ....G 212 239-4411
  New York *(G-10256)*
Luxerdame Co Inc ....E 718 752-9800
  Long Island City *(G-7507)*
Natori Company Incorporated ....E 212 532-7796
  New York *(G-10891)*
Only Hearts Ltd ....E 212 268-0886
  New York *(G-11046)*
Wickers Sportswear Inc ....G 631 543-1700
  Commack *(G-3707)*

CLOTHING: Uniforms & Vestments

Craft Clerical Clothes Inc ....G 212 764-6122
  New York *(G-9416)*
JM Studio Inc ....F 646 546-5514
  New York *(G-10345)*
NY Orthopedic Usa Inc ....D 718 852-5330
  Brooklyn *(G-2279)*

RA Newhouse Inc ....D 516 248-6670
  Mineola *(G-8244)*
White Plains Coat Apron Co Inc ....G 914 736-2610
  Peekskill *(G-12931)*

CLOTHING: Uniforms, Ex Athletic, Women's, Misses' & Juniors'

Adar Medical Uniform LLC ....F 718 935-1197
  Brooklyn *(G-1481)*
Bestec Concept Inc ....G 718 937-5848
  Brooklyn *(G-1604)*
Elie Tahari Ltd ....D 212 763-2000
  New York *(G-9647)*
Lady Brass Co Inc ....G 516 887-8040
  Hewlett *(G-6047)*
Marlou Garments Inc ....F 516 739-7100
  New Hyde Park *(G-8549)*
Shane Tex Inc ....F 516 486-7522
  Woodmere *(G-16642)*
Uniforms By Park Coats Inc ....E 718 499-1182
  Brooklyn *(G-2600)*

CLOTHING: Uniforms, Men's & Boys'

Bestec Concept Inc ....G 718 937-5848
  Brooklyn *(G-1604)*
Occunomix International LLC ....E 631 741-1940
  Port Jeff STA *(G-13216)*
Otex Protective Inc ....G 585 232-7160
  Rochester *(G-13998)*
Uniforms By Park Coats Inc ....E 718 499-1182
  Brooklyn *(G-2600)*
Urban Textiles Inc ....F 212 777-1900
  New York *(G-11970)*
Vf Imagewear Inc ....E 718 352-2363
  Bayside *(G-751)*

CLOTHING: Uniforms, Military, Men/Youth, Purchased Materials

Crye Precision LLC ....C 718 246-3838
  Brooklyn *(G-1736)*
Med-Eng LLC ....E 315 713-0103
  Ogdensburg *(G-12577)*

CLOTHING: Uniforms, Policemen's, From Purchased Materials

Strong Group Inc ....G 516 766-6300
  Oceanside *(G-12558)*

CLOTHING: Uniforms, Team Athletic

American Challenge Enterprises ....G 631 595-7171
  New Hyde Park *(G-8515)*
Mayberry Shoe Company Inc ....G 315 692-4086
  Manlius *(G-7780)*
Nepenthes America Inc ....G 212 343-4262
  Long Island City *(G-7536)*
Pti-Pacific Inc ....G 212 414-8495
  New York *(G-11271)*
R J Liebe Athletic Company ....D 585 237-6111
  Perry *(G-12970)*
Tamka Sport LLC ....G 718 224-7820
  Douglaston *(G-4142)*

CLOTHING: Uniforms, Work

Best Medical Wear Ltd ....G 718 858-5544
  Brooklyn *(G-1603)*
Bestec Concept Inc ....G 718 937-5848
  Brooklyn *(G-1604)*
Lady Brass Co Inc ....G 516 887-8040
  Hewlett *(G-6047)*
Vf Imagewear Inc ....E 718 352-2363
  Bayside *(G-751)*

CLOTHING: Warm Weather Knit Outerwear, Including Beachwear

Warm ....F 212 925-1200
  New York *(G-12069)*

CLOTHING: Waterproof Outerwear

A W R Group Inc ....F 718 729-0412
  Long Island City *(G-7363)*
Float Tech Inc ....G 518 266-0964
  Troy *(G-15605)*
Top Fortune Usa Ltd ....G 516 608-2694
  Lynbrook *(G-7676)*

CLOTHING: Work Apparel, Exc Uniforms

Enzo Manzoni LLC ....G 212 464-7000
  Brooklyn *(G-1839)*

CLOTHING: Work, Men's

5 Star Apparel LLC ....G 212 563-1233
  New York *(G-8681)*
American Apparel Ltd ....G 516 504-4559
  Great Neck *(G-5533)*
Badgley Mischka Licensing LLC ....E 212 921-1585
  New York *(G-8999)*
Billion Tower Intl LLC ....F 212 220-0608
  New York *(G-9082)*
Broadway Knitting Mills Inc ....G 716 692-4421
  North Tonawanda *(G-12418)*
Dalcom USA Ltd ....F 516 466-7733
  Great Neck *(G-5549)*
Doral Apparel Group Inc ....G 917 208-5652
  New York *(G-9558)*
Du Monde Trading Inc ....E 212 944-1306
  New York *(G-9581)*
E J Manufacturing Inc ....G 516 313-9380
  Merrick *(G-8097)*
Far East Industries Inc ....E 718 687-2482
  New Hyde Park *(G-8534)*
Ferris USA LLC ....G 617 895-8102
  New York *(G-9796)*
Hillary Merchant Inc ....G 646 575-9242
  New York *(G-10099)*
Kollage Work Too Ltd ....G 212 695-1821
  New York *(G-10466)*
LLC Major Major ....E 212 354-8550
  New York *(G-10586)*
Medline Industries Inc ....B 845 344-3301
  Middletown *(G-8163)*
Mesh LLC ....E 646 839-7000
  New York *(G-10780)*
New York Hospital Disposable ....E 718 384-1620
  Brooklyn *(G-2262)*
Occunomix International LLC ....E 631 741-1940
  Port Jeff STA *(G-13216)*
Penfli Industries Inc ....F 212 947-6080
  Great Neck *(G-5581)*
Pico Direct LLC ....E 212 947-8969
  Roslyn *(G-14450)*
Rag & Bone Industries LLC ....D 212 278-8214
  New York *(G-11316)*
S & H Uniform Corp ....D 914 937-6800
  White Plains *(G-16500)*
Shanghai Harmony AP Intl LLC ....E 646 569-5680
  New Rochelle *(G-8628)*
Untuckit LLC ....E 201 214-9054
  New York *(G-11965)*
Untuckit LLC ....C 646 724-1857
  New York *(G-11966)*
Ventura Enterprise Co Inc ....E 212 391-0170
  New York *(G-12006)*

CLUTCHES OR BRAKES: Electromagnetic

American Precision Inds Inc ....C 716 691-9100
  Amherst *(G-214)*
Fortitude Industries Inc ....D 607 324-1500
  Hornell *(G-6298)*

CLUTCHES, EXC VEHICULAR

Machine Components Corp ....E 516 694-7222
  Plainview *(G-13071)*
Magtrol Inc ....E 716 668-5555
  Buffalo *(G-2935)*

COAL MINING SERVICES

Desku Group Inc ....G 646 436-1464
  Brooklyn *(G-1771)*
Dowa International Corp ....F 212 697-3217
  New York *(G-9566)*
Starfuels Inc ....G 914 289-4800
  White Plains *(G-16507)*
Trimet Coal LLC ....E 718 951-3654
  Brooklyn *(G-2585)*

COAL MINING SVCS: Bituminous, Contract Basis

Lessoilcom ....G 516 319-5052
  Franklin Square *(G-5118)*

PRODUCT SECTION

COMMERCIAL & INDL SHELVING WHOLESALERS

COATING COMPOUNDS: Tar

Aremco Products Inc .... F 845 268-0039
  Valley Cottage *(G-15752)*
Polyset Company Inc .... E 518 664-6000
  Mechanicville *(G-7932)*
Spray-Tech Finishing Inc .... F 716 664-6317
  Jamestown *(G-6749)*

COATING OR WRAPPING SVC: Steel Pipe

Specialty Bldg Solutions Inc .... G 631 393-6918
  West Babylon *(G-16195)*

COATING SVC

Cnv Architectural Coatings Inc .... G 718 418-9584
  Brooklyn *(G-1702)*
Kwong CHI Metal Fabrication .... G 718 369-6429
  Brooklyn *(G-2086)*

COATING SVC: Aluminum, Metal Prdts

72 Steel and Aluminium Work .... G 917 667-3033
  Brooklyn *(G-1445)*
Micromatter Tech Inc USA .... G 631 580-2522
  Holbrook *(G-6201)*

COATING SVC: Electrodes

Chepaume Industries LLC .... G 315 829-6400
  Vernon *(G-15803)*
Hilord Chemical Corporation .... E 631 234-7373
  Hauppauge *(G-5845)*

COATING SVC: Hot Dip, Metals Or Formed Prdts

Paradigm Group LLC .... G 718 860-1538
  Bronx *(G-1351)*

COATING SVC: Metals & Formed Prdts

Advanced Surface Finishing .... E 516 876-9710
  Westbury *(G-16310)*
Applause Coating LLC .... F 631 231-5223
  Brentwood *(G-1127)*
Barson Composites Corporation .... E 516 752-7882
  Old Bethpage *(G-12583)*
Deloka LLC .... G 315 946-6910
  Lyons *(G-7684)*
Dynocoat Inc .... F 631 244-9344
  Holbrook *(G-6183)*
Electronic Coating Tech Inc .... F 518 688-2048
  Cohoes *(G-3610)*
Elegance Coating Ltd .... E 386 668-8379
  Champlain *(G-3408)*
Future Spray Finishing Co .... G 631 242-6252
  Deer Park *(G-3980)*
Greene Technologies Inc .... D 607 656-4166
  Greene *(G-5615)*
Master Craft Finishers Inc .... E 631 586-0540
  Deer Park *(G-4007)*
Modern Coating and Research .... F 315 597-3517
  Palmyra *(G-12858)*
Oerlikon Blzers Cating USA Inc .... E 716 270-2228
  Amherst *(G-243)*
Oerlikon Blzers Cating USA Inc .... E 716 270-2228
  Amherst *(G-244)*
Oerlikon Blzers Cating USA Inc .... E 716 564-8557
  Buffalo *(G-2978)*
Qualicoat Inc .... D 585 293-2650
  Churchville *(G-3512)*
Sentry Metal Blast Inc .... E 716 285-5241
  Lockport *(G-7331)*
Sequa Corporation .... E 201 343-1122
  Orangeburg *(G-12692)*
Solidus Industries Inc .... D 607 749-4540
  Homer *(G-6259)*
Swain Technology Inc .... F 585 889-2786
  Scottsville *(G-14754)*
Trojan Metal Fabrication Inc .... E 631 968-5040
  Bay Shore *(G-732)*
W W Custom Clad Inc .... D 518 673-3322
  Canajoharie *(G-3209)*

COATING SVC: Metals, With Plastic Or Resins

Heany Industries Inc .... D 585 889-2700
  Scottsville *(G-14750)*
Hudson Valley Coatings LLC .... G 845 398-1778
  Congers *(G-3717)*

Metal Cladding Inc .... D 716 434-5513
  Lockport *(G-7316)*
Piper Plastics Corp .... E 631 842-6889
  Copiague *(G-3772)*
Pro-Teck Coating Inc .... F 716 537-2619
  Holland *(G-6221)*
Tj Powder Coaters LLC .... G 607 724-4779
  Binghamton *(G-920)*

COATING SVC: Rust Preventative

Hubbell Galvanizing Inc .... G 315 736-8311
  Yorkville *(G-16827)*
Monroe County Auto Svcs Inc .... E 585 764-3741
  Rochester *(G-13953)*

COATING SVC: Silicon

Momentive Performance Mtls Inc ...... E 518 237-3330
  Waterford *(G-15981)*
Momentive Prfmce Mtls Holdings ...... A 518 237-3330
  Waterford *(G-15982)*
Mpm Holdings Inc .... E 518 237-3330
  Waterford *(G-15984)*
Mpm Intermediate Holdings Inc .... G 518 237-3330
  Waterford *(G-15985)*

COATINGS: Air Curing

Enecon Corporation .... D 516 349-0022
  Medford *(G-7946)*

COATINGS: Epoxy

Delta Polymers Inc .... G 631 254-6240
  Bay Shore *(G-681)*
Designer Epoxy Finishes Inc .... F 646 943-6044
  Melville *(G-8015)*
Robert Greenburg .... G 845 586-2226
  Margaretville *(G-7799)*

COATINGS: Polyurethane

Absolute Coatings Inc .... E 914 636-0700
  New Rochelle *(G-8586)*
Paint Over Rust Products Inc .... E 914 636-0700
  New Rochelle *(G-8621)*

COFFEE SVCS

Adirondack Ice & Air Inc .... F 518 483-4340
  Malone *(G-7717)*

COILS & TRANSFORMERS

Aeroflex Incorporated .... B 516 694-6700
  Plainview *(G-13032)*
All Shore Industries Inc .... F 718 720-0018
  Staten Island *(G-15042)*
American Trans-Coil Corp .... F 516 922-9640
  Oyster Bay *(G-12809)*
Bel Transformer Inc .... D 516 239-5777
  Inwood *(G-6487)*
Electron Coil Inc .... D 607 336-7414
  Norwich *(G-12485)*
Ems Development Corporation .... D 631 345-6200
  Yaphank *(G-16709)*
Ems Development Corporation .... D 631 924-4736
  Yaphank *(G-16708)*
Eni Technology Inc .... B 585 427-8300
  Rochester *(G-13787)*
Es Beta Inc .... E 631 582-6740
  Ronkonkoma *(G-14339)*
Fuse Electronics Inc .... G 607 352-3222
  Kirkwood *(G-6940)*
Gowanda - Bti LLC .... D 716 492-4081
  Arcade *(G-384)*
Hipotronics Inc .... C 845 279-8091
  Brewster *(G-1167)*
M F L B Inc .... F 631 254-8300
  Bay Shore *(G-697)*
Magnetic Technologies Corp .... D 585 385-9010
  Rochester *(G-13924)*
Mini-Circuits Fort Wayne LLC .... B 718 934-4500
  Brooklyn *(G-2210)*
Misonix Inc .... D 631 694-9555
  Farmingdale *(G-4828)*
Mitchell Electronics Corp .... E 914 699-3800
  Mount Vernon *(G-8422)*
New York Fan Coil LLC .... G 646 580-1344
  Coram *(G-3801)*
Rdi Inc .... F 914 773-1000
  Mount Kisco *(G-8357)*

Sag Harbor Industries Inc .... E 631 725-0440
  Sag Harbor *(G-14502)*

COILS: Electric Motors Or Generators

Electron Coil Inc .... D 607 336-7414
  Norwich *(G-12485)*
P1 Generator Windings LLC .... G 518 930-2879
  Schenectady *(G-14702)*
Sag Harbor Industries Inc .... E 631 725-0440
  Sag Harbor *(G-14502)*

COILS: Pipe

Falcon Perspectives Inc .... G 718 706-9168
  Long Island City *(G-7444)*

COIN OPERATED LAUNDRIES & DRYCLEANERS

Oxford Cleaners .... G 212 734-0006
  New York *(G-11075)*

COIN-OPERATED LAUNDRY

Reynolds Drapery Service Inc .... F 315 845-8632
  Newport *(G-12256)*
Sky Laundromat Inc .... E 718 639-7070
  Jamaica *(G-6677)*

COKE: Calcined Petroleum, Made From Purchased Materials

Hh Liquidating Corp .... A 646 282-2500
  New York *(G-10092)*

COKE: Produced In Chemical Recovery Coke Ovens

Tonawanda Coke Corporation .... C 716 876-6222
  Tonawanda *(G-15582)*

COLLECTION AGENCY, EXC REAL ESTATE

Nyt Capital LLC .... F 212 556-1234
  New York *(G-11021)*

COLLEGES, UNIVERSITIES & PROFESSIONAL SCHOOLS

Stony Brook University .... E 631 632-6434
  Stony Brook *(G-15169)*

COLLETS

Hardinge Inc .... B 607 734-2281
  Elmira *(G-4490)*

COLOGNES

Classique Perfumes Inc .... G 718 657-8200
  Jamaica *(G-6637)*

COLOR SEPARATION: Photographic & Movie Film

Applied Image Inc .... E 585 482-0300
  Rochester *(G-13637)*
Eastern Color Stripping Inc .... F 631 563-3700
  Bohemia *(G-1018)*

COLORS: Pigments, Inorganic

Heany Industries Inc .... D 585 889-2700
  Scottsville *(G-14750)*

COLORS: Pigments, Organic

Sml Brothers Holding Corp .... D 718 402-2000
  Bronx *(G-1387)*

COMFORTERS & QUILTS, FROM MANMADE FIBER OR SILK

Ess Bee Industries Inc .... E 718 894-5202
  Brooklyn *(G-1850)*

COMMERCIAL & INDL SHELVING WHOLESALERS

Tri-Boro Shelving Inc .... F 718 782-8527
  Ridgewood *(G-13557)*

Employee Codes: A=Over 500 employees, B=251-500
C=101-250, D=51-100, E=20-50, F=10-19, G=5-9

COMMERCIAL & OFFICE BUILDINGS RENOVATION & REPAIR

Kng Construction Co Inc .... F 212 595-1451
  Warwick (G-15956)

COMMERCIAL ART & GRAPHIC DESIGN SVCS

Art Digital Technologies LLC .... F 646 649-4820
  Brooklyn (G-1557)
Artscroll Printing Corp .... E 212 929-2413
  New York (G-8926)
Avalon Copy Centers Amer Inc .... D 315 471-3333
  Syracuse (G-15251)
Avalon Copy Centers Amer Inc .... E 716 995-7777
  Buffalo (G-2717)
Clinton Signs Inc .... G 585 482-1620
  Webster (G-16080)
David Helsing .... G 607 796-2681
  Horseheads (G-6311)
Dowd - Witbeck Printing Corp .... F 518 274-2421
  Troy (G-15604)
Dynamic Photography Inc .... G 516 381-2951
  Roslyn (G-14446)
F X Graphix Inc .... G 716 871-1511
  Buffalo (G-2823)
Jay Turoff .... F 718 856-7300
  Brooklyn (G-2035)
Kjckd Inc .... G 518 435-9696
  Latham (G-7078)
Messenger Press .... G 518 885-9231
  Ballston Spa (G-591)
Patrick Rohan .... G 718 781-2573
  Monticello (G-8323)
Resonant Legal Media LLC .... E 212 687-7100
  New York (G-11368)
Riverwood Signs By Dandev Desi .... G 845 229-0282
  Hyde Park (G-6471)
Scan-A-Chrome Color Inc .... G 631 532-6146
  Copiague (G-3779)
Zacmel Graphics LLC .... G 631 944-6031
  Deer Park (G-4066)

COMMERCIAL EQPT WHOLESALERS, NEC

Hamlet Products Inc .... F 914 665-0307
  Mount Vernon (G-8405)

COMMERCIAL EQPT, WHOLESALE: Bakery Eqpt & Splys

Pfeil & Holing Inc .... D 718 545-4600
  Woodside (G-16671)

COMMERCIAL EQPT, WHOLESALE: Comm Cooking & Food Svc Eqpt

Genpak LLC .... C 845 343-7971
  Middletown (G-8155)
Mar-A-Thon Filters Inc .... G 631 957-4774
  Lindenhurst (G-7177)
Meades Welding and Fabricating .... G 631 581-1555
  Islip (G-6548)
Modern Craft Bar Rest Equip .... G 631 226-5647
  Lindenhurst (G-7181)
S & D Welding Corp .... G 631 454-0383
  West Babylon (G-16189)

COMMERCIAL EQPT, WHOLESALE: Display Eqpt, Exc Refrigerated

Bfma Holding Corporation .... G 607 753-6746
  Cortland (G-3862)
Marietta Corporation .... A 323 589-8181
  Cortland (G-3883)

COMMERCIAL EQPT, WHOLESALE: Mannequins

Lifestyle-Trimco .... E 718 257-9101
  Brooklyn (G-2118)
R P M Industries Inc .... E 315 255-1105
  Auburn (G-497)

COMMERCIAL EQPT, WHOLESALE: Restaurant, NEC

Bari Engineering Corp .... E 212 966-2080
  New York (G-9017)

R-S Restaurant Eqp Mfg Corp .... F 212 925-0335
  New York (G-11314)
Roger & Sons Inc .... G 212 226-4734
  New York (G-11422)

COMMERCIAL EQPT, WHOLESALE: Scales, Exc Laboratory

A & K Equipment Incorporated .... G 705 428-3573
  Watertown (G-15999)
Itin Scale Co Inc .... E 718 336-5900
  Brooklyn (G-2019)

COMMERCIAL EQPT, WHOLESALE: Store Fixtures & Display Eqpt

Manhattan Display Inc .... G 718 392-1365
  Long Island City (G-7514)

COMMERCIAL LAUNDRY EQPT

Fowler Route Co Inc .... D 917 653-4640
  Yonkers (G-16760)

COMMERCIAL PRINTING & NEWSPAPER PUBLISHING COMBINED

Amnewyork .... D 212 239-5555
  New York (G-8845)
Aspect Printing Inc .... E 347 789-4284
  Brooklyn (G-1564)
Bleezarde Publishing Inc .... G 518 756-2030
  Ravena (G-13452)
Buffalo Standard Printing Corp .... F 716 835-9454
  Buffalo (G-2753)
Capital Region Wkly Newspapers .... E 518 877-7160
  Albany (G-55)
Catskill Delaware Publications .... F 845 887-5200
  Callicoon (G-3160)
City Newspaper .... G 585 244-3329
  Rochester (G-13711)
Community News Group LLC .... C 718 260-2500
  Brooklyn (G-1710)
Daily Gazette Company .... B 518 374-4141
  Schenectady (G-14667)
Daily News LP .... A 212 210-2100
  New York (G-9455)
Daily World Press Inc .... F 212 922-9201
  New York (G-9458)
Denton Publications Inc .... D 518 873-6368
  Elizabethtown (G-4430)
Denton Publications Inc .... E 518 561-9680
  Plattsburgh (G-13119)
E W Smith Publishing Co .... G 845 562-1218
  New Windsor (G-8643)
Eagle Media Partners LP .... E 315 434-8889
  Syracuse (G-15309)
East Hampton Star Inc .... G 631 324-0002
  East Hampton (G-4236)
Gatehuse Media PA Holdings Inc .... E 585 598-0030
  Pittsford (G-13014)
Herald Newspapers Company Inc .... A 315 470-0011
  Syracuse (G-15340)
Holdens Screen Supply Corp .... G 212 627-2727
  New York (G-10114)
Home Reporter Inc .... E 718 238-6600
  Brooklyn (G-1982)
Huersch Marketing Group LLC .... F 518 874-1045
  Green Island (G-5607)
Ithaca Journal News Co Inc .... E 607 272-2321
  Ithaca (G-6588)
Johnson Acquisition Corp .... F 518 828-1616
  Hudson (G-6360)
Kch Publications Inc .... E 516 671-2360
  Glen Cove (G-5369)
LI Community Newspapers Inc .... G 516 747-8282
  Mineola (G-8233)
Local Media Group Inc .... D 845 341-1100
  Middletown (G-8161)
Local Media Group Holdings LLC .... G 585 598-0030
  Pittsford (G-13019)
Long Island Cmnty Nwsppers Inc .... D 516 482-4490
  Mineola (G-8235)
Lowville Newspaper Corporation .... G 315 376-3525
  Lowville (G-7653)
Mid York Weekly & Pennysaver .... G 315 792-4990
  Utica (G-15721)
Ming Pao (new York) Inc .... D 718 786-2888
  Long Island City (G-7526)
Neighbor Newspapers .... G 631 226-2636
  Farmingdale (G-4833)

New York Times Company .... F 718 281-7000
  Flushing (G-5029)
News India Usa LLC .... G 212 675-7515
  New York (G-10953)
News of The Highlands Inc .... F 845 534-7771
  Cornwall (G-3836)
Newsday LLC .... B 631 843-4050
  Melville (G-8050)
Nyc Trade Printers Corp .... F 718 606-0610
  Woodside (G-16668)
Nyp Holdings Inc .... A 212 997-9272
  New York (G-11018)
Ogden Newspapers Inc .... C 716 487-1111
  Jamestown (G-6741)
Owego Pennysaver Press Inc .... F 607 687-2434
  Owego (G-12802)
Post Journal .... F 716 487-1111
  Jamestown (G-6742)
Prometheus International Inc .... F 718 472-0700
  Long Island City (G-7561)
R W Publications Div of Wtrhs .... E 716 714-5620
  Elma (G-4457)
Record .... G 518 270-1200
  Saratoga Springs (G-14595)
Richner Communications Inc .... C 516 569-4000
  Garden City (G-5278)
Ridgewood Times Prtg & Pubg .... F 718 821-7500
  Ridgewood (G-13549)
Seneca County Area Shopper .... G 607 532-4333
  Ovid (G-12792)
Service Advertising Group Inc .... F 718 361-6161
  Long Island City (G-7588)
South Shore Tribune Inc .... G 516 431-5628
  Island Park (G-6518)
St Lawrence County Newspapers .... D 315 393-1003
  Canton (G-3258)
Ubm LLC .... F 516 562-5000
  New York (G-11930)
Ulster County Press Office .... G 845 687-4480
  High Falls (G-6141)
Vnovom Svete .... G 212 302-9480
  New York (G-12050)
Weisbeck Publishing Printing .... G 716 937-9226
  Alden (G-178)
William B Collins Company .... D 518 773-8272
  Gloversville (G-5473)
William Boyd Printing Co Inc .... C 518 339-5832
  Latham (G-7098)
Williamsburg Bulletin .... G 718 387-0123
  Brooklyn (G-2650)
Wolfe Publications Inc .... G 585 394-0770
  Canandaigua (G-3236)
Zenith Color Comm Group Inc .... E 212 989-4400
  Long Island City (G-7648)

COMMON SAND MINING

E F Lippert Co Inc .... F 716 373-1100
  Allegany (G-189)
Hanson Aggregates East LLC .... G 315 536-9391
  Penn Yan (G-12957)
Hanson Aggregates PA Inc .... G 315 858-1100
  Jordanville (G-6844)
Hanson Aggregates PA Inc .... F 518 568-2444
  Saint Johnsville (G-14518)
Hanson Aggregates PA LLC .... E 315 469-5501
  Jamesville (G-6768)
Hanson Aggregates PA LLC .... E 315 685-3321
  Skaneateles (G-14875)
Hanson Aggregates PA LLC .... F 315 821-7222
  Oriskany Falls (G-12767)
Smith Sand & Gravel Inc .... G 315 673-4124
  Marcellus (G-7795)

COMMUNICATION HEADGEAR: Telephone

Prager Metis Cpas LLC .... F 212 972-7555
  New York (G-11226)
Rus Industries Inc .... E 716 284-7828
  Niagara Falls (G-12331)

COMMUNICATIONS CARRIER: Wired

Comsec Ventures International .... G 518 523-1600
  Lake Placid (G-6975)
Fiberdyne Labs Inc .... D 315 895-8470
  Frankfort (G-5107)

COMMUNICATIONS EQPT & SYSTEMS, NEC

Light Phone Inc .... G 415 595-0044
  Brooklyn (G-2120)

PRODUCT SECTION
COMPUTER & COMPUTER SOFTWARE STORES: Software, Computer Game

Lik LLC .... F 516 848-5135
　Northport *(G-12471)*

COMMUNICATIONS EQPT REPAIR & MAINTENANCE

Unitone Communication Systems .... G 212 777-9090
　New York *(G-11957)*
Zetek Corporation .... F 212 668-1485
　New York *(G-12174)*

COMMUNICATIONS EQPT WHOLESALERS

AES Electronics Inc .... G 212 371-8120
　New York *(G-8763)*
Caravan International Corp .... G 212 223-7190
　New York *(G-9205)*
Communication Power Corp .... E 631 434-7306
　Hauppauge *(G-5796)*
Global Technologies Inc .... D 631 243-7924
　Deer Park *(G-3982)*
Sinclair Technologies Inc .... E 716 874-3682
　Hamburg *(G-5695)*

COMMUNICATIONS EQPT: Microwave

Amplitech Inc .... G 631 521-7738
　Bohemia *(G-978)*
Amplitech Group Inc .... G 631 521-7831
　Bohemia *(G-979)*
Comtech PST Corp .... E 631 777-8900
　Melville *(G-8011)*
Comtech Telecom Corp .... E 631 962-7000
　Melville *(G-8012)*
Specialty Microwave Corp .... F 631 737-2175
　Ronkonkoma *(G-14415)*
United Satcom Inc .... G 718 359-4100
　Flushing *(G-5057)*

COMMUNICATIONS EQPT: Radio, Marine

Maritime Broadband Inc .... E 347 404-6041
　Long Island City *(G-7515)*

COMMUNICATIONS SVCS

Aspire One Communications LLC .... F 201 281-2998
　Cornwall *(G-3830)*
Forerunner Technologies Inc .... E 631 337-2100
　Edgewood *(G-4401)*

COMMUNICATIONS SVCS: Cellular

Bayside Beepers & Cellular .... G 718 343-3888
　Glen Oaks *(G-5386)*

COMMUNICATIONS SVCS: Data

Forerunner Technologies Inc .... E 631 337-2100
　Edgewood *(G-4401)*

COMMUNICATIONS SVCS: Facsimile Transmission

Alternative Technology Corp .... G 914 478-5900
　Hastings On Hudson *(G-5747)*
Key Computer Svcs of Chelsea .... D 212 206-8060
　New York *(G-10438)*

COMMUNICATIONS SVCS: Internet Host Svcs

Nyemac Inc .... G 631 668-1303
　Montauk *(G-8307)*

COMMUNICATIONS SVCS: Online Svc Providers

Beauty America LLC .... E 917 744-1430
　Great Neck *(G-5539)*
Martha Stewart Living .... C 212 827-8000
　New York *(G-10717)*

COMMUNICATIONS SVCS: Proprietary Online Svcs Networks

Working Mother Media Inc .... D 212 351-6400
　New York *(G-12134)*

COMMUNICATIONS SVCS: Satellite Earth Stations

Loral Space Communications Inc .... E 212 697-1105
　New York *(G-10604)*

COMMUNICATIONS SVCS: Signal Enhancement Network Svcs

Fiberdyne Labs Inc .... D 315 895-8470
　Frankfort *(G-5107)*

COMMUNICATIONS SVCS: Telephone, Data

Akoustis Inc .... E 585 919-3073
　Canandaigua *(G-3210)*

COMMUNICATIONS SVCS: Telephone, Local

Highcrest Investors LLC .... D 212 702-4323
　New York *(G-10096)*

COMMUNICATIONS SVCS: Telephone, Voice

ABS Talkx Inc .... G 631 254-9100
　Bay Shore *(G-651)*

COMMUTATORS: Electronic

Amron Electronics Inc .... E 631 737-1234
　Ronkonkoma *(G-14309)*

COMPACT DISCS OR CD'S, WHOLESALE

Universal Mus Group Hldngs Inc .... E 212 333-8000
　New York *(G-11961)*

COMPACT LASER DISCS: Prerecorded

A To Z Media Inc .... E 212 260-0237
　New York *(G-8699)*
Atlantic Recording Corp .... B 212 707-2000
　New York *(G-8951)*
Bertelsmann Inc .... E 212 782-1000
　New York *(G-9055)*
Historic TW Inc .... E 212 484-8000
　New York *(G-10106)*
Media Technologies Ltd .... F 631 467-7900
　Eastport *(G-4385)*
Sony Corporation of America .... C 212 833-8000
　New York *(G-11645)*
Time Warner Companies Inc .... E 212 484-8000
　New York *(G-11845)*
Vaire LLC .... G 631 271-4933
　Huntington Station *(G-6463)*

COMPACTORS: Trash & Garbage, Residential

A Gatty Products Inc .... G 914 592-3903
　Elmsford *(G-4527)*

COMPARATORS: Optical

Quality Vision Services Inc .... D 585 544-0450
　Rochester *(G-14062)*

COMPOSITION STONE: Plastic

Seaway Mats Inc .... G 518 483-2560
　Malone *(G-7726)*

COMPOST

Long Island Compost Corp .... C 516 334-6600
　Westbury *(G-16351)*

COMPRESSORS, AIR CONDITIONING: Wholesalers

Toshiba America Inc .... E 212 596-0600
　New York *(G-11872)*

COMPRESSORS: Air & Gas

Buffalo Compressed Air Inc .... G 716 783-8673
　Cheektowaga *(G-3436)*
Chapin International Inc .... C 585 343-3140
　Batavia *(G-617)*
Chapin Manufacturing Inc .... C 585 343-3140
　Batavia *(G-618)*
Comairco Equipment Inc .... G 716 656-0211
　Cheektowaga *(G-3437)*
Cooper Turbocompressor Inc .... B 716 896-6600
　Buffalo *(G-2781)*
Crosman Corporation .... E 585 657-6161
　Bloomfield *(G-951)*
Crosman Corporation .... E 585 398-3920
　Farmington *(G-4911)*
Cyclone Air Power Inc .... E 718 447-3038
　Staten Island *(G-15067)*
Dresser-Rand (delaware) LLC .... E 607 937-2011
　Painted Post *(G-12839)*
Dresser-Rand Group Inc .... D 716 375-3000
　Olean *(G-12599)*
Gas Tchnlgy Enrgy Cncepts LLC .... G 716 831-9695
　Buffalo *(G-2841)*
GM Components Holdings LLC .... B 716 439-2463
　Lockport *(G-7305)*
GM Components Holdings LLC .... B 716 439-2011
　Lockport *(G-7306)*
Ingersoll-Rand Company .... B 716 896-6600
　Buffalo *(G-2884)*
Mahle Indstrbeteiligungen GMBH .... B 716 319-6700
　Amherst *(G-237)*
Screw Compressor Tech Inc .... F 716 827-6600
　Buffalo *(G-3060)*
Turbopro Inc .... G 716 681-8651
　Alden *(G-177)*

COMPRESSORS: Air & Gas, Including Vacuum Pumps

Air Techniques Inc .... B 516 433-7676
　Melville *(G-8000)*
Atlas Copco Comptec LLC .... B 518 765-3344
　Voorheesville *(G-15879)*
Eastern Air Products LLC .... F 716 391-1866
　Lancaster *(G-7017)*

COMPRESSORS: Refrigeration & Air Conditioning Eqpt

Graham Corporation .... B 585 343-2216
　Batavia *(G-626)*
Standard Motor Products Inc .... B 718 392-0200
　Long Island City *(G-7598)*

COMPRESSORS: Wholesalers

Archrock Inc .... F 716 763-1553
　Lakewood *(G-6988)*

COMPUTER & COMPUTER SOFTWARE STORES

A I T Computers Inc .... G 518 266-9010
　Troy *(G-15599)*
Astrodyne Inc .... G 516 536-5755
　Oceanside *(G-12532)*
Biofeedback Instrument Corp .... G 212 222-5665
　New York *(G-9087)*
G S Communications USA Inc .... E 718 389-7371
　Brooklyn *(G-1913)*
J & N Computer Services Inc .... F 585 388-8780
　Fairport *(G-4636)*
Lasertech Crtridge RE-Builders .... G 518 373-1246
　Clifton Park *(G-3569)*
Maia Systems LLC .... G 718 206-0100
　Jamaica *(G-6658)*
Taste and See Entrmt Inc .... G 516 285-3010
　Valley Stream *(G-15799)*
Tpa Computer Corp .... F 877 866-6044
　Carmel *(G-3282)*

COMPUTER & COMPUTER SOFTWARE STORES: Peripheral Eqpt

Cables and Chips Inc .... E 212 619-3132
　New York *(G-9173)*

COMPUTER & COMPUTER SOFTWARE STORES: Software, Bus/Non-Game

Noetic Partners Inc .... F 212 836-4351
　New York *(G-10984)*
Pointman LLC .... G 716 842-1439
　Buffalo *(G-3008)*

COMPUTER & COMPUTER SOFTWARE STORES: Software, Computer Game

Sony Broadband Entertainment .... F 212 833-6800
　New York *(G-11644)*

COMPUTER & OFFICE MACHINE MAINTENANCE & REPAIR

COMPUTER & OFFICE MACHINE MAINTENANCE & REPAIR

Innovative Systems of New York .... G 516 541-7410
Massapequa Park *(G-7892)*

COMPUTER DISKETTES WHOLESALERS

Formats Unlimited Inc .... F 631 249-9200
Deer Park *(G-3978)*

COMPUTER FORMS

Boces Business Office .... F 607 763-3300
Binghamton *(G-869)*
Multi Packaging Solutions Inc .... E 646 885-0005
New York *(G-10858)*
Specialized Printed Forms Inc .... F 585 538-2381
Caledonia *(G-3158)*

COMPUTER GRAPHICS SVCS

Belsito Communications Inc .... F 845 534-9700
New Windsor *(G-8636)*
Beyer Graphics Inc .... D 631 543-3900
Commack *(G-3682)*
Christian Bus Endeavors Inc .... F 315 788-8560
Watertown *(G-16007)*
Star Composition Services Inc .... G 212 684-4001
Brooklyn *(G-2509)*

COMPUTER HARDWARE REQUIREMENTS ANALYSIS

Quality and Asrn Tech Corp .... G 646 450-6762
Ridge *(G-13523)*

COMPUTER INTERFACE EQPT: Indl Process

Anchor Commerce Trading Corp .... G 516 881-3485
Atlantic Beach *(G-455)*
Aspex Incorporated .... E 212 966-0410
New York *(G-8936)*
ATI Trading Inc .... F 718 888-7918
Flushing *(G-4987)*
Cosa Xentaur Corporation .... E 631 345-3434
Yaphank *(G-16707)*
Industrial Machine Repair .... G 607 272-0717
Ithaca *(G-6584)*
Macrolink Inc .... E 631 924-8200
Medford *(G-7960)*
Sixnet LLC .... D 518 877-5173
Ballston Lake *(G-571)*
Vetra Systems Corporation .... G 631 434-3185
Hauppauge *(G-5969)*

COMPUTER PERIPHERAL EQPT REPAIR & MAINTENANCE

Xerox Corporation .... C 585 427-4500
Rochester *(G-14214)*

COMPUTER PERIPHERAL EQPT, NEC

A I T Computers Inc .... G 518 266-9010
Troy *(G-15599)*
Aalborg Instrs & Contrls Inc .... D 845 398-3160
Orangeburg *(G-12667)*
Aero-Vision Technologies Inc .... G 631 643-8349
Melville *(G-7998)*
Aeroflex Plainview Inc .... C 631 231-9100
Hauppauge *(G-5756)*
Andrea Electronics Corporation .... G 631 719-1800
Bohemia *(G-980)*
Anorad Corporation .... C 631 344-6600
Shirley *(G-14827)*
Aruba Networks Inc .... G 732 343-1305
New York *(G-8927)*
Atlaz International Ltd .... F 516 239-1854
Lawrence *(G-7102)*
Aventura Technologies Inc .... E 631 300-4000
Commack *(G-3680)*
B V M Associates .... G 631 254-6220
Shirley *(G-14831)*
Chemung Cnty Chpter Nysarc Inc .... C 607 734-6151
Elmira *(G-4477)*
Clayton Dubilier & Rice Fun .... E 212 407-5200
New York *(G-9324)*
Datatran Labs Inc .... G 845 856-4313
Port Jervis *(G-13227)*
Digiorange Inc .... G 718 787-1500
Brooklyn *(G-1776)*
Dynamic Decisions Inc .... F 908 755-5000
Fresh Meadows *(G-5196)*
Eastman Kodak Company .... B 585 724-4000
Rochester *(G-13761)*
Ems Development Corporation .... D 631 345-6200
Yaphank *(G-16709)*
Epicor Software Corporation .... E 805 496-6789
Schenectady *(G-14673)*
Gasoft Equipment Inc .... F 845 863-1010
Newburgh *(G-12223)*
Glowa Manufacturing Inc .... E 607 770-0811
Binghamton *(G-887)*
Hauppauge Computer Works Inc .... E 631 434-1600
Hauppauge *(G-5841)*
Hauppauge Digital Inc .... E 631 434-1600
Hauppauge *(G-5842)*
Hergo Ergonomic Support .... E 718 894-0639
Maspeth *(G-7851)*
Hitachi Metals America Ltd .... E 914 694-9200
Purchase *(G-13390)*
Humanscale Corporation .... E 212 725-4749
New York *(G-10150)*
IBM World Trade Corporation .... G 914 765-1900
Armonk *(G-403)*
Innovative Systems of New York .... G 516 541-7410
Massapequa Park *(G-7892)*
Kantek Inc .... E 516 594-4600
Oceanside *(G-12544)*
Luminescent Systems Inc .... B 716 655-0800
East Aurora *(G-4204)*
Macrolink Inc .... E 631 924-8200
Medford *(G-7960)*
Maia Systems LLC .... G 718 206-0100
Jamaica *(G-6658)*
Marco Manufacturing Inc .... E 845 485-1571
Poughkeepsie *(G-13353)*
Mirion Technologies Ist Corp .... D 607 562-4300
Horseheads *(G-6321)*
NCR Corporation .... C 607 273-5310
Ithaca *(G-6599)*
Norazza Inc .... G 716 706-1160
Buffalo *(G-2973)*
O Rama Light Inc .... E 518 539-9000
South Glens Falls *(G-14940)*
Office Grabs LLC .... G 347 678-3993
Brooklyn *(G-2284)*
Orbit International Corp .... D 631 435-8300
Hauppauge *(G-5907)*
Performance Technologies Inc .... E 585 256-0200
Rochester *(G-14012)*
Phoenix Venture Fund LLC .... F 212 759-1909
New York *(G-11185)*
QED Technologies Intl Inc .... E 585 256-6540
Rochester *(G-14056)*
Rdi Inc .... F 914 773-1000
Mount Kisco *(G-8357)*
Reliable Elec Mt Vernon Inc .... E 914 668-4440
Mount Vernon *(G-8439)*
Rodale Wireless Inc .... G 631 231-0044
Hauppauge *(G-5929)*
Ruhle Companies Inc .... E 914 287-4000
Valhalla *(G-15747)*
S G I .... G 917 386-0385
New York *(G-11457)*
Sima Technologies LLC .... G 412 828-9130
Hauppauge *(G-5940)*
Sony Corporation of America .... C 212 833-8000
New York *(G-11645)*
Symbol Technologies LLC .... F 631 738-2400
Bohemia *(G-1093)*
Technomag Inc .... G 631 246-6142
East Setauket *(G-4311)*
Todd Enterprises Inc .... G 516 773-8087
Great Neck *(G-5595)*
Torrent Ems LLC .... F 716 312-4099
Lockport *(G-7337)*
Toshiba Amer Info Systems Inc .... B 949 583-3000
New York *(G-11871)*
Vader Systems LLC .... E 716 688-1600
Getzville *(G-5355)*
Vishay Thin Film LLC .... F 716 283-4025
Niagara Falls *(G-12348)*
Vuzix Corporation .... E 585 359-5900
West Henrietta *(G-16253)*
Wantagh Computer Center .... E 516 826-2189
Wantagh *(G-15927)*
Welch Allyn Inc .... A 315 685-4100
Skaneateles Falls *(G-14882)*
Wilson & Wilson Group .... E 212 729-4736
Forest Hills *(G-5082)*
Xerox Corporation .... C 585 427-4500
Rochester *(G-14214)*
Z-Axis Inc .... D 315 548-5000
Phelps *(G-12984)*
Zebra Technologies Entp Corp .... E 800 722-6234
Holtsville *(G-6251)*

COMPUTER PERIPHERAL EQPT, WHOLESALE

Atlaz International Ltd .... F 516 239-1854
Lawrence *(G-7102)*
Cbord Group Inc .... C 607 257-2410
Ithaca *(G-6571)*
CS Business Systems Inc .... E 716 886-6521
Buffalo *(G-2786)*
Digicom International Inc .... F 631 249-8999
Farmingdale *(G-4751)*
Doar Inc .... G 516 872-8140
Lynbrook *(G-7664)*

COMPUTER PERIPHERAL EQPT: Encoders

Iweb Design Inc .... F 805 243-8305
Bronx *(G-1299)*

COMPUTER PERIPHERAL EQPT: Film Reader Devices

P C Rfrs Radiology .... G 212 586-5700
Long Island City *(G-7544)*

COMPUTER PERIPHERAL EQPT: Graphic Displays, Exc Terminals

Binghamton Simulator Co Inc .... E 607 321-2980
Binghamton *(G-868)*
Medsim-Eagle Simulation Inc .... F 607 658-9354
Endicott *(G-4601)*
Mp Displays LLC .... G 845 268-4113
Valley Cottage *(G-15760)*
Watson Productions LLC .... F 516 334-9766
Hauppauge *(G-5973)*

COMPUTER PERIPHERAL EQPT: Input Or Output

Pda Panache Corp .... G 631 776-0523
Bohemia *(G-1073)*

COMPUTER PROGRAMMING SVCS

Atomic Information Systems .... E 716 713-5402
Unadilla *(G-15661)*
Billing Blocks Inc .... F 718 442-5006
Staten Island *(G-15050)*
Cdml Computer Services Ltd .... G 718 428-9063
Fresh Meadows *(G-5195)*
Data Key Communication LLC .... F 315 445-2347
Fayetteville *(G-4927)*
Defran Systems Inc .... E 212 727-8342
New York *(G-9496)*
Digitronik Labs Inc .... F 585 360-0043
Rochester *(G-13741)*
Doar Inc .... G 516 872-8140
Lynbrook *(G-7664)*
Fidesa US Corporation .... B 212 269-9000
New York *(G-9800)*
Fog Creek Software Inc .... G 866 364-2733
New York *(G-9820)*
Fuel Data Systems Inc .... G 800 447-7870
Middletown *(G-8153)*
Hauppauge Computer Works Inc .... E 631 434-1600
Hauppauge *(G-5841)*
Hudson Software Corporation .... E 914 773-0400
Elmsford *(G-4544)*
Infinity Augmented Reality Inc .... F 917 677-2084
New York *(G-10203)*
Irv Inc .... E 212 334-4507
New York *(G-10273)*
Lockheed Martin Corporation .... D 315 793-5800
New Hartford *(G-8507)*
Matrixcare Inc .... G 518 583-6400
New York *(G-10729)*
Openfin Inc .... G 917 450-8822
New York *(G-11048)*
PC Solutions & Consulting .... G 607 735-0466
Elmira *(G-4499)*
Qlogix Entertainment LLC .... G 215 459-6315
New York *(G-11292)*

PRODUCT SECTION

COMPUTERS, PERIPHERALS & SOFTWARE, WHOLESALE: Software

Safe Passage International Inc .... F 585 292-4910
  Rochester *(G-14108)*
Suite Solutions Inc .... E 716 929-3050
  Amherst *(G-252)*
Syrasoft LLC .... F 315 708-0341
  Baldwinsville *(G-564)*
Wetpaintcom Inc .... E 206 859-6300
  New York *(G-12098)*
X Function Inc .... E 212 231-0092
  New York *(G-12147)*
Ziff Davis Publishing LLC .... D 212 503-3500
  New York *(G-12177)*

COMPUTER PROGRAMMING SVCS: Custom

Endava Inc .... F 212 920-7240
  New York *(G-9675)*
Modern Farmer Media Inc .... F 518 828-7447
  Hudson *(G-6365)*
US Beverage Net Inc .... F 315 579-2025
  Syracuse *(G-15450)*

COMPUTER RELATED MAINTENANCE SVCS

Century Direct LLC .... C 212 763-0600
  Islandia *(G-6524)*
Global Applctions Solution LLC .... G 212 741-9595
  New York *(G-9937)*
IBM World Trade Corporation .... G 914 765-1900
  Armonk *(G-403)*
Laurus Development Inc .... F 716 823-1202
  Buffalo *(G-2922)*

COMPUTER SERVICE BUREAU

Datalink Computer Products .... F 914 666-2358
  Mount Kisco *(G-8341)*
Hudson Software Corporation .... E 914 773-0400
  Elmsford *(G-4544)*

COMPUTER SOFTWARE DEVELOPMENT

Advanced Barcode Tech Inc .... F 516 570-8100
  Great Neck *(G-5527)*
Falconstor Software Inc .... C 631 777-5188
  Melville *(G-8023)*
Geoweb3d Inc .... F 607 323-1114
  Vestal *(G-15817)*
Lake Image Systems Inc .... F 585 321-3630
  Henrietta *(G-6034)*
Os33 Inc .... G 708 336-3466
  New York *(G-11064)*
Sale 121 Corp .... D 240 855-8988
  New York *(G-11467)*
Standard Analytics Io Inc .... G 917 882-5422
  New York *(G-11691)*
Structuredweb Inc .... E 201 325-3110
  New York *(G-11725)*
Williamson Law Book Co .... F 585 924-3400
  Victor *(G-15878)*

COMPUTER SOFTWARE DEVELOPMENT & APPLICATIONS

Amcom Software Inc .... G 212 951-7600
  New York *(G-8817)*
Forerunner Technologies Inc .... E 631 337-2100
  Edgewood *(G-4401)*
Hearst Digital Studios Inc .... E 212 969-7552
  New York *(G-10071)*
Innovation In Motion Inc .... G 407 878-7561
  Long Beach *(G-7359)*
Ipsidy Inc .... F 407 951-8640
  Long Beach *(G-7360)*
Kingboard Holdings Limited .... A 705 844-1993
  New York *(G-10452)*
Magsoft Corporation .... G 518 877-8390
  Ballston Spa *(G-589)*
Orpheo USA Corp .... G 212 464-8255
  New York *(G-11062)*
Post Road .... F 203 545-2122
  New York *(G-11224)*
Randall Loeffler Inc .... E 212 226-8787
  New York *(G-11326)*
Vepo Solutions LLC .... G 914 384-2121
  Cross River *(G-3910)*

COMPUTER SOFTWARE SYSTEMS ANALYSIS & DESIGN: Custom

Complex Biosystems Inc .... G 315 464-8007
  Baldwinsville *(G-553)*

Inprotopia Corporation .... F 917 338-7501
  New York *(G-10224)*
Laurus Development Inc .... F 716 823-1202
  Buffalo *(G-2922)*
Live Vote II Inc .... G 646 343-9053
  New York *(G-10583)*
New York Computer Consulting .... G 516 921-1932
  Woodbury *(G-16626)*
Vizbee Inc .... G 650 787-1424
  New York *(G-12048)*
Vormittag Associates Inc .... G 800 824-7776
  Ronkonkoma *(G-14428)*

COMPUTER STORAGE DEVICES, NEC

Datalink Computer Products .... F 914 666-2358
  Mount Kisco *(G-8341)*
EMC Corporation .... C 212 564-6866
  New York *(G-9666)*
Emcs LLC .... G 716 523-2002
  Hamburg *(G-5678)*
Garland Technology LLC .... E 716 242-8500
  Buffalo *(G-2840)*
Gim Electronics Corp .... F 516 942-3382
  Hicksville *(G-6090)*
Quantum Asset Recovery .... G 716 393-2712
  Buffalo *(G-3026)*
Quantum Knowledge LLC .... G 631 727-6111
  Riverhead *(G-13580)*
Quantum Logic Corp .... G 516 746-1380
  New Hyde Park *(G-8560)*
Quantum Mechanics Ny LLC .... G 917 519-7077
  Huntington *(G-6408)*
Sony Corporation of America .... C 212 833-8000
  New York *(G-11645)*
Technologies Application LLC .... F 607 275-0345
  Cortland *(G-3896)*
Todd Enterprises Inc .... D 516 773-8087
  Great Neck *(G-5595)*
William S Hein & Co Inc .... C 716 882-2600
  Getzville *(G-5356)*

COMPUTER TERMINALS

AG Neovo Professional Inc .... F 212 647-9080
  New York *(G-8767)*
Clayton Dubilier & Rice Fun .... E 212 407-5200
  New York *(G-9324)*
Doar Inc .... G 516 872-8140
  Lynbrook *(G-7664)*
Igt Global Solutions Corp .... D 518 382-2900
  Schenectady *(G-14689)*
Nu - Communitek LLC .... F 516 433-3553
  Hicksville *(G-6115)*
Orbit International Corp .... D 631 435-8300
  Hauppauge *(G-5907)*
Symbio Technologies LLC .... G 914 576-1205
  White Plains *(G-16510)*

COMPUTER TERMINALS: CRT

Cine Design Group LLC .... G 646 747-0734
  New York *(G-9299)*

COMPUTER-AIDED DESIGN SYSTEMS SVCS

Circuits & Systems Inc .... E 516 593-4301
  East Rockaway *(G-4293)*
Trident Precision Mfg Inc .... D 585 265-2010
  Webster *(G-16103)*

COMPUTER-AIDED ENGINEERING SYSTEMS SVCS

Complex Biosystems Inc .... G 315 464-8007
  Baldwinsville *(G-553)*

COMPUTERS, NEC

Argon Corp .... F 516 487-5314
  Great Neck *(G-5536)*
Arnouse Digital Devices Corp .... D 516 673-4444
  New Hyde Park *(G-8517)*
Bak USA Technologies Corp .... E 716 248-2704
  Buffalo *(G-2722)*
Binghamton Simulator Co Inc .... E 607 321-2980
  Binghamton *(G-868)*
Computer Conversions Corp .... F 631 261-3300
  East Northport *(G-4261)*
Critical Link LLC .... G 315 425-4045
  Syracuse *(G-15294)*
Data-Pac Mailing Systems Corp .... F 585 671-0210
  Webster *(G-16081)*

Datacom Systems Inc .... E 315 463-9541
  East Syracuse *(G-4334)*
Dees Audio & Vision .... G 585 719-9256
  Rochester *(G-13738)*
Digicom International Inc .... F 631 249-8999
  Farmingdale *(G-4751)*
Doar Inc .... G 516 872-8140
  Lynbrook *(G-7664)*
Dynamic Decisions Inc .... G 908 755-5000
  Fresh Meadows *(G-5196)*
E-Systems Group LLC .... F 607 775-1100
  Conklin *(G-3727)*
Ebc Technologies LLC .... D 631 729-8182
  Hauppauge *(G-5817)*
Electronic Systems Inc .... G 631 589-4389
  Holbrook *(G-6184)*
Envent Systems Inc .... G 646 294-6980
  Pelham *(G-12935)*
H&L Computers Inc .... E 516 873-8088
  Flushing *(G-5005)*
Hand Held Products Inc .... B 315 554-6000
  Skaneateles Falls *(G-14879)*
Hi-Tech Advanced Solutions Inc .... F 718 926-3488
  Forest Hills *(G-5075)*
Human Electronics Inc .... G 315 724-9850
  Utica *(G-15710)*
IBM World Trade Corporation .... G 914 765-1900
  Armonk *(G-403)*
Irpenscom .... G 585 507-7997
  Penfield *(G-12941)*
J & N Computer Services Inc .... F 585 388-8780
  Fairport *(G-4636)*
Kemp Technologies Inc .... E 631 345-5292
  New York *(G-10429)*
M&C Associates LLC .... E 631 467-8760
  Hauppauge *(G-5875)*
Medsim-Eagle Simulation Inc .... F 607 658-9354
  Endicott *(G-4601)*
N & G of America Inc .... E 516 428-3414
  Plainview *(G-13076)*
N & L Instruments Inc .... F 631 471-4000
  Ronkonkoma *(G-14382)*
NCR Corporation .... C 516 876-7200
  Jericho *(G-6795)*
Photon Vision Systems Inc .... F 607 749-2689
  Homer *(G-6258)*
Qualtronic Devices Inc .... F 631 360-0859
  Smithtown *(G-14908)*
Revivn Public Benefit Corp .... F 347 762-8193
  Brooklyn *(G-2399)*
Todd Enterprises Inc .... D 516 773-8087
  Great Neck *(G-5595)*
Toshiba Amer Info Systems Inc .... B 949 583-3000
  New York *(G-11871)*
Transland Sourcing LLC .... G 718 596-5704
  Brooklyn *(G-2580)*
Wantagh Computer Center .... G 516 826-2189
  Wantagh *(G-15927)*
Yellow E House Inc .... G 718 888-2000
  Flushing *(G-5061)*

COMPUTERS, NEC, WHOLESALE

Todd Enterprises Inc .... D 516 773-8087
  Great Neck *(G-5595)*

COMPUTERS, PERIPHERALS & SOFTWARE, WHOLESALE: Disk Drives

Formats Unlimited Inc .... F 631 249-9200
  Deer Park *(G-3978)*

COMPUTERS, PERIPHERALS & SOFTWARE, WHOLESALE: Printers

Newport Business Solutions Inc .... F 631 319-6129
  Bohemia *(G-1064)*
Printer Components Inc .... G 585 924-5190
  Fairport *(G-4651)*

COMPUTERS, PERIPHERALS & SOFTWARE, WHOLESALE: Software

Base Systems Inc .... G 845 278-1991
  Brewster *(G-1158)*
Cgi Technologies Solutions Inc .... F 212 682-7411
  New York *(G-9254)*
Escholar LLC .... G 914 989-2900
  White Plains *(G-16446)*
Infinite Software Solutions .... F 718 982-1315
  Staten Island *(G-15090)*

Employee Codes: A=Over 500 employees, B=251-500
C=101-250, D=51-100, E=20-50, F=10-19, G=5-9

COMPUTERS, PERIPHERALS & SOFTWARE, WHOLESALE: Software

Interntnl Publcatns Media Grup ....G...... 917 604-9602
  New York *(G-10252)*
Kse Sportsman Media Inc ....D...... 212 852-6600
  New York *(G-10483)*
Pointman LLC ....G...... 716 842-1439
  Buffalo *(G-3008)*
United Data Systems Inc ....G...... 631 549-6900
  Huntington *(G-6423)*
Visible Systems Corporation ....E...... 508 628-1510
  Oneida *(G-12623)*

COMPUTERS: Indl, Process, Gas Flow

Pneumercator Company Inc ....E...... 631 293-8450
  Hauppauge *(G-5917)*

COMPUTERS: Mainframe

Partech Inc ....C...... 315 738-0600
  New Hartford *(G-8509)*
Policy ADM Solutions Inc ....E...... 914 332-4320
  Tarrytown *(G-15486)*

COMPUTERS: Personal

Apple Commuter Inc ....G...... 917 299-0066
  New Hyde Park *(G-8516)*
Apple Healing & Relaxation ....G...... 718 278-1089
  Long Island City *(G-7382)*
Apple Med Urgent Care PC ....G...... 914 523-5965
  Mount Vernon *(G-8377)*
G S Communications USA Inc ....E...... 718 389-7371
  Brooklyn *(G-1913)*
Go Go Apple Inc ....G...... 646 264-8909
  Elmhurst *(G-4465)*
HP Inc ....G...... 650 857-1501
  Albany *(G-85)*
HP Inc ....F...... 650 857-1501
  New York *(G-10140)*
Stargate Computer Corp ....G...... 516 474-4799
  Port Jeff STA *(G-13217)*
Telxon Corporation ....E...... 631 738-2400
  Holtsville *(G-6248)*
Toshiba America Inc ....E...... 212 596-0600
  New York *(G-11872)*
Wilcro Inc ....G...... 716 632-4204
  Buffalo *(G-3130)*

CONCENTRATES, DRINK

Constellation Brands Inc ....D...... 585 678-7100
  Victor *(G-15837)*
Mr Smoothie ....G...... 845 296-1686
  Poughkeepsie *(G-13357)*
Roar Beverages LLC ....E...... 631 683-5565
  Huntington *(G-6410)*
Sabila Corp ....G...... 845 981-7128
  Pine Island *(G-13003)*

CONCENTRATES, FLAVORING, EXC DRINK

Consumer Flavoring Extract Co ....F...... 718 435-0201
  Brooklyn *(G-1712)*

CONCRETE CURING & HARDENING COMPOUNDS

Hanson Aggregates PA LLC ....F...... 585 436-3250
  Rochester *(G-13852)*
Watson Bowman Acme Corp ....C...... 716 691-8162
  Amherst *(G-260)*

CONCRETE MIXERS

X-Treme Ready Mix Inc ....G...... 718 739-3384
  Jamaica *(G-6692)*

CONCRETE PLANTS

Oneida Sales & Service Inc ....E...... 716 822-8205
  Buffalo *(G-2980)*
Seville Central Mix Corp ....D...... 516 293-6190
  Old Bethpage *(G-12587)*

CONCRETE PRDTS

Alpine Building Supply Inc ....G...... 718 456-2522
  Ridgewood *(G-13529)*
Arnan Development Corp ....D...... 607 432-8391
  Oneonta *(G-12625)*
Baliva Concrete Products Inc ....G...... 585 328-8442
  Rochester *(G-13653)*
Barrett Paving Materials Inc ....F...... 315 737-9471
  Clayville *(G-3554)*

Bonsal American Inc ....F...... 585 343-4741
  Batavia *(G-614)*
Bonsal American Inc ....E...... 631 208-8073
  Calverton *(G-3162)*
Buffalo Crushed Stone Inc ....E...... 716 826-7310
  Buffalo *(G-2742)*
City Mason Corp ....F...... 718 658-3796
  Jamaica *(G-6635)*
Coronado ....G...... 718 386-7425
  Brooklyn *(G-1719)*
Elderlee Incorporated ....C...... 315 789-6670
  Oaks Corners *(G-12527)*
Express Concrete Inc ....G...... 631 273-4224
  Brentwood *(G-1133)*
Get Real Surfaces Inc ....G...... 845 337-4483
  Poughkeepsie *(G-13340)*
Grace Associates Inc ....G...... 718 767-9000
  Harrison *(G-5729)*
Great ATL Pr-Cast Con Statuary ....G...... 718 948-5677
  Staten Island *(G-15083)*
Jab Concrete Supply Corp ....G...... 718 842-5250
  Bronx *(G-1300)*
Jenna Concrete Corporation ....G...... 718 842-5250
  Bronx *(G-1302)*
Jenna Harlem River Inc ....G...... 718 842-5997
  Bronx *(G-1303)*
John E Potente & Sons Inc ....E...... 516 935-8585
  Hicksville *(G-6097)*
Lafarge North America Inc ....E...... 518 756-5000
  Ravena *(G-13454)*
Long Island Geotech ....G...... 631 473-1044
  Port Jefferson *(G-13221)*
M K Ulrich Construction Inc ....F...... 716 893-5777
  Buffalo *(G-2930)*
Nicolia Concrete Products Inc ....D...... 631 669-0700
  Lindenhurst *(G-7185)*
Nicolock Paving Stones LLC ....D...... 631 669-0700
  Lindenhurst *(G-7188)*
NY Tempering LLC ....G...... 718 326-8989
  Maspeth *(G-7864)*
Quikrete Companies LLC ....E...... 716 213-2027
  Lackawanna *(G-6951)*
Quikrete Companies LLC ....E...... 315 673-2020
  Marcellus *(G-7794)*
Riefler Concrete Products LLC ....C...... 716 649-3260
  Hamburg *(G-5693)*
Stag Brothers Cast Stone Co ....G...... 718 629-0975
  Brooklyn *(G-2507)*
Taylor Concrete Products Inc ....E...... 315 788-2191
  Watertown *(G-16034)*
Towne House Restorations Inc ....G...... 718 497-9200
  Long Island City *(G-7619)*
Trinic LLC ....F...... 607 655-1517
  Kirkwood *(G-6941)*
Unilock New York Inc ....G...... 845 278-6700
  Brewster *(G-1175)*
Upstone Materials Inc ....G...... 518 483-2671
  Malone *(G-7729)*
Upstone Materials Inc ....G...... 518 873-2275
  Lewis *(G-7137)*

CONCRETE PRDTS, PRECAST, NEC

A & R Concrete Products LLC ....E...... 845 562-0640
  New Windsor *(G-8633)*
Afco Precast Sales Corp ....D...... 631 924-7114
  Middle Island *(G-8116)*
Callanan Industries Inc ....G...... 315 697-9569
  Canastota *(G-3241)*
Callanan Industries Inc ....C...... 518 374-2222
  Albany *(G-54)*
Callanan Industries Inc ....E...... 845 331-6868
  Kingston *(G-6892)*
Callanan Industries Inc ....G...... 518 785-5666
  Latham *(G-7068)*
Castek Inc ....G...... 914 636-1000
  New Rochelle *(G-8595)*
Coastal Pipeline Products Corp ....E...... 631 369-4000
  Calverton *(G-3163)*
David Kucera Inc ....E...... 845 255-1044
  Gardiner *(G-5293)*
Dillner Precast Inc ....G...... 631 421-9130
  Lloyd Harbor *(G-7279)*
Dillner Precast Inc ....G...... 631 421-9130
  Huntington Station *(G-6439)*
Dynasty Metal Works Inc ....G...... 631 284-3719
  Riverhead *(G-13567)*
East Main Associates ....D...... 585 624-1990
  Lima *(G-7151)*
Fort Miller Group Inc ....B...... 518 695-5000
  Greenwich *(G-5639)*

Fort Miller Service Corp ....F...... 518 695-5000
  Greenwich *(G-5640)*
Gamble & Gamble Inc ....G...... 716 731-3239
  Sanborn *(G-14546)*
Glens Falls Ready Mix Inc ....F...... 518 793-1695
  Queensbury *(G-13426)*
Glenwood Cast Stone Inc ....G...... 718 859-6500
  Brooklyn *(G-1931)*
Guardian Concrete Inc ....F...... 518 372-0080
  Schenectady *(G-14686)*
Island Ready Mix Inc ....E...... 631 874-3777
  Center Moriches *(G-3339)*
Lakelands Concrete Pdts Inc ....E...... 585 624-1990
  Lima *(G-7152)*
Lhv Precast Inc ....G...... 845 336-8880
  Kingston *(G-6907)*
Long Island Precast Inc ....E...... 631 286-0240
  Brookhaven *(G-1431)*
Mid-Hudson Concrete Pdts Inc ....F...... 845 265-3141
  Cold Spring *(G-3625)*
Oldcastle Precast Inc ....E...... 518 767-2116
  South Bethlehem *(G-14924)*
Oldcastle Precast Inc ....E...... 518 767-2112
  Selkirk *(G-14769)*
P J R Industries Inc ....E...... 716 825-9300
  Buffalo *(G-2984)*
Pelkowski Precast Corp ....E...... 631 269-5727
  Kings Park *(G-6885)*
Robinson Concrete Inc ....E...... 315 253-6666
  Auburn *(G-498)*
Sunnycrest Inc ....E...... 315 252-7214
  Auburn *(G-501)*
Transpo Industries Inc ....E...... 914 636-1000
  New Rochelle *(G-8630)*
Urban Precast LLC ....E...... 845 331-6299
  Kingston *(G-6928)*
Wel Made Enterprises Inc ....F...... 631 752-1238
  Farmingdale *(G-4906)*
Woodards Concrete Products Inc ....E...... 845 361-3471
  Bullville *(G-3139)*

CONCRETE: Asphaltic, Not From Refineries

Monticello Black Top Corp ....G...... 845 434-7280
  Thompsonville *(G-15500)*
Peckham Industries Inc ....E...... 914 949-2000
  White Plains *(G-16488)*
Peckham Industries Inc ....F...... 518 943-0155
  Catskill *(G-3308)*
Peckham Industries Inc ....F...... 518 893-2176
  Greenfield Center *(G-5619)*
PSI Transit Mix Corp ....G...... 631 382-7930
  Smithtown *(G-14907)*
Swift River Associates Inc ....G...... 716 875-0902
  Tonawanda *(G-15581)*

CONCRETE: Bituminous

Barrett Paving Materials Inc ....E...... 315 353-6611
  Norwood *(G-12495)*
Pallette Stone Corporation ....E...... 518 584-2421
  Gansevoort *(G-5244)*

CONCRETE: Ready-Mixed

Advanced Ready Mix Corp ....F...... 718 497-5020
  Brooklyn *(G-1488)*
Advanced Transit Mix Corp ....G...... 718 497-5020
  Brooklyn *(G-1489)*
All American Transit Mix Corp ....G...... 718 417-3654
  Brooklyn *(G-1507)*
Anbriella Sand & Gravel Corp ....E...... 631 586-2111
  Bay Shore *(G-657)*
Atlas Concrete Batching Corp ....D...... 718 523-3000
  Jamaica *(G-6627)*
Atlas Transit Mix Corp ....C...... 718 523-3000
  Jamaica *(G-6628)*
Barney & Dickenson Inc ....E...... 607 729-1536
  Vestal *(G-15809)*
Barrett Paving Materials Inc ....F...... 315 788-2037
  Watertown *(G-16001)*
Best Concrete Mix Corp ....E...... 718 463-5500
  Flushing *(G-4988)*
Bonded Concrete Inc ....E...... 518 273-5800
  Watervliet *(G-16042)*
Bonded Concrete Inc ....E...... 518 674-2854
  West Sand Lake *(G-16284)*
Brewster Transit Mix Corp ....D...... 845 279-3738
  Brewster *(G-1160)*
Brewster Transit Mix Corp ....E...... 845 279-3738
  Brewster *(G-1161)*

PRODUCT SECTION

CONDENSERS: Heat Transfer Eqpt, Evaporative

Byram Concrete & Supply LLC ....F 914 682-4477
  White Plains (G-16433)
C & C Ready-Mix Corporation ....E 607 797-5108
  Vestal (G-15812)
C & C Ready-Mix Corporation ....F 607 687-1690
  Owego (G-12796)
Capital Concrete Inc ....G 716 648-8001
  Hamburg (G-5673)
Casa Redimix Concrete Corp ....F 718 589-1555
  Bronx (G-1235)
Ccz Ready Mix Concrete Corp ....F 516 579-7352
  Levittown (G-7132)
Cemex Cement Inc ....D 212 317-6000
  New York (G-9237)
Century Ready Mix Inc ....G 631 888-2200
  West Babylon (G-16145)
Champion Materials Inc ....G 315 493-2654
  Carthage (G-3289)
Chenango Concrete Corp ....F 518 294-9964
  Richmondville (G-13518)
Clark Concrete Co Inc ....G 315 478-4101
  Syracuse (G-15279)
Clemente Latham Concrete Corp ....D 518 374-2222
  Schenectady (G-14663)
Cobleskill Red E Mix & Supply ....F 518 234-2015
  Amsterdam (G-332)
Corona Ready Mix Inc ....F 718 271-5940
  Corona (G-3842)
Cortland Ready Mix Inc ....F 607 753-3063
  Cortland (G-3870)
Cossitt Concrete Products Inc ....F 315 824-2700
  Hamilton (G-5698)
Costanza Ready Mix Inc ....F 516 783-4444
  North Bellmore (G-12375)
Cranesville Block Co Inc ....E 315 732-2135
  Utica (G-15688)
Cranesville Block Co Inc ....F 845 292-1585
  Liberty (G-7143)
Cranesville Block Co Inc ....F 845 896-5687
  Fishkill (G-4944)
Cranesville Block Co Inc ....F 845 331-1775
  Kingston (G-6896)
Cranesville Block Co Inc ....G 315 384-4000
  Norfolk (G-12357)
Cranesville Block Co Inc ....E 518 684-6154
  Amsterdam (G-333)
Cranesville Block Co Inc ....E 315 773-2296
  Felts Mills (G-4930)
Custom Mix Inc ....G 516 797-7090
  Massapequa Park (G-7889)
Dalrymple Grav & Contg Co Inc ....F 607 739-0391
  Pine City (G-12999)
Dalrymple Holding Corp ....E 607 737-6200
  Pine City (G-13000)
Deer Park Sand & Gravel Corp ....E 631 586-2323
  Bay Shore (G-680)
Dicks Concrete Co Inc ....E 845 374-5966
  New Hampton (G-8499)
Dunkirk Construction Products ....G 716 366-5220
  Dunkirk (G-4166)
E Tetz & Sons Inc ....D 845 692-4486
  Middletown (G-8148)
East Coast Spring Mix Inc ....G 845 355-1215
  New Hampton (G-8500)
Elam Materials Inc ....F 585 658-2248
  Mount Morris (G-8366)
Electric City Concrete Co Inc ....E 518 887-5560
  Amsterdam (G-335)
Elm Transit Mix Corporation ....F 516 333-6144
  Westbury (G-16327)
Empire Transit Mix Inc ....E 718 384-3000
  Brooklyn (G-1834)
F H Stickles & Son Inc ....F 518 851-9048
  Livingston (G-7275)
Ferrara Bros LLC ....F 718 939-3030
  Flushing (G-4999)
Frey Concrete Inc ....G 716 213-5832
  North Tonawanda (G-12428)
Fulmont Ready-Mix Company Inc ....F 518 887-5560
  Amsterdam (G-338)
G & J Rdymx & Masnry Sup Inc ....F 718 454-0800
  Hollis (G-6234)
Glens Falls Ready Mix Inc ....F 518 793-1695
  Queensbury (G-13426)
Grandview Concrete Corp ....E 518 346-7981
  Schenectady (G-14684)
Haley Concrete Inc ....F 716 492-0849
  Delevan (G-4070)
Hanson Aggregates East LLC ....F 585 798-0762
  Medina (G-7980)

Hanson Aggregates East LLC ....F 716 372-1574
  Falconer (G-4679)
Hanson Aggregates New York LLC ....F 716 665-4620
  Jamestown (G-6721)
Hanson Aggregates New York LLC ....F 585 638-5841
  Pavilion (G-12889)
Hanson Aggregates New York LLC ....C 315 469-5501
  Jamesville (G-6767)
Inwood Material ....F 516 371-1842
  Inwood (G-6493)
Iroquois Rock Products Inc ....F 585 381-7010
  Rochester (G-13887)
Island Ready Mix Inc ....E 631 874-3777
  Center Moriches (G-3339)
James Town Macadam Inc ....D 716 665-4504
  Falconer (G-4683)
Jenna Concrete Corporation ....E 718 842-5250
  Bronx (G-1302)
Jenna Harlem River Inc ....E 718 842-5997
  Bronx (G-1303)
Jet Redi Mix Concrete Inc ....F 631 580-3640
  Ronkonkoma (G-14358)
King Road Materials Inc ....F 518 382-5354
  Albany (G-92)
Kings Park Ready Mix Corp ....F 631 269-4330
  Kings Park (G-6884)
Kings Ready Mix Inc ....F 718 853-4644
  Roslyn Heights (G-14458)
Knight Sttlement Sand Grav LLC ....F 607 776-2048
  Bath (G-646)
Lafarge North America Inc ....E 518 756-5000
  Ravena (G-13454)
Lage Industries Corporation ....F 718 342-3400
  Brooklyn (G-2090)
Lakeside Concrete Services Inc ....G 716 681-7510
  Lancaster (G-7028)
Lazarek Inc ....G 315 343-1242
  Oswego (G-12780)
Lehigh Cement Company ....E 518 943-5940
  Catskill (G-3305)
Liberty Ready Mix Inc ....F 718 526-1700
  Jamaica (G-6655)
Long Island Ready Mix ....G 516 485-5260
  Hempstead (G-6018)
Manitou Concrete ....D 585 424-6040
  Rochester (G-13925)
Manzione Ready Mix Corp ....F 718 628-3837
  Brooklyn (G-2162)
Mastro Concrete Inc ....F 718 528-6788
  Rosedale (G-14441)
Mix N Mac LLC ....F 845 381-5536
  Middletown (G-8165)
N Y Western Concrete Corp ....G 585 343-6850
  Batavia (G-631)
New Atlantic Ready Mix Corp ....G 718 812-0739
  Hollis (G-6235)
Nex-Gen Ready Mix Corp ....G 347 231-0073
  Bronx (G-1342)
Nicolia Ready Mix Inc ....D 631 669-7000
  Lindenhurst (G-7186)
Nicolia Ready Mix Inc ....F 631 669-7000
  Lindenhurst (G-7187)
Northern Ready Mix LLC ....F 315 336-7900
  North Syracuse (G-12408)
Oldcastle Materials Inc ....F 585 424-6410
  Rochester (G-13984)
Oldcastle Precast Inc ....F 518 767-2116
  South Bethlehem (G-14924)
Otsego Ready Mix Inc ....F 607 432-3400
  Oneonta (G-12643)
Precision Ready Mix Corp ....G 718 658-5600
  Jamaica (G-6668)
Presti Ready Mix Concrete Inc ....F 516 378-6006
  Freeport (G-5175)
Quality Ready Mix Inc ....F 516 437-0100
  New Hyde Park (G-8559)
Queens Ready Mix Inc ....F 718 526-4919
  Jamaica (G-6670)
Residential Fences Corp ....E 631 205-9758
  Ridge (G-13524)
Richmond Ready Mix Corp ....F 917 731-8400
  Staten Island (G-15130)
Richmond Ready Mix Corp II ....F 917 731-8400
  Staten Island (G-15131)
Riefler Concrete Products LLC ....C 716 649-3260
  Hamburg (G-5693)
Robinson Concrete Inc ....F 315 253-6666
  Auburn (G-498)
Robinson Concrete Inc ....C 315 676-4333
  West Monroe (G-16262)

Robinson Concrete Inc ....F 315 492-6200
  Jamesville (G-6770)
Robinson Concrete Inc ....F 315 676-4662
  Brewerton (G-1152)
Rochester Asphalt Materials ....D 585 924-7360
  Farmington (G-4918)
Rochester Asphalt Materials ....G 585 381-7010
  Rochester (G-14079)
Rural Hill Sand and Grav Corp ....F 315 846-5212
  Woodville (G-16689)
Russian Mix Inc ....G 347 385-7198
  Brooklyn (G-2428)
Saunders Concrete Co Inc ....F 607 756-7905
  Cortland (G-3893)
Scara-Mix Inc ....F 718 442-7357
  Staten Island (G-15132)
Seville Central Mix Corp ....D 516 868-3000
  Freeport (G-5183)
Seville Central Mix Corp ....D 516 293-6190
  Old Bethpage (G-12587)
Seville Central Mix Corp ....E 516 239-8333
  Lawrence (G-7109)
South Shore Ready Mix Inc ....G 516 872-3049
  Valley Stream (G-15798)
Star Ready Mix East Inc ....F 631 289-8787
  East Hampton (G-4243)
Star Ready Mix Inc ....F 631 289-8787
  Medford (G-7966)
Stephen Miller Gen Contrs Inc ....E 518 661-5601
  Gloversville (G-5467)
Suffolk Cement Precast Inc ....G 631 727-4432
  Calverton (G-3172)
Suffolk Cement Products Inc ....E 631 727-2317
  Calverton (G-3173)
Sullivan Concrete Inc ....F 845 888-2235
  Cochecton (G-3608)
T Mix Inc ....G 646 379-6814
  Brooklyn (G-2549)
TEC - Crete Transit Mix Corp ....E 718 657-6880
  Ridgewood (G-13554)
Thousand Island Ready Mix Con ....G 315 686-3203
  La Fargeville (G-6944)
Torrington Industries Inc ....F 315 676-4662
  Central Square (G-3392)
United Materials LLC ....D 716 683-1432
  North Tonawanda (G-12461)
United Materials LLC ....E 716 731-2332
  Sanborn (G-14556)
United Materials LLC ....G 716 662-0564
  Orchard Park (G-12748)
United Transit Mix Inc ....F 718 416-3400
  Brooklyn (G-2604)
Upstone Materials Inc ....F 315 265-8036
  Plattsburgh (G-13166)
Upstone Materials Inc ....G 315 764-0251
  Massena (G-7910)
Upstone Materials Inc ....E 518 873-2275
  Lewis (G-7137)
Upstone Materials Inc ....D 518 561-5321
  Plattsburgh (G-13165)
US Concrete Inc ....E 718 853-4644
  Roslyn Heights (G-14461)
US Concrete Inc ....E 718 438-6800
  Brooklyn (G-2612)
W F Saunders & Sons Inc ....F 315 469-3217
  Nedrow (G-8480)
W F Saunders & Sons Inc ....G 607 257-6930
  Etna (G-4623)
Watertown Concrete Inc ....F 315 788-1040
  Watertown (G-16036)

CONDENSERS & CONDENSING UNITS: Air Conditioner

Motivair Corporation ....E 716 691-9222
  Amherst (G-239)

CONDENSERS: Fixed Or Variable

Viking Technologies Ltd ....E 631 957-8000
  Lindenhurst (G-7204)

CONDENSERS: Heat Transfer Eqpt, Evaporative

Roemac Industrial Sales Inc ....G 716 692-7332
  North Tonawanda (G-12448)
Rubicon Industries Corp ....E 718 434-4700
  Brooklyn (G-2425)

Employee Codes: A=Over 500 employees, B=251-500
C=101-250, D=51-100, E=20-50, F=10-19, G=5-9

CONDENSERS: Motors Or Generators

Company		Phone
GM Components Holdings LLC	B	716 439-2463
Lockport *(G-7305)*		
GM Components Holdings LLC	B	716 439-2011
Lockport *(G-7306)*		

CONDUITS & FITTINGS: Electric

Company		Phone
Highland Valley Supply Inc	F	845 849-2863
Wappingers Falls *(G-15934)*		
Producto Electric Corp	E	845 359-4900
Orangeburg *(G-12688)*		
Quadristi LLC	F	585 279-3318
Rochester *(G-14059)*		
Superflex Ltd	E	718 768-1400
Brooklyn *(G-2535)*		

CONDUITS: Pressed Pulp Fiber, Made From Purchased Materials

Company		Phone
Stanley Paper Co Inc	F	518 489-1131
Albany *(G-129)*		

CONFECTIONERY PRDTS WHOLESALERS

Company		Phone
Mrchocolatecom LLC	F	718 875-9772
Brooklyn *(G-2235)*		
Roger L Urban Inc	E	716 693-5391
North Tonawanda *(G-12449)*		

CONFECTIONS & CANDY

Company		Phone
5th Avenue Chocolatiere Ltd	G	212 935-5454
Freeport *(G-5134)*		
Anyas Licorice Inc	G	917 935-1916
Brooklyn *(G-1538)*		
Bader Enterprise Inc	G	718 965-9434
Brooklyn *(G-1583)*		
C Howard Company Inc	G	631 286-7940
Bellport *(G-800)*		
Calico Cottage Inc	E	631 841-2100
Amityville *(G-266)*		
Chocolat Moderne LLC	G	212 229-4797
New York *(G-9287)*		
Chocolations LLC	G	914 777-3600
Mamaroneck *(G-7738)*		
Dilese International Inc	F	716 855-3500
Buffalo *(G-2801)*		
Fairbanks Mfg LLC	C	845 341-0002
Middletown *(G-8152)*		
Gertrude Hawk Chocolates Inc	E	
Watertown *(G-16014)*		
Godiva Chocolatier Inc	E	212 984-5900
New York *(G-9950)*		
Gourmet Nut Inc	E	877 830-9030
Brooklyn *(G-1943)*		
Gravymaster Inc	G	203 453-1893
Canajoharie *(G-3207)*		
Handsome Dans LLC	G	917 965-2499
New York *(G-10030)*		
Hercules Candy Co	G	315 463-4339
East Syracuse *(G-4346)*		
Hudson Valley Chocolatier Inc	F	845 831-8240
Beacon *(G-759)*		
In Room Plus Inc	E	716 838-9433
Buffalo *(G-2882)*		
Jo-Mart Candies Corp	F	718 375-1277
Brooklyn *(G-2041)*		
Koppers Choclat Specialty Inc	G	917 834-2290
New York *(G-10469)*		
L A Burdick Chocolates	G	212 796-0143
New York *(G-10492)*		
Lady-N-Th-wndow Chocolates Inc	F	631 549-1059
Huntington *(G-6403)*		
Lanco Corporation	C	631 231-2300
Ronkonkoma *(G-14368)*		
Landies Candies Co Inc	F	716 834-8212
Buffalo *(G-2920)*		
Little Bird Chocolates Inc	G	646 620-6395
Plainview *(G-13070)*		
Momn Pops Inc	E	845 567-0640
Cornwall *(G-3834)*		
Mrchocolatecom LLC	F	718 875-9772
Brooklyn *(G-2235)*		
Nassau Candy Distributors Inc	C	516 433-7100
Hicksville *(G-6113)*		
Noras Candy Shop	F	315 337-4530
Rome *(G-14262)*		
Pachanga Inc	F	212 832-0022
New York *(G-11087)*		
Papa Bubble	G	212 966-2599
New York *(G-11100)*		
Premium Sweets USA Inc	G	718 739-6000
Jamaica *(G-6669)*		
Rajbhog Foods Inc	E	718 358-5105
Flushing *(G-5042)*		
Richardson Brands Company	C	800 839-8938
Canajoharie *(G-3208)*		
Roger L Urban Inc	E	716 693-5391
North Tonawanda *(G-12449)*		
Salty Road Inc		347 673-3925
Brooklyn *(G-2446)*		
Satin Fine Foods Inc	D	845 469-1034
Chester *(G-3483)*		
Scaccianoce Inc	F	718 991-4462
Bronx *(G-1382)*		
Seaward Candies	G	585 638-6761
Holley *(G-6229)*		
Settons Intl Foods Inc	D	631 543-8090
Commack *(G-3702)*		
Simply Natural Foods LLC	C	631 543-9600
Commack *(G-3703)*		
Star Brands North America Inc	E	914 355-9750
White Plains *(G-16506)*		
Steve & Andys Organics Inc	G	718 499-7933
Brooklyn *(G-2521)*		
Stones Homemade Candies Inc	G	315 343-8401
Oswego *(G-12789)*		
Sweetworks Inc	F	716 634-4545
Buffalo *(G-3082)*		
Tomric Systems Inc	F	716 854-6050
Buffalo *(G-3098)*		
Valenti Distributing	G	716 824-2304
Blasdell *(G-932)*		
Vidal Candies USA Inc	G	609 781-8169
New York *(G-12030)*		
Wellspring Corp	G	212 529-5454
New York *(G-12092)*		

CONFINEMENT SURVEILLANCE SYS MAINTENANCE & MONITORING SVCS

Company		Phone
Par Technology Corporation	D	315 738-0600
New Hartford *(G-8508)*		

CONNECTORS & TERMINALS: Electrical Device Uses

Company		Phone
Fiber Instrument Sales Inc	C	315 736-2206
Oriskany *(G-12757)*		
International Key Supply LLC	F	631 983-6096
Farmingdale *(G-4788)*		
Zierick Manufacturing Corp	D	800 882-8020
Mount Kisco *(G-8361)*		

CONNECTORS: Cord, Electric

Company		Phone
Crown Die Casting Corp	E	914 667-5400
Mount Vernon *(G-8392)*		
EB Acquisitions LLC	D	212 355-3310
New York *(G-9614)*		

CONNECTORS: Electrical

Company		Phone
Automatic Connector Inc	F	631 543-5000
Hauppauge *(G-5774)*		
Command Components Corporation	G	631 666-4411
Bay Shore *(G-675)*		

CONNECTORS: Electronic

Company		Phone
Accessories For Electronics	E	631 847-0158
South Hempstead *(G-14941)*		
Amphenol Aerospace France Inc	C	800 678-0141
Sidney *(G-14849)*		
Amphenol Cables On Demand Corp	F	607 321-2115
Endicott *(G-4581)*		
Amphenol Corporation	B	607 563-5364
Sidney *(G-14850)*		
Amphenol Corporation	A	607 563-5011
Sidney *(G-14851)*		
Automatic Connector Inc	F	631 543-5000
Hauppauge *(G-5774)*		
Belden Inc	B	607 796-5600
Horseheads *(G-6306)*		
Casa Innovations Inc	G	718 965-6600
Brooklyn *(G-1682)*		
CS Business Systems Inc	F	716 886-6521
Buffalo *(G-2786)*		
EBY Electro Inc	E	516 576-7777
Plainview *(G-13053)*		
Executive Machines Inc	E	718 965-6600
Brooklyn *(G-1858)*		
Felchar Manufacturing Corp	A	607 723-3106
Binghamton *(G-884)*		
I Trade Technology Ltd	E	845 357-4943
Airmont *(G-13)*		
I Trade Technology Ltd	C	615 348-7233
Suffern *(G-15191)*		
Ieh Corporation	C	718 492-4440
Brooklyn *(G-1994)*		
Keystone Electronics Corp	C	516 328-7500
New Hyde Park *(G-8546)*		
Kirtas Inc	C	585 924-5999
Victor *(G-15852)*		
Kirtas Inc	E	585 924-2420
Victor *(G-15853)*		
Leviton Manufacturing Co Inc	B	631 812-6000
Melville *(G-8043)*		
Mason Industries Inc	B	631 348-0282
Hauppauge *(G-5881)*		
Mill-Max Mfg Corp	C	516 922-6000
Oyster Bay *(G-12815)*		
Mini-Circuits Fort Wayne LLC	B	718 934-4500
Brooklyn *(G-2210)*		
NEa Manufacturing Corp	E	516 371-4200
Inwood *(G-6497)*		
Pei/Genesis Inc	G	631 256-1747
Farmingville *(G-4925)*		
Power Connector Inc	E	631 563-7878
Bohemia *(G-1075)*		
Ppc Broadband Inc	B	315 431-7200
East Syracuse *(G-4363)*		
Princetel Inc	F	914 579-2410
Hawthorne *(G-5996)*		
Rdi Inc	F	914 773-1000
Mount Kisco *(G-8357)*		
Resonance Technologies Inc	E	631 237-4901
Ronkonkoma *(G-14406)*		
Sitewatch Technology LLC	G	207 778-3246
East Quogue *(G-4279)*		
Supplynet Inc	G	800 826-0279
Valley Cottage *(G-15768)*		
Taro Manufacturing Company Inc	F	315 252-9430
Auburn *(G-503)*		
Universal Remote Control Inc	D	914 630-4343
Harrison *(G-5738)*		
Whirlwind Music Distrs Inc	D	800 733-9473
Rochester *(G-14207)*		

CONNECTORS: Solderless, Electric-Wiring Devices

Company		Phone
Andros Manufacturing Corp	F	585 663-5700
Rochester *(G-13633)*		

CONSTRUCTION & MINING MACHINERY WHOLESALERS

Company		Phone
Gone South Concrete Block Inc	E	315 598-2141
Fulton *(G-5218)*		

CONSTRUCTION & ROAD MAINTENANCE EQPT: Drags, Road

Company		Phone
Drillco National Group Inc	E	718 726-9801
Long Island City *(G-7428)*		
Highway Garage	G	518 568-2837
Saint Johnsville *(G-14520)*		

CONSTRUCTION EQPT: Attachments

Company		Phone
Primoplast Inc	F	631 750-0680
Bohemia *(G-1078)*		

CONSTRUCTION EQPT: Attachments, Snow Plow

Company		Phone
Cives Corporation	D	315 543-2321
Harrisville *(G-5740)*		
Pro-Tech Wldg Fabrication Inc	E	585 436-9855
Rochester *(G-14047)*		
Town of Ohio	E	315 392-2055
Forestport *(G-5084)*		

CONSTRUCTION EQPT: Crane Carriers

Company		Phone
Crane Equipment & Service Inc	G	716 689-5400
Amherst *(G-223)*		

PRODUCT SECTION — CONSTRUCTION MATERIALS, WHOLESALE: Stone, Crushed Or Broken

CONSTRUCTION EQPT: Cranes
Dave Sandel Cranes Inc .... G 631 325-5588
 Westhampton *(G-16401)*
Kinedyne Inc .... F 716 667-6833
 Orchard Park *(G-12724)*

CONSTRUCTION EQPT: Dozers, Tractor Mounted, Material Moving
Rapistak Corporation .... G 716 822-2804
 Blasdell *(G-927)*

CONSTRUCTION EQPT: Hammer Mills, Port, Incl Rock/Ore Crush
Schutte-Buffalo Hammermill LLC .... E 716 855-1202
 Buffalo *(G-3059)*

CONSTRUCTION EQPT: Rakes, Land Clearing, Mechanical
Got Wood LLC .... G 315 440-8857
 Cleveland *(G-3561)*

CONSTRUCTION EQPT: Rollers, Sheepsfoot & Vibratory
S R & R Industries Inc .... G 845 692-8329
 Middletown *(G-8175)*

CONSTRUCTION EQPT: SCRAPERS, GRADERS, ROLLERS & SIMILAR EQPT
Gei International Inc .... E 315 463-9261
 East Syracuse *(G-4342)*

CONSTRUCTION EQPT: Wrecker Hoists, Automobile
Pauls Rods & Restos Inc .... G 631 665-7637
 Deer Park *(G-4023)*
Vanhouten Motorsports .... G 315 387-6312
 Lacona *(G-6955)*

CONSTRUCTION MATERIALS, WHOLESALE: Aggregate
Twin County Recycling Corp .... F 516 827-6900
 Westbury *(G-16383)*

CONSTRUCTION MATERIALS, WHOLESALE: Awnings
Acme Awning Co Inc .... F 718 409-1881
 Bronx *(G-1210)*
Kassis Superior Sign Co Inc .... F 315 463-7446
 Syracuse *(G-15354)*

CONSTRUCTION MATERIALS, WHOLESALE: Block, Concrete & Cinder
Lazarek Inc .... G 315 343-1242
 Oswego *(G-12780)*
Taylor Concrete Products Inc .... E 315 788-2191
 Watertown *(G-16034)*

CONSTRUCTION MATERIALS, WHOLESALE: Blocks, Building, NEC
Sg Blocks Inc .... G 615 585-2639
 Brooklyn *(G-2460)*

CONSTRUCTION MATERIALS, WHOLESALE: Building Stone, Granite
Glen Plaza Marble & Gran Inc .... G 516 671-1100
 Glen Cove *(G-5368)*
MCM Natural Stone Inc .... F 585 586-6510
 Rochester *(G-13934)*

CONSTRUCTION MATERIALS, WHOLESALE: Building Stone, Marble
Stone & Terrazzo World Inc .... G 718 361-6899
 Long Island City *(G-7605)*

CONSTRUCTION MATERIALS, WHOLESALE: Building, Exterior
Bestway Enterprises Inc .... E 607 753-8261
 Cortland *(G-3860)*
Bob Murphy Inc .... F 607 729-3553
 Vestal *(G-15811)*
Dolomite Products Company Inc .... E 315 524-1998
 Rochester *(G-13749)*
Tri-State Brick & Stone NY Inc .... D 212 366-0300
 New York *(G-11895)*

CONSTRUCTION MATERIALS, WHOLESALE: Building, Interior
Great American Industries Inc .... E 607 729-9331
 Vestal *(G-15818)*
Nanz Custom Hardware Inc .... E 212 367-7000
 New York *(G-10873)*
Nanz Custom Hardware Inc .... C 212 367-7000
 Deer Park *(G-4012)*

CONSTRUCTION MATERIALS, WHOLESALE: Cement
Dicks Concrete Co Inc .... E 845 374-5966
 New Hampton *(G-8499)*
Lehigh Cement Company .... E 518 943-5940
 Catskill *(G-3305)*

CONSTRUCTION MATERIALS, WHOLESALE: Clay, Exc Refractory
Walsh & Hughes Inc .... G 631 427-5904
 Huntington Station *(G-6464)*

CONSTRUCTION MATERIALS, WHOLESALE: Concrete Mixtures
Barney & Dickenson Inc .... E 607 729-1536
 Vestal *(G-15809)*

CONSTRUCTION MATERIALS, WHOLESALE: Door Frames
Lif Industries Inc .... D 516 390-6800
 Port Washington *(G-13281)*
Lif Industries Inc .... E 718 767-8800
 Whitestone *(G-16545)*
Milanese Commercial Door LLC .... F 518 658-0398
 Berlin *(G-832)*

CONSTRUCTION MATERIALS, WHOLESALE: Glass
Twin Pane Insulated GL Co Inc .... F 631 924-1060
 Yaphank *(G-16725)*

CONSTRUCTION MATERIALS, WHOLESALE: Gravel
Brewster Transit Mix Corp .... D 845 279-3738
 Brewster *(G-1160)*
Deer Park Sand & Gravel Corp .... E 631 586-2323
 Bay Shore *(G-680)*
Jamestown Macadam Inc .... F 716 664-5108
 Jamestown *(G-6730)*

CONSTRUCTION MATERIALS, WHOLESALE: Lime Building Prdts
Specialty Minerals Inc .... E 212 878-1800
 New York *(G-11661)*

CONSTRUCTION MATERIALS, WHOLESALE: Limestone
Minerals Technologies Inc .... E 212 878-1800
 New York *(G-10817)*

CONSTRUCTION MATERIALS, WHOLESALE: Masons' Materials
Colonie Block and Supply Co .... G 518 869-8411
 Colonie *(G-3677)*
Grandview Block & Supply Co .... E 518 346-7981
 Schenectady *(G-14683)*

CONSTRUCTION MATERIALS, WHOLESALE: Millwork
I Meglio Corp .... E 631 617-6900
 Brentwood *(G-1135)*
Metalocke Industries Inc .... G 718 267-9200
 Woodside *(G-16663)*

CONSTRUCTION MATERIALS, WHOLESALE: Molding, All Materials
Globmarble LLC .... G 347 717-4088
 Brooklyn *(G-1933)*
Jaxson Rollforming Inc .... E 631 842-7775
 Amityville *(G-290)*

CONSTRUCTION MATERIALS, WHOLESALE: Paving Materials
Barrett Paving Materials Inc .... E 315 353-6611
 Norwood *(G-12495)*

CONSTRUCTION MATERIALS, WHOLESALE: Paving Mixtures
Peckham Materials Corp .... D 914 686-2045
 White Plains *(G-16489)*

CONSTRUCTION MATERIALS, WHOLESALE: Prefabricated Structures
Morton Buildings Inc .... E 585 786-8191
 Warsaw *(G-15945)*

CONSTRUCTION MATERIALS, WHOLESALE: Roof, Asphalt/Sheet Metal
Jordan Panel Systems Corp .... E 631 754-4900
 East Northport *(G-4266)*

CONSTRUCTION MATERIALS, WHOLESALE: Roofing & Siding Material
Marathon Roofing Products Inc .... F 716 685-3340
 Orchard Park *(G-12728)*
Park Ave Bldg & Roofg Sups LLC .... E 718 403-0100
 Brooklyn *(G-2304)*
S & J Sheet Metal Supply .... G 718 384-0800
 Brooklyn *(G-2431)*

CONSTRUCTION MATERIALS, WHOLESALE: Sand
F H Stickles & Son Inc .... F 518 851-9048
 Livingston *(G-7275)*
Monticello Black Top Corp .... F 845 434-7280
 Thompsonville *(G-15500)*

CONSTRUCTION MATERIALS, WHOLESALE: Septic Tanks
Guardian Concrete Inc .... F 518 372-0080
 Schenectady *(G-14686)*

CONSTRUCTION MATERIALS, WHOLESALE: Siding, Exc Wood
Pal Aluminum Inc .... G 516 937-1990
 Hicksville *(G-6121)*

CONSTRUCTION MATERIALS, WHOLESALE: Stone, Crushed Or Broken
Buffalo Crushed Stone Inc .... F 716 566-9636
 Franklinville *(G-5122)*
Callahan & Nannini Quarry Inc .... G 845 496-4323
 Salisbury Mills *(G-14539)*
Callanan Industries Inc .... E 845 457-3158
 Montgomery *(G-8309)*
Dalrymple Grav & Contg Co Inc .... E 607 529-3235
 Chemung *(G-3463)*
Grosso Materials Inc .... F 845 361-5211
 Montgomery *(G-8312)*
Hanson Aggregates PA LLC .... F 315 782-2300
 Watertown *(G-16015)*
Pallette Stone Corporation .... E 518 584-2421
 Gansevoort *(G-5244)*
Seneca Stone Corporation .... F 315 549-8253
 Fayette *(G-4926)*

Employee Codes: A=Over 500 employees, B=251-500
C=101-250, D=51-100, E=20-50, F=10-19, G=5-9

CONSTRUCTION MATERIALS, WHOLESALE: Stone, Crushed Or Broken

Troy Sand & Gravel Co Inc .... F 518 674-2854
West Sand Lake *(G-16286)*

CONSTRUCTION MATERIALS, WHOLESALE: Tile, Clay/Other Ceramic

Foro Marble Co Inc .... E 718 852-2322
Brooklyn *(G-1898)*
Kowa American Corporation .... E 212 303-7800
New York *(G-10474)*

CONSTRUCTION MATERIALS, WHOLESALE: Windows

Excel Aluminum Products Inc .... G 315 471-0925
Syracuse *(G-15321)*
Express Building Supply Inc .... E 516 608-0379
Oceanside *(G-12537)*
New Bgnnngs Win Door Dstrs LLC .... F 845 214-0698
Poughkeepsie *(G-13358)*

CONSTRUCTION MATLS, WHOL: Lumber, Rough, Dressed/Finished

Berry Industrial Group Inc .... G 845 353-8338
Nyack *(G-12501)*
Georgia-Pacific LLC .... E 631 924-7401
Yaphank *(G-16712)*

CONSTRUCTION MATLS, WHOLESALE: Soil Erosion Cntrl Fabrics

Traffic Lane Closures LLC .... F 845 228-6100
Carmel *(G-3283)*

CONSTRUCTION SAND MINING

Buffalo Crushed Stone Inc .... G 607 587-8102
Alfred Station *(G-186)*
Country Side Sand & Gravel .... F 716 988-3271
South Dayton *(G-14929)*
Elam Sand & Gravel Corp .... E 585 657-8000
Bloomfield *(G-953)*
John Vespa Inc .... F 315 788-6330
Watertown *(G-16019)*
Lazarek Inc .... G 315 343-1242
Oswego *(G-12780)*
Little Valley Sand & Gravel .... G 716 938-6676
Little Valley *(G-7221)*
Ruby Engineering LLC .... G 646 391-4600
Brooklyn *(G-2426)*
Rural Hill Sand and Grav Corp .... F 315 846-5212
Woodville *(G-16689)*
Syracusa Sand and Gravel Inc .... F 585 924-7146
Victor *(G-15870)*

CONSTRUCTION SITE PREPARATION SVCS

Kevin Regan Logging Ltd .... G 315 245-3890
Camden *(G-3190)*

CONSTRUCTION: Bridge

Dalrymple Holding Corp .... E 607 737-6200
Pine City *(G-13000)*
Tiki Industries Inc .... G 516 779-3629
Riverhead *(G-13586)*

CONSTRUCTION: Commercial & Institutional Building

Dynasty Stainless Steel & Meta .... E 718 205-6623
Maspeth *(G-7839)*
Stephen Miller Gen Contrs Inc .... E 518 661-5601
Gloversville *(G-5467)*

CONSTRUCTION: Concrete Patio

Concrete Designs Inc .... G 607 738-0309
Elmira *(G-4479)*

CONSTRUCTION: Dry Cleaning Plant

Genco John .... G 716 483-5446
Jamestown *(G-6717)*

CONSTRUCTION: Food Prdts Manufacturing or Packing Plant

Patla Enterprises Inc .... F 315 367-0237
Sherrill *(G-14821)*

Sidco Food Distribution Corp .... F 718 733-3939
Bronx *(G-1383)*

CONSTRUCTION: Guardrails, Highway

Elderlee Incorporated .... C 315 789-6670
Oaks Corners *(G-12527)*

CONSTRUCTION: Heavy Highway & Street

A Colarusso and Son Inc .... E 518 828-3218
Hudson *(G-6336)*
Barrett Paving Materials Inc .... F 315 788-2037
Watertown *(G-16001)*
Dalrymple Holding Corp .... E 607 737-6200
Pine City *(G-13000)*
Peckham Materials Corp .... E 518 747-3353
Hudson Falls *(G-6384)*
Suit-Kote Corporation .... E 607 535-2743
Watkins Glen *(G-16061)*

CONSTRUCTION: Indl Building & Warehouse

Siemens Industry Inc .... E 716 568-0983
Buffalo *(G-3065)*

CONSTRUCTION: Indl Building, Prefabricated

R & B Fabrication Inc .... E 315 640-9901
Cicero *(G-3522)*
Zebra Technologies Entp Corp .... E 800 722-6234
Holtsville *(G-6251)*

CONSTRUCTION: Indl Buildings, New, NEC

Orange County Ironworks LLC .... E 845 769-3000
Montgomery *(G-8315)*
Stephen Miller Gen Contrs Inc .... E 518 661-5601
Gloversville *(G-5467)*

CONSTRUCTION: Pharmaceutical Manufacturing Plant

Knf Clean Room Products Corp .... E 631 588-7000
Ronkonkoma *(G-14362)*

CONSTRUCTION: Power & Communication Transmission Tower

Ducon Technologies Inc .... F 631 694-1700
New York *(G-9584)*

CONSTRUCTION: Power Plant

Ducon Technologies Inc .... F 631 694-1700
New York *(G-9584)*

CONSTRUCTION: Religious Building

Makarenko Studios Inc .... G 914 968-7673
Yorktown Heights *(G-16818)*

CONSTRUCTION: Residential, Nec

WD Certified Contracting LLC .... F 516 493-9319
Westbury *(G-16387)*

CONSTRUCTION: Single-Family Housing

Frost Publications Inc .... G 845 726-3232
Westtown *(G-16413)*
Kasson & Keller Inc .... A 518 853-3421
Fonda *(G-5065)*

CONSTRUCTION: Single-family Housing, New

Capitol Restoration Corp .... G 516 783-1425
North Bellmore *(G-12373)*

CONSTRUCTION: Steel Buildings

Steele Truss Company Inc .... E 518 562-4663
Plattsburgh *(G-13158)*

CONSTRUCTION: Street Surfacing & Paving

Barrett Paving Materials Inc .... E 315 353-6611
Norwood *(G-12495)*
Cofire Paving Corporation .... E 718 463-1403
Flushing *(G-4993)*
John T Montecalvo Inc .... G 631 325-1492
Speonk *(G-14986)*

PRODUCT SECTION

Lomin Construction Company .... G 516 759-5734
Glen Head *(G-5382)*

CONSTRUCTION: Tennis Court

Lomin Construction Company .... G 516 759-5734
Glen Head *(G-5382)*

CONSTRUCTION: Warehouse

Tech Park Food Services LLC .... G 585 295-1250
Rochester *(G-14161)*

CONSULTING SVC: Business, NEC

Batavia Precision Glass LLC .... G 585 343-6050
Buffalo *(G-2724)*
Cambridge Whos Who Pubg Inc .... E 516 833-8440
Uniondale *(G-15663)*
Chromagraphics Press Inc .... G 631 367-6160
Melville *(G-8007)*
Doar Inc .... E 516 872-8140
Lynbrook *(G-7664)*
Holmes Group The Inc .... G 212 333-2300
New York *(G-10118)*
Integrated Graphics Inc .... E 212 592-5600
New York *(G-10231)*
Marketplace Slutions Group LLC .... E 631 868-0111
Holbrook *(G-6198)*
Milmar Food Group II LLC .... C 845 294-5400
Goshen *(G-5482)*
Next Step Publishing Inc .... F 585 742-1260
Victor *(G-15859)*
Resonant Legal Media LLC .... E 212 687-7100
New York *(G-11368)*
Trendsformers Ltd Liability Co .... G 888 700-2423
New York *(G-11891)*
UI Information & Insights Inc .... E 518 640-9200
Latham *(G-7096)*

CONSULTING SVC: Computer

Caminus Corporation .... D 212 515-3600
New York *(G-9187)*
Cgi Technologies Solutions Inc .... F 212 682-7411
New York *(G-9254)*
Classroom Inc .... E 212 545-8400
New York *(G-9323)*
Dohnsco Inc .... G 516 773-4800
Manhasset *(G-7766)*
Pegasystems Inc .... E 212 626-6550
New York *(G-11141)*

CONSULTING SVC: Educational

National Rding Styles Inst Inc .... F 516 921-5500
Syosset *(G-15225)*

CONSULTING SVC: Engineering

Complex Biosystems Inc .... G 315 464-8007
Baldwinsville *(G-553)*
Exergy LLC .... E 516 832-9300
Garden City *(G-5260)*
General Composites Inc .... E 518 963-7333
Willsboro *(G-16599)*
Glasgow Products Inc .... E 516 374-5937
Woodmere *(G-16641)*
Hudson Valley Tech Dev Ctr Inc .... F 845 391-8214
Highland *(G-6144)*
Innovation Associates Inc .... C 607 798-9376
Johnson City *(G-6811)*
Laser & Electron Beam Inc .... G 603 626-6080
New York *(G-10520)*
Procomponents Inc .... E 516 683-0909
Westbury *(G-16368)*
Select Controls Inc .... E 631 567-9010
Bohemia *(G-1087)*
Skae Power Solutions LLC .... E 845 365-9103
Palisades *(G-12847)*

CONSULTING SVC: Financial Management

Principia Partners LLC .... D 212 480-2270
New York *(G-11244)*

CONSULTING SVC: Human Resource

Chequedcom Inc .... E 888 412-0699
Saratoga Springs *(G-14575)*

CONSULTING SVC: Management

Altius Aviation LLC ....G....... 315 455-7555
  Syracuse *(G-15242)*
Barker Steel LLC ....E....... 518 465-6221
  Albany *(G-44)*
Beer Marketers Insights Inc ....G....... 845 507-0040
  Suffern *(G-15186)*
Ca Inc ....A....... 800 225-5224
  New York *(G-9171)*
Gary Roth & Associates Ltd ....E....... 516 333-1000
  Westbury *(G-16355)*
Marketplace Slutions Group LLC ....E....... 631 868-0111
  Holbrook *(G-6198)*

CONSULTING SVC: Marketing Management

In-Step Marketing Inc ....F....... 212 797-3450
  New York *(G-10191)*
Incro Marketing USA Corp ....G....... 917 365-5552
  New York *(G-10194)*
Maven Marketing LLC ....G....... 615 510-3248
  New York *(G-10731)*
Rainforest Inc ....F....... 212 575-7620
  New York *(G-11319)*
Ramsbury Property Us Inc ....F....... 212 223-6250
  New York *(G-11322)*
Rfn Inc ....F....... 516 764-5100
  Bay Shore *(G-714)*
Sales Hacker Inc ....G....... 516 660-2836
  New York *(G-11469)*
Tri-Force Sales LLC ....E....... 732 261-5507
  New York *(G-11892)*
Zacks Enterprises Inc ....G....... 800 366-4924
  Orangeburg *(G-12693)*

CONSULTING SVC: Online Technology

Orthstar Enterprises Inc ....D....... 607 562-2100
  Horseheads *(G-6323)*

CONSULTING SVC: Sales Management

Island Marketing Corp ....G....... 516 739-0500
  Mineola *(G-8229)*
Karp Overseas Corporation ....E....... 718 784-2105
  Maspeth *(G-7856)*

CONSULTING SVCS, BUSINESS: Communications

L3 Technologies Inc ....D....... 631 231-1700
  Hauppauge *(G-5861)*
Redcom Laboratories Inc ....C....... 585 924-6567
  Victor *(G-15865)*

CONSULTING SVCS, BUSINESS: Energy Conservation

Gotham Energy 360 LLC ....F....... 917 338-1023
  New York *(G-9960)*
Project Energy Savers LLC ....F....... 718 596-4231
  Brooklyn *(G-2356)*
Rle Industries LLC ....E....... 973 276-1444
  New York *(G-11402)*
Western Oil and Gas JV Inc ....G....... 914 967-4758
  Rye *(G-14489)*

CONSULTING SVCS, BUSINESS: Publishing

Mnn Holding Company LLC ....F....... 404 558-5251
  Brooklyn *(G-2220)*
Slosson Eductl Publications ....F....... 716 652-0930
  East Aurora *(G-4210)*

CONSULTING SVCS, BUSINESS: Safety Training Svcs

Bullex Inc ....F....... 518 689-2023
  Albany *(G-51)*

CONSULTING SVCS, BUSINESS: Sys Engnrg, Exc Computer/Prof

Laurus Development Inc ....F....... 716 823-1202
  Buffalo *(G-2922)*
Parlor Labs Inc ....G....... 866 801-7323
  New York *(G-11118)*
Sale 121 Corp ....D....... 240 855-8988
  New York *(G-11467)*

CONSULTING SVCS, BUSINESS: Systems Analysis & Engineering

Syntel Inc ....F....... 212 785-9810
  New York *(G-11765)*

CONSULTING SVCS, BUSINESS: Systems Analysis Or Design

Relx Inc ....E....... 212 309-8100
  New York *(G-11355)*
Visible Systems Corporation ....E....... 508 628-1510
  Oneida *(G-12623)*

CONSULTING SVCS, BUSINESS: Test Development & Evaluation

Micro Semicdtr Researches LLC ....G....... 646 863-6070
  New York *(G-10796)*

CONSULTING SVCS, BUSINESS: Testing, Educational Or Personnel

Bright Kids Nyc Inc ....E....... 917 539-4575
  New York *(G-9140)*

CONSULTING SVCS: Oil

Gotham Energy 360 LLC ....F....... 917 338-1023
  New York *(G-9960)*

CONSULTING SVCS: Scientific

Cognigen Corporation ....D....... 716 633-3463
  Buffalo *(G-2770)*
Guosa Life Sciences Inc ....F....... 718 813-7806
  New York *(G-10010)*
Prime Research Solutions LLC ....F....... 917 836-7941
  Flushing *(G-5040)*
Xactiv Inc ....F....... 585 288-7220
  Fairport *(G-4668)*

CONTACT LENSES

Acuity Polymers Inc ....G....... 585 458-8409
  Rochester *(G-13601)*
Alden Optical Laboratory Inc ....F....... 716 937-9181
  Lancaster *(G-7006)*
Coopervision Inc ....A....... 585 385-6810
  West Henrietta *(G-16235)*
Coopervision Inc ....A....... 585 889-3301
  Scottsville *(G-14749)*
Coopervision Inc ....C....... 585 385-6810
  Victor *(G-15838)*
Coopervision Inc ....D....... 585 385-6810
  Victor *(G-15839)*
Corneal Design Corporation ....F....... 301 670-7076
  Lima *(G-7150)*
J I Intrntnal Contact Lens Lab ....G....... 718 997-1212
  Rego Park *(G-13462)*

CONTACTS: Electrical

Micro Contacts Inc ....E....... 516 433-4830
  Hicksville *(G-6109)*

CONTAINERS, GLASS: Cosmetic Jars

Baralan Usa Inc ....E....... 718 849-5768
  Richmond Hill *(G-13497)*

CONTAINERS, GLASS: Food

Pennsauken Packing Company LLC .....G....... 585 377-7700
  Fairport *(G-4649)*
Saint Gobain Grains & Powders ....A....... 716 731-8200
  Niagara Falls *(G-12332)*

CONTAINERS, GLASS: Medicine Bottles

Velvet Healing By Alma Corp ....G....... 347 271-4220
  Bronx *(G-1414)*

CONTAINERS: Cargo, Wood & Metal Combination

219 South West ....G....... 315 474-2065
  Syracuse *(G-15235)*
Sg Blocks Inc ....G....... 615 585-2639
  Brooklyn *(G-2460)*

CONTAINERS: Cargo, Wood & Wood With Metal

Airline Container Services ....G....... 516 371-4125
  Lido Beach *(G-7147)*
Concord Express Cargo Inc ....G....... 718 276-7200
  Jamaica *(G-6638)*

CONTAINERS: Corrugated

Ares Printing and Packg Corp ....C....... 718 858-8760
  Brooklyn *(G-1550)*
Brand Box USA LLC ....G....... 607 584-7682
  Binghamton *(G-871)*
Cascades New York Inc ....C....... 518 346-6151
  Schenectady *(G-14660)*
Color Carton Corp ....D....... 718 665-0840
  Bronx *(G-1243)*
Fiber USA Corp ....G....... 718 888-1512
  Flushing *(G-5000)*
Gavin Mfg Corp ....E....... 631 467-0040
  Farmingdale *(G-4770)*
International Paper Company ....F....... 716 852-2144
  Buffalo *(G-2888)*
Key Container Corp ....G....... 631 582-3847
  East Islip *(G-4244)*
M C Packaging Corporation ....E....... 631 643-3763
  Babylon *(G-529)*
Orange Die Cutting Corp ....C....... 845 562-0900
  Newburgh *(G-12238)*
Pactiv LLC ....E....... 585 248-1213
  Pittsford *(G-13025)*
Parlor City Paper Box Co Inc ....D....... 607 772-0600
  Binghamton *(G-909)*
Specialized Packg Group Inc ....G....... 315 638-4355
  Baldwinsville *(G-561)*
Track 7 Inc ....G....... 845 544-1810
  Warwick *(G-15960)*
Westrock Rkt LLC ....F....... 315 487-6111
  Camillus *(G-3201)*

CONTAINERS: Foil, Bakery Goods & Frozen Foods

De Luxe Packaging Corp ....E....... 416 754-4633
  Saugerties *(G-14606)*
Tri-State Food Jobbers Inc ....G....... 718 921-1211
  Brooklyn *(G-2582)*

CONTAINERS: Food & Beverage

Cmc-Kuhnke Inc ....F....... 518 694-3310
  Albany *(G-60)*
Marley Spoon Inc ....C....... 646 934-6970
  New York *(G-10714)*
Tio Foods LLC ....F....... 917 946-1160
  New York *(G-11849)*

CONTAINERS: Food, Folding, Made From Purchased Materials

Diamond Packaging Holdings LLC ......G....... 585 334-8030
  Rochester *(G-13739)*
Genpak Industries Inc ....E....... 518 798-9511
  Middletown *(G-8154)*
Mod-Pac Corp ....C....... 716 898-8480
  Buffalo *(G-2951)*
Pactiv LLC ....C....... 518 562-6101
  Plattsburgh *(G-13142)*

CONTAINERS: Food, Liquid Tight, Including Milk

International Paper Company ....C....... 607 775-1550
  Conklin *(G-3728)*

CONTAINERS: Food, Metal

Silgan Containers Mfg Corp ....C....... 315 946-4826
  Lyons *(G-7687)*

CONTAINERS: Glass

Anchor Glass Container Corp ....B....... 607 737-1933
  Elmira Heights *(G-4509)*
Certainteed Corporation ....C....... 716 823-3684
  Lackawanna *(G-6948)*
Intrapac International Corp ....C....... 518 561-2030
  Plattsburgh *(G-13126)*
Owens-Brockway Glass Cont Inc ....C....... 315 258-3211
  Auburn *(G-494)*

Employee Codes: A=Over 500 employees, B=251-500
C=101-250, D=51-100, E=20-50, F=10-19, G=5-9

CONTAINERS: Glass

Rocco Bormioli Glass Co Inc ....E 212 719-0606
  New York *(G-11413)*
Schott Corporation ....D 914 831-2200
  Elmsford *(G-4564)*
SGD North America ....E 212 753-4200
  New York *(G-11549)*
SGD Pharma Packaging Inc ....G 212 223-7100
  New York *(G-11550)*

CONTAINERS: Laminated Phenolic & Vulcanized Fiber

Diemolding Corporation ....G 315 363-4710
  Wampsville *(G-15917)*
Skydyne Company ....D 845 858-6400
  Port Jervis *(G-13237)*

CONTAINERS: Liquid Tight Fiber, From Purchased Materials

Acran Spill Containment Inc ....F 631 841-2300
  Massapequa *(G-7877)*
Custom Manufacturing Inc ....G 607 569-2738
  Hammondsport *(G-5703)*

CONTAINERS: Metal

Abbot & Abbot Box Corp ....F 888 930-5972
  Long Island City *(G-7365)*
Erie Engineered Products Inc ....E 716 206-0204
  Lancaster *(G-7018)*
Hornet Group Inc ....D 845 858-6400
  Port Jervis *(G-13230)*
J R Cooperage Co Inc ....G 718 387-1664
  Brooklyn *(G-2027)*
Medi-Ray Inc ....D 877 898-3003
  Tuckahoe *(G-15644)*
Mobile Mini Inc ....F 315 732-4555
  Utica *(G-15723)*
Westrock - Southern Cont LLC ....C 315 487-6111
  Camillus *(G-3200)*
Westrock CP LLC ....C 716 694-1000
  North Tonawanda *(G-12463)*

CONTAINERS: Plastic

A R Arena Products Inc ....E 585 277-1680
  Rochester *(G-13591)*
Albea Cosmetics America Inc ....E 212 371-5100
  New York *(G-8784)*
Amcor Rigid Plastics Usa LLC ....E 716 366-2440
  Dunkirk *(G-4162)*
Baralan Usa Inc ....E 718 849-5768
  Richmond Hill *(G-13497)*
Billie-Ann Plastics Pkg Corp ....E 718 497-3409
  Brooklyn *(G-1612)*
Chem-Tainer Industries Inc ....E 631 422-8300
  West Babylon *(G-16147)*
Consolidated Container Co LLC ....F 585 343-9351
  Batavia *(G-620)*
Erie Engineered Products Inc ....E 716 206-0204
  Lancaster *(G-7018)*
Form A Rockland Plastics Inc ....G 315 848-3300
  Cranberry Lake *(G-3907)*
Forteq North America Inc ....D 585 427-9410
  West Henrietta *(G-16239)*
Gary Plastic Packaging Corp ....B 718 893-2200
  Bronx *(G-1279)*
GSE Composites Inc ....F 631 389-1300
  Hauppauge *(G-5837)*
Ingenious Designs LLC ....C 631 254-3376
  Ronkonkoma *(G-14353)*
Iridium Industries Inc ....E 516 504-9700
  Great Neck *(G-5563)*
Jamestown Plastics Inc ....D 716 792-4144
  Brocton *(G-1196)*
Kenney Manufacturing Displays ....F 631 231-5563
  Brentwood *(G-1139)*
Kernow North America ....F 585 586-3590
  Pittsford *(G-13017)*
M I T Poly-Cart Corp ....G 212 724-7290
  New York *(G-10640)*
Micromold Products Inc ....E 914 969-2850
  Yonkers *(G-16784)*
Neo Plastics LLC ....F 646 542-1499
  Brooklyn *(G-2253)*
Oneida Molded Plastics LLC ....D 315 363-7990
  Oneida *(G-12617)*
Ontario Plastics Inc ....E 585 663-2644
  Rochester *(G-13989)*

Pactiv LLC ....G 847 482-2000
  Canandaigua *(G-3229)*
Pactiv LLC ....C 518 562-6120
  Plattsburgh *(G-13143)*
Pactiv LLC ....C 518 793-2524
  Glens Falls *(G-5439)*
Plastic Solutions Inc ....E 631 234-9013
  Bayport *(G-738)*
Plastic Sys/Gr Bflo Inc ....G 716 835-7555
  Buffalo *(G-3007)*
Plasticware LLC ....F 845 267-0790
  Monsey *(G-8293)*
Powertex Inc ....E 518 297-4000
  Rouses Point *(G-14469)*
Precision Packaging Pdts Inc ....C 585 638-8200
  Holley *(G-6228)*
Protective Lining Corp ....D 718 854-3838
  Brooklyn *(G-2358)*
Quoin LLC ....A 914 967-9400
  Rye *(G-14487)*
Silgan Plastics LLC ....C 315 536-5690
  Penn Yan *(G-12966)*
Summit Manufacturing LLC ....E 631 952-1570
  Bay Shore *(G-728)*
Visitainer Corp ....E 718 636-0300
  Brooklyn *(G-2629)*
Weber Intl Packg Co LLC ....D 518 561-8282
  Plattsburgh *(G-13168)*

CONTAINERS: Sanitary, Food

Consolidated Container Co LLC ....C 585 262-6470
  Rochester *(G-13721)*

CONTAINERS: Shipping & Mailing, Fiber

American Intrmdal Cont Mfg LLC ....G 631 774-6790
  Hauppauge *(G-5767)*

CONTAINERS: Shipping, Bombs, Metal Plate

828 Express Inc ....G 917 577-9019
  Staten Island *(G-15036)*
Erie Engineered Products Inc ....E 716 206-0204
  Lancaster *(G-7018)*
Vship Co ....F 718 706-8566
  Astoria *(G-447)*
Wayne Integrated Tech Corp ....E 631 242-0213
  Edgewood *(G-4423)*

CONTAINERS: Shipping, Wood

Hood Industries Inc ....F 716 836-0301
  Buffalo *(G-2874)*

CONTAINERS: Wood

Abbot & Abbot Box Corp ....F 888 930-5972
  Long Island City *(G-7365)*
David Isseks & Sons Inc ....E 212 966-8694
  New York *(G-9481)*
Essex Box & Pallet Co Inc ....E 518 834-7279
  Keeseville *(G-6850)*
Great Lakes Specialties ....E 716 672-4622
  Fredonia *(G-5127)*
Pluribus Products Inc ....E 718 852-1614
  Bayville *(G-753)*

CONTRACT FOOD SVCS

Herris Gourmet Inc ....G 917 578-2308
  Brooklyn *(G-1976)*

CONTRACTOR: Framing

Timber Frames Inc ....G 585 374-6405
  Canandaigua *(G-3235)*

CONTRACTORS: Acoustical & Ceiling Work

Newmat Northeast Corp ....F 631 253-9277
  West Babylon *(G-16179)*

CONTRACTORS: Acoustical & Insulation Work

New York State Foam Enrgy LLC ....G 845 534-4656
  Cornwall *(G-3835)*

CONTRACTORS: Antenna Installation

Fred A Nudd Corporation ....D 315 524-2531
  Ontario *(G-12653)*

Gti America Inc ....G 716 332-6151
  Buffalo *(G-2859)*

CONTRACTORS: Awning Installation

Awning Mart Inc ....G 315 699-5928
  Cicero *(G-3514)*
Space Sign ....F 718 961-1112
  College Point *(G-3667)*

CONTRACTORS: Boiler & Furnace

Empire Industrial Systems Corp ....F 631 242-4619
  Bay Shore *(G-685)*

CONTRACTORS: Boiler Maintenance Contractor

Empire Industrial Burner Svc ....F 631 242-4619
  Deer Park *(G-3974)*

CONTRACTORS: Building Eqpt & Machinery Installation

Advanced Door Solutions Inc ....G 631 773-6100
  Holbrook *(G-6169)*
Assa Abloy Entrance Systems US ......E 315 492-6600
  East Syracuse *(G-4323)*
Bargold Storage Systems LLC ....E 718 247-7000
  Long Island City *(G-7398)*
Otis Elevator Company ....E 917 339-9600
  New York *(G-11069)*
Schindler Elevator Corporation ....C 212 708-1000
  New York *(G-11503)*
Windowman Inc (usa) ....F 718 246-2626
  Brooklyn *(G-2652)*

CONTRACTORS: Building Sign Installation & Mntnce

Adirondack Sign Company LLC ....F 518 409-7446
  Saratoga Springs *(G-14566)*
Alley Cat Signs Inc ....F 631 924-7446
  Middle Island *(G-8117)*
Clinton Signs Inc ....G 585 482-1620
  Webster *(G-16080)*
Flexlume Sign Corporation ....G 716 884-2020
  Buffalo *(G-2830)*
Gloede Neon Signs Ltd Inc ....F 845 471-4366
  Poughkeepsie *(G-13341)*
Jem Sign Corp ....G 516 867-4466
  Hempstead *(G-6015)*
Lanza Corp ....G 914 937-6360
  Port Chester *(G-13204)*
North Shore Neon Sign Co Inc ....E 718 937-4848
  Flushing *(G-5031)*
Rapp Signs Inc ....F 607 656-8167
  Greene *(G-5616)*
Ray Sign Inc ....F 518 377-1371
  Schenectady *(G-14707)*
Rgm Signs Inc ....G 718 442-0598
  Staten Island *(G-15129)*
Sign Works Incorporated ....E 914 592-0700
  Elmsford *(G-4569)*
T J Signs Unlimited LLC ....F 631 273-4800
  Islip *(G-6551)*

CONTRACTORS: Carpentry Work

EZ Lift Operator Corp ....F 845 356-1676
  Spring Valley *(G-14990)*
Innova Interiors Inc ....E 718 401-2122
  Bronx *(G-1298)*
Mestel Brothers Stairs & Rails ....C 516 496-4127
  Syosset *(G-15222)*

CONTRACTORS: Carpentry, Cabinet & Finish Work

Cabinet Shapes Corp ....F 718 784-6255
  Long Island City *(G-7404)*
Capital Kit Cab & Door Mfrs ....G 718 886-0303
  College Point *(G-3641)*
Central Kitchen Corp ....F 631 283-1029
  Southampton *(G-14951)*
Dak Mica and Wood Products ....G 631 467-0749
  Ronkonkoma *(G-14332)*
Eugenia Selective Living Inc ....F 631 277-1461
  Islip *(G-6546)*
Hennig Custom Woodwork Corp ....G 516 536-3460
  Oceanside *(G-12540)*

PRODUCT SECTION

CONTRACTORS: Heating & Air Conditioning

Johnny Mica Inc .... G 631 225-5213
  Lindenhurst *(G-7173)*
Jq Woodworking Inc .... G 516 766-3424
  Oceanside *(G-12543)*
M & C Furniture .... G 718 422-2136
  Brooklyn *(G-2140)*
Metro Kitchens Corp .... F 718 434-1166
  Brooklyn *(G-2200)*
Ralph Payne .... G 718 222-4200
  Brooklyn *(G-2383)*

CONTRACTORS: Carpentry, Cabinet Building & Installation

Auburn-Watson Corp .... F 716 876-8000
  Depew *(G-4079)*
Daniel Demarco and Assoc Inc .... E 631 598-7000
  Amityville *(G-271)*
Fontrick Door Inc .... E 585 345-6032
  Batavia *(G-624)*
Home Ideal Inc .... G 718 762-8998
  Flushing *(G-5009)*
Koeppels Kustom Kitchens Inc .... G 518 489-0092
  Albany *(G-93)*
Manhattan Cabinets Inc .... G 212 548-2436
  New York *(G-10684)*
Precision Dental Cabinets Inc .... F 631 543-3870
  Smithtown *(G-14906)*
Yost Neon Displays Inc .... G 716 674-6780
  West Seneca *(G-16304)*

CONTRACTORS: Carpentry, Finish & Trim Work

Millwright Wdwrk Installation .... E 631 587-2635
  West Babylon *(G-16177)*

CONTRACTORS: Ceramic Floor Tile Installation

Icestone LLC .... E 718 624-4900
  Brooklyn *(G-1993)*

CONTRACTORS: Closed Circuit Television Installation

Sartek Industries Inc .... G 631 473-3555
  East Setauket *(G-4309)*

CONTRACTORS: Commercial & Office Building

United Steel Products Inc .... D 718 478-5330
  Corona *(G-3856)*

CONTRACTORS: Communications Svcs

Professional Technology Inc .... G 315 337-4156
  Rome *(G-14267)*

CONTRACTORS: Concrete

A Colarusso and Son Inc .... E 518 828-3218
  Hudson *(G-6336)*
Geneva Granite Co Inc .... F 315 789-8142
  Geneva *(G-5325)*
Seneca Stone Corporation .... G 607 737-6200
  Pine City *(G-13001)*

CONTRACTORS: Concrete Pumping

Barney & Dickenson Inc .... E 607 729-1536
  Vestal *(G-15809)*

CONTRACTORS: Concrete Repair

Capitol Restoration Corp .... G 516 783-1425
  North Bellmore *(G-12373)*

CONTRACTORS: Construction Site Cleanup

Darrell Mitchell .... G 646 659-7075
  Arverne *(G-414)*

CONTRACTORS: Countertop Installation

Contempra Design Inc .... G 718 984-8586
  Staten Island *(G-15065)*
Countertops & Cabinets Inc .... G 315 433-1038
  Syracuse *(G-15292)*
FX INC .... F 212 244-2240
  New York *(G-9865)*
Johnny Mica Inc .... G 631 225-5213
  Lindenhurst *(G-7173)*
Joseph Fedele .... G 718 448-3658
  Staten Island *(G-15097)*
Rochester Countertop Inc .... F 585 338-2260
  Rochester *(G-14085)*
Thornwood Products Ltd .... E 914 769-9161
  Thornwood *(G-15508)*

CONTRACTORS: Demountable Partition Installation

Able Steel Equipment Co Inc .... F 718 361-9240
  Long Island City *(G-7366)*

CONTRACTORS: Directional Oil & Gas Well Drilling Svc

Turner Undgrd Instllations Inc .... F 585 739-0238
  Henrietta *(G-6038)*

CONTRACTORS: Drywall

L & J Interiors Inc .... G 631 218-0838
  Bohemia *(G-1044)*
Nordic Interior Inc .... C 718 456-7000
  Brooklyn *(G-2272)*

CONTRACTORS: Electrical

331 Holding Inc .... E 585 924-1740
  Victor *(G-15827)*
A & S Electric .... G 212 228-2030
  Brooklyn *(G-1452)*
C & G Video Systems Inc .... G 315 452-1490
  Liverpool *(G-7226)*
Cooperfriedman Elc Sup Co Inc .... G 718 269-4906
  Long Island City *(G-7415)*
Mitsubishi Elc Pwr Pdts Inc .... G 516 962-2813
  Melville *(G-8048)*
Schuler-Haas Electric Corp .... G 607 936-3514
  Painted Post *(G-12840)*
Siemens Industry Inc .... E 585 797-2300
  Rochester *(G-14126)*
Spectrum Cable Corporation .... G 585 235-7714
  Rochester *(G-14137)*

CONTRACTORS: Electronic Controls Installation

Emco Electric Services LLC .... G 212 420-9766
  New York *(G-9667)*
Qsf Inc .... G 585 247-6200
  Gates *(G-5311)*
Zeppelin Electric Company Inc .... G 631 928-9467
  East Setauket *(G-4315)*

CONTRACTORS: Energy Management Control

Ihi Inc .... E 212 599-8100
  New York *(G-10179)*
T S B A Group Inc .... E 718 565-6000
  Sunnyside *(G-15206)*

CONTRACTORS: Excavating

Ribble Lumber Inc .... G 315 536-6221
  Penn Yan *(G-12964)*

CONTRACTORS: Excavating Slush Pits & Cellars Svcs

Alice Perkins .... G 716 378-5100
  Salamanca *(G-14523)*

CONTRACTORS: Exterior Wall System Installation

Plant-Tech2o Inc .... G 516 483-7845
  Hempstead *(G-6023)*

CONTRACTORS: Fence Construction

City Store Gates Mfg Corp .... E 718 939-9700
  College Point *(G-3642)*
Fence Plaza Corp .... G 718 469-2200
  Brooklyn *(G-1874)*
Fort Miller Service Corp .... F 518 695-5000
  Greenwich *(G-5640)*
Interstate Wood Products Inc .... E 631 842-4488
  Amityville *(G-288)*
Master-Halco Inc .... F 631 585-8150
  Yaphank *(G-16717)*
Metro Door Inc .... D 800 669-3667
  Islandia *(G-6535)*
Oneida Sales & Service Inc .... E 716 822-8205
  Buffalo *(G-2980)*
Ourem Iron Works Inc .... F 914 476-4856
  Yonkers *(G-16789)*
Universal Steel Fabricators .... E 718 342-0782
  Brooklyn *(G-2610)*
Wood Innovations of Suffolk .... G 631 698-2345
  Medford *(G-7969)*

CONTRACTORS: Fiber Optic Cable Installation

Complete Fiber Solutions Inc .... G 718 828-8900
  Bronx *(G-1245)*

CONTRACTORS: Fire Detection & Burglar Alarm Systems

Detekion Security Systems Inc .... F 607 729-7179
  Vestal *(G-15815)*
Johnson Controls .... G 845 774-4120
  Harriman *(G-5720)*
Sentry Devices Corp .... G 631 491-3191
  Dix Hills *(G-4126)*

CONTRACTORS: Fire Escape Installation

Firecom Inc .... C 718 899-6100
  Woodside *(G-16655)*
Triboro Iron Works Inc .... G 718 361-9600
  Long Island City *(G-7621)*

CONTRACTORS: Fire Sprinkler System Installation Svcs

Johnson Controls .... G 845 774-4120
  Harriman *(G-5720)*

CONTRACTORS: Floor Laying & Other Floor Work

Delta Polymers Inc .... G 631 254-6240
  Bay Shore *(G-681)*
Designer Epoxy Finishes Inc .... G 646 943-6044
  Melville *(G-8015)*

CONTRACTORS: Garage Doors

Griffon Corporation .... E 212 957-5000
  New York *(G-9988)*

CONTRACTORS: Gas Field Svcs, NEC

Petro Inc .... G 516 686-1717
  Plainview *(G-13082)*
Schmitt Sales Inc .... G 716 632-8595
  Williamsville *(G-16585)*
T A S Sales Service LLC .... E 518 234-4919
  Cobleskill *(G-3604)*

CONTRACTORS: Gasoline Condensation Removal Svcs

Gas Recovery Systems LLC .... F 914 421-4903
  White Plains *(G-16453)*

CONTRACTORS: Glass, Glazing & Tinting

A&B McKeon Glass Inc .... G 718 525-2152
  Staten Island *(G-15038)*
Advanced Door Solutions Inc .... G 631 773-6100
  Holbrook *(G-6169)*
Benson Industries Inc .... F 212 779-3230
  New York *(G-9046)*
Global Glass Corp .... G 516 681-2309
  Hicksville *(G-6091)*
Jordan Panel Systems Corp .... E 631 754-4900
  East Northport *(G-4266)*
Lafayette Mirror & Glass Co .... G 718 768-0660
  New Hyde Park *(G-8547)*
Upstate Insulated Glass Inc .... G 315 475-4960
  Central Square *(G-3393)*

CONTRACTORS: Heating & Air Conditioning

Automated Control Logic Inc .... F 914 769-8880
  Thornwood *(G-15501)*

Employee Codes: A=Over 500 employees, B=251-500
C=101-250, D=51-100, E=20-50, F=10-19, G=5-9

CONTRACTORS: Heating & Air Conditioning

City Cooling Enterprises Inc..................G........ 718 331-7400
 Brooklyn *(G-1694)*
Layton Manufacturing Corp..................E........ 718 498-6000
 Brooklyn *(G-2095)*
Nelson Air Device Corporation...............C........ 718 729-3801
 Maspeth *(G-7862)*
Prokosch and Sonn Sheet Metal...........E........ 845 562-4211
 Newburgh *(G-12243)*
Robin Industries Ltd...............................F........ 718 218-9616
 Brooklyn *(G-2410)*
Vincent Genovese..................................G........ 631 281-8170
 Mastic Beach *(G-7912)*

CONTRACTORS: Highway & Street Construction, General

Tiki Industries Inc.................................G........ 516 779-3629
 Riverhead *(G-13586)*

CONTRACTORS: Highway & Street Paving

Pavco Asphalt Inc..................................E........ 631 289-3223
 Holtsville *(G-6242)*
Peckham Materials Corp.......................D........ 914 686-2045
 White Plains *(G-16489)*
Suit-Kote Corporation............................C........ 607 753-1100
 Cortland *(G-3895)*
Suit-Kote Corporation............................C........ 716 664-3750
 Jamestown *(G-6752)*

CONTRACTORS: Highway Sign & Guardrail Construction & Install

Traffic Lane Closures LLC....................F........ 845 228-6100
 Carmel *(G-3283)*

CONTRACTORS: Home & Office Intrs Finish, Furnish/Remodel

Drapery Industries Inc..........................F........ 585 232-2992
 Rochester *(G-13750)*
Griffon Corporation................................E........ 212 957-5000
 New York *(G-9988)*

CONTRACTORS: Hydraulic Eqpt Installation & Svcs

A Gatty Products Inc.............................G........ 914 592-3903
 Elmsford *(G-4527)*

CONTRACTORS: Hydronics Heating

Corona Plumbing & Htg Sup Inc...........G........ 718 424-4133
 Corona *(G-3841)*

CONTRACTORS: Insulation Installation, Building

Advanced Comfort Systems Inc............F........ 518 884-8444
 Ballston Spa *(G-574)*

CONTRACTORS: Kitchen & Bathroom Remodeling

Di Fiore and Sons Custom Wdwkg.......G........ 718 278-1663
 Long Island City *(G-7425)*
Triad Counter Corp................................E........ 631 750-0615
 Bohemia *(G-1098)*

CONTRACTORS: Lighting Syst

Az-Light Inc..G........ 716 837-5533
 Buffalo *(G-2719)*
Light Blue USA LLC..............................G........ 718 475-2515
 Brooklyn *(G-2119)*
Vincent Conigliaro.................................F........ 845 340-0489
 Kingston *(G-6931)*

CONTRACTORS: Machinery Installation

Finger Lakes Conveyors Inc.................G........ 315 539-9246
 Waterloo *(G-15992)*
Re-Al Industrial Corp............................G........ 716 542-4556
 Akron *(G-22)*

CONTRACTORS: Marble Installation, Interior

Aurora Stone Group LLC......................F........ 315 471-6869
 East Syracuse *(G-4324)*

CONTRACTORS: Masonry & Stonework

Tiki Industries Inc.................................G........ 516 779-3629
 Riverhead *(G-13586)*

CONTRACTORS: Mechanical

All-City Metal Inc...................................E........ 718 937-3975
 Maspeth *(G-7817)*
Joy Edward Company...........................E........ 315 474-3360
 Syracuse *(G-15351)*
Metro Duct Systems Inc.......................F........ 718 278-4294
 Long Island City *(G-7522)*

CONTRACTORS: Multi-Family Home Remodeling

Rob Herschenfeld Design Inc..............F........ 718 456-6801
 Brooklyn *(G-2408)*

CONTRACTORS: Office Furniture Installation

Evans & Paul LLC.................................E........ 516 576-0800
 Plainview *(G-13056)*

CONTRACTORS: Oil & Gas Building, Repairing & Dismantling Svc

Cotton Well Drilling Co Inc...................G........ 716 672-2788
 Sheridan *(G-14814)*
Steel Excel Inc.......................................G........ 914 461-1300
 White Plains *(G-16508)*

CONTRACTORS: Oil & Gas Field Fire Fighting Svcs

Uniformed Fire Officer Assoiat.............F........ 212 293-9300
 New York *(G-11942)*

CONTRACTORS: Oil & Gas Field Geological Exploration Svcs

Aquifer Drilling & Testing Inc................D........ 516 616-6026
 Mineola *(G-8204)*
Aterra Exploration LLC..........................E........ 212 315-0030
 New York *(G-8947)*

CONTRACTORS: Oil & Gas Field Geophysical Exploration Svcs

Schlumberger Technology Corp...........C........ 607 378-0105
 Horseheads *(G-6328)*
Smith International Inc..........................D........ 212 350-9400
 New York *(G-11625)*

CONTRACTORS: Oil & Gas Well Casing Cement Svcs

Sabre Energy Services LLC.................F........ 518 514-1572
 Slingerlands *(G-14890)*

CONTRACTORS: Oil & Gas Well Drilling Svc

Alden Aurora Gas Company Inc...........G........ 716 937-9484
 Alden *(G-167)*
Copper Ridge Oil Inc............................G........ 716 372-4021
 Jamestown *(G-6710)*
Geotechnical Drilling Inc......................D........ 516 616-6055
 Mineola *(G-8224)*
Lenape Energy Inc................................G........ 585 344-1200
 Alexander *(G-179)*
Lukoil North America LLC.....................E........ 212 421-4141
 New York *(G-10629)*
Schneider Amalco Inc..........................F........ 917 470-9674
 New York *(G-11507)*
Steel Partners Holdings LP..................D........ 212 520-2300
 New York *(G-11699)*
U S Energy Development Corp.............D........ 716 636-0401
 Getzville *(G-5354)*
Western Oil and Gas JV Inc.................G........ 914 967-4758
 Rye *(G-14489)*

CONTRACTORS: Oil & Gas Wells Svcs

I & S of NY Inc......................................F........ 716 373-7001
 Allegany *(G-191)*
Superior Energy Services Inc..............G........ 716 483-0100
 Jamestown *(G-6754)*

CONTRACTORS: Oil Field Haulage Svcs

Lenape Energy Inc................................G........ 585 344-1200
 Alexander *(G-179)*

CONTRACTORS: Oil Field Lease Tanks: Erectg, Clng/Rprg Svcs

Wellspring Omni Holdings Corp...........A........ 212 318-9800
 New York *(G-12093)*

CONTRACTORS: Oil Sampling Svcs

P & C Gas Measurements Service........F........ 716 257-3412
 Cattaraugus *(G-3313)*

CONTRACTORS: Oil/Gas Well Construction, Rpr/Dismantling Svcs

A & Mt Realty Group LLC.....................F........ 718 974-5871
 Brooklyn *(G-1451)*
Arm Construction Company Inc...........G........ 646 235-6520
 East Elmhurst *(G-4217)*
Babula Construction Inc.......................G........ 716 681-0886
 Lancaster *(G-7009)*
Barber & Deline Enrgy Svcs LLC.........F........ 315 696-8961
 Tully *(G-15648)*
Darrell Mitchell......................................G........ 646 659-7075
 Arverne *(G-414)*
Fame Construction Inc.........................E........ 718 626-1000
 Astoria *(G-429)*
Professional Remodelers Inc...............G........ 516 565-9300
 West Hempstead *(G-16224)*

CONTRACTORS: On-Site Welding

303 Contracting Inc..............................E........ 716 896-2122
 Orchard Park *(G-12694)*
Abdo Shtmtl & Fabrication Inc.............G........ 315 894-4664
 Barneveld *(G-601)*
AG Tech Welding Corp.........................G........ 845 398-0005
 Tappan *(G-15465)*
Bridgehampton Steel & Wldg Inc........F........ 631 537-2486
 Bridgehampton *(G-1179)*
Crownbrook ACC LLC..........................E........ 718 626-0760
 Brooklyn *(G-1734)*
Dorgan Welding Service.......................G........ 315 462-9030
 Phelps *(G-12976)*
Flushing Boiler & Welding Co...............G........ 718 463-1266
 Brooklyn *(G-1893)*
G & C Welding Co Inc...........................G........ 516 883-3228
 Port Washington *(G-13261)*
Glenridge Fabricators Inc....................F........ 718 456-2297
 Glendale *(G-5402)*
Hadfield Inc...F........ 631 981-4314
 Ronkonkoma *(G-14350)*
Hagner Industries Inc...........................G........ 716 873-5720
 Buffalo *(G-2862)*
Hallock Fabricating Corp......................G........ 631 727-2441
 Riverhead *(G-13569)*
Jacksons Welding LLC..........................G........ 607 756-2725
 Cortland *(G-3878)*
Kleinfelder John....................................G........ 716 753-3163
 Mayville *(G-7921)*
Marine Boiler & Welding Inc................G........ 718 378-1900
 Bronx *(G-1322)*
Reliable Welding & Fabrication............G........ 631 758-2637
 Patchogue *(G-12876)*
S & D Welding Corp..............................G........ 631 454-0383
 West Babylon *(G-16189)*
Tioga Tool Inc..F........ 607 785-6005
 Endicott *(G-4611)*

CONTRACTORS: Ornamental Metal Work

Bonura and Sons Iron Works...............F........ 718 381-4100
 Franklin Square *(G-5115)*
E F Iron Works & Construction.............G........ 631 242-4766
 Bay Shore *(G-684)*
GCM Metal Industries Inc....................F........ 718 386-4059
 Brooklyn *(G-1919)*
Irony Limited Inc....................................G........ 631 329-4065
 East Hampton *(G-4238)*
M K Ulrich Construction Inc.................F........ 716 893-5777
 Buffalo *(G-2930)*

CONTRACTORS: Painting & Wall Covering

Abdo Shtmtl & Fabrication Inc.............G........ 315 894-4664
 Barneveld *(G-601)*
D & I Finishing Inc................................G........ 631 471-3034
 Bohemia *(G-1007)*

PRODUCT SECTION

CONTRACTORS: Parking Facility Eqpt Installation

Parkmatic Car Prkg Systems LLC .... G 516 224-7700
  Long Island City (G-7548)

CONTRACTORS: Pipe Laying

AAA Welding and Fabrication of .... G 585 254-2830
  Rochester (G-13592)

CONTRACTORS: Plastering, Plain or Ornamental

Foster Reeve & Associates Inc .... G 718 609-0090
  Brooklyn (G-1900)

CONTRACTORS: Plumbing

Aquifer Drilling & Testing Inc .... D 516 616-6026
  Mineola (G-8204)
Metro City Group Inc .... G 516 781-2500
  Bellmore (G-789)

CONTRACTORS: Power Generating Eqpt Installation

Ls Power Equity Partners LP .... G 212 615-3456
  New York (G-10622)

CONTRACTORS: Prefabricated Fireplace Installation

Chimney Doctors Americas Corp .... G 631 868-3586
  Bayport (G-737)

CONTRACTORS: Prefabricated Window & Door Installation

Pace Window and Door Corp .... E 585 924-8350
  Victor (G-15860)
Pella Corporation .... C 631 208-0710
  Calverton (G-3168)
Proof Industries Inc .... G 631 694-7663
  Farmingdale (G-4859)
Royal Windows Mfg Corp .... E 631 435-8888
  Bay Shore (G-718)
Tri-State Window Factory Corp .... D 631 667-8600
  Deer Park (G-4052)

CONTRACTORS: Roofing

H Klein & Sons Inc .... E 516 746-0163
  Mineola (G-8225)
Tiedemann Waldemar Inc .... F 716 875-5665
  Buffalo (G-3095)

CONTRACTORS: Roustabout Svcs

Jemcap Servicing LLC .... G 212 213-9353
  New York (G-10325)
Legal Servicing LLC .... G 716 565-9300
  Williamsville (G-16581)
Sovereign Servicing System LLC .... F 914 779-1400
  Bronxville (G-1426)

CONTRACTORS: Safety & Security Eqpt

Napco Security Tech Inc .... C 631 842-9400
  Amityville (G-304)
Windowman Inc (usa) .... G 718 246-2626
  Brooklyn (G-2652)

CONTRACTORS: Sandblasting Svc, Building Exteriors

Bruce Pierce .... G 716 731-9310
  Sanborn (G-14542)
Miller Metal Fabricating Inc .... G 585 359-3400
  Rochester (G-13945)
North Shore Monuments Inc .... G 516 759-2156
  Glen Head (G-5385)

CONTRACTORS: Seismograph Survey Svcs

Wellspring Omni Holdings Corp .... A 212 318-9800
  New York (G-12093)

CONTRACTORS: Sheet Metal Work, NEC

Aabco Sheet Metal Co Inc .... D 718 821-1166
  Ridgewood (G-13527)

B & R Sheet .... G 718 558-5544
  Jamaica (G-6629)
Berjen Metal Industries Ltd .... G 631 673-7979
  Huntington (G-6394)
Broadalbin Manufacturing Corp .... E 518 883-5313
  Broadalbin (G-1187)
Goergen-Mackwirth Co Inc .... E 716 874-4800
  Buffalo (G-2852)
Lodolce Machine Co Inc .... E 845 246-7017
  Saugerties (G-14610)
Pro Metal of NY Corp .... G 516 285-0440
  Valley Stream (G-15791)

CONTRACTORS: Sheet metal Work, Architectural

A&B McKeon Glass Inc .... G 718 525-2152
  Staten Island (G-15038)
Morgik Metal Designs .... F 212 463-0304
  New York (G-10842)

CONTRACTORS: Siding

Tri-State Window Factory Corp .... D 631 667-8600
  Deer Park (G-4052)

CONTRACTORS: Single-family Home General Remodeling

Bator Bintor Inc .... F 347 546-6503
  Brooklyn (G-1590)
Deakon Homes and Interiors .... F 518 271-0342
  Troy (G-15603)
Kng Construction Co Inc .... F 212 595-1451
  Warwick (G-15956)
Texas Home Security Inc .... E 516 747-2100
  New Hyde Park (G-8566)

CONTRACTORS: Solar Energy Eqpt

Solar Energy Systems LLC .... F 718 389-1545
  Brooklyn (G-2495)

CONTRACTORS: Sound Eqpt Installation

L A R Electronics Corp .... G 716 285-0555
  Niagara Falls (G-12304)
Telephone Sales & Service Co .... E 212 233-8505
  New York (G-11796)

CONTRACTORS: Stone Masonry

Stuart-Dean Co Inc .... F 718 472-1326
  Long Island City (G-7606)

CONTRACTORS: Store Fixture Installation

Mass Mdsg Self Selection Eqp .... E 631 234-3300
  Bohemia (G-1056)

CONTRACTORS: Store Front Construction

A&B McKeon Glass Inc .... G 718 525-2152
  Staten Island (G-15038)

CONTRACTORS: Structural Iron Work, Structural

M & L Steel & Ornamental Iron .... F 718 816-8660
  Staten Island (G-15102)
Miscellnous Ir Fabricators Inc .... E 518 355-1822
  Schenectady (G-14699)
Moon Gates Company .... G 718 426-0023
  East Elmhurst (G-4224)
Neversink Steel Corp .... G 845 292-4611
  Liberty (G-7146)
Roman Iron Works Inc .... G 516 621-1903
  Greenvale (G-5631)
Triboro Iron Works Inc .... G 718 361-9600
  Long Island City (G-7621)

CONTRACTORS: Structural Steel Erection

Barry Steel Fabrication Inc .... E 716 433-2144
  Lockport (G-7286)
Cives Corporation .... C 315 287-2200
  Gouverneur (G-5488)
GCM Metal Industries Inc .... F 718 386-4059
  Brooklyn (G-1919)
Irv Schroder & Sons Inc .... E 518 828-0194
  Stottville (G-15181)
Rochester Structural LLC .... E 585 436-1250
  Rochester (G-14097)

CONTRACTORS: Windows & Doors

Roth Design & Consulting Inc .... E 718 209-0193
  Brooklyn (G-2417)

CONTRACTORS: Svc Station Eqpt Installation, Maint & Repair

North American Svcs Group LLC .... F 518 885-1820
  Ballston Spa (G-592)

CONTRACTORS: Svc Well Drilling Svcs

Barber & Deline LLC .... F 607 749-2619
  Tully (G-15649)

CONTRACTORS: Textile Warping

Tli Import Inc .... G 917 578-4568
  Brooklyn (G-2568)

CONTRACTORS: Tile Installation, Ceramic

Alp Stone Inc .... F 718 706-6166
  Long Island City (G-7373)
Quality Carpet One Floor & HM .... F 718 941-4200
  Brooklyn (G-2365)

CONTRACTORS: Ventilation & Duct Work

Aabco Sheet Metal Co Inc .... D 718 821-1166
  Ridgewood (G-13527)
Aeroduct Inc .... E 516 248-9550
  Mineola (G-8201)
American Std Shtmtl Sup Corp .... F 718 888-9350
  Flushing (G-4985)
Liffey Sheet Metal Corp .... F 347 381-1134
  Long Island City (G-7498)
Merz Metal & Machine Corp .... F 716 893-7786
  Buffalo (G-2944)

CONTRACTORS: Water Intake Well Drilling Svc

Barber & Deline Enrgy Svcs LLC .... F 315 696-8961
  Tully (G-15648)
US Pump Corp .... G 516 303-7799
  West Hempstead (G-16226)

CONTRACTORS: Water Well Drilling

Barber & Deline LLC .... F 607 749-2619
  Tully (G-15649)

CONTRACTORS: Water Well Servicing

Yr Blanc & Co LLC .... G 716 800-3999
  Buffalo (G-3137)

CONTRACTORS: Waterproofing

Tiki Industries Inc .... G 516 779-3629
  Riverhead (G-13586)

CONTRACTORS: Well Chemical Treating Svcs

Metro Group Inc .... D 718 729-7200
  Long Island City (G-7523)

CONTRACTORS: Well Logging Svcs

Jay Little Oil Well Servi .... G 716 925-8905
  Limestone (G-7158)
Schlumberger Technology Corp .... C 607 378-0105
  Horseheads (G-6328)
Smith International Inc .... D 212 350-9400
  New York (G-11625)

CONTRACTORS: Window Treatment Installation

Instant Verticals Inc .... F 631 501-0001
  Farmingdale (G-4786)
Majestic Curtains LLC .... G 718 898-0774
  Elmhurst (G-4469)

CONTRACTORS: Windows & Doors

Advanced Door Solutions Inc .... G 631 773-6100
  Holbrook (G-6169)
D Best Service Co Inc .... G 718 972-6133
  Brooklyn (G-1746)
Ecker Window Corp .... D 914 776-0000
  Yonkers (G-16753)

Employee Codes: A=Over 500 employees, B=251-500
C=101-250, D=51-100, E=20-50, F=10-19, G=5-9

CONTRACTORS: Windows & Doors

Triple H Construction Inc .... E 516 280-8252
 East Meadow *(G-4256)*
Window-Fix Inc .... E 718 854-3475
 Brooklyn *(G-2651)*
Windowman Inc (usa) .... G 718 246-2626
 Brooklyn *(G-2652)*

CONTRACTORS: Wood Floor Installation & Refinishing

Stuart-Dean Co Inc .... F 718 472-1326
 Long Island City *(G-7606)*
Sunrise Tile Inc .... G 718 939-0538
 Flushing *(G-5050)*
Zahk Sales Inc .... G 631 851-0851
 Islandia *(G-6541)*

CONTROL CIRCUIT DEVICES

Inertia Switch Inc .... E 845 359-8300
 Orangeburg *(G-12679)*

CONTROL EQPT: Electric

Addex Inc .... G 315 331-7700
 Newark *(G-12191)*
Altronix Corp .... D 718 567-8181
 Brooklyn *(G-1515)*
Calia Technical Inc .... G 718 447-3928
 Staten Island *(G-15060)*
Conic Systems Inc .... F 845 856-4053
 Port Jervis *(G-13226)*
Continental Instruments LLC .... E 631 842-9400
 Amityville *(G-268)*
Edo LLC .... C 631 630-4000
 Amityville *(G-274)*
Electronic Machine Parts LLC .... F 631 434-3700
 Hauppauge *(G-5818)*
Goddard Design Co .... G 718 599-0170
 Brooklyn *(G-1936)*
ITT Corp .... E 716 662-1900
 Orchard Park *(G-12719)*
ITT Corporation .... E 585 269-7109
 Hemlock *(G-6004)*
ITT Corporation .... D 866 448-8372
 Seneca Falls *(G-14776)*
ITT Corporation .... D 315 568-2811
 Seneca Falls *(G-14777)*
ITT Inc .... E 914 641-2000
 White Plains *(G-16464)*
ITT International Holdings Inc .... G 914 641-2000
 White Plains *(G-16466)*
ITT LLC .... G 315 568-4733
 Seneca Falls *(G-14780)*
ITT LLC .... D 315 258-4904
 Auburn *(G-484)*
ITT LLC .... D 914 641-2000
 Seneca Falls *(G-14781)*
ITT LLC .... B 914 641-2000
 White Plains *(G-16467)*
Kussmaul Electronics Co Inc .... E 631 218-0298
 West Sayville *(G-16290)*
N E Controls LLC .... F 315 626-2480
 Syracuse *(G-15379)*
Nitram Energy Inc .... E 716 662-6540
 Orchard Park *(G-12732)*
Peraton Inc .... E 315 838-7000
 Rome *(G-14266)*
Ruhle Companies Inc .... E 914 287-4000
 Valhalla *(G-15747)*
Weldcomputer Corporation .... F 518 283-2897
 Troy *(G-15636)*

CONTROL EQPT: Noise

Burgess-Manning Inc .... D 716 662-6540
 Orchard Park *(G-12704)*
I D E Processes Corporation .... F 718 544-1177
 Kew Gardens *(G-6873)*
Mason Industries Inc .... B 631 348-0282
 Hauppauge *(G-5881)*
Mason Industries Inc .... G 631 348-0282
 Hauppauge *(G-5882)*
Soundcoat Company Inc .... D 631 242-2200
 Deer Park *(G-4047)*
Techniflo Corporation .... G 716 741-3500
 Clarence Center *(G-3549)*
Vibration & Noise Engrg Corp .... G 716 827-4959
 Orchard Park *(G-12972)*
Vibration Eliminator Co Inc .... E 631 841-4000
 Copiague *(G-3791)*

CONTROL PANELS: Electrical

Abasco Inc .... E 716 649-4790
 Hamburg *(G-5672)*
Avanti Control Systems Inc .... G 518 921-4368
 Gloversville *(G-5452)*
Benfield Control Systems Inc .... F 914 948-6660
 White Plains *(G-16428)*
Boulay Fabrication Inc .... F 315 677-5247
 La Fayette *(G-6945)*
Custom Controls .... G 315 253-4785
 Scipio Center *(G-14736)*
Link Control Systems Inc .... F 631 471-3950
 Ronkonkoma *(G-14370)*
Micro Instrument Corp .... G 585 458-3150
 Rochester *(G-13939)*
Odyssey Controls Inc .... G 585 548-9800
 Bergen *(G-826)*
Se-Mar Electric Co Inc .... E 716 674-7404
 West Seneca *(G-16302)*
Smith Control Systems Inc .... F 518 828-7646
 Hudson *(G-6373)*
Transit Air Inc .... E 607 324-0216
 Hornell *(G-6304)*

CONTROLS & ACCESS: Indl, Electric

Afi Cybernetics Corporation .... E 607 732-3244
 Elmira *(G-4472)*
Bomac Inc .... F 315 433-9181
 Syracuse *(G-15260)*
Entertron Industries Inc .... E 716 772-7216
 Lockport *(G-7299)*
G C Controls Inc .... E 607 656-4117
 Greene *(G-5614)*
Gemtrol Inc .... G 716 894-0716
 Buffalo *(G-2844)*
General Oil Equipment Co Inc .... E 716 691-7012
 Amherst *(G-229)*
ICM Controls Corp .... F 315 233-5266
 North Syracuse *(G-12405)*
Interntnal Cntrls Msrmnts Corp ...... G 315 233-5266
 North Syracuse *(G-12406)*
Morris Products Inc .... F 518 743-0523
 Queensbury *(G-13434)*
Panelogic Inc .... E 607 962-6319
 Corning *(G-3823)*
Soft-Noze Usa Inc .... G 315 732-2726
 Frankfort *(G-5112)*

CONTROLS & ACCESS: Motor

Designatronics Incorporated .... B 516 328-3300
 Hicksville *(G-6080)*
Eaton Corporation .... C 516 353-3017
 East Meadow *(G-4251)*
Eatons Crouse Hinds Business .... F 315 477-7000
 Syracuse *(G-15313)*
ITT Aerospace Controls LLC .... G 914 641-2000
 White Plains *(G-16463)*
Kaman Automation Inc .... D 585 254-8840
 Rochester *(G-13903)*
Powr-UPS Corp .... E 631 345-5700
 Shirley *(G-14843)*
Teknic Inc .... E 585 784-7454
 Victor *(G-15871)*

CONTROLS: Access, Motor

Bakery Innovative Tech Corp .... F 631 758-3081
 Patchogue *(G-12861)*
Bemco of Western Ny Inc .... G 716 823-8400
 Buffalo *(G-2730)*
Schmersal Inc .... E 914 347-4775
 Hawthorne *(G-5997)*

CONTROLS: Automatic Temperature

Advantex Solutions Inc .... G 718 278-2290
 Bellerose *(G-780)*
Automated Bldg MGT Systems Inc . E 516 216-5603
 Floral Park *(G-4956)*
Automated Building Controls .... G 914 381-2860
 Mamaroneck *(G-7734)*
Day Automation Systems Inc .... D 585 924-4630
 Victor *(G-15841)*
Intellidyne LLC .... F 516 676-0777
 Plainview *(G-13064)*
Intrepid Control Service Inc .... G 718 886-8771
 Flushing *(G-5012)*
Johnson Controls Inc .... E 585 924-9346
 Rochester *(G-13896)*
Logical Control Solutions Inc .... F 585 424-5340
 Victor *(G-15855)*
Pii Holdings Inc .... G 716 876-9951
 Buffalo *(G-3004)*
Protective Industries Inc .... D 716 876-9951
 Buffalo *(G-3019)*
Protective Industries Inc .... C 716 876-9951
 Buffalo *(G-3017)*
Siemens Industry Inc .... E 585 797-2300
 Rochester *(G-14126)*
T S B A Group Inc .... E 718 565-6000
 Sunnyside *(G-15206)*
Use Acquisition LLC .... F 516 812-6800
 New Hyde Park *(G-8572)*

CONTROLS: Electric Motor

Dyson-Kissner-Moran Corp .... E 212 661-4600
 Poughkeepsie *(G-13335)*
US Drives Inc .... D 716 731-1606
 Niagara Falls *(G-12346)*

CONTROLS: Environmental

Anderson Instrument Co Inc .... D 518 922-5315
 Fultonville *(G-5234)*
Cascade Technical Services LLC ... F 516 596-6300
 Lynbrook *(G-7663)*
Cascade Technical Services LLC ... G 518 355-2201
 Schenectady *(G-14659)*
Clean Room Depot Inc .... F 631 589-3033
 Holbrook *(G-6177)*
Cox & Company Inc .... C 212 366-0200
 Plainview *(G-13048)*
Daikin Applied Americas Inc .... G 315 253-2771
 Auburn *(G-475)*
E Global Solutions Inc .... G 516 767-5138
 Port Washington *(G-13256)*
East Hudson Watershed Corp .... G 845 319-6349
 Patterson *(G-12881)*
Fuel Watchman Sales & Service .... F 718 665-6100
 Bronx *(G-1276)*
Grillmaster Inc .... E 718 272-9191
 Howard Beach *(G-6330)*
Heating & Burner Supply Inc .... G 718 665-0006
 Bronx *(G-1290)*
Infitec Inc .... D 315 433-1150
 East Syracuse *(G-4352)*
Johnson Controls Inc .... E 716 688-7340
 Buffalo *(G-2896)*
Leo Schultz .... G 716 969-0945
 Cheektowaga *(G-3451)*
Long Island Analytical Labs .... F 631 472-3400
 Holbrook *(G-6196)*
Microb Phase Services .... F 518 877-8948
 Clifton Park *(G-3571)*
Pulsafeeder Inc .... C 585 292-8000
 Rochester *(G-14054)*
RE Hansen Industries Inc .... G 631 471-2900
 Saint James *(G-14514)*
Transit Air Inc .... E 607 324-0216
 Hornell *(G-6304)*
Zebra Environmental Corp .... F 516 596-6300
 Lynbrook *(G-7678)*

CONTROLS: Marine & Navy, Auxiliary

L-3 Cmmnctons Ntronix Holdings . D 212 697-1111
 New York *(G-10496)*

CONTROLS: Numerical

Teale Machine Company Inc .... D 585 244-6700
 Rochester *(G-14160)*

CONTROLS: Relay & Ind

Air Crafters Inc .... C 631 471-7788
 Ronkonkoma *(G-14295)*
Anderson Instrument Co Inc .... D 518 922-5315
 Fultonville *(G-5234)*
Baco Controls Inc .... F 315 635-2500
 Baldwinsville *(G-551)*
Con Rel Auto Electric Inc .... E 518 356-1646
 Schenectady *(G-14666)*
Cox & Company Inc .... C 212 366-0200
 Plainview *(G-13048)*
Designatronics Incorporated .... G 516 328-3300
 Hicksville *(G-6079)*
Deutsch Relays .... F 631 342-1700
 Hauppauge *(G-5810)*
Enetics Inc .... G 585 924-5010
 Victor *(G-15844)*

PRODUCT SECTION

Exfo Burleigh Pdts Group Inc .... D 585 301-1530
  Canandaigua *(G-3220)*
I E D Corp .... F 631 348-0424
  Islandia *(G-6529)*
Industrial Indxing Systems Inc .... E 585 924-9181
  Victor *(G-15850)*
JE Miller Inc .... F 315 437-6811
  East Syracuse *(G-4355)*
Kearney-National Inc .... F 212 661-4600
  New York *(G-10427)*
Linde LLC .... D 716 773-7552
  Grand Island *(G-5506)*
Logitek Inc .... D 631 567-1100
  Bohemia *(G-1048)*
Magnus Precision Mfg Inc .... D 315 548-8032
  Phelps *(G-12978)*
Moog Inc .... E 716 687-4778
  Elma *(G-4454)*
Moog Inc .... A 716 652-2000
  Elma *(G-4453)*
Nas-Tra Automotive Inds Inc .... C 631 225-1225
  Lindenhurst *(G-7182)*
National Time Recording Eqp Co .... F 212 227-3310
  New York *(G-10887)*
North Point Technology LLC .... F 866 885-3377
  Endicott *(G-4605)*
Nsi Industries LLC .... C 800 841-2505
  Mount Vernon *(G-8426)*
Omntec Mfg Inc .... E 631 981-2001
  Ronkonkoma *(G-14391)*
Peerless Instrument Co Inc .... C 631 396-6500
  Farmingdale *(G-4845)*
Precision Mechanisms Corp .... E 516 333-5955
  Westbury *(G-16366)*
Pulsafeeder Inc .... C 585 292-8000
  Rochester *(G-14054)*
Rochester Industrial Ctrl Inc .... D 315 524-4555
  Ontario *(G-12663)*
Rockwell Automation Inc .... E 585 487-2700
  Pittsford *(G-13026)*
Service Mfg Group Inc .... F 716 893-1482
  Buffalo *(G-3063)*
Ssac Inc .... E 800 843-8848
  Baldwinsville *(G-563)*
Stetron International Inc .... F 716 854-3443
  Buffalo *(G-3077)*
Unimar Inc .... F 315 699-4400
  Syracuse *(G-15448)*
Zeppelin Electric Company Inc .... G 631 928-9467
  East Setauket *(G-4315)*

CONTROLS: Thermostats, Exc Built-in

Bilbee Controls Inc .... F 518 622-3033
  Cairo *(G-3147)*

CONTROLS: Voice

Voices For All LLC .... G 518 261-1664
  Mechanicville *(G-7935)*

CONVENIENCE STORES

Patla Enterprises Inc .... F 315 367-0237
  Sherrill *(G-14821)*
Schaefer Logging Inc .... F 607 467-4990
  Deposit *(G-4111)*
Stewarts Shops Corp .... F 518 499-9376
  Whitehall *(G-16524)*

CONVENTION & TRADE SHOW SVCS

Mechanical Displays Inc .... G 718 258-5588
  Brooklyn *(G-2185)*

CONVERTERS: Data

Annese & Associates Inc .... G 716 972-0076
  Buffalo *(G-2701)*
Cisco Systems Inc .... C 212 714-4000
  New York *(G-9304)*
Data Device Corporation .... B 631 567-5600
  Bohemia *(G-1008)*
Scroll Media Inc .... G 617 395-8904
  New York *(G-11524)*

CONVERTERS: Frequency

Applied Power Systems Inc .... E 516 935-2230
  Hicksville *(G-6059)*

CONVERTERS: Phase Or Rotary, Electrical

Automation Source Technologies .... F 631 643-1678
  West Babylon *(G-16136)*

CONVERTERS: Power, AC to DC

Curtis/Palmer Hydroelectric LP .... F 518 654-6297
  Corinth *(G-3808)*
Endicott Research Group Inc .... D 607 754-9187
  Endicott *(G-4590)*
G B International Trdg Co Ltd .... C 607 785-0938
  Endicott *(G-4594)*

CONVERTERS: Torque, Exc Auto

American Torque Inc .... F 718 526-2433
  Jamaica *(G-6625)*

CONVEYOR SYSTEMS: Belt, General Indl Use

American Material Processing .... F 315 318-0017
  Phoenix *(G-12988)*
Desmi-Afti Inc .... E 716 662-0632
  Orchard Park *(G-12713)*
Hohl Machine & Conveyor Co Inc ...... E 716 882-7210
  Buffalo *(G-2873)*

CONVEYOR SYSTEMS: Bulk Handling

Ward Industrial Equipment Inc .... G 716 856-6966
  Buffalo *(G-3123)*

CONVEYOR SYSTEMS: Pneumatic Tube

Shako Inc .... G 315 437-1294
  East Syracuse *(G-4370)*

CONVEYOR SYSTEMS: Robotic

International Robotics Inc .... F 914 630-1060
  Larchmont *(G-7057)*

CONVEYORS & CONVEYING EQPT

Automated Biomass Systems LLC ..... F 607 849-7800
  Marathon *(G-7788)*
Chemprene Inc .... C 845 831-2800
  Beacon *(G-755)*
Chemprene Holding Inc .... C 845 831-2800
  Beacon *(G-756)*
Columbus McKinnon Corporation ...... C 716 689-5400
  Getzville *(G-5344)*
Columbus McKinnon Corporation ...... C 716 689-5400
  Getzville *(G-5345)*
Columbus McKinnon Corporation ...... C 716 689-5400
  Getzville *(G-5346)*
Crownbrook ACC LLC .... E 718 626-0760
  Brooklyn *(G-1734)*
Dairy Conveyor Corp .... D 845 278-7878
  Brewster *(G-1162)*
Excel Conveyor LLC .... F 718 474-0001
  Rockaway Beach *(G-14225)*
General Splice Corporation .... G 914 271-5131
  Croton On Hudson *(G-3914)*
Glasgow Products Inc .... E 516 374-5937
  Woodmere *(G-16641)*
Green Conveyor & Mch Group LLC ... G 607 692-7050
  Whitney Point *(G-16555)*
Haines Equipment Inc .... E 607 566-8531
  Avoca *(G-516)*
I J White Corporation .... D 631 293-3788
  Farmingdale *(G-4783)*
J D Handling Systems Inc .... F 518 828-9676
  Ghent *(G-5357)*
Joldeson One Aerospace Inds .... D 718 848-7396
  Ozone Park *(G-12827)*
Kinematic Technologies Inc .... E 518 346-7686
  Niskayuna *(G-12355)*
Nerak Systems Inc .... F 914 763-8259
  Fishkill *(G-4951)*
Northeast Conveyors Inc .... F 585 768-8912
  Lima *(G-7153)*
Noto Industrial Corp .... G 631 736-7600
  Coram *(G-3802)*
Pacline Conveyors Inc .... F 716 932-7858
  Buffalo *(G-2989)*
Raymond Corporation .... A 607 656-2311
  Greene *(G-5617)*
Raymond Corporation .... E 315 643-5000
  East Syracuse *(G-4364)*

COOLING TOWERS: Metal

Re-Al Industrial Corp .... G 716 542-4556
  Akron *(G-22)*
Renold Inc .... D 716 326-3121
  Westfield *(G-16396)*
Rlp Holdings Inc .... G 716 852-0832
  Buffalo *(G-3039)*
Rota Pack Inc .... F 631 274-1037
  Farmingdale *(G-4869)*
Speedways Conveyors Inc .... G 716 893-2222
  Buffalo *(G-3075)*
Troy Belting and Supply Co .... D 518 272-4920
  Watervliet *(G-16053)*

COOKING & FOOD WARMING EQPT: Commercial

Advance Tabco Inc .... D 631 242-8270
  Edgewood *(G-4394)*
Attias Oven Corp .... G 718 499-0145
  Brooklyn *(G-1573)*
Bakers Pride Oven Co Inc .... C 914 576-0200
  New Rochelle *(G-8591)*
Carts Mobile Food Eqp Corp .... F 718 788-5540
  Brooklyn *(G-1680)*
IMC Teddy Food Service .... E 631 789-8881
  Amityville *(G-286)*
Kinplex Corp .... C 631 242-4800
  Edgewood *(G-4407)*
Kinplex Corp .... C 631 242-4800
  Edgewood *(G-4408)*
Korin Japanese Trading Corp .... E 212 587-7021
  New York *(G-10471)*
R-S Restaurant Eqp Mfg Corp .... F 212 925-0335
  New York *(G-11314)*
Roger & Sons Inc .... F 212 226-4734
  New York *(G-11422)*
Toga Manufacturing Inc .... C 631 242-4800
  Edgewood *(G-4421)*

COOKING & FOODWARMING EQPT: Coffee Brewing

Arista Coffee Inc .... F 347 531-0813
  Maspeth *(G-7823)*

COOKING & FOODWARMING EQPT: Commercial

Advance Food Service Co Inc .... C 631 242-4800
  Edgewood *(G-4393)*

COOKING WARE, EXC PORCELAIN ENAMELED

Allied Metal Spinning Corp .... D 718 893-3300
  Bronx *(G-1216)*

COOKING WARE: Cooking Ware, Porcelain Enameled

Schiller Stores Inc .... G 631 208-9400
  Riverhead *(G-13583)*
Wilmax Usa LLC .... F 917 388-2790
  New York *(G-12116)*

COOKWARE, STONEWARE: Coarse Earthenware & Pottery

Schiller Stores Inc .... G 845 928-4316
  Central Valley *(G-3397)*

COOKWARE: Fine Earthenware

Lifetime Stainless Steel Corp .... G 585 924-9393
  Victor *(G-15854)*
Mackenzie-Childs LLC .... C 315 364-6118
  Aurora *(G-511)*
Williams-Sonoma Stores Inc .... F 212 633-2203
  New York *(G-12114)*

COOLING TOWERS: Metal

Manhattan Cooling Towers Inc .... F 212 279-1045
  Long Island City *(G-7513)*
SPX Corporation .... E 631 467-2632
  Ronkonkoma *(G-14417)*
SPX Corporation .... B 585 436-5550
  Rochester *(G-14139)*

Employee Codes: A=Over 500 employees, B=251-500
C=101-250, D=51-100, E=20-50, F=10-19, G=5-9

COPPER ORES

Global Gold Corporation ....F 914 925-0020
Rye *(G-14481)*

COPPER PRDTS: Refined, Primary

Hengyuan Copper USA Inc ....G 718 357-6666
Whitestone *(G-16542)*

COPPER: Rolling & Drawing

Aurubis Buffalo Inc ....F 716 879-6700
Buffalo *(G-2714)*
Aurubis Buffalo Inc ....B 716 879-6700
Buffalo *(G-2715)*
Continental Cordage Corp ....D 315 655-9800
Cazenovia *(G-3317)*

COPYRIGHT BUYING & LICENSING

Abkco Music & Records Inc ....E 212 399-0300
New York *(G-8710)*
Penhouse Media Group Inc ....C 212 702-6000
New York *(G-11149)*
Scholastic Corporation ....E 212 343-6100
New York *(G-11513)*
Universal Mus Group Hldngs Inc ....E 212 333-8000
New York *(G-11961)*

CORD & TWINE

Albany International Corp ....C 607 749-7226
Homer *(G-6252)*

CORE WASH OR WAX

Beyond Beauty Basics LLC ....F 516 731-7100
Levittown *(G-7131)*

CORES: Magnetic

Fair-Rite Products Corp ....C 845 895-2055
Wallkill *(G-15904)*

CORK & CORK PRDTS: Tiles

Globus Cork Inc ....F 347 963-4059
Bronx *(G-1282)*

CORRESPONDENCE SCHOOLS

Boardman Simons Publishing ....E 212 620-7200
New York *(G-9115)*
Simmons-Boardman Pubg Corp ....E 212 620-7200
New York *(G-11594)*

CORRUGATED PRDTS: Boxes, Partition, Display Items, Sheet/Pad

Dory Enterprises Inc ....F 607 565-7079
Waverly *(G-16064)*
Land Packaging Corp ....F 914 472-5976
Scarsdale *(G-14640)*
Technical Library Service Inc ....F 212 219-0770
Brooklyn *(G-2558)*

COSMETIC PREPARATIONS

Albion Cosmetics America Inc ....G 212 869-1052
New York *(G-8785)*
Ardex Cosmetics of America ....E 518 283-6700
Troy *(G-15601)*
Bare Escentuals Inc ....G 646 537-0070
New York *(G-9016)*
Becca Inc ....D 646 568-6250
New York *(G-9033)*
Brucci Ltd ....E 914 965-0707
Yonkers *(G-16741)*
Bycmac Corp ....E 845 255-0884
Gardiner *(G-5292)*
California Fragrance Company ....E 631 424-4023
Huntington Station *(G-6435)*
Clark Botanicals Inc ....F 914 826-4319
Bronxville *(G-1424)*
Clean Beauty Collective Inc ....E 212 269-1387
New York *(G-9325)*
Clinique Laboratories LLC ....G 212 572-4200
New York *(G-9327)*
Clinique Services Inc ....G 212 572-4200
New York *(G-9328)*
D & H Amazing Deals Inc ....G 347 318-3805
Brooklyn *(G-1745)*

Dermatech Labs Inc ....F 631 225-1700
Lindenhurst *(G-7169)*
Epic Beauty Co LLC ....G 212 327-3059
New York *(G-9693)*
Estee Lauder Companies Inc ....E 212 572-4200
New York *(G-9715)*
Estee Lauder Companies Inc ....E 212 756-4800
New York *(G-9716)*
Estee Lauder Companies Inc ....A 212 572-4200
New York *(G-9718)*
Ex-It Medical Devices Inc ....A 212 653-0637
New York *(G-9746)*
Forsythe Cosmetic Group Ltd ....E 516 239-4200
Freeport *(G-5156)*
Inter Parfums Inc ....D 212 983-2640
New York *(G-10234)*
Intercos America Inc ....G 845 732-3900
West Nyack *(G-16271)*
Jackel Inc ....E 908 359-2039
New York *(G-10291)*
June Jacobs Labs LLC ....D 212 471-4830
New York *(G-10381)*
Kantian Skincare LLC ....G 631 780-4711
Smithtown *(G-14902)*
Klg Usa LLC ....A 845 856-5311
Port Jervis *(G-13233)*
Lady Burd Exclusive Cosmt Inc ....C 631 454-0444
Farmingdale *(G-4807)*
Lechler Laboratories Inc ....E 845 426-6800
Spring Valley *(G-14998)*
Liddell Corporation ....F 716 297-8557
Niagara Falls *(G-12305)*
Lornamead Inc ....D 646 745-3643
Tonawanda *(G-15555)*
Lornamead Inc ....D 716 874-7190
New York *(G-10611)*
Malin + Goetz Inc ....F 212 244-7771
New York *(G-10678)*
Mana Products Inc ....B 718 361-2550
Long Island City *(G-7510)*
Marietta Corporation ....B 607 753-6746
Cortland *(G-3881)*
Maybelline Inc ....A 212 885-1310
New York *(G-10735)*
Mehron Inc ....E 845 426-1700
Chestnut Ridge *(G-3493)*
Nature Only Inc ....G 917 922-6539
Forest Hills *(G-5078)*
Naturpathica Holistic Hlth Inc ....D 631 329-8792
East Hampton *(G-4241)*
New Avon LLC ....B 212 282-6000
New York *(G-10918)*
Newburgh Distribution Corp ....G 845 561-6330
New Windsor *(G-8652)*
Oasis Cosmetic Labs Inc ....F 631 758-0038
Holtsville *(G-6241)*
Olan Laboratories Inc ....G 631 582-2082
Hauppauge *(G-5904)*
Peppermints Salon Inc ....F 718 357-6304
Whitestone *(G-16547)*
Peter Thomas Roth Labs LLC ....E 212 581-5800
New York *(G-11170)*
Plastic & Reconstructive Svcs ....G 914 584-5605
Mount Kisco *(G-8355)*
Redken 5th Avenue NYC LLC ....C 212 818-1500
New York *(G-11343)*
Redken 5th Avenue Nyc LLC ....G 212 984-5113
New York *(G-11344)*
Revlon Inc ....B 212 527-4000
New York *(G-11376)*
Revlon Consumer Products Corp ....B 212 527-4000
New York *(G-11377)*
Scientific Solutions Globl LLC ....F 516 543-3376
Carle Place *(G-3272)*
Shiseido Americas Corporation ....G 212 805-2300
New York *(G-11570)*
Solabia USA Inc ....G 212 847-2397
New York *(G-11638)*
Sundial Brands LLC ....C 631 842-8800
Amityville *(G-318)*
Sundial Group LLC ....E 631 842-8800
Amityville *(G-320)*
Temptu Inc ....G 718 937-9503
Long Island City *(G-7613)*
Topiderm Inc ....G 631 226-7979
Amityville *(G-321)*
Universal Packg Systems Inc ....A 631 543-2277
Hauppauge *(G-5966)*
Verla International Ltd ....B 845 561-2440
New Windsor *(G-8663)*

Victoria Albi International ....F 212 689-2600
New York *(G-12028)*
Xania Labs Inc ....G 718 361-2550
Long Island City *(G-7644)*
Zela International Co ....E 518 436-1833
Albany *(G-145)*

COSMETICS & TOILETRIES

AEP Environmental LLC ....F 716 446-0739
Buffalo *(G-2690)*
Alabu Inc ....G 518 665-0411
Mechanicville *(G-7929)*
Alexandria Professional LLC ....F 716 242-8514
Williamsville *(G-16567)*
Allan John Company ....F 212 940-2210
New York *(G-8796)*
Antimony New York LLC ....G 917 232-1836
New York *(G-8878)*
Bio-Botanica Inc ....D 631 231-0987
Hauppauge *(G-5780)*
Borghese Inc ....E 212 659-5318
New York *(G-9123)*
China Huaren Organic Pdts Inc ....G 212 232-0120
New York *(G-9278)*
Common Sense Natural Soap ....E 518 677-0224
Cambridge *(G-3179)*
Conopco Inc ....E 585 647-8322
Rochester *(G-13720)*
Coty Inc ....E 212 389-7000
New York *(G-9404)*
Elite Parfums Ltd ....D 212 983-2640
New York *(G-9651)*
Elizabeth Arden Inc ....C 845 810-2175
Central Valley *(G-3396)*
Estee Lauder Companies Inc ....A 917 606-3240
New York *(G-9714)*
Estee Lauder Companies Inc ....F 646 762-7718
New York *(G-9717)*
Estee Lauder Companies Inc ....D 631 694-2601
Melville *(G-8020)*
Estee Lauder Companies Inc ....A 212 572-4200
Melville *(G-8021)*
Estee Lauder Companies Inc ....A 646 602-7590
New York *(G-9719)*
Eternal Love Parfums Corp ....G 516 921-6100
Syosset *(G-15216)*
Four Paws Products Ltd ....D 631 436-7421
Ronkonkoma *(G-14343)*
Hain Celestial Group Inc ....C 516 587-5000
New Hyde Park *(G-8538)*
HFC Prestige Intl US LLC ....A 212 389-7800
New York *(G-10091)*
Hnc Enterprises LLC ....G 904 448-9387
Brooklyn *(G-1979)*
Iles Formula Inc ....G 315 834-2478
New York *(G-10182)*
Intercos America Inc ....G 845 732-3910
West Nyack *(G-16272)*
Interntnal Flvors Frgrnces Inc ....C 212 765-5500
New York *(G-10251)*
Judith N Graham Inc ....G 914 921-5446
Rye *(G-14484)*
Kind Group LLC ....G 212 645-0800
New York *(G-10448)*
LOreal Usa Inc ....B 917 606-9554
New York *(G-10607)*
Mana Products Inc ....B 718 361-5204
Long Island City *(G-7511)*
Marvellissima Intl Ltd ....G 212 682-7306
New York *(G-10720)*
Medisonic Inc ....F 516 653-2345
Great Neck *(G-5572)*
Mentholatum Company ....E 716 677-2500
Orchard Park *(G-12730)*
New Avon LLC ....F 716 572-4842
Buffalo *(G-2962)*
Paula Dorf Cosmetics Inc ....E 212 582-0073
New York *(G-11124)*
Pdk Labs Inc ....D 631 273-2630
Hauppauge *(G-5910)*
Prescriptives Inc ....G 212 572-4400
New York *(G-11234)*
Professional Buty Holdings Inc ....F 631 787-8576
Hauppauge *(G-5924)*
Provisions 5 Corp ....G 718 809-5292
New Hyde Park *(G-8558)*
Quality King Distributors Inc ....C 631 439-2027
Ronkonkoma *(G-14402)*
REB Lybss Inc ....G 845 238-5633
Monroe *(G-8280)*

Robert Racine .... E 518 677-0224
  Cambridge *(G-3183)*
Scent-A-Vision Inc .... E 631 424-4905
  Huntington Station *(G-6457)*
Skin Atelier Inc .... F 845 294-1202
  Goshen *(G-5483)*
Sml Acquisition LLC .... C 914 592-3130
  Elmsford *(G-4570)*
Sundial Brands .... G 631 842-8800
  Farmingdale *(G-4883)*
Tomia Beauty Brands LLC .... G 917 301-0125
  New York *(G-11862)*
Unilever United States Inc .... G 212 546-0200
  New York *(G-11944)*
Unilever United States Inc .... C 212 546-0200
  New York *(G-11945)*
United-Guardian Inc .... E 631 273-0900
  Hauppauge *(G-5965)*

COSMETICS WHOLESALERS

Abbe Laboratories Inc .... F 631 756-2223
  Farmingdale *(G-4707)*
Borghese Inc .... E 212 659-5318
  New York *(G-9123)*
Clean Beauty Collective Inc .... E 212 269-1387
  New York *(G-9325)*
Clinique Laboratories LLC .... G 212 572-4200
  New York *(G-9327)*
Dermatech Labs Inc .... F 631 225-1700
  Lindenhurst *(G-7169)*
Essie Cosmetics Ltd .... D 212 818-1500
  New York *(G-9713)*
Hnc Enterprises LLC .... G 904 448-9387
  Brooklyn *(G-1979)*
Lotta Luv Beauty LLC .... F 646 786-2847
  New York *(G-10614)*
Mana Products Inc .... B 718 361-2550
  Long Island City *(G-7510)*
Marvellissima Intl Ltd .... G. 212 682-7306
  New York *(G-10720)*
New Avon LLC .... B 212 282-6000
  New York *(G-10918)*
Shiseido Americas Corporation .. G 212 805-2300
  New York *(G-11570)*
Xania Labs Inc .... B 718 361-2550
  Long Island City *(G-7644)*
Zela International Co .... E 518 436-1833
  Albany *(G-145)*

COSTUME JEWELRY & NOVELTIES: Apparel, Exc Precious Metals

Jj Fantasia Inc .... G 212 868-1198
  New York *(G-10343)*
Kenneth J Lane LLC .... F 212 868-1780
  New York *(G-10432)*
Mercado Global Inc .... G 718 838-9908
  Brooklyn *(G-2193)*
Von Musulin Patricia .... G 212 206-8345
  New York *(G-12053)*

COSTUME JEWELRY & NOVELTIES: Bracelets, Exc Precious Metals

Aniiwe Inc .... G 347 683-1891
  Brooklyn *(G-1535)*
Vitafede .... F 213 488-0136
  New York *(G-12044)*

COSTUME JEWELRY & NOVELTIES: Costume Novelties

Jay Turoff .... F 718 856-7300
  Brooklyn *(G-2035)*

COSTUME JEWELRY & NOVELTIES: Earrings, Exc Precious Metals

Fashion Accents LLC .... F 401 331-6626
  New York *(G-9784)*

COSTUME JEWELRY & NOVELTIES: Exc Semi & Precious

Accessory Plays LLC .... E 212 564-7301
  New York *(G-8720)*
Barrera Jose & Maria Co Ltd ...... E 212 239-1994
  New York *(G-9021)*
Carol For Eva Graham Inc .... F 212 889-8686
  New York *(G-9211)*

Catherine Stein Designs Inc .... E 212 840-1188
  New York *(G-9230)*
Ciner Manufacturing Co Inc .... E 212 947-3770
  New York *(G-9301)*
Dabby-Reid Ltd .... F 212 356-0040
  New York *(G-9452)*
Erickson Beamon Ltd .... E 212 643-4810
  New York *(G-9701)*
Fantasia Jewelry Inc .... E 212 921-9590
  New York *(G-9781)*
J & H Creations Inc .... E 212 465-0962
  New York *(G-10281)*
Jaymar Jewelry Co Inc .... E 212 564-4788
  New York *(G-10315)*
Lesilu Productions Inc .... G 212 947-6419
  New York *(G-10554)*
Magic Novelty Co Inc .... E 212 304-2777
  New York *(G-10667)*
Marlborough Jewels Inc .... G 718 768-2000
  Brooklyn *(G-2170)*
Mwsi Inc .... D 914 347-4200
  Hawthorne *(G-5993)*
Salmco Jewelry Corp .... F 212 695-8792
  New York *(G-11471)*
Steezys LLC .... G 646 276-5333
  New York *(G-11700)*
Stephan & Company ACC Ltd .... E 212 481-3888
  New York *(G-11705)*

COUGH MEDICINES

Purine Pharma LLC .... E 315 705-4030
  Mount Vernon *(G-8436)*

COUNTER & SINK TOPS

Arcy Plastic Laminates Inc .... E 518 235-0753
  Albany *(G-42)*
Auratic Inc .... G 914 413-8154
  New York *(G-8964)*
Countertops & Cabinets Inc .... G 315 433-1038
  Syracuse *(G-15292)*
Delocon Wholesale Inc .... F 716 592-2711
  Springville *(G-15015)*
Empire Fabricators Inc .... G 585 235-3050
  Rochester *(G-13779)*
Frank J Martello .... G 585 235-2780
  Rochester *(G-13816)*
Icestone LLC .... E 718 624-4900
  Brooklyn *(G-1993)*
Joseph Fedele .... G 718 448-3658
  Staten Island *(G-15097)*
Koeppels Kustom Kitchens Inc .. E 518 489-0092
  Albany *(G-93)*
Metropolitan Granite & MBL Inc . G 585 342-7020
  Rochester *(G-13937)*
Nlr Counter Tops LLC .... G 347 295-0410
  New York *(G-10980)*
Pine Hill Fabricators .... F 716 823-2474
  Buffalo *(G-3005)*
Precision Built Tops LLC .... G 607 336-5417
  Norwich *(G-12491)*
Ridge Cabinet & Showcase Inc .. G 585 663-0560
  Rochester *(G-14073)*
Rochester Countertop Inc .... F 585 338-2260
  Rochester *(G-14085)*
Solid Surfaces Inc .... D 585 292-5340
  Rochester *(G-14134)*
Triad Counter Corp .... E 631 750-0615
  Bohemia *(G-1098)*
Wilbedone Inc .... E 607 756-8813
  Cortland *(G-3897)*
Wolak Inc .... G 315 839-5366
  Clayville *(G-3560)*

COUNTERS & COUNTING DEVICES

Cmp Advnced Mech Sltons NY LLC .. C 607 352-1712
  Binghamton *(G-875)*
Designatronics Incorporated ...... E 516 328-3300
  Hicksville *(G-6079)*
Encore Electronics Inc .... E 518 584-5354
  Saratoga Springs *(G-14577)*
Environment-One Corporation ... C 518 346-6161
  Schenectady *(G-14672)*

COUNTERS OR COUNTER DISPLAY CASES, EXC WOOD

GF Packaging LLC .... E 716 692-2705
  Cheektowaga *(G-3447)*

Glasbau Hahn America LLC .... G 845 566-3331
  Newburgh *(G-12224)*
Stone Expo & Cabinetry LLC ..... F 516 292-2988
  West Hempstead *(G-16225)*

COUNTERS OR COUNTER DISPLAY CASES, WOOD

Bloch Industries LLC .... D 585 334-9600
  Rochester *(G-13666)*
Creative Counter Tops Inc .... F 845 471-6480
  Poughkeepsie *(G-13333)*
Serway Bros Inc .... E 315 337-0601
  Rome *(G-14274)*

COUNTERS: Mechanical

Melland Gear Instr of Huppauge .. E 631 234-0100
  Hauppauge *(G-5885)*

COUNTING DEVICES: Controls, Revolution & Timing

Schlumberger Technology Corp .. C 607 378-0105
  Horseheads *(G-6328)*

COUNTING DEVICES: Electromechanical

K-Technologies Inc .... E 716 828-4444
  Buffalo *(G-2901)*
Vantage Mfg & Assembly LLC ... E 845 471-5290
  Poughkeepsie *(G-13371)*

COUNTING DEVICES: Speed Indicators & Recorders, Vehicle

Curtis Instruments Inc .... C 914 666-2971
  Mount Kisco *(G-8339)*

COUPLINGS: Shaft

Howden North America Inc .... D 803 741-2700
  Depew *(G-4092)*
Kinemotive Corporation .... E 631 249-6440
  Farmingdale *(G-4803)*
Renold Inc .... D 716 326-3121
  Westfield *(G-16396)*

COUPON REDEMPTION SVCS

Syracuse Letter Company Inc .... F 315 476-8328
  Bridgeport *(G-1184)*

COURIER SVCS: Ground

Comsec Ventures International .. G 518 523-1600
  Lake Placid *(G-6975)*

COVERS: Automobile Seat

Mc Coy Tops and Interiors Inc ... G 718 458-5800
  Woodside *(G-16662)*

COVERS: Automotive, Exc Seat & Tire

Automtve Uphl Cnvertible Tops .. G 914 961-4242
  Tuckahoe *(G-15642)*
Kamali Group Inc .... G 516 627-4000
  Great Neck *(G-5567)*

COVERS: Canvas

Covergrip Corporation .... G 855 268-3747
  Manorville *(G-7783)*
Custom Canvas Manufacturing Co .. E 716 852-6372
  Buffalo *(G-2789)*

COVERS: Hot Tub & Spa

Commercial Fabrics Inc .... F 716 694-0641
  North Tonawanda *(G-12422)*
Wave Float Rooms LLC .... G 844 356-2876
  Clarence *(G-3542)*

COVERS: Slip Made Of Fabric, Plastic, Etc.

Superior Decorators Inc .... F 718 381-4793
  Glendale *(G-5408)*

CRANE & AERIAL LIFT SVCS

Neversink Steel Corp .... G 845 292-4611
  Liberty *(G-7146)*

CRANE & AERIAL LIFT SVCS

Snyders Neon Displays Inc .... G 518 857-4100
  Colonie *(G-3679)*

CRANES & MONORAIL SYSTEMS

Debrucque Cleveland Tramrail S .... G 315 697-5160
  Canastota *(G-3243)*

CRANES: Indl Plant

Gorbel Inc .... C 585 924-6262
  Fishers *(G-4940)*
Konecranes Inc .... F 585 359-4450
  Henrietta *(G-6033)*

CRANKSHAFTS & CAMSHAFTS: Machining

Peko Precision Products Inc .... F 585 301-1386
  Rochester *(G-14010)*
Westchstr Crnkshft Grndng .... G 718 651-3900
  East Elmhurst *(G-4226)*

CRATES: Fruit, Wood Wirebound

Wolfe Lumber Mill Inc .... G 716 772-7750
  Gasport *(G-5309)*

CREDIT BUREAUS

Nyt Capital LLC .... F 212 556-1234
  New York *(G-11021)*

CROWNS & CLOSURES

Protocase Incorporated .... C 866 849-3911
  Lewiston *(G-7141)*
Reynolds Packaging McHy Inc .... D 716 358-6451
  Falconer *(G-4690)*

CRUDE PETROLEUM & NATURAL GAS PRODUCTION

Hess Energy Exploration Ltd .... G 732 750-6500
  New York *(G-10086)*
Hess Explrtion Prod Hldngs Ltd .... G 732 750-6000
  New York *(G-10087)*

CRUDE PETROLEUM & NATURAL GAS PRODUCTION

Dlh Energy Service LLC .... G 716 410-0028
  Lakewood *(G-6994)*
Lukoil Americas Corporation .... C 212 421-4141
  New York *(G-10628)*
MRC Global (us) Inc .... F 607 739-8575
  Horseheads *(G-6322)*
Rocket Tech Fuel Corp .... F 516 810-8947
  Bay Shore *(G-716)*
Zenith Energy US Logistics .... G 212 993-1280
  New York *(G-12173)*

CRUDE PETROLEUM PRODUCTION

Chanse Petroleum Corporation .... G 212 682-3789
  New York *(G-9259)*
China N E Petro Holdings Ltd .... A 212 307-3568
  New York *(G-9281)*
Hess Corporation .... B 212 997-8500
  New York *(G-10085)*
Hess Pipeline Corporation .... C 212 997-8500
  New York *(G-10089)*
Resource PTRlm&ptrochmcl Intl .... E 212 537-3856
  New York *(G-11370)*
Speedway LLC .... F 631 738-2536
  Lake Grove *(G-6969)*
Stedman Energy Inc .... G 716 789-3018
  Mayville *(G-7924)*

CRUDES: Cyclic, Organic

Magic Tank LLC .... G 877 646-2442
  New York *(G-10669)*

CRYOGENIC COOLING DEVICES: Infrared Detectors, Masers

Philips Medical Systems Mr .... B 518 782-1122
  Latham *(G-7089)*

CRYSTALS

Crystal Is Inc .... E 518 271-7375
  Green Island *(G-5604)*

Edo LLC .... G 631 630-4000
  Amityville *(G-272)*
Momentive Performance Mtls Inc .... E 518 237-3330
  Waterford *(G-15981)*
Mpm Holdings Inc .... G 518 237-3330
  Waterford *(G-15984)*
Mpm Intermediate Holdings Inc .... G 518 237-3330
  Waterford *(G-15985)*

CULTURE MEDIA

Angus Chemical Company .... E 716 283-1434
  Niagara Falls *(G-12263)*
Debmar-Mercury .... D 212 669-5025
  New York *(G-9494)*
Man of World .... G 212 915-0017
  New York *(G-10681)*
Stemcultures LLC .... E 518 621-0848
  Rensselaer *(G-13478)*

CULVERTS: Metal Plate

Lane Enterprises Inc .... F 607 776-3366
  Bath *(G-647)*

CUPS: Plastic Exc Polystyrene Foam

Capitol Cups Inc .... E 518 627-0051
  Amsterdam *(G-330)*

CURBING: Granite Or Stone

Granite Works LLC .... E 607 565-7012
  Waverly *(G-16065)*
Stone & Terrazzo World Inc .... G 718 361-6899
  Long Island City *(G-7605)*

CURTAIN & DRAPERY FIXTURES: Poles, Rods & Rollers

Abalene Decorating Services .... E 718 782-2000
  New York *(G-8705)*
P E Guerin .... D 212 243-5270
  New York *(G-11084)*
Pj Decorators Inc 516 735-9693
  East Meadow *(G-4255)*
Wcd Window Coverings Inc .... E 845 336-4511
  Lake Katrine *(G-6973)*

CURTAIN WALLS: Building, Steel

AM Architectural Metal & Glass .... E 845 942-8848
  Garnerville *(G-5299)*

CURTAINS & BEDDING: Knit

Commonwealth Home Fashion Inc ...... D 514 384-8290
  Willsboro *(G-16598)*

CURTAINS & CURTAIN FABRICS: Lace

Mary Bright Inc .... G 212 677-1970
  New York *(G-10721)*

CURTAINS: Cottage Sets, From Purchased Materials

Northast Coml Win Trtments Inc .... D 845 331-0148
  Kingston *(G-6912)*

CURTAINS: Shower

Catalina Products Corp .... E 718 336-8288
  Brooklyn *(G-1683)*
Showeray Co .... D 718 965-3633
  Brooklyn *(G-2466)*

CURTAINS: Window, From Purchased Materials

Belle Maison USA Ltd .... E 718 805-0200
  Richmond Hill *(G-13498)*
Drapery Industries Inc .... F 585 232-2992
  Rochester *(G-13750)*

CUSHIONS & PILLOWS

Alexandra Ferguson LLC 718 788-7768
  New Rochelle *(G-8587)*
Anhui Skyworth LLC .... D 917 940-6903
  Hempstead *(G-6005)*
Franks Cushions Inc 718 848-1216
  Maspeth *(G-7847)*

Hollander Sleep Products LLC .... D 212 575-0400
  New York *(G-10117)*
Soft-Tex International Inc .... D 800 366-2324
  Waterford *(G-15987)*

CUSHIONS & PILLOWS: Bed, From Purchased Materials

Arlee Home Fashions Inc .... D 212 689-0020
  New York *(G-8908)*
Hollander HM Fshons Hldngs LLC ..... F 212 575-0400
  New York *(G-10116)*
Home Fashions Intl LLC .... E 212 689-3579
  New York *(G-10119)*
Home Fashions Intl LLC .... F 212 684-0091
  New York *(G-10120)*
Place Vendome Holding Co Inc .... E 212 696-0765
  New York *(G-11205)*
R & M Industries Inc .... F 212 366-6414
  New York *(G-11309)*

CUSHIONS: Textile, Exc Spring & Carpet

Advanced Medical Mfg Corp .... E 845 369-7535
  Suffern *(G-15184)*
Jakes Sneakers Inc 718 233-1132
  Brooklyn *(G-2033)*
Wayne Decorators Inc .... G 718 529-4200
  Jamaica *(G-6690)*

CUSTOM COMPOUNDING OF RUBBER MATERIALS

Pawling Corporation .... C 845 855-1000
  Pawling *(G-12893)*
Tire Conversion Tech Inc .... E 518 372-1600
  Latham *(G-7093)*

CUT STONE & STONE PRODUCTS

Alart Inc .... G 212 840-1508
  New York *(G-8782)*
Barra & Trumbore Inc 845 626-5442
  Kerhonkson *(G-6867)*
Busch Products Inc .... E 315 474-8422
  Syracuse *(G-15264)*
Crown Hill Stone Inc .... E 716 326-4601
  Westfield *(G-16393)*
Denton Stoneworks Inc .... F 516 746-1500
  Garden City Park *(G-5285)*
Devonian Stone New York Inc .... F 607 655-2600
  Windsor *(G-16604)*
European Marble Works Co Inc .... F 718 387-9778
  Garden City *(G-5259)*
First Presbyterian Church 315 252-3861
  Auburn *(G-479)*
Fordham Marble Co Inc .... F 914 682-6699
  White Plains *(G-16451)*
Hilltop Slate Inc .... E 518 642-1453
  Middle Granville *(G-8110)*
Masonville Stone Incorporated .... G 607 265-3597
  Masonville *(G-7815)*
Pallette Stone Corporation .... E 518 584-2421
  Gansevoort *(G-5244)*
Sanford Stone LLC .... E 607 467-1313
  Deposit *(G-4109)*
Seneca Stone Corporation .... F 315 549-8253
  Fayette *(G-4926)*
Seneca Stone Corporation .... G 607 737-6200
  Pine City *(G-13001)*
Vermont Structural Slate Co .... F 518 499-1912
  Whitehall *(G-16525)*
W F Saunders & Sons Inc 315 469-3217
  Nedrow *(G-8480)*

CUTLERY

Advanced Machine Design Co Inc ..... E 716 826-2000
  Buffalo *(G-2689)*
Korin Japanese Trading Corp .... E 212 587-7021
  New York *(G-10471)*
Lifetime Brands Inc .... B 516 683-6000
  Garden City *(G-5265)*
Novelty Crystal Corp .... D 718 458-6700
  Long Island City *(G-7540)*
Oneida International Inc 315 361-3000
  Oneida *(G-12615)*
Oneida Silversmiths Inc .... G 315 361-3000
  Oneida *(G-12619)*
Schilling Forge Inc .... E 315 454-4421
  Syracuse *(G-15417)*

PRODUCT SECTION

DAIRY PRDTS: Frozen Desserts & Novelties

Servotronics Inc..................................C...... 716 655-5990
  Elma (G-4458)
Sherrill Manufacturing Inc..................C...... 315 280-0727
  Sherrill (G-14822)
Warren Cutlery Corp...........................F...... 845 876-3444
  Rhinebeck (G-13490)
Woods Knife Corporation....................E...... 516 798-4972
  Massapequa (G-7888)

CUTLERY WHOLESALERS

Utica Cutlery Company.......................D...... 315 733-4663
  Utica (G-15737)
Warren Cutlery Corp...........................F...... 845 876-3444
  Rhinebeck (G-13490)

CUTOUTS: Cardboard, Die-Cut, Made From Purchased Materials

Lion Die-Cutting Co Inc......................E...... 718 383-8841
  Brooklyn (G-2127)

CUTOUTS: Distribution

Junior Achevement of Eastrn NY.......G...... 518 783-4336
  Latham (G-7076)
Product Station Inc.............................F...... 516 942-4220
  Jericho (G-6796)

CUTTING SVC: Paper, Exc Die-Cut

A-1 Products Inc..................................G...... 718 789-1818
  Brooklyn (G-1462)
J Mackenzie Ltd..................................E...... 585 321-1770
  Rochester (G-13888)

CYCLIC CRUDES & INTERMEDIATES

Chemours Company Fc LLC................E...... 716 278-5100
  Niagara Falls (G-12271)
Durez Corporation...............................F...... 716 286-0100
  Niagara Falls (G-12279)
Micro Powders Inc...............................E...... 914 332-6400
  Tarrytown (G-15483)
Mitsui Chemicals America Inc...........D...... 914 253-0777
  Rye Brook (G-14493)
Premier Brands of America Inc.........E...... 718 325-3000
  Mount Vernon (G-8433)

CYLINDER & ACTUATORS: Fluid Power

A K Allen Co Inc..................................C...... 516 747-5450
  Melville (G-7996)
Ameritool Mfg Inc................................E...... 315 668-2172
  Central Square (G-3390)
ITT Enidine Inc.....................................B...... 716 662-1900
  Orchard Park (G-12720)
Precision Mechanisms Corp..............E...... 516 333-5955
  Westbury (G-16366)
Triumph Actuation Systems LLC......D...... 516 378-0162
  Freeport (G-5188)
Young & Franklin Inc..........................D...... 315 457-3110
  Liverpool (G-7274)

CYLINDERS: Pressure

A K Allen Co Inc..................................C...... 516 747-5450
  Melville (G-7996)

DAIRY EQPT

Richard Stewart..................................G...... 518 632-5363
  Hartford (G-5741)

DAIRY PRDTS STORE: Cheese

Artisanal Brands Inc...........................E...... 914 441-3591
  Bronxville (G-1423)

DAIRY PRDTS STORE: Ice Cream, Packaged

Bleecker Pastry Tartufo Inc................G...... 718 937-9830
  Long Island City (G-7402)
Blue Marble Ice Cream LLC...............E...... 718 858-5551
  Brooklyn (G-1619)
Delicioso Coco Helado Inc................F...... 718 292-1930
  Bronx (G-1257)
Marvel Dairy Whip Inc........................G...... 516 889-4232
  Lido Beach (G-7148)

DAIRY PRDTS STORES

Crosswinds Farm & Creamery..........G...... 607 327-0363
  Ovid (G-12790)

DAIRY PRDTS WHOLESALERS: Fresh

HP Hood LLC.......................................C...... 315 363-3870
  Oneida (G-12611)
Upstate Niagara Coop Inc..................E...... 716 484-7178
  Jamestown (G-6759)

DAIRY PRDTS: Bakers' Cheese

P & F Bakers Inc.................................G...... 516 931-6821
  Hicksville (G-6120)

DAIRY PRDTS: Bottled Baby Formula

Infant Formula Laboratory Svc..........F...... 718 257-3000
  Brooklyn (G-2001)

DAIRY PRDTS: Butter

O-At-Ka Milk Products Coop Inc........B...... 585 343-0536
  Batavia (G-632)
Pure Ghee Inc.....................................G...... 718 224-7399
  Flushing (G-5041)
Vulto Creamery LLC............................G...... 607 865-7059
  Walton (G-15913)

DAIRY PRDTS: Canned Baby Formula

Danone Nutricia Early.........................E...... 914 872-8556
  White Plains (G-16441)

DAIRY PRDTS: Cheese

Castelli America LLC..........................D...... 716 782-2101
  Ashville (G-415)
Emkay Trading Corp............................G...... 914 592-9000
  Elmsford (G-4541)
Emkay Trading Corp............................E...... 585 492-3800
  Arcade (G-382)
Empire Cheese Inc.............................C...... 585 968-1552
  Cuba (G-3919)
F Cappiello Dairy Pdts Inc..................E...... 518 374-5064
  Schenectady (G-14674)
Fly Creek Cder Mill Orchrd Inc..........G...... 607 547-9692
  Fly Creek (G-5064)
Friendship Dairies LLC.......................C...... 585 973-3031
  Friendship (G-5210)
Gharana Industries LLC......................G...... 315 651-4004
  Waterloo (G-15994)
Great Lakes Cheese NY Inc..............D...... 315 232-4511
  Adams (G-3)
HP Hood LLC.......................................D...... 607 295-8134
  Arkport (G-399)
Hudson Valley Creamery LLC...........F...... 518 851-2570
  Hudson (G-6356)
Instantwhip of Buffalo Inc..................E...... 716 892-7031
  Buffalo (G-2885)
Kraft Heinz Foods Company..............B...... 315 376-6575
  Lowville (G-7651)
Kraft Heinz Foods Company..............B...... 607 527-4584
  Campbell (G-3204)
Kraft Heinz Foods Company..............C...... 607 865-7131
  Walton (G-15911)
Mondelez Global LLC.........................G...... 845 567-4701
  Newburgh (G-12234)
Mozzarella Fresca Incorporated.......G...... 559 752-4823
  Buffalo (G-2954)
Rainbeau Ridge Farm........................G...... 914 234-2197
  Bedford Hills (G-779)
Wny Cheese Enterprise LLC.............E...... 585 243-6516
  Pavilion (G-12890)

DAIRY PRDTS: Cheese, Cottage

Garelick Farms LLC............................C...... 518 283-0820
  East Greenbush (G-4229)
HP Hood LLC.......................................D...... 607 295-8134
  Arkport (G-399)

DAIRY PRDTS: Concentrated Skim Milk

O-At-Ka Milk Products Coop Inc........B...... 585 343-0536
  Batavia (G-632)

DAIRY PRDTS: Cream Substitutes

Sugar Foods Corporation...................E...... 212 753-6900
  New York (G-11734)

DAIRY PRDTS: Cream, Sweet

Emkay Trading Corp............................E...... 585 492-3800
  Arcade (G-382)

HP Hood LLC.......................................D...... 315 829-3339
  Vernon (G-15805)

DAIRY PRDTS: Dairy Based Desserts, Frozen

Chobani Idaho LLC..............................G...... 208 432-2248
  Norwich (G-12482)
Indulge Desserts Holdings LLC..........G...... 212 231-8600
  New York (G-10201)
Sweet Melodys LLC............................E...... 716 580-3227
  East Amherst (G-4192)

DAIRY PRDTS: Dietary Supplements, Dairy & Non-Dairy Based

America Health Corp..........................G...... 800 860-1868
  New York (G-8821)
Century Tom Inc..................................G...... 347 654-3179
  Jamaica (G-6632)
Dynatabs LLC......................................F...... 718 376-6084
  Brooklyn (G-1801)
El-Gen LLC...G...... 631 218-3400
  Bohemia (G-1021)
GNI Commerce Inc.............................G...... 347 275-1155
  Brooklyn (G-1935)
Vitakem Nutraceutical Inc..................C...... 631 956-8343
  Smithtown (G-14911)

DAIRY PRDTS: Dips & Spreads, Cheese Based

East Hill Creamery LLC......................G...... 585 237-3622
  Perry (G-12968)
Lumazu LLC...G...... 518 623-3372
  Warrensburg (G-15940)
Lumazu LLC...F...... 518 623-3372
  Warrensburg (G-15941)
Taam Tov Foods Inc............................G...... 718 788-8880
  Brooklyn (G-2551)

DAIRY PRDTS: Dried & Powdered Milk & Milk Prdts

Hain Celestial Group Inc....................C...... 516 587-5000
  New Hyde Park (G-8538)

DAIRY PRDTS: Evaporated Milk

Nestle Usa Inc.....................................C...... 914 272-4021
  White Plains (G-16479)
Nestle Usa Inc.....................................C...... 212 688-2490
  New York (G-10910)

DAIRY PRDTS: Farmers' Cheese

Dwyer Farm LLC..................................G...... 914 456-2742
  Walden (G-15893)

DAIRY PRDTS: Fermented & Cultured Milk Prdts

Crowley Foods Inc..............................E...... 800 637-0019
  Binghamton (G-877)
HP Hood LLC.......................................A...... 607 772-6580
  Binghamton (G-890)
Kong Kee Food Corp..........................E...... 718 937-2746
  Long Island City (G-7490)
Kraft Heinz Foods Company..............C...... 607 865-7131
  Walton (G-15911)
Upstate Niagara Coop Inc..................D...... 716 892-3156
  Buffalo (G-3113)

DAIRY PRDTS: Frozen Desserts & Novelties

Ample Hills Creamery Inc..................E...... 347 725-4061
  Brooklyn (G-1531)
Ample Hills Creamery Inc..................E...... 718 809-1678
  Brooklyn (G-1532)
Ample Hills Holdings Inc....................E...... 347 725-4061
  Brooklyn (G-1533)
Blue Pig Ice Cream Factory...............G...... 914 271-3850
  Croton On Hudson (G-3912)
Carols Polar Parlor.............................G...... 315 468-3404
  Syracuse (G-15270)
Crepini LLC..E...... 347 422-0829
  Brooklyn (G-1730)
Crowley Foods Inc..............................E...... 800 637-0019
  Binghamton (G-877)
Df Mavens Inc.....................................E...... 347 813-4705
  Astoria (G-424)
Ffc Holding Corp Subsidiaries..........F...... 716 366-5400
  Dunkirk (G-4170)

Employee Codes: A=Over 500 employees, B=251-500
C=101-250, D=51-100, E=20-50, F=10-19, G=5-9

DAIRY PRDTS: Frozen Desserts & Novelties

Fresh Ice Cream Company LLC..............F...... 347 603-6021
  Brooklyn (G-1908)
HP Hood LLC..D...... 315 829-3339
  Vernon (G-15805)
HP Hood LLC..A...... 607 772-6580
  Binghamton (G-890)
Jones Humdinger......................................F...... 607 771-6501
  Binghamton (G-900)
Kan Pak LLC..G...... 620 440-2319
  Penn Yan (G-12961)
Kozy Shack Enterprises LLC..................C...... 516 870-3000
  Hicksville (G-6100)
LArte Del Gelato Gruppo Inc...................F...... 718 383-6600
  Long Island City (G-7496)
Lickity Splits..G...... 585 345-6091
  Batavia (G-629)
Macadoodles..G...... 607 652-9019
  Stamford (G-15031)
Main Street Sweets..................................F...... 914 332-5757
  Tarrytown (G-15480)
Ninas Custard...E...... 716 636-0345
  Getzville (G-5350)
Nutrifast LLC..G...... 347 671-3181
  New York (G-11010)
Phyljohn Distributors Inc.........................F...... 518 459-2775
  Albany (G-115)
Quaker Bonnet Inc...................................G...... 716 885-7208
  Buffalo (G-3024)
Ralphs Famous Italian Ices....................G...... 718 605-5052
  Staten Island (G-15123)
Ralphs Ices of Levittown.........................F...... 516 520-0618
  Oceanside (G-12553)
Tia Lattrell..G...... 845 373-9494
  Amenia (G-207)
Unilever United States Inc......................G...... 212 546-0200
  New York (G-11944)
Unilever United States Inc......................G...... 212 546-0200
  New York (G-11945)
Van Leeuwen Artisan Ice Cream............G...... 718 701-1630
  Brooklyn (G-2616)
Wicked Spoon Inc....................................F...... 646 335-2890
  New York (G-12107)

DAIRY PRDTS: Ice Cream & Ice Milk

MSQ Corporation......................................G...... 718 465-0900
  Queens Village (G-13411)
Stewarts Processing Corp......................D...... 518 581-1200
  Ballston Spa (G-597)
Stewarts Shops Corp...............................F...... 518 499-9376
  Whitehall (G-16524)
TLC-Lc Inc..E...... 212 756-8900
  New York (G-11852)
Vanilla Sky LLC..G...... 347 738-4195
  Long Island City (G-7628)
Washburns Dairy Inc...............................E...... 518 725-0629
  Gloversville (G-5472)

DAIRY PRDTS: Ice Cream, Bulk

Bleecker Pastry Tartufo Inc....................G...... 718 937-9830
  Long Island City (G-7402)
Blue Marble Ice Cream LLC...................G...... 718 858-5551
  Brooklyn (G-1619)
Delicioso Coco Helado Inc.....................F...... 718 292-1930
  Bronx (G-1257)
Fieldbrook Foods Corporation..............B...... 716 366-5400
  Dunkirk (G-4171)
G Pesso & Sons Inc.................................G...... 718 224-9130
  Bayside (G-746)
Grom Columbus LLC...............................G...... 212 974-3444
  New York (G-9995)
Ice Cream Man Inc...................................E...... 518 692-8382
  Greenwich (G-5642)
La Cremeria..G...... 212 226-6758
  New York (G-10500)
Macedonia Ltd...F...... 718 462-3596
  Brooklyn (G-2149)
Marina Ice Cream.....................................G...... 718 235-3000
  Brooklyn (G-2168)
Marvel Dairy Whip Inc.............................G...... 516 889-4232
  Lido Beach (G-7148)
Paleteria Fernandez Inc..........................F...... 914 315-1598
  Mamaroneck (G-7752)
Paleteria Fernandez Inc..........................G...... 914 939-3694
  Port Chester (G-13206)
Perrys Ice Cream Company Inc.............B...... 716 542-5492
  Akron (G-21)
Piazzas Ice Cream Ice Hse Inc..............F...... 718 818-8811
  Staten Island (G-15115)
Purity Ice Cream Co Inc..........................F...... 607 272-1545
  Ithaca (G-6607)

Quality Dairy Farms Inc..........................E...... 315 942-2611
  Boonville (G-1120)
Scoops R US Incorporated.....................G...... 212 730-7959
  New York (G-11521)
Smartys Corner..G...... 607 239-5276
  Endicott (G-4610)
Victory Garden...G...... 212 206-7273
  New York (G-12029)

DAIRY PRDTS: Ice Cream, Packaged, Molded, On Sticks, Etc.

Beyond Better Foods LLC......................G...... 212 888-1120
  Bronx (G-1228)
Byrne Dairy Inc...B...... 315 475-2121
  La Fayette (G-6946)

DAIRY PRDTS: Milk, Condensed & Evaporated

Alpina Foods Inc......................................F...... 855 886-1914
  Batavia (G-609)
Friendship Dairies LLC...........................C...... 585 973-3031
  Friendship (G-5210)
FriesIndcmpina Ingrdnts N Amer...........E...... 607 746-0196
  Delhi (G-4074)
Kerry Bfnctnal Ingredients Inc...............D...... 608 363-1200
  Norwich (G-12488)
Nationwide Dairy Inc..............................G...... 347 689-8148
  Brooklyn (G-2247)
Rich Products Corporation....................A...... 716 878-8000
  Buffalo (G-3037)
Solivaira Specialties Inc.........................D...... 716 693-4009
  North Tonawanda (G-12452)

DAIRY PRDTS: Milk, Fluid

Dairy Farmers America Inc....................D...... 585 409-2200
  Batavia (G-622)
Finger Lakes Cheese Trail......................F...... 607 857-5726
  Odessa (G-12567)
HP Hood LLC..C...... 315 363-3870
  Oneida (G-12611)
HP Hood LLC..B...... 315 658-2132
  La Fargeville (G-6942)
HP Hood LLC..B...... 518 218-9097
  Schenectady (G-14688)
Instantwhip of Buffalo Inc.......................E...... 716 892-7031
  Buffalo (G-2885)
Kesso Foods Inc......................................G...... 718 777-5303
  East Elmhurst (G-4222)
Kraft Heinz Foods Company...................B...... 607 527-4584
  Campbell (G-3204)
O-At-Ka Milk Products Coop Inc............B...... 585 343-0536
  Batavia (G-632)
Purity Ice Cream Co Inc..........................F...... 607 272-1545
  Ithaca (G-6607)
Stewarts Processing Corp......................D...... 518 581-1200
  Ballston Spa (G-597)
Upstate Niagara Coop Inc......................D...... 315 389-5111
  North Lawrence (G-12393)
Upstate Niagara Coop Inc......................C...... 716 892-2121
  Buffalo (G-3114)

DAIRY PRDTS: Milk, Processed, Pasteurized, Homogenized/Btld

Byrne Dairy Inc...B...... 315 475-2121
  La Fayette (G-6946)
Dairy Farmers America Inc....................E...... 816 801-6440
  East Syracuse (G-4333)
Dean Foods Company.............................D...... 315 452-5001
  East Syracuse (G-4335)
Midland Farms Inc...................................D...... 518 436-7038
  Menands (G-8089)
Mountain Side Farms Inc.......................E...... 718 526-3442
  Jamaica (G-6664)
Saputo Dairy Foods Usa LLC.................D...... 607 746-2141
  Delhi (G-4075)
Steuben Foods Incorporated................C...... 716 655-4000
  Elma (G-4460)
Upstate Niagara Coop Inc......................D...... 585 458-1880
  Rochester (G-14193)
Upstate Niagara Coop Inc......................E...... 716 484-7178
  Jamestown (G-6759)
Wny Enterprise LLC................................G...... 585 243-6514
  Pavilion (G-12891)

DAIRY PRDTS: Natural Cheese

Agri-Mark Inc...D...... 518 497-6644
  Chateaugay (G-3426)
Artisanal Brands Inc...............................E...... 914 441-3591
  Bronxville (G-1423)
Cemac Foods Corp...................................F...... 914 835-0526
  Harrison (G-5724)
Crosswinds Farm & Creamery................G...... 607 327-0363
  Ovid (G-12790)
Euphrates Inc...D...... 518 762-3488
  Johnstown (G-6827)
Four Fat Fowl Inc.....................................F...... 518 733-5230
  Stephentown (G-15155)
Lactalis American Group Inc.................D...... 716 827-2622
  Buffalo (G-2916)
Lactalis American Group Inc.................B...... 716 823-6262
  Buffalo (G-2917)
Leprino Foods Company.........................C...... 570 888-9658
  Waverly (G-16067)
Losurdo Foods Inc..................................C...... 315 344-2444
  Heuvelton (G-6044)
Mongiello Sales Inc.................................E...... 845 436-4200
  Hurleyville (G-6466)
Original Hrkmer Cnty Chese Inc............D...... 315 895-7428
  Ilion (G-6477)
Pecoraro Dairy Products Inc..................F...... 718 388-2379
  Brooklyn (G-2308)
Sandvoss Farms LLC..............................G...... 585 297-7044
  East Bethany (G-4213)
Sargento Foods Inc.................................C...... 920 893-8484
  New York (G-11489)
Sorrento Lactalis Inc..............................G...... 716 823-6262
  Buffalo (G-3072)
World Cheese Co Inc...............................F...... 718 965-1700
  Brooklyn (G-2657)

DAIRY PRDTS: Processed Cheese

Habco Corp...E...... 631 789-1400
  Amityville (G-279)
HP Hood LLC..D...... 315 829-3339
  Vernon (G-15805)
Upstate Farms Cheese LLC...................C...... 607 527-4584
  Campbell (G-3205)

DAIRY PRDTS: Pudding Pops, Frozen

Allied Food Products Inc........................F...... 718 230-4227
  Brooklyn (G-1510)

DAIRY PRDTS: Sherbets, Dairy Based

Lumazu LLC..G...... 518 623-3372
  Warrensburg (G-15940)
Lumazu LLC..G...... 518 623-3372
  Warrensburg (G-15941)

DAIRY PRDTS: Spreads, Cheese

Noga Dairies Inc......................................F...... 516 293-5448
  Farmingdale (G-4837)

DAIRY PRDTS: Whipped Topping, Exc Frozen Or Dry Mix

Hanan Products Company Inc...............E...... 516 938-1000
  Hicksville (G-6094)

DAIRY PRDTS: Yogurt, Exc Frozen

Bliss Foods Inc..G...... 212 732-8888
  New York (G-9100)
Bliss Foods Inc..F...... 212 732-8888
  New York (G-9101)
Chobani LLC..C...... 607 337-1246
  Norwich (G-12481)
Chobani LLC..C...... 607 847-6181
  New Berlin (G-8487)
Currant Company LLC............................G...... 845 266-8999
  Staatsburg (G-15022)
Danone Us LLC..D...... 914 872-8400
  White Plains (G-16442)
Fage USA Dairy Industry Inc.................B...... 518 762-5912
  Johnstown (G-6828)
Fage USA Holdings..................................D...... 518 762-5912
  Johnstown (G-6829)
Maple Hill Creamery LLC........................E...... 518 758-7777
  Stuyvesant (G-15182)
Maple Hill Creamery LLC........................D...... 518 758-7777
  Kinderhook (G-6880)
Noga Dairies Inc......................................F...... 516 293-5448
  Farmingdale (G-4837)

PRODUCT SECTION   DENTAL EQPT & SPLYS: Sterilizers

Steuben Foods Incorporated ....F 718 291-3333
  Elma (G-4459)
Swirls Twirls Incorporated ....G 516 541-9400
  Massapequa (G-7887)
Twist It Top It ....F 718 793-8947
  Forest Hills (G-5081)
Whitney Foods Inc ....F 718 291-3333
  Jamaica (G-6691)
Yogolicious Inc ....G 914 236-3455
  Briarcliff Manor (G-1178)

DAIRY PRDTS: Yogurt, Frozen

NY Froyo LLC ....G 516 312-4588
  Deer Park (G-4020)
Swirl Bliss LLC ....G 516 867-9475
  North Baldwin (G-12368)

DATA PROCESSING & PREPARATION SVCS

Data Palette Info Svcs LLC ....D 718 433-1060
  Port Washington (G-13251)
Informa Solutions Inc ....E 516 543-3733
  New York (G-10212)
Rational Retention LLC ....E 518 489-3000
  Albany (G-123)
Relx Inc ....E 212 309-8100
  New York (G-11355)
Standard Anaiytics Io Inc ....G 917 882-5422
  New York (G-11691)

DATA PROCESSING SVCS

DP Murphy Co Inc ....D 631 673-9400
  Deer Park (G-3968)
Thomas Publishing Company LLC ......B 212 695-0500
  New York (G-11810)

DATABASE INFORMATION RETRIEVAL SVCS

Reuters Loan Pricing Corp ....D 212 833-9200
  New York (G-11374)

DECORATIVE WOOD & WOODWORK

A Van Hoek Woodworking Limited ......G 718 599-4388
  Brooklyn (G-1459)
Adams Interior Fabrications ....F 631 249-8282
  Massapequa (G-7878)
Andike Millwork Inc ....G 718 894-1796
  Maspeth (G-7821)
Art Essentials of New York ....G 845 368-1100
  Airmont (G-11)
Atelier Viollet Corp ....G 718 782-1727
  Brooklyn (G-1568)
Brooks Woodworking Inc ....F 914 666-2029
  Mount Kisco (G-8338)
Budd Woodwork Inc ....F 718 389-1110
  Brooklyn (G-1654)
Cabinet Shapes Corp ....F 718 784-6255
  Long Island City (G-7404)
Craz Woodworking Assoc Inc ....F 631 205-1890
  Bellport (G-801)
Daniel Demarco and Assoc Inc ....E 631 598-7000
  Amityville (G-271)
Di Fiore and Sons Custom Wdwkg .....F 718 278-1663
  Long Island City (G-7425)
Digital Fabrication Wkshp Inc ....G 518 249-6500
  Hudson (G-6346)
Ed Negron Fine Woodworking ....G 718 246-1016
  Brooklyn (G-1812)
Elephants Custom Furniture Inc ....D 917 509-3581
  Brooklyn (G-1826)
Furniture Dsign By Knossos Inc ....E 718 729-0404
  Woodside (G-16657)
Hennig Custom Woodwork Corp ....G 516 536-3460
  Oceanside (G-12540)
Innova Interiors Inc ....E 718 401-2122
  Bronx (G-1298)
Ivan Horning ....G 315 536-3028
  Penn Yan (G-12959)
Jeffrey John ....G 631 842-2850
  Amityville (G-291)
Jordache Woodworking Corp ....F 718 349-3733
  Brooklyn (G-2045)
K & B Woodworking Inc ....G 518 634-7253
  Cairo (G-3150)
M & R Woodworking & Finishing ....G 718 486-5480
  Brooklyn (G-2143)
McGraw Wood Products LLC ....E 607 836-6465
  Mc Graw (G-7928)
N Sketch Build Inc ....G 800 975-0597
  Fishkill (G-4950)
Northern Forest Pdts Co Inc ....G 315 942-6955
  Boonville (G-1118)
Pdj Components Inc ....E 845 469-9191
  Chester (G-3479)
Pella Corporation ....C 631 208-0710
  Calverton (G-3168)
Pgs Millwork Inc ....D 518 828-2608
  Hudson (G-6368)
Piccini Mnm Inc ....G 845 741-6770
  West Nyack (G-16279)
Prime Wood Products ....G 518 792-1407
  Queensbury (G-13438)
Richard Rothbard Inc ....G 845 355-2300
  Slate Hill (G-14885)
Windsor United Industries LLC ....E 607 655-3300
  Windsor (G-16605)
Wood Innovations of Suffolk ....G 631 698-2345
  Medford (G-7969)
Woodmotif ....F 516 564-8325
  Hempstead (G-6028)
Woodtronics Inc ....G 914 962-5205
  Yorktown Heights (G-16825)

DEFENSE SYSTEMS & EQPT

Eastern Strategic Materials ....E 212 332-1619
  New York (G-9612)
UNI Source Technology ....F 514 748-8888
  Champlain (G-3415)

DEGREASING MACHINES

Cleaning Tech Group LLC ....E 716 665-2340
  Jamestown (G-6707)

DEHYDRATION EQPT

Purvi Enterprises Incorporated ....G 347 808-9448
  Maspeth (G-7868)

DELAY LINES

Allen Avionics Inc ....E 516 248-8080
  Mineola (G-8203)
Esc Control Electronics LLC ....E 631 467-5328
  Sayville (G-14627)

DENTAL EQPT

Boehm Surgical Instrument Corp ....F 585 436-6584
  Rochester (G-13671)
Brandt Equipment LLC ....G 718 994-0800
  Bronx (G-1232)
Buffalo Dental Mfg Co Inc ....E 516 496-7200
  Syosset (G-15210)
J H M Engineering ....E 718 871-1810
  Brooklyn (G-2023)
Kay See Dental Mfg Co ....F 816 842-2817
  New York (G-10421)
Lucas Dental Equipment Co Inc ....F 631 244-2807
  Bohemia (G-1052)

DENTAL EQPT & SPLYS

Air Techniques Inc ....B 516 433-7676
  Melville (G-8000)
Avalonbay Communities Inc ....E 516 484-7766
  Glen Cove (G-5362)
Cmp Export Co Inc ....E 518 434-3147
  Albany (G-61)
Cmp Industries LLC ....E 518 434-3147
  Albany (G-62)
Columbia Dentoform Corporation ......D 718 482-1569
  Long Island City (G-7414)
Crosstex International Inc ....D 631 582-6777
  Hauppauge (G-5805)
Crosstex International Inc ....F 631 582-6777
  Hauppauge (G-5806)
Cynosure Inc ....G 516 594-3333
  Hicksville (G-6078)
Darby Dental Supply ....G 516 688-6421
  Jericho (G-6785)
Dedeco International Sales Inc ....E 845 887-4840
  Long Eddy (G-7361)
DenTek Oral Care Inc ....D 865 983-1300
  Tarrytown (G-15477)
Glaxosmithkline LLC ....D 518 239-6901
  East Durham (G-4216)
Henry Schein Fincl Svcs LLC ....G 631 843-5500
  Melville (G-8030)
Impladent Ltd ....E 718 465-1810
  Jamaica (G-6651)
JM Murray Center Inc ....C 607 756-9913
  Cortland (G-3879)
JM Murray Center Inc ....C 607 756-0246
  Cortland (G-3880)
Lelab Dental Laboratory Inc ....G 516 561-5050
  Valley Stream (G-15785)
Light Dental Labs Inc ....G 516 785-7730
  Massapequa (G-7881)
Luitpold Pharmaceuticals Inc ....E 631 924-4000
  Shirley (G-14839)
Mini-Max Dntl Repr Eqpmnts Inc ....G 631 242-0322
  Deer Park (G-4010)
Oramaax Dental Products Inc ....F 516 771-8514
  Freeport (G-5172)
Precision Dental Ceramics of B ....F 716 681-4133
  Bowmansville (G-1122)
Professional Manufacturers ....F 631 586-2440
  Deer Park (G-4030)
Schilling Forge Inc ....E 315 454-4421
  Syracuse (G-15417)
Temrex Corporation ....E 516 868-6221
  Freeport (G-5186)
Tiger Supply Inc ....G 631 293-2700
  Farmingdale (G-4895)
Total Dntl Implant Sltions LLC ....G 212 877-3777
  Valley Stream (G-15800)
Valplast International Corp ....F 516 442-3923
  Westbury (G-16385)

DENTAL EQPT & SPLYS WHOLESALERS

Impladent Ltd ....E 718 465-1810
  Jamaica (G-6651)
Oramaax Dental Products Inc ....F 516 771-8514
  Freeport (G-5172)

DENTAL EQPT & SPLYS: Cabinets

Precision Dental Cabinets Inc ....F 631 543-3870
  Smithtown (G-14906)
Stylecraft Interiors Inc ....F 516 487-2133
  Great Neck (G-5594)

DENTAL EQPT & SPLYS: Compounds

Lornamead Inc ....D 716 874-7190
  New York (G-10611)

DENTAL EQPT & SPLYS: Cutting Instruments

Smile Specialists ....G 877 337-6135
  New York (G-11623)

DENTAL EQPT & SPLYS: Dental Materials

Grasers Dental Ceramics ....G 716 649-5100
  Orchard Park (G-12717)
Marotta Dental Studio Inc ....E 631 249-7520
  Farmingdale (G-4816)
Safe-Dent Enterprises LLC ....G 845 362-0141
  Monsey (G-8296)

DENTAL EQPT & SPLYS: Enamels

Gallery 57 Dental ....E 212 246-8700
  New York (G-9877)
Gan Kavod Inc ....G 315 797-3114
  New Hartford (G-8505)
Jeffrey D Menoff ....F 716 665-1468
  Jamestown (G-6733)

DENTAL EQPT & SPLYS: Laboratory

Cmp Industries LLC ....G 518 434-3147
  Albany (G-63)
Nu Life Restorations of L I ....D 516 489-5200
  Old Westbury (G-12591)

DENTAL EQPT & SPLYS: Orthodontic Appliances

Cettel Studio of New York Inc ....G 518 494-3622
  Chestertown (G-3490)
Vincent Martino Dental Lab ....F 716 674-7800
  Buffalo (G-3119)

DENTAL EQPT & SPLYS: Sterilizers

Cpac Equipment Inc ....F 585 382-3223
  Leicester (G-7127)

Employee Codes: A=Over 500 employees, B=251-500
C=101-250, D=51-100, E=20-50, F=10-19, G=5-9

DENTAL EQPT & SPLYS: Teeth, Artificial, Exc In Dental Labs

PRODUCT SECTION

DENTAL EQPT & SPLYS: Teeth, Artificial, Exc In Dental Labs
Martins Dental Studio .... G 315 788-0800
  Watertown *(G-16026)*

DENTAL EQPT & SPLYS: Wax
Corning Rubber Company Inc .... F 631 738-0041
  Ronkonkoma *(G-14329)*

DENTISTS' OFFICES & CLINICS
Comprehensive Dental Tech .... G 607 467-4456
  Hancock *(G-5711)*
Marotta Dental Studio Inc .... E 631 249-7520
  Farmingdale *(G-4816)*

DEODORANTS: Personal
Procter & Gamble Company .... C 646 885-4201
  New York *(G-11254)*

DEPILATORIES, COSMETIC
LOreal Usa Inc .... E 212 389-4201
  New York *(G-10608)*
Shop Sky Inc .... F 347 686-4616
  South Richmond Hill *(G-14947)*

DERMATOLOGICALS
Skincare Products Inc .... G 917 837-5255
  New York *(G-11609)*

DERRICKS: Oil & Gas Field
Derrick Corporation .... B 716 685-4892
  Cheektowaga *(G-3440)*

DESALTER KITS: Sea Water
Luxfer Magtech Inc .... D 631 727-8600
  Riverhead *(G-13576)*

DESIGN SVCS, NEC
1 Atelier LLC .... G 917 916-2968
  New York *(G-8664)*
A To Z Media Inc .... E 212 260-0237
  New York *(G-8699)*
Acad Design Corp .... F 585 254-6960
  Rochester *(G-13594)*
Holland & Sherry Inc .... E 212 542-8410
  New York *(G-10115)*
International Direct Group Inc .... E 212 921-9036
  New York *(G-10246)*
Internodal International Inc .... E 631 765-0037
  Southold *(G-14969)*
Jinglebell Inc .... G 914 219-5395
  Armonk *(G-406)*
Leo D Bernstein & Sons Inc .... E 212 337-9578
  New York *(G-10548)*
Linita Design & Mfg Corp .... E 716 566-7753
  Lackawanna *(G-6949)*
Northern Design & Bldg Assoc .... E 518 747-2200
  Queensbury *(G-13435)*
Peerless Instrument Co Inc .... C 631 396-6500
  Farmingdale *(G-4845)*
Polymag Tek Inc .... F 585 235-8390
  Rochester *(G-14026)*
Skincare Products Inc .... G 917 837-5255
  New York *(G-11609)*
Twcc Product and Sales .... E 212 614-9364
  New York *(G-11917)*

DESIGN SVCS: Commercial & Indl
New Dimensions Research Corp .... C 631 694-1356
  Melville *(G-8049)*
Precision Systems Mfg Inc .... E 315 451-3480
  Liverpool *(G-7257)*
Prim Hall Enterprises Inc .... F 518 561-7408
  Plattsburgh *(G-13150)*
Riverwood Signs By Dandev Desi .... G 845 229-0282
  Hyde Park *(G-6471)*
Voss Manufacturing Inc .... D 716 731-5062
  Sanborn *(G-14557)*

DESIGN SVCS: Computer Integrated Systems
331 Holding Inc .... E 585 924-1740
  Victor *(G-15827)*

Cisco Systems Inc .... C 212 714-4000
  New York *(G-9304)*
Informa Solutions Inc .... E 516 543-3733
  New York *(G-10212)*
Innovative Systems of New York .... G 516 541-7410
  Massapequa Park *(G-7892)*
Kld Labs Inc .... E 631 549-4222
  Hauppauge *(G-5857)*
Performance Technologies Inc .... E 585 256-0200
  Rochester *(G-14012)*
Siemens Industry Inc .... E 716 568-0983
  Buffalo *(G-3065)*

DESIGN SVCS: Shoe
Soludos LLC .... F 212 219-1101
  New York *(G-11642)*

DETECTION APPARATUS: Electronic/Magnetic Field, Light/Heat
Sensormatic Electronics LLC .... F 845 365-3125
  Orangeburg *(G-12691)*
Sentry Technology Corporation .... E 631 739-2000
  Ronkonkoma *(G-14410)*
Sentry Technology Corporation .... F 800 645-4224
  Ronkonkoma *(G-14411)*

DIAGNOSTIC SUBSTANCES
Bella International Inc .... G 716 484-0102
  Jamestown *(G-6700)*
Biochemical Diagnostics Inc .... E 631 595-9200
  Edgewood *(G-4397)*
Biopool Us Inc .... G 716 483-3851
  Jamestown *(G-6701)*
Chembio Diagnostic Systems Inc .... C 631 924-1135
  Medford *(G-7941)*
Chembio Diagnostics Inc .... C 631 924-1135
  Medford *(G-7942)*
Clark Laboratories Inc .... F 716 483-3851
  Jamestown *(G-6706)*
Danisco US Inc .... D 585 256-5200
  Rochester *(G-13733)*
E-Z-Em Inc .... E 609 524-2864
  Melville *(G-8018)*
Enzo Life Sciences Inc .... E 631 694-7070
  Farmingdale *(G-4760)*
Immco Diagnostics Inc .... G 716 691-0091
  Buffalo *(G-2881)*
Kannalife Sciences Inc .... G 516 669-3219
  Lloyd Harbor *(G-7280)*
Lesanne Life Sciences LLC .... G 914 234-0860
  Bedford *(G-770)*
Lifelink Monitoring Corp .... F 845 336-2098
  Bearsville *(G-764)*
Petnet Solutions Inc .... G 865 218-2000
  New York *(G-11171)*
Siemens Hlthcare Dgnostics Inc .... E 914 631-0475
  Tarrytown *(G-15492)*
US Diagnostics Inc .... E 866 216-5308
  New York *(G-11975)*
Welch Allyn Inc .... A 315 685-4100
  Skaneateles Falls *(G-14883)*

DIAGNOSTIC SUBSTANCES OR AGENTS: Blood Derivative
Lifescan Inc .... B 516 557-2693
  Wantagh *(G-15923)*
Ortho-Clinical Diagnostics Inc .... E 716 631-1281
  Williamsville *(G-16582)*
Ortho-Clinical Diagnostics Inc .... E 585 453-3000
  Rochester *(G-13995)*

DIAGNOSTIC SUBSTANCES OR AGENTS: In Vivo
Ken-Ton Open Mri PC .... G 716 876-7000
  Kenmore *(G-6863)*

DIAGNOSTIC SUBSTANCES OR AGENTS: Microbiology & Virology
Tiziana Therapeutics Inc .... G 646 396-4970
  New York *(G-11851)*
Ufc Biotechnology .... G 716 777-3776
  Amherst *(G-258)*

DIAGNOSTIC SUBSTANCES OR AGENTS: Veterinary
Gotham Veterinary Center PC .... E 212 222-1900
  New York *(G-9961)*

DIAMOND MINING SVCS: Indl
Romance & Co Inc .... G 212 382-0337
  New York *(G-11427)*
Signature Diamond Entps LLC .... E 212 869-5115
  New York *(G-11587)*

DIAMOND SETTER SVCS
Crystal Ceres Industries Inc .... D 716 283-0445
  Niagara Falls *(G-12275)*

DIAMONDS, GEMS, WHOLESALE
Antwerp Diamond Distributors .... F 212 319-3300
  New York *(G-8879)*
David Weisz & Sons USA LLC .... G 212 840-4747
  New York *(G-9487)*
Diamex Inc .... E 212 575-8145
  New York *(G-9520)*
Diamond Constellation Corp .... G 212 819-0324
  New York *(G-9521)*
E Schreiber Inc .... E 212 382-0280
  New York *(G-9597)*
Eugene Biro Corp .... E 212 997-0146
  New York *(G-9726)*
Fine Cut Diamonds Corporation .... G 212 575-8780
  New York *(G-9803)*
Fischler Diamonds Inc .... E 212 921-8196
  New York *(G-9811)*
Forever Grown Diamonds Inc .... G 212 354-2827
  New York *(G-9823)*
Global Gem Corporation .... G 212 350-9936
  New York *(G-9941)*
Gold & Diamonds Wholesale Outl .... G 718 438-7888
  Brooklyn *(G-1937)*
Herkimer Diamond Mines Inc .... E 315 891-7355
  Herkimer *(G-6041)*
Leo Schachter & Co Inc .... D 212 688-2000
  New York *(G-10551)*
Miller & Veit Inc .... E 212 247-2275
  New York *(G-10810)*
Romance & Co Inc .... G 212 382-0337
  New York *(G-11427)*
Rosy Blue Inc .... E 212 687-8838
  New York *(G-11435)*
T M W Diamonds Mfg Co .... G 212 869-8444
  New York *(G-11769)*
United Gemdiam Inc .... E 718 851-5083
  Brooklyn *(G-2602)*
Waldman Alexander M Diamond Co .... E 212 921-8098
  New York *(G-12065)*

DIAMONDS: Cutting & Polishing
Ace Diamond Corp .... G 212 730-8231
  New York *(G-8725)*
Antwerp Diamond Distributors .... F 212 319-3300
  New York *(G-8879)*
Antwerp Sales Intl Inc .... F 212 354-6515
  New York *(G-8880)*
Baroka Creations Inc .... E 212 768-0527
  New York *(G-9019)*
Dialase Inc .... G 212 575-8833
  New York *(G-9519)*
Diamex Inc .... E 212 575-8145
  New York *(G-9520)*
Diamond Constellation Corp .... G 212 819-0324
  New York *(G-9521)*
Dresdiam Inc .... E 212 819-2217
  New York *(G-9575)*
E Schreiber Inc .... E 212 382-0280
  New York *(G-9597)*
Eugene Biro Corp .... E 212 997-0146
  New York *(G-9726)*
Fine Cut Diamonds Corporation .... G 212 575-8780
  New York *(G-9803)*
Fischler Diamonds Inc .... E 212 921-8196
  New York *(G-9811)*
Forever Grown Diamonds Inc .... G 212 354-2827
  New York *(G-9823)*
Guild Diamond Products Inc .... F 212 871-0007
  New York *(G-10007)*
Hershel Horowitz Corp .... G 212 719-1710
  New York *(G-10084)*

J A G Diamond Manufacturers ... G ... 212 575-0660
New York *(G-10284)*
Julius Klein Group ... E ... 212 719-1811
New York *(G-10376)*
Kaleko Bros ... G ... 212 819-0100
New York *(G-10397)*
Lazare Kaplan Intl Inc ... D ... 212 972-9700
New York *(G-10525)*
Levi Shabtai ... G ... 212 302-7393
New York *(G-10556)*
Miller & Veit Inc ... F ... 212 247-2275
New York *(G-10810)*
Precision Diamond Cutters Inc ... G ... 212 719-4438
Brooklyn *(G-2334)*
Shah Diamonds Inc ... F ... 212 888-9393
New York *(G-11553)*
T M W Diamonds Mfg Co ... G ... 212 869-8444
New York *(G-11769)*
United Gemdiam Inc ... E ... 718 851-5083
Brooklyn *(G-2602)*
Waldman Alexander M Diamond Co ... E ... 212 921-8098
New York *(G-12065)*
William Goldberg Diamond Corp ... E ... 212 980-4343
New York *(G-12110)*
Windiam Usa Inc ... G ... 212 542-0949
New York *(G-12117)*

DIAPERS: Cloth

Becks Classic Mfg Inc ... D ... 631 435-3800
Brentwood *(G-1128)*

DIAPERS: Disposable

Bentley Manufacturing Inc ... G ... 212 714-1800
New York *(G-9047)*
Mr Disposable Inc ... F ... 718 388-8574
Brooklyn *(G-2231)*

DIE CUTTING SVC: Paper

Able National Corp ... E ... 718 386-8801
Brooklyn *(G-1471)*

DIE SETS: Presses, Metal Stamping

Gay Sheet Metal Dies Inc ... G ... 716 877-0208
Buffalo *(G-2842)*

DIES & TOOLS: Special

Ace Specialty Co Inc ... G ... 716 874-3670
Tonawanda *(G-15518)*
All Out Die Cutting Inc ... E ... 718 346-6666
Brook'yn *(G-1508)*
Allstate Tool and Die Inc ... D ... 585 426-0400
Rochester *(G-13618)*
Amada Tool America Inc ... D ... 585 344-3900
Batavia *(G-610)*
Anka Tool & Die Inc ... E ... 845 268-4116
Congers *(G-3709)*
Arro Tool & Die Inc ... F ... 716 763-6203
Lakewood *(G-6990)*
Art Precision Metal Products ... F ... 631 842-8889
Copiague *(G-3752)*
Barron Metal Products Inc ... E ... 914 965-1232
Yonkers *(G-16738)*
Bel-Bee Products Incorporated ... F ... 845 353-0300
West Nyack *(G-16265)*
Bennett Die & Tool Inc ... E ... 607 739-5629
Horseheads *(G-6307)*
Brayley Tool & Machine Inc ... G ... 585 342-7190
Rochester *(G-13675)*
Brighton Tool & Die Designers ... F ... 716 876-0879
Tonawanda *(G-15530)*
Carbaugh Tool Company Inc ... E ... 607 739-3293
Elmira *(C-4475)*
Chamtek Mfg Inc ... F ... 585 328-4900
Rochester *(G-13707)*
Charles A Rogers Entps Inc ... E ... 585 924-6400
Victor *(G-15835)*
Cosmo Electronic Machine Corp ... E ... 631 249-2535
Farmingdale *(G-4739)*
Cuddeback Machining Inc ... G ... 585 392-5889
Hilton *(G-6156)*
Dependable Tool & Die Co Inc ... G ... 315 453-5696
Syracuse *(G-15305)*
Diemax of Rochester Inc ... G ... 585 288-3912
Rochester *(G-13740)*
Diemolding Corporation ... F ... 315 363-4710
Wampsville *(G-15918)*
Eden Tool & Die Inc ... G ... 716 992-4240
Eden *(G-4388)*
Electronic Die Corp ... F ... 718 455-3200
Brooklyn *(G-1821)*
Enhanced Tool Inc ... E ... 716 691-5200
Amherst *(G-225)*
Etna Tool & Die Corporation ... F ... 212 475-4350
New York *(G-9723)*
F M EDM Inc ... G ... 716 655-1784
East Aurora *(G-4200)*
Intri-Cut Inc ... F ... 716 691-5200
Amherst *(G-233)*
James Wire Die Co ... G ... 315 894-3233
Ilion *(G-6476)*
K D M Die Company Inc ... F ... 716 828-9000
Buffalo *(G-2900)*
Keyes Machine Works Inc ... G ... 585 426-5059
Gates *(G-5310)*
Long Island Tool & Die Inc ... G ... 631 225-0600
Copiague *(G-3767)*
M J M Tooling Corp ... G ... 718 292-3590
Bronx *(G-1320)*
Machinecraft Inc ... E ... 585 436-1070
Rochester *(G-13920)*
Magnus Precision Mfg Inc ... D ... 315 548-8032
Phelps *(G-12978)*
Mantel & Mantel Stamping Corp ... G ... 631 467-1916
Ronkonkoma *(G-14374)*
Manufacturers Tool & Die Co ... G ... 585 352-1080
Spencerport *(G-14981)*
May Tool & Die Inc ... G ... 716 695-1033
Tonawanda *(G-15557)*
Micron Inds Rochester Inc ... G ... 585 247-6130
Rochester *(G-13944)*
Ms Machining Inc ... G ... 607 723-1105
Binghamton *(G-907)*
Multifold Die Ctng Finshg Corp ... G ... 631 232-1235
Hauppauge *(G-5898)*
Mustang-Major Tool & Die Co ... G ... 716 992-9200
Eden *(G-4390)*
Niagara Punch & Die Corp ... G ... 716 896-7619
Buffalo *(G-2969)*
Nijon Tool Co Inc ... F ... 631 242-3434
Deer Park *(G-4016)*
P & R Industries Inc ... E ... 585 266-6725
Rochester *(G-14001)*
P & R Industries Inc ... F ... 585 544-1811
Rochester *(G-14002)*
P Tool & Die Co Inc ... E ... 585 889-1340
North Chili *(G-12382)*
Pacific Die Cast Inc ... F ... 845 778-6374
Walden *(G-15894)*
Palma Tool & Die Company Inc ... E ... 716 681-4464
Lancaster *(G-7035)*
Phelinger Tool & Die Corp ... G ... 716 685-1780
Alden *(G-174)*
Precision Grinding & Mfg Corp ... C ... 585 458-4300
Rochester *(G-14035)*
Precision Machining and Mfg ... G ... 845 647-5380
Wawarsing *(G-16069)*
Pronto Tool & Die Co Inc ... E ... 631 981-8920
Ronkonkoma *(G-14401)*
Raloid Tool Co Inc ... F ... 518 664-4261
Mechanicville *(G-7933)*
Rid Lom Precision Mfg ... E ... 585 594-8600
Rochester *(G-14072)*
Rochester Stampings Inc ... F ... 585 467-5241
Rochester *(G-14095)*
S B Whistler & Sons Inc ... E ... 585 798-3000
Medina *(G-7988)*
Stamp Rite Tool & Die Inc ... G ... 718 752-0334
Long Island City *(G-7597)*
Synergy Tooling Systems Inc ... E ... 716 834-4457
Amherst *(G-253)*
Thayer Tool & Die Inc ... F ... 716 782-4841
Ashville *(G-418)*
Tips & Dies Inc ... F ... 315 337-4161
Rome *(G-14275)*
Tools & Stamping Corp ... G ... 718 392-4040
Brooklyn *(G-2570)*
Trinity Tools Inc ... E ... 716 694-1111
North Tonawanda *(G-12460)*
Ultimate Prcision Met Pdts Inc ... C ... 631 249-9441
Farmingdale *(G-4901)*
Xli Corporation ... D ... 585 436-2250
Rochester *(G-14216)*

DIES: Cutting, Exc Metal

Royal Molds Inc ... F ... 718 382-7686
Brooklyn *(G-2422)*

DIES: Extrusion

D Maldari & Sons Inc ... E ... 718 499-3555
Brooklyn *(G-1747)*

DIES: Paper Cutting

Evergreen Corp Central NY ... F ... 315 454-4175
Syracuse *(G-15320)*

DIES: Plastic Forming

Alliance Precision Plas Corp ... C ... 585 426-5310
Rochester *(G-13616)*
Alliance Precision Plas Corp ... E ... 585 426-5310
Rochester *(G-13617)*
Quality Lineals Usa Inc ... E ... 516 378-6577
Freeport *(G-5177)*

DIES: Steel Rule

Dixon Tool and Manufacturing ... F ... 585 235-1352
Rochester *(G-13746)*
Dynamic Dies Inc ... F ... 585 247-4010
Rochester *(G-13754)*
Great Lakes Pressed Steel Corp ... E ... 716 885-4037
Buffalo *(G-2857)*
National Steel Rule Die Inc ... F ... 718 402-1396
Bronx *(G-1339)*
Paragon Steel Rule Dies Inc ... F ... 585 254-3395
Rochester *(G-14008)*

DIODES: Light Emitting

Acolyte Technologies Corp ... F ... 212 629-3239
New York *(G-8728)*
Data Display USA Inc ... C ... 631 218-2130
Holbrook *(G-6182)*
Emagin Corporation ... D ... 845 838-7900
Hopewell Junction *(G-6284)*
General Led Holdings LLC ... F ... 212 629-6830
New York *(G-9900)*
Green Logic Led Elec Sup Inc ... E ... 516 280-2854
Farmingdale *(G-4775)*
Hisun Optoelectronics Co Ltd ... F ... 718 886-6966
Flushing *(G-5008)*
Light Blue USA LLC ... G ... 718 475-2515
Brooklyn *(G-2119)*
Oledworks LLC ... E ... 585 287-6802
Rochester *(G-13985)*
S3j Electronics LLC ... E ... 716 206-1309
Lancaster *(G-7047)*
Tarsier Ltd ... C ... 646 880-8680
New York *(G-11785)*
Veriled Inc ... G ... 877 521-5520
New York *(G-12011)*

DIODES: Solid State, Germanium, Silicon, Etc

Leviton Manufacturing Co Inc ... B ... 631 812-6000
Melville *(G-8043)*
SMC Diode Solutions LLC ... G ... 631 965-0869
Plainview *(G-13088)*

DIRECT SELLING ESTABLISHMENTS: Beverage Svcs

Tao Group LLC ... G ... 646 625-4818
New York *(G-11781)*

DIRECT SELLING ESTABLISHMENTS: Food Svcs

New Dynamics Corporation ... E ... 845 692-0022
Middletown *(G-8167)*

DISCOUNT DEPARTMENT STORES

First Choice News Inc ... G ... 212 477-2044
New York *(G-9806)*

DISCS & TAPE: Optical, Blank

L & M Optical Disc LLC ... D ... 718 649-3500
New York *(G-10491)*
Sony Corporation of America ... C ... 212 833-8000
New York *(G-11645)*
Sony Dadc US Inc ... B ... 212 833-8800
New York *(G-11646)*

DISHWASHING EQPT: Commercial

Hobart Corporation .... E 585 427-9000
Rochester *(G-13871)*
Strategies North America Inc .... G 716 945-6053
Salamanca *(G-14534)*

DISINFECTING SVCS

Vital Vio Inc .... F 914 245-6048
Troy *(G-15632)*

DISK & DRUM DRIVES & COMPONENTS: Computers

Globalfoundries US Inc .... D 518 305-9013
Malta *(G-7730)*

DISK DRIVES: Computer

Formats Unlimited Inc .... F 631 249-9200
Deer Park *(G-3978)*
Sale 121 Corp .... D 240 855-8988
New York *(G-11467)*
Toshiba Amer Info Systems Inc .... B 949 583-3000
New York *(G-11871)*

DISPENSING EQPT & PARTS, BEVERAGE: Fountain/Other Beverage

Chudnow Manufacturing Co Inc .... E 516 593-4222
Oceanside *(G-12533)*
Klearbar Inc .... G 516 684-9892
Port Washington *(G-13277)*

DISPENSING EQPT & SYSTEMS, BEVERAGE: Liquor

Oyster Bay Pump Works Inc .... F 516 933-4500
Hicksville *(G-6119)*

DISPLAY CASES: Refrigerated

Mohawk Cabinet Company Inc .... F 518 725-0645
Gloversville *(G-5462)*

DISPLAY FIXTURES: Showcases, Wood, Exc Refrigerated

R H Guest Incorporated .... G 718 675-7600
Brooklyn *(G-2376)*

DISPLAY FIXTURES: Wood

All Merchandise Display Corp .... G 718 257-2221
Highland Mills *(G-6150)*
David Flatt Furniture Ltd .... F 718 937-7944
Long Island City *(G-7421)*
Gotham City Industries Inc .... E 914 713-0979
Scarsdale *(G-14638)*
Hunter Metal Industries Inc .... D 631 475-5900
East Patchogue *(G-4275)*
J M P Display Fixture Co Inc .... G 718 649-0333
Brooklyn *(G-2026)*
Marplex Furniture Corporation .... G 914 969-7755
Yonkers *(G-16783)*
Specialty Services .... G 585 728-5650
Wayland *(G-16072)*

DISPLAY ITEMS: Corrugated, Made From Purchased Materials

Calpac Incorporated .... F 631 789-0502
Amityville *(G-267)*
Displays & Beyond Inc .... F 718 805-7786
Glendale *(G-5398)*
General Die and Die Cutng Inc .... D 516 665-3584
Massapequa Park *(G-7890)*
Mp Displays LLC .... G 845 268-4113
Valley Cottage *(G-15760)*
Spaeth Design Inc .... G 718 606-9685
Woodside *(G-16677)*

DISPLAY STANDS: Merchandise, Exc Wood

Trylon Wire & Metal Works Inc .... E 718 542-4472
Bronx *(G-1409)*

DISTILLATES: Hardwood

Tioga Hardwoods Inc .... G 607 657-8686
Berkshire *(G-828)*

DOCK OPERATION SVCS, INCL BLDGS, FACILITIES, OPERS & MAINT

Kleinfelder John .... G 716 753-3163
Mayville *(G-7921)*

DOCKS: Floating, Wood

Meeco Sullivan LLC .... C 800 232-3625
Warwick *(G-15959)*

DOCKS: Prefabricated Metal

Guardian Booth LLC .... F 844 992-6684
Spring Valley *(G-14994)*
Metallic Ladder Mfg Corp .... F 716 358-6201
Randolph *(G-13448)*
T Shore Products Ltd .... G 315 252-9174
Auburn *(G-502)*

DOCUMENT EMBOSSING SVCS

Batavia Press LLC .... E 585 343-4429
Batavia *(G-612)*

DOLLIES: Mechanics'

Durall Dolly LLC .... F 802 728-7122
Brooklyn *(G-1796)*

DOLOMITE: Crushed & Broken

Dolomite Products Company Inc .... E 315 524-1998
Rochester *(G-13749)*

DOLOMITIC MARBLE: Crushed & Broken

Rock Iroquois Products Inc .... E 585 637-6834
Brockport *(G-1194)*
Tilcon New York Inc .... D 845 480-3249
Flushing *(G-5053)*
Tilcon New York Inc .... D 845 615-0216
Goshen *(G-5484)*
Tilcon New York Inc .... D 845 457-3158
Montgomery *(G-8318)*

DOMESTIC HELP SVCS

Custom Klean Corp .... F 315 865-8101
Holland Patent *(G-6224)*

DOOR & WINDOW REPAIR SVCS

Lif Industries Inc .... E 718 767-8800
Whitestone *(G-16545)*
United Steel Products Inc .... D 718 478-5330
Corona *(G-3856)*

DOOR OPERATING SYSTEMS: Electric

Assa Abloy Entrance Systems US ..... E 315 492-6600
East Syracuse *(G-4323)*
EZ Lift Operator Corp .... F 845 356-1676
Spring Valley *(G-14990)*
V E Power Door Co Inc .... E 631 231-4500
Brentwood *(G-1148)*
Windowman Inc (usa) .... G 718 246-2626
Brooklyn *(G-2652)*

DOORS & WINDOWS WHOLESALERS: All Materials

Pella Corporation .... C 631 208-0710
Calverton *(G-3168)*
Royal Windows Mfg Corp .... E 631 435-8888
Bay Shore *(G-718)*
Structural Wood Corporation .... E 315 388-4442
Waddington *(G-15882)*

DOORS & WINDOWS: Screen & Storm

I Fix Screen .... G 631 421-1938
Centereach *(G-3344)*
Optimum Window Mfg Corp .... E 845 647-1900
Ellenville *(G-4441)*

DOORS & WINDOWS: Storm, Metal

A & S Window Associates Inc .... E 718 275-7900
Glendale *(G-5389)*
Air Tite Manufacturing Inc .... C 516 897-0295
Long Beach *(G-7356)*
All United Window Corp .... E 718 624-0490
Brooklyn *(G-1509)*

DOORS: Dormers, Wood

Corkhill Manufacturing Co Inc .... G 718 528-7413
Jamaica *(G-6639)*
Excel Aluminum Products Inc .... G 315 471-0925
Syracuse *(G-15321)*
Karey Kassl Corp .... E 516 349-8484
Plainview *(G-13067)*
Pal Manufacturing Corp .... E 516 937-1990
Hicksville *(G-6122)*
Pioneer Window Holdings Inc .... F 516 822-7000
Hicksville *(G-6127)*
Pioneer Window Holdings Inc .... E 518 762-5526
Johnstown *(G-6837)*
Texas Home Security Inc .... E 516 747-2100
New Hyde Park *(G-8566)*

DOORS: Dormers, Wood

Dorm Company Corporation .... G 502 551-6195
Cheektowaga *(G-3441)*

DOORS: Fire, Metal

Ace Fire Door Corp .... E 718 901-0001
Bronx *(G-1209)*
Altype Fire Door Corporation .... G 718 292-3500
Bronx *(G-1218)*
General Fire-Proof Door Corp .... E 718 893-5500
Bronx *(G-1280)*
International Fireproof Door .... F 718 783-1310
Brooklyn *(G-2010)*
Lif Industries Inc .... E 718 767-8800
Whitestone *(G-16545)*
M & D Installers Inc .... D 718 782-6978
Brooklyn *(G-2141)*
Mercury Lock and Door Service .... E 718 542-7048
Bronx *(G-1327)*
Metalline Fire Door Co Inc .... E 718 583-2320
Bronx *(G-1328)*
Schwab Corp .... E 585 381-4900
Rochester *(G-14116)*
Statewide Fireproof Door Co .... F 845 268-6043
Valley Cottage *(G-15766)*
Supreme Fire Proof Door Co .... F 718 665-4224
Bronx *(G-1396)*
Universal Fire Proof Door .... E 718 455-8442
Brooklyn *(G-2607)*

DOORS: Folding, Plastic Or Plastic Coated Fabric

Custom Door & Mirror Inc .... E 631 414-7725
Farmingdale *(G-4745)*
Perma Tech Inc .... E 716 854-0707
Buffalo *(G-3000)*

DOORS: Garage, Overhead, Metal

Amarr Company .... F 585 426-8290
Rochester *(G-13622)*
Griffon Corporation .... E 212 957-5000
New York *(G-9988)*
L & L Overhead Garage Doors .... E 718 721-2518
Long Island City *(G-7494)*
Overhead Door Corporation .... D 518 828-7652
Hudson *(G-6366)*
Roly Door Sales Inc .... E 716 877-1515
Hamburg *(G-5694)*

DOORS: Garage, Overhead, Wood

Griffon Corporation .... E 212 957-5000
New York *(G-9988)*

DOORS: Glass

Executive Mirror Doors Inc .... G 631 234-1090
Ronkonkoma *(G-14340)*
Hecht & Sohn Glass Co Inc .... G 718 782-8295
Brooklyn *(G-1971)*
RB Wyatt Mfg Co Inc .... F 718 209-9682
Brooklyn *(G-2387)*

DOORS: Rolling, Indl Building Or Warehouse, Metal

American Steel Gate Corp .... G 718 291-4050
Jamaica *(G-6624)*
Robert-Masters Corp .... G 718 545-1030
Woodside *(G-16676)*
Steelmasters Inc .... E 718 498-2854
Brooklyn *(G-2518)*

PRODUCT SECTION

DRUGS ACTING ON THE CENTRAL NERVOUS SYSTEM & SENSE ORGANS

Thompson Overhead Door Co Inc .... F 718 788-2470
  Brooklyn *(G-2566)*
United Steel Products Inc .... D 914 968-7782
  Flushing *(G-5058)*

DOORS: Wooden

Ace Fire Door Corp .... E 718 901-0001
  Bronx *(G-1209)*
Burt Millwork Corporation .... E 718 257-4601
  Albertson *(G-147)*
Capital Kit Cab & Door Mfrs .... G 718 886-0303
  College Point *(G-3641)*
Chautauqua Woods Corporation .... E 716 366-3808
  Dunkirk *(G-4164)*
Cuccio-Zanetti Inc .... G 518 587-1363
  Middle Grove *(G-8115)*
D R Cornue Woodworks .... G 315 655-9463
  Cazenovia *(G-3318)*
Living Doors Inc .... F 631 924-5393
  Medford *(G-7958)*
Overhead Door Corporation .... D 518 828-7652
  Hudson *(G-6366)*
Quality Millwork Corp .... E 718 892-2250
  Bronx *(G-1369)*
Rj Millworkers Inc .... E 607 433-0525
  Oneonta *(G-12645)*
Rochester Lumber Company .... E 585 924-7171
  Farmington *(G-4919)*
Select Interior Door Ltd .... E 585 535-9900
  North Java *(G-12392)*
Yesteryears Vintage Doors LLC .... G 315 324-5250
  Hammond *(G-5701)*

DOWN FEATHERS

Eastern Feather & Down Corp .... G 718 387-4100
  Brooklyn *(G-1809)*

DRAPERIES & CURTAINS

Abalene Decorating Services .... E 718 782-2000
  New York *(G-8705)*
Associated Drapery & Equipment .... F 516 671-5245
  Monroe *(G-8263)*
Baby Signature Inc .... G 212 686-1700
  New York *(G-8996)*
Bettertex Inc .... F 212 431-3373
  New York *(G-9062)*
Bramson House Inc .... C 516 764-5006
  Freeport *(G-5146)*
C & G of Kingston Inc .... D 845 331-0148
  Kingston *(G-6890)*
Cabriole Designs Inc .... G 212 593-4528
  New York *(G-9174)*
J Edlin Interiors Ltd .... F 212 243-2111
  New York *(G-10285)*
Jo-Vin Decorators Inc .... E 718 441-9350
  Woodhaven *(G-16636)*
Laregence Inc .... E 212 736-2548
  New York *(G-10517)*
Majestic Curtains LLC .... G 718 898-0774
  Elmhurst *(G-4469)*
Mason Contract Products LLC .... D 516 328-6900
  New Hyde Park *(G-8550)*
Mistdoda Inc .... E 919 735-7111
  New York *(G-10824)*
Mutual Sales Corp .... E 718 361-8373
  Long Island City *(G-7530)*
Richloom Fabrics Corp .... F 212 685-5400
  New York *(G-11391)*
Richloom Fabrics Group Inc .... G 212 685-5400
  New York *(G-11392)*
Seaway Mats Inc .... G 518 483-2560
  Malone *(G-7726)*
Showeray Co .... D 718 965-3633
  Brooklyn *(G-2466)*
Shyam Ahuja Limited .... G 212 644-5910
  New York *(G-11573)*
Terbo Ltd .... G 718 847-2860
  Richmond Hill *(G-13516)*
White Workroom Inc .... G 212 941-5910
  New York *(G-12104)*

DRAPERIES & DRAPERY FABRICS, COTTON

Designway Ltd .... G 212 254-2220
  New York *(G-9509)*
Versailles Drapery Upholstery .... F 212 533-2059
  Long Island City *(G-7631)*
Wallace Home Design Ctr .... G 631 765-3890
  Southold *(G-14971)*

DRAPERIES: Plastic & Textile, From Purchased Materials

Anthony Lawrence of New York .... E 212 206-8820
  Long Island City *(G-7380)*
County Draperies Inc .... E 845 342-9009
  Middletown *(G-8144)*
Deangelis Ltd .... E 212 348-8225
  Glen Head *(G-5379)*
Fabric Quilters Unlimited Inc .... E 516 333-2866
  Westbury *(G-16330)*
Laminated Window Products Inc .... E 631 242-6883
  Bay Shore *(G-693)*
Revman International Inc .... E 212 894-3100
  New York *(G-11378)*
Reynolds Drapery Service Inc .... F 315 845-8632
  Newport *(G-12256)*
Wayne Decorators Inc .... E 718 529-4200
  Jamaica *(G-6690)*
Wcd Window Coverings Inc .... E 845 336-4511
  Lake Katrine *(G-6973)*

DRAPERY & UPHOLSTERY STORES: Draperies

Albert Menin Interiors Ltd .... F 212 876-3041
  Bronx *(G-1215)*
Reynolds Drapery Service Inc .... F 315 845-8632
  Newport *(G-12256)*
Versailles Drapery Upholstery .... F 212 533-2059
  Long Island City *(G-7631)*

DRAPES & DRAPERY FABRICS, FROM MANMADE FIBER

Pierce Arrow Drapery Mfg .... G 716 876-3023
  Buffalo *(G-3003)*
Unique Quality Fabrics Inc .... G 845 343-3070
  Middletown *(G-8182)*

DRIED FRUITS WHOLESALERS

Sahadi Fine Foods Inc .... E 718 369-0100
  Brooklyn *(G-2445)*

DRILL BITS

Mibro Group .... D 716 631-5713
  Buffalo *(G-2945)*

DRILLING MACHINERY & EQPT: Water Well

Blue Tee Corp .... G 212 598-0880
  New York *(G-9109)*

DRINK MIXES, NONALCOHOLIC: Cocktail

American Juice Company LLC 347 620-0252
  New York *(G-8833)*
Motts LLP .... C 972 673-8088
  Elmsford *(G-4552)*

DRINKING PLACES: Alcoholic Beverages

Kurrier Inc .... G 718 389-3018
  Brooklyn *(G-2082)*
Lafayette Pub Inc .... E 212 925-4242
  New York *(G-10507)*

DRINKING PLACES: Night Clubs

Flushing Pharmacy Inc .... C 718 260-8999
  Brooklyn *(G-1894)*

DRINKING PLACES: Wine Bar

Wolffer Estate Vineyard Inc .... E 631 537-5106
  Sagaponack *(G-14505)*

DRINKING WATER COOLERS WHOLESALERS: Mechanical

Pure Planet Waters LLC .... F 718 676-7900
  Brooklyn *(G-2362)*
Yr Blanc & Co LLC .... G 716 800-3999
  Buffalo *(G-3137)*

DRIVE SHAFTS

Deer Park Driveshaft & Hose .... G 631 667-4091
  Deer Park *(G-3963)*
Dennys Drive Shaft Service .... G 716 875-6640
  Kenmore *(G-6858)*
Drive Shaft Shop Inc .... F 631 348-1818
  Hauppauge *(G-5816)*
K M Drive Line Inc .... G 718 599-0628
  Brooklyn *(G-2064)*

DRIVES: High Speed Indl, Exc Hydrostatic

Magna Products Corp .... E 585 647-2280
  Rochester *(G-13923)*
Nidec Indus Automtn USA LLC .... E 716 774-1193
  Grand Island *(G-5507)*

DRONES: Target, Used By Ships, Metal

Dz9 Power LLC .... G 877 533-5530
  Olean *(G-12601)*

DROP CLOTHS: Fabric

Ace Drop Cloth Canvas Pdts Inc .... E 718 731-1550
  Bronx *(G-1208)*

DRUG TESTING KITS: Blood & Urine

Yr Blanc & Co LLC .... G 716 800-3999
  Buffalo *(G-3137)*

DRUGS & DRUG PROPRIETARIES, WHOL: Biologicals/Allied Prdts

Roar Biomedical Inc .... G 631 591-2749
  Calverton *(G-3170)*

DRUGS & DRUG PROPRIETARIES, WHOLESALE

Alo Acquisition LLC .... G 518 464-0279
  Albany *(G-39)*
Ip Med Inc .... G 516 766-3800
  Oceanside *(G-12541)*

DRUGS & DRUG PROPRIETARIES, WHOLESALE: Pharmaceuticals

Amneal Pharmaceuticals LLC .... E 631 952-0214
  Brookhaven *(G-1428)*
Amneal Pharmaceuticals NY LLC .... E 908 947-3120
  Brookhaven *(G-1429)*
Derm-Buro Inc .... E 516 694-8300
  Plainview *(G-13050)*
Forest Laboratories LLC .... C 212 421-7850
  New York *(G-9822)*
G C Hanford Manufacturing Co .... G 315 476-7418
  Syracuse *(G-15328)*
Generics Bidco I LLC .... G 256 859-4011
  Chestnut Ridge *(G-3492)*
Invagen Pharmaceuticals Inc .... B 631 231-3233
  Hauppauge *(G-5851)*
Nutra-Scientifics LLC .... G 917 238-8510
  Pomona *(G-13186)*
Polygen Pharmaceuticals Inc .... E 631 392-4044
  Edgewood *(G-4411)*
Prestige Consmr Healthcare Inc .... D 914 524-6800
  Tarrytown *(G-15488)*
Tocare LLC .... F 718 767-0618
  Whitestone *(G-16549)*
Ucb Pharma Inc .... B 919 767-2555
  Rochester *(G-14183)*
Vyera Pharmaceuticals LLC .... E 646 356-5577
  New York *(G-12059)*
You First Services Inc .... F 716 204-7215
  Buffalo *(G-3135)*

DRUGS & DRUG PROPRIETARIES, WHOLESALE: Vitamins & Minerals

Healthy N Fit Intl Inc .... F 800 338-5200
  Brewster *(G-1166)*
Natures Bounty Co .... D 631 244-2021
  Ronkonkoma *(G-14385)*
Nbty Manufacturing LLC .... G 631 567-9500
  Ronkonkoma *(G-14386)*
Unipharm Inc .... D 212 594-3260
  New York *(G-11947)*
Wellquest International Inc .... G 212 689-9094
  New York *(G-12091)*

DRUGS ACTING ON THE CENTRAL NERVOUS SYSTEM & SENSE ORGANS

Acorda Therapeutics Inc .... C 914 347-4300
  Ardsley *(G-392)*

Employee Codes: A=Over 500 employees, B=251-500
C=101-250, D=51-100, E=20-50, F=10-19, G=5-9

DRUGS AFFECTING NEOPLASMS & ENDOCRINE SYSTEMS

DRUGS AFFECTING NEOPLASMS & ENDOCRINE SYSTEMS

OSI Pharmaceuticals LLC .... D 631 847-0175
  Farmingdale *(G-4842)*
OSI Pharmaceuticals LLC .... G 631 962-2000
  Farmingdale *(G-4843)*

DRUGS/DRUG PROPRIETARIES, WHOL: Proprietary/Patent Medicines

Apothecus Pharmaceutical Corp .... F 516 624-8200
  Oyster Bay *(G-12810)*

DRUGS: Parasitic & Infective Disease Affecting

Safetec of America Inc .... D 716 895-1822
  Buffalo *(G-3054)*

DRUMS: Fiber

Greif Inc .... D 716 836-4200
  Tonawanda *(G-15545)*

DRYCLEANING EQPT & SPLYS: Commercial

Q Omni Inc .... G 914 962-2726
  Yorktown Heights *(G-16821)*
Thermopatch Corporation .... D 315 446-8110
  Syracuse *(G-15443)*

DRYCLEANING SVC: Drapery & Curtain

Abalene Decorating Services .... E 718 782-2000
  New York *(G-8705)*
Reynolds Drapery Service Inc .... F 315 845-8632
  Newport *(G-12256)*

DUCTING: Plastic

Vpulse Inc .... G 646 729-5675
  Brooklyn *(G-2635)*

DUCTS: Sheet Metal

Aabco Sheet Metal Co Inc .... D 718 821-1166
  Ridgewood *(G-13527)*
Accurate Specialty Metal Fabri .... E 718 418-6895
  Middle Village *(G-8119)*
D and D Sheet Metal Corp .... F 718 465-7585
  Jamaica *(G-6641)*
Delta Sheet Metal Corp .... C 718 429-5805
  Long Island City *(G-7422)*
Karo Sheet Metal Inc .... E 718 542-8420
  Brooklyn *(G-2067)*
Liffey Sheet Metal Corp .... F 347 381-1134
  Long Island City *(G-7498)*
Nelson Air Device Corporation .... C 718 729-3801
  Maspeth *(G-7862)*
United Sheet Metal Corp .... E 718 482-1197
  Long Island City *(G-7624)*

DUMPSTERS: Garbage

Mount Kisco Transfer Stn Inc .... G 914 666-6350
  Mount Kisco *(G-8350)*
Wastequip Manufacturing Co LLC ...... E 800 235-0734
  New Lebanon *(G-8574)*

DYES & PIGMENTS: Organic

East Cast Clor Compounding Inc .... G 631 491-9000
  West Babylon *(G-16154)*
F M Group Inc .... F 845 589-0102
  Congers *(G-3716)*

DYES: Synthetic Organic

Jos H Lowenstein and Sons Inc .... D 718 388-5410
  Brooklyn *(G-2046)*

EATING PLACES

A T A Bagel Shoppe Inc .... G 718 352-4948
  Bayside *(G-741)*
Brooklynwrap Inc .... G 718 258-8088
  Brooklyn *(G-1652)*
Capco Marketing .... F 315 699-1687
  Baldwinsville *(G-552)*
Cascade Mountain Winery & Rest ...... F 845 373-9021
  Amenia *(G-205)*
Food Gems Ltd .... E 718 296-7788
  Ozone Park *(G-12826)*

Gilded Otter Brewing Co .... D 845 256-1700
  New Paltz *(G-8577)*
Heron Hill Vineyards Inc .... E 607 868-4241
  Hammondsport *(G-5705)*
Hyde Park Brewing Co Inc .... E 845 229-8277
  Hyde Park *(G-6469)*
Lakeside Cider Mill Farm Inc .... G 518 399-8359
  Ballston Lake *(G-568)*
Malina Management Company Inc ..... E 607 535-9614
  Montour Falls *(G-8326)*
Piemonte Home Made Ravioli Co .... F 718 429-1972
  Woodside *(G-16672)*
Rawpothecary Inc .... G 917 783-7770
  Brooklyn *(G-2385)*
Rosina Food Products Inc .... C 716 668-0123
  Buffalo *(G-3045)*
Sign Company .... G 212 967-2113
  New York *(G-11585)*

EDUCATIONAL PROGRAMS ADMINISTRATION SVCS

Stony Brook University .... E 631 632-6434
  Stony Brook *(G-15169)*
Suny At Binghamton .... D 607 777-2316
  Binghamton *(G-916)*

EDUCATIONAL SVCS

Rainbeau Ridge Farm .... G 914 234-2197
  Bedford Hills *(G-779)*
Social Science Electronic Pubg .... F 585 442-8170
  Rochester *(G-14132)*

EDUCATIONAL SVCS, NONDEGREE GRANTING: Continuing Education

Conference Board Inc .... C 212 759-0900
  New York *(G-9377)*

ELASTOMERS

Elastomers Inc .... G 716 633-4883
  Williamsville *(G-16578)*
Everfab Inc .... D 716 655-1550
  East Aurora *(G-4198)*
Rodgard Corporation .... E 716 852-1435
  Buffalo *(G-3043)*

ELECTRIC MOTOR REPAIR SVCS

A & C/Furia Electric Motors .... F 914 949-0585
  White Plains *(G-16416)*
Armor Machining Services, Inc. .... E 716 825-0190
  Buffalo *(G-2709)*
Bayshore Electric Motors .... G 631 475-1397
  Patchogue *(G-12862)*
Daves Electric Motors & Pumps .... G 212 982-2930
  New York *(G-9478)*
Electric Motor Specialty Inc .... G 716 487-1458
  Jamestown *(G-6714)*
General Electric Company .... E 315 456-3304
  Syracuse *(G-15332)*
General Electric Company .... E 518 459-4110
  Albany *(G-77)*
Genesis Electrical Motors .... F 718 274-7030
  Woodside *(G-16658)*
Lawtons Electric Motor Service .... G 315 393-2728
  Ogdensburg *(G-12576)*
Longo New York Inc .... F 212 929-7128
  New York *(G-10597)*
Power-Flo Technologies Inc .... F 585 426-4607
  Rochester *(G-14029)*
Prime Electric Motors Inc .... G 718 784-1124
  Long Island City *(G-7559)*
Tis Ansonia LLC .... F 518 272-4920
  Watervliet *(G-16052)*
Troy Belting and Supply Co .... D 518 272-4920
  Watervliet *(G-16053)*
Troy Industrial Solutions .... F 518 272-4920
  Watervliet *(G-16054)*
United Richter Electrical Mtrs .... F 716 855-1945
  Buffalo *(G-3112)*

ELECTRIC SERVICES

Besicorp Ltd .... F 845 336-7700
  Kingston *(G-6889)*
County Energy Corp .... G 718 626-7000
  Brooklyn *(G-1723)*

ELECTRIC SVCS, NEC Power Transmission

Hess Corporation .... B 212 997-8500
  New York *(G-10085)*

ELECTRIC SVCS, NEC: Power Generation

Caithness Equities Corporation .... E 212 599-2112
  New York *(G-9178)*

ELECTRICAL APPARATUS & EQPT WHOLESALERS

Aerospace Lighting Corporation .... D 631 563-6400
  Bohemia *(G-974)*
Amertac Holdings Inc .... G 610 336-1330
  Monsey *(G-8284)*
Bombardier Trnsp Holdings USA .... D 607 776-4791
  Bath *(G-641)*
Cummins Northeast LLC .... E 315 437-2296
  Syracuse *(G-15297)*
Edison Price Lighting Inc .... D 718 685-0700
  Long Island City *(G-7434)*
Ener-G-Rotors Inc .... G 518 372-2608
  Schenectady *(G-14670)*
Hammond Manufacturing Co Inc .... F 716 630-7030
  Cheektowaga *(G-3448)*
Linear Lighting Corporation .... C 718 361-7552
  Long Island City *(G-7500)*
LSI Lightron Inc .... A 845 562-5500
  New Windsor *(G-8649)*
Medi-Ray Inc .... D 877 898-3003
  Tuckahoe *(G-15644)*
On Line Power Technologies 914 968-4440
  Yonkers *(G-16787)*
Pcb Piezotronics Inc .... B 716 684-0003
  Depew *(G-4102)*
Pompian Manufacturing Co Inc .... G 914 476-7076
  Yonkers *(G-16793)*
Powr-UPS Corp .... E 631 345-5700
  Shirley *(G-14843)*
S & J Trading Inc 718 347-1323
  Floral Park *(G-4967)*
Stk Electronics Inc .... E 315 655-8476
  Cazenovia *(G-3327)*

ELECTRICAL APPLIANCES, TELEVISIONS & RADIOS WHOLESALERS

AVI-Spl Employee .... B 212 840-4801
  New York *(G-8977)*

ELECTRICAL CONSTRUCTION MATERIALS WHOLESALERS

All-Lifts Incorporated .... E 518 465-3461
  Albany *(G-38)*
Citadel Electrical Sup Co Inc .... G 646 705-0333
  Tappan *(G-15467)*
Morris Products Inc .... F 518 743-0523
  Queensbury *(G-13434)*

ELECTRICAL CURRENT CARRYING WIRING DEVICES

Alstom Signaling Inc .... E 585 274-8700
  Schenectady *(G-14648)*
Associated Lightning Rod Co .... F 845 373-8309
  Millerton *(G-8192)*
Atc Plastics LLC .... E 212 375-2515
  New York *(G-8943)*
Belden Inc .... B 607 796-5600
  Horseheads *(G-6306)*
C A M Graphics Co Inc .... G 631 842-3400
  Farmingdale *(G-4731)*
Charlton Precision Products .... G 845 338-2351
  Kingston *(G-6894)*
Cooper Power Systems LLC .... B 716 375-7100
  Olean *(G-12597)*
Cox & Company Inc .... C 212 366-0200
  Plainview *(G-13048)*
Exxelia-Raf Tabtronics LLC .... E 585 243-4331
  Piffard *(G-12996)*
Hubbell Inc .... E 845 586-2707
  Margaretville *(G-7798)*
Inertia Switch Inc .... E 845 359-8300
  Orangeburg *(G-12679)*
Jaguar Industries Inc .... F 845 947-1800
  Haverstraw *(G-5979)*
Joldeson One Aerospace Inds .... D 718 848-7396
  Ozone Park *(G-12827)*

PRODUCT SECTION

ELECTRICAL GOODS, WHOLESALE: Capacitors

Kelta Inc .... E 631 789-5000
  Edgewood (G-4406)
L3 Technologies Inc .... A 631 436-7400
  Hauppauge (G-5859)
Lighting Holdings Intl LLC .... A 845 306-1850
  Purchase (G-13391)
Lite Brite Manufacturing Inc .... F 718 855-9797
  Brooklyn (G-2129)
Lourdes Industries Inc .... D 631 234-6600
  Hauppauge (G-5873)
Mini-Circuits Fort Wayne LLC .... B 718 934-4500
  Brooklyn (G-2210)
Mono-Systems Inc .... E 716 821-1344
  Buffalo (G-2953)
NEa Manufacturing Corp .... E 516 371-4200
  Inwood (G-6497)
Orbit International Corp .... D 631 435-8300
  Hauppauge (G-5907)
Pass & Seymour Inc .... B 315 468-6211
  Syracuse (G-15394)
Reynolds Packaging McHy Inc .... D 716 358-6451
  Falconer (G-4690)
Rodale Wireless Inc .... E 631 231-0044
  Hauppauge (G-5029)
Saturn Industries Inc .... E 518 828-9956
  Hudson (G-6370)
Sinclair Technologies Inc .... E 716 874-3682
  Hamburg (G-5695)
Stever-Locke Industries Inc .... G 585 624-3450
  Honeoye Falls (G-6274)
Superpower Inc .... E 518 346-1414
  Schenectady (G-14718)
Switching Power Inc .... D 631 981-7231
  Ronkonkoma (G-14420)
Swivelier Company Inc .... D 845 353-1455
  Blauvelt (G-941)
Tappan Wire & Cable Inc .... C 845 353-9000
  Blauvelt (G-942)
Utility Systems Tech Inc .... F 518 326-4142
  Watervliet (G-16055)
Whirlwind Music Distrs Inc .... D 800 733-9473
  Rochester (G-14207)

ELECTRICAL DISCHARGE MACHINING, EDM

Fermer Precision Inc .... D 315 822-6371
  Ilion (G-6474)
Hoercher Industries Inc .... G 585 398-2982
  East Rochester (G-4286)
K & H Industries Inc .... F 716 312-0088
  Hamburg (G-5683)
Ppi Corp .... D 585 243-0300
  Rochester (G-14032)

ELECTRICAL EQPT & SPLYS

303 Contracting Inc .... E 716 896-2122
  Orchard Park (G-12694)
331 Holding Inc .... E 585 924-1740
  Victor (G-15827)
A & S Electric .... G 212 228-2030
  Brooklyn (G-1452)
Advanced Mfg Techniques .... G 518 877-8560
  Clifton Park (G-3562)
Allcom Electric Corp .... G 914 803-0433
  Yonkers (G-16731)
Altaquip LLC .... G 631 580-4740
  Ronkonkoma (G-14304)
American Avionic Tech Corp .... D 631 924-8200
  Medford (G-7937)
Amertac Holdings Inc .... G 610 336-1330
  Monsey (G-8284)
Ametek Inc .... D 585 263-7700
  Rochester (G-13630)
Atlas Switch Co Inc .... E 516 222-6280
  Garden City (G-5251)
B & H Electronics Corp .... E 845 782-5000
  Monroe (G-8264)
Binghamton Simulator Co Inc .... F 607 321-2980
  Binghamton (G-868)
Bombardier Trnsp Holdings USA .... D 607 776-4791
  Bath (G-641)
Bren-Tronics Inc .... C 631 499-5155
  Commack (G-3685)
Buffalo Filter LLC .... D 716 835-7000
  Lancaster (G-7011)
Castle Power Solutions LLC .... F 518 743-1000
  South Glens Falls (G-14935)
Cathay Global Co Inc .... G 718 229-0920
  Bayside Hills (G-752)
Citadel Electrical Sup Co Inc .... G 646 705-0333
  Tappan (G-15467)
Cooper Industries LLC .... E 315 477-7000
  Syracuse (G-15291)
Cooper Power Systems LLC .... B 716 375-7100
  Olean (G-12597)
Cooperfriedman Elc Sup Co Inc .... G 718 269-4906
  Long Island City (G-7415)
Da Electric .... E 347 270-3422
  Bronx (G-1252)
Dahill Distributors Inc .... G 347 371-9453
  Brooklyn (G-1750)
Denmar Electric .... F 845 624-4430
  Nanuet (G-8463)
Dorsey Metrology Intl Inc .... E 845 229-2929
  Poughkeepsie (G-13334)
Eastco Manufacturing Corp .... F 914 738-5667
  Pelham (G-12934)
Edo LLC .... A 631 630-4200
  Amityville (G-273)
Emco Electric Services LLC .... G 212 420-9766
  New York (G-9667)
Emcom Inc .... G 315 255-5300
  Auburn (G-477)
General Electric Company .... G 315 554-2000
  Skaneateles (G-14872)
Gerome Technologies Inc .... E 518 463-1324
  Menands (G-8085)
Green Island Power Authority .... F 518 273-0661
  Green Island (G-5606)
Gsa Upstate NY .... G 631 244-5744
  Oakdale (G-12517)
Guardian Systems Tech Inc .... F 716 481-5597
  East Aurora (G-4202)
Hergo Ergonomic Support .... E 718 894-0639
  Maspeth (G-7851)
Htf Components Inc .... G 914 703-6795
  White Plains (G-16461)
Iconix Inc .... F 516 513-1420
  Hauppauge (G-5848)
Intelligent Ctrl Systems LLC .... G 516 340-1011
  Farmingdale (G-4787)
Itin Scale Co Inc .... E 718 336-5900
  Brooklyn (G-2019)
J H M Engineering .... E 718 871-1810
  Brooklyn (G-2023)
Knf Clean Room Products Corp .... E 631 588-7000
  Ronkonkoma (G-14362)
Koregon Enterprises Inc .... G 450 218-6836
  Champlain (G-3411)
Kyle R Lawrence Electric Inc .... G 315 502-4181
  Palmyra (G-12856)
Lucas Electric .... G 516 809-8619
  Seaford (G-14759)
Madison Electric .... F 718 358-4121
  Cambria Heights (G-3176)
Manhattan Scientifics Inc .... F 212 541-2405
  New York (G-10688)
Manor Electric Supply Corp .... F 718 648-8003
  Brooklyn (G-2161)
Manufacturing Solutions Inc .... E 585 235-3320
  Rochester (G-13927)
Marzullo Electric LLC .... G 315 455-1050
  Syracuse (G-15367)
Mitsubishi Elc Pwr Pdts Inc .... G 516 962-2813
  Melville (G-8048)
Multi Tech Electric .... F 718 606-2695
  Woodside (G-16665)
Nbn Technologies LLC .... G 585 355-5556
  Rochester (G-13966)
Nk Electric LLC .... G 914 271-0222
  Croton On Hudson (G-3915)
OEM Solutions Inc .... G 716 864-9324
  Clarence (G-3536)
Optimum Applied Systems Inc .... F 845 471-3333
  Poughkeepsie (G-13361)
Piller Power Systems Inc .... G 845 695-6658
  Middletown (G-8170)
Pinpoint Systems Intl Inc .... D 631 775-2100
  Bellport (G-812)
Power Metrics Intl Inc .... F 718 524-4370
  Staten Island (G-15118)
Ross Electronics Ltd .... E 718 569-6643
  Haverstraw (G-5981)
Schuler-Haas Electric Corp .... E 607 936-3514
  Painted Post (G-12840)
Sima Technologies LLC .... G 412 828-9130
  Hauppauge (G-5940)
Simulaids Inc .... D 845 679-2475
  Saugerties (G-14616)
Skae Power Solutions LLC .... E 845 365-9103
  Palisades (G-12847)
Smithers Tools & Mch Pdts Inc .... D 845 876-3063
  Rhinebeck (G-13488)
Sunwire Electric Corp .... G 718 456-7500
  Brooklyn (G-2533)
T Jn Electric .... F 917 560-0981
  Mahopac (G-7714)
T Jn Electric Inc .... G 845 628-6970
  Mahopac (G-7715)
Tory Electric .... G 914 292-5036
  Bedford (G-771)
Triborough Electric .... G 718 321-2144
  Whitestone (G-16551)
U E Systems Incorporated .... E 914 592-1220
  Elmsford (G-4575)
United Technologies Corp .... B 866 788-5095
  Pittsford (G-13027)
Werner Brothers Electric Inc .... G 518 377-3056
  Rexford (G-13484)
Z-Axis Inc .... D 315 548-5000
  Phelps (G-12984)

ELECTRICAL EQPT FOR ENGINES

Delphi Powertrain Systems LLC .... B 585 359-6000
  West Henrietta (G-16237)
Fairbanks Morse Engine .... G 608 364-8465
  Palmyra (G-12850)
Kearney-National Inc .... F 212 661-4600
  New York (G-10427)
Leviton Manufacturing Co Inc .... B 631 812-6000
  Melville (G-8043)
Nas-Tra Automotive Inds Inc .... C 631 225-1225
  Lindenhurst (G-7182)
Sopark Corp .... D 716 822-0434
  Buffalo (G-3070)

ELECTRICAL EQPT REPAIR & MAINTENANCE

A L Eastmond & Sons Inc .... D 718 378-3000
  Bronx (G-1201)
Hobart Corporation .... E 631 864-3440
  Commack (G-3695)
Strecks Inc .... E 518 273-4410
  Watervliet (G-16051)

ELECTRICAL EQPT REPAIR SVCS

Siemens Industry Inc .... E 585 797-2300
  Rochester (G-14126)
Zetek Corporation .... F 212 668-1485
  New York (G-12174)

ELECTRICAL EQPT: Automotive, NEC

Autel US Inc .... G 631 923-2620
  Farmingdale (G-4724)
Ev-Box North America Inc .... G 646 930-6305
  New York (G-9732)
International Key Supply LLC .... F 631 983-6096
  Farmingdale (G-4788)

ELECTRICAL EQPT: Household

Kinetic Marketing Inc .... G 212 620-0600
  New York (G-10450)
World Trading Center Inc .... G 631 273-3330
  Hauppauge (G-5978)

ELECTRICAL GOODS, WHOLESALE: Batteries, Dry Cell

Lyntronics Inc .... E 631 205-1061
  Yaphank (G-16715)

ELECTRICAL GOODS, WHOLESALE: Burglar Alarm Systems

Altronix Corp .... D 718 567-8181
  Brooklyn (G-1515)
Detekion Security Systems Inc .... F 607 729-7179
  Vestal (G-15815)

ELECTRICAL GOODS, WHOLESALE: Capacitors

AVX Corporation .... D 716 372-6611
  Olean (G-12592)

Employee Codes: A=Over 500 employees, B=251-500
C=101-250, D=51-100, E=20-50, F=10-19, G=5-9

ELECTRICAL GOODS, WHOLESALE: Connectors

Cables and Chips Inc .... E 212 619-3132
  New York (G-9173)
I Trade Technology Ltd .... G 615 348-7233
  Suffern (G-15191)

ELECTRICAL GOODS, WHOLESALE: Electronic Parts

Falconer Electronics Inc .... D 716 665-4176
  Falconer (G-4678)
Intex Company Inc .... D 516 223-0200
  Freeport (G-5162)
Oakdale Industrial Elec Corp .... F 631 737-4090
  Ronkonkoma (G-14388)
Sj Associates Inc .... E 516 942-3232
  Jericho (G-6804)
Veja Electronics Inc .... D 631 321-6086
  Deer Park (G-4058)

ELECTRICAL GOODS, WHOLESALE: Facsimile Or Fax Eqpt

Alternative Technology Corp .... G 914 478-5900
  Hastings On Hudson (G-5747)

ELECTRICAL GOODS, WHOLESALE: Fans, Household

Canarm Ltd .... G 800 267-4427
  Ogdensburg (G-12572)

ELECTRICAL GOODS, WHOLESALE: Fittings & Construction Mat

Veja Electronics Inc .... D 631 321-6086
  Deer Park (G-4058)

ELECTRICAL GOODS, WHOLESALE: Intercommunication Eqpt

Apple Core Electronics Inc .... F 718 628-4068
  Brooklyn (G-1542)
Elite Cellular Accessories Inc .... E 877 390-2502
  Deer Park (G-3972)
Ingham Industries Inc .... G 631 242-2493
  Holbrook (G-6189)

ELECTRICAL GOODS, WHOLESALE: Light Bulbs & Related Splys

Led Waves Inc .... F 347 416-6182
  Brooklyn (G-2103)
Olive Led Lighting Inc .... G 718 746-0830
  College Point (G-3658)
Sir Industries Inc .... G 631 234-2444
  Hauppauge (G-5941)

ELECTRICAL GOODS, WHOLESALE: Lighting Fittings & Access

Gagne Associates Inc .... E 800 800-5954
  Johnson City (G-6808)
Jed Lights Inc .... F 516 812-5001
  Deer Park (G-3992)

ELECTRICAL GOODS, WHOLESALE: Lighting Fixtures, Comm & Indl

Canarm Ltd .... G 800 267-4427
  Ogdensburg (G-12572)
Creative Stage Lighting Co Inc .... E 518 251-3302
  North Creek (G-12391)
Unimar Inc .... F 315 699-4400
  Syracuse (G-15448)

ELECTRICAL GOODS, WHOLESALE: Lighting Fixtures, Residential

Prestigeline Inc .... D 631 273-3636
  Bay Shore (G-710)
Rapid-Lite Fixture Corporation .... F 347 599-2600
  Brooklyn (G-2384)

ELECTRICAL GOODS, WHOLESALE: Mobile telephone Eqpt

U2o Usa LLC .... G 516 813-9500
  Plainview (G-13094)

ELECTRICAL GOODS, WHOLESALE: Motors

Armor Machining Services, Inc. .... E 716 825-0190
  Buffalo (G-2709)
Electric Motor Specialty Inc .... G 716 487-1458
  Jamestown (G-6714)
Empire Division Inc .... D 315 476-6273
  Syracuse (G-15318)
Heating & Burner Supply Inc .... G 718 665-0006
  Bronx (G-1290)

ELECTRICAL GOODS, WHOLESALE: Semiconductor Devices

Enplas America Inc .... G 646 892-7811
  New York (G-9686)
Lakestar Semi Inc .... F 212 974-6254
  New York (G-10510)

ELECTRICAL GOODS, WHOLESALE: Signaling, Eqpt

BNo Intl Trdg Co Inc .... G 716 487-1900
  Jamestown (G-6703)

ELECTRICAL GOODS, WHOLESALE: Sound Eqpt

L A R Electronics Corp .... G 716 285-0555
  Niagara Falls (G-12304)
Magic Tech Co Ltd .... G 516 539-7944
  West Hempstead (G-16221)
Samson Technologies Corp .... D 631 784-2200
  Hicksville (G-6130)

ELECTRICAL GOODS, WHOLESALE: Telephone Eqpt

Harris Corporation .... F 718 767-1100
  Whitestone (G-16541)

ELECTRICAL GOODS, WHOLESALE: Transformers

Buffalo Power Electronics Ctr .... F 716 651-1600
  Depew (G-4083)

ELECTRICAL GOODS, WHOLESALE: VCR & Access

Toshiba America Inc .... E 212 596-0600
  New York (G-11872)

ELECTRICAL GOODS, WHOLESALE: Vacuum Cleaners, Household

Empire Division Inc .... D 315 476-6273
  Syracuse (G-15318)

ELECTRICAL GOODS, WHOLESALE: Video Eqpt

Bescor Video Accessories Ltd .... F 631 420-1717
  Farmingdale (G-4727)

ELECTRICAL GOODS, WHOLESALE: Wire & Cable

Cortland Company Inc .... D 607 753-8276
  Cortland (G-3866)
Cygnus Automation Inc .... E 631 981-0909
  Bohemia (G-1006)
Hyperline Systems Inc .... G 613 736-8500
  Brooklyn (G-1991)

ELECTRICAL GOODS, WHOLESALE: Wire & Cable, Electronic

Cables and Chips Inc .... E 212 619-3132
  New York (G-9173)
Cables Unlimited Inc .... E 631 563-6363
  Yaphank (G-16705)
Dsr International Corp .... G 631 427-2600
  Great Neck (G-5550)

Global Technologies Inc .... D 631 243-7924
  Deer Park (G-3982)

ELECTRICAL INDL APPARATUS, NEC

Calibration Technologies Inc .... G 631 676-6133
  Centereach (G-3343)
Energy Harvesters LLC .... G 617 325-9852
  Rochester (G-13783)
Key Signals .... G 631 433-2962
  East Moriches (G-4257)

ELECTRICAL SPLYS

Cooper Industries LLC .... E 315 477-7000
  Syracuse (G-15291)
Rwb Controls Inc .... G 716 897-4341
  Buffalo (G-3050)
Tudor Electrical Supply Co Inc .... G 212 867-7550
  New York (G-11912)

ELECTRICAL SUPPLIES: Porcelain

Cetek Inc .... E 845 452-3510
  Poughkeepsie (G-13331)
Corning Incorporated .... E 607 974-1274
  Painted Post (G-12836)
Ferro Electronics Materials .... C 716 278-9400
  Niagara Falls (G-12285)
Ferro Electronics Materials .... C 315 536-3357
  Penn Yan (G-12954)
Ferro Electronics Materials .... C 315 536-3357
  Penn Yan (G-12955)
Filtros Ltd 585 586-8770
  East Rochester (G-4285)

ELECTRODES: Fluorescent Lamps

Preston Glass Industries Inc .... E 718 997-8888
  Forest Hills (G-5080)

ELECTRODES: Indl Process

Vermont Medical Inc .... C 802 463-9976
  Buffalo (G-3118)

ELECTRODES: Thermal & Electrolytic

J V Precision Inc .... G 518 851-3200
  Hudson (G-6357)
Saturn Industries Inc .... E 518 828-9956
  Hudson (G-6370)

ELECTROMEDICAL EQPT

Argon Medical Devices Inc .... G 585 321-1130
  Henrietta (G-6031)
C R Bard Inc .... A 518 793-2531
  Glens Falls (G-5420)
Caliber Imaging Diagnostics Inc .... E 585 239-9800
  Rochester (G-13687)
Conmed Corporation .... D 315 797-8375
  Utica (G-15686)
Excel Technology Inc .... F 212 355-3400
  New York (G-9749)
Fonar Corporation .... C 631 694-2929
  Melville (G-8025)
Forest Medical LLC .... G 315 434-9000
  East Syracuse (G-4341)
Infimed Inc .... D 315 453-4545
  Liverpool (G-7236)
Infimed Inc .... G 585 383-1710
  Pittsford (G-13016)
J H M Engineering .... E 718 871-1810
  Brooklyn (G-2023)
Jaracz Jr Joseph Paul .... G 716 533-1377
  Orchard Park (G-12722)
Kal Manufacturing Corporation .... E 585 265-4310
  Webster (G-16088)
Med Services Inc .... D 631 218-6450
  Bohemia (G-1058)
Misonix Inc .... D 631 694-9555
  Farmingdale (G-4828)
Natus Medical Incorporated .... G 631 457-4430
  Hauppauge (G-5899)
Netech Corporation .... F 631 531-0100
  Farmingdale (G-4836)
Pharmadva LLC .... G 585 469-1410
  Rochester (G-14018)
Radiancy Inc .... F 845 398-1647
  Orangeburg (G-12690)
Ray Medica Inc .... E 952 885-0500
  New York (G-11331)

PRODUCT SECTION — EMBROIDERING & ART NEEDLEWORK FOR THE TRADE

Sonomed Inc .... E 516 354-0900
  New Hyde Park *(G-8564)*
Soterix Medical Inc .... F 888 990-8327
  New York *(G-11652)*
Sun Scientific Inc .... G 914 473-5108
  Dobbs Ferry *(G-4131)*
Ultradian Diagnostics LLC .... G 518 618-0046
  Rensselaer *(G-13479)*
Vasomedical Inc .... E 516 997-4600
  Plainview *(G-13096)*
Vermed Inc .... D 800 669-6905
  Buffalo *(G-3117)*
Vermont Medical Inc .... C 802 463-9976
  Buffalo *(G-3118)*
Z-Axis Inc .... D 315 548-5000
  Phelps *(G-12984)*

ELECTRON TUBES

Harris Corporation .... E 585 244-5830
  Rochester *(G-13858)*
Y & Z Precision Inc .... F 516 349-8243
  Plainview *(G-13104)*

ELECTRON TUBES: Cathode Ray

Passur Aerospace Inc .... G 631 589-6800
  Bohemia *(G-1072)*
Thomas Electronics Inc .... C 315 923-2051
  Clyde *(G-3598)*

ELECTRONIC COMPONENTS

Bud Barger Assoc Inc .... G 631 696-6703
  Farmingville *(G-4923)*
Haynes Roberts Inc .... F 212 989-1901
  New York *(G-10053)*
Lighthouse Components .... E 917 993-6820
  New York *(G-10570)*
Marcon Electronic Systems LLC .... G 516 633-6396
  Freeport *(G-5164)*
Mezmeriz Inc .... G 607 216-8140
  Ithaca *(G-6595)*
MLS Sales .... G 516 681-2736
  Bethpage *(G-848)*
Sln Group Inc .... G 718 677-5969
  Brooklyn *(G-2486)*
Space Coast Semiconductor Inc .... F 631 414-7131
  Farmingdale *(G-4878)*

ELECTRONIC DETECTION SYSTEMS: Aeronautical

Accutrak Inc .... F 212 925-5330
  New York *(G-8723)*

ELECTRONIC DEVICES: Solid State, NEC

Autodyne Manufacturing Co Inc .... F 631 957-5858
  Lindenhurst *(G-7163)*
Automated Control Logic Inc .... F 914 769-8880
  Thornwood *(G-15501)*
Bharat Electronics Limited .... G 516 248-4021
  Garden City *(G-5252)*
DJS Nyc Inc .... G 845 445-8618
  Monsey *(G-8287)*
Enrg Inc .... F 716 873-2939
  Buffalo *(G-2820)*
Orbit International Corp .... D 631 435-8300
  Hauppauge *(G-5907)*
Piezo Electronics Research .... F 845 735-9349
  Pearl River *(G-12907)*
Sonotec US Inc .... C 631 415-4758
  Islandia *(G-6539)*
Thermo Cidtec Inc .... E 315 451-9410
  Liverpool *(G-7267)*

ELECTRONIC EQPT REPAIR SVCS

Ah Elctronic Test Eqp Repr Ctr .... F 631 234-8979
  Central Islip *(G-3354)*
Alexy Associates Inc .... E 845 482-3000
  Bethel *(G-834)*
Custom Sound and Video .... E 585 424-5000
  Rochester *(G-13730)*

ELECTRONIC LOADS & POWER SPLYS

Berkshire Transformer .... G 631 467-5328
  Central Islip *(G-3359)*
D & S Supplies Inc .... F 718 721-5256
  Astoria *(G-422)*

Engagement Technology LLC .... F 914 591-7600
  Elmsford *(G-4542)*
Eni Technology Inc .... B 585 427-8300
  Rochester *(G-13787)*
Mechanical Pwr Conversion LLC .... F 607 766-9620
  Binghamton *(G-903)*
New York Digital Corporation .... F 631 630-9798
  Huntington Station *(G-6453)*
Pvi Solar Inc .... G 212 280-2100
  New York *(G-11286)*
SC Textiles Inc .... F 631 944-6262
  Huntington *(G-6414)*
Spellman Hgh-Voltage Elec Corp .... B 631 630-3000
  Hauppauge *(G-5947)*
Superior Motion Controls Inc .... E 516 420-2921
  Farmingdale *(G-4885)*
Three Five III-V Materials Inc .... F 212 213-8290
  New York *(G-11828)*
Ultralife Corporation .... B 315 332-7100
  Newark *(G-12209)*

ELECTRONIC PARTS & EQPT WHOLESALERS

Apex Signal Corporation .... D 631 567-1100
  Bohemia *(G-981)*
Apollo Display Tech Corp .... E 631 580-4360
  Ronkonkoma *(G-14310)*
Becker Electronics Inc .... F 631 619-9100
  Ronkonkoma *(G-14318)*
Canfield Electronics Inc .... F 631 585-4100
  Lindenhurst *(G-7165)*
Claddagh Electronics Ltd .... E 718 784-0571
  Long Island City *(G-7410)*
Cypress Semiconductor Corp .... F 631 261-1358
  Northport *(G-12467)*
Electronic Devices Inc .... E 914 965-4400
  Yonkers *(G-16755)*
Forerunner Technologies Inc .... F 631 337-2100
  Edgewood *(G-4401)*
G B International Trdg Co Ltd .... C 607 785-0938
  Endicott *(G-4594)*
General Microwave Corporation .... F 516 802-0900
  Syosset *(G-15219)*
High Frequency Tech Co Inc .... F 631 242-3020
  Bohemia *(G-1032)*
Htf Components Inc .... G 914 703-6795
  White Plains *(G-16461)*
Iba Industrial Inc .... E 631 254-6800
  Edgewood *(G-4403)*
Iconix Inc .... F 516 513-1420
  Hauppauge *(G-5848)*
Jaguar Industries Inc .... F 845 947-1800
  Haverstraw *(G-5979)*
Kinetic Marketing Inc .... G 212 620-0600
  New York *(G-10450)*
L K Manufacturing Corp .... E 631 243-6910
  West Babylon *(G-16169)*
Mill-Max Mfg Corp .... C 516 922-6000
  Oyster Bay *(G-12815)*
New Sensor Corporation .... D 718 937-8300
  Long Island City *(G-7538)*
Omntec Mfg Inc .... E 631 981-2001
  Ronkonkoma *(G-14391)*
Ramsey Electronics LLC .... E 585 924-4560
  Victor *(G-15863)*
Sag Harbor Industries Inc .... E 631 725-0440
  Sag Harbor *(G-14502)*
Semitronics Corp .... E 516 223-0200
  Freeport *(G-5182)*
Switching Power Inc .... D 631 981-7231
  Ronkonkoma *(G-14420)*
Ultravolt Inc .... D 631 471-4444
  Ronkonkoma *(G-14426)*
Ying Ke Youth Age Group Inc .... F 929 402-8458
  Dix Hills *(G-4128)*

ELECTRONIC SHOPPING

Runs Capital Inc .... E 212 618-1201
  New York *(G-11448)*
Scientifics Direct Inc .... F 716 773-7500
  Tonawanda *(G-15576)*

ELECTRONIC TRAINING DEVICES

Ces Industries Inc .... E 631 782-7088
  Islandia *(G-6525)*
Full Circle Studios LLC .... G 716 875-7740
  Buffalo *(G-2837)*
Telephonics Corporation .... D 631 755-7000
  Farmingdale *(G-4893)*

Telephonics Corporation .... D 631 470-8800
  Huntington *(G-6420)*

ELECTROPLATING & PLATING SVC

General Galvanizing Sup Co Inc .... D 718 589-4300
  Bronx *(G-1281)*
Psb Ltd .... F 585 654-7078
  Rochester *(G-14052)*

ELEVATORS & EQPT

A & D Entrances LLC .... F 718 989-2441
  Wyandanch *(G-16690)*
Access Elevator & Lift Inc .... G 716 483-3696
  Jamestown *(G-6694)*
An Excelsior Elevator Corp .... F 516 408-3070
  Westbury *(G-16316)*
Bhi Elevator Cabs Inc .... F 516 431-5665
  Island Park *(G-6512)*
Big Apple Elevtr Srv & Consult .... G 212 279-0700
  New York *(G-9075)*
CEC Elevator Cab Corp .... D 718 328-3632
  Bronx *(G-1236)*
Dural Door Company Inc .... F 718 729-1333
  Long Island City *(G-7430)*
E Z Entry Doors Inc .... F 716 434-3440
  Lockport *(G-7297)*
Elevator Accessories Mfg .... F 914 739-7004
  Peekskill *(G-12919)*
Elevator Interiors Inc .... E 315 218-7186
  Syracuse *(G-15314)*
Interface Products Co Inc .... G 631 242-4605
  Bay Shore *(G-690)*
Monitor Elevator Products LLC .... D 516 543-4334
  Hauppauge *(G-5897)*
National Elev Cab & Door Corp .... E 718 478-5900
  Woodside *(G-16666)*
Northern Lifts Elevator Co LLC .... F 518 644-2831
  Bolton Landing *(G-1112)*
Otis Elevator Company .... F 315 736-0167
  Yorkville *(G-16831)*
Otis Elevator Company .... F 917 339-9600
  New York *(G-11069)*
Schindler Elevator Corporation .... C 212 708-1000
  New York *(G-11503)*
Schindler Elevator Corporation .... E 800 225-3123
  New York *(G-11504)*
Velis Associates Inc .... G 631 225-4220
  Lindenhurst *(G-7202)*

ELEVATORS WHOLESALERS

An Excelsior Elevator Corp .... F 516 408-3070
  Westbury *(G-16316)*
EZ Lift Operator Corp .... F 845 356-1676
  Spring Valley *(G-14990)*

ELEVATORS: Installation & Conversion

Schindler Elevator Corporation .... E 800 225-3123
  New York *(G-11504)*

ELEVATORS: Stair, Motor Powered

S & H Enterprises Inc .... G 888 323-8755
  Queensbury *(G-13440)*

EMBLEMS: Embroidered

Eagle Regalia Co Inc .... F 845 425-2245
  Spring Valley *(G-14989)*
Glenda Inc .... G 718 442-8981
  Staten Island *(G-15079)*
Quist Industries Ltd .... F 718 243-2800
  Brooklyn *(G-2373)*
Voyager Emblems Inc .... C 416 255-3421
  Buffalo *(G-3121)*

EMBOSSING SVC: Paper

Gailer Stamping Diecutting LLC .... F 212 243-5662
  Long Island City *(G-7453)*

EMBROIDERING & ART NEEDLEWORK FOR THE TRADE

Active World Solutions Inc .... G 718 922-9404
  Brooklyn *(G-1480)*
All American Awards Inc .... F 631 567-2025
  Bohemia *(G-975)*
Control Research Inc .... G 631 225-1111
  Amityville *(G-269)*

Employee Codes: A=Over 500 employees, B=251-500
C=101-250, D=51-100, E=20-50, F=10-19, G=5-9

EMBROIDERING & ART NEEDLEWORK FOR THE TRADE

Custom Patches Inc .... E 845 679-6320
  Woodstock *(G-16685)*
Design Archives Inc .... G 212 768-0617
  New York *(G-9504)*
Eiseman-Ludmar Co Inc .... F 516 932-6990
  Hicksville *(G-6083)*
Holland & Sherry Inc .... E 212 542-8410
  New York *(G-10115)*
Kabrics .... G 607 962-6344
  Corning *(G-3821)*
Karishma Fashions Inc .... G 718 565-5404
  Jackson Heights *(G-6620)*
Loremanss Embroidery Engrav .... F 518 834-9205
  Keeseville *(G-6852)*
Mrinalini Inc .... G 646 510-2747
  New York *(G-10852)*
NY Embroidery Inc .... G 516 822-6456
  Hicksville *(G-6116)*
Point Canvas Company Inc .... G 607 692-4381
  Whitney Point *(G-16556)*
Ross L Sports Screening Inc .... F 716 824-5350
  Buffalo *(G-3047)*
Round Top Knit & Screening .... G 518 622-3600
  Round Top *(G-14466)*
Royal Tees Inc .... G 845 357-9448
  Suffern *(G-15197)*
Sand Hill Industries Inc .... G 518 885-7991
  Ballston Spa *(G-595)*
Screen Gems Inc .... G 845 561-0036
  New Windsor *(G-8659)*
Shykat Promotions .... G 866 574-2757
  Forestville *(G-5088)*
Stephen M Kiernan .... E 716 836-6300
  Buffalo *(G-3076)*
U All Inc .... E 518 438-2558
  Albany *(G-136)*
Uniform Namemakers Inc .... F 716 626-5474
  Buffalo *(G-3110)*
Wicked Smart LLC .... F 518 459-2855
  Watervliet *(G-16057)*

EMBROIDERING SVC

Aditiany Inc .... G 212 997-8440
  New York *(G-8738)*
All About Art Inc .... F 718 321-0755
  Flushing *(G-4983)*
American Quality Embroidery .... G 631 467-3200
  Ronkonkoma *(G-14306)*
Arena Graphics Inc .... G 516 767-5108
  Port Washington *(G-13244)*
Casual Friday Inc .... F 585 544-9470
  Rochester *(G-13695)*
East Coast Embroidery Ltd .... G 631 254-3878
  Deer Park *(G-3969)*
Expressions Punching & Digitiz .... G 718 291-1177
  Jamaica *(G-6642)*
F X Graphix Inc .... G 716 871-1511
  Buffalo *(G-2823)*
Hosel & Ackerson Inc .... G 212 575-1490
  New York *(G-10125)*
Human Technologies Corporation .... F 315 735-3532
  Utica *(G-15711)*
Instant Monogramming Inc .... G 585 654-5550
  Rochester *(G-13882)*
Kevin J Kassman .... G 585 529-4245
  Rochester *(G-13904)*
Mainly Monograms Inc .... G 845 624-4923
  West Nyack *(G-16275)*
Milaaya Inc .... G 212 764-6386
  New York *(G-10806)*
Northeast Stitches & Ink Inc .... E 518 798-5549
  South Glens Falls *(G-14939)*
On The Job Embroidery & AP .... G 914 381-3556
  Mamaroneck *(G-7750)*
Penn & Fletcher Inc .... F 212 239-6868
  Long Island City *(G-7553)*
Planet Embroidery .... F 718 381-4827
  Ridgewood *(G-13546)*
Rescuestuff Inc .... G 718 318-7570
  Peekskill *(G-12923)*
Sciane Enterprises Inc .... G 845 452-2400
  Poughkeepsie *(G-13366)*

EMBROIDERING SVC: Schiffli Machine

American Images Inc .... F 716 825-8888
  Buffalo *(G-2696)*
Rmb Embroidery Service .... G 585 271-5560
  Rochester *(G-14075)*

EMBROIDERING: Swiss Loom

Stucki Embroidery Works Inc .... F 845 657-2308
  Boiceville *(G-1110)*

EMBROIDERY ADVERTISING SVCS

Dray Enterprises Inc .... F 585 768-2201
  Le Roy *(G-7116)*
Northeast Promotional Group In .... G 518 793-1024
  South Glens Falls *(G-14938)*

EMERGENCY ALARMS

All Metro Emrgncy Response Sys .... G 516 750-9100
  Lynbrook *(G-7659)*
Johnson Controls .... D 585 288-6200
  Rochester *(G-13895)*
Johnson Controls .... E 518 952-6040
  Clifton Park *(G-3568)*
Johnson Controls .... E 845 774-4120
  Harriman *(G-5720)*
Johnson Controls .... F 607 338-5100
  East Syracuse *(G-4356)*
Lifewatch Inc .... F 800 716-1433
  Hewlett *(G-6048)*
Napco Security Tech Inc .... C 631 842-9400
  Amityville *(G-304)*
Octopus Advanced Systems Inc .... G 914 771-6110
  Yonkers *(G-16786)*
Synergx Systems Inc .... D 516 433-4700
  Woodside *(G-16681)*
Telemergency Ltd .... G 914 629-4222
  White Plains *(G-16511)*
Telephonics Corporation .... F 631 755-7000
  Huntington *(G-6419)*

EMPLOYMENT AGENCY SVCS

Equal Opprtnity Pblcations Inc .... F 631 421-9421
  Melville *(G-8019)*
Symphony Talent LLC .... D 212 999-9000
  New York *(G-11759)*
Vaultcom Inc .... E 212 366-4212
  New York *(G-12001)*

ENAMELING SVC: Metal Prdts, Including Porcelain

F & H Metal Finishing Co Inc .... F 585 798-2151
  Medina *(G-7977)*

ENAMELS

Si Group Inc .... C 518 347-4200
  Schenectady *(G-14713)*

ENCLOSURES: Electronic

Compac Development Corporation .... D 631 881-4903
  Hauppauge *(G-5797)*
Kerns Manufacturing Corp .... C 718 784-4044
  Long Island City *(G-7488)*
National Computer & Electronic .... C 631 242-7222
  Deer Park *(G-4013)*

ENCODERS: Digital

Digifab Systems Inc .... G 212 944-9882
  New York *(G-9525)*
Silverlight Digital LLC .... G 646 650-5330
  New York *(G-11591)*

ENERGY MEASUREMENT EQPT

New York Enrgy Synthetics Inc .... G 212 634-4787
  New York *(G-10937)*
Performance Systems Contg Inc .... E 607 277-6240
  Ithaca *(G-6603)*

ENGINE REBUILDING: Diesel

D & W Diesel Inc .... F 518 437-1300
  Latham *(G-7070)*
Jack W Miller .... G 585 538-2399
  Scottsville *(G-14751)*

ENGINE REBUILDING: Gas

Washer Solutions Inc .... E 585 742-6388
  Victor *(G-15877)*

ENGINEERING SVCS

Acad Design Corp .... F 585 254-6960
  Rochester *(G-13594)*
Acme Engineering Products Inc .... E 518 236-5659
  Mooers *(G-8330)*
American Avionic Tech Corp .... D 631 924-8200
  Medford *(G-7937)*
Atlantic Industrial Tech Inc .... E 631 234-3131
  Shirley *(G-14830)*
Avanti Control Systems Inc .... G 518 921-4368
  Gloversville *(G-5452)*
Beltran Technologies Inc .... E 718 338-3311
  Brooklyn *(G-1596)*
Benfield Control Systems Inc .... F 914 948-6660
  White Plains *(G-16428)*
Bombardier Trnsp Holdings USA .... D 607 776-4791
  Bath *(G-641)*
Bsu Inc .... E 607 272-8100
  Ithaca *(G-6569)*
Critical Link LLC .... E 315 425-4045
  Syracuse *(G-15294)*
Dayton T Brown Inc .... B 631 589-6300
  Bohemia *(G-1011)*
Della Systems Inc .... F 631 580-0010
  Ronkonkoma *(G-14333)*
Digitronik Labs Inc .... F 585 360-0043
  Rochester *(G-13741)*
H S Assembly Inc .... E 585 266-4287
  Rochester *(G-13849)*
Howden North America Inc .... D 716 817-6900
  Depew *(G-4093)*
Interntnal Elctronic Mchs Corp .... E 518 268-1636
  Troy *(G-15610)*
Linita Design & Mfg Corp .... E 716 566-7753
  Lackawanna *(G-6949)*
Lourdes Industries Inc .... D 631 234-6600
  Hauppauge *(G-5873)*
Millennium Antenna Corp .... E 315 798-9374
  Utica *(G-15722)*
Mohawk Innovative Tech Inc .... F 518 862-4290
  Albany *(G-99)*
Photon Gear Inc .... F 585 265-3360
  Ontario *(G-12660)*
Remington Arms Company LLC .... A 315 895-3482
  Ilion *(G-6478)*
Rt Solutions LLC .... E 585 245-3456
  Rochester *(G-14107)*
Sg Blocks Inc .... E 615 585-2639
  Brooklyn *(G-2460)*
Stone Well Bodies & Mch Inc .... E 315 497-3512
  Genoa *(G-5338)*
Xactiv Inc .... F 585 288-7220
  Fairport *(G-4668)*

ENGINEERING SVCS: Building Construction

Roth Design & Consulting Inc .... E 718 209-0193
  Brooklyn *(G-2417)*

ENGINEERING SVCS: Electrical Or Electronic

Advanced Testing Tech Inc .... C 631 231-8777
  Hauppauge *(G-5755)*
C Speed LLC .... E 315 453-1043
  Liverpool *(G-7227)*
Nervve Technologies Inc .... E 716 800-2250
  New York *(G-10907)*
Tkm Technologies Inc .... E 631 474-4700
  Port Jeff STA *(G-13219)*

ENGINEERING SVCS: Heating & Ventilation

Vincent Genovese .... G 631 281-8170
  Mastic Beach *(G-7912)*

ENGINEERING SVCS: Industrial

Advanced Machine Design Co Inc .... E 716 826-2000
  Buffalo *(G-2689)*

ENGINEERING SVCS: Marine

L-3 Cmmnctns Ntronix Holdings .... D 212 697-1111
  New York *(G-10496)*

ENGINEERING SVCS: Mechanical

Calvary Design Team Inc .... C 585 347-6127
  Webster *(G-16076)*

PRODUCT SECTION

ENGINEERING SVCS: Pollution Control
Clean Gas Systems Inc ....E 631 467-1600
  Commack *(G-3686)*

ENGINEERING SVCS: Professional
Nasiff Associates Inc ....G 315 676-2346
  Central Square *(G-3391)*

ENGINEERING SVCS: Sanitary
Nes Bearing Company Inc ....E 716 372-6532
  Olean *(G-12605)*

ENGINEERING SVCS: Structural
Marovato Industries Inc ....F 718 389-0800
  Brooklyn *(G-2173)*
Tebbens Steel LLC ....F 631 208-8330
  Calverton *(G-3174)*

ENGINES: Internal Combustion, NEC
AB Engine ....G 518 557-3510
  Latham *(G-7061)*
Briggs & Stratton Corporation ......F 315 495-0100
  Sherrill *(G-14818)*
Briggs & Stratton Corporation ......C 315 495-0100
  Munnsville *(G-8457)*
Cummins - Allison Corp ....D 718 263-2482
  Kew Gardens *(G-6871)*
Cummins Inc ....D 716 456-2676
  Lakewood *(G-6992)*
Cummins Inc ....A 716 456-2111
  Lakewood *(G-6993)*
Cummins Northeast LLC ....E 315 437-2296
  Syracuse *(G-15297)*
Cummins-Wagner-Siewert LLC ...E 585 482-9640
  Rochester *(G-13728)*
Mannesmann Corporation ....D 212 258-4000
  New York *(G-10691)*
Perkins International Inc ....G 309 675-1000
  Buffalo *(G-2999)*

ENGRAVING SVC, NEC
Aldine Inc (ny) ....D 212 226-2870
  New York *(G-8788)*
Bates Jackson Engraving Co Inc ...E 716 854-3000
  Buffalo *(G-2725)*
Tripi Engraving Co Inc ....E 718 383-6500
  Brooklyn *(G-2586)*

ENGRAVING SVC: Jewelry & Personal Goods
Eastern Silver of Boro Park ....G 718 854-5600
  Brooklyn *(G-1810)*
Rayana Designs Inc ....E 718 786-2040
  Long Island City *(G-7573)*
With You Designs LLC ....G 800 413-0670
  Red Hook *(G-13460)*

ENGRAVING SVCS
Loremanss Embroidery Engrav ....F 518 834-9205
  Keeseville *(G-6852)*
Mooney-Keehley Inc ....G 585 271-1573
  Rochester *(G-13955)*

ENGRAVING: Steel line, For The Printing Trade
Lgn Materials & Solutions ....F 888 414-0005
  Mount Vernon *(G-8418)*

ENGRAVINGS: Plastic
Custom House Engravers Inc ....G 631 567-3004
  Bohemia *(G-1004)*

ENTERTAINERS & ENTERTAINMENT GROUPS
Comsec Ventures International .....G 518 523-1600
  Lake Placid *(G-6975)*
G Schirmer Inc ....G 212 254-2100
  New York *(G-9868)*
Tele-Pak Inc ....E 845 426-2300
  Monsey *(G-8302)*

ENTERTAINMENT SVCS
Marvel Entertainment LLC ....C 212 576-4000
  New York *(G-10719)*

ENVELOPES
3dflam Inc ....F 631 647-2694
  Bay Shore *(G-650)*
Apec Paper Industries Ltd ....G 212 730-0088
  New York *(G-8882)*
Buffalo Envelope Inc ....F 716 686-0100
  Depew *(G-4082)*
Cambridge-Pacific Inc ....E 518 677-5988
  Cambridge *(G-3178)*
Conformer Products Inc ....F 516 504-6300
  Great Neck *(G-5547)*
East Cast Envlope Graphics LLC ...E 718 326-2424
  Maspeth *(G-7840)*
Jacmax Industries LLC ....E 718 439-3743
  Brooklyn *(G-2029)*
Kleer-Fax Inc ....D 631 225-1100
  Amityville *(G-295)*
Mercury Envelope Co Inc ....D 516 678-6744
  Rockville Centre *(G-14236)*
Poly-Pak Industries Inc ....B 631 293-6767
  Melville *(G-8057)*
Premier Packaging Corporation ...E 585 924-8460
  Victor *(G-15861)*
Rochester 100 Inc ....C 585 475-0200
  Rochester *(G-14078)*
Westrock Mwv LLC ....C 212 688-5000
  New York *(G-12097)*
X-L Envelope and Printing Inc .....F 716 852-2135
  Buffalo *(G-3134)*

ENVELOPES WHOLESALERS
Apec Paper Industries Ltd ....G 212 730-0088
  New York *(G-8882)*
Buffalo Envelope Inc ....F 716 686-0100
  Depew *(G-4082)*
Diversified Envelope Ltd ....F 585 615-4697
  Rochester *(G-13745)*
Matt Industries Inc ....C 315 472-1316
  Syracuse *(G-15368)*
Prestige Envelope & Lithograph ...F 631 521-7043
  Merrick *(G-8105)*

ENVIRONMENTAL QUALITY PROGS ADMIN, GOVT: Waste Management
City of New York ....C 718 236-2693
  Brooklyn *(G-1696)*

ENZYMES
D-Best Equipment Corp ....E 516 358-0965
  West Hempstead *(G-16215)*
Zymtrnix Catalytic Systems Inc ....G 607 351-2639
  Ithaca *(G-6617)*

EPOXY RESINS
American Epoxy and Metal Inc ....G 718 828-7828
  Scarsdale *(G-14636)*
John C Dolph Company Inc ....E 732 329-2333
  Schenectady *(G-14692)*

EQUIPMENT: Pedestrian Traffic Control
Cq Traffic Control Devices LLC ...G 518 767-0057
  Selkirk *(G-14767)*
Lifeway Network Inc ....G 718 779-8075
  Rego Park *(G-13464)*

EQUIPMENT: Rental & Leasing, NEC
Beck Vault Company ....G 315 337-7590
  Rome *(G-14248)*
G E Inspection Technologies LP ...C 315 554-2000
  Skaneateles *(G-14871)*
Millennium Stl Rack Rntals Inc ....G 718 965-4736
  Brooklyn *(G-2208)*
Mobile Mini Inc ....F 315 732-4555
  Utica *(G-15723)*
Raymond Corporation ....A 607 656-2311
  Greene *(G-5617)*
Raymond Corporation ....E 315 643-5000
  East Syracuse *(G-4364)*

ESCALATORS: Passenger & Freight
Allround Logistics Inc ....G 718 544-8945
  Forest Hills *(G-5071)*

ETCHING & ENGRAVING SVC
Accurate Pnt Powdr Coating Inc ...F 585 235-1650
  Rochester *(G-13597)*
Advanced Coating Service LLC ...G 585 247-3970
  Rochester *(G-13605)*
Ascribe Inc ....E 585 413-0298
  Rochester *(G-13646)*
Custom House Engravers Inc ......G 631 567-3004
  Bohemia *(G-1004)*
Custom Laser Inc ....E 716 434-8600
  Lockport *(G-7292)*
Pro-Tech Catings Solutions Inc ...G 631 707-9400
  Edgewood *(G-4412)*
Steel Partners Holdings LP ....D 212 520-2300
  New York *(G-11699)*
Stuart-Dean Co Inc ....F 718 472-1326
  Long Island City *(G-7606)*

ETCHING SVC: Metal
Jamestown Bronze Works Inc .....G 716 665-2302
  Jamestown *(G-6727)*

ETCHING SVC: Photochemical
Newchem Inc ....E 315 331-7680
  Ithaca *(G-6601)*

ETHANOLAMINES
Western New York Energy LLC ...E 585 798-9693
  Medina *(G-7992)*

ETHYLENE-PROPYLENE RUBBERS: EPDM Polymers
Formosa Polymer Corporation .....G 718 326-1769
  Maspeth *(G-7846)*
Hilord Chemical Corporation ....E 631 234-7373
  Hauppauge *(G-5845)*

EXCAVATING EQPT
Kinshofer Usa Inc ....E 716 731-4333
  Sanborn *(G-14549)*

EXERCISE EQPT STORES
TDS Fitness Equipment Corp ......F 607 733-6789
  Elmira *(G-4505)*

EXHAUST HOOD OR FAN CLEANING SVCS
Jr Engineering Enterprise LLC .....G 716 909-2693
  Grand Island *(G-5504)*

EXHAUST SYSTEMS: Eqpt & Parts
Classic & Performance Spc ....E 716 759-1800
  Lancaster *(G-7014)*

EXPANSION JOINTS: Rubber
Mercer Rubber Co ....C 631 348-0282
  Hauppauge *(G-5886)*

EXPLOSIVES
Dyno Nobel Inc ....D 845 338-2144
  Ulster Park *(G-15658)*

EXPLOSIVES, EXC AMMO & FIREWORKS WHOLESALERS
Island Ordnance Systems LLC ....F 516 746-2100
  Mineola *(G-8230)*

EXTENSION CORDS
Ncc Ny LLC ....E 718 943-7000
  Brooklyn *(G-2251)*

EXTRACTS, FLAVORING
Baldwin Richardson Foods Co ....C 315 986-2727
  Macedon *(G-7695)*
Craftmaster Flavor Technology ....F 631 789-8607
  Amityville *(G-270)*

EXTRACTS, FLAVORING

Esense LLC ....F 718 887-9779
Long Island City *(G-7439)*

Virginia Dare Extract Co Inc.................C 718 788-6320
Brooklyn *(G-2626)*

EXTRACTS: Dying Or Tanning, Natural

Prismatic Dyeing & Finshg Inc ....D 845 561-1800
Newburgh *(G-12242)*

EYEGLASSES

Colors In Optics Ltd...............................D 718 845-0300
New Hyde Park *(G-8523)*

Corinne McCormack Inc..........................F 212 868-7919
New York *(G-9401)*

Eponym Inc..G 646 918-4586
Brooklyn *(G-1843)*

Essilor Laboratories Amer Inc................E 845 365-6700
Orangeburg *(G-12676)*

Frame Works America Inc......................E 631 288-1300
Westhampton Beach *(G-16403)*

Hirsch Optical Corp.................................D 516 752-2211
Farmingdale *(G-4780)*

Humanware USA Inc...............................E 800 722-3393
Champlain *(G-3410)*

M Factory USA Inc...................................G 917 410-7878
Brooklyn *(G-2147)*

Optogenics of Syracuse Inc..................D 315 446-3000
Syracuse *(G-15388)*

Parker Warby Retail Inc..........................G 646 517-5223
New York *(G-11117)*

EYEGLASSES: Sunglasses

Glasses USA LLC....................................F 212 784-6094
New York *(G-9932)*

Xinya International Trading Co...............G 212 216-9681
New York *(G-12152)*

EYES: Artificial

Mager & Gougelman Inc..........................G 212 661-3939
New York *(G-10663)*

Mager & Gougelman Inc..........................G 212 661-3939
Hempstead *(G-6019)*

Mager & Gougelman Inc..........................G 516 489-0202
Hempstead *(G-6020)*

Mark F Rosenhaft N A O ....G 516 374-1010
Cedarhurst *(G-3334)*

Strauss Eye Prosthetics Inc...................G 585 424-1350
Rochester *(G-14146)*

FABRIC FINISHING: Mending, Wool

Woolmark Americas Inc.........................G 347 767-3160
New York *(G-12133)*

FABRIC STORES

Creation Baumann USA Inc....................E 516 764-7431
Rockville Centre *(G-14231)*

Missiontex Inc..G 718 532-9053
Brooklyn *(G-2215)*

Shengkun North America Inc.................F 212 217-2460
New York *(G-11563)*

FABRICATED METAL PRODUCTS, NEC

Brooklyn Cstm Met Fbrction Inc............G 718 499-1573
Brooklyn *(G-1641)*

Factory East ....E 718 280-1558
Brooklyn *(G-1864)*

James D Rubino Inc.................................E 631 244-8730
Bohemia *(G-1039)*

Kwong CHI Metal Fabrication ....G 718 369-6429
Brooklyn *(G-2086)*

PBL Industries Corp ....F 631 979-4266
Smithtown *(G-14904)*

Range Repair Warehouse 585 235-0980
Penfield *(G-12943)*

Total Metal Resource ....F 718 384-7818
Brooklyn *(G-2575)*

FABRICS & CLOTH: Quilted

American Country Quilts & Lin...............G 631 283-5466
Southampton *(G-14949)*

Pink Inc ....E 212 352-8282
New York *(G-11197)*

FABRICS: Alpacas, Mohair, Woven

Alicia Adams Alpaca Inc.........................G 845 868-3366
Millbrook *(G-8187)*

FABRICS: Apparel & Outerwear, Broadwoven

Interaxissourcingcom Inc ....E 212 905-6001
New York *(G-10236)*

Light House Hill Marketing.....................F 212 354-1338
New York *(G-10567)*

Nazim Izzak Inc..G 212 920-5546
Long Island City *(G-7534)*

Oakhurst Partners LLC...........................G 212 502-3220
New York *(G-11024)*

Pinder International Inc..........................G 631 273-0324
Hauppauge *(G-5915)*

Yarnz International Inc...........................G 212 868-5883
New York *(G-12160)*

FABRICS: Apparel & Outerwear, Cotton

A and J Apparel Corp ....G 212 398-8899
New York *(G-8690)*

A3 Apparel LLC..G 888 403-9669
New York *(G-8701)*

Accolade USA Inc....................................C 866 423-5071
Cheektowaga *(G-3434)*

Advanced Fashions Technology............G 212 221-0606
New York *(G-8755)*

Bandier Corp...G 212 242-5400
New York *(G-9011)*

Basileus Company LLC..........................F 315 963-3516
Manlius *(G-7774)*

Benartex LLC..G 212 840-3250
New York *(G-9043)*

Charming Fashion Inc............................G 212 730-2872
New York *(G-9266)*

Comet Intl Trdg Co Inc............................F 731 599-2430
Brooklyn *(G-1708)*

Creation Baumann USA Inc ....E 516 764-7431
Rockville Centre *(G-14231)*

Cy Fashion Corp ....G 212 730-8600
New York *(G-9440)*

Equipment Apparel LLC ....D 212 502-1890
New York *(G-9697)*

Erin Snow Ltd ....G 212 675-7762
New York *(G-9703)*

H Group LLC...F 212 719-5500
New York *(G-10015)*

Hanesbrands Inc ....G 212 576-9300
New York *(G-10032)*

Horizon Apparel Mfg Inc.........................G 516 361-4878
Atlantic Beach *(G-456)*

Internationl Studios Inc..........................G 212 819-1616
New York *(G-10250)*

Knightly Endeavors ....F 845 340-0949
Kingston *(G-6905)*

Magic Brands International LLC.............F 212 563-4999
New York *(G-10666)*

Melwood Partners Inc............................F 631 923-0134
Melville *(G-8045)*

Pacific City International ....F 646 309-1250
New York *(G-11090)*

Phoenix Usa LLC ....G 646 351-6598
New York *(G-11184)*

Premium 5 Kids LLC................................F 212 563-4999
New York *(G-11231)*

Shahin Designs Ltd ....G 212 737-7225
New York *(G-11554)*

Success Apparel LLC..............................G 212 502-1890
New York *(G-11733)*

US Design Group Ltd..............................F 212 354-4070
New York *(G-11974)*

Vf Services LLC.......................................G 212 575-7820
New York *(G-12022)*

FABRICS: Apparel & Outerwear, From Manmade Fiber Or Silk

Concepts Nyc Inc.....................................E 212 244-1033
New York *(G-9372)*

JM Manufacturer Inc................................G 212 869-0626
New York *(G-10344)*

New York Poplin LLC...............................G 718 768-3296
Brooklyn *(G-2264)*

FABRICS: Automotive, From Manmade Fiber

Maharam Fabric Corporation..................G 631 582-3434
Yaphank *(G-16716)*

FABRICS: Bags & Bagging, Cotton

Nochairs Inc ....G 917 748-8731
New York *(G-10983)*

FABRICS: Broad Woven, Goods, Cotton

Beyond Loom Inc.....................................G 212 575-3100
New York *(G-9064)*

Gerli & Co Inc..B 212 213-1919
New York *(G-9913)*

Lydall Performance Mtl Inc ....C 518 273-6320
Green Island *(G-5609)*

FABRICS: Broadwoven, Cotton

Ann Gish Inc..G 212 969-9200
New York *(G-8871)*

Joy of Learning ....G 718 443-6463
Brooklyn *(G-2050)*

Marsha Fleisher ....F 845 679-6500
Woodstock *(G-16686)*

Scalamandre Wallpaper Inc ....B 631 467-8800
Hauppauge *(G-5934)*

Schneider Mills Inc.................................C 828 632-0801
New York *(G-11511)*

FABRICS: Broadwoven, Synthetic Manmade Fiber & Silk

Apex Texicon Inc......................................E 516 239-4400
New York *(G-8883)*

Creation Baumann USA Inc ....E 516 764-7431
Rockville Centre *(G-14231)*

Eastern Silk Mills Inc..............................G 212 730-1300
New York *(G-9611)*

Fabric Resources Intl Ltd.......................F 516 829-4550
Great Neck *(G-5554)*

Fibrix LLC..E 716 683-4100
Depew *(G-4089)*

Gerli & Co Inc..B 212 213-1919
New York *(G-9913)*

Ivi Services Inc..D 607 729-5111
Binghamton *(G-897)*

Jag Manufacturing Inc............................E 518 762-9558
Johnstown *(G-6832)*

Jakob Schlaepfer Inc...............................G 212 221-2323
New York *(G-10302)*

Scalamandre Wallpaper Inc ....B 631 467-8800
Hauppauge *(G-5934)*

Schneider Mills Inc.................................C 828 632-0801
New York *(G-11511)*

Superior Fiber Mills Inc..........................E 718 782-7500
Brooklyn *(G-2538)*

Toltec Fabrics Inc....................................C 212 706-9310
New York *(G-11857)*

Toray Industries Inc................................G 212 697-8150
New York *(G-11869)*

FABRICS: Broadwoven, Wool

Acker & LI Mills Corporation..................G 212 307-7247
New York *(G-8727)*

Citisource Industries Inc ....E 212 683-1033
New York *(G-9307)*

Fabric Resources Intl Ltd.......................F 516 829-4550
Great Neck *(G-5554)*

Hawkins Fabrics Inc................................E 518 773-9550
Johnstown *(G-6830)*

Scalamandre Wallpaper Inc ....B 631 467-8800
Hauppauge *(G-5934)*

FABRICS: Brocade, Cotton

La Lame Inc..G 212 921-9770
New York *(G-10502)*

FABRICS: Canvas

Geordie Magee Uphl & Canvas...............G 315 676-7679
Brewerton *(G-1150)*

Sita Finishing Inc ....F 718 417-5295
Brooklyn *(G-2482)*

FABRICS: Chemically Coated & Treated

Kiltronx Enviro Systems LLC ....E 917 971-7177
Hauppauge *(G-5855)*

Perry Plastics Inc ....F 718 747-5600
Flushing *(G-5037)*

PRODUCT SECTION FABRICS: Trimmings

FABRICS: Coated Or Treated

Breton Industries Inc..................................C....... 518 842-3030
Amsterdam *(G-329)*
Chemprene Inc..C....... 845 831-2800
Beacon *(G-755)*
Chemprene Holding Inc.............................C....... 845 831-2800
Beacon *(G-756)*
Comfort Care Textiles Inc........................E....... 631 543-0531
Commack *(G-3687)*
Eurotex Inc..F....... 716 205-8861
Niagara Falls *(G-12282)*
Fabric Resources Intl Ltd..........................F....... 516 829-4550
Great Neck *(G-5554)*
Newtex Industries Inc................................E....... 585 924-9135
Victor *(G-15858)*
Precision Custom Coatings LLC..............C....... 212 868-5770
New York *(G-11228)*

FABRICS: Cords

Schoen Trimming & Cord Co Inc.............F....... 212 255-3949
New York *(G-11512)*

FABRICS: Corduroys, Cotton

Paramount Cord & Brackets......................G....... 212 325-9100
White Plains *(G-16484)*

FABRICS: Denims

Axis Na LLC..F....... 212 840-4005
New York *(G-8984)*
Brooklyn Denim Co......................................F....... 718 782-2600
Brooklyn *(G-1642)*
Jrg Apparel Group Company Ltd.............E....... 212 997-0900
New York *(G-10372)*
SD Eagle Global Inc...................................G....... 516 822-1778
Jericho *(G-6803)*
Xing Lin USA Intl Corp...............................G....... 212 947-4846
New York *(G-12151)*

FABRICS: Elastic, From Manmade Fiber Or Silk

A B C Elastic Corp......................................G....... 718 388-2953
Brooklyn *(G-1453)*

FABRICS: Fiberglass, Broadwoven

Fiber Glass Industries Inc........................D....... 518 842-4000
Amsterdam *(G-337)*
Newtex Industries Inc................................E....... 585 924-9135
Victor *(G-15858)*
Polytex Inc..D....... 716 549-5100
Angola *(G-370)*

FABRICS: Glass, Narrow

Mergence Studios Ltd................................F....... 212 288-5616
Hauppauge *(G-5887)*

FABRICS: Glove, Lining

J & M Textile Co Inc..................................F....... 212 268-8000
New York *(G-10282)*

FABRICS: Hand Woven

Thistle Hill Weavers....................................G....... 518 284-2729
Cherry Valley *(G-3466)*

FABRICS: Handkerchief, Cotton

Northpoint Trading Inc..............................F....... 212 481-8001
New York *(G-10997)*

FABRICS: Jean

Apollo Apparel Group LLC........................F....... 212 398-6585
New York *(G-8885)*

FABRICS: Jersey Cloth

Cap USA Jerseyman Harlem Inc.............G....... 212 222-7942
New York *(G-9200)*

FABRICS: Lace & Decorative Trim, Narrow

Eiseman-Ludmar Co Inc............................F....... 516 932-6990
Hicksville *(G-6083)*

FABRICS: Lace & Lace Prdts

Orbit Industries LLC..................................F....... 914 244-1500
Mount Kisco *(G-8353)*
Solstiss Inc...G....... 212 719-9194
New York *(G-11641)*
Super-Trim Inc...E....... 212 255-2370
New York *(G-11747)*

FABRICS: Lace, Knit, NEC

Hosel & Ackerson Inc................................G....... 212 575-1490
New York *(G-10125)*
Klauber Brothers Inc..................................G....... 212 686-2531
New York *(G-10457)*

FABRICS: Laminated

A-One Laminating Corp.............................G....... 718 266-6002
Brooklyn *(G-1464)*
A-One Moving & Storage Inc...................E....... 718 266-6002
Brooklyn *(G-1465)*
New York Cutting & Gumming Co...........E....... 212 563-4146
Middletown *(G-8168)*
Tpi Industries LLC......................................E....... 845 692-2820
Middletown *(G-8179)*

FABRICS: Linings & Interlinings, Cotton

Navas Designs Inc.....................................E....... 818 988-9050
New York *(G-10898)*

FABRICS: Long Cloth, Cotton

Haleys Comet Seafood Corp....................E....... 212 571-1828
New York *(G-10022)*

FABRICS: Nonwoven

Albany International Corp.........................C....... 518 445-2200
Rensselaer *(G-13470)*
Fabrication Enterprises Inc......................E....... 914 591-9300
Elmsford *(G-4543)*
Legendary Auto Interiors Ltd..................E....... 315 331-1212
Newark *(G-12198)*
Mgk Group Inc..E....... 212 989-2732
New York *(G-10788)*
Saint-Gobain Adfors Amer Inc................D....... 716 775-3900
Grand Island *(G-5512)*
Saint-Gobain Adfors Amer Inc................E....... 585 589-4401
Albion *(G-163)*

FABRICS: Nylon, Broadwoven

Kragel Co Inc...G....... 716 648-1344
Hamburg *(G-5685)*

FABRICS: Paper, Broadwoven

Albany International Corp.........................C....... 518 445-2200
Rensselaer *(G-13470)*

FABRICS: Pile Warp or Flat Knit

George Knitting Mills Corp.......................G....... 212 242-3300
New York *(G-9910)*

FABRICS: Pile, Circular Knit

Hill Knitting Mills Inc.................................E....... 718 846-5000
Richmond Hill *(G-13504)*

FABRICS: Pocketing Twill, Cotton

Cai Inc..E....... 212 819-0008
New York *(G-9176)*

FABRICS: Polyester, Broadwoven

Marly Home Industries USA Inc..............G....... 718 388-3030
Brooklyn *(G-2172)*

FABRICS: Print, Cotton

Neilson International Inc..........................G....... 631 454-0400
Farmingdale *(G-4834)*
Perfect Print Inc...E....... 718 832-5280
Brooklyn *(G-2313)*

FABRICS: Resin Or Plastic Coated

GE Polymershapes......................................F....... 516 433-4092
Hicksville *(G-6089)*
Kaneka America LLC.................................D....... 212 705-4340
New York *(G-10404)*

Tonoga Inc...C....... 518 658-3202
Petersburg *(G-12973)*

FABRICS: Rubberized

Chemprene Inc..C....... 845 831-2800
Beacon *(G-755)*
Chemprene Holding Inc.............................C....... 845 831-2800
Beacon *(G-756)*
Kelson Products Inc..................................G....... 716 825-2585
Orchard Park *(G-12723)*

FABRICS: Shirting, Cotton

Gotham T-Shirt Corp..................................G....... 516 676-0900
Sea Cliff *(G-14755)*

FABRICS: Shoe

Avitto Leather Goods Inc.........................G....... 212 219-7501
New York *(G-8979)*

FABRICS: Silk, Broadwoven

Beyond Loom Inc..G....... 212 575-3100
New York *(G-9064)*
Himatsingka America Inc.........................E....... 212 252-0802
New York *(G-10102)*

FABRICS: Silk, Narrow

Solstiss Inc...G....... 212 719-9194
New York *(G-11641)*

FABRICS: Spandex, Broadwoven

La Lame Inc...G....... 212 921-9770
New York *(G-10502)*

FABRICS: Specialty Including Twisted Weaves, Broadwoven

Intertex USA Inc...F....... 212 279-3601
New York *(G-10253)*

FABRICS: Stretch, Cotton

Shindo Usa Inc..G....... 212 868-9311
New York *(G-11567)*

FABRICS: Surgical Fabrics, Cotton

Medline Industries Inc..............................B....... 845 344-3301
Middletown *(G-8163)*

FABRICS: Tapestry, Cotton

Renaissnce Crpt Tapestries Inc..............F....... 212 696-0080
New York *(G-11360)*

FABRICS: Tricot

Hudson Fabrics LLC...................................F....... 518 671-6100
Hudson *(G-6355)*
Litchfield Fabrics of NC............................G....... 518 773-9500
Gloversville *(G-5461)*
Veratex Inc...F....... 212 683-9300
New York *(G-12009)*

FABRICS: Trimmings

Albert Siy...G....... 718 359-0389
Flushing *(G-4982)*
American Spray-On Corp..........................E....... 212 929-2100
New York *(G-8837)*
Angel Textiles Inc......................................G....... 212 532-0900
New York *(G-8862)*
Athletic Cap Co Inc....................................E....... 718 398-1300
Staten Island *(G-15045)*
Barnaby Prints Inc.....................................F....... 845 477-2501
Greenwood Lake *(G-5648)*
Bondy Printing Corp..................................G....... 631 242-1510
Bay Shore *(G-666)*
C H Thompson Company Inc...................D....... 607 724-1094
Binghamton *(G-874)*
Coe Displays Inc...G....... 718 937-5658
Long Island City *(G-7412)*
Cooper & Clement Inc...............................E....... 315 454-8135
Syracuse *(G-15289)*
D & R Silk Screening Ltd.........................F....... 631 234-7464
Central Islip *(G-3367)*
Decal Makers Inc.......................................E....... 516 221-7200
Bellmore *(G-788)*
Eagle Lace Dyeing Corp...........................F....... 212 947-2712
New York *(G-9603)*

Employee Codes: A=Over 500 employees, B=251-500
C=101-250, D=51-100, E=20-50, F=10-19, G=5-9

FABRICS: Trimmings

Company		Phone
Emtron Hybrids Inc	F	631 924-9668
Yaphank *(G-16710)*		
Flp Group LLC	F	315 252-7583
Auburn *(G-480)*		
Folder Factory Inc	F	540 477-3852
Amityville *(G-275)*		
Freeport Screen & Stamping		516 379-0330
Freeport *(G-5157)*		
Ihd Motorsports LLC	F	979 690-1669
Binghamton *(G-894)*		
Jack J Florio Jr	G	716 434-9123
Lockport *(G-7311)*		
Kenmar Shirts Inc	E	718 824-3880
Bronx *(G-1307)*		
L I C Screen Printing Inc		516 546-7289
Merrick *(G-8100)*		
Loremanss Embroidery Engrav	F	518 834-9205
Keeseville *(G-6852)*		
Master Craft Finishers Inc	E	631 586-0540
Deer Park *(G-4007)*		
Master Image Printing Inc	G	914 347-4400
Elmsford *(G-4550)*		
New York Binding Co Inc	E	718 729-2454
Long Island City *(G-7539)*		
Northeast Stitches & Ink Inc	E	518 798-5549
South Glens Falls *(G-14939)*		
Round Top Knit & Screening	G	518 622-3600
Round Top *(G-14466)*		
Sellco Industries Inc	E	607 756-7594
Cortland *(G-3894)*		
Solidus Industries Inc	D	607 749-4540
Homer *(G-6259)*		
Todd Walbridge	G	585 254-3018
Rochester *(G-14171)*		
U All Inc	E	518 438-2558
Albany *(G-136)*		

FABRICS: Trimmings, Textile

Company		Phone
American Trim Mfg Inc	E	518 239-8151
Durham *(G-4183)*		
Bardwil Industries Inc	C	212 944-1870
New York *(G-9014)*		
Champion Zipper Corp	G	212 239-0414
New York *(G-9258)*		
Danray Textiles Corp	F	212 354-5213
New York *(G-9470)*		
Jakob Schlaepfer Inc	G	212 221-2323
New York *(G-10302)*		
Marketing Action Xecutives Inc	G	212 971-9155
New York *(G-10712)*		
Scalamandre Silks Inc	D	212 980-3888
New York *(G-11499)*		

FABRICS: Upholstery, Cotton

Company		Phone
Meder Textile Co Inc	G	516 883-0409
Port Washington *(G-13284)*		
Mgk Group Inc	E	212 989-2732
New York *(G-10788)*		
N Y Contract Seating Inc	G	718 417-9298
Maspeth *(G-7860)*		

FABRICS: Varnished Glass & Coated Fiberglass

Company		Phone
Architectural Fiberglass Corp	E	631 842-4772
Copiague *(G-3750)*		

FABRICS: Wall Covering, From Manmade Fiber Or Silk

Company		Phone
Art People Inc	G	212 431-4865
New York *(G-8915)*		
Mgk Group Inc	E	212 989-2732
New York *(G-10788)*		
National Contract Industries	G	212 249-0045
New York *(G-10881)*		

FABRICS: Warp & Flat Knit Prdts

Company		Phone
Fab Industries Corp	B	516 498-3200
Great Neck *(G-5553)*		
Gehring Tricot Corporation	C	315 429-8551
Dolgeville *(G-4134)*		
Ssjjj Manufacturing LLC	B	516 498-3200
Great Neck *(G-5590)*		

FABRICS: Warp Knit, Lace & Netting

Company		Phone
Apex Aridyne Corp	G	516 239-4400
Inwood *(G-6484)*		

Company		Phone
Helmont Mills Inc	G	518 568-7913
Saint Johnsville *(G-14519)*		
Mohawk Fabric Company Inc	F	518 842-3090
Amsterdam *(G-350)*		
Somerset Industries Inc	E	518 773-7383
Gloversville *(G-5466)*		
Sunwin Global Industry Inc	G	646 370-6196
New York *(G-11745)*		

FABRICS: Weft Or Circular Knit

Company		Phone
Apex Aridyne Corp	G	516 239-4400
Inwood *(G-6484)*		
Apex Texicon Inc	E	516 239-4400
New York *(G-8883)*		
Lemral Knitwear Inc	D	718 210-0175
Brooklyn *(G-2109)*		
S & W Knitting Mills Inc	E	718 237-2416
Brooklyn *(G-2436)*		

FABRICS: Woven, Narrow Cotton, Wool, Silk

Company		Phone
Albany International Corp	E	518 445-2200
Rensselaer *(G-13470)*		
American Canvas Binders Corp	G	914 969-0300
Yonkers *(G-16734)*		
Breton Industries Inc	C	518 842-3030
Amsterdam *(G-329)*		
Depot Label Company Inc	G	631 467-2952
Patchogue *(G-12864)*		
Labeltex Mills Inc		212 279-6165
New York *(G-10505)*		
Newtex Industries Inc		585 924-9135
Victor *(G-15858)*		
Skil-Care Corporation		914 963-2040
Yonkers *(G-16798)*		
Valley Industrial Products Inc	E	631 385-9300
Huntington *(G-6424)*		

FACILITIES SUPPORT SVCS

Company		Phone
Johnson Controls Inc	C	585 724-2232
Rochester *(G-13897)*		

FACSIMILE COMMUNICATION EQPT

Company		Phone
Alternative Technology Corp	G	914 478-5900
Hastings On Hudson *(G-5747)*		

FAMILY CLOTHING STORES

Company		Phone
Kate Spade & Company LLC	B	212 354-4900
New York *(G-10415)*		
Land n Sea Inc	D	212 444-6000
New York *(G-10513)*		
Missiontex Inc	G	718 532-9053
Brooklyn *(G-2215)*		
Ramsbury Property Us Inc	F	212 223-6250
New York *(G-11322)*		
Round Top Knit & Screening	G	518 622-3600
Round Top *(G-14466)*		
S & T Knitting Co Inc	E	607 722-7558
Conklin *(G-3732)*		

FANS, BLOWING: Indl Or Commercial

Company		Phone
Apgn Inc	E	518 324-4150
Plattsburgh *(G-13106)*		
Canarm Ltd	G	800 267-4427
Ogdensburg *(G-12572)*		
Oestreich Metal Works Inc	G	315 463-4268
Syracuse *(G-15384)*		
Rapid Fan & Blower Inc	F	718 786-2060
Long Island City *(G-7571)*		

FANS, EXHAUST: Indl Or Commercial

Company		Phone
Howden North America Inc	D	803 741-2700
Depew *(G-4092)*		
Jr Engineering Enterprise LLC	G	716 909-2693
Grand Island *(G-5504)*		

FANS, VENTILATING: Indl Or Commercial

Company		Phone
Howden North America Inc	D	716 817-6900
Depew *(G-4093)*		

FARM & GARDEN MACHINERY WHOLESALERS

Company		Phone
Oxbo International Corporation	D	585 548-2665
Byron *(G-3145)*		
Saxby Implement Corp	F	585 624-2938
Mendon *(G-8094)*		

FARM PRDTS, RAW MATERIALS, WHOLESALE: Bristles

Company		Phone
Cenibra Inc	G	212 818-8242
New York *(G-9239)*		

FARM PRDTS, RAW MATERIALS, WHOLESALE: Hides

Company		Phone
Hastings Hide Inc	G	516 295-2400
Inwood *(G-6492)*		

FARM SPLY STORES

Company		Phone
Bailey Boonville Mills Inc	G	315 942-2131
Boonville *(G-1114)*		
Gramco Inc		716 592-2845
Springville *(G-15017)*		
Lowville Farmers Coop Inc	E	315 376-6587
Lowville *(G-7652)*		

FARM SPLYS, WHOLESALE: Beekeeping Splys, Nondurable

Company		Phone
Northast Ctr For Bekeeping LLC	F	800 632-3379
Greenwich *(G-5643)*		

FASTENERS: Metal

Company		Phone
John Hassall LLC	D	516 334-6200
Westbury *(G-16344)*		
Pmb Precision Products Inc	F	631 491-6753
West Babylon *(G-16182)*		
Universal Metals Inc	G	516 829-0896
Great Neck *(G-5598)*		

FASTENERS: Metal

Company		Phone
D Best Service Co Inc	G	718 972-6133
Brooklyn *(G-1746)*		
Southco Inc	B	585 624-2545
Honeoye Falls *(G-6273)*		

FASTENERS: Notions, NEC

Company		Phone
American Pride Fasteners LLC	E	631 940-8292
Bay Shore *(G-656)*		
CPI of Falconer Inc	E	716 664-4444
Falconer *(G-4674)*		
Cw Fasteners & Zippers Corp	F	212 594-3203
New York *(G-9439)*		
Jem Threading Specialties Inc	G	718 665-3341
Bronx *(G-1301)*		
Kenwin Sales Corp		516 933-7553
Deer Park *(G-3995)*		

FASTENERS: Notions, Snaps

Company		Phone
M H Stryke Co Inc	F	631 242-2660
Deer Park *(G-4005)*		
Rings Wire Inc	G	212 741-9779
New York *(G-11393)*		

FASTENERS: Notions, Zippers

Company		Phone
Champion Zipper Corp		212 239-0414
New York *(G-9258)*		
Riri USA Inc	G	212 268-3866
New York *(G-11394)*		

FAUCETS & SPIGOTS: Metal & Plastic

Company		Phone
Faucets and More Incorporated	G	734 328-2387
Brooklyn *(G-1869)*		
Giagni Enterprises LLC	G	914 699-6500
Mount Vernon *(G-8400)*		
Giagni International Corp	G	914 699-6500
Mount Vernon *(G-8401)*		
Hanco Metal Products Inc	F	212 787-5992
Brooklyn *(G-1965)*		
I W Industries Inc	C	631 293-9494
Melville *(G-8036)*		

FEATHERS: Renovating

Company		Phone
Eser Realty Corp	E	718 383-0565
Brooklyn *(G-1847)*		

FELT: Acoustic

Company		Phone
Ghani Textiles Inc		718 859-4561
Brooklyn *(G-1925)*		
Soundcoat Company Inc	D	631 242-2200
Deer Park *(G-4047)*		

PRODUCT SECTION

FENCE POSTS: Iron & Steel

Bonura and Sons Iron Works ....F 718 381-4100
  Franklin Square *(G-5115)*

FENCES & FENCING MATERIALS

Rose Fence Inc ....E 516 223-0717
  Freeport *(G-5179)*
Rose Fence Inc ....D 516 790-2308
  Halesite *(G-5659)*
Sunward Electronics Inc ....F 518 687-0030
  Troy *(G-15629)*

FENCES OR POSTS: Ornamental Iron Or Steel

786 Iron Works Corp ....G 718 418-4808
  Brooklyn *(G-1446)*
Empire Steel Works Inc ....F 516 561-3500
  Hicksville *(G-6084)*
Fence Plaza Corp ....G 718 469-2200
  Brooklyn *(G-1874)*
Jamaica Iron Works Inc ....F 718 657-4849
  Jamaica *(G-6653)*
McAllisters Precision Wldg Inc ......F 518 221-3455
  Menands *(G-8087)*
Ourem Iron Works Inc ....F 914 476-4856
  Yonkers *(G-16789)*
Tee Pee Fence and Railing ....F 718 658-8323
  Jamaica *(G-6683)*
Triple H Construction Inc ....E 516 280-8252
  East Meadow *(G-4256)*

FENCING DEALERS

A & T Iron Works Inc ....E 914 632-8992
  New Rochelle *(G-8585)*
Fence Plaza Corp ....G 718 469-2200
  Brooklyn *(G-1874)*
Long Lumber and Supply Corp .....F 518 439-1661
  Slingerlands *(G-14889)*
Rose Fence Inc ....F 516 223-0777
  Baldwin *(G-541)*
Walpole Woodworkers Inc ....G 631 726-2859
  Water Mill *(G-15971)*

FENCING MATERIALS: Docks & Other Outdoor Prdts, Wood

Atlas Fence & Railing Co Inc ....E 718 767-2200
  Whitestone *(G-16535)*
Cffco USA Inc ....G 718 747-1118
  Jericho *(G-6781)*

FENCING MATERIALS: Plastic

Amadeo Serrano ....G 516 608-8359
  Freeport *(G-5142)*
Atlas Fence & Railing Co Inc ....E 718 767-2200
  Whitestone *(G-16535)*
Oneonta Fence ....G 607 433-6707
  Oneonta *(G-12642)*

FENCING MATERIALS: Wood

Interstate Wood Products Inc ....E 631 842-4488
  Amityville *(G-288)*
Long Lumber and Supply Corp .....F 518 439-1661
  Slingerlands *(G-14889)*
Rose Fence Inc ....F 516 223-0777
  Baldwin *(G-541)*
Walpole Woodworkers Inc ....G 631 726-2859
  Water Mill *(G-15971)*

FENCING: Chain Link

Master-Halco Inc ....F 631 585-8150
  Yaphank *(G-16717)*

FERRITES

Hoosier Magnetics Inc ....E 315 323-5832
  Ogdensburg *(G-12575)*

FERROALLOYS

CCA Holding Inc ....C 716 446-8800
  Amherst *(G-220)*
Medima LLC ....C 716 741-0400
  Clarence *(G-3535)*
Thyssenkrupp Materials NA Inc ....F 212 972-8800
  New York *(G-11829)*

FERROMANGANESE, NOT MADE IN BLAST FURNACES

Globe Metallurgical Inc ....D 716 804-0862
  Niagara Falls *(G-12288)*

FERTILIZERS: NEC

Biosoil Farm Inc ....G 518 344-4920
  Glenville *(G-5444)*
Carolina Eastern-Vail Inc ....E 518 854-9785
  Salem *(G-14537)*
Commodity Resource Corporation ....F 585 538-9500
  Caledonia *(G-3154)*

FERTILIZERS: Nitrogenous

Growth Products Ltd ....E 914 428-1316
  White Plains *(G-16456)*
Rt Solutions LLC ....G 585 245-3456
  Rochester *(G-14107)*

FERTILIZERS: Phosphatic

Occidental Chemical Corp ....C 716 278-7794
  Niagara Falls *(G-12319)*

FIBER & FIBER PRDTS: Acrylic

Solid Surface Acrylics LLC ....F 716 743-1870
  North Tonawanda *(G-12451)*

FIBER & FIBER PRDTS: Fluorocarbon

Dynax Corporation ....G 914 764-0202
  Pound Ridge *(G-13376)*

FIBER & FIBER PRDTS: Organic, Noncellulose

Dal-Tile Corporation ....G 718 894-9574
  Maspeth *(G-7834)*
Fibrix LLC ....E 716 683-4100
  Depew *(G-4089)*
Solutia Business Entps Inc ....F 314 674-1000
  New York *(G-11643)*

FIBER & FIBER PRDTS: Polyester

Marly Home Industries USA Inc ....G 718 388-3030
  Brooklyn *(G-2172)*
Stein Fibers Ltd ....F 518 489-5700
  Albany *(G-130)*

FIBER & FIBER PRDTS: Synthetic Cellulosic

3M Company ....B 716 876-1596
  Tonawanda *(G-15517)*
Cortland Cable Company Inc ....E 607 753-8276
  Cortland *(G-3865)*
Cytec Industries Inc ....D 716 372-9650
  Olean *(G-12598)*
E I Du Pont De Nemours & Co ....E 716 876-4420
  Buffalo *(G-2807)*
International Fiber Corp ....E 716 693-4040
  North Tonawanda *(G-12433)*
Solivaira Specialties Inc ....D 716 693-4009
  North Tonawanda *(G-12452)*
Solvaira Specialties Inc ....C 716 693-4040
  North Tonawanda *(G-12453)*
Solvaira Specialty LP ....E 716 693-4040
  North Tonawanda *(G-12454)*
Solvaira Specialty LP ....D 716 693-4040
  North Tonawanda *(G-12455)*

FIBER OPTICS

Biolitec Inc ....E 413 525-0600
  New York *(G-9088)*
Complete Fiber Solutions Inc ....G 718 828-8900
  Bronx *(G-1245)*
Photonic Controls LLC ....F 607 562-4585
  Horseheads *(G-6324)*

FIBERS: Carbon & Graphite

Metal Coated Fibers Inc ....E 518 280-8514
  Schenectady *(G-14697)*

FILLERS & SEALERS: Wood

Uc Coatings LLC ....E 716 833-9366
  Buffalo *(G-3108)*

FILM & SHEET: Unsuppported Plastic

American Acrylic Corporation ......E 631 422-2200
  West Babylon *(G-16133)*
API Industries Inc ....B 845 365-2200
  Orangeburg *(G-12668)*
API Industries Inc ....C 845 365-2200
  Orangeburg *(G-12669)*
Berry Global Inc ....C 315 986-2161
  Macedon *(G-7696)*
Berry Global Inc 315 484-0397
  Solvay *(G-14916)*
Berry Plastics Corporation ....B 315 986-6270
  Macedon *(G-7697)*
Comco Plastics Inc ....E 718 849-9000
  Huntington Station *(G-6436)*
Ecoplast & Packaging LLC ....G 718 996-0800
  Brooklyn *(G-1811)*
Excellent Poly Inc ....F 718 768-6555
  Brooklyn *(G-1856)*
Franklin Poly Film Inc ....F 718 492-3523
  Brooklyn *(G-1904)*
Great Lakes Plastics Co Inc ....E 716 896-3100
  Buffalo *(G-2856)*
Kent Chemical Corporation ....E 212 521-1700
  New York *(G-10436)*
Knf Clean Room Products Corp ..E 631 588-7000
  Ronkonkoma *(G-14362)*
Msi Inc ....F 845 639-6683
  New City *(G-8494)*
Nova Packaging Ltd Inc ....E 914 232-8406
  Katonah *(G-6845)*
Oaklee International Inc ....D 631 436-7900
  Ronkonkoma *(G-14389)*
Pliant LLC ....B 315 986-6286
  Macedon *(G-7703)*
R & F Boards & Dividers Inc ....E 718 331-1529
  Brooklyn *(G-2374)*
Rainbow Poly Bag Co Inc ....E 718 386-3500
  Brooklyn *(G-2382)*
Sand Hill Industries Inc ....F 518 885-7991
  Ballston Spa *(G-595)*
Scapa North America ....E 315 413-1111
  Liverpool *(G-7261)*
Swimline Corp ....C 631 254-2155
  Edgewood *(G-4416)*
Toray Industries Inc ....G 212 697-8150
  New York *(G-11869)*
Trinity Packaging Corporation .....E 716 668-3111
  Buffalo *(G-3103)*
Turner Bellows Inc ....E 585 235-4456
  Rochester *(G-14181)*

FILM BASE: Cellulose Acetate Or Nitrocellulose Plastics

Bfgg Investors Group LLC ....G 585 424-3456
  Rochester *(G-13662)*
Island Pyrochemical Inds Corp ....C 516 746-2100
  Mineola *(G-8231)*

FILM: Motion Picture

Big Indie - Beautiful Boy LLC ....G 917 464-5599
  Woodstock *(G-16684)*
Dolby Laboratories Inc ....F 212 767-1700
  New York *(G-9546)*

FILTERS

Acme Engineering Products Inc ....E 518 236-5659
  Mooers *(G-8330)*
Burnett Process Inc ....E 585 277-1623
  Rochester *(G-13684)*
Drasgow Inc ....E 585 786-3603
  Gainesville *(G-5240)*
Foseco Inc ....F 914 345-4760
  Tarrytown *(G-15478)*
Hilliard Corporation ....B 607 733-7121
  Elmira *(G-4492)*
Hilliard Corporation ....C 607 733-7121
  Elmira *(G-4493)*
Lydall Performance Mtls Inc ....F 518 273-6320
  Green Island *(G-5610)*
Pall Corporation ....A 516 484-5400
  Port Washington *(G-13295)*
Pall Corporation ....A 607 753-6041
  Cortland *(G-3885)*
Parker-Hannifin Corporation ....D 716 685-4040
  Lancaster *(G-7037)*
Peregrine Industries Inc ....G 631 838-2870
  New York *(G-11153)*

Employee Codes: A=Over 500 employees, B=251-500
C=101-250, D=51-100, E=20-50, F=10-19, G=5-9

FILTERS

PRODUCT SECTION

Pyrotek Incorporated .... E 716 731-3221
　Sanborn (G-14552)
SC Supply Chain Management LLC .....G 212 344-3322
　New York (G-11498)
Sinclair International Company .... D 518 798-2361
　Queensbury (G-13442)
Stavo Industries Inc .... E 845 331-5389
　Kingston (G-6921)

FILTERS & SOFTENERS: Water, Household

H2o Solutions Inc .... F 518 527-0915
　Stillwater (G-15158)
Menpin Supply Corp .... F 718 415-4168
　Brooklyn (G-2190)
Pure Planet Waters LLC .... F 718 676-7900
　Brooklyn (G-2362)
Water Technologies Inc .... G 315 986-0000
　Macedon (G-7705)

FILTERS: Air

Air Engineering Filters Inc .... G 914 238-5945
　Chappaqua (G-3419)
Air Export Mechanical .... G 917 709-5310
　Flushing (G-4981)
Filta Clean Co Inc .... E 718 495-3800
　Brooklyn (G-1880)
Healthway Home Products Inc .... E 315 298-2904
　Pulaski (G-13385)
Isolation Systems Inc .... F 716 694-6390
　North Tonawanda (G-12435)
Nexstar Holding Corp .... G 716 929-9000
　Amherst (G-240)
Northland Filter Intl LLC .... E 315 207-1410
　Oswego (G-12782)
Pliotron Company America LLC .... G 716 298-4457
　Niagara Falls (G-12323)
R P Fedder Corp .... E 585 288-1600
　Rochester (G-14066)
Roome Technologies Inc .... G 585 229-4437
　Honeoye (G-6261)

FILTERS: Air Intake, Internal Combustion Engine, Exc Auto

Modern-TEC Manufacturing Inc .... G 716 625-8700
　Lockport (G-7319)
Pall Corporation .... A 607 753-6041
　Cortland (G-3885)
Pall Corporation .... A 516 484-5400
　Port Washington (G-13295)

FILTERS: General Line, Indl

Adams Sfc Inc .... E 716 877-2608
　Tonawanda (G-15519)
American Felt & Filter Co Inc .... D 845 561-3560
　New Windsor (G-8635)
American Filtration Tech Inc .... F 585 359-4130
　West Henrietta (G-16228)
Cross Filtration Ltd Lblty Co .... G 315 412-1539
　Moravia (G-8333)
Filter Tech Inc .... D 315 682-8815
　Manlius (G-7777)
Graver Technologies LLC .... E 585 624-1330
　Honeoye Falls (G-6265)
North American Filter Corp .... D 800 265-8943
　Newark (G-12203)
Service Filtration Corp .... E 716 877-2608
　Tonawanda (G-15577)
Sidco Filter Corporation .... E 585 289-3100
　Manchester (G-7762)
Stavo Industries Inc .... F 845 331-4552
　Kingston (G-6920)

FILTERS: Motor Vehicle

P & F Industries Inc .... E 631 694-9800
　Melville (G-8055)
Pall Corporation .... A 516 484-5400
　Port Washington (G-13295)
Pall Corporation .... A 607 753-6041
　Cortland (G-3885)

FILTERS: Paper

Folia Water Inc .... G 412 802-5083
　New York (G-9821)

FILTRATION DEVICES: Electronic

Allen Avionics Inc .... E 516 248-8080
　Mineola (G-8203)
Fil-Coil (fc) Corp .... E 631 467-5328
　Sayville (G-14628)
Frequency Selective Networks .... F 718 424-7500
　Valley Stream (G-15780)
Microwave Filter Company Inc .... E 315 438-4700
　East Syracuse (G-4358)
MTK Electronics Inc .... E 631 924-7666
　Medford (G-7962)
Service Filtration Corp .... E 716 877-2608
　Tonawanda (G-15577)
Tte Filters LLC .... F 716 532-2234
　Gowanda (G-5493)

FINANCIAL INVESTMENT ACTIVITIES, NEC: Financial Reporting

Dow Jones & Company Inc .... E 212 597-5983
　New York (G-9564)
Ruby Newco LLC .... G 212 852-7000
　New York (G-11445)

FINANCIAL INVESTMENT ADVICE

Bernhard Arnold & Company Inc .... G 212 907-1500
　New York (G-9054)
Envy Publishing Group Inc .... G 212 253-9874
　New York (G-9691)
Investors Business Daily Inc .... F 212 626-7676
　New York (G-10264)
Moneypaper Inc .... F 914 925-0022
　Rye (G-14486)
Swaps Monitor Publications Inc .... F 212 742-8550
　New York (G-11754)

FINANCIAL SVCS

Sixteen Markets Inc .... F 347 759-1024
　New York (G-11603)

FINDINGS & TRIMMINGS Fabric, NEC

Lending Trimming Co Inc .... D 212 242-7502
　New York (G-10544)

FINDINGS & TRIMMINGS Waistbands, Trouser

Cai Inc .... E 212 819-0008
　New York (G-9176)

FINDINGS & TRIMMINGS: Apparel

Eagle Finishing .... E 718 497-7875
　Brooklyn (G-1807)
Mas Cutting Inc .... G 212 869-0826
　New York (G-10722)

FINDINGS & TRIMMINGS: Fabric

Legendary Auto Interiors Ltd .... E 315 331-1212
　Newark (G-12198)

FINGERNAILS, ARTIFICIAL

Ivy Enterprises Inc .... B 516 621-9779
　Port Washington (G-13271)

FINGERPRINT EQPT

Fingerprint America Inc .... G 518 435-1609
　Albany (G-74)

FINISHING AGENTS: Leather

Androme Leather Inc .... F 518 773-7945
　Gloversville (G-5451)

FIRE ARMS, SMALL: Guns Or Gun Parts, 30 mm & Below

Magpump LLC .... G 585 444-9812
　Henrietta (G-6035)
Oriskany Arms Inc .... F 315 737-2196
　Oriskany (G-12760)
Remington Arms Company LLC .... A 315 895-3482
　Ilion (G-6478)

FIRE ARMS, SMALL: Pellet & BB guns

Crosman Corporation .... E 585 657-6161
　Bloomfield (G-951)
Crosman Corporation .... E 585 398-3920
　Farmington (G-4911)

FIRE ARMS, SMALL: Rifles Or Rifle Parts, 30 mm & below

Hart Rifle Barrel Inc .... G 315 677-9841
　Syracuse (G-15339)
Kyntec Corporation .... G 716 810-6956
　Buffalo (G-2913)

FIRE CONTROL OR BOMBING EQPT: Electronic

Cooper Crouse-Hinds LLC .... B 315 477-7000
　Syracuse (G-15290)

FIRE DETECTION SYSTEMS

Firecom Inc .... C 718 899-6100
　Woodside (G-16655)
Firetronics Inc .... G 516 997-5151
　Jericho (G-6789)
Zetek Corporation .... F 212 668-1485
　New York (G-12174)

FIRE ESCAPES

Jamestown Fab Stl & Sup Inc .... G 716 665-2227
　Jamestown (G-6728)

FIRE EXTINGUISHERS: Portable

Bullex Inc .... E 518 689-2023
　Albany (G-52)
Nubian Heritage .... G 631 265-3551
　Hauppauge (G-5903)
Trove Inc .... F 212 268-2046
　Brooklyn (G-2589)

FIRE OR BURGLARY RESISTIVE PRDTS

Clad Industries LLC .... G 585 413-4359
　Macedon (G-7698)
Crystalizations Systems Inc .... F 631 467-0090
　Holbrook (G-6180)
Empire Metal Finishing Inc .... E 718 545-6700
　Astoria (G-427)
Finger Lakes Conveyors Inc .... G 315 539-9246
　Waterloo (G-15992)
Maximum Security Products Corp .... E 518 233-1800
　Waterford (G-15977)
Nrd LLC .... E 716 773-7634
　Grand Island (G-5508)
Thyssenkrupp Materials NA Inc .... F 212 972-8800
　New York (G-11829)

FIRE PROTECTION EQPT

First Due Fire Equipment Inc .... F 845 222-1329
　Garnerville (G-5300)
Lifc Corp .... G 516 426-5737
　Port Washington (G-13282)
Sigelock Systems LLC .... G 888 744-3562
　Oceanside (G-12557)

FIREARMS & AMMUNITION, EXC SPORTING, WHOLESALE

Island Ordnance Systems LLC .... F 516 746-2100
　Mineola (G-8230)

FIREARMS: Small, 30mm or Less

Benjamin Sheridan Corporation .... G 585 657-6161
　Bloomfield (G-947)
Dan Wesson Corp .... F 607 336-1174
　Norwich (G-12484)
Redding-Hunter Inc .... E 607 753-3331
　Cortland (G-3892)
Sycamore Hill Designs Inc .... G 585 820-7322
　Victor (G-15869)
Tri-Technologies Inc .... E 914 699-2001
　Mount Vernon (G-8449)

FIREFIGHTING APPARATUS

Bullex Inc .... F 518 689-2023
　Albany (G-51)

PRODUCT SECTION
FLOWER POTS Plastic

Eastern Precision Mfg .... G 845 358-1951
　Nyack *(G-12506)*
Fountainhead Group Inc .... C 315 736-0037
　New York Mills *(G-12186)*
William R Shoemaker Inc .... G 716 649-0511
　Hamburg *(G-5697)*

FIREPLACE & CHIMNEY MATERIAL: Concrete

Chim-Cap Corp .... E 800 262-9622
　Farmingdale *(G-4734)*
Chimney Doctors Americas Corp .... G 631 868-3586
　Bayport *(G-737)*

FIREPLACE EQPT & ACCESS

William H Jackson Company .... G 718 784-4482
　Long Island City *(G-7639)*

FIREWORKS

Alonzo Fire Works Display Inc .... G 518 664-9994
　Mechanicville *(G-7930)*
Fireworks By Grucci Inc .... E 631 286-0088
　Bellport *(G-804)*
Young Explosives Corp .... D 585 394-1783
　Canandaigua *(G-3237)*

FIREWORKS DISPLAY SVCS

Alonzo Fire Works Display Inc .... G 518 664-9994
　Mechanicville *(G-7930)*
Young Explosives Corp .... D 585 394-1783
　Canandaigua *(G-3237)*

FISH & SEAFOOD PROCESSORS: Canned Or Cured

Blue Ocean Food Trading LLC .... G 718 689-4291
　Brooklyn *(G-1620)*
Incro Marketing USA Corp .... G 917 365-5552
　New York *(G-10194)*
Sangster Foods Inc .... F 212 993-9129
　Brooklyn *(G-2447)*

FISH & SEAFOOD PROCESSORS: Fresh Or Frozen

6th Ave Gourmet Inc .... G 845 782-9067
　Monroe *(G-8262)*
AB Seafood Trading Inc .... G 718 353-8848
　Flushing *(G-4978)*
Rich Products Corporation .... A 716 878-8000
　Buffalo *(G-3037)*

FISHING EQPT: Lures

Bruynswick Sales Inc .... F 845 789-2049
　New Paltz *(G-8576)*
Heads & Tails Lure Co .... G 607 739-7900
　Horseheads *(G-6318)*
Northern King Lures Inc .... G 585 865-3373
　Rochester *(G-13982)*

FITTINGS & ASSEMBLIES: Hose & Tube, Hydraulic Or Pneumatic

KSA Manufacturing LLC .... F 315 488-0809
　Camillus *(G-3196)*

FITTINGS: Pipe

Legacy Valve LLC .... F 914 403-5075
　Valhalla *(G-15742)*
United Pipe Nipple Co Inc .... F 516 295-2468
　Hewlett *(G-6052)*

FITTINGS: Pipe, Fabricated

D & G Welding Inc .... G 716 873-3088
　Buffalo *(G-2790)*

FIXTURES & EQPT: Kitchen, Metal, Exc Cast Aluminum

Acme Kitchenettes Corp .... E 518 828-4191
　Hudson *(G-6337)*
Vanity Fair Bathmart Inc .... F 718 584-6700
　Bronx *(G-1413)*

FIXTURES: Bank, Metal, Ornamental

Jonathan Metal & Glass Ltd .... C 718 846-8000
　Jamaica *(G-6654)*

FIXTURES: Cut Stone

Jamestown Kitchen & Bath Inc .... G 716 665-2299
　Jamestown *(G-6729)*

FLAGPOLES

Flagpoles Incorporated .... D 631 751-5500
　East Setauket *(G-4301)*
Pole-Tech Co Inc .... F 631 689-5525
　East Setauket *(G-4307)*

FLAGS: Fabric

AAa Amercn Flag Dctg Co Inc .... G 212 279-3524
　New York *(G-8702)*
City Signs Inc .... G 718 375-5933
　Brooklyn *(G-1697)*
Eagle Regalia Co Inc .... F 845 425-2245
　Spring Valley *(G-14989)*
National Flag & Display Co Inc .... G 212 228-6600
　New York *(G-10882)*

FLAT GLASS: Antique

Munn Works LLC .... E 914 665-6100
　Mount Vernon *(G-8424)*

FLAT GLASS: Building

Lazer Marble & Granite Corp .... G 718 859-9644
　Brooklyn *(G-2096)*
Tempco Glass Fabrication LLC .... D 718 461-6888
　Flushing *(G-5052)*

FLAT GLASS: Construction

RG Glass Creations Inc .... E 212 675-0030
　New York *(G-11383)*
Twin Pane Insulated GL Co Inc .... F 631 924-1060
　Yaphank *(G-16725)*

FLAT GLASS: Laminated

Glass Apps LLC .... F 310 987-1536
　New York *(G-9930)*

FLAT GLASS: Plate, Polished & Rough

Lafayette Mirror & Glass Co .... G 718 768-0660
　New Hyde Park *(G-8547)*
Zered Inc .... F 718 353-7464
　College Point *(G-3670)*

FLAT GLASS: Strengthened Or Reinforced

Saxon Glass Technologies Inc .... F 607 587-9630
　Alfred *(G-184)*

FLAT GLASS: Tempered

Mr Glass Tempering LLC .... F 718 576-3826
　Brooklyn *(G-2232)*

FLAT GLASS: Window, Clear & Colored

Express Building Supply Inc .... E 516 608-0379
　Oceanside *(G-12537)*
Manhattan Shade & Glass Co Inc .... E 212 288-5616
　Great Neck *(G-5570)*
Manhattan Shade & Glass Co Inc .... E 212 288-5616
　Hauppauge *(G-5880)*
South Seneca Vinyl LLC .... G 315 585-6050
　Romulus *(G-14282)*
Window-Fix Inc .... E 718 854-3475
　Brooklyn *(G-2651)*

FLATWARE, STAINLESS STEEL

Utica Cutlery Company .... D 315 733-4663
　Utica *(G-15737)*

FLAVORS OR FLAVORING MATERIALS: Synthetic

Classic Flavors Fragrances Inc .... G 212 777-0004
　New York *(G-9320)*
Comax Aromatics Corporation .... E 631 249-0505
　Melville *(G-8009)*

Craftmaster Flavor Technology .... F 631 789-8607
　Amityville *(G-270)*
Interntnal Flvors Frgrnces Inc .... C 212 765-5500
　New York *(G-10251)*
Kent Chemical Corporation .... E 212 521-1700
　New York *(G-10436)*
Mafco Consolidated Group Inc .... F 212 572-8600
　New York *(G-10659)*

FLOOR COMPOSITION: Magnesite

Vescom Structural Systems Inc .... F 516 876-8100
　Westbury *(G-16386)*

FLOOR COVERING STORES

North Sunshine LLC .... F 307 027-1634
　Valley Cottage *(G-15761)*

FLOOR COVERING STORES: Carpets

Albert Menin Interiors Ltd .... F 212 876-3041
　Bronx *(G-1215)*
Elizabeth Eakins Inc .... F 212 628-1950
　New York *(G-9653)*
Wallace Home Design Ctr .... G 631 765-3890
　Southold *(G-14971)*

FLOOR COVERING: Plastic

Engineered Composites Inc .... E 716 362-0295
　Buffalo *(G-2819)*
H Risch Inc .... D 585 442-0110
　Rochester *(G-13848)*

FLOOR COVERINGS WHOLESALERS

Carpet Fabrications Intl .... F 914 381-6060
　Mamaroneck *(G-7736)*
Quality Carpet One Floor & HM .... F 718 941-4200
　Brooklyn *(G-2365)*

FLOOR COVERINGS: Tile, Support Plastic

Engineered Plastics Inc .... E 800 682-2525
　Williamsville *(G-16579)*

FLOORING & GRATINGS: Open, Construction Applications

Oldcastle Precast Inc .... F 518 767-2116
　South Bethlehem *(G-14924)*

FLOORING: Hard Surface

East To West Architectural Pdts .... G 631 433-9690
　East Northport *(G-4262)*
Heritage Contract Flooring LLC .... E 716 853-1555
　Buffalo *(G-2871)*

FLOORING: Hardwood

Custom Woodwork Ltd .... F 631 727-5260
　Riverhead *(G-13566)*
Fountain Tile Outlet Inc .... G 718 927-4555
　Brooklyn *(G-1901)*
Legno Veneto USA .... G 716 651-9169
　Depew *(G-4094)*
Madison & Dunn .... G 585 563-7760
　Rochester *(G-13922)*
MP Caroll Inc .... G 716 683-8520
　Cheektowaga *(G-3452)*
Mullican Flooring LP .... E 716 537-2642
　Holland *(G-6220)*
Tectonic Flooring USA LLC .... G 212 686-2700
　New York *(G-11795)*
Wood Floor Expo Inc .... G 212 472-0671
　New York *(G-12132)*

FLORISTS

M & S Schmalberg Inc .... F 212 244-2090
　New York *(G-10635)*

FLOWER ARRANGEMENTS: Artificial

Nsj Group Ltd .... F 631 893-9300
　Babylon *(G-530)*

FLOWER POTS Plastic

TVI Imports LLC .... G 631 793-3077
　Massapequa Park *(G-7895)*

FLOWERS: Artificial & Preserved

FLOWERS: Artificial & Preserved
Faster-Form Corp .... D 800 327-3676
  New Hartford *(G-8504)*
M & S Schmalberg Inc .... F 212 244-2090
  New York *(G-10635)*

FLUID METERS & COUNTING DEVICES
Aalborg Instrs & Contrls Inc .... D 845 398-3160
  Orangeburg *(G-12667)*
Computer Instruments Corp .... E 516 876-8400
  Westbury *(G-16321)*
East Hills Instrument Inc .... F 516 621-8686
  Westbury *(G-16325)*

FLUID POWER PUMPS & MOTORS
Atlantic Industrial Tech Inc .... E 631 234-3131
  Shirley *(G-14830)*
Huck International Inc .... C 845 331-7300
  Kingston *(G-6902)*
Hydroacoustics Inc .... F 585 359-1000
  Henrietta *(G-6032)*
ITT Corporation .... D 315 568-2811
  Seneca Falls *(G-14777)*
ITT Inc .... E 914 641-2000
  White Plains *(G-16464)*
ITT LLC .... B 914 641-2000
  White Plains *(G-16467)*
Parker-Hannifin Corporation .... B 631 231-3737
  Hauppauge *(G-5909)*
Parker-Hannifin Corporation .... C 585 425-7000
  Fairport *(G-4647)*
Trench & Marine Pump Co Inc .... E 212 423-9098
  Bronx *(G-1405)*
Triumph Actuation Systems LLC .... D 516 378-0162
  Freeport *(G-5188)*

FLUID POWER VALVES & HOSE FITTINGS
A K Allen Co Inc .... C 516 747-5450
  Melville *(G-7996)*
Aalborg Instrs & Contrls Inc .... D 845 398-3160
  Orangeburg *(G-12667)*
Key High Vacuum Products Inc .... E 631 584-5959
  Nesconset *(G-8485)*
Kinemotive Corporation .... C 631 249-6440
  Farmingdale *(G-4803)*
Lourdes Industries Inc .... E 631 234-6600
  Hauppauge *(G-5873)*
Moog Inc .... B 716 687-4954
  East Aurora *(G-4207)*
Own Instrument Inc .... E 914 668-6546
  Mount Vernon *(G-8427)*
Steel & Obrien Mfg Inc .... C 585 492-5800
  Arcade *(G-389)*
Upstate Tube Inc .... E 315 488-5636
  Camillus *(G-3199)*

FLUORO RUBBERS
Dynax Corporation .... G 914 764-0202
  Pound Ridge *(G-13376)*

FLUXES
Aufhauser Corporation .... F 516 694-8696
  Plainview *(G-13038)*
Johnson Manufacturing Company .... F 716 881-3030
  Buffalo *(G-2897)*

FOAM CHARGE MIXTURES
C P Chemical Co Inc .... G 914 428-2517
  White Plains *(G-16434)*
Concrete Designs Inc .... G 607 738-0309
  Elmira *(G-4479)*
Icynene US Acquisition Corp .... G 800 758-7325
  Buffalo *(G-2879)*

FOAM RUBBER
Foam Products Inc .... E 718 292-4830
  Bronx *(G-1273)*
Mhxco Foam Company LLC .... F 518 843-8400
  Amsterdam *(G-347)*
Par-Foam Products Inc .... C 716 855-2066
  Buffalo *(G-2990)*
Turner Bellows Inc .... E 585 235-4456
  Rochester *(G-14181)*

FOIL & LEAF: Metal
American Packaging Corporation .... G 585 254-2002
  Rochester *(G-13625)*
American Packaging Corporation .... C 585 254-9500
  Rochester *(G-13626)*
Pactiv LLC .... C 518 793-2524
  Glens Falls *(G-5439)*
Quick Roll Leaf Mfg Co Inc .... E 845 457-1500
  Montgomery *(G-8316)*
Thermal Process Cnstr Co .... E 631 293-6400
  Farmingdale *(G-4894)*

FOIL, ALUMINUM, HOUSEHOLD, WHOLESALE
Golden Argosy LLC .... G 212 268-0003
  New York *(G-9953)*

FOIL: Aluminum
Alufoil Products Co Inc .... F 631 231-4141
  Hauppauge *(G-5762)*

FOIL: Copper
Oak-Mitsui Inc .... D 518 686-8060
  Hoosick Falls *(G-6278)*
Oak-Mitsui Technologies LLC .... E 518 686-4961
  Hoosick Falls *(G-6279)*
Steel Partners Holdings LP .... D 212 520-2300
  New York *(G-11699)*

FOIL: Laminated To Paper Or Other Materials
Alufoil Products Co Inc .... F 631 231-4141
  Hauppauge *(G-5762)*

FOOD CASINGS: Plastic
Pactiv LLC .... C 585 394-5125
  Canandaigua *(G-3228)*

FOOD PRDTS, BREAKFAST: Cereal, Infants' Food
Group International LLC .... G 718 475-8805
  Flushing *(G-5003)*
Sangster Foods Inc .... F 212 993-9129
  Brooklyn *(G-2447)*

FOOD PRDTS, BREAKFAST: Cereal, Wheat Flakes
General Mills Inc .... D 716 856-6060
  Buffalo *(G-2846)*

FOOD PRDTS, CANNED OR FRESH PACK: Fruit Juices
Apple & Eve LLC .... D 516 621-1122
  Port Washington *(G-13243)*
Mizkan America Inc .... D 585 765-9171
  Lyndonville *(G-7680)*
Motts LLP .... C 972 673-8088
  Elmsford *(G-4552)*
National Grape Coop Assn Inc .... E 716 326-5200
  Westfield *(G-16394)*
Pressed Juice LLC .... G 646 573-9157
  Brooklyn *(G-2339)*
US Juice Partners LLC .... G 516 621-1122
  Port Washington *(G-13312)*
Welch Foods Inc A Cooperative .... C 716 326-5252
  Westfield *(G-16398)*

FOOD PRDTS, CANNED OR FRESH PACK: Vegetable Juices
Jus By Julie LLC .... G 718 266-3906
  Brooklyn *(G-2060)*

FOOD PRDTS, CANNED OR FRESH PACK: Vegetable Juices
Life Juice Brands LLC .... G 585 944-7982
  Pittsford *(G-13018)*

FOOD PRDTS, CANNED: Baby Food
Beech-Nut Nutrition Company .... B 518 839-0300
  Amsterdam *(G-328)*

FOOD PRDTS, CANNED: Barbecue Sauce
Jets Lefrois Corp .... G 585 637-5003
  Brockport *(G-1193)*
Labarba-Q LLC .... F 845 806-6227
  Warwick *(G-15957)*

FOOD PRDTS, CANNED: Beans & Bean Sprouts
Sahadi Fine Foods Inc .... E 718 369-0100
  Brooklyn *(G-2445)*

FOOD PRDTS, CANNED: Catsup
Kensington & Sons LLC .... E 646 430-8298
  New York *(G-10433)*

FOOD PRDTS, CANNED: Ethnic
Delicious Foods Inc .... F 718 446-9352
  Corona *(G-3843)*
Sangster Foods Inc .... F 212 993-9129
  Brooklyn *(G-2447)*

FOOD PRDTS, CANNED: Fruit Juices, Concentrated
Old Dutch Mustard Co Inc .... G 516 466-0522
  Great Neck *(G-5576)*

FOOD PRDTS, CANNED: Fruit Juices, Fresh
Cahoon Farms Inc .... E 315 594-8081
  Wolcott *(G-16608)*
Cheribundi Inc .... E 800 699-0460
  Geneva *(G-5320)*
Cliffstar LLC .... A 716 366-6100
  Dunkirk *(G-4165)*
Fresh Fanatic Inc .... G 516 521-6574
  Brooklyn *(G-1907)*
Mayer Bros Apple Products Inc .... D 716 668-1787
  West Seneca *(G-16301)*

FOOD PRDTS, CANNED: Fruits
Andros Bowman Products LLC .... G 540 217-4100
  Lyndonville *(G-7679)*
Fruitcrown Products Corp .... E 631 694-5800
  Farmingdale *(G-4767)*
Lagoner Farms Inc .... D 315 904-4109
  Williamson *(G-16560)*

FOOD PRDTS, CANNED: Fruits
Fly Creek Cder Mill Orchrd Inc .... G 607 547-9692
  Fly Creek *(G-5064)*
Goya Foods Inc .... D 716 549-0076
  Angola *(G-369)*
Hc Brill Co Inc .... E 716 685-4000
  Lancaster *(G-7023)*
Lidestri Foods Inc .... B 585 377-7700
  Fairport *(G-4639)*
Victoria Fine Foods LLC .... E 718 649-1635
  Brooklyn *(G-2621)*
Victoria Fine Foods Holding Co .... G 718 649-1635
  Brooklyn *(G-2622)*
Welch Foods Inc A Cooperative .... E 716 326-3131
  Westfield *(G-16399)*

FOOD PRDTS, CANNED: Fruits & Fruit Prdts
Amiram Dror Inc .... F 212 979-9505
  Brooklyn *(G-1529)*
Spf Holdings II LLC .... G 212 750-8300
  New York *(G-11668)*

FOOD PRDTS, CANNED: Italian
A & G Food Distributors LLC .... G 917 939-3457
  Bayside *(G-740)*
Antico Casale Usa LLC .... G 914 760-1100
  Whitestone *(G-16533)*
Edesia World Wide LLC .... E 646 705-3505
  New York *(G-9626)*
Indira Foods Inc .... F 718 343-1500
  Floral Park *(G-4966)*
Marketplace Slutions Group LLC .... E 631 868-0111
  Holbrook *(G-6198)*

PRODUCT SECTION

FOOD PRDTS, CANNED: Jams, Including Imitation
Sbk Preserves Inc .... E 800 773-7378
Bronx *(G-1381)*

FOOD PRDTS, CANNED: Jams, Jellies & Preserves
Eleanors Best .... F 845 809-5621
Garrison *(G-5303)*
Sarabeths Kitchen LLC .... G 718 589-2900
Bronx *(G-1380)*

FOOD PRDTS, CANNED: Maraschino Cherries
Dells Cherries LLC .... E 718 624-4380
Brooklyn *(G-1765)*
Dells Cherries LLC .... E 718 624-4380
Brooklyn *(G-1766)*

FOOD PRDTS, CANNED: Mexican, NEC
Eve Sales Corp .... F 718 589-6800
Bronx *(G-1269)*

FOOD PRDTS, CANNED: Olives
L and S Packing Co .... D 631 845-1717
Farmingdale *(G-4804)*
Olive Branch Foods LLC .... G 631 343-7070
Islandia *(G-6536)*

FOOD PRDTS, CANNED: Puddings, Exc Meat
Steuben Foods Incorporated .... F 718 291-3333
Elma *(G-4459)*

FOOD PRDTS, CANNED: Ravioli
Borgattis Ravioli Egg Noodles .... G 718 367-3799
Bronx *(G-1231)*

FOOD PRDTS, CANNED: Sauerkraut
Glk Foods LLC .... E 585 289-4414
Shortsville *(G-14847)*
Seneca Foods Corporation .... C 315 781-8733
Geneva *(G-5332)*

FOOD PRDTS, CANNED: Soup, Chicken
Morris Kitchen Inc .... F 646 413-5186
Brooklyn *(G-2227)*

FOOD PRDTS, CANNED: Spaghetti & Other Pasta Sauce
Brooklyns Best Pasta Co Inc .... G 917 881-3007
Brooklyn *(G-1651)*
Kaltech Food Packaging Inc .... E 845 856-1210
Port Jervis *(G-13232)*
New York Pasta Authority Inc .... F 347 787-2130
Brooklyn *(G-2263)*
Sneaky Chef Foods LLC .... F 914 301-3277
Tarrytown *(G-15493)*
Wolfgang B Gourmet Foods Inc .... F 518 719-1727
Catskill *(G-3310)*

FOOD PRDTS, CANNED: Tomato Sauce.
Vincents Food Corp .... F 516 481-3544
Carle Place *(G-3273)*

FOOD PRDTS, CANNED: Tomatoes
Giovanni Food Co Inc .... D 315 457-2373
Baldwinsville *(G-555)*
Morris Kitchen Inc .... F 646 413-5186
Brooklyn *(G-2227)*

FOOD PRDTS, CANNED: Vegetables
Green Valley Foods LLC .... G 315 926-4280
Marion *(G-7801)*
Seneca Foods Corporation .... E 315 926-8100
Marion *(G-7806)*
Seneca Foods Corporation .... F 315 926-4277
Marion *(G-7808)*
Seneca Foods Corporation .... E 585 658-2211
Leicester *(G-7129)*

FOOD PRDTS, CONFECTIONERY, WHOLESALE: Candy
Chocolat Moderne LLC .... G 212 229-4797
New York *(G-9287)*
OH How Cute Inc .... G 347 838-6031
Staten Island *(G-15113)*
Premium Sweets USA Inc .... G 718 739-6000
Jamaica *(G-6669)*

FOOD PRDTS, CONFECTIONERY, WHOLESALE: Nuts, Salted/Roasted
Sahadi Fine Foods Inc .... E 718 369-0100
Brooklyn *(G-2445)*

FOOD PRDTS, CONFECTIONERY, WHOLESALE: Snack Foods
Materne North America Corp .... B 212 675-7881
New York *(G-10727)*
Perrys Ice Cream Company Inc .... B 716 542-5492
Akron *(G-21)*

FOOD PRDTS, FISH & SEAFOOD, WHOLESALE: Fresh
Fresh Fanatic Inc .... G 516 521-6574
Brooklyn *(G-1907)*
Montauk Inlet Seafood Inc .... G 631 668-3419
Montauk *(G-8306)*

FOOD PRDTS, FISH & SEAFOOD: Canned & Jarred, Etc
Harbors Maine Lobster LLC .... E 516 775-2400
New Hyde Park *(G-8540)*
Premium Ocean LLC .... F 917 231-1061
Bronx *(G-1365)*

FOOD PRDTS, FISH & SEAFOOD: Fish, Fresh, Prepared
Foo Yuan Food Products Co Inc .... G 212 925-2840
Long Island City *(G-7451)*
Montauk Inlet Seafood Inc .... G 631 668-3419
Montauk *(G-8306)*

FOOD PRDTS, FISH & SEAFOOD: Fish, Smoked
Acme Smoked Fish Corp .... D 954 942-5598
Brooklyn *(G-1479)*
Banner Smoked Fish Inc .... D 718 449-1992
Brooklyn *(G-1584)*
Samaki Inc .... G 845 858-1012
Port Jervis *(G-13236)*

FOOD PRDTS, FISH & SEAFOOD: Fresh/Frozen Chowder, Soup/Stew
Shine Foods USA Inc .... G 516 784-9674
Glen Oaks *(G-5387)*

FOOD PRDTS, FISH & SEAFOOD: Salmon, Smoked
Catsmo LLC .... F 845 895-2296
Wallkill *(G-15903)*

FOOD PRDTS, FISH & SEAFOOD: Seafood, Frozen, Prepared
Oceans Cuisine Ltd .... F 631 209-9200
Ridge *(G-13522)*
Sea Breeze Fish & Seafood of S .... F 718 984-0447
Staten Island *(G-15133)*

FOOD PRDTS, FROZEN: Breakfasts, Packaged
Beetnpath LLC .... G 607 319-5585
Ithaca *(G-6558)*
Juno Chefs .... D 845 294-5400
Goshen *(G-5480)*

FOOD PRDTS, FROZEN: Dinners, Packaged
Alle Processing Corp .... C 718 894-2000
Maspeth *(G-7818)*

FOOD PRDTS, FROZEN: Ethnic Foods, NEC
America NY RI Wang Fd Group Co .... E 718 628-8999
Maspeth *(G-7820)*
Delicious Foods Inc .... F 718 446-9352
Corona *(G-3843)*
Hain Refrigerated Foods Inc .... F 425 485-2476
New Hyde Park *(G-8539)*
Rhosey LLC .... G 718 382-1226
Brooklyn *(G-2400)*

FOOD PRDTS, FROZEN: Fruits & Vegetables
Atlantic Farm & Food Inc .... F 718 441-3152
Richmond Hill *(G-13496)*

FOOD PRDTS, FROZEN: Fruits, Juices & Vegetables
Blend Smoothie Bar .... G 845 568-7366
New Windsor *(G-8637)*
Bonduelle USA Inc .... G 585 434-0399
Rochester *(G-13672)*
C O P R A Inc .... G 917 224-1727
New York *(G-9170)*
Cahoon Farms Inc .... E 315 594-8081
Wolcott *(G-16608)*
Fly Creek Cder Mill Orchrd Inc .... G 607 547-9692
Fly Creek *(G-5064)*
H&F Products Inc .... G 845 651-6100
Monroe *(G-8271)*
Kj Astoria Gourmet Inc .... G 718 545-6900
Astoria *(G-432)*
National Grape Coop Assn Inc .... E 716 326-5200
Westfield *(G-16394)*
Smoothies Strawberry Nysf .... G 315 406-4250
Syracuse *(G-15426)*
T & Smoothie Inc .... G 631 804-6653
Patchogue *(G-12878)*

FOOD PRDTS, FROZEN: NEC
Codinos Limited Inc .... E 518 372-3308
Schenectady *(G-14665)*
Dufour Pastry Kitchens Inc .... E 718 402-8800
Bronx *(G-1260)*
Dvash Foods Inc .... F 845 578-1959
Monsey *(G-8288)*
Finger Food Products Inc .... G 716 297-4888
Sanborn *(G-14545)*
Food Basket USA Company Ltd .... E 631 231-8999
Bay Shore *(G-687)*
Freeze-Dry Foods Inc .... E 585 589-6399
Albion *(G-157)*
Julians Recipe LLC .... G 888 640-8880
Brooklyn *(G-2057)*
Macabee Foods LLC .... G 845 623-1300
West Nyack *(G-16274)*
Milmar Food Group II LLC .... C 845 294-5400
Goshen *(G-5482)*
Seviroli Foods Inc .... C 516 222-6220
Garden City *(G-5281)*
Tami Great Food Corp .... G 845 352-7901
Monsey *(G-8301)*
Tuv Taam Corp .... E 718 855-2207
Brooklyn *(G-2594)*
Unilever United States Inc .... G 212 546-0200
New York *(G-11944)*
Unilever United States Inc .... G 212 546-0200
New York *(G-11945)*
Wlf Founders Corporation .... D 718 777-8899
Astoria *(G-450)*

FOOD PRDTS, FROZEN: Pizza
D R M Management Inc .... E 716 668-0333
Depew *(G-4086)*
F & R Enterprises Inc .... G 315 841-8189
Waterville *(G-16039)*
Salarinos Italian Foods Inc .... F 315 697-9766
Canastota *(G-3247)*

FOOD PRDTS, FROZEN: Snack Items
Les Chateaux De France Inc .... E 516 239-6795
Inwood *(G-6494)*

FOOD PRDTS, FROZEN: Vegetables, Exc Potato Prdts
Birds Eye Foods Inc .... G 716 988-3218
South Dayton *(G-14927)*

Employee Codes: A=Over 500 employees, B=251-500
C=101-250, D=51-100, E=20-50, F=10-19, G=5-9

2019 Harris
New York Manufacturers Directory

FOOD PRDTS, FROZEN: Vegetables, Exc Potato Prdts

Prime Food Processing Corp ....D...... 718 963-2323
  Brooklyn *(G-2342)*
Seneca Foods Corporation ....E...... 315 926-8100
  Marion *(G-7806)*
Tami Great Food Corp ....G...... 845 352-7901
  Monsey *(G-8301)*

FOOD PRDTS, FROZEN: Whipped Topping

Kraft Heinz Foods Company ....B...... 585 226-4400
  Avon *(G-519)*

FOOD PRDTS, MEAT & MEAT PRDTS, WHOLESALE: Brokers

Lancaster Quality Pork Inc ....F...... 718 439-8822
  Brooklyn *(G-2093)*

FOOD PRDTS, MEAT & MEAT PRDTS, WHOLESALE: Fresh

Alps Provision Co Inc ....E...... 718 721-4477
  Astoria *(G-421)*
Camellia General Provision Co .....E...... 716 893-5352
  Buffalo *(G-2760)*
Kamerys Wholesale Meats Inc ......G...... 716 372-6756
  Olean *(G-12603)*
Reliable Brothers Inc ....E...... 518 273-6732
  Green Island *(G-5611)*

FOOD PRDTS, WHOL: Canned Goods, Fruit, Veg, Seafood/Meats

Frank Wardynski & Sons Inc ....E...... 716 854-6083
  Buffalo *(G-2833)*
Spf Holdings II LLC ....G...... 212 750-8300
  New York *(G-11668)*
Wonton Food Inc ....C...... 718 628-6868
  Brooklyn *(G-2655)*

FOOD PRDTS, WHOLESALE: Beverage Concentrates

Motts LLP ....C...... 972 673-8088
  Elmsford *(G-4552)*

FOOD PRDTS, WHOLESALE: Beverages, Exc Coffee & Tea

A Health Obsession LLC ....E...... 347 850-4587
  Brooklyn *(G-1457)*
Pepsi-Cola Sales and Dist Inc ....G...... 914 253-2000
  Purchase *(G-13394)*
Pepsico Sales Inc ....G...... 914 253-2000
  Purchase *(G-13399)*
TLC-Lc Inc ....E...... 212 756-8900
  New York *(G-11852)*

FOOD PRDTS, WHOLESALE: Chocolate

Amiram Dror Inc ....F...... 212 979-9505
  Brooklyn *(G-1529)*
Chocolate Pizza Company Inc ....F...... 315 673-4098
  Marcellus *(G-7793)*
Commodore Chocolatier USA Inc ..F...... 845 561-3960
  Newburgh *(G-12218)*
Godiva Chocolatier Inc ....E...... 212 984-5900
  New York *(G-9950)*
Hercules Candy Co ....G...... 315 463-4339
  East Syracuse *(G-4346)*
Lanco Corporation ....C...... 631 231-2300
  Ronkonkoma *(G-14368)*

FOOD PRDTS, WHOLESALE: Coffee & Tea

Cham Cold Brew LLC ....G...... 646 926-0206
  New York *(G-9257)*
Talmu NY LLC ....G...... 347 434-6700
  Brooklyn *(G-2555)*

FOOD PRDTS, WHOLESALE: Coffee, Green Or Roasted

Coffee Holding Co Inc ....D...... 718 832-0800
  Staten Island *(G-15064)*
Elite Roasters Inc ....F...... 716 626-0307
  East Amherst *(G-4189)*
Orens Daily Roast Inc ....E...... 212 348-5400
  New York *(G-11061)*
Paul De Lima Company Inc ....D...... 315 457-3725
  Liverpool *(G-7253)*

Pintail Coffee Inc ....G...... 631 396-0808
  Farmingdale *(G-4849)*

FOOD PRDTS, WHOLESALE: Condiments

Kensington & Sons LLC ....E...... 646 430-8298
  New York *(G-10433)*

FOOD PRDTS, WHOLESALE: Cookies

212kiddish Inc ....G...... 718 705-7227
  Brooklyn *(G-1434)*

FOOD PRDTS, WHOLESALE: Flour

Archer-Daniels-Midland Company ..D...... 518 828-4691
  Hudson *(G-6340)*

FOOD PRDTS, WHOLESALE: Grains

Chia Usa LLC ....G...... 212 226-7512
  New York *(G-9274)*

FOOD PRDTS, WHOLESALE: Health

Sangster Foods Inc ....F...... 212 993-9129
  Brooklyn *(G-2447)*

FOOD PRDTS, WHOLESALE: Juices

Schutt Cider Mill ....F...... 585 872-2924
  Webster *(G-16097)*

FOOD PRDTS, WHOLESALE: Organic & Diet

Natural Lab Inc ....G...... 718 321-8848
  Flushing *(G-5026)*

FOOD PRDTS, WHOLESALE: Pasta & Rice

Brooklyns Best Pasta Co Inc ....G...... 917 881-3007
  Brooklyn *(G-1651)*
Deer Park Macaroni Co Inc ....F...... 631 667-4600
  Deer Park *(G-3965)*
Great Eastern Pasta Works LLC ....E...... 631 956-0889
  West Babylon *(G-16157)*
New York Ravioli Pasta Co Inc ......E...... 516 270-2852
  New Hyde Park *(G-8553)*
Steinway Pasta & Gelati Inc ....F...... 718 246-5414
  Lindenhurst *(G-7194)*
Victoria Fine Foods LLC ....G...... 718 649-1635
  Brooklyn *(G-2621)*
Victoria Fine Foods Holding Co .....G...... 718 649-1635
  Brooklyn *(G-2622)*

FOOD PRDTS, WHOLESALE: Sandwiches

Fresh Fanatic Inc ....G...... 516 521-6574
  Brooklyn *(G-1907)*

FOOD PRDTS, WHOLESALE: Sausage Casings

DRG New York Holdings Corp ....C...... 914 668-9000
  Mount Vernon *(G-8395)*

FOOD PRDTS, WHOLESALE: Specialty

Castella Imports Inc ....C...... 631 231-5500
  Edgewood *(G-4398)*
Fanshawe Foods LLC ....F...... 212 757-3130
  New York *(G-9780)*

FOOD PRDTS, WHOLESALE: Tea

Harney & Sons Tea Corp ....C...... 518 789-2100
  Millerton *(G-8193)*
White Coffee Corp ....D...... 718 204-7900
  Astoria *(G-449)*

FOOD PRDTS: Almond Pastes

American Almond Pdts Co Inc ....D...... 718 875-8310
  Brooklyn *(G-1519)*

FOOD PRDTS: Animal & marine fats & oils

Darling Ingredients Inc ....F...... 716 895-0655
  Buffalo *(G-2793)*
Ellenburg Recyclers ....F...... 518 594-3900
  Ellenburg Depot *(G-4436)*

FOOD PRDTS: Bran, Rice

Gassho Body & Mind Inc ....G...... 518 695-9991
  Schuylerville *(G-14734)*

FOOD PRDTS: Bread Crumbs, Exc Made In Bakeries

Gourmet Toast Corp ....G...... 718 852-4536
  Brooklyn *(G-1944)*
H & S Edible Products Corp ....E...... 914 413-3489
  Mount Vernon *(G-8404)*

FOOD PRDTS: Breakfast Bars

Keep Healthy Inc ....F...... 631 651-9090
  Northport *(G-12469)*

FOOD PRDTS: Cane Syrup, From Purchased Raw Sugar

Cane Sugar LLC ....G...... 212 329-2695
  New York *(G-9195)*

FOOD PRDTS: Cereals

Associated Brands Inc ....B...... 585 798-3475
  Medina *(G-7970)*
Chia Usa LLC ....G...... 212 226-7512
  New York *(G-9274)*
Gabila Food Products Inc ....E...... 631 789-2220
  Copiague *(G-3760)*
Pepsico Inc ....A...... 914 253-2000
  Purchase *(G-13395)*
Sanzdranz LLC ....G...... 518 894-8625
  Delmar *(G-4078)*
Sanzdranz LLC ....G...... 518 894-8625
  Schenectady *(G-14710)*

FOOD PRDTS: Cheese Curls & Puffs

Emmi USA Inc ....F...... 845 268-9990
  Orangeburg *(G-12675)*

FOOD PRDTS: Chicken, Processed, Frozen

K&Ns Foods Usa LLC ....E...... 315 598-8080
  Fulton *(G-5224)*

FOOD PRDTS: Chocolate Bars, Solid

Amiram Dror Inc ....F...... 212 979-9505
  Brooklyn *(G-1529)*
Cemoi Inc ....G...... 212 583-4920
  New York *(G-9238)*
Chocomize Inc ....F...... 631 506-6085
  Long Island City *(G-7408)*
Max Brenner Union Square LLC ....G...... 646 467-8803
  New York *(G-10733)*
Mbny LLC ....F...... 646 467-8810
  New York *(G-10737)*
Micosta Enterprises Inc 518 822-9708
  Hudson *(G-6364)*
Parkside Candy Co Inc ....F...... 716 833-7540
  Buffalo *(G-2992)*

FOOD PRDTS: Chocolate Coatings & Syrup

Fox 416 Corp ....E...... 718 385-4600
  Brooklyn *(G-1903)*

FOOD PRDTS: Coconut Oil

Jax Coco USA LLC ....G...... 347 688-8198
  New York *(G-10311)*

FOOD PRDTS: Coconut, Desiccated & Shredded

Far Eastern Coconut Company .....F...... 631 851-8800
  Central Islip *(G-3369)*

FOOD PRDTS: Coffee

Arista Coffee Inc ....F...... 347 531-0813
  Maspeth *(G-7823)*
Birch Guys LLC ....G...... 917 763-0751
  Long Island City *(G-7400)*
Cafe Kubal ....G...... 315 278-2812
  Syracuse *(G-15267)*
Coffee Holding Co Inc ....D...... 718 832-0800
  Staten Island *(G-15064)*
Coffee Holding Company Inc ....G...... 718 832-0800
  Brooklyn *(G-1704)*
Elite Roasters Inc ....F...... 716 626-0307
  East Amherst *(G-4189)*
Irving Farm Coffee Co Inc ....G...... 212 206-0707
  New York *(G-10274)*

Jonathan Brose.................................G....... 716 417-8978
  Lockport (G-7312)
List & Beisler GMBH..........................E....... 646 866-6960
  New York (G-10577)
P Pascal Inc....................................E....... 914 969-7933
  Yonkers (G-16790)
Paul De Lima Company Inc...............E....... 315 457-3725
  Cicero (G-3520)
Paul Delima Coffee Company.............E....... 315 457-3725
  Cicero (G-3521)
Star Mountain JFK Inc........................G....... 718 553-6787
  Jamaica (G-6679)
Vega Coffee Inc................................G....... 415 881-7969
  New York (G-12003)

FOOD PRDTS: Coffee Extracts

Brooklyn Roasting Works LLC.............G....... 718 855-1000
  Brooklyn (G-1647)
Death Wish Coffee Company LLC........F....... 518 400-1050
  Ballston Spa (G-579)
Eldorado Coffee Roasters Ltd.............D....... 718 418-4100
  Maspeth (G-7842)

FOOD PRDTS: Coffee Roasting, Exc Wholesale Grocers

Bh Coffee Company LLC...................D....... 914 377-2500
  Elmsford (G-4532)
BK Associates Intl Inc........................F....... 607 432-1499
  Oneonta (G-12626)
Empire Coffee Company Inc...............E....... 914 934-1100
  Port Chester (G-13199)
Gillies Coffee Company......................E....... 718 499-7766
  Brooklyn (G-1927)
John A Vassilaros & Son Inc...............E....... 718 886-4140
  Flushing (G-5014)
Paul De Lima Company Inc................D....... 315 457-3725
  Liverpool (G-7253)
Peaks Coffee Company......................E....... 315 565-1900
  Cazenovia (G-3325)
Pintail Coffee Inc...............................G....... 631 396-0808
  Farmingdale (G-4849)
Regal Trading Inc..............................E....... 914 694-6100
  Purchase (G-13400)
S J McCullagh Inc..............................E....... 716 856-3473
  Buffalo (G-3053)
Where Is Utica Cof Rasting Inc...........F....... 315 269-8898
  Utica (G-15739)
White Coffee Corp.............................D....... 718 204-7900
  Astoria (G-449)

FOOD PRDTS: Cole Slaw, Bulk

UFS Industries Inc.............................D....... 718 822-1100
  Mount Vernon (G-8452)

FOOD PRDTS: Cooking Oils, Refined Vegetable, Exc Corn

C B S Food Products Corp..................F....... 718 452-2500
  Brooklyn (G-1663)
Gourmet Factory Inc.........................G....... 631 231-4548
  Hauppauge (G-5836)
Healthy Brand Oil Corp......................E....... 718 937-0806
  Long Island City (G-7467)

FOOD PRDTS: Corn Oil Prdts

Sunoco Inc.......................................G....... 315 593-0500
  Fulton (G-5232)

FOOD PRDTS: Cottonseed Lecithin

Perimondo LLC.................................G....... 212 749-0721
  New York (G-11157)

FOOD PRDTS: Dessert Mixes & Fillings

Brooklynwrap Inc...............................G....... 718 258-8088
  Brooklyn (G-1652)
Deedee Desserts LLC......................G....... 716 627-2330
  Lake View (G-6982)
Lucky Lous Inc..................................G....... 631 672-1932
  Lake Grove (G-6967)
Noaspence Inc..................................G....... 516 433-7848
  Hicksville (G-6114)
Rich Products Corporation.................A....... 716 878-8000
  Buffalo (G-3037)
VIP Foods Inc...................................E....... 718 821-5330
  Ridgewood (G-13558)

FOOD PRDTS: Desserts, Ready-To-Mix

Butterwood Desserts Inc....................E....... 716 652-0131
  West Falls (G-16208)
Kozy Shack Enterprises LLC.............C....... 516 870-3000
  Hicksville (G-6099)
Kozy Shack Enterprises LLC.............C....... 516 870-3000
  Hicksville (G-6100)
Omg Desserts Inc.............................F....... 585 698-1561
  Rochester (G-13986)

FOOD PRDTS: Dough, Pizza, Prepared

Ohio Baking Company Inc..................E....... 315 724-2033
  Utica (G-15728)
Pizza Blends LLC..............................G....... 518 356-6650
  Schenectady (G-14704)

FOOD PRDTS: Doughs & Batters

Losurdo Foods Inc.............................E....... 518 842-1500
  Amsterdam (G-345)

FOOD PRDTS: Doughs & Batters From Purchased Flour

Cohens Bakery Inc............................E....... 716 892-8149
  Buffalo (G-2771)

FOOD PRDTS: Doughs, Frozen Or Refrig From Purchased Flour

Rhosey LLC......................................G....... 718 382-1226
  Brooklyn (G-2400)

FOOD PRDTS: Dressings, Salad, Raw & Cooked Exc Dry Mixes

Mizkan America Inc...........................F....... 585 798-5720
  Medina (G-7985)

FOOD PRDTS: Dried & Dehydrated Fruits, Vegetables & Soup Mix

Goya Foods Inc.................................D....... 716 549-0076
  Angola (G-369)
Shoreline Fruit LLC............................D....... 585 765-2639
  Lyndonville (G-7681)

FOOD PRDTS: Ducks, Processed, Fresh

Crescent Duck Farm Inc....................E....... 631 722-8700
  Aquebogue (G-374)

FOOD PRDTS: Ducks, Processed, NEC

Hudson Valley Foie Gras LLC............F....... 845 292-2500
  Ferndale (G-4934)

FOOD PRDTS: Edible Oil Prdts, Exc Corn Oil

Consumer Flavoring Extract Co..........F....... 718 435-0201
  Brooklyn (G-1712)

FOOD PRDTS: Edible fats & oils

Bunge Limited Finance Corp..............D....... 914 684-2800
  White Plains (G-16432)
Kerry Bfnctnal Ingredients Inc............D....... 608 363-1200
  Norwich (G-12488)

FOOD PRDTS: Egg Substitutes, Made From Eggs

Egg Low Farms Inc...........................F....... 607 674-4653
  Sherburne (G-14805)

FOOD PRDTS: Eggs, Processed

Ready Egg Farms Inc........................G....... 607 674-4653
  Sherburne (G-14808)

FOOD PRDTS: Emulsifiers

Chemicolloid Laboratories Inc............F....... 516 747-2666
  New Hyde Park (G-8522)
Momentive Performance Mtls Inc.......D....... 914 784-4807
  Tarrytown (G-15484)
Redland Foods Corp..........................F....... 716 288-9061
  Cheektowaga (G-3457)

FOOD PRDTS: Flavored Ices, Frozen

Elegant Desserts By Metro Inc...........F....... 718 388-1323
  Brooklyn (G-1822)
Four Brothers Italian Bakery...............G....... 914 741-5434
  Hawthorne (G-5986)
JMS Ices Inc.....................................F....... 718 448-0853
  Staten Island (G-15095)
My Most Favorite Food......................G....... 212 580-5130
  New York (G-10864)
Olympic Ice Cream Co Inc.................E....... 718 849-6200
  Richmond Hill (G-13507)
Primo Frozen Desserts Inc.................G....... 718 252-2312
  Brooklyn (G-2343)

FOOD PRDTS: Flour & Other Grain Mill Products

Archer-Daniels-Midland Company.......D....... 716 849-7333
  Buffalo (G-2708)
Archer-Daniels-Midland Company.......E....... 518 828-4691
  Hudson (G-6339)
Archer-Daniels-Midland Company.......D....... 518 828-4691
  Hudson (G-6340)
Archer-Daniels-Midland Company.......G....... 585 346-2311
  Lakeville (G-6984)
Ardent Mills LLC................................D....... 518 447-1700
  Albany (G-43)
Birkett Mills......................................G....... 315 536-3311
  Penn Yan (G-12949)
Birkett Mills......................................E....... 315 536-4112
  Penn Yan (G-12950)
Champlain Valley Mil Corp Inc...........G....... 518 963-7650
  Willsboro (G-16597)
Cochecton Mills Inc...........................E....... 845 932-8282
  Cochecton (G-3605)
Sheppard Grain Enterprises LLC........E....... 315 548-9271
  Phelps (G-12981)

FOOD PRDTS: Flour Mixes & Doughs

Aryzta LLC.......................................D....... 310 417-4700
  Rochester (G-13644)
Bektrom Foods Inc...........................G....... 516 802-3800
  Syosset (G-15209)
Lollipop Tree Inc...............................E....... 845 471-8733
  Auburn (G-488)
Pizza Blends LLC..............................G....... 518 356-6650
  Schenectady (G-14704)

FOOD PRDTS: Fruit Juices

Cheribundi Inc...................................E....... 800 699-0460
  Geneva (G-5320)
Dynamic Health Labs Inc...................E....... 718 858-0100
  Brooklyn (G-1799)
Hain Blueprint Inc..............................F....... 212 414-5741
  New Hyde Park (G-8537)
Pepsico Inc.......................................A....... 914 253-2000
  Purchase (G-13395)
Pura Fruta LLC..................................F....... 415 279-5727
  Long Island City (G-7563)
Zoe Sakoutis LLC..............................F....... 212 414-5741
  New York (G-12181)

FOOD PRDTS: Fruits & Vegetables, Pickled

United Farm Processing Corp.............C....... 718 933-6060
  Bronx (G-1411)

FOOD PRDTS: Fruits, Dehydrated Or Dried

Settons Intl Foods Inc........................D....... 631 543-8090
  Commack (G-3702)

FOOD PRDTS: Fruits, Dried Or Dehydrated, Exc Freeze-Dried

Associated Brands Inc......................B....... 585 798-3475
  Medina (G-7970)
Marshall Ingredients LLC...................G....... 800 796-9353
  Wolcott (G-16611)

FOOD PRDTS: Gelatin Dessert Preparations

Original Hrkmer Cnty Chese Inc.........D....... 315 895-7428
  Ilion (G-6477)

FOOD PRDTS: Gluten Meal

Anthony Gigi Inc................................G....... 860 984-1943
  Shirley (G-14828)

FOOD PRDTS: Granulated Cane Sugar
US Sweeteners Corp ....E...... 718 854-8714
  Brooklyn (G-2613)

FOOD PRDTS: Horseradish, Exc Sauce
Whalens Horseradish Products ....G...... 518 587-6404
  Galway (G-5241)

FOOD PRDTS: Ice, Blocks
Clayville Ice Co Inc ....G...... 315 839-5405
  Clayville (G-3556)
Huntington Ice & Cube Corp ....F...... 718 456-2013
  Brooklyn (G-1988)

FOOD PRDTS: Ice, Cubes
Henry Newman LLC ....F...... 607 273-8512
  Ithaca (G-6581)
Ice Cube Inc ....G...... 613 254-0071
  Deer Park (G-3986)

FOOD PRDTS: Instant Coffee
Altaro Corp ....F...... 855 674-2455
  Tarrytown (G-15473)
Orens Daily Roast Inc ....G...... 212 348-5400
  New York (G-11061)
Sangster Foods Inc ....F...... 212 993-9129
  Brooklyn (G-2447)

FOOD PRDTS: Jelly, Corncob
Larte Del Gelato Inc ....G...... 212 366-0570
  New York (G-10519)

FOOD PRDTS: Juice Pops, Frozen
Zings Company LLC ....G...... 631 454-0339
  Farmingdale (G-4908)

FOOD PRDTS: Macaroni Prdts, Dry, Alphabet, Rings Or Shells
Piemonte Home Made Ravioli Co ....F...... 718 429-1972
  Woodside (G-16672)
Queen Ann Macaroni Mfg Co Inc ....G...... 718 256-1061
  Brooklyn (G-2371)
Wing Kei Noodle Inc ....F...... 212 226-1644
  New York (G-12120)

FOOD PRDTS: Macaroni, Noodles, Spaghetti, Pasta, Etc
Cassinelli Food Products Inc ....G...... 718 274-4881
  Long Island City (G-7406)
Deer Park Macaroni Co Inc ....F...... 631 667-4600
  Deer Park (G-3964)
Ravioli Store Inc ....G...... 718 729-9300
  Long Island City (G-7572)

FOOD PRDTS: Malt
Great Western Malting Co ....G...... 800 496-7732
  Champlain (G-3409)
Queen City Malting LLC ....G...... 716 481-1313
  Buffalo (G-3027)

FOOD PRDTS: Mayonnaise & Dressings, Exc Tomato Based
Kensington & Sons LLC ....E...... 646 430-8298
  New York (G-10433)

FOOD PRDTS: Mixes, Bread & Roll From Purchased Flour
Elis Bread (eli Zabar) Inc ....F...... 212 772-2011
  New York (G-9649)

FOOD PRDTS: Mixes, Doughnut From Purchased Flour
Dawn Food Products Inc ....C...... 716 830-8214
  Williamsville (G-16577)

FOOD PRDTS: Mixes, Pancake From Purchased Flour
New Hope Mills Inc ....F...... 315 252-2676
  Auburn (G-491)

FOOD PRDTS: Mixes, Sauces, Dry
Casablanca Foods LLC ....G...... 212 317-1111
  New York (G-9221)

FOOD PRDTS: Mixes, Seasonings, Dry
Kerry Bfnctnal Ingredients Inc ....D...... 608 363-1200
  Norwich (G-12488)

FOOD PRDTS: Mustard, Prepared
Old Dutch Mustard Co Inc ....G...... 516 466-0522
  Great Neck (G-5576)

FOOD PRDTS: Nuts & Seeds
American Almond Pdts Co Inc ....D...... 718 875-8310
  Brooklyn (G-1519)
Our Daily Eats LLC ....F...... 518 810-8412
  Albany (G-109)
Scaccianoce Inc ....F...... 718 991-4462
  Bronx (G-1382)
Sugar Foods Corporation ....E...... 212 753-6900
  New York (G-11734)
Whitsons Food Svc Bronx Corp ....B...... 631 424-2700
  Islandia (G-6540)

FOOD PRDTS: Olive Oil
Bonelli Foods LLC ....G...... 212 346-0942
  New York (G-9119)
F Olivers LLC ....G...... 585 244-2585
  Rochester (G-13801)
L LLC ....E...... 716 885-3918
  Buffalo (G-2914)
Lesieur Cristal Inc ....G...... 646 604-4314
  Long Island City (G-7497)
Pietro Demarco Importers Inc ....F...... 914 969-3201
  Yonkers (G-16792)
Pinos Press Inc ....G...... 315 935-0110
  Syracuse (G-15396)

FOOD PRDTS: Oriental Noodles
Lams Foods Inc ....F...... 718 217-0476
  Queens Village (G-13410)
Twin Marquis Inc ....D...... 718 386-6868
  Brooklyn (G-2596)
Wonton Food Inc ....E...... 718 784-8178
  Long Island City (G-7642)
Wonton Food Inc ....C...... 718 628-6868
  Brooklyn (G-2655)
Wonton Food Inc ....G...... 212 677-8865
  New York (G-12131)

FOOD PRDTS: Pasta, Rice/Potatoes, Uncooked, Pkgd
Barilla America Ny Inc ....C...... 585 226-5600
  Avon (G-518)
Bektrom Foods Inc ....G...... 516 802-3800
  Syosset (G-15209)
New York Ravioli Pasta Co Inc ....E...... 516 270-2852
  New Hyde Park (G-8553)
Steinway Pasta & Gelati Inc ....F...... 718 246-5414
  Lindenhurst (G-7194)

FOOD PRDTS: Pasta, Uncooked, Packaged With Other Ingredients
Brooklyns Best Pasta Co Inc ....G...... 917 881-3007
  Brooklyn (G-1651)
Great Eastern Pasta Works LLC ....E...... 631 956-0889
  West Babylon (G-16157)
Johns Ravioli Company Inc ....F...... 914 576-7030
  New Rochelle (G-8618)
Labella Pasta Inc ....G...... 845 331-9130
  Kingston (G-6906)
Sfoglini LLC ....E...... 646 872-1035
  Brooklyn (G-2459)

FOOD PRDTS: Peanut Butter
ABC Peanut Butter LLC ....B...... 212 661-6886
  New York (G-8707)
Capitol City Specialties Co ....G...... 518 486-8935
  Albany (G-56)
Once Again Nut Butter Collectv ....D...... 585 468-2535
  Nunda (G-12497)
Peanut Butter & Co Inc ....E...... 212 757-3130
  New York (G-11128)

FOOD PRDTS: Pickles, Vinegar
Allen Pickle Works Inc ....F...... 516 676-0640
  Glen Cove (G-5359)
Batampte Pickle Products Inc ....D...... 718 251-2100
  Brooklyn (G-1589)
French Associates Inc ....F...... 718 387-9880
  Fresh Meadows (G-5198)
Heintz & Weber Co Inc ....G...... 716 852-7171
  Buffalo (G-2870)
Moldova Pickles & Salads Inc ....G...... 718 284-2220
  Brooklyn (G-2223)

FOOD PRDTS: Pizza, Refrigerated
D R M Management Inc ....E...... 716 668-0333
  Depew (G-4086)
Ultra Thin Ready To Bake Pizza ....E...... 516 679-6655
  Deer Park (G-4053)

FOOD PRDTS: Popcorn, Popped
Saratoga Chips LLC ....G...... 877 901-6950
  Saratoga Springs (G-14597)

FOOD PRDTS: Popcorn, Unpopped
Sunrise Snacks Rockland Inc ....F...... 845 352-2676
  Monsey (G-8298)

FOOD PRDTS: Potato & Corn Chips & Similar Prdts
BSD Top Direct Inc ....G...... 646 468-0156
  West Babylon (G-16141)
Hain Celestial Group Inc ....C...... 516 587-5000
  New Hyde Park (G-8538)
Ideal Snacks Corporation ....C...... 845 292-7000
  Liberty (G-7144)
Pepsico Inc ....A...... 914 253-2000
  Purchase (G-13395)
Pepsico Inc ....B...... 914 253-2000
  White Plains (G-16493)
Pepsico Inc ....D...... 914 767-6976
  White Plains (G-16495)
Proformance Foods Inc ....G...... 703 869-3413
  Brooklyn (G-2355)
Robs Really Good LLC ....F...... 516 671-4411
  Sea Cliff (G-14756)
Switch Beverage Company LLC ....F...... 203 202-7383
  Port Washington (G-13310)
TLC-Lc Inc ....E...... 212 756-8900
  New York (G-11852)
Tortilleria Chinantla Inc ....G...... 718 302-0101
  Brooklyn (G-2574)

FOOD PRDTS: Potato Chips & Other Potato-Based Snacks
Frito-Lay North America Inc ....D...... 607 775-7000
  Binghamton (G-886)
Terrells Potato Chip Co Inc ....D...... 315 437-2786
  Syracuse (G-15442)

FOOD PRDTS: Potatoes, Dried, Packaged With Other Ingredients
Martens Country Kit Pdts LLC ....F...... 315 776-8821
  Port Byron (G-13188)

FOOD PRDTS: Poultry, Processed, NEC
Wendels Poultry Farm ....G...... 716 592-2299
  East Concord (G-4215)

FOOD PRDTS: Poultry, Slaughtered & Dressed
Sing Ah Poultry ....G...... 718 625-7253
  Brooklyn (G-2479)

FOOD PRDTS: Preparations
212kiddish Inc ....G...... 718 705-7227
  Brooklyn (G-1434)
3v Company Inc ....E...... 718 858-7333
  Brooklyn (G-1440)

FOOD PRDTS: Sneaky Chef / Wonder
Sneaky Chef Foods LLC ....F...... 914 301-3277
  Tarrytown (G-15493)
Wonder Natural Foods Corp ....G...... 631 726-4433
  Water Mill (G-15972)

PRODUCT SECTION

FOOD PRDTS: Sugar, Corn

Ahhmigo LLC .... F 212 315-1818
  New York *(G-8772)*
Andros Bowman Products LLC .... G 540 217-4100
  Lyndonville *(G-7679)*
Armour Bearer Group Inc .... G 646 812-4487
  Arverne *(G-413)*
Aryzta LLC .... D 310 417-4700
  Rochester *(G-13644)*
Associated Brands Inc .... B 585 798-3475
  Medina *(G-7970)*
Bainbridge & Knight LLC .... E 212 986-5100
  New York *(G-9005)*
Baldwin Richardson Foods Co .... C 315 986-2727
  Macedon *(G-7695)*
Beths Farm Kitchen .... G 518 799-3414
  Stuyvesant Falls *(G-15183)*
Bombay Kitchen Foods Inc .... F 516 767-7401
  Port Washington *(G-13246)*
Brightline Ventures I LLC .... E 212 626-6829
  New York *(G-9141)*
Bud Ravioli Center Inc .... G 718 356-4600
  Staten Island *(G-15056)*
Bylada Foods LLC .... E 845 623-1300
  West Nyack *(G-16267)*
Cafe Spice Gct Inc .... C 845 863-0910
  New Windsor *(G-9638)*
Castella Imports Inc .... C 631 231-5500
  Edgewood *(G-4398)*
Chan & Chan (usa) Corp .... G 718 388-9633
  Brooklyn *(G-1688)*
Child Nutrition Prog Dept Ed .... D 212 371-1000
  New York *(G-9275)*
China Huaren Organic Pdts Inc .... G 212 232-0120
  New York *(G-9278)*
Cookiebaker LLC .... G 716 878-8000
  Buffalo *(G-2780)*
Damn Good Foods Inc .... F 518 664-1414
  Stillwater *(G-15157)*
Dundee Foods LLC .... F 585 377-7700
  Fairport *(G-4632)*
Event Services Corporation .... G 315 488-9357
  Solvay *(G-14918)*
Fanshawe Foods LLC .... F 212 757-3130
  New York *(G-9780)*
Flik International/Compass .... E 212 450-4750
  New York *(G-9817)*
Frito-Lay North America Inc .... D 607 775-7000
  Binghamton *(G-886)*
Glenn Foods Inc .... F 516 377-1400
  Freeport *(G-5158)*
Gourmet Boutique LLC .... C 718 977-1200
  Jamaica *(G-6647)*
Gourmet Crafts Inc .... F 718 372-0505
  Brooklyn *(G-1942)*
Gravymaster Inc .... E 203 453-1893
  Canajoharie *(G-3207)*
Heinz Mr .... G 718 761-3997
  Staten Island *(G-15084)*
HP Hood LLC .... D 607 295-8134
  Arkport *(G-399)*
Instantwhip of Buffalo Inc .... E 716 892-7031
  Buffalo *(G-2885)*
Joyva Corp .... D 718 497-0170
  Brooklyn *(G-2052)*
Kale Factory Inc .... G 917 363-6361
  Brooklyn *(G-2066)*
Kaneka America LLC .... D 212 705-4340
  New York *(G-10404)*
Kraft Heinz Foods Company .... B 585 226-4400
  Avon *(G-519)*
Land OLakes Inc .... G 516 681-2980
  Hicksville *(G-6102)*
Lollipop Tree Inc .... E 845 471-8733
  Auburn *(G-488)*
Lugo Nutrition Inc .... G 302 573-2503
  Nyack *(G-12509)*
Mandalay Food Products Inc .... G 718 230-3370
  Brooklyn *(G-2155)*
Mediterrean Dyro Company .... E 718 786-4888
  Long Island City *(G-7521)*
Merb LLC .... F 631 393-3621
  Farmingdale *(G-4820)*
Meta-Therm Corp .... F 914 697-4840
  White Plains *(G-16476)*
Mighty Quinns Barbeque LLC .... C 973 777-8430
  New York *(G-10802)*
Milnot Holding Corporation .... G 518 839-0300
  Amsterdam *(G-349)*
Mizkan America Inc .... D 585 765-9171
  Lyndonville *(G-7680)*

Moira New Hope Food Pantry .... E 518 529-6524
  Moira *(G-8261)*
Mondelez Global LLC .... G 585 345-3300
  Batavia *(G-630)*
Morris Kitchen Inc .... F 646 413-5186
  Brooklyn *(G-2227)*
Natural Lab Inc .... F 718 321-8848
  Flushing *(G-5026)*
Natural Matters Inc .... G 212 337-3077
  New York *(G-10892)*
Naturally Free Food Inc .... G 631 361-9710
  Smithtown *(G-14903)*
Nestle Healthcare Ntrtn Inc .... G 516 249-5085
  Farmingdale *(G-4835)*
North Shore Farms Two Ltd .... G 516 280-6880
  Mineola *(G-8239)*
Parnasa International Inc .... G 516 394-0400
  Valley Stream *(G-15789)*
Pelican Bay Ltd .... F 718 729-9300
  Long Island City *(G-7552)*
Pellicano Specialty Foods Inc .... F 716 822-2366
  Buffalo *(G-2995)*
Ponti Rossi Inc .... G 347 506-9616
  Brooklyn *(G-2327)*
Private Lbel Fods Rchester Inc .... E 585 254-9205
  Rochester *(G-14046)*
Pure Functional Foods Inc .... E 315 294-0733
  Savannah *(G-14624)*
Pure Golds Family Corp .... D 516 483-5600
  Hempstead *(G-6024)*
Qualitea Imports Inc .... G 917 624-6750
  Suffern *(G-15195)*
Raw Indulgence Ltd .... F 866 498-4671
  Elmsford *(G-4561)*
Rob Salamida Company Inc .... F 607 729-4868
  Johnson City *(G-6821)*
Royal Kosher Foods LLC .... G 347 221-1867
  Brooklyn *(G-2421)*
Salvador Colletti Blank .... F 718 217-6725
  Douglaston *(G-4139)*
Sapienza Pastry Inc .... E 516 352-5232
  Elmont *(G-4525)*
Settons Intl Foods Inc .... D 631 543-8090
  Commack *(G-3702)*
Whitsons Food Svc Bronx Corp .... B 631 424-2700
  Islandia *(G-6540)*
Win-Holt Equipment Corp .... E 516 222-0335
  Woodbury *(G-16634)*

FOOD PRDTS: Prepared Meat Sauces Exc Tomato & Dry

American Specialty Mfg Co .... F 585 544-5600
  Rochester *(G-13627)*

FOOD PRDTS: Prepared Sauces, Exc Tomato Based

Bushwick Kitchen LLC .... G 917 297-1045
  Brooklyn *(G-1659)*
Elwood International Inc .... F 631 842-6600
  Copiague *(G-3757)*
Gravymaster Inc .... E 203 453-1893
  Canajoharie *(G-3207)*
Mandarin Soy Sauce Inc .... E 845 343-1505
  Middletown *(G-8162)*
Pure Golds Family Corp .... D 516 483-5600
  Hempstead *(G-6024)*
Rob Salamida Company Inc .... F 607 729-4868
  Johnson City *(G-6821)*
T RS Great American Rest .... F 516 294-1680
  Williston Park *(G-16596)*

FOOD PRDTS: Raw cane sugar

Supreme Chocolatier LLC .... E 718 761-9600
  Staten Island *(G-15143)*

FOOD PRDTS: Relishes, Vinegar

Jets Lefrois Corp .... G 585 637-5003
  Brockport *(G-1193)*

FOOD PRDTS: Rice, Milled

Real Co Inc .... G 347 433-8549
  Valley Cottage *(G-15762)*

FOOD PRDTS: Salads

Golden Taste Inc .... E 845 356-4133
  Spring Valley *(G-14993)*

Koppert Cress USA LLC .... E 631 779-3640
  Riverhead *(G-13571)*
M & M Food Products Inc .... F 718 821-1970
  Brooklyn *(G-2142)*
Pride Pak Inc .... D 905 828-2149
  Medina *(G-7986)*
Radicle Farm LLC .... G 315 226-3294
  New York *(G-11315)*

FOOD PRDTS: Sandwiches

Spread-Mmms LLC .... G 917 727-8116
  Brooklyn *(G-2504)*

FOOD PRDTS: Sauerkraut, Bulk

Glk Foods LLC .... E 585 289-4414
  Shortsville *(G-14847)*

FOOD PRDTS: Seasonings & Spices

Aromasong Usa Inc .... F 718 838-9669
  Brooklyn *(G-1555)*
Diva Farms Ltd .... G 315 735-4397
  Utica *(G-15697)*
La Flor Products Company Inc .... E 631 851-9601
  Hauppauge *(G-5863)*
Pennant Ingredients Inc .... D 585 235-8160
  Rochester *(G-14011)*

FOOD PRDTS: Soup Mixes, Dried

Allied Food Products Inc .... F 718 230-4227
  Brooklyn *(G-1510)*

FOOD PRDTS: Soy Sauce

Wanjashan International LLC .... F 845 343-1505
  Middletown *(G-8183)*

FOOD PRDTS: Spices, Including Ground

Extreme Spices Inc .... G 917 496-4081
  Maspeth *(G-7843)*
Manhattan Milling & Drying Co .... E 516 496-1041
  Woodbury *(G-16625)*
Victoria Fine Foods LLC .... D 718 649-1635
  Brooklyn *(G-2621)*
Victoria Fine Foods Holding Co .... G 718 649-1635
  Brooklyn *(G-2622)*
Wm E Martin and Sons Co Inc .... E 516 605-2444
  Roslyn *(G-14452)*

FOOD PRDTS: Spreads, Sandwich, Salad Dressing Base

Sabra Dipping Company LLC .... D 914 372-3900
  White Plains *(G-16501)*

FOOD PRDTS: Starches

Machoonjdgroup .... G 856 345-4689
  Medford *(G-7959)*

FOOD PRDTS: Sugar

Real Co Inc .... G 347 433-8549
  Valley Cottage *(G-15762)*
Sugar Foods Corporation .... E 212 753-6900
  New York *(G-11734)*
Sugar Shack Desert Company Inc .... E 518 523-7540
  Lake Placid *(G-6978)*
U S Sugar Co Inc .... E 716 828-1170
  Buffalo *(G-3107)*

FOOD PRDTS: Sugar, Beet

Beets Love Production LLC .... E 585 270-2471
  Rochester *(G-13659)*

FOOD PRDTS: Sugar, Cane

American Sugar Refining Inc .... F 914 376-3386
  Yonkers *(G-16735)*
Refined Sugars Inc .... G 914 963-2400
  Yonkers *(G-16795)*
Sweeteners Plus Inc .... D 585 728-3770
  Lakeville *(G-6987)*

FOOD PRDTS: Sugar, Corn

Sweetwater Energy Inc .... G 585 647-5760
  Rochester *(G-14149)*

Employee Codes: A=Over 500 employees, B=251-500
C=101-250, D=51-100, E=20-50, F=10-19, G=5-9

FOOD PRDTS: Sugar, Granulated Cane, Purchd Raw Sugar/Syrup

Domino Foods Inc .... F 800 729-4840
Yonkers *(G-16752)*

FOOD PRDTS: Syrup, Maple

Peaceful Valley Maple Farm .... G 518 762-0491
Johnstown *(G-6835)*

FOOD PRDTS: Syrups

Spf Holdings II LLC .... G 212 750-8300
New York *(G-11668)*

FOOD PRDTS: Tea

Farmers Hub LLC .... G 914 380-2945
White Plains *(G-16450)*
Gillies Coffee Company .... E 718 499-7766
Brooklyn *(G-1927)*
Harney & Sons Tea Corp .... C 518 789-2100
Millerton *(G-8193)*
Tea Life LLC .... G 516 365-7711
Manhasset *(G-7773)*

FOOD PRDTS: Tofu Desserts, Frozen

Pulmuone Foods Usa Inc .... E 845 365-3300
Tappan *(G-15470)*

FOOD PRDTS: Tofu, Exc Frozen Desserts

Chan Kee Dried Bean Curd Inc .... G 718 622-0820
Brooklyn *(G-1689)*
Seasons Soyfood Inc .... G 718 797-9896
Brooklyn *(G-2454)*

FOOD PRDTS: Tortillas

Blue Tortilla LLC .... G 631 451-0100
Selden *(G-14760)*
Buna Besta Tortillas .... G 347 987-3995
Brooklyn *(G-1655)*
La Escondida Inc .... G 845 562-1387
Newburgh *(G-12230)*
Maizteca Foods Inc .... E 718 641-3933
South Richmond Hill *(G-14946)*
Tortilla Heaven Inc .... E 845 339-1550
Kingston *(G-6924)*
Tortilleria Oaxaca .... G 347 355-7336
Staten Island *(G-15148)*
Tuv Taam Corp .... E 718 855-2207
Brooklyn *(G-2594)*

FOOD PRDTS: Vegetables, Dried or Dehydrated Exc Freeze-Dried

Wm E Martin and Sons Co Inc .... E 516 605-2444
Roslyn *(G-14452)*

FOOD PRDTS: Vegetables, Pickled

United Pickle Products Corp .... E 718 933-6060
Bronx *(G-1412)*

FOOD PRDTS: Vinegar

Fleischmanns Vinegar Co Inc .... E 315 587-4414
North Rose *(G-12394)*
Mizkan America Inc .... F 585 798-5720
Medina *(G-7985)*
Mizkan Americas Inc .... F 315 483-6944
Sodus *(G-14913)*
Old Dutch Mustard Co Inc .... G 516 466-0522
Great Neck *(G-5576)*
Vinegar Hill Asset LLC .... G 718 469-0342
Brooklyn *(G-2624)*

FOOD PRODUCTS MACHINERY

Ag-Pak Inc .... F 716 772-2651
Gasport *(G-5304)*
Bake-Rite International Inc .... E 518 395-3340
Schenectady *(G-14652)*
Bakers Pride Oven Co Inc .... C 914 576-0200
New Rochelle *(G-8591)*
Bari Engineering Corp .... E 212 966-2080
New York *(G-9017)*
Buflovak LLC .... E 716 895-2100
Buffalo *(G-2755)*
C-Flex Bearing Co Inc .... F 315 895-7454
Frankfort *(G-5104)*

Carts Mobile Food Eqp Corp .... E 718 788-5540
Brooklyn *(G-1680)*
Chester-Jensen Company .... E 610 876-6276
Cattaraugus *(G-3312)*
Delsur Parts .... G 631 630-1606
Brentwood *(G-1131)*
Esquire Mechanical Corp .... E 718 625-4006
Brooklyn *(G-1849)*
Haines Equipment Inc .... E 607 566-8531
Avoca *(G-516)*
I J White Corporation .... D 631 293-3788
Farmingdale *(G-4783)*
Kinplex Corp .... E 631 242-4800
Edgewood *(G-4408)*
Lyophilization Systems Inc .... G 845 338-0456
New Paltz *(G-8579)*
Olmstead Products Corp .... F 516 681-3700
Hicksville *(G-6117)*
P & M LLC .... E 631 842-2200
Amityville *(G-310)*
Precision N Amer Fd McHy LLC .... F 518 462-3387
Albany *(G-118)*
Sidco Food Distribution Corp .... F 718 733-3939
Bronx *(G-1383)*
Simply Natural Foods LLC .... C 631 543-9600
Commack *(G-3703)*
SPX Flow Us LLC .... A 716 692-3000
Getzville *(G-5353)*
Vr Food Equipment Inc .... F 315 531-8133
Farmington *(G-4921)*

FOOD STORES: Delicatessen

Cassinelli Food Products Inc .... G 718 274-4881
Long Island City *(G-7406)*
Jim Romas Bakery Inc .... E 607 748-7425
Endicott *(G-4600)*
Mds Hot Bagels Deli Inc .... G 718 438-5650
Brooklyn *(G-2184)*
Sam A Lupo & Sons Inc .... G 800 388-5352
Endicott *(G-4609)*

FOOD STORES: Grocery, Independent

Mandalay Food Products Inc .... E 718 230-3370
Brooklyn *(G-2155)*

FOOD STORES: Supermarkets

Hana Pastries Inc .... G 718 369-7593
Brooklyn *(G-1964)*
Reisman Bros Bakery Inc .... F 718 331-1975
Brooklyn *(G-2394)*

FOOTWEAR, WHOLESALE: Athletic

Air Skate & Air Jump Corp .... G 212 967-1201
New York *(G-8778)*
Air Skate & Air Jump Corp .... F 212 967-1201
Brooklyn *(G-1496)*

FOOTWEAR, WHOLESALE: Shoe Access

Aniiwe Inc .... G 347 683-1891
Brooklyn *(G-1535)*
Bfma Holding Corporation .... G 607 753-6746
Cortland *(G-3862)*
Marietta Corporation .... A 323 589-8181
Cortland *(G-3883)*

FOOTWEAR, WHOLESALE: Shoes

Anthony L & S LLC .... G 212 386-7245
New York *(G-8877)*
Onia LLC .... E 646 701-0008
New York *(G-11045)*

FOOTWEAR: Cut Stock

Age Manufacturers Inc .... D 718 927-0048
Brooklyn *(G-1494)*
Premier Brands America Inc .... C 914 667-6200
Mount Vernon *(G-8432)*
Premier Brands of America Inc .... G 718 325-3000
Bronx *(G-1364)*

FORGINGS

Biltron Automotive Products .... E 631 928-8613
Port Jeff STA *(G-13212)*
Borgwarner Morse TEC LLC .... C 607 257-6700
Ithaca *(G-6568)*
Burke Frging Heat Treating Inc .... E 585 235-6060
Rochester *(G-13682)*

Delaware Valley Forge Co Inc .... G 716 447-9140
Buffalo *(G-2796)*
Delaware Valley Forge Inc .... E 716 447-9140
Buffalo *(G-2797)*
Designatronics Incorporated .... E 516 328-3300
Hicksville *(G-6079)*
Hammond & Irving Inc .... D 315 253-6265
Auburn *(G-482)*
Hohmann & Barnard Inc .... E 631 234-0600
Hauppauge *(G-5846)*
Hohmann & Barnard Inc .... E 518 357-9757
Schenectady *(G-14687)*
Jrlon Inc .... D 315 597-4067
Palmyra *(G-12855)*
Mattessich Iron LLC .... G 315 409-8496
Memphis *(G-8076)*
Peck & Hale LLC .... E 631 589-2510
West Sayville *(G-16291)*
Schilling Forge Inc .... G 315 454-4421
Syracuse *(G-15417)*
Special Metals Corporation .... D 716 366-5663
Dunkirk *(G-4180)*
Stoffel Polygon Systems Inc .... F 914 961-2000
Tuckahoe *(G-15646)*
Superior Motion Controls Inc .... E 516 420-2921
Farmingdale *(G-4885)*
Viking Iron Works Inc .... F 845 471-5010
Poughkeepsie *(G-13373)*
W J Albro Machine Works Inc .... G 631 345-0657
Yaphank *(G-16728)*
York Industries Inc .... E 516 746-3736
Garden City Park *(G-5290)*

FORGINGS: Aircraft, Ferrous

Firth Rixson Inc .... D 585 328-1383
Rochester *(G-13805)*

FORGINGS: Aluminum

Arconic Inc .... D 212 836-2758
New York *(G-8903)*
Arconic Inc .... G 315 764-4011
Massena *(G-7900)*

FORGINGS: Gear & Chain

Ball Chain Mfg Co Inc .... D 914 664-7500
Mount Vernon *(G-8379)*
Kurz and Zobel Inc .... G 585 254-9060
Rochester *(G-13908)*

FORGINGS: Machinery, Ferrous

Alry Tool and Die Co Inc .... E 716 693-2419
Tonawanda *(G-15521)*

FORGINGS: Nonferrous

Nak International Corp .... D 516 334-6245
Jericho *(G-6794)*
Special Metals Corporation .... D 716 366-5663
Dunkirk *(G-4180)*

FORGINGS: Pump & compressor, Nonferrous

Penn State Metal Fabri .... G 718 786-8814
Brooklyn *(G-2311)*

FORMS: Concrete, Sheet Metal

Gt Innovations LLC .... G 585 739-7659
Bergen *(G-820)*

FOUNDRIES: Aluminum

American Blade Mfg LLC .... F 607 432-4518
Oneonta *(G-12624)*
American Blade Mfg LLC .... G 607 656-4204
Greene *(G-5612)*
Amt Incorporated .... E 518 284-2910
Sharon Springs *(G-14797)*
Consoldted Precision Pdts Corp .... B 315 687-0014
Chittenango *(G-3502)*
Crown Die Casting Corp .... E 914 667-5400
Mount Vernon *(G-8392)*
East Pattern & Model Corp .... E 585 461-3240
Rochester *(G-13756)*
East Pattern & Model Corp .... F 585 461-3240
Rochester *(G-13757)*
Massena Metals Inc .... F 315 769-3846
Massena *(G-7905)*

PRODUCT SECTION — FUELS: Ethanol

Meloon Foundries LLC .... E 315 454-3231
  Syracuse *(G-15369)*
Micro Instrument Corp .... D 585 458-3150
  Rochester *(G-13939)*
Pyrotek Incorporated .... D 607 756-3050
  Cortland *(G-3890)*
Wolff & Dungey Inc .... E 315 475-2105
  Syracuse *(G-15460)*

FOUNDRIES: Brass, Bronze & Copper

David Fehlman .... G 315 455-8888
  Syracuse *(G-15303)*
Meloon Foundries LLC .... E 315 454-3231
  Syracuse *(G-15369)*
Omega Wire Inc .... E 315 337-4300
  Rome *(G-14265)*
Omega Wire Inc .... D 315 689-7115
  Jordan *(G-6842)*

FOUNDRIES: Gray & Ductile Iron

En Tech Corp .... F 845 398-0776
  Tappan *(G-15468)*
Matrix Steel Company Inc .... G 718 381-6800
  Brooklyn *(G-2180)*
McWane Inc .... B 607 734-2211
  Elmira *(G-4497)*

FOUNDRIES: Iron

Eastern Company .... D 315 468-6251
  Solvay *(G-14917)*
Emcom Industries Inc .... G 716 852-3711
  Buffalo *(G-2817)*
Noresco Industrial Group Inc .... E 516 759-3355
  Glen Cove *(G-5371)*
Plattco Corporation .... E 518 563-4640
  Plattsburgh *(G-13145)*

FOUNDRIES: Nonferrous

Allstar Casting Corporation .... E 212 563-0909
  New York *(G-8801)*
Argos Inc .... E 845 528-0576
  Putnam Valley *(G-13401)*
Carrera Casting Corp .... C 212 382-3296
  New York *(G-9215)*
Cast-All Corporation .... E 516 741-4025
  Mineola *(G-8211)*
Cpp-Syracuse Inc .... E 315 687-0014
  Chittenango *(G-3504)*
Crown Die Casting Corp .... E 914 667-5400
  Mount Vernon *(G-8392)*
Globalfoundries US Inc .... D 518 305-9013
  Malta *(G-7730)*
Globalfoundries US Inc .... F 408 462-3900
  Ballston Spa *(G-583)*
Greenfield Die Casting Corp .... E 516 623-9230
  Freeport *(G-5159)*
J & J Bronze & Aluminum Cast .... E 718 383-2111
  Brooklyn *(G-2021)*
Jamestown Bronze Works Inc .... G 716 665-2302
  Jamestown *(G-6727)*
K & H Precision Products Inc .... E 585 624-4894
  Honeoye Falls *(G-6269)*
Karbra Company .... C 212 736-9300
  New York *(G-10407)*
Kelly Foundry & Machine Co .... E 315 732-8313
  Utica *(G-15717)*
Medi-Ray Inc .... D 877 898-3003
  Tuckahoe *(G-15644)*
Plattco Corporation .... F 518 563-4640
  Plattsburgh *(G-13146)*
Polich Tallix Inc .... D 845 567-9464
  Walden *(G-15895)*
Wemco Casting LLC .... D 631 563-8050
  Bohemia *(G-1108)*

FOUNDRIES: Steel

Amt Incorporated .... E 518 284-2910
  Sharon Springs *(G-14797)*
Brinkman Intl Group Inc .... G 585 429-5000
  Rochester *(G-13676)*
C J Winter Machine Tech .... E 585 429-5000
  Rochester *(G-13685)*
Eastern Industrial Steel Corp .... F 845 639-9749
  New City *(G-8493)*
Frazer & Jones Co .... D 315 468-6251
  Syracuse *(G-15325)*
Steel Craft Rolling Door .... F 631 608-8662
  Copiague *(G-3783)*

FOUNDRIES: Steel Investment

Consoldted Precision Pdts Corp .... B 315 687-0014
  Chittenango *(G-3502)*
Jbf Stainless LLC .... E 315 569-2800
  Frankfort *(G-5108)*
Quality Castings Inc .... E 732 409-3203
  Long Island City *(G-7566)*

FRAMES & FRAMING WHOLESALE

AC Moore Incorporated .... G 516 796-5831
  Bethpage *(G-838)*
Framerica Corporation .... D 631 650-1000
  Yaphank *(G-16711)*
Galas Framing Services .... F 718 706-0007
  Long Island City *(G-7454)*
General Art Company Inc .... F 212 255-1298
  New York *(G-9899)*
Inter Pacific Consulting Corp .... G 718 460-2787
  Flushing *(G-5010)*

FRANCHISES, SELLING OR LICENSING

Authentic Brands Group LLC .... C 212 760-2410
  New York *(G-8966)*
Hugo Boss Usa Inc .... F 212 940-0600
  New York *(G-10146)*
Nautica Opco LLC .... B 212 541-5757
  New York *(G-10896)*
Perry Ellis International Inc .... F 212 536-5400
  New York *(G-11160)*

FREIGHT CONSOLIDATION SVCS

ITT Industries Holdings Inc .... G 914 641-2000
  White Plains *(G-16465)*

FREIGHT FORWARDING ARRANGEMENTS

Janel Corporation .... G 516 256-8143
  Lynbrook *(G-7666)*
Marken LLP .... G 631 396-7454
  Farmingdale *(G-4815)*

FRICTION MATERIAL, MADE FROM POWDERED METAL

Materion Brewster LLC .... D 845 279-0900
  Brewster *(G-1171)*
Raytech Corp Asbestos Personal .... A 516 747-0300
  Mineola *(G-8245)*

FRUIT & VEGETABLE MARKETS

Lagoner Farms Inc .... D 315 904-4109
  Williamson *(G-16560)*

FUEL ADDITIVES

E-Zoil Products Inc .... E 716 213-0106
  Tonawanda *(G-15537)*
Fppf Chemical Co Inc .... G 716 856-9607
  Buffalo *(G-2832)*
Kinetic Fuel Technology Inc .... E 716 745-1461
  Youngstown *(G-16836)*

FUEL BRIQUETTES & WAXES

Costello Bros Petroleum Corp .... G 914 237-3189
  Yonkers *(G-16747)*

FUEL BRIQUETTES OR BOULETS, MADE WITH PETROLEUM BINDER

Cooks Intl Ltd Lblty Co .... G 212 741-4407
  New York *(G-9394)*

FUEL CELL FORMS: Cardboard, Made From Purchased Materials

Emergent Power Inc .... G 201 441-3590
  Latham *(G-7072)*
Plug Power Inc .... B 518 782-7700
  Latham *(G-7091)*

FUEL CELLS: Solid State

Plug Power Inc .... B 518 782-7700
  Latham *(G-7091)*
Plug Power Inc .... G 585 474-3993
  Rochester *(G-14024)*

FUEL DEALERS: Wood

B & J Lumber Co Inc .... G 518 677-3845
  Cambridge *(G-3177)*

FUEL OIL DEALERS

Bluebar Oil Co Inc .... F 315 245-4328
  Blossvale *(G-963)*
Costello Bros Petroleum Corp .... G 914 237-3189
  Yonkers *(G-16747)*
Montauk Inlet Seafood Inc .... G 631 668-3419
  Montauk *(G-8306)*

FUELS: Diesel

Algafuel America .... G 516 295-2257
  Hewlett *(G-6046)*
Northern Biodiesel Inc .... G 585 545-4534
  Ontario *(G-12657)*
Performance Diesel Service LLC .... F 315 854-5269
  Plattsburgh *(G-13144)*

FUELS: Ethanol

A and L Home Fuel LLC .... G 607 638-1994
  Schenevus *(G-14729)*
Avstar Fuel Systems Inc .... G 315 255-1955
  Auburn *(G-468)*
Castle Fuels Corporation .... E 914 381-6600
  Harrison *(G-5723)*
Centar Fuel Co Inc .... G 516 538-2424
  West Hempstead *(G-16214)*
Consolidated Edison Co NY Inc .... F 914 933-2936
  Rye *(G-14478)*
Degennaro Fuel Service LLC .... F 518 239-6350
  Medusa *(G-7993)*
Dib Managmnt Inc .... F 718 439-8190
  Brooklyn *(G-1774)*
Family Fuel Co Inc .... G 718 232-2009
  Brooklyn *(G-1867)*
Fire Island Fuel .... G 631 772-1482
  Shirley *(G-14834)*
Friendly Fuel Incorporated .... G 518 581-7036
  Saratoga Springs *(G-14581)*
Friendly Star Fuel Inc .... G 718 369-8801
  Brooklyn *(G-1909)*
Fuel Energy Services USA Ltd .... E 607 846-2650
  Horseheads *(G-6316)*
Fuel Soul .... G 516 379-0810
  Merrick *(G-8098)*
Golden Renewable Energy LLC .... G 914 920-9800
  Yonkers *(G-16763)*
Highrange Fuels Inc .... G 914 930-8300
  Cortlandt Manor *(G-3902)*
J&R Fuel of LI Inc .... G 631 234-1959
  Central Islip *(G-3375)*
Jmg Fuel Inc .... G 631 579-4319
  Ronkonkoma *(G-14359)*
JRs Fuels Inc .... G 518 622-9939
  Cairo *(G-3149)*
Kore Infrastructure LLC .... G 646 532-9060
  Glen Cove *(G-5370)*
Leroux Fuels .... F 518 563-3653
  Plattsburgh *(G-13131)*
Liberty Food and Fuel .... G 315 299-4039
  Syracuse *(G-15360)*
Lift Safe - Fuel Safe Inc .... G 315 423-7702
  Syracuse *(G-15361)*
Lo-Co Fuel Corp .... G 631 929-5086
  Wading River *(G-15885)*
Logo .... G 212 846-2568
  New York *(G-10592)*
Maio Fuel Company LP .... G 914 683-1154
  White Plains *(G-16474)*
Metro Fuel LLC .... C 212 836-9608
  New York *(G-10785)*
MNS Fuel Corp .... F 516 735-3835
  Ronkonkoma *(G-14380)*
Mt Fuel Corp .... G 631 445-2047
  Stony Brook *(G-15168)*
N & L Fuel Corp .... G 718 863-3538
  Bronx *(G-1337)*
Nagle Fuel Corporation .... G 212 304-4618
  New York *(G-10871)*
North East Fuel Group Inc .... G 718 984-6774
  Staten Island *(G-15111)*
Northeastern Fuel Corp .... G 917 560-6241
  Staten Island *(G-15112)*
Oceanconnect Marine Inc .... G 203 328-3117
  New York *(G-11028)*

FUELS: Ethanol

Patdan Fuel Corporation .... G 718 326-3668
  Middle Village *(G-8126)*
Pretty Fuel Inc .... G 315 823-4063
  Little Falls *(G-7212)*
Provident Fuel Inc .... G 516 224-4427
  Woodbury *(G-16629)*
Quality Fuel 1 Corporation .... G 631 392-4090
  North Babylon *(G-12361)*
Remsen Fuel Inc .... G 718 984-9551
  Staten Island *(G-15127)*
S&B Alternative Fuels Inc .... G 631 585-6637
  Lake Grove *(G-6968)*
Southbay Fuel Injectors .... G 516 442-4707
  Rockville Centre *(G-14242)*
Yankee Fuel Inc .... G 631 880-8810
  West Babylon *(G-16205)*
York Fuel Incorporated .... G 718 951-0202
  Brooklyn *(G-2666)*

FUELS: Oil

209 Discount Oil .... E 845 386-2090
  Middletown *(G-8135)*
Ergun Inc .... G 631 721-0049
  Roslyn Heights *(G-14454)*
Fuel Energy Services USA Ltd .... E 607 846-2650
  Horseheads *(G-6316)*
Heat USA II LLC .... E 212 564-4328
  New York *(G-10076)*
Hygrade Fuel Inc .... G 516 741-0723
  Mineola *(G-8228)*
Starfuels Inc .... G 914 289-4800
  White Plains *(G-16507)*

FUNDRAISING SVCS

Consumer Reports Inc .... B 914 378-2000
  Yonkers *(G-16746)*

FUNERAL HOMES & SVCS

Sunnycrest Inc .... E 315 252-7214
  Auburn *(G-501)*

FUNGICIDES OR HERBICIDES

Bioworks Inc .... G 585 924-4362
  Victor *(G-15832)*

FUR APPAREL STORES

Missiontex Inc .... G 718 532-9053
  Brooklyn *(G-2215)*

FUR CLOTHING WHOLESALERS

Blum & Fink Inc .... F 212 695-2606
  New York *(G-9112)*
Georgy Creative Fashions Inc .... G 212 279-4885
  New York *(G-9912)*

FUR FINISHING & LINING: For The Fur Goods Trade

Steves Original Furs Inc .... E 212 967-8007
  New York *(G-11711)*

FUR: Apparel

Arbeit Bros Inc .... G 212 736-9761
  New York *(G-8898)*
CPT Usa LLC .... E 212 575-1616
  New York *(G-9414)*
Fox Unlimited Inc .... G 212 736-3071
  New York *(G-9835)*
Jerry Sorbara Furs Inc .... F 212 594-3897
  New York *(G-10328)*
Mink Mart Inc .... G 212 868-2785
  New York *(G-10819)*
Superior Furs Inc .... F 516 365-4123
  Manhasset *(G-7772)*
Xanadu .... G 212 465-0580
  New York *(G-12149)*

FUR: Coats

Stallion Inc .... E 718 706-0111
  Long Island City *(G-7596)*

FUR: Coats & Other Apparel

Blum & Fink Inc .... F 212 695-2606
  New York *(G-9112)*

J Percy For Mrvin Rchards Ltd .... E 212 944-5300
  New York *(G-10286)*
Mksf Inc .... F 212 563-3877
  New York *(G-10827)*
Moschos Furs Inc .... G 212 244-0255
  New York *(G-10845)*
Samuel Schulman Furs Inc .... E 212 736-5550
  New York *(G-11478)*

FUR: Hats

Best Brands Consumer Pdts Inc ...... G 212 684-7456
  New York *(G-9057)*
Kaitery Furs Ltd .... G 718 204-1396
  Long Island City *(G-7486)*

FUR: Jackets

Anage Inc .... F 212 944-6533
  New York *(G-8852)*

FURNACES & OVENS: Indl

Buflovak LLC .... E 716 895-2100
  Buffalo *(G-2755)*
Cosmos Electronic Machine Corp .... E 631 249-2535
  Farmingdale *(G-4740)*
Embassy Industries Inc .... C 631 435-0209
  Hauppauge *(G-5820)*
Harper International Corp .... D 716 276-9900
  Buffalo *(G-2868)*
Harper International Corp .... G 716 276-9900
  Depew *(G-4091)*
Hpi Co Inc .... G 718 851-2753
  Brooklyn *(G-1986)*
J H Buhrmaster Company Inc .... G 518 843-1700
  Amsterdam *(G-341)*
Linde LLC .... D 716 773-7552
  Grand Island *(G-5506)*
Parker-Hannifin Corporation .... D 716 685-4040
  Lancaster *(G-7038)*
Vincent Genovese .... G 631 281-8170
  Mastic Beach *(G-7912)*

FURNACES: Indl, Electric

Cooks Intl Ltd Lblty Co .... G 212 741-4407
  New York *(G-9394)*

FURNITURE & CABINET STORES: Cabinets, Custom Work

A Van Hoek Woodworking Limited ... G 718 599-4388
  Brooklyn *(G-1459)*
Central Kitchen Corp .... F 631 283-1029
  Southampton *(G-14951)*
Custom Woodcraft LLC .... F 315 843-4234
  Munnsville *(G-8458)*
Di Fiore and Sons Custom Wdwkg ... G 718 278-1663
  Long Island City *(G-7425)*
Jamestown Kitchen & Bath Inc .... G 716 665-2299
  Jamestown *(G-6729)*
Time Base Corporation .... E 631 293-4068
  Edgewood *(G-4420)*
Ultimate Styles of America .... F 631 254-0219
  Bay Shore *(G-733)*

FURNITURE & CABINET STORES: Custom

Red White & Blue Entps Corp .... G 718 565-8080
  Woodside *(G-16675)*

FURNITURE & FIXTURES Factory

Adirondack Scenic Inc .... D 518 638-8000
  Argyle *(G-398)*
Arper USA Inc .... G 212 647-8900
  New York *(G-8910)*
Artistry In Wood of Syracuse .... F 315 431-4022
  East Syracuse *(G-4322)*
Futon City Discounters Inc .... F 315 437-1328
  Syracuse *(G-15326)*
Interiors-Pft Inc .... E 212 244-9600
  Long Island City *(G-7476)*
J P Installations Warehouse .... G 914 576-3188
  New Rochelle *(G-8617)*
Modu-Craft Inc .... G 716 694-0709
  North Tonawanda *(G-12438)*
Modu-Craft Inc .... G 716 694-0709
  Tonawanda *(G-15559)*
T-Company LLC .... G 646 290-6365
  Smithtown *(G-14910)*

FURNITURE PARTS: Metal

Dimar Manufacturing Corp .... C 716 759-0351
  Clarence *(G-3527)*
Icestone LLC .... E 718 624-4900
  Brooklyn *(G-1993)*
Protocase Incorporated .... C 866 849-3911
  Lewiston *(G-7141)*
Seetin Design Group Inc .... F 718 486-5610
  Brooklyn *(G-2455)*

FURNITURE REFINISHING SVCS

FX INC .... F 212 244-2240
  New York *(G-9865)*
Telesca-Heyman Inc .... F 212 534-3442
  New York *(G-11797)*

FURNITURE STOCK & PARTS: Carvings, Wood

Essequattro USA Inc .... G 917 862-0005
  New York *(G-9711)*
Jim Quinn .... F 518 356-0398
  Schenectady *(G-14691)*
Mason Carvings Inc .... G 716 484-7884
  Jamestown *(G-6737)*

FURNITURE STOCK & PARTS: Dimension Stock, Hardwood

Fitzpatrick and Weller Inc .... D 716 699-2393
  Ellicottville *(G-4446)*
North Hudson Woodcraft Corp .... E 315 429-3105
  Dolgeville *(G-4135)*
Randolph Dimension Corporation ... F 716 358-6901
  Randolph *(G-13449)*

FURNITURE STOCK & PARTS: Frames, Upholstered Furniture, Wood

Artistic Frame Corp .... C 212 289-2100
  New York *(G-8921)*
Vitobob Furniture Inc .... G 516 676-1696
  Long Island City *(G-7632)*

FURNITURE STOCK & PARTS: Hardwood

Guldenschuh Logging & Lbr LLC .... G 585 538-4750
  Caledonia *(G-3155)*

FURNITURE STORES

Classic Sofa Ltd .... D 212 620-0485
  New York *(G-9321)*
D & W Design Inc .... E 845 343-3366
  Middletown *(G-8146)*
French & Itln Furn Craftsmen .... G 718 599-5000
  Brooklyn *(G-1906)*
Furniture Doctor Inc .... G 585 657-6941
  Bloomfield *(G-954)*
Futon City Discounters Inc .... F 315 437-1328
  Syracuse *(G-15326)*
Gothic Cabinet Craft Inc .... D 347 881-1420
  Maspeth *(G-7848)*
Little Wolf Cabinet Shop Inc .... E 212 734-1116
  New York *(G-10581)*
Long Lumber and Supply Corp .... F 518 439-1661
  Slingerlands *(G-14889)*
Manhattan Comfort Inc .... G 908 888-0818
  Brooklyn *(G-2157)*
Omega Furniture Manufacturing ...... F 315 463-7428
  Syracuse *(G-15385)*
Pillow Perfections Ltd Inc .... G 718 383-2259
  Brooklyn *(G-2318)*
Recycled Brooklyn Group LLC .... F 917 902-0662
  Brooklyn *(G-2391)*
Safavieh Inc .... A 516 945-1900
  Port Washington *(G-13302)*
Smart Space Products LLC .... G 877 777-2441
  New York *(G-11622)*
Studio 21 LA Inc .... E 718 965-6579
  Brooklyn *(G-2525)*
Upstate Cabinet Company Inc .... F 585 429-5090
  Rochester *(G-14191)*
Yepes Fine Furniture .... E 718 383-0221
  Brooklyn *(G-2663)*

PRODUCT SECTION   FURNITURE: Household, Metal

FURNITURE STORES: Cabinets, Kitchen, Exc Custom Made
Home Ideal Inc .... G 718 762-8998
  Flushing *(G-5009)*

FURNITURE STORES: Custom Made, Exc Cabinets
Atelier Viollet Corp .... G 718 782-1727
  Brooklyn *(G-1568)*
Designway Ltd .... G 212 254-2220
  New York *(G-9509)*
John Langenbacher Co Inc .... E 718 328-0141
  Bronx *(G-1304)*

FURNITURE STORES: Juvenile
Casa Collection Inc .... G 718 694-0272
  Brooklyn *(G-1681)*

FURNITURE STORES: Office
FX INC .... F 212 244-2240
  New York *(G-9865)*

FURNITURE STORES: Outdoor & Garden
Walpole Woodworkers Inc .... G 631 726-2859
  Water Mill *(G-15971)*
Wood Innovations of Suffolk .... G 631 698-2345
  Medford *(G-7969)*

FURNITURE STORES: Unfinished
Universal Designs Inc .... G 718 721-1111
  Long Island City *(G-7625)*

FURNITURE WHOLESALERS
Etna Products Co Inc .... F 212 989-7591
  New York *(G-9722)*
Furniture Doctor Inc .... G 585 657-6941
  Bloomfield *(G-954)*
Harden Furniture LLC .... C 315 675-3600
  Mc Connellsville *(G-7925)*
Holland & Sherry Inc .... E 212 542-8410
  New York *(G-10115)*
Marretti USA Inc .... G 212 255-5565
  New York *(G-10716)*

FURNITURE, HOUSEHOLD: Wholesalers
Steinbock-Braff Inc .... E 718 972-6500
  Brooklyn *(G-2520)*
Two Worlds Arts Ltd .... G 212 929-2210
  New York *(G-11920)*

FURNITURE, OFFICE: Wholesalers
Artistic Frame Corp .... C 212 289-2100
  New York *(G-8921)*
Kas-Ray Industries Inc .... F 212 620-3144
  New York *(G-10410)*
Workplace Interiors LLC .... E 585 425-7420
  Fairport *(G-4667)*

FURNITURE, WHOLESALE: Beds & Bedding
Jdt International LLC .... G 212 400-7570
  New York *(G-10321)*
Wcd Window Coverings Inc .... E 845 336-4511
  Lake Katrine *(G-6973)*

FURNITURE, WHOLESALE: Racks
ASAP Rack Rental Inc .... G 718 499-4995
  Brooklyn *(G-1561)*
Reliable Welding & Fabrication .... G 631 758-2637
  Patchogue *(G-12876)*

FURNITURE, WHOLESALE: Tables, Occasional
Vaughan Designs Inc .... F 212 319-7070
  New York *(G-12000)*

FURNITURE: Bed Frames & Headboards, Wood
Inova LLC .... E 866 528-2804
  Guilderland Center *(G-5656)*

FURNITURE: Bedroom, Wood
Fiber-Seal of New York Inc .... C 212 888-5580
  New York *(G-9797)*
Your Furniture Designers Inc .... G 845 947-3046
  West Haverstraw *(G-16211)*

FURNITURE: Beds, Household, Incl Folding & Cabinet, Metal
Charles P Rogers Brass Beds .... F 212 675-4400
  New York *(G-9264)*

FURNITURE: Bookcases, Office, Wood
F E Hale Mfg Co .... D 315 894-5490
  Frankfort *(G-5106)*

FURNITURE: Box Springs, Assembled
Charles H Beckley Inc .... F 718 665-2218
  Bronx *(G-1239)*

FURNITURE: Cabinets & Filing Drawers, Office, Exc Wood
Falvo Manufacturing Co Inc .... F 315 724-7925
  Utica *(G-15700)*
Ulrich Planfiling Eqp Corp .... E 716 763-1815
  Lakewood *(G-6998)*

FURNITURE: Cabinets & Vanities, Medicine, Metal
Glissade New York LLC .... E 631 756-4800
  Farmingdale *(G-4772)*

FURNITURE: Chairs & Couches, Wood, Upholstered
Jackson Dakota Inc .... F 718 786-8600
  New York *(G-10293)*
Sleepable Sofas Ltd .... D 973 546-4502
  New York *(G-11617)*

FURNITURE: Chairs, Household Upholstered
Avanti Furniture Corp .... F 516 293-8220
  Farmingdale *(G-4725)*

FURNITURE: Chairs, Household Wood
Custom Display Manufacture .... G 516 783-6491
  North Bellmore *(G-12377)*
El Greco Woodworking Inc .... E 716 483-0315
  Jamestown *(G-6713)*
Hunt Country Furniture Inc .... D 845 832-6601
  Wingdale *(G-16606)*
Manchester Wood Inc .... C 518 642-9518
  Granville *(G-5521)*

FURNITURE: Chairs, Office Exc Wood
Poppin Inc .... D 212 391-7200
  New York *(G-11219)*
Vitra Inc .... F 212 463-5700
  New York *(G-12047)*

FURNITURE: Chairs, Office Wood
Interior Solutions of Wny LLC .... G 716 332-0372
  Buffalo *(G-2887)*

FURNITURE: China Closets
Raff Enterprises .... G 518 218-7883
  Albany *(G-122)*

FURNITURE: Church
American Bptst Chrches Mtro NY .... G 212 870-3195
  New York *(G-8824)*

FURNITURE: Console Tables, Wood
Forecast Consoles Inc .... E 631 253-9000
  Hauppauge *(G-5827)*

FURNITURE: Couches, Sofa/Davenport, Upholstered Wood Frames
Classic Sofa Ltd .... D 212 620-0485
  New York *(G-9321)*

FURNITURE: Cribs, Metal
Hard Manufacturing Co Inc .... E 716 893-1800
  Buffalo *(G-2865)*
NK Medical Products Inc .... G 716 759-7200
  Amherst *(G-241)*
Novum Medical Products Inc .... F 716 759-7200
  Amherst *(G-242)*

FURNITURE: Cut Stone
A&A Marble & Granite .... F 347 810-9595
  Bronx *(G-1202)*
Puccio Design International .... F 516 248-6426
  Garden City *(G-5277)*

FURNITURE: Desks & Tables, Office, Wood
Centre Interiors Wdwkg Co Inc .... E 718 323-1343
  Ozone Park *(G-12822)*

FURNITURE: Desks, Metal
Artistic Products LLC .... E 631 435-0200
  Hauppauge *(G-5771)*

FURNITURE: Desks, Wood
Bush Industries Inc .... C 716 665-2000
  Jamestown *(G-6704)*
Ccn International Inc .... D 315 789-4400
  Geneva *(G-5319)*

FURNITURE: Dinette Sets, Metal
Embassy Dinettes Inc .... G 631 253-2292
  Deer Park *(G-3973)*

FURNITURE: Dining Room, Wood
Falcon Chair and Table Inc .... E 716 664-7136
  Falconer *(G-4677)*
Harden Furniture LLC .... C 315 675-3600
  Mc Connellsville *(G-7925)*

FURNITURE: Fiberglass & Plastic
Universal Interiors LLC .... F 518 298-4400
  Champlain *(G-3417)*

FURNITURE: Foundations & Platforms
Acworth Foundation .... G 631 784-7802
  Huntington *(G-6389)*
Ideal Manufacturing Inc .... E 585 872-7190
  East Rochester *(G-4287)*

FURNITURE: Garden, Exc Wood, Metal, Stone Or Concrete
Anandamali Inc .... F 212 343-8964
  New York *(G-8854)*
Holland & Sherry Inc .... E 212 542-8410
  New York *(G-10115)*

FURNITURE: Hospital
AFC Industries Inc .... D 718 747-0237
  College Point *(G-3638)*
Brandt Equipment LLC .... G 718 994-0800
  Bronx *(G-1232)*
Evans & Paul LLC .... E 516 576-0800
  Plainview *(G-13056)*

FURNITURE: Hotel
Inova LLC .... E 866 528-2804
  Guilderland Center *(G-5656)*
N3a Corporation .... D 516 284-6799
  Inwood *(G-6496)*
Ramler International Ltd .... E 516 353-3106
  Syosset *(G-15229)*
Smart Space Products LLC .... G 877 777-2441
  New York *(G-11622)*
Timeless Decor LLC .... C 315 782-5759
  Watertown *(G-16035)*

FURNITURE: Household, Metal
Brueton Industries Inc .... D 516 379-3400
  Freeport *(G-5147)*
D & W Design Inc .... E 845 343-3366
  Middletown *(G-8146)*
F&M Ornamental Designs LLC .... G 212 353-2600
  New York *(G-9763)*

Employee Codes: A=Over 500 employees, B=251-500
C=101-250, D=51-100, E=20-50, F=10-19, G=5-9

2019 Harris
New York Manufacturers Directory

FURNITURE: Household, Metal

F&M Ornamental Designs LLC ....F...... 908 241-1776
  New York *(G-9764)*
Furniture Doctor Inc ....G...... 585 657-6941
  Bloomfield *(G-954)*
La Forge Francaise Ltd Inc ....G...... 631 591-0572
  Riverhead *(G-13572)*
Meeker Sales Corp ....G...... 718 384-5400
  Brooklyn *(G-2188)*
Royal Metal Products Inc ....E...... 518 966-4442
  Surprise *(G-15207)*
Slava Industries Incorporated ....G...... 718 499-4850
  Brooklyn *(G-2483)*

FURNITURE: Household, NEC

Matthew Shively LLC ....G...... 914 937-3531
  Port Chester *(G-13205)*
Safcore LLC ....F...... 917 627-5263
  Brooklyn *(G-2443)*

FURNITURE: Household, Upholstered On Metal Frames

Precision Orna Ir Works Inc ....G...... 718 379-5200
  Bronx *(G-1363)*

FURNITURE: Household, Upholstered, Exc Wood Or Metal

3phase Industries LLC ....G...... 347 763-2942
  Brooklyn *(G-1438)*
Albert Menin Interiors Ltd ....F...... 212 876-3041
  Bronx *(G-1215)*
Culin/Colella Inc ....G...... 914 698-7727
  Mamaroneck *(G-7741)*
Harome Designs LLC ....E...... 631 864-1900
  Commack *(G-3694)*
L & JG Stickley Incorporated ....A...... 315 682-5500
  Manlius *(G-7779)*
Mbh Furniture Innovations Inc ....G...... 845 354-8202
  Spring Valley *(G-15002)*
Olollo Inc ....G...... 877 701-0110
  Brooklyn *(G-2287)*
Ready To Assemble Company Inc ....E...... 516 825-4397
  Valley Stream *(G-15794)*
Two Worlds Arts Ltd ....G...... 212 929-2210
  New York *(G-11920)*
Yogibo LLC ....F...... 518 456-1762
  Albany *(G-144)*

FURNITURE: Household, Wood

A & S Woodworking Inc ....G...... 518 821-0832
  Hudson *(G-6335)*
A-1 Manhattan Custom Furn Inc ....E...... 718 937-4780
  Island Park *(G-6511)*
Anthony Lawrence of New York ....E...... 212 206-8820
  Long Island City *(G-7380)*
Arthur Brown W Mfg Co ....F...... 631 243-5594
  Deer Park *(G-3946)*
Arthur Lauer Inc ....E...... 845 255-7871
  Gardiner *(G-5291)*
Artisan Woodworking Ltd ....G...... 516 486-0818
  West Hempstead *(G-16212)*
Atelier Viollet Corp ....E...... 718 782-1727
  Brooklyn *(G-1568)*
Benchmark Furniture Mfg ....D...... 718 257-4707
  Brooklyn *(G-1597)*
Black River Woodworking LLC ....G...... 315 376-8405
  Castorland *(G-3298)*
Brueton Industries Inc ....D...... 516 379-3400
  Freeport *(G-5147)*
Bush Industries Inc ....C...... 716 665-2000
  Jamestown *(G-6704)*
Carlos & Alex Atelier Inc ....E...... 718 441-8911
  Richmond Hill *(G-13500)*
Carver Creek Enterprises Inc ....G...... 585 657-7511
  Bloomfield *(G-949)*
Charles H Beckley Inc ....F...... 718 665-2218
  Bronx *(G-1239)*
Comerford Hennessy At Home Inc .....G...... 631 537-6200
  Bridgehampton *(G-1180)*
Concepts In Wood of CNY ....E...... 315 463-8084
  Syracuse *(G-15286)*
Conesus Lake Association Inc ....E...... 585 346-6864
  Lakeville *(G-6985)*
Cousins Furniture & Hm Imprvs ....E...... 631 254-3752
  Deer Park *(G-3959)*
Custom Woodcraft LLC ....F...... 315 843-4234
  Munnsville *(G-8458)*

D & W Design Inc ....E...... 845 343-3366
  Middletown *(G-8146)*
David Sutherland Showrooms - N ....G...... 212 871-9717
  New York *(G-9485)*
Dbs Interiors Corp ....F...... 631 491-3013
  West Babylon *(G-16152)*
Dcl Furniture Manufacturing ....E...... 516 248-2683
  Mineola *(G-8215)*
Deakon Homes and Interiors ....F...... 518 271-0342
  Troy *(G-15603)*
Designs By Robert Scott Inc ....E...... 718 609-2535
  Brooklyn *(G-1770)*
Dessin/Fournir Inc ....F...... 212 758-0844
  New York *(G-9510)*
Dune Inc ....F...... 212 925-6171
  New York *(G-9585)*
Eclectic Cntract Furn Inds Inc ....F...... 212 967-5504
  New York *(G-9622)*
Emilia Interiors Inc ....F...... 718 629-4202
  Brooklyn *(G-1831)*
Eugenia Selective Living Inc ....F...... 631 277-1461
  Islip *(G-6546)*
Fenix Furniture Co ....E...... 631 273-3500
  Bay Shore *(G-686)*
Final Dimension Inc ....G...... 718 786-0100
  Maspeth *(G-7845)*
Fine Arts Furniture Inc ....G...... 212 744-9139
  Long Island City *(G-7447)*
Franz Fischer Inc ....F...... 718 821-1300
  Brooklyn *(G-1905)*
Fred Schulz Inc ....G...... 845 724-3409
  Poughquag *(G-13374)*
French & Itln Furn Craftsmen ....F...... 718 599-5000
  Brooklyn *(G-1906)*
Furniture Doctor Inc ....G...... 585 657-6941
  Bloomfield *(G-954)*
Glendale Architectural WD Pdts ....E...... 718 326-2700
  Glendale *(G-5401)*
Hard Manufacturing Co Inc ....E...... 716 893-1800
  Buffalo *(G-2865)*
Hayman-Chaffey Designs Inc ....F...... 212 889-7771
  New York *(G-10050)*
Icon Design LLC ....E...... 585 768-6040
  Le Roy *(G-10050)*
Inter Craft Custom Furniture ....G...... 718 278-2573
  Astoria *(G-431)*
J Percoco Industries Inc ....G...... 631 312-4572
  Bohemia *(G-1038)*
K & B Woodworking Inc ....E...... 518 634-7253
  Cairo *(G-3150)*
Kazac Inc ....G...... 631 249-7299
  Farmingdale *(G-4799)*
Kittinger Company Inc ....F...... 716 876-1000
  Buffalo *(G-2907)*
Knoll Inc ....D...... 212 343-4124
  New York *(G-10460)*
L& JG Stickley Incorporated ....A...... 315 682-5500
  Manlius *(G-7779)*
Lanoves Inc ....E...... 718 384-1880
  Brooklyn *(G-2094)*
Little Wolf Cabinet Shop Inc ....E...... 212 734-1116
  New York *(G-10581)*
M & C Furniture ....G...... 718 422-2136
  Brooklyn *(G-2140)*
M T D Corporation ....F...... 631 491-3905
  West Babylon *(G-16172)*
Mackenzie-Childs LLC ....C...... 315 364-6118
  Aurora *(G-511)*
Mica International Ltd ....F...... 516 378-3400
  Freeport *(G-5167)*
New Day Woodwork Inc ....E...... 718 275-1721
  Glendale *(G-5404)*
Nicholas Dfine Furn Decorators ....E...... 914 245-8982
  Bronx *(G-1343)*
Patrick Mackin Custom Furn ....G...... 718 237-2592
  Brooklyn *(G-2307)*
Piccini Industries Ltd ....E...... 845 365-0614
  Orangeburg *(G-12685)*
Pillow Perfections Ltd Inc ....F...... 718 383-2259
  Brooklyn *(G-2318)*
Plexi Craft Quality Products ....F...... 212 924-3244
  New York *(G-11211)*
Premier Woodcraft Ltd ....E...... 610 383-6624
  White Plains *(G-16499)*
Recycled Brooklyn Group LLC ....F...... 917 902-0662
  Brooklyn *(G-2391)*
Reis D Furniture Mfg ....E...... 516 248-5676
  Mineola *(G-8246)*
Renco Group Inc ....G...... 212 541-6000
  New York *(G-11361)*

Triple J Bedding LLC ....G...... 718 643-8005
  Brooklyn *(G-2587)*
Universal Designs Inc ....G...... 718 721-1111
  Long Island City *(G-7625)*
Wallace Home Design Ctr ....G...... 631 765-3890
  Southold *(G-14971)*
Walpole Woodworkers Inc ....G...... 631 726-2859
  Water Mill *(G-15971)*
Walter P Sauer LLC ....E...... 718 937-0600
  Brooklyn *(G-2638)*
William Somerville Maintenance ....D...... 212 534-4600
  New York *(G-12113)*
Woodmotif Inc ....F...... 516 564-8325
  Hempstead *(G-6028)*
World Trading Center Inc ....G...... 631 273-3330
  Hauppauge *(G-5978)*

FURNITURE: Hydraulic Barber & Beauty Shop Chairs

Pyrotek Incorporated ....E...... 716 731-3221
  Sanborn *(G-14552)*
Zebrowski Industries Inc ....G...... 716 532-3911
  Collins *(G-3676)*

FURNITURE: Institutional, Exc Wood

Able Steel Equipment Co Inc ....F...... 718 361-9240
  Long Island City *(G-7366)*
Artistry In Wood of Syracuse ....F...... 315 431-4022
  East Syracuse *(G-4322)*
Artone LLC ....D...... 716 664-2232
  Jamestown *(G-6699)*
Forecast Consoles Inc ....E...... 631 253-9000
  Hauppauge *(G-5827)*
Maximum Security Products Corp .....E...... 518 233-1800
  Waterford *(G-15977)*
Maxsecure Systems Inc ....G...... 800 657-4336
  Buffalo *(G-2940)*
N Y Elli Design Corp ....F...... 718 228-0014
  Ridgewood *(G-13543)*
Pluribus Products Inc ....E...... 718 852-1614
  Bayville *(G-753)*
Rosenwach Tank Co Inc ....E...... 212 972-4411
  Astoria *(G-442)*
Seating Inc ....E...... 800 468-2475
  Nunda *(G-12498)*
Testori Interiors Inc ....G...... 518 298-4400
  Champlain *(G-3414)*
Unifor Inc ....F...... 212 673-3434
  New York *(G-11941)*
Universal Interiors LLC ....G...... 518 298-4400
  Champlain *(G-3417)*

FURNITURE: Juvenile, Wood

Community Products LLC ....C...... 845 658-8799
  Rifton *(G-13559)*
Ducduc LLC ....F...... 212 226-1868
  New York *(G-9582)*

FURNITURE: Kitchen & Dining Room

Cab-Network Inc ....G...... 516 334-8666
  Westbury *(G-16320)*
Catskill Craftsmen Inc ....D...... 607 652-7321
  Stamford *(G-15030)*
Dinette Depot Ltd ....D...... 516 515-9623
  Brooklyn *(G-1780)*
Innovant Inc ....G...... 212 929-4883
  New York *(G-10218)*
Lemode Concepts Inc ....G...... 631 841-0796
  Amityville *(G-297)*
Professional Cab Detailing Co ....F...... 845 436-7282
  Woodridge *(G-16643)*

FURNITURE: Kitchen & Dining Room, Metal

Renco Group Inc ....G...... 212 541-6000
  New York *(G-11361)*

FURNITURE: Laboratory

J H C Fabrications Inc ....E...... 718 649-0065
  Brooklyn *(G-2022)*
Modu-Craft Inc ....G...... 716 694-0709
  Tonawanda *(G-15559)*
Modu-Craft Inc ....G...... 716 694-0709
  North Tonawanda *(G-12438)*

PRODUCT SECTION

FURNITURE: Living Room, Upholstered On Wood Frames

Hallagan Manufacturing Co Inc ....D 315 331-4640
  Newark *(G-12195)*

FURNITURE: Mattresses & Foundations

M R C Industries Inc ....C 516 328-6900
  Port Washington *(G-13283)*
Steinbock-Braff Inc ....E 718 972-6500
  Brooklyn *(G-2520)*
VSM Investors LLC ....G 212 351-1600
  New York *(G-12057)*

FURNITURE: Mattresses, Box & Bedsprings

Brook North Farms Inc ....F 315 834-9390
  Auburn *(G-472)*
Duxiana Dux Bed ....G 212 755-2600
  New York *(G-9588)*
Hard Manufacturing Co Inc ....E 716 893-1800
  Buffalo *(G-2865)*
Metro Mattress Corp ....E 716 205-2300
  Niagara Falls *(G-12310)*
Natural Dreams LLC ....G 718 760-4202
  Corona *(G-3852)*

FURNITURE: Mattresses, Innerspring Or Box Spring

KKR Millennium GP LLC ....A 212 750-8300
  New York *(G-10454)*
Otis Bedding Mfg Co Inc ....E 716 825-2599
  Buffalo *(G-2983)*
Royal Bedding Co Buffalo Inc ....E 716 895-1414
  Buffalo *(G-3049)*
Sealy Mattress Co Albany Inc ....B 518 880-1600
  Troy *(G-15598)*

FURNITURE: NEC

Dellet Industries Inc ....F 718 965-0101
  Brooklyn *(G-1764)*
Inova LLC ....F 518 861-3400
  Altamont *(G-198)*

FURNITURE: Novelty, Wood

Feinkind Inc ....G 800 289-6136
  Irvington *(G-6504)*

FURNITURE: Office Panel Systems, Exc Wood

Afco Systems Inc ....C 631 249-9441
  Farmingdale *(G-4708)*
Aztec Industries Inc ....G 631 585-1331
  Ronkonkoma *(G-14313)*
Knoll Inc ....D 212 343-4124
  New York *(G-10460)*

FURNITURE: Office Panel Systems, Wood

New Dimensions Office Group ....D 718 387-0995
  Brooklyn *(G-2259)*

FURNITURE: Office, Exc Wood

3phase Industries LLC ....G 347 763-2942
  Brooklyn *(G-1438)*
Able Steel Equipment Co Inc ....F 718 361-9240
  Long Island City *(G-7366)*
Allcraft Fabricators Inc ....D 631 951-4100
  Hauppauge *(G-5760)*
Aronowitz Metal Works ....G 845 356-1660
  Monsey *(G-8285)*
Artone LLC ....D 716 664-2232
  Jamestown *(G-6699)*
Bisley Inc ....G 212 675-3055
  New York *(G-9091)*
Brueton Industries Inc ....D 516 379-3400
  Freeport *(G-5147)*
Davies Office Refurbishing Inc ....C 518 426-7188
  Albany *(G-67)*
Davinci Designs Inc ....F 631 595-1095
  Deer Park *(G-3962)*
Dcl Furniture Manufacturing ....E 516 248-2683
  Mineola *(G-8215)*
Deakon Homes and Interiors ....F 518 271-0342
  Troy *(G-15603)*
E-Systems Group LLC ....E 607 775-1100
  Conklin *(G-3727)*
Eugenia Selective Living Inc ....F 631 277-1461
  Islip *(G-6546)*
Exhibit Corporation America ....E 718 937-2600
  Long Island City *(G-7441)*
Forecast Consoles Inc ....E 631 253-9000
  Hauppauge *(G-5827)*
FX INC ....F 212 244-2240
  New York *(G-9865)*
Hergo Ergonomic Support ....E 718 894-0639
  Maspeth *(G-7851)*
Hudson Valley Office Furn Inc ....G 845 565-6673
  Newburgh *(G-12227)*
Inscape Inc ....E 716 665-6210
  Falconer *(G-4682)*
Integrated Tech Support Svcs ....G 718 454-2497
  Saint Albans *(G-14508)*
International Office ....G 212 334-4617
  New York *(G-10249)*
Larson Metal Manufacturing Co ....G 716 665-6807
  Jamestown *(G-6736)*
Lucia Group Inc ....G 631 392-4900
  Deer Park *(G-4004)*
Modern Metal Fabricators Inc ....G 518 966-4142
  Hannacroix *(G-5716)*
New Dimensions Office Group ....D 718 387-0995
  Brooklyn *(G-2259)*
Piccini Industries Ltd ....E 845 365-0614
  Orangeburg *(G-12685)*
Premier Woodcraft Ltd ....E 610 383-6624
  White Plains *(G-16499)*
Roberts Office Furn Cncpts Inc ....E 315 451-9185
  Liverpool *(G-7260)*
Royal Metal Products Inc ....G 518 966-4442
  Surprise *(G-15207)*
Workplace Interiors LLC ....E 585 425-7420
  Fairport *(G-4667)*
Zographos Designs Ltd ....G 212 545-0227
  New York *(G-12182)*

FURNITURE: Office, Wood

Artone LLC ....D 716 664-2232
  Jamestown *(G-6699)*
B D B Typewriter Supply Works ....E 718 232-4800
  Brooklyn *(G-1580)*
Bauerschmidt & Sons Inc ....D 718 528-3500
  Jamaica *(G-6630)*
Bloch Industries LLC ....D 585 334-9600
  Rochester *(G-13666)*
Brueton Industries Inc ....D 516 379-3400
  Freeport *(G-5147)*
DAF Office Networks Inc ....G 315 699-7070
  Cicero *(G-3516)*
Davinci Designs Inc ....F 631 595-1095
  Deer Park *(G-3962)*
Dcl Furniture Manufacturing ....E 516 248-2683
  Mineola *(G-8215)*
Deakon Homes and Interiors ....F 518 271-0342
  Troy *(G-15603)*
Designs By Robert Scott Inc ....E 718 609-2535
  Brooklyn *(G-1770)*
Divine Art Furniture Inc ....G 718 834-0111
  Brooklyn *(G-1782)*
E-Systems Group LLC ....E 607 775-1100
  Conklin *(G-3727)*
Eugenia Selective Living Inc ....F 631 277-1461
  Islip *(G-6546)*
Exhibit Corporation America ....E 718 937-2600
  Long Island City *(G-7441)*
Forecast Consoles Inc ....E 631 253-9000
  Hauppauge *(G-5827)*
Furniture By Craftmaster Ltd ....G 631 750-0658
  Bohemia *(G-1025)*
Glendale Architectural WD Pdts ....E 718 326-2700
  Glendale *(G-5401)*
Gunlocke Company LLC ....C 585 728-5111
  Wayland *(G-16071)*
H Freund Woodworking Co Inc ....F 516 334-3774
  Westbury *(G-16337)*
Harden Furniture LLC ....C 315 675-3600
  Mc Connellsville *(G-7925)*
Heartwood Specialties Inc ....G 607 654-0102
  Hammondsport *(G-5704)*
Hni Corporation ....C 212 683-2232
  New York *(G-10110)*
Humanscale Corporation ....E 212 725-4749
  New York *(G-10150)*
Innovant Inc ....G 631 348-1900
  Islandia *(G-6531)*
Kazac Inc ....G 631 249-7299
  Farmingdale *(G-4799)*
Kimball Office Inc ....E 212 753-6161
  New York *(G-10446)*
Kittinger Company Inc ....E 716 876-1000
  Buffalo *(G-2907)*
Knoll Inc ....D 716 891-1700
  Buffalo *(G-2908)*
Knoll Inc ....D 212 343-4124
  New York *(G-10460)*
Lake Country Woodworkers Ltd ....E 585 374-6353
  Naples *(G-8472)*
Longo Commercial Cabinets Inc ....E 631 225-4290
  Lindenhurst *(G-7176)*
M T D Corporation ....F 631 491-3905
  West Babylon *(G-16172)*
Manhattan Comfort Inc ....G 908 888-0818
  Brooklyn *(G-2157)*
Matteo & Antonio Bartolotta ....F 315 252-2220
  Auburn *(G-490)*
Miller Blaker Inc ....D 718 665-0500
  Bronx *(G-1332)*
Millers Millworks Inc ....E 585 494-1420
  Bergen *(G-825)*
Nicholas Dfine Furn Decorators ....F 914 245-8982
  Bronx *(G-1343)*
Omega Furniture Manufacturing ....F 315 463-7428
  Syracuse *(G-15385)*
Phoenix Custom Furniture Ltd ....E 212 727-2648
  Long Island City *(G-7555)*
Piccini Industries Ltd ....E 845 365-0614
  Orangeburg *(G-12685)*
Premier Woodcraft Ltd ....E 610 383-6624
  White Plains *(G-16499)*
Princeton Upholstery Co Inc ....D 845 343-2196
  Middletown *(G-8172)*
Saraval Industries ....G 516 768-9033
  Nyack *(G-12510)*
Technology Desking Inc ....E 212 257-6998
  New York *(G-11794)*
Universal Designs Inc ....G 718 721-1111
  Long Island City *(G-7625)*
Upstate Office Liquidators Inc ....F 607 722-9234
  Johnson City *(G-6822)*
WD Certified Contracting LLC ....E 516 493-9319
  Westbury *(G-16387)*
Woodmotif Inc ....F 516 564-8325
  Hempstead *(G-6028)*
Your Furniture Designers Inc ....G 845 947-3046
  West Haverstraw *(G-16211)*
Zographos Designs Ltd ....G 212 545-0227
  New York *(G-12182)*

FURNITURE: Outdoor, Wood

Long Lumber and Supply Corp ....F 518 439-1661
  Slingerlands *(G-14889)*
Sitecraft Inc ....G 718 729-4900
  Astoria *(G-444)*
Sundown Ski & Sport Shop Inc ....E 631 737-8600
  Lake Grove *(G-6970)*

FURNITURE: Pews, Church

Keck Group Inc ....F 845 988-5757
  Warwick *(G-15954)*

FURNITURE: Picnic Tables Or Benches, Park

Hartford Hwy Dept ....G 315 724-0654
  New Hartford *(G-8506)*
Studio 21 LA Inc ....E 718 965-6579
  Brooklyn *(G-2525)*
Town of Amherst ....E 716 631-7113
  Williamsville *(G-16591)*
Tymor Park ....G 845 724-5691
  Lagrangeville *(G-6963)*

FURNITURE: Rattan

Bielecky Bros Inc ....E 718 424-4764
  Woodside *(G-16646)*

FURNITURE: Restaurant

Dine Rite Seating Products Inc ....E 631 226-8899
  Lindenhurst *(G-7170)*
Hunt Country Furniture Inc ....D 845 832-6601
  Wingdale *(G-16606)*
L & D Manufacturing Corp ....G 718 665-5226
  Bronx *(G-1311)*
Lb Furniture Industries LLC ....C 518 828-1501
  Hudson *(G-6362)*
Maxsun Corporation ....F 718 418-6800
  Maspeth *(G-7859)*

Employee Codes: A=Over 500 employees, B=251-500
C=101-250, D=51-100, E=20-50, F=10-19, G=5-9

FURNITURE: Restaurant

Rollhaus Seating Products Inc .... F 718 729-9111
Long Island City *(G-7577)*

FURNITURE: School

Inova LLC .... E 866 528-2804
Guilderland Center *(G-5656)*

FURNITURE: Ship

Starliner Shipping & Travel .... G 718 385-1515
Brooklyn *(G-2513)*

FURNITURE: Silverware Chests, Wood

McGraw Wood Products LLC .... E 607 836-6465
Mc Graw *(G-7928)*

FURNITURE: Sleep

Sleep Improvement Center Inc .... F 516 536-5799
Rockville Centre *(G-14240)*

FURNITURE: Sofa Beds Or Convertible Sofas)

Sleepable Sofas Ltd .... D 973 546-4502
New York *(G-11617)*

FURNITURE: Storage Chests, Household, Wood

Premiere Living Products LLC .... F 631 873-4337
Dix Hills *(G-4123)*

FURNITURE: Tables & Table Tops, Wood

Ercole Nyc Inc .... F 212 675-2218
Brooklyn *(G-1846)*

FURNITURE: Theater

Steeldeck Ny Inc .... F 718 599-3700
Brooklyn *(G-2517)*

FURNITURE: Unfinished, Wood

Stillwater Wood & Iron .... G 518 664-4501
Stillwater *(G-15159)*

FURNITURE: Upholstered

Arthur Lauer Inc .... E 845 255-7871
Gardiner *(G-5291)*
Artone LLC .... D 716 664-2232
Jamestown *(G-6699)*
August Studios .... G 718 706-6487
Long Island City *(G-7395)*
Deangelis Ltd .... E 212 348-8225
Glen Head *(G-5379)*
Doreen Interiors Ltd .... E 212 255-9008
New Hyde Park *(G-8528)*
Elan Upholstery Inc .... F 631 563-0650
Bohemia *(G-1022)*
Falvo Manufacturing Co Inc .... F 315 724-7925
Utica *(G-15700)*
Fiber-Seal of New York Inc .... C 212 888-5580
New York *(G-9797)*
Furniture By Craftmaster Ltd .... G 631 750-0658
Bohemia *(G-1025)*
H & H Furniture Co .... F 718 850-5252
Jamaica *(G-6648)*
Harden Furniture LLC .... C 315 675-3600
Mc Connellsville *(G-7925)*
Jackson Dakota Inc .... G 212 838-9444
New York *(G-10294)*
Jays Furniture Products Inc .... E 716 876-8854
Buffalo *(G-2890)*
Kittinger Company Inc .... F 716 876-1000
Buffalo *(G-2907)*
Mackenzie-Childs LLC .... C 315 364-6118
Aurora *(G-511)*
Matteo & Antonio Bartolotta .... F 315 252-2220
Auburn *(G-490)*
Mazza Classics Incorporated .... F 631 390-9060
Farmingdale *(G-4818)*
Nicholas Dfine Furn Decorators .... F 914 245-8982
Bronx *(G-1343)*
Pheonix Custom Furniture Ltd .... E 212 727-2648
Long Island City *(G-7555)*
Princeton Upholstery Co Inc .... D 845 343-2196
Middletown *(G-8172)*
Rob Herschenfeld Design Inc .... F 718 456-6801
Brooklyn *(G-2408)*

Simon S Decorating Inc .... G 718 339-2931
Brooklyn *(G-2476)*
Slava Industries Incorporated .... G 718 499-4850
Brooklyn *(G-2483)*
Smith & Watson .... E 212 686-6444
New York *(G-11624)*
Two Worlds Arts Ltd .... G 212 929-2210
Brooklyn *(G-2597)*
Versailles Drapery Upholstery .... F 212 533-2059
Long Island City *(G-7631)*
Wallace Home Design Ctr .... G 631 765-3890
Southold *(G-14971)*
Yepes Fine Furniture .... E 718 383-0221
Brooklyn *(G-2663)*

FURNITURE: Vehicle

Stidd Systems Inc .... E 631 477-2400
Greenport *(G-5626)*

FURRIERS

Anastasia Furs International .... G 212 868-9241
New York *(G-8855)*
Superior Furs Inc .... F 516 365-4123
Manhasset *(G-7772)*

FUSES: Electric

Leviton Manufacturing Co Inc .... B 631 812-6000
Melville *(G-8043)*
Soc America Inc .... F 631 472-6666
Ronkonkoma *(G-14414)*

GAMES & TOYS: Airplanes

Jupiter Creations Inc .... G 917 493-9393
New York *(G-10382)*

GAMES & TOYS: Baby Carriages & Restraint Seats

Babysafe Usa LLC .... G 877 367-4141
Afton *(G-7)*

GAMES & TOYS: Banks

E C C Corp .... G 518 873-6494
Elizabethtown *(G-4431)*

GAMES & TOYS: Child Restraint Seats, Automotive

Pidyon Controls Inc .... F 212 683-9523
New York *(G-11191)*

GAMES & TOYS: Craft & Hobby Kits & Sets

Design Works Craft Inc .... F 631 244-5749
Bohemia *(G-1015)*
Innovative Designs LLC .... E 212 695-0892
New York *(G-10219)*
Master Art Corp .... G 845 362-6430
Spring Valley *(G-15001)*
R F Giardina Co .... F 516 922-1364
Oyster Bay *(G-12820)*
Spectrum Crafts Inc .... E 631 244-5749
Bohemia *(G-1091)*

GAMES & TOYS: Doll Hats

Beila Group Inc .... F 212 260-1948
New York *(G-9038)*

GAMES & TOYS: Dolls & Doll Clothing

Goldberger Company LLC .... F 212 924-1194
New York *(G-9952)*

GAMES & TOYS: Dolls, Exc Stuffed Toy Animals

ADC Dolls Inc .... C 212 244-4500
New York *(G-8734)*
Lovee Doll & Toy Co Inc .... G 212 242-1545
New York *(G-10619)*
Madame Alexander Doll 2018 LLC .... G 917 576-8381
New York *(G-10653)*
Madame Alexander Doll Co LLC .... D 212 244-4500
New York *(G-10654)*
Mattel Inc .... F 716 714-8514
East Aurora *(G-4205)*

Toy Admiration Co Inc .... E 914 963-9400
Yonkers *(G-16804)*

GAMES & TOYS: Electronic

212 Db Corp .... E 212 652-5600
New York *(G-8670)*
Barron Games Intl Co LLC .... F 716 630-0054
Buffalo *(G-2723)*
Kidz Toyz Inc .... G 914 261-4453
Mount Kisco *(G-8347)*
Marvel Entertainment LLC .... E 212 576-4000
New York *(G-10719)*

GAMES & TOYS: Game Machines, Exc Coin-Operated

Ellis Products Corp .... G 516 791-3732
Valley Stream *(G-15778)*

GAMES & TOYS: Miniature Dolls, Collectors'

Tonner Doll Company Inc .... E 845 339-9537
Kingston *(G-6923)*

GAMES & TOYS: Puzzles

Compoz A Puzzle Inc .... G 516 883-2311
Port Washington *(G-13250)*
Tucker Jones House Inc .... E 631 642-9092
East Setauket *(G-4313)*

GAMES & TOYS: Scooters, Children's

Dakott LLC .... G 888 805-6795
New York *(G-9460)*
Famous Box Scooter Co .... G 631 943-2013
West Babylon *(G-16155)*

GAMES & TOYS: Trains & Eqpt, Electric & Mechanical

Gargraves Trackage Corporation .... G 315 483-6577
North Rose *(G-12395)*
Mechanical Displays Inc .... G 718 258-5588
Brooklyn *(G-2185)*
Pride Lines Ltd .... G 631 225-0033
Lindenhurst *(G-7190)*

GARBAGE CONTAINERS: Plastic

CT Industrial Supply Co Inc .... F 718 417-3226
Brooklyn *(G-1737)*
Rainbow Plastics Inc .... F 718 218-7288
Brooklyn *(G-2381)*
Think Green Junk Removal Inc .... G 845 297-7771
Wappingers Falls *(G-15937)*

GARBAGE DISPOSALS: Household

Platinum Carting Corp .... F 631 649-4322
Bay Shore *(G-706)*

GARBAGE DISPOSERS & COMPACTORS: Commercial

240 Michigan Street Inc .... F 716 434-6010
Buffalo *(G-2675)*
Blue Tee Corp .... G 212 598-0880
New York *(G-9109)*

GARNET MINING SVCS

Barton Mines Company LLC .... C 518 798-5462
Glens Falls *(G-5418)*

GAS & OIL FIELD EXPLORATION SVCS

Able Environmental Services .... G 631 567-6585
Bohemia *(G-968)*
Aegis Oil Limited Ventures LLC .... F 646 233-4900
New York *(G-8762)*
America Capital Energy Corp .... G 212 983-8316
New York *(G-8820)*
Bistate Oil Management Corp .... F 212 935-4110
New York *(G-9092)*
FT Seismic Support Inc .... C 607 527-8595
Campbell *(G-3203)*
Hess Energy Exploration Ltd .... G 732 750-6500
New York *(G-10086)*
Hess Explrtion Prod Hldngs Ltd .... G 732 750-6000
New York *(G-10087)*

KKR Ntral Rsources Fund I-A LP ....G....... 212 750-8300
  New York *(G-10455)*
Lenape Energy Inc............................G....... 585 344-1200
  Alexander *(G-179)*
Lenape Resources Inc.......................F....... 585 344-1200
  Alexander *(G-180)*
Madoff Energy III LLC........................G....... 212 744-1918
  New York *(G-10658)*
Native Amercn Enrgy Group Inc..........G....... 718 408-2323
  Forest Hills *(G-5077)*
Norse Energy Corp USA.....................G....... 716 568-2048
  Buffalo *(G-2974)*
Occidental Energy Mktg Inc................G....... 212 632-4950
  New York *(G-11026)*
Range Rsources - Appalachia LLC......E....... 716 753-3395
  Mayville *(G-7923)*
Sanguine Gas Exploration LLC...........E....... 212 582-8555
  New York *(G-11483)*
Seneca Resources Company LLC......F....... 716 630-6750
  Williamsville *(G-16586)*
Somerset Production Co LLC..............G....... 716 932-6480
  Buffalo *(G-3068)*
Springfield Oil Services Inc.................F....... 914 315-6812
  Harrison *(G-5734)*
U S Energy Development Corp............D....... 716 636-0401
  Getzville *(G-5354)*
Waffenbauch USA................................E....... 716 326-4508
  Westfield *(G-16397)*
Warren Energy Services LLC.............G....... 212 697-9660
  New York *(G-12075)*

GAS & OIL FIELD SVCS, NEC

Case Brothers Inc.............................G....... 716 925-7172
  Limestone *(G-7157)*
Essar Americas..................................G....... 212 292-2600
  New York *(G-9706)*

GAS STATIONS

Marina Holding Corp...........................F....... 718 646-9283
  Brooklyn *(G-2167)*

GAS: Refinery

Shell Pipe Line Corporation................G....... 212 740-8786
  New York *(G-11561)*

GASES & LIQUIFIED PETROLEUM GASES

Osaka Gas Energy America Corp........F....... 914 253-5500
  White Plains *(G-16483)*

GASES: Carbon Dioxide

Linde Merchant Production Inc...........G....... 315 593-1360
  Fulton *(G-5227)*

GASES: Flourinated Hydrocarbon

Hudson Technologies Company..........E....... 845 735-6000
  Pearl River *(G-12900)*

GASES: Indl

Airgas Usa LLC...................................F....... 585 436-7781
  Rochester *(G-13610)*
Praxair Inc..F....... 716 879-2000
  Tonawanda *(G-15570)*
Praxair Inc..E....... 716 649-1600
  Hamburg *(G-5690)*
Praxair Inc..E....... 518 482-4360
  Albany *(G-117)*
Praxair Inc..E....... 716 286-4600
  Niagara Falls *(G-12324)*
Praxair Inc..C....... 845 359-4200
  Orangeburg *(G-12686)*
Praxair Inc..E....... 716 879-4000
  Tonawanda *(G-15571)*

GASES: Neon

Neon..F....... 212 727-5628
  New York *(G-10905)*

GASES: Nitrogen

Linde Gas North America LLC............E....... 518 713-2015
  Cohoes *(G-3612)*
Linde Gas North America LLC............F....... 315 431-4081
  Syracuse *(G-15362)*
Linde LLC...E....... 716 847-0748
  Buffalo *(G-2924)*

Linde LLC...D....... 518 439-8187
  Feura Bush *(G-4935)*
Matheson Tri-Gas Inc.........................G....... 518 203-5003
  Cohoes *(G-3613)*

GASES: Oxygen

Air Products and Chemicals Inc..........D....... 518 463-4273
  Glenmont *(G-5410)*
Airgas Inc...F....... 518 690-0068
  Albany *(G-30)*
Oxair Ltd..G....... 716 298-8288
  Niagara Falls *(G-12321)*
Praxair Distribution Inc......................G....... 315 457-5821
  Liverpool *(G-7256)*
Praxair Distribution Inc......................F....... 315 735-6153
  Marcy *(G-7797)*

GASKET MATERIALS

Hollingsworth & Vose Company..........C....... 518 695-8000
  Greenwich *(G-5641)*
Jed Lights Inc.....................................F....... 516 812-5001
  Deer Park *(G-3992)*
Noroc Enterprises Inc........................C....... 718 585-3230
  Bronx *(G-1344)*

GASKETS

Allstate Gasket & Packing Inc.............F....... 631 254-4050
  Deer Park *(G-3937)*
Boonville Manufacturing Corp.............G....... 315 942-4368
  Boonville *(G-1116)*
Everlast Seals and Supply LLC..........F....... 718 388-7373
  Brooklyn *(G-1855)*
Frank Lowe Rbr & Gasket Co Inc........E....... 631 777-2707
  Shirley *(G-14835)*
SAS Industries Inc.............................F....... 631 727-1441
  Manorville *(G-7785)*
Seal & Design Inc..............................E....... 315 432-8021
  Syracuse *(G-15420)*

GASKETS & SEALING DEVICES

A L Sealing..G....... 315 699-6900
  Chittenango *(G-3500)*
GM Components Holdings LLC..........D....... 716 439-2402
  Lockport *(G-7307)*
John Crane Inc...................................D....... 315 593-6237
  Fulton *(G-5223)*
Schlegel Electronic Mtls Inc................F....... 585 295-2030
  Rochester *(G-14114)*
SKF USA Inc......................................D....... 716 661-2600
  Jamestown *(G-6747)*
Temper Corporation............................E....... 518 853-3467
  Fonda *(G-5067)*
USA Sealing Inc.................................E....... 716 288-9952
  Cheektowaga *(G-3462)*
Web Seal Inc......................................E....... 585 546-1320
  Rochester *(G-14204)*
Xto Incorporated.................................D....... 315 451-7807
  Liverpool *(G-7273)*

GASOLINE FILLING STATIONS

Hess Corporation................................B....... 212 997-8500
  New York *(G-10085)*
Lukoil North America LLC..................E....... 212 421-4141
  New York *(G-10629)*

GASOLINE WHOLESALERS

Bluebar Oil Co Inc..............................F....... 315 245-4328
  Blossvale *(G-963)*
Seneca Nation Enterprise..................F....... 716 934-7430
  Irving *(G-6501)*

GATES: Dam, Metal Plate

Linita Design & Mfg Corp...................E....... 716 566-7753
  Lackawanna *(G-6949)*
Riverside Iron LLC............................F....... 315 535-4864
  Gouverneur *(G-5492)*
Rw Gate Company.............................F....... 518 874-4750
  Troy *(G-15622)*
Rw Gate Company.............................D....... 518 874-4750
  Troy *(G-15623)*

GATES: Ornamental Metal

City Store Gates Mfg Corp..................E....... 718 939-9700
  College Point *(G-3642)*
E & J Iron Works Inc..........................E....... 718 665-6040
  Bronx *(G-1262)*

Inter-Fence Co Inc.............................E....... 718 939-9700
  College Point *(G-3648)*
Lopopolo Iron Works Inc....................G....... 718 339-0572
  Brooklyn *(G-2135)*
Moon Gates Company........................G....... 718 426-0023
  East Elmhurst *(G-4224)*
United Steel Products Inc..................D....... 914 968-7782
  Flushing *(G-5058)*
Vr Containment LLC...........................G....... 917 972-3441
  Fresh Meadows *(G-5205)*

GAUGES

Dorsey Metrology Intl Inc...................E....... 845 229-2929
  Poughkeepsie *(G-13334)*
Trinity Tools Inc..................................E....... 716 694-1111
  North Tonawanda *(G-12460)*

GEARS

Gear Motions Incorporated.................E....... 716 885-1080
  Buffalo *(G-2843)*
Gear Motions Incorporated.................E....... 315 488-0100
  Syracuse *(G-15331)*
Great Lakes Gear Co Inc....................G....... 716 694-0715
  Tonawanda *(G-15542)*
Industrial Mch Gear Works LLC..........E....... 516 695-4442
  Rockville Centre *(G-14234)*
Perfect Gear & Instrument..................F....... 516 328-3330
  Hicksville *(G-6125)*
Perfect Gear & Instrument..................E....... 516 873-6122
  Garden City Park *(G-5287)*
Pro-Gear Co Inc.................................G....... 716 684-3811
  Buffalo *(G-3016)*
Riley Gear Corporation.......................E....... 716 694-0900
  North Tonawanda *(G-12446)*
S R & R Industries Inc.......................G....... 845 692-8329
  Middletown *(G-8175)*
Secs Inc...E....... 914 667-5600
  Mount Vernon *(G-8441)*
Secs Inc...E....... 914 667-5600
  Mount Vernon *(G-8442)*
Superite Gear Instr of Hppauge..........G....... 631 234-0100
  Hauppauge *(G-5953)*

GEARS & GEAR UNITS: Reduction, Exc Auto

Perfection Gear Inc............................C....... 716 592-9310
  Springville *(G-15020)*

GEARS: Power Transmission, Exc Auto

Buffalo Gear Inc.................................E....... 716 731-2100
  Sanborn *(G-14543)*
Gleason Works...................................A....... 585 473-1000
  Rochester *(G-13840)*
Jrlon Inc...D....... 315 597-4067
  Palmyra *(G-12855)*
Khk Usa Inc..G....... 516 248-3850
  Mineola *(G-8232)*
McGuigan Inc.....................................E....... 631 750-6222
  Bohemia *(G-1057)*
Niagara Gear Corporation..................E....... 716 874-3131
  Buffalo *(G-2967)*
Nuttall Gear L L C..............................E....... 716 298-4100
  Niagara Falls *(G-12317)*
Oliver Gear Inc...................................E....... 716 885-1080
  Buffalo *(G-2979)*
Peerless-Winsmith Inc.......................C....... 716 592-9311
  Springville *(G-15019)*
Precipart Corporation.........................C....... 631 694-3100
  Farmingdale *(G-4855)*
Precision Mechanisms Corp...............E....... 516 333-5955
  Westbury *(G-16366)*
Rochester Gear Inc............................E....... 585 254-5442
  Rochester *(G-14087)*

GELATIN

Geliko LLC...E....... 212 876-5620
  New York *(G-9895)*

GEM STONES MINING, NEC: Natural

Ray Griffiths Inc.................................G....... 212 689-7209
  New York *(G-11330)*

GEMSTONE & INDL DIAMOND MINING SVCS

Avs Gem Stone Corp..........................G....... 212 944-6380
  New York *(G-8981)*
Didco Inc..F....... 212 997-5022
  Rego Park *(G-13461)*

GEMSTONE & INDL DIAMOND MINING SVCS

PRODUCT SECTION

Herkimer Diamond Mines Inc .... E 315 891-7355
  Herkimer *(G-6041)*
Kotel Importers Inc .... F 212 245-6200
  New York *(G-10473)*

GENERAL & INDUSTRIAL LOAN INSTITUTIONS

Mitsui Chemicals America Inc .... E 914 253-0777
  Rye Brook *(G-14493)*

GENERAL MERCHANDISE, NONDURABLE, WHOLESALE

Dahill Distributors Inc .... G 347 371-9453
  Brooklyn *(G-1750)*
French Associates Inc .... F 718 387-9880
  Fresh Meadows *(G-5198)*
Lokai Holdings LLC .... F 646 979-3474
  New York *(G-10594)*
Specialty Products Inc .... E 866 869-4335
  Center Moriches *(G-3341)*

GENERATING APPARATUS & PARTS: Electrical

Industrial Test Eqp Co Inc .... E 516 883-6423
  Port Washington *(G-13269)*
Mks Medical Electronics .... C 585 292-7400
  Rochester *(G-13950)*

GENERATION EQPT: Electronic

Alliance Control Systems Inc .... G 845 279-4430
  Brewster *(G-1156)*
C & M Circuits Inc .... E 631 589-0208
  Bohemia *(G-992)*
Curtis Instruments Inc .... C 914 666-2971
  Mount Kisco *(G-8339)*
Cygnus Automation Inc .... G 631 981-0909
  Bohemia *(G-1006)*
General Electric Company .... E 518 459-4110
  Albany *(G-77)*
GW Lisk Company Inc .... E 315 548-2165
  Phelps *(G-12977)*
Tonoga Inc .... C 518 658-3202
  Petersburg *(G-12973)*

GENERATORS: Electric

Cellgen Inc .... G 516 889-9300
  Freeport *(G-5149)*
Getec Inc .... F 845 292-0800
  Ferndale *(G-4933)*

GENERATORS: Electrochemical, Fuel Cell

Plug Power Inc .... G 585 474-3993
  Rochester *(G-14024)*

GENERATORS: Gas

Better Power Inc .... G 585 475-1321
  Rochester *(G-13661)*

GENERATORS: Ultrasonic

Uncharted Power Inc .... E 646 675-7783
  New York *(G-11936)*

GIFT SHOP

Csi International Inc .... E 800 441-2895
  Niagara Falls *(G-12276)*
Exotic Print and Paper Inc .... F 212 807-0465
  New York *(G-9753)*
Fly Creek Cder Mill Orchrd Inc .... G 607 547-9692
  Fly Creek *(G-5064)*
Frame Shoppe & Art Gallery .... G 516 365-6014
  Manhasset *(G-7767)*

GIFT, NOVELTY & SOUVENIR STORES: Artcraft & carvings

Kleinfelder John .... G 716 753-3163
  Mayville *(G-7921)*

GIFT, NOVELTY & SOUVENIR STORES: Gifts & Novelties

Issacs Yisroel .... G 718 851-7430
  Brooklyn *(G-2016)*

Mainly Monograms Inc .... E 845 624-4923
  West Nyack *(G-16275)*
Rip Van Wafels Inc .... E 415 529-5403
  Brooklyn *(G-2404)*

GIFTS & NOVELTIES: Wholesalers

Cannizzaro Seal & Engraving Co .... G 718 513-6125
  Brooklyn *(G-1673)*
Full Circle Home LLC .... G 212 432-0001
  New York *(G-9860)*
Justa Company .... G 718 932-6139
  Long Island City *(G-7484)*
Mountain T-Shirts Inc .... G 518 943-4533
  Catskill *(G-3307)*
Nubian Heritage .... G 631 265-3551
  Hauppauge *(G-5903)*
OH How Cute Inc .... G 347 838-6031
  Staten Island *(G-15113)*
Studio Silversmiths Inc .... E 718 418-6785
  Ridgewood *(G-13553)*
Trove Inc .... F 212 268-2046
  Brooklyn *(G-2589)*

GIFTWARE: Brass

Lr Paris LLC .... F 212 634-9372
  New York *(G-10621)*

GLASS FABRICATORS

Benson Industries Inc .... F 212 779-3230
  New York *(G-9046)*
Community Glass Inc .... G 607 737-8860
  Elmira *(G-4478)*
Dillmeier Enterprises Inc .... F 800 325-0596
  Garden City *(G-5255)*
Glassfab Inc .... E 585 262-4000
  Rochester *(G-13836)*
Global Glass Corp .... G 516 681-2309
  Hicksville *(G-6091)*
Granville Glass & Granite .... G 518 812-0492
  Hudson Falls *(G-6381)*
Gray Glass Inc .... E 718 217-2943
  Queens Village *(G-13406)*
Kasson & Keller Inc .... A 518 853-3421
  Fonda *(G-5065)*
Manhattan Shade & Glass Co Inc .... E 212 288-5616
  Hauppauge *(G-5880)*
Michbi Doors Inc .... D 631 231-9050
  Brentwood *(G-1142)*
Oldcastle Building Envelope .... F 212 957-5400
  New York *(G-11036)*
Pal Manufacturing Corp .... E 516 937-1990
  Hicksville *(G-6122)*
Quality Enclosures Inc .... G 631 234-0115
  Central Islip *(G-3382)*
Royal Metal Products Inc .... E 518 966-4442
  Surprise *(G-15207)*
Select Interior Door Ltd .... E 585 535-9900
  North Java *(G-12392)*
Vitarose Corp of America .... G 718 951-9700
  Brooklyn *(G-2630)*
Vitrix Inc .... G 607 936-8707
  Corning *(G-3828)*

GLASS PRDTS, FROM PURCHASED GLASS: Art

Carvart Glass Inc .... E 212 675-0030
  New York *(G-9218)*

GLASS PRDTS, FROM PURCHASED GLASS: Glass Beads, Reflecting

Potters Industries LLC .... E 315 265-4920
  Norwood *(G-12496)*

GLASS PRDTS, FROM PURCHASED GLASS: Glassware

Exquisite Glass & Stone Inc .... G 718 937-9266
  Astoria *(G-428)*
Gmd Industries Inc .... G 718 445-8779
  College Point *(G-3645)*

GLASS PRDTS, FROM PURCHASED GLASS: Insulating

Dunlea Whl GL & Mirror Inc .... G 914 664-5277
  Mount Vernon *(G-8397)*

Press Glass Na Inc .... G 212 631-3044
  New York *(G-11235)*
Rochester Insulated Glass Inc .... D 585 289-3611
  Manchester *(G-7761)*

GLASS PRDTS, FROM PURCHASED GLASS: Mirrored

Depp Glass Inc .... F 718 784-8500
  Long Island City *(G-7424)*
Dundy Glass & Mirror Corp .... E 718 723-5800
  Springfield Gardens *(G-15014)*
G & M Clearview Inc .... G 845 781-4877
  Monroe *(G-8270)*
Lafayette Mirror & Glass Co .... G 718 768-0660
  New Hyde Park *(G-8547)*
Mirror-Tech Manufacturing Co .... F 914 965-1232
  Yonkers *(G-16785)*

GLASS PRDTS, FROM PURCHASED GLASS: Mirrors, Framed

Apf Management Company LLC .... C 914 665-5400
  Yonkers *(G-16736)*
Apf Manufacturing Company LLC .... E 914 963-6300
  Yonkers *(G-16737)*
Munn Works LLC .... G 914 665-6100
  Mount Vernon *(G-8424)*
Timeless Decor LLC .... C 315 782-5759
  Watertown *(G-16035)*

GLASS PRDTS, FROM PURCHASED GLASS: Mosaics

Avenue Mosaic Company .... G 216 245-6306
  New York *(G-8974)*

GLASS PRDTS, FROM PURCHASED GLASS: Ornaments, Christmas Tree

Jinglebell Inc .... G 914 219-5395
  Armonk *(G-406)*
Rauch Industries Inc .... E 704 867-5333
  Tarrytown *(G-15489)*

GLASS PRDTS, FROM PURCHASED GLASS: Sheet, Bent

Flickinger Glassworks Inc .... G 718 875-1531
  Brooklyn *(G-1892)*

GLASS PRDTS, FROM PURCHASED GLASS: Watch Crystals

Jimmy Crystal New York Co Ltd .... E 212 594-0858
  New York *(G-10340)*
Lalique North America Inc .... E 212 355-6550
  New York *(G-10512)*

GLASS PRDTS, FROM PURCHASED GLASS: Windshields

Taylor Made Group LLC .... E 518 725-0681
  Gloversville *(G-5468)*

GLASS PRDTS, FROM PURCHD GLASS: Strengthened Or Reinforced

Campus Crafts Inc .... G 585 328-6780
  Rochester *(G-13688)*
Rochester Colonial Mfg Corp .... D 585 254-8191
  Rochester *(G-14084)*

GLASS PRDTS, PRESSED OR BLOWN: Bulbs, Electric Lights

Daylight Technology USA Inc .... G 973 255-8100
  Maspeth *(G-7835)*
Led Lumina USA LLC .... G 631 750-4433
  Bohemia *(G-1045)*

GLASS PRDTS, PRESSED OR BLOWN: Glassware, Art Or Decorative

Architectural Glass Inc .... F 845 831-3116
  Beacon *(G-754)*
Bedford Downing Glass .... G 718 418-6409
  Brooklyn *(G-1593)*
Jay Strongwater Holdings LLC .... A 646 657-0558
  New York *(G-10312)*

PRODUCT SECTION

GLOVES: Plastic

King Research Inc............................E.......718 788-0122
  Brooklyn *(G-2072)*

GLASS PRDTS, PRESSED OR BLOWN: Glassware, Novelty

Glass Menagerie Inc............................G.......845 754-8344
  Westbrookville *(G-16307)*

GLASS PRDTS, PRESSED OR BLOWN: Lens Blanks, Optical

Ion Optics Inc............................F.......518 339-6853
  Albany *(G-86)*

GLASS PRDTS, PRESSED OR BLOWN: Lighting Eqpt Parts

Niche Design Inc............................F.......212 777-2101
  Beacon *(G-761)*

GLASS PRDTS, PRESSED OR BLOWN: Optical

Match Eyewear LLC............................E.......516 877-0170
  Westbury *(G-16354)*
Semrok Inc............................D.......585 594-7050
  Rochester *(G-14121)*

GLASS PRDTS, PRESSED OR BLOWN: Ornaments, Christmas Tree

Formcraft Display Products............................G.......914 632-1410
  New Rochelle *(G-8603)*
Jinglebell Inc............................G.......914 219-5395
  Armonk *(G-406)*

GLASS PRDTS, PRESSED OR BLOWN: Scientific Glassware

Scientifics Direct Inc............................F.......716 773-7500
  Tonawanda *(G-15576)*

GLASS PRDTS, PRESSED/BLOWN: Glassware, Art, Decor/Novelty

Bronx Wstchester Tempering Inc............................E.......914 663-9400
  Mount Vernon *(G-8383)*
Pasabahce USA............................G.......212 683-1600
  New York *(G-11119)*

GLASS PRDTS, PURCHASED GLASS: Glassware, Scientific/Tech

Swift Glass Co Inc............................D.......607 733-7166
  Elmira Heights *(G-4515)*

GLASS PRDTS, PURCHASED GLASS: Insulating, Multiple-Glazed

Upstate Insulated Glass Inc............................G.......315 475-4960
  Central Square *(G-3393)*

GLASS PRDTS, PURCHD GLASS: Furniture Top, Cut, Beveld/Polshd

Our Terms Fabricators Inc............................E.......631 752-1517
  West Babylon *(G-16180)*

GLASS PRDTS, PURCHSD GLASS: Ornamental, Cut, Engraved/Décor

Oneida International Inc............................G.......315 361-3000
  Oneida *(G-12615)*
Oneida Silversmiths Inc............................G.......315 361-3000
  Oneida *(G-12619)*

GLASS STORE: Leaded Or Stained

Flickinger Glassworks Inc............................G.......718 875-1531
  Brooklyn *(G-1892)*

GLASS STORES

Global Glass Corp............................G.......516 681-2309
  Hicksville *(G-6091)*
Oldcastle Buildingenvelope Inc............................C.......631 234-2200
  Hauppauge *(G-5905)*
Upstate Insulated Glass Inc............................G.......315 475-4960
  Central Square *(G-3393)*

GLASS: Fiber

Corning Incorporated............................A.......607 974-9000
  Corning *(G-3809)*
Corning Incorporated............................E.......607 974-1274
  Painted Post *(G-12836)*
Corning Incorporated............................E.......607 248-1200
  Corning *(G-3812)*
Corning Specialty Mtls Inc............................G.......607 974-9000
  Corning *(G-3817)*
New York Enrgy Synthetics Inc............................G.......212 634-4787
  New York *(G-10937)*
Schott Corporation............................D.......914 831-2200
  Elmsford *(G-4564)*
Volpi Manufacturing USA Co Inc............................E.......315 255-1737
  Auburn *(G-508)*

GLASS: Flat

A Sunshine Glass & Aluminum............................E.......718 932-8080
  Woodside *(G-16644)*
Corning Incorporated............................D.......315 379-3200
  Canton *(G-3256)*
Corning Incorporated............................G.......607 974-6729
  Painted Post *(G-12837)*
Global Glass Corp............................G.......516 681-2309
  Hicksville *(G-6091)*
Guardian Industries LLC............................B.......315 787-7000
  Geneva *(G-5327)*
Hecht & Sohn Glass Co Inc............................G.......718 782-8295
  Brooklyn *(G-1971)*
Pilkington North America Inc............................C.......315 438-3341
  Syracuse *(G-15395)*
Schott Corporation............................D.......914 831-2200
  Elmsford *(G-4564)*
Schott Gemtron Corporation............................C.......423 337-3522
  Elmsford *(G-4565)*
Schott Solar Pv Inc............................G.......888 457-6527
  Elmsford *(G-4568)*
Stefan Sydor Optics Inc............................E.......585 271-7300
  Rochester *(G-14143)*

GLASS: Leaded

Batavia Precision Glass LLC............................G.......585 343-6050
  Buffalo *(G-2724)*

GLASS: Pressed & Blown, NEC

Co-Optics America Lab Inc............................E.......607 432-0557
  Oneonta *(G-12631)*
Corning Incorporated............................D.......607 974-9000
  Corning *(G-3810)*
Corning Incorporated............................E.......607 974-9000
  Corning *(G-3811)*
Corning Incorporated............................D.......315 379-3200
  Canton *(G-3256)*
Corning Incorporated............................E.......607 433-3100
  Oneonta *(G-12635)*
Corning Incorporated............................G.......646 521-9600
  New York *(G-9402)*
Corning Incorporated............................F.......607 962-6036
  Painted Post *(G-12838)*
Corning Incorporated............................G.......607 974-4488
  Corning *(G-3813)*
Corning Incorporated............................E.......607 974-8496
  Corning *(G-3814)*
Corning Incorporated............................G.......607 974-6729
  Painted Post *(G-12837)*
Corning International Corp............................G.......607 974-9000
  Corning *(G-3815)*
Corning Tropel Corporation............................C.......585 377-3200
  Fairport *(G-4629)*
Corning Vitro Corporation............................A.......607 974-8605
  Corning *(G-3818)*
Germanow-Simon Corporation............................E.......585 232-1440
  Rochester *(G-13832)*
Gillinder Brothers Inc............................D.......845 856-5375
  Port Jervis *(G-13229)*
Glasteel Parts & Services Inc............................E.......585 235-1010
  Rochester *(G-13837)*
Lighting Holdings Intl LLC............................A.......845 306-1850
  Purchase *(G-13391)*
Navitar Inc............................D.......585 359-4000
  Rochester *(G-13965)*
Owens Corning Sales LLC............................B.......518 475-3600
  Feura Bush *(G-4936)*
Schott Corporation............................D.......315 255-2791
  Auburn *(G-499)*
Schott North America Inc............................D.......914 831-2200
  Elmsford *(G-4567)*

Stefan Sydor Optics Inc............................E.......585 271-7300
  Rochester *(G-14143)*

GLASS: Stained

Adirondack Stained Glass Works............................G.......518 725-0387
  Gloversville *(G-5449)*
Makarenko Studios Inc............................G.......914 968-7673
  Yorktown Heights *(G-16818)*
Rohlfs Stined Leaded GL Studio............................E.......914 699-4848
  Mount Vernon *(G-8440)*
Somers Stain Glass Inc............................F.......631 586-7772
  Deer Park *(G-4046)*
Sunburst Studios Inc............................G.......718 768-6360
  Brooklyn *(G-2532)*

GLASS: Structural

Europrojects Intl Inc............................F.......917 262-0795
  New York *(G-9731)*

GLASS: Tempered

Oldcastle Buildingenvelope Inc............................C.......631 234-2200
  Hauppauge *(G-5905)*
Taylor Products Inc............................G.......518 773-9312
  Gloversville *(G-5469)*

GLASSWARE STORES

Vitrix Inc............................G.......607 936-8707
  Corning *(G-3828)*

GLASSWARE WHOLESALERS

A Sunshine Glass & Aluminum............................E.......718 932-8080
  Woodside *(G-16644)*

GLASSWARE: Laboratory

TEC Glass & Inst LLC............................G.......315 926-7639
  Marion *(G-7809)*

GLASSWARE: Laboratory & Medical

Immco Diagnostics Inc............................G.......716 691-0091
  Buffalo *(G-2881)*
Mri Northtowns Group PC............................F.......716 836-4646
  Buffalo *(G-2955)*

GLOBAL POSITIONING SYSTEMS & EQPT

Evado Filip............................F.......917 774-8666
  New York *(G-9733)*
Intelibs Inc............................G.......877 213-2640
  Stony Brook *(G-15167)*
Rehabilitation International............................G.......212 420-1500
  Jamaica *(G-6674)*

GLOVES: Fabric

Falls Manufacturing Inc............................G.......518 672-7189
  Philmont *(G-12986)*
Gce International Inc............................F.......212 868-0500
  New York *(G-9891)*

GLOVES: Leather

American Target Marketing Inc............................E.......518 725-4369
  Gloversville *(G-5450)*
Fieldtex Products Inc............................C.......585 427-2940
  Rochester *(G-13803)*
J & D Walter Distributors Inc............................F.......518 449-1606
  Glenmont *(G-5413)*
USA Sewing Inc............................E.......315 792-8017
  Utica *(G-15736)*

GLOVES: Leather, Dress Or Semidress

Fownes Brothers & Co Inc............................E.......212 683-0150
  New York *(G-9834)*
Fownes Brothers & Co Inc............................E.......518 752-4411
  Gloversville *(G-5456)*
Samco LLC............................E.......518 725-4705
  Gloversville *(G-5464)*

GLOVES: Leather, Work

Protech (llc)............................E.......518 725-7785
  Gloversville *(G-5463)*

GLOVES: Plastic

Elara Fdsrvice Disposables LLC............................G.......877 893-3244
  Jericho *(G-6786)*

GLOVES: Safety

GLOVES: Safety
Hand Care Inc ....G...... 516 747-5649
  Roslyn *(G-14447)*
Superior Glove Works USA Ltd ....E...... 716 626-9500
  Cheektowaga *(G-3460)*

GLOVES: Work
Manzella Knitting ....G...... 716 825-0808
  Orchard Park *(G-12727)*

GLOVES: Woven Or Knit, From Purchased Materials
Fownes Brothers & Co Inc ....E...... 212 683-0150
  New York *(G-9834)*
Fownes Brothers & Co Inc ....E...... 518 752-4411
  Gloversville *(G-5456)*

GLUE
Hudson Industries Corporation ....E...... 518 762-4638
  Johnstown *(G-6831)*

GOLD ORE MINING
Andes Gold Corporation ....D...... 212 541-2495
  New York *(G-8856)*
Capital Gold Corporation ....G...... 212 668-0842
  New York *(G-9203)*

GOLD ORES
Global Gold Corporation ....F...... 914 925-0020
  Rye *(G-14481)*
Gncc Capital Inc ....G...... 702 951-9793
  New York *(G-9949)*

GOLD RECOVERY FROM TAILINGS
Fuda Group (usa) Corporation ....G...... 646 751-7488
  New York *(G-9858)*

GOLD STAMPING, EXC BOOKS
John Gailer Inc ....E...... 212 243-5662
  Long Island City *(G-7480)*

GOLF EQPT
Jag Manufacturing Inc ....E...... 518 762-9558
  Johnstown *(G-6832)*
Morris Golf Ventures ....E...... 631 283-0559
  Southampton *(G-14957)*

GOURMET FOOD STORES
Herris Gourmet Inc ....G...... 917 578-2308
  Brooklyn *(G-1976)*
Johns Ravioli Company Inc ....F...... 914 576-7030
  New Rochelle *(G-8618)*
New York Ravioli Pasta Co Inc ....E...... 516 270-2852
  New Hyde Park *(G-8553)*
Queen Ann Macaroni Mfg Co Inc ....G...... 718 256-1061
  Brooklyn *(G-2371)*

GOVERNMENT, EXECUTIVE OFFICES: Mayors'
City of Olean ....G...... 716 376-5694
  Olean *(G-12595)*
City of Oneonta 607 433-3470
  Oneonta *(G-12630)*
Hartford Hwy Dept ....G...... 315 724-0654
  New Hartford *(G-8506)*
Town of Amherst ....E...... 716 631-7113
  Williamsville *(G-16591)*

GOVERNMENT, GENERAL: Administration
City of New York ....E...... 718 965-8787
  Brooklyn *(G-1695)*

GRANITE: Crushed & Broken
MCM Natural Stone Inc ....F...... 585 586-6510
  Rochester *(G-13934)*
Suffolk Granite Manufacturing ....E...... 631 226-4774
  Lindenhurst *(G-7197)*
Tilcon New York Inc ....D...... 845 358-3100
  West Nyack *(G-16282)*

GRANITE: Cut & Shaped
6478 Ridge Road LLC ....G...... 716 625-8400
  Lockport *(G-7282)*
6478 Ridge Road LLC ....F...... 716 625-8400
  Lockport *(G-7283)*
Adirondack Precision Cut Stone ....F...... 518 681-3060
  Queensbury *(G-13414)*
Amendola MBL & Stone Ctr Inc ....D...... 914 997-7968
  White Plains *(G-16419)*
American Bluestone LLC ....F...... 607 369-2235
  Sidney *(G-14848)*
Aurora Stone Group LLC ....F...... 315 471-6869
  East Syracuse *(G-4324)*
Capital Stone LLC ....G...... 518 382-7588
  Schenectady *(G-14658)*
Capital Stone Saratoga LLC ....G...... 518 226-8677
  Saratoga Springs *(G-14573)*
Glen Plaza Marble & Gran Inc ....G...... 516 671-1100
  Glen Cove *(G-5368)*
Granite & Marble Works Inc ....E...... 518 584-2800
  Gansevoort *(G-5243)*
Granite Tops Inc ....G...... 914 699-2909
  Mount Vernon *(G-8403)*
House of Stone Inc ....G...... 845 782-7271
  Monroe *(G-8272)*
Marble Works Inc ....G...... 914 376-3653
  Yonkers *(G-16782)*
MCM Natural Stone Inc ....F...... 585 586-6510
  Rochester *(G-13934)*
New York Quarries Inc ....F...... 518 756-3138
  Alcove *(G-165)*
North Shore Monuments Inc ....G...... 516 759-2156
  Glen Head *(G-5385)*
PR & Stone & Tile Inc ....G...... 718 383-1115
  Brooklyn *(G-2333)*
Royal Marble & Granite Inc ....G...... 516 536-5900
  Oceanside *(G-12555)*

GRANITE: Dimension
Imerys Usa Inc ....F...... 315 287-0780
  Gouverneur *(G-5491)*

GRANITE: Dimension
Alice Perkins ....G...... 716 378-5100
  Salamanca *(G-14523)*
Euro Marmol Gran ....G...... 631 940-9165
  Deer Park *(G-3975)*
Hillburn Granite Company Inc ....G...... 845 357-8900
  Hillburn *(G-6153)*

GRAPHIC ARTS & RELATED DESIGN SVCS
Accent Label & Tag Co Inc ....G...... 631 244-7066
  Ronkonkoma *(G-14287)*
Ad-Vantage Printing Inc ....F...... 718 820-0688
  Kew Gardens *(G-6870)*
Adcomm Graphics Inc ....E...... 212 645-1298
  West Babylon *(G-16128)*
Alabaster Group Inc ....G...... 516 867-8223
  Freeport *(G-5138)*
Beebie Printing & Art Agcy Inc ....E...... 518 725-4528
  Gloversville *(G-5453)*
Desktop Publishing Concepts ....F...... 631 752-1934
  Farmingdale *(G-4750)*
Digital Evolution Inc ....E...... 212 732-2722
  New York *(G-9527)*
Eastern Metal of Elmira Inc ....D...... 607 734-2295
  Elmira *(G-4482)*
Gg Design and Printing ....G...... 718 321-3220
  New York *(G-9916)*
Horne Organization Inc ....F...... 914 572-1330
  Yonkers *(G-16769)*
Middletown Press ....G...... 845 343-1895
  Middletown *(G-8164)*
North American Graphics Inc ....F...... 212 725-2200
  New York *(G-10991)*
Pic A Poc Enterprises Inc ....G...... 631 981-2094
  Ronkonkoma *(G-14399)*
Play-It Productions Inc ....F...... 212 695-6530
  Port Washington *(G-13297)*
Proof 7 Ltd ....F...... 212 680-1843
  New York *(G-11264)*
Resonant Legal Media LLC ....D...... 800 781-3591
  New York *(G-11369)*
Tri Kolor Printing & Sty ....F...... 315 474-6753
  Syracuse *(G-15446)*
Vital Signs & Graphics Co Inc ....G...... 518 237-8372
  Cohoes *(G-3623)*

GRAPHIC LAYOUT SVCS: Printed Circuitry
J N White Associates Inc ....D...... 585 237-5191
  Perry *(G-12969)*

GRASSES: Artificial & Preserved
Techgrass ....F...... 646 719-2000
  New York *(G-11793)*

GRAVE MARKERS: Concrete
Woodside Granite Industries ....G...... 585 589-6500
  Albion *(G-164)*

GRAVEL MINING
Buffalo Crushed Stone Inc ....F...... 716 566-9636
  Franklinville *(G-5122)*
Central Dover Development ....G...... 917 709-3266
  Dover Plains *(G-4143)*
Dalrymple Grav & Contg Co Inc ....E...... 607 529-3235
  Chemung *(G-3463)*
Diehl Development Inc ....G...... 585 494-2920
  Bergen *(G-819)*
Hanson Aggregates PA LLC ....E...... 585 624-1220
  Honeoye Falls *(G-6267)*
Hanson Aggregates PA LLC ....F...... 315 782-2300
  Watertown *(G-16015)*
Hanson Aggregates PA LLC ....G...... 315 789-6202
  Oaks Corners *(G-12528)*
Hanson Aggregates PA LLC ....E...... 585 624-3800
  Honeoye Falls *(G-6266)*
Hanson Aggregates PA LLC ....F...... 585 436-3250
  Rochester *(G-13852)*
IA Construction Corporation ....G...... 716 933-8787
  Portville *(G-13316)*
Rock Mountain Farms Inc ....G...... 845 647-9084
  Ellenville *(G-4443)*
Seven Springs Gravel Pdts LLC ....G...... 585 343-4336
  Batavia *(G-634)*
Shelby Crushed Stone Inc ....E...... 585 798-4501
  Medina *(G-7989)*

GREASE CUPS: Metal
Blue Manufacturing Co Inc ....G...... 607 796-2463
  Millport *(G-8195)*

GREASE TRAPS: Concrete
Long Island Green Guys ....G...... 631 664-4306
  Riverhead *(G-13575)*

GREENHOUSES: Prefabricated Metal
Fillmore Greenhouses Inc ....E...... 585 567-2678
  Portageville *(G-13314)*

GREETING CARDS WHOLESALERS
Paper House Productions Inc ....E...... 845 246-7261
  Saugerties *(G-14612)*

GRINDING BALLS: Ceramic
Malyn Industrial Ceramics Inc ....G...... 716 741-1510
  Clarence Center *(G-3548)*

GRINDING SVC: Precision, Commercial Or Indl
Acme Industries of W Babylon ....F...... 631 737-5231
  Ronkonkoma *(G-14289)*
Ascribe Inc ....E...... 585 413-0298
  Rochester *(G-13646)*
Dean Manufacturing Inc ....F...... 607 770-1300
  Vestal *(G-15814)*
Micro Instrument Corp ....D...... 585 458-3150
  Rochester *(G-13939)*
Temrick Inc 631 567-8860
  Bohemia *(G-1095)*

GRINDING SVCS: Ophthalmic Lens, Exc Prescription
Empire Optical Inc ....F...... 585 454-4470
  Rochester *(G-13781)*

GRINDS: Electric
Arise At Marshall Farms Inc ....G...... 315 687-6727
  Chittenango *(G-3501)*

PRODUCT SECTION

GRIT: Steel

Smm - North America Trade Corp ....G...... 212 604-0710
New York (G-11627)

GRITS: Crushed & Broken

Hanson Aggregates PA LLC ....F 315 393-3743
Ogdensburg (G-12574)
Hanson Aggregates PA LLC ....F 315 821-7222
Oriskany Falls (G-12767)
Masten Enterprises LLC ....C 845 932-8206
Cochecton (G-3607)
Upstone Materials Inc ....D 518 561-5321
Plattsburgh (G-13165)

GROCERIES WHOLESALERS, NEC

Bimbo Bakeries Usa Inc ....C 718 463-6300
Maspeth (G-7828)
Bimbo Bakeries Usa Inc ....E 800 856-8544
Vestal (G-15810)
Bimbo Bakeries Usa Inc ....F 845 294-5282
Goshen (G-5476)
Coca-Cola Btlg Co of NY Inc ....F 518 459-2010
Albany (G-64)
Coca-Cola Refreshments USA Inc ....E 718 401-5200
Bronx (G-1242)
Cohens Bakery Inc ....E 716 892-8149
Buffalo (G-2771)
French Associates Inc ....F 718 387-9880
Fresh Meadows (G-5198)
Infant Formula Laboratory Svc ....F 718 257-3000
Brooklyn (G-2001)
Kozy Shack Enterprises LLC ....C 516 870-3000
Hicksville (G-6099)
Kozy Shack Enterprises LLC ....C 516 870-3000
Hicksville (G-6100)
Luxfer Magtech Inc ....D 631 727-8600
Riverhead (G-13576)
Mandarin Soy Sauce Inc ....E 845 343-1505
Middletown (G-8162)
Rochester Coca Cola Bottling ....D 585 546-3900
Rochester (G-14083)
S J McCullagh Inc ....E 716 856-3473
Buffalo (G-3053)
Shine Foods USA Inc ....G 516 784-9674
Glen Oaks (G-5387)
Wellspring Corp ....G 212 529-5454
New York (G-12092)

GROCERIES, GENERAL LINE WHOLESALERS

Kong Kee Food Corp ....E 718 937-2746
Long Island City (G-7490)
Mondelez Global LLC ....G 585 345-3300
Batavia (G-630)

GUARDRAILS

Elderlee Incorporated ....C 315 789-6670
Oaks Corners (G-12527)

GUIDANCE SYSTEMS & EQPT: Space Vehicle

Harris Corporation ....A 585 269-6600
Rochester (G-13854)
Harris Corporation ....B 585 269-5001
Rochester (G-13855)
Harris Corporation ....C 585 269-5000
Rochester (G-13857)

GUIDED MISSILES & SPACE VEHICLES

Drt Power Systems LLC ....G 585 247-5940
Rochester (G-13751)
Edo LLC ....A 631 630-4200
Amityville (G-273)
Lockheed Martin Corporation ....A 607 751-2000
Owego (G-12799)

GUM & WOOD CHEMICALS

Metro Products & Services LLC ....F 866 846-8486
Brooklyn (G-2201)
Westrock Mwv LLC ....C 212 688-5000
New York (G-12097)

GUN STOCKS: Wood

Revival Industries Inc ....F 315 868-1085
Ilion (G-6479)

GUNSMITHS

Precision Arms Inc ....G 845 225-1130
Carmel (G-3280)

GUTTERS: Sheet Metal

Alfred B Parella ....G 518 872-1238
Altamont (G-194)
Genesee Building Products LLC ....F 585 548-2726
Stafford (G-15026)

GYPSUM PRDTS

East Pattern & Model Corp ....E 585 461-3240
Rochester (G-13756)
Lafarge North America Inc ....D 914 930-3027
Buchanan (G-2673)
United States Gypsum Company ....C 585 948-5221
Oakfield (G-12525)

HAIR & HAIR BASED PRDTS

Age Manufacturers Inc ....D 718 927-0048
Brooklyn (G-1494)
American Culture Hair Inc ....E 631 242-3142
Huntington Station (G-6429)
De Meo Brothers Inc ....G 212 268-1400
New York (G-9493)
Hair Color Research Group Inc ....E 718 445-6026
Flushing (G-5006)
Jason & Jean Products Inc ....F 718 271-8300
Corona (G-3846)
Malouf Colette Inc ....F 212 941-9588
New York (G-10680)
Mgd Brands Inc ....E 516 545-0150
Plainview (G-13075)
Miss Jessies LLC ....G 718 643-9016
New York (G-10823)
Premium Assure Inc ....E 605 252-9999
Brooklyn (G-2338)
Spartan Brands Inc ....F 212 340-0320
New York (G-11660)
Tactica International Inc ....E 212 575-0500
New York (G-11774)

HAIR ACCESS WHOLESALERS

Mgd Brands Inc ....E 516 545-0150
Plainview (G-13075)

HAIR CARE PRDTS

All Cultures Inc ....E 631 293-3143
Greenlawn (G-5620)
Belmay Holding Corporation ....E 914 376-1515
Yonkers (G-16740)
Hair Ventures LLC ....F 718 664-7689
Irvington (G-6506)
LOreal Usa Inc ....B 212 818-1500
New York (G-10606)
Pureology Research LLC ....F 212 984-4360
New York (G-11279)
Unike Products Inc ....G 347 686-4616
Jamaica (G-6687)
Zotos International Inc ....B 315 781-3207
Geneva (G-5337)

HAIR CARE PRDTS: Hair Coloring Preparations

LOreal USA Products Inc ....G 212 818-1500
New York (G-10609)
Salonclick LLC ....F 718 643-6793
New York (G-11472)

HAIRPIN MOUNTINGS

Lemetric Hair Centers Inc ....F 212 986-5620
New York (G-10543)
Shake-N-Go Fashion Inc ....E 516 944-7777
Port Washington (G-13306)
Shake-N-Go Fashion Inc ....C 516 944-7777
Port Washington (G-13307)

HANDBAG STORES

Quilted Koala Ltd ....F 800 223-5678
New York (G-11302)
Steven Madden Ltd ....B 718 446-1800
Long Island City (G-7604)

HANDBAGS

Affordable Luxury Group Inc ....G 631 523-9266
New York (G-8765)
Ahq LLC ....E 212 328-1560
New York (G-8773)
Akh Group LLC ....G 646 320-8720
New York (G-8780)
Bagznyc Corp ....F 212 643-8202
New York (G-9003)
Essex Manufacturing Inc ....D 212 239-0080
New York (G-9712)
Jag Footwear ACC & Ret Corp ....A 800 999-1877
New York (G-10299)
McM Products USA Inc ....E 646 756-4090
New York (G-10744)
Pure Trade Us Inc ....E 212 256-1600
New York (G-11276)
Quilted Koala Ltd ....F 800 223-5678
New York (G-11302)
Rodem Incorporated ....F 212 779-7122
New York (G-11418)

HANDBAGS: Women's

Atalla Handbags Inc ....G 718 965-5500
Brooklyn (G-1567)
Baikal Inc ....D 212 239-4650
New York (G-9004)
Coach Inc ....F 718 760-0624
Elmhurst (G-4463)
Coach Leatherware Intl ....G 212 594-1850
New York (G-9339)
Coach Services Inc ....G 212 594-1850
New York (G-9340)
Dani Accessories Inc ....E 631 692-4505
Cold Spring Harbor (G-3630)
Deux Lux Inc ....G 212 620-0801
New York (G-9513)
Kcp Holdco Inc ....F 212 265-1500
New York (G-10426)
Kenneth Cole Productions Inc ....B 212 265-1500
New York (G-10431)
Paradiso Cnsld Entps LLC ....E 585 924-3937
Rochester (G-14007)
Renco Group Inc ....G 212 541-6000
New York (G-11361)
Roadie Products Inc ....E 631 567-8588
Holbrook (G-6206)
Tapestry Inc ....G 212 615-2082
New York (G-11783)
Tapestry Inc ....G 212 594-1850
New York (G-11784)

HANDCUFFS & LEG IRONS

Boa Security Technologies Corp ....G 516 576-0295
Huntington (G-6395)

HANDLES: Brush Or Tool, Plastic

Allen Field Co Inc ....F 631 665-2782
Brightwaters (G-1185)

HANDLES: Wood

Fibron Products Inc ....E 716 886-2378
Buffalo (G-2826)

HANGERS: Garment, Plastic

American Intl Trimming ....G 718 369-9643
Brooklyn (G-1522)
Capco Wai Shing LLC ....G 212 268-1976
New York (G-9201)
Prestige Hangers Str Fixs Corp ....G 718 522-6777
Brooklyn (G-2341)

HANGERS: Garment, Wire

Styles Manufacturing Corp ....G 516 763-5303
Oceanside (G-12559)

HANGERS: Garment, Wire

American Intl Trimming ....G 718 369-9643
Brooklyn (G-1522)

HARDBOARD & FIBERBOARD PRDTS

Hi-Temp Fabrication Inc ....F 716 852-5655
Buffalo (G-2872)

HARDWARE

HARDWARE

Advantage Wholesale Supply LLC.........D..... 718 284-5346
  Brooklyn *(G-1490)*
American Casting and Mfg Corp ....G..... 516 349-7010
  Plainview *(G-13036)*
Amertac Holdings Inc ....G..... 610 336-1330
  Monsey *(G-8284)*
Barry Industries Inc ....F..... 212 242-5200
  New York *(G-9022)*
Brio USA ....G..... 585 319-5599
  Rochester *(G-13678)*
Cast-All Corporation ....E..... 516 741-4025
  Mineola *(G-8211)*
City Store Gates Mfg Corp ....E..... 718 939-9700
  College Point *(G-3642)*
Designatronics Incorporated ....B..... 516 328-3300
  Hicksville *(G-6080)*
Dico Products Corporation ....F..... 315 797-0470
  Utica *(G-15694)*
ER Butler & Co Inc ....E..... 212 925-3565
  New York *(G-9699)*
Excelco Developments Inc ....E..... 716 934-2651
  Silver Creek *(G-14861)*
Grow Computer Inc ....G..... 646 535-2037
  Brooklyn *(G-1953)*
H A Guden Company Inc ....E..... 631 737-2900
  Ronkonkoma *(G-14349)*
Industrial Electronic Hardware ....D..... 718 492-4440
  Brooklyn *(G-1999)*
Ingham Industries Inc ....G..... 631 242-2493
  Holbrook *(G-6189)*
ITR Industries Inc ....E..... 914 964-7063
  Yonkers *(G-16771)*
Jaquith Industries Inc ....E..... 315 478-5700
  Syracuse *(G-15346)*
Key High Vacuum Products Inc ....E..... 631 584-5959
  Nesconset *(G-8485)*
Kilian Manufacturing Corp ....G..... 315 432-0700
  Syracuse *(G-15355)*
Legendary Auto Interiors Ltd ....E..... 315 331-1212
  Newark *(G-12198)*
Liberty Brass Turning Co Inc ....E..... 718 784-2911
  Westbury *(G-16350)*
Lif Industries Inc ....E..... 718 767-8800
  Whitestone *(G-16545)*
Metalocke Industries Inc ....G..... 718 267-9200
  Woodside *(G-16663)*
Orbital Holdings Inc ....E..... 951 360-7100
  Buffalo *(G-2982)*
P & F Industries Inc ....E..... 631 694-9800
  Melville *(G-8055)*
Rosco Inc ....C..... 718 526-2601
  Jamaica *(G-6675)*
Syraco Products Inc ....F..... 315 476-5306
  Syracuse *(G-15433)*
Tattersall Industries LLC ....E..... 518 381-4270
  Schenectady *(G-14720)*
Truth Hardware Corporation ....G..... 585 627-5964
  Rochester *(G-14180)*
Yaloz Mould & Die Co Inc ....E..... 718 389-1131
  Brooklyn *(G-2662)*
York Industries Inc ....E..... 516 746-3736
  Garden City Park *(G-5290)*

HARDWARE & BUILDING PRDTS: Plastic

Abbott Industries Inc ....B..... 718 291-0800
  Jamaica *(G-6622)*
Cementex Latex Corp ....F..... 212 741-1770
  New York *(G-9236)*
Dortronics Systems Inc ....E..... 631 725-0505
  Sag Harbor *(G-14499)*
Gagne Associates Inc ....E..... 800 800-5954
  Johnson City *(G-6808)*
Kelta Inc ....E..... 631 789-5000
  Edgewood *(G-4406)*
Markwik Corp ....F..... 516 470-1990
  Hicksville *(G-6108)*
Metal Cladding Inc ....D..... 716 434-5513
  Lockport *(G-7316)*
Pace Window and Door Corp ....E..... 585 924-8350
  Victor *(G-15860)*
Performance Advantage Co Inc ....F..... 716 683-7413
  Lancaster *(G-7039)*
Schlegel Systems Inc ....C..... 585 427-7200
  Rochester *(G-14115)*
Space Age Plstic Fbrcators Inc ....F..... 718 324-4062
  Bronx *(G-1388)*
Tii Technologies Inc ....E..... 516 364-9300
  Edgewood *(G-4419)*

Transpo Industries Inc..........................E..... 914 636-1000
  New Rochelle *(G-8630)*

HARDWARE & EQPT: Stage, Exc Lighting

Props Displays & Interiors ....F..... 212 620-3840
  New York *(G-11266)*
Steeldeck Ny Inc ....F..... 718 599-3700
  Brooklyn *(G-2517)*

HARDWARE CLOTH: Woven Wire, Made From Purchased Wire

Dico Products Corporation ....F..... 315 797-0470
  Utica *(G-15694)*

HARDWARE STORES

International Fireproof Door ....F..... 718 783-1310
  Brooklyn *(G-2010)*
Lowville Farmers Coop Inc ....E..... 315 376-6587
  Lowville *(G-7652)*
Syracuse Industrial Sls Co Ltd ....F..... 315 478-5751
  Syracuse *(G-15438)*

HARDWARE STORES: Builders'

Ingham Industries Inc ....G..... 631 242-2493
  Holbrook *(G-6189)*

HARDWARE STORES: Pumps & Pumping Eqpt

A & C/Furia Electric Motors ....F..... 914 949-0585
  White Plains *(G-16416)*

HARDWARE STORES: Snowblowers

Elitsac Inc ....F..... 585 493-2628
  Castile *(G-3293)*

HARDWARE STORES: Tools

Boro Park Cutting Tool Corp ....E..... 718 720-0610
  Staten Island *(G-15053)*
Parker Machine Company Inc ....F..... 518 747-0675
  Fort Edward *(G-5098)*
Zak Jewelry Tools Inc ....F..... 212 768-8122
  New York *(G-12168)*

HARDWARE WHOLESALERS

Amertac Holdings Inc ....G..... 610 336-1330
  Monsey *(G-8284)*
Barry Industries Inc ....F..... 212 242-5200
  New York *(G-9022)*
Best Way Tools By Anderson Inc ....G..... 631 586-4702
  Deer Park *(G-3950)*
Expo Furniture Designs Inc ....F..... 516 674-1420
  Glen Cove *(G-5365)*
Globe Electronic Hardware Inc ....F..... 718 457-0303
  Woodside *(G-16659)*
H A Guden Company Inc ....E..... 631 737-2900
  Ronkonkoma *(G-14349)*
Metalline Fire Door Co Inc ....F..... 718 583-2320
  Bronx *(G-1328)*
Steel-Brite Ltd ....F..... 631 589-4044
  Oakdale *(G-12522)*
Sure Flow Equipment Inc ....E..... 800 263-8251
  Tonawanda *(G-15580)*

HARDWARE, WHOLESALE: Bolts

Park-Ohio Inds Trsry Co Inc ....F..... 212 966-3310
  Albany *(G-110)*

HARDWARE, WHOLESALE: Builders', NEC

ER Butler & Co Inc ....E..... 212 925-3565
  New York *(G-9699)*
P E Guerin ....D..... 212 243-5270
  New York *(G-11084)*
S A Baxter LLC ....G..... 845 469-7995
  Chester *(G-3482)*

HARDWARE, WHOLESALE: Chains

Extreme Shale Performance LLC ....G..... 814 688-7956
  Elmira *(G-4485)*

HARDWARE, WHOLESALE: Security Devices, Locks

Shield Security Doors Ltd ....G..... 202 468-3308
  Brooklyn *(G-2465)*

HARDWARE: Aircraft

Fastener Dimensions Inc ....E..... 718 847-6321
  Ozone Park *(G-12825)*
Kyntec Corporation ....G..... 716 810-6956
  Buffalo *(G-2913)*
Magellan Aerospace Processing ....G..... 631 694-1818
  West Babylon *(G-16173)*
Mpi Consulting Incorporated ....F..... 631 253-2377
  West Babylon *(G-16178)*

HARDWARE: Builders'

Northknight Logistics Inc ....F..... 716 283-3090
  Niagara Falls *(G-12316)*
Pk30 System LLC ....F..... 212 473-8050
  Stone Ridge *(G-15162)*
Progressive Hardware Co Inc ....G..... 631 445-1826
  East Northport *(G-4269)*

HARDWARE: Cabinet

Daniel Demarco and Assoc Inc ....E..... 631 598-7000
  Amityville *(G-271)*
Darman Manufacturing Coinc ....F..... 315 724-9632
  Utica *(G-15692)*
Kenstan Lock & Hardware Co Inc ....E..... 631 423-1977
  Plainview *(G-13068)*

HARDWARE: Door Opening & Closing Devices, Exc Electrical

Nanz Custom Hardware Inc ....E..... 212 367-7000
  New York *(G-10873)*
Nanz Custom Hardware Inc ....C..... 212 367-7000
  Deer Park *(G-4012)*

HARDWARE: Furniture

Real Design Inc ....F..... 315 429-3071
  Dolgeville *(G-4137)*
Water Street Brass Corporation ....E..... 716 763-0059
  Lakewood *(G-6999)*
Weber-Knapp Company ....C..... 716 484-9135
  Jamestown *(G-6761)*

HARDWARE: Furniture, Builders' & Other Household

Classic Brass Inc ....D..... 716 763-1400
  Lakewood *(G-6991)*
Decorative Hardware ....F..... 914 238-5251
  Chappaqua *(G-3421)*
Morgik Metal Designs ....F..... 212 463-0304
  New York *(G-10842)*

HARDWARE: Luggage

Crest Lock Co Inc ....F..... 718 345-9898
  Brooklyn *(G-1731)*
Tools & Stamping Corp ....G..... 718 392-4040
  Brooklyn *(G-2570)*

HARDWARE: Piano

Samscreen Inc ....E..... 607 722-3979
  Conklin *(G-3733)*

HARNESS ASSEMBLIES: Cable & Wire

Advanced Interconnect Mfg Inc ....D..... 585 742-2220
  Victor *(G-15828)*
Altec Datacom LLC ....G..... 631 242-2417
  Bay Shore *(G-655)*
Amphenol Intrconnect Pdts Corp ....G..... 607 754-4444
  Endicott *(G-4582)*
Apx Technologies Inc ....E..... 516 433-1313
  Hicksville *(G-6060)*
Arnold-Davis LLC ....C..... 607 772-1201
  Binghamton *(G-863)*
B3cg Interconnect Usa Inc ....F..... 450 491-4040
  Plattsburgh *(G-13108)*
Badger Technologies Inc ....E..... 585 869-7101
  Farmington *(G-4909)*
Becker Electronics Inc ....D..... 631 619-9100
  Ronkonkoma *(G-14318)*

PRODUCT SECTION

Cables Unlimited Inc..............................E......631 563-6363
 Yaphank *(G-16705)*
Condor Electronics Corp........................E......585 235-1500
 Rochester *(G-13717)*
Hazlow Electronics Inc..........................E......585 325-5323
 Rochester *(G-13863)*
I3 Assembly LLC....................................D......607 238-7077
 Binghamton *(G-892)*
Lyntronics Inc..E......631 205-1061
 Yaphank *(G-16715)*
North Hills Signal Proc Corp..................E......631 244-7393
 Bohemia *(G-1067)*
Paal Technologies Inc............................G......631 319-6262
 Ronkonkoma *(G-14394)*
Sayeda Manufacturing Corp...................F......631 345-2525
 Medford *(G-7965)*
Sturges Elec Pdts Co Inc.......................E......607 844-8604
 Dryden *(G-4152)*
Sturges Electronics LLC.........................F......607 844-8604
 Dryden *(G-4153)*
TCS Electronics Inc...............................E......585 337-4301
 Farmington *(G-4920)*
Tony Baird Electronics Inc......................G......315 422-4430
 Syracuse *(G-15445)*

HARNESSES, HALTERS, SADDLERY & STRAPS

Equicenter Inc..E......585 742-2522
 Honeoye Falls *(G-6264)*
Import-Export Corporation......................F......718 707-0880
 Long Island City *(G-7473)*
Unique Overseas Inc.............................G......516 466-9792
 Great Neck *(G-5597)*

HEADPHONES: Radio

Gotenna Inc...F......415 894-2616
 Brooklyn *(G-1941)*

HEALTH AIDS: Exercise Eqpt

D Squared Technologies Inc..................G......516 932-7319
 Jericho *(G-6784)*
Gym Store Inc.......................................G......718 366-7804
 Maspeth *(G-7850)*
Hypoxico Inc..G......212 972-1009
 New York *(G-10156)*
Physicalmind Institute............................F......212 343-2150
 New York *(G-11186)*
TDS Foundry Corporation......................G......607 733-6789
 Elmira *(G-4506)*

HEALTH SCREENING SVCS

Pharma-Smart International Inc..............E......585 427-0730
 Rochester *(G-14017)*

HEARING AIDS

Atlantic Er Inc..E......516 294-3200
 New Hyde Park *(G-8518)*
Beltone Corporation...............................G......716 565-1015
 Williamsville *(G-16570)*
Benway-Haworth-Lwlr-Iacosta He..........F......518 432-4070
 Albany *(G-46)*
Buffalo Hearg & Speech........................E......716 558-1105
 West Seneca *(G-16295)*
Family Hearing Center...........................G......845 897-3059
 Fishkill *(G-4946)*
Hearing Spech Ctr of Rochester............E......585 286-9373
 Webster *(G-16086)*
Roner Inc..G......718 392-6020
 Long Island City *(G-7579)*
Roner Inc..C......718 392-6020
 Long Island City *(G-7580)*
Todt Hill Audiological Svcs....................G......718 816-1952
 Staten Island *(G-15147)*
Widex Usa Inc.......................................D......718 360-1000
 Hauppauge *(G-5975)*
William H Shapiro..................................G......212 263-7037
 New York *(G-12112)*

HEAT EMISSION OPERATING APPARATUS

Zappone Chrysler Jeep Ddge Inc..........F......518 982-0610
 Halfmoon *(G-5670)*

HEAT EXCHANGERS

Aerco International Inc..........................C......845 580-8000
 Blauvelt *(G-933)*

Costanzos Welding Inc..........................E......716 282-0845
 Niagara Falls *(G-12274)*
Fross Industries Inc...............................E......716 297-0652
 Niagara Falls *(G-12287)*
Schwabel Fabricating Co Inc.................E......716 876-2086
 Tonawanda *(G-15575)*
Yula Corporation....................................E......718 991-0900
 Bronx *(G-1421)*

HEAT EXCHANGERS: After Or Inter Coolers Or Condensers, Etc

American Precision Inds Inc..................C......716 691-9100
 Amherst *(G-214)*
API Heat Transf Thermasys Corp..........A......716 684-6700
 Buffalo *(G-2704)*
API Heat Transfer Company..................G......716 684-6700
 Buffalo *(G-2705)*
API Heat Transfer Inc............................E......585 496-5755
 Arcade *(G-377)*
Nitram Energy Inc.................................E......716 662-6540
 Orchard Park *(G-12732)*
Slantco Manufacturing Inc.....................G......516 484-2600
 Greenvale *(G-5633)*

HEAT TREATING: Metal

A1 International Heat Treating................G......718 863-5552
 Bronx *(G-1204)*
Aterian Investment Partners LP.............E......212 547-2806
 New York *(G-8946)*
B & W Heat Treating Company.............F......716 876-8184
 Tonawanda *(G-15525)*
Bodycote Syracuse Heat Treatin...........E......315 451-0000
 Liverpool *(G-7224)*
Bodycote Thermal Proc Inc...................F......585 436-7876
 Rochester *(G-13670)*
BSV Metal Finishers Inc........................E......585 747-7070
 Rochester *(G-13680)*
Buffalo Armory LLC................................G......716 935-6346
 Buffalo *(G-2740)*
Burke Frging Heat Treating Inc..............E......585 235-6060
 Rochester *(G-13682)*
Burton Industries Inc..............................E......631 643-6660
 West Babylon *(G-16142)*
Cpp - Steel Treaters..............................E......315 736-3081
 Oriskany *(G-12755)*
Expedient Heat Treating Corp...............G......716 433-1177
 North Tonawanda *(G-12426)*
Gibraltar Industries Inc..........................D......716 826-6500
 Buffalo *(G-2849)*
Graywood Companies Inc......................E......585 254-7000
 Rochester *(G-13845)*
Great Lakes Metal Treating...................F......716 694-1240
 Tonawanda *(G-15543)*
Hercules Heat Treating Corp..................E......718 625-1266
 Brooklyn *(G-1973)*
International Ord Tech Inc.....................D......716 664-1100
 Jamestown *(G-6724)*
Jasco Heat Treating Inc........................E......585 388-0071
 Fairport *(G-4637)*
Kittredge & Sons Inc..............................D......978 567-0998
 Niagara Falls *(G-12303)*
Parfuse Corp...E......516 997-8888
 Westbury *(G-16363)*
Rochester Steel Treating Works............F......585 546-3348
 Rochester *(G-14096)*
Rough Brothers Holding Co...................E......716 826-6500
 Buffalo *(G-3048)*

HEATERS: Space, Exc Electric

American Comfort Direct LLC................E......201 364-8309
 New York *(G-8825)*

HEATERS: Swimming Pool, Oil Or Gas

Jus-Sar Fuel Inc....................................G......845 791-8900
 Harris *(G-5722)*

HEATERS: Unit, Domestic

Chicken Hawk Racing Inc......................G......845 758-0700
 Red Hook *(G-13457)*
Roberts-Gordon LLC..............................D......716 852-4400
 Buffalo *(G-3040)*

HEATING & AIR CONDITIONING EQPT & SPLYS WHOLESALERS

Pronto Gas Heating Sups Inc................G......718 292-0707
 Bronx *(G-1366)*

HEATING UNITS & DEVICES: Indl, Electric

Siemens Industry Inc.............................E......585 797-2300
 Rochester *(G-14126)*
Split Systems Corp................................G......516 223-5511
 North Baldwin *(G-12367)*

HEATING & AIR CONDITIONING UNITS, COMBINATION

Colburns AC Rfrgn.................................F......716 569-3695
 Frewsburg *(G-5207)*
Daikin Applied Americas Inc..................D......315 253-2771
 Auburn *(G-475)*
Enviromaster International LLC.............D......315 336-3716
 Rome *(G-14250)*
John F Krell Jr......................................G......315 492-3201
 Syracuse *(G-15348)*
Keeler Services.....................................G......607 776-5757
 Bath *(G-645)*
Northern Air Systems Inc......................E......585 594-5050
 Rochester *(G-13980)*
Pro Metal of NY Corp............................G......516 285-0440
 Valley Stream *(G-15791)*

HEATING EQPT & SPLYS

A Nuclimate Qulty Systems Inc.............F......315 431-0226
 Syracuse *(G-15236)*
Carrier Corporation................................B......315 432-6000
 Syracuse *(G-15272)*
Chentronics Corporation........................E......607 334-5531
 Norwich *(G-12480)*
CIDC Corp...F......718 342-5820
 Glendale *(G-5395)*
Dandelion Energy Inc............................F......603 781-2663
 Brooklyn *(G-1754)*
Economy Pump & Motor Repr Inc.........G......718 433-2600
 Astoria *(G-425)*
Embassy Industries Inc.........................C......631 435-0209
 Hauppauge *(G-5820)*
Fisonic Corp..G......212 732-3777
 Long Island City *(G-7450)*
Fisonic Corp..F......716 763-0295
 New York *(G-9814)*
Fulton Volcanic Inc................................D......315 298-5121
 Pulaski *(G-13384)*
Juniper Elbow Co Inc............................F......718 326-2546
 Middle Village *(G-8124)*
North Pk Innovations Group Inc............E......716 699-2031
 Ellicottville *(G-4447)*
Omega Heater Company Inc................D......631 588-8820
 Ronkonkoma *(G-14390)*
RE Hansen Industries Inc......................G......631 471-2900
 Saint James *(G-14514)*
Slant/Fin Corporation.............................B......516 484-2600
 Greenvale *(G-5632)*
Vincent Genovese.................................G......631 281-8170
 Mastic Beach *(G-7912)*

HEATING EQPT: Complete

A Nuclimate Qulty Systems Inc.............F......315 431-0226
 Syracuse *(G-15236)*
Coil Craft Inc...G......718 369-1210
 Ozone Park *(G-12823)*
Dundas-Jafine Inc..................................E......716 681-9690
 Alden *(G-170)*
Siemens Industry Inc.............................E......716 568-0983
 Buffalo *(G-3065)*
Specified Air Solutions LLC...................E......716 852-4400
 Buffalo *(G-3074)*
Thomson Industries Inc.........................F......716 691-9100
 Amherst *(G-255)*

HEATING EQPT: Induction

Ambrell Corporation...............................F......585 889-0236
 Rochester *(G-13623)*
Ultraflex Power Technologies................G......631 467-6814
 Ronkonkoma *(G-14425)*

HEATING SYSTEMS: Radiant, Indl Process

Radiant Pro Ltd.....................................G......516 763-5678
 Oceanside *(G-12552)*

HEATING UNITS & DEVICES: Indl, Electric

Cvd Equipment Corporation...................F......631 582-4365
 Central Islip *(G-3366)*
Fulton Volcanic Inc................................D......315 298-5121
 Pulaski *(G-13384)*
Igniter Systems Inc................................E......716 542-5511
 Akron *(G-19)*

HELICOPTERS
CIC International Ltd.............................D...... 212 213-0089
  Brooklyn *(G-1692)*

HELMETS: Athletic
Cascade Helmets Holdings Inc...........G...... 315 453-3073
  Liverpool *(G-7229)*
Performance Lacrosse Group Inc ....G...... 315 453-3073
  Liverpool *(G-7254)*

HIGH ENERGY PARTICLE PHYSICS EQPT
Advance Energy Systems NY LLC........G...... 315 735-5125
  Utica *(G-15676)*
Spirent Inc...G...... 631 208-0680
  Riverhead *(G-13585)*

HIGHWAY SIGNALS: Electric
BNo Intl Trdg Co Inc ....G...... 716 487-1900
  Jamestown *(G-6703)*
Traffic Lane Closures LLC ....F...... 845 228-6100
  Carmel *(G-3283)*

HOBBY & CRAFT SPLY STORES
Paper House Productions Inc..............E...... 845 246-7261
  Saugerties *(G-14612)*

HOBBY, TOY & GAME STORES: Ceramics Splys
Corning International Corp ....G...... 607 974-9000
  Corning *(G-3815)*

HOBBY, TOY & GAME STORES: Toys & Games
Minted Green Inc..................................G...... 845 458-1845
  Airmont *(G-15)*

HOISTS
Columbus McKinnon Corporation ....C...... 716 689-5400
  Getzville *(G-5344)*
Columbus McKinnon Corporation ....C...... 716 689-5400
  Getzville *(G-5345)*
Columbus McKinnon Corporation ....C...... 716 689-5400
  Getzville *(G-5346)*
Mannesmann Corporation ....D...... 212 258-4000
  New York *(G-10691)*
Marros Equipment & Trucks ....F...... 315 539-8702
  Waterloo *(G-15996)*
Mohawk Resources Ltd ....D...... 518 842-1431
  Amsterdam *(G-351)*
Reimann & Georger Corporation..........E...... 716 895-1156
  Buffalo *(G-3034)*
T Shore Products Ltd ....G...... 315 252-9174
  Auburn *(G-502)*
Thego Corporation................................G...... 631 776-2472
  Bellport *(G-814)*

HOLDING COMPANIES: Banks
Flavors Holdings Inc.............................F...... 212 572-8677
  New York *(G-9816)*

HOLDING COMPANIES: Investment, Exc Banks
Ample Hills Holdings Inc......................G...... 347 725-4061
  Brooklyn *(G-1533)*
Chemprene Inc......................................C...... 845 831-2800
  Beacon *(G-755)*
Geritrex Holdings Inc...........................G...... 914 668-4003
  Mount Vernon *(G-8399)*
Global Video LLC................................D...... 516 222-2600
  Woodbury *(G-16620)*
Graphic Controls Holdings Inc.............F...... 716 853-7500
  Buffalo *(G-2854)*
Hw Holdings Inc ....G...... 212 399-1000
  New York *(G-10153)*
Noco Incorporated................................G...... 716 833-6626
  Tonawanda *(G-15565)*
Pii Holdings Inc....................................G...... 716 876-9951
  Buffalo *(G-3004)*
Skip Hop Holdings Inc.........................G...... 212 868-9850
  New York *(G-11611)*

HOLDING COMPANIES: Personal, Exc Banks
Spf Holdings II LLC..............................G...... 212 750-8300
  New York *(G-11668)*

HOME DELIVERY NEWSPAPER ROUTES
Nyt Capital LLC ....F...... 212 556-1234
  New York *(G-11021)*

HOME ENTERTAINMENT EQPT: Electronic, NEC
Request Inc...E...... 518 899-1254
  Halfmoon *(G-5667)*
Request Serious Play LLC ....E...... 518 899-1254
  Halfmoon *(G-5668)*
Shyk International Corp ....G...... 212 663-3302
  New York *(G-11574)*
Sing Trix...F...... 212 352-1500
  New York *(G-11599)*

HOME FOR THE MENTALLY RETARDED
Chemung Cnty Chpter Nysarc Inc........C...... 607 734-6151
  Elmira *(G-4477)*

HOME FURNISHINGS WHOLESALERS
Feldman Company Inc..........................F...... 212 966-1303
  New York *(G-9792)*
Lifetime Brands Inc..............................B...... 516 683-6000
  Garden City *(G-5265)*

HOMEBUILDERS & OTHER OPERATIVE BUILDERS
Hope International Productions ....F...... 212 247-3188
  New York *(G-10122)*

HOMEFURNISHING STORES: Beddings & Linens
Duxiana Dux Bed ....G...... 212 755-2600
  New York *(G-9588)*
Metro Mattress Corp ....E...... 716 205-2300
  Niagara Falls *(G-12310)*

HOMEFURNISHING STORES: Cookware, Exc Aluminum
Comet Intl Trdg Co Inc.........................F...... 731 599-2430
  Brooklyn *(G-1708)*

HOMEFURNISHING STORES: Lighting Fixtures
David Weeks Studio..............................F...... 212 966-3433
  New York *(G-9486)*
Edison Power & Light Co Inc...............F...... 718 522-0002
  Brooklyn *(G-1814)*
Maxsun Corporation.............................F...... 718 418-6800
  Maspeth *(G-7859)*
Rapid-Lite Fixture Corporation.............F...... 347 599-2600
  Brooklyn *(G-2384)*
Serway Bros Inc ....E...... 315 337-0601
  Rome *(G-14274)*
Sir Industries Inc..................................G...... 631 234-2444
  Hauppauge *(G-5941)*

HOMEFURNISHING STORES: Mirrors
Global Glass Corp.................................G...... 516 681-2309
  Hicksville *(G-6091)*

HOMEFURNISHING STORES: Vertical Blinds
Pj Decorators Inc..................................E...... 516 735-9693
  East Meadow *(G-4255)*

HOMEFURNISHING STORES: Window Furnishings
Blinds To Go (us) Inc...........................E...... 718 477-9523
  Staten Island *(G-15051)*
Wallace Home Design Ctr ....G...... 631 765-3890
  Southold *(G-14971)*

HOMEFURNISHINGS & SPLYS, WHOLESALE: Decorative
Cioccolato 7 LLC..................................G...... 347 240-7115
  Brooklyn *(G-1693)*
Mistdoda Inc ....E...... 919 735-7111
  New York *(G-10824)*
Secret Celebrity Licensing LLC............G...... 212 812-9277
  New York *(G-11528)*

HOMEFURNISHINGS, WHOLESALE: Bedspreads
Ess Bee Industries Inc..........................E...... 718 894-5202
  Brooklyn *(G-1850)*

HOMEFURNISHINGS, WHOLESALE: Blinds, Venetian
D & D Window Tech Inc ....G...... 212 308-2822
  New York *(G-9446)*

HOMEFURNISHINGS, WHOLESALE: Blinds, Vertical
Pj Decorators Inc..................................E...... 516 735-9693
  East Meadow *(G-4255)*

HOMEFURNISHINGS, WHOLESALE: Carpets
Albert Menin Interiors Ltd ....F...... 212 876-3041
  Bronx *(G-1215)*
Elizabeth Eakins Inc.............................F...... 212 628-1950
  New York *(G-9653)*

HOMEFURNISHINGS, WHOLESALE: Curtains
Baby Signature Inc...............................G...... 212 686-1700
  New York *(G-8996)*

HOMEFURNISHINGS, WHOLESALE: Draperies
Reynolds Drapery Service Inc ....F...... 315 845-8632
  Newport *(G-12256)*

HOMEFURNISHINGS, WHOLESALE: Kitchenware
Lifetime Chimney Supply LLC.............G...... 516 576-8144
  Plainview *(G-13069)*
Madison Lifestyle Ny LLC ....G...... 212 725-4002
  New York *(G-10657)*
Vanity Fair Bathmart Inc.......................F...... 718 584-6700
  Bronx *(G-1413)*

HOMEFURNISHINGS, WHOLESALE: Linens, Table
Lintex Linens Inc..................................B...... 212 679-8046
  New York *(G-10574)*

HOMEFURNISHINGS, WHOLESALE: Pillowcases
Anhui Skyworth LLC.............................D...... 917 940-6903
  Hempstead *(G-6005)*

HOMEFURNISHINGS, WHOLESALE: Rugs
Lorena Canals USA Inc.........................G...... 844 567-3622
  Hastings On Hudson *(G-5751)*

HOMEFURNISHINGS, WHOLESALE: Stainless Steel Flatware
Utica Cutlery Company ....D...... 315 733-4663
  Utica *(G-15737)*

HOMEFURNISHINGS, WHOLESALE: Window Covering Parts & Access
Chf Industries Inc.................................E...... 212 951-7800
  New York *(G-9273)*
P E Guerin Inc......................................D...... 212 243-5270
  New York *(G-11084)*

HOMEFURNISHINGS, WHOLESALE: Wood Flooring

Wego International Floors LLC ....F 516 487-3510
  Great Neck *(G-5600)*

HOMES, MODULAR: Wooden

Best Mdlr IIMS Afrbe P Q& S In ....F 631 204-0049
  Southampton *(G-14950)*
Bill Lake Homes Construction ....D 518 673-2424
  Sprakers *(G-14987)*
Westchester Modular Homes Inc ....C 845 832-9400
  Wingdale *(G-16607)*
Whitley East LLC ....D 718 403-0050
  Brooklyn *(G-2644)*

HOMES: Log Cabins

Alta Industries Ltd ....F 845 586-3336
  Halcottsville *(G-5657)*
Beaver Mountain Log Homes Inc ......G 607 467-2700
  Hancock *(G-5709)*
Northern Design & Bldg Assoc ....E 518 747-2200
  Queensbury *(G-13435)*
Timberbuilt Inc ....F 716 337-0012
  North Collins *(G-12389)*

HONES

09 Flshy Bll/Dsert Sunrise LLC ....G 518 583-6638
  Saratoga Springs *(G-14565)*

HORMONE PREPARATIONS

American Hormones Inc ....F 845 471-7272
  Poughkeepsie *(G-13325)*
Erika T Schwartz MD PC ....G 212 873-3420
  New York *(G-9702)*

HORSE & PET ACCESSORIES: Textile

Saratoga Horseworks Ltd ....E 518 843-6756
  Amsterdam *(G-359)*
Triple E Manufacturing ....F 716 761-6996
  Sherman *(G-14817)*

HORSE ACCESS: Harnesses & Riding Crops, Etc, Exc Leather

Hampton Transport Inc ....F 631 716-4445
  Coram *(G-3798)*
Stonegate Stabless ....G 518 746-7133
  Fort Edward *(G-5101)*

HOSE: Automobile, Plastic

Deer Park Driveshaft & Hose ....G 631 667-4091
  Deer Park *(G-3963)*

HOSE: Fire, Rubber

Cataract Hose Co ....E 914 941-9019
  Ossining *(G-12769)*

HOSE: Flexible Metal

Flex-Hose Company Inc ....E 315 437-1903
  East Syracuse *(G-4340)*
TI Group Auto Systems LLC ....G 315 568-7042
  Seneca Falls *(G-14787)*

HOSE: Plastic

Jain Irrigation Inc ....D 315 755-4400
  Watertown *(G-16017)*
Superflex Ltd ....E 718 768-1400
  Brooklyn *(G-2535)*
TI Group Auto Systems LLC ....G 315 568-7042
  Seneca Falls *(G-14787)*

HOSE: Pneumatic, Rubber Or Rubberized Fabric, NEC

Moreland Hose & Belting Corp ....G 631 563-7071
  Oakdale *(G-12519)*

HOSE: Rubber

Mason Industries Inc ....B 631 348-0282
  Hauppauge *(G-5881)*
Mercer Rubber Co ....C 631 348-0282
  Hauppauge *(G-5886)*

HOSE: Vacuum Cleaner, Rubber

Anchor Tech Products Corp ....E 914 592-0240
  Elmsford *(G-4529)*

HOSES & BELTING: Rubber & Plastic

Flex Enterprises Inc ....E 585 742-1000
  Victor *(G-15846)*
Habasit America Inc ....D 716 824-8484
  Buffalo *(G-2860)*
Hitachi Cable America Inc ....F 914 694-9200
  Purchase *(G-13388)*
Index Incorporated ....F 440 632-5400
  Bronx *(G-1295)*
Jed Lights Inc ....F 516 812-5001
  Deer Park *(G-3992)*
Peraflex Hose Inc ....F 716 876-8806
  Buffalo *(G-2998)*
Standard Motor Products Inc ....B 718 392-0200
  Long Island City *(G-7598)*
Troy Belting and Supply Co ....D 518 272-4920
  Watervliet *(G-16053)*
WF Lake Corp ....E 518 798-9934
  Queensbury *(G-13445)*

HOSPITALS: Cancer

Actinium Pharmaceuticals Inc ....E 646 677-3870
  New York *(G-8730)*

HOSPITALS: Medical & Surgical

Norcorp Inc ....E 914 666-1310
  Mount Kisco *(G-8352)*

HOT TUBS

D & M Enterprises Incorporated ....G 914 937-6430
  Port Chester *(G-13195)*

HOT TUBS: Plastic & Fiberglass

D & M Enterprises Incorporated ....G 914 937-6430
  Port Chester *(G-13195)*
Independent Home Products LLC .....E 718 541-1256
  West Hempstead *(G-16216)*

HOUSEHOLD APPLIANCE STORES: Air Cond Rm Units, Self-Contnd

RE Hansen Industries Inc ....C 631 471-2900
  Saint James *(G-14514)*

HOUSEHOLD APPLIANCE STORES: Fans, Electric

A & C/Furia Electric Motors ....F 914 949-0585
  White Plains *(G-16416)*

HOUSEHOLD APPLIANCE STORES: Garbage Disposals

Mount Kisco Transfer Stn Inc ....G 914 666-6350
  Mount Kisco *(G-8350)*

HOUSEHOLD ARTICLES: Metal

Di Highway Sign Structure Corp ....E 315 736-8312
  New York Mills *(G-12185)*
Hatfield Metal Fab Inc ....E 845 454-9078
  Poughkeepsie *(G-13345)*
L D Flecken Inc ....F 631 777-4881
  Yaphank *(G-16714)*
New York Manufactured Products .....F 585 254-9353
  Rochester *(G-13967)*
Ulster County Iron Works LLC ....G 845 255-0003
  New Paltz *(G-8582)*

HOUSEHOLD FURNISHINGS, NEC

388 Associates Inc ....G 267 367-0990
  Brooklyn *(G-1437)*
AEP Environmental LLC ....F 716 446-0739
  Buffalo *(G-2690)*
Ann Gish Inc ....G 212 969-9200
  New York *(G-8871)*
Area Inc ....G 212 924-7084
  New York *(G-8904)*
August Silk Inc ....G 212 643-2400
  New York *(G-8961)*
August Silk Inc ....G 212 643-2400
  New York *(G-8962)*

Caddy Concepts Inc ....F 516 570-6279
  Great Neck *(G-5541)*
Creative Home Furnishings ....G 631 582-8000
  Central Islip *(G-3364)*
Creative Scents USA Inc ....G 718 522-5901
  Brooklyn *(G-1729)*
Dico Products Corporation ....F 315 797-0470
  Utica *(G-15694)*
Ess Bee Industries Inc ....E 718 894-5202
  Brooklyn *(G-1850)*
Kartell Us Inc ....G 212 966-6665
  New York *(G-10409)*
Kim Seybert Inc ....F 212 564-7850
  New York *(G-10445)*
Medline Industries Inc ....B 845 344-3301
  Middletown *(G-8163)*
Mgk Group Inc ....E 212 989-2732
  New York *(G-10788)*
MMS H& F Inc ....G 718 785-6663
  Jamaica *(G-6663)*
Moga Trading Company Inc ....G 718 760-2966
  Corona *(G-3851)*
Nationwide Tarps Incorporated ....D 518 843-1545
  Amsterdam *(G-353)*
Nbets Corporation ....G 516 785-1259
  Wantagh *(G-15925)*
Paramount Textiles Inc ....F 212 966-1040
  New York *(G-11109)*
Performance Sourcing Group Inc .....G 914 636-2100
  Scarsdale *(G-14642)*
Q Squared Design LLC ....E 212 686-8860
  New York *(G-11290)*
Richloom Fabrics Corp ....F 212 685-5400
  New York *(G-11391)*
Silly Phillie Creations Inc ....E 718 492-6300
  Brooklyn *(G-2471)*
Skil-Care Corporation ....E 914 963-2040
  Yonkers *(G-16798)*
Sleepable Sofas Ltd ....D 973 546-4502
  New York *(G-11617)*
Sleeping Partners Intl Inc ....F 212 254-1515
  Brooklyn *(G-2484)*
Sure Fit Inc ....E 212 395-9340
  New York *(G-11749)*
Terbo Ltd ....G 718 847-2860
  Richmond Hill *(G-13516)*
William Harvey Studio Inc ....G 718 599-4343
  Brooklyn *(G-2648)*

HOUSEWARE STORES

Swissmar Inc ....G 905 764-1121
  Niagara Falls *(G-12339)*

HOUSEWARES, ELECTRIC, EXC COOKING APPLIANCES & UTENSILS

Bino Products LLC ....E 212 689-6008
  New York *(G-9085)*
Brumis Imports Inc ....D 646 845-6000
  New York *(G-9152)*
World Trading Center Inc ....G 631 273-3330
  Hauppauge *(G-5978)*

HOUSEWARES, ELECTRIC: Cooking Appliances

Peek A Boo USA Inc ....G 201 533-8700
  New York *(G-11135)*

HOUSEWARES, ELECTRIC: Extractors, Juice

Goodnature Products Inc ....E 716 855-3325
  Orchard Park *(G-12716)*
Sundance Industries Inc ....G 845 795-5809
  Milton *(G-8198)*

HOUSEWARES, ELECTRIC: Fryers

Abbott Industries Inc ....B 718 291-0800
  Jamaica *(G-6622)*

HOUSEWARES, ELECTRIC: Heaters, Sauna

US Health Equipment Company ....E 845 658-7576
  Kingston *(G-6929)*

HOUSEWARES, ELECTRIC: Heaters, Space

Valad Electric Heating Corp ....F 888 509-4927
  Montgomery *(G-8319)*

HOUSEWARES, ELECTRIC: Heating, Bsbrd/Wall, Radiant Heat

Vincent Genovese .... G 631 281-8170
  Mastic Beach *(G-7912)*

HOUSEWARES, ELECTRIC: Humidifiers, Household

Dampits International Inc .... G 212 581-3047
  New York *(G-9461)*
Remedies Surgical Supplies .... G 718 599-5301
  Brooklyn *(G-2396)*

HOUSEWARES, ELECTRIC: Massage Machines, Exc Beauty/Barber

Advanced Response Corporation .... G 212 459-0887
  New York *(G-8757)*
Quality Life Inc .... F 718 939-5787
  College Point *(G-3662)*

HOUSEWARES: Dishes, China

Jill Fagin Enterprises Inc .... G 212 674-9383
  New York *(G-10337)*
Korin Japanese Trading Corp .... E 212 587-7021
  New York *(G-10471)*
Oneida International Inc .... G 315 361-3000
  Oneida *(G-12615)*
Oneida Silversmiths Inc .... G 315 361-3000
  Oneida *(G-12619)*

HOUSEWARES: Dishes, Earthenware

Ceramica Varm .... G 914 381-6215
  New Rochelle *(G-8596)*

HOUSEWARES: Dishes, Plastic

Comet Intl Trdg Co Inc .... F 731 599-2430
  Brooklyn *(G-1708)*
Digitac Inc .... F 732 215-4020
  Brooklyn *(G-1777)*
Etna Products Co Inc .... F 212 989-7591
  New York *(G-9722)*
Howard Charles Inc .... G 917 902-6934
  Woodbury *(G-16621)*
J M R Plastics Corporation .... G 718 898-9825
  Middle Village *(G-8122)*
Madison Lifestyle Ny LLC .... G 212 725-4002
  New York *(G-10657)*
Novelty Crystal Corp .... D 718 458-6700
  Long Island City *(G-7540)*
Ocala Group LLC .... F 516 233-2750
  New Hyde Park *(G-8555)*
Peek A Boo USA Inc .... G 201 533-8700
  New York *(G-11135)*
Robinson Knife .... F 716 685-6300
  Buffalo *(G-3041)*
Villeroy & Boch Usa Inc .... F 212 213-8149
  New York *(G-12035)*
Waddington North America Inc .... F 585 638-8200
  Holley *(G-6230)*

HOUSEWARES: Kettles & Skillets, Cast Iron

Field Wares LLC .... G 508 380-6545
  Brooklyn *(G-1878)*
S M S C Inc .... G 315 942-4394
  Boonville *(G-1121)*

HUMIDIFIERS & DEHUMIDIFIERS

Alfa Laval Kathabar Inc .... C 716 875-2000
  Tonawanda *(G-15520)*
MSP Technologycom LLC .... G 631 424-7542
  Centerport *(G-3351)*

HYDRAULIC EQPT REPAIR SVC

Mooradian Hydraulics & Eqp Co .... F 518 766-3866
  Castleton On Hudson *(G-3296)*

Hard Rubber & Molded Rubber Prdts

Apple Rubber Products Inc .... C 716 684-7649
  Lancaster *(G-7008)*
Mason Industries Inc .... B 631 348-0282
  Hauppauge *(G-5881)*
Prince Rubber & Plas Co Inc .... E 225 272-1653
  Buffalo *(G-3014)*

ICE

Adirondack Ice & Air Inc .... F 518 483-4340
  Malone *(G-7717)*
Annies Ice .... G 585 593-5605
  Wellsville *(G-16111)*
Arctic Glacier Newburgh Inc .... G 718 456-2013
  Brooklyn *(G-1548)*
Arctic Glacier Newburgh Inc .... F 845 561-0549
  Newburgh *(G-12215)*
Mamitas Ices Ltd .... F 718 738-3238
  Ozone Park *(G-12830)*
Maplewood Ice Co Inc .... F 518 499-2345
  Whitehall *(G-16523)*
South Shore Ice Co Inc .... F 516 379-2056
  Roosevelt *(G-14437)*

ICE CREAM & ICES WHOLESALERS

Four Brothers Italian Bakery .... G 914 741-5434
  Hawthorne *(G-5986)*
Fresh Ice Cream Company LLC .... F 347 603-6021
  Brooklyn *(G-1908)*
Macedonia Ltd .... F 718 462-3596
  Brooklyn *(G-2149)*
Marina Ice Cream .... G 718 235-3000
  Brooklyn *(G-2168)*
Purity Ice Cream Co Inc .... F 607 272-1545
  Ithaca *(G-6607)*
Ralphs Famous Italian Ices .... F 718 605-5052
  Staten Island *(G-15123)*
Washburns Dairy Inc .... E 518 725-0629
  Gloversville *(G-5472)*

IDENTIFICATION TAGS, EXC PAPER

Ketchum Manufacturing Co Inc .... F 518 696-3331
  Lake Luzerne *(G-6974)*

IGNEOUS ROCK: Crushed & Broken

Barrett Paving Materials Inc .... F 315 737-9471
  Clayville *(G-3554)*
Peckham Materials Corp .... E 518 747-3353
  Hudson Falls *(G-6384)*

IGNITION APPARATUS & DISTRIBUTORS

Magnum Shielding Corporation .... E 585 381-9957
  Pittsford *(G-13020)*
Martinez Specialties Inc .... G 607 898-3053
  Groton *(G-5652)*
Taro Manufacturing Company Inc .... F 315 252-9430
  Auburn *(G-503)*

IGNITION SYSTEMS: High Frequency

Standard Motor Products Inc .... B 718 392-0200
  Long Island City *(G-7598)*
Zenith Autoparts Corp .... E 845 344-1382
  Middletown *(G-8185)*

IGNITION SYSTEMS: Internal Combustion Engine

Zierick Manufacturing Corp .... D 800 882-8020
  Mount Kisco *(G-8361)*

INCINERATORS

Thermal Process Cnstr Co .... E 631 293-6400
  Farmingdale *(G-4894)*

INDICATORS: Cabin Environment

Excelsior Mlt-Cltural Inst Inc .... F 706 627-4285
  Flushing *(G-4998)*

INDL & PERSONAL SVC PAPER WHOLESALERS

Felix Schoeller North Amer Inc .... D 315 298-8425
  Pulaski *(G-13379)*
Josh Packaging Inc .... F 631 822-1660
  Hauppauge *(G-5854)*
Stanley Paper Co Inc .... F 518 489-1131
  Albany *(G-129)*

INDL & PERSONAL SVC PAPER, WHOL: Bags, Paper/Disp Plastic

Dawn Paper Co Inc .... F 516 596-9110
  East Rockaway *(G-4294)*

Dory Enterprises Inc .... F 607 565-7079
  Waverly *(G-16064)*
Dynamic Packaging Inc .... F 718 388-0800
  Brooklyn *(G-1800)*
Elara Fdsrvice Disposables LLC .... G 877 893-3244
  Jericho *(G-6786)*
Garb-O-Liner Inc .... G 914 235-1585
  New Rochelle *(G-8607)*
Golden Group International Ltd .... G 845 440-1025
  Patterson *(G-12882)*
M C Packaging Corporation .... E 631 643-3763
  Babylon *(G-529)*
Paramount Equipment Inc .... E 631 981-4422
  Ronkonkoma *(G-14395)*
Poly Craft Industries Corp .... E 631 630-6731
  Hauppauge *(G-5918)*
Primo Plastics Inc .... E 718 349-1000
  Brooklyn *(G-2344)*
Westrock Rkt LLC .... C 631 586-6000
  Deer Park *(G-4062)*

INDL & PERSONAL SVC PAPER, WHOL: Boxes, Corrugtd/Solid Fiber

Cattaraugus Containers Inc .... E 716 676-2000
  Franklinville *(G-5123)*
Technical Packaging Inc .... F 516 223-2300
  Baldwin *(G-545)*

INDL & PERSONAL SVC PAPER, WHOL: Container, Paper/Plastic

Pactiv LLC .... C 585 394-5125
  Canandaigua *(G-3228)*

INDL & PERSONAL SVC PAPER, WHOL: Cups, Disp, Plastic/Paper

S J McCullagh Inc .... E 716 856-3473
  Buffalo *(G-3053)*

INDL & PERSONAL SVC PAPER, WHOLESALE: Paperboard & Prdts

G F Labels LLC .... F 518 798-6643
  Queensbury *(G-13424)*

INDL & PERSONAL SVC PAPER, WHOLESALE: Press Sensitive Tape

Edco Supply Corporation .... D 718 788-8108
  Brooklyn *(G-1813)*
Tape-It Inc .... E 631 243-4100
  Bay Shore *(G-730)*

INDL EQPT SVCS

Burnett Process Inc .... G 585 254-8080
  Rochester *(G-13683)*
Eis Inc .... E 585 426-5330
  Rochester *(G-13774)*
Keyes Machine Works Inc .... G 585 426-5059
  Gates *(G-5310)*
Oliver Gear Inc .... E 716 885-1080
  Buffalo *(G-2979)*
R & B Fabrication Inc .... F 315 640-9901
  Cicero *(G-3522)*

INDL GASES WHOLESALERS

Haun Welding Supply Inc .... G 607 846-2289
  Elmira *(G-4491)*

INDL MACHINERY & EQPT WHOLESALERS

Accurate Industrial Machining .... E 631 242-0566
  Holbrook *(G-6168)*
Advanced Photonics Inc .... F 631 471-3693
  Ronkonkoma *(G-14293)*
Analog Digital Technology LLC .... G 585 698-1845
  Rochester *(G-13631)*
Anderson Instrument Co Inc .... D 518 922-5315
  Fultonville *(G-5234)*
Anthony Manufacturing Inc .... G 631 957-9424
  Lindenhurst *(G-7161)*
Arbe Machinery Inc .... F 631 756-2477
  Farmingdale *(G-4722)*
Brinkman Products Inc .... G 585 235-4545
  Rochester *(G-13677)*
Brooklyn Brew Shop LLC .... F 718 874-0119
  Brooklyn *(G-1638)*

PRODUCT SECTION

INDL SPLYS, WHOLESALE: Abrasives

Buflovak LLC .... E 716 895-2100
  Buffalo *(G-2755)*
Charles Ross & Son Company .... D 631 234-0500
  Hauppauge *(G-5788)*
Conrad Blasius Equipment Co .... E 516 753-1200
  Plainview *(G-13044)*
DI Manufacturing Inc .... E 315 432-8977
  North Syracuse *(G-12400)*
Dorsey Metrology Intl Inc .... E 845 229-2929
  Poughkeepsie *(G-13334)*
Filling Equipment Co Inc .... F 718 445-2111
  College Point *(G-3644)*
Genesee Manufacturing Co Inc .... G 585 266-3201
  Rochester *(G-13829)*
Goulds Pumps LLC .... A 315 568-2811
  Seneca Falls *(G-14774)*
Hades Manufacturing Corp .... F 631 249-4244
  Farmingdale *(G-4778)*
Halpern Tool Corp .... F 914 633-0038
  New Rochelle *(G-8611)*
Hunter Douglas Inc .... D 845 664-7000
  Pearl River *(G-12901)*
Innotech Graphic Eqp Corp .... E 845 268-6900
  Valley Cottage *(G-15755)*
ITT Goulds Pumps Inc .... A 914 641-2129
  Seneca Falls *(G-14779)*
John N Fehlinger Inc .... F 212 233-5656
  New York *(G-10353)*
Khk Usa Inc .... G 516 248-3850
  Mineola *(G-8232)*
Kps Capital Partners LP .... E 212 338-5100
  New York *(G-10476)*
Makerbot Industries LLC .... C 347 334-6800
  Brooklyn *(G-2153)*
Mark - 10 Corporation .... E 631 842-9200
  Copiague *(G-3769)*
N E Controls LLC .... F 315 626-2480
  Syracuse *(G-15379)*
Noresco Industrial Group Inc .... E 516 759-3355
  Glen Cove *(G-5371)*
Rapid Fan & Blower Inc .... F 718 786-2060
  Long Island City *(G-7571)*
Riverside Machinery Company .... E 718 492-7400
  Brooklyn *(G-2407)*
Rs Automation .... F 585 589-0199
  Albion *(G-162)*
Simmons Machine Tool Corp .... C 518 462-5431
  Menands *(G-8091)*
Specialty Steel Fabg Corp .... F 718 893-6326
  Bronx *(G-1390)*
Speedways Conveyors Inc .... E 716 893-2222
  Buffalo *(G-3075)*
Thread Check Inc .... D 631 231-1515
  Hauppauge *(G-5958)*
Troy Belting and Supply Co .... D 518 272-4920
  Watervliet *(G-16053)*
Uneeda Enterprizes Inc .... C 800 431-2494
  Spring Valley *(G-15011)*
Unicell Body Company Inc .... F 716 853-8628
  Schenectady *(G-14723)*
Viatran Corporation .... E 716 564-7813
  Tonawanda *(G-15589)*
Vibration & Noise Engrg Corp .... G 716 827-4959
  Orchard Park *(G-12749)*
Ward Industrial Equipment Inc .... G 716 856-6966
  Buffalo *(G-3123)*

INDL MACHINERY REPAIR & MAINTENANCE

Alternative Service Inc .... F 631 345-9500
  Bellport *(G-798)*
Atlantic Industrial Tech Inc .... E 631 234-3131
  Shirley *(G-14830)*
Dairy Conveyor Corp .... D 845 278-7878
  Brewster *(G-1162)*
Demartini Oil Equipment Svc .... G 518 463-5752
  Glenmont *(G-5411)*
Excel Conveyor LLC .... F 718 474-0001
  Rockaway Beach *(G-14225)*
General Oil Equipment Co Inc .... E 716 691-7012
  Amherst *(G-229)*
Konecranes Inc .... F 585 359-4450
  Henrietta *(G-6033)*
Locker Masters Inc .... F 518 288-3203
  Granville *(G-5519)*
Prim Hall Enterprises Inc .... F 518 561-7408
  Plattsburgh *(G-13150)*
Tchnologies N MRC Ameerica LLC ..... G 716 822-4300
  Buffalo *(G-3087)*

INDL PATTERNS: Foundry Patternmaking

G Haynes Holdings Inc .... G 607 538-1160
  Bloomville *(G-961)*
Studio One Leather Design Inc .... F 212 760-1701
  New York *(G-11728)*

INDL PROCESS INSTRUMENT: Potentiomtrc Self-Bal, Exc XY Plot

Betapast Holdings LLC .... D 631 582-6740
  Hauppauge *(G-5779)*

INDL PROCESS INSTRUMENTS: Analyzers

Vibro-Laser Instrs Corp LLC .... G 518 874-2700
  Glens Falls *(G-5443)*

INDL PROCESS INSTRUMENTS: Control

Automation Evolution LLC .... G 585 241-6010
  Webster *(G-16075)*
Conax Technologies LLC .... C 716 684-4500
  Buffalo *(G-2777)*
Electrcal Instrumentation Ctrl .... F 518 861-5789
  Delanson *(G-4068)*
Inficon Inc .... C 315 434-1100
  East Syracuse *(G-4350)*
Inficon Holding AG .... G 315 434-1100
  East Syracuse *(G-4351)*
Micromod Automtn & Cntrls Inc .... C 585 321-9209
  Rochester *(G-13943)*
Nidec Indus Automtn USA LLC .... E 716 774-1193
  Grand Island *(G-5507)*
Partlow Corporation .... G 518 922-5315
  Fultonville *(G-5238)*
Rwb Controls Inc .... G 716 897-4341
  Buffalo *(G-3050)*

INDL PROCESS INSTRUMENTS: Controllers, Process Variables

Anderson Instrument Co Inc .... D 518 922-5315
  Fultonville *(G-5234)*
Applied Power Systems Inc .... E 516 935-2230
  Hicksville *(G-6059)*
Classic Automation LLC .... E 585 241-6010
  Webster *(G-16079)*
Digitronik Labs Inc .... F 585 360-0043
  Rochester *(G-13741)*
New Scale Technologies Inc .... E 585 924-4450
  Victor *(G-15857)*
Ormec Systems Corp .... E 585 385-3520
  Rochester *(G-13991)*

INDL PROCESS INSTRUMENTS: Digital Display, Process Variables

Display Logic USA Inc .... G 631 406-1922
  Hauppauge *(G-5813)*
Webinfinity Americas Inc .... F 516 331-5180
  Huntington *(G-6427)*

INDL PROCESS INSTRUMENTS: Elements, Primary

Aalborg Instrs & Cntrls Inc .... D 845 398-3160
  Orangeburg *(G-12667)*

INDL PROCESS INSTRUMENTS: Fluidic Devices, Circuit & Systems

ITT Corporation .... D 315 568-2811
  Seneca Falls *(G-14777)*
ITT Inc .... E 914 641-2000
  White Plains *(G-16464)*
ITT LLC .... D 914 641-2000
  Seneca Falls *(G-14781)*
ITT LLC .... E 914 641-2000
  White Plains *(G-16467)*
Swagelok Western NY .... G 585 359-8470
  West Henrietta *(G-16252)*

INDL PROCESS INSTRUMENTS: Indl Flow & Measuring

Computer Instruments Corp .... E 516 876-8400
  Westbury *(G-16321)*
Select Controls Inc .... E 631 567-9010
  Bohemia *(G-1087)*

INDL PROCESS INSTRUMENTS: Level & Bulk Measuring

Gizmo Products Inc .... G 585 301-0970
  Stanley *(G-15034)*

INDL PROCESS INSTRUMENTS: On-Stream Gas Or Liquid Analysis

Calibrated Instruments Inc .... F 914 741-5700
  Manhasset *(G-7765)*

INDL PROCESS INSTRUMENTS: Temperature

Weiss Instruments Inc .... D 631 207-1200
  Holtsville *(G-6250)*

INDL PROCESS INSTRUMENTS: Water Quality Monitoring/Cntrl Sys

Blue Tee Corp .... G 212 598-0880
  New York *(G-9109)*
Danaher Corporation .... C 516 443-9432
  New York *(G-9464)*
Ewt Holdings III Corp .... F 212 644-5900
  New York *(G-9744)*
Roessel & Co Inc .... G 585 458-5560
  Rochester *(G-14101)*

INDL SALTS WHOLESALERS

American Rock Salt Company LLC ...... E 585 991-6878
  Retsof *(G-13480)*

INDL SPLYS WHOLESALERS

Allstate Gasket & Packing Inc .... F 631 254-4050
  Deer Park *(G-3937)*
Applince Installation Svc Corp .... E 716 884-7425
  Buffalo *(G-2707)*
Bfg Marine Inc .... F 631 586-5500
  Bay Shore *(G-662)*
D K Machine Inc .... F 518 747-0626
  Fort Edward *(G-5095)*
Dura-Mill Inc .... D 518 899-2255
  Ballston Spa *(G-582)*
Executive Mirror Doors Inc .... G 631 234-1090
  Ronkonkoma *(G-14340)*
Flex Enterprises Inc .... E 585 742-1000
  Victor *(G-15846)*
Ford Regulator Valve Corp .... G 718 497-3255
  Brooklyn *(G-1897)*
Jar Metals Inc .... F 845 425-8901
  Nanuet *(G-8464)*
Macinnes Tool Corporation .... E 585 467-1920
  Rochester *(G-13921)*
Marks Corpex Banknote Co .... E 631 968-0277
  Bay Shore *(G-698)*
Peraflex Hose Inc .... F 716 876-8806
  Buffalo *(G-2998)*
Rollers Inc .... G 716 837-0700
  Buffalo *(G-3044)*
SAS Industries Inc .... F 631 727-1441
  Manorville *(G-7785)*
Troy Belting and Supply Co .... D 518 272-4920
  Watervliet *(G-16053)*

INDL SPLYS, WHOL: Fasteners, Incl Nuts, Bolts, Screws, Etc

Fastener Dimensions Inc .... E 718 847-6321
  Ozone Park *(G-12825)*
Reddi Car Inc .... G 631 589-3141
  Sayville *(G-14634)*
SD Christie Associates Inc .... G 914 734-1800
  Peekskill *(G-12925)*

INDL SPLYS, WHOLESALE: Abrasives

Barton Mines Company LLC .... C 518 798-5462
  Glens Falls *(G-5418)*
Sunbelt Industries Inc .... F 315 823-2947
  Little Falls *(G-7214)*
Uneeda Enterprizes Inc .... C 800 431-2494
  Spring Valley *(G-15011)*
Warren Cutlery Corp .... F 845 876-3444
  Rhinebeck *(G-13490)*

Employee Codes: A=Over 500 employees, B=251-500
C=101-250, D=51-100, E=20-50, F=10-19, G=5-9

INDL SPLYS, WHOLESALE: Adhesives, Tape & Plasters
Xto Incorporated ....D...... 315 451-7807
Liverpool *(G-7273)*

INDL SPLYS, WHOLESALE: Bearings
Raydon Precision Bearing Co ....G...... 516 887-2582
Lynbrook *(G-7671)*

INDL SPLYS, WHOLESALE: Bins & Containers, Storage
McIntosh Box & Pallet Co Inc ....E...... 315 446-9350
Rome *(G-14257)*

INDL SPLYS, WHOLESALE: Brushes, Indl
Braun Bros Brushes Inc.........................G...... 631 667-2179
Valley Stream *(G-15775)*

INDL SPLYS, WHOLESALE: Clean Room Splys
Air Crafters Inc......................................C...... 631 471-7788
Ronkonkoma *(G-14295)*
Knf Clean Room Products Corp ....E...... 631 588-7000
Ronkonkoma *(G-14362)*

INDL SPLYS, WHOLESALE: Fasteners & Fastening Eqpt
American Pride Fasteners LLC............E...... 631 940-8292
Bay Shore *(G-656)*
General Galvanizing Sup Co Inc..........D...... 718 589-4300
Bronx *(G-1281)*

INDL SPLYS, WHOLESALE: Gears
Khk Usa Inc ....G...... 516 248-3850
Mineola *(G-8232)*

INDL SPLYS, WHOLESALE: Knives, Indl
Save O Seal Corporation Inc................G...... 914 592-3031
Elmsford *(G-4563)*

INDL SPLYS, WHOLESALE: Mill Splys
Polymag Tek Inc...................................F...... 585 235-8390
Rochester *(G-14026)*

INDL SPLYS, WHOLESALE: Rubber Goods, Mechanical
Tattersall Industries LLC ....E...... 518 381-4270
Schenectady *(G-14720)*
Triangle Rubber Co Inc ....E...... 631 589-9400
Bohemia *(G-1099)*

INDL SPLYS, WHOLESALE: Seals
American Casting and Mfg Corp ....D...... 800 342-0333
Plainview *(G-13035)*
Web Seal Inc ....E...... 585 546-1320
Rochester *(G-14204)*

INDL SPLYS, WHOLESALE: Springs
Lee Spring Company LLC ....C...... 718 362-5183
Brooklyn *(G-2105)*

INDL SPLYS, WHOLESALE: Tools
Dinosaw Inc..E...... 518 828-9942
Hudson *(G-6347)*

INDL SPLYS, WHOLESALE: Valves & Fittings
John N Fehlinger Co Inc.......................F...... 212 233-5656
New York *(G-10353)*
McWane Inc ....B...... 607 734-2211
Elmira *(G-4497)*
Trident Valve Actuator Co ....F...... 914 698-2650
Mamaroneck *(G-7759)*

INDUCTORS
Island Audio Engineering.....................G...... 631 543-2372
Commack *(G-3696)*

INFORMATION RETRIEVAL SERVICES
Alternative Technology Corp................G...... 914 478-5900
Hastings On Hudson *(G-5747)*
Aquifer Drilling & Testing Inc...............D...... 516 616-6026
Mineola *(G-8204)*
Avalon Copy Centers Amer Inc ....D...... 315 471-3333
Syracuse *(G-15251)*
Avalon Copy Centers Amer Inc ....E...... 716 995-7777
Buffalo *(G-2717)*
Chakra Communications Inc ....E...... 716 505-7300
Lancaster *(G-7013)*
Data Key Communication LLC ....F...... 315 445-2347
Fayetteville *(G-4927)*
IAC Search LLC ....E...... 212 314-7300
New York *(G-10163)*
Iac/Interactivecorp...............................A...... 212 314-7300
New York *(G-10164)*
New York Times Company ....B...... 212 556-1234
New York *(G-10944)*
Realtimetraderscom ....E...... 716 632-6600
Buffalo *(G-3033)*

INFRARED OBJECT DETECTION EQPT
Infrared Components Corp ....E...... 315 732-1544
Utica *(G-15715)*

INGOT: Aluminum
Novelis Inc...E...... 315 349-0121
Oswego *(G-12785)*

INK OR WRITING FLUIDS
American Electronic Products..............F...... 631 924-1299
Yaphank *(G-16704)*
F M Group Inc ....F...... 845 589-0102
Congers *(G-3716)*
Specialty Ink Co Inc ....F...... 631 586-3666
Blue Point *(G-965)*

INK: Letterpress Or Offset
Bishop Print Shop Inc ....G...... 607 965-8155
Edmeston *(G-4425)*

INK: Printing
Atlas Coatings Corp ....D...... 718 402-2000
Bronx *(G-1222)*
Calchem Corporation ....G...... 631 423-5696
Ronkonkoma *(G-14324)*
Flint Group Incorporated......................E...... 585 458-1223
Rochester *(G-13807)*
Gotham Ink & Color Co Inc ....E...... 845 947-4000
Stony Point *(G-15172)*
Inglis Co Inc...G...... 315 475-1315
Syracuse *(G-15343)*
Intrinsiq Materials Inc ....G...... 585 301-4432
Rochester *(G-13886)*
INX International Ink Co ....E...... 716 366-6010
Dunkirk *(G-4172)*
Micro Powders Inc................................E...... 914 332-6400
Tarrytown *(G-15483)*
Millennium Rmnfctred Toner Inc ....F...... 718 585-9887
Bronx *(G-1331)*
Mitsubishi Chemical Amer Inc ....E...... 212 223-3043
New York *(G-10825)*
Specialty Ink Co Inc ....F...... 631 586-3666
Blue Point *(G-965)*
Superior Printing Ink Co Inc ....G...... 716 877-0250
Tonawanda *(G-15579)*
Wikoff Color Corporation ....F...... 585 458-0653
Rochester *(G-14209)*

INK: Screen process
Standard Screen Supply Corp ....F...... 212 627-2727
New York *(G-11693)*

INSECTICIDES
Island Marketing Corp..........................G...... 516 739-0500
Mineola *(G-8229)*
Noble Pine Products Co Inc.................E...... 914 664-5877
Mount Vernon *(G-8425)*

INSPECTION & TESTING SVCS
Cs Automation Inc ....F...... 315 524-5123
Ontario *(G-12650)*

INSTR, MEASURE & CONTROL: Gauge, Oil Pressure & Water Temp
Make-Waves Instrument Corp ....E...... 716 681-7524
Buffalo *(G-2936)*

INSTRUMENTS & METERS: Measuring, Electric
Herman H Sticht Company Inc ....G...... 718 852-7602
Brooklyn *(G-1974)*
Pulsafeeder Inc ....C...... 585 292-8000
Rochester *(G-14054)*
S R Instruments Inc.............................E...... 716 693-5977
Tonawanda *(G-15573)*
Schlumberger Technology Corp ....C...... 607 378-0105
Horseheads *(G-6328)*

INSTRUMENTS, LABORATORY: Differential Thermal Analysis
East Coast Envmtl Group Inc ....G...... 516 352-1946
Farmingdale *(G-4757)*

INSTRUMENTS, LABORATORY: Magnetic/Elec Properties Measuring
CTB Enterprise LLC.............................F...... 631 563-0088
Holbrook *(G-6181)*
MMC Enterprises Corp ....G...... 800 435-1088
Hauppauge *(G-5894)*

INSTRUMENTS, LABORATORY: Mass Spectrometers
Advion Inc..E...... 607 266-9162
Ithaca *(G-6555)*

INSTRUMENTS, LABORATORY: Protein Analyzers
Elementar Americas Inc ....G...... 856 787-0022
Ronkonkoma *(G-14338)*

INSTRUMENTS, LABORATORY: Spectrometers
Spectra Vista Corporation....................G...... 845 471-7007
Poughkeepsie *(G-13367)*

INSTRUMENTS, MEASURING & CNTRL: Radiation & Testing, Nuclear
L N D Incorporated..............................E...... 516 678-6141
Oceanside *(G-12545)*
Mirion Tech Conax Nuclear Inc...........E...... 716 681-1973
Buffalo *(G-2948)*
Mirion Technologies Ist Corp ....D...... 607 562-4300
Horseheads *(G-6321)*
VJ Technologies Inc ....E...... 631 589-8800
Bohemia *(G-1106)*

INSTRUMENTS, MEASURING & CNTRL: Testing, Abrasion, Etc
Magnetic Analysis Corporation ....D...... 914 530-2000
Elmsford *(G-4549)*

INSTRUMENTS, MEASURING & CNTRLG: Aircraft & Motor Vehicle
James A Staley Co Inc........................F...... 845 878-3344
Carmel *(G-3277)*
Magtrol Inc...E...... 716 668-5555
Buffalo *(G-2935)*

INSTRUMENTS, MEASURING & CNTRLG: Stress, Strain & Measure
Mechanical Technology Inc ....E...... 518 218-2550
Albany *(G-98)*
MTI Instruments Inc ....F...... 518 218-2550
Albany *(G-101)*

INSTRUMENTS, MEASURING & CNTRLG: Tensile Strength Testing
Andor Design Corp..............................G...... 516 364-1619
Syosset *(G-15208)*

PRODUCT SECTION — INSTRUMENTS: Analytical

INSTRUMENTS, MEASURING & CNTRLG: Thermometers/Temp Sensors
Qhi Group Incorporated ....G....... 646 512-5727
  New York *(G-11291)*

INSTRUMENTS, MEASURING & CONTROLLING: Gas Detectors
Industrial Test Eqp Co Inc..................E...... 516 883-6423
  Port Washington *(G-13269)*

INSTRUMENTS, MEASURING & CONTROLLING: Magnetometers
Vector Magnetics LLC ....E...... 607 273-8351
  Ithaca *(G-6616)*

INSTRUMENTS, MEASURING & CONTROLLING: Photogrammetrical
Elsag North America LLC ....G....... 877 773-5724
  Brewster *(G-1164)*

INSTRUMENTS, MEASURING & CONTROLLING: Toll Booths, Automatic
Highway Toll ADM LLC ....F...... 516 684-9584
  Roslyn Heights *(G-14455)*

INSTRUMENTS, MEASURING & CONTROLLING: Ultrasonic Testing
Aurora Technical Services Ltd ....G....... 716 652-1463
  East Aurora *(G-4195)*
U E Systems Incorporated ....E...... 914 592-1220
  Elmsford *(G-4575)*

INSTRUMENTS, MEASURING/CNTRL: Hydrometers, Exc Indl Process
Mobius Labs Inc ....G....... 518 961-2600
  Rexford *(G-13481)*
Peyser Instrument Corporation ....E...... 631 841-3600
  West Babylon *(G-16181)*

INSTRUMENTS, MEASURING/CNTRLG: Fare Registers, St Cars/Buses
Cubic Trnsp Systems Inc ....F...... 212 255-1810
  New York *(G-9431)*

INSTRUMENTS, MEASURING/CNTRLNG: Med Diagnostic Sys, Nuclear
Amarantus Bscence Holdings Inc.........F...... 917 686-5317
  New York *(G-8816)*
Eastern Niagra Radiology ....E...... 716 882-6544
  Buffalo *(G-2811)*
H D M Labs Inc ....G....... 516 431-8357
  Island Park *(G-6515)*
Nuclear Diagnostic Pdts NY Inc ....G....... 516 575-4201
  Plainview *(G-13079)*
Oyster Bay Pump Works Inc ....F...... 516 933-4500
  Hicksville *(G-6119)*

INSTRUMENTS, OPTICAL: Borescopes
Machida Incorporated ....G....... 845 365-0600
  Orangeburg *(G-12683)*

INSTRUMENTS, OPTICAL: Elements & Assemblies, Exc Ophthalmic
Applied Coatings Holding Corp.............G....... 585 482-0300
  Rochester *(G-13636)*
Photon Gear Inc ....F...... 585 265-3360
  Ontario *(G-12660)*

INSTRUMENTS, OPTICAL: Gratings, Diffraction
Newport Rochester Inc......................D...... 585 262-1325
  Rochester *(G-13971)*

INSTRUMENTS, OPTICAL: Grinding, Lens Exc Ophthalmic
Cnc Systems 2000 Inc ....E...... 585 265-0160
  Ontario *(G-12649)*

INSTRUMENTS, OPTICAL: Lenses, All Types Exc Ophthalmic
21st Century Optics Inc........................E...... 347 527-1079
  Long Island City *(G-7362)*
Advanced Glass Industries Inc.............D...... 585 458-8040
  Rochester *(G-13606)*
Enplas America Inc............................G....... 646 892-7811
  New York *(G-9686)*
Jml Optical Industries LLC ....D...... 585 248-8900
  Rochester *(G-13894)*
Lens Triptar Co Inc ....G....... 585 473-4470
  Rochester *(G-13911)*
Optics Technology Inc........................G....... 585 586-0950
  Pittsford *(G-13023)*
Optimax Systems Inc.........................C....... 585 265-1020
  Ontario *(G-12658)*
Rochester Precision Optics LLC...........C....... 585 292-5450
  West Henrietta *(G-16249)*
Spectrum Thin Films Inc ....E...... 631 901-1010
  Hauppauge *(G-5946)*

INSTRUMENTS, OPTICAL: Mirrors
Hudson Mirror LLC ....E...... 914 930-8906
  Peekskill *(G-12922)*
North American Enclosures Inc ....E...... 631 234-9500
  Central Islip *(G-3381)*

INSTRUMENTS, OPTICAL: Prisms
Ariel Optics Inc.................................G....... 585 265-4820
  Ontario *(G-12647)*

INSTRUMENTS, OPTICAL: Spyglasses
Digitac Inc..F...... 732 215-4020
  Brooklyn *(G-1777)*

INSTRUMENTS, OPTICAL: Test & Inspection
Quality Vision Intl Inc ....B...... 585 544-0450
  Rochester *(G-14061)*
Videk Inc ....E...... 585 377-0377
  Fairport *(G-4665)*

INSTRUMENTS, SURGICAL & MEDICAL: Blood & Bone Work
Drive Medical Spv LLC ....G....... 516 998-4600
  Port Washington *(G-13255)*
Future Diagnostics LLC ....E...... 347 434-6700
  Brooklyn *(G-1910)*
Manhattan Eastside Dev Corp ....F...... 212 305-3275
  New York *(G-10685)*

INSTRUMENTS, SURGICAL & MEDICAL: Blood Pressure
American Diagnostic Corp..................D...... 631 273-6155
  Hauppauge *(G-5765)*
N Y B P Inc ....G....... 585 624-2541
  Mendon *(G-8093)*
W A Baum Co Inc ....E...... 631 226-3940
  Copiague *(G-3793)*

INSTRUMENTS, SURGICAL & MEDICAL: Catheters
Angiodynamics Inc ....C....... 706 846-3126
  Glens Falls *(G-5417)*
Nasco Enterprises Inc ....G....... 516 921-9696
  Syosset *(G-15223)*
Novamed-Usa Inc..............................E...... 914 789-2100
  Elmsford *(G-4556)*
Vante Inc ....F...... 716 778-7691
  Newfane *(G-12254)*

INSTRUMENTS, SURGICAL & MEDICAL: IV Transfusion
Sigma Intl Gen Med Apprtus LLC ....B...... 585 798-3901
  Medina *(G-7990)*

INSTRUMENTS, SURGICAL & MEDICAL: Inhalation Therapy
Beacon Spch Lnge Pthlgy Phys ....F...... 516 626-1635
  Roslyn *(G-14443)*

INSTRUMENTS, SURGICAL & MEDICAL: Inhalators
Ip Med Inc ....G....... 516 766-3800
  Oceanside *(G-12541)*

INSTRUMENTS, SURGICAL & MEDICAL: Knives
Huron TI Cutter Grinding Inc ....E...... 631 420-7000
  Farmingdale *(G-4782)*

INSTRUMENTS, SURGICAL & MEDICAL: Lasers, Surgical
Aerolase Corporation ....D...... 914 345-8300
  Tarrytown *(G-15472)*
Clerio Vision Inc.................................F...... 617 216-7881
  Rochester *(G-13714)*

INSTRUMENTS, SURGICAL & MEDICAL: Muscle Exercise, Ophthalmic
Biodex Medical Systems Inc ....C....... 631 924-9000
  Shirley *(G-14832)*
Biodex Medical Systems Inc ....E...... 631 924-3146
  Shirley *(G-14833)*

INSTRUMENTS, SURGICAL & MEDICAL: Ophthalmic
Bausch & Lomb Incorporated..............B...... 585 338-6000
  Rochester *(G-13655)*
Corning Tropel Corporation ....C....... 585 377-3200
  Fairport *(G-4629)*
Sonomed Inc ....E...... 516 354-0900
  New Hyde Park *(G-8564)*

INSTRUMENTS, SURGICAL & MEDICAL: Physiotherapy, Electrical
Fabrication Enterprises Inc..................E...... 914 591-9300
  Elmsford *(G-4543)*

INSTRUMENTS, SURGICAL & MEDICAL: Skin Grafting
Skyler Brand Ventures LLC ....G....... 646 979-5904
  New York *(G-11615)*

INSTRUMENTS, SURGICAL & MEDICAL: Suction Therapy
Njr Medical Devices ....E...... 440 258-8204
  Cedarhurst *(G-3336)*
Repro Med Systems Inc ....D...... 845 469-2042
  Chester *(G-3480)*

INSTRUMENTS: Analytical
A S A Precision Co Inc.......................G....... 845 482-4870
  Jeffersonville *(G-6778)*
Advanced Mtl Analytics LLC ....G....... 321 684-0528
  Vestal *(G-15808)*
Bristol Instruments Inc ....G....... 585 924-2620
  Victor *(G-15833)*
Brookhaven Instruments Corp ....E...... 631 758-3200
  Holtsville *(G-6237)*
Carl Zeiss Inc....................................C....... 914 747-1800
  Thornwood *(G-15502)*
Ceres Technologies Inc......................D...... 845 247-4701
  Saugerties *(G-14604)*
Chromosense LLC ....G....... 646 541-2302
  Rye Brook *(G-14490)*
Corning Incorporated ....G....... 607 974-6729
  Painted Post *(G-12837)*
East Hills Instrument Inc ....F...... 516 621-8686
  Westbury *(G-16325)*
Equine Imaging LLC ....E...... 414 326-0665
  Port Washington *(G-13258)*
General Microwave Corporation..........F...... 516 802-0900
  Syosset *(G-15219)*
High Voltage Inc ....E...... 518 329-3275
  Copake *(G-3746)*
Ion-Tof Usa Inc ....G....... 845 352-8082
  Spring Valley *(G-14996)*
Life Technologies Corporation ....D...... 716 774-6700
  Grand Island *(G-5505)*
Multiwire Laboratories Ltd ....G....... 607 257-3378
  Ithaca *(G-6598)*

Employee Codes: A=Over 500 employees, B=251-500
C=101-250, D=51-100, E=20-50, F=10-19, G=5-9

2019 Harris
New York Manufacturers Directory

INSTRUMENTS: Analytical

Nanotronics Imaging Inc ....E...... 212 401-6209
Brooklyn *(G-2242)*
Nikon Instruments Inc ....D...... 631 547-4200
Melville *(G-8052)*
Photonics Industries Intl Inc ....D...... 631 218-2240
Ronkonkoma *(G-14398)*
Rheonix Inc ....D...... 607 257-1242
Ithaca *(G-6608)*
Smartpill Corporation ....E...... 716 882-0701
Buffalo *(G-3067)*
Thermo Fisher Scientific Inc ....E...... 585 899-7780
Penfield *(G-12946)*
Thermo Fisher Scientific Inc ....G...... 716 774-6700
Grand Island *(G-5515)*
Thermo Fisher Scientific Inc ....B...... 585 458-8008
Rochester *(G-14166)*
Thermo Fisher Scientific Inc ....A...... 585 899-7610
Rochester *(G-14167)*
Veeco Instruments Inc ....C...... 516 677-0200
Woodbury *(G-16633)*
Velp Scientific Inc ....G...... 631 573-6002
Bohemia *(G-1105)*

INSTRUMENTS: Colonoscopes, Electromedical

Gravity East Village Inc ....G...... 212 388-9788
New York *(G-9979)*

INSTRUMENTS: Combustion Control, Indl

Aureonic ....G...... 518 791-9331
Gansevoort *(G-5242)*

INSTRUMENTS: Electrocardiographs

Integrated Medical Devices ....G...... 315 457-4200
Liverpool *(G-7238)*

INSTRUMENTS: Electrolytic Conductivity, Indl

Mark - 10 Corporation ....E...... 631 842-9200
Copiague *(G-3769)*

INSTRUMENTS: Endoscopic Eqpt, Electromedical

Elizabeth Wood ....G...... 315 492-5470
Syracuse *(G-15315)*

INSTRUMENTS: Function Generators

Allied Motion Technologies Inc ....C...... 716 242-8634
Amherst *(G-211)*

INSTRUMENTS: Generators Tachometer

Make-Waves Instrument Corp ....E...... 716 681-7524
Buffalo *(G-2936)*

INSTRUMENTS: Indl Process Control

Ametek Inc ....D...... 585 263-7700
Rochester *(G-13630)*
Betatronix Inc ....E...... 631 582-6740
Ronkonkoma *(G-14319)*
Ceres Technologies Inc ....D...... 845 247-4701
Saugerties *(G-14604)*
Defelsko Corporation ....D...... 315 393-4450
Ogdensburg *(G-12573)*
Digital Analysis Corporation ....F...... 315 685-0760
Skaneateles *(G-14869)*
Dyna-Empire Inc ....C...... 516 222-2700
Garden City *(G-5256)*
East Hills Instrument Inc ....F...... 516 621-8686
Westbury *(G-16325)*
Electronic Machine Parts LLC ....E...... 631 434-3700
Hauppauge *(G-5818)*
Emerson Electric Co ....E...... 212 244-2490
New York *(G-9668)*
Fts Systems Inc ....D...... 845 687-5300
Stone Ridge *(G-15161)*
Gurley Precision Instrs Corp ....C...... 518 272-6300
Troy *(G-15607)*
Hades Manufacturing Corp ....F...... 631 249-4244
Farmingdale *(G-4778)*
Herman H Sticht Company Inc ....G...... 718 852-7602
Brooklyn *(G-1974)*
Hilliard Corporation ....B...... 607 733-7121
Elmira *(G-4492)*

Hilliard Corporation ....G...... 607 733-7121
Elmira *(G-4493)*
Integrated Control Corp ....E...... 631 673-5100
Huntington *(G-6400)*
Koehler Instrument Company Inc ...D...... 631 589-3800
Holtsville *(G-6240)*
Magtrol Inc ....F...... 716 668-5555
Buffalo *(G-2935)*
Mausner Equipment Co Inc ....C...... 631 689-7358
Setauket *(G-14795)*
Mks Instruments Inc ....E...... 585 292-7472
Rochester *(G-13949)*
Nutec Components Inc ....F...... 631 242-1224
Deer Park *(G-4018)*
Orthstar Enterprises Inc ....D...... 607 562-2100
Horseheads *(G-6323)*
Parrington Instruments ....G...... 518 373-8420
Rexford *(G-13482)*
Pcb Group Inc ....E...... 716 684-0001
Depew *(G-4100)*
Poseidon Systems LLC ....F...... 585 239-6025
Rochester *(G-14028)*
Pulsafeeder Inc ....C...... 585 292-8000
Rochester *(G-14054)*
R K B Opto-Electronics Inc ....F...... 315 455-6636
Syracuse *(G-15400)*
Rotronic Instrument Corp ....G...... 631 427-3898
Huntington *(G-6413)*
Schneider Elc Systems USA Inc ....F...... 214 527-3099
New York *(G-11508)*
Sixnet Holdings LLC ....G...... 518 877-5173
Ballston Lake *(G-572)*
Solar Metrology LLC ....G...... 845 247-4701
Holbrook *(G-6209)*
Tel-Tru Inc ....C...... 585 232-1440
Rochester *(G-14162)*
Telog Instruments Inc ....E...... 585 742-3000
Victor *(G-15872)*
Thread Check Inc ....D...... 631 231-1515
Hauppauge *(G-5958)*
Transtech Systems Inc ....E...... 518 370-5558
Latham *(G-7095)*
Vacuum Instrument Corporation .....D...... 631 737-0900
Ronkonkoma *(G-14427)*
Veeco Instruments Inc ....C...... 516 677-0200
Woodbury *(G-16633)*
Vertiv Corporation ....G...... 516 349-8500
Plainview *(G-13101)*
Winters Instruments Inc ....E...... 281 880-8607
Buffalo *(G-3133)*
Xentaur Corporation ....E...... 631 345-3434
Yaphank *(G-16729)*

INSTRUMENTS: Laser, Scientific & Engineering

Cambridge Manufacturing LLC ....G...... 516 326-1350
New Hyde Park *(G-8521)*
Gemprint Corporation ....E...... 212 997-0007
New York *(G-9897)*
Micro Photo Acoustics Inc ....E...... 631 750-6035
Ronkonkoma *(G-14377)*
Porous Materials Inc ....F...... 607 257-5544
Ithaca *(G-6605)*
Uptek Solutions Corp ....E...... 631 256-5565
Bohemia *(G-1104)*

INSTRUMENTS: Measurement, Indl Process

Packaging Tech & Insptn LLC ....E...... 914 337-2005
Tuckahoe *(G-15645)*
Riverhawk Company LP ....E...... 315 624-7171
New Hartford *(G-8510)*
Robat Inc ....G...... 518 812-6244
Clifton Park *(G-3575)*

INSTRUMENTS: Measuring & Controlling

Aspex Incorporated ....E...... 212 966-0410
New York *(G-8936)*
Biodesign Inc of New York ....F...... 845 454-6610
Carmel *(G-3274)*
Carl Zeiss Inc ....C...... 914 747-1800
Thornwood *(G-15502)*
Circor Aerospace Inc ....D...... 631 737-1900
Hauppauge *(G-5789)*
Computer Instruments Corp ....E...... 516 876-8400
Westbury *(G-16321)*
Cosense Inc ....G...... 516 364-9161
Syosset *(G-15212)*
Dayton T Brown Inc ....B...... 631 589-6300
Bohemia *(G-1011)*

Defelsko Corporation ....D...... 315 393-4450
Ogdensburg *(G-12573)*
Dispersion Technology Inc ....G...... 914 241-4777
Bedford Hills *(G-775)*
Dyna-Empire Inc ....C...... 516 222-2700
Garden City *(G-5256)*
Dynamic Systems Inc ....E...... 518 283-5350
Poestenkill *(G-13180)*
East Hills Instrument Inc ....F...... 516 621-8686
Westbury *(G-16325)*
Electrical Controls Link ....E...... 585 924-7010
Victor *(G-15843)*
Electro-Optical Products Corp ....G...... 718 456-6000
Ridgewood *(G-13535)*
Erbessd Reliability LLC ....E...... 518 874-2700
Glens Falls *(G-5424)*
Fougera Pharmaceuticals Inc ....F...... 631 454-7677
Melville *(G-8026)*
Freeman Technology Inc ....E...... 732 829-8345
Bayside *(G-745)*
Gei International Inc ....G...... 315 463-9261
East Syracuse *(G-4342)*
Hci Engineering ....G...... 315 336-3450
Rome *(G-14252)*
Herman H Sticht Company Inc ....G...... 718 852-7602
Brooklyn *(G-1974)*
Hipotronics Inc ....C...... 845 279-8091
Brewster *(G-1167)*
Images Si Inc ....F...... 718 966-3694
Staten Island *(G-15089)*
Imaginant Inc ....E...... 585 264-0480
Pittsford *(G-13015)*
Itin Scale Co Inc ....F...... 718 336-5900
Brooklyn *(G-2019)*
Kem Medical Products Corp ....G...... 631 454-6565
Farmingdale *(G-4802)*
Kistler Instrument Corporation ....D...... 716 691-5100
Amherst *(G-234)*
Kld Labs Inc ....E...... 631 549-4222
Hauppauge *(G-5857)*
Liberty Controls Inc ....G...... 718 461-0600
College Point *(G-3653)*
Machine Technology Inc ....G...... 845 454-4030
Poughkeepsie *(G-13352)*
Mason Industries Inc ....B...... 631 348-0282
Hauppauge *(G-5881)*
Orolia Usa Inc ....E...... 585 321-5800
Rochester *(G-13992)*
Pcb Piezotronics Inc ....F...... 716 684-0001
Depew *(G-4101)*
Peerless Instrument Co Inc ....C...... 631 396-6500
Farmingdale *(G-4845)*
Poseidon Systems LLC ....F...... 585 239-6025
Rochester *(G-14028)*
Precision Design Systems Inc ....E...... 585 426-4500
Rochester *(G-14034)*
Pronto Gas Heating Sups Inc ....G...... 718 292-0707
Bronx *(G-1366)*
Qualitrol Company LLC ....C...... 586 643-3717
Fairport *(G-4653)*
Research Frontiers Inc ....C...... 516 364-1902
Woodbury *(G-16630)*
Riverhawk Company LP ....E...... 315 624-7171
New Hartford *(G-8510)*
RJ Harvey Instrument Corp ....F...... 845 359-3943
Tappan *(G-15471)*
Schenck Corporation ....D...... 631 242-4010
Deer Park *(G-4040)*
Schenck Trebel Corp ....D...... 631 242-4010
Deer Park *(G-4041)*
Schott Corporation ....D...... 914 831-2200
Elmsford *(G-4564)*
Teledyne Lecroy Inc ....C...... 845 425-2000
Chestnut Ridge *(G-3497)*
Telog Instruments Inc ....E...... 585 742-3000
Victor *(G-15872)*
Vacuum Instrument Corporation .....E...... 631 737-0900
Ronkonkoma *(G-14427)*
Videk Inc ....E...... 585 377-0377
Fairport *(G-4665)*
Weiss Instruments Inc ....D...... 631 207-1200
Holtsville *(G-6250)*
Xeku Corporation ....F...... 607 761-1447
Vestal *(G-15826)*
York Industries Inc ....E...... 516 746-3736
Garden City Park *(G-5290)*
Zomega Terahertz Corporation ....F...... 585 347-4337
Webster *(G-16109)*

INSTRUMENTS: Measuring Electricity

Agilent Technologies Inc ....A....... 877 424-4536
New York *(G-8769)*

American Quality Technology ....F....... 607 777-9488
Binghamton *(G-861)*

Ametek Inc ....D....... 585 263-7700
Rochester *(G-13630)*

C Speed LLC ....E....... 315 453-1043
Liverpool *(G-7227)*

C-Flex Bearing Co Inc ....F....... 315 895-7454
Frankfort *(G-5104)*

Cetek Inc ....E....... 845 452-3510
Poughkeepsie *(G-13331)*

East Hills Instrument Inc ....F....... 516 621-8686
Westbury *(G-16325)*

Edo LLC ....F....... 631 218-1413
Bohemia *(G-1020)*

Edo LLC ....A....... 631 630-4200
Amityville *(G-273)*

Ems Development Corporation ....D....... 631 924-4736
Yaphank *(G-16708)*

Enertiv Inc ....G....... 646 350-3525
New York *(G-9682)*

Interntnal Elctronic Mchs Corp ....E....... 518 268-1636
Troy *(G-15610)*

Larry Kings Corporation ....G....... 718 481-8741
Rosedale *(G-14440)*

Linde LLC ....D....... 716 773-7552
Grand Island *(G-5506)*

Logitek Inc ....D....... 631 567-1100
Bohemia *(G-1048)*

Ludl Electronic Products Ltd ....E....... 914 769-6111
Hawthorne *(G-5992)*

Magnetic Analysis Corporation ....D....... 914 530-2000
Elmsford *(G-4549)*

Magtrol Inc ....E....... 716 668-5555
Buffalo *(G-2935)*

North Atlantic Industries Inc ....E....... 631 567-1100
Bohemia *(G-1065)*

North Atlantic Industries Inc ....C....... 631 567-1100
Bohemia *(G-1066)*

Peerless Instrument Co Inc ....C....... 631 396-6500
Farmingdale *(G-4845)*

R K B Opto-Electronics Inc ....F....... 315 455-6636
Syracuse *(G-15400)*

Rodale Wireless Inc ....E....... 631 231-0044
Hauppauge *(G-5929)*

Scientific Components Corp ....E....... 631 243-4901
Deer Park *(G-4042)*

Transcat Inc ....B....... 585 352-7777
Rochester *(G-14175)*

Trek Inc ....F....... 716 438-7555
Lockport *(G-7338)*

Viatran Corporation ....E....... 716 564-7813
Tonawanda *(G-15589)*

W & W Manufacturing Co ....F....... 516 942-0011
West Islip *(G-16261)*

Zumbach Electronics Corp ....D....... 914 241-7080
Mount Kisco *(G-8362)*

INSTRUMENTS: Measuring, Electrical Energy

Apogee Power Usa Inc ....F....... 202 746-2890
Hartsdale *(G-5742)*

Quadlogic Controls Corporation ....D....... 212 930-9300
Long Island City *(G-7565)*

INSTRUMENTS: Measuring, Electrical Power

Allied Motion Systems Corp ....F....... 716 691-5868
Amherst *(G-210)*

Primesouth Inc ....F....... 585 567-4191
Fillmore *(G-4938)*

INSTRUMENTS: Measuring, Electrical Quantities

Vermed Inc ....D....... 800 669-6905
Buffalo *(G-3117)*

INSTRUMENTS: Medical & Surgical

A Titan Instruments Inc ....F....... 716 667-9211
Orchard Park *(G-12696)*

Advanced Placement LLC ....E....... 949 281-9086
Holbrook *(G-6170)*

Ala Scientific Instruments Inc ....F....... 631 393-6401
Farmingdale *(G-4712)*

Alconox Inc ....G....... 914 948-4040
White Plains *(G-16418)*

AM Bickford Inc ....F....... 716 652-1590
Wales Center *(G-15900)*

American Healthcare Supply Inc ....F....... 212 674-3636
New York *(G-8828)*

Angiodynamics Inc ....E....... 518 761-6867
Queensbury *(G-13417)*

Angiodynamics Inc ....B....... 518 975-1400
Queensbury *(G-13418)*

Angiodynamics Inc ....B....... 518 792-4112
Glens Falls *(G-5416)*

Angiodynamics Inc ....B....... 518 742-4430
Queensbury *(G-13419)*

Angiodynamics Inc ....B....... 518 795-1400
Latham *(G-7063)*

Argon Medical Devices Inc ....G....... 585 321-1130
Henrietta *(G-6031)*

Astra Tool & Instrument Mfg ....E....... 914 747-3863
Hawthorne *(G-5983)*

Bioresearch Inc ....G....... 212 734-5315
Pound Ridge *(G-13375)*

Boehm Surgical Instrument Corp ....F....... 585 436-6584
Rochester *(G-13671)*

Buffalo Filter LLC ....D....... 716 835-7000
Lancaster *(G-7011)*

Buxton Medical Equipment Corp ....E....... 631 957-4500
Lindenhurst *(G-7164)*

C R Bard Inc ....B....... 518 793-2531
Queensbury *(G-13421)*

C R Bard Inc ....A....... 518 793-2531
Glens Falls *(G-5420)*

Caliber Imging Diagnostics Inc ....E....... 585 239-9800
Rochester *(G-13687)*

CN Group Incorporated ....A....... 914 358-5690
White Plains *(G-16438)*

Cognitiveflow Sensor Tech ....G....... 631 513-9369
Stony Brook *(G-15164)*

Common Sense Marketing Inc ....G....... 516 282-1214
Mineola *(G-8213)*

Conmed Corporation ....D....... 315 797-8375
Utica *(G-15686)*

Cynosure Inc ....G....... 516 594-3333
Hicksville *(G-6078)*

Daxor Corporation ....F....... 212 330-8500
New York *(G-9492)*

Delcath Systems Inc ....E....... 212 489-2100
New York *(G-9497)*

Derm-Buro Inc ....E....... 516 694-8300
Plainview *(G-13050)*

Designs For Vision Inc ....C....... 631 585-3300
Bohemia *(G-1016)*

Elliquence LLC ....F....... 516 277-9000
Baldwin *(G-538)*

Endovor Inc ....G....... 214 679-7385
New York *(G-9676)*

Endovor LLC ....G....... 214 679-7385
New York *(G-9677)*

Esc Control Electronics LLC ....E....... 631 467-5328
Sayville *(G-14627)*

Extek Inc ....E....... 585 533-1672
Rush *(G-14472)*

Eyeglass Service Industries ....G....... 914 666-3150
Bedford Hills *(G-776)*

Flexbar Machine Corporation ....E....... 631 582-8440
Islandia *(G-6528)*

Flowmedica Inc ....F....... 800 772-6446
Queensbury *(G-13423)*

Fluorologic Inc ....G....... 585 248-2796
Pittsford *(G-13012)*

Ftt Medical Inc ....G....... 585 444-0980
Rochester *(G-13819)*

Gaymar Industries Inc ....B....... 800 828-7341
Orchard Park *(G-12715)*

Getinge Usa Inc ....C....... 800 475-9040
Rochester *(G-13834)*

Harmac Medical Products Inc ....B....... 716 897-4500
Buffalo *(G-2866)*

Hogil Pharmaceutical Corp ....F....... 914 681-1800
White Plains *(G-16460)*

Hurryworks LLC ....D....... 516 998-4600
Port Washington *(G-13266)*

Incredible Scents Inc ....G....... 516 656-3300
Greenvale *(G-5630)*

J H M Engineering ....E....... 718 871-1810
Brooklyn *(G-2023)*

J Jamner Surgical Instrs Inc ....E....... 914 592-9051
Hawthorne *(G-5988)*

Jaracz Jr Joseph Paul ....G....... 716 533-1377
Orchard Park *(G-12722)*

Liberty Install Inc ....F....... 631 651-5655
Centerport *(G-3350)*

Medical Depot Inc ....C....... 516 998-4600
Port Washington *(G-13285)*

Medical Technology Products ....G....... 631 285-6640
Greenlawn *(G-5624)*

Medline Industries Inc ....B....... 845 344-3301
Middletown *(G-8163)*

Medsource Technologies LLC ....D....... 716 662-5025
Orchard Park *(G-12729)*

Misonix Inc ....D....... 631 694-9555
Farmingdale *(G-4828)*

Modular Medical Corp ....E....... 718 829-2626
Bronx *(G-1334)*

Moog Inc ....A....... 716 652-2000
Elma *(G-4453)*

Nano Vibronix Inc ....G....... 516 374-8330
Cedarhurst *(G-3335)*

Navilyst Medical Inc ....A....... 800 833-9973
Glens Falls *(G-5436)*

Ocala Group LLC ....F....... 516 233-2750
New Hyde Park *(G-8555)*

Orics Industries Inc ....E....... 718 461-8613
Farmingdale *(G-4839)*

Ortho Medical Products ....E....... 212 879-3700
New York *(G-11063)*

Orthocon Inc ....E....... 914 357-2600
Irvington *(G-6508)*

P-Ryton Corp ....F....... 718 937-7052
Long Island City *(G-7545)*

Pall Corporation ....A....... 516 484-5400
Port Washington *(G-13295)*

Pall Corporation ....A....... 607 753-6041
Cortland *(G-3885)*

Parace Bionics LLC ....G....... 877 727-2231
New York *(G-11105)*

Parkchester Dps LLC ....C....... 718 823-4411
Bronx *(G-1352)*

Pavmed Inc ....G....... 212 401-1951
New York *(G-11127)*

Peter Digioia ....G....... 516 644-5517
Plainview *(G-13081)*

Precimed Inc ....E....... 716 759-5600
Clarence *(G-3539)*

Professional Medical Devices ....F....... 914 835-0614
Harrison *(G-5733)*

Progressive Orthotics Ltd ....G....... 631 732-5556
Selden *(G-14766)*

Rdd Pharma Inc ....G....... 302 319-9970
New York *(G-11337)*

Reichert Inc ....C....... 716 686-4500
Depew *(G-4104)*

Responselink Inc ....G....... 518 424-7776
Latham *(G-7092)*

Retia Medical LLC ....G....... 914 594-1986
Valhalla *(G-15746)*

Robert Bosch LLC ....E....... 315 733-3312
Utica *(G-15731)*

Seedlngs Lf Scnce Ventures LLC ....G....... 917 913-8511
New York *(G-11532)*

Seneca TEC Inc ....G....... 585 381-2645
Fairport *(G-4658)*

Simulaids Inc ....D....... 845 679-2475
Saugerties *(G-14616)*

Solid-Look Corporation ....G....... 917 683-1780
Douglaston *(G-4140)*

Soniquence LLC ....F....... 516 267-6400
Baldwin *(G-543)*

St Silicones Corporation ....F....... 518 406-3208
Clifton Park *(G-3578)*

Striker Orthopedics ....E....... 585 381-1773
Rochester *(G-14147)*

Symmetry Medical Inc ....G....... 845 368-4573
Hillburn *(G-6155)*

Tril Inc ....G....... 631 645-7989
Copiague *(G-3789)*

Vasomedical Inc ....E....... 516 997-4600
Plainview *(G-13096)*

Viterion Corporation ....F....... 914 333-6033
Elmsford *(G-4576)*

Vizio Medical Devices LLC ....F....... 646 845-7382
New York *(G-12049)*

Wyeth Holdings LLC ....D....... 845 602-5000
Pearl River *(G-12913)*

INSTRUMENTS: Meteorological

Climatronics Corp ....F....... 541 471-7111
Bohemia *(G-994)*

INSTRUMENTS: Microwave Test

Hamilton Marketing Corporation ....G....... 585 395-0678
Brockport *(G-1191)*

PRODUCT

Employee Codes: A=Over 500 employees, B=251-500
C=101-250, D=51-100, E=20-50, F=10-19, G=5-9

INSTRUMENTS: Optical, Analytical

INSTRUMENTS: Optical, Analytical
- Applied Image Inc ....E....... 585 482-0300
  Rochester *(G-13637)*
- Exfo Burleigh Pdts Group Inc ....D....... 585 301-1530
  Canandaigua *(G-3220)*
- Qioptiq, Inc. ....E....... 585 223-2370
  Fairport *(G-4652)*

INSTRUMENTS: Oscillographs & Oscilloscopes
- Teledyne Lecroy Inc..............................C....... 845 425-2000
  Chestnut Ridge *(G-3497)*

INSTRUMENTS: Pressure Measurement, Indl
- Taber Acquisition Corp ....D....... 716 694-4000
  North Tonawanda *(G-12458)*
- Viatran Corporation ....E....... 716 564-7813
  Tonawanda *(G-15589)*

INSTRUMENTS: Radar Testing, Electric
- Anmar Acquisition LLC ....G....... 585 352-7777
  Rochester *(G-13634)*

INSTRUMENTS: Radio Frequency Measuring
- Omni-ID Usa Inc ....E....... 585 697-9913
  Rochester *(G-13987)*
- T & C Power Conversion Inc ....F....... 585 482-5551
  Rochester *(G-14154)*
- W D Technology Inc.............................G....... 914 779-8738
  Eastchester *(G-4383)*

INSTRUMENTS: Standards & Calibration, Electrical Measuring
- Ah Elctronic Test Eqp Repr Ctr ....F....... 631 234-8979
  Central Islip *(G-3354)*

INSTRUMENTS: Telemetering, Indl Process
- Medsafe Systems Inc...........................G....... 516 883-8222
  Port Washington *(G-13287)*

INSTRUMENTS: Temperature Measurement, Indl
- Rotronic Instrument Corp ....F....... 631 348-6844
  Hauppauge *(G-5930)*
- Springfield Control Systems................G....... 718 631-0870
  Douglaston *(G-4141)*
- Tel-Tru Inc ....D....... 585 295-0225
  Rochester *(G-14163)*

INSTRUMENTS: Test, Electrical, Engine
- Practical Instrument Elec Inc...............F....... 585 872-9350
  Webster *(G-16092)*

INSTRUMENTS: Test, Electronic & Electric Measurement
- Advanced Testing Tech Inc ....C....... 631 231-8777
  Hauppauge *(G-5755)*
- Avanel Industries Inc ....F....... 516 333-0990
  Westbury *(G-16318)*
- Clayton Dubilier & Rice Fun................E....... 212 407-5200
  New York *(G-9324)*
- Comtech PST Corp ....C....... 631 777-8900
  Melville *(G-8011)*
- John Ramsey Elec Svcs LLC ....G....... 585 298-9596
  Victor *(G-15851)*
- Millivac Instruments Inc ....G....... 518 355-8300
  Schenectady *(G-14698)*
- Nas CP Corp ....E....... 718 961-6757
  College Point *(G-3657)*
- Northeast Metrology Corp...................F....... 716 827-3770
  Depew *(G-4098)*
- Optimized Devices Inc........................F....... 914 769-6100
  Pleasantville *(G-13175)*
- Photonix Technologies Inc ....F....... 607 786-4600
  Endicott *(G-4608)*
- Precision Filters Inc.............................E....... 607 277-3550
  Ithaca *(G-6606)*
- Ramsey Electronics LLC ....E....... 585 924-4560
  Victor *(G-15863)*
- Scj Associates Inc ....E....... 585 359-0600
  Rochester *(G-14117)*

INSTRUMENTS: Test, Electronic & Electrical Circuits
- Automated Control Logic Inc..............F....... 914 769-8880
  Thornwood *(G-15501)*
- Automation Correct LLC......................G....... 315 299-3589
  Syracuse *(G-15249)*
- Avcom of Virginia Inc ....D....... 585 924-4560
  Victor *(G-15830)*
- Clarke Hess Communication RES.......G....... 631 698-3350
  Medford *(G-7944)*
- General Microwave Corporation ....F....... 516 802-0900
  Syosset *(G-15219)*
- Hipotronics Inc ....C....... 845 279-8091
  Brewster *(G-1167)*
- Iet Labs Inc ....F....... 516 334-5959
  Roslyn Heights *(G-14456)*
- Lexan Industries Inc ....F....... 631 434-7586
  Bay Shore *(G-696)*
- Pulsar Technology Systems Inc ....G....... 718 361-9292
  Long Island City *(G-7562)*

INSTRUMENTS: Testing, Semiconductor
- Pragmatics Technology Inc ....G....... 845 795-5071
  Milton *(G-8196)*

INSTRUMENTS: Thermal Conductive, Indl
- Ktk Thermal Technologies Inc ....E....... 585 678-9025
  Macedon *(G-7700)*

INSTRUMENTS: Vibration
- SKF USA Inc ....D....... 716 661-2600
  Jamestown *(G-6747)*

INSTRUMENTS: Viscometer, Indl Process
- Beauty America LLC.............................E....... 917 744-1430
  Great Neck *(G-5539)*

INSULATION & CUSHIONING FOAM: Polystyrene
- C P Chemical Co Inc ....G....... 914 428-2517
  White Plains *(G-16434)*
- Carlisle Construction Mtls LLC ....D....... 386 753-0786
  Montgomery *(G-8310)*
- Foam Products Inc...............................E....... 718 292-4830
  Bronx *(G-1273)*
- New York State Foam Enrgy LLC ....G....... 845 534-4656
  Cornwall *(G-3835)*
- Shelter Enterprises Inc........................D....... 518 237-4100
  Cohoes *(G-3621)*
- Soundcoat Company Inc ....G....... 631 242-2200
  Deer Park *(G-4047)*
- Thermal Foams/Syracuse Inc ....G....... 716 874-6474
  Buffalo *(G-3093)*

INSULATION MATERIALS WHOLESALERS
- Regional MGT & Consulting Inc ....F....... 718 599-3718
  Brooklyn *(G-2393)*

INSULATION: Felt
- Shannon Entps Wstn NY Inc................D....... 716 693-7954
  North Tonawanda *(G-12450)*

INSULATION: Fiberglass
- Burnett Process Inc.............................G....... 585 254-8080
  Rochester *(G-13683)*
- Elliot Industries Inc ....F....... 716 287-3100
  Ellington *(G-4448)*
- Fbm Galaxy Inc ....F....... 315 463-5144
  East Syracuse *(G-4338)*
- Richlar Industries Inc ....F....... 315 463-5144
  East Syracuse *(G-4366)*

INSULATORS & INSULATION MATERIALS: Electrical
- Gerome Technologies Inc ....D....... 518 463-1324
  Menands *(G-8085)*
- J H C Fabrications Inc ....F....... 718 649-0065
  Brooklyn *(G-2022)*
- Varflex Corporation ....C....... 315 336-4400
  Rome *(G-14278)*
- Volt Tek Inc ....F....... 585 377-2050
  Fairport *(G-4666)*
- Von Roll Usa Inc...................................C....... 518 344-7100
  Schenectady *(G-14727)*

INSULATORS, PORCELAIN: Electrical
- Pfisterer Lapp LLC................................C....... 585 768-6221
  Le Roy *(G-7124)*
- Victor Insulators Inc ....C....... 585 924-2127
  Victor *(G-15875)*

INTEGRATED CIRCUITS, SEMICONDUCTOR NETWORKS, ETC
- Akoustis Inc..E....... 585 919-3073
  Canandaigua *(G-3210)*
- Artemis Inc..G....... 631 232-2424
  Hauppauge *(G-5770)*
- Central Semiconductor Corp ....D....... 631 435-1110
  Hauppauge *(G-5786)*
- Dionics-Usa Inc ....G....... 516 997-7474
  Westbury *(G-16323)*
- Elite Semi Conductor Products ....G....... 631 884-8400
  Lindenhurst *(G-7172)*
- Globalfoundries US Inc ....F....... 408 462-3900
  Ballston Spa *(G-583)*
- LSI Computer Systems.........................E....... 631 271-0400
  Melville *(G-8044)*
- Philips Medical Systems Mr ....B....... 518 782-1122
  Latham *(G-7089)*
- Plures Technologies Inc ....G....... 585 905-0554
  Canandaigua *(G-3231)*
- Pvi Solar Inc ....G....... 212 280-2100
  New York *(G-11286)*
- RSM Electron Power Inc ....D....... 631 586-7600
  Deer Park *(G-4039)*

INTERCOMMUNICATIONS SYSTEMS: Electric
- Andrea Systems LLC ....E....... 631 390-3140
  Farmingdale *(G-4721)*
- Apple Core Electronics Inc ....F....... 718 628-4068
  Brooklyn *(G-1542)*
- AVI-Spl Employee ....B....... 212 840-4801
  New York *(G-8977)*
- Capstream Technologies LLC ....G....... 716 945-7100
  Salamanca *(G-14524)*
- Curbell Medical Products Inc..............F....... 716 667-2520
  Orchard Park *(G-12711)*
- Curbell Medical Products Inc..............F....... 716 667-2520
  Orchard Park *(G-12712)*
- Frequency Electronics Inc ....C....... 516 794-4500
  Uniondale *(G-15668)*
- Global Technologies Inc......................D....... 631 243-7924
  Deer Park *(G-3982)*
- Goddard Design Co ....G....... 718 599-0170
  Brooklyn *(G-1936)*
- McDowell Research Co Inc ....D....... 315 332-7100
  Newark *(G-12200)*
- Nu2 Systems LLC ....F....... 914 719-7272
  White Plains *(G-16481)*
- Response Care Inc ....G....... 585 671-4144
  Webster *(G-16096)*
- Roanwell Corporation...........................E....... 718 401-0288
  Bronx *(G-1373)*
- Simrex Corporation ....G....... 716 206-0174
  Buffalo *(G-3066)*
- Telephonics Corporation......................A....... 631 755-7000
  Farmingdale *(G-4892)*
- Tokenize Inc..F....... 585 981-9919
  Rochester *(G-14172)*
- TX Rx Systems Inc ....C....... 716 549-4700
  Angola *(G-371)*
- Visiontron Corp ....E....... 631 582-8600
  Hauppauge *(G-5971)*

INTERIOR DECORATING SVCS
- Furniture Doctor Inc.............................G....... 585 657-6941
  Bloomfield *(G-954)*

INTERIOR DESIGN SVCS, NEC
- Ann Gish Inc..G....... 212 969-9200
  New York *(G-8871)*

INTERIOR DESIGNING SVCS
- Exhibit Corporation America ....E....... 718 937-2600
  Long Island City *(G-7441)*

PRODUCT SECTION

JEWELRY FINDINGS & LAPIDARY WORK

INTERIOR REPAIR SVCS
Auto-Mat Company Inc .... E 516 938-7373
Hicksville *(G-6062)*

INTRAVENOUS SOLUTIONS
Mercer Milling Co .... E 315 701-1334
Liverpool *(G-7246)*
Zenith Solutions .... G 718 575-8570
Flushing *(G-5062)*

INVERTERS: Nonrotating Electrical
Applied Power Systems Inc .... E 516 935-2230
Hicksville *(G-6059)*

INVERTERS: Rotating Electrical
IEC Holden Corporation .... F 518 213-3991
Plattsburgh *(G-13125)*

INVESTMENT ADVISORY SVCS
Nsgv Inc .... E 212 367-3167
New York *(G-11003)*
Value Line Inc .... D 212 907-1500
New York *(G-11988)*

INVESTMENT FUNDS: Open-Ended
Altius Aviation LLC .... G 315 455-7555
Syracuse *(G-15242)*
Kps Capital Partners LP .... E 212 338-5100
New York *(G-10476)*

INVESTORS: Security Speculators For Own Account
Acf Industries Holding LLC .... G 212 702-4363
New York *(G-8726)*

IRON & STEEL PRDTS: Hot-Rolled
A-1 Iron Works Inc .... G 718 927-4766
Brooklyn *(G-1461)*
Bebitz USA Inc .... G 516 280-8378
Hicksville *(G-6065)*
Hudson Valley Steel Products .... G 845 565-2270
Newburgh *(G-12229)*
Image Iron Works Inc .... G 718 592-8276
Corona *(G-3845)*
N C Iron Works Inc .... G 718 633-4660
Brooklyn *(G-2240)*

IRON & STEEL: Corrugating, Cold-Rolled
Renco Group Inc .... G 212 541-6000
New York *(G-11361)*

IRON ORE MINING
Essar Steel Minnesota LLC .... F 212 292-2600
New York *(G-9707)*

IRON OXIDES
Applied Minerals Inc .... F 212 226-4265
Brooklyn *(G-1543)*

IRONING BOARDS
Garment Care Systems LLC .... G 518 674-1826
Averill Park *(G-514)*

IRRADIATION EQPT: Nuclear
R M F Health Management L L C .... E 718 854-5400
Wantagh *(G-15926)*

IRRIGATION SYSTEMS, NEC Water Distribution Or Sply Systems
Sigelock Systems LLC .... G 888 744-3562
Oceanside *(G-12557)*

JANITORIAL & CUSTODIAL SVCS
New Dynamics Corporation .... E 845 692-0022
Middletown *(G-8167)*
R H Crown Co Inc .... E 518 762-4589
Johnstown *(G-6838)*

JANITORIAL EQPT & SPLYS WHOLESALERS
Emulso Corp .... G 716 854-2889
Tonawanda *(G-15538)*
Nationwide Sales and Service .... F 631 491-6625
Farmingdale *(G-4832)*

JEWELERS' FINDINGS & MATERIALS
Boucheron Joaillerie USA Inc .... G 212 715-7330
New York *(G-9126)*
Goldmark Inc .... E 718 438-0295
Brooklyn *(G-1939)*
Nathan Berrie & Sons Inc .... G 516 432-8500
Island Park *(G-6516)*
New York Findings Corp .... F 212 925-5745
New York *(G-10938)*
Renco Manufacturing Inc .... E 718 392-8877
Long Island City *(G-7575)*

JEWELERS' FINDINGS & MATERIALS: Castings
A J M Enterprises .... F 716 626-7294
Buffalo *(G-2679)*
Allstar Casting Corporation .... E 212 563-0909
New York *(G-8801)*
Ampex Casting Corporation .... E 212 719-1318
New York *(G-8847)*
Asco Castings Inc .... G 212 719-9800
Long Island City *(G-7389)*
Asur Jewelry Inc .... G 718 472-1687
Long Island City *(G-7393)*
Carrera Casting Corp .... C 212 382-3296
New York *(G-9215)*
D M J Casting Corp .... G 212 719-1951
New York *(G-9448)*
Frank Billanti Casting Co Inc .... F 212 221-0440
New York *(G-9840)*
Jaguar Casting Co Inc .... E 212 869-0197
New York *(G-10300)*
Jewelry Arts Manufacturing .... E 212 382-3583
New York *(G-10329)*
Karbra Company .... C 212 736-9300
New York *(G-10407)*
Satco Castings Service Inc .... E 516 354-1500
New Hyde Park *(G-8561)*

JEWELERS' FINDINGS & MATERIALS: Parts, Unassembled
Asa Manufacturing Inc .... E 718 853-3033
Brooklyn *(G-1560)*
Kemp Metal Products Inc .... E 516 997-8860
Westbury *(G-16348)*

JEWELERS' FINDINGS & MTLS: Jewel Prep, Instr, Tools, Watches
A J C Jewelry Contracting Inc .... G 212 594-3703
New York *(G-8696)*
D R S Watch Materials .... E 212 819-0470
New York *(G-9450)*
Zak Jewelry Tools Inc .... F 212 768-8122
New York *(G-12168)*

JEWELERS' FINDINGS/MTRLS: Gem Prep, Settings, Real/Imitation
Jim Wachtler Inc .... G 212 755-4367
New York *(G-10338)*
Nyman Jewelry Inc .... G 212 944-1976
New York *(G-11017)*

JEWELRY & PRECIOUS STONES WHOLESALERS
Ace Diamond Corp .... G 212 730-8451
New York *(G-8725)*
Clyde Duneier Inc .... D 212 398-1122
New York *(G-9336)*
Dabby-Reid Ltd .... F 212 356-0040
New York *(G-9452)*
Gemoro Inc .... G 212 768-8844
New York *(G-9896)*
Jayden Star LLC .... E 212 686-0400
New York *(G-10314)*
Justperfectmsp Ltd .... E 877 201-0005
New York *(G-10386)*
Leo Schachter Diamonds LLC .... D 212 688-2000
New York *(G-10552)*

Mark King Jewelry Inc .... G 212 921-0746
New York *(G-10705)*
Midura Jewels Inc .... G 213 265-8090
New York *(G-10801)*
Neil Savalia Inc .... F 212 869-0123
New York *(G-10903)*
Precision International Co Inc .... E 212 268-9090
New York *(G-11229)*
William Goldberg Diamond Corp .... E 212 980-4343
New York *(G-12110)*

JEWELRY APPAREL
Ale Viola LLC .... D 212 868-3808
New York *(G-8789)*
All The Rage Inc .... G 516 605-2001
Hicksville *(G-6058)*
Ateliers Tamalet Corp .... E 929 325-7976
New York *(G-8944)*
CJ Jewelry Inc .... F 212 719-2464
New York *(G-9316)*
Eastern Jewelry Mfg Co Inc .... E 212 840-0001
New York *(G-9610)*
Efron Designs Ltd .... G 718 482-8440
Long Island City *(G-7436)*
Fam Creations .... E 212 869-4833
New York *(G-9777)*
Fuzion Creations Intl LLC .... E 718 369-8800
Brooklyn *(G-1912)*
Gramercy Jewelry Mfg Corp .... E 212 268-0461
New York *(G-9969)*
H C Kionka & Co Inc .... F 212 227-3155
New York *(G-10014)*
Jaguar Jewelry Casting NY Inc .... G 212 768-4848
New York *(G-10301)*
Jayden Star LLC .... E 212 686-0400
New York *(G-10314)*
JC Crystal Inc .... E 212 594-0858
New York *(G-10318)*
Jewelry By Sarah Belle .... G 518 793-1626
Fort Ann *(G-5089)*
Le Hook Rouge LLC .... E 212 947-6272
Brooklyn *(G-2099)*
Leo Schachter & Co Inc .... E 212 688-2000
New York *(G-10551)*
Love Bright Jewelry Inc .... E 516 620-2509
Oceanside *(G-12546)*
MB Plastics Inc .... F 718 523-1180
Greenlawn *(G-5623)*
Park West Jewelry Inc .... E 646 329-6145
New York *(G-11116)*
R & R Grosbard Inc .... E 212 575-0077
New York *(G-11311)*
Riva Jewelry Manufacturing Inc .... C 718 361-3100
Brooklyn *(G-2405)*
Sterling Possessions Ltd .... G 212 594-0418
New York *(G-11707)*
Thomas Sasson Co Inc .... E 212 697-4998
New York *(G-11822)*
Whitney Boin Studio Inc .... E 914 377-4385
Yonkers *(G-16807)*

JEWELRY FINDINGS & LAPIDARY WORK
Christopher Designs Inc .... E 212 382-1013
New York *(G-9294)*
Creative Tools & Supply Inc .... G 212 279-7077
New York *(G-9422)*
Danhier Co LLC .... F 212 563-7683
New York *(G-9465)*
Gemini Manufactures .... F 716 633-0306
Cheektowaga *(G-3446)*
Kaprielian Enterprises Inc .... D 212 645-6623
New York *(G-10406)*
Leo Schachter Diamonds LLC .... D 212 688-2000
New York *(G-10552)*
Magic Novelty Co Inc .... E 212 304-2777
New York *(G-10667)*
Max Kahan Inc .... F 212 575-4646
New York *(G-10734)*
ME & Ro Inc .... G 212 431-8744
New York *(G-10748)*
R G Flair Co Inc .... E 631 586-7311
Bay Shore *(G-712)*
Townley Inc .... E 212 779-0544
New York *(G-11877)*
Via America Fine Jewelry Inc .... G 212 302-1218
New York *(G-12025)*
Zirconia Creations Intl .... G 212 239-3730
New York *(G-12179)*

Employee Codes: A=Over 500 employees, B=251-500
C=101-250, D=51-100, E=20-50, F=10-19, G=5-9

JEWELRY FINDINGS WHOLESALERS | PRODUCT SECTION

JEWELRY FINDINGS WHOLESALERS

Cardona Industries USA Ltd .... G 516 466-5200
 Great Neck *(G-5542)*
D R S Inc .... E 212 819-0237
 New York *(G-9449)*
New York Findings Corp .... F 212 925-5745
 New York *(G-10938)*

JEWELRY REPAIR SVCS

Burke & Bannayan .... G 585 723-1010
 Rochester *(G-13681)*
Carr Manufacturing Jewelers .... G 518 783-6093
 Latham *(G-7069)*
Richards & West Inc .... D 585 461-4088
 East Rochester *(G-4291)*

JEWELRY STORES

Burke & Bannayan .... G 585 723-1010
 Rochester *(G-13681)*
Carr Manufacturing Jewelers .... G 518 783-6093
 Latham *(G-7069)*
Charles Perrella Inc .... E 845 348-4777
 Nyack *(G-12502)*
Diamond Boutique .... G 516 444-3373
 Port Washington *(G-13252)*
Golden Integrity Inc .... E 212 764-6753
 New York *(G-9955)*
Henry Dunay Designs Inc .... E 212 768-9700
 New York *(G-10080)*
Iriniri Designs Ltd .... F 845 469-7934
 Sugar Loaf *(G-15200)*
Joan Boyce Ltd .... G 212 867-7474
 New York *(G-10346)*
Julius Cohen Jewelers Inc .... G 212 371-3050
 Brooklyn *(G-2058)*
Love Bright Jewelry Inc .... E 516 620-2509
 Oceanside *(G-12546)*
Mimi So International LLC .... E 212 300-8600
 New York *(G-10815)*
Neil Savalia Inc .... F 212 869-0123
 New York *(G-10903)*
Nyman Jewelry Inc .... G 212 944-1976
 New York *(G-11017)*
Royal Jewelry Mfg Inc .... D 212 302-2500
 Great Neck *(G-5586)*
Stanmark Jewelry Inc .... G 212 730-2557
 New York *(G-11694)*
Suna Bros Inc .... E 212 869-5670
 New York *(G-11741)*

JEWELRY STORES: Precious Stones & Precious Metals

Aaron Group LLC .... D 718 392-5454
 Mount Vernon *(G-8372)*
Atr Jewelry Inc .... F 212 819-0075
 New York *(G-8957)*
Bourghol Brothers Inc .... G 845 268-9752
 Congers *(G-3712)*
David S Diamonds Inc .... F 212 921-8029
 New York *(G-9484)*
Harry Winston Inc .... C 212 399-1000
 New York *(G-10043)*
Hw Holdings Inc .... G 212 399-1000
 New York *(G-10153)*
Jim Wachtler Inc .... G 212 755-4367
 New York *(G-10338)*
Mellem Corporation .... F 607 723-0001
 Binghamton *(G-904)*
Midura Jewels Inc .... G 213 265-8090
 New York *(G-10801)*
Nicolo Raineri .... G 212 925-6128
 New York *(G-10965)*
Peter Atman Inc .... F 212 644-8882
 New York *(G-11167)*
Reinhold Brothers Inc .... E 212 867-8310
 New York *(G-11351)*
Richards & West Inc .... D 585 461-4088
 East Rochester *(G-4291)*
Shining Creations Inc .... G 845 358-4911
 New City *(G-8495)*

JEWELRY, PREC METAL: Mountings, Pens, Lthr, Etc, Gold/Silver

Leo Ingwer Inc .... E 212 719-1342
 New York *(G-10549)*

JEWELRY, PRECIOUS METAL: Bracelets

Alex Sepkus Inc .... F 212 391-8466
 New York *(G-8792)*
Hammerman Bros Inc .... G 212 956-2800
 New York *(G-10026)*
Innovative Jewelry Inc .... G 718 408-8950
 Valley Cottage *(G-15756)*
Jacoby Enterprises LLC .... G 718 435-0289
 Brooklyn *(G-2032)*
Julius Cohen Jewelers Inc .... G 212 371-3050
 Brooklyn *(G-2058)*
Lokai Holdings LLC .... F 646 979-3474
 New York *(G-10594)*
Master Craft Jewelry Co Inc .... D 516 599-1012
 Lynbrook *(G-7668)*

JEWELRY, PRECIOUS METAL: Cases

Albea Cosmetics America Inc .... E 212 371-5100
 New York *(G-8784)*

JEWELRY, PRECIOUS METAL: Cigar & Cigarette Access

Cigar Oasis LLC .... G 516 520-5258
 Farmingdale *(G-4735)*

JEWELRY, PRECIOUS METAL: Earrings

Indonesian Imports Inc .... E 888 800-5899
 New York *(G-10200)*
Jay-Aimee Designs Inc .... C 718 609-0333
 Great Neck *(G-5564)*
Richline Group Inc .... E 212 643-2908
 New York *(G-11388)*

JEWELRY, PRECIOUS METAL: Medals, Precious Or Semiprecious

Eagle Regalia Co Inc .... F 845 425-2245
 Spring Valley *(G-14989)*
Jacmel Jewelry Inc .... C 718 349-4300
 New York *(G-10296)*
Leon Mege Inc .... F 212 768-3868
 New York *(G-10553)*
Sarkisians Jewelry Co .... G 212 869-1060
 New York *(G-11491)*

JEWELRY, PRECIOUS METAL: Mountings & Trimmings

Shining Creations Inc .... G 845 358-4911
 New City *(G-8495)*

JEWELRY, PRECIOUS METAL: Necklaces

Feldman Jewelry Creations Inc .... G 718 438-8895
 Brooklyn *(G-1872)*
Iridesse Inc .... F 212 230-6000
 New York *(G-10269)*

JEWELRY, PRECIOUS METAL: Pearl, Natural Or Cultured

Clyde Duneier Inc .... D 212 398-1122
 New York *(G-9336)*
Dweck Industries Inc .... G 718 615-1695
 Brooklyn *(G-1797)*
Lali Jewelry Inc .... G 212 944-2277
 New York *(G-10511)*
Robin Stanley Inc .... G 212 871-0007
 New York *(G-11411)*

JEWELRY, PRECIOUS METAL: Pins

M H Manufacturing Incorporated .... G 212 461-6900
 New York *(G-10637)*

JEWELRY, PRECIOUS METAL: Rings, Finger

Alfred Butler Inc .... F 516 829-7460
 Great Neck *(G-5529)*
D R S Inc .... E 212 819-0237
 New York *(G-9449)*
Grandeur Creations Inc .... G 212 643-1277
 New York *(G-9972)*
Hjn Inc .... F 212 398-9564
 New York *(G-10107)*
Jeff Cooper Inc .... F 516 333-8200
 Carle Place *(G-3266)*
S & M Ring Corp .... F 212 382-0900
 Hewlett *(G-6050)*
Standard Wedding Band Co .... G 516 294-0954
 Garden City *(G-5282)*
W & B Mazza & Sons Inc .... E 516 379-4130
 North Baldwin *(G-12371)*

JEWELRY, PRECIOUS METAL: Rosaries/Other Sm Religious Article

Rand & Paseka Mfg Co Inc .... E 516 867-1500
 Freeport *(G-5178)*
Yofah Religious Articles Inc .... F 718 435-3288
 Brooklyn *(G-2664)*

JEWELRY, PRECIOUS METAL: Settings & Mountings

AF Design Inc .... G 347 548-5273
 New York *(G-8764)*
Gold & Diamonds Wholesale Outl .... G 718 438-7888
 Brooklyn *(G-1937)*
Golden Integrity Inc .... E 212 764-6753
 New York *(G-9955)*
Kaprielian Enterprises Inc .... D 212 645-6623
 New York *(G-10406)*
Reinhold Brothers Inc .... E 212 867-8310
 New York *(G-11351)*

JEWELRY, PRECIOUS METAL: Trimmings, Canes, Umbrellas, Etc

Houles USA Inc .... G 212 935-3900
 New York *(G-10132)*

JEWELRY, WHOLESALE

Aaron Group LLC .... D 718 392-5454
 Mount Vernon *(G-8372)*
AF Design Inc .... G 347 548-5273
 New York *(G-8764)*
American Originals Corporation .... G 212 836-4155
 New York *(G-8835)*
Anatoli Inc .... F 845 334-9000
 West Hurley *(G-16256)*
Classic Medallics Inc .... E 718 392-5410
 Mount Vernon *(G-8388)*
Crown Jewelers Intl Inc .... G 212 420-7800
 New York *(G-9426)*
Diana Kane Incorporated .... G 718 638-6520
 Brooklyn *(G-1772)*
Formart Corp .... F 212 819-1819
 New York *(G-9824)*
Fuzion Creations Intl LLC .... E 718 369-8800
 Brooklyn *(G-1912)*
J & H Creations Inc .... E 212 465-0962
 New York *(G-10281)*
J R Gold Designs Ltd .... F 212 922-9292
 New York *(G-10287)*
Keith Lewis Studio Inc .... G 845 339-5629
 Rifton *(G-13561)*
Love Bright Jewelry Inc .... E 516 620-2509
 Oceanside *(G-12546)*
Magic Novelty Co Inc .... E 212 304-2777
 New York *(G-10667)*
Marlborough Jewels Inc .... G 718 768-2000
 Brooklyn *(G-2170)*
Mgd Brands Inc .... E 516 545-0150
 Plainview *(G-13075)*
Michael Bondanza Inc .... E 212 869-0043
 New York *(G-10791)*
Mimi So International LLC .... E 212 300-8600
 New York *(G-10815)*
Mwsi Inc .... D 914 347-4200
 Hawthorne *(G-5993)*
Pesselnik & Cohen Inc .... G 212 925-0287
 New York *(G-11165)*
Q Ed Creations .... E 212 391-1155
 New York *(G-11289)*
R M Reynolds .... G 315 789-7365
 Geneva *(G-5331)*
Richline Group Inc .... C 212 764-8454
 New York *(G-11389)*
Royal Jewelry Mfg Inc .... D 212 302-2500
 Great Neck *(G-5586)*
Select Jewelry Inc .... D 718 784-3626
 Long Island City *(G-7587)*
Shah Diamonds Inc .... F 212 888-9393
 New York *(G-11553)*
Shanu Gems Inc .... F 212 921-4470
 New York *(G-11556)*

JEWELRY: Decorative, Fashion & Costume

Sterling Possessions Ltd ....G...... 212 594-0418
  New York (G-11707)
UNI Jewelry Inc ....G...... 212 398-1818
  New York (G-11938)

JEWELRY: Decorative, Fashion & Costume

Allure Jewelry and ACC LLC ....F...... 646 226-8057
  New York (G-8802)
Anatoli Inc ....F...... 845 334-9000
  West Hurley (G-16256)
Beth Ward Studios LLC ....F...... 646 922-7575
  New York (G-9060)
Bnns Co Inc ....G...... 212 302-1844
  New York (G-9114)
Carvin French Jewelers Inc ....E...... 212 755-6474
  New York (G-9219)
Columbus Trading Corp ....F..... 212 564-1780
  New York (G-9361)
Ema Jewelry Inc ....D..... 212 575-8989
  New York (G-9662)
Eu Design LLC ....G..... 212 420-7788
  New York (G-9725)
Five Star Creations Inc ....E..... 845 783-1187
  Monroe (G-8269)
Formart Corp ....F..... 212 819-1819
  New York (G-9824)
Greenbeads Llc ....G..... 212 327-2765
  New York (G-9984)
Holbrooke Inc ....G..... 646 397-4674
  New York (G-10113)
I Love Accessories Inc ....F..... 212 239-1875
  New York (G-10158)
International Inspirations Ltd ....D..... 212 465-8500
  New York (G-10247)
J J Creations Inc ....E..... 718 392-2828
  Long Island City (G-7477)
Jewelry Arts Manufacturing ....E..... 212 382-3583
  New York (G-10329)
Jill Fagin Enterprises Inc ....G..... 212 674-9383
  New York (G-10337)
K2 International Corp ....G..... 212 947-1734
  New York (G-10392)
Mataci Inc ....D..... 212 502-1899
  New York (G-10725)
Maurice Max Inc ....E..... 212 334-6573
  New York (G-10730)
Mel Bernie and Company Inc ....G..... 212 889-8570
  New York (G-10768)
Nes Jewelry Inc ....D..... 212 502-0025
  New York (G-10908)
Noir Jewelry LLC ....G..... 212 465-8500
  New York (G-10986)
Pearl Erwin Inc ....E..... 212 889-7410
  New York (G-11129)
Pepe Creations Inc ....F..... 212 391-1514
  New York (G-11151)
Pincharming Inc ....F..... 516 663-5115
  Garden City (G-5274)
Reino Manufacturing Co Inc ....F..... 914 636-8990
  New Rochelle (G-8625)
Rush Gold Manufacturing Ltd ....D..... 516 781-3155
  Bellmore (G-793)
Sanoy Inc ....E..... 212 695-6384
  New York (G-11484)
Sarina Accessories LLC ....F..... 212 239-8106
  New York (G-11490)
Shira Accessories Ltd ....F..... 212 594-4455
  New York (G-11568)
Swarovski North America Ltd ....G..... 212 695-1502
  New York (G-11755)
Toho Shoji (new York) Inc ....F..... 212 868-7466
  New York (G-11856)
Tycoon International Inc ....G..... 212 563-7107
  New York (G-11922)
Vetta Jewelry Inc ....E..... 212 564-8250
  New York (G-12020)
Yacoubian Jewelers Inc ....E..... 212 302-6729
  New York (G-12157)

JEWELRY: Precious Metal

1ktgold Inc ....F..... 212 302-8200
  White Plains (G-16415)
A & V Castings Inc ....G..... 212 997-0042
  New York (G-8689)
A Jaffe Inc ....C..... 212 843-7464
  New York (G-8697)
Aaron Group LLC ....D..... 718 392-5454
  Mount Vernon (G-8372)
Abraham Jwly Designers & Mfrs ....F..... 212 944-1149
  New York (G-8713)
Abrimian Bros Corp ....F..... 212 382-1106
  New York (G-8714)
Adamor Inc ....G..... 212 688-8885
  New York (G-8733)
Alart Inc ....G..... 212 840-1508
  New York (G-8782)
Alchemy Simya Inc ....E..... 646 230-1122
  New York (G-8786)
Alex Archer Designs Ltd ....G..... 212 219-8664
  New York (G-8791)
Alexander Primak Jewelry Inc ....D..... 212 398-0287
  New York (G-8793)
Almond Jewelers Inc ....F..... 516 933-6000
  Port Washington (G-13242)
Alpine Creations Ltd ....G..... 212 308-9353
  New York (G-8813)
Ambras Fine Jewelry Inc ....E..... 718 784-5252
  Long Island City (G-7375)
American Craft Jewelers Inc ....G..... 718 972-0945
  Brooklyn (G-1520)
American Originals Corporation ....G..... 212 836-4155
  New York (G-8835)
Anatoli Inc ....F..... 845 334-9000
  West Hurley (G-16256)
Anima Group LLC ....G..... 917 913-2053
  New York (G-8868)
Apicella Jewelers Inc ....E..... 212 840-2024
  New York (G-8884)
AR & AR Jewelry Inc ....E..... 212 764-7916
  New York (G-8895)
Arringement International Inc ....G..... 347 323-7974
  Flushing (G-4986)
Art-TEC Jewelry Designs Ltd ....E..... 212 719-2941
  New York (G-8918)
Ateret LLC ....G..... 212 819-0777
  New York (G-8945)
Atlantic Precious Metal Cast ....G..... 718 937-7100
  Long Island City (G-7394)
Atr Jewelry Inc ....F..... 212 819-0075
  New York (G-8957)
B K Jewelry Contractor Inc ....E..... 212 398-9093
  New York (G-8989)
Barber Brothers Jewelry Mfg ....F..... 212 819-0666
  New York (G-9013)
Baroka Creations Inc ....F..... 212 768-0527
  New York (G-9019)
Bartholomew Mazza Ltd Inc ....E..... 212 935-4530
  New York (G-9023)
Bellataire Diamonds Inc ....F..... 212 687-8881
  New York (G-9039)
Benlee Enterprises LLC ....E..... 718 730-7330
  Long Island City (G-7399)
BH Multi Com Corp ....E..... 212 944-0020
  New York (G-9069)
Bielka Inc ....G..... 212 980-6841
  New York (G-9074)
Billanti Casting Co Inc ....E..... 516 775-4800
  New Hyde Park (G-8520)
BJG Services LLC ....F..... 516 592-5692
  New York (G-9095)
Bourghol Brothers Inc ....G..... 845 268-9752
  Congers (G-3712)
Bral Nader Fine Jewelry Inc ....G..... 800 493-1222
  New York (G-9134)
Brannkey Inc ....D..... 212 371-1515
  New York (G-9135)
Brilliant Jewelers/Mjj Inc ....G..... 212 353-2326
  New York (G-9142)
Brilliant Stars Collection Inc ....F..... 516 365-9000
  Great Neck (G-5540)
Bristol Seamless Ring Corp ....F..... 212 874-2645
  New York (G-9143)
Burke & Bannayan ....G..... 585 723-1010
  Rochester (G-13681)
Carlo Monte Designs Inc ....G..... 212 935-5611
  New York (G-9209)
Carr Manufacturing Jewelers ....G..... 518 783-6093
  Latham (G-7069)
Carvin French Jewelers Inc ....E..... 212 755-6474
  New York (G-9219)
Chaindom Enterprises Inc ....F..... 212 719-4778
  New York (G-9256)
Chameleon Gems Inc ....F..... 516 829-3333
  Great Neck (G-5544)
Charis & Mae Inc ....G..... 212 641-0816
  New York (G-9261)
Charles Krypell Inc ....F..... 212 752-3313
  New York (G-9263)
Charles Perrella Inc ....E..... 845 348-4777
  Nyack (G-12502)
Charles Vaillant Inc ....G..... 212 752-4832
  New York (G-9265)
Christopher Designs Inc ....E..... 212 382-1013
  New York (G-9294)
Concord Jewelry Mfg Co LLC ....E..... 212 719-4030
  New York (G-9373)
Creative Gold LLC ....E..... 718 686-2225
  Brooklyn (G-1728)
Crown Jewelers Intl Inc ....G..... 212 420-7800
  New York (G-9426)
Csi International Inc ....E..... 800 441-2895
  Niagara Falls (G-12276)
David Friedman Chain Co Inc ....F..... 212 684-1760
  New York (G-9480)
David Howell Product Design ....G..... 914 666-4080
  Bedford Hills (G-774)
David S Diamonds Inc ....F..... 212 921-8029
  New York (G-9484)
David Weisz & Sons USA LLC ....G..... 212 840-4747
  New York (G-9487)
David Yurman Enterprises LLC ....G..... 914 539-4444
  White Plains (G-16443)
David Yurman Enterprises LLC ....B..... 212 896-1550
  New York (G-9488)
David Yurman Enterprises LLC ....G..... 845 928-8660
  Central Valley (G-3395)
David Yurman Retail LLC ....G..... 877 226-1400
  New York (G-9489)
Diamond Distributors Inc ....G..... 212 921-9188
  New York (G-9522)
Diana Kane Incorporated ....G..... 718 638-6520
  Brooklyn (G-1772)
Dimoda Designs Inc ....E..... 212 355-8166
  New York (G-9530)
Donna Distefano Ltd ....G..... 212 594-3757
  New York (G-9548)
Doris Panos Designs Ltd ....E..... 631 245-0580
  Melville (G-8017)
Duran Jewelry Inc ....F..... 212 431-1959
  New York (G-9586)
Earring King Jewelry Mfg Inc ....G..... 718 544-7947
  New York (G-9606)
Echo Group Inc ....F..... 917 608-7440
  New York (G-9621)
Eclipse Collection Jewelers ....G..... 212 764-6883
  New York (G-9623)
Ed Levin Inc ....E..... 518 677-8595
  Cambridge (G-3181)
Elegant Jewelers Mfg Co Inc ....F..... 212 869-4951
  New York (G-9643)
Ema Jewelry Inc ....D..... 212 575-8989
  New York (G-9662)
Emsaru USA Corp ....G..... 212 459-9355
  New York (G-9669)
Eternal Line ....E..... 845 856-1999
  Sparrow Bush (G-14972)
Euro Bands Inc ....F..... 212 719-9777
  New York (G-9728)
F M Abdulky Inc ....F..... 607 272-7373
  Ithaca (G-6576)
F M Abdulky Inc ....F..... 607 272-7373
  Ithaca (G-6577)
Fantasia Jewelry Inc ....E..... 212 921-9590
  New York (G-9781)
Five Star Creations Inc ....E..... 845 783-1187
  Monroe (G-8269)
Frank Blancato Inc ....F..... 212 768-1495
  New York (G-9841)
Gemoro Inc ....F..... 212 768-8844
  New York (G-9896)
Gemveto Jewelry Company Inc ....E..... 212 755-2522
  New York (G-9898)
George Lederman Inc ....G..... 212 753-4556
  New York (G-9911)
Giovane Ltd ....E..... 212 332-7373
  New York (G-9923)
Global Gem Corporation ....G..... 212 350-9936
  New York (G-9941)
Goldarama Company Inc ....G..... 212 730-7299
  New York (G-9951)
Goldmark Products Inc ....E..... 631 777-3343
  Farmingdale (G-4773)
Gorga Fehren Fine Jewelry LLC ....G..... 646 861-3595
  New York (G-9959)
Gottlieb & Sons Inc ....E..... 212 575-1907
  New York (G-9962)
Grinnell Designs Inc ....E..... 212 391-5277
  New York (G-9991)
Guild Diamond Products Inc ....F..... 212 871-0007
  New York (G-10007)

Employee Codes: A=Over 500 employees, B=251-500
C=101-250, D=51-100, E=20-50, F=10-19, G=5-9

JEWELRY: Precious Metal

H & T Goldman Corporation ....G...... 800 822-0272
  New York *(G-10012)*
Hanna Altinis Co Inc ....E...... 718 706-1134
  Long Island City *(G-7466)*
Hansa Usa LLC ....E...... 646 412-6407
  New York *(G-10034)*
Harry Winston Inc ....C...... 212 399-1000
  New York *(G-10043)*
Haskell Jewels Ltd ....E...... 212 764-3332
  New York *(G-10048)*
Henry Design Studios Inc ....G...... 516 801-2760
  Locust Valley *(G-7349)*
Henry Dunay Designs Inc ....E...... 212 768-9700
  New York *(G-10080)*
Horo Creations LLC ....G...... 212 719-4818
  New York *(G-10124)*
Hw Holdings Inc ....G...... 212 399-1000
  New York *(G-10153)*
Ilico Jewelry Inc ....G...... 516 482-0201
  Great Neck *(G-5561)*
Imena Jewelry Manufacturer Inc ....F...... 212 827-0073
  New York *(G-10184)*
Incon Gems Inc ....F...... 212 221-8560
  New York *(G-10193)*
Inori Jewels ....F...... 347 703-5078
  New York *(G-10223)*
Intentions Jewelry LLC ....G...... 845 226-4650
  Lagrangeville *(G-6957)*
Iradj Moini Couture Ltd ....E...... 212 594-9242
  New York *(G-10268)*
Iriniri Designs Ltd ....F...... 845 469-7934
  Sugar Loaf *(G-15200)*
J J Creations Inc ....E...... 718 392-2828
  Long Island City *(G-7477)*
J R Gold Designs Ltd ....F...... 212 922-9292
  New York *(G-10287)*
Jacobs & Cohen Inc ....E...... 212 714-2702
  New York *(G-10298)*
Jaguar Casting Co Inc ....E...... 212 869-0197
  New York *(G-10300)*
Jane Bohan Inc ....G...... 212 529-6090
  New York *(G-10305)*
Jasani Designs Usa Inc ....G...... 212 257-6465
  New York *(G-10310)*
Jay Strongwater Holdings LLC ....A...... 646 657-0558
  New York *(G-10312)*
Jewelry Arts Manufacturing ....E...... 212 382-3583
  New York *(G-10329)*
Jewels By Star Ltd ....E...... 212 308-3490
  New York *(G-10330)*
Jeweltex Mfg Corp ....F...... 212 921-8188
  New York *(G-10331)*
Jimmy Crystal New York Co Ltd ....E...... 212 594-0858
  New York *(G-10340)*
JK Manufacturing Inc ....G...... 212 683-3535
  Locust Valley *(G-7350)*
Joan Boyce Ltd ....G...... 212 867-7474
  New York *(G-10346)*
Jordan Scott Designs Ltd ....E...... 212 947-4250
  New York *(G-10362)*
Jotaly Inc ....A...... 212 886-6000
  New York *(G-10367)*
Justin Ashley Designs Inc ....G...... 718 707-0200
  Long Island City *(G-7485)*
Justperfectmsp Ltd ....E...... 877 201-0005
  New York *(G-10386)*
Justyna Kaminska NY Inc ....G...... 917 423-5527
  New York *(G-10387)*
Karbra Company ....C...... 212 736-9300
  New York *(G-10407)*
Keith Lewis Studio Inc ....G...... 845 339-5629
  Rifton *(G-13561)*
Krainz Creations Inc ....E...... 212 583-1555
  New York *(G-10477)*
Krasner Group Inc ....G...... 212 268-4100
  New York *(G-10479)*
Kurt Gaum Inc ....F...... 212 719-2836
  New York *(G-10487)*
La Fina Design Inc ....G...... 212 689-6725
  New York *(G-10501)*
Le Paveh Ltd ....F...... 212 736-6110
  New York *(G-10527)*
Le Vian Corp ....D...... 516 466-7200
  Great Neck *(G-5568)*
Le Vian Corp ....E...... 516 466-7200
  New York *(G-10528)*
Leser Enterprises Ltd ....F...... 212 644-8921
  Yonkers *(G-16778)*
M & S Quality Co Ltd ....F...... 212 302-8757
  New York *(G-10634)*

M A R A Metals Ltd ....G...... 718 786-7868
  Long Island City *(G-7508)*
M Heskia Company Inc ....G...... 212 768-1845
  New York *(G-10638)*
M S Riviera Inc ....E...... 212 391-0206
  New York *(G-10643)*
Magnum Creation Inc ....F...... 212 642-0993
  New York *(G-10671)*
Manny Grunberg Inc ....E...... 212 302-6173
  New York *(G-10692)*
Marco Moore Inc ....M...... 212 575-2090
  Great Neck *(G-5571)*
Marina Jewelry Co Inc ....G...... 212 354-5027
  New York *(G-10703)*
Mark King Jewelry Inc ....G...... 212 921-0746
  New York *(G-10705)*
Mark Robinson Inc ....G...... 212 223-3515
  New York *(G-10708)*
Markowitz Jewelry Co Inc ....E...... 845 774-1175
  Monroe *(G-8276)*
Marlborough Jewels Inc ....G...... 718 768-2000
  Brooklyn *(G-2170)*
Maxine Denker Inc ....G...... 212 689-1440
  Staten Island *(G-15103)*
ME & Ro Inc ....G...... 212 431-8744
  New York *(G-10748)*
Mellem Corporation ....F...... 607 723-0001
  Binghamton *(G-904)*
Mer Gems Corp ....G...... 212 714-9129
  New York *(G-10772)*
Mgd Brands Inc ....E...... 516 545-0150
  Plainview *(G-13075)*
Michael Bondanza Inc ....G...... 212 869-0043
  New York *(G-10791)*
Midura Jewels Inc ....G...... 213 265-8090
  New York *(G-10801)*
Mimi So International LLC ....E...... 212 300-8600
  New York *(G-10815)*
Min Ho Designs Inc ....G...... 212 838-3667
  New York *(G-10816)*
MJM Jewelry Corp ....D...... 212 354-5014
  New York *(G-10826)*
MJM Jewelry Corp ....D...... 718 596-1600
  Brooklyn *(G-2218)*
Monelle Jewelry ....G...... 212 977-9535
  New York *(G-10838)*
Mwsi Inc ....D...... 914 347-4200
  Hawthorne *(G-5993)*
N Y Bijoux Corp ....G...... 212 244-9585
  Port Washington *(G-13290)*
Neil Savalia Inc ....F...... 212 869-0123
  New York *(G-10903)*
Nicolo Raineri ....G...... 212 925-6128
  New York *(G-10965)*
Oscar Heyman & Bros Inc ....E...... 212 593-0400
  New York *(G-11065)*
Osnat Gad Inc ....G...... 212 957-0535
  New York *(G-11066)*
Overnight Mountings Inc ....D...... 516 865-3000
  New Hyde Park *(G-8556)*
Parijat Jewels Inc ....G...... 212 302-2549
  New York *(G-11112)*
Patuga LLC ....F...... 716 204-7220
  Williamsville *(G-16583)*
Pearl Erwin Inc ....E...... 212 889-7410
  New York *(G-11129)*
Pesselnik & Cohen Inc ....E...... 212 925-0287
  New York *(G-11165)*
Peter Atman Inc ....F...... 212 644-8882
  New York *(G-11167)*
PHC Restoration Holdings LLC ....F...... 212 643-0517
  New York *(G-11180)*
Photograve Corporation ....E...... 718 667-4825
  Staten Island *(G-15114)*
Pink Box Accessories LLC ....G...... 718 435-2821
  Brooklyn *(G-2319)*
Premier Jewelry Designs LLC ....G...... 212 391-8778
  New York *(G-11230)*
Pronto Jewelry Inc ....G...... 212 719-9455
  New York *(G-11263)*
Q Ed Creations ....G...... 212 391-1155
  New York *(G-11289)*
R Klein Jewelry Co Inc ....D...... 516 482-3260
  Massapequa *(G-7884)*
R M Reynolds ....G...... 315 789-7365
  Geneva *(G-5331)*
Regal Jewelry Inc ....E...... 212 382-1695
  New York *(G-11348)*
Renaissance Bijou Ltd ....G...... 212 869-1969
  New York *(G-11359)*

Richards & West Inc ....D...... 585 461-4088
  East Rochester *(G-4291)*
Richline Group Inc ....C...... 212 764-8454
  New York *(G-11389)*
Richline Group Inc ....C...... 914 699-0000
  New York *(G-11390)*
Robert Bartholomew Ltd ....E...... 516 767-2970
  Port Washington *(G-13301)*
Rosy Blue Inc ....E...... 212 687-8838
  New York *(G-11435)*
Royal Jewelry Mfg Inc ....D...... 212 302-2500
  Great Neck *(G-5586)*
Royal Miracle Corp ....E...... 212 921-5797
  New York *(G-11438)*
Rubinstein Jewelry Mfg Co ....F...... 718 784-8650
  Long Island City *(G-7581)*
Rudolf Friedman Inc ....F...... 212 869-5070
  New York *(G-11446)*
Rumson Acquisition LLC ....E...... 718 349-4300
  New York *(G-11447)*
Ryan Gems Inc ....E...... 212 697-0149
  New York *(G-11452)*
S Kashi & Sons Inc ....F...... 212 869-9393
  Great Neck *(G-5587)*
S Scharf Inc ....F...... 516 541-9552
  Massapequa *(G-7885)*
Samuel B Collection Inc ....G...... 516 466-1826
  Great Neck *(G-5588)*
Sanoy Inc ....E...... 212 695-6384
  New York *(G-11484)*
Satco Castings Service Inc ....E...... 516 354-1500
  New Hyde Park *(G-8561)*
Satellite Incorporated ....G...... 212 221-6687
  New York *(G-11492)*
Select Jewelry Inc ....D...... 718 784-3626
  Long Island City *(G-7587)*
Shah Diamonds Inc ....F...... 212 888-9393
  New York *(G-11553)*
Shanu Gems Inc ....F...... 212 921-4470
  New York *(G-11556)*
Sharodine Inc ....G...... 516 767-3548
  Port Washington *(G-13308)*
Shiro Limited ....G...... 212 780-0007
  New York *(G-11569)*
Simka Diamond Corp ....F...... 212 921-4420
  New York *(G-11593)*
Somerset Manufacturers Inc ....E...... 516 626-3832
  Roslyn Heights *(G-14460)*
Spark Creations Inc ....F...... 212 575-8385
  New York *(G-11657)*
Stanley Creations Inc ....C...... 718 361-6100
  Long Island City *(G-7599)*
Stanmark Jewelry Inc ....G...... 212 730-2557
  New York *(G-11694)*
Stone House Associates Inc ....E...... 212 221-7447
  New York *(G-11714)*
Sube Inc ....E...... 212 243-6930
  New York *(G-11732)*
Sumer Gold Ltd ....G...... 212 354-8677
  New York *(G-11737)*
Suna Bros Inc ....E...... 212 869-5070
  New York *(G-11741)*
Sunrise Jewelers of NY Inc ....G...... 516 541-1302
  Massapequa *(G-7886)*
Tambetti Inc ....G...... 212 751-9584
  New York *(G-11778)*
Tamsen Z LLC ....E...... 212 292-6412
  New York *(G-11779)*
Tanagro Jewelry Corp ....E...... 212 753-2817
  New York *(G-11780)*
Technical Service Industries ....E...... 212 719-9800
  Jamaica *(G-6682)*
Teena Creations Inc ....E...... 516 867-1500
  Freeport *(G-5185)*
Temple St Clair LLC ....E...... 212 219-8664
  New York *(G-11799)*
Tiga Holdings Inc ....G...... 845 838-3000
  Beacon *(G-763)*
Trianon Collection Inc ....E...... 212 921-9450
  New York *(G-11896)*
Ultra Fine Jewelry Mfg ....E...... 516 349-2848
  Plainview *(G-13095)*
UNI Jewelry Inc ....G...... 212 398-1818
  New York *(G-11938)*
Unique Designs Inc ....F...... 212 575-7701
  New York *(G-11949)*
United Brothers Jewelry Inc ....E...... 212 921-2558
  New York *(G-11952)*
Valentin & Kalich Jwly Mfg Ltd ....E...... 212 575-9044
  New York *(G-11984)*

PRODUCT SECTION

LABORATORIES: Biological Research

Valentine Jewelry Mfg Co Inc .... E 212 382-0606
New York *(G-11985)*
Variety Gem Co Inc .... F 212 921-1820
Great Neck *(G-5599)*
Viktor Gold Enterprise Corp .... G 212 768-8885
New York *(G-12033)*
Von Musulin Patricia .... E 212 206-8345
New York *(G-12053)*
Weisco Inc .... F 212 575-8989
New York *(G-12088)*
William Goldberg Diamond Corp .... E 212 980-1343
New York *(G-12110)*
Xomox Jewelry Inc .... G 212 944-8428
New York *(G-12154)*
Zeeba Jewelry Mfg Inc .... G 212 997-1009
New York *(G-12172)*
Zelman & Friedman Jwly Mfg Co .... E 718 349-3400
Long Island City *(G-7647)*

JIGS & FIXTURES

Amsco Inc .... F 716 823-4213
Buffalo *(G-2699)*
Knise & Krick Inc .... E 315 422-3516
Syracuse *(G-15357)*
Manhasset Tool & Die Co Inc .... F 716 684-6066
Lancaster *(G-7031)*
Prime Tool & Die LLC .... G 607 334-5435
Norwich *(G-12492)*

JOB PRINTING & NEWSPAPER PUBLISHING COMBINED

Adirondack Publishing Co Inc .... E 518 891-2600
Saranac Lake *(G-14560)*
Albion-Holley Pennysaver Inc .... E 585 589-5641
Albion *(G-154)*
Empire State Weeklies Inc .... E 585 671-1533
Webster *(G-16084)*
Mexico Independent Inc .... E 315 963-3763
Watertown *(G-16027)*
Thousand Islands Printing Co .... G 315 482-2581
Alexandria Bay *(G-182)*

JOB TRAINING & VOCATIONAL REHABILITATION SVCS

Avcom of Virginia Inc .... D 585 924-4560
Victor *(G-15830)*
Chemung Cnty Chpter Nysarc Inc .... C 607 734-6151
Elmira *(G-4477)*

JOINTS: Ball Except aircraft & Auto

Advanced Thermal Systems Inc .... E 716 681-1800
Lancaster *(G-7002)*
York Industries Inc .... E 516 746-3736
Garden City Park *(G-5290)*

JOINTS: Expansion

Adsco Manufacturing Corp .... D 716 827-5450
Buffalo *(G-2688)*
Mageba USA LLC .... E 212 317-1991
New York *(G-10662)*
Mount Vernon Iron Works Inc .... G 914 668-7064
Mount Vernon *(G-8423)*
Vulcraft of New York Inc .... C 607 529-9000
Chemung *(G-3464)*
Watson Bowman Acme Corp .... C 716 691-8162
Amherst *(G-260)*

JOINTS: Expansion, Pipe

Advanced Thermal Systems Inc .... E 716 681-1800
Lancaster *(G-7002)*

KEYBOARDS: Computer Or Office Machine

Wey Inc .... G 212 532-3299
New York *(G-12099)*

KEYS, KEY BLANKS

International Key Supply LLC .... F 631 983-6096
Farmingdale *(G-4788)*

KITCHEN CABINET STORES, EXC CUSTOM

Carefree Kitchens Inc .... G 631 567-2120
Holbrook *(G-6175)*
Custom Design Kitchens Inc .... F 518 355-4446
Duanesburg *(G-4155)*

Joseph Fedele .... G 718 448-3658
Staten Island *(G-15097)*
Michael P Mmarr .... G 315 623-9380
Constantia *(G-3740)*
Mind Designs Inc .... G 631 563-3644
Farmingville *(G-4924)*
S & K Counter Tops Inc .... G 716 662-7986
Orchard Park *(G-12743)*
Serway Bros Inc .... G 315 337-0601
Rome *(G-14274)*

KITCHEN CABINETS WHOLESALERS

Capital Kit Cab & Door Mfrs .... G 718 886-0303
College Point *(G-3641)*
Carefree Kitchens Inc .... G 631 567-2120
Holbrook *(G-6175)*
Central Kitchen Corp .... F 631 283-1029
Southampton *(G-14951)*
Custom Design Kitchens Inc .... F 518 355-4446
Duanesburg *(G-4155)*
Dak Mica and Wood Products .... G 631 467-0749
Ronkonkoma *(G-14332)*
Deer Pk Stair Bldg Mllwk Inc .... E 631 363-5000
Blue Point *(G-964)*
Di Fiore and Sons Custom Wdwkg .... G 718 278-1663
Long Island City *(G-7425)*
Hennig Custom Woodwork Corp .... G 516 536-3460
Oceanside *(G-12540)*
Johnny Mica Inc .... G 631 225-5213
Lindenhurst *(G-7173)*
Joseph Fedele .... G 718 448-3658
Staten Island *(G-15097)*
M & C Furniture .... G 718 422-2136
Brooklyn *(G-2140)*
Metro Kitchens Corp .... F 718 434-1166
Brooklyn *(G-2200)*
Rochester Countertop Inc .... F 585 338-2260
Rochester *(G-14085)*
Triad Counter Corp .... G 631 750-0615
Bohemia *(G-1098)*

KITCHEN TOOLS & UTENSILS WHOLESALERS

Ashco Management Inc .... F 212 960-8428
Brooklyn *(G-1562)*

KITCHEN UTENSILS: Bakers' Eqpt, Wood

Charles Freihofer Baking Co .... G 518 463-2221
Albany *(G-58)*
Unisource Food Eqp Systems Inc .... G 516 681-0537
Holbrook *(G-6217)*

KITCHEN UTENSILS: Food Handling & Processing Prdts, Wood

Channel Manufacturing Inc .... E 516 944-6271
Port Washington *(G-13247)*

KITCHEN UTENSILS: Wooden

Abbott Industries Inc .... B 718 291-0800
Jamaica *(G-6622)*
Catskill Craftsmen Inc .... D 607 652-7321
Stamford *(G-15030)*
Imperial Frames & Albums LLC .... G 718 832-9793
Brooklyn *(G-1995)*
Thomas Matthews Wdwkg Ltd .... F 631 287-3657
Southampton *(G-14964)*
Thomas Matthews Wdwkg Ltd .... G 631 287-2023
Southampton *(G-14965)*

KITCHENWARE STORES

Lalique North America Inc .... E 212 355-6550
New York *(G-10512)*
Lifetime Brands Inc .... B 516 683-6000
Garden City *(G-5265)*
Nash Metalware Co Inc .... G 315 339-5794
Rome *(G-14260)*
Roger & Sons Inc .... G 212 226-4734
New York *(G-11422)*

KITCHENWARE: Plastic

L K Manufacturing Corp .... E 631 243-6910
West Babylon *(G-16169)*

KNIT GOODS, WHOLESALE

A & B Finishing Inc .... E 718 522-4702
Brooklyn *(G-1449)*
North Star Knitting Mills Inc .... G 718 894-4848
Glendale *(G-5405)*
Premier Knits Ltd .... F 718 323-8264
Ozone Park *(G-12831)*

KNIT OUTERWEAR DYEING & FINISHING, EXC HOSIERY & GLOVE

Grand Processing Inc .... E 718 388-0600
Brooklyn *(G-1948)*

KNIVES: Agricultural Or indl

Lancaster Knives Inc .... E 716 683-5050
Lancaster *(G-7029)*
Woods Knife Corporation .... E 516 798-4972
Massapequa *(G-7888)*

LABELS: Cotton, Printed

Sml USA Inc .... E 212 736-8800
New York *(G-11626)*

LABELS: Paper, Made From Purchased Materials

Accent Label & Tag Co Inc .... G 631 244-7066
Ronkonkoma *(G-14287)*
Apexx Omni-Graphics Inc .... D 718 326-3330
Maspeth *(G-7822)*
Master Image Printing Inc .... G 914 347-4400
Elmsford *(G-4550)*
Precision Label Corporation .... F 631 270-4490
Farmingdale *(G-4857)*
Quadra Flex Corp .... G 607 758-7066
Cortland *(G-3891)*
Quality Circle Products Inc .... D 914 736-6600
Montrose *(G-8329)*
Stoney Croft Converters Inc .... F 718 608-9800
Staten Island *(G-15140)*
Tri-Flex Label Corp .... E 631 293-0411
Farmingdale *(G-4898)*
Web-Tech Packaging Inc .... F 716 684-4520
Lancaster *(G-7054)*

LABELS: Woven

Colonial Tag & Label Co Inc .... F 516 482-0508
Great Neck *(G-5546)*
Imperial-Harvard Label Co .... F 212 736-8420
New York *(G-10186)*
Itc Mfg Group Inc .... F 212 684-3696
New York *(G-10278)*
Label Source Inc .... G 212 244-1403
New York *(G-10503)*
Labels Inter-Global Inc .... F 212 398-0006
New York *(G-10504)*
R-Pac International Corp .... F 212 465-1818
New York *(G-11313)*
Sml USA Inc .... E 212 736-8800
New York *(G-11626)*
Triangle Label Tag Inc .... G 718 875-3030
Brooklyn *(G-2583)*

LABORATORIES, TESTING: Forensic

Siemens Hlthcare Dgnostics Inc .... E 914 631-0475
Tarrytown *(G-15492)*

LABORATORIES, TESTING: Product Testing, Safety/Performance

Custom Sports Lab Inc .... G 212 832-1648
New York *(G-9436)*

LABORATORIES: Biological Research

Advance Biofactures Corp .... E 516 593-7000
Lynbrook *(G-7658)*
Cleveland Biolabs Inc .... E 716 849-6810
Buffalo *(G-2768)*
Eyenovia Inc .... G 917 289-1117
New York *(G-9760)*
Folia Water Inc .... E 412 802-5083
New York *(G-9821)*
Neurotrope Inc .... G 973 242-0005
New York *(G-10915)*
Synergy Pharmaceuticals Inc .... G 212 227-8611
New York *(G-11763)*

LABORATORIES: Biotechnology

LABORATORIES: Biotechnology
Acorda Therapeutics Inc .... C 914 347-4300
   Ardsley *(G-392)*
Albany Molecular Research Inc .... B 518 512-2000
   Albany *(G-35)*

LABORATORIES: Commercial Nonphysical Research
Ubm Inc .... A 212 600-3000
   New York *(G-11929)*

LABORATORIES: Dental
Marotta Dental Studio Inc .... E 631 249-7520
   Farmingdale *(G-4816)*
Martins Dental Studio .... G 315 788-0800
   Watertown *(G-16026)*

LABORATORIES: Dental Orthodontic Appliance Production
Vincent Martino Dental Lab .... F 716 674-7800
   Buffalo *(G-3119)*

LABORATORIES: Electronic Research
C & D Assembly Inc .... E 607 898-4275
   Groton *(G-5650)*
GE Aviation Systems LLC .... D 513 243-9104
   Bohemia *(G-1027)*
Intrinsiq Materials Inc .... G 585 301-4432
   Rochester *(G-13886)*
Mark - 10 Corporation .... E 631 842-9200
   Copiague *(G-3769)*
Millennium Antenna Corp .... G 315 798-9374
   Utica *(G-15722)*
Terahertz Technologies Inc .... G 315 736-3642
   Oriskany *(G-12765)*

LABORATORIES: Medical
Immco Diagnostics Inc .... G 716 691-0091
   Buffalo *(G-2881)*

LABORATORIES: Noncommercial Research
American Institute Physics Inc .... C 516 576-2410
   Melville *(G-8002)*
Human Life Foundation Inc .... G 212 685-5210
   New York *(G-10148)*

LABORATORIES: Physical Research, Commercial
Advanced Biomedical Tech Inc .... G 718 766-7898
   New York *(G-8752)*
Akzo Nobel Chemicals LLC .... C 914 674-5008
   Dobbs Ferry *(G-4129)*
Albany Molecular Research Inc .... B 518 512-2234
   Albany *(G-34)*
Conmed Corporation .... D 315 797-8375
   Utica *(G-15686)*
Danisco US Inc .... D 585 256-5200
   Rochester *(G-13733)*
Delphi Powertrain Systems LLC .... B 585 359-6000
   West Henrietta *(G-16237)*
Durata Therapeutics Inc .... G 646 871-6400
   New York *(G-9587)*
Easton Pharmaceuticals Inc .... G 347 284-0192
   Lewiston *(G-7139)*
Fujitsu Ntwrk Cmmnications Inc .... F 845 731-2000
   Pearl River *(G-12897)*
Grumman Field Support Services ...... D 516 575-0574
   Bethpage *(G-842)*
Interdgital Communications LLC .... C 631 622-4000
   Melville *(G-8038)*
International Aids Vaccine Ini .... D 646 381-8066
   Brooklyn *(G-2009)*
International Aids Vccne Inttv .... D 212 847-1111
   New York *(G-10242)*
International Paper Company .... C 845 986-6409
   Tuxedo Park *(G-15657)*
Islechem LLC .... E 716 773-4501
   Grand Island *(G-5503)*
Momentive Performance Mtls Inc ...... D 914 784-4807
   Tarrytown *(G-15484)*
Northrop Grumman Systems Corp ...... A 516 575-0574
   Bethpage *(G-850)*
OSI Pharmaceuticals LLC .... G 631 962-2000
   Farmingdale *(G-4843)*

Starfire Systems Inc .... F 518 899-9336
   Glenville *(G-5447)*
Transtech Systems Inc .... E 518 370-5558
   Latham *(G-7095)*
Xactiv Inc .... F 585 288-7220
   Fairport *(G-4668)*

LABORATORIES: Testing
Ken-Ton Open Mri PC .... G 716 876-7000
   Kenmore *(G-6863)*

LABORATORIES: Testing
A & Z Pharmaceutical Inc .... D 631 952-3802
   Hauppauge *(G-5752)*
B & H Electronics Corp .... E 845 782-5000
   Monroe *(G-8264)*
Bga Technology LLC .... E 631 750-4600
   Bohemia *(G-988)*
Dayton T Brown Inc .... B 631 589-6300
   Bohemia *(G-1011)*
G E Inspection Technologies LP .... D 315 554-2000
   Skaneateles *(G-14871)*
Kyra Communications Corp .... F 516 783-6244
   Seaford *(G-14758)*
Laser & Electron Beam Inc .... G 603 626-6080
   New York *(G-10520)*
Northeast Metrology Corp .... F 716 827-3770
   Depew *(G-4098)*
Stetron International Inc .... G 716 854-3443
   Buffalo *(G-3077)*

LABORATORY APPARATUS & FURNITURE
Biodesign Inc of New York .... F 845 454-6610
   Carmel *(G-3274)*
Dynamica Inc .... F 212 818-1900
   New York *(G-9594)*
Fungilab Inc .... G 631 750-6361
   Hauppauge *(G-5829)*
Healthalliance Hospital .... G 845 338-2500
   Kingston *(G-6901)*
Hyman Podrusnick Co Inc .... G 718 853-4502
   Brooklyn *(G-1990)*
Instrumentation Laboratory Co .... C 845 680-0028
   Orangeburg *(G-12681)*
Integrted Work Envronments LLC ...... G 716 725-5088
   East Amherst *(G-4190)*
Itin Scale Co Inc .... E 718 336-5900
   Brooklyn *(G-2019)*
Maripharm Laboratories .... F 716 984-6520
   Niagara Falls *(G-12308)*
Nalge Nunc International Corp .... A 585 498-2661
   Rochester *(G-13962)*
Newport Corporation .... E 585 248-4246
   Rochester *(G-13970)*
Radon Testing Corp of America .... F 914 345-3380
   Elmsford *(G-4559)*
S P Industries Inc .... G 845 255-5000
   Gardiner *(G-5295)*
Staplex Company Inc .... E 718 768-3333
   Brooklyn *(G-2508)*
VWR Education LLC .... C 585 359-2502
   West Henrietta *(G-16254)*

LABORATORY APPARATUS: Furnaces
Crystal Linton Technologies .... F 585 444-8784
   Rochester *(G-13726)*

LABORATORY APPARATUS: Pipettes, Hemocytometer
Vistalab Technologies Inc .... E 914 244-6226
   Brewster *(G-1176)*

LABORATORY APPARATUS: Shakers & Stirrers
Scientific Industries Inc .... E 631 567-4700
   Bohemia *(G-1085)*

LABORATORY EQPT, EXC MEDICAL: Wholesalers
Ankom Technology Corp .... E 315 986-8090
   Macedon *(G-7693)*
Enzo Life Sciences Inc .... E 631 694-7070
   Farmingdale *(G-4760)*
Eugenia Selective Living Inc .... F 631 277-1461
   Islip *(G-6546)*

Integrted Work Envronments LLC ...... G 716 725-5088
   East Amherst *(G-4190)*
Lab Crafters Inc .... E 631 471-7755
   Ronkonkoma *(G-14365)*
Magic Touch Icewares Intl .... G 212 794-2852
   New York *(G-10670)*
TEC Glass & Inst LLC .... G 315 926-7639
   Marion *(G-7809)*

LABORATORY EQPT: Chemical
Integrated Liner Tech Inc .... E 518 621-7422
   Rensselaer *(G-13475)*

LABORATORY EQPT: Clinical Instruments Exc Medical
Next Advance Inc .... F 518 674-3510
   Troy *(G-15611)*

LABORATORY EQPT: Measuring
East Hills Instrument Inc .... F 516 621-8686
   Westbury *(G-16325)*

LABORATORY EQPT: Sterilizers
Steriliz LLC .... G 585 415-5411
   Rochester *(G-14144)*

LACE GOODS & WARP KNIT FABRIC DYEING & FINISHING
Eagle Lace Dyeing Corp .... F 212 947-2712
   New York *(G-9603)*
Gehring Tricot Corporation .... D 315 429-8551
   Dolgeville *(G-4133)*
Somerset Dyeing & Finishing .... E 518 773-7383
   Gloversville *(G-5465)*

LACQUERING SVC: Metal Prdts
Berkman Bros Inc .... E 718 782-1827
   Brooklyn *(G-1601)*

LADDERS: Metal
Brakewell Stl Fabricators Inc .... E 845 469-9131
   Chester *(G-3469)*

LADDERS: Portable, Metal
Metallic Ladder Mfg Corp .... F 716 358-6201
   Randolph *(G-13448)*

LADDERS: Wood
Babcock Co Inc .... E 607 776-3341
   Bath *(G-640)*
Putnam Rolling Ladder Co Inc .... F 212 226-5147
   New York *(G-11280)*
Putnam Rolling Ladder Co Inc .... F 718 381-8219
   Brooklyn *(G-2363)*

LAMINATED PLASTICS: Plate, Sheet, Rod & Tubes
American Acrylic Corporation .... E 631 422-2200
   West Babylon *(G-16133)*
Architctral Dsgn Elements LLC .... G 718 218-7800
   Brooklyn *(G-1546)*
Displays By Rioux Inc .... E 315 458-3639
   North Syracuse *(G-12399)*
Favorite Plastic Corp .... C 718 253-7000
   Brooklyn *(G-1870)*
Griffon Corporation .... E 212 957-5000
   New York *(G-9988)*
Inland Paper Products Corp .... E 718 827-8150
   Brooklyn *(G-2005)*
Iridium Industries Inc .... E 516 504-9700
   Great Neck *(G-5563)*
Jaguar Industries Inc .... F 845 947-1800
   Haverstraw *(G-5979)*
Nalge Nunc International Corp .... A 585 498-2661
   Rochester *(G-13962)*
Strux Corp .... E 516 768-3969
   Lindenhurst *(G-7196)*

LAMINATING SVCS
Copy Room Inc .... F 212 371-8600
   New York *(G-9397)*

PRODUCT SECTION — LEAD & ZINC

Hennig Custom Woodwork Corp............G..... 516 536-3460
  Oceanside *(G-12540)*

LAMP & LIGHT BULBS & TUBES

Kreon Inc..G..... 516 470-9522
  Bethpage *(G-844)*
La Mar Lighting Co Inc........................E..... 631 777-7700
  Farmingdale *(G-4806)*
Led Waves Inc.......................................F..... 347 416-6182
  Brooklyn *(G-2103)*
Lowel-Light Manufacturing Inc...........E..... 718 921-0600
  Brooklyn *(G-2137)*
Make-Waves Instrument Corp............E..... 716 681-7524
  Buffalo *(G-2936)*
Oledworks LLC......................................E..... 585 287-6802
  Rochester *(G-13985)*
Philips Elec N Amer Corp....................C..... 607 776-3692
  Bath *(G-648)*
Ric-Lo Productions Ltd.......................E..... 845 469-2285
  Chester *(G-3481)*
Satco Products Inc..............................D..... 631 243-2022
  Edgewood *(G-4415)*
Siemens Corporation...........................F..... 202 434-7800
  New York *(G-11577)*
Siemens USA Holdings Inc.................B..... 212 258-4000
  New York *(G-11580)*
Welch Allyn Inc......................................A..... 315 685-4347
  Skaneateles Falls *(G-14884)*
Westron Corporation............................E..... 516 678-2300
  Oceanside *(G-12565)*

LAMP BULBS & TUBES, ELECTRIC: For Specialized Applications

Boehm Surgical Instrument Corp........F..... 585 436-6584
  Rochester *(G-13671)*

LAMP BULBS & TUBES, ELECTRIC: Light, Complete

Emitled Inc...G..... 516 531-3533
  Westbury *(G-16328)*
Goldstar Lighting LLC..........................F..... 646 543-6811
  New York *(G-9956)*

LAMP BULBS & TUBES/PARTS, ELECTRIC: Generalized Applications

General Electric Company...................A..... 518 385-4022
  Schenectady *(G-14675)*
Lighting Holdings Intl LLC...................A..... 845 306-1850
  Purchase *(G-13391)*
Saratoga Lighting Holdings LLC........A..... 212 906-7800
  New York *(G-11487)*

LAMP FRAMES: Wire

Lyn Jo Enterprises Ltd.........................G..... 716 753-2776
  Mayville *(G-7922)*

LAMP SHADES: Glass

Depp Glass Inc......................................F..... 718 784-8500
  Long Island City *(G-7424)*
Somers Stain Glass Inc.......................F..... 631 586-7772
  Deer Park *(G-4046)*

LAMP SHADES: Metal

Judis Lampshades Inc.........................G..... 917 561-3921
  Brooklyn *(G-2055)*

LAMP STORES

Custom Lampshades Inc.....................F..... 718 254-0500
  Brooklyn *(G-1742)*
Lighting Holdings Intl LLC...................A..... 845 306-1850
  Purchase *(G-13391)*

LAMPS: Arc Units, Electrotherapeutic

Isimulate LLC...G..... 877 947-2831
  Albany *(G-87)*

LAMPS: Floor, Residential

Adesso Inc..E..... 212 736-4440
  New York *(G-8735)*

LAMPS: Fluorescent

K & H Industries Inc..............................F..... 716 312-0088
  Hamburg *(G-5683)*
K & H Industries Inc..............................E..... 716 312-0088
  Hamburg *(G-5684)*

LAMPS: Table, Residential

Jimco Lamp & Manufacturing Co........G..... 631 218-2152
  Islip *(G-6547)*
Two Worlds Arts Ltd..............................G..... 212 929-2210
  New York *(G-11920)*

LAMPS: Ultraviolet

Atlantic Ultraviolet Corp......................E..... 631 234-3275
  Hauppauge *(G-5773)*

LAND SUBDIVIDERS & DEVELOPERS: Commercial

Micro Instrument Corp.........................D..... 585 458-3150
  Rochester *(G-13939)*

LAND SUBDIVISION & DEVELOPMENT

Nsgv Inc..E..... 212 367-3167
  New York *(G-11003)*

LANGUAGE SCHOOLS

Japan America Learning Ctr Inc..........F..... 914 723-7600
  Scarsdale *(G-14639)*

LANTERNS

Mjk Enterprises LLC..............................G..... 917 653-9042
  Brooklyn *(G-2217)*

LAPIDARY WORK & DIAMOND CUTTING & POLISHING

Engelack Gem Corporation.................G..... 212 719-3094
  New York *(G-9683)*
Fischer Diamonds Inc..........................F..... 212 869-1990
  New York *(G-9810)*
Sunshine Diamond Cutter Inc.............G..... 212 221-1028
  New York *(G-11744)*

LAPIDARY WORK: Contract Or Other

Dweck Industries Inc............................E..... 718 615-1695
  Brooklyn *(G-1798)*

LAPIDARY WORK: Jewel Cut, Drill, Polish, Recut/Setting

Classic Creations Inc...........................G..... 516 498-1991
  Great Neck *(G-5545)*
Diamond Boutique.................................G..... 516 444-3373
  Port Washington *(G-13252)*
Perma Glow Ltd Inc...............................F..... 212 575-9677
  New York *(G-11158)*
Stephen J Lipkins Inc...........................G..... 631 249-8866
  Farmingdale *(G-4881)*
Touch Adjust Clip Co Inc.....................G..... 631 589-3077
  Bohemia *(G-1096)*

LARD: From Slaughtering Plants

Bliss-Poston The Second Wind..........G..... 212 481-1055
  New York *(G-9102)*

LASER SYSTEMS & EQPT

Advanced Photonics Inc......................F..... 631 471-3693
  Ronkonkoma *(G-14293)*
Bare Beauty Laser Hair Removal........G..... 718 278-2273
  New York *(G-9015)*
Exfo Burleigh Pdts Group Inc.............D..... 585 301-1530
  Canandaigua *(G-3220)*
Gb Group Inc..G..... 212 594-3748
  New York *(G-9885)*
Idex Health & Science LLC.................D..... 585 244-7220
  Rochester *(G-13875)*
Lasermax Inc..D..... 585 272-5420
  Rochester *(G-13909)*
Navitar Inc..D..... 585 359-4000
  Rochester *(G-13965)*
Teledyne Optech Inc.............................F..... 585 427-8310
  Rochester *(G-14164)*
Uptek Solutions Corp...........................F..... 631 256-5565
  Bohemia *(G-1104)*

LASERS: Welding, Drilling & Cutting Eqpt

Empire Plastics Inc...............................E..... 607 754-9132
  Endwell *(G-4616)*
Trident Precision Mfg Inc....................D..... 585 265-2010
  Webster *(G-16103)*

LAUNDRY & GARMENT SVCS, NEC: Fur Cleaning, Repairing/Storage

Anastasia Furs International..............G..... 212 868-9241
  New York *(G-8855)*

LAUNDRY & GARMENT SVCS, NEC: Garment Alteration & Repair

Connie French Cleaners Inc...............G..... 516 487-1343
  Great Neck *(G-5548)*

LAUNDRY EQPT: Commercial

G A Braun Inc...E..... 315 475-3123
  Syracuse *(G-15327)*
Lb Laundry Inc.......................................G..... 347 399-8030
  Flushing *(G-5021)*

LAUNDRY EQPT: Household

AES Electronics Inc..............................G..... 212 371-8120
  New York *(G-8763)*
Coinmach Service Corp.......................A..... 516 349-8555
  Plainview *(G-13042)*
CSC SW Holdco Inc..............................G..... 516 349-8555
  Plainview *(G-13049)*
Penn Enterprises Inc............................F..... 845 446-0765
  West Point *(G-16283)*
Spin Holdco Inc.....................................G..... 516 349-8555
  Plainview *(G-13089)*

LAUNDRY SVC: Wiping Towel Sply

Hygrade..G..... 718 488-9000
  Brooklyn *(G-1989)*
Yankee Corp...F..... 718 589-1377
  Bronx *(G-1420)*

LAWN & GARDEN EQPT

Briggs & Stratton Corporation............C..... 315 495-0100
  Munnsville *(G-8457)*
Chapin International Inc......................C..... 585 343-3140
  Batavia *(G-617)*
Chapin Manufacturing Inc...................C..... 585 343-3140
  Batavia *(G-618)*
Clopay Ames True Temper...................F..... 212 957-5096
  New York *(G-9330)*
Fradan Manufacturing Corp................F..... 914 632-3653
  New Rochelle *(G-8605)*
Real Bark Mulch LLC............................G..... 518 747-3650
  Fort Edward *(G-5099)*
Rhett M Clark Inc...................................G..... 585 538-9570
  Caledonia *(G-3157)*

LAWN & GARDEN EQPT STORES

Nelson Holdings Ltd.............................G..... 607 772-1794
  Binghamton *(G-908)*

LAWN & GARDEN EQPT: Tractors & Eqpt

Eaton Brothers Corp.............................G..... 716 649-8250
  Hamburg *(G-5676)*
Saxby Implement Corp.........................F..... 585 624-2938
  Mendon *(G-8094)*

LAWN & GARDEN EQPT: Trimmers

Capital E Financial Group...................F..... 212 319-6550
  New York *(G-9202)*

LAWN MOWER REPAIR SHOP

Nelson Holdings Ltd.............................G..... 607 772-1794
  Binghamton *(G-908)*

LEAD & ZINC

Hh Liquidating Corp.............................A..... 646 282-2500
  New York *(G-10092)*
T L Diamond & Company Inc..............G..... 212 249-6660
  New York *(G-11768)*

Employee Codes: A=Over 500 employees, B=251-500, C=101-250, D=51-100, E=20-50, F=10-19, G=5-9

2019 Harris New York Manufacturers Directory

LEAD PENCILS & ART GOODS

Aakron Rule Corp ....C 716 542-5483
  Akron *(G-16)*
R & F Handmade Paints Inc ....F 845 331-3112
  Kingston *(G-6915)*

LEASING & RENTAL SVCS: Cranes & Aerial Lift Eqpt

R & B Fabrication Inc........................F 315 640-9901
  Cicero *(G-3522)*

LEASING & RENTAL SVCS: Earth Moving Eqpt

Duke Company..G 607 347-4455
  Ithaca *(G-6575)*

LEASING & RENTAL: Computers & Eqpt

IBM World Trade Corporation ....G 914 765-1900
  Armonk *(G-403)*
Key Computer Svcs of Chelsea............D 212 206-8060
  New York *(G-10438)*
Systems Trading Inc............................G 718 261-8900
  Melville *(G-8068)*

LEASING & RENTAL: Construction & Mining Eqpt

Christian Fabrication LLC....................G 315 822-0135
  West Winfield *(G-16305)*

LEASING & RENTAL: Other Real Estate Property

Beardslee Realty..................................G 516 747-5557
  Mineola *(G-8206)*

LEASING: Laundry Eqpt

Thermopatch Corporation....................D 315 446-8110
  Syracuse *(G-15443)*

LEASING: Shipping Container

A R Arena Products Inc ....E 585 277-1680
  Rochester *(G-13591)*
Shiprite Software Inc ....G 315 733-6191
  Utica *(G-15733)*

LEATHER GOODS, EXC FOOTWEAR, GLOVES, LUGGAGE/BELTING, WHOL

Pan American Leathers Inc................G 978 741-4150
  New York *(G-11097)*

LEATHER GOODS: Belt Laces

McM Products USA Inc.......................E 646 756-4090
  New York *(G-10744)*

LEATHER GOODS: Belting & Strapping

Fahrenheit NY Inc ....G 212 354-6554
  New York *(G-9772)*

LEATHER GOODS: Boxes

Kamali Leather LLC ....G 518 762-2522
  Johnstown *(G-6833)*

LEATHER GOODS: Cases

Slim Line Case Co Inc ....F 585 546-3639
  Rochester *(G-14131)*

LEATHER GOODS: Corners, Luggage

Deluxe Travel Store Inc ....G 718 435-8111
  Brooklyn *(G-1767)*

LEATHER GOODS: Cosmetic Bags

Baker Products Inc ....G 212 459-2323
  White Plains *(G-16425)*
M G New York Inc ....F 212 371-5566
  New York *(G-10636)*
Penthouse Manufacturing Co Inc........B 516 379-1300
  Freeport *(G-5173)*

LEATHER GOODS: Desk Sets

Star Desk Pad Co Inc..........................E 914 963-9400
  Yonkers *(G-16800)*

LEATHER GOODS: Garments

Dvf Studio LLC ....D 212 741-6607
  New York *(G-9589)*
Dvf Studio LLC ....G 646 576-8009
  New York *(G-9590)*
East West Global Sourcing Inc............G 917 887-2286
  Brooklyn *(G-1808)*
First Manufacturing Co Inc ....E 516 763-0400
  Oceanside *(G-12538)*
Perrone Leather LLC ....D 518 853-4300
  Fultonville *(G-5239)*
Tucano Usa Inc....................................G 212 966-9211
  New York *(G-11911)*

LEATHER GOODS: Holsters

Adirondack Leather Pdts Inc ....F 607 547-5798
  Fly Creek *(G-5063)*
Courtlandt Boot Jack Co Inc................G 718 445-6200
  Flushing *(G-4994)*
Helgen Industries Inc..........................C 631 841-6300
  Amityville *(G-283)*

LEATHER GOODS: Key Cases

Atlantic Specialty Co Inc ....E 845 356-2502
  Monsey *(G-8286)*
Form A Rockland Plastics Inc..............G 315 848-3300
  Cranberry Lake *(G-3907)*

LEATHER GOODS: NEC

Leather Outlet......................................G 518 668-0328
  Lake George *(G-6964)*

LEATHER GOODS: Personal

American Puff Corp ....D 516 379-1300
  Freeport *(G-5143)*
Astucci US Ltd ....F 718 752-9700
  Long Island City *(G-7392)*
Datamax International Inc ....E 212 693-0933
  New York *(G-9476)*
Elco Manufacturing Co Inc..................E 516 767-3577
  Port Washington *(G-13257)*
Excelled Sheepskin & Lea Coat..........F 212 594-5843
  New York *(G-9750)*
Fahrenheit NY Inc ....G 212 354-6554
  New York *(G-9772)*
First Manufacturing Co Inc ....E 516 763-0400
  Oceanside *(G-12538)*
Grownbeans Inc ....G 212 989-3486
  New York *(G-9999)*
Helgen Industries Inc..........................C 631 841-6300
  Amityville *(G-283)*
Hemisphere Novelties Inc ....E 914 378-4100
  Yonkers *(G-16767)*
House of Portfolios Co Inc ....E 212 206-7323
  New York *(G-10136)*
House of Portfolios Co Inc ....E 212 206-7323
  New York *(G-10137)*
Just Brass Inc ....G 212 724-5447
  New York *(G-10384)*
Leather Artisan....................................G 518 359-3102
  Childwold *(G-3499)*
Merzon Leather Co Inc ....C 718 782-6260
  Brooklyn *(G-2197)*
Neumann Jutta New York Inc..............F 212 982-7048
  New York *(G-10914)*
Tapestry Inc...B 212 594-1850
  New York *(G-11784)*

LEATHER GOODS: Transmission Belting

Sampla Belting North Amer LLC ....E 716 667-7450
  Lackawanna *(G-6953)*

LEATHER GOODS: Wallets

L Y Z Creations Ltd Inc ....E 718 768-2977
  Brooklyn *(G-2088)*
Randa Accessories Lea Gds LLC.......D 212 354-5100
  New York *(G-11325)*
Trafalgar Company LLC ....E 212 768-8800
  New York *(G-11885)*

LEATHER TANNING & FINISHING

Aston Leather Inc................................G 212 481-2760
  New York *(G-8940)*
Corium Corporation ....F 914 381-0100
  Mamaroneck *(G-7740)*
Edsim Leather Co Inc ....E 212 695-8500
  New York *(G-9630)*
Hastings Hide Inc................................G 516 295-2400
  Inwood *(G-6492)*
Legendary Auto Interiors Ltd..............E 315 331-1212
  Newark *(G-12198)*
Pearl Leather Finishers Inc ....F 518 762-4543
  Johnstown *(G-6836)*
Studio One Leather Design Inc...........F 212 760-1701
  New York *(G-11728)*

LEATHER, LEATHER GOODS & FURS, WHOLESALE

Leather Artisan....................................G 518 359-3102
  Childwold *(G-3499)*
Tandy Leather Factory Inc ....G 845 480-3588
  Nyack *(G-12511)*

LEATHER: Accessory Prdts

Adam Scott Designs Inc......................E 212 420-8866
  New York *(G-8732)*
Ariel Tian LLC......................................G 212 457-1266
  Forest Hills *(G-5072)*
Automotive Leather Group LLC ....F 516 627-4000
  Great Neck *(G-5537)*
Centric Brands Inc ....D 323 890-1800
  New York *(G-9246)*
Justin Gregory Inc ....G 631 249-5187
  Deer Park *(G-3994)*
Kamali Group Inc ....G 516 627-4000
  Great Neck *(G-5567)*
Pacific Worldwide Inc ....G 212 502-3360
  New York *(G-11091)*
Tandy Leather Factory Inc ....G 845 480-3588
  Nyack *(G-12511)*
Vic Demayos Inc ....G 845 626-4343
  Accord *(G-1)*

LEATHER: Artificial

Beckmann Converting Inc...................E 518 842-0073
  Amsterdam *(G-327)*

LEATHER: Bag

Givi Inc...F 212 586-5029
  New York *(G-9926)*
Hat Attack Inc......................................E 718 994-1000
  Bronx *(G-1288)*

LEATHER: Bookbinders'

Graphic Image Associates LLC ....D 631 249-9600
  Melville *(G-8028)*
System of AME Binding ....G 631 390-8560
  Central Islip *(G-3386)*

LEATHER: Case

Baker Products Inc ....G 212 459-2323
  White Plains *(G-16425)*

LEATHER: Colored

Mohawk River Leather Works..............F 518 853-3900
  Fultonville *(G-5237)*

LEATHER: Cut

A-1 Products Inc ....G 718 789-1818
  Brooklyn *(G-1462)*
Hohenforst Splitting Co Inc ....G 518 725-0012
  Gloversville *(G-5458)*

LEATHER: Die-cut

John Gailer Inc.....................................E 212 243-5662
  Long Island City *(G-7480)*

LEATHER: Embossed

Rainbow Leather Inc............................F 718 939-8762
  College Point *(G-3663)*

PRODUCT SECTION

LIGHTING FIXTURES: Indl & Commercial

LEATHER: Finished
- Androme Leather Inc .... F 518 773-7945
  Gloversville *(G-5451)*
- Arrow Leather Finishing Inc .... E 518 762-3121
  Johnstown *(G-6823)*
- Pan American Leathers Inc .... G 978 741-4150
  New York *(G-11097)*

LEATHER: Glove
- Shadal LLC .... G 212 319-5946
  New York *(G-11551)*

LEATHER: Handbag
- Street Smart Designs Inc .... G 646 865-0056
  New York *(G-11720)*

LEATHER: Processed
- Pearl Leather Group LLC .... E 516 627-4047
  Great Neck *(G-5580)*

LEATHER: Upholstery
- Kamali Automotive Group Inc .... F 516 627-4000
  Great Neck *(G-5566)*

LEGAL & TAX SVCS
- Westchester Law Journal Inc .... G 914 948-0715
  White Plains *(G-16518)*

LEGAL OFFICES & SVCS
- Dick Bailey Service Inc .... F 718 522-4363
  Brooklyn *(G-1775)*
- Thomson Reuters Corporation ...... A 646 223-4000
  New York *(G-11825)*
- Wave Publishing Co Inc .... F 718 634-4000
  Rockaway Beach *(G-14226)*

LEGITIMATE LIVE THEATER PRODUCERS
- Abkco Music & Records Inc .... E 212 399-0300
  New York *(G-8710)*

LENS COATING: Ophthalmic
- Equicheck LLC .... G 631 987-6356
  Patchogue *(G-12865)*
- Optisource International Inc .... E 631 924-8360
  Bellport *(G-810)*

LENSES: Plastic, Exc Optical
- Bin Optics .... G 604 257-3200
  Ithaca *(G-6561)*

LESSORS: Landholding Office
- Rock Mountain Farms Inc .... G 845 647-9084
  Ellenville *(G-4443)*

LIFESAVING & SURVIVAL EQPT, EXC MEDICAL, WHOLESALE
- Aero Healthcare (us) LLC .... G 855 225-2376
  Valley Cottage *(G-15751)*

LIGHT SENSITIVE DEVICES
- Nsi Industries LLC .... C 800 841-2505
  Mount Vernon *(G-8426)*
- Tork Inc .... D 914 664-3542
  Mount Vernon *(G-8446)*

LIGHTING EQPT: Flashlights
- Psg Innovations Inc .... F 917 299-8986
  Valley Stream *(G-15792)*

LIGHTING EQPT: Motor Vehicle, Headlights
- Licenders .... G 212 759-5200
  New York *(G-10561)*

LIGHTING EQPT: Motor Vehicle, NEC
- Mobile Fleet Inc .... G 631 206-2920
  Hauppauge *(G-5896)*

LIGHTING EQPT: Outdoor
- Northern Air Technology Inc .... G 585 594-5050
  Rochester *(G-13981)*

LIGHTING EQPT: Reflectors, Metal, For Lighting Eqpt
- Island Lite Louvers Inc .... E 631 608-4250
  Amityville *(G-289)*

LIGHTING EQPT: Streetcar Fixtures
- Power and Cnstr Group Inc .... E 585 889-6020
  Scottsville *(G-14752)*

LIGHTING EQPT: Strobe Lighting Systems
- Star Headlight Lantern Co Inc .... C 585 226-9500
  Avon *(G-522)*

LIGHTING FIXTURES WHOLESALERS
- Expo Furniture Designs Inc .... F 516 674-1420
  Glen Cove *(G-5365)*
- Global Lighting Inc .... G 914 591-4095
  Yonkers *(G-16762)*
- Lighting Holdings Intl LLC .... A 845 306-1850
  Purchase *(G-13391)*
- Matov Industries Inc .... E 718 392-5060
  Long Island City *(G-7518)*
- Quality HM Brands Holdings LLC .. G 718 292-2024
  Bronx *(G-1368)*
- Quoizel Inc .... E 631 436-4402
  Hauppauge *(G-5927)*
- Satco Products Inc .... D 631 243-2022
  Edgewood *(G-4415)*
- Solarwaterway Inc .... E 888 998-5337
  Brooklyn *(G-2496)*
- Visual Effects Inc .... F 718 324-0011
  Jamaica *(G-6689)*

LIGHTING FIXTURES, NEC
- Broadway National Group LLC ..... D 800 797-4467
  Ronkonkoma *(G-14321)*
- Cooper Industries LLC .... E 315 477-7000
  Syracuse *(G-15291)*
- Creative Stage Lighting Co Inc ..... E 518 251-3302
  North Creek *(G-12391)*
- Edison Power & Light Co Inc .... F 718 522-0002
  Brooklyn *(G-1814)*
- Fabbian USA Corp .... G 973 882-3824
  New York *(G-9769)*
- General Led Corp .... G 516 280-2854
  Mineola *(G-8223)*
- Goddard Design Co .... G 718 599-0170
  Brooklyn *(G-1936)*
- Gordon S Anderson Mfg Co .... G 845 677-3304
  Millbrook *(G-8188)*
- Gti Graphic Technology Inc .... E 845 562-7066
  Newburgh *(G-12225)*
- J M Canty Inc .... E 716 625-4227
  Lockport *(G-7310)*
- Jag Lighting .... G 917 226-3575
  Maspeth *(G-7855)*
- Jaquith Industries Inc .... E 315 478-5700
  Syracuse *(G-15346)*
- Jed Lights Inc .... F 516 812-5001
  Deer Park *(G-3992)*
- Jt Roselle Lighting & Sup Inc .... F 914 666-3700
  Mount Kisco *(G-8346)*
- Julian A McDermott Corporation ... E 718 456-3606
  Ridgewood *(G-13540)*
- La Mar Lighting Co Inc .... E 631 777-7700
  Farmingdale *(G-4806)*
- Lamparts Co Inc .... F 914 723-8986
  Mount Vernon *(G-8416)*
- Light Blue USA LLC .... G 718 475-2515
  Brooklyn *(G-2119)*
- Lighting N Beyond LLC .... G 718 669-9142
  Blauvelt *(G-937)*
- Lighting Sculptures Inc .... F 631 242-3387
  Deer Park *(G-4002)*
- Luminescent Systems Inc .... B 716 655-0800
  East Aurora *(G-4204)*
- Olive Led Lighting Inc .... G 718 746-0830
  College Point *(G-3658)*
- Rodac USA Corp .... F 716 741-3931
  Clarence *(G-3541)*
- Saratoga Lighting Holdings LLC ... A 212 906-7800
  New York *(G-11487)*
- Sensio America .... F 877 501-5337
  Clifton Park *(G-3576)*
- Sensio America LLC .... F 877 501-5337
  Clifton Park *(G-3577)*
- Shakuff LLC .... G 212 675-0383
  Brooklyn *(G-2462)*
- Siemens Electro Industrial Sa ...... A 212 258-4000
  New York *(G-11578)*
- Strider Global LLC .... G 212 726-1302
  New York *(G-11723)*
- Tecnolux Incorporated .... G 718 369-3900
  Brooklyn *(G-2560)*
- Times Square Stage Ltg Co Inc ... E 845 947-3034
  Stony Point *(G-15177)*
- Truck-Lite Co LLC .... F 716 665-2614
  Falconer *(G-4695)*
- Vertex Innovative Solutions .... F 315 437-6711
  Syracuse *(G-15452)*
- Vincent Conigliaro .... F 845 340-0489
  Kingston *(G-6931)*
- Visual Effects Inc .... F 718 324-0011
  Jamaica *(G-6689)*
- Vivid Rgb Lighting LLC .... G 718 635-0817
  Peekskill *(G-12926)*

LIGHTING FIXTURES: Airport
- Eaton Crouse-Hinds .... C 315 477-7000
  Syracuse *(G-15312)*

LIGHTING FIXTURES: Decorative Area
- Enchante Lites LLC .... G 212 602-1818
  New York *(G-9673)*
- Secret Celebrity Licensing LLC ..... G 212 812-9277
  New York *(G-11528)*

LIGHTING FIXTURES: Fluorescent, Commercial
- La Mar Lighting Co Inc .... E 631 777-7700
  Farmingdale *(G-4806)*
- Legion Lighting Co Inc .... E 718 498-1770
  Brooklyn *(G-2107)*
- Lite Brite Manufacturing Inc .... E 718 855-9797
  Brooklyn *(G-2129)*
- Spectronics Corporation .... C 516 333-4840
  Westbury *(G-16373)*
- Vision Quest Lighting Inc .... E 631 737-4800
  East Setauket *(G-4314)*

LIGHTING FIXTURES: Fluorescent, Residential
- Az-Light Inc .... G 716 837-5533
  Buffalo *(G-2719)*
- Eaton Corporation .... E 315 579-2872
  Syracuse *(G-15311)*

LIGHTING FIXTURES: Indl & Commercial
- A-1 Stamping & Spinning Corp ..... F 718 388-2626
  Rockaway Park *(G-14227)*
- AEP Environmental LLC .... F 716 446-0739
  Buffalo *(G-2690)*
- Aesthonics Inc .... D 646 723-2463
  Brooklyn *(G-1492)*
- Altman Stage Lighting Co Inc .... C 914 476-7987
  Yonkers *(G-16733)*
- Apogee Translite Inc .... E 631 254-6975
  Deer Park *(G-3944)*
- Apparatus Studio .... E 646 527-9732
  New York *(G-8887)*
- Aquarii Inc .... G 315 672-8807
  Camillus *(G-3194)*
- Aristocrat Lighting Inc .... F 718 522-0003
  Brooklyn *(G-1553)*
- Arlee Lighting Corp .... G 516 595-8558
  Inwood *(G-6485)*
- Big Shine Worldwide Inc .... G 845 444-5255
  Newburgh *(G-12216)*
- Canarm Ltd .... G 800 267-4427
  Ogdensburg *(G-12572)*
- Coldstream Group Inc .... F 914 698-5959
  Mamaroneck *(G-7739)*
- Contemporary Visions LLC .... G 845 926-5469
  Wappingers Falls *(G-15928)*
- Cooper Industries LLC .... C 315 477-7000
  Syracuse *(G-15291)*
- Cooper Lighting LLC .... C 516 470-1000
  Hicksville *(G-6071)*

Employee Codes: A=Over 500 employees, B=251-500
C=101-250, D=51-100, E=20-50, F=10-19, G=5-9

2019 Harris
New York Manufacturers Directory

Dreyfus Ashby Inc ....E.... 212 818-0770
New York *(G-9578)*
E-Ffinergy Group LLC ....G.... 845 547-2424
Suffern *(G-15189)*
Edison Price Lighting Inc ....C.... 718 685-0700
Long Island City *(G-7433)*
Edison Price Lighting Inc ....D.... 718 685-0700
Long Island City *(G-7434)*
Electric Lighting Agencies ....E.... 212 645-4580
New York *(G-9640)*
Energy Conservation & Sup Inc ....E.... 718 855-5888
Brooklyn *(G-1836)*
G&G Led LLC ....E.... 800 285-6780
Clifton Park *(G-3566)*
Green Energy Concepts Inc ....G.... 845 238-2574
Chester *(G-3476)*
Hudson Valley Lighting Inc ....D.... 845 561-0300
Wappingers Falls *(G-15935)*
Ideoli Group Inc ....F.... 212 705-8769
Port Washington *(G-13268)*
Jesco Lighting Inc ....E.... 718 366-3211
Port Washington *(G-13273)*
Jesco Lighting Group LLC ....E.... 718 366-3211
Port Washington *(G-13274)*
LDI Lighting Inc ....G.... 718 384-4490
Brooklyn *(G-2098)*
Light Waves Concept Inc ....F.... 212 677-6400
Brooklyn *(G-2121)*
Lighting By Dom Yonkers Inc ....G.... 914 968-8700
Yonkers *(G-16779)*
Lighting Services Inc ....D.... 845 942-2800
Stony Point *(G-15174)*
Linear Lighting Corporation ....C.... 718 361-7552
Long Island City *(G-7500)*
Litelab Corp ....G.... 718 361-6829
Long Island City *(G-7502)*
Litelab Corp ....C.... 716 856-4300
Buffalo *(G-2926)*
LSI Lightron Inc ....A.... 845 562-5500
New Windsor *(G-8649)*
Lukas Lighting Inc ....E.... 800 841-4011
Long Island City *(G-7506)*
Luminatta Inc ....G.... 914 664-3600
Mount Vernon *(G-8419)*
Luminescent Systems Inc ....B.... 716 655-0800
East Aurora *(G-4204)*
Magniflood Inc ....E.... 631 226-1000
Amityville *(G-301)*
Matov Industries Inc ....E.... 718 392-5060
Long Island City *(G-7518)*
Modulightor Inc ....F.... 212 371-0336
New York *(G-10832)*
Mtz Enterprises Inc ....F.... 347 834-2716
Brooklyn *(G-2237)*
North American Mfg Entps Inc ....E.... 718 524-4370
Staten Island *(G-15109)*
North American Mfg Entps Inc ....F.... 718 524-4370
Staten Island *(G-15110)*
Nulux Inc ....E.... 718 383-1112
Ridgewood *(G-13544)*
Oledworks LLC ....E.... 585 287-6802
Rochester *(G-13985)*
Philips Lighting N Amer Corp ....C.... 646 265-7170
New York *(G-11182)*
Preciseled Inc ....F.... 516 418-5337
Valley Stream *(G-15790)*
Primelite Manufacturing Corp ....G.... 516 868-4411
Freeport *(G-5176)*
Rapid-Lite Fixture Corporation ....F.... 347 599-2600
Brooklyn *(G-2384)*
Remains Lighting ....E.... 212 675-8051
New York *(G-11358)*
S E A Supplies Ltd ....F.... 516 694-6677
Plainview *(G-13086)*
Sandy Littman Inc ....G.... 845 562-1112
Newburgh *(G-12245)*
Saratoga Lighting Holdings LLC ....A.... 212 906-7800
New York *(G-11487)*
Savenergy Inc ....G.... 516 239-1958
Garden City *(G-5280)*
Savwatt Usa Inc ....G.... 646 478-2676
New York *(G-11494)*
Selux Corporation ....C.... 845 691-7723
Highland *(G-6147)*
Solarpath Inc ....G.... 201 490-4499
New York *(G-11639)*
Solarwaterway Inc ....E.... 888 998-5337
Brooklyn *(G-2496)*
Swivelier Company Inc ....D.... 845 353-1455
Blauvelt *(G-941)*
Twinkle Lighting Inc ....G.... 718 225-0939
Flushing *(G-5056)*
Versaponents Inc ....F.... 631 242-3387
Deer Park *(G-4059)*
Vital Vio Inc ....F.... 914 245-6048
Troy *(G-15632)*
Xeleum Lighting LLC ....F.... 954 617-8170
Mount Kisco *(G-8360)*
Zumtobel Lighting Inc ....C.... 845 691-6262
Highland *(G-6148)*

LIGHTING FIXTURES: Motor Vehicle

Copy Cat ....G.... 718 934-2192
Brooklyn *(G-1716)*
Truck-Lite Co LLC ....E.... 716 665-2614
Falconer *(G-4695)*
Truck-Lite Co LLC ....B.... 716 665-6214
Falconer *(G-4696)*
Wolo Mfg Corp ....E.... 631 242-0333
Deer Park *(G-4064)*

LIGHTING FIXTURES: Ornamental, Commercial

LDI Lighting Inc ....G.... 718 384-4490
Brooklyn *(G-2097)*
Rle Industries LLC ....E.... 973 276-1444
New York *(G-11402)*

LIGHTING FIXTURES: Public

CEIT Corp ....F.... 518 825-0649
Plattsburgh *(G-13116)*
Tarsier Ltd ....C.... 646 880-8680
New York *(G-11785)*
USA Illumination Inc ....E.... 845 565-8500
New Windsor *(G-8662)*

LIGHTING FIXTURES: Residential

A-1 Stamping & Spinning Corp ....F.... 718 388-2626
Rockaway Park *(G-14227)*
Aesthonics Inc ....D.... 646 723-2463
Brooklyn *(G-1492)*
Artemis Studios Inc ....D.... 718 788-6022
Brooklyn *(G-1558)*
Canarm Ltd ....G.... 800 267-4427
Ogdensburg *(G-12572)*
Cooper Lighting LLC ....C.... 516 470-1000
Hicksville *(G-6071)*
David Weeks Studio ....F.... 212 966-3433
New York *(G-9486)*
ER Butler & Co Inc ....E.... 212 925-3565
New York *(G-9699)*
Hudson Valley Lighting Inc ....D.... 845 561-0300
Wappingers Falls *(G-15935)*
Jamaica Lamp Corp ....E.... 718 776-5039
Queens Village *(G-13409)*
Litelab Corp ....C.... 716 856-4300
Buffalo *(G-2926)*
Matov Industries Inc ....E.... 718 392-5060
Long Island City *(G-7518)*
Modulightor Inc ....F.... 212 371-0336
New York *(G-10832)*
New Generation Lighting Inc ....F.... 212 966-0328
New York *(G-10923)*
Nulux Inc ....E.... 718 383-1112
Ridgewood *(G-13544)*
Philips Elec N Amer Corp ....C.... 607 776-3692
Bath *(G-648)*
Pompian Manufacturing Co Inc ....G.... 914 476-7076
Yonkers *(G-16793)*
Preciseled Inc ....F.... 516 418-5337
Valley Stream *(G-15790)*
Prestigeline Inc ....D.... 631 273-3636
Bay Shore *(G-710)*
Quality HM Brands Holdings LLC ....G.... 718 292-2024
Bronx *(G-1368)*
Quoizel Inc ....E.... 631 436-4402
Hauppauge *(G-5927)*
Rapid-Lite Fixture Corporation ....F.... 347 599-2600
Brooklyn *(G-2384)*
Remains Lighting ....E.... 212 675-8051
New York *(G-11358)*
Sandy Littman Inc ....G.... 845 562-1112
Newburgh *(G-12245)*
Saratoga Lighting Holdings LLC ....A.... 212 906-7800
New York *(G-11487)*
Satco Products Inc ....D.... 631 243-2022
Edgewood *(G-4415)*
Savwatt Usa Inc ....G.... 646 478-2676
New York *(G-11494)*
Solarwaterway Inc ....E.... 888 998-5337
Brooklyn *(G-2496)*
Swarovski Lighting Ltd ....B.... 518 563-7500
Plattsburgh *(G-13161)*
Swivelier Company Inc ....D.... 845 353-1455
Blauvelt *(G-941)*
Tarsier Ltd ....C.... 646 880-8680
New York *(G-11785)*
Tudor Electrical Supply Co Inc ....G.... 212 867-7550
New York *(G-11912)*
Ulster Precision Inc ....E.... 845 338-0995
Kingston *(G-6925)*
Vaughan Designs Inc ....F.... 212 319-7070
New York *(G-12000)*
Vision Quest Lighting Inc ....E.... 631 737-4800
East Setauket *(G-4314)*
Wainland Inc ....E.... 718 626-2233
Astoria *(G-448)*

LIGHTING FIXTURES: Residential, Electric

Expo Furniture Designs Inc ....F.... 516 674-1420
Glen Cove *(G-5365)*
Lighting Collaborative Inc ....G.... 212 253-7220
Brooklyn *(G-2122)*
Serway Bros Inc ....E.... 315 337-0601
Rome *(G-14274)*

LIGHTING FIXTURES: Street

Eluminocity US Inc ....G.... 651 528-1165
New York *(G-9660)*
Power and Cnstr Group Inc ....E.... 585 889-6020
Scottsville *(G-14752)*

LIGHTS: Trouble lights

Lyn Jo Enterprises Ltd ....G.... 716 753-2776
Mayville *(G-7922)*

LIME

Lime Energy Co ....G.... 704 892-4442
Buffalo *(G-2923)*

LIME: Agricultural

Masick Soil Conservation Co ....F.... 518 827-5354
Schoharie *(G-14732)*

LIMESTONE & MARBLE: Dimension

Domoteck Interiors Inc ....G.... 718 433-4300
Woodside *(G-16653)*
Minerals Technologies Inc ....E.... 212 878-1800
New York *(G-10817)*

LIMESTONE: Crushed & Broken

Barrett Paving Materials Inc ....F.... 315 737-9471
Clayville *(G-3554)*
Buffalo Crushed Stone Inc ....E.... 716 632-6963
Clarence *(G-3526)*
Cayuga Crushed Stone Inc ....E.... 607 533-4273
Lansing *(G-7055)*
Cobleskill Stone Products Inc ....F.... 518 299-3066
Prattsville *(G-13378)*
Cobleskill Stone Products Inc ....F.... 518 295-7121
Schoharie *(G-14731)*
Cobleskill Stone Products Inc ....F.... 518 234-0221
Cobleskill *(G-3601)*
Cobleskill Stone Products Inc ....F.... 607 637-4271
Hancock *(G-5710)*
Hanson Aggregates PA Inc ....E.... 315 858-1100
Jordanville *(G-6844)*
Hanson Aggregates PA LLC ....E.... 315 469-5501
Jamesville *(G-6768)*
Hanson Aggregates PA LLC ....E.... 315 685-3321
Skaneateles *(G-14875)*
Hanson Aggregates PA LLC ....E.... 585 624-1220
Honeoye Falls *(G-6267)*
Hanson Aggregates PA LLC ....F.... 315 821-7222
Oriskany Falls *(G-12767)*
Hanson Aggregates PA LLC ....E.... 315 789-6202
Oaks Corners *(G-12528)*
Jml Quarries Inc ....E.... 845 932-8206
Cochecton *(G-3606)*
John Vespa Inc ....F.... 315 788-6330
Watertown *(G-16019)*
Lilac Quarries LLC ....G.... 607 867-4016
Mount Upton *(G-8371)*

PRODUCT SECTION — LOGGING CAMPS & CONTRACTORS

Patterson Materials Corp .... E 845 832-6000
  New Windsor *(G-8654)*
Shelby Crushed Stone Inc .... E 585 798-4501
  Medina *(G-7989)*
Specialty Minerals Inc .... E 212 878-1800
  New York *(G-11661)*
Upstone Materials Inc .... E 518 891-0236
  Saranac Lake *(G-14564)*

LIMESTONE: Cut & Shaped

Hanson Aggregates East LLC .... F 315 493-3721
  Great Bend *(G-5526)*
Minerals Technologies Inc .... E 212 878-1800
  New York *(G-10817)*

LIMESTONE: Dimension

New York Quarries Inc .... F 518 756-3138
  Alcove *(G-165)*

LIMESTONE: Ground

Hanson Aggregates PA Inc .... F 518 568-2444
  Saint Johnsville *(G-14518)*
Hanson Aggregates PA LLC .... F 315 393-3743
  Ogdensburg *(G-12574)*

LINEN SPLY SVC: Apron

White Plains Coat Apron Co Inc .... G 914 736-2610
  Peekskill *(G-12931)*

LINEN SPLY SVC: Coat

Maple Grove Corp .... E 585 492-5286
  Arcade *(G-386)*

LINENS & TOWELS WHOLESALERS

American Country Quilts & Lin .... G 631 283-5466
  Southampton *(G-14949)*
David King Linen Inc .... F 718 241-7298
  New York *(G-9482)*
E & F Home Fashions Inc .... F 718 968-9719
  Brooklyn *(G-1802)*
Paramount Textiles Inc .... F 212 966-1040
  New York *(G-11109)*

LINENS: Napkins, Fabric & Nonwoven, From Purchased Materials

Bardwil Industries Inc .... C 212 944-1870
  New York *(G-9014)*

LINENS: Tablecloths, From Purchased Materials

Josie Accessories Inc .... D 212 889-6376
  New York *(G-10366)*
Michael Stuart Inc .... E 718 821-0704
  Brooklyn *(G-2204)*
Premier Skirting Products Inc .... F 516 239-6581
  Lawrence *(G-7107)*
Repellem Consumer Pdts Corp .... F 631 273-3992
  Bohemia *(G-1082)*
Tablecloths For Granted Ltd .... F 518 370-5481
  Schenectady *(G-14719)*
University Table Cloth Company .... F 845 371-3876
  Spring Valley *(G-15012)*

LINERS & COVERS: Fabric

Kragel Co Inc .... G 716 648-1344
  Hamburg *(G-5685)*
Meyco Products Inc .... E 631 421-9800
  Melville *(G-8046)*
Vinyl Works Inc .... E 518 786-1200
  Latham *(G-7097)*

LINERS & LINING

Themis Chimney Inc .... F 718 937-4716
  Brooklyn *(G-2565)*

LINERS: Indl, Metal Plate

Lifetime Chimney Supply LLC .... G 516 576-8144
  Plainview *(G-13069)*

LINIMENTS

Ges Ges .... G 631 291-9624
  Hauppauge *(G-5834)*

LININGS: Apparel, Made From Purchased Materials

Bpe Studio Inc .... G 212 868-9896
  New York *(G-9131)*

LININGS: Fabric, Apparel & Other, Exc Millinery

Amoseastern Apparel Inc .... F 212 921-1859
  New York *(G-8846)*
Pangea Brands LLC .... F 617 638-0001
  New York *(G-11098)*
Pangea Brands LLC .... F 617 638-0001
  New York *(G-11099)*
Polkadot Usa Inc .... G 914 835-3697
  Mamaroneck *(G-7754)*

LIP BALMS

Lotta Luv Beauty LLC .... F 646 786-2847
  New York *(G-10614)*

LIPSTICK

Precision Cosmetics Mfg Co .... G 914 667-1200
  Mount Vernon *(G-8431)*

LIQUEFIED PETROLEUM GAS DEALERS

Praxair Distribution Inc .... G 315 457-5821
  Liverpool *(G-7256)*

LIQUID CRYSTAL DISPLAYS

Apollo Display Tech Corp .... E 631 580-4360
  Ronkonkoma *(G-14310)*
Dimension Technologies Inc .... G 585 436-3530
  Rochester *(G-13742)*
Orthogonal .... G 585 254-2775
  Rochester *(G-13996)*
Plura Broadcast Inc .... G 516 997-5675
  Massapequa *(G-7882)*
W D Technology Inc .... G 914 779-8738
  Eastchester *(G-4383)*

LITHOGRAPHIC PLATES

Chakra Communications Inc .... E 716 505-7300
  Lancaster *(G-7013)*

LOCK & KEY SVCS

Advanced Door Solutions Inc .... G 631 773-6100
  Holbrook *(G-6169)*

LOCKERS

Locker Masters Inc .... F 518 288-3203
  Granville *(G-5519)*

LOCKERS: Refrigerated

Carrier Corporation .... B 315 432-3844
  East Syracuse *(G-4330)*

LOCKS

A & L Doors & Hardware LLC .... F 718 585-8400
  Bronx *(G-1199)*
Delta Lock Company LLC .... F 631 238-7035
  Bohemia *(G-1012)*
Dortronics Systems Inc .... E 631 725-0505
  Sag Harbor *(G-14499)*
Eazy Locks LLC .... G 718 327-7770
  Far Rockaway *(G-4699)*
G Marks Hdwr Liquidating Corp .... D 631 225-5400
  Amityville *(G-276)*
Safe Skies LLC .... G 888 632-5027
  New York *(G-11464)*

LOCKS: Coin-Operated

American Lckr SEC Systems Inc .... E 716 699-2773
  Ellicottville *(G-4444)*

LOCKS: Safe & Vault, Metal

Secureit Tactical Inc .... A 800 651-8835
  Syracuse *(G-15421)*

LOCKSMITHS

A & L Doors & Hardware LLC .... F 718 585-8400
  Bronx *(G-1199)*

LOCOMOTIVES & PARTS

Higher Power Industries Inc .... G 914 709-9800
  Yonkers *(G-16768)*

LOG LOADING & UNLOADING SVCS

Bart Ostrander Trckg Log Corp .... G 518 661-6535
  Mayfield *(G-7919)*
Seaway Timber Harvesting Inc .... D 315 769-5970
  Massena *(G-7908)*

LOGGING

Attica Package Company Inc .... F 585 591-0510
  Attica *(G-459)*
B & B Forest Products Ltd .... F 518 622-0811
  Cairo *(G-3146)*
Bart Ostrander Trckg Log Corp .... G 518 661-6535
  Mayfield *(G-7919)*
C J Logging Equipment Inc .... E 315 942-5431
  Boonville *(G-1117)*
Central Timber Co Inc .... G 518 638-6338
  Granville *(G-5518)*
Chad Pierson .... G 518 251-0186
  Bakers Mills *(G-537)*
Clearlake Land Co Inc .... F 315 848-2427
  Star Lake *(G-15035)*
Daniel & Lois Lyndaker Logging .... G 315 346-6527
  Castorland *(G-3299)*
Davis Logging & Lumber .... G 315 245-1040
  Camden *(G-3187)*
Donald Snyder Jr .... F 315 265-4485
  Potsdam *(G-13318)*
Ed Beach Forest Management .... G 607 538-1745
  Bloomville *(G-960)*
Finger Lakes Timber Co Inc .... G 585 346-2990
  Livonia *(G-7278)*
Guldenschuh Logging & Lbr LLC .... G 585 538-4750
  Caledonia *(G-3155)*
Harris Logging Inc .... E 518 792-1083
  Queensbury *(G-13427)*
Kevin Regan Logging Ltd .... G 315 245-3890
  Camden *(G-3190)*
Mountain Forest Products Inc .... G 518 597-3674
  Crown Point *(G-3916)*
Northern Timber Harvesting LLC .... F 585 233-7330
  Alfred Station *(G-187)*
Oak Valley Logging Inc .... G 518 622-8249
  Cairo *(G-3151)*
Peters LLC .... G 607 637-5470
  Hancock *(G-5713)*
Russell Bass .... F 607 637-5253
  Hancock *(G-5714)*
Schaefer Logging Inc .... F 607 467-4990
  Deposit *(G-4111)*
Seaway Timber Harvesting Inc .... D 315 769-5970
  Massena *(G-7908)*
Tim Cretin Logging & Sawmill .... F 315 946-4476
  Lyons *(G-7688)*
Timothy L Simpson .... G 518 234-1401
  Sharon Springs *(G-14799)*
Van Cpeters Logging Inc .... G 607 637-3574
  Hancock *(G-5715)*
William Ward Logging .... F 518 946-7826
  Jay *(G-6775)*

LOGGING CAMPS & CONTRACTORS

Baker Logging & Firewood .... G 585 374-5733
  Naples *(G-8470)*
Couture Timber Harvesting .... G 607 836-4719
  Mc Graw *(G-7926)*
Decker Forest Products Inc .... G 607 563-2345
  Sidney *(G-14852)*
George Chilson Logging .... G 607 732-1558
  Elmira *(G-4488)*
Homer Logging Contractor .... G 607 753-8553
  Homer *(G-6257)*
J & S Logging Inc .... E 315 262-2112
  South Colton *(G-14925)*
Klein & Sons Logging Inc .... F 845 292-6682
  Wht Sphr Spgs *(G-16557)*
Lizotte Logging Inc .... G 518 359-2200
  Tupper Lake *(G-15650)*
Matteson Logging Inc .... G 585 593-3037
  Wellsville *(G-16118)*
Murray Logging LLC .... G 518 834-7372
  Keeseville *(G-6853)*
Paul J Mitchell Logging Inc .... E 518 359-7029
  Tupper Lake *(G-15652)*

Employee Codes: A=Over 500 employees, B=251-500
C=101-250, D=51-100, E=20-50, F=10-19, G=5-9

2019 Harris
New York Manufacturers Directory

LOGGING CAMPS & CONTRACTORS

Richard Bauer Logging ....G...... 585 343-4149
  Alexander *(G-181)*
Richards Logging LLC ....F...... 518 359-2775
  Tupper Lake *(G-15653)*
Robert W Butts Logging Co ....G...... 518 643-2897
  Peru *(G-12972)*
Smoothbore International Inc ....G...... 315 754-8124
  Red Creek *(G-13455)*
Snyder Logging ....F...... 315 265-1462
  Potsdam *(G-13323)*
Wadsworth Logging Inc ....F...... 518 863-6870
  Gloversville *(G-5471)*

LOGGING: Timber, Cut At Logging Camp

GL & RL Logging Inc ....F...... 518 883-3936
  Broadalbin *(G-1189)*
Got Wood LLC ....G...... 315 440-8857
  Cleveland *(G-3561)*
Lyndaker Timber Harvesting LLC ....F...... 315 346-1328
  Castorland *(G-3300)*
Tonche Timber LLC ....G...... 845 389-3489
  Amsterdam *(G-360)*

LOGGING: Wood Chips, Produced In The Field

Chip It All Ltd ....G...... 631 473-2040
  Port Jefferson *(G-13220)*

LOGGING: Wooden Logs

Kapstone Container Corporation ....D...... 518 842-2450
  Amsterdam *(G-342)*

LOOSELEAF BINDERS

Acco Brands USA LLC ....C...... 847 541-9500
  Ogdensburg *(G-12568)*
Brewer-Cantelmo Co Inc ....E...... 212 244-4600
  New York *(G-9138)*
Consolidated Loose Leaf Inc ....E...... 212 924-5800
  New York *(G-9384)*
Sellco Industries Inc ....E...... 607 756-7594
  Cortland *(G-3894)*

LOTIONS OR CREAMS: Face

Abbe Laboratories Inc ....F...... 631 756-2223
  Farmingdale *(G-4707)*
Distribio USA LLC ....G...... 212 989-6077
  New York *(G-9540)*
EL Erman International Ltd ....G...... 212 444-9440
  Brooklyn *(G-1819)*
Estee Lauder International Inc ....G...... 212 572-4200
  New York *(G-9720)*
Fsr Beauty Ltd ....G...... 212 447-0036
  New York *(G-9855)*
Gassho Body & Mind Inc ....G...... 518 695-9991
  Schuylerville *(G-14734)*
Restorsea LLC ....G...... 212 828-8878
  New York *(G-11372)*

LOTIONS: SHAVING

Glacee Skincare LLC ....G...... 212 690-7632
  New York *(G-9927)*

LOUDSPEAKERS

Global Market Development Inc ....E...... 631 667-1000
  Edgewood *(G-4402)*
Speaqua Corp ....E...... 858 334-9042
  Deer Park *(G-4048)*

LOUVERS: Ventilating

Airflex Industrial Inc ....E...... 631 752-1234
  Farmingdale *(G-4710)*
Airflex Industrial Inc ....D...... 631 752-1234
  Farmingdale *(G-4711)*
Imperial Damper & Louver Co ....E...... 718 731-3800
  Bronx *(G-1294)*

LOZENGES: Pharmaceutical

HHS Pharmaceuticals Inc ....F...... 347 674-1670
  New York *(G-10093)*

LUBRICANTS: Corrosion Preventive

Engineering Maint Pdts Inc ....F...... 516 624-9774
  Oyster Bay *(G-12813)*

Reliance Fluid Tech LLC ....E...... 716 332-0988
  Niagara Falls *(G-12329)*

LUBRICATING EQPT: Indl

Advanced Tchncal Solutions Inc ....F...... 914 214-8230
  Mahopac *(G-7707)*

LUBRICATING OIL & GREASE WHOLESALERS

Chemlube International LLC ....F...... 914 381-5800
  Harrison *(G-5725)*
Chemlube Marketing Inc ....F...... 914 381-5800
  Harrison *(G-5726)*

LUBRICATION SYSTEMS & EQPT

Bowen Products Corporation ....G...... 315 498-4481
  Nedrow *(G-8478)*

LUGGAGE & BRIEFCASES

Adam Scott Designs Inc ....E...... 212 420-8866
  New York *(G-8732)*
Atlantic Specialty Co Inc ....E...... 845 356-2502
  Monsey *(G-8286)*
Bragley Mfg Co Inc ....E...... 718 622-7469
  Brooklyn *(G-1631)*
Deluxe Travel Store Inc ....G...... 718 435-8111
  Brooklyn *(G-1767)*
Fish & Crown Ltd ....D...... 212 707-9603
  New York *(G-9813)*
Golden Bridge Group Inc ....G...... 718 335-8882
  Elmhurst *(G-4467)*
Goyard NM Beverly Hills LLC ....G...... 212 355-3872
  New York *(G-9965)*
Hornet Group Inc ....D...... 845 858-6400
  Port Jervis *(G-13230)*
Prepac Designs Inc ....G...... 914 524-7800
  Yonkers *(G-16794)*
Rhino Trunk & Case Inc ....F...... 585 244-4553
  Rochester *(G-14071)*
Royal Industries Inc ....E...... 718 369-3046
  Brooklyn *(G-2420)*
Trunk & Trolley LLC ....G...... 212 947-9001
  New York *(G-11905)*

LUGGAGE & LEATHER GOODS STORES: Leather, Exc Luggage & Shoes

House of Portfolios Co Inc ....E...... 212 206-7323
  New York *(G-10136)*
Tandy Leather Factory Inc ....G...... 845 480-3588
  Nyack *(G-12511)*

LUGGAGE WHOLESALERS

Deluxe Travel Store Inc ....G...... 718 435-8111
  Brooklyn *(G-1767)*

LUGGAGE: Traveling Bags

Aka Sport Inc ....F...... 631 858-9888
  Dix Hills *(G-4118)*
Carry-All Canvas Bag Co Inc ....G...... 718 375-4230
  Brooklyn *(G-1678)*
Lo & Sons Inc ....F...... 917 775-4025
  Brooklyn *(G-2132)*

LUGGAGE: Wardrobe Bags

Goyard Inc ....G...... 212 813-0005
  New York *(G-9963)*
Goyard Miami LLC ....G...... 212 813-0005
  New York *(G-9964)*

LUMBER & BLDG MATLS DEALER, RET: Garage Doors, Sell/Install

Amarr Company ....F...... 585 426-8290
  Rochester *(G-13622)*
EZ Lift Operator Corp ....F...... 845 356-1676
  Spring Valley *(G-14990)*
L & L Overhead Garage Doors ....G...... 718 721-2518
  Long Island City *(G-7494)*

LUMBER & BLDG MATRLS DEALERS, RET: Bath Fixtures, Eqpt/Sply

Vaire LLC ....G...... 631 271-4933
  Huntington Station *(G-6463)*

PRODUCT SECTION

LUMBER & BLDG MTRLS DEALERS, RET: Doors, Storm, Wood/Metal

Finger Lakes Trellis Supply ....G...... 315 904-4007
  Williamson *(G-16558)*

LUMBER & BLDG MTRLS DEALERS, RET: Windows, Storm, Wood/Metal

All United Window Corp ....E...... 718 624-0490
  Brooklyn *(G-1509)*
Express Building Supply Inc ....E...... 516 608-0379
  Oceanside *(G-12537)*

LUMBER & BUILDING MATERIAL DEALERS, RETAIL: Roofing Material

Hri Metals LLC ....G...... 518 822-1013
  Hudson *(G-6354)*

LUMBER & BUILDING MATERIALS DEALER, RET: Door & Window Prdts

City Store Gates Mfg Corp ....E...... 718 939-9700
  College Point *(G-3642)*
D D & L Inc ....F...... 607 729-9131
  Binghamton *(G-878)*
Executive Mirror Doors Inc ....G...... 631 234-1090
  Ronkonkoma *(G-14340)*
Lif Industries Inc ....E...... 718 767-8800
  Whitestone *(G-16545)*
M & D Installers Inc ....D...... 718 782-6978
  Brooklyn *(G-2141)*
Thompson Overhead Door Co Inc ....F...... 718 788-2470
  Brooklyn *(G-2566)*

LUMBER & BUILDING MATERIALS DEALER, RET: Masonry Matls/Splys

Afco Precast Sales Corp ....D...... 631 924-7114
  Middle Island *(G-8116)*
Cranesville Block Co Inc ....G...... 315 384-4000
  Norfolk *(G-12357)*
Ferrara Bros LLC ....E...... 718 939-3030
  Flushing *(G-4999)*
Guardian Concrete Inc ....F...... 518 372-0080
  Schenectady *(G-14686)*
Nicolia Concrete Products Inc ....D...... 631 669-0700
  Lindenhurst *(G-7185)*
Palumbo Block Co Inc ....E...... 845 832-6100
  Dover Plains *(G-4145)*

LUMBER & BUILDING MATERIALS DEALERS, RETAIL: Brick

Barrasso & Sons Trucking Inc ....E...... 631 581-0360
  Islip Terrace *(G-6552)*
Brick-It Inc ....G...... 631 244-3993
  Hauppauge *(G-5783)*

LUMBER & BUILDING MATERIALS DEALERS, RETAIL: Countertops

Nlr Counter Tops LLC ....G...... 347 295-0410
  New York *(G-10980)*
NY Cabinet Factory Inc ....F...... 718 256-6541
  Brooklyn *(G-2278)*

LUMBER & BUILDING MATERIALS DEALERS, RETAIL: Paving Stones

Pallette Stone Corporation ....E...... 518 584-2421
  Gansevoort *(G-5244)*
Unilock New York Inc ....G...... 845 278-6700
  Brewster *(G-1175)*

LUMBER & BUILDING MATERIALS DEALERS, RETAIL: Sand & Gravel

Champion Materials Inc ....G...... 315 493-2654
  Carthage *(G-3289)*

LUMBER & BUILDING MATERIALS DEALERS, RETAIL: Tile, Ceramic

Amendola MBL & Stone Ctr Inc ....D...... 914 997-7968
  White Plains *(G-16419)*
Glen Plaza Marble & Gran Inc ....G...... 516 671-1100
  Glen Cove *(G-5368)*

PRODUCT SECTION

LUMBER & BUILDING MATERIALS RET DEALERS: Millwork & Lumber

Andike Millwork Inc .... G 718 894-1796
  Maspeth *(G-7821)*
Attica Package Company Inc .... F 585 591-0510
  Attica *(G-459)*
Island Street Lumber Co Inc .... G 716 692-4127
  North Tonawanda *(G-12434)*
Meltz Lumber Co of Mellenville .... E 518 672-7021
  Hudson *(G-6363)*
Metalocke Industries Inc .... G 718 267-9200
  Woodside *(G-16663)*
Pella Corporation .... C 631 208-0710
  Calverton *(G-3168)*
Pgs Millwork Inc .... D 518 828-2608
  Hudson *(G-6368)*
Stephenson Lumber Company Inc .... G 518 548-7521
  Speculator *(G-14973)*

LUMBER & BUILDING MATLS DEALERS, RET: Concrete/Cinder Block

Cranesville Block Co Inc .... E 518 684-6154
  Amsterdam *(G-333)*
Duke Concrete Products Inc .... E 518 793-7743
  Queensbury *(G-13422)*
Fort Miller Service Corp .... F 518 695-5000
  Greenwich *(G-5640)*
Taylor Concrete Products Inc .... E 315 788-2191
  Watertown *(G-16034)*

LUMBER: Dimension, Hardwood

Norton-Smith Hardwoods Inc .... G 716 945-0346
  Salamanca *(G-14529)*
Wrights Hardwoods Inc .... E 716 595-2345
  Cassadaga *(G-3291)*

LUMBER: Fiberboard

Niagara Fiberboard Inc .... E 716 434-8881
  Lockport *(G-7322)*

LUMBER: Fuelwood, From Mill Waste

GM Palmer Inc .... F 585 492-2990
  Arcade *(G-383)*
PA Pellets LLC .... F 814 848-9970
  Pittsford *(G-13024)*

LUMBER: Furniture Dimension Stock, Softwood

Hennig Custom Woodwork Corp .... G 516 536-3460
  Oceanside *(G-12540)*

LUMBER: Hardwood Dimension

A D Bowman & Son Lumber Co .... E 607 692-2595
  Castle Creek *(G-3294)*
Carlson Wood Products Inc .... G 716 287-2923
  Sinclairville *(G-14864)*
Gutchess Lumber Co Inc .... C 607 753-3393
  Cortland *(G-3876)*

LUMBER: Hardwood Dimension & Flooring Mills

B & B Lumber Company Inc .... C 866 282-0582
  Jamesville *(G-6763)*
Clements Burrville Sawmill .... G 315 782-4549
  Watertown *(G-16008)*
Donver Incorporated .... F 716 945-1910
  Kill Buck *(G-6878)*
Fibron Products Inc .... E 716 886-2378
  Buffalo *(G-2826)*
H B Millwork Inc .... E 631 289-8086
  Medford *(G-7949)*
Horizon Floors I LLC .... G 212 509-9686
  New York *(G-10123)*
J & J Log & Lumber Corp .... D 845 832-6535
  Dover Plains *(G-4144)*
J A Yansick Lumber Co Inc .... E 585 492-4312
  Arcade *(G-385)*
Mm of East Aurora LLC .... F 716 651-9663
  Buffalo *(G-2949)*
Petteys Lumber .... G 518 792-5943
  Fort Ann *(G-5090)*
Potter Lumber Co Inc .... E 716 373-1260
  Allegany *(G-192)*

Premier Hardwood Products Inc .... E 315 492-1786
  Jamesville *(G-6769)*
S Donadic Inc .... D 718 361-9888
  Sunnyside *(G-15205)*
Tupper Lake Hardwoods Inc .... E 518 359-8248
  Tupper Lake *(G-15655)*
Wagner Millwork Inc .... D 607 687-5362
  Owego *(G-12805)*

LUMBER: Kiln Dried

Carlson Wood Products Inc .... G 716 287-2923
  Sinclairville *(G-14864)*
Mallery Lumber LLC .... E 607 637-2236
  Hancock *(G-5712)*
Salamanca Lumber Company Inc .... E 716 945-4810
  Salamanca *(G-14530)*

LUMBER: Plywood, Hardwood

Veneer One Inc .... E 516 536-6480
  Oceanside *(G-12563)*

LUMBER: Plywood, Hardwood or Hardwood Faced

Kings Quartet Corp .... G 845 986-9090
  Warwick *(G-15955)*

LUMBER: Plywood, Prefinished, Hardwood

Geonex International Corp .... G 212 473-4555
  New York *(G-9909)*

LUMBER: Plywood, Softwood

H B Millwork Inc .... E 631 289-8086
  Medford *(G-7949)*

LUMBER: Poles, Wood, Untreated

3b Timber Company Inc .... F 315 942-6580
  Boonville *(G-1113)*

LUMBER: Siding, Dressed

Weather Tight Exteriors .... G 631 375-5108
  Ridge *(G-13525)*

LUMBER: Silo Stock, Sawn

Machina Deus Lex Inc .... G 917 577-0972
  Jamaica *(G-6657)*

LUMBER: Treated

Donver Incorporated .... F 716 945-1910
  Kill Buck *(G-6878)*
Northeast Treaters Inc .... E 518 945-2660
  Athens *(G-451)*

LUNCHROOMS & CAFETERIAS

Wired Coffee and Bagel Inc .... F 518 506-3194
  Malta *(G-7733)*

MACHINE PARTS: Stamped Or Pressed Metal

Allen Machine Products Inc .... E 631 630-8800
  Hauppauge *(G-5761)*
Belrix Industries Inc .... G 716 821-5964
  Buffalo *(G-2729)*
Brach Machine Inc .... F 585 343-9134
  Batavia *(G-615)*
Cgs Fabrication LLC .... F 585 347-6127
  Webster *(G-16078)*
Colonial Precision Machinery .... G 631 249-0738
  Farmingdale *(G-4737)*
Creative Design and Mch Inc .... E 845 778-9001
  Rock Tavern *(G-14224)*
Custom Metal Incorporated .... F 631 643-4075
  West Babylon *(G-16151)*
Electric Motors and Pumps Inc .... G 718 935-9118
  Brooklyn *(G-1820)*
Forkey Construction & Fabg Inc .... E 607 849-4879
  Cortland *(G-3872)*
G A Richards & Co Inc .... F 516 334-5412
  Westbury *(G-16334)*
German Machine & Assembly Inc .... E 585 546-4200
  Rochester *(G-13831)*
Lancaster Knives Inc .... G 716 683-5050
  Lancaster *(G-7029)*
M F Manufacturing Enterprises .... G 516 822-5135
  Hicksville *(G-6104)*

MACHINE SHOPS

Maehr Industries Inc .... G 631 924-1661
  Bellport *(G-807)*
Mega Tool & Mfg Corp .... E 607 734-8398
  Elmira *(G-4498)*
Pervi Precision Company Inc .... G 631 589-5557
  Bohemia *(G-1074)*
Rayco Manufacturing Co Inc .... F 516 431-2006
  Jamaica *(G-6672)*
Reynolds Manufacturing Inc .... F 607 562-8936
  Big Flats *(G-856)*
Sharon Manufacturing Co Inc .... G 631 242-8870
  Deer Park *(G-4045)*
Solidus Industries Inc .... D 607 749-4540
  Homer *(G-6259)*
Twinco Mfg Co Inc .... E 631 231-0022
  Hauppauge *(G-5963)*
Vosky Precision Machining Corp .... F 631 737-3200
  Ronkonkoma *(G-14429)*
Wessie Machine Inc .... G 315 926-4060
  Marion *(G-7811)*
Zeta Machine Corp .... G 631 471-8832
  Ronkonkoma *(G-14433)*

MACHINE SHOPS

Acad Design Corp .... F 585 254-6960
  Rochester *(G-13594)*
Allied Industrial Products Co .... G 716 664-3893
  Jamestown *(G-6697)*
Applied Technology Mfg Corp .... E 607 687-2200
  Owego *(G-12795)*
Architectural Coatings Inc .... F 718 418-9584
  Brooklyn *(G-1547)*
Birch Machine & Tool Inc .... G 716 735-9802
  Middleport *(G-8131)*
Bms Manufacturing Co Inc .... E 607 535-2426
  Watkins Glen *(G-16058)*
Carballo Contract Machining .... G 315 594-2511
  Wolcott *(G-16609)*
Carbaugh Tool Company Inc .... E 607 739-3293
  Elmira *(G-4475)*
Cem Machine Inc .... E 315 493-4258
  Carthage *(G-3288)*
Centerless Technology Inc .... F 585 436-2240
  Rochester *(G-13700)*
Conesus Lake Association Inc .... E 585 346-6864
  Lakeville *(G-6985)*
Crowley Fabg Machining Co Inc .... E 607 484-0299
  Endicott *(G-4585)*
David Fehlman .... G 315 455-8888
  Syracuse *(G-15303)*
DMD Machining Technology Inc .... G 585 659-8180
  Kendall *(G-6856)*
Elite Precise Manufacturer LLC .... G 518 993-3040
  Fort Plain *(G-5102)*
Engineering Mfg Tech LLC .... D 607 754-7111
  Endicott *(G-4591)*
Euro Gear (usa) Inc .... E 518 578-1775
  Plattsburgh *(G-13120)*
Everfab Inc .... D 716 655-1550
  East Aurora *(G-4198)*
Fortech Inc .... G 315 478-2048
  Syracuse *(G-15324)*
Harwitt Industries Inc .... F 516 623-9787
  Freeport *(G-5161)*
Hohl Machine & Conveyor Co Inc .... E 716 882-7210
  Buffalo *(G-2873)*
Indian Springs Mfg Co Inc .... F 315 635-6101
  Baldwinsville *(G-556)*
Industrial Services of Wny .... G 716 799-7788
  Niagara Falls *(G-12299)*
Island Machine Inc .... G 518 562-1232
  Plattsburgh *(G-13127)*
ISO Plastics Corp .... D 914 663-8300
  Mount Vernon *(G-8410)*
Johnnys Machine Shop .... G 631 338-9733
  West Babylon *(G-16166)*
Jordan Machine Inc .... G 585 647-3585
  Rochester *(G-13898)*
Kal Manufacturing Corporation .... E 585 265-4310
  Webster *(G-16088)*
KMA Corporation .... G 518 743-1330
  Glens Falls *(G-5430)*
Knise & Krick Inc .... E 315 422-3516
  Syracuse *(G-15357)*
M & S Precision Machine Co LLC .... F 518 747-1193
  Queensbury *(G-13433)*
Magellan Aerospace Bethel Inc .... C 203 798-9373
  Corona *(G-3848)*
Mar-A-Thon Filters Inc .... G 631 957-4774
  Lindenhurst *(G-7177)*

MACHINE SHOPS — PRODUCT SECTION

Mount Vernon Machine Inc .... E 845 268-9400
  Valley Cottage (G-15759)
Ms Spares LLC .... G 607 223-3024
  Clay (G-3551)
Optics Technology Inc .... G 585 586-0950
  Pittsford (G-13023)
Precision Metals Corp .... E 631 586-5032
  Bay Shore (G-709)
Pronto Tool & Die Co Inc .... E 631 981-8920
  Ronkonkoma (G-14401)
Roccera LLC .... F 585 426-0887
  Rochester (G-14077)
Saturn Industries Inc .... E 518 828-9956
  Hudson (G-6370)
Sick Inc .... E 585 347-2000
  Webster (G-16098)
Source Technologies .... F 718 708-0305
  Brooklyn (G-2500)
Tioga Tool Inc .... F 607 785-6005
  Endicott (G-4611)
Tobeyco Manufacturing Co Inc .... F 607 962-2446
  Corning (G-3827)
Triple Point Manufacturing .... G 631 218-4988
  Bohemia (G-1101)
Twinco Mfg Co Inc .... G 631 231-0022
  Hauppauge (G-5963)
V Lake Industries Inc .... G 716 885-9141
  Buffalo (G-3115)
Vader Systems LLC .... F 716 688-1600
  Getzville (G-5355)
Van Thomas Inc .... E 585 426-1414
  Rochester (G-14199)
Verns Machine Co Inc .... E 315 926-4223
  Marion (G-7810)
Village Decoration Ltd .... E 315 437-2522
  East Syracuse (G-4380)

MACHINE TOOL ACCESS: Balancing Machines

Schenck Corporation .... D 631 242-4010
  Deer Park (G-4040)
Schenck Trebel Corp .... D 631 242-4010
  Deer Park (G-4041)

MACHINE TOOL ACCESS: Cams

Designatronics Incorporated .... G 516 328-3300
  Hicksville (G-6079)

MACHINE TOOL ACCESS: Cutting

Ameri-Cut Tool Grinding Inc .... G 716 692-3900
  North Tonawanda (G-12410)
Boro Park Cutting Tool Corp .... E 718 720-0610
  Staten Island (G-15053)
Champion Cutting Tool Corp .... E 516 536-8200
  Rockville Centre (G-14230)
Dura-Mill Inc .... E 518 899-2255
  Ballston Spa (G-582)
Genesee Manufacturing Co Inc .... G 585 266-3201
  Rochester (G-13829)
Griffin Manufacturing Company .... E 585 265-1991
  Webster (G-16085)
Macinnes Tool Corporation .... E 585 467-1920
  Rochester (G-13921)
Morgood Tools Inc .... D 585 436-8828
  Rochester (G-13956)
Rota File Corporation .... E 516 496-7200
  Syosset (G-15231)
Steiner Technologies Inc .... F 585 425-5910
  Fairport (G-4660)

MACHINE TOOL ACCESS: Diamond Cutting, For Turning, Etc

Advance D Tech Inc .... F 845 534-8248
  Cornwall (G-3829)

MACHINE TOOL ACCESS: Dies, Thread Cutting

Brinkman Intl Group Inc .... G 585 429-5000
  Rochester (G-13676)
C J Winter Machine Tech .... E 585 429-5000
  Rochester (G-13685)

MACHINE TOOL ACCESS: Dressing/Wheel Crushing Attach, Diamond

Scomac Inc .... F 585 494-2200
  Bergen (G-827)

MACHINE TOOL ACCESS: Drills

Truebite Inc .... F 607 786-3184
  Endicott (G-4613)

MACHINE TOOL ACCESS: Knives, Shear

Lancaster Knives Inc .... E 716 683-5050
  Lancaster (G-7029)

MACHINE TOOL ACCESS: Milling Machine Attachments

Innex Industries Inc .... E 585 247-3575
  Rochester (G-13880)

MACHINE TOOL ACCESS: Sockets

Socket Products Mfg Corp .... G 631 232-9870
  Islandia (G-6538)

MACHINE TOOL ACCESS: Tool Holders

New Market Products LLC .... E 607 292-6226
  Wayne (G-16073)
Robert J Faraone .... G 585 232-7160
  Rochester (G-14076)

MACHINE TOOL ACCESS: Tools & Access

Fred M Velepec Co Inc .... E 718 821-6636
  Glendale (G-5400)
Huron TI Cutter Grinding Inc .... E 631 420-7000
  Farmingdale (G-4782)
JD Tool Inc .... E 607 786-3129
  Endicott (G-4599)
Methods Tooling & Mfg Inc .... E 845 246-7100
  Mount Marion (G-8364)
Rochling Advent Tool & Mold LP .... D 585 254-2000
  Rochester (G-14100)

MACHINE TOOL ATTACHMENTS & ACCESS

Curran Manufacturing Corp .... E 631 273-1010
  Hauppauge (G-5807)
Curran Manufacturing Corp .... G 631 273-1010
  Hauppauge (G-5808)
Flexbar Machine Corporation .... F 631 582-8440
  Islandia (G-6528)
Innovative Automation Inc .... F 631 439-3300
  Farmingdale (G-4785)
Jem Tool & Die Corp .... F 631 539-8734
  West Islip (G-16259)
Prz Technologies Inc .... F 716 683-1300
  Lancaster (G-7042)
Thuro Metal Products Inc .... E 631 435-0444
  Brentwood (G-1145)
Velmex Inc .... E 585 657-6151
  Bloomfield (G-958)

MACHINE TOOLS & ACCESS

Acu-Rite Companies Inc .... G 716 661-1700
  Jamestown (G-6695)
Ale-Techniques Inc .... F 845 687-7200
  High Falls (G-6139)
American Linear Manufacturers .... F 516 333-1351
  Westbury (G-16314)
Baldwin Machine Works Inc .... G 631 842-9110
  Copiague (G-3754)
Bdp Industries Inc .... E 518 695-6851
  Greenwich (G-5636)
Bnm Product Service .... G 631 750-1586
  Holbrook (G-6172)
Circo File Corp .... G 516 922-1848
  Oyster Bay (G-12811)
Custom Service Solutions Inc .... G 585 637-3760
  Brockport (G-1190)
Dinosaw Inc .... E 518 828-9942
  Hudson (G-6347)
Dock Hardware Incorporated .... F 585 266-7920
  Rochester (G-13747)
Everfab Inc .... D 716 655-1550
  East Aurora (G-4198)
F W Roberts Mfg Co Inc .... F 716 434-3555
  Lockport (G-7300)
Flashflo Manufacturing Inc .... F 716 826-9500
  Buffalo (G-2827)
Gardei Industries LLC .... F 716 693-7100
  North Tonawanda (G-12429)
Germanow-Simon Corporation .... E 585 232-1440
  Rochester (G-13832)
Graywood Companies Inc .... E 585 254-7000
  Rochester (G-13845)
Helmel Engineering Pdts Inc .... E 716 297-8644
  Niagara Falls (G-12293)
J H Robotics Inc .... E 607 729-3758
  Johnson City (G-6812)
Kps Capital Partners LP .... E 212 338-5100
  New York (G-10476)
Linde LLC .... D 716 773-7552
  Grand Island (G-5506)
M & S Precision Machine Co LLC ..... F 518 747-1193
  Queensbury (G-13433)
Make-Waves Instrument Corp .... E 716 681-7524
  Buffalo (G-2936)
Michael Fiore Ltd .... G 516 561-8238
  Valley Stream (G-15786)
Myles Tool Company Inc .... E 716 731-1300
  Sanborn (G-14550)
Omega Tool Measuring Mchs Inc ...... E 585 598-7800
  Fairport (G-4645)
Parlec LLC .... D 585 425-4400
  Fairport (G-4648)
Precision Mechanisms Corp .... E 516 333-5955
  Westbury (G-16366)
Production Metal Cutting Inc .... F 585 458-7136
  Rochester (G-14050)
Ross JC Inc .... G 716 439-1161
  Lockport (G-7328)
S & S Machinery Corp .... E 718 492-7400
  Brooklyn (G-2432)
S S Precision Gear & Instr .... G 718 457-7474
  Corona (G-5342)
Seneca Falls Machine Tool Co .... D 315 568-5804
  Seneca Falls (G-14785)
Sinn-Tech Industries Inc .... F 631 643-1171
  West Babylon (G-16192)
Strippit Inc .... E 716 542-4511
  Akron (G-23)
Transport National Dev Inc .... E 716 662-0270
  Orchard Park (G-12747)
Trident Precision Mfg Inc .... D 585 265-2010
  Webster (G-16103)
Universal Tooling Corporation .... F 716 985-4691
  Gerry (G-5342)
Vandilay Industries Inc .... E 631 226-3064
  West Babylon (G-16202)

MACHINE TOOLS, METAL CUTTING: Centering

Rush Machinery Inc .... G 585 554-3070
  Rushville (G-14477)

MACHINE TOOLS, METAL CUTTING: Exotic, Including Explosive

High Speed Hammer Company Inc .... F 585 266-4287
  Rochester (G-13869)

MACHINE TOOLS, METAL CUTTING: Grind, Polish, Buff, Lapp

Hartchrom Inc .... F 518 880-0411
  Watervliet (G-16047)
Mortech Industries Inc .... G 845 628-6138
  Mahopac (G-7709)

MACHINE TOOLS, METAL CUTTING: Lathes

Zyp Precision LLC .... G 315 539-3667
  Waterloo (G-15998)

MACHINE TOOLS, METAL CUTTING: Numerically Controlled

Omega Tool Measuring Mchs Inc ...... E 585 598-7800
  Fairport (G-4645)
Ppi Corp .... E 585 880-7277
  Rochester (G-14031)
Ppi Corp .... D 585 243-0300
  Rochester (G-14032)
Precise Tool & Mfg Inc .... D 585 247-0700
  Rochester (G-14033)

PRODUCT SECTION   MACHINERY & EQPT, INDL, WHOLESALE: Countersinks

MACHINE TOOLS, METAL CUTTING: Tool Replacement & Rpr Parts

Advanced Machine Design Co Inc .... E 716 826-2000
 Buffalo *(G-2689)*
Welch Machine Inc .... G 585 647-3578
 Rochester *(G-14205)*

MACHINE TOOLS, METAL FORMING: Die Casting & Extruding

Raloid Tool Co Inc .... F 518 664-4261
 Mechanicville *(G-7933)*

MACHINE TOOLS, METAL FORMING: Electroforming

Precision Eforming LLC .... F 607 753-7730
 Cortland *(G-3889)*

MACHINE TOOLS, METAL FORMING: Forging Machinery & Hammers

Special Metals Corporation .... D 716 366-5663
 Dunkirk *(G-4180)*
Trueforge Global McHy Corp .... G 516 825-7040
 Rockville Centre *(G-14243)*

MACHINE TOOLS, METAL FORMING: Forming, Metal Deposit

Vader Systems LLC .... F 716 688-1600
 Getzville *(G-5355)*

MACHINE TOOLS, METAL FORMING: Headers

American Racing Headers Inc .... E 631 608-1427
 Deer Park *(G-3940)*

MACHINE TOOLS, METAL FORMING: High Energy Rate

Arconic Inc .... G 716 358-6451
 Falconer *(G-4671)*
Smart High Voltage Solutions .... F 631 563-6724
 Bohemia *(G-1090)*

MACHINE TOOLS, METAL FORMING: Presses, Hyd & Pneumatic

Servotec Usa LLC .... G 518 671-6120
 Hudson *(G-6372)*

MACHINE TOOLS, METAL FORMING: Pressing

Mpi Incorporated .... C 845 471-7630
 Poughkeepsie *(G-13356)*

MACHINE TOOLS, METAL FORMING: Punching & Shearing

Manhasset Tool & Die Co Inc .... F 716 684-6066
 Lancaster *(G-7031)*

MACHINE TOOLS, METAL FORMING: Rebuilt

Uhmac Inc .... F 716 537-2343
 Holland *(G-6223)*

MACHINE TOOLS, METAL FORMING: Spinning, Spline Rollg/Windg

Gemcor Automation LLC .... D 716 674-9300
 West Seneca *(G-16298)*

MACHINE TOOLS: Metal Cutting

Abtex Corporation .... E 315 536-7403
 Dresden *(G-4146)*
Alpine Machine Inc .... F 607 272-1344
 Ithaca *(G-6556)*
Alternative Service Inc .... F 631 345-9500
 Bellport *(G-798)*
Alton Manufacturing Inc .... D 585 458-2600
 Rochester *(G-13621)*
Ascension Industries Inc .... C 716 693-9381
 North Tonawanda *(G-12413)*
Aztec Mfg of Rochester .... G 585 352-8112
 Spencerport *(G-14975)*
Brinkman Products Inc .... B 585 235-4545
 Rochester *(G-13677)*
Coastel Cable Tools Inc .... E 315 471-5361
 Syracuse *(G-15283)*
Dinosaw Inc .... E 518 828-9942
 Hudson *(G-6347)*
Dunlap Machine LLC .... F 315 926-1013
 Marion *(G-7800)*
Gallery of Machines LLC .... G 607 849-6028
 Marathon *(G-7789)*
Gb Aero Engine LLC .... B 914 925-9600
 Rye *(G-14480)*
Genco John .... G 716 483-5446
 Jamestown *(G-6717)*
Gleason Corporation .... A 585 473-1000
 Rochester *(G-13839)*
H S Assembly Inc .... G 585 266-4287
 Rochester *(G-13849)*
Halpern Tool Corp .... F 914 633-0038
 New Rochelle *(G-8611)*
Hardinge Inc .... B 607 734-2281
 Elmira *(G-4490)*
IPC/Razor LLC .... D 212 551-4500
 New York *(G-10266)*
J Vogler Enterprise LLC .... F 585 247-1625
 Rochester *(G-13889)*
Jalex Industries Ltd .... F 631 491-5072
 West Babylon *(G-16163)*
Kodiak Cutting Tools LLC .... G 800 892-1006
 Syracuse *(G-15358)*
Kps Capital Partners LP .... E 212 338-5100
 New York *(G-10476)*
Kyocera Precision Tools Inc .... F 607 687-0012
 Owego *(G-12798)*
Lancaster Knives Inc .... E 716 683-5050
 Lancaster *(G-7029)*
Lk Industries Inc .... E 716 941-9202
 Glenwood *(G-5448)*
Montrose Equipment Sales Inc .... F 718 388-7446
 Brooklyn *(G-2225)*
Multimatic Products Inc .... D 800 767-7633
 Ronkonkoma *(G-14381)*
Munson Machinery Company Inc .... E 315 797-0090
 Utica *(G-15724)*
Myles Tool Company Inc .... E 716 731-1300
 Sanborn *(G-14550)*
Nifty Bar Grinding & Cutting .... E 585 381-0450
 Penfield *(G-12942)*
Omega Consolidated Corporation .... E 585 392-9262
 Hilton *(G-6158)*
P & R Industries Inc .... E 585 266-6725
 Rochester *(G-14001)*
Producto Corporation .... C 716 484-7131
 Jamestown *(G-6744)*
R Steiner Technologies Inc .... E 585 425-5912
 Fairport *(G-4655)*
Rapid Precision Machining Inc .... D 585 467-0780
 Rochester *(G-14069)*
S & S Machinery Corp .... E 718 492-7400
 Brooklyn *(G-2432)*
S & S Machinery Corp .... E 718 492-7400
 Brooklyn *(G-2433)*
Selflock Screw Products Co Inc .... E 315 541-4464
 Syracuse *(G-15422)*
Seneca Falls Capital Inc .... G 315 568-5804
 Seneca Falls *(G-14784)*
Seneca Falls Machine Tool Co .... D 315 568-5804
 Seneca Falls *(G-14785)*
Simmons Machine Tool Corp .... C 518 462-5431
 Menands *(G-8091)*
Teka Precision Inc .... G 845 753-1900
 Nyack *(G-12512)*
Transport National Dev Inc .... E 716 662-0270
 Orchard Park *(G-12746)*
Truemade Products Inc .... G 631 981-4755
 Ronkonkoma *(G-14422)*
Verns Machine Co Inc .... E 315 926-4223
 Marion *(G-7810)*
World LLC .... F 631 940-9121
 Deer Park *(G-4065)*
Zwack Incorporated .... E 518 733-5135
 Stephentown *(G-15156)*

MACHINE TOOLS: Metal Forming

Adaptive Mfg Tech Inc .... E 631 580-5400
 Ronkonkoma *(G-14290)*
Advanced Machine Design Co Inc .... E 716 826-2000
 Buffalo *(G-2689)*
Advantage Metalwork Finshg LLC .... D 585 454-0160
 Rochester *(G-13608)*
Austin Industries Inc .... G 585 589-1353
 Albion *(G-155)*
Bdp Industries Inc .... E 518 695-6851
 Greenwich *(G-5636)*
Brinkman Intl Group Inc .... G 585 429-5000
 Rochester *(G-13676)*
Buffalo Machine Tls of Niagara .... F 716 201-1310
 Lockport *(G-7288)*
C & T Tool & Instrument Co .... E 718 429-1253
 Woodside *(G-16648)*
C J Winter Machine Tech .... E 585 429-5000
 Rochester *(G-13685)*
Commodore Manufactring Corp .... E 718 788-2600
 Brooklyn *(G-1709)*
Dover Global Holdings Inc .... F 212 922-1640
 New York *(G-9562)*
Dunlap Machine LLC .... F 315 926-1013
 Marion *(G-7800)*
Ecko Fin & Tooling Inc .... F 716 487-0200
 Jamestown *(G-6712)*
Gh Induction Atmospheres LLC .... E 585 368-2120
 Rochester *(G-13835)*
Hawthorne Garden Company .... F 516 883-6550
 Port Washington *(G-13263)*
Hydramec Inc .... E 585 593-5190
 Scio *(G-14735)*
Lourdes Systems Inc .... F 631 234-7077
 Hauppauge *(G-5874)*
Miller Mechanical Services Inc .... E 518 792-0430
 Glens Falls *(G-5434)*
Prim Hall Enterprises Inc .... F 518 561-7408
 Plattsburgh *(G-13150)*
Producto Corporation .... C 716 484-7131
 Jamestown *(G-6744)*
Schaefer Machine Co Inc .... E 516 248-6880
 Mineola *(G-8249)*
Standard Paper Box Machine Co .... E 718 328-3300
 Bronx *(G-1392)*
Strippit Inc .... C 716 542-4511
 Akron *(G-23)*
Taumel Metalforming Corp .... G 845 878-3100
 Patterson *(G-12886)*

MACHINERY & EQPT, AGRICULTURAL, WHOLESALE: Dairy

Brook North Farms Inc .... F 315 834-9390
 Auburn *(G-472)*

MACHINERY & EQPT, AGRICULTURAL, WHOLESALE: Landscaping Eqpt

Upstone Materials Inc .... F 315 265-8036
 Plattsburgh *(G-13166)*

MACHINERY & EQPT, AGRICULTURAL, WHOLESALE: Lawn & Garden

Rhett M Clark Inc .... G 585 538-9570
 Caledonia *(G-3157)*

MACHINERY & EQPT, INDL, WHOL: Controlling Instruments/Access

Unimar Inc .... F 315 699-4400
 Syracuse *(G-15448)*

MACHINERY & EQPT, INDL, WHOL: Recording Instruments/Access

His Productions USA Inc .... G 212 594-3737
 New York *(G-10105)*

MACHINERY & EQPT, INDL, WHOLESALE: Conveyor Systems

Vetra Systems Corporation .... G 631 434-3185
 Hauppauge *(G-5969)*

MACHINERY & EQPT, INDL, WHOLESALE: Countersinks

Empire Fabricators Inc .... G 585 235-3050
 Rochester *(G-13779)*
Nlr Counter Tops LLC .... G 347 295-0410
 New York *(G-10980)*

Employee Codes: A=Over 500 employees, B=251-500
C=101-250, D=51-100, E=20-50, F=10-19, G=5-9

MACHINERY & EQPT, INDL, WHOLESALE: Cranes

Armor Machining Services, Inc. .... E 716 825-0190
Buffalo (G-2709)

MACHINERY & EQPT, INDL, WHOLESALE: Fans

Canarm Ltd .... G 800 267-4427
Ogdensburg (G-12572)

MACHINERY & EQPT, INDL, WHOLESALE: Food Manufacturing

Vr Food Equipment Inc .... F 315 531-8133
Farmington (G-4921)

MACHINERY & EQPT, INDL, WHOLESALE: Food Product Manufacturng

Crepini LLC .... E 347 422-0829
Brooklyn (G-1730)
ET Oakes Corporation .... E 631 232-0002
Hauppauge (G-5821)
Hobart Corporation .... E 631 864-3440
Commack (G-3695)

MACHINERY & EQPT, INDL, WHOLESALE: Heat Exchange

Aavid Niagara LLC .... E 716 297-0652
Niagara Falls (G-12257)

MACHINERY & EQPT, INDL, WHOLESALE: Hydraulic Systems

Ener-G-Rotors Inc .... G 518 372-2608
Schenectady (G-14670)
Triumph Actuation Systems LLC .... D 516 378-0162
Freeport (G-5188)

MACHINERY & EQPT, INDL, WHOLESALE: Indl Machine Parts

Alternative Service Inc .... F 631 345-9500
Bellport (G-798)
Rpb Distributors LLC .... G 914 244-3600
Mount Kisco (G-8358)

MACHINERY & EQPT, INDL, WHOLESALE: Instruments & Cntrl Eqpt

Carl Zeiss Inc .... C 914 747-1800
Thornwood (G-15502)
Winters Instruments Inc .... E 281 880-8607
Buffalo (G-3133)

MACHINERY & EQPT, INDL, WHOLESALE: Machine Tools & Access

Cementex Latex Corp .... F 212 741-1770
New York (G-9236)
Curran Manufacturing Corp .... E 631 273-1010
Hauppauge (G-5807)
S & S Machinery Corp .... E 718 492-7400
Brooklyn (G-2433)

MACHINERY & EQPT, INDL, WHOLESALE: Measure/Test, Electric

Mausner Equipment Co Inc .... C 631 689-7358
Setauket (G-14795)

MACHINERY & EQPT, INDL, WHOLESALE: Packaging

Millwood Inc .... F 518 233-1475
Waterford (G-15978)
Modern Packaging Inc .... D 631 595-2437
Deer Park (G-4011)

MACHINERY & EQPT, INDL, WHOLESALE: Paint Spray

Inglis Co Inc .... G 315 475-1315
Syracuse (G-15343)

MACHINERY & EQPT, INDL, WHOLESALE: Pneumatic Tools

U S Air Tool Co Inc .... F 631 471-3300
Ronkonkoma (G-14423)

MACHINERY & EQPT, INDL, WHOLESALE: Power Plant Machinery

Ultravolt Inc .... D 631 471-4444
Ronkonkoma (G-14426)

MACHINERY & EQPT, INDL, WHOLESALE: Processing & Packaging

National Equipment Corporation .... F 718 585-0200
Harrison (G-5731)
National Equipment Corporation .... E 718 585-0200
Bronx (G-1338)

MACHINERY & EQPT, INDL, WHOLESALE: Robots

Automated Cells & Eqp Inc .... E 607 936-1341
Painted Post (G-12835)

MACHINERY & EQPT, INDL, WHOLESALE: Safety Eqpt

Traffic Logix Corporation .... G 866 915-6449
Spring Valley (G-15009)

MACHINERY & EQPT, INDL, WHOLESALE: Textile

John A Eberly Inc .... G 315 449-3034
Syracuse (G-15347)
Sml USA Inc .... E 212 736-8800
New York (G-11626)

MACHINERY & EQPT, INDL, WHOLESALE: Tire Recapping Machinery

Loomis Root Inc .... F 716 564-7668
Amherst (G-236)

MACHINERY & EQPT, INDL, WHOLESALE: Water Pumps

Air Flow Pump Corp .... G 718 241-2800
Brooklyn (G-1495)

MACHINERY & EQPT, INDL, WHOLESALE: Woodworking

Putnam Rolling Ladder Co Inc .... F 212 226-5147
New York (G-11280)

MACHINERY & EQPT, WHOLESALE: Construction, General

Zwack Incorporated .... E 518 733-5135
Stephentown (G-15156)

MACHINERY & EQPT, WHOLESALE: Crushing, Pulverizng & Screeng

American Material Processing .... F 315 318-0017
Phoenix (G-12988)

MACHINERY & EQPT, WHOLESALE: Masonry

Arnan Development Corp .... D 607 432-8391
Oneonta (G-12625)
Duke Concrete Products Inc .... E 518 793-7743
Queensbury (G-13422)
Inwood Material .... F 516 371-1842
Inwood (G-6493)
Palumbo Block Co Inc .... E 845 832-6100
Dover Plains (G-4145)

MACHINERY & EQPT, WHOLESALE: Road Construction & Maintenance

Ducon Technologies Inc .... F 631 694-1700
New York (G-9584)

MACHINERY & EQPT: Electroplating

Caswell Inc .... F 315 946-1213
Lyons (G-7682)
Digital Matrix Corp .... E 516 481-7990
Farmingdale (G-4752)
Precision Process Inc .... D 716 731-1587
Niagara Falls (G-12327)
Sonicor Inc .... F 631 920-6555
West Babylon (G-16194)
Technic Inc .... F 516 349-0700
Plainview (G-13092)

MACHINERY & EQPT: Farm

Don Beck Inc .... G 585 493-3040
Castile (G-3292)
Eastern Welding Inc .... E 631 727-0306
Riverhead (G-13568)
Haines Equipment Inc .... E 607 566-8531
Avoca (G-516)
House of The Foaming Case Inc .... G 718 454-0101
Saint Albans (G-14507)
Landpro Equipment LLC .... E 716 665-3110
Falconer (G-4686)
Oxbo International Corporation .... E 585 548-2665
Byron (G-3145)
Plant-Tech2o Inc .... G 516 483-7845
Hempstead (G-6023)
Road Cases USA Inc .... E 631 563-0633
Bohemia (G-1083)
Zappala Farms AG Systems Inc .... E 315 626-6293
Cato (G-3301)

MACHINERY & EQPT: Gas Producers, Generators/Other Rltd Eqpt

ACI Controls Inc .... F 800 333-7519
West Seneca (G-16293)
Audubon Machinery Corporation .... D 716 564-5165
North Tonawanda (G-12414)

MACHINERY & EQPT: Liquid Automation

Javlyn Process Systems LLC .... E 585 424-5580
Rochester (G-13893)

MACHINERY & EQPT: Metal Finishing, Plating Etc

Cameo Metal Products Inc .... E 718 788-1106
Brooklyn (G-1670)
P K G Equipment Incorporated .... E 585 436-4650
Rochester (G-14003)
Qes Solutions Inc .... D 585 783-1455
Rochester (G-14057)
R & B Machinery Corp .... G 716 894-3332
Buffalo (G-3030)

MACHINERY BASES

American Standard Mfg Inc .... E 518 868-2512
Central Bridge (G-3353)
Cleveland Polymer Tech LLC .... G 518 326-9146
Schenectady (G-14664)
Kefa Industries Group Inc .... G 718 568-9297
Rego Park (G-13463)
Machinery Mountings Inc .... F 631 851-0480
Hauppauge (G-5876)

MACHINERY, COMMERCIAL LAUNDRY: Dryers, Incl Coin-Operated

Maxi Companies Inc .... G 315 446-1002
De Witt (G-3930)

MACHINERY, COMMERCIAL LAUNDRY: Washing, Incl Coin-Operated

G A Braun Inc .... C 315 475-3123
North Syracuse (G-12401)
Lynx Product Group LLC .... E 716 751-3100
Wilson (G-16601)

MACHINERY, EQPT & SUPPLIES: Parking Facility

Automotion Parking Systems LLC .... G 516 565-5600
West Hempstead (G-16213)
Park Assist LLC .... D 646 666-7525
New York (G-11115)

PRODUCT SECTION

MACHINERY, TEXTILE: Embroidery

Parkmatic Car Prkg Systems LLC ....G....... 516 224-7700
  Long Island City *(G-7548)*
Parkmatic Car Prkg Systems LLC ....G....... 800 422-5438
  College Point *(G-3659)*

MACHINERY, FLOOR SANDING: Commercial

Hubco Inc..G....... 716 683-5940
  Alden *(G-172)*

MACHINERY, FOOD PRDTS: Beverage

Brooklyn Brew Shop LLC..................F....... 718 874-0119
  Brooklyn *(G-1638)*
Kedco Inc..F....... 516 454-7800
  Farmingdale *(G-4800)*
US Beverage Net Inc............................F....... 315 579-2025
  Syracuse *(G-15450)*

MACHINERY, FOOD PRDTS: Choppers, Commercial

Mary F Morse....................................G....... 315 866-2741
  Mohawk *(G-8255)*

MACHINERY, FOOD PRDTS: Confectionery

National Equipment Corporation..........F....... 718 585-0200
  Harrison *(G-5731)*
National Equipment Corporation..........E....... 718 585-0200
  Bronx *(G-1338)*

MACHINERY, FOOD PRDTS: Cutting, Chopping, Grinding, Mixing

ET Oakes Corporation.........................E....... 631 232-0002
  Hauppauge *(G-5821)*
Janel Corporation.................................G....... 516 256-8143
  Lynbrook *(G-7666)*

MACHINERY, FOOD PRDTS: Dairy & Milk

Chemicolloid Laboratories Inc ....F....... 516 747-2666
  New Hyde Park *(G-8522)*

MACHINERY, FOOD PRDTS: Dairy, Pasteurizing

Goodnature Products Inc ....E....... 716 855-3325
  Orchard Park *(G-12716)*

MACHINERY, FOOD PRDTS: Food Processing, Smokers

Bonduelle USA Inc.............................E....... 585 948-5252
  Oakfield *(G-12523)*
Los Olivos Ltd...................................C....... 631 773-6439
  Farmingdale *(G-4811)*

MACHINERY, FOOD PRDTS: Juice Extractors, Fruit & Veg, Comm

Acai of America Inc...........................G....... 862 205-9334
  New York *(G-8717)*

MACHINERY, FOOD PRDTS: Milk Processing, NEC

Delaval Inc..F....... 585 599-4696
  Corfu *(G-3806)*

MACHINERY, FOOD PRDTS: Mixers, Commercial

Expert Industries Inc ....E....... 718 434-6060
  Brooklyn *(G-1859)*

MACHINERY, FOOD PRDTS: Oilseed Crushing & Extracting

Caravella Food Corp...........................F....... 646 552-0455
  Whitestone *(G-16537)*

MACHINERY, FOOD PRDTS: Ovens, Bakery

Home Maide Inc.................................F....... 845 837-1700
  Harriman *(G-5719)*
Mohawk Valley Manufacturing............G....... 315 797-0851
  Frankfort *(G-5110)*

MACHINERY, FOOD PRDTS: Packing House

Desu Machinery Corporation................D....... 716 681-5798
  Depew *(G-4087)*

MACHINERY, FOOD PRDTS: Presses, Cheese, Beet, Cider & Sugar

Blue Toad Hard Cider ....E....... 585 424-5508
  Rochester *(G-13668)*

MACHINERY, FOOD PRDTS: Roasting, Coffee, Peanut, Etc.

Wired Coffee and Bagel Inc ....F....... 518 506-3194
  Malta *(G-7733)*

MACHINERY, MAILING: Canceling

Action Technologies Inc......................G....... 718 278-1000
  Long Island City *(G-7367)*

MACHINERY, MAILING: Mailing

Pitney Bowes Inc................................C....... 518 283-0345
  Troy *(G-15616)*

MACHINERY, MAILING: Postage Meters

Neopost USA Inc................................E....... 631 435-9100
  Hauppauge *(G-5900)*
Pitney Bowes Inc................................E....... 212 564-7548
  New York *(G-11200)*
Pitney Bowes Inc................................E....... 203 356-5000
  New York *(G-11201)*
Pitney Bowes Inc................................E....... 516 822-0900
  Jericho *(G-6797)*

MACHINERY, METALWORKING: Assembly, Including Robotic

Alliance Automation Systems ....C....... 585 426-2700
  Rochester *(G-13615)*
Hover-Davis Inc..................................C....... 585 352-9590
  Rochester *(G-13872)*
Manufacturing Resources Inc..............E....... 631 481-0041
  Rochester *(G-13926)*
Mold-A-Matic Corporation..................F....... 607 433-2121
  Oneonta *(G-12641)*
Standard Bots Company ....G....... 646 876-2687
  Locust Valley *(G-7351)*
Tessy Plastics Corp.............................B....... 315 689-3924
  Skaneateles *(G-14878)*
Unidex Corporation Western NY ....F....... 585 786-3170
  Warsaw *(G-15946)*
Van Blarcom Closures Inc...................C....... 718 855-3810
  Brooklyn *(G-2615)*
You First Services Inc........................F....... 716 204-7215
  Buffalo *(G-3135)*

MACHINERY, METALWORKING: Cutting & Slitting

Expert Metal Slitters Corp...................G....... 718 361-2735
  Long Island City *(G-7443)*

MACHINERY, OFFICE: Perforators

Cummins - Allison Corp ....D....... 718 263-2482
  Kew Gardens *(G-6871)*

MACHINERY, OFFICE: Stapling, Hand Or Power

Staplex Company Inc..........................E....... 718 768-3333
  Brooklyn *(G-2508)*

MACHINERY, OFFICE: Time Clocks & Time Recording Devices

Central Time Clock Inc ....F....... 718 784-4900
  Long Island City *(G-7407)*
Gradual LLC......................................F....... 347 293-0974
  Long Island City *(G-7459)*
Widmer Time Recorder Company ....F....... 212 227-0405
  New York *(G-12108)*

MACHINERY, PACKAGING: Canning, Food

Reynolds Packaging McHy Inc ....D....... 716 358-6451
  Falconer *(G-4690)*

MACHINERY, PACKAGING: Carton Packing

Niagara Scientific Inc..........................D....... 315 437-0821
  East Syracuse *(G-4360)*

MACHINERY, PACKAGING: Packing & Wrapping

Fourteen Arnold Ave Corp ....F....... 315 272-1700
  Utica *(G-15703)*
Turbofil Packaging Mchs LLC ....F....... 914 239-3878
  Mount Vernon *(G-8451)*
Vetroelite Inc......................................G....... 925 724-7900
  New York *(G-12019)*

MACHINERY, PAPER INDUSTRY: Converting, Die Cutting & Stampng

Fbm Galaxy Inc..................................F....... 315 463-5144
  East Syracuse *(G-4338)*
Gailer Stamping Diecutting LLC..........F....... 212 243-5662
  Long Island City *(G-7453)*
Richlar Industries Inc..........................F....... 315 463-5144
  East Syracuse *(G-4366)*
Rsb Associates Inc..............................F....... 518 281-5067
  Altamont *(G-202)*

MACHINERY, PAPER INDUSTRY: Paper Mill, Plating, Etc

F W Roberts Mfg Co Inc ....F....... 716 434-3555
  Lockport *(G-7300)*
Sonicor Inc...F....... 631 920-6555
  West Babylon *(G-16194)*

MACHINERY, PRINTING TRADES: Copy Holders

Copy4les Inc......................................F....... 212 487-9778
  New York *(G-9398)*
Exacta LLC..G....... 716 406-2303
  Clarence Center *(G-3544)*

MACHINERY, PRINTING TRADES: Plates

C M E Corp.......................................F....... 315 451-7101
  Syracuse *(G-15266)*
Csw Inc..F....... 585 247-4010
  Rochester *(G-13727)*
Impressions International Inc ....F....... 585 442-5240
  Rochester *(G-13879)*
Rubber Stamps Inc..............................E....... 212 675-1180
  Mineola *(G-8247)*

MACHINERY, PRINTING TRADES: Plates, Offset

Apexx Omni-Graphics Inc...................D....... 718 326-3330
  Maspeth *(G-7822)*

MACHINERY, PRINTING TRADES: Printing Trade Parts & Attchts

Lexar Global LLC..............................G....... 845 352-9700
  Valley Cottage *(G-15758)*
Rollers Inc..G....... 716 837-0700
  Buffalo *(G-3044)*

MACHINERY, PRINTING TRADES: Sticks

Bmp America Inc................................C....... 585 798-0950
  Medina *(G-7973)*

MACHINERY, SEWING: Sewing & Hat & Zipper Making

Cvd Equipment Corporation ....E....... 845 246-3631
  Saugerties *(G-14605)*
Jado Sewing Machines Inc ....E....... 718 784-2314
  Long Island City *(G-7478)*

MACHINERY, TEXTILE: Card Cutting, Jacquard

Mjk Cutting Inc..................................F....... 718 384-7613
  Brooklyn *(G-2216)*

MACHINERY, TEXTILE: Embroidery

Herrmann Group LLC.........................G....... 716 876-9798
  Kenmore *(G-6860)*

Employee Codes: A=Over 500 employees, B=251-500
C=101-250, D=51-100, E=20-50, F=10-19, G=5-9

MACHINERY, TEXTILE: Silk Screens

Company		Phone
Angel Textiles Inc	G	212 532-0900
New York (G-8862)		
Big Apple Sign Corp	E	631 342-0303
Islandia (G-6522)		
Screen Team Inc	F	718 786-2424
Long Island City (G-7586)		

MACHINERY, TEXTILE: Thread Making Or Spinning

Thread Check Inc	D	631 231-1515
Hauppauge (G-5958)		

MACHINERY, WOODWORKING: Bandsaws

Phoenix Wood Wrights Ltd	F	631 727-9691
Riverhead (G-13579)		

MACHINERY, WOODWORKING: Cabinet Makers'

901 D LLC	E	845 369-1111
Airmont (G-10)		
Hat Factory Furniture Co	G	914 788-6288
Peekskill (G-12921)		

MACHINERY, WOODWORKING: Furniture Makers

Downtown Interiors Inc	F	212 337-0230
New York (G-9567)		

MACHINERY, WOODWORKING: Lathes, Wood Turning Includes Access

Hardinge Inc	B	607 734-2281
Elmira (G-4490)		

MACHINERY, WOODWORKING: Pattern Makers'

Corbett Stves Pttern Works Inc	E	585 546-7109
Rochester (G-13722)		

MACHINERY, WOODWORKING: Sanding, Exc Portable Floor Sanders

US Sander LLC	G	518 875-9157
Esperance (G-4622)		

MACHINERY: Ammunition & Explosives Loading

Eastend Enforcement Products	G	631 878-8424
Smithtown (G-14898)		

MACHINERY: Assembly, Exc Metalworking

Alliance Automation Systems	C	585 426-2700
Rochester (G-13615)		
Distech Systems Inc	G	585 254-7020
Rochester (G-13744)		
Dynamasters Inc	G	585 458-9970
Rochester (G-13753)		
Hubco Inc	G	716 683-5940
Alden (G-172)		
New Vision Industries Inc	F	607 687-7700
Endicott (G-4604)		
Quality Manufacturing Sys LLC	G	716 763-0988
Lakewood (G-6995)		
Rfb Associates Inc	F	518 271-0551
Fort Edward (G-5100)		
Trident Precision Mfg Inc	D	585 265-2010
Webster (G-16103)		
Veeco Process Equipment Inc	C	516 677-0200
Plainview (G-13100)		

MACHINERY: Automotive Maintenance

Blue Star Products Inc	F	631 952-3204
Hauppauge (G-5782)		
T-Rex Supply Corporation	G	516 308-0505
Hempstead (G-6026)		

MACHINERY: Automotive Related

B&K Precision Corporation	G	631 369-2665
Manorville (G-7782)		
Eltee Tool & Die Co	F	607 748-4301
Endicott (G-4587)		
Hitachi Metals America Ltd	E	914 694-9200
Purchase (G-13390)		
Reefer Tek Llc	F	347 590-1067
Bronx (G-1371)		
Rfb Associates Inc	F	518 271-0551
Fort Edward (G-5100)		
Riverview Associates Inc	F	585 235-5980
Rochester (G-14074)		

MACHINERY: Billing

Gary Roth & Associates Ltd	E	516 333-1000
Westbury (G-16335)		

MACHINERY: Brewery & Malting

Kings Cnty Brwers Cllctive LLC	F	917 207-2739
Brooklyn (G-2075)		
Singlecut Beersmiths LLC	F	718 606-0788
Astoria (G-443)		

MACHINERY: Bridge Or Gate, Hydraulic

Island Automated Gate Co LLC	G	631 425-0196
Huntington Station (G-6448)		

MACHINERY: Concrete Prdts

Nycon Diamond & Tools Corp	G	855 937-6922
Bohemia (G-1069)		

MACHINERY: Construction

AAAA York Inc	F	718 784-6666
Long Island City (G-7364)		
Air-Flo Mfg Co Inc	D	607 733-8284
Elmira (G-4473)		
Anderson Equipment Company	D	716 877-1992
Tonawanda (G-15522)		
BW Elliott Mfg Co LLC	B	607 772-0404
Binghamton (G-873)		
Capitol Eq 2 LLC	G	518 886-8341
Saratoga Springs (G-14574)		
CCS Machinery Inc	F	631 968-0900
Bay Shore (G-668)		
Ceno Technologies Inc	G	716 885-5050
Buffalo (G-2763)		
Cooper Industries LLC	E	315 477-7000
Syracuse (G-15291)		
Diamond Coring & Cutting Inc	G	718 381-4545
Maspeth (G-7836)		
Dover Global Holdings Inc	F	212 922-1640
New York (G-9562)		
ET Oakes Corporation	E	631 232-0002
Hauppauge (G-5821)		
Line Ward Corporation	G	716 675-7373
Buffalo (G-2925)		
Northrock Industries Inc	E	631 924-6130
Bohemia (G-1068)		
Oswald Manufacturing Co Inc	G	516 883-8850
Port Washington (G-13292)		
Penn State Metal Fabri	G	718 786-8814
Brooklyn (G-2311)		
Pier-Tech Inc	G	516 442-5420
Oceanside (G-12550)		
Precision Product Inc	G	718 852-7127
Brooklyn (G-2336)		
Rockland Manufacturing Co	G	845 358-6000
West Nyack (G-16281)		
Ziegler Truck & Diesl Repr Inc	G	315 782-7278
Watertown (G-16037)		

MACHINERY: Cryogenic, Industrial

Cryomech Inc	D	315 455-2555
Syracuse (G-15296)		
General Cryogenic Tech LLC	F	516 334-8200
Westbury (G-16336)		

MACHINERY: Custom

Accede Mold & Tool Co Inc	D	585 254-6490
Rochester (G-13595)		
Adaptive Mfg Tech Inc	E	631 580-5400
Ronkonkoma (G-14290)		
Aloi Solutions LLC	E	585 292-0920
Rochester (G-13619)		
American Linear Manufacturers	F	516 333-1351
Westbury (G-16314)		
Armstrong Mold Corporation	D	315 437-1517
East Syracuse (G-4321)		
Auburn Bearing & Mfg Inc	G	315 986-7600
Macedon (G-7694)		
Calvary Design Team Inc	C	585 347-6127
Webster (G-16076)		
Chocovision Corporation	F	845 473-4970
Poughkeepsie (G-13332)		
Converter Design Inc	G	518 745-7138
Glens Falls (G-5421)		
Duetto Integrated Systems Inc	F	631 851-0102
Islandia (G-6527)		
Dynak Inc	F	585 271-2255
Churchville (G-3509)		
Endicott Precision Inc	C	607 754-7076
Endicott (G-4589)		
Finesse Creations Inc	F	718 692-2100
Brooklyn (G-1883)		
Hebeler Process Solutions LLC	E	716 873-9300
Tonawanda (G-15548)		
Interactive Instruments Inc	G	518 347-0955
Scotia (G-14742)		
International Climbing Mchs	G	607 288-4001
Ithaca (G-6586)		
Jet Sew Corporation	F	315 896-2683
Barneveld (G-602)		
Keller Technology Corporation	G	716 693-3840
Tonawanda (G-15553)		
Keyes Machine Works Inc	G	585 426-5059
Gates (G-5310)		
McGuigan Inc	G	631 750-6222
Bohemia (G-1057)		
Modern Packaging Inc	D	631 595-2437
Deer Park (G-4011)		
Ms Machining Inc	G	607 723-1105
Binghamton (G-907)		
Northern Tier Cnc Inc	G	518 236-4702
Mooers Forks (G-8331)		
R E F Precision Products	G	631 242-4471
Deer Park (G-4032)		
Rand Machine Products, Inc.	C	716 665-5217
Falconer (G-4688)		
Roboshop Inc	G	315 437-6454
Syracuse (G-15408)		
Tricon Machine LLC	G	585 671-0679
Webster (G-16102)		
Voss Manufacturing Inc	D	716 731-5062
Sanborn (G-14557)		
W H Jones & Son Inc	F	716 875-8233
Kenmore (G-6864)		
W J Albro Machine Works Inc	G	631 345-0657
Yaphank (G-16728)		
Washburn Manufacturing Tech	G	607 387-3991
Trumansburg (G-15641)		
Wendt Corporation	D	716 391-1200
Buffalo (G-3127)		
Willemin-Macodel Inc	G	914 345-3504
Elmsford (G-4579)		

MACHINERY: Drill Presses

Baldwin Machine Works Inc	G	631 842-9110
Copiague (G-3754)		

MACHINERY: Electronic Component Making

CBA Group LLC	A	607 779-7522
Conklin (G-3725)		
Designatronics Incorporated	G	516 328-3300
Hicksville (G-6079)		
James Morris	E	315 824-8519
Hamilton (G-5699)		
Sj Associates Inc	E	516 942-3232
Jericho (G-6804)		
Ui Acquisition Holding Co	G	607 779-7522
Conklin (G-3736)		
Ui Holding Company	G	607 779-7522
Conklin (G-3737)		
Universal Instruments Corp	C	800 842-9732
Conklin (G-3738)		

MACHINERY: Engraving

Bartizan Data Systems LLC	E	914 965-7977
Yonkers (G-16739)		

MACHINERY: Extruding

Kobe Steel USA Holdings Inc	G	212 751-9400
New York (G-10462)		

MACHINERY: Fiber Optics Strand Coating

Accurate McHning Incorporation	F	315 689-1428
Elbridge (G-4426)		

PRODUCT SECTION

MACHINERY: Gear Cutting & Finishing

Gleason Works .... A 585 473-1000
  Rochester *(G-13840)*

MACHINERY: General, Industrial, NEC

Markpericom .... G 516 208-6824
  Oceanside *(G-12548)*

MACHINERY: Glassmaking

Emhart Glass Manufacturing Inc .... C 607 734-3671
  Horseheads *(G-6314)*
Wilt Industries Inc .... G 518 548-4961
  Lake Pleasant *(G-6979)*

MACHINERY: Grinding

Connex Grinding & Machining .... G 315 946-4340
  Lyons *(G-7683)*
East Coast Tool & Mfg .... G 716 826-5183
  Buffalo *(G-2810)*
Stephen Bader Company Inc .... F 518 753-4456
  Valley Falls *(G-15770)*

MACHINERY: Ice Cream

Pic Nic LLC .... G 914 245-6500
  Amawalk *(G-204)*

MACHINERY: Ice Crushers

American Material Processing .... F 315 318-0017
  Phoenix *(G-12988)*

MACHINERY: Ice Making

Hoshizaki Nrtheastern Dist Ctr .... G 516 605-1411
  Plainview *(G-13060)*
Mgr Equipment Corp .... E 516 239-3030
  Inwood *(G-6495)*

MACHINERY: Industrial, NEC

A P Manufacturing .... G 909 228-3049
  Bohemia *(G-966)*
Exigo Precision Inc .... G 585 254-5818
  Rochester *(G-13798)*
Northeast Hardware Specialties .... F 516 487-6868
  Mineola *(G-8240)*
Semi-Linear Inc .... G 212 243-2108
  New York *(G-11541)*

MACHINERY: Jewelers

Arbe Machinery Inc .... F 631 756-2477
  Farmingdale *(G-4722)*

MACHINERY: Marking, Metalworking

Autostat Corporation .... F 516 379-9447
  Roosevelt *(G-14434)*

MACHINERY: Metalworking

Advanced Machine Design Co Inc .... E 716 826-2000
  Buffalo *(G-2689)*
Bartell Machinery Systems LLC .... C 315 336-7600
  Rome *(G-14246)*
Charles A Rogers Entps Inc .... E 585 924-6400
  Victor *(G-15835)*
Duall Finishing Inc .... G 716 827-1707
  Buffalo *(G-2804)*
Esm II Inc .... E 716 446-8888
  Amherst *(G-227)*
Hardinge Inc .... B 607 734-2281
  Elmira *(G-4490)*
Hje Company Inc .... G 518 792-8733
  Queensbury *(G-13428)*
Mono-Systems Inc .... E 716 821-1344
  Buffalo *(G-2953)*
Mtwli Precision Corp .... G 631 244-3767
  Bohemia *(G-1061)*
Munson Machinery Company Inc .... E 315 797-0090
  Utica *(G-15724)*
Pems Tool & Machine Inc .... E 315 823-3595
  Little Falls *(G-7211)*
Precision Systems Mfg Inc .... E 315 451-3480
  Liverpool *(G-7257)*
Reelex Packaging Solutions Inc .... E 845 878-7878
  Patterson *(G-12884)*
Riverside Machinery Company .... E 718 492-7400
  Brooklyn *(G-2407)*

S & S Machinery Corp .... E 718 492-7400
  Brooklyn *(G-2432)*
S & S Machinery Corp .... E 718 492-7400
  Brooklyn *(G-2433)*
Serge Duct Designs Inc .... E 718 783-7799
  Brooklyn *(G-2457)*
Strippit Inc .... C 716 542-4511
  Akron *(G-23)*
Vader Systems LLC .... F 716 688-1600
  Getzville *(G-5355)*
Voss Manufacturing Inc .... D 716 731-5062
  Sanborn *(G-14557)*
Xto Incorporated .... D 315 451-7807
  Liverpool *(G-7273)*

MACHINERY: Milling

Five Star Tool Co Inc .... E 585 328-9580
  Rochester *(G-13806)*

MACHINERY: Mining

Flatcut LLC .... G 212 542-5732
  Brooklyn *(G-1888)*
Universal Metal Fabricators .... F 845 331-8248
  Kingston *(G-6927)*

MACHINERY: Optical Lens

Optipro Systems LLC .... D 585 265-0160
  Ontario *(G-12659)*
Universal Thin Film Lab Corp .... G 845 562-0601
  Newburgh *(G-12249)*

MACHINERY: Ozone

Queenaire Technologies Inc .... G 315 393-5454
  Ogdensburg *(G-12578)*

MACHINERY: Packaging

A & G Heat Sealing .... G 631 724-7764
  Smithtown *(G-14893)*
All Packaging McHy & Sups Corp .... F 631 588-7310
  Ronkonkoma *(G-14300)*
Automecha International Ltd .... E 607 843-2235
  Oxford *(G-12807)*
Crandall Filling Machinery Inc .... C 716 897-3486
  Buffalo *(G-2783)*
Dover Global Holdings Inc .... F 212 922-1640
  New York *(G-9562)*
Elmar Industries Inc .... D 716 681-5650
  Depew *(G-4088)*
Haines Equipment Inc .... E 607 566-8531
  Avoca *(G-516)*
Kabar Manufacturing Corp .... E 631 694-6857
  Farmingdale *(G-4797)*
Millwood Inc .... F 518 233-1475
  Waterford *(G-15978)*
Modern Packaging Inc .... D 631 595-2437
  Deer Park *(G-4011)*
National Equipment Corporation .... E 718 585-0200
  Bronx *(G-1338)*
Orics Industries Inc .... E 718 461-8613
  Farmingdale *(G-4839)*
Overhead Door Corporation .... D 518 828-7652
  Hudson *(G-6366)*
Pacemaker Packaging Corp .... F 718 458-1188
  Woodside *(G-16670)*
Packaging Dynamics Ltd .... F 631 563-4499
  Bohemia *(G-1071)*
Rfb Associates Inc .... F 518 271-0551
  Fort Edward *(G-5100)*
Rota Pack Inc .... F 631 274-1037
  Farmingdale *(G-4869)*
Save O Seal Corporation Inc .... G 914 592-3031
  Elmsford *(G-4563)*
Utleys Incorporated .... E 718 956-1661
  Woodside *(G-16682)*
Volckening Inc .... E 718 748-0294
  Brooklyn *(G-2633)*

MACHINERY: Paper Industry Miscellaneous

Automecha International Ltd .... E 607 843-2235
  Oxford *(G-12807)*
Cyclotherm of Watertown Inc .... E 315 782-1100
  Watertown *(G-16011)*
GL&v USA Inc .... C 518 747-2444
  Hudson Falls *(G-6380)*
Haanen Packard Machinery Inc .... G 518 747-2330
  Hudson Falls *(G-6382)*

Jacob Inc .... E 646 450-3067
  Brooklyn *(G-2030)*
Johnston Dandy Company .... G 315 455-5773
  Syracuse *(G-15349)*
Kadant Inc .... F 518 793-8801
  Glens Falls *(G-5429)*
Lake Image Systems Inc .... F 585 321-3630
  Henrietta *(G-6034)*
Sinclair International Company .... D 518 798-2361
  Queensbury *(G-13442)*
Verso Corporation .... B 212 599-2700
  New York *(G-12014)*

MACHINERY: Pharmaciutical

George Ponte Inc .... G 914 243-4202
  Jefferson Valley *(G-6776)*
Gordon S Anderson Mfg Co .... G 845 677-3304
  Millbrook *(G-8188)*
Innovation Associates Inc .... C 607 798-9376
  Johnson City *(G-6811)*
Michael Benalt Inc .... E 845 628-1008
  Mahopac *(G-7708)*

MACHINERY: Photographic Reproduction

Qls Solutions Group Inc .... E 716 852-2203
  Buffalo *(G-3022)*
Xerox Corporation .... A 585 422-4564
  Webster *(G-16108)*

MACHINERY: Plastic Working

Addex Inc .... G 781 344-5800
  Newark *(G-12192)*
Century-Tech Inc .... E 516 493-9800
  Hempstead *(G-6010)*
Germanow-Simon Corporation .... E 585 232-1440
  Rochester *(G-13832)*
Haanen Packard Machinery Inc .... G 518 747-2330
  Hudson Falls *(G-6382)*
High Frequency Tech Co Inc .... F 631 242-3020
  Bohemia *(G-1032)*
Illinois Tool Works Inc .... C 716 681-8222
  Lancaster *(G-7024)*
Kabar Manufacturing Corp .... E 631 694-1036
  Farmingdale *(G-4798)*
Kabar Manufacturing Corp .... E 631 694-6857
  Farmingdale *(G-4797)*
Pearl Technologies Inc .... E 315 365-3742
  Savannah *(G-14623)*
Quality Strapping Inc .... D 718 418-1111
  Brooklyn *(G-2369)*
Ultrepet LLC .... D 781 275-6400
  Albany *(G-138)*
Valplast International Corp .... F 516 442-3923
  Westbury *(G-16385)*

MACHINERY: Printing Presses

Advance Grafix Equipment Inc .... G 917 202-4593
  Wyandanch *(G-16692)*
Halm Instrument Co Inc .... D 516 676-6700
  Glen Head *(G-5380)*

MACHINERY: Recycling

Adirondack Plas & Recycl Inc .... E 518 746-9212
  Argyle *(G-397)*
Andela Tool & Machine Inc .... G 315 858-0055
  Richfield Springs *(G-13492)*
Ben Weitsman of Albany LLC .... E 518 462-4444
  Albany *(G-45)*
Crumbrubber Technology Inc .... F 718 468-3988
  Hollis *(G-6233)*

MACHINERY: Riveting

High Speed Hammer Company Inc .... F 585 266-4287
  Rochester *(G-13869)*

MACHINERY: Road Construction & Maintenance

City of Jamestown .... D 716 483-7545
  Jamestown *(G-6705)*
Professional Pavers Corp .... E 718 784-7853
  Rego Park *(G-13468)*

MACHINERY: Rubber Working

Curtin-Hebert Co Inc .... F 518 725-7157
  Gloversville *(G-5455)*

MACHINERY: Screening Eqpt, Electric

Innovation In Motion Inc...............G...... 407 878-7561
  Long Beach *(G-7359)*

MACHINERY: Semiconductor Manufacturing

Applied Materials Inc..................E...... 845 227-5000
  Hopewell Junction *(G-6282)*
Cvd Equipment Corporation..........F...... 631 582-4365
  Central Islip *(G-3366)*
Globalfoundries US Inc.................E...... 512 457-3900
  Hopewell Junction *(G-6287)*
Lam Research Corporation...........E...... 845 896-0606
  Fishkill *(G-4947)*
Veeco Instruments Inc..................B...... 516 677-0200
  Plainview *(G-13099)*
Vistec Lithography, Inc..................E...... 518 874-3000
  Watervliet *(G-16056)*

MACHINERY: Separation Eqpt, Magnetic

Innovative Cleaning Solutions........G...... 716 731-4408
  Sanborn *(G-14547)*

MACHINERY: Sheet Metal Working

U S Air Tool Co Inc......................F...... 631 471-3300
  Ronkonkoma *(G-14423)*

MACHINERY: Specialty

Force Dynamics Inc.....................F...... 607 546-5023
  Trumansburg *(G-15640)*

MACHINERY: Textile

Aglika Trade LLC.........................F...... 727 424-1944
  Middle Village *(G-8120)*
Corbertex LLC............................G...... 212 971-0008
  New York *(G-9399)*
Eastman Machine Company..........C...... 716 856-2200
  Buffalo *(G-2812)*
Herr Manufacturing Co Inc............E...... 716 754-4341
  Tonawanda *(G-15549)*
Mohawk Valley Knt McHy Co Inc....F...... 315 736-3038
  New York Mills *(G-12189)*
Rfb Associates Inc......................F...... 518 271-0551
  Fort Edward *(G-5100)*
Schwabel Fabricating Co Inc..........E...... 716 876-2086
  Tonawanda *(G-15575)*
Simtec Industries Corporation........G...... 631 293-0080
  Farmingdale *(G-4874)*

MACHINERY: Tire Shredding

Northeast Data...........................G...... 845 331-5554
  Kingston *(G-6913)*
Shred Center.............................G...... 716 664-3052
  Jamestown *(G-6746)*

MACHINERY: Wire Drawing

Carpenter Manufacturing Co..........E...... 315 682-9176
  Manlius *(G-7775)*
MGS Manufacturing Inc................F...... 315 337-3350
  Rome *(G-14258)*

MACHINERY: Woodworking

James L Taylor Mfg Co.................E...... 845 452-3780
  Poughkeepsie *(G-13348)*
James L Taylor Mfg Co.................G...... 845 452-3780
  Poughkeepsie *(G-13349)*
Merritt Machinery LLC..................F...... 716 434-5558
  Lockport *(G-7315)*
Oneida Air Systems Inc................E...... 315 476-5151
  Syracuse *(G-15387)*
Wood-Mizer Holdings Inc..............G...... 315 564-5722
  Hannibal *(G-5718)*

MACHINES: Forming, Sheet Metal

Cetek Inc.................................E...... 845 452-3510
  Poughkeepsie *(G-13331)*
Product Integration & Mfg Inc........F...... 585 436-6260
  Rochester *(G-14049)*

MACHINISTS' TOOLS: Measuring, Precision

Mausner Equipment Co Inc............C...... 631 689-7358
  Setauket *(G-14795)*

MACHINISTS' TOOLS: Precision

Arch Globl Prcsion Rchster LLC.....D...... 585 254-7000
  Rochester *(G-13638)*
Drt Power Systems LLC...............G...... 585 247-5940
  Rochester *(G-13751)*
Egli Machine Company Inc............E...... 607 563-3663
  Sidney *(G-14853)*
Hubbard Tool and Die Corp............E...... 315 337-7840
  Rome *(G-14253)*
Melland Gear Instr of Huppauge.....E...... 631 234-0100
  Hauppauge *(G-5885)*
Miller Metal Fabricating Inc............G...... 585 359-3400
  Rochester *(G-13945)*
Novatech Inc..............................E...... 716 892-6682
  Cheektowaga *(G-3455)*
Park Enterprises Rochester Inc......C...... 585 546-4200
  Rochester *(G-14009)*
Ppi Corp...................................G...... 585 243-0300
  Rochester *(G-14032)*
Precision Grinding & Mfg Corp........C...... 585 458-4300
  Rochester *(G-14035)*
Ptc Precision LLC.......................E...... 607 748-8294
  Endwell *(G-4620)*
Streamline Precision Inc...............G...... 585 421-9050
  Fairport *(G-4661)*
Streamline Precision Inc...............G...... 585 421-9050
  Fairport *(G-4662)*
Townline Machine Co Inc..............G...... 315 462-3413
  Clifton Springs *(G-3584)*
Trimaster/Htech Holding LLC........G...... 212 257-6772
  New York *(G-11899)*
Xactra Technologies Inc................D...... 585 426-2030
  Rochester *(G-14213)*

MAGAZINES, WHOLESALE

Economist Newspaper NA Inc........E...... 212 554-0676
  New York *(G-9625)*
Global Finance Media Inc..............F...... 212 447-7900
  New York *(G-9939)*

MAGNETIC INK & OPTICAL SCANNING EQPT

Hand Held Products Inc................B...... 315 554-6000
  Skaneateles Falls *(G-14879)*
Hand Held Products Inc................G...... 315 554-6000
  Skaneateles Falls *(G-14880)*
Peoples Choice M R I..................F...... 716 681-7377
  Buffalo *(G-2997)*
Symbol Technologies LLC.............F...... 631 218-3907
  Holbrook *(G-6214)*

MAGNETIC RESONANCE IMAGING DEVICES: Nonmedical

Finger Lakes Radiology LLC...........G...... 315 787-5399
  Geneva *(G-5324)*
Islandia Mri Associates PC.............F...... 631 234-2828
  Central Islip *(G-3374)*

MAGNETIC TAPE, AUDIO: Prerecorded

Universal Mus Group Hldngs Inc.....E...... 212 333-8000
  New York *(G-11961)*

MAGNETOHYDRODYNAMIC DEVICES OR MHD

Passive-Plus Inc.........................F...... 631 425-0938
  Huntington *(G-6407)*

MAGNETS: Ceramic

Arnold Magnetic Tech Corp............C...... 585 385-9010
  Rochester *(G-13640)*
Eneflux Armtek Magnetics Inc........G...... 516 576-3434
  Medford *(G-7947)*
Hitachi Metals America Ltd..........E...... 914 694-9200
  Purchase *(G-13390)*

MAGNETS: Permanent

Arnold Magnetic Tech Corp............C...... 585 385-9010
  Rochester *(G-13640)*
Carpentier Industries LLC.............F...... 585 385-5550
  East Rochester *(G-4281)*
Magnaworks Technology Inc.........G...... 631 218-3431
  Bohemia *(G-1054)*
Magnetic Aids Inc.......................G...... 845 863-1400
  Newburgh *(G-12231)*

MMC Magnetics Corp..................F...... 631 435-9888
  Hauppauge *(G-5895)*
Polymag Inc..............................E...... 631 286-4111
  Bellport *(G-813)*
Precision Magnetics LLC...............E...... 585 385-9010
  Rochester *(G-14038)*
Technomag Inc..........................G...... 631 246-6142
  East Setauket *(G-4311)*
Truebite Inc..............................E...... 607 785-7664
  Vestal *(G-15824)*

MAGNIFIERS

Edroy Products Co Inc.................G...... 845 358-6600
  Nyack *(G-12507)*

MAIL-ORDER BOOK CLUBS

Global Video LLC........................D...... 516 222-2600
  Woodbury *(G-16620)*
Station Hill of Barrytown...............G...... 845 758-5293
  Barrytown *(G-606)*

MAIL-ORDER HOUSE, NEC

American Country Quilts & Lin........G...... 631 283-5466
  Southampton *(G-14949)*
Chocolat Moderne LLC.................G...... 212 229-4797
  New York *(G-9287)*
Collinite Corporation....................G...... 315 732-2282
  Utica *(G-15684)*
Hamtronics Inc..........................G...... 585 392-9430
  Rochester *(G-13851)*
Hubray Inc...............................F...... 800 645-2855
  North Baldwin *(G-12364)*
Quaker Boy Inc.........................E...... 716 662-3979
  Orchard Park *(G-12740)*
TRM Linen Inc..........................G...... 718 686-6075
  Brooklyn *(G-2588)*

MAIL-ORDER HOUSES: Book & Record Clubs

Oxford University Press LLC..........B...... 212 726-6000
  New York *(G-11078)*
Oxford University Press LLC..........G...... 212 726-6000
  New York *(G-11079)*

MAIL-ORDER HOUSES: Books, Exc Book Clubs

Anthroposophic Press Inc.............G...... 518 851-2054
  Clifton Park *(G-3563)*
Looseleaf Law Publications Inc......F...... 718 359-5559
  Flushing *(G-5025)*
Rizzoli Intl Publications Inc.............E...... 212 387-3400
  New York *(G-11398)*
Syracuse Cultural Workers Prj........F...... 315 474-1132
  Syracuse *(G-15437)*
Trusted Media Brands Inc............A...... 914 238-1000
  New York *(G-11907)*
Trusted Media Brands Inc............F...... 914 244-5244
  White Plains *(G-16513)*

MAIL-ORDER HOUSES: Cards

Color Card LLC.........................F...... 631 232-1300
  Central Islip *(G-3363)*

MAIL-ORDER HOUSES: Clothing, Exc Women's

Cockpit Usa Inc.........................F...... 212 575-1616
  New York *(G-9343)*

MAIL-ORDER HOUSES: Computer Eqpt & Electronics

Gim Electronics Corp..................F...... 516 942-3382
  Hicksville *(G-6090)*

MAIL-ORDER HOUSES: Cosmetics & Perfumes

Borghese Inc............................E...... 212 659-5318
  New York *(G-9123)*

MAIL-ORDER HOUSES: Fitness & Sporting Goods

KD Dids Inc..............................E...... 718 402-2012
  Bronx *(G-1305)*

PRODUCT SECTION

MAIL-ORDER HOUSES: Food
Sbk Preserves Inc ....E 800 773-7378
Bronx *(G-1381)*

MAIL-ORDER HOUSES: Furniture & Furnishings
Charles P Rogers Brass Beds ....F 212 675-4400
New York *(G-9264)*
Wink Inc ....E 212 389-1382
New York *(G-12121)*

MAIL-ORDER HOUSES: Gift Items
Jomar Industries Inc ....E 845 357-5773
Airmont *(G-14)*

MAIL-ORDER HOUSES: Jewelry
Indonesian Imports Inc ....E 888 800-5899
New York *(G-10200)*

MAIL-ORDER HOUSES: Magazines
Dlc Comprehensive Medical PC ....F 718 857-1200
Brooklyn *(G-1783)*

MAILING LIST: Brokers
Luria Communications Inc ....G 631 329-4922
East Hampton *(G-4240)*

MAILING LIST: Compilers
Select Information Exchange ....F 212 496-6435
New York *(G-11538)*

MAILING SVCS, NEC
Data Palette Info Svcs LLC ....D 718 433-1060
Port Washington *(G-13251)*
Dispatch Graphics Inc ....F 212 307-5943
New York *(G-9536)*
DP Murphy Co Inc ....D 631 673-9400
Deer Park *(G-3968)*
Five Star Prtg & Mailing Svcs ....F 212 929-0300
New York *(G-9815)*
Hart Reproduction Services ....G 212 704-0556
New York *(G-10046)*
Hugh F McPherson Inc ....G 716 668-6107
Cheektowaga *(G-3450)*
Mason & Gore Inc ....E 914 921-1025
Rye *(G-14485)*
PDQ Shipping Services ....G 845 255-5500
New Paltz *(G-8580)*
The Nugent Organization Inc ....F 212 645-6600
Oceanside *(G-12561)*
Westchester Mailing Service ....E 914 948-1116
White Plains *(G-16519)*

MANAGEMENT CONSULTING SVCS: Automation & Robotics
Cs Automation Inc ....F 315 524-5123
Ontario *(G-12650)*
Javlyn Process Systems LLC ....E 585 424-5580
Rochester *(G-13893)*

MANAGEMENT CONSULTING SVCS: Business
Hargrave Development ....F 716 877-7880
Kenmore *(G-6859)*
Security Letter ....G 212 348-1553
New York *(G-11531)*
Universal Mus Group Hldngs Inc ....E 212 333-8000
New York *(G-11961)*
Yale Robbins Inc ....D 212 683-5700
New York *(G-12158)*

MANAGEMENT CONSULTING SVCS: Construction Project
Darrell Mitchell ....G 646 659-7075
Arverne *(G-414)*

MANAGEMENT CONSULTING SVCS: Distribution Channels
Standard Analytics Io Inc ....G 917 882-5422
New York *(G-11691)*

MANAGEMENT CONSULTING SVCS: Food & Beverage
Marley Spoon Inc ....C 646 934-6970
New York *(G-10714)*
SPX Flow Us LLC ....A 716 692-3000
Getzville *(G-5353)*

MANAGEMENT CONSULTING SVCS: Industrial
GE Global Research ....A 518 387-5000
Niskayuna *(G-12353)*

MANAGEMENT CONSULTING SVCS: Industrial & Labor
Terahertz Technologies Inc ....G 315 736-3642
Oriskany *(G-12765)*

MANAGEMENT CONSULTING SVCS: Industry Specialist
ER Butler & Co Inc ....E 212 925-3565
New York *(G-9699)*

MANAGEMENT CONSULTING SVCS: New Products & Svcs
L D Weiss Inc ....G 212 697-3023
New York *(G-10493)*

MANAGEMENT CONSULTING SVCS: Real Estate
SC Building Solutions LLC ....D 800 564-1152
New York *(G-11497)*

MANAGEMENT CONSULTING SVCS: Training & Development
Calia Technical Inc ....G 718 447-3928
Staten Island *(G-15060)*

MANAGEMENT SERVICES
A & Mt Realty Group LLC ....F 718 974-5871
Brooklyn *(G-1451)*
Arnan Development Corp ....D 607 432-8391
Oneonta *(G-12625)*
Elie Tahari Ltd ....D 212 398-2622
New York *(G-9646)*
Fonar Corporation ....C 631 694-2929
Melville *(G-8025)*
International Center For Postg ....G 607 257-5860
Ithaca *(G-6585)*
Quoizel Inc ....E 631 436-4402
Hauppauge *(G-5927)*

MANAGEMENT SVCS: Administrative
Supermedia LLC ....D 212 513-9700
New York *(G-11748)*
Tdk USA Corporation ....D 516 535-2600
Uniondale *(G-15672)*

MANAGEMENT SVCS: Circuit, Motion Picture Theaters
Dolomite Products Company Inc ....E 315 524-1998
Rochester *(G-13749)*

MANAGEMENT SVCS: Construction
Darrell Mitchell ....G 646 659-7075
Arverne *(G-414)*
Sg Blocks Inc ....G 615 585-2639
Brooklyn *(G-2460)*

MANAGEMENT SVCS: Restaurant
D R M Management Inc ....E 716 668-0333
Depew *(G-4086)*

MANDRELS
Carl Safina Center Inc ....G 808 888-9440
Setauket *(G-14793)*

MANHOLES COVERS: Concrete
Jefferson Concrete Corp ....D 315 788-4171
Watertown *(G-16018)*

MANICURE PREPARATIONS
Angel Tips Nail Salon ....G 718 225-8300
Little Neck *(G-7217)*
Essie Cosmetics Ltd ....D 212 818-1500
New York *(G-9713)*

MANIFOLDS: Pipe, Fabricated From Purchased Pipe
M Manastrip-M Corporation ....G 518 664-2089
Clifton Park *(G-3570)*

MANNEQUINS
Adel Rootstein (usa) Inc ....E 718 499-5650
Brooklyn *(G-1482)*
Columbia Dentoform Corporation ....D 718 482-1569
Long Island City *(G-7414)*
Genesis Mannequins USA II Inc ....G 212 505-6600
New York *(G-9903)*
Lifestyle-Trimco ....E 718 257-9101
Brooklyn *(G-2118)*
Siegel & Stockman Inc ....G 212 633-1508
New York *(G-11576)*

MANUFACTURING INDUSTRIES, NEC
A & W Metal Works Inc ....F 845 352-2346
Garnerville *(G-5298)*
A Fire Inc ....G 631 897-9449
Ronkonkoma *(G-14285)*
A&M Model Makers LLC ....G 626 813-9661
Macedon *(G-7691)*
Accessible Bath Tech LLC ....F 518 937-1518
Albany *(G-27)*
AFP Manufacturing Corp ....F 516 466-6464
Great Neck *(G-5528)*
Atlas Metal Industries Inc ....G 607 776-2048
Hammondsport *(G-5702)*
B F G Elcpltg and Mfg Co ....E 716 362-0888
Blasdell *(G-924)*
Bee Green Industries Inc ....G 516 334-3525
Carle Place *(G-3262)*
Bushwick Bottling LLC ....F 929 666-3618
Brooklyn *(G-1658)*
Cemecon Inc ....E 607 562-2363
Horseheads *(G-6309)*
Consolidated Spring LLC ....F 845 391-8855
Newburgh *(G-12219)*
Dark Storm Industries LLC ....G 631 967-3170
Oakdale *(G-12515)*
Dj Pirrone Industries Inc ....G 518 864-5496
Pattersonville *(G-12888)*
Dolmen ....F 912 596-1537
Conklin *(G-3726)*
Dyco Manufacturing LLC ....D 607 324-2030
Hornell *(G-6297)*
E-Z Global Wholesale Inc ....G 888 769-7888
Brooklyn *(G-1806)*
Essex Industries ....G 518 942-6671
Mineville *(G-8253)*
Everstone Industries LLC ....E 347 777-8150
New York *(G-9739)*
Feraco Industries ....G 631 547-8120
Huntington Station *(G-6440)*
Fun Industries of NY ....F 631 845-3805
Farmingdale *(G-4768)*
Hudson Eastern Industries Inc ....G 917 295-5818
Whitestone *(G-16543)*
Ilc Industries Inc ....E 631 567-5600
Bohemia *(G-1035)*
Impressart ....F 631 940-9530
Edgewood *(G-4404)*
J & R Unique Giftware ....E 718 821-0398
Maspeth *(G-7853)*
John Prior ....G 516 520-9801
East Meadow *(G-4254)*
Just Right Carbines LLC ....G 585 261-5331
Canandaigua *(G-3224)*
K Dymond Industries Inc ....F 631 828-0826
Medford *(G-7956)*
Kafko (us) Corp ....G 877 721-7665
Latham *(G-7077)*
Kaylon Industries LLC ....G 315 303-2119
Baldwinsville *(G-557)*

Employee Codes: A=Over 500 employees, B=251-500
C=101-250, D=51-100, E=20-50, F=10-19, G=5-9

MANUFACTURING INDUSTRIES, NEC — PRODUCT SECTION

Lois Kitchen LLC ....G...... 216 308-9335
  New York (G-10593)
Madison Mfg & Mch Inc ....G...... 315 922-4476
  Erieville (G-4621)
Mitco Manufacturing ....G...... 800 338-8908
  Garden City (G-5272)
O Brien Gere Mfg Inc ....G...... 315 437-6100
  Liverpool (G-7250)
Ogd V-Hvac Inc ....E...... 315 858-1002
  Van Hornesville (G-15802)
Omicron Technologies Inc ....E...... 631 434-7697
  Holbrook (G-6204)
Oriskany Manufacturing LLC ....F...... 315 732-4962
  Yorkville (G-16829)
Oso Industries Inc ....G...... 917 709-2050
  Brooklyn (G-2294)
Performance Precision Mfg LLC ....G...... 518 993-3033
  Fort Plain (G-5103)
Quest Manufacturing Inc ....E...... 716 312-8000
  Hamburg (G-5692)
Rockwell Video Solutions LLC ....F...... 631 745-0582
  Southampton (G-14960)
Rutcarele Inc ....G...... 347 830-5353
  Corona (G-3853)
Select Industries New York Inc ....F...... 800 723-5333
  New York (G-11537)
Shenzhen Xnhdingsheng Tech Ltd ....E...... 510 506-5753
  Flushing (G-5045)
Sonaal Industries Inc ....G...... 718 383-3860
  Brooklyn (G-2499)
Specialists Ltd ....F...... 212 941-7696
  Ridgewood (G-13552)
Stasi Industries Inc ....G...... 516 334-2742
  Old Bethpage (G-12588)
Talisman Industries LLC ....G...... 908 433-7116
  New York (G-11777)
Tii Industries Inc ....F...... 631 789-5000
  Copiague (G-3787)
Tiki Industries Inc ....G...... 516 779-3629
  Riverhead (G-13586)
Topoo Industries Incorporated ....G...... 718 331-3755
  Brooklyn (G-2572)
Unistel LLC ....D...... 585 341-4600
  Webster (G-16105)
Water Splash Inc ....G...... 800 936-3430
  Champlain (G-3418)
Woodfalls Industries ....F...... 518 236-7201
  Plattsburgh (G-13170)
Zmz Mfg Inc ....G...... 518 234-4336
  Warnerville (G-15939)

MAPS

Mapeasy Inc ....F...... 631 537-6213
  Wainscott (G-15889)

MARBLE BOARD

Amendola MBL & Stone Ctr Inc ....D...... 914 997-7968
  White Plains (G-16419)

MARBLE, BUILDING: Cut & Shaped

Dicamillo Marble and Granite ....E...... 845 878-0078
  Patterson (G-12880)
International Stone Accessrs ....G...... 718 522-5399
  Brooklyn (G-2012)
Italian Marble & Granite Inc ....F...... 716 741-1800
  Clarence Center (G-3545)
Monroe Industries Inc ....G...... 585 226-8230
  Avon (G-520)
Salsburg Dimensional Stone ....F...... 631 653-6790
  Brookhaven (G-1432)
Unique MBL Gran Orgnztion Corp ....G...... 718 482-0440
  Long Island City (G-7622)
White Plains Marble Inc ....G...... 914 347-6000
  Elmsford (G-4578)

MARBLE: Crushed & Broken

Sparclean MBL Refinishing Inc ....G...... 718 445-2451
  Ridgewood (G-13551)

MARINAS

Meeco Sullivan LLC ....C...... 800 232-3625
  Warwick (G-15959)

MARINE HARDWARE

Bfg Marine Inc ....F...... 631 586-5500
  Bay Shore (G-662)

Dover Marine Mfg & Sup Co Inc ....G...... 631 667-4300
  Deer Park (G-3967)
Hesperus Nauticals Inc ....G...... 516 974-3016
  Hicksville (G-6095)
Rollson Inc ....E...... 631 423-9578
  Huntington (G-6412)
Taylor Made Group LLC ....E...... 518 725-0681
  Gloversville (G-5468)

MARINE RELATED EQPT

Kyntec Corporation ....G...... 716 810-6956
  Buffalo (G-2913)

MARINE SVC STATIONS

Accurate Marine Specialties ....G...... 631 589-5502
  Bohemia (G-970)

MARKERS

Mark Dri Products Inc ....C...... 516 484-6200
  Bethpage (G-846)

MARKETS: Meat & fish

Schaller Manufacturing Corp ....D...... 718 721-5480
  New York (G-11501)

MARKING DEVICES

Bianca Group Ltd ....G...... 212 768-3011
  New York (G-9070)
C M E Corp ....F...... 315 451-7101
  Syracuse (G-15266)
East Coast Thermographers Inc ....E...... 718 321-3211
  College Point (G-3643)
Hampton Art LLC ....E...... 631 924-1335
  Medford (G-7950)
Hodgins Engraving Co Inc ....D...... 585 343-4444
  Batavia (G-628)
Kelly Foundry & Machine Co ....E...... 315 732-8313
  Utica (G-15717)
Krengel Manufacturing Co Inc ....F...... 212 227-1901
  Fulton (G-5226)
Samoss Group Ltd ....E...... 212 239-6677
  New York (G-11476)
Tech Products Inc ....E...... 718 442-4900
  Staten Island (G-15146)
UI Corp ....G...... 201 203-4453
  Bayside (G-750)
United Sttes Brnze Sign of Fla ....E...... 516 352-5155
  New Hyde Park (G-8570)

MARKING DEVICES: Date Stamps, Hand, Rubber Or Metal

Koehlr-Gibson Mkg Graphics Inc ....E...... 716 838-5960
  Buffalo (G-2910)
Long Island Stamp & Seal Co ....F...... 718 628-8550
  Ridgewood (G-13542)

MARKING DEVICES: Embossing Seals & Hand Stamps

A & M Steel Stamps Inc ....E...... 516 741-6223
  Mineola (G-8199)
Cannizzaro Seal & Engraving Co ....G...... 718 513-6125
  Brooklyn (G-1673)
Joseph Treu Successors Inc ....E...... 212 691-7026
  New York (G-10365)
New York Marking Devices Corp ....G...... 585 454-5188
  Rochester (G-13969)
New York Marking Devices Corp ....F...... 315 463-8641
  Syracuse (G-15381)
Rubber Stamp X Press ....G...... 631 423-1322
  Huntington Station (G-6456)

MARKING DEVICES: Embossing Seals, Corporate & Official

Sales Tax Asset Rceivable Corp ....G...... 212 788-5874
  New York (G-11470)

MARKING DEVICES: Figures, Metal

Thermopatch Corporation ....D...... 315 446-8110
  Syracuse (G-15443)

MARKING DEVICES: Irons, Marking Or Branding

Name Base Inc ....G...... 212 545-1400
  New York (G-10872)

MARKING DEVICES: Letters, Metal

I & I Systems ....G...... 845 753-9126
  Tuxedo Park (G-15656)

MARKING DEVICES: Numbering Machines

National Time Recording Eqp Co ....F...... 212 227-3310
  New York (G-10887)

MARKING DEVICES: Pads, Inking & Stamping

Dab-O-Matic Corp ....D...... 914 699-7070
  Mount Vernon (G-8394)
Specialty Ink Co Inc ....F...... 631 586-3666
  Blue Point (G-965)
United Silicone Inc ....D...... 716 681-8222
  Lancaster (G-7052)

MARKING DEVICES: Postmark Stamps, Hand, Rubber Or Metal

Rubber Stamps Inc ....E...... 212 675-1180
  Mineola (G-8247)

MARKING DEVICES: Screens, Textile Printing

Michael Todd Stevens ....G...... 585 436-9957
  Rochester (G-13938)
Ward Sales Co Inc ....G...... 315 476-5276
  Syracuse (G-15454)

MASKS: Gas

Go Blue Technologies Ltd ....G...... 631 404-6285
  North Babylon (G-12360)

MASQUERADE OR THEATRICAL COSTUMES STORES

D-C Theatricks ....G...... 716 847-0180
  Buffalo (G-2791)
Moresca Clothing and Costume ....F...... 845 331-6012
  Ulster Park (G-15659)

MASTIC ROOFING COMPOSITION

Savage & Son Installations LLC ....E...... 585 342-7533
  Rochester (G-14113)

MATERIALS HANDLING EQPT WHOLESALERS

Four-Way Pallet Corp ....E...... 631 351-3401
  Huntington Station (G-6442)
George Ponte Inc ....G...... 914 243-4202
  Jefferson Valley (G-6776)
High Frequency Tech Co Inc ....F...... 631 242-3020
  Bohemia (G-1032)
Koke Inc ....E...... 800 535-5303
  Queensbury (G-13432)
Nerak Systems Inc ....F...... 914 763-8259
  Fishkill (G-4951)
Overhead Door Corporation ....D...... 518 828-7652
  Hudson (G-6366)
Raymond Sales Corporation ....G...... 607 656-2311
  Greene (G-5618)
Tri-Boro Shelving Inc ....F...... 718 782-8527
  Ridgewood (G-13557)

MATS & MATTING, MADE FROM PURCHASED WIRE

Brook North Farms Inc ....F...... 315 834-9390
  Auburn (G-472)

MATS OR MATTING, NEC: Rubber

Seaway Mats Inc ....G...... 518 483-2560
  Malone (G-7726)

PRODUCT SECTION

MATS, MATTING & PADS: Auto, Floor, Exc Rubber Or Plastic

Auto-Mat Company Inc .... E 516 938-7373
Hicksville *(G-6062)*

MATS, MATTING & PADS: Nonwoven

North Sunshine LLC .... F 307 027-1634
Valley Cottage *(G-15761)*

MATS: Blasting, Rope

T M International LLC .... G 718 842-0949
Bronx *(G-1399)*

MATTRESS STORES

Otis Bedding Mfg Co Inc .... E 716 825-2599
Buffalo *(G-2983)*

MEAT & FISH MARKETS: Fish

Sea Breeze Fish & Seafood of S ..... F 718 984-0447
Staten Island *(G-15133)*

MEAT & MEAT PRDTS WHOLESALERS

Brooklyn Bangers LLC .... F 718 875-3535
Brooklyn *(G-1637)*
Elmgang Enterprises I Inc .... F 212 868-4142
New York *(G-9657)*
Tri-Town Packing Corp .... F 315 389-5101
Brasher Falls *(G-1125)*

MEAT CUTTING & PACKING

A To Z Kosher Meat Products Co .... E 718 384-7400
Brooklyn *(G-1458)*
Caribbean Foods Delight Inc .... D 845 398-3000
Tappan *(G-15466)*
Chefs Delight Packing Co .... F 718 388-8581
Brooklyn *(G-1691)*
Crescent Duck Farm Inc .... E 631 722-8700
Aquebogue *(G-374)*
Domestic Casing Co .... G 718 522-1902
Brooklyn *(G-1787)*
DRG New York Holdings Corp .... C 914 668-9000
Mount Vernon *(G-8395)*
Frank Wardynski & Sons Inc .... E 716 854-6083
Buffalo *(G-2833)*
Gold Medal Packing Inc .... D 315 337-1911
Criskany *(G-12758)*
Ives Farm Market .... G 315 592-4880
Fulton *(G-5222)*
Kamerys Wholesale Meats Inc ...... G 716 372-6756
Olean *(G-12603)*
Orleans Custom Packing Inc .... G 585 314-8227
Holley *(G-6227)*
Side Hill Farmers Coop Inc .... G 315 447-4693
Canastota *(G-3248)*
The Smoke House of Catskills ...... G 845 246-8767
Saugerties *(G-14619)*
Tri-Town Packing Corp .... F 315 389-5101
Brasher Falls *(G-1125)*
We Work .... G 877 673-6628
New York *(G-12083)*

MEAT MARKETS

Ives Farm Market .... G 315 592-4880
Fulton *(G-5222)*
Lancaster Quality Pork Inc .... F 718 439-8822
Brooklyn *(G-2093)*
Mineo & Sapio Meats Inc .... G 716 884-2398
Buffalo *(G-2947)*
The Smoke House of Catskills ...... G 845 246-8767
Saugerties *(G-14619)*
Wilson Beef Farms LLC .... F 607 545-8308
Canaseraga *(G-3239)*

MEAT PRDTS: Bologna, From Purchased Meat

Atlantic Pork & Provisions Inc .... E 718 272-9550
Jamaica *(G-6626)*

MEAT PRDTS: Boneless Meat, From Purchased Meat

Tower Isles Frozen Foods Ltd .... D 718 495-2626
Brooklyn *(G-2577)*

MEAT PRDTS: Dried Beef, From Purchased Meat

Patla Enterprises Inc .... F 315 367-0237
Sherrill *(G-14821)*

MEAT PRDTS: Frankfurters, From Purchased Meat

Marathon Enterprises Inc .... D 718 665-2560
Bronx *(G-1321)*
White Eagle Packing Co Inc .... F 518 374-4366
Schenectady *(G-14728)*

MEAT PRDTS: Frozen

Caribbean Foods Delight Inc .... D 845 398-3000
Tappan *(G-15466)*
Life Earth Company .... G 310 751-0627
New York *(G-10562)*
Original Crunch Roll Fctry LLC ..... G 716 402-5030
Amherst *(G-247)*
Prime Food Processing Corp .... D 718 963-2323
Brooklyn *(G-2342)*

MEAT PRDTS: Meat By-Prdts, From Slaughtered Meat

Cni Meat & Produce Inc .... G 516 599-5929
Valley Stream *(G-15777)*
Joel Kiryas Meat Market Corp ...... F 845 782-9194
Monroe *(G-8273)*
Robert & William Inc .... G 631 727-5780
Riverhead *(G-13582)*
Sam A Lupo & Sons Inc .... G 800 388-5352
Endicott *(G-4609)*
USA Halal Foods Inc .... G 718 291-9111
Long Island City *(G-7626)*

MEAT PRDTS: Meat Extracts, From Purchased Meat

Reliable Brothers Inc .... E 518 273-6732
Green Island *(G-5611)*

MEAT PRDTS: Pork, From Slaughtered Meat

Hilltown Pork Inc .... E 518 781-4050
Canaan *(G-3206)*

MEAT PRDTS: Prepared Beef Prdts From Purchased Beef

Alle Processing Corp .... C 718 894-2000
Maspeth *(G-7818)*
Julian Freirich Company Inc .... E 718 361-9111
Long Island City *(G-7482)*

MEAT PRDTS: Prepared Pork Prdts, From Purchased Meat

Lancaster Quality Pork Inc .... F 718 439-8822
Brooklyn *(G-2093)*
Schaller Manufacturing Corp .... D 718 721-5480
New York *(G-11501)*
Syracuse Casing Co Inc .... F 315 475-0309
Syracuse *(G-15434)*

MEAT PRDTS: Sausage Casings, Natural

Brooklyn Casing Co Inc .... G 718 522-0866
Brooklyn *(G-1639)*
Camellia General Provision Co .... E 716 893-5352
Buffalo *(G-2760)*
Domestic Casing Co .... G 718 522-1902
Brooklyn *(G-1787)*
Frank Wardynski & Sons Inc .... E 716 854-6083
Buffalo *(G-2833)*
Niagara Tying Service Inc .... G 716 825-0066
Buffalo *(G-2971)*
Rapa Independent North America ... G 518 561-0513
Plattsburgh *(G-13153)*

MEAT PRDTS: Sausages & Related Prdts, From Purchased Meat

Dinos Sausage & Meat Co Inc ..... F 315 732-2661
Utica *(G-15696)*
Elmgang Enterprises I Inc .... F 212 868-4142
New York *(G-9657)*

MEAT PRDTS: Sausages, From Purchased Meat

Arnolds Meat Food Products .... E 718 384-8071
Brooklyn *(G-1554)*
Buffalo Provisions Co Inc .... F 718 292-4300
Elmhurst *(G-4462)*
De Ans Pork Products Inc .... E 718 788-2464
Brooklyn *(G-1762)*
Grossglockner Inc .... G 585 266-4960
Canandaigua *(G-3223)*
Salarinos Italian Foods Inc .... F 315 697-9766
Canastota *(G-3247)*
Schonwetter Enterprises Inc ...... E 518 237-0171
Cohoes *(G-3620)*
Zweigles Inc .... D 585 546-1740
Rochester *(G-14221)*

MEAT PRDTS: Sausages, From Slaughtered Meat

Sahlen Packing Company Inc ..... D 716 852-8677
Buffalo *(G-3056)*

MEAT PRDTS: Snack Sticks, Incl Jerky, From Purchased Meat

Big Johns Adirondack Inc .... G 518 587-3680
Saratoga Springs *(G-14571)*
Holy Cow Kosher LLC .... G 347 788-8620
Spring Valley *(G-14995)*
Provisionaire & Co LLC .... E 646 681-8600
Brooklyn *(G-2360)*

MEAT PROCESSED FROM PURCHASED CARCASSES

Alps Provision Co Inc .... E 718 721-4477
Astoria *(G-421)*
Brooklyn Bangers LLC .... F 718 875-3535
Brooklyn *(G-1637)*
Cni Meat & Produce Inc .... G 516 599-5929
Valley Stream *(G-15777)*
Hilltown Pork Inc .... E 518 781-4050
Canaan *(G-3206)*
Jacks Gourmet LLC .... F 718 954-4681
Brooklyn *(G-2028)*
Milan Provision Co Inc .... E 718 899-7678
Corona *(G-3850)*
Mineo & Sapio Meats Inc .... G 716 884-2398
Buffalo *(G-2947)*
Mr Pierogi LLC .... F 718 499-7821
Brooklyn *(G-2233)*
Orchard Sausages Inc .... F 718 381-9388
Brooklyn *(G-2290)*
Picone Meat Specialties Ltd .... G 914 381-3002
Mamaroneck *(G-7753)*
Pork King Sausage Inc .... E 718 542-2810
Bronx *(G-1362)*
Rosina Food Products Inc .... C 716 668-0123
Buffalo *(G-3045)*
Rosina Holding Inc .... G 716 668-0123
Buffalo *(G-3046)*
Schaller Manufacturing Corp ...... F 212 879-3047
New York *(G-11502)*
Schrader Meat Market .... F 607 869-6328
Romulus *(G-14281)*
Sun Ming Jan Inc .... F 718 418-8221
Brooklyn *(G-2531)*
Wilson Beef Farms LLC .... F 607 545-8308
Canaseraga *(G-3239)*

MED, DENTAL & HOSPITAL EQPT, WHOL: Incontinent Prdts/Splys

Koregon Enterprises Inc .... G 450 218-6836
Champlain *(G-3411)*

MEDIA BUYING AGENCIES

Medizine Operating LLC .... D 212 695-2223
New York *(G-10761)*
Selby Marketing Associates Inc ... F 585 377-0750
Rochester *(G-14120)*
Silverlight Digital LLC .... G 646 650-5330
New York *(G-11591)*
Ubm LLC .... D 516 562-7800
New Hyde Park *(G-8568)*

MEDIA: Magnetic & Optical Recording

Aarfid LLC .... G 716 992-3999
 Eden *(G-4386)*
BMA Media Services Inc .... E 585 385-2060
 Rochester *(G-13669)*
Dm2 Media LLC .... E 646 419-4357
 New York *(G-9542)*
Ember Media Corporation .... F 212 695-1919
 New York *(G-9664)*
Next Big Sound Inc .... G 646 657-9837
 New York *(G-10958)*
Stamper Technology Inc .... G 585 247-8370
 Rochester *(G-14141)*

MEDICAL & HOSPITAL EQPT WHOLESALERS

AEP Environmental LLC .... F 716 446-0739
 Buffalo *(G-2690)*
Allied Pharmacy Products Inc .... G 516 374-8862
 Woodmere *(G-16639)*
Angiodynamics Inc .... C 706 846-3126
 Glens Falls *(G-5417)*
Boehm Surgical Instrument Corp .... F 585 436-6584
 Rochester *(G-13671)*
Hogil Pharmaceutical Corp .... F 914 681-1800
 White Plains *(G-16460)*
Nova Health Systems Inc .... G 315 798-9018
 Utica *(G-15727)*
Occunomix International LLC .... E 631 741-1940
 Port Jeff STA *(G-13216)*
Precimed Inc .... G 716 759-5600
 Clarence *(G-3539)*
Progressive Orthotics Ltd .... G 631 732-5556
 Selden *(G-14766)*
Roner Inc .... G 718 392-6020
 Long Island City *(G-7579)*
TSS Foam Industries Corp .... F 585 538-2321
 Caledonia *(G-3159)*

MEDICAL & HOSPITAL SPLYS: Radiation Shielding Garments

Biodex Medical Systems Inc .... C 631 924-9000
 Shirley *(G-14832)*
Biodex Medical Systems Inc .... E 631 924-3146
 Shirley *(G-14833)*
Xylon Industries Inc .... G 631 293-4717
 Farmingdale *(G-4907)*

MEDICAL & SURGICAL SPLYS: Bandages & Dressings

Aero Healthcare (us) LLC .... G 855 225-2376
 Valley Cottage *(G-15751)*
Euromed Inc .... D 845 359-4039
 Orangeburg *(G-12677)*

MEDICAL & SURGICAL SPLYS: Braces, Orthopedic

Complete Orthopedic Svcs Inc .... E 516 357-9113
 East Meadow *(G-4248)*
Eschen Prosthetic & Orthotic L .... E 212 606-1262
 New York *(G-9704)*
Langer Biomechanics Inc .... D 800 645-5520
 Ronkonkoma *(G-14369)*
Lorelei Orthotics Prosthetics .... G 212 727-2011
 New York *(G-10610)*

MEDICAL & SURGICAL SPLYS: Canes, Orthopedic

Harvy Surgical Supply Corp .... E 718 939-1122
 Flushing *(G-5007)*

MEDICAL & SURGICAL SPLYS: Clothing, Fire Resistant & Protect

Crye Precision LLC .... C 718 246-3838
 Brooklyn *(G-1736)*
Elwood Specialty Products Inc .... F 716 877-6622
 Buffalo *(G-2815)*
Hakson Safety Wears Inc .... F 613 667-3015
 Buffalo *(G-2863)*

MEDICAL & SURGICAL SPLYS: Cotton & Cotton Applicators

Advanced Enterprises Inc .... F 845 342-1009
 Middletown *(G-8136)*

MEDICAL & SURGICAL SPLYS: Ear Plugs

Cirrus Healthcare Products LLC .... E 631 692-7600
 Cold Spring Harbor *(G-3629)*
New Dynamics Corporation .... E 845 692-0022
 Middletown *(G-8167)*

MEDICAL & SURGICAL SPLYS: Foot Appliances, Orthopedic

Brannock Device Co Inc .... E 315 475-9862
 Liverpool *(G-7225)*
Fiber Foot Appliances Inc .... F 631 465-9199
 Farmingdale *(G-4765)*
Schuster & Richard Labortories .... G 718 358-8607
 College Point *(G-3664)*

MEDICAL & SURGICAL SPLYS: Gynecological Splys & Appliances

Cityscape Ob/Gyn PLLC .... F 212 683-3595
 New York *(G-9314)*
Womens Health Care PC .... G 718 850-0009
 Richmond Hill *(G-13517)*

MEDICAL & SURGICAL SPLYS: Limbs, Artificial

Aaaaar Orthopedics Inc 845 278-4938
 Brewster *(G-1153)*
Creative Orthotics & Prosthet .... F 607 734-7215
 Elmira *(G-4481)*
Creative Orthotics Prosthetics .... G 607 771-4672
 Binghamton *(G-876)*
Gfh Orthotic & Prosthetic Labs .... G 631 467-3725
 Bohemia *(G-1028)*
Goldberg Prosthetic & Orthotic .... F 631 689-6606
 East Setauket *(G-4302)*
Great Lakes Orthpd Labs Inc .... G 716 878-7307
 Buffalo *(G-2855)*
Green Prosthetics & Orthotics .... E 716 484-1088
 Jamestown *(G-6719)*
Hanger Prsthetcs & Ortho Inc .... G 607 771-4672
 Binghamton *(G-889)*
Hanger Prsthetcs & Ortho Inc .... D 607 795-1220
 Elmira *(G-4489)*
Hanger Prsthetcs & Ortho Inc 315 789-4810
 Geneva *(G-5328)*
J-K Prosthetics & Orthotics .... E 914 699-2077
 Mount Vernon *(G-8411)*
Lehneis Orthotics Prosthetic 516 790-1897
 Hauppauge *(G-5864)*
Lehneis Orthotics Prosthetic .... G 631 369-3115
 Riverhead *(G-13573)*
National Prosthetic Orthot .... G 718 767-8400
 Bayside *(G-748)*
New England Orthotic & Prost 212 682-9313
 New York *(G-10922)*
North Shore Orthtics Prsthtics 631 928-3040
 Port Jeff STA *(G-13215)*
Orthocraft Inc 718 951-1700
 Brooklyn *(G-2292)*
Orthopedic Arts Laboratory Inc .... G 718 858-2400
 Brooklyn *(G-2293)*
Orthopedic Treatment Facility 718 898-7326
 Woodside *(G-16669)*
Progressive Orthotics Ltd 631 732-5556
 Selden *(G-14766)*
Prosthetic Rehabilitation Ctr 845 565-8255
 Newburgh *(G-12244)*
Prosthetics By Nelson Inc .... F 716 894-6666
 Cheektowaga *(G-3456)*
Robert Cohen .... G 718 789-0996
 Ozone Park *(G-12832)*
Rochester Orthopedic Labs 585 272-1060
 Rochester *(G-14089)*
Sampsons Prsthtic Orthotic Lab .... E 518 374-6011
 Schenectady *(G-14709)*
Stafford Labs Orthotics/Prosth .... F 845 692-5227
 Middletown *(G-8176)*
Tonawanda Limb & Brace Inc 716 695-1131
 Tonawanda *(G-15583)*

MEDICAL & SURGICAL SPLYS: Models, Anatomical

Columbia Dentoform Corporation .... D 718 482-1569
 Long Island City *(G-7414)*

MEDICAL & SURGICAL SPLYS: Orthopedic Appliances

Advantage Orthotics Inc .... G 631 368-1754
 East Northport *(G-4259)*
Apollo Orthotics Corp 516 333-3223
 Carle Place *(G-3261)*
Arimed Orthotics Prosthetics .... F 718 875-8754
 Brooklyn *(G-1551)*
Church Communities NY Inc .... E 518 589-5103
 Elka Park *(G-4433)*
Church Communities NY Inc .... E 518 589-5103
 Elka Park *(G-4434)*
Community Products LLC .... C 845 658-8799
 Rifton *(G-13559)*
Community Products LLC .... E 845 572-3433
 Chester *(G-3472)*
Cranial Technologies Inc .... G 914 472-0975
 Scarsdale *(G-14637)*
Custom Sports Lab Inc .... G 212 832-1648
 New York *(G-9436)*
East Cast Orthtics Prosthetics .... F 716 856-5192
 Buffalo *(G-2809)*
East Coast Orthoic & Pros Cor .... D 516 248-5566
 Deer Park *(G-3970)*
East Coast Orthoic & Pros Cor 212 923-2161
 New York *(G-9608)*
Hanger Prsthetcs & Ortho Inc .... G 607 776-8013
 Bath *(G-644)*
Hersco-Orthotic Labs Corp .... E 718 391-0416
 Long Island City *(G-7469)*
Higgins Supply Company Inc .... D 607 836-6474
 Mc Graw *(G-7927)*
Klemmt Orthotics & Prosthetics 607 770-4400
 Johnson City *(G-6813)*
Latorre Orthopedic Laboratory 518 786-8655
 Latham *(G-7085)*
M H Mandelbaum Orthotic .... F 631 473-8668
 Port Jefferson *(G-13222)*
Medi-Ray Inc .... D 877 898-3003
 Tuckahoe *(G-15644)*
Ortho Medical Products .... E 212 879-3700
 New York *(G-11063)*
Orthotics & Prosthetics Dept .... F 585 341-9299
 Rochester *(G-13997)*
Premier Brands of America Inc .... G 718 325-3000
 Bronx *(G-1364)*
Profoot Inc .... E 718 965-8600
 Brooklyn *(G-2354)*
Progressive Orthotics Ltd .... F 631 447-3860
 East Patchogue *(G-4276)*
Rehablitation Tech of Syracuse .... G 315 426-9920
 Syracuse *(G-15406)*
Stj Orthotic Services Inc .... F 631 956-0181
 Lindenhurst *(G-7195)*

MEDICAL & SURGICAL SPLYS: Personal Safety Eqpt

Bio-Chem Barrier Systems LLC .... G 631 261-2682
 Northport *(G-12464)*
Hygrade .... G 718 488-9000
 Brooklyn *(G-1989)*
Kem Medical Products Corp .... G 631 454-6565
 Farmingdale *(G-4802)*
Lakeland Industries Inc .... E 631 981-9700
 Ronkonkoma *(G-14367)*
NY Orthopedic Usa Inc .... D 718 852-5330
 Brooklyn *(G-2279)*
Occunomix International LLC .... E 631 741-1940
 Port Jeff STA *(G-13216)*
Queue Solutions LLC .... F 631 750-6440
 Bohemia *(G-1081)*

MEDICAL & SURGICAL SPLYS: Prosthetic Appliances

Advanced Prosthetics Orthotics .... F 516 365-7225
 Manhasset *(G-7763)*
Center For Prosthetic .... G 845 336-7762
 Kingston *(G-6893)*
Flo-Tech Orthotic & Prosthetic .... G 607 387-3070
 Trumansburg *(G-15639)*

PRODUCT SECTION

MELAMINE RESINS: Melamine-Formaldehyde

New York Rhbilitative Svcs LLC ....F...... 516 239-0990
  Valley Stream (G-15787)
Peak Performance Design LLC............G...... 518 302-9198
  Lake Placid (G-6977)
Syracuse Prosthetic Center Inc............G...... 315 476-9697
  Syracuse (G-15440)
Ultrapedics Ltd............................G...... 718 748-4806
  Brooklyn (G-2598)

MEDICAL & SURGICAL SPLYS: Respiratory Protect Eqpt, Personal

Monaghan Medical Corporation............G...... 315 472-2136
  Syracuse (G-15376)
Venture Respiratory Inc............F...... 718 437-3633
  Brooklyn (G-2618)

MEDICAL & SURGICAL SPLYS: Sponges

Medical Action Industries Inc............C...... 631 231-4600
  Hauppauge (G-5884)

MEDICAL & SURGICAL SPLYS: Suspensories

Ortho Rite Inc............................E...... 914 235-9100
  Mamaroneck (G-7751)

MEDICAL & SURGICAL SPLYS: Technical Aids, Handicapped

Orcam Inc............................F...... 800 713-3741
  New York (G-11056)
Thomas F Egan............................E...... 607 669-4822
  Binghamton (G-919)

MEDICAL EQPT REPAIR SVCS, NON-ELECTRIC

Med Services Inc............................D...... 631 218-6450
  Bohemia (G-1058)

MEDICAL EQPT: Diagnostic

Advantage Plus Diagnostics Inc............G...... 631 393-5044
  Melville (G-7997)
American Bio Medica Corp............D...... 518 758-8158
  Kinderhook (G-6879)
Becton Dickinson and Company............B...... 845 353-3371
  Nyack (G-12500)
Biochemical Diagnostics Inc............E...... 631 595-9200
  Edgewood (G-4397)
E-Z-Em Inc............................ 609 524-2864
  Melville (G-8018)
Ken-Ton Open Mri PC............G...... 716 876-7000
  Kenmore (G-6863)
Memory Md Inc............................G...... 917 318-0215
  New York (G-10770)
Nanobionovum LLC............................F...... 518 581-1171
  Saratoga Springs (G-14591)
Nasiff Associates Inc............................G...... 315 676-2346
  Central Square (G-3391)
Ortho-Clinical Diagnostics Inc............B...... 585 453-4771
  Rochester (G-13993)
Ortho-Clinical Diagnostics Inc............F...... 585 453-5200
  Rochester (G-13994)
Ovitz Corporation............................G...... 585 474-4695
  West Henrietta (G-16246)
Pharma-Smart International Inc............E...... 585 427-0730
  Rochester (G-14017)
Praxis Powder Technology Inc............E...... 518 812-0112
  Queensbury (G-13437)
Proactive Medical Products LLC............G...... 845 205-6004
  Mount Vernon (G-8435)
RJ Harvey Instrument Corp............ 845 359-3943
  Tappan (G-15471)
Vasomedical Solutions Inc............D...... 516 997-4600
  Plainview (G-13097)
Welch Allyn Inc............................A...... 315 685-4100
  Skaneateles Falls (G-14882)
Welch Allyn Inc............................A...... 315 685-4100
  Skaneateles Falls (G-14883)
Welch Allyn Inc............................A...... 315 685-4347
  Skaneateles Falls (G-14884)

MEDICAL EQPT: Electromedical Apparatus

Biofeedback Instrument Corp............G...... 212 222-5665
  New York (G-9087)
Conmed Andover Medical Inc............F...... 315 797-8375
  Utica (G-15685)

Conmed Corporation............................B...... 315 797-8375
  Utica (G-15687)
Health Care Originals Inc............G...... 585 471-8215
  Rochester (G-13864)
Qrs Technologies Inc............................G...... 315 457-5300
  Liverpool (G-7259)

MEDICAL EQPT: Electrotherapeutic Apparatus

Complex Biosystems Inc............G...... 315 464-8007
  Baldwinsville (G-553)

MEDICAL EQPT: Heart-Lung Machines, Exc Iron Lungs

Advd Heart Phys & Surgs............F...... 212 434-3000
  New York (G-8759)
Gary Gelbfish MD............................G...... 718 258-3004
  Brooklyn (G-1918)
Jarvik Heart Inc............................E...... 212 397-3911
  New York (G-10309)

MEDICAL EQPT: Laser Systems

Buffalo Filter LLC............................D...... 716 835-7000
  Lancaster (G-7011)
Ddc Technologies Inc............................ 516 594-1533
  Oceanside (G-12535)
Juvly Aesthetics Inc............................D...... 614 686-3627
  New York (G-10388)
Laser and Varicose Vein Trtmnt............G...... 718 667-1777
  Staten Island (G-15100)
New Primecare............................G...... 516 822-4031
  Hewlett (G-6049)
New York Laser & Aestheticks............G...... 516 627-7777
  Roslyn (G-14448)
Teledyne Optech Inc............................F...... 585 427-8310
  Rochester (G-14164)
University of Rochester............................B...... 585 275-3483
  Rochester (G-14190)

MEDICAL EQPT: MRI/Magnetic Resonance Imaging Devs, Nuclear

City Sports Imaging Inc............E...... 212 481-3600
  New York (G-9313)
Philips Medical Systems Mr............B...... 518 782-1122
  Latham (G-7089)

MEDICAL EQPT: PET Or Position Emission Tomography Scanners

Nirx Medical Technologies LLC............F...... 516 676-6479
  Glen Head (G-5384)

MEDICAL EQPT: Patient Monitoring

Equivital Inc............................E...... 646 513-4169
  New York (G-9698)
Novamed-Usa Inc............................E...... 914 789-2100
  Elmsford (G-4556)
Ocean Cardiac Monitoring............................ 631 777-3700
  Deer Park (G-4021)
Quadrant Biosciences Inc............G...... 315 614-2325
  Syracuse (G-15399)

MEDICAL EQPT: Sterilizers

Getinge Group Logistics Ameri............C...... 585 475-1400
  Rochester (G-13833)
Getinge Usa Inc............................C...... 800 475-9040
  Rochester (G-13834)
SPS Medical Supply Corp............F...... 585 968-2377
  Cuba (G-3920)
Steriliz LLC............................ 585 415-5411
  Rochester (G-14144)

MEDICAL EQPT: Ultrasonic Scanning Devices

Empire Open Mri............................G...... 914 961-1777
  Yonkers (G-16756)
Global Instrumentation LLC............F...... 315 682-0272
  Manlius (G-7778)
Imacor Inc............................E...... 516 393-0970
  Garden City (G-5262)

MEDICAL EQPT: Ultrasonic, Exc Cleaning

Nanovibronix Inc............................F...... 914 233-3004
  Elmsford (G-4554)

MEDICAL EQPT: X-Ray Apparatus & Tubes, Radiographic

Genesis Digital Imaging Inc............G...... 310 305-7358
  Rochester (G-13830)
Quantum Medical Imaging LLC............D...... 631 567-5800
  Rochester (G-14063)
Siemens Corporation............................F...... 202 434-7800
  New York (G-11577)
Siemens USA Holdings Inc............B...... 212 258-4000
  New York (G-11580)

MEDICAL EQPT: X-Ray Apparatus & Tubes, Therapeutic

Community Products LLC............C...... 845 658-8799
  Rifton (G-13559)

MEDICAL PHOTOGRAPHY & ART SVCS

Burns Archive Photographic Dis............G...... 212 889-1938
  New York (G-9160)

MEDICAL, DENTAL & HOSPITAL EQPT, WHOL: Dentists' Prof Splys

Crosstex International Inc............D...... 631 582-6777
  Hauppauge (G-5805)

MEDICAL, DENTAL & HOSPITAL EQPT, WHOL: Hosptl Eqpt/Furniture

Creative Orthotics & Prosthet............F...... 607 734-7215
  Elmira (G-4481)
Medical Action Industries Inc............C...... 631 231-4600
  Hauppauge (G-5884)

MEDICAL, DENTAL & HOSPITAL EQPT, WHOL: Surgical Eqpt & Splys

Medline Industries Inc............................B...... 845 344-3301
  Middletown (G-8163)
Paramount Textiles Inc............................F...... 212 966-1040
  New York (G-11109)

MEDICAL, DENTAL & HOSPITAL EQPT, WHOLESALE: Diagnostic, Med

Memory Md Inc............................G...... 917 318-0215
  New York (G-10770)
Pharma-Smart International Inc............E...... 585 427-0730
  Rochester (G-14017)

MEDICAL, DENTAL & HOSPITAL EQPT, WHOLESALE: Med Eqpt & Splys

Ala Scientific Instruments Inc............F...... 631 393-6401
  Farmingdale (G-4712)
American Healthcare Supply Inc............F...... 212 674-3636
  New York (G-8828)
Basil S Kadhim............................G...... 888 520-5192
  New York (G-9024)
Brinkman Precision Inc............................D...... 585 429-5001
  West Henrietta (G-16233)
Lehneis Orthotics Prosthetic............ 516 790-1897
  Hauppauge (G-5864)
Lehneis Orthotics Prosthetic............G...... 631 369-3115
  Riverhead (G-13573)
Peter Digioia............................G...... 516 644-5517
  Plainview (G-13081)
Quantum Medical Imaging LLC............D...... 631 567-5800
  Rochester (G-14063)

MEDICAL, DENTAL & HOSPITAL EQPT, WHOLESALE: Medical Lab

Integrted Work Envronments LLC............G...... 716 725-5088
  East Amherst (G-4190)

MELAMINE RESINS: Melamine-Formaldehyde

Hexion Inc............................E...... 518 792-8040
  South Glens Falls (G-14936)
Queen City Manufacturing Inc............G...... 716 877-1102
  Buffalo (G-3028)

MEMBERSHIP ORGS, BUSINESS: Growers' Marketing Advisory Svc

Atlantic Farm & Food Inc .... F 718 441-3152
Richmond Hill *(G-13496)*

MEMBERSHIP ORGS, CIVIC, SOCIAL/FRAT: Educator's Assoc

Modern Language Assn Amer Inc .... C 646 576-5000
New York *(G-10829)*

MEMORY DEVICES: Magnetic Bubble

Dynamic Photography Inc .... G 516 381-2951
Roslyn *(G-14446)*

MEN'S & BOYS' CLOTHING ACCESS STORES

Broadway Knitting Mills Inc .... G 716 692-4421
North Tonawanda *(G-12418)*
Giliberto Designs Inc .... E 212 695-0216
New York *(G-9920)*
Swank Inc .... B 212 867-2600
New York *(G-11753)*

MEN'S & BOYS' CLOTHING STORES

By Robert James .... G 212 253-2121
New York *(G-9165)*
Elie Tahari Ltd .... G 212 398-2622
New York *(G-9645)*
Grunt Apparel Inc .... G 646 878-6171
New York *(G-10002)*
Hugo Boss Usa Inc .... D 212 940-0600
New York *(G-10146)*
Kcp Holdco Inc .... F 212 265-1500
New York *(G-10426)*
Kenneth Cole Productions Inc .... B 212 265-1500
New York *(G-10431)*
Mee Accessories LLC .... B 917 262-1000
New York *(G-10762)*
Mega Sourcing Inc .... G 646 682-0304
Merrick *(G-8103)*
Michael Andrews LLC .... F 212 677-1755
New York *(G-10790)*
Perrone Leather LLC .... D 518 853-4300
Fultonville *(G-5239)*
Perry Ellis Menswear LLC .... C 212 221-7500
New York *(G-11162)*
Phillips-Van Heusen Europe .... F 212 381-3500
New York *(G-11183)*
Pvh Corp .... D 212 381-3500
New York *(G-11281)*
Pvh Corp .... G 212 549-6000
New York *(G-11282)*
Sanctuary Brands LLC .... G 212 704-4014
New York *(G-11479)*

MEN'S & BOYS' CLOTHING WHOLESALERS, NEC

All Net Ltd .... F 516 504-4559
Great Neck *(G-5531)*
Billion Tower Intl LLC .... F 212 220-0608
New York *(G-9082)*
D-C Theatricks .... G 716 847-0180
Buffalo *(G-2791)*
Enzo Manzoni LLC .... G 212 464-7000
Brooklyn *(G-1839)*
G-III Apparel Group Ltd .... B 212 403-0500
New York *(G-9869)*
Herrmann Group LLC .... G 716 876-9798
Kenmore *(G-6860)*
Jeans Inc .... G 646 223-1122
New York *(G-10324)*
Kate Spade & Company LLC .... B 212 354-4900
New York *(G-10415)*
Kenmar Shirts Inc .... E 718 824-3880
Bronx *(G-1307)*
M Hidary & Co Inc .... D 212 736-6540
New York *(G-10639)*
Moresca Clothing and Costume .... F 845 331-6012
Ulster Park *(G-15659)*
Mountain T-Shirts Inc .... G 518 943-4533
Catskill *(G-3307)*
Onia LLC .... G 646 701-0008
New York *(G-11045)*
Penfli Industries Inc .... F 212 947-6080
Great Neck *(G-5581)*

Ryba General Merchandise Inc .... G 718 522-2028
Brooklyn *(G-2430)*
Sanctuary Brands LLC .... G 212 704-4014
New York *(G-11479)*
United Knitwear International .... G 212 354-2920
New York *(G-11953)*
Universal Mus Group Hldngs Inc .... E 212 333-8000
New York *(G-11961)*
Wp Lavori USA Inc .... G 212 244-6074
New York *(G-12143)*

MEN'S & BOYS' SPORTSWEAR CLOTHING STORES

Authentic Brands Group LLC .... C 212 760-2410
New York *(G-8966)*
Cockpit Usa Inc .... F 212 575-1616
New York *(G-9343)*
Foot Locker Retail Inc .... F 516 827-5306
Hicksville *(G-6087)*
Herrmann Group LLC .... G 716 876-9798
Kenmore *(G-6860)*
Mainly Monograms Inc .... E 845 624-4923
West Nyack *(G-16275)*
Nautica Opco LLC .... B 212 541-5757
New York *(G-10896)*
Royal Tees Inc .... G 845 357-9448
Suffern *(G-15197)*

MEN'S & BOYS' SPORTSWEAR WHOLESALERS

Bandit International Ltd .... F 718 402-2100
Bronx *(G-1225)*
Cockpit Usa Inc .... F 212 575-1616
New York *(G-9343)*
Mee Accessories LLC .... B 917 262-1000
New York *(G-10762)*
Sterling Possessions Ltd .... G 212 594-0418
New York *(G-11707)*

MEN'S & BOYS' UNDERWEAR WHOLESALERS

Apparel Partnership Group LLC .... G 212 302-7722
New York *(G-8889)*

MEN'S SUITS STORES

Kozinn+sons Merchant Tailors .... E 212 643-1916
New York *(G-10475)*
Royal Clothing Corp .... G 718 436-5841
Brooklyn *(G-2418)*

MESSAGE CONCENTRATORS

Gac Express Inc .... F 718 438-2227
Brooklyn *(G-1915)*

METAL & STEEL PRDTS: Abrasive

Datum Alloys Inc .... G 607 239-6274
Endicott *(G-4586)*
Pellets LLC .... F 716 693-1750
North Tonawanda *(G-12441)*
Raulli and Sons Inc .... G 315 479-2515
Syracuse *(G-15404)*

METAL COMPONENTS: Prefabricated

Precision Fabrication LLC .... G 585 591-3449
Attica *(G-461)*

METAL CUTTING SVCS

Elmsford Sheet Metal Works Inc .... D 914 739-6300
Cortlandt Manor *(G-3900)*
Knise & Krick Inc .... E 315 422-3516
Syracuse *(G-15357)*
S & S Prtg Die-Cutting Co Inc .... F 718 388-8990
Brooklyn *(G-2434)*

METAL FABRICATORS: Architechtural

A & T Iron Works Inc .... E 914 632-8992
New Rochelle *(G-8585)*
A1 Ornamental Iron Works Inc .... F 718 265-3055
Brooklyn *(G-1467)*
Accurate Welding Service Inc .... G 516 333-1730
Westbury *(G-16308)*
Aero-Data Metal Crafters Inc .... C 631 471-7733
Ronkonkoma *(G-14294)*

Airflex Corp .... D 631 752-1219
Farmingdale *(G-4709)*
Aldos Iron Works Inc .... G 718 834-0408
Brooklyn *(G-1503)*
All American Metal Corporation .... E 516 623-0222
Freeport *(G-5140)*
Babylon Iron Works Inc .... F 631 643-3311
West Babylon *(G-16137)*
Bobrick Washroom Equipment Inc ..... D 518 877-7444
Clifton Park *(G-3565)*
Cabezon Design Group Inc .... G 718 488-9868
Brooklyn *(G-1667)*
Caliper Studio Inc .... E 718 302-2427
Brooklyn *(G-1669)*
Creative Metal Fabricators .... G 631 567-2266
Bohemia *(G-1002)*
E F Iron Works & Construction .... G 631 242-4766
Bay Shore *(G-684)*
Ej Group Inc .... E 315 699-2601
Cicero *(G-3517)*
Elevator Accessories Mfg .... F 914 739-7004
Peekskill *(G-12919)*
Flushing Iron Weld Inc .... E 718 359-2208
Flushing *(G-5001)*
Forest Iron Works Inc .... G 516 671-4229
Locust Valley *(G-7348)*
Giumenta Corp .... E 718 832-1200
Brooklyn *(G-1930)*
Global Steel Products Corp .... C 631 586-3455
Deer Park *(G-3981)*
Grillmaster Inc .... E 718 272-9191
Howard Beach *(G-6330)*
Hi-Tech Metals Inc .... E 718 894-1212
Maspeth *(G-7852)*
ITR Industries Inc .... E 914 964-7063
Yonkers *(G-16771)*
Jerry Cardullo Iron Works Inc .... F 631 242-8881
Bay Shore *(G-692)*
Kenal Services Corp .... G 315 788-9226
Watertown *(G-16020)*
Keuka Studios Inc .... E 585 624-5960
Rush *(G-14475)*
Kms Contracting Inc .... F 718 495-6500
Brooklyn *(G-2077)*
M B C Metal Inc .... F 718 384-6713
Brooklyn *(G-2145)*
Martin Orna Ir Works II Inc .... G 516 354-3923
Elmont *(G-4542)*
Material Process Systems Inc .... F 718 302-3081
Brooklyn *(G-2179)*
Mestel Brothers Stairs & Rails .... C 516 496-4127
Syosset *(G-15222)*
Metalworks Inc .... E 718 319-0011
Bronx *(G-1329)*
Milgo Industrial Inc .... D 718 388-6476
Brooklyn *(G-2206)*
Milgo Industrial Inc .... G 718 387-0406
Brooklyn *(G-2207)*
Mison Concepts Inc .... E 516 933-8000
Hicksville *(G-6110)*
Modern Art Foundry Inc .... E 718 728-2030
Astoria *(G-436)*
Morgik Metal Designs .... F 212 463-0304
New York *(G-10842)*
Moro Corporation .... E 607 724-4241
Binghamton *(G-906)*
New Dimensions Office Group .... D 718 387-0995
Brooklyn *(G-2259)*
Old Dutchmans Wrough Iron Inc .... G 716 688-2034
Getzville *(G-5351)*
Pawling Corporation .... D 845 373-9300
Wassaic *(G-15965)*
Peconic Ironworks Ltd .... F 631 204-0323
Southampton *(G-14959)*
Phoenix Metal Designs Inc .... G 516 597-4100
Brooklyn *(G-2315)*
Pk30 System LLC .... F 212 473-8050
Stone Ridge *(G-15162)*
Railings By New Star Brass .... E 516 358-1153
Brooklyn *(G-2380)*
Raulli and Sons Inc .... D 315 479-6693
Syracuse *(G-15402)*
Riverside Iron LLC .... F 315 535-4864
Gouverneur *(G-5492)*
Rollson Inc .... E 631 423-9578
Huntington *(G-6412)*
Roman Iron Works Inc .... F 516 621-1103
Greenvale *(G-5631)*
Royal Metal Products Inc .... E 518 966-4442
Surprise *(G-15207)*

S A Baxter LLC ....G.... 845 469-7995
Chester *(G-3482)*
Steel Sales Inc ....E.... 607 674-6363
Sherburne *(G-14811)*
Steel Work Inc ....G.... 585 232-1555
Rochester *(G-14142)*
Steps Plus Inc ....D.... 315 432-0885
Syracuse *(G-15430)*
Studio 40 Inc ....G.... 212 420-8631
Brooklyn *(G-2526)*
Superior Metal & Woodwork Inc ....E.... 631 465-9004
Farmingdale *(G-4884)*
Tonys Ornamental Ir Works Inc ....E.... 315 337-3730
Rome *(G-14276)*
Tropical Driftwood Originals ....G.... 516 623-0980
Roosevelt *(G-14438)*
United Iron Inc ....E.... 914 667-5700
Mount Vernon *(G-8453)*
Universal Steel Fabricators ....F.... 718 342-0782
Brooklyn *(G-2610)*
Village Wrought Iron Inc ....F.... 315 683-5589
Fabius *(G-4624)*
West End Iron Works Inc ....G.... 518 456-1105
Albany *(G-141)*
Z-Studios Dsign Fbrication LLC ....G.... 347 512-4210
Brooklyn *(G-2668)*

METAL FABRICATORS: Plate

Acro Industries Inc ....C.... 585 254-3661
Rochester *(G-13600)*
Aero-Data Metal Crafters Inc ....C.... 631 471-7733
Ronkonkoma *(G-14294)*
Allstate Gasket & Packing Inc ....F.... 631 254-4050
Deer Park *(G-3937)*
American Boiler Tank Wldg Inc ....E.... 518 463-5012
Albany *(G-40)*
Arvos Inc ....C.... 785 243-3300
Wellsville *(G-16112)*
Atlantic Industrial Tech Inc ....E.... 631 234-3131
Shirley *(G-14830)*
Bellmore Steel Products Corp ....F.... 516 785-9667
Bellmore *(G-786)*
Blackstone Advanced Tech LLC ....C.... 716 665-5410
Jamestown *(G-6702)*
Breton Industries Inc ....C.... 518 842-3030
Amsterdam *(G-329)*
Bridgehampton Steel & Wldg Inc ....F.... 631 537-2486
Bridgehampton *(G-1179)*
Bruce Pierce ....G.... 716 731-9310
Sanborn *(G-14542)*
Buflovak LLC ....E.... 716 895-2100
Buffalo *(G-2755)*
C & F Fabricators & Erectors ....G.... 607 432-3520
Colliersville *(G-3671)*
Charles Ross & Son Company ....D.... 631 234-0500
Hauppauge *(G-5788)*
Chart Industries Inc ....E.... 716 691-0202
Amherst *(G-222)*
Cigar Box Studios Inc ....F.... 845 236-9283
Marlboro *(G-7812)*
Contech Engnered Solutions LLC ....F.... 716 870-9091
Orchard Park *(G-12710)*
Direkt Force LLC ....E.... 716 652-3022
East Aurora *(G-4197)*
Easco Boiler Corp ....E.... 718 378-3000
Bronx *(G-1264)*
ECR International Inc ....D.... 315 797-1310
Utica *(G-15699)*
ECR International Inc ....C.... 716 366-5500
Dunkirk *(G-4169)*
Endicott Precision Inc ....C.... 607 754-7076
Endicott *(G-4589)*
Fulton Boiler Works Inc ....C.... 315 298-5121
Pulaski *(G-13381)*
Fulton China LLC ....G.... 315 298-0112
Pulaski *(G-13382)*
Global Steel Products Corp ....C.... 631 586-3455
Deer Park *(G-3981)*
Inex Inc ....G.... 716 537-2270
Holland *(G-6219)*
Jaquith Industries Inc ....E.... 315 478-5700
Syracuse *(G-15346)*
Marex Aquisition Corp ....C.... 585 458-3940
Rochester *(G-13930)*
Methods Tooling & Mfg Inc ....E.... 845 246-7100
Mount Marion *(G-8364)*
Mitsubishi Chemical Amer Inc ....E.... 212 223-3043
New York *(G-10825)*
Niagara Cooler Inc ....G.... 716 434-1235
Lockport *(G-7321)*

Pfaudler US Inc ....C.... 585 235-1000
Rochester *(G-14015)*
Roemac Industrial Sales Inc ....G.... 716 692-7332
North Tonawanda *(G-12448)*
Rosenwach Tank Co Inc ....E.... 212 972-4411
Astoria *(G-442)*
Seibel Modern Mfg & Wldg Corp ....D.... 716 683-1536
Lancaster *(G-7049)*
Slant/Fin Corporation ....B.... 516 484-2600
Greenvale *(G-5632)*
SPX Cooling Technologies Inc ....G.... 914 697-5030
White Plains *(G-16505)*

METAL FABRICATORS: Sheet

303 Contracting Inc ....E.... 716 896-2122
Orchard Park *(G-12694)*
A & L Shtmtl Fabrications Corp ....E.... 718 842-1600
Bronx *(G-1200)*
Accra Sheetmetal LLC ....G.... 631 643-2100
Wyandanch *(G-16691)*
Acme Architectural Pdts Inc ....D.... 718 384-7800
Brooklyn *(G-1477)*
Acro-Fab Ltd ....E.... 315 564-6688
Hannibal *(G-5717)*
Advanced Precision Technology ....F.... 845 279-3540
Brewster *(G-1154)*
Advantech Industries Inc ....C.... 585 247-0701
Rochester *(G-13609)*
Aero Trades Mfg Corp ....E.... 516 746-3360
Mineola *(G-8200)*
Aeroduct Inc ....E.... 516 248-9550
Mineola *(G-8201)*
Afco Systems Inc ....C.... 631 249-9441
Farmingdale *(G-4708)*
Aj Genco Mch Sp McHy Rdout Svc ....F.... 716 664-4925
Falconer *(G-4669)*
Ajl Manufacturing Inc ....C.... 585 254-1128
Rochester *(G-13611)*
Albany Mtal Fbrcation Holdings ....G.... 518 463-5161
Albany *(G-36)*
Aldo Frustacci Iron Works Inc ....F.... 718 768-0707
Brooklyn *(G-1502)*
Aleta Industries Inc ....F.... 718 349-0040
Brooklyn *(G-1504)*
Alkemy Machine LLC ....G.... 585 436-8730
Rochester *(G-13613)*
All Around Spiral Inc ....G.... 631 588-0220
Ronkonkoma *(G-14299)*
All Metal Specialties Inc ....E.... 716 664-6009
Jamestown *(G-6696)*
All Star Carts & Vehicles Inc ....D.... 631 666-5581
Bay Shore *(G-654)*
All Star Sheet Metal Inc ....F.... 718 456-1567
Farmingdale *(G-4715)*
Allen Machine Products Inc ....E.... 631 630-8800
Hauppauge *(G-5761)*
Alliance Welding & Steel Fabg ....F.... 516 775-7600
Floral Park *(G-4954)*
Allure Metal Works Inc ....F.... 631 588-0220
Ronkonkoma *(G-14302)*
Alpine Machine Inc ....F.... 607 272-1344
Ithaca *(G-6556)*
Alternative Service Inc ....F.... 631 345-9500
Bellport *(G-798)*
American Std Shtmtl Sup Corp ....F.... 718 888-9350
Flushing *(G-4985)*
Amsco Inc ....F.... 716 823-4213
Buffalo *(G-2699)*
Arcadia Mfg Group Inc ....E.... 518 434-6213
Green Island *(G-5602)*
Arcadia Mfg Group Inc ....G.... 518 434-6213
Menands *(G-8081)*
Art Precision Metal Products ....F.... 631 842-8889
Copiague *(G-3752)*
Ascension Industries Inc ....C.... 716 693-9381
North Tonawanda *(G-12413)*
Atech-Seh Metal Fabricator ....E.... 716 895-8888
Buffalo *(G-2711)*
Atlantis Equipment Corporation ....E.... 518 733-5910
Stephentown *(G-15154)*
Auburn Tank & Manufacturing Co ....F.... 315 255-2788
Auburn *(G-466)*
B & R Sheet ....G.... 718 558-5544
Jamaica *(G-6629)*
Bargold Storage Systems LLC ....E.... 718 247-7000
Long Island City *(G-7398)*
Batavia Enclosures Inc ....G.... 585 344-1797
Arcade *(G-378)*
Berjen Metal Industries Ltd ....G.... 631 673-7979
Huntington *(G-6394)*

Best Tinsmith Supply Inc ....G.... 518 863-2541
Northville *(G-12476)*
Blackstone Advanced Tech LLC ....C.... 716 665-5410
Jamestown *(G-6702)*
Bmg Systems ....F.... 716 432-5160
Depew *(G-4081)*
Broadway Neon Sign Corp ....F.... 908 241-4177
Ronkonkoma *(G-14322)*
Brzozka Industries Inc ....F.... 631 588-8164
Holbrook *(G-6173)*
C & T Tool & Instrument Co ....E.... 718 429-1253
Woodside *(G-16648)*
C J & C Sheet Metal Corp ....F.... 631 376-9425
West Babylon *(G-16144)*
Cameron Mfg & Design Inc ....C.... 607 739-3606
Horseheads *(G-6308)*
Cannon Industries Inc ....D.... 585 254-8080
Rochester *(G-13690)*
CBM Fabrications Inc ....E.... 518 399-8023
Ballston Lake *(G-567)*
Center Sheet Metal Inc ....C.... 718 378-4476
Bronx *(G-1237)*
Chamtek Mfg Inc ....F.... 585 328-4900
Rochester *(G-13707)*
Chutes and Compactors of NY ....F.... 718 494-2247
Staten Island *(G-15062)*
City Cooling Enterprises Inc ....G.... 718 331-7400
Brooklyn *(G-1694)*
Clark Specialty Co Inc ....E.... 607 776-3193
Bath *(G-642)*
CPI Industries Inc ....D.... 631 909-3434
Manorville *(G-7784)*
Crown Die Casting Corp ....E.... 914 667-5400
Mount Vernon *(G-8392)*
Cutting Edge Metal Works ....E.... 631 981-8333
Holtsville *(G-6239)*
Cw Metals Inc ....E.... 917 416-7906
Long Island City *(G-7419)*
D & G Sheet Metal Co Inc ....F.... 718 326-9111
Maspeth *(G-7833)*
Dawson Metal Company Inc ....C.... 716 664-3811
Jamestown *(G-6711)*
Dimar Manufacturing Corp ....C.... 716 759-0351
Clarence *(G-3527)*
Dj Acquisition Management Corp ....D.... 585 265-3000
Ontario *(G-12652)*
Doortec Archtctural Met GL LLC ....E.... 718 567-2730
Brooklyn *(G-1789)*
Dundas-Jafine Inc ....E.... 716 681-9690
Alden *(G-170)*
Dynasty Stainless Steel & Meta ....E.... 718 205-6623
Maspeth *(G-7839)*
Elevator Accessories Mfg ....F.... 914 739-7004
Peekskill *(G-12919)*
Empire Air Specialties Inc ....E.... 518 689-4440
Albany *(G-72)*
Endicott Precision Inc ....C.... 607 754-7076
Endicott *(G-4589)*
Engineering Mfg Tech LLC ....D.... 607 754-7111
Endicott *(G-4591)*
Expert Industries Inc ....E.... 718 434-6060
Brooklyn *(G-1859)*
F M L Industries Inc ....G.... 607 749-7273
Homer *(G-6254)*
Federal Sheet Metal Works Inc ....F.... 315 735-4730
Utica *(G-15702)*
Five Star Industries Inc ....E.... 716 674-2589
West Seneca *(G-16297)*
Fred A Nudd Corporation ....D.... 315 524-2531
Ontario *(G-12653)*
Goergen-Mackwirth Co Inc ....E.... 716 874-4800
Buffalo *(G-2852)*
Greene Technologies Inc ....D.... 607 656-4166
Greene *(G-5615)*
H Klein & Sons Inc ....E.... 516 746-0163
Mineola *(G-8225)*
Hana Sheet Metal Inc ....G.... 914 377-0773
Yonkers *(G-16766)*
Hansen Steel ....E.... 585 398-2020
Farmington *(G-4915)*
Hergo Ergonomic Support ....E.... 718 894-0639
Maspeth *(G-7851)*
Hermann Gerdens Inc ....G.... 631 841-3132
Copiague *(G-3763)*
Hi-Tech Industries NY Inc ....E.... 607 217-7361
Johnson City *(G-6810)*
Hrd Metal Products Inc ....G.... 631 243-6700
Deer Park *(G-3985)*
Hunter Douglas Inc ....D.... 845 664-7000
Pearl River *(G-12901)*

PRODUCT

Employee Codes: A=Over 500 employees, B=251-500
C=101-250, D=51-100, E=20-50, F=10-19, G=5-9
2019 Harris
New York Manufacturers Directory
1187

METAL FABRICATORS: Sheet

I Rauchs Sons Inc .... E 718 507-8844
  East Elmhurst (G-4221)
IEC Electronics Corp .... D 585 647-1760
  Rochester (G-13876)
Industrial Fabricating Corp .... E 315 437-3353
  East Syracuse (G-4348)
Intellimetal Inc .... D 585 424-3260
  Rochester (G-13883)
Jamestown Advanced Pdts Corp .... E 716 483-3406
  Jamestown (G-6725)
Jaquith Industries Inc .... E 315 478-5700
  Syracuse (G-15346)
Jar Metals Inc .... F 845 425-8901
  Nanuet (G-8464)
Kal Manufacturing Corporation .... E 585 265-4310
  Webster (G-16088)
Kassis Superior Sign Co Inc .... F 315 463-7446
  Syracuse (G-15354)
Kittredge & Sons Inc .... D 978 567-0998
  Niagara Falls (G-12303)
Ksm Group Ltd .... G 716 751-6006
  Newfane (G-12252)
Leader Sheet Metal Inc .... F 347 271-4961
  Bronx (G-1314)
Manufacturing Resources Inc .... E 631 481-0041
  Rochester (G-13926)
Marex Aquisition Corp .... C 585 458-3940
  Rochester (G-13930)
Mariah Metal Products Inc .... G 516 938-9783
  Hicksville (G-6106)
McHone Industries Inc .... D 716 945-3380
  Salamanca (G-14526)
MD International Industries .... E 631 254-3100
  Deer Park (G-4009)
Melto Metal Products Co Inc .... E 516 546-8866
  Freeport (G-5166)
Merz Metal & Machine Corp .... E 716 893-7786
  Buffalo (G-2944)
Metal Solutions Inc .... E 315 732-6271
  Utica (G-15719)
Metallogix Design Fabrication .... E 315 738-4554
  Utica (G-15720)
Metalsmith Inc .... G 631 467-1500
  Holbrook (G-6200)
Methods Tooling & Mfg Inc .... E 845 246-7100
  Mount Marion (G-8364)
Metro Duct Systems Inc .... F 718 278-4294
  Long Island City (G-7522)
Mitsubishi Chemical Amer Inc .... E 212 223-3043
  New York (G-10825)
Monarch Metal Fabrication Inc .... G 631 563-8967
  Bohemia (G-1059)
Monroe Piping & Shtmtl LLC .... D 585 482-0200
  Rochester (G-13954)
Ms Spares LLC .... G 607 223-3024
  Clay (G-3551)
N & L Instruments Inc .... F 631 471-4000
  Ronkonkoma (G-14382)
Nci Group Inc .... D 315 339-1245
  Rome (G-14261)
North Coast Outfitters Ltd .... E 631 727-5580
  Riverhead (G-13578)
Northeast Fabricators LLC .... D 607 865-4031
  Walton (G-15912)
Northern Awning & Sign Company .... G 315 782-8515
  Watertown (G-16030)
Olympic Manufacturing Inc .... E 631 231-8900
  Hauppauge (G-5906)
Omc Inc .... C 718 731-5001
  Bronx (G-1347)
Pathfinder Industries Inc .... E 315 593-2483
  Fulton (G-5231)
PDQ Manufacturing Co Inc .... G 845 889-3123
  Rhinebeck (G-13487)
Phoenix Envmtl Svcs Corp .... F 718 381-8100
  Glendale (G-5406)
Pirnat Precise Metals Inc .... G 631 293-9169
  Farmingdale (G-4850)
Plattsburgh Sheet Metal Inc .... G 518 561-4930
  Plattsburgh (G-13147)
Precision Fabrication LLC .... G 585 591-3449
  Attica (G-461)
Precision Metals Corp .... E 631 586-5032
  Bay Shore (G-709)
Precision Mtl Fabricators Inc .... F 718 832-8645
  Brooklyn (G-2335)
Precision Systems Mfg Inc .... E 315 451-3480
  Liverpool (G-7257)
Protofast Holding Corp .... G 631 753-2549
  Copiague (G-3775)

R & J Sheet Metal Distributors .... G 518 433-1525
  Albany (G-120)
Rayco Manufacturing Co Inc .... F 516 431-2006
  Jamaica (G-6672)
Reynolds Manufacturing Inc .... F 607 562-8936
  Big Flats (G-856)
Rigidized Metals Corporation .... E 716 849-4703
  Buffalo (G-3038)
Robert E Derecktor Inc .... F 914 698-0962
  Mamaroneck (G-7756)
Rochester Colonial Mfg Corp .... D 585 254-8191
  Rochester (G-14084)
Rollson Inc .... E 631 423-9578
  Huntington (G-6412)
Royal Metal Products Inc .... E 518 966-4442
  Surprise (G-15207)
S & J Sheet Metal Supply .... G 718 384-0800
  Brooklyn (G-2431)
Service Mfg Group Inc .... E 716 893-1482
  Buffalo (G-3064)
Simmons Fabricating Svc Inc .... G 845 635-3755
  Pleasant Valley (G-13172)
Smg Metal Products LLC .... G 716 633-6439
  Cheektowaga (G-3458)
Solidus Industries Inc .... D 607 749-4540
  Homer (G-6259)
Standard Industrial Works Inc .... F 631 888-0130
  Bay Shore (G-726)
Steel Sales Inc .... E 607 674-6363
  Sherburne (G-14811)
Steel Work Inc .... G 585 232-1555
  Rochester (G-14142)
Sterling Industries Inc .... E 631 753-3070
  Farmingdale (G-4882)
T Lemme Mechanical Inc .... E 518 436-4136
  Menands (G-8092)
Tatra Mfg Corporation .... F 631 691-1184
  Copiague (G-3786)
TCS Industries Inc .... D 585 426-1160
  Rochester (G-14158)
Themis Chimney Inc .... F 718 937-4716
  Brooklyn (G-2565)
Tri-Technologies Inc .... E 914 699-2001
  Mount Vernon (G-8449)
Trident Precision Mfg Inc .... D 585 265-2010
  Webster (G-16103)
Tripar Manufacturing Co Inc .... G 631 563-0855
  Bohemia (G-1100)
Truform Manufacturing Corp .... D 585 458-1090
  Rochester (G-14179)
Trylon Wire & Metal Works Inc .... E 718 542-4472
  Bronx (G-1409)
Ucr Steel Group LLC .... F 718 764-3414
  Ronkonkoma (G-14424)
Ultimate Prcision Met Pdts Inc .... C 631 249-9441
  Farmingdale (G-4901)
Unadilla Silo Company Inc .... D 607 369-9341
  Sidney (G-14857)
Universal Shielding Corp .... E 631 667-7900
  Deer Park (G-4055)
Vance Metal Fabricators Inc .... D 315 789-5626
  Geneva (G-5335)
Voss Manufacturing Inc .... D 716 731-5062
  Sanborn (G-14557)
Wainland Inc .... E 718 626-2233
  Astoria (G-448)
Wenig Corporation .... E 718 542-3600
  Bronx (G-1419)
Wg Sheet Metal Corp .... G 718 235-3093
  Brooklyn (G-2643)
William Kanes Mfg Corp .... E 718 346-1515
  Brooklyn (G-2649)
Zahk Sales Inc .... G 631 851-0851
  Islandia (G-6541)

METAL FABRICATORS: Structural, Ship

Cameron Bridge Works LLC .... E 607 734-9456
  Elmira (G-4474)
Miller Metal Fabricating Inc .... G 585 359-3400
  Rochester (G-13945)

METAL FINISHING SVCS

21st Century Finishes Inc .... F 516 221-7000
  North Bellmore (G-12372)
ABS Metal Corp .... G 646 302-9018
  Hewlett (G-6045)
Anthony River Inc .... F 315 475-1315
  Syracuse (G-15244)
D & I Finishing Inc .... G 631 471-3034
  Bohemia (G-1007)

D & W Enterprises LLC .... F 585 590-6727
  Medina (G-7976)
Ever-Nu-Metal Products Inc .... F 646 423-5833
  Brooklyn (G-1854)
First Impressions Finishing .... G 631 467-2244
  Ronkonkoma (G-14341)
Halmark Architectural Finshg .... E 718 272-1831
  Brooklyn (G-1961)
I W Industries Inc .... C 631 293-9494
  Melville (G-8036)
L W S Inc .... E 631 580-0472
  Ronkonkoma (G-14364)
Maracle Industrial Finshg Co .... E 585 387-9077
  Rochester (G-13928)
Master Craft Finishers Inc .... E 631 586-0540
  Deer Park (G-4007)
McAlpin Industries Inc .... E 585 544-5335
  Rochester (G-13933)
Multitone Finishing Co Inc .... G 516 485-1043
  West Hempstead (G-16222)
North East Finishing Co Inc .... F 631 789-8000
  Copiague (G-3771)
Oerlikon Blzers Cating USA Inc .... E 716 564-8557
  Buffalo (G-2978)
Paradigm Group LLC .... G 718 860-1538
  Bronx (G-1351)
Rainbow Powder Coating Corp .... G 631 586-4019
  Deer Park (G-4034)
Saccomize Inc .... G 818 287-3000
  Bronx (G-1378)
Surface Finish Technology .... E 607 732-2909
  Elmira (G-4504)
Vibra Tech Industries Inc .... F 914 946-1916
  White Plains (G-16515)

METAL RESHAPING & REPLATING SVCS

Elmsford Sheet Metal Works Inc .... D 914 739-6300
  Cortlandt Manor (G-3900)
Miscellnous Ir Fabricators Inc .... E 518 355-1822
  Schenectady (G-14699)

METAL SERVICE CENTERS & OFFICES

Albea Cosmetics America Inc .... E 212 371-5100
  New York (G-8784)
Aufhauser Corporation .... F 516 694-8696
  Plainview (G-13038)
Cannon Industries Inc .... D 585 254-8080
  Rochester (G-13690)
Specialty Steel Fabg Corp .... F 718 893-6326
  Bronx (G-1390)
Steel Sales Inc .... E 607 674-6363
  Sherburne (G-14811)

METAL SPINNING FOR THE TRADE

Acme Architectural Products .... B 718 360-0700
  Brooklyn (G-1476)
American Metal Spinning Pdts .... G 631 454-6276
  West Babylon (G-16134)
Art Precision Metal Products .... F 631 842-8889
  Copiague (G-3752)
Bridgeport Metalcraft Inc .... G 315 623-9597
  Constantia (G-3739)
Gem Metal Spinning & Stamping .... G 718 729-7014
  Long Island City (G-7456)
Hy-Grade Metal Products Corp .... G 315 475-4221
  Syracuse (G-15341)
Koch Metal Spinning Co Inc .... D 716 835-3631
  Buffalo (G-2909)
Long Island Metalform Inc .... F 631 242-9088
  Deer Park (G-4003)
Russco Metal Spinning Co Inc .... F 516 872-6055
  Baldwin (G-542)
S D Z Metal Spinning Stamping .... F 718 778-3600
  Brooklyn (G-2439)

METAL STAMPING, FOR THE TRADE

4m Precision Industries Inc .... E 315 252-8415
  Auburn (G-462)
A-1 Stamping & Spinning Corp .... F 718 388-2626
  Rockaway Park (G-14227)
Albest Metal Stamping Corp .... D 718 388-6000
  Brooklyn (G-1500)
Alton Manufacturing Inc .... D 585 458-2600
  Rochester (G-13621)
American Mtal Stmping Spinning .... F 718 384-1500
  Brooklyn (G-1524)
Belmet Products Inc .... E 718 542-8220
  Bronx (G-1227)

PRODUCT SECTION

METALWORK: Miscellaneous

Cep Technologies Corporation............E...... 914 968-4100
  Yonkers *(G-16744)*
Charles A Rogers Entps Inc...............E...... 585 924-6400
  Victor *(G-15835)*
Crosby Company....................................E...... 716 852-3522
  Buffalo *(G-2784)*
D-K Manufacturing Corp....................E...... 315 592-4327
  Fulton *(G-5214)*
Dayton Industries Inc..........................E...... 718 542-8144
  Bronx *(G-1254)*
Dayton Rogers New York LLC..........D...... 585 349-4040
  Rochester *(G-13735)*
Die-Matic Products LLC.....................E...... 516 433-7900
  Plainview *(G-13051)*
Falso Industries Inc............................E...... 315 463-0266
  Syracuse *(G-15322)*
Feldware Inc...E...... 718 372-0486
  Brooklyn *(G-1873)*
Gasser & Sons Inc..............................C...... 631 543-6600
  Commack *(G-3692)*
Gay Sheet Metal Dies Inc..................E...... 716 877-0208
  Buffalo *(G-2842)*
Genesee Metal Stampings Inc.........G...... 585 475-0450
  West Henrietta *(G-16240)*
Great Lakes Pressed Steel Corp.....E...... 716 885-4037
  Buffalo *(G-2857)*
P&G Metal Components Corp.........D...... 716 896-7900
  Buffalo *(G-2986)*
Quality Metal Stamping LLC.............E...... 516 255-9000
  Rockville Centre *(G-14239)*
R G Flair Co Inc..................................E...... 631 586-7311
  Bay Shore *(G-712)*
Richter Metalcraft Corporation.........E...... 845 895-2025
  Wallkill *(G-15907)*
Rolite Mfg Inc......................................E...... 716 683-0259
  Lancaster *(G-7046)*
S & S Prtg Die-Cutting Co Inc.........F...... 718 388-8990
  Brooklyn *(G-2434)*
Smithers Tools & Mch Pdts Inc.......D...... 845 876-3063
  Rhinebeck *(G-13488)*
Square Stamping Mfg Corp...............E...... 315 896-2641
  Barneveld *(G-605)*
Stamped Fittings Inc..........................E...... 607 733-9988
  Elmira Heights *(G-4514)*
Tooling Enterprises Inc......................F...... 716 842-0445
  Buffalo *(G-3099)*
Tools & Stamping Corp......................G...... 718 392-4040
  Brooklyn *(G-2570)*
Trident Precision Mfg Inc..................D...... 585 265-2010
  Webster *(G-16103)*
Ultimate Prcision Met Pdts Inc........C...... 631 249-9441
  Farmingdale *(G-4901)*
Van Reenen Tool & Die Inc...............F...... 585 288-6000
  Rochester *(G-14198)*
Volkert Precision Tech Inc.................E...... 718 464-9500
  Queens Village *(G-13412)*
W & H Stampings Inc.........................E...... 631 234-6161
  Hauppauge *(G-5972)*

METAL STAMPINGS: Patterned

Corbett Stves Pttern Works Inc........E...... 585 546-7109
  Rochester *(G-13722)*

METAL STAMPINGS: Perforated

Erdle Perforating Holdings Inc........D...... 585 247-4700
  Rochester *(G-13789)*
National Wire & Metal Tech Inc.......E...... 716 661-9180
  Jamestown *(G-6740)*
Pall Corporation..................................A...... 607 753-6041
  Cortland *(G-3885)*

METAL STAMPINGS: Rigidized

Rigidized Metals Corporation............E...... 716 849-4703
  Buffalo *(G-3038)*

METAL TREATING COMPOUNDS

Foseco Inc..F...... 914 345-4760
  Tarrytown *(G-15478)*
Technic Inc...F...... 516 349-0700
  Plainview *(G-13092)*

METAL, TITANIUM: Sponge & Granules

Saes Smart Materials Inc..................E...... 315 266-2026
  New Hartford *(G-8511)*

METAL: Heavy, Perforated

Perforated Screen Surfaces..............E...... 866 866-8690
  Conklin *(G-3731)*

METALLIC ORES WHOLESALERS

Umicore USA Inc.................................E...... 919 874-7171
  Glens Falls *(G-5442)*

METALS SVC CENTERS & WHOL: Structural Shapes, Iron Or Steel

Blue Tee Corp......................................G...... 212 598-0880
  New York *(G-9109)*
GCM Metal Industries Inc.................F...... 718 386-4059
  Brooklyn *(G-1919)*
Reliable Welding & Fabrication........G...... 631 758-2637
  Patchogue *(G-12876)*
Supreme Steel Inc..............................F...... 631 884-1320
  Lindenhurst *(G-7200)*
Universal Steel Fabricators...............F...... 718 342-0782
  Brooklyn *(G-2610)*

METALS SVC CENTERS & WHOLESALERS: Cable, Wire

Ultra Clarity Corp................................G...... 719 470-1010
  Spring Valley *(G-15010)*

METALS SVC CENTERS & WHOLESALERS: Iron & Steel Prdt, Ferrous

Apollo Management V LP..................E...... 914 467-6510
  Purchase *(G-13386)*
Ewt Holdings III Corp.........................F...... 212 644-5900
  New York *(G-9744)*

METALS SVC CENTERS & WHOLESALERS: Misc Nonferrous Prdts

Amt Incorporated.................................E...... 518 284-2910
  Sharon Springs *(G-14797)*

METALS SVC CENTERS & WHOLESALERS: Nonferrous Sheets, Etc

Umicore USA Inc.................................E...... 919 874-7171
  Glens Falls *(G-5442)*

METALS SVC CENTERS & WHOLESALERS: Pipe & Tubing, Steel

Accord Pipe Fabricators Inc.............E...... 718 657-3900
  Jamaica *(G-6623)*
ASAP Rack Rental Inc.......................G...... 718 499-4495
  Brooklyn *(G-1561)*

METALS SVC CENTERS & WHOLESALERS: Sheets, Metal

Hatfield Metal Fab Inc.......................E...... 845 454-9078
  Poughkeepsie *(G-13345)*

METALS SVC CENTERS & WHOLESALERS: Steel

Asm USA Inc...F...... 212 925-2906
  New York *(G-8934)*
DAgostino Iron Works Inc..................G...... 585 235-8850
  Rochester *(G-13731)*
Hitachi Metals America Ltd..............G...... 914 694-9200
  Purchase *(G-13390)*
Massena Metals Inc............................F...... 315 769-3846
  Massena *(G-7905)*
Nathan Steel Corp...............................F...... 315 797-1335
  Utica *(G-15725)*
R & S Machine Center Inc................F...... 518 563-4016
  Plattsburgh *(G-13151)*
Ta Chen International Inc..................F...... 845 352-5300
  Monsey *(G-8300)*

METALS SVC CENTERS & WHOLESALERS: Tin & Tin Base Metals

Tin Box Company of America Inc....E...... 631 845-1600
  Farmingdale *(G-4897)*

METALS SVC CENTERS & WHOLESALERS: Tubing, Metal

Tube Fabrication Company Inc........F...... 716 673-1871
  Fredonia *(G-5128)*

METALS: Honeycombed

Unicel Corporation..............................E...... 760 741-3912
  Deer Park *(G-4054)*

METALS: Precious NEC

All American Funding & Ref LLC.....G...... 516 978-7531
  Farmingdale *(G-4713)*
Doral Refining Corp............................E...... 516 223-3684
  Freeport *(G-5151)*
Eco-Bat America LLC.........................C...... 845 692-4414
  Middletown *(G-8150)*
Euro Pacific Precious Metals...........G...... 212 481-0310
  New York *(G-9729)*
Handy & Harman Ltd..........................A...... 212 520-2300
  New York *(G-10031)*
Sph Group Holdings LLC....................F...... 212 520-2300
  New York *(G-11669)*
Starfuels Inc...G...... 914 289-4800
  White Plains *(G-16507)*
Wallace Refiners Inc..........................E...... 212 391-2649
  New York *(G-12068)*

METALS: Precious, Secondary

Encore Refining and Recycling........G...... 631 319-1910
  Holbrook *(G-6185)*
Sabin Metal Corporation...................F...... 631 329-1695
  East Hampton *(G-4242)*
Sabin Metal Corporation...................C...... 585 538-2194
  Scottsville *(G-14753)*

METALS: Primary Nonferrous, NEC

Ames Goldsmith Corp........................F...... 518 792-7435
  Glens Falls *(G-5414)*
Billanti Casting Co Inc.......................E...... 516 775-4800
  New Hyde Park *(G-8520)*
Goldmark Products Inc......................E...... 631 777-3343
  Farmingdale *(G-4773)*
Marina Jewelry Co Inc.......................G...... 212 354-5027
  New York *(G-10703)*
Materion Advanced Materials..........G...... 800 327-1355
  Brewster *(G-1170)*
S & W Metal Trading Corp.................E...... 212 719-5070
  Brooklyn *(G-2438)*
Sabin Metal Corporation...................C...... 585 538-2194
  Scottsville *(G-14753)*
Sigmund Cohn Corp...........................D...... 914 664-5300
  Mount Vernon *(G-8443)*
Tdy Industries LLC..............................E...... 716 433-4411
  Lockport *(G-7334)*

METALWORK: Miscellaneous

Abasco Inc..E...... 716 649-4790
  Hamburg *(G-5672)*
Accurate Metal Weather Strip..........G...... 914 668-6042
  Mount Vernon *(G-8375)*
Coral Management Corp....................G...... 718 893-9286
  Bronx *(G-1246)*
Empire Metal Finishing Inc...............E...... 718 545-6700
  Astoria *(G-427)*
Halmark Architectural Finshg..........E...... 718 272-1831
  Brooklyn *(G-1961)*
Hornet Group Inc................................D...... 845 858-6400
  Port Jervis *(G-13230)*
Janed Enterprises..............................F...... 631 694-4494
  Farmingdale *(G-4792)*
Jpl Designs Ltd...................................G...... 212 689-7096
  New York *(G-10371)*
Kraman Iron Works Inc......................F...... 212 460-8400
  New York *(G-10478)*
Lane Enterprises Inc..........................E...... 518 885-4385
  Ballston Spa *(G-587)*
Longstem Organizers Inc..................G...... 914 777-2174
  Jefferson Valley *(G-6777)*
Metal Products Intl LLC.....................G...... 716 215-1930
  Niagara Falls *(G-12309)*
Northern Metalworks Corp................G...... 646 523-1689
  Selden *(G-14765)*
Orange County Ironworks LLC.......E...... 845 769-3000
  Montgomery *(G-8315)*
Orbital Holdings Inc...........................G...... 951 360-7100
  Buffalo *(G-2982)*

METALWORK: Miscellaneous

Paragon Aquatics .... E 845 452-5500
Lagrangeville *(G-6960)*
Ppi Corp .... E 585 880-7277
Rochester *(G-14031)*
Risa Management Corp .... E 718 361-2606
Maspeth *(G-7870)*
Riverside Iron LLC .... F 315 535-4864
Gouverneur *(G-5492)*
Semans Enterprises Inc .... F 585 444-0097
West Henrietta *(G-16250)*
Signature Metal MBL Maint LLC .... D 718 292-8280
Bronx *(G-1385)*
Sims Steel Corporation .... E 631 587-8670
Lindenhurst *(G-7192)*
Tebbens Steel LLC .... F 631 208-8330
Calverton *(G-3174)*
Tonys Ornamental Ir Works Inc .... E 315 337-3730
Rome *(G-14276)*
United Iron Inc .... E 914 667-5700
Mount Vernon *(G-8453)*
West Metal Works Inc .... E 716 895-4900
Buffalo *(G-3128)*

METALWORK: Ornamental

Allied Bronze Corp (del Corp) .... E 646 421-6400
New York *(G-8798)*
Arcadia Mfg Group Inc .... E 518 434-6213
Green Island *(G-5602)*
Arcadia Mfg Group Inc .... G 518 434-6213
Menands *(G-8081)*
Armento Incorporated .... G 716 875-2423
Kenmore *(G-6857)*
Duke of Iron Inc .... G 631 543-3600
Smithtown *(G-14897)*
Giumenta Corp .... E 718 832-1200
Brooklyn *(G-1929)*
Iron Art Inc .... G 914 592-7977
Elmsford *(G-4546)*
Kendi Iron Works Inc .... E 718 821-2722
Brooklyn *(G-2068)*
Kleinfelder John .... G 716 753-3163
Mayville *(G-7921)*
Koenig Iron Works Inc .... E 718 433-0900
Long Island City *(G-7489)*
Kryten Iron Works Inc .... G 914 345-0990
Hawthorne *(G-5990)*
Raulli Iron Works Inc .... F 315 337-8070
Rome *(G-14269)*
Shanker Industries Realty Inc .... G 631 940-9889
Deer Park *(G-4044)*
Tensator Inc .... D 631 666-0300
Bay Shore *(G-731)*

METALWORKING MACHINERY WHOLESALERS

S & S Machinery Corp .... E 718 492-7400
Brooklyn *(G-2432)*

METER READERS: Remote

Quadlogic Controls Corporation .... D 212 930-9300
Long Island City *(G-7565)*

METERING DEVICES: Flow Meters, Impeller & Counter Driven

Flexim Americas Corporation .... F 631 492-2300
Edgewood *(G-4400)*
SPX Flow Us LLC .... D 585 436-5550
Rochester *(G-14140)*
Turbo Machined Products LLC .... E 315 895-3010
Frankfort *(G-5113)*

METERING DEVICES: Totalizing, Consumption

Siemens Industry Inc .... C 631 231-3600
Hauppauge *(G-5938)*

METERING DEVICES: Water Quality Monitoring & Control Systems

Gurley Precision Instrs Inc .... C 518 272-6300
Troy *(G-15607)*
Vepo Solutions LLC .... G 914 384-2121
Cross River *(G-3910)*

METERS: Elasped Time

Curtis Instruments Inc .... C 914 666-2971
Mount Kisco *(G-8339)*
Frequency Electronics Inc .... E 516 794-4500
Uniondale *(G-15668)*

METERS: Liquid

Walter R Tucker Entps Ltd .... E 607 467-2866
Deposit *(G-4112)*

METHANOL: Natural

Oci USA Inc .... G 646 589-6180
New York *(G-11029)*
Ocip Holding LLC .... G 646 589-6180
New York *(G-11030)*

MICA PRDTS

Fra-Rik Formica Fabg Co Inc .... G 718 597-3335
Bronx *(G-1275)*
Reliance Mica Co Inc .... G 718 788-0282
Rockaway Park *(G-14229)*
S & J Trading Inc .... E 718 347-1323
Floral Park *(G-4967)*

MICROCIRCUITS, INTEGRATED: Semiconductor

Aeroflex Incorporated .... B 516 694-6700
Plainview *(G-13032)*
Aeroflex Plainview Inc .... B 516 694-6700
Plainview *(G-13033)*
Imperium Partners Group LLC .... C 212 433-1360
New York *(G-10187)*
Microchip Technology Inc .... E 631 233-3280
Hauppauge *(G-5890)*
Park Electrochemical Corp .... D 631 465-3600
Melville *(G-8056)*
Standard Microsystems Corp .... D 631 435-6000
Hauppauge *(G-5948)*
Telephonics Tlsi Corp .... E 631 470-8854
Huntington *(G-6421)*

MICROFILM EQPT

Mekatronics Incorporated .... E 516 883-6805
Port Washington *(G-13288)*

MICROMANIPULATOR

Anaren Microwave Inc .... G 315 432-8909
East Syracuse *(G-4319)*

MICROPHONES

Andrea Electronics Corporation .... G 631 719-1800
Bohemia *(G-980)*
New Audio LLC .... E 212 213-6060
New York *(G-10917)*
Theodore A Rapp Associates .... G 845 469-2100
Chester *(G-3488)*

MICROPROCESSORS

Adco Circuits Inc .... G 716 668-6600
Buffalo *(G-2685)*
Eversan Inc .... F 315 736-3967
Whitesboro *(G-16527)*
I E D Corp .... F 631 348-0424
Islandia *(G-6529)*
INTEL Corporation .... D 408 765-8080
Getzville *(G-5348)*

MICROWAVE COMPONENTS

Antenna & Radome Res Assoc .... E 631 231-8400
Bay Shore *(G-658)*
Cobham Holdings (us) Inc .... A 716 662-0006
Orchard Park *(G-12707)*
Cobham Holdings Inc .... E 716 662-0006
Orchard Park *(G-12708)*
Frequency Electronics Inc .... C 516 794-4500
Uniondale *(G-15668)*
General Microwave Corporation .... F 516 802-0900
Syosset *(G-15219)*
L3 Foreign Holdings Inc .... D 212 697-1111
New York *(G-10497)*
L3 Technologies Inc .... E 631 289-0363
Patchogue *(G-12870)*
L3 Technologies Inc .... B 212 697-1111
New York *(G-10498)*
Lexan Industries Inc .... F 631 434-7586
Bay Shore *(G-696)*
Microwave Filter Company Inc .... E 315 438-4700
East Syracuse *(G-4358)*
Passive-Plus Inc .... F 631 425-0938
Huntington *(G-6407)*
Sendec Corp .... E 585 425-5965
Fairport *(G-4657)*
Transistor Power Tech Inc .... E 631 491-0265
Stony Brook *(G-15170)*
Werlatone Inc .... E 845 278-2220
Patterson *(G-12887)*

MICROWAVE OVENS: Household

Toshiba America Inc .... E 212 596-0600
New York *(G-11872)*

MILITARY INSIGNIA

Baldwin Ribbon & Stamping Corp .... F 718 335-6700
Woodside *(G-16645)*

MILITARY INSIGNIA, TEXTILE

Skd Tactical Inc .... G 845 897-2889
Highland Falls *(G-6149)*
Tulmar Manufacturing Inc .... G 315 393-7191
Ogdensburg *(G-12580)*

MILL PRDTS: Structural & Rail

Matrix Steel Company Inc .... G 718 381-6800
Brooklyn *(G-2180)*

MILLINERY SUPPLIES: Veils & Veiling, Bridal, Funeral, Etc

Paula Varsalona Ltd .... F 212 570-9100
New York *(G-11125)*

MILLING: Chemical

Falk Precision Inc .... E 315 437-4545
East Syracuse *(G-4337)*

MILLING: Grains, Exc Rice

ADM Milling Co .... D 716 849-7333
Buffalo *(G-2686)*

MILLWORK

Adams Interior Fabrications .... F 631 249-8282
Massapequa *(G-7878)*
Amstutze Woodworking .... G 518 946-8206
Upper Jay *(G-15674)*
Architctral Mllwk Installation .... E 631 499-0755
East Northport *(G-4260)*
Architectural Enhancements Inc .... F 845 343-9663
Middletown *(G-8137)*
Attica Millwork Inc .... F 585 591-2333
Attica *(G-458)*
Auburn Custom Millwork Inc .... G 315 253-3843
Auburn *(G-463)*
Bloch Industries LLC .... D 585 334-9600
Rochester *(G-13666)*
BNC Innovative Woodworking .... F 718 277-2800
Brooklyn *(G-1624)*
Braga Woodworks .... G 845 342-4636
Middletown *(G-8139)*
Broadway Neon Sign Corp .... F 908 241-4177
Ronkonkoma *(G-14322)*
Carob Industries Inc .... F 631 225-0900
Lindenhurst *(G-7166)*
Champion Millwork Inc .... E 315 463-0711
Syracuse *(G-15275)*
Christiana Millwork Inc .... E 315 492-9099
Jamesville *(G-6765)*
City Store Gates Mfg Corp .... E 718 939-9700
College Point *(G-3642)*
Clearwood Custom Carpentry and .... E 315 432-8422
East Syracuse *(G-4331)*
Columbus Woodworking Inc .... G 607 674-4546
Sherburne *(G-14804)*
Concepts In Wood of CNY .... E 315 463-8084
Syracuse *(G-15286)*
Cousins Furniture & Hm Imprvs .... E 631 254-3752
Deer Park *(G-3959)*
Craftsmen Woodworkers Ltd .... E 718 326-3350
Maspeth *(G-7832)*
Crown Mill Work Corp .... G 845 371-2200
Nanuet *(G-8462)*

Crown Woodworking Corp G 718 974-6415
Brooklyn *(G-1733)*
Custom Door & Mirror Inc E 631 414-7725
Farmingdale *(G-4745)*
Dbs Interiors Corp F 631 491-3013
West Babylon *(G-16152)*
Dimaio Millwork Corporation E 914 476-1937
Yonkers *(G-16750)*
Duncan & Son Carpentry Inc E 914 664-4311
Mount Vernon *(G-8396)*
Ed Negron Fine Woodworking G 718 246-1016
Brooklyn *(G-1812)*
Efj Inc D 518 234-4799
Cobleskill *(G-3602)*
EM Pfaff & Son Inc F 607 739-3691
Horseheads *(G-6313)*
Excelsior Wood Products LLC F 845 339-6630
Kingston *(G-6900)*
Five Star Millwork LLC F 845 920-0247
Pearl River *(G-12896)*
Grace Ryan & Magnus Mllwk LLC D 914 665-0902
Mount Vernon *(G-8402)*
Gw Manufacturing E 718 386-8078
Ridgewood *(G-13538)*
H B Millwork Inc E 631 289-8086
Medford *(G-7949)*
H B Millwork Inc G 631 924-4195
Yaphank *(G-16713)*
Highland Organization Corp E 631 991-3240
Deer Park *(G-3984)*
Hulley Holding Company Inc F 716 332-3982
Kenmore *(G-6862)*
Humboldt Woodworking G 718 707-0022
Long Island City *(G-7471)*
I Meglio Corp E 631 617-6900
Brentwood *(G-1135)*
Island Street Lumber Co Inc G 716 692-4127
North Tonawanda *(G-12434)*
J Percoco Industries Inc G 631 312-4572
Bohemia *(G-1038)*
Jacobs Woodworking LLC G 315 427-8999
Syracuse *(G-15345)*
James King Woodworking Inc G 518 761-6091
Queensbury *(G-13429)*
Jays Furniture Products Inc E 716 876-8854
Buffalo *(G-2890)*
John Langenbacher Co Inc E 718 328-0141
Bronx *(G-1304)*
KB Millwork Inc G 516 280-2183
Levittown *(G-7135)*
M & D Millwork LLC F 631 789-1439
Amityville *(G-299)*
Mack Wood Working G 845 657-6625
Shokan *(G-14846)*
Mason Woodworks LLC G 917 363-7052
Brooklyn *(G-2176)*
Medina Millworks LLC G 585 798-2969
Medina *(G-7983)*
Mensch Mill & Lumber Corp E 718 359-7500
Bronx *(G-1326)*
Metalocke Industries Inc G 718 267-9200
Woodside *(G-16663)*
Michbi Doors Inc D 631 231-9050
Brentwood *(G-1142)*
Millco Woodworking LLC F 585 526-6844
Hall *(G-5671)*
Millwright Wdwrk Installetion E 631 587-2635
West Babylon *(G-16177)*
North Fork Wood Works Inc G 631 255-4028
Mattituck *(G-7915)*
Northern Forest Pdts Co Inc G 315 942-6955
Boonville *(G-1118)*
Pella Corporation C 631 208-0710
Calverton *(G-3168)*
Peter Productions Devivi Inc F 315 568-8484
Waterloo *(G-15997)*
Piccini Industries Ltd E 845 365-0614
Orangeburg *(G-12685)*
Professional Cab Detailing Co F 845 436-7282
Woodridge *(G-16643)*
Randolph Dimension Corporation F 716 358-6901
Randolph *(G-13449)*
Richard Anthony Corp E 914 922-7141
Yorktown Heights *(G-16822)*
Robert Strahan Custom Wdwkg G 718 349-3570
Brooklyn *(G-2409)*
Roode Hoek & Co Inc F 718 522-5921
Brooklyn *(G-2413)*
S Donadic Inc D 718 361-9888
Sunnyside *(G-15205)*
Shawmut Woodworking & Sup Inc C 212 920-8900
New York *(G-11560)*
Specialty Services G 585 728-5650
Wayland *(G-16072)*
Syracuse Industrial Sls Co Ltd F 315 478-5751
Syracuse *(G-15438)*
TDS Woodworking Inc F 718 442-5298
Staten Island *(G-15144)*
Three R Enterprises Inc E 585 254-5050
Rochester *(G-14169)*
Tiedemann Waldemar Inc F 716 875-5665
Buffalo *(G-3095)*
Unicenter Millwork Inc G 716 741-8201
Clarence Center *(G-3550)*
Universal Custom Millwork Inc D 518 330-6622
Amsterdam *(G-362)*
Urban Woodworks Ltd G 718 827-1570
Brooklyn *(G-2611)*
Wagner Millwork Inc D 607 687-5362
Owego *(G-12805)*
Wolfe Lumber Mill Inc G 716 772-7750
Gasport *(G-5309)*
Xylon Industries Inc G 631 293-4717
Farmingdale *(G-4907)*
Zanzano Woodworking Inc F 914 725-6025
Scarsdale *(G-14646)*

MINE DEVELOPMENT SVCS: Nonmetallic Minerals

Resource Capital Funds LP G 631 692-9111
Jericho *(G-6799)*

MINERAL ABRASIVES MINING SVCS

Capital Gold Corporation G 212 668-0842
New York *(G-9203)*

MINERAL MINING: Nonmetallic

Hargrave Development F 716 877-7880
Kenmore *(G-6859)*

MINERAL PRODUCTS

American Crmic Process RES LLC G 315 828-6268
Phelps *(G-12974)*

MINERAL WOOL

Owens Corning Sales LLC B 518 475-3600
Feura Bush *(G-4936)*
Soundcoat Company Inc D 631 242-2200
Deer Park *(G-4047)*
Unifrax I LLC C 716 696-3000
Tonawanda *(G-15586)*

MINERAL WOOL INSULATION PRDTS

Unifrax Corporation E 716 278-3800
Niagara Falls *(G-12345)*

MINERALS: Ground Or Otherwise Treated

Minerals Technologies Inc E 212 878-1800
New York *(G-10817)*
Nutech Biosciences Inc F 315 505-6500
Oneida *(G-12613)*

MINERALS: Ground or Treated

Allied Aero Services Inc G 631 277-9368
Brentwood *(G-1126)*
DSM Nutritional Products LLC C 518 372-5155
Schenectady *(G-14669)*
DSM Nutritional Products LLC C 518 372-5155
Glenville *(G-5445)*
Mineralbious Corp F 516 498-9715
Westbury *(G-16357)*
Northeast Solite Corporation E 845 246-2646
Saugerties *(G-14611)*
Northeast Solite Corporation E 845 246-2177
Mount Marion *(G-8365)*
Oro Avanti Inc G 516 487-5185
Great Neck *(G-5577)*

MINIATURES

Islip Miniture Golf G 631 940-8900
Bay Shore *(G-691)*

MINING EXPLORATION & DEVELOPMENT SVCS

Advanced Biomedical Tech Inc G 718 766-7898
New York *(G-8752)*
Coremet Trading Inc G 212 964-3600
New York *(G-9400)*

MINING SVCS, NEC: Lignite

US Pump Corp G 516 303-7799
West Hempstead *(G-16226)*

MIRROR REPAIR SHOP

D Best Service Co Inc G 718 972-6133
Brooklyn *(G-1746)*

MIRRORS: Motor Vehicle

Rosco Inc C 718 526-2601
Jamaica *(G-6675)*

MIXING EQPT

Munson Machinery Company Inc E 315 797-0090
Utica *(G-15724)*

MIXTURES & BLOCKS: Asphalt Paving

Advanced Pavement Group Corp G 631 277-8400
Islip *(G-6543)*
Albany Asp & Aggregates Corp E 518 436-8916
Albany *(G-31)*
Barrett Paving Materials Inc E 315 652-4585
Liverpool *(G-7222)*
Barrett Paving Materials Inc F 315 737-8310
Clayville *(G-3555)*
Barrett Paving Materials Inc F 315 788-2037
Watertown *(G-16001)*
Bross Quality Paving G 845 532-7116
Ellenville *(G-4437)*
C & C Ready-Mix Corporation F 607 687-1690
Owego *(G-12796)*
Callanan Industries Inc C 518 374-2222
Albany *(G-54)*
Callanan Industries Inc E 845 331-6868
Kingston *(G-6892)*
Canal Asphalt Inc F 914 667-8500
Mount Vernon *(G-8384)*
Cofire Paving Corporation E 718 463-1403
Flushing *(G-4993)*
Cold Mix Manufacturing Corp F 718 463-1444
Mount Vernon *(G-8389)*
Deans Paving Inc G 315 736-7601
Marcy *(G-7796)*
Doctor Pavers G 516 342-6016
Commack *(G-3689)*
Dolomite Products Company Inc F 585 352-0460
Spencerport *(G-14978)*
Gernatt Asphalt Products Inc G 716 496-5111
Springville *(G-15016)*
Grace Associates Inc G 718 767-9000
Harrison *(G-5729)*
Graymont Materials Inc E 518 561-5200
Plattsburgh *(G-13122)*
Hanson Aggregates East LLC E 585 343-1787
Stafford *(G-15027)*
J Pahura Contractors G 585 589-5793
Albion *(G-158)*
Jamestown Macadam Inc F 716 664-5108
Jamestown *(G-6730)*
Jet-Black Sealers Inc G 716 891-4197
Buffalo *(G-2895)*
John T Montecalvo Inc G 631 325-1492
Speonk *(G-14986)*
Kal-Harbour Inc F 518 266-0690
Albany *(G-90)*
Lafarge North America Inc E 518 756-5000
Ravena *(G-13454)*
McConnaughay Technologies G 607 753-1100
Cortland *(G-3884)*
Nicolia Concrete Products Inc D 631 669-0700
Lindenhurst *(G-7185)*
Northeastern Sealcoat Inc F 585 544-4372
Rochester *(G-13979)*
Patterson Blacktop Corp E 914 949-2000
White Plains *(G-16485)*
Patterson Materials Corp F 914 949-2000
White Plains *(G-16486)*
Pavco Asphalt Inc E 631 289-3223
Holtsville *(G-6242)*

PRODUCT

Employee Codes: A=Over 500 employees, B=251-500
C=101-250, D=51-100, E=20-50, F=10-19, G=5-9
2019 Harris
New York Manufacturers Directory
1191

MIXTURES & BLOCKS: Asphalt Paving

Peckham Industries Inc .... G 518 945-1120
  Athens *(G-453)*
Peckham Materials Corp .... E 518 945-1120
  Athens *(G-454)*
Peckham Materials Corp .... F 518 494-2313
  Chestertown *(G-3491)*
Peckham Materials Corp .... E 518 747-3353
  Hudson Falls *(G-6384)*
Peckham Road Corp .... E 518 792-3157
  Queensbury *(G-13436)*
Prima Asphalt and Concrete .... F 631 289-3223
  Holtsville *(G-6243)*
Rochester Seal Pro LLC .... G 585 594-3818
  Rochester *(G-14092)*
Sheldon Slate Products Co Inc .... E 518 642-1280
  Middle Granville *(G-8112)*
Suit-Kote Corporation .... G 315 735-8501
  Oriskany *(G-12763)*
Suit-Kote Corporation .... E 607 535-2743
  Watkins Glen *(G-16061)*
Thalle Industries Inc .... E 914 762-3415
  Briarcliff Manor *(G-1177)*
Tilcon New York Inc .... D 845 638-3594
  Haverstraw *(G-5982)*
Tri City Highway Products Inc .... E 607 722-2967
  Binghamton *(G-921)*
Tri-City Highway Products Inc .... E 518 294-9964
  Richmondville *(G-13519)*
Twin County Recycling Corp .... G 516 827-6900
  Westbury *(G-16383)*
Ultimate Pavers Corp .... E 917 417-2652
  Staten Island *(G-15149)*
Unilock New York Inc .... G 845 278-6700
  Brewster *(G-1175)*
Universal Ready Mix Inc .... G 516 746-4535
  New Hyde Park *(G-8571)*
Upstone Materials Inc .... E 518 873-2275
  Lewis *(G-7137)*
Zielinskis Asphalt Inc .... F 315 306-4057
  Oriskany Falls *(G-12768)*

MOBILE COMMUNICATIONS EQPT

2p Agency Usa Inc .... G 212 203-5586
  Brooklyn *(G-1436)*
Andrea Electronics Corporation .... G 631 719-1800
  Bohemia *(G-980)*
Cmb Wireless Group LLC .... B 631 750-4700
  Bohemia *(G-996)*
Elite Cellular Accessories Inc .... E 877 390-2502
  Deer Park *(G-3972)*
Flycell Inc .... D 212 400-1212
  New York *(G-9818)*
Icell Inc .... C 516 590-0007
  Hempstead *(G-6014)*
Innovation In Motion Inc .... G 407 878-7561
  Long Beach *(G-7359)*
Toura LLC .... F 646 652-8668
  Brooklyn *(G-2576)*

MOBILE HOMES

All Star Carts & Vehicles Inc .... D 631 666-5581
  Bay Shore *(G-654)*
Champion Home Builders Inc .... C 315 841-4122
  Sangerfield *(G-14559)*
Leatherstocking Mobile Home PA .... G 315 839-5691
  Sauquoit *(G-14622)*

MOBILE HOMES WHOLESALERS

Century Ready Mix Inc .... G 631 888-2200
  West Babylon *(G-16145)*

MODELS

Copesetic Inc .... F 315 684-7780
  Morrisville *(G-8336)*
Tri-Force Sales LLC .... E 732 261-5507
  New York *(G-11892)*

MODELS: General, Exc Toy

Active Manufacturing Inc .... F 607 775-3162
  Kirkwood *(G-6937)*
Creative Models & Prototypes .... E 516 433-6828
  Hicksville *(G-6075)*
J T Systematic .... G 607 754-0929
  Endwell *(G-4617)*

MODULES: Computer Logic

Intech 21 Inc .... F 516 626-7221
  Port Washington *(G-13270)*
International Bus Mchs Corp .... E 212 324-5000
  New York *(G-10243)*

MODULES: Solid State

Data Device Corporation .... B 631 567-5600
  Bohemia *(G-1008)*

MOLDED RUBBER PRDTS

Apple Rubber Products Inc .... C 716 684-6560
  Lancaster *(G-7007)*
Buffalo Lining & Fabricating .... G 716 883-6500
  Buffalo *(G-2746)*
Enviroform Recycled Pdts Inc .... G 315 789-1810
  Geneva *(G-5322)*
Moldtech Inc .... E 716 685-3344
  Lancaster *(G-7033)*
SD Christie Associates Inc .... G 914 734-1800
  Peekskill *(G-12925)*
Short Jj Associates Inc .... F 315 986-3511
  Macedon *(G-7704)*
Traffic Logix Corporation .... G 866 915-6449
  Spring Valley *(G-15009)*
Triangle Rubber Co Inc .... E 631 589-9400
  Bohemia *(G-1099)*

MOLDING COMPOUNDS

Coda Resources Ltd .... D 718 649-1666
  Brooklyn *(G-1703)*
Craftech .... D 518 828-5011
  Chatham *(G-3427)*
Hanet Plastics Usa Inc .... G 518 324-5850
  Plattsburgh *(G-13123)*
Imperial Polymers Inc .... G 718 387-4741
  Brooklyn *(G-1996)*
Jrlon Inc .... D 315 597-4067
  Palmyra *(G-12855)*
Majestic Mold & Tool Inc .... F 315 695-2079
  Phoenix *(G-12990)*
Plaslok Corp .... E 716 681-7755
  Buffalo *(G-3006)*

MOLDINGS, ARCHITECTURAL: Plaster Of Paris

Foster Reeve & Associates Inc .... G 718 609-0090
  Brooklyn *(G-1900)*

MOLDINGS: Picture Frame

AC Moore Incorporated .... G 516 796-5831
  Bethpage *(G-838)*
Amci Ltd .... D 718 937-5858
  Long Island City *(G-7376)*
Drummond Framing Inc .... F 212 647-1701
  New York *(G-9580)*
Frame Shoppe & Art Gallery .... E 516 365-6014
  Manhasset *(G-7767)*
Framerica Corporation .... D 631 650-1000
  Yaphank *(G-16711)*
General Art Company Inc .... F 212 255-1298
  New York *(G-9899)*
Julius Lowy Frame Restoring Co .... E 212 861-8585
  New York *(G-10377)*
Lco Destiny LLC .... B 315 782-3302
  Watertown *(G-16025)*
P B & H Moulding Corporation .... E 315 455-1756
  Fayetteville *(G-4929)*
Quattro Frameworks Inc .... E 718 361-2620
  Long Island City *(G-7569)*
Sky Frame & Art Inc .... F 212 925-7856
  New York *(G-11613)*
Structural Industries Inc .... C 631 471-5200
  Bohemia *(G-1092)*

MOLDS: Indl

Allmetal Chocolate Mold Co Inc .... F 631 752-2888
  West Babylon *(G-16131)*
American Orthotic Lab Co Inc .... G 718 961-6487
  College Point *(G-3639)*
Blue Chip Mold Inc .... F 585 647-1790
  Rochester *(G-13667)*
Century Mold Company Inc .... D 585 352-8600
  Rochester *(G-13701)*
Chenango Valley Tech Inc .... F 607 674-4115
  Sherburne *(G-14803)*
East Pattern & Model Corp .... E 585 461-3240
  Rochester *(G-13756)*
G N R Plastics Inc .... G 631 724-8758
  Smithtown *(G-14899)*
Gatti Tool & Mold Inc .... F 585 328-1350
  Rochester *(G-13823)*
Globmarble LLC .... G 347 717-4088
  Brooklyn *(G-1933)*
HNST Mold Inspections LLC .... G 845 215-9258
  Pearl River *(G-12899)*
Hy-Tech Mold Inc .... F 585 247-2450
  Rochester *(G-13873)*
J T Systematic .... G 607 754-0929
  Endwell *(G-4617)*
James B Crowell & Sons Inc .... G 845 895-3464
  Wallkill *(G-15905)*
Nicoform Inc .... E 585 454-5530
  Rochester *(G-13973)*
Nordon Inc .... D 585 546-6200
  Rochester *(G-13974)*
Nordon Inc .... E 585 546-6200
  Rochester *(G-13975)*
Nordon Inc .... E 585 546-6200
  Rochester *(G-13976)*
PMI Industries LLC .... E 585 464-8050
  Rochester *(G-14025)*
Polyshot Corporation .... E 585 292-5010
  West Henrietta *(G-16248)*
Rochester Tool and Mold Inc .... F 585 464-9336
  Rochester *(G-14098)*
Rochling Advent Tool & Mold LP .... D 585 254-2000
  Rochester *(G-14100)*
Romold Inc .... E 585 529-4440
  Rochester *(G-14103)*
Royal Molds Inc .... F 718 382-7686
  Brooklyn *(G-2422)*
Sb Molds LLC .... D 845 352-3700
  Monsey *(G-8297)*
Specialty Model & Mold Inc .... G 631 475-0840
  Ronkonkoma *(G-14416)*
Star Mold Co Inc .... G 631 694-2283
  Farmingdale *(G-4880)*
Stuart Tool & Die Inc .... E 716 488-1975
  Falconer *(G-4694)*
Syntec Technologies Inc .... F 585 464-9336
  Rochester *(G-14153)*
T A Tool & Molding Inc .... E 631 293-0172
  Farmingdale *(G-4888)*
W N R Pattern & Tool Inc .... E 716 681-9334
  Lancaster *(G-7053)*

MOLDS: Plastic Working & Foundry

A & D Tool Inc .... G 631 243-4339
  Dix Hills *(G-4117)*
Accede Mold & Tool Co Inc .... D 585 254-6490
  Rochester *(G-13595)*
Clifford H Jones Inc .... F 716 693-2444
  Tonawanda *(G-15534)*
Inter Molds Inc .... G 631 667-8580
  Bay Shore *(G-689)*
Moldcraft Inc .... F 716 684-1126
  Depew *(G-4096)*
Northern Design Inc .... G 716 652-7071
  East Aurora *(G-4209)*
Universal Tooling Corporation .... F 716 985-4691
  Gerry *(G-5342)*

MONUMENTS & GRAVE MARKERS, EXC TERRAZZO

Galle & Zinter Inc .... G 716 833-4212
  Buffalo *(G-2839)*

MONUMENTS: Concrete

Presbrey-Leland Inc .... G 914 949-2264
  Valhalla *(G-15745)*
St Raymond Monument Co .... G 718 824-3600
  Bronx *(G-1391)*

MONUMENTS: Cut Stone, Exc Finishing Or Lettering Only

Dominic De Nigris Inc .... E 718 597-4460
  Bronx *(G-1258)*
Suffolk Granite Manufacturing .... E 631 226-4774
  Lindenhurst *(G-7197)*

PRODUCT SECTION

MOPS: Floor & Dust

Cpac Inc .... E 585 382-3223
  Leicester *(G-7126)*
Ingenious Designs LLC .... C 631 254-3376
  Ronkonkoma *(G-14353)*
National Wire & Metal Tech Inc .... E 716 661-9180
  Jamestown *(G-6740)*
Perfex Corporation .... F 315 826-3600
  Poland *(G-13184)*

MORTGAGE BANKERS

Caithness Equities Corporation .... E 212 599-2112
  New York *(G-9178)*

MOTION PICTURE & VIDEO PRODUCTION SVCS

Chakra Communications Inc .... E 716 505-7300
  Lancaster *(G-7013)*
Crain Communications Inc .... C 212 210-0100
  New York *(G-9418)*
Entertainment Weekly Inc .... C 212 522-5600
  New York *(G-9688)*
Laird Telemedia .... C 845 339-9555
  Mount Marion *(G-8363)*
North Six Inc .... F 212 463-7227
  New York *(G-10994)*
Taste and See Entrmt Inc .... G 516 285-3010
  Valley Stream *(G-15799)*

MOTION PICTURE & VIDEO PRODUCTION SVCS: Non-Theatrical, TV

Scholastic Corporation .... G 212 343-6100
  New York *(G-11513)*

MOTION PICTURE PRODUCTION & DISTRIBUTION

21st Century Fox America Inc .... D 212 852-7000
  New York *(G-8673)*
Historic TW Inc .... E 212 484-8000
  New York *(G-10106)*
Sony Broadband Entertainment .... F 212 833-6800
  New York *(G-11644)*
Time Warner Companies Inc .... D 212 484-8000
  New York *(G-11845)*

MOTION PICTURE PRODUCTION & DISTRIBUTION: Television

Martha Stewart Living .... C 212 827-8000
  New York *(G-10717)*

MOTION PICTURE PRODUCTION ALLIED SVCS

Yam TV LLC .... G 917 932-5418
  New York *(G-12159)*

MOTION PICTURE PRODUCTION SVCS

Abkco Music & Records Inc .... E 212 399-0300
  New York *(G-8710)*

MOTOR & GENERATOR PARTS: Electric

Allied Motion Technologies Inc .... C 315 782-5910
  Watertown *(G-16000)*
Ems Development Corporation .... D 631 924-4736
  Yaphank *(G-16708)*
Hes Inc .... G 607 359-2974
  Addison *(G-6)*
Moley Magnetics Inc .... F 716 434-4023
  Lockport *(G-7320)*
Power and Composite Tech LLC .... D 518 843-6825
  Amsterdam *(G-357)*
Stature Electric Inc .... D 716 242-7535
  Amherst *(G-251)*

MOTOR HOMES

Authority Transportation Inc .... F 888 933-1268
  Dix Hills *(G-4120)*

MOTOR REPAIR SVCS

Accurate Marine Specialties .... G 631 589-5502
  Bohemia *(G-970)*

Premco Inc .... F 914 636-7095
  New Rochelle *(G-8623)*
RC Entps Bus & Trck Inc .... G 518 568-5753
  Saint Johnsville *(G-14521)*

MOTOR SCOOTERS & PARTS

Piaggio Group Americas Inc .... E 212 380-4400
  New York *(G-11187)*
Ying Ke Youth Age Group Inc .... F 929 402-8458
  Dix Hills *(G-4128)*

MOTOR VEHICLE ASSEMBLY, COMPLETE: Autos, Incl Specialty

Auto Sport Designs Inc .... F 631 425-1555
  Huntington Station *(G-6433)*
Cabot Coach Builders Inc .... G 516 625-4000
  Roslyn Heights *(G-14453)*
Marcovicci-Wenz Engineering .... G 631 467-9040
  Ronkonkoma *(G-14375)*
Medical Coaches Incorporated .... E 607 432-1333
  Oneonta *(G-12640)*
Pcb Coach Builders Corp .... G 718 897-7606
  Rego Park *(G-13467)*
Troyer Inc .... F 585 352-5590
  Rochester *(G-14177)*

MOTOR VEHICLE ASSEMBLY, COMPLETE: Buses, All Types

Leonard Bus Sales Inc .... G 607 467-3100
  Rome *(G-14256)*
Prevost Car (us) Inc .... C 518 957-2052
  Plattsburgh *(G-13148)*

MOTOR VEHICLE ASSEMBLY, COMPLETE: Cars, Armored

Armor Dynamics Inc .... F 845 658-9200
  Kingston *(G-6888)*

MOTOR VEHICLE ASSEMBLY, COMPLETE: Fire Department Vehicles

AB Fire Inc .... G 917 416-6444
  Brooklyn *(G-1468)*
Global Fire Corporation .... E 888 320-1799
  New York *(G-9940)*
Kovatch Mobile Equipment Corp .... F 518 785-0900
  Latham *(G-7079)*
Schenvus Fire Dist .... D 607 638-9017
  Schenevus *(G-14730)*

MOTOR VEHICLE ASSEMBLY, COMPLETE: Military Motor Vehicle

CIC International Ltd .... D 212 213-0089
  Brooklyn *(G-1692)*

MOTOR VEHICLE ASSEMBLY, COMPLETE: Motor Buses

Daimler Buses North Amer Inc .... A 315 768-8101
  Oriskany *(G-12756)*

MOTOR VEHICLE ASSEMBLY, COMPLETE: Snow Plows

Brothers-In-Lawn Property .... G 716 279-6191
  Tonawanda *(G-15531)*
Sabre Enterprises Inc .... G 315 430-3127
  Syracuse *(G-15413)*
Smart Systems Inc .... E 607 776-5380
  Bath *(G-649)*

MOTOR VEHICLE ASSEMBLY, COMPLETE: Truck & Tractor Trucks

Dejana Trck Utility Eqp Co LLC .... C 631 544-9000
  Kings Park *(G-6882)*
Tee Pee Auto Sales Corp .... F 516 338-9333
  Westbury *(G-16376)*

MOTOR VEHICLE ASSEMBLY, COMPLETE: Trucks, Pickup

Dejana Trck Utility Eqp Co LLC .... E 631 549-0944
  Huntington *(G-6397)*

MOTOR VEHICLE DEALERS: Automobiles, New & Used

Cabot Coach Builders Inc .... G 516 625-4000
  Roslyn Heights *(G-14453)*
Split Rock Trading Co Inc .... G 631 929-3261
  Wading River *(G-15887)*

MOTOR VEHICLE PARTS & ACCESS: Acceleration Eqpt

Lemans Corporation .... G 518 885-7500
  Ballston Spa *(G-588)*

MOTOR VEHICLE PARTS & ACCESS: Air Conditioner Parts

GM Components Holdings LLC .... C 716 439-2237
  Lockport *(G-7304)*
Titanx Engine Cooling Inc .... B 716 665-7129
  Jamestown *(G-6758)*
Transcedar Industries Ltd .... G 716 731-6442
  Niagara Falls *(G-12343)*

MOTOR VEHICLE PARTS & ACCESS: Axel Housings & Shafts

Mohawk Innovative Tech Inc .... F 518 862-4290
  Albany *(G-99)*

MOTOR VEHICLE PARTS & ACCESS: Bearings

Fcmp Inc .... F 716 692-4623
  Tonawanda *(G-15539)*

MOTOR VEHICLE PARTS & ACCESS: Body Components & Frames

Johnson Controls Inc .... C 585 724-2232
  Rochester *(G-13897)*

MOTOR VEHICLE PARTS & ACCESS: Cylinder Heads

M2 Race Systems Inc .... G 607 882-9078
  Ithaca *(G-6591)*

MOTOR VEHICLE PARTS & ACCESS: Electrical Eqpt

Katikati Inc .... G 585 678-1764
  West Henrietta *(G-16243)*
Nassau Auto Remanufacturer .... G 516 485-4500
  North Bellmore *(G-12380)*

MOTOR VEHICLE PARTS & ACCESS: Engines & Parts

ARC Remanufacturing Inc .... D 718 728-0701
  Long Island City *(G-7384)*
Curtis L Maclean L C .... B 716 898-7800
  Buffalo *(G-2787)*
Marcovicci-Wenz Engineering .... G 631 467-9040
  Ronkonkoma *(G-14375)*
Standard Motor Products Inc .... B 718 392-0200
  Long Island City *(G-7598)*

MOTOR VEHICLE PARTS & ACCESS: Fuel Systems & Parts

Kearney-National Inc .... F 212 661-4600
  New York *(G-10427)*
TI Group Auto Systems LLC .... G 315 568-7042
  Seneca Falls *(G-14787)*

MOTOR VEHICLE PARTS & ACCESS: Gears

Enplas America Inc .... G 646 892-7811
  New York *(G-9686)*
Gleason Works .... A 585 473-1000
  Rochester *(G-13840)*

MOTOR VEHICLE PARTS & ACCESS: Power Steering Eqpt

CRS Remanufacturing Co Inc .... F 718 739-1720
  Jamaica *(G-6640)*

MOTOR VEHICLE PARTS & ACCESS: Propane Conversion Eqpt

Kurtz Truck Equipment Inc .... F 607 849-3468
Marathon *(G-7790)*

MOTOR VEHICLE PARTS & ACCESS: Sanders, Safety

Smith Metal Works Newark Inc .... E 315 331-1651
Newark *(G-12206)*
Vehicle Safety Dept .... F 315 458-6683
Syracuse *(G-15451)*
Zwack Incorporated .... E 518 733-5135
Stephentown *(G-15156)*

MOTOR VEHICLE PARTS & ACCESS: Tops

Electron Top Mfg Co Inc .... E 718 846-7400
Richmond Hill *(G-13501)*

MOTOR VEHICLE PARTS & ACCESS: Transmission Housings Or Parts

Northeastern Transparts Inc .... F 716 833-0792
Hamburg *(G-5688)*

MOTOR VEHICLE PARTS & ACCESS: Transmissions

Banner Transmission & Eng Co .... F 516 221-9459
Melville *(G-8004)*

MOTOR VEHICLE PARTS & ACCESS: Wheel rims

Extreme Auto Accessories Corp .... F 718 978-6722
Mineola *(G-8221)*

MOTOR VEHICLE PARTS & ACCESS: Wiring Harness Sets

Agri Services Co .... G 716 937-6618
Alden *(G-166)*

MOTOR VEHICLE SPLYS & PARTS WHOLESALERS: New

American Auto ACC Incrporation ..... E 718 886-6600
Flushing *(G-4984)*
K M Drive Line Inc .... G 718 599-0628
Brooklyn *(G-2064)*
Knorr Brake Holding Corp .... G 315 786-5356
Watertown *(G-16022)*
Trading Services International .... F 212 501-0142
New York *(G-11884)*
Walter R Tucker Entps Ltd .... E 607 467-2866
Deposit *(G-4112)*

MOTOR VEHICLE: Hardware

Fuccillo Ford Nelliston Inc .... G 518 993-5555
Nelliston *(G-8482)*
Wolo Mfg Corp .... E 631 242-0333
Deer Park *(G-4064)*
Zip Products Inc .... F 585 482-0044
Rochester *(G-14220)*

MOTOR VEHICLE: Radiators

API Heat Transf Thermasys Corp .... A 716 684-6700
Buffalo *(G-2704)*

MOTOR VEHICLE: Steering Mechanisms

Automotive Accessories Group .... B 212 736-8100
New York *(G-8967)*
Biltron Automotive Products .... E 631 928-8613
Port Jeff STA *(G-13212)*
Steering Columns Galore Inc .... G 845 278-5762
Mahopac *(G-7713)*

MOTOR VEHICLES & CAR BODIES

Antonicelli Vito Race Car .... G 716 684-2205
Buffalo *(G-2703)*
Jtekt Torsen North America .... F 585 464-5000
Rochester *(G-13899)*
North Eastern Rescue Vehicles ...... G 315 414-9999
Syracuse *(G-15382)*
Ranger Design Us Inc .... E 800 565-5321
Ontario *(G-12662)*

Roberts Nichols Fire Apparatus .... G 518 431-1945
Cohoes *(G-3619)*
Siemens Mobility Inc .... G 916 717-8174
New York *(G-11579)*
Tesla Motors Inc .... A 212 206-1204
New York *(G-11803)*
Transprttion Collaborative Inc .... E 845 988-2333
Warwick *(G-15961)*

MOTOR VEHICLES, WHOLESALE: Recreational, All-Terrain

Adirondack Power Sports .... G 518 481-6269
Malone *(G-7718)*

MOTOR VEHICLES, WHOLESALE: Truck bodies

Smart Systems Inc .... E 607 776-5380
Bath *(G-649)*

MOTORCYCLE ACCESS

Chicken Hawk Racing Inc .... G 845 758-0700
Red Hook *(G-13457)*

MOTORCYCLE DEALERS

Se-Mar Electric Co Inc .... E 716 674-7404
West Seneca *(G-16302)*
Split Rock Trading Co Inc .... G 631 929-3261
Wading River *(G-15887)*

MOTORCYCLE DEALERS: Bicycles, Motorized

Bignay Inc .... G 786 346-1673
New York *(G-9080)*

MOTORCYCLE PARTS: Wholesalers

J & D Walter Distributors Inc .... F 518 449-1606
Glenmont *(G-5413)*

MOTORCYCLES & RELATED PARTS

Golub Corporation .... E 518 943-3903
Catskill *(G-3303)*
Golub Corporation .... E 518 899-6063
Malta *(G-7731)*
Golub Corporation .... E 315 363-0679
Oneida *(G-12609)*
Golub Corporation .... E 607 336-2588
Norwich *(G-12486)*
Golub Corporation .... E 518 583-3697
Saratoga Springs *(G-14582)*
Golub Corporation .... E 518 822-0076
Hudson *(G-6351)*
Golub Corporation .... E 607 235-7240
Binghamton *(G-888)*
Golub Corporation .... E 845 344-0327
Middletown *(G-8157)*
Ihd Motorsports LLC .... F 979 690-1669
Binghamton *(G-894)*
Indian Larry Legacy .... G 718 609-9184
Brooklyn *(G-1998)*
Orange County Choppers Inc .... G 845 522-5200
Newburgh *(G-12237)*
Price Chopper Operating Co .... F 518 562-3565
Plattsburgh *(G-13149)*
Price Chopper Operating Co .... E 518 456-5115
Guilderland *(G-5655)*
Robs Cycle Supply .... G 315 292-6878
Syracuse *(G-15409)*
Sumax Cycle Products Inc .... F 315 768-1058
Oriskany *(G-12764)*
Super Price Chopper Inc .... F 716 893-3323
Buffalo *(G-3080)*

MOTORS: Electric

Aeroflex Plainview Inc .... B 516 694-6700
Plainview *(G-13033)*
Allied Motion Technologies Inc .... C 716 242-8634
Amherst *(G-211)*
ARC Systems Inc .... E 631 582-8020
Hauppauge *(G-5768)*
Current Applications Inc .... E 315 788-4689
Watertown *(G-16010)*
Elton El Mantle Inc .... G 315 432-9067
Syracuse *(G-15316)*

Empire Division Inc .... D 315 476-6273
Syracuse *(G-15318)*
Faradyne Motors LLC .... F 315 331-5985
Palmyra *(G-12851)*
Franklin Electric Co Inc .... A 718 244-7744
Jamaica *(G-6645)*
Island Components Group Inc .... F 631 563-4224
Holbrook *(G-6191)*
John G Rubino Inc .... E 315 253-7396
Auburn *(G-486)*
Nidec Motor Corporation .... F 315 434-9303
East Syracuse *(G-4361)*
Sopark Corp .... D 716 822-0434
Buffalo *(G-3070)*

MOTORS: Generators

Aeroflex Plainview Inc .... C 631 231-9100
Hauppauge *(G-5756)*
Allied Motion Control Corp .... G 716 242-7535
Amherst *(G-209)*
American Precision Inds Inc .... C 716 691-9100
Amherst *(G-214)*
Ametek Inc .... G 631 467-8400
Ronkonkoma *(G-14307)*
Ametek Inc .... D 607 763-4700
Binghamton *(G-862)*
Ametek Inc .... D 585 263-7700
Rochester *(G-13630)*
D & D Motor Systems Inc .... E 315 701-0861
Syracuse *(G-15299)*
Designatronics Incorporated .... B 516 328-3300
Hicksville *(G-6080)*
Emes Motor Inc .... G 718 387-2445
Brooklyn *(G-1830)*
Ener-G-Rotors Inc .... G 518 372-2608
Schenectady *(G-14670)*
Eni Technology Inc .... B 585 427-8300
Rochester *(G-13787)*
Felchar Manufacturing Corp .... A 607 723-3106
Binghamton *(G-884)*
General Electric Company .... B 518 385-2211
Schenectady *(G-14679)*
General Electric Intl Inc .... G 518 385-2211
Schenectady *(G-14682)*
Generation Power LLC .... G 315 234-2451
Syracuse *(G-15333)*
Got Power Inc .... G 631 767-9493
Ronkonkoma *(G-14347)*
Kaddis Manufacturing Corp .... G 585 624-3070
Honeoye Falls *(G-6270)*
Lcdrives Corp .... F 860 712-8926
Potsdam *(G-13319)*
Makerbot Industries LLC .... C 347 334-6800
Brooklyn *(G-2153)*
Modular Devices Inc .... D 631 345-3100
Shirley *(G-14841)*
Premco Inc .... F 914 636-7095
New Rochelle *(G-8623)*
Protective Power Systms & Cntr .... F 845 721-1875
Staatsburg *(G-15024)*
Ruhle Companies Inc .... E 914 287-4000
Valhalla *(G-15747)*
Sima Technologies LLC .... C 412 828-9130
Hauppauge *(G-5940)*
Supergen Products LLC .... G 315 573-7887
Newark *(G-12208)*
Troy Belting and Supply Co .... D 518 272-4920
Watervliet *(G-16053)*
W J Albro Machine Works Inc .... G 631 345-0657
Yaphank *(G-16728)*

MOTORS: Torque

Aeroflex Incorporated .... B 516 694-6700
Plainview *(G-13032)*

MOVIE THEATERS, EXC DRIVE-IN

Sony Broadband Entertainment ...... F 212 833-6800
New York *(G-11644)*
Taste and See Entrmt Inc .... G 516 285-3010
Valley Stream *(G-15799)*

MOWERS & ACCESSORIES

Benishty Brothers Corp .... G 646 339-9991
Woodmere *(G-16640)*

MULTIPLEXERS: Telephone & Telegraph

Toshiba America Inc .... E 212 596-0600
New York *(G-11872)*

PRODUCT SECTION   NATURAL GAS TRANSMISSION & DISTRIBUTION

MUSEUMS & ART GALLERIES
Njf Publishing Corp ....G....... 631 345-5200
　Shirley (G-14842)

MUSIC BROADCASTING SVCS
Michael Karp Music Inc ....G....... 212 840-3285
　New York (G-10792)

MUSIC COPYING SVCS
Boosey and Hawkes Inc ....E....... 212 358-5300
　New York (G-9122)

MUSIC DISTRIBUTION APPARATUS
Nykon Inc ....G....... 315 483-0504
　Sodus (G-14914)
Tunecore Inc ....E....... 646 651-1060
　Brooklyn (G-2591)

MUSIC LICENSING & ROYALTIES
Warner Music Group Corp ....B....... 212 275-2000
　New York (G-12072)

MUSIC LICENSING TO RADIO STATIONS
Historic TW Inc ....E....... 212 484-8000
　New York (G-10106)
Time Warner Companies Inc ....D....... 212 484-8000
　New York (G-11845)

MUSIC RECORDING PRODUCER
Euphorbia Productions Ltd ....G....... 212 533-1700
　New York (G-9727)

MUSICAL ENTERTAINERS
Wmg Acquisition Corp ....F....... 212 275-2000
　New York (G-12126)

MUSICAL INSTRUMENT PARTS & ACCESS, WHOLESALE
Carl Fischer LLC ....E....... 212 777-0900
　New York (G-9208)

MUSICAL INSTRUMENT REPAIR
Guitar Specialist Inc ....G....... 914 401-9052
　Goldens Bridge (G-5475)
Sadowsky Guitars Ltd ....F....... 718 433-1990
　Long Island City (G-7584)

MUSICAL INSTRUMENTS & ACCESS: Carrying Cases
Roadie Products Inc ....E....... 631 567-8588
　Holbrook (G-6206)
Xstatic Pro Inc ....F....... 718 237-2299
　Brooklyn (G-2660)

MUSICAL INSTRUMENTS & ACCESS: NEC
DAddario & Company Inc ....E....... 718 599-6660
　Brooklyn (G-1749)
DAndrea Inc ....E....... 516 496-2200
　Syosset (G-15214)
Magic Reed ....F....... 914 630-4005
　Larchmont (G-7058)
Muzet Inc ....F....... 315 452-0050
　Syracuse (G-15378)
Nathan Love LLC ....F....... 212 925-7111
　New York (G-10877)
Roli USA Inc ....F....... 412 600-4840
　New York (G-11424)
Samson Technologies Corp ....D....... 631 784-2200
　Hicksville (G-6130)
Sound Source Inc ....G....... 585 271-5370
　Rochester (G-14135)
Steinway Musical Instrs Inc ....E....... 781 894-9770
　New York (G-11702)

MUSICAL INSTRUMENTS & ACCESS: Pianos
Steinway Inc ....A....... 718 721-2600
　Long Island City (G-7601)
Steinway and Sons ....C....... 718 721-2600
　Long Island City (G-7602)

MUSICAL INSTRUMENTS & ACCESS: Pipe Organs
Kerner and Merchant ....G....... 315 463-8023
　East Syracuse (G-4357)

MUSICAL INSTRUMENTS & PARTS: Brass
Siegfrieds Call Inc ....G....... 845 765-2275
　Beacon (G-762)

MUSICAL INSTRUMENTS & PARTS: String
DAddario & Company Inc ....D....... 631 439-3300
　Melville (G-8014)
Sadowsky Guitars Ltd ....F....... 718 433-1990
　Long Island City (G-7584)

MUSICAL INSTRUMENTS & SPLYS STORES
Albert Augustine Ltd ....D....... 718 913-9635
　Mount Vernon (G-8376)
Barbera Transduser Systems ....F....... 718 816-3025
　Staten Island (G-15048)
Carl Fischer LLC ....E....... 212 777-0900
　New York (G-9208)
DAndrea Inc ....E....... 516 496-2200
　Syosset (G-15214)
Hipshot Products Inc ....F....... 607 532-9404
　Interlaken (G-6481)

MUSICAL INSTRUMENTS & SPLYS STORES: Pianos
Steinway Inc ....A....... 718 721-2600
　Long Island City (G-7601)
Steinway and Sons ....C....... 718 721-2600
　Long Island City (G-7602)

MUSICAL INSTRUMENTS WHOLESALERS
Samson Technologies Corp ....D....... 631 784-2200
　Hicksville (G-6130)

MUSICAL INSTRUMENTS: Electric & Electronic
New Sensor Corporation ....D....... 718 937-8300
　Long Island City (G-7538)

MUSICAL INSTRUMENTS: Guitars & Parts, Electric & Acoustic
Barbera Transduser Systems ....F....... 718 816-3025
　Staten Island (G-15048)
DAddario & Company Inc ....A....... 631 439-3300
　Farmingdale (G-4747)
Dimarzio Inc ....E....... 718 442-6655
　Staten Island (G-15069)
Guitar Specialist Inc ....G....... 914 401-9052
　Goldens Bridge (G-5475)
Hipshot Products Inc ....F....... 607 532-9404
　Interlaken (G-6481)
J D Calato Manufacturing Co ....E....... 716 285-3546
　Niagara Falls (G-12300)
Stuart Spector Designs Ltd ....G....... 845 246-6124
　Saugerties (G-14618)

MUSICAL INSTRUMENTS: Harmonicas
Jason Ladanye Guitar Piano & H ....E....... 518 527-3973
　Albany (G-88)

MUSICAL INSTRUMENTS: Heads, Drum
Evans Manufacturing LLC ....D....... 631 439-3300
　Farmingdale (G-4762)

MUSICAL INSTRUMENTS: Organs
Gluck Orgelbau Inc ....G....... 212 233-2684
　New York (G-9947)
Leonard Carlson ....G....... 518 477-4710
　East Greenbush (G-4230)

MUSICAL INSTRUMENTS: Strings, Instrument
Albert Augustine Ltd ....D....... 718 913-9635
　Mount Vernon (G-8376)
E & O Mari Inc ....D....... 845 562-4400
　Newburgh (G-12220)

Mari Strings Inc ....F....... 212 799-6781
　New York (G-10701)

NAIL SALONS
Angel Tips Nail Salon ....G....... 718 225-8300
　Little Neck (G-7217)

NAME PLATES: Engraved Or Etched
Advanced Graphics Company ....F....... 607 692-7875
　Whitney Point (G-16554)
C & M Products Inc ....G....... 315 471-3303
　Syracuse (G-15265)
Champion America Inc ....A....... 716 626-1616
　Williamsville (G-16575)
Harold Wood Co Inc ....G....... 716 873-1535
　Buffalo (G-2867)
Nameplate Mfrs of Amer ....E....... 631 752-0055
　Farmingdale (G-4831)
Precision Design Systems Inc ....E....... 585 426-4500
　Rochester (G-14034)
The Gramecy Group ....G....... 518 348-1325
　Clifton Park (G-3579)
Tricor Direct Inc ....G....... 716 626-1616
　Williamsville (G-16592)

NAMEPLATES
Decal Makers Inc ....E....... 516 221-7200
　Bellmore (G-788)
Island Nameplate Inc ....G....... 845 651-4005
　Florida (G-4971)
Modern Decal Co ....G....... 315 622-2778
　Liverpool (G-7248)
Signature Name Plate Co Inc ....G....... 585 321-9960
　Rochester (G-14128)

NATIONAL SECURITY FORCES
Universal Armor Systems Corp ....E....... 631 838-1836
　Levittown (G-7136)

NATURAL BUTANE PRODUCTION
Center State Propane LLC ....G....... 315 841-4044
　Waterville (G-16038)
Green Buffalo Fuel LLC ....F....... 716 768-0600
　Tonawanda (G-15544)

NATURAL GAS COMPRESSING SVC, On-Site
Archrock Inc ....F....... 716 763-1553
　Lakewood (G-6988)

NATURAL GAS DISTRIBUTION TO CONSUMERS
Noco Incorporated ....G....... 716 833-6626
　Tonawanda (G-15565)

NATURAL GAS LIQUIDS PRODUCTION
Nfe Management LLC ....F....... 212 798-6100
　New York (G-10960)
Okra Energy LLC ....G....... 206 495-7574
　New York (G-11035)
Western Oil and Gas JV Inc ....G....... 914 967-4758
　Rye (G-14489)

NATURAL GAS PRODUCTION
County Energy Corp ....G....... 718 626-7000
　Brooklyn (G-1723)
Flownet LLC ....G....... 716 685-4036
　Lancaster (G-7020)
Green Buffalo Fuel LLC ....F....... 716 768-0600
　Tonawanda (G-15544)
Repsol Oil & Gas Usa LLC ....G....... 607 562-4000
　Horseheads (G-6325)
Reserve Gas Company Inc ....G....... 716 937-9484
　Alden (G-175)

NATURAL GAS TRANSMISSION & DISTRIBUTION
Lenape Energy Inc ....G....... 585 344-1200
　Alexander (G-179)
Lenape Resources Inc ....F....... 585 344-1200
　Alexander (G-180)

NATURAL GASOLINE PRODUCTION

20 Bliss St Inc .... G 716 326-2790
Westfield *(G-16390)*

NAVIGATIONAL SYSTEMS & INSTRUMENTS

Lockheed Martin Corporation .... A 315 456-0123
Liverpool *(G-7242)*

NET & NETTING PRDTS

Apex Texicon Inc .... E 516 239-4400
New York *(G-8883)*

NETS: Laundry

Sky Laundromat Inc .... E 718 639-7070
Jamaica *(G-6677)*

NEW & USED CAR DEALERS

Auto Sport Designs Inc .... F 631 425-1555
Huntington Station *(G-6433)*
Fuccillo Ford Nelliston Inc .... G 518 993-5555
Nelliston *(G-8482)*
Zappone Chrysler Jeep Ddge Inc .... F 518 982-0610
Halfmoon *(G-5670)*

NEWS DEALERS & NEWSSTANDS

Chronicle Express .... F 315 536-4422
Penn Yan *(G-12951)*

NEWS FEATURE SYNDICATES

Hearst Business Media Corp .... F 631 650-4441
New York *(G-10056)*
Hearst Corporation .... A 212 649-2000
New York *(G-10061)*
New York Times Company .... B 212 556-1234
New York *(G-10944)*

NEWS PICTURES GATHERING & DISTRIBUTING SVCS

Kraus Organization Limited .... D 212 686-5411
New York *(G-10481)*

NEWS SYNDICATES

Thomson Reuters Corporation .... A 646 223-4000
New York *(G-11825)*

NEWSPAPERS & PERIODICALS NEWS REPORTING SVCS

Dow Jones & Company Inc .... E 212 597-5983
New York *(G-9564)*

NEWSPAPERS, WHOLESALE

Nyt Capital LLC .... F 212 556-1234
New York *(G-11021)*

NICKEL ALLOY

Nickel City Studios Photo Jour .... G 716 200-0956
Buffalo *(G-2972)*

NONCURRENT CARRYING WIRING DEVICES

Chase Corporation .... F 631 827-0476
Northport *(G-12466)*
Complete SEC & Contrls Inc .... F 631 421-7200
Huntington Station *(G-6437)*
Pfisterer Lapp LLC .... C 585 768-6221
Le Roy *(G-7124)*
Von Roll Usa Inc .... E 203 562-2171
Schenectady *(G-14726)*
Zierick Manufacturing Corp .... D 800 882-8020
Mount Kisco *(G-8361)*

NONFERROUS: Rolling & Drawing, NEC

Arlon Viscor Ltd .... A 914 461-1300
White Plains *(G-16422)*
Continental Cordage Corp .... D 315 655-9800
Cazenovia *(G-3317)*
Cpp-Syracuse Inc .... E 315 687-0014
Chittenango *(G-3504)*
Eco-Bat America LLC .... C 845 692-4414
Middletown *(G-8150)*
Medi-Ray Inc .... D 877 898-3003
Tuckahoe *(G-15644)*

Nationwide Precision Pdts Corp .... B 585 272-7100
Rochester *(G-13964)*
Selectrode Industries Inc .... D 631 547-5470
Huntington Station *(G-6458)*

NONMETALLIC MINERALS: Support Activities, Exc Fuels

Crystal Ceres Industries Inc .... D 716 283-0445
Niagara Falls *(G-12275)*

NOTARIES PUBLIC

Chesu Inc .... F 239 564-2803
East Hampton *(G-4234)*

NOTEBOOKS, MADE FROM PURCHASED MATERIALS

Anne Taintor Inc .... G 718 483-9312
Brooklyn *(G-1536)*

NOTIONS: Button Blanks & Molds

Connection Mold Inc .... G 585 458-6463
Rochester *(G-13719)*

NOTIONS: Pins, Straight, Steel Or Brass

Karp Overseas Corporation .... E 718 784-2105
Maspeth *(G-7856)*

NOTIONS: Studs, Shirt, Exc Precious/Semi Metal/Stone

Columbia Button Nailhead Corp .... F 718 386-3414
Brooklyn *(G-1706)*

NOVELTIES

Best Priced Products Inc .... G 914 345-3800
Elmsford *(G-4531)*
Fish & Crown Ltd .... D 212 707-9603
New York *(G-9813)*
Jacobs Juice Corp .... G 646 255-2860
Brooklyn *(G-2031)*
Jpm Fine Woodworking LLC .... G 516 236-7605
Jericho *(G-6792)*
Orlandi Inc .... D 631 756-0110
Farmingdale *(G-4840)*
Orlandi Inc .... E 631 756-0110
Farmingdale *(G-4841)*

NOVELTIES & SPECIALTIES: Metal

Buttons & Trimcom Inc .... F 212 868-1971
New York *(G-9164)*
Criterion Bell & Specialty .... E 718 788-2600
Brooklyn *(G-1732)*
Polich Tallix Inc .... D 845 567-9464
Walden *(G-15895)*
Split Rock Trading Co Inc .... G 631 929-3261
Wading River *(G-15887)*
Stylebuilt Accessories Inc .... F 917 439-0578
East Rockaway *(G-4297)*

NOVELTIES: Paper, Made From Purchased Materials

National Advertising & Prtg .... G 212 629-7650
New York *(G-10880)*
P C I Paper Conversions Inc .... F 315 437-1641
Syracuse *(G-15392)*

NOVELTIES: Plastic

Buttons & Trimcom Inc .... F 212 868-1971
New York *(G-9164)*
Frisch Plastics Corp .... E 973 685-5936
Hartsdale *(G-5743)*
GPM Associates LLC .... E 585 335-3940
Dansville *(G-3926)*
Kling Magnetics Inc .... E 518 392-4000
Chatham *(G-3428)*
Pelican Products Co Inc .... E 718 860-3220
Bronx *(G-1354)*
Pleasure Chest Sales Ltd .... E 212 242-2158
New York *(G-11209)*
Royal Industries Inc .... E 718 369-3046
Brooklyn *(G-2420)*
Skd Distribution Corp .... E 718 525-6000
Jericho *(G-6805)*

NOVELTY SHOPS

Mgd Brands Inc .... E 516 545-0150
Plainview *(G-13075)*

NOZZLES & SPRINKLERS Lawn Hose

Artys Sprnklr Svc Instllation .... F 516 538-4371
East Meadow *(G-4246)*

NOZZLES: Spray, Aerosol, Paint Or Insecticide

Sono-Tek Corporation .... D 845 795-2020
Milton *(G-8197)*

NUCLEAR REACTORS: Military Or Indl

Energy Nuclear Operations .... E 315 342-0055
Oswego *(G-12777)*

NURSERIES & LAWN & GARDEN SPLY STORES, RETAIL: Sod

E F Lippert Co Inc .... F 716 373-1100
Allegany *(G-189)*

NURSERIES & LAWN & GARDEN SPLY STORES, RETAIL: Top Soil

East Coast Mines Ltd .... E 631 653-5445
East Quogue *(G-4277)*
Grosso Materials Inc .... F 845 361-5211
Montgomery *(G-8312)*
Hampton Sand Corp .... G 631 325-5533
Westhampton *(G-16402)*

NURSERIES & LAWN/GARDEN SPLY STORE, RET: Lawnmowers/Tractors

Kelley Farm & Garden Inc .... E 518 234-2332
Cobleskill *(G-3603)*

NURSERY & GARDEN CENTERS

Birkett Mills .... G 315 536-3311
Penn Yan *(G-12949)*

NUTS: Metal

Buckley Qc Fasteners Inc .... E 716 662-1490
Orchard Park *(G-12702)*
Dependable Acme Threaded Pdts ...... G 516 338-4700
Westbury *(G-16322)*
Zierick Manufacturing Corp .... D 800 882-8020
Mount Kisco *(G-8361)*

NYLON RESINS

Sk Capital Partners II LP .... F 212 826-2700
New York *(G-11604)*
Sk Titan Holdings LLC .... G 212 826-2700
New York *(G-11605)*

OFFICE EQPT WHOLESALERS

Automecha International Ltd .... E 607 843-2235
Oxford *(G-12807)*
DAF Office Networks Inc .... G 315 699-7070
Cicero *(G-3516)*
Finesse Creations Inc .... F 718 692-2100
Brooklyn *(G-1883)*

OFFICE EQPT, WHOLESALE: Duplicating Machines

Media Technologies Ltd .... F 631 467-7900
Eastport *(G-4385)*

OFFICE FIXTURES: Exc Wood

Air Crafters Inc .... C 631 471-7788
Ronkonkoma *(G-14295)*
Evans & Paul LLC .... E 516 576-0800
Plainview *(G-13056)*

OFFICE FIXTURES: Wood

Bauerschmidt & Sons Inc .... D 718 528-3500
Jamaica *(G-6630)*

PRODUCT SECTION OPHTHALMIC GOODS WHOLESALERS

OFFICE FURNITURE REPAIR & MAINTENANCE SVCS

Davies Office Refurbishing Inc..............C...... 518 426-7188
  Albany (G-67)
Jim Quinn..F...... 518 356-0398
  Schenectady (G-14691)
Roberts Office Furn Cncpts Inc...........E...... 315 451-9185
  Liverpool (G-7260)

OFFICE SPLY & STATIONERY STORES

American Office Supply Inc..................F...... 516 294-9444
  Westbury (G-16315)
Flynns Inc..E...... 212 339-8700
  New York (G-9819)
Tripi Engraving Co Inc........................E...... 718 383-6500
  Brooklyn (G-2586)

OFFICE SPLY & STATIONERY STORES: Office Forms & Splys

Datagraphic Business Systems...........G...... 516 485-9069
  Brentwood (G-1130)
Grant Hamilton..................................F...... 716 652-0320
  East Aurora (G-4201)
J P Printing Inc..................................G...... 516 293-6110
  Farmingdale (G-4790)
Kleer-Fax Inc....................................D...... 631 225-1100
  Amityville (G-295)
Richard Ruffner................................F...... 631 234-4600
  Central Islip (G-3383)
Rmd Holding Inc................................G...... 845 628-0030
  Mahopac (G-7712)
Short Run Forms Inc.........................D...... 631 567-7171
  Bohemia (G-1089)
Tannens..G...... 718 292-4646
  Bronx (G-1400)

OFFICE SPLYS, NEC, WHOLESALE

DAF Office Networks Inc....................G...... 315 699-7070
  Cicero (G-3516)
Rike Enterprises Inc.........................F...... 631 277-8338
  Islip (G-6550)
Robert Tabatznik Assoc Inc...............F...... 845 336-4555
  Kingston (G-6916)

OFFICES & CLINICS OF DENTISTS: Prosthodontist

Goldberg Prosthetic & Orthotic..........F...... 631 689-6606
  East Setauket (G-4302)

OFFICES & CLINICS OF DRS, MED: Specialized Practitioners

Erika T Schwartz MD PC..................G...... 212 873-3420
  New York (G-9702)

OFFICES & CLINICS OF HEALTH PRACTITIONERS: Nutritionist

Everlast Worldwide Inc......................E...... 212 239-0990
  New York (G-9738)

OIL & GAS FIELD MACHINERY

Basin Holdings LLC............................E...... 212 695-7376
  New York (G-9026)
Derrick Corporation............................C...... 716 683-9010
  Buffalo (G-2799)
Schlumberger Technology Corp..........C...... 607 378-0105
  Horseheads (G-6328)
Smith International Inc......................F...... 585 265-2330
  Ontario (G-12666)

OIL FIELD MACHINERY & EQPT

Anchor Commerce Trading Corp........G...... 516 881-3485
  Atlantic Beach (G-455)
Desmi-Afti Inc...................................E...... 716 662-0632
  Orchard Park (G-12713)

OIL FIELD SVCS, NEC

Alba Fuel Corp..................................G...... 718 931-1700
  Bronx (G-1214)
Bass Oil & Chemical Llc....................F...... 718 628-4444
  Brooklyn (G-1587)
Bluebar Oil Co Inc..............................F...... 315 245-4328
  Blossvale (G-963)

Fuel Energy Services USA Ltd...........E...... 607 846-2650
  Horseheads (G-6316)
Gas Field Specialists Inc...................D...... 716 378-6422
  Horseheads (G-6317)
Grit Energy Services Inc...................E...... 212 701-4500
  New York (G-9992)
Marcellus Energy Services LLC........E...... 607 236-0038
  Candor (G-3253)
Petro Inc..G...... 516 686-1900
  Hicksville (G-6126)
Rpc Inc...E...... 347 873-3935
  Elmont (G-4524)
Schlumberger Foundation Inc............G...... 212 350-9400
  New York (G-11505)
Schneider Amalco Inc........................F...... 917 470-9674
  New York (G-11507)
U S Energy Development Corp..........D...... 716 636-0401
  Getzville (G-5354)

OIL ROYALTY TRADERS

Schneider Amalco Inc........................F...... 917 470-9674
  New York (G-11507)

OILS & GREASES: Blended & Compounded

Battenfeld Grease Oil Corp NY..........E...... 716 695-2100
  North Tonawanda (G-12417)
Battenfeld-American Inc...................F...... 716 822-8410
  Buffalo (G-2726)
High Line Lube LLC..........................G...... 914 684-0170
  White Plains (G-16459)
Tribology Inc....................................E...... 631 345-3000
  Yaphank (G-16724)

OILS & GREASES: Lubricating

Baums Castorine Company Inc.........G...... 315 336-8154
  Rome (G-14247)
Beka World LP..................................G...... 905 821-1050
  Buffalo (G-2728)
Bestline International RES Inc..........G...... 518 631-2177
  Schenectady (G-14654)
Castoleum Corporation.....................F...... 914 664-5877
  Mount Vernon (G-8385)
Chemlube International LLC.............F...... 914 381-5800
  Harrison (G-5725)
Chemlube Marketing Inc...................F...... 914 381-5800
  Harrison (G-5726)
Finish Line Technologies Inc.............E...... 631 666-7300
  Hauppauge (G-5824)
Inland Vacuum Industries Inc...........F...... 585 293-3330
  Churchville (G-3510)
Interdynamics..................................F...... 914 241-1423
  Mount Kisco (G-8344)
Loobrica International Corp..............G...... 347 997-0296
  Staten Island (G-15101)
Noco Incorporated............................G...... 716 833-6626
  Tonawanda (G-15565)
Oil and Lubricant Depot LLC.............F...... 718 258-9220
  Amityville (G-308)
Polycast Industries Inc......................G...... 631 595-2530
  Bay Shore (G-708)
Specialty Silicone Pdts Inc................D...... 518 885-8826
  Ballston Spa (G-596)
Summit Lubricants Inc......................E...... 585 815-0798
  Batavia (G-636)
US Global Lubricants Inc..................F...... 845 271-4277
  Stony Point (G-15178)

OILS: Anise

Von Roll Usa Inc..............................E...... 203 562-2171
  Schenectady (G-14726)

OILS: Essential

Natures Warehouse...........................F...... 800 215-4372
  Philadelphia (G-12985)
Torre Products Co Inc......................G...... 212 925-8989
  New York (G-11870)

OILS: Lubricating

Oil Solutions Intl Inc.........................G...... 631 608-8889
  Amityville (G-309)
R H Crown Co Inc.............................E...... 518 762-4589
  Johnstown (G-6838)

OILS: Lubricating

Black Bear Company Inc..................E...... 718 784-7330
  Valley Stream (G-15774)

Blaser Production Inc.......................F...... 845 294-3200
  Goshen (G-5477)
Blaser Swisslube Holding Corp.........F...... 845 294-3200
  Goshen (G-5478)
Mdi Holdings LLC..............................A...... 212 559-1127
  New York (G-10747)
Monroe Fluid Technology Inc............E...... 585 392-3434
  Hilton (G-6157)

OILS: Orange

Solvents Company Inc......................F...... 631 595-9300
  Kingston (G-6917)

OILS: Still

E and V Energy Corporation..............F...... 315 786-2067
  Watertown (G-16013)

OINTMENTS

Easton Pharmaceuticals Inc..............G...... 347 284-0192
  Lewiston (G-7139)
Perrigo New York Inc.......................F...... 718 901-2800
  Bronx (G-1357)
Perrigo New York Inc.......................B...... 718 960-9900
  Bronx (G-1358)

ON-LINE DATABASE INFORMATION RETRIEVAL SVCS

Endava Inc......................................F...... 212 920-7240
  New York (G-9675)
Informa Media Inc............................B...... 212 204-4200
  New York (G-10210)
News Corporation.............................C...... 212 416-3400
  New York (G-10952)
Optionline LLC..................................E...... 516 218-3225
  Garden City (G-5273)
Sparta Commercial Services Inc.......F...... 212 239-2666
  New York (G-11658)

OPEN PIT GOLD MINING

Surtic Mining Company LLC.............F...... 718 434-0477
  Brooklyn (G-2544)

OPERATOR: Apartment Buildings

Gallagher Printing Inc......................E...... 716 873-2434
  Buffalo (G-2838)
Hospitality Inc..................................E...... 212 268-1930
  New York (G-10128)

OPHTHALMIC GOODS

21st Century Optics Inc....................E...... 347 527-1079
  Long Island City (G-7362)
Bausch & Lomb Holdings Inc............G...... 585 338-6000
  New York (G-9028)
Bausch & Lomb Incorporated............B...... 585 338-6000
  Rochester (G-13655)
Bausch & Lomb Incorporated............D...... 585 338-6000
  Rochester (G-13656)
Bausch & Lomb Incorporated............B...... 585 338-6000
  Rochester (G-13657)
Designs For Vision Inc.....................C...... 631 585-3300
  Bohemia (G-1016)
Doug Lambertson Od........................G...... 718 698-9300
  Staten Island (G-15070)
Esc Control Electronics LLC.............E...... 631 467-5328
  Sayville (G-14627)
Eyeworks Inc...................................G...... 585 454-4470
  Rochester (G-13800)
Lens Lab..G...... 718 379-2020
  Bronx (G-1317)
Lens Lab Express.............................G...... 718 921-5488
  Brooklyn (G-2110)
Lens Lab Express of Graham Ave....G...... 718 486-0117
  Brooklyn (G-2111)
Lens Lab Express Southern Blvd.....G...... 718 626-5184
  Astoria (G-434)
North Bronx Retinal & Ophthlmi........G...... 347 535-4932
  Bronx (G-1345)
Surgical Design Corp........................F...... 914 273-2445
  Armonk (G-410)
Wyeth Holdings LLC.........................D...... 845 602-5000
  Pearl River (G-12913)

OPHTHALMIC GOODS WHOLESALERS

21st Century Optics Inc....................E...... 347 527-1079
  Long Island City (G-7362)

Employee Codes: A=Over 500 employees, B=251-500
C=101-250, D=51-100, E=20-50, F=10-19, G=5-9

2019 Harris
New York Manufacturers Directory

OPHTHALMIC GOODS WHOLESALERS

Lens Lab Express Southern Blvd..........G........ 718 626-5184
  Astoria (G-434)
Winchester Optical Company................E...... 607 734-4251
  Elmira (G-4507)

OPHTHALMIC GOODS: Eyewear, Protective

Provision Supply LLC...............................F....... 347 623-0237
  Brooklyn (G-2359)

OPHTHALMIC GOODS: Frames & Parts, Eyeglass & Spectacle

Art-Craft Optical Company Inc ....E....... 585 546-6640
  Rochester (G-13643)
His Vision Inc ....E....... 585 254-0022
  Rochester (G-13870)
Zyloware Corporation ....D...... 914 708-1200
  Port Chester (G-13211)

OPHTHALMIC GOODS: Frames, Lenses & Parts, Eyeglasses

Moscot Wholesale Corp ....G....... 212 647-1550
  New York (G-10846)
Optika Eyes Ltd ....E....... 631 567-8852
  Sayville (G-14633)
Winchester Optical Company ....E....... 607 734-4251
  Elmira (G-4507)

OPHTHALMIC GOODS: Lenses, Ophthalmic

Co-Optics America Lab Inc ....E....... 607 432-0557
  Oneonta (G-12631)
Tri-Supreme Optical LLC ....D...... 631 249-2020
  Farmingdale (G-4899)

OPHTHALMIC GOODS: Spectacles

Modo Retail LLC ....E....... 212 965-4900
  New York (G-10830)
Spectacle Optical Inc ....G....... 646 706-1015
  Rego Park (G-13469)

OPHTHALMIC GOODS: Temples & Fronts, Ophthalmic

Kathmando Valley Preservation ....F....... 212 727-0074
  New York (G-10417)

OPTICAL GOODS STORES

Hart Specialties Inc ....D...... 631 226-5600
  Amityville (G-281)
Match Eyewear LLC ....E....... 516 877-0170
  Westbury (G-16354)
Optika Eyes Ltd ....G....... 631 567-8852
  Sayville (G-14633)
Parker Warby Retail Inc ....E....... 646 517-5223
  New York (G-11117)

OPTICAL GOODS STORES: Opticians

Eyeglass Service Industries ....G....... 914 666-3150
  Bedford Hills (G-776)
Lens Lab Express ....G....... 718 921-5488
  Brooklyn (G-2110)

OPTICAL INSTRUMENTS & APPARATUS

Aeroflex Incorporated.............................B....... 516 694-6700
  Plainview (G-13032)
Applied Image Inc ....E....... 585 482-0300
  Rochester (G-13637)
Carl Zeiss Inc..C....... 914 747-1800
  Thornwood (G-15502)
Gradient Lens Corporation ....E....... 585 235-2620
  Rochester (G-13844)
Halo Optical Products Inc ....D...... 518 773-4256
  Gloversville (G-5457)
Hart Specialties Inc ....D...... 631 226-5600
  Amityville (G-281)
Idex Health & Science LLC....................D...... 585 244-7220
  Rochester (G-13875)
Isp Optics Corporation ....D...... 914 591-3070
  Irvington (G-6507)
Kevin Freeman ....G....... 631 447-5421
  Patchogue (G-12869)
Leica Microsystems Inc ....G....... 716 686-3000
  Depew (G-4095)
Lumetrics Inc..F....... 585 214-2455
  Rochester (G-13918)

Plx Inc ....E....... 631 586-4190
  Deer Park (G-4026)
RPC Photonics Inc ....F....... 585 272-2840
  Rochester (G-14106)
Spectral Systems LLC ....E....... 845 896-2200
  Hopewell Junction (G-6293)
Stefan Sydor Optics Inc ....E....... 585 271-7300
  Rochester (G-14143)
Tele-Vue Optics Inc ....E....... 845 469-4551
  Chester (G-3487)
Westchester Technologies Inc ....E....... 914 736-1034
  Peekskill (G-12929)

OPTICAL INSTRUMENTS & LENSES

Accu Coat Inc...G....... 585 288-2330
  Rochester (G-13596)
Aeroflex Plainview Inc ....B....... 516 694-6700
  Plainview (G-13033)
Anorad Corporation ....C....... 631 344-6600
  Shirley (G-14827)
Apollo Optical Systems Inc ....E....... 585 272-6170
  West Henrietta (G-16229)
Binoptics LLC..E....... 607 257-3200
  Ithaca (G-6562)
Caliber Imging Diagnostics Inc ....E....... 585 239-9800
  Rochester (G-13687)
Carl Zeiss Microscopy LLC ....B....... 914 747-1800
  Thornwood (G-15503)
Carl Zeiss Sbe LLC ....E....... 914 747-1132
  Thornwood (G-15504)
Cartiheal Inc ....G....... 917 703-6992
  New York (G-9217)
CK Coatings ....G....... 585 502-0425
  Le Roy (G-7114)
Corning Tropel Corporation ....C....... 585 377-3200
  Fairport (G-4629)
Cross Bronx Optical ....G....... 917 667-6611
  Bronx (G-1248)
Dorsey Metrology Intl Inc ....E....... 845 229-2929
  Poughkeepsie (G-13334)
Dynamic Laboratories Inc ....E....... 631 231-7474
  Ronkonkoma (G-14334)
Exfo Burleigh Pdts Group Inc ....D...... 585 301-1530
  Canandaigua (G-3220)
Gurley Precision Instrs Inc ....C....... 518 272-6300
  Troy (G-15607)
Keon Optics Inc......................................F....... 845 429-7103
  Stony Point (G-15173)
Match Eyewear LLC ....E....... 516 877-0170
  Westbury (G-16354)
Micatu Inc ....G....... 888 705-8836
  Horseheads (G-6319)
Navitar Inc..D...... 585 359-4000
  Rochester (G-13965)
Optipro Systems LLC ....D...... 585 265-0160
  Ontario (G-12659)
Orafol Americas Inc ....F....... 585 272-0290
  West Henrietta (G-16244)
Planar Optics Inc....................................G....... 585 671-0100
  Webster (G-16091)
Qioptiq, Inc. ....E....... 585 223-2370
  Fairport (G-4652)
Rochester Photonics Corp ....D...... 585 387-0674
  Rochester (G-14091)
Santa Fe Manufacturing Corp.................G....... 631 234-0100
  Hauppauge (G-5932)
Schneider Optics Inc ....E....... 631 761-5000
  Hauppauge (G-5935)
Schott Corporation ....D...... 315 255-2791
  Auburn (G-499)
Steven John Opticians ....G....... 718 543-3336
  Bronx (G-1394)
Surgical Design Corp ....F....... 914 273-2445
  Armonk (G-410)
Va Inc ....E....... 585 385-5930
  Rochester (G-14195)
Welch Allyn Inc.......................................A....... 315 685-4100
  Skaneateles Falls (G-14883)

OPTICAL SCANNING SVCS

Kjckd Inc ....G....... 518 435-9696
  Latham (G-7078)
Printech Business Systems Inc..............F....... 212 290-2542
  New York (G-11249)

OPTOMETRIC EQPT & SPLYS WHOLESALERS

Orafol Americas Inc ....F....... 585 272-0290
  West Henrietta (G-16244)

ORAL PREPARATIONS

Good Home Co Inc..................................G....... 212 352-1509
  New York (G-9957)
Robell Research Inc...............................G....... 212 755-6577
  New York (G-11405)

ORDNANCE

Dyno Nobel Inc.......................................D...... 845 338-2144
  Ulster Park (G-15658)
Island Ordnance Systems LLC ....F....... 516 746-2100
  Mineola (G-8230)
Magellan Aerospace NY Inc ....C....... 718 699-4000
  Corona (G-3849)

ORGAN TUNING & REPAIR SVCS

Kerner and Merchant..............................G....... 315 463-8023
  East Syracuse (G-4357)

ORGANIZATIONS, NEC

New York State Assoc ....F....... 518 434-2281
  Albany (G-102)

ORGANIZATIONS: Medical Research

Encysive Pharmaceuticals Inc................E....... 212 733-2323
  New York (G-9674)

ORGANIZATIONS: Professional

Physicalmind Institute............................F....... 212 343-2150
  New York (G-11186)
Public Relations Soc Amer Inc ....G....... 212 460-1400
  New York (G-11273)

ORGANIZATIONS: Religious

Albany Catholic Press Assoc ....G....... 518 453-6688
  Albany (G-32)
American Jewish Congress Inc ....E....... 212 879-4500
  New York (G-8832)
Nationwide Custom Services..................G....... 845 365-0414
  Tappan (G-15469)
Seneca Media Inc ....C....... 607 324-1425
  Hornell (G-6302)
United Synggue Cnsrvtive Jdism...........E....... 212 533-7800
  New York (G-11956)

ORGANIZATIONS: Research Institute

Alo Acquisition LLC................................G....... 518 464-0279
  Albany (G-39)
Katikati Inc..G....... 585 678-1764
  West Henrietta (G-16243)

ORGANIZATIONS: Scientific Research Agency

Loobrica International Corp....................G....... 347 997-0296
  Staten Island (G-15101)

ORGANIZERS, CLOSET & DRAWER Plastic

Plascoline Inc..F....... 917 410-5754
  New York (G-11206)

ORNAMENTS: Christmas Tree, Exc Electrical & Glass

Criterion Bell & Specialty ....E....... 718 788-2600
  Brooklyn (G-1732)
Patience Brewster Inc............................F....... 315 685-8336
  Skaneateles (G-14876)

ORTHOPEDIC SUNDRIES: Molded Rubber

Advanced Back Technologies ....G....... 631 231-0076
  Hauppauge (G-5754)
Certified Health Products Inc.................E....... 718 339-7498
  Brooklyn (G-1686)
Newyork Pedorthic Associates ....G....... 718 236-7700
  Brooklyn (G-2268)

OSCILLATORS

Centroid Inc..E....... 516 349-0070
  Plainview (G-13040)

OUTLETS: Electric, Convenience

99cent World and Variety Corp ....G....... 212 740-0010
  New York (G-8686)

PRODUCT SECTION

PACKING & CRATING SVCS: Containerized Goods For Shipping

Another 99 Cent Paradise .... G 718 786-4578
  Sunnyside *(G-15201)*
Bronx New Way Corp .... G 347 431-1385
  Bronx *(G-1233)*
Dollar Popular Inc .... G 914 375-0361
  Yonkers *(G-16751)*
RE 99 Cents Inc .... G 718 639-2325
  Woodside *(G-16674)*

OVENS: Paint Baking & Drying

Specified Air Solutions LLC .... E 716 852-4400
  Buffalo *(G-3074)*

PACKAGE DESIGN SVCS

Dolco LLC .... E 585 657-7777
  Bloomfield *(G-952)*
Force Digital Media Inc .... G 631 243-0243
  Deer Park *(G-3977)*
Hcrnet Group Inc .... D 845 858-6400
  Port Jervis *(G-13230)*
Titherington Design & Mfg .... F 518 324-2205
  Plattsburgh *(G-13163)*

PACKAGED FROZEN FOODS WHOLESALERS, NEC

Bagelovers Inc .... F 607 844-3683
  Dryden *(G-4149)*
Rhosey LLC .... G 718 382-1226
  Brooklyn *(G-2400)*

PACKAGING & LABELING SVCS

Atlantic Essential Pdts Inc .... D 631 434-8333
  Hauppauge *(G-5772)*
Bfma Holding Corporation .... G 607 753-6746
  Cortland *(G-3862)*
Ccmi Inc .... G 315 781-3270
  Geneva *(G-5318)*
Elite Roasters Inc .... F 716 626-0307
  East Amherst *(G-4189)*
F M Howell & Company .... D 607 734-6291
  Elmira *(G-4486)*
Klg Usa LLC .... A 845 856-5311
  Port Jervis *(G-13233)*
Marietta Corporation .... B 607 753-0982
  Cortland *(G-3882)*
Marietta Corporation .... A 323 589-8181
  Cortland *(G-3883)*
Nice-Pak Products Inc .... B 845 365-2772
  Orangeburg *(G-12684)*
Nutra Solutions USA Inc .... E 631 392-1900
  Deer Park *(G-4019)*
Orlandi Inc .... D 631 756-0110
  Farmingdale *(G-4840)*
Orlandi Inc .... E 631 756-0110
  Farmingdale *(G-4841)*
Paul Michael Group Inc .... G 631 585-5700
  Ronkonkoma *(G-14397)*
Piezo Electronics Research .... F 845 735-9349
  Pearl River *(G-12907)*
Princeton Label & Packaging .... E 609 490-0800
  Patchogue *(G-12875)*
Professional Disposables Inc .... A 845 365-1700
  Orangeburg *(G-12689)*
Sugar Foods Corporation .... E 212 753-6900
  New York *(G-11734)*
Universal Packg Systems Inc .... A 631 543-2277
  Hauppauge *(G-5966)*
Valentine Packaging Corp .... F 718 418-6000
  Maspeth *(G-7875)*
Weather Products Corporation .... G 315 474-8593
  Syracuse *(G-15455)*

PACKAGING MATERIALS, INDL: Wholesalers

Philpac Corporation .... E 716 875-8005
  Buffalo *(G-3002)*

PACKAGING MATERIALS, WHOLESALE

Patco Tapes Inc .... G 718 497-1527
  Maspeth *(G-7867)*
Technical Library Service Inc .... F 212 219-0770
  Brooklyn *(G-2558)*
Technical Packaging Inc .... F 516 223-2300
  Baldwin *(G-545)*
Terphane Holdings LLC .... G 585 657-5800
  Bloomfield *(G-956)*
W N Vanalstine & Sons Inc .... D 518 237-1436
  Cohoes *(G-3624)*

PACKAGING MATERIALS: Paper

Anasia Inc .... G 718 588-1407
  Bronx *(G-1220)*
Apexx Omni-Graphics Inc .... D 718 326-3330
  Maspeth *(G-7822)*
Ares Box LLC .... D 718 858-8760
  Brooklyn *(G-1549)*
Berry Plastics Corporation .... B 315 986-6270
  Macedon *(G-7697)*
CCL Label Inc .... C 716 852-2155
  Buffalo *(G-2762)*
Classic Labels Inc .... E 631 467-2300
  Patchogue *(G-12863)*
Colad Group LLC .... D 716 961-1776
  Buffalo *(G-2772)*
Craft Packaging Inc .... G 718 633-4045
  Brooklyn *(G-1725)*
De Luxe Packaging Corp .... E 416 754-4633
  Saugerties *(G-14606)*
Depot Label Company Inc .... G 631 467-2952
  Patchogue *(G-12864)*
Dolco LLC .... E 585 657-7777
  Bloomfield *(G-952)*
General Fibre Products Corp .... D 516 358-7500
  New Hyde Park *(G-8536)*
General Trade Mark La .... E 718 979-7261
  Staten Island *(G-15078)*
Idesco Corp .... F 212 889-2530
  New York *(G-10174)*
International Paper Company .... C 585 663-1000
  Rochester *(G-13884)*
K Sidrane Inc .... E 631 393-6974
  Farmingdale *(G-4796)*
Multi Packaging Solutions Inc .... C 516 488-2000
  Hicksville *(G-6112)*
Multi Packaging Solutions Inc .... E 646 885-0005
  New York *(G-10858)*
Nameplate Mfrs of Amer .... E 631 752-0055
  Farmingdale *(G-4831)*
Nova Packaging Ltd Inc .... E 914 232-8406
  Katonah *(G-6845)*
Pactiv LLC .... C 518 562-6101
  Plattsburgh *(G-13142)*
Paperworks Industries Inc .... F 913 621-0922
  Baldwinsville *(G-559)*
Penta-Tech Coated Products LLC ..... F 315 986-4098
  Macedon *(G-7702)*
Pliant LLC .... B 315 986-6286
  Macedon *(G-7703)*
Printex Packaging Corporation .... D 631 234-4300
  Islandia *(G-6537)*
Quality Circle Products Inc .... D 914 736-6600
  Montrose *(G-8329)*
Saint-Gobain Prfmce Plas Corp .... C 518 642-2200
  Granville *(G-5524)*
Shaant Industries Inc .... E 716 366-3654
  Dunkirk *(G-4179)*
Time Release Sciences Inc .... E 716 823-4580
  Buffalo *(G-3096)*
Transcntinental Ultra Flex Inc .... B 718 272-9100
  Brooklyn *(G-2579)*
Valley Industrial Products Inc .... E 631 385-9300
  Huntington *(G-6424)*
Westrock Mwv LLC .... C 212 688-5000
  New York *(G-12097)*

PACKAGING MATERIALS: Paper, Coated Or Laminated

American Packaging Corporation ...... C 585 537-4650
  Churchville *(G-3506)*
American Packaging Corporation ...... G 585 254-2002
  Rochester *(G-13625)*
American Packaging Corporation ...... C 585 254-9500
  Rochester *(G-13626)*
Cove Point Holdings LLC .... E 212 599-3388
  New York *(G-9413)*
Patco Tapes Inc .... G 718 497-1527
  Maspeth *(G-7867)*
Tri-Plex Packaging Corporation .... E 212 481-6070
  New York *(G-11894)*

PACKAGING MATERIALS: Paper, Thermoplastic Coated

F M Howell & Company .... D 607 734-6291
  Elmira *(G-4486)*
Smart USA Inc .... F 631 969-1111
  Bay Shore *(G-724)*

PACKAGING MATERIALS: Plastic Film, Coated Or Laminated

Allied Converters Inc .... E 914 235-1585
  New Rochelle *(G-8589)*
Brook & Whittle Limited .... E 716 691-4348
  Amherst *(G-219)*
Brook & Whittle Limited .... C 716 853-1688
  Buffalo *(G-2736)*
Ecoplast & Packaging LLC .... E 718 996-0800
  Brooklyn *(G-1811)*
Folene Packaging LLC .... E 917 626-6740
  Brooklyn *(G-1895)*
Mason Transparent Package Inc .... E 718 792-6000
  Bronx *(G-1324)*
RMS Packaging Inc .... F 914 205-2070
  Peekskill *(G-12924)*
Universal Packg Systems Inc .... A 631 543-2277
  Hauppauge *(G-5966)*
W E W Container Corporation .... E 718 827-8150
  Brooklyn *(G-2637)*

PACKAGING MATERIALS: Polystyrene Foam

24 Seven Enterprises Inc .... G 845 563-9033
  New Windsor *(G-8632)*
ABI Packaging Inc .... E 716 677-2900
  West Seneca *(G-16292)*
Barclay Brown Corp .... F 718 376-7166
  Brooklyn *(G-1586)*
Calpac Incorporated .... F 631 789-0502
  Amityville *(G-267)*
Chesu Inc .... F 239 564-2803
  East Hampton *(G-4234)*
Fedex Ground Package Sys Inc .... G 800 463-3339
  Plattsburgh *(G-13121)*
First Qlty Packg Solutions LLC .... F 516 829-3030
  Great Neck *(G-5555)*
Interntnal Bus Cmmncations Inc .... E 516 352-4505
  New Hyde Park *(G-8542)*
Jamestown Container Corp .... C 716 665-4623
  Falconer *(G-4684)*
Jem Container Corp .... E 800 521-0145
  Plainview *(G-13066)*
Knoll Printing & Packaging Inc .... E 516 621-0100
  Syosset *(G-15220)*
Lamar Plastics Packaging Ltd .... D 516 378-2500
  Freeport *(G-5163)*
Lewis & Myers Inc .... G 585 494-1410
  Bergen *(G-823)*
Printex Packaging Corporation .... D 631 234-4300
  Islandia *(G-6537)*
R D A Container Corporation .... E 585 247-2323
  Gates *(G-5312)*
Shell Containers Inc (ny) .... E 516 352-4505
  New Hyde Park *(G-8562)*
Snow Craft Co Inc .... E 516 739-1399
  New Hyde Park *(G-8563)*
Technical Packaging Inc .... F 516 223-2300
  Baldwin *(G-545)*
TSS Foam Industries Corp .... F 585 538-2321
  Caledonia *(G-3159)*
W Stuart Smith Inc .... E 585 742-3310
  Victor *(G-15876)*
Walnut Packaging Inc .... E 631 293-3836
  Farmingdale *(G-4905)*

PACKAGING MATERIALS: Resinous Impregnated Paper

Cameo Process Corp .... G 914 948-0082
  White Plains *(G-16435)*

PACKAGING: Blister Or Bubble Formed, Plastic

Di Domenico Packaging Co Inc .... G 718 727-5454
  Staten Island *(G-15068)*
Formatix Corp .... E 631 467-3399
  Ronkonkoma *(G-14342)*

PACKING & CRATING SVC

Precision Techniques Inc .... D 718 991-1440
  Stony Point *(G-15175)*

PACKING & CRATING SVCS: Containerized Goods For Shipping

New York Air Brake LLC .... E 315 786-5576
  Watertown *(G-16028)*

Employee Codes: A=Over 500 employees, B=251-500
C=101-250, D=51-100, E=20-50, F=10-19, G=5-9

PACKING MATERIALS: Mechanical   PRODUCT SECTION

PACKING MATERIALS: Mechanical

Bag Arts Ltd .... G 212 684-7020
  New York *(G-9000)*
Gaddis Industrial Equipment .... F 516 759-3100
  Glen Cove *(G-5367)*
Technical Packaging Inc .... F 516 223-2300
  Baldwin *(G-545)*
Unique Packaging Corporation .... G 514 341-5872
  Champlain *(G-3416)*

PACKING: Metallic

Commercial Gaskets New York .... F 212 244-8130
  New York *(G-9365)*

PADDING: Foamed Plastics

Arm Rochester Inc .... F 585 354-5077
  Rochester *(G-13639)*
Philpac Corporation .... E 716 875-8005
  Buffalo *(G-3002)*

PADS: Desk, Exc Paper

Star Desk Pad Co Inc .... E 914 963-9400
  Yonkers *(G-16800)*

PADS: Desk, Paper, Made From Purchased Materials

General Diaries Corporation .... F 516 371-2244
  Inwood *(G-6491)*

PADS: Mattress

Continental Quilting Co Inc .... E 718 499-9100
  New Hyde Park *(G-8525)*
Excellent Art Mfg Corp .... F 718 388-7075
  Inwood *(G-6489)*

PAGERS: One-way

Bayside Beepers & Cellular .... G 718 343-3888
  Glen Oaks *(G-5386)*

PAINT STORE

Atlas Coatings Group Corp .... D 718 469-8787
  Brooklyn *(G-1572)*
Mercury Paint Corporation .... D 718 469-8787
  Brooklyn *(G-2194)*
Nautical Marine Paint Corp .... E 718 462-7000
  Brooklyn *(G-2249)*
Starlite Pnt & Varnish Co Inc .... G 718 292-6420
  Bronx *(G-1393)*

PAINTING SVC: Metal Prdts

Aircraft Finishing Corp .... F 631 422-5000
  West Babylon *(G-16130)*
Buffalo Finishing Works Inc .... G 716 893-5266
  Buffalo *(G-2743)*
Buffalo Metal Finishing Co .... G 716 883-2751
  Buffalo *(G-2749)*
Color Craft Finishing Corp .... F 631 563-3230
  Bohemia *(G-998)*
D & I Finishing Inc .... G 631 471-3034
  Bohemia *(G-1007)*
Duzmor Painting Inc .... G 585 768-4760
  Le Roy *(G-7117)*
Industrial Paint Services Corp .... F 607 687-0107
  Owego *(G-12797)*
Keymark Corporation .... A 518 853-3421
  Fonda *(G-5066)*
Mac Artspray Finishing Corp .... F 718 649-3800
  Brooklyn *(G-2148)*
Rims Like New Inc .... F 845 537-0396
  Middletown *(G-8174)*
Tailored Coatings Inc .... E 716 893-4869
  Buffalo *(G-3086)*

PAINTS & ADDITIVES

Atlas Coatings Group Corp .... D 718 469-8787
  Brooklyn *(G-1572)*
Fougera Pharmaceuticals Inc .... C 631 454-7677
  Melville *(G-8026)*
General Coatings Tech Inc .... E 718 821-1232
  Ridgewood *(G-13537)*
Inglis Co Inc .... G 315 475-1315
  Syracuse *(G-15343)*
Liberty Panel Center Inc .... F 718 647-2763
  Brooklyn *(G-2116)*
Mercury Paint Corporation .... D 718 469-8787
  Brooklyn *(G-2194)*
Reddi Car Corp .... G 631 589-3141
  Sayville *(G-14634)*
Sml Brothers Holding Corp .... D 718 402-2000
  Bronx *(G-1387)*
Starlite Pnt & Varnish Co Inc .... G 718 292-6420
  Bronx *(G-1393)*
T C Dunham Paint Company Inc .... E 914 969-4202
  Yonkers *(G-16801)*
T J Ronan Paint Corp .... E 718 292-1100
  Bronx *(G-1398)*

PAINTS & ALLIED PRODUCTS

A & B Color Corp (del) .... G 718 441-5482
  Kew Gardens *(G-6869)*
Angiotech Biocoatings Corp .... E 585 321-1130
  Henrietta *(G-6030)*
Anthony River Inc .... F 315 475-1315
  Syracuse *(G-15244)*
Atc Plastics LLC .... E 212 375-2515
  New York *(G-8943)*
B & F Architectural Support Gr .... E 212 279-6488
  New York *(G-8987)*
Barson Composites Corporation .... E 516 752-7882
  Old Bethpage *(G-12583)*
Benjamin Moore & Co .... E 518 736-1723
  Johnstown *(G-6824)*
Cytec Industries Inc .... D 716 372-9650
  Olean *(G-12598)*
Eric S Turner & Company Inc .... F 914 235-7114
  New Rochelle *(G-8602)*
Fayette Street Coatings Inc .... E 315 488-5401
  Liverpool *(G-7233)*
Garco Manufacturing Corp Inc .... G 718 287-3330
  Brooklyn *(G-1917)*
Heany Industries Inc .... D 585 889-2700
  Scottsville *(G-14750)*
Jrlon Inc .... D 315 597-4067
  Palmyra *(G-12855)*
Nautical Marine Paint Corp .... E 718 462-7000
  Brooklyn *(G-2249)*
Nortek Powder Coating LLC .... F 315 337-2339
  Rome *(G-14263)*
Peter Kwasny Inc .... G 727 641-1462
  Hauppauge *(G-5913)*
Yewtree Millworks Corp .... G 914 320-5851
  Yonkers *(G-16809)*

PAINTS & VARNISHES: Plastics Based

Industrial Finishing Products .... F 718 342-4871
  Brooklyn *(G-2000)*

PAINTS, VARNISHES & SPLYS, WHOLESALE: Paints

A & B Color Corp (del) .... G 718 441-5482
  Kew Gardens *(G-6869)*
Benjamin Moore & Co .... E 518 736-1723
  Johnstown *(G-6824)*

PALLET REPAIR SVCS

Four-Way Pallet Corp .... E 631 351-3401
  Huntington Station *(G-6442)*

PALLETS

A D Bowman & Son Lumber Co .... E 607 692-2595
  Castle Creek *(G-3294)*
Best Pallet & Crate LLC .... G 518 438-2945
  Albany *(G-47)*
Four-Way Pallet Corp .... E 631 351-3401
  Huntington Station *(G-6442)*
Just Wood Pallets Inc .... G 718 644-7013
  New Windsor *(G-8647)*
North Shore Pallet Inc .... G 631 673-4700
  Huntington Station *(G-6454)*
Pooran Pallet Inc .... G 718 938-7970
  Bronx *(G-1361)*
Sanjay Pallets Inc .... G 347 590-2485
  Bronx *(G-1379)*
Steven Coffey Pallet S Inc .... G 585 261-6783
  Rochester *(G-14145)*

PALLETS & SKIDS: Wood

Chemung Cnty Chpter Nysarc Inc .... C 607 734-1625
  Elmira *(G-4477)*
Dimensional Mills Inc .... E 518 746-1047
  Hudson Falls *(G-6377)*
McIntosh Box & Pallet Co Inc .... F 315 789-8750
  Geneva *(G-5329)*
McIntosh Box & Pallet Co Inc .... E 315 446-9350
  Rome *(G-14257)*
Nefab Packaging North East LLC .... E 518 346-9105
  Scotia *(G-14744)*
Ongweoweh Corp .... D 607 266-7070
  Ithaca *(G-6602)*
Pallet Services Inc .... C 716 873-7700
  Clarence *(G-3537)*
Reuter Pallet Pkg Sys Inc .... G 845 457-9937
  Montgomery *(G-8317)*

PALLETS: Wood & Metal Combination

Pallet Division Inc .... G 585 328-3780
  Rochester *(G-14004)*

PALLETS: Wooden

Abbot & Abbot Box Corp .... F 888 930-5972
  Long Island City *(G-7365)*
B & B Lumber Company Inc .... C 866 282-0582
  Jamesville *(G-6763)*
B&B Albany Pallet Company LLC .... E 315 492-1786
  Jamesville *(G-6764)*
Berry Industrial Group Inc .... G 845 353-8338
  Nyack *(G-12501)*
CDF Indstrial Pckg Sltions Inc .... F 716 672-2984
  Fredonia *(G-5125)*
Clements Burrville Sawmill .... G 315 782-4549
  Watertown *(G-16008)*
Custom Shipping Products Inc .... F 716 355-4437
  Clymer *(G-3599)*
Dwa Pallet Inc .... G 518 746-1047
  Hudson Falls *(G-6378)*
Essex Box & Pallet Co Inc .... E 518 834-7279
  Keeseville *(G-6850)*
Great Lakes Specialites .... G 716 672-4622
  Fredonia *(G-5127)*
Lindley Wood Works Inc .... F 607 523-7786
  Lindley *(G-7207)*
McIntosh Box & Pallet Co Inc .... G 716 825-4122
  Buffalo *(G-2942)*
McIntosh Box & Pallet Co Inc .... D 315 675-8511
  Bernhards Bay *(G-833)*
Neville Mfg Svc & Dist Inc .... E 716 834-3038
  Cheektowaga *(G-3454)*
Northeast Pallet & Cont Co Inc .... F 518 271-0535
  Troy *(G-15613)*
Orleans Pallet Company Inc .... F 585 589-0781
  Albion *(G-160)*
Pallet Services Inc .... E 585 647-4020
  Rochester *(G-14005)*
Pallets Inc .... E 518 747-4177
  Fort Edward *(G-5097)*
Pallets R US Inc .... E 631 758-2360
  Bellport *(G-811)*
Paul Bunyan Products Inc .... G 315 696-6164
  Cortland *(G-3888)*
Peco Pallet Inc .... E 914 376-5444
  Irvington *(G-6509)*
Peter C Herman Inc .... E 315 926-4100
  Marion *(G-7805)*
Taylor Brothers Inc .... F 607 625-2828
  Apalachin *(G-372)*
Vansantis Development Inc .... E 315 461-0113
  Liverpool *(G-7268)*
Wolfe Lumber Mill Inc .... G 716 772-7750
  Gasport *(G-5309)*

PANEL & DISTRIBUTION BOARDS: Electric

Allied Circuits LLC .... E 716 551-0285
  Buffalo *(G-2692)*
Claddagh Electronics Ltd .... E 718 784-0571
  Long Island City *(G-7410)*

PANELS: Building, Wood

Harvest Homes Inc .... E 518 895-2341
  Delanson *(G-4069)*

PANELS: Cardboard, Die-Cut, Made From Purchased Materials

Hubray Inc .... F 800 645-2855
  North Baldwin *(G-12364)*

PAPER & BOARD: Die-cut

All Out Die Cutting Inc .... E 718 346-6666
  Brooklyn *(G-1508)*

PAPER: Adding Machine Rolls, Made From Purchased Materials

Company	Code	Phone
American Dsplay Die Ctters Inc New York *(G-8826)*	E	212 645-1274
Art Industries of New York New York *(G-8914)*	E	212 633-9200
Borden & Riley Paper Co Inc Hollis *(G-6231)*	E	718 454-9494
Dia New York *(G-9518)*	G	212 675-4097
General Die and Die Cutng Inc Massapequa Park *(G-7890)*	D	516 665-3584
General Fibre Products Corp New Hyde Park *(G-8536)*	D	516 358-7500
Kleer-Fax Inc Amityville *(G-295)*	D	631 225-1100
Leather Indexes Corp Hicksville *(G-6103)*	D	516 827-1900
Manufacturers Indexing Pdts Halesite *(G-5658)*	G	631 271-0956
Mid Island Die Cutting Corp Farmingdale *(G-4823)*	C	631 293-0180
Miken Companies Inc Buffalo *(G-2946)*	D	716 668-6311
New York Cutting & Gumming Co Middletown *(G-8168)*	E	212 563-4146
Norampac New York City Inc Maspeth *(G-7863)*	C	718 340-2100
Paperworld Inc Bellmore *(G-790)*	E	516 221-2702
Premier Packaging Corporation Victor *(G-15861)*	E	585 924-8460
S & S Prtg Die-Cutting Co Inc Brooklyn *(G-2434)*	F	718 388-8990
Spectrum Prtg Lithography Inc New York *(G-11665)*	E	212 255-3131

PAPER CONVERTING

Company	Code	Phone
Aigner Label Holder Corp New Windsor *(G-8634)*	F	845 562-4510
Beetins Wholesale Inc Staten Island *(G-15049)*	F	718 524-0899
Best Time Processor LLC Richmond Hill *(G-13499)*	G	917 455-4126
Eagles Nest Holdings LLC New York *(G-9604)*	E	513 874-5270
Gardei Industries LLC North Tonawanda *(G-12429)*	F	716 693-7100
Gavin Mfg Corp Farmingdale *(G-4770)*	E	631 467-0040
Graphic Cntrls Acqisition Corp Buffalo *(G-2853)*	B	716 853-7500
Graphic Controls Holdings Inc Buffalo *(G-2854)*	F	716 853-7500
Interface Performance Mtls Beaver Falls *(G-766)*	F	315 346-3100
Katz Group Americas Inc Sanborn *(G-14548)*	E	716 995-3059
Marketing Group International Northport *(G-12472)*	G	631 754-8095
Noteworthy Industries Inc Amsterdam *(G-356)*	C	518 842-2662
P C I Paper Conversions Inc Syracuse *(G-15389)*	C	315 437-1641
Pack America Corp New York *(G-11092)*	G	212 508-6666
Paradigm Mktg Consortium Inc Syosset *(G-15227)*	E	516 496-0000
RB Converting Inc Binghamton *(G-911)*	G	607 777-1325
Sappi North America Inc White Plains *(G-16503)*	D	914 696-5544
Trinity Packaging Corporation Armonk *(G-411)*	F	914 273-4111
Waymor1 Inc Cambridge *(G-3184)*	E	518 677-8511

PAPER MANUFACTURERS: Exc Newsprint

Company	Code	Phone
Albany International Corp Menands *(G-8079)*	C	518 445-2230
Ampac Paper LLC Walden *(G-15890)*	G	845 713-6600
Atlas Recycling LLC New York *(G-8956)*	G	212 925-3280
Bestwall LLC Plattsburgh *(G-13109)*	A	518 561-3500
Burrows Paper Corporation Little Falls *(G-7208)*	D	315 823-2300
Carta Usa LLC Rochester *(G-13693)*	E	585 436-3012
Clearwater Paper Corporation Gouverneur *(G-5489)*	D	315 287-1200
Daniel O Reich Incorporated Brooklyn *(G-1756)*	F	718 748-6000
Dunmore Corporation Brewster *(G-1163)*	D	845 279-5061
Essity Prof Hygiene N Amer LLC Saratoga Springs *(G-14579)*	C	518 583-2785
Euro Fine Paper Inc Garden City *(G-5258)*	G	516 238-5253
Freeport Paper Industries Inc Central Islip *(G-3370)*	D	631 851-1555
Global Tissue Group Inc Medford *(G-7948)*	E	631 924-3019
International Paper Company Ticonderoga *(G-15511)*	A	518 585-6761
International Paper Company Tuxedo Park *(G-15657)*	C	845 986-6409
International Paper Company Utica *(G-15716)*	C	315 797-5120
Lenaro Paper Co Inc Central Islip *(G-3376)*	F	631 439-8800
Linden Meyr Munroe Inc Latham *(G-7086)*	F	518 471-5111
Minimill Technologies Inc Syracuse *(G-15374)*	F	315 692-4557
Mohawk Fine Papers Inc Cohoes *(G-3615)*	E	518 237-1741
Mohawk Fine Papers Inc Cohoes *(G-3614)*	B	518 237-1740
Omniafiltra LLC Beaver Falls *(G-767)*	E	315 346-7300
Potsdam Specialty Paper Inc Potsdam *(G-13321)*	C	315 265-4000
Twin Rivers Paper Company LLC Little Falls *(G-7215)*	A	315 823-2300
US Alliance Paper Inc Edgewood *(G-4422)*	C	631 254-3030
Verso Corporation New York *(G-12014)*	B	212 599-2700
Verso Paper Management LP New York *(G-12015)*	A	781 320-8660
Verso Paper Management LP New York *(G-12016)*	C	212 599-2700

PAPER PRDTS

Company	Code	Phone
Bigname Commerce LLC Amityville *(G-265)*	D	631 693-1070

PAPER PRDTS: Feminine Hygiene Prdts

Company	Code	Phone
Corman USA Inc Staten Island *(G-15066)*	G	718 727-7455
Maxim Hygiene Products Inc Mineola *(G-8236)*	F	516 621-3323
Rochester Midland Corporation Rochester *(G-14088)*	C	585 336-2200

PAPER PRDTS: Infant & Baby Prdts

Company	Code	Phone
Kas Direct LLC Westbury *(G-16347)*	E	516 934-0541
Kimberly-Clark Corporation New York *(G-10447)*	D	212 554-4252
Skip Hop Inc New York *(G-11610)*	E	646 902-9874
Skip Hop Holdings Inc New York *(G-11611)*	G	212 868-9850

PAPER PRDTS: Napkin Stock

Company	Code	Phone
Essity Prof Hygiene N Amer LLC Greenwich *(G-5638)*	E	518 692-8434

PAPER PRDTS: Napkins, Sanitary, Made From Purchased Material

Company	Code	Phone
Precare Corp Hauppauge *(G-5920)*	G	631 667-1055

PAPER PRDTS: Pattern Tissue

Company	Code	Phone
Stephen Singer Pattern Co Inc New York *(G-11706)*	F	212 947-2902

PAPER PRDTS: Pressed Pulp Prdts

Company	Code	Phone
Huhtamaki Inc Fulton *(G-5220)*	A	315 593-5311

PAPER PRDTS: Sanitary

Company	Code	Phone
Attends Healthcare Inc New York *(G-8958)*	A	212 338-5100
Becks Classic Mfg Inc Brentwood *(G-1128)*	D	631 435-3800
Bestwall LLC Plattsburgh *(G-13109)*	A	518 561-3500
Cellu Tissue - Long Island LLC Central Islip *(G-3361)*	C	631 232-2626
Crosstex International Inc Hauppauge *(G-5805)*	D	631 582-6777
First Quality Products Inc Great Neck *(G-5557)*	F	516 829-4949
Monthly Gift Inc New York *(G-10840)*	G	888 444-9661
Nice-Pak Products Inc Orangeburg *(G-12684)*	B	845 365-2772
Nutek Disposables Inc Great Neck *(G-5574)*	D	516 829-3030
Precare Corp Hauppauge *(G-5919)*	G	631 524-5171
Professional Disposables Inc Orangeburg *(G-12689)*	A	845 365-1700
Sqp Inc Schenectady *(G-14716)*	C	518 831-6800
Waymor1 Inc Cambridge *(G-3184)*	E	518 677-8511

PAPER PRDTS: Sanitary Tissue Paper

Company	Code	Phone
Kimberly-Clark Corporation New York *(G-10447)*	D	212 554-4252

PAPER PRDTS: Tampons, Sanitary, Made From Purchased Material

Company	Code	Phone
Alyk Inc New York *(G-8815)*	F	917 968-2552
L VII Resilient LLC Medford *(G-7957)*	F	631 987-5819

PAPER PRDTS: Toilet Paper, Made From Purchased Materials

Company	Code	Phone
Deluxe Packaging Corp Saugerties *(G-14607)*	F	845 246-6090

PAPER PRDTS: Toweling Tissue

Company	Code	Phone
Crosstex International Inc Hauppauge *(G-5805)*	D	631 582-6777

PAPER PRDTS: Towels, Napkins/Tissue Paper, From Purchd Mtrls

Company	Code	Phone
Cascades Tssue Group-Sales Inc Waterford *(G-15973)*	D	518 238-1900
First Quality Hygienic Inc Great Neck *(G-5556)*	G	516 829-3030
Florelle Tissue Corporation Brownville *(G-2671)*	E	647 997-7405
HFC Prestige Intl US LLC New York *(G-10091)*	A	212 389-7800
N3a Corporation Inwood *(G-6496)*	G	516 284-6799
Select Products Holdings LLC Huntington *(G-6416)*	E	631 421-6000

PAPER, WHOLESALE: Fine

Company	Code	Phone
Lenaro Paper Co Inc Central Islip *(G-3376)*	F	631 439-8800
Xerox Corporation Rochester *(G-14214)*	C	585 427-4500

PAPER, WHOLESALE: Printing

Company	Code	Phone
Chesu Inc East Hampton *(G-4234)*	F	239 564-2803
Malone Industrial Press Inc Malone *(G-7724)*	G	518 483-5880

PAPER: Absorbent

Company	Code	Phone
Cascades Tssue Group-Sales Inc Waterford *(G-15974)*	E	819 363-5100
National Paper Converting Inc Owego *(G-12800)*	G	607 687-6049

PAPER: Adding Machine Rolls, Made From Purchased Materials

Company	Code	Phone
Gaylord Bros Inc North Syracuse *(G-12402)*	D	315 457-5070

Employee Codes: A=Over 500 employees, B=251-500, C=101-250, D=51-100, E=20-50, F=10-19, G=5-9

PAPER: Adding Machine Rolls, Made From Purchased Materials — PRODUCT SECTION

Paperworld Inc .... E 516 221-2702
  Bellmore *(G-790)*

PAPER: Adhesive

CCL Label Inc .... C 716 852-2155
  Buffalo *(G-2762)*
Cove Point Holdings LLC .... E 212 599-3388
  New York *(G-9413)*
Oaklee International Inc .... D 631 436-7900
  Ronkonkoma *(G-14389)*
Rochester 100 Inc .... C 585 475-0200
  Rochester *(G-14078)*
Triangle Label Tag Inc .... G 718 875-3030
  Brooklyn *(G-2583)*

PAPER: Art

Donne Dieu Paper Mill Inc .... G 212 226-0573
  Brooklyn *(G-1788)*

PAPER: Bristols

Bristol Core Inc .... F 585 919-0302
  Canandaigua *(G-3212)*
Bristol/White Plains .... G 914 681-1800
  White Plains *(G-16431)*

PAPER: Building, Insulating & Packaging

CCT (us) Inc .... F 716 297-7509
  Niagara Falls *(G-12269)*
Howard J Moore Company Inc .... E 631 351-8467
  Plainview *(G-13062)*

PAPER: Business Form

Bigrow Paper Mfg Corp .... F 718 624-4439
  Brooklyn *(G-1611)*
Datagraphic Business Systems .... G 516 485-9069
  Brentwood *(G-1130)*

PAPER: Card

Lion Die-Cutting Co Inc .... E 718 383-8841
  Brooklyn *(G-2127)*

PAPER: Chemically Treated, Made From Purchased Materials

Micro Essential Laboratory .... E 718 338-3618
  Brooklyn *(G-2205)*

PAPER: Cigarette

Schweitzer-Mauduit Intl Inc .... C 518 329-4222
  Ancram *(G-365)*

PAPER: Cloth, Lined, Made From Purchased Materials

Albany International Corp .... D 518 447-6400
  Menands *(G-8080)*

PAPER: Coated & Laminated, NEC

A-One Laminating Corp .... G 718 266-6002
  Brooklyn *(G-1464)*
C & R De Santis Inc .... E 718 447-5076
  Staten Island *(G-15057)*
Classic Labels Inc .... E 631 467-2300
  Patchogue *(G-12863)*
Clp Holdings LLC .... G 917 846-5094
  New York *(G-9334)*
Dunmore Corporation .... D 845 279-5061
  Brewster *(G-1163)*
Felix Schoeller North Amer Inc .... D 315 298-8425
  Pulaski *(G-13379)*
Greenbush Tape & Label Inc .... E 518 465-2389
  Albany *(G-79)*
K Sidrane Inc .... E 631 393-6974
  Farmingdale *(G-4796)*
Liberty Label Mfg Inc .... F 631 737-2365
  Holbrook *(G-6195)*
Miken Companies Inc .... D 716 668-6311
  Buffalo *(G-2946)*
Mohawk Fine Papers Inc .... B 518 237-1740
  Cohoes *(G-3614)*
Neenah Northeast LLC .... C 315 376-3571
  Lowville *(G-7654)*
New York Cutting & Gumming Co ... E 212 563-4146
  Middletown *(G-8168)*
P C I Paper Conversions Inc .... C 315 437-1641
  Syracuse *(G-15389)*

Princeton Label & Packaging .... E 609 490-0800
  Patchogue *(G-12875)*
S & S Prtg Die-Cutting Co Inc .... F 718 388-8990
  Brooklyn *(G-2434)*
Uniflex Holdings LLC .... F 516 932-2000
  Hauppauge *(G-5964)*

PAPER: Coated, Exc Photographic, Carbon Or Abrasive

Janice Moses Represents .... G 212 898-4898
  New York *(G-10307)*

PAPER: Corrugated

General Fibre Products Corp .... D 516 358-7500
  New Hyde Park *(G-8536)*

PAPER: Envelope

Tag Envelope Co Inc .... E 718 389-6844
  College Point *(G-3669)*

PAPER: Filter

Andex Corp .... E 585 328-3790
  Rochester *(G-13632)*
Hollingsworth & Vose Company .... C 518 695-8000
  Greenwich *(G-5641)*
Knowlton Technologies LLC .... C 315 782-0600
  Watertown *(G-16024)*

PAPER: Kraft

APC Paper Company Inc .... D 315 384-4225
  Norfolk *(G-12356)*
Kapstone Container Corporation ..... D 518 842-2450
  Amsterdam *(G-342)*
Scalamandre Wallpaper Inc .... B 631 467-8800
  Hauppauge *(G-5934)*

PAPER: Parchment

Palisades Paper Inc .... G 845 354-0333
  Spring Valley *(G-15004)*

PAPER: Printer

International Paper Company .... C 607 775-1550
  Conklin *(G-3728)*
Summit Fincl Disclosure LLC .... E 212 913-0510
  New York *(G-11739)*

PAPER: Specialty

Cottrell Paper Company Inc .... E 518 885-1702
  Rock City Falls *(G-14222)*
Dunn Paper - Natural Dam Inc .... D 315 287-1200
  Gouverneur *(G-5490)*
Gratitude & Company Inc .... E 607 277-3188
  Ithaca *(G-6579)*

PAPER: Tissue

Burrows Paper Corporation .... D 315 823-2300
  Little Falls *(G-7209)*
Morcon Inc .... D 518 677-8511
  Cambridge *(G-3182)*
North End Paper Co Inc .... G 315 593-8100
  Fulton *(G-5229)*
Precare Corp .... G 631 667-1055
  Hauppauge *(G-5920)*
Twin Rivers Paper Company LLC .... E 315 348-8491
  Lyons Falls *(G-7690)*

PAPER: Wrapping

Flower Cy Tissue Mills Co Inc .... E 585 458-9200
  Rochester *(G-13810)*

PAPER: Wrapping & Packaging

Gooding Co Inc .... E 716 266-6252
  Lockport *(G-7308)*

PAPER: Writing

Automation Papers Inc .... G 315 432-0565
  Syracuse *(G-15250)*

PAPERBOARD

Alpine Paper Box Co Inc .... E 718 345-4040
  Brooklyn *(G-1514)*

American Wire Tie Inc .... E 716 337-2412
  North Collins *(G-12383)*
Carthage Specialty Pprbd Inc .... G 315 493-2120
  Carthage *(G-3287)*
Interface Performance Mtls Inc .... D 518 686-3400
  Hoosick Falls *(G-6276)*
Ms Paper Products Co Inc .... G 718 624-0248
  Brooklyn *(G-2236)*
Niagara Fiberboard Inc .... E 716 434-8881
  Lockport *(G-7322)*
Professional Packg Svcs Inc .... E 518 677-5100
  Eagle Bridge *(G-4185)*
Sonoco Products Company .... D 518 392-2000
  Chatham *(G-3430)*

PAPERBOARD CONVERTING

Allied Converters Inc .... E 914 235-1585
  New Rochelle *(G-8589)*
Mid-York Press Inc .... D 607 674-4491
  Sherburne *(G-14807)*
Setterstix Inc .... E 716 257-3451
  Cattaraugus *(G-3314)*

PAPERBOARD PRDTS: Building Insulating & Packaging

Shell Containers Inc (ny) .... E 516 352-4505
  New Hyde Park *(G-8562)*

PAPERBOARD PRDTS: Container Board

Kapstone Container Corporation ..... D 518 842-2450
  Amsterdam *(G-342)*
Pactiv LLC .... E 585 248-1213
  Pittsford *(G-13025)*
Westrock - Solvay Llc .... C 315 484-9050
  Syracuse *(G-15456)*
Westrock CP LLC .... C 315 484-9050
  Syracuse *(G-15457)*

PAPERBOARD PRDTS: Folding Boxboard

Burt Rigid Box Inc .... F 607 433-2510
  Oneonta *(G-12629)*
Di Domenico Packaging Co Inc .... G 718 727-5454
  Staten Island *(G-15068)*
Enterprise Folding Box Co Inc .... E 716 876-6421
  Buffalo *(G-2821)*
Paper Box Corp .... D 212 226-7490
  New York *(G-11101)*
Westrock Rkt Company .... C 770 448-2193
  Syracuse *(G-15458)*

PAPERBOARD PRDTS: Kraft Linerboard

Continental Kraft Corp .... G 516 681-9090
  Jericho *(G-6783)*

PAPERBOARD PRDTS: Packaging Board

Farrington Packaging Corp .... E 315 733-4600
  Utica *(G-15701)*

PAPERBOARD: Boxboard

Prestige Box Corporation .... E 516 773-3115
  Great Neck *(G-5583)*

PAPERBOARD: Liner Board

Cascades New York Inc .... C 716 285-3681
  Niagara Falls *(G-12268)*
Greenpac Mill LLC .... C 716 299-0560
  Niagara Falls *(G-12291)*
Westrock Mwv LLC .... C 212 688-5000
  New York *(G-12097)*

PAPIER-MACHE PRDTS, EXC STATUARY & ART GOODS

Specialty Quality Packg LLC .... D 914 580-3200
  Scotia *(G-14747)*

PARACHUTES

National Parachute Industries .... E 908 782-1646
  Palenville *(G-12844)*
Yoland Corporation .... E 718 499-4803
  Brooklyn *(G-2665)*

PRODUCT SECTION   PERFUMES

PARKING LOTS

Deans Paving Inc .... G 315 736-7601
  Marcy *(G-7796)*

PARTITIONS & FIXTURES: Except Wood

All American Metal Corporation .... E 516 623-0222
  Freeport *(G-5140)*
American Standard Mfg Inc .... E 518 868-2512
  Central Bridge *(G-3353)*
Avf Group Inc .... F 951 360-7111
  Cheektowaga *(G-3435)*
Bobrick Washroom Equipment Inc .... D 518 877-7444
  Clifton Park *(G-3565)*
Bridge Metal Industries LLC .... C 914 663-9200
  Mount Vernon *(G-8382)*
Core Group Displays Inc .... E 845 876-5109
  Rhinebeck *(G-13485)*
Dakota Systems Mfg Corp .... G 631 249-5811
  Farmingdale *(G-4748)*
E-Systems Group LLC .... E 607 775-1100
  Conklin *(G-3727)*
Fifty Door Partners LLC .... E 845 562-3332
  New Windsor *(G-8644)*
Hergo Ergonomic Support .... E 718 894-0639
  Maspeth *(G-7851)*
Inscape Inc .... E 716 665-6210
  Falconer *(G-4682)*
Joldeson One Aerospace Inds .... D 718 848-7396
  Ozone Park *(G-12827)*
Mass Mdsg Self Selection Eqp .... E 631 234-3300
  Bohemia *(G-1056)*
Maximum Security Products Corp ..... E 518 233-1800
  Waterford *(G-15977)*
Milton Merl & Associates Inc .... G 212 634-9292
  New York *(G-10812)*
Mobile Media Inc .... E 845 744-8080
  Pine Bush *(G-12997)*
Modu-Craft Inc .... G 716 694-0709
  Tonawanda *(G-15559)*
Storflex Holdings Inc .... C 607 962-2137
  Corning *(G-3826)*
Sturdy Store Displays Inc .... E 718 389-9919
  Brooklyn *(G-2528)*
Traco Manufacturing Inc .... C 585 343-2434
  Batavia *(G-638)*

PARTITIONS: Nonwood, Floor Attached

All American Metal Corporation .... G 516 223-1760
  Freeport *(G-5139)*
Global Steel Products Corp .... C 631 586-3455
  Deer Park *(G-3981)*
Inscape (new York) Inc .... D 716 665-6210
  Falconer *(G-4C81)*
Knickerbocker Partition Corp .... C 516 546-0550
  Melville *(G-8042)*

PARTITIONS: Solid Fiber, Made From Purchased Materials

Westrock Rkt Company .... C 770 448-2193
  Camillus *(G-3202)*

PARTITIONS: Wood & Fixtures

Artone LLC .... D 716 664-2232
  Jamestown *(G-6699)*
Custom Countertops Inc .... G 716 685-2871
  Depew *(G-4085)*
Dbs Interiors Corp .... F 631 491-3013
  West Babylon *(G-16152)*
Deakon Homes and Interiors .... F 518 271-0342
  Troy *(G-15603)*
Encore Retail Systems Inc .... F 718 385-3443
  Mamaroneck *(G-7743)*
Farrington Packaging Corp .... E 315 733-4600
  Utica *(G-15701)*
Fina Cabinet Corp .... G 718 409-2900
  Mount Vernon *(G-8398)*
Gaughan Construction Corp .... G 718 850-9577
  Richmond Hill *(G-13503)*
Greenleaf Cabinet Makers LLC .... F 315 432-4600
  Syracuse *(G-15335)*
Hamlet Products Inc .... G 914 665-0307
  Mount Vernon *(G-8405)*
Heartwood Specialties Inc .... G 607 654-0102
  Hammondsport *(G-5704)*
Home Ideal Inc .... G 718 762-8998
  Flushing *(G-5009)*

Industrial Support Inc .... D 716 662-2954
  Buffalo *(G-2883)*
Integrated Wood Components Inc .... E 607 467-1739
  Deposit *(G-4108)*
Inter State Laminates Inc .... E 518 283-8355
  Poestenkill *(G-13181)*
Michael P Mmarr .... G 315 623-9380
  Constantia *(G-3740)*
New Dimensions Office Group .... D 718 387-0995
  Brooklyn *(G-2259)*
Premier Woodworking Inc .... F 631 236-4100
  Hauppauge *(G-5922)*
Steelcraft Manufacturing Co .... F 718 277-2404
  Brooklyn *(G-2516)*
Stein Industries Inc .... F 631 789-2222
  Amityville *(G-316)*
Universal Designs Inc .... G 718 721-1111
  Long Island City *(G-7625)*
Wineracksscom Inc .... F 845 658-7181
  Tillson *(G-15515)*

PARTITIONS: Wood, Floor Attached

Steeldeck Ny Inc .... F 718 599-3700
  Brooklyn *(G-2517)*

PARTS: Metal

All-State Diversified Pdts Inc .... E 315 472-4728
  Syracuse *(G-15239)*
Ross Metal Fabricators Inc .... F 631 586-7000
  Deer Park *(G-4038)*
Zone Fabricators Inc .... F 718 272-0200
  Ozone Park *(G-12834)*

PARTY & SPECIAL EVENT PLANNING SVCS

Proof 7 Ltd .... F 212 680-1843
  New York *(G-11264)*

PASTES, FLAVORING

American Almond Pdts Co Inc .... D 718 875-8310
  Brooklyn *(G-1519)*

PATENT OWNERS & LESSORS

Compositech Ltd .... C 516 835-1458
  Woodbury *(G-16615)*
Eagle Telephonics Inc .... F 631 471-3600
  Bohemia *(G-1017)*
General Microwave Corporation .... F 516 802-0900
  Syosset *(G-15219)*
Rainforest Inc .... F 212 575-7620
  New York *(G-11319)*

PATTERNS: Indl

A & T Tooling LLC .... G 716 601-7299
  Lancaster *(G-7000)*
Armstrong Mold Corporation .... E 315 437-1517
  East Syracuse *(G-4320)*
Armstrong Mold Corporation .... D 315 437-1517
  East Syracuse *(G-4321)*
Bianca Group Ltd .... G 212 768-3011
  New York *(G-9070)*
City Pattern Shop Inc .... F 315 463-5239
  Syracuse *(G-15278)*
K & H Precision Products Inc .... E 585 624-4894
  Honeoye Falls *(G-6269)*
W N R Pattern & Tool Inc .... G 716 681-9334
  Lancaster *(G-7053)*
Wolff & Dungey Inc .... G 315 475-2105
  Syracuse *(G-15460)*
Woodward Industries Inc .... G 716 692-2242
  Tonawanda *(G-15591)*

PAVERS

Lomin Construction Company .... G 516 759-5734
  Glen Head *(G-5382)*
Technopaving New York Inc .... G 631 351-6472
  Huntington Station *(G-6461)*

PAVING MATERIALS: Prefabricated, Concrete

Copeland Coating Company Inc .... F 518 766-2932
  Nassau *(G-8477)*

PAVING MIXTURES

Dolomite Products Company Inc .... E 315 524-1998
  Rochester *(G-13749)*

Dolomite Products Company Inc .... F 607 324-3636
  Hornell *(G-6295)*
Dolomite Products Company Inc .... F 585 768-7295
  Le Roy *(G-7115)*
Iroquois Rock Products Inc .... F 585 381-7010
  Rochester *(G-13887)*

PENCILS & PENS WHOLESALERS

Mark Dri Products Inc .... C 516 484-6200
  Bethpage *(G-846)*
Pda Panache Corp .... G 631 776-0523
  Bohemia *(G-1073)*

PENS & PARTS: Ball Point

Mercury Pen Company Inc .... G 518 899-9653
  Ballston Lake *(G-569)*

PENS & PARTS: Cartridges, Refill, Ball Point

STS Refill America LLC .... G 516 934-8008
  Hicksville *(G-6133)*

PENS & PENCILS: Mechanical, NEC

Aakron Rule Corp .... C 716 542-5483
  Akron *(G-16)*
Harper Products Ltd .... F 516 997-2330
  Westbury *(G-16340)*
Henry Morgan .... F 718 317-5013
  Staten Island *(G-15085)*
Pelican Products Co Inc .... F 718 860-3220
  Bronx *(G-1354)*
Pintrill LLC .... F 718 782-1000
  Brooklyn *(G-2320)*

PERFUME: Concentrated

Inter Parfums Usa LLC .... G 212 983-2640
  New York *(G-10235)*
Nr Fragrances & Cosmetics Inc .... G 212 686-4006
  New York *(G-11002)*
Thompson Ferrier LLC .... G 212 244-2212
  New York *(G-11823)*

PERFUME: Perfumes, Natural Or Synthetic

Christian Dior Perfumes LLC .... E 212 931-2200
  New York *(G-9291)*
Delbia Do Company Inc .... E 718 585-2226
  Bronx *(G-1255)*
Elias Fragrances Inc .... F 718 693-6400
  Rye Brook *(G-14491)*

PERFUMES

Alan F Bourguet .... F 516 883-4315
  Port Washington *(G-13241)*
Cassini Parfums Ltd .... G 212 753-7540
  New York *(G-9222)*
Coty Inc .... G 212 389-7300
  New York *(G-9405)*
Coty US LLC .... C 212 389-7000
  New York *(G-9406)*
Coty US LLC .... B 212 389-7000
  Uniondale *(G-15664)*
Delbia Do Company Inc .... F 718 585-2226
  Bronx *(G-1256)*
Editions De Prfums Madison LLC ...... F 646 666-0527
  New York *(G-9628)*
Estee Lauder Inc .... F 631 531-1000
  Melville *(G-8022)*
F L Demeter Inc .... E 516 487-5187
  Great Neck *(G-5552)*
Fragrance Acquisitions LLC .... D 845 534-9172
  Newburgh *(G-12222)*
Hogan Flavors & Fragrances .... E 212 598-4310
  New York *(G-10112)*
Jean Philippe Fragrances LLC .... E 212 983-2640
  New York *(G-10322)*
JP Filling Inc .... D 845 534-4793
  Mountainville *(G-8456)*
Le Labo Holding LLC .... E 646 490-6200
  Brooklyn *(G-2100)*
Le Labo Holding LLC .... E 646 719-1740
  Brooklyn *(G-2101)*
Perfume Amrcana Whlesalers Inc ..... F 212 683-8029
  New York *(G-11155)*
Perfumers Workshop Intl Ltd .... F 212 644-8950
  New York *(G-11156)*
Selective Beauty Corporation .... F 585 336-7600
  New York *(G-11539)*

Employee Codes: A=Over 500 employees, B=251-500
C=101-250, D=51-100, E=20-50, F=10-19, G=5-9

2019 Harris
New York Manufacturers Directory

PERFUMES

Sixthscents Paper Products Ltd..........G...... 212 627-5066
Long Island City *(G-7592)*

PERLITE: Processed

Skyline LLC..........E...... 631 403-4131
East Setauket *(G-4310)*

PERSONAL APPEARANCE SVCS

Womens Health Care PC..........G...... 718 850-0009
Richmond Hill *(G-13517)*

PERSONAL CREDIT INSTITUTIONS: Consumer Finance Companies

Steel Partners Holdings LP..........D...... 212 520-2300
New York *(G-11699)*

PEST CONTROL SVCS

Hawthorne Garden Company..........F...... 516 883-6550
Port Washington *(G-13263)*

PET ACCESS: Collars, Leashes, Etc, Exc Leather

American Leather Specialties..........D...... 800 556-6488
Brooklyn *(G-1523)*

PET COLLARS, LEASHES, MUZZLES & HARNESSES: Leather

Dog Good Products LLC..........G...... 212 789-7000
New York *(G-9545)*
Finger Lakes Lea Crafters LLC..........F...... 315 252-4107
Auburn *(G-478)*
Max 200 Performance Dog Eqp..........E...... 315 776-9588
Port Byron *(G-13189)*

PET SPLYS

Animal Pantry..........G...... 631 673-3666
Huntington *(G-6391)*
Clara Papa..........G...... 315 733-2660
Utica *(G-15682)*
Four Paws Products Ltd..........D...... 631 436-7421
Ronkonkoma *(G-14343)*
Grand Island Animal Hospital..........E...... 716 773-7645
Grand Island *(G-5502)*
Image Tech..........F...... 716 635-0167
Buffalo *(G-2880)*
Kittywalk Systems Inc..........G...... 516 627-8418
Port Washington *(G-13276)*
Skaffles Group LLC..........F...... 212 944-9494
New York *(G-11606)*
Soggy Doggy Productions LLC..........G...... 877 504-4811
Larchmont *(G-7059)*
Spectrum Brands Inc..........B...... 631 232-1200
Hauppauge *(G-5945)*
Unique Petz LLC..........E...... 212 714-1800
New York *(G-11950)*

PET SPLYS WHOLESALERS

American Leather Specialties..........D...... 800 556-6488
Brooklyn *(G-1523)*
Clara Papa..........G...... 315 733-2660
Utica *(G-15682)*

PETROLEUM & PETROLEUM PRDTS, WHOLESALE Engine Fuels & Oils

Bass Oil Company Inc..........E...... 718 628-4444
Brooklyn *(G-1588)*

PETROLEUM & PETROLEUM PRDTS, WHOLESALE Fuel Oil

Alba Fuel Corp..........G...... 718 931-1700
Bronx *(G-1214)*

PETROLEUM & PETROLEUM PRDTS, WHOLESALE: Bulk Stations

Hess Corporation..........B...... 212 997-8500
New York *(G-10085)*

PETROLEUM PRDTS WHOLESALERS

Industrial Raw Materials LLC..........F...... 212 688-8080
Plainview *(G-13063)*

Noco Incorporated..........G...... 716 833-6626
Tonawanda *(G-15565)*

PEWTER WARE

Quest Bead & Cast Inc..........G...... 212 354-1737
New York *(G-11300)*
Silver City Group Inc..........G...... 315 363-0344
Sherrill *(G-14823)*

PHARMACEUTICAL PREPARATIONS: Adrenal

Central Islip Pharmacy Inc..........G...... 631 234-6039
Central Islip *(G-3362)*

PHARMACEUTICAL PREPARATIONS: Barbituric Acid

872 Hunts Point Pharmacy Inc..........G...... 718 991-3519
Bronx *(G-1198)*

PHARMACEUTICAL PREPARATIONS: Digitalis

Intstrux LLC..........E...... 646 688-2782
New York *(G-10261)*

PHARMACEUTICAL PREPARATIONS: Druggists' Preparations

Actavis Laboratories Ny Inc..........D...... 631 693-8000
Copiague *(G-3747)*
Advance Pharmaceutical Inc..........D...... 631 981-4600
Holtsville *(G-6236)*
Akari Therapeutics PLC..........F...... 646 350-0702
New York *(G-8779)*
Asence Inc..........E...... 347 335-2606
New York *(G-8930)*
Biomed Pharmaceuticals Inc..........G...... 914 592-0525
Hawthorne *(G-5984)*
Biotie Therapies Inc..........G...... 650 244-4850
Ardsley *(G-394)*
Bristol-Myers Squibb Company..........E...... 315 432-2000
East Syracuse *(G-4327)*
Century Grand Inc..........G...... 212 925-3838
New York *(G-9250)*
Cognigen Corporation..........D...... 716 633-3463
Buffalo *(G-2770)*
Flushing Pharmacy Inc..........C...... 718 260-8999
Brooklyn *(G-1894)*
Fougera Pharmaceuticals Inc..........C...... 631 454-7677
Melville *(G-8026)*
Fougera Pharmaceuticals Inc..........C...... 631 454-7677
Hicksville *(G-6088)*
Global Alliance For Tb..........E...... 212 227-7540
New York *(G-9935)*
Hospira Inc..........C...... 716 684-9400
Buffalo *(G-2875)*
Ima Life North America Inc..........C...... 716 695-6354
Tonawanda *(G-15550)*
Jerome Stvens Phrmcuticals Inc..........F...... 631 567-1113
Bohemia *(G-1041)*
JRS Pharma LP..........E...... 845 878-8300
Patterson *(G-12883)*
Kingston Pharma LLC..........D...... 315 705-4019
Massena *(G-7904)*
Luitpold Pharmaceuticals Inc..........B...... 631 924-4000
Shirley *(G-14838)*
Marietta Corporation..........B...... 607 753-6746
Cortland *(G-3881)*
Nutrascience Labs Inc..........E...... 631 247-0660
Farmingdale *(G-4838)*
Ony Inc Baird Researchpark..........E...... 716 636-9096
Buffalo *(G-2981)*
Pace Up Pharmaceuticals LLC..........G...... 631 450-4495
Lindenhurst *(G-7189)*
Par Pharmaceutical Inc..........B...... 845 573-5500
Chestnut Ridge *(G-3494)*
Pharbest Pharmaceuticals Inc..........E...... 631 249-5130
Farmingdale *(G-4846)*
Pharmavantage LLC..........G...... 631 321-8171
Babylon *(G-531)*
Strativa Pharmaceuticals..........F...... 201 802-4000
Spring Valley *(G-15008)*
Triceutical Inc..........F...... 631 249-0003
Bronx *(G-1406)*
Wavodyne Therapeutics Inc..........G...... 954 632-6630
West Henrietta *(G-16255)*

PHARMACEUTICAL PREPARATIONS: Medicines, Capsule Or Ampule

Futurebiotics LLC..........E...... 631 273-6300
Hauppauge *(G-5830)*
Nanorx Inc..........G...... 914 671-0224
Chappaqua *(G-3423)*

PHARMACEUTICAL PREPARATIONS: Penicillin

G C Hanford Manufacturing Co..........C...... 315 476-7418
Syracuse *(G-15328)*

PHARMACEUTICAL PREPARATIONS: Pills

A & Z Pharmaceutical Inc..........D...... 631 952-3802
Hauppauge *(G-5752)*

PHARMACEUTICAL PREPARATIONS: Powders

Athenex Pharmaceutical Div LLC..........F...... 877 463-7823
Buffalo *(G-2713)*

PHARMACEUTICAL PREPARATIONS: Procaine

Glaxosmithkline LLC..........D...... 518 239-6901
East Durham *(G-4216)*

PHARMACEUTICAL PREPARATIONS: Proprietary Drug PRDTS

Ip Med Inc..........G...... 516 766-3800
Oceanside *(G-12541)*
Time-Cap Laboratories Inc..........C...... 631 753-9090
Farmingdale *(G-4896)*

PHARMACEUTICAL PREPARATIONS: Solutions

Container Tstg Solutions LLC..........F...... 716 487-3300
Jamestown *(G-6709)*
Container Tstg Solutions LLC..........F...... 716 487-3300
Sinclairville *(G-14865)*
Guosa Life Sciences Inc..........F...... 718 813-7806
New York *(G-10010)*
Kent Chemical Corporation..........E...... 212 521-1700
New York *(G-10436)*
Medek Laboratories Inc..........E...... 845 943-4988
Monroe *(G-8277)*
Pall Corporation..........A...... 516 484-5400
Port Washington *(G-13295)*
R J S Direct Marketing Inc..........F...... 631 667-5768
Deer Park *(G-4033)*
Sterrx LLC..........E...... 518 324-7879
Plattsburgh *(G-13159)*
You First Services Inc..........F...... 716 204-7215
Buffalo *(G-3135)*
Zitomer LLC..........G...... 212 737-5560
New York *(G-12180)*

PHARMACEUTICAL PREPARATIONS: Tablets

Aiping Pharmaceutical Inc..........G...... 631 952-3802
Hauppauge *(G-5757)*
Bli International Inc..........C...... 631 940-9000
Deer Park *(G-3952)*
Chartwell Pharma Nda B2 Holdin..........G...... 845 268-5000
Congers *(G-3713)*
Innovative Labs LLC..........D...... 631 231-5522
Hauppauge *(G-5849)*
Invagen Pharmaceuticals Inc..........C...... 631 949-6367
Central Islip *(G-3372)*
Marken LLP..........G...... 631 396-7454
Farmingdale *(G-4815)*
Satnam Distributors LLC..........G...... 516 802-0600
Jericho *(G-6801)*

PHARMACEUTICALS

3v Company Inc..........E...... 718 858-7333
Brooklyn *(G-1440)*
5th Avenue Pharmacy Inc..........G...... 718 439-8585
Brooklyn *(G-1443)*
888 Pharmacy Inc..........F...... 718 871-8833
Brooklyn *(G-1447)*
Abbott Laboratories..........F...... 716 633-1904
Williamsville *(G-16566)*

Abeona Therapeutics Inc ....E....... 646 813-4712
New York *(G-8709)*
Abh Pharma Inc ....D....... 866 922-4669
Edgewood *(G-4392)*
Abraxis Bioscience LLC ....G....... 716 773-0800
Grand Island *(G-5494)*
Actinium Pharmaceuticals Inc ....E....... 646 677-3870
New York *(G-8730)*
Affymax Inc ....G....... 650 812-8700
New York *(G-8766)*
Alfred Khalily Inc ....F....... 516 504-0059
Great Neck *(G-5530)*
Allied Pharmacy Products Inc ....G....... 516 374-8862
Woodmere *(G-16639)*
Altaire Pharmaceuticals Inc ....C....... 631 722-5988
Aquebogue *(G-373)*
Amarantus Bscence Holdings Inc ....F....... 917 686-5317
New York *(G-8816)*
American Bio Medica Corp ....D....... 518 758-8158
Kinderhook *(G-6879)*
American Regent Inc ....B....... 631 924-4000
Shirley *(G-14826)*
Amneal Pharmaceuticals LLC ....E....... 908 231-1911
Brookhaven *(G-1427)*
Amneal Pharmaceuticals LLC ....E....... 631 952-0214
Brookhaven *(G-1428)*
Amneal Pharmaceuticals NY LLC ....E....... 908 947-3120
Brookhaven *(G-1429)*
Anacor Pharmaceuticals Inc ....E....... 212 733-2323
New York *(G-8851)*
Angiogenex Inc ....G....... 347 468-6799
New York *(G-8864)*
Anterios Inc ....G....... 212 303-1683
New York *(G-8876)*
Apothecus Pharmaceutical Corp ....F....... 516 624-8200
Oyster Bay *(G-12810)*
Ascent Pharmaceuticals Inc ....D....... 631 851-0550
Central Islip *(G-3356)*
Athenex Inc ....D....... 716 427-2950
Buffalo *(G-2712)*
Athenex Pharma Solutions LLC ....G....... 877 463-7823
Clarence *(G-3525)*
Auven Therapeutics MGT LP ....F....... 212 616-4000
New York *(G-8968)*
Avenue Therapeutics Inc ....G....... 781 652-4500
New York *(G-8975)*
Axim Biotechnologies Inc ....F....... 212 751-0001
New York *(G-8983)*
Azurrx Biopharma Inc ....F....... 646 699-7855
Brooklyn *(G-1577)*
Barc Usa Inc ....E....... 516 719-1052
New Hyde Park *(G-8519)*
Bausch & Lomb Holdings Inc ....G....... 585 338-6000
New York *(G-9028)*
Bausch & Lomb Incorporated ....B....... 585 338-6000
Rochester *(G-13655)*
Baxter Healthcare Corporation ....B....... 800 356-3454
Medina *(G-7972)*
Baxter International Inc ....G....... 845 457-9370
Montgomery *(G-8308)*
Beyondspring Inc ....E....... 646 305-6387
New York *(G-9066)*
Beyondspring Phrmceuticals Inc ....F....... 646 305-6387
New York *(G-9067)*
Biospecifics Technologies Corp ....G....... 516 593-7000
Lynbrook *(G-7662)*
Bristol-Myers Squibb Company ....C....... 516 832-2191
Garden City *(G-5253)*
Campbell Alliance Group Inc ....E....... 212 377-2740
New York *(G-9188)*
Cas Biosciences LLC ....C....... 844 227-2467
New York *(G-9220)*
Cellectis Inc ....F....... 347 809-5980
New York *(G-9235)*
Cerovene Inc ....F....... 845 359-1101
Orangeburg *(G-12671)*
Cerovene Inc ....F....... 845 267-2055
Valley Cottage *(G-15753)*
Chartwell Pharmaceuticals LLC ....D....... 845 268-5000
Congers *(G-3714)*
Chartwell Rx LLC ....E....... 845 268-5000
Congers *(G-3715)*
Citypharma Inc ....G....... 917 832-6035
Jackson Heights *(G-6619)*
Cleveland Biolabs Inc ....E....... 716 849-6810
Buffalo *(G-2768)*
Combe Incorporated ....C....... 914 694-5454
White Plains *(G-16439)*
Contract Pharmacal Corp ....E....... 631 231-4610
Hauppauge *(G-5798)*
Contract Pharmacal Corp ....C....... 631 231-4610
Hauppauge *(G-5799)*
Contract Pharmacal Corp ....E....... 631 231-4610
Hauppauge *(G-5800)*
Contract Pharmacal Corp ....D....... 631 231-4610
Hauppauge *(G-5801)*
Contract Pharmacal Corp ....F....... 631 231-4610
Hauppauge *(G-5803)*
Contract Phrmctcals Ltd Nagara ....C....... 716 887-3400
Buffalo *(G-2779)*
Coopersurgical Inc ....F....... 716 693-6230
North Tonawanda *(G-12424)*
CRS Nuclear Services LLC ....F....... 716 810-0688
Cheektowaga *(G-3438)*
Delcath Systems Inc ....E....... 212 489-2100
New York *(G-9497)*
Dr Reddys Laboratories NY Inc ....E....... 518 827-7702
Middleburgh *(G-8129)*
Edlaw Pharmaceuticals Inc ....E....... 631 454-6888
Farmingdale *(G-4758)*
Eli Lilly and Company ....F....... 516 622-2244
New Hyde Park *(G-8532)*
Emilior Phrm Compounding Inc ....E....... 855 426-6768
Bronx *(G-1268)*
Emphascience ....G....... 585 348-9415
Pittsford *(G-13011)*
Encysive Pharmaceuticals Inc ....E....... 212 733-2323
New York *(G-9674)*
Enumeral Biomedical Corp ....G....... 347 227-4787
New York *(G-9690)*
Enzo Life Sciences Inc ....E....... 631 694-7070
Farmingdale *(G-4760)*
Enzo Life Sciences Intl Inc ....E....... 610 941-0430
Farmingdale *(G-4761)*
Eon Labs Inc ....F....... 516 478-9700
New Hyde Park *(G-8533)*
Epic Pharma LLC ....C....... 718 276-8600
Laurelton *(G-7099)*
Equinox Aegis LLC ....G....... 212 316-9078
New York *(G-9696)*
Eyenovia Inc ....G....... 917 289-1117
New York *(G-9760)*
Fera Pharmaceuticals LLC ....F....... 516 277-1449
Locust Valley *(G-7346)*
Forest Laboratories LLC ....C....... 212 421-7850
New York *(G-9822)*
Forest Laboratories LLC ....D....... 212 421-7850
Hauppauge *(G-5828)*
Forest Labs ....G....... 631 755-1185
Farmingdale *(G-4766)*
Forest Research Institute Inc ....F....... 631 858-5200
Commack *(G-3691)*
Fortress Biotech Inc ....E....... 781 652-4500
New York *(G-9825)*
Fresenius Kabi Usa LLC ....B....... 716 773-0053
Grand Island *(G-5500)*
Fresenius Kabi USA LLC ....E....... 716 773-0800
Grand Island *(G-5501)*
Gemini Pharmaceuticals Inc ....B....... 631 543-3334
Commack *(G-3693)*
Generic Pharmaceutical Svcs ....E....... 631 348-6900
Hauppauge *(G-5832)*
Generics Bidco I LLC ....G....... 256 859-4011
Chestnut Ridge *(G-3492)*
Genzyme Corporation ....D....... 212 698-0300
New York *(G-9907)*
Geritrex LLC ....E....... 914 668-4003
Middletown *(G-8156)*
Geritrex Holdings Inc ....G....... 914 668-4003
Mount Vernon *(G-8399)*
Glaxosmithkline LLC ....E....... 845 341-7590
Montgomery *(G-8311)*
Glaxosmithkline LLC ....E....... 845 797-3259
Wappingers Falls *(G-15933)*
Glaxosmithkline LLC ....E....... 585 738-9025
Rochester *(G-13838)*
Glaxosmithkline LLC ....E....... 716 913-5679
Buffalo *(G-2850)*
Glaxosmithkline LLC ....E....... 518 852-9637
Mechanicville *(G-7931)*
Glycobia Inc ....G....... 607 339-0051
Ithaca *(G-6578)*
Greenkissny Inc ....G....... 914 304-4323
White Plains *(G-16455)*
Greentree Pharmacy Inc ....F....... 718 768-2700
Brooklyn *(G-1952)*
Health Care Products ....G....... 631 789-8228
Amityville *(G-282)*
Healthone Pharmacy Inc ....F....... 718 495-9015
Brooklyn *(G-1969)*
Hi-Tech Pharmacal Co Inc ....C....... 631 789-8228
Amityville *(G-284)*
Hi-Tech Pharmacal Co Inc ....F....... 631 789-8228
Amityville *(G-285)*
Hoffmann-La Roche Inc ....G....... 973 890-2291
New York *(G-10111)*
Hogil Pharmaceutical Corp ....F....... 914 681-1800
White Plains *(G-16460)*
Ibio Inc ....E....... 302 355-0650
New York *(G-10165)*
Innogenix Inc ....F....... 631 450-4704
Amityville *(G-287)*
Intercept Pharmaceuticals Inc ....D....... 646 747-1000
New York *(G-10238)*
Intra-Cellular Therapies Inc ....E....... 646 440-9333
New York *(G-10257)*
Invagen Pharmaceuticals Inc ....B....... 631 231-3233
Hauppauge *(G-5851)*
Irx Therapeutics Inc ....G....... 347 442-0640
Brooklyn *(G-2015)*
Izun Pharmaceuticals Corp ....F....... 212 618-6357
New York *(G-10280)*
Kadmon Corporation LLC ....F....... 212 308-6000
New York *(G-10393)*
Kadmon Holdings Inc ....D....... 212 308-6000
New York *(G-10394)*
Kaneka America LLC ....D....... 212 705-4340
New York *(G-10404)*
Kannalife Sciences Inc ....G....... 516 669-3219
Lloyd Harbor *(G-7280)*
Kbl Healthcare LP ....G....... 212 319-5555
New York *(G-10424)*
Klg Usa LLC ....A....... 845 856-5311
Port Jervis *(G-13233)*
Life Pill Laboratories LLC ....G....... 914 682-2146
White Plains *(G-16472)*
Liptis Pharmaceuticals USA Inc ....A....... 845 627-0260
Spring Valley *(G-14999)*
LNK International Inc ....D....... 631 435-3500
Hauppauge *(G-5867)*
LNK International Inc ....D....... 631 435-3500
Hauppauge *(G-5868)*
LNK International Inc ....D....... 631 435-3500
Hauppauge *(G-5869)*
LNK International Inc ....D....... 631 543-3787
Hauppauge *(G-5870)*
LNK International Inc ....D....... 631 435-3500
Hauppauge *(G-5871)*
LNK International Inc ....D....... 631 231-4020
Hauppauge *(G-5872)*
Makers Nutrition LLC ....E....... 631 456-5397
Hauppauge *(G-5879)*
Maks Pharma & Diagnostics Inc ....G....... 631 270-1528
Baldwin *(G-540)*
Medtech Products Inc ....F....... 914 524-6810
Tarrytown *(G-15482)*
Moleclar Insght Phrmctcals Inc ....G....... 914 789-2800
Sleepy Hollow *(G-14886)*
Mustang Bio Inc ....G....... 781 652-4500
New York *(G-10862)*
Mylan Health Management LLC ....G....... 917 262-2950
New York *(G-10867)*
Neurotrope Inc ....G....... 973 242-0005
New York *(G-10915)*
Noho Health Inc ....E....... 877 227-3631
New York *(G-10985)*
Norwich Pharmaceuticals Inc ....B....... 607 335-3000
Norwich *(G-12490)*
Novartis AG ....C....... 617 435-0469
Port Washington *(G-13291)*
Novartis Corporation ....D....... 718 276-8600
Laurelton *(G-7100)*
Novartis Pharmaceuticals Corp ....G....... 888 669-6682
New York *(G-11000)*
Novartis Pharmaceuticals Corp ....G....... 718 276-8600
Laurelton *(G-7101)*
Noven Pharmaceuticals Inc ....E....... 212 682-4420
New York *(G-11001)*
Nutra-Scientifics LLC ....G....... 917 238-8510
Pomona *(G-13186)*
Nutratech Labs Inc ....G....... 315 695-2256
Phoenix *(G-12991)*
NY Phrmacy Compounding Ctr Inc ....G....... 201 403-5151
Astoria *(G-438)*
Ony Biotech Inc ....E....... 716 636-9096
Amherst *(G-246)*
Ophthotech Corporation ....C....... 212 845-8200
New York *(G-11051)*
Orenova Group LLC ....G....... 914 517-3000
White Plains *(G-16482)*

PRODUCT

Employee Codes: A=Over 500 employees, B=251-500
C=101-250, D=51-100, E=20-50, F=10-19, G=5-9
2019 Harris
New York Manufacturers Directory
1205

PHARMACEUTICALS — PRODUCT SECTION

Ovid Therapeutics Inc ....E...... 646 661-7661
  New York *(G-11072)*
P & L Development LLC ....D...... 516 986-1700
  Westbury *(G-16360)*
P & L Development LLC ....D...... 516 986-1700
  Westbury *(G-16361)*
P & L Development LLC ....D...... 516 986-1700
  Westbury *(G-16362)*
Par Phrmceutical Companies Inc ....E...... 845 573-5500
  Chestnut Ridge *(G-3495)*
Par Sterile Products LLC ....E...... 845 573-5500
  Chestnut Ridge *(G-3496)*
Pfizer HCP Corporation ....F...... 212 733-2323
  New York *(G-11173)*
Pfizer Inc ....B...... 518 297-6611
  Rouses Point *(G-14468)*
Pfizer Inc ....C...... 914 437-5868
  White Plains *(G-16497)*
Pfizer Inc ....C...... 937 746-3603
  New York *(G-11175)*
Pfizer Inc ....D...... 212 733-6276
  New York *(G-11176)*
Pfizer Inc ....E...... 212 733-2323
  New York *(G-11177)*
Pfizer Overseas LLC ....G...... 212 733-2323
  New York *(G-11178)*
PH David J Rossi ....G...... 585 455-1160
  Rochester *(G-14016)*
Pharmaceutic Labs LLC ....F...... 518 608-1060
  Albany *(G-114)*
Polygen Pharmaceuticals Inc ....E...... 631 392-4044
  Edgewood *(G-4411)*
Precision Pharma Services Inc ....C...... 631 752-7314
  Melville *(G-8058)*
Prestige Brands Intl LLC ....F...... 914 524-6800
  Tarrytown *(G-15487)*
Prestige Consmr Healthcare Inc ....D...... 914 524-6800
  Tarrytown *(G-15488)*
Prime Pack LLC ....F...... 732 253-7734
  New York *(G-11241)*
Progenics Pharmaceuticals Inc ....D...... 646 975-2500
  New York *(G-11257)*
Protein Sciences Corporation ....E...... 203 686-0800
  Pearl River *(G-12908)*
Purinepharma LLC ....G...... 732 485-1400
  Massena *(G-7907)*
Quogue Capital LLC ....G...... 212 554-4475
  New York *(G-11304)*
Quva Pharma Inc ....G...... 973 224-7795
  New York *(G-11306)*
Regeneron Pharmaceuticals Inc ....B...... 914 847-7000
  Tarrytown *(G-15490)*
Regeneron Pharmaceuticals Inc ....E...... 518 488-6000
  Rensselaer *(G-13477)*
Regenlab USA LLC ....G...... 800 220-9082
  New York *(G-11350)*
Regenron Hlthcare Slutions Inc ....A...... 914 847-7000
  Tarrytown *(G-15491)*
Relmada Therapeutics Inc ....F...... 646 677-3853
  New York *(G-11354)*
Retrophin LLC ....G...... 646 564-3680
  New York *(G-11373)*
Rij Pharmaceutical Corporation ....E...... 845 692-5799
  Middletown *(G-8173)*
Rk Pharma Inc ....G...... 646 884-3765
  Pearl River *(G-12910)*
Rls Holdings Inc ....G...... 716 418-7274
  Clarence *(G-3540)*
Roche Tcrc Inc ....G...... 800 626-3553
  New York *(G-11414)*
Ropack USA Inc ....F...... 631 482-7777
  Commack *(G-3700)*
S1 Biopharma Inc ....G...... 201 839-0941
  New York *(G-11460)*
Salutem Group LLC ....G...... 347 620-2640
  New York *(G-11473)*
Saptalis Pharmaceuticals LLC ....E...... 631 231-2751
  Hauppauge *(G-5933)*
Scarguard Labs LLC ....F...... 516 482-8050
  Great Neck *(G-5589)*
Sciarra Laboratories Inc ....G...... 516 933-7853
  Hicksville *(G-6131)*
Scienta Pharmaceuticals LLC ....G...... 845 589-0774
  Valley Cottage *(G-15764)*
Seidlin Consulting ....G...... 212 496-2043
  New York *(G-11535)*
Sellas Life Sciences Group Inc ....F...... 917 438-4353
  New York *(G-11540)*
Shennong Pharmaceuticals Inc ....E...... 347 422-2200
  New York *(G-11564)*

Shrineeta Pharmacy ....G...... 212 234-7959
  New York *(G-11571)*
Shrineeta Pharmacy Inc ....E...... 212 234-7959
  New York *(G-11572)*
Siga Technologies Inc ....E...... 212 672-9100
  New York *(G-11582)*
Silarx Pharmaceuticals Inc ....D...... 845 352-4020
  Carmel *(G-3281)*
Silver Oak Pharmacy Inc ....G...... 718 922-3400
  Brooklyn *(G-2472)*
Sincerus LLC ....G...... 800 419-2804
  Brooklyn *(G-2478)*
Skills Alliance Inc ....G...... 646 492-5300
  New York *(G-11608)*
Specgx LLC ....A...... 607 538-9124
  Hobart *(G-6164)*
Stemline Therapeutics Inc ....E...... 646 502-2311
  New York *(G-11703)*
Steri-Pharma LLC ....E...... 315 473-7180
  Syracuse *(G-15431)*
Sunquest Pharmaceuticals Inc ....F...... 855 478-6779
  Hicksville *(G-6135)*
Synergy Pharmaceuticals Inc ....B...... 212 297-0020
  New York *(G-11764)*
Syntho Pharmaceuticals Inc ....G...... 631 755-9898
  Farmingdale *(G-4887)*
Teva Pharmaceuticals Usa Inc ....G...... 212 259-2030
  New York *(G-11804)*
Tg Therapeutics Inc ....D...... 212 554-4484
  New York *(G-11806)*
Tmp Technologies Inc ....D...... 716 895-6100
  Buffalo *(G-3097)*
Tocare LLC ....F...... 718 767-0618
  Whitestone *(G-16549)*
Tongli Pharmaceuticals USA Inc ....F...... 212 842-8837
  Flushing *(G-5054)*
Tonix Pharmaceuticals Inc ....G...... 212 980-9155
  New York *(G-11865)*
Tonix Phrmceuticals Holdg Corp ....F...... 212 980-9155
  New York *(G-11866)*
Topiderm Inc ....C...... 631 226-7979
  Amityville *(G-321)*
Topix Pharmaceuticals Inc ....C...... 631 226-7979
  Amityville *(G-322)*
Tyme Inc ....G...... 646 205-1603
  New York *(G-11924)*
Tyme Technologies Inc ....F...... 212 461-2315
  New York *(G-11925)*
Ucb Pharma Inc ....G...... 919 767-2555
  Rochester *(G-14183)*
United-Guardian Inc ....E...... 631 273-0900
  Hauppauge *(G-5965)*
Unither Manufacturing LLC ....C...... 585 475-9000
  Rochester *(G-14187)*
Unither Manufacturing LLC ....F...... 585 274-5430
  Rochester *(G-14188)*
Vaccinex Inc ....E...... 585 271-2700
  Rochester *(G-14196)*
Ventrus Biosciences Inc ....G...... 646 706-5208
  New York *(G-12005)*
Verona Pharma Inc ....F...... 914 797-5007
  White Plains *(G-16514)*
Viropro Inc ....E...... 650 300-5190
  New York *(G-12039)*
Vitalis LLC ....G...... 646 831-7338
  New York *(G-12045)*
Vitane Pharmaceuticals Inc ....E...... 845 267-6700
  Congers *(G-3722)*
Vvs International Inc ....G...... 212 302-5410
  New York *(G-12058)*
Watson Laboratories Inc ....F...... 951 493-5300
  Carmel *(G-3284)*
Wyeth Holdings LLC ....D...... 845 602-5000
  Pearl River *(G-12913)*
X-Gen Pharmaceuticals Inc ....G...... 607 562-2700
  Big Flats *(G-857)*
X-Gen Pharmaceuticals Inc ....E...... 631 261-8188
  Northport *(G-12475)*
Xstelos Holdings Inc ....G...... 212 729-4962
  New York *(G-12155)*
Y-Mabs Therapeutics Inc ....F...... 917 817-2992
  New York *(G-12156)*
Ys Marketing Inc ....E...... 718 778-6080
  Brooklyn *(G-2667)*

PHARMACEUTICALS: Mail-Order Svc

Generics Bidco I LLC ....G...... 256 859-4011
  Chestnut Ridge *(G-3492)*
Greentree Pharmacy Inc ....F...... 718 768-2700
  Brooklyn *(G-1952)*

Natures Bounty Co ....D...... 631 244-2021
  Ronkonkoma *(G-14385)*

PHARMACEUTICALS: Medicinal & Botanical Prdts

Accredo Health Incorporated ....G...... 718 353-3012
  Flushing *(G-4979)*
Albany Molecular Research Inc ....F...... 518 433-7700
  Rensselaer *(G-13471)*
Albany Molecular Research Inc ....F...... 518 512-2000
  Rensselaer *(G-13472)*
Alo Acquisition LLC ....G...... 518 464-0279
  Albany *(G-39)*
Conversion Labs Inc ....F...... 866 351-5907
  New York *(G-9392)*
GE Healthcare Inc ....F...... 516 626-2799
  Port Washington *(G-13262)*
Kannalife Sciences Inc ....G...... 516 669-3219
  Lloyd Harbor *(G-7280)*
Nbty Inc ....G...... 631 200-2062
  Holbrook *(G-6203)*
Setauket Manufacturing Co ....G...... 631 231-7272
  Ronkonkoma *(G-14412)*

PHARMACIES & DRUG STORES

Biomed Pharmaceuticals Inc ....G...... 914 592-0525
  Hawthorne *(G-5984)*
Emilior Phrm Compounding Inc ....E...... 855 426-6768
  Bronx *(G-1268)*
Far Rockaway Drugs Inc ....F...... 718 471-2500
  Far Rockaway *(G-4701)*
J P R Pharmacy Inc ....F...... 718 327-0600
  Far Rockaway *(G-4702)*
Nucare Pharmacy Inc ....G...... 212 426-9300
  New York *(G-11005)*
Nucare Pharmacy West LLC ....F...... 212 462-2525
  New York *(G-11006)*

PHONOGRAPH NEEDLES

Grado Laboratories Inc ....F...... 718 435-5340
  Brooklyn *(G-1946)*

PHONOGRAPH RECORDS WHOLESALERS

Hope International Productions ....F...... 212 247-3188
  New York *(G-10122)*
Sony Music Holdings Inc ....A...... 212 833-8000
  New York *(G-11649)*

PHONOGRAPH RECORDS: Prerecorded

Abkco Music & Records Inc ....E...... 212 399-0300
  New York *(G-8710)*
Eks Manufacturing Inc ....F...... 917 217-0784
  Brooklyn *(G-1817)*
Hope International Productions ....F...... 212 247-3188
  New York *(G-10122)*
Warner Music Inc ....D...... 212 275-2000
  New York *(G-12073)*

PHOSPHATES

International Ord Tech Inc ....D...... 716 664-1100
  Jamestown *(G-6724)*
Mdi Holdings LLC ....A...... 212 559-1127
  New York *(G-10747)*

PHOTOCOPY MACHINES

Cannon Industries Inc ....D...... 585 254-8080
  Rochester *(G-13690)*
Facsimile Cmmncations Inds Inc ....D...... 212 741-6400
  New York *(G-9770)*
Xerox Corporation ....D...... 212 330-1386
  New York *(G-12150)*
Xerox Corporation ....C...... 585 427-4500
  Rochester *(G-14214)*

PHOTOCOPYING & DUPLICATING SVCS

A Q P Inc ....G...... 585 256-1690
  Rochester *(G-13590)*
Apple Press ....G...... 914 723-6660
  White Plains *(G-16421)*
Avalon Copy Centers Amer Inc ....D...... 315 471-3333
  Syracuse *(G-15251)*
Avalon Copy Centers Amer Inc ....E...... 716 995-7777
  Buffalo *(G-2717)*
Business Never Stops LLC ....G...... 888 479-3111
  South Richmond Hill *(G-14945)*

PRODUCT SECTION

PHOTOGRAPHIC LIBRARY SVCS

Capital Dst Print & Imaging..........G......518 456-6773
  Schenectady (G-14657)
Carges Entps of Canandaigua......G......585 394-2600
  Canandaigua (G-3214)
Cds Productions Inc.....................F......518 385-8255
  Schenectady (G-14661)
Chakra Communications Inc........E......607 748-7491
  Endicott (G-4584)
Clarion Publications Inc................F......585 243-3530
  Geneseo (G-5313)
Clarsons Corp.............................F......585 235-8775
  Rochester (G-13713)
Constas Printing Corporation.......G......315 474-2176
  Syracuse (G-15287)
Evolution Impressions Inc.............D......585 473-6600
  Rochester (G-13795)
Fairmount Press..........................G......212 255-2300
  New York (G-9775)
Fambus Inc.................................G......607 785-3700
  Endicott (G-4592)
Fedex Office & Print Svcs Inc......G......718 982-5223
  Staten Island (G-15076)
Graphic Fabrications Inc..............G......516 763-3222
  Rockville Centre (G-14232)
Graphicomm Inc..........................G......716 283-0830
  Niagara Falls (G-12289)
Jon Lyn Ink Inc...........................G......516 546-2312
  Merrick (G-8099)
Kjckd Inc....................................G......518 435-9696
  Latham (G-7078)
Leader Printing Inc.....................F......516 546-1544
  Merrick (G-8101)
Mercury Print Productions Inc.....C......585 458-7900
  Rochester (G-13936)
Multiple Imprssons of Rchester....G......585 546-1160
  Rochester (G-13960)
National Reproductions Inc..........E......212 619-3800
  New York (G-10884)
North Delaware Printing Inc........G......716 692-0576
  Tonawanda (G-15566)
Persch Service Print Inc..............G......716 366-2677
  Dunkirk (G-4176)
R & L Press of SI Inc..................G......718 667-3258
  Staten Island (G-15122)
Rapid Print and Marketing Inc.....G......585 924-1520
  Victor (G-15864)
Shipmtes/Printmates Holdg Corp..D......518 370-1158
  Scotia (G-14746)
Shiprite Software Inc...................G......315 733-6191
  Utica (G-15733)
Silver Griffin Inc.........................F......518 272-7771
  Troy (G-15627)
Twin Counties Pro Printers Inc....F......518 828-3278
  Hudson (G-6374)
William J Ryan...........................G......585 392-6200
  Hilton (G-6159)
Woodbury Printing Plus + Inc......G......845 928-6610
  Central Valley (G-3399)

PHOTOELECTRIC DEVICES: Magnetic

MMC Magnetics Corp..................F......631 435-9888
  Hauppauge (G-5895)
Truebite Inc................................E......607 785-7664
  Vestal (G-15824)

PHOTOENGRAVING SVC

Koehlr-Gibson Mkg Graphics Inc..E......716 838-5960
  Buffalo (G-2910)
Rapid Service Engraving Co........G......716 896-4555
  Buffalo (G-3032)

PHOTOFINISHING LABORATORIES

Eastman Kodak Company............B......585 724-4000
  Rochester (G-13761)

PHOTOGRAPH DEVELOPING & RETOUCHING SVCS

Digital Evolution Inc...................E......212 732-2722
  New York (G-9527)

PHOTOGRAPHIC EQPT & SPLY: Sound Recordg/Reprod Eqpt, Motion

Kelmar Systems Inc....................F......631 421-1230
  Huntington Station (G-6450)

PHOTOGRAPHIC EQPT & SPLYS

Astrodyne Inc.............................G......516 536-5755
  Oceanside (G-12532)
AVI-Spl Employee.......................B......212 840-4801
  New York (G-8977)
Carestream Health Inc................B......585 627-1800
  Rochester (G-13692)
Chemung Cnty Chpter Nysarc Inc..C......607 734-6151
  Elmira (G-4477)
Cpac Inc.....................................E......585 382-3223
  Leicester (G-7126)
Creatron Services Inc.................E......516 437-5119
  Floral Park (G-4961)
Eastman Kodak Company............G......585 724-4000
  Rochester (G-13771)
Ebsco Industries Inc....................G......585 398-2000
  Farmington (G-4912)
Emda Inc....................................F......631 243-6363
  Plainview (G-13055)
Garys Loft..................................G......212 244-0970
  New York (G-9884)
Henrys Deals Inc........................E......347 821-4685
  Brooklyn (G-1972)
Kodak Alaris Inc.........................B......585 290-2891
  Rochester (G-13906)
Kodak Graphic Communications..F......585 724-4000
  Rochester (G-13907)
Labgrafix Printing Inc.................G......516 280-8300
  Lynbrook (G-7667)
Lowel-Light Manufacturing Inc....E......718 921-0600
  Brooklyn (G-2137)
Mirion Technologies Ist Corp......D......607 562-4300
  Horseheads (G-6321)
Norazza Inc................................G......716 706-1160
  Buffalo (G-2973)
Rockland Colloid Corp.................G......845 359-5559
  Piermont (G-12994)
Stallion Technologies Inc............G......315 622-1176
  Liverpool (G-7263)
Thermo Cidtec Inc......................E......315 451-9410
  Liverpool (G-7267)
Tiffen Company LLC...................G......631 273-2500
  Hauppauge (G-5959)
Tiffen Company LLC...................D......631 273-2500
  Hauppauge (G-5960)
Vishay Thin Film LLC..................C......716 283-4025
  Niagara Falls (G-12348)
Xerox Corporation......................E......518 434-6543
  Albany (G-143)
Xerox Corporation......................C......585 264-5584
  Rochester (G-14215)

PHOTOGRAPHIC EQPT & SPLYS WHOLESALERS

AVI-Spl Employee.......................B......212 840-4801
  New York (G-8977)
Rockland Colloid Corp.................G......845 359-5559
  Piermont (G-12994)

PHOTOGRAPHIC EQPT & SPLYS, WHOLESALE: Motion Picture

Doar Inc.....................................G......516 872-8140
  Lynbrook (G-7664)

PHOTOGRAPHIC EQPT & SPLYS: Cameras, Aerial

Fluxdata Incorporated................G......800 425-0176
  Rochester (G-13811)
Geospatial Systems Inc...............F......585 427-8310
  West Henrietta (G-16241)

PHOTOGRAPHIC EQPT & SPLYS: Cameras, Still & Motion Pictures

Critical Imaging LLC..................E......315 732-5020
  Utica (G-15689)

PHOTOGRAPHIC EQPT & SPLYS: Editing Eqpt, Motion Picture

Avid Technology Inc...................E......212 983-2424
  New York (G-8978)
Kyle Editing LLC.........................G......212 675-3464
  New York (G-10490)

PHOTOGRAPHIC EQPT & SPLYS: Film, Sensitized

Eastman Kodak Company............D......585 722-2187
  Rochester (G-13760)
Eastman Kodak Company............B......585 724-4000
  Rochester (G-13761)
Eastman Kodak Company............B......585 724-5600
  Rochester (G-13762)
Eastman Kodak Company............D......585 722-9695
  Pittsford (G-13010)
Eastman Kodak Company............B......585 726-6261
  Rochester (G-13763)
Eastman Kodak Company............D......585 724-4000
  Rochester (G-13764)
Eastman Kodak Company............F......800 698-3324
  Rochester (G-13765)
Eastman Kodak Company............D......585 722-4385
  Rochester (G-13766)
Eastman Kodak Company............B......585 588-5598
  Rochester (G-13767)
Eastman Kodak Company............C......585 726-7000
  Rochester (G-13768)
Eastman Kodak Company............B......585 722-4007
  Rochester (G-13769)
Eastman Kodak Company............D......585 588-3896
  Rochester (G-13770)
Eastman Park Micrographics Inc..G......866 934-4376
  Rochester (G-13772)
Truesense Imaging Inc................C......585 784-5500
  Rochester (G-14178)

PHOTOGRAPHIC EQPT & SPLYS: Graphic Arts Plates, Sensitized

Gpc International Inc.................C......631 752-9600
  Melville (G-8027)

PHOTOGRAPHIC EQPT & SPLYS: Plates, Sensitized

Apexx Omni-Graphics Inc............D......718 326-3330
  Maspeth (G-7822)

PHOTOGRAPHIC EQPT & SPLYS: Printing Eqpt

Jack L Popkin & Co Inc..............G......718 361-6700
  Kew Gardens (G-6875)
Printer Components Inc..............G......585 924-5190
  Fairport (G-4651)

PHOTOGRAPHIC EQPT & SPLYS: Processing Eqpt

All-Pro Imaging Corp..................E......516 433-7676
  Melville (G-8001)

PHOTOGRAPHIC EQPT & SPLYS: Shutters, Camera

Va Inc..E......585 385-5930
  Rochester (G-14195)

PHOTOGRAPHIC EQPT & SPLYS: Toners, Prprd, Not Chem Plnts

Efam Enterprises LLC.................E......718 204-1760
  Long Island City (G-7435)
Hilord Chemical Corporation.......E......631 234-7373
  Hauppauge (G-5845)
Konica Mnolta Sups Mfg USA Inc..D......845 294-8400
  Goshen (G-5481)
Lasertech Crtridge RE-Builders...G......518 373-1246
  Clifton Park (G-3569)
Toner-N-More Inc.......................G......718 232-6200
  Brooklyn (G-2569)

PHOTOGRAPHIC EQPT/SPLYS, WHOL: Cameras/Projectors/Eqpt/Splys

Bescor Video Accessories Ltd.....F......631 420-1717
  Farmingdale (G-4727)

PHOTOGRAPHIC LIBRARY SVCS

Kraus Organization Limited.........D......212 686-5411
  New York (G-10481)

PHOTOGRAPHIC PEOCESSING CHEMICALS
Champion Photochemistry Inc .... D 585 760-6444
  Rochester *(G-13706)*

PHOTOGRAPHIC PROCESSING EQPT & CHEMICALS
Air Techniques Inc .... B 516 433-7676
  Melville *(G-8000)*
Cine Magnetics Inc .... E 914 667-6707
  Mount Vernon *(G-8387)*
Seneca TEC Inc .... G 585 381-2645
  Fairport *(G-4658)*
Sima Technologies LLC .... G 412 828-9130
  Hauppauge *(G-5940)*

PHOTOGRAPHIC SENSITIZED GOODS, NEC
Turner Bellows Inc .... E 585 235-4456
  Rochester *(G-14181)*

PHOTOGRAPHIC SVCS
Labgrafix Printing Inc .... G 516 280-8300
  Lynbrook *(G-7667)*

PHOTOGRAPHY SVCS: Commercial
Cobico Productions Inc .... G 347 417-5883
  New York *(G-9342)*
Folio Graphics Co Inc .... G 718 763-2076
  Brooklyn *(G-1896)*
Untitled Media .... E 212 780-0960
  New York *(G-11964)*

PHOTOGRAPHY SVCS: Portrait Studios
Classic Album .... E 718 388-2818
  Brooklyn *(G-1699)*
Classic Album LLC .... D 718 388-2818
  Brooklyn *(G-1700)*

PHOTOGRAPHY SVCS: Still Or Video
Dynamic Photography Inc .... G 516 381-2951
  Roslyn *(G-14446)*

PHOTOTYPESETTING SVC
Digital Color Concepts Inc .... E 212 989-4888
  New York *(G-9526)*

PHOTOVOLTAIC Solid State
Besicorp Ltd .... F 845 336-7700
  Kingston *(G-6889)*
Onyx Solar Group LLC .... G 917 951-9732
  New York *(G-11047)*
Solar Thin Films Inc .... E 212 629-8260
  Cedarhurst *(G-3337)*

PHYSICAL FITNESS CENTERS
Womens Health Care PC .... G 718 850-0009
  Richmond Hill *(G-13517)*

PHYSICIANS' OFFICES & CLINICS: Medical doctors
M H Mandelbaum Orthotic .... F 631 473-8668
  Port Jefferson *(G-13222)*

PICTURE FRAMES: Metal
Access Display Group Inc .... F 516 678-7772
  Freeport *(G-5136)*
Bristol Gift Co Inc .... F 845 496-2821
  Washingtonville *(G-15963)*
Custom Frame & Molding Co .... F 631 491-9091
  West Babylon *(G-16150)*
Dobrin Industries Inc .... G 800 353-2229
  Lockport *(G-7295)*
Elias Artmetal Inc .... F 516 873-7501
  Mineola *(G-8217)*
Frame Shoppe & Art Gallery .... G 516 365-6014
  Manhasset *(G-7767)*
Inter Pacific Consulting Corp .... G 718 460-2787
  Flushing *(G-5010)*
Jay Strongwater Holdings LLC .... A 646 657-0558
  New York *(G-10312)*
Picture Perfect Framing .... G 718 851-1884
  Brooklyn *(G-2316)*
Structural Industries Inc .... C 631 471-5200
  Bohemia *(G-1092)*

PICTURE FRAMES: Wood
Apf Manufacturing Company LLC ..... E 914 963-6300
  Yonkers *(G-16737)*
FG Galassi Moulding Co Inc .... G 845 258-2100
  Goshen *(G-5479)*
Fred M Lawrence Co Inc .... E 718 786-7227
  Bay Shore *(G-688)*
Galas Framing Services .... F 718 706-0007
  Long Island City *(G-7454)*
Grant-Noren .... G 845 726-4281
  Westtown *(G-16414)*
House of Heydenryk Jr Inc .... F 212 206-9611
  New York *(G-10135)*
Hubray Inc .... F 800 645-2855
  North Baldwin *(G-12364)*
Interntonal Consmr Connections ...... F 516 481-3438
  West Hempstead *(G-16217)*
North American Enclosures Inc .... E 631 234-9500
  Central Islip *(G-3381)*
Picture Perfect Framing .... G 718 851-1884
  Brooklyn *(G-2316)*
Regence Picture Frames Inc .... E 718 779-0888
  Lynbrook *(G-7672)*

PICTURE FRAMING SVCS, CUSTOM
Frame Shoppe & Art Gallery .... G 516 365-6014
  Manhasset *(G-7767)*
Galas Framing Services .... F 718 706-0007
  Long Island City *(G-7454)*
Interntonal Consmr Connections ...... F 516 481-3438
  West Hempstead *(G-16217)*
Timeless Decor LLC .... C 315 782-5759
  Watertown *(G-16035)*

PICTURE PROJECTION EQPT
Just Lamps of New York Inc .... F 716 626-2240
  Buffalo *(G-2898)*

PIECE GOODS & NOTIONS WHOLESALERS
Hpk Industries LLC .... F 315 724-0196
  Utica *(G-15709)*
J & M Textile Co Inc .... F 212 268-8000
  New York *(G-10282)*
Triangle Label Tag Inc .... G 718 875-3030
  Brooklyn *(G-2583)*

PIECE GOODS, NOTIONS & DRY GOODS, WHOL: Textile Converters
Bank-Miller Co Inc .... E 914 227-9357
  Pelham *(G-12933)*
Klauber Brothers Inc .... E 212 686-2531
  New York *(G-10457)*
La Lame Inc .... E 212 921-9770
  New York *(G-10502)*

PIECE GOODS, NOTIONS & DRY GOODS, WHOL: Textiles, Woven
Kowa American Corporation .... E 212 303-7800
  New York *(G-10474)*
Mutual Sales Corp .... E 718 361-8373
  Long Island City *(G-7530)*
Shengkun North America Inc .... E 212 217-2460
  New York *(G-11563)*
Zorlu USA Inc .... D 212 689-4622
  New York *(G-12184)*

PIECE GOODS, NOTIONS & DRY GOODS, WHOLESALE: Fabrics, Knit
Continental Knitting Mills .... G 631 242-5330
  Deer Park *(G-3958)*

PIECE GOODS, NOTIONS & DRY GOODS, WHOLESALE: Fabrics, Lace
Penn & Fletcher Inc .... F 212 239-6868
  Long Island City *(G-7553)*
Super-Trim Inc .... E 212 255-2370
  New York *(G-11747)*

PIECE GOODS, NOTIONS & DRY GOODS, WHOLESALE: Sewing Access
Bfma Holding Corporation .... G 607 753-6746
  Cortland *(G-3862)*
Marietta Corporation .... A 323 589-8181
  Cortland *(G-3883)*

PIECE GOODS, NOTIONS & OTHER DRY GOODS, WHOLESALE: Buttons
Emsig Manufacturing Corp .... F 518 828-7301
  Hudson *(G-6348)*
Hemisphere Novelties Inc .... E 914 378-4100
  Yonkers *(G-16767)*

PIECE GOODS, NOTIONS & OTHER DRY GOODS, WHOLESALE: Fabrics
Creation Baumann USA Inc .... E 516 764-7431
  Rockville Centre *(G-14231)*
Eu Design LLC .... G 212 420-7788
  New York *(G-9725)*
Sifonya Inc .... G 212 620-4512
  New York *(G-11581)*

PIECE GOODS, NOTIONS & OTHER DRY GOODS, WHOLESALE: Woven
Citisource Industries Inc .... E 212 683-1033
  New York *(G-9307)*

PIECE GOODS, NOTIONS/DRY GOODS, WHOL: Drapery Mtrl, Woven
Richloom Fabrics Corp .... F 212 685-5400
  New York *(G-11391)*
Scalamandre Silks Inc .... D 212 980-3888
  New York *(G-11499)*

PIECE GOODS, NOTIONS/DRY GOODS, WHOL: Linen Piece, Woven
Simple Elegance New York Inc .... F 718 360-1947
  Brooklyn *(G-2477)*

PIECE GOODS, NOTIONS/DRY GOODS, WHOL: Sewing Splys/Notions
Artistic Ribbon Novelty Co Inc .... E 212 255-4224
  New York *(G-8922)*

PILLOW FILLING MTRLS: Curled Hair, Cotton Waste, Moss
American Home Mfg LLC .... G 212 643-0680
  New York *(G-8829)*

PILLOWS: Sponge Rubber
Schlegel Systems Inc .... C 585 427-7200
  Rochester *(G-14115)*

PINS
Pin Pharma Inc .... G 212 543-2583
  New York *(G-11195)*
Pins N Needles .... F 212 535-6222
  New York *(G-11199)*
Pni Capital Partners .... G 516 466-7120
  Westbury *(G-16364)*

PIPE & FITTING: Fabrication
Accord Pipe Fabricators Inc .... E 718 657-3900
  Jamaica *(G-6623)*
Advanced Thermal Systems Inc .... E 716 681-1800
  Lancaster *(G-7002)*
Arcadia Mfg Group Inc .... E 518 434-6213
  Green Island *(G-5602)*
Arcadia Mfg Group Inc .... G 518 434-6213
  Menands *(G-8081)*
Cobey Inc .... C 716 362-9550
  Buffalo *(G-2769)*
Daikin Applied Americas Inc .... D 315 253-2771
  Auburn *(G-475)*
Flatcut LLC .... G 212 542-5732
  Brooklyn *(G-1888)*
H & H Metal Specialty Inc .... E 716 665-2110
  Jamestown *(G-6720)*

PRODUCT SECTION

PLASTICS FINISHED PRDTS: Laminated

J D Steward Inc .... G 718 358-0169
   Flushing *(G-5013)*
James Woerner Inc .... G 631 454-9330
   Farmingdale *(G-4791)*
Juniper Elbow Co Inc .... C 718 326-2546
   Middle Village *(G-8124)*
Juniper Industries Florida Inc .... G 718 326-2546
   Middle Village *(G-8125)*
Leo International Inc .... E 718 290-8005
   Brooklyn *(G-2112)*
Leroy Plastics Inc .... D 585 768-8158
   Le Roy *(G-7121)*
Long Island Pipe Supply Inc .... E 516 222-8008
   Garden City *(G-5267)*
Long Island Pipe Supply Inc .... G 718 456-7877
   Flushing *(G-5024)*
Long Island Pipe Supply Inc .... G 518 270-2159
   Troy *(G-15597)*
Long Island Pipe Supply Inc .... E 516 222-8008
   Garden City *(G-5268)*
Met Weld International LLC .... D 518 765-2318
   Altamont *(G-199)*
Micromold Products Inc .... E 914 969-2850
   Yonkers *(G-16784)*
Rochester Tube Fabricators .... F 585 254-0290
   Rochester *(G-14099)*
Tag Flange & Machining Inc .... G 516 536-1300
   Oceanside *(G-12560)*
Total Piping Solutions Inc .... F 716 372-0160
   Olean *(G-12608)*
Truly Tubular Fitting Corp .... F 914 664-8686
   Mount Vernon *(G-8450)*

PIPE & FITTINGS: Cast Iron

Cpp - Guaymas .... C 315 687-0014
   Chittenango *(G-3503)*
Dragon Trading Inc .... G 212 717-1496
   New York *(G-9572)*

PIPE & FITTINGS: Pressure, Cast Iron

Acme Nipple Mfg Co Inc .... G 716 873-7491
   Buffalo *(G-2683)*
Penner Elbow Company Inc .... F 718 526-9000
   Elmhurst *(G-4470)*

PIPE CLEANERS

R V Dow Enterprises Inc .... F 585 454-5862
   Rochester *(G-14067)*

PIPE JOINT COMPOUNDS

Continental Buchanan LLC .... D 703 480-3800
   Buchanan *(G-2672)*

PIPE: Concrete

Binghamton Precast & Sup Corp .... E 607 722-0334
   Binghamton *(G-867)*
Roman Stone Construction Co .... E 631 667-0566
   Bay Shore *(G-717)*

PIPE: Extruded, Aluminum

North American Pipe Corp .... F 516 338-2863
   East Williston *(G-4382)*

PIPE: Plastic

BMC LLC .... E 716 681-7755
   Buffalo *(G-2735)*
Hancor Inc .... D 607 565-3033
   Waverly *(G-16066)*
Micromold Products Inc .... E 914 969-2850
   Yonkers *(G-16784)*
National Pipe & Plastics Inc .... C 607 729-9381
   Vestal *(G-15820)*
North American Pipe Corp .... F 516 338-2863
   East Williston *(G-4382)*
Prince Rubber & Plas Co Inc .... E 225 272-1653
   Buffalo *(G-3014)*

PIPE: Sheet Metal

Lane Enterprises Inc .... E 518 885-4385
   Ballston Spa *(G-587)*

PIPES & TUBES: Steel

Coventry Manufacturing Co Inc .... G 914 668-2212
   Mount Vernon *(G-8391)*
Liberty Pipe Incorporated .... G 516 747-2472
   Mineola *(G-8234)*
Markin Tubing LP .... F 585 495-6211
   Buffalo *(G-2937)*
McHone Industries Inc .... D 716 945-3380
   Salamanca *(G-14526)*
Micromold Products Inc .... E 914 969-2850
   Yonkers *(G-16784)*
Stony Brook Mfg Co Inc .... G 631 369-9530
   Calverton *(G-3171)*
Super Steelworks Corporation .... G 718 386-4770
   Deer Park *(G-4050)*
Tricon Piping Systems Inc .... F 315 697-8787
   Canastota *(G-3250)*
Welded Tube Usa Inc .... D 716 828-1111
   Lackawanna *(G-6954)*

PIPES & TUBES: Welded

Oriskany Mfg Tech LLC .... E 315 732-4962
   Yorkville *(G-16830)*

PIPES: Steel & Iron

Lino International Inc .... G 516 482-7100
   Great Neck *(G-5569)*

PIPES: Tobacco

Ryers Creek Corp .... E 607 523-6617
   Corning *(G-3825)*

PISTONS & PISTON RINGS

Fcmp Inc .... F 716 692-4623
   Tonawanda *(G-15539)*

PLACEMATS: Plastic Or Textile

Baby Signature Inc .... G 212 686-1700
   New York *(G-8996)*
NY Cutting Inc .... G 646 434-1355
   Suffern *(G-15194)*
Sterling Shelf Liners Inc .... G 631 676-5175
   Holbrook *(G-6211)*

PLANING MILLS: Independent, Exc Millwork

Embassy Millwork Inc .... F 518 839-0965
   Amsterdam *(G-336)*

PLANING MILLS: Millwork

Mind Designs Inc .... G 631 563-3644
   Farmingville *(G-4924)*

PLANT CARE SVCS

Plant-Tech2o Inc .... G 516 483-7845
   Hempstead *(G-6023)*

PLAQUES: Clay, Plaster/Papier-Mache, Factory Production

B & R Promotional Products .... G 212 563-0040
   New York *(G-8988)*

PLAQUES: Picture, Laminated

B & R Promotional Products .... G 212 563-0040
   New York *(G-8988)*
Donorwall Inc .... F 212 766-9670
   New York *(G-9557)*
Kelly Foundry & Machine Co .... E 315 732-8313
   Utica *(G-15717)*

PLASMAS

Coral Blood Service .... F 800 483-4888
   Elmsford *(G-4538)*
D C I Plasma Center Inc .... G 914 241-1646
   Mount Kisco *(G-8340)*
Lake Immunogenics Inc .... F 585 265-1973
   Ontario *(G-12656)*

PLASTER WORK: Ornamental & Architectural

American Wood Column Corp .... G 718 782-3163
   Brooklyn *(G-1528)*

PLASTIC COLORING & FINISHING

Color Craft Finishing Corp .... F 631 563-3230
   Bohemia *(G-998)*

PLASTIC PRDTS

Castino Corporation .... G 845 229-0341
   Hyde Park *(G-6468)*
G and G Service .... G 518 785-9247
   Latham *(G-7073)*
Global Hanger & Display Inc .... G 631 475-5900
   East Patchogue *(G-4274)*
Kc Tag Co .... G 518 842-6666
   Amsterdam *(G-343)*

PLASTIC PRDTS REPAIR SVCS

All Spec Finishing Inc .... E 607 770-9174
   Binghamton *(G-860)*

PLASTICIZERS, ORGANIC: Cyclic & Acyclic

Wecare Organics LLC .... E 315 689-1937
   Jordan *(G-6843)*

PLASTICS FILM & SHEET

Albert F Stager Inc .... G 315 434-7240
   East Syracuse *(G-4316)*
Astra Products Inc .... E 631 464-4747
   Copiague *(G-3753)*
Dunmore Corporation .... D 845 279-5061
   Brewster *(G-1163)*
Farber Plastics Inc .... E 516 378-4860
   Freeport *(G-5153)*
Farber Trucking Corp .... E 516 378-4860
   Freeport *(G-5154)*
Favorite Plastic Corp .... C 718 253-7000
   Brooklyn *(G-1870)*
Integument Technologies Inc .... F 716 873-1199
   Tonawanda *(G-15552)*
Kings Film & Sheet Inc .... E 718 624-7510
   Brooklyn *(G-2076)*
Maco Bag Corporation .... C 315 226-1000
   Newark *(G-12199)*

PLASTICS FILM & SHEET: Polyethylene

Clear View Bag Company Inc .... C 518 458-7153
   Albany *(G-59)*
Nationwide Tarps Incorporated .... D 518 843-1545
   Amsterdam *(G-353)*
Pace Polyethylene Mfg Co Inc .... E 914 381-3000
   Harrison *(G-5732)*
Potential Poly Bag Inc .... G 718 258-0800
   Brooklyn *(G-2329)*
Sentinel Products Corp .... F 518 568-7036
   Saint Johnsville *(G-14522)*

PLASTICS FILM & SHEET: Polyvinyl

Georgia-Pacific LLC .... E 845 986-2011
   Warwick *(G-15953)*
Shaant Industries Inc .... E 716 366-3654
   Dunkirk *(G-4179)*

PLASTICS FILM & SHEET: Vinyl

Ace Canvas & Tent Corp .... F 631 648-0614
   Ronkonkoma *(G-14288)*
Latham International Inc .... F 518 346-5292
   Schenectady *(G-14695)*
Latham International Inc .... G 518 783-7776
   Latham *(G-7080)*
Orafol Americas Inc .... E 585 272-0309
   Henrietta *(G-6036)*
Plascal Corp .... G 516 249-2200
   Farmingdale *(G-4851)*
Robeco/Ascot Products Inc .... G 516 248-1521
   Garden City *(G-5279)*
Vinyl Materials Inc .... E 631 586-9444
   Deer Park *(G-4060)*

PLASTICS FINISHED PRDTS: Laminated

Anthony River Inc .... F 315 475-1315
   Syracuse *(G-15244)*
Blue Sky Plastic Production .... F 718 366-3966
   Brooklyn *(G-1621)*
Clear Cast Technologies Inc .... E 914 945-0848
   Ossining *(G-12770)*
Inter State Laminates Inc .... E 518 283-8355
   Poestenkill *(G-13181)*
Synthetic Textiles Inc .... G 716 842-2598
   Buffalo *(G-3083)*
Unico Special Products Inc .... E 845 562-9255
   Newburgh *(G-12248)*

Employee Codes: A=Over 500 employees, B=251-500
C=101-250, D=51-100, E=20-50, F=10-19, G=5-9

PLASTICS MATERIAL & RESINS — PRODUCT SECTION

PLASTICS MATERIAL & RESINS

American Acrylic Corporation .... E 631 422-2200
   West Babylon *(G-16133)*
Ampacet Corporation .... A 914 631-6600
   Tarrytown *(G-15474)*
Ashley Resin Corp .... G 718 851-8111
   Brooklyn *(G-1563)*
Atc Plastics LLC .... E 212 375-2515
   New York *(G-8943)*
Bairnco Corporation .... E 914 461-1300
   White Plains *(G-16424)*
Barrett Bronze Inc .... E 914 699-6060
   Mount Vernon *(G-8380)*
Ccmi Inc .... G 315 781-3270
   Geneva *(G-5318)*
Clarence Resins and Chemicals .... G 716 406-9804
   Clarence Center *(G-3543)*
CN Group Incorporated .... A 914 358-5690
   White Plains *(G-16438)*
Cytec Industries Inc .... D 716 372-9650
   Olean *(G-12598)*
Dice America Inc .... G 585 869-6200
   Victor *(G-15842)*
Durez Corporation .... F 716 286-0100
   Niagara Falls *(G-12279)*
E I Du Pont De Nemours & Co .... E 716 876-4420
   Buffalo *(G-2807)*
Eastman Chemical Company .... D 585 722-2905
   Rochester *(G-13759)*
Endurart Inc .... E 212 473-7000
   New York *(G-9679)*
GE Plastics .... G 518 475-5011
   Selkirk *(G-14768)*
General Vy-Coat LLC .... E 718 266-6002
   Brooklyn *(G-1921)*
Global Plastics LP .... E 800 417-4605
   New York *(G-9944)*
Imbibitive Tech Amer Corp .... G 888 843-2323
   Niagara Falls *(G-12294)*
Imbibitive Technologies Corp .... G 888 843-2323
   Niagara Falls *(G-12295)*
International Casein Corp Cal .... E 516 466-4363
   Great Neck *(G-5562)*
Kuraray America Inc .... F 212 986-2230
   New York *(G-10486)*
Macneil Polymers Inc .... F 716 681-7755
   Buffalo *(G-2932)*
Maviano Corp .... G 845 494-2598
   Monsey *(G-8290)*
MB Plastics Inc .... F 718 523-1180
   Greenlawn *(G-5623)*
Momentive Performance Mtls Inc .... D 914 784-4807
   Tarrytown *(G-15484)*
Nationwide Tarps Incorporated .... D 518 843-1545
   Amsterdam *(G-353)*
Parker-Hannifin Corporation .... E 315 926-4211
   Marion *(G-7804)*
Polycast Industries Inc .... G 631 595-2530
   Bay Shore *(G-708)*
Polymers Merona Inc .... F 631 862-8010
   Saint James *(G-14513)*
Sabic Innovative Plas US LLC .... B 518 475-5011
   Selkirk *(G-14771)*
Sabic Innovative Plastics .... E 713 448-7474
   East Greenbush *(G-4231)*
Saga International Recycl LLC .... G 718 621-5900
   Brooklyn *(G-2444)*
Saint-Gobain Prfmce Plas Corp .... C 518 686-7301
   Hoosick Falls *(G-6280)*
Saint-Gobain Prfmce Plas Corp .... C 518 642-2200
   Granville *(G-5524)*
SC Medical Overseas Inc .... E 516 935-8500
   Jericho *(G-6802)*
Solepoxy Inc .... D 716 372-6300
   Olean *(G-12607)*
Solid Surfaces Inc .... D 585 292-5340
   Rochester *(G-14134)*
Telechemische Inc .... G 845 561-3237
   Newburgh *(G-12247)*
Terphane Holdings LLC .... G 585 657-5800
   Bloomfield *(G-956)*
Tmp Technologies Inc .... D 716 895-6100
   Buffalo *(G-3097)*
Toray Holding (usa) Inc .... E 212 697-8150
   New York *(G-11868)*
Toray Industries Inc .... E 212 697-8150
   New York *(G-11869)*
Transpo Industries Inc .... E 914 636-1000
   New Rochelle *(G-8630)*
Tri-Seal Holdings Inc .... D 845 353-3300
   Blauvelt *(G-943)*
Wilsonart Intl Holdings LLC .... E 516 935-6980
   Bethpage *(G-854)*
WR Smith & Sons Inc .... G 845 620-9400
   Nanuet *(G-8469)*

PLASTICS MATERIALS, BASIC FORMS & SHAPES WHOLESALERS

Fibre Materials Corp .... E 516 349-1660
   Plainview *(G-13058)*
Imbibitive Tech Amer Corp .... G 888 843-2323
   Niagara Falls *(G-12294)*
Imbibitive Technologies Corp .... G 888 843-2323
   Niagara Falls *(G-12295)*
Plastic-Craft Products Corp .... E 845 358-3010
   West Nyack *(G-16280)*

PLASTICS PROCESSING

A & G Heat Sealing .... G 631 724-7764
   Smithtown *(G-14893)*
A-1 Products Inc .... G 718 789-1818
   Brooklyn *(G-1462)*
Adirondack Plas & Recycl Inc .... E 518 746-9212
   Argyle *(G-397)*
American Visuals Inc .... G 631 694-6104
   Farmingdale *(G-4720)*
Centro Inc .... B 212 791-9450
   New York *(G-9249)*
Continental Latex Corp .... F 718 783-7883
   Brooklyn *(G-1713)*
CSP Technologies Inc .... E 518 627-0051
   Amsterdam *(G-334)*
Dacobe Enterprises LLC .... F 315 368-0093
   Utica *(G-15691)*
Dawnex Industries Inc .... F 718 384-0199
   Brooklyn *(G-1760)*
Fbm Galaxy Inc .... F 315 463-5144
   East Syracuse *(G-4338)*
Fei Products LLC .... G 716 693-6230
   North Tonawanda *(G-12427)*
Formed Plastics Inc .... D 516 334-2300
   Carle Place *(G-3264)*
Genpak LLC .... C 845 343-7971
   Middletown *(G-8155)*
Germanow-Simon Corporation .... E 585 232-1440
   Rochester *(G-13832)*
Imperial Polymers Inc .... G 718 387-4741
   Brooklyn *(G-1996)*
L I C Screen Printing Inc .... E 516 546-7289
   Merrick *(G-8100)*
Major-IPC Inc .... G 845 292-2200
   Liberty *(G-7145)*
Mettowee Lumber & Plastics Co .... C 518 642-1100
   Granville *(G-5522)*
Mold-A-Matic Corporation .... E 607 433-2121
   Oneonta *(G-12641)*
Nalge Nunc International Corp .... A 585 498-2661
   Rochester *(G-13962)*
Patmian LLC .... B 212 758-0770
   New York *(G-11122)*
Plasticycle Corporation .... E 914 997-6882
   White Plains *(G-16498)*
Prince Rubber & Plas Co Inc .... E 225 272-1653
   Buffalo *(G-3014)*
Richlar Industries Inc .... F 315 463-5144
   East Syracuse *(G-4366)*
Rimco Plastics Corp .... G 607 739-3864
   Horseheads *(G-6326)*
Royal Plastics Corp .... F 718 647-7500
   Brooklyn *(G-2423)*
Royce Associates A Ltd Partnr .... E 516 367-6298
   Jericho *(G-6800)*
Shamrock Plastic Corporation .... G 585 328-6040
   Rochester *(G-14124)*
Shamrock Plastics & Tool Inc .... E 585 328-6040
   Rochester *(G-14125)*
Silvatrim Corp .... C 212 675-0933
   New York *(G-11590)*
Specialty Products Inc .... E 866 869-4335
   Center Moriches *(G-3341)*
Structural Industries Inc. .... C 631 471-5200
   Bohemia *(G-1092)*
Toray Industries Inc .... E 212 697-8150
   New York *(G-11869)*
United Plastics Inc .... G 718 389-2255
   Brooklyn *(G-2603)*
Vinyl Materials Inc .... E 631 586-9444
   Deer Park *(G-4060)*
Zone Fabricators Inc .... F 718 272-0200
   Ozone Park *(G-12834)*

PLASTICS SHEET: Packing Materials

Edco Supply Corporation .... D 718 788-8108
   Brooklyn *(G-1813)*
Knoll Printing & Packaging Inc .... E 516 621-0100
   Syosset *(G-15220)*
Tri-Seal Holdings Inc .... D 845 353-3300
   Blauvelt *(G-943)*

PLASTICS: Blow Molded

Bst United Corp .... F 631 777-2110
   Farmingdale *(G-4729)*
Confer Plastics Inc .... C 800 635-3213
   North Tonawanda *(G-12423)*

PLASTICS: Cast

Albest Metal Stamping Corp .... D 718 388-6000
   Brooklyn *(G-1500)*
Discover Casting Inc .... F 212 302-5060
   New York *(G-9534)*
Miller Technology Inc .... G 631 694-2224
   Farmingdale *(G-4826)*

PLASTICS: Extruded

Albany International Corp .... C 607 749-7226
   Homer *(G-6252)*
Burnham Polymeric Inc .... G 518 792-3040
   Fort Edward *(G-5094)*
Certainteed Corporation .... B 716 827-7560
   Buffalo *(G-2764)*
Christi Plastics Inc .... G 585 436-8510
   Rochester *(G-13710)*
E & T Plastic Mfg Co Inc .... E 718 729-6226
   Long Island City *(G-7432)*
East Cast Clor Compounding Inc .... G 631 491-9000
   West Babylon *(G-16154)*
Eastern Industrial Steel Corp .... F 845 639-9749
   New City *(G-8493)*
Finger Lakes Extrusion Corp .... E 585 905-0632
   Canandaigua *(G-3221)*
Kleer-Fax Inc .... D 631 225-1100
   Amityville *(G-295)*
Pawling Engineered Pdts Inc .... C 845 855-1000
   Pawling *(G-12894)*

PLASTICS: Finished Injection Molded

A R V Precision Mfg Inc .... G 631 293-9643
   Farmingdale *(G-4705)*
Alliance Precision Plas Corp .... C 585 426-5310
   Rochester *(G-13616)*
Alliance Precision Plas Corp .... E 585 426-5310
   Rochester *(G-13617)*
Aluminum Injection Mold Co LLC .... G 585 502-6087
   Le Roy *(G-7112)*
Anna Young Assoc Ltd .... C 516 546-4400
   Freeport *(G-5144)*
Aztec Tool Co Inc .... E 631 243-1144
   Edgewood *(G-4396)*
Epp Team Inc .... D 585 454-4995
   Rochester *(G-13788)*
Everblock Systems LLC .... G 844 422-5625
   New York *(G-9734)*
H & H Hulls Inc .... G 518 828-1339
   Hudson *(G-6352)*
Harbec Inc .... D 585 265-0010
   Ontario *(G-12654)*
J T Systematic .... G 607 754-0929
   Endwell *(G-4617)*
Joe Pietryka Incorporated .... E 845 855-1201
   Pawling *(G-12892)*
K & H Precision Products Inc .... E 585 624-4894
   Honeoye Falls *(G-6269)*
Leidel Corporation .... E 631 244-0900
   Bohemia *(G-1047)*
M & M Molding Corp .... E 631 582-1900
   Central Islip *(G-3377)*
PMI Industries LLC .... E 585 464-8050
   Rochester *(G-14025)*
Primoplast Inc .... F 631 750-0680
   Bohemia *(G-1078)*
Sterling Molded Products Inc .... E 845 344-4546
   Middletown *(G-8177)*

PRODUCT SECTION

PLASTICS: Polystyrene Foam

PLASTICS: Injection Molded

Company	Code	Phone
Aaron Tool & Mold Inc	G	585 426-5100
Rochester (G-13593)		
American Casting and Mfg Corp	D	800 342-0333
Plainview (G-13035)		
American Casting and Mfg Corp	G	516 349-7010
Plainview (G-13036)		
American Spacer Technologies	G	518 828-1339
Hudson (G-6338)		
Anka Tool & Die Inc	E	845 268-4116
Congers (G-3709)		
Armstrong Mold Corporation	G	315 437-1517
East Syracuse (G-4320)		
Armstrong Mold Corporation	D	315 437-1517
East Syracuse (G-4321)		
Auburn Vacuum Forming Co Inc	F	315 253-2440
Auburn (G-467)		
Autronic Plastics Inc	D	516 333-7577
Central Islip (G-3357)		
Avanti Advanced Mfg Corp	F	716 791-9001
Buffalo (G-2718)		
Avanti U S A Ltd	F	716 695-5800
Tonawanda (G-15524)		
Barton Tool Inc	G	716 665-2801
Falconer (G-4672)		
Brandys Mold and Tool Ctr Ltd	F	585 334-8333
West Henrietta (G-16232)		
Buffalo Polymer Processors Inc	E	716 537-3153
Holland (G-6218)		
Cambridge Security Seals LLC	E	845 520-4111
Pomona (G-13185)		
Carolina Precision Plas LLC	D	631 981-0743
Ronkonkoma (G-14326)		
Cast-All Corporation	E	516 741-4025
Mineola (G-8211)		
Cast-All Corporation	E	516 741-4025
Mineola (G-8212)		
Cdj Stamping Inc	G	585 224-8120
Rochester (G-13696)		
Century Mold Company Inc	D	585 352-8600
Rochester (G-13701)		
Century Mold Mexico LLC	G	585 352-8600
Rochester (G-13702)		
Champlain Plastics Inc	D	518 297-3700
Rouses Point (G-14467)		
Chenango Valley Tech Inc	E	607 674-4115
Sherburne (G-14803)		
Clifford H Jones Inc	F	716 693-2444
Tonawanda (G-15534)		
Colonie Plastics Corp	C	631 434-6969
Bay Shore (G-673)		
CPI of Falconer Inc	E	716 664-4444
Falconer (G-4674)		
Craftech Industries Inc	D	518 828-5001
Hudson (G-6344)		
Currier Plastics Inc	D	315 255-1779
Auburn (G-474)		
Custom Lucite Creations Inc	F	718 871-2000
Brooklyn (G-1743)		
Custom Molding Solutions Inc	E	585 293-1702
Churchville (G-3508)		
Cy Plastics Works Inc	E	585 229-2555
Honeoye (G-6260)		
Dolco LLC	E	585 657-7777
Bloomfield (G-952)		
Dutch!and Plastics LLC	C	315 280-0247
Sherrill (G-14820)		
East Pattern & Model Corp	F	585 461-3240
Rochester (G-13757)		
East Pattern & Model Corp	E	585 461-3240
Rochester (G-13756)		
Eck Plastic Arts Inc	E	607 722-3227
Binghamton (G-880)		
Em-Kay Molds Inc	G	716 895-6180
Buffalo (G-2816)		
Ernie Green Industries Inc	D	585 295-8951
Rochester (G-13790)		
Ernie Green Industries Inc	C	585 647-2300
Rochester (G-13791)		
Ernie Green Industries Inc	D	585 647-2300
Rochester (G-13792)		
Extreme Molding LLC	E	518 326-9319
Watervliet (G-16045)		
Faro Industries Inc	F	585 647-6000
Rochester (G-13802)		
Felchar Manufacturing Corp	A	607 723-3106
Binghamton (G-884)		
G N R Plastics Inc	F	631 724-8758
Smithtown (G-14899)		
Galt Industries Inc	G	212 758-0770
New York (G-9878)		
Gen-West Associates LLC	G	315 255-1779
Auburn (G-481)		
Hansa Plastics Inc	F	631 269-9050
Kings Park (G-6883)		
Highland Injection Molding	D	716 945-2424
Salamanca (G-14525)		
Ilion Plastics Inc	F	315 894-4868
Ilion (G-6475)		
Illinois Tool Works Inc	D	860 435-2574
Millerton (G-8194)		
Imco Inc	E	585 352-7810
Spencerport (G-14979)		
Innovative Plastics Corp	F	845 359-7500
Orangeburg (G-12680)		
Inteva Products LLC	B	248 655-8886
New York (G-10255)		
K & H Industries Inc	F	716 312-0088
Hamburg (G-5683)		
K & H Industries Inc	F	716 312-0088
Hamburg (G-5684)		
Kobe Steel USA Holdings Inc	F	212 751-9400
New York (G-10462)		
Line By Line Design Inc	G	716 655-4680
East Aurora (G-4203)		
Mam Molding Inc	G	607 433-2121
Oneonta (G-12639)		
Mdi East Inc	E	518 747-8730
South Glens Falls (G-14937)		
Midbury Industries Inc	F	516 868-0600
Freeport (G-5168)		
Milne Mfg Inc	F	716 772-2536
Gasport (G-5308)		
Minico Industries Inc	G	631 595-1455
Bay Shore (G-702)		
Mold-Rite Plastics LLC	E	518 561-1812
Plattsburgh (G-13134)		
Natech Plastics Inc	E	631 580-3506
Ronkonkoma (G-14383)		
New York Manufactured Products	F	585 254-9353
Rochester (G-13967)		
Nordon Inc	D	585 546-6200
Rochester (G-13974)		
Nordon Inc	E	585 546-6200
Rochester (G-13975)		
Nordon Inc	E	585 546-6200
Rochester (G-13976)		
Oneida Molded Plastics LLC	C	315 363-7980
Oneida (G-12616)		
P M Plastics Inc	F	716 662-1255
Orchard Park (G-12733)		
Peninsula Plastics Ltd	D	716 854-3050
Buffalo (G-2996)		
Plastic-Craft Products Corp	E	845 358-3010
West Nyack (G-16280)		
Polymer Engineered Pdts Inc	D	585 426-1811
Rochester (G-14027)		
Precision Extrusion Inc	E	518 792-1199
Glens Falls (G-5440)		
Precision Techniques Inc	D	718 991-1440
Stony Point (G-15175)		
Pylantis New York LLC	G	310 429-5911
Groton (G-5653)		
Rochling Advent Tool & Mold LP	D	585 254-2000
Rochester (G-14100)		
Russell Plastics Tech Co Inc	C	631 963-8602
Lindenhurst (G-7191)		
Southern Tier Plastics Inc	D	607 723-2601
Binghamton (G-915)		
Staroba Plastics Inc	C	716 537-3153
Holland (G-6222)		
Stuart Mold & Manufacturing	F	716 488-9765
Falconer (G-4693)		
Surprise Plastics Inc	C	718 492-6355
Brooklyn (G-2543)		
Sweet Tooth Enterprises LLC	E	631 752-2888
West Babylon (G-16199)		
Syntec Technologies Inc	E	585 768-2513
Rochester (G-14152)		
Syracuse Plastics LLC	C	315 637-9881
Liverpool (G-7265)		
T A Tool & Molding Inc	F	631 293-0172
Farmingdale (G-4888)		
Tessy Plastics Corp	B	315 689-3924
Skaneateles (G-14878)		
Tessy Plastics Corp	A	315 689-3924
Elbridge (G-4429)		
Titherington Design & Mfg	F	518 324-2205
Plattsburgh (G-13163)		
Toolroom Express Inc	D	607 723-5373
Conklin (G-3735)		
Trimac Molding Services	F	607 967-2900
Bainbridge (G-535)		
Tulip Molded Plastics Corp	D	716 282-1261
Niagara Falls (G-12344)		
Unifab Inc	E	585 235-1760
Rochester (G-14186)		
Unifuse LLC	F	845 889-4000
Staatsburg (G-15025)		
Usheco Inc	F	845 658-9200
Kingston (G-6930)		
Viele Manufacturing Corp	B	718 893-2200
Bronx (G-1416)		
W Kintz Plastics Inc	F	518 296-8513
Howes Cave (G-6334)		

PLASTICS: Molded

Company	Code	Phone
Abr Molding Andy LLC	F	212 576-1821
Ridgewood (G-13528)		
Ace Molding & Tool Inc	G	631 567-2355
Bohemia (G-972)		
Baird Mold Making Inc	G	631 667-0322
Bay Shore (G-661)		
Craftech	D	518 828-5001
Chatham (G-3427)		
Egli Machine Company Inc	E	607 563-3663
Sidney (G-14853)		
Form-Tec Inc	E	516 867-0200
Freeport (G-5155)		
ISO Plastics Corp	D	914 663-8300
Mount Vernon (G-8410)		
K2 Plastics Inc	F	585 494-2727
Bergen (G-822)		
Mechanical Rubber Pdts Co Inc	F	845 986-2271
Warwick (G-15958)		
Mercury Plastics Corp	E	718 498-5400
Brooklyn (G-2195)		
Mirage Moulding Mfg Inc	F	631 843-6168
Farmingdale (G-4827)		
Monarch Plastics Inc	E	716 569-2175
Frewsburg (G-5209)		
Msi-Molding Solutions Inc	E	315 736-2412
Rome (G-14259)		
Niagara Fiberglass Inc	F	716 822-3921
Buffalo (G-2966)		
P V C Molding Technologies	F	315 331-1212
Newark (G-12204)		
Pawling Corporation	C	845 855-1000
Pawling (G-12893)		
Peconic Plastics Inc	F	631 653-3676
Quogue (G-13446)		
Pii Holdings Inc	G	716 876-9951
Buffalo (G-3004)		
Piper Plastics Corp	E	631 842-6889
Copiague (G-3772)		
Piper Plastics Corp	E	631 842-6889
Copiague (G-3773)		
Plastic Works	G	914 576-2050
New Rochelle (G-8622)		
Polymer Conversions Inc	D	716 662-8550
Orchard Park (G-12737)		
Protective Industries Inc	C	716 876-9951
Buffalo (G-3017)		
Protective Industries Inc	C	716 876-9855
Buffalo (G-3018)		
Pulse Plastics Products Inc	E	718 328-5224
Bronx (G-1367)		
Pvc Container Corporation	C	518 672-7721
Philmont (G-12987)		
Seal Reinforced Fiberglass Inc	E	631 842-2230
Copiague (G-3780)		
Seal Reinforced Fiberglass Inc	G	631 842-2230
Copiague (G-3781)		
Sonoco-Crellin Intl Inc	B	518 392-2000
Chatham (G-3431)		
Termatec Molding Inc	F	315 483-4150
Sodus (G-14915)		
Thermold Corporation	C	315 697-3924
Canastota (G-3249)		

PLASTICS: Polystyrene Foam

Company	Code	Phone
Berry Plastics Corporation	B	315 986-6270
Macedon (G-7697)		
Burnett Process Inc	G	585 254-8080
Rochester (G-13683)		
Cellect Plastics LLC	D	518 568-7036
Saint Johnsville (G-14517)		
China Xd Plastics Company Ltd	G	212 747-1118
New York (G-9284)		

Employee Codes: A=Over 500 employees, B=251-500
C=101-250, D=51-100, E=20-50, F=10-19, G=5-9

PLASTICS: Polystyrene Foam

Company	Col	Phone	Loc
Dura Foam Inc	E	718 894-2488	Maspeth (G-7838)
General Vy-Coat LLC	E	718 266-6002	Brooklyn (G-1921)
Great American Industries Inc	G	607 729-9331	Vestal (G-15818)
J & M Packaging Inc	F	631 608-3069	Hauppauge (G-5852)
Latham International Inc	G	518 783-7776	Latham (G-7080)
Latham Pool Products Inc	E	260 432-8731	Latham (G-7083)
Par-Foam Products Inc	C	716 855-2066	Buffalo (G-2990)
Plastpac Inc	E	908 272-7200	Brooklyn (G-2323)
Pliant LLC	B	315 986-6286	Macedon (G-7703)
Professional Packg Svcs Inc	E	518 677-5100	Eagle Bridge (G-4185)
Rimco Plastics Corp	E	607 739-3864	Horseheads (G-6326)
Saint-Gobain Prfmce Plas Corp	C	518 642-2200	Granville (G-5524)
Skd Distribution Corp	E	718 525-6000	Jericho (G-6805)
Strux Corp	E	516 768-3969	Lindenhurst (G-7196)
Thermal Foams/Syracuse Inc	E	315 699-8734	Cicero (G-3523)
Tmp Technologies Inc	D	716 895-6100	Buffalo (G-3097)

PLASTICS: Thermoformed

Company	Col	Phone	Loc
Bo-Mer Plastics LLC	E	315 252-7216	Auburn (G-471)
Cjk Manufacturing LLC	F	585 663-6370	Rochester (G-13712)
Marval Industries Inc	D	914 381-2400	Mamaroneck (G-7748)
Pactiv Corporation	C	518 743-3100	Glens Falls (G-5438)
Plastitel Usa Inc	G	450 687-0600	Chazy (G-3433)
Specialty Model & Mold Inc	G	631 475-0840	Ronkonkoma (G-14416)
Weather Products Corporation	G	315 474-8593	Syracuse (G-15455)

PLATE WORK: Metalworking Trade

Company	Col	Phone	Loc
West Metal Works Inc	E	716 895-4900	Buffalo (G-3128)

PLATEMAKING SVC: Color Separations, For The Printing Trade

Company	Col	Phone	Loc
Absolute Color Corporation	G	212 868-0404	New York (G-8715)
Eastern Color Stripping Inc	F	631 563-3700	Bohemia (G-1018)
Lazer Incorporated	E	336 744-8047	Rochester (G-13910)
Leo P Callahan Inc	F	607 797-7314	Binghamton (G-902)
Micro Publishing Inc	G	212 533-9180	New York (G-10795)

PLATEMAKING SVC: Embossing, For The Printing Trade

Company	Col	Phone	Loc
Aldine Inc (ny)	D	212 226-2870	New York (G-8788)

PLATEMAKING SVC: Gravure, Plates Or Cylinders

Company	Col	Phone	Loc
Charles Henricks Inc	F	212 243-5800	New York (G-9262)
Miroddi Imaging Inc	G	516 624-6898	Oyster Bay (G-12816)

PLATES

Company	Col	Phone	Loc
Circle Press Inc	D	212 924-4277	New York (G-9303)
Csw Inc	F	585 247-4010	Rochester (G-13727)
David Fehlman	E	315 455-8888	Syracuse (G-15303)
Dowd - Witbeck Printing Corp	F	518 274-2421	Troy (G-15604)
Gallant Graphics Ltd	E	845 868-1166	Stanfordville (G-15033)
Gazette Press Inc	E	914 963-8300	Rye (G-14479)
Karr Graphics Corp	E	212 645-6000	Long Island City (G-7487)
Mutual Engraving Company Inc	D	516 489-0534	West Hempstead (G-16223)
P & H Thermotech Inc	G	585 624-1310	Lima (G-7154)
Rigidized Metals Corporation	E	716 849-4703	Buffalo (G-3038)
Rotation Dynamics Corporation	E	585 352-9023	Spencerport (G-14982)
Syracuse Computer Forms Inc	E	315 478-0108	Syracuse (G-15436)
Tobay Printing Co Inc	E	631 842-3300	Copiague (G-3788)
Tripi Engraving Co Inc	E	718 383-6500	Brooklyn (G-2586)

PLATES: Paper, Made From Purchased Materials

Company	Col	Phone	Loc
Amscan Inc	F	845 469-9116	Chester (G-3468)
Amscan Inc	E	845 782-0490	Newburgh (G-12214)
Apexx Omni-Graphics Inc	D	718 326-3330	Maspeth (G-7822)
Hadp LLC	F	518 831-6824	Scotia (G-14741)
Pactiv LLC	E	518 562-6101	Plattsburgh (G-13142)

PLATES: Plastic Exc Polystyrene Foam

Company	Col	Phone	Loc
Apexx Omni-Graphics Inc	D	718 326-3330	Maspeth (G-7822)

PLATES: Truss, Metal

Company	Col	Phone	Loc
Steele Truss and Panel LLC	G	518 562-4663	Plattsburgh (G-13157)

PLATING & FINISHING SVC: Decorative, Formed Prdts

Company	Col	Phone	Loc
Jay Strongwater Holdings LLC	A	646 657-0558	New York (G-10312)

PLATING & POLISHING SVC

Company	Col	Phone	Loc
Abetter Processing Corp	F	718 252-2223	Brooklyn (G-1469)
Epner Technology Inc	G	718 782-8722	Brooklyn (G-1840)
Epner Technology Incorporated	E	718 782-8722	Brooklyn (G-1842)
Kittredge & Sons Inc	D	978 567-0998	Niagara Falls (G-12303)
Praxair Surface Tech Inc	C	845 398-8322	Orangeburg (G-12687)
Qos Enterprises LLC	G	585 454-0550	Rochester (G-14058)
Square One Coating Systems LLC	F	315 790-5921	Oriskany (G-12762)
Tcmf Inc	D	607 724-1094	Binghamton (G-918)

PLATING COMPOUNDS

Company	Col	Phone	Loc
Coventya Inc	F	315 768-6635	Oriskany (G-12754)
Mdi Holdings LLC	A	212 559-1127	New York (G-10747)

PLATING SVC: Chromium, Metals Or Formed Prdts

Company	Col	Phone	Loc
West Falls Machine Co Inc	F	716 655-0440	East Aurora (G-4211)

PLATING SVC: Electro

Company	Col	Phone	Loc
Airmarine Electroplating Corp	G	516 623-4406	Freeport (G-5137)
Astro Electroplating Inc	E	631 968-0656	Bay Shore (G-660)
Berkman Bros Inc	E	718 782-1827	Brooklyn (G-1601)
Bfg Manufacturing Services Inc	E	716 362-0888	Buffalo (G-2732)
Dan Kane Plating Co Inc	F	212 675-4947	New York (G-9462)
Deming Electro-Plating Corp	G	585 968-2355	Cuba (G-3918)
Dura Spec Inc	F	718 526-3053	North Baldwin (G-12362)
Electro Plating Service Inc	F	914 948-3777	White Plains (G-16445)
Epner Technology Incorporated	E	718 782-5948	Brooklyn (G-1841)
Eric S Turner & Company Inc	F	914 235-7114	New Rochelle (G-8602)
Finest Cc Corp	E	917 574-4525	Bronx (G-1270)
General Plating LLC	E	585 423-0830	Rochester (G-13827)
Greene Technologies Inc	D	607 656-4166	Greene (G-5615)
John Larocca & Son Inc	G	631 423-5256	Huntington Station (G-6449)
Key Tech Finishing	E	716 832-1232	Buffalo (G-2904)
Keystone Corporation	E	716 832-1232	Buffalo (G-2906)
Precious Plate Inc	D	716 283-0690	Niagara Falls (G-12325)
Rayco of Schenectady Inc	F	518 212-5113	Amsterdam (G-358)
Sandys Bumper Mart Inc	G	315 472-8149	Syracuse (G-15415)
T & M Plating Inc	E	212 967-1110	New York (G-11766)
Tompkins Metal Finishing Inc	D	585 344-2600	Batavia (G-637)
Tripp Plating Works Inc	E	716 894-2424	Buffalo (G-3104)
Tronic Plating Co Inc	F	516 293-7883	Farmingdale (G-4900)
Victoria Plating Co Inc	D	718 589-1550	Bronx (G-1415)

PLATING SVC: Gold

Company	Col	Phone	Loc
Empire Metal Finishing Inc	E	718 545-6700	Astoria (G-427)
Sherrill Manufacturing Inc	C	315 280-0727	Sherrill (G-14822)

PLATING SVC: NEC

Company	Col	Phone	Loc
Aircraft Finishing Corp	F	631 422-5000	West Babylon (G-16130)
Buffalo Metal Finishing Co	G	716 883-2751	Buffalo (G-2749)
Coating Technology Inc	E	585 546-7170	Rochester (G-13716)
Eastside Oxide Co	E	607 734-1253	Elmira (G-4483)
Galmer Ltd	G	718 392-4609	Long Island City (G-7455)
Hartchrom Inc	F	518 880-0411	Watervliet (G-16047)
Metal Man Restoration	F	914 662-4218	Mount Vernon (G-8421)
Nas CP Corp	E	718 961-6757	College Point (G-3657)
Nassau Chromium Plating Co Inc	E	516 746-6666	Mineola (G-8238)
Premier Finishing Inc	F	716 484-6271	Jamestown (G-6743)
Reynolds Tech Fabricators Inc	E	315 437-0532	East Syracuse (G-4365)
Rochester Overnight Pltg LLC	D	585 328-4590	Rochester (G-14090)
Silverman & Gorf Inc	G	718 625-1309	Brooklyn (G-2473)
US Electroplating Corp	G	631 293-1998	West Babylon (G-16201)
Vernon Plating Works Inc	F	718 639-1124	Woodside (G-16683)

PLAYGROUND EQPT

Company	Col	Phone	Loc
Bears Management Group Inc	G	585 624-5694	Lima (G-7149)
Billy Beez Usa LLC	F	315 741-5099	Syracuse (G-15257)

PRODUCT SECTION

POWDER: Silver

Billy Beez Usa LLC .... F 646 606-2249
 New York *(G-9084)*
Billy Beez Usa LLC .... E 845 915-4709
 West Nyack *(G-16266)*
Eastern Jungle Gym Inc .... E 845 878-9800
 Carmel *(G-3275)*

PLEATING & STITCHING FOR THE TRADE: Decorative & Novelty

A Trusted Name Inc .... F 716 326-7400
 Westfield *(G-16391)*

PLEATING & STITCHING FOR TRADE: Permanent Pleating/Pressing

Stylist Pleating Corp .... F 718 384-8181
 Brooklyn *(G-2529)*

PLEATING & STITCHING SVC

Athletic Cap Co Inc .... E 718 398-1300
 Staten Island *(G-15045)*
Pass Em-Entries Inc .... F 718 392-0100
 Long Island City *(G-7550)*
Todd Walbridge .... G 585 254-3018
 Rochester *(G-14171)*

PLEATING & TUCKING FOR THE TRADE

Vogue Too Plting Stitching EMB .... F 212 354-1022
 New York *(G-12052)*

PLUGS: Electric

K & H Industries Inc .... F 716 312-0088
 Hamburg *(G-5683)*

PLUMBING & HEATING EQPT & SPLY, WHOL: Htg Eqpt/Panels, Solar

Vincent Genovese .... G 631 281-8170
 Mastic Beach *(G-7912)*

PLUMBING & HEATING EQPT & SPLY, WHOLESALE: Hydronic Htg Eqpt

Flushing Boiler & Welding Co .... G 718 463-1266
 Brooklyn *(G-1893)*

PLUMBING & HEATING EQPT & SPLYS WHOLESALERS

Bobrick Washroom Equipment Inc .... D 518 877-7444
 Clifton Park *(G-3565)*
Pronto Gas Heating Sups Inc .... G 718 292-0707
 Bronx *(G-1366)*
Siemens Industry Inc .... E 585 797-2300
 Rochester *(G-14126)*

PLUMBING & HEATING EQPT & SPLYS, WHOL: Plumbing Fitting/Sply

Great American Industries Inc .... G 607 729-9331
 Vestal *(G-15818)*
Long Island Pipe Supply Inc .... E 516 222-8008
 Garden City *(G-5268)*
P E Guerin .... D 212 243-5270
 New York *(G-11084)*

PLUMBING & HEATING EQPT & SPLYS, WHOL: Plumbng/Heatng Valves

Flow-Safe Inc .... E 716 662-2585
 Orchard Park *(G-12714)*

PLUMBING & HEATING EQPT & SPLYS, WHOL: Water Purif Eqpt

Empire Division Inc .... D 315 476-6273
 Syracuse *(G-15318)*
Neptune Soft Water Inc .... F 315 446-5151
 Syracuse *(G-15380)*
Pure Planet Waters LLC .... F 718 676-7900
 Brooklyn *(G-2362)*

PLUMBING & HEATING EQPT & SPLYS, WHOLESALE: Boilers, Steam

Great Rock Automation Inc .... F 631 270-1508
 Farmingdale *(G-4774)*

PLUMBING & HEATING EQPT & SPLYS, WHOLESALE: Brass/Fittings

Coronet Parts Mfg Co Inc .... E 718 649-1750
 Brooklyn *(G-1720)*

PLUMBING & HEATING EQPT & SPLYS, WHOLESALE: Sanitary Ware

Porcelain Refinishing Corp .... F 516 352-4841
 Flushing *(G-5038)*

PLUMBING FIXTURES

Corona Plumbing & Htg Sup Inc .... G 718 424-4133
 Corona *(G-3841)*
ER Butler & Co Inc .... E 212 925-3565
 New York *(G-9699)*
G Sicuranza Ltd .... G 516 759-0259
 Glen Cove *(G-5366)*
L A S Replacement Parts Inc .... F 718 583-4700
 Bronx *(G-1312)*
Liberty Brass Turning Co Inc .... E 718 784-2911
 Westbury *(G-16350)*
Malyn Industrial Ceramics Inc .... G 716 741-1510
 Clarence Center *(G-3548)*
P E Guerin .... D 212 243-5270
 New York *(G-11084)*
Roccera LLC .... F 585 426-0887
 Rochester *(G-14077)*
Toto USA Inc .... G 917 237-0665
 New York *(G-11874)*
Watermark Designs Holdings Ltd .... D 718 257-2800
 Brooklyn *(G-2640)*

PLUMBING FIXTURES: Brass, Incl Drain Cocks, Faucets/Spigots

A B S Brass Products Inc .... F 718 497-2115
 Brooklyn *(G-1454)*
Acme Parts Inc .... E 718 649-1750
 Brooklyn *(G-1478)*
Coronet Parts Mfg Co Inc .... E 718 649-1750
 Brooklyn *(G-1720)*
Coronet Parts Mfg Co Inc .... E 718 649-1750
 Brooklyn *(G-1721)*

PLUMBING FIXTURES: Plastic

An-Cor Industrial Plastics Inc .... D 716 695-3141
 North Tonawanda *(G-12411)*
Bow Industrial Corporation .... D 518 561-0190
 Champlain *(G-3406)*
Gms Hicks Street Corporation .... E 718 858-1010
 Brooklyn *(G-1934)*
H Rindustries .... G 516 487-3825
 Mineola *(G-8226)*
Quality Enclosures Inc .... E 631 234-0115
 Central Islip *(G-3382)*

POINT OF SALE DEVICES

Kenney Manufacturing Displays .... F 631 231-5563
 Brentwood *(G-1139)*
Powa Technologies Inc .... E 347 344-7848
 New York *(G-11225)*

POLISHING SVC: Metals Or Formed Prdts

Barnes Metal Finishing Inc .... F 585 798-4817
 Medina *(G-7971)*
Cnc Systems 2000 Inc .... E 585 265-0160
 Ontario *(G-12649)*
Control Electropolishing Corp .... F 718 858-6634
 Brooklyn *(G-1714)*

POLYESTERS

Perfect Poly Inc .... E 631 265-0539
 Nesconset *(G-8486)*
Terphane LLC .... D 585 657-5800
 Bloomfield *(G-957)*

POLYETHYLENE RESINS

APS American Polymers Svcs Inc .... G 212 362-7711
 New York *(G-8894)*

POLYTETRAFLUOROETHYLENE RESINS

Saint-Gobain Prfmce Plas Corp .... C 518 686-7301
 Hoosick Falls *(G-6281)*

POLYVINYL CHLORIDE RESINS

Adam Scott Designs Inc .... E 212 420-8866
 New York *(G-8732)*
De Originals Ltd .... G 516 474-6544
 Old Westbury *(G-12590)*
Kent Chemical Corporation .... E 212 521-1700
 New York *(G-10436)*
Newmat Northeast Corp .... F 631 253-9277
 West Babylon *(G-16179)*

POPCORN & SUPPLIES WHOLESALERS

Terrells Potato Chip Co Inc .... D 315 437-2786
 Syracuse *(G-15442)*

POSTERS

Candid Worldwide LLC .... G 212 799-5300
 Farmingdale *(G-4733)*

POTTERY: Laboratory & Indl

Saint Gobain Grains & Powders .... A 716 731-8200
 Niagara Falls *(G-12332)*
Saint-Gbain Advnced Crmics LLC .... C 716 278-6066
 Niagara Falls *(G-12333)*

POULTRY & POULTRY PRDTS WHOLESALERS

Vineland Kosher Poultry Inc .... F 718 921-1347
 Brooklyn *(G-2625)*

POULTRY & SMALL GAME SLAUGHTERING & PROCESSING

Advanced Frozen Foods Inc .... E 516 333-6344
 Westbury *(G-16309)*
Campanellis Poultry Farm Inc .... G 845 482-2222
 Bethel *(G-835)*
Goya Foods Inc .... D 716 549-0076
 Angola *(G-369)*
Hoskie Co Inc .... D 718 628-8672
 Brooklyn *(G-1985)*
JW Consulting Inc .... G 845 325-7070
 Monroe *(G-8274)*
MB Food Processing Inc .... B 845 436-5001
 South Fallsburg *(G-14931)*
Murray Bresky Consultants Ltd .... B 845 436-5001
 South Fallsburg *(G-14932)*
Vineland Kosher Poultry Inc .... F 718 921-1347
 Brooklyn *(G-2625)*

POULTRY SLAUGHTERING & PROCESSING

Alle Processing Corp .... C 718 894-2000
 Maspeth *(G-7818)*
Hlw Acres LLC .... G 585 591-0795
 Attica *(G-460)*

POWDER PUFFS & MITTS

American Puff Corp .... D 516 379-1300
 Freeport *(G-5143)*
Penthouse Manufacturing Co Inc .... B 516 379-1300
 Freeport *(G-5173)*

POWDER: Aluminum Atomized

Aip Mc Holdings LLC .... G 212 627-2360
 New York *(G-8777)*

POWDER: Metal

Buffalo Tungsten Inc .... D 716 683-9170
 Depew *(G-4084)*
Cws Powder Coatings Company LP .... G 845 398-2911
 Blauvelt *(G-934)*
Hje Company Inc .... G 518 792-8733
 Queensbury *(G-13428)*
Imerys Steelcasting Usa Inc .... D 716 278-1634
 Niagara Falls *(G-12298)*
Oerlikon Metco (us) Inc .... G 716 270-2228
 Amherst *(G-245)*
Reed Systems Ltd .... F 845 647-3660
 Ellenville *(G-4442)*
Tam Ceramics Group of Ny LLC .... D 716 278-9400
 Niagara Falls *(G-12340)*

POWDER: Silver

Ames Advanced Materials Corp .... D 518 792-5808
 South Glens Falls *(G-14933)*

POWDER: Silver

Ames Goldsmith Corp .... F 518 792-7435
Glens Falls *(G-5414)*

POWER GENERATORS

Independent Field Svc LLC .... G 315 559-9243
Syracuse *(G-15342)*
Intelligen Power Systems LLC .... G 212 750-0373
Old Bethpage *(G-12586)*
Power Gneration Indus Engs Inc .... E 315 633-9389
Bridgeport *(G-1182)*
Suez Energy Astoria LLC .... C 718 274-7700
Flushing *(G-5049)*

POWER SPLY CONVERTERS: Static, Electronic Applications

Albatros North America Inc .... E 518 381-7100
Ballston Spa *(G-575)*
Orbit International Corp .... D 631 435-8300
Hauppauge *(G-5908)*

POWER SUPPLIES: All Types, Static

3835 Lebron Rest Eqp & Sup Inc .... E 212 942-8258
New York *(G-8679)*
Applied Concepts Inc .... E 315 696-6676
Tully *(G-15647)*
Applied Power Systems Inc .... E 516 935-2230
Hicksville *(G-6059)*
Arstan Products International .... F 516 433-1313
Hicksville *(G-6061)*
BC Systems Inc .... E 631 751-9370
Setauket *(G-14792)*
Espey Mfg & Electronics Corp .... C 518 584-4100
Saratoga Springs *(G-14578)*
Hipotronics Inc .... C 845 279-8091
Brewster *(G-1167)*
Orbit International Corp .... D 631 435-8300
Hauppauge *(G-5907)*
Ultravolt Inc .... D 631 471-4444
Ronkonkoma *(G-14426)*
Walter G Legge Company Inc .... G 914 737-5040
Peekskill *(G-12928)*

POWER SUPPLIES: Transformer, Electronic Type

Applied Power Systems Inc .... E 516 935-2230
Hicksville *(G-6059)*
Bright Way Supply Inc .... F 718 833-2882
Brooklyn *(G-1635)*
Fil-Coil International LLC .... F 631 467-5328
Sayville *(G-14629)*
Hammond Manufacturing Co Inc .... F 716 630-7030
Cheektowaga *(G-3448)*

POWER SWITCHING EQPT

Switching Power Inc .... D 631 981-7231
Ronkonkoma *(G-14420)*

POWER TOOLS, HAND: Grinders, Portable, Electric Or Pneumatic

Dean Manufacturing Inc .... F 607 770-1300
Vestal *(G-15814)*
P & F Industries Inc .... E 631 694-9800
Melville *(G-8055)*

POWER TOOLS, HAND: Guns, Pneumatic, Chip Removal

New York Industrial Works Inc .... F 718 292-0615
Bronx *(G-1341)*

POWER TOOLS, HAND: Hammers, Portable, Elec/Pneumatic, Chip

Rbhammers Corp .... F 845 353-5042
Blauvelt *(G-939)*

POWER TRANSMISSION EQPT WHOLESALERS

Peerless-Winsmith Inc .... C 716 592-9311
Springville *(G-15019)*
United Richter Electrical Mtrs .... F 716 855-1945
Buffalo *(G-3112)*

POWER TRANSMISSION EQPT: Aircraft

Precision Gear Incorporated .... C 718 321-7200
College Point *(G-3661)*

POWER TRANSMISSION EQPT: Mechanical

Babbitt Bearings Incorporated .... D 315 479-6603
Syracuse *(G-15253)*
Borgwarner Morse TEC LLC .... C 607 257-6700
Ithaca *(G-6568)*
Champlain Hudson Power Ex Inc .... G 518 465-0710
Albany *(G-57)*
Designatronics Incorporated .... B 516 328-3300
Hicksville *(G-6080)*
Eaw Electronic Systems Inc .... E 845 471-5290
Poughkeepsie *(G-13336)*
Hudson Power Transmission Co .... C 718 622-3869
Brooklyn *(G-1987)*
Huron TI Cutter Grinding Inc .... E 631 420-7000
Farmingdale *(G-4782)*
Kaddis Manufacturing Corp .... G 585 624-3070
Honeoye Falls *(G-6270)*
Ls Power Equity Partners LP .... G 212 615-3456
New York *(G-10622)*
Metallized Carbon Corporation .... C 914 941-3738
Ossining *(G-12771)*
On Line Power Technologies .... G 914 968-4440
Yonkers *(G-16787)*
Package One Inc .... D 518 344-5425
Schenectady *(G-14703)*
Sepac Inc .... E 607 732-2030
Elmira *(G-4502)*
Watson Bowman Acme Corp .... C 716 691-8162
Amherst *(G-260)*

PRECAST TERRAZZO OR CONCRETE PRDTS

Accurate Precast .... F 718 345-2910
Brooklyn *(G-1473)*
Coral Cast LLC .... E 516 349-1300
Plainview *(G-13046)*
Diamond Precast Products Inc .... F 631 874-3777
Center Moriches *(G-3338)*
Key Cast Stone Company Inc .... F 631 789-2145
Amityville *(G-294)*
Northeast Concrete Pdts Inc .... F 518 563-0700
Plattsburgh *(G-13138)*
Superior Aggregates Supply LLC .... E 516 333-2923
Lindenhurst *(G-7199)*
Superior Walls Upstate NY Inc .... D 585 624-9390
Lima *(G-7156)*
Superior Wlls of Hdson Vly Inc .... E 845 485-4033
Poughkeepsie *(G-13370)*

PRECIOUS METALS

Sigmund Cohn Corp .... D 914 664-5300
Mount Vernon *(G-8443)*

PRECIOUS METALS WHOLESALERS

Wallace Refiners Inc .... G 212 391-2649
New York *(G-12068)*

PRECIOUS STONES & METALS, WHOLESALE

Jacoby Enterprises LLC .... G 718 435-0289
Brooklyn *(G-2032)*
S Kashi & Sons Inc .... F 212 869-9393
Great Neck *(G-5587)*

PRECIOUS STONES WHOLESALERS

Incon Gems Inc .... F 212 221-8560
New York *(G-10193)*
Jim Wachtler Inc .... G 212 755-4367
New York *(G-10338)*

PRECIPITATORS: Electrostatic

Beltran Technologies Inc .... E 718 338-3311
Brooklyn *(G-1596)*

PRERECORDED TAPE, CD & RECORD STORES: Video Discs/Tapes

Sony Broadband Entertainment .... F 212 833-6800
New York *(G-11644)*

PRERECORDED TAPE, CD/RECORD STORES: Video Tapes, Prerecorded

Society For The Study .... G 212 822-8806
New York *(G-11634)*

PRERECORDED TAPE, COMPACT DISC & RECORD STORES

Taste and See Entrmt Inc .... G 516 285-3010
Valley Stream *(G-15799)*

PRERECORDED TAPE, COMPACT DISC & RECORD STORES: Records

Motema Music LLC .... G 212 860-6969
New York *(G-10847)*

PRESSED FIBER & MOLDED PULP PRDTS, EXC FOOD PRDTS

Avco Industries Inc .... F 631 851-1555
Central Islip *(G-3358)*
Interntnal Bus Cmmncations Inc .... E 516 352-4505
New Hyde Park *(G-8542)*

PRESSES

Win Set Technologies LLC .... F 631 234-7077
Centereach *(G-3346)*

PRIMARY METAL PRODUCTS

Bridge Components Inc .... G 716 731-1184
Sanborn *(G-14540)*
Cintube Ltd .... F 518 324-3333
Plattsburgh *(G-13117)*
Specialty Fabricators .... F 631 256-6982
Oakdale *(G-12520)*

PRINT CARTRIDGES: Laser & Other Computer Printers

Guttz Corporation of America .... F 914 591-9600
Irvington *(G-6505)*
Hf Technologies LLC .... E 585 254-5030
Hamlin *(G-5700)*
Northeast Toner Inc .... G 518 899-5545
Ballston Lake *(G-570)*
Printer Components Inc .... E 585 924-5190
Fairport *(G-4651)*
Qls Solutions Group Inc .... E 716 852-2203
Buffalo *(G-3022)*
Smartoners Inc .... F 718 975-0197
Brooklyn *(G-2488)*
Summit Technologies LLC .... E 631 590-1040
Holbrook *(G-6212)*

PRINTED CIRCUIT BOARDS

A A Technology Inc .... D 631 913-0400
Ronkonkoma *(G-14284)*
Adco Circuits Inc .... G 716 668-6600
Buffalo *(G-2685)*
Advance Circuit Technology Inc .... E 585 328-2000
Rochester *(G-13604)*
Advance Micro Power Corp .... F 631 471-6157
Ronkonkoma *(G-14291)*
Advanced Digital Info Corp .... E 607 266-4000
Ithaca *(G-6554)*
Advanced Manufacturing Svc Inc .... E 631 676-5210
Ronkonkoma *(G-14292)*
American Quality Technology .... F 607 777-9488
Binghamton *(G-861)*
American Tchncal Ceramics Corp .... B 631 622-4700
Huntington Station *(G-6430)*
Ansen Corporation .... G 315 393-3573
Ogdensburg *(G-12570)*
Ansen Corporation .... C 315 393-3573
Ogdensburg *(G-12571)*
Badger Technologies Inc .... D 585 869-7101
Farmington *(G-4910)*
BCM Electronics Manuf Services .... G 631 580-9516
Ronkonkoma *(G-14317)*
Bsu Inc .... E 607 272-8100
Ithaca *(G-6569)*
C & D Assembly Inc .... E 607 898-4275
Groton *(G-5650)*
C A M Graphics Co Inc .... E 631 842-3400
Farmingdale *(G-4731)*

PRODUCT SECTION — PRINTING MACHINERY

Chautauqua Circuits Inc .... G 716 366-5771
  Dunkirk (G-4163)
Cygnus Automation Inc .... E 631 981-0909
  Bohemia (G-1006)
Della Systems Inc .... F 631 580-0010
  Ronkonkoma (G-14333)
Electronic Coating Tech Inc .... F 518 688-2048
  Cohoes (G-3610)
Ems Technologies Inc .... E 607 723-3676
  Binghamton (G-882)
Entertron Industries Inc .... E 716 772-7216
  Lockport (G-7299)
Falconer Electronics Inc .... D 716 665-4176
  Falconer (G-4678)
Geometric Circuits Inc .... D 631 249-0230
  Holbrook (G-6186)
Global Technologies Inc .... D 631 243-7924
  Deer Park (G-3982)
Hazlow Electronics Inc .... E 585 325-5323
  Rochester (G-13863)
I 3 Manufacturing Services Inc .... G 607 238-7077
  Binghamton (G-891)
I3 Electronics Inc .... C 607 238-7077
  Binghamton (G-893)
I3 Electronics Inc .... D 607 238-7077
  Endicott (G-4596)
IEC Electronics Corp .... B 315 331-7742
  Newark (G-12196)
IEC Electronics Wire Cable Inc .... D 585 924-9010
  Newark (G-12197)
Irtronics Instruments Inc .... F 914 693-6291
  Ardsley (G-395)
Isine Inc .... E 631 913-4400
  Melville (G-8040)
Jabil Circuit Inc .... B 845 471-9237
  Poughkeepsie (G-13347)
Kingboard Holdings Limited .... A 705 844-1993
  New York (G-10452)
Mpl Inc .... E 607 266-0480
  Ithaca (G-6597)
NEa Manufacturing Corp .... E 516 371-4200
  Inwood (G-6497)
Oakdale Industrial Elec Corp .... F 631 737-4090
  Ronkonkoma (G-14388)
Ormec Systems Corp .... E 585 385-3520
  Rochester (G-13991)
Park Electrochemical Corp .... D 631 465-3600
  Melville (G-8056)
Performance Technologies Inc .... E 585 256-0200
  Rochester (G-14012)
Photonamics Inc .... F 585 247-8990
  Rochester (G-14020)
Procomponents Inc .... E 516 683-0909
  Westbury (G-16368)
Rce Manufacturing LLC .... G 631 856-9005
  Commack (G-3699)
Rochester Industrial Ctrl Inc .... D 315 524-4555
  Ontario (G-12663)
Rumsey Corp .... G 914 751-3640
  Yonkers (G-16797)
S K Circuits Inc .... F 703 376-8718
  Canastota (G-3246)
Sag Harbor Industries Inc .... E 631 725-0440
  Sag Harbor (G-14502)
Sopark Corp .... D 716 822-0434
  Buffalo (G-3070)
Stetron International Inc .... F 716 854-3443
  Buffalo (G-3077)
Surf-Tech Manufacturing Corp .... F 631 589-1194
  Ronkonkoma (G-14419)
Transistor Devices Inc .... E 631 471-7492
  Ronkonkoma (G-14421)
Vexos Inc .... E 855 711-3227
  New York (G-12021)
Windsor Technology LLC .... F 585 461-2500
  Rochester (G-14210)

PRINTERS & PLOTTERS

Blue Skies .... G 631 392-1140
  Deer Park (G-3953)
CNy Business Solutions .... G 315 733-5031
  Utica (G-15683)
Mdi Holdings LLC .... A 212 559-1127
  New York (G-10747)
Mg Imaging .... G 212 704-4073
  New York (G-10787)
Peak Performance Design LLC .... G 518 302-9198
  Lake Placid (G-6977)
X Brand Editions .... G 718 482-7646
  Long Island City (G-7643)

PRINTERS' SVCS: Folding, Collating, Etc

JP Signs .... G 518 569-3907
  Chazy (G-3432)
Shield Press Inc .... G 212 431-7489
  New York (G-11565)

PRINTERS: Computer

Control Logic Corporation .... G 607 965-6423
  West Burlington (G-16206)
Future Star Digatech .... F 718 666-0350
  Brooklyn (G-1911)
Hf Technologies LLC .... E 585 254-5030
  Hamlin (G-5700)
Lsc Peripherals Incorporated .... G 631 244-0707
  Bohemia (G-1051)
Transact Technologies Inc .... D 607 257-8901
  Ithaca (G-6613)

PRINTERS: Magnetic Ink, Bar Code

Advanced Barcode Tech Inc .... F 516 570-8100
  Great Neck (G-5527)
Jadak Technologies Inc .... C 315 701-0678
  North Syracuse (G-12407)

PRINTING & BINDING: Book Music

Bridge Enterprises Inc .... G 718 625-6622
  Brooklyn (G-1633)

PRINTING & BINDING: Books

Book1one LLC .... G 585 458-2101
  Rochester (G-13673)
Hamilton Printing Company Inc .... C 518 732-2161
  Troy (G-15608)
Logical Operations Inc .... C 585 350-7000
  Rochester (G-13916)
Syracuse Cultural Workers Prj .... F 315 474-1132
  Syracuse (G-15437)

PRINTING & BINDING: Pamphlets

Bmg Printing and Promotion LLC .... G 631 231-9200
  Bohemia (G-989)

PRINTING & EMBOSSING: Plastic Fabric Articles

Acorn Products Corp .... F 315 894-4868
  Ilion (G-6473)
Mountain T-Shirts Inc .... G 518 943-4533
  Catskill (G-3307)
Patrick Rohan .... G 718 781-2573
  Monticello (G-8323)
Starline Usa Inc .... C 716 773-0100
  Grand Island (G-5514)

PRINTING & ENGRAVING: Card, Exc Greeting

Abigal Press Inc .... D 718 641-5350
  Ozone Park (G-12821)
Printery .... G 516 922-3250
  Oyster Bay (G-12818)
Proof 7 Ltd .... F 212 680-1843
  New York (G-11264)

PRINTING & ENGRAVING: Financial Notes & Certificates

Doremus FP LLC .... E 212 366-3800
  New York (G-9559)
Merrill New York Company Inc .... C 212 229-6500
  New York (G-10778)
Superior Print On Demand .... G 607 240-5231
  Vestal (G-15823)
Table Tops Paper Corp .... G 718 831-6440
  Brooklyn (G-2552)

PRINTING & ENGRAVING: Invitation & Stationery

Batavia Press LLC .... E 585 343-4429
  Batavia (G-612)
Jon Lyn Ink Inc .... G 516 546-2312
  Merrick (G-8099)
Kurtskraft Inc .... G 516 944-4449
  Port Washington (G-13280)

Lion In The Sun Park Slope Ltd .... G 718 369-4006
  Brooklyn (G-2128)
Print Mall .... G 718 437-7700
  Brooklyn (G-2347)
Shade Tree Greetings Inc .... F 585 442-4580
  Rochester (G-14123)

PRINTING & ENGRAVING: Plateless

K & B Stamping Co Inc .... G 914 664-8555
  Mount Vernon (G-8412)

PRINTING & ENGRAVING: Poster & Decal

BDR Creative Concepts Inc .... F 516 942-7768
  Farmingdale (G-4726)
Stickershopcom Inc .... G 631 563-4323
  Bayport (G-739)

PRINTING & STAMPING: Fabric Articles

Casual Friday Inc .... F 585 544-9470
  Rochester (G-13695)
Hollywood Advertising Banners .... E 631 842-3000
  Copiague (G-3764)

PRINTING & WRITING PAPER WHOLESALERS

Argo Lithographers Inc .... E 718 729-2700
  Long Island City (G-7388)
Shipmtes/Printmates Holdg Corp .... D 518 370-1158
  Scotia (G-14746)
Table Tops Paper Corp .... G 718 831-6440
  Brooklyn (G-2552)

PRINTING EQPT & SUPPLIES: Illustration & Poster Woodcuts

Patrick Rohan .... G 718 781-2573
  Monticello (G-8323)

PRINTING INKS WHOLESALERS

I N K T Inc .... F 212 957-2700
  New York (G-10159)
Interntnl Publcatns Media Grup .... G 917 604-9602
  New York (G-10252)
Won & Lee Inc .... E 516 222-0712
  Garden City (G-5284)

PRINTING MACHINERY

A-Mark Machinery Corp .... F 631 643-6300
  West Babylon (G-16125)
Anand Printing Machinery Inc .... G 631 667-3079
  Deer Park (G-3942)
Awt Supply Corp .... G 516 437-9105
  Elmont (G-4517)
Castlereagh Printcraft Inc .... D 516 623-1728
  Freeport (G-5148)
Daige Products Inc .... G 516 621-2100
  Albertson (G-148)
Davis International Inc .... E 585 421-8175
  Fairport (G-4631)
Hodgins Engraving Co Inc .... D 585 343-4444
  Batavia (G-628)
Innotech Graphic Eqp Corp .... G 845 268-6900
  Valley Cottage (G-15755)
International Imaging Mtls Inc .... B 716 691-6333
  Amherst (G-232)
Mekatronics Incorporated .... E 516 883-6805
  Port Washington (G-13288)
Micro Powders Inc .... E 914 332-6400
  Tarrytown (G-15483)
Mount Vernon Machine Inc .... E 845 268-9400
  Valley Cottage (G-15759)
Newport Business Solutions Inc .... F 631 319-6129
  Bohemia (G-1064)
Package Print Technologies .... F 716 871-9905
  Buffalo (G-2988)
Perretta Graphics Corp .... E 845 473-0550
  Poughkeepsie (G-13362)
Prim Hall Enterprises Inc .... F 518 561-7408
  Plattsburgh (G-13150)
Skandacor Direct Inc .... G 585 265-9020
  Webster (G-16099)
Southern Graphic Systems LLC .... C 315 695-7079
  Phoenix (G-12993)
Specilty Bus Mchs Holdings LLC .... E 212 587-9600
  New York (G-11663)

Employee Codes: A=Over 500 employees, B=251-500
C=101-250, D=51-100, E=20-50, F=10-19, G=5-9

PRINTING MACHINERY — PRODUCT SECTION

Sterling Toggle Inc .... F 631 491-0500
  West Babylon (G-16196)
Super Web Inc .... E 631 643-9100
  West Babylon (G-16198)
Universal Metal Fabricators .... F 845 331-8248
  Kingston (G-6927)
Vits International Inc .... E 845 353-5000
  Blauvelt (G-945)
Voodoo Manufacturing Inc .... E 646 893-8366
  Brooklyn (G-2634)
Woerner Industries Inc .... E 585 436-1934
  Rochester (G-14211)

PRINTING MACHINERY, EQPT & SPLYS: Wholesalers

Boxcar Press Incorporated .... E 315 473-0930
  Syracuse (G-15261)
Davis International Inc .... G 585 421-8175
  Fairport (G-4631)
Info Label Inc .... F 518 664-0791
  Halfmoon (G-5663)
Super Web Inc .... E 631 643-9100
  West Babylon (G-16198)

PRINTING TRADES MACHINERY & EQPT REPAIR SVCS

Efam Enterprises LLC .... E 718 204-1760
  Long Island City (G-7435)
Jack L Popkin & Co Inc .... G 718 361-6700
  Kew Gardens (G-6875)

PRINTING, COMMERCIAL Newspapers, NEC

Buffalo Newspress Inc .... C 716 852-1600
  Buffalo (G-2751)
Expedi-Printing Inc .... C 516 513-0919
  Great Neck (G-5551)
Kim Jae Printing Co Inc .... G 212 691-6289
  Roslyn Heights (G-14457)
Kurrier Inc .... G 718 389-3018
  Brooklyn (G-2082)
Republican Registrar Inc .... G 315 497-1551
  Moravia (G-8334)
Stellar Printing Inc .... D 718 361-1600
  Long Island City (G-7603)
Webster Printing Corporation ..... F 585 671-1533
  Webster (G-16107)

PRINTING, COMMERCIAL: Announcements, NEC

Kates Paperie Ltd .... G 212 966-3904
  New York (G-10416)

PRINTING, COMMERCIAL: Bags, Plastic, NEC

Bags Unlimited Inc .... E 585 436-6282
  Rochester (G-13651)
Dynamic Packaging Inc .... F 718 388-0800
  Brooklyn (G-1800)

PRINTING, COMMERCIAL: Business Forms, NEC

Bfc Print Network Inc .... G 716 838-4532
  Amherst (G-217)
Empire Business Forms Inc .... F 845 562-7780
  Newburgh (G-12221)
General Business Supply Inc .... D 518 720-3939
  Watervliet (G-16046)
Kinaneco Inc .... E 315 468-6201
  Syracuse (G-15356)
McAuliffe Paper Inc .... E 315 453-2222
  Liverpool (G-7245)
Select-A-Form Inc .... D 631 981-3076
  Holbrook (G-6208)
Short Run Forms Inc .... D 631 567-7171
  Bohemia (G-1089)
United Print Group Inc .... F 718 392-4242
  Long Island City (G-7623)
Vez Inc .... G 718 273-7002
  Staten Island (G-15151)
Yoman Madeo Fano .... G 631 438-0246
  Patchogue (G-12879)

PRINTING, COMMERCIAL: Calendars, NEC

Won & Lee Inc .... E 516 222-0712
  Garden City (G-5284)

PRINTING, COMMERCIAL: Cards, Visiting, Incl Business, NEC

Create-A-Card Inc .... G 631 584-2273
  Saint James (G-14510)

PRINTING, COMMERCIAL: Circulars, NEC

Linda Campbell .... G 718 994-4026
  Bronx (G-1318)

PRINTING, COMMERCIAL: Coupons, NEC

Ad Publications Inc .... F 585 248-2888
  Pittsford (G-13007)

PRINTING, COMMERCIAL: Decals, NEC

Love Unlimited NY Inc .... E 718 359-8500
  Westbury (G-16353)
Modern Decal Co .... G 315 622-2778
  Liverpool (G-7248)
Seri Systems Inc .... E 585 272-5515
  Rochester (G-14122)

PRINTING, COMMERCIAL: Envelopes, NEC

Argo Envelope Corp .... D 718 729-2700
  Long Island City (G-7386)
Design Distributors Inc .... D 631 242-2000
  Deer Park (G-3966)
Diversified Envelope Ltd .... F 585 615-4697
  Rochester (G-13745)
Dupli Graphics Corporation .... G 315 422-4732
  Syracuse (G-15307)
Dupli Graphics Corporation .... C 315 234-7286
  Syracuse (G-15306)
Eagle Envelope Company .... G 607 387-3195
  Trumansburg (G-15638)
Ehs Group LLC .... G 914 937-6162
  Port Chester (G-13198)
Federal Envelope Inc .... F 212 243-8380
  New York (G-9790)
Hudson Envelope Corporation ... G 212 473-6666
  New York (G-10142)
Matt Industries Inc .... C 315 472-1316
  Syracuse (G-15368)
Poly-Flex Corp .... F 631 586-9500
  Edgewood (G-4410)
Precision Envelope Co Inc .... G 631 694-3990
  Farmingdale (G-4856)
Sentine Printing Inc .... G 516 334-7400
  Westbury (G-16372)
Shipman Printing Inds Inc .... E 716 504-7700
  Niagara Falls (G-12336)

PRINTING, COMMERCIAL: Imprinting

Burr & Son Inc .... G 315 446-1550
  Syracuse (G-15263)
Imprint Branded Content LLC .... G 212 888-8073
  New York (G-10189)
Issacs Yisroel .... G 718 851-7430
  Brooklyn (G-2016)
Total Solution Graphics Inc .... G 718 706-1540
  Long Island City (G-7617)

PRINTING, COMMERCIAL: Invitations, NEC

Alpine Business Group Inc .... F 212 989-4198
  New York (G-8812)
Color Card LLC .... F 631 232-1300
  Central Islip (G-3363)

PRINTING, COMMERCIAL: Labels & Seals, NEC

American Casting and Mfg Corp ...... D 800 342-0333
  Plainview (G-13035)
Citation Healthcare Labels LLC .... G 631 293-4646
  Hauppauge (G-5790)
Classic Labels Inc .... E 631 467-2300
  Patchogue (G-12863)
Crisray Printing Corp .... E 631 293-3770
  Farmingdale (G-4741)
Franklin Packaging Inc .... G 631 582-8900
  Northport (G-12468)
General Trade Mark La .... E 718 979-7261
  Staten Island (G-15078)
Greenbush Tape & Label Inc ..... E 518 465-2389
  Albany (G-79)
Hammer Packaging Corp .... B 585 424-3880
  West Henrietta (G-16242)
Info Label Inc .... F 518 664-0791
  Halfmoon (G-5663)
Janco Press Inc .... G 631 563-3003
  Bohemia (G-1040)
Labels Inter-Global Inc .... F 212 398-0006
  New York (G-10504)
Magazines & Brochures Inc ...... G 716 875-9699
  Buffalo (G-2933)
Master Image Printing Inc .... G 914 347-4400
  Elmsford (G-4550)
Niagara Label Company Inc ...... F 716 542-3000
  Akron (G-20)
Ontario Label Graphics Inc .... F 716 434-8505
  Lockport (G-7325)
Precision Label Corporation ...... F 631 270-4490
  Farmingdale (G-4857)
Quadra Flex Corp .... G 607 758-7066
  Cortland (G-3891)
Tri Star Label Inc .... G 914 237-4800
  Mount Vernon (G-8448)
Triangle Label Tag Inc .... F 718 875-3030
  Brooklyn (G-2583)

PRINTING, COMMERCIAL: Letterpress & Screen

Drns Corp .... F 718 369-4530
  Brooklyn (G-1795)
Farthing Press Inc .... G 716 852-4674
  Buffalo (G-2825)
L I C Screen Printing Inc .... E 516 546-7289
  Merrick (G-8100)
Quist Industries Ltd .... F 718 243-2800
  Brooklyn (G-2373)

PRINTING, COMMERCIAL: Literature, Advertising, NEC

Bizbash Media Inc .... D 646 638-3602
  New York (G-9093)
Grado Group Inc .... G 718 556-4200
  Staten Island (G-15081)
Landlord Guard Inc .... F 212 695-6505
  New York (G-10514)
Nomad Editions LLC .... F 212 918-0992
  Bronxville (G-1425)
North American DF Inc .... G 718 698-2500
  Staten Island (G-15108)

PRINTING, COMMERCIAL: Magazines, NEC

Aspect Printing Inc .... E 347 789-4284
  Brooklyn (G-1564)
L & M Uniserv Corp .... G 718 854-3700
  Brooklyn (G-2087)

PRINTING, COMMERCIAL: Periodicals, NEC

Willis Mc Donald Co Inc .... F 212 366-1526
  New York (G-12115)

PRINTING, COMMERCIAL: Post Cards, Picture, NEC

4 Over 4com Inc .... G 718 932-2700
  Astoria (G-419)

PRINTING, COMMERCIAL: Promotional

Bobley-Harmann Corporation .... G 516 433-3800
  Ronkonkoma (G-14320)
Cooper & Clement Inc .... E 315 454-8135
  Syracuse (G-15289)
Excell Print & Promotions Inc .... G 914 437-8668
  White Plains (G-16448)
Fulcrum Promotions & Prtg LLC ...... G 203 909-6362
  New York (G-9859)
Gary Stock Corporation .... G 914 276-2700
  Croton Falls (G-3911)
Medallion Associates Inc .... E 212 929-9130
  New York (G-10751)
Newport Business Solutions Inc ...... F 631 319-6129
  Bohemia (G-1064)
PDQ Shipping Services .... G 845 255-5500
  New Paltz (G-8580)

Printech Business Systems Inc .... F 212 290-2542
  New York *(G-11249)*
Scancorp Inc .... F 315 454-5596
  Syracuse *(G-15416)*
Swift Multigraphics LLC .... G 585 442-8000
  Rochester *(G-14150)*
Syracuse Letter Company Inc .... F 315 476-8328
  Bridgeport *(G-1184)*
Xpress Printing Inc .... G 516 605-1000
  Plainview *(G-13103)*

PRINTING, COMMERCIAL: Publications

Advance Finance Group LLC .... D 212 630-5900
  New York *(G-8746)*
Beis Moshiach Inc .... E 718 778-8000
  Brooklyn *(G-1594)*
Check-O-Matic Inc .... G 845 781-7675
  Monroe *(G-8267)*
Dental Tribune America LLC .... F 212 244-7181
  New York *(G-9503)*
Glenn Horowitz Bookseller Inc .... G 212 691-9100
  New York *(G-9934)*
Graphic Printing .... G 718 701-4433
  Bronx *(G-1285)*
Graphics 247 Corp .... G 718 729-2470
  Long Island City *(G-7461)*
J T Printing 21 .... G 718 484-3939
  Staten Island *(G-15093)*
Merchandiser Inc .... G 315 462-6411
  Clifton Springs *(G-3582)*
New York Christan Times Inc .... G 718 638-6397
  Brooklyn *(G-2260)*
Nys Nyu-Cntr Intl Cooperation .... E 212 998-3680
  New York *(G-11020)*
Sephardic Yellow Pages .... E 718 998-0299
  Brooklyn *(G-2456)*

PRINTING, COMMERCIAL: Screen

A Promos USA Inc .... F 516 377-0186
  Freeport *(G-5135)*
A Tradition of Excellence Inc .... G 845 638-4595
  New City *(G-8489)*
Acme Screenprinting .... G 716 565-1052
  Buffalo *(G-2684)*
Active World Solutions Inc .... G 718 922-9404
  Brooklyn *(G-1480)*
Advanced Graphics Company .... F 607 692-7875
  Whitney Point *(G-16554)*
Albert Siy .... G 718 359-0389
  Flushing *(G-4982)*
Alicia F Herdlein .... G 585 344-4411
  Batavia *(G-608)*
AMA Precision Screening Inc .... F 585 293-0820
  Churchville *(G-3505)*
Arca Ink LLC .... G 518 798-0100
  South Glens Falls *(G-14934)*
Arena Graphics Inc .... G 516 767-5108
  Port Washington *(G-13244)*
Artscroll Printing Corp .... E 212 929-2413
  New York *(G-8926)*
Barnaby Prints Inc .... F 845 477-2501
  Greenwood Lake *(G-5648)*
Bartolomeo Publishing Inc .... G 631 420-4949
  West Babylon *(G-16138)*
Bidpress LLC .... G 267 973-8876
  New York *(G-9073)*
C & C Athletic Inc .... G 845 713-4670
  Walden *(G-15891)*
CHv Printed Company .... F 516 997-1101
  East Meadow *(G-4247)*
Cnyshirts .... G 315 432-1789
  Syracuse *(G-15282)*
Con-Tees Custom Printing Ltd .... G 914 664-0251
  Mount Vernon *(G-8390)*
Control Research Inc .... G 631 225-1111
  Amityville *(G-269)*
Custom 101 Prints Inc .... F 718 708-4425
  Bronx *(G-1249)*
Custom Prtrs Guilderland Inc .... F 518 456-2811
  Guilderland *(G-5654)*
Custom Sportswear Corp .... G 914 666-9200
  Bedford Hills *(G-773)*
D B F Associates .... G 718 328-0005
  Bronx *(G-1250)*
DEW Graphics Inc .... E 212 727-8820
  New York *(G-9515)*
Dkm Sales LLC .... E 716 893-7777
  Buffalo *(G-2802)*
Effective Slling Solutions LLC .... G 716 771-8503
  Lake View *(G-6983)*

Efs Designs LLC .... G 718 852-9511
  Brooklyn *(G-1816)*
First2print Inc .... G 212 868-6886
  New York *(G-9809)*
Freeport Screen & Stamping .... E 516 379-0330
  Freeport *(G-5157)*
Fresh Prints LLC .... E 917 826-2752
  New York *(G-9848)*
Graph-Tex Inc .... F 607 756-7791
  Cortland *(G-3873)*
Graph-Tex Inc .... G 607 756-1875
  Cortland *(G-3874)*
Graphics For Industry Inc .... F 212 889-6202
  New York *(G-9977)*
Graphics Plus Printing Inc .... G 607 299-0500
  Cortland *(G-3875)*
Gruber Display Co Inc .... F 718 882-8220
  Bronx *(G-1286)*
Handone Studios Inc .... G 585 421-8175
  Fairport *(G-4634)*
Herrmann Group LLC .... G 716 876-9798
  Kenmore *(G-6860)*
Human Technologies Corporation .... F 315 735-3532
  Utica *(G-15711)*
Impressive Imprints .... F 716 692-0905
  North Tonawanda *(G-12432)*
Island Silkscreen Inc .... E 631 757-4567
  East Northport *(G-4265)*
J Kendall LLC .... E 646 739-4956
  Yonkers *(G-16772)*
J M L Productions Inc .... D 718 643-1674
  Brooklyn *(G-2025)*
J N White Associates Inc .... D 585 237-5191
  Perry *(G-12969)*
Kenmar Shirts Inc .... E 718 824-3880
  Bronx *(G-1307)*
Knucklehead Embroidery Inc .... G 607 797-2725
  Johnson City *(G-6814)*
Logomax Inc .... G 631 420-0484
  Farmingdale *(G-4809)*
Loremanss Embroidery Engrav .... E 518 834-9205
  Keeseville *(G-6852)*
Mart-Tex Athletics Inc .... E 631 454-9583
  Farmingdale *(G-4817)*
Mastercraft Decorators Inc .... G 585 223-5150
  Fairport *(G-4641)*
Mastro Graphic Arts Inc .... G 585 436-7570
  Rochester *(G-13931)*
Matthew-Lee Corporation .... G 631 226-0100
  Lindenhurst *(G-7179)*
Metro Creative Graphics Inc .... F 212 947-5100
  New York *(G-10784)*
Mixture Screen Printing .... G 845 561-2857
  Newburgh *(G-12232)*
Multi Packaging Solutions Inc .... E 646 885-0005
  New York *(G-10858)*
Mv Corp Inc .... C 631 273-8020
  Bay Shore *(G-703)*
Nathan Printing Express Inc .... G 914 472-0914
  Scarsdale *(G-14641)*
New Art Signs Co Inc .... G 718 443-0900
  Glen Head *(G-5383)*
New Buffalo Shirt Factory Inc .... G 716 436-5839
  Buffalo *(G-2963)*
Northwind Graphics .... G 518 899-9651
  Ballston Spa *(G-593)*
Okey Enterprises Inc .... G 212 213-2640
  New York *(G-11034)*
One In A Million Inc .... G 516 829-1111
  Valley Stream *(G-15788)*
Paratore Signs Inc .... G 315 455-5551
  Syracuse *(G-15393)*
Park Avenue Imprints LLC .... G 716 822-5737
  Buffalo *(G-2991)*
Patrick Kraft .... G 315 343-9376
  Oswego *(G-12786)*
PDM Studios Inc .... G 716 694-8337
  Tonawanda *(G-15569)*
Penny Lane Printing Inc .... D 585 226-8111
  Avon *(G-521)*
Personal Graphics Corporation .... G 315 853-3421
  Westmoreland *(G-16408)*
Peter Papastro .... G 607 723-8112
  Binghamton *(G-910)*
Pierrepont Visual Graphics .... G 585 305-9672
  Rochester *(G-14022)*
Premier Ink Systems Inc .... E 845 782-5802
  Harriman *(G-5721)*
Print Shoppe .... G 315 792-9585
  Utica *(G-15730)*

Printed Image .... G 716 821-1880
  Buffalo *(G-3015)*
Printing Max New York Inc .... G 718 692-1400
  Brooklyn *(G-2350)*
Publimax Printing Corp .... G 718 366-7133
  Ridgewood *(G-13548)*
R R Donnelley & Sons Company .... D 518 438-9722
  Albany *(G-121)*
Rainbow Lettering .... G 607 732-5751
  Elmira *(G-4501)*
Regal Screen Printing Intl .... G 845 356-8181
  Spring Valley *(G-15005)*
Richs Stthes EMB Screenprint .... G 845 621-2175
  Mahopac *(G-7711)*
Round Top Knit & Screening .... G 518 622-3600
  Round Top *(G-14466)*
Royal Tees Inc .... G 845 357-9448
  Suffern *(G-15197)*
S L C Industries Incorporated .... F 607 775-2299
  Binghamton *(G-913)*
Sand Hill Industries Inc .... G 518 885-7991
  Ballston Spa *(G-595)*
Screen The World Inc .... F 631 475-0023
  Holtsville *(G-6244)*
Shore Line Monogramming Inc .... F 914 698-8000
  Mamaroneck *(G-7757)*
Shykat Promotions .... G 866 574-2757
  Forestville *(G-5088)*
Sign Shop Inc .... G 631 226-4145
  Copiague *(G-3782)*
Silk Screen Art Inc .... F 518 762-8423
  Johnstown *(G-6839)*
Sino Printing Inc .... G 212 334-6896
  New York *(G-11600)*
Spst Inc .... G 607 798-6952
  Vestal *(G-15822)*
Stromberg Brand Corporation .... F 914 739-7410
  Valley Cottage *(G-15767)*
T L F Graphics Inc .... D 585 272-5500
  Rochester *(G-14156)*
Tara Rific Screen Printing Inc .... G 718 583-6864
  Bronx *(G-1401)*
Todd Walbridge .... G 585 254-3018
  Rochester *(G-14171)*
U All Inc .... E 518 438-2558
  Albany *(G-136)*
Universal Screening Associates .... F 718 232-2744
  Brooklyn *(G-2609)*
Unlimited Ink Inc .... E 631 582-0696
  Hauppauge *(G-5967)*
Viking Athletics Ltd .... G 631 957-8000
  Lindenhurst *(G-7203)*
Voss Signs LLC .... E 315 682-6418
  Manlius *(G-7781)*
Zacks Enterprises Inc .... G 800 366-4924
  Orangeburg *(G-12693)*

PRINTING, COMMERCIAL: Stamps, Trading, NEC

Ashton-Potter USA Ltd .... C 716 633-2000
  Williamsville *(G-16568)*

PRINTING, COMMERCIAL: Stationery, NEC

Hart Reproduction Services .... G 212 704-0556
  New York *(G-10046)*

PRINTING, COMMERCIAL: Tags, NEC

Actioncraft Products Inc .... G 516 883-6423
  Port Washington *(G-13239)*
Colonial Tag & Label Co Inc .... F 516 482-0508
  Great Neck *(G-5546)*
Industrial Test Eqp Co Inc .... E 516 883-6423
  Port Washington *(G-13269)*
Itc Mfg Group Inc .... F 212 684-3696
  New York *(G-10278)*

PRINTING, LITHOGRAPHIC: Advertising Posters

First Displays Inc .... F 347 642-5972
  Long Island City *(G-7449)*
V C N Group Ltd Inc .... G 516 223-4812
  North Baldwin *(G-12369)*

PRINTING, LITHOGRAPHIC: Calendars

Redi Records Payroll .... F 718 854-6990
  Brooklyn *(G-2392)*

PRINTING, LITHOGRAPHIC: Color

Company		Phone
Chakra Communications Inc	E	716 505-7300
Lancaster (G-7013)		
Crawford Print Shop Inc	G	607 359-4970
Addison (G-5)		
Create-A-Card Inc	G	631 584-2273
Saint James (G-14510)		
Digital United Color Prtg Inc	G	845 986-9846
Warwick (G-15950)		
Raith America Inc	E	518 874-3000
Troy (G-15619)		
Select-A-Form Inc	D	631 981-3076
Holbrook (G-6208)		
Spectrum Prtg Lithography Inc	E	212 255-3131
New York (G-11665)		

PRINTING, LITHOGRAPHIC: Decals

Company		Phone
Aro-Graph Corporation	G	315 463-8693
Syracuse (G-15246)		
Decal Makers Inc	E	516 221-7200
Bellmore (G-788)		
Decal Techniques Inc	G	631 491-1800
Bay Shore (G-679)		
Paper House Productions Inc	E	845 246-7261
Saugerties (G-14612)		

PRINTING, LITHOGRAPHIC: Forms & Cards, Business

Company		Phone
Batavia Press LLC	E	585 343-4429
Batavia (G-612)		
Color Card LLC	F	631 232-1300
Central Islip (G-3363)		
Miller Place Printing Inc	G	631 473-1158
Miller Place (G-8191)		
Perfect Forms and Systems Inc	F	631 462-1100
Smithtown (G-14905)		
Webb-Mason Inc	E	716 276-8792
Buffalo (G-3126)		

PRINTING, LITHOGRAPHIC: Forms, Business

Company		Phone
Artina Group Inc	E	914 592-1850
Elmsford (G-4530)		
Precision Envelope Co Inc	G	631 694-3990
Farmingdale (G-4856)		

PRINTING, LITHOGRAPHIC: Letters, Circular Or Form

Company		Phone
Brooklyn Circus	F	718 858-0919
Brooklyn (G-1640)		
F & D Services Inc	F	718 984-1635
Staten Island (G-15075)		

PRINTING, LITHOGRAPHIC: Menus

Company		Phone
Ready Check Glo Inc	G	516 547-1849
East Northport (G-4270)		

PRINTING, LITHOGRAPHIC: Offset & photolithographic printing

Company		Phone
Ace Printing & Publishing Inc	F	718 939-0040
Flushing (G-4980)		
Iron Horse Graphics Ltd	G	631 537-3400
Bridgehampton (G-1181)		
Kaymil Printing Company Inc	G	212 594-3718
New York (G-10422)		
Mdi Holdings LLC	A	212 559-1127
New York (G-10747)		
Nova Inc	G	212 967-1139
New York (G-10999)		
Progressive Color Graphics	E	212 292-8787
Great Neck (G-5584)		
Remsen Graphics Corp	G	718 643-7500
Brooklyn (G-2397)		
Rgm Signs Inc	G	718 442-0598
Staten Island (G-15129)		
Superior Print On Demand	G	607 240-5231
Vestal (G-15823)		

PRINTING, LITHOGRAPHIC: On Metal

Company		Phone
A I P Printing & Stationers	G	631 929-5529
Wading River (G-15883)		
Avon Reproductions Inc	G	631 273-2400
Hauppauge (G-5776)		

Company		Phone
Challenge Graphics Svcs Inc	E	631 586-0171
Deer Park (G-3956)		
Cherry Lane Lithographing Corp	E	516 293-9294
Plainview (G-13041)		
David Helsing	G	607 796-2681
Horseheads (G-6311)		
Denton Advertising Inc	F	631 586-4333
Bohemia (G-1013)		
Hks Printing Company Inc	F	212 675-2529
New York (G-10109)		
Mansfield Press Inc	F	212 265-5411
New York (G-10695)		
Messenger Press	G	518 885-9231
Ballston Spa (G-591)		
Seneca West Printing Inc	G	716 675-8010
West Seneca (G-16303)		

PRINTING, LITHOGRAPHIC: Post Cards, Picture

Company		Phone
Anne Taintor Inc	G	718 483-9312
Brooklyn (G-1536)		

PRINTING, LITHOGRAPHIC: Promotional

Company		Phone
21st Century Fox America Inc	D	212 852-7000
New York (G-8673)		
China Imprint LLC	G	585 563-3391
Rochester (G-13709)		
Gmp LLC	D	914 939-0571
Port Chester (G-13200)		
In-Step Marketing Inc	F	212 797-3450
New York (G-10191)		
R & L Press Inc	F	718 447-8557
Staten Island (G-15121)		

PRINTING, LITHOGRAPHIC: Publications

Company		Phone
Canyon Publishing Inc	F	212 334-0227
New York (G-9199)		
Hudson Park Press Inc	G	212 929-8898
New York (G-10144)		
Post Road	G	203 545-2122
New York (G-11224)		
Print By Premier LLC	G	212 947-1365
New York (G-11245)		

PRINTING, LITHOGRAPHIC: Tags

Company		Phone
Kwik Ticket Inc	F	718 421-3800
Brooklyn (G-2085)		

PRINTING, LITHOGRAPHIC: Tickets

Company		Phone
Worldwide Ticket Craft	D	516 538-6200
Merrick (G-8107)		

PRINTING, LITHOGRAPHIC: Transfers, Decalcomania Or Dry

Company		Phone
Royal Tees Inc	G	845 357-9448
Suffern (G-15197)		

PRINTING: Books

Company		Phone
Cct Inc	G	212 532-3355
New York (G-9233)		
Kravitz Design Inc	G	212 625-1644
New York (G-10482)		
North Country Books Inc	G	315 735-4877
Utica (G-15726)		
Twp America Inc	G	212 274-8090
New York (G-11921)		
Vicks Lithograph & Prtg Corp	C	315 272-2401
Yorkville (G-16832)		

PRINTING: Books

Company		Phone
450 Ridge St Inc	G	716 754-2789
Lewiston (G-7138)		
Bedford Freeman & Worth	C	212 576-9400
New York (G-9034)		
Centrisource Inc	G	716 871-1105
Tonawanda (G-15533)		
E Graphics Corporation	G	718 486-9767
Brooklyn (G-1804)		
Experiment LLC	G	212 889-1659
New York (G-9754)		
Flare Multicopy Corp	E	718 258-8860
Brooklyn (G-1887)		
Hudson Valley Paper Works Inc	F	845 569-8883
Newburgh (G-12228)		

Company		Phone
Hys LLC	F	212 716-6600
New York (G-10157)		
In-House Inc	F	718 445-9007
College Point (G-3646)		
Literary Classics of US	F	212 308-3360
New York (G-10578)		
Printing Factory LLC	F	718 451-0500
Brooklyn (G-2349)		
Promotional Sales Books LLC	G	212 675-0364
New York (G-11260)		
Royal Fireworks Printing Co	F	845 726-3333
Unionville (G-15673)		
Steffen Publishing Inc	D	315 865-4100
Holland Patent (G-6225)		
Sterling Pierce Company Inc	E	516 593-1170
East Rockaway (G-4296)		
Stop Entertainment Inc	F	212 242-7867
Monroe (G-8281)		
The Nugent Organization Inc	F	212 645-6600
Oceanside (G-12561)		
Tobay Printing Co Inc	G	631 842-3300
Copiague (G-3788)		
Vicks Lithograph & Prtg Corp	C	315 736-9344
Yorkville (G-16833)		
Worzalla Publishing Company	C	212 967-7909
New York (G-12141)		

PRINTING: Broadwoven Fabrics. Cotton

Company		Phone
Mountain T-Shirts Inc	G	518 943-4533
Catskill (G-3307)		

PRINTING: Checkbooks

Company		Phone
Datamax International Inc	E	212 693-0933
New York (G-9476)		
Deluxe Corporation	B	845 362-4054
Spring Valley (G-14988)		
Wood Designs Deluxe Corp	G	917 414-4640
Island Park (G-6519)		

PRINTING: Commercial, NEC

Company		Phone
2 1 2 Postcards Inc	E	212 767-8227
New York (G-8667)		
461 New Lots Avenue LLC	G	347 303-9305
Brooklyn (G-1442)		
5 Stars Printing Corp	F	718 461-4612
Flushing (G-4977)		
A & A Graphics II	G	516 735-0078
Seaford (G-14757)		
A Graphic Printing Inc	G	212 233-9696
New York (G-8694)		
Academy Printing Services Inc	G	631 765-3346
Southold (G-14967)		
Accel Printing & Graphics	G	914 241-3369
Mount Kisco (G-8337)		
Action Envelope & Prtg Co Inc	F	631 225-3900
Amityville (G-263)		
Adirondack Pennysaver Inc	E	518 563-0100
Plattsburgh (G-13105)		
Allsafe Technologies Inc	D	716 691-0400
Amherst (G-212)		
Alpina Copyworld Inc	F	212 683-3511
New York (G-8811)		
Always Printing	G	914 481-5209
Port Chester (G-13193)		
American Office Supply Inc	F	516 294-9444
Westbury (G-16315)		
Amerikom Group Inc	D	212 675-1329
New York (G-8842)		
Amstead Press Corp	G	347 416-2373
New York (G-8850)		
Andrew J George	G	518 462-4662
Albany (G-41)		
Ansun Graphics Inc	F	315 437-6869
Syracuse (G-15243)		
Apple Enterprises Inc	E	718 361-2200
Long Island City (G-7381)		
April Printing Co Inc	F	212 685-7455
New York (G-8893)		
Argo Lithographers Inc	E	718 729-2700
Long Island City (G-7388)		
Arista Innovations Inc	E	516 746-2262
Mineola (G-8205)		
Artistic Typography Corp	F	212 463-8880
New York (G-8923)		
Asn Inc	F	718 894-0800
Maspeth (G-7824)		
Balajee Enterprises Inc	G	212 629-6150
New York (G-9006)		

Bedford Freeman & Worth	C	212 576-9400	New York (G-9034)
Beebie Printing & Art Agcy Inc	G	518 725-4528	Gloversville (G-5453)
Benchemark Printing Inc	D	518 393-1361	Schenectady (G-14653)
Berkshire Business Forms Inc	F	518 828-2600	Hudson (G-6343)
Bestmade Printing LLC	F	718 384-0719	Brooklyn (G-1605)
Bestype Digital Imaging LLC	F	212 966-6886	New York (G-9058)
Big Apple Sign Corp	D	212 629-3650	New York (G-9076)
Body Builders Inc	G	718 492-7997	Brooklyn (G-1627)
Bondy Printing Corp	G	631 242-1510	Bay Shore (G-666)
BP Beyond Printing Inc	G	516 323-2700	Hempstead (G-6008)
Bradley Marketing Group Inc	G	212 967-6100	New York (G-9132)
Bridge Fulfillment Inc	G	718 625-6622	Brooklyn (G-1634)
Brooks Litho Digital Group Inc	G	631 789-4500	Deer Park (G-3955)
Cama Graphics Inc	F	718 707-9747	Long Island City (G-7405)
Century Direct LLC	C	212 763-0600	Islandia (G-6524)
Chakra Communications Inc	E	607 748-7491	Endicott (G-4584)
Christian Bus Endeavors Inc	F	315 788-8560	Watertown (G-16007)
Chroma Communications Inc	G	631 289-8871	Medford (G-7943)
Classic Album	E	718 388-2818	Brooklyn (G-1699)
Colad Group LLC	D	716 961-1776	Buffalo (G-2772)
Colonial Label Systems Inc	E	631 254-0111	Bay Shore (G-672)
Comgraph Sales Service	G	716 601-7243	Elma (G-4449)
Commercial Press Inc	G	315 274-0028	Canton (G-3255)
Copy Room Inc	F	212 371-8600	New York (G-9397)
Copy X/Press Ltd	D	631 585-2200	Ronkonkoma (G-14328)
D G M Graphics Inc	F	516 223-2220	Merrick (G-8096)
D3 Repro Group	G	347 507-1075	Long Island City (G-7420)
DArcy Printing and Lithog	G	212 924-1554	New York (G-9471)
Dash Printing Inc	G	212 643-8534	New York (G-9472)
Data Flow Inc	G	631 436-9200	Medford (G-7945)
Delft Printing Inc	G	716 683-1100	Lancaster (G-7015)
Digital Evolution Inc	E	212 732-2722	New York (G-9527)
Direct Print Inc	F	212 987-6003	New York (G-9532)
Dit Prints Incorporated	G	518 885-4400	Ballston Spa (G-581)
Division Den-Bar Enterprises	G	914 381-2220	Mamaroneck (G-7742)
Donald Bruhnke	F	212 600-1260	New York (G-9547)
Dutchess Plumbing & Heating	G	845 889-8255	Staatsburg (G-15023)
E&I Printing	F	212 206-0506	New York (G-9599)
Elm Graphics Inc	G	315 737-5984	New Hartford (G-8503)
Enterprise Press Inc	C	212 741-2111	New York (G-9687)
Evergreen Corp Central NY	F	315 454-4175	Syracuse (G-15320)
Excellent Printing Inc	G	718 384-7272	Brooklyn (G-1857)
Exotic Print and Paper Inc	F	212 807-0465	New York (G-9753)
Fedex Office & Print Svcs Inc	G	718 982-5223	Staten Island (G-15076)
Fleaheart Inc	F	718 521-4958	Brooklyn (G-1890)
Flp Group LLC	F	315 252-7583	Auburn (G-480)
Folder Factory Inc	F	540 477-3852	Amityville (G-275)
Force Digital Media Inc	G	631 243-0243	Deer Park (G-3977)
Freeville Publishing Co Inc	F	607 844-9119	Freeville (G-5191)
G&J Graphics Inc	G	718 409-9874	Bronx (G-1277)
Gallant Graphics Ltd	E	845 868-1166	Stanfordville (G-15033)
Garrett J Cronin	G	914 761-9299	White Plains (G-16452)
Gatehouse Media LLC	B	585 598-0030	Pittsford (G-13013)
GE Healthcare Fincl Svcs Inc	G	212 713-2000	New York (G-9894)
Gem Reproduction Services Corp	G	845 298-0172	Wappingers Falls (G-15932)
Genie Instant Printing Co Inc	F	212 575-8258	New York (G-9905)
Georgia-Pacific LLC	E	845 986-2011	Warwick (G-15953)
Grand Meridian Printing Inc	E	718 937-3888	Long Island City (G-7460)
Graphic Lab Inc	E	212 682-1815	New York (G-9976)
Graphics Service Bureau Inc	F	212 684-3600	Long Island City (G-7462)
Haig Press Inc	E	631 582-5800	Hauppauge (G-5838)
Hi-Tech Packg World-Wide LLC	G	845 947-1912	New Windsor (G-8646)
Horace J Metz	G	716 873-9103	Kenmore (G-6861)
Hospitality Inc	E	212 268-1930	New York (G-10128)
I N K T Inc	F	212 957-2700	New York (G-10159)
Image Typography Inc	G	631 218-6932	Holbrook (G-6188)
Impress Graphic Technologies	F	516 781-0845	Westbury (G-16342)
Incodema3d LLC	E	607 269-4390	Ithaca (G-6583)
Integrated Graphics Inc	G	212 592-5600	New York (G-10231)
Iron Horse Graphics Ltd	G	631 537-3400	Bridgehampton (G-1181)
Jack J Florio Jr	G	716 434-9123	Lockport (G-7311)
Japan Printing & Graphics Inc	G	212 406-2905	New York (G-10308)
Joed Press	G	212 243-3620	New York (G-10350)
John Auguliaro Printing Co	G	718 382-5283	Brooklyn (G-2043)
Jomar Industries Inc	E	845 357-5773	Airmont (G-14)
Jomart Associates Inc	E	212 627-2153	Islandia (G-6532)
Kallen Corp	G	212 242-1470	New York (G-10399)
Kenan International Trading	G	718 672-4922	Corona (G-3847)
Key Computer Svcs of Chelsea	D	212 206-8060	New York (G-10438)
Lake Placid Advertisers Wkshp	E	518 523-3359	Lake Placid (G-6976)
Lauricella Press Inc	E	516 931-5906	Brentwood (G-1140)
Lennons Litho Inc	F	315 866-3156	Herkimer (G-6043)
Leo Paper Inc	G	917 305-0708	New York (G-10550)
Levon Graphics Corp	D	631 753-2022	Deer Park (G-4001)
Linden Forms & Systems Inc	E	212 219-1100	Brooklyn (G-2126)
Loy L Press Inc	G	716 634-5966	Buffalo (G-2928)
M C Packaging Corporation	E	631 643-3763	Babylon (G-529)
Mason Transparent Package Inc	E	718 792-6000	Bronx (G-1324)
Measurement Incorporated	F	914 682-1969	White Plains (G-16475)
Mega Graphics Inc	G	914 962-1402	Yorktown Heights (G-16819)
Merrill Communications LLC	G	212 620-5600	New York (G-10775)
Merrill Corporation	D	917 934-7300	New York (G-10776)
Middletown Press	G	845 343-1895	Middletown (G-8164)
Miken Companies Inc	D	716 668-6311	Buffalo (G-2946)
Mimeocom Inc	B	212 847-3000	New York (G-10814)
Mini Graphics Inc	D	516 223-6464	Hauppauge (G-5893)
Mpe Graphics Inc	F	631 582-8900	Bohemia (G-1060)
New Deal Printing Corp	G	718 729-5800	New York (G-10919)
New York Legal Publishing	G	518 459-1100	Menands (G-8090)
Niagara Sample Book Co Inc	F	716 284-6151	Niagara Falls (G-12313)
Noble Checks Inc	G	212 537-6241	Brooklyn (G-2271)
North American Graphics Inc	F	212 725-2200	New York (G-10991)
North Six Inc	F	212 463-7227	New York (G-10994)
Pace Editions Inc	G	212 675-7431	New York (G-11086)
Paris Art Label Co Inc	D	631 467-2300	Patchogue (G-12872)
Paulin Investment Company	E	631 957-8500	Amityville (G-311)
Pony Farm Press & Graphics	G	607 432-9020	Oneonta (G-12644)
Presstek Printing LLC	F	585 266-2770	Rochester (G-14043)
Print City Corp	F	212 487-9778	New York (G-11246)
Printfacility Inc	G	212 349-4009	New York (G-11250)
Printing Resources Inc	E	518 482-2470	Albany (G-119)
Printworks Printing & Design	G	315 433-8587	Syracuse (G-15398)
Quality Impressions Inc	G	646 613-0002	Long Island City (G-7567)
Quality Offset LLC	G	347 342-4660	Long Island City (G-7568)
R & M Graphics of New York	F	212 929-0294	New York (G-11308)
R R Donnelley & Sons Company	F	716 763-2613	Lakewood (G-6996)
R R Donnelley & Sons Company	D	716 773-0647	Grand Island (G-5510)
R R Donnelley & Sons Company	G	646 755-8125	New York (G-11312)
Register Graphics Inc	E	716 358-2921	Randolph (G-13450)
Rfn Inc	F	516 764-5100	Bay Shore (G-714)
Richard Ruffner	F	631 234-4600	Central Islip (G-3383)
Rike Enterprises Inc	F	631 277-8338	Islip (G-6550)
RIT Printing Corp	F	631 586-6220	Bay Shore (G-715)
Rose Graphics LLC	F	516 547-6142	West Babylon (G-16188)
Salamanca Press Penny Saver	E	716 945-1500	Salamanca (G-14531)
Scan-A-Chrome Color Inc	G	631 532-6146	Copiague (G-3779)
Shapeways Inc	C	914 356-5816	New York (G-11557)
Shapeways Inc	G	646 470-3576	Long Island City (G-7589)
Silver Griffin Inc	F	518 272-7771	Troy (G-15627)
Solarz Bros Printing Corp	G	718 383-1330	Brooklyn (G-2497)
Spaulding Law Printing Inc	G	315 422-4805	Syracuse (G-15427)
Spectrum Prtg Lithography Inc	E	212 255-3131	New York (G-11665)
St James Printing Inc	G	631 981-2095	Ronkonkoma (G-14418)
Standwill Packaging Inc	E	631 752-1236	Farmingdale (G-4879)
Starbrook Incorporated	G	212 514-5212	Brooklyn (G-2512)

PRODUCT

Employee Codes: A=Over 500 employees, B=251-500
C=101-250, D=51-100, E=20-50, F=10-19, G=5-9

PRINTING: Commercial, NEC

Company		Phone
Starfire Printing Inc	G	631 736-1495
Holtsville (G-6245)		
Structured 3d Inc	G	346 704-2614
Amityville (G-317)		
Syracuse Label Co Inc	D	315 422-1037
Syracuse (G-15439)		
T S O General Corp	E	631 952-5320
Brentwood (G-1144)		
T&K Printing Inc	F	718 439-9454
Brooklyn (G-2550)		
T-Base Communications USA Inc	E	315 713-0013
Ogdensburg (G-12579)		
Tapemaker Supply Company LLC		914 693-3407
Hartsdale (G-5745)		
Tc Transcontinental USA Inc	G	818 993-4767
New York (G-11788)		
Tcmf Inc	D	607 724-1094
Binghamton (G-918)		
Tele-Pak Inc	E	845 426-2300
Monsey (G-8302)		
The Gramecy Group	G	518 348-1325
Clifton Park (G-3579)		
Thomson Press (india) Limited	G	646 318-0369
Long Island City (G-7616)		
Toppan Vintage Inc	D	212 596-7747
New York (G-11867)		
Toprint Ltd		718 439-0469
Brooklyn (G-2573)		
Tri-Lon Clor Lithographers Ltd		212 255-6140
New York (G-11893)		
USA Custom Pad Corp	E	607 563-9550
Sidney (G-14858)		
Varick Street Litho Inc		646 843-0800
New York (G-11995)		
Venus Printing Company	F	212 967-8900
Hewlett (G-6053)		
Veterans Offset Printing Inc	G	585 288-2900
Rochester (G-14200)		
Weicro Graphics Inc	E	631 253-3360
West Babylon (G-16204)		
Were Forms Inc	G	585 482-4400
Rochester (G-14206)		
Westypo Printers Inc		914 737-7394
Peekskill (G-12930)		
Willco Fine Art Ltd	F	718 935-9567
New York (G-12109)		
William J Ryan	G	585 392-6200
Hilton (G-6159)		
Wilson Press LLC	E	315 568-9693
Seneca Falls (G-14788)		
Worldwide Ticket Craft	D	516 538-6200
Merrick (G-8107)		
X Myles Mar Inc	E	212 683-2015
New York (G-12148)		
X Press Screen Printing		716 679-7788
Dunkirk (G-4181)		
Xl Graphics Inc	G	212 929-8700
New York (G-12153)		

PRINTING: Engraving & Plate

Company		Phone
Allstate Sign & Plaque Corp	F	631 242-2828
Deer Park (G-3938)		
Custom House Engravers Inc	G	631 567-3004
Bohemia (G-1004)		
D & A Offset Services Inc	F	212 924-0612
New York (G-9445)		

PRINTING: Flexographic

Company		Phone
Astro Label & Tag Ltd	G	718 435-4474
Brooklyn (G-1565)		
Gemson Graphics Inc	G	516 873-8400
Albertson (G-149)		
Marlow Printing Co Inc	E	718 625-4948
Brooklyn (G-2171)		
Transcntinental Ultra Flex Inc	B	718 272-9100
Brooklyn (G-2579)		
W N Vanalstine & Sons Inc	D	518 237-1436
Cohoes (G-3624)		

PRINTING: Gravure, Business Form & Card

Company		Phone
Alamar Printing Inc	F	914 993-9007
White Plains (G-16417)		
Alfa Card Inc	G	718 326-7107
Glendale (G-5390)		

PRINTING: Gravure, Color

Company		Phone
Clarion Publications Inc	F	585 243-3530
Geneseo (G-5313)		
Kinaneco Inc	E	315 468-6201
Syracuse (G-15356)		

PRINTING: Gravure, Forms, Business

Company		Phone
American Print Solutions Inc	G	718 208-2309
Brooklyn (G-1527)		

PRINTING: Gravure, Imprinting

Company		Phone
C C Industries Inc	F	518 581-7633
Saratoga Springs (G-14572)		

PRINTING: Gravure, Job

Company		Phone
Leonardo Printing Corp		914 664-7890
Mount Vernon (G-8417)		
Sommer and Sons Printing Inc	F	716 822-4311
Buffalo (G-3069)		

PRINTING: Gravure, Labels

Company		Phone
Janco Press Inc	F	631 563-3003
Bohemia (G-1040)		
Liberty Label Mfg Inc	F	631 737-2365
Holbrook (G-6195)		
Niagara Label Company Inc		716 542-3000
Akron (G-20)		
Trust of Colum Unive In The Ci	F	212 854-2793
New York (G-11906)		

PRINTING: Gravure, Rotogravure

Company		Phone
Color Industries LLC	G	718 392-8301
Long Island City (G-7413)		
Copy Corner Inc	G	718 388-4545
Brooklyn (G-1717)		
Ecoplast & Packaging LLC	G	718 996-0800
Brooklyn (G-1811)		
Foleys Graphic Center Inc	E	914 245-3625
Yorktown Heights (G-16816)		
Gruner + Jahr USA Group Inc	B	866 323-9336
New York (G-10001)		
Image Sales & Marketing Inc		516 238-7023
Massapequa Park (G-7891)		
Jack J Florio Jr		716 434-9123
Lockport (G-7311)		
Krepe Kraft Inc	B	716 826-7086
Buffalo (G-2912)		
McG Graphics Inc		631 499-0730
Dix Hills (G-4122)		
Mod-Pac Corp	D	716 447-9013
Buffalo (G-2952)		
Paya Printing of NY Inc		516 625-8346
Albertson (G-151)		
SRC Liquidation Company	G	716 631-3900
Williamsville (G-16588)		
Tele-Pak Inc	E	845 426-2300
Monsey (G-8302)		

PRINTING: Gravure, Stamps, Trading

Company		Phone
Ashton-Potter USA Ltd	C	716 633-2000
Williamsville (G-16568)		

PRINTING: Gravure, Stationery

Company		Phone
Karr Graphics Corp	E	212 645-6000
Long Island City (G-7487)		
Mrs John L Strong & Co LLC	F	212 838-3775
New York (G-10853)		
Mutual Engraving Company Inc	D	516 489-0534
West Hempstead (G-16223)		

PRINTING: Laser

Company		Phone
Amsterdam Printing & Litho Inc	F	518 792-6501
Queensbury (G-13416)		
Batavia Legal Printing Inc	G	585 768-2100
Le Roy (G-7113)		
Data Palette Info Svcs LLC	D	718 433-1060
Port Washington (G-13251)		
Diamond Inscription Tech	F	646 366-7944
New York (G-9523)		
Doctor Print Inc	E	631 873-4560
Hauppauge (G-5814)		
Miller Place Printing Inc	G	631 473-1158
Miller Place (G-8191)		

PRINTING: Letterpress

Company		Phone
6727 11th Ave Corp	F	718 837-8787
Brooklyn (G-1444)		
Amax Printing Inc	F	718 384-8600
Maspeth (G-7819)		
Bella Figura Letterpress	G	866 699-6040
Syracuse (G-15255)		
Brodock Press Inc	D	315 735-9577
Utica (G-15681)		
Chenango Union Printing Inc	G	607 334-2112
Norwich (G-12479)		
Craig Envelope Corp	E	718 786-4277
Hicksville (G-6074)		
Curtis Prtg Co The Del Press	G	518 477-4820
East Greenbush (G-4228)		
Eastwood Litho Inc	E	315 437-2626
Syracuse (G-15310)		
Edgian Press Inc	G	516 931-2114
Hicksville (G-6082)		
Efficiency Printing Co Inc	F	914 949-8611
White Plains (G-16444)		
F & B Photo Offset Co Inc	G	516 431-5433
Island Park (G-6514)		
Fairmount Press	G	212 255-2300
New York (G-9775)		
Forward Enterprises Inc		585 235-7670
Rochester (G-13814)		
Frederick Coon Inc	E	716 683-6812
Elma (G-4450)		
Gazette Press Inc	E	914 963-8300
Rye (G-14479)		
Golos Printing Inc	G	607 732-1896
Elmira Heights (G-4511)		
Grover Cleveland Press Inc	F	716 564-2222
Amherst (G-230)		
H T L & S Ltd	F	718 435-4474
Brooklyn (G-1957)		
Harmon and Castella Printing	F	845 471-9163
Poughkeepsie (G-13344)		
HI Speed Envelope Co Inc	F	718 617-1600
Mount Vernon (G-8406)		
Hill Crest Press	G	518 943-0671
Catskill (G-3304)		
Johnnys Ideal Printing Co		518 828-6666
Hudson (G-6359)		
Judith Lewis Printer Inc	G	516 997-7777
Westbury (G-16346)		
Kaufman Brothers Printing		212 563-1854
New York (G-10419)		
Kaymil Printing Company Inc		212 594-3718
New York (G-10422)		
Linco Printing Inc	E	718 937-5141
Long Island City (G-7499)		
Louis Heindl & Son Inc	G	585 454-5080
Rochester (G-13917)		
M T M Printing Co Inc	F	718 353-3297
College Point (G-3654)		
Malone Industrial Press Inc	G	518 483-5880
Malone (G-7724)		
Mark T Westinghouse		518 678-3262
Catskill (G-3306)		
Maspeth Press Inc		718 429-2363
Maspeth (G-7857)		
Midgley Printing Corp		315 475-1864
Syracuse (G-15372)		
Mines Press Inc	C	914 788-1800
Cortlandt Manor (G-3903)		
Moore Printing Company Inc		585 394-1533
Canandaigua (G-3225)		
P & W Press Inc	E	646 486-3417
New York (G-11083)		
Patrick Ryans Modern Press	F	518 434-2921
Albany (G-111)		
S & S Prtg Die-Cutting Co Inc	F	718 388-8990
Brooklyn (G-2434)		
Scotti Graphics Inc	E	212 367-9602
Long Island City (G-7585)		
Seneca West Printing Inc	G	716 675-8010
West Seneca (G-16303)		
Soho Letterpress Inc		718 788-2518
Brooklyn (G-2493)		
Source Envelope Inc	G	866 284-0707
Farmingdale (G-4877)		
Star Press Pearl River Inc	G	845 268-2294
Valley Cottage (G-15765)		
Starcraft Press Inc	G	718 383-6700
Long Island City (G-7600)		
Stony Point Graphics Ltd	G	845 786-3322
Stony Point (G-15176)		
Tannens	G	718 292-4646
Bronx (G-1400)		
Tovie Asarese Royal Prtg Co	G	716 885-7692
Buffalo (G-3100)		

Tri Kolor Printing & Sty ... F ... 315 474-6753
Syracuse *(G-15446)*
Weeks & Reichel Printing Inc ... G ... 631 589-1443
Sayville *(G-14635)*
William Charles Prtg Co Inc ... E ... 516 349-0900
Plainview *(G-13102)*

PRINTING: Lithographic

12pt Printing LLC ... G ... 718 376-2120
Brooklyn *(G-1433)*
2 1 2 Postcards Inc ... E ... 212 767-8227
New York *(G-8667)*
2 X 4 Inc ... E ... 212 647-1170
New York *(G-8668)*
450 Ridge St Inc ... G ... 716 754-2789
Lewiston *(G-7138)*
518 Prints LLC ... G ... 518 674-5346
Averill Park *(G-512)*
A Esteban & Company Inc ... E ... 212 714-2227
New York *(G-8692)*
A M & J Digital ... G ... 518 434-2579
Menands *(G-8077)*
A National Printing Co Inc ... G ... 631 243-3395
Farmingville *(G-4922)*
Adirondack Publishing Co Inc ... E ... 518 891-2600
Saranac Lake *(G-14560)*
Advance Publications Inc ... D ... 718 981-1234
Staten Island *(G-15040)*
Advanced Business Group Inc ... F ... 212 398-1010
New York *(G-8753)*
Advanced Digital Printing LLC ... E ... 718 649-1500
New York *(G-8754)*
Advertising Lithographers ... F ... 212 966-7771
Long Island City *(G-7368)*
Albert Siy ... G ... 718 359-0389
Flushing *(G-4982)*
All Color Business Spc Ltd ... G ... 516 420-0649
Deer Park *(G-3936)*
Alpina Copyworld Inc ... F ... 212 683-3511
New York *(G-8811)*
Alpine Business Group Inc ... F ... 212 989-4198
New York *(G-8812)*
Amax Printing Inc ... F ... 718 384-8600
Maspeth *(G-7819)*
American Business Forms Inc ... E ... 716 836-5111
Amherst *(G-213)*
American Icon Industries Inc ... G ... 845 561-1299
Newburgh *(G-12213)*
Amsterdam Printing & Litho Inc ... F ... 518 842-6000
Amsterdam *(G-325)*
Amsterdam Printing & Litho Inc ... E ... 518 842-6000
Amsterdam *(G-326)*
Answer Printing Inc ... F ... 212 922-2922
New York *(G-8875)*
Argo Envelope Corp ... D ... 718 729-2700
Long Island City *(G-7386)*
Art Digital Technologies LLC ... F ... 646 649-4820
Brooklyn *(G-1557)*
Artscroll Printing Corp ... E ... 212 929-2413
New York *(G-8926)*
Asn Inc ... E ... 718 894-0800
Maspeth *(G-7824)*
Avm Printing Inc ... F ... 631 351-1331
Hauppauge *(G-5775)*
B D B Typewriter Supply Works ... E ... 718 232-4800
Brooklyn *(G-1580)*
Beastons Budget Printing ... G ... 585 244-2721
Rochester *(G-13658)*
Benjamin Printing Inc ... F ... 315 788-7922
Adams *(G-2)*
Bennett Multimedia Inc ... F ... 718 629-1454
Brooklyn *(G-1598)*
Bevilacque Group LLC ... F ... 212 414-8858
Port Washington *(G-13245)*
Billing Coding and Prtg Inc ... G ... 718 827-9409
Brooklyn *(G-1613)*
Bittner Company LLC ... F ... 585 214-1790
Rochester *(G-13664)*
Bk Printing Inc ... G ... 315 565-5396
East Syracuse *(G-4326)*
Bklynfavors Party Print ... G ... 718 277-0233
Brooklyn *(G-1617)*
Bluesoho ... F ... 646 805-2583
New York *(G-9111)*
Boka Printing Inc ... G ... 607 725-3235
Binghamton *(G-870)*
Brigar X-Press Solutions Inc ... D ... 518 438-7817
Albany *(G-50)*
Brodock Press Inc ... D ... 315 735-9577
Utica *(G-15681)*
Business Card Express Inc ... E ... 631 669-3400
West Babylon *(G-16143)*
C K Printing ... G ... 718 965-0388
Brooklyn *(G-1664)*
C To C Design & Print Inc ... F ... 631 885-4020
Ronkonkoma *(G-14323)*
Canandaigua Msgnr Incorporated ... C ... 585 394-0770
Canandaigua *(G-3213)*
Castlereagh Printcraft Inc ... D ... 516 623-1728
Freeport *(G-5148)*
Catskill Delaware Publications ... F ... 845 887-5200
Callicoon *(G-3160)*
Cazar Printing & Advertising ... G ... 718 446-4606
Corona *(G-3840)*
Cds Productions Inc ... F ... 518 385-8255
Schenectady *(G-14661)*
Chromagraphics Press Inc ... G ... 631 367-6160
Melville *(G-8007)*
Circle Press Inc ... D ... 212 924-4277
New York *(G-9303)*
Classic Business Solutions ... G ... 212 563-9100
New York *(G-9318)*
Classic Color Graphics Inc ... G ... 516 822-9090
Hicksville *(G-6069)*
Cloud Printing ... G ... 212 775-0888
New York *(G-9331)*
Cobico Productions Inc ... G ... 347 417-5883
New York *(G-9342)*
Colad Group LLC ... D ... 716 961-1776
Buffalo *(G-2772)*
Color-Aid Corporation ... G ... 212 673-5500
Hudson Falls *(G-6376)*
Community Media LLC ... E ... 212 229-1890
New York *(G-9368)*
Community Newspaper Group LLC ... F ... 607 432-1000
Oneonta *(G-12633)*
Cronin Enterprises Inc ... G ... 914 345-9600
Elmsford *(G-4540)*
Daily Record ... F ... 585 232-2035
Rochester *(G-13732)*
Dark Star Lithograph Corp ... G ... 845 634-3780
New City *(G-8490)*
Datorib Inc ... G ... 631 698-6222
Selden *(G-14763)*
Dawn Paper Co Inc ... F ... 516 596-9110
East Rockaway *(G-4294)*
Denton Publications Inc ... D ... 518 873-6368
Elizabethtown *(G-4430)*
Dependable Lithographers Inc ... F ... 718 472-4200
Long Island City *(G-7423)*
Design Distributors Inc ... D ... 631 242-2000
Deer Park *(G-3966)*
Designlogocom Inc ... G ... 212 564-0200
New York *(G-9508)*
Digital Color Concepts Inc ... E ... 212 989-4888
New York *(G-9526)*
Digital Imaging Tech LLC ... G ... 518 885-4400
Ballston Spa *(G-580)*
Diversified Envelope Ltd ... F ... 585 615-4697
Rochester *(G-13745)*
Donnelley Financial LLC ... B ... 212 425-0298
New York *(G-9555)*
Donnelley Financial LLC ... D ... 212 351-9000
New York *(G-9556)*
Dovelin Printing Company Inc ... F ... 718 302-3951
Brooklyn *(G-1790)*
Dual Print & Mail LLC ... D ... 716 775-8001
Grand Island *(G-5497)*
Dual Print & Mail LLC ... D ... 716 684-3825
Cheektowaga *(G-3442)*
Dupli Graphics Corporation ... C ... 315 234-7286
Syracuse *(G-15306)*
Dyenamix Inc ... G ... 212 941-6642
New York *(G-9593)*
E B B Graphics Inc ... F ... 516 750-5510
Westbury *(G-16324)*
E W Smith Publishing Co ... F ... 845 562-1218
New Windsor *(G-8643)*
Eagle Graphics Inc ... G ... 585 244-5006
Rochester *(G-13755)*
Earth Enterprises Inc ... E ... 212 741-3999
New York *(G-9607)*
East Coast Business Forms Inc ... G ... 631 231-9300
Saint James *(G-14512)*
East Coast Thermographers Inc ... E ... 718 321-3211
College Point *(G-3643)*
Eastwood Litho Inc ... E ... 315 437-2626
Syracuse *(G-15310)*
Edwards Graphic Co Inc ... G ... 718 548-6858
Bronx *(G-1267)*
Efficiency Printing Co Inc ... F ... 914 949-8611
White Plains *(G-16444)*
Electronic Printing Inc ... G ... 631 218-2200
Hauppauge *(G-5819)*
Endeavor Printing LLC ... G ... 718 570-2720
Long Island City *(G-7438)*
Entermarket ... G ... 914 437-7268
Mount Kisco *(G-8342)*
Enterprise Press Inc ... C ... 212 741-2111
New York *(G-9687)*
Evenhouse Printing ... G ... 716 649-2666
Hamburg *(G-5679)*
Evolution Impressions Inc ... D ... 585 473-6600
Rochester *(G-13795)*
Excelsus Solutions LLC ... E ... 585 533-0003
Rochester *(G-13797)*
F5 Networks Inc ... G ... 888 882-7535
New York *(G-9768)*
Final Touch Printing Inc ... F ... 845 352-2677
Spring Valley *(G-14991)*
Flower City Printing Inc ... G ... 585 512-1235
Rochester *(G-13809)*
Flynns Inc ... E ... 212 339-8700
New York *(G-9819)*
Foleys Graphic Center Inc ... E ... 914 245-3625
Yorktown Heights *(G-16816)*
G F Labels LLC ... F ... 518 798-6643
Queensbury *(G-13424)*
Gannett Stllite Info Ntwrk LLC ... E ... 845 578-2300
West Nyack *(G-16269)*
Gatehouse Media LLC ... D ... 585 394-0770
Canandaigua *(G-3222)*
Gazette Press Inc ... E ... 914 963-8300
Rye *(G-14479)*
Global Graphics Inc ... F ... 718 939-4967
Flushing *(G-5002)*
Government Data Publication ... E ... 347 789-8719
Brooklyn *(G-1945)*
GPM Associates LLC ... E ... 585 335-3940
Dansville *(G-3926)*
Grafconect Corp ... G ... 212 714-1795
New York *(G-9968)*
Great Eastern Color Lith ... C ... 845 454-7420
Poughkeepsie *(G-13342)*
Green Girl Prtg & Msgnr Inc ... G ... 212 575-0357
New York *(G-9983)*
Guaranteed Printing Svc Co Inc ... E ... 212 929-2410
Long Island City *(G-7464)*
Hamptons Magazine ... E ... 631 283-7125
Southampton *(G-14955)*
Hearst Corporation ... A ... 518 454-5694
Albany *(G-82)*
Hooek Produktion Inc ... G ... 212 367-9111
New York *(G-10121)*
Horne Organization Inc ... F ... 914 572-1330
Yonkers *(G-16769)*
Huckleberry Inc ... G ... 631 630-5450
Hauppauge *(G-5847)*
Ink Well ... G ... 718 253-9736
Brooklyn *(G-2004)*
Inland Printing Company Inc ... G ... 516 367-4700
Woodbury *(G-16622)*
Instant Again LLC ... E ... 585 436-8003
Rochester *(G-13881)*
Instant Stream Inc ... E ... 917 438-7182
New York *(G-10227)*
Insty-Prints of Buffalo Inc ... G ... 716 853-6483
Buffalo *(G-2886)*
Interstate Litho Corp ... D ... 631 232-6025
Brentwood *(G-1136)*
J A T Printing Inc ... G ... 631 427-1155
Huntington *(G-6401)*
J F B & Sons Lithographers ... D ... 631 467-1444
Lake Ronkonkoma *(G-6981)*
J V Haring & Son ... F ... 718 720-1947
Staten Island *(G-15094)*
J3 Printing Inc ... G ... 516 304-6103
Queens Village *(G-13408)*
Jam Printing Publishing Inc ... G ... 914 345-8400
Elmsford *(G-4547)*
Japan Printing & Graphics Inc ... G ... 212 406-2905
New York *(G-10308)*
Joseph Paul ... G ... 718 693-4269
Brooklyn *(G-2047)*
Kaleidoscope Imaging Inc ... E ... 212 631-9947
New York *(G-10396)*
Karr Graphics Corp ... E ... 212 645-6000
Long Island City *(G-7487)*
Keeners East End Litho Inc ... G ... 631 324-8565
East Hampton *(G-4239)*

Employee Codes: A=Over 500 employees, B=251-500
C=101-250, D=51-100, E=20-50, F=10-19, G=5-9

2019 Harris
New York Manufacturers Directory

1221

Key Brand Entertainment Inc................C....... 212 966-5400
New York (G-10437)
Kim Jae Printing Co Inc..........................G....... 212 691-6289
Roslyn Heights (G-14457)
King Lithographers Inc............................E....... 914 667-4200
Mount Vernon (G-8414)
Kling Magnetics Inc...............................E....... 518 392-4000
Chatham (G-3428)
L & K Graphics Inc..................................G....... 631 667-2269
Deer Park (G-3997)
Label Gallery Inc....................................E....... 607 334-3244
Norwich (G-12489)
Lake Placid Advertisers Wkshp.............E....... 518 523-3359
Lake Placid (G-6976)
Laser Printer Checks Corp.....................G....... 845 782-5837
Monroe (G-8275)
LI Script LLC...E....... 631 321-3850
Woodbury (G-16624)
Liberty Label Mfg Inc...............................F....... 631 737-2365
Holbrook (G-6195)
Litmor Publishing Corp...........................F....... 516 931-0012
Garden City (G-5266)
Lmg National Publishing Inc.................E....... 585 598-6874
Fairport (G-4640)
Logo Print Company................................G....... 607 324-5403
Hornell (G-6301)
Love Unlimited NY Inc............................E....... 718 359-8500
Westbury (G-16353)
Magazines & Brochures Inc...................G....... 716 875-9699
Buffalo (G-2933)
Marlow Printing Co Inc...........................E....... 718 625-4948
Brooklyn (G-2171)
Master Image Printing Inc......................G....... 914 347-4400
Elmsford (G-4550)
McG Graphics Inc....................................G....... 631 499-0730
Dix Hills (G-4122)
Mdr Printing Corp....................................G....... 516 627-3221
Manhasset (G-7769)
Merrill New York Company Inc..............C....... 212 229-6500
New York (G-10778)
Mickelberry Communications Inc..........G....... 212 832-0303
New York (G-10794)
Midgley Printing Corp.............................G....... 315 475-1864
Syracuse (G-15372)
Miken Companies Inc.............................D....... 716 668-6311
Buffalo (G-2946)
Minuteman Press Inc..............................G....... 845 623-2277
Nanuet (G-8466)
Minuteman Press Intl Inc.......................G....... 718 343-5440
Jamaica (G-6662)
Mod-Pac Corp...D....... 716 447-9013
Buffalo (G-2952)
Moneast Inc..G....... 845 298-8898
Wappingers Falls (G-15936)
Mutual Engraving Company Inc............D....... 516 489-0534
West Hempstead (G-16223)
Nameplate Mfrs of Amer.........................E....... 631 752-0055
Farmingdale (G-4831)
Nash Printing Inc.....................................F....... 516 935-4567
Plainview (G-13077)
NCR Corporation......................................C....... 607 273-5310
Ithaca (G-6599)
New Goldstar 1 Printing Corp................G....... 212 343-3909
New York (G-10924)
Northern NY Newspapers Corp.............C....... 315 782-1000
Watertown (G-16031)
Observer Daily Sunday Newsppr..........D....... 716 366-3000
Dunkirk (G-4175)
Office Grabs NY Inc................................G....... 212 444-1331
Brooklyn (G-2285)
Orlandi Inc..D....... 631 756-0110
Farmingdale (G-4840)
Orlandi Inc..E....... 631 756-0110
Farmingdale (G-4841)
Pace Editions Inc.....................................G....... 212 675-7431
New York (G-11086)
Paladino Prtg & Graphics Inc................G....... 718 279-6000
Flushing (G-5033)
Pama Enterprises Inc.............................G....... 516 504-6300
Great Neck (G-5579)
Parkside Printing Co Inc........................F....... 516 933-5423
Jericho (G-6796)
Paya Printing of NY Inc..........................G....... 516 625-8346
Albertson (G-151)
Phillip Tissicher.......................................F....... 718 282-3310
Brooklyn (G-2314)
Platinum Printing & Graphics................G....... 631 249-3325
Farmingdale (G-4852)
Play-It Productions Inc...........................F....... 212 695-6530
Port Washington (G-13297)

Pre Cycled Inc..G....... 845 278-7611
Brewster (G-1174)
Preebro Printing.......................................G....... 718 633-7300
Brooklyn (G-2337)
Presstek Printing LLC.............................F....... 585 266-2770
Rochester (G-14043)
Pricet Printing..G....... 315 655-0369
Cazenovia (G-3326)
Print Better Inc...G....... 347 348-1841
Ridgewood (G-13547)
Print Center Inc..G....... 718 643-9559
Cold Spring Harbor (G-3632)
Print Cottage LLC....................................F....... 516 369-1749
Massapequa Park (G-7894)
Print House Inc...D....... 718 443-7500
Brooklyn (G-2346)
Print It Here..G....... 516 308-7785
Massapequa (G-7883)
Print It Inc...G....... 845 371-2227
Monsey (G-8294)
Print Management Group Inc.................G....... 212 213-1555
New York (G-11247)
Print Market Inc..G....... 631 940-8181
Deer Park (G-4029)
Print On Demand Initiative Inc..............F....... 585 239-6044
Rochester (G-14044)
Print Seforim Bzul Inc.............................G....... 718 679-1011
Brooklyn (G-2348)
Printech Business Systems Inc.............F....... 212 290-2542
New York (G-11249)
Printing Prmtnal Solutions LLC.............F....... 315 474-1110
Syracuse (G-15397)
Printing Resources Inc............................E....... 518 482-2470
Albany (G-119)
Printz and Patternz LLC..........................G....... 518 944-6020
Schenectady (G-14705)
Professional Solutions Print...................G....... 631 231-9300
Hauppauge (G-5925)
Psychonomic Society Inc........................E....... 512 381-1494
New York (G-11270)
R & J Graphics Inc...................................F....... 631 293-6611
Farmingdale (G-4863)
Rapid Service Engraving Co...................G....... 716 896-4555
Buffalo (G-3032)
Resonant Legal Media LLC.....................E....... 212 687-7100
New York (G-11368)
Richard Ruffner...F....... 631 234-4600
Central Islip (G-3383)
Rmf Printing Technologies Inc..............E....... 716 683-7500
Lancaster (G-7045)
Rosen Mandell & Immerman Inc...........E....... 212 691-2277
New York (G-11431)
Rv Printing..G....... 631 567-8658
Holbrook (G-6207)
Sample News Group LLC........................D....... 315 343-3800
Oswego (G-12787)
Seaboard Graphic Services LLC............E....... 315 652-4200
East Syracuse (G-4369)
Seifert Graphics Inc.................................F....... 315 736-2744
Oriskany (G-12761)
Sentine Printing Inc.................................G....... 516 334-7400
Westbury (G-16372)
Sign Shop Inc..G....... 631 226-4145
Copiague (G-3782)
Sign World Inc..E....... 212 619-9000
Brooklyn (G-2469)
Sloane Design Inc.....................................G....... 212 539-0184
Brooklyn (G-2487)
Source Envelope Inc.................................G....... 866 284-0707
Farmingdale (G-4877)
Speedcard Inc..G....... 631 472-1904
Holbrook (G-6210)
Speedy Enterprise of USA Corp.............G....... 718 463-3000
Flushing (G-5047)
Sputnick 84 LLC...G....... 844 667-7468
New York (G-11686)
St James Printing Inc...............................G....... 631 981-2095
Ronkonkoma (G-14418)
St Lawrence County Newspapers..........D....... 315 393-1003
Canton (G-3258)
Star Press Pearl River Inc.......................G....... 845 268-2294
Valley Cottage (G-15765)
Steffen Publishing Inc.............................D....... 315 865-4100
Holland Patent (G-6225)
Sterling Pierce Company Inc..................E....... 516 593-1170
East Rockaway (G-4296)
Stony Brook University............................E....... 631 632-6434
Stony Brook (G-15169)
Studio 22 Print..G....... 212 679-2656
New York (G-11726)

Sun Printing Incorporated.......................E....... 607 337-3034
Norwich (G-12493)
Syracuse Computer Forms Inc...............E....... 315 478-0108
Syracuse (G-15436)
Sz - Design & Print Inc.............................F....... 845 659-2273
Monsey (G-8299)
Taylor Communications Inc....................G....... 718 361-1000
Long Island City (G-7612)
Technipoly Manufacturing Inc................E....... 718 383-0363
Brooklyn (G-2559)
Teller Printing Corp..................................G....... 718 486-3662
Brooklyn (G-2562)
Tobay Printing Co Inc...............................E....... 631 842-3300
Copiague (G-3788)
Transaction Printer Group........................G....... 607 274-2500
Ithaca (G-6614)
Transcntinental Ultra Flex Inc................B....... 718 272-9100
Brooklyn (G-2579)
Transcontinental Printing GP..................G....... 716 626-3078
Amherst (G-256)
Tripi Engraving Co Inc.............................E....... 718 383-6500
Brooklyn (G-2586)
Troy Sign & Printing.................................G....... 718 994-4482
Bronx (G-1407)
Vic-Gina Printing Company Inc..............G....... 914 636-0200
New Rochelle (G-8631)
Vicks Lithograph & Prtg Corp.................C....... 315 736-9344
Yorkville (G-16833)
Vicks Lithograph & Prtg Corp.................C....... 315 272-2401
Yorkville (G-16832)
VIP Printing...G....... 718 641-9361
Howard Beach (G-6332)
Virgil Mountain Inc....................................G....... 212 378-0007
New York (G-12037)
Wallkill Valley Publications......................E....... 845 561-0170
Newburgh (G-12251)
Wappingers Falls Shopper Inc.................E....... 845 297-3723
Wappingers Falls (G-15938)
Webster Printing Corporation..................F....... 585 671-1533
Webster (G-16107)
Westmore Litho Corp.................................G....... 718 361-9403
Long Island City (G-7636)
Whitestone Dev Group LLC......................G....... 585 482-7770
Rochester (G-14208)
William Boyd Printing Co Inc...................C....... 518 339-5832
Latham (G-7098)
William J Kline & Son Inc.........................D....... 518 843-1100
Amsterdam (G-364)
William J Ryan..G....... 585 392-6200
Hilton (G-6159)
Won & Lee Inc..E....... 516 222-0712
Garden City (G-5284)
X Myles Mar Inc...E....... 212 683-2015
New York (G-12148)
X-L Envelope and Printing Inc.................F....... 716 852-2135
Buffalo (G-3134)
Zacmel Graphics LLC................................G....... 631 944-6031
Deer Park (G-4066)
Zenger Group Inc.......................................E....... 716 871-1058
Tonawanda (G-15593)

PRINTING: Offset

514 Adams Corporation.............................G....... 516 352-6948
Franklin Square (G-5114)
6727 11th Ave Corp.....................................F....... 718 837-8787
Brooklyn (G-1444)
A & M Litho Inc...E....... 516 342-9727
Bethpage (G-836)
A Esteban & Company Inc........................E....... 212 989-7000
New York (G-8691)
A Q P Inc...G....... 585 256-1690
Rochester (G-13590)
Accuprint..G....... 518 456-2431
Albany (G-28)
Act Communications Group Inc...............F....... 631 669-2403
West Islip (G-16257)
Ad-Vantage Printing Inc............................F....... 718 820-0688
Kew Gardens (G-6870)
Ads-N-Color Inc...E....... 718 797-0900
Brooklyn (G-1485)
Advanced Printing New York Inc.............G....... 212 840-8108
New York (G-8756)
Advantage Press Inc..................................F....... 518 584-3405
Saratoga Springs (G-14568)
Advantage Quick Print Inc........................G....... 212 989-5644
New York (G-8758)
Agrecolor Inc..F....... 516 741-8700
Mineola (G-8202)
Ahw Printing Corp......................................F....... 516 536-3600
Oceanside (G-12531)

PRINTING: Offset

Company	Code	Phone
Alamar Printing Inc	F	914 993-9007
White Plains (G-16417)		
Albany Letter Shop Inc	G	518 434-1172
Albany (G-33)		
Aldine Inc (ny)	D	212 226-2870
New York (G-8788)		
All Color Offset Printers Inc	G	516 420-0649
Farmingdale (G-4714)		
All Time Products Inc	G	718 464-1400
Queens Village (G-13402)		
Allen William & Company Inc	C	212 675-6461
Glendale (G-5391)		
Allied Reproductions Inc	E	212 255-2472
New York (G-8799)		
Allstatebannerscom Corporation	G	718 300-1256
Long Island City (G-7372)		
Alpha Printing Corp	F	315 454-5507
Syracuse (G-15241)		
Alpina Color Graphics Inc	G	212 285-2700
New York (G-8810)		
American Print Solutions Inc	G	718 246-7800
Brooklyn (G-1526)		
Amsterdam Printing & Litho Inc	F	518 792-6501
Queensbury (G-13415)		
Apple Press	G	914 723-6660
White Plains (G-16421)		
Ares Printing and Packg Corp	C	718 858-8760
Brooklyn (G-1550)		
Argo Lithographers Inc	E	718 729-2700
Long Island City (G-7388)		
Arista Innovations Inc	E	516 746-2262
Mineola (G-8205)		
Arnold Printing Corp	E	607 272-7800
Ithaca (G-6557)		
Arnold Taylor Printing Inc	G	516 781-0564
Bellmore (G-785)		
Art Scroll Printing Corp	F	212 929-2413
New York (G-8917)		
At Copy Inc	G	718 624-6136
Brooklyn (G-1566)		
Atlantic Color Corp	E	631 345-3800
Shirley (G-14829)		
Atlas Print Solutions Inc	E	212 949-8775
New York (G-8955)		
B & P Jays Inc	G	716 668-8408
Buffalo (G-2721)		
B Q P Inc	G	518 793-4999
Queensbury (G-13420)		
Bajan Group Inc	G	518 464-2884
Latham (G-7064)		
Ballantrae Lithographers Inc	G	914 592-3275
White Plains (G-16426)		
Barone Offset Printing Corp	G	212 989-5500
Mohegan Lake (G-8257)		
Bartolomeo Publishing Inc	G	631 420-4949
West Babylon (G-16138)		
Bates Jackson Engraving Co Inc	E	716 854-3000
Buffalo (G-2725)		
Baum Christine and John Corp	G	585 621-8910
Rochester (G-13654)		
Beacon Press Inc	E	212 691-5050
White Plains (G-16427)		
Beehive Press Inc	G	718 654-1200
Bronx (G-1226)		
Bel Aire Offset Corp	G	718 539-8333
College Point (G-3640)		
Benchemark Printing Inc	F	518 393-1361
Schenectady (G-14653)		
Benchmark Graphics Ltd	F	212 683-1711
New York (G-9044)		
Bennett Printing Corporation	F	718 629-1454
Brooklyn (G-1599)		
Bernard Hall	G	585 425-3340
Fairport (G-4625)		
Beyer Graphics Inc	D	631 543-3900
Commack (G-3682)		
Bishop Print Shop Inc	G	607 965-8155
Edmeston (G-4425)		
Bmg Printing and Promotion LLC	G	631 231-9200
Bohemia (G-989)		
Boncraft Inc	D	716 662-9720
Tonawanda (G-15528)		
Bondy Printing Corp	G	631 242-1510
Bay Shore (G-666)		
Boulevard Printing	G	716 837-3800
Tonawanda (G-15529)		
Boxcar Press Incorporated	E	315 473-0930
Syracuse (G-15261)		
BP Beyond Printing Inc	G	516 328-2700
Hempstead (G-6008)		
Brennans Quick Print Inc	G	518 793-4999
Glens Falls (G-5419)		
Bridge Printing Inc	G	212 243-5390
Long Island City (G-7403)		
Brooks Litho Digital Group Inc	G	631 789-4500
Deer Park (G-3955)		
Brown Printing Company	E	212 782-7800
New York (G-9149)		
C & R De Santis Inc	G	718 447-5076
Staten Island (G-15057)		
Cabba Printing Incorporated	G	212 319-4747
New York (G-9172)		
Caboodle Printing Inc	G	716 693-6000
Williamsville (G-16573)		
Canaan Printing Inc	G	718 729-3100
Bayside (G-744)		
Canastota Publishing Co Inc	G	315 697-9010
Canastota (G-3242)		
Candid Litho Printing Ltd	G	212 431-3800
Farmingdale (G-4732)		
Canfield & Tack Inc	D	585 235-7710
Rochester (G-13689)		
Capital Dst Print & Imaging	G	518 456-6773
Schenectady (G-14657)		
Carges Entps of Canandaigua	G	585 394-2600
Canandaigua (G-3214)		
Carlara Group Ltd	G	914 769-2020
Pleasantville (G-13173)		
Carnels Printing Inc	G	516 883-3355
Great Neck (G-5543)		
Carr Communications Group LLC	F	607 748-0481
Vestal (G-15813)		
Cathedral Corporation	G	315 338-0021
Rome (G-14249)		
Cayuga Press Cortland Inc	E	888 229-8421
Liverpool (G-7230)		
Cedar West Inc	D	631 467-1444
Ronkonkoma (G-14327)		
Chakra Communications Inc	E	607 748-7491
Endicott (G-4584)		
Chenango Union Printing Inc	G	607 334-2112
Norwich (G-12479)		
Cilyox Inc	F	716 853-3809
Buffalo (G-2766)		
Clarsons Corp	G	585 235-8775
Rochester (G-13713)		
Classic Color Graphics Inc	G	516 822-9090
Hicksville (G-6068)		
Cody Printing Corp	G	718 651-8854
Woodside (G-16651)		
Coe Displays Inc	G	718 937-5658
Long Island City (G-7412)		
Cohber Press Inc	D	585 475-9100
West Henrietta (G-16234)		
Color Carton Corp	G	718 665-0840
Bronx (G-1243)		
Colorfast	F	212 929-2440
New York (G-9354)		
Colorfully Yours Inc	G	631 242-8600
Bay Shore (G-674)		
Combine Graphics Corp	G	212 695-4044
Forest Hills (G-5073)		
Commerce Offset Ltd	G	914 769-6671
Thornwood (G-15505)		
Commercial Press Inc	G	315 274-0028
Canton (G-3255)		
Commercial Print & Imaging	G	716 597-0100
Buffalo (G-2774)		
Compass Printing Plus	F	518 523-3308
Saranac Lake (G-14561)		
Complemar Print LLC	F	716 875-7238
Buffalo (G-2776)		
Composite Forms Inc	F	914 937-1808
Port Chester (G-13194)		
Compucolor Associates Inc	E	516 358-0000
New Hyde Park (G-8524)		
Concept Printing Inc	G	845 353-4040
Nyack (G-12503)		
Consolidated Color Press Inc	F	212 929-8197
New York (G-9382)		
Constas Printing Corporation	G	315 474-2176
Syracuse (G-15287)		
Copy Stop Inc	G	914 428-5188
White Plains (G-16440)		
Coral Color Process Ltd	G	631 543-5200
Commack (G-3688)		
Coral Graphic Services Inc	G	516 576-2100
Hicksville (G-6072)		
Coral Graphic Services Inc	C	516 576-2100
Hicksville (G-6073)		
Cosmos Communications Inc	C	718 482-1800
Long Island City (G-7416)		
Courier Printing Corp	E	607 467-2191
Deposit (G-4107)		
Craig Envelope Corp	E	718 786-4277
Hicksville (G-6074)		
Crater Service Group Inc	G	585 482-7770
Rochester (G-13724)		
Creative Forms Inc	E	212 431-7540
New York (G-9420)		
Creative Printing Corp	E	212 226-3870
New York (G-9421)		
D W S Associates Inc	E	631 667-6666
Deer Park (G-3961)		
Dan Trent Company Inc	G	716 822-1422
Buffalo (G-2792)		
Deanco Digital Printing LLC	E	212 371-2025
Sunnyside (G-15202)		
Dell Communications Inc	G	212 989-3434
New York (G-9498)		
Delta Press Inc	E	212 989-3445
High Falls (G-6140)		
Design Lithographers Inc	F	212 645-8900
New York (G-9505)		
Dick Bailey Service Inc	F	718 522-4363
Brooklyn (G-1775)		
Dispatch Graphics Inc	F	212 307-5943
New York (G-9536)		
Distinctive Printing Inc	F	212 727-3000
New York (G-9539)		
Doco Quick Print Inc	F	315 782-6623
Watertown (G-16012)		
Donmar Printing Co	F	516 280-2239
Mineola (G-8216)		
Dowd - Witbeck Printing Corp	F	518 274-2421
Troy (G-15604)		
DP Murphy Co Inc	D	631 673-9400
Deer Park (G-3968)		
Dupli Graphics Corporation	G	315 422-4732
Syracuse (G-15307)		
E L Smith Printing Co Inc	E	201 373-0111
New City (G-8492)		
East Ridge Quick Print	F	585 266-4911
Rochester (G-13758)		
Eastern Hills Printing	G	716 741-3300
Clarence (G-3530)		
Echo Appellate Press Inc	E	516 432-3601
Long Beach (G-7358)		
Edgian Press Inc	G	516 931-2114
Hicksville (G-6082)		
Elmat Quality Printing Ltd	F	516 569-5722
Cedarhurst (G-3331)		
Empire Press Co	G	718 756-9500
Brooklyn (G-1833)		
Engrav-O-Type Press Inc	F	585 262-7590
Rochester (G-13785)		
Excel Graphics Services Inc	F	212 929-2183
New York (G-9748)		
Excelsior Graphics Inc	G	212 730-6200
New York (G-9751)		
F & B Photo Offset Co Inc	G	516 431-5433
Island Park (G-6514)		
F & T Graphics Inc	G	631 643-1000
Hauppauge (G-5822)		
F J Remey Co Inc	E	516 741-5112
Mineola (G-8222)		
Fambus Inc	G	607 785-3700
Endicott (G-4592)		
Farthing Press Inc	G	716 852-4674
Buffalo (G-2825)		
Fasprint	G	518 483-4631
Malone (G-7721)		
Federal Envelope Inc	E	212 243-8380
New York (G-9790)		
Finer Touch Printing Corp	F	516 944-8000
Port Washington (G-13259)		
First Line Printing Inc	F	718 606-0860
Woodside (G-16656)		
Five Star Prtg & Mailing Svcs	F	212 929-0300
New York (G-9815)		
Flare Multicopy Corp	E	718 258-8860
Brooklyn (G-1887)		
Flower City Printing Inc	C	585 663-9000
Rochester (G-13808)		
Flp Group LLC	G	315 252-7583
Auburn (G-480)		
Folder Factory Inc	F	540 477-3852
Amityville (G-275)		
Fort Orange Press Inc	E	518 489-3233
Albany (G-75)		

Employee Codes: A=Over 500 employees, B=251-500
C=101-250, D=51-100, E=20-50, F=10-19, G=5-9

PRINTING: Offset

Company	Loc	Phone
Forward Enterprises Inc — Rochester (G-13814)	F	585 235-7670
Francis Emory Fitch Inc — New York (G-9838)	E	212 619-3800
Frederick Coon Inc — Elma (G-4450)	E	716 683-6812
Freeville Publishing Co Inc — Freeville (G-5191)	F	607 844-9119
Fulton Newspapers Inc — Fulton (G-5216)	E	315 598-6397
G & P Printing Inc — New York (G-9866)	G	212 274-8092
G W Canfield & Son Inc — Utica (G-15704)	G	315 735-5522
Gallagher Printing Inc — Buffalo (G-2838)	G	716 873-2434
Gallant Graphics Ltd — Stanfordville (G-15033)	E	845 868-1166
Gateway Prtg & Graphics Inc — Hamburg (G-5680)	E	716 823-3873
Gem Reproduction Services Corp — Wappingers Falls (G-15932)	G	845 298-0172
Gemson Graphics Inc — Albertson (G-149)	E	516 873-8400
General Business Supply Inc — Watervliet (G-16046)	D	518 720-3939
Geneva Printing Company Inc — Geneva (G-5326)	G	315 789-8191
Glens Falls Printing LLC — Glens Falls (G-5427)	F	518 793-0555
Gn Printing — Long Island City (G-7457)	G	718 784-1713
Golos Printing Inc — Elmira Heights (G-4511)	G	607 732-1896
Gooding Co Inc — Lockport (G-7308)	E	716 266-6252
Grand Meridian Printing Inc — Long Island City (G-7460)	E	718 937-3888
Grand Prix Litho Inc — Holbrook (G-6187)	E	631 242-4182
Graphic Fabrications Inc — Rockville Centre (G-14232)	G	516 763-3222
Graphicomm Inc — Niagara Falls (G-12289)	G	716 283-0830
Graphics Plus Printing Inc — Cortland (G-3875)	E	607 299-0500
Grover Cleveland Press Inc — Amherst (G-230)	F	716 564-2222
H T L & S Ltd — Brooklyn (G-1957)	F	718 435-4474
H&E Service Corp — Garden City (G-5261)	D	646 472-1936
Haig Press Inc — Hauppauge (G-5838)	E	631 582-5800
Harmon and Castella Printing — Poughkeepsie (G-13344)	F	845 471-9163
Hempstead Sentinel Inc — Hempstead (G-6013)	F	516 486-5000
Heritage Printing Center — Plattsburgh (G-13124)	G	518 563-8240
HI Speed Envelope Co Inc — Mount Vernon (G-8406)	F	718 617-1600
High End Print Solutions Inc — Rochester (G-13866)	F	585 325-5320
Hill Crest Press — Catskill (G-3304)	G	518 943-0671
Hillside Printing Inc — Jamaica (G-6650)	F	718 658-6719
Hospitality Graphics Inc — New York (G-10127)	G	212 643-6700
Hudson Envelope Corporation — New York (G-10142)	E	212 473-6666
Hudson Printing Co Inc — New York (G-10145)	F	718 937-8600
Hugh F McPherson Inc — Cheektowaga (G-3450)	G	716 668-6107
I 2 Print Inc — Long Island City (G-7472)	F	718 937-8800
Impala Press Ltd — Ronkonkoma (G-14352)	G	631 588-4262
In-House Inc — College Point (G-3646)	F	718 445-9007
Ink-It Printing Inc — College Point (G-3647)	G	718 229-5590
International Newsppr Prtg Co — Glen Head (G-5381)	E	516 626-6095
Iver Printing Inc — New Hyde Park (G-8543)	G	718 275-2070
J & J Printing Inc — Syracuse (G-15344)	G	315 458-7411
J P Printing Inc — Farmingdale (G-4790)	G	516 293-6110
Jack J Florio Jr — Lockport (G-7311)	G	716 434-9123
Jacobs Press Inc — Auburn (G-485)	F	315 252-4861
James Conolly Printing Co — Rochester (G-13891)	E	585 426-4150
Jane Lewis — Binghamton (G-898)	F	607 722-0584
JDS Graphics Inc — New York (G-10320)	F	973 330-3300
Johnnys Ideal Printing Co — Hudson (G-6359)	G	518 828-6666
Jon Lyn Ink Inc — Merrick (G-8099)	G	516 546-2312
Judith Lewis Printer Inc — Westbury (G-16346)	G	516 997-7777
Jurist Company Inc — Long Island City (G-7483)	G	212 243-8008
Just Press Print LLC — Rochester (G-13901)	G	585 783-1300
Kas-Ray Industries Inc — New York (G-10410)	F	212 620-3144
Kaufman Brothers Printing — New York (G-10419)	G	212 563-1854
Keller Bros & Miller Inc — Buffalo (G-2903)	F	716 854-2374
Kent Associates Inc — New York (G-10435)	E	212 675-0722
Kenyon Press Inc — Sherburne (G-14806)	E	607 674-9066
Kinaneco Inc — Syracuse (G-15356)	E	315 468-6201
Kingsbury Printing Co Inc — Queensbury (G-13431)	G	518 747-6606
Kurtskraft Inc — Port Washington (G-13280)	F	516 944-4449
L I F Publishing Corp — Shirley (G-14837)	D	631 345-5200
L K Printing Corp — White Plains (G-16470)	F	914 761-1944
L M N Printing Company Inc — Valley Stream (G-15784)	E	516 285-8526
Lee Printing Inc — Brooklyn (G-2104)	G	718 237-1651
Lehmann Printing Company Inc — Whitestone (G-16542)	G	212 929-2395
Leigh Scott Enterprises Inc — Bellerose (G-781)	G	718 343-5440
Lennons Litho Inc — Herkimer (G-6043)	F	315 866-3156
Levon Graphics Corp — Deer Park (G-4001)	D	631 753-2022
Litho Dynamics Inc — Hawthorne (G-5991)	E	914 769-1759
Lithomatic Business Forms Inc — New York (G-10579)	G	212 255-6700
Loudon Ltd — East Northport (G-4267)	E	631 757-4447
Louis Heindl & Son Inc — Rochester (G-13917)	G	585 454-5080
Loy L Press Inc — Buffalo (G-2928)	G	716 634-5966
Lynmar Printing Corp — Amityville (G-298)	G	631 957-8500
M L Design Inc — New York (G-10641)	F	212 233-0213
M T M Printing Co Inc — College Point (G-3654)	F	718 353-3297
M&M Printing Inc — Carle Place (G-3269)	F	516 796-3020
Madison Printing Corp — Ithaca (G-6592)	G	607 273-3535
Mahin Impressions Inc — Riverhead (G-13577)	G	212 871-9777
Malone Industrial Press Inc — Malone (G-7724)	G	518 483-5880
Manifestation-Glow Press Inc — Fresh Meadows (G-5202)	G	718 380-5259
Marcal Printing Inc — Hicksville (G-6105)	G	516 942-9500
Marcy Printing Inc — Brooklyn (G-2166)	G	718 935-9100
Mark T Westinghouse — Catskill (G-3306)	G	518 678-3262
Marks Corpex Banknote Co — Bay Shore (G-698)	G	631 968-0277
Marsid Group Ltd — Carle Place (G-3271)	G	516 334-1603
Mason & Gore Inc — Rye (G-14485)	E	914 921-1025
Mc Squared Nyc Inc — New York (G-10738)	F	212 947-2260
McPc Inc — New York (G-10746)	D	212 583-6000
Medallion Associates Inc — New York (G-10751)	E	212 929-9130
Mercury Print Productions Inc — Rochester (G-13936)	C	585 458-7900
Michael K Lennon Inc — Westhampton Beach (G-16404)	E	631 288-5200
Microera Printers Inc — Rochester (G-13941)	E	585 783-1300
Mid Atlantic Graphics Corp — Shirley (G-14840)	E	631 345-3800
Mid-York Press Inc — Sherburne (G-14807)	D	607 674-4491
Middletown Press — Middletown (G-8164)	G	845 343-1895
Midstate Printing Corp — Liverpool (G-7247)	E	315 475-4101
Mikam Graphics LLC — New York (G-10805)	D	212 684-9393
Miller Printing & Litho Inc — Amsterdam (G-348)	G	518 842-0001
Mines Press Inc — Cortlandt Manor (G-3903)	C	914 788-1800
Mitchell Prtg & Mailing Inc — Oswego (G-12781)	F	315 343-3531
MJB Printing Corp — Islip (G-6549)	G	631 581-0177
Monarch Graphics Inc — Central Islip (G-3378)	F	631 232-1300
Monte Press Inc — Bronx (G-1336)	G	718 325-4999
Moore Printing Company Inc — Canandaigua (G-3225)	G	585 394-1533
Multimedia Services Inc — Corning (G-3822)	E	607 936-3186
Multiple Imprssons of Rchester — Rochester (G-13960)	G	585 546-1160
Nesher Printing Inc — New York (G-10909)	G	212 760-2521
New Horizon Graphics Inc — Hauppauge (G-5901)	E	631 231-8055
New York Digital Print Center — Whitestone (G-16546)	G	718 767-1953
New York Typing & Printing Co — Forest Hills (G-5079)	G	718 268-7900
Newburgh Envelope Corp — Newburgh (G-12236)	G	845 566-4211
Newport Graphics Inc — New York (G-10950)	E	212 924-2600
North Delaware Printing Inc — Tonawanda (G-15566)	G	716 692-0576
Northeast Commercial Prtg Inc — Albany (G-106)	G	518 459-5047
Northeast Prtg & Dist Co Inc — Plattsburgh (G-13141)	G	518 563-8214
Official Offset Corporation — Amityville (G-307)	E	631 957-8500
Olympic Press Inc — New York (G-11038)	F	212 242-4934
Orbis Brynmore Lithographics — New York (G-11055)	G	212 987-2100
Orffeo Printing & Imaging Inc — Lancaster (G-7034)	G	716 681-5757
Ozipko Enterprises Inc — Rochester (G-13999)	G	585 424-6740
P & W Press Inc — New York (G-11083)	E	646 486-3417
P D R Inc — Plainview (G-13080)	G	516 829-5300
Panther Graphics Inc — Rochester (G-14006)	E	585 546-7163
Park Slope Copy Center — Brooklyn (G-2306)	G	718 783-0268
Parrinello Printing Inc — Buffalo (G-2993)	F	716 633-7780
Patrick Ryans Modern Press — Albany (G-111)	F	518 434-2921
Paul Michael Group Inc — Ronkonkoma (G-14397)	G	631 585-5700
PBR Graphics Inc — Albany (G-112)	G	518 458-2909
Peachtree Enterprises Inc — Long Island City (G-7551)	E	212 989-3445
Persch Service Print Inc — Dunkirk (G-4176)	G	716 366-2677

Petcap Press Corporation......F...... 718 609-0910
Long Island City *(G-7554)*
Petit Printing Corp......G...... 716 871-9490
Getzville *(G-5352)*
Phoenix Graphics Inc......E...... 585 232-4040
Rochester *(G-14019)*
Pic A Poc Enterprises Inc......G...... 631 981-2094
Ronkonkoma *(G-14399)*
Pine Bush Printing Co Inc......G...... 518 456-2431
Albany *(G-116)*
Pioneer Printers Inc......F...... 716 693-7100
North Tonawanda *(G-12442)*
PIP Inc......G...... 518 861-0133
Latham *(G-7090)*
Pixos Print......G...... 585 500-4600
Rochester *(G-14023)*
Pollack Graphics Inc......G...... 212 727-8400
New York *(G-11216)*
Pop Printing Incorporated......F...... 212 808-7800
Brooklyn *(G-2328)*
Positive Print Litho Offset......G...... 212 431-4850
New York *(G-11223)*
Presstek Printing......G...... 585 266-2770
Rochester *(G-14041)*
Presstek Printing LLC......F...... 585 467-8140
Rochester *(G-14042)*
Prestige Envelope & Lithograph......F...... 631 521-7043
Merrick *(G-8105)*
Prestone Press LLC......C...... 347 468-7900
Long Island City *(G-7558)*
Print & Graphics Group......G...... 518 371-4649
Clifton Park *(G-3573)*
Print Early LLC......E...... 718 915-7368
Westbury *(G-16367)*
Print Media Inc......D...... 212 563-4040
New York *(G-11248)*
Print Solutions Plus Inc......G...... 315 234-3801
Liverpool *(G-7258)*
Printcorp Inc......E...... 631 696-0641
Ronkonkoma *(G-14400)*
Printers 3 Inc......F...... 631 351-1331
Hauppauge *(G-5923)*
Printing Sales Group Limited......E...... 718 258-8860
Brooklyn *(G-2351)*
Printing Spectrum Inc......F...... 631 689-1010
East Setauket *(G-4308)*
Printing X Press Ions......G...... 631 242-1992
Dix Hills *(G-4124)*
Printinghouse Press Ltd......G...... 212 719-0990
New York *(G-11251)*
Printroc Inc......F...... 585 461-2556
Rochester *(G-14045)*
Printutopia......F...... 718 788-1545
Brooklyn *(G-2352)*
Pro Printing......G...... 516 561-9700
Lynbrook *(G-7670)*
Profile Printing & Graphics......G...... 631 273-2727
Hauppauge *(G-5926)*
Progressive Graphics & Prtg......G...... 315 331-3635
Newark *(G-12205)*
Prompt Printing Inc......G...... 631 454-6524
Farmingdale *(G-4858)*
Quad/Graphics Inc......A...... 518 581-4000
Saratoga Springs *(G-14594)*
Quad/Graphics Inc......C...... 212 672-1300
New York *(G-11294)*
Quad/Graphics Inc......A...... 212 206-5535
New York *(G-11295)*
Quad/Graphics Inc......A...... 212 741-1001
New York *(G-11296)*
Quadrangle Quickprints Ltd......G...... 631 694-4464
Melville *(G-8060)*
Quality Graphics Tri State......G...... 845 735-2523
Pearl River *(G-12909)*
Quicker Printer Inc......G...... 607 734-8622
Elmira *(G-4500)*
Quickprint......G...... 585 394-2600
Canandaigua *(G-3232)*
R & L Press of SI Inc......G...... 718 667-3258
Staten Island *(G-15122)*
R D Printing Associates Inc......F...... 631 390-5964
Farmingdale *(G-4864)*
R Hochman Papers Incorporated......F...... 516 466-6414
Brooklyn *(G-2377)*
Rapid Print and Marketing Inc......G...... 585 924-1520
Victor *(G-15864)*
Rapid Reproductions LLC......G...... 607 843-2221
Oxford *(G-12808)*
Rasco Graphics Inc......G...... 212 206-0447
New York *(G-11327)*

Reflex Offset Inc......G...... 516 746-4142
Deer Park *(G-4035)*
REM Printing Inc......G...... 518 438-7338
Albany *(G-125)*
Resonant Legal Media LLC......D...... 800 781-3591
New York *(G-11369)*
RIT Printing Corp......F...... 631 586-6220
Bay Shore *(G-715)*
Rmd Holding Inc......G...... 845 628-0030
Mahopac *(G-7712)*
Rmf Print Management Group......F...... 716 683-4351
Depew *(G-4105)*
Robert Tabatznik Assoc Inc......F...... 845 336-4555
Kingston *(G-6916)*
Rosemont Press Incorporated......E...... 212 239-4770
New York *(G-11430)*
Ryan Printing Inc......E...... 845 535-3235
Blauvelt *(G-940)*
Sand Hill Industries Inc......G...... 518 885-7991
Ballston Spa *(G-595)*
Sanford Printing Inc......G...... 718 461-1202
Flushing *(G-5044)*
Scotti Graphics Inc......E...... 212 367-9602
Long Island City *(G-7585)*
Searles Graphics Inc......E...... 631 345-2202
Yaphank *(G-16720)*
Security Offset Services Inc......G...... 631 944-6031
Huntington *(G-6415)*
Sharp Printing Inc......G...... 716 731-3994
Sanborn *(G-14553)*
Shield Press Inc......G...... 212 431-7489
New York *(G-11565)*
Shipman Printing Inds Inc......E...... 716 504-7700
Niagara Falls *(G-12336)*
Shipman Printing Inds Inc......G...... 716 504-7700
Sanborn *(G-14554)*
Shipmtes/Printmates Holdg Corp......D...... 518 370-1158
Scotia *(G-14746)*
Shoreline Publishing Inc......G...... 914 738-7869
Pelham *(G-12938)*
Sizzal LLC......E...... 212 354-6123
Long Island City *(G-7593)*
South Bridge Press Inc......G...... 212 233-4047
New York *(G-11654)*
Speedway Press Inc......G...... 315 343-3531
Oswego *(G-12788)*
Standwill Packaging Inc......E...... 631 752-1236
Farmingdale *(G-4879)*
Star Quality Printing Inc......F...... 631 273-1900
Hauppauge *(G-5949)*
Sterling North America Inc......E...... 631 243-6933
Hauppauge *(G-5950)*
Steval Graphics Concepts Inc......F...... 516 576-0220
Plainview *(G-13090)*
Stevens Bandes Graphics Corp......F...... 212 675-1128
New York *(G-11710)*
Stevenson Printing Co Inc......G...... 516 676-1233
Glen Cove *(G-5376)*
Stony Point Graphics Ltd......G...... 845 786-3322
Stony Point *(G-15176)*
Stubbs Printing Inc......G...... 315 769-8641
Massena *(G-7909)*
Studley Printing & Publishing......F...... 518 563-1414
Plattsburgh *(G-13160)*
Stylistic Press Inc......F...... 212 675-0797
New York *(G-11731)*
Suffolk Copy Center Inc......G...... 631 665-0570
Bay Shore *(G-727)*
Summit MSP LLC......G...... 716 433-1014
Lockport *(G-7332)*
Summit Print & Mail LLC......G...... 716 433-1014
Lockport *(G-7333)*
T C Peters Printing Co Inc......G...... 315 724-4149
Utica *(G-15735)*
The Kingsbury Printing Co Inc......G...... 518 747-6606
Queensbury *(G-13443)*
The Nugent Organization Inc......F...... 212 645-6600
Oceanside *(G-12561)*
Thomas Group Inc......F...... 212 947-6400
New York *(G-11817)*
Tom & Jerry Printcraft Forms......E...... 914 777-7468
Mamaroneck *(G-7758)*
Torsaf Printers Inc......G...... 516 569-5577
Hewlett *(G-6051)*
Total Concept Graphic Inc......G...... 212 229-2626
New York *(G-11873)*
Tovie Asarese Royal Prtg Co......G...... 716 885-7692
Buffalo *(G-3100)*
Trade Mark Graphics Inc......G...... 718 306-0001
Brooklyn *(G-2578)*

Tremont Offset Inc......G...... 718 892-7333
Bronx *(G-1404)*
Tri Kolor Printing & Sty......F...... 315 474-6753
Syracuse *(G-15446)*
Tri-Lon Clor Lithographers Ltd......E...... 212 255-6140
New York *(G-11893)*
Tri-Star Offset Corp......E...... 718 894-5555
Maspeth *(G-7873)*
Tri-Town News Inc......E...... 607 561-3515
Sidney *(G-14855)*
Triad Printing Inc......G...... 845 343-2722
Middletown *(G-8180)*
Tropp Printing Corp......G...... 212 233-4519
New York *(G-11903)*
True Type Printing Co Inc......G...... 718 706-6900
Amityville *(G-324)*
Tucker Printers Inc......D...... 585 359-3030
Henrietta *(G-6037)*
Twenty-First Century Press Inc......F...... 716 837-0800
Buffalo *(G-3106)*
Twin Counties Pro Printers Inc......F...... 518 828-3278
Hudson *(G-6374)*
Upstate Printing Inc......F...... 315 475-6140
Syracuse *(G-15449)*
V & J Graphics Inc......G...... 315 363-1933
Oneida *(G-12622)*
Vanguard Graphics LLC......C...... 607 272-1212
Ithaca *(G-6615)*
Variable Graphics LLC......G...... 212 691-2323
New York *(G-11994)*
Veterans Offset Printing Inc......G...... 585 288-2900
Rochester *(G-14200)*
Vincys Printing Ltd......F...... 518 355-4363
Schenectady *(G-14725)*
Vivona Business Printers Inc......G...... 516 496-3453
Syosset *(G-15233)*
Walnut Printing Inc......G...... 718 707-0100
Long Island City *(G-7633)*
Warren Printing Inc......F...... 212 627-5000
Long Island City *(G-7634)*
Wayne Printing Inc......F...... 914 761-2400
White Plains *(G-16517)*
Weeks & Reichel Printing Inc......G...... 631 589-1443
Sayville *(G-14635)*
Weicro Graphics Inc......E...... 631 253-3360
West Babylon *(G-16204)*
Westchester Mailing Service......E...... 914 948-1116
White Plains *(G-16519)*
Westypo Printers Inc......G...... 914 737-7394
Peekskill *(G-12930)*
William Charles Prtg Co Inc......E...... 516 349-0900
Plainview *(G-13102)*
Wilson Press LLC......E...... 315 568-9693
Seneca Falls *(G-14788)*
Winner Press Inc......E...... 718 937-7715
Long Island City *(G-7640)*
Winson Surnamer Inc......G...... 718 729-8787
Long Island City *(G-7641)*
Woodbury Printing Plus + Inc......G...... 845 928-6610
Central Valley *(G-3399)*
Wynco Press One Inc......G...... 516 354-6145
Glen Oaks *(G-5388)*
Yorktown Printing Corp......C...... 914 962-2526
Yorktown Heights *(G-16826)*
Zenger Partners LLC......E...... 716 876-2284
Kenmore *(G-6865)*

PRINTING: Pamphlets

Willis Mc Donald Co Inc......F...... 212 366-1526
New York *(G-12115)*

PRINTING: Photo-Offset

Academy Printing Services Inc......G...... 631 765-3346
Southold *(G-14967)*
D G M Graphics Inc......F...... 516 223-2220
Merrick *(G-8096)*
Genie Instant Printing Co Inc......F...... 212 575-8258
New York *(G-9905)*
Kjckd Inc......G...... 518 435-9696
Latham *(G-7078)*
Leader Printing Inc......F...... 516 546-1544
Merrick *(G-8101)*
National Reproductions Inc......E...... 212 619-3800
New York *(G-10884)*
Pronto Printer......G...... 914 737-0800
Cortlandt Manor *(G-3904)*
Rapid Rays Printing & Copying......G...... 716 852-0550
Buffalo *(G-3031)*
Scriven Duplicating Service......G...... 518 233-8180
Troy *(G-15624)*

Employee Codes: A=Over 500 employees, B=251-500
C=101-250, D=51-100, E=20-50, F=10-19, G=5-9
2019 Harris
New York Manufacturers Directory
1225

PRINTING: Photo-Offset

Three Star Offset Printing ....F 516 867-8223
  Freeport *(G-5187)*

PRINTING: Photogravure

Dijifi LLC ....F 646 519-2447
  Brooklyn *(G-1778)*

PRINTING: Photolithographic

BP Digital Imaging LLC ....G 607 753-0022
  Cortland *(G-3864)*

PRINTING: Rotary Photogravure

Mastro Graphic Arts Inc ....E 585 436-7570
  Rochester *(G-13931)*

PRINTING: Rotogravure

American Packaging Corporation ....C 585 254-9500
  Rochester *(G-13626)*

PRINTING: Screen, Broadwoven Fabrics, Cotton

D & R Silk Screening Ltd ....F 631 234-7464
  Central Islip *(G-3367)*
Dynamic Screenprinting ....G 518 487-4256
  Albany *(G-69)*
Loremanss Embroidery Engrav ....F 518 834-9205
  Keeseville *(G-6852)*
Printery ....G 315 253-7403
  Auburn *(G-496)*
Santee Print Works ....B 212 997-1570
  New York *(G-11485)*
Sciane Enterprises Inc ....G 845 452-2400
  Poughkeepsie *(G-13266)*
Steve Poli Sales ....G 315 487-0394
  Camillus *(G-3197)*
Tramwell Inc ....G 315 789-2762
  Geneva *(G-5334)*
Ward Sales Co Inc ....G 315 476-5276
  Syracuse *(G-15454)*

PRINTING: Screen, Fabric

Apple Imprints Apparel Inc ....E 716 893-1130
  Buffalo *(G-2706)*
Apsco Sports Enterprises Inc ....D 718 965-9500
  Brooklyn *(G-1545)*
Aro-Graph Corporation ....G 315 463-8693
  Syracuse *(G-15246)*
Dirt T Shirts Inc ....E 845 336-4230
  Kingston *(G-6898)*
Galli Shirts and Sports AP ....G 845 226-7305
  Stormville *(G-15179)*
Human Technologies Corporation ....F 315 735-3532
  Utica *(G-15711)*
Irene Cerone ....G 315 668-2899
  Brewerton *(G-1151)*
J M L Productions Inc ....D 718 643-1674
  Brooklyn *(G-2025)*
Kevin J Kassman ....G 585 529-4245
  Rochester *(G-13904)*
Printz and Patternz LLC ....F 518 944-6020
  Schenectady *(G-14705)*
Rainbow Lettering ....G 607 732-5751
  Elmira *(G-4501)*
Randy Sixberry ....G 315 265-6211
  Potsdam *(G-13322)*
Special Tees ....E 718 980-0987
  Staten Island *(G-15136)*
Viewsport International Inc ....G 585 259-1562
  Penfield *(G-12947)*
Wicked Smart LLC ....F 518 459-2855
  Watervliet *(G-16057)*

PRINTING: Screen, Manmade Fiber & Silk, Broadwoven Fabric

Dyenamix Inc ....G 212 941-6642
  New York *(G-9593)*
Efs Designs LLC ....G 718 852-9511
  Brooklyn *(G-1816)*
Intertex USA Inc ....F 212 279-3601
  New York *(G-10253)*
Mv Corp Inc ....C 631 273-8020
  Bay Shore *(G-703)*
Rescuestuff Inc ....G 718 318-7570
  Peekskill *(G-12923)*

Screen Gems Inc ....G 845 561-0036
  New Windsor *(G-8659)*
Valley Stream Sporting Gds Inc ....E 516 593-7800
  Lynbrook *(G-7677)*

PRINTING: Thermography

Bco Industries Western NY Inc ....E 716 877-2800
  Tonawanda *(G-15526)*
Business Card Express Inc ....E 631 669-3400
  West Babylon *(G-16143)*
East Coast Thermographers Inc ....E 718 321-3211
  College Point *(G-3643)*
Fineline Thermographers Inc ....G 718 643-1100
  Brooklyn *(G-1882)*
Karr Graphics Corp ....E 212 645-6000
  Long Island City *(G-7487)*

PROFESSIONAL EQPT & SPLYS, WHOLESALE: Analytical Instruments

Peyser Instrument Corporation ....E 631 841-3600
  West Babylon *(G-16181)*

PROFESSIONAL EQPT & SPLYS, WHOLESALE: Engineers', NEC

Advanced Tchncal Solutions Inc ....F 914 214-8230
  Mahopac *(G-7707)*

PROFESSIONAL EQPT & SPLYS, WHOLESALE: Optical Goods

Carl Zeiss Inc ....C 914 747-1800
  Thornwood *(G-15502)*
Dynamic Laboratories Inc ....E 631 231-7474
  Ronkonkoma *(G-14334)*
Lens Lab Express ....G 718 921-5488
  Brooklyn *(G-2110)*
Moscot Wholesale Corp ....E 212 647-1550
  New York *(G-10846)*
Spectrum Thin Films Inc ....E 631 901-1010
  Hauppauge *(G-5946)*
Tri-Supreme Optical LLC ....D 631 249-2020
  Farmingdale *(G-4899)*

PROFESSIONAL EQPT & SPLYS, WHOLESALE: Scientific & Engineerg

Avanel Industries Inc ....F 516 333-0990
  Westbury *(G-16318)*
Scientifics Direct Inc ....F 716 773-7500
  Tonawanda *(G-15576)*
VWR Education LLC ....C 585 359-2502
  West Henrietta *(G-16254)*

PROFESSIONAL EQPT & SPLYS, WHOLESALE: Theatrical

Steeldeck Ny Inc ....F 718 599-3700
  Brooklyn *(G-2517)*

PROFILE SHAPES: Unsupported Plastics

Chelsea Plastics Inc ....F 212 924-4530
  New York *(G-9269)*
Franklin Poly Film Inc ....E 718 492-3523
  Brooklyn *(G-1904)*
Howard J Moore Company Inc ....E 631 351-8467
  Plainview *(G-13062)*
Mitsui Chemicals America Inc ....E 914 253-0777
  Rye Brook *(G-14493)*
Ontario Plastics Inc ....E 585 663-2644
  Rochester *(G-13989)*

PROGRAM ADMIN, GOVT: Air, Water & Solid Waste Mgmt, Local

City of Kingston ....F 845 331-2490
  Kingston *(G-6895)*

PROMOTION SVCS

Drns Corp ....F 718 369-4530
  Brooklyn *(G-1795)*
Shykat Promotions ....G 866 574-2757
  Forestville *(G-5088)*

PROPERTY DAMAGE INSURANCE

Xerox Corporation ....C 585 427-4500
  Rochester *(G-14214)*

PROTECTION EQPT: Lightning

Heary Bros Lghtning Protection ....E 716 941-6141
  Springville *(G-15018)*
Tii Technologies Inc ....E 516 364-9300
  Edgewood *(G-4419)*

PROTECTIVE FOOTWEAR: Rubber Or Plastic

Lust For Life Footwear LLC ....F 646 732-9742
  Pearl River *(G-12906)*

PUBLIC RELATIONS & PUBLICITY SVCS

Studley Printing & Publishing ....F 518 563-1414
  Plattsburgh *(G-13160)*

PUBLISHERS: Art Copy

Classic Collections Fine Art ....G 914 591-4500
  White Plains *(G-16437)*

PUBLISHERS: Art Copy & Poster

Luminary Publishing Inc ....F 845 334-8600
  Kingston *(G-6909)*
Pace Editions Inc ....E 212 421-3237
  New York *(G-11085)*
Space 150 ....C 612 332-6458
  Brooklyn *(G-2502)*

PUBLISHERS: Atlases

Directory Major Malls Inc ....G 845 348-7000
  Nyack *(G-12505)*

PUBLISHERS: Book

A Lesley Dummett ....G 646 541-1168
  Saint Albans *(G-14506)*
Advance Publications Inc ....D 718 981-1234
  Staten Island *(G-15040)*
Alm Media LLC ....B 212 457-9400
  New York *(G-8805)*
Alm Media Holdings Inc ....B 212 457-9400
  New York *(G-8806)*
American Inst Chem Engineers ....D 646 495-1355
  New York *(G-8830)*
Assouline Publishing Inc ....F 212 989-6769
  New York *(G-8939)*
Ateres Publishing & Bk Bindery ....F 718 935-9355
  Brooklyn *(G-1569)*
Atlas & Company LLC ....G 212 234-3100
  New York *(G-8953)*
Beauty Fashion Inc ....E 212 840-8800
  New York *(G-9032)*
Bedrock Communications ....G 212 532-4150
  New York *(G-9037)*
Benchmark Education Co LLC ....D 914 637-7200
  New Rochelle *(G-8592)*
Bobley-Harmann Corporation ....G 516 433-3800
  Ronkonkoma *(G-14320)*
Burns Archive Photographic Dis ....E 212 889-1938
  New York *(G-9160)*
Byliner Inc ....E 415 680-3608
  New York *(G-9168)*
Canopy Books LLC ....G 516 354-4888
  Massapequa *(G-7879)*
CCC Publications Inc ....F 718 306-1008
  Brooklyn *(G-1684)*
Changdu Technology (usa) Co ....F 917 340-1976
  North Bellmore *(G-12374)*
Curriculum Associates LLC ....F 978 313-1355
  Brooklyn *(G-1740)*
Der Yid Inc ....E 718 797-3900
  Brooklyn *(G-1769)*
Divine Phoenix LLC ....A 585 737-1482
  Skaneateles *(G-14870)*
Eagle Art Publishing Inc ....G 212 685-7411
  New York *(G-9602)*
Entertainment Weekly Inc ....C 212 522-5600
  New York *(G-9688)*
F P H Communications ....G 212 528-1728
  New York *(G-9762)*
Fairchild Publications Inc ....A 212 630-4000
  New York *(G-9773)*
Family Publishing Group Inc ....G 914 381-7474
  Mamaroneck *(G-7744)*
Feminist Press Inc ....E 212 817-7915
  New York *(G-9794)*
Franklin Report LLC ....G 212 639-9100
  New York *(G-9843)*

Gq Magazine....G....212 286-2860
New York (G-9966)
Grey House Publishing Inc....E....518 789-8700
Amenia (G-206)
Grolier International Inc....G....212 343-6100
New York (G-9994)
Guilford Publications Inc....G....800 365-7006
New York (G-10009)
Haights Cross Operating Co....E....914 289-9400
White Plains (G-16457)
Harpercollins Publishers LLC....E....212 553-4200
New York (G-10039)
Harvard University Press....D....212 337-0280
New York (G-10047)
Informa Business Media Inc....F....914 949-8500
White Plains (G-16462)
Kwesi Legesse LLC....G....347 581-9872
Brooklyn (G-2084)
Learningexpress LLC....E....646 274-6454
New York (G-10532)
Legal Strategies Inc....G....516 377-3940
Merrick (G-8102)
Lexis Publishing....C....518 487-3000
Menands (G-8086)
Living Well Innovations Inc....G....646 517-3200
Hauppauge (G-5866)
Macmillan Audio....G....646 600-7856
New York (G-10648)
Macmillan College Pubg Co Inc....F....212 702-2000
New York (G-10649)
Martha Stewart Living....C....212 827-8000
New York (G-10717)
Mathisen Ventures Inc....G....212 986-1025
New York (G-10728)
McGraw-Hill School Educatn LLC....A....646 766-2060
New York (G-10743)
Mediaplanet Publishing Hse Inc....E....646 922-1400
New York (G-10755)
Meegenius Inc....G....212 283-7285
New York (G-10763)
Micro Publishing Inc....G....212 533-9180
New York (G-10795)
N A R Associates Inc....G....845 557-8713
Barryville (G-607)
NBM Publishing Inc....G....646 559-4681
New York (G-10900)
NC Audience Exchange LLC....F....212 416-3400
New York (G-10901)
New York Legal Publishing....G....518 459-1100
Menands (G-8090)
New York Qrtrly Foundation Inc....F....917 843-8825
Brooklyn (G-2265)
News Corporation....C....212 416-3400
New York (G-10952)
Nova Science Publishers Inc....F....631 231-7269
Hauppauge (G-5902)
Origin Press Inc....G....516 746-2262
Mineola (G-8243)
Oxford University Press LLC....G....212 726-6000
New York (G-11079)
Ozmodyl Ltd....G....212 226-0622
New York (G-11081)
Pace Walkers of America Inc....F....631 444-2147
Port Jefferson (G-13223)
Pearson Education Inc....E....845 340-8700
Kingston (G-6914)
Pearson Education Inc....F....212 782-3337
New York (G-11130)
Pearson Education Inc....E....212 366-2000
New York (G-11131)
Pearson Education Inc....F....201 236-7000
West Nyack (G-16278)
Pegasus Books NY Ltd....G....646 343-9502
New York (G-11140)
Poetry Mailing List Marsh Hawk....G....516 766-1891
Oceanside (G-12551)
Poets House Inc....F....212 431-7920
New York (G-11215)
Powerhouse Cultural Entrmt Inc....F....212 604-9074
Brooklyn (G-2330)
Preserving Chrstn Publications....G....315 942-6617
Boonville (G-1119)
Rda Holding Co....E....914 238-1000
New York (G-11336)
Readers Dgest Yung Fmilies Inc....E....914 238-1000
Pleasantville (G-13176)
Repertoire International De Ll....E....212 817-1990
New York (G-11364)
Rizzoli Intl Publications Inc....F....212 387-3572
New York (G-11399)
S P Books Inc....G....212 431-5011
New York (G-11458)
Scholastic Inc....E....212 343-6100
New York (G-11515)
Scholium International Inc....G....516 883-8032
Port Washington (G-13305)
Sheridan House Inc....G....914 725-5431
Scarsdale (G-14645)
Simon Schuster Digital Sls Inc....D....212 698-4391
New York (G-11597)
Springer Customer Svc Ctr LLC....B....212 460-1500
New York (G-11682)
Station Hill of Barrytown....G....845 758-5293
Barrytown (G-606)
Steffen Publishing Inc....D....315 865-4100
Holland Patent (G-6225)
Stonesong Press LLC....G....212 929-4600
New York (G-11715)
Storybooks Forever....F....716 822-7845
Buffalo (G-3078)
Studio Fun International Inc....E....914 238-1000
White Plains (G-16509)
Sweet Mouth Inc....E....800 433-7758
New York (G-11757)
Targum Press USA Inc....G....248 355-2266
Brooklyn (G-2556)
Taylor & Francis Group LLC....C....212 216-7800
New York (G-11786)
Thornwillow Press Ltd....G....212 980-0738
New York (G-11826)
Time Home Entertainment Inc....E....212 522-1212
New York (G-11836)
Time Inc....E....212 522-1212
New York (G-11837)
Verso Inc....G....718 246-8160
Brooklyn (G-2619)
W W Norton & Company Inc....G....212 354-5500
New York (G-12062)
Woodward/White Inc....F....718 509-6082
Brooklyn (G-2656)
Ziff Davis Publishing LLC....D....212 503-3500
New York (G-12177)
Zinepak LLC....F....212 706-8621
New York (G-12178)

PUBLISHERS: Book Clubs, No Printing

Humana Press Inc....E....212 460-1500
New York (G-10149)

PUBLISHERS: Books, No Printing

Abbeville Press Inc....E....212 366-5585
New York (G-8706)
Aip Publishing LLC....C....516 576-2200
Melville (G-7999)
Alba House Publishers....E....718 698-2759
Staten Island (G-15041)
Amereon Ltd....G....631 298-5100
Mattituck (G-7913)
American Institute Physics Inc....C....516 576-2410
Melville (G-8002)
Amherst Media Inc....G....716 874-4450
Buffalo (G-2698)
Annuals Publishing Co Inc....G....212 505-0950
New York (G-8874)
Anthroposophic Press Inc....G....518 851-2054
Clifton Park (G-3563)
Barrons Educational Series Inc....C....631 434-3311
Hauppauge (G-5778)
Bertelsmann Pubg Group Inc....A....212 782-1000
New York (G-9056)
Bicker Inc....F....212 688-0085
New York (G-9072)
Bloomsbury Publishing Inc....D....212 419-5300
New York (G-9104)
Bmg Rights Management (us) LLC....E....212 561-3000
New York (G-9113)
Boardman Simons Publishing....E....212 620-7200
New York (G-9115)
Bonnier Publishing Usa Inc....E....212 321-0237
New York (G-9120)
British American Publishing....D....518 786-6000
Latham (G-7065)
Cambridge University Press....D....212 337-5000
New York (G-9186)
Campus Course Paks Inc....G....516 877-3967
Garden City (G-5254)
Castle Connolly Medical Ltd....E....212 367-8400
New York (G-9224)
CB Publishing LLC....G....516 354-4888
Floral Park (G-4959)
Central Cnfrnce of Amrcn Rbbis....F....212 972-3636
New York (G-9243)
Chain Store Age Magazine....G....212 756-5000
New York (G-9255)
Church Publishing Incorporated....G....212 592-1800
New York (G-9296)
Cinderella Press Ltd....G....212 431-3130
New York (G-9298)
Clarkson N Potter Inc....F....212 782-9000
New York (G-9317)
Columbia University Press....E....212 459-0600
New York (G-9358)
Columbia University Press....E....212 459-0600
New York (G-9359)
Columbia University Press....E....212 459-0600
New York (G-9360)
Confrtrnity of Prescious Blood....G....718 436-1120
Brooklyn (G-1711)
Continuum Intl Pubg Group Inc....F....646 649-4215
New York (G-9390)
Daheshist Publishing Co Ltd....F....212 581-8360
New York (G-9453)
Definition Press Inc....F....212 777-4490
New York (G-9495)
Delaney Books Inc....F....516 921-8888
Syosset (G-15215)
Demos Medical Publishing LLC....F....516 889-1791
New York (G-9499)
Dorling Kindersley Publishing....D....212 213-4800
New York (G-9560)
Edwin Mellen Press Inc....E....716 754-2796
Lewiston (G-7140)
Egmont US Inc....G....212 685-0102
New York (G-9635)
Folio Graphics Co Inc....G....718 763-2076
Brooklyn (G-1896)
Four M Studios....D....515 284-2157
New York (G-9831)
Foxhill Press Inc....E....212 995-9620
New York (G-9836)
Frank Merriwell Inc....F....516 921-8888
Syosset (G-15218)
Ggp Publishing Inc....F....914 834-8896
Harrison (G-5728)
Government Data Publication....E....347 789-8719
Brooklyn (G-1945)
Grand Central Publishing....C....212 364-1200
New York (G-9970)
Graphis Inc....F....212 532-9387
New York (G-9978)
Grey House Publishing Inc....E....845 483-3535
Poughkeepsie (G-13343)
Guilford Publications Inc....D....212 431-9800
New York (G-10008)
Hachette Book Group Inc....B....800 759-0190
New York (G-10016)
Hachette Book Group USA....E....212 364-1200
New York (G-10017)
Harpercollins....F....212 207-7000
New York (G-10037)
Harpercollins Publishers LLC....A....212 207-7000
New York (G-10038)
Harry N Abrams Incorporated....D....212 206-7715
New York (G-10042)
Hearst Business Media Corp....F....631 650-4441
New York (G-10056)
Hearst Corporation....A....212 649-2000
New York (G-10061)
Hearst Corporation....E....212 649-2275
New York (G-10070)
Henry Holt and Company LLC....D....646 307-5095
New York (G-10081)
Highline Media LLC....C....859 692-2100
New York (G-10097)
Hudson Park Press Inc....G....212 929-8898
New York (G-10144)
Infobase Holdings Inc....D....212 967-8800
New York (G-10206)
Infobase Publishing Company....G....212 967-8800
New York (G-10207)
Ir Media Group (usa) Inc....E....212 425-9649
New York (G-10267)
Jonathan David Publishers Inc....F....718 456-8611
Middle Village (G-8123)
Judaica Press Inc....G....718 972-6202
Brooklyn (G-2054)
Juris Publishing Inc....F....631 351-5430
Huntington (G-6402)
K T A V Publishing House Inc....F....201 963-9524
Brooklyn (G-2065)

PRODUCT

Employee Codes: A=Over 500 employees, B=251-500
C=101-250, D=51-100, E=20-50, F=10-19, G=5-9
2019 Harris
New York Manufacturers Directory
1227

Kaplan Inc E 212 752-1840
New York *(G-10405)*
Kensington Publishing Corp D 212 407-1500
New York *(G-10434)*
Kodansha USA Inc G 917 322-6200
New York *(G-10464)*
Le Book Publishing Inc G 212 334-5252
New York *(G-10526)*
Lee & Low Books Incorporated F 212 779-4400
New York *(G-10537)*
Lippincott Massie McQuilkin L F 212 352-2055
New York *(G-10576)*
Literary Classics of US F 212 308-3360
New York *(G-10578)*
Liveright Publishing Corp G 212 354-5500
New York *(G-10584)*
Looseleaf Law Publications Inc F 718 359-5559
Flushing *(G-5025)*
Macmillan Publishers Inc A 646 307-5151
New York *(G-10651)*
Macmillan Publishing Group LLC B 212 674-5145
New York *(G-10652)*
Malhame Publs & Importers Inc E 631 694-8600
Bohemia *(G-1055)*
Marshall Cavendish Corp E 914 332-8888
Tarrytown *(G-15481)*
Mary Ann Liebert Inc D 914 740-2100
New Rochelle *(G-8620)*
McBooks Press Inc G 607 272-2114
Ithaca *(G-6594)*
McGraw-Hill Education Inc D 646 766-2000
New York *(G-10741)*
McGraw-Hill School Education H B 646 766-2000
New York *(G-10742)*
Medikidz Usa Inc G 646 895-9319
New York *(G-10759)*
Melcher Media Inc F 212 727-2322
New York *(G-10769)*
Merkos Llnyonei Chinuch Inc E 718 778-0226
Brooklyn *(G-2196)*
Mesorah Publications Ltd E 718 921-9000
Brooklyn *(G-2198)*
Modern Language Assn Amer Inc C 646 576-5000
New York *(G-10829)*
Monacelli Press LLC G 212 229-9925
New York *(G-10836)*
Mondo Publishing Inc E 212 268-3560
New York *(G-10837)*
Moznaim Publishing Co Inc G 718 853-0525
Brooklyn *(G-2229)*
Mud Puddle Books Inc G 212 647-9168
New York *(G-10856)*
New City Press Inc G 845 229-0335
Hyde Park *(G-6470)*
New Directions Publishing F 212 255-0230
New York *(G-10920)*
New Press E 212 629-8802
New York *(G-10928)*
North Shore Home Improver F 631 474-2824
Port Jeff STA *(G-13214)*
North-South Books Inc E 212 706-4545
New York *(G-10995)*
Other Press LLC G 212 414-0054
New York *(G-11068)*
Oxford University Press LLC B 212 726-6000
New York *(G-11078)*
P J D Publications Ltd G 516 626-0650
New Hyde Park *(G-8557)*
Palgrave Macmillan Ltd G 646 307-5028
New York *(G-11095)*
Papercutz Inc G 646 559-4681
New York *(G-11104)*
Parachute Publishing LLC E 212 337-6743
New York *(G-11106)*
Penguin Putnam Inc G 212 366-2000
New York *(G-11144)*
Penguin Random House LLC E 212 782-1000
New York *(G-11145)*
Penguin Random House LLC B 212 782-9000
New York *(G-11146)*
Penguin Random House LLC A 212 572-6162
New York *(G-11147)*
Penguin Random House LLC A 212 782-9000
New York *(G-11148)*
Penguin Random House LLC C 212 366-2377
Albany *(G-113)*
Peter Mayer Publishers Inc F 212 673-2210
New York *(G-11169)*
Peter Pauper Press Inc E 914 681-0144
White Plains *(G-16496)*
Phaidon Press Inc E 212 652-5400
New York *(G-11179)*
Philipp Feldheim Inc G 845 356-2282
Nanuet *(G-8467)*
Picador USA F 646 307-5629
New York *(G-11189)*
Prestel Publishing LLC G 212 995-2720
New York *(G-11236)*
Princton Archtctural Press LLC F 518 671-6100
Hudson *(G-6369)*
Prometheus Books Inc E 716 691-2158
Amherst *(G-248)*
PSR Press Ltd F 716 754-2266
Lewiston *(G-7142)*
Quarto Group Inc E 212 779-0700
New York *(G-11299)*
Rapid Intellect Group Inc F 518 929-3210
Chatham *(G-3429)*
Relx Inc E 212 309-8100
New York *(G-11355)*
Research Centre of Kabbalah G 718 805-0380
Richmond Hill *(G-13509)*
Richard C Owen Publishers Inc F 914 232-3903
Somers *(G-14922)*
Rizzoli Intl Publications Inc E 212 387-3400
New York *(G-11398)*
Rosen Publishing Group Inc C 212 777-3017
New York *(G-11432)*
Ryland Peters & Small Inc G 646 791-5410
New York *(G-11453)*
Scholastic Corporation G 212 343-6100
New York *(G-11513)*
Scholastic Inc A 800 724-6527
New York *(G-11514)*
Second Chance Press Inc G 631 725-1101
Sag Harbor *(G-14503)*
Seven Stories Press Inc G 212 226-8760
New York *(G-11547)*
Simon & Schuster Inc D 212 698-7000
New York *(G-11595)*
Skyhorse Publishing Inc E 212 643-6816
New York *(G-11614)*
Social Register Association F 646 612-7314
New York *(G-11633)*
Soho Press Inc G 212 260-1900
New York *(G-11637)*
Springer Adis Us LLC F 212 460-1500
New York *(G-11681)*
Springer Publishing Co LLC E 212 431-4370
New York *(G-11684)*
Springer Scnce + Bus Media LLC D 212 460-1500
New York *(G-11685)*
Square One Publishers Inc F 516 535-2010
Garden City Park *(G-5288)*
STf Services Inc E 315 463-8506
East Syracuse *(G-4371)*
Suny At Binghamton D 607 777-2316
Binghamton *(G-916)*
Syracuse University Press Inc E 315 443-5534
Syracuse *(G-15441)*
Tom Doherty Associates Inc E 212 388-0100
New York *(G-11859)*
Trusted Media Brands Inc A 914 238-1000
New York *(G-11907)*
Trusted Media Brands Inc F 914 244-5244
White Plains *(G-16513)*
Unisystems Inc E 212 826-0850
New York *(G-11951)*
United Synggue Cnsrvtive Jdism E 212 533-7800
New York *(G-11956)*
Vaad LHafotzas Sichoes F 718 778-5436
Brooklyn *(G-2614)*
Vandam Inc F 212 929-0416
Long Island City *(G-7627)*
Vaultcom Inc E 212 366-4212
New York *(G-12001)*
William H Sadlier Inc C 212 233-3646
New York *(G-12111)*
William S Hein & Co Inc C 716 882-2600
Getzville *(G-5356)*
William S Hein & Co Inc D 716 882-2600
Buffalo *(G-3132)*
Wolters Kluwer US Inc F 212 894-8920
New York *(G-12129)*
Workman Publishing Co Inc C 212 254-5900
New York *(G-12135)*
Workman Publishing Co Inc C 212 254-5900
New York *(G-12136)*
YS Publishing Co Inc G 212 682-9360
New York *(G-12166)*

PUBLISHERS: Catalogs

Christopher Anthony Pubg Co F 516 826-9205
Wantagh *(G-15920)*
Select Information Exchange F 212 496-6435
New York *(G-11538)*

PUBLISHERS: Comic Books, No Printing

Archie Comic Publications Inc D 914 381-5155
Pelham *(G-12932)*
Clp Pb LLC E 212 340-8100
New York *(G-9335)*
Continuity Publishing Inc F 212 869-4170
New York *(G-9388)*
Interntnl Publcatns Media Grup G 917 604-9602
New York *(G-10252)*
Marvel Entertainment LLC C 212 576-4000
New York *(G-10719)*
Valiant Entertainment LLC E 212 972-0361
New York *(G-11986)*

PUBLISHERS: Directories, NEC

Black Book Photography Inc F 212 979-6700
New York *(G-9096)*
Catholic News Publishing Co F 914 632-7771
Mamaroneck *(G-7737)*
Easy Book Publishing Inc G 518 459-6281
Albany *(G-70)*
Foundation Center Inc C 212 620-4230
New York *(G-9826)*
Hearst Business Media D 516 227-1300
Uniondale *(G-15669)*
Highline Media LLC C 859 692-2100
New York *(G-10097)*
Leadership Directories Inc D 212 627-4140
New York *(G-10530)*
Supermedia LLC D 212 513-9700
New York *(G-11748)*
Thomas Publishing Company LLC B 212 695-0500
New York *(G-11818)*

PUBLISHERS: Directories, Telephone

Associated Publishing Company E 325 676-4032
Buffalo *(G-2710)*
Hola Publishing Co G 718 424-3129
Long Island City *(G-7470)*
Mac Innes Enterprises Inc E 325 676-4032
Buffalo *(G-2931)*

PUBLISHERS: Guides

Family Publications Ltd F 212 947-2177
New York *(G-9778)*
Fredonia Pennysaver Inc G 716 679-1509
Fredonia *(G-5126)*
Metro Group Inc G 716 434-4055
Lockport *(G-7317)*
Mt Morris Shopper Inc G 585 658-3520
Mount Morris *(G-8367)*

PUBLISHERS: Magazines, No Printing

21st Century Fox America Inc D 212 852-7000
New York *(G-8673)*
2600 Enterprises Inc F 631 474-2677
Saint James *(G-14509)*
A Guideposts Church Corp C 212 251-8100
New York *(G-8695)*
Abp International Inc E 212 490-3999
New York *(G-8712)*
Adirondack Life Inc F 518 946-2191
Jay *(G-6773)*
Adirondack Life Inc G 518 946-2191
Jay *(G-6774)*
Advance Magazine Publs Inc C 212 450-7000
New York *(G-8750)*
Advanced Research Media Inc F 631 751-9696
Setauket *(G-14791)*
Adventure Publishing Group E 212 575-4510
New York *(G-8760)*
Aeon America Inc G 914 584-0275
Brooklyn *(G-1491)*
Alm Media LLC B 212 457-9400
New York *(G-8805)*
Alm Media Holdings Inc B 212 457-9400
New York *(G-8806)*
America Press Inc E 212 581-4640
New York *(G-8822)*
American Inst Chem Engineers D 646 495-1355
New York *(G-8830)*

PRODUCT SECTION
PUBLISHERS: Magazines, No Printing

Company	Code	Phone
American Jewish Committee — New York (G-8831)	G	212 891-1400
American Towman Network Inc — Warwick (G-15948)	F	845 986-4546
Analysts In Media (aim) Inc — New York (G-8853)	E	212 488-1777
Animal Fair Media Inc — New York (G-8869)	F	212 629-0392
Atlantic Monthly Group Inc — New York (G-8950)	E	202 266-7000
Backstage LLC — Brooklyn (G-1582)	E	212 493-4243
Beauty Fashion Inc — New York (G-9032)	E	212 840-8800
Bedford Communications Inc — New York (G-9036)	E	212 807-8220
Bellerophon Publications Inc — New York (G-9040)	E	212 627-9977
Bertelsmann Pubg Group Inc — New York (G-9056)	A	212 782-1000
Beverage Media Group Inc — New York (G-9063)	F	212 571-3232
Blue Horizon Media Inc — New York (G-9108)	F	212 661-7878
Bnei Aram Soba Inc — Brooklyn (G-1625)	F	718 645-4460
Buffalo Spree Publishing Inc — Buffalo (G-2752)	E	716 783-9119
Bust Inc — Brooklyn (G-1662)	G	212 675-1707
C Q Communications Inc — Hicksville (G-6066)	E	516 681-2922
Carol Group Ltd — New York (G-9212)	G	212 505-2030
Centennial Media LLC — New York (G-9240)	F	646 527-7320
Center For Inquiry Inc — Amherst (G-221)	F	716 636-4869
Cfo Publishing LLC — New York (G-9253)	E	212 459-3004
Coda Media Inc — New York (G-9345)	G	917 478-2565
College Calendar Company — Whitesboro (G-16526)	F	315 768-8242
Commonweal Foundation Inc — New York (G-9366)	F	212 662-4200
Consumer Reports Inc — Yonkers (G-16746)	B	914 378-2000
Crain Communications Inc — New York (G-9418)	C	212 210-0100
Crains New York Business — New York (G-9419)	E	212 210-0250
Daily Beast Company LLC — New York (G-9454)	E	212 445-4600
Data Key Communication LLC — Fayetteville (G-4927)	F	315 445-2347
Dennis Publishing Inc — New York (G-9502)	D	646 717-9500
Discover Media LLC — New York (G-9535)	E	212 624-4800
Dissent Magazine — New York (G-9538)	F	212 316-3120
Dj Publishing Inc — Port Washington (G-13253)	E	516 767-2500
Doctorow Communications Inc — New City (G-8491)	F	845 708-5166
Dotto Wagner — Oswego (G-12776)	G	315 342-8020
Dow Jones & Company Inc — New York (G-9564)	E	212 597-5983
E W Williams Publications — New York (G-9598)	G	212 661-1516
Earl G Graves Pubg Co Inc — New York (G-9605)	D	212 242-8000
Essence Communications Inc — Brooklyn (G-1851)	C	212 522-1212
Essence Ventures LLC — New York (G-9708)	C	212 522-1212
Executive Business Media Inc — Westbury (G-16329)	E	516 334-3030
Faces Magazine Inc — Poughkeepsie (G-13337)	F	201 843-4004
Fader Inc — New York (G-9771)	F	212 741-7100
Fahy-Williams Publishing Inc — Geneva (G-5323)	F	315 781-6820
Family Publishing Group Inc — Mamaroneck (G-7744)	E	914 381-7474
Four M Studios — New York (G-9830)	F	212 499-2000
Fridge Magazine Inc — New York (G-9850)	G	212 997-7673
Frozen Food Digest Inc — New York (G-9852)	G	212 557-8600
Fun Media Inc — New York (G-9861)	E	646 472-0135
Genomeweb LLC — New York (G-9906)	F	212 651-5636
Getting The Word Out Inc — Saranac Lake (G-14562)	G	518 891-9352
Golfing Magazine — Hicksville (G-6093)	G	516 822-5446
Grants Financial Publishing — New York (G-9975)	F	212 809-7994
Graphis Inc — New York (G-9978)	F	212 532-9387
Gruner + Jahr Prtg & Pubg Co — New York (G-10000)	C	212 463-1000
Halcyon Business Publications — Westbury (G-16338)	F	800 735-2732
Hamptons Magazine — Southampton (G-14955)	E	631 283-7125
Hamptons Media LLC — Southampton (G-14956)	G	631 283-6900
Harpers Magazine Foundation — New York (G-10040)	E	212 420-5720
Hart Energy Publishing Lllp — New York (G-10045)	F	212 621-4621
Haymarket Group Ltd — New York (G-10051)	F	212 239-0855
Haymarket Media Inc — New York (G-10052)	C	646 638-6000
Hearst Bus Communications Inc — New York (G-10055)	G	212 649-2000
Hearst Business Media — Uniondale (G-15669)	D	516 227-1300
Hearst Business Media Corp — Great River (G-5601)	G	631 650-6151
Hearst Business Media Corp — New York (G-10056)	F	631 650-4441
Hearst Business Publishing Inc — New York (G-10057)	F	212 969-7500
Hearst Communications Inc — New York (G-10060)	C	212 649-2000
Hearst Corporation — New York (G-10061)	A	212 649-2000
Hearst Corporation — New York (G-10062)	E	212 649-3100
Hearst Corporation — New York (G-10063)	E	212 903-5366
Hearst Corporation — New York (G-10064)	B	212 767-5800
Hearst Corporation — New York (G-10065)	D	516 382-4580
Hearst Corporation — New York (G-10066)	D	212 649-4271
Hearst Corporation — New York (G-10067)	D	212 204-4300
Hearst Corporation — New York (G-10069)	E	212 649-3204
Hearst Corporation — New York (G-10070)	E	212 649-2275
Hearst Holdings Inc — New York (G-10072)	F	212 649-2000
Herman Hall Communications — Brooklyn (G-1975)	F	718 941-1879
Historic TW Inc — New York (G-10106)	E	212 484-8000
Icd Publications Inc — Islandia (G-6530)	F	631 246-9300
Imek Media LLC — New York (G-10183)	E	212 422-9000
Informa Business Media Inc — New York (G-10209)	C	212 204-4200
Informa Media Inc — New York (G-10210)	B	212 204-4200
Ink Publishing Corporation — Brooklyn (G-2003)	G	347 294-1220
Intelligne The Ftr Cmptng Nwsl — New York (G-10232)	F	212 222-1123
Intellitravel Media Inc — New York (G-10233)	G	646 695-6700
Interhellenic Publishing Inc — New York (G-10241)	G	212 967-5016
Interview New York — New York (G-10254)	G	857 928-4120
Irish America Inc — New York (G-10270)	E	212 725-2993
JSD Communications Inc — Bedford (G-769)	F	914 588-1841
Kids Discover LLC — New York (G-10439)	G	212 677-4457
L I F Publishing Corp — Shirley (G-14837)	D	631 345-5200
Lagardere North America Inc — New York (G-10508)	E	212 477-7373
Locations Magazine — New York (G-10589)	G	212 288-4745
Long Island Catholic Newspaper — Rockville Centre (G-14235)	E	516 594-1212
Macfadden Cmmnctions Group LLC — New York (G-10647)	C	212 979-4800
Macmillan Holdings LLC — New York (G-10650)	F	212 576-9428
Mag Inc — Ithaca (G-6593)	E	607 257-6970
Manhattan Media LLC — New York (G-10686)	F	212 268-8600
Mann Publications Inc — New York (G-10690)	F	212 840-6266
Mansueto Ventures LLC — New York (G-10696)	E	212 389-5300
Maritime Activity Reports — New York (G-10704)	E	212 477-6700
Mark Levine — New York (G-10706)	F	212 677-4457
Martha Stewart Living — New York (G-10717)	C	212 827-8000
Martha Stewart Living Omni LLC — New York (G-10718)	B	212 827-8000
Martinelli Holdings LLC — Harrison (G-5730)	E	302 504-1361
Mass Appeal Magazine — Brooklyn (G-2177)	G	718 858-0979
Mergent Inc — New York (G-10773)	B	212 413-7700
Miami Media LLC — New York (G-10789)	F	212 268-8600
Modern Farmer Media Inc — Hudson (G-6365)	F	518 828-7447
Music & Sound Retailer Inc — Port Washington (G-13289)	E	516 767-2500
Nation Company LLC — New York (G-10878)	E	212 209-5400
Nation Magazine — New York (G-10879)	E	212 209-5400
National Review Inc — New York (G-10885)	E	212 679-7330
Nature America Inc — New York (G-10893)	B	212 726-9200
Nervecom Inc — New York (G-10906)	F	212 625-9914
New Art Publications Inc — Brooklyn (G-2256)	F	718 636-9100
New York Media LLC — New York (G-10940)	C	212 508-0700
Next Step Publishing Inc — Victor (G-15859)	F	585 742-1260
Nickelodeon Magazines Inc — New York (G-10964)	G	212 541-1949
Nova Science Publishers Inc — Hauppauge (G-5902)	F	631 231-7269
Nsgv Inc — New York (G-11003)	E	212 367-3167
Nsgv Inc — New York (G-11004)	E	212 367-3100
Nyemac Inc — Montauk (G-8307)	G	631 668-1303
Nylon LLc — New York (G-11015)	E	212 226-6454
Nyrev Inc — New York (G-11019)	E	212 757-8070
Paper Publishing Company Inc — New York (G-11103)	E	212 226-4405
Parade Publications Inc — New York (G-11107)	E	212 450-7000
Parents Guide Network Corp — New York (G-11110)	E	212 213-8840
Penhouse Media Group Inc — New York (G-11149)	C	212 702-6000
Periodical Services Co Inc — Hudson (G-6367)	F	518 822-9300
Photo Industry Inc — Woodbury (G-16628)	F	516 364-0016
Preparatory Magazine Group — Staten Island (G-15119)	D	718 761-4800
Prescribing Reference Inc — New York (G-11233)	D	646 638-6000
Professnl Spt Pblications Inc — New York (G-11256)	D	212 697-1460

Employee Codes: A=Over 500 employees, B=251-500
C=101-250, D=51-100, E=20-50, F=10-19, G=5-9

2019 Harris
New York Manufacturers Directory

1229

Q Communications Inc....G.... 212 594-6520
New York (G-11288)
Quest Media Llc....F.... 646 840-3404
New York (G-11301)
Raharney Capital LLC....G.... 212 220-9084
Brooklyn (G-2379)
Ralph Martinelli....E.... 914 345-3055
Elmsford (G-4560)
Ramholtz Publishing Inc....D.... 718 761-4800
Staten Island (G-15124)
Readers Digest Assn Incthe....F.... 414 423-0100
New York (G-11338)
Real Estate Media Inc....E.... 212 929-6976
New York (G-11339)
Relx Inc....E.... 212 463-6644
New York (G-11356)
Rfp LLC....E.... 212 838-7733
New York (G-11381)
Risk Society Management Pubg....E.... 212 286-9364
New York (G-11396)
Rough Draft Publishing LLC....F.... 212 741-4773
New York (G-11436)
Rsl Media LLC....G.... 212 307-6760
New York (G-11443)
Ruby Newco LLC....G.... 212 852-7000
New York (G-11445)
Sandow Media LLC....F.... 646 805-0200
New York (G-11481)
Scholastic Corporation....G.... 212 343-6100
New York (G-11513)
Scholastic Inc....A.... 800 724-6527
New York (G-11514)
Shoreline Publishing Inc....G.... 914 738-7869
Pelham (G-12938)
Simmons-Boardman Pubg Corp....E.... 212 620-7200
New York (G-11594)
Smart & Strong LLC....E.... 212 938-2051
New York (G-11621)
Smooth Magazine....F.... 212 925-1150
New York (G-11629)
Society For The Study....G.... 212 822-8806
New York (G-11634)
Sound Communications Inc....E.... 516 767-2500
Port Washington (G-13309)
Spin Magazine Media....E.... 212 231-7400
New York (G-11670)
Sports Illustrated For Kids....E.... 212 522-1212
New York (G-11674)
Spotlight Publications LLC....G.... 914 345-9473
Elmsford (G-4571)
Staten Island Parent Magazine....G.... 718 761-4800
Staten Island (G-15138)
Suburban Publishing Inc....F.... 845 463-0542
Fishkill (G-4952)
Testa Communications Inc....E.... 516 767-2500
Port Washington (G-13311)
Thomas Publishing Company LLC....G.... 212 695-0500
New York (G-11820)
Time Inc....A.... 212 522-1212
New York (G-11838)
Time Inc....E.... 212 522-0361
New York (G-11839)
Time Inc Affluent Media Group....B.... 212 382-5600
New York (G-11840)
Time Inc Affluent Media Group....G.... 212 382-5600
New York (G-11841)
Time Warner Companies Inc....D.... 212 484-8000
New York (G-11845)
Trusted Media Brands Inc....A.... 914 238-1000
New York (G-11907)
Trusted Media Brands Inc....F.... 914 244-5244
White Plains (G-16513)
TV Guide Magazine Group Inc....D.... 212 852-7500
New York (G-11916)
U S Japan Publication NY Inc....G.... 212 252-8833
New York (G-11926)
Ulster Publishing Co Inc....E.... 845 334-8205
Kingston (G-6926)
Untitled Media....E.... 212 780-0960
New York (G-11964)
US Frontline News Inc....E.... 212 922-9090
New York (G-11976)
US Weekly LLC....D.... 212 484-1616
New York (G-11979)
Value Line Inc....D.... 212 907-1500
New York (G-11988)
Vending Times Inc....F.... 516 442-1850
Rockville Centre (G-14244)
Veranda Publications Inc....G.... 212 903-5206
New York (G-12008)
Visionaire Publishing LLC....E.... 646 434-6091
New York (G-12043)
Weider Publications LLC....C.... 212 545-4800
New York (G-12087)
Welcome Magazine Inc....F.... 716 839-3121
Amherst (G-261)
Western New York Family Mag....G.... 716 836-3486
Buffalo (G-3129)
Wine & Spirits Magazine Inc....G.... 212 695-4660
New York (G-12118)
Womens E News Inc....G.... 212 244-1720
New York (G-12130)
Working Mother Media Inc....D.... 212 351-6400
New York (G-12134)
World Guide Publishing....E.... 800 331-7840
New York (G-12137)
Wsn Inc....G.... 212 924-7620
New York (G-12145)

PUBLISHERS: Maps

Vandam Inc....F.... 212 929-0416
Long Island City (G-7627)

PUBLISHERS: Miscellaneous

212 Media LLC....E.... 212 710-3092
New York (G-8671)
ABRA Media Inc....G.... 518 398-1010
Pine Plains (G-13004)
Absolute Color Corporation....G.... 212 868-0404
New York (G-8715)
Adcomm Graphics Inc....E.... 212 645-1298
West Babylon (G-16128)
Add Associates Inc....G.... 315 449-3474
Cicero (G-3513)
Albany Student Press Inc....E.... 518 442-5665
Albany (G-37)
Albion-Holley Pennysaver Inc....E.... 585 589-5641
Albion (G-154)
Alfred Mainzer Inc....E.... 718 392-4200
Long Island City (G-7370)
American Hsptals Patient Guide....F.... 518 346-1099
Schenectady (G-14649)
Amy Pak Publishing Inc....G.... 585 964-8188
Holley (G-6226)
Art Asiapacific Publishing LLC....G.... 212 255-6003
New York (G-8913)
Award Publishing Limited....G.... 212 246-0405
New York (G-8982)
Bear Port Publishing Company....F.... 877 337-8577
New York (G-9031)
Blood Moon Productions Ltd....G.... 718 556-9410
Staten Island (G-15052)
Brownstone Publishers Inc....E.... 212 473-8200
New York (G-9151)
Bucksense Inc....E.... 877 710-2825
New York (G-9154)
Bulkley Dunton....E.... 212 863-1800
New York (G-9155)
Burdick Publications Inc....G.... 315 685-9500
Skaneateles (G-14867)
Business Expert Press LLC....F.... 212 661-8810
New York (G-9161)
Bys Publishing LLC....G.... 315 655-9431
Cazenovia (G-3316)
Cambridge Whos Who Pubg Inc....E.... 516 833-8440
Uniondale (G-15663)
Castle Connolly Medical Ltd....E.... 212 367-8400
New York (G-9224)
Cayuga Press Cortland Inc....E.... 888 229-8421
Liverpool (G-7230)
Cherry Lane Magazine LLC....D.... 212 561-3000
New York (G-9271)
City Post Express Inc....G.... 718 995-8690
Jamaica (G-6636)
Cnhi LLC....D.... 716 282-2311
Niagara Falls (G-12273)
Coastal Publications Inc....F.... 631 725-1700
Sag Harbor (G-14498)
Community Cpons Frnchising Inc....E.... 516 277-1968
Glen Cove (G-5363)
Complete Publishing Solutions....G.... 212 242-7321
New York (G-9370)
Comps Inc....F.... 516 676-0400
Glen Cove (G-5364)
Consumer Reports Inc....B.... 914 378-2000
Yonkers (G-16746)
Couture Press....F.... 310 734-4831
New York (G-9412)
D C I Technical Inc....F.... 516 355-0464
Franklin Square (G-5116)
Dailycandy Inc....E.... 646 230-8719
New York (G-9459)
Dapper Dads Inc....G.... 917 903-8045
Brooklyn (G-1757)
Dezawy LLC....G.... 917 436-8820
New York (G-9516)
DK Publishing....F.... 212 366-2000
New York (G-9541)
Dlc Comprehensive Medical PC....F.... 718 857-1200
Brooklyn (G-1783)
Draper Associates Incorporated....F.... 212 255-2727
New York (G-9573)
Dryve LLC....G.... 646 279-3648
Bronx (G-1259)
Dwell Life Inc....E.... 212 382-2010
New York (G-9591)
Enjoy City North Inc....D.... 607 584-5061
Binghamton (G-883)
Ethis Communications Inc....G.... 212 791-1440
White Plains (G-16447)
Experiment Publishing LLC....G.... 212 889-1273
New York (G-9755)
F+w Media Inc....G.... 212 447-1400
New York (G-9765)
Fantasy Sports Media Group Inc....E.... 416 917-6002
New York (G-9782)
First Games Publr Netwrk Inc....D.... 212 983-0501
New York (G-9807)
Fitzgerald Publishing Co Inc....G.... 914 793-5016
Yonkers (G-16758)
Galison Publishing LLC....E.... 212 354-8840
New York (G-9876)
Gannett Co Inc....D.... 607 352-2702
Johnson City (G-6809)
Gen Publishing Inc....D.... 914 834-3880
New Rochelle (G-8608)
Genius Media Group Inc....F.... 509 670-7502
Brooklyn (G-1922)
Glassview LLC....E.... 646 844-4922
New York (G-9933)
Global Grind Digital....E.... 212 840-9399
New York (G-9943)
Government Data Publication....E.... 347 789-8719
Brooklyn (G-1945)
Grey House Publishing Inc....E.... 518 789-8700
Amenia (G-206)
Grey House Publishing Inc....E.... 845 483-3535
Poughkeepsie (G-13343)
Guest Informat LLC....F.... 212 557-3010
New York (G-10005)
Guilford Publications Inc....D.... 212 431-9800
New York (G-10008)
Guilford Publications Inc....G.... 800 365-7006
New York (G-10009)
Hagedorn Communications Inc....G.... 914 636-7400
New York (G-10020)
Hampton Press Incorporated....G.... 646 638-3800
New York (G-10028)
Harborside Press....G.... 631 470-4967
Huntington (G-6399)
Hearst Communications Inc....G.... 212 247-1014
New York (G-10059)
Helium Media Inc....G.... 917 596-4081
New York (G-10078)
Helvetica Press Incorporated....G.... 212 737-1857
New York (G-10079)
Hibert Publishing LLC....G.... 914 381-7474
Rye (G-14482)
Holmes Group The Inc....G.... 212 333-2300
New York (G-10118)
Humor Rainbow Inc....E.... 646 402-9113
New York (G-10151)
International Society For Medl....G.... 520 820-8594
Tarrytown (G-15479)
Intuition Publishing Limited....G.... 212 838-7115
New York (G-10262)
Jewish Heritage For Blind....G.... 718 338-4999
Brooklyn (G-2038)
Jobson Medical Information LLC....C.... 212 274-7000
New York (G-10347)
John Szoke Graphics Inc....G.... 212 219-8300
New York (G-10354)
Kalel Partners LLC....F.... 347 561-7804
Flushing (G-5015)
Korangy Publishing Inc....C.... 212 260-1332
New York (G-10470)
Kraus Organization Limited....D.... 212 686-5411
New York (G-10481)
Kyra Communications Corp....F.... 516 783-6244
Seaford (G-14758)

Language and Graphics Inc....................G....... 212 315-5266
New York (G-10516)
Lightbulb Press Inc....................E....... 212 485-8800
New York (G-10569)
Lino Press Inc....................E....... 718 665-2625
Bronx (G-1319)
Llcs Publishing Corp....................F....... 718 569-2703
Brooklyn (G-2131)
Lucky Peach LLC....................G....... 212 228-0031
New York (G-10626)
Mailers-Pblsher Wlfare Tr Fund....................G....... 212 869-5986
New York (G-10673)
Market Partners International....................G....... 212 447-0855
New York (G-10711)
Marketresearchcom Inc....................F....... 212 807-2600
New York (G-10713)
Mary Ann Liebert Inc....................D....... 914 740-2100
New Rochelle (G-8620)
Media Transcripts Inc....................E....... 212 362-1481
New York (G-10753)
Medical Information Systems....................G....... 516 621-7200
Port Washington (G-13286)
Mens Journal LLC....................G....... 212 484-1616
New York (G-10771)
Menucha Publishers Inc....................F....... 718 232-0856
Brooklyn (G-2192)
Merrill Corporation....................D....... 212 620-5600
New York (G-10777)
Millennium Medical Publishing....................F....... 212 995-2211
New York (G-10807)
Minyanville Media Inc....................E....... 212 991-6200
New York (G-10821)
Morey Publishing....................E....... 516 284-3300
Farmingdale (G-4830)
Mortgage Press Ltd....................E....... 516 409-1400
Wantagh (G-15924)
Mtm Publishing Inc....................G....... 212 242-6930
New York (G-10855)
Multi-Health Systems Inc....................D....... 800 456-3003
Cheektowaga (G-3453)
My Publisher Inc....................G....... 212 935-5215
New York (G-10865)
National Health Prom Assoc....................E....... 914 421-2525
White Plains (G-16478)
National Rding Styles Inst Inc....................F....... 516 921-5500
Syosset (G-15225)
Nature Publishing Co....................G....... 212 726-9200
New York (G-10894)
New York Legal Publishing....................G....... 518 459-1100
Menands (G-8090)
New York Times Company....................G....... 212 556-1200
New York (G-10945)
Newbay Media LLC....................D....... 212 378-0400
New York (G-10949)
O Val Nick Music Co Inc....................G....... 212 873-2179
New York (G-11023)
Oakwood Publishing Co....................G....... 516 482-7720
Great Neck (G-5575)
One Story Inc....................G....... 917 816-3659
Brooklyn (G-2289)
Openroad Integrated Media Inc....................E....... 212 691-0900
New York (G-11049)
Osprey Publishing Inc....................G....... 212 419-5300
New York (G-11067)
Outreach Publishing Corp....................G....... 718 773-0525
Brooklyn (G-2296)
Pace Editions Inc....................G....... 212 675-7431
New York (G-11086)
Paragon Publishing Inc....................G....... 718 302-2093
Brooklyn (G-2303)
Per Annum Inc....................E....... 212 647-8700
New York (G-11152)
Press Express....................G....... 914 592-3790
Elmsford (G-4558)
Primary Wave Publishing LLC....................G....... 212 661-6990
New York (G-11240)
Professnal Spt Pblications Inc....................E....... 516 327-9500
Elmont (G-4522)
Publishers Clearing House LLC....................E....... 516 249-4063
Melville (G-8059)
Pwxyz LLC....................E....... 212 377-5500
New York (G-11287)
Qtalk Publishing LLC....................G....... 877 549-1841
New York (G-11293)
Quality Patterns Inc....................D....... 212 704-0355
New York (G-11297)
R W Publications Div of Wtrhs....................E....... 716 714-5620
Elma (G-4456)
Rda Holding Co....................E....... 914 238-1000
New York (G-11336)
Refinery 29 Inc....................D....... 212 966-3112
New York (G-11346)
Regan Arts LLC....................F....... 646 488-6610
New York (G-11349)
Reliable Press II Inc....................F....... 718 840-5812
Hempstead (G-6025)
Repertoire International De Ll....................E....... 212 817-1990
New York (G-11364)
Reuters Loan Pricing Corp....................D....... 212 833-9200
New York (G-11374)
Rolling Stone Magazine....................G....... 212 484-1616
New York (G-11425)
Rosemont Press Incorporated....................G....... 212 239-4770
Deer Park (G-4037)
Rough Guides US Ltd....................D....... 212 414-3635
New York (G-11437)
Rsl Media LLC....................G....... 212 307-6760
New York (G-11443)
Sacks and Company New York....................G....... 212 741-1000
New York (G-11463)
Sag Harbor Express....................G....... 631 725-1700
Sag Harbor (G-14501)
Scepter Publishers Inc....................G....... 212 354-0670
New Rochelle (G-8627)
Seabay Media Holdings LLC....................G....... 212 457-7790
New York (G-11525)
Selby Marketing Associates Inc....................F....... 585 377-0750
Rochester (G-14120)
Sephardic Yellow Pages....................E....... 718 998-0299
Brooklyn (G-2456)
Sharedbook Inc....................E....... 646 442-8840
New York (G-11559)
Sing Tao Newspapers NY Ltd....................E....... 212 699-3800
New York (G-11598)
Slosson Eductl Publications....................F....... 716 652-0930
East Aurora (G-4210)
Social Science Electronic Pubg....................F....... 585 442-8170
Rochester (G-14132)
Sony Music Holdings Inc....................A....... 212 833-8000
New York (G-11649)
Southampton Town Newspapers....................E....... 631 283-4100
Southampton (G-14962)
Stephen Singer Pattern Co Inc....................F....... 212 947-2902
New York (G-11706)
STf Services Inc....................E....... 315 463-8506
East Syracuse (G-4371)
Straight Arrow Publishing Co....................C....... 212 484-1616
New York (G-11717)
Strathmore Directories Ltd....................E....... 516 997-2525
Westbury (G-16374)
Student Lifeline Inc....................E....... 516 327-0800
Franklin Square (G-5121)
Summit Communications....................G....... 914 273-5504
Armonk (G-409)
Super Express USA Pubg Corp....................F....... 212 227-5800
Richmond Hill (G-13515)
Tablet Publishing Company Inc....................E....... 718 965-7333
Brooklyn (G-2553)
Te Neues Publishing Company....................F....... 212 627-9090
New York (G-11790)
Thomson Reuters Corporation....................F....... 212 393-9461
New York (G-11824)
Thomson Reuters Corporation....................A....... 646 223-4000
New York (G-11825)
Trader Interntnal Publications....................G....... 914 631-6856
Sleepy Hollow (G-14887)
Tradewins Publishing Corp....................G....... 631 361-6916
Saint James (G-14516)
Treiman Publications Corp....................G....... 607 657-8473
Berkshire (G-829)
Tribune Entertainment Co Del....................E....... 203 866-2204
New York (G-11897)
Tribune Media Services Inc....................B....... 518 792-9914
Queensbury (G-13444)
Triumph Learning LLC....................E....... 212 652-0200
New York (G-11902)
Trusted Media Brands Inc....................A....... 914 238-1000
New York (G-11907)
Trusted Media Brands Inc....................F....... 914 244-5244
White Plains (G-16513)
Tunecore Inc....................F....... 646 651-1060
Brooklyn (G-2592)
Turbo Express Inc....................G....... 718 723-3686
Jamaica (G-6686)
Two Palms Press Inc....................F....... 212 965-8598
New York (G-11919)
Ucc Guide Inc....................F....... 518 434-0909
Albany (G-137)
Underline Communications LLC....................F....... 212 994-4340
New York (G-11937)
USA Custom Pad Corp....................E....... 607 563-9550
Sidney (G-14858)
Value Line Inc....................D....... 212 907-1500
New York (G-11988)
Vending Times Inc....................F....... 516 442-1850
Rockville Centre (G-14244)
Vendome Group LLC....................D....... 646 795-3899
New York (G-12004)
Viamedia Corporation....................G....... 718 485-7792
Brooklyn (G-2620)
Viewfinder Inc....................G....... 212 831-0939
New York (G-12032)
Vincys Printing Ltd....................F....... 518 355-4363
Schenectady (G-14725)
VWR Education LLC....................C....... 585 359-2502
West Henrietta (G-16254)
Watchanish LLC....................F....... 917 558-0404
New York (G-12078)
Wayuga Community Newspapers....................E....... 315 754-6229
Red Creek (G-13456)
Welcome Rain Publishers LLC....................G....... 212 686-1909
New York (G-12089)
Won & Lee Inc....................E....... 516 222-0712
Garden City (G-5284)
Yam TV LLC....................G....... 917 932-5418
New York (G-12159)

PUBLISHERS: Music Book

Boydell & Brewer Inc....................F....... 585 275-0419
Rochester (G-13674)
Congress For Jewish Culture....................G....... 212 505-8040
New York (G-9379)
Simmons-Boardman Pubg Corp....................E....... 212 620-7200
New York (G-11594)

PUBLISHERS: Music Book & Sheet Music

Alphonse Lduc - Rbert King Inc....................G....... 508 238-8118
New York (G-8809)
Boosey and Hawkes Inc....................E....... 212 358-5300
New York (G-9122)
C F Peters Corp....................E....... 718 416-7800
Glendale (G-5394)
Carbert Music Inc....................E....... 212 725-9277
New York (G-9206)
Downtown Music LLC....................G....... 212 625-2980
New York (G-9569)
Franklin-Douglas Inc....................F....... 516 883-0121
Port Washington (G-13260)
Lagunatic Music & Filmworks....................F....... 212 353-9600
Brooklyn (G-2091)
Lefrak Entertainment Co Ltd....................G....... 212 586-3600
New York (G-10540)
Reservoir Media Management Inc....................F....... 212 675-0541
New York (G-11367)
Sony/Atv Music Publishing LLC....................E....... 212 833-7730
New York (G-11650)

PUBLISHERS: Music, Book

Euphorbia Productions Ltd....................G....... 212 533-1700
New York (G-9727)
G Schirmer Inc....................G....... 212 254-2100
New York (G-9868)
G Schirmer Inc....................E....... 845 469-4699
Chester (G-3475)
Largo Music Inc....................G....... 212 756-5080
New York (G-10518)
Music Sales Corporation....................G....... 212 254-2100
New York (G-10861)
Peer International Corp....................E....... 212 265-3910
New York (G-11136)
Peermusic III Ltd....................F....... 212 265-3910
New York (G-11138)
Peermusic Ltd....................F....... 212 265-3910
New York (G-11139)

PUBLISHERS: Music, Sheet

Abkco Music & Records Inc....................E....... 212 399-0300
New York (G-8710)
Bourne Music Publishers....................F....... 212 391-4300
New York (G-9129)
Charing Cross Music Inc....................G....... 212 541-7571
New York (G-9260)
Historic TW Inc....................E....... 212 484-8000
New York (G-10106)
Integrated Copyright Group....................E....... 615 329-3999
New York (G-10230)
Ludlow Music Inc....................F....... 212 594-9795
New York (G-10627)

Employee Codes: A=Over 500 employees, B=251-500
C=101-250, D=51-100, E=20-50, F=10-19, G=5-9

PUBLISHERS: Music, Sheet

Michael Karp Music Inc .... G 212 840-3285
  New York *(G-10792)*
Mom Dad Publishing Inc .... E 646 476-9170
  New York *(G-10834)*
Screen Gems-EMI Music Inc .... D 212 786-8000
  New York *(G-11523)*
Shapiro Bernstein & Co Inc .... F 212 588-0878
  New York *(G-11558)*
Time Warner Companies Inc .... D 212 484-8000
  New York *(G-11845)*

PUBLISHERS: Newsletter

Alm Media LLC .... B 212 457-9400
  New York *(G-8805)*
Alm Media Holdings Inc .... B 212 457-9400
  New York *(G-8806)*
Energy Intelligence Group Inc .... D 212 532-1112
  New York *(G-9681)*
Fischler Hockey Service .... F 212 749-4152
  New York *(G-9812)*
Grant Hamilton .... F 716 652-0320
  East Aurora *(G-4201)*
Hart Energy Publishing Lllp .... G 212 621-4621
  New York *(G-10045)*
Ledes Group Inc .... F 212 840-8800
  New York *(G-10536)*
London Theater News Ltd .... F 212 517-8608
  New York *(G-10596)*
Mathisen Ventures Inc .... G 212 986-1025
  New York *(G-10728)*
Redspring Communications Inc .... E 518 587-0547
  Saratoga Springs *(G-14596)*

PUBLISHERS: Newspaper

Advance Magazine Publs Inc .... C 212 450-7000
  New York *(G-8750)*
Advertiser Perceptions Inc .... G 212 626-6683
  New York *(G-8761)*
Advertiser Publications Inc .... F 845 783-1111
  Chester *(G-3467)*
Afro Times Newspaper .... F 718 636-9500
  Brooklyn *(G-1493)*
Albany Student Press Inc .... E 518 442-5665
  Albany *(G-37)*
All Times Publishing LLC .... E 315 422-7011
  Syracuse *(G-15238)*
Bangla Patrika Inc .... G 718 482-9923
  Long Island City *(G-7397)*
Brooklyn Rail Inc .... F 718 349-8427
  Brooklyn *(G-1645)*
Bureau of National Affairs Inc .... E 212 687-4530
  New York *(G-9158)*
Business Journals .... F 212 790-5100
  New York *(G-9163)*
China Daily Distribution Corp .... E 212 537-8888
  New York *(G-9277)*
China Newsweek Corporation .... F 212 481-2510
  New York *(G-9282)*
Chinese Medical Report Inc .... G 718 359-5676
  Flushing *(G-4990)*
Citywire LLC .... F 646 503-2216
  New York *(G-9315)*
Country Folks .... G 585 343-9721
  Batavia *(G-621)*
Digital One USA Inc .... F 718 396-4890
  Flushing *(G-4996)*
Economist Newspaper NA Inc .... E 212 554-0676
  New York *(G-9625)*
Fairchild Publications Inc .... A 212 630-4000
  New York *(G-9773)*
Gallagher Printing Inc .... E 716 873-2434
  Buffalo *(G-2838)*
Gannett Co Inc .... D 607 798-1234
  Vestal *(G-15816)*
General Media Strategies Inc .... E 212 586-4141
  New York *(G-9901)*
Hagedorn Communications Inc .... E 914 636-7400
  New York *(G-10020)*
Haitian Times Inc .... G 718 230-8700
  New Rochelle *(G-8610)*
Hearst Corporation .... A 518 454-5694
  Albany *(G-82)*
Informa Uk Ltd .... G 646 957-8966
  New York *(G-10213)*
Jewish Journal .... G 718 630-9350
  Brooklyn *(G-2039)*
Lmg National Publishing Inc .... E 585 598-6874
  Fairport *(G-4640)*
Long Island Catholic Newspaper .... E 516 594-1212
  Rockville Centre *(G-14235)*

Long Islander Newspapers LLC .... G 631 427-7000
  Huntington *(G-6405)*
Market Place Publications .... E 516 997-7909
  Carle Place *(G-3270)*
Merchandiser Inc .... G 315 462-6411
  Clifton Springs *(G-3582)*
Ming Pao (new York) Inc .... E 718 786-2888
  Long Island City *(G-7525)*
Mortgage Press Ltd .... E 516 409-1400
  Wantagh *(G-15924)*
Newspaper Delivery Solutions .... G 718 370-1111
  Staten Island *(G-15107)*
Nick Lugo Inc .... F 212 348-2100
  New York *(G-10963)*
Noticia Hispanoamericana Inc .... E 516 223-5678
  North Baldwin *(G-12365)*
Observer Daily Sunday Newsppr .... D 716 366-3000
  Dunkirk *(G-4175)*
Panagraphics Inc .... G 716 312-8088
  Orchard Park *(G-12734)*
Pearson Inc .... D 212 641-2400
  New York *(G-11133)*
Realtimetraderscom .... E 716 632-6600
  Buffalo *(G-3033)*
Record Advertiser .... E 716 693-1000
  North Tonawanda *(G-12445)*
River Valley Paper Company .... F 330 631-8320
  Syracuse *(G-15407)*
Rizzoli Intl Publications Inc .... F 212 308-2000
  New York *(G-11400)*
Rochester Democrat & Chronicle .... E 585 232-7100
  Rochester *(G-14086)*
Sag Harbor Express .... E 631 725-1700
  Sag Harbor *(G-14501)*
Salamanca Press Penny Saver .... E 716 945-1500
  Salamanca *(G-14531)*
Sample News Group LLC .... D 315 343-3800
  Oswego *(G-12787)*
Sing Tao Newspapers NY Ltd .... F 212 431-9030
  Brooklyn *(G-2480)*
SM News Plus Incorporated .... G 212 888-0153
  New York *(G-11620)*
Smithtown News Inc .... E 631 265-2100
  Smithtown *(G-14909)*
Star Sports Corp .... E 516 773-4075
  Great Neck *(G-5593)*
Stratconglobal Inc .... G 212 989-2355
  New York *(G-11718)*
Straus Newspapers Inc .... E 845 782-4000
  Chester *(G-3486)*
Syracuse Catholic Press Assn .... G 315 422-8153
  Syracuse *(G-15435)*
Tegna Inc .... C 716 849-2222
  Buffalo *(G-3089)*
Tenney Media Group .... D 315 853-5569
  Clinton *(G-3589)*
The Sandhar Corp .... G 718 523-0819
  Jamaica *(G-6684)*
Tompkins Weekly Inc .... G 607 539-7100
  Ithaca *(G-6612)*
Tryp Times Square .... G 212 246-8800
  New York *(G-11908)*
Ubm Inc .... A 212 600-3000
  New York *(G-11929)*
Ubm LLC .... D 516 562-7800
  New Hyde Park *(G-8568)*
Urdu Times .... G 718 297-8700
  Jamaica *(G-6688)*
USA Today International Corp .... G 703 854-3400
  New York *(G-11980)*
Wallkill Lodge No 627 F&Am .... F 845 778-7148
  Walden *(G-15899)*
Webster Ontrio Wlwrth Pnnysver .... F 585 265-3620
  Webster *(G-16106)*
Weekly Ajkal .... F 718 565-2100
  Jackson Heights *(G-6621)*
West Seneca Bee Inc .... D 716 632-4700
  Williamsville *(G-16593)*

PUBLISHERS: Newspapers, No Printing

A C J Communications Inc .... F 631 587-5612
  Babylon *(G-523)*
Albany Catholic Press Assoc .... G 518 453-6688
  Albany *(G-32)*
Algemeiner Journal Inc .... G 718 771-0400
  Brooklyn *(G-1505)*
Alm Media LLC .... B 212 457-9400
  New York *(G-8805)*
Alm Media Holdings Inc .... B 212 457-9400
  New York *(G-8806)*

American City Bus Journals Inc .... E 716 541-1654
  Buffalo *(G-2694)*
American Sports Media LLC .... G 585 377-9636
  Rochester *(G-13628)*
Angel Media and Publishing .... G 845 727-4949
  West Nyack *(G-16264)*
Architects Newspaper LLC .... F 212 966-0630
  New York *(G-8900)*
Auburn Publishing Co .... D 315 253-5311
  Auburn *(G-465)*
Bee Publications Inc .... D 716 632-4700
  Williamsville *(G-16569)*
Belsito Communications Inc .... E 845 534-9700
  New Windsor *(G-8636)*
Blue and White Publishing Inc .... F 215 431-3339
  New York *(G-9106)*
Buffalo Law Journal .... G 716 541-1600
  Buffalo *(G-2745)*
Business First of New York .... E 716 854-5822
  Buffalo *(G-2756)*
Business First of New York .... E 518 640-6800
  Latham *(G-7067)*
Camden News Inc .... G 315 245-1849
  Camden *(G-3185)*
Canandaigua Msgnr Incorporated .... C 585 394-0770
  Canandaigua *(G-3213)*
Catskill Mountain Publishing .... F 845 586-2601
  Arkville *(G-400)*
Chase Media Group .... F 914 962-3871
  Yorktown Heights *(G-16814)*
Clarion Publications Inc .... F 585 243-3530
  Geneseo *(G-5313)*
Cnhi LLC .... E 585 798-1400
  Medina *(G-7975)*
Cnhi LLC .... D 716 693-1000
  Niagara Falls *(G-12272)*
Cnhi LLC .... D 716 282-2311
  Niagara Falls *(G-12273)*
Cnhi LLC .... E 716 439-9222
  Lockport *(G-7291)*
CNY Business Review Inc .... F 315 472-3104
  Syracuse *(G-15281)*
Community Newspaper Group LLC ..... F 607 432-1000
  Oneonta *(G-12633)*
Community Newspaper Group LLC ..... F 518 565-4114
  Plattsburgh *(G-13118)*
Cortland Standard Printing Co .... D 607 756-5665
  Cortland *(G-3871)*
Courier-Life Inc .... C 718 260-2500
  Brooklyn *(G-1724)*
CT Publications Co .... G 718 592-2196
  Whitestone *(G-16539)*
Daily Cornell Sun .... E 607 273-0746
  Ithaca *(G-6574)*
Daily Orange Corporation .... E 315 443-2314
  Syracuse *(G-15301)*
Dale Press Inc .... E 718 543-6200
  Bronx *(G-1253)*
Danet Inc .... F 718 266-4444
  Brooklyn *(G-1755)*
Dans Paper Inc .... D 631 537-0500
  Southampton *(G-14952)*
Das Yidishe Licht Inc .... G 718 387-3166
  Brooklyn *(G-1758)*
Dbg Media .... G 718 599-6828
  Brooklyn *(G-1761)*
Delaware County Times Inc .... G 607 746-2176
  Delhi *(G-4072)*
Dray Enterprises Inc .... F 585 768-2201
  Le Roy *(G-7116)*
Ecclesiastical Communications .... F 212 688-2399
  New York *(G-9620)*
Ecuador News Inc .... F 718 205-7014
  Woodside *(G-16654)*
Empire Publishing Inc .... F 516 829-4000
  Far Rockaway *(G-4700)*
Expositor Newspapers Inc .... G 585 427-2468
  Rochester *(G-13799)*
Five Islands Publishing Inc .... F 631 583-5345
  Bronx *(G-1271)*
Four Directions Inc .... E 315 829-8388
  Vernon *(G-15804)*
Freetime Magazine Inc .... G 585 473-2266
  Rochester *(G-13817)*
French Morning LLC .... G 646 290-7463
  New York *(G-9847)*
FT Publications Inc .... E 212 641-2420
  New York *(G-9857)*
Fulton Newspapers Inc .... E 315 598-6397
  Fulton *(G-5216)*

Gannett Co Inc ....G.... 585 924-3406
Farmington *(G-4914)*

Gannett Stllite Info Ntwrk Inc ....E.... 914 965-5000
Yonkers *(G-16761)*

Gannett Stllite Info Ntwrk LLC ....E.... 845 578-2300
West Nyack *(G-16269)*

Good Health Healthcare Newsppr ....F.... 585 421-8109
Victor *(G-15848)*

Guest of A Guest Inc ....G.... 212 206-0397
New York *(G-10006)*

Hagedorn Communications Inc ....D.... 914 636-7400
New Rochelle *(G-8609)*

Highline Media LLC ....C.... 859 692-2100
New York *(G-10097)*

Hudson Valley Black Press ....G.... 845 562-1313
Newburgh *(G-12226)*

Impremedia LLC ....D.... 212 807-4600
Brooklyn *(G-1997)*

India Abroad Publications Inc ....D.... 212 929-1727
New York *(G-10198)*

Irish Echo Newspaper Corp ....F.... 212 482-4818
New York *(G-10271)*

Jewish Press Inc ....C.... 718 330-1100
Brooklyn *(G-2040)*

Jewish Week Inc ....E.... 212 921-7822
New York *(G-10332)*

John Lor Publishing Ltd ....E.... 631 475-1000
Patchogue *(G-12868)*

Johnson Newspaper Corporation ....E.... 518 483-4700
Malone *(G-7722)*

Journal Register Company ....D.... 518 584-4242
Saratoga Springs *(G-14589)*

Korea Times New York Inc ....D.... 718 784-4526
Long Island City *(G-7492)*

Korea Times New York Inc ....G.... 718 961-7979
Flushing *(G-5019)*

L & M Publications Inc ....E.... 516 378-3133
Garden City *(G-5264)*

Lee Enterprises Incorporated ....C.... 518 792-3131
Glens Falls *(G-5431)*

Local Media Group Inc ....B.... 845 341-1100
Middletown *(G-8159)*

Local Media Group Inc ....E.... 845 341-1100
Middletown *(G-8160)*

Local Media Group Inc ....F.... 845 340-4910
Kingston *(G-6908)*

Manchester Newspaper Inc ....E.... 518 642-1234
Granville *(G-5520)*

Manhattan Media LLC ....F.... 212 268-8600
New York *(G-10686)*

Manhattan Times Inc ....F.... 212 569-5800
New York *(G-10689)*

Massapequa Post ....E.... 516 798-5100
Massapequa Park *(G-7893)*

McClary Media Inc ....G.... 800 453-6397
Amsterdam *(G-346)*

Miami Media LLC ....F.... 212 268-8600
New York *(G-10789)*

Nassau County Publications ....G.... 516 481-5400
Hempstead *(G-6022)*

National Herald Inc ....E.... 718 784-5255
Long Island City *(G-7533)*

Neighbor To Neighbor News Inc ....G.... 585 492-2525
Arcade *(G-387)*

New Ski Inc ....E.... 607 277-7000
Ithaca *(G-6600)*

New York Cvl Srvc Emplys Pblsh ....F.... 212 962-2690
New York *(G-10934)*

New York Daily Challenge Inc ....E.... 718 636-9500
Brooklyn *(G-2261)*

New York IL Bo Inc ....F.... 718 961-1538
Flushing *(G-5028)*

News Communications Inc ....F.... 212 689-2500
New York *(G-10951)*

News Report Inc ....E.... 718 851-6607
Brooklyn *(G-2267)*

Newspaper Publisher LLC ....F.... 607 775-0472
Conklin *(G-3730)*

Newsweek LLC ....G.... 646 867-7100
New York *(G-10956)*

Nordic Press Inc ....G.... 212 686-3356
New York *(G-10988)*

North Country This Week ....G.... 315 265-1000
Potsdam *(G-13320)*

Northern NY Newspapers Corp ....C.... 315 782-1000
Watertown *(G-16031)*

Northern Tier Publishing Corp ....F.... 914 962-4748
Yorktown Heights *(G-16820)*

Novoye Rsskoye Slovo Pubg Corp ....D.... 646 460-4566
Brooklyn *(G-2276)*

Oak Lone Publishing Co Inc ....E.... 518 792-1126
Glens Falls *(G-5437)*

Page Front Group Inc ....G.... 716 823-8222
Lackawanna *(G-6950)*

Patchogue Advance Inc ....E.... 631 475-1000
Patchogue *(G-12873)*

Peace Times Weekly Inc ....G.... 718 762-6500
Flushing *(G-5036)*

Publishing Group America Inc ....F.... 646 658-0550
New York *(G-11274)*

Putnam Cnty News Recorder LLC ....F.... 845 265-2468
Cold Spring *(G-3626)*

Quality Guides ....G.... 716 326-3163
Westfield *(G-16395)*

Richner Communications Inc ....G.... 516 569-4000
Lawrence *(G-7108)*

Rochester Business Journal ....E.... 585 546-8303
Rochester *(G-14081)*

Rochester Catholic Press ....F.... 585 529-9530
Rochester *(G-14082)*

S I Communications Inc ....F.... 914 725-2500
Scarsdale *(G-14644)*

Seneca Media Inc ....F.... 585 593-5300
Wellsville *(G-16122)*

Sing Tao Newspapers NY Ltd ....E.... 212 699-3800
New York *(G-11598)*

Southampton Town Newspapers ....E.... 631 283-4100
Southampton *(G-14962)*

Southampton Town Newspapers ....F.... 631 288-1100
Westhampton Beach *(G-16406)*

Spartacist Publishing Co ....E.... 212 732-7860
New York *(G-11659)*

Steffen Publishing Inc ....D.... 315 865-4100
Holland Patent *(G-6225)*

Stuart Communications Inc ....F.... 845 252-7414
Narrowsburg *(G-8475)*

Tablet Publishing Company Inc ....E.... 718 965-7333
Brooklyn *(G-2553)*

Thestreet Inc ....D.... 212 321-5000
New York *(G-11814)*

Times Beacon Record Newspapers ....F.... 631 331-1154
East Setauket *(G-4312)*

Times Review Newspaper Corp ....E.... 631 354-8031
Mattituck *(G-7918)*

Tioga County Courier ....G.... 607 687-0108
Owego *(G-12804)*

Tri-Village Publishers Inc ....D.... 518 843-1100
Amsterdam *(G-361)*

Tribco LLC ....E.... 718 357-7400
Whitestone *(G-16550)*

Tricycle Foundation Inc ....G.... 800 873-9871
New York *(G-11898)*

Ulster Publishing Co Inc ....E.... 845 334-8205
Kingston *(G-6926)*

Ulster Publishing Co Inc ....F.... 845 255-7005
New Paltz *(G-8583)*

Wallkill Valley Publications ....E.... 845 561-0170
Newburgh *(G-12251)*

Wappingers Falls Shopper Inc ....E.... 845 297-3723
Wappingers Falls *(G-15938)*

Wave Publishing Co Inc ....F.... 718 634-4000
Rockaway Beach *(G-14226)*

Westfair Communications Inc ....E.... 914 694-3600
White Plains *(G-16521)*

Westside News Inc ....F.... 585 352-3411
Spencerport *(G-14983)*

William J Kline & Son Inc ....D.... 518 843-1100
Amsterdam *(G-364)*

Yated Neeman Inc ....F.... 845 369-1600
Monsey *(G-8303)*

Yonkers Time Publishing Co ....F.... 914 965-4000
Yonkers *(G-16811)*

PUBLISHERS: Pamphlets, No Printing

Spartacist Publishing Co ....E.... 212 732-7860
New York *(G-11659)*

PUBLISHERS: Periodical, With Printing

Artifex Press LLC ....F.... 212 414-1482
New York *(G-8920)*

Bizbash Media Inc ....D.... 646 638-3602
New York *(G-9093)*

Eidosmedia Inc ....E.... 646 795-2100
New York *(G-9636)*

Frost Publications Inc ....G.... 845 726-3232
Westtown *(G-16413)*

Gruner + Jahr USA Group Inc ....B.... 866 323-9336
New York *(G-10001)*

H W Wilson Company Inc ....B.... 718 588-8635
Bronx *(G-1287)*

Impact Journals LLC ....G.... 800 922-0957
Orchard Park *(G-12718)*

Sky Art Media Inc ....G.... 917 355-9022
New York *(G-11612)*

The PRS Group Inc ....F.... 315 431-0511
East Syracuse *(G-4373)*

Yale Robbins Inc ....D.... 212 683-5700
New York *(G-12158)*

PUBLISHERS: Periodicals, Magazines

21st Century Fox America Inc ....D.... 212 447-4600
New York *(G-8674)*

Annointed Buty Ministries LLC ....G.... 646 867-3796
Brooklyn *(G-1537)*

Archaelogy Magazine ....E.... 718 472-3050
Long Island City *(G-7385)*

Bedford Freeman & Worth ....C.... 212 576-9400
New York *(G-9034)*

Berger & Wild LLC ....G.... 646 415-8459
New York *(G-9050)*

BJ Magazines Inc ....G.... 212 367-9705
New York *(G-9094)*

Cambridge University Press ....D.... 212 337-5000
New York *(G-9186)*

Canopy Canopy Canopy Inc ....G.... 347 529-5182
New York *(G-9196)*

Choice Magazine Listening Inc ....G.... 516 883-8280
Port Washington *(G-13249)*

CNY Business Review Inc ....F.... 315 472-3104
Syracuse *(G-15281)*

Cornell University ....E.... 607 254-2473
Ithaca *(G-6573)*

Delaware County Times Inc ....G.... 607 746-2176
Delhi *(G-4072)*

Denton Publications Inc ....E.... 518 561-9680
Plattsburgh *(G-13119)*

Dow Jones Aer Company Inc ....A.... 212 416-2000
New York *(G-9565)*

Downtown Media Group LLC ....F.... 646 723-4510
New York *(G-9568)*

Envy Publishing Group Inc ....G.... 212 253-9874
New York *(G-9691)*

Fairchild Publications Inc ....A.... 212 630-4000
New York *(G-9773)*

Fairchild Publishing LLC ....G.... 212 286-3897
New York *(G-9774)*

Fashion Calendar International ....G.... 212 289-0420
New York *(G-9787)*

Four M Studios ....D.... 212 557-6600
New York *(G-9829)*

Frontiers Unlimited Inc ....G.... 631 283-4663
Southampton *(G-14953)*

Global Finance Magazine ....G.... 212 524-3223
New York *(G-9938)*

Global Finance Media Inc ....F.... 212 447-7900
New York *(G-9939)*

Guernica ....F.... 914 414-7318
Brooklyn *(G-1954)*

Healthy Way of Life Magazine ....G.... 718 616-1681
Brooklyn *(G-1970)*

I On Youth ....G.... 716 832-6509
Buffalo *(G-2878)*

Jerome Levy Forecasting Center ....G.... 914 244-8617
Mount Kisco *(G-8345)*

L F International Inc ....D.... 212 756-5000
New York *(G-10495)*

Laurtom Inc ....E.... 914 273-2233
Mount Kisco *(G-8349)*

Lucky Magazine ....F.... 212 286-6220
New York *(G-10625)*

Magazine I Spectrum E ....E.... 212 419-7555
New York *(G-10661)*

Magnificat Inc ....F.... 914 502-1820
Yonkers *(G-16781)*

Media Press Corp ....E.... 212 791-6347
New York *(G-10752)*

Njf Publishing Corp ....G.... 631 345-5200
Shirley *(G-14842)*

Northeast Group ....D.... 518 563-8214
Plattsburgh *(G-13139)*

Northeast Prtg & Dist Co Inc ....G.... 514 577-3545
Plattsburgh *(G-13140)*

Paris Review Foundation Inc ....G.... 212 343-1333
New York *(G-11113)*

Pearson Education Inc ....F.... 201 236-7000
West Nyack *(G-16278)*

Professnal Spt Pblications Inc ....D.... 516 327-9500
Elmont *(G-4523)*

Rda Holding Co ....E.... 914 238-1000
New York *(G-11336)*

Employee Codes: A=Over 500 employees, B=251-500
C=101-250, D=51-100, E=20-50, F=10-19, G=5-9

2019 Harris
New York Manufacturers Directory

1233

PUBLISHERS: Periodicals, Magazines

Readers Digest Sls & Svcs Inc .... C 914 238-1000
  Pleasantville *(G-13177)*
Relx Inc .... B 212 633-3900
  New York *(G-11357)*
Rolling Stone Magazine .... G 212 484-1616
  New York *(G-11425)*
Rye Record .... G 914 713-3213
  Rye *(G-14488)*
Small Business Advisors Inc .... F 516 374-1387
  Atlantic Beach *(G-457)*
Springer Healthcare LLC .... E 212 460-1500
  New York *(G-11683)*
Standard Analytics Io Inc .... G 917 882-5422
  New York *(G-11691)*
Steffen Publishing Inc .... D 315 865-4100
  Holland Patent *(G-6225)*
Surface Magazine .... E 646 805-0200
  New York *(G-11751)*
Swaps Monitor Publications Inc .... F 212 742-8550
  New York *(G-11754)*
Time Out New York Partners LP .... D 646 432-3000
  New York *(G-11843)*
TMC Usa LLC .... G 518 587-8920
  Saratoga Springs *(G-14600)*
Trend Pot Inc .... E 212 431-9970
  New York *(G-11890)*
Ubm Inc .... A 212 600-3000
  New York *(G-11929)*
US China Magazine .... E 212 663-4333
  New York *(G-11973)*
Vibe Media Group LLC .... D 212 448-7300
  New York *(G-12026)*
Vickers Stock Research Corp .... E 212 425-7500
  New York *(G-12027)*
Wallkill Valley Publications .... E 845 561-0170
  Newburgh *(G-12251)*
Westfair Communications Inc .... E 914 694-3600
  White Plains *(G-16521)*
Winsight LLC .... G 646 708-7309
  New York *(G-12123)*
Ziff Davis Publishing LLC .... D 212 503-3500
  New York *(G-12177)*

PUBLISHERS: Periodicals, No Printing

Academy of Political Science .... G 212 870-2500
  New York *(G-8716)*
Alcoholics Anonymous Grapevine .... F 212 870-3400
  New York *(G-8787)*
Association For Cmpt McHy Inc .... D 212 869-7440
  New York *(G-8938)*
Athlon Spt Communications Inc .... E 212 478-1910
  New York *(G-8949)*
Bernhard Arnold & Company Inc .... G 212 907-1500
  New York *(G-9054)*
Boardman Simons Publishing .... E 212 620-7200
  New York *(G-9115)*
Brownstone Publishers Inc .... E 212 473-8200
  New York *(G-9151)*
Capital Reg Wkly Newsppr Group .... F 518 674-2841
  Averill Park *(G-513)*
Conference Board Inc .... C 212 759-0900
  New York *(G-9377)*
Congress For Jewish Culture .... G 212 505-8040
  New York *(G-9379)*
Creative Magazine Inc .... G 516 378-0800
  Merrick *(G-8095)*
Economist Intelligence Unit NA .... D 212 554-0600
  New York *(G-9624)*
Francis Emory Fitch Inc .... E 212 619-3800
  New York *(G-9838)*
Global Entity Media Inc .... G 631 580-7772
  Ronkonkoma *(G-14346)*
Government Data Publication .... E 347 789-8719
  Brooklyn *(G-1945)*
Hearst Corporation .... A 518 454-5694
  Albany *(G-82)*
Highline Media LLC .... C 859 692-2100
  New York *(G-10097)*
Human Life Foundation Inc .... G 212 685-5210
  New York *(G-10148)*
Impressions Inc .... G 212 594-5954
  New York *(G-10188)*
International Center For Postg .... G 607 257-5860
  Ithaca *(G-6585)*
Leadership Directories Inc .... D 212 627-4140
  New York *(G-10530)*
Mathisen Ventures Inc .... G 212 986-1025
  New York *(G-10728)*
McCarthy LLC .... F 646 862-5354
  New York *(G-10740)*

Optionline LLC .... E 516 218-3225
  Garden City *(G-5273)*
Pati Corp .... F 718 244-6788
  Jamaica *(G-6667)*
Pointwise Information Service 315 457-4111
  Liverpool *(G-7255)*
Psychonomic Society Inc .... E 512 381-1494
  New York *(G-11270)*
Real Est Book of Long Island .... F 516 364-5000
  Syosset *(G-15230)*
Shugar Publishing .... G 631 288-4404
  Westhampton Beach *(G-16405)*
Suffolk Community Council Inc .... G 631 434-9277
  Deer Park *(G-4049)*
Swift Fulfillment Services .... G 516 593-1198
  Lynbrook *(G-7675)*
Thestreet Inc .... D 212 321-5000
  New York *(G-11814)*
Trader Interntnal Publications .... G 914 631-6856
  Sleepy Hollow *(G-14887)*
Ubm LLC .... D 516 562-7800
  New Hyde Park *(G-8568)*
Value Line Publishing LLC .... C 201 842-8054
  New York *(G-11989)*

PUBLISHERS: Posters

History Publishing Company LLC .... G 845 398-8161
  Palisades *(G-12846)*

PUBLISHERS: Sheet Music

Carl Fischer LLC .... E 212 777-0900
  New York *(G-9208)*
Kendor Music Inc .... F 716 492-1254
  Delevan *(G-4071)*
Warner Music Inc .... D 212 275-2000
  New York *(G-12073)*

PUBLISHERS: Shopping News

Freeville Publishing Co Inc .... F 607 844-9119
  Freeville *(G-5191)*
Service Advertising Group Inc 718 361-6161
  Long Island City *(G-7588)*
Skylark Publications Ltd .... G 607 535-9866
  Watkins Glen *(G-16060)*
Sneaker News Inc .... G 347 687-1588
  New York *(G-11630)*

PUBLISHERS: Technical Manuals

Dayton T Brown Inc .... B 631 589-6300
  Bohemia *(G-1011)*
Elsevier Inc .... B 212 989-5800
  New York *(G-9659)*
Mosby Holdings Corp .... G 212 309-8100
  New York *(G-10844)*

PUBLISHERS: Technical Manuals & Papers

Cambridge Info Group Inc .... F 301 961-6700
  New York *(G-9185)*
Clearstep Technologies LLC .... G 315 952-3628
  Camillus *(G-3195)*

PUBLISHERS: Technical Papers

Humana Press Inc .... E 212 460-1500
  New York *(G-10149)*

PUBLISHERS: Telephone & Other Directory

Auto Market Publications Inc .... G 631 667-0500
  Deer Park *(G-3949)*
Business Directory Inc .... F 718 486-8099
  Brooklyn *(G-1660)*
Fashiondex Inc .... G 914 271-6121
  New York *(G-9788)*
Golf Directories USA Inc .... G 516 365-5351
  Manhasset *(G-7768)*
Infoservices International .... F 631 549-1805
  Cold Spring Harbor *(G-3631)*
Israeli Yellow Pages .... E 718 520-1000
  Kew Gardens *(G-6874)*
Korean Yellow Pages .... F 718 461-0073
  Flushing *(G-5020)*
Long Islands Best Inc .... G 855 542-3785
  Bohemia *(G-1049)*
Yellow Pages Inc .... G 845 639-6060
  New City *(G-8496)*

PUBLISHERS: Textbooks, No Printing

Allworth Communications Inc .... F 212 777-8395
  New York *(G-8803)*
Amsco School Publications Inc .... D 212 886-6500
  New York *(G-8849)*
Bedford Freeman & Worth .... D 212 375-7000
  New York *(G-9035)*
Bedford Freeman & Worth .... E 212 576-9400
  New York *(G-9034)*
Booklinks Publishing Svcs LLC .... G 718 852-2116
  Brooklyn *(G-1628)*
Brown Publishing Network Inc .... E 212 682-3330
  New York *(G-9150)*
Cornell University 607 277-2338
  Ithaca *(G-6572)*
E W Williams Publications .... G 212 661-1516
  New York *(G-9598)*
Hippocrene Books Inc .... E 212 685-4371
  New York *(G-10104)*
Houghton Mifflin Harcourt Pubg .... E 212 420-5800
  New York *(G-10131)*
Houghton Mifflin Harcourt Pubg .... C 914 747-2709
  Thornwood *(G-15507)*
John Wiley & Sons Inc .... D 845 457-6250
  Montgomery *(G-8313)*
Oxford Book Company Inc .... C 212 227-2120
  New York *(G-11074)*
Peter Lang Publishing Inc .... F 212 647-7700
  New York *(G-11168)*
Project Energy Savers LLC .... F 718 596-4231
  Brooklyn *(G-2356)*
W W Norton & Company Inc .... C 212 354-5500
  New York *(G-12061)*
Waldman Publishing Corporation .... F 212 730-9590
  New York *(G-12066)*
Wordwise Inc .... G 914 232-5366
  Katonah *(G-6848)*
Worth Publishers Inc .... C 212 475-6000
  New York *(G-12140)*

PUBLISHERS: Trade journals, No Printing

Access Intelligence LLC .... A 212 204-4269
  New York *(G-8719)*
American Institute Physics Inc 516 576-2410
  Melville *(G-8002)*
American Physical Society .... D 631 591-4025
  Ridge *(G-13521)*
Demos Medical Publishing LLC .... F 516 889-1791
  New York *(G-9499)*
Direct Mktg Edctl Fndation Inc .... G 212 790-1512
  New York *(G-9531)*
Elmont North Little League .... E 516 775-8210
  Elmont *(G-4518)*
Hatherleigh Company Ltd .... G 607 538-1092
  Hobart *(G-6163)*
Humana Press Inc .... E 212 460-1500
  New York *(G-10149)*
International Data Group Inc .... E 212 331-7883
  New York *(G-10244)*
Japan America Learning Ctr Inc .... F 914 723-7600
  Scarsdale *(G-14639)*
Luria Communications Inc .... G 631 329-4922
  East Hampton *(G-4240)*
Mary Ann Liebert Inc 914 740-2100
  New Rochelle *(G-8620)*
McMahon Group LLC .... D 212 957-5300
  New York *(G-10745)*
NCM Publishers Inc .... G 212 691-9100
  New York *(G-10902)*
Public Relations Soc Amer Inc .... E 212 460-1400
  New York *(G-11273)*
Relx Inc .... E 212 309-8100
  New York *(G-11355)*
Security Letter .... G 212 348-1553
  New York *(G-11531)*
Springer Adis Us LLC .... F 212 460-1500
  New York *(G-11681)*
Springer Publishing Co LLC 212 431-4370
  New York *(G-11684)*
Springer Scnce + Bus Media LLC .... D 212 460-1500
  New York *(G-11685)*
Thomas Publishing Company LLC ...... B 212 695-0500
  New York *(G-11818)*
Westchester Law Journal Inc .... G 914 948-0715
  White Plains *(G-16518)*

PUBLISHING & BROADCASTING: Internet Only

Adsmain LLC ... G ... 347 560-5060 — Brooklyn *(G-1486)*
Ai Media Group Inc ... F ... 212 660-2400 — New York *(G-8775)*
Aleteia Usa Inc ... G ... 914 502-1855 — Yonkers *(G-16730)*
Bdg Media Inc ... C ... 917 551-6510 — New York *(G-9030)*
Bright Line Eting Slutions LLC ... E ... 585 245-2956 — Pittsford *(G-13009)*
Business Never Stops LLC ... G ... 888 479-3111 — South Richmond Hill *(G-14945)*
Byliner Inc ... E ... 415 680-3608 — New York *(G-9168)*
Classpass Inc ... E ... 888 493-5953 — New York *(G-9322)*
East Meet East Inc ... G ... 646 481-0033 — New York *(G-9609)*
Elite Daily Inc ... F ... 212 402-9097 — New York *(G-9650)*
Entrainant Inc ... G ... 212 946-4724 — New York *(G-9689)*
Epost International Inc ... G ... 212 352-9390 — New York *(G-9694)*
Equityarcade LLC ... G ... 678 232-1301 — Brooklyn *(G-1845)*
Gds Publishing Inc ... F ... 212 796-2000 — New York *(G-9893)*
Golden Eagle Marketing LLC ... G ... 212 726-1242 — New York *(G-9954)*
Hearst Digital Studios Inc ... E ... 212 969-7552 — New York *(G-10071)*
Heed LLC ... E ... 646 708-7111 — New York *(G-10077)*
Media Trust LLC ... G ... 212 802-1162 — New York *(G-10754)*
Medical Daily Inc ... E ... 646 867-7100 — New York *(G-10757)*
Mindbodygreen LLC ... E ... 347 529-6952 — Brooklyn *(G-2209)*
Napean LLC ... G ... 917 968-6757 — New York *(G-10874)*
Narratively Inc ... E ... 203 536-0332 — Brooklyn *(G-2244)*
News Now Waverly ... F ... 607 296-6769 — Waverly *(G-16068)*
Newsweek Media Group Inc ... E ... 646 867-7100 — New York *(G-10957)*
Nimbletv Inc ... F ... 646 502-7010 — New York *(G-10970)*
Panoply Media LLC ... E ... 646 382-5423 — Brooklyn *(G-2300)*
Pictoure Inc ... G ... 212 641-0098 — New York *(G-11190)*
Playlife LLC ... G ... 646 207-9082 — New York *(G-11208)*
Pro Publica Inc ... D ... 212 514-5250 — New York *(G-11253)*
Qworldstar Inc ... G ... 212 768-4500 — New York *(G-11307)*
Renegade Nation Online LLC ... G ... 212 868-9000 — New York *(G-11363)*
Riot New Media Group Inc ... G ... 604 700-4896 — Brooklyn *(G-2403)*
Sagelife Parenting LLC ... G ... 315 299-5713 — Syracuse *(G-15414)*
Shepherds Pl LLC ... G ... 516 647-8151 — Valley Stream *(G-15797)*
Sportsgrid Inc ... F ... 646 849-4085 — New York *(G-11678)*
Standard Analytics Io Inc ... G ... 917 882-5422 — New York *(G-11691)*
Statebook LLC ... G ... 845 383-1991 — Kingston *(G-6919)*
Thehuffingtonpostcom Inc ... E ... 212 245-7844 — New York *(G-11809)*
Theskimm Inc ... F ... 646 213-4754 — New York *(G-11813)*
Total Webcasting Inc ... G ... 845 883-0909 — New Paltz *(G-8581)*
Trading Edge Ltd ... G ... 347 699-7079 — Ridgewood *(G-13556)*
Vinous Group LLC ... G ... 917 275-5184 — New York *(G-12036)*
Winterwheat Corp ... G ... 212 203-2064 — New York *(G-12124)*
Zazoom LLC ... F ... 212 321-2100 — New York *(G-12170)*

PUBLISHING & PRINTING: Art Copy

Avalon Copy Centers Amer Inc ... D ... 315 471-3333 — Syracuse *(G-15251)*
Avalon Copy Centers Amer Inc ... E ... 716 995-7777 — Buffalo *(G-2717)*
Color Unlimited Inc ... G ... 212 802-7547 — New York *(G-9353)*
Soho Editions Inc ... E ... 914 591-5100 — Mohegan Lake *(G-8260)*

PUBLISHING & PRINTING: Book Clubs

Dreams To Print ... G ... 718 483-8020 — Brooklyn *(G-1793)*
National Learning Corp ... F ... 516 921-8888 — Syosset *(G-15224)*

PUBLISHING & PRINTING: Book Music

Ai Entertainment Holdings LLC ... F ... 212 247-6400 — New York *(G-8774)*
Alfred Publishing Co Inc ... D ... 315 736-1572 — Oriskany *(G-12750)*
Faces Magazine Inc ... D ... 845 454-7420 — Poughkeepsie *(G-13338)*
Kobalt Music Pubg Amer Inc ... D ... 212 247-6204 — New York *(G-10461)*

PUBLISHING & PRINTING: Books

450 Ridge St Inc ... G ... 716 754-2789 — Lewiston *(G-7138)*
Adir Publishing Co ... F ... 718 633-9437 — Brooklyn *(G-1483)*
Apollo Investment Fund VII LP ... G ... 212 515-3200 — New York *(G-8886)*
Bertelsmann Inc ... E ... 212 782-1000 — New York *(G-9055)*
Booklyn Artists Alliance Inc ... G ... 718 383-9621 — Brooklyn *(G-1629)*
Callaway Arts & Entrmt Inc ... F ... 646 465-4667 — New York *(G-9181)*
Crabtree Publishing Inc ... E ... 212 496-5040 — New York *(G-9415)*
D C I Technical Inc ... F ... 516 355-0464 — Franklin Square *(G-5116)*
H W Wilson Company Inc ... B ... 718 588-8635 — Bronx *(G-1287)*
Interntnl Publcatns Media Grup ... G ... 917 604-9602 — New York *(G-10252)*
James Morgan Publishing ... G ... 212 655-5470 — New York *(G-10303)*
Klutz ... E ... 650 687-2600 — New York *(G-10458)*
Metro Creative Graphics Inc ... E ... 212 947-5100 — New York *(G-10784)*
Multi Packaging Solutions Inc ... E ... 646 885-0005 — New York *(G-10858)*
Nationwide Custom Services ... G ... 845 365-0414 — Tappan *(G-15469)*
Natural E Creative LLC ... F ... 516 488-1143 — New Hyde Park *(G-8551)*
News India USA Inc ... F ... 212 675-7515 — New York *(G-10954)*
Pearson Inc ... D ... 212 641-2400 — New York *(G-11133)*
Pearson Longman LLC ... C ... 917 981-2200 — New York *(G-11134)*
Pearson Longman LLC ... E ... 212 641-2400 — White Plains *(G-16487)*
Samuel French Inc ... E ... 212 206-8990 — New York *(G-11477)*
T G S Inc ... G ... 516 629-6905 — Locust Valley *(G-7352)*
Windows Media Publishing LLC ... E ... 917 732-7892 — Brooklyn *(G-2653)*

PUBLISHING & PRINTING: Catalogs

Global Video LLC ... D ... 516 222-2600 — Woodbury *(G-16620)*
Gooding & Associates Inc ... F ... 631 749-3313 — Shelter Island *(G-14801)*
Mexico Independent Inc ... E ... 315 963-3763 — Watertown *(G-16027)*
Sentinel Printing Services Inc ... D ... 845 562-1218 — New Windsor *(G-8660)*
Thomas Publishing Company LLC ... D ... 212 695-0500 — New York *(G-11819)*

PUBLISHING & PRINTING: Comic Books

Medikidz Usa Inc ... G ... 646 895-9319 — New York *(G-10759)*

PUBLISHING & PRINTING: Directories, NEC

Hibu Inc ... C ... 516 730-1900 — East Meadow *(G-4253)*
Want-Ad Digest Inc ... F ... 518 279-1181 — Troy *(G-15634)*

PUBLISHING & PRINTING: Guides

Open-Xchange Inc ... F ... 914 332-5720 — Tarrytown *(G-15485)*

PUBLISHING & PRINTING: Magazines: publishing & printing

Advance Magazine Publs Inc ... A ... 212 286-2860 — New York *(G-8747)*
Advance Magazine Publs Inc ... D ... 212 790-4422 — New York *(G-8748)*
Advance Magazine Publs Inc ... D ... 212 286-2860 — New York *(G-8749)*
Advance Magazine Publs Inc ... D ... 212 697-0126 — New York *(G-8751)*
Advance Publications Inc ... D ... 718 981-1234 — Staten Island *(G-15040)*
Alpha Media Group Inc ... B ... 212 302-2626 — New York *(G-8808)*
American Graphic Design Awards ... G ... 212 696-4380 — New York *(G-8827)*
American Intl Media LLC ... F ... 845 359-4225 — White Plains *(G-16420)*
American Jewish Congress Inc ... E ... 212 879-4500 — New York *(G-8832)*
Artnews Ltd ... F ... 212 398-1690 — New York *(G-8925)*
Aspire One Communications LLC ... F ... 201 281-2998 — Cornwall *(G-3830)*
Aspire One Communications Inc ... G ... 845 534-6110 — Cornwall *(G-3831)*
Bazaar ... G ... 212 903-5497 — New York *(G-9029)*
Bertelsmann Inc ... E ... 212 782-1000 — New York *(G-9055)*
Binah Magazines Corp ... E ... 718 305-5200 — Brooklyn *(G-1614)*
Blackbook Media Corp ... E ... 212 334-1800 — New York *(G-9097)*
Bullett Media LLC ... F ... 212 242-2123 — New York *(G-9157)*
Bz Media LLC ... F ... 631 421-4158 — Melville *(G-8005)*
Capco Marketing ... F ... 315 699-1687 — Baldwinsville *(G-552)*
City and State Ny LLC ... E ... 212 268-0442 — New York *(G-9309)*
City Real Estate Book Inc ... G ... 516 593-2949 — Valley Stream *(G-15776)*
Civil Svc Rtred Employees Assn ... F ... 718 937-0290 — Long Island City *(G-7409)*
Clarion Publications Inc ... F ... 585 243-3530 — Geneseo *(G-5313)*
CMX Media LLC ... E ... 917 793-5831 — New York *(G-9338)*
Commentary Inc ... F ... 212 891-1400 — New York *(G-9364)*
Complex Media Inc ... E ... 917 793-5831 — New York *(G-9371)*
Conde Nast Entertainment LLC ... A ... 212 286-2860 — New York *(G-9375)*
Convenience Store News ... G ... 214 217-7800 — New York *(G-9391)*
Cosmopolitan Magazine ... G ... 212 649-2000 — New York *(G-9403)*
Credit Union Journal Inc ... G ... 212 803-8200 — New York *(G-9423)*
Davler Media Group LLC ... E ... 212 315-0800 — New York *(G-9490)*
Distinction Magazine Inc ... E ... 631 843-3522 — Melville *(G-8016)*
Dow Jones & Company Inc ... B ... 609 627-2999 — New York *(G-9563)*
Ebner Publishing International ... G ... 646 742-0740 — New York *(G-9617)*
Elite Traveler LLC ... F ... 646 430-7900 — New York *(G-9652)*
Equal Opprtnity Pblcations Inc ... F ... 631 421-9421 — Melville *(G-8019)*

PRODUCT

PUBLISHING & PRINTING: Magazines: publishing & printing

Essential Publications US LLC ....G...... 646 707-0898
 New York *(G-9709)*
Excelsior Publications ....G...... 607 746-7600
 Delhi *(G-4073)*
Foundtion For A Mndful Soc Inc ....G...... 902 431-8062
 New York *(G-9827)*
Four M Studios ....C...... 212 557-6600
 New York *(G-9828)*
Four M Studios ....D...... 515 284-2157
 New York *(G-9831)*
Glamour Magazine ....G...... 212 286-2860
 New York *(G-9928)*
Green Apple Courage Inc ....G...... 716 614-4673
 Buffalo *(G-2858)*
Hearst Corporation ....D...... 212 903-5000
 New York *(G-10068)*
Homesell Inc ....F...... 718 514-0346
 Staten Island *(G-15086)*
Icarus Enterprises Inc ....G...... 917 969-4461
 New York *(G-10167)*
Index Magazine ....G...... 212 243-1428
 New York *(G-10197)*
Informa Media Inc ....G...... 212 204-4200
 New York *(G-10211)*
Intercultural Alliance Artists ....G...... 917 406-1202
 Flushing *(G-5011)*
Jobson Medical Information LLC ....C...... 212 274-7000
 New York *(G-10347)*
Kbs Communications LLC ....F...... 212 765-7124
 New York *(G-10425)*
Latina Media Ventures LLC ....E...... 212 642-0200
 New York *(G-10522)*
Livid Magazine ....F...... 929 340-7123
 Brooklyn *(G-2130)*
Ltb Media (usa) Inc ....D...... 212 447-9555
 New York *(G-10624)*
Luminary Publishing Inc ....F...... 845 334-8600
 Kingston *(G-6909)*
M Shanken Communications Inc ....C...... 212 684-4224
 New York *(G-10644)*
Marie Claire USA ....D...... 212 841-8493
 New York *(G-10702)*
Medizine Operating LLC ....D...... 212 695-2223
 New York *(G-10761)*
Metrosource Publishing Inc ....F...... 212 691-5127
 New York *(G-10786)*
Mishpacha Magazine Inc ....G...... 718 686-9339
 Brooklyn *(G-2211)*
National Ggraphic Partners LLC ....G...... 212 656-0726
 New York *(G-10883)*
Nautilusthink Inc ....G...... 646 239-6858
 New York *(G-10897)*
New Hope Media LLC ....G...... 646 366-0830
 New York *(G-10926)*
New York Fshion Week Guide LLC ....F...... 646 757-9119
 New York *(G-10939)*
Niche Media Holdings LLC ....E...... 702 990-2500
 New York *(G-10961)*
Northside Media Group LLC ....F...... 917 318-6513
 Brooklyn *(G-2273)*
Northside Media Group LLC ....E...... 917 318-6513
 Brooklyn *(G-2274)*
Nylon Media Inc ....F...... 212 226-6454
 New York *(G-11016)*
Odyssey Mag Pubg Group Inc ....G...... 212 545-4800
 New York *(G-11033)*
Pensions & Investments ....E...... 212 210-0763
 New York *(G-11150)*
Playbill Incorporated ....C...... 212 557-5757
 New York *(G-11207)*
Ragozin Data ....E...... 212 674-3123
 Long Island City *(G-7570)*
Redbook Magazine ....F...... 212 649-3331
 New York *(G-11342)*
Rnd Enterprises Inc ....G...... 212 627-0165
 New York *(G-11403)*
Rodale Inc ....B...... 212 697-2040
 New York *(G-11417)*
Romantic Times Inc ....F...... 718 237-1097
 Brooklyn *(G-2412)*
Ross Communications Associates ....F...... 631 393-5089
 Melville *(G-8062)*
Saveur Magazine ....E...... 212 219-7400
 New York *(G-11493)*
Securities Data Publishing Inc ....G...... 212 631-1411
 New York *(G-11530)*
Source Media LLC ....C...... 212 803-8200
 New York *(G-11653)*
Stuff Magazine ....G...... 212 302-2626
 New York *(G-11729)*
Suburban Publishing Inc ....G...... 914 345-0601
 Elmsford *(G-4572)*
Summit Professional Networks ....D...... 212 557-7480
 New York *(G-11740)*
Sussex Publishers LLC ....E...... 212 260-7210
 New York *(G-11752)*
T V Trade Media Inc ....F...... 212 288-3933
 New York *(G-11772)*
Thomas Publishing Company LLC ....G...... 212 695-0500
 New York *(G-11821)*
Time Inc ....E...... 212 522-1212
 New York *(G-11837)*
Time Out America LLC ....C...... 646 432-3000
 New York *(G-11842)*
Towse Publishing Co ....F...... 914 235-3095
 New Rochelle *(G-8629)*
Trans-High Corporation ....E...... 212 387-0500
 New York *(G-11886)*
TV Guide Magazine LLC ....G...... 800 866-1400
 New York *(G-11915)*
Ubm LLC ....F...... 516 562-5000
 New York *(G-11930)*
Universal Cmmncations of Miami ....C...... 212 986-5100
 New York *(G-11958)*
Uptown Media Group LLC ....E...... 212 360-5073
 New York *(G-11967)*
Urbandaddy Inc ....F...... 212 929-7905
 New York *(G-11971)*
US News & World Report Inc ....C...... 212 716-6800
 New York *(G-11978)*
Valassis Communications Inc ....G...... 585 627-4138
 Rochester *(G-14197)*
Vanity Fair ....F...... 212 286-6052
 New York *(G-11991)*
Wall Street Reporter Magazine ....D...... 212 363-2600
 New York *(G-12067)*
Watch Journal LLC ....G...... 212 229-1500
 New York *(G-12077)*
Wenner Media LLC ....C...... 212 484-1616
 New York *(G-12094)*
World Business Media LLC ....F...... 212 344-0759
 Massapequa Park *(G-7896)*

PUBLISHING & PRINTING: Music, Book

Alley Music Corp ....E...... 212 779-7977
 New York *(G-8797)*
Atlas Music Publishing LLC ....G...... 646 502-5170
 New York *(G-8954)*
Johnny Bienstock Music ....E...... 212 779-7977
 New York *(G-10355)*
Princess Music Publishing Co ....D...... 212 586-0240
 New York *(G-11243)*
Spirit Music Group Inc ....E...... 212 533-7672
 New York *(G-11671)*
Universal Edition Inc ....D...... 917 213-2177
 New York *(G-11959)*
Wmg Acquisition Corp ....F...... 212 275-2000
 New York *(G-12126)*

PUBLISHING & PRINTING: Newsletters, Business Svc

An Group Inc ....G...... 631 549-4090
 Melville *(G-8003)*
Answer Printing Inc ....F...... 212 922-2922
 New York *(G-8875)*
Ceo Cast Inc ....F...... 212 732-4300
 New York *(G-9251)*
Church Bulletin Inc ....F...... 631 249-4994
 West Babylon *(G-16148)*
Froebe Group LLC ....G...... 646 649-2150
 New York *(G-9851)*
Portfolio Media Inc ....C...... 646 783-7100
 New York *(G-11221)*
Scholastic Inc ....D...... 212 343-7100
 New York *(G-11516)*
Shop Smart Central Inc ....G...... 914 962-3871
 Yorktown Heights *(G-16823)*
Ubm Inc ....A...... 212 600-3000
 New York *(G-11929)*

PUBLISHING & PRINTING: Newspapers

21st Century Fox America Inc ....G...... 212 782-8000
 New York *(G-8672)*
50+ Lifestyle ....G...... 631 286-0058
 Bellport *(G-796)*
A Zimmer Ltd ....D...... 315 422-7011
 Syracuse *(G-15237)*
Advance Publications Inc ....D...... 718 981-1234
 Staten Island *(G-15040)*
After 50 Inc ....G...... 716 832-9300
 Lancaster *(G-7003)*
All Island Media Inc ....C...... 631 698-8400
 Edgewood *(G-4395)*
All Island Media Inc ....E...... 516 942-8400
 Hicksville *(G-6057)*
American Sports Media ....G...... 585 924-4250
 Victor *(G-15829)*
Amnews Corporation ....E...... 212 932-7400
 New York *(G-8844)*
Angola Penny Saver Inc ....F...... 716 549-1164
 Angola *(G-368)*
AR Publishing Company Inc ....F...... 212 482-0303
 New York *(G-8896)*
Asahi Shimbun America Inc ....F...... 212 398-0257
 New York *(G-8929)*
Beth Kobliner Company LLC ....G...... 212 501-8407
 New York *(G-9059)*
BNH Lead Examiner Corp ....G...... 718 807-1365
 Brooklyn *(G-1626)*
Boonville Herald Inc ....G...... 315 942-4449
 Boonville *(G-1115)*
Bornomala USA Inc ....G...... 347 753-2355
 Jackson Heights *(G-6618)*
Bradford Publications Inc ....C...... 716 373-2500
 Olean *(G-12594)*
Brasilans Press Pblcations Inc ....E...... 212 764-6161
 New York *(G-9136)*
Brooklyn Journal Publications ....E...... 718 422-7400
 Brooklyn *(G-1644)*
Buffalo News Inc ....A...... 716 849-4401
 Buffalo *(G-2750)*
Canarsie Courier Inc ....F...... 718 257-0600
 Brooklyn *(G-1671)*
Chester West County Press ....G...... 914 684-0006
 Mount Vernon *(G-8386)*
Christian Press Inc ....G...... 718 886-4400
 Flushing *(G-4991)*
Chronicle Express ....F...... 315 536-4422
 Penn Yan *(G-12951)*
Citizen Publishing Corp ....F...... 845 627-1414
 Nanuet *(G-8461)*
Columbia Daily Spectator ....E...... 212 854-9550
 New York *(G-9356)*
Community Media Group Inc ....D...... 315 789-3333
 Geneva *(G-5321)*
Community Media Group LLC ....E...... 518 439-4949
 Delmar *(G-4077)*
Community Media LLC ....E...... 212 229-1890
 New York *(G-9368)*
Copia Interactive LLC ....F...... 212 481-0520
 New York *(G-9396)*
Daily Freeman ....F...... 845 331-5000
 Kingston *(G-6897)*
Daily Gazette Company ....C...... 518 395-3060
 Schenectady *(G-14668)*
Daily Mail & Greene Cnty News ....F...... 518 943-2100
 Hudson *(G-6345)*
Daily Racing Form Inc ....C...... 212 366-7600
 New York *(G-9456)*
Daily Racing Form LLC ....F...... 212 514-2180
 New York *(G-9457)*
Daily Record ....F...... 585 232-2035
 Rochester *(G-13732)*
Der Blatt Inc ....F...... 845 783-1148
 Monroe *(G-8268)*
Document Journal Inc ....G...... 646 586-3099
 New York *(G-9544)*
DOT Publishing ....F...... 315 593-2510
 Fulton *(G-5215)*
Dow Jones & Company Inc ....B...... 609 627-2999
 New York *(G-9563)*
Dow Jones & Company Inc ....E...... 212 597-5983
 New York *(G-9564)*
East Hampton Ind News Inc ....E...... 631 324-2500
 East Hampton *(G-4235)*
El Diario LLC ....C...... 212 807-4600
 Brooklyn *(G-1818)*
Event Journal Inc ....F...... 516 470-1811
 Jericho *(G-6787)*
Evercore Partners Svcs E LLC ....A...... 212 857-3100
 New York *(G-9735)*
Exhibits & More ....G...... 585 924-4040
 Victor *(G-15845)*
Finger Lakes Media Inc ....F...... 607 243-7600
 Dundee *(G-4157)*
Fire Island Tide Publication ....F...... 631 567-7470
 Sayville *(G-14630)*
Firefighters Journal ....E...... 718 391-0283
 Long Island City *(G-7448)*

PRODUCT SECTION

PUBLISHING & PRINTING: Posters

Company	Code	Phone
First Choice News Inc	G	212 477-2044
New York (G-9806)		
Francepress LLC	G	646 202-9828
New York (G-9837)		
Fredonia Pennysaver Inc	G	716 679-1509
Fredonia (G-5126)		
FT Publications Inc	D	212 641-6500
New York (G-9856)		
Gannett Co Inc	D	585 232-7100
Rochester (G-13822)		
Gannett Co Inc	E	914 278-9315
New Rochelle (G-8606)		
Gannett Stllite Info Ntwrk Inc	D	585 798-1400
Medina (G-7978)		
Gannett Stllite Info Ntwrk LLC	C	845 454-2000
Poughkeepsie (G-13339)		
Gannett Stllite Info Ntwrk LLC	F	914 381-3400
Mamaroneck (G-7745)		
Gatehouse Media LLC	B	585 598-0030
Pittsford (G-13013)		
Gatehouse Media LLC	E	315 792-5000
Utica (G-15706)		
Gatehouse Media LLC	G	607 776-2121
Bath (G-643)		
Gatehouse Media LLC	F	315 866-2220
Herkimer (G-6039)		
Gatehouse Media LLC	G	607 936-4651
Corning (G-3819)		
Gatehouse Media LLC	D	585 394-0770
Canandaigua (G-3222)		
Gatehouse Media LLC	C	607 324-1425
Hornell (G-6299)		
Gleaner Company Ltd	G	718 657-0788
Jamaica (G-6646)		
Glens Falls Newspapers Inc	G	518 792-3131
Glens Falls (G-5426)		
Guardian News & Media LLC	E	917 900-4663
New York (G-10004)		
Guidance Group Inc	G	631 619-2600
Bohemia (G-1031)		
Guidance Group Inc	F	631 756-4618
Melville (G-8029)		
Hamodia Corp	G	718 338-5637
Brooklyn (G-1962)		
Hamodia Corp	F	718 853-9094
Brooklyn (G-1963)		
Hearst Business Media Corp	F	631 650-4441
New York (G-10056)		
Hearst Communications Inc	A	212 649-2000
New York (G-10058)		
Hearst Corporation	A	212 649-2000
New York (G-10061)		
Hearst Corporation	E	212 649-2275
New York (G-10070)		
Herald Publishing Company LLC	G	315 470-2022
New York (G-10082)		
High Ridge News LLC	G	718 548-7412
Bronx (G-1292)		
Hudson News Inc	G	212 971-6800
New York (G-10143)		
IMG The Daily	G	212 541-5640
New York (G-10185)		
Investment News	E	212 210-0100
New York (G-10263)		
Investors Business Daily Inc	F	212 626-7676
New York (G-10264)		
Irish Tribune Inc	G	212 684-3366
New York (G-10272)		
Jobs Weekly Inc	F	716 648-5627
Hamburg (G-5682)		
Journal News	G	914 694-5000
White Plains (G-16468)		
Journal News	G	845 578-2324
West Nyack (G-16273)		
Journal Register Company	E	212 257-7212
New York (G-10368)		
Korea Central Daily News Inc	D	718 361-7700
Long Island City (G-7491)		
Korea Times New York Inc	G	718 729-5555
Long Island City (G-7493)		
Lee Newspapers Inc	F	518 673-3237
Palatine Bridge (G-12842)		
Lee Publications Inc	D	518 673-3237
Palatine Bridge (G-12843)		
Litmor Publishing Corp	F	516 931-0012
Garden City (G-5266)		
Livingston County News	G	585 243-1234
Geneseo (G-5315)		
Local Media Group Inc	F	845 794-3712
Monticello (G-8321)		
Long Island Business News	E	631 737-1700
Ronkonkoma (G-14371)		
Long Island Cmnty Nwsppers Inc	F	631 427-7000
Huntington (G-6404)		
Los Angles Tmes Cmmnctions LLC	E	212 418-9600
New York (G-10612)		
Louis Vuitton North Amer Inc	G	212 644-2574
New York (G-10617)		
Made Fresh Daily	G	212 285-2253
New York (G-10655)		
Main Street Connect LLC	F	203 803-4110
Armonk (G-407)		
Mark I Publications Inc	E	718 205-8000
Glendale (G-5403)		
Melmont Fine Pringng/Graphics	G	516 939-2253
Bethpage (G-847)		
Mid-York Press Inc	D	607 674-4491
Sherburne (G-14807)		
Ming Pao (new York) Inc	F	212 334-2220
New York (G-10818)		
Minority Reporter Inc	G	585 225-3628
Rochester (G-13946)		
Moneypaper Inc	F	914 925-0022
Rye (G-14486)		
NC Audience Exchange LLC	F	212 416-3400
New York (G-10901)		
New Living Inc	G	631 751-8819
Patchogue (G-12871)		
New Media Investment Group Inc	B	212 479-3160
New York (G-10927)		
New Republic	G	212 989-8200
New York (G-10929)		
New York Daily News	G	212 248-2100
New York (G-10935)		
New York Press Inc	E	212 268-8600
New York (G-10941)		
New York Times Company	G	212 556-1234
New York (G-10944)		
New York Times Company	F	212 556-4300
New York (G-10946)		
New York University	E	212 998-4300
New York (G-10947)		
New York1 News Operations	F	212 379-3311
New York (G-10948)		
News Corporation	C	212 416-3400
New York (G-10952)		
News India USA Inc	F	212 675-7515
New York (G-10954)		
News Now Waverly	F	607 296-6769
Waverly (G-16068)		
Newsday LLC	C	631 843-3135
Melville (G-8051)		
Newspaper Times Union	F	518 454-5676
Albany (G-104)		
Nikkei America Inc	E	212 261-6200
New York (G-10968)		
Nikkei America Holdings Inc	D	212 261-6200
New York (G-10969)		
Nyc Community Media LLC	F	212 229-1890
Brooklyn (G-2281)		
Nyp Holdings Inc	D	718 260-2500
Brooklyn (G-2282)		
Nyt Capital LLC	F	212 556-1234
New York (G-11021)		
Nytimes Corporate	G	212 556-1234
New York (G-11022)		
Observer Media LLC	F	212 755-2400
New York (G-11025)		
Oneida Publications Inc	E	315 363-5100
Oneida (G-12618)		
Ottaway Newspapers Inc	G	845 343-2181
Middletown (G-8169)		
Pearson Longman LLC	E	212 641-2400
White Plains (G-16487)		
Pennysaver Group Inc	F	914 966-1400
Yonkers (G-16791)		
Permanent Observer Mission	G	212 883-0140
New York (G-11159)		
Prospect News Inc	F	212 374-2800
New York (G-11267)		
Queens Ldgr/Grenpoint Star Inc	F	718 639-7000
Maspeth (G-7869)		
R W Publications Div of Wtrhs	E	716 714-5620
Elma (G-4456)		
Record Review LLC	F	914 244-0533
Katonah (G-6846)		
Rocket Communications Inc	F	716 873-2594
Buffalo (G-3042)		
Rome Main Street Alliance Inc	G	315 271-8356
Rome (G-14270)		
Royal News Corp	F	212 564-8972
New York (G-11439)		
Rtt News	E	716 632-3400
Williamsville (G-16584)		
Ruby Newco LLC	G	212 852-7000
New York (G-11445)		
Russkaya Reklama LLC	E	718 769-3000
Brooklyn (G-2429)		
S G New York LLC	F	631 698-8400
Edgewood (G-4414)		
S G New York LLC	F	631 665-4000
Bohemia (G-1084)		
Sb New York Inc	D	212 457-7790
New York (G-11496)		
Schneps Publications Inc	E	718 224-5863
Bayside (G-749)		
Seabay Media Holdings LLC	G	212 457-7790
New York (G-11525)		
Second Amendment Foundation	G	716 885-6408
Buffalo (G-3061)		
Seneca Media Inc	C	607 324-1425
Hornell (G-6302)		
Shelter Island Reporter Inc	G	631 749-1000
Shelter Island (G-14802)		
Sing Tao Newspapers NY Ltd	E	718 821-0123
Brooklyn (G-2481)		
Spartan Publishing Inc	F	716 664-7373
Jamestown (G-6748)		
Sports Pblications Prod NY LLC	D	212 366-7700
New York (G-11675)		
Sports Reporter Inc	G	212 737-2750
New York (G-11677)		
Spring Publishing Corporation	F	718 782-0881
Brooklyn (G-2505)		
Ssrja LLC	F	718 725-7020
Jamaica (G-6678)		
Star Community Publishing	C	631 843-4050
Melville (G-8065)		
Star-Gazette Fund Inc	C	607 734-5151
Elmira (G-4503)		
Straus Communications	F	845 782-4000
Chester (G-3485)		
Sun-Times Media Group Inc	E	716 945-1644
Salamanca (G-14535)		
The Earth Times Foundation	G	718 297-0488
Brooklyn (G-2564)		
Tri-Town News Inc	F	607 561-3515
Sidney (G-14855)		
Tribune Entertainment Co Del	E	203 866-2204
New York (G-11897)		
Trilake Three Press Corp	G	518 359-2462
Tupper Lake (G-15654)		
Unified Media Inc	F	917 595-2710
New York (G-11940)		
Village Herald	G	516 569-4403
Lawrence (G-7111)		
Vpj Publication Inc	E	718 845-3221
Howard Beach (G-6333)		
W H White Publications Inc	G	914 725-2500
Dobbs Ferry (G-4132)		
W M T Publications Inc	F	585 244-3329
Rochester (G-14202)		
Wayuga Community Newspapers	E	315 754-6229
Red Creek (G-13456)		
Wayuga Community Newspapers	G	315 594-2506
Wolcott (G-16612)		
Weekly Business News Corp	G	212 689-5888
New York (G-12086)		
Westbury Times	D	516 747-8282
Mineola (G-8252)		
World Journal LLC	C	718 746-8889
Whitestone (G-16553)		
World Journal LLC	F	718 871-5000
Brooklyn (G-2658)		
Wp Company LLC	G	212 445-5050
New York (G-12142)		

PUBLISHING & PRINTING: Pamphlets

Company	Code	Phone
Newkirk Products Inc	C	518 862-3200
Albany (G-103)		

PUBLISHING & PRINTING: Patterns, Paper

Company	Code	Phone
Royalty Network Inc	G	212 967-4300
New York (G-11441)		

PUBLISHING & PRINTING: Posters

Company	Code	Phone
Enhance A Colour Corp	E	212 490-3620
New York (G-9684)		

Employee Codes: A=Over 500 employees, B=251-500
C=101-250, D=51-100, E=20-50, F=10-19, G=5-9

2019 Harris
New York Manufacturers Directory

PUBLISHING & PRINTING: Posters

Kjckd Inc .... G 518 435-9696
  Latham (G-7078)

PUBLISHING & PRINTING: Shopping News

Adirondack Pennysaver Inc .... E 518 563-0100
  Plattsburgh (G-13105)
City of New York .... E 718 965-8787
  Brooklyn (G-1695)
S G New York LLC .... E 631 665-4000
  Bohemia (G-1084)
Salamanca Press Penny Saver ...... E 716 945-1500
  Salamanca (G-14531)
Tenney Media Group .... D 315 853-5569
  Clinton (G-3589)

PUBLISHING & PRINTING: Technical Manuals

Dohnsco Inc .... G 516 773-4800
  Manhasset (G-7766)
Service Education Incorporated ..... G 585 264-9240
  Victor (G-15867)

PUBLISHING & PRINTING: Textbooks

Bright Kids Nyc Inc .... E 917 539-4575
  New York (G-9140)
Codesters Inc .... G 646 232-1025
  New York (G-9346)
Iat Interactive LLC .... E 914 273-2233
  Mount Kisco (G-8343)
Pearson Education Holdings Inc .... A 201 236-6716
  New York (G-11132)
Peri-Facts Academy .... G 585 275-6037
  Rochester (G-14013)
Warodean Corporation .... G 718 359-5559
  Flushing (G-5059)

PUBLISHING & PRINTING: Trade Journals

Beer Marketers Insights Inc .... G 845 507-0040
  Suffern (G-15186)
Forum Publishing Co .... G 631 754-5000
  Centerport (G-3348)
Guilford Publications Inc .... D 212 431-9800
  New York (G-10008)
H F W Communications Inc .... F 315 703-7979
  East Syracuse (G-4344)
Institute of Electrical and El .... E 212 705-8900
  New York (G-10228)
Lockwood Trade Journal Co Inc .... E 212 391-2060
  Long Island City (G-7503)
Med Reviews LLC .... E 212 239-5860
  New York (G-10750)
Pageant Media US Limited .... E 646 891-2110
  New York (G-11093)
Strathmore Directories Ltd .... E 516 997-2525
  Westbury (G-16374)

PUBLISHING & PRINTING: Yearbooks

Herff Jones LLC .... E 607 936-2366
  Corning (G-3820)
Visant Secondary Holdings Corp ... E 914 595-8200
  Armonk (G-412)

PULP MILLS

APC Paper Company Inc .... D 315 384-4225
  Norfolk (G-12356)
Cenibra Inc .... G 212 818-8242
  New York (G-9239)
Georgia-Pacific LLC .... E 631 924-7401
  Yaphank (G-16712)
International Paper Company .... C 607 775-1550
  Conklin (G-3728)
ITT Industries Holdings Inc .... G 914 641-2000
  White Plains (G-16465)
Parsons & Whittemore Inc .... B 914 937-9009
  Port Chester (G-13207)
Parsons Whittemore Entps Corp ... E 914 937-9009
  Port Chester (G-13208)

PULP MILLS: Mech Pulp, Incl Groundwood & Thermomechanical

Norton Pulpstones Incorporated .... G 716 433-9400
  Lockport (G-7324)

PULP MILLS: Mechanical & Recycling Processing

Advanced Recovery & Recycl LLC ... F 315 450-3301
  Baldwinsville (G-548)
Central Nat Pulp & Ppr Sls Inc ...... A 914 696-9000
  Purchase (G-13387)
Hamlin Bottle & Can Return Inc .... G 585 259-1301
  Brockport (G-1192)
Suffolk Indus Recovery Corp .... D 631 732-6403
  Coram (G-3805)

PULP MILLS: Soda Pulp

R D S Mountain View Trucking ...... G 315 823-4265
  Little Falls (G-7213)

PUMICE

A&B Conservation LLC .... G 845 282-7272
  Monsey (G-8283)

PUMP GOVERNORS: Gas Machines

Dormitory Authority - State NY ...... G 631 434-1487
  Brentwood (G-1132)

PUMPS

Air Flow Pump Corp .... G 718 241-2800
  Brooklyn (G-1495)
Air Techniques Inc .... B 516 433-7676
  Melville (G-8000)
Curaegis Technologies Inc .... E 585 254-1100
  Rochester (G-13729)
Daikin Applied Americas Inc .... D 315 253-2771
  Auburn (G-475)
Fisonic Corp .... F 716 763-0295
  New York (G-9814)
Fluid Handling LLC .... G 716 897-2800
  Cheektowaga (G-3445)
Goulds Pumps (ipg) LLC .... G 315 568-2811
  Seneca Falls (G-14773)
Goulds Pumps LLC .... A 315 568-2811
  Seneca Falls (G-14774)
Goulds Pumps LLC .... E 315 568-2811
  Seneca Falls (G-14775)
ITT Corporation .... D 315 568-2811
  Seneca Falls (G-14777)
ITT Goulds Pumps Inc .... A 914 641-2129
  Seneca Falls (G-14789)
John N Fehlinger Co Inc .... D 212 233-5656
  New York (G-10353)
Ketcham Pump Co Inc .... F 718 457-0800
  Woodside (G-16660)
Lanco Manufacturing Co .... G 516 292-8953
  West Hempstead (G-16220)
Linde LLC .... D 716 773-7552
  Grand Island (G-5506)
Mannesmann Corporation .... D 212 258-4000
  New York (G-10691)
McWane Inc .... B 607 734-2211
  Elmira (G-4497)
Oyster Bay Pump Works Inc .... F 516 933-4500
  Hicksville (G-6119)
Pumpcrete Corporation .... G 716 667-7867
  Orchard Park (G-12739)
Voss Usa Inc .... C 212 995-2255
  New York (G-12056)
Wastecorp Pumps LLC .... F 888 829-2783
  New York (G-12076)
Xylem Inc .... F 716 862-4123
  Seneca Falls (G-14789)
Xylem Inc .... C 315 258-4949
  Auburn (G-510)
Xylem Inc .... D 315 239-2499
  Seneca Falls (G-14790)
Xylem Inc .... B 914 323-5700
  Rye Brook (G-14496)

PUMPS & PARTS: Indl

Armstrong Pumps Inc .... D 716 693-8813
  North Tonawanda (G-12412)
Buffalo Pumps Inc .... C 716 693-1850
  North Tonawanda (G-12420)
Century-Tech Inc .... F 718 326-9400
  Hempstead (G-6009)
Federal Pump Corporation .... E 718 451-2000
  New York (G-9791)
Fisonic Corp .... G 212 732-3777
  Long Island City (G-7450)

Gardner Dnver Oberdorfer Pumps ... E 315 437-0361
  Syracuse (G-15330)
Oberdorfer Pumps Inc .... E 315 437-0361
  Syracuse (G-15383)
Pulsafeeder Inc .... E 585 292-8000
  Rochester (G-14054)
Sihi Pumps Inc .... E 716 773-6450
  Grand Island (G-5513)
Stavo Industries Inc .... F 845 331-4552
  Kingston (G-6920)
Westmoor Ltd .... F 315 363-1500
  Sherrill (G-14825)

PUMPS & PUMPING EQPT REPAIR SVCS

A & C/Furia Electric Motors .... F 914 949-0585
  White Plains (G-16416)
Daves Electric Motors & Pumps .... G 212 982-2930
  New York (G-9478)
Fuel Energy Services USA Ltd ...... E 607 846-2650
  Horseheads (G-6316)
Sunset Ridge Holdings Inc .... G 716 487-1458
  Jamestown (G-6753)

PUMPS & PUMPING EQPT WHOLESALERS

Cummins-Wagner-Siewert LLC ...... E 585 482-9640
  Rochester (G-13728)
Electric Motors and Pumps Inc ..... G 718 935-9118
  Brooklyn (G-1820)

PUMPS, HEAT: Electric

Economy Pump & Motor Repr Inc ... G 718 433-2600
  Astoria (G-425)

PUMPS: Domestic, Water Or Sump

Flow Control LLC .... C 914 323-5700
  Rye Brook (G-14492)
Geopump Inc .... G 585 798-6666
  Medina (G-7979)
Liberty Pumps Inc .... C 800 543-2550
  Bergen (G-824)
Pentair Water Pool and Spa Inc .... E 845 452-5500
  Lagrangeville (G-6961)
Trench & Marine Pump Co Inc ...... E 212 423-9098
  Bronx (G-1405)
Water Cooling Corp .... G 718 723-6500
  Rosedale (G-14442)

PUMPS: Fluid Power

Parker-Hannifin Corporation .... C 716 686-6400
  Lancaster (G-7036)

PUMPS: Measuring & Dispensing

Aptargroup Inc .... C 845 639-3700
  Congers (G-3710)
Charles Ross & Son Company .... D 631 234-0500
  Hauppauge (G-5788)
Economy Pump & Motor Repr Inc ... G 718 433-2600
  Astoria (G-425)
Pulsafeeder Inc .... E 585 292-8000
  Rochester (G-14054)
Schlumberger Technology Corp ..... C 607 378-0105
  Horseheads (G-6328)
Valois of America Inc .... C 845 639-3700
  Congers (G-3721)

PUMPS: Vacuum, Exc Laboratory

Graham Corporation .... B 585 343-2216
  Batavia (G-626)
Precision Plus Vacuum Parts .... D 716 297-2039
  Sanborn (G-14551)

PUNCHES: Forming & Stamping

Arro Manufacturing LLC .... F 716 763-6203
  Lakewood (G-6989)
Pivot Punch Corporation .... D 716 625-8000
  Lockport (G-7326)
Precise Punch Corporation .... F 716 625-8000
  Lockport (G-7327)

PURIFICATION & DUST COLLECTION EQPT

Hilliard Corporation .... B 607 733-7121
  Elmira (G-4492)
Hilliard Corporation .... G 607 733-7121
  Elmira (G-4493)

PRODUCT SECTION — RAILROAD CAR RENTING & LEASING SVCS

Low-Cost Mfg Co Inc .... G 516 627-3282
  Carle Place (G-3268)
Oneida Air Systems Inc .... E 315 476-5151
  Syracuse (G-15387)

PURSES: Women's

Formart Corp .... F 212 819-1819
  New York (G-9824)

PUSHCARTS & WHEELBARROWS

Truxton Corp .... G 718 842-6000
  Bronx (G-1408)

QUICKLIME

Minerals Technologies Inc .... E 212 878-1800
  New York (G-10817)

RACE TRACK OPERATION

P S M Group Inc .... E 716 532-6686
  Forestville (G-5087)

RACEWAYS

Speedzone Inc .... G 631 750-1973
  Oakdale (G-12521)

RACKS & SHELVING: Household, Wood

American Epoxy and Metal Inc .... G 718 828-7828
  Scarsdale (G-14636)

RACKS: Garment, Exc Wood

ASAP Rack Rental Inc .... G 718 499-4495
  Brooklyn (G-1561)
Lifestyle-Trimco .... E 718 257-9101
  Brooklyn (G-2118)
Millennium Stl Rack Rntals Inc .... G 718 965-4736
  Brooklyn (G-2208)

RACKS: Garment, Wood

Lifestyle-Trimco .... E 718 257-9101
  Brooklyn (G-2118)

RACKS: Pallet, Exc Wood

Frazier Industrial Company .... D 315 539-9256
  Waterloo (G-15993)

RADAR SYSTEMS & EQPT

Artemis Inc .... G 631 232-2424
  Hauppauge (G-5770)
ITT Corporation .... D 315 568-2811
  Seneca Falls (G-14777)
ITT Inc .... E 914 641-2000
  White Plains (G-16464)
ITT LLC .... B 914 641-2000
  White Plains (G-16467)
ITT LLC .... D 914 641-2000
  Seneca Falls (G-14781)
Laufer Wind Group LLC .... F 212 792-3912
  New York (G-10523)
Penetradar Corporation .... F 716 731-2629
  Niagara Falls (G-12322)
Systems Drs C3 Inc .... B 716 631-6200
  Buffalo (G-3084)
Telephonics Corporation .... A 631 755-7000
  Farmingdale (G-4892)
Traffic Logix Corporation .... G 866 915-6449
  Spring Valley (G-15009)

RADIO & TELEVISION COMMUNICATIONS EQUIPMENT

Airnet Communications Corp .... F 516 338-0008
  Westbury (G-16312)
Ashly Audio Inc .... E 585 872-0010
  Webster (G-16074)
AVI-Spl Employee .... B 212 840-4801
  New York (G-8977)
Benchmark Media Systems Inc .... F 315 437-6300
  Syracuse (G-15256)
Chyronhego Corporation .... C 631 845-2000
  Melville (G-8008)
CJ Component Products LLC .... G 631 567-3733
  Oakdale (G-12514)
Clever Devices Ltd .... E 516 433-6100
  Woodbury (G-16614)
Edo LLC .... A 631 630-4200
  Amityville (G-273)
Electro-Metrics Corporation .... E 518 762-2600
  Johnstown (G-6825)
Eni Technology Inc .... B 585 427-8300
  Rochester (G-13787)
Fujitsu Ntwrk Cmmnications Inc .... F 845 731-2000
  Pearl River (G-12897)
GE Mds LLC .... C 585 242-9600
  Rochester (G-13824)
Griffon Corporation .... E 212 957-5000
  New York (G-9988)
Gurley Precision Instrs Inc .... C 518 272-6300
  Troy (G-15607)
Hand Held Products Inc .... B 315 554-6000
  Skaneateles Falls (G-14879)
Harris Corporation .... A 585 244-5830
  Rochester (G-13853)
Harris Corporation .... E 585 244-5830
  Rochester (G-13859)
Harris Corporation .... F 718 767-1100
  Whitestone (G-16541)
Harris Corporation .... E 585 244-5830
  Rochester (G-13860)
It Commodity Sourcing Inc .... G 718 677-1577
  Brooklyn (G-2017)
L3 Technologies Inc .... A 631 436-7400
  Hauppauge (G-5859)
Listec Video Corp .... G 631 273-3029
  Hauppauge (G-5865)
Mark Peri International .... F 516 208-6824
  Oceanside (G-12547)
Mini-Circuits Fort Wayne LLC .... B 718 934-4500
  Brooklyn (G-2210)
Mirion Tech Imaging LLC .... E 607 562-4300
  Horseheads (G-6320)
Mitel Networks Inc .... G 877 654-3573
  Rochester (G-13948)
Motorola Solutions Inc .... E 518 869-9517
  Albany (G-100)
Movin On Sounds and SEC Inc .... E 516 489-2350
  Franklin Square (G-5119)
Navitar Inc .... D 585 359-4000
  Rochester (G-13965)
Quanta Electronics Inc .... F 631 961-9953
  Centereach (G-3345)
Quintel Usa Inc .... E 585 420-8364
  Rochester (G-14065)
Rodale Wireless Inc .... G 631 231-0044
  Hauppauge (G-5929)
Ruhle Companies Inc .... E 914 287-4000
  Valhalla (G-15747)
Sdr Technology Inc .... G 716 583-1249
  Alden (G-176)
Spectracom Corporation .... E 585 321-5800
  Rochester (G-14136)
Telebyte Inc .... E 631 423-3232
  Hauppauge (G-5957)
Telephonics Corporation .... A 631 755-7000
  Farmingdale (G-4892)
Telxon Corporation .... E 631 738-2400
  Holtsville (G-6248)
Thewave Communications LLC .... G 646 973-8294
  Bronx (G-1402)
W & W Manufacturing Co .... F 516 942-0011
  West Islip (G-16261)
Whirlwind Music Distrs Inc .... D 800 733-9473
  Rochester (G-14207)
Zetek Corporation .... F 212 668-1485
  New York (G-12174)

RADIO & TELEVISION REPAIR

NCR Corporation .... C 516 876-7200
  Jericho (G-6795)

RADIO BROADCASTING & COMMUNICATIONS EQPT

Apex Airtronics Inc .... E 718 485-8560
  Brooklyn (G-1539)
Appairent Technologies Inc .... G 585 214-2460
  West Henrietta (G-16230)
Fleetcom Inc .... F 914 776-5582
  Yonkers (G-16759)
Hamtronics Inc .... G 585 392-9430
  Rochester (G-13851)
L3 Technologies Inc .... D 631 436-7400
  Hauppauge (G-5862)
Motorola Solutions Inc .... C 518 348-0833
  Halfmoon (G-5665)
North American MBL Systems Inc .... E 718 898-8700
  Woodside (G-16667)
Persistent Systems LLC .... E 212 561-5895
  New York (G-11164)
Wireless Communications Inc .... G 845 353-5921
  Nyack (G-12513)

RADIO BROADCASTING STATIONS

Hearst Business Media Corp .... F 631 650-4441
  New York (G-10056)
Hearst Corporation .... A 212 649-2000
  New York (G-10061)
Iheartcommunications Inc .... C 585 454-4884
  Rochester (G-13877)
New York Times Company .... B 212 556-1234
  New York (G-10944)

RADIO COMMUNICATIONS: Airborne Eqpt

Eni Mks Products Group .... F 585 427-8300
  Rochester (G-13786)

RADIO RECEIVER NETWORKS

Cntry Cross Communications LLC .... F 386 758-9696
  Jamestown (G-6708)
Iheartcommunications Inc .... C 585 454-4884
  Rochester (G-13877)
Iheartcommunications Inc .... E 212 603-4660
  New York (G-10178)

RADIO, TELEVISION & CONSUMER ELECTRONICS STORES: Eqpt, NEC

Electrotech Service Eqp Corp .... E 718 626-7700
  Astoria (G-426)
Pass & Seymour Inc .... B 315 468-6211
  Syracuse (G-15394)
Sound Source Inc .... G 585 271-5370
  Rochester (G-14135)

RADIO, TV & CONSUMER ELEC STORES: Automotive Sound Eqpt

Ghostek LLC .... F 855 310-3439
  Brooklyn (G-1926)

RADIO, TV & CONSUMER ELECTRONICS: VCR & Access

Elite Cellular Accessories Inc .... E 877 390-2502
  Deer Park (G-3972)

RADIO, TV/CONSUMER ELEC STORES: Antennas, Satellite Dish

L3 Technologies Inc .... D 631 231-1700
  Hauppauge (G-5861)

RAILINGS: Prefabricated, Metal

D V S Iron & Aluminum Works .... G 718 768-7961
  Brooklyn (G-1748)
Paragon Aquatics .... E 845 452-5500
  Lagrangeville (G-6960)

RAILINGS: Wood

Blooming Grove Stair Co .... F 845 783-4245
  Monroe (G-8265)
Blooming Grove Stair Co .... G 845 791-4016
  Monticello (G-8320)
D K P Wood Railings & Stairs .... F 631 665-8656
  Bay Shore (G-677)
Deer Pk Stair Bldg Mllwk Inc .... E 631 363-5000
  Blue Point (G-964)
Rockaway Stairs Ltd .... G 718 945-0047
  Far Rockaway (G-4703)
Stairworld Inc .... G 718 441-9722
  Richmond Hill (G-13514)

RAILROAD CAR RENTING & LEASING SVCS

Acf Industries Holding LLC .... G 212 702-4363
  New York (G-8726)
Highcrest Investors LLC .... E 212 702-4323
  New York (G-10096)
Starfire Holding Corporation .... E 914 614-7000
  New York (G-11697)

Employee Codes: A=Over 500 employees, B=251-500
C=101-250, D=51-100, E=20-50, F=10-19, G=5-9

2019 Harris
New York Manufacturers Directory

RAILROAD CAR REPAIR SVCS

RAILROAD CAR REPAIR SVCS
Acf Industries Holding LLC..................G.... 212 702-4363
  New York *(G-8726)*
Ebenezer Railcar Services Inc................D.... 716 674-5650
  West Seneca *(G-16296)*
Highcrest Investors LLC........................D.... 212 702-4323
  New York *(G-10096)*
Starfire Holding Corporation..................E.... 914 614-7000
  New York *(G-11697)*

RAILROAD CARGO LOADING & UNLOADING SVCS
Brook & Whittle Limited........................C.... 716 853-1688
  Buffalo *(G-2736)*

RAILROAD EQPT
Alstom Signaling Inc............................E.... 585 274-8700
  Schenectady *(G-14648)*
Bombardier Mass Transit Corp................B.... 518 566-0150
  Plattsburgh *(G-13112)*
CAF Usa Inc...D.... 607 737-3004
  Elmira Heights *(G-4510)*
Cox & Company Inc..............................C.... 212 366-0200
  Plainview *(G-13048)*
Eagle Bridge Machine & TI Inc...............E.... 518 686-4541
  Eagle Bridge *(G-4184)*
Ebenezer Railcar Services Inc................D.... 716 674-5650
  West Seneca *(G-16296)*
Gray Manufacturing Inds LLC.................F.... 607 281-1325
  Hornell *(G-6300)*
Horne Products Inc..............................G.... 631 293-0773
  Farmingdale *(G-4781)*
Hudson Machine Works Inc...................C.... 845 279-1413
  Brewster *(G-1168)*
Knorr Brake Holding Corp.....................G.... 315 786-5356
  Watertown *(G-16022)*
Matrix Railway Corp.............................G.... 631 643-1483
  West Babylon *(G-16175)*
Peck & Hale LLC.................................E.... 631 589-2510
  West Sayville *(G-16291)*
Semec Corp..F.... 518 825-0160
  Plattsburgh *(G-13155)*
Strato Transit Components LLC.............G.... 518 686-4541
  Eagle Bridge *(G-4187)*
Transco Railway Products Inc...............E.... 716 825-1663
  Buffalo *(G-3102)*
Twinco Mfg Co Inc...............................E.... 631 231-0022
  Hauppauge *(G-5963)*
Westcode Incorporated.........................E.... 607 766-9881
  Binghamton *(G-923)*

RAILROAD EQPT & SPLYS WHOLESALERS
Horne Products Inc..............................G.... 631 293-0773
  Farmingdale *(G-4781)*

RAILROAD EQPT, EXC LOCOMOTIVES
Bombardier Transportation.....................D.... 607 324-0216
  Hornell *(G-6294)*
Kawasaki Rail Car Inc..........................C.... 914 376-4700
  Yonkers *(G-16774)*
Transco Railway Products Inc...............E.... 716 824-1219
  Blasdell *(G-931)*

RAILROAD EQPT: Brakes, Air & Vacuum
Knorr Brake Company LLC.....................G.... 518 561-1387
  Plattsburgh *(G-13129)*
Knorr Brake Truck Systems Co..............B.... 315 786-5200
  Watertown *(G-16023)*
New York Air Brake LLC........................E.... 315 786-5576
  Watertown *(G-16028)*
New York Air Brake LLC........................C.... 315 786-5219
  Watertown *(G-16029)*
Westinghouse A Brake Tech Corp..........D.... 518 561-0044
  Plattsburgh *(G-13169)*

RAILROAD EQPT: Cars & Eqpt, Dining
Acf Industries Holding LLC..................G.... 212 702-4363
  New York *(G-8726)*
Highcrest Investors LLC........................D.... 212 702-4323
  New York *(G-10096)*
Starfire Holding Corporation..................E.... 914 614-7000
  New York *(G-11697)*

RAILROAD EQPT: Cars & Eqpt, Rapid Transit
Seisenbacher Inc.................................F.... 585 730-4960
  Rochester *(G-14119)*
Westinghouse A Brake Tech Corp..........F.... 914 347-8650
  Elmsford *(G-4577)*

RAILROAD EQPT: Cars, Maintenance
Koshii Maxelum America Inc..................E.... 845 471-0500
  Poughkeepsie *(G-13350)*

RAILROAD EQPT: Cars, Motor
Siemens Mobility Inc............................G.... 916 717-8174
  New York *(G-11579)*

RAILROAD EQPT: Locomotives & Parts, Indl
Rand Machine Products, Inc...................C.... 716 665-5217
  Falconer *(G-4688)*

RAILROAD RELATED EQPT: Railway Track
Applied Technology Mfg Corp.................E.... 607 687-2200
  Owego *(G-12795)*
Railworks Transit Systems Inc...............E.... 212 502-7900
  New York *(G-11317)*

RAILS: Steel Or Iron
Artistic Iron Works Inc..........................G.... 631 665-4285
  Bay Shore *(G-659)*

RAMPS: Prefabricated Metal
Landmark Group Inc.............................E.... 845 358-0350
  Valley Cottage *(G-15757)*

RAZORS, RAZOR BLADES
HFC Prestige Intl US LLC......................A.... 212 389-7800
  New York *(G-10091)*

RAZORS: Electric
Harrys Inc...D.... 888 212-6855
  New York *(G-10044)*

REAL ESTATE AGENCIES & BROKERS
Yale Robbins Inc..................................D.... 212 683-5700
  New York *(G-12158)*

REAL ESTATE AGENTS & MANAGERS
Directory Major Malls Inc......................G.... 845 348-7000
  Nyack *(G-12505)*

REAL ESTATE OPERATORS, EXC DEVELOPERS: Apartment Hotel
Atlas Bituminous Co Inc........................F.... 315 457-2394
  Syracuse *(G-15248)*

REAL ESTATE OPERATORS, EXC DEVELOPERS: Commercial/Indl Bldg
Bertelsmann Inc..................................E.... 212 782-1000
  New York *(G-9055)*
E F Thresh Inc....................................E.... 315 437-7301
  East Syracuse *(G-4336)*
Penhouse Media Group Inc....................C.... 212 702-6000
  New York *(G-11149)*

RECEIVERS: Radio Communications
Harris Globl Cmmunications Inc.............A.... 585 244-5830
  Rochester *(G-13861)*

RECLAIMED RUBBER: Reworked By Manufacturing Process
Hti Recycling LLC................................E.... 716 433-9294
  Lockport *(G-7309)*
Rubberform Recycled Pdts LLC.............E.... 716 478-0404
  Lockport *(G-7330)*

RECORD BLANKS: Phonographic
Chesky Records Inc.............................F.... 212 586-7799
  New York *(G-9272)*
Europadisk LLC...................................E.... 718 407-7300
  Long Island City *(G-7440)*

RECORDING HEADS: Speech & Musical Eqpt
Felluss Recording.................................G.... 212 727-8055
  New York *(G-9793)*
Fine Sounds Group Inc.........................F.... 212 364-0219
  New York *(G-9805)*

RECORDS & TAPES: Prerecorded
Columbia Records Inc..........................F.... 212 833-8000
  New York *(G-9357)*
Cult Records LLC................................G.... 718 395-2077
  New York *(G-9432)*
Dorling Kindersley Publishing.................D.... 212 213-4800
  New York *(G-9560)*
Emusiccom Inc....................................E.... 212 201-9240
  New York *(G-9672)*
Extreme Group Holdings LLC.................F.... 212 833-8000
  New York *(G-9757)*
High Quality Video Inc..........................F.... 212 686-9534
  New York *(G-10095)*
His Productions USA Inc.......................F.... 212 594-3737
  New York *(G-10105)*
Lefrak Entertainment Co Ltd..................G.... 212 586-3600
  New York *(G-10540)*
Pete Levin Music Inc............................G.... 845 247-9211
  Saugerties *(G-14614)*
Pivot Records LLC...............................F.... 718 417-1213
  Brooklyn *(G-2322)*
Recorded Anthology of Amrcn Mus.........F.... 212 290-1695
  Brooklyn *(G-2390)*
Roadrunner Records Inc.......................E.... 212 274-7500
  New York *(G-11404)*
Side Hustle Music Group LLC...............F.... 800 219-4003
  New York *(G-11575)*
Sony Broadband Entertainment..............F.... 212 833-6800
  New York *(G-11644)*
Sony Music Entertainment....................A.... 212 833-8000
  New York *(G-11647)*
Sony Music Entertainment Inc...............E.... 212 833-5057
  New York *(G-11648)*
Sony Music Holdings Inc.......................A.... 212 833-8000
  New York *(G-11649)*
Taste and See Entrmt Inc.....................G.... 516 285-3010
  Valley Stream *(G-15799)*
Universal Music Group Inc....................F.... 212 333-8237
  New York *(G-11962)*
Warner Music Group Corp.....................B.... 212 275-2000
  New York *(G-12072)*

RECORDS OR TAPES: Masters
Bridge Records Inc..............................G.... 914 654-9270
  New Rochelle *(G-8594)*
Masterdisk Corporation.........................F.... 212 541-5022
  Elmsford *(G-4551)*
Peer-Southern Productions Inc..............E.... 212 265-3910
  New York *(G-11137)*
Sterling Sound Inc...............................E.... 212 604-9433
  New York *(G-11708)*
Wea International Inc...........................D.... 212 275-1300
  New York *(G-12084)*

RECOVERY SVC: Iron Ore, From Open Hearth Slag
Robert J Deluca Associates..................G.... 845 357-3212
  New York *(G-11408)*

RECOVERY SVCS: Metal
Island Recycling Corp...........................G.... 631 234-6688
  Central Islip *(G-3373)*

RECREATIONAL & SPORTING CAMPS
Steel Excel Inc....................................G.... 914 461-1300
  White Plains *(G-16508)*

RECTIFIERS: Electrical Apparatus
Ems Development Corporation..............D.... 631 924-4736
  Yaphank *(G-16708)*
Solid Sealing Technology Inc................E.... 518 874-3600
  Watervliet *(G-16050)*

RECTIFIERS: Solid State
Electronic Devices Inc.........................E.... 914 965-4400
  Yonkers *(G-16755)*

PRODUCT SECTION

RECYCLABLE SCRAP & WASTE MATERIALS WHOLESALERS

Metalico Aluminum Recovery Inc .... E 315 463-9500
  Syracuse (G-15370)

RECYCLING: Paper

Andritz Inc .... E 518 745-2988
  Glens Falls (G-5415)
Fcr LLC .... G 845 926-1071
  Beacon (G-758)
Georgia-Pacific Corrugated LLC .... D 585 343-3800
  Batavia (G-625)
Harvest Technologies Inc .... G 518 899-7124
  Ballston Spa (G-585)
Repapers Corporation .... F 305 691-1635
  Hicksville (G-6128)
Sierra Processing LLC .... F 518 433-0020
  Schenectady (G-14714)

REELS: Cable, Metal

Hannay Reels Inc .... C 518 797-3791
  Westerlo (G-16389)
Reelcology Inc .... F 845 258-1880
  Pine Island (G-13002)

REFINERS & SMELTERS: Aluminum

Metalico Aluminum Recovery Inc .... E 315 463-9500
  Syracuse (G-15370)

REFINERS & SMELTERS: Antimony, Primary

Zerovalent Nanometals Inc .... G 585 298-8592
  Rochester (G-14219)

REFINERS & SMELTERS: Cobalt, Primary

Umicore USA Inc .... E 919 874-7171
  Glens Falls (G-5442)

REFINERS & SMELTERS: Copper

Sherburne Metal Sales Inc .... F 607 674-4441
  Sherburne (G-14809)
Tecnofil Chenango SAC .... E 607 674-4441
  Sherburne (G-14812)

REFINERS & SMELTERS: Copper, Secondary

Ben Weitsman of Albany LLC .... E 518 462-4444
  Albany (G-45)

REFINERS & SMELTERS: Gold

Electro Alloy Recovery Inc .... G 631 879-7530
  Bohemia (G-1023)
General Refining & Smelting .... G 516 533-4747
  Hempstead (G-6011)
General Refining Corporation .... G 516 538-4747
  Hempstead (G-6012)

REFINERS & SMELTERS: Lead, Secondary

Eco-Bat America LLC .... C 845 692-4414
  Middletown (G-8150)

REFINERS & SMELTERS: Nonferrous Metal

Advanced Precision Technology .... F 845 279-3540
  Brewster (G-1154)
Amt Incorporated .... E 518 284-2910
  Sharon Springs (G-14797)
Cora Materials Corp .... F 516 488-6300
  New Hyde Park (G-8526)
General Refining & Smelting .... G 516 538-4747
  Hempstead (G-6011)
Germanium Corp America Inc .... F 315 853-4900
  Clinton (G-3585)
Karbra Company .... C 212 736-9300
  New York (G-10407)
Parfuse Corp .... E 516 997-8888
  Westbury (G-16363)
Pluribus Products Inc .... E 718 852-1614
  Bayville (G-753)
S & W Metal Trading Corp .... G 212 719-5070
  Brooklyn (G-2438)
Scepter Inc .... E 315 568-4225
  Seneca Falls (G-14783)
Sims Group USA Holdings Corp .... F 718 786-6031
  Long Island City (G-7591)

Special Metals Corporation .... D 716 366-5663
  Dunkirk (G-4180)

REFINERS & SMELTERS: Platinum Group Metal Refining, Primary

AAA Catalytic Recycling Inc .... F 631 920-7944
  Farmingdale (G-4706)

REFINERS & SMELTERS: Silicon, Primary, Over 99% Pure

Globe Metallurgical Inc .... D 716 804-0862
  Niagara Falls (G-12288)

REFINERS & SMELTERS: Silver

Rochester Silver Works LLC .... G 585 743-1610
  Rochester (G-14094)
Umicore Technical Materials .... C 518 792-7700
  Glens Falls (G-5441)

REFINERS & SMELTERS: Zinc, Primary, Including Slabs & Dust

Hh Liquidating Corp .... A 646 282-2500
  New York (G-10092)

REFINING LUBRICATING OILS & GREASES, NEC

Industrial Oil Tank Service .... F 315 736-6080
  Oriskany (G-12759)
Safety-Kleen Systems Inc .... F 716 855-2212
  Buffalo (G-3055)

REFINING: Petroleum

California Petro Trnspt Corp .... G 212 302-5151
  New York (G-9179)
Hess Corporation .... B 212 997-8500
  New York (G-10085)
Hess Oil Virgin Island Corp .... A 212 997-8500
  New York (G-10088)
Hess Pipeline Corporation .... B 212 997-8500
  New York (G-10089)
Iep Energy Holding LLC .... A 212 702-4300
  New York (G-10175)
Koch Supply & Trading LP .... G 212 319-4895
  New York (G-10463)
Petre Alii Petroleum .... G 315 785-1037
  Watertown (G-16032)

REFRACTORIES: Alumina Fused

Global Alumina Services Co .... B 212 309-8060
  New York (G-9936)

REFRACTORIES: Brick

Capitol Restoration Corp .... G 516 783-1425
  North Bellmore (G-12373)

REFRACTORIES: Brick

Saint-Gobain Strl Ceramics .... A 716 278-6233
  Niagara Falls (G-12335)

REFRACTORIES: Clay

Filtros Ltd .... E 585 586-8770
  East Rochester (G-4285)
Upstate Refractory Svcs Inc .... E 315 331-2955
  Newark (G-12210)

REFRACTORIES: Graphite, Carbon Or Ceramic Bond

Blasch Precision Ceramics Inc .... D 518 436-1263
  Menands (G-8083)
Surmet Ceramics Corporation .... F 716 875-4091
  Buffalo (G-3081)

REFRACTORIES: Nonclay

Filtros Ltd .... E 585 586-8770
  East Rochester (G-4285)
Lucideon .... F 518 382-0082
  Schenectady (G-14696)
Monofrax LLC .... C 716 483-7200
  Falconer (G-4687)
Rembar Company LLC .... E 914 693-2620
  Dobbs Ferry (G-4130)

REFRIGERATION EQPT: Complete

Saint-Gobain Dynamics Inc .... F 716 278-6007
  Niagara Falls (G-12334)
Unifrax I LLC .... C 716 696-3000
  Tonawanda (G-15586)
Zircar Ceramics Inc .... G 845 651-6600
  Florida (G-4973)
Zircar Refr Composites Inc .... G 845 651-4481
  Florida (G-4975)
Zircar Zirconia Inc .... G 845 651-3040
  Florida (G-4976)

REFRACTORY CASTABLES

Hanyan & Higgins Company Inc .... G 315 769-8838
  Massena (G-7903)

REFRACTORY MATERIALS WHOLESALERS

Upstate Refractory Svcs Inc .... E 315 331-2955
  Newark (G-12210)

REFRIGERATION & HEATING EQUIPMENT

A&S Refrigeration Equipment .... G 718 993-6030
  Bronx (G-1203)
Besicorp Ltd .... F 845 336-7700
  Kingston (G-6889)
Bombardier Trnsp Holdings USA .... D 607 776-4791
  Bath (G-641)
Carrier Corporation .... A 315 432-6000
  Syracuse (G-15273)
Carrier Corporation .... B 315 432-6000
  Syracuse (G-15272)
Columbia Pool Accessories Inc .... G 718 993-0389
  Bronx (G-1244)
Environmental Temp Systems LLC .... G 516 640-5818
  Mineola (G-8218)
Fts Systems Inc .... D 845 687-5300
  Stone Ridge (G-15161)
GM Components Holdings LLC .... B 716 439-2463
  Lockport (G-7305)
GM Components Holdings LLC .... B 716 439-2011
  Lockport (G-7306)
Healthway Products Company .... E 315 207-1410
  Oswego (G-12778)
Hydro-Air Components Inc .... C 716 827-6510
  Buffalo (G-2877)
Kedco Inc .... F 516 454-7800
  Farmingdale (G-4800)
Manning Lewis Div Rubicon Inds .... E 908 687-2400
  Brooklyn (G-2160)
Nationwide Coils Inc .... G 914 277-7396
  Mount Kisco (G-8351)
Parker-Hannifin Corporation .... D 716 685-4040
  Lancaster (G-7038)
Pfannenberg Manufacturing LLC .... D 716 685-6866
  Lancaster (G-7041)
Supermarket Equipment Depo Inc .... G 718 665-6200
  Bronx (G-1395)
Trane US Inc .... D 718 721-8844
  Long Island City (G-7620)
Trane US Inc .... G 914 593-0303
  Elmsford (G-4573)
Trane US Inc .... E 315 234-1500
  East Syracuse (G-4375)
Trane US Inc .... E 518 785-1315
  Latham (G-7094)
Trane US Inc .... E 585 256-2500
  Rochester (G-14174)
Trane US Inc .... E 716 626-1260
  Buffalo (G-3101)
Trane US Inc .... E 631 952-9477
  Plainview (G-13093)
Universal Parent and Youth .... F 917 754-2426
  Brooklyn (G-2608)
York International Corporation .... D 718 389-4152
  Long Island City (G-7645)

REFRIGERATION EQPT & SPLYS WHOLESALERS

Maplewood Ice Co Inc .... E 518 499-2345
  Whitehall (G-16523)

REFRIGERATION EQPT: Complete

American Refrigeration Inc .... G 212 699-4000
  New York (G-8836)
Atmost Refrigeration Co Inc .... E 518 828-2180
  Hudson (G-6342)
Cleanroom Systems Inc .... E 315 452-7400
  North Syracuse (G-12398)

Employee Codes: A=Over 500 employees, B=251-500
C=101-250, D=51-100, E=20-50, F=10-19, G=5-9

REFRIGERATION EQPT: Complete

Foster Refrigerators Entp....F....518 671-6036
Hudson *(G-6350)*

Millrock Technology Inc....E....845 339-5700
Kingston *(G-6911)*

S & V Restaurant Eqp Mfrs Inc....E....718 220-1140
Bronx *(G-1377)*

REFRIGERATION REPAIR SVCS

Colburns AC Rfrgn....F....716 569-3695
Frewsburg *(G-5207)*

REFRIGERATION SVC & REPAIR

Foster Refrigerators Entp....F....518 671-6036
Hudson *(G-6350)*

Medi-Ray Inc....D....877 898-3003
Tuckahoe *(G-15644)*

REFRIGERATORS & FREEZERS WHOLESALERS

Acme Kitchenettes Corp....E....518 828-4191
Hudson *(G-6337)*

REFUSE SYSTEMS

APC Paper Company Inc....D....315 384-4225
Norfolk *(G-12356)*

REGULATORS: Generator Voltage

Marvel Equipment Corp Inc....G....718 383-6597
Brooklyn *(G-2175)*

REGULATORS: Power

Trac Regulators Inc....E....914 699-9352
Mount Vernon *(G-8447)*

REGULATORS: Transmission & Distribution Voltage

Telephone Sales & Service Co....E....212 233-8505
New York *(G-11796)*

REGULATORS: Transmission & Distribution Voltage

Precision Electronics Inc....F....631 842-4900
Copiague *(G-3774)*

RELAYS & SWITCHES: Indl, Electric

C D A Inc....G....631 473-1595
Nesconset *(G-8483)*

Select Controls Inc....E....631 567-9010
Bohemia *(G-1087)*

RELAYS: Electronic Usage

Dri Relays Inc....D....631 342-1700
Hauppauge *(G-5815)*

Hasco Componets....E....516 328-9292
New Hyde Park *(G-8541)*

Precision Electronics Inc....F....631 842-4900
Copiague *(G-3774)*

RELIGIOUS SPLYS WHOLESALERS

Cathedral Candle Co....D....315 422-9119
Syracuse *(G-15274)*

Leiter Sukkahs Inc....G....718 436-0303
Brooklyn *(G-2108)*

Malhame Publs & Importers Inc....E....631 694-8600
Bohemia *(G-1055)*

Rose Solomon Co....E....718 855-1788
Brooklyn *(G-2415)*

REMOVERS & CLEANERS

G & M Dege Inc....F....631 475-1450
East Patchogue *(G-4273)*

Rapid Removal LLC....F....716 665-4663
Falconer *(G-4689)*

RENTAL CENTERS: General

Grayhawk Leasing LLC....G....914 767-6000
Somers *(G-14920)*

RENTAL SVCS: Business Machine & Electronic Eqpt

Neopost USA Inc....E....631 435-9100
Hauppauge *(G-5900)*

Pitney Bowes Inc....E....212 564-7548
New York *(G-11200)*

Pitney Bowes Inc....E....203 356-5000
New York *(G-11201)*

Pitney Bowes Inc....E....516 822-0900
Jericho *(G-6797)*

RENTAL SVCS: Costume

Rubies Costume Company Inc....B....718 846-1008
Richmond Hill *(G-13510)*

Rubies Costume Company Inc....D....631 777-3300
Bay Shore *(G-719)*

Rubies Costume Company Inc....C....631 951-3688
Bay Shore *(G-720)*

Rubies Costume Company Inc....C....718 846-1008
Richmond Hill *(G-13512)*

Rubies Costume Company Inc....E....516 326-1500
Bay Shore *(G-722)*

RENTAL SVCS: Electronic Eqpt, Exc Computers

Sentry Technology Corporation....E....631 739-2000
Ronkonkoma *(G-14410)*

RENTAL SVCS: Eqpt, Theatrical

Mutual Sales Corp....E....718 361-8373
Long Island City *(G-7530)*

Production Resource Group LLC....D....877 774-7088
Armonk *(G-408)*

Production Resource Group LLC....E....845 567-5700
New Windsor *(G-8655)*

RENTAL SVCS: Invalid Splys

Konrad Prosthetics & Orthotics....F....516 485-9164
West Hempstead *(G-16219)*

RENTAL SVCS: Live Plant

Plant-Tech2o Inc....G....516 483-7845
Hempstead *(G-6023)*

RENTAL SVCS: Pallet

Peco Pallet Inc....E....914 376-5444
Irvington *(G-6509)*

RENTAL SVCS: Stores & Yards Eqpt

Elitsac Inc....F....585 493-2628
Castile *(G-3293)*

RENTAL SVCS: Tent & Tarpaulin

Ace Canvas & Tent Corp....F....631 648-0614
Ronkonkoma *(G-14288)*

Classic Awnings Inc....F....716 649-0390
Hamburg *(G-5674)*

RENTAL SVCS: Work Zone Traffic Eqpt, Flags, Cones, Etc

Traffic Lane Closures LLC....F....845 228-6100
Carmel *(G-3283)*

RENTAL: Video Tape & Disc

Simulaids Inc....D....845 679-2475
Saugerties *(G-14616)*

REPEATERS: Passive

Innovative Power Products Inc....E....631 563-0088
Holbrook *(G-6190)*

REPRODUCTION SVCS: Video Tape Or Disk

Bertelsmann Inc....E....212 782-1000
New York *(G-9055)*

Play-It Productions Inc....F....212 695-6530
Port Washington *(G-13297)*

Professional Tape Corporation....E....516 656-5519
Glen Cove *(G-5373)*

RESEARCH, DEV & TESTING SVCS, COMM: Chem Lab, Exc Testing

Advanced Polymer Solutions LLC....G....516 621-5800
Port Washington *(G-13240)*

RESEARCH, DEVELOPMENT & TEST SVCS, COMM: Business Analysis

Economist Intelligence Unit NA....D....212 554-0600
New York *(G-9624)*

RESEARCH, DEVELOPMENT & TEST SVCS, COMM: Cmptr Hardware Dev

Argon Inc....F....516 487-5314
Great Neck *(G-5536)*

Digitronik Labs Inc....F....585 360-0043
Rochester *(G-13741)*

Mitsui Chemicals America Inc....E....914 253-0777
Rye Brook *(G-14493)*

Tokenize Inc....F....585 981-9919
Rochester *(G-14172)*

RESEARCH, DEVELOPMENT & TEST SVCS, COMM: Research, Exc Lab

Dowa International Corp....F....212 697-3217
New York *(G-9566)*

Intra-Cellular Therapies Inc....E....646 440-9333
New York *(G-10257)*

RESEARCH, DEVELOPMENT & TESTING SVCS, COMM: Research Lab

MTI Instruments Inc....F....518 218-2550
Albany *(G-101)*

RESEARCH, DEVELOPMENT & TESTING SVCS, COMMERCIAL: Medical

Athenex Inc....D....716 427-2950
Buffalo *(G-2712)*

Health Care Originals Inc....G....585 471-8215
Rochester *(G-13864)*

RESEARCH, DVLPMT & TESTING SVCS, COMM: Merger, Acq & Reorg

Toppan Vintage Inc....D....212 596-7747
New York *(G-11867)*

RESEARCH, DVLPT & TEST SVCS, COMM: Mkt Analysis or Research

International Data Group Inc....E....212 331-7883
New York *(G-10244)*

RESIDENTIAL REMODELERS

Andike Millwork Inc....G....718 894-1796
Maspeth *(G-7821)*

Di Fiore and Sons Custom Wdwkg....G....718 278-1663
Long Island City *(G-7425)*

Majestic Home Imprvs Distr....G....718 853-5079
Brooklyn *(G-2152)*

RESINS: Custom Compound Purchased

Advance Chemicals Usa Inc....G....718 633-1030
Brooklyn *(G-1487)*

Atc Plastics LLC....E....212 375-2515
New York *(G-8943)*

Cryovac Inc....C....585 436-3211
Rochester *(G-13725)*

Lahr Recycling & Resins Inc....F....585 425-8608
Fairport *(G-4638)*

Marval Industries Inc....D....914 381-2400
Mamaroneck *(G-7748)*

Polyset Company Inc....E....518 664-6000
Mechanicville *(G-7932)*

Si Group Inc....C....518 347-4200
Schenectady *(G-14713)*

RESISTORS

Betapast Holdings LLC....D....631 582-6740
Hauppauge *(G-5779)*

Microgen Systems Inc....G....585 214-2426
Fairport *(G-4642)*

PRODUCT SECTION
RETAIL STORES: Cosmetics

Micropen Technologies Corp .... D 585 624-2610
  Honeoye Falls *(G-6271)*
Passive-Plus Inc .... F 631 425-0938
  Huntington *(G-6407)*
Stetron International Inc .... F 716 854-3443
  Buffalo *(G-3077)*
Vishay Thin Film LLC .... C 716 283-4025
  Niagara Falls *(G-12348)*

RESISTORS & RESISTOR UNITS

Micropen Technologies Corp .... D 585 624-2610
  Honeoye Falls *(G-6271)*

RESORT HOTELS

Quinn and Co of NY Ltd .... D 212 868-1900
  New York *(G-11303)*

RESPIRATORS

Medical Acoustics LLC .... F 716 218-7353
  Buffalo *(G-2943)*

RESTAURANT EQPT REPAIR SVCS

Applince Installation Svc Corp .... E 716 884-7425
  Buffalo *(G-2707)*
Hobart Corporation .... E 631 864-3440
  Commack *(G-3695)*
Ronbar Laboratories Inc .... F 718 937-6755
  Long Island City *(G-7578)*

RESTAURANT EQPT: Carts

A-Plus Restaurant Equipment .... G 718 522-2656
  Brooklyn *(G-1466)*
All Star Carts & Vehicles Inc .... D 631 666-5581
  Bay Shore *(G-654)*

RESTAURANT EQPT: Food Wagons

Carts Mobile Food Eqp Corp .... E 718 788-5540
  Brooklyn *(G-1680)*
Kinplex Corp .... E 631 242-4800
  Edgewood *(G-4408)*
Restaurant 570 8th Avenue LLC .... F 646 722-8191
  New York *(G-11371)*
Tao Group LLC .... G 646 625-4818
  New York *(G-11781)*

RESTAURANT EQPT: Sheet Metal

E G M Restaurant Equipment Mfg .... G 718 782-9800
  Brooklyn *(G-1803)*
Middleby Corporation .... E 631 226-6688
  Lindenhurst *(G-7180)*
Shanghai Stove Inc .... F 718 599-4583
  Brooklyn *(G-2464)*

RESTAURANTS: Full Svc, American

Empire Brewing Company Inc .... D 315 925-8308
  Syracuse *(G-15317)*

RESTAURANTS: Full Svc, Mexican

Tortilla Heaven Inc .... E 845 339-1550
  Kingston *(G-6924)*

RESTAURANTS: Full Svc, Seafood

Fire Island Sea Clam Co Inc .... G 631 589-2199
  West Sayville *(G-16289)*

RESTAURANTS: Limited Svc, Coffee Shop

Aphrodities .... G 718 224-1774
  Whitestone *(G-16534)*
Jonathan Brose .... G 716 417-8978
  Lockport *(G-7312)*

RESTAURANTS: Limited Svc, Ice Cream Stands Or Dairy Bars

Blue Pig Ice Cream Factory .... G 914 271-3850
  Croton On Hudson *(G-3912)*
Purity Ice Cream Co Inc .... F 607 272-1545
  Ithaca *(G-6607)*

RESTAURANTS: Limited Svc, Lunch Counter

Roslyn Bread Company Inc .... E 516 625-1470
  Roslyn Heights *(G-14459)*

RESTAURANTS: Ltd Svc, Ice Cream, Soft Drink/Fountain Stands

Nestle Healthcare Ntrtn Inc .... G 516 249-5085
  Farmingdale *(G-4835)*

RESUME WRITING SVCS

Key Computer Svcs of Chelsea .... D 212 206-8060
  New York *(G-10438)*

RETAIL BAKERY: Bagels

999 Bagels Inc .... G 718 915-0742
  Brooklyn *(G-1448)*
A T A Bagel Shoppe Inc .... G 718 352-4948
  Bayside *(G-741)*
Bagel Grove Inc .... E 315 724-8015
  Utica *(G-15679)*
M & M Bagel Corp .... G 516 295-1222
  Cedarhurst *(G-3333)*
Mds Hot Bagels Deli Inc .... G 718 438-5650
  Brooklyn *(G-2184)*

RETAIL BAKERY: Bread

Addeo Bakers Inc .... F 718 367-8316
  Bronx *(G-1212)*
Giovanni Bakery Corp .... F 212 695-4296
  New York *(G-9924)*
Harrison Bakery West .... G 315 422-1468
  Syracuse *(G-15338)*
Rock Hill Bakehouse Ltd .... E 518 743-1627
  Gansevoort *(G-5246)*
Roslyn Bread Company Inc .... E 516 625-1470
  Roslyn Heights *(G-14459)*

RETAIL BAKERY: Cookies

Mannys Cheesecake Inc .... G 315 732-0639
  Utica *(G-15718)*

RETAIL LUMBER YARDS

Axtell Bradtke Lumber Co .... G 607 265-3850
  Masonville *(G-7814)*
Deer Pk Stair Bldg Mllwk Inc .... E 631 363-5000
  Blue Point *(G-964)*
Georgia-Pacific LLC .... G 631 924-7401
  Yaphank *(G-16712)*
Guldenschuh Logging & Lbr LLC .... G 585 538-4750
  Caledonia *(G-3155)*
Lowville Farmers Coop Inc .... E 315 376-6587
  Lowville *(G-7652)*
Mensch Mill & Lumber Corp .... E 718 359-7500
  Bronx *(G-1326)*

RETAIL STORES, NEC

Exhibits & More .... G 585 924-4040
  Victor *(G-15845)*
Mark F Rosenhaft N A O .... G 516 374-1010
  Cedarhurst *(G-3334)*

RETAIL STORES: Alarm Signal Systems

Lifewatch Inc .... F 800 716-1433
  Hewlett *(G-6048)*
Table Tops Paper Corp .... G 718 831-6440
  Brooklyn *(G-2552)*

RETAIL STORES: Alcoholic Beverage Making Eqpt & Splys

DAgostino Iron Works Inc .... G 585 235-8850
  Rochester *(G-13731)*
Dutch Spirits LLC .... F 518 398-1022
  Pine Plains *(G-13005)*
Foster - Gordon Manufacturing .... G 631 589-6776
  Bohemia *(G-1024)*

RETAIL STORES: Aquarium Splys

C B Management Services Inc .... F 845 735-2300
  Pearl River *(G-12895)*

RETAIL STORES: Artificial Limbs

Creative Orthotics & Prosthet .... F 607 734-7215
  Elmira *(G-4481)*
Goldberg Prosthetic & Orthotic .... F 631 689-6606
  East Setauket *(G-4302)*
Green Prosthetics & Orthotics .... G 716 484-1088
  Jamestown *(G-6719)*
Hanger Inc .... G 718 575-5504
  Forest Hills *(G-5074)*
Konrad Prosthetics & Orthotics .... F 516 485-9164
  West Hempstead *(G-16219)*
Lehneis Orthotics Prosthetic .... G 516 790-1897
  Hauppauge *(G-5864)*
Lehneis Orthotics Prosthetic .... G 631 369-3115
  Riverhead *(G-13573)*
M H Mandelbaum Orthotic .... F 631 473-8668
  Port Jefferson *(G-13222)*
North Shore Orthtics Prsthtics .... G 631 928-3040
  Port Jeff STA *(G-13215)*
Prosthetic Rehabilitation Ctr .... G 845 565-8255
  Newburgh *(G-12244)*
Ultrapedics Ltd .... G 718 748-4806
  Brooklyn *(G-2598)*

RETAIL STORES: Audio-Visual Eqpt & Splys

Audio Video Invasion Inc .... F 516 345-2636
  Plainview *(G-13037)*
Tony Baird Electronics Inc .... G 315 422-4430
  Syracuse *(G-15445)*

RETAIL STORES: Awnings

Acme Awning Co Inc .... F 718 409-1881
  Bronx *(G-1210)*
Alley Cat Signs Inc .... F 631 924-7446
  Middle Island *(G-8117)*
Awning Mart Inc .... G 315 699-5928
  Cicero *(G-3514)*
City Signs Inc .... G 718 375-5933
  Brooklyn *(G-1697)*
Dart Awning Inc .... G 516 544-2082
  Freeport *(G-5150)*
Di Sanos Creative Canvas Inc .... G 315 894-3137
  Frankfort *(G-5105)*
Graphic Signs & Awnings Ltd .... G 718 227-6000
  Staten Island *(G-15082)*
Kenan International Trading .... G 718 672-4922
  Corona *(G-3847)*
Lanza Corp .... G 914 937-6360
  Port Chester *(G-13204)*
Lotus Awnings Enterprises Inc .... G 718 965-4824
  Brooklyn *(G-2136)*
Mauceri Sign Inc .... G 718 656-7700
  Jamaica *(G-6659)*
Proof Industries Inc .... G 631 694-7663
  Farmingdale *(G-4859)*
Rgm Signs Inc .... G 718 442-0598
  Staten Island *(G-15129)*
Space Sign .... F 718 961-1112
  College Point *(G-3667)*
Steinway Awning II LLC .... G 718 729-2965
  Astoria *(G-446)*

RETAIL STORES: Cake Decorating Splys

Pfeil & Holing Inc .... D 718 545-4600
  Woodside *(G-16671)*

RETAIL STORES: Canvas Prdts

Brock Awnings Ltd .... F 631 765-5200
  Hampton Bays *(G-5708)*
Geordie Magee Uphl & Canvas .... G 315 676-7679
  Brewerton *(G-1150)*

RETAIL STORES: Cleaning Eqpt & Splys

Collinite Corporation .... G 315 732-2282
  Utica *(G-15684)*
Empire Division Inc .... D 315 476-6273
  Syracuse *(G-15318)*
Mortech Industries Inc .... G 845 628-6138
  Mahopac *(G-7709)*

RETAIL STORES: Concrete Prdts, Precast

Riefler Concrete Products LLC .... C 716 649-3260
  Hamburg *(G-5693)*

RETAIL STORES: Cosmetics

Borghese Inc .... E 212 659-5318
  New York *(G-9123)*
Malin + Goetz Inc .... F 212 244-7771
  New York *(G-10678)*
New Avon LLC .... B 212 282-6000
  New York *(G-10918)*

Employee Codes: A=Over 500 employees, B=251-500
C=101-250, D=51-100, E=20-50, F=10-19, G=5-9

RETAIL STORES: Electronic Parts & Eqpt

G B International Trdg Co Ltd .... C 607 785-0938
  Endicott *(G-4594)*
I Trade Technology Ltd .... G 615 348-7233
  Suffern *(G-15191)*
Industrial Support Inc .... D 716 662-2954
  Buffalo *(G-2883)*
Ross Electronics Ltd .... E 718 569-6643
  Haverstraw *(G-5981)*

RETAIL STORES: Engine & Motor Eqpt & Splys

Electric Motors and Pumps Inc .... G 718 935-9118
  Brooklyn *(G-1820)*

RETAIL STORES: Farm Eqpt & Splys

Birkett Mills .... G 315 536-3311
  Penn Yan *(G-12949)*

RETAIL STORES: Fiberglass Materials, Exc Insulation

Architectural Fiberglass Corp .... E 631 842-4772
  Copiague *(G-3750)*

RETAIL STORES: Fire Extinguishers

C E King & Sons Inc .... G 631 324-4944
  East Hampton *(G-4233)*
Sausbiers Awning Shop Inc .... G 518 828-3748
  Hudson *(G-6371)*

RETAIL STORES: Gravestones, Finished

Woodside Granite Industries .... G 585 589-6500
  Albion *(G-164)*

RETAIL STORES: Hearing Aids

Benway-Haworth-Lwlr-Iacosta He ...... F 518 432-4070
  Albany *(G-46)*

RETAIL STORES: Ice

Henry Newman LLC .... F 607 273-8512
  Ithaca *(G-6581)*
South Shore Ice Co Inc .... F 516 379-2056
  Roosevelt *(G-14437)*

RETAIL STORES: Infant Furnishings & Eqpt

Mam USA Corporation .... F 914 269-2500
  Purchase *(G-13392)*

RETAIL STORES: Medical Apparatus & Splys

Goodman Main Stopper Mfg Co .... F 718 875-5140
  Brooklyn *(G-1940)*
Medical Action Industries Inc .... C 631 231-4600
  Hauppauge *(G-5884)*
NY Orthopedic Usa Inc .... D 718 852-5330
  Brooklyn *(G-2279)*

RETAIL STORES: Mobile Telephones & Eqpt

2p Agency Usa Inc .... G 212 203-5586
  Brooklyn *(G-1436)*
Sima Technologies LLC .... G 412 828-9130
  Hauppauge *(G-5940)*

RETAIL STORES: Monuments, Finished To Custom Order

Presbrey-Leland Inc .... G 914 949-2264
  Valhalla *(G-15745)*
St Raymond Monument Co .... G 718 824-3600
  Bronx *(G-1391)*

RETAIL STORES: Motors, Electric

A & C/Furia Electric Motors .... F 914 949-0585
  White Plains *(G-16416)*
Economy Pump & Motor Repr Inc ...... G 718 433-2600
  Astoria *(G-425)*
Emes Motor Inc .... G 718 387-2445
  Brooklyn *(G-1830)*

RETAIL STORES: Orthopedic & Prosthesis Applications

Arimed Orthotics Prosthetics .... F 718 875-8754
  Brooklyn *(G-1551)*
Creative Orthotics Prosthetics .... G 607 771-4672
  Binghamton *(G-876)*
Klemmt Orthotics & Prosthetics .... G 607 770-4400
  Johnson City *(G-6813)*
Ortho Medical Products .... E 212 879-3700
  New York *(G-11063)*
Orthocraft Inc .... F 718 951-1700
  Brooklyn *(G-2292)*
Progressive Orthotics Ltd .... F 631 447-3860
  East Patchogue *(G-4276)*
Progressive Orthotics Ltd .... F 631 732-5556
  Selden *(G-14766)*
Prosthetics By Nelson Inc .... F 716 894-6666
  Cheektowaga *(G-3456)*
Sampsons Prsthtic Orthotic Lab .... E 518 374-6011
  Schenectady *(G-14709)*

RETAIL STORES: Photocopy Machines

Printer Components Inc .... G 585 924-5190
  Fairport *(G-4651)*

RETAIL STORES: Religious Goods

A-1 Skull Cap Corp .... E 718 633-9333
  Brooklyn *(G-1463)*
J Lowy Co .... G 718 338-7324
  Brooklyn *(G-2024)*
Moznaim Publishing Co Inc .... G 718 853-0525
  Brooklyn *(G-2229)*
Y & A Trading Inc .... F 718 436-6333
  Brooklyn *(G-2661)*

RETAIL STORES: Stones, Crystalline, Rough

Amendola MBL & Stone Ctr Inc .... D 914 997-7968
  White Plains *(G-16419)*
Hanson Aggregates PA LLC .... E 585 624-1220
  Honeoye Falls *(G-6267)*

RETAIL STORES: Telephone Eqpt & Systems

ABS Talkx Inc .... G 631 254-9100
  Bay Shore *(G-651)*

RETAIL STORES: Tents

Leiter Sukkahs Inc .... G 718 436-0303
  Brooklyn *(G-2108)*

RETAIL STORES: Water Purification Eqpt

Neptune Soft Water Inc .... F 315 446-5151
  Syracuse *(G-15380)*
Pure Planet Waters LLC .... F 718 676-7900
  Brooklyn *(G-2362)*

RETAIL STORES: Welding Splys

Haun Welding Supply Inc .... G 607 846-2289
  Elmira *(G-4491)*

REUPHOLSTERY & FURNITURE REPAIR

Furniture Doctor Inc .... G 585 657-6941
  Bloomfield *(G-954)*
KPP Ltd .... G 516 338-5201
  Jericho *(G-6793)*

REUPHOLSTERY SVCS

Anthony Lawrence of New York .... E 212 206-8820
  Long Island City *(G-7380)*

RIBBONS & BOWS

Artistic Ribbon Novelty Co Inc .... E 212 255-4224
  New York *(G-8922)*

RIBBONS, NEC

Essential Ribbons Inc .... G 212 967-4173
  New York *(G-9710)*
Fashion Ribbon Co Inc .... E 718 482-0100
  Long Island City *(G-7445)*

RIBBONS: Machine, Inked Or Carbon

International Imaging Mtls Inc .... B 716 691-6333
  Amherst *(G-232)*

RIDING APPAREL STORES

Robert Viggiani .... G 914 423-4046
  Yonkers *(G-16796)*

RIVETS: Metal

John Hassall LLC .... D 516 334-6200
  Westbury *(G-16344)*

ROAD MATERIALS: Bituminous, Not From Refineries

Alliance Paving Materials Inc .... G 315 337-0795
  Rome *(G-14245)*
R Schleider Contracting Corp .... G 631 269-4249
  Kings Park *(G-6886)*
Rochester Asphalt Materials .... G 585 381-7010
  Rochester *(G-14079)*

ROBOTS: Assembly Line

Automated Cells & Eqp Inc .... E 607 936-1341
  Painted Post *(G-12835)*
Honeybee Robotics Ltd .... E 212 966-0661
  Brooklyn *(G-1984)*
J H Robotics Inc .... E 607 729-3758
  Johnson City *(G-6812)*
McHone Industries Inc .... D 716 945-3380
  Salamanca *(G-14526)*

ROCK SALT MINING

American Rock Salt Company LLC ..... E 585 991-6878
  Retsof *(G-13480)*
Steel City Salt LLC .... G 716 532-0000
  Collins *(G-3675)*

ROCKET LAUNCHERS

CIC International Ltd .... D 212 213-0089
  Brooklyn *(G-1692)*

ROCKETS: Space & Military

Lockheed Martin Corporation .... A 315 456-0123
  Liverpool *(G-7242)*

RODS: Extruded, Aluminum

Jem Threading Specialties Inc .... G 718 665-3341
  Bronx *(G-1301)*

RODS: Plastic

Comco Plastics Inc .... E 718 849-9000
  Huntington Station *(G-6436)*
Great Lakes Plastics Co Inc .... E 716 896-3100
  Buffalo *(G-2856)*

RODS: Steel & Iron, Made In Steel Mills

Hitachi Metals America Ltd .... E 914 694-9200
  Purchase *(G-13389)*
Mardek LLC .... G 585 735-9333
  Pittsford *(G-13021)*

RODS: Welding

Aufhauser Corporation .... F 516 694-8696
  Plainview *(G-13038)*
Aufhauser Manufacturing Corp .... E 516 694-8696
  Plainview *(G-13039)*

ROLL COVERINGS: Rubber

Finzer Holding LLC .... E 315 597-1147
  Palmyra *(G-12852)*

ROLL FORMED SHAPES: Custom

Inscape (new York) Inc .... D 716 665-6210
  Falconer *(G-4681)*
Lakeside Capital Corporation .... E 716 664-2555
  Jamestown *(G-6735)*
Rolite Mfg Inc .... E 716 683-0259
  Lancaster *(G-7046)*
Rollform of Jamestown Inc .... F 716 665-5310
  Jamestown *(G-6745)*

ROLLED OR DRAWN SHAPES, NEC: Copper & Copper Alloy

Sherburne Metal Sales Inc .... F 607 674-4441
  Sherburne *(G-14809)*

PRODUCT SECTION

ROLLERS & FITTINGS: Window Shade

Windowtex Inc ....F....... 877 294-3580
  New Hyde Park *(G-8573)*

ROLLING MILL MACHINERY

Anthony Manufacturing Inc ....G....... 631 957-9424
  Lindenhurst *(G-7161)*
Ivy Classic Industries Inc ....E....... 914 632-8200
  New Rochelle *(G-8616)*
Johnston Dandy Company ....G....... 315 455-5773
  Syracuse *(G-15349)*
Mannesmann Corporation ....D....... 212 258-4000
  New York *(G-10691)*
Polymag Tek Inc ....F....... 585 235-8390
  Rochester *(G-14026)*

ROLLS & BLANKETS, PRINTERS': Rubber Or Rubberized Fabric

Enbi Indiana Inc ....E....... 585 647-1627
  Rochester *(G-13782)*
Package Print Technologies ....F....... 716 871-9905
  Buffalo *(G-2988)*

ROLLS: Rubber, Solid Or Covered

Idg LLC ....E....... 315 797-1000
  Utica *(G-15712)*
Rotation Dynamics Corporation ....E....... 585 352-9023
  Spencerport *(G-14982)*

ROOFING MATERIALS: Asphalt

Johns Manville Corporation ....E....... 518 565-3000
  Plattsburgh *(G-13128)*
Marathon Roofing Products Inc ....F....... 716 685-3340
  Orchard Park *(G-12728)*

ROOFING MATERIALS: Sheet Metal

Brothers Roofing Supplies Co ....E....... 718 779-0280
  East Elmhurst *(G-4218)*
Elitsac Inc ....F....... 585 493-2628
  Castile *(G-3293)*
Hri Metals LLC ....G....... 518 822-1013
  Hudson *(G-6354)*
Pal Aluminum Inc ....G....... 516 937-1990
  Hicksville *(G-6121)*
Pal Aluminum Inc ....E....... 718 262-0091
  Jamaica *(G-6666)*

ROPE

Gladding Braided Products LLC ....E....... 315 653-7211
  South Otselic *(G-14943)*

ROTORS: Motor

Taro Manufacturing Company Inc ......F....... 315 252-9430
  Auburn *(G-503)*

RUBBER

David Fehlman ....G....... 315 455-8888
  Syracuse *(G-15303)*
Integrated Liner Tech Inc ....E....... 518 621-7422
  Rensselaer *(G-13475)*
Release Coatings New York Inc ....G....... 585 593-2335
  Wellsville *(G-16120)*

RUBBER PRDTS: Automotive, Mechanical

Bridgestone APM Company ....D....... 419 423-9552
  Sanborn *(G-14541)*

RUBBER PRDTS: Mechanical

Apple Rubber Products Inc ....C....... 716 684-7649
  Lancaster *(G-7008)*
Delford Industries Inc ....D....... 845 342-3901
  Middletown *(G-8147)*
Finzer Holding LLC ....E....... 315 597-1147
  Palmyra *(G-12852)*
Mechanical Rubber Pdts Co Inc ....F....... 845 986-2271
  Warwick *(G-15958)*
Moldtech Inc ....E....... 716 685-3344
  Lancaster *(G-7033)*
Ms Spares LLC ....G....... 607 223-3024
  Clay *(G-3551)*
Pawling Corporation ....C....... 845 855-1000
  Pawling *(G-12893)*

Pawling Corporation ....D....... 845 373-9300
  Wassaic *(G-15965)*
Pawling Engineered Pdts Inc ....C....... 845 855-1000
  Pawling *(G-12894)*
Pilot Products Inc ....F....... 718 728-2141
  Long Island City *(G-7556)*
R & A Industrial Products ....F....... 716 823-4300
  Buffalo *(G-3029)*
The Centro Company Inc ....G....... 914 533-2200
  South Salem *(G-14948)*
Triangle Rubber Co Inc ....E....... 631 589-9400
  Bohemia *(G-1099)*

RUBBER PRDTS: Oil & Gas Field Machinery, Mechanical

Camso Manufacturing Usa Ltd ....D....... 518 561-7528
  Plattsburgh *(G-13115)*

RUBBER PRDTS: Reclaimed

Cementex Latex Corp ....F....... 212 741-1770
  New York *(G-9236)*

RUBBER PRDTS: Silicone

Canton Bio-Medical Inc ....E....... 518 283-5963
  Poestenkill *(G-13179)*
Depco Inc ....F....... 631 582-1995
  Hauppauge *(G-5809)*
Silicone Products & Technology ....C....... 716 684-1155
  Lancaster *(G-7050)*
Specialty Silicone Pdts Inc ....D....... 518 885-8826
  Ballston Spa *(G-596)*
Vasquez Tito ....F....... 212 944-0441
  New York *(G-11999)*

RUBBER PRDTS: Sponge

Tmp Technologies Inc ....D....... 716 895-6100
  Buffalo *(G-3097)*

RUBBER PRDTS: Wet Suits

Great American Industries Inc ....G....... 607 729-9331
  Vestal *(G-15818)*

RUBBER STRUCTURES: Air-Supported

Continental Latex Corp ....F....... 718 783-7883
  Brooklyn *(G-1713)*

RUGS: Hand & Machine Made

Mark Nelson Designs LLC ....F....... 646 422-7020
  New York *(G-10707)*
Mgk Group Inc ....E....... 212 989-2732
  New York *(G-10788)*
Renaissnce Crpt Tapestries Inc ....F....... 212 696-0080
  New York *(G-11360)*
Safavieh Inc ....A....... 516 945-1900
  Port Washington *(G-13302)*

RULERS: Metal

Gei International Inc ....E....... 315 463-9261
  East Syracuse *(G-4342)*

SAFES & VAULTS: Metal

Gardall Safe Corporation ....E....... 315 432-9115
  Syracuse *(G-15329)*
Schwab Corp ....E....... 585 381-4900
  Rochester *(G-14116)*

SAFETY EQPT & SPLYS WHOLESALERS

Human Condition Safety Inc ....F....... 646 867-0644
  New York *(G-10147)*

SAILBOAT BUILDING & REPAIR

Allen Boat Co Inc ....G....... 716 842-0800
  Buffalo *(G-2691)*

SAILS

Allen Boat Co Inc ....G....... 716 842-0800
  Buffalo *(G-2691)*
Melbourne C Fisher Yacht Sails ....G....... 631 673-5055
  Huntington Station *(G-6451)*
Ulmer Sales LLC ....F....... 718 885-1700
  Port Chester *(G-13210)*

SALES PROMOTION SVCS

Platinum Sales Promotion Inc ....G....... 718 361-0200
  Long Island City *(G-7557)*

SALT

Real Co Inc ....G....... 347 433-8549
  Valley Cottage *(G-15762)*
Roto Salt Company Inc ....E....... 315 536-3742
  Penn Yan *(G-12965)*
Topaz Industries Inc ....F....... 631 207-0700
  Holtsville *(G-6249)*
US Salt LLC ....D....... 607 535-2721
  Watkins Glen *(G-16062)*

SALT & SULFUR MINING

Morton Salt Inc ....F....... 585 493-2511
  Silver Springs *(G-14863)*

SAMPLE BOOKS

Federal Sample Card Corp ....D....... 718 458-1344
  Elmhurst *(G-4464)*
Niagara Sample Book Co Inc ....F....... 716 284-6151
  Niagara Falls *(G-12313)*

SAND & GRAVEL

110 Sand Company ....E....... 631 694-2822
  Melville *(G-7994)*
110 Sand Company ....E....... 631 694-2822
  West Babylon *(G-16124)*
A Colarusso and Son Inc ....E....... 518 828-3218
  Hudson *(G-6336)*
Barrett Paving Materials Inc ....G....... 607 723-5367
  Binghamton *(G-864)*
Belangers Gravel & Stone Inc ....E....... 585 728-3906
  Wayland *(G-16070)*
Callanan Industries Inc ....E....... 845 331-6868
  Kingston *(G-6892)*
Carver Sand & Gravel LLC ....E....... 518 355-6034
  Altamont *(G-196)*
Dalrymple Grav & Contg Co Inc ....E....... 607 739-0391
  Pine City *(G-12999)*
Dalrymple Holding Corp ....E....... 607 737-6200
  Pine City *(G-13000)*
E Tetz & Sons Inc ....D....... 845 692-4486
  Middletown *(G-8148)*
East Coast Mines Ltd ....E....... 631 653-5445
  East Quogue *(G-4277)*
Frew Run Gravel Products Inc ....G....... 716 569-4712
  Frewsburg *(G-5208)*
Genoa Sand & Gravel Lnsg ....G....... 607 533-4551
  Freeville *(G-5192)*
Gernatt Asphalt Products Inc ....E....... 716 532-3371
  Collins *(G-3674)*
Greenebuild LLC ....F....... 917 562-0556
  Brooklyn *(G-1951)*
Johnson S Sand Gravel Inc ....G....... 315 771-1450
  La Fargeville *(G-6943)*
Lafarge North America Inc ....E....... 716 651-9235
  Lancaster *(G-7027)*
Lafarge North America Inc ....E....... 518 756-5000
  Ravena *(G-13454)*
McEwan Trucking & Grav Produc .....G....... 716 609-1828
  East Concord *(G-4214)*
Milestone Construction Corp ....E....... 718 459-8500
  Rego Park *(G-13466)*
Mitchell Stone Products LLC ....E....... 518 359-7029
  Tupper Lake *(G-15651)*
Northeast Solite Corporation ....E....... 845 246-2177
  Mount Marion *(G-8365)*
R K King General Construction ....G....... 315 583-3560
  Adams Center *(G-4)*
R J Valente Gravel Inc ....D....... 518 432-4470
  Troy *(G-15618)*
R J Valente Gravel Inc ....E....... 518 279-1001
  Cropseyville *(G-3909)*
R J Valente Gravel Inc ....F....... 518 432-4470
  Rensselaer *(G-13476)*
Rd2 Construction & Dem LLC ....F....... 718 980-1650
  Staten Island *(G-15125)*
Republic Construction Co Inc ....G....... 914 235-3654
  New Rochelle *(G-8626)*
Robinson Concrete Inc ....E....... 315 253-6666
  Auburn *(G-498)*
Seneca Stone Corporation ....G....... 607 737-6200
  Pine City *(G-13001)*
Speyside Holdings LLC ....E....... 845 928-2221
  Highland Mills *(G-6152)*

SAND & GRAVEL

Tilcon New York Inc ....D...... 845 358-3100
  West Nyack *(G-16282)*
Titus Mountain Sand & Grav LLC ....G...... 518 483-3740
  Malone *(G-7728)*
Tri City Highway Products Inc ....E...... 607 722-2967
  Binghamton *(G-921)*
Tri-City Highway Products Inc ....E...... 518 294-9964
  Richmondville *(G-13519)*
Troy Sand & Gravel Co Inc ....F...... 518 674-2854
  West Sand Lake *(G-16286)*
United Materials Inc ....G...... 716 662-0564
  Orchard Park *(G-12748)*
US Allegro Inc ....E...... 347 408-6601
  Maspeth *(G-7874)*

SAND MINING

Country Side Sand & Gravel ....G...... 716 988-3271
  Collins *(G-3672)*
Dicks Concrete Co Inc ....E...... 845 374-5966
  New Hampton *(G-8499)*
H L Robinson Sand & Gravel ....F...... 607 659-5153
  Candor *(G-3252)*
Hampton Sand Corp ....G...... 631 325-5533
  Westhampton *(G-16402)*
Rush Gravel Corp ....G...... 585 533-1740
  Honeoye Falls *(G-6272)*
Sparrow Mining Co ....G...... 718 519-6600
  Bronx *(G-1389)*
Tilcon New York Inc ....E...... 845 942-0602
  Tomkins Cove *(G-15516)*
Troy Sand & Gravel Co Inc ....G...... 518 203-5115
  West Sand Lake *(G-16285)*

SAND: Hygrade

New Jersey Pulverizing Co Inc ....G...... 516 921-9595
  Syosset *(G-15226)*
Precision Elctro Mnrl Pmco Inc ....E...... 716 284-2484
  Niagara Falls *(G-12326)*

SANDSTONE: Crushed & Broken

County Line Stone Co Inc ....E...... 716 542-5435
  Akron *(G-17)*
Shelby Crushed Stone Inc ....E...... 585 798-4501
  Medina *(G-7989)*

SANITARY SVCS: Environmental Cleanup

Hygrade..G...... 718 488-9000
  Brooklyn *(G-1989)*

SANITARY SVCS: Waste Materials, Recycling

Crumbrubber Technology Inc ....F...... 718 468-3988
  Hollis *(G-6233)*
Hampton Sand Corp ....G...... 631 325-5533
  Westhampton *(G-16402)*
Ivi Services Inc ....D...... 607 729-5111
  Binghamton *(G-897)*
Kore Infrastructure LLC ....G...... 646 532-9060
  Glen Cove *(G-5370)*
Twin County Recycling Corp ....F...... 516 827-6900
  Westbury *(G-16383)*

SANITARY WARE: Metal

Advance Tabco Inc ....D...... 631 242-8270
  Edgewood *(G-4394)*
Kenbenco Inc ....F...... 845 246-3066
  Saugerties *(G-14609)*
Metpar Corp ....D...... 516 333-2600
  Westbury *(G-16356)*

SANITATION CHEMICALS & CLEANING AGENTS

Bennett Manufacturing Co Inc ....C...... 716 937-9161
  Alden *(G-168)*
Cleanse TEC ....E...... 718 346-9111
  Brooklyn *(G-1701)*
Colgate-Palmolive Company ....A...... 212 310-2000
  New York *(G-9349)*
Crosstex International Inc ....D...... 631 582-6777
  Hauppauge *(G-5805)*
James Richard Specialty Chem ....G...... 914 478-7500
  Hastings On Hudson *(G-5750)*
Micro Powders Inc ....E...... 914 332-6400
  Tarrytown *(G-15483)*
Olin Chlor Alkali Logistics ....C...... 716 278-6411
  Niagara Falls *(G-12320)*

P S M Group Inc ....E...... 716 532-6686
  Forestville *(G-5087)*
Pure Green LLC..G...... 800 306-9122
  Oyster Bay *(G-12819)*
Rochester Midland Corporation ....C...... 585 336-2200
  Rochester *(G-14088)*
Safetec of America Inc ....D...... 716 895-1822
  Buffalo *(G-3054)*
Tribology Inc..E...... 631 345-3000
  Yaphank *(G-16724)*
US Nonwovens Corp ....A...... 631 952-0100
  Brentwood *(G-1147)*

SASHES: Door Or Window, Metal

A G M Deco Inc ....F...... 718 624-6200
  Brooklyn *(G-1455)*
A G M Deco Inc ....D...... 718 624-6200
  Brooklyn *(G-1456)*
Hopes Windows Inc ....C...... 716 665-5124
  Jamestown *(G-6722)*
Revival Sash & Door LLC ....G...... 973 500-4242
  New York *(G-11375)*
Thermal Tech Doors Inc ....E...... 516 745-0100
  Garden City *(G-5283)*

SATCHELS

Barclay Brown Corp ....F...... 718 376-7166
  Brooklyn *(G-1586)*

SATELLITES: Communications

Geosync Microwave Inc ....G...... 631 760-5567
  Hauppauge *(G-5833)*
Icon Enterprises Intl Inc ....E...... 718 752-9764
  Mohegan Lake *(G-8258)*
Loral Space & Commncts Holdng ....E...... 212 697-1105
  New York *(G-10603)*
Loral Space Communications Inc ....E...... 212 697-1105
  New York *(G-10604)*
Loral Spacecom Corporation ....E...... 212 697-1105
  New York *(G-10605)*
Orbcomm Inc ....F...... 703 433-6396
  Utica *(G-15729)*
Village Video Productions Inc ....G...... 631 752-9311
  West Babylon *(G-16203)*

SAW BLADES

Allway Tools Inc ....D...... 718 792-3636
  Bronx *(G-1217)*
Amana Tool Corp ....D...... 631 752-1300
  Farmingdale *(G-4718)*
Diamond Saw Works Inc ....E...... 716 496-7417
  Chaffee *(G-3402)*
Dinosaw Inc ....E...... 518 828-9942
  Hudson *(G-6347)*
Suffolk McHy & Pwr Tl Corp ....G...... 631 289-7153
  Patchogue *(G-12877)*

SAWDUST & SHAVINGS

Bono Sawdust Supply Co Inc ....G...... 718 446-1374
  Corona *(G-3839)*

SAWDUST, WHOLESALE

Attica Package Company Inc ....F...... 585 591-0510
  Attica *(G-459)*

SAWING & PLANING MILLS

A D Bowman & Son Lumber Co ....E...... 607 692-2595
  Castle Creek *(G-3294)*
Angelica Forest Products Inc ....G...... 585 466-3205
  Angelica *(G-366)*
Axtell Bradtke Lumber Co........................G...... 607 265-3850
  Masonville *(G-7814)*
B & J Lumber Co Inc................................G...... 518 677-3845
  Cambridge *(G-3177)*
Bissel-Babcock Millwork Inc ....F...... 716 761-6976
  Sherman *(G-14815)*
Cannonsville Lumber Inc ....G...... 607 467-3380
  Deposit *(G-4106)*
Capital Sawmill Service ....G...... 518 479-0729
  Nassau *(G-8476)*
Clements Burrville Sawmill ....G...... 315 782-4549
  Watertown *(G-16008)*
Cote Hardwood Products Inc ....F...... 607 898-5737
  Locke *(G-7281)*
Curran Renewable Energy LLC ....E...... 315 769-2000
  Massena *(G-7901)*

Dlr Enterprises LLC ....G...... 315 813-2911
  Sherrill *(G-14819)*
Donver Incorporated..................................F...... 716 945-1910
  Kill Buck *(G-6878)*
Farney Lumber Corporation ....G...... 315 346-6013
  Lowville *(G-7650)*
Gutchess Lumber Co Inc ....E...... 716 492-2824
  Freedom *(G-5132)*
J & J Log & Lumber Corp........................D...... 845 832-6535
  Dover Plains *(G-4144)*
McDonough Hardwoods Ltd ....E...... 315 829-3449
  Vernon Center *(G-15807)*
Meltz Lumber Co of Mellenville ....E...... 518 672-7021
  Hudson *(G-6363)*
Mettowee Lumber & Plastics Co ....C...... 518 642-1100
  Granville *(G-5522)*
Owletts Saw Mills......................................G...... 607 525-6340
  Woodhull *(G-16638)*
Pallets Inc..E...... 518 747-4177
  Fort Edward *(G-5097)*
Piccini Industries Ltd ....E...... 845 365-0614
  Orangeburg *(G-12685)*
Rudy Stempel & Family Sawmill............G...... 518 872-0431
  East Berne *(G-4212)*
Russell Bass..F...... 607 637-5253
  Hancock *(G-5714)*
S Donadic Inc ....D...... 718 361-9888
  Sunnyside *(G-15205)*
Saw Mill Pediatrics Pllc ....G...... 914 449-6064
  Pleasantville *(G-13178)*
Simplicity Bandsaw Inc ....G...... 716 557-8805
  Hinsdale *(G-6162)*
Sirianni Hardwoods Inc ....E...... 607 962-4688
  Painted Post *(G-12841)*
Spiegel Woodworks Inc............................F...... 845 336-8090
  Kingston *(G-6918)*
St Lawrence Lumber Inc ....G...... 315 649-2990
  Three Mile Bay *(G-15509)*
Swanson Lumber ....G...... 716 499-1726
  Gerry *(G-5341)*
Tupper Lake Hardwoods Inc ....E...... 518 359-8248
  Tupper Lake *(G-15655)*
Urrey Lumber ....G...... 518 827-4851
  Middleburgh *(G-8130)*
Wagner Hardwoods LLC ....C...... 607 594-3321
  Cayuta *(G-3315)*
Wagner Hardwoods LLC ....G...... 607 229-8198
  Friendship *(G-5211)*
Wagner Millwork Inc ....D...... 607 687-5362
  Owego *(G-12805)*
Wagner Nineveh Inc..................................F...... 607 693-2689
  Afton *(G-9)*

SAWING & PLANING MILLS: Custom

Gutchess Freedom Inc ....D...... 716 492-2824
  Freedom *(G-5131)*

SAWS & SAWING EQPT

Kelley Farm & Garden Inc ....E...... 518 234-2332
  Cobleskill *(G-3603)*

SCALES & BALANCES, EXC LABORATORY

A & K Equipment Incorporated ....G...... 705 428-3573
  Watertown *(G-15999)*
Circuits & Systems Inc ....E...... 516 593-4301
  East Rockaway *(G-4293)*
Itin Scale Co Inc ....E...... 718 336-5900
  Brooklyn *(G-2019)*

SCALES: Baby

Scale-Tronix Inc ....E...... 914 948-8117
  Skaneateles *(G-14877)*

SCALP TREATMENT SVCS

British Science Corporation ....G...... 212 980-8700
  Staten Island *(G-15055)*

SCANNING DEVICES: Optical

Broadnet Technologies Inc ....F...... 315 443-3694
  Syracuse *(G-15262)*
Symbol Technologies LLC ....A...... 631 737-6851
  Holtsville *(G-6246)*
T&K Printing Inc ....F...... 718 439-9454
  Brooklyn *(G-2550)*

PRODUCT SECTION

SCHOOLS & EDUCATIONAL SVCS, NEC

Codesters Inc .... G 646 232-1025
  New York *(G-9346)*

SCIENTIFIC EQPT REPAIR SVCS

Transcat Inc .... B 585 352-7777
  Rochester *(G-14175)*

SCISSORS: Hand

Klein Cutlery LLC .... D 585 928-2500
  Bolivar *(G-1111)*

SCRAP & WASTE MATERIALS, WHOLESALE: Ferrous Metal

Blue Tee Corp .... G 212 598-0880
  New York *(G-9109)*
Massena Metals Inc .... F 315 769-3846
  Massena *(G-7905)*

SCRAP & WASTE MATERIALS, WHOLESALE: Metal

All American Funding & Ref LLC .... G 516 978-7531
  Farmingdale *(G-4713)*
Umicore USA Inc .... E 919 874-7171
  Glens Falls *(G-5442)*

SCRAP & WASTE MATERIALS, WHOLESALE: Plastics Scrap

Fiber USA Corp .... G 718 888-1512
  Flushing *(G-5200)*

SCRAP & WASTE MATERIALS, WHOLESALE: Rags

Yankee Corp .... F 718 589-1377
  Bronx *(G-1420)*

SCREENS: Projection

Dnp Electronics America LLC .... D 212 503-1060
  New York *(G-9543)*

SCREENS: Window, Metal

Alumil Fabrication Inc .... F 845 469-2874
  Newburgh *(G-12212)*
Window Tech Systems Inc .... E 518 899-9000
  Ballston Spa *(G-598)*

SCREENS: Woven Wire

Star Wire Mesh Fabricators .... G 212 831-4133
  New York *(G-11696)*

SCREW MACHINE PRDTS

Acme Precision Screw Pdts Inc .... F 585 328-2028
  Rochester *(G-13599)*
Action Machined Products Inc .... F 631 842-2333
  Copiague *(G-3748)*
Albert Gates Inc .... D 585 594-9401
  North Chili *(G-12381)*
All Type Screw Machine Pdts .... G 516 334-5100
  Westbury *(G-16313)*
Alpha Fasteners Corp .... G 516 867-6188
  Freeport *(G-5141)*
American-Swiss Products Co Inc .... G 585 292-1720
  Pittsford *(G-13008)*
Anderson Precision Inc .... D 716 484-1148
  Jamestown *(G-6698)*
Andros Manufacturing Corp .... F 585 663-5700
  Rochester *(G-13633)*
Brinkman Intl Group Inc .... G 585 429-5000
  Rochester *(G-13676)*
Broda Machine Co Inc .... F 716 297-3221
  Niagara Falls *(G-12266)*
C R C Manufacturing Inc .... F 585 254-8820
  Rochester *(G-13686)*
C&C Automatics Inc .... E 315 331-1436
  Newark *(G-12193)*
Century Metal Parts Corp .... E 631 667-0800
  Bay Shore *(G-669)*
Craftech Industries Inc .... D 518 828-5001
  Hudson *(G-6344)*
Curtis Screw Co Inc .... E 716 898-7800
  Buffalo *(G-2788)*

Emory Machine & Tool Co Inc .... E 585 436-9610
  Farmington *(G-4913)*
Five Star Tool Co Inc .... E 585 328-9580
  Rochester *(G-13806)*
Globe Electronic Hardware Inc .... F 718 457-0303
  Woodside *(G-16659)*
Gsp Components Inc .... D 585 436-3377
  Rochester *(G-13846)*
Hanco Metal Products Inc .... F 212 787-5992
  Brooklyn *(G-1965)*
I W Industries Inc .... C 631 293-9494
  Melville *(G-8036)*
J & J Swiss Precision Inc .... E 631 243-5584
  Deer Park *(G-3988)*
Kaddis Manufacturing Corp 585 624-3070
  Honeoye Falls *(G-6270)*
Kathleen B Mead 585 247-0146
  Webster *(G-16089)*
Lexington Machining LLC .... C 585 235-0880
  Rochester *(G-13912)*
Lexington Machining LLC .... C 585 235-0880
  Rochester *(G-13913)*
Liberty Brass Turning Co Inc .... E 718 784-2911
  Westbury *(G-16350)*
M Manastrip-M Corporation 518 664-2089
  Clifton Park *(G-3570)*
Manacraft Precision Inc .... F 914 654-0967
  Pelham *(G-12937)*
Manth-Brownell Inc .... C 315 687-7263
  Kirkville *(G-6934)*
Marmach Machine Inc .... G 585 768-8800
  Le Roy *(G-7122)*
Micro Threaded Products Inc .... G 585 288-0080
  Rochester *(G-13940)*
Miggins Screw Products Inc .... G 845 279-2307
  Brewster *(G-1172)*
Muller Tool Inc .... E 716 895-3658
  Buffalo *(G-2956)*
Multimatic Products Inc .... D 800 767-7633
  Ronkonkoma *(G-14381)*
Murphy Manufacturing Co Inc .... G 585 223-0100
  Fairport *(G-4644)*
Norwood Screw Machine Parts .... F 516 481-6644
  Mineola *(G-8241)*
Park-Ohio Inds Trsry Co Inc .... F 212 966-3310
  Albany *(G-110)*
Ppi Corp .... D 585 243-0300
  Rochester *(G-14032)*
R P M Machine Co .... G 585 671-3744
  Webster *(G-16094)*
Ranney Precision .... F 716 731-6418
  Niagara Falls *(G-12328)*
Selflock Screw Products Co Inc .... E 315 541-4464
  Syracuse *(G-15422)*
Supreme Screw Products Inc .... D 718 293-6600
  Plainview *(G-13091)*
T & L Automatics Inc 585 647-3717
  Rochester *(G-14155)*
TAC Screw Products Inc .... F 585 663-5840
  Rochester *(G-14157)*
Taylor Metalworks Inc .... C 716 662-3113
  Orchard Park *(G-12745)*
Teale Machine Company Inc .... D 585 244-6700
  Rochester *(G-14160)*
Thuro Metal Products Inc .... E 631 435-0444
  Brentwood *(G-1145)*
Tri-Technologies Inc .... E 914 699-2001
  Mount Vernon *(G-8449)*
Trihex Manufacturing Inc .... G 315 589-9331
  Williamson *(G-16563)*
Triple Point Manufacturing .... G 631 218-4988
  Bohemia *(G-1101)*
Umbro Machine & Tool Co Inc .... F 845 876-4669
  Rhinebeck *(G-13489)*
Vanguard Metals Inc .... F 631 234-6500
  Central Islip *(G-3388)*
Verns Machine Co Inc .... E 315 926-4223
  Marion *(G-7810)*

SCREW MACHINES

Johnson Mch & Fibr Pdts Co Inc .... F 716 665-2003
  Jamestown *(G-6734)*
Swiss Specialties Inc .... F 631 567-8800
  Wading River *(G-15888)*

SCREWS: Metal

Anthony Manno & Co Inc .... G 631 445-1834
  Deer Park *(G-3943)*
John F Rafter Inc .... G 716 992-3425
  Eden *(G-4389)*

Kinemotive Corporation .... E 631 249-6440
  Farmingdale *(G-4803)*
Radax Industries Inc .... E 585 265-2055
  Webster *(G-16095)*
Socket Products Mfg Corp .... G 631 232-9870
  Islandia *(G-6538)*
Tamperproof Screw Company Inc ...... F 516 931-1616
  Hicksville *(G-6136)*

SEALANTS

Deal International Inc .... E 585 288-4444
  Rochester *(G-13737)*
J M Canty Inc .... E 716 625-4227
  Lockport *(G-7310)*
R-Co Products Corporation .... F 800 854-7657
  Lakewood *(G-6997)*
Saint-Gobain Prfmce Plas Corp .... C 518 642-2200
  Granville *(G-5524)*
Walsh & Hughes Inc .... G 631 427-5904
  Huntington Station *(G-6464)*

SEALING COMPOUNDS: Sealing, synthetic rubber or plastic

USA Sealing Inc .... E 716 288-9952
  Cheektowaga *(G-3462)*

SEARCH & DETECTION SYSTEMS, EXC RADAR

Frequency Electronics Inc .... C 516 794-4500
  Uniondale *(G-15668)*
Saab Defense and SEC USA LLC ...... F 315 445-5009
  East Syracuse *(G-4367)*
U S Tech Corporation .... F 315 437-7207
  East Syracuse *(G-4377)*
Virtualapt Corp .... F 917 293-3173
  Brooklyn *(G-2627)*
VJ Technologies Inc .... E 631 589-8800
  Bohemia *(G-1106)*

SEARCH & NAVIGATION SYSTEMS

Accipiter Radar Corporation .... G 716 508-4432
  Orchard Park *(G-12697)*
Ametek Inc .... D 585 263-7700
  Rochester *(G-13630)*
Aventura Technologies Inc .... E 631 300-4000
  Commack *(G-3680)*
B/E Aerospace Inc .... C 631 589-0877
  Bohemia *(G-986)*
Bae Systems Info & Elec Sys .... G 631 912-1525
  Greenlawn *(G-5621)*
Bae Systems PLC .... E 631 261-7000
  Greenlawn *(G-5622)*
C Speed LLC 315 453-1043
  Liverpool *(G-7227)*
C-Flex Bearing Co Inc .... F 315 895-7454
  Frankfort *(G-5104)*
CIT Aerospace LLC 212 461-5200
  New York *(G-9305)*
Clayton Dubilier & Rice Fun .... E 212 407-5200
  New York *(G-9324)*
Cobham Management Services Inc ... A 716 662-0006
  Orchard Park *(G-12709)*
Computer Instruments Corp .... E 516 876-8400
  Westbury *(G-16321)*
Cox & Company Inc .... C 212 366-0200
  Plainview *(G-13048)*
Dyna-Empire Inc .... C 516 222-2700
  Garden City *(G-5256)*
Edo LLC .... A 631 630-4200
  Amityville *(G-273)*
Flightline Electronics Inc .... D 585 924-4000
  Victor *(G-15847)*
GE Aviation Systems LLC .... D 513 243-9104
  Bohemia *(G-1027)*
Harris Corporation .... E 631 630-4000
  Amityville *(G-280)*
Inficon Inc .... C 315 434-1100
  East Syracuse *(G-4350)*
Joldeson One Aerospace Inds .... D 718 848-7396
  Ozone Park *(G-12827)*
Kerns Manufacturing Corp .... C 718 784-4044
  Long Island City *(G-7488)*
Klx Inc .... F 845 534-0401
  Cornwall *(G-3833)*
L3 Foreign Holdings Inc .... D 212 697-1111
  New York *(G-10497)*

SEARCH & NAVIGATION SYSTEMS

L3 Technologies Inc..............................B...... 212 697-1111
   New York (G-10498)
L3 Technologies Inc..............................G...... 631 231-3994
   Hauppauge (G-5860)
Lockheed Martin Corporation................G...... 212 953-1510
   New York (G-10590)
Lockheed Martin Corporation................C...... 516 228-2000
   Uniondale (G-15670)
Lockheed Martin Corporation................A...... 607 751-2000
   Owego (G-12799)
Lockheed Martin Corporation................D...... 212 697-1105
   New York (G-10591)
Lockheed Martin Corporation................E...... 716 297-1000
   Niagara Falls (G-12307)
Lockheed Martin Global Inc...................E...... 315 456-2982
   Liverpool (G-7243)
Lockheed Martin Integrtd Systm.............E...... 315 456-3333
   Syracuse (G-15364)
Logitek Inc..D...... 631 567-1100
   Bohemia (G-1048)
Magellan Aerospace NY Inc...................C...... 718 699-4000
   Corona (G-3849)
Metro Dynamics Scie..............................F...... 631 842-4300
   West Babylon (G-16176)
Mirion Technologies Ist Corp..................D...... 607 562-4300
   Horseheads (G-6321)
Moog Inc...C...... 716 805-8100
   East Aurora (G-4208)
Northrop Grumman Corporation.............A...... 703 280-2900
   Bethpage (G-849)
Orthstar Enterprises Inc.........................D...... 607 562-2100
   Horseheads (G-6323)
Rodale Wireless Inc................................E...... 631 231-0044
   Hauppauge (G-5929)
Transistor Devices Inc............................E...... 631 471-7492
   Ronkonkoma (G-14421)
Tusk Manufacturing Inc..........................F...... 631 567-3349
   Bohemia (G-1102)
U E Systems Incorporated.......................E...... 914 592-1220
   Elmsford (G-4575)
Vacuum Instrument Corporation.............D...... 631 737-0900
   Ronkonkoma (G-14427)
Worldwide Arntcal Cmpnents Inc............E...... 631 842-3780
   Copiague (G-3794)
Worldwide Arntcal Cmpnents Inc............G...... 631 842-3780
   Copiague (G-3795)

SEATING: Bleacher, Portable

E & D Specialty Stands Inc.....................E...... 716 337-0161
   North Collins (G-12785)

SECRETARIAL SVCS

New York Typing & Printing Co...............G...... 718 268-7900
   Forest Hills (G-5079)

SECURITY CONTROL EQPT & SYSTEMS

Aabacs Group Inc....................................F...... 718 961-3577
   College Point (G-3635)
Albatros North America Inc.....................E...... 518 381-7100
   Ballston Spa (G-575)
Altronix Corp..D...... 718 567-8181
   Brooklyn (G-1515)
Ameta International Co Ltd......................G...... 416 992-8036
   Buffalo (G-2697)
Atlantic Electronic Tech LLC....................G...... 800 296-2177
   Brooklyn (G-1570)
Auraspace Inc...G...... 212 905-6100
   New York (G-8963)
C & G Video Systems Inc........................G...... 315 452-1490
   Liverpool (G-7226)
Comsec Ventures International...............G...... 518 523-1600
   Lake Placid (G-6975)
Detekion Security Systems Inc................F...... 607 729-7179
   Vestal (G-15815)
Eyelock Corporation................................G...... 855 393-5625
   New York (G-9758)
Eyelock LLC..F...... 855 393-5625
   New York (G-9759)
Fire Fox Security Corp............................G...... 917 981-9280
   Brooklyn (G-1884)
Forte Network..E...... 631 390-9050
   East Northport (G-4264)
Innovative Video Tech Inc.......................G...... 631 388-5700
   Hauppauge (G-5850)
Issco Corporation....................................F...... 212 732-8748
   Garden City (G-5263)
Mkj Communications Corp......................F...... 212 206-0072
   Brooklyn (G-2219)

Napco Security Tech Inc.........................C...... 631 842-9400
   Amityville (G-304)
National Security Systems Inc................E...... 516 627-2222
   Manhasset (G-7770)
Protex International Corp........................D...... 631 563-4250
   Bohemia (G-1080)
Security Dynamics Inc............................F...... 631 392-1701
   Bohemia (G-1086)
Shield Security Doors Ltd.......................G...... 202 468-3308
   Brooklyn (G-2465)

SECURITY DEVICES

Canary Connect Inc................................C...... 212 390-8576
   New York (G-9192)
Custom Sound and Video........................E...... 585 424-5000
   Rochester (G-13730)
Dyson-Kissner-Moran Corp.....................E...... 212 661-4600
   Poughkeepsie (G-13335)
Fairview Bell and Intercom......................E...... 718 627-8621
   Brooklyn (G-1865)
Fiber Instrument Sales Inc......................C...... 315 736-2206
   Oriskany (G-12757)
Hampton Technologies LLC....................E...... 631 924-1335
   Medford (G-7951)
Hawk-I Security Inc.................................E...... 631 656-1056
   Hauppauge (G-5843)
Highlander Realty Inc..............................E...... 914 235-8073
   New Rochelle (G-8614)
Intellicheck Inc..E...... 516 992-1900
   Melville (G-8037)
Manhole Brrier SEC Systems Inc...........E...... 516 741-1032
   Kew Gardens (G-6877)
News/Sprts Microwave Rentl Inc.............E...... 619 670-0572
   New York (G-10955)
Parabit Systems Inc................................E...... 516 378-4800
   Bellmore (G-791)
Scorpion Security Products Inc...............E...... 607 724-9999
   Vestal (G-15821)
Security Defense System........................G...... 718 769-7900
   Whitestone (G-16548)

SECURITY EQPT STORES

Mod-Pac Corp...C...... 716 898-8480
   Buffalo (G-2951)

SECURITY PROTECTIVE DEVICES MAINTENANCE & MONITORING SVCS

Basil S Kadhim.......................................G...... 888 520-5192
   New York (G-9024)
Security Defense System........................G...... 718 769-7900
   Whitestone (G-16548)

SECURITY SYSTEMS SERVICES

Indegy Inc...E...... 866 801-5394
   New York (G-10196)
Intralinks Holdings Inc.............................E...... 212 543-7700
   New York (G-10258)
Synergx Systems Inc..............................D...... 516 433-4700
   Woodside (G-16681)
Verint Systems Inc..................................E...... 631 962-9600
   Melville (G-8075)
World Business Media LLC...................F...... 212 344-0759
   Massapequa Park (G-7896)

SEMICONDUCTOR & RELATED DEVICES: Read-Only Memory Or ROM

Monolithic Coatings Inc..........................G...... 914 621-2765
   Sharon Springs (G-14798)

SEMICONDUCTOR CIRCUIT NETWORKS

Nanomas Technologies Inc....................F...... 607 821-4208
   Endicott (G-4603)

SEMICONDUCTOR DEVICES: Wafers

Thermoaura Inc.......................................F...... 518 813-4997
   Albany (G-134)

SEMICONDUCTORS & RELATED DEVICES

Able Electronics Inc................................F...... 631 924-5386
   Bellport (G-797)
Accumetrics Associates Inc....................F...... 518 393-2200
   Latham (G-7062)
Advis Inc...G...... 585 568-0100
   Caledonia (G-3152)

Aeroflex Holding Corp.............................A...... 516 694-6700
   Plainview (G-13031)
Aeroflex Plainview Inc.............................C...... 631 231-9100
   Hauppauge (G-5756)
Applied Materials Inc..............................G...... 518 245-1400
   Ballston Spa (G-577)
Atlantis Energy Systems Inc...................G...... 916 438-2930
   Poughkeepsie (G-13329)
Beech Grove Technology Inc..................G...... 845 223-6844
   Hopewell Junction (G-6283)
Bga Technology LLC...............................E...... 631 750-4600
   Bohemia (G-988)
Ceres Technologies Inc..........................D...... 845 247-4701
   Saugerties (G-14604)
Cold Springs R & D Inc...........................F...... 315 413-1237
   Syracuse (G-15285)
Compositech Ltd....................................C...... 516 835-1458
   Woodbury (G-16615)
Convergent Med MGT Svcs LLC............G...... 718 921-6159
   Brooklyn (G-1715)
Cooper Power Systems LLC...................B...... 716 375-7100
   Olean (G-12597)
Corning Incorporated..............................E...... 607 248-1200
   Corning (G-3812)
Corning Incorporated..............................A...... 607 974-9000
   Corning (G-3809)
Corning Incorporated..............................F...... 607 974-6729
   Painted Post (G-12837)
Corning Specialty Mtls Inc......................G...... 607 974-9000
   Corning (G-3817)
Crystalonics of New York Inc..................F...... 631 981-6140
   Ronkonkoma (G-14331)
Curtiss-Wright Controls..........................F...... 631 756-4740
   Farmingdale (G-4742)
Cvd Equipment Corporation....................C...... 631 981-7081
   Central Islip (G-3365)
Cypress Semiconductor Corp.................F...... 631 261-1358
   Northport (G-12467)
Endicott Interconnect Tech Inc................A...... 866 820-4820
   Endicott (G-4588)
Energy Materials Corporation.................G...... 315 247-0880
   Rochester (G-13784)
Exceltech Inc..F...... 718 423-7262
   Fresh Meadows (G-5197)
General Semiconductor Inc....................G...... 631 300-3818
   Hauppauge (G-5831)
Globalfoundries US 2 LLC......................C...... 512 457-3900
   Hopewell Junction (G-6286)
Globalfoundries US Inc..........................C...... 512 457-3900
   Hopewell Junction (G-6287)
Gurley Precision Instrs Inc......................C...... 518 272-6300
   Troy (G-15607)
H K Technologies Inc.............................G...... 718 255-1898
   Long Island City (G-7465)
Hi-Tron Semiconductor Corp..................E...... 631 231-1500
   Hauppauge (G-5844)
Hipotronics Inc..C...... 845 279-8091
   Brewster (G-1167)
Ilc Holdings Inc.......................................G...... 631 567-5600
   Bohemia (G-1034)
Ilc Industries LLC...................................F...... 631 567-5600
   Bohemia (G-1036)
International Bus Mchs Corp...................C...... 800 426-4968
   Hopewell Junction (G-6289)
Intex Company Inc..................................D...... 516 223-0200
   Freeport (G-5162)
Isine Inc..E...... 631 913-4400
   Melville (G-8040)
J H Rhodes Company Inc.......................F...... 315 829-3600
   Vernon (G-15806)
Kionix Inc..C...... 607 257-1080
   Ithaca (G-6590)
KLA-Tencor Corporation.........................F...... 845 897-1723
   Hopewell Junction (G-6290)
Lakestar Semi Inc...................................F...... 212 974-6254
   New York (G-10510)
Lasermax Inc..D...... 585 272-5420
   Rochester (G-13909)
Lightspin Technologies Inc.....................G...... 301 656-7600
   Endwell (G-4618)
Logitek Inc..D...... 631 567-1100
   Bohemia (G-1048)
M C Products..E...... 631 471-4070
   Holbrook (G-6197)
Marcon Services.....................................G...... 516 223-8019
   Freeport (G-5165)
Marktech International Corp...................E...... 518 956-2980
   Latham (G-7087)
Materion Advanced Materials..................C...... 800 327-1355
   Buffalo (G-2939)

PRODUCT SECTION — SHEET METAL SPECIALTIES, EXC STAMPED

Materion Brewster LLC .... D 845 279-0900
  Brewster *(G-1171)*
McG Electronics Inc .... E 631 586-5125
  Deer Park *(G-4008)*
Micro Contract Manufacturing .... D 631 738-7874
  Medford *(G-7961)*
Micro Semicdtr Researches LLC ..... G 646 863-6070
  New York *(G-10796)*
Microchip Technology Inc .... C 607 785-5992
  Endicott *(G-4602)*
Micromem Technologies .... F 212 672-1806
  New York *(G-10797)*
Mini-Circuits Fort Wayne LLC .... B 718 934-4500
  Brooklyn *(G-2210)*
Mosaic Microsystems LLC .... G 585 314-7441
  Rochester *(G-13958)*
Moser Baer Technologies Inc .... F 585 749-0480
  Fairport *(G-4643)*
Navitar Inc .... D 585 359-4000
  Rochester *(G-13965)*
On Semiconductor Corporation ...... G 585 784-5770
  Rochester *(G-13988)*
Procomponents Inc .... E 516 683-0909
  Westbury *(G-16368)*
Riverhawk Company LP .... E 315 624-7171
  New Hartford *(G-8510)*
RSM Electron Power Inc .... D 631 586-7600
  Hauppauge *(G-5931)*
Ruhle Companies Inc .... E 914 287-4000
  Valhalla *(G-15747)*
Sanrex Corporation .... F 516 625-1313
  Port Washington *(G-13304)*
Schott Corporation .... D 315 255-2791
  Auburn *(G-499)*
Schott Lithotec USA Corp .... D 845 463-5300
  Elmsford *(G-4566)*
Semitronics Corp .... E 516 223-0200
  Freeport *(G-5182)*
Sendyne Corp .... G 212 966-0663
  New York *(G-11542)*
Sinclair Technologies Inc .... E 716 874-3682
  Hamburg *(G-5695)*
Solid Cell Inc .... F 585 426-5000
  Rochester *(G-14133)*
Spectron Glass & Electronics .... F 631 582-5600
  Hauppauge *(G-5943)*
Spectron Systems Technology .... F 631 582-5600
  Hauppauge *(G-5944)*
Spellman High Vltage Elec Corp .... D 914 686-3600
  Valhalla *(G-15748)*
Stetron International Inc .... F 716 854-3443
  Buffalo *(G-3077)*
Sumitomo Elc USA Holdings Inc .... C 212 490-6610
  New York *(G-11738)*
Super Conductor Materials Inc .... F 845 368-0240
  Suffern *(G-15198)*
Swissbit Na Inc .... G 914 935-1400
  Port Chester *(G-13209)*
Symwave Inc .... G 949 542-4400
  Hauppauge *(G-5954)*
Tel Technology Center Amer LLC .. E 512 424-4200
  Albany *(G-133)*
Telephonics Corporation .... E 631 549-6000
  Huntington *(G-6418)*
Thales Laser SA .... D 585 223-2370
  Fairport *(G-4664)*
Tlsi Incorporated .... D 631 470-8880
  Huntington *(G-6422)*
Tokyo Electron America Inc .... G 518 289-3100
  Malta *(G-7732)*
Tokyo Electron America Inc .... G 518 292-4200
  Albany *(G-135)*
Vgg Holding LLC .... G 212 415-6700
  New York *(G-12023)*
Viking Technologies Ltd .... E 631 957-8000
  Lindenhurst *(G-7204)*
Washington Foundries Inc .... D 516 374-8447
  Hewlett *(G-6054)*
Zastech Inc .... E 516 496-4777
  Syosset *(G-15234)*

SENSORS: Temperature For Motor Windings

Irtronics Instruments Inc .... F 914 693-6291
  Ardsley *(G-395)*

SENSORS: Temperature, Exc Indl Process

Titan Controls Inc .... F 516 358-2407
  New York *(G-11850)*

SEPARATORS: Metal Plate

Motivair Corporation .... E 716 691-9222
  Amherst *(G-239)*

SEPTIC TANKS: Concrete

Bistrian Cement Corporation .... F 631 324-1123
  East Hampton *(G-4232)*
H F Cary & Sons .... G 607 598-2563
  Lockwood *(G-7344)*

SEPTIC TANKS: Plastic

Roth Global Plastics Inc .... E 315 475-0100
  Syracuse *(G-15410)*

SERVICES, NEC

G and G Service .... G 518 785-9247
  Latham *(G-7073)*

SERVOMOTORS: Electric

Magna Products Corp .... E 585 647-2280
  Rochester *(G-13923)*

SEWAGE & WATER TREATMENT EQPT

City of Kingston .... F 845 331-2490
  Kingston *(G-6895)*
Ewt Holdings III Corp .... F 212 644-5900
  New York *(G-9744)*
Ferguson Enterprises Inc .... G 800 437-1146
  New Hyde Park *(G-8535)*
Yr Blanc & Co LLC .... G 716 800-3999
  Buffalo *(G-3137)*

SEWAGE TREATMENT SYSTEMS & EQPT

Environment-One Corporation .... C 518 346-6161
  Schenectady *(G-14672)*

SEWER CLEANING EQPT: Power

Dyna-Vac Equipment Inc .... F 315 865-8084
  Stittville *(G-15160)*
Pathfinder 103 Inc .... G 315 363-4260
  Oneida *(G-12620)*

SEWING CONTRACTORS

TSS Foam Industries Corp .... F 585 538-2321
  Caledonia *(G-3159)*

SEWING MACHINES & PARTS: Indl

Herbert Jaffe Inc .... G 718 392-1956
  Long Island City *(G-7468)*
Tompkins Srm LLC .... C 315 422-8763
  Syracuse *(G-15444)*

SEWING, NEEDLEWORK & PIECE GOODS STORE: Needlework Gds/Sply

Viking Athletics Ltd .... E 631 957-8000
  Lindenhurst *(G-7203)*

SEWING, NEEDLEWORK & PIECE GOODS STORES: Sewing & Needlework

Great Adirondack Yarn Company .... F 518 943-3381
  Amsterdam *(G-339)*

SHADES: Lamp & Light, Residential

Custom Lampshades Inc .... F 718 254-0500
  Brooklyn *(G-1742)*
Dreyfus Ashby Inc .... E 212 818-0770
  New York *(G-9578)*

SHADES: Lamp Or Candle

Artemis Studios Inc .... D 718 788-6022
  Brooklyn *(G-1558)*
Blanche P Field LLC .... E 212 355-6616
  New York *(G-9099)*
Diane Studios Inc .... D 718 788-6007
  Brooklyn *(G-1773)*
Jamaica Lamp Corp .... E 718 776-5039
  Queens Village *(G-13409)*
Jimco Lamp & Manufacturing Co ... G 631 218-2152
  Islip *(G-6547)*
Our Own Candle Company Inc .... F 716 769-5000
  Findley Lake *(G-4939)*

Ray Gold Shade Inc .... F 718 377-8892
  Brooklyn *(G-2386)*

SHADES: Window

Mechoshade Systems Inc .... C 718 729-2020
  Long Island City *(G-7520)*
Solar Screen Co Inc .... E 718 592-8222
  Corona *(G-3855)*
Windowcraft Inc .... E 516 294-3580
  Garden City Park *(G-5289)*

SHAFTS: Flexible

BW Elliott Mfg Co LLC .... B 607 772-0404
  Binghamton *(G-873)*
Fait Usa Inc .... G 215 674-5310
  New York *(G-9776)*

SHALE MINING, COMMON

Callahan & Nannini Quarry Inc .... G 845 496-4323
  Salisbury Mills *(G-14539)*
Grosso Materials Inc .... F 845 361-5211
  Montgomery *(G-8312)*

SHALE: Expanded

Norlite LLC .... B 518 235-0030
  Cohoes *(G-3616)*

SHAPES & PILINGS, STRUCTURAL: Steel

Empire Steel Works Inc .... F 516 561-3500
  Hicksville *(G-6084)*
Markin Tubing Inc .... C 585 495-6211
  Wyoming *(G-16700)*
Rochester Structural LLC .... E 585 436-1250
  Rochester *(G-14097)*

SHEATHING: Paper

Sabin Robbins Paper Company ...... E 513 874-5270
  New York *(G-11462)*

SHEET METAL SPECIALTIES, EXC STAMPED

Abdo Shtmtl & Fabrication Inc .... G 315 894-4664
  Barneveld *(G-601)*
Aberdeen Blower & Shtmtl Works .. G 631 661-6100
  West Babylon *(G-16127)*
Aero-Data Metal Crafters Inc .... C 631 471-7733
  Ronkonkoma *(G-14294)*
All Island Blower & Shtmtl .... F 631 567-7070
  Bohemia *(G-976)*
Apparatus Mfg Inc .... G 845 471-5116
  Poughkeepsie *(G-13326)*
Architctral Shetmetal Pdts Inc .... E 518 381-6144
  Scotia *(G-14738)*
Arlan Damper Corporation .... E 631 589-7431
  Bohemia *(G-983)*
Asm USA Inc .... F 212 925-2906
  New York *(G-8934)*
Asp Industries Inc .... E 585 254-9130
  Rochester *(G-13647)*
Avalanche Fabrication Inc .... F 585 545-4000
  Ontario *(G-12648)*
B & B Sheet Metal Inc .... E 718 433-2501
  Long Island City *(G-7396)*
B & H Precision Fabricators .... F 631 563-9620
  Bohemia *(G-984)*
Banner Metalcraft Inc .... D 631 563-7303
  Ronkonkoma *(G-14316)*
Boss Precision Ltd .... D 585 352-7070
  Spencerport *(G-14976)*
Construction Parts Whse Inc .... G 315 445-1310
  East Syracuse *(G-4332)*
Custom Sheet Metal Corp .... G 315 463-9105
  Syracuse *(G-15298)*
Dayton T Brown Inc .... F 631 589-6300
  Bohemia *(G-1011)*
Elmsford Sheet Metal Works Inc .... D 914 739-6300
  Cortlandt Manor *(G-3900)*
Franchet Metal Craft Inc .... E 718 658-6400
  Jamaica *(G-6644)*
Hatfield Metal Fab Inc .... G 845 454-9078
  Poughkeepsie *(G-13345)*
Incodema Inc .... E 607 277-7070
  Ithaca *(G-6582)*
K Barthelmes Mfg Co Inc .... F 585 328-8140
  Rochester *(G-13902)*
McAlpin Industries Inc .... C 585 266-3060
  Rochester *(G-13932)*

Employee Codes: A=Over 500 employees, B=251-500
C=101-250, D=51-100, E=20-50, F=10-19, G=5-9

2019 Harris
New York Manufacturers Directory

SHEET METAL SPECIALTIES, EXC STAMPED

Metal Tek Products .... G 516 586-4514
  Plainview *(G-13073)*
P R B Metal Products Inc .... F 631 467-1800
  Ronkonkoma *(G-14393)*
Prokosch and Sonn Sheet Metal .... E 845 562-4211
  Newburgh *(G-12243)*
Read Manufacturing Company Inc .... E 631 567-4487
  Holbrook *(G-6205)*
S & B Machine Works Inc .... E 516 997-2666
  Westbury *(G-16371)*
S & T Machine Inc .... F 718 272-2484
  Brooklyn *(G-2435)*
Service Mfg Group Inc .... F 716 893-1482
  Buffalo *(G-3063)*
Technimetal Precision Inds .... E 631 231-8900
  Hauppauge *(G-5956)*
Tri-Metal Industries Inc .... E 716 691-3323
  Amherst *(G-257)*
Ulster Precision Inc .... E 845 338-0995
  Kingston *(G-6925)*
Universal Precision Corp .... E 585 321-9760
  Rochester *(G-14189)*
Vin Mar Precision Metals Inc .... F 631 563-6608
  Copiague *(G-3792)*
VM Choppy & Sons LLC .... E 518 266-1444
  Troy *(G-15633)*

SHEET MUSIC STORES

Golfing Magazine .... G 516 822-5446
  Hicksville *(G-6093)*

SHEET MUSIC, WHOLESALE

Carl Fischer LLC .... E 212 777-0900
  New York *(G-9208)*

SHEETING: Laminated Plastic

Advanced Structures Corp .... F 631 667-5000
  Deer Park *(G-3934)*
Allred & Associates Inc .... E 315 252-2559
  Elbridge *(G-4427)*

SHEETS & STRIPS: Aluminum

Alcoa Fastening Systems .... G 585 368-5049
  Rochester *(G-13612)*
Arconic Inc .... D 212 836-2758
  New York *(G-8903)*
Arconic Inc .... G 315 764-4011
  Massena *(G-7900)*

SHEETS: Fabric, From Purchased Materials

Elegant Linen Inc .... E 718 492-0297
  Brooklyn *(G-1823)*

SHELVES & SHELVING: Wood

Forecast Consoles Inc .... E 631 253-9000
  Hauppauge *(G-5827)*
Karp Associates Inc .... D 631 768-8300
  Melville *(G-8041)*

SHELVING: Office & Store, Exc Wood

Abaco Steel Products Inc .... E 631 589-1800
  Bohemia *(G-967)*
Amscor Inc .... F 800 825-9800
  West Babylon *(G-16135)*
Jack Luckner Steel Shelving Co .... D 718 363-0500
  Maspeth *(G-7854)*
Lucia Group Inc .... G 631 392-4900
  Deer Park *(G-4004)*
Sterling Shelf Liners Inc .... E 631 676-5175
  Holbrook *(G-6211)*
Tri-Boro Shelving Inc .... F 718 782-8527
  Ridgewood *(G-13557)*
Your Furniture Designers Inc .... G 845 947-3046
  West Haverstraw *(G-16211)*

SHERARDIZING SVC: Metals Or Metal Prdts

Superior Metals & Processing .... G 718 545-7500
  Long Island City *(G-7609)*

SHIELDS OR ENCLOSURES: Radiator, Sheet Metal

Interior Metals .... E 718 439-7324
  Brooklyn *(G-2008)*
Radiation Shielding Systems .... F 888 631-2278
  Suffern *(G-15196)*

Rand Products Manufacturing Co .... G 518 374-9871
  Schenectady *(G-14706)*
Steelcraft Manufacturing Co .... F 718 277-2404
  Brooklyn *(G-2516)*

SHIMS: Metal

McD Metals LLC .... F 518 456-9694
  Albany *(G-97)*
Romac Electronics Inc .... E 516 349-7900
  Plainview *(G-13085)*

SHIP BUILDING & REPAIRING: Cargo Vessels

Reynolds Shipyard Corporation .... F 718 981-2800
  Staten Island *(G-15128)*

SHIP BUILDING & REPAIRING: Cargo, Commercial

Steelways Inc .... E 845 562-0860
  Newburgh *(G-12246)*

SHIP BUILDING & REPAIRING: Ferryboats

Robert E Derecktor Inc .... D 914 698-0962
  Mamaroneck *(G-7756)*

SHIP BUILDING & REPAIRING: Lighthouse Tenders

Highland Museum & Lighthouse .... F 508 487-1121
  Cairo *(G-3148)*

SHIP BUILDING & REPAIRING: Offshore Sply Boats

Weldrite Closures Inc .... E 585 429-8790
  Pittsford *(G-13028)*

SHIP BUILDING & REPAIRING: Rigging, Marine

Dragon Trading Inc .... E 212 717-1496
  New York *(G-9572)*

SHIP BUILDING & REPAIRING: Tankers

McQuilling Partners Inc .... E 516 227-5718
  Garden City *(G-5270)*

SHIPBUILDING & REPAIR

Caddell Dry Dock & Repr Co Inc .... C 718 442-2112
  Staten Island *(G-15059)*
Excelco Developments Inc .... E 716 934-2651
  Silver Creek *(G-14861)*
Excelco/Newbrook Inc .... D 716 934-2644
  Silver Creek *(G-14862)*
Huntington Ingalls Inc .... E 518 884-3834
  Saratoga Springs *(G-14587)*
May Ship Repair Contg Corp .... E 718 442-9700
  Staten Island *(G-15104)*
Metalcraft Marine Us Inc .... F 315 501-4015
  Cape Vincent *(G-3259)*
Moran Shipyard Corporation .... C 718 981-5600
  Staten Island *(G-15106)*
Port Everglades Machine Works .... F 516 367-2280
  Plainview *(G-13083)*
Viking Mar Wldg Ship Repr LLC .... F 718 758-4116
  Brooklyn *(G-2623)*
World Maritime News .... G 212 477-6700
  New York *(G-12138)*

SHIPPING AGENTS

Hastings Hide Inc .... G 516 295-2400
  Inwood *(G-6492)*

SHOCK ABSORBERS: Indl

Kyntec Corporation .... G 716 810-6956
  Buffalo *(G-2913)*
Taylor Devices Inc .... C 716 694-0800
  North Tonawanda *(G-12459)*

SHOE & BOOT ACCESS

Randall Loeffler Inc .... E 212 226-8787
  New York *(G-11326)*

SHOE MATERIALS: Counters

Counter Evolution .... G 212 647-7505
  New York *(G-9407)*
Custom Countertops Inc .... G 716 685-2871
  Depew *(G-4085)*
Custom Design Kitchens Inc .... F 518 355-4446
  Duanesburg *(G-4155)*

SHOE MATERIALS: Plastic

311 Industries Corp .... G 607 846-4520
  Endicott *(G-4580)*

SHOE MATERIALS: Quarters

Priscilla Quart Co Firts .... G 516 365-2755
  Manhasset *(G-7771)*
Wash Quarters LLC .... G 989 802-2017
  Wallkill *(G-15909)*

SHOE MATERIALS: Sole Parts

MBA Orthotics Inc .... G 631 392-4755
  Bay Shore *(G-699)*

SHOE MATERIALS: Uppers

Northwest Urgent Care .... G 646 870-6406
  New York *(G-10998)*

SHOE REPAIR SHOP

Arimed Orthotics Prosthetics .... F 718 875-8754
  Brooklyn *(G-1551)*

SHOE STORES

GH Bass & Co .... E 646 768-4600
  New York *(G-9917)*
Givi Inc .... F 212 586-5029
  New York *(G-9926)*
Jag Footwear ACC & Ret Corp .... A 800 999-1877
  New York *(G-10299)*
Kcp Holdco Inc .... F 212 265-1500
  New York *(G-10426)*
Kenneth Cole Productions Inc .... B 212 265-1500
  New York *(G-10431)*

SHOE STORES: Children's

Jakes Sneakers Inc .... G 718 233-1132
  Brooklyn *(G-2033)*

SHOE STORES: Custom

Bandier Corp .... G 212 242-5400
  New York *(G-9011)*

SHOE STORES: Orthopedic

Arimed Orthotics Prosthetics .... F 718 875-8754
  Brooklyn *(G-1551)*

SHOE STORES: Women's

Lsil & Co Inc .... G 914 761-0998
  White Plains *(G-16473)*

SHOES & BOOTS WHOLESALERS

Ashko Group LLC .... F 212 594-6050
  New York *(G-8931)*
Jag Footwear ACC & Ret Corp .... A 800 999-1877
  New York *(G-10299)*
Lust For Life Footwear LLC .... F 646 732-9742
  Pearl River *(G-12906)*

SHOES: Athletic, Exc Rubber Or Plastic

Custom Sports Lab Inc .... G 212 832-1648
  New York *(G-9436)*
Kicks Closet Sportswear Inc .... G 347 577-0857
  Bronx *(G-1308)*
Mango Usa Inc .... E 718 998-6050
  Brooklyn *(G-2156)*
Mayberry Shoe Company Inc .... G 315 692-4086
  Manlius *(G-7780)*
McM Products USA Inc .... G 646 756-4090
  New York *(G-10744)*
Reebok International Ltd .... C 718 370-0471
  Staten Island *(G-15126)*
Vsg International LLC .... G 718 300-8171
  Brooklyn *(G-2636)*

PRODUCT SECTION

SIGNS & ADVERTISING SPECIALTIES

SHOES: Ballet Slippers
La Strada Dance Footwear Inc ....G...... 631 242-1401
  Deer Park *(G-3999)*

SHOES: Canvas, Rubber Soled
Inkkas LLC ....G...... 646 845-9803
  New York *(G-10216)*
Little Eric Shoes On Madison ....G...... 212 717-1513
  New York *(G-10580)*
Mango Usa Inc ....E....... 718 998-6050
  Brooklyn *(G-2156)*
Vans Inc ....F....... 631 724-1011
  Lake Grove *(G-6971)*
Vans Inc ....F....... 718 349-2311
  Brooklyn *(G-2617)*

SHOES: Infants' & Children's
Everlast Worldwide Inc ....E...... 212 239-0990
  New York *(G-9738)*
GH Bass & Co ....E...... 646 768-4600
  New York *(G-9917)*
Steven Madden Ltd ....B...... 718 446-1800
  Long Island City *(G-7604)*

SHOES: Men's
Air Skate & Air Jump Corp ....G...... 212 967-1201
  New York *(G-8778)*
Air Skate & Air Jump Corp ....F....... 212 967-1201
  Brooklyn *(G-1496)*
Detny Footwear Inc ....G...... 212 423-1040
  New York *(G-9511)*
GH Bass & Co ....E...... 646 768-4600
  New York *(G-9917)*
Kcp Holdco Inc ....F....... 212 265-1500
  New York *(G-10426)*
Kenneth Cole Productions LP ....E...... 212 265-1500
  New York *(G-10430)*
Kenneth Cole Productions Inc ....B...... 212 265-1500
  New York *(G-10431)*
Lake View Manufacturing LLC ....F....... 315 364-7892
  King Ferry *(G-6881)*
Nicholas Kirkwood LLC ....G...... 646 559-5239
  New York *(G-10962)*
Phillips-Van Heusen Europe ....F....... 212 381-3500
  New York *(G-11183)*
Pvh Corp ....D...... 212 381-3500
  New York *(G-11281)*
Pvh Corp ....G...... 212 549-6000
  New York *(G-11282)*
Steven Madden Ltd ....B...... 718 446-1800
  Long Island City *(G-7604)*
T O Dey Service Corp ....F....... 212 683-6300
  New York *(G-11770)*
Tapestry Inc ....B...... 212 594-1850
  New York *(G-11784)*
Tic TAC Toes Mfg Corp ....D...... 518 773-8187
  Gloversville *(G-5470)*

SHOES: Men's, Sandals
Neumann Jutta New York Inc ....F....... 212 982-7048
  New York *(G-10914)*

SHOES: Orthopedic, Men's
Jerry Miller Molded Shoes Inc ....F....... 716 881-3920
  Buffalo *(G-2893)*
Pedifix Inc ....E...... 845 277-2850
  Brewster *(G-1173)*
Tru Mold Shoes Inc ....F....... 716 881-4484
  Buffalo *(G-3105)*

SHOES: Orthopedic, Women's
Jerry Miller Molded Shoes Inc ....F....... 716 881-3920
  Buffalo *(G-2893)*
Pedifix Inc ....E...... 845 277-2850
  Brewster *(G-1173)*
T O Dey Service Corp ....F....... 212 683-6300
  New York *(G-11770)*
Tru Mold Shoes Inc ....F....... 716 881-4484
  Buffalo *(G-3105)*

SHOES: Plastic Or Rubber
Anthony L & S LLC ....G...... 212 386-7245
  New York *(G-8877)*
Detny Footwear Inc ....G...... 212 423-1040
  New York *(G-9511)*

Homegrown For Good LLC ....F....... 857 540-6361
  New Rochelle *(G-8615)*
Nike Inc ....E...... 212 226-5433
  New York *(G-10967)*
Nike Inc ....E...... 631 242-3014
  Deer Park *(G-4017)*
Nike Inc ....E...... 631 960-0184
  Islip Terrace *(G-6553)*
Nike Inc ....E...... 716 298-5615
  Niagara Falls *(G-12314)*
Skechers USA Inc ....F....... 718 585-3024
  Bronx *(G-1386)*
Timing Group LLC ....F....... 646 878-2600
  New York *(G-11848)*

SHOES: Plastic Or Rubber Soles With Fabric Uppers
Soludos LLC ....F....... 212 219-1101
  New York *(G-11642)*

SHOES: Rubber Or Rubber Soled Fabric Uppers
Crocs Inc ....F....... 845 928-3002
  Central Valley *(G-3394)*

SHOES: Women's
Akh Group LLC ....G...... 646 320-8720
  New York *(G-8780)*
Alpargatas Usa Inc ....E...... 646 277-7171
  New York *(G-8807)*
Detny Footwear Inc ....G...... 212 423-1040
  New York *(G-9511)*
Everlast Worldwide Inc ....E...... 212 239-0990
  New York *(G-9738)*
GH Bass & Co ....E...... 646 768-4600
  New York *(G-9917)*
Kenneth Cole Productions Inc ....B...... 212 265-1500
  New York *(G-10431)*
Lake View Manufacturing LLC ....F....... 315 364-7892
  King Ferry *(G-6881)*
Nicholas Kirkwood LLC ....G...... 646 559-5239
  New York *(G-10962)*
Nine West Holdings Inc ....F....... 212 642-3860
  New York *(G-10976)*
Steven Madden Ltd ....B...... 718 446-1800
  Long Island City *(G-7604)*
Tapestry Inc ....B...... 212 594-1850
  New York *(G-11784)*
Tic TAC Toes Mfg Corp ....D...... 518 773-8187
  Gloversville *(G-5470)*

SHOES: Women's, Dress
Adl Design Inc ....G...... 516 949-6658
  Huntington *(G-6390)*
Attitudes Footwear Inc ....G...... 212 754-9113
  New York *(G-8959)*
Mango Usa Inc ....E...... 718 998-6050
  Brooklyn *(G-2156)*
Scott Silverstein Llc ....G...... 212 781-1818
  New York *(G-11522)*

SHOES: Women's, Sandals
Neumann Jutta New York Inc ....F....... 212 982-7048
  New York *(G-10914)*

SHOPPING CENTERS & MALLS
Northpoint Trading Inc ....F....... 212 481-8001
  New York *(G-10997)*

SHOT PEENING SVC
Metal Improvement Company LLC ......F....... 631 567-2610
  Bay Shore *(G-700)*
Metal Improvement Company LLC ......D...... 607 533-7000
  Lansing *(G-7056)*

SHOWCASES & DISPLAY FIXTURES: Office & Store
Aarco Products Inc ....F....... 631 924-5461
  Yaphank *(G-16703)*
Abbott Industries Inc ....B...... 718 291-0800
  Jamaica *(G-6622)*
Four S Showcase Manufacturing ....G...... 718 649-4900
  Brooklyn *(G-1902)*

Glaro Inc ....D...... 631 234-1717
  Hauppauge *(G-5835)*
Ledan Inc ....E...... 631 239-1226
  Northport *(G-12470)*
Manhattan Display Inc ....G...... 718 392-1365
  Long Island City *(G-7514)*
Steven Kraus Associates Inc ....G...... 631 923-2033
  Huntington *(G-6417)*
Visual Millwork & Fix Mfg Inc ....D...... 718 267-7800
  Deer Park *(G-4061)*

SHOWER STALLS: Metal
ITR Industries Inc ....E...... 914 964-7063
  Yonkers *(G-16771)*

SHOWER STALLS: Plastic & Fiberglass
ITR Industries Inc ....E...... 914 964-7063
  Yonkers *(G-16771)*

SIDING & STRUCTURAL MATERIALS: Wood
Greater Niagara Bldg Ctr Inc ....F....... 716 299-0543
  Niagara Falls *(G-12290)*
Gutchess Lumber Co Inc ....C...... 607 753-3393
  Cortland *(G-3876)*
L J Valente Inc ....G...... 518 674-3750
  Averill Park *(G-515)*
Mohawk Metal Mfg & Sls ....G...... 315 853-7663
  Westmoreland *(G-16407)*
One Tree Dist ....G...... 315 701-2924
  Syracuse *(G-15386)*
Tri-State Brick & Stone NY Inc ....D...... 212 366-0300
  New York *(G-11895)*
Upstate Increte Incorporated ....G...... 585 254-2010
  Rochester *(G-14192)*

SIGN LETTERING & PAINTING SVCS
Sign Shop Inc ....G...... 631 226-4145
  Copiague *(G-3782)*

SIGN PAINTING & LETTERING SHOP
Clinton Signs Inc ....G...... 585 482-1620
  Webster *(G-16080)*
Lanza Corp ....G...... 914 937-6360
  Port Chester *(G-13204)*
Paratore Signs Inc ....G...... 315 455-5551
  Syracuse *(G-15393)*
Ray Sign Inc ....F....... 518 377-1371
  Schenectady *(G-14707)*

SIGNALING APPARATUS: Electric
Intelligent Traffic Systems ....G...... 631 567-5994
  Bohemia *(G-1037)*
L3 Foreign Holdings Inc ....D...... 212 697-1111
  New York *(G-10497)*
L3 Technologies Inc ....B...... 212 697-1111
  New York *(G-10498)*
Werma (usa) Inc ....G...... 315 414-0200
  East Syracuse *(G-4381)*

SIGNALING DEVICES: Sound, Electrical
Sensor Films Incorporated ....E...... 585 738-3500
  Victor *(G-15866)*

SIGNALS: Railroad, Electric
Alstom Signaling Inc ....B...... 585 783-2000
  West Henrietta *(G-16227)*
Alstom Signaling Inc ....E...... 585 274-8700
  Schenectady *(G-14648)*
Star Headlight Lantern Co Inc ....C...... 585 226-9500
  Avon *(G-522)*
Twinco Mfg Co Inc ....E...... 631 231-0022
  Hauppauge *(G-5963)*

SIGNALS: Traffic Control, Electric
Apex Signal Corporation ....D...... 631 567-1100
  Bohemia *(G-981)*
Comet Flasher Inc ....G...... 716 821-9595
  Buffalo *(G-2773)*
Power Line Constructors Inc ....E...... 315 853-6183
  Clinton *(G-3587)*

SIGNS & ADVERTISING SPECIALTIES
A M S Sign Designs ....G...... 631 467-7722
  Centereach *(G-3342)*

Employee Codes: A=Over 500 employees, B=251-500
C=101-250, D=51-100, E=20-50, F=10-19, G=5-9

Aakron Rule Corp .... C 716 542-5483
Akron ***(G-16)***

Accurate Signs & Awnings Inc .... F 718 788-0302
Brooklyn ***(G-1474)***

Acme Signs of Baldwinsville .... G 315 638-4865
Baldwinsville ***(G-547)***

Ad Makers Long Island Inc .... F 631 595-9100
Deer Park ***(G-3933)***

Allied Maker .... F 516 200-9145
Glen Cove ***(G-5360)***

Allstar Graphics Ltd .... E 718 740-2240
Queens Village ***(G-13403)***

Aric Signs & Awnings Inc .... G 516 350-0409
Hempstead ***(G-6006)***

Artscroll Printing Corp .... E 212 929-2413
New York ***(G-8926)***

Asi Sign Systems Inc .... G 646 742-1320
New York ***(G-8932)***

Asi Sign Systems Inc .... G 716 775-0104
Grand Island ***(G-5495)***

BC Communications Inc .... G 631 549-8833
Huntington Station ***(G-6434)***

Bedford Precision Parts Corp .... E 914 241-2211
Bedford Hills ***(G-772)***

Bmg Printing and Promotion LLC .... G 631 231-9200
Bohemia ***(G-989)***

Broadway National Group LLC .... D 800 797-4467
Ronkonkoma ***(G-14321)***

Buckeye Corrugated Inc .... D 585 924-1600
Victor ***(G-15834)***

Central Rede Sign Co Inc .... G 716 213-0797
Tonawanda ***(G-15532)***

Chautauqua Sign Co Inc .... G 716 665-2222
Falconer ***(G-4673)***

Climax Packaging Inc .... C 315 376-8000
Lowville ***(G-7649)***

Coe Displays Inc .... G 718 937-5658
Long Island City ***(G-7412)***

Colad Group LLC .... D 716 961-1776
Buffalo ***(G-2772)***

Colonial Redi Record Corp .... E 718 972-7433
Brooklyn ***(G-1705)***

Community Products LLC .... E 845 658-8351
Rifton ***(G-13560)***

Custom Display Manufacture .... G 516 783-6491
North Bellmore ***(G-12377)***

Designplex LLC .... G 845 358-6647
Nyack ***(G-12504)***

Displays & Beyond Inc .... F 718 805-7786
Glendale ***(G-5398)***

Eastern Metal of Elmira Inc .... D 607 734-2295
Elmira ***(G-4482)***

Elderlee Incorporated .... C 315 789-6670
Oaks Corners ***(G-12527)***

Exhibit Corporation America .... E 718 937-2600
Long Island City ***(G-7441)***

Fastsigns .... F 518 456-7446
Albany ***(G-73)***

Five Star Prtg & Mailing Svcs .... F 212 929-0300
New York ***(G-9815)***

Fletcher Enterprises Inc .... G 716 837-7446
Buffalo ***(G-2828)***

Forrest Engraving Co Inc .... F 845 228-0200
New Rochelle ***(G-8604)***

Fortune Sign .... G 646 383-8682
Brooklyn ***(G-1899)***

G I Certified Inc .... G 212 397-1945
New York ***(G-9867)***

Graphitek Inc .... F 518 686-5966
Hoosick Falls ***(G-6275)***

Greyline Signs Inc .... G 716 947-4526
Derby ***(G-4113)***

Gupp Signs Inc .... G 585 244-5070
Rochester ***(G-13847)***

Hollywood Signs Inc .... G 917 577-7333
Brooklyn ***(G-1980)***

Hospitality Graphic Systems .... F 212 563-9334
New York ***(G-10126)***

Ideal Signs Inc .... G 718 292-9196
Bronx ***(G-1293)***

Image360 .... G 585 272-1234
Rochester ***(G-13878)***

Impressive Imprints Inc .... G 631 293-6161
Farmingdale ***(G-4784)***

Jaf Converters Inc .... E 631 842-3131
Copiague ***(G-3766)***

Jal Signs Inc .... F 516 536-7280
Baldwin ***(G-539)***

Jay Turoff .... F 718 856-7300
Brooklyn ***(G-2035)***

JP Signs .... G 518 569-3907
Chazy ***(G-3432)***

Kenan International Trading .... G 718 672-4922
Corona ***(G-3847)***

Kennyetto Graphics Inc .... E 518 883-6360
Gloversville ***(G-5460)***

KP Industries Inc .... F 516 679-3161
North Bellmore ***(G-12379)***

Kraus & Sons Inc .... F 212 620-0408
New York ***(G-10480)***

L I C Screen Printing Inc .... E 516 546-7289
Merrick ***(G-8100)***

L Miller Design Inc .... G 631 242-1163
Deer Park ***(G-3998)***

L Y Z Creations Ltd Inc .... E 718 768-2977
Brooklyn ***(G-2088)***

Lanco Corporation .... C 631 231-2300
Ronkonkoma ***(G-14368)***

Letterama Inc .... G 516 349-0800
West Babylon ***(G-16170)***

Lifestyle-Trimco .... E 718 257-9101
Brooklyn ***(G-2118)***

Marigold Signs Inc .... F 516 433-7446
Hicksville ***(G-6107)***

Mekanism Inc .... E 212 226-2772
New York ***(G-10767)***

Millennium Signs & Display Inc .... E 516 292-8000
Hempstead ***(G-6021)***

Mixture Screen Printing .... G 845 561-2857
Newburgh ***(G-12232)***

Monasani Signs Inc .... G 631 266-2635
East Northport ***(G-4268)***

Morris Brothers Sign Svc Inc .... G 212 675-9130
New York ***(G-10843)***

Movinads & Signs LLC .... G 518 378-3000
Halfmoon ***(G-5666)***

Mr Sign Usa Inc .... F 718 218-3321
Brooklyn ***(G-2234)***

Nameplate Mfrs of Amer .... E 631 752-0055
Farmingdale ***(G-4831)***

New Art Signs Co Inc .... G 718 443-0900
Glen Head ***(G-5383)***

New Dimensions Research Corp .... C 631 694-1356
Melville ***(G-8049)***

New Kit On The Block .... G 631 757-5655
Bohemia ***(G-1063)***

Noel Assoc .... G 516 371-5420
Inwood ***(G-6498)***

Norampac New York City Inc .... C 718 340-2100
Maspeth ***(G-7863)***

Northeastern Sign Corp .... G 315 265-6657
South Colton ***(G-14926)***

Northern Awning & Sign Company .... G 315 782-8515
Watertown ***(G-16030)***

Nysco Products LLC .... D 718 792-9000
Hawthorne ***(G-5994)***

On The Mark Digital Printing & .... G 716 823-3373
Hamburg ***(G-5689)***

Orlandi Inc .... D 631 756-0110
Farmingdale ***(G-4840)***

Orlandi Inc .... E 631 756-0110
Farmingdale ***(G-4841)***

Promotional Development Inc .... D 718 485-8550
Brooklyn ***(G-2357)***

Quick Sign F X .... F 516 249-6531
Farmingdale ***(G-4862)***

Resonant Legal Media LLC .... D 800 781-3591
New York ***(G-11369)***

Riverwood Signs By Dandev Desi .... G 845 229-0282
Hyde Park ***(G-6471)***

Rpf Associates Inc .... G 631 462-7446
Commack ***(G-3701)***

Saxton Corporation .... E 518 732-7705
Castleton On Hudson ***(G-3297)***

Sellco Industries Inc .... E 607 756-7594
Cortland ***(G-3894)***

Seneca Signs LLC .... G 315 446-9420
Syracuse ***(G-15423)***

Sign A Rama Inc .... G 631 952-3324
Hauppauge ***(G-5939)***

Sign A Rama of Syracuse .... G 315 446-9420
Syracuse ***(G-15425)***

Sign City of New York Inc .... G 718 661-1118
College Point ***(G-3666)***

Sign Company .... G 212 967-2113
New York ***(G-11585)***

Sign Here Enterprises LLC .... G 914 328-3111
Hartsdale ***(G-5744)***

Sign World Inc .... E 212 619-9000
Brooklyn ***(G-2469)***

Signature Industries Inc .... F 516 679-5177
Freeport ***(G-5184)***

Signexpo Enterprises Inc .... F 212 925-8585
New York ***(G-11588)***

Signs Inc .... G 518 483-4759
Malone ***(G-7727)***

Smith Graphics Inc .... G 631 420-4180
Farmingdale ***(G-4876)***

Snyders Neon Displays Inc .... G 518 857-4100
Colonie ***(G-3679)***

Spanjer Corp .... G 347 448-8033
Long Island City ***(G-7595)***

Specialty Signs Co Inc .... F 212 243-8521
New York ***(G-11662)***

Speedy Sign A Rama USA Inc .... G 516 783-1075
Bellmore ***(G-795)***

Sportsdepot Inc .... G 516 543-5018
Baldwin ***(G-544)***

Starlite Media LLC .... G 212 909-7700
New York ***(G-11698)***

Stepping Stones One Day Signs .... G 518 237-5774
Waterford ***(G-15988)***

Tech Products Inc .... E 718 442-4900
Staten Island ***(G-15146)***

Three Gems Inc .... G 516 248-0388
New Hyde Park ***(G-8567)***

Timely Signs of Kingston Inc .... F 845 331-8710
Kingston ***(G-6922)***

Tj Signs Unlimited LLC .... C 631 273-4800
Hicksville ***(G-6137)***

Todd Walbridge .... G 585 254-3018
Rochester ***(G-14171)***

Tru-Art Sign Co Inc .... F 718 658-5068
Jamaica ***(G-6685)***

United Sttes Brnze Sign of Fla .... E 516 352-5155
New Hyde Park ***(G-8570)***

USA Signs of America Inc .... D 631 254-6900
Deer Park ***(G-4057)***

Vez Inc .... G 718 273-7002
Staten Island ***(G-15151)***

Viana Signs Corp .... F 516 887-2000
Oceanside ***(G-12564)***

Visual ID Source Inc .... F 516 307-9759
Mineola ***(G-8251)***

Visual Impact Graphics Inc .... G 585 548-7118
Batavia ***(G-639)***

Voss Signs LLC .... E 315 682-6418
Manlius ***(G-7781)***

Westchester Signs Inc .... G 914 666-7446
Mount Kisco ***(G-8359)***

Wl Concepts & Production Inc .... G 516 538-5300
Freeport ***(G-5190)***

Woodbury Printing Plus + Inc .... G 845 928-6610
Central Valley ***(G-3399)***

Yellowpagecitycom .... F 585 410-6688
Rochester ***(G-14217)***

Z-Car-D Corp .... E 631 424-2077
Huntington Station ***(G-6465)***

SIGNS & ADVERTISING SPECIALTIES: Artwork, Advertising

Adstream America LLC .... E 212 804-8498
New York ***(G-8743)***

Liberty Awnings & Signs Inc .... G 347 203-1470
East Elmhurst ***(G-4223)***

National Prfmce Solutions Inc .... D 718 833-4767
Brooklyn ***(G-2246)***

Pereira & ODell LLC .... G 212 897-1000
New York ***(G-11154)***

Pyx Inc .... G 718 469-4253
Brooklyn ***(G-2364)***

Rocket Fuel Inc .... F 212 594-8888
New York ***(G-11415)***

Rsquared Ny Inc .... D 631 521-8700
Edgewood ***(G-4413)***

United Print Group Inc .... F 718 392-4242
Long Island City ***(G-7623)***

Whispr Group Inc .... F 212 924-3979
New York ***(G-12101)***

SIGNS & ADVERTISING SPECIALTIES: Displays, Paint Process

Chameleon Color Cards Ltd .... D 716 625-9452
Lockport ***(G-7290)***

Faster-Form Corp .... D 800 327-3676
New Hartford ***(G-8504)***

Props Displays & Interiors .... F 212 620-3840
New York ***(G-11266)***

SIGNS & ADVERTISING SPECIALTIES: Letters For Signs, Metal

Brooklyn Signs LLC ......G 718 252-7575
Brooklyn *(G-1648)*

Stickershopcom Inc ......G 631 563-4323
Bayport *(G-739)*

SIGNS & ADVERTISING SPECIALTIES: Novelties

Amsterdam Printing & Litho Inc ......F 518 842-6000
Amsterdam *(G-325)*

Amsterdam Printing & Litho Inc ......E 518 842-6000
Amsterdam *(G-326)*

Dkm Sales LLC ......E 716 893-7777
Buffalo *(G-2802)*

Jomar Industries Inc ......E 845 357-5773
Airmont *(G-14)*

Keep America Beautiful Inc ......G 518 842-4388
Amsterdam *(G-344)*

Kling Magnetics Inc ......E 518 392-4000
Chatham *(G-3428)*

Mastercraft Manufacturing Co ......G 718 729-5620
Long Island City *(G-7517)*

National Advertising & Prtg ......G 212 629-7650
New York *(G-10880)*

Northeast Promotional Group In ......G 518 793-1024
South Glens Falls *(G-14938)*

Pama Enterprises Inc ......G 516 504-6300
Great Neck *(G-5579)*

Sign Men ......G 718 227-7446
Staten Island *(G-15135)*

Tempo Industries Inc ......G 516 334-6900
Westbury *(G-16377)*

Von Pok & Chang New York Inc ......G 212 599-0556
New York *(G-12054)*

SIGNS & ADVERTISING SPECIALTIES: Scoreboards, Electric

Eversan Inc ......F 315 736-3967
Whitesboro *(G-16527)*

SIGNS & ADVERTISING SPECIALTIES: Signs

ABC Windows and Signs Corp ......F 718 353-6210
College Point *(G-3636)*

Adirondack Sign Company LLC ......F 518 409-7446
Saratoga Springs *(G-14566)*

Allstate Sign & Plaque Corp ......F 631 242-2828
Deer Park *(G-3938)*

Art Parts Signs Inc ......G 585 381-2134
East Rochester *(G-4280)*

Big Apple Sign Corp ......E 631 342-0303
Islandia *(G-6522)*

Big Apple Sign Corp ......D 212 629-3650
New York *(G-9076)*

Cab Signs Inc ......E 718 479-2424
Brooklyn *(G-1666)*

Checklist Boards Corporation ......G 585 586-0152
Rochester *(G-13708)*

City Signs Inc ......G 718 375-5933
Brooklyn *(G-1697)*

Crown Sign Systems Inc ......F 914 375-2118
Mount Vernon *(G-8393)*

Decree Signs & Graphics Inc ......F 973 278-3603
Floral Park *(G-4902)*

Dura Engraving Corporation ......E 718 706-6400
Long Island City *(G-7429)*

East End Sign Design Inc ......G 631 399-2574
Mastic *(G-7911)*

Eastern Concepts Ltd ......F 718 472-3377
Sunnyside *(G-15203)*

Executive Sign Corp ......G 212 397-4050
Cornwall On Hudson *(G-3838)*

Executive Sign Corporation ......G 212 397-4050
New York *(G-9752)*

Flado Enterprises Inc ......G 716 668-6400
Depew *(G-4090)*

Fossil Industries Inc ......E 631 254-9200
Deer Park *(G-3979)*

Graphic Signs & Awnings Ltd ......G 718 227-6000
Staten Island *(G-15082)*

Hanson Sign Screen Prcess Corp ......E 716 661-3900
Falconer *(G-4680)*

Hermosa Corp ......E 315 768-4320
New York Mills *(G-12188)*

HI Tech Signs of NY Inc ......G 516 794-7880
East Meadow *(G-4252)*

L S Sign Co Inc ......F 718 469-8600
Ridgewood *(G-13541)*

Linear Signs Inc ......F 631 532-5330
Lindenhurst *(G-7175)*

Mauceri Sign Inc ......F 718 656-7700
Jamaica *(G-6659)*

Modulex New York Inc ......G 646 742-1320
New York *(G-10831)*

Mohawk Sign Systems Inc ......E 518 842-5303
Amsterdam *(G-352)*

Nas Quick Sign Inc ......G 716 876-7599
Buffalo *(G-2961)*

Penn Signs Inc ......E 718 797-1112
Brooklyn *(G-2310)*

Poncio Signs ......G 718 543-4851
Bronx *(G-1360)*

Precision Signscom Inc ......D 631 841-7500
Amityville *(G-314)*

Quorum Group LLC ......D 585 798-8888
Medina *(G-7987)*

Rapp Signs Inc ......F 607 656-8167
Greene *(G-5616)*

Rgm Signs Inc ......G 718 442-0598
Staten Island *(G-15129)*

Rome Sign & Display Co ......G 315 336-0550
Rome *(G-14271)*

Sign Center Inc ......F 212 967-2113
New York *(G-11584)*

Sign Impressions Inc ......G 585 723-0420
Rochester *(G-14127)*

Sign Language Inc ......G 585 237-2620
Perry *(G-12971)*

Sign Studio Inc ......F 518 266-0877
Troy *(G-15626)*

Sign Works Incorporated ......E 914 592-0700
Elmsford *(G-4569)*

Signs of Success Ltd ......F 516 295-6000
Lynbrook *(G-7674)*

Suma Industries Inc ......G 646 436-5202
New York *(G-11736)*

Universal 3d Innovation Inc ......F 516 837-9423
Valley Stream *(G-15801)*

Universal Signs and Svc Inc ......E 631 446-1121
Deer Park *(G-4056)*

Valley Creek Side Inc ......G 315 839-5526
Clayville *(G-3559)*

Victory Signs Inc ......G 315 762-0220
Canastota *(G-3251)*

Vital Signs & Graphics Co Inc ......G 518 237-8372
Cohoes *(G-3623)*

Wizard Equipment Inc ......G 315 414-9999
Syracuse *(G-15459)*

SIGNS & ADVERTSG SPECIALTIES: Displays/Cutouts Window/Lobby

American Visuals Inc ......G 631 694-6104
Farmingdale *(G-4720)*

Creative Solutions Group Inc ......B 914 771-4200
Yonkers *(G-16748)*

Display Marketing Group Inc ......E 631 348-4450
Islandia *(G-6526)*

Display Presentations Ltd ......D 631 951-4050
Brooklyn *(G-1781)*

Display Producers Inc ......C 718 904-1200
New Rochelle *(G-8599)*

DSI Group Inc ......C 800 553-2202
Maspeth *(G-7837)*

Edge Display Group Entp Inc ......F 631 498-1373
Bellport *(G-803)*

Flair Display Inc ......D 718 324-9330
Bronx *(G-1272)*

Hadley Exhibits Inc ......D 716 874-3666
Buffalo *(G-2861)*

Joseph Struhl Co Inc ......F 516 741-3660
New Hyde Park *(G-8544)*

King Displays Inc ......F 212 629-8455
New York *(G-10451)*

Lamar Plastics Packaging Ltd ......D 516 378-2500
Freeport *(G-5163)*

Miller Mohr Display Inc ......G 631 941-2769
East Setauket *(G-4304)*

Mystic Display Co Inc ......G 718 485-2651
Brooklyn *(G-2239)*

Nationwide Exhibitor Svcs Inc ......F 631 467-2034
Central Islip *(G-3379)*

New Style Signs Limited Inc ......F 212 242-7848
New York *(G-10930)*

Newline Products Inc ......C 972 881-3318
New Windsor *(G-8653)*

Platinum Sales Promotion Inc ......G 718 361-0200
Long Island City *(G-7557)*

Polyplastic Forms Inc ......E 631 249-5011
Farmingdale *(G-4853)*

R & J Displays Inc ......E 631 491-3500
West Babylon *(G-16185)*

Royal Promotion Group Inc ......D 212 246-3780
New York *(G-11440)*

Signs & Decal Corp ......E 718 486-6400
Brooklyn *(G-2470)*

Steel-Brite Ltd ......F 631 589-4044
Oakdale *(G-12522)*

Substrate LLC ......E 212 913-9600
Long Island City *(G-7607)*

Timely Signs Inc ......G 516 285-5339
Elmont *(G-4526)*

Unique Display Mfg Corp ......G 516 546-3800
Freeport *(G-5189)*

Visual Citi Inc ......C 631 482-3030
Lindenhurst *(G-7206)*

SIGNS, EXC ELECTRIC, WHOLESALE

Fedex Office & Print Svcs Inc ......G 718 982-5223
Staten Island *(G-15076)*

Mixture Screen Printing ......G 845 561-2857
Newburgh *(G-12232)*

New Kit On The Block ......G 631 757-5655
Bohemia *(G-1063)*

SIGNS: Electrical

A B C Mc Cleary Sign Co Inc ......F 315 493-3550
Carthage *(G-3285)*

Adirondack Sign Perfect Inc ......G 518 409-7446
Saratoga Springs *(G-14567)*

All Signs ......G 973 736-2113
Staten Island *(G-15043)*

Alley Cat Signs Inc ......F 631 924-7446
Middle Island *(G-8117)*

Allied Decorations Co Inc ......F 315 637-0273
Syracuse *(G-15240)*

American Car Signs Inc ......G 518 227-1173
Duanesburg *(G-4154)*

Architectural Sign Group Inc ......G 516 326-1800
Elmont *(G-4516)*

Artkraft Strauss LLC ......E 212 265-5155
New York *(G-8924)*

Clinton Signs Inc ......G 585 482-1620
Webster *(G-16080)*

Flexlume Sign Corporation ......G 716 884-2020
Buffalo *(G-2830)*

Gloede Neon Signs Ltd Inc ......F 845 471-4366
Poughkeepsie *(G-13341)*

ID Signsystems Inc ......E 585 266-5750
Rochester *(G-13874)*

Jax Signs and Neon Inc ......G 607 727-3420
Endicott *(G-4598)*

Jem Sign Corp ......G 516 867-4466
Hempstead *(G-6015)*

Lanza Corp ......G 914 937-6360
Port Chester *(G-13204)*

M Santoliquido Corp ......F 914 375-6674
Yonkers *(G-16780)*

Metropolitan Signs Inc ......F 315 638-1448
Baldwinsville *(G-558)*

Motion Message Inc ......F 631 924-9500
Bellport *(G-809)*

North Shore Neon Sign Co Inc ......E 718 937-4848
Flushing *(G-5031)*

Olson Sign Company Inc ......G 518 370-2118
Schenectady *(G-14701)*

Premier Sign Systems LLC ......E 585 235-0390
Rochester *(G-14040)*

Ray Sign Inc ......F 518 377-1371
Schenectady *(G-14707)*

Sign & Signs ......G 718 941-6200
Brooklyn *(G-2467)*

Sign Design Group New York Inc ......F 718 392-0779
Long Island City *(G-7590)*

Sign Group Inc ......E 718 438-7103
Brooklyn *(G-2468)*

Signs Ink Ltd ......F 914 739-9059
Yorktown Heights *(G-16824)*

Space Sign ......F 718 961-1112
College Point *(G-3667)*

Spectrum On Broadway ......F 718 932-5388
Woodside *(G-16678)*

Spectrum Signs Inc ......E 631 756-1010
Woodside *(G-16679)*

Strategic Signage Sourcing LLC ......F 518 450-1093
Saratoga Springs *(G-14599)*

Employee Codes: A=Over 500 employees, B=251-500
C=101-250, D=51-100, E=20-50, F=10-19, G=5-9

2019 Harris
New York Manufacturers Directory

1253

SIGNS: Electrical

T J Signs Unlimited LLC................E...... 631 273-4800
  Islip *(G-6551)*
Trans-Lux Corporation................D...... 800 243-5544
  New York *(G-11887)*
Ultimate Signs & Designs Inc..........E...... 516 481-0800
  Hempstead *(G-6027)*
Valle Signs and Awnings..............F...... 516 408-3440
  Copiague *(G-3790)*
Visual Effects Inc...................F...... 718 324-0011
  Jamaica *(G-6689)*
Wedel Sign Company Inc..............G...... 631 727-4577
  Riverhead *(G-13588)*

SIGNS: Neon

Bannerboy Corporation................G...... 646 691-6524
  Brooklyn *(G-1585)*
Broadway Neon Sign Corp..............F...... 908 241-4177
  Ronkonkoma *(G-14322)*
K & B Stamping Co Inc................G...... 914 664-8555
  Mount Vernon *(G-8412)*
Manhattan Neon Sign Corp.............F...... 212 714-0430
  New York *(G-10687)*
Super Neon Light Co Inc..............G...... 718 236-5667
  Brooklyn *(G-2534)*
Turoff Tower Graphics Inc............F...... 718 856-7300
  Brooklyn *(G-2593)*
Ulrich Sign Co Inc...................E...... 716 434-0167
  Lockport *(G-7340)*
Yost Neon Displays Inc...............G...... 716 674-6780
  West Seneca *(G-16304)*

SILICA MINING

American Minerals Inc................F...... 646 747-4222
  New York *(G-8834)*
St Silicones Inc.....................G...... 518 664-0745
  Mechanicville *(G-7934)*

SILICON & CHROMIUM

Medima LLC...........................C...... 716 741-0400
  Clarence *(G-3535)*

SILICON WAFERS: Chemically Doped

Isonics Corporation..................G...... 212 356-7400
  New York *(G-10277)*

SILICONE RESINS

George M Dujack......................G...... 518 279-1303
  Troy *(G-15606)*
Meliorum Technologies Inc............G...... 585 313-0616
  Rochester *(G-13935)*
Pawling Corporation..................C...... 845 855-1000
  Pawling *(G-12893)*

SILICONES

Crown Delta Corporation..............E...... 914 245-8910
  Yorktown Heights *(G-16815)*
Momentive Performance Mtls Inc.......A...... 614 986-2495
  Waterford *(G-15980)*
Momentive Performance Mtls Inc.......E...... 518 237-3330
  Waterford *(G-15981)*
Momentive Prfmce Mtls Holdings.......A...... 518 237-3330
  Waterford *(G-15982)*
Mpm Holdings Inc.....................B...... 518 237-3330
  Waterford *(G-15983)*
Mpm Holdings Inc.....................G...... 518 237-3330
  Waterford *(G-15984)*
Mpm Intermediate Holdings Inc........G...... 518 237-3330
  Waterford *(G-15985)*
Mpm Silicones LLC....................A...... 518 233-3330
  Waterford *(G-15986)*
Specialty Silicone Pdts Inc..........D...... 518 885-8620
  Ballston Spa *(G-596)*

SILK SCREEN DESIGN SVCS

Buffalo Circuits Inc.................G...... 716 662-2113
  Orchard Park *(G-12703)*
Mainly Monograms Inc.................E...... 845 624-4923
  West Nyack *(G-16275)*

SILVER ORES

Global Gold Corporation..............F...... 914 925-0020
  Rye *(G-14481)*

SILVER ORES PROCESSING

Rochester Silver Works LLC...........E...... 585 477-9501
  Rochester *(G-14093)*

SILVERSMITHS

D W Haber & Son Inc..................E...... 718 993-6405
  Bronx *(G-1251)*
Denvin Inc...........................E...... 718 232-3389
  Brooklyn *(G-1768)*
R Goldsmith..........................F...... 718 239-1396
  Bronx *(G-1370)*

SILVERWARE

Studio Silversmiths Inc..............E...... 718 418-6785
  Ridgewood *(G-13553)*

SILVERWARE & PLATED WARE

Oneida International Inc.............G...... 315 361-3000
  Oneida *(G-12615)*
Oneida Silversmiths Inc..............G...... 315 361-3000
  Oneida *(G-12619)*

SILVERWARE, SILVER PLATED

Sherrill Manufacturing Inc...........C...... 315 280-0727
  Sherrill *(G-14822)*

SIMULATORS: Electronic Countermeasure

Rodale Wireless Inc..................E...... 631 231-0044
  Hauppauge *(G-5929)*

SIMULATORS: Flight

BSC Associates LLC...................F...... 607 321-2980
  Binghamton *(G-872)*
Northrop Grumman Intl Trdg Inc.......G...... 716 626-7233
  Buffalo *(G-2975)*

SINKS: Vitreous China

Kraus USA Inc........................F...... 800 775-0703
  Port Washington *(G-13278)*

SKIN CARE PRDTS: Suntan Lotions & Oils

St Tropez Inc........................G...... 800 366-6383
  New York *(G-11690)*

SKYLIGHTS

Citros Building Materials Co.........E...... 718 779-0727
  East Elmhurst *(G-4219)*
Gottlieb Schwartz Family.............E...... 718 761-2010
  Staten Island *(G-15080)*

SLAB & TILE: Precast Concrete, Floor

Duranm Inc...........................G...... 914 774-3367
  Cortlandt Manor *(G-3899)*
Rain Catchers Seamless Gutters.......G...... 516 520-1956
  Bethpage *(G-852)*

SLABS: Steel

Safespan Platform Systems Inc........E...... 716 694-1100
  Tonawanda *(G-15574)*

SLATE PRDTS

Evergreen Slate Company Inc..........D...... 518 642-2530
  Middle Granville *(G-8109)*
North American Slate Inc.............G...... 518 642-1702
  Granville *(G-5523)*
Northeast Solite Corporation.........E...... 845 246-2177
  Mount Marion *(G-8365)*
Sheldon Slate Products Co Inc........E...... 518 642-1280
  Middle Granville *(G-8112)*
Vermont Natural Stoneworks...........E...... 518 642-2460
  Middle Granville *(G-8114)*

SLATE: Dimension

Vermont Multicolor Slate.............G...... 518 642-2400
  Middle Granville *(G-8113)*

SLINGS: Rope

All-Lifts Incorporated...............E...... 518 465-3461
  Albany *(G-38)*

SLIP RINGS

Princetel Inc........................F...... 914 579-2410
  Hawthorne *(G-5996)*

SLIPPERS: House

RG Barry Corporation.................F...... 212 244-3145
  New York *(G-11382)*

SMOKE DETECTORS

Fuel Watchman Sales & Service........F...... 718 665-6100
  Bronx *(G-1276)*
Nrd LLC..............................E...... 716 773-7634
  Grand Island *(G-5508)*

SNOW PLOWING SVCS

Northeastern Sealcoat Inc............F...... 585 544-4372
  Rochester *(G-13979)*

SOAPS & DETERGENTS

Aura Detergent LLC...................G...... 718 824-2162
  Bronx *(G-1223)*
Baums Castorine Company Inc..........G...... 315 336-8154
  Rome *(G-14247)*
Colgate-Palmolive Company............A...... 212 310-2000
  New York *(G-9349)*
Colgate-Palmolive Nj Inc.............E...... 212 310-2000
  New York *(G-9350)*
Cosco Enterprises Inc................G...... 718 383-4488
  Ridgewood *(G-13533)*
Cosco Interprises Inc................E...... 718 417-8995
  Ridgewood *(G-13534)*
Cpac Inc.............................E...... 585 382-3223
  Leicester *(G-7126)*
Crosstex International Inc...........D...... 631 582-6777
  Hauppauge *(G-5805)*
Dr Jacobs Naturals LLC...............E...... 718 265-1522
  Brooklyn *(G-1791)*
Ecolab Inc...........................F...... 716 683-6298
  Cheektowaga *(G-3443)*
Enviro Service & Supply Corp.........F...... 347 838-6500
  Staten Island *(G-15074)*
Gfl USA Inc..........................G...... 917 297-8701
  Brooklyn *(G-1924)*
Greenmaker Industries LLC............F...... 866 684-7800
  Farmingdale *(G-4776)*
H & H Laboratories Inc...............F...... 718 624-8041
  Brooklyn *(G-1955)*
H & H Laboratories Inc...............F...... 718 624-8041
  Brooklyn *(G-1956)*
Medtech Products Inc.................F...... 914 524-6810
  Tarrytown *(G-15482)*
Monroe Fluid Technology Inc..........E...... 585 392-3434
  Hilton *(G-6157)*
Natures Warehouse....................F...... 800 215-4372
  Philadelphia *(G-12985)*
Pro-Line Solutions Inc...............G...... 914 664-0002
  Mount Vernon *(G-8434)*
Robert Racine........................E...... 518 677-0224
  Cambridge *(G-3183)*
Sunfeather Natural Soap Co Inc.......G...... 315 265-1776
  Potsdam *(G-13324)*

SOAPS & DETERGENTS: Textile

T S Pink Corp........................F...... 607 432-1100
  Oneonta *(G-12646)*

SOCIAL SERVICES INFORMATION EXCHANGE

Human Life Foundation Inc............G...... 212 685-5210
  New York *(G-10148)*

SOCIAL SVCS, HANDICAPPED

Choice Magazine Listening Inc........G...... 516 883-8280
  Port Washington *(G-13249)*

SOCIAL SVCS: Individual & Family

Maramont Corporation.................B...... 718 439-8900
  Brooklyn *(G-2163)*
Suffolk Community Council Inc........G...... 631 434-9277
  Deer Park *(G-4049)*

SOFT DRINKS WHOLESALERS

Load/N/Go Beverage Corp..............F...... 585 218-4019
  Rochester *(G-13915)*

Save More Beverage Corp .....G..... 518 371-2520
Halfmoon *(G-5669)*

SOFTWARE PUBLISHERS: Application

30dc Inc .....F..... 212 962-4400
New York *(G-8677)*
Adobe Systems Incorporated .....E..... 212 471-0904
New York *(G-8741)*
Advanced Comfort Systems Inc .....F..... 518 884-8444
Ballston Spa *(G-574)*
Aimsun Inc .....G..... 917 267-8534
New York *(G-8776)*
Amcom Software Inc .....G..... 212 951-7600
New York *(G-8817)*
Ansa Systems of USA Inc .....G..... 718 835-3743
Valley Stream *(G-15772)*
Automated & MGT Solutions LLC .....G..... 518 833-0315
East Greenbush *(G-4227)*
Big White Wall Holding Inc .....F..... 917 281-2649
New York *(G-9079)*
Bigwood Systems Inc .....G..... 607 257-0915
Ithaca *(G-6560)*
Birdsigns Inc .....G..... 201 388-7613
New York *(G-9089)*
Braze Inc .....E..... 504 327-7269
New York *(G-9137)*
Bull Street LLC .....G..... 212 495-9855
New York *(G-9156)*
C S I G Inc .....G..... 845 383-3800
Kingston *(G-6891)*
Callaway Digital Arts Inc .....E..... 212 675-3050
New York *(G-9182)*
Capital Programs Inc .....G..... 212 842-4640
New York *(G-9204)*
Catalyst Group Inc .....G..... 212 243-7777
New York *(G-9226)*
Catch Ventures Inc .....F..... 347 620-4351
New York *(G-9228)*
Cbord Group Inc .....C..... 607 257-2410
Ithaca *(G-6571)*
Ceipal LLC .....G..... 585 584-1316
Rochester *(G-13698)*
Citic Intl (usa) Travel Inc .....G..... 718 888-9577
Flushing *(G-4992)*
Cloud Rock Group LLC .....G..... 516 967-6023
Roslyn *(G-14444)*
Cloudparc Inc .....G..... 954 665-5962
New York *(G-9332)*
Contactive Inc .....E..... 646 476-9059
New York *(G-9387)*
Crowd Media Inc .....G..... 212 497-1100
New York *(G-9424)*
Customshow Inc .....G..... 800 255-5303
New York *(G-9438)*
Dbase LLC .....G..... 607 729-0234
Binghamton *(G-879)*
Document Strategies LLC .....F..... 585 506-9000
Rochester *(G-13748)*
Dwnld Inc .....E..... 484 483-6572
New York *(G-9592)*
Eft Analytics Inc .....G..... 212 290-2300
New York *(G-9634)*
Elepath Inc .....G..... 347 417-4975
Brooklyn *(G-1825)*
Empire Innovation Group LLC .....F..... 716 852-5000
Buffalo *(G-2818)*
Evidon Inc .....D..... 917 262-2530
New York *(G-9740)*
Evocate Media LLC .....F..... 646 361-3014
New York *(G-9741)*
Exchange My Mail Inc .....F..... 516 605-1835
Jericho *(G-6788)*
Express Checkout LLC .....G..... 646 512-2068
New York *(G-9756)*
Filestream Inc .....F..... 516 759-4100
Locust Valley *(G-7347)*
Financial Technologies 360 Inc .....G..... 862 200-1164
Whitestone *(G-16540)*
Freshop Inc .....E..... 585 738-6035
Rochester *(G-13818)*
Galaxy Software LLC .....G..... 631 244-8405
Oakdale *(G-12516)*
Geoweb3d Inc .....F..... 607 323-1114
Vestal *(G-15817)*
Grantoo LLC .....G..... 646 356-0460
New York *(G-9974)*
Gresham Technologies (us) Inc .....F..... 646 943-5955
New York *(G-9985)*
High Performance Sftwr USA Inc .....E..... 866 616-4958
Valley Stream *(G-15782)*
Hvr Mso LLC .....G..... 833 345-6974
Poughkeepsie *(G-13346)*
Hydrogen Technology Corp .....E..... 800 315-9554
New York *(G-10154)*
Identifycom Inc .....G..... 212 235-0000
New York *(G-10173)*
Incentivate Health LLC .....G..... 518 469-8491
Saratoga Springs *(G-14588)*
Incycle Software Corp .....F..... 212 626-2608
New York *(G-10195)*
Infomir LLC .....F..... 631 482-6636
Brooklyn *(G-2002)*
Innofun Digital Entrmt LLC .....F..... 347 708-0078
New York *(G-10217)*
INTEL Corporation .....D..... 408 765-8080
Getzville *(G-5348)*
Intraworlds Inc .....G..... 631 602-5333
New York *(G-10259)*
Jump Ramp Games Inc .....E..... 212 500-1456
New York *(G-10379)*
Jvl Ventures LLC .....D..... 212 365-7555
New York *(G-10389)*
Kik Us Inc .....F..... 519 505-7616
New York *(G-10443)*
Knight Life Entertainment .....G..... 646 733-8911
Brooklyn *(G-2078)*
Live Vote II Inc .....G..... 646 343-9053
New York *(G-10583)*
Lookbooks Media Inc .....F..... 646 737-3360
New York *(G-10600)*
Lovingly LLC .....E..... 845 977-0775
Fishkill *(G-4948)*
Lubbu Inc .....G..... 917 693-9600
Sag Harbor *(G-14500)*
Luluvise Inc .....E..... 914 309-7812
New York *(G-10630)*
Madhat Inc .....G..... 518 947-0732
New York *(G-10656)*
Mall Inc .....G..... 315 751-9490
Cazenovia *(G-3322)*
Marcus Goldman Inc .....F..... 212 431-0707
New York *(G-10700)*
Medidata Solutions Inc .....B..... 212 918-1800
New York *(G-10758)*
Mej Beats LLC .....G..... 516 707-6655
New York *(G-10766)*
Microsoft Corporation .....A..... 914 323-2150
White Plains *(G-16477)*
Microsoft Corporation .....F..... 212 245-2100
New York *(G-10798)*
Microsoft Corporation .....D..... 516 380-1531
Hauppauge *(G-5891)*
Microstrategy Incorporated .....F..... 888 537-8135
New York *(G-10799)*
Mml Software Ltd .....E..... 631 941-1313
East Setauket *(G-4305)*
Molabs Inc .....G..... 310 721-6828
New York *(G-10833)*
Nervve Technologies Inc .....E..... 716 800-2250
New York *(G-10907)*
New York State Assoc .....F..... 518 434-2281
Albany *(G-102)*
Omx (us) Inc .....A..... 646 428-2800
New York *(G-11040)*
One-Blue LLC .....G..... 212 223-4380
New York *(G-11044)*
P8h Inc .....E..... 212 343-1142
Brooklyn *(G-2298)*
Pexip Inc .....E..... 703 338-3544
New York *(G-11172)*
Piano Software Inc .....D..... 646 350-1999
New York *(G-11188)*
Pingmd Inc .....G..... 212 632-2665
New York *(G-11196)*
Piwik Pro LLC .....E..... 888 444-0049
New York *(G-11202)*
Playground NY Inc .....F..... 505 920-7236
Brooklyn *(G-2325)*
Plectica LLC .....G..... 917 304-7052
New York *(G-11210)*
Preplay Inc .....G..... 917 297-7428
New York *(G-11232)*
Proginet Corporation .....E..... 516 535-3600
Garden City *(G-5276)*
Pts Financial Technology LLC .....E..... 844 825-7634
New York *(G-11272)*
Raleigh and Drake Pbc .....F..... 212 625-8212
New York *(G-11320)*
Revivn Public Benefit Corp .....F..... 347 762-8193
Brooklyn *(G-2399)*
Robert Ehrlich .....G..... 516 353-4617
New York *(G-11407)*
Robot Fruit Inc .....F..... 631 423-7250
Huntington *(G-6411)*
Runs Capital Inc .....E..... 212 618-1201
New York *(G-11448)*
Runs Inc .....E..... 212 618-1201
New York *(G-11449)*
SC Building Solutions LLC .....D..... 800 564-1152
New York *(G-11497)*
Signpost Inc .....C..... 877 334-2837
New York *(G-11589)*
Splacer Inc .....G..... 646 853-9789
New York *(G-11672)*
Spring Inc .....G..... 646 732-0323
New York *(G-11680)*
Streetcred Nyc LLC .....G..... 646 675-0073
New York *(G-11721)*
Striata Inc .....D..... 212 918-4677
New York *(G-11722)*
Synced Inc .....G..... 917 565-5591
New York *(G-11761)*
Tabi Inc .....G..... 347 701-1051
Flushing *(G-5051)*
Theirapp LLC .....E..... 212 896-1255
New York *(G-11810)*
Thing Daemon Inc .....E..... 917 746-9895
New York *(G-11815)*
Tootter Inc .....E..... 212 204-7937
Brooklyn *(G-2571)*
Tpa Computer Corp .....F..... 877 866-6044
Carmel *(G-3282)*
Trac Medical Solutions Inc .....G..... 518 346-7799
Schenectady *(G-14722)*
Treauu Inc .....G..... 703 731-0196
New York *(G-11889)*
Usq Group LLC .....G..... 212 777-7751
New York *(G-11982)*
Vhx Corporation .....F..... 347 689-1446
New York *(G-12024)*
Virtual Frameworks Inc .....F..... 646 690-8207
New York *(G-12040)*
Vision Logic Inc .....G..... 212 729-4606
New York *(G-12042)*
West Internet Trading Company .....G..... 415 484-5848
New York *(G-12095)*
White Label Partners LLC .....G..... 917 445-6650
New York *(G-12103)*
Whiteboard Ventures Inc .....F..... 855 972-6346
New York *(G-12105)*
Winesoft International Corp .....G..... 914 400-6247
Yonkers *(G-16808)*
Wink Inc .....E..... 212 389-1382
New York *(G-12121)*
Wink Labs Inc .....E..... 916 717-0437
New York *(G-12122)*
Xborder Entertainment LLC .....G..... 518 726-7036
Plattsburgh *(G-13171)*
Zipari Inc .....E..... 855 558-7884
Brooklyn *(G-2669)*

SOFTWARE PUBLISHERS: Business & Professional

Aarfid LLC .....G..... 716 992-3999
Eden *(G-4386)*
Abacus Labs Inc .....E..... 917 426-6642
New York *(G-8704)*
Abel Noser Solutions LLC .....E..... 646 432-4000
New York *(G-8708)*
Adfin Solutions Inc .....F..... 650 464-0742
New York *(G-8736)*
Adgorithmics LLC .....G..... 646 277-8728
New York *(G-8737)*
Adl Data Systems Inc .....E..... 914 591-1800
Elmsford *(G-4528)*
Agrinetix Cmpt Systems LLC .....F..... 877 978-5477
Henrietta *(G-6029)*
Amplience Inc .....G..... 917 410-7189
New York *(G-8848)*
Andigo New Media Inc .....G..... 212 727-8445
New York *(G-8857)*
Appfigures Inc .....F..... 212 343-7900
New York *(G-8891)*
Application Security Inc .....D..... 212 912-4100
New York *(G-8892)*
Apprenda Inc .....D..... 518 383-2130
Troy *(G-15600)*
Articulate Global Inc .....C..... 800 861-4880
New York *(G-8919)*

PRODUCT

Employee Codes: A=Over 500 employees, B=251-500
C=101-250, D=51-100, E=20-50, F=10-19, G=5-9
2019 Harris
New York Manufacturers Directory
1255

SOFTWARE PUBLISHERS: Business & Professional — PRODUCT SECTION

Company	Code	Phone
Aspen Research Group Ltd — New York *(G-8935)*	G	212 425-9588
Augury Inc — New York *(G-8960)*	E	866 432-0976
Automated Office Systems Inc — Valley Stream *(G-15773)*	F	516 396-5555
Aycan Medical Systems LLC — Rochester *(G-13649)*	F	585 271-3078
B601 V2 Inc — New York *(G-8995)*	G	646 391-6431
Beyondly Inc — New York *(G-9065)*	E	646 658-3665
Big Data Bizviz LLC — West Seneca *(G-16294)*	G	716 803-2367
Blue Wolf Group LLC — New York *(G-9110)*	D	866 455-9653
Botify Corporation — New York *(G-9124)*	G	617 576-2005
Boundless Spatial Inc — New York *(G-9128)*	E	646 831-5531
Broadway Technology LLC — New York *(G-9146)*	E	646 912-6450
Business Integrity Inc — New York *(G-9162)*	G	718 238-2008
Business Management Systems — Brooklyn *(G-1661)*	F	914 245-8558
Ca Inc — New York *(G-9171)*	A	800 225-5224
Ca Inc — Islandia *(G-6523)*	A	800 225-5224
Callidus Software Inc — New York *(G-9183)*	F	212 554-7300
Caminus Corporation — New York *(G-9187)*	D	212 515-3600
Candex Solutions Inc — New York *(G-9193)*	G	215 650-3214
Careconnector — Brooklyn *(G-1677)*	G	919 360-2987
Chequedcom Inc — Saratoga Springs *(G-14575)*	E	888 412-0699
Clearview Social Inc — Buffalo *(G-2767)*	G	801 414-7675
Cloudscale365 Inc — Jericho *(G-6782)*	G	888 608-6245
Condeco Software Inc — New York *(G-9376)*	E	408 508-7330
Confiant Inc — New York *(G-9378)*	F	646 397-4198
Continuity Software Inc — New York *(G-9389)*	E	646 216-8628
Cross Border Transactions LLC — Tarrytown *(G-15476)*	F	646 767-7342
Crunched Inc — New York *(G-9427)*	G	415 484-9909
Cuffs Planning & Models Ltd — New Rochelle *(G-8597)*	G	914 632-1883
Curaegis Technologies Inc — Rochester *(G-13729)*	E	585 254-1100
Cureatr Inc — New York *(G-9435)*	E	212 203-3927
Dartcom Incorporated — New Hartford *(G-8502)*	G	315 790-5456
Diligent Corporation — New York *(G-9529)*	C	212 741-8181
Dow Jones & Company Inc — New York *(G-9564)*	E	212 597-5983
Dropcar Operating Company Inc — New York *(G-9579)*	G	646 342-1595
EBM Care Inc — New York *(G-9616)*	F	212 500-5000
Ebrevia Inc — New York *(G-9618)*	E	203 870-3000
Eccella Corporation — New York *(G-9619)*	G	718 612-0451
Efront Financial Solutions Inc — New York *(G-9633)*	E	212 220-0660
Elodina Inc — New York *(G-9658)*	G	646 402-5202
Endava Inc — New York *(G-9675)*	F	212 920-7240
Equilend Holdings LLC — New York *(G-9695)*	E	212 901-2200
Exact Solutions Inc — New York *(G-9747)*	F	212 707-8627
EZ Systems US Inc — Brooklyn *(G-1862)*	C	929 295-0699
F-O-R Software LLC — White Plains *(G-16449)*	E	914 220-8800
Fastnet Software Intl Inc — East Northport *(G-4263)*	F	888 740-7790
Findmine Inc — New York *(G-9802)*	F	925 787-6181
Flextrade Systems Inc — Great Neck *(G-5558)*	C	516 627-8993
Frazer Computing Inc — Canton *(G-3257)*	E	315 379-3500
Gifts Software Inc — New York *(G-9918)*	E	904 438-6000
Glassbox US Inc — New York *(G-9931)*	D	917 378-2933
Globalquest Solutions Inc — Buffalo *(G-2851)*	F	716 601-3524
Happy Software LLC — Saratoga Springs *(G-14586)*	G	518 584-4668
Heartland Commerce Inc — Pearl River *(G-12898)*	E	845 920-0800
Highside Inc — New York *(G-10098)*	F	917 525-3340
Hovee Inc — New York *(G-10139)*	F	646 249-6200
Igambit Inc — Smithtown *(G-14900)*	G	631 670-6777
Innroad Inc — New York *(G-10220)*	E	631 458-1437
Inprotopia Corporation — New York *(G-10224)*	F	917 338-7501
Ivalua Inc — Brooklyn *(G-2020)*	F	650 930-9710
Kasisto Inc — New York *(G-10412)*	E	917 734-4750
Kindling Inc — New York *(G-10449)*	F	212 400-6296
Klara Technologies Inc — New York *(G-10456)*	F	844 215-5272
Latchable Inc — New York *(G-10521)*	E	646 833-0604
Laurus Development Inc — Buffalo *(G-2922)*	F	716 823-1202
Liftforward Inc — New York *(G-10566)*	F	917 693-4993
Livetiles Corp — New York *(G-10585)*	F	917 472-7887
Loyaltyplant Inc — Forest Hills *(G-5076)*	F	551 221-2701
Market Factory Inc — New York *(G-10709)*	F	212 625-9988
Medius Software Inc — New York *(G-10760)*	F	877 295-0058
Micro Systems Specialists Inc — Millbrook *(G-8189)*	G	845 677-6150
Mobo Systems Inc — New York *(G-10828)*	D	212 260-0895
Navatar Group Inc — New York *(G-10899)*	F	212 863-9655
Network Infrstructure Tech Inc — New York *(G-10913)*	C	212 404-7340
Neverware Inc — New York *(G-10916)*	F	516 302-3223
Nift Group Inc — Brooklyn *(G-2269)*	F	504 505-1144
Nikish Software Corp — Northport *(G-12473)*	F	631 754-1618
Noetic Partners Inc — New York *(G-10984)*	F	212 836-4351
Numerix LLC — New York *(G-11007)*	D	212 302-2220
Operative Media Inc — New York *(G-11050)*	F	212 994-8930
Oracle Corporation — New York *(G-11053)*	C	212 508-7700
Orangenius Inc — New York *(G-11054)*	F	631 742-0648
Ordergroove Inc — New York *(G-11060)*	E	866 253-1261
Orthstar Enterprises Inc — Horseheads *(G-6323)*	D	607 562-2100
Ougra Inc — Long Island City *(G-7543)*	G	646 342-4575
Pb Mapinfo Corporation — Troy *(G-15614)*	A	518 285-6000
Pegasystems Inc — New York *(G-11141)*	F	212 626-6550
Pilot Inc — New York *(G-11193)*	G	212 951-1133
Pilot Inc — New York *(G-11194)*	G	212 951-1133
Pointman LLC — Buffalo *(G-3008)*	G	716 842-1439
Powa Technologies Inc — New York *(G-11225)*	F	347 344-7848
Premier Heart LLC — Port Washington *(G-13298)*	G	516 883-3383
Pricing Engine Inc — New York *(G-11238)*	F	917 549-3289
Principia Partners LLC — New York *(G-11244)*	D	212 480-2270
Purebase Networks Inc — New York *(G-11277)*	G	646 670-8964
Quality and Asrn Tech Corp — Ridge *(G-13523)*	G	646 450-6762
Rational Retention LLC — Albany *(G-123)*	E	518 489-3000
Ray Theta Inc — New York *(G-11332)*	G	646 757-4956
Reality Analytics Inc — New York *(G-11340)*	G	347 363-2200
Relavis Corporation — New York *(G-11352)*	E	212 995-2900
Ringlead Inc — Melville *(G-8061)*	F	310 906-0545
Rision Inc — New York *(G-11395)*	E	212 987-2628
Ritnoa Inc — Bellerose *(G-782)*	E	212 660-2148
RPS Holdings Inc — Ithaca *(G-6609)*	E	607 257-7778
Sakonnet Technology LLC — New York *(G-11466)*	E	212 849-9267
Sales Hacker Inc — New York *(G-11469)*	G	516 660-2836
Sapphire Systems Inc — New York *(G-11486)*	F	212 905-0100
Sefaira Inc — New York *(G-11533)*	E	855 733-2472
Serraview America Inc — New York *(G-11545)*	D	800 903-3716
Servicenow Inc — New York *(G-11546)*	F	914 318-1168
Shake Inc — New York *(G-11555)*	F	650 544-5479
Siemens Product Life Mgmt Sftw — Fairport *(G-4659)*	E	585 389-8699
Sixteen Markets Inc — New York *(G-11603)*	F	347 759-1024
Skystem LLC — New York *(G-11616)*	G	877 778-3320
Solve Advisors Inc — Rockville Centre *(G-14241)*	G	646 699-5041
Stop N Shop LLC — Albany *(G-131)*	G	518 512-9657
Structured Retail Products — New York *(G-11724)*		212 224-3692
Structuredweb Inc — New York *(G-11725)*	E	201 325-3110
Styleclick Inc — New York *(G-11730)*	D	212 329-0300
Symphony Talent LLC — New York *(G-11759)*		212 999-9000
Synergy Resources Inc — Central Islip *(G-3385)*	D	631 665-2050
Syntel Inc — New York *(G-11765)*		212 785-9810
Team Builders Inc — Staten Island *(G-15145)*	F	718 979-1005
Tech Software LLC — Melville *(G-8070)*		516 986-3050
Telmar Information Services — New York *(G-11798)*	E	212 725-3000
Thinktrek Inc — New York *(G-11816)*	F	212 884-8399
Tika Mobile Inc — New York *(G-11834)*		646 650-5545
Touchcare P LLC — New York *(G-11875)*	F	646 824-5373
Transportgistics Inc — Mount Sinai *(G-8370)*	F	631 567-4100
Trueex LLC — New York *(G-11904)*	E	646 786-8526
Trustfort LLC — Holbrook *(G-6216)*	G	781 787-0906
Tyme Global Technologies LLC — New York *(G-11923)*	E	212 796-1950
UI Information & Insights Inc — Latham *(G-7096)*	E	518 640-9200
Ullink Inc — New York *(G-11935)*	F	646 565-6675
Unqork Inc — New York *(G-11963)*		844 486-7675
Varnish Software Inc — New York *(G-11996)*	G	201 857-2832

Varonis Systems Inc .... D 877 292-8767
New York (G-11997)
Varsity Monitor LLC .... G 212 691-6292
New York (G-11998)
Virtuvent Inc .... G 855 672-8677
Brooklyn (G-2628)
Vita Rara Inc .... G 518 369-7356
Troy (G-15631)
Whentech LLC .... F 212 571-0042
New York (G-12100)
Wochit Inc .... G 212 979-8343
New York (G-12128)
Ypis of Staten Island Inc .... G 718 815-4557
Staten Island (G-15153)
Zoomifier Corporation .... D 800 255-5303
New York (G-12183)

SOFTWARE PUBLISHERS: Computer Utilities

Vline Inc .... G 512 222-5464
Brooklyn (G-2632)
Wagner Technical Services Inc .... F 845 566-4018
Newburgh (G-12250)

SOFTWARE PUBLISHERS: Education

Accelify Solutions LLC .... E 888 922-2354
New York (G-8718)
Assessment Technologies Inc .... G 646 530-8666
New York (G-8937)
Brainpop LLC .... E 212 574-6017
New York (G-9133)
Childrens Progress Inc .... E 212 730-0905
New York (G-9276)
Classroom Inc .... E 212 545-8400
New York (G-9323)
Coalition On Positive Health .... F 212 633-2500
New York (G-9341)
Cognotion Inc .... G 347 692-0640
New York (G-9347)
Educational Networks Inc .... G 866 526-0200
New York (G-9631)
Health Care Compliance .... F 516 478-4100
Jericho (G-6790)
Jumprope Inc .... G 347 927-5867
New York (G-10380)
Learningateway LLC .... G 212 920-7969
Brooklyn (G-2102)
Maven Marketing LLC .... G 615 510-3248
New York (G-10731)
Multimedia Plus Inc .... F 212 982-3229
New York (G-10860)
Nemaris Inc .... E 646 794-8648
New York (G-10904)
Parlor Labs Inc .... G 866 801-7323
New York (G-11118)
Playfitness Corp .... G 917 497-5443
Staten Island (G-15116)
Prime Research Solutions LLC .... F 917 836-7941
Flushing (G-5040)
Qlogix Entertainment LLC .... G 215 459-6315
New York (G-11292)
San Jae Educational Resou .... G 845 364-5458
Pomona (G-13187)
Scholastic Corporation .... G 212 343-6100
New York (G-11513)
Scholastic Inc .... A 800 724-6527
New York (G-11514)
Schoolnet Inc .... C 646 496-9000
New York (G-11517)
Sciterra LLC .... G 646 883-3724
New York (G-11520)
Skillsoft Corporation .... F 585 240-7500
Rochester (G-14130)
Skyop LLC .... F 585 598-4737
Canandaigua (G-3234)
Special Circle Inc .... F 516 595-9988
New Hyde Park (G-8565)
Teachergaming LLC .... F 866 644-9323
New York (G-11791)
Teachley LLC .... G 347 552-1272
New York (G-11792)
Tequipment Inc .... D 516 922-3508
Huntington Station (G-6462)
Time To Know Inc .... F 212 230-1210
New York (G-11844)
Virtusphere Inc .... F 607 760-2207
Binghamton (G-922)

SOFTWARE PUBLISHERS: Home Entertainment

Avalanche Studios New York Inc .... D 212 993-6447
New York (G-8970)
Boulevard Arts Inc .... G 917 968-8693
New York (G-9127)
Clever Goats Media LLC .... G 917 512-0340
New York (G-9326)
E H Hurwitz & Associates .... G 718 884-3766
Bronx (G-1263)
Magic Numbers Inc .... G 646 839-8578
New York (G-10668)
Mdcare911 LLC .... G 917 640-4869
Brooklyn (G-2183)
Reentry Games Inc .... G 646 421-0080
New York (G-11345)
Remarkety Inc .... G 800 570-7564
Brooklyn (G-2395)
Udisense Inc .... F 866 696-2648
New York (G-11931)
Urthworx Inc .... G 646 373-7535
New York (G-11972)
Vizbee Inc .... G 650 787-1424
New York (G-12048)

SOFTWARE PUBLISHERS: NEC

2k Inc .... G 646 536-3007
New York (G-8675)
30dc Inc .... F 212 962-4400
New York (G-8676)
A K A Computer Consulting Inc .... G 718 351-5200
Staten Island (G-15037)
A2ia Corp .... G 917 237-0390
New York (G-8700)
Ableton Inc .... G 646 723-4586
New York (G-8711)
Accela Inc .... F 631 563-5005
Ronkonkoma (G-14286)
Adobe Systems Inc .... E 212 471-0904
New York (G-8739)
Adobe Systems Incorporated .... C 212 592-1400
New York (G-8740)
Adtech Us Inc .... C 212 402-4840
New York (G-8744)
Advanced Cmpt Sftwr Consulting .... G 718 300-3577
Bronx (G-1213)
Amenity Analytics Inc .... E 646 786-8316
New York (G-8818)
Anju Sylogent LLC .... F 480 326-2358
New York (G-8870)
Anyvision US Inc .... F 606 901-4894
New York (G-8881)
Application Resources Inc .... G 516 636-6200
Great Neck (G-5534)
Appsbidder Inc .... G 917 880-4269
Brooklyn (G-1544)
APS Enterprise Software Inc .... E 631 784-7720
Huntington (G-6392)
Archive360 Inc .... E 212 731-2438
New York (G-8902)
Articulate .... F 646 706-7596
Sagaponack (G-14504)
Arumai Technologies Inc .... F 914 217-0038
Armonk (G-401)
Asite LLC .... D 203 545-3089
New York (G-8933)
AT&T Corp .... F 212 317-7048
New York (G-8942)
Atomic Information Systems .... E 716 713-5402
Unadilla (G-15661)
AVM Software Inc .... F 646 381-2468
New York (G-8980)
Base Systems Inc .... G 845 278-1991
Brewster (G-1158)
Billing Blocks Inc .... F 718 442-5006
Staten Island (G-15050)
Bluebird Transportation LLC .... F 716 395-0000
Williamsville (G-16571)
Brigadoon Software Inc .... G 845 624-0909
Nanuet (G-8459)
Buncee LLC .... F 631 591-1390
Speonk (G-14984)
Byte Consulting Inc .... G 646 500-8606
New York (G-9169)
California US Holdings Inc .... A 212 726-6500
New York (G-9180)
Cdml Computer Services Ltd .... G 718 428-9063
Fresh Meadows (G-5195)
Ceipal LLC .... G 585 351-2934
Rochester (G-13697)
Celonis Inc .... G 941 615-9670
Brooklyn (G-1685)
Cgi Technologies Solutions Inc .... F 212 682-7411
New York (G-9254)
Cinch Technologies Inc .... G 212 266-0022
New York (G-9297)
Cinedigm Software .... G 212 206-9001
New York (G-9300)
Citixsys Technologies Inc .... G 212 745-1365
New York (G-9308)
Clayton Dubilier & Rice Fun .... E 212 407-5200
New York (G-9324)
Cloudsense Inc .... G 917 880-6195
New York (G-9333)
Cmnty Corporation .... G 646 712-9949
New York (G-9337)
Commercehub Inc .... F 518 810-0700
Albany (G-66)
Comprehensive Dental Tech .... G 607 467-4456
Hancock (G-5711)
Construction Technology Inc .... E 914 747-8900
Chappaqua (G-3420)
Coocoo SMS Inc .... F 646 459-4260
Huntington (G-6396)
CTI Software Inc .... F 631 253-3550
Deer Park (G-3960)
Cultureiq Inc .... E 212 755-8633
New York (G-9433)
Cybersports Inc .... G 315 737-7150
Utica (G-15690)
Dakota Software Corporation .... G 216 765-7100
Victor (G-15840)
Dashlane Inc .... E 212 596-7510
New York (G-9473)
Data Implementation Inc .... G 212 979-2015
New York (G-9474)
Davel Systems Inc .... G 718 382-6024
Brooklyn (G-1759)
Defran Systems Inc .... E 212 727-8342
New York (G-9496)
Deniz Information Systems .... G 212 750-5199
New York (G-9500)
Diligent Board Member Svcs LLC .... E 212 741-8181
New York (G-9528)
Dynamo Development Inc .... G 212 385-1552
New York (G-9595)
Eastnets Americas Corp .... F 212 631-0666
New York (G-9613)
Easy Analytic Software Inc .... G 718 740-7930
Flushing (G-4997)
Ebeling Associates Inc .... F 518 688-8700
Halfmoon (G-5662)
Econometric Software Inc .... G 516 938-5254
Plainview (G-13054)
Electronic Arts Inc .... G 212 672-0722
New York (G-9641)
Elevondata Labs Inc .... E 470 222-5438
New York (G-9644)
Emblaze Systems Inc .... C 212 371-1100
New York (G-9665)
Enterprise Tech Group Inc .... F 914 588-0327
New Rochelle (G-8601)
Ert Software Inc .... G 845 358-5721
Blauvelt (G-935)
Ex El Enterprises Ltd .... F 212 489-4500
New York (G-9745)
EZ Newsletter LLC .... F 412 943-7777
Brooklyn (G-1861)
F R A M Technologies Inc .... G 718 338-6230
Brooklyn (G-1863)
F-O-R Software LLC .... F 212 231-9506
New York (G-9766)
F-O-R Software LLC .... G 212 724-3920
New York (G-9767)
Falconstor Software Inc .... C 631 777-5188
Melville (G-8023)
Femtech Women Powered Software .... D 516 328-2631
Franklin Square (G-5117)
Fidelus Technologies LLC .... D 212 616-7800
New York (G-9799)
Fidesa US Corporation .... B 212 269-9000
New York (G-9800)
Flogic Inc .... F 914 478-1352
Hastings On Hudson (G-5748)
Fog Creek Software Inc .... G 866 364-2733
New York (G-9820)
Formats Unlimited Inc .... F 631 249-9200
Deer Park (G-3978)

Employee Codes: A=Over 500 employees, B=251-500
C=101-250, D=51-100, E=20-50, F=10-19, G=5-9

2019 Harris
New York Manufacturers Directory

1257

SOFTWARE PUBLISHERS: NEC

Company		Phone
Fruit St Hlth Pub Beneft Corp	G	347 960-6400
New York (G-9854)		
Fuel Data Systems Inc	G	800 447-7870
Middletown (G-8153)		
Fusion Connect Inc	C	212 201-2400
New York (G-9863)		
Gameclub Inc	G	415 359-5742
New York (G-9880)		
Games For Change Inc	G	212 242-4922
New York (G-9881)		
Gcom Software Inc	E	518 869-1671
Albany (G-76)		
Glitnir Ticketing Inc	G	516 390-5168
Levittown (G-7134)		
Global Applctions Solution LLC	G	212 741-9595
New York (G-9937)		
Great Dane Parent LLC	G	518 810-0700
Albany (G-78)		
Group Commerce Inc	F	646 346-0598
New York (G-9996)		
Hailo Network Usa Inc	G	646 561-8552
New York (G-10021)		
Hallmark Hlth Care Sltions LLC	F	516 513-0959
Hauppauge (G-5839)		
Heineck Associates Inc	G	631 207-2347
Bellport (G-805)		
Hinge Inc	G	502 445-3111
New York (G-10103)		
Hourglass Interactive LLC	F	954 254-2853
New York (G-10134)		
Hudson Software Corporation	E	914 773-0400
Elmsford (G-4544)		
Human Condition Safety Inc	F	646 867-0644
New York (G-10147)		
Huntington Services Inc	G	516 795-8500
Massapequa (G-7880)		
IAC Search LLC	E	212 314-7300
New York (G-10163)		
Iac/Interactivecorp	A	212 314-7300
New York (G-10164)		
Indegy Inc	E	866 801-5394
New York (G-10196)		
Infinity Augmented Reality Inc	G	917 677-2084
New York (G-10203)		
Info Quick Solutions	E	315 463-1400
Liverpool (G-7237)		
Infobase Holdings Inc	D	212 967-8800
New York (G-10206)		
Infobase Publishing Company	G	212 967-8800
New York (G-10207)		
Infor Global Solutions Inc	D	646 336-1700
New York (G-10208)		
Informa Solutions Inc	E	516 543-3733
New York (G-10212)		
Informatica LLC	F	212 845-7650
New York (G-10214)		
Informerly Inc	G	646 238-7137
New York (G-10215)		
Innovation MGT Group Inc	F	800 889-0987
Shirley (G-14836)		
Insight Unlimited Inc	G	914 861-2090
Chappaqua (G-3422)		
Insight Venture Partners IV	C	212 230-9200
New York (G-10225)		
Inspired Entertainment Inc	F	646 565-3861
New York (G-10226)		
International Bus Mchs Corp	E	914 345-5219
Armonk (G-404)		
International Bus Mchs Corp	G	914 499-2000
Armonk (G-405)		
International Identity LLC	G	787 864-0379
Brooklyn (G-2011)		
International MGT Netwrk	F	646 401-0032
New York (G-10248)		
Internodal International Inc	E	631 765-0037
Southold (G-14969)		
Intralinks Holdings Inc	F	212 543-7700
New York (G-10258)		
Invision Inc	G	212 557-5554
New York (G-10265)		
Ipsidy Inc	F	407 951-8640
Long Beach (G-7360)		
Irv Inc	E	212 334-4507
New York (G-10273)		
Isisnet LLC	G	212 239-1205
New York (G-10276)		
Joseph A Filippazzo Software	G	718 987-1626
Staten Island (G-15096)		
Kaseya US Sales LLC	D	415 694-5700
New York (G-10411)		
Kastor Consulting Inc	G	718 224-9109
Bayside (G-747)		
Key Computer Svcs of Chelsea	D	212 206-8060
New York (G-10438)		
Keynote Systems Corporation	G	716 564-1332
Buffalo (G-2905)		
Kronos Incorporated	E	518 459-5545
Albany (G-94)		
Latham Software Sciences Inc	F	518 785-1100
Latham (G-7084)		
Lincdoc LLC	G	585 563-1669
East Rochester (G-4290)		
Lmt Technology Solutions	F	585 784-7470
Rochester (G-13914)		
Magsoft Corporation	G	518 877-8390
Ballston Spa (G-589)		
Maler Technologies Inc	G	212 391-2070
New York (G-10677)		
Market Logic Software Inc	F	646 405-1041
New York (G-10710)		
Matrixcare Inc	G	518 583-6400
New York (G-10729)		
Mealplan Corp	G	909 706-8398
New York (G-10749)		
Medforce Technologies Inc	F	845 426-0459
Suffern (G-15193)		
Meta Pharmacy Systems Inc	E	516 488-6189
Garden City (G-5271)		
Microcad Trning Consulting Inc	G	617 923-0500
Lagrangeville (G-6959)		
Microcad Trning Consulting Inc	G	631 291-9484
Hauppauge (G-5889)		
Microsoft Corporation	G	631 760-2340
Huntington Station (G-6452)		
Midas Mdici Group Holdings Inc	G	212 792-0920
New York (G-10800)		
Mitel Networks Inc	G	877 654-3573
Rochester (G-13948)		
Mobileapp Systems LLC	G	716 667-2780
Buffalo (G-2950)		
Mongodb Inc	C	646 727-4092
New York (G-10839)		
Mymee Inc	F	917 476-4122
New York (G-10868)		
Nastel Technologies Inc	E	631 761-9100
Plainview (G-13078)		
Netegrity Inc	C	631 342-6000
Central Islip (G-3380)		
Netologic Inc	E	212 269-3796
New York (G-10911)		
Netsuite Inc	G	646 652-5700
New York (G-10912)		
New Triad For Collaborative	E	212 873-9610
New York (G-10931)		
New York Computer Consulting	G	516 921-1932
Woodbury (G-16626)		
Obout Software Inc	F	212 380-3500
Brooklyn (G-2283)		
Olympic Software & Consulting	G	631 351-0655
Melville (G-8053)		
Open Text Inc	E	585 424-1950
Rochester (G-13990)		
Openfin Inc	G	917 450-8822
New York (G-11048)		
Operateit Inc	G	631 259-4777
Ronkonkoma (G-14392)		
Oracle America Inc	D	518 427-9353
Albany (G-108)		
Oracle America Inc	D	585 317-4648
Fairport (G-4646)		
Orchard Platform Advisors LLC	E	888 217-2718
New York (G-11058)		
Os33 Inc	D	708 336-3466
New York (G-11064)		
Overture Media Inc	G	917 446-7455
New York (G-11071)		
Pap Chat Inc	G	516 350-1888
Brooklyn (G-2301)		
Par Technology Corporation	D	315 738-0600
New Hartford (G-8508)		
Pareteum Corporation	F	212 984-1096
New York (G-11111)		
Patient Portal Tech Inc	F	315 638-2030
Baldwinsville (G-560)		
Peer Software Incorporated	G	631 979-1770
Hauppauge (G-5912)		
Perry Street Software Inc	G	415 935-1429
New York (G-11163)		
Plain Digital Inc	G	914 310-0280
Scarsdale (G-14643)		
Platform Experts Inc	G	646 843-7100
Brooklyn (G-2324)		
Portfolio Decisionware Inc	E	212 947-1326
New York (G-11220)		
Portware LLC	D	212 425-5233
New York (G-11222)		
Practicepro Software Systems	G	516 222-0010
Garden City (G-5275)		
Quartet Financial Systems Inc	F	845 358-6071
New York (G-11298)		
Radnor-Wallace	G	516 767-2131
Port Washington (G-13300)		
Ramsey Solutions LLC	F	888 329-1055
New York (G-11323)		
Rational Retention LLC	G	518 489-3000
Albany (G-124)		
Red Oak Software Inc	G	585 454-3170
Rochester (G-14070)		
Reliant Security	E	917 338-2200
New York (G-11353)		
Robly Digital Marketing LLC	E	917 238-0730
New York (G-11412)		
Robocom Us LLC	F	631 861-2045
Farmingdale (G-4867)		
Rockport Pa LLC	F	212 482-8580
New York (G-11416)		
Ryba Software Inc	G	718 264-9352
Fresh Meadows (G-5203)		
Safe Passage International Inc	F	585 292-4910
Rochester (G-14108)		
Salentica Corp	E	212 672-1777
New York (G-11468)		
Secured Services Inc	G	866 419-3900
New York (G-11529)		
Segovia Technology Co	F	212 868-4412
New York (G-11534)		
Shiprite Software Inc	G	315 733-6191
Utica (G-15733)		
Siemens Product Life Mgmt Sftw	B	631 549-2300
Melville (G-8063)		
Similarweb Inc	F	347 685-5422
New York (G-11592)		
Slidebean Incorporated	F	866 365-0588
New York (G-11619)		
Slyde Inc	F	917 331-2114
Long Island City (G-7594)		
Sneakers Software Inc	F	800 877-9221
New York (G-11631)		
Social Bicycles Inc	E	917 746-7624
Brooklyn (G-2490)		
Softlink International	E	914 574-8197
White Plains (G-16504)		
Software & General Services Co	G	315 986-4184
Walworth (G-15916)		
Somml Health Inc	G	518 880-2170
Albany (G-128)		
Soroc Technology Corp	G	716 849-5913
Buffalo (G-3071)		
Sparta Commercial Services Inc	F	212 239-2666
New York (G-11658)		
SS&c Financial Services LLC	C	914 670-3600
Harrison (G-5735)		
Stensul Inc	G	212 380-8620
New York (G-11704)		
Strada Soft Inc	G	718 556-6940
Staten Island (G-15141)		
Successware Inc	F	716 565-2338
Williamsville (G-16589)		
Suite Solutions Inc	E	716 929-3050
Amherst (G-252)		
Sutton Place Software Inc	G	631 421-1737
Melville (G-8067)		
Symantec Corporation	D	646 487-6000
New York (G-11758)		
Synco Technologies Inc	G	212 255-2031
New York (G-11762)		
Syrasoft LLC	F	315 708-0341
Baldwinsville (G-564)		
Systems Trading Inc	G	718 261-8900
Melville (G-8068)		
Tap2play LLC	G	914 960-6232
New York (G-11782)		
Targetprocess Inc	F	877 718-2617
Amherst (G-254)		
Tel Tech International	E	516 393-5174
Melville (G-8071)		
Tensa Software	F	914 686-5376
White Plains (G-16512)		
Terranua US Corp	F	212 852-9028
New York (G-11802)		

PRODUCT SECTION

SPECIALTY FOOD STORES: Health & Dietetic Food

Thomson Reuters Corporation .... A 646 223-4000
  New York *(G-11825)*
Tibco Software Inc .... G 646 495-2600
  New York *(G-11830)*
Total Defense Inc .... D 631 257-3258
  Hauppauge *(G-5961)*
Tradepaq Corporation .... F 914 332-9174
  Tarrytown *(G-15497)*
Ttg LLC .... G 917 777-0959
  New York *(G-11910)*
Tunaverse Media Inc .... G 631 778-8350
  Hauppauge *(G-5962)*
U X World Inc .... G 914 375-6167
  Hawthorne *(G-5998)*
United Data Systems Inc .... G 631 549-6900
  Huntington *(G-6423)*
Upstate Records Management LLC ... G 518 834-1144
  Keeseville *(G-6855)*
Uxc Eclipse (usa) Inc .... D 212 965-6400
  New York *(G-11983)*
Value Spring Technology Inc .... F 917 705-4658
  Harrison *(G-5739)*
Vehicle Tracking Solutions LLC .... E 631 586-7400
  Commack *(G-3704)*
Verint Americas Inc .... F 631 962-9334
  Melville *(G-8073)*
Verint SEC Intelligence Inc .... D 631 962-9300
  Melville *(G-8074)*
Verint Systems Inc .... C 631 962-9600
  Melville *(G-8075)*
Verris Inc .... G 201 565-1648
  New York *(G-12012)*
Vertana Group LLC .... G 646 430-8226
  New York *(G-12017)*
Viridis Learning Inc .... G 347 420-9181
  New York *(G-12038)*
Visible Systems Corporation .... E 508 628-1510
  Oneida *(G-12623)*
Vormittag Associates Inc .... G 800 824-7776
  Ronkonkoma *(G-14428)*
Water Oracle .... G 845 876-8327
  Rhinebeck *(G-13491)*
Wetpaintcom Inc .... E 206 859-6300
  New York *(G-12098)*
Wizq Inc .... F 586 381-9048
  New York *(G-12125)*
Woodbury Systems Group Inc .... G 516 364-2653
  Woodbury *(G-16635)*
Wrkbook LLC .... F 914 355-1293
  White Plains *(G-16522)*
X Function Inc .... E 212 231-0092
  New York *(G-12147)*
Zedge Inc .... D 330 577-3424
  New York *(G-12171)*
Zydoc Med Transcription LLC .... F 631 273-1963
  Islandia *(G-6542)*

SOFTWARE PUBLISHERS: Operating Systems

Advanced Cyber Security Corp .... E 866 417-9155
  Bohemia *(G-973)*
J9 Technologies Inc .... E 412 586-5038
  New York *(G-10289)*
Northrop Grumman Systems Corp .... E 315 336-0500
  Rome *(G-14264)*
Reason Software Company Inc .... F 646 664-1038
  New York *(G-11341)*

SOFTWARE PUBLISHERS: Publisher's

Catholic News Publishing Co .... F 914 632-7771
  Mamaroneck *(G-7737)*
Ceros Inc .... E 347 744-9250
  New York *(G-9252)*
Datadog Inc .... E 866 329-4466
  New York *(G-9475)*
Digital Associates LLC .... G 631 983-6075
  Smithtown *(G-14896)*
Hyperlaw Inc .... F 212 873-6982
  New York *(G-10155)*
Maz Systems Inc .... F 855 629-3444
  New York *(G-10736)*
Mediapost Communications LLC ...... E 212 204-2000
  New York *(G-10756)*
Mnn Holding Company LLC .... F 404 558-5251
  Brooklyn *(G-2220)*
On Demand Books LLC .... G 212 966-2222
  New York *(G-11041)*
Spektrix Inc .... G 646 741-5110
  New York *(G-11666)*

Vortex Ventures Inc .... G 516 946-8345
  North Baldwin *(G-12370)*

SOFTWARE PUBLISHERS: Word Processing

Cegid Corporation .... F 212 757-9038
  New York *(G-9234)*

SOFTWARE TRAINING, COMPUTER

Microcad Trning Consulting Inc .... G 617 923-0500
  Lagrangeville *(G-6959)*

SOLAR CELLS

Atlantis Energy Systems Inc .... E 845 486-4052
  Poughkeepsie *(G-13328)*
Ely Beach Solar LLC .... G 718 796-9400
  New York *(G-9661)*
Idalia Solar Technologies LLC .... G 212 792-3913
  New York *(G-10170)*
Nationwide Tarps Incorporated .... D 518 843-1545
  Amsterdam *(G-353)*
Renewable Energy Inc .... G 718 690-2691
  Little Neck *(G-7220)*
Schott Solar Pv Inc .... G 888 457-6527
  Elmsford *(G-4568)*
Warner Energy LLC .... G 315 457-3828
  Liverpool *(G-7271)*

SOLAR HEATING EQPT

Atlantis Energy Systems Inc .... G 916 438-2930
  Poughkeepsie *(G-13329)*
Atlantis Solar Inc .... F 916 226-9183
  Potsdam *(G-13317)*
General Electric Intl Inc .... G 518 385-2211
  Schenectady *(G-14682)*
I-Evolve Techonology Services .... F 801 566-5268
  Amherst *(G-231)*
Integrated Solar Tech LLC .... G 914 249-9364
  Port Chester *(G-13202)*
Mx Solar USA LLC .... C 732 356-7300
  New York *(G-10863)*
Nanopv Corporation .... C 609 851-3666
  Liverpool *(G-7249)*
New Energy Systems Group .... C 917 573-0302
  New York *(G-10921)*
Prism Solar Technologies Inc .... E 845 883-4200
  Highland *(G-6146)*
Solar Energy Systems LLC .... F 718 389-1545
  Brooklyn *(G-2495)*

SOLDERS

Braze Alloy Inc .... G 718 815-5757
  Staten Island *(G-15054)*
Indium Corporation of America .... E 800 446-3486
  Clinton *(G-3586)*
Indium Corporation of America .... E 315 793-8200
  Utica *(G-15713)*
Indium Corporation of America .... E 315 381-2330
  Utica *(G-15714)*
Jewelers Solder Supply Inc .... F 718 637-1256
  Brooklyn *(G-2037)*

SOLVENTS

Solvents Company Inc .... F 631 595-9300
  Kingston *(G-6917)*

SONAR SYSTEMS & EQPT

Edo LLC .... G 631 630-4000
  Amityville *(G-272)*
Lockheed Martin Corporation .... E 315 456-6604
  Syracuse *(G-15363)*
Lockheed Martin Overseas .... F 315 456-0123
  Liverpool *(G-7244)*

SOUND EQPT: Electric

Audible Difference Inc .... E 212 662-4848
  Brooklyn *(G-1574)*
Audible Difference Inc .... G 212 662-4848
  Brooklyn *(G-1575)*
Isolation Technology Inc .... G 631 253-3314
  West Babylon *(G-16159)*
Magic Tech Co Ltd .... G 516 539-7944
  West Hempstead *(G-16221)*

SOUND EQPT: Underwater

L-3 Cmmnctons Ntronix Holdings .... D 212 697-1111
  New York *(G-10496)*

SOUND REPRODUCING EQPT

Samson Technologies Corp .... D 631 784-2200
  Hicksville *(G-6130)*
Vtb Holdings Inc .... G 914 345-4255
  Valhalla *(G-15749)*

SPACE VEHICLE EQPT

Gb Aero Engine LLC .... B 914 925-9600
  Rye *(G-14480)*
GKN Aerospace Monitor Inc .... B 562 619-8558
  Amityville *(G-277)*
L3 Foreign Holdings Inc .... D 212 697-1111
  New York *(G-10497)*
L3 Technologies Inc .... A 631 436-7400
  Hauppauge *(G-5859)*
L3 Technologies Inc .... B 212 697-1111
  New York *(G-10498)*
Lockheed Martin Corporation .... E 716 297-1000
  Niagara Falls *(G-12307)*
Magellan Aerospace NY Inc .... C 718 699-4000
  Corona *(G-3849)*
Moog Inc .... A 716 652-2000
  Elma *(G-4453)*
Saturn Industries Inc .... E 518 828-9956
  Hudson *(G-6370)*
Servotronics Inc .... C 716 655-5990
  Elma *(G-4458)*
SKF USA Inc .... D 716 661-2869
  Falconer *(G-4691)*
SKF USA Inc .... D 716 661-2600
  Falconer *(G-4692)*
Turbine Engine Comp Utica .... A 315 768-8070
  Whitesboro *(G-16531)*
Unison Industries LLC .... B 607 335-5000
  Norwich *(G-12494)*

SPARK PLUGS: Internal Combustion Engines

Karlyn Industries Inc .... F 845 351-2249
  Southfields *(G-14966)*

SPAS

461 New Lots Avenue LLC .... G 347 303-9305
  Brooklyn *(G-1442)*
Epic Beauty Co LLC .... G 212 327-3059
  New York *(G-9693)*
Skincare Products Inc .... G 917 837-5255
  New York *(G-11609)*

SPEAKER SYSTEMS

Accent Speaker Technology Ltd .... G 631 738-2540
  Holbrook *(G-6167)*
Covington Sound .... G 646 256-7486
  Bronx *(G-1247)*
L A R Electronics Corp .... G 716 285-0555
  Niagara Falls *(G-12304)*
Professional Technology Inc .... G 315 337-4156
  Rome *(G-14267)*
Pure Acoustics Inc .... G 718 788-4411
  Brooklyn *(G-2361)*
Widgetworks Unlimited LLC .... G 914 666-6395
  Chappaqua *(G-3424)*

SPECIAL EVENTS DECORATION SVCS

Allied Decorations Co Inc .... F 315 637-0273
  Syracuse *(G-15240)*
Ubm LLC .... D 516 562-7800
  New Hyde Park *(G-8568)*

SPECIALTY FOOD STORES: Coffee

Death Wish Coffee Company LLC ..... F 518 400-1050
  Ballston Spa *(G-579)*
Orens Daily Roast Inc .... G 212 348-5400
  New York *(G-11061)*

SPECIALTY FOOD STORES: Health & Dietetic Food

Ajes Pharmaceuticals LLC .... E 631 608-1728
  Copiague *(G-3749)*

Employee Codes: A=Over 500 employees, B=251-500
C=101-250, D=51-100, E=20-50, F=10-19, G=5-9

SPECIALTY FOOD STORES: Health & Dietetic Food

Cosmic Enterprise .... G 718 342-6257
  Brooklyn (G-1722)
Natures Bounty Co .... D 631 244-2021
  Ronkonkoma (G-14385)
Only Natural Inc .... F 516 897-7001
  Oceanside (G-12549)
Setauket Manufacturing Co .... G 631 231-7272
  Ronkonkoma (G-14412)

SPECIALTY FOOD STORES: Juices, Fruit Or Vegetable

Mayer Bros Apple Products Inc .... D 716 668-1787
  West Seneca (G-16301)
Nantucket Allserve Inc .... B 914 612-4000
  Elmsford (G-4555)
Schutt Cider Mill .... F 585 872-2924
  Webster (G-16097)

SPECIALTY FOOD STORES: Tea

Harney & Sons Tea Corp .... C 518 789-2100
  Millerton (G-8193)

SPECIALTY FOOD STORES: Vitamin

Natures Warehouse .... F 800 215-4372
  Philadelphia (G-12985)

SPERM BANK

Daxor Corporation .... F 212 330-8500
  New York (G-9492)

SPONGES: Plastic

3M Company .... B 716 876-1596
  Tonawanda (G-15517)

SPOOLS: Fiber, Made From Purchased Materials

Syraco Products Inc .... F 315 476-5306
  Syracuse (G-15433)

SPOOLS: Indl

McIntosh Box & Pallet Co Inc .... E 315 446-9350
  Rome (G-14257)

SPORTING & ATHLETIC GOODS: Bags, Golf

Athalon Sportgear Inc .... G 212 268-8070
  New York (G-8948)

SPORTING & ATHLETIC GOODS: Bowling Pins

Qubicaamf Worldwide LLC .... C 315 376-6541
  Lowville (G-7655)

SPORTING & ATHLETIC GOODS: Bows, Archery

Perfect Form Manufacturing LLC .... G 585 500-5923
  West Henrietta (G-16247)

SPORTING & ATHLETIC GOODS: Boxing Eqpt & Splys, NEC

Everlast Worldwide Inc .... E 212 239-0990
  New York (G-9738)

SPORTING & ATHLETIC GOODS: Camping Eqpt & Splys

Adirondack Outdoor Center LLC .... G 315 369-2300
  Old Forge (G-12589)
J R Products Inc .... G 716 633-7565
  Clarence Center (G-3546)

SPORTING & ATHLETIC GOODS: Cartridge Belts

Car Doctor Motor Sports LLC .... G 631 537-1548
  Water Mill (G-15968)

SPORTING & ATHLETIC GOODS: Driving Ranges, Golf, Electronic

Paddock Chevrolet Golf Dome .... E 716 504-4059
  Tonawanda (G-15568)

SPORTING & ATHLETIC GOODS: Dumbbells & Other Weight Eqpt

TDS Fitness Equipment Corp .... F 607 733-6789
  Elmira (G-4505)

SPORTING & ATHLETIC GOODS: Fishing Bait, Artificial

Fishing Valley LLC .... G 716 523-6158
  Lockport (G-7301)
Makiplastic .... G 716 772-2222
  Gasport (G-5307)

SPORTING & ATHLETIC GOODS: Fishing Eqpt

Cortland Line Mfg LLC .... E 607 756-2851
  Cortland (G-3867)
Fly-Tyers Carry-All LLC .... G 607 821-1460
  Charlotteville (G-3425)
Rome Specialty Company Inc .... E 315 337-8200
  Rome (G-14272)

SPORTING & ATHLETIC GOODS: Fishing Tackle, General

Sea Isle Custom Rod Builders .... G 516 868-8855
  Freeport (G-5181)

SPORTING & ATHLETIC GOODS: Game Calls

Quaker Boy Inc .... E 716 662-3979
  Orchard Park (G-12740)

SPORTING & ATHLETIC GOODS: Gymnasium Eqpt

Peloton Interactive Inc .... F 866 679-9129
  New York (G-11142)
Peloton Interactive Inc 866 650-1996
  New York (G-11143)

SPORTING & ATHLETIC GOODS: Hockey Eqpt & Splys, NEC

Hart Sports Inc .... G 631 385-1805
  Huntington Station (G-6443)
Kohlberg Sports Group Inc 914 241-7430
  Mount Kisco (G-8348)

SPORTING & ATHLETIC GOODS: Lacrosse Eqpt & Splys, NEC

Maverik Lacrosse LLC .... A 516 213-3050
  New York (G-10732)
Tosch Products Ltd .... G 315 672-3040
  Camillus (G-3198)

SPORTING & ATHLETIC GOODS: Pools, Swimming, Exc Plastic

Charm Mfg Co Inc .... E 607 565-8161
  Waverly (G-16063)
Imperial Pools Inc .... C 518 786-1200
  Latham (G-7075)
Latham International Mfg Corp .... B 800 833-3800
  Latham (G-7081)
Latham Pool Products Inc .... C 518 951-1000
  Latham (G-7082)
Polytech Pool Mfg Inc .... F 718 492-8991
  Brooklyn (G-2326)

SPORTING & ATHLETIC GOODS: Pools, Swimming, Plastic

Florida North Inc .... F 518 868-2888
  Sloansville (G-14891)
Hinspergers Poly Industries .... E 585 798-6625
  Medina (G-7981)
Swimline Corp .... C 631 254-2155
  Edgewood (G-4416)
Wilbar International Inc .... D 631 951-9800
  Hauppauge (G-5976)

SPORTING & ATHLETIC GOODS: Shooting Eqpt & Splys, General

Otis Products Inc .... C 315 348-4300
  Lyons Falls (G-7689)

SPORTING & ATHLETIC GOODS: Skateboards

Blades .... F 212 477-1059
  New York (G-9098)

SPORTING & ATHLETIC GOODS: Skates & Parts, Roller

Chapman Skateboard Co Inc .... G 631 321-4773
  Deer Park (G-3957)

SPORTING & ATHLETIC GOODS: Target Shooting Eqpt

Devin Mfg Inc .... F 585 496-5770
  Arcade (G-381)

SPORTING & ATHLETIC GOODS: Team Sports Eqpt

Adpro Sports LLC .... D 716 854-5116
  Buffalo (G-2687)

SPORTING & ATHLETIC GOODS: Tennis Eqpt & Splys

Rottkamp Tennis Inc .... E 631 421-0040
  Huntington Station (G-6455)

SPORTING & REC GOODS, WHOLESALE: Camping Eqpt & Splys

Adirondack Outdoor Center LLC .... G 315 369-2300
  Old Forge (G-12589)
Johnson Outdoors Inc .... C 607 779-2200
  Binghamton (G-899)

SPORTING & RECREATIONAL GOODS & SPLYS WHOLESALERS

Everlast Sports Mfg Corp .... E 212 239-0990
  New York (G-9737)
Graph-Tex Inc .... G 607 756-1875
  Cortland (G-3874)
Walsh & Hughes Inc .... G 631 427-5904
  Huntington Station (G-6464)

SPORTING & RECREATIONAL GOODS, WHOL: Sharpeners, Sporting

Dead Ringer LLC .... G 585 355-4685
  Rochester (G-13736)

SPORTING & RECREATIONAL GOODS, WHOLESALE: Boat Access & Part

Brock Awnings Ltd .... F 631 765-5200
  Hampton Bays (G-5708)
Di Sanos Creative Canvas Inc .... G 315 894-3137
  Frankfort (G-5105)
Katherine Blizniak .... G 716 674-8545
  West Seneca (G-16300)

SPORTING & RECREATIONAL GOODS, WHOLESALE: Exercise

TDS Fitness Equipment Corp .... F 607 733-6789
  Elmira (G-4505)

SPORTING & RECREATIONAL GOODS, WHOLESALE: Fishing

Fly-Tyers Carry-All LLC .... G 607 821-1460
  Charlotteville (G-3425)

SPORTING & RECREATIONAL GOODS, WHOLESALE: Fishing Tackle

Hemisphere Novelties Inc .... E 914 378-4100
  Yonkers (G-16767)

SPORTING & RECREATIONAL GOODS, WHOLESALE: Hot Tubs

Charm Mfg Co Inc .... E 607 565-8161
  Waverly (G-16063)

PRODUCT SECTION

SPRINKLING SYSTEMS: Fire Control

SPORTING & RECREATIONAL GOODS, WHOLESALE: Skiing

Sundown Ski & Sport Shop Inc .... E 631 737-8600
  Lake Grove *(G-6970)*

SPORTING & RECREATIONAL GOODS, WHOLESALE: Watersports

Great American Industries Inc .... G 607 729-9331
  Vestal *(G-15818)*

SPORTING GOODS

Absolute Fitness US Corp .... D 732 979-8582
  Bayside *(G-742)*
Apparel Production Inc .... E 212 278-8362
  New York *(G-8890)*
Azibi Ltd .... F 212 869-6550
  New York *(G-8986)*
Burnt Mill Smithing .... G 585 293-2380
  Churchville *(G-3507)*
Burton Corporation .... D 802 862-4500
  Champlain *(G-3407)*
City Sports Inc .... G 212 730-2009
  New York *(G-9312)*
Cy Plastics Works Inc .... E 585 229-2555
  Honeoye *(G-6260)*
Everlast Sports Mfg Corp .... E 212 239-0990
  New York *(G-9737)*
Excellent Art Mfg Corp .... F 718 388-7075
  Inwood *(G-6489)*
Fitsmo LLC .... G 585 519-1956
  Fairport *(G-4633)*
Good Show Sportwear Inc .... F 212 334-8751
  New York *(G-9958)*
Grand Slam Safety LLC .... G 315 766-7008
  Croghan *(G-3908)*
Hana Sportswear Inc .... E 315 639-6332
  Dexter *(G-4115)*
Hector Pt Sr Rehab Svc Pllc .... G 518 371-5554
  Clifton Park *(G-3567)*
Herrmann Group LLC .... G 716 876-9798
  Kenmore *(G-6860)*
Johnson Outdoors Inc .... C 607 779-2200
  Binghamton *(G-899)*
Mattel Inc .... F 716 714-8514
  East Aurora *(G-4205)*
Nalge Nunc International Corp .... A 585 498-2661
  Rochester *(G-13962)*
North Coast Outfitters Ltd .... E 631 727-5580
  Riverhead *(G-13578)*
Pilates Designs LLC .... G 718 721-5929
  Astoria *(G-440)*
PNC Sports .... G 516 665-2244
  Deer Park *(G-4027)*
PRC Liquidating Company .... E 212 823-9626
  New York *(G-11227)*
Rawlings Sporting Goods Co Inc .... D 315 429-8511
  Dolgeville *(G-4136)*
Rising Stars Soccer Club CNY .... F 315 381-3096
  Westmoreland *(G-16409)*
Sportsfield Specialties Inc .... E 607 746-8911
  Delhi *(G-4076)*
Stephenson Custom Case Company .... E 905 542-8762
  Niagara Falls *(G-12338)*
Vertical Lax Inc .... G 518 669-3699
  Albany *(G-140)*
Viking Athletics Ltd .... E 631 957-8000
  Lindenhurst *(G-7203)*
Watson Adventures LLC .... G 212 564-8293
  New York *(G-12081)*
World Best Sporting Goods Inc .... F 800 489-0908
  Westbury *(G-16388)*

SPORTING GOODS STORES, NEC

A Trusted Name Inc .... F 716 326-7400
  Westfield *(G-16391)*
Arena Graphics Inc .... G 516 767-5108
  Port Washington *(G-13244)*
Burnt Mill Smithing .... G 585 293-2380
  Churchville *(G-3507)*
Glenda Inc .... G 718 442-8981
  Staten Island *(G-15079)*
Graph-Tex Inc .... G 607 756-1875
  Cortland *(G-3874)*
Great American Bicycle LLC .... E 518 584-8100
  Saratoga Springs *(G-14583)*
Pda Panache Corp .... G 631 776-0523
  Bohemia *(G-1073)*

Shore Line Monogramming Inc .... F 914 698-8000
  Mamaroneck *(G-7757)*
Vic Demayos Inc .... G 845 626-4343
  Accord *(G-1)*

SPORTING GOODS STORES: Camping Eqpt

Johnson Outdoors Inc .... C 607 779-2200
  Binghamton *(G-899)*

SPORTING GOODS STORES: Fishing Eqpt

Sea Isle Custom Rod Builders .... G 516 868-8855
  Freeport *(G-5181)*

SPORTING GOODS STORES: Playground Eqpt

Eastern Jungle Gym Inc .... E 845 878-9800
  Carmel *(G-3275)*

SPORTING GOODS STORES: Skateboarding Eqpt

Chapman Skateboard Co Inc .... G 631 321-4773
  Deer Park *(G-3957)*

SPORTING GOODS STORES: Tennis Goods & Eqpt

Walsh & Hughes Inc .... G 631 427-5904
  Huntington Station *(G-6464)*

SPORTING GOODS: Archery

Copper John Corporation .... F 315 258-9269
  Auburn *(G-473)*
Outdoor Group LLC .... C 877 503-5483
  West Henrietta *(G-16245)*
Shehawken Archery Co Inc .... F 607 967-8333
  Bainbridge *(G-534)*

SPORTING GOODS: Fishing Nets

Koring Bros Inc .... G 888 233-1292
  New Rochelle *(G-8619)*
Osprey Boat .... G 631 331-4153
  Mount Sinai *(G-8369)*

SPORTING GOODS: Sailboards

Alternatives For Children .... E 631 271-0977
  Dix Hills *(G-4119)*

SPORTING GOODS: Skin Diving Eqpt

Sunny Scuba Inc .... G 212 333-4915
  New York *(G-11743)*

SPORTING GOODS: Surfboards

Bungers Surf Shop .... G 631 244-3646
  Sayville *(G-14626)*
Pilgrim Surf & Supply .... G 718 218-7456
  Brooklyn *(G-2317)*

SPORTING/ATHLETIC GOODS: Gloves, Boxing, Handball, Etc

Fownes Brothers & Co Inc .... E 212 683-0150
  New York *(G-9834)*
Fownes Brothers & Co Inc .... E 518 752-4411
  Gloversville *(G-5456)*
Olympia Sports Company Inc .... F 914 347-4737
  Elmsford *(G-4557)*

SPORTS APPAREL STORES

Gametime Sportswear Plus LLC .... G 315 724-5893
  Utica *(G-15705)*
Hanesbrands Inc .... G 212 576-9300
  New York *(G-10032)*
JM Studio Inc .... F 646 546-5514
  New York *(G-10345)*
Unlimited Ink Inc .... G 631 582-0696
  Hauppauge *(G-5967)*

SPORTS PROMOTION SVCS

Professnal Spt Pblications Inc .... D 212 697-1460
  New York *(G-11256)*

SPOUTING: Plastic & Fiberglass Reinforced

Saint-Gobain Prfmce Plas Corp .... E 518 283-5963
  Poestenkill *(G-13182)*

SPRAYING & DUSTING EQPT

Spfm Corp .... G 718 788-6800
  Brooklyn *(G-2503)*

SPRAYING EQPT: Agricultural

Fountainhead Group Inc .... C 315 736-0037
  New York Mills *(G-12186)*

SPRAYS: Artificial & Preserved

Jenray Products Inc .... E 914 375-5596
  Yonkers *(G-16773)*

SPRINGS: Coiled Flat

Angelica Spring Company Inc .... F 585 466-7892
  Angelica *(G-367)*
Whiting Door Mfg Corp .... D 716 542-3070
  Akron *(G-25)*

SPRINGS: Leaf, Automobile, Locomotive, Etc

Red Onyx Industrial Pdts LLC .... G 516 459-6035
  Huntington *(G-6409)*
Whitesboro Spring & Alignment .... F 315 736-4441
  Whitesboro *(G-16532)*

SPRINGS: Mechanical, Precision

Lee Spring Company LLC .... C 718 362-5183
  Brooklyn *(G-2105)*
Unimex Corporation .... C 718 236-2222
  Brooklyn *(G-2601)*

SPRINGS: Precision

Fennell Spring Company LLC .... D 607 739-3541
  Horseheads *(G-6315)*
Kinemotive Corporation .... E 631 249-6440
  Farmingdale *(G-4803)*

SPRINGS: Sash Balances

Pullman Mfg Corporation .... G 585 334-1350
  Rochester *(G-14053)*

SPRINGS: Steel

Isolation Dynamics Corp .... E 631 491-5670
  West Babylon *(G-16158)*
Lee Spring Company LLC .... C 718 362-5183
  Brooklyn *(G-2105)*
Midstate Spring Inc .... E 315 437-2623
  Syracuse *(G-15373)*
Temper Corporation .... E 518 853-3467
  Fonda *(G-5067)*

SPRINGS: Wire

Ajax Wire Specialty Co Inc .... F 516 935-2333
  Hicksville *(G-6056)*
Barnes Group Inc .... G 315 457-9200
  Syracuse *(G-15254)*
Commerce Spring Corp .... F 631 293-4844
  Farmingdale *(G-4738)*
Commercial Communications LLC .... G 845 343-9078
  Middletown *(G-8143)*
Lee Spring LLC .... F 718 236-2222
  Brooklyn *(G-2106)*
Midstate Spring Inc .... E 315 437-2623
  Syracuse *(G-15373)*
Teka Precision Inc .... G 845 753-1900
  Nyack *(G-12512)*
The Caldwell Manufacturing Co .... D 585 352-3790
  Rochester *(G-14165)*
The Caldwell Manufacturing Co .... G 585 352-2803
  Victor *(G-15873)*
Unimex Corporation .... D 212 755-8800
  New York *(G-11946)*

SPRINKLING SYSTEMS: Fire Control

Allied Inspection Services LLC .... F 716 489-3199
  Falconer *(G-4670)*
Reliable Autmtc Sprnklr Co Inc .... B 800 431-1588
  Elmsford *(G-4562)*
Sentry Automatic Sprinkler .... F 631 723-3095
  Riverhead *(G-13584)*

SPRINKLING SYSTEMS: Fire Control

Tyco Simplexgrinnell .... E 315 437-9664
 East Syracuse (G-4376)

STAGE LIGHTING SYSTEMS

Altman Stage Lighting Co Inc .... C 914 476-7987
 Yonkers (G-16733)
Methods Tooling & Mfg Inc .... E 845 246-7100
 Mount Marion (G-8364)
Ric-Lo Productions Ltd .... E 845 469-2285
 Chester (G-3481)
Sir Industries Inc .... G 631 234-2444
 Hauppauge (G-5941)

STAINLESS STEEL

Allvac .... F 716 433-4411
 Lockport (G-7284)
American Chimney Supplies Inc .... G 631 434-2020
 Hauppauge (G-5764)
Dakota Systems Mfg Corp .... G 631 249-5811
 Farmingdale (G-4748)
Dunkirk Specialty Steel LLC .... C 716 366-1000
 Dunkirk (G-4168)
Hallock Fabricating Corp .... G 631 727-2441
 Riverhead (G-13569)
Nucor Steel Auburn Inc .... B 315 253-4561
 Auburn (G-493)
Qsf Inc .... G 585 247-6200
 Gates (G-5311)
Quality Stainless Steel NY Inc .... F 718 748-1785
 Brooklyn (G-2368)
Quest Manufacturing Inc .... E 716 312-8000
 Hamburg (G-5691)
Recon Construction Corp .... F 718 939-1305
 Little Neck (G-7219)
Sims Group USA Holdings Corp .... D 718 786-6031
 Long Island City (G-7591)
Tdy Industries LLC .... E 716 433-4411
 Lockport (G-7334)
Viraj - USA Inc .... G 516 280-8380
 Hicksville (G-6138)

STAIRCASES & STAIRS, WOOD

A W Hamel Stair Mfg Inc .... F 518 346-3031
 Schenectady (G-14647)
Adirondack Stairs Inc .... F 845 246-2525
 Saugerties (G-14602)
Bennett Stair Company Inc .... G 518 384-1554
 Ballston Lake (G-566)
Capital District Stairs Inc .... G 518 383-2449
 Halfmoon (G-5661)
Custom Stair & Millwork Co .... G 315 839-5793
 Sauquoit (G-14621)
Ideal Wood Products Inc .... E 315 823-1124
 Little Falls (G-7210)
Island Stairs Corp .... G 347 645-0560
 Staten Island (G-15091)
Mestel Brothers Stairs & Rails .... C 516 496-4127
 Syosset (G-15222)
Monroe Stair Products Inc .... E 845 783-4245
 Monroe (G-8278)
Monroe Stair Products Inc .... G 845 791-4016
 Monticello (G-8322)
Ne & Ws Inc .... G 718 326-4699
 Maspeth (G-7861)
Quality Stair Builders Inc .... F 631 694-0711
 Farmingdale (G-4861)
R C Henderson Stair Builders .... F 516 876-9898
 Westbury (G-16369)
S R Sloan Inc .... D 315 736-7730
 Whitesboro (G-16529)
Staten Island Stair Inc .... G 718 317-9276
 Staten Island (G-15139)
United Rockland Holding Co Inc .... E 845 357-1900
 Suffern (G-15199)

STAMPED ART GOODS FOR EMBROIDERING

Dirt T Shirts Inc .... E 845 336-4230
 Kingston (G-6898)

STAMPING SVC: Book, Gold

Mines Press Inc .... C 914 788-1800
 Cortlandt Manor (G-3903)

STAMPINGS: Automotive

P R B Metal Products Inc .... F 631 467-1800
 Ronkonkoma (G-14393)

Thyssenkrupp Materials NA Inc .... G 585 279-0000
 Rochester (G-14170)

STAMPINGS: Metal

Able National Corp .... E 718 386-8801
 Brooklyn (G-1471)
Acro Industries Inc .... C 585 254-3661
 Rochester (G-13600)
Advanced Structures Corp .... F 631 667-5000
 Deer Park (G-3934)
Afco Systems Inc .... C 631 249-9441
 Farmingdale (G-4708)
All Out Die Cutting Inc .... E 718 346-6666
 Brooklyn (G-1508)
Arnell Inc .... G 516 486-7098
 Hempstead (G-6007)
Arro Manufacturing LLC .... E 716 763-6203
 Lakewood (G-6989)
Arro Tool & Die Inc .... F 716 763-6203
 Lakewood (G-6990)
B & R Tool Inc .... E 718 948-2729
 Staten Island (G-15046)
B H M Metal Products Co .... G 845 292-5297
 Kauneonga Lake (G-6849)
Bailey Manufacturing Co LLC .... E 716 965-2731
 Forestville (G-5085)
Barnes Group Inc .... G 315 457-9200
 Syracuse (G-15254)
Barron Metal Products Inc .... E 914 965-1232
 Yonkers (G-16738)
Bcs Access Systems Us LLC .... B 315 258-3469
 Auburn (G-469)
Bowen Products Corporation .... G 315 498-4481
 Nedrow (G-8478)
C & H Precision Tools Inc .... E 631 758-3806
 Holtsville (G-6238)
Cameo Metal Products Inc .... E 718 788-1106
 Brooklyn (G-1670)
Cannon Industries Inc .... D 585 254-8080
 Rochester (G-13690)
Check-Mate Industries Inc .... E 631 491-1777
 West Babylon (G-16146)
Chivvis Enterprises Inc .... F 631 842-9055
 Copiague (G-3755)
Cobbe Industries Inc .... E 716 287-2661
 Gerry (G-5340)
Coda Resources Ltd .... D 718 649-1666
 Brooklyn (G-1703)
Coil Stamping Inc .... F 631 588-3040
 Holbrook (G-6178)
Compar Manufacturing Corp .... E 212 304-2777
 New York (G-9369)
Dunkirk Metal Products Wny LLC .... E 716 366-2555
 Dunkirk (G-4167)
Endicott Precision Inc .... C 607 754-7076
 Endicott (G-4589)
Engineering Mfg Tech LLC .... D 607 754-7111
 Endicott (G-4591)
Forsyth Industries Inc .... E 716 652-1070
 Buffalo (G-2831)
Freeport Screen & Stamping .... E 516 379-0330
 Freeport (G-5157)
Gleason Works .... A 585 473-1000
 Rochester (G-13840)
Greene Technologies Inc .... D 607 656-4166
 Greene (G-5615)
International Ord Tech Inc .... D 716 664-1100
 Jamestown (G-6724)
J T D Stamping Co Inc .... E 631 643-4144
 West Babylon (G-16162)
Johnson & Hoffman LLC .... D 516 742-3333
 Carle Place (G-3267)
Lamparts Co Inc .... F 914 723-8986
 Mount Vernon (G-8416)
Magic Novelty Co Inc .... E 212 304-2777
 New York (G-10667)
Mantel & Mantel Stamping Corp .... G 631 467-1916
 Ronkonkoma (G-14374)
Marex Aquisition Corp .... C 585 458-3940
 Rochester (G-13930)
Matov Industries Inc .... E 718 392-5060
 Long Island City (G-7518)
McHone Industries Inc .... D 716 945-3380
 Salamanca (G-14526)
National Die & Button Mould Co .... E 201 939-7800
 Brooklyn (G-2245)
OEM Solutions Inc .... G 716 864-9324
 Clarence (G-3536)
P R B Metal Products Inc .... E 631 467-1800
 Ronkonkoma (G-14393)

P&G Steel Inc .... F 716 896-7900
 Buffalo (G-2987)
Phoenix Metal Products Inc .... F 516 546-4200
 Freeport (G-5174)
Precision Photo-Fab Inc .... D 716 821-9393
 Buffalo (G-3011)
Premier Metals Group .... E 585 436-4020
 Rochester (G-14039)
Pronto Tool & Die Co Inc .... E 631 981-8920
 Ronkonkoma (G-14401)
Richter Charles Metal STMp&sp .... E 845 895-2025
 Wallkill (G-15906)
Rochester Stampings Inc .... F 585 467-5241
 Rochester (G-14095)
Simplex Manufacturing Co Inc .... F 315 252-7524
 Auburn (G-500)
Stampcrete International Ltd .... E 315 451-2837
 Liverpool (G-7264)
Stever-Locke Industries Inc .... G 585 624-3450
 Honeoye Falls (G-6274)
Tri-Technologies Inc .... E 914 699-2001
 Mount Vernon (G-8449)
TRW Automotive Inc .... B 315 255-3311
 Auburn (G-506)
Universal Shielding Corp .... E 631 667-7900
 Deer Park (G-4055)
Web Associates Inc .... G 716 883-3377
 Buffalo (G-3125)
WR Smith & Sons Inc .... G 845 620-9400
 Nanuet (G-8469)

STANDS & RACKS: Engine, Metal

Devin Mfg Inc .... F 585 496-5770
 Arcade (G-381)

STARTERS: Motor

Con Rel Auto Electric Inc .... E 518 356-1646
 Schenectady (G-14666)

STATIC ELIMINATORS: Ind

Nrd LLC .... E 716 773-7634
 Grand Island (G-5508)

STATIONARY & OFFICE SPLYS, WHOLESALE: Blank Books

Foster - Gordon Manufacturing .... G 631 589-6776
 Bohemia (G-1024)

STATIONARY & OFFICE SPLYS, WHOLESALE: Laser Printer Splys

Interntnl Publcatns Media Grup .... G 917 604-9602
 New York (G-10252)
Printer Components Inc .... G 585 924-5190
 Fairport (G-4651)

STATIONARY & OFFICE SPLYS, WHOLESALE: Stationery

F J Remey Co Inc .... E 516 741-5112
 Mineola (G-8222)
One In A Million Inc .... G 516 829-1111
 Valley Stream (G-15788)
Tripi Engraving Co Inc .... E 718 383-6500
 Brooklyn (G-2586)

STATIONER'S SUNDRIES: Rubber

Hampton Art LLC .... E 631 924-1335
 Medford (G-7950)
Rubber Stamps Inc .... E 212 675-1180
 Mineola (G-8247)

STATIONERY & OFFICE SPLYS WHOLESALERS

Argo Lithographers Inc .... E 718 729-2700
 Long Island City (G-7388)
Atlaz International Ltd .... F 516 239-1854
 Lawrence (G-7102)
Kas-Ray Industries Inc .... F 212 620-3144
 New York (G-10410)
Labels Inter-Global Inc .... F 212 398-0006
 New York (G-10504)

PRODUCT SECTION

STEEL FABRICATORS

STATIONERY PRDTS

Cos TEC Manufacturing Corp .... G 631 589-7170
  Bohemia *(G-999)*
Drimark .... F 516 484-6200
  Bethpage *(G-841)*
Dynamic Intl Mfrs & Distrs Inc .... F 347 993-1914
  Suffern *(G-15188)*
Innovative Designs LLC .... E 212 695-0892
  New York *(G-10219)*
International Design Assoc Ltd .... G 212 687-0333
  New York *(G-10245)*
Kleer-Fax Inc .... D 631 225-1100
  Amityville *(G-295)*
Leather Indexes Corp .... D 516 827-1900
  Hicksville *(G-6103)*
P C I Paper Conversions Inc .... C 315 437-1641
  Syracuse *(G-15389)*
Paper Magic Group Inc .... B 631 521-3682
  New York *(G-11102)*
Princton Archtctural Press LLC .... F 518 671-6100
  Hudson *(G-6369)*
Westrock Mwv LLC .... C 212 688-5000
  New York *(G-12097)*

STATIONERY: Made From Purchased Materials

Allen William & Company Inc .... C 212 675-6461
  Glendale *(G-5391)*

STATUARY & OTHER DECORATIVE PRDTS: Nonmetallic

Design Research Ltd .... C 212 228-7675
  New York *(G-9506)*

STATUES: Nonmetal

Barrett Bronze Inc .... E 914 699-6060
  Mount Vernon *(G-8380)*
Dream Statuary Inc .... G 718 647-2024
  Brooklyn *(G-1792)*
Jonas Louis Paul Studios Inc .... G 518 851-2211
  Hudson *(G-6361)*

STEAM SPLY SYSTEMS SVCS INCLUDING GEOTHERMAL

Caithness Equities Corporation .... E 212 599-2112
  New York *(G-9178)*

STEAM, HEAT & AIR CONDITIONING DISTRIBUTION SVC

P&G Metal Components Corp .... D 716 896-7900
  Buffalo *(G-2986)*

STEEL & ALLOYS: Tool & Die

B H M Metal Products Co .... G 845 292-5297
  Kauneonga Lake *(G-6849)*
Fuller Tool Incorporated .... F 315 891-3183
  Newport *(G-12255)*
Spin-Rite Corporation .... F 585 266-5200
  Rochester *(G-14138)*

STEEL FABRICATORS

760 NI Holdings .... E 716 821-1391
  Buffalo *(G-2678)*
A & T Iron Works Inc .... E 914 632-8992
  New Rochelle *(G-8585)*
A-Fab Initiatives Inc .... F 716 877-5257
  Buffalo *(G-2680)*
A/C Design & Fabrication Corp .... E 718 227-8100
  Staten Island *(G-15039)*
AAA Welding and Fabrication of .... G 585 254-2830
  Rochester *(G-13592)*
Abalon Precision Mfg Corp .... E 914 665-7700
  Mount Vernon *(G-8373)*
Abalon Precision Mfg Corp .... F 718 589-5682
  Mount Vernon *(G-8374)*
Acadia Stairs .... G 845 765-8600
  Fishkill *(G-4942)*
Accucut Inc .... G 631 567-2868
  West Sayville *(G-16287)*
Ackroyd Metal Fabricators Inc .... F 518 434-1281
  Menands *(G-8078)*
Advanced Thermal Systems Inc .... E 716 681-1800
  Lancaster *(G-7002)*

Advantage Machining Inc .... F 716 731-6418
  Niagara Falls *(G-12258)*
Aero-Data Metal Crafters Inc .... C 631 471-7733
  Ronkonkoma *(G-14294)*
Aldo Frustacci Iron Works Inc .... F 718 768-0707
  Brooklyn *(G-1502)*
Alken Industries Inc .... E 631 467-2000
  Ronkonkoma *(G-14298)*
All-City Metal Inc .... F 718 937-3975
  Maspeth *(G-7817)*
Alpha Iron Works LLC .... F 585 424-7260
  Rochester *(G-13620)*
American Aerogel Corporation .... E 585 328-2140
  Rochester *(G-13624)*
Asp Industries Inc .... E 585 254-9130
  Rochester *(G-13647)*
Atlantis Equipment Corporation .... E 518 733-5910
  Stephentown *(G-15154)*
B H M Metal Products Co .... G 845 292-5297
  Kauneonga Lake *(G-6849)*
B P Nash Co Inc .... F 315 445-1310
  East Syracuse *(G-4325)*
Barber Welding Inc .... G 315 834-6645
  Weedsport *(G-16110)*
Barker Steel LLC .... E 518 465-6221
  Albany *(G-44)*
Barry Steel Fabrication Inc .... E 716 433-2144
  Lockport *(G-7286)*
Bear Metal Works Inc .... F 716 824-4350
  Buffalo *(G-2727)*
Bennett Manufacturing Co Inc .... C 716 937-9161
  Alden *(G-168)*
Bereza Iron Works Inc .... F 585 254-6311
  Rochester *(G-13660)*
Blackstone Advanced Tech LLC .... C 716 665-5410
  Jamestown *(G-6702)*
Bms Manufacturing Co Inc .... E 607 535-2426
  Watkins Glen *(G-16058)*
Bob Murphy Inc .... F 607 729-3553
  Vestal *(G-15811)*
Bombardier Transportation .... D 607 324-0216
  Hornell *(G-6294)*
Bombardier Trnsp Holdings USA .... D 607 776-4791
  Bath *(G-641)*
Bristol Metals Inc .... F 585 657-7665
  Bloomfield *(G-948)*
Buffalo Metal Fabricating Corp .... F 716 892-7800
  Buffalo *(G-2748)*
Buffalo Structural Steel Inc .... E 814 827-1350
  Buffalo *(G-2754)*
Burnt Hills Fabricators Inc .... F 518 885-1115
  Ballston Spa *(G-578)*
C & C Custom Metal Fabricators .... G 631 235-9646
  Hauppauge *(G-5785)*
C & C Metal Fabrications Inc .... F 315 598-7607
  Fulton *(G-5212)*
C & T Tool & Instrument Co .... E 718 429-1253
  Woodside *(G-16648)*
Carpenter Industries Inc .... F 315 463-4284
  Syracuse *(G-15271)*
CBM Fabrications Inc .... E 518 399-8023
  Ballston Lake *(G-567)*
Chautauqua Machine Spc LLC .... F 716 782-3276
  Ashville *(G-416)*
Christian Fabrication LLC .... G 315 822-0135
  West Winfield *(G-16305)*
Cives Corporation .... C 315 287-2200
  Gouverneur *(G-5488)*
Cobbe Industries Inc .... E 716 287-2661
  Gerry *(G-5340)*
Cobra Operating Industries LLC .... G 607 639-1700
  Afton *(G-8)*
Coco Architectureal Grilles .... G 631 482-9449
  Farmingdale *(G-4736)*
Computerized Metal Bending Ser .... F 631 249-1177
  West Babylon *(G-16149)*
Cottonwood Metals Inc .... G 646 807-8674
  Bohemia *(G-1000)*
County Fabricators .... F 914 741-0219
  Pleasantville *(G-13174)*
Cyncal Steel Fabricators Inc .... F 631 254-5600
  Bay Shore *(G-676)*
Dennies Manufacturing Inc .... E 585 393-4646
  Canandaigua *(G-3218)*
Diversified Manufacturing Inc .... F 716 681-7670
  Lancaster *(G-7016)*
Donald Stefan .... G 716 492-1110
  Chaffee *(G-3403)*
Dynasty Metal Works Inc .... G 631 284-3719
  Riverhead *(G-13567)*

E B Atlas Steel Corp .... F 716 876-0900
  Buffalo *(G-2806)*
Eastern Manufacturing Inc .... F 716 741-4572
  Clarence *(G-3531)*
Eastern Welding Inc .... F 631 727-0306
  Riverhead *(G-13568)*
Elevator Accessories Mfg .... F 914 739-7004
  Peekskill *(G-12919)*
Empire Industrial Systems Corp .... F 631 242-4619
  Bay Shore *(G-685)*
Empire Metal Fabricators Inc .... G 585 288-2140
  Rochester *(G-13780)*
Empro Niagara Inc .... G 716 433-2769
  Lockport *(G-7298)*
Eps Iron Works Inc .... G 516 294-5840
  Mineola *(G-8219)*
Erie Engineered Products Inc .... E 716 206-0204
  Lancaster *(G-7018)*
Everfab Inc .... D 716 655-1550
  East Aurora *(G-4198)*
Excel Industries Inc .... G 716 542-5468
  Clarence *(G-3533)*
Farmingdale Iron Works Inc .... G 631 249-5995
  Farmingdale *(G-4763)*
Feinstein Iron Works Inc .... F 516 997-8300
  Westbury *(G-16331)*
Fence Plaza Corp .... G 718 469-2200
  Brooklyn *(G-1874)*
Five Corners Repair Inc .... E 585 322-7369
  Bliss *(G-946)*
Flagpoles Incorporated .... D 631 751-5500
  East Setauket *(G-4301)*
Fort Miller Group Inc .... B 518 695-5000
  Greenwich *(G-5639)*
Framing Technology Inc .... E 585 464-8470
  Rochester *(G-13815)*
Frazier Industrial Company .... D 315 539-9256
  Waterloo *(G-15993)*
Fred Santucci Inc .... F 716 483-1411
  Jamestown *(G-6716)*
Gasport Welding & Fabg Inc .... F 716 772-7205
  Gasport *(G-5306)*
Genesee Metal Products Inc .... E 585 968-6000
  Wellsville *(G-16117)*
George Industries LLC .... D 607 748-3371
  Endicott *(G-4595)*
Gibraltar Industries Inc .... D 716 826-6500
  Buffalo *(G-2849)*
Glenridge Fabricators Inc .... F 718 456-2297
  Glendale *(G-5402)*
Hallock Fabricating Corp .... G 631 727-2441
  Riverhead *(G-13569)*
Hansen Steel .... E 585 398-2020
  Farmington *(G-4915)*
Hebeler LLC .... F 716 873-9300
  Tonawanda *(G-15547)*
Homer Iron Works LLC .... F 607 749-3963
  Homer *(G-6256)*
Industrial Fabricating Corp .... E 315 437-3353
  East Syracuse *(G-4348)*
Industrial Support Inc .... D 716 662-2954
  Buffalo *(G-2883)*
Inscape (new York) Inc .... D 716 665-6210
  Falconer *(G-4681)*
Inter Metal Fabricators Inc .... F 718 852-4000
  Brooklyn *(G-2007)*
Irony Limited Inc .... G 631 329-4065
  East Hampton *(G-4238)*
Irv Schroder & Sons Inc .... E 518 828-0194
  Stottville *(G-15181)*
Irving Woodlands LLC .... E 607 723-4862
  Conklin *(G-3729)*
J F M Sheet Metal Inc .... G 631 737-8494
  Ronkonkoma *(G-14355)*
J M Haley Corp .... C 631 845-5200
  Farmingdale *(G-4789)*
Jaab Precision Inc .... G 631 218-3725
  Ronkonkoma *(G-14357)*
James Woerner Inc .... G 631 454-9330
  Farmingdale *(G-4791)*
Jbs LLC .... E 518 346-0001
  Scotia *(G-14743)*
Jentsch & Co Inc .... G 716 852-4111
  Buffalo *(G-2892)*
Joy Edward Company .... E 315 474-3360
  Syracuse *(G-15351)*
Jpw Structural Contracting Inc .... E 315 432-1111
  Syracuse *(G-15352)*
K & E Fabricating Company Inc .... F 716 829-1829
  Buffalo *(G-2899)*

Employee Codes: A=Over 500 employees, B=251-500
C=101-250, D=51-100, E=20-50, F=10-19, G=5-9

2019 Harris
New York Manufacturers Directory

STEEL FABRICATORS | PRODUCT SECTION

Kal Manufacturing Corporation............E....... 585 265-4310
  Webster *(G-16088)*
KDO Industries Inc..................................G....... 631 608-4612
  Amityville *(G-293)*
King Steel Iron Work Corp...................F....... 718 384-7500
  Brooklyn *(G-2074)*
Kleinfelder John......................................G....... 716 753-3163
  Mayville *(G-7921)*
Knj Fabricators LLC................................F....... 347 234-6985
  Bronx *(G-1310)*
Koenig Iron Works Inc............................E....... 718 433-0900
  Long Island City *(G-7489)*
Kryten Iron Works Inc............................G....... 914 345-0990
  Hawthorne *(G-5990)*
Lindenhurst Fabricators Inc..................G....... 631 226-3737
  Lindenhurst *(G-7174)*
M & E Mfg Co Inc....................................D....... 845 331-7890
  Kingston *(G-6910)*
M & L Steel & Ornamental Iron............F....... 718 816-8660
  Staten Island *(G-15102)*
Major-IPC Inc..G....... 845 292-2200
  Liberty *(G-7145)*
Marex Aquisition Corp...........................C....... 585 458-3940
  Rochester *(G-13930)*
Mason Industries Inc.............................B....... 631 348-0282
  Hauppauge *(G-5881)*
Maspeth Steel Fabricators Inc..............G....... 718 361-9192
  Long Island City *(G-7516)*
Maspeth Welding Inc.............................E....... 718 497-5430
  Maspeth *(G-7858)*
Metal Concepts......................................G....... 845 592-1863
  Beacon *(G-760)*
Metal Crafts Inc......................................E....... 718 443-3333
  Brooklyn *(G-2199)*
Metal Fab LLC..G....... 607 775-3200
  Binghamton *(G-905)*
Metal Works of NY Inc...........................E....... 718 525-9440
  Jamaica *(G-6660)*
Metro Iron Corp......................................G....... 631 842-5929
  Amityville *(G-303)*
Miscellnous Ir Fabricators Inc..............E....... 518 355-1822
  Schenectady *(G-14699)*
Mobile Mini Inc......................................F....... 315 732-4555
  Utica *(G-15723)*
Nathan Steel Corp..................................E....... 315 797-1335
  Utica *(G-15725)*
Nb Elctrcal Enclsures Mfrs Inc.............G....... 718 272-8792
  Brooklyn *(G-2250)*
Nci Group Inc...D....... 315 339-1245
  Rome *(G-14261)*
Neversink Steel Corp.............................E....... 845 292-4611
  Liberty *(G-7146)*
New Vision Industries Inc.....................F....... 607 687-7700
  Endicott *(G-4604)*
New York Manufactured Products.......F....... 585 254-9353
  Rochester *(G-13967)*
North E Rggers Erectors NY Inc..........E....... 518 842-6377
  Amsterdam *(G-354)*
North Eastern Fabricators Inc..............E....... 718 542-0450
  New York *(G-10993)*
Northeast Fabricators LLC....................D....... 607 865-4031
  Walton *(G-15912)*
Oehlers Wldg & Fabrication Inc...........F....... 716 821-1800
  Buffalo *(G-2977)*
Orange County Ironworks LLC.............E....... 845 769-3000
  Montgomery *(G-8315)*
Oriskany Mfg Tech LLC.........................E....... 315 732-4962
  Yorkville *(G-16830)*
P K G Equipment Incorporated............E....... 585 436-4650
  Rochester *(G-14003)*
Patsy Strocchia & Sons Iron Wo..........F....... 516 625-8800
  Albertson *(G-150)*
Pcx Aerostructures LLC........................E....... 631 467-2632
  Farmingdale *(G-4844)*
Pecker Iron Works LLC.........................G....... 914 665-0100
  Mount Kisco *(G-8354)*
Penasack Machine Company Inc.........E....... 585 589-7044
  Albion *(G-161)*
Peralta Metal Works Inc........................G....... 718 649-8661
  Brooklyn *(G-2312)*
Perma Tech Inc......................................E....... 716 854-0707
  Buffalo *(G-3000)*
Pierce Industries LLC...........................E....... 585 458-0888
  Rochester *(G-14021)*
Pierce Steel Fabricators Inc.................F....... 716 372-7652
  Olean *(G-12606)*
Pirod Inc...E....... 631 231-7660
  Hauppauge *(G-5916)*
Portfab LLC..E....... 718 542-3600
  Amityville *(G-313)*

Precision Metals Corp...........................E....... 631 586-5032
  Bay Shore *(G-709)*
Precision Polish LLC.............................E....... 315 894-3792
  Frankfort *(G-5111)*
Prime Materials Recovery Inc..............G....... 315 697-5251
  Canastota *(G-3245)*
Productand Design Inc.........................F....... 718 858-2440
  Brooklyn *(G-2353)*
Raulli and Sons Inc...............................D....... 315 479-6693
  Syracuse *(G-15402)*
REO Welding Inc...................................F....... 518 238-1022
  Cohoes *(G-3618)*
Risa Management Corp........................E....... 718 361-2606
  Maspeth *(G-7870)*
RJ Precision LLC...................................E....... 585 768-8030
  Stafford *(G-15028)*
Robert E Derecktor Inc.........................D....... 914 698-0962
  Mamaroneck *(G-7756)*
Roman Iron Works Inc..........................F....... 516 621-1103
  Greenvale *(G-5631)*
Romar Contracting Inc.........................G....... 845 778-2737
  Walden *(G-15896)*
Roth Design & Consulting Inc.............E....... 718 209-0193
  Brooklyn *(G-2417)*
Rothe Welding Inc................................G....... 845 246-3051
  Saugerties *(G-14615)*
Rough Brothers Holding Co.................G....... 716 826-6500
  Buffalo *(G-3048)*
Rs Automation.......................................F....... 585 589-0199
  Albion *(G-162)*
Rus Industries Inc.................................E....... 716 284-7828
  Niagara Falls *(G-12331)*
Salit Specialty Rebar Inc......................E....... 716 299-1990
  Buffalo *(G-3057)*
Savaco Inc..G....... 716 751-9455
  Newfane *(G-12253)*
Schneider Brothers Corporation..........E....... 315 458-8369
  Syracuse *(G-15418)*
Schuler-Subra Inc..................................G....... 716 893-3100
  Buffalo *(G-3058)*
Seibel Modern Mfg & Wldg Corp.........D....... 716 683-1536
  Lancaster *(G-7049)*
Sentry Metal Blast Inc..........................E....... 716 285-5241
  Lockport *(G-7331)*
Silverstone Shtmtl Fbrications.............E....... 718 422-0380
  Brooklyn *(G-2474)*
Specialty Steel Fabg Corp....................F....... 718 893-6326
  Bronx *(G-1390)*
Specialty Wldg & Fabg NY Inc.............D....... 315 426-1807
  Syracuse *(G-15428)*
Steel Tech SA LLC.................................G....... 845 786-3691
  Thiells *(G-15499)*
Stone Well Bodies & Mch Inc..............E....... 315 497-3512
  Genoa *(G-5338)*
Supreme Steel Inc.................................F....... 631 884-1320
  Lindenhurst *(G-7200)*
Team Fabrication Inc............................G....... 716 655-4038
  West Falls *(G-16209)*
Tms Structures Inc................................C....... 646 740-7646
  New York *(G-11854)*
Triboro Iron Works Inc..........................G....... 718 361-9600
  Long Island City *(G-7621)*
Triton Builders Inc................................E....... 631 841-2534
  Amityville *(G-323)*
Tropical Driftwood Originals...............G....... 516 623-0980
  Roosevelt *(G-14438)*
Tymetal Corp..E....... 518 692-9930
  Greenwich *(G-5646)*
Ulster Precision Inc..............................E....... 845 338-0995
  Kingston *(G-6925)*
United Iron Inc......................................E....... 914 667-5700
  Mount Vernon *(G-8453)*
United Structure Solution Inc..............F....... 347 227-7526
  New York *(G-11955)*
Universal Metal Works LLC..................F....... 315 598-7607
  Fulton *(G-5233)*
Vance Metal Fabricators Inc................D....... 315 789-5626
  Geneva *(G-5335)*
Vulcan Iron Works Inc..........................E....... 631 395-6846
  Manorville *(G-7787)*
Waverly Iron Corp.................................E....... 631 732-2800
  Medford *(G-7968)*
Welding Metallurgy Inc........................E....... 631 253-0500
  Hauppauge *(G-5974)*
Whitacre Engineering Company..........G....... 315 622-1075
  Liverpool *(G-7272)*
Winters Railroad Service Inc...............G....... 716 337-2668
  North Collins *(G-12390)*

STEEL MILLS

Albaluz Films LLC.................................G....... 347 613-2321
  New York *(G-8783)*
Baker Tool & Die....................................G....... 716 694-2025
  North Tonawanda *(G-12415)*
Belmet Products Inc.............................E....... 718 542-8220
  Bronx *(G-1227)*
China Industrial Steel Inc....................C....... 646 328-1502
  New York *(G-9279)*
Coventry Manufacturing Co Inc..........E....... 914 668-2212
  Mount Vernon *(G-8391)*
David Fehlman......................................E....... 315 455-8888
  Syracuse *(G-15303)*
Hmi Metal Powders...............................C....... 315 839-5421
  Clayville *(G-3557)*
Jaquith Industries Inc..........................E....... 315 478-5700
  Syracuse *(G-15346)*
Juniper Elbow Co Inc...........................C....... 718 326-2546
  Middle Village *(G-8124)*
Kenbenco Inc...F....... 845 246-3066
  Saugerties *(G-14609)*
Republic Steel Inc................................B....... 716 827-2800
  Blasdell *(G-928)*
Samuel Son & Co Inc...........................G....... 716 856-6500
  Blasdell *(G-929)*
Tms International LLC.........................G....... 315 253-8925
  Auburn *(G-504)*

STEEL, COLD-ROLLED: Sheet Or Strip, From Own Hot-Rolled

Renco Group Inc...................................G....... 212 541-6000
  New York *(G-11361)*

STEEL, COLD-ROLLED: Strip NEC, From Purchased Hot-Rolled

Worthington Industries Inc.................D....... 315 336-5500
  Rome *(G-14279)*

STEEL, HOT-ROLLED: Sheet Or Strip

Jfe Engineering Corporation...............F....... 212 310-9320
  New York *(G-10333)*
Jfe Steel America Inc...........................G....... 212 310-9320
  New York *(G-10334)*

STEEL: Cold-Rolled

Aero-Data Metal Crafters Inc..............C....... 631 471-7733
  Ronkonkoma *(G-14294)*
Clover Wire Forming Co Inc................E....... 914 375-0400
  Yonkers *(G-16745)*
Gibraltar Industries Inc.......................D....... 716 826-6500
  Buffalo *(G-2849)*
Hitachi Metals America Ltd................E....... 914 694-9200
  Purchase *(G-13389)*
Northeast Cnstr Inds Inc.....................F....... 845 565-1000
  Montgomery *(G-8314)*
Rough Brothers Holding Co.................G....... 716 826-6500
  Buffalo *(G-3048)*

STEEL: Galvanized

Elderlee Incorporated...........................C....... 315 789-6670
  Oaks Corners *(G-12527)*

STEEL: Laminated

Advantech Industries Inc....................C....... 585 247-0701
  Rochester *(G-13609)*

STENCIL BOARD: Die-Cut, Made From Purchased Materials

Precision Diecutting Inc......................G....... 315 776-8465
  Port Byron *(G-13190)*

STENCILS

Crafters Workshop Inc.........................G....... 914 345-2838
  Elmsford *(G-4539)*

STONE: Cast Concrete

Alp Stone Inc...F....... 718 706-6166
  Long Island City *(G-7373)*
Corinthian Cast Stone Inc...................E....... 631 920-2340
  Wyandanch *(G-16694)*

PRODUCT SECTION

STONE: Crushed & Broken, NEC
Labrador Stone Inc .... G 570 465-2120
  Binghamton *(G-901)*

STONE: Dimension, NEC
Dominic De Nigris Inc .... E 718 597-4460
  Bronx *(G-1258)*
Suffolk Granite Manufacturing .... E 631 226-4774
  Lindenhurst *(G-7197)*

STONE: Quarrying & Processing, Own Stone Prdts
Callanan Industries Inc .... E 845 331-6868
  Kingston *(G-6892)*
Dalrymple Holding Corp .... E 607 737-6200
  Pine City *(G-13000)*
Graymont Materials Inc .... E 518 561-5200
  Plattsburgh *(G-13122)*
Hanson Aggregates PA LLC .... E 315 789-6202
  Oaks Corners *(G-12528)*
Iroquois Rock Products Inc .... F 585 381-7010
  Rochester *(G-13887)*
Thalle Industries Inc .... E 914 762-3415
  Briarcliff Manor *(G-1177)*

STONEWARE CLAY MINING
Devonian Stone New York Inc .... E 607 655-2600
  Windsor *(G-16604)*

STORE FIXTURES, EXC REFRIGERATED: Wholesalers
Alrod Associates Inc .... F 631 981-2193
  Ronkonkoma *(G-14303)*
Artistry In Wood of Syracuse .... F 315 431-4022
  East Syracuse *(G-4322)*
Leo D Bernstein & Sons Inc .... E 212 337-9578
  New York *(G-10548)*

STORE FIXTURES: Exc Wood
Alrod Associates Inc .... F 631 981-2193
  Ronkonkoma *(G-14303)*
Fixtures 2000 Inc .... B 631 236-4100
  Hauppauge *(G-5825)*
Hamlet Products Inc .... F 914 665-0307
  Mount Vernon *(G-8405)*
Yaloz Mould & Die Co Inc .... E 718 389-1131
  Brooklyn *(G-2662)*

STORE FIXTURES: Wood
Abbott Industries Inc .... B 718 291-0800
  Jamaica *(G-6622)*
Alrod Associates Inc .... F 631 981-2193
  Ronkonkoma *(G-14303)*
Custom Wood Inc .... G 718 927-4700
  Brooklyn *(G-1744)*
Falvo Manufacturing Co Inc .... F 315 724-7925
  Utica *(G-15700)*
L & J Interiors Inc .... G 631 218-0838
  Bohemia *(G-1044)*
Longo Commercial Cabinets Inc .... E 631 225-4290
  Lindenhurst *(G-7176)*
Madjek Inc .... D 631 842-4475
  Amityville *(G-300)*
Three R Enterprises Inc .... E 585 254-5050
  Rochester *(G-14169)*

STORE FRONTS: Prefabricated, Metal
Eastern Storefronts & Mtls Inc .... F 631 471-7065
  Ronkonkoma *(G-14336)*
Empire Archtctural Systems Inc .... F 518 773-5109
  Johnstown *(G-6826)*
Gamma North Corporation .... E 716 902-5100
  Alden *(G-171)*
Pk30 System LLC .... F 212 473-8050
  Stone Ridge *(G-15162)*

STORE FRONTS: Prefabricated, Wood
Empire Archtctural Systems Inc .... F 518 773-5109
  Johnstown *(G-6826)*

STRAPPING
Gibraltar Industries Inc .... D 716 826-6500
  Buffalo *(G-2849)*

Precision Spclty Fbrctions LLC .... E 716 824-2108
  Buffalo *(G-3012)*
Rough Brothers Holding Co .... G 716 826-6500
  Buffalo *(G-3048)*

STRAPS: Bindings, Textile
Ambind Corp .... G 716 836-4365
  Buffalo *(G-2693)*
New York Binding Co Inc .... E 718 729-2454
  Long Island City *(G-7539)*

STRAPS: Braids, Textile
La Lame Inc .... G 212 921-9770
  New York *(G-10502)*

STRAPS: Cotton Webbing
Sturges Manufacturing Co Inc .... D 315 732-6159
  Utica *(G-15734)*

STRAWS: Drinking, Made From Purchased Materials
Last Straw Inc .... E 516 371-2727
  Lawrence *(G-7104)*
Plastirun Corporation .... E 631 273-2626
  Brentwood *(G-1143)*
Sqp Inc .... C 518 831-6800
  Schenectady *(G-14716)*

STRINGING BEADS
Toho Company Limited .... G 212 391-9058
  New York *(G-11855)*

STRUCTURAL SUPPORT & BUILDING MATERIAL: Concrete
Cossitt Concrete Products Inc .... F 315 824-2700
  Hamilton *(G-5698)*
Geotech Associates Ltd .... G 631 286-0251
  Brookhaven *(G-1430)*

STUDIOS: Artist's
Donne Dieu Paper Mill Inc .... G 212 226-0573
  Brooklyn *(G-1788)*
Eskayel Inc .... G 347 703-8084
  Brooklyn *(G-1848)*

STUDIOS: Sculptor's
Surving Studios .... F 845 355-1430
  Middletown *(G-8178)*

STUDS & JOISTS: Sheet Metal
Studco Building Systems US LLC .... E 585 545-3000
  Webster *(G-16100)*

SUBSCRIPTION FULFILLMENT SVCS: Magazine, Newspaper, Etc
Time Inc Affluent Media Group .... G 212 382-5600
  New York *(G-11841)*

SUGAR SUBSTITUTES: Organic
American Hlth Formulations Inc .... G 631 392-1756
  Hauppauge *(G-5766)*
Cumberland Packing Corp .... B 718 858-4200
  Brooklyn *(G-1739)*
Dulcette Technologies LLC .... G 631 752-8700
  Lindenhurst *(G-7171)*
Flavors Holdings Inc .... F 212 572-8677
  New York *(G-9816)*
Sugar Foods Corporation .... E 212 753-6900
  New York *(G-11734)*

SUNDRIES & RELATED PRDTS: Medical & Laboratory, Rubber
Geri-Gentle Corporation .... G 917 804-7807
  Brooklyn *(G-1923)*
Hutchinson Industries Inc .... E 716 852-1435
  Buffalo *(G-2876)*
Impladent Ltd .... E 718 465-1810
  Jamaica *(G-6651)*
Jamestown Scientific Inds LLC .... F 716 665-3224
  Jamestown *(G-6732)*

SURGICAL APPLIANCES & SPLYS

Life Medical Technologies LLC .... F 845 894-2121
  Hopewell Junction *(G-6291)*
Remedies Surgical Supplies .... G 718 599-5301
  Brooklyn *(G-2396)*
Tmp Technologies Inc .... D 585 495-6231
  Wyoming *(G-16702)*

SUNROOMS: Prefabricated Metal
Latium USA Trading LLC .... D 631 563-4000
  Holbrook *(G-6193)*
Sunbilt Solar Pdts By Sussman .... D 718 297-0228
  Jamaica *(G-6681)*

SUPERMARKETS & OTHER GROCERY STORES
Ives Farm Market .... G 315 592-4880
  Fulton *(G-5222)*
Melita Corp .... C 718 392-7280
  Astoria *(G-435)*
Ravioli Store Inc .... G 718 729-9300
  Long Island City *(G-7572)*
TLC-Lc Inc .... E 212 756-8900
  New York *(G-11852)*

SURFACE ACTIVE AGENTS
Bigsky Technologies LLC .... G 585 270-5282
  Rochester *(G-13663)*
Halmark Architectural Finshg .... E 718 272-1831
  Brooklyn *(G-1961)*
Medisca Inc .... E 514 333-7811
  Plattsburgh *(G-13133)*
Momentive Performance Mtls Inc .... D 914 784-4807
  Tarrytown *(G-15484)*
Suit-Kote Corporation .... F 716 683-8850
  Buffalo *(G-3079)*

SURFACE ACTIVE AGENTS: Oils & Greases
Comander Terminals LLC .... E 516 922-7600
  Oyster Bay *(G-12812)*

SURGICAL & MEDICAL INSTRUMENTS WHOLESALERS
Derm-Buro Inc .... E 516 694-8300
  Plainview *(G-13050)*
Ppi Corp .... D 585 243-0300
  Rochester *(G-14032)*

SURGICAL APPLIANCES & SPLYS
Proficient Surgical Eqp Inc .... G 516 487-1175
  Port Washington *(G-13299)*
Steris Corporation .... G 877 887-1788
  Melville *(G-8066)*

SURGICAL APPLIANCES & SPLYS
ACS Custom USA LLC .... G 646 559-5642
  New York *(G-8729)*
Argon Medical Devices Inc .... G 585 321-1130
  Henrietta *(G-6031)*
Avanti U S A Ltd .... F 716 695-5800
  Tonawanda *(G-15524)*
Backtech Inc .... G 973 279-0838
  New York *(G-8998)*
Byer California .... G 212 944-8989
  New York *(G-9167)*
Centinel Spine LLC .... G 212 583-9700
  New York *(G-9241)*
Community Products LLC .... E 845 658-7720
  Chester *(G-3471)*
Community Products LLC .... G 518 589-5103
  Elka Park *(G-4435)*
Creative Orthotics Prosthetics .... G 607 431-2526
  Oneonta *(G-12636)*
Cy Plastics Works Inc .... E 585 229-2555
  Honeoye *(G-6260)*
Depuy Synthes Inc .... C 607 271-2500
  Horseheads *(G-6312)*
Derm-Buro Inc .... E 516 694-8300
  Plainview *(G-13050)*
Eschen Prsthetic Orthotic Labs .... F 516 871-0029
  Hicksville *(G-6085)*
Far Rockaway Drugs Inc .... F 718 471-2500
  Far Rockaway *(G-4701)*
Flexible Lifeline Systems Inc .... E 716 896-4949
  Buffalo *(G-2829)*

Employee Codes: A=Over 500 employees, B=251-500
C=101-250, D=51-100, E=20-50, F=10-19, G=5-9

SURGICAL APPLIANCES & SPLYS

Grand Slam Holdings LLC .... E 212 583-5000
  New York *(G-9971)*
Hanger Inc .... E 518 435-0840
  Albany *(G-81)*
Hanger Inc .... E 518 438-4546
  East Syracuse *(G-4345)*
Hanger Inc .... G 718 575-5504
  Forest Hills *(G-5074)*
Hanger Inc .... F 516 678-3650
  Rockville Centre *(G-14233)*
Hanger Prsthetcs & Ortho Inc .... G 631 751-6966
  Stony Brook *(G-15166)*
Hanger Prsthetcs & Ortho Inc .... G 516 338-4466
  Westbury *(G-16339)*
Hanger Prsthetcs & Ortho Inc .... F 607 277-6620
  Ithaca *(G-6580)*
Hanger Prsthetcs & Ortho Inc .... G 315 472-5200
  Syracuse *(G-15337)*
Hanger Prsthetcs & Ortho Inc .... G 607 334-3320
  Norwich *(G-12487)*
Howmedica Osteonics Corp .... E 518 783-1880
  Latham *(G-7074)*
Howmedica Osteonics Corp .... G 516 484-0897
  Port Washington *(G-13265)*
Instrumentation Laboratory Co .... G 845 680-0028
  Orangeburg *(G-12681)*
Integer Holdings Corporation .... D 716 759-5200
  Clarence *(G-3534)*
J P R Pharmacy Inc .... F 718 327-0600
  Far Rockaway *(G-4702)*
Konrad Prosthetics & Orthotics .... F 516 485-9164
  West Hempstead *(G-16219)*
Mayflower Splint Co .... E 631 549-5131
  Dix Hills *(G-4121)*
Medline Industries Inc .... B 845 344-3301
  Middletown *(G-8163)*
Monaghan Medical Corporation .... D 518 561-7330
  Plattsburgh *(G-13135)*
Nova Health Systems Inc .... G 315 798-9018
  Utica *(G-15727)*
Nucare Pharmacy Inc .... F 212 426-9300
  New York *(G-11005)*
Nucare Pharmacy West LLC .... F 212 462-2525
  New York *(G-11006)*
Overhead Door Corporation .... D 518 828-7652
  Hudson *(G-6366)*
Pall Biomedical Inc .... C 516 484-3600
  Port Washington *(G-13294)*
Pall Corporation .... A 607 753-6041
  Cortland *(G-3885)*
Pall Corporation .... A 607 753-6041
  Cortland *(G-3886)*
Pall Corporation .... A 516 484-2818
  Port Washington *(G-13296)*
Pall Corporation .... A 607 753-6041
  Cortland *(G-3887)*
Premier Brands America Inc .... C 914 667-6200
  Mount Vernon *(G-8432)*
Scientific Plastics Inc .... F 212 967-1199
  New York *(G-11519)*
Silipos Holding LLC .... G 716 283-0700
  Niagara Falls *(G-12337)*
SPS Medical Supply Corp .... D 585 359-0130
  Rush *(G-14476)*
Steris Corporation .... G 845 469-4087
  Chester *(G-3484)*
Tumble Forms Inc .... E 315 429-3101
  Dolgeville *(G-4138)*
Turbine Engine Comp Utica .... A 315 768-8070
  Whitesboro *(G-16531)*
Wyeth Holdings LLC .... D 845 602-5000
  Pearl River *(G-12913)*

SURGICAL EQPT: See Also Instruments

Abyrx Inc .... F 914 357-2600
  Irvington *(G-6502)*
Avery Biomedical Devices Inc .... F 631 864-1600
  Commack *(G-3681)*
Conmed Corporation .... B 315 797-8375
  Utica *(G-15687)*
Integer Holdings Corporation .... D 716 759-5200
  Clarence *(G-3534)*
Lake Region Medical Inc .... C 716 662-5025
  Orchard Park *(G-12725)*
Medipoint Inc .... F 516 294-8822
  Mineola *(G-8237)*
Schilling Forge Inc .... E 315 454-4421
  Syracuse *(G-15417)*
Surgical Design Corp .... F 914 273-2445
  Armonk *(G-410)*

T G M Products Inc .... G 631 491-0515
  Wyandanch *(G-16696)*

SURGICAL IMPLANTS

Agnovos Healthcare LLC .... F 646 502-5860
  New York *(G-8770)*
Bionic Eye Technologies Inc .... G 845 505-5254
  Fishkill *(G-4943)*
Paradigm Spine LLC .... E 888 273-9897
  New York *(G-11108)*

SURVEYING SVCS: Aerial Digital Imaging

Systems Drs C3 Inc .... B 716 631-6200
  Buffalo *(G-3084)*

SVC ESTABLISHMENT EQPT & SPLYS WHOLESALERS

Architectural Textiles USA Inc .... E 212 213-6972
  New York *(G-8901)*
Licenders .... G 212 759-5200
  New York *(G-10561)*
Mirandy Products Ltd .... E 516 489-6800
  South Hempstead *(G-14942)*

SVC ESTABLISHMENT EQPT, WHOL: Cleaning & Maint Eqpt & Splys

Jad Corp of America .... E 718 762-8900
  College Point *(G-3650)*
Paradigm Mktg Consortium Inc .... E 516 496-0000
  Syosset *(G-15227)*

SVC ESTABLISHMENT EQPT, WHOLESALE: Beauty Parlor Eqpt & Sply

Ivy Enterprises Inc .... B 516 621-9779
  Port Washington *(G-13271)*
Ralph Payne .... G 718 222-4200
  Brooklyn *(G-2383)*

SVC ESTABLISHMENT EQPT, WHOLESALE: Firefighting Eqpt

Johnson Controls .... G 845 774-4120
  Harriman *(G-5720)*

SVC ESTABLISHMENT EQPT, WHOLESALE: Laundry Eqpt & Splys

Coinmach Service Corp .... A 516 349-8555
  Plainview *(G-13042)*
CSC SW Holdco Inc .... D 516 349-8555
  Plainview *(G-13049)*
G A Braun Inc .... C 315 475-3123
  North Syracuse *(G-12401)*
Low-Cost Mfg Co Inc .... G 516 627-3282
  Carle Place *(G-3268)*
Spin Holdco Inc .... G 516 349-8555
  Plainview *(G-13089)*

SWEEPING COMPOUNDS

Bono Sawdust Supply Co Inc .... G 718 446-1374
  Corona *(G-3839)*

SWIMMING POOL ACCESS: Leaf Skimmers Or Pool Rakes

Swimline International Corp .... C 631 254-2155
  Edgewood *(G-4417)*

SWIMMING POOL EQPT: Filters & Water Conditioning Systems

Abe Pool Service .... G 845 473-7730
  Hyde Park *(G-6467)*
Pentair Water Pool and Spa Inc .... E 845 452-5500
  Lagrangeville *(G-6961)*
Pleatco LLC .... D 516 609-0200
  Glen Cove *(G-5372)*

SWIMMING POOL SPLY STORES

Clean All of Syracuse LLC .... G 315 472-9189
  Syracuse *(G-15280)*

SWIMMING POOLS, EQPT & SPLYS: Wholesalers

Imperial Pools Inc .... C 518 786-1200
  Latham *(G-7075)*

SWITCHBOARDS & PARTS: Power

Electric Swtchbard Sltions LLC .... G 718 643-1105
  New Hyde Park *(G-8531)*

SWITCHES

Sector Microwave Inds Inc .... D 631 242-2245
  Deer Park *(G-4043)*

SWITCHES: Electric Power

Adeptronics Incorporated .... G 631 667-0659
  Bay Shore *(G-652)*
Marquardt Switches Inc .... C 315 655-8050
  Cazenovia *(G-3323)*
Tork Inc .... D 914 664-3542
  Mount Vernon *(G-8446)*
Transistor Devices Inc .... G 631 471-7492
  Ronkonkoma *(G-14421)*

SWITCHES: Electric Power, Exc Snap, Push Button, Etc

Atlas Switch Co Inc .... E 516 222-6280
  Garden City *(G-5251)*

SWITCHES: Electronic

C A M Graphics Co Inc .... E 631 842-3400
  Farmingdale *(G-4731)*
Dortronics Systems Inc .... E 631 725-0505
  Sag Harbor *(G-14499)*
Kearney-National Inc .... F 212 661-4600
  New York *(G-10427)*
NEa Manufacturing Corp .... E 516 371-4200
  Inwood *(G-6497)*
Scientific Components Corp .... B 718 934-4500
  Brooklyn *(G-2452)*
Secs Inc .... G 914 667-5600
  Mount Vernon *(G-8442)*
Spectron Glass & Electronics .... F 631 582-5600
  Hauppauge *(G-5943)*

SWITCHES: Electronic Applications

Dortronics Systems Inc .... E 631 725-0505
  Sag Harbor *(G-14499)*
Machine Components Corp .... E 516 694-7222
  Plainview *(G-13071)*
Switches and Sensors Inc .... F 631 924-2167
  Yaphank *(G-16723)*

SWITCHES: Silicon Control

Senera Co Inc .... F 516 639-3774
  Valley Stream *(G-15796)*

SWITCHES: Starting, Fluorescent

Monarch Electric Products Inc .... G 718 583-7996
  Bronx *(G-1335)*

SWITCHES: Time, Electrical Switchgear Apparatus

Citadel Electrical Sup Co Inc .... G 646 705-0333
  Tappan *(G-15467)*
Ems Development Corporation .... D 631 924-4736
  Yaphank *(G-16708)*

SWITCHGEAR & SWITCHBOARD APPARATUS

All City Switchboard Corp .... E 718 956-7244
  Long Island City *(G-7371)*
C A M Graphics Co Inc .... E 631 842-3400
  Farmingdale *(G-4731)*
Cooper Power Systems LLC .... B 716 375-7100
  Olean *(G-12597)*
Inertia Switch Inc .... E 845 359-8300
  Orangeburg *(G-12679)*
Marquardt Switches Inc .... C 315 655-8050
  Cazenovia *(G-3323)*
Pacs Switchgear LLC .... G 516 465-7100
  Bethpage *(G-851)*

PRODUCT SECTION

TAPE DRIVES

Schneider Electric Usa Inc..............C....... 646 335-0220
New York *(G-11510)*
Select Controls Inc........................E....... 631 567-9010
Bohemia *(G-1087)*
Sinclair Technologies Inc...............E....... 716 874-3682
Hamburg *(G-5695)*

SWITCHGEAR & SWITCHGEAR ACCESS, NEC

Cooper Industries LLC..................E....... 315 477-7000
Syracuse *(G-15291)*
Electrotech Service Eqp Corp..........E....... 718 626-7700
Astoria *(G-426)*

SWORDS

Starfire Swords Ltd Inc..................E....... 607 589-7244
Spencer *(G-14974)*

SYNTHETIC RESIN FINISHED PRDTS, NEC

General Composites Inc.................E....... 518 963-7333
Willsboro *(G-16599)*
Kaneka America LLC.....................D....... 212 705-4340
New York *(G-10404)*

SYRUPS, DRINK

Pepsi-Cola Metro Btlg Co Inc...........G....... 914 767-6000
White Plains *(G-16491)*

SYRUPS, FLAVORING, EXC DRINK

3v Company Inc.............................E....... 718 858-7333
Brooklyn *(G-1440)*
Fox 416 Corp..................................E....... 718 385-4600
Brooklyn *(G-1903)*
Mapleland Farms LLC.....................G....... 518 854-7669
Salem *(G-14538)*

SYSTEMS INTEGRATION SVCS

Binghamton Simulator Co Inc..........E....... 607 321-2980
Binghamton *(G-868)*
Medsim-Eagle Simulation Inc..........F....... 607 658-9354
Endicott *(G-4601)*
New Media Investment Group Inc....B....... 212 479-3160
New York *(G-10927)*
Telxon Corporation........................E....... 631 738-2400
Holtsville *(G-6248)*

SYSTEMS INTEGRATION SVCS: Local Area Network

Cables and Chips Inc......................E....... 212 619-3132
New York *(G-9173)*

SYSTEMS SOFTWARE DEVELOPMENT SVCS

Ex El Enterprises Ltd......................F....... 212 489-4500
New York *(G-9745)*
Inprotopia Corporation...................F....... 917 338-7501
New York *(G-10224)*
Napco Security Tech Inc................C....... 631 842-9400
Amityville *(G-304)*
Sale 121 Corp...............................D....... 240 855-8988
New York *(G-11467)*
Schoolnet Inc.................................C....... 646 496-9000
New York *(G-11517)*
Verint Systems Inc........................C....... 631 962-9600
Melville *(G-8075)*

TABLE OR COUNTERTOPS, PLASTIC LAMINATED

Allegany Laminating and Supply.....G....... 716 372-2424
Allegany *(G-188)*
Contempra Design Inc...................G....... 718 984-8586
Staten Island *(G-15065)*
Kitchen Specialty Craftsmen..........G....... 607 739-0833
Elmira *(G-4496)*
Lif Distributing Inc.........................F....... 631 630-6900
Islandia *(G-6533)*
Red White & Blue Entps Corp........G....... 718 565-8080
Woodside *(G-16675)*
Wilsonart Intl Holdings LLC............E....... 516 935-6980
Bethpage *(G-854)*

TABLECLOTHS & SETTINGS

Broder Mfg Inc...............................G....... 718 366-1667
Brooklyn *(G-1636)*
E & F Home Fashions Inc...............G....... 718 968-9719
Brooklyn *(G-1802)*
Royal Copenhagen Inc...................F....... 845 454-4442
Poughkeepsie *(G-13364)*

TABLES: Lift, Hydraulic

Columbus McKinnon Corporation....C....... 716 689-5400
Getzville *(G-5344)*
Columbus McKinnon Corporation....C....... 716 689-5400
Getzville *(G-5345)*
Columbus McKinnon Corporation....C....... 716 689-5400
Getzville *(G-5346)*

TABLETS & PADS: Book & Writing, Made From Purchased Material

Duck Flats Pharma.........................G....... 315 689-3407
Elbridge *(G-4428)*
USA Custom Pad Corp....................E....... 607 563-9550
Sidney *(G-14858)*

TABLEWARE OR KITCHEN ARTICLES: Commercial, Fine Earthenware

Green Wave International Inc.........G....... 718 499-3371
Brooklyn *(G-1950)*
Korin Japanese Trading Corp.........E....... 212 587-7021
New York *(G-10471)*

TABLEWARE: Plastic

Pactiv LLC....................................A....... 585 393-3149
Canandaigua *(G-3230)*
Q Squared Design LLC..................E....... 212 686-8860
New York *(G-11290)*
Supreme Poultry Inc......................G....... 718 472-0300
Long Island City *(G-7610)*

TAGS & LABELS: Paper

Auto Data Systems Inc...................E....... 631 667-2382
Deer Park *(G-3948)*
Depot Label Company Inc..............G....... 631 467-2952
Patchogue *(G-12864)*
Gooding Co Inc..............................E....... 716 266-6252
Lockport *(G-7308)*
K Sidrane Inc................................E....... 631 393-6974
Farmingdale *(G-4796)*
Sml USA Inc..................................E....... 212 736-8800
New York *(G-11626)*
Stickershopcom Inc.......................G....... 631 563-4323
Bayport *(G-739)*

TAGS: Paper, Blank, Made From Purchased Paper

Jerry Tomaselli..............................F....... 718 965-1400
Brooklyn *(G-2036)*
Tag Envelope Co Inc......................E....... 718 389-6844
College Point *(G-3669)*

TAILORS: Custom

Adrian Jules Ltd............................D....... 585 342-5886
Rochester *(G-13603)*

TALLOW: Animal

Baker Commodities Inc..................E....... 585 482-1880
Rochester *(G-13652)*

TANK REPAIR SVCS

David Isseks & Sons Inc.................E....... 212 966-8694
New York *(G-9481)*

TANK TOWERS: Metal Plate

Vertarib Inc..................................G....... 561 683-0888
Jericho *(G-6806)*

TANKS & OTHER TRACKED VEHICLE CMPNTS

Lourdes Industries Inc...................D....... 631 234-6600
Hauppauge *(G-5873)*
Tecmotiv (usa) Inc........................E....... 905 669-5911
Niagara Falls *(G-12342)*

TANKS: Concrete

Preload Concrete Structures...........E....... 631 231-8100
Hauppauge *(G-5921)*

TANKS: Cryogenic, Metal

North American Svcs Group LLC....F....... 518 885-1820
Ballston Spa *(G-592)*

TANKS: Fuel, Including Oil & Gas, Metal Plate

Cardinal Tank Corp........................E....... 718 625-4350
Brooklyn *(G-1676)*
Crown Tank Company LLC............F....... 855 276-9682
Horseheads *(G-6310)*
Stutzman Management Corp.........F....... 800 735-2013
Lancaster *(G-7051)*

TANKS: Lined, Metal

Amherst Stnless Fbrication LLC.....E....... 716 691-7012
Amherst *(G-215)*
General Oil Equipment Co Inc........E....... 716 691-7012
Amherst *(G-229)*
Modutank Inc................................F....... 718 392-1112
Long Island City *(G-7528)*

TANKS: Plastic & Fiberglass

An-Cor Industrial Plastics Inc.........D....... 716 695-3141
North Tonawanda *(G-12411)*
Chem-Tek Systems Inc.................F....... 631 253-3010
Bay Shore *(G-670)*
Norwesco Inc................................F....... 607 687-8081
Owego *(G-12801)*

TANKS: Standard Or Custom Fabricated, Metal Plate

Expert Industries Inc......................E....... 718 434-6060
Brooklyn *(G-1859)*
Feldmeier Equipment Inc...............D....... 315 823-2000
Syracuse *(G-15323)*
Gasport Welding & Fabg Inc..........F....... 716 772-7205
Gasport *(G-5306)*
K Industries Inc............................G....... 631 897-2125
Bellport *(G-806)*
Stainless Metals Inc.......................F....... 718 784-1454
Woodside *(G-16680)*
Stavo Industries Inc.......................F....... 845 331-4552
Kingston *(G-6920)*
Steelways Inc................................E....... 845 562-0860
Newburgh *(G-12246)*
Taylor Tank Company Inc..............E....... 718 434-1300
Brooklyn *(G-2557)*

TANKS: Storage, Farm, Metal Plate

Bigbee Steel and Tank Company....E....... 518 273-0801
Watervliet *(G-16041)*

TANKS: Water, Metal Plate

David Isseks & Sons Inc.................E....... 212 966-8694
New York *(G-9481)*
Jbren Corp....................................F....... 716 332-5928
Buffalo *(G-2891)*
Water Cooling Corp.......................G....... 718 723-6500
Rosedale *(G-14442)*

TANKS: Wood

Rosenwach Tank Co Inc.................E....... 212 972-4411
Astoria *(G-442)*

TANNERIES: Leather

Colonial Tanning Corporation.........G....... 518 725-7171
Gloversville *(G-5454)*
Myers Group LLC..........................G....... 973 761-6414
New York *(G-10866)*
Simco Leather Corporation............E....... 518 762-7100
Johnstown *(G-6840)*
Wood & Hyde Leather Co Inc........E....... 518 725-7105
Gloversville *(G-5474)*

TAPE DRIVES

Matrox Graphics Inc......................G....... 518 561-4417
Plattsburgh *(G-13132)*

Employee Codes: A=Over 500 employees, B=251-500
C=101-250, D=51-100, E=20-50, F=10-19, G=5-9

2019 Harris
New York Manufacturers Directory

TAPES, ADHESIVE: Medical

Eis Inc .... E 585 426-5330
  Rochester *(G-13774)*
Tape Systems Inc .... F 914 668-3700
  Mount Vernon *(G-8444)*

TAPES: Audio Range, Blank

Orpheo USA Corp .... G 212 464-8255
  New York *(G-11062)*

TAPES: Coated Fiberglass, Pipe Sealing Or Insulating

GM Insulation Corp .... F 516 354-6000
  Elmont *(G-4519)*

TAPES: Gummed, Cloth Or Paper Based, From Purchased Matls

Patco Tapes Inc .... G 718 497-1527
  Maspeth *(G-7867)*

TAPES: Magnetic

Professional Tape Corporation .... G 516 656-5519
  Glen Cove *(G-5373)*

TAPES: Pressure Sensitive

Berry Specialty Tapes LLC .... C 631 727-6000
  Riverhead *(G-13565)*
Kleen Stik Industries Inc .... F 718 984-5031
  Staten Island *(G-15098)*
Merco Hackensack Inc .... G 845 357-3699
  Hillburn *(G-6154)*
T L F Graphics Inc .... D 585 272-5500
  Rochester *(G-14156)*
Tape-It Inc .... E 631 243-4100
  Bay Shore *(G-730)*
Valley Industrial Products Inc .... E 631 385-9300
  Huntington *(G-6424)*

TARGET DRONES

Enlighten Air Inc .... G 917 656-1248
  New York *(G-9685)*

TARPAULINS

Breton Industries Inc .... C 518 842-3030
  Amsterdam *(G-329)*

TELECOMMUNICATION SYSTEMS & EQPT

Aines Manufacturing Corp .... E 631 471-3900
  Islip *(G-6544)*
Alcatel-Lucent USA Inc .... D 516 349-4900
  Plainview *(G-13034)*
Clayton Dubilier & Rice Fun .... E 212 407-5200
  New York *(G-9324)*
Corning Incorporated .... E 607 248-1200
  Corning *(G-3812)*
Corning Incorporated .... G 607 974-6729
  Painted Post *(G-12837)*
Corning Incorporated .... A 607 974-9000
  Corning *(G-3809)*
ESi Cases & Accessories Inc .... E 212 883-8838
  New York *(G-9705)*
Forerunner Technologies Inc .... E 631 337-2100
  Edgewood *(G-4401)*
Harris Corporation .... E 585 244-5830
  Rochester *(G-13858)*
Interdigital Communications LLC .... C 631 622-4000
  Melville *(G-8038)*
Kelta Inc .... E 631 789-5000
  Edgewood *(G-4406)*
L3 Technologies Inc .... A 631 436-7400
  Hauppauge *(G-5859)*
Mitel Networks Inc .... G 877 654-3573
  Rochester *(G-13948)*
Parabit Systems Inc .... E 516 378-4800
  Bellmore *(G-791)*
Performance Technologies Inc .... E 585 256-0200
  Rochester *(G-14012)*
Snake Tray International LLC .... E 631 674-0004
  Bay Shore *(G-725)*
Telephonics Corporation .... D 631 755-7659
  Farmingdale *(G-4891)*
Telephonics Corporation .... A 631 755-7000
  Farmingdale *(G-4892)*

Tii Technologies Inc .... E 516 364-9300
  Edgewood *(G-4419)*

TELECOMMUNICATIONS CARRIERS & SVCS: Wired

Forerunner Technologies Inc .... E 631 337-2100
  Edgewood *(G-4401)*
Fusion Connect Inc .... G 212 201-2400
  New York *(G-9863)*
Human Electronics Inc .... G 315 724-9850
  Utica *(G-15710)*
Key Computer Svcs of Chelsea ...... D 212 206-8060
  New York *(G-10438)*

TELEMARKETING BUREAUS

S & H Uniform Corp .... D 914 937-6800
  White Plains *(G-16500)*

TELEMETERING EQPT

L3 Foreign Holdings Inc .... D 212 697-1111
  New York *(G-10497)*
L3 Technologies Inc .... B 631 231-1700
  Hauppauge *(G-5858)*
L3 Technologies Inc .... D 631 231-1700
  Hauppauge *(G-5861)*
L3 Technologies Inc .... B 212 697-1111
  New York *(G-10498)*

TELEPHONE ANSWERING SVCS

Milne Mfg Inc .... F 716 772-2536
  Gasport *(G-5308)*

TELEPHONE BOOTHS, EXC WOOD

Clark Specialty Co Inc .... E 607 776-3193
  Bath *(G-642)*
Parabit Systems Inc .... E 516 378-4800
  Bellmore *(G-791)*

TELEPHONE EQPT INSTALLATION

Telecommunication Concepts .... G 315 736-8523
  Whitesboro *(G-16530)*

TELEPHONE EQPT: Modems

Simrex Corporation .... G 716 206-0174
  Buffalo *(G-3066)*

TELEPHONE EQPT: NEC

ABS Talkx Inc .... G 631 254-9100
  Bay Shore *(G-651)*
Access 24 .... G 845 358-5397
  Valley Cottage *(G-15750)*
Audio-Sears Corp .... D 607 652-7305
  Stamford *(G-15029)*
Avaya Services Inc .... G 866 462-8292
  New York *(G-8973)*
Call Forwarding Technologies .... G 516 621-3600
  Greenvale *(G-5628)*
Eagle Telephonics Inc .... F 631 471-3600
  Bohemia *(G-1017)*
I D Tel Corp .... F 718 876-6000
  Staten Island *(G-15087)*
Luxcore Networks Inc .... F 212 618-1724
  New York *(G-10631)*
R I R Communications Systems ...... E 718 706-9957
  Mount Vernon *(G-8437)*
Siemens Corporation .... F 202 434-7800
  New York *(G-11577)*
Siemens USA Holdings Inc .... B 212 258-4000
  New York *(G-11580)*
Telecommunication Concepts .... G 315 736-8523
  Whitesboro *(G-16530)*
Toshiba Amer Info Systems Inc ...... B 949 583-3000
  New York *(G-11871)*

TELEPHONE SVCS

Tempo Industries Inc .... G 516 334-6900
  Westbury *(G-16377)*

TELEPHONE SWITCHING EQPT

Redcom Laboratories Inc .... C 585 924-6567
  Victor *(G-15865)*

TELEPHONE: Fiber Optic Systems

Fiber Instrument Sales Inc .... C 315 736-2206
  Oriskany *(G-12757)*
Fiberwave Corporation .... C 718 802-9011
  Brooklyn *(G-1877)*
Fujitsu Ntwrk Cmmnications Inc ..... F 845 731-2000
  Pearl River *(G-12897)*
Sandstone Technologies Corp .... G 585 785-5537
  Rochester *(G-14110)*
Sandstone Technologies Corp .... G 585 785-5537
  Rochester *(G-14111)*
Splice Technologies Inc .... G 631 924-8108
  Manorville *(G-7786)*
Terahertz Technologies Inc .... G 315 736-3642
  Oriskany *(G-12765)*

TELEPHONE: Headsets

Quality One Wireless LLC .... C 631 233-3337
  Ronkonkoma *(G-14403)*
U2o Usa LLC .... G 516 813-9500
  Plainview *(G-13094)*

TELEPHONE: Sets, Exc Cellular Radio

Maia Systems LLC .... G 718 206-0100
  Jamaica *(G-6658)*
Powermate Cellular .... G 718 833-9400
  Brooklyn *(G-2331)*

TELEVISION BROADCASTING & COMMUNICATIONS EQPT

Basil S Kadhim .... G 888 520-5192
  New York *(G-9024)*
Prime View USA Inc .... G 212 730-4905
  New York *(G-11242)*

TELEVISION BROADCASTING STATIONS

21st Century Fox America Inc .... D 212 852-7000
  New York *(G-8673)*
General Electric Company .... A 518 385-4022
  Schenectady *(G-14675)*
Hearst Business Media Corp .... F 631 650-4441
  New York *(G-10056)*
Hearst Corporation .... A 212 649-2000
  New York *(G-10061)*
New York Times Company .... B 212 556-1234
  New York *(G-10944)*
Tegna Inc .... C 716 849-2222
  Buffalo *(G-3089)*
Tribune Entertainment Co Del .... E 203 866-2204
  New York *(G-11897)*

TELEVISION SETS

Jwin Electronics Corp .... C 516 626-7188
  Port Washington *(G-13275)*
Toshiba America Inc .... E 212 596-0600
  New York *(G-11872)*

TELEVISION: Closed Circuit Eqpt

Click It Inc .... D 631 686-2900
  Hauppauge *(G-5791)*
Sartek Industries Inc .... G 631 473-3555
  East Setauket *(G-4309)*
Sentry Technology Corporation .... F 800 645-4224
  Ronkonkoma *(G-14411)*
Vicon Industries Inc .... C 631 952-2288
  Hauppauge *(G-5970)*

TEMPERING: Metal

Elmira Heat Treating Inc .... E 607 734-1577
  Elmira *(G-4484)*

TENT REPAIR SHOP

Custom Canvas Manufacturing Co .. E 716 852-6372
  Buffalo *(G-2789)*

TENTS: All Materials

Air Structures Amercn Tech Inc ...... E 914 937-4500
  Port Chester *(G-13191)*
AMS Star Structures Inc .... G 914 584-0898
  Nyack *(G-12499)*
Dhs Systems LLC .... F 845 359-6066
  Orangeburg *(G-12674)*
Johnson Outdoors Inc .... C 607 779-2200
  Binghamton *(G-899)*

PRODUCT SECTION

Kraus & Sons Inc .... F 212 620-0408
  New York *(G-10480)*
Leiter Sukkahs Inc .... G 718 436-0303
  Brooklyn *(G-2108)*
Select Fabricators Inc .... F 585 393-0650
  Canandaigua *(G-3233)*
Toptec Products LLC .... F 631 421-9800
  Melville *(G-8072)*

TERMINAL BOARDS

Veja Electronics Inc .... D 631 321-6086
  Deer Park *(G-4058)*

TERRA COTTA: Architectural

Boston Valley Pottery Inc .... D 716 649-7490
  Orchard Park *(G-12701)*

TEST KITS: Pregnancy

Inolife Tchnlgies Oprtions Inc .... G 212 386-5575
  New York *(G-10222)*
Ithaca Pregancy Center .... G 607 753-3909
  Cortland *(G-3877)*
Northeast Doulas .... G 845 621-0654
  Mahopac *(G-7710)*
Working Family Solutions Inc .... G 845 802-6182
  Saugerties *(G-14620)*

TESTERS: Battery

Sorfin Yoshimura Ltd .... G 516 802-4600
  Woodbury *(G-16632)*
Walter R Tucker Entps Ltd .... E 607 467-2866
  Deposit *(G-4112)*

TESTERS: Environmental

Caltex International Ltd .... E 315 425-1040
  Syracuse *(G-15268)*
Nexgen Enviro Systems Inc .... G 631 226-2930
  Lindenhurst *(G-7184)*
Niagara Scientific Inc .... D 315 437-0821
  East Syracuse *(G-4360)*

TESTERS: Integrated Circuit

Epoch Microelectronics Inc .... G 914 332-8570
  Valhalla *(G-15741)*
Xelic Incorporated .... F 585 415-2764
  Pittsford *(G-13029)*

TESTERS: Physical Property

G E Inspection Technologies LP ... C 315 554-2000
  Skaneateles *(G-14871)*
Gleason Corporation .... A 585 473-1000
  Rochester *(G-13839)*
Gleason Works .... A 585 473-1000
  Rochester *(G-13840)*
Gurley Precision Instrs Inc .... C 518 272-6300
  Troy *(G-15607)*

TESTERS: Water, Exc Indl Process

Ewt Holdings III Corp .... F 212 644-5900
  New York *(G-9744)*
Industrial Municipal Equipment ..... F 631 665-6712
  Brightwaters *(G-1186)*

TEXTILE & APPAREL SVCS

Crye Precision LLC .... C 718 246-3838
  Brooklyn *(G-1736)*
Newcastle Fabrics Corp .... G 718 388-6600
  Brooklyn *(G-2266)*
RAK Finishing Corp .... E 718 416-4242
  Howard Beach *(G-6331)*

TEXTILE BAGS WHOLESALERS

Adam Scott Designs Inc .... E 212 420-8866
  New York *(G-8732)*
Nochairs Inc .... G 917 748-9731
  New York *(G-10983)*

TEXTILE CONVERTERS: Knit Goods

Bank-Miller Co Inc .... E 914 227-9357
  Pelham *(G-12933)*
Sextet Fabrics Inc .... F 516 593-0608
  East Rockaway *(G-4295)*

TEXTILE FABRICATORS

Dream Green Productions .... G 917 267-8920
  Warwick *(G-15951)*

TEXTILE FINISH: Chem Coat/Treat, Fire Resist, Manmade

American Spray-On Corp .... E 212 929-2100
  New York *(G-8837)*
Beckmann Converting Inc .... E 518 842-0073
  Amsterdam *(G-327)*

TEXTILE FINISHING: Chemical Coating Or Treating

Reynolds Drapery Service Inc ..... F 315 845-8632
  Newport *(G-12256)*

TEXTILE FINISHING: Decorative, Man Fiber & Silk, Broadwoven

Toltec Fabrics Inc .... C 212 706-9310
  New York *(G-11857)*

TEXTILE FINISHING: Dyeing, Broadwoven, Cotton

B & K Dye Cutting Inc .... G 718 497-5216
  Brooklyn *(G-1579)*
Dyenamix Inc .... G 212 941-6642
  New York *(G-9593)*

TEXTILE FINISHING: Dyeing, Finishing & Printng, Linen Fabric

American Country Quilts & Lin .... G 631 283-5466
  Southampton *(G-14949)*
China Ting Fashion Group (usa) .. G 212 716-1600
  New York *(G-9283)*
Duck River Textiles Inc .... F 212 679-2980
  New York *(G-9583)*

TEXTILE FINISHING: Dyeing, Manmade Fiber & Silk, Broadwoven

Eastern Silk Mills Inc .... G 212 730-1300
  New York *(G-9611)*

TEXTILE FINISHING: Embossing, Cotton, Broadwoven

Lee Dyeing Company NC Inc ...... F 518 736-5232
  Johnstown *(G-6834)*

TEXTILE FINISHING: Embossing, Man Fiber & Silk, Broadwoven

Knucklehead Embroidery Inc ...... G 607 797-2725
  Johnson City *(G-6814)*

TEXTILE FINISHING: Silk, Broadwoven

Raxon Fabrics Corp .... F 212 532-6816
  New York *(G-11329)*

TEXTILE FINISHING: Sponging, Cotton, Broadwoven, Trade

Basiloff LLC .... G 646 671-0353
  New York *(G-9025)*

TEXTILE PRDTS: Hand Woven & Crocheted

HMS Productions LLC .... G 212 719-9190
  Mineola *(G-8227)*

TEXTILE: Finishing, Cotton Broadwoven

All About Art Inc .... F 718 321-0755
  Flushing *(G-4983)*
Carolyn Ray Inc .... G 914 476-0619
  Yonkers *(G-16743)*
Central Textiles Inc .... F 212 213-8740
  New York *(G-9245)*
Marcel Finishing Corp .... E 718 381-2889
  Plainview *(G-13072)*
Prismatic Dyeing & Finshg Inc ... D 845 561-1800
  Newburgh *(G-12242)*

TEXTILE: Finishing, Raw Stock NEC

Ben-Sak Textile Inc .... G 212 279-5122
  New York *(G-9042)*
Hosel & Ackerson Inc .... G 212 575-1490
  New York *(G-10125)*
Majestic Rayon Corporation .... E 212 929-6443
  New York *(G-10675)*
Marcel Finishing Corp .... E 718 381-2889
  Plainview *(G-13072)*
National Spinning Co Inc .... E 212 382-6400
  New York *(G-10886)*
Newcastle Fabrics Corp .... G 718 388-6600
  Brooklyn *(G-2266)*
Prismatic Dyeing & Finshg Inc ... D 845 561-1800
  Newburgh *(G-12242)*
Skin Prints Inc .... E 845 920-8755
  Pearl River *(G-12911)*

TEXTILE: Goods, NEC

Southern Adrndck Fbr Prdcrs CP ... G 518 692-2700
  Greenwich *(G-5645)*

TEXTILES

Stern & Stern Industries Inc .... D 607 324-4485
  Hornell *(G-6303)*

TEXTILES: Bagging, Jute

Ivi Services Inc .... D 607 729-5111
  Binghamton *(G-897)*

TEXTILES: Fibers, Textile, Rcvrd From Mill Waste/Rags

Ace Drop Cloth Canvas Pdts Inc ... E 718 731-1550
  Bronx *(G-1208)*

TEXTILES: Flock

Solivaira Specialties Inc .... D 716 693-4009
  North Tonawanda *(G-12452)*
Solvaira Specialties Inc .... C 716 693-4040
  North Tonawanda *(G-12453)*
Solvaira Specialty LP .... E 716 693-4040
  North Tonawanda *(G-12454)*
Solvaira Specialty LP .... D 716 693-4040
  North Tonawanda *(G-12455)*

TEXTILES: Linen Fabrics

David King Linen Inc .... F 718 241-7298
  New York *(G-9482)*
Novita Fabrics Furnishing Corp ... F 516 299-4500
  Mineola *(G-8242)*
Sabbsons International Inc .... F 718 360-1947
  Brooklyn *(G-2442)*
Sam Salem & Son LLC .... F 212 695-6020
  New York *(G-11475)*
Simple Elegance New York Inc ... F 718 360-1947
  Brooklyn *(G-2477)*
TRM Linen Inc .... G 718 686-6075
  Brooklyn *(G-2588)*

TEXTILES: Mill Waste & Remnant

Dean Trading Corp .... F 718 485-0600
  Brooklyn *(G-1763)*
S Hellerman Inc .... F 718 622-2995
  Brooklyn *(G-2440)*

TEXTILES: Tops & Top Processing, Manmade Or Other Fiber

Jo-Vin Decorators Inc .... E 718 441-9350
  Woodhaven *(G-16636)*

THEATRICAL LIGHTING SVCS

Creative Stage Lighting Co Inc ... E 518 251-3302
  North Creek *(G-12391)*

THEATRICAL PRODUCERS & SVCS

Congress For Jewish Culture ...... G 212 505-8040
  New York *(G-9379)*
Peermusic Ltd .... F 212 265-3910
  New York *(G-11139)*

THEATRICAL SCENERY

Company		Phone
Center Line Studios Inc .... G		845 534-7143
New Windsor *(G-8639)*		
Center Line Studios Inc .... F		845 534-7143
New Windsor *(G-8640)*		
Costume Armour Inc .... F		845 534-9120
Cornwall *(G-3832)*		
Hudson Scenic Studio Inc C		914 375-0900
Yonkers *(G-16770)*		
King Displays Inc .... F		212 629-8455
New York *(G-10451)*		
Production Resource Group LLC .... D		877 774-7088
Armonk *(G-408)*		
Production Resource Group LLC .... E		845 567-5700
New Windsor *(G-8655)*		
Stiegelbauer Associates Inc .... E		718 624-0835
Brooklyn *(G-2522)*		

THERMOMETERS: Indl

Kessler Thermometer Corp .... G 631 841-5500
West Babylon *(G-16167)*
Oden Machinery Inc .... E 716 874-3000
Tonawanda *(G-15567)*

THERMOMETERS: Liquid-In-Glass & Bimetal

Germanow-Simon Corporation .... E 585 232-1440
Rochester *(G-13832)*

THERMOMETERS: Medical, Digital

Accuvein Inc .... D 816 997-9400
Medford *(G-7936)*

THERMOPLASTIC MATERIALS

Bso Energy Corp .... F 212 520-1827
New York *(G-9153)*

THERMOPLASTICS

ADC Acquisition Company .... E 518 377-6471
Niskayuna *(G-12352)*
On Time Plastics Inc .... G 516 442-4280
Freeport *(G-5170)*

THERMOSETTING MATERIALS

Empire Plastics Inc .... E 607 754-9132
Endwell *(G-4616)*

THIN FILM CIRCUITS

CAM Touchview Products Inc .... F 631 842-3400
Sag Harbor *(G-14497)*

THREAD: All Fibers

Albany International Corp .... C 607 749-7226
Homer *(G-6252)*
United Thread Mills Corp .... G 516 536-3900
Oceanside *(G-12562)*

THREAD: Embroidery

American Quality Embroidery .... G 631 467-3200
Ronkonkoma *(G-14306)*
One In A Million Inc .... G 516 829-1111
Valley Stream *(G-15788)*

TICKET OFFICES & AGENCIES: Theatrical

London Theater News Ltd .... F 212 517-8608
New York *(G-10596)*

TIES, FORM: Metal

American Wire Tie Inc .... E 716 337-2412
North Collins *(G-12383)*

TILE: Asphalt, Floor

Shenfield Studio LLC .... F 315 436-8869
Syracuse *(G-15424)*

TILE: Brick & Structural, Clay

Stone and Bath Gallery .... G 718 438-4500
Brooklyn *(G-2523)*

TILE: Drain, Clay

Bistrian Cement Corporation .... F 631 324-1123
East Hampton *(G-4232)*

TILE: Fireproofing, Clay

Certified Flameproofing Corp .... G 631 265-4824
Smithtown *(G-14895)*
Noroc Enterprises Inc .... C 718 585-3230
Bronx *(G-1344)*

TILE: Mosaic, Ceramic

Artsaics Studios Inc .... G 631 254-2558
Deer Park *(G-3947)*
Avenue Mosaic Company .... G 216 245-6306
New York *(G-8974)*

TILE: Stamped Metal, Floor Or Wall

Surving Studios .... F 845 355-1430
Middletown *(G-8178)*

TILE: Terrazzo Or Concrete, Precast

Foro Marble Co Inc .... E 718 852-2322
Brooklyn *(G-1898)*
Walter G Legge Company Inc .... G 914 737-5040
Peekskill *(G-12928)*

TILE: Wall & Floor, Ceramic

Aremco Products Inc .... F 845 268-0039
Valley Cottage *(G-15752)*
Dal-Tile Corporation .... G 914 835-1801
Harrison *(G-5727)*
Lazer Marble & Granite Corp .... G 718 859-9644
Brooklyn *(G-2096)*

TILE: Wall & Floor, clay

Quality Components Framing Sys .... F 315 768-1167
Whitesboro *(G-16528)*

TIMBER PRDTS WHOLESALERS

Guldenschuh Logging & Lbr LLC .... G 585 538-4750
Caledonia *(G-3155)*

TIMING DEVICES: Electronic

Eversan Inc .... F 315 736-3967
Whitesboro *(G-16527)*
Infitec Inc .... D 315 433-1150
East Syracuse *(G-4352)*

TIN

Mustard Tin .... G 315 769-8409
Massena *(G-7906)*

TIRE & INNER TUBE MATERIALS & RELATED PRDTS

Handy & Harman Ltd .... A 212 520-2300
New York *(G-10031)*
Roli Retreads Inc .... E 631 694-7670
Farmingdale *(G-4868)*
Sph Group Holdings LLC .... F 212 520-2300
New York *(G-11669)*

TIRE & TUBE REPAIR MATERIALS, WHOLESALE

Loomis Root Inc .... F 716 564-7668
Amherst *(G-236)*

TIRE CORD & FABRIC

Albany International Corp .... C 518 445-2230
Menands *(G-8079)*
Designatronics Incorporated .... B 516 328-3300
Hicksville *(G-6080)*
Haines Equipment Inc .... E 607 566-8531
Avoca *(G-516)*
York Industries Inc .... F 516 746-3736
Garden City Park *(G-5290)*

TIRE INFLATORS: Hand Or Compressor Operated

Vac Air Service Inc .... F 716 665-2206
Jamestown *(G-6760)*

TIRES & INNER TUBES

East Coast Intl Tire Inc .... G 718 386-9088
Maspeth *(G-7841)*

New York CT Loc246 Seiu Wel BF .... G 212 233-0616
New York *(G-10933)*

TIRES: Auto

McCarthy Tire Svc Co NY Inc .... F 518 449-5185
Menands *(G-8088)*

TITANIUM MILL PRDTS

Titanium Dem Remediation Group .... F 716 433-4100
Lockport *(G-7336)*

TOBACCO LEAF PROCESSING

Schweitzer-Mauduit Intl Inc .... C 518 329-4222
Ancram *(G-365)*

TOBACCO: Chewing

National Tobacco Company LP .... F 212 253-8185
New York *(G-10888)*

TOBACCO: Chewing & Snuff

Elab Smokers Boutique .... G 585 865-4513
Rochester *(G-13775)*
Standard Diversified Inc .... G 302 824-7062
Mineola *(G-8250)*

TOBACCO: Cigarettes

East End .... F 716 532-2622
Collins *(G-3673)*
Epuffer Inc .... G 718 374-6030
Brooklyn *(G-1844)*
Jacobs Tobacco Company .... E 518 358-4948
Hogansburg *(G-6165)*
Onondaga Nation .... G 315 469-3230
Nedrow *(G-8479)*
Philip Morris Intl Inc .... D 917 663-2000
New York *(G-11181)*
PMI Global Services Inc .... E 917 663-2000
New York *(G-11213)*
R J Reynolds Tobacco Company .... C 716 871-1553
Tonawanda *(G-15572)*
Schweitzer-Mauduit Intl Inc .... C 518 329-4222
Ancram *(G-365)*
Seneca Manufacturing Company .... G 716 945-4400
Salamanca *(G-14532)*
Seneca Nation Enterprise .... F 716 934-7430
Irving *(G-6501)*
Vector Group Ltd .... B 212 409-2800
New York *(G-12002)*

TOBACCO: Cigars

American Cigar .... G 718 969-0008
Fresh Meadows *(G-5194)*
Mafco Consolidated Group Inc .... F 212 572-8600
New York *(G-10659)*

TOBACCO: Smoking

Mafco Consolidated Group Inc .... F 212 572-8600
New York *(G-10659)*

TOILET FIXTURES: Plastic

Metpar Corp .... D 516 333-2600
Westbury *(G-16356)*

TOILET PREPARATIONS

H & H Laboratories Inc .... F 718 624-8041
Brooklyn *(G-1955)*
H & H Laboratories Inc .... G 718 624-8041
Brooklyn *(G-1956)*
King Research Inc .... E 718 788-0122
Brooklyn *(G-2072)*
MZB Accessories LLC .... D 718 472-7500
Long Island City *(G-7531)*

TOILETRIES, COSMETICS & PERFUME STORES

Estee Lauder Inc .... D 631 531-1000
Melville *(G-8022)*
International Design Assoc Ltd .... G 212 687-0333
New York *(G-10245)*

TOILETRIES, WHOLESALE: Hair Preparations

EL Erman International Ltd .... G 212 444-9440
  Brooklyn (G-1819)

TOILETRIES, WHOLESALE: Perfumes

Elias Fragrances Inc .... F 718 693-6400
  Rye Brook (G-14491)
Elite Parfums Ltd .... D 212 983-2640
  New York (G-9651)
Eternal Love Parfums Corp .... G 516 921-6100
  Syosset (G-15216)
Scent-A-Vision Inc .... E 631 424-4905
  Huntington Station (G-6457)
Sundial Fragrances & Flavors .... E 631 842-8800
  Amityville (G-319)

TOILETRIES, WHOLESALE: Toilet Preparations

Bare Escentuals Inc .... G 646 537-0070
  New York (G-9016)
Quality King Distributors Inc .... C 631 439-2027
  Ronkonkoma (G-14402)

TOILETRIES, WHOLESALE: Toiletries

Bfma Holding Corporation .... G 607 753-6746
  Cortland (G-3862)
Gassho Body & Mind Inc .... G 518 695-9991
  Schuylerville (G-14734)
Marietta Corporation .... A 323 589-8181
  Cortland (G-3883)
Robell Research Inc .... G 212 755-6577
  New York (G-11405)

TOMBSTONES: Terrazzo Or Concrete, Precast

Eaton Brothers Corp .... G 716 649-8250
  Hamburg (G-5676)

TOOL & DIE STEEL

Baker Tool & Die & Die .... G 716 694-2025
  North Tonawanda (G-12416)

TOOLS: Carpenters', Including Levels & Chisels, Exc Saws

Nyc District Council Ubcja .... G 212 366-7500
  New York (G-11012)

TOOLS: Hand

Allway Tools Inc .... D 718 792-3636
  Bronx (G-1217)
Ames Companies Inc .... E 607 739-4544
  Pine Valley (G-13006)
Best Way Tools By Anderson Inc .... G 631 586-4702
  Deer Park (G-3950)
Coastal Cable Tools Inc .... E 315 471-5361
  Syracuse (G-15283)
Dead Ringer LLC .... G 585 355-4685
  Rochester (G-13736)
Dresser-Argus Inc .... G 718 643-1540
  Brooklyn (G-1794)
Huron TI Cutter Grinding Inc .... E 631 420-7000
  Farmingdale (G-4782)
Hydramec Inc .... E 585 593-5190
  Scio (G-14735)
Ivy Classic Industries Inc .... E 914 632-8200
  New Rochelle (G-8616)
Robinson Tools LLC .... G 585 586-5432
  Penfield (G-12944)
Schilling Forge Inc .... E 315 454-4421
  Syracuse (G-15417)
Snyder Manufacturing Inc .... E 716 945-0354
  Salamanca (G-14533)
U S Air Tool Co Inc .... F 631 471-3300
  Ronkonkoma (G-14423)
Winters Railroad Service Inc .... G 716 337-2668
  North Collins (G-12390)
York Industries Inc .... E 516 746-3736
  Garden City Park (G-5290)

TOOLS: Hand, Engravers'

Edward C Lyons Company Inc .... G 718 515-5361
  Bronx (G-1265)

Edward C Muller Corp .... F 718 881-7270
  Bronx (G-1266)

TOOLS: Hand, Jewelers'

Boucheron Joaillerie USA Inc .... G 212 715-7330
  New York (G-9126)
Empire Devleopment .... G 716 789-2097
  Mayville (G-7920)

TOOLS: Hand, Mechanics

Classic Tool Design Inc .... E 845 562-8700
  New Windsor (G-8641)

TOOLS: Hand, Plumbers'

Design Source By Lg Inc .... E 212 274-0022
  New York (G-9507)
Metro City Group Inc .... G 516 781-2500
  Bellmore (G-789)

TOOLS: Hand, Power

Allied Motion Technologies Inc .... C 315 782-5910
  Watertown (G-16000)
Awt Supply Corp .... G 516 437-9105
  Elmont (G-4517)
Black & Decker (us) Inc .... B 914 235-6300
  Brewster (G-1159)
Black & Decker (us) Inc .... G 716 884-6220
  Buffalo (G-2734)
Black & Decker (us) Inc .... G 631 952-2008
  Hauppauge (G-5781)
Black & Decker Corporation .... G 718 335-1042
  Woodside (G-16647)
Dynabrade Inc .... C 716 631-0100
  Clarence (G-3529)
Great American Tool Co Inc .... G 716 646-5700
  Hamburg (G-5681)
Huck International Inc .... C 845 331-7300
  Kingston (G-6902)
Ivy Classic Industries Inc .... E 914 632-8200
  New Rochelle (G-8616)
Meritool LLC .... E 716 699-6005
  Salamanca (G-14527)
Reimann & Georger Corporation .... E 716 895-1156
  Buffalo (G-3034)
Stature Electric Inc .... D 716 242-7535
  Amherst (G-251)
Thomas C Wilson LLC .... E 718 729-3360
  Long Island City (G-7615)

TOOTHBRUSHES: Electric

Quip Nyc Inc .... G 917 331-3993
  Brooklyn (G-2372)

TOOTHBRUSHES: Exc Electric

Colgate-Palmolive Company .... A 212 310-2000
  New York (G-9349)

TOOTHPASTES, GELS & TOOTHPOWDERS

Colgat-Plmolive Centl Amer Inc .... G 212 310-2000
  New York (G-9348)
Colgate-Palmolive Company .... A 212 310-2000
  New York (G-9349)
Colgate-Palmolive Company .... B 718 506-3961
  Queens Village (G-13404)
Quip Nyc Inc .... G 917 331-3993
  Brooklyn (G-2372)

TOWELS: Indl

Blu Sand LLC .... G 212 564-1147
  New York (G-9105)

TOWELS: Linen & Linen & Cotton Mixtures

Blc Textiles Inc .... E 844 500-7900
  Mineola (G-8208)

TOWERS, SECTIONS: Transmission, Radio & Television

Fred A Nudd Corporation .... D 315 524-2531
  Ontario (G-12653)

TOYS

Buffalo Games LLC .... D 716 827-8393
  Buffalo (G-2744)

Church Communities NY Inc .... E 518 589-5103
  Elka Park (G-4433)
Church Communities NY Inc .... E 518 589-5103
  Elka Park (G-4434)
Cioccolato 7 LLC .... G 347 240-7115
  Brooklyn (G-1693)
Dana Michele LLC .... G 917 757-7777
  New York (G-9463)
Drescher Paper Box Inc .... F 716 854-0288
  Clarence (G-3528)
Haba USA .... G 800 468-6873
  Skaneateles (G-14873)
Habermaass Corporation .... F 315 685-8919
  Skaneateles (G-14874)
Joel Zelcer .... F 917 525-6790
  Brooklyn (G-2042)
Kidtellect Inc .... G 617 803-1456
  New York (G-10440)
Kling Magnetics Inc .... E 518 392-4000
  Chatham (G-3428)
Master Juvenile Products Inc .... F 845 647-8400
  Ellenville (G-4440)
Matel LLC .... G 646 825-6760
  New York (G-10726)
Mattel Inc .... F 716 714-8514
  East Aurora (G-4205)
Mattel Inc .... E 310 252-2000
  East Aurora (G-4206)
Ogosport LLC .... G 718 554-0777
  Brooklyn (G-2286)
Sandbox Brands Inc .... G 212 647-8877
  New York (G-11480)
Toymax Inc .... G 212 633-6611
  New York (G-11878)
Vogel Applied Technologies .... G 212 677-3136
  New York (G-12051)
Way Out Toys Inc .... G 212 689-9094
  New York (G-12082)
Whats Next Manufacturing Inc .... E 585 492-1014
  Arcade (G-391)

TOYS & HOBBY GOODS & SPLYS, WHOLESALE: Arts/Crafts Eqpt/Sply

Multi Packaging Solutions Inc .... E 646 885-0005
  New York (G-10858)

TOYS & HOBBY GOODS & SPLYS, WHOLESALE: Balloons, Novelty

OH How Cute Inc .... G 347 838-6031
  Staten Island (G-15113)

TOYS & HOBBY GOODS & SPLYS, WHOLESALE: Educational Toys

Global Video LLC .... D 516 222-2600
  Woodbury (G-16620)

TOYS & HOBBY GOODS & SPLYS, WHOLESALE: Toys & Games

Last Straw Inc .... E 516 371-2727
  Lawrence (G-7104)
Minted Green Inc .... G 845 458-1845
  Airmont (G-15)
Way Out Toys Inc .... G 212 689-9094
  New York (G-12082)

TOYS & HOBBY GOODS & SPLYS, WHOLESALE: Toys, NEC

Toymax Inc .... G 212 633-6611
  New York (G-11878)

TOYS & HOBBY GOODS & SPLYS, WHOLESALE: Video Games

Barron Games Intl Co LLC .... F 716 630-0054
  Buffalo (G-2723)

TOYS, HOBBY GOODS & SPLYS WHOLESALERS

Fierce Fun Toys LLC .... G 646 322-7172
  New York (G-9801)
Habermaass Corporation .... F 315 685-8919
  Skaneateles (G-14874)

TOYS: Dolls, Stuffed Animals & Parts

Community Products LLC .... G 518 589-5103
 Elka Park *(G-4435)*
Cosmetics Plus Ltd .... G 516 768-7250
 Amagansett *(G-203)*
Dana Michele LLC .... G 917 757-7777
 New York *(G-9463)*
Jupiter Creations Inc .... G 917 493-9393
 New York *(G-10382)*
Minted Green Inc .... G 845 458-1845
 Airmont *(G-15)*

TOYS: Electronic

Littlebits Electronics Inc .... E 917 464-4577
 New York *(G-10582)*
Wobbleworks Inc .... E 718 618-9904
 New York *(G-12127)*

TOYS: Video Game Machines

C T A Digital Inc .... F 718 963-9845
 Brooklyn *(G-1665)*
C T A Digital Inc .... E 845 513-0433
 Monroe *(G-8266)*

TRADE SHOW ARRANGEMENT SVCS

Alm Media LLC .... B 212 457-9400
 New York *(G-8805)*
Alm Media Holdings Inc .... B 212 457-9400
 New York *(G-8806)*
International Data Group Inc .... E 212 331-7883
 New York *(G-10244)*
Relx Inc .... E 212 309-8100
 New York *(G-11355)*

TRADERS: Commodity, Contracts

De Meo Brothers Inc .... G 212 268-1400
 New York *(G-9493)*

TRAILERS & PARTS: Boat

Performance Custom Trailer .... G 518 504-4021
 Lake George *(G-6965)*

TRAILERS & PARTS: Truck & Semi's

Cross Country Mfg Inc .... F 607 656-4103
 Greene *(G-5613)*
Davis Trailer World LLC .... F 585 538-6640
 York *(G-16813)*
G L 7 Sales Plus Ltd .... G 631 696-8290
 Coram *(G-3797)*
General Welding & Fabg Inc .... G 716 652-0033
 Elma *(G-4451)*
Seneca Truck & Trailer Inc .... G 315 781-1100
 Geneva *(G-5333)*
Stone Well Bodies & Mch Inc ...... G 315 497-3512
 Genoa *(G-5338)*

TRAILERS & TRAILER EQPT

Rolling Star Manufacturing Inc .... E 315 896-4767
 Barneveld *(G-604)*

TRAILERS: Semitrailers, Truck Tractors

Blue Tee Corp .... G 212 598-0880
 New York *(G-9109)*

TRANSDUCERS: Electrical Properties

American Aerospace Contrls Inc .. E 631 694-5100
 Farmingdale *(G-4719)*
Pcb Group Inc .... E 716 684-0001
 Depew *(G-4100)*
Ruhle Companies Inc .... E 914 287-4000
 Valhalla *(G-15747)*

TRANSDUCERS: Pressure

Dylix Corporation .... E 719 773-2985
 Grand Island *(G-5498)*
Kinemotive Corporation .... E 631 249-6440
 Farmingdale *(G-4803)*

TRANSFORMERS: Control

Current Controls Inc .... C 585 593-1544
 Wellsville *(G-16114)*

TRANSFORMERS: Distribution

Electron Coil Inc .... D 607 336-7414
 Norwich *(G-12485)*
Ems Development Corporation ... D 631 345-6200
 Yaphank *(G-16709)*
Kepco Inc .... C 718 461-7000
 Flushing *(G-5016)*
Kepco Inc .... D 718 461-7000
 Flushing *(G-5017)*
Kepco Inc .... E 718 461-7000
 Flushing *(G-5018)*
Schneider Electric It Corp .... F 646 335-0216
 New York *(G-11509)*

TRANSFORMERS: Distribution, Electric

Hale Electrical Dist Svcs Inc .... G 716 818-7595
 Wales Center *(G-15901)*
Siemens Corporation .... F 202 434-7800
 New York *(G-11577)*
Siemens USA Holdings Inc .... B 212 258-4000
 New York *(G-11580)*

TRANSFORMERS: Electric

Niagara Transformer Corp .... D 716 896-6500
 Buffalo *(G-2970)*
Transistor Devices Inc .... E 631 471-7492
 Ronkonkoma *(G-14421)*

TRANSFORMERS: Electronic

Atlantic Transformer Inc .... F 716 795-3258
 Barker *(G-599)*
Beta Transformer Tech Corp .... E 631 244-7393
 Bohemia *(G-987)*
Data Device Corporation .... B 631 567-5600
 Bohemia *(G-1008)*
Esc Control Electronics LLC .... E 631 467-5328
 Sayville *(G-14627)*
Exxelia-Raf Tabtronics LLC .... E 585 243-4331
 Piffard *(G-12996)*
NEa Manufacturing Corp .... E 516 371-4200
 Inwood *(G-6497)*
Todd Systems Inc .... D 914 963-3400
 Yonkers *(G-16802)*
Urban Technologies Inc .... G 716 672-2709
 Fredonia *(G-5129)*

TRANSFORMERS: Ignition, Domestic Fuel Burners

Frederick Cowan & Company Inc .. F 631 369-0360
 Wading River *(G-15884)*

TRANSFORMERS: Power Related

Arstan Products International .... F 516 433-1313
 Hicksville *(G-6061)*
Berkshire Transformer .... G 631 467-5328
 Central Islip *(G-3359)*
Buffalo Power Electronics Ctr ...... F 716 651-1600
 Depew *(G-4083)*
Caddell Burns Manufacturing Co .. E 631 757-1772
 Northport *(G-12465)*
Cooper Power Systems LLC .... B 716 375-7100
 Olean *(G-12597)*
Exxelia-Raf Tabtronics LLC .... E 585 243-4331
 Piffard *(G-12996)*
K Road Power Management LLC .. G 212 351-0535
 New York *(G-10390)*
Piller Power Systems Inc .... E 845 695-6658
 Middletown *(G-8170)*
Ram Transformer Technologies .. F 914 632-3988
 New Rochelle *(G-8624)*
Reenergy Black River LLC .... E 315 773-2314
 Fort Drum *(G-5092)*
Sag Harbor Industries Inc .... E 631 725-0440
 Sag Harbor *(G-14502)*
Schneider Electric Usa Inc .... E 585 377-1313
 Penfield *(G-12945)*
Spence Engineering Company Inc .. C 845 778-5566
 Walden *(G-15897)*
Sunward Electronics Inc .... E 518 687-0030
 Troy *(G-15629)*
Switching Power Inc .... D 631 981-7231
 Ronkonkoma *(G-14420)*
Veeco Instruments Inc .... E 516 349-8300
 Plainview *(G-13098)*

TRANSFORMERS: Signaling Transformers, Electric

Railworks Corporation .... G 904 296-5055
 Farmingdale *(G-4865)*

TRANSFORMERS: Specialty

Dyco Electronics Inc .... D 607 324-2030
 Hornell *(G-6296)*
Mitchell Electronics Corp .... E 914 699-3800
 Mount Vernon *(G-8422)*

TRANSLATION & INTERPRETATION SVCS

Language and Graphics Inc .... G 212 315-5266
 New York *(G-10516)*

TRANSMISSIONS: Motor Vehicle

A-Line Technologies Inc .... F 607 772-2439
 Binghamton *(G-858)*
Auburn Bearing & Mfg Inc .... G 315 986-7600
 Macedon *(G-7694)*
Pro Torque .... E 631 218-8700
 Bohemia *(G-1079)*

TRANSPORTATION EPQT & SPLYS, WHOLESALE: Acft/Space Vehicle

Nell-Joy Industries Inc .... E 631 842-8989
 Copiague *(G-3770)*

TRANSPORTATION EQPT & SPLYS WHOLESALERS, NEC

Worldwide Arntcal Cmpnents Inc ... G 631 842-3780
 Copiague *(G-3795)*
Zebra Technologies Entp Corp .... E 800 722-6234
 Holtsville *(G-6251)*

TRANSPORTATION EQUIPMENT, NEC

Truck-Lite Sub Inc .... G 800 888-7095
 Falconer *(G-4697)*

TRANSPORTATION: Local Passenger, NEC

Hampton Transport Inc .... F 631 716-4445
 Coram *(G-3798)*

TRAP ROCK: Crushed & Broken

Dolomite Products Company Inc .. E 585 586-2568
 Penfield *(G-12940)*
Tilcon New York Inc .... E 845 778-5591
 Walden *(G-15898)*
Tilcon New York Inc .... D 845 358-3100
 West Nyack *(G-16282)*

TRAPS: Animal & Fish, Wire

Cuba Specialty Mfg Co Inc .... F 585 567-4176
 Fillmore *(G-4937)*

TRAPS: Stem

John N Fehlinger Co Inc .... F 212 233-5656
 New York *(G-10353)*

TRAVEL AGENCIES

Citic Intl (usa) Travel Inc .... G 718 888-9577
 Flushing *(G-4992)*
Mapeasy Inc .... F 631 537-6213
 Wainscott *(G-15889)*
Quinn and Co of NY Ltd .... D 212 868-1900
 New York *(G-11303)*
Rfp LLC .... E 212 838-7733
 New York *(G-11381)*

TRAVEL TRAILERS & CAMPERS

All Star Carts & Vehicles Inc .... D 631 666-5581
 Bay Shore *(G-654)*

TRAYS: Cable, Metal Plate

Mono-Systems Inc .... E 716 821-1344
 Buffalo *(G-2953)*

TRAYS: Plastic

Commodore Machine Co Inc .... E 585 657-6916
 Bloomfield *(G-950)*

PRODUCT SECTION

TUBING: Plastic

SAV Thermo Inc .... F 631 249-9444
  West Babylon (G-16191)
Tully Products Inc .... G 716 773-3166
  Grand Island (G-5516)

TROPHIES, NEC

All American Awards Inc .... F 631 567-2025
  Bohemia (G-975)
Dwm International Inc .... F 646 290-7448
  Long Island City (G-7431)
Endurart Inc .... E 212 473-7000
  New York (G-9679)

TROPHIES, PEWTER

Valerie Bohigian .... G 914 631-8866
  Sleepy Hollow (G-14888)

TROPHIES, PLATED, ALL METALS

Csi International Inc .... E 800 441-2895
  Niagara Falls (G-12276)

TROPHIES, SILVER

Atlantic Trophy Co Inc .... G 212 684-6020
  New York (G-8952)

TROPHIES: Metal, Exc Silver

C & M Products Inc .... G 315 471-3303
  Syracuse (G-15265)
Classic Medallics Inc .... E 718 392-5410
  Mount Vernon (G-8388)
New Dimension Awards Inc .... G 718 236-8200
  Brooklyn (G-2258)

TROPHY & PLAQUE STORES

Displays & Beyond Inc .... F 718 805-7786
  Glendale (G-5398)
Jem Sign Corp .... G 516 867-4466
  Hempstead (G-6015)

TRUCK & BUS BODIES: Ambulance

Jeffersonville Volunteer .... E 845 482-3110
  Jeffersonville (G-6779)

TRUCK & BUS BODIES: Motor Vehicle, Specialty

Kurtz Truck Equipment Inc .... F 607 849-3468
  Marathon (G-7790)
Rexford Services Inc .... G 716 366-6671
  Dunkirk (G-4178)

TRUCK & BUS BODIES: Truck, Motor Vehicle

Demartini Oil Equipment Svc .... G 518 463-5752
  Glenmont (G-5411)
Eastern Welding Inc .... G 631 727-0306
  Riverhead (G-13568)
Marros Equipment & Trucks .... F 315 539-8702
  Waterloo (G-15996)
Renaldos Sales & Service Ctr .... G 716 337-3760
  North Collins (G-12388)
Unicell Body Company Inc .... E 716 853-8628
  Buffalo (G-3109)
Unicell Body Company Inc .... F 585 424-2660
  Rochester (G-14185)
USA Body Inc .... G 315 852-6123
  De Ruyter (G-3929)
Weld-Built Body Co Inc .... E 631 643-9700
  Wyandanch (G-16697)

TRUCK BODIES: Body Parts

Brunner International Inc .... C 585 798-6000
  Medina (G-7974)
Concrete Mixer Supplycom Inc .... G 716 375-5565
  Olean (G-12596)
Ekostinger Inc .... F 585 739-0450
  East Rochester (G-4283)
General Welding & Fabg Inc .... F 585 697-7660
  Rochester (G-13828)
Tectran Mfg Inc .... D 800 776-5549
  Buffalo (G-3088)
Unicell Body Company Inc .... F 716 853-8628
  Schenectady (G-14723)

TRUCK GENERAL REPAIR SVC

Bick & Heintz Inc .... F 315 733-7577
  Utica (G-15680)
Riverview Industries Inc .... G 845 265-5284
  Cold Spring (G-3627)

TRUCK PAINTING & LETTERING SVCS

Jem Sign Corp .... G 516 867-4466
  Hempstead (G-6015)
Monasani Signs Inc .... G 631 266-2635
  East Northport (G-4268)

TRUCK PARTS & ACCESSORIES: Wholesalers

Unicell Body Company Inc .... E 716 853-8628
  Buffalo (G-3109)

TRUCKING & HAULING SVCS: Garbage, Collect/Transport Only

Suffolk Indus Recovery Corp .... D 631 732-6403
  Coram (G-3805)

TRUCKING, DUMP

Alice Perkins .... G 716 378-5100
  Salamanca (G-14523)
Ribble Lumber Inc .... G 315 536-6221
  Penn Yan (G-12964)

TRUCKING: Except Local

Platinum Sales Promotion Inc .... G 718 361-0200
  Long Island City (G-7557)

TRUCKING: Local, Without Storage

Clark Concrete Co Inc .... G 315 478-4101
  Syracuse (G-15279)
Haley Concrete Inc .... F 716 492-0849
  Delevan (G-4070)
J & S Logging Inc .... E 315 262-2112
  South Colton (G-14925)
Little Valley Sand & Gravel .... G 716 938-6676
  Little Valley (G-7221)

TRUCKS & TRACTORS: Industrial

ASAP Rack Rental Inc .... G 718 499-4495
  Brooklyn (G-1561)
Channel Manufacturing Inc .... E 516 944-6271
  Port Washington (G-13247)
Ducon Technologies Inc .... F 631 694-1700
  New York (G-9584)
Ducon Technologies Inc .... E 631 420-4900
  Farmingdale (G-4753)
E-One Inc .... D 716 646-6790
  Hamburg (G-5675)
Raymond Corporation .... E 315 643-5000
  East Syracuse (G-4364)
Speedways Conveyors Inc .... E 716 893-2222
  Buffalo (G-3075)

TRUCKS: Forklift

Continental Lift Truck Inc .... F 718 738-4738
  South Ozone Park (G-14944)
Raymond Sales Corporation .... F 607 656-2311
  Greene (G-5618)
Stanley Industrial Eqp LLC .... G 315 656-8733
  Kirkville (G-6935)

TRUCKS: Indl

Meteor Express Inc .... F 718 551-9177
  Jamaica (G-6661)
Pb08 Inc .... G 347 866-7353
  Hicksville (G-6123)
Ward Lafrance Truck Corp .... F 518 893-1865
  Saratoga Springs (G-14601)

TRUNKS

Junk In My Trunk Inc .... G 631 420-5865
  Farmingdale (G-4795)
Rose Trunk Mfg Co Inc .... F 516 766-6686
  Oceanside (G-12554)

TRUSSES: Wood, Roof

Faulkner Truss Company Inc .... G 315 536-8894
  Dresden (G-4147)
Pdj Components Inc .... E 845 469-9191
  Chester (G-3479)
Proof Industries Inc .... E 631 694-7663
  Farmingdale (G-4859)
Rochester Lumber Company .... E 585 924-7171
  Farmington (G-4919)
S R Sloan Inc .... D 315 736-7730
  Whitesboro (G-16529)
Steele Truss Company Inc .... E 518 562-4663
  Plattsburgh (G-13158)
Structural Wood Corporation .... E 315 388-4442
  Waddington (G-15882)
Ufp New York LLC .... E 716 496-5484
  Chaffee (G-3405)
Ufp New York LLC .... E 518 828-2888
  Hudson (G-6375)
Ufp New York LLC .... E 315 253-2758
  Auburn (G-507)

TUBE & TUBING FABRICATORS

Albany Nipple and Pipe Mfg .... E 518 270-2162
  Troy (G-15594)
Coventry Manufacturing Co Inc ...... E 914 668-2212
  Mount Vernon (G-8391)
Ram Fabricating LLC .... E 315 437-6654
  Syracuse (G-15401)
Spinco Metal Products Inc .... D 315 331-6285
  Newark (G-12207)
Star Tubing Corp .... G 716 483-1703
  Jamestown (G-6750)
Tube Fabrication Company Inc .... F 716 673-1871
  Fredonia (G-5128)

TUBES: Finned, For Heat Transfer

CMS Heat Transfer Division Inc ...... E 631 968-0084
  Bohemia (G-997)

TUBES: Generator, Electron Beam, Beta Ray

E-Beam Services Inc .... G 516 622-1422
  Hicksville (G-6081)

TUBES: Paper

Caraustar Industries Inc .... G 716 874-0393
  Buffalo (G-2761)

TUBES: Paper Or Fiber, Chemical Or Electrical Uses

Industrial Paper Tube Inc .... F 718 893-5000
  Bronx (G-1296)

TUBES: Steel & Iron

Markin Tubing LP .... F 585 495-6211
  Buffalo (G-2937)
TI Group Auto Systems LLC .... E 315 568-7042
  Seneca Falls (G-14787)

TUBES: Vacuum

New Sensor Corporation .... D 718 937-8300
  Long Island City (G-7538)

TUBES: Wrought, Welded Or Lock Joint

Markin Tubing LP .... C 585 495-6211
  Wyoming (G-16699)
Markin Tubing Inc .... C 585 495-6211
  Wyoming (G-16700)
Thyssenkrupp Materials NA Inc ..... G 585 279-0000
  Rochester (G-14170)

TUBING: Flexible, Metallic

Conrad Blasius Equipment Co .... G 516 753-1200
  Plainview (G-13044)

TUBING: Glass

Gray Glass Inc .... E 718 217-2943
  Queens Village (G-13406)

TUBING: Plastic

Finger Lakes Extrusion Corp .... E 585 905-0632
  Canandaigua (G-3221)

Employee Codes: A=Over 500 employees, B=251-500
C=101-250, D=51-100, E=20-50, F=10-19, G=5-9

TUBING: Plastic

Hancor Inc .... D 607 565-3033
  Waverly (G-16066)

TUBING: Seamless

TI Group Auto Systems LLC .... G 315 568-7042
  Seneca Falls (G-14787)

TUNGSTEN CARBIDE

Buffalo Tungsten Inc .... D 716 683-9170
  Depew (G-4084)
Niagara Refining LLC .... E 716 706-1400
  Depew (G-4097)

TUNGSTEN CARBIDE POWDER

Golden Egret LLC .... G 516 922-2839
  East Norwich (G-4272)

TURBINE GENERATOR SET UNITS: Hydraulic, Complete

Hdm Hydraulics LLC .... D 716 694-8004
  Tonawanda (G-15546)
Signa Chemistry Inc .... F 212 933-4101
  New York (G-11586)

TURBINES & TURBINE GENERATOR SET UNITS: Gas, Complete

General Electric Company .... B 518 385-3716
  Schenectady (G-14678)
General Electric Company .... B 518 385-2211
  Schenectady (G-14679)
General Electric Intl Inc .... B 518 385-2211
  Schenectady (G-14682)

TURBINES & TURBINE GENERATOR SETS

Awr Energy Inc .... F 585 469-7750
  Plattsburgh (G-13107)
Beowawe Binary LLC .... E 646 829-3900
  New York (G-9049)
Cooper Turbocompressor Inc .... B 716 896-6600
  Buffalo (G-2781)
Dresser-Rand Company .... A 585 596-3100
  Wellsville (G-16116)
Dresser-Rand Group Inc .... D 716 375-3000
  Olean (G-12599)
Gas Turbine Controls Corp .... E 914 693-0830
  Hawthorne (G-5987)
GE Global Research .... A 518 387-5000
  Niskayuna (G-12353)
General Electric Company .... B 518 385-2211
  Schenectady (G-14676)
General Electric Company .... B 203 373-2756
  Schenectady (G-14677)
General Electric Company .... B 518 387-5000
  Schenectady (G-14680)
General Electric Company .... G 518 385-3439
  Schenectady (G-14681)
Mission Critical Energy Inc .... G 716 276-8465
  Getzville (G-5349)
Prime Turbine Parts LLC .... G 518 306-7306
  Saratoga Springs (G-14593)
Stork H & E Turbo Blading Inc .... C 607 277-4968
  Ithaca (G-6610)
Tgp Flying Cloud Holdings LLC .... E 646 829-3900
  New York (G-11807)
Tuthill Corporation .... B 631 727-1097
  Riverhead (G-13587)
Weaver Wind Energy LLC .... G 607 379-9463
  Freeville (G-5193)
Worldwide Gas Turbine Pdts Inc .... G 518 877-7200
  Clifton Park (G-3581)

TURBINES & TURBINE GENERATOR SETS & PARTS

Intersource Management Group .... G 518 372-6798
  Halfmoon (G-5664)
Intersource Management Group .... E 518 372-6798
  Schenectady (G-14690)
Siemens Government Tech Inc .... B 585 593-1234
  Wellsville (G-16123)
Turbine Engine Comp Utica .... A 315 768-8070
  Whitesboro (G-16531)
Turbo Machined Products LLC .... E 315 895-3010
  Frankfort (G-5113)

TURBINES: Hydraulic, Complete

Atlantic Projects Company Inc .... F 518 878-2065
  Clifton Park (G-3564)
Frontier Hydraulics Corp .... F 716 694-2070
  Buffalo (G-2836)

TURBINES: Steam

General Electric Company .... A 518 385-4022
  Schenectady (G-14675)
General Electric Company .... E 518 385-7620
  Niskayuna (G-12354)

TURBO-GENERATORS

Mannesmann Corporation .... D 212 258-4000
  New York (G-10691)

TYPESETTING SVC

514 Adams Corporation .... G 516 352-6948
  Franklin Square (G-5114)
Act Communications Group Inc .... F 631 669-2403
  West Islip (G-16257)
Advance Publications Inc .... D 718 981-1234
  Staten Island (G-15040)
Agrecolor Inc .... F 516 741-8700
  Mineola (G-8202)
Alabaster Group Inc .... G 516 867-8223
  Freeport (G-5138)
Albion-Holley Pennysaver Inc .... E 585 589-5641
  Albion (G-154)
Arista Innovations Inc .... F 516 746-2262
  Mineola (G-8205)
Art Resources Transfer Inc .... G 212 255-2919
  New York (G-8916)
Artscroll Printing Corp .... F 212 929-2413
  New York (G-8926)
Bates Jackson Engraving Co Inc .... E 716 854-3000
  Buffalo (G-2725)
Baum Christine and John Corp .... G 585 621-8910
  Rochester (G-13654)
Bco Industries Western NY Inc .... E 716 877-2800
  Tonawanda (G-15526)
Beastons Budget Printing .... G 585 244-2721
  Rochester (G-13658)
Beehive Press Inc .... G 718 654-1200
  Bronx (G-1226)
Benchemark Printing Inc .... D 518 393-1361
  Schenectady (G-14653)
Bernard Hall .... G 585 425-3340
  Fairport (G-4625)
Beyer Graphics Inc .... D 631 543-3900
  Commack (G-3682)
Boncraft Inc .... D 716 662-9720
  Tonawanda (G-15528)
Bondy Printing Corp .... G 631 242-1510
  Bay Shore (G-666)
Brodock Press Inc .... D 315 735-9577
  Utica (G-15681)
Brooks Litho Digital Group Inc .... G 631 789-4500
  Deer Park (G-3955)
Bytheway Publishing Services .... F 607 334-8365
  Norwich (G-12477)
Carlara Group Ltd .... G 914 769-2020
  Pleasantville (G-13173)
Carnels Printing Inc .... G 516 883-3355
  Great Neck (G-5543)
Castlereagh Printcraft Inc .... D 516 623-1728
  Freeport (G-5148)
Chakra Communications Inc .... E 716 505-7300
  Lancaster (G-7013)
Chakra Communications Inc .... E 607 748-7491
  Endicott (G-4584)
Challenge Graphics Svcs Inc .... E 631 586-0171
  Deer Park (G-3956)
Clarsons Corp .... F 585 235-8775
  Rochester (G-13713)
Cohber Press Inc .... D 585 475-9100
  West Henrietta (G-16234)
Consolidated Color Press Inc .... F 212 929-8197
  New York (G-9382)
Cortland Standard Printing Co .... D 607 756-5665
  Cortland (G-3871)
Cosmos Communications Inc .... C 718 482-1800
  Long Island City (G-7416)
Csw Inc .... F 585 247-4010
  Rochester (G-13727)
D G M Graphics Inc .... F 516 223-2220
  Merrick (G-8096)
Desktop Publishing Concepts .... F 631 752-1934
  Farmingdale (G-4750)
Digital Page LLC .... F 518 446-9129
  Albany (G-68)
Dispatch Graphics Inc .... F 212 307-5943
  New York (G-9536)
Dowd - Witbeck Printing Corp .... F 518 274-2421
  Troy (G-15604)
DP Murphy Co Inc .... D 631 673-9400
  Deer Park (G-3968)
Draper Associates Incorporated .... F 212 255-2727
  New York (G-9573)
E B B Graphics Inc .... F 516 750-5510
  Westbury (G-16324)
Eastwood Litho Inc .... E 315 437-2626
  Syracuse (G-15310)
Empire Press Co .... G 718 756-9500
  Brooklyn (G-1833)
Flare Multicopy Corp .... G 718 258-8860
  Brooklyn (G-1887)
Flp Group LLC .... F 315 252-7583
  Auburn (G-480)
Foleys Graphic Center Inc .... E 914 245-3625
  Yorktown Heights (G-16816)
Fort Orange Press Inc .... E 518 489-3233
  Albany (G-75)
Fulton Newspapers Inc .... E 315 598-6397
  Fulton (G-5216)
Gallant Graphics Ltd .... E 845 868-1166
  Stanfordville (G-15033)
Gateway Prtg & Graphics Inc .... E 716 823-3873
  Hamburg (G-5680)
Gazette Press Inc .... E 914 963-8300
  Rye (G-14479)
Gg Design and Printing .... G 718 321-3220
  New York (G-9916)
Graphic Fabrications Inc .... G 516 763-3222
  Rockville Centre (G-14232)
Graphicomm Inc .... G 716 283-0830
  Niagara Falls (G-12289)
Grid Typographic Services Inc .... F 212 627-0303
  New York (G-9987)
Hamptons Magazine .... E 631 283-7125
  Southampton (G-14955)
Hks Printing Company Inc .... F 212 675-2529
  New York (G-10109)
Hugh F McPherson Inc .... G 716 668-6107
  Cheektowaga (G-3450)
In-House Inc .... F 718 445-9007
  College Point (G-3646)
Interstate Litho Corp .... D 631 232-6025
  Brentwood (G-1136)
Jack J Florio Jr .... G 716 434-9123
  Lockport (G-7311)
James Conolly Printing Co .... E 585 426-4150
  Rochester (G-13891)
Jane Lewis .... G 607 722-0584
  Binghamton (G-898)
Johnnys Ideal Printing Co .... G 518 828-6666
  Hudson (G-6359)
Jon Lyn Ink Inc .... G 516 546-2312
  Merrick (G-8099)
L M N Printing Company Inc .... E 516 285-8526
  Valley Stream (G-15784)
Lake Placid Advertisers Wkshp .... E 518 523-3359
  Lake Placid (G-6976)
Leigh Scott Enterprises Inc .... G 718 343-5440
  Bellerose (G-781)
Litmor Publishing Corp .... F 516 931-0012
  Garden City (G-5266)
Loudon Ltd .... G 631 757-4447
  East Northport (G-4267)
Louis Heindl & Son Inc .... G 585 454-5080
  Rochester (G-13917)
Loy L Press Inc .... G 716 634-5966
  Buffalo (G-2928)
Mechon Beiss Uvas .... G 718 436-1489
  Brooklyn (G-2186)
Medallion Associates Inc .... E 212 929-9130
  New York (G-10751)
Mercury Print Productions Inc .... C 585 458-7900
  Rochester (G-13936)
Midgley Printing Corp .... G 315 475-1864
  Syracuse (G-15372)
Mines Press Inc .... C 914 788-1800
  Cortlandt Manor (G-3903)
Moneast Inc .... G 845 298-8898
  Wappingers Falls (G-15936)
Multiple Imprssons of Rchester .... G 585 546-1160
  Rochester (G-13960)

PRODUCT SECTION

VALVES

Mutual Engraving Company Inc .... D 516 489-0534
   West Hempstead *(G-16223)*
News India USA Inc .... F 212 675-7515
   New York *(G-10954)*
Newspaper Publisher LLC .... F 607 775-0472
   Conklin *(G-3730)*
Official Offset Corporation .... E 631 957-8500
   Amityville *(G-307)*
P D R Inc .... G 516 829-5300
   Plainview *(G-13080)*
Panagraphics Inc .... G 716 312-8088
   Orchard Park *(G-12734)*
Patrick Ryans Modern Press .... F 518 434-2921
   Albany *(G-111)*
Presstek Printing LLC .... F 585 467-8140
   Rochester *(G-14042)*
Prestige Envelope & Lithograph .... F 631 521-7043
   Merrick *(G-8105)*
Printery .... G 516 922-3250
   Oyster Bay *(G-12818)*
Printing Resources Inc .... E 518 482-2470
   Albany *(G-119)*
Pro Printing .... G 516 561-9700
   Lynbrook *(G-7670)*
Progressive Graphics & Prtg .... G 315 331-3635
   Newark *(G-12205)*
Publishing Synthesis Ltd .... G 212 219-0135
   New York *(G-11275)*
Quad/Graphics Inc .... A 518 581-4000
   Saratoga Springs *(G-14594)*
Quicker Printer Inc .... G 607 734-8622
   Elmira *(G-4500)*
Rmd Holding Inc .... G 845 628-0030
   Mahopac *(G-7712)*
Scotti Graphics Inc .... E 212 367-9602
   Long Island City *(G-7585)*
Sentine Printing Inc .... G 516 334-7400
   Westbury *(G-16372)*
Stone Crest Industries Inc .... G 607 652-2665
   Stamford *(G-15032)*
Syracuse Computer Forms Inc .... E 315 478-0108
   Syracuse *(G-15436)*
Thomas Group Inc .... F 212 947-6400
   New York *(G-11817)*
Times Review Newspaper Corp .... E 631 354-8031
   Mattituck *(G-7918)*
Tobay Printing Co Inc .... E 631 842-3300
   Copiague *(G-3788)*
Tom & Jerry Printcraft Forms .... E 914 777-7468
   Mamaroneck *(G-7758)*
Torsaf Printers Inc .... G 516 569-5577
   Hewlett *(G-6051)*
Tri Kolor Printing & Sty .... F 315 474-6753
   Syracuse *(G-15446)*
Tri-Lon Clor Lithographers Ltd .... E 212 255-6140
   New York *(G-11893)*
Tripi Engraving Co Inc .... E 718 383-6500
   Brooklyn *(G-2586)*
Voss Signs LLC .... E 315 682-6418
   Manlius *(G-7781)*
Wallkill Valley Publications .... E 845 561-0170
   Newburgh *(G-12251)*
Webster Printing Corporation .... F 585 671-1533
   Webster *(G-16107)*
Westchester Mailing Service .... E 914 948-1116
   White Plains *(G-16519)*
Wilson Press LLC .... E 315 568-9693
   Seneca Falls *(G-14788)*
Woodbury Printing Plus + Inc .... G 845 928-6610
   Central Valley *(G-3399)*
Worldwide Ticket Craft .... D 516 538-6200
   Merrick *(G-8107)*
Wynco Press One Inc .... F 516 354-6145
   Glen Oaks *(G-5388)*
X Myles Mar Inc .... E 212 683-2015
   New York *(G-12148)*
Zenger Partners LLC .... E 716 876-2284
   Kenmore *(G-6865)*

TYPESETTING SVC: Computer

Cds Productions Inc .... F 518 385-8255
   Schenectady *(G-14661)*
Star Composition Services Inc .... G 212 684-4001
   Brooklyn *(G-2509)*

TYPOGRAPHY

Artistic Typography Corp .... F 212 463-8880
   New York *(G-8923)*
Rubber Stamps Inc .... E 212 675-1180
   Mineola *(G-8247)*

ULTRASONIC EQPT: Cleaning, Exc Med & Dental

Alexy Associates Inc .... E 845 482-3000
   Bethel *(G-834)*
Branson Ultrasonics Corp .... E 585 624-8000
   Honeoye Falls *(G-6262)*
Tectran Inc .... G 800 776-5549
   Cheektowaga *(G-3461)*

UMBRELLAS & CANES

Essex Manufacturing Inc .... D 212 239-0080
   New York *(G-9712)*
Gustbuster Ltd .... G 631 391-9000
   Farmingdale *(G-4777)*

UMBRELLAS: Garden Or Wagon

Zip-Jack Industries Ltd .... E 914 592-2000
   Tarrytown *(G-15498)*

UNIFORM STORES

Craft Clerical Clothes Inc .... G 212 764-6122
   New York *(G-9416)*

UNIVERSITY

Cornell University .... D 607 277-2338
   Ithaca *(G-6572)*
Cornell University .... E 607 254-2473
   Ithaca *(G-6573)*
New York University .... E 212 998-4300
   New York *(G-10947)*
Suny At Binghamton .... D 607 777-2316
   Binghamton *(G-916)*
Trust of Colum Unive In The Ci .... F 212 854-2793
   New York *(G-11906)*
University of Rochester .... B 585 275-3483
   Rochester *(G-14190)*

UNSUPPORTED PLASTICS: Floor Or Wall Covering

Pacific Designs Intl Inc .... G 718 364-2867
   Bronx *(G-1350)*

UPHOLSTERY FILLING MATERIALS

Global Resources Sg Inc .... F 212 686-1411
   New York *(G-9945)*
Manrico Usa Inc .... G 212 794-4200
   New York *(G-10694)*

UPHOLSTERY MATERIALS, BROADWOVEN

Scalamandre Silks Inc .... D 212 980-3888
   New York *(G-11499)*

UPHOLSTERY WORK SVCS

August Studios .... G 718 706-6487
   Long Island City *(G-7395)*
Bettertex Inc .... F 212 431-3973
   New York *(G-9062)*
Dine Rite Seating Products Inc .... E 631 226-8899
   Lindenhurst *(G-7170)*
Elan Upholstery Inc .... F 631 563-0650
   Bohemia *(G-1022)*
Terbo Ltd .... G 718 847-2860
   Richmond Hill *(G-13516)*

URANIUM ORE MINING, NEC

Global Gold Corporation .... F 914 925-0020
   Rye *(G-14481)*

USED CAR DEALERS

A Zimmer Ltd .... D 315 422-7011
   Syracuse *(G-15237)*
Want-Ad Digest Inc .... F 518 279-1181
   Troy *(G-15634)*

USED MERCHANDISE STORES: Building Materials

Veeco Instruments Inc .... C 516 349-8300
   Plainview *(G-13098)*

USED MERCHANDISE STORES: Rare Books

Glenn Horowitz Bookseller Inc .... G 212 691-9100
   New York *(G-9934)*

UTENSILS: Cast Aluminum, Cooking Or Kitchen

August Thomsen Corp .... E 516 676-7100
   Glen Cove *(G-5361)*
Smart USA Inc .... F 631 969-1111
   Bay Shore *(G-724)*

UTENSILS: Household, Cooking & Kitchen, Metal

Corning Vitro Corporation .... A 607 974-8605
   Corning *(G-3818)*
Lb Furniture Industries LLC .... C 518 828-1501
   Hudson *(G-6362)*
Nash Metalware Co Inc .... F 315 339-5794
   Rome *(G-14260)*
Oxo International Inc .... C 212 242-3333
   New York *(G-11080)*
Progressus Company Inc .... F 516 255-0245
   Rockville Centre *(G-14238)*

UTENSILS: Household, Cooking & Kitchen, Porcelain Enameled

Hyman Podrusnick Co Inc .... G 718 853-4502
   Brooklyn *(G-1990)*

UTENSILS: Household, Metal, Exc Cast

Korin Japanese Trading Corp .... E 212 587-7021
   New York *(G-10471)*

UTENSILS: Household, Porcelain Enameled

Seneca Ceramics Corp .... G 315 781-0100
   Phelps *(G-12980)*

UTILITY TRAILER DEALERS

J D Handling Systems Inc .... F 518 828-9676
   Ghent *(G-5357)*

VACUUM CLEANER STORES

Nationwide Sales and Service .... F 631 491-6625
   Farmingdale *(G-4832)*

VACUUM CLEANERS: Household

American Comfort Direct LLC .... E 201 364-8309
   New York *(G-8825)*
D & C Cleaning Inc .... F 631 789-5659
   Copiague *(G-3756)*
Global Resources Sg Inc .... F 212 686-1411
   New York *(G-9945)*
Nationwide Sales and Service .... F 631 491-6625
   Farmingdale *(G-4832)*
Tri County Custom Vacuum .... G 845 774-7595
   Monroe *(G-8282)*

VACUUM CLEANERS: Indl Type

Empire Division Inc .... D 315 476-6273
   Syracuse *(G-15318)*
Key High Vacuum Products Inc .... E 631 584-5959
   Nesconset *(G-8485)*
National Vac Envmtl Svcs Corp .... E 518 743-0563
   Glens Falls *(G-5435)*

VACUUM SYSTEMS: Air Extraction, Indl

Adams Sfc Inc .... E 716 877-2608
   Tonawanda *(G-15519)*
Edwards Vacuum LLC .... D 800 848-9800
   Sanborn *(G-14544)*

VALUE-ADDED RESELLERS: Computer Systems

Graphics Slution Providers Inc .... F 845 677-5088
   Lagrangeville *(G-6956)*
Vision Logic Inc .... G 212 729-4606
   New York *(G-12042)*

VALVES

ITT Engineered Valves LLC .... D 662 257-6982
   Seneca Falls *(G-14778)*

Employee Codes: A=Over 500 employees, B=251-500
C=101-250, D=51-100, E=20-50, F=10-19, G=5-9

VALVES & PIPE FITTINGS

VALVES & PIPE FITTINGS

A K Allen Co Inc	C	516 747-5450	
Melville *(G-7996)*			
Aalborg Instrs & Contrls Inc	D	845 398-3160	
Orangeburg *(G-12667)*			
Anderson Precision Inc	D	716 484-1148	
Jamestown *(G-6698)*			
Curtiss-Wright Flow Ctrl Corp	C	631 293-3800	
Farmingdale *(G-4743)*			
Devin Mfg Inc	F	585 496-5770	
Arcade *(G-381)*			
Flomatic Corporation	E	518 761-9797	
Glens Falls *(G-5425)*			
Ford Regulator Valve Corp	G	718 497-3255	
Brooklyn *(G-1897)*			
Goodman Main Stopper Mfg Co	F	718 875-5140	
Brooklyn *(G-1940)*			
Holyoke Fittings Inc	F	718 649-0710	
Brooklyn *(G-1981)*			
J H Robotics Inc	E	607 729-3758	
Johnson City *(G-6812)*			
Key High Vacuum Products Inc	E	631 584-5959	
Nesconset *(G-8485)*			
Kingston Hoops Summer	G	845 401-6830	
Kingston *(G-6904)*			
Lance Valves	G	716 681-5825	
Lancaster *(G-7030)*			
M Manastrip-M Corporation	E	518 664-2089	
Clifton Park *(G-3570)*			
Make-Waves Instrument Corp	E	716 681-7524	
Buffalo *(G-2936)*			
Micromold Products Inc	E	914 969-2850	
Yonkers *(G-16784)*			
Rand Machine Products, Inc.	C	716 665-5217	
Falconer *(G-4688)*			
Ross Valve Mfg	G	518 274-0961	
Troy *(G-15621)*			
Sigmamotor Inc	E	716 735-3115	
Middleport *(G-8134)*			
Spence Engineering Company Inc	C	845 778-5566	
Walden *(G-15897)*			
Steel & Obrien Mfg Inc	D	585 492-5800	
Arcade *(G-389)*			
Sure Flow Equipment Inc	E	800 263-8251	
Tonawanda *(G-15580)*			
Westchester Valve & Fitting Co	G	914 762-6600	
Clifton Park *(G-3580)*			
William E William Valve Corp	E	718 392-1660	
Long Island City *(G-7637)*			
William E Williams Valve Corp	E	718 392-1660	
Long Island City *(G-7638)*			

VALVES & REGULATORS: Pressure, Indl

Doyle & Roth Mfg Co Inc	D	212 269-7840	
New York *(G-9570)*			
Spence Engineering Company Inc	C	845 778-5566	
Walden *(G-15897)*			
Total Energy Fabrication Corp	G	580 363-1500	
North Salem *(G-12397)*			

VALVES: Aerosol, Metal

Chapin International Inc	C	585 343-3140	
Batavia *(G-617)*			
Chapin Manufacturing Inc	C	585 343-3140	
Batavia *(G-618)*			
Jordan Panel Systems Corp	E	631 754-4900	
East Northport *(G-4266)*			
Mpl Metal Inc	G	718 338-4952	
Brooklyn *(G-2230)*			
Peak Motion Inc	G	716 534-4925	
Clarence *(G-3538)*			
Peelle Company	G	631 231-6000	
Hauppauge *(G-5911)*			

VALVES: Aircraft

Valvetech Inc	E	315 548-4551	
Phelps *(G-12983)*			

VALVES: Aircraft, Control, Hydraulic & Pneumatic

Young & Franklin Inc	D	315 457-3110	
Liverpool *(G-7274)*			

VALVES: Aircraft, Fluid Power

Dmic Inc	G	716 743-4360	
North Tonawanda *(G-12425)*			

Moog Inc	A	716 652-2000	
Elma *(G-4453)*			
Tactair Fluid Controls Inc	C	315 451-3928	
Liverpool *(G-7266)*			

VALVES: Control, Automatic

ADC Industries Inc	E	516 596-1304	
Valley Stream *(G-15771)*			

VALVES: Electrohydraulic Servo, Metal

Servotronics Inc	C	716 655-5990	
Elma *(G-4458)*			

VALVES: Fluid Power, Control, Hydraulic & pneumatic

Aerco International Inc	C	845 580-8000	
Blauvelt *(G-933)*			
BW Elliott Mfg Co LLC	B	607 772-0404	
Binghamton *(G-873)*			
Direkt Force LLC	E	716 652-3022	
East Aurora *(G-4197)*			
Dynamic Sealing Tech Inc	G	716 376-0708	
Olean *(G-12600)*			

VALVES: Gas Cylinder, Compressed

Caithness Equities Corporation	E	212 599-2112	
New York *(G-9178)*			

VALVES: Hard Rubber

Inflation Systems Inc	E	914 381-8070	
Mamaroneck *(G-7746)*			

VALVES: Indl

Air System Products Inc	F	716 683-0435	
Lancaster *(G-7004)*			
Byelocorp Scientific Inc	E	212 785-2580	
New York *(G-9166)*			
Curtiss-Wright Flow Ctrl Corp	C	631 293-3800	
Farmingdale *(G-4743)*			
Curtiss-Wright Flow Ctrl Corp	C	631 293-3800	
Farmingdale *(G-4744)*			
Dresser-Rand Company	A	585 596-3100	
Wellsville *(G-16116)*			
Flow-Safe Inc	E	716 662-2585	
Orchard Park *(G-12714)*			
Hy Cert Services Inc	G	631 231-7005	
Brentwood *(G-1134)*			
J H Buscher Inc	G	716 667-2003	
Orchard Park *(G-12721)*			
McWane Inc	B	607 734-2211	
Elmira *(G-4497)*			
Murphy Manufacturing Co Inc	G	585 223-0100	
Fairport *(G-4644)*			
Plattco Corporation	E	518 563-4640	
Plattsburgh *(G-13145)*			
Precision Valve & Automtn Inc	C	518 371-2684	
Cohoes *(G-3617)*			
Syraco Products Inc	F	315 476-5306	
Syracuse *(G-15433)*			
Trac Regulators Inc	E	914 699-9352	
Mount Vernon *(G-8447)*			
William E Williams Valve Corp	E	718 392-1660	
Long Island City *(G-7638)*			

VALVES: Plumbing & Heating

Lemode Plumbing & Heating	E	718 545-3336	
Astoria *(G-433)*			
Venco Sales Inc	E	631 754-0782	
Huntington *(G-6426)*			

VALVES: Regulating & Control, Automatic

Curtiss-Wright Electro-	E	585 596-3482	
Wellsville *(G-16115)*			
Digital Home Creations Inc	G	585 576-7070	
Webster *(G-16082)*			
Tyco Simplexgrinnell	E	315 437-9664	
East Syracuse *(G-4376)*			

VALVES: Water Works

Flomatic Corporation	E	518 761-9797	
Glens Falls *(G-5425)*			

VARNISHES, NEC

John C Dolph Company Inc	E	732 329-2333	
Schenectady *(G-14692)*			
Royce Associates A Ltd Partnr	G	516 367-6298	
Jericho *(G-6800)*			
Si Group Inc	C	518 347-4200	
Rotterdam Junction *(G-14463)*			

VEGETABLE STANDS OR MARKETS

Lakeside Cider Mill Farm Inc	G	518 399-8359	
Ballston Lake *(G-568)*			

VEHICLES: All Terrain

Kens Service & Sales Inc	F	716 683-1155	
Elma *(G-4452)*			

VEHICLES: Recreational

Adirondack Power Sports	G	518 481-6269	
Malone *(G-7718)*			
Bullet Industries Inc	G	585 352-0836	
Spencerport *(G-14977)*			

VENDING MACHINES & PARTS

Cubic Trnsp Systems Inc	F	212 255-1810	
New York *(G-9431)*			
Green Enviro Machine LLC	G	407 461-6412	
Schenectady *(G-14685)*			
Vengo Inc	G	866 526-7054	
Bethpage *(G-853)*			

VENTILATING EQPT: Metal

Air Louver & Damper Inc	F	718 392-3232	
Long Island City *(G-7369)*			
Imperial Damper & Louver Co	E	718 731-3800	
Bronx *(G-1294)*			
M&G Duravent Inc	E	518 463-7284	
Albany *(G-96)*			
Spence Engineering Company Inc	C	845 778-5566	
Walden *(G-15897)*			

VENTILATING EQPT: Sheet Metal

Empire Ventilation Eqp Co Inc	F	718 728-2143	
Florida *(G-4970)*			
Lambro Industries Inc	D	631 842-8088	
Amityville *(G-296)*			

VENTURE CAPITAL COMPANIES

Capital E Financial Group	F	212 319-6550	
New York *(G-9202)*			
Circle Peak Capital MGT LLC	E	646 230-8812	
New York *(G-9302)*			

VETERINARY PHARMACEUTICAL PREPARATIONS

Ark Sciences Inc	G	646 943-1520	
Islandia *(G-6521)*			
H W Naylor Co Inc	F	607 263-5145	
Morris *(G-8335)*			
Inolife Tchnlgies Oprtions Inc	G	212 386-5575	
New York *(G-10222)*			

VIBRATORS: Concrete Construction

Ozteck Industries Inc	E	516 883-8857	
Port Washington *(G-13293)*			

VIDEO & AUDIO EQPT, WHOLESALE

Listec Video Corp	G	631 273-3029	
Hauppauge *(G-5865)*			
Professional Tape Corporation	G	516 656-5519	
Glen Cove *(G-5373)*			
Video Technology Services Inc	F	516 937-9700	
Syosset *(G-15232)*			

VIDEO CAMERA-AUDIO RECORDERS: Household Use

Bayit Home Automation Corp	E	973 988-2638	
Brooklyn *(G-1591)*			
Digitac Inc	F	732 215-4020	
Brooklyn *(G-1777)*			

PRODUCT SECTION

VIDEO EQPT
Video Technology Services Inc .... F 516 937-9700
  Syosset *(G-15232)*

VIDEO PRODUCTION SVCS
Amherst Media Inc .... G 716 874-4450
  Buffalo *(G-2698)*
Scholastic Inc .... A 800 724-6527
  New York *(G-11514)*
Wochit Inc .... G 212 979-8343
  New York *(G-12128)*

VIDEO REPAIR SVCS
Video Technology Services Inc .... F 516 937-9700
  Syosset *(G-15232)*

VIDEO TAPE PRODUCTION SVCS
NCM Publishers Inc .... G 212 691-9100
  New York *(G-10902)*
Physicalmind Institute .... F 212 343-2150
  New York *(G-11186)*

VINYL RESINS, NEC
Manufacturers Indexing Pdts .... G 631 271-0956
  Halesite *(G-5658)*

VISUAL COMMUNICATIONS SYSTEMS
Vicon Industries Inc .... C 631 952-2288
  Hauppauge *(G-5970)*

VITAMINS: Natural Or Synthetic, Uncompounded, Bulk
Abh Natures Products Inc .... E 631 249-5783
  Edgewood *(G-4391)*
Ajes Pharmaceuticals LLC .... E 631 608-1728
  Copiague *(G-3749)*
Country Life LLC .... C 631 231-1031
  Hauppauge *(G-5804)*
Gemini Pharmaceuticals Inc .... B 631 543-3334
  Commack *(G-3693)*
Healthee Endeavors Inc .... G 718 653-5499
  Bronx *(G-1289)*
Healthy N Fit Intl Inc .... F 800 338-5200
  Brewster *(G-1166)*
Natures Bounty Co .... D 631 244-2021
  Ronkonkoma *(G-14385)*
Natures Bounty Co .... F 631 588-3492
  Holbrook *(G-6202)*
Nbty Manufacturing LLC .... F 631 567-9500
  Ronkonkoma *(G-14386)*
Nutra Solutions USA Inc .... E 631 392-1900
  Deer Park *(G-4019)*
Nutraqueen LLC .... F 347 368-6568
  New York *(G-11009)*
Only Natural Inc .... F 516 897-7001
  Oceanside *(G-12549)*
Vitalize Labs LLC .... G 212 966-6130
  New York *(G-12046)*
Wellquest International Inc .... G 212 689-9094
  New York *(G-12091)*

VITAMINS: Pharmaceutical Preparations
American Hlth Formulations Inc .... G 631 392-1756
  Hauppauge *(G-5766)*
Atlantic Essential Pdts Inc .... D 631 434-8333
  Hauppauge *(G-5772)*
Bactolac Pharmaceutical Inc .... B 631 951-4908
  Hauppauge *(G-5777)*
Bi Nutraceuticals Inc .... D 631 232-1105
  Central Islip *(G-3360)*
Contract Pharmacal Corp .... C 631 231-4610
  Hauppauge *(G-5802)*
Danbury Pharma LLC .... E 631 393-6333
  Farmingdale *(G-4749)*
FB Laboratories Inc .... F 631 750-0000
  Hauppauge *(G-5823)*
Kabco Pharmaceuticals Inc .... G 631 842-3600
  Amityville *(G-292)*
Natural Organics Labs Inc .... B 631 957-5600
  Amityville *(G-305)*
Natures Bounty (ny) Inc .... G 631 567-9500
  Bohemia *(G-1062)*
Natures Bounty (ny) Inc .... A 631 200-2000
  Ronkonkoma *(G-14384)*

Natures Value Inc .... B 631 846-2500
  Coram *(G-3800)*
Nutraceutical Wellness LLC .... G 888 454-3320
  New York *(G-11008)*
Premium Processing Corp .... D 631 232-1105
  Babylon *(G-533)*
Sciegen Pharmaceuticals Inc .... D 631 434-2723
  Hauppauge *(G-5936)*
Tishcon Corp .... C 516 333-3056
  Westbury *(G-16378)*
Tishcon Corp .... C 516 333-3056
  Westbury *(G-16379)*
Tishcon Corp .... C 516 333-3050
  Westbury *(G-16380)*
Tishcon Corp .... C 516 333-3050
  Westbury *(G-16381)*
Unipharm Inc .... D 212 594-3260
  New York *(G-11947)*
Wellmill LLC .... E 631 465-9245
  Commack *(G-3706)*

WALL COVERINGS WHOLESALERS
Scalamandre Wallpaper Inc .... B 631 467-8800
  Hauppauge *(G-5934)*

WALLBOARD: Decorated, Made From Purchased Materials
Aniiwe Inc .... G 347 683-1891
  Brooklyn *(G-1535)*

WALLPAPER & WALL COVERINGS
Adelphi Paper Hangings .... G 518 284-9066
  Sharon Springs *(G-14796)*
Eskayel Inc .... G 347 703-8084
  Brooklyn *(G-1848)*
Flavor Paper Ltd .... F 718 422-0230
  Brooklyn *(G-1889)*
Gerald McGlone .... G 518 482-2613
  Colonie *(G-3678)*
Larkin Anya Ltd .... G 718 361-1827
  Long Island City *(G-7495)*
Sunnyside Decorative Prints Co .... G 516 671-1935
  Glen Cove *(G-5377)*

WALLS: Curtain, Metal
A&B McKeon Glass Inc .... G 718 525-2152
  Staten Island *(G-15038)*
Metalsigma Usa Inc .... G 212 731-4346
  New York *(G-10783)*

WAREHOUSE CLUBS STORES
Brucci Ltd .... E 914 965-0707
  Yonkers *(G-16741)*

WAREHOUSING & STORAGE FACILITIES, NEC
Acme Signs of Baldwinsville .... G 315 638-4865
  Baldwinsville *(G-547)*
Cambridge University Press .... D 212 337-5000
  New York *(G-9186)*
Eastern Welding Inc .... G 631 727-0306
  Riverhead *(G-13568)*
Medical Action Industries Inc .... C 631 231-4600
  Hauppauge *(G-5884)*

WAREHOUSING & STORAGE, REFRIGERATED: Frozen Or Refrig Goods
Adirondack Ice & Air Inc .... F 518 483-4340
  Malone *(G-7717)*

WAREHOUSING & STORAGE: General
Ivi Services Inc .... D 607 729-5111
  Binghamton *(G-897)*
Lighting Holdings Intl LLC .... A 845 306-1850
  Purchase *(G-13391)*
Platinum Sales Promotion Inc .... G 718 361-0200
  Long Island City *(G-7557)*
Wayuga Community Newspapers .... G 315 594-2506
  Wolcott *(G-16612)*

WAREHOUSING & STORAGE: General
Canfield & Tack Inc .... D 585 235-7710
  Rochester *(G-13689)*

Dayleen Intimates Inc .... E 914 969-5900
  Yonkers *(G-16749)*

WAREHOUSING & STORAGE: Refrigerated
Crescent Duck Farm Inc .... E 631 722-8700
  Aquebogue *(G-374)*

WARM AIR HEATING & AC EQPT & SPLYS, WHOLESALE Air Filters
R P Fedder Corp .... E 585 288-1600
  Rochester *(G-14066)*

WARM AIR HEATING/AC EQPT/SPLYS, WHOL Dehumidifiers, Exc Port
MSP Technologycom LLC .... G 631 424-7542
  Centerport *(G-3351)*

WARM AIR HEATING/AC EQPT/SPLYS, WHOL: Ventilating Eqpt/Sply
DI Manufacturing Inc .... E 315 432-8977
  North Syracuse *(G-12400)*

WASHCLOTHS
1510 Associates LLC .... G 212 828-8720
  New York *(G-8665)*

WASHERS: Metal
Superior Washer & Gasket Corp .... D 631 273-8282
  Hauppauge *(G-5952)*

WASHERS: Plastic
Fibre Materials Corp .... E 516 349-1660
  Plainview *(G-13058)*

WATCH STRAPS, EXC METAL
International Time Products .... G 516 931-0005
  Jericho *(G-6791)*
Roma Industries LLC .... G 212 268-0723
  New York *(G-11426)*

WATCHCASES
American Time Mfg Ltd .... F 585 266-5120
  Rochester *(G-13629)*

WATCHES
Croton Watch Co Inc .... E 800 443-7639
  West Nyack *(G-16268)*
E Gluck Corporation .... C 718 784-0700
  Little Neck *(G-7218)*
First Sbf Holding Inc .... E 845 425-9882
  Valley Cottage *(G-15754)*
Geneva Watch Company Inc .... E 212 221-1177
  New York *(G-9904)*
Life Watch Technology Inc .... D 917 669-2428
  Flushing *(G-5023)*

WATCHES & PARTS, WHOLESALE
E Gluck Corporation .... C 718 784-0700
  Little Neck *(G-7218)*

WATER PURIFICATION EQPT: Household
Airgle Corporation .... E 866 501-7750
  Ronkonkoma *(G-14296)*
Atlantic Ultraviolet Corp .... E 631 234-3275
  Hauppauge *(G-5773)*
Water Energy Systems LLC .... G 844 822-7665
  New York *(G-12079)*

WATER SUPPLY
Ewt Holdings III Corp .... F 212 644-5900
  New York *(G-9744)*

WATER TREATMENT EQPT: Indl
Bolton Point Wtr Trtmnt Plant .... G 607 277-0660
  Ithaca *(G-6563)*
Business Advisory Services .... G 718 337-3740
  Far Rockaway *(G-4698)*
City of Olean .... G 716 376-5694
  Olean *(G-12595)*

WATER TREATMENT EQPT: Indl

City of Oneonta .... G 607 433-3470
  Oneonta *(G-12630)*
Clearcove Systems Inc .... F 585 734-3012
  Victor *(G-15836)*
Integrated Water Management .... G 607 844-4276
  Dryden *(G-4150)*
Metro Group Inc .... D 718 729-7200
  Long Island City *(G-7523)*
Neptune Soft Water Inc .... F 315 446-5151
  Syracuse *(G-15380)*
New Windsor Waste Water Plant ..... F 845 561-2550
  New Windsor *(G-8651)*
Ossining Village of Inc .... G 914 202-9668
  Ossining *(G-12773)*
R C Kolstad Water Corp .... G 585 216-2230
  Ontario *(G-12661)*

WATER: Mineral, Carbonated, Canned & Bottled, Etc

Alpha Wolf LLC .... G 516 778-5812
  Carle Place *(G-3260)*
Global Brands Inc .... G 845 358-1212
  Nyack *(G-12508)*
Just Beverages LLC .... F 480 388-1133
  Glens Falls *(G-5428)*
New York Spring Water Inc .... E 212 777-4649
  New York *(G-10942)*
Nirvana Inc .... C 315 942-4900
  Forestport *(G-5083)*
Saratoga Spring Water Company ..... E 518 584-6363
  Saratoga Springs *(G-14598)*

WATER: Pasteurized & Mineral, Bottled & Canned

Ariesun Inc .... E 866 274-3049
  Mount Vernon *(G-8378)*
Mayer Bros Apple Products Inc .... D 716 668-1787
  West Seneca *(G-16301)*

WATER: Pasteurized, Canned & Bottled, Etc

Crystal Rock LLC .... E 716 626-7460
  Buffalo *(G-2785)*
Just Goods Inc .... F 917 294-0043
  New York *(G-10385)*
Superleaf LLC .... G 888 887-4318
  Brooklyn *(G-2539)*

WATERPROOFING COMPOUNDS

Penetron International Ltd .... F 631 941-9700
  East Setauket *(G-4306)*

WAVEGUIDES & FITTINGS

M W Microwave Corp .... F 516 295-1814
  Lawrence *(G-7105)*

WAXES: Mineral, Natural

Koster Keunen Waxes Ltd .... F 631 589-0400
  Sayville *(G-14632)*

WAXES: Paraffin

Industrial Raw Materials LLC .... F 212 688-8080
  Plainview *(G-13063)*
Kent Chemical Corporation .... E 212 521-1700
  New York *(G-10436)*

WAXES: Petroleum, Not Produced In Petroleum Refineries

Industrial Raw Materials LLC .... G 212 688-8080
  New York *(G-10202)*
Premier Ingridients Inc .... G 516 641-6763
  Great Neck *(G-5582)*

WEATHER STRIPS: Metal

Accurate Metal Weather Strip .... G 914 668-6042
  Mount Vernon *(G-8375)*

WEAVING MILL, BROADWOVEN FABRICS: Wool Or Similar Fabric

Loomstate LLC .... E 212 219-2300
  New York *(G-10602)*

WEDDING CHAPEL: Privately Operated

Silver Griffin Inc .... F 518 272-7771
  Troy *(G-15627)*

WEIGHING MACHINERY & APPARATUS

Measupro Inc .... F 845 425-8777
  Spring Valley *(G-15003)*
S R Instruments Inc .... E 716 693-5977
  Tonawanda *(G-15573)*
Weighing & Systems Tech Inc .... G 518 274-2797
  Troy *(G-15635)*

WELDING & CUTTING APPARATUS & ACCESS, NEC

McAllisters Precision Wldg Inc .... F 518 221-3455
  Menands *(G-8087)*

WELDING EQPT

Apogee Translite Inc .... E 631 254-6975
  Deer Park *(G-3944)*
Riverview Industries Inc .... G 845 265-5284
  Cold Spring *(G-3627)*
Vante Inc .... F 716 778-7691
  Newfane *(G-12254)*

WELDING EQPT & SPLYS WHOLESALERS

Haun Welding Supply Inc .... G 315 592-5012
  Fulton *(G-5219)*
Jacksons Welding LLC .... G 607 756-2725
  Cortland *(G-3878)*

WELDING EQPT: Electrical

3krf LLC .... G 516 208-6824
  Oceanside *(G-12529)*

WELDING MACHINES & EQPT: Ultrasonic

Sonicor Inc .... F 631 920-6555
  West Babylon *(G-16194)*

WELDING REPAIR SVC

303 Contracting Inc .... E 716 896-2122
  Orchard Park *(G-12694)*
A & J Machine & Welding Inc .... F 631 845-7586
  Farmingdale *(G-4704)*
AAA Welding and Fabrication of ...... G 585 254-2830
  Rochester *(G-13592)*
Accurate Welding Service Inc .... G 516 333-1730
  Westbury *(G-16308)*
Acro-Fab Ltd .... E 315 564-6688
  Hannibal *(G-5717)*
Airweld Inc .... G 631 924-6366
  Ridge *(G-13520)*
Aj Genco Mch Sp McHy Rdout Svc .. F 716 664-4925
  Falconer *(G-4669)*
Allen Tool Phoenix Inc .... E 315 463-7533
  East Syracuse *(G-4317)*
Alliance Services Corp .... G 516 775-7600
  Floral Park *(G-4953)*
Alliance Welding & Steel Fabg .... F 516 775-7600
  Floral Park *(G-4954)*
Alloy Metal Works Inc .... G 631 694-8163
  Farmingdale *(G-4716)*
Alpine Machine Inc .... F 607 272-1344
  Ithaca *(G-6556)*
Andersens Spring & Wldg Corp .... G 516 785-7337
  Bellmore *(G-784)*
ARC TEC Wldg & Fabrication Inc .... G 718 982-9274
  Staten Island *(G-15044)*
Atlantis Equipment Corporation .... E 518 733-5910
  Stephentown *(G-15154)*
Barber Welding Inc .... E 315 834-6645
  Weedsport *(G-16110)*
Benemy Welding & Fabrication .... G 315 548-8500
  Phelps *(G-12975)*
Bms Manufacturing Co Inc .... E 607 535-2426
  Watkins Glen *(G-16058)*
Boilermatic Welding Inds Inc .... E 631 654-1341
  Medford *(G-7940)*
Bracci Ironworks Inc .... F 718 629-2374
  Brooklyn *(G-1630)*
Brenseke George Wldg Ir Works ..... G 631 271-4870
  Deer Park *(G-3954)*
Broadalbin Manufacturing Corp .... E 518 883-5313
  Broadalbin *(G-1187)*
Bruce Pierce .... G 716 731-9310
  Sanborn *(G-14542)*
C G & Son Machining Inc .... G 315 964-2430
  Williamstown *(G-16564)*
CBM Fabrications Inc .... E 518 399-8023
  Ballston Lake *(G-567)*
Competicion Mower Repair .... G 516 280-6584
  Mineola *(G-8214)*
Cs Automation Inc .... E 315 524-5123
  Ontario *(G-12650)*
Custom Laser Inc .... E 716 434-8600
  Lockport *(G-7292)*
D & G Welding Inc .... G 716 873-3088
  Buffalo *(G-2790)*
DC Fabrication & Welding Inc .... G 845 295-0215
  Ferndale *(G-4932)*
Deck Bros Inc .... E 716 852-0262
  Buffalo *(G-2795)*
Dennies Manufacturing Inc .... E 585 393-4646
  Canandaigua *(G-3218)*
Donald Stefan .... G 716 492-1110
  Chaffee *(G-3403)*
Dorgan Welding Service .... G 315 462-9030
  Phelps *(G-12976)*
E B Industries LLC .... E 631 293-8565
  Farmingdale *(G-4754)*
E B Industries LLC .... E 631 293-8565
  Farmingdale *(G-4755)*
Eagle Welding Machine .... G 315 594-1845
  Wolcott *(G-16610)*
Etna Tool & Die Corporation .... F 212 475-4350
  New York *(G-9723)*
Excelco/Newbrook Inc .... D 716 934-2644
  Silver Creek *(G-14862)*
F M L Industries Inc .... G 607 749-7273
  Homer *(G-6254)*
Flushing Boiler & Welding Co .... G 718 463-1266
  Brooklyn *(G-1893)*
Formac Welding Inc .... G 631 421-5525
  Huntington Station *(G-6441)*
Fred Santucci Inc .... F 716 483-1411
  Jamestown *(G-6716)*
G & C Welding Co Inc .... G 516 883-3228
  Port Washington *(G-13261)*
Gasport Welding & Fabg Inc .... F 716 772-7205
  Gasport *(G-5306)*
Gc Mobile Services Inc .... G 914 736-9730
  Cortlandt Manor *(G-3901)*
Genco John .... G 716 483-5446
  Jamestown *(G-6717)*
General Welding & Fabg Inc .... G 716 652-0033
  Elma *(G-4451)*
Guthrie Heli-ARC Inc .... G 585 548-5053
  Bergen *(G-821)*
Hadfield Inc .... F 631 981-4314
  Ronkonkoma *(G-14350)*
Hadleys Fab-Weld Inc .... G 315 926-5101
  Marion *(G-7802)*
Hansen Steel .... E 585 398-2020
  Farmington *(G-4915)*
Hartman Enterprises Inc .... D 315 363-7300
  Oneida *(G-12610)*
Haskell Machine & Tool Inc .... F 607 749-2421
  Homer *(G-6255)*
Haun Welding Supply Inc .... G 607 846-2289
  Elmira *(G-4491)*
Haun Welding Supply Inc .... G 315 592-5012
  Fulton *(G-5219)*
Homer Iron Works LLC .... G 607 749-3963
  Homer *(G-6256)*
Huntington Welding & Iron .... G 631 423-3331
  Huntington Station *(G-6445)*
Ingleside Machine Co Inc .... D 585 924-3046
  Farmington *(G-4916)*
Jacksons Welding LLC .... G 607 756-2725
  Cortland *(G-3878)*
Kon Tat Group Corporation .... G 718 207-5022
  Brooklyn *(G-2081)*
L & S Metals Inc .... E 716 692-6865
  North Tonawanda *(G-12436)*
Lagasse Works Inc .... G 315 946-9202
  Lyons *(G-7685)*
Linita Design & Mfg Corp .... E 716 566-7753
  Lackawanna *(G-6949)*
M M Welding .... E 315 363-3980
  Oneida *(G-12612)*
Maple Grove Corp .... E 585 492-5286
  Arcade *(G-386)*
Maria Dionisio Welding Inc .... G 631 956-0815
  Lindenhurst *(G-7178)*

PRODUCT SECTION

WIRE

Maspeth Welding Inc .... E 718 497-5430		
Maspeth *(G-7858)*		
Meades Welding and Fabricating .... G 631 581-1555		
Islip *(G-6548)*		
Mega Tool & Mfg Corp .... E 607 734-8398		
Elmira *(G-4498)*		
Miller Metal Fabricating Inc .... G 585 359-3400		
Rochester *(G-13945)*		
Modern Mechanical Fab Inc .... G 518 298-5177		
Champlain *(G-3412)*		
Mooradian Hydraulics & Eqp Co .... F 518 766-3866		
Castleton On Hudson *(G-3296)*		
Ms Spares LLC .... G 607 223-3024		
Clay *(G-3551)*		
New Age Ironworks Inc .... F 718 277-1895		
Brooklyn *(G-2255)*		
NY Iron Inc .... F 718 302-9000		
Long Island City *(G-7541)*		
Phillip J Ortiz Manufacturing .... G 845 226-7030		
Hopewell Junction *(G-6292)*		
Phoenix Welding & Fabg Inc .... G 315 695-2223		
Phoenix *(G-12992)*		
Precision Laser Technology LLC .... F 585 458-6208		
Rochester *(G-14036)*		
Pro-Tech Wldg Fabrication Inc .... E 585 436-9855		
Rochester *(G-14047)*		
Qsf Inc .... G 585 247-6200		
Gates *(G-5311)*		
Quality Industrial Services .... F 716 667-7703		
Orchard Park *(G-12742)*		
R & B Fabrication Inc .... F 315 640-9901		
Cicero *(G-3522)*		
Reliable Welding & Fabrication .... G 631 758-2637		
Patchogue *(G-12876)*		
REO Welding Inc .... F 518 238-1022		
Cohoes *(G-3618)*		
Rini Tank & Truck Service .... F 718 384-6606		
Brooklyn *(G-2402)*		
Rj Welding & Fabricating Inc .... G 315 523-1288		
Clifton Springs *(G-3583)*		
Robert M Brown .... F 607 426-6250		
Montour Falls *(G-8327)*		
Rothe Welding Inc .... G 845 246-3051		
Saugerties *(G-14615)*		
S & D Welding Corp .... G 631 454-0383		
West Babylon *(G-16189)*		
S J B Fabrication .... F 716 895-0281		
Buffalo *(G-3052)*		
Sierson Crane Inc .... F 315 723-6914		
Westmoreland *(G-16411)*		
Sierson Welding Inc .... G 315 724-3903		
Westmoreland *(G-16412)*		
Smithers Tools & Mch Pdts Inc .... D 845 876-3063		
Rhinebeck *(G-13488)*		
Strecks Inc .... E 518 273-4410		
Watervliet *(G-16051)*		
Tracey Welding Co Inc .... G 518 756-6309		
Coeymans *(G-3609)*		
Walters & Walters Inc .... G 347 202-8535		
Bronx *(G-1418)*		
Watkins Welding and Mch Sp Inc .... G 914 949-6168		
White Plains *(G-16516)*		
Welding Chapter of New York .... G 212 481-1496		
New York *(G-12090)*		
West Metal Works Inc .... E 716 895-4900		
Buffalo *(G-3128)*		

WELDING SPLYS, EXC GASES: Wholesalers

Austin Industries Inc .... G 585 589-1353
Albion *(G-155)*

WELDING TIPS: Heat Resistant, Metal

JE Monahan Fabrications LLC .... F 518 761-0414
Queensbury *(G-13430)*
National Maint Contg Corp .... D 716 285-1583
Niagara Falls *(G-12312)*

WELDMENTS

Glenridge Fabricators Inc .... F 718 456-2297
Glendale *(G-5402)*
Industrial Fabricating Corp .... F 315 437-8234
East Syracuse *(G-4349)*
Miller Metal Fabricating Inc .... G 585 359-3400
Rochester *(G-13945)*

WHEELBARROWS

Clopay Ames True Temper .... F 212 957-5096
New York *(G-9330)*

WHEELCHAIR LIFTS

S & H Enterprises Inc .... G 888 323-8755
Queensbury *(G-13440)*
Thomas F Egan .... E 607 669-4822
Binghamton *(G-919)*

WHEELCHAIRS

Crosley Medical Products Inc .... F 631 595-2547
Syosset *(G-15213)*
Gadabout USA Wheelchairs Inc .... F 585 338-2110
Rochester *(G-13821)*
Palmer Industries Inc .... G 607 754-8741
Endicott *(G-4606)*
Palmer Industries Inc .... E 607 754-2957
Endicott *(G-4607)*
Skil-Care Corporation .... C 914 963-2040
Yonkers *(G-16798)*
Vcp Mobility Inc .... B 718 356-7827
Staten Island *(G-15150)*
VSM Investors LLC .... G 212 351-1600
New York *(G-12057)*

WHEELS & PARTS

Bam Enterprises Inc .... G 716 773-7634
Grand Island *(G-5496)*
Factory Wheel Warehouse Inc .... G 516 605-2131
Plainview *(G-13057)*
Motor Components LLC .... D 607 737-8011
Elmira Heights *(G-4512)*

WHEELS: Abrasive

Jta USA Inc .... G 718 722-0902
Brooklyn *(G-2053)*

WHEELS: Buffing & Polishing

Barker Brothers Incorporated .... D 718 456-6400
Ridgewood *(G-13530)*
Dimanco Inc .... G 315 797-0470
Utica *(G-15695)*
Divine Brothers Company .... C 315 797-0470
Utica *(G-15698)*

WHEELS: Iron & Steel, Locomotive & Car

Nitro Wheels Inc .... F 716 337-0709
North Collins *(G-12387)*

WIGS & HAIRPIECES

M and J Hair Center Inc .... F 516 872-1010
Garden City *(G-5269)*
Moti Inc .... F 718 436-4280
Brooklyn *(G-2228)*

WIND TUNNELS

United Wind Inc .... F 888 313-3353
Brooklyn *(G-2605)*

WINDINGS: Coil, Electronic

American Precision Inds Inc .... C 716 691-9100
Amherst *(G-214)*
American Precision Inds Inc .... D 716 652-3600
East Aurora *(G-4193)*
American Precision Inds Inc .... D 585 496-5755
Arcade *(G-376)*
Caddell Burns Manufacturing Co .... E 631 757-1772
Northport *(G-12465)*
Mohawk Electro Techniques Inc .... D 315 896-2661
Barneveld *(G-603)*
Precision Electronics Inc .... F 631 842-4900
Copiague *(G-3774)*

WINDMILLS: Electric Power Generation

EDP Renewables North Amer LLC .... G 518 426-1650
Albany *(G-71)*

WINDOW & DOOR FRAMES

Action Bullet Resistant .... F 631 422-0888
West Islip *(G-16258)*
D D & L Inc .... F 607 729-9131
Binghamton *(G-878)*
Interstate Window Corporation .... D 631 231-0800
Brentwood *(G-1137)*
J Sussman Inc .... E 718 297-0228
Jamaica *(G-6652)*
Jaidan Industries Inc .... F 516 944-3650
Port Washington *(G-13272)*
Kasson & Keller Inc .... A 518 853-3421
Fonda *(G-5065)*
Munschauer Inc .... F 716 895-8888
Buffalo *(G-2959)*
New Bgnnngs Win Door Dstrs LLC ...... F 845 214-0698
Poughkeepsie *(G-13358)*
Sunrise Door Solutions .... G 631 464-4139
Copiague *(G-3784)*

WINDOW BLIND REPAIR SVCS

Window-Fix Inc .... E 718 854-3475
Brooklyn *(G-2651)*

WINDOW FRAMES & SASHES: Plastic

Hart To Hart Industries Inc .... G 716 492-2709
Chaffee *(G-3404)*
JSM Vinyl Products Inc .... F 516 775-4520
New Hyde Park *(G-8545)*

WINDOW FRAMES, MOLDING & TRIM: Vinyl

Eastern Enterprise Corp .... F 718 727-8600
Staten Island *(G-15073)*
Kasson & Keller Inc .... A 518 853-3421
Fonda *(G-5065)*
Northeast Windows Usa Inc .... F 516 378-6577
Merrick *(G-8104)*
Pvc Industries Inc .... F 518 877-8670
Clifton Park *(G-3574)*
Tri-State Window Factory Corp .... D 631 667-8600
Deer Park *(G-4052)*
Vinyline Window and Door Inc .... F 914 476-3500
Yonkers *(G-16806)*
Window Tech Systems Inc .... E 518 899-9000
Ballston Spa *(G-598)*

WINDOW TRIMMING SVCS

New Business Solutions Inc .... E 631 789-1500
Amityville *(G-306)*

WINDOWS: Wood

Kelly Window Systems Inc .... E 631 420-8500
Farmingdale *(G-4801)*
Pella Corporation .... B 607 223-2023
Johnson City *(G-6816)*
Pella Corporation .... B 607 231-8550
Johnson City *(G-6817)*
Pella Corporation .... B 607 238-2812
Johnson City *(G-6818)*
Pella Corporation .... B 516 385-3622
Albertson *(G-152)*
Pella Corporation .... B 607 238-2812
Johnson City *(G-6819)*
Pella Corporation .... B 516 385-3622
Albertson *(G-153)*
Pella Corporation .... B 607 231-8550
Johnson City *(G-6820)*
Royal Windows Mfg Corp .... E 631 435-8888
Bay Shore *(G-718)*
Stealth Archtctral Windows Inc .... F 718 821-6666
Brooklyn *(G-2514)*

WINE & DISTILLED ALCOHOLIC BEVERAGES WHOLESALERS

Constellation Brands Inc .... D 585 678-7100
Victor *(G-15837)*
Liquid Management Partners LLC .... F 516 775-5050
New Hyde Park *(G-8548)*

WINE CELLARS, BONDED: Wine, Blended

Hickory Road Land Co LLC .... G 607 243-9114
Dundee *(G-4161)*
Solstars Inc .... G 212 605-0430
New York *(G-11640)*
Tickle Hill Winery .... G 607 546-7740
Hector *(G-6003)*
Wine Services Inc .... G 631 722-3800
Riverhead *(G-13589)*

WIRE

Bekaert Corporation .... E 716 830-1321
Amherst *(G-216)*
CFS Enterprises Inc .... E 718 585-0500
Bronx *(G-1238)*

WIRE

PRODUCT SECTION

EB Acquisitions LLC ....D.... 212 355-3310
  New York *(G-9614)*
Island Industries Corp ....G.... 631 451-8825
  Coram *(G-3799)*
Lee Spring Company LLC ....C.... 718 362-5183
  Brooklyn *(G-2105)*
Liberty Fabrication Inc ....G.... 718 495-5735
  Brooklyn *(G-2115)*
Nupro Technologies LLC ....F.... 412 422-5922
  Canandaigua *(G-3227)*
Spectrum Cable Corporation 585 235-7714
  Rochester *(G-14137)*
Tappan Wire & Cable Inc ....C.... 845 353-9000
  Blauvelt *(G-942)*
Web Associates Inc ....G.... 716 883-3377
  Buffalo *(G-3125)*

WIRE & CABLE: Aluminum

Irtronics Instruments Inc ....F.... 914 693-6291
  Ardsley *(G-395)*
SI Partners Inc ....G.... 516 433-1415
  Hicksville *(G-6132)*

WIRE & WIRE PRDTS

369 River Road Inc ....E.... 716 694-5001
  North Tonawanda *(G-12409)*
Abbott Industries Inc ....B.... 718 291-0800
  Jamaica *(G-6622)*
Albest Metal Stamping Corp ......D.... 718 388-6000
  Brooklyn *(G-1500)*
American Wire Tie Inc ....E.... 716 337-2412
  North Collins *(G-12383)*
Angelica Spring Company Inc ....F.... 585 466-7892
  Angelica *(G-367)*
Bayshore Wire Products Corp ....F.... 631 451-8825
  Coram *(G-3796)*
Better Wire Products Inc ....E.... 716 883-3377
  Buffalo *(G-2731)*
Bison Steel Incorporated ....G.... 716 683-0900
  Depew *(G-4080)*
Cable Management Solutions Inc ....E.... 631 674-0004
  Bay Shore *(G-667)*
Clover Wire Forming Co Inc ......E.... 914 375-0400
  Yonkers *(G-16745)*
Compar Manufacturing Corp ......E.... 212 304-2777
  New York *(G-9369)*
Continental Cordage Corp ....D.... 315 655-9800
  Cazenovia *(G-3317)*
Cuddeback Machining Inc ....G.... 585 392-5889
  Hilton *(G-6156)*
Engineering Mfg Tech LLC ....D.... 607 754-7111
  Endicott *(G-4591)*
Flanagans Creative Disp Inc ....E.... 845 858-2542
  Port Jervis *(G-13228)*
Flatcut LLC ....G.... 212 542-5732
  Brooklyn *(G-1888)*
Hanes Supply Inc ....F.... 518 438-0139
  Albany *(G-80)*
Hitachi Metals America Ltd ....E.... 914 694-9200
  Purchase *(G-13389)*
Interstate Wood Products Inc .....E.... 631 842-4488
  Amityville *(G-288)*
Kehr-Buffalo Wire Frame Co Inc ....E.... 716 897-2288
  Buffalo *(G-2902)*
Magic Novelty Co Inc ....E.... 212 304-2777
  New York *(G-10667)*
Oneida Sales & Service Inc ....E.... 716 822-8205
  Buffalo *(G-2980)*
Owl Wire & Cable LLC ....C.... 315 697-2011
  Canastota *(G-3244)*
Peck & Hale LLC ....E.... 631 589-2510
  West Sayville *(G-16291)*
Quality Industrial Services ....F.... 716 667-7703
  Orchard Park *(G-12742)*
Rose Fence Inc ....F.... 516 223-0777
  Baldwin *(G-541)*
SCI Bore Inc ....G.... 212 674-7128
  New York *(G-11518)*
Selectrode Industries Inc ....D.... 631 547-5470
  Huntington Station *(G-6458)*
Sigmund Cohn Corp ....D.... 914 664-5300
  Mount Vernon *(G-8443)*
Teka Precision Inc ....G.... 845 753-1900
  Nyack *(G-12512)*
Trylon Wire & Metal Works Inc ....E.... 718 542-4472
  Bronx *(G-1409)*
Utility Engineering Co ....F.... 845 735-8900
  Pearl River *(G-12912)*

WIRE CLOTH & WOVEN WIRE PRDTS, MADE FROM PURCHASED WIRE

G Bopp USA Inc ....G.... 845 296-1065
  Wappingers Falls *(G-15931)*
Sinclair International Company ...D.... 518 798-2361
  Queensbury *(G-13442)*

WIRE FABRIC: Welded Steel

Technical Wldg Fabricators LLC ....F.... 518 463-2229
  Albany *(G-132)*

WIRE FENCING & ACCESS WHOLESALERS

Master-Halco Inc ....F.... 631 585-8150
  Yaphank *(G-16717)*

WIRE MATERIALS: Copper

Camden Wire Co Inc ....A.... 315 245-3800
  Camden *(G-3186)*
International Wire Group ....F.... 315 245-3800
  Camden *(G-3188)*
Jaguar Industries Inc ....F.... 845 947-1800
  Haverstraw *(G-5979)*
Omega Wire Inc ....D.... 315 689-7115
  Jordan *(G-6842)*
Omega Wire Inc ....B.... 315 245-3800
  Camden *(G-3191)*
Owl Corporation ....G.... 315 245-4305
  Camden *(G-3192)*

WIRE MATERIALS: Steel

American Wire Tie Inc ....E.... 716 337-2412
  North Collins *(G-12383)*
Continental Cordage Corp ....D.... 315 655-9800
  Cazenovia *(G-3317)*
Hitachi Metals America Ltd ....E.... 914 694-9200
  Purchase *(G-13389)*
Hohmann & Barnard Inc ....D.... 631 234-0600
  Hauppauge *(G-5846)*
Omega Wire Inc ....D.... 315 689-7115
  Jordan *(G-6842)*
Rolling Gate Supply Corp ....G.... 718 366-5258
  Glendale *(G-5407)*
Rose Fence Inc ....F.... 516 223-0777
  Baldwin *(G-541)*
Sigmund Cohn Corp ....D.... 914 664-5300
  Mount Vernon *(G-8443)*

WIRE PRDTS: Ferrous Or Iron, Made In Wiredrawing Plants

Forsyth Industries Inc ....E.... 716 652-1070
  Buffalo *(G-2831)*

WIRE PRDTS: Steel & Iron

Handy & Harman Ltd ....A.... 212 520-2300
  New York *(G-10031)*
Sph Group Holdings LLC ....F.... 212 520-2300
  New York *(G-11669)*

WIRE WHOLESALERS

Awt Supply Corp ....G.... 516 437-9105
  Elmont *(G-4517)*

WIRE: Barbed

Cobra Systems Inc ....F.... 845 338-6675
  Bloomington *(G-959)*

WIRE: Barbed & Twisted

Cobra Manufacturing Corp ....G.... 845 514-2505
  Lake Katrine *(G-6972)*

WIRE: Communication

Caldwell Bennett Inc ....E.... 315 337-8540
  Oriskany *(G-12752)*
Corning Optcal Cmmncations LLC ....F.... 607 974-7543
  Corning *(G-3816)*
Global Technologies Inc ....D.... 631 243-7924
  Deer Park *(G-3982)*

WIRE: Mesh

Aeroflex Incorporated ....B.... 516 694-6700
  Plainview *(G-13032)*

WIRE: Nonferrous

Camden Wire Co Inc ....A.... 315 245-3800
  Camden *(G-3186)*
Colonial Wire & Cable Co Inc .....D.... 631 234-8500
  Hauppauge *(G-5793)*
Colonial Wire Cable Co NJ Inc ....G.... 631 234-8500
  Hauppauge *(G-5794)*
Continental Cordage Corp ....D.... 315 655-9800
  Cazenovia *(G-3317)*
Convergent Cnnctivity Tech Inc ....G.... 845 651-5250
  Florida *(G-4969)*
Cortland Cable Company Inc .....E.... 607 753-8276
  Cortland *(G-3865)*
CS Business Systems Inc ....E.... 716 886-6521
  Buffalo *(G-2786)*
Fiberall Corp ....E.... 516 371-5200
  Inwood *(G-6490)*
International Wire Group Inc ....B.... 315 245-2000
  Camden *(G-3189)*
Jaguar Industries Inc ....F.... 845 947-1800
  Haverstraw *(G-5979)*
Leviton Manufacturing Co Inc .....B.... 631 812-6000
  Melville *(G-8043)*
Performance Wire & Cable Inc ....F.... 315 245-2594
  Camden *(G-3193)*
Rdi Inc ....F.... 914 773-1000
  Mount Kisco *(G-8357)*
Remee Products Corp ....D.... 845 651-4431
  Florida *(G-4972)*
Rockland Insulated Wire Cable ....G.... 845 429-3103
  Haverstraw *(G-5980)*
Siemens Corporation ....F.... 202 434-7800
  New York *(G-11577)*
Siemens USA Holdings Inc ....B.... 212 258-4000
  New York *(G-11580)*
Sinclair Technologies Inc ....E.... 716 874-3682
  Hamburg *(G-5695)*
Steelflex Electro Corp ....D.... 516 226-4466
  Lindenhurst *(G-7193)*
Tappan Wire & Cable Inc ....C.... 845 353-9000
  Blauvelt *(G-942)*
United Wire Technologies Inc .....F.... 315 623-7203
  Constantia *(G-3741)*
Universal Builders Supply Inc .....F.... 845 758-8801
  Red Hook *(G-13459)*
Whirlwind Music Distrs Inc ....D.... 800 733-9473
  Rochester *(G-14207)*

WIRE: Nonferrous, Appliance Fixture

Kris-Tech Wire Company Inc .....E.... 315 339-5268
  Rome *(G-14255)*

WIRE: Steel, Insulated Or Armored

Able Industries Inc ....F.... 914 739-5685
  Cortlandt Manor *(G-3898)*
Aerospace Wire & Cable Inc .....E.... 718 358-2345
  College Point *(G-3637)*

WOMEN'S & CHILDREN'S CLOTHING WHOLESALERS, NEC

Alpha 6 Distributions LLC ....F.... 516 801-8290
  Locust Valley *(G-7345)*
Bilco Industries Inc ....F.... 917 783-5008
  New York *(G-9081)*
D-C Theatricks ....G.... 716 847-0180
  Buffalo *(G-2791)*
Design Archives Inc ....G.... 212 768-0617
  New York *(G-9504)*
Eb Couture Ltd ....E.... 212 912-0190
  New York *(G-9615)*
Grand Knitting Mills Inc ....E.... 631 226-5000
  Amityville *(G-278)*
Halmode Apparel Inc ....A.... 212 819-9114
  New York *(G-10023)*
Hampshire Sub II Inc ....D.... 631 321-0923
  New York *(G-10027)*
JM Originals Inc ....C.... 845 647-3003
  Ellenville *(G-4439)*
Kate Spade & Company LLC ....B.... 212 354-4900
  New York *(G-10415)*
Kenmar Shirts Inc ....E.... 718 824-3880
  Bronx *(G-1307)*
Lloyds Fashions Inc ....D.... 631 435-3353
  Brentwood *(G-1141)*
M Hidary & Co Inc ....D.... 212 736-6540
  New York *(G-10639)*
Maggy Boutique Ltd ....E.... 212 997-5222
  New York *(G-10664)*

Mango Usa Inc .... E 718 998-6050
  Brooklyn *(G-2156)*
Moresca Clothing and Costume .... F 845 331-6012
  Ulster Park *(G-15659)*
Nlhe LLC .... E 212 594-0012
  Brooklyn *(G-2270)*
Onia LLC .... E 646 701-0008
  New York *(G-11045)*
Only Hearts Ltd .... E 212 268-0886
  New York *(G-11046)*
Penfli Industries Inc .... F 212 947-6080
  Great Neck *(G-5581)*
Soho Apparel Ltd .... G 212 840-1109
  New York *(G-11636)*
Therese The Childrens Collectn .... G 518 346-2315
  Schenectady *(G-14721)*
United Knitwear International .... G 212 354-2920
  New York *(G-11953)*
Universal Mus Group Hldngs Inc .... E 212 333-8000
  New York *(G-11961)*
Ying Ke Youth Age Group Inc .... F 929 402-8458
  Dix Hills *(G-4128)*

WOMEN'S & GIRLS' SPORTSWEAR WHOLESALERS

Argee America Inc .... G 212 768-9840
  New York *(G-8905)*
Casuals Etc Inc .... D 212 838-1319
  New York *(G-9225)*
Danice Stores Inc .... F 212 665-0389
  New York *(G-9467)*
F & J Designs Inc .... G 212 302-8755
  New York *(G-9761)*
Jaxis Inc .... G 212 302-7611
  Brooklyn *(G-2034)*
Lollytogs Ltd .... D 212 502-6000
  New York *(G-10595)*
Morelle Products Ltd .... F 212 391-8070
  New York *(G-10841)*
Noah Enterprises Ltd .... E 212 736-2888
  New York *(G-10982)*
S2 Sportswear Inc .... F 347 335-0713
  Brooklyn *(G-2441)*
Sterling Possessions Ltd .... G 212 594-0418
  New York *(G-11707)*

WOMEN'S CLOTHING STORES

6 Shore Road LLC .... G 212 274-9666
  New York *(G-8683)*
Amj DOT LLC .... G 718 775-3288
  Brooklyn *(G-1530)*
Caribbean Fashion Group Inc .... G 212 706-8851
  New York *(G-9207)*
Elie Tahari Ltd .... G 212 398-2622
  New York *(G-9645)*
Joseph (uk) Inc .... G 212 570-0077
  New York *(G-10363)*
Kozinn+sons Merchant Tailors .... E 212 643-1916
  New York *(G-10475)*
Mee Accessories LLC .... B 917 262-1000
  New York *(G-10762)*
Mega Sourcing Inc .... G 646 682-0304
  Merrick *(G-8103)*
Uniqlo USA LLC .... F 877 486-4756
  New York *(G-11948)*

WOMEN'S CLOTHING STORES: Ready-To-Wear

Ferris USA LLC .... G 617 895-8102
  New York *(G-9796)*
Hillary Merchant Inc .... G 646 575-9242
  New York *(G-10099)*
Phillips-Van Heusen Europe .... F 212 381-3500
  New York *(G-11183)*
Pvh Corp .... D 212 381-3500
  New York *(G-11281)*
Pvh Corp .... G 212 549-6000
  New York *(G-11282)*
Stallion Inc .... E 718 706-0111
  Long Island City *(G-7596)*

WOMEN'S SPECIALTY CLOTHING STORES

B S J Limited .... E 212 764-4600
  New York *(G-8990)*
Dvf Studio LLC .... D 212 741-6607
  New York *(G-9589)*

Dvf Studio LLC .... G 646 576-8009
  New York *(G-9590)*

WOMEN'S SPORTSWEAR STORES

Central Apparel Group Ltd .... F 212 868-6505
  New York *(G-9242)*
Mainly Monograms Inc .... E 845 624-4923
  West Nyack *(G-16275)*
Royal Tees Inc .... G 845 357-9448
  Suffern *(G-15197)*

WOOD FENCING WHOLESALERS

Interstate Wood Products Inc .... E 631 842-4488
  Amityville *(G-288)*
Master-Halco Inc .... F 631 585-8150
  Yaphank *(G-16717)*

WOOD PRDTS: Beekeeping Splys

Betterbee Inc .... F 518 314-0575
  Greenwich *(G-5637)*
Northast Ctr For Bekeeping LLC .... F 800 632-3379
  Greenwich *(G-5643)*

WOOD PRDTS: Clothespins

Green Renewable Inc .... E 518 658-2233
  Berlin *(G-831)*

WOOD PRDTS: Display Forms, Boot & Shoe

Encore Retail Systems Inc .... F 718 385-3443
  Mamaroneck *(G-7743)*

WOOD PRDTS: Engraved

Lanwood Industries Inc .... E 718 786-3000
  Bay Shore *(G-694)*

WOOD PRDTS: Furniture Inlays, Veneers

American Woods & Veneers Works .... E 718 937-2195
  Long Island City *(G-7378)*

WOOD PRDTS: Jalousies, Glass, Wood Framed

Paul David Enterprises Inc .... G 646 667-5530
  New York *(G-11123)*

WOOD PRDTS: Ladders & Stepladders

York Ladder Inc .... F 718 784-6666
  Long Island City *(G-7646)*

WOOD PRDTS: Laundry

American Casino Equipment Mfg .... F 631 242-2440
  Deer Park *(G-3939)*
Grohe America Inc .... G 212 206-8820
  New York *(G-9993)*

WOOD PRDTS: Moldings, Unfinished & Prefinished

Adriatic Wood Products Inc .... E 718 922-4621
  Brooklyn *(G-1484)*
Deerfield Millwork Inc .... F 631 726-9663
  Water Mill *(G-15969)*
Fire Island Sea Clam Co Inc .... G 631 589-2199
  West Sayville *(G-16289)*
Old World Mouldings Inc .... G 631 563-8660
  Bohemia *(G-1070)*
Regal Windows & Doors LLC .... F 201 934-0100
  Spring Valley *(G-15006)*
Scanga Woodworking Corp .... E 845 265-9115
  Cold Spring *(G-3628)*
Spiegel Woodworks Inc .... F 845 336-8090
  Kingston *(G-6918)*

WOOD PRDTS: Mulch Or Sawdust

Premium Mulch & Materials Inc .... F 631 320-3666
  Coram *(G-3803)*
Wholesale Mulch & Sawdust Inc .... G 607 687-2637
  Owego *(G-12806)*

WOOD PRDTS: Novelties, Fiber

Cowee Forest Products Inc .... E 518 658-2233
  Berlin *(G-830)*
Graphics Slution Providers Inc .... F 845 677-5088
  Lagrangeville *(G-6956)*

Ryers Creek Corp .... E 607 523-6617
  Corning *(G-3825)*

WOOD PRDTS: Outdoor, Structural

Amish Structure .... F 607 257-1070
  Dryden *(G-4148)*
Wolski Wood Works Inc .... G 718 577-9816
  Flushing *(G-5060)*

WOOD PRDTS: Panel Work

Empire Building Products Inc .... G 518 695-6094
  Schuylerville *(G-14733)*

WOOD PRDTS: Pedestals & Statuary

Mrp Supports LLC .... F 716 332-7673
  Orchard Park *(G-12731)*

WOOD PRDTS: Rulers & Rules

Aakron Rule Corp .... C 716 542-5483
  Akron *(G-16)*

WOOD PRDTS: Shavings & Packaging, Excelsior

RWS Manufacturing Inc .... G 518 361-1657
  Queensbury *(G-13439)*

WOOD PRDTS: Shoe Trees

R P M Industries Inc .... E 315 255-1105
  Auburn *(G-497)*

WOOD PRDTS: Signboards

Paramount Graphix .... G 845 367-5003
  Port Jervis *(G-13234)*
Sentine Printing Inc .... G 516 334-7400
  Westbury *(G-16372)*

WOOD PRDTS: Silo Staves

Unadilla Silo Company Inc .... D 607 369-9341
  Sidney *(G-14857)*

WOOD PRDTS: Survey Stakes

T Eason Land Surveyor .... G 631 474-2200
  Port Jeff STA *(G-13218)*

WOOD PRDTS: Trellises

Finger Lakes Trellis Supply .... G 315 904-4007
  Williamson *(G-16558)*

WOOD PRDTS: Trophy Bases

Cherry Creek Woodcraft Inc .... E 716 988-3211
  South Dayton *(G-14928)*
M A Moslow & Bros Inc .... E 716 896-2950
  Buffalo *(G-2929)*

WOOD PRDTS: Window Backs, Store Or Lunchroom, Prefabricated

Vitarose Corp of America .... G 718 951-9700
  Brooklyn *(G-2630)*

WOOD PRDTS: Yard Sticks

Cfp Purchasing Inc .... G 705 806-0383
  Flushing *(G-4989)*

WOOD PRODUCTS: Reconstituted

Bedford Wdwrk Instllations Inc .... G 914 764-9434
  Bedford *(G-768)*
Northeastern Products Corp .... E 518 623-3161
  Warrensburg *(G-15942)*
Zircar Refr Composites Inc .... F 845 651-2200
  Florida *(G-4974)*

WOOD TREATING: Creosoting

Colorspec Coatings Intl Inc .... F 631 472-8251
  Holbrook *(G-6179)*
Osmose Holdings Inc .... A 716 882-5905
  Depew *(G-4099)*

WOOD TREATING: Flooring, Block

Wego International Floors LLC .... F 516 487-3510
  Great Neck *(G-5600)*

WOOD TREATING: Structural Lumber & Timber

Bestway Enterprises Inc .... E 607 753-8261
  Cortland (G-3860)
Bestway of New York Inc .... G 607 753-8261
  Cortland (G-3861)
Genesee Reserve Buffalo LLC .... E 716 824-3116
  Buffalo (G-2848)
Northeast Treaters NY LLC .... E 518 945-2660
  Athens (G-452)

WOODWORK & TRIM: Interior & Ornamental

Beaver Creek Industries Inc .... G 607 545-6382
  Canaseraga (G-3238)
Inform Studio Inc .... F 718 401-6149
  Bronx (G-1297)
Miller Blaker Inc .... D 718 665-0500
  Bronx (G-1332)
P H Custom Woodworking Corp .... E 917 801-1444
  Bronx (G-1349)
Props Displays & Interiors .... F 212 620-3840
  New York (G-11266)
RB Woodcraft Inc .... E 315 474-2429
  Syracuse (G-15405)
Upstate Door Inc .... D 585 786-3880
  Warsaw (G-15947)
Vander Heyden Woodworking .... G 212 242-0525
  New York (G-11990)
Wood Innovations of Suffolk .... G 631 698-2345
  Medford (G-7969)

WOODWORK: Carved & Turned

Architectural Dctg Co LLC .... E 845 483-1340
  Poughkeepsie (G-13327)
Lanza Corp .... G 914 937-6360
  Port Chester (G-13204)
Regal Windows & Doors LLC .... F 201 934-0100
  Spring Valley (G-15006)
Superior Wood Turnings .... F 716 483-1254
  Jamestown (G-6756)

WOODWORK: Interior & Ornamental, NEC

A Losee & Sons .... G 516 676-3060
  Glen Cove (G-5358)
American Wood Column Corp .... G 718 782-3163
  Brooklyn (G-1528)
Bauerschmidt & Sons Inc .... D 718 528-3500
  Jamaica (G-6630)
Brauen Construction .... G 585 492-0042
  Arcade (G-380)
Custom Wood Inc .... G 718 927-4700
  Brooklyn (G-1744)
DAngelo Home Collections Inc .... G 917 267-8920
  Warwick (G-15949)
DC Contracting & Building Corp .... F 631 385-1117
  Huntington Station (G-6438)
Ignelzi Interiors Inc .... E 718 464-0279
  Queens Village (G-13407)
Kng Construction Co Inc .... F 212 595-1451
  Warwick (G-15956)
Michael Bernstein Design Assoc .... E 718 456-9277
  Brooklyn (G-2203)
Nordic Interior Inc .... C 718 456-7000
  Brooklyn (G-2272)
Pgs Millwork Inc .... D 518 828-2608
  Hudson (G-6368)
Zeller Woodworks LLC .... F 585 254-7607
  Rochester (G-14218)

WOVEN WIRE PRDTS, NEC

Joldeson One Aerospace Inds .... D 718 848-7396
  Ozone Park (G-12827)

WRITING FOR PUBLICATION SVCS

Mosby Holdings Corp .... G 212 309-8100
  New York (G-10844)

X-RAY EQPT & TUBES

Air Techniques Inc .... B 516 433-7676
  Melville (G-8000)
American Access Care LLC .... F 631 582-9729
  Hauppauge (G-5763)
Biodex Medical Systems Inc .... C 631 924-9000
  Shirley (G-14832)
Dra Imaging PC .... E 845 296-1057
  Wappingers Falls (G-15929)
Flow X Ray Corporation .... D 631 242-9729
  Deer Park (G-3976)
Mitegen LLC .... G 607 266-8877
  Ithaca (G-6596)
Multiwire Laboratories Ltd .... G 607 257-3378
  Ithaca (G-6598)
New York Imaging Service Inc .... F 716 834-8022
  Tonawanda (G-15561)
Phantom Laboratory Inc .... F 518 692-1190
  Greenwich (G-5644)
Photo Medic Equipment Inc .... D 631 242-6600
  Deer Park (G-4025)
Surescan Corporation .... E 607 321-0042
  Binghamton (G-917)
Varex Imaging Corporation .... A 315 234-6853
  Liverpool (G-7269)
VJ Technologies Inc .... E 631 589-8800
  Bohemia (G-1106)
Wolf X-Ray Corporation .... D 631 242-9729
  Deer Park (G-4063)

YARN & YARN SPINNING

Advanced Yarn Technologies Inc ...... E 518 239-6600
  Durham (G-4182)
Colortex Inc .... G 212 564-2000
  New York (G-9355)
Missiontex Inc .... G 718 532-9053
  Brooklyn (G-2215)
National Spinning Co Inc .... E 212 382-6400
  New York (G-10886)
United Thread Mills Corp .... G 516 536-3900
  Oceanside (G-12562)

YARN MILLS: Twisting

Majestic Rayon Corporation .... E 212 929-6443
  New York (G-10675)

YARN WHOLESALERS

Colortex Inc .... G 212 564-2000
  New York (G-9355)
Great Adirondack Yarn Company ...... F 518 843-3381
  Amsterdam (G-339)
National Spinning Co Inc .... E 212 382-6400
  New York (G-10886)

YARN: Embroidery, Spun

Printz and Patternz LLC .... G 518 944-6020
  Schenectady (G-14705)

YARN: Natural & Animal Fiber, Spun

Great Adirondack Yarn Company ...... F 518 843-3381
  Amsterdam (G-339)

YARN: Specialty & Novelty

A Thousand Cranes Inc .... F 212 724-9596
  New York (G-8698)
K F I Inc .... G 516 546-2904
  Roosevelt (G-14436)
La Lame Inc .... G 212 921-9770
  New York (G-10502)

YARN: Weaving, Twisting, Winding Or Spooling

Marsha Fleisher .... F 845 679-6500
  Woodstock (G-16686)

YOGURT WHOLESALERS

Fage USA Holdings .... G 518 762-5912
  Johnstown (G-6829)
Kesso Foods Inc .... G 718 777-5303
  East Elmhurst (G-4222)